BUTTERWORTHS
COMPANY LAW
HANDBOOK

 KT-590-562

BUTTERWORTHS
COMPANY LAW
HANDBOOK

Twenty-fifth edition

Consultant Editor

KEITH WALMSLEY LLB, FCIS, Barrister

Members of the LexisNexis Group worldwide

United Kingdom	LexisNexis, a Division of Reed Elsevier (UK) Ltd, Halsbury House, 35 Chancery Lane, London, WC2A 1EL, and London House, 20–22 East London Street, Edinburgh EH7 4BQ
Australia	LexisNexis Butterworths, Chatswood, New South Wales
Austria	LexisNexis Verlag ARD Orac GmbH & Co KG, Vienna
Benelux	LexisNexis Benelux, Amsterdam
Canada	LexisNexis Canada, Markham, Ontario
China	LexisNexis China, Beijing and Shanghai
France	LexisNexis SA, Paris
Germany	LexisNexis Deutschland GmbH, Munster
Hong Kong	LexisNexis Hong Kong, Hong Kong
India	LexisNexis India, New Delhi
Italy	Giuffrè Editore, Milan
Japan	LexisNexis Japan, Tokyo
Malaysia	Malayan Law Journal Sdn Bhd, Kuala Lumpur
New Zealand	LexisNexis NZ Ltd, Wellington
Poland	Wydawnictwo Prawnicze LexisNexis Sp, Warsaw
Singapore	LexisNexis Singapore, Singapore
South Africa	LexisNexis Butterworths, Durban
USA	LexisNexis, Dayton, Ohio

© Reed Elsevier (UK) Ltd 2011
Published by LexisNexis

This is a Butterworths title

All rights reserved. No part of this publication may be reproduced in any material form (including photocopying or storing it in any medium by electronic means and whether or not transiently or incidentally to some other use of this publication) without the written permission of the copyright owner except in accordance with the provisions of the Copyright, Designs and Patents Act 1988 or under the terms of a licence issued by the Copyright Licensing Agency Ltd, Saffron House, 6–10 Kirby Street, London EC1N 8TS. Applications for the copyright owner's written permission to reproduce any part of this publication should be addressed to the publisher.
Warning: The doing of an unauthorised act in relation to a copyright work may result in both a civil claim for damages and criminal prosecution.

Crown copyright material is reproduced with the permission of the Controller of HMSO and the Queen's Printer for Scotland. Any European material in this work which has been reproduced from EUR-lex, the official European Union legislation website, is European Union copyright.

A CIP Catalogue record for this book is available from the British Library.

ISBN: 978 1 4057 5752 2

Printed and bound by CPI Group (UK) Ltd, Croydon, CR0 4YY

Visit LexisNexis at www.lexisnexis.co.uk

EDITOR'S INTRODUCTION TO THE TWENTY-FIFTH EDITION

In this, the twenty-fifth edition of *Butterworths Company Law Handbook*, the various Parts of the Handbook have been restructured to complete the transition of the contents from those of the 1985 Act regime to those of the 2006 Act regime. In relation to the 1985 Act material, the Handbook now only includes (in Parts 5 and 6) those provisions which remain in full force. Users needing access to the full 1985 Act materials, prior to the 2006 Act related repeals (eg, when dealing with corporate events occurring prior to 1 October 2009) should consult the special one-off archival edition of the Handbook published in 2010 (*Butterworths Company Law Handbook: The Companies Act 1985 Regime*). See below regarding the inclusion of some of the 1985 Act regime materials in the electronic version of the Handbook.

Recent developments which have been included and reflected in the twenty-fifth edition include the Companies Act 2006 (Consequential Amendments and Transitional Provisions) Order 2011 (which effects a "final" tidying-up of some loose ends remaining in the move from the 1985 Act regime to the 2006 Act regime) and the Companies Act 2006 (Annual Returns) Regulations 2011 (affecting ss 855–856B of the 2006 Act and making important changes to the contents of companies' annual returns from 1 October 2011). The numerous amendments (particularly to Part 27 of the 2006 Act – Mergers and Divisions of Public Companies) made by the Companies (Reporting Requirements in Mergers and Divisions) Regulations 2011 which were laid before Parliament on the Handbook's cut-off date of 1 July 2011 are also included.

The Handbook also now includes (in Part 9) the text of the Bribery Act 2010, which came into force on 1 July 2011.

It should also be noted that the Statutory Auditors and Third Country Auditors (Amendment) Regulations 2011 (SI 2011/1856) were published on 27 July 2011 just before this edition of *Butterworths Company Law Handbook* went to press. As the majority of the pages for this edition had already been set at that date, there was not sufficient time to incorporate the amendments made by the 2011 Regulations in the Companies Act 2006, the Companies (Audit, Investigations and Community Enterprise) Act 2004, or the Statutory Auditors and Third Country Auditors Regulations 2007 (SI 2007/3494). Accordingly, the 2011 Regulations are set out *in full text* at the end of Part 4. Note also that, for the same reason, the 2011 Regulations are not listed in the complete list of Companies Act 2006 statutory instruments at the start of that Part.

Contents of this Handbook

The aim of this Handbook is to make available, in a convenient and up-to-date form, the full text of the most important company law statutes, statutory instruments and European legislation. The Handbook is published annually. The book is now divided into 12 main Parts—

- Part 1 — The Companies Act 2006
- Part 2 — Companies Act 2006 commencement orders, etc
- Part 3 — Companies Act 2006 supporting materials
- Part 4 — Companies Act 2006 statutory instruments
- Part 5 — Pre-2006 companies primary legislation
- Part 6 — Statutory instruments made under pre-2006 companies legislation
- Part 7 — The Financial Services and Markets Act 2000
- Part 8 — Financial Services and Markets Act 2000 statutory instruments
- Part 9 — Miscellaneous other primary legislation
- Part 10 — Miscellaneous other statutory instruments
- Part 11 — EU material
- Appendices

Within each Part, the contents are printed in chronological order. A list of all the amending provisions is provided at the beginning of each statute, statutory instrument and European Regulation/Directive. A purely amending or repealing provision is not normally reproduced; instead, the amendments etc are incorporated into the affected provision (see further the note on house style of amendments below). In some cases (ie, where an amending only statutory instrument is deemed to be of exceptional importance) a detailed note is provided for that SI.

An index and glossary are also provided in this Handbook. References in the index and glossary are to the unique paragraph number given to each provision – not its page number.

The contents are reproduced as amended to include materials published at 1 July 2011, though later materials have been included, and later amendments have been noted, where possible.

Companies Act 2006 (Part 1)

This Part contains the complete fully-updated version of the 2006 Act.

Companies Act 2006 commencement orders, etc (Part 2)

All eight commencement orders for the 2006 Act are set out in chronological order. Included at the end of the Part is a fully-updated table of commencements for the 2006 Act with commencement details for all of the original provisions plus details for all added, substituted and repealed provisions.

Companies Act 2006 supporting materials (Part 3)

This Part contains the explanatory notes to the Companies Act 2006, the table of origins for the 2006 Act, the tables of destinations for the Companies Acts 1985 and 1989, and the Ministerial statements on duties of directors.

Companies Act 2006 statutory instruments (Part 4)

A complete list of all statutory instruments made under the 2006 Act is included at the start of this Part. It also contains the companies statutory instruments made under the 2006 Act (with the exception of the commencement orders included in Part 2). Note that some statutory instruments that were made under the 2006 Act are not included in this Part. Ie, where the subject matter of such instruments is not company law (eg, where it *only* concerns the law relating to LLPs) the statutory instruments are set out in Part 10 instead.

Pre-2006 companies primary legislation (Part 5)

This Part contains the Companies Act 1985 (as remaining in full force at 1 July 2011). Note that repealed provisions are not reproduced but details of the repeal are given, together with details of any relevant savings or transitional provisions and cross-references to the relevant savings provision. It also contains the Company Directors Disqualification Act 1986, the unrepealed provisions of the Companies Act 1989, the relevant provisions of the Criminal Justice Act 1993, and the Companies (Audit, Investigations and Community Enterprise) Act 2004.

Statutory instruments made under pre-2006 companies legislation (Part 6)

This Part contains the statutory instruments made under the primary legislation contained in Part 5. Again, it should be noted that where an instrument is made under the authority of more than one Act, the instrument will be included in its most appropriate Part. For example, the Insolvent Companies (Disqualification of Unfit Directors) Proceedings Rules 1987 were made partly under the Company Directors Disqualification Act 1986 and partly under the Insolvency Act 1986. These Rules are set out in Part 10 as it is felt that the subject matter of the statutory instrument is insolvency law rather than company law.

The Financial Services and Markets Act 2000 (Part 7)

Selected provisions of the Financial Services and Markets Act 2000 are reproduced in Part 7. It should be emphasised that this edition of *Butterworths Company Law Handbook* (unlike some of its predecessors) does not contain the full text of FSMA 2000. It is felt that, because of the pressure on space in this work, such material is more appropriately contained in volumes dealing with financial services law, as opposed to company law. Where a provision has been omitted for reasons of space, a note is included to that effect. Those users of this work who need such material are referred to this Handbook's companion works such as *Butterworths Banking Law Handbook* and, in particular, *Butterworths Securities & Financial Services Law Handbook* (which is published annually in the first quarter of the year). Rules, Regulations and Guidance made by the FSA are not reproduced. They can be accessed at *www.fsa.gov.uk/Pages/handbook/* or through the Lexis®Library online service at *www.lexisnexis.com/uk/legal.*

Financial Services and Markets Act 2000 statutory instruments (Part 8)

This Part includes the texts of those statutory instruments made under FSMA 2000 that are most relevant to corporate lawyers.

Miscellaneous other primary legislation (Part 9)

This Part includes a variety of other primary legislation covering such subject areas as partnerships, limited liability partnerships and insolvency. Also included are the relevant provisions relating to fraud, bribery and theft.

Miscellaneous other statutory instruments (Part 10)

The most relevant statutory instruments made under the Acts included in Part 9 are set out here.

EU materials (Part 11)

Part 11 contains a wide-ranging selection of European Regulations and Directives covering such areas as insolvency, market abuse, takeovers, and transparency etc.

Appendices

Appendix 1 contains the Companies Act 2006 Model Articles. The text of the Companies Act 1948 Table A is reproduced because this version of Table A continues to apply to many companies incorporated prior to 1 July 1985 (Appendix 3). For convenience, the Companies Act 1985 Table A is set out in Appendix 2.

House style for amendments

Amendments are indicated using the house style of the Handbooks series as follows: in force repeals/revocations are indicated by an ellipsis; insertions and in force substitutions are in square brackets; and prospective repeals/revocations or substitutions are in italics with, in the case of substitutions, the text to be substituted set out in the notes. Details of the provenance of changes are given in the notes, together with the effective date. Text that has been repealed or revoked with savings in relation to its continued application is also in italics (with full details of the relevant savings or transitional provisions set out in the notes). A summary follows—

in force repeal or revocation	. . .
prospective repeal or revocation	*text in italics*
insertion (in force and prospective)	[text in square brackets]
in force substitution	[text in square brackets]
prospective substitution	*text in italics* (with new text set out in notes)
repealed/revoked with savings or transitional provisions	*text in italics* (with details of savings, etc, set out in notes)

Electronic versions of this Handbook

Butterworths Company Law Handbook is included as part of the Lexis®Library service (at *www.lexisnexis.com/uk/legal*). The Handbook is updated fortnightly on this service.

There is also a CD version of this work that is updated monthly and which can be ordered from the LexisNexis Customer Services Department.

Note that both electronic versions of the Handbook contain certain extra material that has not been included in the hardcopy version simply because there is not the space to fit it all into a one volume work. This material is as follows:
- Appendix 4 — Companies Act 1985 (at 7 November 2006)
- Appendix 5 — Companies Act 1985 (at 1 October 2010)
- Appendix 6 — Companies Act 1985 Fees and Forms

Standard Scale; Statutory Maximum

There are numerous references to the standard scale, and to the statutory maximum, throughout the legislation contained in this Handbook. For reasons of space, notes have not been made at every place where the references appear, but users should refer back to this note.

The standard scale is the scale set out in the Criminal Justice Act 1982, s 37(2), but different amounts may be substituted by order under the Magistrates' Courts Act 1980, s 143. The scale (as substituted by the Criminal Justice Act 1991, s 17(1), as from 1 October 1992) is—

level 1: £200;

level 2: £500;

level 3: £1,000;

level 4: £2,500; and

level 5: £5,000.

The statutory maximum is the prescribed sum within the meaning of the Magistrates' Courts Act 1980, s 32. Section 32(9) of the 1980 Act (as amended by the Criminal Justice Act 1991, s 17(2)(c), as from 1 October 1992), provides that the prescribed sum is £5,000, but a different sum may be substituted by order under s 143 of the 1980 Act.

Keith Walmsley, July 2011

CONTENTS

Introduction (including the glossary of words and phrases)   **page v**

PART 9 — MISCELLANEOUS OTHER PRIMARY LEGISLATION

PART 10 — MISCELLANEOUS OTHER STATUTORY INSTRUMENTS

PART 11 — EU LEGISLATION

APPENDICES

Glossary of Words and Phrases

accounting documents, **[4.390]**

accounting standards, **[1.464]**

act as insolvency practitioner, **[9.350]**

administrative receiver, **[9.347]**

advertisement, **[11.401]**

ancillary document, **[5.41]**

annual accounts, **[1.471]**

annuities on human life, **[8.3]**

applicant, **[7.328]**

application, **[7.328]**

appropriate audit authority, **[1.525]**

appropriate deposit, **[10.846]**

appropriate rate, **[1.592]**, **[1.609]**, **[9.398]**

appropriates, **[9.82]**

approved exchange, **[8.241]**

Article 21 relief application, **[10.964]**, **[10.976]**

asset backed securities, **[11.401]**

assets requirement, **[7.50]**

associate, **[1.345]**, **[1.1260]**, **[9.398]**

associated pension scheme, **[4.222]**

audit working papers, **[1.1261]**

authorised deposit-taker, **[10.668]**

authorised insurance company, **[10.1034]**

authorised unit trust scheme, **[7.223]**

bank, **[10.722]**

banking company, **[1.1164]**, **[10.1034]**

banking group, **[1.1164]**

banking LLP, **[10.1034]**

belonging to another, **[9.84]**

body corporate, **[7.359]**

building, **[9.155]**

building block, **[11.401]**

building operations, **[9.155]**

business, **[9.44]**

business day, **[9.347]**, **[10.669]**, **[6.35]**

called-up share capital, **[1.547]**

central bank, **[10.777]**

PART 1
THE COMPANIES ACT 2006

COMPANIES ACT 2006

(2006 c 46)

NOTES

Commencement: the commencement of this Act is provided for by s 1300 at **[1.1300]** and the Orders made under that section. For a summary of all commencement information, see the Table of commencements for the Companies Act 2006 at **[2.92]**.

General saving for existing companies etc: the Companies Act 2006 (Commencement No 8, Transitional Provisions and Savings) Order 2008, SI 2008/2860, Sch 2, para 1(1) (at **[2.91]**) provides that nothing in this Act affects: (a) the registration or re-registration of a company under the former Companies Acts, or the continued existence of a company by virtue of such registration or re-registration, or (b) the application in relation to an existing company of (i) Table B in the Joint Stock Companies Act 1856, (ii) Table A in any of the former Companies Acts, or the Companies (Tables A to F) Regulations 1985 or the Companies (Tables A to F) Regulations (Northern Ireland) 1986.

Application of this Act to old public companies:
The Companies Act 2006 (Consequential Amendments and Transitional Provisions) Order 2011, SI 2011/1265, Sch 1, para 2 provides as follows (for further provision as to old public companies see paras 1, 3–9 of that Schedule at **[4.651]**)—

"2　Application of Companies Acts to old public companies
(1)　References in the Companies Acts to—
　(a)　a public company, or
　(b)　a company other than a private company,
are to be read (unless the context otherwise requires) as including an old public company.
(2)　References in the Companies Acts to a private company are to be read accordingly.
(3)　Sub-paragraphs (1) and (2)—
　(a)　do not apply in relation to—
　　(i)　Part 7 of the Companies Act 2006 (re-registration as a means of altering a company's status), and
　　(ii)　sections 662 to 669 of that Act (treatment of shares held by or for public company) (see paragraph 7(1) and (2) below), and
　(b)　do not restrict the power to make provision by regulations under section 65 of that Act (inappropriate use of indications of company type or legal form).".

References to companies registered or re-registered under earlier legislation: see the note to s 1297 at **[1.1297]**.

Offences under the Companies Acts: see, generally, Part 36 of this Act at **[1.1121]** et seq. See also the Companies Act 2006 (Commencement No 8, Transitional Provisions and Savings) Order 2008, SI 2008/2860, art 7 at **[2.88]** (prosecution of offences in transitional cases). As to offences under the Companies Act 1985, see also Sch 2, para 116 to the 2008 Order at **[2.91]** (savings for provisions relating to offences).

Application to limited liability partnerships: as to the application of this Act to LLPs, see:
　•　(i) the Limited Liability Partnerships (Accounts and Audit) (Application of Companies Act 2006) Regulations 2008, SI 2008/1911 at **[10.1003]**; (ii) the Limited Liability Partnerships (Application of Companies Act 2006) Regulations 2009, SI 2009/1804 at **[10.1097]**. The 2008 Regulations apply provisions on the accounts and audit of companies contained in this Act to LLPs, with modifications. The 2009 Regulations apply the remaining provisions of this Act (in so far as appropriate) to LLPs with modifications. Both sets of Regulations replace certain provisions in the Limited Liability Partnerships Regulations 2001, SI 2001/1090 (which applied the Companies Act 1985 to LLPs). Both sets of Regulations also set out, in full, the applied provisions of this Act in so far as they apply to LLPs.
　•　As to LLPs, see also the Small Limited Liability Partnerships (Accounts) Regulations 2008, SI 2008/1912 at **[10.1061]**, and the Large and Medium-sized Limited Liability Partnerships (Accounts) Regulations 2008, SI 2008/1913 at **[10.1078]**. These Regulations specify the form and content of the accounts of LLPs by applying, with modifications, provisions of the Small Companies and Groups (Accounts and Directors' Report) Regulations 2008 (SI 2008/409) and the Large and Medium-sized Companies and Groups (Accounts and Reports) Regulations 2008 (SI 2008/410).
See also the Companies (Late Filing Penalties) and Limited Liability Partnerships (Filing Periods and Late Filing Penalties) Regulations 2008, SI 2008/497, reg 6(1) and Schedule, Pt 1 at **[4.255]** and **[4.256]**.

Application to overseas companies: as to the application of this Act to overseas companies, see the Overseas Companies Regulations 2009, SI 2009/1801 at **[10.1096]**, and the Overseas Companies (Execution of Documents and Registration of Charges) Regulations 2009, SI 2009/1917 at **[4.500]**.

Application to unregistered companies: as to the application of certain parts of this Act to unregistered companies, see the Unregistered Companies Regulations 2009, SI 2009/2436 at **[4.594]** et seq. Note that these Regulations revoked and replaced (as from 1 October 2009 but subject to transitional provisions and savings) the Companies Acts (Unregistered Companies) Regulations 2007, SI 2007/318.

Application to partnerships: as to the application of the accounts and audit provisions of this Act to partnerships, see the Partnerships (Accounts) Regulations 2008, SI 2008/569 at **[10.984]**.

Application to European Economic Interest Groupings: certain provisions of this Act are applied with modifications to EEIGs registered, or in the process of being registered, under the European Economic Interest Grouping Regulations 1989, SI 1989/638; see reg 18 of, and Sch 4 to, the 1989 Regulations at **[10.696]** et seq (as amended by the European Economic Interest Grouping (Amendment) Regulations 2009, SI 2009/2399).

Application to Societas Europaea: as to the application of certain provisions of this Act to SEs, see the European Public Limited-Liability Company Regulations 2004, SI 2004/2326 at **[10.851]** (as amended by the European Public Limited-Liability Company (Amendment) Regulations 2009, SI 2009/2400). See in particular, Sch 2 (provisions of this Act applying to the registration of SEs) at **[10.908]**, and Sch 4 (modifications of this Act and the Insolvency Act 1986) at **[10.909]**.

Application to insurance undertakings: as to the application of the accounts and audit provisions of this Act to specified insurance undertakings, see the Insurance Accounts Directive (Miscellaneous Insurance Undertakings) Regulations 2008, SI 2008/565 (see the note at **[10.982]**). See also, the Insurance Accounts Directive (Lloyd's Syndicate and Aggregate Accounts) Regulations 2008, SI 2008/1950.

Application to banks: as to the application of the accounts and audit provisions of this Act to banks, see the Bank Accounts Directive (Miscellaneous Banks) Regulations 2008, SI 2008/567 (see the note at **[10.983]**). As to the application of this Act to bank insolvency and administration, see the Banking Act 2009 and the Orders etc made under that Act. As to the application of certain provisions of this Act to particular banks, see also the Banking (Special Provisions) Act 2008 and the Banking Act 2009, and the Orders made under those Acts. As to the application of this Act to Banks authorised to issue banknotes in Scotland and Northern Ireland (other than the Bank of England), see the Scottish and Northern Ireland Banknote Regulations 2009, SI 2009/3056.

Civil Procedure Rules: the Civil Procedure Rules 1998, SI 1998/3132, rule 49 (as amended), states that those Rules apply to proceedings under this Act subject to the provisions of the relevant practice direction which applies to those proceedings.

This Act is reproduced as amended by the following Acts:

2009	Finance Act 2009.
2010	Corporation Tax Act 2010.
2011	Budget Responsibility and National Audit Act 2011; Damages (Scotland) Act 2011.

This Act is reproduced as amended by the following SIs:

2007	Companies (EEA State) Regulations 2007, SI 2007/732; Government of Wales Act 2006 (Consequential Modifications and Transitional Provisions) Order 2007, SI 2007/1388; Markets in Financial Instruments Directive (Consequential Amendments) Regulations 2007, SI 2007/2932; Reinsurance Directive Regulations 2007, SI 2007/3253; Statutory Auditors and Third Country Auditors Regulations 2007, SI 2007/3494.
2008	Companies Act 2006 (Amendment) (Accounts and Reports) Regulations 2008, SI 2008/393; Insurance Accounts Directive (Miscellaneous Insurance Undertakings) Regulations 2008, SI 2008/565; Bank Accounts Directive (Miscellaneous Banks) Regulations 2008, SI 2008/567; Companies (Mergers and Divisions of Public Companies) (Amendment) Regulations 2008, SI 2008/690; Companies Act 2006 (Consequential Amendments etc) Order 2008, SI 2008/948; Consumer Protection from Unfair Trading Regulations 2008, SI 2008/1277; Insurance Accounts Directive (Lloyd's Syndicate and Aggregate Accounts) Regulations 2008, SI 2008/1950.
2009	Companies Act 2006 (Amendment of Schedule 2) Order 2009, SI 2009/202; Companies Act 2006 (Amendment of Schedule 2) (No 2) Order 2009, SI 2009/1208; Financial Services and Markets Act 2000 (Regulated Activities) (Amendment) Order 2009, SI 2009/1342; Companies Act 2006 (Accounts, Reports and Audit) Regulations 2009, SI 2009/1581; Companies (Shareholders' Rights) Regulations 2009, SI 2009/1632; Companies Act 2006 (Part 35) (Consequential Amendments, Transitional Provisions and Savings) Order 2009, SI 2009/1802; Companies Act 2006 (Consequential Amendments, Transitional Provisions and Savings) Order 2009, SI 2009/1941; Companies (Share Capital and Acquisition by Company of its Own Shares) Regulations 2009, SI 2009/2022; Companies Act 2006 (Allotment of Shares and Right of Pre-emption) (Amendment) Regulations 2009, SI 2009/2561; Government of Wales Act 2006 (Consequential Modifications, Transitional Provisions and Saving) Order 2009, SI 2009/2958; Companies Act 2006 (Amendment of Section 413) Regulations 2009, SI 2009/3022; Companies Act 2006 (Substitution of Section 1201) Regulations 2009, SI 2009/3182.
2010	Transfer of Tribunal Functions Order 2010, SI 2010/22; Companies Act 2006 (Transfer of Audit Working Papers to Third Countries) Regulations 2010, SI 2010/2537.
2011	Electronic Money Regulations 2011, SI 2011/99; Companies Act 2006 (Consequential Amendments and Transitional Provisions) Order 2011, SI 2011/1265; Companies Act 2006 (Annual Returns) Regulations 2011, SI 2011/1487; Companies (Reporting Requirements in Mergers and Divisions) Regulations 2011, SI 2011/1606.

References to the "European Community", "Community", etc: see the Treaty of Lisbon (Changes in Terminology) Order 2011, SI 2011/1043, which provides (with effect from 22 April 2011): (1) that for references to the "European Communities" or to the "European Community" (including references to "the Communities", "the Community", "the EC" or "the EEC") substitute references to the European Union; and (2) that "EU" should be substituted for the word "Community" (subject to certain exceptions) in references to "Community treaties", "Community customs duty", "Community institution", "Community instrument", "Community obligation", "enforceable Community right", "Community law", "Community legislation", and "Community provision". Also, where such a term is preceded by the word "a", for "a" substitute "an".

ARRANGEMENT OF SECTIONS

PART 1
GENERAL INTRODUCTORY PROVISIONS

Companies and Companies Acts

Types of company

PART 2
COMPANY FORMATION

General

PART 5
A COMPANY'S NAME

CHAPTER 1
GENERAL REQUIREMENTS

Prohibited names

Sensitive words and expressions

Permitted characters etc

CHAPTER 2
INDICATIONS OF COMPANY TYPE OR LEGAL FORM

Required indications for limited companies

Inappropriate use of indications of company type or legal form

CHAPTER 3
SIMILARITY TO OTHER NAMES

Similarity to other name on registrar's index

Similarity to other name in which person has goodwill

CHAPTER 4
OTHER POWERS OF THE SECRETARY OF STATE

CHAPTER 5
CHANGE OF NAME

PART 10
A COMPANY'S DIRECTORS

CHAPTER 1
APPOINTMENT AND REMOVAL OF DIRECTORS

CHAPTER 2
GENERAL DUTIES OF DIRECTORS

CHAPTER 3
DECLARATION OF INTEREST IN EXISTING TRANSACTION OR ARRANGEMENT

CHAPTER 4
TRANSACTIONS WITH DIRECTORS REQUIRING APPROVAL OF MEMBERS

CHAPTER 5
DIRECTORS' SERVICE CONTRACTS

CHAPTER 6
CONTRACTS WITH SOLE MEMBERS WHO ARE DIRECTORS

CHAPTER 7
DIRECTORS' LIABILITIES

CHAPTER 8
DIRECTORS' RESIDENTIAL ADDRESSES: PROTECTION FROM DISCLOSURE

CHAPTER 9
SUPPLEMENTARY PROVISIONS

Provision for employees on cessation or transfer of business

Records of meetings of directors

Meaning of "director" and "shadow director"

Other definitions

General

PART 11
DERIVATIVE CLAIMS AND PROCEEDINGS BY MEMBERS

CHAPTER 1
DERIVATIVE CLAIMS IN ENGLAND AND WALES OR NORTHERN IRELAND

CHAPTER 2
DERIVATIVE PROCEEDINGS IN SCOTLAND

PART 12
COMPANY SECRETARIES

Private companies

Public companies

Provisions applying to private companies with a secretary and to public companies

CHAPTER 3
FUNCTIONS OF AUDITOR

CHAPTER 6
AUDITORS' LIABILITY

CHAPTER 7
SUPPLEMENTARY PROVISIONS

PART 17
A COMPANY'S SHARE CAPITAL

CHAPTER 1
SHARES AND SHARE CAPITAL OF A COMPANY

CHAPTER 2
ALLOTMENT OF SHARES: GENERAL PROVISIONS

CHAPTER 3
ALLOTMENT OF EQUITY SECURITIES: EXISTING SHAREHOLDERS' RIGHT OF PRE-EMPTION

PART 23
DISTRIBUTIONS

CHAPTER 1
RESTRICTIONS ON WHEN DISTRIBUTIONS MAY BE MADE

Introductory

General rules

Distributions by investment companies

CHAPTER 2
JUSTIFICATION OF DISTRIBUTION BY REFERENCE TO ACCOUNTS

Justification of distribution by reference to accounts

Requirements applicable in relation to relevant accounts

Part 1   The Companies Act 2006

PART 37
COMPANIES: SUPPLEMENTARY PROVISIONS

Company records

Service addresses

Sending or supplying documents or information

Requirements as to independent valuation

Notice of appointment of certain officers

Courts and legal proceedings

PART 38
COMPANIES: INTERPRETATION

Meaning of "UK-registered company"

Meaning of "subsidiary" and related expressions

Meaning of "undertaking" and related expressions

Other definitions

General

PART 42
STATUTORY AUDITORS

CHAPTER 1
INTRODUCTORY

CHAPTER 2
INDIVIDUALS AND FIRMS

Eligibility for appointment

Independence requirement

Effect of appointment of a partnership

Supervisory bodies

Professional qualifications

Information

Enforcement

CHAPTER 3
AUDITORS GENERAL

Eligibility for appointment

Conduct of audits

The Independent Supervisor

Supervision of Auditors General

Reporting requirement

Information

Enforcement

Proceedings

An Act to reform company law and restate the greater part of the enactments relating to companies; to make other provision relating to companies and other forms of business organisation; to make provision about directors' disqualification, business names, auditors and actuaries; to amend Part 9 of the Enterprise Act 2002; and for connected purposes

[8 November 2006]

PART 1
GENERAL INTRODUCTORY PROVISIONS

Companies and Companies Acts

[1.1]
1 Companies

(1) In the Companies Acts, unless the context otherwise requires—

"company" means a company formed and registered under this Act, that is—

> (a)　a company so formed and registered after the commencement of this Part, or
> (b)　a company that immediately before the commencement of this Part—
> > (i)　was formed and registered under the Companies Act 1985 (c 6) or the Companies (Northern Ireland) Order 1986 (SI 1986/1032 (NI 6)), or
> > (ii)　was an existing company for the purposes of that Act or that Order,
> > (which is to be treated on commencement as if formed and registered under this Act).
> (2)　Certain provisions of the Companies Acts apply to—
> > (a)　companies registered, but not formed, under this Act (see Chapter 1 of Part 33), and
> > (b)　bodies incorporated in the United Kingdom but not registered under this Act (see Chapter 2 of that Part).
> (3)　For provisions applying to companies incorporated outside the United Kingdom, see Part 34 (overseas companies).

NOTES

Commencement: 1 October 2009.

Transitional provisions: as to the definition of "company" see further the transitional provisions note to s 7 at **[1.7]**.

[1.2]
2　The Companies Acts
(1)　In this Act "the Companies Acts" means—
　(a)　the company law provisions of this Act,
　(b)　Part 2 of the Companies (Audit, Investigations and Community Enterprise) Act 2004 (c 27) (community interest companies), and
　(c)　the provisions of the Companies Act 1985 (c 6) and the Companies Consolidation (Consequential Provisions) Act 1985 (c 9) that remain in force.
(2)　The company law provisions of this Act are—
　(a)　the provisions of Parts 1 to 39 of this Act, and
　(b)　the provisions of Parts 45 to 47 of this Act so far as they apply for the purposes of those Parts.

NOTES

Commencement: 1 January 2007 (certain purposes); 20 January 2007 (certain purposes); 6 April 2007 (otherwise) (see the note below).

Commencement (transitional adaptations): art 5 of the Companies Act 2006 (Commencement No 1, Transitional Provisions and Savings) Order 2006, SI 2006/3428 provides that the provisions brought into force by arts 2–4 of 2006 Order shall have effect subject to any transitional adaptations specified in Sch 1 to that Order. Schedule 1, para 1 to the 2006 Order (at **[2.9]**) provided for such transitional adaptations (note that this paragraph was revoked by the Companies Act 2006 (Commencement No 8, Transitional Provisions and Savings) Order 2008, SI 2008/2860, art 6, as from 1 October 2009 (subject to any relevant transitional provision or saving in Sch 2 to that Order)).

Commencement (transitional adaptations): art 3 of the Companies Act 2006 (Commencement No 2, Consequential Amendments, Transitional Provisions and Savings) Order 2007, SI 2007/1093 provides that the provisions brought into force by art 2 of 2007 Order shall have effect subject to any transitional adaptations specified in Sch 1 to that Order. Schedule 1, para 1 to the 2007 Order (at **[2.27]**) provided for such transitional adaptations (note that this paragraph was revoked by the Companies Act 2006 (Commencement No 8, Transitional Provisions and Savings) Order 2008, SI 2008/2860, art 6, as from 1 October 2009 (subject to any relevant transitional provision or saving in Sch 2 to that Order)).

Commencement (note): the Companies Act 2006 (Commencement No 1, Transitional Provisions and Savings) Order 2006, SI 2006/3428, arts 2(2), 3(2) provide that this section shall come into force on 1 January 2007 and 20 January 2007 respectively so far as is necessary for the purposes of the provisions of this Act brought into force on those dates by arts 2(1), 3(1) of that Order (see **[2.2]**, **[2.3]**).

Types of company

[1.3]
3　Limited and unlimited companies
(1)　A company is a "limited company" if the liability of its members is limited by its constitution. It may be limited by shares or limited by guarantee.
(2)　If their liability is limited to the amount, if any, unpaid on the shares held by them, the company is "limited by shares".
(3)　If their liability is limited to such amount as the members undertake to contribute to the assets of the company in the event of its being wound up, the company is "limited by guarantee".
(4)　If there is no limit on the liability of its members, the company is an "unlimited company".

NOTES

Commencement: 1 October 2009.

[1.4]
4　Private and public companies
(1)　A "private company" is any company that is not a public company.
(2)　A "public company" is a company limited by shares or limited by guarantee and having a share capital—
　(a)　whose certificate of incorporation states that it is a public company, and

(b)   in relation to which the requirements of this Act, or the former Companies Acts, as to registration or re-registration as a public company have been complied with on or after the relevant date.

(3)   For the purposes of subsection (2)(b) the relevant date is—

(a)   in relation to registration or re-registration in Great Britain, 22nd December 1980;

(b)   in relation to registration or re-registration in Northern Ireland, 1st July 1983.

(4)   For the two major differences between private and public companies, see Part 20.

NOTES
Commencement: 1 October 2009.

[1.5]
5   Companies limited by guarantee and having share capital

(1)   A company cannot be formed as, or become, a company limited by guarantee with a share capital.

(2)   Provision to this effect has been in force—

(a)   in Great Britain since 22nd December 1980, and

(b)   in Northern Ireland since 1st July 1983.

(3)   Any provision in the constitution of a company limited by guarantee that purports to divide the company's undertaking into shares or interests is a provision for a share capital.

This applies whether or not the nominal value or number of the shares or interests is specified by the provision.

NOTES
Commencement: 1 October 2009.

[1.6]
6   Community interest companies

(1)   In accordance with Part 2 of the Companies (Audit, Investigations and Community Enterprise) Act 2004 (c 27)—

(a)   a company limited by shares or a company limited by guarantee and not having a share capital may be formed as or become a community interest company, and

(b)   a company limited by guarantee and having a share capital may become a community interest company.

(2)   The other provisions of the Companies Acts have effect subject to that Part.

NOTES
Commencement: 1 October 2009.

PART 2
COMPANY FORMATION
General

[1.7]
7   Method of forming company

(1)   A company is formed under this Act by one or more persons—

(a)   subscribing their names to a memorandum of association (see section 8), and

(b)   complying with the requirements of this Act as to registration (see sections 9 to 13).

(2)   A company may not be so formed for an unlawful purpose.

NOTES
Commencement: 1 October 2009.
Commencement (transitional provisions): Sch 2, para 2 to the Companies Act 2006 (Commencement No 8, Transitional Provisions and Savings) Order 2008, SI 2008/2860 (at **[2.91]**) provides as follows—

"Company formation (ss 7 to 16)
2.—(1)   Sections 7 to 16 of the Companies Act 2006 (company formation) apply to applications for registration received by the registrar on or after 1st October 2009.

(2)   Any application for registration under those provisions received by the registrar before that date shall not be entertained.

(3)   The corresponding provisions of the 1985 Act or 1986 Order continue to apply to an application for registration if—

(a)   it is received by the registrar, and

(b)   the requirements as to registration are met in relation to it,

before 1st October 2009.

(4)   Any application for registration under that Act or Order in relation to which the requirements as to registration are not met before that date shall be treated as withdrawn.

(5)   For the purposes of section 1297(3) of the Companies Act 2006 (continuity of the law) as it applies to treat a company formed and registered under Part 1 of the 1985 Act or Part 2 of the 1986 Order as if formed and registered under the corresponding provisions of the Companies Act 2006, the registration of a company on an application to which sub-paragraph (3) above applies is to be regarded as in force and effective immediately before the commencement of Part 1 of the Companies Act 2006.

(6)   In the definition of "company" in section 1 of the Companies Act 2006—

(a)   the reference to a company formed and registered after the commencement of Part 1 of that Act shall be read as a reference to a company formed and registered on an application to which sub-paragraph (1) above applies, and

(b)   the reference to a company formed and registered under the 1985 Act or 1986 Order immediately before the commencement of Part 1 of the Companies Act 2006 includes a company formed and registered on an application to which sub-paragraph (3) above applies.".

[1.8]
8   Memorandum of association
(1)   A memorandum of association is a memorandum stating that the subscribers—
   (a)   wish to form a company under this Act, and
   (b)   agree to become members of the company and, in the case of a company that is to have a share capital, to take at least one share each.
(2)   The memorandum must be in the prescribed form and must be authenticated by each subscriber.

NOTES
   Commencement: 20 January 2007 (for the purpose of enabling the exercise of powers to make Orders or Regulations by statutory instrument); 1 October 2009 (otherwise).
   Commencement (transitional provisions): see the note to s 7 at **[1.7]**.
   Regulations: the Companies (Registration) Regulations 2008, SI 2008/3014 at **[4.329]**.

Requirements for registration
[1.9]
9   Registration documents
(1)   The memorandum of association must be delivered to the registrar together with an application for registration of the company, the documents required by this section and a statement of compliance.
(2)   The application for registration must state—
   (a)   the company's proposed name,
   (b)   whether the company's registered office is to be situated in England and Wales (or in Wales), in Scotland or in Northern Ireland,
   (c)   whether the liability of the members of the company is to be limited, and if so whether it is to be limited by shares or by guarantee, and
   (d)   whether the company is to be a private or a public company.
(3)   If the application is delivered by a person as agent for the subscribers to the memorandum of association, it must state his name and address.
(4)   The application must contain—
   (a)   in the case of a company that is to have a share capital, a statement of capital and initial shareholdings (see section 10);
   (b)   in the case of a company that is to be limited by guarantee, a statement of guarantee (see section 11);
   (c)   a statement of the company's proposed officers (see section 12).
(5)   The application must also contain—
   (a)   a statement of the intended address of the company's registered office; and
   (b)   a copy of any proposed articles of association (to the extent that these are not supplied by the default application of model articles: see section 20).
(6)   The application must be delivered—
   (a)   to the registrar of companies for England and Wales, if the registered office of the company is to be situated in England and Wales (or in Wales);
   (b)   to the registrar of companies for Scotland, if the registered office of the company is to be situated in Scotland;
   (c)   to the registrar of companies for Northern Ireland, if the registered office of the company is to be situated in Northern Ireland.

NOTES
   Commencement: 1 October 2009.
   Commencement (transitional provisions): see the note to s 7 at **[1.7]**.

[1.10]
10   Statement of capital and initial shareholdings
(1)   The statement of capital and initial shareholdings required to be delivered in the case of a company that is to have a share capital must comply with this section.
(2)   It must state—
   (a)   the total number of shares of the company to be taken on formation by the subscribers to the memorandum of association,
   (b)   the aggregate nominal value of those shares,
   (c)   for each class of shares—
      (i)   prescribed particulars of the rights attached to the shares,
      (ii)   the total number of shares of that class, and
      (iii)   the aggregate nominal value of shares of that class, and

(d)   the amount to be paid up and the amount (if any) to be unpaid on each share (whether on account of the nominal value of the share or by way of premium).

(3)   It must contain such information as may be prescribed for the purpose of identifying the subscribers to the memorandum of association.

(4)   It must state, with respect to each subscriber to the memorandum—

    (a)   the number, nominal value (of each share) and class of shares to be taken by him on formation, and

    (b)   the amount to be paid up and the amount (if any) to be unpaid on each share (whether on account of the nominal value of the share or by way of premium).

(5)   Where a subscriber to the memorandum is to take shares of more than one class, the information required under subsection (4)(a) is required for each class.

NOTES

Commencement: 20 January 2007 (for the purpose of enabling the exercise of powers to make Orders or Regulations by statutory instrument); 1 October 2009 (otherwise).
Commencement (transitional provisions): see the note to s 7 at [**1.7**].
Regulations: the Companies (Registration) Regulations 2008, SI 2008/3014 at [**4.329**].
Orders: the Companies (Shares and Share Capital) Order 2009, SI 2009/388 at [**4.364**].

[1.11]
11   Statement of guarantee

(1)   The statement of guarantee required to be delivered in the case of a company that is to be limited by guarantee must comply with this section.

(2)   It must contain such information as may be prescribed for the purpose of identifying the subscribers to the memorandum of association.

(3)   It must state that each member undertakes that, if the company is wound up while he is a member, or within one year after he ceases to be a member, he will contribute to the assets of the company such amount as may be required for—

    (a)   payment of the debts and liabilities of the company contracted before he ceases to be a member,

    (b)   payment of the costs, charges and expenses of winding up, and

    (c)   adjustment of the rights of the contributories among themselves,

not exceeding a specified amount.

NOTES

Commencement: 20 January 2007 (for the purpose of enabling the exercise of powers to make Orders or Regulations by statutory instrument); 1 October 2009 (otherwise).
Commencement (transitional provisions): see the note to s 7 at [**1.7**].
Regulations: the Companies (Registration) Regulations 2008, SI 2008/3014 at [**4.329**].

[1.12]
12   Statement of proposed officers

(1)   The statement of the company's proposed officers required to be delivered to the registrar must contain the required particulars of—

    (a)   the person who is, or persons who are, to be the first director or directors of the company;

    (b)   in the case of a company that is to be a private company, any person who is (or any persons who are) to be the first secretary (or joint secretaries) of the company;

    (c)   in the case of a company that is to be a public company, the person who is (or the persons who are) to be the first secretary (or joint secretaries) of the company.

(2)   The required particulars are the particulars that will be required to be stated—

    (a)   in the case of a director, in the company's register of directors and register of directors' residential addresses (see sections 162 to 166);

    (b)   in the case of a secretary, in the company's register of secretaries (see sections 277 to 279).

(3)   The statement must also contain a consent by each of the persons named as a director, as secretary or as one of joint secretaries, to act in the relevant capacity.

If all the partners in a firm are to be joint secretaries, consent may be given by one partner on behalf of all of them.

NOTES

Commencement: 1 October 2009.
Commencement (transitional provisions): see the note to s 7 at [**1.7**].

[1.13]
13   Statement of compliance

(1)   The statement of compliance required to be delivered to the registrar is a statement that the requirements of this Act as to registration have been complied with.

(2)   The registrar may accept the statement of compliance as sufficient evidence of compliance.

NOTES

Commencement: 1 October 2009.

Commencement (transitional provisions): see the note to s 7 at **[1.7]**.

Registration and its effect

[1.14]
14 Registration
If the registrar is satisfied that the requirements of this Act as to registration are complied with, he shall register the documents delivered to him.

NOTES
Commencement: 1 October 2009.
Commencement (transitional provisions): see the note to s 7 at **[1.7]**.

[1.15]
15 Issue of certificate of incorporation
(1)   On the registration of a company, the registrar of companies shall give a certificate that the company is incorporated.
(2)   The certificate must state—
  (a)   the name and registered number of the company,
  (b)   the date of its incorporation,
  (c)   whether it is a limited or unlimited company, and if it is limited whether it is limited by shares or limited by guarantee,
  (d)   whether it is a private or a public company, and
  (e)   whether the company's registered office is situated in England and Wales (or in Wales), in Scotland or in Northern Ireland.
(3)   The certificate must be signed by the registrar or authenticated by the registrar's official seal.
(4)   The certificate is conclusive evidence that the requirements of this Act as to registration have been complied with and that the company is duly registered under this Act.

NOTES
Commencement: 1 October 2009.
Commencement (transitional provisions): see the note to s 7 at **[1.7]**.

[1.16]
16 Effect of registration
(1)   The registration of a company has the following effects as from the date of incorporation.
(2)   The subscribers to the memorandum, together with such other persons as may from time to time become members of the company, are a body corporate by the name stated in the certificate of incorporation.
(3)   That body corporate is capable of exercising all the functions of an incorporated company.
(4)   The status and registered office of the company are as stated in, or in connection with, the application for registration.
(5)   In the case of a company having a share capital, the subscribers to the memorandum become holders of the shares specified in the statement of capital and initial shareholdings.
(6)   The persons named in the statement of proposed officers—
  (a)   as director, or
  (b)   as secretary or joint secretary of the company,
are deemed to have been appointed to that office.

NOTES
Commencement: 1 October 2009.
Commencement (transitional provisions): see the note to s 7 at **[1.7]**.

PART 3
A COMPANY'S CONSTITUTION

CHAPTER 1
INTRODUCTORY

[1.17]
17 A company's constitution
Unless the context otherwise requires, references in the Companies Acts to a company's constitution include—
  (a)   the company's articles, and
  (b)   any resolutions and agreements to which Chapter 3 applies (see section 29).

NOTES
Commencement: 1 October 2007 (certain purposes); 6 April 2008 (certain purposes); 1 October 2009 (otherwise) (see the notes below).
Commencement (transitional adaptations): art 6 of the Companies Act 2006 (Commencement No 3, Consequential Amendments, Transitional Provisions and Savings) Order 2007, SI 2007/2194 provides that the provisions brought into force by

that Order shall have effect subject to any transitional adaptations specified in Sch 1 to that Order. Schedule 1, para 1 to the Order (at **[2.43]**) provided for such transitional adaptations (note that this paragraph was revoked by the Companies Act 2006 (Commencement No 8, Transitional Provisions and Savings) Order 2008, SI 2008/2860, art 6, as from 1 October 2009 (subject to any relevant transitional provision or saving in Sch 2 to that Order)).

Commencement (note): the Companies Act 2006 (Commencement No 3, Consequential Amendments, Transitional Provisions and Savings) Order 2007, SI 2007/2194, art 2(3) provides that this section shall come into force on 1 October 2007 so far as is necessary for the purposes of the provisions of this Act brought into force on that date by art 2(1), (2) of that Order (see **[2.32]**).

Commencement (note): the Companies Act 2006 (Commencement No 5, Transitional Provisions and Savings) Order 2007, SI 2007/3495, art 3(3) provides that this section shall come into force on 6 April 2008 so far as is necessary for the purposes of the provisions of this Act brought into force on that date by art 3(1)(a)–(t), (2) of that Order (see **[2.52]**).

CHAPTER 2
ARTICLES OF ASSOCIATION

General

[1.18]
18 Articles of association
(1)   A company must have articles of association prescribing regulations for the company.
(2)   Unless it is a company to which model articles apply by virtue of section 20 (default application of model articles in case of limited company), it must register articles of association.
(3)   Articles of association registered by a company must—
  (a)   be contained in a single document, and
  (b)   be divided into paragraphs numbered consecutively.
(4)   References in the Companies Acts to a company's "articles" are to its articles of association.

NOTES
Commencement: 1 October 2009.
Commencement (transitional provisions): Sch 2, para 3 to the Companies Act 2006 (Commencement No 8, Transitional Provisions and Savings) Order 2008, SI 2008/2860 (at **[2.91]**) provides as follows—

"Articles of association (ss 18 to 20)
3.—(1)   Sections 7 and 8 of the 1985 Act or Articles 18 and 19 of the 1986 Order (articles of association) apply, and sections 18 to 20 of the Companies Act 2006 do not apply, to a company formed and registered under the 1985 Act or 1986 Order on an application to which paragraph 2(3) above applies.
(2)   Nothing in section 18(3) of the Companies Act 2006 (articles to be contained in single document divided into consecutively numbered paragraphs) is to be read as affecting the operation of section 28 of that Act (under which certain provisions are to be treated as part of a company's articles).".

Application to which paragraph 2(3) above applies: see further s 7 at **[1.7]**.

[1.19]
19 Power of Secretary of State to prescribe model articles
(1)   The Secretary of State may by regulations prescribe model articles of association for companies.
(2)   Different model articles may be prescribed for different descriptions of company.
(3)   A company may adopt all or any of the provisions of model articles.
(4)   Any amendment of model articles by regulations under this section does not affect a company registered before the amendment takes effect.
   "Amendment" here includes addition, alteration or repeal.
(5)   Regulations under this section are subject to negative resolution procedure.

NOTES
Commencement: 20 January 2007 (for the purpose of enabling the exercise of powers to make Orders or Regulations by statutory instrument); 1 October 2009 (otherwise).
Commencement (transitional provisions): see the note to s 18 at **[1.18]**.
Regulations: the Companies (Model Articles) Regulations 2008, SI 2008/3229 at **[4.340]**.

[1.20]
20 Default application of model articles
(1)   On the formation of a limited company—
  (a)   if articles are not registered, or
  (b)   if articles are registered, in so far as they do not exclude or modify the relevant model articles,
the relevant model articles (so far as applicable) form part of the company's articles in the same manner and to the same extent as if articles in the form of those articles had been duly registered.
(2)   The "relevant model articles" means the model articles prescribed for a company of that description as in force at the date on which the company is registered.

NOTES
Commencement: 1 October 2009.
Commencement (transitional provisions): see the note to s 18 at **[1.18]**.

Alteration of articles

[1.21]
21   Amendment of articles
(1)   A company may amend its articles by special resolution.
(2)   In the case of a company that is a charity, this is subject to—
   (a)   in England and Wales, section 64 of the Charities Act 1993 (c 10);
   (b)   in Northern Ireland, Article 9 of the Charities (Northern Ireland) Order 1987 (SI 1987/2048 (NI 19)).
(3)   In the case of a company that is registered in the Scottish Charity Register, this is subject to—
   (a)   section 112 of the Companies Act 1989 (c 40), and
   (b)   section 16 of the Charities and Trustee Investment (Scotland) Act 2005 (asp 10).

NOTES
Commencement: 1 October 2009.
Commencement (transitional provisions): Sch 2, para 4 to the Companies Act 2006 (Commencement No 8, Transitional Provisions and Savings) Order 2008, SI 2008/2860 (at **[2.91]**) provides as follows—

"Amendment of provisions of articles (ss 21 and 22)
4.—(1)   The power conferred by section 21(1) of the Companies Act 2006 (amendment of company's articles by special resolution) does not apply—
   (a)   to provisions of the articles of an existing company that were not capable of being so amended immediately before 1st October 2009; or
   (b)   to provisions of the articles of a transitional company that were not capable of being so amended under the company's constitution on its registration or re-registration (as the case may be).
(2)   The power conferred by section 22(3)(a) of that Act (amendment of entrenched provisions of articles by agreement of all the members of the company) does not apply—
   (a)   to provisions of the articles of an existing company that were not capable of being so amended immediately before 1st October 2009; or
   (b)   to provisions of the articles of a transitional company that were not capable of being so amended under the company's constitution on its registration or re-registration (as the case may be).
(3)   References in this paragraph to provisions of the articles of an existing or transitional company include provisions of the company's memorandum that are to be treated by virtue of section 28 of that Act as provisions of its articles.
(4)   A special resolution passed before 1st October 2009 removing or amending with effect from that date any provision that as from that date is treated by virtue of section 28 of that Act as a provision of the company's articles, has effect as if passed on that date.".

[1.22]
22   Entrenched provisions of the articles
(1)   A company's articles may contain provision ("provision for entrenchment") to the effect that specified provisions of the articles may be amended or repealed only if conditions are met, or procedures are complied with, that are more restrictive than those applicable in the case of a special resolution.
(2)   Provision for entrenchment may only be made—
   (a)   in the company's articles on formation, or
   (b)   by an amendment of the company's articles agreed to by all the members of the company.
(3)   Provision for entrenchment does not prevent amendment of the company's articles—
   (a)   by agreement of all the members of the company, or
   (b)   by order of a court or other authority having power to alter the company's articles.
(4)   Nothing in this section affects any power of a court or other authority to alter a company's articles.

NOTES
Commencement: 1 October 2009 (sub-ss (1), (3), (4)); to be appointed (otherwise). See further the final note below.
Commencement (transitional provisions): see the note to s 21 at **[1.21]**.
Note: the Companies Act 2006 (Commencement No 8, Transitional Provisions and Savings) Order 2008, SI 2008/2860, art 3(c) originally provided that this section would come into force for all purposes on 1 October 2009. That article was subsequently amended by the Companies Act 2006 and Limited Liability Partnerships (Transitional Provisions and Savings) (Amendment) Regulations 2009, SI 2009/2476, art 2(1), (2) which substituted the words "sections 18 to 21, 22(1), (3) and (4) and 23 to 28" for the original words "sections 18 to 28" in art 3(c) (as from 30 September 2009). The effect of this amendment was to prevent sub-s (2) above coming into force on 1 October 2009.

[1.23]
23   Notice to registrar of existence of restriction on amendment of articles
(1)   Where a company's articles—
   (a)   on formation contain provision for entrenchment,
   (b)   are amended so as to include such provision, or
   (c)   are altered by order of a court or other authority so as to restrict or exclude the power of the company to amend its articles,
the company must give notice of that fact to the registrar.
(2)   Where a company's articles—
   (a)   are amended so as to remove provision for entrenchment, or
   (b)   are altered by order of a court or other authority—

(i)   so as to remove such provision, or

(ii)   so as to remove any other restriction on, or any exclusion of, the power of the company to amend its articles,

the company must give notice of that fact to the registrar.

NOTES

Commencement: 1 October 2009.

Commencement (transitional provisions): Sch 2, para 5 to the Companies Act 2006 (Commencement No 8, Transitional Provisions and Savings) Order 2008, SI 2008/2860 (at **[2.91]**) provides as follows—

"**Notice to registrar of existence of restrictions on amendment of articles (s 23)**

5.   Section 23(1)(a) of the Companies Act 2006 (notice to registrar of fact that company's articles on formation contain provision for entrenchment) does not apply to a transitional company.".

[1.24]

24   Statement of compliance where amendment of articles restricted

(1)   This section applies where a company's articles are subject—

(a)   to provision for entrenchment, or

(b)   to an order of a court or other authority restricting or excluding the company's power to amend the articles.

(2)   If the company—

(a)   amends its articles, and

(b)   is required to send to the registrar a document making or evidencing the amendment,

the company must deliver with that document a statement of compliance.

(3)   The statement of compliance required is a statement certifying that the amendment has been made in accordance with the company's articles and, where relevant, any applicable order of a court or other authority.

(4)   The registrar may rely on the statement of compliance as sufficient evidence of the matters stated in it.

NOTES

Commencement: 1 October 2009.

[1.25]

25   Effect of alteration of articles on company's members

(1)   A member of a company is not bound by an alteration to its articles after the date on which he became a member, if and so far as the alteration—

(a)   requires him to take or subscribe for more shares than the number held by him at the date on which the alteration is made, or

(b)   in any way increases his liability as at that date to contribute to the company's share capital or otherwise to pay money to the company.

(2)   Subsection (1) does not apply in a case where the member agrees in writing, either before or after the alteration is made, to be bound by the alteration.

NOTES

Commencement: 1 October 2009.

[1.26]

26   Registrar to be sent copy of amended articles

(1)   Where a company amends its articles it must send to the registrar a copy of the articles as amended not later than 15 days after the amendment takes effect.

(2)   This section does not require a company to set out in its articles any provisions of model articles that—

(a)   are applied by the articles, or

(b)   apply by virtue of section 20 (default application of model articles).

(3)   If a company fails to comply with this section an offence is committed by—

(a)   the company, and

(b)   every officer of the company who is in default.

(4)   A person guilty of an offence under this section is liable on summary conviction to a fine not exceeding level 3 on the standard scale and, for continued contravention, a daily default fine not exceeding one-tenth of level 3 on the standard scale.

NOTES

Commencement: 1 October 2009.

Commencement (transitional provisions): Sch 2, para 6 to the Companies Act 2006 (Commencement No 8, Transitional Provisions and Savings) Order 2008, SI 2008/2860 (at **[2.91]**) provides as follows—

"**Registrar to be sent copy of amended articles (s 26)**

6.—(1)   Section 26 of the Companies Act 2006 (registrar to be sent copy of amended articles) applies in relation to amendments taking effect on or after 1st October 2009.

(2)　Section 18(2) and (3) of the 1985 Act or Article 29(2) and (3) of the 1986 Order continue to apply in relation to amendments taking effect before that date.".

[1.27]
27　Registrar's notice to comply in case of failure with respect to amended articles
(1)　If it appears to the registrar that a company has failed to comply with any enactment requiring it—
  (a)　to send to the registrar a document making or evidencing an alteration in the company's articles, or
  (b)　to send to the registrar a copy of the company's articles as amended,
the registrar may give notice to the company requiring it to comply.
(2)　The notice must—
  (a)　state the date on which it is issued, and
  (b)　require the company to comply within 28 days from that date.
(3)　If the company complies with the notice within the specified time, no criminal proceedings may be brought in respect of the failure to comply with the enactment mentioned in subsection (1).
(4)　If the company does not comply with the notice within the specified time, it is liable to a civil penalty of £200.
  This is in addition to any liability to criminal proceedings in respect of the failure mentioned in subsection (1).
(5)　The penalty may be recovered by the registrar and is to be paid into the Consolidated Fund.

NOTES
Commencement: 1 October 2009.

Supplementary

[1.28]
28　Existing companies: provisions of memorandum treated as provisions of articles
(1)　Provisions that immediately before the commencement of this Part were contained in a company's memorandum but are not provisions of the kind mentioned in section 8 (provisions of new-style memorandum) are to be treated after the commencement of this Part as provisions of the company's articles.
(2)　This applies not only to substantive provisions but also to provision for entrenchment (as defined in section 22).
(3)　The provisions of this Part about provision for entrenchment apply to such provision as they apply to provision made on the company's formation, except that the duty under section 23(1)(a) to give notice to the registrar does not apply.

NOTES
Commencement: 1 October 2009.
Commencement (transitional provisions): Sch 2, paras 7–10 to the Companies Act 2006 (Commencement No 8, Transitional Provisions and Savings) Order 2008, SI 2008/2860 (at **[2.91]**) provide as follows—

"Provisions of memorandum treated as provisions of articles (s 28)
7.—(1)　Section 28 of the Companies Act 2006 (existing companies: provisions of memorandum treated as provisions of articles) applies not only to an existing company but also to a transitional company.
(2)　In its application to a transitional company the reference to provisions that were contained in the company's memorandum immediately before the commencement of Part 3 shall be read as a reference to provisions that are contained in the company's memorandum on its registration or re-registration (as the case may be).
(3)　Subject to sub-paragraphs (1) and (2), in subsection (1) of that section—
  (a)　"before the commencement of this Part" means before 1st October 2009, and
  (b)　"after the commencement of this Part" means on or after that date.
8.　Nothing in section 28 of the Companies Act 2006 requires a company to give notice to the registrar of an alteration of its articles.
9.—(1)　A company whose articles are deemed by virtue of section 28 of the Companies Act 2006 to contain provisions formerly in its memorandum may comply with any obligation to send a person a copy of its articles—
  (a)　by appending to a copy of the other provisions of the articles a copy of the provisions of its old-style memorandum that are deemed to be provisions of the articles, or
  (b)　by sending together with a copy of the other provisions of the articles a copy of its old-style memorandum indicating the provisions that are deemed to be provisions of the articles.
(2)　References in sub-paragraph (1) to a company's "old-style memorandum" are—
  (a)　in the case of an existing company, to its memorandum of association as it stood immediately before 1st October 2009;
  (b)　in the case of a transitional company, to its memorandum of association as it stood on its registration or re-registration (as the case may be) apart from the operation of section 28.
10.　Nothing in the Companies Act 2006 shall be read as enabling a company to amend or omit provisions of its articles that were formerly in its memorandum so as to change its status as a limited or unlimited company otherwise than in accordance with the relevant provisions of Part 7 of that Act (re-registration as a means of changing company's status).".

Transitional provisions: for transitional provisions where, in the case of an existing or transitional company, the company's articles are deemed to contain a statement of its name by virtue of this section, and the company changes its name (by any means) on or after 1 October 2009, see the Companies Act 2006 (Consequential Amendments, Transitional Provisions and Savings) Order 2009, SI 2009/1941, art 5 (at **[4.532]**).

See also SI 2008/2860, Sch 2, para 110 which provides that where an application is made under s 5 of the 1985 Act or Art 16 of the 1986 Order (application to court for cancellation of alteration) and on or after 1 October 2009 (a) the alteration is confirmed (either wholly or in part) by the court, or (b) the court by order alters the company's memorandum under s 5(5) or Art 16(5) (alteration in consequence of provision for purchase by company of shares of members of the company), the alteration has effect, in accordance with this section as an alteration of the company's articles of association.

CHAPTER 3
RESOLUTIONS AND AGREEMENTS AFFECTING A COMPANY'S CONSTITUTION

[1.29]
29 Resolutions and agreements affecting a company's constitution
(1) This Chapter applies to—
   (a) any special resolution;
   (b) any resolution or agreement agreed to by all the members of a company that, if not so agreed to, would not have been effective for its purpose unless passed as a special resolution;
   (c) any resolution or agreement agreed to by all the members of a class of shareholders that, if not so agreed to, would not have been effective for its purpose unless passed by some particular majority or otherwise in some particular manner;
   (d) any resolution or agreement that effectively binds all members of a class of shareholders though not agreed to by all those members;
   (e) any other resolution or agreement to which this Chapter applies by virtue of any enactment.
(2) References in subsection (1) to a member of a company, or of a class of members of a company, do not include the company itself where it is such a member by virtue only of its holding shares as treasury shares.

NOTES
Commencement: 1 October 2007.
Commencement (transitional provisions): Sch 3, para 1 to the Companies Act 2006 (Commencement No 3, Consequential Amendments, Transitional Provisions and Savings) Order 2007, SI 2007/2194 (at **[2.45]**) provides as follows—

> "**1 Resolutions and agreements affecting a company's constitution (ss 29 and 30)**
> (1) Sections 29 and 30 of the Companies Act 2006 (resolutions and agreements affecting a company's constitution) apply to resolutions passed and agreements made on or after 1st October 2007.
> (2) The provisions of section 380(1) and (5) of the 1985 Act or Article 388(1) and (5) of the 1986 Order continue to apply in relation to resolutions passed and agreements made, but not forwarded to the registrar, before that date.
>   This does not affect the operation of section 1297 of the Companies Act 2006 (continuity of the law) in relation to things done under those provisions.".

[1.30]
30 Copies of resolutions or agreements to be forwarded to registrar
(1) A copy of every resolution or agreement to which this Chapter applies, or (in the case of a resolution or agreement that is not in writing) a written memorandum setting out its terms, must be forwarded to the registrar within 15 days after it is passed or made.
(2) If a company fails to comply with this section, an offence is committed by—
   (a) the company, and
   (b) every officer of it who is in default.
(3) A person guilty of an offence under this section is liable on summary conviction to a fine not exceeding level 3 on the standard scale and, for continued contravention, a daily default fine not exceeding one-tenth of level 3 on the standard scale.
(4) For the purposes of this section, a liquidator of the company is treated as an officer of it.

NOTES
Commencement: 1 October 2007
Commencement (transitional provisions): see the note to s 29 at **[1.29]**.

CHAPTER 4
MISCELLANEOUS AND SUPPLEMENTARY PROVISIONS
Statement of company's objects
[1.31]
31 Statement of company's objects
(1) Unless a company's articles specifically restrict the objects of the company, its objects are unrestricted.
(2) Where a company amends its articles so as to add, remove or alter a statement of the company's objects—
   (a) it must give notice to the registrar,
   (b) on receipt of the notice, the registrar shall register it, and
   (c) the amendment is not effective until entry of that notice on the register.
(3) Any such amendment does not affect any rights or obligations of the company or render defective any legal proceedings by or against it.

(4)   In the case of a company that is a charity, the provisions of this section have effect subject to—

    (a)   in England and Wales, section 64 of the Charities Act 1993 (c 10);

    (b)   in Northern Ireland, Article 9 of the Charities (Northern Ireland) Order 1987 (SI 1987/2048 (NI 19)).

(5)   In the case of a company that is entered in the Scottish Charity Register, the provisions of this section have effect subject to the provisions of the Charities and Trustee Investment (Scotland) Act 2005 (asp 10).

NOTES

Commencement: 1 October 2009.

Other provisions with respect to a company's constitution

[1.32]

32   Constitutional documents to be provided to members

(1)   A company must, on request by any member, send to him the following documents—

    (a)   an up-to-date copy of the company's articles;

    (b)   a copy of any resolution or agreement relating to the company to which Chapter 3 applies (resolutions and agreements affecting a company's constitution) and that is for the time being in force;

    (c)   a copy of any document required to be sent to the registrar under—

        (i)   section 34(2) (notice where company's constitution altered by enactment), or

        (ii)   section 35(2)(a) (notice where order of court or other authority alters company's constitution);

    (d)   a copy of any court order under section 899 (order sanctioning compromise or arrangement) or section 900 (order facilitating reconstruction or amalgamation);

    (e)   a copy of any court order under section 996 (protection of members against unfair prejudice: powers of the court) that alters the company's constitution;

    (f)   a copy of the company's current certificate of incorporation, and of any past certificates of incorporation;

    (g)   in the case of a company with a share capital, a current statement of capital;

    (h)   in the case of a company limited by guarantee, a copy of the statement of guarantee.

(2)   The statement of capital required by subsection (1)(g) is a statement of—

    (a)   the total number of shares of the company,

    (b)   the aggregate nominal value of those shares,

    (c)   for each class of shares—

        (i)   prescribed particulars of the rights attached to the shares,

        (ii)   the total number of shares of that class, and

        (iii)   the aggregate nominal value of shares of that class, and

    (d)   the amount paid up and the amount (if any) unpaid on each share (whether on account of the nominal value of the share or by way of premium).

(3)   If a company makes default in complying with this section, an offence is committed by every officer of the company who is in default.

(4)   A person guilty of an offence under this section is liable on summary conviction to a fine not exceeding level 3 on the standard scale.

NOTES

Commencement: 20 January 2007 (for the purpose of enabling the exercise of powers to make Orders or Regulations by statutory instrument); 1 October 2009 (otherwise).

Commencement (transitional provisions): Sch 2, para 11 to the Companies Act 2006 (Commencement No 8, Transitional Provisions and Savings) Order 2008, SI 2008/2860 (at **[2.91]**) provides as follows—

"Constitutional documents to be provided to members (s 32)

11.—(1)   Section 32 of the Companies Act 2006 (constitutional documents to be provided to members) applies where the request is received by the company on or after 1st October 2009.

(2)   Section 19 of the 1985 Act or Article 30 of the 1986 Order continues to apply where the request was received by the company before that date.".

Orders: the Companies (Shares and Share Capital) Order 2009, SI 2009/388 at **[4.364]**.

[1.33]

33   Effect of company's constitution

(1)   The provisions of a company's constitution bind the company and its members to the same extent as if there were covenants on the part of the company and of each member to observe those provisions.

(2)   Money payable by a member to the company under its constitution is a debt due from him to the company.

In England and Wales and Northern Ireland it is of the nature of an ordinary contract debt.

NOTES

Commencement: 1 October 2009.

Saving for provisions relating to nature of liability of member or contributory: the Companies Act 2006 (Consequential Amendments, Transitional Provisions and Savings) Order 2009, SI 2009/1941, art 11 (at **[4.538]**) provides that the new provisions as to the nature of a member's or contributory's liability (ie, sub-s (2) above and, in England and Wales, s 80 of the Insolvency Act 1986 as amended by that Order) apply to liabilities arising on or after 1 October 2009, and the old provisions (ie, CA 1985, s 14(2) and s 80 of the 1986 Act as it had effect prior to that amendment) continue to apply to liabilities arising before that date. Note also that for the purposes of art 11, a liability is treated as arising when the limitation period starts to run for the purposes of the Limitation Act 1980.

Contractual rights of third parties: the Contracts (Rights of Third Parties) Act 1999, s 1, confers no rights on a third party in the case of any contract binding on a company and its members under this section; see s 6(2) of the 1999 Act (as amended).

[1.34]
34 Notice to registrar where company's constitution altered by enactment

(1) This section applies where a company's constitution is altered by an enactment, other than an enactment amending the general law.

(2) The company must give notice of the alteration to the registrar, specifying the enactment, not later than 15 days after the enactment comes into force.

In the case of a special enactment the notice must be accompanied by a copy of the enactment.

(3) If the enactment amends—

(a) the company's articles, or

(b) a resolution or agreement to which Chapter 3 applies (resolutions and agreements affecting a company's constitution),

the notice must be accompanied by a copy of the company's articles, or the resolution or agreement in question, as amended.

(4) A "special enactment" means an enactment that is not a public general enactment, and includes—

(a) an Act for confirming a provisional order,

(b) any provision of a public general Act in relation to the passing of which any of the standing orders of the House of Lords or the House of Commons relating to Private Business applied, or

(c) any enactment to the extent that it is incorporated in or applied for the purposes of a special enactment.

(5) If a company fails to comply with this section an offence is committed by—

(a) the company, and

(b) every officer of the company who is in default.

(6) A person guilty of an offence under this section is liable on summary conviction to a fine not exceeding level 3 on the standard scale and, for continued contravention, a daily default fine not exceeding one-tenth of level 3 on the standard scale.

NOTES

Commencement: 1 October 2009.

Commencement (transitional provisions): Sch 2, para 12 to the Companies Act 2006 (Commencement No 8, Transitional Provisions and Savings) Order 2008, SI 2008/2860 (at **[2.91]**) provides as follows—

"Notice to registrar where company's constitution altered by enactment (s 34)

12.—(1) Section 34 of the Companies Act 2006 (notice to registrar where company's constitution altered by enactment) applies where the enactment in question comes into force on or after 1st October 2009.

(2) Section 18(1) and (3) of the 1985 Act or Article 29(1) and (3) of the 1986 Order continue to apply in relation to alterations made by statutory provisions coming into force before that date.".

[1.35]
35 Notice to registrar where company's constitution altered by order

(1) Where a company's constitution is altered by an order of a court or other authority, the company must give notice to the registrar of the alteration not later than 15 days after the alteration takes effect.

(2) The notice must be accompanied by—

(a) a copy of the order, and

(b) if the order amends—

(i) the company's articles, or

(ii) a resolution or agreement to which Chapter 3 applies (resolutions and agreements affecting the company's constitution),

a copy of the company's articles, or the resolution or agreement in question, as amended.

(3) If a company fails to comply with this section an offence is committed by—

(a) the company, and

(b) every officer of the company who is in default.

(4) A person guilty of an offence under this section is liable on summary conviction to a fine not exceeding level 3 on the standard scale and, for continued contravention, a daily default fine not exceeding one-tenth of level 3 on the standard scale.

(5) This section does not apply where provision is made by another enactment for the delivery to the registrar of a copy of the order in question.

NOTES

Commencement: 1 October 2009.

Commencement (transitional provisions): Sch 2, para 13 to the Companies Act 2006 (Commencement No 8, Transitional Provisions and Savings) Order 2008, SI 2008/2860 (at **[2.91]**) provides as follows—

"Notice to registrar where company's constitution altered by order (s 35)

13. Section 35 of the Companies Act 2006 (notice to registrar where company's constitution altered by order) applies in relation to orders made on or after 1st October 2009.".

[1.36]

36   Documents to be incorporated in or accompany copies of articles issued by company

(1)   Every copy of a company's articles issued by the company must be accompanied by—

    (a)   a copy of any resolution or agreement relating to the company to which Chapter 3 applies (resolutions and agreements affecting a company's constitution),

    (b)   where the company has been required to give notice to the registrar under section 34(2) (notice where company's constitution altered by enactment), a statement that the enactment in question alters the effect of the company's constitution,

    (c)   where the company's constitution is altered by a special enactment (see section 34(4)), a copy of the enactment, and

    (d)   a copy of any order required to be sent to the registrar under section 35(2)(a) (order of court or other authority altering company's constitution).

(2)   This does not require the articles to be accompanied by a copy of a document or by a statement if—

    (a)   the effect of the resolution, agreement, enactment or order (as the case may be) on the company's constitution has been incorporated into the articles by amendment, or

    (b)   the resolution, agreement, enactment or order (as the case may be) is not for the time being in force.

(3)   If the company fails to comply with this section, an offence is committed by every officer of the company who is in default.

(4)   A person guilty of an offence under this section is liable on summary conviction to a fine not exceeding level 3 on the standard scale for each occasion on which copies are issued, or, as the case may be, requested.

(5)   For the purposes of this section, a liquidator of the company is treated as an officer of it.

NOTES

Commencement: 1 October 2009.

Commencement (transitional provisions): Sch 2, para 14 to the Companies Act 2006 (Commencement No 8, Transitional Provisions and Savings) Order 2008, SI 2008/2860 (at **[2.91]**) provides as follows—

"Documents to be incorporated in or accompany copies of articles issued by company (s 36)

14.—(1)   Section 36 of the Companies Act 2006 (documents to be incorporated in or accompany copies of articles issued by company) applies to copies of a company's articles issued on or after 1st October 2009.

(2)   Section 380(2), (6) and (7) of the 1985 Act or Article 388(2), (6) and (7) of the 1986 Order continue to apply to copies issued before that date.".

Supplementary provisions

[1.37]

37   Right to participate in profits otherwise than as member void

In the case of a company limited by guarantee and not having a share capital any provision in the company's articles, or in any resolution of the company, purporting to give a person a right to participate in the divisible profits of the company otherwise than as a member is void.

NOTES

Commencement: 1 October 2009.

[1.38]

38   Application to single member companies of enactments and rules of law

Any enactment or rule of law applicable to companies formed by two or more persons or having two or more members applies with any necessary modification in relation to a company formed by one person or having only one person as a member.

NOTES

Commencement: 1 October 2009.

PART 4
A COMPANY'S CAPACITY AND RELATED MATTERS

Capacity of company and power of directors to bind it

[1.39]

39   A company's capacity

(1)   The validity of an act done by a company shall not be called into question on the ground of lack of capacity by reason of anything in the company's constitution.

(2)   This section has effect subject to section 42 (companies that are charities).

NOTES

Commencement: 1 October 2009.

Commencement (transitional provisions): Sch 2, para 15 to the Companies Act 2006 (Commencement No 8, Transitional Provisions and Savings) Order 2008, SI 2008/2860 (at **[2.91]**) provides as follows—

"A company's capacity (s 39)

15.—(1)   Section 39 of the Companies Act 2006 (a company's capacity) applies to acts of a company done on or after 1st October 2009.

(2)   Section 35 of the 1985 Act or Article 45 of the 1986 Order continues to apply to acts of a company done before that date.".

[1.40]

40   Power of directors to bind the company

(1)   In favour of a person dealing with a company in good faith, the power of the directors to bind the company, or authorise others to do so, is deemed to be free of any limitation under the company's constitution.

(2)   For this purpose—

   (a)   a person "deals with" a company if he is a party to any transaction or other act to which the company is a party,

   (b)   a person dealing with a company—

      (i)   is not bound to enquire as to any limitation on the powers of the directors to bind the company or authorise others to do so,

      (ii)   is presumed to have acted in good faith unless the contrary is proved, and

      (iii)   is not to be regarded as acting in bad faith by reason only of his knowing that an act is beyond the powers of the directors under the company's constitution.

(3)   The references above to limitations on the directors' powers under the company's constitution include limitations deriving—

   (a)   from a resolution of the company or of any class of shareholders, or

   (b)   from any agreement between the members of the company or of any class of shareholders.

(4)   This section does not affect any right of a member of the company to bring proceedings to restrain the doing of an action that is beyond the powers of the directors.

But no such proceedings lie in respect of an act to be done in fulfilment of a legal obligation arising from a previous act of the company.

(5)   This section does not affect any liability incurred by the directors, or any other person, by reason of the directors' exceeding their powers.

(6)   This section has effect subject to—

   section 41 (transactions with directors or their associates), and

   section 42 (companies that are charities).

NOTES

Commencement: 1 October 2009.

[1.41]

41   Constitutional limitations: transactions involving directors or their associates

(1)   This section applies to a transaction if or to the extent that its validity depends on section 40 (power of directors deemed to be free of limitations under company's constitution in favour of person dealing with company in good faith).

Nothing in this section shall be read as excluding the operation of any other enactment or rule of law by virtue of which the transaction may be called in question or any liability to the company may arise.

(2)   Where—

   (a)   a company enters into such a transaction, and

   (b)   the parties to the transaction include—

      (i)   a director of the company or of its holding company, or

      (ii)   a person connected with any such director,

the transaction is voidable at the instance of the company.

(3)   Whether or not it is avoided, any such party to the transaction as is mentioned in subsection (2)(b)(i) or (ii), and any director of the company who authorised the transaction, is liable—

Part 1   The Companies Act 2006

(a)   to account to the company for any gain he has made directly or indirectly by the transaction, and

(b)   to indemnify the company for any loss or damage resulting from the transaction.

(4)   The transaction ceases to be voidable if—

(a)   restitution of any money or other asset which was the subject matter of the transaction is no longer possible, or

(b)   the company is indemnified for any loss or damage resulting from the transaction, or

(c)   rights acquired bona fide for value and without actual notice of the directors' exceeding their powers by a person who is not party to the transaction would be affected by the avoidance, or

(d)   the transaction is affirmed by the company.

(5)   A person other than a director of the company is not liable under subsection (3) if he shows that at the time the transaction was entered into he did not know that the directors were exceeding their powers.

(6)   Nothing in the preceding provisions of this section affects the rights of any party to the transaction not within subsection (2)(b)(i) or (ii).

But the court may, on the application of the company or any such party, make an order affirming, severing or setting aside the transaction on such terms as appear to the court to be just.

(7)   In this section—

(a)   "transaction" includes any act; and

(b)   the reference to a person connected with a director has the same meaning as in Part 10 (company directors).

NOTES

Commencement: 1 October 2009.

[1.42]

42   Constitutional limitations: companies that are charities

(1)   Sections 39 and 40 (company's capacity and power of directors to bind company) do not apply to the acts of a company that is a charity except in favour of a person who—

(a)   does not know at the time the act is done that the company is a charity, or

(b)   gives full consideration in money or money's worth in relation to the act in question and does not know (as the case may be)—

(i)   that the act is not permitted by the company's constitution, or

(ii)   that the act is beyond the powers of the directors.

(2)   Where a company that is a charity purports to transfer or grant an interest in property, the fact that (as the case may be)—

(a)   the act was not permitted by the company's constitution, or

(b)   the directors in connection with the act exceeded any limitation on their powers under the company's constitution,

does not affect the title of a person who subsequently acquires the property or any interest in it for full consideration without actual notice of any such circumstances affecting the validity of the company's act.

(3)   In any proceedings arising out of subsection (1) or (2) the burden of proving—

(a)   that a person knew that the company was a charity, or

(b)   that a person knew that an act was not permitted by the company's constitution or was beyond the powers of the directors,

lies on the person asserting that fact.

(4)   In the case of a company that is a charity the affirmation of a transaction to which section 41 applies (transactions with directors or their associates) is ineffective without the prior written consent of—

(a)   in England and Wales, the Charity Commission;

(b)   in Northern Ireland, the Department for Social Development.

(5)   This section does not extend to Scotland (but see section 112 of the Companies Act 1989 (c 40)).

NOTES

Commencement: 1 October 2009.

Transitional provisions: the Companies Act 2006 (Consequential Amendments, Transitional Provisions and Savings) Order 2009, SI 2009/1941, art 6 (at **[4.533]**) provides as follows—

"**6   Companies that are charities: requirement of consent for affirmation of certain transactions**

(1)   Section 42(4) of the Companies Act 2006 (companies that are charities: requirement of consent for affirmation of certain transactions with directors or their associates) applies where the request for consent is received on or after 1st October 2009.

(2)   Any request for consent under section 65(4) of the Charities Act 1993 or Article 9A(4) of the Charities (Northern Ireland) Order 1987 received but not determined before that date is treated as if made under section 42(4) of the Companies Act 2006.

(3)   In relation to a decision under section 65(4) of the Charities Act 1993 made before 1st October 2009 the provisions of that Act as to appeals continue to have effect without the amendments made by this Order.".

Formalities of doing business under the law of England and Wales or Northern Ireland

[1.43]

43   Company contracts

(1)   Under the law of England and Wales or Northern Ireland a contract may be made—

   (a)   by a company, by writing under its common seal, or

   (b)   on behalf of a company, by a person acting under its authority, express or implied.

(2)   Any formalities required by law in the case of a contract made by an individual also apply, unless a contrary intention appears, to a contract made by or on behalf of a company.

NOTES

Commencement: 1 October 2009.

[1.44]

44   Execution of documents

(1)   Under the law of England and Wales or Northern Ireland a document is executed by a company—

   (a)   by the affixing of its common seal, or

   (b)   by signature in accordance with the following provisions.

(2)   A document is validly executed by a company if it is signed on behalf of the company—

   (a)   by two authorised signatories, or

   (b)   by a director of the company in the presence of a witness who attests the signature.

(3)   The following are "authorised signatories" for the purposes of subsection (2)—

   (a)   every director of the company, and

   (b)   in the case of a private company with a secretary or a public company, the secretary (or any joint secretary) of the company.

(4)   A document signed in accordance with subsection (2) and expressed, in whatever words, to be executed by the company has the same effect as if executed under the common seal of the company.

(5)   In favour of a purchaser a document is deemed to have been duly executed by a company if it purports to be signed in accordance with subsection (2).

A "purchaser" means a purchaser in good faith for valuable consideration and includes a lessee, mortgagee or other person who for valuable consideration acquires an interest in property.

(6)   Where a document is to be signed by a person on behalf of more than one company, it is not duly signed by that person for the purposes of this section unless he signs it separately in each capacity.

(7)   References in this section to a document being (or purporting to be) signed by a director or secretary are to be read, in a case where that office is held by a firm, as references to its being (or purporting to be) signed by an individual authorised by the firm to sign on its behalf.

(8)   This section applies to a document that is (or purports to be) executed by a company in the name of or on behalf of another person whether or not that person is also a company.

NOTES

Commencement: 6 April 2008.

Commencement (transitional provisions): Sch 4, Pt 1, para 1 to the Companies Act 2006 (Commencement No 5, Transitional Provisions and Savings) Order 2007, SI 2007/3495 (at **[2.66]**) provides as follows—

"Execution of documents (s 44)

1.—(1)   Section 44 of the Companies Act 2006 (execution of documents) applies in relation to the execution of documents on or after 6th April 2008.

(2)   Section 36A of the 1985 Act or Article 46A of the 1986 Order continues to apply in relation to documents executed before that date.

(3)   For the purposes of this paragraph a document signed by one authorised signatory before 6th April 2008 and by another on or after that date is treated as executed on or after 6th April 2008.".

[1.45]

45   Common seal

(1)   A company may have a common seal, but need not have one.

(2)   A company which has a common seal shall have its name engraved in legible characters on the seal.

(3)   If a company fails to comply with subsection (2) an offence is committed by—

   (a)   the company, and

   (b)   every officer of the company who is in default.

(4)   An officer of a company, or a person acting on behalf of a company, commits an offence if he uses, or authorises the use of, a seal purporting to be a seal of the company on which its name is not engraved as required by subsection (2).

(5)   A person guilty of an offence under this section is liable on summary conviction to a fine not exceeding level 3 on the standard scale.

(6)   This section does not form part of the law of Scotland.

NOTES

Commencement: 1 October 2009.

[1.46]
46   Execution of deeds
(1)   A document is validly executed by a company as a deed for the purposes of section 1(2)(b) of the Law of Property (Miscellaneous Provisions) Act 1989 (c 34) and for the purposes of the law of Northern Ireland if, and only if—
  (a)   it is duly executed by the company, and
  (b)   it is delivered as a deed.
(2)   For the purposes of subsection (1)(b) a document is presumed to be delivered upon its being executed, unless a contrary intention is proved.

NOTES
  Commencement: 1 October 2009.

[1.47]
47   Execution of deeds or other documents by attorney
(1)   Under the law of England and Wales or Northern Ireland a company may, by instrument executed as a deed, empower a person, either generally or in respect of specified matters, as its attorney to execute deeds or other documents on its behalf.
(2)   A deed or other document so executed, whether in the United Kingdom or elsewhere, has effect as if executed by the company.

NOTES
  Commencement: 1 October 2009.
  Commencement (transitional provisions): Sch 2, para 16 to the Companies Act 2006 (Commencement No 8, Transitional Provisions and Savings) Order 2008, SI 2008/2860 (at **[2.91]**) provides as follows—

  "Execution of deeds or other documents by attorney (s 47)
  16.—(1)   Section 47 of the Companies Act 2006 (execution of deeds or other documents by attorney) applies where the instrument empowering a person to act as a company's attorney is executed on or after 1st October 2009.
  (2)   Section 38 of the 1985 Act or Article 48 of the 1986 Order continues to have effect where the power to act as a company's attorney was conferred before that date (including in relation to instruments executed by the attorney on behalf of the company on or after that date).".

Formalities of doing business under the law of Scotland

[1.48]
48   Execution of documents by companies
(1)   The following provisions form part of the law of Scotland only.
(2)   Notwithstanding the provisions of any enactment, a company need not have a company seal.
(3)   For the purposes of any enactment—
  (a)   providing for a document to be executed by a company by affixing its common seal, or
  (b)   referring (in whatever terms) to a document so executed,
a document signed or subscribed by or on behalf of the company in accordance with the provisions of the Requirements of Writing (Scotland) Act 1995 (c 7) has effect as if so executed.

NOTES
  Commencement: 1 October 2009.

Other matters

[1.49]
49   Official seal for use abroad
(1)   A company that has a common seal may have an official seal for use outside the United Kingdom.
(2)   The official seal must be a facsimile of the company's common seal, with the addition on its face of the place or places where it is to be used.
(3)   The official seal when duly affixed to a document has the same effect as the company's common seal.
  This subsection does not extend to Scotland.
(4)   A company having an official seal for use outside the United Kingdom may—
  (a)   by writing under its common seal, or
  (b)   as respects Scotland, by writing subscribed in accordance with the Requirements of Writing (Scotland) Act 1995,
authorise any person appointed for the purpose to affix the official seal to any deed or other document to which the company is party.
(5)   As between the company and a person dealing with such an agent, the agent's authority continues—
  (a)   during the period mentioned in the instrument conferring the authority, or
  (b)   if no period is mentioned, until notice of the revocation or termination of the agent's authority has been given to the person dealing with him.
(6)   The person affixing the official seal must certify in writing on the deed or other document to which the seal is affixed the date on which, and place at which, it is affixed.

NOTES
Commencement: 1 October 2009.

[1.50]
50 Official seal for share certificates etc
(1)   A company that has a common seal may have an official seal for use—
  (a)   for sealing securities issued by the company, or
  (b)   for sealing documents creating or evidencing securities so issued.
(2)   The official seal—
  (a)   must be a facsimile of the company's common seal, with the addition on its face of the word "Securities", and
  (b)   when duly affixed to the document has the same effect as the company's common seal.

NOTES
Commencement: 1 October 2009.

[1.51]
51 Pre-incorporation contracts, deeds and obligations
(1)   A contract that purports to be made by or on behalf of a company at a time when the company has not been formed has effect, subject to any agreement to the contrary, as one made with the person purporting to act for the company or as agent for it, and he is personally liable on the contract accordingly.
(2)   Subsection (1) applies—
  (a)   to the making of a deed under the law of England and Wales or Northern Ireland, and
  (b)   to the undertaking of an obligation under the law of Scotland,
as it applies to the making of a contract.

NOTES
Commencement: 1 October 2009.

[1.52]
52 Bills of exchange and promissory notes
A bill of exchange or promissory note is deemed to have been made, accepted or endorsed on behalf of a company if made, accepted or endorsed in the name of, or by or on behalf or on account of, the company by a person acting under its authority.

NOTES
Commencement: 1 October 2009.

PART 5
A COMPANY'S NAME

CHAPTER 1
GENERAL REQUIREMENTS

Prohibited names

[1.53]
53 Prohibited names
A company must not be registered under this Act by a name if, in the opinion of the Secretary of State—
  (a)   its use by the company would constitute an offence, or
  (b)   it is offensive.

NOTES
Commencement: 1 October 2009.

Sensitive words and expressions

[1.54]
54 Names suggesting connection with government or public authority
(1)   The approval of the Secretary of State is required for a company to be registered under this Act by a name that would be likely to give the impression that the company is connected with—
  (a)   Her Majesty's Government, any part of the Scottish administration[, the Welsh Assembly Government] or Her Majesty's Government in Northern Ireland,
  (b)   a local authority, or
  (c)   any public authority specified for the purposes of this section by regulations made by the Secretary of State.
(2)   For the purposes of this section—
  "local authority" means—

    (a)   a local authority within the meaning of the Local Government Act 1972 (c 70), the Common Council of the City of London or the Council of the Isles of Scilly,

    (b)   a council constituted under section 2 of the Local Government etc (Scotland) Act 1994 (c 39), or

    (c)   a district council in Northern Ireland;

"public authority" includes any person or body having functions of a public nature.

(3)   Regulations under this section are subject to affirmative resolution procedure.

NOTES

Commencement: 20 January 2007 (for the purpose of enabling the exercise of powers to make Orders or Regulations by statutory instrument); 1 October 2009 (otherwise).

Commencement (transitional provisions): Sch 2, paras 17, 18 to the Companies Act 2006 (Commencement No 8, Transitional Provisions and Savings) Order 2008, SI 2008/2860 (at **[2.91]**) provide as follows—

"A company's name (ss 53 to 81)

17.—(1)   The following provisions of the Companies Act 2006 do not affect the continued registration of a company by a name by which it was duly registered—

    (a)   in the case of an existing company, immediately before 1st October 2009, or

    (b)   in the case of a transitional company, on its registration or re-registration (as the case may be).

(2)   The provisions are—

    (a)   section 54 (name suggesting connection with government or public authority);

    (b)   section 55 (other sensitive words or expressions);

    (c)   section 57 (permitted characters etc);

    (d)   section 65 (inappropriate use of indications of company type or legal form);

    (e)   section 66 (name not to be the same as another in registrar's index).

18.—(1)   Sections 54 to 56 of the Companies Act 2006 (sensitive words and expressions) apply to applications for approval received by the Secretary of State on or after 1st October 2009.

(2)   Section 29 of the 1985 Act or Article 39 of the 1986 Order continues to apply in relation to applications received by the Secretary of State or the Department of Enterprise, Trade and Investment in Northern Ireland before that date."

Sub-s (1): words in square brackets inserted by the Government of Wales Act 2006 (Consequential Modifications, Transitional Provisions and Saving) Order 2009, SI 2009/2958, arts 8, 9, as from 6 November 2009.

Regulations: the Company, Limited Liability Partnership and Business Names (Public Authorities) Regulations 2009, SI 2009/2982 at **[4.641]**.

[1.55]

55   Other sensitive words or expressions

(1)   The approval of the Secretary of State is required for a company to be registered under this Act by a name that includes a word or expression for the time being specified in regulations made by the Secretary of State under this section.

(2)   Regulations under this section are subject to approval after being made.

NOTES

Commencement: 20 January 2007 (for the purpose of enabling the exercise of powers to make Orders or Regulations by statutory instrument); 1 October 2009 (otherwise).

Commencement (transitional provisions): see the note to s 54 at **[1.54]**.

Chamber of commerce: by the Company and Business Names (Chamber of Commerce, etc) Act 1999, s 1 (as amended), the Secretary of State is required to include the title "chamber of commerce" (and its Welsh equivalent) in the list of controlled titles maintained in accordance with regulations made under this section.

Regulations: the Company, Limited Liability Partnership and Business Names (Sensitive Words and Expressions) Regulations 2009, SI 2009/2615 at **[4.630]**.

[1.56]

56   Duty to seek comments of government department or other specified body

(1)   The Secretary of State may by regulations under—

    (a)   section 54 (name suggesting connection with government or public authority), or

    (b)   section 55 (other sensitive words or expressions),

require that, in connection with an application for the approval of the Secretary of State under that section, the applicant must seek the view of a specified Government department or other body.

(2)   Where such a requirement applies, the applicant must request the specified department or other body (in writing) to indicate whether (and if so why) it has any objections to the proposed name.

(3)   Where a request under this section is made in connection with an application for the registration of a company under this Act, the application must—

    (a)   include a statement that a request under this section has been made, and

    (b)   be accompanied by a copy of any response received.

(4)   Where a request under this section is made in connection with a change in a company's name, the notice of the change sent to the registrar must be accompanied by—

    (a)   a statement by a director or secretary of the company that a request under this section has been made, and

    (b)   a copy of any response received.

(5)   In this section "specified" means specified in the regulations.

NOTES

Commencement: 20 January 2007 (for the purpose of enabling the exercise of powers to make Orders or Regulations by statutory instrument); 1 October 2009 (otherwise).

Commencement (transitional provisions): see the note to s 54 at **[1.54]**.

Regulations: the Company, Limited Liability Partnership and Business Names (Sensitive Words and Expressions) Regulations 2009, SI 2009/2615 at **[4.630]**; the Company, Limited Liability Partnership and Business Names (Public Authorities) Regulations 2009, SI 2009/2982 at **[4.641]**.

Permitted characters etc

[1.57]

57   Permitted characters etc

(1)   The Secretary of State may make provision by regulations—

    (a)   as to the letters or other characters, signs or symbols (including accents and other diacritical marks) and punctuation that may be used in the name of a company registered under this Act; and

    (b)   specifying a standard style or format for the name of a company for the purposes of registration.

(2)   The regulations may prohibit the use of specified characters, signs or symbols when appearing in a specified position (in particular, at the beginning of a name).

(3)   A company may not be registered under this Act by a name that consists of or includes anything that is not permitted in accordance with regulations under this section.

(4)   Regulations under this section are subject to negative resolution procedure.

(5)   In this section "specified" means specified in the regulations.

NOTES

Commencement: 20 January 2007 (for the purpose of enabling the exercise of powers to make Orders or Regulations by statutory instrument); 1 October 2009 (otherwise).

Commencement (transitional provisions): see the note to s 54 at **[1.54]**.

Regulations: the Company and Business Names (Miscellaneous Provisions) Regulations 2009, SI 2009/1085 at **[4.369]**.

CHAPTER 2

INDICATIONS OF COMPANY TYPE OR LEGAL FORM

Required indications for limited companies

[1.58]

58   Public limited companies

(1)   The name of a limited company that is a public company must end with "public limited company" or "p.l.c.".

(2)   In the case of a Welsh company, its name may instead end with "cwmni cyfyngedig cyhoeddus" or "c.c.c.".

(3)   This section does not apply to community interest companies (but see section 33(3) and (4) of the Companies (Audit, Investigations and Community Enterprise) Act 2004 (c 27)).

NOTES

Commencement: 1 October 2009.

[1.59]

59   Private limited companies

(1)   The name of a limited company that is a private company must end with "limited" or "ltd.".

(2)   In the case of a Welsh company, its name may instead end with "cyfyngedig" or "cyf.".

(3)   Certain companies are exempt from this requirement (see section 60).

(4)   This section does not apply to community interest companies (but see section 33(1) and (2) of the Companies (Audit, Investigations and Community Enterprise) Act 2004).

NOTES

Commencement: 1 October 2009.

[1.60]

60   Exemption from requirement as to use of "limited"

(1)   A private company is exempt from section 59 (requirement to have name ending with "limited" or permitted alternative) if—

    (a)   it is a charity,

    (b)   it is exempted from the requirement of that section by regulations made by the Secretary of State, or

    (c)   it meets the conditions specified in—

        section 61 (continuation of existing exemption: companies limited by shares), or

        section 62 (continuation of existing exemption: companies limited by guarantee).

(2)   The registrar may refuse to register a private limited company by a name that does not include the word "limited" (or a permitted alternative) unless a statement has been delivered to him that the company meets the conditions for exemption.

(3)   The registrar may accept the statement as sufficient evidence of the matters stated in it.

(4)   Regulations under this section are subject to negative resolution procedure.

NOTES

   Commencement: 20 January 2007 (for the purpose of enabling the exercise of powers to make Orders or Regulations by statutory instrument); 1 October 2009 (otherwise).

   Regulations: the Company and Business Names (Miscellaneous Provisions) Regulations 2009, SI 2009/1085 at **[4.369]**.

[1.61]

61   Continuation of existing exemption: companies limited by shares

(1)   This section applies to a private company limited by shares—

     (a)   that on 25th February 1982—

         (i)   was registered in Great Britain, and

         (ii)   had a name that, by virtue of a licence under section 19 of the Companies Act 1948 (c 38) (or corresponding earlier legislation), did not include the word "limited" or any of the permitted alternatives, or

     (b)   that on 30th June 1983—

         (i)   was registered in Northern Ireland, and

         (ii)   had a name that, by virtue of a licence under section 19 of the Companies Act (Northern Ireland) 1960 (c 22 (NI)) (or corresponding earlier legislation), did not include the word "limited" or any of the permitted alternatives.

(2)   A company to which this section applies is exempt from section 59 (requirement to have name ending with "limited" or permitted alternative) so long as—

     (a)   it continues to meet the following two conditions, and

     (b)   it does not change its name.

(3)   The first condition is that the objects of the company are the promotion of commerce, art, science, education, religion, charity or any profession, and anything incidental or conducive to any of those objects.

(4)   The second condition is that the company's articles—

     (a)   require its income to be applied in promoting its objects,

     (b)   prohibit the payment of dividends, or any return of capital, to its members, and

     (c)   require all the assets that would otherwise be available to its members generally to be transferred on its winding up either—

         (i)   to another body with objects similar to its own, or

         (ii)   to another body the objects of which are the promotion of charity and anything incidental or conducive thereto,

     (whether or not the body is a member of the company).

NOTES

   Commencement: 1 October 2009.

[1.62]

62   Continuation of existing exemption: companies limited by guarantee

(1)   A private company limited by guarantee that immediately before the commencement of this Part—

     (a)   was exempt by virtue of section 30 of the Companies Act 1985 (c 6) or Article 40 of the Companies (Northern Ireland) Order 1986 (SI 1986/ 1032 (NI 6)) from the requirement to have a name including the word "limited" or a permitted alternative, and

     (b)   had a name that did not include the word "limited" or any of the permitted alternatives,

is exempt from section 59 (requirement to have name ending with "limited" or permitted alternative) so long as it continues to meet the following two conditions and does not change its name.

(2)   The first condition is that the objects of the company are the promotion of commerce, art, science, education, religion, charity or any profession, and anything incidental or conducive to any of those objects.

(3)   The second condition is that the company's articles—

     (a)   require its income to be applied in promoting its objects,

     (b)   prohibit the payment of dividends to its members, and

     (c)   require all the assets that would otherwise be available to its members generally to be transferred on its winding up either—

         (i)   to another body with objects similar to its own, or

         (ii)   to another body the objects of which are the promotion of charity and anything incidental or conducive thereto,

     (whether or not the body is a member of the company).

NOTES
Commencement: 1 October 2009.

[1.63]
63 Exempt company: restriction on amendment of articles
(1)   A private company—
  (a)   that is exempt under section 61 or 62 from the requirement to use "limited" (or a permitted alternative) as part of its name, and
  (b)   whose name does not include "limited" or any of the permitted alternatives,
must not amend its articles so that it ceases to comply with the conditions for exemption under that section.
(2)   If subsection (1) above is contravened an offence is committed by—
  (a)   the company, and
  (b)   every officer of the company who is in default.
  For this purpose a shadow director is treated as an officer of the company.
(3)   A person guilty of an offence under this section is liable on summary conviction to a fine not exceeding level 5 on the standard scale and, for continued contravention, a daily default fine not exceeding one-tenth of level 5 on the standard scale.
(4)   Where immediately before the commencement of this section—
  (a)   a company was exempt by virtue of section 30 of the Companies Act 1985 (c 6) or Article 40 of the Companies (Northern Ireland) Order 1986 (SI 1986/1032 (NI 6)) from the requirement to have a name including the word "limited" (or a permitted alternative), and
  (b)   the company's memorandum or articles contained provision preventing an alteration of them without the approval of—
    (i)   the Board of Trade or a Northern Ireland department (or any other department or Minister), or
    (ii)   the Charity Commission,
that provision, and any condition of any such licence as is mentioned in section 61(1)(a)(ii) or (b)(ii) requiring such provision, shall cease to have effect.
  This does not apply if, or to the extent that, the provision is required by or under any other enactment.
(5)   It is hereby declared that any such provision as is mentioned in subsection (4)(b) formerly contained in a company's memorandum was at all material times capable, with the appropriate approval, of being altered or removed under section 17 of the Companies Act 1985 or Article 28 of the Companies (Northern Ireland) Order 1986 (SI 1986/1032 (NI 6)) (or corresponding earlier enactments).

NOTES
Commencement: 1 October 2009.

[1.64]
64 Power to direct change of name in case of company ceasing to be entitled to exemption
(1)   If it appears to the Secretary of State that a company whose name does not include "limited" or any of the permitted alternatives—
  (a)   has ceased to be entitled to exemption under section 60(1)(a) or (b), or
  (b)   in the case of a company within section 61 or 62 (which impose conditions as to the objects and articles of the company)—
    (i)   has carried on any business other than the promotion of any of the objects mentioned in subsection (3) of section 61 or, as the case may be, subsection (2) of section 62, or
    (ii)   has acted inconsistently with the provision required by subsection (4)(a) or (b) of section 61 or, as the case may be, subsection (3)(a) or (b) of section 62,
the Secretary of State may direct the company to change its name so that it ends with "limited" or one of the permitted alternatives.
(2)   The direction must be in writing and must specify the period within which the company is to change its name.
(3)   A change of name in order to comply with a direction under this section may be made by resolution of the directors.
  This is without prejudice to any other method of changing the company's name.
(4)   Where a resolution of the directors is passed in accordance with subsection (3), the company must give notice to the registrar of the change.
  Sections 80 and 81 apply as regards the registration and effect of the change.
(5)   If the company fails to comply with a direction under this section an offence is committed by—
  (a)   the company, and
  (b)   every officer of the company who is in default.
(6)   A person guilty of an offence under this section is liable on summary conviction to a fine not exceeding level 5 on the standard scale and, for continued contravention, a daily default fine not exceeding one-tenth of level 5 on the standard scale.

(7) A company that has been directed to change its name under this section may not, without the approval of the Secretary of State, subsequently change its name so that it does not include "limited" or one of the permitted alternatives. This does not apply to a change of name on re-registration or on conversion to a community interest company.

NOTES

Commencement: 1 October 2009.

Inappropriate use of indications of company type or legal form

[1.65]

65   Inappropriate use of indications of company type or legal form

(1) The Secretary of State may make provision by regulations prohibiting the use in a company name of specified words, expressions or other indications —

  (a)   that are associated with a particular type of company or form of organisation, or

  (b)   that are similar to words, expressions or other indications associated with a particular type of company or form of organisation.

(2) The regulations may prohibit the use of words, expressions or other indications—

  (a)   in a specified part, or otherwise than in a specified part, of a company's name;

  (b)   in conjunction with, or otherwise than in conjunction with, such other words, expressions or indications as may be specified.

(3) A company must not be registered under this Act by a name that consists of or includes anything prohibited by regulations under this section.

(4) In this section "specified" means specified in the regulations.

(5) Regulations under this section are subject to negative resolution procedure.

NOTES

Commencement: 20 January 2007 (for the purpose of enabling the exercise of powers to make Orders or Regulations by statutory instrument); 1 October 2009 (otherwise).

Commencement (transitional provisions): see the note to s 54 at **[1.54]**.

Regulations: the Company and Business Names (Miscellaneous Provisions) Regulations 2009, SI 2009/1085 at **[4.369]**; the Company, Limited Liability Partnership and Business Names (Miscellaneous Provisions) (Amendment) Regulations 2009, SI 2009/2404.

CHAPTER 3
SIMILARITY TO OTHER NAMES

Similarity to other name on registrar's index

[1.66]

66   Name not to be the same as another in the index

(1) A company must not be registered under this Act by a name that is the same as another name appearing in the registrar's index of company names.

(2) The Secretary of State may make provision by regulations supplementing this section.

(3) The regulations may make provision—

  (a)   as to matters that are to be disregarded, and

  (b)   as to words, expressions, signs or symbols that are, or are not, to be regarded as the same, for the purposes of this section.

(4) The regulations may provide—

  (a)   that registration by a name that would otherwise be prohibited under this section is permitted—

    (i)   in specified circumstances, or

    (ii)   with specified consent, and

  (b)   that if those circumstances obtain or that consent is given at the time a company is registered by a name, a subsequent change of circumstances or withdrawal of consent does not affect the registration.

(5) Regulations under this section are subject to negative resolution procedure.

(6) In this section "specified" means specified in the regulations.

NOTES

Commencement: 20 January 2007 (for the purpose of enabling the exercise of powers to make Orders or Regulations by statutory instrument); 1 October 2009 (otherwise).

Commencement (transitional provisions): see the note to s 54 at **[1.54]**.

Regulations: the Company and Business Names (Miscellaneous Provisions) Regulations 2009, SI 2009/1085 at **[4.369]**; the Company, Limited Liability Partnership and Business Names (Miscellaneous Provisions) (Amendment) Regulations 2009, SI 2009/2404.

[1.67]

67   Power to direct change of name in case of similarity to existing name

(1) The Secretary of State may direct a company to change its name if it has been registered in a name that is the same as or, in the opinion of the Secretary of State, too like—

(a)   a name appearing at the time of the registration in the registrar's index of company names, or

(b)   a name that should have appeared in that index at that time.

(2)   The Secretary of State may make provision by regulations supplementing this section.

(3)   The regulations may make provision—

(a)   as to matters that are to be disregarded, and

(b)   as to words, expressions, signs or symbols that are, or are not, to be regarded as the same, for the purposes of this section.

(4)   The regulations may provide—

(a)   that no direction is to be given under this section in respect of a name—

(i)   in specified circumstances, or

(ii)   if specified consent is given, and

(b)   that a subsequent change of circumstances or withdrawal of consent does not give rise to grounds for a direction under this section.

(5)   Regulations under this section are subject to negative resolution procedure.

(6)   In this section "specified" means specified in the regulations.

NOTES

Commencement: 20 January 2007 (for the purpose of enabling the exercise of powers to make Orders or Regulations by statutory instrument); 1 October 2009 (otherwise).

[1.68]

68   Direction to change name: supplementary provisions

(1)   The following provisions have effect in relation to a direction under section 67 (power to direct change of name in case of similarity to existing name).

(2)   Any such direction—

(a)   must be given within twelve months of the company's registration by the name in question, and

(b)   must specify the period within which the company is to change its name.

(3)   The Secretary of State may by a further direction extend that period.

Any such direction must be given before the end of the period for the time being specified.

(4)   A direction under section 67 or this section must be in writing.

(5)   If a company fails to comply with the direction, an offence is committed by—

(a)   the company, and

(b)   every officer of the company who is in default.

For this purpose a shadow director is treated as an officer of the company.

(6)   A person guilty of an offence under this section is liable on summary conviction to a fine not exceeding level 3 on the standard scale and, for continued contravention, a daily default fine not exceeding one-tenth of level 3 on the standard scale.

NOTES

Commencement: 1 October 2009.

Similarity to other name in which person has goodwill

[1.69]

69   Objection to company's registered name

(1)   A person ("the applicant") may object to a company's registered name on the ground—

(a)   that it is the same as a name associated with the applicant in which he has goodwill, or

(b)   that it is sufficiently similar to such a name that its use in the United Kingdom would be likely to mislead by suggesting a connection between the company and the applicant.

(2)   The objection must be made by application to a company names adjudicator (see section 70).

(3)   The company concerned shall be the primary respondent to the application. Any of its members or directors may be joined as respondents.

(4)   If the ground specified in subsection (1)(a) or (b) is established, it is for the respondents to show—

(a)   that the name was registered before the commencement of the activities on which the applicant relies to show goodwill; or

(b)   that the company—

(i)   is operating under the name, or

(ii)   is proposing to do so and has incurred substantial start-up costs in preparation, or

(iii) was formerly operating under the name and is now dormant; or

(c)   that the name was registered in the ordinary course of a company formation business and the company is available for sale to the applicant on the standard terms of that business; or

(d)   that the name was adopted in good faith; or

(e)   that the interests of the applicant are not adversely affected to any significant extent.

If none of those is shown, the objection shall be upheld.

(5) If the facts mentioned in subsection (4)(a), (b) or (c) are established, the objection shall nevertheless be upheld if the applicant shows that the main purpose of the respondents (or any of them) in registering the name was to obtain money (or other consideration) from the applicant or prevent him from registering the name.

(6) If the objection is not upheld under subsection (4) or (5), it shall be dismissed.

(7) In this section "goodwill" includes reputation of any description.

NOTES

Commencement: 1 October 2008.

[1.70]
70 Company names adjudicators
(1) The Secretary of State shall appoint persons to be company names adjudicators.

(2) The persons appointed must have such legal or other experience as, in the Secretary of State's opinion, makes them suitable for appointment.

(3) An adjudicator—

    (a) holds office in accordance with the terms of his appointment,

    (b) is eligible for re-appointment when his term of office ends,

    (c) may resign at any time by notice in writing given to the Secretary of State, and

    (d) may be dismissed by the Secretary of State on the ground of incapacity or misconduct.

(4) One of the adjudicators shall be appointed Chief Adjudicator.

He shall perform such functions as the Secretary of State may assign to him.

(5) The other adjudicators shall undertake such duties as the Chief Adjudicator may determine.

(6) The Secretary of State may—

    (a) appoint staff for the adjudicators;

    (b) pay remuneration and expenses to the adjudicators and their staff;

    (c) defray other costs arising in relation to the performance by the adjudicators of their functions;

    (d) compensate persons for ceasing to be adjudicators.

NOTES

Commencement: 1 October 2008.

[1.71]
71 Procedural rules
(1) The Secretary of State may make rules about proceedings before a company names adjudicator.

(2) The rules may, in particular, make provision—

    (a) as to how an application is to be made and the form and content of an application or other documents;

    (b) for fees to be charged;

    (c) about the service of documents and the consequences of failure to serve them;

    (d) as to the form and manner in which evidence is to be given;

    (e) for circumstances in which hearings are required and those in which they are not;

    (f) for cases to be heard by more than one adjudicator;

    (g) setting time limits for anything required to be done in connection with the proceedings (and allowing for such limits to be extended, even if they have expired);

    (h) enabling the adjudicator to strike out an application, or any defence, in whole or in part—

        (i) on the ground that it is vexatious, has no reasonable prospect of success or is otherwise misconceived, or

        (ii) for failure to comply with the requirements of the rules;

    (i) conferring power to order security for costs (in Scotland, caution for expenses);

    (j) as to how far proceedings are to be held in public;

    (k) requiring one party to bear the costs (in Scotland, expenses) of another and as to the taxing (or settling) the amount of such costs (or expenses).

(3) The rules may confer on the Chief Adjudicator power to determine any matter that could be the subject of provision in the rules.

(4) Rules under this section shall be made by statutory instrument which shall be subject to annulment in pursuance of a resolution of either House of Parliament.

NOTES

Commencement: 1 October 2008.

Rules: the Company Names Adjudicator Rules 2008, SI 2008/1738 at **[4.287]**.

[1.72]
72 Decision of adjudicator to be made available to public
(1) A company names adjudicator must, within 90 days of determining an application under section 69, make his decision and his reasons for it available to the public.

(2) He may do so by means of a website or by such other means as appear to him to be appropriate.

NOTES
Commencement: 1 October 2008.

[1.73]
73 Order requiring name to be changed
(1) If an application under section 69 is upheld, the adjudicator shall make an order—
  (a) requiring the respondent company to change its name to one that is not an offending name, and
  (b) requiring all the respondents—
    (i) to take all such steps as are within their power to make, or facilitate the making, of that change, and
    (ii) not to cause or permit any steps to be taken calculated to result in another company being registered with a name that is an offending name.
(2) An "offending name" means a name that, by reason of its similarity to the name associated with the applicant in which he claims goodwill, would be likely—
  (a) to be the subject of a direction under section 67 (power of Secretary of State to direct change of name), or
  (b) to give rise to a further application under section 69.
(3) The order must specify a date by which the respondent company's name is to be changed and may be enforced—
  (a) in England and Wales or Northern Ireland, in the same way as an order of the High Court;
  (b) in Scotland, in the same way as a decree of the Court of Session.
(4) If the respondent company's name is not changed in accordance with the order by the specified date, the adjudicator may determine a new name for the company.
(5) If the adjudicator determines a new name for the respondent company he must give notice of his determination—
  (a) to the applicant,
  (b) to the respondents, and
  (c) to the registrar.
(6) For the purposes of this section a company's name is changed when the change takes effect in accordance with section 81(1) (on the issue of the new certification of incorporation).

NOTES
Commencement: 1 October 2008.
Commencement (transitional adaptations): art 6 of the Companies Act 2006 (Commencement No 5, Transitional Provisions and Savings) Order 2007, SI 2007/3495 provides that the provisions brought into force by arts 3 and 5 of that Order shall have effect subject to any transitional adaptations specified in Sch 1 to that Order. Schedule 1, Pt 2, para 22 to the Order (at **[2.63]**) provided for such transitional adaptations (note that this paragraph was revoked by the Companies Act 2006 (Commencement No 8, Transitional Provisions and Savings) Order 2008, SI 2008/2860, art 6, as from 1 October 2009 (subject to any relevant transitional provision or saving in Sch 2 to that Order)).

[1.74]
74 Appeal from adjudicator's decision
(1) An appeal lies to the court from any decision of a company names adjudicator to uphold or dismiss an application under section 69.
(2) Notice of appeal against a decision upholding an application must be given before the date specified in the adjudicator's order by which the respondent company's name is to be changed.
(3) If notice of appeal is given against a decision upholding an application, the effect of the adjudicator's order is suspended.
(4) If on appeal the court—
  (a) affirms the decision of the adjudicator to uphold the application, or
  (b) reverses the decision of the adjudicator to dismiss the application,
the court may (as the case may require) specify the date by which the adjudicator's order is to be complied with, remit the matter to the adjudicator or make any order or determination that the adjudicator might have made.
(5) If the court determines a new name for the company it must give notice of the determination—
  (a) to the parties to the appeal, and
  (b) to the registrar.

NOTES
Commencement: 1 October 2008.

CHAPTER 4
OTHER POWERS OF THE SECRETARY OF STATE

[1.75]
75 Provision of misleading information etc
(1) If it appears to the Secretary of State—
    (a) that misleading information has been given for the purposes of a company's registration by a particular name, or
    (b) that an undertaking or assurance has been given for that purpose and has not been fulfilled,
the Secretary of State may direct the company to change its name.
(2) Any such direction—
    (a) must be given within five years of the company's registration by that name, and
    (b) must specify the period within which the company is to change its name.
(3) The Secretary of State may by a further direction extend the period within which the company is to change its name.
Any such direction must be given before the end of the period for the time being specified.
(4) A direction under this section must be in writing.
(5) If a company fails to comply with a direction under this section, an offence is committed by—
    (a) the company, and
    (b) every officer of the company who is in default.
For this purpose a shadow director is treated as an officer of the company.
(6) A person guilty of an offence under this section is liable on summary conviction to a fine not exceeding level 3 on the standard scale and, for continued contravention, a daily default fine not exceeding one-tenth of level 3 on the standard scale.

NOTES
Commencement: 1 October 2009.

[1.76]
76 Misleading indication of activities
(1) If in the opinion of the Secretary of State the name by which a company is registered gives so misleading an indication of the nature of its activities as to be likely to cause harm to the public, the Secretary of State may direct the company to change its name.
(2) The direction must be in writing.
(3) The direction must be complied with within a period of six weeks from the date of the direction or such longer period as the Secretary of State may think fit to allow.
This does not apply if an application is duly made to the court under the following provisions.
(4) The company may apply to the court to set the direction aside.
The application must be made within the period of three weeks from the date of the direction.
(5) The court may set the direction aside or confirm it.
If the direction is confirmed, the court shall specify the period within which the direction is to be complied with.
(6) If a company fails to comply with a direction under this section, an offence is committed by—
    (a) the company, and
    (b) every officer of the company who is in default.
For this purpose a shadow director is treated as an officer of the company.
(7) A person guilty of an offence under this section is liable on summary conviction to a fine not exceeding level 3 on the standard scale and, for continued contravention, a daily default fine not exceeding one-tenth of level 3 on the standard scale.

NOTES
Commencement: 1 October 2009.

CHAPTER 5
CHANGE OF NAME

[1.77]
77 Change of name
(1) A company may change its name—
    (a) by special resolution (see section 78), or
    (b) by other means provided for by the company's articles (see section 79).
(2) The name of a company may also be changed—
    (a) by resolution of the directors acting under section 64 (change of name to comply with direction of Secretary of State under that section);
    (b) on the determination of a new name by a company names adjudicator under section 73 (powers of adjudicator on upholding objection to company name);
    (c) on the determination of a new name by the court under section 74 (appeal against decision of company names adjudicator);
    (d) under section 1033 (company's name on restoration to the register).

NOTES

Commencement: 1 October 2009.

Commencement (transitional provisions): Sch 2, para 19 to the Companies Act 2006 (Commencement No 8, Transitional Provisions and Savings) Order 2008, SI 2008/2860 (at **[2.91]**) provides as follows—

"19.—(1)   Sections 77(1)(a) and 78 of the Companies Act 2006 (change of name by special resolution), and sections 80 and 81 of that Act so far as relating to a change of name by special resolution, apply where—

    (a)   the resolution is passed on or after 1st October 2009, or

    (b)   the resolution is passed before that date but no copy of the resolution is received by the registrar under section 30 of that Act (resolution affecting a company's constitution) before that date.

(2)   Section 28(1), (6) and (7) of the 1985 Act or Article 38(1), (6) and (7) of the 1986 Order continue to apply to resolutions of which a copy is received by the registrar before that date.".

[1.78]

78   Change of name by special resolution

(1)   Where a change of name has been agreed to by a company by special resolution, the company must give notice to the registrar.

This is in addition to the obligation to forward a copy of the resolution to the registrar.

(2)   Where a change of name by special resolution is conditional on the occurrence of an event, the notice given to the registrar of the change must—

    (a)   specify that the change is conditional, and

    (b)   state whether the event has occurred.

(3)   If the notice states that the event has not occurred—

    (a)   the registrar is not required to act under section 80 (registration and issue of new certificate of incorporation) until further notice,

    (b)   when the event occurs, the company must give notice to the registrar stating that it has occurred, and

    (c)   the registrar may rely on the statement as sufficient evidence of the matters stated in it.

NOTES

Commencement: 1 October 2009.

Commencement (transitional provisions): see the note to s 77 at **[1.77]**.

[1.79]

79   Change of name by means provided for in company's articles

(1)   Where a change of a company's name has been made by other means provided for by its articles—

    (a)   the company must give notice to the registrar, and

    (b)   the notice must be accompanied by a statement that the change of name has been made by means provided for by the company's articles.

(2)   The registrar may rely on the statement as sufficient evidence of the matters stated in it.

NOTES

Commencement: 1 October 2009.

[1.80]

80   Change of name: registration and issue of new certificate of incorporation

(1)   This section applies where the registrar receives notice of a change of a company's name.

(2)   If the registrar is satisfied—

    (a)   that the new name complies with the requirements of this Part, and

    (b)   that the requirements of the Companies Acts, and any relevant requirements of the company's articles, with respect to a change of name are complied with,

the registrar must enter the new name on the register in place of the former name.

(3)   On the registration of the new name, the registrar must issue a certificate of incorporation altered to meet the circumstances of the case.

NOTES

Commencement: 1 October 2009.

Commencement (transitional provisions): see the note to s 77 at **[1.77]**.

[1.81]

81   Change of name: effect

(1)   A change of a company's name has effect from the date on which the new certificate of incorporation is issued.

(2)   The change does not affect any rights or obligations of the company or render defective any legal proceedings by or against it.

(3)   Any legal proceedings that might have been continued or commenced against it by its former name may be continued or commenced against it by its new name.

NOTES
Commencement: 1 October 2009.
Commencement (transitional provisions): see the note to s 77 at **[1.77]**.

CHAPTER 6
TRADING DISCLOSURES

[1.82]
82 Requirement to disclose company name etc

(1) The Secretary of State may by regulations make provision requiring companies—
  (a) to display specified information in specified locations,
  (b) to state specified information in specified descriptions of document or communication, and
  (c) to provide specified information on request to those they deal with in the course of their business.
(2) The regulations—
  (a) must in every case require disclosure of the name of the company, and
  (b) may make provision as to the manner in which any specified information is to be displayed, stated or provided.
(3) The regulations may provide that, for the purposes of any requirement to disclose a company's name, any variation between a word or words required to be part of the name and a permitted abbreviation of that word or those words (or vice versa) shall be disregarded.
(4) In this section "specified" means specified in the regulations.
(5) Regulations under this section are subject to affirmative resolution procedure.

NOTES
Commencement: 20 January 2007 (for the purpose of enabling the exercise of powers to make Orders or Regulations by statutory instrument); 1 October 2008 (otherwise).
Regulations: the Companies (Trading Disclosures) Regulations 2008, SI 2008/495 at **[4.230]**; the Companies (Trading Disclosures) (Amendment) Regulations 2009, SI 2009/218.

[1.83]
83 Civil consequences of failure to make required disclosure

(1) This section applies to any legal proceedings brought by a company to which section 82 applies (requirement to disclose company name etc) to enforce a right arising out of a contract made in the course of a business in respect of which the company was, at the time the contract was made, in breach of regulations under that section.
(2) The proceedings shall be dismissed if the defendant (in Scotland, the defender) to the proceedings shows—
  (a) that he has a claim against the claimant (pursuer) arising out of the contract that he has been unable to pursue by reason of the latter's breach of the regulations, or
  (b) that he has suffered some financial loss in connection with the contract by reason of the claimant's (pursuer's) breach of the regulations,
unless the court before which the proceedings are brought is satisfied that it is just and equitable to permit the proceedings to continue.
(3) This section does not affect the right of any person to enforce such rights as he may have against another person in any proceedings brought by that person.

NOTES
Commencement: 1 October 2008.

[1.84]
84 Criminal consequences of failure to make required disclosures

(1) Regulations under section 82 may provide—
  (a) that where a company fails, without reasonable excuse, to comply with any specified requirement of regulations under that section an offence is committed by—
    (i)   the company, and
    (ii)   every officer of the company who is in default;
  (b) that a person guilty of such an offence is liable on summary conviction to a fine not exceeding level 3 on the standard scale and, for continued contravention, a daily default fine not exceeding one-tenth of level 3 on the standard scale.
(2) The regulations may provide that, for the purposes of any provision made under subsection (1), a shadow director of the company is to be treated as an officer of the company.
(3) In subsection (1)(a) "specified" means specified in the regulations.

NOTES
Commencement: 20 January 2007 (for the purpose of enabling the exercise of powers to make Orders or Regulations by statutory instrument); 1 October 2008 (otherwise).
Regulations under section 82: see the notes to that section at **[1.82]**.

[1.85]
85 Minor variations in form of name to be left out of account
(1)   For the purposes of this Chapter, in considering a company's name no account is to be taken of—
- (a)   whether upper or lower case characters (or a combination of the two) are used,
- (b)   whether diacritical marks or punctuation are present or absent,
- (c)   whether the name is in the same format or style as is specified under section 57(1)(b) for the purposes of registration,

provided there is no real likelihood of names differing only in those respects being taken to be different names.
(2)   This does not affect the operation of regulations under section 57(1)(a) permitting only specified characters, diacritical marks or punctuation.

NOTES
Commencement: 1 October 2008.
Commencement (transitional adaptations): art 6 of the Companies Act 2006 (Commencement No 5, Transitional Provisions and Savings) Order 2007, SI 2007/3495 provides that the provisions brought into force by arts 3 and 5 of that Order shall have effect subject to any transitional adaptations specified in Sch 1 to that Order. Schedule 1, Pt 2, para 23 to the Order (at **[2.63]**) provided for such transitional adaptations (note that this paragraph was revoked by the Companies Act 2006 (Commencement No 8, Transitional Provisions and Savings) Order 2008, SI 2008/2860, art 6, as from 1 October 2009 (subject to any relevant transitional provision or saving in Sch 2 to that Order)).

PART 6
A COMPANY'S REGISTERED OFFICE
General

[1.86]
86   A company's registered office
A company must at all times have a registered office to which all communications and notices may be addressed.

NOTES
Commencement: 1 October 2009.

[1.87]
87   Change of address of registered office
(1)   A company may change the address of its registered office by giving notice to the registrar.
(2)   The change takes effect upon the notice being registered by the registrar, but until the end of the period of 14 days beginning with the date on which it is registered a person may validly serve any document on the company at the address previously registered.
(3)   For the purposes of any duty of a company—
- (a)   to keep available for inspection at its registered office any register, index or other document, or
- (b)   to mention the address of its registered office in any document,

a company that has given notice to the registrar of a change in the address of its registered office may act on the change as from such date, not more than 14 days after the notice is given, as it may determine.
(4)   Where a company unavoidably ceases to perform at its registered office any such duty as is mentioned in subsection (3)(a) in circumstances in which it was not practicable to give prior notice to the registrar of a change in the address of its registered office, but—
- (a)   resumes performance of that duty at other premises as soon as practicable, and
- (b)   gives notice accordingly to the registrar of a change in the situation of its registered office within 14 days of doing so,

it is not to be treated as having failed to comply with that duty.

NOTES
Commencement: 1 October 2009.

Welsh companies

[1.88]
88   Welsh companies
(1)   In the Companies Acts a "Welsh company" means a company as to which it is stated in the register that its registered office is to be situated in Wales.
(2)   A company—
- (a)   whose registered office is in Wales, and
- (b)   as to which it is stated in the register that its registered office is to be situated in England and Wales,

may by special resolution require the register to be amended so that it states that the company's registered office is to be situated in Wales.
(3)   A company—

(a)   whose registered office is in Wales, and

(b)   as to which it is stated in the register that its registered office is to be situated in Wales,

may by special resolution require the register to be amended so that it states that the company's registered office is to be situated in England and Wales.

(4)   Where a company passes a resolution under this section it must give notice to the registrar, who shall—

(a)   amend the register accordingly, and

(b)   issue a new certificate of incorporation altered to meet the circumstances of the case.

NOTES

Commencement: 1 October 2009.

PART 7
RE-REGISTRATION AS A MEANS OF ALTERING A COMPANY'S STATUS

NOTES

As to the application of this Part to old public companies, see the introductory notes to this Act and the Companies Act 2006 (Consequential Amendments and Transitional Provisions) Order 2011, SI 2011/1265, Sch 1 at **[4.651]**.

Introductory

[1.89]
89   Alteration of status by re-registration

A company may by re-registration under this Part alter its status—

(a)   from a private company to a public company (see sections 90 to 96);

(b)   from a public company to a private company (see sections 97 to 101);

(c)   from a private limited company to an unlimited company (see sections 102 to 104);

(d)   from an unlimited private company to a limited company (see sections 105 to 108);

(e)   from a public company to an unlimited private company (see sections 109 to 111).

NOTES

Commencement: 1 October 2009.

Commencement (transitional provisions): Sch 2, para 22 to the Companies Act 2006 (Commencement No 8, Transitional Provisions and Savings) Order 2008, SI 2008/2860 (at **[2.91]**) provides as follows—

"Re-registration as a means of altering a company's status (ss 89 to 108)

22.—(1)   Sections 89 to 108 of the Companies Act 2006 (re-registration as a means of altering a company's status) apply to applications for re-registration received by the registrar on or after 1st October 2009.

(2)   Any application for re-registration under those provisions received by the registrar before that date shall not be entertained.

(3)   The corresponding provisions of the 1985 Act or 1986 Order continue to apply to an application for re-registration if—

(a)   it is received by the registrar, and

(b)   the requirements for re-registration are met in relation to it,

before 1st October 2009.

(4)   Any application for re-registration under that Act or Order in relation to which the requirements as to re-registration are not met before that date shall be treated as withdrawn.

(5)   On an application to which sub-paragraph (1) above applies a resolution agreed to, or other thing done, before 1st October 2009 may be relied on for the purpose of meeting the requirements of the Companies Act 2006.

(6)   For the purposes of section 1297(3) of the Companies Act 2006 (continuity of the law) as it applies to treat a company re-registered under the 1985 Act or the 1986 Order as if re-registered under the corresponding provisions of the Companies Act 2006, the re-registration of a company on an application to which sub-paragraph (3) above applies is to be regarded as in force and effective immediately before the commencement of Part 7 of the Companies Act 2006.".

Old public companies: see the note preceding s 89 at **[1.89]**.

Private company becoming public

[1.90]
90   Re-registration of private company as public

(1)   A private company (whether limited or unlimited) may be re-registered as a public company limited by shares if—

(a)   a special resolution that it should be so re-registered is passed,

(b)   the conditions specified below are met, and

(c)   an application for re-registration is delivered to the registrar in accordance with section 94, together with—

(i)   the other documents required by that section, and

(ii)   a statement of compliance.

(2)   The conditions are—

(a)   that the company has a share capital;

(b)   that the requirements of section 91 are met as regards its share capital;

(c)   that the requirements of section 92 are met as regards its net assets;

(d)   if section 93 applies (recent allotment of shares for non-cash consideration), that the requirements of that section are met; and

(e)   that the company has not previously been re-registered as unlimited.
(3)   The company must make such changes—
   (a)   in its name, and
   (b)   in its articles,
as are necessary in connection with its becoming a public company.
(4)   If the company is unlimited it must also make such changes in its articles as are necessary in connection with its becoming a company limited by shares.

NOTES

Commencement: 1 October 2009.
Commencement (transitional provisions): see the note to s 89 at **[1.89]**.
Old public companies: see the note preceding s 89 at **[1.89]**.

[1.91]
91   Requirements as to share capital
(1)   The following requirements must be met at the time the special resolution is passed that the company should be re-registered as a public company—
   (a)   the nominal value of the company's allotted share capital must be not less than the authorised minimum;
   (b)   each of the company's allotted shares must be paid up at least as to one-quarter of the nominal value of that share and the whole of any premium on it;
   (c)   if any shares in the company or any premium on them have been fully or partly paid up by an undertaking given by any person that he or another should do work or perform services (whether for the company or any other person), the undertaking must have been performed or otherwise discharged;
   (d)   if shares have been allotted as fully or partly paid up as to their nominal value or any premium on them otherwise than in cash, and the consideration for the allotment consists of or includes an undertaking to the company (other than one to which paragraph (c) applies), then either—
      (i)   the undertaking must have been performed or otherwise discharged, or
      (ii)   there must be a contract between the company and some person pursuant to which the undertaking is to be performed within five years from the time the special resolution is passed.
(2)   For the purpose of determining whether the requirements in subsection (1)(b), (c) and (d) are met, the following may be disregarded—
   (a)   shares allotted—
      (i)   before 22nd June 1982 in the case of a company then registered in Great Britain, or
      (ii)   before 31st December 1984 in the case of a company then registered in Northern Ireland;
   (b)   shares allotted in pursuance of an employees' share scheme by reason of which the company would, but for this subsection, be precluded under subsection (1)(b) (but not otherwise) from being re-registered as a public company.
(3)   No more than one-tenth of the nominal value of the company's allotted share capital is to be disregarded under subsection (2)(a).
   For this purpose the allotted share capital is treated as not including shares disregarded under subsection (2)(b).
(4)   Shares disregarded under subsection (2) are treated as not forming part of the allotted share capital for the purposes of subsection (1)(a).
(5)   A company must not be re-registered as a public company if it appears to the registrar that—
   (a)   the company has resolved to reduce its share capital,
   (b)   the reduction—
      (i)   is made under section 626 (reduction in connection with redenomination of share capital),
      (ii)   is supported by a solvency statement in accordance with section 643, or
      (iii)   has been confirmed by an order of the court under section 648, and
   (c)   the effect of the reduction is, or will be, that the nominal value of the company's allotted share capital is below the authorised minimum.

NOTES

Commencement: 1 October 2009.
Commencement (transitional provisions): see the note to s 89 at **[1.89]**.
Old public companies: see the note preceding s 89 at **[1.89]**.

[1.92]
92   Requirements as to net assets
(1)   A company applying to re-register as a public company must obtain—
   (a)   a balance sheet prepared as at a date not more than seven months before the date on which the application is delivered to the registrar,
   (b)   an unqualified report by the company's auditor on that balance sheet, and

(c)   a written statement by the company's auditor that in his opinion at the balance sheet date the amount of the company's net assets was not less than the aggregate of its called-up share capital and undistributable reserves.

(2)   Between the balance sheet date and the date on which the application for re-registration is delivered to the registrar, there must be no change in the company's financial position that results in the amount of its net assets becoming less than the aggregate of its called-up share capital and undistributable reserves.

(3)   In subsection (1)(b) an "unqualified report" means—

(a)   if the balance sheet was prepared for a financial year of the company, a report stating without material qualification the auditor's opinion that the balance sheet has been properly prepared in accordance with the requirements of this Act;

(b)   if the balance sheet was not prepared for a financial year of the company, a report stating without material qualification the auditor's opinion that the balance sheet has been properly prepared in accordance with the provisions of this Act which would have applied if it had been prepared for a financial year of the company.

(4)   For the purposes of an auditor's report on a balance sheet that was not prepared for a financial year of the company, the provisions of this Act apply with such modifications as are necessary by reason of that fact.

(5)   For the purposes of subsection (3) a qualification is material unless the auditor states in his report that the matter giving rise to the qualification is not material for the purpose of determining (by reference to the company's balance sheet) whether at the balance sheet date the amount of the company's net assets was not less than the aggregate of its called-up share capital and undistributable reserves.

(6)   In this Part "net assets" and "undistributable reserves" have the same meaning as in section 831 (net asset restriction on distributions by public companies).

NOTES

Commencement: 1 October 2009.

Commencement (transitional provisions): see the note to s 89 at **[1.89]**.

Old public companies: see the note preceding s 89 at **[1.89]**.

[1.93]

93   Recent allotment of shares for non-cash consideration

(1)   This section applies where—

(a)   shares are allotted by the company in the period between the date as at which the balance sheet required by section 92 is prepared and the passing of the resolution that the company should re-register as a public company, and

(b)   the shares are allotted as fully or partly paid up as to their nominal value or any premium on them otherwise than in cash.

(2)   The registrar shall not entertain an application by the company for re-registration as a public company unless—

(a)   the requirements of section 593(1)(a) and (b) have been complied with (independent valuation of non-cash consideration; valuer's report to company not more than six months before allotment), or

(b)   the allotment is in connection with—

(i)   a share exchange (see subsections (3) to (5) below), or

(ii)   a proposed merger with another company (see subsection (6) below).

(3)   An allotment is in connection with a share exchange if—

(a)   the shares are allotted in connection with an arrangement under which the whole or part of the consideration for the shares allotted is provided by—

(i)   the transfer to the company allotting the shares of shares (or shares of a particular class) in another company, or

(ii)   the cancellation of shares (or shares of a particular class) in another company; and

(b)   the allotment is open to all the holders of the shares of the other company in question (or, where the arrangement applies only to shares of a particular class, to all the holders of the company's shares of that class) to take part in the arrangement in connection with which the shares are allotted.

(4)   In determining whether a person is a holder of shares for the purposes of subsection (3), there shall be disregarded—

(a)   shares held by, or by a nominee of, the company allotting the shares;

(b)   shares held by, or by a nominee of—

(i)   the holding company of the company allotting the shares,

(ii)   a subsidiary of the company allotting the shares, or

(iii)   a subsidiary of the holding company of the company allotting the shares.

(5)   It is immaterial, for the purposes of deciding whether an allotment is in connection with a share exchange, whether or not the arrangement in connection with which the shares are allotted involves the issue to the company allotting the shares of shares (or shares of a particular class) in the other company.

(6)   There is a proposed merger with another company if one of the companies concerned proposes to acquire all the assets and liabilities of the other in exchange for the issue of its shares or other securities to shareholders of the other (whether or not accompanied by a cash payment).

"Another company" includes any body corporate.

(7)   For the purposes of this section—

   (a)   the consideration for an allotment does not include any amount standing to the credit of any of the company's reserve accounts, or of its profit and loss account, that has been applied in paying up (to any extent) any of the shares allotted or any premium on those shares; and

   (b)   "arrangement" means any agreement, scheme or arrangement, (including an arrangement sanctioned in accordance with—

      (i)   Part 26 of this Act (arrangements and reconstructions), or

      (ii)   section 110 of the Insolvency Act 1986 (c 45) or Article 96 of the Insolvency (Northern Ireland) Order 1989 (SI 1989/2405 (NI 19)) (liquidator in winding up accepting shares as consideration for sale of company's property)).

NOTES

Commencement: 1 October 2009.

Commencement (transitional provisions): see the note to s 89 at **[1.89]**.

Old public companies: see the note preceding s 89 at **[1.89]**.

[1.94]

94   Application and accompanying documents

(1)   An application for re-registration as a public company must contain—

   (a)   a statement of the company's proposed name on re-registration; and

   (b)   in the case of a company without a secretary, a statement of the company's proposed secretary (see section 95).

(2)   The application must be accompanied by—

   (a)   a copy of the special resolution that the company should re-register as a public company (unless a copy has already been forwarded to the registrar under Chapter 3 of Part 3);

   (b)   a copy of the company's articles as proposed to be amended;

   (c)   a copy of the balance sheet and other documents referred to in section 92(1); and

   (d)   if section 93 applies (recent allotment of shares for non-cash consideration), a copy of the valuation report (if any) under subsection (2)(a) of that section.

(3)   The statement of compliance required to be delivered together with the application is a statement that the requirements of this Part as to re-registration as a public company have been complied with.

(4)   The registrar may accept the statement of compliance as sufficient evidence that the company is entitled to be re-registered as a public company.

NOTES

Commencement: 1 October 2009.

Commencement (transitional provisions): see the note to s 89 at **[1.89]**.

Old public companies: see the note preceding s 89 at **[1.89]**.

[1.95]

95   Statement of proposed secretary

(1)   The statement of the company's proposed secretary must contain the required particulars of the person who is or the persons who are to be the secretary or joint secretaries of the company.

(2)   The required particulars are the particulars that will be required to be stated in the company's register of secretaries (see sections 277 to 279).

(3)   The statement must also contain a consent by the person named as secretary, or each of the persons named as joint secretaries, to act in the relevant capacity. If all the partners in a firm are to be joint secretaries, consent may be given by one partner on behalf of all of them.

NOTES

Commencement: 1 October 2009.

Commencement (transitional provisions): see the note to s 89 at **[1.89]**.

Old public companies: see the note preceding s 89 at **[1.89]**.

[1.96]

96   Issue of certificate of incorporation on re-registration

(1)   If on an application for re-registration as a public company the registrar is satisfied that the company is entitled to be so re-registered, the company shall be re-registered accordingly.

(2)   The registrar must issue a certificate of incorporation altered to meet the circumstances of the case.

(3)   The certificate must state that it is issued on re-registration and the date on which it is issued.

(4)   On the issue of the certificate—

   (a)   the company by virtue of the issue of the certificate becomes a public company,

   (b)   the changes in the company's name and articles take effect, and

(c)   where the application contained a statement under section 95 (statement of proposed secretary), the person or persons named in the statement as secretary or joint secretary of the company are deemed to have been appointed to that office.

(5)   The certificate is conclusive evidence that the requirements of this Act as to re-registration have been complied with.

NOTES

Commencement: 1 October 2009.

Commencement (transitional provisions): see the note to s 89 at **[1.89]**.

Old public companies: see the note preceding s 89 at **[1.89]**.

Public company becoming private

[1.97]

97   Re-registration of public company as private limited company

(1)   A public company may be re-registered as a private limited company if—

     (a)   a special resolution that it should be so re-registered is passed,

     (b)   the conditions specified below are met, and

     (c)   an application for re-registration is delivered to the registrar in accordance with section 100, together with—

         (i)   the other documents required by that section, and

         (ii)   a statement of compliance.

(2)   The conditions are that—

     (a)   where no application under section 98 for cancellation of the resolution has been made—

         (i)   having regard to the number of members who consented to or voted in favour of the resolution, no such application may be made, or

         (ii)   the period within which such an application could be made has expired, or

     (b)   where such an application has been made—

         (i)   the application has been withdrawn, or

         (ii)   an order has been made confirming the resolution and a copy of that order has been delivered to the registrar.

(3)   The company must make such changes—

     (a)   in its name, and

     (b)   in its articles,

as are necessary in connection with its becoming a private company limited by shares or, as the case may be, by guarantee.

NOTES

Commencement: 1 October 2009.

Commencement (transitional provisions): see the note to s 89 at **[1.89]**.

Old public companies: see the note preceding s 89 at **[1.89]**.

[1.98]

98   Application to court to cancel resolution

(1)   Where a special resolution by a public company to be re-registered as a private limited company has been passed, an application to the court for the cancellation of the resolution may be made—

     (a)   by the holders of not less in the aggregate than 5% in nominal value of the company's issued share capital or any class of the company's issued share capital (disregarding any shares held by the company as treasury shares);

     (b)   if the company is not limited by shares, by not less than 5% of its members; or

     (c)   by not less than 50 of the company's members;

but not by a person who has consented to or voted in favour of the resolution.

(2)   The application must be made within 28 days after the passing of the resolution and may be made on behalf of the persons entitled to make it by such one or more of their number as they may appoint for the purpose.

(3)   On the hearing of the application the court shall make an order either cancelling or confirming the resolution.

(4)   The court may—

     (a)   make that order on such terms and conditions as it thinks fit,

     (b)   if it thinks fit adjourn the proceedings in order that an arrangement may be made to the satisfaction of the court for the purchase of the interests of dissentient members, and

     (c)   give such directions, and make such orders, as it thinks expedient for facilitating or carrying into effect any such arrangement.

(5)   The court's order may, if the court thinks fit—

     (a)   provide for the purchase by the company of the shares of any of its members and for the reduction accordingly of the company's capital; and

     (b)   make such alteration in the company's articles as may be required in consequence of that provision.

(6) The court's order may, if the court thinks fit, require the company not to make any, or any specified, amendments to its articles without the leave of the court.

NOTES
Commencement: 1 October 2009.
Commencement (transitional provisions): see the note to s 89 at **[1.89]**.
Old public companies: see the note preceding s 89 at **[1.89]**.

[1.99]
99 Notice to registrar of court application or order
(1) On making an application under section 98 (application to court to cancel resolution) the applicants, or the person making the application on their behalf, must immediately give notice to the registrar.

This is without prejudice to any provision of rules of court as to service of notice of the application.
(2) On being served with notice of any such application, the company must immediately give notice to the registrar.
(3) Within 15 days of the making of the court's order on the application, or such longer period as the court may at any time direct, the company must deliver to the registrar a copy of the order.
(4) If a company fails to comply with subsection (2) or (3) an offence is committed by—
   (a) the company, and
   (b) every officer of the company who is in default.
(5) A person guilty of an offence under this section is liable on summary conviction to a fine not exceeding level 3 on the standard scale and, for continued contravention, a daily default fine not exceeding one-tenth of level 3 on the standard scale.

NOTES
Commencement: 1 October 2009.
Commencement (transitional provisions): see the note to s 89 at **[1.89]**.
Old public companies: see the note preceding s 89 at **[1.89]**.

[1.100]
100 Application and accompanying documents
(1) An application for re-registration as a private limited company must contain a statement of the company's proposed name on re-registration.
(2) The application must be accompanied by—
   (a) a copy of the resolution that the company should re-register as a private limited company (unless a copy has already been forwarded to the registrar under Chapter 3 of Part 3); and
   (b) a copy of the company's articles as proposed to be amended.
(3) The statement of compliance required to be delivered together with the application is a statement that the requirements of this Part as to re-registration as a private limited company have been complied with.
(4) The registrar may accept the statement of compliance as sufficient evidence that the company is entitled to be re-registered as a private limited company.

NOTES
Commencement: 1 October 2009.
Commencement (transitional provisions): see the note to s 89 at **[1.89]**.
Old public companies: see the note preceding s 89 at **[1.89]**.

[1.101]
101 Issue of certificate of incorporation on re-registration
(1) If on an application for re-registration as a private limited company the registrar is satisfied that the company is entitled to be so re-registered, the company shall be re-registered accordingly.
(2) The registrar must issue a certificate of incorporation altered to meet the circumstances of the case.
(3) The certificate must state that it is issued on re-registration and the date on which it is issued.
(4) On the issue of the certificate—
   (a) the company by virtue of the issue of the certificate becomes a private limited company, and
   (b) the changes in the company's name and articles take effect.
(5) The certificate is conclusive evidence that the requirements of this Act as to re-registration have been complied with.

NOTES
Commencement: 1 October 2009.
Commencement (transitional provisions): see the note to s 89 at **[1.89]**.
Old public companies: see the note preceding s 89 at **[1.89]**.

Private limited company becoming unlimited

[1.102]

102　Re-registration of private limited company as unlimited

(1)　A private limited company may be re-registered as an unlimited company if—

   (a)　all the members of the company have assented to its being so re-registered,

   (b)　the condition specified below is met, and

   (c)　an application for re-registration is delivered to the registrar in accordance with section 103, together with—

      (i)　the other documents required by that section, and

      (ii)　a statement of compliance.

(2)　The condition is that the company has not previously been re-registered as limited.

(3)　The company must make such changes in its name and its articles—

   (a)　as are necessary in connection with its becoming an unlimited company; and

   (b)　if it is to have a share capital, as are necessary in connection with its becoming an unlimited company having a share capital.

(4)　For the purposes of this section—

   (a)　a trustee in bankruptcy of a member of the company is entitled, to the exclusion of the member, to assent to the company's becoming unlimited; and

   (b)　the personal representative of a deceased member of the company may assent on behalf of the deceased.

(5)　In subsection (4)(a), "a trustee in bankruptcy of a member of the company" includes—

   (a)　a permanent trustee or an interim trustee (within the meaning of the Bankruptcy (Scotland) Act 1985 (c 66)) on the sequestrated estate of a member of the company;

   (b)　a trustee under a protected trustee deed (within the meaning of the Bankruptcy (Scotland) Act 1985) granted by a member of the company.

NOTES

Commencement: 1 October 2009.

Commencement (transitional provisions): see the note to s 89 at **[1.89]**.

Old public companies: see the note preceding s 89 at **[1.89]**.

[1.103]

103　Application and accompanying documents

(1)　An application for re-registration as an unlimited company must contain a statement of the company's proposed name on re-registration.

(2)　The application must be accompanied by—

   (a)　the prescribed form of assent to the company's being registered as an unlimited company, authenticated by or on behalf of all the members of the company;

   (b)　a copy of the company's articles as proposed to be amended.

(3)　The statement of compliance required to be delivered together with the application is a statement that the requirements of this Part as to re-registration as an unlimited company have been complied with.

(4)　The statement must contain a statement by the directors of the company—

   (a)　that the persons by whom or on whose behalf the form of assent is authenticated constitute the whole membership of the company, and

   (b)　if any of the members have not authenticated that form themselves, that the directors have taken all reasonable steps to satisfy themselves that each person who authenticated it on behalf of a member was lawfully empowered to do so.

(5)　The registrar may accept the statement of compliance as sufficient evidence that the company is entitled to be re-registered as an unlimited company.

NOTES

Commencement: 20 January 2007 (for the purpose of enabling the exercise of powers to make Orders or Regulations by statutory instrument); 1 October 2009 (otherwise).

Commencement (transitional provisions): see the note to s 89 at **[1.89]**.

Old public companies: see the note preceding s 89 at **[1.89]**.

Regulations: the Companies (Registration) Regulations 2008, SI 2008/3014 at **[4.329]**.

[1.104]

104　Issue of certificate of incorporation on re-registration

(1)　If on an application for re-registration of a private limited company as an unlimited company the registrar is satisfied that the company is entitled to be so re-registered, the company shall be re-registered accordingly.

(2)　The registrar must issue a certificate of incorporation altered to meet the circumstances of the case.

(3)　The certificate must state that it is issued on re-registration and the date on which it is issued.

(4)　On the issue of the certificate—

   (a)　the company by virtue of the issue of the certificate becomes an unlimited company, and

   (b)　the changes in the company's name and articles take effect.

(5) The certificate is conclusive evidence that the requirements of this Act as to re-registration have been complied with.

NOTES

Commencement: 1 October 2009.
Commencement (transitional provisions): see the note to s 89 at **[1.89]**.
Old public companies: see the note preceding s 89 at **[1.89]**.

Unlimited private company becoming limited

[1.105]
105 Re-registration of unlimited company as limited
(1) An unlimited company may be re-registered as a private limited company if—
  (a) a special resolution that it should be so re-registered is passed,
  (b) the condition specified below is met, and
  (c) an application for re-registration is delivered to the registrar in accordance with section 106, together with—
    (i) the other documents required by that section, and
    (ii) a statement of compliance.
(2) The condition is that the company has not previously been re-registered as unlimited.
(3) The special resolution must state whether the company is to be limited by shares or by guarantee.
(4) The company must make such changes—
  (a) in its name, and
  (b) in its articles,
as are necessary in connection with its becoming a company limited by shares or, as the case may be, by guarantee.

NOTES

Commencement: 1 October 2009.
Commencement (transitional provisions): see the note to s 89 at **[1.89]**.
Old public companies: see the note preceding s 89 at **[1.89]**.

[1.106]
106 Application and accompanying documents
(1) An application for re-registration as a limited company must contain a statement of the company's proposed name on re-registration.
(2) The application must be accompanied by—
  (a) a copy of the resolution that the company should re-register as a private limited company (unless a copy has already been forwarded to the registrar under Chapter 3 of Part 3);
  (b) if the company is to be limited by guarantee, a statement of guarantee;
  (c) a copy of the company's articles as proposed to be amended.
(3) The statement of guarantee required to be delivered in the case of a company that is to be limited by guarantee must state that each member undertakes that, if the company is wound up while he is a member, or within one year after he ceases to be a member, he will contribute to the assets of the company such amount as may be required for—
  (a) payment of the debts and liabilities of the company contracted before he ceases to be a member,
  (b) payment of the costs, charges and expenses of winding up, and
  (c) adjustment of the rights of the contributories among themselves,
not exceeding a specified amount.
(4) The statement of compliance required to be delivered together with the application is a statement that the requirements of this Part as to re-registration as a limited company have been complied with.
(5) The registrar may accept the statement of compliance as sufficient evidence that the company is entitled to be re-registered as a limited company.

NOTES

Commencement: 1 October 2009.
Commencement (transitional provisions): see the note to s 89 at **[1.89]**.
Old public companies: see the note preceding s 89 at **[1.89]**.

[1.107]
107 Issue of certificate of incorporation on re-registration
(1) If on an application for re-registration of an unlimited company as a limited company the registrar is satisfied that the company is entitled to be so re-registered, the company shall be re-registered accordingly.
(2) The registrar must issue a certificate of incorporation altered to meet the circumstances of the case.
(3) The certificate must state that it is issued on re-registration and the date on which it is so issued.

(4) On the issue of the certificate—

    (a)   the company by virtue of the issue of the certificate becomes a limited company, and

    (b)   the changes in the company's name and articles take effect.

(5) The certificate is conclusive evidence that the requirements of this Act as to re-registration have been complied with.

NOTES

Commencement: 1 October 2009.

Commencement (transitional provisions): see the note to s 89 at **[1.89]**.

Old public companies: see the note preceding s 89 at **[1.89]**.

[1.108]

108 Statement of capital required where company already has share capital

(1) A company which on re-registration under section 107 already has allotted share capital must within 15 days after the re-registration deliver a statement of capital to the registrar.

(2) This does not apply if the information which would be included in the statement has already been sent to the registrar in—

    (a)   a statement of capital and initial shareholdings (see section 10), or

    (b)   a statement of capital contained in an annual return (see section 856(2)).

(3) The statement of capital must state with respect to the company's share capital on re-registration—

    (a)   the total number of shares of the company,

    (b)   the aggregate nominal value of those shares,

    (c)   for each class of shares—

        (i)   prescribed particulars of the rights attached to the shares,

        (ii)   the total number of shares of that class, and

        (iii) the aggregate nominal value of shares of that class, and

    (d)   the amount paid up and the amount (if any) unpaid on each share (whether on account of the nominal value of the share or by way of premium).

(4) If default is made in complying with this section, an offence is committed by—

    (a)   the company, and

    (b)   every officer of the company who is in default.

(5) A person guilty of an offence under this section is liable on summary conviction to a fine not exceeding level 3 on the standard scale and, for continued contravention, a daily default fine not exceeding one-tenth of level 3 on the standard scale.

NOTES

Commencement: 20 January 2007 (for the purpose of enabling the exercise of powers to make Orders or Regulations by statutory instrument); 1 October 2009 (otherwise).

Commencement (transitional provisions): see the note to s 89 at **[1.89]**.

Old public companies: see the note preceding s 89 at **[1.89]**.

Orders: the Companies (Shares and Share Capital) Order 2009, SI 2009/388 at **[4.364]**.

Public company becoming private and unlimited

[1.109]

109 Re-registration of public company as private and unlimited

(1) A public company limited by shares may be re-registered as an unlimited private company with a share capital if—

    (a)   all the members of the company have assented to its being so re-registered,

    (b)   the condition specified below is met, and

    (c)   an application for re-registration is delivered to the registrar in accordance with section 110, together with—

        (i)   the other documents required by that section, and

        (ii)   a statement of compliance.

(2) The condition is that the company has not previously been re-registered—

    (a)   as limited, or

    (b)   as unlimited.

(3) The company must make such changes—

    (a)   in its name, and

    (b)   in its articles,

as are necessary in connection with its becoming an unlimited private company.

(4) For the purposes of this section—

    (a)   a trustee in bankruptcy of a member of the company is entitled, to the exclusion of the member, to assent to the company's re-registration; and

    (b)   the personal representative of a deceased member of the company may assent on behalf of the deceased.

(5) In subsection (4)(a), "a trustee in bankruptcy of a member of the company" includes—

    (a)   a permanent trustee or an interim trustee (within the meaning of the Bankruptcy (Scotland) Act 1985 (c 66)) on the sequestrated estate of a member of the company;

(b)   a trustee under a protected trustee deed (within the meaning of the Bankruptcy (Scotland) Act 1985) granted by a member of the company.

NOTES
Commencement: 1 October 2009.
Old public companies: see the note preceding s 89 at [**1.89**].

[1.110]
110   Application and accompanying documents
(1)   An application for re-registration of a public company as an unlimited private company must contain a statement of the company's proposed name on re-registration.
(2)   The application must be accompanied by—
(a)   the prescribed form of assent to the company's being registered as an unlimited company, authenticated by or on behalf of all the members of the company, and
(b)   a copy of the company's articles as proposed to be amended.
(3)   The statement of compliance required to be delivered together with the application is a statement that the requirements of this Part as to re-registration as an unlimited private company have been complied with.
(4)   The statement must contain a statement by the directors of the company—
(a)   that the persons by whom or on whose behalf the form of assent is authenticated constitute the whole membership of the company, and
(b)   if any of the members have not authenticated that form themselves, that the directors have taken all reasonable steps to satisfy themselves that each person who authenticated it on behalf of a member was lawfully empowered to do so.
(5)   The registrar may accept the statement of compliance as sufficient evidence that the company is entitled to be re-registered as an unlimited private company.

NOTES
Commencement: 20 January 2007 (for the purpose of enabling the exercise of powers to make Orders or Regulations by statutory instrument); 1 October 2009 (otherwise).
Old public companies: see the note preceding s 89 at [**1.89**].
Regulations: the Companies (Registration) Regulations 2008, SI 2008/3014 at [**4.329**].

[1.111]
111   Issue of certificate of incorporation on re-registration
(1)   If on an application for re-registration of a public company as an unlimited private company the registrar is satisfied that the company is entitled to be so re-registered, the company shall be re-registered accordingly.
(2)   The registrar must issue a certificate of incorporation altered to meet the circumstances of the case.
(3)   The certificate must state that it is issued on re-registration and the date on which it is so issued.
(4)   On the issue of the certificate—
(a)   the company by virtue of the issue of the certificate becomes an unlimited private company, and
(b)   the changes in the company's name and articles take effect.
(5)   The certificate is conclusive evidence that the requirements of this Act as to re-registration have been complied with.

NOTES
Commencement: 1 October 2009.
Old public companies: see the note preceding s 89 at [**1.89**].

PART 8
A COMPANY'S MEMBERS

CHAPTER 1
THE MEMBERS OF A COMPANY

[1.112]
112   The members of a company
(1)   The subscribers of a company's memorandum are deemed to have agreed to become members of the company, and on its registration become members and must be entered as such in its register of members.
(2)   Every other person who agrees to become a member of a company, and whose name is entered in its register of members, is a member of the company.

NOTES
Commencement: 1 October 2009.

CHAPTER 2
REGISTER OF MEMBERS
General

[1.113]
113 Register of members

(1)   Every company must keep a register of its members.

(2)   There must be entered in the register—

  (a)   the names and addresses of the members,

  (b)   the date on which each person was registered as a member, and

  (c)   the date at which any person ceased to be a member.

(3)   In the case of a company having a share capital, there must be entered in the register, with the names and addresses of the members, a statement of—

  (a)   the shares held by each member, distinguishing each share—

    (i)   by its number (so long as the share has a number), and

    (ii)   where the company has more than one class of issued shares, by its class, and

  (b)   the amount paid or agreed to be considered as paid on the shares of each member.

(4)   If the company has converted any of its shares into stock, and given notice of the conversion to the registrar, the register of members must show the amount and class of stock held by each member instead of the amount of shares and the particulars relating to shares specified above.

(5)   In the case of joint holders of shares or stock in a company, the company's register of members must state the names of each joint holder.

In other respects joint holders are regarded for the purposes of this Chapter as a single member (so that the register must show a single address).

(6)   In the case of a company that does not have a share capital but has more than one class of members, there must be entered in the register, with the names and addresses of the members, a statement of the class to which each member belongs.

(7)   If a company makes default in complying with this section an offence is committed by—

  (a)   the company, and

  (b)   every officer of the company who is in default.

(8)   A person guilty of an offence under this section is liable on summary conviction to a fine not exceeding level 3 on the standard scale and, for continued contravention, a daily default fine not exceeding one-tenth of level 3 on the standard scale.

NOTES

Commencement: 1 October 2009.

[1.114]
114 Register to be kept available for inspection

(1)   A company's register of members must be kept available for inspection—

  (a)   at its registered office, or

  (b)   at a place specified in regulations under section 1136.

(2)   A company must give notice to the registrar of the place where its register of members is kept available for inspection and of any change in that place.

(3)   No such notice is required if the register has, at all times since it came into existence (or, in the case of a register in existence on the relevant date, at all times since then) been kept available for inspection at the company's registered office.

(4)   The relevant date for the purposes of subsection (3) is—

  (a)   1st July 1948 in the case of a company registered in Great Britain, and

  (b)   1st April 1961 in the case of a company registered in Northern Ireland.

(5)   If a company makes default for 14 days in complying with subsection (2), an offence is committed by—

  (a)   the company, and

  (b)   every officer of the company who is in default.

(6)   A person guilty of an offence under this section is liable on summary conviction to a fine not exceeding level 3 on the standard scale and, for continued contravention, a daily default fine not exceeding one-tenth of level 3 on the standard scale.

NOTES

Commencement: 1 October 2009.

[1.115]
115 Index of members

(1)   Every company having more than 50 members must keep an index of the names of the members of the company, unless the register of members is in such a form as to constitute in itself an index.

(2)   The company must make any necessary alteration in the index within 14 days after the date on which any alteration is made in the register of members.

(3)   The index must contain, in respect of each member, a sufficient indication to enable the account of that member in the register to be readily found.

(4)   The index must be at all times kept available for inspection at the same place as the register of members.

(5)   If default is made in complying with this section, an offence is committed by—
  (a)   the company, and
  (b)   every officer of the company who is in default.

(6)   A person guilty of an offence under this section is liable on summary conviction to a fine not exceeding level 3 on the standard scale and, for continued contravention, a daily default fine not exceeding one-tenth of level 3 on the standard scale.

NOTES

Commencement: 1 October 2009.

[1.116]
116   Rights to inspect and require copies

(1)   The register and the index of members' names must be open to the inspection—
  (a)   of any member of the company without charge, and
  (b)   of any other person on payment of such fee as may be prescribed.

(2)   Any person may require a copy of a company's register of members, or of any part of it, on payment of such fee as may be prescribed.

(3)   A person seeking to exercise either of the rights conferred by this section must make a request to the company to that effect.

(4)   The request must contain the following information—
  (a)   in the case of an individual, his name and address;
  (b)   in the case of an organisation, the name and address of an individual responsible for making the request on behalf of the organisation;
  (c)   the purpose for which the information is to be used; and
  (d)   whether the information will be disclosed to any other person, and if so—
    (i)   where that person is an individual, his name and address,
    (ii)   where that person is an organisation, the name and address of an individual responsible for receiving the information on its behalf, and
    (iii)   the purpose for which the information is to be used by that person.

NOTES

Commencement: 20 January 2007 (for the purpose of enabling the exercise of powers to make Orders or Regulations by statutory instrument); 1 October 2007 (otherwise).

Commencement (transitional provisions): Sch 3, para 2 to the Companies Act 2006 (Commencement No 3, Consequential Amendments, Transitional Provisions and Savings) Order 2007, SI 2007/2194 (at **[2.45]**) provides as follows—

"**2   Inspection of register of members (ss 116 to 119)**
  (1)   Sections 116 to 119 of the Companies Act 2006 (inspection of register of members) apply where—
    (a)   the request is made on or after 1st October 2007, and
    (b)   the company is not obliged to deliver an annual return under section 363 of the 1985 Act or Article 371 of the 1986 Order made up to a date before 1st October 2008.
  (2)   Sections 356 and 357 of the 1985 Act or Articles 364 and 365 of the 1986 Order continue to apply to requests made before 1st October 2007 or after that date to a company that is so obliged.".

Commencement (transitional adaptations): art 6 of the Companies Act 2006 (Commencement No 3, Consequential Amendments, Transitional Provisions and Savings) Order 2007, SI 2007/2194 provides that the provisions brought into force by that Order shall have effect subject to any transitional adaptations specified in Sch 1 to that Order. Schedule 1, para 2 to the Order (at **[2.43]**) provided for such transitional adaptations (note that this paragraph was revoked by the Companies Act 2006 (Commencement No 8, Transitional Provisions and Savings) Order 2008, SI 2008/2860, art 6, as from 1 October 2009 (subject to any relevant transitional provision or saving in Sch 2 to that Order)).

Regulations: the Companies (Fees for Inspection and Copying of Company Records) Regulations 2007, SI 2007/2612 at **[4.12]**.

[1.117]
117   Register of members: response to request for inspection or copy

(1)   Where a company receives a request under section 116 (register of members: right to inspect and require copy), it must within five working days either—
  (a)   comply with the request, or
  (b)   apply to the court.

(2)   If it applies to the court it must notify the person making the request.

(3)   If on an application under this section the court is satisfied that the inspection or copy is not sought for a proper purpose—
  (a)   it shall direct the company not to comply with the request, and
  (b)   it may further order that the company's costs (in Scotland, expenses) on the application be paid in whole or in part by the person who made the request, even if he is not a party to the application.

(4)   If the court makes such a direction and it appears to the court that the company is or may be subject to other requests made for a similar purpose (whether made by the same person or different persons), it may direct that the company is not to comply with any such request.

The order must contain such provision as appears to the court appropriate to identify the requests to which it applies.

(5)   If on an application under this section the court does not direct the company not to comply with the request, the company must comply with the request immediately upon the court giving its decision or, as the case may be, the proceedings being discontinued.

NOTES
Commencement: 1 October 2007.
Commencement (transitional provisions): see the note to s 116 at **[1.116]**.

[1.118]
118   Register of members: refusal of inspection or default in providing copy

(1)   If an inspection required under section 116 (register of members: right to inspect and require copy) is refused or default is made in providing a copy required under that section, otherwise than in accordance with an order of the court, an offence is committed by—
  (a)   the company, and
  (b)   every officer of the company who is in default.
(2)   A person guilty of an offence under this section is liable on summary conviction to a fine not exceeding level 3 on the standard scale and, for continued contravention, a daily default fine not exceeding one-tenth of level 3 on the standard scale.
(3)   In the case of any such refusal or default the court may by order compel an immediate inspection or, as the case may be, direct that the copy required be sent to the person requesting it.

NOTES
Commencement: 1 October 2007.
Commencement (transitional provisions): see the note to s 116 at **[1.116]**.

[1.119]
119   Register of members: offences in connection with request for or disclosure of information

(1)   It is an offence for a person knowingly or recklessly to make in a request under section 116 (register of members: right to inspect or require copy) a statement that is misleading, false or deceptive in a material particular.
(2)   It is an offence for a person in possession of information obtained by exercise of either of the rights conferred by that section—
  (a)   to do anything that results in the information being disclosed to another person, or
  (b)   to fail to do anything with the result that the information is disclosed to another person,
knowing, or having reason to suspect, that person may use the information for a purpose that is not a proper purpose.
(3)   A person guilty of an offence under this section is liable—
  (a)   on conviction on indictment, to imprisonment for a term not exceeding two years or a fine (or both);
  (b)   on summary conviction—
    (i)   in England and Wales, to imprisonment for a term not exceeding twelve months or to a fine not exceeding the statutory maximum (or both);
    (ii)   in Scotland or Northern Ireland, to imprisonment for a term not exceeding six months, or to a fine not exceeding the statutory maximum (or both).

NOTES
Commencement: 1 October 2007.
Commencement (transitional provisions): see the note to s 116 at **[1.116]**.
Offences under this section: see further s 1131 at **[1.1131]**.

[1.120]
120   Information as to state of register and index

(1)   When a person inspects the register, or the company provides him with a copy of the register or any part of it, the company must inform him of the most recent date (if any) on which alterations were made to the register and there were no further alterations to be made.
(2)   When a person inspects the index of members' names, the company must inform him whether there is any alteration to the register that is not reflected in the index.
(3)   If a company fails to provide the information required under subsection (1) or (2), an offence is committed by—
  (a)   the company, and
  (b)   every officer of the company who is in default.
(4)   A person guilty of an offence under this section is liable on summary conviction to a fine not exceeding level 3 on the standard scale.

NOTES

Commencement: 1 October 2009.

Commencement (transitional provisions): Sch 2, para 23 to the Companies Act 2006 (Commencement No 8, Transitional Provisions and Savings) Order 2008, SI 2008/2860 (at **[2.91]**) provides as follows—

"Register of members: information as to state of register and index (s 120)

23. Section 120 of the Companies Act 2006 (information as to state of register or index) applies where a person—
    (a) inspects a company's register of members or index of members' names on or after 1st October 2009, or
    (b) is provided by a company on or after that date with a copy of the company's register of members or any part of it,

whether the person's request to inspect, or be provided with a copy, was made before, on or after that date.".

[1.121]
121 Removal of entries relating to former members
An entry relating to a former member of the company may be removed from the register after the expiration of ten years from the date on which he ceased to be a member.

NOTES

Commencement: 6 April 2008.

Commencement (transitional provisions): Sch 4, Pt 1, para 2 to the Companies Act 2006 (Commencement No 5, Transitional Provisions and Savings) Order 2007, SI 2007/3495 (at **[2.66]**) (as amended by the Companies Act 2006 (Commencement No 6, Saving and Commencement Nos 3 and 5 (Amendment)) Order 2008, SI 2008/674, art 5, Sch 3, para 6(1), (2), as from 6 April 2008) provides as follows—

"Register of members: removal of entries relating to former members (s 121)

2.—(1) The power conferred by section 121 of the Companies Act 2006 (removal after ten years of entries relating to former members) is exercisable on and after 6th April 2008, whenever the period of ten years referred to in that provision expired.

(2) A copy of any details that were included in the register immediately before that date and that are removed from the register under that power must be retained by the company until 6th April [2018] or, if earlier, 20 years after the member concerned ceased to be a member.".

Special cases

[1.122]
122 Share warrants
(1) On the issue of a share warrant the company must—
    (a) enter in the register of members—
        (i) the fact of the issue of the warrant,
        (ii) a statement of the shares included in the warrant, distinguishing each share by its number so long as the share has a number, and
        (iii) the date of the issue of the warrant,
        and
    (b) amend the register, if necessary, so that no person is named on the register as the holder of the shares specified in the warrant.
(2) Until the warrant is surrendered, the particulars specified in subsection (1)(a) are deemed to be those required by this Act to be entered in the register of members.
(3) The bearer of a share warrant may, if the articles of the company so provide, be deemed a member of the company within the meaning of this Act, either to the full extent or for any purposes defined in the articles.
(4) Subject to the company's articles, the bearer of a share warrant is entitled, on surrendering it for cancellation, to have his name entered as a member in the register of members.
(5) The company is responsible for any loss incurred by any person by reason of the company entering in the register the name of a bearer of a share warrant in respect of the shares specified in it without the warrant being surrendered and cancelled.
(6) On the surrender of a share warrant, the date of the surrender must be entered in the register.

NOTES

Commencement: 1 October 2009.

[1.123]
123 Single member companies
(1) If a limited company is formed under this Act with only one member there shall be entered in the company's register of members, with the name and address of the sole member, a statement that the company has only one member.
(2) If the number of members of a limited company falls to one, or if an unlimited company with only one member becomes a limited company on re-registration, there shall upon the occurrence of that event be entered in the company's register of members, with the name and address of the sole member—
    (a) a statement that the company has only one member, and
    (b) the date on which the company became a company having only one member.

(3) If the membership of a limited company increases from one to two or more members, there shall upon the occurrence of that event be entered in the company's register of members, with the name and address of the person who was formerly the sole member—

  (a) a statement that the company has ceased to have only one member, and

  (b) the date on which that event occurred.

(4) If a company makes default in complying with this section, an offence is committed by—

  (a) the company, and

  (b) every officer of the company who is in default.

(5) A person guilty of an offence under this section is liable on summary conviction to a fine not exceeding level 3 on the standard scale and, for continued contravention, a daily default fine not exceeding one-tenth of level 3 on the standard scale.

NOTES

Commencement: 1 October 2009.

[1.124]

124 Company holding its own shares as treasury shares

(1) Where a company purchases its own shares in circumstances in which section 724 (treasury shares) applies—

  (a) the requirements of section 113 (register of members) need not be complied with if the company cancels all of the shares forthwith after the purchase, and

  (b) if the company does not cancel all of the shares forthwith after the purchase, any share that is so cancelled shall be disregarded for the purposes of that section.

(2) Subject to subsection (1), where a company holds shares as treasury shares the company must be entered in the register as the member holding those shares.

NOTES

Commencement: 1 October 2009.

Supplementary

[1.125]

125 Power of court to rectify register

(1) If—

  (a) the name of any person is, without sufficient cause, entered in or omitted from a company's register of members, or

  (b) default is made or unnecessary delay takes place in entering on the register the fact of any person having ceased to be a member,

the person aggrieved, or any member of the company, or the company, may apply to the court for rectification of the register.

(2) The court may either refuse the application or may order rectification of the register and payment by the company of any damages sustained by any party aggrieved.

(3) On such an application the court may decide any question relating to the title of a person who is a party to the application to have his name entered in or omitted from the register, whether the question arises between members or alleged members, or between members or alleged members on the one hand and the company on the other hand, and generally may decide any question necessary or expedient to be decided for rectification of the register.

(4) In the case of a company required by this Act to send a list of its members to the registrar of companies, the court, when making an order for rectification of the register, shall by its order direct notice of the rectification to be given to the registrar.

NOTES

Commencement: 1 October 2009.

[1.126]

126 Trusts not to be entered on register

No notice of any trust, expressed, implied or constructive, shall be entered on the register of members of a company registered in England and Wales or Northern Ireland, or be receivable by the registrar.

NOTES

Commencement: 1 October 2009.

[1.127]

127 Register to be evidence

The register of members is prima facie evidence of any matters which are by this Act directed or authorised to be inserted in it.

NOTES

Commencement: 1 October 2009.

[1.128]
128 Time limit for claims arising from entry in register
(1)   Liability incurred by a company—
   (a)   from the making or deletion of an entry in the register of members, or
   (b)   from a failure to make or delete any such entry,
is not enforceable more than ten years after the date on which the entry was made or deleted or, as the case may be, the failure first occurred.
(2)   This is without prejudice to any lesser period of limitation (and, in Scotland, to any rule that the obligation giving rise to the liability prescribes before the expiry of that period).

NOTES
   Commencement: 6 April 2008.
   Commencement (transitional provisions): Sch 4, Pt 1, para 3 to the Companies Act 2006 (Commencement No 5, Transitional Provisions and Savings) Order 2007, SI 2007/3495 (at **[2.66]**) provides as follows—

"Register of members: time limit for claims arising from entry (s 128)
   3.—(1)   Section 128 of the Companies Act 2006 (ten year time limit for claims arising from entry in register of members) applies to causes of action arising on or after 6th April 2008.
   (2)   The time limit for causes of action arising before that date is—
      (a)   ten years from 6th April 2008, or
      (b)   20 years (as provided by section 352(7) of the 1985 Act or Article 360(7) of the 1986 Order) from when the cause of action arose,
   whichever expires first.
   (3)   This is without prejudice to any lesser period of limitation (and, in Scotland, to any rule that the obligation giving rise to the liability prescribes before the expiry of that period).".

CHAPTER 3
OVERSEAS BRANCH REGISTERS

[1.129]
129 Overseas branch registers
(1)   A company having a share capital may, if it transacts business in a country or territory to which this Chapter applies, cause to be kept there a branch register of members resident there (an "overseas branch register").
(2)   This Chapter applies to—
   (a)   any part of Her Majesty's dominions outside the United Kingdom, the Channel Islands and the Isle of Man, and
   (b)   the countries or territories listed below.

Bangladesh	Malaysia
Cyprus	Malta
Dominica	Nigeria
The Gambia	Pakistan
Ghana	Seychelles
Guyana	Sierra Leone
The Hong Kong Special Administrative Region of the People's Republic of China	Singapore
	South Africa
India	Sri Lanka
Ireland	Swaziland
Kenya	Trinidad and Tobago
Kiribati	Uganda
Lesotho	Zimbabwe
Malawi	

(3)   The Secretary of State may make provision by regulations as to the circumstances in which a company is to be regarded as keeping a register in a particular country or territory.
(4)   Regulations under this section are subject to negative resolution procedure.
(5)   References—
   (a)   in any Act or instrument (including, in particular, a company's articles) to a dominion register, or
   (b)   in articles registered before 1st November 1929 to a colonial register,
are to be read (unless the context otherwise requires) as a reference to an overseas branch register kept under this section.

NOTES
   Commencement: 20 January 2007 (for the purpose of enabling the exercise of powers to make Orders or Regulations by statutory instrument); 1 October 2009 (otherwise).

[1.130]
130 Notice of opening of overseas branch register
(1) A company that begins to keep an overseas branch register must give notice to the registrar within 14 days of doing so, stating the country or territory in which the register is kept.
(2) If default is made in complying with subsection (1), an offence is committed by—
    (a)   the company, and
    (b)   every officer of the company who is in default.
(3) A person guilty of an offence under subsection (2) is liable on summary conviction to a fine not exceeding level 3 on the standard scale and, for continued contravention, a daily default fine not exceeding one-tenth of level 3 on the standard scale.

NOTES
   Commencement: 1 October 2009.

[1.131]
131 Keeping of overseas branch register
(1) An overseas branch register is regarded as part of the company's register of members ("the main register").
(2) The Secretary of State may make provision by regulations modifying any provision of Chapter 2 (register of members) as it applies in relation to an overseas branch register.
(3) Regulations under this section are subject to negative resolution procedure.
(4) Subject to the provisions of this Act, a company may by its articles make such provision as it thinks fit as to the keeping of overseas branch registers.

NOTES
   Commencement: 20 January 2007 (for the purpose of enabling the exercise of powers to make Orders or Regulations by statutory instrument); 1 October 2009 (otherwise).

[1.132]
132 Register or duplicate to be kept available for inspection in UK
(1) A company that keeps an overseas branch register must keep available for inspection—
    (a)   the register, or
    (b)   a duplicate of the register duly entered up from time to time,
at the place in the United Kingdom where the company's main register is kept available for inspection.
(2) Any such duplicate is treated for all purposes of this Act as part of the main register.
(3) If default is made in complying with subsection (1), an offence is committed by—
    (a)   the company, and
    (b)   every officer of the company who is in default.
(4) A person guilty of an offence under subsection (3) is liable on summary conviction to a fine not exceeding level 3 on the standard scale and, for continued contravention, a daily default fine not exceeding one-tenth of level 3 on the standard scale.

NOTES
   Commencement: 1 October 2009.

[1.133]
133 Transactions in shares registered in overseas branch register
(1) Shares registered in an overseas branch register must be distinguished from those registered in the main register.
(2) No transaction with respect to shares registered in an overseas branch register may be registered in any other register.
(3) An instrument of transfer of a share registered in an overseas branch register—
    (a)   is regarded as a transfer of property situated outside the United Kingdom, and
    (b)   unless executed in a part of the United Kingdom, is exempt from stamp duty.

NOTES
   Commencement: 1 October 2009.

[1.134]
134 Jurisdiction of local courts
(1) A competent court in a country or territory where an overseas branch register is kept may exercise the same jurisdiction as is exercisable by a court in the United Kingdom—
    (a)   to rectify the register (see section 125), or
    (b)   in relation to a request for inspection or a copy of the register (see section 117).
(2) The offences—
    (a)   of refusing inspection or failing to provide a copy of the register (see section 118), and
    (b)   of making a false, misleading or deceptive statement in a request for inspection or a copy (see section 119),

may be prosecuted summarily before any tribunal having summary criminal jurisdiction in the country or territory where the register is kept.

(3) This section extends only to those countries and territories to which paragraph 3 of Schedule 14 to the Companies Act 1985 (c 6) (which made similar provision) extended immediately before the coming into force of this Chapter.

NOTES
Commencement: 1 October 2009.

[1.135]
135 Discontinuance of overseas branch register
(1)   A company may discontinue an overseas branch register.
(2)   If it does so all the entries in that register must be transferred—
   (a)   to some other overseas branch register kept in the same country or territory, or
   (b)   to the main register.
(3)   The company must give notice to the registrar within 14 days of the discontinuance.
(4)   If default is made in complying with subsection (3), an offence is committed by—
   (a)   the company, and
   (b)   every officer of the company who is in default.
(5)   A person guilty of an offence under subsection (4) is liable on summary conviction to a fine not exceeding level 3 on the standard scale and, for continued contravention, a daily default fine not exceeding one-tenth of level 3 on the standard scale.

NOTES
Commencement: 1 October 2009.

CHAPTER 4
PROHIBITION ON SUBSIDIARY BEING MEMBER OF ITS HOLDING COMPANY
General prohibition

[1.136]
136 Prohibition on subsidiary being a member of its holding company
(1)   Except as provided by this Chapter—
   (a)   a body corporate cannot be a member of a company that is its holding company, and
   (b)   any allotment or transfer of shares in a company to its subsidiary is void.
(2)   The exceptions are provided for in—
   section 138 (subsidiary acting as personal representative or trustee), and
   section 141 (subsidiary acting as authorised dealer in securities).

NOTES
Commencement: 1 October 2009.

[1.137]
137 Shares acquired before prohibition became applicable
(1)   Where a body corporate became a holder of shares in a company—
   (a)   before the relevant date, or
   (b)   on or after that date and before the commencement of this Chapter in circumstances in which the prohibition in section 23(1) of the Companies Act 1985 or Article 33(1) of the Companies (Northern Ireland) Order 1986 (SI 1986/1032 (NI 6)) (or any corresponding earlier enactment), as it then had effect, did not apply, or
   (c)   on or after the commencement of this Chapter in circumstances in which the prohibition in section 136 did not apply,
it may continue to be a member of the company.
(2)   The relevant date for the purposes of subsection (1)(a) is—
   (a)   1st July 1948 in the case of a company registered in Great Britain, and
   (b)   1st April 1961 in the case of a company registered in Northern Ireland.
(3)   So long as it is permitted to continue as a member of a company by virtue of this section, an allotment to it of fully paid shares in the company may be validly made by way of capitalisation of reserves of the company.
(4)   But, so long as the prohibition in section 136 would (apart from this section) apply, it has no right to vote in respect of the shares mentioned in subsection (1) above, or any shares allotted as mentioned in subsection (3) above, on a written resolution or at meetings of the company or of any class of its members.

NOTES
Commencement: 1 October 2009.

Part 1 The Companies Act 2006

Subsidiary acting as personal representative or trustee

[1.138]
138 Subsidiary acting as personal representative or trustee
(1) The prohibition in section 136 (prohibition on subsidiary being a member of its holding company) does not apply where the subsidiary is concerned only—
    (a)   as personal representative, or
    (b)   as trustee,
unless, in the latter case, the holding company or a subsidiary of it is beneficially interested under the trust.
(2) For the purpose of ascertaining whether the holding company or a subsidiary is so interested, there shall be disregarded—
    (a)   any interest held only by way of security for the purposes of a transaction entered into by the holding company or subsidiary in the ordinary course of a business that includes the lending of money;
    (b)   any interest within—
        section 139 (interests to be disregarded: residual interest under pension scheme or employees' share scheme), or
        section 140 (interests to be disregarded: employer's rights of recovery under pension scheme or employees' share scheme);
    (c)   any rights that the company or subsidiary has in its capacity as trustee, including in particular—
        (i)   any right to recover its expenses or be remunerated out of the trust property, and
        (ii) any right to be indemnified out of the trust property for any liability incurred by reason of any act or omission in the performance of its duties as trustee.

NOTES
Commencement: 1 October 2009.

[1.139]
139 Interests to be disregarded: residual interest under pension scheme or employees' share scheme
(1) Where shares in a company are held on trust for the purposes of a pension scheme or employees' share scheme, there shall be disregarded for the purposes of section 138 any residual interest that has not vested in possession.
(2) A "residual interest" means a right of the company or subsidiary ("the residual beneficiary") to receive any of the trust property in the event of—
    (a)   all the liabilities arising under the scheme having been satisfied or provided for, or
    (b)   the residual beneficiary ceasing to participate in the scheme, or
    (c)   the trust property at any time exceeding what is necessary for satisfying the liabilities arising or expected to arise under the scheme.
(3) In subsection (2)—
    (a)   the reference to a right includes a right dependent on the exercise of a discretion vested by the scheme in the trustee or another person, and
    (b)   the reference to liabilities arising under a scheme includes liabilities that have resulted, or may result, from the exercise of any such discretion.
(4) For the purposes of this section a residual interest vests in possession—
    (a)   in a case within subsection (2)(a), on the occurrence of the event mentioned there (whether or not the amount of the property receivable pursuant to the right is ascertained);
    (b)   in a case within subsection (2)(b) or (c), when the residual beneficiary becomes entitled to require the trustee to transfer to him any of the property receivable pursuant to the right.
(5) In this section "pension scheme" means a scheme for the provision of benefits consisting of or including relevant benefits for or in respect of employees or former employees.
(6) In subsection (5)—
    (a)   "relevant benefits" means any pension, lump sum, gratuity or other like benefit given or to be given on retirement or on death or in anticipation of retirement or, in connection with past service, after retirement or death; and
    (b)   "employee" shall be read as if a director of a company were employed by it.

NOTES
Commencement: 1 October 2009.

[1.140]
140 Interests to be disregarded: employer's rights of recovery under pension scheme or employees' share scheme
(1) Where shares in a company are held on trust for the purposes of a pension scheme or employees' share scheme, there shall be disregarded for the purposes of section 138 any charge or lien on, or set-off against, any benefit or other right or interest under the scheme for the purpose of enabling the employer or former employer of a member of the scheme to obtain the discharge of a monetary obligation due to him from the member.

(2) In the case of a trust for the purposes of a pension scheme there shall also be disregarded any right to receive from the trustee of the scheme, or as trustee of the scheme to retain, an amount that can be recovered or retained, under section 61 of the Pension Schemes Act 1993 (c 48) or section 57 of the Pension Schemes (Northern Ireland) Act 1993 (c 49) (deduction of contributions equivalent premium from refund of scheme contributions) or otherwise, as reimbursement or partial reimbursement for any contributions equivalent premium paid in connection with the scheme under Part 3 of that Act.

(3) In this section "pension scheme" means a scheme for the provision of benefits consisting of or including relevant benefits for or in respect of employees or former employees.

"Relevant benefits" here means any pension, lump sum, gratuity or other like benefit given or to be given on retirement or on death or in anticipation of retirement or, in connection with past service, after retirement or death.

(4) In this section "employer" and "employee" shall be read as if a director of a company were employed by it.

NOTES

Commencement: 1 October 2009.

Subsidiary acting as dealer in securities

[1.141]

141 Subsidiary acting as authorised dealer in securities

(1) The prohibition in section 136 (prohibition on subsidiary being a member of its holding company) does not apply where the shares are held by the subsidiary in the ordinary course of its business as an intermediary.

(2) For this purpose a person is an intermediary if he—
   (a) carries on a bona fide business of dealing in securities,
   (b) is a member of or has access to a regulated market, and
   (c) does not carry on an excluded business.

(3) The following are excluded businesses—
   (a) a business that consists wholly or mainly in the making or managing of investments;
   (b) a business that consists wholly or mainly in, or is carried on wholly or mainly for the purposes of, providing services to persons who are connected with the person carrying on the business;
   (c) a business that consists in insurance business;
   (d) a business that consists in managing or acting as trustee in relation to a pension scheme, or that is carried on by the manager or trustee of such a scheme in connection with or for the purposes of the scheme;
   (e) a business that consists in operating or acting as trustee in relation to a collective investment scheme, or that is carried on by the operator or trustee of such a scheme in connection with and for the purposes of the scheme.

(4) For the purposes of this section—
   (a) the question whether a person is connected with another shall be determined in accordance with [section 1122 of the Corporation Tax Act 2010];
   (b) "collective investment scheme" has the meaning given in section 235 of the Financial Services and Markets Act 2000 (c 8);
   (c) "insurance business" means business that consists in the effecting or carrying out of contracts of insurance;
   (d) "securities" includes—
      (i) options,
      (ii) futures, and
      (iii) contracts for differences,
      and rights or interests in those investments;
   (e) "trustee" and "the operator" in relation to a collective investment scheme shall be construed in accordance with section 237(2) of the Financial Services and Markets Act 2000 (c 8).

(5) Expressions used in this section that are also used in the provisions regulating activities under the Financial Services and Markets Act 2000 have the same meaning here as they do in those provisions.

See section 22 of that Act, orders made under that section and Schedule 2 to that Act.

NOTES

Commencement: 1 October 2009.

Sub-s (4): words in square brackets in para (a) substituted by the Corporation Tax Act 2010, s 1177, Sch 1, Pt 2, paras 487, 488 (note that the 2010 Act comes into force on 1 April 2010 and has effect, for corporation tax purposes for accounting periods ending on or after that day, and for income tax and capital gains tax purposes for the tax year 2010–11 and subsequent tax years; see s 1184(1) of the 2010 Act (and for transitional provisions and savings, see Sch 2 to that Act)).

[1.142]
142 Protection of third parties in other cases where subsidiary acting as dealer in securities
(1) This section applies where—
- (a) a subsidiary that is a dealer in securities has purportedly acquired shares in its holding company in contravention of the prohibition in section 136, and
- (b) a person acting in good faith has agreed, for value and without notice of the contravention, to acquire shares in the holding company—
  - (i) from the subsidiary, or
  - (ii) from someone who has purportedly acquired the shares after their disposal by the subsidiary.

(2) A transfer to that person of the shares mentioned in subsection (1)(a) has the same effect as it would have had if their original acquisition by the subsidiary had not been in contravention of the prohibition.

NOTES
Commencement: 1 October 2009.

Supplementary

[1.143]
143 Application of provisions to companies not limited by shares
In relation to a company other than a company limited by shares, the references in this Chapter to shares shall be read as references to the interest of its members as such, whatever the form of that interest.

NOTES
Commencement: 1 October 2009.

[1.144]
144 Application of provisions to nominees
The provisions of this Chapter apply to a nominee acting on behalf of a subsidiary as to the subsidiary itself.

NOTES
Commencement: 1 October 2009.

PART 9
EXERCISE OF MEMBERS' RIGHTS

Effect of provisions in company's articles

[1.145]
145 Effect of provisions of articles as to enjoyment or exercise of members' rights
(1) This section applies where provision is made by a company's articles enabling a member to nominate another person or persons as entitled to enjoy or exercise all or any specified rights of the member in relation to the company.
(2) So far as is necessary to give effect to that provision, anything required or authorised by any provision of the Companies Acts to be done by or in relation to the member shall instead be done, or (as the case may be) may instead be done, by or in relation to the nominated person (or each of them) as if he were a member of the company.
(3) This applies, in particular, to the rights conferred by—
- (a) sections 291 and 293 (right to be sent proposed written resolution);
- (b) section 292 (right to require circulation of written resolution);
- (c) section 303 (right to require directors to call general meeting);
- (d) section 310 (right to notice of general meetings);
- (e) section 314 (right to require circulation of a statement);
- [(ea) section 319A (right to ask question at meeting of traded company);]
- (f) section 324 (right to appoint proxy to act at meeting);
- (g) section 338 (right to require circulation of resolution for AGM of public company); and
- [(ga) section 338A (traded companies: members' power to include matters in business dealt with at AGM);]
- (h) section 423 (right to be sent a copy of annual accounts and reports).

(4) This section and any such provision as is mentioned in subsection (1)—
- (a) do not confer rights enforceable against the company by anyone other than the member, and
- (b) do not affect the requirements for an effective transfer or other disposition of the whole or part of a member's interest in the company.

NOTES
Commencement: 1 October 2007.
Commencement (transitional provisions): Sch 3, para 3 to the Companies Act 2006 (Commencement No 3, Consequential Amendments, Transitional Provisions and Savings) Order 2007, SI 2007/2194 (at **[2.45]**) provides as follows—

"3 Exercise of members' rights (ss 145 to 153)

(1)   Section 145 of the Companies Act 2006 (effect of provisions of articles as to enjoyment or exercise of members' rights) applies in relation to things required or authorised to be done as mentioned in subsection (2) of that section on or after 1st October 2007.

(2)   Nominations under section 146 of that Act (traded companies: nomination of persons to enjoy information rights) may be made at any time on or after 1st October 2007.

A company is not required to act on a nomination before 1st January 2008; but if it does so, sections 147 to 150 apply.

(3)   Section 152 of that Act (exercise of rights where shares held on behalf of others: exercise in different ways) applies in relation to the exercise of rights on or after 1st October 2007.

(4)   A request may be made under section 153 of that Act (exercise of rights where shares held on behalf of others: members' requests) at any time on or after 1st October 2007.".

Commencement (transitional adaptations): the transitional adaptations of this section contained in the Companies Act 2006 (Commencement No 3, Consequential Amendments, Transitional Provisions and Savings) Order 2007, SI 2007/2194, Sch 1, para 3 were revoked by the Companies Act 2006 (Commencement No 5, Transitional Provisions and Savings) Order 2007, SI 2007/3495, art 10(1), (3), as from 6 April 2008 (subject to any transitional provisions and savings as apply, in accordance with Sch 4 to that Order, in relation to the repeal of any provision of the 1985 Act referred to in the adaptation). See **[2.43]**.

Sub-s (3): paras (ea), (ga) inserted by the Companies (Shareholders' Rights) Regulations 2009, SI 2009/1632, regs 12(2), 17(2), as from 3 August 2009, in relation to meetings of which notice is given, or first given, on or after that date.

Information rights

[1.146]

146 Traded companies: nomination of persons to enjoy information rights

(1)   This section applies to a company whose shares are admitted to trading on a regulated market.

(2)   A member of such a company who holds shares on behalf of another person may nominate that person to enjoy information rights.

(3)   "Information rights" means—

(a)   the right to receive a copy of all communications that the company sends to its members generally or to any class of its members that includes the person making the nomination, and

(b)   the rights conferred by—

    (i)   section 431 or 432 (right to require copies of accounts and reports), and

    (ii) section 1145 (right to require hard copy version of document or information provided in another form).

(4)   The reference in subsection (3)(a) to communications that a company sends to its members generally includes the company's annual accounts and reports. For the application of section 426 (option to provide summary financial statement) in relation to a person nominated to enjoy information rights, see subsection (5) of that section.

(5)   A company need not act on a nomination purporting to relate to certain information rights only.

NOTES

Commencement: 1 October 2007.

Commencement (transitional provisions): see the note to s 145 at **[1.145]**.

Commencement (transitional adaptations): the transitional adaptations of this section contained in the Companies Act 2006 (Commencement No 3, Consequential Amendments, Transitional Provisions and Savings) Order 2007, SI 2007/2194, Sch 1, para 4 were revoked by the Companies Act 2006 (Commencement No 5, Transitional Provisions and Savings) Order 2007, SI 2007/3495, art 10(1), (3), as from 6 April 2008 (subject to any transitional provisions and savings as apply, in accordance with Sch 4 to that Order, in relation to the repeal of any provision of the 1985 Act referred to in the adaptation). See **[2.43]**.

[1.147]

147 Information rights: form in which copies to be provided

(1)   This section applies as regards the form in which copies are to be provided to a person nominated under section 146 (nomination of person to enjoy information rights).

(2)   If the person to be nominated wishes to receive hard copy communications, he must—

(a)   request the person making the nomination to notify the company of that fact, and

(b)   provide an address to which such copies may be sent.

This must be done before the nomination is made.

(3)   If having received such a request the person making the nomination—

(a)   notifies the company that the nominated person wishes to receive hard copy communications, and

(b)   provides the company with that address,

the right of the nominated person is to receive hard copy communications accordingly.

(4)   This is subject to the provisions of Parts 3 and 4 of Schedule 5 (communications by company) under which the company may take steps to enable it to communicate in electronic form or by means of a website.

(5)   If no such notification is given (or no address is provided), the nominated person is taken to have agreed that documents or information may be sent or supplied to him by the company by means of a website.

(6)   That agreement—

(a)   may be revoked by the nominated person, and

(b)   does not affect his right under section 1145 to require a hard copy version of a document or information provided in any other form.

NOTES
Commencement: 1 October 2007.
Commencement (transitional provisions): see the note to s 145 at **[1.145]**.

[1.148]

148   Termination or suspension of nomination

(1)   The following provisions have effect in relation to a nomination under section 146 (nomination of person to enjoy information rights).

(2)   The nomination may be terminated at the request of the member or of the nominated person.

(3)   The nomination ceases to have effect on the occurrence in relation to the member or the nominated person of any of the following—

(a)   in the case of an individual, death or bankruptcy;

(b)   in the case of a body corporate, dissolution or the making of an order for the winding up of the body otherwise than for the purposes of reconstruction.

(4)   In subsection (3)—

(a)   the reference to bankruptcy includes—

(i)   the sequestration of a person's estate, and

(ii)   a person's estate being the subject of a protected trust deed (within the meaning of the Bankruptcy (Scotland) Act 1985 (c 66)); and

(b)   the reference to the making of an order for winding up is to—

(i)   the making of such an order under the Insolvency Act 1986 (c 45) or the Insolvency (Northern Ireland) Order 1989 (SI 1989/2405 (NI 19)), or

(ii)   any corresponding proceeding under the law of a country or territory outside the United Kingdom.

(5)   The effect of any nominations made by a member is suspended at any time when there are more nominated persons than the member has shares in the company.

(6)   Where—

(a)   the member holds different classes of shares with different information rights, and

(b)   there are more nominated persons than he has shares conferring a particular right,

the effect of any nominations made by him is suspended to the extent that they confer that right.

(7)   Where the company—

(a)   enquires of a nominated person whether he wishes to retain information rights, and

(b)   does not receive a response within the period of 28 days beginning with the date on which the company's enquiry was sent,

the nomination ceases to have effect at the end of that period.

Such an enquiry is not to be made of a person more than once in any twelve-month period.

(8)   The termination or suspension of a nomination means that the company is not required to act on it.

It does not prevent the company from continuing to do so, to such extent or for such period as it thinks fit.

NOTES
Commencement: 1 October 2007.
Commencement (transitional provisions): see the note to s 145 at **[1.145]**.

[1.149]

149   Information as to possible rights in relation to voting

(1)   This section applies where a company sends a copy of a notice of a meeting to a person nominated under section 146 (nomination of person to enjoy information rights).

(2)   The copy of the notice must be accompanied by a statement that—

(a)   he may have a right under an agreement between him and the member by whom he was nominated to be appointed, or to have someone else appointed, as a proxy for the meeting, and

(b)   if he has no such right or does not wish to exercise it, he may have a right under such an agreement to give instructions to the member as to the exercise of voting rights.

(3)   Section 325 (notice of meeting to contain statement of member's rights in relation to appointment of proxy) does not apply to the copy, and the company must either—

(a)   omit the notice required by that section, or

(b)   include it but state that it does not apply to the nominated person.

NOTES
Commencement: 1 October 2007.
Commencement (transitional provisions): see the note to s 145 at **[1.145]**.

[1.150]
150 Information rights: status of rights
(1) This section has effect as regards the rights conferred by a nomination under section 146 (nomination of person to enjoy information rights).

(2) Enjoyment by the nominated person of the rights conferred by the nomination is enforceable against the company by the member as if they were rights conferred by the company's articles.

(3) Any enactment, and any provision of the company's articles, having effect in relation to communications with members has a corresponding effect (subject to any necessary adaptations) in relation to communications with the nominated person.

(4) In particular—
    (a) where under any enactment, or any provision of the company's articles, the members of a company entitled to receive a document or information are determined as at a date or time before it is sent or supplied, the company need not send or supply it to a nominated person—
        (i) whose nomination was received by the company after that date or time, or
        (ii) if that date or time falls in a period of suspension of his nomination; and
    (b) where under any enactment, or any provision of the company's articles, the right of a member to receive a document or information depends on the company having a current address for him, the same applies to any person nominated by him.

(5) The rights conferred by the nomination—
    (a) are in addition to the rights of the member himself, and
    (b) do not affect any rights exercisable by virtue of any such provision as is mentioned in section 145 (provisions of company's articles as to enjoyment or exercise of members' rights).

(6) A failure to give effect to the rights conferred by the nomination does not affect the validity of anything done by or on behalf of the company.

(7) References in this section to the rights conferred by the nomination are to—
    (a) the rights referred to in section 146(3) (information rights), and
    (b) where applicable, the rights conferred by section 147(3) (right to hard copy communications) and section 149 (information as to possible voting rights).

NOTES
Commencement: 1 October 2007.
Commencement (transitional provisions): see the note to s 145 at **[1.145]**.

[1.151]
151 Information rights: power to amend
(1) The Secretary of State may by regulations amend the provisions of sections 146 to 150 (information rights) so as to—
    (a) extend or restrict the classes of companies to which section 146 applies,
    (b) make other provision as to the circumstances in which a nomination may be made under that section, or
    (c) extend or restrict the rights conferred by such a nomination.

(2) The regulations may make such consequential modifications of any other provisions of this Part, or of any other enactment, as appear to the Secretary of State to be necessary.

(3) Regulations under this section are subject to affirmative resolution procedure.

NOTES
Commencement: 20 January 2007 (for the purpose of enabling the exercise of powers to make Orders or Regulations by statutory instrument); 1 October 2007 (otherwise).
Commencement (transitional provisions): see the note to s 145 at **[1.145]**.

Exercise of rights where shares held on behalf of others

[1.152]
152 Exercise of rights where shares held on behalf of others: exercise in different ways
(1) Where a member holds shares in a company on behalf of more than one person—
    (a) rights attached to the shares, and
    (b) rights under any enactment exercisable by virtue of holding the shares,
need not all be exercised, and if exercised, need not all be exercised in the same way.

(2) A member who exercises such rights but does not exercise all his rights, must inform the company to what extent he is exercising the rights.

(3) A member who exercises such rights in different ways must inform the company of the ways in which he is exercising them and to what extent they are exercised in each way.

(4) If a member exercises such rights without informing the company—
    (a) that he is not exercising all his rights, or
    (b) that he is exercising his rights in different ways,
the company is entitled to assume that he is exercising all his rights and is exercising them in the same way.

NOTES

Commencement: 1 October 2007.

Commencement (transitional provisions): see the note to s 145 at **[1.145]**.

[1.153]
153 Exercise of rights where shares held on behalf of others: members' requests

(1) This section applies for the purposes of—

(a) section 314 (power to require circulation of statement),

(b) section 338 (public companies: power to require circulation of resolution for AGM),

[(ba) section 338A (traded companies: members' power to include matters in business dealt with at AGM),]

(c) section 342 (power to require independent report on poll), and

(d) section 527 (power to require website publication of audit concerns).

(2) A company is required to act under any of those sections if it receives a request in relation to which the following conditions are met—

(a) it is made by at least 100 persons;

(b) it is authenticated by all the persons making it;

(c) in the case of any of those persons who is not a member of the company, it is accompanied by a statement—

(i) of the full name and address of a person ("the member") who is a member of the company and holds shares on behalf of that person,

(ii) that the member is holding those shares on behalf of that person in the course of a business,

(iii) of the number of shares in the company that the member holds on behalf of that person,

(iv) of the total amount paid up on those shares,

(v) that those shares are not held on behalf of anyone else or, if they are, that the other person or persons are not among the other persons making the request,

(vi) that some or all of those shares confer voting rights that are relevant for the purposes of making a request under the section in question, and

(vii) that the person has the right to instruct the member how to exercise those rights;

(d) in the case of any of those persons who is a member of the company, it is accompanied by a statement—

(i) that he holds shares otherwise than on behalf of another person, or

(ii) that he holds shares on behalf of one or more other persons but those persons are not among the other persons making the request;

(e) it is accompanied by such evidence as the company may reasonably require of the matters mentioned in paragraph (c) and (d);

(f) the total amount of the sums paid up on—

(i) shares held as mentioned in paragraph (c), and

(ii) shares held as mentioned in paragraph (d),

divided by the number of persons making the request, is not less than £100;

(g) the request complies with any other requirements of the section in question as to contents, timing and otherwise.

NOTES

Commencement: 1 October 2007.

Commencement (transitional provisions): see the note to s 145 at **[1.145]**.

Commencement (transitional adaptations): the transitional adaptations of this section contained in the Companies Act 2006 (Commencement No 3, Consequential Amendments, Transitional Provisions and Savings) Order 2007, SI 2007/2194, Sch 1, para 5 were revoked by the Companies Act 2006 (Commencement No 5, Transitional Provisions and Savings) Order 2007, SI 2007/3495, art 10(1), as from 6 April 2008. See **[2.43]**.

Sub-s (1): para (ba) inserted by the Companies (Shareholders' Rights) Regulations 2009, SI 2009/1632, reg 17(3), as from 3 August 2009, in relation to meetings of which notice is given, or first given, on or after that date.

PART 10
A COMPANY'S DIRECTORS

CHAPTER 1
APPOINTMENT AND REMOVAL OF DIRECTORS

Requirement to have directors

[1.154]
154 Companies required to have directors

(1) A private company must have at least one director.

(2) A public company must have at least two directors.

NOTES

Commencement: 1 October 2007.

[1.155]

155 Companies required to have at least one director who is a natural person

(1) A company must have at least one director who is a natural person.

(2) This requirement is met if the office of director is held by a natural person as a corporation sole or otherwise by virtue of an office.

NOTES

Commencement: 1 October 2008.

Commencement (transitional provisions): Sch 4, Pt 3, para 46 to the Companies Act 2006 (Commencement No 5, Transitional Provisions and Savings) Order 2007, SI 2007/3495 (at **[2.68]**) provides as follows—

"**Requirement to have at least one director who is a natural person (s 155)**

46. If on 8th November 2006—
   (a) none of a company's directors were natural persons, and
   (b) section 282 of the 1985 Act or Article 290 of the 1986 Order (requirement as to number of directors) was complied with in relation to the company,

section 155 of the Companies Act 2006 (companies required to have at least one director who is a natural person) does not apply to the company until 1st October 2010.".

[1.156]

156 Direction requiring company to make appointment

(1) If it appears to the Secretary of State that a company is in breach of—

section 154 (requirements as to number of directors), or

section 155 (requirement to have at least one director who is a natural person),

the Secretary of State may give the company a direction under this section.

(2) The direction must specify—

(a) the statutory requirement the company appears to be in breach of,

(b) what the company must do in order to comply with the direction, and

(c) the period within which it must do so.

That period must be not less than one month or more than three months after the date on which the direction is given.

(3) The direction must also inform the company of the consequences of failing to comply.

(4) Where the company is in breach of section 154 or 155 it must comply with the direction by—

(a) making the necessary appointment or appointments, and

(b) giving notice of them under section 167,

before the end of the period specified in the direction.

(5) If the company has already made the necessary appointment or appointments (or so far as it has done so), it must comply with the direction by giving notice of them under section 167 before the end of the period specified in the direction.

(6) If a company fails to comply with a direction under this section, an offence is committed by—

(a) the company, and

(b) every officer of the company who is in default.

For this purpose a shadow director is treated as an officer of the company.

(7) A person guilty of an offence under this section is liable on summary conviction to a fine not exceeding level 5 on the standard scale and, for continued contravention, a daily default fine not exceeding one-tenth of level 5 on the standard scale.

NOTES

Commencement: 1 October 2008.

Commencement (transitional adaptations): art 6 of the Companies Act 2006 (Commencement No 5, Transitional Provisions and Savings) Order 2007, SI 2007/3495 provides that the provisions brought into force by arts 3 and 5 of that Order shall have effect subject to any transitional adaptations specified in Sch 1 to that Order. Schedule 1, Pt 2, para 24 to the Order (at **[2.63]**) provided for such transitional adaptations (note that this paragraph was revoked by the Companies Act 2006 (Commencement No 8, Transitional Provisions and Savings) Order 2008, SI 2008/2860, art 6, as from 1 October 2009 (subject to any relevant transitional provision or saving in Sch 2 to that Order)).

Appointment

[1.157]

157 Minimum age for appointment as director

(1) A person may not be appointed a director of a company unless he has attained the age of 16 years.

(2) This does not affect the validity of an appointment that is not to take effect until the person appointed attains that age.

(3) Where the office of director of a company is held by a corporation sole, or otherwise by virtue of another office, the appointment to that other office of a person who has not attained the age of 16 years is not effective also to make him a director of the company until he attains the age of 16 years.

(4) An appointment made in contravention of this section is void.

(5) Nothing in this section affects any liability of a person under any provision of the Companies Acts if he—

    (a) purports to act as director, or

    (b) acts as a shadow director,

although he could not, by virtue of this section, be validly appointed as a director.

(6) This section has effect subject to section 158 (power to provide for exceptions from minimum age requirement).

NOTES

Commencement: 1 October 2008.

[1.158]
158 Power to provide for exceptions from minimum age requirement

(1) The Secretary of State may make provision by regulations for cases in which a person who has not attained the age of 16 years may be appointed a director of a company.

(2) The regulations must specify the circumstances in which, and any conditions subject to which, the appointment may be made.

(3) If the specified circumstances cease to obtain, or any specified conditions cease to be met, a person who was appointed by virtue of the regulations and who has not since attained the age of 16 years ceases to hold office.

(4) The regulations may make different provision for different parts of the United Kingdom.

This is without prejudice to the general power to make different provision for different cases.

(5) Regulations under this section are subject to negative resolution procedure.

NOTES

Commencement: 20 January 2007 (for the purpose of enabling the exercise of powers to make Orders or Regulations by statutory instrument); 1 October 2008 (otherwise).

[1.159]
159 Existing under-age directors

(1) This section applies where—

    (a) a person appointed a director of a company before section 157 (minimum age for appointment as director) comes into force has not attained the age of 16 when that section comes into force, or

    (b) the office of director of a company is held by a corporation sole, or otherwise by virtue of another office, and the person appointed to that other office has not attained the age of 16 years when that section comes into force,

and the case is not one excepted from that section by regulations under section 158.

(2) That person ceases to be a director on section 157 coming into force.

(3) The company must make the necessary consequential alteration in its register of directors but need not give notice to the registrar of the change.

(4) If it appears to the registrar (from other information) that a person has ceased by virtue of this section to be a director of a company, the registrar shall note that fact on the register.

NOTES

Commencement: 1 October 2008.

[1.160]
160 Appointment of directors of public company to be voted on individually

(1) At a general meeting of a public company a motion for the appointment of two or more persons as directors of the company by a single resolution must not be made unless a resolution that it should be so made has first been agreed to by the meeting without any vote being given against it.

(2) A resolution moved in contravention of this section is void, whether or not its being so moved was objected to at the time.

But where a resolution so moved is passed, no provision for the automatic reappointment of retiring directors in default of another appointment applies.

(3) For the purposes of this section a motion for approving a person's appointment, or for nominating a person for appointment, is treated as a motion for his appointment.

(4) Nothing in this section applies to a resolution amending the company's articles.

NOTES

Commencement: 1 October 2007.

[1.161]
161 Validity of acts of directors

(1) The acts of a person acting as a director are valid notwithstanding that it is afterwards discovered—

    (a) that there was a defect in his appointment;

    (b)   that he was disqualified from holding office;

    (c)   that he had ceased to hold office;

    (d)   that he was not entitled to vote on the matter in question.

(2)   This applies even if the resolution for his appointment is void under section 160 (appointment of directors of public company to be voted on individually).

NOTES

Commencement: 1 October 2007.

Commencement (transitional provisions): Sch 3, para 4 to the Companies Act 2006 (Commencement No 3, Consequential Amendments, Transitional Provisions and Savings) Order 2007, SI 2007/2194 (at **[2.45]**) provides that this section applies to acts done on or after 1 October 2007 (and that s 285 of the 1985 Act continues to apply to acts done before that date).

Register of directors, etc

[1.162]

162   Register of directors

(1)   Every company must keep a register of its directors.

(2)   The register must contain the required particulars (see sections 163, 164 and 166) of each person who is a director of the company.

(3)   The register must be kept available for inspection—

    (a)   at the company's registered office, or

    (b)   at a place specified in regulations under section 1136.

(4)   The company must give notice to the registrar—

    (a)   of the place at which the register is kept available for inspection, and

    (b)   of any change in that place,

unless it has at all times been kept at the company's registered office.

(5)   The register must be open to the inspection—

    (a)   of any member of the company without charge, and

    (b)   of any other person on payment of such fee as may be prescribed.

(6)   If default is made in complying with subsection (1), (2) or (3) or if default is made for 14 days in complying with subsection (4), or if an inspection required under subsection (5) is refused, an offence is committed by—

    (a)   the company, and

    (b)   every officer of the company who is in default.

For this purpose a shadow director is treated as an officer of the company.

(7)   A person guilty of an offence under this section is liable on summary conviction to a fine not exceeding level 5 on the standard scale and, for continued contravention, a daily default fine not exceeding one-tenth of level 5 on the standard scale.

(8)   In the case of a refusal of inspection of the register, the court may by order compel an immediate inspection of it.

NOTES

Commencement: 20 January 2007 (for the purpose of enabling the exercise of powers to make Orders or Regulations by statutory instrument); 1 October 2009 (otherwise).

Commencement (transitional provisions): Sch 2, paras 25–39 to the Companies Act 2006 (Commencement No 8, Transitional Provisions and Savings) Order 2008, SI 2008/2860 (at **[2.91]**) contain a variety of transitional provisions in connection with the registers of directors and secretaries, the particulars to be registered, protection from disclosure, etc. Those paragraphs provide as follows—

"Registers of directors and secretaries (ss 162 and 275)

25.   On and after 1st October 2009 the register of directors and secretaries kept by a company under section 288(1) of the 1985 Act or Article 296(1) of the 1986 Order shall be treated as two separate registers—

    (a)   a register of directors kept under and for the purposes of section 162 of the Companies Act 2006, and

    (b)   a register of secretaries kept under and for the purposes of section 275 of that Act.

Particulars to be registered (ss 163, 164 and 166 and 277 to 279)

26.—(1)   Subject to the following provisions, an existing company need not comply with any provision of the Companies Act 2006 requiring the company's register of directors or secretaries to contain particulars additional to those required by the 1985 Act or the 1986 Order until the earlier of—

    (a)   the date to which the company makes up its first annual return made up to a date on or after 1st October 2009, and

    (b)   the last date to which the company should have made up that return.

(2)   Sub-paragraph (1) does not apply in relation to a director or secretary of whom particulars are first registered on or after 1st October 2009 (whether the director or secretary was appointed before, on or after that date).

(3)   Sub-paragraph (1) ceases to apply in relation to a director or secretary whose registered particulars fall to be altered on or after 1st October 2009 because they have changed (whether the change occurred before, on or after that date).

(4)   This paragraph does not affect the particulars required to be included in the company's annual return.

27.—(1)   In the case of an existing company—

    (a)   the relevant existing address of a director or secretary is deemed, on and after 1st October 2009, to be a service address, and

    (b)   any entry in the company's register of directors or secretaries stating that address is treated, on and after that date, as complying with the obligation in section 163(1)(b) or 277(1)(b) of the Companies Act 2006 to state a service address.

(2)   The relevant existing address is—

(a)   the address that immediately before 1st October 2009 appeared in the company's register of directors and secretaries as having been notified to the company under section 289(1A) or 290(1A) of the 1985 Act (service address notified by individual applying for confidentiality order in respect of usual residential address), or

(b)   if no such address appeared, the address that immediately before that date appeared in the company's register of directors and secretaries as the director's or secretary's usual residential address.

(3)   Any notification of a change of a relevant existing address occurring before 1st October 2009 that is received by the company on or after that date is treated as being or, as the case may be, including notification of a change of service address.

(4)   The operation of this paragraph does not give rise to any duty to notify the registrar under section 167 or 276 of the Companies Act 2006 (duty to notify registrar of changes in particulars contained in register).

28.—(1)   An existing company must remove from its register of directors on 1st October 2009 any entry relating to a shadow director.

(2)   Section 167 of the Companies Act 2006 (duty to notify registrar of changes) applies as if the shadow director had ceased to be a director on that date.

29.   The removal by an existing company from its register of directors or secretaries on or after 1st October 2009 of particulars required by the 1985 Act or the 1986 Order but not required by the Companies Act 2006 does not give rise to any duty to notify the registrar under section 167 or 276 of the Companies Act 2006 (duty to notify registrar of changes in particulars contained in register).

Register of directors' residential addresses (s 165)

30.—(1)   The duty of a company to keep a register of directors' residential addresses has effect on and after 1st October 2009.

(2)   The entry on that register of information that immediately before that date was contained in the company's register of directors and secretaries does not give rise to any duty to notify the registrar under section 167 of the Companies Act 2006 (duty to notify registrar of changes in particulars contained in register).

Duty to notify registrar of changes (ss 167 and 276)

31.—(1)   Sections 167 and 276 of the Companies Act 2006 (duty to notify registrar of changes) apply in relation to—

(a)   a change among a company's directors or in its secretaries, or

(b)   a change in the particulars contained in the register,

occurring on or after 1st October 2009.

(2)   Sections 288(2), (4) and (6), 289 and 290 of the 1985 Act or Articles 296(2), (4) and (6), 297 and 298 of the 1986 Order (notification to registrar of changes) continue to apply in relation to a change occurring before that date.

Directors and secretaries: entries on the register of companies

32.—(1)   The registrar may make such entries in the register as appear to be appropriate having regard to paragraphs 26 to 30 and the information appearing on the register immediately before 1st October 2009 or notified to the registrar in accordance with paragraph 31(2).

(2)   In particular, the registrar may record as a service address—

(a)   a relevant existing address (within the meaning of paragraph 27), or

(b)   in the case of a company formed and registered on an application to which paragraph 2(3) applies, an address notified to the registrar in connection with that application as a director's or secretary's usual residential address.

(3)   Any notification of a change of a relevant existing address occurring before 1st October 2009 that is received by the registrar on or after that date is treated as being or, as the case may be, including notification of a change of service address.

Directors' residential addresses: protection from disclosure (ss 240 to 246)

33.   Where a director's usual residential address appears as a service address—

(a)   in the company's register of directors by virtue of paragraph 27, or

(b)   in the register of companies by virtue of paragraph 32,

that address is not protected information for the purposes of Chapter 8 of Part 10 of the Companies Act 2006.

34.—(1)   Section 242(1) of the Companies Act 2006 (duty of registrar to omit protected information from material available for inspection) does not apply—

(a)   to material delivered to the registrar before 1st October 2009, or

(b)   to material delivered to the registrar on or after 1st October 2009 by virtue of paragraph 31(2) (notification of change occurring before that date).

(2)   In section 242(2)(b) of the Companies Act 2006 (exclusion of material registered before commencement) the reference to things registered before Chapter 8 of Part 10 of that Act comes into force is treated as including anything registered as a result of a notification in accordance with paragraph 31(2) (notification on or after 1st October 2009 of change occurring before that date).

(3)   Sub-paragraphs (1) and (2) have effect subject to paragraph 36 below (which provides for the continued protection of information formerly protected by a confidentiality order).

35.   In determining under section 245(1) of the Companies Act 2006 whether to put a director's usual residential address on the public record, the registrar may take into account only—

(a)   communications sent by the registrar on or after 1st October 2009, and

(b)   evidence as to the effectiveness of service coming to the registrar's attention on or after that date.

Continuation of protection afforded by confidentiality orders under the 1985 Act

36.—(1)   A director or secretary in relation to whom a confidentiality order under section 723B of the 1985 Act was in force immediately before 1st October 2009 is treated on and after that date as if—

(a)   they had made an application under section 1088 of the Companies Act 2006 (application to make address unavailable for public inspection) in respect of any address that immediately before that date was contained in "confidential records" as defined in section 723D(3) of the 1985 Act, and

(b)   that application had been determined by the registrar in their favour.

(2)   The provisions of regulations under section 1088 relating to decisions of the registrar in favour of an applicant (in particular, as to the duration and revocation of such a decision) apply accordingly.

(3)   As those regulations apply in accordance with this paragraph any reference to an offence under section 1112 of the Companies Act 2006 (false statement) shall be read as a reference to an offence under regulations under section 723E(1)(a) of the 1985 Act in relation to the application for the confidentiality order.

37.—(1) A director in relation to whom a confidentiality order under section 723B of the 1985 Act was in force immediately before 1st October 2009 is treated on and after that date as if—

    (a)   they had made an application under section 243(4) of the Companies Act 2006 (application to prevent disclosure of protected information by registrar to credit reference agency), and

    (b)   that application had been determined by the registrar in their favour.

(2)   The provisions of regulations under section 243(4) relating to decisions of the registrar in favour of an applicant (in particular, as to the duration and revocation of such a decision) apply accordingly.

(3)   As those regulations apply in accordance with this paragraph any reference to an offence under section 1112 (false statement) shall be read as a reference to an offence under regulations under section 723E(1)(a) of the 1985 Act in relation to the application for the confidentiality order.

38.   Where a confidentiality order under section 723B of the 1985 Act was in force immediately before 1st October 2009 in relation to a director or secretary of a company—

    (a)   section 162(5) and (8) of the Companies Act 2006 (inspection of company's register of directors), or

    (b)   section 275(5) and (8) of that Act (inspection of company's register of secretaries),

do not apply in relation to the part of the company's register containing particulars of the usual residential address of the individual that before that date were protected from disclosure by section 288(5A) of the 1985 Act.

Effect of pending application for confidentiality order

39.—(1)   Section 723B(3) to (8) of the 1985 Act (application for confidentiality order) continue to apply in relation to an application for a confidentiality order made before 1st October 2009.

(2)   Paragraphs 36 to 38 (continuation of protection afforded by confidentiality orders) apply to a person in respect of whom such an application has been made, and has not been determined or withdrawn, as to a person in relation to whom a confidentiality order was in force immediately before that date.

(3)   If the application is dismissed or withdrawn, those paragraphs cease to apply.

(4)   If the application is successful those paragraphs continue to apply as in the case of an individual in relation to whom a confidentiality order was in force immediately before 1st October 2009.

Regulations: the Companies (Fees for Inspection of Company Records) Regulations 2008, SI 2008/3007 at **[4.327]**.

[1.163]
163 Particulars of directors to be registered: individuals

(1)   A company's register of directors must contain the following particulars in the case of an individual—

    (a)   name and any former name;

    (b)   a service address;

    (c)   the country or state (or part of the United Kingdom) in which he is usually resident;

    (d)   nationality;

    (e)   business occupation (if any);

    (f)   date of birth.

(2)   For the purposes of this section "name" means a person's Christian name (or other forename) and surname, except that in the case of—

    (a)   a peer, or

    (b)   an individual usually known by a title,

the title may be stated instead of his Christian name (or other forename) and surname or in addition to either or both of them.

(3)   For the purposes of this section a "former name" means a name by which the individual was formerly known for business purposes.

Where a person is or was formerly known by more than one such name, each of them must be stated.

(4)   It is not necessary for the register to contain particulars of a former name in the following cases—

    (a)   in the case of a peer or an individual normally known by a British title, where the name is one by which the person was known previous to the adoption of or succession to the title;

    (b)   in the case of any person, where the former name—

        (i)   was changed or disused before the person attained the age of 16 years, or

        (ii)   has been changed or disused for 20 years or more.

(5)   A person's service address may be stated to be "The company's registered office".

NOTES

Commencement: 1 October 2009.

Commencement (transitional provisions): see the note to s 162 at **[1.162]**.

[1.164]
164 Particulars of directors to be registered: corporate directors and firms

A company's register of directors must contain the following particulars in the case of a body corporate, or a firm that is a legal person under the law by which it is governed—

    (a)   corporate or firm name;

    (b)   registered or principal office;

    (c)   in the case of an EEA company to which the First Company Law Directive (68/151/EEC) applies, particulars of—

        (i)   the register in which the company file mentioned in Article 3 of that Directive is kept (including details of the relevant state), and

    (ii)   the registration number in that register;

(d)   in any other case, particulars of—

    (i)   the legal form of the company or firm and the law by which it is governed, and

    (ii)   if applicable, the register in which it is entered (including details of the state) and its registration number in that register.

NOTES

Commencement: 1 October 2009.

Commencement (transitional provisions): see the note to s 162 at **[1.162]**.

[1.165]

165   Register of directors' residential addresses

(1)   Every company must keep a register of directors' residential addresses.

(2)   The register must state the usual residential address of each of the company's directors.

(3)   If a director's usual residential address is the same as his service address (as stated in the company's register of directors), the register of directors' residential addresses need only contain an entry to that effect.

    This does not apply if his service address is stated to be "The company's registered office".

(4)   If default is made in complying with this section, an offence is committed by—

    (a)   the company, and

    (b)   every officer of the company who is in default.

    For this purpose a shadow director is treated as an officer of the company.

(5)   A person guilty of an offence under this section is liable on summary conviction to a fine not exceeding level 5 on the standard scale and, for continued contravention, a daily default fine not exceeding one-tenth of level 5 on the standard scale.

(6)   This section applies only to directors who are individuals, not where the director is a body corporate or a firm that is a legal person under the law by which it is governed.

NOTES

Commencement: 1 October 2009.

Commencement (transitional provisions): see the note to s 162 at **[1.162]**.

[1.166]

166   Particulars of directors to be registered: power to make regulations

(1)   The Secretary of State may make provision by regulations amending—

    section 163 (particulars of directors to be registered: individuals),

    section 164 (particulars of directors to be registered: corporate directors and firms), or

    section 165 (register of directors' residential addresses),

so as to add to or remove items from the particulars required to be contained in a company's register of directors or register of directors' residential addresses.

(2)   Regulations under this section are subject to affirmative resolution procedure.

NOTES

Commencement: 20 January 2007 (for the purpose of enabling the exercise of powers to make Orders or Regulations by statutory instrument); 1 October 2009 (otherwise).

Commencement (transitional provisions): see the note to s 162 at **[1.162]**.

[1.167]

167   Duty to notify registrar of changes

(1)   A company must, within the period of 14 days from—

    (a)   a person becoming or ceasing to be a director, or

    (b)   the occurrence of any change in the particulars contained in its register of directors or its register of directors' residential addresses,

give notice to the registrar of the change and of the date on which it occurred.

(2)   Notice of a person having become a director of the company must—

    (a)   contain a statement of the particulars of the new director that are required to be included in the company's register of directors and its register of directors' residential addresses, and

    (b)   be accompanied by a consent, by that person, to act in that capacity.

(3)   Where—

    (a)   a company gives notice of a change of a director's service address as stated in the company's register of directors, and

    (b)   the notice is not accompanied by notice of any resulting change in the particulars contained in the company's register of directors' residential addresses,

the notice must be accompanied by a statement that no such change is required.

(4)   If default is made in complying with this section, an offence is committed by—

    (a)   the company, and

    (b)   every officer of the company who is in default.

For this purpose a shadow director is treated as an officer of the company.

(5) A person guilty of an offence under this section is liable on summary conviction to a fine not exceeding level 5 on the standard scale and, for continued contravention, a daily default fine not exceeding one-tenth of level 5 on the standard scale.

NOTES

Commencement: 1 October 2009.

Commencement (transitional provisions): see the note to s 162 at **[1.162]**.

Removal

[1.168]

168   Resolution to remove director

(1)   A company may by ordinary resolution at a meeting remove a director before the expiration of his period of office, notwithstanding anything in any agreement between it and him.

(2)   Special notice is required of a resolution to remove a director under this section or to appoint somebody instead of a director so removed at the meeting at which he is removed.

(3)   A vacancy created by the removal of a director under this section, if not filled at the meeting at which he is removed, may be filled as a casual vacancy.

(4)   A person appointed director in place of a person removed under this section is treated, for the purpose of determining the time at which he or any other director is to retire, as if he had become director on the day on which the person in whose place he is appointed was last appointed a director.

(5)   This section is not to be taken—

  (a)   as depriving a person removed under it of compensation or damages payable to him in respect of the termination of his appointment as director or of any appointment terminating with that as director, or

  (b)   as derogating from any power to remove a director that may exist apart from this section.

NOTES

Commencement: 1 October 2007.

[1.169]

169   Director's right to protest against removal

(1)   On receipt of notice of an intended resolution to remove a director under section 168, the company must forthwith send a copy of the notice to the director concerned.

(2)   The director (whether or not a member of the company) is entitled to be heard on the resolution at the meeting.

(3)   Where notice is given of an intended resolution to remove a director under that section, and the director concerned makes with respect to it representations in writing to the company (not exceeding a reasonable length) and requests their notification to members of the company, the company shall, unless the representations are received by it too late for it to do so—

  (a)   in any notice of the resolution given to members of the company state the fact of the representations having been made; and

  (b)   send a copy of the representations to every member of the company to whom notice of the meeting is sent (whether before or after receipt of the representations by the company).

(4)   If a copy of the representations is not sent as required by subsection (3) because received too late or because of the company's default, the director may (without prejudice to his right to be heard orally) require that the representations shall be read out at the meeting.

(5)   Copies of the representations need not be sent out and the representations need not be read out at the meeting if, on the application either of the company or of any other person who claims to be aggrieved, the court is satisfied that the rights conferred by this section are being abused.

(6)   The court may order the company's costs (in Scotland, expenses) on an application under subsection (5) to be paid in whole or in part by the director, notwithstanding that he is not a party to the application.

NOTES

Commencement: 1 October 2007.

Commencement (transitional provisions): Sch 3, para 5 to the Companies Act 2006 (Commencement No 3, Consequential Amendments, Transitional Provisions and Savings) Order 2007, SI 2007/2194 (at **[2.45]**) provides that sub-s (5) above applies where the representations are received by the company on or after 1 October 2007 (and that s 304(4) of the 1985 Act continues to apply where the representations are received by the company before that date).

CHAPTER 2

GENERAL DUTIES OF DIRECTORS

Introductory

[1.170]

170   Scope and nature of general duties

(1)   The general duties specified in sections 171 to 177 are owed by a director of a company to the company.

(2)   A person who ceases to be a director continues to be subject—

  (a)   to the duty in section 175 (duty to avoid conflicts of interest) as regards the exploitation of any property, information or opportunity of which he became aware at a time when he was a director, and

  (b)   to the duty in section 176 (duty not to accept benefits from third parties) as regards things done or omitted by him before he ceased to be a director.

To that extent those duties apply to a former director as to a director, subject to any necessary adaptations.

(3)   The general duties are based on certain common law rules and equitable principles as they apply in relation to directors and have effect in place of those rules and principles as regards the duties owed to a company by a director.

(4)   The general duties shall be interpreted and applied in the same way as common law rules or equitable principles, and regard shall be had to the corresponding common law rules and equitable principles in interpreting and applying the general duties.

(5)   The general duties apply to shadow directors where, and to the extent that, the corresponding common law rules or equitable principles so apply.

NOTES

Commencement: 1 October 2007.

Commencement (transitional adaptations): the transitional adaptations of this section contained in the Companies Act 2006 (Commencement No 3, Consequential Amendments, Transitional Provisions and Savings) Order 2007, SI 2007/2194, Sch 1, para 6 were revoked by the Companies Act 2006 (Commencement No 5, Transitional Provisions and Savings) Order 2007, SI 2007/3495, art 10(1), as from 1 October 2008. See **[2.43]**.

The general duties

[1.171]
171 Duty to act within powers
A director of a company must—

  (a)   act in accordance with the company's constitution, and

  (b)   only exercise powers for the purposes for which they are conferred.

NOTES

Commencement: 1 October 2007.

[1.172]
172 Duty to promote the success of the company
(1)   A director of a company must act in the way he considers, in good faith, would be most likely to promote the success of the company for the benefit of its members as a whole, and in doing so have regard (amongst other matters) to—

  (a)   the likely consequences of any decision in the long term,

  (b)   the interests of the company's employees,

  (c)   the need to foster the company's business relationships with suppliers, customers and others,

  (d)   the impact of the company's operations on the community and the environment,

  (e)   the desirability of the company maintaining a reputation for high standards of business conduct, and

  (f)   the need to act fairly as between members of the company.

(2)   Where or to the extent that the purposes of the company consist of or include purposes other than the benefit of its members, subsection (1) has effect as if the reference to promoting the success of the company for the benefit of its members were to achieving those purposes.

(3)   The duty imposed by this section has effect subject to any enactment or rule of law requiring directors, in certain circumstances, to consider or act in the interests of creditors of the company.

NOTES

Commencement: 1 October 2007.

[1.173]
173 Duty to exercise independent judgment
(1)   A director of a company must exercise independent judgment.

(2)   This duty is not infringed by his acting—

  (a)   in accordance with an agreement duly entered into by the company that restricts the future exercise of discretion by its directors, or

  (b)   in a way authorised by the company's constitution.

NOTES

Commencement: 1 October 2007.

[1.174]
174 Duty to exercise reasonable care, skill and diligence
(1)   A director of a company must exercise reasonable care, skill and diligence.

(2) This means the care, skill and diligence that would be exercised by a reasonably diligent person with—

    (a) the general knowledge, skill and experience that may reasonably be expected of a person carrying out the functions carried out by the director in relation to the company, and

    (b) the general knowledge, skill and experience that the director has.

NOTES

Commencement: 1 October 2007.

[1.175]

175 Duty to avoid conflicts of interest

(1) A director of a company must avoid a situation in which he has, or can have, a direct or indirect interest that conflicts, or possibly may conflict, with the interests of the company.

(2) This applies in particular to the exploitation of any property, information or opportunity (and it is immaterial whether the company could take advantage of the property, information or opportunity).

(3) This duty does not apply to a conflict of interest arising in relation to a transaction or arrangement with the company.

(4) This duty is not infringed—

    (a) if the situation cannot reasonably be regarded as likely to give rise to a conflict of interest; or

    (b) if the matter has been authorised by the directors.

(5) Authorisation may be given by the directors—

    (a) where the company is a private company and nothing in the company's constitution invalidates such authorisation, by the matter being proposed to and authorised by the directors; or

    (b) where the company is a public company and its constitution includes provision enabling the directors to authorise the matter, by the matter being proposed to and authorised by them in accordance with the constitution.

(6) The authorisation is effective only if—

    (a) any requirement as to the quorum at the meeting at which the matter is considered is met without counting the director in question or any other interested director, and

    (b) the matter was agreed to without their voting or would have been agreed to if their votes had not been counted.

(7) Any reference in this section to a conflict of interest includes a conflict of interest and duty and a conflict of duties.

NOTES

Commencement: 1 October 2008.

Commencement (transitional provisions): Sch 4, Pt 3, para 47 to the Companies Act 2006 (Commencement No 5, Transitional Provisions and Savings) Order 2007, SI 2007/3495 (at **[2.68]**) provides as follows—

"Duty of directors to avoid conflicts of interest (s 175)

47.—(1) Section 175 of the Companies Act 2006 (duty to avoid conflicts of interest) applies where the situation described in subsection (1) of that section arises on or after 1st October 2008.

(2) The law that applied before that date continues to apply to such a situation that arose before that date.

(3) Section 175(5)(a) of that Act (private companies: authorisation by directors) applies—

    (a) to companies incorporated on or after 1st October 2008, and

    (b) to companies incorporated before that date where the members of the company have resolved (before, on or after 1st October 2008) that authorisation may be given in accordance with that provision.

(4) Chapter 3 of Part 3 of the Companies Act 2006 (resolutions and agreements affecting a company's constitution) applies to any such resolution.

(5) For the purposes of section 30 of that Act (copies of resolutions to be forwarded to registrar) such a resolution passed before 1st October 2008 is treated as if passed on that date.".

[1.176]

176 Duty not to accept benefits from third parties

(1) A director of a company must not accept a benefit from a third party conferred by reason of—

    (a) his being a director, or

    (b) his doing (or not doing) anything as director.

(2) A "third party" means a person other than the company, an associated body corporate or a person acting on behalf of the company or an associated body corporate.

(3) Benefits received by a director from a person by whom his services (as a director or otherwise) are provided to the company are not regarded as conferred by a third party.

(4) This duty is not infringed if the acceptance of the benefit cannot reasonably be regarded as likely to give rise to a conflict of interest.

(5) Any reference in this section to a conflict of interest includes a conflict of interest and duty and a conflict of duties.

NOTES

Commencement: 1 October 2008.

Part 1   The Companies Act 2006

[1.177]
177   Duty to declare interest in proposed transaction or arrangement
(1)   If a director of a company is in any way, directly or indirectly, interested in a proposed transaction or arrangement with the company, he must declare the nature and extent of that interest to the other directors.
(2)   The declaration may (but need not) be made—
  (a)   at a meeting of the directors, or
  (b)   by notice to the directors in accordance with—
    (i)   section 184 (notice in writing), or
    (ii)   section 185 (general notice).
(3)   If a declaration of interest under this section proves to be, or becomes, inaccurate or incomplete, a further declaration must be made.
(4)   Any declaration required by this section must be made before the company enters into the transaction or arrangement.
(5)   This section does not require a declaration of an interest of which the director is not aware or where the director is not aware of the transaction or arrangement in question.
  For this purpose a director is treated as being aware of matters of which he ought reasonably to be aware.
(6)   A director need not declare an interest—
  (a)   if it cannot reasonably be regarded as likely to give rise to a conflict of interest;
  (b)   if, or to the extent that, the other directors are already aware of it (and for this purpose the other directors are treated as aware of anything of which they ought reasonably to be aware); or
  (c)   if, or to the extent that, it concerns terms of his service contract that have been or are to be considered—
    (i)   by a meeting of the directors, or
    (ii)   by a committee of the directors appointed for the purpose under the company's constitution.

NOTES
Commencement: 1 October 2008.
Commencement (transitional provisions): Sch 4, Pt 3, para 48 to the Companies Act 2006 (Commencement No 5, Transitional Provisions and Savings) Order 2007, SI 2007/3495 (at **[2.68]**) provides as follows—

"Declaration by directors of interest in proposed transaction or arrangement (s 177)
48.—(1)   Section 177(1) of the Companies Act 2006 (duty of director to declare interest in proposed transaction or arrangement) applies where the duty to declare an interest arises on or after 1st October 2008.
(2)   Section 317 of the 1985 Act or Article 325 of the 1986 Order continues to apply in relation to a duty arising before that date.
(3)   For the purposes of section 177(3) of the Companies Act 2006 (previous declaration under that section proving or becoming inadequate), a declaration of interest in relation to a proposed transaction or arrangement made before 1st October 2008 under section 317 of the 1985 Act or Article 325 of the 1986 Order is treated on and after that date as if made under section 177 of the Companies Act 2006.".

Supplementary provisions

[1.178]
178   Civil consequences of breach of general duties
(1)   The consequences of breach (or threatened breach) of sections 171 to 177 are the same as would apply if the corresponding common law rule or equitable principle applied.
(2)   The duties in those sections (with the exception of section 174 (duty to exercise reasonable care, skill and diligence)) are, accordingly, enforceable in the same way as any other fiduciary duty owed to a company by its directors.

NOTES
Commencement: 1 October 2007.
Commencement (transitional adaptations): the transitional adaptations of this section contained in the Companies Act 2006 (Commencement No 3, Consequential Amendments, Transitional Provisions and Savings) Order 2007, SI 2007/2194, Sch 1, para 7 were revoked by the Companies Act 2006 (Commencement No 5, Transitional Provisions and Savings) Order 2007, SI 2007/3495, art 10(1), as from 1 October 2008. See **[2.43]**.

[1.179]
179   Cases within more than one of the general duties
Except as otherwise provided, more than one of the general duties may apply in any given case.

NOTES
Commencement: 1 October 2007.

[1.180]
180   Consent, approval or authorisation by members
(1)   In a case where—

(a)   section 175 (duty to avoid conflicts of interest) is complied with by authorisation by the directors, or

(b)   section 177 (duty to declare interest in proposed transaction or arrangement) is complied with,

the transaction or arrangement is not liable to be set aside by virtue of any common law rule or equitable principle requiring the consent or approval of the members of the company.

This is without prejudice to any enactment, or provision of the company's constitution, requiring such consent or approval.

(2)   The application of the general duties is not affected by the fact that the case also falls within Chapter 4 (transactions requiring approval of members), except that where that Chapter applies and— (a) approval is given under that Chapter, or (b) the matter is one as to which it is provided that approval is not needed, it is not necessary also to comply with section 175 (duty to avoid conflicts of interest) or section 176 (duty not to accept benefits from third parties).

(3)   Compliance with the general duties does not remove the need for approval under any applicable provision of Chapter 4 (transactions requiring approval of members).

(4)   The general duties—

(a)   have effect subject to any rule of law enabling the company to give authority, specifically or generally, for anything to be done (or omitted) by the directors, or any of them, that would otherwise be a breach of duty, and

(b)   where the company's articles contain provisions for dealing with conflicts of interest, are not infringed by anything done (or omitted) by the directors, or any of them, in accordance with those provisions.

(5)   Otherwise, the general duties have effect (except as otherwise provided or the context otherwise requires) notwithstanding any enactment or rule of law.

NOTES

Commencement: 1 October 2007.

Commencement (transitional provisions): Sch 4, Pt 3, para 49 to the Companies Act 2006 (Commencement No 5, Transitional Provisions and Savings) Order 2007, SI 2007/3495 (at **[2.68]**) provides as follows—

"General duties of directors: approval by members (s 180(2))

49.   The reference in section 180(2) of the Companies Act 2006 (exclusion of general duties where approval of members given) to approval given under Chapter 4 of Part 10 of that Act (transactions requiring approval of members) includes approval given by a resolution passed before 1st October 2007 that is effective by virtue of paragraph 6(2), 7(2), 8(2) or 12(2) of Schedule 3 to the Companies Act 2006 (Commencement No 3, Consequential Amendments, Transitional Provisions and Savings) Order 2007.".

Commencement (transitional adaptations): the transitional adaptations of this section contained in the Companies Act 2006 (Commencement No 3, Consequential Amendments, Transitional Provisions and Savings) Order 2007, SI 2007/2194, Sch 1, para 8 were revoked by the Companies Act 2006 (Commencement No 5, Transitional Provisions and Savings) Order 2007, SI 2007/3495, art 10(1), as from 1 October 2008. See **[2.43]**.

[1.181]
181   Modification of provisions in relation to charitable companies

(1)   In their application to a company that is a charity, the provisions of this Chapter have effect subject to this section.

(2)   Section 175 (duty to avoid conflicts of interest) has effect as if—

(a)   for subsection (3) (which disapplies the duty to avoid conflicts of interest in the case of a transaction or arrangement with the company) there were substituted—

"(3)   This duty does not apply to a conflict of interest arising in relation to a transaction or arrangement with the company if or to the extent that the company's articles allow that duty to be so disapplied, which they may do only in relation to descriptions of transaction or arrangement specified in the company's articles.";

(b)   for subsection (5) (which specifies how directors of a company may give authority under that section for a transaction or arrangement) there were substituted—

"(5)   Authorisation may be given by the directors where the company's constitution includes provision enabling them to authorise the matter, by the matter being proposed to and authorised by them in accordance with the constitution.".

(3)   Section 180(2)(b) (which disapplies certain duties under this Chapter in relation to cases excepted from requirement to obtain approval by members under Chapter 4) applies only if or to the extent that the company's articles allow those duties to be so disapplied, which they may do only in relation to descriptions of transaction or arrangement specified in the company's articles.

(4)   *(Inserts the Charities Act 1993, s 26(5A) (outside the scope of this work).)*

(5)   This section does not extend to Scotland.

NOTES

Commencement: 1 October 2007.

Commencement (transitional adaptations): the transitional adaptations of this section contained in the Companies Act 2006 (Commencement No 3, Consequential Amendments, Transitional Provisions and Savings) Order 2007, SI 2007/2194, Sch 1, para 9 were revoked by the Companies Act 2006 (Commencement No 5, Transitional Provisions and Savings) Order 2007, SI 2007/3495, art 10(1), as from 1 October 2008. See **[2.43]**.

CHAPTER 3
DECLARATION OF INTEREST IN EXISTING TRANSACTION OR ARRANGEMENT

[1.182]
182   Declaration of interest in existing transaction or arrangement
(1)   Where a director of a company is in any way, directly or indirectly, interested in a transaction or arrangement that has been entered into by the company, he must declare the nature and extent of the interest to the other directors in accordance with this section.

This section does not apply if or to the extent that the interest has been declared under section 177 (duty to declare interest in proposed transaction or arrangement).

(2)   The declaration must be made—
    (a)   at a meeting of the directors, or
    (b)   by notice in writing (see section 184), or
    (c)   by general notice (see section 185).

(3)   If a declaration of interest under this section proves to be, or becomes, inaccurate or incomplete, a further declaration must be made.

(4)   Any declaration required by this section must be made as soon as is reasonably practicable.

Failure to comply with this requirement does not affect the underlying duty to make the declaration.

(5)   This section does not require a declaration of an interest of which the director is not aware or where the director is not aware of the transaction or arrangement in question.

For this purpose a director is treated as being aware of matters of which he ought reasonably to be aware.

(6)   A director need not declare an interest under this section—
    (a)   if it cannot reasonably be regarded as likely to give rise to a conflict of interest;
    (b)   if, or to the extent that, the other directors are already aware of it (and for this purpose the other directors are treated as aware of anything of which they ought reasonably to be aware); or
    (c)   if, or to the extent that, it concerns terms of his service contract that have been or are to be considered—
        (i)   by a meeting of the directors, or
        (ii)   by a committee of the directors appointed for the purpose under the company's constitution.

NOTES

Commencement: 1 October 2008.

Commencement (transitional provisions): Sch 4, Pt 3, para 50 to the Companies Act 2006 (Commencement No 5, Transitional Provisions and Savings) Order 2007, SI 2007/3495 (at **[2.68]**) provides as follows—

"Declaration of interest in existing transaction or arrangement (ss 182 to 187)

50.—(1)   Sections 182 to 187 of the Companies Act 2006 (declaration by director of interest in existing transaction or arrangement) apply in relation to transactions or arrangements entered into by a company on or after 1st October 2008.

(2)   Section 317 of the 1985 Act or Article 325 of the 1986 Order continues to apply in relation to transactions or arrangements entered into before that date.

(3)   For the purposes of section 182(1) of the Companies Act 2006 (declaration of interest in existing transaction not previously declared under section 177), a declaration of interest made before 1st October 2008 under section 317 of the 1985 Act or Article 325 of the 1986 Order is treated on and after that date as if made under section 177.

(4)   For the purposes of section 182(3) of the Companies Act 2006 (previous declaration under that section proving or becoming inadequate), a declaration of interest made before 1st October 2008 under section 317 of the 1985 Act or Article 325 of the 1986 Order is treated on and after that date as if made under section 182.".

[1.183]
183   Offence of failure to declare interest
(1)   A director who fails to comply with the requirements of section 182 (declaration of interest in existing transaction or arrangement) commits an offence.

(2)   A person guilty of an offence under this section is liable—
    (a)   on conviction on indictment, to a fine;
    (b)   on summary conviction, to a fine not exceeding the statutory maximum.

NOTES

Commencement: 1 October 2008.

Commencement (transitional provisions): see the note to s 182 at **[1.182]**.

[1.184]
184   Declaration made by notice in writing
(1)   This section applies to a declaration of interest made by notice in writing.

(2)   The director must send the notice to the other directors.

(3)   The notice may be sent in hard copy form or, if the recipient has agreed to receive it in electronic form, in an agreed electronic form.

(4)   The notice may be sent—

   (a)   by hand or by post, or

   (b)   if the recipient has agreed to receive it by electronic means, by agreed electronic means.

(5)   Where a director declares an interest by notice in writing in accordance with this section—

   (a)   the making of the declaration is deemed to form part of the proceedings at the next meeting of the directors after the notice is given, and

   (b)   the provisions of section 248 (minutes of meetings of directors) apply as if the declaration had been made at that meeting.

NOTES

Commencement: 1 October 2008.

Commencement (transitional provisions): see the note to s 182 at **[1.182]**.

[1.185]

185   General notice treated as sufficient declaration

(1)   General notice in accordance with this section is a sufficient declaration of interest in relation to the matters to which it relates.

(2)   General notice is notice given to the directors of a company to the effect that the director—

   (a)   has an interest (as member, officer, employee or otherwise) in a specified body corporate or firm and is to be regarded as interested in any transaction or arrangement that may, after the date of the notice, be made with that body corporate or firm, or

   (b)   is connected with a specified person (other than a body corporate or firm) and is to be regarded as interested in any transaction or arrangement that may, after the date of the notice, be made with that person.

(3)   The notice must state the nature and extent of the director's interest in the body corporate or firm or, as the case may be, the nature of his connection with the person.

(4)   General notice is not effective unless—

   (a)   it is given at a meeting of the directors, or

   (b)   the director takes reasonable steps to secure that it is brought up and read at the next meeting of the directors after it is given.

NOTES

Commencement: 1 October 2008.

Commencement (transitional provisions): see the note to s 182 at **[1.182]**.

[1.186]

186   Declaration of interest in case of company with sole director

(1)   Where a declaration of interest under section 182 (duty to declare interest in existing transaction or arrangement) is required of a sole director of a company that is required to have more than one director—

   (a)   the declaration must be recorded in writing,

   (b)   the making of the declaration is deemed to form part of the proceedings at the next meeting of the directors after the notice is given, and

   (c)   the provisions of section 248 (minutes of meetings of directors) apply as if the declaration had been made at that meeting.

(2)   Nothing in this section affects the operation of section 231 (contract with sole member who is also a director: terms to be set out in writing or recorded in minutes).

NOTES

Commencement: 1 October 2008.

Commencement (transitional provisions): see the note to s 182 at **[1.182]**.

[1.187]

187   Declaration of interest in existing transaction by shadow director

(1)   The provisions of this Chapter relating to the duty under section 182 (duty to declare interest in existing transaction or arrangement) apply to a shadow director as to a director, but with the following adaptations.

(2)   Subsection (2)(a) of that section (declaration at meeting of directors) does not apply.

(3)   In section 185 (general notice treated as sufficient declaration), subsection (4) (notice to be given at or brought up and read at meeting of directors) does not apply.

(4)   General notice by a shadow director is not effective unless given by notice in writing in accordance with section 184.

NOTES

Commencement: 1 October 2008.

Commencement (transitional provisions): see the note to s 182 at **[1.182]**.

CHAPTER 4
TRANSACTIONS WITH DIRECTORS REQUIRING APPROVAL OF MEMBERS

Service contracts

[1.188]
188   Directors' long-term service contracts: requirement of members' approval
(1)   This section applies to provision under which the guaranteed term of a director's employment—
  (a)   with the company of which he is a director, or
  (b)   where he is the director of a holding company, within the group consisting of that company and its subsidiaries,
is, or may be, longer than two years.
(2)   A company may not agree to such provision unless it has been approved—
  (a)   by resolution of the members of the company, and
  (b)   in the case of a director of a holding company, by resolution of the members of that company.
(3)   The guaranteed term of a director's employment is—
  (a)   the period (if any) during which the director's employment—
      (i)   is to continue, or may be continued otherwise than at the instance of the company (whether under the original agreement or under a new agreement entered into in pursuance of it), and
      (ii)   cannot be terminated by the company by notice, or can be so terminated only in specified circumstances, or
  (b)   in the case of employment terminable by the company by notice, the period of notice required to be given,
or, in the case of employment having a period within paragraph (a) and a period within paragraph (b), the aggregate of those periods.
(4)   If more than six months before the end of the guaranteed term of a director's employment the company enters into a further service contract (otherwise than in pursuance of a right conferred, by or under the original contract, on the other party to it), this section applies as if there were added to the guaranteed term of the new contract the unexpired period of the guaranteed term of the original contract.
(5)   A resolution approving provision to which this section applies must not be passed unless a memorandum setting out the proposed contract incorporating the provision is made available to members—
  (a)   in the case of a written resolution, by being sent or submitted to every eligible member at or before the time at which the proposed resolution is sent or submitted to him;
  (b)   in the case of a resolution at a meeting, by being made available for inspection by members of the company both—
      (i)   at the company's registered office for not less than 15 days ending with the date of the meeting, and
      (ii)   at the meeting itself.
(6)   No approval is required under this section on the part of the members of a body corporate that—
  (a)   is not a UK-registered company, or
  (b)   is a wholly-owned subsidiary of another body corporate.
(7)   In this section "employment" means any employment under a director's service contract.

NOTES
  Commencement: 1 October 2007.
  Commencement (transitional provisions): Sch 3, para 6 to the Companies Act 2006 (Commencement No 3, Consequential Amendments, Transitional Provisions and Savings) Order 2007, SI 2007/2194 (at **[2.45]**) provides as follows—

  "**6   Transactions requiring members' approval: directors' long-term service contracts (ss 188 and 189)**
  (1)   Sections 188 and 189 of the Companies Act 2006 (directors' long-term service contracts: requirement of members' approval) apply to agreements made on or after 1st October 2007.
  (2)   A resolution passed before that date approving the provision made by such an agreement is effective for the purposes of those sections if it complies with the requirements of those sections.
  (3)   Section 188(4) (addition of unexpired period of earlier contract in determining guaranteed period under new contract) applies whether the original contract (within the meaning of that provision) was entered into before or after that date.
  (4)   Section 319 of the 1985 Act or Article 327 of the 1986 Order continues to apply to agreements made before that date.".

[1.189]
189   Directors' long-term service contracts: civil consequences of contravention
If a company agrees to provision in contravention of section 188 (directors' long-term service contracts: requirement of members' approval)—
  (a)   the provision is void, to the extent of the contravention, and
  (b)   the contract is deemed to contain a term entitling the company to terminate it at any time by the giving of reasonable notice.

NOTES
Commencement: 1 October 2007.
Commencement (transitional provisions): see the note to s 188 at **[1.188]**.

Substantial property transactions

[1.190]
190 Substantial property transactions: requirement of members' approval
(1) A company may not enter into an arrangement under which—
   (a) a director of the company or of its holding company, or a person connected with such a director, acquires or is to acquire from the company (directly or indirectly) a substantial non-cash asset, or
   (b) the company acquires or is to acquire a substantial non-cash asset (directly or indirectly) from such a director or a person so connected,
unless the arrangement has been approved by a resolution of the members of the company or is conditional on such approval being obtained.
   For the meaning of "substantial non-cash asset" see section 191.
(2) If the director or connected person is a director of the company's holding company or a person connected with such a director, the arrangement must also have been approved by a resolution of the members of the holding company or be conditional on such approval being obtained.
(3) A company shall not be subject to any liability by reason of a failure to obtain approval required by this section.
(4) No approval is required under this section on the part of the members of a body corporate that—
   (a) is not a UK-registered company, or
   (b) is a wholly-owned subsidiary of another body corporate.
(5) For the purposes of this section—
   (a) an arrangement involving more than one non-cash asset, or
   (b) an arrangement that is one of a series involving non-cash assets,
shall be treated as if they involved a non-cash asset of a value equal to the aggregate value of all the non-cash assets involved in the arrangement or, as the case may be, the series.
(6) This section does not apply to a transaction so far as it relates—
   (a) to anything to which a director of a company is entitled under his service contract, or
   (b) to payment for loss of office as defined in section 215 (payments requiring members' approval).

NOTES
Commencement: 1 October 2007.
Commencement (transitional provisions): Sch 3, para 7 to the Companies Act 2006 (Commencement No 3, Consequential Amendments, Transitional Provisions and Savings) Order 2007, SI 2007/2194 (at **[2.45]**) provides as follows—

"**7 Transactions requiring members' approval: substantial property transactions (ss 190 to 196)**
(1) Sections 190 to 196 of the Companies Act 2006 (substantial property transactions: requirement of members' approval) apply to arrangements or transactions entered into on or after 1st October 2007.
(2) A resolution passed before that date approving an arrangement or transaction is effective for the purposes of those sections if it complies with the requirements of those sections.
(3) Sections 320 to 322 of the 1985 Act or Articles 328 to 330 of the 1986 Order continue to apply in relation to arrangements or transactions entered into before that date.".

[1.191]
191 Meaning of "substantial"
(1) This section explains what is meant in section 190 (requirement of approval for substantial property transactions) by a "substantial" non-cash asset.
(2) An asset is a substantial asset in relation to a company if its value—
   (a) exceeds 10% of the company's asset value and is more than £5,000, or
   (b) exceeds £100,000.
(3) For this purpose a company's "asset value" at any time is—
   (a) the value of the company's net assets determined by reference to its most recent statutory accounts, or
   (b) if no statutory accounts have been prepared, the amount of the company's called-up share capital.
(4) A company's "statutory accounts" means its annual accounts prepared in accordance with Part 15, and its "most recent" statutory accounts means those in relation to which the time for sending them out to members (see section 424) is most recent.
(5) Whether an asset is a substantial asset shall be determined as at the time the arrangement is entered into.

NOTES
Commencement: 1 October 2007.
Commencement (transitional provisions): see the note to s 190 at **[1.190]**.

Commencement (transitional adaptations): the transitional adaptations of this section contained in the Companies Act 2006 (Commencement No 3, Consequential Amendments, Transitional Provisions and Savings) Order 2007, SI 2007/2194, Sch 1, para 10 were revoked by the Companies Act 2006 (Commencement No 5, Transitional Provisions and Savings) Order 2007, SI 2007/3495, art 10(1), (3), as from 6 April 2008 (subject to any transitional provisions and savings as apply, in accordance with Sch 4 to that Order, in relation to the repeal of any provision of the 1985 Act referred to in the adaptation). See **[2.43]**.

[1.192]
192   Exception for transactions with members or other group companies
Approval is not required under section 190 (requirement of members' approval for substantial property transactions)—
(a)   for a transaction between a company and a person in his character as a member of that company, or
(b)   for a transaction between—
    (i)   a holding company and its wholly-owned subsidiary, or
    (ii)   two wholly-owned subsidiaries of the same holding company.

NOTES
Commencement: 1 October 2007.
Commencement (transitional provisions): see the note to s 190 at **[1.190]**.

[1.193]
193   Exception in case of company in winding up or administration
(1)   This section applies to a company—
(a)   that is being wound up (unless the winding up is a members' voluntary winding up), or
(b)   that is in administration within the meaning of Schedule B1 to the Insolvency Act 1986 (c 45) or the Insolvency (Northern Ireland) Order 1989 (SI 1989/2405 (NI 19)).
(2)   Approval is not required under section 190 (requirement of members' approval for substantial property transactions)—
(a)   on the part of the members of a company to which this section applies, or
(b)   for an arrangement entered into by a company to which this section applies.

NOTES
Commencement: 1 October 2007.
Commencement (transitional provisions): see the note to s 190 at **[1.190]**.

[1.194]
194   Exception for transactions on recognised investment exchange
(1)   Approval is not required under section 190 (requirement of members' approval for substantial property transactions) for a transaction on a recognised investment exchange effected by a director, or a person connected with him, through the agency of a person who in relation to the transaction acts as an independent broker.
(2)   For this purpose—
(a)   "independent broker" means a person who, independently of the director or any person connected with him, selects the person with whom the transaction is to be effected; and
(b)   "recognised investment exchange" has the same meaning as in Part 18 of the Financial Services and Markets Act 2000 (c 8).

NOTES
Commencement: 1 October 2007.
Commencement (transitional provisions): see the note to s 190 at **[1.190]**.

[1.195]
195   Property transactions: civil consequences of contravention
(1)   This section applies where a company enters into an arrangement in contravention of section 190 (requirement of members' approval for substantial property transactions).
(2)   The arrangement, and any transaction entered into in pursuance of the arrangement (whether by the company or any other person), is voidable at the instance of the company, unless—
(a)   restitution of any money or other asset that was the subject matter of the arrangement or transaction is no longer possible,
(b)   the company has been indemnified in pursuance of this section by any other persons for the loss or damage suffered by it, or
(c)   rights acquired in good faith, for value and without actual notice of the contravention by a person who is not a party to the arrangement or transaction would be affected by the avoidance.
(3)   Whether or not the arrangement or any such transaction has been avoided, each of the persons specified in subsection (4) is liable—
(a)   to account to the company for any gain that he has made directly or indirectly by the arrangement or transaction, and
(b)   (jointly and severally with any other person so liable under this section) to indemnify the company for any loss or damage resulting from the arrangement or transaction.

(4) The persons so liable are—
- (a) any director of the company or of its holding company with whom the company entered into the arrangement in contravention of section 190,
- (b) any person with whom the company entered into the arrangement in contravention of that section who is connected with a director of the company or of its holding company,
- (c) the director of the company or of its holding company with whom any such person is connected, and
- (d) any other director of the company who authorised the arrangement or any transaction entered into in pursuance of such an arrangement.

(5) Subsections (3) and (4) are subject to the following two subsections.

(6) In the case of an arrangement entered into by a company in contravention of section 190 with a person connected with a director of the company or of its holding company, that director is not liable by virtue of subsection (4)(c) if he shows that he took all reasonable steps to secure the company's compliance with that section.

(7) In any case—
- (a) a person so connected is not liable by virtue of subsection (4)(b), and
- (b) a director is not liable by virtue of subsection (4)(d),

if he shows that, at the time the arrangement was entered into, he did not know the relevant circumstances constituting the contravention.

(8) Nothing in this section shall be read as excluding the operation of any other enactment or rule of law by virtue of which the arrangement or transaction may be called in question or any liability to the company may arise.

NOTES

Commencement: 1 October 2007.
Commencement (transitional provisions): see the note to s 190 at **[1.190]**.

[1.196]
196 Property transactions: effect of subsequent affirmation

Where a transaction or arrangement is entered into by a company in contravention of section 190 (requirement of members' approval) but, within a reasonable period, it is affirmed—
- (a) in the case of a contravention of subsection (1) of that section, by resolution of the members of the company, and
- (b) in the case of a contravention of subsection (2) of that section, by resolution of the members of the holding company,

the transaction or arrangement may no longer be avoided under section 195.

NOTES

Commencement: 1 October 2007.
Commencement (transitional provisions): see the note to s 190 at **[1.190]**.

Loans, quasi-loans and credit transactions

[1.197]
197 Loans to directors: requirement of members' approval

(1) A company may not—
- (a) make a loan to a director of the company or of its holding company, or
- (b) give a guarantee or provide security in connection with a loan made by any person to such a director,

unless the transaction has been approved by a resolution of the members of the company.

(2) If the director is a director of the company's holding company, the transaction must also have been approved by a resolution of the members of the holding company.

(3) A resolution approving a transaction to which this section applies must not be passed unless a memorandum setting out the matters mentioned in subsection (4) is made available to members—
- (a) in the case of a written resolution, by being sent or submitted to every eligible member at or before the time at which the proposed resolution is sent or submitted to him;
- (b) in the case of a resolution at a meeting, by being made available for inspection by members of the company both—
  - (i) at the company's registered office for not less than 15 days ending with the date of the meeting, and
  - (ii) at the meeting itself.

(4) The matters to be disclosed are—
- (a) the nature of the transaction,
- (b) the amount of the loan and the purpose for which it is required, and
- (c) the extent of the company's liability under any transaction connected with the loan.

(5) No approval is required under this section on the part of the members of a body corporate that—
- (a) is not a UK-registered company, or
- (b) is a wholly-owned subsidiary of another body corporate.

NOTES

Commencement: 1 October 2007.

Commencement (transitional provisions): Sch 3, paras 8–11 to the Companies Act 2006 (Commencement No 3, Consequential Amendments, Transitional Provisions and Savings) Order 2007, SI 2007/2194 (at **[2.45]**) provides as follows—

"**Transactions requiring members' approval: loans, quasi-loans and credit transactions (ss 197 to 214)**

8.—(1) Sections 197 to 214 of the Companies Act 2006 (loans, quasi-loans and credit transactions: requirement of members' approval) apply to transactions or arrangements entered into on or after 1st October 2007.

(2) A resolution passed before that date approving a transaction or arrangement is effective for the purposes of those sections if it complies with the requirements of those sections.

(3) Sections 330 to 342 of the 1985 Act or Articles 338 to 350 of the 1986 Order continue to apply in relation to a contravention occurring before that date.

9. Approval is not required under section 197, 198, 200 or 201 of the Companies Act 2006 (requirement of members' approval for loans etc) for anything done by a company in pursuance of an agreement entered into before 1st October 2007 that, by virtue of section 337A of the 1985 Act or Article 345A of the 1986 Order (funding of director's expenditure on defending proceedings), would not have required approval if done before that date.

10.—(1) This paragraph applies where before 1st October 2007 a company has done anything—

(a)　pursuant to section 337(1) or (2) of the 1985 Act or Article 345(1) or (2) of the 1986 Order (funding of director's expenditure on duty to company), and

(b)　on the condition mentioned in section 337(3)(b) of that Act or Article 345(3)(b) of that Order (condition requiring repayment of loan etc if approval of company in general meeting not given within six months).

(2) If that condition has not been satisfied before that date, it continues to apply notwithstanding the repeal of that section or that Article, but subject as follows.

(3) In the case of a private company that by reason of the repeal of section 366 of the 1985 Act or Article 374 of the 1986 Order with effect from that date ceases to be required to hold an annual general meeting, the condition shall be read as if it provided—

(a)　that the approval of the company is required on or before the last date on which the company would have been required to hold an annual general meeting but for the repeal, and

(b)　that the loan is to be repaid within six months from that date if such approval is not forthcoming.

11.—(1) This paragraph applies where before 1st October 2007 a company has done anything—

(a)　pursuant to section 337A(1) or (3) of the 1985 Act or Article 345A(1) or (3) of the 1986 Order (funding of director's expenditure on defending proceedings), and

(b)　on the terms mentioned in section 337A(4) of that Act or Article 345A(4) of that Order (terms requiring repayment of loan etc if defendant convicted, has judgment given against him or refused relief).

(2) If immediately before that date—

(a)　it is not yet known whether repayment will be required, or

(b)　repayment is required but had not been made,

those terms continue to apply notwithstanding the repeal of that section or that Article.".

[1.198]

198 Quasi-loans to directors: requirement of members' approval

(1) This section applies to a company if it is—

(a)　a public company, or

(b)　a company associated with a public company.

(2) A company to which this section applies may not—

(a)　make a quasi-loan to a director of the company or of its holding company, or

(b)　give a guarantee or provide security in connection with a quasi-loan made by any person to such a director,

unless the transaction has been approved by a resolution of the members of the company.

(3) If the director is a director of the company's holding company, the transaction must also have been approved by a resolution of the members of the holding company.

(4) A resolution approving a transaction to which this section applies must not be passed unless a memorandum setting out the matters mentioned in subsection (5) is made available to members—

(a)　in the case of a written resolution, by being sent or submitted to every eligible member at or before the time at which the proposed resolution is sent or submitted to him;

(b)　in the case of a resolution at a meeting, by being made available for inspection by members of the company both—

(i)　at the company's registered office for not less than 15 days ending with the date of the meeting, and

(ii)　at the meeting itself.

(5) The matters to be disclosed are—

(a)　the nature of the transaction,

(b)　the amount of the quasi-loan and the purpose for which it is required, and

(c)　the extent of the company's liability under any transaction connected with the quasi-loan.

(6) No approval is required under this section on the part of the members of a body corporate that—

(a)　is not a UK-registered company, or

(b)　is a wholly-owned subsidiary of another body corporate.

NOTES

Commencement: 1 October 2007.

Commencement (transitional provisions): see the note to s 197 at **[1.197]**.

[1.199]
199 Meaning of "quasi-loan" and related expressions

(1) A "quasi-loan" is a transaction under which one party ("the creditor") agrees to pay, or pays otherwise than in pursuance of an agreement, a sum for another ("the borrower") or agrees to reimburse, or reimburses otherwise than in pursuance of an agreement, expenditure incurred by another party for another ("the borrower")—

  (a) on terms that the borrower (or a person on his behalf) will reimburse the creditor; or

  (b) in circumstances giving rise to a liability on the borrower to reimburse the creditor.

(2) Any reference to the person to whom a quasi-loan is made is a reference to the borrower.

(3) The liabilities of the borrower under a quasi-loan include the liabilities of any person who has agreed to reimburse the creditor on behalf of the borrower.

NOTES

Commencement: 1 October 2007.

Commencement (transitional provisions): see the note to s 197 at **[1.197]**.

[1.200]
200 Loans or quasi-loans to persons connected with directors: requirement of members' approval

(1) This section applies to a company if it is—

  (a) a public company, or

  (b) a company associated with a public company.

(2) A company to which this section applies may not—

  (a) make a loan or quasi-loan to a person connected with a director of the company or of its holding company, or

  (b) give a guarantee or provide security in connection with a loan or quasi-loan made by any person to a person connected with such a director,

unless the transaction has been approved by a resolution of the members of the company.

(3) If the connected person is a person connected with a director of the company's holding company, the transaction must also have been approved by a resolution of the members of the holding company.

(4) A resolution approving a transaction to which this section applies must not be passed unless a memorandum setting out the matters mentioned in subsection (5) is made available to members—

  (a) in the case of a written resolution, by being sent or submitted to every eligible member at or before the time at which the proposed resolution is sent or submitted to him;

  (b) in the case of a resolution at a meeting, by being made available for inspection by members of the company both—

    (i) at the company's registered office for not less than 15 days ending with the date of the meeting, and

    (ii) at the meeting itself.

(5) The matters to be disclosed are—

  (a) the nature of the transaction,

  (b) the amount of the loan or quasi-loan and the purpose for which it is required, and

  (c) the extent of the company's liability under any transaction connected with the loan or quasi-loan.

(6) No approval is required under this section on the part of the members of a body corporate that—

  (a) is not a UK-registered company, or

  (b) is a wholly-owned subsidiary of another body corporate.

NOTES

Commencement: 1 October 2007.

Commencement (transitional provisions): see the note to s 197 at **[1.197]**.

[1.201]
201 Credit transactions: requirement of members' approval

(1) This section applies to a company if it is—

  (a) a public company, or

  (b) a company associated with a public company.

(2) A company to which this section applies may not—

  (a) enter into a credit transaction as creditor for the benefit of a director of the company or of its holding company, or a person connected with such a director, or

  (b) give a guarantee or provide security in connection with a credit transaction entered into by any person for the benefit of such a director, or a person connected with such a director,

unless the transaction (that is, the credit transaction, the giving of the guarantee or the provision of security, as the case may be) has been approved by a resolution of the members of the company.

(3)   If the director or connected person is a director of its holding company or a person connected with such a director, the transaction must also have been approved by a resolution of the members of the holding company.

(4)   A resolution approving a transaction to which this section applies must not be passed unless a memorandum setting out the matters mentioned in subsection (5) is made available to members—

- (a)   in the case of a written resolution, by being sent or submitted to every eligible member at or before the time at which the proposed resolution is sent or submitted to him;
- (b)   in the case of a resolution at a meeting, by being made available for inspection by members of the company both—
  - (i)   at the company's registered office for not less than 15 days ending with the date of the meeting, and
  - (ii)   at the meeting itself.

(5)   The matters to be disclosed are—

- (a)   the nature of the transaction,
- (b)   the value of the credit transaction and the purpose for which the land, goods or services sold or otherwise disposed of, leased, hired or supplied under the credit transaction are required, and
- (c)   the extent of the company's liability under any transaction connected with the credit transaction.

(6)   No approval is required under this section on the part of the members of a body corporate that—

- (a)   is not a UK-registered company, or
- (b)   is a wholly-owned subsidiary of another body corporate.

NOTES

Commencement: 1 October 2007.
Commencement (transitional provisions): see the note to s 197 at **[1.197]**.

[1.202]
202   Meaning of "credit transaction"

(1)   A "credit transaction" is a transaction under which one party ("the creditor")—

- (a)   supplies any goods or sells any land under a hire-purchase agreement or a conditional sale agreement,
- (b)   leases or hires any land or goods in return for periodical payments, or
- (c)   otherwise disposes of land or supplies goods or services on the understanding that payment (whether in a lump sum or instalments or by way of periodical payments or otherwise) is to be deferred.

(2)   Any reference to the person for whose benefit a credit transaction is entered into is to the person to whom goods, land or services are supplied, sold, leased, hired or otherwise disposed of under the transaction.

(3)   In this section—

"conditional sale agreement" has the same meaning as in the Consumer Credit Act 1974 (c 39); and

"services" means anything other than goods or land.

NOTES

Commencement: 1 October 2007.
Commencement (transitional provisions): see the note to s 197 at **[1.197]**.

[1.203]
203   Related arrangements: requirement of members' approval

(1)   A company may not—

- (a)   take part in an arrangement under which—
  - (i)   another person enters into a transaction that, if it had been entered into by the company, would have required approval under section 197, 198, 200 or 201, and
  - (ii)   that person, in pursuance of the arrangement, obtains a benefit from the company or a body corporate associated with it, or
- (b)   arrange for the assignment to it, or assumption by it, of any rights, obligations or liabilities under a transaction that, if it had been entered into by the company, would have required such approval,

unless the arrangement in question has been approved by a resolution of the members of the company.

(2)   If the director or connected person for whom the transaction is entered into is a director of its holding company or a person connected with such a director, the arrangement must also have been approved by a resolution of the members of the holding company.

(3)   A resolution approving an arrangement to which this section applies must not be passed unless a memorandum setting out the matters mentioned in subsection (4) is made available to members—

- (a)   in the case of a written resolution, by being sent or submitted to every eligible member at or before the time at which the proposed resolution is sent or submitted to him;

(b) in the case of a resolution at a meeting, by being made available for inspection by members of the company both—

    (i) at the company's registered office for not less than 15 days ending with the date of the meeting, and

    (ii) at the meeting itself.

(4) The matters to be disclosed are—

  (a) the matters that would have to be disclosed if the company were seeking approval of the transaction to which the arrangement relates,

  (b) the nature of the arrangement, and

  (c) the extent of the company's liability under the arrangement or any transaction connected with it.

(5) No approval is required under this section on the part of the members of a body corporate that—

  (a) is not a UK-registered company, or

  (b) is a wholly-owned subsidiary of another body corporate.

(6) In determining for the purposes of this section whether a transaction is one that would have required approval under section 197, 198, 200 or 201 if it had been entered into by the company, the transaction shall be treated as having been entered into on the date of the arrangement.

NOTES

Commencement: 1 October 2007.

Commencement (transitional provisions): see the note to s 197 at **[1.197]**.

[1.204]
204 Exception for expenditure on company business

(1) Approval is not required under section 197, 198, 200 or 201 (requirement of members' approval for loans etc) for anything done by a company—

  (a) to provide a director of the company or of its holding company, or a person connected with any such director, with funds to meet expenditure incurred or to be incurred by him—

    (i) for the purposes of the company, or

    (ii) for the purpose of enabling him properly to perform his duties as an officer of the company, or

  (b) to enable any such person to avoid incurring such expenditure.

(2) This section does not authorise a company to enter into a transaction if the aggregate of—

  (a) the value of the transaction in question, and

  (b) the value of any other relevant transactions or arrangements,

exceeds £50,000.

NOTES

Commencement: 1 October 2007.

Commencement (transitional provisions): see the note to s 197 at **[1.197]**.

[1.205]
205 Exception for expenditure on defending proceedings etc

(1) Approval is not required under section 197, 198, 200 or 201 (requirement of members' approval for loans etc) for anything done by a company—

  (a) to provide a director of the company or of its holding company with funds to meet expenditure incurred or to be incurred by him—

    (i) in defending any criminal or civil proceedings in connection with any alleged negligence, default, breach of duty or breach of trust by him in relation to the company or an associated company, or

    (ii) in connection with an application for relief (see subsection (5)), or

  (b) to enable any such director to avoid incurring such expenditure,

if it is done on the following terms.

(2) The terms are—

  (a) that the loan is to be repaid, or (as the case may be) any liability of the company incurred under any transaction connected with the thing done is to be discharged, in the event of—

    (i) the director being convicted in the proceedings,

    (ii) judgment being given against him in the proceedings, or

    (iii) the court refusing to grant him relief on the application; and

  (b) that it is to be so repaid or discharged not later than—

    (i) the date when the conviction becomes final,

    (ii) the date when the judgment becomes final, or

    (iii) the date when the refusal of relief becomes final.

(3) For this purpose a conviction, judgment or refusal of relief becomes final—

  (a) if not appealed against, at the end of the period for bringing an appeal;

  (b) if appealed against, when the appeal (or any further appeal) is disposed of.

(4) An appeal is disposed of—

  (a) if it is determined and the period for bringing any further appeal has ended, or

(b)   if it is abandoned or otherwise ceases to have effect.
(5)   The reference in subsection (1)(a)(ii) to an application for relief is to an application for relief under—

section 661(3) or (4) (power of court to grant relief in case of acquisition of shares by innocent nominee), or

section 1157 (general power of court to grant relief in case of honest and reasonable conduct).

NOTES

Commencement: 1 October 2007.

Commencement (transitional provisions): see the note to s 197 at **[1.197]**.

Commencement (transitional adaptations): the transitional adaptations of this section contained in the Companies Act 2006 (Commencement No 3, Consequential Amendments, Transitional Provisions and Savings) Order 2007, SI 2007/2194, Sch 1, para 11 were revoked by the Companies Act 2006 (Commencement No 5, Transitional Provisions and Savings) Order 2007, SI 2007/3495, art 10(1), (3), as from 1 October 2008 (subject to any transitional provisions and savings as apply, in accordance with Sch 4 to that Order, in relation to the repeal of any provision of the 1985 Act referred to in the adaptation) (see **[2.43]**). The transitional adaptation contained in the Companies Act 2006 (Commencement No 5, Transitional Provisions and Savings) Order 2007, SI 2007/3495, Sch 1, para 1 was revoked by the Companies Act 2006 (Commencement No 6, Saving and Commencement Nos 3 and 5 (Amendment)) Order 2008, SI 2008/674, art 5, Sch 3, para 5, as from 6 April 2008 (ie, without ever coming into force; see **[2.62]**). The transitional adaptation contained in the Companies Act 2006 (Commencement No 6, Saving and Commencement Nos 3 and 5 (Amendment)) Order 2008, SI 2008/674, art 5, Sch 3, para 1(1)(b) was revoked by the Companies Act 2006 (Commencement No 8, Transitional Provisions and Savings) Order 2008, SI 2008/2860, art 6, as from 1 October 2009 (see **[2.74]**).

[1.206]
206   Exception for expenditure in connection with regulatory action or investigation
Approval is not required under section 197, 198, 200 or 201 (requirement of members' approval for loans etc) for anything done by a company—

(a)   to provide a director of the company or of its holding company with funds to meet expenditure incurred or to be incurred by him in defending himself—
(i)   in an investigation by a regulatory authority, or
(ii)   against action proposed to be taken by a regulatory authority,
in connection with any alleged negligence, default, breach of duty or breach of trust by him in relation to the company or an associated company, or

(b)   to enable any such director to avoid incurring such expenditure.

NOTES

Commencement: 1 October 2007.

Commencement (transitional provisions): see the note to s 197 at **[1.197]**.

[1.207]
207   Exceptions for minor and business transactions
(1)   Approval is not required under section 197, 198 or 200 for a company to make a loan or quasi-loan, or to give a guarantee or provide security in connection with a loan or quasi-loan, if the aggregate of—

(a)   the value of the transaction, and
(b)   the value of any other relevant transactions or arrangements,
does not exceed £10,000.
(2)   Approval is not required under section 201 for a company to enter into a credit transaction, or to give a guarantee or provide security in connection with a credit transaction, if the aggregate of—

(a)   the value of the transaction (that is, of the credit transaction, guarantee or security), and
(b)   the value of any other relevant transactions or arrangements,
does not exceed £15,000.
(3)   Approval is not required under section 201 for a company to enter into a credit transaction, or to give a guarantee or provide security in connection with a credit transaction, if—

(a)   the transaction is entered into by the company in the ordinary course of the company's business, and
(b)   the value of the transaction is not greater, and the terms on which it is entered into are not more favourable, than it is reasonable to expect the company would have offered to, or in respect of, a person of the same financial standing but unconnected with the company.

NOTES

Commencement: 1 October 2007.

Commencement (transitional provisions): see the note to s 197 at **[1.197]**.

[1.208]
208   Exceptions for intra-group transactions
(1)   Approval is not required under section 197, 198 or 200 for—

(a)   the making of a loan or quasi-loan to an associated body corporate, or
(b)   the giving of a guarantee or provision of security in connection with a loan or quasi-loan made to an associated body corporate.
(2)   Approval is not required under section 201—

(a)   to enter into a credit transaction as creditor for the benefit of an associated body corporate, or

(b)   to give a guarantee or provide security in connection with a credit transaction entered into by any person for the benefit of an associated body corporate.

NOTES

Commencement: 1 October 2007.

Commencement (transitional provisions): see the note to s 197 at **[1.197]**.

[1.209]
209   Exceptions for money-lending companies

(1)   Approval is not required under section 197, 198 or 200 for the making of a loan or quasi-loan, or the giving of a guarantee or provision of security in connection with a loan or quasi-loan, by a money-lending company if—

(a)   the transaction (that is, the loan, quasi-loan, guarantee or security) is entered into by the company in the ordinary course of the company's business, and

(b)   the value of the transaction is not greater, and its terms are not more favourable, than it is reasonable to expect the company would have offered to a person of the same financial standing but unconnected with the company.

(2)   A "money-lending company" means a company whose ordinary business includes the making of loans or quasi-loans, or the giving of guarantees or provision of security in connection with loans or quasi-loans.

(3)   The condition specified in subsection (1)(b) does not of itself prevent a company from making a home loan—

(a)   to a director of the company or of its holding company, or

(b)   to an employee of the company,

if loans of that description are ordinarily made by the company to its employees and the terms of the loan in question are no more favourable than those on which such loans are ordinarily made.

(4)   For the purposes of subsection (3) a "home loan" means a loan—

(a)   for the purpose of facilitating the purchase, for use as the only or main residence of the person to whom the loan is made, of the whole or part of any dwelling-house together with any land to be occupied and enjoyed with it,

(b)   for the purpose of improving a dwelling-house or part of a dwelling-house so used or any land occupied and enjoyed with it, or

(c)   in substitution for any loan made by any person and falling within paragraph (a) or (b).

NOTES

Commencement: 1 October 2007.

Commencement (transitional provisions): see the note to s 197 at **[1.197]**.

[1.210]
210   Other relevant transactions or arrangements

(1)   This section has effect for determining what are "other relevant transactions or arrangements" for the purposes of any exception to section 197, 198, 200 or 201. In the following provisions "the relevant exception" means the exception for the purposes of which that falls to be determined.

(2)   Other relevant transactions or arrangements are those previously entered into, or entered into at the same time as the transaction or arrangement in question in relation to which the following conditions are met.

(3)   Where the transaction or arrangement in question is entered into—

(a)   for a director of the company entering into it, or

(b)   for a person connected with such a director,

the conditions are that the transaction or arrangement was (or is) entered into for that director, or a person connected with him, by virtue of the relevant exception by that company or by any of its subsidiaries.

(4)   Where the transaction or arrangement in question is entered into—

(a)   for a director of the holding company of the company entering into it, or

(b)   for a person connected with such a director,

the conditions are that the transaction or arrangement was (or is) entered into for that director, or a person connected with him, by virtue of the relevant exception by the holding company or by any of its subsidiaries.

(5)   A transaction or arrangement entered into by a company that at the time it was entered into—

(a)   was a subsidiary of the company entering into the transaction or arrangement in question, or

(b)   was a subsidiary of that company's holding company,

is not a relevant transaction or arrangement if, at the time the question arises whether the transaction or arrangement in question falls within a relevant exception, it is no longer such a subsidiary.

NOTES

Commencement: 1 October 2007.

Commencement (transitional provisions): see the note to s 197 at **[1.197]**.

[1.211]
211 The value of transactions and arrangements
(1) For the purposes of sections 197 to 214 (loans etc)—
  (a) the value of a transaction or arrangement is determined as follows, and
  (b) the value of any other relevant transaction or arrangement is taken to be the value so determined reduced by any amount by which the liabilities of the person for whom the transaction or arrangement was made have been reduced.
(2) The value of a loan is the amount of its principal.
(3) The value of a quasi-loan is the amount, or maximum amount, that the person to whom the quasi-loan is made is liable to reimburse the creditor.
(4) The value of a credit transaction is the price that it is reasonable to expect could be obtained for the goods, services or land to which the transaction relates if they had been supplied (at the time the transaction is entered into) in the ordinary course of business and on the same terms (apart from price) as they have been supplied, or are to be supplied, under the transaction in question.
(5) The value of a guarantee or security is the amount guaranteed or secured.
(6) The value of an arrangement to which section 203 (related arrangements) applies is the value of the transaction to which the arrangement relates.
(7) If the value of a transaction or arrangement is not capable of being expressed as a specific sum of money—
  (a) whether because the amount of any liability arising under the transaction or arrangement is unascertainable, or for any other reason, and
  (b) whether or not any liability under the transaction or arrangement has been reduced,
its value is deemed to exceed £50,000.

NOTES
Commencement: 1 October 2007.
Commencement (transitional provisions): see the note to s 197 at **[1.197]**.

[1.212]
212 The person for whom a transaction or arrangement is entered into
For the purposes of sections 197 to 214 (loans etc) the person for whom a transaction or arrangement is entered into is—
  (a) in the case of a loan or quasi-loan, the person to whom it is made;
  (b) in the case of a credit transaction, the person to whom goods, land or services are supplied, sold, hired, leased or otherwise disposed of under the transaction;
  (c) in the case of a guarantee or security, the person for whom the transaction is made in connection with which the guarantee or security is entered into;
  (d) in the case of an arrangement within section 203 (related arrangements), the person for whom the transaction is made to which the arrangement relates.

NOTES
Commencement: 1 October 2007.
Commencement (transitional provisions): see the note to s 197 at **[1.197]**.

[1.213]
213 Loans etc: civil consequences of contravention
(1) This section applies where a company enters into a transaction or arrangement in contravention of section 197, 198, 200, 201 or 203 (requirement of members' approval for loans etc).
(2) The transaction or arrangement is voidable at the instance of the company, unless—
  (a) restitution of any money or other asset that was the subject matter of the transaction or arrangement is no longer possible,
  (b) the company has been indemnified for any loss or damage resulting from the transaction or arrangement, or
  (c) rights acquired in good faith, for value and without actual notice of the contravention by a person who is not a party to the transaction or arrangement would be affected by the avoidance.
(3) Whether or not the transaction or arrangement has been avoided, each of the persons specified in subsection (4) is liable—
  (a) to account to the company for any gain that he has made directly or indirectly by the transaction or arrangement, and
  (b) (jointly and severally with any other person so liable under this section) to indemnify the company for any loss or damage resulting from the transaction or arrangement.
(4) The persons so liable are—
  (a) any director of the company or of its holding company with whom the company entered into the transaction or arrangement in contravention of section 197, 198, 201 or 203,

(b)   any person with whom the company entered into the transaction or arrangement in contravention of any of those sections who is connected with a director of the company or of its holding company,

(c)   the director of the company or of its holding company with whom any such person is connected, and

(d)   any other director of the company who authorised the transaction or arrangement.

(5)   Subsections (3) and (4) are subject to the following two subsections.

(6)   In the case of a transaction or arrangement entered into by a company in contravention of section 200, 201 or 203 with a person connected with a director of the company or of its holding company, that director is not liable by virtue of subsection (4)(c) if he shows that he took all reasonable steps to secure the company's compliance with the section concerned.

(7)   In any case—

(a)   a person so connected is not liable by virtue of subsection (4)(b), and

(b)   a director is not liable by virtue of subsection (4)(d),

if he shows that, at the time the transaction or arrangement was entered into, he did not know the relevant circumstances constituting the contravention.

(8)   Nothing in this section shall be read as excluding the operation of any other enactment or rule of law by virtue of which the transaction or arrangement may be called in question or any liability to the company may arise.

NOTES

Commencement: 1 October 2007.
Commencement (transitional provisions): see the note to s 197 at **[1.197]**.

[1.214]
214   Loans etc: effect of subsequent affirmation

Where a transaction or arrangement is entered into by a company in contravention of section 197, 198, 200, 201 or 203 (requirement of members' approval for loans etc) but, within a reasonable period, it is affirmed—

(a)   in the case of a contravention of the requirement for a resolution of the members of the company, by a resolution of the members of the company, and

(b)   in the case of a contravention of the requirement for a resolution of the members of the company's holding company, by a resolution of the members of the holding company,

the transaction or arrangement may no longer be avoided under section 213.

NOTES

Commencement: 1 October 2007.
Commencement (transitional provisions): see the note to s 197 at **[1.197]**.

Payments for loss of office

[1.215]
215   Payments for loss of office

(1)   In this Chapter a "payment for loss of office" means a payment made to a director or past director of a company—

(a)   by way of compensation for loss of office as director of the company,

(b)   by way of compensation for loss, while director of the company or in connection with his ceasing to be a director of it, of—

  (i)   any other office or employment in connection with the management of the affairs of the company, or

  (ii)   any office (as director or otherwise) or employment in connection with the management of the affairs of any subsidiary undertaking of the company,

(c)   as consideration for or in connection with his retirement from his office as director of the company, or

(d)   as consideration for or in connection with his retirement, while director of the company or in connection with his ceasing to be a director of it, from—

  (i)   any other office or employment in connection with the management of the affairs of the company, or

  (ii)   any office (as director or otherwise) or employment in connection with the management of the affairs of any subsidiary undertaking of the company.

(2)   The references to compensation and consideration include benefits otherwise than in cash and references in this Chapter to payment have a corresponding meaning.

(3)   For the purposes of sections 217 to 221 (payments requiring members' approval)—

(a)   payment to a person connected with a director, or

(b)   payment to any person at the direction of, or for the benefit of, a director or a person connected with him,

is treated as payment to the director.

(4)   References in those sections to payment by a person include payment by another person at the direction of, or on behalf of, the person referred to.

NOTES

Commencement: 1 October 2007.

Commencement (transitional provisions): Sch 3, para 12 to the Companies Act 2006 (Commencement No 3, Consequential Amendments, Transitional Provisions and Savings) Order 2007, SI 2007/2194 (at **[2.45]**) provides as follows—

"12 Transactions requiring members' approval: payments for loss of office (ss 215 to 222)

(1) Sections 215 to 222 of the Companies Act 2006 (payments for loss of office: requirement of members' approval) apply in relation to any such loss of office or employment as is mentioned in section 215(1)(a) or (b), or any such retirement as is mentioned in section 215(1)(c) or (d), occurring on or after 1st October 2007.

(2) A resolution passed before that date approving a payment is effective for the purposes of those sections if it complies with the requirements of those sections.

(3) Sections 312 to 316 of the 1985 Act or Articles 320 to 324 of the 1986 Order continue to apply in relation to loss of office or retirement within the meaning of those provisions occurring before that date.

(4) For the purposes of this paragraph loss of office or retirement is regarded as occurring—

(a) in the case of a directorship, when the person ceases to be a director;

(b) in the case of any other office, when the person ceases to hold that office;

(c) in the case of employment, when the employment comes to an end.".

[1.216]

216 Amounts taken to be payments for loss of office

(1) This section applies where in connection with any such transfer as is mentioned in section 218 or 219 (payment in connection with transfer of undertaking, property or shares) a director of the company—

(a) is to cease to hold office, or

(b) is to cease to be the holder of—

(i) any other office or employment in connection with the management of the affairs of the company, or

(ii) any office (as director or otherwise) or employment in connection with the management of the affairs of any subsidiary undertaking of the company.

(2) If in connection with any such transfer—

(a) the price to be paid to the director for any shares in the company held by him is in excess of the price which could at the time have been obtained by other holders of like shares, or

(b) any valuable consideration is given to the director by a person other than the company,

the excess or, as the case may be, the money value of the consideration is taken for the purposes of those sections to have been a payment for loss of office.

NOTES

Commencement: 1 October 2007.

Commencement (transitional provisions): see the note to s 215 at **[1.215]**.

[1.217]

217 Payment by company: requirement of members' approval

(1) A company may not make a payment for loss of office to a director of the company unless the payment has been approved by a resolution of the members of the company.

(2) A company may not make a payment for loss of office to a director of its holding company unless the payment has been approved by a resolution of the members of each of those companies.

(3) A resolution approving a payment to which this section applies must not be passed unless a memorandum setting out particulars of the proposed payment (including its amount) is made available to the members of the company whose approval is sought—

(a) in the case of a written resolution, by being sent or submitted to every eligible member at or before the time at which the proposed resolution is sent or submitted to him;

(b) in the case of a resolution at a meeting, by being made available for inspection by the members both—

(i) at the company's registered office for not less than 15 days ending with the date of the meeting, and

(ii) at the meeting itself.

(4) No approval is required under this section on the part of the members of a body corporate that—

(a) is not a UK-registered company, or

(b) is a wholly-owned subsidiary of another body corporate.

NOTES

Commencement: 1 October 2007.

Commencement (transitional provisions): see the note to s 215 at **[1.215]**.

[1.218]
218 Payment in connection with transfer of undertaking etc: requirement of members' approval
(1) No payment for loss of office may be made by any person to a director of a company in connection with the transfer of the whole or any part of the undertaking or property of the company unless the payment has been approved by a resolution of the members of the company.
(2) No payment for loss of office may be made by any person to a director of a company in connection with the transfer of the whole or any part of the undertaking or property of a subsidiary of the company unless the payment has been approved by a resolution of the members of each of the companies.
(3) A resolution approving a payment to which this section applies must not be passed unless a memorandum setting out particulars of the proposed payment (including its amount) is made available to the members of the company whose approval is sought—
   (a) in the case of a written resolution, by being sent or submitted to every eligible member at or before the time at which the proposed resolution is sent or submitted to him;
   (b) in the case of a resolution at a meeting, by being made available for inspection by the members both—
       (i) at the company's registered office for not less than 15 days ending with the date of the meeting, and
       (ii) at the meeting itself.
(4) No approval is required under this section on the part of the members of a body corporate that—
   (a) is not a UK-registered company, or
   (b) is a wholly-owned subsidiary of another body corporate.
(5) A payment made in pursuance of an arrangement—
   (a) entered into as part of the agreement for the transfer in question, or within one year before or two years after that agreement, and
   (b) to which the company whose undertaking or property is transferred, or any person to whom the transfer is made, is privy,
is presumed, except in so far as the contrary is shown, to be a payment to which this section applies.

NOTES
   Commencement: 1 October 2007.
   Commencement (transitional provisions): see the note to s 215 at **[1.215]**.

[1.219]
219 Payment in connection with share transfer: requirement of members' approval
(1) No payment for loss of office may be made by any person to a director of a company in connection with a transfer of shares in the company, or in a subsidiary of the company, resulting from a takeover bid unless the payment has been approved by a resolution of the relevant shareholders.
(2) The relevant shareholders are the holders of the shares to which the bid relates and any holders of shares of the same class as any of those shares.
(3) A resolution approving a payment to which this section applies must not be passed unless a memorandum setting out particulars of the proposed payment (including its amount) is made available to the members of the company whose approval is sought—
   (a) in the case of a written resolution, by being sent or submitted to every eligible member at or before the time at which the proposed resolution is sent or submitted to him;
   (b) in the case of a resolution at a meeting, by being made available for inspection by the members both—
       (i) at the company's registered office for not less than 15 days ending with the date of the meeting, and
       (ii) at the meeting itself.
(4) Neither the person making the offer, nor any associate of his (as defined in section 988), is entitled to vote on the resolution, but—
   (a) where the resolution is proposed as a written resolution, they are entitled (if they would otherwise be so entitled) to be sent a copy of it, and
   (b) at any meeting to consider the resolution they are entitled (if they would otherwise be so entitled) to be given notice of the meeting, to attend and speak and if present (in person or by proxy) to count towards the quorum.
(5) If at a meeting to consider the resolution a quorum is not present, and after the meeting has been adjourned to a later date a quorum is again not present, the payment is (for the purposes of this section) deemed to have been approved.
(6) No approval is required under this section on the part of shareholders in a body corporate that—
   (a) is not a UK-registered company, or
   (b) is a wholly-owned subsidiary of another body corporate.
(7) A payment made in pursuance of an arrangement—

(a)   entered into as part of the agreement for the transfer in question, or within one year before or two years after that agreement, and

(b)   to which the company whose shares are the subject of the bid, or any person to whom the transfer is made, is privy,

is presumed, except in so far as the contrary is shown, to be a payment to which this section applies.

NOTES
Commencement: 1 October 2007.
Commencement (transitional provisions): see the note to s 215 at **[1.215]**.

[1.220]
220   Exception for payments in discharge of legal obligations etc
(1)   Approval is not required under section 217, 218 or 219 (payments requiring members' approval) for a payment made in good faith—
(a)   in discharge of an existing legal obligation (as defined below),
(b)   by way of damages for breach of such an obligation,
(c)   by way of settlement or compromise of any claim arising in connection with the termination of a person's office or employment, or
(d)   by way of pension in respect of past services.
(2)   In relation to a payment within section 217 (payment by company) an existing legal obligation means an obligation of the company, or any body corporate associated with it, that was not entered into in connection with, or in consequence of, the event giving rise to the payment for loss of office.
(3)   In relation to a payment within section 218 or 219 (payment in connection with transfer of undertaking, property or shares) an existing legal obligation means an obligation of the person making the payment that was not entered into for the purposes of, in connection with or in consequence of, the transfer in question.
(4)   In the case of a payment within both section 217 and section 218, or within both section 217 and section 219, subsection (2) above applies and not subsection (3).
(5)   A payment part of which falls within subsection (1) above and part of which does not is treated as if the parts were separate payments.

NOTES
Commencement: 1 October 2007.
Commencement (transitional provisions): see the note to s 215 at **[1.215]**.

[1.221]
221   Exception for small payments
(1)   Approval is not required under section 217, 218 or 219 (payments requiring members' approval) if—
(a)   the payment in question is made by the company or any of its subsidiaries, and
(b)   the amount or value of the payment, together with the amount or value of any other relevant payments, does not exceed £200.
(2)   For this purpose "other relevant payments" are payments for loss of office in relation to which the following conditions are met.
(3)   Where the payment in question is one to which section 217 (payment by company) applies, the conditions are that the other payment was or is paid—
(a)   by the company making the payment in question or any of its subsidiaries,
(b)   to the director to whom that payment is made, and
(c)   in connection with the same event.
(4)   Where the payment in question is one to which section 218 or 219 applies (payment in connection with transfer of undertaking, property or shares), the conditions are that the other payment was (or is) paid in connection with the same transfer—
(a)   to the director to whom the payment in question was made, and
(b)   by the company making the payment or any of its subsidiaries.

NOTES
Commencement: 1 October 2007.
Commencement (transitional provisions): see the note to s 215 at **[1.215]**.

[1.222]
222   Payments made without approval: civil consequences
(1)   If a payment is made in contravention of section 217 (payment by company)—
(a)   it is held by the recipient on trust for the company making the payment, and
(b)   any director who authorised the payment is jointly and severally liable to indemnify the company that made the payment for any loss resulting from it.
(2)   If a payment is made in contravention of section 218 (payment in connection with transfer of undertaking etc), it is held by the recipient on trust for the company whose undertaking or property is or is proposed to be transferred.
(3)   If a payment is made in contravention of section 219 (payment in connection with share transfer)—

(a)   it is held by the recipient on trust for persons who have sold their shares as a result of the offer made, and

(b)   the expenses incurred by the recipient in distributing that sum amongst those persons shall be borne by him and not retained out of that sum.

(4)   If a payment is in contravention of section 217 and section 218, subsection (2) of this section applies rather than subsection (1).

(5)   If a payment is in contravention of section 217 and section 219, subsection (3) of this section applies rather than subsection (1), unless the court directs otherwise.

NOTES

Commencement: 1 October 2007.
Commencement (transitional provisions): see the note to s 215 at **[1.215]**.

Supplementary

[1.223]
223   Transactions requiring members' approval: application of provisions to shadow directors
(1)   For the purposes of—
   (a)   sections 188 and 189 (directors' service contracts),
   (b)   sections 190 to 196 (property transactions),
   (c)   sections 197 to 214 (loans etc), and
   (d)   sections 215 to 222 (payments for loss of office),
a shadow director is treated as a director.
(2)   Any reference in those provisions to loss of office as a director does not apply in relation to loss of a person's status as a shadow director.

NOTES

Commencement: 1 October 2007.

[1.224]
224   Approval by written resolution: accidental failure to send memorandum
(1)   Where—
   (a)   approval under this Chapter is sought by written resolution, and
   (b)   a memorandum is required under this Chapter to be sent or submitted to every eligible member before the resolution is passed,
any accidental failure to send or submit the memorandum to one or more members shall be disregarded for the purpose of determining whether the requirement has been met.
(2)   Subsection (1) has effect subject to any provision of the company's articles.

NOTES

Commencement: 1 October 2007.

[1.225]
225   Cases where approval is required under more than one provision
(1)   Approval may be required under more than one provision of this Chapter.
(2)   If so, the requirements of each applicable provision must be met.
(3)   This does not require a separate resolution for the purposes of each provision.

NOTES

Commencement: 1 October 2007.

[1.226]
226   Requirement of consent of Charity Commission: companies that are charities
(Substitutes the Charities Act 1993, ss 66, 66A for original s 66 (outside the scope of this work.)

NOTES

Commencement: 1 October 2007.

CHAPTER 5
DIRECTORS' SERVICE CONTRACTS

[1.227]
227   Directors' service contracts
(1)   For the purposes of this Part a director's "service contract", in relation to a company, means a contract under which—
   (a)   a director of the company undertakes personally to perform services (as director or otherwise) for the company, or for a subsidiary of the company, or
   (b)   services (as director or otherwise) that a director of the company undertakes personally to perform are made available by a third party to the company, or to a subsidiary of the company.

(2)   The provisions of this Part relating to directors' service contracts apply to the terms of a person's appointment as a director of a company.

They are not restricted to contracts for the performance of services outside the scope of the ordinary duties of a director.

NOTES
Commencement: 1 October 2007.

[1.228]
228   Copy of contract or memorandum of terms to be available for inspection
(1)   A company must keep available for inspection—
  (a)   a copy of every director's service contract with the company or with a subsidiary of the company, or
  (b)   if the contract is not in writing, a written memorandum setting out the terms of the contract.
(2)   All the copies and memoranda must be kept available for inspection at—
  (a)   the company's registered office, or
  (b)   a place specified in regulations under section 1136.
(3)   The copies and memoranda must be retained by the company for at least one year from the date of termination or expiry of the contract and must be kept available for inspection during that time.
(4)   The company must give notice to the registrar—
  (a)   of the place at which the copies and memoranda are kept available for inspection, and
  (b)   of any change in that place,
unless they have at all times been kept at the company's registered office.
(5)   If default is made in complying with subsection (1), (2) or (3), or default is made for 14 days in complying with subsection (4), an offence is committed by every officer of the company who is in default.
(6)   A person guilty of an offence under this section is liable on summary conviction to a fine not exceeding level 3 on the standard scale and, for continued contravention, a daily default fine not exceeding one-tenth of level 3 on the standard scale.
(7)   The provisions of this section apply to a variation of a director's service contract as they apply to the original contract.

NOTES
Commencement: 1 October 2007.
Commencement (transitional provisions): Sch 3, para 13 to the Companies Act 2006 (Commencement No 3, Consequential Amendments, Transitional Provisions and Savings) Order 2007, SI 2007/2194 (at **[2.45]**) (as amended by the Companies Act 2006 (Commencement No 5, Transitional Provisions and Savings) Order 2007, SI 2007/3495, art 11, Sch 5, para 2(1), (3), as from 14 January 2008) provides as follows—

> **"13   Directors' service contracts (ss 227 to 230)**
> (1)   Sections 228 to 230 of the Companies Act 2006 (directors' service contracts) apply to—
>   (a)   contracts within section 227(1) of that Act entered into on or after 1st October 2007,
>   (b)   appointments within section 227(2) of that Act made on or after that date, and
>   (c)   contracts to which section 318(1) of the 1985 Act or Article 326(1) of the 1986 Order applied immediately before that date.
> (2)   Until regulations under section 1136 of the Companies Act 2006 [come into force] specifying a place for the purposes of section 228(2)(b), the copies and memoranda referred to in section 228 may be kept by a company—
>   (a)   at any place where its register of members is kept, or
>   (b)   at its principal place of business,
> provided that place is situated in the part of the United Kingdom in which the company is registered.
> (3)   Until section 1068(1) of the Companies Act 2006 comes into force the notice referred to in section 228(4) must be given on the form prescribed for the purposes of section 318(4) of the 1985 Act or Article 326(4) of the 1986 Order.
> (4)   The provisions of section 318 of the 1985 Act or Article 326 of the 1986 Order continue to apply in relation to—
>   (a)   any default before 1st October 2007 in complying with section 318(1) or (5) or Article 326(1) or (5);
>   (b)   any request for inspection under section 318(7) or Article 326(7) made before that date;
>   (c)   any duty to give notice under section 318(4) or Article 326(4) arising before that date.".

[1.229]
229   Right of member to inspect and request copy
(1)   Every copy or memorandum required to be kept under section 228 must be open to inspection by any member of the company without charge.
(2)   Any member of the company is entitled, on request and on payment of such fee as may be prescribed, to be provided with a copy of any such copy or memorandum.

The copy must be provided within seven days after the request is received by the company.
(3)   If an inspection required under subsection (1) is refused, or default is made in complying with subsection (2), an offence is committed by every officer of the company who is in default.
(4)   A person guilty of an offence under this section is liable on summary conviction to a fine not exceeding level 3 on the standard scale and, for continued contravention, a daily default fine not exceeding one-tenth of level 3 on the standard scale.

(5) In the case of any such refusal or default the court may by order compel an immediate inspection or, as the case may be, direct that the copy required be sent to the person requiring it.

NOTES

Commencement: 20 January 2007 (for the purpose of enabling the exercise of powers to make Orders or Regulations by statutory instrument); 1 October 2007 (otherwise).

Commencement (transitional provisions): see the note to s 228 at **[1.228]**.

Regulations: the Companies (Fees for Inspection and Copying of Company Records) Regulations 2007, SI 2007/2612 at **[4.12]**.

[1.230]
230   Directors' service contracts: application of provisions to shadow directors
A shadow director is treated as a director for the purposes of the provisions of this Chapter.

NOTES

Commencement: 1 October 2007.

Commencement (transitional provisions): see the note to s 228 at **[1.228]**.

CHAPTER 6
CONTRACTS WITH SOLE MEMBERS WHO ARE DIRECTORS

[1.231]
231   Contract with sole member who is also a director
(1)   This section applies where—
  (a)   a limited company having only one member enters into a contract with the sole member,
  (b)   the sole member is also a director of the company, and
  (c)   the contract is not entered into in the ordinary course of the company's business.
(2)   The company must, unless the contract is in writing, ensure that the terms of the contract are either—
  (a)   set out in a written memorandum, or
  (b)   recorded in the minutes of the first meeting of the directors of the company following the making of the contract.
(3)   If a company fails to comply with this section an offence is committed by every officer of the company who is in default.
(4)   A person guilty of an offence under this section is liable on summary conviction to a fine not exceeding level 5 on the standard scale.
(5)   For the purposes of this section a shadow director is treated as a director.
(6)   Failure to comply with this section in relation to a contract does not affect the validity of the contract.
(7)   Nothing in this section shall be read as excluding the operation of any other enactment or rule of law applying to contracts between a company and a director of the company.

NOTES

Commencement: 1 October 2007.

Commencement (transitional provisions): Sch 3, para 14 to the Companies Act 2006 (Commencement No 3, Consequential Amendments, Transitional Provisions and Savings) Order 2007, SI 2007/2194 (at **[2.45]**) provides that this section applies to contracts entered into on or after 1 October 2007 (and that s 322B of the 1985 Act continues to apply to contracts entered into before that date).

CHAPTER 7
DIRECTORS' LIABILITIES

Provision protecting directors from liability

[1.232]
232   Provisions protecting directors from liability
(1)   Any provision that purports to exempt a director of a company (to any extent) from any liability that would otherwise attach to him in connection with any negligence, default, breach of duty or breach of trust in relation to the company is void.
(2)   Any provision by which a company directly or indirectly provides an indemnity (to any extent) for a director of the company, or of an associated company, against any liability attaching to him in connection with any negligence, default, breach of duty or breach of trust in relation to the company of which he is a director is void, except as permitted by—
  (a)   section 233 (provision of insurance),
  (b)   section 234 (qualifying third party indemnity provision), or
  (c)   section 235 (qualifying pension scheme indemnity provision).
(3)   This section applies to any provision, whether contained in a company's articles or in any contract with the company or otherwise.
(4)   Nothing in this section prevents a company's articles from making such provision as has previously been lawful for dealing with conflicts of interest.

NOTES

Commencement: 1 October 2007.

Commencement (transitional provisions): Sch 3, paras 15–17 to the Companies Act 2006 (Commencement No 3, Consequential Amendments, Transitional Provisions and Savings) Order 2007, SI 2007/2194 (at **[2.45]**) (as amended, in the case of para 16, by the Companies Act 2006 (Commencement No 5, Transitional Provisions and Savings) Order 2007, SI 2007/3495, art 11, Sch 5, para 2(1), (3), as from 14 January 2008) provide as follows—

"Directors' liabilities (ss 232 to 239)

15.—(1)   Sections 232 to 236 of the Companies Act 2006 (restrictions on provision protecting directors from liability) apply to any provision made on or after 1st October 2007.

(2)   Sections 309A, 309B and 309C(1) to (3) and (6) of the 1985 Act or Article 318 of the 1986 Order (so far as it relates to directors) continue to apply in relation to any provision to which they applied immediately before that date.

16.—(1)   Sections 237 and 238 of the Companies Act 2006 (copies of qualifying indemnity provision to be available for inspection etc) apply to—

(a)   qualifying indemnity provision within the meaning of section 237 made on or after 1st October 2007, and

(b)   qualifying third party indemnity provision within the meaning of section 309B(1) of the 1985 Act to which section 309C(4) and (5) of that Act applied immediately before that date.

(2)   Until regulations under section 1136 of the Companies Act 2006 [come into force] specifying a place for the purposes of section 237(3)(b), the copies and memoranda referred to in section 237 may be kept by a company—

(a)   at any place where its register of members is kept, or

(b)   at its principal place of business,

provided that place is situated in the part of the United Kingdom in which the company is registered.

(3)   Until section 1068(1) of the Companies Act 2006 comes into force the notice referred to in section 237(5) must be given on the form prescribed for the purposes of section 318(4) of the 1985 Act or Article 326(4) of the 1986 Order.

(4)   The provisions of section 318 of the 1985 Act, as applied by section 309C(4) and (5), continue to apply in relation to—

(a)   any default before 1st October 2007 in complying with section 318(1) or (5), as so applied;

(b)   any request for inspection under section 318(7), as so applied, made before that date;

(c)·   any duty to give notice under section 318(4), as so applied, arising before that date.

17.—(1)   Section 239 of the Companies Act 2006 (ratification of acts of directors giving rise to liability) applies to conduct by a director on or after 1st October 2007.

(2)   Conduct by a director before that date is subject to the law relating to ratification that applied immediately before that date.".

[1.233]

233   Provision of insurance

Section 232(2) (voidness of provisions for indemnifying directors) does not prevent a company from purchasing and maintaining for a director of the company, or of an associated company, insurance against any such liability as is mentioned in that subsection.

NOTES

Commencement: 1 October 2007.

Commencement (transitional provisions): see the note to s 232 at **[1.232]**.

[1.234]

234   Qualifying third party indemnity provision

(1)   Section 232(2) (voidness of provisions for indemnifying directors) does not apply to qualifying third party indemnity provision.

(2)   Third party indemnity provision means provision for indemnity against liability incurred by the director to a person other than the company or an associated company.

Such provision is qualifying third party indemnity provision if the following requirements are met.

(3)   The provision must not provide any indemnity against—

(a)   any liability of the director to pay—

   (i)   a fine imposed in criminal proceedings, or

   (ii)   a sum payable to a regulatory authority by way of a penalty in respect of non-compliance with any requirement of a regulatory nature (however arising); or

(b)   any liability incurred by the director—

   (i)   in defending criminal proceedings in which he is convicted, or

   (ii)   in defending civil proceedings brought by the company, or an associated company, in which judgment is given against him, or

   (iii)   in connection with an application for relief (see subsection (6)) in which the court refuses to grant him relief.

(4)   The references in subsection (3)(b) to a conviction, judgment or refusal of relief are to the final decision in the proceedings.

(5)   For this purpose—

(a)   a conviction, judgment or refusal of relief becomes final—

   (i)   if not appealed against, at the end of the period for bringing an appeal, or

   (ii)   if appealed against, at the time when the appeal (or any further appeal) is disposed of; and

(b)   an appeal is disposed of—

(i)   if it is determined and the period for bringing any further appeal has ended, or

(ii)   if it is abandoned or otherwise ceases to have effect.

(6)   The reference in subsection (3)(b)(iii) to an application for relief is to an application for relief under—

section 661(3) or (4) (power of court to grant relief in case of acquisition of shares by innocent nominee), or

section 1157 (general power of court to grant relief in case of honest and reasonable conduct).

NOTES

Commencement: 1 October 2007.

Commencement (transitional provisions): see the note to s 232 at **[1.232]**.

Commencement (transitional adaptations): the transitional adaptations of this section contained in the Companies Act 2006 (Commencement No 3, Consequential Amendments, Transitional Provisions and Savings) Order 2007, SI 2007/2194, Sch 1, para 12 were revoked by the Companies Act 2006 (Commencement No 5, Transitional Provisions and Savings) Order 2007, SI 2007/3495, art 10(1), (3), as from 1 October 2008 (subject to any transitional provisions and savings as apply, in accordance with Sch 4 to that Order, in relation to the repeal of any provision of the 1985 Act referred to in the adaptation; see **[2.43]**). The transitional adaptation contained in the Companies Act 2006 (Commencement No 5, Transitional Provisions and Savings) Order 2007, SI 2007/3495, Sch 1, para 2 was revoked by the Companies Act 2006 (Commencement No 6, Saving and Commencement Nos 3 and 5 (Amendment)) Order 2008, SI 2008/674, art 5, Sch 3, para 5, as from 6 April 2008 (ie, without ever coming into force; see **[2.62]**). The transitional adaptation contained in the Companies Act 2006 (Commencement No 6, Saving and Commencement Nos 3 and 5 (Amendment)) Order 2008, SI 2008/674, art 5, Sch 3, para 1(1)(b) was revoked by the Companies Act 2006 (Commencement No 8, Transitional Provisions and Savings) Order 2008, SI 2008/2860, art 6, as from 1 October 2009 (see **[2.74]**).

[1.235]
235   Qualifying pension scheme indemnity provision

(1)   Section 232(2) (voidness of provisions for indemnifying directors) does not apply to qualifying pension scheme indemnity provision.

(2)   Pension scheme indemnity provision means provision indemnifying a director of a company that is a trustee of an occupational pension scheme against liability incurred in connection with the company's activities as trustee of the scheme.

Such provision is qualifying pension scheme indemnity provision if the following requirements are met.

(3)   The provision must not provide any indemnity against—

(a)   any liability of the director to pay—

(i)   a fine imposed in criminal proceedings, or

(ii)   a sum payable to a regulatory authority by way of a penalty in respect of non-compliance with any requirement of a regulatory nature (however arising); or

(b)   any liability incurred by the director in defending criminal proceedings in which he is convicted.

(4)   The reference in subsection (3)(b) to a conviction is to the final decision in the proceedings.

(5)   For this purpose—

(a)   a conviction becomes final—

(i)   if not appealed against, at the end of the period for bringing an appeal, or

(ii)   if appealed against, at the time when the appeal (or any further appeal) is disposed of; and

(b)   an appeal is disposed of—

(i)   if it is determined and the period for bringing any further appeal has ended, or

(ii)   if it is abandoned or otherwise ceases to have effect.

(6)   In this section "occupational pension scheme" means an occupational pension scheme as defined in section 150(5) of the Finance Act 2004 (c 12) that is established under a trust.

NOTES

Commencement: 1 October 2007.

Commencement (transitional provisions): see the note to s 232 at **[1.232]**.

[1.236]
236   Qualifying indemnity provision to be disclosed in directors' report

(1)   This section requires disclosure in the directors' report of—

(a)   qualifying third party indemnity provision, and

(b)   qualifying pension scheme indemnity provision.

Such provision is referred to in this section as "qualifying indemnity provision".

(2)   If when a directors' report is approved any qualifying indemnity provision (whether made by the company or otherwise) is in force for the benefit of one or more directors of the company, the report must state that such provision is in force.

(3)   If at any time during the financial year to which a directors' report relates any such provision was in force for the benefit of one or more persons who were then directors of the company, the report must state that such provision was in force.

(4) If when a directors' report is approved qualifying indemnity provision made by the company is in force for the benefit of one or more directors of an associated company, the report must state that such provision is in force.

(5) If at any time during the financial year to which a directors' report relates any such provision was in force for the benefit of one or more persons who were then directors of an associated company, the report must state that such provision was in force.

NOTES

Commencement: 1 October 2007.

Commencement (transitional provisions): see the note to s 232 at **[1.232]**.

[1.237]
237 Copy of qualifying indemnity provision to be available for inspection

(1) This section has effect where qualifying indemnity provision is made for a director of a company, and applies—

    (a) to the company of which he is a director (whether the provision is made by that company or an associated company), and

    (b) where the provision is made by an associated company, to that company.

(2) That company or, as the case may be, each of them must keep available for inspection—

    (a) a copy of the qualifying indemnity provision, or

    (b) if the provision is not in writing, a written memorandum setting out its terms.

(3) The copy or memorandum must be kept available for inspection at—

    (a) the company's registered office, or

    (b) a place specified in regulations under section 1136.

(4) The copy or memorandum must be retained by the company for at least one year from the date of termination or expiry of the provision and must be kept available for inspection during that time.

(5) The company must give notice to the registrar—

    (a) of the place at which the copy or memorandum is kept available for inspection, and

    (b) of any change in that place,

unless it has at all times been kept at the company's registered office.

(6) If default is made in complying with subsection (2), (3) or (4), or default is made for 14 days in complying with subsection (5), an offence is committed by every officer of the company who is in default.

(7) A person guilty of an offence under this section is liable on summary conviction to a fine not exceeding level 3 on the standard scale and, for continued contravention, a daily default fine not exceeding one-tenth of level 3 on the standard scale.

(8) The provisions of this section apply to a variation of a qualifying indemnity provision as they apply to the original provision.

(9) In this section "qualifying indemnity provision" means—

    (a) qualifying third party indemnity provision, and

    (b) qualifying pension scheme indemnity provision.

NOTES

Commencement: 1 October 2007.

Commencement (transitional provisions): see the note to s 232 at **[1.232]**.

[1.238]
238 Right of member to inspect and request copy

(1) Every copy or memorandum required to be kept by a company under section 237 must be open to inspection by any member of the company without charge.

(2) Any member of the company is entitled, on request and on payment of such fee as may be prescribed, to be provided with a copy of any such copy or memorandum.

The copy must be provided within seven days after the request is received by the company.

(3) If an inspection required under subsection (1) is refused, or default is made in complying with subsection (2), an offence is committed by every officer of the company who is in default.

(4) A person guilty of an offence under this section is liable on summary conviction to a fine not exceeding level 3 on the standard scale and, for continued contravention, a daily default fine not exceeding one-tenth of level 3 on the standard scale.

(5) In the case of any such refusal or default the court may by order compel an immediate inspection or, as the case may be, direct that the copy required be sent to the person requiring it.

NOTES

Commencement: 20 January 2007 (for the purpose of enabling the exercise of powers to make Orders or Regulations by statutory instrument); 1 October 2007 (otherwise).

Commencement (transitional provisions): see the note to s 232 at **[1.232]**.

Regulations: the Companies (Fees for Inspection and Copying of Company Records) Regulations 2007, SI 2007/2612 at **[4.12]**.

Ratification of acts giving rise to liability

[1.239]

239 Ratification of acts of directors

(1) This section applies to the ratification by a company of conduct by a director amounting to negligence, default, breach of duty or breach of trust in relation to the company.

(2) The decision of the company to ratify such conduct must be made by resolution of the members of the company.

(3) Where the resolution is proposed as a written resolution neither the director (if a member of the company) nor any member connected with him is an eligible member.

(4) Where the resolution is proposed at a meeting, it is passed only if the necessary majority is obtained disregarding votes in favour of the resolution by the director (if a member of the company) and any member connected with him. This does not prevent the director or any such member from attending, being counted towards the quorum and taking part in the proceedings at any meeting at which the decision is considered.

(5) For the purposes of this section—

    (a) "conduct" includes acts and omissions;

    (b) "director" includes a former director;

    (c) a shadow director is treated as a director; and

    (d) in section 252 (meaning of "connected person"), subsection (3) does not apply (exclusion of person who is himself a director).

(6) Nothing in this section affects—

    (a) the validity of a decision taken by unanimous consent of the members of the company, or

    (b) any power of the directors to agree not to sue, or to settle or release a claim made by them on behalf of the company.

(7) This section does not affect any other enactment or rule of law imposing additional requirements for valid ratification or any rule of law as to acts that are incapable of being ratified by the company.

NOTES

Commencement: 1 October 2007.

Commencement (transitional provisions): see the note to s 232 at **[1.232]**.

CHAPTER 8
DIRECTORS' RESIDENTIAL ADDRESSES: PROTECTION FROM DISCLOSURE

[1.240]

240 Protected information

(1) This Chapter makes provision for protecting, in the case of a company director who is an individual—

    (a) information as to his usual residential address;

    (b) the information that his service address is his usual residential address.

(2) That information is referred to in this Chapter as "protected information".

(3) Information does not cease to be protected information on the individual ceasing to be a director of the company.

References in this Chapter to a director include, to that extent, a former director.

NOTES

Commencement: 1 October 2009.

Commencement (transitional provisions): see the note to s 162 at **[1.162]**.

[1.241]

241 Protected information: restriction on use or disclosure by company

(1) A company must not use or disclose protected information about any of its directors, except—

    (a) for communicating with the director concerned,

    (b) in order to comply with any requirement of the Companies Acts as to particulars to be sent to the registrar, or

    (c) in accordance with section 244 (disclosure under court order).

(2) Subsection (1) does not prohibit any use or disclosure of protected information with the consent of the director concerned.

NOTES

Commencement: 1 October 2009.

Commencement (transitional provisions): see the note to s 162 at **[1.162]**.

[1.242]

242 Protected information: restriction on use or disclosure by registrar

(1) The registrar must omit protected information from the material on the register that is available for inspection where—

(a)   it is contained in a document delivered to him in which such information is required to be stated, and

(b)   in the case of a document having more than one part, it is contained in a part of the document in which such information is required to be stated.

(2)   The registrar is not obliged—

(a)   to check other documents or (as the case may be) other parts of the document to ensure the absence of protected information, or

(b)   to omit from the material that is available for public inspection anything registered before this Chapter comes into force.

(3)   The registrar must not use or disclose protected information except—

(a)   as permitted by section 243 (permitted use or disclosure by registrar), or

(b)   in accordance with section 244 (disclosure under court order).

NOTES

Commencement: 1 October 2009.

Commencement (transitional provisions): see the note to s 162 at **[1.162]**.

[1.243]
243   Permitted use or disclosure by the registrar

(1)   The registrar may use protected information for communicating with the director in question.

(2)   The registrar may disclose protected information—

(a)   to a public authority specified for the purposes of this section by regulations made by the Secretary of State, or

(b)   to a credit reference agency.

(3)   The Secretary of State may make provision by regulations—

(a)   specifying conditions for the disclosure of protected information in accordance with this section, and

(b)   providing for the charging of fees.

(4)   The Secretary of State may make provision by regulations requiring the registrar, on application, to refrain from disclosing protected information relating to a director to a credit reference agency.

(5)   Regulations under subsection (4) may make provision as to—

(a)   who may make an application,

(b)   the grounds on which an application may be made,

(c)   the information to be included in and documents to accompany an application, and

(d)   how an application is to be determined.

(6)   Provision under subsection (5)(d) may in particular—

(a)   confer a discretion on the registrar;

(b)   provide for a question to be referred to a person other than the registrar for the purposes of determining the application.

(7)   In this section—

"credit reference agency" means a person carrying on a business comprising the furnishing of information relevant to the financial standing of individuals, being information collected by the agency for that purpose; and

"public authority" includes any person or body having functions of a public nature.

(8)   Regulations under this section are subject to negative resolution procedure.

NOTES

Commencement: 20 January 2007 (for the purpose of enabling the exercise of powers to make Orders or Regulations by statutory instrument); 1 October 2009 (otherwise).

Commencement (transitional provisions): see the note to s 162 at **[1.162]**.

Regulations: the Companies (Disclosure of Address) Regulations 2009, SI 2009/214 at **[4.344]**; the Registrar of Companies (Fees) (Companies, Overseas Companies and Limited Liability Partnerships) Regulations 2009, SI 2009/2101 at **[4.543]**; the Companies (Disclosure of Address) (Amendment) Regulations 2010, SI 2010/2156; the Registrar of Companies (Fees) (Companies, Overseas Companies and Limited Liability Partnerships) (Amendment) Regulations 2011, SI 2011/309.

[1.244]
244   Disclosure under court order

(1)   The court may make an order for the disclosure of protected information by the company or by the registrar if—

(a)   there is evidence that service of documents at a service address other than the director's usual residential address is not effective to bring them to the notice of the director, or

(b)   it is necessary or expedient for the information to be provided in connection with the enforcement of an order or decree of the court,

and the court is otherwise satisfied that it is appropriate to make the order.

(2)   An order for disclosure by the registrar is to be made only if the company—

(a)   does not have the director's usual residential address, or

(b)   has been dissolved.

(3) The order may be made on the application of a liquidator, creditor or member of the company, or any other person appearing to the court to have a sufficient interest.

(4) The order must specify the persons to whom, and purposes for which, disclosure is authorised.

NOTES

Commencement: 1 October 2009.

Commencement (transitional provisions): see the note to s 162 at **[1.162]**.

[1.245]
245 Circumstances in which registrar may put address on the public record

(1) The registrar may put a director's usual residential address on the public record if—
   (a) communications sent by the registrar to the director and requiring a response within a specified period remain unanswered, or
   (b) there is evidence that service of documents at a service address provided in place of the director's usual residential address is not effective to bring them to the notice of the director.

(2) The registrar must give notice of the proposal—
   (a) to the director, and
   (b) to every company of which the registrar has been notified that the individual is a director.

(3) The notice must—
   (a) state the grounds on which it is proposed to put the director's usual residential address on the public record, and
   (b) specify a period within which representations may be made before that is done.

(4) It must be sent to the director at his usual residential address, unless it appears to the registrar that service at that address may be ineffective to bring it to the individual's notice, in which case it may be sent to any service address provided in place of that address.

(5) The registrar must take account of any representations received within the specified period.

(6) What is meant by putting the address on the public record is explained in section 246.

NOTES

Commencement: 1 October 2009.

Commencement (transitional provisions): see the note to s 162 at **[1.162]**.

[1.246]
246 Putting the address on the public record

(1) The registrar, on deciding in accordance with section 245 that a director's usual residential address is to be put on the public record, shall proceed as if notice of a change of registered particulars had been given—
   (a) stating that address as the director's service address, and
   (b) stating that the director's usual residential address is the same as his service address.

(2) The registrar must give notice of having done so—
   (a) to the director, and
   (b) to the company.

(3) On receipt of the notice the company must—
   (a) enter the director's usual residential address in its register of directors as his service address, and
   (b) state in its register of directors' residential addresses that his usual residential address is the same as his service address.

(4) If the company has been notified by the director in question of a more recent address as his usual residential address, it must—
   (a) enter that address in its register of directors as the director's service address, and
   (b) give notice to the registrar as on a change of registered particulars.

(5) If a company fails to comply with subsection (3) or (4), an offence is committed by—
   (a) the company, and
   (b) every officer of the company who is in default.

(6) A person guilty of an offence under subsection (5) is liable on summary conviction to a fine not exceeding level 5 on the standard scale and, for continued contravention, a daily default fine not exceeding one-tenth of level 5 on the standard scale.

(7) A director whose usual residential address has been put on the public record by the registrar under this section may not register a service address other than his usual residential address for a period of five years from the date of the registrar's decision.

NOTES

Commencement: 1 October 2009.

Commencement (transitional provisions): see the note to s 162 at **[1.162]**.

CHAPTER 9
SUPPLEMENTARY PROVISIONS
Provision for employees on cessation or transfer of business

[1.247]
247 Power to make provision for employees on cessation or transfer of business

(1) The powers of the directors of a company include (if they would not otherwise do so) power to make provision for the benefit of persons employed or formerly employed by the company, or any of its subsidiaries, in connection with the cessation or the transfer to any person of the whole or part of the undertaking of the company or that subsidiary.

(2) This power is exercisable notwithstanding the general duty imposed by section 172 (duty to promote the success of the company).

(3) In the case of a company that is a charity it is exercisable notwithstanding any restrictions on the directors' powers (or the company's capacity) flowing from the objects of the company.

(4) The power may only be exercised if sanctioned—
 (a) by a resolution of the company, or
 (b) by a resolution of the directors,
in accordance with the following provisions.

(5) A resolution of the directors—
 (a) must be authorised by the company's articles, and
 (b) is not sufficient sanction for payments to or for the benefit of directors, former directors or shadow directors.

(6) Any other requirements of the company's articles as to the exercise of the power conferred by this section must be complied with.

(7) Any payment under this section must be made—
 (a) before the commencement of any winding up of the company, and
 (b) out of profits of the company that are available for dividend.

NOTES
Commencement: 1 October 2009.

Commencement (transitional provisions): Sch 2, para 40 to the Companies Act 2006 (Commencement No 8, Transitional Provisions and Savings) Order 2008, SI 2008/2860 (at **[2.91]**) provides as follows—

"Power to make provision for employees on cessation or transfer of business (s 247)
40.—(1) Section 247 of the Companies Act 2006 (power to make provision for employees on cessation or transfer of business) applies to provision made on or after 1st October 2009 (subject to sub-paragraph (2)(b)).
(2) Section 719 of the 1985 Act or Article 668 of the 1986 Order continues to apply—
 (a) to provision made before that date, and
 (b) to anything sanctioned in accordance with subsection (3) of that section or paragraph (3) of that Article before that date.".

Note: the Companies Act 2006 (Commencement No 3, Consequential Amendments, Transitional Provisions and Savings) Order 2007, SI 2007/2194, art 2(1)(d) originally provided that this section would come into force on 1 October 2007 (subject to transitional provisions in Sch 3, para 18 to that Order). Article 2(1)(d) was subsequently amended by the Companies Act 2006 (Commencement No 4 and Commencement No 3 (Amendment)) Order 2007, SI 2007/2607, art 4(1) (with effect from 30 September 2007) so that the commencement of this section on 1 October 2007 was reversed. The transitional provisions in Sch 3, para 18 were revoked at the same time.

Records of meetings of directors

[1.248]
248 Minutes of directors' meetings

(1) Every company must cause minutes of all proceedings at meetings of its directors to be recorded.

(2) The records must be kept for at least ten years from the date of the meeting.

(3) If a company fails to comply with this section, an offence is committed by every officer of the company who is in default.

(4) A person guilty of an offence under this section is liable on summary conviction to a fine not exceeding level 3 on the standard scale and, for continued contravention, a daily default fine not exceeding one-tenth of level 3 on the standard scale.

NOTES
Commencement: 1 October 2007.

Commencement (transitional provisions): Sch 3, para 19 to the Companies Act 2006 (Commencement No 3, Consequential Amendments, Transitional Provisions and Savings) Order 2007, SI 2007/2194 (at **[2.45]**) provides that this section and s 249 apply to meetings held on or after 1 October 2007 (and that s 382 of the 1985 Act continues to apply to meetings of directors held before that date).

[1.249]
249 Minutes as evidence

(1) Minutes recorded in accordance with section 248, if purporting to be authenticated by the chairman of the meeting or by the chairman of the next directors' meeting, are evidence (in Scotland, sufficient evidence) of the proceedings at the meeting.

(2)   Where minutes have been made in accordance with that section of the proceedings of a meeting of directors, then, until the contrary is proved—

(a)   the meeting is deemed duly held and convened,

(b)   all proceedings at the meeting are deemed to have duly taken place, and

(c)   all appointments at the meeting are deemed valid.

NOTES

Commencement: 1 October 2007.

Commencement (transitional provisions): see the note to s 248 at **[1.248]**.

Meaning of "director" and "shadow director"

[1.250]

250   "Director"

In the Companies Acts "director" includes any person occupying the position of director, by whatever name called.

NOTES

Commencement: 1 October 2007.

[1.251]

251   "Shadow director"

(1)   In the Companies Acts "shadow director", in relation to a company, means a person in accordance with whose directions or instructions the directors of the company are accustomed to act.

(2)   A person is not to be regarded as a shadow director by reason only that the directors act on advice given by him in a professional capacity.

(3)   A body corporate is not to be regarded as a shadow director of any of its subsidiary companies for the purposes of—

Chapter 2 (general duties of directors),

Chapter 4 (transactions requiring members' approval), or

Chapter 6 (contract with sole member who is also a director),

by reason only that the directors of the subsidiary are accustomed to act in accordance with its directions or instructions.

NOTES

Commencement: 1 October 2007.

Other definitions

[1.252]

252   Persons connected with a director

(1)   This section defines what is meant by references in this Part to a person being "connected" with a director of a company (or a director being "connected" with a person).

(2)   The following persons (and only those persons) are connected with a director of a company—

(a)   members of the director's family (see section 253);

(b)   a body corporate with which the director is connected (as defined in section 254);

(c)   a person acting in his capacity as trustee of a trust—

(i)   the beneficiaries of which include the director or a person who by virtue of paragraph (a) or (b) is connected with him, or

(ii)   the terms of which confer a power on the trustees that may be exercised for the benefit of the director or any such person,

other than a trust for the purposes of an employees' share scheme or a pension scheme;

(d)   a person acting in his capacity as partner—

(i)   of the director, or

(ii)   of a person who, by virtue of paragraph (a), (b) or (c), is connected with that director;

(e)   a firm that is a legal person under the law by which it is governed and in which—

(i)   the director is a partner,

(ii)   a partner is a person who, by virtue of paragraph (a), (b) or (c) is connected with the director, or

(iii)   a partner is a firm in which the director is a partner or in which there is a partner who, by virtue of paragraph (a), (b) or (c), is connected with the director.

(3)   References in this Part to a person connected with a director of a company do not include a person who is himself a director of the company.

NOTES

Commencement: 1 October 2007.

(3) A derivative claim under this Chapter may be brought only in respect of a cause of action arising from an actual or proposed act or omission involving negligence, default, breach of duty or breach of trust by a director of the company.

The cause of action may be against the director or another person (or both).

(4) It is immaterial whether the cause of action arose before or after the person seeking to bring or continue the derivative claim became a member of the company.

(5) For the purposes of this Chapter—

    (a) "director" includes a former director;

    (b) a shadow director is treated as a director; and

    (c) references to a member of a company include a person who is not a member but to whom shares in the company have been transferred or transmitted by operation of law.

NOTES

Commencement: 1 October 2007.

Commencement (transitional provisions): Sch 3, paras 20, 21 to the Companies Act 2006 (Commencement No 3, Consequential Amendments, Transitional Provisions and Savings) Order 2007, SI 2007/2194 (at **[2.45]**) provide as follows—

"Derivative claims and proceedings by members (ss 260 to 269)

20.—(1) On and after 1st October 2007 sections 260 to 264 of the Companies Act 2006 (derivative claims in England and Wales or Northern Ireland) apply to all derivative claims, subject to the following provisions.

(2) Those sections do not apply, and the law in force immediately before 1st October 2007 continues to apply, where the claimant (in Northern Ireland, the plaintiff) has applied for permission (in Northern Ireland, leave) to continue the claim before that date.

(3) If, or to the extent that, the claim arises from acts or omissions that occurred before 1st October 2007, the court must exercise its powers under those sections so as to secure that the claim is allowed to proceed as a derivative claim only if, or to the extent that, it would have been allowed to proceed as a derivative claim under the law in force immediately before that date.

21.—(1) This paragraph applies where an application is made under section 266 or 267 (derivative proceedings in Scotland).

(2) If the cause of action arises, wholly or to any extent, from an act or omission that occurred before 1st October 2007, the court shall exercise its powers under those sections so as to secure that the proceedings in respect of that act or omission are allowed to proceed as derivative proceedings only to the extent that they could have been pursued by the applicant under the law in force immediately before that date.".

[1.261]

261 Application for permission to continue derivative claim

(1) A member of a company who brings a derivative claim under this Chapter must apply to the court for permission (in Northern Ireland, leave) to continue it.

(2) If it appears to the court that the application and the evidence filed by the applicant in support of it do not disclose a prima facie case for giving permission (or leave), the court—

    (a) must dismiss the application, and

    (b) may make any consequential order it considers appropriate.

(3) If the application is not dismissed under subsection (2), the court—

    (a) may give directions as to the evidence to be provided by the company, and

    (b) may adjourn the proceedings to enable the evidence to be obtained.

(4) On hearing the application, the court may—

    (a) give permission (or leave) to continue the claim on such terms as it thinks fit,

    (b) refuse permission (or leave) and dismiss the claim, or

    (c) adjourn the proceedings on the application and give such directions as it thinks fit.

NOTES

Commencement: 1 October 2007.

Commencement (transitional provisions): see the note to s 260 at **[1.260]**.

[1.262]

262 Application for permission to continue claim as a derivative claim

(1) This section applies where—

    (a) a company has brought a claim, and

    (b) the cause of action on which the claim is based could be pursued as a derivative claim under this Chapter.

(2) A member of the company may apply to the court for permission (in Northern Ireland, leave) to continue the claim as a derivative claim on the ground that—

    (a) the manner in which the company commenced or continued the claim amounts to an abuse of the process of the court,

    (b) the company has failed to prosecute the claim diligently, and

    (c) it is appropriate for the member to continue the claim as a derivative claim.

(3) If it appears to the court that the application and the evidence filed by the applicant in support of it do not disclose a prima facie case for giving permission (or leave), the court—

    (a) must dismiss the application, and

    (b) may make any consequential order it considers appropriate.

(4)   If the application is not dismissed under subsection (3), the court—
   (a)   may give directions as to the evidence to be provided by the company, and
   (b)   may adjourn the proceedings to enable the evidence to be obtained.
(5)   On hearing the application, the court may—
   (a)   give permission (or leave) to continue the claim as a derivative claim on such terms as it thinks fit,
   (b)   refuse permission (or leave) and dismiss the application, or
   (c)   adjourn the proceedings on the application and give such directions as it thinks fit.

NOTES

Commencement: 1 October 2007.
Commencement (transitional provisions): see the note to s 260 at **[1.260]**.

[1.263]
263   Whether permission to be given
(1)   The following provisions have effect where a member of a company applies for permission (in Northern Ireland, leave) under section 261 or 262.
(2)   Permission (or leave) must be refused if the court is satisfied—
   (a)   that a person acting in accordance with section 172 (duty to promote the success of the company) would not seek to continue the claim, or
   (b)   where the cause of action arises from an act or omission that is yet to occur, that the act or omission has been authorised by the company, or
   (c)   where the cause of action arises from an act or omission that has already occurred, that the act or omission—
      (i)   was authorised by the company before it occurred, or
      (ii)   has been ratified by the company since it occurred.
(3)   In considering whether to give permission (or leave) the court must take into account, in particular—
   (a)   whether the member is acting in good faith in seeking to continue the claim;
   (b)   the importance that a person acting in accordance with section 172 (duty to promote the success of the company) would attach to continuing it;
   (c)   where the cause of action results from an act or omission that is yet to occur, whether the act or omission could be, and in the circumstances would be likely to be—
      (i)   authorised by the company before it occurs, or
      (ii)   ratified by the company after it occurs;
   (d)   where the cause of action arises from an act or omission that has already occurred, whether the act or omission could be, and in the circumstances would be likely to be, ratified by the company;
   (e)   whether the company has decided not to pursue the claim;
   (f)   whether the act or omission in respect of which the claim is brought gives rise to a cause of action that the member could pursue in his own right rather than on behalf of the company.
(4)   In considering whether to give permission (or leave) the court shall have particular regard to any evidence before it as to the views of members of the company who have no personal interest, direct or indirect, in the matter.
(5)   The Secretary of State may by regulations—
   (a)   amend subsection (2) so as to alter or add to the circumstances in which permission (or leave) is to be refused;
   (b)   amend subsection (3) so as to alter or add to the matters that the court is required to take into account in considering whether to give permission (or leave).
(6)   Before making any such regulations the Secretary of State shall consult such persons as he considers appropriate.
(7)   Regulations under this section are subject to affirmative resolution procedure.

NOTES

Commencement: 20 January 2007 (for the purpose of enabling the exercise of powers to make Orders or Regulations by statutory instrument); 1 October 2007 (otherwise).
Commencement (transitional provisions): see the note to s 260 at **[1.260]**.

[1.264]
264   Application for permission to continue derivative claim brought by another member
(1)   This section applies where a member of a company ("the claimant")—
   (a)   has brought a derivative claim,
   (b)   has continued as a derivative claim a claim brought by the company, or
   (c)   has continued a derivative claim under this section.
(2)   Another member of the company ("the applicant") may apply to the court for permission (in Northern Ireland, leave) to continue the claim on the ground that—
   (a)   the manner in which the proceedings have been commenced or continued by the claimant amounts to an abuse of the process of the court,

(b)   the claimant has failed to prosecute the claim diligently, and
(c)   it is appropriate for the applicant to continue the claim as a derivative claim.
(3)   If it appears to the court that the application and the evidence filed by the applicant in support of it do not disclose a prima facie case for giving permission (or leave), the court—
(a)   must dismiss the application, and
(b)   may make any consequential order it considers appropriate.
(4)   If the application is not dismissed under subsection (3), the court—
(a)   may give directions as to the evidence to be provided by the company, and
(b)   may adjourn the proceedings to enable the evidence to be obtained.
(5)   On hearing the application, the court may—
(a)   give permission (or leave) to continue the claim on such terms as it thinks fit,
(b)   refuse permission (or leave) and dismiss the application, or
(c)   adjourn the proceedings on the application and give such directions as it thinks fit.

NOTES

Commencement: 1 October 2007.
Commencement (transitional provisions): see the note to s 260 at **[1.260]**.

CHAPTER 2
DERIVATIVE PROCEEDINGS IN SCOTLAND

[1.265]
265   Derivative proceedings
(1)   In Scotland, a member of a company may raise proceedings in respect of an act or omission specified in subsection (3) in order to protect the interests of the company and obtain a remedy on its behalf.
(2)   A member of a company may raise such proceedings only under subsection (1).
(3)   The act or omission referred to in subsection (1) is any actual or proposed act or omission involving negligence, default, breach of duty or breach of trust by a director of the company.
(4)   Proceedings may be raised under subsection (1) against (either or both)—
(a)   the director referred to in subsection (3), or
(b)   another person.
(5)   It is immaterial whether the act or omission in respect of which the proceedings are to be raised or, in the case of continuing proceedings under section 267 or 269, are raised, arose before or after the person seeking to raise or continue them became a member of the company.
(6)   This section does not affect—
(a)   any right of a member of a company to raise proceedings in respect of an act or omission specified in subsection (3) in order to protect his own interests and obtain a remedy on his own behalf, or
(b)   the court's power to make an order under section 996(2)(c) or anything done under such an order.
(7)   In this Chapter—
(a)   proceedings raised under subsection (1) are referred to as "derivative proceedings",
(b)   the act or omission in respect of which they are raised is referred to as the "cause of action",
(c)   "director" includes a former director,
(d)   references to a director include a shadow director, and
(e)   references to a member of a company include a person who is not a member but to whom shares in the company have been transferred or transmitted by operation of law.

NOTES

Commencement: 1 October 2007.

[1.266]
266   Requirement for leave and notice
(1)   Derivative proceedings may be raised by a member of a company only with the leave of the court.
(2)   An application for leave must—
(a)   specify the cause of action, and
(b)   summarise the facts on which the derivative proceedings are to be based.
(3)   If it appears to the court that the application and the evidence produced by the applicant in support of it do not disclose a prima facie case for granting it, the court—
(a)   must refuse the application, and
(b)   may make any consequential order it considers appropriate.
(4)   If the application is not refused under subsection (3)—
(a)   the applicant must serve the application on the company,
(b)   the court—
(i)   may make an order requiring evidence to be produced by the company, and

     (ii)   may adjourn the proceedings on the application to enable the evidence to be obtained, and

  (c)   the company is entitled to take part in the further proceedings on the application.

(5) On hearing the application, the court may—

  (a)   grant the application on such terms as it thinks fit,

  (b)   refuse the application, or

  (c)   adjourn the proceedings on the application and make such order as to further procedure as it thinks fit.

NOTES

Commencement: 1 October 2007.

Commencement (transitional provisions): see the note to s 260 at **[1.260]**.

[1.267]

267　Application to continue proceedings as derivative proceedings

(1) This section applies where—

  (a)   a company has raised proceedings, and

  (b)   the proceedings are in respect of an act or omission which could be the basis for derivative proceedings.

(2) A member of the company may apply to the court to be substituted for the company in the proceedings, and for the proceedings to continue in consequence as derivative proceedings, on the ground that—

  (a)   the manner in which the company commenced or continued the proceedings amounts to an abuse of the process of the court,

  (b)   the company has failed to prosecute the proceedings diligently, and

  (c)   it is appropriate for the member to be substituted for the company in the proceedings.

(3) If it appears to the court that the application and the evidence produced by the applicant in support of it do not disclose a prima facie case for granting it, the court—

  (a)   must refuse the application, and

  (b)   may make any consequential order it considers appropriate.

(4) If the application is not refused under subsection (3)—

  (a)   the applicant must serve the application on the company,

  (b)   the court—

     (i)   may make an order requiring evidence to be produced by the company, and

     (ii)   may adjourn the proceedings on the application to enable the evidence to be obtained, and

  (c)   the company is entitled to take part in the further proceedings on the application.

(5) On hearing the application, the court may—

  (a)   grant the application on such terms as it thinks fit,

  (b)   refuse the application, or

  (c)   adjourn the proceedings on the application and make such order as to further procedure as it thinks fit.

NOTES

Commencement: 1 October 2007.

Commencement (transitional provisions): see the note to s 260 at **[1.260]**.

[1.268]

268　Granting of leave

(1) The court must refuse leave to raise derivative proceedings or an application under section 267 if satisfied—

  (a)   that a person acting in accordance with section 172 (duty to promote the success of the company) would not seek to raise or continue the proceedings (as the case may be), or

  (b)   where the cause of action is an act or omission that is yet to occur, that the act or omission has been authorised by the company, or

  (c)   where the cause of action is an act or omission that has already occurred, that the act or omission—

     (i)   was authorised by the company before it occurred, or

     (ii)   has been ratified by the company since it occurred.

(2) In considering whether to grant leave to raise derivative proceedings or an application under section 267, the court must take into account, in particular—

  (a)   whether the member is acting in good faith in seeking to raise or continue the proceedings (as the case may be),

  (b)   the importance that a person acting in accordance with section 172 (duty to promote the success of the company) would attach to raising or continuing them (as the case may be),

  (c)   where the cause of action is an act or omission that is yet to occur, whether the act or omission could be, and in the circumstances would be likely to be—

     (i)   authorised by the company before it occurs, or

     (ii)   ratified by the company after it occurs,

(d)   where the cause of action is an act or omission that has already occurred, whether the act or omission could be, and in the circumstances would be likely to be, ratified by the company,

(e)   whether the company has decided not to raise proceedings in respect of the same cause of action or to persist in the proceedings (as the case may be),

(f)   whether the cause of action is one which the member could pursue in his own right rather than on behalf of the company.

(3)   In considering whether to grant leave to raise derivative proceedings or an application under section 267, the court shall have particular regard to any evidence before it as to the views of members of the company who have no personal interest, direct or indirect, in the matter.

(4)   The Secretary of State may by regulations—

(a)   amend subsection (1) so as to alter or add to the circumstances in which leave or an application is to be refused,

(b)   amend subsection (2) so as to alter or add to the matters that the court is required to take into account in considering whether to grant leave or an application.

(5)   Before making any such regulations the Secretary of State shall consult such persons as he considers appropriate.

(6)   Regulations under this section are subject to affirmative resolution procedure.

NOTES

Commencement: 20 January 2007 (for the purpose of enabling the exercise of powers to make Orders or Regulations by statutory instrument); 1 October 2007 (otherwise).

[1.269]
269   Application by member to be substituted for member pursuing derivative proceedings

(1)   This section applies where a member of a company ("the claimant")—

(a)   has raised derivative proceedings,

(b)   has continued as derivative proceedings raised by the company, or

(c)   has continued derivative proceedings under this section.

(2)   Another member of the company ("the applicant") may apply to the court to be substituted for the claimant in the action on the ground that—

(a)   the manner in which the proceedings have been commenced or continued by the claimant amounts to an abuse of the process of the court,

(b)   the claimant has failed to prosecute the proceedings diligently, and

(c)   it is appropriate for the applicant to be substituted for the claimant in the proceedings.

(3)   If it appears to the court that the application and the evidence produced by the applicant in support of it do not disclose a prima facie case for granting it, the court—

(a)   must refuse the application, and

(b)   may make any consequential order it considers appropriate.

(4)   If the application is not refused under subsection (3)—

(a)   the applicant must serve the application on the company,

(b)   the court—

(i)   may make an order requiring evidence to be produced by the company, and

(ii)   may adjourn the proceedings on the application to enable the evidence to be obtained, and

(c)   the company is entitled to take part in the further proceedings on the application.

(5)   On hearing the application, the court may—

(a)   grant the application on such terms as it thinks fit,

(b)   refuse the application, or

(c)   adjourn the proceedings on the application and make such order as to further procedure as it thinks fit.

NOTES

Commencement: 1 October 2007.

PART 12
COMPANY SECRETARIES

Private companies

[1.270]
270   Private company not required to have secretary

(1)   A private company is not required to have a secretary.

(2)   References in the Companies Acts to a private company "without a secretary" are to a private company that for the time being is taking advantage of the exemption in subsection (1); and references to a private company "with a secretary" shall be construed accordingly.

(3)   In the case of a private company without a secretary—

(a)   anything authorised or required to be given or sent to, or served on, the company by being sent to its secretary—

(i)   may be given or sent to, or served on, the company itself, and

(ii)   if addressed to the secretary shall be treated as addressed to the company; and

(b)   anything else required or authorised to be done by or to the secretary of the company may be done by or to—

(i)   a director, or

(ii)   a person authorised generally or specifically in that behalf by the directors.

NOTES

Commencement: 6 April 2008.

Commencement (transitional provisions): Sch 4, Pt 1, para 4 to the Companies Act 2006 (Commencement No 5, Transitional Provisions and Savings) Order 2007, SI 2007/3495 (at **[2.66]**) provides as follows—

"Company secretaries (ss 270 to 274 and 280)

4.—(1)   A private company whose articles immediately before 6th April 2008 expressly required it to have a secretary is a company "with a secretary" for the purposes of section 270(2) until its articles are amended to remove the requirement.

(2)   For this purpose a provision—

(a)   requiring or authorising things to be done by or in relation to a secretary, or

(b)   as to the manner in which, or terms on which, a secretary is to be appointed or removed,

is not a provision expressly requiring the company to have a secretary.".

Commencement (transitional adaptations): art 6 of the Companies Act 2006 (Commencement No 5, Transitional Provisions and Savings) Order 2007, SI 2007/3495 provides that the provisions brought into force by arts 3 and 5 of that Order shall have effect subject to any transitional adaptations specified in Sch 1 to that Order. Schedule 1, Pt 1, para 3 to the Order (at **[2.62]**) provided for such transitional adaptations (note that this paragraph was revoked by the Companies Act 2006 (Commencement No 8, Transitional Provisions and Savings) Order 2008, SI 2008/2860, art 6, as from 1 October 2009 (subject to any relevant transitional provision or saving in Sch 2 to that Order)).

Public companies

[1.271]

271   Public company required to have secretary

A public company must have a secretary.

NOTES

Commencement: 6 April 2008.

[1.272]

272   Direction requiring public company to appoint secretary

(1)   If it appears to the Secretary of State that a public company is in breach of section 271 (requirement to have secretary), the Secretary of State may give the company a direction under this section.

(2)   The direction must state that the company appears to be in breach of that section and specify—

(a)   what the company must do in order to comply with the direction, and

(b)   the period within which it must do so.

That period must be not less than one month or more than three months after the date on which the direction is given.

(3)   The direction must also inform the company of the consequences of failing to comply.

(4)   Where the company is in breach of section 271 it must comply with the direction by—

(a)   making the necessary appointment, and

(b)   giving notice of it under section 276,

before the end of the period specified in the direction.

(5)   If the company has already made the necessary appointment, it must comply with the direction by giving notice of it under section 276 before the end of the period specified in the direction.

(6)   If a company fails to comply with a direction under this section, an offence is committed by—

(a)   the company, and

(b)   every officer of the company who is in default.

For this purpose a shadow director is treated as an officer of the company.

(7)   A person guilty of an offence under this section is liable on summary conviction to a fine not exceeding level 5 on the standard scale and, for continued contravention, a daily default fine not exceeding one-tenth of level 5 on the standard scale.

NOTES

Commencement: 6 April 2008.

Commencement (transitional adaptations): art 6 of the Companies Act 2006 (Commencement No 5, Transitional Provisions and Savings) Order 2007, SI 2007/3495 provides that the provisions brought into force by arts 3 and 5 of that Order shall have effect subject to any transitional adaptations specified in Sch 1 to that Order. Schedule 1, Pt 1, para 4 to the Order (at **[2.62]**) provided for such transitional adaptations (note that this paragraph was revoked by the Companies Act 2006 (Commencement No 8, Transitional Provisions and Savings) Order 2008, SI 2008/2860, art 6, as from 1 October 2009 (subject to any relevant transitional provision or saving in Sch 2 to that Order)).

[1.273]

273   Qualifications of secretaries of public companies

(1)   It is the duty of the directors of a public company to take all reasonable steps to secure that the secretary (or each joint secretary) of the company—

   (a)   is a person who appears to them to have the requisite knowledge and experience to discharge the functions of secretary of the company, and

   (b)   has one or more of the following qualifications.

(2)   The qualifications are—

   (a)   that he has held the office of secretary of a public company for at least three of the five years immediately preceding his appointment as secretary;

   (b)   that he is a member of any of the bodies specified in subsection (3);

   (c)   that he is a barrister, advocate or solicitor called or admitted in any part of the United Kingdom;

   (d)   that he is a person who, by virtue of his holding or having held any other position or his being a member of any other body, appears to the directors to be capable of discharging the functions of secretary of the company.

(3)   The bodies referred to in subsection (2)(b) are—

   (a)   the Institute of Chartered Accountants in England and Wales;

   (b)   the Institute of Chartered Accountants of Scotland;

   (c)   the Association of Chartered Certified Accountants;

   (d)   the Institute of Chartered Accountants in Ireland;

   (e)   the Institute of Chartered Secretaries and Administrators;

   (f)   the Chartered Institute of Management Accountants;

   (g)   the Chartered Institute of Public Finance and Accountancy.

NOTES

Commencement: 6 April 2008.

Commencement (transitional provisions): Sch 4, Pt 1, para 5 to the Companies Act 2006 (Commencement No 5, Transitional Provisions and Savings) Order 2007, SI 2007/3495 (at **[2.66]**) provides that this section applies in relation to company secretaries appointed on or after 6 April 2008 (and that s 286 of the 1985 Act continues to apply in relation to company secretaries appointed before that date).

Provisions applying to private companies with a secretary and to public companies

[1.274]

274   Discharge of functions where office vacant or secretary unable to act

Where in the case of any company the office of secretary is vacant, or there is for any other reason no secretary capable of acting, anything required or authorised to be done by or to the secretary may be done—

   (a)   by or to an assistant or deputy secretary (if any), or

   (b)   if there is no assistant or deputy secretary or none capable of acting, by or to any person authorised generally or specifically in that behalf by the directors.

NOTES

Commencement: 6 April 2008.

Commencement (transitional adaptations): art 6 of the Companies Act 2006 (Commencement No 5, Transitional Provisions and Savings) Order 2007, SI 2007/3495 provides that the provisions brought into force by arts 3 and 5 of that Order shall have effect subject to any transitional adaptations specified in Sch 1 to that Order. Schedule 1, Pt 1, para 5 to the Order (at **[2.62]**) provided for such transitional adaptations (note that this paragraph was revoked by the Companies Act 2006 (Commencement No 8, Transitional Provisions and Savings) Order 2008, SI 2008/2860, art 6, as from 1 October 2009 (subject to any relevant transitional provision or saving in Sch 2 to that Order)).

[1.275]

275   Duty to keep register of secretaries

(1)   A company must keep a register of its secretaries.

(2)   The register must contain the required particulars (see sections 277 to 279) of the person who is, or persons who are, the secretary or joint secretaries of the company.

(3)   The register must be kept available for inspection—

   (a)   at the company's registered office, or

   (b)   at a place specified in regulations under section 1136.

(4)   The company must give notice to the registrar—

   (a)   of the place at which the register is kept available for inspection, and

   (b)   of any change in that place,

unless it has at all times been kept at the company's registered office.

(5)   The register must be open to the inspection—

   (a)   of any member of the company without charge, and

   (b)   of any other person on payment of such fee as may be prescribed.

(6)   If default is made in complying with subsection (1), (2) or (3), or if default is made for 14 days in complying with subsection (4), or if an inspection required under subsection (5) is refused, an offence is committed by—

   (a)   the company, and

(b)   every officer of the company who is in default.

For this purpose a shadow director is treated as an officer of the company.

(7)   A person guilty of an offence under this section is liable on summary conviction to a fine not exceeding level 5 on the standard scale and, for continued contravention, a daily default fine not exceeding one-tenth of level 5 on the standard scale.

(8)   In the case of a refusal of inspection of the register, the court may by order compel an immediate inspection of it.

NOTES

Commencement: 20 January 2007 (for the purpose of enabling the exercise of powers to make Orders or Regulations by statutory instrument); 1 October 2009 (otherwise).

Commencement (transitional provisions): see the note to s 162 at **[1.162]**.

Regulations: the Companies (Fees for Inspection of Company Records) Regulations 2008, SI 2008/3007 at **[4.327]**.

[1.276]
276   Duty to notify registrar of changes
(1)   A company must, within the period of 14 days from—
   (a)   a person becoming or ceasing to be its secretary or one of its joint secretaries, or
   (b)   the occurrence of any change in the particulars contained in its register of secretaries,
give notice to the registrar of the change and of the date on which it occurred.
(2)   Notice of a person having become secretary, or one of joint secretaries, of the company must be accompanied by a consent by that person to act in the relevant capacity.
(3)   If default is made in complying with this section, an offence is committed by every officer of the company who is in default.

For this purpose a shadow director is treated as an officer of the company.
(4)   A person guilty of an offence under this section is liable on summary conviction to a fine not exceeding level 5 on the standard scale and, for continued contravention, a daily default fine not exceeding one-tenth of level 5 on the standard scale.

NOTES

Commencement: 1 October 2009.

Commencement (transitional provisions): see the note to s 162 at **[1.162]**.

[1.277]
277   Particulars of secretaries to be registered: individuals
(1)   A company's register of secretaries must contain the following particulars in the case of an individual—
   (a)   name and any former name;
   (b)   address.
(2)   For the purposes of this section "name" means a person's Christian name (or other forename) and surname, except that in the case of—
   (a)   a peer, or
   (b)   an individual usually known by a title,
the title may be stated instead of his Christian name (or other forename) and surname or in addition to either or both of them.
(3)   For the purposes of this section a "former name" means a name by which the individual was formerly known for business purposes.

Where a person is or was formerly known by more than one such name, each of them must be stated.
(4)   It is not necessary for the register to contain particulars of a former name in the following cases—
   (a)   in the case of a peer or an individual normally known by a British title, where the name is one by which the person was known previous to the adoption of or succession to the title;
   (b)   in the case of any person, where the former name—
     (i)   was changed or disused before the person attained the age of 16 years, or
     (ii)   has been changed or disused for 20 years or more.
(5)   The address required to be stated in the register is a service address. This may be stated to be "The company's registered office".

NOTES

Commencement: 1 October 2009.

Commencement (transitional provisions): see the note to s 162 at **[1.162]**.

[1.278]
278   Particulars of secretaries to be registered: corporate secretaries and firms
(1)   A company's register of secretaries must contain the following particulars in the case of a body corporate, or a firm that is a legal person under the law by which it is governed—
   (a)   corporate or firm name;
   (b)   registered or principal office;

    (c)   in the case of an EEA company to which the First Company Law Directive (68/151/EEC) applies, particulars of—

        (i)   the register in which the company file mentioned in Article 3 of that Directive is kept (including details of the relevant state), and

        (ii) the registration number in that register;

    (d)   in any other case, particulars of—

        (i)   the legal form of the company or firm and the law by which it is governed, and

        (ii) if applicable, the register in which it is entered (including details of the state) and its registration number in that register.

(2)   If all the partners in a firm are joint secretaries it is sufficient to state the particulars that would be required if the firm were a legal person and the firm had been appointed secretary.

NOTES

Commencement: 1 October 2009.

Commencement (transitional provisions): see the note to s 162 at **[1.162]**.

[1.279]

279 Particulars of secretaries to be registered: power to make regulations

(1)   The Secretary of State may make provision by regulations amending—

section 277 (particulars of secretaries to be registered: individuals), or

section 278 (particulars of secretaries to be registered: corporate secretaries and firms),

so as to add to or remove items from the particulars required to be contained in a company's register of secretaries.

(2)   Regulations under this section are subject to affirmative resolution procedure.

NOTES

Commencement: 20 January 2007 (for the purpose of enabling the exercise of powers to make Orders or Regulations by statutory instrument); 1 October 2009 (otherwise).

Commencement (transitional provisions): see the note to s 162 at **[1.162]**.

[1.280]

280 Acts done by person in dual capacity

A provision requiring or authorising a thing to be done by or to a director and the secretary of a company is not satisfied by its being done by or to the same person acting both as director and as, or in place of, the secretary.

NOTES

Commencement: 6 April 2008.

PART 13
RESOLUTIONS AND MEETINGS

CHAPTER 1
GENERAL PROVISIONS ABOUT RESOLUTIONS

[1.281]

281 Resolutions

(1)   A resolution of the members (or of a class of members) of a private company must be passed—

    (a)   as a written resolution in accordance with Chapter 2, or

    (b)   at a meeting of the members (to which the provisions of Chapter 3 apply).

(2)   A resolution of the members (or of a class of members) of a public company must be passed at a meeting of the members (to which the provisions of Chapter 3 and, where relevant, Chapter 4 apply).

(3)   Where a provision of the Companies Acts—

    (a)   requires a resolution of a company, or of the members (or a class of members) of a company, and

    (b)   does not specify what kind of resolution is required,

what is required is an ordinary resolution unless the company's articles require a higher majority (or unanimity).

(4)   Nothing in this Part affects any enactment or rule of law as to—

    (a)   things done otherwise than by passing a resolution,

    (b)   circumstances in which a resolution is or is not treated as having been passed, or

    (c)   cases in which a person is precluded from alleging that a resolution has not been duly passed.

NOTES

Commencement: 1 October 2007.

Commencement (transitional provisions): Sch 3, paras 22, 23, 23A to the Companies Act 2006 (Commencement No 3, Consequential Amendments, Transitional Provisions and Savings) Order 2007, SI 2007/2194 (at **[2.45]**) (as amended by the Companies Act 2006 (Commencement No 5, Transitional Provisions and Savings) Order 2007, SI 2007/3495, art 11, Sch 5, para 2(1), (4), (5), as from 14 January 2008, and the Companies (Shareholders' Rights) Regulations 2009, SI 2009/1632, reg 22, as from 3 August 2009, in relation to meetings of which notice is given, or first given, on or after that date) provide as follows—

"General provisions about resolutions (ss 281 to 287)

22.—(1)   Sections 281 to 287 of the Companies Act 2006 (general provisions about resolutions), apply—
  (a)   to written resolutions to which sections 288 to 300 of that Act apply (see paragraph 24);
  (b)   to resolutions (other than written resolutions)—
    (i)   of which notice is given on or after 1st October 2007, or
    (ii)   that are proposed at a meeting of which notice is given on or after 1st October 2007, other than a meeting convened in pursuance of a requisition made under section 368 or 376 of the 1985 Act or Article 376 or 384 of the 1986 Order made before that date.
(2)   The provisions of the 1985 Act or 1986 Order continue to apply to resolutions (other than written resolutions)—
  (a)   of which notice is given before 1st October 2007, or
  (b)   that are proposed at a meeting—
    (i)   of which notice was given before 1st October 2007, or
    (ii)   that is convened in pursuance of a requisition under section 368 or 376 of the 1985 Act or Article 376 or 384 of the 1986 Order made before that date.
(3)   The provisions referred to in sub-paragraph (2) include—
  section 370(6) of the 1985 Act or Article 378(6) of the 1986 Order (voting entitlement of members); and
  section 378 of the 1985 Act or Article 386 of the 1986 Order (extraordinary and special resolutions).
(4)   Where notice of a meeting is given over more than one day, it is treated for the purposes of this paragraph as given on the first of those days.
(5)   Where copies of a requisition are deposited on more than one day, the references in this paragraph to the day on which the requisition is made shall be read as references to the first day on which the copies deposited are sufficient to require the company to act.
23.—[(1)]   Any reference to an extraordinary resolution in a provision—
  (a)   of a company's memorandum or articles, or
  (b)   of a contract,
continues to have effect and shall continue to be construed in accordance with section 378 of the 1985 Act or Article 386 of the 1986 Order as if that section or Article had not been repealed.
[(2)   Chapter 3 of Part 3 of the Companies Act 2006 (resolutions affecting a company's constitution) applies to any such resolution.]
[23A.—(1)   This paragraph applies where, immediately before 1st October 2007, the articles of a company provided that in the event of equality of votes on an ordinary resolution, whether on a show of hands or on a poll, the chairman should have a casting vote in addition to any other vote that the chairman might have.
(2)   If that provision has not been removed by a subsequent alteration of the articles, it continues to have effect notwithstanding sections 281(3) and 282.
(3)   If that provision has been removed by a subsequent alteration of the articles, the company may at any time restore that provision, which shall have effect notwithstanding sections 281(3) and 282.
[(4)   Nothing in this paragraph applies in relation to a traded company (as defined by section 360C of the Companies Act 2006).]]".

[1.282]
282   Ordinary resolutions
(1)   An ordinary resolution of the members (or of a class of members) of a company means a resolution that is passed by a simple majority.
(2)   A written resolution is passed by a simple majority if it is passed by members representing a simple majority of the total voting rights of eligible members (see Chapter 2).
(3)   A resolution passed at a meeting on a show of hands is passed by a simple majority if it is passed by [a simple majority of the votes cast by those entitled to vote].
(4)   A resolution passed on a poll taken at a meeting is passed by a simple majority if it is passed by members representing a simple majority of the total voting rights of members who (being entitled to do so) vote [in person, by proxy or in advance (see section 322A)] on the resolution.
(5)   Anything that may be done by ordinary resolution may also be done by special resolution.

NOTES
  Commencement: 1 October 2007.
  Commencement (transitional provisions): see the note to s 281 at **[1.281]**.
  Sub-ss (3), (4): words in square brackets substituted by the Companies (Shareholders' Rights) Regulations 2009, SI 2009/1632, regs 2(1), 5(2), as from 3 August 2009, in relation to meetings of which notice is given, or first given, on or after that date.

[1.283]
283   Special resolutions
(1)   A special resolution of the members (or of a class of members) of a company means a resolution passed by a majority of not less than 75%.
(2)   A written resolution is passed by a majority of not less than 75% if it is passed by members representing not less than 75% of the total voting rights of eligible members (see Chapter 2).
(3)   Where a resolution of a private company is passed as a written resolution—
  (a)   the resolution is not a special resolution unless it stated that it was proposed as a special resolution, and
  (b)   if the resolution so stated, it may only be passed as a special resolution.

(4)   A resolution passed at a meeting on a show of hands is passed by a majority of not less than 75% if it is passed by [not less than 75% of the votes cast by those entitled to vote]

(5)   A resolution passed on a poll taken at a meeting is passed by a majority of not less than 75% if it is passed by members representing not less than 75% of the total voting rights of the members who (being entitled to do so) vote [in person, by proxy or in advance (see section 322A)] on the resolution.

(6)   Where a resolution is passed at a meeting—

    (a)   the resolution is not a special resolution unless the notice of the meeting included the text of the resolution and specified the intention to propose the resolution as a special resolution, and

    (b)   if the notice of the meeting so specified, the resolution may only be passed as a special resolution.

NOTES

Commencement: 1 October 2007.

Commencement (transitional provisions): see the note to s 281 at **[1.281]**.

Sub-ss (4), (5): words in square brackets substituted by the Companies (Shareholders' Rights) Regulations 2009, SI 2009/1632, reg 2(2), 5(2), as from 3 August 2009, in relation to meetings of which notice is given, or first given, on or after that date.

[1.284]

284   Votes: general rules

(1)   On a vote on a written resolution—

    (a)   in the case of a company having a share capital, every member has one vote in respect of each share or each £10 of stock held by him, and

    (b)   in any other case, every member has one vote.

[(2)   On a vote on a resolution on a show of hands at a meeting, each member present in person has one vote.]

(3)   On a vote on a resolution on a poll taken at a meeting—

    (a)   in the case of a company having a share capital, every member has one vote in respect of each share or each £10 of stock held by him, and

    (b)   in any other case, every member has one vote.

(4)   The provisions of this section have effect subject to any provision of the company's articles.

[(5)   Nothing in this section is to be read as restricting the effect of—

    section 152 (exercise of rights by nominees),

    section 285 (voting by proxy),

    section 322 (exercise of voting rights on poll),

    section 322A (voting on a poll: votes cast in advance), or

    section 323 (representation of corporations at meetings).]

NOTES

Commencement: 1 October 2007.

Commencement (transitional provisions): see the note to s 281 at **[1.281]**.

Sub-s (2): substituted by the Companies (Shareholders' Rights) Regulations 2009, SI 2009/1632, reg 2(3), as from 3 August 2009, in relation to meetings of which notice is given, or first given, on or after that date.

Sub-s (5): added by SI 2009/1632, reg 2(4), as from 3 August 2009, in relation to meetings of which notice is given, or first given, on or after that date.

[1.285]

[285   Voting by proxy

(1)   On a vote on a resolution on a show of hands at a meeting, every proxy present who has been duly appointed by one or more members entitled to vote on the resolution has one vote.

    This is subject to subsection (2).

(2)   On a vote on a resolution on a show of hands at a meeting, a proxy has one vote for and one vote against the resolution if—

    (a)   the proxy has been duly appointed by more than one member entitled to vote on the resolution, and

    (b)   the proxy has been instructed by one or more of those members to vote for the resolution and by one or more other of those members to vote against it.

(3)   On a poll taken at a meeting of a company all or any of the voting rights of a member may be exercised by one or more duly appointed proxies.

(4)   Where a member appoints more than one proxy, subsection (3) does not authorise the exercise by the proxies taken together of more extensive voting rights than could be exercised by the member in person.

(5)   Subsections (1) and (2) have effect subject to any provision of the company's articles.]

NOTES

Commencement: 3 August 2009.

Commencement (transitional provisions): see the note to s 281 at **[1.281]**.

Substituted, together with s 285A (for the original s 285), by the Companies (Shareholders' Rights) Regulations 2009, SI 2009/1632, reg 3, as from 3 August 2009, in relation to meetings of which notice is given, or first given, on or after that date.

[1.285A]
[285A   Voting rights on poll or written resolution
In relation to a resolution required or authorised by an enactment, if a private company's articles provide that a member has a different number of votes in relation to a resolution when it is passed as a written resolution and when it is passed on a poll taken at a meeting—
   (a)   the provision about how many votes a member has in relation to the resolution passed on a poll is void, and
   (b)   a member has the same number of votes in relation to the resolution when it is passed on a poll as the member has when it is passed as a written resolution.]

NOTES
Commencement: 3 August 2009.
Substituted as noted to s 285 at **[1.285]**.

[1.286]
286   Votes of joint holders of shares
(1)   In the case of joint holders of shares of a company, only the vote of the senior holder who votes (and any proxies duly authorised by him) may be counted by the company.
(2)   For the purposes of this section, the senior holder of a share is determined by the order in which the names of the joint holders appear in the register of members.
(3)   Subsections (1) and (2) have effect subject to any provision of the company's articles.

NOTES
Commencement: 1 October 2007.
Commencement (transitional provisions): see the note to s 281 at **[1.281]**.

[1.287]
287   Saving for provisions of articles as to determination of entitlement to vote
Nothing in this Chapter affects—
   (a)   any provision of a company's articles—
      (i)   requiring an objection to a person's entitlement to vote on a resolution to be made in accordance with the articles, and
     (ii)   for the determination of any such objection to be final and conclusive, or
   (b)   the grounds on which such a determination may be questioned in legal proceedings.

NOTES
Commencement: 1 October 2007.
Commencement (transitional provisions): see the note to s 281 at **[1.281]**.

CHAPTER 2
WRITTEN RESOLUTIONS

General provisions about written resolutions

[1.288]
288   Written resolutions of private companies
(1)   In the Companies Acts a "written resolution" means a resolution of a private company proposed and passed in accordance with this Chapter.
(2)   The following may not be passed as a written resolution—
   (a)   a resolution under section 168 removing a director before the expiration of his period of office;
   (b)   a resolution under section 510 removing an auditor before the expiration of his term of office.
(3)   A resolution may be proposed as a written resolution—
   (a)   by the directors of a private company (see section 291), or
   (b)   by the members of a private company (see sections 292 to 295).
(4)   References in enactments passed or made before this Chapter comes into force to—
   (a)   a resolution of a company in general meeting, or
   (b)   a resolution of a meeting of a class of members of the company,
have effect as if they included references to a written resolution of the members, or of a class of members, of a private company (as appropriate).
(5)   A written resolution of a private company has effect as if passed (as the case may be)—
   (a)   by the company in general meeting, or
   (b)   by a meeting of a class of members of the company,
and references in enactments passed or made before this section comes into force to a meeting at which a resolution is passed or to members voting in favour of a resolution shall be construed accordingly.

NOTES

Commencement: 1 October 2007.

Commencement (transitional provisions): Sch 3, para 24 to the Companies Act 2006 (Commencement No 3, Consequential Amendments, Transitional Provisions and Savings) Order 2007, SI 2007/2194 (at **[2.45]**) provides as follows—

"**24   Written resolutions (ss 288 to 300)**

(1)   Sections 288 to 300 of the Companies Act 2006 (written resolutions) apply to resolutions for which the circulation date (see section 290) is on or after 1st October 2007.

(2)   Section 381A to 381C of, and Schedule 15A to, the 1985 Act or Article 389A to 389C of, and Schedule 15A to, the 1986 Order continue to apply to resolutions sent or circulated to any relevant member before that date.

A "relevant member" means one whose signature is required by section 381A(1) or Article 389A(1).".

Commencement (transitional adaptations): art 6 of the Companies Act 2006 (Commencement No 3, Consequential Amendments, Transitional Provisions and Savings) Order 2007, SI 2007/2194 provides that the provisions brought into force by that Order shall have effect subject to any transitional adaptations specified in Sch 1 to that Order. Schedule 1, para 13(1)–(3) to the Order (at **[2.43]**) provided for such transitional adaptations. Note, however, that sub-para 13(2)(a) was revoked by the Companies Act 2006 (Commencement No 5, Transitional Provisions and Savings) Order 2007, SI 2007/3495, art 10(1), (3), as from 6 April 2008 (subject to any transitional provisions and savings as apply, in accordance with Sch 4 to that Order, in relation to the repeal of any provision of the 1985 Act referred to in the adaptation). Note also that the whole of this paragraph was revoked by the Companies Act 2006 (Commencement No 8, Transitional Provisions and Savings) Order 2008, SI 2008/2860, art 6, as from 1 October 2009 (subject to any relevant transitional provision or saving in Sch 2 to that Order).

[1.289]

289   Eligible members

(1)   In relation to a resolution proposed as a written resolution of a private company, the eligible members are the members who would have been entitled to vote on the resolution on the circulation date of the resolution (see section 290).

(2)   If the persons entitled to vote on a written resolution change during the course of the day that is the circulation date of the resolution, the eligible members are the persons entitled to vote on the resolution at the time that the first copy of the resolution is sent or submitted to a member for his agreement.

NOTES

Commencement: 1 October 2007.

Commencement (transitional provisions): see the note to s 288 at **[1.288]**.

Circulation of written resolutions

[1.290]

290   Circulation date

References in this Part to the circulation date of a written resolution are to the date on which copies of it are sent or submitted to members in accordance with this Chapter (or if copies are sent or submitted to members on different days, to the first of those days).

NOTES

Commencement: 1 October 2007.

Commencement (transitional provisions): see the note to s 288 at **[1.288]**.

[1.291]

291   Circulation of written resolutions proposed by directors

(1)   This section applies to a resolution proposed as a written resolution by the directors of the company.

(2)   The company must send or submit a copy of the resolution to every eligible member.

(3)   The company must do so—

     (a)   by sending copies at the same time (so far as reasonably practicable) to all eligible members in hard copy form, in electronic form or by means of a website, or

     (b)   if it is possible to do so without undue delay, by submitting the same copy to each eligible member in turn (or different copies to each of a number of eligible members in turn),

or by sending copies to some members in accordance with paragraph (a) and submitting a copy or copies to other members in accordance with paragraph (b).

(4)   The copy of the resolution must be accompanied by a statement informing the member—

     (a)   how to signify agreement to the resolution (see section 296), and

     (b)   as to the date by which the resolution must be passed if it is not to lapse (see section 297).

(5)   In the event of default in complying with this section, an offence is committed by every officer of the company who is in default.

(6)   A person guilty of an offence under this section is liable—

     (a)   on conviction on indictment, to a fine;

     (b)   on summary conviction, to a fine not exceeding the statutory maximum.

(7)   The validity of the resolution, if passed, is not affected by a failure to comply with this section.

NOTES

Commencement: 1 October 2007.

Commencement (transitional provisions): see the note to s 288 at **[1.288]**.

[1.292]
292   Members' power to require circulation of written resolution
(1)   The members of a private company may require the company to circulate a resolution that may properly be moved and is proposed to be moved as a written resolution.
(2)   Any resolution may properly be moved as a written resolution unless—
  (a)   it would, if passed, be ineffective (whether by reason of inconsistency with any enactment or the company's constitution or otherwise),
  (b)   it is defamatory of any person, or
  (c)   it is frivolous or vexatious.
(3)   Where the members require a company to circulate a resolution they may require the company to circulate with it a statement of not more than 1,000 words on the subject matter of the resolution.
(4)   A company is required to circulate the resolution and any accompanying statement once it has received requests that it do so from members representing not less than the requisite percentage of the total voting rights of all members entitled to vote on the resolution.
(5)   The "requisite percentage" is 5% or such lower percentage as is specified for this purpose in the company's articles.
(6)   A request—
  (a)   may be in hard copy form or in electronic form,
  (b)   must identify the resolution and any accompanying statement, and
  (c)   must be authenticated by the person or persons making it.

NOTES

Commencement: 1 October 2007.

Commencement (transitional provisions): see the note to s 288 at **[1.288]**.

[1.293]
293   Circulation of written resolution proposed by members
(1)   A company that is required under section 292 to circulate a resolution must send or submit to every eligible member—
  (a)   a copy of the resolution, and
  (b)   a copy of any accompanying statement.
This is subject to section 294(2) (deposit or tender of sum in respect of expenses of circulation) and section 295 (application not to circulate members' statement).
(2)   The company must do so—
  (a)   by sending copies at the same time (so far as reasonably practicable) to all eligible members in hard copy form, in electronic form or by means of a website, or
  (b)   if it is possible to do so without undue delay, by submitting the same copy to each eligible member in turn (or different copies to each of a number of eligible members in turn),
or by sending copies to some members in accordance with paragraph (a) and submitting a copy or copies to other members in accordance with paragraph (b).
(3)   The company must send or submit the copies (or, if copies are sent or submitted to members on different days, the first of those copies) not more than 21 days after it becomes subject to the requirement under section 292 to circulate the resolution.
(4)   The copy of the resolution must be accompanied by guidance as to—
  (a)   how to signify agreement to the resolution (see section 296), and
  (b)   the date by which the resolution must be passed if it is not to lapse (see section 297).
(5)   In the event of default in complying with this section, an offence is committed by every officer of the company who is in default.
(6)   A person guilty of an offence under this section is liable—
  (a)   on conviction on indictment, to a fine;
  (b)   on summary conviction, to a fine not exceeding the statutory maximum.
(7)   The validity of the resolution, if passed, is not affected by a failure to comply with this section.

NOTES

Commencement: 1 October 2007.

Commencement (transitional provisions): see the note to s 288 at **[1.288]**.

[1.294]
294   Expenses of circulation
(1)   The expenses of the company in complying with section 293 must be paid by the members who requested the circulation of the resolution unless the company resolves otherwise.

(2) Unless the company has previously so resolved, it is not bound to comply with that section unless there is deposited with or tendered to it a sum reasonably sufficient to meet its expenses in doing so.

NOTES

Commencement: 1 October 2007.
Commencement (transitional provisions): see the note to s 288 at **[1.288]**.

[1.295]
295   Application not to circulate members' statement

(1) A company is not required to circulate a members' statement under section 293 if, on an application by the company or another person who claims to be aggrieved, the court is satisfied that the rights conferred by section 292 and that section are being abused.

(2) The court may order the members who requested the circulation of the statement to pay the whole or part of the company's costs (in Scotland, expenses) on such an application, even if they are not parties to the application.

NOTES

Commencement: 1 October 2007.
Commencement (transitional provisions): see the note to s 288 at **[1.288]**.

Agreeing to written resolutions

[1.296]
296   Procedure for signifying agreement to written resolution

(1) A member signifies his agreement to a proposed written resolution when the company receives from him (or from someone acting on his behalf) an authenticated document—
    (a)   identifying the resolution to which it relates, and
    (b)   indicating his agreement to the resolution.

(2) The document must be sent to the company in hard copy form or in electronic form.

(3) A member's agreement to a written resolution, once signified, may not be revoked.

(4) A written resolution is passed when the required majority of eligible members have signified their agreement to it.

NOTES

Commencement: 1 October 2007.
Commencement (transitional provisions): see the note to s 288 at **[1.288]**.

[1.297]
297   Period for agreeing to written resolution

(1) A proposed written resolution lapses if it is not passed before the end of—
    (a)   the period specified for this purpose in the company's articles, or
    (b)   if none is specified, the period of 28 days beginning with the circulation date.

(2) The agreement of a member to a written resolution is ineffective if signified after the expiry of that period.

NOTES

Commencement: 1 October 2007.
Commencement (transitional provisions): see the note to s 288 at **[1.288]**.

Supplementary

[1.298]
298   Sending documents relating to written resolutions by electronic means

(1) Where a company has given an electronic address in any document containing or accompanying a proposed written resolution, it is deemed to have agreed that any document or information relating to that resolution may be sent by electronic means to that address (subject to any conditions or limitations specified in the document).

(2) In this section "electronic address" means any address or number used for the purposes of sending or receiving documents or information by electronic means.

NOTES

Commencement: 1 October 2007.
Commencement (transitional provisions): see the note to s 288 at **[1.288]**.

[1.299]
299   Publication of written resolution on website

(1) This section applies where a company sends—
    (a)   a written resolution, or
    (b)   a statement relating to a written resolution,
to a person by means of a website.

(2)   The resolution or statement is not validly sent for the purposes of this Chapter unless the resolution is available on the website throughout the period beginning with the circulation date and ending on the date on which the resolution lapses under section 297.

NOTES
Commencement: 1 October 2007.
Commencement (transitional provisions): see the note to s 288 at **[1.288]**.

[1.300]
300   Relationship between this Chapter and provisions of company's articles
A provision of the articles of a private company is void in so far as it would have the effect that a resolution that is required by or otherwise provided for in an enactment could not be proposed and passed as a written resolution.

NOTES
Commencement: 1 October 2007.
Commencement (transitional provisions): see the note to s 288 at **[1.288]**.
Commencement (transitional adaptations): art 6 of the Companies Act 2006 (Commencement No 3, Consequential Amendments, Transitional Provisions and Savings) Order 2007, SI 2007/2194 provides that the provisions brought into force by that Order shall have effect subject to any transitional adaptations specified in Sch 1 to that Order. Schedule 1, para 13(4) to the Order (at **[2.43]**) provided for such transitional adaptations (ie, the transitional insertion of ss 300A–300D). Note that para 13(4) was revoked by the Companies Act 2006 (Commencement No 8, Transitional Provisions and Savings) Order 2008, SI 2008/2860, art 6, as from 1 October 2009 (subject to any relevant transitional provision or saving in Sch 2 to that Order).

CHAPTER 3
RESOLUTIONS AT MEETINGS

General provisions about resolutions at meetings

[1.301]
301   Resolutions at general meetings
A resolution of the members of a company is validly passed at a general meeting if—
(a)   notice of the meeting and of the resolution is given, and
(b)   the meeting is held and conducted,
in accordance with the provisions of this Chapter (and, where relevant, Chapter 4) and the company's articles.

NOTES
Commencement: 1 October 2007.

Calling meetings

[1.302]
302   Directors' power to call general meetings
The directors of a company may call a general meeting of the company.

NOTES
Commencement: 1 October 2007.

[1.303]
303   Members' power to require directors to call general meeting
(1)   The members of a company may require the directors to call a general meeting of the company.
(2)   The directors are required to call a general meeting once the company has received requests to do so from—
(a)   members representing at least [5%] of such of the paid-up capital of the company as carries the right of voting at general meetings of the company (excluding any paid-up capital held as treasury shares); or
(b)   in the case of a company not having a share capital, members who represent at least [5%] of the total voting rights of all the members having a right to vote at general meetings.
(3)   . . .
(4)   A request—
(a)   must state the general nature of the business to be dealt with at the meeting, and
(b)   may include the text of a resolution that may properly be moved and is intended to be moved at the meeting.
(5)   A resolution may properly be moved at a meeting unless—
(a)   it would, if passed, be ineffective (whether by reason of inconsistency with any enactment or the company's constitution or otherwise),
(b)   it is defamatory of any person, or
(c)   it is frivolous or vexatious.
(6)   A request—
(a)   may be in hard copy form or in electronic form, and

(b)　must be authenticated by the person or persons making it.

NOTES

Commencement: 1 October 2007.

Commencement (transitional provisions): Sch 3, para 25 to the Companies Act 2006 (Commencement No 3, Consequential Amendments, Transitional Provisions and Savings) Order 2007, SI 2007/2194 (at **[2.45]**) provides as follows—

> **"25　Members' power to require directors to call meeting (ss 303 to 305)**
> (1)　Sections 303 to 305 of the Companies Act 2006 (meetings required by members) apply to requests made on or after 1st October 2007.
> (2)　Section 368 of the 1985 Act or Article 376 of the 1986 Order continues to apply to requisitions made before that date.
> (3)　Where requests are made or copies of a requisition are deposited on more than one day, the references in this paragraph to the day on which the request or requisition is made shall be read as references to the first day on which the requests made or copies deposited are sufficient to require the company to act.".

Sub-s (2): the figure "5%" in square brackets in paras (a) and (b) was substituted by the Companies (Shareholders' Rights) Regulations 2009, SI 2009/1632, reg 4(1), (2), as from 3 August 2009, in relation to meetings of which notice is given, or first given, on or after that date.

Sub-s (3): repealed by SI 2009/1632, reg 4(1), (3), as from 3 August 2009, in relation to meetings of which notice is given, or first given, on or after that date.

[1.304]
304　Directors' duty to call meetings required by members
(1)　Directors required under section 303 to call a general meeting of the company must call a meeting—
　　(a)　within 21 days from the date on which they become subject to the requirement, and
　　(b)　to be held on a date not more than 28 days after the date of the notice convening the meeting.
(2)　If the requests received by the company identify a resolution intended to be moved at the meeting, the notice of the meeting must include notice of the resolution.
(3)　The business that may be dealt with at the meeting includes a resolution of which notice is given in accordance with this section.
(4)　If the resolution is to be proposed as a special resolution, the directors are treated as not having duly called the meeting if they do not give the required notice of the resolution in accordance with section 283.

NOTES

Commencement: 1 October 2007.

Commencement (transitional provisions): see the note to s 303 at **[1.303]**.

[1.305]
305　Power of members to call meeting at company's expense
(1)　If the directors—
　　(a)　are required under section 303 to call a meeting, and
　　(b)　do not do so in accordance with section 304,
the members who requested the meeting, or any of them representing more than one half of the total voting rights of all of them, may themselves call a general meeting.
(2)　Where the requests received by the company included the text of a resolution intended to be moved at the meeting, the notice of the meeting must include notice of the resolution.
(3)　The meeting must be called for a date not more than three months after the date on which the directors become subject to the requirement to call a meeting.
(4)　The meeting must be called in the same manner, as nearly as possible, as that in which meetings are required to be called by directors of the company.
(5)　The business which may be dealt with at the meeting includes a resolution of which notice is given in accordance with this section.
(6)　Any reasonable expenses incurred by the members requesting the meeting by reason of the failure of the directors duly to call a meeting must be reimbursed by the company.
(7)　Any sum so reimbursed shall be retained by the company out of any sums due or to become due from the company by way of fees or other remuneration in respect of the services of such of the directors as were in default.

NOTES

Commencement: 1 October 2007.

Commencement (transitional provisions): see the note to s 303 at **[1.303]**.

[1.306]
306　Power of court to order meeting
(1)　This section applies if for any reason it is impracticable—
　　(a)　to call a meeting of a company in any manner in which meetings of that company may be called, or
　　(b)　to conduct the meeting in the manner prescribed by the company's articles or this Act.
(2)　The court may, either of its own motion or on the application—

(a)   of a director of the company, or

(b)   of a member of the company who would be entitled to vote at the meeting,

order a meeting to be called, held and conducted in any manner the court thinks fit.

(3)   Where such an order is made, the court may give such ancillary or consequential directions as it thinks expedient.

(4)   Such directions may include a direction that one member of the company present at the meeting be deemed to constitute a quorum.

(5)   A meeting called, held and conducted in accordance with an order under this section is deemed for all purposes to be a meeting of the company duly called, held and conducted.

NOTES

Commencement: 1 October 2007.

Commencement (transitional adaptations): art 6 of the Companies Act 2006 (Commencement No 3, Consequential Amendments, Transitional Provisions and Savings) Order 2007, SI 2007/2194 provides that the provisions brought into force by that Order shall have effect subject to any transitional adaptations specified in Sch 1 to that Order. Schedule 1, para 14 to the Order (at **[2.43]**) provided for such transitional adaptations (note that this paragraph was revoked by the Companies Act 2006 (Commencement No 8, Transitional Provisions and Savings) Order 2008, SI 2008/2860, art 6, as from 1 October 2009 (subject to any relevant transitional provision or saving in Sch 2 to that Order)).

Notice of meetings

[1.307]

307   Notice required of general meeting

[(A1)   This section applies to—

(a)   a general meeting of a company that is not a traded company; and

(b)   a general meeting of a traded company that is an opted-in company (as defined by section 971(1)), where—

(i)   the meeting is held to decide whether to take any action that might result in the frustration of a takeover bid for the company; or

(ii)   the meeting is held by virtue of section 969 (power of offeror to require general meeting to be held).

(A2)   For corresponding provision in relation to general meetings of traded companies (other than meetings within subsection (A1)(b)), see section 307A.]

(1)   A general meeting of a private company (other than an adjourned meeting) must be called by notice of at least 14 days.

(2)   A general meeting of a public company (other than an adjourned meeting) must be called by notice of—

(a)   in the case of an annual general meeting, at least 21 days, and

(b)   in any other case, at least 14 days.

(3)   The company's articles may require a longer period of notice than that specified in subsection (1) or (2).

(4)   A general meeting may be called by shorter notice than that otherwise required if shorter notice is agreed by the members.

(5)   The shorter notice must be agreed to by a majority in number of the members having a right to attend and vote at the meeting, being a majority who—

(a)   together hold not less than the requisite percentage in nominal value of the shares giving a right to attend and vote at the meeting (excluding any shares in the company held as treasury shares), or

(b)   in the case of a company not having a share capital, together represent not less than the requisite percentage of the total voting rights at that meeting of all the members.

(6)   The requisite percentage is—

(a)   in the case of a private company, 90% or such higher percentage (not exceeding 95%) as may be specified in the company's articles;

(b)   in the case of a public company, 95%.

(7)   Subsections (5) and (6) do not apply to an annual general meeting of a public company (see instead section 337(2)).

NOTES

Commencement: 1 October 2007.

Commencement (transitional provisions): Sch 3, paras 26, 26A to the Companies Act 2006 (Commencement No 3, Consequential Amendments, Transitional Provisions and Savings) Order 2007, SI 2007/2194 (at **[2.45]**) provides as follows (note that para 26A was inserted by the Companies Act 2006 (Commencement No 6, Saving and Commencement Nos 3 and 5 (Amendment)) Order 2008, SI 2008/674, art 5, Sch 3, para 2(1), (2), as from 6 April 2008)—

"Notice of meetings (ss 307, 310 and 311)

26.—(1)   Sections 307, 310 and 311 of the Companies Act 2006 (notice of meetings) apply in relation to meetings of which notice is given on or after 1st October 2007.

(2)   The provisions of the 1985 Act or the 1986 Order continue to apply in relation to a meeting of which notice was given before that date.

(3)   The provisions referred to in sub-paragraph (2) include sections 369 and 370(2) of the 1985 Act or Articles 377 and 378(2) of the 1986 Order.

(4)   Where notice of a meeting is given over more than one day, it is treated for the purposes of this paragraph as given

on the first of those days.

26A.—(1)   The following provisions have effect for the purposes of section 307(6)(a) of the Companies Act 2006 (private company: requisite percentage for calling general meeting at short notice).

(2)   If immediately before 1st October 2007 there was in force in relation to a company a resolution under section 369(4) of the 1985 Act or Article 377(4) of the 1986 Order—

    (a)   specifying 90%, or

    (b)   under which the company in general meeting had determined that the percentage should be 90%,

any provision of the company's articles specifying a higher percentage shall be disregarded.

(3)   If immediately before 1st October 2007 there was in force in relation to a company a resolution under section 369(4) of the 1985 Act or Article 377(4) of the 1986 Order—

    (a)   specifying a percentage greater than 90% but less than 95%, or

    (b)   under which the company in general meeting had determined a percentage greater than 90% but less than 95%,

any provision of the company's articles specifying a different percentage shall be disregarded.

(4)   Sub-paragraph (2) or (3) does not apply in relation to provisions of the company's articles adopted on or after 1st October 2007.".

Sub-s (A1), (A2): inserted by the Companies (Shareholders' Rights) Regulations 2009, SI 2009/1632, reg 9(1), as from 3 August 2009, in relation to meetings of which notice is given, or first given, on or after that date.

[1.307A]
[307A   Notice required of general meeting: certain meetings of traded companies

(1)   A general meeting of a traded company must be called by notice of—

    (a)   in a case where conditions A to C (set out below) are met, at least 14 days;

    (b)   in any other case, at least 21 days.

(2)   Condition A is that the general meeting is not an annual general meeting.

(3)   Condition B is that the company offers the facility for members to vote by electronic means accessible to all members who hold shares that carry rights to vote at general meetings.

This condition is met if there is a facility, offered by the company and accessible to all such members, to appoint a proxy by means of a website.

(4)   Condition C is that a special resolution reducing the period of notice to not less than 14 days has been passed—

    (a)   at the immediately preceding annual general meeting, or

    (b)   at a general meeting held since that annual general meeting.

(5)   In the case of a company which has not yet held an annual general meeting, condition C is that a special resolution reducing the period of notice to not less than 14 days has been passed at a general meeting.

(6)   The company's articles may require a longer period of notice than that specified in subsection (1).

(7)   Where a general meeting is adjourned, the adjourned meeting may be called by shorter notice than required by subsection (1).

But in the case of an adjournment for lack of a quorum this subsection applies only if—

    (a)   no business is to be dealt with at the adjourned meeting the general nature of which was not stated in the notice of the original meeting, and

    (b)   the adjourned meeting is to be held at least 10 days after the original meeting.

(8)   Nothing in this section applies in relation to a general meeting of a kind mentioned in section 307(A1)(b) (certain meetings regarding takeover of opted-in company).]

NOTES

Commencement: 3 August 2009.

Inserted by the Companies (Shareholders' Rights) Regulations 2009, SI 2009/1632, reg 9(2), as from 3 August 2009, in relation to meetings of which notice is given, or first given, on or after that date (for transitional provisions, see the note below).

Transitional provisions: SI 2009/1632, reg 23 provides that in sub-ss (4) and (5) above, references to annual general meetings and general meetings include ones held before 3 August 2009.

[1.308]
308   Manner in which notice to be given

Notice of a general meeting of a company must be given—

    (a)   in hard copy form,

    (b)   in electronic form, or

    (c)   by means of a website (see section 309),

or partly by one such means and partly by another.

NOTES

Commencement: 20 January 2007.

[1.309]
309   Publication of notice of meeting on website

(1)   Notice of a meeting is not validly given by a company by means of a website unless it is given in accordance with this section.

(2)   When the company notifies a member of the presence of the notice on the website the notification must—

(a) state that it concerns a notice of a company meeting,
(b) specify the place, date and time of the meeting, and
(c) in the case of a public company, state whether the meeting will be an annual general meeting.

(3) The notice must be available on the website throughout the period beginning with the date of that notification and ending with the conclusion of the meeting.

NOTES
Commencement: 20 January 2007.

[1.310]
310 Persons entitled to receive notice of meetings
(1) Notice of a general meeting of a company must be sent to—
(a) every member of the company, and
(b) every director.
(2) In subsection (1), the reference to members includes any person who is entitled to a share in consequence of the death or bankruptcy of a member, if the company has been notified of their entitlement.
(3) In subsection (2), the reference to the bankruptcy of a member includes—
(a) the sequestration of the estate of a member;
(b) a member's estate being the subject of a protected trust deed (within the meaning of the Bankruptcy (Scotland) Act 1985 (c 66)).
(4) This section has effect subject to—
(a) any enactment, and
(b) any provision of the company's articles.

NOTES
Commencement: 1 October 2007.
Commencement (transitional provisions): see the note to s 307 at **[1.307]**.

[1.311]
311 Contents of notices of meetings
(1) Notice of a general meeting of a company must state—
(a) the time and date of the meeting, and
(b) the place of the meeting.
(2) Notice of a general meeting of a company must state the general nature of the business to be dealt with at the meeting.
[In relation to a company other than a traded company, this subsection has effect subject to any provision of the company's articles].
[(3) Notice of a general meeting of a traded company must also include—
(a) a statement giving the address of the website on which the information required by section 311A (traded companies: publication of information in advance of general meeting) is published;
(b) a statement—
(i) that the right to vote at the meeting is determined by reference to the register of members, and
(ii) of the time when that right will be determined in accordance with section 360B(2) (traded companies: share dealings before general meetings);
(c) a statement of the procedures with which members must comply in order to be able to attend and vote at the meeting (including the date by which they must comply);
(d) a statement giving details of any forms to be used for the appointment of a proxy;
(e) where the company offers the facility for members to vote in advance (see section 322A) or by electronic means (see section 360A), a statement of the procedure for doing so (including the date by which it must be done, and details of any forms to be used); and
(f) a statement of the right of members to ask questions in accordance with section 319A (traded companies: questions at meetings).]

NOTES
Commencement: 1 October 2007.
Commencement (transitional provisions): see the note to s 307 at **[1.307]**.
Sub-s (2): words in square brackets substituted by the Companies (Shareholders' Rights) Regulations 2009, SI 2009/1632, reg 10(1), (2), as from 3 August 2009, in relation to meetings of which notice is given, or first given, on or after that date.
Sub-s (3): added by SI 2009/1632, reg 10(1), (3), as from 3 August 2009, in relation to meetings of which notice is given, or first given, on or after that date.

[1.311A]
[311A Traded companies: publication of information in advance of general meeting
(1) A traded company must ensure that the following information relating to a general meeting of the company is made available on a website—
(a) the matters set out in the notice of the meeting;

(b)   the total numbers of—
     (i)   shares in the company, and
     (ii)   shares of each class,
     in respect of which members are entitled to exercise voting rights at the meeting;
(c)   the totals of the voting rights that members are entitled to exercise at the meeting in respect of the shares of each class;
(d)   members' statements, members' resolutions and members' matters of business received by the company after the first date on which notice of the meeting is given.
(2)   The information must be made available on a website that—
   (a)   is maintained by or on behalf of the company, and
   (b)   identifies the company.
(3)   Access to the information on the website, and the ability to obtain a hard copy of the information from the website, must not be conditional on payment of a fee or otherwise restricted.
(4)   The information—
   (a)   must be made available—
     (i)   in the case of information required by subsection (1)(a) to (c), on or before the first date on which notice of the meeting is given, and
     (ii)   in the case of information required by subsection (1)(d), as soon as reasonably practicable, and
   (b)   must be kept available throughout the period of two years beginning with the date on which it is first made available on a website in accordance with this section.
(5)   A failure to make information available throughout the period specified in subsection (4)(b) is disregarded if—
   (a)   the information is made available on the website for part of that period, and
   (b)   the failure is wholly attributable to circumstances that it would not be reasonable to have expected the company to prevent or avoid.
(6)   The amounts mentioned in subsection (1)(b) and (c) must be ascertained at the latest practicable time before the first date on which notice of the meeting is given.
(7)   Failure to comply with this section does not affect the validity of the meeting or of anything done at the meeting.
(8)   If this section is not complied with as respects any meeting, an offence is committed by every officer of the company who is in default.
(9)   A person guilty of an offence under this section is liable on summary conviction to a fine not exceeding level 3 on the standard scale.]

NOTES

Commencement: 3 August 2009.

Inserted by the Companies (Shareholders' Rights) Regulations 2009, SI 2009/1632, reg 11, as from 3 August 2009, in relation to meetings of which notice is given, or first given, on or after that date.

[1.312]
312   Resolution requiring special notice
(1)   Where by any provision of the Companies Acts special notice is required of a resolution, the resolution is not effective unless notice of the intention to move it has been given to the company at least 28 days before the meeting at which it is moved.
(2)   The company must, where practicable, give its members notice of any such resolution in the same manner and at the same time as it gives notice of the meeting.
(3)   Where that is not practicable, the company must give its members notice at least 14 days before the meeting—
   (a)   by advertisement in a newspaper having an appropriate circulation, or
   (b)   in any other manner allowed by the company's articles.
(4)   If, after notice of the intention to move such a resolution has been given to the company, a meeting is called for a date 28 days or less after the notice has been given, the notice is deemed to have been properly given, though not given within the time required.

NOTES

Commencement: 1 October 2007.

Commencement (transitional provisions): Sch 3, para 27 to the Companies Act 2006 (Commencement No 3, Consequential Amendments, Transitional Provisions and Savings) Order 2007, SI 2007/2194 (at **[2.45]**) provides as follows—

"**27**   **Special notice (s 312)**
(1)   Section 312 of the Companies Act 2006 (special notice) applies in relation to resolutions for which special notice is required where notice of the intention to move the resolution is given to the company on or after 1st October 2007.
(2)   Section 379 of the 1985 Act or Article 387 of the 1986 Order continues to apply to resolutions for which special notice is required where notice of the intention to move the resolution is given to the company before that date.".

[1.313]
313   Accidental failure to give notice of resolution or meeting
(1)   Where a company gives notice of—
   (a)   a general meeting, or

(b)   a resolution intended to be moved at a general meeting,

any accidental failure to give notice to one or more persons shall be disregarded for the purpose of determining whether notice of the meeting or resolution (as the case may be) is duly given.

(2)   Except in relation to notice given under—

(a)   section 304 (notice of meetings required by members),

(b)   section 305 (notice of meetings called by members), or

(c)   section 339 (notice of resolutions at AGMs proposed by members),

subsection (1) has effect subject to any provision of the company's articles.

NOTES

Commencement: 1 October 2007.

Commencement (transitional provisions): Sch 3, para 28 to the Companies Act 2006 (Commencement No 3, Consequential Amendments, Transitional Provisions and Savings) Order 2007, SI 2007/2194 (at **[2.45]**) provides as follows—

"28   Accidental failure to give notice of resolution or meeting (s 313)

(1)   Section 313 of the Companies Act 2006 (accidental failure to give notice of resolution or meeting) applies to resolutions or meetings of which notice is given on or after 1st October 2007.

(2)   The reference in sub-paragraph (1) to cases in which notice is given on or after 1st October 2007 includes cases in which notice would be regarded as so given if section 313 applied.".

Members' statements

[1.314]

314   Members' power to require circulation of statements

(1)   The members of a company may require the company to circulate, to members of the company entitled to receive notice of a general meeting, a statement of not more than 1,000 words with respect to—

(a)   a matter referred to in a proposed resolution to be dealt with at that meeting, or

(b)   other business to be dealt with at that meeting.

(2)   A company is required to circulate a statement once it has received requests to do so from—

(a)   members representing at least 5% of the total voting rights of all the members who have a relevant right to vote (excluding any voting rights attached to any shares in the company held as treasury shares), or

(b)   at least 100 members who have a relevant right to vote and hold shares in the company on which there has been paid up an average sum, per member, of at least £100.

See also section 153 (exercise of rights where shares held on behalf of others).

(3)   In subsection (2), a "relevant right to vote" means—

(a)   in relation to a statement with respect to a matter referred to in a proposed resolution, a right to vote on that resolution at the meeting to which the requests relate, and

(b)   in relation to any other statement, a right to vote at the meeting to which the requests relate.

(4)   A request—

(a)   may be in hard copy form or in electronic form,

(b)   must identify the statement to be circulated,

(c)   must be authenticated by the person or persons making it, and

(d)   must be received by the company at least one week before the meeting to which it relates.

NOTES

Commencement: 1 October 2007.

Commencement (transitional provisions): Sch 3, para 29 to the Companies Act 2006 (Commencement No 3, Consequential Amendments, Transitional Provisions and Savings) Order 2007, SI 2007/2194 (at **[2.45]**) provides as follows—

"29   Circulation of members' statements (ss 314 to 317)

(1)   Sections 314 to 317 of the Companies Act 2006 (circulation of members' statements) apply to requests made on or after 1st October 2007.

(2)   Sections 376 and 377 of the 1985 Act or Articles 384 and 385 of the 1986 Order continue to apply in relation to requisitions made before that date.

(3)   So long as such a requisition made to a private company under section 376(1)(b) or Article 384(1)(b) is not complied with, section 366 of the 1985 Act or Article 374 of the 1986 Order (duty to hold annual general meeting) continues to apply in relation to the company.

This does not apply if the company is not required to comply with the requisition (see section 377 of the 1985 Act or Article 385 of the 1986 Order).

(4)   Where requests are made or copies of a requisition are deposited on more than one day, the references in this paragraph to the day on which the request or requisition is made shall be read as references to the first day on which the requests made or copies deposited are sufficient to require the company to act.".

[1.315]

315   Company's duty to circulate members' statement

(1)   A company that is required under section 314, to circulate a statement must send a copy of it to each member of the company entitled to receive notice of the meeting—

(a)   in the same manner as the notice of the meeting, and

(b)   at the same time as, or as soon as reasonably practicable after, it gives notice of the meeting.

(2)   Subsection (1) has effect subject to section 316(2) (deposit or tender of sum in respect of expenses of circulation) and section 317 (application not to circulate members' statement).

(3)   In the event of default in complying with this section, an offence is committed by every officer of the company who is in default.

(4)   A person guilty of an offence under this section is liable—

    (a)   on conviction on indictment, to a fine;

    (b)   on summary conviction, to a fine not exceeding the statutory maximum.

NOTES

Commencement: 1 October 2007.

Commencement (transitional provisions): see the note to s 314 at **[1.314]**.

[1.316]
316   Expenses of circulating members' statement

(1)   The expenses of the company in complying with section 315 need not be paid by the members who requested the circulation of the statement if—

    (a)   the meeting to which the requests relate is an annual general meeting of a public company, and

    (b)   requests sufficient to require the company to circulate the statement are received before the end of the financial year preceding the meeting.

(2)   Otherwise—

    (a)   the expenses of the company in complying with that section must be paid by the members who requested the circulation of the statement unless the company resolves otherwise, and

    (b)   unless the company has previously so resolved, it is not bound to comply with that section unless there is deposited with or tendered to it, not later than one week before the meeting, a sum reasonably sufficient to meet its expenses in doing so.

NOTES

Commencement: 1 October 2007.

Commencement (transitional provisions): see the note to s 314 at **[1.314]**.

[1.317]
317   Application not to circulate members' statement

(1)   A company is not required to circulate a members' statement under section 315 if, on an application by the company or another person who claims to be aggrieved, the court is satisfied that the rights conferred by section 314 and that section are being abused.

(2)   The court may order the members who requested the circulation of the statement to pay the whole or part of the company's costs (in Scotland, expenses) on such an application, even if they are not parties to the application.

NOTES

Commencement: 1 October 2007.

Commencement (transitional provisions): see the note to s 314 at **[1.314]**.

Procedure at meetings

[1.318]
318   Quorum at meetings

(1)   In the case of a company limited by shares or guarantee and having only one member, one qualifying person present at a meeting is a quorum.

(2)   In any other case, subject to the provisions of the company's articles, two qualifying persons present at a meeting are a quorum, unless—

    (a)   each is a qualifying person only because he is authorised under section 323 to act as the representative of a corporation in relation to the meeting, and they are representatives of the same corporation; or

    (b)   each is a qualifying person only because he is appointed as proxy of a member in relation to the meeting, and they are proxies of the same member.

(3)   For the purposes of this section a "qualifying person" means—

    (a)   an individual who is a member of the company,

    (b)   a person authorised under section 323 (representation of corporations at meetings) to act as the representative of a corporation in relation to the meeting, or

    (c)   a person appointed as proxy of a member in relation to the meeting.

NOTES

Commencement: 1 October 2007.

Commencement (transitional provisions): Sch 3, para 30 to the Companies Act 2006 (Commencement No 3, Consequential Amendments, Transitional Provisions and Savings) Order 2007, SI 2007/2194 (at **[2.45]**) provides as follows—

"30   Procedure at meetings and proxies (ss 318 to 331)

(1)   Sections 318 to 323 of the Companies Act 2006 (procedure at meetings) and sections 324 to 331 (proxies) apply to meetings of which notice is given on or after 1st October 2007.

(2)   The provisions of the 1985 Act or the 1986 Order continue to apply to meetings of which notice was given before

that date.

(3)   The provisions referred to in sub-paragraph (2) include sections 370, 370A, 372 to 375 and 378(4) of the 1985 Act or Articles 378, 378A, 380 to 383 and 386(4) of the 1986 Order.

(4)   Where notice of a meeting is given over more than one day, it is treated for the purposes of this paragraph as given on the first of those days.".

[1.319]
319   Chairman of meeting

(1)   A member may be elected to be the chairman of a general meeting by a resolution of the company passed at the meeting.

(2)   Subsection (1) is subject to any provision of the company's articles that states who may or may not be chairman.

NOTES

Commencement: 1 October 2007.

Commencement (transitional provisions): see the note to s 318 at **[1.318]**.

[1.319A]
[319A   Traded companies: questions at meetings

(1)   At a general meeting of a traded company, the company must cause to be answered any question relating to the business being dealt with at the meeting put by a member attending the meeting.

(2)   No such answer need be given—
  (a)   if to do so would—
      (i)   interfere unduly with the preparation for the meeting, or
      (ii)   involve the disclosure of confidential information;
  (b)   if the answer has already been given on a website in the form of an answer to a question; or
  (c)   if it is undesirable in the interests of the company or the good order of the meeting that the question be answered.]

NOTES

Commencement: 3 August 2009.

Inserted by the Companies (Shareholders' Rights) Regulations 2009, SI 2009/1632, reg 12(1), as from 3 August 2009, in relation to meetings of which notice is given, or first given, on or after that date.

[1.320]
320   Declaration by chairman on a show of hands

(1)   On a vote on a resolution at a meeting on a show of hands, a declaration by the chairman that the resolution—
  (a)   has or has not been passed, or
  (b)   passed with a particular majority,
is conclusive evidence of that fact without proof of the number or proportion of the votes recorded in favour of or against the resolution.

(2)   An entry in respect of such a declaration in minutes of the meeting recorded in accordance with section 355 is also conclusive evidence of that fact without such proof.

(3)   This section does not have effect if a poll is demanded in respect of the resolution (and the demand is not subsequently withdrawn).

NOTES

Commencement: 1 October 2007.

Commencement (transitional provisions): see the note to s 318 at **[1.318]**.

[1.321]
321   Right to demand a poll

(1)   A provision of a company's articles is void in so far as it would have the effect of excluding the right to demand a poll at a general meeting on any question other than—
  (a)   the election of the chairman of the meeting, or
  (b)   the adjournment of the meeting.

(2)   A provision of a company's articles is void in so far as it would have the effect of making ineffective a demand for a poll on any such question which is made—
  (a)   by not less than 5 members having the right to vote on the resolution; or
  (b)   by a member or members representing not less than 10% of the total voting rights of all the members having the right to vote on the resolution (excluding any voting rights attached to any shares in the company held as treasury shares); or
  (c)   by a member or members holding shares in the company conferring a right to vote on the resolution, being shares on which an aggregate sum has been paid up equal to not less than 10% of the total sum paid up on all the shares conferring that right (excluding shares in the company conferring a right to vote on the resolution which are held as treasury shares).

NOTES

Commencement: 1 October 2007.

Commencement (transitional provisions): see the note to s 318 at **[1.318]**.

[1.322]

322   Voting on a poll

On a poll taken at a general meeting of a company, a member entitled to more than one vote need not, if he votes, use all his votes or cast all the votes he uses in the same way.

NOTES

Commencement: 1 October 2007.

Commencement (transitional provisions): see the note to s 318 at **[1.318]**.

[1.322A]

[322A   Voting on a poll: votes cast in advance

(1)   A company's articles may contain provision to the effect that on a vote on a resolution on a poll taken at a meeting, the votes may include votes cast in advance.

(2)   In the case of a traded company any such provision in relation to voting at a general meeting may be made subject only to such requirements and restrictions as are—

(a)   necessary to ensure the identification of the person voting, and

(b)   proportionate to the achievement of that objective.

Nothing in this subsection affects any power of a company to require reasonable evidence of the entitlement of any person who is not a member to vote.

(3)   Any provision of a company's articles is void in so far as it would have the effect of requiring any document casting a vote in advance to be received by the company or another person earlier than the following time—

(a)   in the case of a poll taken more than 48 hours after it was demanded, 24 hours before the time appointed for the taking of the poll;

(b)   in the case of any other poll, 48 hours before the time for holding the meeting or adjourned meeting.

(4)   In calculating the periods mentioned in subsection (3), no account is to be taken of any part of a day that is not a working day.]

NOTES

Commencement: 3 August 2009.

Inserted by the Companies (Shareholders' Rights) Regulations 2009, SI 2009/1632, reg 5(1), as from 3 August 2009, in relation to meetings of which notice is given, or first given, on or after that date.

[1.323]

323   Representation of corporations at meetings

(1)   If a corporation (whether or not a company within the meaning of this Act) is a member of a company, it may by resolution of its directors or other governing body authorise a person or persons to act as its representative or representatives at any meeting of the company.

[(2)   A person authorised by a corporation is entitled to exercise (on behalf of the corporation) the same powers as the corporation could exercise if it were an individual member of the company.

Where a corporation authorises more than one person, this subsection is subject to subsections (3) and (4).

(3)   On a vote on a resolution on a show of hands at a meeting of the company, each authorised person has the same voting rights as the corporation would be entitled to.

(4)   Where subsection (3) does not apply and more than one authorised person purport to exercise a power under subsection (2) in respect of the same shares—

(a)   if they purport to exercise the power in the same way as each other, the power is treated as exercised in that way;

(b)   if they do not purport to exercise the power in the same way as each other, the power is treated as not exercised.]

NOTES

Commencement: 1 October 2007.

Commencement (transitional provisions): see the note to s 318 at **[1.318]**.

Sub-ss (2)–(4): substituted by the Companies (Shareholders' Rights) Regulations 2009, SI 2009/1632, reg 6, as from 3 August 2009, in relation to meetings of which notice is given, or first given, on or after that date.

Proxies

[1.324]

324   Rights to appoint proxies

(1)   A member of a company is entitled to appoint another person as his proxy to exercise all or any of his rights to attend and to speak and vote at a meeting of the company.

(2) In the case of a company having a share capital, a member may appoint more than one proxy in relation to a meeting, provided that each proxy is appointed to exercise the rights attached to a different share or shares held by him, or (as the case may be) to a different £10, or multiple of £10, of stock held by him.

NOTES

Commencement: 1 October 2007.

Commencement (transitional provisions): see the note to s 318 at **[1.318]**.

[1.324A]
[324A Obligation of proxy to vote in accordance with instructions
A proxy must vote in accordance with any instructions given by the member by whom the proxy is appointed.]

NOTES

Commencement: 3 August 2009.

Inserted by the Companies (Shareholders' Rights) Regulations 2009, SI 2009/1632, reg 7, as from 3 August 2009, in relation to meetings of which notice is given, or first given, on or after that date.

[1.325]
325 Notice of meeting to contain statement of rights
(1) In every notice calling a meeting of a company there must appear, with reasonable prominence, a statement informing the member of—
   (a) his rights under section 324, and
   (b) any more extensive rights conferred by the company's articles to appoint more than one proxy.
(2) Failure to comply with this section does not affect the validity of the meeting or of anything done at the meeting.
(3) If this section is not complied with as respects any meeting, an offence is committed by every officer of the company who is in default.
(4) A person guilty of an offence under this section is liable on summary conviction to a fine not exceeding level 3 on the standard scale.

NOTES

Commencement: 1 October 2007.

Commencement (transitional provisions): see the note to s 318 at **[1.318]**.

[1.326]
326 Company-sponsored invitations to appoint proxies
(1) If for the purposes of a meeting there are issued at the company's expense invitations to members to appoint as proxy a specified person or a number of specified persons, the invitations must be issued to all members entitled to vote at the meeting.
(2) Subsection (1) is not contravened if—
   (a) there is issued to a member at his request a form of appointment naming the proxy or a list of persons willing to act as proxy, and
   (b) the form or list is available on request to all members entitled to vote at the meeting.
(3) If subsection (1) is contravened as respects a meeting, an offence is committed by every officer of the company who is in default.
(4) A person guilty of an offence under this section is liable on summary conviction to a fine not exceeding level 3 on the standard scale.

NOTES

Commencement: 1 October 2007.

Commencement (transitional provisions): see the note to s 318 at **[1.318]**.

[1.327]
327 Notice required of appointment of proxy etc
[(A1) In the case of a traded company—
   (a) the appointment of a person as proxy for a member must be notified to the company in writing;
   (b) where such an appointment is made, the company may require reasonable evidence of—
       (i) the identity of the member and of the proxy,
       (ii) the member's instructions (if any) as to how the proxy is to vote, and
       (iii) where the proxy is appointed by a person acting on behalf of the member, authority of that person to make the appointment;
       but may not require to be provided with anything else relating to the appointment.]
(1) [The following provisions apply in the case of traded companies and other companies as regards]—
   (a) the appointment of a proxy, and

(b)   any document necessary to show the validity of, or otherwise relating to, the appointment of a proxy.

(2)   Any provision of the company's articles is void in so far as it would have the effect of requiring any such appointment or document to be received by the company or another person earlier than the following time—

     (a)   in the case of a meeting or adjourned meeting, 48 hours before the time for holding the meeting or adjourned meeting;

     (b)   in the case of a poll taken more than 48 hours after it was demanded, 24 hours before the time appointed for the taking of the poll;

     (c)   in the case of a poll taken not more than 48 hours after it was demanded, the time at which it was demanded.

(3)   In calculating the periods mentioned in subsection (2) no account shall be taken of any part of a day that is not a working day.

NOTES

Commencement: 1 October 2007 (except sub-s (2)(c)); to be appointed (otherwise).

Commencement (transitional provisions): see the note to s 318 at **[1.318]**.

Commencement (note): the government have announced that they do not intend to commence sub-s (2)(c) of this section or s 330(6)(c) and that they will be repealed in due course; see the written ministerial statements for 6 November 2008.

Sub-s (A1): inserted by the Companies (Shareholders' Rights) Regulations 2009, SI 2009/1632, reg 13(1), as from 3 August 2009, in relation to meetings of which notice is given, or first given, on or after that date.

Sub-s (1): words in square brackets substituted by SI 2009/1632, reg 13(2), as from 3 August 2009, in relation to meetings of which notice is given, or first given, on or after that date.

[1.328]

328   Chairing meetings

(1)   A proxy may be elected to be the chairman of a general meeting by a resolution of the company passed at the meeting.

(2)   Subsection (1) is subject to any provision of the company's articles that states who may or who may not be chairman.

NOTES

Commencement: 1 October 2007.

Commencement (transitional provisions): see the note to s 318 at **[1.318]**.

[1.329]

329   Right of proxy to demand a poll

(1)   The appointment of a proxy to vote on a matter at a meeting of a company authorises the proxy to demand, or join in demanding, a poll on that matter.

(2)   In applying the provisions of section 321(2) (requirements for effective demand), a demand by a proxy counts—

     (a)   for the purposes of paragraph (a), as a demand by the member;

     (b)   for the purposes of paragraph (b), as a demand by a member representing the voting rights that the proxy is authorised to exercise;

     (c)   for the purposes of paragraph (c), as a demand by a member holding the shares to which those rights are attached.

NOTES

Commencement: 1 October 2007.

Commencement (transitional provisions): see the note to s 318 at **[1.318]**.

[1.330]

330   Notice required of termination of proxy's authority

[(A1)   In the case of a traded company the termination of the authority of a person to act as proxy must be notified to the company in writing.]

(1)   [The following provisions apply in the case of traded companies and other companies as regards] notice that the authority of a person to act as proxy is terminated ("notice of termination").

(2)   The termination of the authority of a person to act as proxy does not affect—

     (a)   whether he counts in deciding whether there is a quorum at a meeting,

     (b)   the validity of anything he does as chairman of a meeting, or

     (c)   the validity of a poll demanded by him at a meeting,

unless the company receives notice of the termination before the commencement of the meeting.

(3)   The termination of the authority of a person to act as proxy does not affect the validity of a vote given by that person unless the company receives notice of the termination—

     (a)   before the commencement of the meeting or adjourned meeting at which the vote is given, or

     (b)   in the case of a poll taken more than 48 hours after it is demanded, before the time appointed for taking the poll.

(4) If the company's articles require or permit members to give notice of termination to a person other than the company, the references above to the company receiving notice have effect as if they were or (as the case may be) included a reference to that person.

(5) Subsections (2) and (3) have effect subject to any provision of the company's articles which has the effect of requiring notice of termination to be received by the company or another person at a time earlier than that specified in those subsections.

This is subject to subsection (6).

(6) Any provision of the company's articles is void in so far as it would have the effect of requiring notice of termination to be received by the company or another person earlier than the following time—

   (a) in the case of a meeting or adjourned meeting, 48 hours before the time for holding the meeting or adjourned meeting;

   (b) in the case of a poll taken more than 48 hours after it was demanded, 24 hours before the time appointed for the taking of the poll;

   (c) in the case of a poll taken not more than 48 hours after it was demanded, the time at which it was demanded.

(7) In calculating the periods mentioned in subsections (3)(b) and (6) no account shall be taken of any part of a day that is not a working day.

NOTES

Commencement: 1 October 2007 (except sub-s (6)(c)); to be appointed (otherwise).

Commencement (transitional provisions): see the note to s 318 at **[1.318]**.

Commencement (note): see the note to s 327 at **[1.327]**.

Sub-s (A1): inserted by the Companies (Shareholders' Rights) Regulations 2009, SI 2009/1632, reg 13(3)(a), as from 3 August 2009, in relation to meetings of which notice is given, or first given, on or after that date.

Sub-s (1): words in square brackets substituted by SI 2009/1632, reg 13(3)(b), as from 3 August 2009, in relation to meetings of which notice is given, or first given, on or after that date.

[1.331]
331 Saving for more extensive rights conferred by articles

Nothing in sections 324 to 330 (proxies) prevents a company's articles from conferring more extensive rights on members or proxies than are conferred by those sections.

NOTES

Commencement: 1 October 2007.

Commencement (transitional provisions): see the note to s 318 at **[1.318]**.

Adjourned meetings

[1.332]
332 Resolution passed at adjourned meeting

Where a resolution is passed at an adjourned meeting of a company, the resolution is for all purposes to be treated as having been passed on the date on which it was in fact passed, and is not to be deemed passed on any earlier date.

NOTES

Commencement: 1 October 2007.

Electronic communications

[1.333]
333 Sending documents relating to meetings etc in electronic form

(1) Where a company has given an electronic address in a notice calling a meeting, it is deemed to have agreed that any document or information relating to proceedings at the meeting may be sent by electronic means to that address (subject to any conditions or limitations specified in the notice).

(2) Where a company has given an electronic address—

   (a) in an instrument of proxy sent out by the company in relation to the meeting, or

   (b) in an invitation to appoint a proxy issued by the company in relation to the meeting,

it is deemed to have agreed that any document or information relating to proxies for that meeting may be sent by electronic means to that address (subject to any conditions or limitations specified in the notice).

(3) In subsection (2), documents relating to proxies include—

   (a) the appointment of a proxy in relation to a meeting,

   (b) any document necessary to show the validity of, or otherwise relating to, the appointment of a proxy, and

   (c) notice of the termination of the authority of a proxy.

(4) In this section "electronic address" means any address or number used for the purposes of sending or receiving documents or information by electronic means.

NOTES

Commencement: 20 January 2007.

[1.333A]
[333A   Traded company: duty to provide electronic address for receipt of proxies etc
(1)   A traded company must provide an electronic address for the receipt of any document or information relating to proxies for a general meeting.
(2)   The company must provide the address either—
    (a)   by giving it when sending out an instrument of proxy for the purposes of the meeting or issuing an invitation to appoint a proxy for those purposes; or
    (b)   by ensuring that it is made available, throughout the period beginning with the first date on which notice of the meeting is given and ending with the conclusion of the meeting, on the website on which the information required by section 311A(1) is made available.
(3)   The company is deemed to have agreed that any document or information relating to proxies for the meeting may be sent by electronic means to the address provided (subject to any limitations specified by the company when providing the address).
(4)   In this section—
    (a)   documents relating to proxies include—
        (i)   the appointment of a proxy for a meeting,
        (ii)   any document necessary to show the validity of, or otherwise relating to, the appointment of a proxy, and
        (iii)   notice of the termination of the authority of a proxy;
    (b)   "electronic address" has the meaning given by section 333(4).]

NOTES
Commencement: 3 August 2009.
Inserted by the Companies (Shareholders' Rights) Regulations 2009, SI 2009/1632, reg 13(4), as from 3 August 2009, in relation to meetings of which notice is given, or first given, on or after that date.

Application to class meetings
[1.334]
334   Application to class meetings
(1)   The provisions of this Chapter apply (with necessary modifications) in relation to a meeting of holders of a class of shares as they apply in relation to a general meeting.
    This is subject to subsections [(2) to (3)].
(2)   The following provisions of this Chapter do not apply in relation to a meeting of holders of a class of shares—
    (a)   sections 303 to 305 (members' power to require directors to call general meeting),   . . .
    (b)   section 306 (power of court to order meeting)[, and
    (c)   sections 311(3), 311A, 319A, 327(A1), 330(A1) and 333A (additional requirements relating to traded companies)].
[(2A)   Section 307(1) to (6) apply in relation to a meeting of holders of a class of shares in a traded company as they apply in relation to a meeting of holders of a class of shares in a company other than a traded company (and, accordingly, section 307A does not apply in relation to such a meeting).]
(3)   The following provisions (in addition to those mentioned in subsection (2)) do not apply in relation to a meeting in connection with the variation of rights attached to a class of shares (a "variation of class rights meeting")—
    (a)   section 318 (quorum), and
    (b)   section 321 (right to demand a poll).
(4)   The quorum for a variation of class rights meeting is—
    (a)   for a meeting other than an adjourned meeting, two persons present holding at least one-third in nominal value of the issued shares of the class in question (excluding any shares of that class held as treasury shares);
    (b)   for an adjourned meeting, one person present holding shares of the class in question.
(5)   For the purposes of subsection (4), where a person is present by proxy or proxies, he is treated as holding only the shares in respect of which those proxies are authorised to exercise voting rights.
(6)   At a variation of class rights meeting, any holder of shares of the class in question present may demand a poll.
(7)   For the purposes of this section—
    (a)   any amendment of a provision contained in a company's articles for the variation of the rights attached to a class of shares, or the insertion of any such provision into the articles, is itself to be treated as a variation of those rights, and
    (b)   references to the variation of rights attached to a class of shares include references to their abrogation.

NOTES
Commencement: 1 October 2007.
Commencement (transitional provisions): Sch 3, para 31 to the Companies Act 2006 (Commencement No 3, Consequential Amendments, Transitional Provisions and Savings) Order 2007, SI 2007/2194 (at **[2.45]**) provides as follows—

"**31   Application of provisions to class meetings (ss 334 and 335)**
(1)   Sections 334 and 335 of the Companies Act 2006 (application of provisions of Chapter 3 to class meetings) apply to

requests and meetings in relation to which the provisions applied by those sections have effect.

(2) Section 125(6) of the 1985 Act or Article 135(6) of the 1986 Order continues to apply to meetings of which notice is given before 1st October 2007.

(3) Where notice of a meeting is given over more than one day, it is treated for the purposes of sub-paragraph (2) as given on the first of those days.".

Sub-s (1): words in square brackets substituted by the Companies (Shareholders' Rights) Regulations 2009, SI 2009/1632, reg 14(1), (2), as from 3 August 2009, in relation to meetings of which notice is given, or first given, on or after that date.

Sub-s (2): the word omitted from para (a) was repealed, and para (c) (and the preceding word) was inserted, by SI 2009/1632, reg 14(1), (3), as from 3 August 2009, in relation to meetings of which notice is given, or first given, on or after that date.

Sub-s (2A): inserted by SI 2009/1632, reg 14(1), (4), as from 3 August 2009, in relation to meetings of which notice is given, or first given, on or after that date.

[1.335]
335 Application to class meetings: companies without a share capital

(1) The provisions of this Chapter apply (with necessary modifications) in relation to a meeting of a class of members of a company without a share capital as they apply in relation to a general meeting.

This is subject to subsections (2) and (3).

(2) The following provisions of this Chapter do not apply in relation to a meeting of a class of members—

(a) sections 303 to 305 (members' power to require directors to call general meeting), and

(b) section 306 (power of court to order meeting).

(3) The following provisions (in addition to those mentioned in subsection (2)) do not apply in relation to a meeting in connection with the variation of the rights of a class of members (a "variation of class rights meeting")—

(a) section 318 (quorum), and

(b) section 321 (right to demand a poll).

(4) The quorum for a variation of class rights meeting is—

(a) for a meeting other than an adjourned meeting, two members of the class present (in person or by proxy) who together represent at least one-third of the voting rights of the class;

(b) for an adjourned meeting, one member of the class present (in person or by proxy).

(5) At a variation of class rights meeting, any member present (in person or by proxy) may demand a poll.

(6) For the purposes of this section—

(a) any amendment of a provision contained in a company's articles for the variation of the rights of a class of members, or the insertion of any such provision into the articles, is itself to be treated as a variation of those rights, and

(b) references to the variation of rights of a class of members include references to their abrogation.

NOTES

Commencement: 1 October 2007.

Commencement (transitional provisions): see the note to s 334 at **[1.334]**.

CHAPTER 4
PUBLIC COMPANIES [AND TRADED COMPANIES]:
ADDITIONAL REQUIREMENTS FOR AGMS

NOTES

Words in square brackets in the Chapter heading inserted by the Companies (Shareholders' Rights) Regulations 2009, SI 2009/1632, reg 15(5), as from 3 August 2009, in relation to meetings of which notice is given, or first given, on or after that date.

[1.336]
336 Public companies [and traded companies]: annual general meeting

(1) Every public company must hold a general meeting as its annual general meeting in each period of 6 months beginning with the day following its accounting reference date (in addition to any other meetings held during that period).

[(1A) Every private company that is a traded company must hold a general meeting as its annual general meeting in each period of 9 months beginning with the day following its accounting reference date (in addition to any other meetings held during that period).]

(2) A company that fails to comply with subsection (1) [or (1A)] as a result of giving notice under section 392 (alteration of accounting reference date)—

(a) specifying a new accounting reference date, and

(b) stating that the current accounting reference period or the previous accounting reference period is to be shortened,

shall be treated as if it had complied with subsection (1) [or (1A)] if it holds a general meeting as its annual general meeting within 3 months of giving that notice.

(3) If a company fails to comply with subsection (1) [or (1A)], an offence is committed by every officer of the company who is in default.

(4)   A person guilty of an offence under this section is liable—

   (a)   on conviction on indictment, to a fine;

   (b)   on summary conviction, to a fine not exceeding the statutory maximum.

NOTES

Commencement: 1 October 2007.

Commencement (transitional provisions): Sch 3, paras 32–38 to the Companies Act 2006 (Commencement No 3, Consequential Amendments, Transitional Provisions and Savings) Order 2007, SI 2007/2194 (at **[2.45]**) (as amended by the Companies Act 2006 (Commencement No 5, Transitional Provisions and Savings) Order 2007, SI 2007/3495, art 11, Sch 5, para 2(1), (6), as from 31 December 2007) provide as follows—

"Annual general meetings (ss 336 to 340)

32.—(1)   The repeal of section 366 of the 1985 Act or Article 374 of the 1986 Order (duty to hold annual general meeting) does not affect any provision of a private company's memorandum or articles that expressly requires the company to hold an annual general meeting.

(2)   Any such provision continues to have such effect as it had immediately before 1st October 2007.

(3)   Provision specifying that one or more directors are to retire at an annual general meeting of the company is not provision expressly requiring the company to hold an annual general meeting.

[(4)   A company is not to be treated as one whose articles expressly require it to hold an annual general meeting if immediately before 1st October 2007 there was in force in relation to the company a resolution under section 366A of the 1985 Act or Article 374A of the 1986 Order (election to dispense with annual general meeting).]

33.   The repeal of section 367 of the 1985 Act (default power of Secretary of State to call AGM) has effect in relation to a private company as from 1st October 2007, even if an application under that section has been made, or the Secretary of State has called or directed the calling of a meeting under that section, before that date.

34.—(1)   The repeal of sections 376 and 377 of the 1985 Act or Articles 384 and 385 of the 1986 Order does not affect their application in relation to a requisition under section 376(1)(a) or Article 384(1)(a) made to a private company before 1st October 2007.

(2)   So long as such a requisition has not been complied with, section 366 of the 1985 Act or Article 374 of the 1986 Order (duty to hold annual general meeting) continues to apply in relation to the company.

This does not apply if the company is not required to comply with the requisition (see section 377 of the 1985 Act or Article 385 of the 1986 Order).

(3)   Where copies of the requisition are deposited on more than one day, the reference in sub-paragraph (1) to the day on which the request or requisition is made shall be read as a reference to the first day on which the copies deposited are sufficient to require the company to act.

35.—(1)   In the case of an existing public company—

   (a)   section 366 of the 1985 Act or Article 374 of the 1986 Order (duty to hold annual general meeting) continues to apply to determine the date by which the company must hold its first annual general meeting after 30th September 2007, and

   (b)   section 336 of the Companies Act 2006 (public companies: annual general meeting) applies in relation to subsequent annual general meetings.

(2)   An "existing public company" means a company formed and registered before 1st October 2007 that is a public company immediately before that date.

36.   The repeal of section 367 of the 1985 Act (default power of Secretary of State to call AGM) does not affect the operation of that section in relation to a public company where an application under that section was made before 1st October 2007.

37.—(1)   Section 337 of the Companies Act 2006 (public companies: notice of AGM) applies to meetings of which notice is given on or after 1st October 2007.

(2)   Section 369 of the 1985 Act or Article 377 of the 1986 Order continues to apply in relation to meetings of which notice is given before that date.

(3)   Where notice of a meeting is given over more than one day, it is treated for the purposes of this paragraph as given on the first of those days.

38.—(1)   Sections 338 to 340 of the Companies Act 2006 (public companies: members' power to require circulation of resolutions for AGMs) apply to requests made on or after 1st October 2007.

(2)   Sections 376 and 377 of the 1985 Act or Articles 384 and 385 of the 1986 Order continue to apply to requisitions made to a public company before that date.

(3)   Where requests are made or copies of a requisition are deposited on more than one day, the references in this paragraph to the day on which the request or requisition is made shall be read as references to the first day on which the requests made or copies deposited are sufficient to require the company to act.".

Commencement (transitional adaptations): the transitional adaptations of this section contained in the Companies Act 2006 (Commencement No 3, Consequential Amendments, Transitional Provisions and Savings) Order 2007, SI 2007/2194, Sch 1, para 15 were revoked by the Companies Act 2006 (Commencement No 5, Transitional Provisions and Savings) Order 2007, SI 2007/3495, art 10(1), (3), as from 6 April 2008 (subject to any transitional provisions and savings as apply, in accordance with Sch 4 to that Order, in relation to the repeal of any provision of the 1985 Act referred to in the adaptation; see **[2.43]**). Note also that the Companies Act 2006 (Commencement No 6, Saving and Commencement Nos 3 and 5 (Amendment)) Order 2008, SI 2008/674, Sch 3, para 4 (at **[2.74]**) provides that the revocation of para 15 (as noted above) does not have effect in relation to a company until: (a) the directors of the company have complied with CA 1985, s 241 in respect of the last financial year of the company beginning before 6 April 2008, or (b) the first financial year of the company beginning on or after that date comes to an end.

Words in square brackets in the section heading and sub-ss (2), (3) inserted, and sub-s (1A) inserted, by the Companies (Shareholders' Rights) Regulations 2009, SI 2009/1632, reg 15(1)–(4), as from 3 August 2009, in relation to meetings of which notice is given, or first given, on or after that date.

[1.337]
337 Public companies [and traded companies]: notice of AGM

(1) A notice calling an annual general meeting of a public company [or a private company that is a traded company] must state that the meeting is an annual general meeting.

(2) An annual general meeting [of a public company that is not a traded company] may be called by shorter notice than that required by section 307(2) or by the company's articles (as the case may be), if all the members entitled to attend and vote at the meeting agree to the shorter notice.

[(3) Where a notice calling an annual general meeting of a traded company is given more than 6 weeks before the meeting, the notice must include—

    (a) if the company is a public company, a statement of the right under section 338 to require the company to give notice of a resolution to be moved at the meeting, and

    (b) whether or not the company is a public company, a statement of the right under section 338A to require the company to include a matter in the business to be dealt with at the meeting.]

NOTES
Commencement: 1 October 2007.
Commencement (transitional provisions): see the note to s 336 at **[1.336]**.
Words in square brackets in the section heading and sub-ss (1), (2) inserted, and sub-s (3) added, by the Companies (Shareholders' Rights) Regulations 2009, SI 2009/1632, reg 16(1)–(5), as from 3 August 2009, in relation to meetings of which notice is given, or first given, on or after that date.

[1.338]
338 Public companies: members' power to require circulation of resolutions for AGMs

(1) The members of a public company may require the company to give, to members of the company entitled to receive notice of the next annual general meeting, notice of a resolution which may properly be moved and is intended to be moved at that meeting.

(2) A resolution may properly be moved at an annual general meeting unless—

    (a) it would, if passed, be ineffective (whether by reason of inconsistency with any enactment or the company's constitution or otherwise),

    (b) it is defamatory of any person, or

    (c) it is frivolous or vexatious.

(3) A company is required to give notice of a resolution once it has received requests that it do so from—

    (a) members representing at least 5% of the total voting rights of all the members who have a right to vote on the resolution at the annual general meeting to which the requests relate (excluding any voting rights attached to any shares in the company held as treasury shares), or

    (b) at least 100 members who have a right to vote on the resolution at the annual general meeting to which the requests relate and hold shares in the company on which there has been paid up an average sum, per member, of at least £100.

See also section 153 (exercise of rights where shares held on behalf of others).

(4) A request—

    (a) may be in hard copy form or in electronic form,

    (b) must identify the resolution of which notice is to be given,

    (c) must be authenticated by the person or persons making it, and

    (d) must be received by the company not later than—

        (i) 6 weeks before the annual general meeting to which the requests relate, or

        (ii) if later, the time at which notice is given of that meeting.

NOTES
Commencement: 1 October 2007.
Commencement (transitional provisions): see the note to s 336 at **[1.336]**.

[1.338A]
[338A Traded companies: members' power to include other matters in business dealt with at AGM

(1) The members of a traded company may request the company to include in the business to be dealt with at an annual general meeting any matter (other than a proposed resolution) which may properly be included in the business.

(2) A matter may properly be included in the business at an annual general meeting unless—

    (a) it is defamatory of any person, or

    (b) it is frivolous or vexatious.

(3) A company is required to include such a matter once it has received requests that it do so from—

    (a) members representing at least 5% of the total voting rights of all the members who have a right to vote at the meeting, or

    (b) at least 100 members who have a right to vote at the meeting and hold shares in the company on which there has been paid up an average sum, per member, of at least £100.

See also section 153 (exercise of rights where shares held on behalf of others).

(4) A request—
(a) may be in hard copy form or in electronic form,
(b) must identify the matter to be included in the business,
(c) must be accompanied by a statement setting out the grounds for the request, and
(d) must be authenticated by the person or persons making it.
(5) A request must be received by the company not later than—
(a) 6 weeks before the meeting, or
(b) if later, the time at which notice is given of the meeting.]

NOTES
Commencement: 3 August 2009.
Inserted by the Companies (Shareholders' Rights) Regulations 2009, SI 2009/1632, reg 17(1), as from 3 August 2009, in relation to meetings of which notice is given, or first given, on or after that date.

[1.339]
339 Public companies: company's duty to circulate members' resolutions for AGMs
(1) A company that is required under section 338 to give notice of a resolution must send a copy of it to each member of the company entitled to receive notice of the annual general meeting—
(a) in the same manner as notice of the meeting, and
(b) at the same time as, or as soon as reasonably practicable after, it gives notice of the meeting.
(2) Subsection (1) has effect subject to section 340(2) (deposit or tender of sum in respect of expenses of circulation).
(3) The business which may be dealt with at an annual general meeting includes a resolution of which notice is given in accordance with this section.
(4) In the event of default in complying with this section, an offence is committed by every officer of the company who is in default.
(5) A person guilty of an offence under this section is liable—
(a) on conviction on indictment, to a fine;
(b) on summary conviction, to a fine not exceeding the statutory maximum.

NOTES
Commencement: 1 October 2007.
Commencement (transitional provisions): see the note to s 336 at **[1.336]**.

[1.340]
340 Public companies: expenses of circulating members' resolutions for AGM
(1) The expenses of the company in complying with section 339 need not be paid by the members who requested the circulation of the resolution if requests sufficient to require the company to circulate it are received before the end of the financial year preceding the meeting.
(2) Otherwise—
(a) the expenses of the company in complying with that section must be paid by the members who requested the circulation of the resolution unless the company resolves otherwise, and
(b) unless the company has previously so resolved, it is not bound to comply with that section unless there is deposited with or tendered to it, not later than—
(i) six weeks before the annual general meeting to which the requests relate, or
(ii) if later, the time at which notice is given of that meeting,
a sum reasonably sufficient to meet its expenses in complying with that section.

NOTES
Commencement: 1 October 2007.
Commencement (transitional provisions): see the note to s 336 at **[1.336]**.

[1.340A]
[340A Traded companies: duty to circulate members' matters for AGM
(1) A company that is required under section 338A to include any matter in the business to be dealt with at an annual general meeting must—
(a) give notice of it to each member of the company entitled to receive notice of the annual general meeting—
(i) in the same manner as notice of the meeting, and
(ii) at the same time as, or as soon as reasonably practicable after, it gives notice of the meeting, and
(b) publish it on the same website as that on which the company published the information required by section 311A.
(2) Subsection (1) has effect subject to section 340B(2) (deposit or tender of sum in respect of expenses of circulation).
(3) In the event of default in complying with this section, an offence is committed by every officer of the company who is in default.
(4) A person guilty of an offence under this section is liable—
(a) on conviction on indictment, to a fine;

(b)   on summary conviction, to a fine not exceeding the statutory maximum.]

NOTES
Commencement: 3 August 2009.
Inserted, together with s 340B, by the Companies (Shareholders' Rights) Regulations 2009, SI 2009/1632, reg 18(1), as from 3 August 2009, in relation to meetings of which notice is given, or first given, on or after that date.

[1.340B]
[340B   Traded companies: expenses of circulating members' matters to be dealt with at AGM
(1)   The expenses of the company in complying with section 340A need not be paid by the members who requested the inclusion of the matter in the business to be dealt with at the annual general meeting if requests sufficient to require the company to include the matter are received before the end of the financial year preceding the meeting.
(2)   Otherwise—
    (a)   the expenses of the company in complying with that section must be paid by the members who requested the inclusion of the matter unless the company resolves otherwise, and
    (b)   unless the company has previously so resolved, it is not bound to comply with that section unless there is deposited with or tendered to it, not later than—
        (i)   six weeks before the annual general meeting to which the requests relate, or
        (ii)   if later, the time at which notice is given of that meeting,
    a sum reasonably sufficient to meet its expenses in complying with that section.]

NOTES
Commencement: 3 August 2009.
Inserted as noted to s 340A at **[1.340A]**.

CHAPTER 5
ADDITIONAL REQUIREMENTS FOR QUOTED COMPANIES
[AND TRADED COMPANIES]

NOTES
Words in square brackets in the Chapter heading inserted by the Companies (Shareholders' Rights) Regulations 2009, SI 2009/1632, reg 19(5), as from 3 August 2009, in relation to meetings of which notice is given, or first given, on or after that date.

Website publication of poll results
[1.341]
341   Results of poll to be made available on website
(1)   Where a poll is taken at a general meeting of a quoted company [that is not a traded company], the company must ensure that the following information is made available on a website—
    (a)   the date of the meeting,
    (b)   the text of the resolution or, as the case may be, a description of the subject matter of the poll,
    (c)   the number of votes cast in favour, and
    (d)   the number of votes cast against.
[(1A)   Where a poll is taken at a general meeting of a traded company, the company must ensure that the following information is made available on a website—
    (a)   the date of the meeting,
    (b)   the text of the resolution or, as the case may be, a description of the subject matter of the poll,
    (c)   the number of votes validly cast,
    (d)   the proportion of the company's issued share capital (determined at the time at which the right to vote is determined under section 360B(2)) represented by those votes,
    (e)   the number of votes cast in favour,
    (f)   the number of votes cast against, and
    (g)   the number of abstentions (if counted).
(1B)   A traded company must comply with subsection (1A) by—
    (a)   the end of 16 days beginning with the day of the meeting, or
    (b)   if later, the end of the first working day after the day on which the result of the poll is declared.]
(2)   The provisions of section 353 (requirements as to website availability) apply.
(3)   In the event of default in complying with this section (or with the requirements of section 353 as it applies for the purposes of this section), an offence is committed by every officer of the company who is in default.
(4)   A person guilty of an offence under subsection (3) is liable on summary conviction to a fine not exceeding level 3 on the standard scale.
(5)   Failure to comply with this section (or the requirements of section 353) does not affect the validity of—

(a)　the poll, or

(b)　the resolution or other business (if passed or agreed to) to which the poll relates.

(6)　This section only applies to polls taken after this section comes into force.

NOTES

Commencement: 1 October 2007.

Sub-s (1): words in square brackets inserted by the Companies (Shareholders' Rights) Regulations 2009, SI 2009/1632, reg 19(1), (2), as from 3 August 2009, in relation to meetings of which notice is given, or first given, on or after that date.

Sub-ss (1A), (1B): inserted by SI 2009/1632, reg 19(1), (3), as from 3 August 2009, in relation to meetings of which notice is given, or first given, on or after that date.

Independent report on poll

[1.342]
342　Members' power to require independent report on poll

(1)　The members of a quoted company may require the directors to obtain an independent report on any poll taken, or to be taken, at a general meeting of the company.

(2)　The directors are required to obtain an independent report if they receive requests to do so from—

(a)　members representing not less than 5% of the total voting rights of all the members who have a right to vote on the matter to which the poll relates (excluding any voting rights attached to any shares in the company held as treasury shares), or

(b)　not less than 100 members who have a right to vote on the matter to which the poll relates and hold shares in the company on which there has been paid up an average sum, per member, of not less than £100.

See also section 153 (exercise of rights where shares held on behalf of others).

(3)　Where the requests relate to more than one poll, subsection (2) must be satisfied in relation to each of them.

(4)　A request—

(a)　may be in hard copy form or in electronic form,

(b)　must identify the poll or polls to which it relates,

(c)　must be authenticated by the person or persons making it, and

(d)　must be received by the company not later than one week after the date on which the poll is taken.

NOTES

Commencement: 1 October 2007.

Commencement (transitional provisions): Sch 3, para 39 to the Companies Act 2006 (Commencement No 3, Consequential Amendments, Transitional Provisions and Savings) Order 2007, SI 2007/2194 (at **[2.45]**) provides as follows—

"39　Additional requirements for quoted companies (ss 342 to 354)

(1)　Sections 342 to 354 of the Companies Act 2006 apply to polls taken at meetings of which notice was given on or after 1st October 2007.

(2)　Where notice of a meeting is given over more than one day, it is treated for the purposes of this paragraph as given on the first of those days.".

[1.343]
343　Appointment of independent assessor

(1)　Directors who are required under section 342 to obtain an independent report on a poll or polls must appoint a person they consider to be appropriate (an "independent assessor") to prepare a report for the company on it or them.

(2)　The appointment must be made within one week after the company being required to obtain the report.

(3)　The directors must not appoint a person who—

(a)　does not meet the independence requirement in section 344, or

(b)　has another role in relation to any poll on which he is to report (including, in particular, a role in connection with collecting or counting votes or with the appointment of proxies).

(4)　In the event of default in complying with this section, an offence is committed by every officer of the company who is in default.

(5)　A person guilty of an offence under this section is liable on summary conviction to a fine not exceeding level 5 on the standard scale.

(6)　If at the meeting no poll on which a report is required is taken—

(a)　the directors are not required to obtain a report from the independent assessor, and

(b)　his appointment ceases (but without prejudice to any right to be paid for work done before the appointment ceased).

NOTES

Commencement: 1 October 2007.

Commencement (transitional provisions): see the note to s 342 at **[1.342]**.

[1.344]

344 Independence requirement

(1) A person may not be appointed as an independent assessor—
   (a) if he is—
      (i) an officer or employee of the company, or
      (ii) a partner or employee of such a person, or a partnership of which such a person is a partner;
   (b) if he is—
      (i) an officer or employee of an associated undertaking of the company, or
      (ii) a partner or employee of such a person, or a partnership of which such a person is a partner;
   (c) if there exists between— (i) the person or an associate of his, and (ii) the company or an associated undertaking of the company, a connection of any such description as may be specified by regulations made by the Secretary of State.

(2) An auditor of the company is not regarded as an officer or employee of the company for this purpose.

(3) In this section—
   "associated undertaking" means—
      (a) a parent undertaking or subsidiary undertaking of the company, or
      (b) a subsidiary undertaking of a parent undertaking of the company; and
   "associate" has the meaning given by section 345.

(4) Regulations under this section are subject to negative resolution procedure.

NOTES

Commencement: 20 January 2007 (for the purpose of enabling the exercise of powers to make Orders or Regulations by statutory instrument); 1 October 2007 (otherwise).

Commencement (transitional provisions): see the note to s 342 at **[1.342]**.

[1.345]

345 Meaning of "associate"

(1) This section defines "associate" for the purposes of section 344 (independence requirement).

(2) In relation to an individual, "associate" means—
   (a) that individual's spouse or civil partner or minor child or step-child,
   (b) any body corporate of which that individual is a director, and
   (c) any employee or partner of that individual.

(3) In relation to a body corporate, "associate" means—
   (a) any body corporate of which that body is a director,
   (b) any body corporate in the same group as that body, and
   (c) any employee or partner of that body or of any body corporate in the same group.

(4) In relation to a partnership that is a legal person under the law by which it is governed, "associate" means—
   (a) any body corporate of which that partnership is a director,
   (b) any employee of or partner in that partnership, and
   (c) any person who is an associate of a partner in that partnership.

(5) In relation to a partnership that is not a legal person under the law by which it is governed, "associate" means any person who is an associate of any of the partners.

(6) In this section, in relation to a limited liability partnership, for "director" read "member".

NOTES

Commencement: 1 October 2007.

Commencement (transitional provisions): see the note to s 342 at **[1.342]**.

[1.346]

346 Effect of appointment of a partnership

(1) This section applies where a partnership that is not a legal person under the law by which it is governed is appointed as an independent assessor.

(2) Unless a contrary intention appears, the appointment is of the partnership as such and not of the partners.

(3) Where the partnership ceases, the appointment is to be treated as extending to—
   (a) any partnership that succeeds to the practice of that partnership, or
   (b) any other person who succeeds to that practice having previously carried it on in partnership.

(4) For the purposes of subsection (3)—
   (a) a partnership is regarded as succeeding to the practice of another partnership only if the members of the successor partnership are substantially the same as those of the former partnership, and
   (b) a partnership or other person is regarded as succeeding to the practice of a partnership only if it or he succeeds to the whole or substantially the whole of the business of the former partnership.

(5) Where the partnership ceases and the appointment is not treated under subsection (3) as extending to any partnership or other person, the appointment may with the consent of the company be treated as extending to a partnership, or other person, who succeeds to—
   (a) the business of the former partnership, or
   (b) such part of it as is agreed by the company is to be treated as comprising the appointment.

NOTES
Commencement: 1 October 2007.
Commencement (transitional provisions): see the note to s 342 at **[1.342]**.

[1.347]
347 The independent assessor's report
(1) The report of the independent assessor must state his opinion whether—
   (a) the procedures adopted in connection with the poll or polls were adequate;
   (b) the votes cast (including proxy votes) were fairly and accurately recorded and counted;
   (c) the validity of members' appointments of proxies was fairly assessed;
   (d) the notice of the meeting complied with section 325 (notice of meeting to contain statement of rights to appoint proxy);
   (e) section 326 (company-sponsored invitations to appoint proxies) was complied with in relation to the meeting.
(2) The report must give his reasons for the opinions stated.
(3) If he is unable to form an opinion on any of those matters, the report must record that fact and state the reasons for it.
(4) The report must state the name of the independent assessor.

NOTES
Commencement: 1 October 2007.
Commencement (transitional provisions): see the note to s 342 at **[1.342]**.

[1.348]
348 Rights of independent assessor: right to attend meeting etc
(1) Where an independent assessor has been appointed to report on a poll, he is entitled to attend—
   (a) the meeting at which the poll may be taken, and
   (b) any subsequent proceedings in connection with the poll.
(2) He is also entitled to be provided by the company with a copy of—
   (a) the notice of the meeting, and
   (b) any other communication provided by the company in connection with the meeting to persons who have a right to vote on the matter to which the poll relates.
(3) The rights conferred by this section are only to be exercised to the extent that the independent assessor considers necessary for the preparation of his report.
(4) If the independent assessor is a firm, the right under subsection (1) to attend the meeting and any subsequent proceedings in connection with the poll is exercisable by an individual authorised by the firm in writing to act as its representative for that purpose.

NOTES
Commencement: 1 October 2007.
Commencement (transitional provisions): see the note to s 342 at **[1.342]**.

[1.349]
349 Rights of independent assessor: right to information
(1) The independent assessor is entitled to access to the company's records relating to—
   (a) any poll on which he is to report;
   (b) the meeting at which the poll or polls may be, or were, taken.
(2) The independent assessor may require anyone who at any material time was—
   (a) a director or secretary of the company,
   (b) an employee of the company,
   (c) a person holding or accountable for any of the company's records,
   (d) a member of the company, or
   (e) an agent of the company,
to provide him with information or explanations for the purpose of preparing his report.
(3) For this purpose "agent" includes the company's bankers, solicitors and auditor.
(4) A statement made by a person in response to a requirement under this section may not be used in evidence against him in criminal proceedings except proceedings for an offence under section 350 (offences relating to provision of information).
(5) A person is not required by this section to disclose information in respect of which a claim to legal professional privilege (in Scotland, to confidentiality of communications) could be maintained in legal proceedings.

NOTES
Commencement: 1 October 2007.
Commencement (transitional provisions): see the note to s 342 at **[1.342]**.

[1.350]
350 Offences relating to provision of information
(1) A person who fails to comply with a requirement under section 349 without delay commits an offence unless it was not reasonably practicable for him to provide the required information or explanation.

(2) A person guilty of an offence under subsection (1) is liable on summary conviction to a fine not exceeding level 3 on the standard scale.

(3) A person commits an offence who knowingly or recklessly makes to an independent assessor a statement (oral or written) that—
  (a) conveys or purports to convey any information or explanations which the independent assessor requires, or is entitled to require, under section 349, and
  (b) is misleading, false or deceptive in a material particular.

(4) A person guilty of an offence under subsection (3) is liable—
  (a) on conviction on indictment, to imprisonment for a term not exceeding two years or a fine (or both);
  (b) on summary conviction—
    (i) in England and Wales, to imprisonment for a term not exceeding twelve months or to a fine not exceeding the statutory maximum (or both);
    (ii) in Scotland or Northern Ireland, to imprisonment for a term not exceeding six months, or to a fine not exceeding the statutory maximum (or both).

(5) Nothing in this section affects any right of an independent assessor to apply for an injunction (in Scotland, an interdict or an order for specific performance) to enforce any of his rights under section 348 or 349.

NOTES
Commencement: 1 October 2007.
Commencement (transitional provisions): see the note to s 342 at **[1.342]**.

[1.351]
351 Information to be made available on website
(1) Where an independent assessor has been appointed to report on a poll, the company must ensure that the following information is made available on a website—
  (a) the fact of his appointment,
  (b) his identity,
  (c) the text of the resolution or, as the case may be, a description of the subject matter of the poll to which his appointment relates, and
  (d) a copy of a report by him which complies with section 347.

(2) The provisions of section 353 (requirements as to website availability) apply.

(3) In the event of default in complying with this section (or with the requirements of section 353 as it applies for the purposes of this section), an offence is committed by every officer of the company who is in default.

(4) A person guilty of an offence under subsection (3) is liable on summary conviction to a fine not exceeding level 3 on the standard scale.

(5) Failure to comply with this section (or the requirements of section 353) does not affect the validity of—
  (a) the poll, or
  (b) the resolution or other business (if passed or agreed to) to which the poll relates.

NOTES
Commencement: 1 October 2007.
Commencement (transitional provisions): see the note to s 342 at **[1.342]**.

Supplementary

[1.352]
352 Application of provisions to class meetings
[(1) The provisions of section 341 (results of poll to be made available on website) apply (with any necessary modifications) in relation to a meeting of holders of a class of shares of a quoted company or traded company in connection with the variation of the rights attached to such shares as they apply in relation to a general meeting of the company.

(1A) The provisions of section 342 to 351 (independent report on poll) apply (with any necessary modifications) in relation to a meeting of holders of a class of shares of a quoted company in connection with the variation of the rights attached to such shares as they apply in relation to a general meeting of the company.]

(2) For the purposes of this section—

(a)   any amendment of a provision contained in a company's articles for the variation of the rights attached to a class of shares, or the insertion of any such provision into the articles, is itself to be treated as a variation of those rights, and

(b)   references to the variation of rights attached to a class of shares include references to their abrogation.

NOTES

Commencement: 1 October 2007.

Commencement (transitional provisions): see the note to s 342 at **[1.342]**.

Sub-ss (1), (1A): substituted, for the original sub-s (1), by the Companies (Shareholders' Rights) Regulations 2009, SI 2009/1632, reg 19(4), as from 3 August 2009, in relation to meetings of which notice is given, or first given, on or after that date.

[1.353]

353   Requirements as to website availability

(1)   The following provisions apply for the purposes of—

section 341 (results of poll to be made available on website), and

section 351 (report of independent observer to be made available on website).

(2)   The information must be made available on a website that—

(a)   is maintained by or on behalf of the company, and

(b)   identifies the company in question.

(3)   Access to the information on the website, and the ability to obtain a hard copy of the information from the website, must not be conditional on the payment of a fee or otherwise restricted.

(4)   The information—

(a)   must be made available as soon as reasonably practicable, and

(b)   must be kept available throughout the period of two years beginning with the date on which it is first made available on a website in accordance with this section.

(5)   A failure to make information available on a website throughout the period specified in subsection (4)(b) is disregarded if—

(a)   the information is made available on the website for part of that period, and

(b)   the failure is wholly attributable to circumstances that it would not be reasonable to have expected the company to prevent or avoid.

NOTES

Commencement: 1 October 2007.

Commencement (transitional provisions): see the note to s 342 at **[1.342]**.

[1.354]

354   Power to limit or extend the types of company to which provisions of this Chapter apply

(1)   The Secretary of State may by regulations—

(a)   limit the types of company to which some or all of the provisions of this Chapter apply, or

(b)   extend some or all of the provisions of this Chapter to additional types of company.

(2)   Regulations under this section extending the application of any provision of this Chapter are subject to affirmative resolution procedure.

(3)   Any other regulations under this section are subject to negative resolution procedure.

(4)   Regulations under this section may—

(a)   amend the provisions of this Chapter (apart from this section);

(b)   repeal and re-enact provisions of this Chapter with modifications of form or arrangement, whether or not they are modified in substance;

(c)   contain such consequential, incidental and supplementary provisions (including provisions amending, repealing or revoking enactments) as the Secretary of State thinks fit.

NOTES

Commencement: 20 January 2007 (for the purpose of enabling the exercise of powers to make Orders or Regulations by statutory instrument); 1 October 2007 (otherwise).

Commencement (transitional provisions): see the note to s 342 at **[1.342]**.

CHAPTER 6

RECORDS OF RESOLUTIONS AND MEETINGS

[1.355]

355   Records of resolutions and meetings etc

(1)   Every company must keep records comprising—

(a)   copies of all resolutions of members passed otherwise than at general meetings,

(b)   minutes of all proceedings of general meetings, and

(c)   details provided to the company in accordance with section 357 (decisions of sole member).

(2)   The records must be kept for at least ten years from the date of the resolution, meeting or decision (as appropriate).

(3) If a company fails to comply with this section, an offence is committed by every officer of the company who is in default.

(4) A person guilty of an offence under this section is liable on summary conviction to a fine not exceeding level 3 on the standard scale and, for continued contravention, a daily default fine not exceeding one-tenth of level 3 on the standard scale.

NOTES

Commencement: 1 October 2007.

Commencement (transitional provisions): Sch 3, para 40 to the Companies Act 2006 (Commencement No 3, Consequential Amendments, Transitional Provisions and Savings) Order 2007, SI 2007/2194 (at **[2.45]**) provides that ss 355–359 of this Act apply to resolutions passed, meetings held or decisions taken on or after 1 October 2007 (and that ss 382, 382A, 382B and 383 of the 1985 Act continue to apply to resolutions passed, meetings held or decisions taken before that date).

[1.356]
356 Records as evidence of resolutions etc
(1) This section applies to the records kept in accordance with section 355.
(2) The record of a resolution passed otherwise than at a general meeting, if purporting to be signed by a director of the company or by the company secretary, is evidence (in Scotland, sufficient evidence) of the passing of the resolution.
(3) Where there is a record of a written resolution of a private company, the requirements of this Act with respect to the passing of the resolution are deemed to be complied with unless the contrary is proved.
(4) The minutes of proceedings of a general meeting, if purporting to be signed by the chairman of that meeting or by the chairman of the next general meeting, are evidence (in Scotland, sufficient evidence) of the proceedings at the meeting.
(5) Where there is a record of proceedings of a general meeting of a company, then, until the contrary is proved—
  (a) the meeting is deemed duly held and convened,
  (b) all proceedings at the meeting are deemed to have duly taken place, and
  (c) all appointments at the meeting are deemed valid.

NOTES
Commencement: 1 October 2007.
Commencement (transitional provisions): see the note to s 355 at **[1.355]**.

[1.357]
357 Records of decisions by sole member
(1) This section applies to a company limited by shares or by guarantee that has only one member.
(2) Where the member takes any decision that—
  (a) may be taken by the company in general meeting, and
  (b) has effect as if agreed by the company in general meeting,
he must (unless that decision is taken by way of a written resolution) provide the company with details of that decision.
(3) If a person fails to comply with this section he commits an offence.
(4) A person guilty of an offence under this section is liable on summary conviction to a fine not exceeding level 2 on the standard scale.
(5) Failure to comply with this section does not affect the validity of any decision referred to in subsection (2).

NOTES
Commencement: 1 October 2007.
Commencement (transitional provisions): see the note to s 355 at **[1.355]**.

[1.358]
358 Inspection of records of resolutions and meetings
(1) The records referred to in section 355 (records of resolutions etc) relating to the previous ten years must be kept available for inspection—
  (a) at the company's registered office, or
  (b) at a place specified in regulations under section 1136.
(2) The company must give notice to the registrar—
  (a) of the place at which the records are kept available for inspection, and
  (b) of any change in that place,
unless they have at all times been kept at the company's registered office.
(3) The records must be open to the inspection of any member of the company without charge.
(4) Any member may require a copy of any of the records on payment of such fee as may be prescribed.
(5) If default is made for 14 days in complying with subsection (2) or an inspection required under subsection (3) is refused, or a copy requested under subsection (4) is not sent, an offence is committed by every officer of the company who is in default.

(6)   A person guilty of an offence under this section is liable on summary conviction to a fine not exceeding level 3 on the standard scale and, for continued contravention, a daily default fine not exceeding one-tenth of level 3 on the standard scale.

(7)   In a case in which an inspection required under subsection (3) is refused or a copy requested under subsection (4) is not sent, the court may by order compel an immediate inspection of the records or direct that the copies required be sent to the persons who requested them.

NOTES

Commencement: 20 January 2007 (for the purpose of enabling the exercise of powers to make Orders or Regulations by statutory instrument); 1 October 2007 (otherwise).

Commencement (transitional provisions): see the note to s 355 at **[1.355]**.

Regulations: the Companies (Fees for Inspection and Copying of Company Records) Regulations 2007, SI 2007/2612 at **[4.12]**.

[1.359]
359   Records of resolutions and meetings of class of members
The provisions of this Chapter apply (with necessary modifications) in relation to resolutions and meetings of—

     (a)   holders of a class of shares, and

     (b)   in the case of a company without a share capital, a class of members,

as they apply in relation to resolutions of members generally and to general meetings.

NOTES

Commencement: 1 October 2007.

Commencement (transitional provisions): see the note to s 355 at **[1.355]**.

CHAPTER 7
SUPPLEMENTARY PROVISIONS

[1.360]
360   Computation of periods of notice etc: clear day rule
(1)   This section applies for the purposes of the following provisions of this Part—

     section 307(1) and (2) (notice required of general meeting),

     [section 307A(1), (4), (5) and (7)(b) (notice required of general meeting of traded company),]

     section 312(1) and (3) (resolution requiring special notice),

     section 314(4)(d) (request to circulate members' statement),

     section 316(2)(b) (expenses of circulating statement to be deposited or tendered before meeting),

     [section 337(3) (contents of notice of AGM of traded company),]

     section 338(4)(d)(i) (request to circulate member's resolution at AGM of public company), . . .

     [section 338A(5) (request to include matter in the business to be dealt with at AGM of traded company),]

     section 340(2)(b)(i) (expenses of circulating statement to be deposited or tendered before meeting),

     [section 340B(2)(b) (traded companies: duty to circulate members' matters for AGM)].

(2)   Any reference in those provisions to a period of notice, or to a period before a meeting by which a request must be received or sum deposited or tendered, is to a period of the specified length excluding—

     (a)   the day of the meeting, and

     (b)   the day on which the notice is given, the request received or the sum deposited or tendered.

NOTES

Commencement: 1 October 2007.

Sub-s (1): words in square brackets inserted, and word omitted repealed, by the Companies (Shareholders' Rights) Regulations 2009, SI 2009/1632, regs 9(3), 16(6), 17(4), 18(2), as from 3 August 2009, in relation to meetings of which notice is given, or first given, on or after that date.

[1.360A]
[360A   Electronic meetings and voting
(1)   Nothing in this Part is to be taken to preclude the holding and conducting of a meeting in such a way that persons who are not present together at the same place may by electronic means attend and speak and vote at it.

(2)   In the case of a traded company the use of electronic means for the purpose of enabling members to participate in a general meeting may be made subject only to such requirements and restrictions as are—

     (a)   necessary to ensure the identification of those taking part and the security of the electronic communication, and

     (b)   proportionate to the achievement of those objectives.

(3) Nothing in subsection (2) affects any power of a company to require reasonable evidence of the entitlement of any person who is not a member to participate in the meeting.]

NOTES

Commencement: 3 August 2009.

Inserted by the Companies (Shareholders' Rights) Regulations 2009, SI 2009/1632, reg 8, as from 3 August 2009, in relation to meetings of which notice is given, or first given, on or after that date.

[1.360B]
[360B Traded companies: requirements for participating in and voting at general meetings
(1) Any provision of a traded company's articles is void in so far as it would have the effect of—
(a) imposing a restriction on a right of a member to participate in and vote at a general meeting of the company unless the member's shares have (after having been acquired by the member and before the meeting) been deposited with, or transferred to, or registered in the name of another person, or
(b) imposing a restriction on the right of a member to transfer shares in the company during the period of 48 hours before the time for the holding of a general meeting of the company if that right would not otherwise be subject to that restriction.
(2) A traded company must determine the right to vote at a general meeting of the company by reference to the register of members as at a time (determined by the company) that is not more than 48 hours before the time for the holding of the meeting.
(3) In calculating the period mentioned in subsection (1)(b) or (2), no account is to be taken of any part of a day that is not a working day.
(4) Nothing in this section affects—
(a) the operation of—
(i) Part 22 of this Act (information about interests in a company's shares),
(ii) Part 15 of the Companies Act 1985 (orders imposing restrictions on shares), or
(iii) any provision in a company's articles relating to the application of any provision of either of those Parts; or
(b) the validity of articles prescribed, or to the same effect as articles prescribed, under section 19 of this Act (power of Secretary of State to prescribe model articles).]

NOTES

Commencement: 3 August 2009.

Inserted by the Companies (Shareholders' Rights) Regulations 2009, SI 2009/1632, reg 20, as from 3 August 2009, in relation to meetings of which notice is given, or first given, on or after that date.

[1.360C]
[360C Meaning of "traded company"
In this Part, "traded company" means a company any shares of which—
(a) carry rights to vote at general meetings, and
(b) are admitted to trading on a regulated market in an EEA State by or with the consent of the company.]

NOTES

Commencement: 3 August 2009.

Inserted by the Companies (Shareholders' Rights) Regulations 2009, SI 2009/1632, reg 21(1), as from 3 August 2009, in relation to meetings of which notice is given, or first given, on or after that date.

[1.361]
361 Meaning of "quoted company"
In this Part "quoted company" has the same meaning as in Part 15 of this Act.

NOTES

Commencement: 1 October 2007.

PART 14
CONTROL OF POLITICAL DONATIONS AND EXPENDITURE
Introductory

[1.362]
362 Introductory
This Part has effect for controlling—
(a) political donations made by companies to political parties, to other political organisations and to independent election candidates, and
(b) political expenditure incurred by companies.

NOTES

Commencement: 1 October 2007 (in relation to Great Britain (subject to the exception noted below)); 1 November 2007 (in relation to Northern Ireland (subject to the exception noted below)); 1 October 2008 (otherwise).

Commencement (transitional provisions): the Companies Act 2006 (Commencement No 3, Consequential Amendments,

Transitional Provisions and Savings) Order 2007, SI 2007/2194, Sch 3, paras 41, 42 (at **[2.45]**) provide as follows—

"Political donations and expenditure (ss 362 to 379)

41.—(1)   Sections 362 to 379 of the Companies Act 2006 (political donations and expenditure) apply to donations made or expenditure incurred on or after 1st October 2007.

Section 379(2) of that Act applies as to the time when a donation is regarded as made or expenditure as incurred, including where it is made or incurred in pursuance of a contract entered into before that date.

(2)   Part 10A of the 1985 Act continues to apply to donations or expenditure in relation to which the relevant time, as defined in section 347A(10) of that Act, is before that date.

(3)   The repeal of that Part does not affect paragraph 3(4) of Schedule 7 to the 1985 Act (matters to be dealt with in directors' report: expressions to have same meaning as in Part 10A).

42.   An approval resolution passed in accordance with section 347C of the 1985 Act before 1st October 2007 is treated as complying with the requirements of section 367 of the Companies Act 2006 (form of authorising resolution) although it does not comply with the requirements of that section as to the heads under which donations and expenditure are to be stated.".

Commencement (note): the Companies Act 2006 (Commencement No 3, Consequential Amendments, Transitional Provisions and Savings) Order 2007, SI 2007/2194, arts 2(2), 3(1) provide that this section shall come into force on 1 October 2007 (in Great Britain) and 1 November 2007 (in Northern Ireland) with the exception of the provisions specified in art 5 of that Order (which relate to independent election candidates and which shall come into force on 1 October 2008). Article 5 provides that in this section, the words "and to independent election candidates" in para (a) shall come into force on 1 October 2008 (see that Order at **[2.31]** et seq).

Donations and expenditure to which this Part applies

[1.363]

363   Political parties, organisations etc to which this Part applies

(1)   This Part applies to a political party if—

   (a)   it is registered under Part 2 of the Political Parties, Elections and Referendums Act 2000 (c 41), or

   (b)   it carries on, or proposes to carry on, activities for the purposes of or in connection with the participation of the party in any election or elections to public office held in a member State other than the United Kingdom.

(2)   This Part applies to an organisation (a "political organisation") if it carries on, or proposes to carry on, activities that are capable of being reasonably regarded as intended—

   (a)   to affect public support for a political party to which, or an independent election candidate to whom, this Part applies, or

   (b)   to influence voters in relation to any national or regional referendum held under the law of the United Kingdom or another member State.

(3)   This Part applies to an independent election candidate at any election to public office held in the United Kingdom or another member State.

(4)   Any reference in the following provisions of this Part to a political party, political organisation or independent election candidate, or to political expenditure, is to a party, organisation, independent candidate or expenditure to which this Part applies.

NOTES

Commencement: 1 October 2007 (in relation to Great Britain (subject to the exception noted below)); 1 November 2007 (in relation to Northern Ireland (subject to the exception noted below)); 1 October 2008 (otherwise).

Commencement (transitional provisions): see the note to s 362 at **[1.362]**.

Commencement (note): the Companies Act 2006 (Commencement No 3, Consequential Amendments, Transitional Provisions and Savings) Order 2007, SI 2007/2194, arts 2(2), 3(1) provide that this section shall come into force on 1 October 2007 (in Great Britain) and 1 November 2007 (in Northern Ireland) with the exception of the provisions specified in art 5 of that Order (which relate to independent election candidates and which shall come into force on 1 October 2008). Article 5 provides that in this section, (i) the words "or an independent election candidate to whom" in sub-s (2)(a); (ii) all of sub-s (3); and (iii) the words "or independent election candidate" and "independent candidate" in sub-s (4) shall come into force on 1 October 2008 (see that Order at **[2.31]** et seq).

[1.364]

364   Meaning of "political donation"

(1)   The following provisions have effect for the purposes of this Part as regards the meaning of "political donation".

(2)   In relation to a political party or other political organisation—

   (a)   "political donation" means anything that in accordance with sections 50 to 52 of the Political Parties, Elections and Referendums Act 2000—

      (i)   constitutes a donation for the purposes of Chapter 1 of Part 4 of that Act (control of donations to registered parties), or

      (ii)   would constitute such a donation reading references in those sections to a registered party as references to any political party or other political organisation,

   and

   (b)   section 53 of that Act applies, in the same way, for the purpose of determining the value of a donation.

(3)   In relation to an independent election candidate—

   (a)   "political donation" means anything that, in accordance with sections 50 to 52 of that Act, would constitute a donation for the purposes of Chapter 1 of Part 4 of that Act (control of donations to registered parties) reading references in those sections to a registered party as references to the independent election candidate, and

   (b)   section 53 of that Act applies, in the same way, for the purpose of determining the value of a donation.

(4)   For the purposes of this section, sections 50 and 53 of the Political Parties, Elections and Referendums Act 2000 (c 41) (definition of "donation" and value of donations) shall be treated as if the amendments to those sections made by the Electoral Administration Act 2006 (which remove from the definition of "donation" loans made otherwise than on commercial terms) had not been made.

NOTES

Commencement: 1 October 2007 (in relation to Great Britain (subject to the exception noted below)); 1 November 2007 (in relation to Northern Ireland (subject to the exception noted below)); 1 October 2008 (otherwise).

Commencement (transitional provisions): see the note to s 362 at **[1.362]**.

Commencement (note): the Companies Act 2006 (Commencement No 3, Consequential Amendments, Transitional Provisions and Savings) Order 2007, SI 2007/2194, arts 2(2), 3(1) provide that this section shall come into force on 1 October 2007 (in Great Britain) and 1 November 2007 (in Northern Ireland) with the exception of the provisions specified in art 5 of that Order (which relate to independent election candidates and which shall come into force on 1 October 2008). Article 5 provides that in this section, sub-s (3) shall come into force on 1 October 2008 (see that Order at **[2.31]** et seq).

[1.365]
365 Meaning of "political expenditure"

(1)   In this Part "political expenditure", in relation to a company, means expenditure incurred by the company on—

   (a)   the preparation, publication or dissemination of advertising or other promotional or publicity material—

      (i)   of whatever nature, and

      (ii)   however published or otherwise disseminated,

      that, at the time of publication or dissemination, is capable of being reasonably regarded as intended to affect public support for a political party or other political organisation, or an independent election candidate, or

   (b)   activities on the part of the company that are capable of being reasonably regarded as intended—

      (i)   to affect public support for a political party or other political organisation, or an independent election candidate, or

      (ii)   to influence voters in relation to any national or regional referendum held under the law of a member State.

(2)   For the purposes of this Part a political donation does not count as political expenditure.

NOTES

Commencement: 1 October 2007 (in relation to Great Britain (subject to the exception noted below)); 1 November 2007 (in relation to Northern Ireland (subject to the exception noted below)); 1 October 2008 (otherwise).

Commencement (transitional provisions): see the note to s 362 at **[1.362]**.

Commencement (note): the Companies Act 2006 (Commencement No 3, Consequential Amendments, Transitional Provisions and Savings) Order 2007, SI 2007/2194, arts 2(2), 3(1) provide that this section shall come into force on 1 October 2007 (in Great Britain) and 1 November 2007 (in Northern Ireland) with the exception of the provisions specified in art 5 of that Order (which relate to independent election candidates and which shall come into force on 1 October 2008). Article 5 provides that in this section, the words "or an independent election candidate" in sub-s (1)(a), (b)(i) shall come into force on 1 October 2008 (see that Order at **[2.31]** et seq).

Authorisation required for donations or expenditure

[1.366]
366 Authorisation required for donations or expenditure

(1)   A company must not—

   (a)   make a political donation to a political party or other political organisation, or to an independent election candidate, or

   (b)   incur any political expenditure,

unless the donation or expenditure is authorised in accordance with the following provisions.

(2)   The donation or expenditure must be authorised—

   (a)   in the case of a company that is not a subsidiary of another company, by a resolution of the members of the company;

   (b)   in the case of a company that is a subsidiary of another company by—

      (i)   a resolution of the members of the company, and

      (ii)   a resolution of the members of any relevant holding company.

(3)   No resolution is required on the part of a company that is a wholly-owned subsidiary of a UK-registered company.

(4)   For the purposes of subsection (2)(b)(ii) a "relevant holding company" means a company that, at the time the donation was made or the expenditure was incurred—

(a)   was a holding company of the company by which the donation was made or the expenditure was incurred,

(b)   was a UK-registered company, and

(c)   was not a subsidiary of another UK-registered company.

(5)   The resolution or resolutions required by this section—

(a)   must comply with section 367 (form of authorising resolution), and

(b)   must be passed before the donation is made or the expenditure incurred.

(6)   Nothing in this section enables a company to be authorised to do anything that it could not lawfully do apart from this section.

NOTES

Commencement: 1 October 2007 (in relation to Great Britain (subject to the exception noted below)); 1 November 2007 (in relation to Northern Ireland (subject to the exception noted below)); 1 October 2008 (otherwise).

Commencement (transitional provisions): see the note to s 362 at **[1.362]**.

Commencement (note): the Companies Act 2006 (Commencement No 3, Consequential Amendments, Transitional Provisions and Savings) Order 2007, SI 2007/2194, arts 2(2), 3(1) provide that this section shall come into force on 1 October 2007 (in Great Britain) and 1 November 2007 (in Northern Ireland) with the exception of the provisions specified in art 5 of that Order (which relate to independent election candidates and which shall come into force on 1 October 2008). Article 5 provides that in this section, the words "or to an independent election candidate" in sub-s (1)(a) shall come into force on 1 October 2008 (see that Order at **[2.31]** et seq).

[1.367]
367   Form of authorising resolution

(1)   A resolution conferring authorisation for the purposes of this Part may relate to—

(a)   the company passing the resolution,

(b)   one or more subsidiaries of that company, or

(c)   the company passing the resolution and one or more subsidiaries of that company.

(2)   A resolution may be expressed to relate to all companies that are subsidiaries of the company passing the resolution—

(a)   at the time the resolution is passed, or

(b)   at any time during the period for which the resolution has effect,

without identifying them individually.

(3)   The resolution may authorise donations or expenditure under one or more of the following heads—

(a)   donations to political parties or independent election candidates;

(b)   donations to political organisations other than political parties;

(c)   political expenditure.

(4)   The resolution must specify a head or heads—

(a)   in the case of a resolution under subsection (2), for all of the companies to which it relates taken together;

(b)   in the case of any other resolution, for each company to which it relates.

(5)   The resolution must be expressed in general terms conforming with [subsection (3)] and must not purport to authorise particular donations or expenditure.

(6)   For each of the specified heads the resolution must authorise donations or, as the case may be, expenditure up to a specified amount in the period for which the resolution has effect (see section 368).

(7)   The resolution must specify such amounts—

(a)   in the case of a resolution under subsection (2), for all of the companies to which it relates taken together;

(b)   in the case of any other resolution, for each company to which it relates.

NOTES

Commencement: 1 October 2007 (in relation to Great Britain (subject to the exception noted below)); 1 November 2007 (in relation to Northern Ireland (subject to the exception noted below)); 1 October 2008 (otherwise).

Commencement (transitional provisions): see the note to s 362 at **[1.362]**.

Commencement (note): the Companies Act 2006 (Commencement No 3, Consequential Amendments, Transitional Provisions and Savings) Order 2007, SI 2007/2194, arts 2(2), 3(1) provide that this section shall come into force on 1 October 2007 (in Great Britain) and 1 November 2007 (in Northern Ireland) with the exception of the provisions specified in art 5 of that Order (which relate to independent election candidates and which shall come into force on 1 October 2008). Article 5 provides that in this section, the words "or independent election candidates" in sub-s (3)(a) shall come into force on 1 October 2008 (see that Order at **[2.31]** et seq).

Sub-s (5): words in square brackets substituted by the Companies Act 2006 (Consequential Amendments, Transitional Provisions and Savings) Order 2009, SI 2009/1941, art 2(1), Sch 1, para 260(1), (2), as from 1 October 2009.

[1.368]
368   Period for which resolution has effect

(1)   A resolution conferring authorisation for the purposes of this Part has effect for a period of four years beginning with the date on which it is passed unless the directors determine, or the articles require, that it is to have effect for a shorter period beginning with that date.

(2)   The power of the directors to make a determination under this section is subject to any provision of the articles that operates to prevent them from doing so.

NOTES

Commencement: 1 October 2007 (in relation to Great Britain); 1 November 2007 (in relation to Northern Ireland).
Commencement (transitional provisions): see the note to s 362 at **[1.362]**.

Remedies in case of unauthorised donations or expenditure

[1.369]
369 Liability of directors in case of unauthorised donation or expenditure

(1) This section applies where a company has made a political donation or incurred political expenditure without the authorisation required by this Part.

(2) The directors in default are jointly and severally liable—
  (a) to make good to the company the amount of the unauthorised donation or expenditure, with interest, and
  (b) to compensate the company for any loss or damage sustained by it as a result of the unauthorised donation or expenditure having been made.

(3) The directors in default are—
  (a) those who, at the time the unauthorised donation was made or the unauthorised expenditure was incurred, were directors of the company by which the donation was made or the expenditure was incurred, and
  (b) where—
    (i)   that company was a subsidiary of a relevant holding company, and
    (ii) the directors of the relevant holding company failed to take all reasonable steps to prevent the donation being made or the expenditure being incurred,
  the directors of the relevant holding company.

(4) For the purposes of subsection (3)(b) a "relevant holding company" means a company that, at the time the donation was made or the expenditure was incurred—
  (a) was a holding company of the company by which the donation was made or the expenditure was incurred,
  (b) was a UK-registered company, and
  (c) was not a subsidiary of another UK-registered company.

(5) The interest referred to in subsection (2)(a) is interest on the amount of the unauthorised donation or expenditure, so far as not made good to the company—
  (a) in respect of the period beginning with the date when the donation was made or the expenditure was incurred, and
  (b) at such rate as the Secretary of State may prescribe by regulations.

Section 379(2) (construction of references to date when donation made or expenditure incurred) does not apply for the purposes of this subsection.

(6) Where only part of a donation or expenditure was unauthorised, this section applies only to so much of it as was unauthorised.

NOTES

Commencement: 20 January 2007 (for the purpose of enabling the exercise of powers to make Orders or Regulations by statutory instrument); 1 October 2007 (otherwise, in relation to Great Britain); 1 November 2007 (otherwise, in relation to Northern Ireland).
Commencement (transitional provisions): see the note to s 362 at **[1.362]**.
Regulations: the Companies (Interest Rate for Unauthorised Political Donation or Expenditure) Regulations 2007, SI 2007/2242 at **[4.11]**.

[1.370]
370 Enforcement of directors' liabilities by shareholder action

(1) Any liability of a director under section 369 is enforceable—
  (a) in the case of a liability of a director of a company to that company, by proceedings brought under this section in the name of the company by an authorised group of its members;
  (b) in the case of a liability of a director of a holding company to a subsidiary, by proceedings brought under this section in the name of the subsidiary by—
    (i)   an authorised group of members of the subsidiary, or
    (ii) an authorised group of members of the holding company.

(2) This is in addition to the right of the company to which the liability is owed to bring proceedings itself to enforce the liability.

(3) An "authorised group" of members of a company means—
  (a) the holders of not less than 5% in nominal value of the company's issued share capital,
  (b) if the company is not limited by shares, not less than 5% of its members, or
  (c) not less than 50 of the company's members.

(4) The right to bring proceedings under this section is subject to the provisions of section 371.

(5) Nothing in this section affects any right of a member of a company to bring or continue proceedings under Part 11 (derivative claims or proceedings).

NOTES
Commencement: 1 October 2007 (in relation to Great Britain); 1 November 2007 (in relation to Northern Ireland).
Commencement (transitional provisions): see the note to s 362 at **[1.362]**.

[1.371]
371　Enforcement of directors' liabilities by shareholder action: supplementary

(1)　A group of members may not bring proceedings under section 370 in the name of a company unless—

  (a)　the group has given written notice to the company stating—

    (i)　the cause of action and a summary of the facts on which the proceedings are to be based,

    (ii)　the names and addresses of the members comprising the group, and

    (iii)　the grounds on which it is alleged that those members constitute an authorised group; and

  (b)　not less than 28 days have elapsed between the date of the giving of the notice to the company and the bringing of the proceedings.

(2)　Where such a notice is given to a company, any director of the company may apply to the court within the period of 28 days beginning with the date of the giving of the notice for an order directing that the proposed proceedings shall not be brought, on one or more of the following grounds—

  (a)　that the unauthorised amount has been made good to the company;

  (b)　that proceedings to enforce the liability have been brought, and are being pursued with due diligence, by the company;

  (c)　that the members proposing to bring proceedings under this section do not constitute an authorised group.

(3)　Where an application is made on the ground mentioned in subsection (2)(b), the court may as an alternative to directing that the proposed proceedings under section 370 are not to be brought, direct—

  (a)　that such proceedings may be brought on such terms and conditions as the court thinks fit, and

  (b)　that the proceedings brought by the company—

    (i)　shall be discontinued, or

    (ii)　may be continued on such terms and conditions as the court thinks fit.

(4)　The members by whom proceedings are brought under section 370 owe to the company in whose name they are brought the same duties in relation to the proceedings as would be owed by the company's directors if the proceedings were being brought by the company.

But proceedings to enforce any such duty may be brought by the company only with the permission of the court.

(5)　Proceedings brought under section 370 may not be discontinued or settled by the group except with the permission of the court, which may be given on such terms as the court thinks fit.

NOTES
Commencement: 1 October 2007 (in relation to Great Britain); 1 November 2007 (in relation to Northern Ireland).
Commencement (transitional provisions): see the note to s 362 at **[1.362]**.

[1.372]
372　Costs of shareholder action

(1)　This section applies in relation to proceedings brought under section 370 in the name of a company ("the company") by an authorised group ("the group").

(2)　The group may apply to the court for an order directing the company to indemnify the group in respect of costs incurred or to be incurred by the group in connection with the proceedings.

The court may make such an order on such terms as it thinks fit.

(3)　The group is not entitled to be paid any such costs out of the assets of the company except by virtue of such an order.

(4)　If no such order has been made with respect to the proceedings, then—

  (a)　if the company is awarded costs in connection with the proceedings, or it is agreed that costs incurred by the company in connection with the proceedings should be paid by any defendant, the costs shall be paid to the group; and

  (b)　if any defendant is awarded costs in connection with the proceedings, or it is agreed that any defendant should be paid costs incurred by him in connection with the proceedings, the costs shall be paid by the group.

(5)　In the application of this section to Scotland for "costs" read "expenses" and for "defendant" read "defender".

NOTES
Commencement: 1 October 2007 (in relation to Great Britain); 1 November 2007 (in relation to Northern Ireland).
Commencement (transitional provisions): see the note to s 362 at **[1.362]**.

[1.373]

373 Information for purposes of shareholder action

(1) Where proceedings have been brought under section 370 in the name of a company by an authorised group, the group is entitled to require the company to provide it with all information relating to the subject matter of the proceedings that is in the company's possession or under its control or which is reasonably obtainable by it.

(2) If the company, having been required by the group to do so, refuses to provide the group with all or any of that information, the court may, on an application made by the group, make an order directing—

    (a)   the company, and

    (b)   any of its officers or employees specified in the application,

to provide the group with the information in question in such form and by such means as the court may direct.

NOTES

Commencement: 1 October 2007 (in relation to Great Britain); 1 November 2007 (in relation to Northern Ireland).
Commencement (transitional provisions): see the note to s 362 at **[1.362]**.

Exemptions

[1.374]

374 Trade unions

(1) A donation to a trade union, other than a contribution to the union's political fund, is not a political donation for the purposes of this Part.

(2) A trade union is not a political organisation for the purposes of section 365 (meaning of "political expenditure").

(3) In this section—

"trade union" has the meaning given by section 1 of Trade Union and Labour Relations (Consolidation) Act 1992 (c 52) or Article 3 of the Industrial Relations (Northern Ireland) Order 1992 (SI 1992/807 (NI 5));

"political fund" means the fund from which payments by a trade union in the furtherance of political objects are required to be made by virtue of section 82(1)(a) of that Act or Article 57(2)(a) of that Order.

NOTES

Commencement: 1 October 2007 (in relation to Great Britain); 1 November 2007 (in relation to Northern Ireland).
Commencement (transitional provisions): see the note to s 362 at **[1.362]**.

[1.375]

375 Subscription for membership of trade association

(1) A subscription paid to a trade association for membership of the association is not a political donation for the purposes of this Part.

(2) For this purpose—

"trade association" means an organisation formed for the purpose of furthering the trade interests of its members, or of persons represented by its members, and

"subscription" does not include a payment to the association to the extent that it is made for the purpose of financing any particular activity of the association.

NOTES

Commencement: 1 October 2007 (in relation to Great Britain); 1 November 2007 (in relation to Northern Ireland).
Commencement (transitional provisions): see the note to s 362 at **[1.362]**.

[1.376]

376 All-party parliamentary groups

(1) An all-party parliamentary group is not a political organisation for the purposes of this Part.

(2) An "all-party parliamentary group" means an all-party group composed of members of one or both of the Houses of Parliament (or of such members and other persons).

NOTES

Commencement: 1 October 2007 (in relation to Great Britain); 1 November 2007 (in relation to Northern Ireland).
Commencement (transitional provisions): see the note to s 362 at **[1.362]**.

[1.377]

377 Political expenditure exempted by order

(1) Authorisation under this Part is not needed for political expenditure that is exempt by virtue of an order of the Secretary of State under this section.

(2) An order may confer an exemption in relation to—

    (a)   companies of any description or category specified in the order, or

    (b)   expenditure of any description or category so specified (whether framed by reference to goods, services or other matters in respect of which such expenditure is incurred or otherwise), or both.

(3)   If or to the extent that expenditure is exempt from the requirement of authorisation under this Part by virtue of an order under this section, it shall be disregarded in determining what donations are authorised by any resolution of the company passed for the purposes of this Part.

(4)   An order under this section is subject to affirmative resolution procedure.

NOTES

Commencement: 20 January 2007 (for the purpose of enabling the exercise of powers to make Orders or Regulations by statutory instrument); 1 October 2007 (otherwise, in relation to Great Britain); 1 November 2007 (otherwise, in relation to Northern Ireland).

Commencement (transitional provisions): see the note to s 362 at **[1.362]**.

Orders: the Companies (Political Expenditure Exemption) Order 2007, SI 2007/2081 at **[4.7]**.

[1.378]
378   Donations not amounting to more than £5,000 in any twelve month period

(1)   Authorisation under this Part is not needed for a donation except to the extent that the total amount of—

   (a)   that donation, and

   (b)   other relevant donations made in the period of 12 months ending with the date on which that donation is made,

exceeds £5,000.

(2)   In this section—

"donation" means a donation to a political party or other political organisation or to an independent election candidate; and

"other relevant donations" means—

   (a)   in relation to a donation made by a company that is not a subsidiary, any other donations made by that company or by any of its subsidiaries;

   (b)   in relation to a donation made by a company that is a subsidiary, any other donations made by that company, by any holding company of that company or by any other subsidiary of any such holding company.

(3)   If or to the extent that a donation is exempt by virtue of this section from the requirement of authorisation under this Part, it shall be disregarded in determining what donations are authorised by any resolution passed for the purposes of this Part.

NOTES

Commencement: 1 October 2007 (in relation to Great Britain (subject to the exception noted below)); 1 November 2007 (in relation to Northern Ireland (subject to the exception noted below)); 1 October 2008 (otherwise).

Commencement (transitional provisions): see the note to s 362 at **[1.362]**.

Commencement (note): the Companies Act 2006 (Commencement No 3, Consequential Amendments, Transitional Provisions and Savings) Order 2007, SI 2007/2194, arts 2(2), 3(1) provide that this section shall come into force on 1 October 2007 (in Great Britain) and 1 November 2007 (in Northern Ireland) with the exception of the provisions specified in art 5 of that Order (which relate to independent election candidates and which shall come into force on 1 October 2008). Article 5 provides that in this section, the words "or to an independent election candidate" in sub-s (2) shall come into force on 1 October 2008 (see that Order at **[2.31]** et seq).

Supplementary provisions

[1.379]
379   Minor definitions

(1)   In this Part—

"director" includes shadow director; and

"organisation" includes any body corporate or unincorporated association and any combination of persons.

(2)   Except as otherwise provided, any reference in this Part to the time at which a donation is made or expenditure is incurred is, in a case where the donation is made or expenditure incurred in pursuance of a contract, any earlier time at which that contract is entered into by the company.

NOTES

Commencement: 1 October 2007 (in relation to Great Britain); 1 November 2007 (in relation to Northern Ireland).

Commencement (transitional provisions): see the note to s 362 at **[1.362]**.

PART 15
ACCOUNTS AND REPORTS

NOTES

See further the Finance Act 2009, s 93, Sch 46 in relation to the duty of the senior accounting officer of a qualifying company to take reasonable steps to ensure that the company establishes and maintains appropriate tax accounting arrangements. A company is a "qualifying company" for these purposes if the company's turnover exceeds £200 million or if the company's balance sheet total exceeds £2 billion (or both) (see Sch 46, para 15).

CHAPTER 1
INTRODUCTION
General

[1.380]
380   Scheme of this Part
(1)   The requirements of this Part as to accounts and reports apply in relation to each financial year of a company.
(2)   In certain respects different provisions apply to different kinds of company.
(3)   The main distinctions for this purpose are—
  (a)   between companies subject to the small companies regime (see section 381) and companies that are not subject to that regime; and
  (b)   between quoted companies (see section 385) and companies that are not quoted.
(4)   In this Part, where provisions do not apply to all kinds of company—
  (a)   provisions applying to companies subject to the small companies regime appear before the provisions applying to other companies,
  (b)   provisions applying to private companies appear before the provisions applying to public companies, and
  (c)   provisions applying to quoted companies appear after the provisions applying to other companies.

NOTES
Commencement: 6 April 2008.
Commencement (transitional provisions): Sch 4, Pt 1, paras 6–8 to the Companies Act 2006 (Commencement No 5, Transitional Provisions and Savings) Order 2007, SI 2007/3495 (at **[2.66]**) provide as follows—

"Accounts and reports (ss 380 to 389, 393 to 416, 418 to 462 and 464 to 474)
6.—(1)   Sections 380 to 389, 393 to 416, 418 to 462 and 464 to 474 of the Companies Act 2006 (accounts and reports) apply to accounts and reports for financial years beginning on or after 6th April 2008.
(2)   The corresponding provisions of the 1985 Act or the 1986 Order continue to apply to accounts and reports for financial years beginning before that date.
7.   Any question whether—
  (a)   for the purposes of section 382, 383, 384(3) or 467(3) of the Companies Act 2006 a company or group qualified as small in a financial year beginning before 6th April 2008, or
  (b)   for the purposes of section 465 or 466 of that Act a company or group qualified as medium-sized in any such financial year,
is to be determined by reference to the corresponding provisions of the 1985 Act or the 1986 Order.
8.   Until section 1068(1) of the Companies Act 2006 comes into force, the notice referred to in section 392 of that Act (notice of alteration of accounting reference date) must be given in the form prescribed for the purposes of section 225(1) of the 1985 Act or Article 233(1) of the 1986 Order.".

Companies subject to the small companies regime

[1.381]
381   Companies subject to the small companies regime
The small companies regime   .   .   .   applies to a company for a financial year in relation to which the company—
  (a)   qualifies as small (see sections 382 and 383), and
  (b)   is not excluded from the regime (see section 384).

NOTES
Commencement: 6 April 2008.
Commencement (transitional provisions): see the note to s 380 at **[1.380]**.
Words omitted repealed by the Companies Act 2006 (Amendment) (Accounts and Reports) Regulations 2008, SI 2008/393, reg 6(1), as from 6 April 2008, in relation to financial years beginning on or after that date.

[1.382]
382   Companies qualifying as small: general
(1)   A company qualifies as small in relation to its first financial year if the qualifying conditions are met in that year.
(2)   A company qualifies as small in relation to a subsequent financial year—
  (a)   if the qualifying conditions are met in that year and the preceding financial year;
  (b)   if the qualifying conditions are met in that year and the company qualified as small in relation to the preceding financial year;
  (c)   if the qualifying conditions were met in the preceding financial year and the company qualified as small in relation to that year.
(3)   The qualifying conditions are met by a company in a year in which it satisfies two or more of the following requirements—

1 Turnover	[Not more than £6.5 million]
2 Balance sheet total	[Not more than £3.26 million]
3 Number of employees	Not more than 50

(4)   For a period that is a company's financial year but not in fact a year the maximum figures for turnover must be proportionately adjusted.

(5)   The balance sheet total means the aggregate of the amounts shown as assets in the company's balance sheet.

(6)   The number of employees means the average number of persons employed by the company in the year, determined as follows—

    (a)   find for each month in the financial year the number of persons employed under contracts of service by the company in that month (whether throughout the month or not),

    (b)   add together the monthly totals, and

    (c)   divide by the number of months in the financial year.

(7)   This section is subject to section 383 (companies qualifying as small: parent companies).

NOTES

Commencement: 6 April 2008.

Commencement (transitional provisions): see the note to s 380 at **[1.380]**.

Sub-s (3): words in square brackets substituted by the Companies Act 2006 (Amendment) (Accounts and Reports) Regulations 2008, SI 2008/393, reg 3(1), as from 6 April 2008, in relation to financial years beginning on or after that date (as to whether a company qualifies as small for the purposes of this section, see further reg 2(3) of the 2008 Regulations at **[4.141]**).

[1.383]

383   Companies qualifying as small: parent companies

(1)   A parent company qualifies as a small company in relation to a financial year only if the group headed by it qualifies as a small group.

(2)   A group qualifies as small in relation to the parent company's first financial year if the qualifying conditions are met in that year.

(3)   A group qualifies as small in relation to a subsequent financial year of the parent company—

    (a)   if the qualifying conditions are met in that year and the preceding financial year;

    (b)   if the qualifying conditions are met in that year and the group qualified as small in relation to the preceding financial year;

    (c)   if the qualifying conditions were met in the preceding financial year and the group qualified as small in relation to that year.

(4)   The qualifying conditions are met by a group in a year in which it satisfies two or more of the following requirements—

1. Aggregate turnover	[Not more than £6.5 million net (or £7.8 million gross)]
2. Aggregate balance sheet total	[Not more than £3.26 million net (or £3.9 million gross)]
3. Aggregate number of employees	Not more than 50

(5)   The aggregate figures are ascertained by aggregating the relevant figures determined in accordance with section 382 for each member of the group.

(6)   In relation to the aggregate figures for turnover and balance sheet total—

    "net" means after any set-offs and other adjustments made to eliminate group transactions—

    (a)   in the case of Companies Act accounts, in accordance with regulations under section 404,

    (b)   in the case of IAS accounts, in accordance with international accounting standards; and

    "gross" means without those set-offs and other adjustments.

A company may satisfy any relevant requirement on the basis of either the net or the gross figure.

(7)   The figures for each subsidiary undertaking shall be those included in its individual accounts for the relevant financial year, that is—

    (a)   if its financial year ends with that of the parent company, that financial year, and

    (b)   if not, its financial year ending last before the end of the financial year of the parent company.

If those figures cannot be obtained without disproportionate expense or undue delay, the latest available figures shall be taken.

NOTES

Commencement: 6 April 2008.

Commencement (transitional provisions): see the note to s 380 at **[1.380]**.

Sub-s (4): words in square brackets substituted by the Companies Act 2006 (Amendment) (Accounts and Reports) Regulations 2008, SI 2008/393, reg 3(2), as from 6 April 2008, in relation to financial years beginning on or after that date (as to whether a group qualifies as small for the purposes of this section, see further reg 2(3) of the 2008 Regulations at **[4.141]**).

[1.384]

384 Companies excluded from the small companies regime

(1) The small companies regime does not apply to a company that is, or was at any time within the financial year to which the accounts relate—

    (a) a public company,

    (b) a company that—

        (i) is an authorised insurance company, a banking company, an e-money issuer, [a MiFID investment firm] or a UCITS management company, or

        (ii) carries on insurance market activity, or

    (c) a member of an ineligible group.

(2) A group is ineligible if any of its members is—

    (a) a public company,

    (b) a body corporate (other than a company) whose shares are admitted to trading on a regulated market in an EEA State,

    (c) a person (other than a small company) who has permission under Part 4 of the Financial Services and Markets Act 2000 (c 8) to carry on a regulated activity,

    (d) a small company that is an authorised insurance company, a banking company, an e-money issuer, [a MiFID investment firm] or a UCITS management company, or

    (e) a person who carries on insurance market activity.

(3) A company is a small company for the purposes of subsection (2) if it qualified as small in relation to its last financial year ending on or before the end of the financial year to which the accounts relate.

NOTES

Commencement: 6 April 2008.

Commencement (transitional provisions): see the note to s 380 at **[1.380]**.

Sub-ss (1), (2): words in square brackets substituted by the Markets in Financial Instruments Directive (Consequential Amendments) Regulations 2007, SI 2007/2932, reg 3(1), (2), as from 1 November 2007.

Quoted and unquoted companies

[1.385]

385 Quoted and unquoted companies

(1) For the purposes of this Part a company is a quoted company in relation to a financial year if it is a quoted company immediately before the end of the accounting reference period by reference to which that financial year was determined.

(2) A "quoted company" means a company whose equity share capital—

    (a) has been included in the official list in accordance with the provisions of Part 6 of the Financial Services and Markets Act 2000 (c 8), or

    (b) is officially listed in an EEA State, or

    (c) is admitted to dealing on either the New York Stock Exchange or the exchange known as Nasdaq.

In paragraph (a) "the official list" has the meaning given by section 103(1) of the Financial Services and Markets Act 2000.

(3) An "unquoted company" means a company that is not a quoted company.

(4) The Secretary of State may by regulations amend or replace the provisions of subsections (1) to (2) so as to limit or extend the application of some or all of the provisions of this Part that are expressed to apply to quoted companies.

(5) Regulations under this section extending the application of any such provision of this Part are subject to affirmative resolution procedure.

(6) Any other regulations under this section are subject to negative resolution procedure.

NOTES

Commencement: 20 January 2007 (for the purpose of enabling the exercise of powers to make Orders or Regulations by statutory instrument); 1 October 2007 (certain purposes); 6 April 2008 (otherwise) (see the note below).

Commencement (transitional provisions): see the note to s 380 at **[1.380]**.

Commencement (note): the Companies Act 2006 (Commencement No 3, Consequential Amendments, Transitional Provisions and Savings) Order 2007, SI 2007/2194, art 2(3) provides that this section shall come into force on 1 October 2007 so far as is necessary for the purposes of the provisions of this Act brought into force on that date by art 2(1), (2) of that Order (see **[2.32]**).

CHAPTER 2
ACCOUNTING RECORDS

[1.386]

386 Duty to keep accounting records

(1) Every company must keep adequate accounting records.

(2) Adequate accounting records means records that are sufficient—

    (a) to show and explain the company's transactions,

    (b) to disclose with reasonable accuracy, at any time, the financial position of the company at that time, and

(c)   to enable the directors to ensure that any accounts required to be prepared comply with the requirements of this Act (and, where applicable, of Article 4 of the IAS Regulation).

(3)   Accounting records must, in particular, contain—

(a)   entries from day to day of all sums of money received and expended by the company and the matters in respect of which the receipt and expenditure takes place, and

(b)   a record of the assets and liabilities of the company.

(4)   If the company's business involves dealing in goods, the accounting records must contain—

(a)   statements of stock held by the company at the end of each financial year of the company,

(b)   all statements of stocktakings from which any statement of stock as is mentioned in paragraph (a) has been or is to be prepared, and

(c)   except in the case of goods sold by way of ordinary retail trade, statements of all goods sold and purchased, showing the goods and the buyers and sellers in sufficient detail to enable all these to be identified.

(5)   A parent company that has a subsidiary undertaking in relation to which the above requirements do not apply must take reasonable steps to secure that the undertaking keeps such accounting records as to enable the directors of the parent company to ensure that any accounts required to be prepared under this Part comply with the requirements of this Act (and, where applicable, of Article 4 of the IAS Regulation).

NOTES

Commencement: 6 April 2008.

Commencement (transitional provisions): see the note to s 380 at **[1.380]**.

[1.387]

387   Duty to keep accounting records: offence

(1)   If a company fails to comply with any provision of section 386 (duty to keep accounting records), an offence is committed by every officer of the company who is in default.

(2)   It is a defence for a person charged with such an offence to show that he acted honestly and that in the circumstances in which the company's business was carried on the default was excusable.

(3)   A person guilty of an offence under this section is liable—

(a)   on conviction on indictment, to imprisonment for a term not exceeding two years or a fine (or both);

(b)   on summary conviction—

     (i)   in England and Wales, to imprisonment for a term not exceeding twelve months or to a fine not exceeding the statutory maximum (or both);

     (ii)   in Scotland or Northern Ireland, to imprisonment for a term not exceeding six months, or to a fine not exceeding the statutory maximum (or both).

NOTES

Commencement: 6 April 2008.

Commencement (transitional provisions): see the note to s 380 at **[1.380]**.

Offences under this section: see further s 1131 at **[1.1131]**.

[1.388]

388   Where and for how long records to be kept

(1)   A company's accounting records—

(a)   must be kept at its registered office or such other place as the directors think fit, and

(b)   must at all times be open to inspection by the company's officers.

(2)   If accounting records are kept at a place outside the United Kingdom, accounts and returns with respect to the business dealt with in the accounting records so kept must be sent to, and kept at, a place in the United Kingdom, and must at all times be open to such inspection.

(3)   The accounts and returns to be sent to the United Kingdom must be such as to—

(a)   disclose with reasonable accuracy the financial position of the business in question at intervals of not more than six months, and

(b)   enable the directors to ensure that the accounts required to be prepared under this Part comply with the requirements of this Act (and, where applicable, of Article 4 of the IAS Regulation).

(4)   Accounting records that a company is required by section 386 to keep must be preserved by it—

(a)   in the case of a private company, for three years from the date on which they are made;

(b)   in the case of a public company, for six years from the date on which they are made.

(5)   Subsection (4) is subject to any provision contained in rules made under section 411 of the Insolvency Act 1986 (c 45) (company insolvency rules) or Article 359 of the Insolvency (Northern Ireland) Order 1989 (SI 1989/2405 (NI 19)).

NOTES

Commencement: 6 April 2008.

Commencement (transitional provisions): see the note to s 380 at **[1.380]**.

[1.389]
389   Where and for how long records to be kept: offences
(1)   If a company fails to comply with any provision of subsections (1) to (3) of section 388 (requirements as to keeping of accounting records), an offence is committed by every officer of the company who is in default.

(2)   It is a defence for a person charged with such an offence to show that he acted honestly and that in the circumstances in which the company's business was carried on the default was excusable.

(3)   An officer of a company commits an offence if he—
- (a)   fails to take all reasonable steps for securing compliance by the company with subsection (4) of that section (period for which records to be preserved), or
- (b)   intentionally causes any default by the company under that subsection.

(4)   A person guilty of an offence under this section is liable—
- (a)   on conviction on indictment, to imprisonment for a term not exceeding two years or a fine (or both);
- (b)   on summary conviction—
  - (i)   in England and Wales, to imprisonment for a term not exceeding twelve months or to a fine not exceeding the statutory maximum (or both);
  - (ii)   in Scotland or Northern Ireland, to imprisonment for a term not exceeding six months, or to a fine not exceeding the statutory maximum (or both).

NOTES

Commencement: 6 April 2008.

Commencement (transitional provisions): see the note to s 380 at **[1.380]**.

Offences under this section: see further s 1131 at **[1.1131]**.

CHAPTER 3
A COMPANY'S FINANCIAL YEAR

[1.390]
390   A company's financial year
(1)   A company's financial year is determined as follows.

(2)   Its first financial year—
- (a)   begins with the first day of its first accounting reference period, and
- (b)   ends with the last day of that period or such other date, not more than seven days before or after the end of that period, as the directors may determine.

(3)   Subsequent financial years—
- (a)   begin with the day immediately following the end of the company's previous financial year, and
- (b)   end with the last day of its next accounting reference period or such other date, not more than seven days before or after the end of that period, as the directors may determine.

(4)   In relation to an undertaking that is not a company, references in this Act to its financial year are to any period in respect of which a profit and loss account of the undertaking is required to be made up (by its constitution or by the law under which it is established), whether that period is a year or not.

(5)   The directors of a parent company must secure that, except where in their opinion there are good reasons against it, the financial year of each of its subsidiary undertakings coincides with the company's own financial year.

NOTES

Commencement: 6 April 2008.

[1.391]
391   Accounting reference periods and accounting reference date
(1)   A company's accounting reference periods are determined according to its accounting reference date in each calendar year.

(2)   The accounting reference date of a company incorporated in Great Britain before 1st April 1996 is—
- (a)   the date specified by notice to the registrar in accordance with section 224(2) of the Companies Act 1985 (c 6) (notice specifying accounting reference date given within nine months of incorporation), or
- (b)   failing such notice—
  - (i)   in the case of a company incorporated before 1st April 1990, 31st March, and
  - (ii)   in the case of a company incorporated on or after 1st April 1990, the last day of the month in which the anniversary of its incorporation falls.

(3)   The accounting reference date of a company incorporated in Northern Ireland before 22nd August 1997 is—

(a)   the date specified by notice to the registrar in accordance with article 232(2) of the Companies (Northern Ireland) Order 1986 (SI 1986/1032 (NI 6)) (notice specifying accounting reference date given within nine months of incorporation), or

(b)   failing such notice—

  (i)   in the case of a company incorporated before the coming into operation of Article 5 of the Companies (Northern Ireland) Order 1990 (SI 1990/593 (NI 5)), 31st March, and

  (ii)   in the case of a company incorporated after the coming into operation of that Article, the last day of the month in which the anniversary of its incorporation falls.

(4)   The accounting reference date of a company incorporated—

  (a)   in Great Britain on or after 1st April 1996 and before the commencement of this Act,

  (b)   in Northern Ireland on or after 22nd August 1997 and before the commencement of this Act, or

  (c)   after the commencement of this Act,

is the last day of the month in which the anniversary of its incorporation falls.

(5)   A company's first accounting reference period is the period of more than six months, but not more than 18 months, beginning with the date of its incorporation and ending with its accounting reference date.

(6)   Its subsequent accounting reference periods are successive periods of twelve months beginning immediately after the end of the previous accounting reference period and ending with its accounting reference date.

(7)   This section has effect subject to the provisions of section 392 (alteration of accounting reference date).

NOTES

Commencement: 6 April 2008.

[1.392]
392   Alteration of accounting reference date

(1)   A company may by notice given to the registrar specify a new accounting reference date having effect in relation to—

  (a)   the company's current accounting reference period and subsequent periods, or

  (b)   the company's previous accounting reference period and subsequent periods.

A company's "previous accounting reference period" means the one immediately preceding its current accounting reference period.

(2)   The notice must state whether the current or previous accounting reference period—

  (a)   is to be shortened, so as to come to an end on the first occasion on which the new accounting reference date falls or fell after the beginning of the period, or

  (b)   is to be extended, so as to come to an end on the second occasion on which that date falls or fell after the beginning of the period.

(3)   A notice extending a company's current or previous accounting reference period is not effective if given less than five years after the end of an earlier accounting reference period of the company that was extended under this section.

This does not apply—

  (a)   to a notice given by a company that is a subsidiary undertaking or parent undertaking of another EEA undertaking if the new accounting reference date coincides with that of the other EEA undertaking or, where that undertaking is not a company, with the last day of its financial year, or

  (b)   where the company is in administration under Part 2 of the Insolvency Act 1986 (c 45) or Part 3 of the Insolvency (Northern Ireland) Order 1989 (SI 1989/2405 (NI 19)), or

  (c)   where the Secretary of State directs that it should not apply, which he may do with respect to a notice that has been given or that may be given.

(4)   A notice under this section may not be given in respect of a previous accounting reference period if the period for filing accounts and reports for the financial year determined by reference to that accounting reference period has already expired.

(5)   An accounting reference period may not be extended so as to exceed 18 months and a notice under this section is ineffective if the current or previous accounting reference period as extended in accordance with the notice would exceed that limit.

This does not apply where the company is in administration under Part 2 of the Insolvency Act 1986 (c 45) or Part 3 of the Insolvency (Northern Ireland) Order 1989 (SI 1989/2405 (NI 19)).

(6)   In this section "EEA undertaking" means an undertaking established under the law of any part of the United Kingdom or the law of any other EEA State.

NOTES

Commencement: 6 April 2008.
Commencement (transitional provisions): see the note to s 380 at **[1.380]**.

CHAPTER 4
ANNUAL ACCOUNTS
General

[1.393]
393 Accounts to give true and fair view
(1) The directors of a company must not approve accounts for the purposes of this Chapter unless they are satisfied that they give a true and fair view of the assets, liabilities, financial position and profit or loss—
  (a) in the case of the company's individual accounts, of the company;
  (b) in the case of the company's group accounts, of the undertakings included in the consolidation as a whole, so far as concerns members of the company.
(2) The auditor of a company in carrying out his functions under this Act in relation to the company's annual accounts must have regard to the directors' duty under subsection (1).

NOTES
Commencement: 6 April 2008.
Commencement (transitional provisions): see the note to s 380 at **[1.380]**.

Individual accounts

[1.394]
394 Duty to prepare individual accounts
The directors of every company must prepare accounts for the company for each of its financial years.
Those accounts are referred to as the company's "individual accounts".

NOTES
Commencement: 6 April 2008.
Commencement (transitional provisions): see the note to s 380 at **[1.380]**.

[1.395]
395 Individual accounts: applicable accounting framework
(1) A company's individual accounts may be prepared—
  (a) in accordance with section 396 ("Companies Act individual accounts"), or
  (b) in accordance with international accounting standards ("IAS individual accounts").
  This is subject to the following provisions of this section and to section 407 (consistency of financial reporting within group).
(2) The individual accounts of a company that is a charity must be Companies Act individual accounts.
(3) After the first financial year in which the directors of a company prepare IAS individual accounts ("the first IAS year"), all subsequent individual accounts of the company must be prepared in accordance with international accounting standards unless there is a relevant change of circumstance.
(4) There is a relevant change of circumstance if, at any time during or after the first IAS year—
  (a) the company becomes a subsidiary undertaking of another undertaking that does not prepare IAS individual accounts,
  [(aa) the company ceases to be a subsidiary undertaking,]
  (b) the company ceases to be a company with securities admitted to trading on a regulated market in an EEA State, or
  (c) a parent undertaking of the company ceases to be an undertaking with securities admitted to trading on a regulated market in an EEA State.
(5) If, having changed to preparing Companies Act individual accounts following a relevant change of circumstance, the directors again prepare IAS individual accounts for the company, subsections (3) and (4) apply again as if the first financial year for which such accounts are again prepared were the first IAS year.

NOTES
Commencement: 6 April 2008.
Commencement (transitional provisions): see the note to s 380 at **[1.380]**.
Sub-s (4): para (aa) inserted by the Companies Act 2006 (Amendment) (Accounts and Reports) Regulations 2008, SI 2008/393, reg 9, as from 6 April 2008, in relation to financial years beginning on or after that date.

[1.396]
396 Companies Act individual accounts
(1) Companies Act individual accounts must comprise—
  (a) a balance sheet as at the last day of the financial year, and
  (b) a profit and loss account.
(2) The accounts must—
  (a) in the case of the balance sheet, give a true and fair view of the state of affairs of the company as at the end of the financial year, and

(b)   in the case of the profit and loss account, give a true and fair view of the profit or loss of the company for the financial year.

(3)   The accounts must comply with provision made by the Secretary of State by regulations as to—

(a)   the form and content of the balance sheet and profit and loss account, and

(b)   additional information to be provided by way of notes to the accounts.

(4)   If compliance with the regulations, and any other provision made by or under this Act as to the matters to be included in a company's individual accounts or in notes to those accounts, would not be sufficient to give a true and fair view, the necessary additional information must be given in the accounts or in a note to them.

(5)   If in special circumstances compliance with any of those provisions is inconsistent with the requirement to give a true and fair view, the directors must depart from that provision to the extent necessary to give a true and fair view.

Particulars of any such departure, the reasons for it and its effect must be given in a note to the accounts.

NOTES

Commencement: 20 January 2007 (for the purpose of enabling the exercise of powers to make Orders or Regulations by statutory instrument); 6 April 2008 (otherwise).

Commencement (transitional provisions): see the note to s 380 at **[1.380]**.

Regulations: the Small Companies and Groups (Accounts and Directors' Report) Regulations 2008, SI 2008/409 at **[4.142]**; the Large and Medium-sized Companies and Groups (Accounts and Reports) Regulations 2008, SI 2008/410 at **[4.170]**.

[1.397]
397   IAS individual accounts
Where the directors of a company prepare IAS individual accounts, they must state in the notes to the accounts that the accounts have been prepared in accordance with international accounting standards.

NOTES

Commencement: 6 April 2008.

Commencement (transitional provisions): see the note to s 380 at **[1.380]**.

Group accounts: small companies

[1.398]
398   Option to prepare group accounts
If at the end of a financial year a company subject to the small companies regime is a parent company the directors, as well as preparing individual accounts for the year, may prepare group accounts for the year.

NOTES

Commencement: 6 April 2008.

Commencement (transitional provisions): see the note to s 380 at **[1.380]**.

Group accounts: other companies

[1.399]
399   Duty to prepare group accounts
(1)   This section applies to companies that are not subject to the small companies regime.

(2)   If at the end of a financial year the company is a parent company the directors, as well as preparing individual accounts for the year, must prepare group accounts for the year unless the company is exempt from that requirement.

(3)   There are exemptions under-
section 400 (company included in EEA accounts of larger group),
section 401 (company included in non-EEA accounts of larger group), and
section 402 (company none of whose subsidiary undertakings need be included in the consolidation).

(4)   A company to which this section applies but which is exempt from the requirement to prepare group accounts, may do so.

NOTES

Commencement: 6 April 2008.

Commencement (transitional provisions): see the note to s 380 at **[1.380]**.

[1.400]
400   Exemption for company included in EEA group accounts of larger group
(1)   A company is exempt from the requirement to prepare group accounts if it is itself a subsidiary undertaking and its immediate parent undertaking is established under the law of an EEA State, in the following cases—

(a)   where the company is a wholly-owned subsidiary of that parent undertaking;

(b)　where that parent undertaking holds more than 50% of the allotted shares in the company and notice requesting the preparation of group accounts has not been served on the company by shareholders holding in aggregate—
　　(i)　more than half of the remaining allotted shares in the company, or
　　(ii)　5% of the total allotted shares in the company.

Such notice must be served not later than six months after the end of the financial year before that to which it relates.

(2)　Exemption is conditional upon compliance with all of the following conditions—
　(a)　the company must be included in consolidated accounts for a larger group drawn up to the same date, or to an earlier date in the same financial year, by a parent undertaking established under the law of an EEA State;
　(b)　those accounts must be drawn up and audited, and that parent undertaking's annual report must be drawn up, according to that law—
　　(i)　in accordance with the provisions of the Seventh Directive (83/ 349/EEC) (as modified, where relevant, by the provisions of the Bank Accounts Directive (86/635/EEC) or the Insurance Accounts Directive (91/674/EEC)), or
　　(ii)　in accordance with international accounting standards;
　(c)　the company must disclose in its individual accounts that it is exempt from the obligation to prepare and deliver group accounts;
　(d)　the company must state in its individual accounts the name of the parent undertaking that draws up the group accounts referred to above and—
　　(i)　if it is incorporated outside the United Kingdom, the country in which it is incorporated, or
　　(ii)　if it is unincorporated, the address of its principal place of business;
　(e)　the company must deliver to the registrar, within the period for filing its accounts and reports for the financial year in question, copies of—
　　(i)　those group accounts, and
　　(ii)　the parent undertaking's annual report,
　　together with the auditor's report on them;
　(f)　any requirement of Part 35 of this Act as to the delivery to the registrar of a certified translation into English must be met in relation to any document comprised in the accounts and reports delivered in accordance with paragraph (e).

(3)　For the purposes of subsection (1)(b) shares held by a wholly-owned subsidiary of the parent undertaking, or held on behalf of the parent undertaking or a wholly-owned subsidiary, shall be attributed to the parent undertaking.

(4)　The exemption does not apply to a company any of whose securities are admitted to trading on a regulated market in an EEA State.

(5)　Shares held by directors of a company for the purpose of complying with any share qualification requirement shall be disregarded in determining for the purposes of this section whether the company is a wholly-owned subsidiary.

(6)　In subsection (4) "securities" includes—
　(a)　shares and stock,
　(b)　debentures, including debenture stock, loan stock, bonds, certificates of deposit and other instruments creating or acknowledging indebtedness,
　(c)　warrants or other instruments entitling the holder to subscribe for securities falling within paragraph (a) or (b), and
　(d)　certificates or other instruments that confer—
　　(i)　property rights in respect of a security falling within paragraph (a), (b) or (c),
　　(ii)　any right to acquire, dispose of, underwrite or convert a security, being a right to which the holder would be entitled if he held any such security to which the certificate or other instrument relates, or
　　(iii)　a contractual right (other than an option) to acquire any such security otherwise than by subscription.

NOTES

Commencement: 6 April 2008.

Commencement (transitional provisions): see the note to s 380 at **[1.380]**.

[1.401]

401　Exemption for company included in non-EEA group accounts of larger group

(1)　A company is exempt from the requirement to prepare group accounts if it is itself a subsidiary undertaking and its parent undertaking is not established under the law of an EEA State, in the following cases—
　(a)　where the company is a wholly-owned subsidiary of that parent undertaking;
　(b)　where that parent undertaking holds more than 50% of the allotted shares in the company and notice requesting the preparation of group accounts has not been served on the company by shareholders holding in aggregate—
　　(i)　more than half of the remaining allotted shares in the company, or
　　(ii)　5% of the total allotted shares in the company.

Such notice must be served not later than six months after the end of the financial year before that to which it relates.

(2) Exemption is conditional upon compliance with all of the following conditions—

    (a)   the company and all of its subsidiary undertakings must be included in consolidated accounts for a larger group drawn up to the same date, or to an earlier date in the same financial year, by a parent undertaking;

    (b)   those accounts and, where appropriate, the group's annual report, must be drawn up—

        (i)   in accordance with the provisions of the Seventh Directive (83/ 349/EEC) (as modified, where relevant, by the provisions of the Bank Accounts Directive (86/635/EEC) or the Insurance Accounts Directive (91/674/EEC)), or

        (ii)   in a manner equivalent to consolidated accounts and consolidated annual reports so drawn up;

    (c)   the group accounts must be audited by one or more persons authorised to audit accounts under the law under which the parent undertaking which draws them up is established;

    (d)   the company must disclose in its individual accounts that it is exempt from the obligation to prepare and deliver group accounts;

    (e)   the company must state in its individual accounts the name of the parent undertaking which draws up the group accounts referred to above and—

        (i)   if it is incorporated outside the United Kingdom, the country in which it is incorporated, or

        (ii)   if it is unincorporated, the address of its principal place of business;

    (f)   the company must deliver to the registrar, within the period for filing its accounts and reports for the financial year in question, copies of—

        (i)   the group accounts, and

        (ii)   where appropriate, the consolidated annual report,

        together with the auditor's report on them;

    (g)   any requirement of Part 35 of this Act as to the delivery to the registrar of a certified translation into English must be met in relation to any document comprised in the accounts and reports delivered in accordance with paragraph (f).

(3) For the purposes of subsection (1)(b), shares held by a wholly-owned subsidiary of the parent undertaking, or held on behalf of the parent undertaking or a wholly-owned subsidiary, are attributed to the parent undertaking.

(4) The exemption does not apply to a company any of whose securities are admitted to trading on a regulated market in an EEA State.

(5) Shares held by directors of a company for the purpose of complying with any share qualification requirement shall be disregarded in determining for the purposes of this section whether the company is a wholly-owned subsidiary.

(6) In subsection (4) "securities" includes—

    (a)   shares and stock,

    (b)   debentures, including debenture stock, loan stock, bonds, certificates of deposit and other instruments creating or acknowledging indebtedness,

    (c)   warrants or other instruments entitling the holder to subscribe for securities falling within paragraph (a) or (b), and

    (d)   certificates or other instruments that confer—

        (i)   property rights in respect of a security falling within paragraph (a), (b) or (c),

        (ii)   any right to acquire, dispose of, underwrite or convert a security, being a right to which the holder would be entitled if he held any such security to which the certificate or other instrument relates, or

        (iii)   a contractual right (other than an option) to acquire any such security otherwise than by subscription.

NOTES

Commencement: 6 April 2008.

Commencement (transitional provisions): see the note to s 380 at **[1.380]**.

[1.402]

402 Exemption if no subsidiary undertakings need be included in the consolidation

A parent company is exempt from the requirement to prepare group accounts if under section 405 all of its subsidiary undertakings could be excluded from consolidation in Companies Act group accounts.

NOTES

Commencement: 6 April 2008.

Commencement (transitional provisions): see the note to s 380 at **[1.380]**.

Group accounts: general

[1.403]

403   Group accounts: applicable accounting framework

(1)   The group accounts of certain parent companies are required by Article 4 of the IAS Regulation to be prepared in accordance with international accounting standards ("IAS group accounts").

(2)   The group accounts of other companies may be prepared—

  (a)   in accordance with section 404 ("Companies Act group accounts"), or

  (b)   in accordance with international accounting standards ("IAS group accounts").

  This is subject to the following provisions of this section.

(3)   The group accounts of a parent company that is a charity must be Companies Act group accounts.

(4)   After the first financial year in which the directors of a parent company prepare IAS group accounts ("the first IAS year"), all subsequent group accounts of the company must be prepared in accordance with international accounting standards unless there is a relevant change of circumstance.

(5)   There is a relevant change of circumstance if, at any time during or after the first IAS year—

  (a)   the company becomes a subsidiary undertaking of another undertaking that does not prepare IAS group accounts,

  (b)   the company ceases to be a company with securities admitted to trading on a regulated market in an EEA State, or

  (c)   a parent undertaking of the company ceases to be an undertaking with securities admitted to trading on a regulated market in an EEA State.

(6)   If, having changed to preparing Companies Act group accounts following a relevant change of circumstance, the directors again prepare IAS group accounts for the company, subsections (4) and (5) apply again as if the first financial year for which such accounts are again prepared were the first IAS year.

NOTES

Commencement: 6 April 2008.

Commencement (transitional provisions): see the note to s 380 at **[1.380]**.

[1.404]

404   Companies Act group accounts

(1)   Companies Act group accounts must comprise—

  (a)   a consolidated balance sheet dealing with the state of affairs of the parent company and its subsidiary undertakings, and

  (b)   a consolidated profit and loss account dealing with the profit or loss of the parent company and its subsidiary undertakings.

(2)   The accounts must give a true and fair view of the state of affairs as at the end of the financial year, and the profit or loss for the financial year, of the undertakings included in the consolidation as a whole, so far as concerns members of the company.

(3)   The accounts must comply with provision made by the Secretary of State by regulations as to—

  (a)   the form and content of the consolidated balance sheet and consolidated profit and loss account, and

  (b)   additional information to be provided by way of notes to the accounts.

(4)   If compliance with the regulations, and any other provision made by or under this Act as to the matters to be included in a company's group accounts or in notes to those accounts, would not be sufficient to give a true and fair view, the necessary additional information must be given in the accounts or in a note to them.

(5)   If in special circumstances compliance with any of those provisions is inconsistent with the requirement to give a true and fair view, the directors must depart from that provision to the extent necessary to give a true and fair view.

  Particulars of any such departure, the reasons for it and its effect must be given in a note to the accounts.

NOTES

Commencement: 20 January 2007 (for the purpose of enabling the exercise of powers to make Orders or Regulations by statutory instrument); 6 April 2008 (otherwise).

Commencement (transitional provisions): see the note to s 380 at **[1.380]**.

Regulations: the Small Companies and Groups (Accounts and Directors' Report) Regulations 2008, SI 2008/409 at **[4.142]**; the Large and Medium-sized Companies and Groups (Accounts and Reports) Regulations 2008, SI 2008/410 at **[4.170]**.

[1.405]

405   Companies Act group accounts: subsidiary undertakings included in the consolidation

(1)   Where a parent company prepares Companies Act group accounts, all the subsidiary undertakings of the company must be included in the consolidation, subject to the following exceptions.

(2)   A subsidiary undertaking may be excluded from consolidation if its inclusion is not material for the purpose of giving a true and fair view (but two or more undertakings may be excluded only if they are not material taken together).

(3)   A subsidiary undertaking may be excluded from consolidation where—

(a)   severe long-term restrictions substantially hinder the exercise of the rights of the parent company over the assets or management of that undertaking, or

(b)   the information necessary for the preparation of group accounts cannot be obtained without disproportionate expense or undue delay, or

(c)   the interest of the parent company is held exclusively with a view to subsequent resale.

(4)   The reference in subsection (3)(a) to the rights of the parent company and the reference in subsection (3)(c) to the interest of the parent company are, respectively, to rights and interests held by or attributed to the company for the purposes of the definition of "parent undertaking" (see section 1162) in the absence of which it would not be the parent company.

NOTES

Commencement: 6 April 2008.

Commencement (transitional provisions): see the note to s 380 at **[1.380]**.

[1.406]
406   IAS group accounts

Where the directors of a company prepare IAS group accounts, they must state in the notes to those accounts that the accounts have been prepared in accordance with international accounting standards.

NOTES

Commencement: 6 April 2008.

Commencement (transitional provisions): see the note to s 380 at **[1.380]**.

[1.407]
407   Consistency of financial reporting within group

(1)   The directors of a parent company must secure that the individual accounts of—

(a)   the parent company, and

(b)   each of its subsidiary undertakings,

are all prepared using the same financial reporting framework, except to the extent that in their opinion there are good reasons for not doing so.

(2)   Subsection (1) does not apply if the directors do not prepare group accounts for the parent company.

(3)   Subsection (1) only applies to accounts of subsidiary undertakings that are required to be prepared under this Part.

(4)   Subsection (1) does not require accounts of undertakings that are charities to be prepared using the same financial reporting framework as accounts of undertakings which are not charities.

(5)   Subsection (1)(a) does not apply where the directors of a parent company prepare IAS group accounts and IAS individual accounts.

NOTES

Commencement: 6 April 2008.

Commencement (transitional provisions): see the note to s 380 at **[1.380]**.

[1.408]
408   Individual profit and loss account where group accounts prepared

(1)   This section applies where—

(a)   a company prepares group accounts in accordance with this Act, and

(b)   the notes to the company's individual balance sheet show the company's profit or loss for the financial year determined in accordance with this Act.

(2)   [The company's individual profit and loss account] need not contain the information specified in section 411 (information about employee numbers and costs).

(3)   The company's individual profit and loss account must be approved in accordance with section 414(1) (approval by directors) but may be omitted from the company's annual accounts for the purposes of the other provisions of the Companies Acts.

(4)   The exemption conferred by this section is conditional upon its being disclosed in the company's annual accounts that the exemption applies.

NOTES

Commencement: 6 April 2008.

Commencement (transitional provisions): see the note to s 380 at **[1.380]**.

Sub-s (2): words in square brackets substituted by the Companies Act 2006 (Amendment) (Accounts and Reports) Regulations 2008, SI 2008/393, reg 10, as from 6 April 2008, in relation to financial years beginning on or after that date.

Information to be given in notes to the accounts

[1.409]

409 Information about related undertakings

(1) The Secretary of State may make provision by regulations requiring information about related undertakings to be given in notes to a company's annual accounts.

(2) The regulations—

    (a) may make different provision according to whether or not the company prepares group accounts, and

    (b) may specify the descriptions of undertaking in relation to which they apply, and make different provision in relation to different descriptions of related undertaking.

(3) The regulations may provide that information need not be disclosed with respect to an undertaking that—

    (a) is established under the law of a country outside the United Kingdom, or

    (b) carries on business outside the United Kingdom,

if the following conditions are met.

(4) The conditions are—

    (a) that in the opinion of the directors of the company the disclosure would be seriously prejudicial to the business of—

        (i) that undertaking,

        (ii) the company,

        (iii) any of the company's subsidiary undertakings, or

        (iv) any other undertaking which is included in the consolidation;

    (b) that the Secretary of State agrees that the information need not be disclosed.

(5) Where advantage is taken of any such exemption, that fact must be stated in a note to the company's annual accounts.

NOTES

Commencement: 20 January 2007 (for the purpose of enabling the exercise of powers to make Orders or Regulations by statutory instrument); 6 April 2008 (otherwise).

Commencement (transitional provisions): see the note to s 380 at **[1.380]**.

Regulations: the Small Companies and Groups (Accounts and Directors' Report) Regulations 2008, SI 2008/409 at **[4.142]**; the Large and Medium-sized Companies and Groups (Accounts and Reports) Regulations 2008, SI 2008/410 at **[4.170]**.

[1.410]

410 Information about related undertakings: alternative compliance

(1) This section applies where the directors of a company are of the opinion that the number of undertakings in respect of which the company is required to disclose information under any provision of regulations under section 409 (related undertakings) is such that compliance with that provision would result in information of excessive length being given in notes to the company's annual accounts.

(2) The information need only be given in respect of—

    (a) the undertakings whose results or financial position, in the opinion of the directors, principally affected the figures shown in the company's annual accounts, and

    (b) where the company prepares group accounts, undertakings excluded from consolidation under section 405(3) (undertakings excluded on grounds other than materiality).

(3) If advantage is taken of subsection (2)—

    (a) there must be included in the notes to the company's annual accounts a statement that the information is given only with respect to such undertakings as are mentioned in that subsection, and

    (b) the full information (both that which is disclosed in the notes to the accounts and that which is not) must be annexed to the company's next annual return.

For this purpose the "next annual return" means that next delivered to the registrar after the accounts in question have been approved under section 414.

(4) If a company fails to comply with subsection (3)(b), an offence is committed by—

    (a) the company, and

    (b) every officer of the company who is in default.

(5) A person guilty of an offence under subsection (4) is liable on summary conviction to a fine not exceeding level 3 on the standard scale and, for continued contravention, a daily default fine not exceeding one-tenth of level 3 on the standard scale.

NOTES

Commencement: 6 April 2008.

Commencement (transitional provisions): see the note to s 380 at **[1.380]**.

[1.410A]

[410A Information about off-balance sheet arrangements

(1) In the case of a company that is not subject to the small companies regime, if in any financial year—

(a) the company is or has been party to arrangements that are not reflected in its balance sheet, and

(b) at the balance sheet date the risks or benefits arising from those arrangements are material,

the information required by this section must be given in notes to the company's annual accounts.

(2) The information required is—

(a) the nature and business purpose of the arrangements, and

(b) the financial impact of the arrangements on the company.

(3) The information need only be given to the extent necessary for enabling the financial position of the company to be assessed.

(4) If the company qualifies as medium-sized in relation to the financial year (see sections 465 to 467) it need not comply with subsection (2)(b).

(5) This section applies in relation to group accounts as if the undertakings included in the consolidation were a single company.]

NOTES

Commencement: 6 April 2008.

Inserted by the Companies Act 2006 (Amendment) (Accounts and Reports) Regulations 2008, SI 2008/393, reg 8, as from 6 April 2008, in relation to financial years beginning on or after that date.

[1.411]
411 Information about employee numbers and costs

(1) In the case of a company not subject to the small companies regime, the following information with respect to the employees of the company must be given in notes to the company's annual accounts—

(a) the average number of persons employed by the company in the financial year, and

(b) the average number of persons so employed within each category of persons employed by the company.

(2) The categories by reference to which the number required to be disclosed by subsection (1)(b) is to be determined must be such as the directors may select having regard to the manner in which the company's activities are organised.

(3) The average number required by subsection (1)(a) or (b) is determined by dividing the relevant annual number by the number of months in the financial year.

(4) The relevant annual number is determined by ascertaining for each month in the financial year—

(a) for the purposes of subsection (1)(a), the number of persons employed under contracts of service by the company in that month (whether throughout the month or not);

(b) for the purposes of subsection (1)(b), the number of persons in the category in question of persons so employed;

and adding together all the monthly numbers.

(5) In respect of all persons employed by the company during the financial year who are taken into account in determining the relevant annual number for the purposes of subsection (1)(a) there must also be stated the aggregate amounts respectively of—

(a) wages and salaries paid or payable in respect of that year to those persons;

(b) social security costs incurred by the company on their behalf; and

(c) other pension costs so incurred.

This does not apply in so far as those amounts, or any of them, are stated elsewhere in the company's accounts.

(6) In subsection (5)—

"pension costs" includes any costs incurred by the company in respect of—

(a) any pension scheme established for the purpose of providing pensions for persons currently or formerly employed by the company,

(b) any sums set aside for the future payment of pensions directly by the company to current or former employees, and

(c) any pensions paid directly to such persons without having first been set aside;

"social security costs" means any contributions by the company to any state social security or pension scheme, fund or arrangement.

[(7) This section applies in relation to group accounts as if the undertakings included in the consolidation were a single company.]

NOTES

Commencement: 6 April 2008.

Commencement (transitional provisions): see the note to s 380 at **[1.380]**.

Sub-s (7): substituted by the Companies Act 2006 (Amendment) (Accounts and Reports) Regulations 2008, SI 2008/393, reg 11, as from 6 April 2008, in relation to financial years beginning on or after that date.

[1.412]
412 Information about directors' benefits: remuneration

(1) The Secretary of State may make provision by regulations requiring information to be given in notes to a company's annual accounts about directors' remuneration.

(2) The matters about which information may be required include—

(a)   gains made by directors on the exercise of share options;
(b)   benefits received or receivable by directors under long-term incentive schemes;
(c)   payments for loss of office (as defined in section 215);
(d)   benefits receivable, and contributions for the purpose of providing benefits, in respect of past services of a person as director or in any other capacity while director;
(e)   consideration paid to or receivable by third parties for making available the services of a person as director or in any other capacity while director.

(3)   Without prejudice to the generality of subsection (1), regulations under this section may make any such provision as was made immediately before the commencement of this Part by Part 1 of Schedule 6 to the Companies Act 1985 (c 6).

(4)   For the purposes of this section, and regulations made under it, amounts paid to or receivable by—
(a)   a person connected with a director, or
(b)   a body corporate controlled by a director,
are treated as paid to or receivable by the director.
     The expressions "connected with" and "controlled by" in this subsection have the same meaning as in Part 10 (company directors).

(5)   It is the duty of—
(a)   any director of a company, and
(b)   any person who is or has at any time in the preceding five years been a director of the company,
to give notice to the company of such matters relating to himself as may be necessary for the purposes of regulations under this section.

(6)   A person who makes default in complying with subsection (5) commits an offence and is liable on summary conviction to a fine not exceeding level 3 on the standard scale.

NOTES

Commencement: 20 January 2007 (for the purpose of enabling the exercise of powers to make Orders or Regulations by statutory instrument); 6 April 2008 (otherwise).

Commencement (transitional provisions): see the note to s 380 at [**1.380**].

Regulations: the Small Companies and Groups (Accounts and Directors' Report) Regulations 2008, SI 2008/409 at [**4.142**]; the Large and Medium-sized Companies and Groups (Accounts and Reports) Regulations 2008, SI 2008/410 at [**4.170**].

[1.413]
413   Information about directors' benefits: advances, credit and guarantees
(1)   In the case of a company that does not prepare group accounts, details of—
(a)   advances and credits granted by the company to its directors, and
(b)   guarantees of any kind entered into by the company on behalf of its directors,
must be shown in the notes to its individual accounts.

(2)   In the case of a parent company that prepares group accounts, details of—
(a)   advances and credits granted to the directors of the parent company, by that company or by any of its subsidiary undertakings, and
(b)   guarantees of any kind entered into on behalf of the directors of the parent company, by that company or by any of its subsidiary undertakings,
must be shown in the notes to the group accounts.

(3)   The details required of an advance or credit are—
(a)   its amount,
(b)   an indication of the interest rate,
(c)   its main conditions, and
(d)   any amounts repaid.

(4)   The details required of a guarantee are—
(a)   its main terms,
(b)   the amount of the maximum liability that may be incurred by the company (or its subsidiary), and
(c)   any amount paid and any liability incurred by the company (or its subsidiary) for the purpose of fulfilling the guarantee (including any loss incurred by reason of enforcement of the guarantee).

(5)   There must also be stated in the notes to the accounts the totals—
(a)   of amounts stated under subsection (3)(a),
(b)   of amounts stated under subsection (3)(d),
(c)   of amounts stated under subsection (4)(b), and
(d)   of amounts stated under subsection (4)(c).

(6)   References in this section to the directors of a company are to the persons who were a director at any time in the financial year to which the accounts relate.

(7)   The requirements of this section apply in relation to every advance, credit or guarantee subsisting at any time in the financial year to which the accounts relate—
(a)   whenever it was entered into,
(b)   whether or not the person concerned was a director of the company in question at the time it was entered into, and

(c)   in the case of an advance, credit or guarantee involving a subsidiary undertaking of that company, whether or not that undertaking was such a subsidiary undertaking at the time it was entered into.

(8)   Banking companies and the holding companies of credit institutions need only state the details required by [subsection (5)(a) and (c)].

NOTES

Commencement: 6 April 2008.

Commencement (transitional provisions): see the note to s 380 at **[1.380]**.

Sub-s (8): words in square brackets substituted by the Companies Act 2006 (Amendment of Section 413) Regulations 2009, SI 2009/3022, reg 2, as from 23 December 2009, with effect in relation to financial years which end on or after that date.

Approval and signing of accounts

[1.414]

414   Approval and signing of accounts

(1)   A company's annual accounts must be approved by the board of directors and signed on behalf of the board by a director of the company.

(2)   The signature must be on the company's balance sheet.

(3)   If the accounts are prepared in accordance with the provisions applicable to companies subject to the small companies regime, the balance sheet must contain a statement to that effect in a prominent position above the signature.

(4)   If annual accounts are approved that do not comply with the requirements of this Act (and, where applicable, of Article 4 of the IAS Regulation), every director of the company who—

(a)   knew that they did not comply, or was reckless as to whether they complied, and

(b)   failed to take reasonable steps to secure compliance with those requirements or, as the case may be, to prevent the accounts from being approved,

commits an offence.

(5)   A person guilty of an offence under this section is liable—

(a)   on conviction on indictment, to a fine;

(b)   on summary conviction, to a fine not exceeding the statutory maximum.

NOTES

Commencement: 6 April 2008.

Commencement (transitional provisions): see the note to s 380 at **[1.380]**.

CHAPTER 5
DIRECTORS' REPORT

Directors' report

[1.415]

415   Duty to prepare directors' report

(1)   The directors of a company must prepare a directors' report for each financial year of the company.

(2)   For a financial year in which—

(a)   the company is a parent company, and

(b)   the directors of the company prepare group accounts,

the directors' report must be a consolidated report (a "group directors' report") relating to the undertakings included in the consolidation.

(3)   A group directors' report may, where appropriate, give greater emphasis to the matters that are significant to the undertakings included in the consolidation, taken as a whole.

(4)   In the case of failure to comply with the requirement to prepare a directors' report, an offence is committed by every person who—

(a)   was a director of the company immediately before the end of the period for filing accounts and reports for the financial year in question, and

(b)   failed to take all reasonable steps for securing compliance with that requirement.

(5)   A person guilty of an offence under this section is liable—

(a)   on conviction on indictment, to a fine;

(b)   on summary conviction, to a fine not exceeding the statutory maximum.

NOTES

Commencement: 6 April 2008.

Commencement (transitional provisions): see the note to s 380 at **[1.380]**.

Transfer of money held in dormant bank accounts: where (a) directors of a company that is a bank are required by sub-s (1) above to prepare a report for a particular financial year, and (b) in that year the company made transfers in relation to which the Dormant Bank and Building Society Accounts Act 2008, s 2 applied (transfer of balances to charities, with proportion to reclaim fund) the report must identify each of the charities concerned and specify the amount transferred to each of them (as from 12 March 2009). See s 13 of the 2008 Act.

[1.415A]
[415A   Directors' report: small companies exemption
(1)   A company is entitled to small companies exemption in relation to the directors' report for a financial year if—
   (a)   it is entitled to prepare accounts for the year in accordance with the small companies regime, or
   (b)   it would be so entitled but for being or having been a member of an ineligible group.
(2)   The exemption is relevant to—
     section 416(3) (contents of report: statement of amount recommended by way of dividend),
     section 417 (contents of report: business review), and
     sections 444 to 446 (filing obligations of different descriptions of company).]

NOTES
Commencement: 6 April 2008.
Inserted by the Companies Act 2006 (Amendment) (Accounts and Reports) Regulations 2008, SI 2008/393, reg 6(2), as from 6 April 2008, in relation to financial years beginning on or after that date.

[1.416]
416   Contents of directors' report: general
(1)   The directors' report for a financial year must state—
   (a)   the names of the persons who, at any time during the financial year, were directors of the company, and
   (b)   the principal activities of the company in the course of the year.
(2)   In relation to a group directors' report subsection (1)(b) has effect as if the reference to the company was to the undertakings included in the consolidation.
(3)   Except in the case of a company [entitled to the small companies exemption], the report must state the amount (if any) that the directors recommend should be paid by way of dividend.
(4)   The Secretary of State may make provision by regulations as to other matters that must be disclosed in a directors' report.
   Without prejudice to the generality of this power, the regulations may make any such provision as was formerly made by Schedule 7 to the Companies Act 1985.

NOTES
Commencement: 20 January 2007 (for the purpose of enabling the exercise of powers to make Orders or Regulations by statutory instrument); 6 April 2008 (otherwise).
Commencement (transitional provisions): see the note to s 380 at **[1.380]**.
Sub-s (3): words in square brackets substituted by the Companies Act 2006 (Amendment) (Accounts and Reports) Regulations 2008, SI 2008/393, reg 6(3), as from 6 April 2008, in relation to financial years beginning on or after that date.
Regulations: the Small Companies and Groups (Accounts and Directors' Report) Regulations 2008, SI 2008/409 at **[4.142]**; the Large and Medium-sized Companies and Groups (Accounts and Reports) Regulations 2008, SI 2008/410 at **[4.170]**.

[1.417]
417   Contents of directors' report: business review
(1)   Unless the company is [entitled to the small companies exemption], the directors' report must contain a business review.
(2)   The purpose of the business review is to inform members of the company and help them assess how the directors have performed their duty under section 172 (duty to promote the success of the company).
(3)   The business review must contain—
   (a)   a fair review of the company's business, and
   (b)   a description of the principal risks and uncertainties facing the company.
(4)   The review required is a balanced and comprehensive analysis of—
   (a)   the development and performance of the company's business during the financial year, and
   (b)   the position of the company's business at the end of that year,
consistent with the size and complexity of the business.
(5)   In the case of a quoted company the business review must, to the extent necessary for an understanding of the development, performance or position of the company's business, include—
   (a)   the main trends and factors likely to affect the future development, performance and position of the company's business; and
   (b)   information about—
     (i)   environmental matters (including the impact of the company's business on the environment),
     (ii)   the company's employees, and
     (iii)   social and community issues,
     including information about any policies of the company in relation to those matters and the effectiveness of those policies; and
   (c)   subject to subsection (11), information about persons with whom the company has contractual or other arrangements which are essential to the business of the company.
   If the review does not contain information of each kind mentioned in paragraphs (b)(i), (ii) and (iii) and (c), it must state which of those kinds of information it does not contain.

(6) The review must, to the extent necessary for an understanding of the development, performance or position of the company's business, include—

(a) analysis using financial key performance indicators, and

(b) where appropriate, analysis using other key performance indicators, including information relating to environmental matters and employee matters.

"Key performance indicators" means factors by reference to which the development, performance or position of the company's business can be measured effectively.

(7) Where a company qualifies as medium-sized in relation to a financial year (see sections 465 to 467), the directors' report for the year need not comply with the requirements of subsection (6) so far as they relate to non-financial information.

(8) The review must, where appropriate, include references to, and additional explanations of, amounts included in the company's annual accounts.

(9) In relation to a group directors' report this section has effect as if the references to the company were references to the undertakings included in the consolidation.

(10) Nothing in this section requires the disclosure of information about impending developments or matters in the course of negotiation if the disclosure would, in the opinion of the directors, be seriously prejudicial to the interests of the company.

(11) Nothing in subsection (5)(c) requires the disclosure of information about a person if the disclosure would, in the opinion of the directors, be seriously prejudicial to that person and contrary to the public interest.

NOTES

Commencement: 1 October 2007.

Commencement (transitional provisions): Sch 3, para 43 to the Companies Act 2006 (Commencement No 3, Consequential Amendments, Transitional Provisions and Savings) Order 2007, SI 2007/2194 (at **[2.45]**) provides that this section applies to directors' reports for financial years beginning on or after 1 October 2007 (and that ss 234(1)(a), 234ZZB, 246(4)(a) and 246A(2A) of the 1985 Act continue to apply to directors' reports for financial years beginning before that date).

Commencement (transitional adaptations): the transitional adaptations of this section contained in the Companies Act 2006 (Commencement No 3, Consequential Amendments, Transitional Provisions and Savings) Order 2007, SI 2007/2194, Sch 1, para 16 were revoked by the Companies Act 2006 (Commencement No 5, Transitional Provisions and Savings) Order 2007, SI 2007/3495, art 10(1), (3), as from 6 April 2008 (subject to any transitional provisions and savings as apply, in accordance with Sch 4 to that Order, in relation to the repeal of any provision of the 1985 Act referred to in the adaptation). See **[2.43]**.

Sub-s (1): words in square brackets substituted by the Companies Act 2006 (Amendment) (Accounts and Reports) Regulations 2008, SI 2008/393, reg 6(4), as from 6 April 2008, in relation to financial years beginning on or after that date.

[1.418]
418　Contents of directors' report: statement as to disclosure to auditors

(1) This section applies to a company unless—

(a) it is exempt for the financial year in question from the requirements of Part 16 as to audit of accounts, and

(b) the directors take advantage of that exemption.

(2) The directors' report must contain a statement to the effect that, in the case of each of the persons who are directors at the time the report is approved—

(a) so far as the director is aware, there is no relevant audit information of which the company's auditor is unaware, and

(b) he has taken all the steps that he ought to have taken as a director in order to make himself aware of any relevant audit information and to establish that the company's auditor is aware of that information.

(3) "Relevant audit information" means information needed by the company's auditor in connection with preparing his report.

(4) A director is regarded as having taken all the steps that he ought to have taken as a director in order to do the things mentioned in subsection (2)(b) if he has—

(a) made such enquiries of his fellow directors and of the company's auditors for that purpose, and

(b) taken such other steps (if any) for that purpose,

as are required by his duty as a director of the company to exercise reasonable care, skill and diligence.

(5) Where a directors' report containing the statement required by this section is approved but the statement is false, every director of the company who—

(a) knew that the statement was false, or was reckless as to whether it was false, and

(b) failed to take reasonable steps to prevent the report from being approved,

commits an offence.

(6) A person guilty of an offence under subsection (5) is liable—

(a) on conviction on indictment, to imprisonment for a term not exceeding two years or a fine (or both);

(b) on summary conviction—

(i) in England and Wales, to imprisonment for a term not exceeding twelve months or to a fine not exceeding the statutory maximum (or both);

(ii) in Scotland or Northern Ireland, to imprisonment for a term not exceeding six months, or to a fine not exceeding the statutory maximum (or both).

NOTES
Commencement: 6 April 2008.
Commencement (transitional provisions): see the note to s 380 at **[1.380]**.
Offences under this section: see further s 1131 at **[1.1131]**.

[1.419]
419 Approval and signing of directors' report

(1) The directors' report must be approved by the board of directors and signed on behalf of the board by a director or the secretary of the company.

(2) [If in preparing the report advantage is taken of the small companies exemption,] it must contain a statement to that effect in a prominent position above the signature.

(3) If a directors' report is approved that does not comply with the requirements of this Act, every director of the company who—

  (a) knew that it did not comply, or was reckless as to whether it complied, and

  (b) failed to take reasonable steps to secure compliance with those requirements or, as the case may be, to prevent the report from being approved,

commits an offence.

(4) A person guilty of an offence under this section is liable—

  (a) on conviction on indictment, to a fine;

  (b) on summary conviction, to a fine not exceeding the statutory maximum.

NOTES
Commencement: 6 April 2008.
Commencement (transitional provisions): see the note to s 380 at **[1.380]**.
Sub-s (2): words in square brackets substituted by the Companies Act 2006 (Amendment) (Accounts and Reports) Regulations 2008, SI 2008/393, reg 6(5), as from 6 April 2008, in relation to financial years beginning on or after that date.

[1.419A]
[419A Approval and signing of separate corporate governance statement

Any separate corporate governance statement must be approved by the board of directors and signed on behalf of the board by a director or the secretary of the company.]

NOTES
Commencement: 27 June 2009.
Inserted by the Companies Act 2006 (Accounts, Reports and Audit) Regulations 2009, SI 2009/1581, reg 2, as from 27 June 2009, in relation to financial years beginning on or after 29 June 2008 which have not ended before 27 June 2009.

CHAPTER 6
QUOTED COMPANIES: DIRECTORS' REMUNERATION REPORT

[1.420]
420 Duty to prepare directors' remuneration report

(1) The directors of a quoted company must prepare a directors' remuneration report for each financial year of the company.

(2) In the case of failure to comply with the requirement to prepare a directors' remuneration report, every person who—

  (a) was a director of the company immediately before the end of the period for filing accounts and reports for the financial year in question, and

  (b) failed to take all reasonable steps for securing compliance with that requirement,

commits an offence.

(3) A person guilty of an offence under this section is liable—

  (a) on conviction on indictment, to a fine;

  (b) on summary conviction, to a fine not exceeding the statutory maximum.

NOTES
Commencement: 6 April 2008.
Commencement (transitional provisions): see the note to s 380 at **[1.380]**.

[1.421]
421 Contents of directors' remuneration report

(1) The Secretary of State may make provision by regulations as to—

  (a) the information that must be contained in a directors' remuneration report,

  (b) how information is to be set out in the report, and

  (c) what is to be the auditable part of the report.

(2) Without prejudice to the generality of this power, the regulations may make any such provision as was made, immediately before the commencement of this Part, by Schedule 7A to the Companies Act 1985 (c 6).

(3) It is the duty of—

  (a) any director of a company, and

(b)   any person who is or has at any time in the preceding five years been a director of the company,

to give notice to the company of such matters relating to himself as may be necessary for the purposes of regulations under this section.

(4)   A person who makes default in complying with subsection (3) commits an offence and is liable on summary conviction to a fine not exceeding level 3 on the standard scale.

NOTES

Commencement: 20 January 2007 (for the purpose of enabling the exercise of powers to make Orders or Regulations by statutory instrument); 6 April 2008 (otherwise).

Commencement (transitional provisions): see the note to s 380 at **[1.380]**.

Regulations: the Large and Medium-sized Companies and Groups (Accounts and Reports) Regulations 2008, SI 2008/410 at **[4.170]**.

[1.422]

422   Approval and signing of directors' remuneration report

(1)   The directors' remuneration report must be approved by the board of directors and signed on behalf of the board by a director or the secretary of the company.

(2)   If a directors' remuneration report is approved that does not comply with the requirements of this Act, every director of the company who—

    (a)   knew that it did not comply, or was reckless as to whether it complied, and

    (b)   failed to take reasonable steps to secure compliance with those requirements or, as the case may be, to prevent the report from being approved,

commits an offence.

(3)   A person guilty of an offence under this section is liable—

    (a)   on conviction on indictment, to a fine;

    (b)   on summary conviction, to a fine not exceeding the statutory maximum.

NOTES

Commencement: 6 April 2008.

Commencement (transitional provisions): see the note to s 380 at **[1.380]**.

CHAPTER 7
PUBLICATION OF ACCOUNTS AND REPORTS

Duty to circulate copies of accounts and reports

[1.423]

423   Duty to circulate copies of annual accounts and reports

(1)   Every company must send a copy of its annual accounts and reports for each financial year to—

    (a)   every member of the company,

    (b)   every holder of the company's debentures, and

    (c)   every person who is entitled to receive notice of general meetings.

(2)   Copies need not be sent to a person for whom the company does not have a current address.

(3)   A company has a "current address" for a person if—

    (a)   an address has been notified to the company by the person as one at which documents may be sent to him, and

    (b)   the company has no reason to believe that documents sent to him at that address will not reach him.

(4)   In the case of a company not having a share capital, copies need not be sent to anyone who is not entitled to receive notices of general meetings of the company.

(5)   Where copies are sent out over a period of days, references in the Companies Acts to the day on which copies are sent out shall be read as references to the last day of that period.

(6)   This section has effect subject to section 426 (option to provide summary financial statement).

NOTES

Commencement: 6 April 2008.

Commencement (transitional provisions): see the note to s 380 at **[1.380]**.

[1.424]

424   Time allowed for sending out copies of accounts and reports

(1)   The time allowed for sending out copies of the company's annual accounts and reports is as follows.

(2)   A private company must comply with section 423 not later than—

    (a)   the end of the period for filing accounts and reports, or

    (b)   if earlier, the date on which it actually delivers its accounts and reports to the registrar.

(3)   A public company must comply with section 423 at least 21 days before the date of the relevant accounts meeting.

(4) If in the case of a public company copies are sent out later than is required by subsection (3), they shall, despite that, be deemed to have been duly sent if it is so agreed by all the members entitled to attend and vote at the relevant accounts meeting.

(5) Whether the time allowed is that for a private company or a public company is determined by reference to the company's status immediately before the end of the accounting reference period by reference to which the financial year for the accounts in question was determined.

(6) In this section the "relevant accounts meeting" means the accounts meeting of the company at which the accounts and reports in question are to be laid.

NOTES

Commencement: 6 April 2008.

Commencement (transitional provisions): see the note to s 380 at **[1.380]**.

[1.425]
425 Default in sending out copies of accounts and reports: offences
(1) If default is made in complying with section 423 or 424, an offence is committed by—
  (a) the company, and
  (b) every officer of the company who is in default.
(2) A person guilty of an offence under this section is liable—
  (a) on conviction on indictment, to a fine;
  (b) on summary conviction, to a fine not exceeding the statutory maximum.

NOTES

Commencement: 6 April 2008.

Commencement (transitional provisions): see the note to s 380 at **[1.380]**.

Option to provide summary financial statement

[1.426]
426 Option to provide summary financial statement
(1) A company may—
  (a) in such cases as may be specified by regulations made by the Secretary of State, and
  (b) provided any conditions so specified are complied with,
provide a summary financial statement instead of copies of the accounts and reports required to be sent out in accordance with section 423.
(2) Copies of those accounts and reports must, however, be sent to any person entitled to be sent them in accordance with that section and who wishes to receive them.
(3) The Secretary of State may make provision by regulations as to the manner in which it is to be ascertained, whether before or after a person becomes entitled to be sent a copy of those accounts and reports, whether he wishes to receive them.
(4) A summary financial statement must comply with the requirements of—
    section 427 (form and contents of summary financial statement: unquoted companies), or
    section 428 (form and contents of summary financial statement: quoted companies).
(5) This section applies to copies of accounts and reports required to be sent out by virtue of section 146 to a person nominated to enjoy information rights as it applies to copies of accounts and reports required to be sent out in accordance with section 423 to a member of the company.
(6) Regulations under this section are subject to negative resolution procedure.

NOTES

Commencement: 20 January 2007 (for the purpose of enabling the exercise of powers to make Orders or Regulations by statutory instrument); 6 April 2008 (otherwise).

Commencement (transitional provisions): see the note to s 380 at **[1.380]**.

Regulations: the Companies (Summary Financial Statement) Regulations 2008, SI 2008/374 at **[4.120]**.

[1.427]
427 Form and contents of summary financial statement: unquoted companies
(1) A summary financial statement by a company that is not a quoted company must—
  (a) be derived from the company's annual accounts, and
  (b) be prepared in accordance with this section and regulations made under it.
(2) The summary financial statement must be in such form, and contain such information, as the Secretary of State may specify by regulations.
The regulations may require the statement to include information derived from the directors' report.
(3) Nothing in this section or regulations made under it prevents a company from including in a summary financial statement additional information derived from the company's annual accounts or the directors' report.
(4) The summary financial statement must—
  (a) state that it is only a summary of information derived from the company's annual accounts;
  (b) state whether it contains additional information derived from the directors' report and, if so, that it does not contain the full text of that report;

   (c)   state how a person entitled to them can obtain a full copy of the company's annual accounts and the directors' report;

   (d)   contain a statement by the company's auditor of his opinion as to whether the summary financial statement—

      (i)   is consistent with the company's annual accounts and, where information derived from the directors' report is included in the statement, with that report, and

      (ii) complies with the requirements of this section and regulations made under it;

   (e)   state whether the auditor's report on the annual accounts was unqualified or qualified and, if it was qualified, set out the report in full together with any further material needed to understand the qualification;

   (f)   state whether, in that report, the auditor's statement under section 496 (whether directors' report consistent with accounts) was qualified or unqualified and, if it was qualified, set out the qualified statement in full together with any further material needed to understand the qualification;

   (g)   state whether that auditor's report contained a statement under—

      (i)   section 498(2)(a) or (b) (accounting records or returns inadequate or accounts not agreeing with records and returns), or

      (ii) section 498(3) (failure to obtain necessary information and explanations), and if so, set out the statement in full.

(5)   Regulations under this section may provide that any specified material may, instead of being included in the summary financial statement, be sent separately at the same time as the statement.

(6)   Regulations under this section are subject to negative resolution procedure.

NOTES

  Commencement: 20 January 2007 (for the purpose of enabling the exercise of powers to make Orders or Regulations by statutory instrument); 6 April 2008 (otherwise).

  Commencement (transitional provisions): see the note to s 380 at **[1.380]**.

  Regulations: the Companies (Summary Financial Statement) Regulations 2008, SI 2008/374 at **[4.120]**.

[1.428]

428   Form and contents of summary financial statement: quoted companies

(1)   A summary financial statement by a quoted company must—

   (a)   be derived from the company's annual accounts and the directors' remuneration report, and

   (b)   be prepared in accordance with this section and regulations made under it.

(2)   The summary financial statement must be in such form, and contain such information, as the Secretary of State may specify by regulations.

The regulations may require the statement to include information derived from the directors' report.

(3)   Nothing in this section or regulations made under it prevents a company from including in a summary financial statement additional information derived from the company's annual accounts, the directors' remuneration report or the directors' report.

(4)   The summary financial statement must—

   (a)   state that it is only a summary of information derived from the company's annual accounts and the directors' remuneration report;

   (b)   state whether it contains additional information derived from the directors' report and, if so, that it does not contain the full text of that report;

   (c)   state how a person entitled to them can obtain a full copy of the company's annual accounts, the directors' remuneration report or the directors' report;

   (d)   contain a statement by the company's auditor of his opinion as to whether the summary financial statement—

      (i)   is consistent with the company's annual accounts and the directors' remuneration report and, where information derived from the directors' report is included in the statement, with that report, and

      (ii) complies with the requirements of this section and regulations made under it;

   (e)   state whether the auditor's report on the annual accounts and the auditable part of the directors' remuneration report was unqualified or qualified and, if it was qualified, set out the report in full together with any further material needed to understand the qualification;

   (f)   state whether that auditor's report contained a statement under—

      (i)   section 498(2) (accounting records or returns inadequate or accounts or directors' remuneration report not agreeing with records and returns), or

      (ii) section 498(3) (failure to obtain necessary information and explanations), and if so, set out the statement in full;

   (g)   state whether, in that report, the auditor's statement under section 496 (whether directors' report consistent with accounts) was qualified or unqualified and, if it was qualified, set out the qualified statement in full together with any further material needed to understand the qualification.

(5)   Regulations under this section may provide that any specified material may, instead of being included in the summary financial statement, be sent separately at the same time as the statement.

(6)   Regulations under this section are subject to negative resolution procedure.

NOTES

Commencement: 20 January 2007 (for the purpose of enabling the exercise of powers to make Orders or Regulations by statutory instrument); 6 April 2008 (otherwise).

Commencement (transitional provisions): see the note to s 380 at [**1.380**].

Regulations: the Companies (Summary Financial Statement) Regulations 2008, SI 2008/374 at [**4.120**].

[1.429]
429 Summary financial statements: offences
(1) If default is made in complying with any provision of section 426, 427 or 428, or of regulations under any of those sections, an offence is committed by—
   (a) the company, and
   (b) every officer of the company who is in default.
(2) A person guilty of an offence under this section is liable on summary conviction to a fine not exceeding level 3 on the standard scale.

NOTES

Commencement: 6 April 2008.

Commencement (transitional provisions): see the note to s 380 at [**1.380**].

Quoted companies: requirements as to website publication

[1.430]
430 Quoted companies: annual accounts and reports to be made available on website
(1) A quoted company must ensure that its annual accounts and reports—
   (a) are made available on a website, and
   (b) remain so available until the annual accounts and reports for the company's next financial year are made available in accordance with this section.
(2) The annual accounts and reports must be made available on a website that—
   (a) is maintained by or on behalf of the company, and
   (b) identifies the company in question.
(3) Access to the annual accounts and reports on the website, and the ability to obtain a hard copy of the annual accounts and reports from the website, must not be—
   (a) conditional on the payment of a fee, or
   (b) otherwise restricted, except so far as necessary to comply with any enactment or regulatory requirement (in the United Kingdom or elsewhere).
(4) The annual accounts and reports—
   (a) must be made available as soon as reasonably practicable, and
   (b) must be kept available throughout the period specified in subsection (1)(b).
(5) A failure to make the annual accounts and reports available on a website throughout that period is disregarded if—
   (a) the annual accounts and reports are made available on the website for part of that period, and
   (b) the failure is wholly attributable to circumstances that it would not be reasonable to have expected the company to prevent or avoid.
(6) In the event of default in complying with this section, an offence is committed by every officer of the company who is in default.
(7) A person guilty of an offence under subsection (6) is liable on summary conviction to a fine not exceeding level 3 on the standard scale.

NOTES

Commencement: 6 April 2008.

Commencement (transitional provisions): see the note to s 380 at [**1.380**].

Right of member or debenture holder to demand copies of accounts and reports

[1.431]
431 Right of member or debenture holder to copies of accounts and reports: unquoted companies
(1) A member of, or holder of debentures of, an unquoted company is entitled to be provided, on demand and without charge, with a copy of—
   (a) the company's last annual accounts,
   (b) the last directors' report, and
   (c) the auditor's report on those accounts (including the statement on that report).
(2) The entitlement under this section is to a single copy of those documents, but that is in addition to any copy to which a person may be entitled under section 423.
(3) If a demand made under this section is not complied with within seven days of receipt by the company, an offence is committed by—
   (a) the company, and
   (b) every officer of the company who is in default.

(4)   A person guilty of an offence under this section is liable on summary conviction to a fine not exceeding level 3 on the standard scale and, for continued contravention, a daily default fine not exceeding one-tenth of level 3 on the standard scale.

NOTES
Commencement: 6 April 2008.
Commencement (transitional provisions): see the note to s 380 at **[1.380]**.

[1.432]
432   Right of member or debenture holder to copies of accounts and reports: quoted companies
(1)   A member of, or holder of debentures of, a quoted company is entitled to be provided, on demand and without charge, with a copy of—
    (a)   the company's last annual accounts,
    (b)   the last directors' remuneration report,
    (c)   the last directors' report, and
    (d)   the auditor's report on those accounts (including the report on the directors' remuneration report and on the directors' report).
(2)   The entitlement under this section is to a single copy of those documents, but that is in addition to any copy to which a person may be entitled under section 423.
(3)   If a demand made under this section is not complied with within seven days of receipt by the company, an offence is committed by—
    (a)   the company, and
    (b)   every officer of the company who is in default.
(4)   A person guilty of an offence under this section is liable on summary conviction to a fine not exceeding level 3 on the standard scale and, for continued contravention, a daily default fine not exceeding one-tenth of level 3 on the standard scale.

NOTES
Commencement: 6 April 2008.
Commencement (transitional provisions): see the note to s 380 at **[1.380]**.

Requirements in connection with publication of accounts and reports

[1.433]
433   Name of signatory to be stated in published copies of accounts and reports
(1)   Every copy of a document to which this section applies that is published by or on behalf of the company must state the name of the person who signed it on behalf of the board.
(2)   In the case of an unquoted company, this section applies to copies of—
    (a)   the company's balance sheet, and
    (b)   the directors' report.
(3)   In the case of a quoted company, this section applies to copies of—
    (a)   the company's balance sheet,
    (b)   the directors' remuneration report, and
    (c)   the directors' report.
(4)   If a copy is published without the required statement of the signatory's name, an offence is committed by—
    (a)   the company, and
    (b)   every officer of the company who is in default.
(5)   A person guilty of an offence under this section is liable on summary conviction to a fine not exceeding level 3 on the standard scale.

NOTES
Commencement: 6 April 2008.
Commencement (transitional provisions): see the note to s 380 at **[1.380]**.

[1.434]
434   Requirements in connection with publication of statutory accounts
(1)   If a company publishes any of its statutory accounts, they must be accompanied by the auditor's report on those accounts (unless the company is exempt from audit and the directors have taken advantage of that exemption).
(2)   A company that prepares statutory group accounts for a financial year must not publish its statutory individual accounts for that year without also publishing with them its statutory group accounts.
(3)   A company's "statutory accounts" are its accounts for a financial year as required to be delivered to the registrar under section 441.
(4)   If a company contravenes any provision of this section, an offence is committed by—
    (a)   the company, and
    (b)   every officer of the company who is in default.
(5)   A person guilty of an offence under this section is liable on summary conviction to a fine not exceeding level 3 on the standard scale.

(6) This section does not apply in relation to the provision by a company of a summary financial statement (see section 426).

NOTES

Commencement: 6 April 2008.

Commencement (transitional provisions): see the note to s 380 at **[1.380]**.

[1.435]
435 Requirements in connection with publication of non-statutory accounts
(1) If a company publishes non-statutory accounts, it must publish with them a statement indicating—
  (a) that they are not the company's statutory accounts,
  (b) whether statutory accounts dealing with any financial year with which the non-statutory accounts purport to deal have been delivered to the registrar, and
  (c) whether an auditor's report has been made on the company's statutory accounts for any such financial year, and if so whether the report—
    (i) was qualified or unqualified, or included a reference to any matters to which the auditor drew attention by way of emphasis without qualifying the report, or
    (ii) contained a statement under section 498(2) (accounting records or returns inadequate or accounts or directors' remuneration report not agreeing with records and returns), or section 498(3) (failure to obtain necessary information and explanations).
(2) The company must not publish with non-statutory accounts the auditor's report on the company's statutory accounts.
(3) References in this section to the publication by a company of "non-statutory accounts" are to the publication of—
  (a) any balance sheet or profit and loss account relating to, or purporting to deal with, a financial year of the company, or
  (b) an account in any form purporting to be a balance sheet or profit and loss account for a group headed by the company relating to, or purporting to deal with, a financial year of the company,
otherwise than as part of the company's statutory accounts.
(4) In subsection (3)(b) "a group headed by the company" means a group consisting of the company and any other undertaking (regardless of whether it is a subsidiary undertaking of the company) other than a parent undertaking of the company.
(5) If a company contravenes any provision of this section, an offence is committed by—
  (a) the company, and
  (b) every officer of the company who is in default.
(6) A person guilty of an offence under this section is liable on summary conviction to a fine not exceeding level 3 on the standard scale.
(7) This section does not apply in relation to the provision by a company of a summary financial statement (see section 426).

NOTES

Commencement: 6 April 2008.

Commencement (transitional provisions): see the note to s 380 at **[1.380]**.

[1.436]
436 Meaning of "publication" in relation to accounts and reports
(1) This section has effect for the purposes of—
  section 433 (name of signatory to be stated in published copies of accounts and reports),
  section 434 (requirements in connection with publication of statutory accounts), and
  section 435 (requirements in connection with publication of non-statutory accounts).
(2) For the purposes of those sections a company is regarded as publishing a document if it publishes, issues or circulates it or otherwise makes it available for public inspection in a manner calculated to invite members of the public generally, or any class of members of the public, to read it.

NOTES

Commencement: 6 April 2008.

Commencement (transitional provisions): see the note to s 380 at **[1.380]**.

CHAPTER 8
PUBLIC COMPANIES: LAYING OF ACCOUNTS AND REPORTS BEFORE GENERAL MEETING

[1.437]
437 Public companies: laying of accounts and reports before general meeting
(1) The directors of a public company must lay before the company in general meeting copies of its annual accounts and reports.

(2) This section must be complied with not later than the end of the period for filing the accounts and reports in question.

(3) In the Companies Acts "accounts meeting", in relation to a public company, means a general meeting of the company at which the company's annual accounts and reports are (or are to be) laid in accordance with this section.

NOTES

Commencement: 6 April 2008.
Commencement (transitional provisions): see the note to s 380 at **[1.380]**.

[1.438]
438 Public companies: offence of failure to lay accounts and reports

(1) If the requirements of section 437 (public companies: laying of accounts and reports before general meeting) are not complied with before the end of the period allowed, every person who immediately before the end of that period was a director of the company commits an offence.

(2) It is a defence for a person charged with such an offence to prove that he took all reasonable steps for securing that those requirements would be complied with before the end of that period.

(3) It is not a defence to prove that the documents in question were not in fact prepared as required by this Part.

(4) A person guilty of an offence under this section is liable on summary conviction to a fine not exceeding level 5 on the standard scale and, for continued contravention, a daily default fine not exceeding one-tenth of level 5 on the standard scale.

NOTES

Commencement: 6 April 2008.
Commencement (transitional provisions): see the note to s 380 at **[1.380]**.

CHAPTER 9
QUOTED COMPANIES: MEMBERS' APPROVAL OF DIRECTORS'
REMUNERATION REPORT

[1.439]
439 Quoted companies: members' approval of directors' remuneration report

(1) A quoted company must, prior to the accounts meeting, give to the members of the company entitled to be sent notice of the meeting notice of the intention to move at the meeting, as an ordinary resolution, a resolution approving the directors' remuneration report for the financial year.

(2) The notice may be given in any manner permitted for the service on the member of notice of the meeting.

(3) The business that may be dealt with at the accounts meeting includes the resolution.
This is so notwithstanding any default in complying with subsection (1) or (2).

(4) The existing directors must ensure that the resolution is put to the vote of the meeting.

(5) No entitlement of a person to remuneration is made conditional on the resolution being passed by reason only of the provision made by this section.

(6) In this section—

"the accounts meeting" means the general meeting of the company before which the company's annual accounts for the financial year are to be laid; and

"existing director" means a person who is a director of the company immediately before that meeting.

NOTES

Commencement: 6 April 2008.
Commencement (transitional provisions): see the note to s 380 at **[1.380]**.

[1.440]
440 Quoted companies: offences in connection with procedure for approval

(1) In the event of default in complying with section 439(1) (notice to be given of resolution for approval of directors' remuneration report), an offence is committed by every officer of the company who is in default.

(2) If the resolution is not put to the vote of the accounts meeting, an offence is committed by each existing director.

(3) It is a defence for a person charged with an offence under subsection (2) to prove that he took all reasonable steps for securing that the resolution was put to the vote of the meeting.

(4) A person guilty of an offence under this section is liable on summary conviction to a fine not exceeding level 3 on the standard scale.

(5) In this section—

"the accounts meeting" means the general meeting of the company before which the company's annual accounts for the financial year are to be laid; and

"existing director" means a person who is a director of the company immediately before that meeting.

NOTES
Commencement: 6 April 2008.
Commencement (transitional provisions): see the note to s 380 at **[1.380]**.

CHAPTER 10
FILING OF ACCOUNTS AND REPORTS
Duty to file accounts and reports

[1.441]
441   Duty to file accounts and reports with the registrar
(1)   The directors of a company must deliver to the registrar for each financial year the accounts and reports required by—
   section 444 (filing obligations of companies subject to small companies regime),
   [section 444A (filing obligations of companies entitled to small companies exemption in relation to directors' report),]
   section 445 (filing obligations of medium-sized companies),
   section 446 (filing obligations of unquoted companies), or
   section 447 (filing obligations of quoted companies).
(2)   This is subject to section 448 (unlimited companies exempt from filing obligations).

NOTES
Commencement: 6 April 2008.
Commencement (transitional provisions): see the note to s 380 at **[1.380]**.
Sub-s (1): words in square brackets inserted by the Companies Act 2006 (Amendment) (Accounts and Reports) Regulations 2008, SI 2008/393, reg 6(6), as from 6 April 2008, in relation to financial years beginning on or after that date.

[1.442]
442   Period allowed for filing accounts
(1)   This section specifies the period allowed for the directors of a company to comply with their obligation under section 441 to deliver accounts and reports for a financial year to the registrar.
   This is referred to in the Companies Acts as the "period for filing" those accounts and reports.
(2)   The period is—
   (a)   for a private company, nine months after the end of the relevant accounting reference period, and
   (b)   for a public company, six months after the end of that period.
   This is subject to the following provisions of this section.
(3)   If the relevant accounting reference period is the company's first and is a period of more than twelve months, the period is—
   (a)   nine months or six months, as the case may be, from the first anniversary of the incorporation of the company, or
   (b)   three months after the end of the accounting reference period,
whichever last expires.
(4)   If the relevant accounting reference period is treated as shortened by virtue of a notice given by the company under section 392 (alteration of accounting reference date), the period is—
   (a)   that applicable in accordance with the above provisions, or
   (b)   three months from the date of the notice under that section,
whichever last expires.
(5)   If for any special reason the Secretary of State thinks fit he may, on an application made before the expiry of the period otherwise allowed, by notice in writing to a company extend that period by such further period as may be specified in the notice.
(6)   Whether the period allowed is that for a private company or a public company is determined by reference to the company's status immediately before the end of the relevant accounting reference period.
(7)   In this section "the relevant accounting reference period" means the accounting reference period by reference to which the financial year for the accounts in question was determined.

NOTES
Commencement: 6 April 2008.
Commencement (transitional provisions): see the note to s 380 at **[1.380]**.

[1.443]
443   Calculation of period allowed
(1)   This section applies for the purposes of calculating the period for filing a company's accounts and reports which is expressed as a specified number of months from a specified date or after the end of a specified previous period.
(2)   Subject to the following provisions, the period ends with the date in the appropriate month corresponding to the specified date or the last day of the specified previous period.

(3)   If the specified date, or the last day of the specified previous period, is the last day of a month, the period ends with the last day of the appropriate month (whether or not that is the corresponding date).

(4)   If—

    (a)   the specified date, or the last day of the specified previous period, is not the last day of a month but is the 29th or 30th, and

    (b)   the appropriate month is February,

the period ends with the last day of February.

(5)   "The appropriate month" means the month that is the specified number of months after the month in which the specified date, or the end of the specified previous period, falls.

NOTES

Commencement: 6 April 2008.

Commencement (transitional provisions): see the note to s 380 at **[1.380]**.

Filing obligations of different descriptions of company

[1.444]

444   Filing obligations of companies subject to small companies regime

(1)   The directors of a company subject to the small companies regime—

    (a)   must deliver to the registrar for each financial year a copy of a balance sheet drawn up as at the last day of that year, and

    (b)   may also deliver to the registrar—

        (i)   a copy of the company's profit and loss account for that year, and

        (ii)   a copy of the directors' report for that year.

(2)   The directors must also deliver to the registrar a copy of the auditor's report on [the accounts (and any directors' report) that it delivers].

This does not apply if the company is exempt from audit and the directors have taken advantage of that exemption.

(3)   The copies of accounts and reports delivered to the registrar must be copies of the company's annual accounts and reports, except that where the company prepares Companies Act accounts—

    (a)   the directors may deliver to the registrar a copy of a balance sheet drawn up in accordance with regulations made by the Secretary of State, and

    (b)   there may be omitted from the copy profit and loss account delivered to the registrar such items as may be specified by the regulations.

These are referred to in this Part as "abbreviated accounts".

(4)   If abbreviated accounts are delivered to the registrar the obligation to deliver a copy of the auditor's report on the accounts is to deliver a copy of the special auditor's report required by section 449.

(5)   Where the directors of a company subject to the small companies regime deliver to the registrar IAS accounts, or Companies Act accounts that are not abbreviated accounts, and in accordance with this section—

    (a)   do not deliver to the registrar a copy of the company's profit and loss account, or

    (b)   do not deliver to the registrar a copy of the directors' report,

the copy of the balance sheet delivered to the registrar must contain in a prominent position a statement that the company's annual accounts and reports have been delivered in accordance with the provisions applicable to companies subject to the small companies regime.

(6)   The copies of the balance sheet and any directors' report delivered to the registrar under this section must state the name of the person who signed it on behalf of the board.

(7)   The copy of the auditor's report delivered to the registrar under this section must—

    (a)   state the name of the auditor and (where the auditor is a firm) the name of the person who signed it as senior statutory auditor, or

    (b)   if the conditions in section 506 (circumstances in which names may be omitted) are met, state that a resolution has been passed and notified to the Secretary of State in accordance with that section.

NOTES

Commencement: 20 January 2007 (for the purpose of enabling the exercise of powers to make Orders or Regulations by statutory instrument); 6 April 2008 (otherwise).

Commencement (transitional provisions): see the note to s 380 at **[1.380]**.

Commencement (transitional adaptations): art 6 of the Companies Act 2006 (Commencement No 5, Transitional Provisions and Savings) Order 2007, SI 2007/3495 provides that the provisions brought into force by arts 3 and 5 of that Order shall have effect subject to any transitional adaptations specified in Sch 1 to that Order. Schedule 1, Pt 1, para 6 to the Order (at **[2.62]**) provided for such transitional adaptations (note that this paragraph was revoked by the Companies Act 2006 (Commencement No 8, Transitional Provisions and Savings) Order 2008, SI 2008/2860, art 6, as from 1 October 2009 (subject to any relevant transitional provision or saving in Sch 2 to that Order)).

Sub-s (2): words in square brackets substituted by the Companies Act 2006 (Amendment) (Accounts and Reports) Regulations 2008, SI 2008/393, reg 12, as from 6 April 2008, in relation to financial years beginning on or after that date.

Regulations: the Small Companies and Groups (Accounts and Directors' Report) Regulations 2008, SI 2008/409 at **[4.142]**.

[1.444A]
[444A Filing obligations of companies entitled to small companies exemption in relation to directors' report
(1)   The directors of a company that is entitled to small companies exemption in relation to the directors' report for a financial year—
   (a)   must deliver to the registrar a copy of the company's annual accounts for that year, and
   (b)   may also deliver to the registrar a copy of the directors' report.
(2)   The directors must also deliver to the registrar a copy of the auditor's report on the accounts (and any directors' report) that it delivers.
This does not apply if the company is exempt from audit and the directors have taken advantage of that exception.
(3)   The copies of the balance sheet and directors' report delivered to the registrar under this section must state the name of the person who signed it on behalf of the board.
[(4)   The copy of the auditor's report delivered to the registrar under this section must—
   (a)   state the name of the auditor and (where the auditor is a firm) the name of the person who signed it as senior statutory auditor, or
   (b)   if the conditions in section 506 (circumstances in which names may be omitted) are met, state that a resolution has been passed and notified to the Secretary of State in accordance with that section.]
(5)   This section does not apply to companies within section 444 (filing obligations of companies subject to the small companies regime).]

NOTES
Commencement: 6 April 2008.
Inserted by the Companies Act 2006 (Amendment) (Accounts and Reports) Regulations 2008, SI 2008/393, reg 6(7), as from 6 April 2008, in relation to financial years beginning on or after that date.
Sub-s (4): substituted by the Companies Act 2006 (Accounts, Reports and Audit) Regulations 2009, SI 2009/1581, reg 10, as from 1 October 2009.

[1.445]
445   Filing obligations of medium-sized companies
(1)   The directors of a company that qualifies as a medium-sized company in relation to a financial year (see sections 465 to 467) must deliver to the registrar a copy of—
   (a)   the company's annual accounts, and
   (b)   the directors' report.
(2)   They must also deliver to the registrar a copy of the auditor's report on those accounts (and on the directors' report).
This does not apply if the company is exempt from audit and the directors have taken advantage of that exemption.
(3)   Where the company prepares Companies Act accounts, the directors may deliver to the registrar a copy of the company's annual accounts for the financial year—
   (a)   that includes a profit and loss account in which items are combined in accordance with regulations made by the Secretary of State, and
   (b)   that does not contain items whose omission is authorised by the regulations.
These are referred to in this Part as "abbreviated accounts".
(4)   If abbreviated accounts are delivered to the registrar the obligation to deliver a copy of the auditor's report on the accounts is to deliver a copy of the special auditor's report required by section 449.
(5)   The copies of the balance sheet and directors' report delivered to the registrar under this section must state the name of the person who signed it on behalf of the board.
(6)   The copy of the auditor's report delivered to the registrar under this section must—
   (a)   state the name of the auditor and (where the auditor is a firm) the name of the person who signed it as senior statutory auditor, or
   (b)   if the conditions in section 506 (circumstances in which names may be omitted) are met, state that a resolution has been passed and notified to the Secretary of State in accordance with that section.
[(7)   This section does not apply to companies within—
   (a)   section 444 (filing obligations of companies subject to the small companies regime), or
   (b)   section 444A (filing obligations of companies entitled to small companies exemption in relation to directors' report).]

NOTES
Commencement: 20 January 2007 (for the purpose of enabling the exercise of powers to make Orders or Regulations by statutory instrument); 6 April 2008 (otherwise).
Commencement (transitional provisions): see the note to s 380 at **[1.380]**.
Commencement (transitional adaptations): art 6 of the Companies Act 2006 (Commencement No 5, Transitional Provisions and Savings) Order 2007, SI 2007/3495 provides that the provisions brought into force by arts 3 and 5 of that Order shall have effect subject to any transitional adaptations specified in Sch 1 to that Order. Schedule 1, Pt 1, para 7 to the Order (at **[2.62]**)

provided for such transitional adaptations (note that this paragraph was revoked by the Companies Act 2006 (Commencement No 8, Transitional Provisions and Savings) Order 2008, SI 2008/2860, art 6, as from 1 October 2009 (subject to any relevant transitional provision or saving in Sch 2 to that Order)).

Sub-s (7): substituted by the Companies Act 2006 (Amendment) (Accounts and Reports) Regulations 2008, SI 2008/393, reg 6(8), as from 6 April 2008, in relation to financial years beginning on or after that date.

Regulations: the Large and Medium-sized Companies and Groups (Accounts and Reports) Regulations 2008, SI 2008/410 at **[4.170]**.

[1.446]
446   Filing obligations of unquoted companies
(1)   The directors of an unquoted company must deliver to the registrar for each financial year of the company a copy of—
- (a)   the company's annual accounts,   . . .
- (b)   the directors' report[, and
- (c)   any separate corporate governance statement].

(2)   The directors must also deliver to the registrar a copy of the auditor's report on those accounts (and the directors' report [and any separate corporate governance statement]).

This does not apply if the company is exempt from audit and the directors have taken advantage of that exemption.

(3)   The copies of the balance sheet[, directors' report and any separate corporate governance statement] delivered to the registrar under this section must state the name of the person who signed it on behalf of the board.

(4)   The copy of the auditor's report delivered to the registrar under this section must—
- (a)   state the name of the auditor and (where the auditor is a firm) the name of the person who signed it as senior statutory auditor, or
- (b)   if the conditions in section 506 (circumstances in which names may be omitted) are met, state that a resolution has been passed and notified to the Secretary of State in accordance with that section.

(5)   This section does not apply to companies within—
- (a)   section 444 (filing obligations of companies subject to the small companies regime),   . . .
- [(aa)   section 444A (filing obligations of companies entitled to small companies exemption in relation to directors' report), or]
- (b)   section 445 (filing obligations of medium-sized companies).

NOTES

Commencement: 6 April 2008.

Commencement (transitional provisions): see the note to s 380 at **[1.380]**.

Commencement (transitional adaptations): art 6 of the Companies Act 2006 (Commencement No 5, Transitional Provisions and Savings) Order 2007, SI 2007/3495 provides that the provisions brought into force by arts 3 and 5 of that Order shall have effect subject to any transitional adaptations specified in Sch 1 to that Order. Schedule 1, Pt 1, para 8 to the Order (at **[2.62]**) provided for such transitional adaptations (note that this paragraph was revoked by the Companies Act 2006 (Commencement No 8, Transitional Provisions and Savings) Order 2008, SI 2008/2860, art 6, as from 1 October 2009 (subject to any relevant transitional provision or saving in Sch 2 to that Order)).

Sub-s (1): the word omitted from the end of para (a) was repealed, and para (c) (and the word preceding it) was added by the Companies Act 2006 (Accounts, Reports and Audit) Regulations 2009, SI 2009/1581, reg 3(1), (2), as from 27 June 2009, in relation to financial years beginning on or after 29 June 2008 which have not ended before 27 June 2009.

Sub-s (2): words in square brackets inserted by SI 2009/1581, reg 3(1), (3), as from 27 June 2009, in relation to financial years beginning on or after 29 June 2008 which have not ended before 27 June 2009.

Sub-s (3): words in square brackets substituted by SI 2009/1581, reg 3(1), (6), as from 27 June 2009, in relation to financial years beginning on or after 29 June 2008 which have not ended before 27 June 2009. Note that reg 3(6) provides that this amendment has effect after the transitional adaptation mentioned below ceases to have effect.

Sub-s (5): word omitted from para (a) repealed, and para (aa) inserted, by the Companies Act 2006 (Amendment) (Accounts and Reports) Regulations 2008, SI 2008/393, reg 6(9), as from 6 April 2008, in relation to financial years beginning on or after that date.

Note: SI 2009/1581, reg 3(1), (4) provided that a sub-s (3B) should be inserted after sub-s (3A) (which was inserted by way of transitional adaptation by SI 2007/3495, Schedule 1, Pt 1, para 8 as noted above). Reg 3(5) of the 2009 Regulations further provided that sub-s (3B) shall cease to have effect when that transitional adaptation ceases to have effect. That occurred on 1 October 2009.

[1.447]
447   Filing obligations of quoted companies
(1)   The directors of a quoted company must deliver to the registrar for each financial year of the company a copy of—
- (a)   the company's annual accounts,
- (b)   the directors' remuneration report,   . . .
- (c)   the directors' report[, and
- (d)   any separate corporate governance statement].

(2)   They must also deliver a copy of the auditor's report on those accounts (and on the directors' remuneration report[, the directors' report and any separate corporate governance statement]).

(3)   The copies of the balance sheet, the directors' remuneration report[, the directors' report and any separate corporate governance statement] delivered to the registrar under this section must state the name of the person who signed it on behalf of the board.

(4)   The copy of the auditor's report delivered to the registrar under this section must—

(a)   state the name of the auditor and (where the auditor is a firm) the name of the person who signed it as senior statutory auditor, or

(b)   if the conditions in section 506 (circumstances in which names may be omitted) are met, state that a resolution has been passed and notified to the Secretary of State in accordance with that section.

NOTES

Commencement: 6 April 2008.

Commencement (transitional provisions): see the note to s 380 at **[1.380]**.

Commencement (transitional adaptations): art 6 of the Companies Act 2006 (Commencement No 5, Transitional Provisions and Savings) Order 2007, SI 2007/3495 provides that the provisions brought into force by arts 3 and 5 of that Order shall have effect subject to any transitional adaptations specified in Sch 1 to that Order. Schedule 1, Pt 1, para 9 to the Order (at **[2.62]**) provided for such transitional adaptations (note that this paragraph was revoked by the Companies Act 2006 (Commencement No 8, Transitional Provisions and Savings) Order 2008, SI 2008/2860, art 6, as from 1 October 2009 (subject to any relevant transitional provision or saving in Sch 2 to that Order)).

Sub-s (1): the word omitted from the end of para (b) was repealed, and para (d) (and the word preceding it) was added by the Companies Act 2006 (Accounts, Reports and Audit) Regulations 2009, SI 2009/1581, reg 4(1), (2), as from 27 June 2009, in relation to financial years beginning on or after 29 June 2008 which have not ended before 27 June 2009.

Sub-ss (2), (3): words in square brackets substituted by SI 2009/1581, reg 4(1), (3), (6), as from 27 June 2009, in relation to financial years beginning on or after 29 June 2008 which have not ended before 27 June 2009. Note that reg 4(6) (which amends sub-s (3)) also provides that this amendment has effect after the transitional adaptation mentioned below ceases to have effect.

Note: SI 2009/1581, reg 4(1), (4) provided that a sub-s (3C) should be inserted after sub-s (3B) (which was inserted by way of transitional adaptation by SI 2007/3495, Schedule 1, Pt 1, para 9 as noted above). Reg 4(5) of the 2009 Regulations further provided that sub-s (3C) shall cease to have effect when that transitional adaptation ceases to have effect. That occurred on 1 October 2009.

[1.448]

448   Unlimited companies exempt from obligation to file accounts

(1)   The directors of an unlimited company are not required to deliver accounts and reports to the registrar in respect of a financial year if the following conditions are met.

(2)   The conditions are that at no time during the relevant accounting reference period—

(a)   has the company been, to its knowledge, a subsidiary undertaking of an undertaking which was then limited, or

(b)   have there been, to its knowledge, exercisable by or on behalf of two or more undertakings which were then limited, rights which if exercisable by one of them would have made the company a subsidiary undertaking of it, or

(c)   has the company been a parent company of an undertaking which was then limited.

The references above to an undertaking being limited at a particular time are to an undertaking (under whatever law established) the liability of whose members is at that time limited.

(3)   The exemption conferred by this section does not apply if—

(a)   the company is a banking or insurance company or the parent company of a banking or insurance group, or

[(b)   each of the members of the company is—

(i)   a limited company,

(ii)   another unlimited company each of whose members is a limited company, or

(iii)   a Scottish partnership each of whose members is a limited company.]

[The references in paragraph (b) to a limited company, another unlimited company or a Scottish partnership include a comparable undertaking incorporated in or formed under the law of a country or territory outside the United Kingdom.]

(4)   Where a company is exempt by virtue of this section from the obligation to deliver accounts—

(a)   section 434(3) (requirements in connection with publication of statutory accounts: meaning of "statutory accounts") has effect with the substitution for the words "as required to be delivered to the registrar under section 441" of the words "as prepared in accordance with this Part and approved by the board of directors"; and

(b)   section 435(1)(b) (requirements in connection with publication of non-statutory accounts: statement whether statutory accounts delivered) has effect with the substitution for the words from "whether statutory accounts" to "have been delivered to the registrar" of the words "that the company is exempt from the requirement to deliver statutory accounts".

(5)   In this section the "relevant accounting reference period", in relation to a financial year, means the accounting reference period by reference to which that financial year was determined.

NOTES

Commencement: 6 April 2008.

Commencement (transitional provisions): see the note to s 380 at **[1.380]**.

Sub-s (3): para (b) substituted, and final words in square brackets inserted, by the Companies Act 2006 (Amendment) (Accounts and Reports) Regulations 2008, SI 2008/393, reg 13, as from 6 April 2008, in relation to financial years beginning on or after that date.

Requirements where abbreviated accounts delivered

[1.449]
449   Special auditor's report where abbreviated accounts delivered
(1)   This section applies where—
    (a)   the directors of a company deliver abbreviated accounts to the registrar, and
    (b)   the company is not exempt from audit (or the directors have not taken advantage of any such exemption).
(2)   The directors must also deliver to the registrar a copy of a special report of the company's auditor stating that in his opinion—
    (a)   the company is entitled to deliver abbreviated accounts in accordance with the section in question, and
    (b)   the abbreviated accounts to be delivered are properly prepared in accordance with regulations under that section.
(3)   The auditor's report on the company's annual accounts need not be delivered, but—
    (a)   if that report was qualified, the special report must set out that report in full together with any further material necessary to understand the qualification, and
    (b)   if that report contained a statement under—
        (i)   section 498(2)(a) or (b) (accounts, records or returns inadequate or accounts not agreeing with records and returns), or
        (ii)   section 498(3) (failure to obtain necessary information and explanations),
        the special report must set out that statement in full.
(4)   The provisions of—
    sections 503 to 506 (signature of auditor's report), and
    sections 507 to 509 (offences in connection with auditor's report),
apply to a special report under this section as they apply to an auditor's report on the company's annual accounts prepared under Part 16.
(5)   If abbreviated accounts are delivered to the registrar, the references in section 434 or 435 (requirements in connection with publication of accounts) to the auditor's report on the company's annual accounts shall be read as references to the special auditor's report required by this section.

NOTES
    Commencement: 6 April 2008.
    Commencement (transitional provisions): see the note to s 380 at **[1.380]**.
    Commencement (transitional adaptations): art 6 of the Companies Act 2006 (Commencement No 5, Transitional Provisions and Savings) Order 2007, SI 2007/3495 provides that the provisions brought into force by arts 3 and 5 of that Order shall have effect subject to any transitional adaptations specified in Sch 1 to that Order. Schedule 1, Pt 1, para 10 to the Order (at **[2.62]**) provided for such transitional adaptations (note that this paragraph was revoked by the Companies Act 2006 (Commencement No 8, Transitional Provisions and Savings) Order 2008, SI 2008/2860, art 6, as from 1 October 2009 (subject to any relevant transitional provision or saving in Sch 2 to that Order)).

[1.450]
450   Approval and signing of abbreviated accounts
(1)   Abbreviated accounts must be approved by the board of directors and signed on behalf of the board by a director of the company.
(2)   The signature must be on the balance sheet.
(3)   The balance sheet must contain in a prominent position above the signature a statement to the effect that it is prepared in accordance with the special provisions of this Act relating (as the case may be) to companies subject to the small companies regime or to medium-sized companies.
(4)   If abbreviated accounts are approved that do not comply with the requirements of regulations under the relevant section, every director of the company who—
    (a)   knew that they did not comply, or was reckless as to whether they complied, and
    (b)   failed to take reasonable steps to prevent them from being approved,
commits an offence.
(5)   A person guilty of an offence under subsection (4) is liable—
    (a)   on conviction on indictment, to a fine;
    (b)   on summary conviction, to a fine not exceeding the statutory maximum.

NOTES
    Commencement: 6 April 2008.
    Commencement (transitional provisions): see the note to s 380 at **[1.380]**.

Failure to file accounts and reports

[1.451]
451   Default in filing accounts and reports: offences
(1)   If the requirements of section 441 (duty to file accounts and reports) are not complied with in relation to a company's accounts and reports for a financial year before the end of the period for filing those accounts and reports, every person who immediately before the end of that period was a director of the company commits an offence.

(2)   It is a defence for a person charged with such an offence to prove that he took all reasonable steps for securing that those requirements would be complied with before the end of that period.
(3)   It is not a defence to prove that the documents in question were not in fact prepared as required by this Part.
(4)   A person guilty of an offence under this section is liable on summary conviction to a fine not exceeding level 5 on the standard scale and, for continued contravention, a daily default fine not exceeding one-tenth of level 5 on the standard scale.

NOTES
Commencement: 6 April 2008.
Commencement (transitional provisions): see the note to s 380 at **[1.380]**.

[1.452]
452   Default in filing accounts and reports: court order
(1)   If—
  (a)   the requirements of section 441 (duty to file accounts and reports) are not complied with in relation to a company's accounts and reports for a financial year before the end of the period for filing those accounts and reports, and
  (b)   the directors of the company fail to make good the default within 14 days after the service of a notice on them requiring compliance,
the court may, on the application of any member or creditor of the company or of the registrar, make an order directing the directors (or any of them) to make good the default within such time as may be specified in the order.
(2)   The court's order may provide that all costs (in Scotland, expenses) of and incidental to the application are to be borne by the directors.

NOTES
Commencement: 6 April 2008.
Commencement (transitional provisions): see the note to s 380 at **[1.380]**.

[1.453]
453   Civil penalty for failure to file accounts and reports
(1)   Where the requirements of section 441 are not complied with in relation to a company's accounts and reports for a financial year before the end of the period for filing those accounts and reports, the company is liable to a civil penalty.
This is in addition to any liability of the directors under section 451.
(2)   The amount of the penalty shall be determined in accordance with regulations made by the Secretary of State by reference to—
  (a)   the length of the period between the end of the period for filing the accounts and reports in question and the day on which the requirements are complied with, and
  (b)   whether the company is a private or public company.
(3)   The penalty may be recovered by the registrar and is to be paid into the Consolidated Fund.
(4)   It is not a defence in proceedings under this section to prove that the documents in question were not in fact prepared as required by this Part.
(5)   Regulations under this section having the effect of increasing the penalty payable in any case are subject to affirmative resolution procedure. Otherwise, the regulations are subject to negative resolution procedure.

NOTES
Commencement: 20 January 2007 (for the purpose of enabling the exercise of powers to make Orders or Regulations by statutory instrument); 6 April 2008 (otherwise).
Commencement (transitional provisions): see the note to s 380 at **[1.380]**.
Regulations: the Companies (Late Filing Penalties) and Limited Liability Partnerships (Filing Periods and Late Filing Penalties) Regulations 2008, SI 2008/497 at **[4.252]**.

CHAPTER 11
REVISION OF DEFECTIVE ACCOUNTS AND REPORTS

Voluntary revision

[1.454]
454   Voluntary revision of accounts etc
(1)   If it appears to the directors of a company that—
  (a)   the company's annual accounts,
  (b)   the directors' remuneration report or the directors' report, or
  (c)   a summary financial statement of the company,
did not comply with the requirements of this Act (or, where applicable, of Article 4 of the IAS Regulation), they may prepare revised accounts or a revised report or statement.
(2)   Where copies of the previous accounts or report have been sent out to members, delivered to the registrar or (in the case of a public company) laid before the company in general meeting, the revisions must be confined to—

(a)   the correction of those respects in which the previous accounts or report did not comply with the requirements of this Act (or, where applicable, of Article 4 of the IAS Regulation), and

(b)   the making of any necessary consequential alterations.

(3)   The Secretary of State may make provision by regulations as to the application of the provisions of this Act in relation to—

   (a)   revised annual accounts,

   (b)   a revised directors' remuneration report or directors' report, or

   (c)   a revised summary financial statement.

(4)   The regulations may, in particular—

   (a)   make different provision according to whether the previous accounts, report or statement are replaced or are supplemented by a document indicating the corrections to be made;

   (b)   make provision with respect to the functions of the company's auditor in relation to the revised accounts, report or statement;

   (c)   require the directors to take such steps as may be specified in the regulations where the previous accounts or report have been—

      (i)   sent out to members and others under section 423,

      (ii)   laid before the company in general meeting, or

      (iii)   delivered to the registrar,

     or where a summary financial statement containing information derived from the previous accounts or report has been sent to members under section 426;

   (d)   apply the provisions of this Act (including those creating criminal offences) subject to such additions, exceptions and modifications as are specified in the regulations.

(5)   Regulations under this section are subject to negative resolution procedure.

NOTES

Commencement: 20 January 2007 (for the purpose of enabling the exercise of powers to make Orders or Regulations by statutory instrument); 6 April 2008 (otherwise).

Commencement (transitional provisions): see the note to s 380 at **[1.380]**.

Regulations: the Companies (Revision of Defective Accounts and Reports) Regulations 2008, SI 2008/373 at **[4.100]**.

Secretary of State's notice

[1.455]

455   Secretary of State's notice in respect of accounts or reports

(1)   This section applies where—

   (a)   copies of a company's annual accounts or directors' report have been sent out under section 423, or

   (b)   a copy of a company's annual accounts or directors' report has been delivered to the registrar or (in the case of a public company) laid before the company in general meeting,

and it appears to the Secretary of State that there is, or may be, a question whether the accounts or report comply with the requirements of this Act (or, where applicable, of Article 4 of the IAS Regulation).

(2)   The Secretary of State may give notice to the directors of the company indicating the respects in which it appears that such a question arises or may arise.

(3)   The notice must specify a period of not less than one month for the directors to give an explanation of the accounts or report or prepare revised accounts or a revised report.

(4)   If at the end of the specified period, or such longer period as the Secretary of State may allow, it appears to the Secretary of State that the directors have not—

   (a)   given a satisfactory explanation of the accounts or report, or

   (b)   revised the accounts or report so as to comply with the requirements of this Act (or, where applicable, of Article 4 of the IAS Regulation),

the Secretary of State may apply to the court.

(5)   The provisions of this section apply equally to revised annual accounts and revised directors' reports, in which case they have effect as if the references to revised accounts or reports were references to further revised accounts or reports.

NOTES

Commencement: 6 April 2008.

Commencement (transitional provisions): see the note to s 380 at **[1.380]**.

Application to court

[1.456]

456   Application to court in respect of defective accounts or reports

(1)   An application may be made to the court—

   (a)   by the Secretary of State, after having complied with section 455, or

   (b)   by a person authorised by the Secretary of State for the purposes of this section,

for a declaration (in Scotland, a declarator) that the annual accounts of a company do not comply, or a directors' report does not comply, with the requirements of this Act (or, where applicable, of

Article 4 of the IAS Regulation) and for an order requiring the directors of the company to prepare revised accounts or a revised report.

(2)   Notice of the application, together with a general statement of the matters at issue in the proceedings, shall be given by the applicant to the registrar for registration.

(3)   If the court orders the preparation of revised accounts, it may give directions as to—
   (a)   the auditing of the accounts,
   (b)   the revision of any directors' remuneration report, directors' report or summary financial statement, and
   (c)   the taking of steps by the directors to bring the making of the order to the notice of persons likely to rely on the previous accounts,
and such other matters as the court thinks fit.

(4)   If the court orders the preparation of a revised directors' report it may give directions as to—
   (a)   the review of the report by the auditors,
   (b)   the revision of any summary financial statement,
   (c)   the taking of steps by the directors to bring the making of the order to the notice of persons likely to rely on the previous report, and
   (d)   such other matters as the court thinks fit.

(5)   If the court finds that the accounts or report did not comply with the requirements of this Act (or, where applicable, of Article 4 of the IAS Regulation) it may order that all or part of—
   (a)   the costs (in Scotland, expenses) of and incidental to the application, and
   (b)   any reasonable expenses incurred by the company in connection with or in consequence of the preparation of revised accounts or a revised report,
are to be borne by such of the directors as were party to the approval of the defective accounts or report.

For this purpose every director of the company at the time of the approval of the accounts or report shall be taken to have been a party to the approval unless he shows that he took all reasonable steps to prevent that approval.

(6)   Where the court makes an order under subsection (5) it shall have regard to whether the directors party to the approval of the defective accounts or report knew or ought to have known that the accounts or report did not comply with the requirements of this Act (or, where applicable, of Article 4 of the IAS Regulation), and it may exclude one or more directors from the order or order the payment of different amounts by different directors.

(7)   On the conclusion of proceedings on an application under this section, the applicant must send to the registrar for registration a copy of the court order or, as the case may be, give notice to the registrar that the application has failed or been withdrawn.

(8)   The provisions of this section apply equally to revised annual accounts and revised directors' reports, in which case they have effect as if the references to revised accounts or reports were references to further revised accounts or reports.

NOTES

Commencement: 6 April 2008.

Commencement (transitional provisions): see the note to s 380 at **[1.380]**.

[1.457]
457   Other persons authorised to apply to the court
(1)   The Secretary of State may by order (an "authorisation order") authorise for the purposes of section 456 any person appearing to him—
   (a)   to have an interest in, and to have satisfactory procedures directed to securing, compliance by companies with the requirements of this Act (or, where applicable, of Article 4 of the IAS Regulation) relating to accounts and directors' reports,
   (b)   to have satisfactory procedures for receiving and investigating complaints about companies' annual accounts and directors' reports, and
   (c)   otherwise to be a fit and proper person to be authorised.

(2)   A person may be authorised generally or in respect of particular classes of case, and different persons may be authorised in respect of different classes of case.

(3)   The Secretary of State may refuse to authorise a person if he considers that his authorisation is unnecessary having regard to the fact that there are one or more other persons who have been or are likely to be authorised.

(4)   If the authorised person is an unincorporated association, proceedings brought in, or in connection with, the exercise of any function by the association as an authorised person may be brought by or against the association in the name of a body corporate whose constitution provides for the establishment of the association.

(5)   An authorisation order may contain such requirements or other provisions relating to the exercise of functions by the authorised person as appear to the Secretary of State to be appropriate.

No such order is to be made unless it appears to the Secretary of State that the person would, if authorised, exercise his functions as an authorised person in accordance with the provisions proposed.

(6)   Where authorisation is revoked, the revoking order may make such provision as the Secretary of State thinks fit with respect to pending proceedings.

(7)   An order under this section is subject to negative resolution procedure.

Part 1   The Companies Act 2006

NOTES

Commencement: 20 January 2007 (for the purpose of enabling the exercise of powers to make Orders or Regulations by statutory instrument); 6 April 2008 (otherwise).

Commencement (transitional provisions): see the note to s 380 at **[1.380]**.

Orders: the Companies (Defective Accounts and Directors' Reports) (Authorised Person) and Supervision of Accounts and Reports (Prescribed Body) Order 2008, SI 2008/623. Article 2 of this Order (at **[4.259]**) authorises the Financial Reporting Review Panel established under the articles of association of The Financial Reporting Council Limited for the purposes of s 456 of this Act. For transitional provisions in relation to proceedings under the Companies Act 1985, s 245B pending at 6 April 2008, see art 6 of the Order at **[4.263]**.

[1.458]
458   Disclosure of information by tax authorities
(1)   The Commissioners for Her Majesty's Revenue and Customs may disclose information to a person authorised under section 457 for the purpose of facilitating—
  (a)   the taking of steps by that person to discover whether there are grounds for an application to the court under section 456 (application in respect of defective accounts etc), or
  (b)   a decision by the authorised person whether to make such an application.
(2)   This section applies despite any statutory or other restriction on the disclosure of information.
  Provided that, in the case of personal data within the meaning of the Data Protection Act 1998 (c 29), information is not to be disclosed in contravention of that Act.
(3)   Information disclosed to an authorised person under this section—
  (a)   may not be used except in or in connection with—
    (i)   taking steps to discover whether there are grounds for an application to the court under section 456, or
    (ii)   deciding whether or not to make such an application,
    or in, or in connection with, proceedings on such an application; and
  (b)   must not be further disclosed except—
    (i)   to the person to whom the information relates, or
    (ii)   in, or in connection with, proceedings on any such application to the court.
(4)   A person who contravenes subsection (3) commits an offence unless—
  (a)   he did not know, and had no reason to suspect, that the information had been disclosed under this section, or
  (b)   he took all reasonable steps and exercised all due diligence to avoid the commission of the offence.
(5)   A person guilty of an offence under subsection (4) is liable—
  (a)   on conviction on indictment, to imprisonment for a term not exceeding two years or a fine (or both);
  (b)   on summary conviction—
    (i)   in England and Wales, to imprisonment for a term not exceeding twelve months or to a fine not exceeding the statutory maximum (or both);
    (ii)   in Scotland or Northern Ireland, to imprisonment for a term not exceeding six months, or to a fine not exceeding the statutory maximum (or both).
[(6)   Where an offence under this section is committed by a body corporate, every officer of the body who is in default also commits the offence.
  For this purpose—
  (a)   any person who purports to act as director, manager or secretary of the body is treated as an officer of the body, and
  (b)   if the body is a company, any shadow director is treated as an officer of the company.]

NOTES

Commencement: 6 April 2008.

Commencement (transitional provisions): see the note to s 380 at **[1.380]**.

Sub-s (6): added by the Companies Act 2006 (Consequential Amendments etc) Order 2008, SI 2008/948, art 3(1), Sch 1, Pt 2, para 244, as from 6 April 2008.

Offences under this section: see further s 1131 at **[1.1131]**.

Power of authorised person to require documents etc

[1.459]
459   Power of authorised person to require documents, information and explanations
(1)   This section applies where it appears to a person who is authorised under section 457 that there is, or may be, a question whether a company's annual accounts or directors' report comply with the requirements of this Act (or, where applicable, of Article 4 of the IAS Regulation).
(2)   The authorised person may require any of the persons mentioned in subsection (3) to produce any document, or to provide him with any information or explanations, that he may reasonably require for the purpose of—
  (a)   discovering whether there are grounds for an application to the court under section 456, or
  (b)   deciding whether to make such an application.
(3)   Those persons are—

    (a)   the company;

    (b)   any officer, employee, or auditor of the company;

    (c)   any persons who fell within paragraph (b) at a time to which the document or information required by the authorised person relates.

(4)   If a person fails to comply with such a requirement, the authorised person may apply to the court.

(5)   If it appears to the court that the person has failed to comply with a requirement under subsection (2), it may order the person to take such steps as it directs for securing that the documents are produced or the information or explanations are provided.

(6)   A statement made by a person in response to a requirement under subsection (2) or an order under subsection (5) may not be used in evidence against him in any criminal proceedings.

(7)   Nothing in this section compels any person to disclose documents or information in respect of which a claim to legal professional privilege (in Scotland, to confidentiality of communications) could be maintained in legal proceedings.

(8)   In this section "document" includes information recorded in any form.

NOTES

Commencement: 6 April 2008.

Commencement (transitional provisions): see the note to s 380 at **[1.380]**.

[1.460]

460 Restrictions on disclosure of information obtained under compulsory powers

(1)   This section applies to information (in whatever form) obtained in pursuance of a requirement or order under section 459 (power of authorised person to require documents etc) that relates to the private affairs of an individual or to any particular business.

(2)   No such information may, during the lifetime of that individual or so long as that business continues to be carried on, be disclosed without the consent of that individual or the person for the time being carrying on that business.

(3)   This does not apply—

    (a)   to disclosure permitted by section 461 (permitted disclosure of information obtained under compulsory powers), or

    (b)   to the disclosure of information that is or has been available to the public from another source.

(4)   A person who discloses information in contravention of this section commits an offence, unless—

    (a)   he did not know, and had no reason to suspect, that the information had been disclosed under section 459, or

    (b)   he took all reasonable steps and exercised all due diligence to avoid the commission of the offence.

(5)   A person guilty of an offence under this section is liable—

    (a)   on conviction on indictment, to imprisonment for a term not exceeding two years or a fine (or both);

    (b)   on summary conviction—

        (i)   in England and Wales, to imprisonment for a term not exceeding twelve months or to a fine not exceeding the statutory maximum (or both);

        (ii)   in Scotland or Northern Ireland, to imprisonment for a term not exceeding six months, or to a fine not exceeding the statutory maximum (or both).

[(6)   Where an offence under this section is committed by a body corporate, every officer of the body who is in default also commits the offence.

For this purpose—

    (a)   any person who purports to act as director, manager or secretary of the body is treated as an officer of the body, and

    (b)   if the body is a company, any shadow director is treated as an officer of the company.]

NOTES

Commencement: 6 April 2008.

Commencement (transitional provisions): see the note to s 380 at **[1.380]**.

Sub-s (6): added by the Companies Act 2006 (Consequential Amendments etc) Order 2008, SI 2008/948, art 3(1), Sch 1, Pt 2, para 245, as from 6 April 2008.

Offences under this section: see further s 1131 at **[1.1131]**.

[1.461]

461 Permitted disclosure of information obtained under compulsory powers

(1)   The prohibition in section 460 of the disclosure of information obtained in pursuance of a requirement or order under section 459 (power of authorised person to require documents etc) that relates to the private affairs of an individual or to any particular business has effect subject to the following exceptions.

(2)   It does not apply to the disclosure of information for the purpose of facilitating the carrying out by the authorised person of his functions under section 456.

(3)   It does not apply to disclosure to—

(a)   the Secretary of State,

(b)   the Department of Enterprise, Trade and Investment for Northern Ireland,

(c)   the Treasury,

(d)   the Bank of England,

(e)   the Financial Services Authority, or

(f)   the Commissioners for Her Majesty's Revenue and Customs.

(4)   It does not apply to disclosure—

(a)   for the purpose of assisting a body designated by an order under [section 1252] (delegation of functions of the Secretary of State) to exercise its functions under [Part 42];

(b)   with a view to the institution of, or otherwise for the purposes of, disciplinary proceedings relating to the performance by an accountant or auditor of his professional duties;

(c)   for the purpose of enabling or assisting the Secretary of State or the Treasury to exercise any of their functions under any of the following—

     (i)   the Companies Acts,

     (ii)   Part 5 of the Criminal Justice Act 1993 (c 36) (insider dealing),

     (iii)   the Insolvency Act 1986 (c 45) or the Insolvency (Northern Ireland) Order 1989 (SI 1989/2405 (NI 19)),

     (iv)   the Company Directors Disqualification Act 1986 (c 46) or the Company Directors Disqualification (Northern Ireland) Order 2002 (SI 2002/3150 (NI 4)),

     (v)   the Financial Services and Markets Act 2000 (c 8);

(d)   for the purpose of enabling or assisting the Department of Enterprise, Trade and Investment for Northern Ireland to exercise any powers conferred on it by the enactments relating to companies, directors' disqualification or insolvency;

(e)   for the purpose of enabling or assisting the Bank of England to exercise its functions;

(f)   for the purpose of enabling or assisting the Commissioners for Her Majesty's Revenue and Customs to exercise their functions;

(g)   for the purpose of enabling or assisting the Financial Services Authority to exercise its functions under any of the following—

     (i)   the legislation relating to friendly societies or to industrial and provident societies,

     (ii)   the Building Societies Act 1986 (c 53),

     (iii)   Part 7 of the Companies Act 1989 (c 40),

     (iv)   the Financial Services and Markets Act 2000; or

(h)   in pursuance of any Community obligation.

(5)   It does not apply to disclosure to a body exercising functions of a public nature under legislation in any country or territory outside the United Kingdom that appear to the authorised person to be similar to his functions under section 456 for the purpose of enabling or assisting that body to exercise those functions.

(6)   In determining whether to disclose information to a body in accordance with subsection (5), the authorised person must have regard to the following considerations—

(a)   whether the use which the body is likely to make of the information is sufficiently important to justify making the disclosure;

(b)   whether the body has adequate arrangements to prevent the information from being used or further disclosed other than—

     (i)   for the purposes of carrying out the functions mentioned in that subsection, or

     (ii)   for other purposes substantially similar to those for which information disclosed to the authorised person could be used or further disclosed.

(7)   Nothing in this section authorises the making of a disclosure in contravention of the Data Protection Act 1998 (c 29).

NOTES

Commencement: 6 April 2008.

Commencement (transitional provisions): see the note to s 380 at **[1.380]**.

Sub-s (4): words in square brackets substituted by the Companies Act 2006 (Consequential Amendments etc) Order 2008, SI 2008/948, art 3(1), Sch 1, Pt 2, para 246, as from 6 April 2008.

[1.462]
462   Power to amend categories of permitted disclosure

(1)   The Secretary of State may by order amend section 461(3), (4) and (5).

(2)   An order under this section must not—

(a)   amend subsection (3) of that section (UK public authorities) by specifying a person unless the person exercises functions of a public nature (whether or not he exercises any other function);

(b)   amend subsection (4) of that section (purposes for which disclosure permitted) by adding or modifying a description of disclosure unless the purpose for which the disclosure is permitted is likely to facilitate the exercise of a function of a public nature;

(c)   amend subsection (5) of that section (overseas regulatory authorities) so as to have the effect of permitting disclosures to be made to a body other than one that exercises functions of a public nature in a country or territory outside the United Kingdom.

(3)   An order under this section is subject to negative resolution procedure.

NOTES

Commencement: 20 January 2007 (for the purpose of enabling the exercise of powers to make Orders or Regulations by statutory instrument); 6 April 2008 (otherwise).

Commencement (transitional provisions): see the note to s 380 at **[1.380]**.

CHAPTER 12
SUPPLEMENTARY PROVISIONS

Liability for false or misleading statements in reports

[1.463]
463 Liability for false or misleading statements in reports

(1) The reports to which this section applies are—
   (a) the directors' report,
   (b) the directors' remuneration report, and
   (c) a summary financial statement so far as it is derived from either of those reports.

(2) A director of a company is liable to compensate the company for any loss suffered by it as a result of—
   (a) any untrue or misleading statement in a report to which this section applies, or
   (b) the omission from a report to which this section applies of anything required to be included in it.

(3) He is so liable only if—
   (a) he knew the statement to be untrue or misleading or was reckless as to whether it was untrue or misleading, or
   (b) he knew the omission to be dishonest concealment of a material fact.

(4) No person shall be subject to any liability to a person other than the company resulting from reliance, by that person or another, on information in a report to which this section applies.

(5) The reference in subsection (4) to a person being subject to a liability includes a reference to another person being entitled as against him to be granted any civil remedy or to rescind or repudiate an agreement.

(6) This section does not affect—
   (a) liability for a civil penalty, or
   (b) liability for a criminal offence.

NOTES

Commencement: 20 January 2007.

Commencement (transitional provisions): the Companies Act 2006 (Commencement No 1, Transitional Provisions and Savings) Order 2006, SI 2006/3428, Sch 5, Pt 2, para 3 (at **[2.14]**) provides that this section does not apply to a directors' report, directors' remuneration report or summary financial statement first sent to members and others under ss 238 or 251 of the 1985 Act before 20 January 2007.

Accounting and reporting standards

[1.464]
464 Accounting standards

(1) In this Part "accounting standards" means statements of standard accounting practice issued by such body or bodies as may be prescribed by regulations.

(2) References in this Part to accounting standards applicable to a company's annual accounts are to such standards as are, in accordance with their terms, relevant to the company's circumstances and to the accounts.

(3) Regulations under this section may contain such transitional and other supplementary and incidental provisions as appear to the Secretary of State to be appropriate.

NOTES

Commencement: 20 January 2007 (for the purpose of enabling the exercise of powers to make Orders or Regulations by statutory instrument); 6 April 2008 (otherwise).

Commencement (transitional provisions): see the note to s 380 at **[1.380]**.

Orders: the Accounting Standards (Prescribed Body) Regulations 2008, SI 2008/651 at **[4.265]**. Article 2 of that Order (at **[4.266]**) prescribes the body known as the Accounting Standards Board established under the articles of association of The Financial Reporting Council Limited for the purposes of this section. See also art 4 (transitional provisions) at **[4.268]**, which provides that statements of standard accounting practice which immediately before 6 April 2008 have been issued and not withdrawn by the former body known as the Accounting Standards Board for the purposes of s 256 of the 1985 Act shall be treated, on and after that date, as statements of standard accounting practice issued by the Accounting Standards Board for the purposes of this section.

Companies qualifying as medium-sized

[1.465]
465 Companies qualifying as medium-sized: general

(1) A company qualifies as medium-sized in relation to its first financial year if the qualifying conditions are met in that year.

(2) A company qualifies as medium-sized in relation to a subsequent financial year—

(a)   if the qualifying conditions are met in that year and the preceding financial year;

(b)   if the qualifying conditions are met in that year and the company qualified as medium-sized in relation to the preceding financial year;

(c)   if the qualifying conditions were met in the preceding financial year and the company qualified as medium-sized in relation to that year.

(3)   The qualifying conditions are met by a company in a year in which it satisfies two or more of the following requirements—

1 Turnover	[Not more than £25.9 million]
2 Balance sheet total	[Not more than £12.9 million]
3 Number of employees	Not more than 250

(4)   For a period that is a company's financial year but not in fact a year the maximum figures for turnover must be proportionately adjusted.

(5)   The balance sheet total means the aggregate of the amounts shown as assets in the company's balance sheet.

(6)   The number of employees means the average number of persons employed by the company in the year, determined as follows—

(a)   find for each month in the financial year the number of persons employed under contracts of service by the company in that month (whether throughout the month or not),

(b)   add together the monthly totals, and

(c)   divide by the number of months in the financial year.

(7)   This section is subject to section 466 (companies qualifying as medium-sized: parent companies).

NOTES

Commencement: 6 April 2008.

Commencement (transitional provisions): see the note to s 380 at **[1.380]**.

Sub-s (3): words in square brackets substituted by the Companies Act 2006 (Amendment) (Accounts and Reports) Regulations 2008, SI 2008/393, reg 4(1), as from 6 April 2008, in relation to financial years beginning on or after that date (as to whether a company qualifies as medium-sized for the purposes of this section, see further reg 2(3) of the 2008 Regulations at **[4.141]**).

[1.466]

466 Companies qualifying as medium-sized: parent companies

(1)   A parent company qualifies as a medium-sized company in relation to a financial year only if the group headed by it qualifies as a medium-sized group.

(2)   A group qualifies as medium-sized in relation to the parent company's first financial year if the qualifying conditions are met in that year.

(3)   A group qualifies as medium-sized in relation to a subsequent financial year of the parent company—

(a)   if the qualifying conditions are met in that year and the preceding financial year;

(b)   if the qualifying conditions are met in that year and the group qualified as medium-sized in relation to the preceding financial year;

(c)   if the qualifying conditions were met in the preceding financial year and the group qualified as medium-sized in relation to that year.

(4)   The qualifying conditions are met by a group in a year in which it satisfies two or more of the following requirements—

1 Aggregate turnover	[Not more than £25.9 million net (or £31.1 million gross)]
2 Aggregate balance sheet total	[Not more than £12.9 million net (or £15.5 million gross)]
3 Aggregate number of employees	Not more than 250

(5)   The aggregate figures are ascertained by aggregating the relevant figures determined in accordance with section 465 for each member of the group.

(6)   In relation to the aggregate figures for turnover and balance sheet total—

"net" means after any set-offs and other adjustments made to eliminate group transactions—

(a)   in the case of Companies Act accounts, in accordance with regulations under section 404,

(b)   in the case of IAS accounts, in accordance with international accounting standards; and

"gross" means without those set-offs and other adjustments.

A company may satisfy any relevant requirement on the basis of either the net or the gross figure.

(7)   The figures for each subsidiary undertaking shall be those included in its individual accounts for the relevant financial year, that is—

(a)   if its financial year ends with that of the parent company, that financial year, and

(b)   if not, its financial year ending last before the end of the financial year of the parent company.

If those figures cannot be obtained without disproportionate expense or undue delay, the latest available figures shall be taken.

NOTES

Commencement: 6 April 2008.

Commencement (transitional provisions): see the note to s 380 at **[1.380]**.

Sub-s (4): words in square brackets substituted by the Companies Act 2006 (Amendment) (Accounts and Reports) Regulations 2008, SI 2008/393, reg 4(2), as from 6 April 2008, in relation to financial years beginning on or after that date (as to whether a group qualifies as medium-sized for the purposes of this section, see further reg 2(3) of the 2008 Regulations at **[4.141]**).

[1.467]
467   Companies excluded from being treated as medium-sized

(1)   A company is not entitled to take advantage of any of the provisions of this Part relating to companies qualifying as medium-sized if it was at any time within the financial year in question—
    (a)   a public company,
    (b)   a company that—
        (i)   has permission under Part 4 of the Financial Services and Markets Act 2000 (c 8) to carry on a regulated activity, or
        (ii)   carries on insurance market activity, or
    (c)   a member of an ineligible group.

(2)   A group is ineligible if any of its members is—
    (a)   a public company,
    (b)   a body corporate (other than a company) whose shares are admitted to trading on a regulated market,
    (c)   a person (other than a small company) who has permission under Part 4 of the Financial Services and Markets Act 2000 to carry on a regulated activity,
    (d)   a small company that is an authorised insurance company, a banking company, an e-money issuer, [a MiFID investment firm] or a UCITS management company, or
    (e)   a person who carries on insurance market activity.

(3)   A company is a small company for the purposes of subsection (2) if it qualified as small in relation to its last financial year ending on or before the end of the financial year in question.

[(4)   This section does not prevent a company from taking advantage of section 417(7) (business review: non-financial information) by reason only of its having been a member of an ineligible group at any time within the financial year in question.]

NOTES

Commencement: 6 April 2008.

Commencement (transitional provisions): see the note to s 380 at **[1.380]**.

Sub-s (2): words in square brackets in para (d) substituted by the Markets in Financial Instruments Directive (Consequential Amendments) Regulations 2007, SI 2007/2932, reg 3(1), (3), as from 1 November 2007.

Sub-s (4): added by the Companies Act 2006 (Amendment) (Accounts and Reports) Regulations 2008, SI 2008/393, reg 7, as from 6 April 2008, in relation to financial years beginning on or after that date.

General power to make further provision about accounts and reports

[1.468]
468   General power to make further provision about accounts and reports

(1)   The Secretary of State may make provision by regulations about—
    (a)   the accounts and reports that companies are required to prepare;
    (b)   the categories of companies required to prepare accounts and reports of any description;
    (c)   the form and content of the accounts and reports that companies are required to prepare;
    (d)   the obligations of companies and others as regards—
        (i)   the approval of accounts and reports,
        (ii)   the sending of accounts and reports to members and others,
        (iii)   the laying of accounts and reports before the company in general meeting,
        (iv)   the delivery of copies of accounts and reports to the registrar, and
        (v)   the publication of accounts and reports.

(2)   The regulations may amend this Part by adding, altering or repealing provisions.

(3)   But they must not amend (other than consequentially)—
    (a)   section 393 (accounts to give true and fair view), or
    (b)   the provisions of Chapter 11 (revision of defective accounts and reports).

(4)   The regulations may create criminal offences in cases corresponding to those in which an offence is created by an existing provision of this Part.

The maximum penalty for any such offence may not be greater than is provided in relation to an offence under the existing provision.

(5)   The regulations may provide for civil penalties in circumstances corresponding to those within section 453(1) (civil penalty for failure to file accounts and reports).

The provisions of section 453(2) to (5) apply in relation to any such penalty.

Part 1   The Companies Act 2006

NOTES

Commencement: 20 January 2007 (for the purpose of enabling the exercise of powers to make Orders or Regulations by statutory instrument); 6 April 2008 (otherwise).

Commencement (transitional provisions): see the note to s 380 at **[1.380]**.

Regulations: the Companies Act 2006 (Amendment) (Accounts and Reports) Regulations 2008, SI 2008/393 at **[4.140]**; the Companies Act 2006 (Accounts, Reports and Audit) Regulations 2009, SI 2009/1581 at **[4.388]**; the Companies Act 2006 (Amendment of Section 413) Regulations 2009, SI 2009/3022.

Other supplementary provisions

[1.469]

469   Preparation and filing of accounts in euros

(1)   The amounts set out in the annual accounts of a company may also be shown in the same accounts translated into euros.

(2)   When complying with section 441 (duty to file accounts and reports), the directors of a company may deliver to the registrar an additional copy of the company's annual accounts in which the amounts have been translated into euros.

(3)   In both cases—

(a)   the amounts must have been translated at the exchange rate prevailing on the date to which the balance sheet is made up, and

(b)   that rate must be disclosed in the notes to the accounts.

(4)   For the purposes of sections 434 and 435 (requirements in connection with published accounts) any additional copy of the company's annual accounts delivered to the registrar under subsection (2) above shall be treated as statutory accounts of the company.

In the case of such a copy, references in those sections to the auditor's report on the company's annual accounts shall be read as references to the auditor's report on the annual accounts of which it is a copy.

NOTES

Commencement: 6 April 2008.

Commencement (transitional provisions): see the note to s 380 at **[1.380]**.

[1.470]

470   Power to apply provisions to banking partnerships

(1)   The Secretary of State may by regulations apply to banking partnerships, subject to such exceptions, adaptations and modifications as he considers appropriate, the provisions of this Part (and of regulations made under this Part) applying to banking companies.

(2)   A "banking partnership" means a partnership which has permission under Part 4 of the Financial Services and Markets Act 2000 (c 8).

But a partnership is not a banking partnership if it has permission to accept deposits only for the purpose of carrying on another regulated activity in accordance with that permission.

(3)   Expressions used in this section that are also used in the provisions regulating activities under the Financial Services and Markets Act 2000 have the same meaning here as they do in those provisions.

See section 22 of that Act, orders made under that section and Schedule 2 to that Act.

(4)   Regulations under this section are subject to affirmative resolution procedure.

NOTES

Commencement: 20 January 2007 (for the purpose of enabling the exercise of powers to make Orders or Regulations by statutory instrument); 6 April 2008 (otherwise).

Commencement (transitional provisions): see the note to s 380 at **[1.380]**.

[1.471]

471   Meaning of "annual accounts" and related expressions

(1)   In this Part a company's "annual accounts", in relation to a financial year, means—

(a)   the company's individual accounts for that year (see section 394), and

(b)   any group accounts prepared by the company for that year (see sections 398 and 399).

This is subject to section 408 (option to omit individual profit and loss account from annual accounts where information given in group accounts).

(2)   In the case of an unquoted company, its "annual accounts and reports" for a financial year are—

(a)   its annual accounts,

(b)   the directors' report, and

(c)   the auditor's report on those accounts and the directors' report (unless the company is exempt from audit).

(3)   In the case of a quoted company, its "annual accounts and reports" for a financial year are—

(a)   its annual accounts,

(b)   the directors' remuneration report,

(c)   the directors' report, and

(d)   the auditor's report on those accounts, on the auditable part of the directors' remuneration report and on the directors' report.

NOTES

Commencement: 6 April 2008.

Commencement (transitional provisions): see the note to s 380 at **[1.380]**.

[1.472]
472   Notes to the accounts

(1)   Information required by this Part to be given in notes to a company's annual accounts may be contained in the accounts or in a separate document annexed to the accounts.

(2)   References in this Part to a company's annual accounts, or to a balance sheet or profit and loss account, include notes to the accounts giving information which is required by any provision of this Act or international accounting standards, and required or allowed by any such provision to be given in a note to company accounts.

NOTES

Commencement: 6 April 2008.

Commencement (transitional provisions): see the note to s 380 at **[1.380]**.

[1.472A]
[472A   Meaning of "corporate governance statement" etc

(1)   In this Part "corporate governance statement" means the statement required by rules 7.2.1 to 7.2.11 in the Disclosure Rules and Transparency Rules sourcebook issued by the Financial Services Authority.

(2)   Those rules were inserted by Annex C of the Disclosure Rules and Transparency Rules Sourcebook (Corporate Governance Rules) Instrument 2008 made by the Authority on 26th June 2008 (FSA 2008/32).

(3)   A "separate" corporate governance statement means one that is not included in the directors' report.]

NOTES

Commencement: 27 June 2009.

Inserted by the Companies Act 2006 (Accounts, Reports and Audit) Regulations 2009, SI 2009/1581, reg 5, as from 27 June 2009, in relation to financial years beginning on or after 29 June 2008 which have not ended before 27 June 2009.

[1.473]
473   Parliamentary procedure for certain regulations under this Part

(1)   This section applies to regulations under the following provisions of this Part—

section 396 (Companies Act individual accounts),
section 404 (Companies Act group accounts),
section 409 (information about related undertakings),
section 412 (information about directors' benefits: remuneration, pensions and compensation for loss of office),
section 416 (contents of directors' report: general),
section 421 (contents of directors' remuneration report),
section 444 (filing obligations of companies subject to small companies regime),
section 445 (filing obligations of medium-sized companies),
section 468 (general power to make further provision about accounts and reports).

(2)   Any such regulations may make consequential amendments or repeals in other provisions of this Act, or in other enactments.

(3)   Regulations that—

(a)   restrict the classes of company which have the benefit of any exemption, exception or special provision,
(b)   require additional matter to be included in a document of any class, or
(c)   otherwise render the requirements of this Part more onerous,

are subject to affirmative resolution procedure.

(4)   Otherwise, the regulations are subject to negative resolution procedure.

NOTES

Commencement: 20 January 2007 (for the purpose of enabling the exercise of powers to make Orders or Regulations by statutory instrument); 6 April 2008 (otherwise).

Commencement (transitional provisions): see the note to s 380 at **[1.380]**.

As to Regulations made under the sections listed in sub-s (1), see the notes to those sections *ante.*

[1.474]
474   Minor definitions

(1)   In this Part—

"e-money issuer" means a person who has permission under Part 4 of the Financial Services and Markets Act 2000 (c 8) to carry on the activity of issuing electronic money within the meaning of article 9B of the Financial Services and Markets Act 2000 (Regulated Activities) Order 2001 (SI 2001/544);

"group" means a parent undertaking and its subsidiary undertakings;

"IAS Regulation" means EC Regulation No 1606/2002 of the European Parliament and of the Council of 19 July 2002 on the application of international accounting standards;

"included in the consolidation", in relation to group accounts, or "included in consolidated group accounts", means that the undertaking is included in the accounts by the method of full (and not proportional) consolidation, and references to an undertaking excluded from consolidation shall be construed accordingly;

"international accounting standards" means the international accounting standards, within the meaning of the IAS Regulation, adopted from time to time by the European Commission in accordance with that Regulation;

. . .

["MiFID investment firm" means an investment firm within the meaning of Article 4.1.1 of Directive 2004/39/EC of the European Parliament and of the Council of 21 April 2004 on markets in financial instruments, other than—

    (a)   a company to which that Directive does not apply by virtue of Article 2 of that Directive,

    (b)   a company which is an exempt investment firm within the meaning of regulation 4A(3) of the Financial Services and Markets Act 2000 (Markets in Financial Instruments) Regulations 2007, and

    (c)   any other company which fulfils all the requirements set out in regulation 4C(3) of those Regulations;]

"profit and loss account", in relation to a company that prepares IAS accounts, includes an income statement or other equivalent financial statement required to be prepared by international accounting standards;

"regulated activity" has the meaning given in section 22 of the Financial Services and Markets Act 2000, except that it does not include activities of the kind specified in any of the following provisions of the Financial Services and Markets Act 2000 (Regulated Activities) Order 2001 (SI 2001/544)—

    (a)   article 25A (arranging regulated mortgage contracts),

    (b)   article 25B (arranging regulated home reversion plans),

    (c)   article 25C (arranging regulated home purchase plans),

    [(ca) article 25E (arranging regulated sale and rent back agreements),]

    (d)   article 39A (assisting administration and performance of a contract of insurance),

    (e)   article 53A (advising on regulated mortgage contracts),

    (f)   article 53B (advising on regulated home reversion plans),

    (g)   article 53C (advising on regulated home purchase plans),

    [(ga) article 53D (advising on regulated sale and rent back agreements),]

    (h)   article 21 (dealing as agent), article 25 (arranging deals in investments) or article 53 (advising on investments) where the activity concerns relevant investments that are not contractually based investments (within the meaning of article 3 of that Order), or

    (i)   article 64 (agreeing to carry on a regulated activity of the kind mentioned in paragraphs (a) to (h));

"turnover", in relation to a company, means the amounts derived from the provision of goods and services falling within the company's ordinary activities, after deduction of—

    (a)   trade discounts,

    (b)   value added tax, and

    (c)   any other taxes based on the amounts so derived;

"UCITS management company" has the meaning given by the Glossary forming part of the Handbook made by the Financial Services Authority under the Financial Services and Markets Act 2000 (c 8).

(2) In the case of an undertaking not trading for profit, any reference in this Part to a profit and loss account is to an income and expenditure account. References to profit and loss and, in relation to group accounts, to a consolidated profit and loss account shall be construed accordingly.

NOTES

Commencement: 6 April 2008.

Commencement (transitional provisions): see the note to s 380 at **[1.380]**.

Definition "ISD investment firm" (omitted) revoked, and definition "MiFID investment firm" inserted, by the Markets in Financial Instruments Directive (Consequential Amendments) Regulations 2007, SI 2007/2932, reg 3(4), as from 1 November 2007.

In the definition "regulated activity", paras (ca), (ga) inserted by the Financial Services and Markets Act 2000 (Regulated Activities) (Amendment) Order 2009, SI 2009/1342, art 26, as from 1 July 2009 (other than for the purposes of enabling applications to be made for a Part IV permission, or a variation of a Part IV permission, in relation to activities of the kind specified by arts 25E, 53D or 63J or, so far as relevant to any such activity, art 64 of this Order), and as from 30 June 2010 (for those purposes).

PART 16
AUDIT

CHAPTER 1
REQUIREMENT FOR AUDITED ACCOUNTS

Requirement for audited accounts

[1.475]
475 Requirement for audited accounts

(1)   A company's annual accounts for a financial year must be audited in accordance with this Part unless the company—
  (a)   is exempt from audit under—
     section 477 (small companies), or
     section 480 (dormant companies);
     or
  (b)   is exempt from the requirements of this Part under section 482 (non-profit-making companies subject to public sector audit).

(2)   A company is not entitled to any such exemption unless its balance sheet contains a statement by the directors to that effect.

(3)   A company is not entitled to exemption under any of the provisions mentioned in subsection (1)(a) unless its balance sheet contains a statement by the directors to the effect that—
  (a)   the members have not required the company to obtain an audit of its accounts for the year in question in accordance with section 476, and
  (b)   the directors acknowledge their responsibilities for complying with the requirements of this Act with respect to accounting records and the preparation of accounts.

(4)   The statement required by subsection (2) or (3) must appear on the balance sheet above the signature required by section 414.

NOTES
Commencement: 6 April 2008.
Commencement (transitional provisions): Sch 4, Pt 1, para 9 to the Companies Act 2006 (Commencement No 5, Transitional Provisions and Savings) Order 2007, SI 2007/3495 (at **[2.66]**) provides as follows—

"Audit (ss 475 to 484 and 489 to 539)
9.—(1)   In Chapter 1 of Part 16 of the Companies Act 2006 (requirement for audited accounts)—
  (a)   sections 475 to 481 (general provisions) apply to accounts for financial years beginning on or after 6th April 2008;
  (b)   sections 482 and 483 (companies subject to public sector audit) apply to accounts for financial years beginning on or after 1st April 2008;
  (c)   section 484 (general power of amendment by regulations) applies accordingly.
(2)   Sections 235(1), 249A(1), (3) and (6) to (7), 249AA and 249B of the 1985 Act or Articles 243(1), 257A(1), (3) and (6) to (7), 257AA and 257B of the 1986 Order continue to apply to accounts for financial years beginning before 6th April 2008.
(3)   In section 482 of the Companies Act 2006 (non-profit-making companies subject to public sector audit) as it applies in relation to accounts for financial years beginning on or after 1st April 2008 and before 6th April 2008, the reference to the requirements of Part 16 of that Act shall be read as a reference to the requirements of Part 7 of the 1985 Act or Part 8 of the 1986 Order.".

[1.476]
476 Right of members to require audit

(1)   The members of a company that would otherwise be entitled to exemption from audit under any of the provisions mentioned in section 475(1)(a) may by notice under this section require it to obtain an audit of its accounts for a financial year.

(2)   The notice must be given by—
  (a)   members representing not less in total than 10% in nominal value of the company's issued share capital, or any class of it, or
  (b)   if the company does not have a share capital, not less than 10% in number of the members of the company.

(3)   The notice may not be given before the financial year to which it relates and must be given not later than one month before the end of that year.

NOTES
Commencement: 6 April 2008.
Commencement (transitional provisions): see the note to s 475 at **[1.475]**.

Exemption from audit: small companies

[1.477]
477 Small companies: conditions for exemption from audit

(1) A company that meets the following conditions in respect of a financial year is exempt from the requirements of this Act relating to the audit of accounts for that year.

(2) The conditions are—
- (a) that the company qualifies as a small company in relation to that year,
- (b) that its turnover in that year is [not more than £6.5 million], and
- (c) that its balance sheet total for that year is [not more than £3.26 million].

(3) For a period which is a company's financial year but not in fact a year the maximum figure for turnover shall be proportionately adjusted.

(4) For the purposes of this section—
- (a) whether a company qualifies as a small company shall be determined in accordance with section 382(1) to (6), and
- (b) "balance sheet total" has the same meaning as in that section.

(5) This section has effect subject to—
section 475(2) and (3) (requirements as to statements to be contained in balance sheet),
section 476 (right of members to require audit),
section 478 (companies excluded from small companies exemption), and
section 479 (availability of small companies exemption in case of group company).

NOTES
Commencement: 6 April 2008.
Commencement (transitional provisions): see the note to s 475 at **[1.475]**.
Sub-s (2): words in square brackets substituted by the Companies Act 2006 (Amendment) (Accounts and Reports) Regulations 2008, SI 2008/393, reg 5(1), as from 6 April 2008, in relation to financial years beginning on or after that date.

[1.478]
478 Companies excluded from small companies exemption

A company is not entitled to the exemption conferred by section 477 (small companies) if it was at any time within the financial year in question—
- (a) a public company,
- (b) a company that—
  - (i) is an authorised insurance company, a banking company, an e-money issuer, [a MiFID investment firm] or a UCITS management company, or
  - (ii) carries on insurance market activity, or
- (c) a special register body as defined in section 117(1) of the Trade Union and Labour Relations (Consolidation) Act 1992 (c 52) or an employers' association as defined in section 122 of that Act or Article 4 of the Industrial Relations (Northern Ireland) Order 1992 (SI 1992/807 (NI 5)).

NOTES
Commencement: 6 April 2008.
Commencement (transitional provisions): see the note to s 475 at **[1.475]**.
Words in square brackets in para (b)(i) substituted by the Markets in Financial Instruments Directive (Consequential Amendments) Regulations 2007, SI 2007/2932, reg 3(5), as from 1 November 2007.

[1.479]
479 Availability of small companies exemption in case of group company

(1) A company is not entitled to the exemption conferred by section 477 (small companies) in respect of a financial year during any part of which it was a group company unless—
- (a) the conditions specified in subsection (2) below are met, or
- (b) subsection (3) applies.

(2) The conditions are—
- (a) that the group—
  - (i) qualifies as a small group in relation to that financial year, and
  - (ii) was not at any time in that year an ineligible group;
- (b) that the group's aggregate turnover in that year is [not more than £6.5 million net (or £7.8 million gross)];
- (c) that the group's aggregate balance sheet total for that year is [not more than £3.26 million net (or £3.9 million gross)].

(3) A company is not excluded by subsection (1) if, throughout the whole of the period or periods during the financial year when it was a group company, it was both a subsidiary undertaking and dormant.

(4) In this section—
- (a) "group company" means a company that is a parent company or a subsidiary undertaking, and
- (b) "the group", in relation to a group company, means that company together with all its associated undertakings.

For this purpose undertakings are associated if one is a subsidiary undertaking of the other or both are subsidiary undertakings of a third undertaking.

(5) For the purposes of this section—

   (a) whether a group qualifies as small shall be determined in accordance with section 383 (companies qualifying as small: parent companies);

   (b) "ineligible group" has the meaning given by section 384(2) and (3);

   (c) a group's aggregate turnover and aggregate balance sheet total shall be determined as for the purposes of section 383;

   (d) "net" and "gross" have the same meaning as in that section;

   (e) a company may meet any relevant requirement on the basis of either the gross or the net figure.

(6) The provisions mentioned in subsection (5) apply for the purposes of this section as if all the bodies corporate in the group were companies.

NOTES

Commencement: 6 April 2008.

Commencement (transitional provisions): see the note to s 475 at **[1.475]**.

Sub-s (2): words in square brackets substituted by the Companies Act 2006 (Amendment) (Accounts and Reports) Regulations 2008, SI 2008/393, reg 5(2), as from 6 April 2008, in relation to financial years beginning on or after that date.

Exemption from audit: dormant companies

[1.480]

480 Dormant companies: conditions for exemption from audit

(1) A company is exempt from the requirements of this Act relating to the audit of accounts in respect of a financial year if—

   (a) it has been dormant since its formation, or

   (b) it has been dormant since the end of the previous financial year and the following conditions are met.

(2) The conditions are that the company—

   (a) as regards its individual accounts for the financial year in question—

      (i) is entitled to prepare accounts in accordance with the small companies regime (see sections 381 to 384), or

      (ii) would be so entitled but for having been a public company or a member of an ineligible group, and

   (b) is not required to prepare group accounts for that year.

(3) This section has effect subject to—

   section 475(2) and (3) (requirements as to statements to be contained in balance sheet),

   section 476 (right of members to require audit), and

   section 481 (companies excluded from dormant companies exemption).

NOTES

Commencement: 6 April 2008.

Commencement (transitional provisions): see the note to s 475 at **[1.475]**.

[1.481]

481 Companies excluded from dormant companies exemption

A company is not entitled to the exemption conferred by section 480 (dormant companies) if it was at any time within the financial year in question a company that—

   (a) is an authorised insurance company, a banking company, an e-money issuer, [a MiFID investment firm] or a UCITS management company, or

   (b) carries on insurance market activity.

NOTES

Commencement: 6 April 2008.

Commencement (transitional provisions): see the note to s 475 at **[1.475]**.

Words in square brackets in para (a) substituted by the Markets in Financial Instruments Directive (Consequential Amendments) Regulations 2007, SI 2007/2932, reg 3(6), as from 1 November 2007.

Companies subject to public sector audit

[1.482]

482 Non-profit-making companies subject to public sector audit

(1) The requirements of this Part as to audit of accounts do not apply to a company for a financial year if it is non-profit-making and its accounts—

   [(a) are subject to audit by the Comptroller and Auditor General by virtue of an order under section 25(6) of the Government Resources and Accounts Act 2000;

   (ab) are subject to audit by the Auditor General for Wales by virtue of—

      (i) an order under section 144 of the Government of Wales Act 1998, or

      (ii) paragraph 18 of Schedule 8 to the Government of Wales Act 2006;]

   (b) are accounts—

(i)   in relation to which section 21 of the Public Finance and Accountability (Scotland) Act 2000 (asp 1) (audit of accounts: Auditor General for Scotland) applies, or

(ii)   that are subject to audit by the Auditor General for Scotland by virtue of an order under section 483 (Scottish public sector companies: audit by Auditor General for Scotland); or

(c)   are subject to audit by the Comptroller and Auditor General for Northern Ireland by virtue of an order under Article 5(3) of the Audit and Accountability (Northern Ireland) Order 2003 (SI 2003/418 (NI 5)).

(2)   In the case of a company that is a parent company or a subsidiary undertaking, subsection (1) applies only if every group undertaking is non-profit-making.

(3)   In this section "non-profit-making" has the same meaning as in Article 48 of the Treaty establishing the European Community.

(4)   This section has effect subject to section 475(2) (balance sheet to contain statement that company entitled to exemption under this section).

NOTES

Commencement: 6 April 2008.

Commencement (transitional provisions): see the note to s 475 at **[1.475]**.

Sub-s (1): paras (a), (ab) substituted, for the original para (a), by the Government of Wales Act 2006 (Consequential Modifications, Transitional Provisions and Saving) Order 2009, SI 2009/2958, arts 8, 10, as from 6 November 2009.

[1.483]

483   Scottish public sector companies: audit by Auditor General for Scotland

(1)   The Scottish Ministers may by order provide for the accounts of a company having its registered office in Scotland to be audited by the Auditor General for Scotland.

(2)   An order under subsection (1) may be made in relation to a company only if it appears to the Scottish Ministers that the company—

(a)   exercises in or as regards Scotland functions of a public nature none of which relate to reserved matters (within the meaning of the Scotland Act 1998 (c 46)), or

(b)   is entirely or substantially funded from a body having accounts falling within paragraph (a) or (b) of subsection (3).

(3)   Those accounts are—

(a)   accounts in relation to which section 21 of the Public Finance and Accountability (Scotland) Act 2000 (asp 1) (audit of accounts: Auditor General for Scotland) applies,

(b)   accounts which are subject to audit by the Auditor General for Scotland by virtue of an order under this section.

(4)   An order under subsection (1) may make such supplementary or consequential provision (including provision amending an enactment) as the Scottish Ministers think expedient.

(5)   An order under subsection (1) shall not be made unless a draft of the statutory instrument containing it has been laid before, and approved by resolution of, the Scottish Parliament.

NOTES

Commencement: 20 January 2007 (for the purpose of enabling the exercise of powers to make Orders or Regulations by statutory instrument); 6 April 2008 (otherwise).

Commencement (transitional provisions): see the note to s 475 at **[1.475]**.

Orders: the Companies Act 2006 (Scottish public sector companies to be audited by the Auditor General for Scotland) Order 2008, SSI 2008/144. This Order provides that certain companies with registered offices in Scotland are to have their accounts audited by the Auditor General for Scotland. This means that in terms of s 475 of this Act, these companies will be exempt from the auditing of company accounts requirements of Part 16. The companies subject to this Order are non-profit making public sector companies, which appear to Scottish Ministers to carry out functions of a public nature or are funded by bodies audited by the Auditor General for Scotland.

General power of amendment by regulations

[1.484]

484   General power of amendment by regulations

(1)   The Secretary of State may by regulations amend this Chapter or section 539 (minor definitions) so far as applying to this Chapter by adding, altering or repealing provisions.

(2)   The regulations may make consequential amendments or repeals in other provisions of this Act, or in other enactments.

(3)   Regulations under this section imposing new requirements, or rendering existing requirements more onerous, are subject to affirmative resolution procedure.

(4)   Other regulations under this section are subject to negative resolution procedure.

NOTES

Commencement: 20 January 2007 (for the purpose of enabling the exercise of powers to make Orders or Regulations by statutory instrument); 6 April 2008 (otherwise).

Commencement (transitional provisions): see the note to s 475 at **[1.475]**.

Regulations: the Companies Act 2006 (Amendment) (Accounts and Reports) Regulations 2008, SI 2008/393 at **[4.140]**.

CHAPTER 2
APPOINTMENT OF AUDITORS

Private companies

[1.485]
485 Appointment of auditors of private company: general
(1) An auditor or auditors of a private company must be appointed for each financial year of the company, unless the directors reasonably resolve otherwise on the ground that audited accounts are unlikely to be required.
(2) For each financial year for which an auditor or auditors is or are to be appointed (other than the company's first financial year), the appointment must be made before the end of the period of 28 days beginning with—
  (a) the end of the time allowed for sending out copies of the company's annual accounts and reports for the previous financial year (see section 424), or
  (b) if earlier, the day on which copies of the company's annual accounts and reports for the previous financial year are sent out under section 423.
  This is the "period for appointing auditors".
(3) The directors may appoint an auditor or auditors of the company—
  (a) at any time before the company's first period for appointing auditors,
  (b) following a period during which the company (being exempt from audit) did not have any auditor, at any time before the company's next period for appointing auditors, or
  (c) to fill a casual vacancy in the office of auditor.
(4) The members may appoint an auditor or auditors by ordinary resolution—
  (a) during a period for appointing auditors,
  (b) if the company should have appointed an auditor or auditors during a period for appointing auditors but failed to do so, or
  (c) where the directors had power to appoint under subsection (3) but have failed to make an appointment.
(5) An auditor or auditors of a private company may only be appointed—
  (a) in accordance with this section, or
  (b) in accordance with section 486 (default power of Secretary of State).
  This is without prejudice to any deemed re-appointment under section 487.

NOTES
Commencement: 1 October 2007.
Commencement (transitional provisions): Sch 3, paras 44, 45 to the Companies Act 2006 (Commencement No 3, Consequential Amendments, Transitional Provisions and Savings) Order 2007, SI 2007/2194 (at **[2.45]**) provide as follows—

"Appointment of auditors of private companies (ss 485 to 488)
44.—(1) Sections 485 to 488 of the Companies Act 2006 (appointment of auditors of private companies) apply in relation to appointments for financial years beginning on or after 1st October 2007.
(2) Sections 384 to 388A of the 1985 Act or Articles 392 to 396A of the 1986 Order continue to apply in relation to appointments for financial years beginning before that date.
(3) Where—
  (a) a private company has elected under section 386 of the 1985 Act or Article 394 of the 1986 Order to dispense with the annual appointment of auditors, and
  (b) the election is in force immediately before 1st October 2007,
section 487(2)(a) of the Companies Act 2006 (no deemed reappointment of auditors appointed by directors) does not prevent the deemed reappointment under that subsection of auditors first appointed before 1st October 2007.
45.—(1) This paragraph applies where immediately before 1st October 2007 a resolution of a private company under section 390A of the 1985 Act or Article 398A of the 1986 Order (remuneration of auditors) was in force and was expressed (in whatever terms) to continue to have effect so long as a resolution under section 386 of that Act or Article 394 of that Order (election to dispense with annual appointment of auditors) continued in force.
(2) The repeal of section 386 of the 1985 Act or Article 394 of the 1986 Order does not affect the continued operation of the resolution, which shall continue to have effect until—
  (a) it is revoked or superseded by a further resolution,
  (b) the auditors to which it applies cease to hold office, or
  (c) it otherwise ceases to have effect in accordance with its terms.".

Commencement (transitional adaptations): the transitional adaptations of this section contained in the Companies Act 2006 (Commencement No 3, Consequential Amendments, Transitional Provisions and Savings) Order 2007, SI 2007/2194, Sch 1, para 17 were revoked by the Companies Act 2006 (Commencement No 5, Transitional Provisions and Savings) Order 2007, SI 2007/3495, art 10(1), (3), as from 6 April 2008 (subject to any transitional provisions and savings as apply, in accordance with Sch 4 to that Order, in relation to the repeal of any provision of the 1985 Act referred to in the adaptation). See **[2.43]**.

[1.486]
486 Appointment of auditors of private company: default power of Secretary of State
(1) If a private company fails to appoint an auditor or auditors in accordance with section 485, the Secretary of State may appoint one or more persons to fill the vacancy.

(2)   Where subsection (2) of that section applies and the company fails to make the necessary appointment before the end of the period for appointing auditors, the company must within one week of the end of that period give notice to the Secretary of State of his power having become exercisable.

(3)   If a company fails to give the notice required by this section, an offence is committed by—
  (a)   the company, and
  (b)   every officer of the company who is in default.

(4)   A person guilty of an offence under this section is liable on summary conviction to a fine not exceeding level 3 on the standard scale and, for continued contravention, a daily default fine not exceeding one-tenth of level 3 on the standard scale.

NOTES
Commencement: 1 October 2007.
Commencement (transitional provisions): see the note to s 485 at **[1.485]**.

[1.487]
487   Term of office of auditors of private company

(1)   An auditor or auditors of a private company hold office in accordance with the terms of their appointment, subject to the requirements that—
  (a)   they do not take office until any previous auditor or auditors cease to hold office, and
  (b)   they cease to hold office at the end of the next period for appointing auditors unless re-appointed.

(2)   Where no auditor has been appointed by the end of the next period for appointing auditors, any auditor in office immediately before that time is deemed to be re-appointed at that time, unless—
  (a)   he was appointed by the directors, or
  (b)   the company's articles require actual re-appointment, or
  (c)   the deemed re-appointment is prevented by the members under section 488, or
  (d)   the members have resolved that he should not be re-appointed, or
  (e)   the directors have resolved that no auditor or auditors should be appointed for the financial year in question.

(3)   This is without prejudice to the provisions of this Part as to removal and resignation of auditors.

(4)   No account shall be taken of any loss of the opportunity of deemed re-appointment under this section in ascertaining the amount of any compensation or damages payable to an auditor on his ceasing to hold office for any reason.

NOTES
Commencement: 1 October 2007.
Commencement (transitional provisions): see the note to s 485 at **[1.485]**.
Commencement (transitional adaptations): the transitional adaptations of this section contained in the Companies Act 2006 (Commencement No 3, Consequential Amendments, Transitional Provisions and Savings) Order 2007, SI 2007/2194, Sch 1, para 18 were revoked by the Companies Act 2006 (Commencement No 5, Transitional Provisions and Savings) Order 2007, SI 2007/3495, art 10(1), (3), as from 6 April 2008 (subject to any transitional provisions and savings as apply, in accordance with Sch 4 to that Order, in relation to the repeal of any provision of the 1985 Act referred to in the adaptation). See **[2.43]**.

[1.488]
488   Prevention by members of deemed re-appointment of auditor

(1)   An auditor of a private company is not deemed to be re-appointed under section 487(2) if the company has received notices under this section from members representing at least the requisite percentage of the total voting rights of all members who would be entitled to vote on a resolution that the auditor should not be re-appointed.

(2)   The "requisite percentage" is 5%, or such lower percentage as is specified for this purpose in the company's articles.

(3)   A notice under this section—
  (a)   may be in hard copy or electronic form,
  (b)   must be authenticated by the person or persons giving it, and
  (c)   must be received by the company before the end of the accounting reference period immediately preceding the time when the deemed re-appointment would have effect.

NOTES
Commencement: 1 October 2007.
Commencement (transitional provisions): see the note to s 485 at **[1.485]**.

Public companies

[1.489]
489   Appointment of auditors of public company: general

(1)   An auditor or auditors of a public company must be appointed for each financial year of the company, unless the directors reasonably resolve otherwise on the ground that audited accounts are unlikely to be required.

(2) For each financial year for which an auditor or auditors is or are to be appointed (other than the company's first financial year), the appointment must be made before the end of the accounts meeting of the company at which the company's annual accounts and reports for the previous financial year are laid.

(3) The directors may appoint an auditor or auditors of the company—
- (a) at any time before the company's first accounts meeting;
- (b) following a period during which the company (being exempt from audit) did not have any auditor, at any time before the company's next accounts meeting;
- (c) to fill a casual vacancy in the office of auditor.

(4) The members may appoint an auditor or auditors by ordinary resolution—
- (a) at an accounts meeting;
- (b) if the company should have appointed an auditor or auditors at an accounts meeting but failed to do so;
- (c) where the directors had power to appoint under subsection (3) but have failed to make an appointment.

(5) An auditor or auditors of a public company may only be appointed—
- (a) in accordance with this section, or
- (b) in accordance with section 490 (default power of Secretary of State).

NOTES

Commencement: 6 April 2008.

Commencement (transitional provisions): Sch 4, Pt 1, paras 10, 11 to the Companies Act 2006 (Commencement No 5, Transitional Provisions and Savings) Order 2007, SI 2007/3495 (at **[2.66]**) provide as follows—

"10.—(1) In Chapter 2 of Part 16 of that Act (appointment of auditors)—
- (a) sections 489 and 490 (appointment of auditors by public companies) apply to appointments for financial years beginning on or after 6th April 2008;
- (b) section 491 (term of office of auditors of public company) applies to auditors appointed for financial years beginning on or after that date.

(2) Sections 384, 385, 387 and 388(1), (3) and (4) of the 1985 Act or Articles 392, 393, 395 and 396(1), (3) and (4) of the 1986 Order continue to apply to appointments by public companies for financial years beginning before that date.

11.—(1) In that Chapter, the following provisions apply to auditors appointed for financial years beginning on or after 6th April 2008—
section 492 (fixing of auditor's remuneration),
section 493 (disclosure of terms of audit appointment), and
section 494 (disclosure of services provided by auditor or associated and related remuneration).

(2) Sections 390A and 390B of the 1985 Act or Articles 398A and 398B of the 1986 Order continue to apply to auditors appointed for financial years beginning before that date.

(3) The repeal of section 390A of the 1985 Act and Article 398A of the 1986 Order (remuneration of auditors) does not affect the operation of any such resolution as is mentioned in paragraph 45 of Schedule 3 to the Companies Act 2006 (Commencement No 3, Consequential Amendments, Transitional Provisions and Savings) Order 2007.".

[1.490]

490 Appointment of auditors of public company: default power of Secretary of State

(1) If a public company fails to appoint an auditor or auditors in accordance with section 489, the Secretary of State may appoint one or more persons to fill the vacancy.

(2) Where subsection (2) of that section applies and the company fails to make the necessary appointment before the end of the accounts meeting, the company must within one week of the end of that meeting give notice to the Secretary of State of his power having become exercisable.

(3) If a company fails to give the notice required by this section, an offence is committed by—
- (a) the company, and
- (b) every officer of the company who is in default.

(4) A person guilty of an offence under this section is liable on summary conviction to a fine not exceeding level 3 on the standard scale and, for continued contravention, a daily default fine not exceeding one-tenth of level 3 on the standard scale.

NOTES

Commencement: 6 April 2008.

Commencement (transitional provisions): see the note to s 489 at **[1.489]**.

[1.491]

491 Term of office of auditors of public company

(1) The auditor or auditors of a public company hold office in accordance with the terms of their appointment, subject to the requirements that—
- (a) they do not take office until the previous auditor or auditors have ceased to hold office, and
- (b) they cease to hold office at the conclusion of the accounts meeting next following their appointment, unless re-appointed.

(2) This is without prejudice to the provisions of this Part as to removal and resignation of auditors.

NOTES

Commencement: 6 April 2008.

Commencement (transitional provisions): see the note to s 489 at **[1.489]**.

General provisions

[1.492]
492   Fixing of auditor's remuneration
(1)   The remuneration of an auditor appointed by the members of a company must be fixed by the members by ordinary resolution or in such manner as the members may by ordinary resolution determine.

(2)   The remuneration of an auditor appointed by the directors of a company must be fixed by the directors.

(3)   The remuneration of an auditor appointed by the Secretary of State must be fixed by the Secretary of State.

(4)   For the purposes of this section "remuneration" includes sums paid in respect of expenses.

(5)   This section applies in relation to benefits in kind as to payments of money.

NOTES

Commencement: 6 April 2008.

Commencement (transitional provisions): see the note to s 489 at **[1.489]**.

[1.493]
493   Disclosure of terms of audit appointment
(1)   The Secretary of State may make provision by regulations for securing the disclosure of the terms on which a company's auditor is appointed, remunerated or performs his duties.

Nothing in the following provisions of this section affects the generality of this power.

(2)   The regulations may—
    (a)   require disclosure of—
        (i)   a copy of any terms that are in writing, and
        (ii)   a written memorandum setting out any terms that are not in writing;
    (b)   require disclosure to be at such times, in such places and by such means as are specified in the regulations;
    (c)   require the place and means of disclosure to be stated—
        (i)   in a note to the company's annual accounts (in the case of its individual accounts) or in such manner as is specified in the regulations (in the case of group accounts),
        (ii)   in the directors' report, or
        (iii)   in the auditor's report on the company's annual accounts.

(3)   The provisions of this section apply to a variation of the terms mentioned in subsection (1) as they apply to the original terms.

(4)   Regulations under this section are subject to affirmative resolution procedure.

NOTES

Commencement: 20 January 2007 (for the purpose of enabling the exercise of powers to make Orders or Regulations by statutory instrument); 6 April 2008 (otherwise).

Commencement (transitional provisions): see the note to s 489 at **[1.489]**.

[1.494]
494   Disclosure of services provided by auditor or associates and related remuneration
(1)   The Secretary of State may make provision by regulations for securing the disclosure of—
    (a)   the nature of any services provided for a company by the company's auditor (whether in his capacity as auditor or otherwise) or by his associates;
    (b)   the amount of any remuneration received or receivable by a company's auditor, or his associates, in respect of any such services.

Nothing in the following provisions of this section affects the generality of this power.

(2)   The regulations may provide—
    (a)   for disclosure of the nature of any services provided to be made by reference to any class or description of services specified in the regulations (or any combination of services, however described);
    (b)   for the disclosure of amounts of remuneration received or receivable in respect of services of any class or description specified in the regulations (or any combination of services, however described);
    (c)   for the disclosure of separate amounts so received or receivable by the company's auditor or any of his associates, or of aggregate amounts so received or receivable by all or any of those persons.

(3)   The regulations may—
    (a)   provide that "remuneration" includes sums paid in respect of expenses;
    (b)   apply to benefits in kind as well as to payments of money, and require the disclosure of the nature of any such benefits and their estimated money value;
    (c)   apply to services provided for associates of a company as well as to those provided for a company;
    (d)   define "associate" in relation to an auditor and a company respectively.

(4)   The regulations may provide that any disclosure required by the regulations is to be made—
    (a)   in a note to the company's annual accounts (in the case of its individual accounts) or in such manner as is specified in the regulations (in the case of group accounts),
    (b)   in the directors' report, or
    (c)   in the auditor's report on the company's annual accounts.
(5)   If the regulations provide that any such disclosure is to be made as mentioned in subsection (4)(a) or (b), the regulations may require the auditor to supply the directors of the company with any information necessary to enable the disclosure to be made.
(6)   Regulations under this section are subject to negative resolution procedure.

NOTES
    Commencement: 20 January 2007 (for the purpose of enabling the exercise of powers to make Orders or Regulations by statutory instrument); 6 April 2008 (otherwise).
    Commencement (transitional provisions): see the note to s 489 at **[1.489]**.
    Regulations: the Companies (Disclosure of Auditor Remuneration and Liability Limitation Agreements) Regulations 2008, SI 2008/489 at **[4.220]**.

CHAPTER 3
FUNCTIONS OF AUDITOR
Auditor's report

[1.495]
495   Auditor's report on company's annual accounts
(1)   A company's auditor must make a report to the company's members on all annual accounts of the company of which copies are, during his tenure of office—
    (a)   in the case of a private company, to be sent out to members under section 423;
    (b)   in the case of a public company, to be laid before the company in general meeting under section 437.
(2)   The auditor's report must include—
    (a)   an introduction identifying the annual accounts that are the subject of the audit and the financial reporting framework that has been applied in their preparation, and
    (b)   a description of the scope of the audit identifying the auditing standards in accordance with which the audit was conducted.
(3)   The report must state clearly whether, in the auditor's opinion, the annual accounts—
    (a)   give a true and fair view—
        (i)   in the case of an individual balance sheet, of the state of affairs of the company as at the end of the financial year,
        (ii)   in the case of an individual profit and loss account, of the profit or loss of the company for the financial year,
        (iii)   in the case of group accounts, of the state of affairs as at the end of the financial year and of the profit or loss for the financial year of the undertakings included in the consolidation as a whole, so far as concerns members of the company;
    (b)   have been properly prepared in accordance with the relevant financial reporting framework; and
    (c)   have been prepared in accordance with the requirements of this Act (and, where applicable, Article 4 of the IAS Regulation).
Expressions used in this subsection that are defined for the purposes of Part 15 (see section 474) have the same meaning as in that Part.
(4)   The auditor's report—
    (a)   must be either unqualified or qualified, and
    (b)   must include a reference to any matters to which the auditor wishes to draw attention by way of emphasis without qualifying the report.

NOTES
    Commencement: 6 April 2008.
    Commencement (transitional provisions): Sch 4, Pt 1, para 12 to the Companies Act 2006 (Commencement No 5, Transitional Provisions and Savings) Order 2007, SI 2007/3495 (at **[2.66]**) provides as follows—

    "12.—(1)   In Chapter 3 of Part 16 of that Act (functions of auditor)—
      (a)   sections 495 to 498 (auditor's report and duties of auditor) apply to auditors' reports on accounts or reports for financial years beginning on or after 6th April 2008;
      (b)   sections 499 to 501 (rights of auditors) apply to auditors appointed for financial years beginning on or after that date;
      (c)   sections 503 to 509 (signature of auditor's report and offences in connection with auditor's report) apply to auditors' reports on accounts or reports for financial years beginning on or after that date.
    (2)   Sections 235 to 237, 389A and 389B of the 1985 Act or Articles 243 to 245, 397A and 397B of the 1986 Order continue to apply as regards financial years beginning before that date.
    (3)   Section 502 of the Companies Act 2006 (auditor's rights in relation to resolutions and meetings) applies to auditors appointed on or after 6th April 2008.
    (4)   Section 390 of the 1985 Act or Article 398 of the 1986 Order continues to apply to auditors appointed before that date.".

Part 1   The Companies Act 2006

[1.496]
496   Auditor's report on directors' report
The auditor must state in his report on the company's annual accounts whether in his opinion the information given in the directors' report for the financial year for which the accounts are prepared is consistent with those accounts.

NOTES
Commencement: 6 April 2008.
Commencement (transitional provisions): see the note to s 495 at **[1.495]**.

[1.497]
497   Auditor's report on auditable part of directors' remuneration report
(1)   If the company is a quoted company, the auditor, in his report on the company's annual accounts for the financial year, must—
  (a)   report to the company's members on the auditable part of the directors' remuneration report, and
  (b)   state whether in his opinion that part of the directors' remuneration report has been properly prepared in accordance with this Act.
(2)   For the purposes of this Part, "the auditable part" of a directors' remuneration report is the part identified as such by regulations under section 421.

NOTES
Commencement: 6 April 2008.
Commencement (transitional provisions): see the note to s 495 at **[1.495]**.

[1.497A]
[497A   Auditor's report on separate corporate governance statement
(1)   Where the company prepares a separate corporate governance statement in respect of a financial year the auditor must state in his report on the company's annual accounts for that year whether in his opinion the information given in the statement in compliance with rules 7.2.5 and 7.2.6 in the Disclosure Rules and Transparency Rules sourcebook issued by the Financial Services Authority (information about internal control and risk management systems in relation to financial reporting processes and about share capital structures) is consistent with those accounts.
(2)   The rules referred to above were inserted by Annex C of the Disclosure Rules and Transparency Rules Sourcebook (Corporate Governance Rules) Instrument 2008 made by the Authority on 26th June 2008 (FSA 2008/32).]

NOTES
Commencement: 27 June 2009.
 Inserted by the Companies Act 2006 (Accounts, Reports and Audit) Regulations 2009, SI 2009/1581, reg 6, as from 27 June 2009, in relation to financial years beginning on or after 29 June 2008 which have not ended before 27 June 2009.

Duties and rights of auditors
[1.498]
498   Duties of auditor
(1)   A company's auditor, in preparing his report, must carry out such investigations as will enable him to form an opinion as to—
  (a)   whether adequate accounting records have been kept by the company and returns adequate for their audit have been received from branches not visited by him, and
  (b)   whether the company's individual accounts are in agreement with the accounting records and returns, and
  (c)   in the case of a quoted company, whether the auditable part of the company's directors' remuneration report is in agreement with the accounting records and returns.
(2)   If the auditor is of the opinion—
  (a)   that adequate accounting records have not been kept, or that returns adequate for their audit have not been received from branches not visited by him, or
  (b)   that the company's individual accounts are not in agreement with the accounting records and returns, or
  (c)   in the case of a quoted company, that the auditable part of its directors' remuneration report is not in agreement with the accounting records and returns,
the auditor shall state that fact in his report.
(3)   If the auditor fails to obtain all the information and explanations which, to the best of his knowledge and belief, are necessary for the purposes of his audit, he shall state that fact in his report.
(4)   If—
  (a)   the requirements of regulations under section 412 (disclosure of directors' benefits: remuneration, pensions and compensation for loss of office) are not complied with in the annual accounts, or

(b)   in the case of a quoted company, the requirements of regulations under section 421 as to information forming the auditable part of the directors' remuneration report are not complied with in that report,

the auditor must include in his report, so far as he is reasonably able to do so, a statement giving the required particulars.

[(5)   If the directors of the company—

    (a)   have prepared accounts in accordance with the small companies regime, or

    (b)   have taken advantage of small companies exemption in preparing the directors' report,

and in the auditor's opinion they were not entitled to do so, the auditor shall state that fact in his report.]

NOTES

Commencement: 6 April 2008.

Commencement (transitional provisions): see the note to s 495 at [**1.495**].

Sub-s (5): substituted by the Companies Act 2006 (Amendment) (Accounts and Reports) Regulations 2008, SI 2008/393, reg 6(10), as from 6 April 2008, in relation to financial years beginning on or after that date.

[1.498A]
[498A   Auditor's duties in relation to separate corporate governance statement

Where the company is required to prepare a corporate governance statement in respect of a financial year and no such statement is included in the directors' report—

    (a)   the company's auditor, in preparing his report on the company's annual accounts for that year, must ascertain whether a corporate governance statement has been prepared, and

    (b)   if it appears to the auditor that no such statement has been prepared, he must state that fact in his report.]

NOTES

Commencement: 27 June 2009.

Inserted by the Companies Act 2006 (Accounts, Reports and Audit) Regulations 2009, SI 2009/1581, reg 7, as from 27 June 2009, in relation to financial years beginning on or after 29 June 2008 which have not ended before 27 June 2009.

[1.499]
499   Auditor's general right to information

(1)   An auditor of a company—

    (a)   has a right of access at all times to the company's books, accounts and vouchers (in whatever form they are held), and

    (b)   may require any of the following persons to provide him with such information or explanations as he thinks necessary for the performance of his duties as auditor.

(2)   Those persons are—

    (a)   any officer or employee of the company;

    (b)   any person holding or accountable for any of the company's books, accounts or vouchers;

    (c)   any subsidiary undertaking of the company which is a body corporate incorporated in the United Kingdom;

    (d)   any officer, employee or auditor of any such subsidiary undertaking or any person holding or accountable for any books, accounts or vouchers of any such subsidiary undertaking;

    (e)   any person who fell within any of paragraphs (a) to (d) at a time to which the information or explanations required by the auditor relates or relate.

(3)   A statement made by a person in response to a requirement under this section may not be used in evidence against him in criminal proceedings except proceedings for an offence under section 501.

(4)   Nothing in this section compels a person to disclose information in respect of which a claim to legal professional privilege (in Scotland, to confidentiality of communications) could be maintained in legal proceedings.

NOTES

Commencement: 6 April 2008.

Commencement (transitional provisions): see the note to s 495 at [**1.495**].

[1.500]
500   Auditor's right to information from overseas subsidiaries

(1)   Where a parent company has a subsidiary undertaking that is not a body corporate incorporated in the United Kingdom, the auditor of the parent company may require it to obtain from any of the following persons such information or explanations as he may reasonably require for the purposes of his duties as auditor.

(2)   Those persons are—

    (a)   the undertaking;

    (b)   any officer, employee or auditor of the undertaking;

    (c)   any person holding or accountable for any of the undertaking's books, accounts or vouchers;

(d)   any person who fell within paragraph (b) or (c) at a time to which the information or explanations relates or relate.

(3)   If so required, the parent company must take all such steps as are reasonably open to it to obtain the information or explanations from the person concerned.

(4)   A statement made by a person in response to a requirement under this section may not be used in evidence against him in criminal proceedings except proceedings for an offence under section 501.

(5)   Nothing in this section compels a person to disclose information in respect of which a claim to legal professional privilege (in Scotland, to confidentiality of communications) could be maintained in legal proceedings.

NOTES

Commencement: 6 April 2008.
Commencement (transitional provisions): see the note to s 495 at **[1.495]**.

[1.501]
501   Auditor's rights to information: offences

(1)   A person commits an offence who knowingly or recklessly makes to an auditor of a company a statement (oral or written) that—

    (a)   conveys or purports to convey any information or explanations which the auditor requires, or is entitled to require, under section 499, and

    (b)   is misleading, false or deceptive in a material particular.

(2)   A person guilty of an offence under subsection (1) is liable—

    (a)   on conviction on indictment, to imprisonment for a term not exceeding two years or a fine (or both);

    (b)   on summary conviction—

       (i)   in England and Wales, to imprisonment for a term not exceeding twelve months or to a fine not exceeding the statutory maximum (or both);

       (ii)   in Scotland or Northern Ireland, to imprisonment for a term not exceeding six months or to a fine not exceeding the statutory maximum (or both).

(3)   A person who fails to comply with a requirement under section 499 without delay commits an offence unless it was not reasonably practicable for him to provide the required information or explanations.

(4)   If a parent company fails to comply with section 500, an offence is committed by—

    (a)   the company, and

    (b)   every officer of the company who is in default.

(5)   A person guilty of an offence under subsection (3) or (4) is liable on summary conviction to a fine not exceeding level 3 on the standard scale.

(6)   Nothing in this section affects any right of an auditor to apply for an injunction (in Scotland, an interdict or an order for specific performance) to enforce any of his rights under section 499 or 500.

NOTES

Commencement: 6 April 2008.
Commencement (transitional provisions): see the note to s 495 at **[1.495]**.
Offences under this section: see further s 1131 at **[1.1131]**.

[1.502]
502   Auditor's rights in relation to resolutions and meetings

(1)   In relation to a written resolution proposed to be agreed to by a private company, the company's auditor is entitled to receive all such communications relating to the resolution as, by virtue of any provision of Chapter 2 of Part 13 of this Act, are required to be supplied to a member of the company.

(2)   A company's auditor is entitled—

    (a)   to receive all notices of, and other communications relating to, any general meeting which a member of the company is entitled to receive,

    (b)   to attend any general meeting of the company, and

    (c)   to be heard at any general meeting which he attends on any part of the business of the meeting which concerns him as auditor.

(3)   Where the auditor is a firm, the right to attend or be heard at a meeting is exercisable by an individual authorised by the firm in writing to act as its representative at the meeting.

NOTES

Commencement: 6 April 2008.
Commencement (transitional provisions): see the note to s 495 at **[1.495]**.

Signature of auditor's report

[1.503]

503 Signature of auditor's report

(1) The auditor's report must state the name of the auditor and be signed and dated.

(2) Where the auditor is an individual, the report must be signed by him.

(3) Where the auditor is a firm, the report must be signed by the senior statutory auditor in his own name, for and on behalf of the auditor.

NOTES

Commencement: 6 April 2008.

Commencement (transitional provisions): see the note to s 495 at **[1.495]**.

[1.504]

504 Senior statutory auditor

(1) The senior statutory auditor means the individual identified by the firm as senior statutory auditor in relation to the audit in accordance with—

(a) standards issued by the European Commission, or

(b) if there is no applicable standard so issued, any relevant guidance issued by—

  (i) the Secretary of State, or

  (ii) a body appointed by order of the Secretary of State.

(2) The person identified as senior statutory auditor must be eligible for appointment as auditor of the company in question (see Chapter 2 of Part 42 of this Act).

(3) The senior statutory auditor is not, by reason of being named or identified as senior statutory auditor or by reason of his having signed the auditor's report, subject to any civil liability to which he would not otherwise be subject.

(4) An order appointing a body for the purpose of subsection (1)(b)(ii) is subject to negative resolution procedure.

NOTES

Commencement: 20 January 2007 (for the purpose of enabling the exercise of powers to make Orders or Regulations by statutory instrument); 6 April 2008 (otherwise).

Commencement (transitional provisions): see the note to s 495 at **[1.495]**.

Orders: the Statutory Auditors (Delegation of Functions etc) Order 2008, SI 2008/496 at **[4.240]**. Note that art 11 of that Order (at **[4.250]**) provides that the body known as the Auditing Practices Board established under the articles of association of The Financial Reporting Council Limited is appointed for the purposes of sub-s (1)(b)(ii) above.

[1.505]

505 Names to be stated in published copies of auditor's report

(1) Every copy of the auditor's report that is published by or on behalf of the company must—

(a) state the name of the auditor and (where the auditor is a firm) the name of the person who signed it as senior statutory auditor, or

(b) if the conditions in section 506 (circumstances in which names may be omitted) are met, state that a resolution has been passed and notified to the Secretary of State in accordance with that section.

(2) For the purposes of this section a company is regarded as publishing the report if it publishes, issues or circulates it or otherwise makes it available for public inspection in a manner calculated to invite members of the public generally, or any class of members of the public, to read it.

(3) If a copy of the auditor's report is published without the statement required by this section, an offence is committed by—

(a) the company, and

(b) every officer of the company who is in default.

(4) A person guilty of an offence under this section is liable on summary conviction to a fine not exceeding level 3 on the standard scale.

NOTES

Commencement: 6 April 2008.

Commencement (transitional provisions): see the note to s 495 at **[1.495]**.

[1.506]

506 Circumstances in which names may be omitted

(1) The auditor's name and, where the auditor is a firm, the name of the person who signed the report as senior statutory auditor, may be omitted from—

(a) published copies of the report, and

(b) the copy of the report delivered to the registrar under Chapter 10 of Part 15 (filing of accounts and reports),

if the following conditions are met.

(2) The conditions are that the company—

(a) considering on reasonable grounds that statement of the name would create or be likely to create a serious risk that the auditor or senior statutory auditor, or any other person, would be subject to violence or intimidation, has resolved that the name should not be stated, and

(b) has given notice of the resolution to the Secretary of State, stating—
    (i) the name and registered number of the company,
    (ii) the financial year of the company to which the report relates, and
    (iii) the name of the auditor and (where the auditor is a firm) the name of the person who signed the report as senior statutory auditor.

NOTES
Commencement: 6 April 2008.
Commencement (transitional provisions): see the note to s 495 at **[1.495]**.

Offences in connection with auditor's report

[1.507]
507 Offences in connection with auditor's report
(1) A person to whom this section applies commits an offence if he knowingly or recklessly causes a report under section 495 (auditor's report on company's annual accounts) to include any matter that is misleading, false or deceptive in a material particular.
(2) A person to whom this section applies commits an offence if he knowingly or recklessly causes such a report to omit a statement required by—
(a) section 498(2)(b) (statement that company's accounts do not agree with accounting records and returns),
(b) section 498(3) (statement that necessary information and explanations not obtained), or
(c) section 498(5) (statement that directors wrongly took advantage of exemption from obligation to prepare group accounts).
(3) This section applies to—
(a) where the auditor is an individual, that individual and any employee or agent of his who is eligible for appointment as auditor of the company;
(b) where the auditor is a firm, any director, member, employee or agent of the firm who is eligible for appointment as auditor of the company.
(4) A person guilty of an offence under this section is liable—
(a) on conviction on indictment, to a fine;
(b) on summary conviction, to a fine not exceeding the statutory maximum.

NOTES
Commencement: 6 April 2008.
Commencement (transitional provisions): see the note to s 495 at **[1.495]**.

[1.508]
508 Guidance for regulatory and prosecuting authorities: England, Wales and Northern Ireland
(1) The Secretary of State may issue guidance for the purpose of helping relevant regulatory and prosecuting authorities to determine how they should carry out their functions in cases where behaviour occurs that—
(a) appears to involve the commission of an offence under section 507 (offences in connection with auditor's report), and
(b) has been, is being or may be investigated pursuant to arrangements—
    (i) under paragraph 15 of Schedule 10 (investigation of complaints against auditors and supervisory bodies), or
    (ii) of a kind mentioned in paragraph 24 of that Schedule (independent investigation for disciplinary purposes of public interest cases).
(2) The Secretary of State must obtain the consent of the Attorney General before issuing any such guidance.
(3) In this section "relevant regulatory and prosecuting authorities" means—
(a) supervisory bodies within the meaning of Part 42 of this Act,
(b) bodies to which the Secretary of State may make grants under section 16(1) of the Companies (Audit, Investigations and Community Enterprise) Act 2004 (c 27) (bodies concerned with accounting standards etc),
(c) the Director of the Serious Fraud Office,
(d) the Director of Public Prosecutions or the Director of Public Prosecutions for Northern Ireland, and
(e) the Secretary of State.
(4) This section does not apply to Scotland.

NOTES
Commencement: 6 April 2008.
Commencement (transitional provisions): see the note to s 495 at **[1.495]**.

[1.509]
509 Guidance for regulatory authorities: Scotland

(1) The Lord Advocate may issue guidance for the purpose of helping relevant regulatory authorities to determine how they should carry out their functions in cases where behaviour occurs that—
  (a) appears to involve the commission of an offence under section 507 (offences in connection with auditor's report), and
  (b) has been, is being or may be investigated pursuant to arrangements—
    (i) under paragraph 15 of Schedule 10 (investigation of complaints against auditors and supervisory bodies), or
    (ii) of a kind mentioned in paragraph 24 of that Schedule (independent investigation for disciplinary purposes of public interest cases).
(2) The Lord Advocate must consult the Secretary of State before issuing any such guidance.
(3) In this section "relevant regulatory authorities" means—
  (a) supervisory bodies within the meaning of Part 42 of this Act,
  (b) bodies to which the Secretary of State may make grants under section 16(1) of the Companies (Audit, Investigations and Community Enterprise) Act 2004 (c 27) (bodies concerned with accounting standards etc), and
  (c) the Secretary of State.
(4) This section applies only to Scotland.

NOTES
Commencement: 6 April 2008.
Commencement (transitional provisions): see the note to s 495 at **[1.495]**.

CHAPTER 4
REMOVAL, RESIGNATION, ETC OF AUDITORS

Removal of auditor

[1.510]
510 Resolution removing auditor from office

(1) The members of a company may remove an auditor from office at any time.
(2) This power is exercisable only—
  (a) by ordinary resolution at a meeting, and
  (b) in accordance with section 511 (special notice of resolution to remove auditor).
(3) Nothing in this section is to be taken as depriving the person removed of compensation or damages payable to him in respect of the termination—
  (a) of his appointment as auditor, or
  (b) of any appointment terminating with that as auditor.
(4) An auditor may not be removed from office before the expiration of his term of office except by resolution under this section.

NOTES
Commencement: 6 April 2008.
Commencement (transitional provisions): Sch 4, Pt 1, paras 13–17 to the Companies Act 2006 (Commencement No 5, Transitional Provisions and Savings) Order 2007, SI 2007/3495 (at **[2.66]**) (as amended by the Companies Act 2006 (Commencement No 7, Transitional Provisions and Savings) Order 2008, SI 2008/1886, art 8, as from 11 August 2008) provide as follows—

"13.—(1) In Chapter 4 of Part 16 of that Act (removal, resignation, etc of auditors), sections 510 to 513 (removal of auditor) apply where notice of the intended resolution is given to the company on or after 6th April 2008.
(2) Sections 391 and 391A of the 1985 Act or Articles 399 and 399A of the 1986 Order continue to apply where notice of the intended resolution is given to the company before that date.
(3) Until section 1068(1) of the Companies Act 2006 comes into force, the notice referred to in section 512(1) (notice to registrar of resolution removing auditor from office) must be in the form prescribed for the purposes of section 391(2) of the 1985 Act or Article 399(2) of the 1986 Order.
(4) In section 513 (rights of auditor removed from office) as it applies in relation to an auditor appointed before 6th April 2008, the reference to rights under section 502(2) shall be read as a reference to rights under section 390(1) of the 1985 Act or Article 398(1) of the 1986 Order.
14.—(1) In that Chapter, sections 514 and 515 (failure to re-appoint auditor) apply to appointments for financial years beginning on or after 6th April 2008.
(2) Section 391A of the 1985 Act or Article 399A of the 1986 Order continues to apply to appointments for financial years beginning before that date.
15.—(1) In that Chapter, sections 516 to 518 (resignation of auditor) apply to resignations occurring on or after 6th April 2008.
(2) Sections 392 and 392A of the 1985 Act or Articles 400 and 400A of the 1986 Order continue to apply to resignations occurring before that date.
[(3) In section 518 (rights of resigning auditor) as it applies in relation to an auditor appointed before 6th April 2008, the reference to rights under section 502(2) shall be read as a reference to rights under section 390(1) of the 1985 Act or Article 398(1) of the 1986 Order.]
16.—(1) In that Chapter, sections 519 to 525 (statement by auditor ceasing to hold office) apply where the auditor ceases to hold office on or after 6th April 2008.
(2) Sections 394 and 394A of the 1985 Act or Articles 401A and 401B of the 1986 Order continue to apply where the

Part 1 The Companies Act 2006

auditor ceases to hold office before that date.

17.—(1)   In that Chapter, section 526 (effect of casual vacancies) applies where the vacancy occurs on or after 6th April 2008.

(2)   Section 388(2) of the 1985 Act or Article 396(2) of the 1986 Order continues to apply where the vacancy occurred before that date.".

[1.511]
511   Special notice required for resolution removing auditor from office
(1)   Special notice is required for a resolution at a general meeting of a company removing an auditor from office.

(2)   On receipt of notice of such an intended resolution the company must immediately send a copy of it to the auditor proposed to be removed.

(3)   The auditor proposed to be removed may make with respect to the intended resolution representations in writing to the company (not exceeding a reasonable length) and request their notification to members of the company.

(4)   The company must (unless the representations are received by it too late for it to do so)—
   (a)   in any notice of the resolution given to members of the company, state the fact of the representations having been made, and
   (b)   send a copy of the representations to every member of the company to whom notice of the meeting is or has been sent.

(5)   If a copy of any such representations is not sent out as required because received too late or because of the company's default, the auditor may (without prejudice to his right to be heard orally) require that the representations be read out at the meeting.

(6)   Copies of the representations need not be sent out and the representations need not be read at the meeting if, on the application either of the company or of any other person claiming to be aggrieved, the court is satisfied that the auditor is using the provisions of this section to secure needless publicity for defamatory matter.

The court may order the company's costs (in Scotland, expenses) on the application to be paid in whole or in part by the auditor, notwithstanding that he is not a party to the application.

NOTES
Commencement: 6 April 2008.
Commencement (transitional provisions): see the note to s 510 at **[1.510]**.

[1.512]
512   Notice to registrar of resolution removing auditor from office
(1)   Where a resolution is passed under section 510 (resolution removing auditor from office), the company must give notice of that fact to the registrar within 14 days.

(2)   If a company fails to give the notice required by this section, an offence is committed by—
   (a)   the company, and
   (b)   every officer of it who is in default.

(3)   A person guilty of an offence under this section is liable on summary conviction to a fine not exceeding level 3 on the standard scale and, for continued contravention, a daily default fine not exceeding one-tenth of level 3 on the standard scale.

NOTES
Commencement: 6 April 2008.
Commencement (transitional provisions): see the note to s 510 at **[1.510]**.

[1.513]
513   Rights of auditor who has been removed from office
(1)   An auditor who has been removed by resolution under section 510 has, notwithstanding his removal, the rights conferred by section 502(2) in relation to any general meeting of the company—
   (a)   at which his term of office would otherwise have expired, or
   (b)   at which it is proposed to fill the vacancy caused by his removal.

(2)   In such a case the references in that section to matters concerning the auditor as auditor shall be construed as references to matters concerning him as a former auditor.

NOTES
Commencement: 6 April 2008.
Commencement (transitional provisions): see the note to s 510 at **[1.510]**.

Failure to re-appoint auditor

[1.514]
514   Failure to re-appoint auditor: special procedure required for written resolution
(1)   This section applies where a resolution is proposed as a written resolution of a private company whose effect would be to appoint a person as auditor in place of a person (the "outgoing auditor") whose term of office has expired, or is to expire, at the end of the period for appointing auditors.

(2)   The following provisions apply if—

(a)   no period for appointing auditors has ended since the outgoing auditor ceased to hold office, or

(b)   such a period has ended and an auditor or auditors should have been appointed but were not.

(3)   The company must send a copy of the proposed resolution to the person proposed to be appointed and to the outgoing auditor.

(4)   The outgoing auditor may, within 14 days after receiving the notice, make with respect to the proposed resolution representations in writing to the company (not exceeding a reasonable length) and request their circulation to members of the company.

(5)   The company must circulate the representations together with the copy or copies of the resolution circulated in accordance with section 291 (resolution proposed by directors) or section 293 (resolution proposed by members).

(6)   Where subsection (5) applies—

(a)   the period allowed under section 293(3) for service of copies of the proposed resolution is 28 days instead of 21 days, and

(b)   the provisions of section 293(5) and (6) (offences) apply in relation to a failure to comply with that subsection as in relation to a default in complying with that section.

(7)   Copies of the representations need not be circulated if, on the application either of the company or of any other person claiming to be aggrieved, the court is satisfied that the auditor is using the provisions of this section to secure needless publicity for defamatory matter.

The court may order the company's costs (in Scotland, expenses) on the application to be paid in whole or in part by the auditor, notwithstanding that he is not a party to the application.

(8)   If any requirement of this section is not complied with, the resolution is ineffective.

NOTES

Commencement: 6 April 2008.

Commencement (transitional provisions): see the note to s 510 at **[1.510]**.

[1.515]

515   Failure to re-appoint auditor: special notice required for resolution at general meeting

(1)   This section applies to a resolution at a general meeting of a company whose effect would be to appoint a person as auditor in place of a person (the "outgoing auditor") whose term of office has ended, or is to end—

(a)   in the case of a private company, at the end of the period for appointing auditors;

(b)   in the case of a public company, at the end of the next accounts meeting.

(2)   Special notice is required of such a resolution if—

(a)   in the case of a private company—

(i)   no period for appointing auditors has ended since the outgoing auditor ceased to hold office, or

(ii)   such a period has ended and an auditor or auditors should have been appointed but were not;

(b)   in the case of a public company—

(i)   there has been no accounts meeting of the company since the outgoing auditor ceased to hold office, or

(ii)   there has been an accounts meeting at which an auditor or auditors should have been appointed but were not.

(3)   On receipt of notice of such an intended resolution the company shall forthwith send a copy of it to the person proposed to be appointed and to the outgoing auditor.

(4)   The outgoing auditor may make with respect to the intended resolution representations in writing to the company (not exceeding a reasonable length) and request their notification to members of the company.

(5)   The company must (unless the representations are received by it too late for it to do so)—

(a)   in any notice of the resolution given to members of the company, state the fact of the representations having been made, and

(b)   send a copy of the representations to every member of the company to whom notice of the meeting is or has been sent.

(6)   If a copy of any such representations is not sent out as required because received too late or because of the company's default, the outgoing auditor may (without prejudice to his right to be heard orally) require that the representations be read out at the meeting.

(7)   Copies of the representations need not be sent out and the representations need not be read at the meeting if, on the application either of the company or of any other person claiming to be aggrieved, the court is satisfied that the auditor is using the provisions of this section to secure needless publicity for defamatory matter.

The court may order the company's costs (in Scotland, expenses) on the application to be paid in whole or in part by the outgoing auditor, notwithstanding that he is not a party to the application.

NOTES

Commencement: 6 April 2008.

Commencement (transitional provisions): see the note to s 510 at **[1.510]**.

Resignation of auditor

[1.516]
516   Resignation of auditor

(1)   An auditor of a company may resign his office by depositing a notice in writing to that effect at the company's registered office.

(2)   The notice is not effective unless it is accompanied by the statement required by section 519.

(3)   An effective notice of resignation operates to bring the auditor's term of office to an end as of the date on which the notice is deposited or on such later date as may be specified in it.

NOTES
Commencement: 6 April 2008.
Commencement (transitional provisions): see the note to s 510 at **[1.510]**.

[1.517]
517   Notice to registrar of resignation of auditor

(1)   Where an auditor resigns the company must within 14 days of the deposit of a notice of resignation send a copy of the notice to the registrar of companies.

(2)   If default is made in complying with this section, an offence is committed by—
   (a)   the company, and
   (b)   every officer of the company who is in default.

(3)   A person guilty of an offence under this section is liable—
   (a)   on conviction on indictment, to a fine;
   (b)   on summary conviction, to a fine not exceeding the statutory maximum and, for continued contravention, a daily default fine not exceeding one-tenth of the statutory maximum.

NOTES
Commencement: 6 April 2008.
Commencement (transitional provisions): see the note to s 510 at **[1.510]**.

[1.518]
518   Rights of resigning auditor

(1)   This section applies where an auditor's notice of resignation is accompanied by a statement of the circumstances connected with his resignation (see section 519).

(2)   He may deposit with the notice a signed requisition calling on the directors of the company forthwith duly to convene a general meeting of the company for the purpose of receiving and considering such explanation of the circumstances connected with his resignation as he may wish to place before the meeting.

(3)   He may request the company to circulate to its members—
   (a)   before the meeting convened on his requisition, or
   (b)   before any general meeting at which his term of office would otherwise have expired or at which it is proposed to fill the vacancy caused by his resignation,
a statement in writing (not exceeding a reasonable length) of the circumstances connected with his resignation.

(4)   The company must (unless the statement is received too late for it to comply)—
   (a)   in any notice of the meeting given to members of the company, state the fact of the statement having been made, and
   (b)   send a copy of the statement to every member of the company to whom notice of the meeting is or has been sent.

(5)   The directors must within 21 days from the date of the deposit of a requisition under this section proceed duly to convene a meeting for a day not more than 28 days after the date on which the notice convening the meeting is given.

(6)   If default is made in complying with subsection (5), every director who failed to take all reasonable steps to secure that a meeting was convened commits an offence.

(7)   A person guilty of an offence under this section is liable—
   (a)   on conviction on indictment, to a fine;
   (b)   on summary conviction to a fine not exceeding the statutory maximum.

(8)   If a copy of the statement mentioned above is not sent out as required because received too late or because of the company's default, the auditor may (without prejudice to his right to be heard orally) require that the statement be read out at the meeting.

(9)   Copies of a statement need not be sent out and the statement need not be read out at the meeting if, on the application either of the company or of any other person who claims to be aggrieved, the court is satisfied that the auditor is using the provisions of this section to secure needless publicity for defamatory matter.

The court may order the company's costs (in Scotland, expenses) on such an application to be paid in whole or in part by the auditor, notwithstanding that he is not a party to the application.

(10)   An auditor who has resigned has, notwithstanding his resignation, the rights conferred by section 502(2) in relation to any such general meeting of the company as is mentioned in subsection (3)(a) or (b) above.

In such a case the references in that section to matters concerning the auditor as auditor shall be construed as references to matters concerning him as a former auditor.

NOTES

Commencement: 6 April 2008.

Commencement (transitional provisions): see the note to s 510 at **[1.510]**.

Statement by auditor on ceasing to hold office

[1.519]

519 Statement by auditor to be deposited with company

(1) Where an auditor of an unquoted company ceases for any reason to hold office, he must deposit at the company's registered office a statement of the circumstances connected with his ceasing to hold office, unless he considers that there are no circumstances in connection with his ceasing to hold office that need to be brought to the attention of members or creditors of the company.

(2) If he considers that there are no circumstances in connection with his ceasing to hold office that need to be brought to the attention of members or creditors of the company, he must deposit at the company's registered office a statement to that effect.

(3) Where an auditor of a quoted company ceases for any reason to hold office, he must deposit at the company's registered office a statement of the circumstances connected with his ceasing to hold office.

(4) The statement required by this section must be deposited—

   (a) in the case of resignation, along with the notice of resignation;

   (b) in the case of failure to seek re-appointment, not less than 14 days before the end of the time allowed for next appointing an auditor;

   (c) in any other case, not later than the end of the period of 14 days beginning with the date on which he ceases to hold office.

(5) A person ceasing to hold office as auditor who fails to comply with this section commits an offence.

(6) In proceedings for such an offence it is a defence for the person charged to show that he took all reasonable steps and exercised all due diligence to avoid the commission of the offence.

(7) A person guilty of an offence under this section is liable—

   (a) on conviction on indictment, to a fine;

   (b) on summary conviction, to a fine not exceeding the statutory maximum.

[(8) Where an offence under this section is committed by a body corporate, every officer of the body who is in default also commits the offence.

For this purpose—

   (a) any person who purports to act as director, manager or secretary of the body is treated as an officer of the body, and

   (b) if the body is a company, any shadow director is treated as an officer of the company.]

NOTES

Commencement: 6 April 2008.

Commencement (transitional provisions): see the note to s 510 at **[1.510]**.

Sub-s (8): added by the Companies Act 2006 (Consequential Amendments etc) Order 2008, SI 2008/948, art 3(1), Sch 1, Pt 2, para 247, as from 6 April 2008.

[1.520]

520 Company's duties in relation to statement

(1) This section applies where the statement deposited under section 519 states the circumstances connected with the auditor's ceasing to hold office.

(2) The company must within 14 days of the deposit of the statement either—

   (a) send a copy of it to every person who under section 423 is entitled to be sent copies of the accounts, or

   (b) apply to the court.

(3) If it applies to the court, the company must notify the auditor of the application.

(4) If the court is satisfied that the auditor is using the provisions of section 519 to secure needless publicity for defamatory matter—

   (a) it shall direct that copies of the statement need not be sent out, and

   (b) it may further order the company's costs (in Scotland, expenses) on the application to be paid in whole or in part by the auditor, even if he is not a party to the application.

The company must within 14 days of the court's decision send to the persons mentioned in subsection (2)(a) a statement setting out the effect of the order.

(5) If no such direction is made the company must send copies of the statement to the persons mentioned in subsection (2)(a) within 14 days of the court's decision or, as the case may be, of the discontinuance of the proceedings.

(6) In the event of default in complying with this section an offence is committed by every officer of the company who is in default.

(7)   In proceedings for such an offence it is a defence for the person charged to show that he took all reasonable steps and exercised all due diligence to avoid the commission of the offence.

(8)   A person guilty of an offence under this section is liable—

  (a)   on conviction on indictment, to a fine;

  (b)   on summary conviction, to a fine not exceeding the statutory maximum.

NOTES

  Commencement: 6 April 2008.

  Commencement (transitional provisions): see the note to s 510 at **[1.510]**.

[1.521]

521   Copy of statement to be sent to registrar

(1)   Unless within 21 days beginning with the day on which he deposited the statement under section 519 the auditor receives notice of an application to the court under section 520, he must within a further seven days send a copy of the statement to the registrar.

(2)   If an application to the court is made under section 520 and the auditor subsequently receives notice under subsection (5) of that section, he must within seven days of receiving the notice send a copy of the statement to the registrar.

(3)   An auditor who fails to comply with subsection (1) or (2) commits an offence.

(4)   In proceedings for such an offence it is a defence for the person charged to show that he took all reasonable steps and exercised all due diligence to avoid the commission of the offence.

(5)   A person guilty of an offence under this section is liable—

  (a)   on conviction on indictment, to a fine;

  (b)   on summary conviction, to a fine not exceeding the statutory maximum.

[(6)   Where an offence under this section is committed by a body corporate, every officer of the body who is in default also commits the offence.

  For this purpose—

  (a)   any person who purports to act as director, manager or secretary of the body is treated as an officer of the body, and

  (b)   if the body is a company, any shadow director is treated as an officer of the company.]

NOTES

  Commencement: 6 April 2008.

  Commencement (transitional provisions): see the note to s 510 at **[1.510]**.

  Sub-s (6): added by the Companies Act 2006 (Consequential Amendments etc) Order 2008, SI 2008/948, art 3(1), Sch 1, Pt 2, para 248, as from 6 April 2008.

[1.522]

522   Duty of auditor to notify appropriate audit authority

(1)   Where—

  (a)   in the case of a major audit, an auditor ceases for any reason to hold office, or

  (b)   in the case of an audit that is not a major audit, an auditor ceases to hold office before the end of his term of office,

the auditor ceasing to hold office must notify the appropriate audit authority.

(2)   The notice must—

  (a)   inform the appropriate audit authority that he has ceased to hold office, and

  (b)   be accompanied by a copy of the statement deposited by him at the company's registered office in accordance with section 519.

(3)   If the statement so deposited is to the effect that he considers that there are no circumstances in connection with his ceasing to hold office that need to be brought to the attention of members or creditors of the company, the notice must also be accompanied by a statement of the reasons for his ceasing to hold office.

(4)   The auditor must comply with this section—

  (a)   in the case of a major audit, at the same time as he deposits a statement at the company's registered office in accordance with section 519;

  (b)   in the case of an audit that is not a major audit, at such time (not being earlier than the time mentioned in paragraph (a)) as the appropriate audit authority may require.

(5)   A person ceasing to hold office as auditor who fails to comply with this section commits an offence.

(6)   If that person is a firm an offence is committed by—

  (a)   the firm, and

  (b)   every officer of the firm who is in default.

(7)   In proceedings for an offence under this section it is a defence for the person charged to show that he took all reasonable steps and exercised all due diligence to avoid the commission of the offence.

(8)   A person guilty of an offence under this section is liable—

  (a)   on conviction on indictment, to a fine;

  (b)   on summary conviction, to a fine not exceeding the statutory maximum.

NOTES
Commencement: 6 April 2008.
Commencement (transitional provisions): see the note to s 510 at **[1.510]**.

[1.523]
523 Duty of company to notify appropriate audit authority
(1) Where an auditor ceases to hold office before the end of his term of office, the company must notify the appropriate audit authority.
(2) The notice must—
  (a) inform the appropriate audit authority that the auditor has ceased to hold office, and
  (b) be accompanied by—
    (i) a statement by the company of the reasons for his ceasing to hold office, or
    (ii) if the copy of the statement deposited by the auditor at the company's registered office in accordance with section 519 contains a statement of circumstances in connection with his ceasing to hold office that need to be brought to the attention of members or creditors of the company, a copy of that statement.
(3) The company must give notice under this section not later than 14 days after the date on which the auditor's statement is deposited at the company's registered office in accordance with section 519.
(4) If a company fails to comply with this section, an offence is committed by—
  (a) the company, and
  (b) every officer of the company who is in default.
(5) In proceedings for such an offence it is a defence for the person charged to show that he took all reasonable steps and exercised all due diligence to avoid the commission of the offence.
(6) A person guilty of an offence under this section is liable—
  (a) on conviction on indictment, to a fine;
  (b) on summary conviction, to a fine not exceeding the statutory maximum.

NOTES
Commencement: 6 April 2008.
Commencement (transitional provisions): see the note to s 510 at **[1.510]**.

[1.524]
524 Information to be given to accounting authorities
(1) The appropriate audit authority on receiving notice under section 522 or 523 of an auditor's ceasing to hold office—
  (a) must inform the accounting authorities, and
  (b) may if it thinks fit forward to those authorities a copy of the statement or statements accompanying the notice.
(2) The accounting authorities are—
  (a) the Secretary of State, and
  (b) any person authorised by the Secretary of State for the purposes of section 456 (revision of defective accounts: persons authorised to apply to court).
(3) If either of the accounting authorities is also the appropriate audit authority it is only necessary to comply with this section as regards any other accounting authority.
(4) If the court has made an order under section 520(4) directing that copies of the statement need not be sent out by the company, sections 460 and 461 (restriction on further disclosure) apply in relation to the copies sent to the accounting authorities as they apply to information obtained under section 459 (power to require documents etc).

NOTES
Commencement: 6 April 2008.
Commencement (transitional provisions): see the note to s 510 at **[1.510]**.

[1.525]
525 Meaning of "appropriate audit authority" and "major audit"
(1) In sections 522, 523 and 524 "appropriate audit authority" means—
  (a) in the case of a major audit [(other than one conducted by an Auditor General)]—
    (i) the Secretary of State, or
    (ii) if the Secretary of State has delegated functions under section 1252 to a body whose functions include receiving the notice in question, that body;
  (b) in the case of an audit [(other than one conducted by an Auditor General)] that is not a major audit, the relevant supervisory body;
  [(c) in the case of an audit conducted by an Auditor General, the Independent Supervisor.]
["Supervisory body" and "Independent Supervisor" have the same meaning] as in Part 42 (statutory auditors) (see [sections 1217 and 1228]).
(2) In sections 522 and this section "major audit" means a statutory audit conducted in respect of—

   (a)   a company any of whose securities have been admitted to the official list (within the meaning of Part 6 of the Financial Services and Markets Act 2000 (c 8)), or

   (b)   any other person in whose financial condition there is a major public interest.

(3)   In determining whether an audit is a major audit within subsection (2)(b), regard shall be had to any guidance issued by any of the authorities mentioned in subsection (1).

NOTES

Commencement: 6 April 2008.

Commencement (transitional provisions): see the note to s 510 at **[1.510]**.

Sub-s (1): words in square brackets in paras (a), (b), and the whole of para (c) inserted, and other words in square brackets substituted, by the Statutory Auditors and Third Country Auditors Regulations 2007, SI 2007/3494, reg 41, as from 6 April 2008.

As to the delegation of the Secretary of State's functions to the Professional Oversight Board (for the purposes of sub-s (1)(a)(ii) above): see the Statutory Auditors (Delegation of Functions etc) Order 2008, SI 2008/496, art 5 at **[4.244]**.

Supplementary

[1.526]
526   Effect of casual vacancies
If an auditor ceases to hold office for any reason, any surviving or continuing auditor or auditors may continue to act.

NOTES

Commencement: 6 April 2008.

Commencement (transitional provisions): see the note to s 510 at **[1.510]**.

CHAPTER 5
QUOTED COMPANIES: RIGHT OF MEMBERS TO RAISE AUDIT CONCERNS AT ACCOUNTS MEETING

[1.527]
527   Members' power to require website publication of audit concerns
(1)   The members of a quoted company may require the company to publish on a website a statement setting out any matter relating to—

   (a)   the audit of the company's accounts (including the auditor's report and the conduct of the audit) that are to be laid before the next accounts meeting, or

   (b)   any circumstances connected with an auditor of the company ceasing to hold office since the previous accounts meeting,

that the members propose to raise at the next accounts meeting of the company.

(2)   A company is required to do so once it has received requests to that effect from—

   (a)   members representing at least 5% of the total voting rights of all the members who have a relevant right to vote (excluding any voting rights attached to any shares in the company held as treasury shares), or

   (b)   at least 100 members who have a relevant right to vote and hold shares in the company on which there has been paid up an average sum, per member, of at least £100.

See also section 153 (exercise of rights where shares held on behalf of others).

(3)   In subsection (2) a "relevant right to vote" means a right to vote at the accounts meeting.

(4)   A request—

   (a)   may be sent to the company in hard copy or electronic form,

   (b)   must identify the statement to which it relates,

   (c)   must be authenticated by the person or persons making it, and

   (d)   must be received by the company at least one week before the meeting to which it relates.

(5)   A quoted company is not required to place on a website a statement under this section if, on an application by the company or another person who claims to be aggrieved, the court is satisfied that the rights conferred by this section are being abused.

(6)   The court may order the members requesting website publication to pay the whole or part of the company's costs (in Scotland, expenses) on such an application, even if they are not parties to the application.

NOTES

Commencement: 6 April 2008.

Commencement (transitional provisions): Sch 4, Pt 1, para 18 to the Companies Act 2006 (Commencement No 5, Transitional Provisions and Savings) Order 2007, SI 2007/3495 (at **[2.66]**) provides that sub-s (1)(a) above (matters relating to audit of company's accounts) applies to accounts for financial years beginning on or after 6 April 2008, and sub-s (1)(b) above (matters relating to circumstances connected with an auditor of the company) applies to auditors appointed for financial years beginning on or after that date.

[1.528]
528   Requirements as to website availability
(1)   The following provisions apply for the purposes of section 527 (website publication of members' statement of audit concerns).

(2)   The information must be made available on a website that—

(a) is maintained by or on behalf of the company, and
(b) identifies the company in question.

(3) Access to the information on the website, and the ability to obtain a hard copy of the information from the website, must not be conditional on the payment of a fee or otherwise restricted.

(4) The statement—
(a) must be made available within three working days of the company being required to publish it on a website, and
(b) must be kept available until after the meeting to which it relates.

(5) A failure to make information available on a website throughout the period specified in subsection (4)(b) is disregarded if—
(a) the information is made available on the website for part of that period, and
(b) the failure is wholly attributable to circumstances that it would not be reasonable to have expected the company to prevent or avoid.

NOTES
Commencement: 6 April 2008.

[1.529]
529 Website publication: company's supplementary duties
(1) A quoted company must in the notice it gives of the accounts meeting draw attention to—
(a) the possibility of a statement being placed on a website in pursuance of members' requests under section 527, and
(b) the effect of the following provisions of this section.

(2) A company may not require the members requesting website publication to pay its expenses in complying with that section or section 528 (requirements in connection with website publication).

(3) Where a company is required to place a statement on a website under section 527 it must forward the statement to the company's auditor not later than the time when it makes the statement available on the website.

(4) The business which may be dealt with at the accounts meeting includes any statement that the company has been required under section 527 to publish on a website.

NOTES
Commencement: 6 April 2008.

[1.530]
530 Website publication: offences
(1) In the event of default in complying with
(a) section 528 (requirements as to website publication), or
(b) section 529 (companies' supplementary duties in relation to request for website publication),

an offence is committed by every officer of the company who is in default.

(2) A person guilty of an offence under this section is liable—
(a) on conviction on indictment, to a fine;
(b) on summary conviction, to a fine not exceeding the statutory maximum.

NOTES
Commencement: 6 April 2008.

[1.531]
531 Meaning of "quoted company"
(1) For the purposes of this Chapter a company is a quoted company if it is a quoted company in accordance with section 385 (quoted and unquoted companies for the purposes of Part 15) in relation to the financial year to which the accounts to be laid at the next accounts meeting relate.

(2) The provisions of subsections (4) to (6) of that section (power to amend definition by regulations) apply in relation to the provisions of this Chapter as in relation to the provisions of that Part.

NOTES
Commencement: 6 April 2008.

CHAPTER 6
AUDITORS' LIABILITY

Voidness of provisions protecting auditors from liability

[1.532]
532 Voidness of provisions protecting auditors from liability
(1) This section applies to any provision—

(a)   for exempting an auditor of a company (to any extent) from any liability that would otherwise attach to him in connection with any negligence, default, breach of duty or breach of trust in relation to the company occurring in the course of the audit of accounts, or

(b)   by which a company directly or indirectly provides an indemnity (to any extent) for an auditor of the company, or of an associated company, against any liability attaching to him in connection with any negligence, default, breach of duty or breach of trust in relation to the company of which he is auditor occurring in the course of the audit of accounts.

(2)   Any such provision is void, except as permitted by—

(a)   section 533 (indemnity for costs of successfully defending proceedings), or

(b)   sections 534 to 536 (liability limitation agreements).

(3)   This section applies to any provision, whether contained in a company's articles or in any contract with the company or otherwise.

(4)   For the purposes of this section companies are associated if one is a subsidiary of the other or both are subsidiaries of the same body corporate.

NOTES
Commencement: 6 April 2008.

Indemnity for costs of defending proceedings

[1.533]
533   Indemnity for costs of successfully defending proceedings
Section 532 (general voidness of provisions protecting auditors from liability) does not prevent a company from indemnifying an auditor against any liability incurred by him—

(a)   in defending proceedings (whether civil or criminal) in which judgment is given in his favour or he is acquitted, or

(b)   in connection with an application under section 1157 (power of court to grant relief in case of honest and reasonable conduct) in which relief is granted to him by the court.

NOTES
Commencement: 6 April 2008.
Commencement (transitional adaptations): the transitional adaptations of this section contained in the Companies Act 2006 (Commencement No 5, Transitional Provisions and Savings) Order 2007, SI 2007/3495, Sch 1, Pt 1, para 11 were revoked by art 10(2) of that Order, as from 1 October 2008. See **[2.62]**.

Liability limitation agreements

[1.534]
534   Liability limitation agreements
(1)   A "liability limitation agreement" is an agreement that purports to limit the amount of a liability owed to a company by its auditor in respect of any negligence, default, breach of duty or breach of trust, occurring in the course of the audit of accounts, of which the auditor may be guilty in relation to the company.

(2)   Section 532 (general voidness of provisions protecting auditors from liability) does not affect the validity of a liability limitation agreement that—

(a)   complies with section 535 (terms of liability limitation agreement) and of any regulations under that section, and

(b)   is authorised by the members of the company (see section 536).

(3)   Such an agreement—

(a)   is effective to the extent provided by section 537, and

(b)   is not subject—

(i)   in England and Wales or Northern Ireland, to section 2(2) or 3(2)(a) of the Unfair Contract Terms Act 1977 (c 50);

(ii)   in Scotland, to section 16(1)(b) or 17(1)(a) of that Act.

NOTES
Commencement: 6 April 2008.

[1.535]
535   Terms of liability limitation agreement
(1)   A liability limitation agreement—

(a)   must not apply in respect of acts or omissions occurring in the course of the audit of accounts for more than one financial year, and

(b)   must specify the financial year in relation to which it applies.

(2)   The Secretary of State may by regulations—

(a)   require liability limitation agreements to contain specified provisions or provisions of a specified description;

(b)   prohibit liability limitation agreements from containing specified provisions or provisions of a specified description.

"Specified" here means specified in the regulations.

(3)　Without prejudice to the generality of the power conferred by subsection (2), that power may be exercised with a view to preventing adverse effects on competition.

(4)　Subject to the preceding provisions of this section, it is immaterial how a liability limitation agreement is framed.

In particular, the limit on the amount of the auditor's liability need not be a sum of money, or a formula, specified in the agreement.

(5)　Regulations under this section are subject to negative resolution procedure.

NOTES

Commencement: 20 January 2007 (for the purpose of enabling the exercise of powers to make Orders or Regulations by statutory instrument); 6 April 2008 (otherwise).

[1.536]
536 Authorisation of agreement by members of the company

(1)　A liability limitation agreement is authorised by the members of the company if it has been authorised under this section and that authorisation has not been withdrawn.

(2)　A liability limitation agreement between a private company and its auditor may be authorised—

    (a)　by the company passing a resolution, before it enters into the agreement, waiving the need for approval,

    (b)　by the company passing a resolution, before it enters into the agreement, approving the agreement's principal terms, or

    (c)　by the company passing a resolution, after it enters into the agreement, approving the agreement.

(3)　A liability limitation agreement between a public company and its auditor may be authorised—

    (a)　by the company passing a resolution in general meeting, before it enters into the agreement, approving the agreement's principal terms, or

    (b)　by the company passing a resolution in general meeting, after it enters into the agreement, approving the agreement.

(4)　The "principal terms" of an agreement are terms specifying, or relevant to the determination of—

    (a)　the kind (or kinds) of acts or omissions covered,

    (b)　the financial year to which the agreement relates, or

    (c)　the limit to which the auditor's liability is subject.

(5)　Authorisation under this section may be withdrawn by the company passing an ordinary resolution to that effect—

    (a)　at any time before the company enters into the agreement, or

    (b)　if the company has already entered into the agreement, before the beginning of the financial year to which the agreement relates.

Paragraph (b) has effect notwithstanding anything in the agreement.

NOTES

Commencement: 6 April 2008.

Commencement (transitional provisions): Sch 4, Pt 1, para 19 to the Companies Act 2006 (Commencement No 5, Transitional Provisions and Savings) Order 2007, SI 2007/3495 (at **[2.66]**) provides that a resolution passed before 6 April 2008 authorising a liability limitation agreement is effective for the purposes of this section if it complies with the requirements of this section.

[1.537]
537 Effect of liability limitation agreement

(1)　A liability limitation agreement is not effective to limit the auditor's liability to less than such amount as is fair and reasonable in all the circumstances of the case having regard (in particular) to—

    (a)　the auditor's responsibilities under this Part,

    (b)　the nature and purpose of the auditor's contractual obligations to the company, and

    (c)　the professional standards expected of him.

(2)　A liability limitation agreement that purports to limit the auditor's liability to less than the amount mentioned in subsection (1) shall have effect as if it limited his liability to that amount.

(3)　In determining what is fair and reasonable in all the circumstances of the case no account is to be taken of—

    (a)　matters arising after the loss or damage in question has been incurred, or

    (b)　matters (whenever arising) affecting the possibility of recovering compensation from other persons liable in respect of the same loss or damage.

NOTES

Commencement: 6 April 2008.

[1.538]
538 Disclosure of agreement by company
(1) A company which has entered into a liability limitation agreement must make such disclosure in connection with the agreement as the Secretary of State may require by regulations.
(2) The regulations may provide, in particular, that any disclosure required by the regulations shall be made—
  (a) in a note to the company's annual accounts (in the case of its individual accounts) or in such manner as is specified in the regulations (in the case of group accounts), or
  (b) in the directors' report.
(3) Regulations under this section are subject to negative resolution procedure.

NOTES
Commencement: 20 January 2007 (for the purpose of enabling the exercise of powers to make Orders or Regulations by statutory instrument); 6 April 2008 (otherwise).
Regulations: the Companies (Disclosure of Auditor Remuneration and Liability Limitation Agreements) Regulations 2008, SI 2008/489 at **[4.220]**.

CHAPTER 7
SUPPLEMENTARY PROVISIONS

[1.538A]
[538A Meaning of "corporate governance statement" etc
(1) In this Part "corporate governance statement" means the statement required by rules 7.2.1 to 7.2.11 in the Disclosure Rules and Transparency Rules sourcebook issued by the Financial Services Authority.
(2) Those rules were inserted by Annex C of the Disclosure Rules and Transparency Rules Sourcebook (Corporate Governance Rules) Instrument 2008 made by the Authority on 26th June 2008 (FSA 2008/32).
(3) A "separate" corporate governance statement means one that is not included in the directors' report.]

NOTES
Commencement: 27 June 2009.
Inserted by the Companies Act 2006 (Accounts, Reports and Audit) Regulations 2009, SI 2009/1581, reg 8, as from 27 June 2009, in relation to financial years beginning on or after 29 June 2008 which have not ended before 27 June 2009.

[1.539]
539 Minor definitions
In this Part—
  "e-money issuer" means a person who has permission under Part 4 of the Financial Services and Markets Act 2000 (c 8) to carry on the activity of issuing electronic money within the meaning of article 9B of the Financial Services and Markets Act 2000 (Regulated Activities) Order 2001 (SI 2001/544);
  . . . .
  ["MiFID investment firm" means an investment firm within the meaning of Article 4.1.1 of Directive 2004/39/EC of the European Parliament and of the Council of 21 April 2004 on markets in financial instruments, other than—
    (a) a company to which that Directive does not apply by virtue of Article 2 of that Directive,
    (b) a company which is an exempt investment firm within the meaning of regulation 4A(3) of the Financial Services and Markets Act 2000 (Markets in Financial Instruments) Regulations 2007, and
    (c) any other company which fulfils all the requirements set out in regulation 4C(3) of those Regulations;]
  "qualified", in relation to an auditor's report (or a statement contained in an auditor's report), means that the report or statement does not state the auditor's unqualified opinion that the accounts have been properly prepared in accordance with this Act or, in the case of an undertaking not required to prepare accounts in accordance with this Act, under any corresponding legislation under which it is required to prepare accounts;
  "turnover", in relation to a company, means the amounts derived from the provision of goods and services falling within the company's ordinary activities, after deduction of—
    (a) trade discounts,
    (b) value added tax, and
    (c) any other taxes based on the amounts so derived;
  "UCITS management company" has the meaning given by the Glossary forming part of the Handbook made by the Financial Services Authority under the Financial Services and Markets Act 2000.

NOTES
Commencement: 6 April 2008.

Definition "ISD investment firm" (omitted) repealed, and definition "MiFID investment firm" inserted, by the Markets in Financial Instruments Directive (Consequential Amendments) Regulations 2007, SI 2007/2932, reg 3(7), as from 1 November 2007.

PART 17
A COMPANY'S SHARE CAPITAL

CHAPTER 1
SHARES AND SHARE CAPITAL OF A COMPANY

Shares

[1.540]
540 Shares
(1)   In the Companies Acts "share", in relation to a company, means share in the company's share capital.
(2)   A company's shares may no longer be converted into stock.
(3)   Stock created before the commencement of this Part may be reconverted into shares in accordance with section 620.
(4)   In the Companies Acts—
  (a)   references to shares include stock except where a distinction between share and stock is express or implied, and
  (b)   references to a number of shares include an amount of stock where the context admits of the reference to shares being read as including stock.

NOTES
Commencement: 1 October 2007 (sub-ss (1), (4) certain purposes); 6 April 2008 (sub-ss (1), (4) certain purposes); 1 October 2009 (otherwise) (see the notes below).
Commencement (transitional provisions): Sch 2, para 41 to the Companies Act 2006 (Commencement No 8, Transitional Provisions and Savings) Order 2008, SI 2008/2860 (at **[2.91]**) provides as follows—

"Conversion of shares into stock (s 540(2) and (3))
41.—(1)   Section 540(2) of the Companies Act 2006 (prohibition on conversion of shares into stock) does not affect the conversion of shares into stock in pursuance of a resolution of the company in general meeting passed, or a written resolution agreed to, before 1st October 2009.
(2)   The reference in section 540(3) (reconversion) to stock created before the commencement of Part 17 of that Act includes stock created in pursuance of such a resolution.
(3)   Section 122(1)(b) and (2) of the 1985 Act or Article 132(1)(b) and (2) of the 1986 Order (notice to registrar of conversion) continue to apply in relation to the conversion of shares into stock under such a resolution.".

Commencement (note): the Companies Act 2006 (Commencement No 3, Consequential Amendments, Transitional Provisions and Savings) Order 2007, SI 2007/2194, art 2(3) provides that sub-ss (1), (4) shall come into force on 1 October 2007 so far as is necessary for the purposes of the provisions of this Act brought into force on that date by art 2(1), (2) of that Order (see **[2.32]**).
Commencement (note): the Companies Act 2006 (Commencement No 5, Transitional Provisions and Savings) Order 2007, SI 2007/3495, art 3(3) provides that sub-ss (1), (4) shall come into force on 6 April 2008 so far as is necessary for the purposes of the provisions of this Act brought into force on that date by art 3(1)(a)–(t), (2) of that Order (see **[2.52]**).

[1.541]
541 Nature of shares
The shares or other interest of a member in a company are personal property (or, in Scotland, moveable property) and are not in the nature of real estate (or heritage).

NOTES
Commencement: 1 October 2009.

[1.542]
542 Nominal value of shares
(1)   Shares in a limited company having a share capital must each have a fixed nominal value.
(2)   An allotment of a share that does not have a fixed nominal value is void.
(3)   Shares in a limited company having a share capital may be denominated in any currency, and different classes of shares may be denominated in different currencies.
  But see section 765 (initial authorised minimum share capital requirement for public company to be met by reference to share capital denominated in sterling or euros).
(4)   If a company purports to allot shares in contravention of this section, an offence is committed by every officer of the company who is in default.
(5)   A person guilty of an offence under this section is liable—
  (a)   on conviction on indictment, to a fine;
  (b)   on summary conviction, to a fine not exceeding the statutory maximum.

NOTES
Commencement: 1 October 2009.

[1.543]
543 Numbering of shares
(1) Each share in a company having a share capital must be distinguished by its appropriate number, except in the following circumstances.
(2) If at any time—
   (a) all the issued shares in a company are fully paid up and rank *pari passu* for all purposes, or
   (b) all the issued shares of a particular class in a company are fully paid up and rank *pari passu* for all purposes,

none of those shares need thereafter have a distinguishing number so long as it remains fully paid up and ranks *pari passu* for all purposes with all shares of the same class for the time being issued and fully paid up.

NOTES
Commencement: 1 October 2009.

[1.544]
544 Transferability of shares
(1) The shares or other interest of any member in a company are transferable in accordance with the company's articles.
(2) This is subject to—
   (a) the Stock Transfer Act 1963 (c 18) or the Stock Transfer Act (Northern Ireland) 1963 (c 24 (NI)) (which enables securities of certain descriptions to be transferred by a simplified process), and
   (b) regulations under Chapter 2 of Part 21 of this Act (which enable title to securities to be evidenced and transferred without a written instrument).
(3) See Part 21 of this Act generally as regards share transfers.

NOTES
Commencement: 6 April 2008.

[1.545]
545 Companies having a share capital
References in the Companies Acts to a company having a share capital are to a company that has power under its constitution to issue shares.

NOTES
Commencement: 1 October 2007 (certain purposes); 6 April 2008 (certain purposes); 1 October 2009 (otherwise) (see the notes below).
Commencement (note): the Companies Act 2006 (Commencement No 3, Consequential Amendments, Transitional Provisions and Savings) Order 2007, SI 2007/2194, art 2(3) provides that this section shall come into force on 1 October 2007 so far as is necessary for the purposes of the provisions of this Act brought into force on that date by art 2(1), (2) of that Order (see **[2.32]**).
Commencement (note): the Companies Act 2006 (Commencement No 5, Transitional Provisions and Savings) Order 2007, SI 2007/3495, art 3(3) provides that this section shall come into force on 6 April 2008 so far as is necessary for the purposes of the provisions of this Act brought into force on that date by art 3(1)(a)–(t), (2) of that Order (see **[2.52]**).

[1.546]
546 Issued and allotted share capital
(1) References in the Companies Acts—
   (a) to "issued share capital" are to shares of a company that have been issued;
   (b) to "allotted share capital" are to shares of a company that have been allotted.
(2) References in the Companies Acts to issued or allotted shares, or to issued or allotted share capital, include shares taken on the formation of the company by the subscribers to the company's memorandum.

NOTES
Commencement: 6 April 2007 (certain purposes); 1 October 2007 (certain purposes); 1 November 2007 (certain purposes); 6 April 2008 (certain purposes); 1 October 2009 (otherwise) (see the notes below).
Commencement (note): the Companies Act 2006 (Commencement No 2, Consequential Amendments, Transitional Provisions and Savings) Order 2007, SI 2007/1093, art 2(2) provides that this section shall come into force on 6 April 2007 so far as is necessary for the purposes of the provisions of this Act brought into force on that date by art 2(1) of that Order (see **[2.17]**).
Commencement (note): the Companies Act 2006 (Commencement No 3, Consequential Amendments, Transitional Provisions and Savings) Order 2007, SI 2007/2194, arts 2(3) and 3(2) provide that this section shall come into force on 1 October 2007 and 1 November 2007 so far as is necessary for the purposes of the provisions of this Act brought into force on those dates by art 2(1), (2) and art 3(1) of that Order respectively (see **[2.32]** and **[2.33]**).
Commencement (note): the Companies Act 2006 (Commencement No 5, Transitional Provisions and Savings) Order 2007, SI 2007/3495, art 3(3) provides that this section shall come into force on 6 April 2008 so far as is necessary for the purposes of the provisions of this Act brought into force on that date by art 3(1)(a)–(t), (2) of that Order (see **[2.52]**).

Share capital

[1.547]
547 Called-up share capital

In the Companies Acts—

"called-up share capital", in relation to a company, means so much of its share capital as equals the aggregate amount of the calls made on its shares (whether or not those calls have been paid), together with—

(a) any share capital paid up without being called, and

(b) any share capital to be paid on a specified future date under the articles, the terms of allotment of the relevant shares or any other arrangements for payment of those shares; and

"uncalled share capital" is to be construed accordingly.

NOTES

Commencement: 1 October 2009.

[1.548]
548 Equity share capital

In the Companies Acts "equity share capital", in relation to a company, means its issued share capital excluding any part of that capital that, neither as respects dividends nor as respects capital, carries any right to participate beyond a specified amount in a distribution.

NOTES

Commencement: 1 October 2007 (certain purposes); 6 April 2008 (certain purposes); 1 October 2009 (otherwise) (see the notes below).

Commencement (note): the Companies Act 2006 (Commencement No 3, Consequential Amendments, Transitional Provisions and Savings) Order 2007, SI 2007/2194, art 2(3) provides that this section shall come into force on 1 October 2007 so far as is necessary for the purposes of the provisions of this Act brought into force on that date by art 2(1), (2) of that Order (see **[2.32]**).

Commencement (note): the Companies Act 2006 (Commencement No 5, Transitional Provisions and Savings) Order 2007, SI 2007/3495, art 3(3) provides that this section shall come into force on 6 April 2008 so far as is necessary for the purposes of the provisions of this Act brought into force on that date by art 3(1)(a)–(t), (2) of that Order (see **[2.52]**).

CHAPTER 2
ALLOTMENT OF SHARES: GENERAL PROVISIONS

Power of directors to allot shares

[1.549]
549 Exercise by directors of power to allot shares etc

(1) The directors of a company must not exercise any power of the company—

(a) to allot shares in the company, or

(b) to grant rights to subscribe for, or to convert any security into, shares in the company,

except in accordance with section 550 (private company with single class of shares) or section 551 (authorisation by company).

(2) Subsection (1) does not apply—

(a) to the allotment of shares in pursuance of an employees' share scheme, or

(b) to the grant of a right to subscribe for, or to convert any security into, shares so allotted.

[(3) Subsection (1) does not apply to the allotment of shares pursuant to a right to subscribe for, or to convert any security into, shares in the company.]

(4) A director who knowingly contravenes, or permits or authorises a contravention of, this section commits an offence.

(5) A person guilty of an offence under this section is liable—

(a) on conviction on indictment, to a fine;

(b) on summary conviction, to a fine not exceeding the statutory maximum.

(6) Nothing in this section affects the validity of an allotment or other transaction.

NOTES

Commencement: 1 October 2009.

Sub-s (3): substituted by the Companies Act 2006 (Allotment of Shares and Right of Pre-emption) (Amendment) Regulations 2009, SI 2009/2561, reg 2(1), as from 1 October 2009.

[1.550]
550 Power of directors to allot shares etc: private company with only one class of shares

Where a private company has only one class of shares, the directors may exercise any power of the company—

(a) to allot shares of that class, or

(b) to grant rights to subscribe for or to convert any security into such shares,

except to the extent that they are prohibited from doing so by the company's articles.

NOTES

Commencement: 1 October 2009.

Commencement (transitional provisions): Sch 2, paras 43, 44 to the Companies Act 2006 (Commencement No 8, Transitional Provisions and Savings) Order 2008, SI 2008/2860 (at **[2.91]**) provide as follows—

"Power of directors to allot shares etc: private company with only one class of shares (s 550)

43.—(1) Section 550 of the Companies Act 2006 (power of directors to allot shares etc: private company with only one class of shares) applies to an existing or transitional company only if the members of the company have resolved that the directors should have the powers given by that section.

(2) A resolution under this paragraph may be an ordinary resolution (even if it takes the form of an alteration of the company's articles).

(3) Chapter 3 of Part 3 of the Companies Act 2006 (resolutions and agreements affecting a company's constitution) applies to any such resolution.

(4) Any such resolution passed before 1st October 2009 is treated as if passed on that date.

(5) Once the members of the company have resolved as mentioned in sub-paragraph (1), the application of section 550 in relation to the company is not affected by any subsequent resolution, except one altering the company's articles so as to prohibit (to any extent) exercise of the powers mentioned in the section.

44. For the purposes of section 550 of the Companies Act 2006 provisions of the articles of an existing or transitional company—

    (a)   authorising the directors to allot shares in accordance with section 80 of the 1985 Act or Article 90 of the 1986 Order, or

    (b)   added following an elective resolution under section 80A of the 1985 Act or Article 90A of the 1986 Order and authorising the directors to allot shares,

are not to be treated as provisions prohibiting the directors from exercising the powers conferred by section 550 in cases to which the authority does not extend.".

[1.551]

551 Power of directors to allot shares etc: authorisation by company

(1) The directors of a company may exercise a power of the company—

    (a)   to allot shares in the company, or

    (b)   to grant rights to subscribe for or to convert any security into shares in the company,

if they are authorised to do so by the company's articles or by resolution of the company.

(2) Authorisation may be given for a particular exercise of the power or for its exercise generally, and may be unconditional or subject to conditions.

(3) Authorisation must—

    (a)   state the maximum amount of shares that may be allotted under it, and

    (b)   specify the date on which it will expire, which must be not more than five years from—

        (i)   in the case of authorisation contained in the company's articles at the time of its original incorporation, the date of that incorporation;

        (ii)   in any other case, the date on which the resolution is passed by virtue of which the authorisation is given.

(4) Authorisation may—

    (a)   be renewed or further renewed by resolution of the company for a further period not exceeding five years, and

    (b)   be revoked or varied at any time by resolution of the company.

(5) A resolution renewing authorisation must—

    (a)   state (or restate) the maximum amount of shares that may be allotted under the authorisation or, as the case may be, the amount remaining to be allotted under it, and

    (b)   specify the date on which the renewed authorisation will expire.

(6) In relation to rights to subscribe for or to convert any security into shares in the company, references in this section to the maximum amount of shares that may be allotted under the authorisation are to the maximum amount of shares that may be allotted pursuant to the rights.

(7) The directors may allot shares, or grant rights to subscribe for or to convert any security into shares, after authorisation has expired if—

    (a)   the shares are allotted, or the rights are granted, in pursuance of an offer or agreement made by the company before the authorisation expired, and

    (b)   the authorisation allowed the company to make an offer or agreement which would or might require shares to be allotted, or rights to be granted, after the authorisation had expired.

(8) A resolution of a company to give, vary, revoke or renew authorisation under this section may be an ordinary resolution, even though it amends the company's articles.

(9) Chapter 3 of Part 3 (resolutions affecting a company's constitution) applies to a resolution under this section.

NOTES

Commencement: 1 October 2009.

Commencement (transitional provisions): Sch 2, para 51 to the Companies Act 2006 (Commencement No 8, Transitional Provisions and Savings) Order 2008, SI 2008/2860 (at **[2.91]**) provides that an authorisation in force immediately before 1 October 2009 under ss 80 or 80A of the 1985 Act has effect on and after that date as if given under this section.

Prohibition of commissions, discounts and allowances

[1.552]
552 General prohibition of commissions, discounts and allowances
(1)   Except as permitted by section 553 (permitted commission), a company must not apply any of its shares or capital money, either directly or indirectly, in payment of any commission, discount or allowance to any person in consideration of his—
- (a)   subscribing or agreeing to subscribe (whether absolutely or conditionally) for shares in the company, or
- (b)   procuring or agreeing to procure subscriptions (whether absolute or conditional) for shares in the company.

(2)   It is immaterial how the shares or money are so applied, whether by being added to the purchase money of property acquired by the company or to the contract price of work to be executed for the company, or being paid out of the nominal purchase money or contract price, or otherwise.

(3)   Nothing in this section affects the payment of such brokerage as has previously been lawful.

NOTES
Commencement: 1 October 2009.

[1.553]
553 Permitted commission
(1)   A company may, if the following conditions are satisfied, pay a commission to a person in consideration of his subscribing or agreeing to subscribe (whether absolutely or conditionally) for shares in the company, or procuring or agreeing to procure subscriptions (whether absolute or conditional) for shares in the company.

(2)   The conditions are that—
- (a)   the payment of the commission is authorised by the company's articles; and
- (b)   the commission paid or agreed to be paid does not exceed—
  - (i)   10% of the price at which the shares are issued, or
  - (ii)   the amount or rate authorised by the articles,
  whichever is the less.

(3)   A vendor to, or promoter of, or other person who receives payment in money or shares from, a company may apply any part of the money or shares so received in payment of any commission the payment of which directly by the company would be permitted by this section.

NOTES
Commencement: 1 October 2009.

Registration of allotment

[1.554]
554 Registration of allotment
(1)   A company must register an allotment of shares as soon as practicable and in any event within two months after the date of the allotment.

(2)   This does not apply if the company has issued a share warrant in respect of the shares (see section 779).

(3)   If a company fails to comply with this section, an offence is committed by—
- (a)   the company, and
- (b)   every officer of the company who is in default.

(4)   A person guilty of an offence under this section is liable on summary conviction to a fine not exceeding level 3 on the standard scale and, for continued contravention, a daily default fine not exceeding one-tenth of level 3 on the standard scale.

(5)   For the company's duties as to the issue of share certificates etc, see Part 21 (certification and transfer of securities).

NOTES
Commencement: 1 October 2009.
Commencement (transitional provisions): this section applies to shares allotted on or after 1 October 2009; see the Companies Act 2006 (Commencement No 8, Transitional Provisions and Savings) Order 2008, SI 2008/2860, Sch 2, para 46 (at **[2.91]**).

Return of allotment

[1.555]
555 Return of allotment by limited company
(1)   This section applies to a company limited by shares and to a company limited by guarantee and having a share capital.

(2)   The company must, within one month of making an allotment of shares, deliver to the registrar for registration a return of the allotment.

(3)   The return must—
- (a)   contain the prescribed information, and

(b)   be accompanied by a statement of capital.

(4)   The statement of capital must state with respect to the company's share capital at the date to which the return is made up—

(a)   the total number of shares of the company,

(b)   the aggregate nominal value of those shares,

(c)   for each class of shares—

(i)   prescribed particulars of the rights attached to the shares,

(ii)   the total number of shares of that class, and

(iii)   the aggregate nominal value of shares of that class, and

(d)   the amount paid up and the amount (if any) unpaid on each share (whether on account of the nominal value of the share or by way of premium).

NOTES

Commencement: 20 January 2007 (for the purpose of enabling the exercise of powers to make Orders or Regulations by statutory instrument); 1 October 2009 (otherwise).

Commencement (transitional provisions): this section applies to shares allotted on or after 1 October 2009 (and s 88 of the 1985 Act continues to apply to shares allotted before that date); see the Companies Act 2006 (Commencement No 8, Transitional Provisions and Savings) Order 2008, SI 2008/2860, Sch 2, para 47 (at **[2.91]**).

Orders: the Companies (Shares and Share Capital) Order 2009, SI 2009/388 at **[4.364]**.

[1.556]

556   Return of allotment by unlimited company allotting new class of shares

(1)   This section applies to an unlimited company that allots shares of a class with rights that are not in all respects uniform with shares previously allotted.

(2)   The company must, within one month of making such an allotment, deliver to the registrar for registration a return of the allotment.

(3)   The return must contain the prescribed particulars of the rights attached to the shares.

(4)   For the purposes of this section shares are not to be treated as different from shares previously allotted by reason only that the former do not carry the same rights to dividends as the latter during the twelve months immediately following the former's allotment.

NOTES

Commencement: 20 January 2007 (for the purpose of enabling the exercise of powers to make Orders or Regulations by statutory instrument); 1 October 2009 (otherwise).

Commencement (transitional provisions): this section applies to shares allotted on or after 1 October 2009 (and s 128(1), (2), (5) of the 1985 Act continue to apply to shares allotted before that date); see the Companies Act 2006 (Commencement No 8, Transitional Provisions and Savings) Order 2008, SI 2008/2860, Sch 2, para 48 (at **[2.91]**).

Orders: the Companies (Shares and Share Capital) Order 2009, SI 2009/388 at **[4.364]**.

[1.557]

557   Offence of failure to make return

(1)   If a company makes default in complying with—

section 555 (return of allotment of shares by limited company), or

section 556 (return of allotment of new class of shares by unlimited company),

an offence is committed by every officer of the company who is in default.

(2)   A person guilty of an offence under this section is liable—

(a)   on conviction on indictment, to a fine;

(b)   on summary conviction, to a fine not exceeding the statutory maximum and, for continued contravention, a daily default fine not exceeding one-tenth of the statutory maximum.

(3)   In the case of default in delivering to the registrar within one month after the allotment the return required by section 555 or 556—

(a)   any person liable for the default may apply to the court for relief, and

(b)   the court, if satisfied—

(i)   that the omission to deliver the document was accidental or due to inadvertence, or

(ii)   that it is just and equitable to grant relief,

may make an order extending the time for delivery of the document for such period as the court thinks proper.

NOTES

Commencement: 1 October 2009.

Supplementary provisions

[1.558]

558   When shares are allotted

For the purposes of the Companies Acts shares in a company are taken to be allotted when a person acquires the unconditional right to be included in the company's register of members in respect of the shares.

NOTES

Commencement: 6 April 2007 (certain purposes); 1 October 2009 (otherwise) (see the note below).

Commencement (note): the Companies Act 2006 (Commencement No 2, Consequential Amendments, Transitional Provisions and Savings) Order 2007, SI 2007/1093, art 2(2) provides that this section shall come into force on 6 April 2007 so far as is necessary for the purposes of the provisions of this Act brought into force on that date by art 2(1) of that Order (see **[2.17]**).

[1.559]
559 Provisions about allotment not applicable to shares taken on formation
The provisions of this Chapter have no application in relation to the taking of shares by the subscribers to the memorandum on the formation of the company.

NOTES
Commencement: 1 October 2009.

CHAPTER 3
ALLOTMENT OF EQUITY SECURITIES:
EXISTING SHAREHOLDERS' RIGHT OF PRE-EMPTION

Introductory

[1.560]
560 Meaning of "equity securities" and related expressions
(1) In this Chapter—
"equity securities" means—
    (a)   ordinary shares in the company, or
    (b)   rights to subscribe for, or to convert securities into, ordinary shares in the company;
"ordinary shares" means shares other than shares that as respects dividends and capital carry a right to participate only up to a specified amount in a distribution.
[(2) References in this Chapter to the allotment of equity securities—
    (a)   include the grant of a right to subscribe for, or to convert any securities into, ordinary shares in the company, and
    (b)   do not include the allotment of shares pursuant to such a right.
(3) References in this Chapter to the allotment of equity securities include the sale of ordinary shares in the company that immediately before the sale were held by the company as treasury shares.]

NOTES
Commencement: 1 October 2009.
Sub-ss (2), (3): substituted, for the original sub-s (2), by the Companies Act 2006 (Allotment of Shares and Right of Pre-emption) (Amendment) Regulations 2009, SI 2009/2561, reg 2(2), as from 1 October 2009.

Existing shareholders' right of pre-emption

[1.561]
561 Existing shareholders' right of pre-emption
(1) A company must not allot equity securities to a person on any terms unless—
    (a)   it has made an offer to each person who holds ordinary shares in the company to allot to him on the same or more favourable terms a proportion of those securities that is as nearly as practicable equal to the proportion in nominal value held by him of the ordinary share capital of the company, and
    (b)   the period during which any such offer may be accepted has expired or the company has received notice of the acceptance or refusal of every offer so made.
(2) Securities that a company has offered to allot to a holder of ordinary shares may be allotted to him, or anyone in whose favour he has renounced his right to their allotment, without contravening subsection (1)(b).
(3) . . .
(4) Shares held by the company as treasury shares are disregarded for the purposes of this section, so that—
    (a)   the company is not treated as a person who holds ordinary shares, and
    (b)   the shares are not treated as forming part of the ordinary share capital of the company.
(5) This section is subject to—
    (a)   sections 564 to 566 (exceptions to pre-emption right),
    (b)   sections 567 and 568 (exclusion of rights of pre-emption),
    (c)   sections 569 to 573 (disapplication of pre-emption rights), and
    (d)   section 576 (saving for certain older pre-emption procedures).

NOTES
Commencement: 1 October 2009.
Commencement (transitional provisions): Sch 2, paras 49–55 to the Companies Act 2006 (Commencement No 8, Transitional Provisions and Savings) Order 2008, SI 2008/2860 (at **[2.91]**) provide for a wide-range of transitional provisions in connection with the commencement of this Chapter and the repeal of the equivalent provisions of the Companies Act 1985 (ie, ss 89–96 in Part IV). Those paragraphs provide as follows—

"Existing shareholders' right of pre-emption (ss 561 to 577)

49.—(1)   Section 561 of the Companies Act 2006 (prohibition on allotment unless offers made to existing shareholders) applies to the allotment of shares on or after 1st October 2009.

(2)   Where that section applies—

    (a)   section 562 of that Act (communication of pre-emption offers to shareholders) applies to offers made on or after 1st October 2009, and

    (b)   section 90 of the 1985 Act or Article 100 of the 1986 Order continues to apply to offers made before that date,

and the requirements of section 561 may be met by offers within paragraph (a) or (b) above.

(3)   Section 563 of the Companies Act 2006 (consequences of contravention) applies where section 561 applies and the reference to section 562 of that Act shall be read accordingly as including a reference to section 90 of the 1985 Act or Article 100 of the 1986 Order.

50.—(1)   This paragraph applies where provision made by virtue of section 91 of the 1985 Act or Article 101 of the 1986 Order (exclusion of requirements by private company) excluding the requirements of section 89 or 90 or Article 99 or 100 is in force immediately before 1st October 2009.

(2)   That provision has effect on and after that date as if it was or, as the case may be, included provision made by virtue of section 567 of the Companies Act 2006 excluding the corresponding requirements of section 561 or 562 of that Act.

51.—(1)   Section 568 of the Companies Act 2006 (exclusion of statutory pre-emption right where articles confer corresponding right) applies to the allotment of shares on or after 1st October 2009.

(2)   The reference in section 568(3) to section 562 of that Act (communication of pre-emption offers to shareholders) shall be read in relation to offers made before 1st October 2009 as a reference to section 90 of the 1985 Act or Article 100 of the 1986 Order.

(3)   Section 563 of the Companies Act 2006 (consequences of contravention) applies in relation to such an offer as if the reference to section 562 of that Act were a reference to section 90 of the 1985 Act or Article 100 of the 1986 Order.

52.—(1)   This paragraph applies where provision excluding or modifying section 89(1) of the 1985 Act or Article 99(1) of the 1986 Order has been made by virtue of section 95(1) of the 1985 Act or Article 105(1) of the 1986 Order and is in force immediately before 1st October 2009.

(2)   The provision has effect on and after that date as if it had been made by virtue of section 570 of the Companies Act 2006 (disapplication of pre-emption rights: directors acting under general authorisation) and excluded, or made corresponding modifications of, section 561 of that Act.

(3)   The power conferred to allot equity securities may accordingly be renewed under section 570(3).

53.—(1)   This paragraph applies where a special resolution excluding or modifying section 89(1) of the 1985 Act or Article 99(1) of the 1986 Order has been passed by virtue of section 95(2) of the 1985 Act or Article 105(2) of the 1986 Order and is in force immediately before 1st October 2009.

(2)   The resolution has effect on and after that date as if it had been passed by virtue of section 571 of the Companies Act 2006 (disapplication of pre-emption rights by special resolution) and excluded, or made corresponding modifications of, section 561 of that Act.

(3)   The resolution may accordingly be renewed under section 571(3).

54.—(1)   It is immaterial whether the directors' statement required before a resolution can be proposed under section 571 of the Companies Act 2006 (disapplication of pre-emption rights by special resolution) is made, or is sent, submitted or circulated as required by subsection (7) of that section before, on or after 1st October 2009.

(2)   Section 572 of that Act (criminal liability for false statement) applies to a directors' statement that is sent, submitted or circulated to a member on or after 1st October 2009.

(3)   Section 95(6) of the 1985 Act or Article 105(6) of the 1986 Order applies to a directors' statement that is circulated or supplied to a member before that date.

55.—(1)   This paragraph applies where provision excluding or modifying section 89(1) of the 1985 Act or Article 99(1) of the 1986 Order has been made by virtue of section 95(2A) of the 1985 Act or Article 105(2A) of the 1986 Order and is in force immediately before 1st October 2009.

(2)   The provision has effect on and after that date as if it had been made by virtue of section 573 of the Companies Act 2006 (disapplication of pre-emption rights: sale of treasury shares) and excluded, or made corresponding modifications of, section 561 of that Act.

(3)   The power conferred to allot equity securities may accordingly be renewed under section 570(3) or, as the case may be, section 571(3).".

Sub-s (3): repealed by the Companies Act 2006 (Allotment of Shares and Right of Pre-emption) (Amendment) Regulations 2009, SI 2009/2561, reg 2(3), as from 1 October 2009.

[1.562]

562   Communication of pre-emption offers to shareholders

(1)   This section has effect as to the manner in which offers required by section 561 are to be made to holders of a company's shares.

(2)   The offer may be made in hard copy or electronic form.

(3)   If the holder—

    (a)   has no registered address in an EEA State and has not given to the company an address in an EEA State for the service of notices on him, or

    (b)   is the holder of a share warrant,

the offer may be made by causing it, or a notice specifying where a copy of it can be obtained or inspected, to be published in the Gazette.

(4)   The offer must state a period during which it may be accepted and the offer shall not be withdrawn before the end of that period.

(5)   The period must be a period of at least [14 days] beginning—

    (a)   in the case of an offer made in hard copy form, with the date on which the offer is sent or supplied;

    (b)   in the case of an offer made in electronic form, with the date on which the offer is sent;

    (c)   in the case of an offer made by publication in the Gazette, with the date of publication.

(6)   The Secretary of State may by regulations made by statutory instrument—

(a)   reduce the period specified in subsection (5) (but not to less than 14 days), or

(b)   increase that period.

(7)   A statutory instrument containing regulations made under subsection (6) is subject to affirmative resolution procedure.

NOTES

Commencement: 20 January 2007 (for the purpose of enabling the exercise of powers to make Orders or Regulations by statutory instrument); 1 October 2009 (otherwise).

Commencement (transitional provisions): see the note to s 561 at **[1.561]**.

Sub-s (5): words in square brackets substituted by the Companies (Share Capital and Acquisition by Company of its Own Shares) Regulations 2009, SI 2009/2022, reg 2, as from 1 October 2009.

Regulations: the Companies (Share Capital and Acquisition by Company of its Own Shares) Regulations 2009, SI 2009/2022 at **[4.542]**.

[1.563]
563   Liability of company and officers in case of contravention

(1)   This section applies where there is a contravention of—

section 561 (existing shareholders' right of pre-emption), or

section 562 (communication of pre-emption offers to shareholders).

(2)   The company and every officer of it who knowingly authorised or permitted the contravention are jointly and severally liable to compensate any person to whom an offer should have been made in accordance with those provisions for any loss, damage, costs or expenses which the person has sustained or incurred by reason of the contravention.

(3)   No proceedings to recover any such loss, damage, costs or expenses shall be commenced after the expiration of two years—

(a)   from the delivery to the registrar of companies of the return of allotment, or

(b)   where equity securities other than shares are granted, from the date of the grant.

NOTES

Commencement: 1 October 2009.

Commencement (transitional provisions): see the note to s 561 at **[1.561]**.

Exceptions to right of pre-emption

[1.564]
564   Exception to pre-emption right: bonus shares

Section 561(1) (existing shareholders' right of pre-emption) does not apply in relation to the allotment of bonus shares.

NOTES

Commencement: 1 October 2009.

Commencement (transitional provisions): see the note to s 561 at **[1.561]**.

[1.565]
565   Exception to pre-emption right: issue for non-cash consideration

Section 561(1) (existing shareholders' right of pre-emption) does not apply to a particular allotment of equity securities if these are, or are to be, wholly or partly paid up otherwise than in cash.

NOTES

Commencement: 1 October 2009.

Commencement (transitional provisions): see the note to s 561 at **[1.561]**.

[1.566]
[566   Exceptions to pre-emption right: employees' share schemes

Section 561 (existing shareholders' right of pre-emption) does not apply to the allotment of equity securities that would, apart from any renunciation or assignment of the right to their allotment, be held under or allotted or transferred pursuant to an employees' share scheme.]

NOTES

Commencement: 1 October 2009.

Commencement (transitional provisions): see the note to s 561 at **[1.561]**.

Substituted by the Companies Act 2006 (Allotment of Shares and Right of Pre-emption) (Amendment) Regulations 2009, SI 2009/2561, reg 2(4), as from 1 October 2009.

Exclusion of right of pre-emption

[1.567]
567   Exclusion of requirements by private companies

(1)   All or any of the requirements of—

(a)   section 561 (existing shareholders' right of pre-emption), or

(b)   section 562 (communication of pre-emption offers to shareholders)

may be excluded by provision contained in the articles of a private company.

(2)   They may be excluded—

(a) generally in relation to the allotment by the company of equity securities, or

(b) in relation to allotments of a particular description.

(3) Any requirement or authorisation contained in the articles of a private company that is inconsistent with either of those sections is treated for the purposes of this section as a provision excluding that section.

(4) A provision to which section 568 applies (exclusion of pre-emption right: corresponding right conferred by articles) is not to be treated as inconsistent with section 561.

NOTES
Commencement: 1 October 2009.
Commencement (transitional provisions): see the note to s 561 at **[1.561]**.

[1.568]
568 Exclusion of pre-emption right: articles conferring corresponding right

(1) The provisions of this section apply where, in a case in which section 561 (existing shareholders' right of pre-emption) would otherwise apply—

(a) a company's articles contain provision ("pre-emption provision") prohibiting the company from allotting ordinary shares of a particular class unless it has complied with the condition that it makes such an offer as is described in section 561(1) to each person who holds ordinary shares of that class, and

(b) in accordance with that provision—

(i) the company makes an offer to allot shares to such a holder, and

(ii) he or anyone in whose favour he has renounced his right to their allotment accepts the offer.

(2) In that case, section 561 does not apply to the allotment of those shares and the company may allot them accordingly.

(3) The provisions of section 562 (communication of pre-emption offers to shareholders) apply in relation to offers made in pursuance of the pre-emption provision of the company's articles.

This is subject to section 567 (exclusion of requirements by private companies).

(4) If there is a contravention of the pre-emption provision of the company's articles, the company, and every officer of it who knowingly authorised or permitted the contravention, are jointly and severally liable to compensate any person to whom an offer should have been made under the provision for any loss, damage, costs or expenses which the person has sustained or incurred by reason of the contravention.

(5) No proceedings to recover any such loss, damage, costs or expenses may be commenced after the expiration of two years—

(a) from the delivery to the registrar of companies of the return of allotment, or

(b) where equity securities other than shares are granted, from the date of the grant.

NOTES
Commencement: 1 October 2009.
Commencement (transitional provisions): see the note to s 561 at **[1.561]**.

Disapplication of pre-emption rights

[1.569]
569 Disapplication of pre-emption rights: private company with only one class of shares

(1) The directors of a private company that has only one class of shares may be given power by the articles, or by a special resolution of the company, to allot equity securities of that class as if section 561 (existing shareholders' right of pre-emption)—

(a) did not apply to the allotment, or

(b) applied to the allotment with such modifications as the directors may determine.

(2) Where the directors make an allotment under this section, the provisions of this Chapter have effect accordingly.

NOTES
Commencement: 1 October 2009.
Commencement (transitional provisions): see the note to s 561 at **[1.561]**.

[1.570]
570 Disapplication of pre-emption rights: directors acting under general authorisation

(1) Where the directors of a company are generally authorised for the purposes of section 551 (power of directors to allot shares etc: authorisation by company), they may be given power by the articles, or by a special resolution of the company, to allot equity securities pursuant to that authorisation as if section 561 (existing shareholders' right of pre-emption)—

(a) did not apply to the allotment, or

(b) applied to the allotment with such modifications as the directors may determine.

(2) Where the directors make an allotment under this section, the provisions of this Chapter have effect accordingly.

(3)   The power conferred by this section ceases to have effect when the authorisation to which it relates—

(a)   is revoked, or

(b)   would (if not renewed) expire.

But if the authorisation is renewed the power may also be renewed, for a period not longer than that for which the authorisation is renewed, by a special resolution of the company.

(4)   Notwithstanding that the power conferred by this section has expired, the directors may allot equity securities in pursuance of an offer or agreement previously made by the company if the power enabled the company to make an offer or agreement that would or might require equity securities to be allotted after it expired.

NOTES

Commencement: 1 October 2009.

Commencement (transitional provisions): see the note to s 561 at **[1.561]**.

[1.571]

571   Disapplication of pre-emption rights by special resolution

(1)   Where the directors of a company are authorised for the purposes of section 551 (power of directors to allot shares etc: authorisation by company), whether generally or otherwise, the company may by special resolution resolve that section 561 (existing shareholders' right of pre-emption)—

(a)   does not apply to a specified allotment of equity securities to be made pursuant to that authorisation, or

(b)   applies to such an allotment with such modifications as may be specified in the resolution.

(2)   Where such a resolution is passed the provisions of this Chapter have effect accordingly.

(3)   A special resolution under this section ceases to have effect when the authorisation to which it relates—

(a)   is revoked, or

(b)   would (if not renewed) expire.

But if the authorisation is renewed the resolution may also be renewed, for a period not longer than that for which the authorisation is renewed, by a special resolution of the company.

(4)   Notwithstanding that any such resolution has expired, the directors may allot equity securities in pursuance of an offer or agreement previously made by the company if the resolution enabled the company to make an offer or agreement that would or might require equity securities to be allotted after it expired.

(5)   A special resolution under this section, or a special resolution to renew such a resolution, must not be proposed unless—

(a)   it is recommended by the directors, and

(b)   the directors have complied with the following provisions.

(6)   Before such a resolution is proposed, the directors must make a written statement setting out—

(a)   their reasons for making the recommendation,

(b)   the amount to be paid to the company in respect of the equity securities to be allotted, and

(c)   the directors' justification of that amount.

(7)   The directors' statement must—

(a)   if the resolution is proposed as a written resolution, be sent or submitted to every eligible member at or before the time at which the proposed resolution is sent or submitted to him;

(b)   if the resolution is proposed at a general meeting, be circulated to the members entitled to notice of the meeting with that notice.

NOTES

Commencement: 1 October 2009.

Commencement (transitional provisions): see the note to s 561 at **[1.561]**.

[1.572]

572   Liability for false statement in directors' statement

(1)   This section applies in relation to a directors' statement under section 571 (special resolution disapplying pre-emption rights) that is sent, submitted or circulated under subsection (7) of that section.

(2)   A person who knowingly or recklessly authorises or permits the inclusion of any matter that is misleading, false or deceptive in a material particular in such a statement commits an offence.

(3)   A person guilty of an offence under this section is liable—

(a)   on conviction on indictment, to imprisonment for a term not exceeding two years or a fine (or both);

(b)   on summary conviction—

(i)   in England and Wales, to imprisonment for a term not exceeding twelve months or to a fine not exceeding the statutory maximum (or both);

(ii)   in Scotland or Northern Ireland, to imprisonment for a term not exceeding six months, or to a fine not exceeding the statutory maximum (or both).

NOTES

Commencement: 1 October 2009.

Commencement (transitional provisions): see the note to s 561 at **[1.561]**.

Offences under this section: see further s 1131 at **[1.1131]**.

[1.573]
573   Disapplication of pre-emption rights: sale of treasury shares

(1)   This section applies in relation to a sale of shares that is an allotment of equity securities by virtue of [section 560(3)] (sale of shares held by company as treasury shares).

(2)   The directors of a company may be given power by the articles, or by a special resolution of the company, to allot equity securities as if section 561 (existing shareholders' right of pre-emption)—

    (a)   did not apply to the allotment, or

    (b)   applied to the allotment with such modifications as the directors may determine.

(3)   The provisions of section 570(2) and (4) apply in that case as they apply to a case within subsection (1) of that section.

(4)   The company may by special resolution resolve that section 561—

    (a)   shall not apply to a specified allotment of securities, or

    (b)   shall apply to the allotment with such modifications as may be specified in the resolution.

(5)   The provisions of section 571(2) and (4) to (7) apply in that case as they apply to a case within subsection (1) of that section.

NOTES

Commencement: 1 October 2009.

Commencement (transitional provisions): see the note to s 561 at **[1.561]**.

Sub-s (1): words in square brackets substituted by the Companies Act 2006 (Allotment of Shares and Right of Pre-emption) (Amendment) Regulations 2009, SI 2009/2561, reg 2(5), as from 1 October 2009.

Supplementary

[1.574]
574   References to holder of shares in relation to offer

(1)   In this Chapter, in relation to an offer to allot securities required by—

    (a)   section 561 (existing shareholders' right of pre-emption), or

    (b)   any provision to which section 568 applies (articles conferring corresponding right),

a reference (however expressed) to the holder of shares of any description is to whoever was the holder of shares of that description at the close of business on a date to be specified in the offer.

(2)   The specified date must fall within the period of 28 days immediately before the date of the offer.

NOTES

Commencement: 1 October 2009.

Commencement (transitional provisions): see the note to s 561 at **[1.561]**.

[1.575]
575   Saving for other restrictions on offer or allotment

(1)   The provisions of this Chapter are without prejudice to any other enactment by virtue of which a company is prohibited (whether generally or in specified circumstances) from offering or allotting equity securities to any person.

(2)   Where a company cannot by virtue of such an enactment offer or allot equity securities to a holder of ordinary shares of the company, those shares are disregarded for the purposes of section 561 (existing shareholders' right of pre-emption), so that—

    (a)   the person is not treated as a person who holds ordinary shares, and

    (b)   the shares are not treated as forming part of the ordinary share capital of the company.

NOTES

Commencement: 1 October 2009.

Commencement (transitional provisions): see the note to s 561 at **[1.561]**.

[1.576]
576   Saving for certain older pre-emption requirements

(1)   In the case of a public company the provisions of this Chapter do not apply to an allotment of equity securities that are subject to a pre-emption requirement in relation to which section 96(1) of the Companies Act 1985 (c 6) or Article 106(1) of the Companies (Northern Ireland) Order 1986 (SI 1986/1032 (NI 6)) applied immediately before the commencement of this Chapter.

(2)   In the case of a private company a pre-emption requirement to which section 96(3) of the Companies Act 1985 or Article 106(3) of the Companies (Northern Ireland) Order 1986 applied immediately before the commencement of this Chapter shall have effect, so long as the company remains a private company, as if it were contained in the company's articles.

(3) A pre-emption requirement to which section 96(4) of the Companies Act 1985 or Article 106(4) of the Companies (Northern Ireland) Order 1986 applied immediately before the commencement of this section shall be treated for the purposes of this Chapter as if it were contained in the company's articles.

NOTES

Commencement: 1 October 2009.

Commencement (transitional provisions): see the note to s 561 at **[1.561]**.

[1.577]

577 Provisions about pre-emption not applicable to shares taken on formation

The provisions of this Chapter have no application in relation to the taking of shares by the subscribers to the memorandum on the formation of the company.

NOTES

Commencement: 1 October 2009.

Commencement (transitional provisions): see the note to s 561 at **[1.561]**.

CHAPTER 4

PUBLIC COMPANIES: ALLOTMENT WHERE ISSUE NOT FULLY SUBSCRIBED

[1.578]

578 Public companies: allotment where issue not fully subscribed

(1) No allotment shall be made of shares of a public company offered for subscription unless—
  (a) the issue is subscribed for in full, or
  (b) the offer is made on terms that the shares subscribed for may be allotted—
     (i) in any event, or
     (ii) if specified conditions are met (and those conditions are met).

(2) If shares are prohibited from being allotted by subsection (1) and 40 days have elapsed after the first making of the offer, all money received from applicants for shares must be repaid to them forthwith, without interest.

(3) If any of the money is not repaid within 48 days after the first making of the offer, the directors of the company are jointly and severally liable to repay it, with interest at the rate for the time being specified under section 17 of the Judgments Act 1838 (c 110) from the expiration of the 48th day.

A director is not so liable if he proves that the default in the repayment of the money was not due to any misconduct or negligence on his part.

(4) This section applies in the case of shares offered as wholly or partly payable otherwise than in cash as it applies in the case of shares offered for subscription.

(5) In that case—
  (a) the references in subsection (1) to subscription shall be construed accordingly;
  (b) references in subsections (2) and (3) to the repayment of money received from applicants for shares include—
     (i) the return of any other consideration so received (including, if the case so requires, the release of the applicant from any undertaking), or
     (ii) if it is not reasonably practicable to return the consideration, the payment of money equal to its value at the time it was so received;
  (c) references to interest apply accordingly.

(6) Any condition requiring or binding an applicant for shares to waive compliance with any requirement of this section is void.

NOTES

Commencement: 1 October 2009.

Commencement (transitional provisions): Sch 2, para 56 to the Companies Act 2006 (Commencement No 8, Transitional Provisions and Savings) Order 2008, SI 2008/2860 (at **[2.91]**) provides as follows—

"**Public companies: allotment where issue not fully subscribed (ss 578 and 579)**

56.—(1) Sections 578 and 579 of the Companies Act 2006 (public companies: allotment where issue not fully subscribed) apply where the offer is made on or after 1st October 2009, unless a prospectus has been issued before that date.
(2) Sections 84 and 85 of the 1985 Act or Articles 94 and 95 of the 1986 Order continue to apply where the offer was made, or a prospectus issued, before that date.
(3) In the case of an offer made or a prospectus issued on more than one day, the references in this paragraph to the date on which it is made or issued are to the first day on which it was made or issued.
(4) References in this paragraph to a prospectus being issued are to its being made available to the public in accordance with Part 6 of the Financial Services and Markets Act 2000.".

[1.579]

579 Public companies: effect of irregular allotment where issue not fully subscribed

(1) An allotment made by a public company to an applicant in contravention of section 578 (public companies: allotment where issue not fully subscribed) is voidable at the instance of the applicant within one month after the date of the allotment, and not later.

(2)   It is so voidable even if the company is in the course of being wound up.

(3)   A director of a public company who knowingly contravenes, or permits or authorises the contravention of, any provision of section 578 with respect to allotment is liable to compensate the company and the allottee respectively for any loss, damages, costs or expenses that the company or allottee may have sustained or incurred by the contravention.

(4)   Proceedings to recover any such loss, damages, costs or expenses may not be brought more than two years after the date of the allotment.

NOTES
    Commencement: 1 October 2009.
    Commencement (transitional provisions): see the note to s 578 at **[1.578]**.

CHAPTER 5
PAYMENT FOR SHARES
General rules

[1.580]
580   Shares not to be allotted at a discount
(1)   A company's shares must not be allotted at a discount.
(2)   If shares are allotted in contravention of this section, the allottee is liable to pay the company an amount equal to the amount of the discount, with interest at the appropriate rate.

NOTES
    Commencement: 1 October 2009.

[1.581]
581   Provision for different amounts to be paid on shares
A company, if so authorised by its articles, may—
    (a)   make arrangements on the issue of shares for a difference between the shareholders in the amounts and times of payment of calls on their shares;
    (b)   accept from any member the whole or part of the amount remaining unpaid on any shares held by him, although no part of that amount has been called up;
    (c)   pay a dividend in proportion to the amount paid up on each share where a larger amount is paid up on some shares than on others.

NOTES
    Commencement: 1 October 2009.

[1.582]
582   General rule as to means of payment
(1)   Shares allotted by a company, and any premium on them, may be paid up in money or money's worth (including goodwill and know-how).
(2)   This section does not prevent a company—
    (a)   from allotting bonus shares to its members, or
    (b)   from paying up, with sums available for the purpose, any amounts for the time being unpaid on any of its shares (whether on account of the nominal value of the shares or by way of premium).
(3)   This section has effect subject to the following provisions of this Chapter (additional rules for public companies).

NOTES
    Commencement: 1 October 2009.

[1.583]
583   Meaning of payment in cash
(1)   The following provisions have effect for the purposes of the Companies Acts.
(2)   A share in a company is deemed paid up (as to its nominal value or any premium on it) in cash, or allotted for cash, if the consideration received for the allotment or payment up is a cash consideration.
(3)   A "cash consideration" means—
    (a)   cash received by the company,
    (b)   a cheque received by the company in good faith that the directors have no reason for suspecting will not be paid,
    (c)   a release of a liability of the company for a liquidated sum,
    (d)   an undertaking to pay cash to the company at a future date, or
    (e)   payment by any other means giving rise to a present or future entitlement (of the company or a person acting on the company's behalf) to a payment, or credit equivalent to payment, in cash.
(4)   The Secretary of State may by order provide that particular means of payment specified in the order are to be regarded as falling within subsection (3)(e).

(5)   In relation to the allotment or payment up of shares in a company—

(a)   the payment of cash to a person other than the company, or

(b)   an undertaking to pay cash to a person other than the company,

counts as consideration other than cash.

This does not apply for the purposes of Chapter 3 (allotment of equity securities: existing shareholders' right of pre-emption).

(6)   For the purpose of determining whether a share is or is to be allotted for cash, or paid up in cash, "cash" includes foreign currency.

(7)   An order under this section is subject to negative resolution procedure.

NOTES

Commencement: 20 January 2007 (for the purpose of enabling the exercise of powers to make Orders or Regulations by statutory instrument); 1 October 2009 (otherwise).

Commencement (transitional provisions): Sch 2, para 57 to the Companies Act 2006 (Commencement No 8, Transitional Provisions and Savings) Order 2008, SI 2008/2860 (at **[2.91]**) provides as follows—

"Meaning of "cash consideration" for shares (ss 583 and 607)

57.—(1)   Section 583(3)(e) of the Companies Act 2006 (meaning of "cash consideration for shares": other means equivalent to payment in cash) applies only in relation to consideration received in pursuance of an obligation entered into on or after 1st October 2009.

(2)   Section 607 of that Act (penalty for contravention of provisions about valuation of non-cash consideration) applies in relation to consideration received in pursuance of an obligation entered into on or after that date.

(3)   Section 114 of the 1985 Act or Article 124 of the 1986 Order continues to apply in relation to consideration received in pursuance of an obligation entered into before that date.".

Orders: the Companies (Shares and Share Capital) Order 2009, SI 2009/388 at **[4.364]**.

Additional rules for public companies

[1.584]
584   Public companies: shares taken by subscribers of memorandum

Shares taken by a subscriber to the memorandum of a public company in pursuance of an undertaking of his in the memorandum, and any premium on the shares, must be paid up in cash.

NOTES

Commencement: 1 October 2009.

Old public companies: ss 584–587 of this Act apply to an old public company whose directors have passed and not revoked a resolution to be re-registered as a public company, as they apply to a public company; see the introductory notes to this Act and the Companies Act 2006 (Consequential Amendments and Transitional Provisions) Order 2011, SI 2011/1265, Sch 1, para 9 at **[4.651]**.

[1.585]
585   Public companies: must not accept undertaking to do work or perform services

(1)   A public company must not accept at any time, in payment up of its shares or any premium on them, an undertaking given by any person that he or another should do work or perform services for the company or any other person.

(2)   If a public company accepts such an undertaking in payment up of its shares or any premium on them, the holder of the shares when they or the premium are treated as paid up (in whole or in part) by the undertaking is liable—

(a)   to pay the company in respect of those shares an amount equal to their nominal value, together with the whole of any premium or, if the case so requires, such proportion of that amount as is treated as paid up by the undertaking; and

(b)   to pay interest at the appropriate rate on the amount payable under paragraph (a).

(3)   The reference in subsection (2) to the holder of shares includes a person who has an unconditional right—

(a)   to be included in the company's register of members in respect of those shares, or

(b)   to have an instrument of transfer of them executed in his favour.

NOTES

Commencement: 1 October 2009.

Old public companies: see the note to s 584 at **[1.584]**.

[1.586]
586   Public companies: shares must be at least one-quarter paid up

(1)   A public company must not allot a share except as paid up at least as to one-quarter of its nominal value and the whole of any premium on it.

(2)   This does not apply to shares allotted in pursuance of an employees' share scheme.

(3)   If a company allots a share in contravention of this section—

(a)   the share is to be treated as if one-quarter of its nominal value, together with the whole of any premium on it, had been received, and

(b)   the allottee is liable to pay the company the minimum amount which should have been received in respect of the share under subsection (1) (less the value of any consideration actually applied in payment up, to any extent, of the share and any premium on it), with interest at the appropriate rate.

(4)   Subsection (3) does not apply to the allotment of bonus shares, unless the allottee knew or ought to have known the shares were allotted in contravention of this section.

NOTES

Commencement: 1 October 2009.

Old public companies: see the note to s 584 at **[1.584]**.

[1.587]

587   Public companies: payment by long-term undertaking

(1)   A public company must not allot shares as fully or partly paid up (as to their nominal value or any premium on them) otherwise than in cash if the consideration for the allotment is or includes an undertaking which is to be, or may be, performed more than five years after the date of the allotment.

(2)   If a company allots shares in contravention of subsection (1), the allottee is liable to pay the company an amount equal to the aggregate of their nominal value and the whole of any premium (or, if the case so requires, so much of that aggregate as is treated as paid up by the undertaking), with interest at the appropriate rate.

(3)   Where a contract for the allotment of shares does not contravene subsection (1), any variation of the contract that has the effect that the contract would have contravened the subsection, if the terms of the contract as varied had been its original terms, is void.

This applies also to the variation by a public company of the terms of a contract entered into before the company was re-registered as a public company.

(4)   Where—

(a)   a public company allots shares for a consideration which consists of or includes (in accordance with subsection (1)) an undertaking that is to be performed within five years of the allotment, and

(b)   the undertaking is not performed within the period allowed by the contract for the allotment of the shares,

the allottee is liable to pay the company, at the end of the period so allowed, an amount equal to the aggregate of the nominal value of the shares and the whole of any premium (or, if the case so requires, so much of that aggregate as is treated as paid up by the undertaking), with interest at the appropriate rate.

(5)   References in this section to a contract for the allotment of shares include an ancillary contract relating to payment in respect of them.

NOTES

Commencement: 1 October 2009.

Old public companies: see the note to s 584 at **[1.584]**.

Supplementary provisions

[1.588]

588   Liability of subsequent holders of shares

(1)   If a person becomes a holder of shares in respect of which—

(a)   there has been a contravention of any provision of this Chapter, and

(b)   by virtue of that contravention another is liable to pay any amount under the provision contravened,

that person is also liable to pay that amount (jointly and severally with any other person so liable), subject as follows.

(2)   A person otherwise liable under subsection (1) is exempted from that liability if either—

(a)   he is a purchaser for value and, at the time of the purchase, he did not have actual notice of the contravention concerned, or

(b)   he derived title to the shares (directly or indirectly) from a person who became a holder of them after the contravention and was not liable under subsection (1).

(3)   References in this section to a holder, in relation to shares in a company, include any person who has an unconditional right—

(a)   to be included in the company's register of members in respect of those shares, or

(b)   to have an instrument of transfer of the shares executed in his favour.

(4)   This section applies in relation to a failure to carry out a term of a contract as mentioned in section 587(4) (public companies: payment by long-term undertaking) as it applies in relation to a contravention of a provision of this Chapter.

NOTES

Commencement: 1 October 2009.

[1.589]
589 Power of court to grant relief
(1) This section applies in relation to liability under—

section 585(2) (liability of allottee in case of breach by public company of prohibition on accepting undertaking to do work or perform services),

section 587(2) or (4) (liability of allottee in case of breach by public company of prohibition on payment by long-term undertaking), or

section 588 (liability of subsequent holders of shares),

as it applies in relation to a contravention of those sections.

(2) A person who—
- (a) is subject to any such liability to a company in relation to payment in respect of shares in the company, or
- (b) is subject to any such liability to a company by virtue of an undertaking given to it in, or in connection with, payment for shares in the company,

may apply to the court to be exempted in whole or in part from the liability.

(3) In the case of a liability within subsection (2)(a), the court may exempt the applicant from the liability only if and to the extent that it appears to the court just and equitable to do so having regard to—
- (a) whether the applicant has paid, or is liable to pay, any amount in respect of—
  - (i) any other liability arising in relation to those shares under any provision of this Chapter or Chapter 6, or
  - (ii) any liability arising by virtue of any undertaking given in or in connection with payment for those shares;
- (b) whether any person other than the applicant has paid or is likely to pay, whether in pursuance of any order of the court or otherwise, any such amount;
- (c) whether the applicant or any other person—
  - (i) has performed in whole or in part, or is likely so to perform any such undertaking, or
  - (ii) has done or is likely to do any other thing in payment or part payment for the shares.

(4) In the case of a liability within subsection (2)(b), the court may exempt the applicant from the liability only if and to the extent that it appears to the court just and equitable to do so having regard to—
- (a) whether the applicant has paid or is liable to pay any amount in respect of liability arising in relation to the shares under any provision of this Chapter or Chapter 6;
- (b) whether any person other than the applicant has paid or is likely to pay, whether in pursuance of any order of the court or otherwise, any such amount.

(5) In determining whether it should exempt the applicant in whole or in part from any liability, the court must have regard to the following overriding principles—
- (a) a company that has allotted shares should receive money or money's worth at least equal in value to the aggregate of the nominal value of those shares and the whole of any premium or, if the case so requires, so much of that aggregate as is treated as paid up;
- (b) subject to that, where a company would, if the court did not grant the exemption, have more than one remedy against a particular person, it should be for the company to decide which remedy it should remain entitled to pursue.

(6) If a person brings proceedings against another ("the contributor") for a contribution in respect of liability to a company arising under any provision of this Chapter or Chapter 6 and it appears to the court that the contributor is liable to make such a contribution, the court may, if and to the extent that it appears to it just and equitable to do so having regard to the respective culpability (in respect of the liability to the company) of the contributor and the person bringing the proceedings—
- (a) exempt the contributor in whole or in part from his liability to make such a contribution, or
- (b) order the contributor to make a larger contribution than, but for this subsection, he would be liable to make.

NOTES

Commencement: 1 October 2009.

Commencement (transitional provisions): Sch 2, para 58 to the Companies Act 2006 (Commencement No 8, Transitional Provisions and Savings) Order 2008, SI 2008/2860 (at **[2.91]**) provides as follows—

"Power of court to grant relief (ss 589 and 606)
58. In section 589(3) and (4) and section 606(2) and (3) of the Companies Act 2006 (power of court to grant relief from liabilities in connection with payment for shares: matters to be taken into account), the words from "having regard to" to the end of the subsection shall be omitted in relation to a decision whether to grant relief in respect of a liability for interest arising before 1st October 2009.".

[1.590]
590 Penalty for contravention of this Chapter
(1) If a company contravenes any of the provisions of this Chapter, an offence is committed by—
- (a) the company, and
- (b) every officer of the company who is in default.

(2) A person guilty of an offence under this section is liable—
- (a) on conviction on indictment, to a fine;

(b)   on summary conviction, to a fine not exceeding the statutory maximum.

NOTES
Commencement: 1 October 2009.

[1.591]
591   Enforceability of undertakings to do work etc
(1)   An undertaking given by any person, in or in connection with payment for shares in a company, to do work or perform services or to do any other thing, if it is enforceable by the company apart from this Chapter, is so enforceable notwithstanding that there has been a contravention in relation to it of a provision of this Chapter or Chapter 6.
(2)   This is without prejudice to section 589 (power of court to grant relief etc in respect of liabilities).

NOTES
Commencement: 1 October 2009.

[1.592]
592   The appropriate rate of interest
(1)   For the purposes of this Chapter the "appropriate rate" of interest is 5% per annum or such other rate as may be specified by order made by the Secretary of State.
(2)   An order under this section is subject to negative resolution procedure.

NOTES
Commencement: 20 January 2007 (for the purpose of enabling the exercise of powers to make Orders or Regulations by statutory instrument); 1 October 2009 (otherwise).

CHAPTER 6
PUBLIC COMPANIES: INDEPENDENT VALUATION OF NON-CASH CONSIDERATION

Non-cash consideration for shares

[1.593]
593   Public company: valuation of non-cash consideration for shares
(1)   A public company must not allot shares as fully or partly paid up (as to their nominal value or any premium on them) otherwise than in cash unless—
(a)   the consideration for the allotment has been independently valued in accordance with the provisions of this Chapter,
(b)   the valuer's report has been made to the company during the six months immediately preceding the allotment of the shares, and
(c)   a copy of the report has been sent to the proposed allottee.
(2)   For this purpose the application of an amount standing to the credit of—
(a)   any of a company's reserve accounts, or
(b)   its profit and loss account,
in paying up (to any extent) shares allotted to members of the company, or premiums on shares so allotted, does not count as consideration for the allotment.
Accordingly, subsection (1) does not apply in that case.
(3)   If a company allots shares in contravention of subsection (1) and either—
(a)   the allottee has not received the valuer's report required to be sent to him, or
(b)   there has been some other contravention of the requirements of this section or section 596 that the allottee knew or ought to have known amounted to a contravention,
the allottee is liable to pay the company an amount equal to the aggregate of the nominal value of the shares and the whole of any premium (or, if the case so requires, so much of that aggregate as is treated as paid up by the consideration), with interest at the appropriate rate.
(4)   This section has effect subject to—
section 594 (exception to valuation requirement: arrangement with another company), and
section 595 (exception to valuation requirement: merger [or division]).

NOTES
Commencement: 1 October 2009.
Sub-s (4): words in square brackets inserted by the Companies (Reporting Requirements in Mergers and Divisions) Regulations 2011, SI 2011/1606, reg 2(4)(b), as from 1 August 2011 (except in relation to any merger or division the draft terms of which were adopted before that date).

[1.594]
594   Exception to valuation requirement: arrangement with another company
(1)   Section 593 (valuation of non-cash consideration) does not apply to the allotment of shares by a company ("company A") in connection with an arrangement to which this section applies.
(2)   This section applies to an arrangement for the allotment of shares in company A on terms that the whole or part of the consideration for the shares allotted is to be provided by—
(a)   the transfer to that company, or

(b)   the cancellation,

of all or some of the shares, or of all or some of the shares of a particular class, in another company ("company B").

(3)   It is immaterial whether the arrangement provides for the issue to company A of shares, or shares of any particular class, in company B.

(4)   This section applies to an arrangement only if under the arrangement it is open to all the holders of the shares in company B (or, where the arrangement applies only to shares of a particular class, to all the holders of shares of that class) to take part in the arrangement.

(5)   In determining whether that is the case, the following shall be disregarded—
  (a)   shares held by or by a nominee of company A;
  (b)   shares held by or by a nominee of a company which is—
      (i)   the holding company, or a subsidiary, of company A, or
      (ii)   a subsidiary of such a holding company;
  (c)   shares held as treasury shares by company B.

(6)   In this section—
  (a)   "arrangement" means any agreement, scheme or arrangement (including an arrangement sanctioned in accordance with—
      (i)   Part 26 (arrangements and reconstructions), or
      (ii)   section 110 of the Insolvency Act 1986 (c 45) or Article 96 of the Insolvency (Northern Ireland) Order 1989 (SI 1989/2405 (NI 19)) (liquidator in winding up accepting shares as consideration for sale of company property)), and
  (b)   "company", except in reference to company A, includes any body corporate.

NOTES
Commencement: 1 October 2009.

[1.595]
595   Exception to valuation requirement: merger [or division]

(1)   Section 593 (valuation of non-cash consideration) does not apply to the allotment of shares by a company *in connection with a proposed merger with another company.*

(2)   *A proposed merger is where one of the companies proposes to acquire all the assets and liabilities of the other in exchange for the issue of shares or other securities of that one to shareholders of the other, with or without any cash payment to shareholders.*

(3)   *In this section "company", in reference to the other company, includes any body corporate.*

NOTES
Commencement: 1 October 2009.
Section heading: words in square brackets added by by the Companies (Reporting Requirements in Mergers and Divisions) Regulations 2011, SI 2011/1606, reg 2(1), (4)(a), as from 1 August 2011 (except in relation to any merger or division the draft terms of which were adopted before that date).
Sub-s (1): for the words in italics there are substituted the following words by SI 2011/1606, reg 2(1), (2), as from 1 August 2011 (except in relation to any merger or division the draft terms of which were adopted before that date)—

"as part of a scheme to which Part 27 (mergers and divisions of public companies) applies if—
  (a)   in the case of a scheme involving a merger, an expert's report is drawn up as required by section 909, or
  (b)   in the case of a scheme involving a division, an expert's report is drawn up as required by section 924.".

Sub-ss (2), (3): repealed by SI 2011/1606, reg 2(1), (3), as from 1 August 2011 (except in relation to any merger or division the draft terms of which were adopted before that date).

[1.596]
596   Non-cash consideration for shares: requirements as to valuation and report

(1)   The provisions of sections 1150 to 1153 (general provisions as to independent valuation and report) apply to the valuation and report required by section 593 (public company: valuation of non-cash consideration for shares).

(2)   The valuer's report must state—
  (a)   the nominal value of the shares to be wholly or partly paid for by the consideration in question;
  (b)   the amount of any premium payable on the shares;
  (c)   the description of the consideration and, as respects so much of the consideration as he himself has valued, a description of that part of the consideration, the method used to value it and the date of the valuation;
  (d)   the extent to which the nominal value of the shares and any premium are to be treated as paid up—
      (i)   by the consideration;
      (ii)   in cash.

(3)   The valuer's report must contain or be accompanied by a note by him—
  (a)   in the case of a valuation made by a person other than himself, that it appeared to himself reasonable to arrange for it to be so made or to accept a valuation so made,
  (b)   whoever made the valuation, that the method of valuation was reasonable in all the circumstances,

(c)   that it appears to the valuer that there has been no material change in the value of the consideration in question since the valuation, and

(d)   that, on the basis of the valuation, the value of the consideration, together with any cash by which the nominal value of the shares or any premium payable on them is to be paid up, is not less than so much of the aggregate of the nominal value and the whole of any such premium as is treated as paid up by the consideration and any such cash.

(4)   Where the consideration to be valued is accepted partly in payment up of the nominal value of the shares and any premium and partly for some other consideration given by the company, section 593 and the preceding provisions of this section apply as if references to the consideration accepted by the company included the proportion of that consideration that is properly attributable to the payment up of that value and any premium.

(5)   In such a case—

(a)   the valuer must carry out, or arrange for, such other valuations as will enable him to determine that proportion, and

(b)   his report must state what valuations have been made under this subsection and also the reason for, and method and date of, any such valuation and any other matters which may be relevant to that determination.

NOTES

Commencement: 1 October 2009.

[1.597]
597   Copy of report to be delivered to registrar

(1)   A company to which a report is made under section 593 as to the value of any consideration for which, or partly for which, it proposes to allot shares must deliver a copy of the report to the registrar for registration.

(2)   The copy must be delivered at the same time that the company files the return of the allotment of those shares under section 555 (return of allotment by limited company).

(3)   If default is made in complying with subsection (1) or (2), an offence is committed by every officer of the company who is in default.

(4)   A person guilty of an offence under this section is liable—

(a)   on conviction on indictment, to a fine;

(b)   on summary conviction, to a fine not exceeding the statutory maximum and, for continued contravention, a daily default fine not exceeding one-tenth of the statutory maximum.

(5)   In the case of default in delivering to the registrar any document as required by this section, any person liable for the default may apply to the court for relief.

(6)   The court, if satisfied—

(a)   that the omission to deliver the document was accidental or due to inadvertence, or

(b)   that it is just and equitable to grant relief,

may make an order extending the time for delivery of the document for such period as the court thinks proper.

NOTES

Commencement: 1 October 2009.

Transfer of non-cash asset in initial period

[1.598]
598   Public company: agreement for transfer of non-cash asset in initial period

(1)   A public company formed as such must not enter into an agreement—

(a)   with a person who is a subscriber to the company's memorandum,

(b)   for the transfer by him to the company, or another, before the end of the company's initial period of one or more non-cash assets, and

(c)   under which the consideration for the transfer to be given by the company is at the time of the agreement equal in value to one-tenth or more of the company's issued share capital,

unless the conditions referred to below have been complied with.

(2)   The company's "initial period" means the period of two years beginning with the date of the company being issued with a certificate under section 761 (trading certificate).

(3)   The conditions are those specified in—

section 599 (requirement of independent valuation), and

section 601 (requirement of approval by members).

(4)   This section does not apply where—

(a)   it is part of the company's ordinary business to acquire, or arrange for other persons to acquire, assets of a particular description, and

(b)   the agreement is entered into by the company in the ordinary course of that business.

(5)   This section does not apply to an agreement entered into by the company under the supervision of the court or of an officer authorised by the court for the purpose.

NOTES

Commencement: 1 October 2009.

[1.599]
599   Agreement for transfer of non-cash asset: requirement of independent valuation
(1)   The following conditions must have been complied with—
  (a)   the consideration to be received by the company, and any consideration other than cash to be given by the company, must have been independently valued in accordance with the provisions of this Chapter,
  (b)   the valuer's report must have been made to the company during the six months immediately preceding the date of the agreement, and
  (c)   a copy of the report must have been sent to the other party to the proposed agreement not later than the date on which copies have to be circulated to members under section 601(3).
(2)   The reference in subsection (1)(a) to the consideration to be received by the company is to the asset to be transferred to it or, as the case may be, to the advantage to the company of the asset's transfer to another person.
(3)   The reference in subsection (1)(c) to the other party to the proposed agreement is to the person referred to in section 598(1)(a).
  If he has received a copy of the report under section 601 in his capacity as a member of the company, it is not necessary to send another copy under this section.
(4)   This section does not affect any requirement to value any consideration for purposes of section 593 (valuation of non-cash consideration for shares).

NOTES
Commencement: 1 October 2009.

[1.600]
600   Agreement for transfer of non-cash asset: requirements as to valuation and report
(1)   The provisions of sections 1150 to 1153 (general provisions as to independent valuation and report) apply to the valuation and report required by section 599 (public company: transfer of non-cash asset).
(2)   The valuer's report must state—
  (a)   the consideration to be received by the company, describing the asset in question (specifying the amount to be received in cash) and the consideration to be given by the company (specifying the amount to be given in cash), and
  (b)   the method and date of valuation.
(3)   The valuer's report must contain or be accompanied by a note by him—
  (a)   in the case of a valuation made by a person other than himself, that it appeared to himself reasonable to arrange for it to be so made or to accept a valuation so made,
  (b)   whoever made the valuation, that the method of valuation was reasonable in all the circumstances,
  (c)   that it appears to the valuer that there has been no material change in the value of the consideration in question since the valuation, and
  (d)   that, on the basis of the valuation, the value of the consideration to be received by the company is not less than the value of the consideration to be given by it.
(4)   Any reference in section 599 or this section to consideration given for the transfer of an asset includes consideration given partly for its transfer.
(5)   In such a case—
  (a)   the value of any consideration partly so given is to be taken as the proportion of the consideration properly attributable to its transfer,
  (b)   the valuer must carry out or arrange for such valuations of anything else as will enable him to determine that proportion, and
  (c)   his report must state what valuations have been made for that purpose and also the reason for and method and date of any such valuation and any other matters which may be relevant to that determination.

NOTES
Commencement: 1 October 2009.

[1.601]
601   Agreement for transfer of non-cash asset: requirement of approval by members
(1)   The following conditions must have been complied with—
  (a)   the terms of the agreement must have been approved by an ordinary resolution of the company,
  [(b)   copies of the valuer's report must have been circulated to the members entitled to notice of the meeting at which the resolution is proposed, not later than the date on which notice of the meeting is given, and]
  (c)   a copy of the proposed resolution must have been sent to the other party to the proposed agreement.
(2)   The reference in subsection (1)(c) to the other party to the proposed agreement is to the person referred to in section 598(1)(a).
(3)   . . .

NOTES

Commencement: 1 October 2009.

Sub-s (1): para (b) substituted by the Companies Act 2006 (Consequential Amendments, Transitional Provisions and Savings) Order 2009, SI 2009/1941, art 2(1), Sch 1, para 260(1), (3)(a), as from 1 October 2009.

Sub-s (3): repealed by SI 2009/1941, art 2(1), Sch 1, para 260(1), (3)(b), as from 1 October 2009.

[1.602]
602   Copy of resolution to be delivered to registrar
(1)   A company that has passed a resolution under section 601 with respect to the transfer of an asset must, within 15 days of doing so, deliver to the registrar a copy of the resolution together with the valuer's report required by that section.
(2)   If a company fails to comply with subsection (1), an offence is committed by—
  (a)   the company, and
  (b)   every officer of the company who is in default.
(3)   A person guilty of an offence under this section is liable on summary conviction to a fine not exceeding level 3 on the standard scale and, for continued contravention, to a daily default fine not exceeding one-tenth of level 3 on the standard scale.

NOTES

Commencement: 1 October 2009.

[1.603]
603   Adaptation of provisions in relation to company re-registering as public
The provisions of sections 598 to 602 (public companies: transfer of non-cash assets) apply with the following adaptations in relation to a company re-registered as a public company—
  (a)   the reference in section 598(1)(a) to a person who is a subscriber to the company's memorandum shall be read as a reference to a person who is a member of the company on the date of re-registration;
  (b)   the reference in section 598(2) to the date of the company being issued with a certificate under section 761 (trading certificate) shall be read as a reference to the date of re-registration.

NOTES

Commencement: 1 October 2009.

[1.604]
604   Agreement for transfer of non-cash asset: effect of contravention
(1)   This section applies where a public company enters into an agreement in contravention of section 598 and either—
  (a)   the other party to the agreement has not received the valuer's report required to be sent to him, or
  (b)   there has been some other contravention of the requirements of this Chapter that the other party to the agreement knew or ought to have known amounted to a contravention.
(2)   In those circumstances—
  (a)   the company is entitled to recover from that person any consideration given by it under the agreement, or an amount equal to the value of the consideration at the time of the agreement, and
  (b)   the agreement, so far as not carried out, is void.
(3)   If the agreement is or includes an agreement for the allotment of shares in the company, then—
  (a)   whether or not the agreement also contravenes section 593 (valuation of non-cash consideration for shares), this section does not apply to it in so far as it is for the allotment of shares, and
  (b)   the allottee is liable to pay the company an amount equal to the aggregate of the nominal value of the shares and the whole of any premium (or, if the case so requires, so much of that aggregate as is treated as paid up by the consideration), with interest at the appropriate rate.

NOTES

Commencement: 1 October 2009.

Supplementary provisions

[1.605]
605   Liability of subsequent holders of shares
(1)   If a person becomes a holder of shares in respect of which—
  (a)   there has been a contravention of section 593 (public company: valuation of non-cash consideration for shares), and
  (b)   by virtue of that contravention another is liable to pay any amount under the provision contravened,

that person is also liable to pay that amount (jointly and severally with any other person so liable), unless he is exempted from liability under subsection (3) below.

(2)   If a company enters into an agreement in contravention of section 598 (public company: agreement for transfer of non-cash asset in initial period) and—

(a)   the agreement is or includes an agreement for the allotment of shares in the company,

(b)   a person becomes a holder of shares allotted under the agreement, and

(c)   by virtue of the agreement and allotment under it another person is liable to pay an amount under section 604,

the person who becomes the holder of the shares is also liable to pay that amount (jointly and severally with any other person so liable), unless he is exempted from liability under subsection (3) below.

This applies whether or not the agreement also contravenes section 593.

(3)   A person otherwise liable under subsection (1) or (2) is exempted from that liability if either—

(a)   he is a purchaser for value and, at the time of the purchase, he did not have actual notice of the contravention concerned, or

(b)   he derived title to the shares (directly or indirectly) from a person who became a holder of them after the contravention and was not liable under subsection (1) or (2).

(4)   References in this section to a holder, in relation to shares in a company, include any person who has an unconditional right—

(a)   to be included in the company's register of members in respect of those shares, or

(b)   to have an instrument of transfer of the shares executed in his favour.

NOTES
Commencement: 1 October 2009.

[1.606]
606   Power of court to grant relief
(1)   A person who—

(a)   is liable to a company under any provision of this Chapter in relation to payment in respect of any shares in the company, or

(b)   is liable to a company by virtue of an undertaking given to it in, or in connection with, payment for any shares in the company,

may apply to the court to be exempted in whole or in part from the liability.

(2)   In the case of a liability within subsection (1)(a), the court may exempt the applicant from the liability only if and to the extent that it appears to the court just and equitable to do so having regard to—

(a)   whether the applicant has paid, or is liable to pay, any amount in respect of—

(i)   any other liability arising in relation to those shares under any provision of this Chapter or Chapter 5, or

(ii)   any liability arising by virtue of any undertaking given in or in connection with payment for those shares;

(b)   whether any person other than the applicant has paid or is likely to pay, whether in pursuance of any order of the court or otherwise, any such amount;

(c)   whether the applicant or any other person—

(i)   has performed in whole or in part, or is likely so to perform any such undertaking, or

(ii)   has done or is likely to do any other thing in payment or part payment for the shares.

(3)   In the case of a liability within subsection (1)(b), the court may exempt the applicant from the liability only if and to the extent that it appears to the court just and equitable to do so having regard to—

(a)   whether the applicant has paid or is liable to pay any amount in respect of liability arising in relation to the shares under any provision of this Chapter or Chapter 5;

(b)   whether any person other than the applicant has paid or is likely to pay, whether in pursuance of any order of the court or otherwise, any such amount.

(4)   In determining whether it should exempt the applicant in whole or in part from any liability, the court must have regard to the following overriding principles—

(a)   that a company that has allotted shares should receive money or money's worth at least equal in value to the aggregate of the nominal value of those shares and the whole of any premium or, if the case so requires, so much of that aggregate as is treated as paid up;

(b)   subject to this, that where such a company would, if the court did not grant the exemption, have more than one remedy against a particular person, it should be for the company to decide which remedy it should remain entitled to pursue.

(5)   If a person brings proceedings against another ("the contributor") for a contribution in respect of liability to a company arising under any provision of this Chapter or Chapter 5 and it appears to the court that the contributor is liable to make such a contribution, the court may, if and to the extent that it appears to it, just and equitable to do so having regard to the respective culpability (in respect of the liability to the company) of the contributor and the person bringing the proceedings—

(a)   exempt the contributor in whole or in part from his liability to make such a contribution, or

(b)   order the contributor to make a larger contribution than, but for this subsection, he would be liable to make.

Part 1　The Companies Act 2006

(6)　Where a person is liable to a company under section 604(2) (agreement for transfer of non-cash asset: effect of contravention), the court may, on application, exempt him in whole or in part from that liability if and to the extent that it appears to the court to be just and equitable to do so having regard to any benefit accruing to the company by virtue of anything done by him towards the carrying out of the agreement mentioned in that subsection.

NOTES
Commencement: 1 October 2009.
Commencement (transitional provisions): see the note to s 589 at **[1.589]**.

[1.607]
607　Penalty for contravention of this Chapter
(1)　This section applies where a company contravenes—
　　section 593 (public company allotting shares for non-cash consideration), or
　　section 598 (public company entering into agreement for transfer of non-cash asset).
(2)　An offence is committed by—
　(a)　the company, and
　(b)　every officer of the company who is in default.
(3)　A person guilty of an offence under this section is liable—
　(a)　on conviction on indictment, to a fine;
　(b)　on summary conviction, to a fine not exceeding the statutory maximum.

NOTES
Commencement: 1 October 2009.
Commencement (transitional provisions): see the note to s 583 at **[1.583]**.

[1.608]
608　Enforceability of undertakings to do work etc
(1)　An undertaking given by any person, in or in connection with payment for shares in a company, to do work or perform services or to do any other thing, if it is enforceable by the company apart from this Chapter, is so enforceable notwithstanding that there has been a contravention in relation to it of a provision of this Chapter or Chapter 5.
(2)　This is without prejudice to section 606 (power of court to grant relief etc in respect of liabilities).

NOTES
Commencement: 1 October 2009.

[1.609]
609　The appropriate rate of interest
(1)　For the purposes of this Chapter the "appropriate rate" of interest is 5% per annum or such other rate as may be specified by order made by the Secretary of State.
(2)　An order under this section is subject to negative resolution procedure.

NOTES
Commencement: 20 January 2007 (for the purpose of enabling the exercise of powers to make Orders or Regulations by statutory instrument); 1 October 2009 (otherwise).

CHAPTER 7
SHARE PREMIUMS

The share premium account

[1.610]
610　Application of share premiums
(1)　If a company issues shares at a premium, whether for cash or otherwise, a sum equal to the aggregate amount or value of the premiums on those shares must be transferred to an account called "the share premium account".
(2)　Where, on issuing shares, a company has transferred a sum to the share premium account, it may use that sum to write off—
　(a)　the expenses of the issue of those shares;
　(b)　any commission paid on the issue of those shares.
(3)　The company may use the share premium account to pay up new shares to be allotted to members as fully paid bonus shares.
(4)　Subject to subsections (2) and (3), the provisions of the Companies Acts relating to the reduction of a company's share capital apply as if the share premium account were part of its paid up share capital.
(5)　This section has effect subject to—
　　section 611 (group reconstruction relief);
　　section 612 (merger relief);
　　section 614 (power to make further provisions by regulations).

(6) In this Chapter "the issuing company" means the company issuing shares as mentioned in subsection (1) above.

NOTES

Commencement: 1 October 2008 (certain purposes); 1 October 2009 (otherwise) (see the note below).

Commencement (note): the Companies Act 2006 (Commencement No 7, Transitional Provisions and Savings) Order 2008, SI 2008/1886, art 2(c) provides that sub-ss (2)–(4) shall come into force on 1 October 2008 so far as relating to a reduction of capital under ss 641(1)(a), (2)–(6), 642–644 of this Act (see **[2.76]**).

Relief from requirements as to share premiums

[1.611]

611 Group reconstruction relief

(1) This section applies where the issuing company—

    (a)   is a wholly-owned subsidiary of another company ("the holding company"), and

    (b)   allots shares—

        (i)   to the holding company, or

        (ii) to another wholly-owned subsidiary of the holding company,

        in consideration for the transfer to the issuing company of non-cash assets of a company ("the transferor company") that is a member of the group of companies that comprises the holding company and all its wholly-owned subsidiaries.

(2) Where the shares in the issuing company allotted in consideration for the transfer are issued at a premium, the issuing company is not required by section 610 to transfer any amount in excess of the minimum premium value to the share premium account.

(3) The minimum premium value means the amount (if any) by which the base value of the consideration for the shares allotted exceeds the aggregate nominal value of the shares.

(4) The base value of the consideration for the shares allotted is the amount by which the base value of the assets transferred exceeds the base value of any liabilities of the transferor company assumed by the issuing company as part of the consideration for the assets transferred.

(5) For the purposes of this section—

    (a)   the base value of assets transferred is taken as—

        (i)   the cost of those assets to the transferor company, or

        (ii) if less, the amount at which those assets are stated in the transferor company's accounting records immediately before the transfer;

    (b)   the base value of the liabilities assumed is taken as the amount at which they are stated in the transferor company's accounting records immediately before the transfer.

NOTES

Commencement: 1 October 2009.

[1.612]

612 Merger relief

(1) This section applies where the issuing company has secured at least a 90% equity holding in another company in pursuance of an arrangement providing for the allotment of equity shares in the issuing company on terms that the consideration for the shares allotted is to be provided—

    (a)   by the issue or transfer to the issuing company of equity shares in the other company, or

    (b)   by the cancellation of any such shares not held by the issuing company.

(2) If the equity shares in the issuing company allotted in pursuance of the arrangement in consideration for the acquisition or cancellation of equity shares in the other company are issued at a premium, section 610 does not apply to the premiums on those shares.

(3) Where the arrangement also provides for the allotment of any shares in the issuing company on terms that the consideration for those shares is to be provided—

    (a)   by the issue or transfer to the issuing company of non-equity shares in the other company, or

    (b)   by the cancellation of any such shares in that company not held by the issuing company,

relief under subsection (2) extends to any shares in the issuing company allotted on those terms in pursuance of the arrangement.

(4) This section does not apply in a case falling within section 611 (group reconstruction relief).

NOTES

Commencement: 1 October 2009.

[1.613]

613 Merger relief: meaning of 90% equity holding

(1) The following provisions have effect to determine for the purposes of section 612 (merger relief) whether a company ("company A") has secured at least a 90% equity holding in another company ("company B") in pursuance of such an arrangement as is mentioned in subsection (1) of that section.

(2)   Company A has secured at least a 90% equity holding in company B if in consequence of an acquisition or cancellation of equity shares in company B (in pursuance of that arrangement) it holds equity shares in company B of an aggregate amount equal to 90% or more of the nominal value of that company's equity share capital.

(3)   For this purpose—

    (a)   it is immaterial whether any of those shares were acquired in pursuance of the arrangement; and

    (b)   shares in company B held by the company as treasury shares are excluded in determining the nominal value of company B's share capital.

(4)   Where the equity share capital of company B is divided into different classes of shares, company A is not regarded as having secured at least a 90% equity holding in company B unless the requirements of subsection (2) are met in relation to each of those classes of shares taken separately.

(5)   For the purposes of this section shares held by—

    (a)   a company that is company A's holding company or subsidiary, or

    (b)   a subsidiary of company A's holding company, or

    (c)   its or their nominees,

are treated as held by company A.

NOTES

Commencement: 1 October 2009.

[1.614]
614   Power to make further provision by regulations

(1)   The Secretary of State may by regulations make such provision as he thinks appropriate—

    (a)   for relieving companies from the requirements of section 610 (application of share premiums) in relation to premiums other than cash premiums;

    (b)   for restricting or otherwise modifying any relief from those requirements provided by this Chapter.

(2)   Regulations under this section are subject to affirmative resolution procedure.

NOTES

Commencement: 20 January 2007 (for the purpose of enabling the exercise of powers to make Orders or Regulations by statutory instrument); 1 October 2009 (otherwise).

[1.615]
615   Relief may be reflected in company's balance sheet

An amount corresponding to the amount representing the premiums, or part of the premiums, on shares issued by a company that by virtue of any relief under this Chapter is not included in the company's share premium account may also be disregarded in determining the amount at which any shares or other consideration provided for the shares issued is to be included in the company's balance sheet.

NOTES

Commencement: 1 October 2009.

Supplementary provisions

[1.616]
616   Interpretation of this Chapter

(1)   In this Chapter—

"arrangement" means any agreement, scheme or arrangement (including an arrangement sanctioned in accordance with—

    (a)   Part 26 (arrangements and reconstructions), or

    (b)   section 110 of the Insolvency Act 1986 (c 45) or Article 96 of the Insolvency (Northern Ireland) Order 1989 (SI 1989/2405 (NI 19)) (liquidator in winding up accepting shares as consideration for sale of company property));

"company", except in reference to the issuing company, includes any body corporate;

"equity shares" means shares comprised in a company's equity share capital, and "non-equity shares" means shares (of any class) that are not so comprised;

"the issuing company" has the meaning given by section 610(6).

(2)   References in this Chapter (however expressed) to—

    (a)   the acquisition by a company of shares in another company, and

    (b)   the issue or allotment of shares to, or the transfer of shares to or by, a company,

include (respectively) the acquisition of shares by, and the issue or allotment or transfer of shares to or by, a nominee of that company.

The reference in section 611 to the transferor company shall be read accordingly.

(3)   References in this Chapter to the transfer of shares in a company include the transfer of a right to be included in the company's register of members in respect of those shares.

NOTES
Commencement: 1 October 2009.

CHAPTER 8
ALTERATION OF SHARE CAPITAL

How share capital may be altered

[1.617]
617 Alteration of share capital of limited company
(1) A limited company having a share capital may not alter its share capital except in the following ways.
(2) The company may—
  (a) increase its share capital by allotting new shares in accordance with this Part, or
  (b) reduce its share capital in accordance with Chapter 10.
(3) The company may—
  (a) sub-divide or consolidate all or any of its share capital in accordance with section 618, or
  (b) reconvert stock into shares in accordance with section 620.
(4) The company may redenominate all or any of its shares in accordance with section 622, and may reduce its share capital in accordance with section 626 in connection with such a redenomination.
(5) Nothing in this section affects—
  (a) the power of a company to purchase its own shares, or to redeem shares, in accordance with Part 18;
  (b) the power of a company to purchase its own shares in pursuance of an order of the court under—
      (i) section 98 (application to court to cancel resolution for re-registration as a private company),
      (ii) section 721(6) (powers of court on objection to redemption or purchase of shares out of capital),
      (iii) section 759 (remedial order in case of breach of prohibition of public offers by private company), or
      (iv) Part 30 (protection of members against unfair prejudice);
  (c) the forfeiture of shares, or the acceptance of shares surrendered in lieu, in pursuance of the company's articles, for failure to pay any sum payable in respect of the shares;
  (d) the cancellation of shares under section 662 (duty to cancel shares held by or for a public company);
  (e) the power of a company—
      (i) to enter into a compromise or arrangement in accordance with Part 26 (arrangements and reconstructions), or
      (ii) to do anything required to comply with an order of the court on an application under that Part.

NOTES
Commencement: 1 October 2009.

Subdivision or consolidation of shares

[1.618]
618 Sub-division or consolidation of shares
(1) A limited company having a share capital may—
  (a) sub-divide its shares, or any of them, into shares of a smaller nominal amount than its existing shares, or
  (b) consolidate and divide all or any of its share capital into shares of a larger nominal amount than its existing shares.
(2) In any sub-division, consolidation or division of shares under this section, the proportion between the amount paid and the amount (if any) unpaid on each resulting share must be the same as it was in the case of the share from which that share is derived.
(3) A company may exercise a power conferred by this section only if its members have passed a resolution authorising it to do so.
(4) A resolution under subsection (3) may authorise a company—
  (a) to exercise more than one of the powers conferred by this section;
  (b) to exercise a power on more than one occasion;
  (c) to exercise a power at a specified time or in specified circumstances.
(5) The company's articles may exclude or restrict the exercise of any power conferred by this section.

NOTES
Commencement: 1 October 2009.

[1.619]
619 Notice to registrar of sub-division or consolidation

(1) If a company exercises the power conferred by section 618 (sub-division or consolidation of shares) it must within one month after doing so give notice to the registrar, specifying the shares affected.

(2) The notice must be accompanied by a statement of capital.

(3) The statement of capital must state with respect to the company's share capital immediately following the exercise of the power—
 (a) the total number of shares of the company,
 (b) the aggregate nominal value of those shares,
 (c) for each class of shares—
  (i) prescribed particulars of the rights attached to the shares,
  (ii) the total number of shares of that class, and
  (iii) the aggregate nominal value of shares of that class, and
 (d) the amount paid up and the amount (if any) unpaid on each share (whether on account of the nominal value of the share or by way of premium).

(4) If default is made in complying with this section, an offence is committed by—
 (a) the company, and
 (b) every officer of the company who is in default.

(5) A person guilty of an offence under this section is liable on summary conviction to a fine not exceeding level 3 on the standard scale and, for continued contravention, a daily default fine not exceeding one-tenth of level 3 on the standard scale.

NOTES
Commencement: 20 January 2007 (for the purpose of enabling the exercise of powers to make Orders or Regulations by statutory instrument); 1 October 2009 (otherwise).

Orders: the Companies (Shares and Share Capital) Order 2009, SI 2009/388 at **[4.364]**.

Reconversion of stock into shares

[1.620]
620 Reconversion of stock into shares

(1) A limited company that has converted paid-up shares into stock (before the repeal by this Act of the power to do so) may reconvert that stock into paid-up shares of any nominal value.

(2) A company may exercise the power conferred by this section only if its members have passed an ordinary resolution authorising it to do so.

(3) A resolution under subsection (2) may authorise a company to exercise the power conferred by this section—
 (a) on more than one occasion;
 (b) at a specified time or in specified circumstances.

NOTES
Commencement: 1 October 2009.

[1.621]
621 Notice to registrar of reconversion of stock into shares

(1) If a company exercises a power conferred by section 620 (reconversion of stock into shares) it must within one month after doing so give notice to the registrar, specifying the stock affected.

(2) The notice must be accompanied by a statement of capital.

(3) The statement of capital must state with respect to the company's share capital immediately following the exercise of the power—
 (a) the total number of shares of the company,
 (b) the aggregate nominal value of those shares,
 (c) for each class of shares—
  (i) prescribed particulars of the rights attached to the shares,
  (ii) the total number of shares of that class, and
  (iii) the aggregate nominal value of shares of that class, and
 (d) the amount paid up and the amount (if any) unpaid on each share (whether on account of the nominal value of the share or by way of premium).

(4) If default is made in complying with this section, an offence is committed by—
 (a) the company, and
 (b) every officer of the company who is in default.

(5) A person guilty of an offence under this section is liable on summary conviction to a fine not exceeding level 3 on the standard scale and, for continued contravention, a daily default fine not exceeding one-tenth of level 3 on the standard scale.

NOTES
Commencement: 20 January 2007 (for the purpose of enabling the exercise of powers to make Orders or Regulations by statutory instrument); 1 October 2009 (otherwise).

Orders: the Companies (Shares and Share Capital) Order 2009, SI 2009/388 at **[4.364]**.

Redenomination of share capital

[1.622]

622 Redenomination of share capital

(1) A limited company having a share capital may by resolution redenominate its share capital or any class of its share capital.

"Redenominate" means convert shares from having a fixed nominal value in one currency to having a fixed nominal value in another currency.

(2) The conversion must be made at an appropriate spot rate of exchange specified in the resolution.

(3) The rate must be either—

  (a) a rate prevailing on a day specified in the resolution, or

  (b) a rate determined by taking the average of rates prevailing on each consecutive day of a period specified in the resolution.

The day or period specified for the purposes of paragraph (a) or (b) must be within the period of 28 days ending on the day before the resolution is passed.

(4) A resolution under this section may specify conditions which must be met before the redenomination takes effect.

(5) Redenomination in accordance with a resolution under this section takes effect—

  (a) on the day on which the resolution is passed, or

  (b) on such later day as may be determined in accordance with the resolution.

(6) A resolution under this section lapses if the redenomination for which it provides has not taken effect at the end of the period of 28 days beginning on the date on which it is passed.

(7) A company's articles may prohibit or restrict the exercise of the power conferred by this section.

(8) Chapter 3 of Part 3 (resolutions affecting a company's constitution) applies to a resolution under this section.

NOTES

Commencement: 1 October 2009.

[1.623]

623 Calculation of new nominal values

For each class of share the new nominal value of each share is calculated as follows:

Step One

Take the aggregate of the old nominal values of all the shares of that class.

Step Two

Translate that amount into the new currency at the rate of exchange specified in the resolution.

Step Three

Divide that amount by the number of shares in the class.

NOTES

Commencement: 1 October 2009.

[1.624]

624 Effect of redenomination

(1) The redenomination of shares does not affect any rights or obligations of members under the company's constitution, or any restrictions affecting members under the company's constitution.

In particular, it does not affect entitlement to dividends (including entitlement to dividends in a particular currency), voting rights or any liability in respect of amounts unpaid on shares.

(2) For this purpose the company's constitution includes the terms on which any shares of the company are allotted or held.

(3) Subject to subsection (1), references to the old nominal value of the shares in any agreement or statement, or in any deed, instrument or document, shall (unless the context otherwise requires) be read after the resolution takes effect as references to the new nominal value of the shares.

NOTES

Commencement: 1 October 2009.

[1.625]

625 Notice to registrar of redenomination

(1) If a limited company having a share capital redenominates any of its share capital, it must within one month after doing so give notice to the registrar, specifying the shares redenominated.

(2) The notice must—

  (a) state the date on which the resolution was passed, and

  (b) be accompanied by a statement of capital.

(3) The statement of capital must state with respect to the company's share capital as redenominated by the resolution—

  (a) the total number of shares of the company,

  (b) the aggregate nominal value of those shares,

   (c)   for each class of shares—
      (i)   prescribed particulars of the rights attached to the shares,
      (ii)   the total number of shares of that class, and
      (iii)   the aggregate nominal value of shares of that class, and
   (d)   the amount paid up and the amount (if any) unpaid on each share (whether on account of the nominal value of the share or by way of premium).
(4)   If default is made in complying with this section, an offence is committed by—
   (a)   the company, and
   (b)   every officer of the company who is in default.
(5)   A person guilty of an offence under this section is liable on summary conviction to a fine not exceeding level 3 on the standard scale and, for continued contravention, a daily default fine not exceeding one-tenth of level 3 on the standard scale.

NOTES

Commencement: 20 January 2007 (for the purpose of enabling the exercise of powers to make Orders or Regulations by statutory instrument); 1 October 2009 (otherwise).

Orders: the Companies (Shares and Share Capital) Order 2009, SI 2009/388 at **[4.364]**.

[1.626]
626   Reduction of capital in connection with redenomination
(1)   A limited company that passes a resolution redenominating some or all of its shares may, for the purpose of adjusting the nominal values of the redenominated shares to obtain values that are, in the opinion of the company, more suitable, reduce its share capital under this section.
(2)   A reduction of capital under this section requires a special resolution of the company.
(3)   Any such resolution must be passed within three months of the resolution effecting the redenomination.
(4)   The amount by which a company's share capital is reduced under this section must not exceed 10% of the nominal value of the company's allotted share capital immediately after the reduction.
(5)   A reduction of capital under this section does not extinguish or reduce any liability in respect of share capital not paid up.
(6)   Nothing in Chapter 10 applies to a reduction of capital under this section.

NOTES

Commencement: 1 October 2009.

[1.627]
627   Notice to registrar of reduction of capital in connection with redenomination
(1)   A company that passes a resolution under section 626 (reduction of capital in connection with redenomination) must within 15 days after the resolution is passed give notice to the registrar stating—
   (a)   the date of the resolution, and
   (b)   the date of the resolution under section 622 in connection with which it was passed.
   This is in addition to the copies of the resolutions themselves that are required to be delivered to the registrar under Chapter 3 of Part 3.
(2)   The notice must be accompanied by a statement of capital.
(3)   The statement of capital must state with respect to the company's share capital as reduced by the resolution—
   (a)   the total number of shares of the company,
   (b)   the aggregate nominal value of those shares,
   (c)   for each class of shares—
      (i)   prescribed particulars of the rights attached to the shares,
      (ii)   the total number of shares of that class, and
      (iii)   the aggregate nominal value of shares of that class, and
   (d)   the amount paid up and the amount (if any) unpaid on each share (whether on account of the nominal value of the share or by way of premium).
(4)   The registrar must register the notice and the statement on receipt.
(5)   The reduction of capital is not effective until those documents are registered.
(6)   The company must also deliver to the registrar, within 15 days after the resolution is passed, a statement by the directors confirming that the reduction in share capital is in accordance with section 626(4) (reduction of capital not to exceed 10% of nominal value of allotted shares immediately after reduction).
(7)   If default is made in complying with this section, an offence is committed by—
   (a)   the company, and
   (b)   every officer of the company who is in default.
(8)   A person guilty of an offence under this section is liable—
   (a)   on conviction on indictment to a fine, and
   (b)   on summary conviction to a fine not exceeding the statutory maximum.

NOTES

Commencement: 20 January 2007 (for the purpose of enabling the exercise of powers to make Orders or Regulations by statutory instrument); 1 October 2009 (otherwise).

Orders: the Companies (Shares and Share Capital) Order 2009, SI 2009/388 at **[4.364]**.

[1.628]
628 Redenomination reserve

(1)   The amount by which a company's share capital is reduced under section 626 (reduction of capital in connection with redenomination) must be transferred to a reserve, called "the redenomination reserve".

(2)   The redenomination reserve may be applied by the company in paying up shares to be allotted to members as fully paid bonus shares.

(3)   Subject to that, the provisions of the Companies Acts relating to the reduction of a company's share capital apply as if the redenomination reserve were paid-up share capital of the company.

NOTES

Commencement: 1 October 2009.

CHAPTER 9
CLASSES OF SHARE AND CLASS RIGHTS

Introductory

[1.629]
629 Classes of shares

(1)   For the purposes of the Companies Acts shares are of one class if the rights attached to them are in all respects uniform.

(2)   For this purpose the rights attached to shares are not regarded as different from those attached to other shares by reason only that they do not carry the same rights to dividends in the twelve months immediately following their allotment.

NOTES

Commencement: 1 October 2007 (certain purposes); 6 April 2008 (certain purposes); 1 October 2009 (otherwise) (see the notes below).

Commencement (note): the Companies Act 2006 (Commencement No 3, Consequential Amendments, Transitional Provisions and Savings) Order 2007, SI 2007/2194, art 2(3) provides that this section shall come into force on 1 October 2007 so far as is necessary for the purposes of the provisions of this Act brought into force on that date by art 2(1), (2) of that Order (see **[2.32]**).

Commencement (note): the Companies Act 2006 (Commencement No 5, Transitional Provisions and Savings) Order 2007, SI 2007/3495, art 3(3) provides that this section shall come into force on 6 April 2008 so far as is necessary for the purposes of the provisions of this Act brought into force on that date by art 3(1)(a)–(t), (2) of that Order (see **[2.52]**).

Variation of class rights

[1.630]
630 Variation of class rights: companies having a share capital

(1)   This section is concerned with the variation of the rights attached to a class of shares in a company having a share capital.

(2)   Rights attached to a class of a company's shares may only be varied—
   (a)   in accordance with provision in the company's articles for the variation of those rights, or
   (b)   where the company's articles contain no such provision, if the holders of shares of that class consent to the variation in accordance with this section.

(3)   This is without prejudice to any other restrictions on the variation of the rights.

(4)   The consent required for the purposes of this section on the part of the holders of a class of a company's shares is—
   (a)   consent in writing from the holders of at least three-quarters in nominal value of the issued shares of that class (excluding any shares held as treasury shares), or
   (b)   a special resolution passed at a separate general meeting of the holders of that class sanctioning the variation.

(5)   Any amendment of a provision contained in a company's articles for the variation of the rights attached to a class of shares, or the insertion of any such provision into the articles, is itself to be treated as a variation of those rights.

(6)   In this section, and (except where the context otherwise requires) in any provision in a company's articles for the variation of the rights attached to a class of shares, references to the variation of those rights include references to their abrogation.

NOTES

Commencement: 1 October 2009.

[1.631]

631   Variation of class rights: companies without a share capital

(1)   This section is concerned with the variation of the rights of a class of members of a company where the company does not have a share capital.

(2)   Rights of a class of members may only be varied—

    (a)   in accordance with provision in the company's articles for the variation of those rights, or

    (b)   where the company's articles contain no such provision, if the members of that class consent to the variation in accordance with this section.

(3)   This is without prejudice to any other restrictions on the variation of the rights.

(4)   The consent required for the purposes of this section on the part of the members of a class is—

    (a)   consent in writing from at least three-quarters of the members of the class, or

    (b)   a special resolution passed at a separate general meeting of the members of that class sanctioning the variation.

(5)   Any amendment of a provision contained in a company's articles for the variation of the rights of a class of members, or the insertion of any such provision into the articles, is itself to be treated as a variation of those rights.

(6)   In this section, and (except where the context otherwise requires) in any provision in a company's articles for the variation of the rights of a class of members, references to the variation of those rights include references to their abrogation.

NOTES

Commencement: 1 October 2009.

Commencement (transitional provisions): Sch 2, para 61 to the Companies Act 2006 (Commencement No 8, Transitional Provisions and Savings) Order 2008, SI 2008/2860 (at **[2.91]**) provides that nothing in this section or s 634 affects a variation of class rights made (in accordance with provision in the company's memorandum or articles) before 1 October 2009.

[1.632]

632   Variation of class rights: saving for court's powers under other provisions

Nothing in section 630 or 631 (variation of class rights) affects the power of the court under—

    section 98 (application to cancel resolution for public company to be re-registered as private),

    Part 26 (arrangements and reconstructions), or

    Part 30 (protection of members against unfair prejudice).

NOTES

Commencement: 1 October 2009.

[1.633]

633   Right to object to variation: companies having a share capital

(1)   This section applies where the rights attached to any class of shares in a company are varied under section 630 (variation of class rights: companies having a share capital).

(2)   The holders of not less in the aggregate than 15% of the issued shares of the class in question (being persons who did not consent to or vote in favour of the resolution for the variation) may apply to the court to have the variation cancelled.

    For this purpose any of the company's share capital held as treasury shares is disregarded.

(3)   If such an application is made, the variation has no effect unless and until it is confirmed by the court.

(4)   Application to the court—

    (a)   must be made within 21 days after the date on which the consent was given or the resolution was passed (as the case may be), and

    (b)   may be made on behalf of the shareholders entitled to make the application by such one or more of their number as they may appoint in writing for the purpose.

(5)   The court, after hearing the applicant and any other persons who apply to the court to be heard and appear to the court to be interested in the application, may, if satisfied having regard to all the circumstances of the case that the variation would unfairly prejudice the shareholders of the class represented by the applicant, disallow the variation, and shall if not so satisfied confirm it. The decision of the court on any such application is final.

(6)   References in this section to the variation of the rights of holders of a class of shares include references to their abrogation.

NOTES

Commencement: 1 October 2009.

[1.634]

634   Right to object to variation: companies without a share capital

(1)   This section applies where the rights of any class of members of a company are varied under section 631 (variation of class rights: companies without a share capital).

(2)   Members amounting to not less than 15% of the members of the class in question (being persons who did not consent to or vote in favour of the resolution for the variation) may apply to the court to have the variation cancelled.

(3)   If such an application is made, the variation has no effect unless and until it is confirmed by the court.

(4)   Application to the court must be made within 21 days after the date on which the consent was given or the resolution was passed (as the case may be) and may be made on behalf of the members entitled to make the application by such one or more of their number as they may appoint in writing for the purpose.

(5)   The court, after hearing the applicant and any other persons who apply to the court to be heard and appear to the court to be interested in the application, may, if satisfied having regard to all the circumstances of the case that the variation would unfairly prejudice the members of the class represented by the applicant, disallow the variation, and shall if not so satisfied confirm it.

The decision of the court on any such application is final.

(6)   References in this section to the variation of the rights of a class of members include references to their abrogation.

NOTES

Commencement: 1 October 2009.

Commencement (transitional provisions): see the note to s 631 at **[1.631]**.

[1.635]

635   Copy of court order to be forwarded to the registrar

(1)   The company must within 15 days after the making of an order by the court on an application under section 633 or 634 (objection to variation of class rights) forward a copy of the order to the registrar.

(2)   If default is made in complying with this section an offence is committed by—

(a)   the company, and

(b)   every officer of the company who is in default.

(3)   A person guilty of an offence under this section is liable on summary conviction to a fine not exceeding level 3 on the standard scale and, for continued contravention, a daily default fine not exceeding one-tenth of level 3 on the standard scale.

NOTES

Commencement: 1 October 2009.

Matters to be notified to the registrar

[1.636]

636   Notice of name or other designation of class of shares

(1)   Where a company assigns a name or other designation, or a new name or other designation, to any class or description of its shares, it must within one month from doing so deliver to the registrar a notice giving particulars of the name or designation so assigned.

(2)   If default is made in complying with this section, an offence is committed by—

(a)   the company, and

(b)   every officer of the company who is in default.

(3)   A person guilty of an offence under this section is liable on summary conviction to a fine not exceeding level 3 on the standard scale and, for continued contravention, a daily default fine not exceeding one-tenth of level 3 on the standard scale.

NOTES

Commencement: 1 October 2009.

Commencement (transitional provisions): Sch 2, para 62 to the Companies Act 2006 (Commencement No 8, Transitional Provisions and Savings) Order 2008, SI 2008/2860 (at **[2.91]**) provides that this section applies where the new name or other designation is assigned on or after 1 October 2009 (and that s 128(4), (5) of the 1985 Act continue to apply where the new name or other designation was assigned before that date).

[1.637]

637   Notice of particulars of variation of rights attached to shares

(1)   Where the rights attached to any shares of a company are varied, the company must within one month from the date on which the variation is made deliver to the registrar a notice giving particulars of the variation.

(2)   If default is made in complying with this section, an offence is committed by—

(a)   the company, and

(b)   every officer of the company who is in default.

(3)   A person guilty of an offence under this section is liable on summary conviction to a fine not exceeding level 3 on the standard scale and, for continued contravention, a daily default fine not exceeding one-tenth of level 3 on the standard scale.

NOTES

Commencement: 1 October 2009.

Commencement (transitional provisions): Sch 2, para 63 to the Companies Act 2006 (Commencement No 8, Transitional Provisions and Savings) Order 2008, SI 2008/2860 (at **[2.91]**) provides that this section applies where the variation is made on or after 1 October 2009 (and that s 128(3), (5) of the 1985 Act continue to apply where the variation was made before that date).

[1.638]
638 Notice of new class of members
(1)   If a company not having a share capital creates a new class of members, the company must within one month from the date on which the new class is created deliver to the registrar a notice containing particulars of the rights attached to that class.
(2)   If default is made in complying with this section, an offence is committed by—
   (a)   the company, and
   (b)   every officer of the company who is in default.
(3)   A person guilty of an offence under this section is liable on summary conviction to a fine not exceeding level 3 on the standard scale and, for continued contravention, a daily default fine not exceeding one-tenth of level 3 on the standard scale.

NOTES
Commencement: 1 October 2009.
Commencement (transitional provisions): Sch 2, para 64 to the Companies Act 2006 (Commencement No 8, Transitional Provisions and Savings) Order 2008, SI 2008/2860 (at **[2.91]**) provides that this section applies where a new class of members is created on or after 1 October 2009 (and that s 129(1), (4) of the 1985 Act continue to apply where a new class of members was created before that date).

[1.639]
639 Notice of name or other designation of class of members
(1)   Where a company not having a share capital assigns a name or other designation, or a new name or other designation, to any class of its members, it must within one month from doing so deliver to the registrar a notice giving particulars of the name or designation so assigned.
(2)   If default is made in complying with this section, an offence is committed by—
   (a)   the company, and
   (b)   every officer of the company who is in default.
(3)   A person guilty of an offence under this section is liable on summary conviction to a fine not exceeding level 3 on the standard scale and, for continued contravention, a daily default fine not exceeding one-tenth of level 3 on the standard scale.

NOTES
Commencement: 1 October 2009.
Commencement (transitional provisions): Sch 2, para 65 to the Companies Act 2006 (Commencement No 8, Transitional Provisions and Savings) Order 2008, SI 2008/2860 (at **[2.91]**) provides that this section applies where the name or other designation, or new name or other designation, is assigned on or after 1 October 2009 (and that s 129(3), (4) of the 1985 Act continue to apply where the name or other designation, or new name or other designation, was assigned before that date).

[1.640]
640 Notice of particulars of variation of class rights
(1)   If the rights of any class of members of a company not having a share capital are varied, the company must within one month from the date on which the variation is made deliver to the registrar a notice containing particulars of the variation.
(2)   If default is made in complying with this section, an offence is committed by—
   (a)   the company, and
   (b)   every officer of the company who is in default.
(3)   A person guilty of an offence under this section is liable on summary conviction to a fine not exceeding level 3 on the standard scale and, for continued contravention, a daily default fine not exceeding one-tenth of level 3 on the standard scale.

NOTES
Commencement: 1 October 2009.
Commencement (transitional provisions): Sch 2, para 66 to the Companies Act 2006 (Commencement No 8, Transitional Provisions and Savings) Order 2008, SI 2008/2860 (at **[2.91]**) provides that this section applies where the variation is made on or after 1 October 2009 (and that s 129(2), (4) of the 1985 Act continue to apply where the variation was made before that date).

CHAPTER 10
REDUCTION OF SHARE CAPITAL

Introductory

[1.641]
641 Circumstances in which a company may reduce its share capital
(1)   A limited company having a share capital may reduce its share capital—
   (a)   in the case of a private company limited by shares, by special resolution supported by a solvency statement (see sections 642 to 644);
   (b)   in any case, by special resolution confirmed by the court (see sections 645 to 651).
(2)   A company may not reduce its capital under subsection (1)(a) if as a result of the reduction there would no longer be any member of the company holding shares other than redeemable shares.
(3)   Subject to that, a company may reduce its share capital under this section in any way.
(4)   In particular, a company may—

(a) extinguish or reduce the liability on any of its shares in respect of share capital not paid up, or

(b) either with or without extinguishing or reducing liability on any of its shares—
  (i) cancel any paid-up share capital that is lost or unrepresented by available assets, or
  (ii) repay any paid-up share capital in excess of the company's wants.

(5) A special resolution under this section may not provide for a reduction of share capital to take effect later than the date on which the resolution has effect in accordance with this Chapter.

(6) This Chapter (apart from subsection (5) above) has effect subject to any provision of the company's articles restricting or prohibiting the reduction of the company's share capital.

NOTES

Commencement: 1 October 2008 (sub-ss (1)(a), (2)–(6)); 1 October 2009 (otherwise).

Commencement (transitional adaptations): art 3 of the Companies Act 2006 (Commencement No 7, Transitional Provisions and Savings) Order 2008, SI 2008/1886 (at **[2.77]**) provided for transitional adaptations of this section. Note, however, that that article was revoked by the Companies Act 2006 (Commencement No 8, Transitional Provisions and Savings) Order 2008, SI 2008/2860, art 6(1), as from 1 October 2009 (subject to any relevant transitional provision or saving in Sch 2 to that Order)).

Private companies: reduction of capital supported by solvency statement

[1.642]
642 Reduction of capital supported by solvency statement
(1) A resolution for reducing share capital of a private company limited by shares is supported by a solvency statement if—
  (a) the directors of the company make a statement of the solvency of the company in accordance with section 643 (a "solvency statement") not more than 15 days before the date on which the resolution is passed, and
  (b) the resolution and solvency statement are registered in accordance with section 644.

(2) Where the resolution is proposed as a written resolution, a copy of the solvency statement must be sent or submitted to every eligible member at or before the time at which the proposed resolution is sent or submitted to him.

(3) Where the resolution is proposed at a general meeting, a copy of the solvency statement must be made available for inspection by members of the company throughout that meeting.

(4) The validity of a resolution is not affected by a failure to comply with subsection (2) or (3).

NOTES

Commencement: 1 October 2008.

[1.643]
643 Solvency statement
(1) A solvency statement is a statement that each of the directors—
  (a) has formed the opinion, as regards the company's situation at the date of the statement, that there is no ground on which the company could then be found to be unable to pay (or otherwise discharge) its debts; and
  (b) has also formed the opinion—
    (i) if it is intended to commence the winding up of the company within twelve months of that date, that the company will be able to pay (or otherwise discharge) its debts in full within twelve months of the commencement of the winding up; or
    (ii) in any other case, that the company will be able to pay (or otherwise discharge) its debts as they fall due during the year immediately following that date.

(2) In forming those opinions, the directors must take into account all of the company's liabilities (including any contingent or prospective liabilities).

(3) The solvency statement must be in the prescribed form and must state—
  (a) the date on which it is made, and
  (b) the name of each director of the company.

(4) If the directors make a solvency statement without having reasonable grounds for the opinions expressed in it, and the statement is delivered to the registrar, an offence is committed by every director who is in default.

(5) A person guilty of an offence under subsection (4) is liable—
  (a) on conviction on indictment, to imprisonment for a term not exceeding two years or a fine (or both);
  (b) on summary conviction—
    (i) in England and Wales, to imprisonment for a term not exceeding twelve months or to a fine not exceeding the statutory maximum (or both);
    (ii) in Scotland or Northern Ireland, to imprisonment for a term not exceeding six months, or to a fine not exceeding the statutory maximum (or both).

NOTES

Commencement: 20 January 2007 (for the purpose of enabling the exercise of powers to make Orders or Regulations by statutory instrument); 1 October 2008 (otherwise).

Orders: the Companies (Reduction of Share Capital) Order 2008, SI 2008/1915 at **[4.303]**.

Offences under this section: see further s 1131 at **[1.1131]**.

[1.644]
644 Registration of resolution and supporting documents

(1)   Within 15 days after the resolution for reducing share capital is passed the company must deliver to the registrar—
    (a)   a copy of the solvency statement, and
    (b)   a statement of capital.
This is in addition to the copy of the resolution itself that is required to be delivered to the registrar under Chapter 3 of Part 3.

(2)   The statement of capital must state with respect to the company's share capital as reduced by the resolution—
    (a)   the total number of shares of the company,
    (b)   the aggregate nominal value of those shares,
    (c)   for each class of shares—
        (i)   prescribed particulars of the rights attached to the shares,
        (ii)   the total number of shares of that class, and
        (iii)   the aggregate nominal value of shares of that class, and
    (d)   the amount paid up and the amount (if any) unpaid on each share (whether on account of the nominal value of the share or by way of premium).

(3)   The registrar must register the documents delivered to him under subsection (1) on receipt.

(4)   The resolution does not take effect until those documents are registered.

(5)   The company must also deliver to the registrar, within 15 days after the resolution is passed, a statement by the directors confirming that the solvency statement was—
    (a)   made not more than 15 days before the date on which the resolution was passed, and
    (b)   provided to members in accordance with section 642(2) or (3).

(6)   The validity of a resolution is not affected by—
    (a)   a failure to deliver the documents required to be delivered to the registrar under subsection (1) within the time specified in that subsection, or
    (b)   a failure to comply with subsection (5).

(7)   If the company delivers to the registrar a solvency statement that was not provided to members in accordance with section 642(2) or (3), an offence is committed by every officer of the company who is in default.

(8)   If default is made in complying with this section, an offence is committed by—
    (a)   the company, and
    (b)   every officer of the company who is in default.

(9)   A person guilty of an offence under subsection (7) or (8) is liable—
    (a)   on conviction on indictment, to a fine;
    (b)   on summary conviction, to a fine not exceeding the statutory maximum.

NOTES
Commencement: 20 January 2007 (for the purpose of enabling the exercise of powers to make Orders or Regulations by statutory instrument); 1 October 2008 (otherwise).
Commencement (transitional adaptations): art 4 of the Companies Act 2006 (Commencement No 7, Transitional Provisions and Savings) Order 2008, SI 2008/1886 (at **[2.78]**) provided for transitional adaptations of this section. Note, however, that that article was revoked by the Companies Act 2006 (Commencement No 8, Transitional Provisions and Savings) Order 2008, SI 2008/2860, art 6(1), as from 1 October 2009 (subject to any relevant transitional provision or saving in Sch 2 to that Order)).
Orders: the Companies (Shares and Share Capital) Order 2009, SI 2009/388 at **[4.364]**.

Reduction of capital confirmed by the court

[1.645]
645 Application to court for order of confirmation

(1)   Where a company has passed a resolution for reducing share capital, it may apply to the court for an order confirming the reduction.

(2)   If the proposed reduction of capital involves either—
    (a)   diminution of liability in respect of unpaid share capital, or
    (b)   the payment to a shareholder of any paid-up share capital,
section 646 (creditors entitled to object to reduction) applies unless the court directs otherwise.

(3)   The court may, if having regard to any special circumstances of the case it thinks proper to do so, direct that section 646 is not to apply as regards any class or classes of creditors.

(4)   The court may direct that section 646 is to apply in any other case.

NOTES
Commencement: 1 October 2009.
Commencement (transitional provisions): Sch 2, para 68 to the Companies Act 2006 (Commencement No 8, Transitional Provisions and Savings) Order 2008, SI 2008/2860 (at **[2.91]**) provides as follows—

"Reduction of capital confirmed by the court (ss 645 to 653)
68.—(1)   Sections 645 to 651 of the Companies Act 2006 (reduction of capital confirmed by the court) apply where an application to the court is made under section 645(1) on or after 1st October 2009.
(2)   It is immaterial for the purposes of such an application whether the resolution for reducing share capital was agreed to before, on or after 1st October 2009.
(3)   The corresponding provisions of the 1985 Act or the 1986 Order continue to apply where an application to the court

has been made under section 136 of that Act or Article 146 of that Order before that date.

(4)   For the purposes of an application under section 645(1) any amendments of a company's memorandum contained in a resolution agreed to before 1st October 2009 are treated as amendments of the company's articles.".

[1.646]

646   Creditors entitled to object to reduction

(1)   Where this section applies (see section 645(2) and (4)), every creditor of the company who[—

    (a)]   at the date fixed by the court is entitled to any debt or claim that, if that date were the commencement of the winding up of the company would be admissible in proof against the company, [and

    (b)   can show that there is a real likelihood that the reduction would result in the company being unable to discharge his debt or claim when it fell due,]

is entitled to object to the reduction of capital.

(2)   The court shall settle a list of creditors entitled to object.

(3)   For that purpose the court—

    (a)   shall ascertain, as far as possible without requiring an application from any creditor, the names of those creditors and the nature and amount of their debts or claims, and

    (b)   may publish notices fixing a day or days within which creditors not entered on the list are to claim to be so entered or are to be excluded from the right of objecting to the reduction of capital.

(4)   If a creditor entered on the list whose debt or claim is not discharged or has not determined does not consent to the reduction, the court may, if it thinks fit, dispense with the consent of that creditor on the company securing payment of his debt or claim.

(5)   For this purpose the debt or claim must be secured by appropriating (as the court may direct) the following amount—

    (a)   if the company admits the full amount of the debt or claim or, though not admitting it, is willing to provide for it, the full amount of the debt or claim;

    (b)   if the company does not admit, and is not willing to provide for, the full amount of the debt or claim, or if the amount is contingent or not ascertained, an amount fixed by the court after the like enquiry and adjudication as if the company were being wound up by the court.

NOTES

Commencement: 1 October 2009.

Commencement (transitional provisions): see the note to s 645 at **[1.645]**.

Sub-s (1): words in square brackets inserted by the Companies (Share Capital and Acquisition by Company of its Own Shares) Regulations 2009, SI 2009/2022, reg 3, as from 1 October 2009.

[1.647]

647   Offences in connection with list of creditors

(1)   If an officer of the company—

    (a)   intentionally or recklessly—

        (i)   conceals the name of a creditor entitled to object to the reduction of capital, or

        (ii)   misrepresents the nature or amount of the debt or claim of a creditor, or

    (b)   is knowingly concerned in any such concealment or misrepresentation,

he commits an offence.

(2)   A person guilty of an offence under this section is liable—

    (a)   on conviction on indictment, to a fine;

    (b)   on summary conviction, to a fine not exceeding the statutory maximum.

NOTES

Commencement: 1 October 2009.

Commencement (transitional provisions): see the note to s 645 at **[1.645]**.

[1.648]

648   Court order confirming reduction

(1)   The court may make an order confirming the reduction of capital on such terms and conditions as it thinks fit.

(2)   The court must not confirm the reduction unless it is satisfied, with respect to every creditor of the company who is entitled to object to the reduction of capital that either—

    (a)   his consent to the reduction has been obtained, or

    (b)   his debt or claim has been discharged, or has determined or has been secured.

(3)   Where the court confirms the reduction, it may order the company to publish (as the court directs) the reasons for reduction of capital, or such other information in regard to it as the court thinks expedient with a view to giving proper information to the public, and (if the court thinks fit) the causes that led to the reduction.

(4)   The court may, if for any special reason it thinks proper to do so, make an order directing that the company must, during such period (commencing on or at any time after the date of the order) as is specified in the order, add to its name as its last words the words "and reduced".

If such an order is made, those words are, until the end of the period specified in the order, deemed to be part of the company's name.

NOTES

Commencement: 1 October 2009.

Commencement (transitional provisions): see the note to s 645 at **[1.645]**.

[1.649]
649   Registration of order and statement of capital

(1)   The registrar, on production of an order of the court confirming the reduction of a company's share capital and the delivery of a copy of the order and of a statement of capital (approved by the court), shall register the order and statement.

This is subject to section 650 (public company reducing capital below authorised minimum).

(2)   The statement of capital must state with respect to the company's share capital as altered by the order—

    (a)   the total number of shares of the company,

    (b)   the aggregate nominal value of those shares,

    (c)   for each class of shares—

        (i)   prescribed particulars of the rights attached to the shares,

        (ii)   the total number of shares of that class, and

        (iii)   the aggregate nominal value of shares of that class, and

    (d)   the amount paid up and the amount (if any) unpaid on each share (whether on account of the nominal value of the share or by way of premium).

(3)   The resolution for reducing share capital, as confirmed by the court's order, takes effect—

    (a)   in the case of a reduction of share capital that forms part of a compromise or arrangement sanctioned by the court under Part 26 (arrangements and reconstructions)—

        (i)   on delivery of the order and statement of capital to the registrar, or

        (ii)   if the court so orders, on the registration of the order and statement of capital;

    (b)   in any other case, on the registration of the order and statement of capital.

(4)   Notice of the registration of the order and statement of capital must be published in such manner as the court may direct.

(5)   The registrar must certify the registration of the order and statement of capital.

(6)   The certificate—

    (a)   must be signed by the registrar or authenticated by the registrar's official seal, and

    (b)   is conclusive evidence—

        (i)   that the requirements of this Act with respect to the reduction of share capital have been complied with, and

        (ii)   that the company's share capital is as stated in the statement of capital.

NOTES

Commencement: 20 January 2007 (for the purpose of enabling the exercise of powers to make Orders or Regulations by statutory instrument); 1 October 2009 (otherwise).

Commencement (transitional provisions): see the note to s 645 at **[1.645]**.

Orders: the Companies (Shares and Share Capital) Order 2009, SI 2009/388 at **[4.364]**.

See further the Companies (Authorised Minimum) Regulations 2009, SI 2009/2425, reg 5 at **[4.590]** (Registration of a court order confirming a capital reduction: assumptions which may be made by the registrar).

Public company reducing capital below authorised minimum

[1.650]
650   Public company reducing capital below authorised minimum

(1)   This section applies where the court makes an order confirming a reduction of a public company's capital that has the effect of bringing the nominal value of its allotted share capital below the authorised minimum.

(2)   The registrar must not register the order unless either—

    (a)   the court so directs, or

    (b)   the company is first re-registered as a private company.

(3)   Section 651 provides an expedited procedure for re-registration in these circumstances.

NOTES

Commencement: 1 October 2009.

Commencement (transitional provisions): see the note to s 645 at **[1.645]**.

See further the Companies (Authorised Minimum) Regulations 2009, SI 2009/2425, reg 3 (Application of the authorised minimum requirement for certain purposes), and reg 5 (Registration of a court order confirming a capital reduction: assumptions which may be made by the registrar) at **[4.588]** and **[4.590]**.

[1.651]
651   Expedited procedure for re-registration as a private company

(1)   The court may authorise the company to be re-registered as a private company without its having passed the special resolution required by section 97.

(2)   If it does so, the court must specify in the order the changes to the company's name and articles to be made in connection with the re-registration.

(3)   The company may then be re-registered as a private company if an application to that effect is delivered to the registrar together with—

    (a)   a copy of the court's order, and

    (b)   notice of the company's name, and a copy of the company's articles, as altered by the court's order.

(4)   On receipt of such an application the registrar must issue a certificate of incorporation altered to meet the circumstances of the case.

(5)   The certificate must state that it is issued on re-registration and the date on which it is issued.

(6)   On the issue of the certificate—

    (a)   the company by virtue of the issue of the certificate becomes a private company, and

    (b)   the changes in the company's name and articles take effect.

(7)   The certificate is conclusive evidence that the requirements of this Act as to re-registration have been complied with.

NOTES

Commencement: 1 October 2009.

Commencement (transitional provisions): see the note to s 645 at **[1.645]**.

Effect of reduction of capital

[1.652]

652   Liability of members following reduction of capital

(1)   Where a company's share capital is reduced a member of the company (past or present) is not liable in respect of any share to any call or contribution exceeding in amount the difference (if any) between—

    (a)   the nominal amount of the share as notified to the registrar in the statement of capital delivered under section 644 or 649, and

    (b)   the amount paid on the share or the reduced amount (if any) which is deemed to have been paid on it, as the case may be.

(2)   This is subject to section 653 (liability to creditor in case of omission from list).

(3)   Nothing in this section affects the rights of the contributories among themselves.

NOTES

Commencement: 1 October 2008 (certain purposes); 1 October 2009 (otherwise) (see the note below).

Commencement (transitional provisions): Sch 2, para 69 to the Companies Act 2006 (Commencement No 8, Transitional Provisions and Savings) Order 2008, SI 2008/2860 (at **[2.91]**) provides as follows—

"69.—(1)   Nothing in section 652 of the Companies Act 2006 (liability of members following reduction of capital) as it applies in relation to a reduction of capital confirmed by the court, or in section 653 of that Act (liability to creditor in case of omission from list of creditors), applies in relation to a reduction of capital in pursuance of an application to the court made before 1st October 2009.

(2)   The provisions of section 140 of the 1985 Act or Article 150 of the 1986 Order continue to apply in relation to such a reduction.".

Commencement (transitional adaptations): art 5 of the Companies Act 2006 (Commencement No 7, Transitional Provisions and Savings) Order 2008, SI 2008/1886 (at **[2.79]**) provided for transitional adaptations of this section. Note, however, that that article was revoked by the Companies Act 2006 (Commencement No 8, Transitional Provisions and Savings) Order 2008, SI 2008/2860, art 6(1), as from 1 October 2009 (subject to any relevant transitional provision or saving in Sch 2 to that Order)).

Commencement (note): the Companies Act 2006 (Commencement No 7, Transitional Provisions and Savings) Order 2008, SI 2008/1886, art 2(c) provides that sub-ss (1), (3) shall come into force on 1 October 2008 so far as relating to a reduction of capital under ss 641(1)(a), (2)–(6), 642–644 of this Act (see **[2.76]**).

[1.653]

653   Liability to creditor in case of omission from list of creditors

(1)   This section applies where, in the case of a reduction of capital confirmed by the court—

    (a)   a creditor entitled to object to the reduction of share capital is by reason of his ignorance—

        (i)   of the proceedings for reduction of share capital, or

        (ii)   of their nature and effect with respect to his debt or claim,

        not entered on the list of creditors, and

    (b)   after the reduction of capital the company is unable to pay the amount of his debt or claim.

(2)   Every person who was a member of the company at the date on which the resolution for reducing capital took effect under section 649(3) is liable to contribute for the payment of the debt or claim an amount not exceeding that which he would have been liable to contribute if the company had commenced to be wound up on the day before that date.

(3)   If the company is wound up, the court on the application of the creditor in question, and proof of ignorance as mentioned in subsection (1)(a), may if it thinks fit—

    (a)   settle accordingly a list of persons liable to contribute under this section, and

    (b)   make and enforce calls and orders on them as if they were ordinary contributories in a winding up.

(4)   The reference in subsection (1)(b) to a company being unable to pay the amount of a debt or claim has the same meaning as in section 123 of the Insolvency Act 1986 (c 45) or Article 103 of the Insolvency (Northern Ireland) Order 1989 (SI 1989/2405 (NI 19)).

NOTES
Commencement: 1 October 2009.
Commencement (transitional provisions): see the note to s 652 at **[1.652]**.

CHAPTER 11
MISCELLANEOUS AND SUPPLEMENTARY PROVISIONS

[1.654]
654   Treatment of reserve arising from reduction of capital
(1)   A reserve arising from the reduction of a company's share capital is not distributable, subject to any provision made by order under this section.
(2)   The Secretary of State may by order specify cases in which—
  (a)   the prohibition in subsection (1) does not apply, and
  (b)   the reserve is to be treated for the purposes of Part 23 (distributions) as a realised profit.
(3)   An order under this section is subject to affirmative resolution procedure.

NOTES
Commencement: 20 January 2007 (for the purpose of enabling the exercise of powers to make Orders or Regulations by statutory instrument); 1 October 2008 (otherwise).
Commencement (transitional provisions): the Companies Act 2006 (Commencement No 7, Transitional Provisions and Savings) Order 2008, SI 2008/1886, art 7(2) (at **[2.81]**) provides as follows—

"(2)   Section 654 of the Companies Act 2006 (treatment of reserve arising from reduction of capital) and any order made under that section apply in relation to reserves arising from—
  (a)   a reduction of capital under Chapter 4 of Part 5 of the Companies Act 1985 or Chapter 4 of Part 6 of the Companies (Northern Ireland) Order 1986,
  (b)   a reduction of capital under the provisions of the Companies Act 2006 mentioned in article 2(a) above, or
  (c)   a reduction in the capital of an unlimited company not under those provisions,
irrespective of when the reduction occurred or the reserves arose.".

Note that the provisions "mentioned in article 2(a) above" are ss 641(1)(a), (2)–(6) and 642–644 of this Act (see **[2.76]**).
Orders: the Companies (Reduction of Share Capital) Order 2008, SI 2008/1915 at **[4.303]**.

[1.655]
655   Shares no bar to damages against company
A person is not debarred from obtaining damages or other compensation from a company by reason only of his holding or having held shares in the company or any right to apply or subscribe for shares or to be included in the company's register of members in respect of shares.

NOTES
Commencement: 1 October 2009.

[1.656]
656   Public companies: duty of directors to call meeting on serious loss of capital
(1)   Where the net assets of a public company are half or less of its called-up share capital, the directors must call a general meeting of the company to consider whether any, and if so what, steps should be taken to deal with the situation.
(2)   They must do so not later than 28 days from the earliest day on which that fact is known to a director of the company.
(3)   The meeting must be convened for a date not later than 56 days from that day.
(4)   If there is a failure to convene a meeting as required by this section, each of the directors of the company who—
  (a)   knowingly authorises or permits the failure, or
  (b)   after the period during which the meeting should have been convened, knowingly authorises or permits the failure to continue,
commits an offence.
(5)   A person guilty of an offence under this section is liable—
  (a)   on conviction on indictment, to a fine;
  (b)   on summary conviction, to a fine not exceeding the statutory maximum.
(6)   Nothing in this section authorises the consideration at a meeting convened in pursuance of subsection (1) of any matter that could not have been considered at that meeting apart from this section.

NOTES
Commencement: 1 October 2009.

[1.657]

657 General power to make further provision by regulations

(1) The Secretary of State may by regulations modify the following provisions of this Part—

sections 552 and 553 (prohibited commissions, discounts and allowances),

Chapter 5 (payment for shares),

Chapter 6 (public companies: independent valuation of non-cash consideration),

Chapter 7 (share premiums),

sections 622 to 628 (redenomination of share capital),

Chapter 10 (reduction of capital), and

section 656 (public companies: duty of directors to call meeting on serious loss of capital).

(2) The regulations may—

(a) amend or repeal any of those provisions, or

(b) make such other provision as appears to the Secretary of State appropriate in place of any of those provisions.

(3) Regulations under this section may make consequential amendments or repeals in other provisions of this Act, or in other enactments.

(4) Regulations under this section are subject to affirmative resolution procedure.

NOTES

Commencement: 20 January 2007 (for the purpose of enabling the exercise of powers to make Orders or Regulations by statutory instrument); 1 October 2009 (otherwise).

Orders: the Companies Act 2006 (Consequential Amendments, Transitional Provisions and Savings) Order 2009, SI 2009/1941 at **[4.528]**.

Regulations: the Companies (Share Capital and Acquisition by Company of its Own Shares) Regulations 2009, SI 2009/2022 at **[4.542]**.

PART 18
ACQUISITION BY LIMITED COMPANY OF ITS OWN SHARES

CHAPTER 1
GENERAL PROVISIONS

Introductory

[1.658]

658 General rule against limited company acquiring its own shares

(1) A limited company must not acquire its own shares, whether by purchase, subscription or otherwise, except in accordance with the provisions of this Part.

(2) If a company purports to act in contravention of this section—

(a) an offence is committed by—

(i) the company, and

(ii) every officer of the company who is in default, and

(b) the purported acquisition is void.

(3) A person guilty of an offence under this section is liable—

(a) on conviction on indictment, to imprisonment for a term not exceeding two years or a fine (or both);

(b) on summary conviction—

(i) in England and Wales, to imprisonment for a term not exceeding twelve months or a fine not exceeding the statutory maximum (or both);

(ii) in Scotland or Northern Ireland, to imprisonment for a term not exceeding six months or a fine not exceeding the statutory maximum (or both).

NOTES

Commencement: 1 October 2009.

Offences under this section: see further s 1131 at **[1.1131]**.

[1.659]

659 Exceptions to general rule

(1) A limited company may acquire any of its own fully paid shares otherwise than for valuable consideration.

(2) Section 658 does not prohibit—

(a) the acquisition of shares in a reduction of capital duly made;

(b) the purchase of shares in pursuance of an order of the court under—

(i) section 98 (application to court to cancel resolution for re-registration as a private company),

(ii) section 721(6) (powers of court on objection to redemption or purchase of shares out of capital),

(iii) section 759 (remedial order in case of breach of prohibition of public offers by private company), or

(iv) Part 30 (protection of members against unfair prejudice);

(c)   the forfeiture of shares, or the acceptance of shares surrendered in lieu, in pursuance of the company's articles, for failure to pay any sum payable in respect of the shares.

NOTES
Commencement: 1 October 2009.

Shares held by company's nominee

[1.660]
660   Treatment of shares held by nominee

(1)   This section applies where shares in a limited company—
   (a)   are taken by a subscriber to the memorandum as nominee of the company,
   (b)   are issued to a nominee of the company, or
   (c)   are acquired by a nominee of the company, partly paid up, from a third person.
(2)   For all purposes—
   (a)   the shares are to be treated as held by the nominee on his own account, and
   (b)   the company is to be regarded as having no beneficial interest in them.
(3)   This section does not apply—
   (a)   to shares acquired otherwise than by subscription by a nominee of a public company, where—
     (i)   a person acquires shares in the company with financial assistance given to him, directly or indirectly, by the company for the purpose of or in connection with the acquisition, and
     (ii)   the company has a beneficial interest in the shares;
   (b)   to shares acquired by a nominee of the company when the company has no beneficial interest in the shares.

NOTES
Commencement: 1 October 2009.

[1.661]
661   Liability of others where nominee fails to make payment in respect of shares

(1)   This section applies where shares in a limited company—
   (a)   are taken by a subscriber to the memorandum as nominee of the company,
   (b)   are issued to a nominee of the company, or
   (c)   are acquired by a nominee of the company, partly paid up, from a third person.
(2)   If the nominee, having been called on to pay any amount for the purposes of paying up, or paying any premium on, the shares, fails to pay that amount within 21 days from being called on to do so, then—
   (a)   in the case of shares that he agreed to take as subscriber to the memorandum, the other subscribers to the memorandum, and
   (b)   in any other case, the directors of the company when the shares were issued to or acquired by him,
are jointly and severally liable with him to pay that amount.
(3)   If in proceedings for the recovery of an amount under subsection (2) it appears to the court that the subscriber or director—
   (a)   has acted honestly and reasonably, and
   (b)   having regard to all the circumstances of the case, ought fairly to be relieved from liability,
the court may relieve him, either wholly or in part, from his liability on such terms as the court thinks fit.
(4)   If a subscriber to a company's memorandum or a director of a company has reason to apprehend that a claim will or might be made for the recovery of any such amount from him—
   (a)   he may apply to the court for relief, and
   (b)   the court has the same power to relieve him as it would have had in proceedings for recovery of that amount.
(5)   This section does not apply to shares acquired by a nominee of the company when the company has no beneficial interest in the shares.

NOTES
Commencement: 1 October 2009.

Shares held by or for public company

NOTES
As to the application of this group of sections (ie, ss 662–669) to old public companies, see the introductory notes to this Act and the Companies Act 2006 (Consequential Amendments and Transitional Provisions) Order 2011, SI 2011/1265, Sch 1 at **[4.651]**.

[1.662]
662   Duty to cancel shares in public company held by or for the company

(1)   This section applies in the case of a public company—

(a) where shares in the company are forfeited, or surrendered to the company in lieu of forfeiture, in pursuance of the articles, for failure to pay any sum payable in respect of the shares;

(b) where shares in the company are surrendered to the company in pursuance of section 102C(1)(b) of the Building Societies Act 1986 (c 53);

(c) where shares in the company are acquired by it (otherwise than in accordance with this Part or Part 30 (protection of members against unfair prejudice)) and the company has a beneficial interest in the shares;

(d) where a nominee of the company acquires shares in the company from a third party without financial assistance being given directly or indirectly by the company and the company has a beneficial interest in the shares; or

(e) where a person acquires shares in the company, with financial assistance given to him, directly or indirectly, by the company for the purpose of or in connection with the acquisition, and the company has a beneficial interest in the shares.

(2) Unless the shares or any interest of the company in them are previously disposed of, the company must—

(a) cancel the shares and diminish the amount of the company's share capital by the nominal value of the shares cancelled, and

(b) where the effect is that the nominal value of the company's allotted share capital is brought below the authorised minimum, apply for re-registration as a private company, stating the effect of the cancellation.

(3) It must do so no later than—

(a) in a case within subsection (1)(a) or (b), three years from the date of the forfeiture or surrender;

(b) in a case within subsection (1)(c) or (d), three years from the date of the acquisition;

(c) in a case within subsection (1)(e), one year from the date of the acquisition.

(4) The directors of the company may take any steps necessary to enable the company to comply with this section, and may do so without complying with the provisions of Chapter 10 of Part 17 (reduction of capital).

See also section 664 (re-registration as private company in consequence of cancellation).

(5) Neither the company nor, in a case within subsection (1)(d) or (e), the nominee or other shareholder may exercise any voting rights in respect of the shares.

(6) Any purported exercise of those rights is void.

NOTES

Commencement: 1 October 2009.

Commencement (transitional provisions): Sch 2, paras 70–72 to the Companies Act 2006 (Commencement No 8, Transitional Provisions and Savings) Order 2008, SI 2008/2860 (at **[2.91]**) provide as follows—

"Cancellation of shares in public company held by or for the company (ss 662 to 668)

70.—(1) Section 662 of the Companies Act 2006 (duty to cancel shares in public company held by or for the company) applies where an event mentioned in section 662(1) or 668(1)(a) to (d) occurs on or after 1st October 2009.

(2) Section 662 also applies where an event mentioned in section 146(1) or 148(1)(a) to (d) of the 1985 Act or Article 156(1) or 158(1)(a) to (d) of the 1986 Order occurred before 1st October 2009, unless before that date—

(a) the company has complied with section 146(2) or Article 156(2), or

(b) the period for compliance specified in section 146(3) or Article 156(3) has expired.

(3) The provisions of the 1985 Act or 1986 Order continue to apply in those cases where section 662 does not apply.

71.—(1) Section 663 of the Companies Act 2006 (notice of cancellation of shares in public company held by or for the company) applies where the shares referred to in subsection (1) of that section are cancelled on or after 1st October 2009.

(2) Section 122(1)(f) and (2) of the 1985 Act or Article 132(1)(f) and (2) of the 1986 Order continue to apply where the shares referred to in section 122(1)(f) or Article 132(1)(f) are cancelled before that date.

72.—(1) Sections 664 to 667 of the Companies Act 2006 (re-registration as private company in consequence of cancellation) apply in any case where section 662 of that Act applies (see paragraph 70(1) and (2) above).

(2) The corresponding provisions of the 1985 Act or 1986 Order continue to apply in any other case.

(3) For the purposes of an application under section 664 made by virtue of paragraph 70(2) above a resolution agreed to before 1st October 2009 under section 147(2) of the 1985 Act or Article 157(2) of the 1986 Order may be treated as if agreed to under section 664(1) and (2) (and as if amendments of the company's memorandum were amendments of its articles).".

See further the Companies (Authorised Minimum) Regulations 2009, SI 2009/2425, reg 3 at **[4.588]** (Application of the authorised minimum requirement for certain purposes).

Old public companies: see the note preceding s 662 at **[1.662]**.

[1.663]
663 Notice of cancellation of shares

(1) Where a company cancels shares in order to comply with section 662, it must within one month after the shares are cancelled give notice to the registrar, specifying the shares cancelled.

(2) The notice must be accompanied by a statement of capital.

(3) The statement of capital must state with respect to the company's share capital immediately following the cancellation—

(a) the total number of shares of the company,

(b) the aggregate nominal value of those shares,

  (c)   for each class of shares—
      (i)   prescribed particulars of the rights attached to the shares,
      (ii)   the total number of shares of that class, and
      (iii)   the aggregate nominal value of shares of that class, and
  (d)   the amount paid up and the amount (if any) unpaid on each share (whether on account of the nominal value of the share or by way of premium).

(4)   If default is made in complying with this section, an offence is committed by—
  (a)   the company, and
  (b)   every officer of the company who is in default.

(5)   A person guilty of an offence under this section is liable on summary conviction to a fine not exceeding level 3 on the standard scale and, for continued contravention, a daily default fine not exceeding one-tenth of level 3 on the standard scale.

NOTES

Commencement: 20 January 2007 (for the purpose of enabling the exercise of powers to make Orders or Regulations by statutory instrument); 1 October 2009 (otherwise).

Commencement (transitional provisions): see the note to s 662 at **[1.662]**.

Old public companies: see the note preceding s 662 at **[1.662]**.

Orders: the Companies (Shares and Share Capital) Order 2009, SI 2009/388 at **[4.364]**.

[1.664]
664   Re-registration as private company in consequence of cancellation

(1)   Where a company is obliged to re-register as a private company to comply with section 662, the directors may resolve that the company should be so re-registered.

    Chapter 3 of Part 3 (resolutions affecting a company's constitution) applies to any such resolution.

(2)   The resolution may make such changes—
  (a)   in the company's name, and
  (b)   in the company's articles,
as are necessary in connection with its becoming a private company.

(3)   The application for re-registration must contain a statement of the company's proposed name on re-registration.

(4)   The application must be accompanied by—
  (a)   a copy of the resolution (unless a copy has already been forwarded under Chapter 3 of Part 3),
  (b)   a copy of the company's articles as amended by the resolution, and
  (c)   a statement of compliance.

(5)   The statement of compliance required is a statement that the requirements of this section as to re-registration as a private company have been complied with.

(6)   The registrar may accept the statement of compliance as sufficient evidence that the company is entitled to be re-registered as a private company.

NOTES

Commencement: 1 October 2009.

Commencement (transitional provisions): see the note to s 662 at **[1.662]**.

Old public companies: see the note preceding s 662 at **[1.662]**.

[1.665]
665   Issue of certificate of incorporation on re-registration

(1)   If on an application under section 664 the registrar is satisfied that the company is entitled to be re-registered as a private company, the company shall be re-registered accordingly.

(2)   The registrar must issue a certificate of incorporation altered to meet the circumstances of the case.

(3)   The certificate must state that it is issued on re-registration and the date on which it is issued.

(4)   On the issue of the certificate—
  (a)   the company by virtue of the issue of the certificate becomes a private company, and
  (b)   the changes in the company's name and articles take effect.

(5)   The certificate is conclusive evidence that the requirements of this Act as to re-registration have been complied with.

NOTES

Commencement: 1 October 2009.

Commencement (transitional provisions): see the note to s 662 at **[1.662]**.

Old public companies: see the note preceding s 662 at **[1.662]**.

[1.666]
666 Effect of failure to re-register

(1) If a public company that is required by section 662 to apply to be re-registered as a private company fails to do so before the end of the period specified in subsection (3) of that section, Chapter 1 of Part 20 (prohibition of public offers by private company) applies to it as if it were a private company.

(2) Subject to that, the company continues to be treated as a public company until it is so re-registered.

NOTES

Commencement: 1 October 2009.

Commencement (transitional provisions): see the note to s 662 at **[1.662]**.

Old public companies: see the note preceding s 662 at **[1.662]**.

[1.667]
667 Offence in case of failure to cancel shares or re-register

(1) This section applies where a company, when required to do by section 662—
  (a) fails to cancel any shares, or
  (b) fails to make an application for re-registration as a private company,
within the time specified in subsection (3) of that section.

(2) An offence is committed by—
  (a) the company, and
  (b) every officer of the company who is in default.

(3) A person guilty of an offence under this section is liable on summary conviction to a fine not exceeding level 3 on the standard scale and, for continued contravention, a daily default fine not exceeding one-tenth of level 3 on the standard scale.

NOTES

Commencement: 1 October 2009.

Commencement (transitional provisions): see the note to s 662 at **[1.662]**.

See further the Companies (Authorised Minimum) Regulations 2009, SI 2009/2425, reg 6 at **[4.591]** (Determination of exchange rates by the court in certain proceedings)

Old public companies: see the note preceding s 662 at **[1.662]**.

[1.668]
668 Application of provisions to company re-registering as public company

(1) This section applies where, after shares in a private company—
  (a) are forfeited in pursuance of the company's articles or are surrendered to the company in lieu of forfeiture,
  (b) are acquired by the company (otherwise than by any of the methods permitted by this Part or Part 30 (protection of members against unfair prejudice)), the company having a beneficial interest in the shares,
  (c) are acquired by a nominee of the company from a third party without financial assistance being given directly or indirectly by the company, the company having a beneficial interest in the shares, or
  (d) are acquired by a person with financial assistance given to him, directly or indirectly, by the company for the purpose of or in connection with the acquisition, the company having a beneficial interest in the shares,
the company is re-registered as a public company.

(2) In that case the provisions of sections 662 to 667 apply to the company as if it had been a public company at the time of the forfeiture, surrender or acquisition, subject to the following modification.

(3) The modification is that the period specified in section 662(3)(a), (b) or (c) (period for complying with obligations under that section) runs from the date of the re-registration of the company as a public company.

NOTES

Commencement: 1 October 2009.

Commencement (transitional provisions): see the note to s 662 at **[1.662]**.

Old public companies: see the note preceding s 662 at **[1.662]**.

[1.669]
669 Transfer to reserve on acquisition of shares by public company or nominee

(1) Where—
  (a) a public company, or a nominee of a public company, acquires shares in the company, and
  (b) those shares are shown in a balance sheet of the company as an asset,
an amount equal to the value of the shares must be transferred out of profits available for dividend to a reserve fund and is not then available for distribution.

(2) Subsection (1) applies to an interest in shares as it applies to shares.

As it so applies the reference to the value of the shares shall be read as a reference to the value to the company of its interest in the shares.

NOTES

Commencement: 1 October 2009.

Old public companies: see the note preceding s 662 at **[1.662]**.

Charges of public company on own shares

[1.670]

670   Public companies: general rule against lien or charge on own shares

(1) A lien or other charge of a public company on its own shares (whether taken expressly or otherwise) is void, except as permitted by this section.

(2) In the case of any description of company, a charge is permitted if the shares are not fully paid up and the charge is for an amount payable in respect of the shares.

(3) In the case of a company whose ordinary business—

    (a) includes the lending of money, or

    (b) consists of the provision of credit or the bailment (in Scotland, hiring) of goods under a hire-purchase agreement, or both,

a charge is permitted (whether the shares are fully paid or not) if it arises in connection with a transaction entered into by the company in the ordinary course of that business.

(4) In the case of a company that has been re-registered as a public company, a charge is permitted if it was in existence immediately before the application for re-registration.

NOTES

Commencement: 1 October 2009.

Supplementary provisions

[1.671]

671   Interests to be disregarded in determining whether company has beneficial interest

In determining for the purposes of this Chapter whether a company has a beneficial interest in shares, there shall be disregarded any such interest as is mentioned in—

    section 672 (residual interest under pension scheme or employees' share scheme),

    section 673 (employer's charges and other rights of recovery), or

    section 674 (rights as personal representative or trustee).

NOTES

Commencement: 1 October 2009.

[1.672]

672   Residual interest under pension scheme or employees' share scheme

(1) Where the shares are held on trust for the purposes of a pension scheme or employees' share scheme, there shall be disregarded any residual interest of the company that has not vested in possession.

(2) A "residual interest" means a right of the company to receive any of the trust property in the event of—

    (a) all the liabilities arising under the scheme having been satisfied or provided for, or

    (b) the company ceasing to participate in the scheme, or

    (c) the trust property at any time exceeding what is necessary for satisfying the liabilities arising or expected to arise under the scheme.

(3) In subsection (2)—

    (a) the reference to a right includes a right dependent on the exercise of a discretion vested by the scheme in the trustee or another person, and

    (b) the reference to liabilities arising under a scheme includes liabilities that have resulted, or may result, from the exercise of any such discretion.

(4) For the purposes of this section a residual interest vests in possession—

    (a) in a case within subsection (2)(a), on the occurrence of the event mentioned there (whether or not the amount of the property receivable pursuant to the right is ascertained);

    (b) in a case within subsection (2)(b) or (c), when the company becomes entitled to require the trustee to transfer to it any of the property receivable pursuant to that right.

(5) Where by virtue of this section shares are exempt from section 660 or 661 (shares held by company's nominee) at the time they are taken, issued or acquired but the residual interest in question vests in possession before they are disposed of or fully paid up, those sections apply to the shares as if they had been taken, issued or acquired on the date on which that interest vests in possession.

(6) Where by virtue of this section shares are exempt from sections 662 to 668 (shares held by or for public company) at the time they are acquired but the residual interest in question vests in possession before they are disposed of, those sections apply to the shares as if they had been acquired on the date on which the interest vests in possession.

NOTES
Commencement: 1 October 2009.

[1.673]
673 Employer's charges and other rights of recovery
(1) Where the shares are held on trust for the purposes of a pension scheme there shall be disregarded—
   (a) any charge or lien on, or set-off against, any benefit or other right or interest under the scheme for the purpose of enabling the employer or former employer of a member of the scheme to obtain the discharge of a monetary obligation due to him from the member;
   (b) any right to receive from the trustee of the scheme, or as trustee of the scheme to retain, an amount that can be recovered or retained—
      (i) under section 61 of the Pension Schemes Act 1993 (c 48), or otherwise, as reimbursement or partial reimbursement for any contributions equivalent premium paid in connection with the scheme under Part 3 of that Act, or
      (ii) under section 57 of the Pension Schemes (Northern Ireland) Act 1993 (c 49), or otherwise, as reimbursement or partial reimbursement for any contributions equivalent premium paid in connection with the scheme under Part 3 of that Act.
(2) Where the shares are held on trust for the purposes of an employees' share scheme, there shall be disregarded any charge or lien on, or set-off against, any benefit or other right or interest under the scheme for the purpose of enabling the employer or former employer of a member of the scheme to obtain the discharge of a monetary obligation due to him from the member.

NOTES
Commencement: 1 October 2009.

[1.674]
674 Rights as personal representative or trustee
Where the company is a personal representative or trustee, there shall be disregarded any rights that the company has in that capacity including, in particular—
   (a) any right to recover its expenses or be remunerated out of the estate or trust property, and
   (b) any right to be indemnified out of that property for any liability incurred by reason of any act or omission of the company in the performance of its duties as personal representative or trustee.

NOTES
Commencement: 1 October 2009.

[1.675]
675 Meaning of "pension scheme"
(1) In this Chapter "pension scheme" means a scheme for the provision of benefits consisting of or including relevant benefits for or in respect of employees or former employees.
(2) In subsection (1) "relevant benefits" means any pension, lump sum, gratuity or other like benefit given or to be given on retirement or on death or in anticipation of retirement or, in connection with past service, after retirement or death.

NOTES
Commencement: 1 October 2009.

[1.676]
676 Application of provisions to directors
For the purposes of this Chapter references to "employer" and "employee", in the context of a pension scheme or employees' share scheme, shall be read as if a director of a company were employed by it.

NOTES
Commencement: 1 October 2009.

CHAPTER 2
FINANCIAL ASSISTANCE FOR PURCHASE OF OWN SHARES
Introductory

[1.677]
677 Meaning of "financial assistance"
(1) In this Chapter "financial assistance" means—
   (a) financial assistance given by way of gift,
   (b) financial assistance given—

      (i)   by way of guarantee, security or indemnity (other than an indemnity in respect of the indemnifier's own neglect or default), or

      (ii)   by way of release or waiver,

  (c)   financial assistance given—

      (i)   by way of a loan or any other agreement under which any of the obligations of the person giving the assistance are to be fulfilled at a time when in accordance with the agreement any obligation of another party to the agreement remains unfulfilled, or

      (ii)   by way of the novation of, or the assignment (in Scotland, assignation) of rights arising under, a loan or such other agreement, or

  (d)   any other financial assistance given by a company where—

      (i)   the net assets of the company are reduced to a material extent by the giving of the assistance, or

      (ii)   the company has no net assets.

(2) "Net assets" here means the aggregate amount of the company's assets less the aggregate amount of its liabilities.

(3) For this purpose a company's liabilities include—

  (a)   where the company draws up Companies Act individual accounts, any provision of a kind specified for the purposes of this subsection by regulations under section 396, and

  (b)   where the company draws up IAS individual accounts, any provision made in those accounts.

NOTES

Commencement: 1 October 2009.

Regulations under section 396: see the notes to that section at **[1.396]**. See also the Small Companies and Groups (Accounts and Directors' Report) Regulations 2008, SI 2008/409, reg 12 (at **[4.153]**), and the Large and Medium-sized Companies and Groups (Accounts and Reports) Regulations 2008, SI 2008/410, reg 12 (at **[4.181]**) which provide that Sch 7 to SI 2008/409 (at **[4.167]**, **[4.168]**) and Sch 9 to SI 2008/410 (at **[4.217]**, **[4.218]**) define "provisions" for the purpose of those Regulations and for the purposes of sub-s (3)(a) above.

Circumstances in which financial assistance prohibited

[1.678]
678 Assistance for acquisition of shares in public company

(1) Where a person is acquiring or proposing to acquire shares in a public company, it is not lawful for that company, or a company that is a subsidiary of that company, to give financial assistance directly or indirectly for the purpose of the acquisition before or at the same time as the acquisition takes place.

(2) Subsection (1) does not prohibit a company from giving financial assistance for the acquisition of shares in it or its holding company if—

  (a)   the company's principal purpose in giving the assistance is not to give it for the purpose of any such acquisition, or

  (b)   the giving of the assistance for that purpose is only an incidental part of some larger purpose of the company,

and the assistance is given in good faith in the interests of the company.

(3) Where—

  (a)   a person has acquired shares in a company, and

  (b)   a liability has been incurred (by that or another person) for the purpose of the acquisition,

it is not lawful for that company, or a company that is a subsidiary of that company, to give financial assistance directly or indirectly for the purpose of reducing or discharging the liability if, at the time the assistance is given, the company in which the shares were acquired is a public company.

(4) Subsection (3) does not prohibit a company from giving financial assistance if—

  (a)   the company's principal purpose in giving the assistance is not to reduce or discharge any liability incurred by a person for the purpose of the acquisition of shares in the company or its holding company, or

  (b)   the reduction or discharge of any such liability is only an incidental part of some larger purpose of the company,

and the assistance is given in good faith in the interests of the company.

(5) This section has effect subject to sections 681 and 682 (unconditional and conditional exceptions to prohibition).

NOTES

Commencement: 1 October 2009.

[1.679]
679 Assistance by public company for acquisition of shares in its private holding company

(1) Where a person is acquiring or proposing to acquire shares in a private company, it is not lawful for a public company that is a subsidiary of that company to give financial assistance directly or indirectly for the purpose of the acquisition before or at the same time as the acquisition takes place.

(2)   Subsection (1) does not prohibit a company from giving financial assistance for the acquisition of shares in its holding company if—

(a)   the company's principal purpose in giving the assistance is not to give it for the purpose of any such acquisition, or

(b)   the giving of the assistance for that purpose is only an incidental part of some larger purpose of the company,

and the assistance is given in good faith in the interests of the company.

(3)   Where—

(a)   a person has acquired shares in a private company, and

(b)   a liability has been incurred (by that or another person) for the purpose of the acquisition,

it is not lawful for a public company that is a subsidiary of that company to give financial assistance directly or indirectly for the purpose of reducing or discharging the liability.

(4)   Subsection (3) does not prohibit a company from giving financial assistance if—

(a)   the company's principal purpose in giving the assistance is not to reduce or discharge any liability incurred by a person for the purpose of the acquisition of shares in its holding company, or

(b)   the reduction or discharge of any such liability is only an incidental part of some larger purpose of the company,

and the assistance is given in good faith in the interests of the company.

(5)   This section has effect subject to sections 681 and 682 (unconditional and conditional exceptions to prohibition).

NOTES

Commencement: 1 October 2009.

[1.680]

680   Prohibited financial assistance an offence

(1)   If a company contravenes section 678(1) or (3) or section 679(1) or (3) (prohibited financial assistance) an offence is committed by—

(a)   the company, and

(b)   every officer of the company who is in default.

(2)   A person guilty of an offence under this section is liable—

(a)   on conviction on indictment, to imprisonment for a term not exceeding two years or a fine (or both);

(b)   on summary conviction—

(i)   in England and Wales, to imprisonment for a term not exceeding twelve months or to a fine not exceeding the statutory maximum (or both);

(ii)   in Scotland or Northern Ireland, to imprisonment for a term not exceeding six months, or to a fine not exceeding the statutory maximum (or both).

NOTES

Commencement: 1 October 2009.

Offences under this section: see further s 1131 at **[1.1131]**.

Exceptions from prohibition

[1.681]

681   Unconditional exceptions

(1)   Neither section 678 nor section 679 prohibits a transaction to which this section applies.

(2)   Those transactions are—

(a)   a distribution of the company's assets by way of—

(i)   dividend lawfully made, or

(ii)   distribution in the course of a company's winding up;

(b)   an allotment of bonus shares;

(c)   a reduction of capital under Chapter 10 of Part 17;

(d)   a redemption of shares under Chapter 3 or a purchase of shares under Chapter 4 of this Part;

(e)   anything done in pursuance of an order of the court under Part 26 (order sanctioning compromise or arrangement with members or creditors);

(f)   anything done under an arrangement made in pursuance of section 110 of the Insolvency Act 1986 (c 45) or Article 96 of the Insolvency (Northern Ireland) Order 1989 (SI 1989/2405 (NI 19)) (liquidator in winding up accepting shares as consideration for sale of company's property);

(g)   anything done under an arrangement made between a company and its creditors that is binding on the creditors by virtue of Part 1 of the Insolvency Act 1986 or Part 2 of the Insolvency (Northern Ireland) Order 1989 (SI 1989/2405 (NI 19)).

NOTES

Commencement: 1 October 2009.

[1.682]

682 Conditional exceptions

(1) Neither section 678 nor section 679 prohibits a transaction to which this section applies—

    (a) if the company giving the assistance is a private company, or

    (b) if the company giving the assistance is a public company and—

        (i) the company has net assets that are not reduced by the giving of the assistance, or

        (ii) to the extent that those assets are so reduced, the assistance is provided out of distributable profits.

(2) The transactions to which this section applies are—

    (a) where the lending of money is part of the ordinary business of the company, the lending of money in the ordinary course of the company's business;

    (b) the provision by the company, in good faith in the interests of the company or its holding company, of financial assistance for the purposes of an employees' share scheme;

    (c) the provision of financial assistance by the company for the purposes of or in connection with anything done by the company (or another company in the same group) for the purpose of enabling or facilitating transactions in shares in the first-mentioned company or its holding company between, and involving the acquisition of beneficial ownership of those shares by—

        (i) bona fide employees or former employees of that company (or another company in the same group), or

        (ii) spouses or civil partners, widows, widowers or surviving civil partners, or minor children or step-children of any such employees or former employees;

    (d) the making by the company of loans to persons (other than directors) employed in good faith by the company with a view to enabling those persons to acquire fully paid shares in the company or its holding company to be held by them by way of beneficial ownership.

(3) The references in this section to "net assets" are to the amount by which the aggregate of the company's assets exceeds the aggregate of its liabilities.

(4) For this purpose—

    (a) the amount of both assets and liabilities shall be taken to be as stated in the company's accounting records immediately before the financial assistance is given, and

    (b) "liabilities" includes any amount retained as reasonably necessary for the purpose of providing for a liability the nature of which is clearly defined and that is either likely to be incurred or certain to be incurred but uncertain as to amount or as to the date on which it will arise.

(5) For the purposes of subsection (2)(c) a company is in the same group as another company if it is a holding company or subsidiary of that company or a subsidiary of a holding company of that company.

NOTES

Commencement: 1 October 2009.

Supplementary

[1.683]

683 Definitions for this Chapter

(1) In this Chapter—

    "distributable profits", in relation to the giving of any financial assistance—

        (a) means those profits out of which the company could lawfully make a distribution equal in value to that assistance, and

        (b) includes, in a case where the financial assistance consists of or includes, or is treated as arising in consequence of, the sale, transfer or other disposition of a non-cash asset, any profit that, if the company were to make a distribution of that character would be available for that purpose (see section 846); and

    "distribution" has the same meaning as in Part 23 (distributions) (see section 829).

(2) In this Chapter—

    (a) a reference to a person incurring a liability includes his changing his financial position by making an agreement or arrangement (whether enforceable or unenforceable, and whether made on his own account or with any other person) or by any other means, and

    (b) a reference to a company giving financial assistance for the purposes of reducing or discharging a liability incurred by a person for the purpose of the acquisition of shares includes its giving such assistance for the purpose of wholly or partly restoring his financial position to what it was before the acquisition took place.

NOTES

Commencement: 1 October 2009.

CHAPTER 3
REDEEMABLE SHARES

[1.684]
684   Power of limited company to issue redeemable shares

(1)   A limited company having a share capital may issue shares that are to be redeemed or are liable to be redeemed at the option of the company or the shareholder ("redeemable shares"), subject to the following provisions.

(2)   The articles of a private limited company may exclude or restrict the issue of redeemable shares.

(3)   A public limited company may only issue redeemable shares if it is authorised to do so by its articles.

(4)   No redeemable shares may be issued at a time when there are no issued shares of the company that are not redeemable.

NOTES

Commencement: 1 October 2009.

[1.685]
685   Terms and manner of redemption

(1)   The directors of a limited company may determine the terms, conditions and manner of redemption of shares if they are authorised to do so—
    (a)   by the company's articles, or
    (b)   by a resolution of the company.

(2)   A resolution under subsection (1)(b) may be an ordinary resolution, even though it amends the company's articles.

(3)   Where the directors are authorised under subsection (1) to determine the terms, conditions and manner of redemption of shares—
    (a)   they must do so before the shares are allotted, and
    (b)   any obligation of the company to state in a statement of capital the rights attached to the shares extends to the terms, conditions and manner of redemption.

(4)   Where the directors are not so authorised, the terms, conditions and manner of redemption of any redeemable shares must be stated in the company's articles.

NOTES

Commencement: 1 October 2009.

[1.686]
686   Payment for redeemable shares

(1)   Redeemable shares in a limited company may not be redeemed unless they are fully paid.

(2)   The terms of redemption of shares in a limited company may provide that the amount payable on redemption may, by agreement between the company and the holder of the shares, be paid on a date later than the redemption date.

(3)   Unless redeemed in accordance with a provision authorised by subsection (2), the shares must be paid for on redemption.

NOTES

Commencement: 1 October 2009.

Commencement (transitional provisions): Sch 2, para 73 to the Companies Act 2006 (Commencement No 8, Transitional Provisions and Savings) Order 2008, SI 2008/2860 (at **[2.91]**) provides as follows—

"Redeemable shares (ss 684 to 689)

73.—(1)   Section 686(2) of the Companies Act 2006 (terms allowing for payment on date later than redemption date) applies—
    (a)   to shares issued on or after 1st October 2009, and
    (b)   to shares issued before that date where the terms of redemption have been amended on or after that date to allow for payment on a date later than the redemption date.

(2)   So much of section 159(3) of the 1985 Act or Article 169(3) of the 1986 Order as requires payment on redemption continues to apply in any other case.".

[1.687]
687   Financing of redemption

(1)   A private limited company may redeem redeemable shares out of capital in accordance with Chapter 5.

(2)   Subject to that, redeemable shares in a limited company may only be redeemed out of—
    (a)   distributable profits of the company, or
    (b)   the proceeds of a fresh issue of shares made for the purposes of the redemption.

(3)   Any premium payable on redemption of shares in a limited company must be paid out of distributable profits of the company, subject to the following provision.

(4) If the redeemable shares were issued at a premium, any premium payable on their redemption may be paid out of the proceeds of a fresh issue of shares made for the purposes of the redemption, up to an amount equal to—

    (a) the aggregate of the premiums received by the company on the issue of the shares redeemed, or

    (b) the current amount of the company's share premium account (including any sum transferred to that account in respect of premiums on the new shares),

whichever is the less.

(5) The amount of the company's share premium account is reduced by a sum corresponding (or by sums in the aggregate corresponding) to the amount of any payment made under subsection (4).

(6) This section is subject to section 735(4) (terms of redemption enforceable in a winding up).

NOTES

Commencement: 1 October 2009.

[1.688]
688 Redeemed shares treated as cancelled

Where shares in a limited company are redeemed—

    (a) the shares are treated as cancelled, and

    (b) the amount of the company's issued share capital is diminished accordingly by the nominal value of the shares redeemed.

NOTES

Commencement: 1 October 2009.

[1.689]
689 Notice to registrar of redemption

(1) If a limited company redeems any redeemable shares it must within one month after doing so give notice to the registrar, specifying the shares redeemed.

(2) The notice must be accompanied by a statement of capital.

(3) The statement of capital must state with respect to the company's share capital immediately following the redemption—

    (a) the total number of shares of the company,

    (b) the aggregate nominal value of those shares,

    (c) for each class of shares—

        (i) prescribed particulars of the rights attached to the shares,

        (ii) the total number of shares of that class, and

        (iii) the aggregate nominal value of shares of that class, and

    (d) the amount paid up and the amount (if any) unpaid on each share (whether on account of the nominal value of the share or by way of premium).

(4) If default is made in complying with this section, an offence is committed by—

    (a) the company, and

    (b) every officer of the company who is in default.

(5) A person guilty of an offence under this section is liable on summary conviction to a fine not exceeding level 3 on the standard scale and, for continued contravention, a daily default fine not exceeding one-tenth of level 3 on the standard scale.

NOTES

Commencement: 20 January 2007 (for the purpose of enabling the exercise of powers to make Orders or Regulations by statutory instrument); 1 October 2009 (otherwise).

Commencement (transitional provisions): the Companies Act 2006 (Commencement No 8, Transitional Provisions and Savings) Order 2008, SI 2008/2860, Sch 2, para 74 (at **[2.91]**) provides that this section applies where shares are redeemed on or after 1 October 2009 (and that s 122(1)(e), (2) of the 1985 Act continue to apply where shares are redeemed before that date).

Orders: the Companies (Shares and Share Capital) Order 2009, SI 2009/388 at **[4.364]**.

CHAPTER 4

PURCHASE OF OWN SHARES

General provisions

[1.690]
690 Power of limited company to purchase own shares

(1) A limited company having a share capital may purchase its own shares (including any redeemable shares), subject to—

    (a) the following provisions of this Chapter, and

    (b) any restriction or prohibition in the company's articles.

(2) A limited company may not purchase its own shares if as a result of the purchase there would no longer be any issued shares of the company other than redeemable shares or shares held as treasury shares.

NOTES
Commencement: 1 October 2009.

[1.691]
691   Payment for purchase of own shares
(1)   A limited company may not purchase its own shares unless they are fully paid.
(2)   Where a limited company purchases its own shares, the shares must be paid for on purchase.

NOTES
Commencement: 1 October 2009.

[1.692]
692   Financing of purchase of own shares
(1)   A private limited company may purchase its own shares out of capital in accordance with Chapter 5.
(2)   Subject to that—
   (a)   a limited company may only purchase its own shares out of—
      (i)   distributable profits of the company, or
      (ii)   the proceeds of a fresh issue of shares made for the purpose of financing the purchase, and
   (b)   any premium payable on the purchase by a limited company of its own shares must be paid out of distributable profits of the company, subject to subsection (3).
(3)   If the shares to be purchased were issued at a premium, any premium payable on their purchase by the company may be paid out of the proceeds of a fresh issue of shares made for the purpose of financing the purchase, up to an amount equal to—
   (a)   the aggregate of the premiums received by the company on the issue of the shares purchased, or
   (b)   the current amount of the company's share premium account (including any sum transferred to that account in respect of premiums on the new shares),
whichever is the less.
(4)   The amount of the company's share premium account is reduced by a sum corresponding (or by sums in the aggregate corresponding) to the amount of any payment made under subsection (3).
(5)   This section has effect subject to section 735(4) (terms of purchase enforceable in a winding up).

NOTES
Commencement: 1 October 2009.

Authority for purchase of own shares

[1.693]
693   Authority for purchase of own shares
(1)   A limited company may only purchase its own shares—
   (a)   by an off-market purchase, in pursuance of a contract approved in advance in accordance with section 694;
   (b)   by a market purchase, authorised in accordance with section 701.
(2)   A purchase is "off-market" if the shares either—
   (a)   are purchased otherwise than on a recognised investment exchange, or
   (b)   are purchased on a recognised investment exchange but are not subject to a marketing arrangement on the exchange.
(3)   For this purpose a company's shares are subject to a marketing arrangement on a recognised investment exchange if—
   (a)   they are listed under Part 6 of the Financial Services and Markets Act 2000 (c 8), or
   (b)   the company has been afforded facilities for dealings in the shares to take place on the exchange—
      (i)   without prior permission for individual transactions from the authority governing that investment exchange, and
      (ii)   without limit as to the time during which those facilities are to be available.
(4)   A purchase is a "market purchase" if it is made on a recognised investment exchange and is not an off-market purchase by virtue of subsection (2)(b).
(5)   In this section "recognised investment exchange" means a recognised investment exchange (within the meaning of Part 18 of the Financial Services and Markets Act 2000) other than an overseas exchange (within the meaning of that Part).

NOTES
Commencement: 1 October 2009.
Commencement (transitional provisions): Sch 2, paras 75, 76 to the Companies Act 2006 (Commencement No 8, Transitional Provisions and Savings) Order 2008, SI 2008/2860 (at **[2.91]**) provide as follows—

"Purchase of own shares (ss 690 to 708)

75.　Where immediately before 1st October 2009 a resolution is in force having been passed under any provision of—

　(a)　section 164 of the 1985 Act or Article 174 of the 1986 Order (authority for off-market purchase),

　(b)　section 165 of the 1985 Act or Article 175 of the 1986 Order (authority for contingent purchase contract),

　(c)　section 166 of the 1985 Act or Article 176 of the 1986 Order (authority for market purchase), or

　(d)　section 167(2) of the 1985 Act or Article 177(2) of the 1986 Order (release of company's right to purchase own shares),

the resolution has effect on and after that date as if passed under the corresponding provision of the Companies Act 2006 and may be varied, revoked or renewed from time to time accordingly.

76.—(1)　Sections 693(1)(a) and 694 of the Companies Act 2006 (purchase of own shares: authority for off-market purchase) apply—

　(a)　to contracts entered into on or after 1st October 2009, and

　(b)　to contracts entered into before that date that—

　　(i)　provide that no shares may be purchased in pursuance of the contract until its terms have been authorised by a special resolution of the company, and

　　(ii)　are authorised by a special resolution passed on or after that date.

(2)　Sections 164 and 165 of the 1985 Act or Articles 174 and 175 of the 1986 Order continue to apply to any other contract entered into before that date.".

Authority for off-market purchase

[1.694]

694　Authority for off-market purchase

(1)　A company may only make an off-market purchase of its own shares in pursuance of a contract approved prior to the purchase in accordance with this section.

(2)　Either—

　(a)　the terms of the contract must be authorised by a special resolution of the company before the contract is entered into, or

　(b)　the contract must provide that no shares may be purchased in pursuance of the contract until its terms have been authorised by a special resolution of the company.

(3)　The contract may be a contract, entered into by the company and relating to shares in the company, that does not amount to a contract to purchase the shares but under which the company may (subject to any conditions) become entitled or obliged to purchase the shares.

(4)　The authority conferred by a resolution under this section may be varied, revoked or from time to time renewed by a special resolution of the company.

(5)　In the case of a public company a resolution conferring, varying or renewing authority must specify a date on which the authority is to expire, which must not be later than [five years] after the date on which the resolution is passed.

(6)　A resolution conferring, varying, revoking or renewing authority under this section is subject to—

　section 695 (exercise of voting rights), and

　section 696 (disclosure of details of contract).

NOTES

Commencement: 1 October 2009.

Commencement (transitional provisions): see the note to s 693 at **[1.693]**.

Sub-s (5): words in square brackets substituted by the Companies (Share Capital and Acquisition by Company of its Own Shares) Regulations 2009, SI 2009/2022, reg 4(1), as from 1 October 2009.

[1.695]

695　Resolution authorising off-market purchase: exercise of voting rights

(1)　This section applies to a resolution to confer, vary, revoke or renew authority for the purposes of section 694 (authority for off-market purchase of own shares).

(2)　Where the resolution is proposed as a written resolution, a member who holds shares to which the resolution relates is not an eligible member.

(3)　Where the resolution is proposed at a meeting of the company, it is not effective if—

　(a)　any member of the company holding shares to which the resolution relates exercises the voting rights carried by any of those shares in voting on the resolution, and

　(b)　the resolution would not have been passed if he had not done so.

(4)　For this purpose—

　(a)　a member who holds shares to which the resolution relates is regarded as exercising the voting rights carried by those shares not only if he votes in respect of them on a poll on the question whether the resolution shall be passed, but also if he votes on the resolution otherwise than on a poll;

　(b)　any member of the company may demand a poll on that question;

　(c)　a vote and a demand for a poll by a person as proxy for a member are the same respectively as a vote and a demand by the member.

NOTES

Commencement: 1 October 2009.

Commencement (transitional provisions): see the note to s 693 at **[1.693]**.

[1.696]
696 Resolution authorising off-market purchase: disclosure of details of contract
(1)   This section applies in relation to a resolution to confer, vary, revoke or renew authority for the purposes of section 694 (authority for off-market purchase of own shares).
(2)   A copy of the contract (if it is in writing) or a memorandum setting out its terms (if it is not) must be made available to members—
  (a)   in the case of a written resolution, by being sent or submitted to every eligible member at or before the time at which the proposed resolution is sent or submitted to him;
  (b)   in the case of a resolution at a meeting, by being made available for inspection by members of the company both—
    (i)   at the company's registered office for not less than 15 days ending with the date of the meeting, and
    (ii)   at the meeting itself.
(3)   A memorandum of contract terms so made available must include the names of the members holding shares to which the contract relates.
(4)   A copy of the contract so made available must have annexed to it a written memorandum specifying such of those names as do not appear in the contract itself.
(5)   The resolution is not validly passed if the requirements of this section are not complied with.

NOTES
Commencement: 1 October 2009.
Commencement (transitional provisions): see the note to s 693 at **[1.693]**.

[1.697]
697 Variation of contract for off-market purchase
(1)   A company may only agree to a variation of a contract authorised under section 694 (authority for off-market purchase) if the variation is approved in advance in accordance with this section.
(2)   The terms of the variation must be authorised by a special resolution of the company before it is agreed to.
(3)   That authority may be varied, revoked or from time to time renewed by a special resolution of the company.
(4)   In the case of a public company a resolution conferring, varying or renewing authority must specify a date on which the authority is to expire, which must not be later than [five years] after the date on which the resolution is passed.
(5)   A resolution conferring, varying, revoking or renewing authority under this section is subject to—
     section 698 (exercise of voting rights), and
     section 699 (disclosure of details of variation).

NOTES
Commencement: 1 October 2009.
Commencement (transitional provisions): see the note to s 693 at **[1.693]**.
Sub-s (4): words in square brackets substituted by the Companies (Share Capital and Acquisition by Company of its Own Shares) Regulations 2009, SI 2009/2022, reg 4(1), as from 1 October 2009.

[1.698]
698 Resolution authorising variation: exercise of voting rights
(1)   This section applies to a resolution to confer, vary, revoke or renew authority for the purposes of section 697 (variation of contract for off-market purchase of own shares).
(2)   Where the resolution is proposed as a written resolution, a member who holds shares to which the resolution relates is not an eligible member.
(3)   Where the resolution is proposed at a meeting of the company, it is not effective if—
  (a)   any member of the company holding shares to which the resolution relates exercises the voting rights carried by any of those shares in voting on the resolution, and
  (b)   the resolution would not have been passed if he had not done so.
(4)   For this purpose—
  (a)   a member who holds shares to which the resolution relates is regarded as exercising the voting rights carried by those shares not only if he votes in respect of them on a poll on the question whether the resolution shall be passed, but also if he votes on the resolution otherwise than on a poll;
  (b)   any member of the company may demand a poll on that question;
  (c)   a vote and a demand for a poll by a person as proxy for a member are the same respectively as a vote and a demand by the member.

NOTES
Commencement: 1 October 2009.
Commencement (transitional provisions): see the note to s 693 at **[1.693]**.

[1.699]
699   Resolution authorising variation: disclosure of details of variation
(1)   This section applies in relation to a resolution under section 697 (variation of contract for off-market purchase of own shares).
(2)   A copy of the proposed variation (if it is in writing) or a written memorandum giving details of the proposed variation (if it is not) must be made available to members—
  (a)   in the case of a written resolution, by being sent or submitted to every eligible member at or before the time at which the proposed resolution is sent or submitted to him;
  (b)   in the case of a resolution at a meeting, by being made available for inspection by members of the company both—
    (i)   at the company's registered office for not less than 15 days ending with the date of the meeting, and
    (ii)   at the meeting itself.
(3)   There must also be made available as mentioned in subsection (2) a copy of the original contract or, as the case may be, a memorandum of its terms, together with any variations previously made.
(4)   A memorandum of the proposed variation so made available must include the names of the members holding shares to which the variation relates.
(5)   A copy of the proposed variation so made available must have annexed to it a written memorandum specifying such of those names as do not appear in the variation itself.
(6)   The resolution is not validly passed if the requirements of this section are not complied with.

NOTES
Commencement: 1 October 2009.
Commencement (transitional provisions): see the note to s 693 at **[1.693]**.

[1.700]
700   Release of company's rights under contract for off-market purchase
(1)   An agreement by a company to release its rights under a contract approved under section 694 (authorisation of off-market purchase) is void unless the terms of the release agreement are approved in advance in accordance with this section.
(2)   The terms of the proposed agreement must be authorised by a special resolution of the company before the agreement is entered into.
(3)   That authority may be varied, revoked or from time to time renewed by a special resolution of the company.
(4)   In the case of a public company a resolution conferring, varying or renewing authority must specify a date on which the authority is to expire, which must not be later than [five years] after the date on which the resolution is passed.
(5)   The provisions of—
    section 698 (exercise of voting rights), and
    section 699 (disclosure of details of variation),
apply to a resolution authorising a proposed release agreement as they apply to a resolution authorising a proposed variation.

NOTES
Commencement: 1 October 2009.
Commencement (transitional provisions): see the note to s 693 at **[1.693]**.
Sub-s (4): words in square brackets substituted by the Companies (Share Capital and Acquisition by Company of its Own Shares) Regulations 2009, SI 2009/2022, reg 4(1), as from 1 October 2009.

Authority for market purchase

[1.701]
701   Authority for market purchase
(1)   A company may only make a market purchase of its own shares if the purchase has first been authorised by a resolution of the company.
(2)   That authority—
  (a)   may be general or limited to the purchase of shares of a particular class or description, and
  (b)   may be unconditional or subject to conditions.
(3)   The authority must—
  (a)   specify the maximum number of shares authorised to be acquired, and
  (b)   determine both the maximum and minimum prices that may be paid for the shares.
(4)   The authority may be varied, revoked or from time to time renewed by a resolution of the company.
(5)   A resolution conferring, varying or renewing authority must specify a date on which it is to expire, which must not be later than [five years] after the date on which the resolution is passed.
(6)   A company may make a purchase of its own shares after the expiry of the time limit specified if—
  (a)   the contract of purchase was concluded before the authority expired, and

    (b)   the terms of the authority permitted the company to make a contract of purchase that would or might be executed wholly or partly after its expiration.

(7)   A resolution to confer or vary authority under this section may determine either or both the maximum and minimum price for purchase by—

    (a)   specifying a particular sum, or

    (b)   providing a basis or formula for calculating the amount of the price (but without reference to any person's discretion or opinion).

(8)   Chapter 3 of Part 3 (resolutions affecting a company's constitution) applies to a resolution under this section.

NOTES

Commencement: 1 October 2009.

Commencement (transitional provisions): see the note to s 693 at **[1.693]**.

Sub-s (5): words in square brackets substituted by the Companies (Share Capital and Acquisition by Company of its Own Shares) Regulations 2009, SI 2009/2022, reg 4(2), as from 1 October 2009.

Supplementary provisions

[1.702]
702 Copy of contract or memorandum to be available for inspection

(1)   This section applies where a company has entered into—

    (a)   a contract approved under section 694 (authorisation of contract for off-market purchase), or

    (b)   a contract for a purchase authorised under section 701 (authorisation of market purchase).

(2)   The company must keep available for inspection—

    (a)   a copy of the contract, or

    (b)   if the contract is not in writing, a written memorandum setting out its terms.

(3)   The copy or memorandum must be kept available for inspection from the conclusion of the contract until the end of the period of ten years beginning with—

    (a)   the date on which the purchase of all the shares in pursuance of the contract is completed, or

    (b)   the date on which the contract otherwise determines.

(4)   The copy or memorandum must be kept available for inspection—

    (a)   at the company's registered office, or

    (b)   at a place specified in regulations under section 1136.

(5)   The company must give notice to the registrar—

    (a)   of the place at which the copy or memorandum is kept available for inspection, and

    (b)   of any change in that place,

unless it has at all times been kept at the company's registered office.

(6)   Every copy or memorandum required to be kept under this section must be kept open to inspection without charge—

    (a)   by any member of the company, and

    (b)   in the case of a public company, by any other person.

(7)   The provisions of this section apply to a variation of a contract as they apply to the original contract.

NOTES

Commencement: 1 October 2009.

[1.703]
703 Enforcement of right to inspect copy or memorandum

(1)   If default is made in complying with section 702(2), (3) or (4) or default is made for 14 days in complying with section 702(5), or an inspection required under section 702(6) is refused, an offence is committed by—

    (a)   the company, and

    (b)   every officer of the company who is in default.

(2)   A person guilty of an offence under this section is liable on summary conviction to a fine not exceeding level 3 on the standard scale and, for continued contravention, a daily default fine not exceeding one-tenth of level 3 on the standard scale.

(3)   In the case of refusal of an inspection required under section 702(6) the court may by order compel an immediate inspection.

NOTES

Commencement: 1 October 2009.

[1.704]
704 No assignment of company's right to purchase own shares

The rights of a company under a contract authorised under—

    (a)   section 694 (authority for off-market purchase), or

    (b)   section 701 (authority for market purchase)

are not capable of being assigned.

NOTES
Commencement: 1 October 2009.

[1.705]
705   Payments apart from purchase price to be made out of distributable profits
(1)   A payment made by a company in consideration of—
  (a)   acquiring any right with respect to the purchase of its own shares in pursuance of a contingent purchase contract approved under section 694 (authorisation of off-market purchase),
  (b)   the variation of any contract approved under that section, or
  (c)   the release of any of the company's obligations with respect to the purchase of any of its own shares under a contract—
    (i)   approved under section 694, or
    (ii)   authorised under section 701 (authorisation of market purchase),
must be made out of the company's distributable profits.
(2)   If this requirement is not met in relation to a contract, then—
  (a)   in a case within subsection (1)(a), no purchase by the company of its own shares in pursuance of that contract may be made under this Chapter;
  (b)   in a case within subsection (1)(b), no such purchase following the variation may be made under this Chapter;
  (c)   in a case within subsection (1)(c), the purported release is void.

NOTES
Commencement: 1 October 2009.

[1.706]
706   Treatment of shares purchased
Where a limited company makes a purchase of its own shares in accordance with this Chapter, then—
  (a)   if section 724 (treasury shares) applies, the shares may be held and dealt with in accordance with Chapter 6;
  (b)   if that section does not apply—
    (i)   the shares are treated as cancelled, and
    (ii)   the amount of the company's issued share capital is diminished accordingly by the nominal value of the shares cancelled.

NOTES
Commencement: 1 October 2009.

[1.707]
707   Return to registrar of purchase of own shares
(1)   Where a company purchases shares under this Chapter, it must deliver a return to the registrar within the period of 28 days beginning with the date on which the shares are delivered to it.
(2)   The return must distinguish—
  (a)   shares in relation to which section 724 (treasury shares) applies and shares in relation to which that section does not apply, and
  (b)   shares in relation to which that section applies—
    (i)   that are cancelled forthwith (under section 729 (cancellation of treasury shares)), and
    (ii)   that are not so cancelled.
(3)   The return must state, with respect to shares of each class purchased—
  (a)   the number and nominal value of the shares, and
  (b)   the date on which they were delivered to the company.
(4)   In the case of a public company the return must also state—
  (a)   the aggregate amount paid by the company for the shares, and
  (b)   the maximum and minimum prices paid in respect of shares of each class purchased.
(5)   Particulars of shares delivered to the company on different dates and under different contracts may be included in a single return.
    In such a case the amount required to be stated under subsection (4)(a) is the aggregate amount paid by the company for all the shares to which the return relates.
(6)   If default is made in complying with this section an offence is committed by every officer of the company who is in default.
(7)   A person guilty of an offence under this section is liable—
  (a)   on conviction on indictment, to a fine;
  (b)   on summary conviction to a fine not exceeding the statutory maximum and, for continued contravention, a daily default fine not exceeding one-tenth of the statutory maximum.

NOTES
Commencement: 1 October 2009.

Commencement (transitional provisions): Sch 2, para 77 to the Companies Act 2006 (Commencement No 8, Transitional Provisions and Savings) Order 2008, SI 2008/2860 (at **[2.91]**) provides that this section and s 708 apply in relation to shares delivered to the company on or after 1 October 2009 (and that s 169 of the 1985 Act continues to apply in relation to shares delivered to the company before that date).

[1.708]
708 Notice to registrar of cancellation of shares
(1) If on the purchase by a company of any of its own shares in accordance with this Part—
   (a)   section 724 (treasury shares) does not apply (so that the shares are treated as cancelled), or
   (b)   that section applies but the shares are cancelled forthwith (under section 729 (cancellation of treasury shares)),
the company must give notice of cancellation to the registrar, within the period of 28 days beginning with the date on which the shares are delivered to it, specifying the shares cancelled.
(2) The notice must be accompanied by a statement of capital.
(3) The statement of capital must state with respect to the company's share capital immediately following the cancellation—
   (a)   the total number of shares of the company,
   (b)   the aggregate nominal value of those shares,
   (c)   for each class of shares—
      (i)   prescribed particulars of the rights attached to the shares,
      (ii)   the total number of shares of that class, and
      (iii)   the aggregate nominal value of shares of that class, and
   (d)   the amount paid up and the amount (if any) unpaid on each share (whether on account of the nominal value of the share or by way of premium).
(4) If default is made in complying with this section, an offence is committed by—
   (a)   the company, and
   (b)   every officer of the company who is in default.
(5) A person guilty of an offence under this section is liable on summary conviction to a fine not exceeding level 3 on the standard scale and, for continued contravention, a daily default fine not exceeding one-tenth of level 3 on the standard scale.

NOTES
Commencement: 20 January 2007 (for the purpose of enabling the exercise of powers to make Orders or Regulations by statutory instrument); 1 October 2009 (otherwise).
Commencement (transitional provisions): see the note to s 707 at **[1.707]**.
Orders: the Companies (Shares and Share Capital) Order 2009, SI 2009/388 at **[4.364]**.

CHAPTER 5
REDEMPTION OR PURCHASE BY PRIVATE COMPANY OUT OF CAPITAL

Introductory

[1.709]
709 Power of private limited company to redeem or purchase own shares out of capital
(1) A private limited company may in accordance with this Chapter, but subject to any restriction or prohibition in the company's articles, make a payment in respect of the redemption or purchase of its own shares otherwise than out of distributable profits or the proceeds of a fresh issue of shares.
(2) References below in this Chapter to payment out of capital are to any payment so made, whether or not it would be regarded apart from this section as a payment out of capital.

NOTES
Commencement: 1 October 2009.
Commencement (transitional provisions): Sch 2, para 78 to the Companies Act 2006 (Commencement No 8, Transitional Provisions and Savings) Order 2008, SI 2008/2860 (at **[2.91]**) provides as follows—

> **"Power of private company to redeem or purchase own shares out of capital (ss 709 to 723)**
> 78.—(1) Sections 709 to 723 of the Companies Act 2006 (redemption or purchase by private company out of capital) apply where the directors' statement referred to in section 714 is made on or after 1st October 2009.
> (2) Sections 171 to 178 of the 1985 Act or Articles 181 to 188 of the 1986 Order continue to apply where the statutory declaration required by section 173(3) or Article 183(3) was made before that date.".

The permissible capital payment

[1.710]
710 The permissible capital payment
(1) The payment that may, in accordance with this Chapter, be made by a company out of capital in respect of the redemption or purchase of its own shares is such amount as, after applying for that purpose—
   (a)   any available profits of the company, and
   (b)   the proceeds of any fresh issue of shares made for the purposes of the redemption or purchase,

is required to meet the price of redemption or purchase.

(2)   That is referred to below in this Chapter as "the permissible capital payment" for the shares.

NOTES
Commencement: 1 October 2009.
Commencement (transitional provisions): see the note to s 709 at **[1.709]**.

[1.711]
711   Available profits
(1)   For the purposes of this Chapter the available profits of the company, in relation to the redemption or purchase of any shares, are the profits of the company that are available for distribution (within the meaning of Part 23).

(2)   But the question whether a company has any profits so available, and the amount of any such profits, shall be determined in accordance with section 712 instead of in accordance with sections 836 to 842 in that Part.

NOTES
Commencement: 1 October 2009.
Commencement (transitional provisions): see the note to s 709 at **[1.709]**.

[1.712]
712   Determination of available profits
(1)   The available profits of the company are determined as follows.

(2)   First, determine the profits of the company by reference to the following items as stated in the relevant accounts—
   (a)   profits, losses, assets and liabilities,
   (b)   provisions of the following kinds—
      (i)   where the relevant accounts are Companies Act accounts, provisions of a kind specified for the purposes of this subsection by regulations under section 396;
      (ii)   where the relevant accounts are IAS accounts, provisions of any kind;
   (c)   share capital and reserves (including undistributable reserves).

(3)   Second, reduce the amount so determined by the amount of—
   (a)   any distribution lawfully made by the company, and
   (b)   any other relevant payment lawfully made by the company out of distributable profits,
after the date of the relevant accounts and before the end of the relevant period.

(4)   For this purpose "other relevant payment lawfully made" includes—
   (a)   financial assistance lawfully given out of distributable profits in accordance with Chapter 2,
   (b)   payments lawfully made out of distributable profits in respect of the purchase by the company of any shares in the company, and
   (c)   payments of any description specified in section 705 (payments other than purchase price to be made out of distributable profits) lawfully made by the company.

(5)   The resulting figure is the amount of available profits.

(6)   For the purposes of this section "the relevant accounts" are any accounts that—
   (a)   are prepared as at a date within the relevant period, and
   (b)   are such as to enable a reasonable judgment to be made as to the amounts of the items mentioned in subsection (2).

(7)   In this section "the relevant period" means the period of three months ending with the date on which the directors' statement is made in accordance with section 714.

NOTES
Commencement: 1 October 2009.
Commencement (transitional provisions): see the note to s 709 at **[1.709]**.
Regulations under section 396: see the notes to that section at **[1.396]**. See also the Small Companies and Groups (Accounts and Directors' Report) Regulations 2008, SI 2008/409, reg 12 (at **[4.153]**), and the Large and Medium-sized Companies and Groups (Accounts and Reports) Regulations 2008, SI 2008/410, reg 12 (at **[4.181]**) which provide that Sch 7 to SI 2008/409 (at **[4.167]**, **[4.168]**) and Sch 9 to SI 2008/410 (at **[4.217]**, **[4.218]**) define "provisions" for the purpose of those Regulations and for the purposes of sub-s (2)(b)(i) above.

Requirements for payment out of capital

[1.713]
713   Requirements for payment out of capital
(1)   A payment out of capital by a private company for the redemption or purchase of its own shares is not lawful unless the requirements of the following sections are met—
   section 714 (directors' statement and auditor's report);
   section 716 (approval by special resolution);
   section 719 (public notice of proposed payment);
   section 720 (directors' statement and auditor's report to be available for inspection).

(2)   This is subject to any order of the court under section 721 (power of court to extend period for compliance on application by persons objecting to payment).

NOTES

Commencement: 1 October 2009.

Commencement (transitional provisions): see the note to s 709 at **[1.709]**.

[1.714]

714 Directors' statement and auditor's report

(1) The company's directors must make a statement in accordance with this section.

(2) The statement must specify the amount of the permissible capital payment for the shares in question.

(3) It must state that, having made full inquiry into the affairs and prospects of the company, the directors have formed the opinion—

(a) as regards its initial situation immediately following the date on which the payment out of capital is proposed to be made, that there will be no grounds on which the company could then be found unable to pay its debts, and

(b) as regards its prospects for the year immediately following that date, that having regard to—

(i) their intentions with respect to the management of the company's business during that year, and

(ii) the amount and character of the financial resources that will in their view be available to the company during that year,

the company will be able to continue to carry on business as a going concern (and will accordingly be able to pay its debts as they fall due) throughout that year.

(4) In forming their opinion for the purposes of subsection (3)(a), the directors must take into account all of the company's liabilities (including any contingent or prospective liabilities).

(5) The directors' statement must be in the prescribed form and must contain such information with respect to the nature of the company's business as may be prescribed.

(6) It must in addition have annexed to it a report addressed to the directors by the company's auditor stating that—

(a) he has inquired into the company's state of affairs,

(b) the amount specified in the statement as the permissible capital payment for the shares in question is in his view properly determined in accordance with sections 710 to 712, and

(c) he is not aware of anything to indicate that the opinion expressed by the directors in their statement as to any of the matters mentioned in subsection (3) above is unreasonable in all the circumstances.

NOTES

Commencement: 20 January 2007 (for the purpose of enabling the exercise of powers to make Orders or Regulations by statutory instrument); 1 October 2009 (otherwise).

Commencement (transitional provisions): see the note to s 709 at **[1.709]**.

Orders: the Companies (Shares and Share Capital) Order 2009, SI 2009/388 at **[4.364]**.

[1.715]

715 Directors' statement: offence if no reasonable grounds for opinion

(1) If the directors make a statement under section 714 without having reasonable grounds for the opinion expressed in it, an offence is committed by every director who is in default.

(2) A person guilty of an offence under this section is liable—

(a) on conviction on indictment, to imprisonment for a term not exceeding two years or a fine (or both);

(b) on summary conviction—

(i) in England and Wales, to imprisonment for a term not exceeding twelve months or a fine not exceeding the statutory maximum (or both);

(ii) in Scotland or Northern Ireland, to imprisonment for a term not exceeding six months or a fine not exceeding the statutory maximum (or both).

NOTES

Commencement: 1 October 2009.

Commencement (transitional provisions): see the note to s 709 at **[1.709]**.

Offences under this section: see further s 1131 at **[1.1131]**.

[1.716]

716 Payment to be approved by special resolution

(1) The payment out of capital must be approved by a special resolution of the company.

(2) The resolution must be passed on, or within the week immediately following, the date on which the directors make the statement required by section 714.

(3) A resolution under this section is subject to—

section 717 (exercise of voting rights), and

section 718 (disclosure of directors' statement and auditors' report).

Part 1   The Companies Act 2006

NOTES

Commencement: 1 October 2009.

Commencement (transitional provisions): see the note to s 709 at **[1.709]**.

[1.717]

717   Resolution authorising payment: exercise of voting rights

(1)   This section applies to a resolution under section 716 (authority for payment out of capital for redemption or purchase of own shares).

(2)   Where the resolution is proposed as a written resolution, a member who holds shares to which the resolution relates is not an eligible member.

(3)   Where the resolution is proposed at a meeting of the company, it is not effective if—

    (a)   any member of the company holding shares to which the resolution relates exercises the voting rights carried by any of those shares in voting on the resolution, and

    (b)   the resolution would not have been passed if he had not done so.

(4)   For this purpose—

    (a)   a member who holds shares to which the resolution relates is regarded as exercising the voting rights carried by those shares not only if he votes in respect of them on a poll on the question whether the resolution shall be passed, but also if he votes on the resolution otherwise than on a poll;

    (b)   any member of the company may demand a poll on that question;

    (c)   a vote and a demand for a poll by a person as proxy for a member are the same respectively as a vote and a demand by the member.

NOTES

Commencement: 1 October 2009.

Commencement (transitional provisions): see the note to s 709 at **[1.709]**.

[1.718]

718   Resolution authorising payment: disclosure of directors' statement and auditor's report

(1)   This section applies to a resolution under section 716 (resolution authorising payment out of capital for redemption or purchase of own shares).

(2)   A copy of the directors' statement and auditor's report under section 714 must be made available to members—

    (a)   in the case of a written resolution, by being sent or submitted to every eligible member at or before the time at which the proposed resolution is sent or submitted to him;

    (b)   in the case of a resolution at a meeting, by being made available for inspection by members of the company at the meeting.

(3)   The resolution is ineffective if this requirement is not complied with.

NOTES

Commencement: 1 October 2009.

Commencement (transitional provisions): see the note to s 709 at **[1.709]**.

[1.719]

719   Public notice of proposed payment

(1)   Within the week immediately following the date of the resolution under section 716 the company must cause to be published in the Gazette a notice—

    (a)   stating that the company has approved a payment out of capital for the purpose of acquiring its own shares by redemption or purchase or both (as the case may be),

    (b)   specifying—

        (i)   the amount of the permissible capital payment for the shares in question, and

        (ii)   the date of the resolution,

    (c)   stating where the directors' statement and auditor's report required by section 714 are available for inspection, and

    (d)   stating that any creditor of the company may at any time within the five weeks immediately following the date of the resolution apply to the court under section 721 for an order preventing the payment.

(2)   Within the week immediately following the date of the resolution the company must also either—

    (a)   cause a notice to the same effect as that required by subsection (1) to be published in an appropriate national newspaper, or

    (b)   give notice in writing to that effect to each of its creditors.

(3)   "An appropriate national newspaper" means a newspaper circulating throughout the part of the United Kingdom in which the company is registered.

(4)   Not later than the day on which the company—

    (a)   first publishes the notice required by subsection (1), or

    (b)   if earlier, first publishes or gives the notice required by subsection (2), the company must deliver to the registrar a copy of the directors' statement and auditor's report required by section 714.

NOTES

Commencement: 1 October 2009.

Commencement (transitional provisions): see the note to s 709 at **[1.709]**.

[1.720]
720   Directors' statement and auditor's report to be available for inspection
(1)   The directors' statement and auditor's report must be kept available for inspection throughout the period—
    (a)   beginning with the day on which the company—
        (i)   first publishes the notice required by section 719(1), or
        (ii)   if earlier, first publishes or gives the notice required by section 719(2), and
    (b)   ending five weeks after the date of the resolution for payment out of capital.
(2)   They must be kept available for inspection—
    (a)   at the company's registered office, or
    (b)   at a place specified in regulations under section 1136.
(3)   The company must give notice to the registrar—
    (a)   of the place at which the statement and report are kept available for inspection, and
    (b)   of any change in that place,
unless they have at all times been kept at the company's registered office.
(4)   They must be open to the inspection of any member or creditor of the company without charge.
(5)   If default is made for 14 days in complying with subsection (3), or an inspection under subsection (4) is refused, an offence is committed by—
    (a)   the company, and
    (b)   every officer of the company who is in default.
(6)   A person guilty of an offence under this section is liable on summary conviction to a fine not exceeding level 3 on the standard scale and, for continued contravention, a daily default fine not exceeding one-tenth of level 3 on the standard scale.
(7)   In the case of a refusal of an inspection required by subsection (4), the court may by order compel an immediate inspection.

NOTES

Commencement: 1 October 2009.

Commencement (transitional provisions): see the note to s 709 at **[1.709]**.

Objection to payment by members or creditors

[1.721]
721   Application to court to cancel resolution
(1)   Where a private company passes a special resolution approving a payment out of capital for the redemption or purchase of any of its shares—
    (a)   any member of the company (other than one who consented to or voted in favour of the resolution), and
    (b)   any creditor of the company,
may apply to the court for the cancellation of the resolution.
(2)   The application—
    (a)   must be made within five weeks after the passing of the resolution, and
    (b)   may be made on behalf of the persons entitled to make it by such one or more of their number as they may appoint in writing for the purpose.
(3)   On an application under this section the court may if it thinks fit—
    (a)   adjourn the proceedings in order that an arrangement may be made to the satisfaction of the court—
        (i)   for the purchase of the interests of dissentient members, or
        (ii)   for the protection of dissentient creditors, and
    (b)   give such directions and make such orders as it thinks expedient for facilitating or carrying into effect any such arrangement.
(4)   Subject to that, the court must make an order either cancelling or confirming the resolution, and may do so on such terms and conditions as it thinks fit.
(5)   If the court confirms the resolution, it may by order alter or extend any date or period of time specified—
    (a)   in the resolution, or
    (b)   in any provision of this Chapter applying to the redemption or purchase to which the resolution relates.
(6)   The court's order may, if the court thinks fit—
    (a)   provide for the purchase by the company of the shares of any of its members and for the reduction accordingly of the company's capital, and

(b)   make any alteration in the company's articles that may be required in consequence of that provision.

(7)   The court's order may, if the court thinks fit, require the company not to make any, or any specified, amendments of its articles without the leave of the court.

NOTES
Commencement: 1 October 2009.
Commencement (transitional provisions): see the note to s 709 at **[1.709]**.

[1.722]
722   Notice to registrar of court application or order

(1)   On making an application under section 721 (application to court to cancel resolution) the applicants, or the person making the application on their behalf, must immediately give notice to the registrar.

This is without prejudice to any provision of rules of court as to service of notice of the application.

(2)   On being served with notice of any such application, the company must immediately give notice to the registrar.

(3)   Within 15 days of the making of the court's order on the application, or such longer period as the court may at any time direct, the company must deliver to the registrar a copy of the order.

(4)   If a company fails to comply with subsection (2) or (3) an offence is committed by—
    (a)   the company, and
    (b)   every officer of the company who is in default.

(5)   A person guilty of an offence under this section is liable on summary conviction to a fine not exceeding level 3 on the standard scale and, for continued contravention, a daily default fine not exceeding one-tenth of level 3 on the standard scale.

NOTES
Commencement: 1 October 2009.
Commencement (transitional provisions): see the note to s 709 at **[1.709]**.

Supplementary provisions

[1.723]
723   When payment out of capital to be made

(1)   The payment out of capital must be made—
    (a)   no earlier than five weeks after the date on which the resolution under section 716 is passed, and
    (b)   no more than seven weeks after that date.

(2)   This is subject to any exercise of the court's powers under section 721(5) (power to alter or extend time where resolution confirmed after objection).

NOTES
Commencement: 1 October 2009.
Commencement (transitional provisions): see the note to s 709 at **[1.709]**.

CHAPTER 6
TREASURY SHARES

[1.724]
724   Treasury shares

(1)   This section applies where—
    (a)   a limited company makes a purchase of its own shares in accordance with Chapter 4,
    (b)   the purchase is made out of distributable profits, and
    (c)   the shares are qualifying shares.

(2)   For this purpose "qualifying shares" means shares that—
    (a)   are included in the official list in accordance with the provisions of Part 6 of the Financial Services and Markets Act 2000 (c 8),
    (b)   are traded on the market known as the Alternative Investment Market established under the rules of London Stock Exchange plc,
    (c)   are officially listed in an EEA State, or
    (d)   are traded on a regulated market.

In paragraph (a) "the official list" has the meaning given in section 103(1) of the Financial Services and Markets Act 2000.

(3)   Where this section applies the company may—
    (a)   hold the shares (or any of them), or
    (b)   deal with any of them, at any time, in accordance with section 727 or 729.

(4)   Where shares are held by the company, the company must be entered in its register of members as the member holding the shares.

(5)   In the Companies Acts references to a company holding shares as treasury shares are to the company holding shares that—

(a)   were (or are treated as having been) purchased by it in circumstances in which this section applies, and

(b)   have been held by the company continuously since they were so purchased (or treated as purchased).

NOTES
Commencement: 1 October 2009.

[1.725]
725   Treasury shares: maximum holdings
(Repealed as noted below.)

NOTES
Commencement: 1 October 2009.
Repealed by the Companies (Share Capital and Acquisition by Company of its Own Shares) Regulations 2009, SI 2009/2022, reg 5(1), as from 1 October 2009, subject to transitional provisions in paras (2), (3) of that regulation, as follows—

"(2)   Any outstanding obligation to dispose of or cancel excess shares arising under section 725(3) of that Act (duty to dispose of excess shares) shall cease to exist on 1st October 2009, whether or not the period mentioned in that provision has expired, but this is subject to paragraph (3).
(3)   This amendment does not affect any liability under section 732 of that Act (treasury shares: offences) in respect of a failure to comply with section 725(3) where the period mentioned in that provision expired before 1st October 2009.".

Editorial Note: as noted above, this section comes into force and is repealed on the same date and, in practice, events occurring before 1 October 2009 will continue to be governed by the Companies Act 1985, s 162B. The savings in paras (2), (3) above should be read with the Interpretation Act 1978, s 16(1)(e) which provides that the repeal of an enactment does not affect any investigation, legal proceeding or remedy in respect of any such right, privilege, obligation, liability, penalty, forfeiture or punishment, and any such investigation, legal proceeding or remedy may be instituted, continued or enforced, and any such penalty, forfeiture or punishment may be imposed, as if the repealing Act had not been passed

[1.726]
726   Treasury shares: exercise of rights
(1)   This section applies where shares are held by a company as treasury shares.
(2)   The company must not exercise any right in respect of the treasury shares, and any purported exercise of such a right is void.
This applies, in particular, to any right to attend or vote at meetings.
(3)   No dividend may be paid, and no other distribution (whether in cash or otherwise) of the company's assets (including any distribution of assets to members on a winding up) may be made to the company, in respect of the treasury shares.
(4)   Nothing in this section prevents—
(a)   an allotment of shares as fully paid bonus shares in respect of the treasury shares, or
(b)   the payment of any amount payable on the redemption of the treasury shares (if they are redeemable shares).
(5)   Shares allotted as fully paid bonus shares in respect of the treasury shares are treated as if purchased by the company, at the time they were allotted, in circumstances in which section 724(1) (treasury shares) applied.

NOTES
Commencement: 1 October 2009.

[1.727]
727   Treasury shares: disposal
(1)   Where shares are held as treasury shares, the company may at any time—
(a)   sell the shares (or any of them) for a cash consideration, or
(b)   transfer the shares (or any of them) for the purposes of or pursuant to an employees' share scheme.
(2)   In subsection (1)(a) "cash consideration" means—
(a)   cash received by the company, or
(b)   a cheque received by the company in good faith that the directors have no reason for suspecting will not be paid, or
(c)   a release of a liability of the company for a liquidated sum, or
(d)   an undertaking to pay cash to the company on or before a date not more than 90 days after the date on which the company agrees to sell the shares, or
(e)   payment by any other means giving rise to a present or future entitlement (of the company or a person acting on the company's behalf) to a payment, or credit equivalent to payment, in cash.
For this purpose "cash" includes foreign currency.
(3)   The Secretary of State may by order provide that particular means of payment specified in the order are to be regarded as falling within subsection (2)(e).

Part 1   The Companies Act 2006

(4) If the company receives a notice under section 979 (takeover offers: right of offeror to buy out minority shareholders) that a person desires to acquire shares held by the company as treasury shares, the company must not sell or transfer the shares to which the notice relates except to that person.

(5) An order under this section is subject to negative resolution procedure.

NOTES

Commencement: 20 January 2007 (for the purpose of enabling the exercise of powers to make Orders or Regulations by statutory instrument); 1 October 2009 (otherwise).

Commencement (transitional provisions): the Companies Act 2006 (Commencement No 8, Transitional Provisions and Savings) Order 2008, SI 2008/2860, Sch 2, para 79 (Treasury shares: disposal) at **[2.91]** provides that this section applies where the contract for the sale of the shares is entered into on or after 1 October 2009 (and that s 162D(1)(a) of the 1985 Act continues to apply where the contract for the sale of the shares was entered into before that date).

Orders: the Companies (Shares and Share Capital) Order 2009, SI 2009/388 at **[4.364]**.

[1.728]
728 Treasury shares: notice of disposal

(1) Where shares held by a company as treasury shares—
  (a) are sold, or
  (b) are transferred for the purposes of an employees' share scheme,
the company must deliver a return to the registrar not later than 28 days after the shares are disposed of.

(2) The return must state with respect to shares of each class disposed of—
  (a) the number and nominal value of the shares, and
  (b) the date on which they were disposed of.

(3) Particulars of shares disposed of on different dates may be included in a single return.

(4) If default is made in complying with this section an offence is committed by every officer of the company who is in default.

(5) A person guilty of an offence under this section is liable—
  (a) on conviction on indictment, to a fine;
  (b) on summary conviction, to a fine not exceeding the statutory maximum and, for continued contravention, a daily default fine not exceeding one-tenth of the statutory maximum.

NOTES

Commencement: 1 October 2009.

[1.729]
729 Treasury shares: cancellation

(1) Where shares are held as treasury shares, the company may at any time cancel the shares (or any of them).

(2) If shares held as treasury shares cease to be qualifying shares, the company must forthwith cancel the shares.

(3) For this purpose shares are not to be regarded as ceasing to be qualifying shares by virtue only of—
  (a) the suspension of their listing in accordance with the applicable rules in the EEA State in which the shares are officially listed, or
  (b) the suspension of their trading in accordance with—
    (i) in the case of shares traded on the market known as the Alternative Investment Market, the rules of London Stock Exchange plc, and
    (ii) in any other case, the rules of the regulated market on which they are traded.

(4) If company cancels shares held as treasury shares, the amount of the company's share capital is reduced accordingly by the nominal amount of the shares cancelled.

(5) The directors may take any steps required to enable the company to cancel its shares under this section without complying with the provisions of Chapter 10 of Part 17 (reduction of share capital).

NOTES

Commencement: 1 October 2009.

[1.730]
730 Treasury shares: notice of cancellation

(1) Where shares held by a company as treasury shares are cancelled, the company must deliver a return to the registrar not later than 28 days after the shares are cancelled.

This does not apply to shares that are cancelled forthwith on their acquisition by the company (see section 708).

(2) The return must state with respect to shares of each class cancelled—
  (a) the number and nominal value of the shares, and
  (b) the date on which they were cancelled.

(3) Particulars of shares cancelled on different dates may be included in a single return.

(4) The notice must be accompanied by a statement of capital.

(5) The statement of capital must state with respect to the company's share capital immediately following the cancellation—

    (a) the total number of shares of the company,

    (b) the aggregate nominal value of those shares,

    (c) for each class of shares—

        (i) prescribed particulars of the rights attached to the shares,

        (ii) the total number of shares of that class, and

        (iii) the aggregate nominal value of shares of that class, and

    (d) the amount paid up and the amount (if any) unpaid on each share (whether on account of the nominal value of the share or by way of premium).

(6) If default is made in complying with this section, an offence is committed by—

    (a) the company, and

    (b) every officer of the company who is in default.

(7) A person guilty of an offence under this section is liable on summary conviction to a fine not exceeding level 3 on the standard scale and, for continued contravention, a daily default fine not exceeding one-tenth of level 3 on the standard scale.

NOTES

Commencement: 20 January 2007 (for the purpose of enabling the exercise of powers to make Orders or Regulations by statutory instrument); 1 October 2009 (otherwise).

Commencement (transitional provisions): the Companies Act 2006 (Commencement No 8, Transitional Provisions and Savings) Order 2008, SI 2008/2860, Sch 2, para 80 (Treasury shares: notice of cancellation) at **[2.91]** provides that this section applies to shares cancelled on or after 1 October 2009 (and that s 169A of the 1985 Act continues to apply to shares cancelled before that date).

Orders: the Companies (Shares and Share Capital) Order 2009, SI 2009/388 at **[4.364]**.

[1.731]
731 Treasury shares: treatment of proceeds of sale

(1) Where shares held as treasury shares are sold, the proceeds of sale must be dealt with in accordance with this section.

(2) If the proceeds of sale are equal to or less than the purchase price paid by the company for the shares, the proceeds are treated for the purposes of Part 23 (distributions) as a realised profit of the company.

(3) If the proceeds of sale exceed the purchase price paid by the company—

    (a) an amount equal to the purchase price paid is treated as a realised profit of the company for the purposes of that Part, and

    (b) the excess must be transferred to the company's share premium account.

(4) For the purposes of this section—

    (a) the purchase price paid by the company must be determined by the application of a weighted average price method, and

    (b) if the shares were allotted to the company as fully paid bonus shares, the purchase price paid for them is treated as nil.

NOTES

Commencement: 1 October 2009.

[1.732]
732 Treasury shares: offences

(1) If a company contravenes any of the provisions of this Chapter (except section 730 (notice of cancellation)), an offence is committed by—

    (a) the company, and

    (b) every officer of the company who is in default.

(2) A person guilty of an offence under this section is liable—

    (a) on conviction on indictment, to a fine;

    (b) on summary conviction to a fine not exceeding the statutory maximum.

NOTES

Commencement: 1 October 2009.

CHAPTER 7
SUPPLEMENTARY PROVISIONS

[1.733]
733 The capital redemption reserve

(1) In the following circumstances a company must transfer amounts to a reserve, called the "capital redemption reserve".

(2) Where under this Part shares of a limited company are redeemed or purchased wholly out of the company's profits, the amount by which the company's issued share capital is diminished in accordance with—

    (a) section 688(b) (on the cancellation of shares redeemed), or

    (b)   section 706(b)(ii) (on the cancellation of shares purchased),

must be transferred to the capital redemption reserve.

(3)   If—

    (a)   the shares are redeemed or purchased wholly or partly out of the proceeds of a fresh issue, and

    (b)   the aggregate amount of the proceeds is less than the aggregate nominal value of the shares redeemed or purchased,

the amount of the difference must be transferred to the capital redemption reserve.

This does not apply in the case of a private company if, in addition to the proceeds of the fresh issue, the company applies a payment out of capital under Chapter 5 in making the redemption or purchase.

(4)   The amount by which a company's share capital is diminished in accordance with section 729(4) (on the cancellation of shares held as treasury shares) must be transferred to the capital redemption reserve.

(5)   The company may use the capital redemption reserve to pay up new shares to be allotted to members as fully paid bonus shares.

(6)   Subject to that, the provisions of the Companies Acts relating to the reduction of a company's share capital apply as if the capital redemption reserve were part of its paid up share capital.

NOTES

Commencement: 1 October 2008 (certain purposes); 1 October 2009 (otherwise) (see the note below).

Commencement (note): the Companies Act 2006 (Commencement No 7, Transitional Provisions and Savings) Order 2008, SI 2008/1886, art 2(c) provides that sub-ss (5), (6) shall come into force on 1 October 2008 so far as relating to a reduction of capital under ss 641(1)(a), (2)–(6), 642–644 of this Act (see **[2.76]**).

[1.734]
734   Accounting consequences of payment out of capital

(1)   This section applies where a payment out of capital is made in accordance with Chapter 5 (redemption or purchase of own shares by private company out of capital).

(2)   If the permissible capital payment is less than the nominal amount of the shares redeemed or purchased, the amount of the difference must be transferred to the company's capital redemption reserve.

(3)   If the permissible capital payment is greater than the nominal amount of the shares redeemed or purchased—

    (a)   the amount of any capital redemption reserve, share premium account or fully paid share capital of the company, and

    (b)   any amount representing unrealised profits of the company for the time being standing to the credit of any revaluation reserve maintained by the company,

may be reduced by a sum not exceeding (or by sums not in total exceeding) the amount by which the permissible capital payment exceeds the nominal amount of the shares.

(4)   Where the proceeds of a fresh issue are applied by the company in making a redemption or purchase of its own shares in addition to a payment out of capital under this Chapter, the references in subsections (2) and (3) to the permissible capital payment are to be read as referring to the aggregate of that payment and those proceeds.

NOTES

Commencement: 1 October 2009.

[1.735]
735   Effect of company's failure to redeem or purchase

(1)   This section applies where a company—

    (a)   issues shares on terms that they are or are liable to be redeemed, or

    (b)   agrees to purchase any of its shares.

(2)   The company is not liable in damages in respect of any failure on its part to redeem or purchase any of the shares.

This is without prejudice to any right of the holder of the shares other than his right to sue the company for damages in respect of its failure.

(3)   The court shall not grant an order for specific performance of the terms of redemption or purchase if the company shows that it is unable to meet the costs of redeeming or purchasing the shares in question out of distributable profits.

(4)   If the company is wound up and at the commencement of the winding up any of the shares have not been redeemed or purchased, the terms of redemption or purchase may be enforced against the company.

When shares are redeemed or purchased under this subsection, they are treated as cancelled.

(5)   Subsection (4) does not apply if—

    (a)   the terms provided for the redemption or purchase to take place at a date later than that of the commencement of the winding up, or

    (b)   during the period—

> (i)   beginning with the date on which the redemption or purchase was to have taken place, and
>
> (ii)   ending with the commencement of the winding up,
>
> the company could not at any time have lawfully made a distribution equal in value to the price at which the shares were to have been redeemed or purchased.

(6)   There shall be paid in priority to any amount that the company is liable under subsection (4) to pay in respect of any shares—

(a)   all other debts and liabilities of the company (other than any due to members in their character as such), and

(b)   if other shares carry rights (whether as to capital or as to income) that are preferred to the rights as to capital attaching to the first-mentioned shares, any amount due in satisfaction of those preferred rights.

Subject to that, any such amount shall be paid in priority to any amounts due to members in satisfaction of their rights (whether as to capital or income) as members.

NOTES

Commencement: 1 October 2009.

[1.736]
736   Meaning of "distributable profits"

In this Part (except in Chapter 2 (financial assistance): see section 683) "distributable profits", in relation to the making of any payment by a company, means profits out of which the company could lawfully make a distribution (within the meaning given by section 830) equal in value to the payment.

NOTES

Commencement: 1 October 2009.

[1.737]
737   General power to make further provision by regulations

(1)   The Secretary of State may by regulations modify the provisions of this Part.

(2)   The regulations may—

(a)   amend or repeal any of the provisions of this Part, or

(b)   make such other provision as appears to the Secretary of State appropriate in place of any of the provisions of this Part.

(3)   Regulations under this section may make consequential amendments or repeals in other provisions of this Act, or in other enactments.

(4)   Regulations under this section are subject to affirmative resolution procedure.

NOTES

Commencement: 20 January 2007 (for the purpose of enabling the exercise of powers to make Orders or Regulations by statutory instrument); 1 October 2009 (otherwise).

Regulations: the Companies (Share Capital and Acquisition by Company of its Own Shares) Regulations 2009, SI 2009/2022 at **[4.542]**.

PART 19
DEBENTURES

General provisions

[1.738]
738   Meaning of "debenture"

In the Companies Acts "debenture" includes debenture stock, bonds and any other securities of a company, whether or not constituting a charge on the assets of the company.

NOTES

Commencement: 6 April 2008.

[1.739]
739   Perpetual debentures

(1)   A condition contained in debentures, or in a deed for securing debentures, is not invalid by reason only that the debentures are made—

(a)   irredeemable, or

(b)   redeemable only—

> (i)   on the happening of a contingency (however remote), or
>
> (ii)   on the expiration of a period (however long),

any rule of equity to the contrary notwithstanding.

(2)   Subsection (1) applies to debentures whenever issued and to deeds whenever executed.

NOTES

Commencement: 6 April 2008.

[1.740]

740   Enforcement of contract to subscribe for debentures

A contract with a company to take up and pay for debentures of the company may be enforced by an order for specific performance.

NOTES

Commencement: 6 April 2008.

[1.741]

741   Registration of allotment of debentures

(1)   A company must register an allotment of debentures as soon as practicable and in any event within two months after the date of the allotment.

(2)   If a company fails to comply with this section, an offence is committed by—

   (a)   the company, and

   (b)   every officer of the company who is in default.

(3)   A person guilty of an offence under this section is liable on summary conviction to a fine not exceeding level 3 on the standard scale and, for continued contravention, a daily default fine not exceeding one-tenth of level 3 on the standard scale.

(4)   For the duties of the company as to the issue of the debentures, or certificates of debenture stock, see Part 21 (certification and transfer of securities)

NOTES

Commencement: 6 April 2008.

Commencement (transitional provisions): Sch 4, Pt 1, para 20 to the Companies Act 2006 (Commencement No 5, Transitional Provisions and Savings) Order 2007, SI 2007/3495 (at **[2.66]**) provides that this section applies to allotments of debentures made on or after 6 April 2008.

[1.742]

742   Debentures to bearer (Scotland)

Notwithstanding anything in the statute of the Scots Parliament of 1696, chapter 25, debentures to bearer issued in Scotland are valid and binding according to their terms.

NOTES

Commencement: 6 April 2008.

Register of debenture holders

[1.743]

743   Register of debenture holders

(1)   Any register of debenture holders of a company that is kept by the company must be kept available for inspection—

   (a)   at the company's registered office, or

   (b)   at a place specified in regulations under section 1136.

(2)   A company must give notice to the registrar of the place where any such register is kept available for inspection and of any change in that place.

(3)   No such notice is required if the register has, at all times since it came into existence, been kept available for inspection at the company's registered office.

(4)   If a company makes default for 14 days in complying with subsection (2), an offence is committed by—

   (a)   the company, and

   (b)   every officer of the company who is in default.

(5)   A person guilty of an offence under this section is liable on summary conviction to a fine not exceeding level 3 on the standard scale and, for continued contravention, a daily default fine not exceeding one-tenth of level 3 on the standard scale.

(6)   References in this section to a register of debenture holders include a duplicate—

   (a)   of a register of debenture holders that is kept outside the United Kingdom, or

   (b)   of any part of such a register.

NOTES

Commencement: 6 April 2008.

Commencement (transitional provisions): Sch 4, Pt 1, para 21 to the Companies Act 2006 (Commencement No 5, Transitional Provisions and Savings) Order 2007, SI 2007/3495 (at **[2.66]**) provides as follows—

"21.—(1)   Until regulations under section 1136 of the Companies Act 2006 come into force specifying a place for the purposes of section 743(1)(b), a company's register of debenture holders may be kept—

   (a)   at any office of the company at which the work of making it up is done, or

   (b)   if the company arranges with some other person for the making up of the register to be undertaken on its behalf by that other person, at the office of that other person at which the work is done,

provided that place is situated in the part of the United Kingdom in which the company is registered.

(2)   Until section 1068(1) of the Companies Act 2006 comes into force, the notice referred to in section 743(2) (notice of place where register of debenture holders is kept) must be given in the form prescribed for the purposes of section 190(5) of the 1985 Act or Article 199(3) of the 1986 Order.".

[1.744]

744 Register of debenture holders: right to inspect and require copy

(1) Every register of debenture holders of a company must, except when duly closed, be open to the inspection—

    (a) of the registered holder of any such debentures, or any holder of shares in the company, without charge, and

    (b) of any other person on payment of such fee as may be prescribed.

(2) Any person may require a copy of the register, or any part of it, on payment of such fee as may be prescribed.

(3) A person seeking to exercise either of the rights conferred by this section must make a request to the company to that effect.

(4) The request must contain the following information—

    (a) in the case of an individual, his name and address;

    (b) in the case of an organisation, the name and address of an individual responsible for making the request on behalf of the organisation;

    (c) the purpose for which the information is to be used; and

    (d) whether the information will be disclosed to any other person, and if so—

        (i) where that person is an individual, his name and address,

        (ii) where that person is an organisation, the name and address of an individual responsible for receiving the information on its behalf, and

        (iii) the purpose for which the information is to be used by that person.

(5) For the purposes of this section a register is "duly closed" if it is closed in accordance with provision contained—

    (a) in the articles or in the debentures,

    (b) in the case of debenture stock in the stock certificates, or

    (c) in the trust deed or other document securing the debentures or debenture stock.

The total period for which a register is closed in any year must not exceed 30 days.

(6) References in this section to a register of debenture holders include a duplicate—

    (a) of a register of debenture holders that is kept outside the United Kingdom, or

    (b) of any part of such a register.

NOTES

Commencement: 20 January 2007 (for the purpose of enabling the exercise of powers to make Orders or Regulations by statutory instrument); 6 April 2008 (otherwise).

Commencement (transitional provisions): Sch 4, Pt 1, para 22 to the Companies Act 2006 (Commencement No 5, Transitional Provisions and Savings) Order 2007, SI 2007/3495 (at **[2.66]**) provides that ss 744–747, 749 of this Act apply where the request is made on or after 6 April 2008 (and that s 191(1)–(6) of the 1985 Act continue to apply to requests made before that date).

Regulations: the Companies (Fees for Inspection and Copying of Company Records) (No 2) Regulations 2007, SI 2007/3535 at **[4.95]**.

[1.745]

745 Register of debenture holders: response to request for inspection or copy

(1) Where a company receives a request under section 744 (register of debenture holders: right to inspect and require copy), it must within five working days either—

    (a) comply with the request, or

    (b) apply to the court.

(2) If it applies to the court it must notify the person making the request.

(3) If on an application under this section the court is satisfied that the inspection or copy is not sought for a proper purpose—

    (a) it shall direct the company not to comply with the request, and

    (b) it may further order that the company's costs (in Scotland, expenses) on the application be paid in whole or in part by the person who made the request, even if he is not a party to the application.

(4) If the court makes such a direction and it appears to the court that the company is or may be subject to other requests made for a similar purpose (whether made by the same person or different persons), it may direct that the company is not to comply with any such request.

The order must contain such provision as appears to the court appropriate to identify the requests to which it applies.

(5) If on an application under this section the court does not direct the company not to comply with the request, the company must comply with the request immediately upon the court giving its decision or, as the case may be, the proceedings being discontinued.

NOTES

Commencement: 6 April 2008.

Commencement (transitional provisions): see the note to s 744 at **[1.744]**.

[1.746]
746 Register of debenture holders: refusal of inspection or default in providing copy

(1) If an inspection required under section 744 (register of debenture holders: right to inspect and require copy) is refused or default is made in providing a copy required under that section, otherwise than in accordance with an order of the court, an offence is committed by—

    (a)   the company, and

    (b)   every officer of the company who is in default.

(2) A person guilty of an offence under this section is liable on summary conviction to a fine not exceeding level 3 on the standard scale and, for continued contravention, a daily default fine not exceeding one-tenth of level 3 on the standard scale.

(3) In the case of any such refusal or default the court may by order compel an immediate inspection or, as the case may be, direct that the copy required be sent to the person requesting it.

NOTES

Commencement: 6 April 2008.

Commencement (transitional provisions): see the note to s 744 at **[1.744]**.

[1.747]
747 Register of debenture holders: offences in connection with request for or disclosure of information

(1) It is an offence for a person knowingly or recklessly to make in a request under section 744 (register of debenture holders: right to inspect and require copy) a statement that is misleading, false or deceptive in a material particular.

(2) It is an offence for a person in possession of information obtained by exercise of either of the rights conferred by that section—

    (a)   to do anything that results in the information being disclosed to another person, or

    (b)   to fail to do anything with the result that the information is disclosed to another person,

knowing, or having reason to suspect, that person may use the information for a purpose that is not a proper purpose.

(3) A person guilty of an offence under this section is liable—

    (a)   on conviction on indictment, to imprisonment for a term not exceeding two years or a fine (or both);

    (b)   on summary conviction—

        (i)   in England and Wales, to imprisonment for a term not exceeding twelve months or to a fine not exceeding the statutory maximum (or both);

        (ii)   in Scotland or Northern Ireland, to imprisonment for a term not exceeding six months, or to a fine not exceeding the statutory maximum (or both).

NOTES

Commencement: 6 April 2008.

Commencement (transitional provisions): see the note to s 744 at **[1.744]**.

Offences under this section: see further s 1131 at **[1.1131]**.

[1.748]
748 Time limit for claims arising from entry in register

(1) Liability incurred by a company—

    (a)   from the making or deletion of an entry in the register of debenture holders, or

    (b)   from a failure to make or delete any such entry,

is not enforceable more than ten years after the date on which the entry was made or deleted or, as the case may be, the failure first occurred.

(2) This is without prejudice to any lesser period of limitation (and, in Scotland, to any rule that the obligation giving rise to the liability prescribes before the expiry of that period).

NOTES

Commencement: 6 April 2008.

Commencement (transitional provisions): Sch 4, Pt 1, para 23 to the Companies Act 2006 (Commencement No 5, Transitional Provisions and Savings) Order 2007, SI 2007/3495 (at **[2.66]**) provides as follows—

    "23.—(1)   Section 748 of the Companies Act 2006 (ten year time limit for claims arising from entry in register of debenture holders) applies to causes of action arising on or after 6th April 2008.

    (2)   The time limit for causes of action arising before that date is—

        (a)   ten years from 6th April 2008, or

        (b)   20 years (as provided by section 191(7) of the 1985 Act or Article 200(7) of the 1986 Order) from when the cause of action arose,

    whichever expires first.

    (3)   This is without prejudice to any lesser period of limitation (and, in Scotland, to any rule that the obligation giving rise to the liability prescribes before the expiry of that period).".

Supplementary provisions

[1.749]

749 Right of debenture holder to copy of deed

(1)   Any holder of debentures of a company is entitled, on request and on payment of such fee as may be prescribed, to be provided with a copy of any trust deed for securing the debentures.

(2)   If default is made in complying with this section, an offence is committed by every officer of the company who is in default.

(3)   A person guilty of an offence under this section is liable on summary conviction to a fine not exceeding level 3 on the standard scale and, for continued contravention, a daily default fine not exceeding one-tenth of level 3 on the standard scale.

(4)   In the case of any such default the court may direct that the copy required be sent to the person requiring it.

NOTES

Commencement: 20 January 2007 (for the purpose of enabling the exercise of powers to make Orders or Regulations by statutory instrument); 6 April 2008 (otherwise).

Commencement (transitional provisions): see the note to s 744 at **[1.744]**.

Regulations: the Companies (Fees for Inspection and Copying of Company Records) (No 2) Regulations 2007, SI 2007/3535 at **[4.95]**.

[1.750]

750 Liability of trustees of debentures

(1)   Any provision contained in—

   (a)   a trust deed for securing an issue of debentures, or

   (b)   any contract with the holders of debentures secured by a trust deed,

is void in so far as it would have the effect of exempting a trustee of the deed from, or indemnifying him against, liability for breach of trust where he fails to show the degree of care and diligence required of him as trustee, having regard to the provisions of the trust deed conferring on him any powers, authorities or discretions.

(2)   Subsection (1) does not invalidate—

   (a)   a release otherwise validly given in respect of anything done or omitted to be done by a trustee before the giving of the release;

   (b)   any provision enabling such a release to be given—

      (i)   on being agreed to by a majority of not less than 75% in value of the debenture holders present and voting in person or, where proxies are permitted, by proxy at a meeting summoned for the purpose, and

      (ii)   either with respect to specific acts or omissions or on the trustee dying or ceasing to act.

(3)   This section is subject to section 751 (saving for certain older provisions).

NOTES

Commencement: 6 April 2008.

[1.751]

751 Liability of trustees of debentures: saving for certain older provisions

(1)   Section 750 (liability of trustees of debentures) does not operate—

   (a)   to invalidate any provision in force on the relevant date so long as any person—

      (i)   then entitled to the benefit of the provision, or

      (ii)   afterwards given the benefit of the provision under subsection (3) below,

   remains a trustee of the deed in question, or

   (b)   to deprive any person of any exemption or right to be indemnified in respect of anything done or omitted to be done by him while any such provision was in force.

(2)   The relevant date for this purpose is—

   (a)   1st July 1948 in a case where section 192 of the Companies Act 1985 (c 6) applied immediately before the commencement of this section;

   (b)   1st July 1961 in a case where Article 201 of the Companies (Northern Ireland) Order 1986 (SI 1986/1032 (NI 6)) then applied.

(3)   While any trustee of a trust deed remains entitled to the benefit of a provision saved by subsection (1) above the benefit of that provision may be given either—

   (a)   to all trustees of the deed, present and future, or

   (b)   to any named trustees or proposed trustees of it,

by a resolution passed by a majority of not less than 75% in value of the debenture holders present in person or, where proxies are permitted, by proxy at a meeting summoned for the purpose.

(4)   A meeting for that purpose must be summoned in accordance with the provisions of the deed or, if the deed makes no provision for summoning meetings, in a manner approved by the court.

NOTES

Commencement: 6 April 2008.

[1.752]
752 Power to re-issue redeemed debentures

(1)   Where a company has redeemed debentures previously issued, then unless—

    (a)   provision to the contrary (express or implied) is contained in the company's articles or in any contract made by the company, or

    (b)   the company has, by passing a resolution to that effect or by some other act, manifested its intention that the debentures shall be cancelled,

the company may re-issue the debentures, either by re-issuing the same debentures or by issuing new debentures in their place.

This subsection is deemed always to have had effect.

(2)   On a re-issue of redeemed debentures the person entitled to the debentures has (and is deemed always to have had) the same priorities as if the debentures had never been redeemed.

(3)   The re-issue of a debenture or the issue of another debenture in its place under this section is treated as the issue of a new debenture for the purposes of stamp duty.

It is not so treated for the purposes of any provision limiting the amount or number of debentures to be issued.

(4)   A person lending money on the security of a debenture re-issued under this section which appears to be duly stamped may give the debenture in evidence in any proceedings for enforcing his security without payment of the stamp duty or any penalty in respect of it, unless he had notice (or, but for his negligence, might have discovered) that the debenture was not duly stamped. In that case the company is liable to pay the proper stamp duty and penalty.

NOTES
Commencement: 6 April 2008.

[1.753]
753 Deposit of debentures to secure advances

Where a company has deposited any of its debentures to secure advances from time to time on current account or otherwise, the debentures are not treated as redeemed by reason only of the company's account having ceased to be in debit while the debentures remained so deposited.

NOTES
Commencement: 6 April 2008.

[1.754]
754 Priorities where debentures secured by floating charge

(1)   This section applies where debentures of a company registered in England and Wales or Northern Ireland are secured by a charge that, as created, was a floating charge.

(2)   If possession is taken, by or on behalf of the holders of the debentures, of any property comprised in or subject to the charge, and the company is not at that time in the course of being wound up, the company's preferential debts shall be paid out of assets coming to the hands of the persons taking possession in priority to any claims for principal or interest in respect of the debentures.

(3)   "Preferential debts" means the categories of debts listed in Schedule 6 to the Insolvency Act 1986 (c 45) or Schedule 4 to the Insolvency (Northern Ireland) Order 1989 (SI 1989/2405 (NI 19)).

For the purposes of those Schedules "the relevant date" is the date of possession being taken as mentioned in subsection (2).

(4)   Payments under this section shall be recouped, as far as may be, out of the assets of the company available for payment of general creditors.

NOTES
Commencement: 6 April 2008.

PART 20
PRIVATE AND PUBLIC COMPANIES

CHAPTER 1
PROHIBITION OF PUBLIC OFFERS BY PRIVATE COMPANIES

[1.755]
755 Prohibition of public offers by private company

(1)   A private company limited by shares or limited by guarantee and having a share capital must not—

    (a)   offer to the public any securities of the company, or

    (b)   allot or agree to allot any securities of the company with a view to their being offered to the public.

(2)   Unless the contrary is proved, an allotment or agreement to allot securities is presumed to be made with a view to their being offered to the public if an offer of the securities (or any of them) to the public is made—

(a)   within six months after the allotment or agreement to allot, or

(b)   before the receipt by the company of the whole of the consideration to be received by it in respect of the securities.

(3)   A company does not contravene this section if—

(a)   it acts in good faith in pursuance of arrangements under which it is to re-register as a public company before the securities are allotted, or

(b)   as part of the terms of the offer it undertakes to re-register as a public company within a specified period, and that undertaking is complied with.

(4)   The specified period for the purposes of subsection (3)(b) must be a period ending not later than six months after the day on which the offer is made (or, in the case of an offer made on different days, first made).

(5)   In this Chapter "securities" means shares or debentures.

NOTES

Commencement: 6 April 2008.

Commencement (transitional provisions): Sch 4, Pt 1, para 24 to the Companies Act 2006 (Commencement No 5, Transitional Provisions and Savings) Order 2007, SI 2007/3495 (at **[2.66]**) provides that this section and s 756 apply to offers made on or after 6 April 2008 (and that s 81 of the 1985 Act continues to apply to offers made before that date).

[1.756]
756   Meaning of "offer to the public"

(1)   This section explains what is meant in this Chapter by an offer of securities to the public.

(2)   An offer to the public includes an offer to any section of the public, however selected.

(3)   An offer is not regarded as an offer to the public if it can properly be regarded, in all the circumstances, as—

(a)   not being calculated to result, directly or indirectly, in securities of the company becoming available to persons other than those receiving the offer, or

(b)   otherwise being a private concern of the person receiving it and the person making it.

(4)   An offer is to be regarded (unless the contrary is proved) as being a private concern of the person receiving it and the person making it if—

(a)   it is made to a person already connected with the company and, where it is made on terms allowing that person to renounce his rights, the rights may only be renounced in favour of another person already connected with the company; or

(b)   it is an offer to subscribe for securities to be held under an employees' share scheme and, where it is made on terms allowing that person to renounce his rights, the rights may only be renounced in favour of—

(i)   another person entitled to hold securities under the scheme, or

(ii)   a person already connected with the company.

(5)   For the purposes of this section "person already connected with the company" means—

(a)   an existing member or employee of the company,

(b)   a member of the family of a person who is or was a member or employee of the company,

(c)   the widow or widower, or surviving civil partner, of a person who was a member or employee of the company,

(d)   an existing debenture holder of the company, or

(e)   a trustee (acting in his capacity as such) of a trust of which the principal beneficiary is a person within any of paragraphs (a) to (d).

(6)   For the purposes of subsection (5)(b) the members of a person's family are the person's spouse or civil partner and children (including step-children) and their descendants.

NOTES

Commencement: 6 April 2008.

Commencement (transitional provisions): see the note to s 755 at **[1.755]**.

[1.757]
757   Enforcement of prohibition: order restraining proposed contravention

(1)   If it appears to the court—

(a)   on an application under this section, or

(b)   in proceedings under Part 30 (protection of members against unfair prejudice),

that a company is proposing to act in contravention of section 755 (prohibition of public offers by private companies), the court shall make an order under this section.

(2)   An order under this section is an order restraining the company from contravening that section.

(3)   An application for an order under this section may be made by—

(a)   a member or creditor of the company, or

(b)   the Secretary of State.

NOTES

Commencement: 6 April 2008.

With regard to proceedings under this section, see further the Companies (Authorised Minimum) Regulations 2008, SI 2008/729, reg 6 at **[4.273]** (Determination of exchange rates by the court in certain proceedings), and the Companies (Authorised Minimum) Regulations 2009, SI 2009/2425, reg 6 at **[4.591]** (Determination of exchange rates by the court in certain proceedings).

[1.758]

758   Enforcement of prohibition: orders available to the court after contravention

(1)   This section applies if it appears to the court—

    (a)   on an application under this section, or

    (b)   in proceedings under Part 30 (protection of members against unfair prejudice),

that a company has acted in contravention of section 755 (prohibition of public offers by private companies).

(2)   The court must make an order requiring the company to re-register as a public company unless it appears to the court—

    (a)   that the company does not meet the requirements for re-registration as a public company, and

    (b)   that it is impractical or undesirable to require it to take steps to do so.

(3)   If it does not make an order for re-registration, the court may make either or both of the following—

    (a)   a remedial order (see section 759), or

    (b)   an order for the compulsory winding up of the company.

(4)   An application under this section may be made by—

    (a)   a member of the company who—

        (i)   was a member at the time the offer was made (or, if the offer was made over a period, at any time during that period), or

        (ii)   became a member as a result of the offer,

    (b)   a creditor of the company who was a creditor at the time the offer was made (or, if the offer was made over a period, at any time during that period), or

    (c)   the Secretary of State.

NOTES

Commencement: 6 April 2008.

Commencement (transitional provisions): Sch 4, Pt 1, para 25 to the Companies Act 2006 (Commencement No 5, Transitional Provisions and Savings) Order 2007, SI 2007/3495 (at **[2.66]**) provides that this section and s 759 apply to offers made on or after 6 April 2008.

With regard to proceedings under this section, see further the Companies (Authorised Minimum) Regulations 2008, SI 2008/729, reg 6 at **[4.273]** (Determination of exchange rates by the court in certain proceedings), and the Companies (Authorised Minimum) Regulations 2009, SI 2009/2425, reg 6 at **[4.591]** (Determination of exchange rates by the court in certain proceedings).

[1.759]

759   Enforcement of prohibition: remedial order

(1)   A "remedial order" is an order for the purpose of putting a person affected by anything done in contravention of section 755 (prohibition of public offers by private company) in the position he would have been in if it had not been done.

(2)   The following provisions are without prejudice to the generality of the power to make such an order.

(3)   Where a private company has—

    (a)   allotted securities pursuant to an offer to the public, or

    (b)   allotted or agreed to allot securities with a view to their being offered to the public,

a remedial order may require any person knowingly concerned in the contravention of section 755 to offer to purchase any of those securities at such price and on such other terms as the court thinks fit.

(4)   A remedial order may be made—

    (a)   against any person knowingly concerned in the contravention, whether or not an officer of the company;

    (b)   notwithstanding anything in the company's constitution (which includes, for this purpose, the terms on which any securities of the company are allotted or held);

    (c)   whether or not the holder of the securities subject to the order is the person to whom the company allotted or agreed to allot them.

(5)   Where a remedial order is made against the company itself, the court may provide for the reduction of the company's capital accordingly.

NOTES

Commencement: 6 April 2008.

Commencement (transitional provisions): see the note to s 758 at **[1.758]**.

[1.760]
760   Validity of allotment etc not affected
Nothing in this Chapter affects the validity of any allotment or sale of securities or of any agreement to allot or sell securities.

NOTES
Commencement: 6 April 2008.

CHAPTER 2
MINIMUM SHARE CAPITAL REQUIREMENT FOR PUBLIC COMPANIES

[1.761]
761   Public company: requirement as to minimum share capital
(1)   A company that is a public company (otherwise than by virtue of re-registration as a public company) must not do business or exercise any borrowing powers unless the registrar has issued it with a certificate under this section (a "trading certificate").
(2)   The registrar shall issue a trading certificate if, on an application made in accordance with section 762, he is satisfied that the nominal value of the company's allotted share capital is not less than the authorised minimum.
(3)   For this purpose a share allotted in pursuance of an employees' share scheme shall not be taken into account unless paid up as to—
   (a)   at least one-quarter of the nominal value of the share, and
   (b)   the whole of any premium on the share.
(4)   A trading certificate has effect from the date on which it is issued and is conclusive evidence that the company is entitled to do business and exercise any borrowing powers.

NOTES
Commencement: 6 April 2008.
Commencement (transitional provisions): Sch 4, Pt 1, para 26 to the Companies Act 2006 (Commencement No 5, Transitional Provisions and Savings) Order 2007, SI 2007/3495 (at **[2.66]**) provides that a certificate issued under s 117 of the 1985 Act has effect, on and after 6 April 2008, as if issued under this section.

[1.762]
762   Procedure for obtaining certificate
(1)   An application for a certificate under section 761 must—
   (a)   state that the nominal value of the company's allotted share capital is not less than the authorised minimum,
   (b)   specify the amount, or estimated amount, of the company's preliminary expenses,
   (c)   specify any amount or benefit paid or given, or intended to be paid or given, to any promoter of the company, and the consideration for the payment or benefit, and
   (d)   be accompanied by a statement of compliance.
(2)   The statement of compliance is a statement that the company meets the requirements for the issue of a certificate under section 761.
(3)   The registrar may accept the statement of compliance as sufficient evidence of the matters stated in it.

NOTES
Commencement: 6 April 2008.
Commencement (transitional provisions): Sch 4, Pt 1, paras 27, 28 to the Companies Act 2006 (Commencement No 5, Transitional Provisions and Savings) Order 2007, SI 2007/3495 (at **[2.66]**) provide as follows—

"27.—(1)   Section 762 of the Companies Act 2006 (procedure for obtaining trading certificate) applies to applications made on or after 6th April 2008.
(2)   Section 117(1) to (5) and (7A) of the 1985 Act or Article 127(1) to (5) and (7A) of the 1986 Order continue to apply to applications made before 6th April 2008.
(3)   An application is treated as made before 6th April 2008 if—
   (a)   a statutory declaration is delivered to the registrar in accordance with section 117(2) of the 1985 Act or Article 127(2) of the 1986 Order, and
   (b)   the declaration was signed before that date.
28.—(1)   Until section 1068(1) of the Companies Act 2006 comes into force—
   (a)   an application under section 762 of that Act must be in the form prescribed for the purposes of section 117(2) of the 1985 Act or Article 127(2) of the 1986 Order;
   (b)   the statement and information required by section 762(1)(a) to (c) must be provided on the form prescribed for the statutory declaration required by section 117(3) of the 1985 Act or Article 127(3) of the 1986 Order (but not in the form of a statutory declaration and disregarding so much of the form as requires other information);
   (c)   a company seeking to satisfy the minimum share capital requirement in euros may adapt the form accordingly; and
   (d)   the form must be signed by a director or by the company secretary.
(2)   A form completed in accordance with sub-paragraph (1) is treated as the statement of compliance required by section 762(1)(d) and (2).
(3)   By adapting the form as mentioned in paragraph (1)(c) the applicant is treated as electing that euros shall be the currency by reference to which it is determined whether the requirement mentioned in section 765(1) is met.
(4)   By not so adapting the form the applicant is treated as electing that sterling shall be that currency.

(5)   Sub-paragraphs (1)(c), (3) and (4) above also apply in relation to the form prescribed for the purposes of section 43(3) of the 1985 Act or Article 53(3) of the 1986 Order (re-registration or private company as public) where a company seeks to satisfy the minimum share capital requirement in section 45(2)(a) of that Act or Article 55(2)(a) of that Order in euros.".

[1.763]
763   The authorised minimum
(1)   "The authorised minimum", in relation to the nominal value of a public company's allotted share capital is—
  (a)   £50,000, or
  (b)   the prescribed euro equivalent.
(2)   The Secretary of State may by order prescribe the amount in euros that is for the time being to be treated as equivalent to the sterling amount of the authorised minimum.
(3)   This power may be exercised from time to time as appears to the Secretary of State to be appropriate.
(4)   The amount prescribed shall be determined by applying an appropriate spot rate of exchange to the sterling amount and rounding to the nearest 100 euros.
(5)   An order under this section is subject to negative resolution procedure.
(6)   This section has effect subject to any exercise of the power conferred by section 764 (power to alter authorised minimum).

NOTES
  Commencement: 20 January 2007 (for the purpose of enabling the exercise of powers to make Orders or Regulations by statutory instrument); 6 April 2008 (otherwise).
  Regulations: the Companies (Authorised Minimum) Regulations 2008, SI 2008/729 at **[4.269]**; the Companies (Authorised Minimum) Regulations 2009, SI 2009/2425 at **[4.586]** (reg 2 of which prescribes €57,100 as the equivalent amount for the purposes of sub-s (1) (subject to transitional provisions in reg 9 of those Regulations)).

[1.764]
764   Power to alter authorised minimum
(1)   The Secretary of State may by order—
  (a)   alter the sterling amount of the authorised minimum, and
  (b)   make a corresponding alteration of the prescribed euro equivalent.
(2)   The amount of the prescribed euro equivalent shall be determined by applying an appropriate spot rate of exchange to the sterling amount and rounding to the nearest 100 euros.
(3)   An order under this section that increases the authorised minimum may—
  (a)   require a public company having an allotted share capital of which the nominal value is less than the amount specified in the order to—
     (i)   increase that value to not less than that amount, or
     (ii)   re-register as a private company;
  (b)   make provision in connection with any such requirement for any of the matters for which provision is made by this Act relating to—
     (i)   a company's registration, re-registration or change of name,
     (ii)   payment for shares comprised in a company's share capital, and
     (iii)   offers to the public of shares in or debentures of a company,
     including provision as to the consequences (in criminal law or otherwise) of a failure to comply with any requirement of the order;
  (c)   provide for any provision of the order to come into force on different days for different purposes.
(4)   An order under this section is subject to affirmative resolution procedure.

NOTES
  Commencement: 20 January 2007 (for the purpose of enabling the exercise of powers to make Orders or Regulations by statutory instrument); 6 April 2008 (otherwise).

[1.765]
765   Authorised minimum: application of initial requirement
(1)   The initial requirement for a public company to have allotted share capital of a nominal value not less than the authorised minimum, that is—
  (a)   the requirement in section 761(2) for the issue of a trading certificate, or
  (b)   the requirement in section 91(1)(a) for re-registration as a public company,
must be met either by reference to allotted share capital denominated in sterling or by reference to allotted share capital denominated in euros (but not partly in one and partly in the other).
(2)   Whether the requirement is met is determined in the first case by reference to the sterling amount and in the second case by reference to the prescribed euro equivalent.
(3)   No account is to be taken of any allotted share capital of the company denominated in a currency other than sterling or, as the case may be, euros.
(4)   If the company could meet the requirement either by reference to share capital denominated in sterling or by reference to share capital denominated in euros, it must elect in its application for a trading certificate or, as the case may be, for re-registration as a public company which is to be the currency by reference to which the matter is determined.

NOTES

Commencement: 6 April 2008.

Commencement (transitional adaptations): art 6 of the Companies Act 2006 (Commencement No 5, Transitional Provisions and Savings) Order 2007, SI 2007/3495 provides that the provisions brought into force by arts 3 and 5 of that Order shall have effect subject to any transitional adaptations specified in Sch 1 to that Order. Schedule 1, Pt 1, para 12 to the Order (at **[2.62]**) provided for such transitional adaptations (note that this paragraph was revoked by the Companies Act 2006 (Commencement No 8, Transitional Provisions and Savings) Order 2008, SI 2008/2860, art 6, as from 1 October 2009 (subject to any relevant transitional provision or saving in Sch 2 to that Order)).

[1.766]

766 Authorised minimum: application where shares denominated in different currencies etc

(1)   The Secretary of State may make provision by regulations as to the application of the authorised minimum in relation to a public company that—

[(a)   has shares denominated—

(i)   in more than one currency, or

(ii)   in a currency other than sterling or euros,]

(b)   redenominates the whole or part of its allotted share capital, or

(c)   allots new shares.

(2)   The regulations may make provision as to the currencies, exchange rates and dates by reference to which it is to be determined whether the nominal value of the company's allotted share capital is less than the authorised minimum.

(3)   The regulations may provide that where—

(a)   a company has redenominated the whole or part of its allotted share capital, and

(b)   the effect of the redenomination is that the nominal value of the company's allotted share capital is less than the authorised minimum,

the company must re-register as a private company.

(4)   Regulations under subsection (3) may make provision corresponding to any provision made by sections 664 to 667 (re-registration as private company in consequence of cancellation of shares).

(5)   Any regulations under this section have effect subject to section 765 (authorised minimum: application of initial requirement).

(6)   Regulations under this section are subject to negative resolution procedure.

NOTES

Commencement: 20 January 2007 (for the purpose of enabling the exercise of powers to make Orders or Regulations by statutory instrument); 6 April 2008 (otherwise).

Commencement (transitional adaptations): art 6 of the Companies Act 2006 (Commencement No 5, Transitional Provisions and Savings) Order 2007, SI 2007/3495 provides that the provisions brought into force by arts 3 and 5 of that Order shall have effect subject to any transitional adaptations specified in Sch 1 to that Order. Schedule 1, Pt 1, para 13 to the Order (at **[2.62]**) provided for such transitional adaptations (note that this paragraph was revoked by the Companies Act 2006 (Commencement No 8, Transitional Provisions and Savings) Order 2008, SI 2008/2860, art 6, as from 1 October 2009 (subject to any relevant transitional provision or saving in Sch 2 to that Order)).

Sub-s (1): para (a) substituted by the Companies Act 2006 (Consequential Amendments and Transitional Provisions) Order 2011, SI 2011/1265, art 28(1), (2), as from 12 May 2011.

Regulations: the Companies (Authorised Minimum) Regulations 2008, SI 2008/729 at **[4.269]**; the Companies (Authorised Minimum) Regulations 2009, SI 2009/2425 at **[4.586]**.

[1.767]

767 Consequences of doing business etc without a trading certificate

(1)   If a company does business or exercises any borrowing powers in contravention of section 761, an offence is committed by—

(a)   the company, and

(b)   every officer of the company who is in default.

(2)   A person guilty of an offence under subsection (1) is liable—

(a)   on conviction on indictment, to a fine;

(b)   on summary conviction, to a fine not exceeding the statutory maximum.

(3)   A contravention of section 761 does not affect the validity of a transaction entered into by the company, but if a company—

(a)   enters into a transaction in contravention of that section, and

(b)   fails to comply with its obligations in connection with the transaction within 21 days from being called on to do so,

the directors of the company are jointly and severally liable to indemnify any other party to the transaction in respect of any loss or damage suffered by him by reason of the company's failure to comply with its obligations.

(4)   The directors who are so liable are those who were directors at the time the company entered into the transaction.

NOTES

Commencement: 6 April 2008.

Commencement (transitional provisions): Sch 4, Pt 1, para 29 to the Companies Act 2006 (Commencement No 5, Transitional Provisions and Savings) Order 2007, SI 2007/3495 (at **[2.66]**) provides that this section applies in relation to things done on or after 6 April 2008 (and that s 117(6)–(8) of the 1985 Act continue to apply in relation to things done before that date).

PART 21
CERTIFICATION AND TRANSFER OF SECURITIES

CHAPTER 1
CERTIFICATION AND TRANSFER OF SECURITIES: GENERAL

Share certificates

[1.768]
768   Share certificate to be evidence of title
(1)   In the case of a company registered in England and Wales or Northern Ireland, a certificate under the common seal of the company specifying any shares held by a member is prima facie evidence of his title to the shares.
(2)   In the case of a company registered in Scotland—
   (a)   a certificate under the common seal of the company specifying any shares held by a member, or
   (b)   a certificate specifying any shares held by a member and subscribed by the company in accordance with the Requirements of Writing (Scotland) Act 1995 (c 7),
is sufficient evidence, unless the contrary is shown, of his title to the shares.

NOTES
Commencement: 6 April 2008.

Issue of certificates etc on allotment

[1.769]
769   Duty of company as to issue of certificates etc on allotment
(1)   A company must, within two months after the allotment of any of its shares, debentures or debenture stock, complete and have ready for delivery—
   (a)   the certificates of the shares allotted,
   (b)   the debentures allotted, or
   (c)   the certificates of the debenture stock allotted.
(2)   Subsection (1) does not apply—
   (a)   if the conditions of issue of the shares, debentures or debenture stock provide otherwise,
   (b)   in the case of allotment to a financial institution (see section 778), or
   (c)   in the case of an allotment of shares if, following the allotment, the company has issued a share warrant in respect of the shares (see section 779).
(3)   If default is made in complying with subsection (1) an offence is committed by every officer of the company who is in default.
(4)   A person guilty of an offence under subsection (3) is liable on summary conviction to a fine not exceeding level 3 on the standard scale and, for continued contravention, a daily default fine not exceeding one-tenth of level 3 on the standard scale.

NOTES
Commencement: 6 April 2008.

Transfer of securities

[1.770]
770   Registration of transfer
(1)   A company may not register a transfer of shares in or debentures of the company unless—
   (a)   a proper instrument of transfer has been delivered to it, or
   (b)   the transfer—
      (i)   is an exempt transfer within the Stock Transfer Act 1982 (c 41), or
      (ii)   is in accordance with regulations under Chapter 2 of this Part.
(2)   Subsection (1) does not affect any power of the company to register as shareholder or debenture holder a person to whom the right to any shares in or debentures of the company has been transmitted by operation of law.

NOTES
Commencement: 6 April 2008.

[1.771]
771   Procedure on transfer being lodged
(1)   When a transfer of shares in or debentures of a company has been lodged with the company, the company must either—
   (a)   register the transfer, or

   (b)   give the transferee notice of refusal to register the transfer, together with its reasons for the
          refusal,
as soon as practicable and in any event within two months after the date on which the transfer is
lodged with it.
(2)   If the company refuses to register the transfer, it must provide the transferee with such further
information about the reasons for the refusal as the transferee may reasonably request.
   This does not include copies of minutes of meetings of directors.
(3)   If a company fails to comply with this section, an offence is committed by—
   (a)   the company, and
   (b)   every officer of the company who is in default.
(4)   A person guilty of an offence under this section is liable on summary conviction to a fine not
exceeding level 3 on the standard scale and, for continued contravention, a daily default fine not
exceeding one-tenth of level 3 on the standard scale.
(5)   This section does not apply—
   (a)   in relation to a transfer of shares if the company has issued a share warrant in respect of the
          shares (see section 779);
   (b)   in relation to the transmission of shares or debentures by operation of law.

NOTES
   Commencement: 6 April 2008.
   Commencement (transitional provisions): Sch 4, Pt 1, para 30 to the Companies Act 2006 (Commencement No 5,
Transitional Provisions and Savings) Order 2007, SI 2007/3495 (at **[2.66]**) provides that this section applies to transfers lodged
with the company on or after 6 April 2008.

[1.772]
772   Transfer of shares on application of transferor
On the application of the transferor of any share or interest in a company, the company shall enter
in its register of members the name of the transferee in the same manner and subject to the same
conditions as if the application for the entry were made by the transferee.

NOTES
   Commencement: 6 April 2008.

[1.773]
773   Execution of share transfer by personal representative
An instrument of transfer of the share or other interest of a deceased member of a company—
   (a)   may be made by his personal representative although the personal representative is not
          himself a member of the company, and
   (b)   is as effective as if the personal representative had been such a member at the time of the
          execution of the instrument.

NOTES
   Commencement: 6 April 2008.

[1.774]
774   Evidence of grant of probate etc
The production to a company of any document that is by law sufficient evidence of the grant of—
   (a)   probate of the will of a deceased person,
   (b)   letters of administration of the estate of a deceased person, or
   (c)   confirmation as executor of a deceased person,
shall be accepted by the company as sufficient evidence of the grant.

NOTES
   Commencement: 6 April 2008.

[1.775]
755   Certification of instrument of transfer
(1)   The certification by a company of an instrument of transfer of any shares in, or debentures of,
the company is to be taken as a representation by the company to any person acting on the faith of
the certification that there have been produced to the company such documents as on their face
show a prima facie title to the shares or debentures in the transferor named in the instrument.
(2)   The certification is not to be taken as a representation that the transferor has any title to the
shares or debentures.
(3)   Where a person acts on the faith of a false certification by a company made negligently, the
company is under the same liability to him as if the certification had been made fraudulently.
(4)   For the purposes of this section—
   (a)   an instrument of transfer is certificated if it bears the words "certificate lodged" (or words
          to the like effect);
   (b)   the certification of an instrument of transfer is made by a company if—

(i)   the person issuing the instrument is a person authorised to issue certificated instruments of transfer on the company's behalf, and

(ii)   the certification is signed by a person authorised to certificate transfers on the company's behalf or by an officer or employee either of the company or of a body corporate so authorised;

(c)   a certification is treated as signed by a person if—

     (i)   it purports to be authenticated by his signature or initials (whether handwritten or not), and

     (ii)   it is not shown that the signature or initials was or were placed there neither by himself nor by a person authorised to use the signature or initials for the purpose of certificating transfers on the company's behalf.

NOTES

Commencement: 6 April 2008.

Issue of certificates etc on transfer

[1.776]

776   Duty of company as to issue of certificates etc on transfer

(1)   A company must, within two months after the date on which a transfer of any of its shares, debentures or debenture stock is lodged with the company, complete and have ready for delivery—

(a)   the certificates of the shares transferred,

(b)   the debentures transferred, or

(c)   the certificates of the debenture stock transferred.

(2)   For this purpose a "transfer" means—

(a)   a transfer duly stamped and otherwise valid, or

(b)   an exempt transfer within the Stock Transfer Act 1982 (c 41),

but does not include a transfer that the company is for any reason entitled to refuse to register and does not register.

(3)   Subsection (1) does not apply—

(a)   if the conditions of issue of the shares, debentures or debenture stock provide otherwise,

(b)   in the case of a transfer to a financial institution (see section 778), or

(c)   in the case of a transfer of shares if, following the transfer, the company has issued a share warrant in respect of the shares (see section 779).

(4)   Subsection (1) has effect subject to section 777 (cases where the Stock Transfer Act 1982 applies).

(5)   If default is made in complying with subsection (1) an offence is committed by every officer of the company who is in default.

(6)   A person guilty of an offence under this section is liable on summary conviction to a fine not exceeding level 3 on the standard scale and, for continued contravention, a daily default fine not exceeding one-tenth of level 3 on the standard scale.

NOTES

Commencement: 6 April 2008.

[1.777]

777   Issue of certificates etc: cases within the Stock Transfer Act 1982

(1)   Section 776(1) (duty of company as to issue of certificates etc on transfer) does not apply in the case of a transfer to a person where, by virtue of regulations under section 3 of the Stock Transfer Act 1982, he is not entitled to a certificate or other document of or evidencing title in respect of the securities transferred.

(2)   But if in such a case the transferee—

(a)   subsequently becomes entitled to such a certificate or other document by virtue of any provision of those regulations, and

(b)   gives notice in writing of that fact to the company,

section 776 (duty to company as to issue of certificates etc) has effect as if the reference in subsection (1) of that section to the date of the lodging of the transfer were a reference to the date of the notice.

NOTES

Commencement: 6 April 2008.

Issue of certificates etc on allotment or transfer to financial institution

[1.778]

778   Issue of certificates etc: allotment or transfer to financial institution

(1)   A company—

(a)   of which shares or debentures are allotted to a financial institution,

(b)   of which debenture stock is allotted to a financial institution, or

(c)   with which a transfer for transferring shares, debentures or debenture stock to a financial institution is lodged, is not required in consequence of that allotment or transfer to comply with section 769(1) or 776(1) (duty of company as to issue of certificates etc).

(2) A "financial institution" means—

(a) a recognised clearing house acting in relation to a recognised investment exchange, or

(b) a nominee of—

    (i) a recognised clearing house acting in that way, or

    (ii) a recognised investment exchange,

    designated for the purposes of this section in the rules of the recognised investment exchange in question.

(3) Expressions used in subsection (2) have the same meaning as in Part 18 of the Financial Services and Markets Act 2000 (c 8).

NOTES

Commencement: 6 April 2008.

Share warrants

[1.779]
779 Issue and effect of share warrant to bearer

(1) A company limited by shares may, if so authorised by its articles, issue with respect to any fully paid shares a warrant (a "share warrant") stating that the bearer of the warrant is entitled to the shares specified in it.

(2) A share warrant issued under the company's common seal or (in the case of a company registered in Scotland) subscribed in accordance with the Requirements of Writing (Scotland) Act 1995 (c 7) entitles the bearer to the shares specified in it and the shares may be transferred by delivery of the warrant.

(3) A company that issues a share warrant may, if so authorised by its articles, provide (by coupons or otherwise) for the payment of the future dividends on the shares included in the warrant.

NOTES

Commencement: 6 April 2008.

[1.780]
780 Duty of company as to issue of certificates on surrender of share warrant

(1) A company must, within two months of the surrender of a share warrant for cancellation, complete and have ready for delivery the certificates of the shares specified in the warrant.

(2) Subsection (1) does not apply if the company's articles provide otherwise.

(3) If default is made in complying with subsection (1) an offence is committed by every officer of the company who is in default.

(4) A person guilty of an offence under subsection (3) is liable on summary conviction to a fine not exceeding level 3 on the standard scale and, for continued contravention, a daily default fine not exceeding one-tenth of level 3 on the standard scale.

NOTES

Commencement: 6 April 2008.

Commencement (transitional provisions): Sch 4, Pt 1, para 31 to the Companies Act 2006 (Commencement No 5, Transitional Provisions and Savings) Order 2007, SI 2007/3495 (at **[2.66]**) provides that this section applies to share warrants surrendered on or after 6 April 2008.

[1.781]
781 Offences in connection with share warrants (Scotland)

(1) If in Scotland a person—

(a) with intent to defraud, forges or alters, or offers, utters, disposes of, or puts off, knowing the same to be forged or altered, any share warrant or coupon, or any document purporting to be a share warrant or coupon issued in pursuance of this Act, or

(b) by means of any such forged or altered share warrant, coupon or document—

    (i) demands or endeavours to obtain or receive any share or interest in a company under this Act, or

    (ii) demands or endeavours to receive any dividend or money payment in respect of any such share or interest,

    knowing the warrant, coupon or document to be forged or altered,

he commits an offence.

(2) If in Scotland a person without lawful authority or excuse (of which proof lies on him)—

(a) engraves or makes on any plate, wood, stone, or other material, any share warrant or coupon purporting to be—

    (i) a share warrant or coupon issued or made by any particular company in pursuance of this Act, or

    (ii) a blank share warrant or coupon so issued or made, or

    (iii) a part of such a share warrant or coupon, or

(b)   uses any such plate, wood, stone, or other material, for the making or printing of any such share warrant or coupon, or of any such blank share warrant or coupon or of any part of such a share warrant or coupon, or

(c)   knowingly has in his custody or possession any such plate, wood, stone, or other material, he commits an offence.

(3)   A person guilty of an offence under subsection (1) is liable on summary conviction to imprisonment for a term not exceeding six months or to a fine not exceeding level 5 on the standard scale (or both).

(4)   A person guilty of an offence under subsection (2) is liable—

(a)   on conviction on indictment, to imprisonment for a term not exceeding seven years or a fine (or both);

(b)   on summary conviction, to imprisonment for a term not exceeding six months or a fine not exceeding the statutory maximum (or both).

NOTES
Commencement: 6 April 2008.

Supplementary provisions

[1.782]
782   Issue of certificates etc: court order to make good default
(1)   If a company on which a notice has been served requiring it to make good any default in complying with—

(a)   section 769(1) (duty of company as to issue of certificates etc on allotment),

(b)   section 776(1) (duty of company as to issue of certificates etc on transfer), or

(c)   section 780(1) (duty of company as to issue of certificates etc on surrender of share warrant),

fails to make good the default within ten days after service of the notice, the person entitled to have the certificates or the debentures delivered to him may apply to the court.

(2)   The court may on such an application make an order directing the company and any officer of it to make good the default within such time as may be specified in the order.

(3)   The order may provide that all costs (in Scotland, expenses) of and incidental to the application are to be borne by the company or by an officer of it responsible for the default.

NOTES
Commencement: 6 April 2008.

CHAPTER 2
EVIDENCING AND TRANSFER OF TITLE TO SECURITIES WITHOUT WRITTEN INSTRUMENT
Introductory

[1.783]
783   Scope of this Chapter
In this Chapter—

(a)   "securities" means shares, debentures, debenture stock, loan stock, bonds, units of a collective investment scheme within the meaning of the Financial Services and Markets Act 2000 (c 8) and other securities of any description;

(b)   references to title to securities include any legal or equitable interest in securities;

(c)   references to a transfer of title include a transfer by way of security;

(d)   references to transfer without a written instrument include, in relation to bearer securities, transfer without delivery.

NOTES
Commencement: 6 April 2008.

[1.784]
784   Power to make regulations
(1)   The power to make regulations under this Chapter is exercisable by the Treasury and the Secretary of State, either jointly or concurrently.

(2)   References in this Chapter to the authority having power to make regulations shall accordingly be read as references to both or either of them, as the case may require.

(3)   Regulations under this Chapter are subject to affirmative resolution procedure.

NOTES
Commencement: 20 January 2007 (for the purpose of enabling the exercise of powers to make Orders or Regulations by statutory instrument); 6 April 2008 (otherwise).
Regulations: the Companies Act 2006 (Consequential Amendments) (Uncertificated Securities) Order 2009, SI 2009/1889.

Powers exercisable

[1.785]
785 Provision enabling procedures for evidencing and transferring title
(1) Provision may be made by regulations for enabling title to securities to be evidenced and transferred without a written instrument.
(2) The regulations may make provision—
  (a) for procedures for recording and transferring title to securities, and
  (b) for the regulation of those procedures and the persons responsible for or involved in their operation.
(3) The regulations must contain such safeguards as appear to the authority making the regulations appropriate for the protection of investors and for ensuring that competition is not restricted, distorted or prevented.
(4) The regulations may, for the purpose of enabling or facilitating the operation of the procedures provided for by the regulations, make provision with respect to the rights and obligations of persons in relation to securities dealt with under the procedures.
(5) The regulations may include provision for the purpose of giving effect to—
  (a) the transmission of title to securities by operation of law;
  (b) any restriction on the transfer of title to securities arising by virtue of the provisions of any enactment or instrument, court order or agreement;
  (c) any power conferred by any such provision on a person to deal with securities on behalf of the person entitled.
(6) The regulations may make provision with respect to the persons responsible for the operation of the procedures provided for by the regulations—
  (a) as to the consequences of their insolvency or incapacity, or
  (b) as to the transfer from them to other persons of their functions in relation to those procedures.

NOTES
Commencement: 20 January 2007 (for the purpose of enabling the exercise of powers to make Orders or Regulations by statutory instrument); 6 April 2008 (otherwise).
Regulations: the Companies Act 2006 (Consequential Amendments) (Uncertificated Securities) Order 2009, SI 2009/1889. Also, by virtue of s 1297 of this Act (continuity of law) the Uncertificated Securities Regulations 2001, SI 2001/3755 (at **[6.42]**) and the Uncertificated Securities (Amendment) (Eligible Debt Securities) Regulations 2003, SI 2003/1633 (as amended, in both cases, by further SIs made under s 207 of the Companies Act 1989) have effect as if made under this section.

[1.786]
786 Provision enabling or requiring arrangements to be adopted
(1) Regulations under this Chapter may make provision—
  (a) enabling the members of a company or of any designated class of companies to adopt, by ordinary resolution, arrangements under which title to securities is required to be evidenced or transferred (or both) without a written instrument; or
  (b) requiring companies, or any designated class of companies, to adopt such arrangements.
(2) The regulations may make such provision—
  (a) in respect of all securities issued by a company, or
  (b) in respect of all securities of a specified description.
(3) The arrangements provided for by regulations making such provision as is mentioned in subsection (1)—
  (a) must not be such that a person who but for the arrangements would be entitled to have his name entered in the company's register of members ceases to be so entitled, and
  (b) must be such that a person who but for the arrangements would be entitled to exercise any rights in respect of the securities continues to be able effectively to control the exercise of those rights.
(4) The regulations may—
  (a) prohibit the issue of any certificate by the company in respect of the issue or transfer of securities,
  (b) require the provision by the company to holders of securities of statements (at specified intervals or on specified occasions) of the securities held in their name, and
  (c) make provision as to the matters of which any such certificate or statement is, or is not, evidence.
(5) In this section—
  (a) references to a designated class of companies are to a class designated in the regulations or by order under section 787; and
  (b) "specified" means specified in the regulations.

NOTES
Commencement: 20 January 2007 (for the purpose of enabling the exercise of powers to make Orders or Regulations by statutory instrument); 6 April 2008 (otherwise).

[1.787]
787 Provision enabling or requiring arrangements to be adopted: order-making powers
(1) The authority having power to make regulations under this Chapter may by order—
  (a) designate classes of companies for the purposes of section 786 (provision enabling or requiring arrangements to be adopted);
  (b) provide that, in relation to securities of a specified description—
    (i) in a designated class of companies, or
    (ii) in a specified company or class of companies,
    specified provisions of regulations made under this Chapter by virtue of that section either do not apply or apply subject to specified modifications.
(2) In subsection (1) "specified" means specified in the order.
(3) An order under this section is subject to negative resolution procedure.

NOTES
Commencement: 20 January 2007 (for the purpose of enabling the exercise of powers to make Orders or Regulations by statutory instrument); 6 April 2008 (otherwise).

Supplementary

[1.788]
788 Provision that may be included in regulations
Regulations under this Chapter may—
  (a) modify or exclude any provision of any enactment or instrument, or any rule of law;
  (b) apply, with such modifications as may be appropriate, the provisions of any enactment or instrument (including provisions creating criminal offences);
  (c) require the payment of fees, or enable persons to require the payment of fees, of such amounts as may be specified in the regulations or determined in accordance with them;
  (d) empower the authority making the regulations to delegate to any person willing and able to discharge them any functions of the authority under the regulations.

NOTES
Commencement: 20 January 2007 (for the purpose of enabling the exercise of powers to make Orders or Regulations by statutory instrument); 6 April 2008 (otherwise).
Regulations: the Companies Act 2006 (Consequential Amendments) (Uncertificated Securities) Order 2009, SI 2009/1889. Also, by virtue of s 1297 of this Act (continuity of law) the Uncertificated Securities Regulations 2001, SI 2001/3755 (at **[6.42]**) and the Uncertificated Securities (Amendment) (Eligible Debt Securities) Regulations 2003, SI 2003/1633 (as amended, in both cases, by further SIs made under s 207 of the Companies Act 1989) have effect as if made under this section.

[1.789]
789 Duty to consult
Before making—
  (a) regulations under this Chapter, or
  (b) any order under section 787,
the authority having power to make regulations under this Chapter must carry out such consultation as appears to it to be appropriate.

NOTES
Commencement: 20 January 2007 (for the purpose of enabling the exercise of powers to make Orders or Regulations by statutory instrument); 6 April 2008 (otherwise).

[1.790]
790 Resolutions to be forwarded to registrar
Chapter 3 of Part 3 (resolutions affecting a company's constitution) applies to a resolution passed by virtue of regulations under this Chapter.

NOTES
Commencement: 6 April 2008.

PART 22
INFORMATION ABOUT INTERESTS IN A COMPANY'S SHARES
Introductory

[1.791]
791 Companies to which this Part applies
This Part applies only to public companies.

NOTES
Commencement: 20 January 2007.

[1.792]
792 Shares to which this Part applies
(1) References in this Part to a company's shares are to the company's issued shares of a class carrying rights to vote in all circumstances at general meetings of the company (including any shares held as treasury shares).
(2) The temporary suspension of voting rights in respect of any shares does not affect the application of this Part in relation to interests in those or any other shares.

NOTES
Commencement: 20 January 2007.

Notice requiring information about interests in shares

[1.793]
793 Notice by company requiring information about interests in its shares
(1) A public company may give notice under this section to any person whom the company knows or has reasonable cause to believe—
    (a)   to be interested in the company's shares, or
    (b)   to have been so interested at any time during the three years immediately preceding the date on which the notice is issued.
(2) The notice may require the person—
    (a)   to confirm that fact or (as the case may be) to state whether or not it is the case, and
    (b)   if he holds, or has during that time held, any such interest, to give such further information as may be required in accordance with the following provisions of this section.
(3) The notice may require the person to whom it is addressed to give particulars of his own present or past interest in the company's shares (held by him at any time during the three year period mentioned in subsection (1)(b)).
(4) The notice may require the person to whom it is addressed, where—
    (a)   his interest is a present interest and another interest in the shares subsists, or
    (b)   another interest in the shares subsisted during that three year period at a time when his interest subsisted,
to give, so far as lies within his knowledge, such particulars with respect to that other interest as may be required by the notice.
(5) The particulars referred to in subsections (3) and (4) include—
    (a)   the identity of persons interested in the shares in question, and
    (b)   whether persons interested in the same shares are or were parties to—
        (i)   an agreement to which section 824 applies (certain share acquisition agreements), or
        (ii)   an agreement or arrangement relating to the exercise of any rights conferred by the holding of the shares.
(6) The notice may require the person to whom it is addressed, where his interest is a past interest, to give (so far as lies within his knowledge) particulars of the identity of the person who held that interest immediately upon his ceasing to hold it.
(7) The information required by the notice must be given within such reasonable time as may be specified in the notice.

NOTES
Commencement: 20 January 2007.

[1.794]
794 Notice requiring information: order imposing restrictions on shares
(1) Where—
    (a)   a notice under section 793 (notice requiring information about interests in company's shares) is served by a company on a person who is or was interested in shares in the company, and
    (b)   that person fails to give the company the information required by the notice within the time specified in it,
the company may apply to the court for an order directing that the shares in question be subject to restrictions.
    For the effect of such an order see section 797.
(2) If the court is satisfied that such an order may unfairly affect the rights of third parties in respect of the shares, the court may, for the purpose of protecting those rights and subject to such terms as it thinks fit, direct that such acts by such persons or descriptions of persons and for such purposes as may be set out in the order shall not constitute a breach of the restrictions.
(3) On an application under this section the court may make an interim order. Any such order may be made unconditionally or on such terms as the court thinks fit.
(4) Sections 798 to 802 make further provision about orders under this section.

NOTES
Commencement: 20 January 2007.

[1.795]
795 Notice requiring information: offences
(1)   A person who—
  (a)   fails to comply with a notice under section 793 (notice requiring information about interests in company's shares), or
  (b)   in purported compliance with such a notice—
    (i)   makes a statement that he knows to be false in a material particular, or
    (ii)   recklessly makes a statement that is false in a material particular,
commits an offence.
(2)   A person does not commit an offence under subsection (1)(a) if he proves that the requirement to give information was frivolous or vexatious.
(3)   A person guilty of an offence under this section is liable—
  (a)   on conviction on indictment, to imprisonment for a term not exceeding two years or a fine (or both);
  (b)   on summary conviction—
    (i)   in England and Wales, to imprisonment for a term not exceeding twelve months or to a fine not exceeding the statutory maximum (or both);
    (ii)   in Scotland or Northern Ireland, to imprisonment for a term not exceeding six months, or to a fine not exceeding the statutory maximum (or both).

NOTES
Commencement: 20 January 2007.
Offences under this section: see further s 1131 at **[1.1131]**.

[1.796]
796 Notice requiring information: persons exempted from obligation to comply
(1)   A person is not obliged to comply with a notice under section 793 (notice requiring information about interests in company's shares) if he is for the time being exempted by the Secretary of State from the operation of that section.
(2)   The Secretary of State must not grant any such exemption unless—
  (a)   he has consulted the Governor of the Bank of England, and
  (b)   he (the Secretary of State) is satisfied that, having regard to any undertaking given by the person in question with respect to any interest held or to be held by him in any shares, there are special reasons why that person should not be subject to the obligations imposed by that section.

NOTES
Commencement: 20 January 2007.

Orders imposing restrictions on shares

[1.797]
797 Consequences of order imposing restrictions
(1)   The effect of an order under section 794 that shares are subject to restrictions is as follows—
  (a)   any transfer of the shares is void;
  (b)   no voting rights are exercisable in respect of the shares;
  (c)   no further shares may be issued in right of the shares or in pursuance of an offer made to their holder;
  (d)   except in a liquidation, no payment may be made of sums due from the company on the shares, whether in respect of capital or otherwise.
(2)   Where shares are subject to the restriction in subsection (1)(a), an agreement to transfer the shares is void.
This does not apply to an agreement to transfer the shares on the making of an order under section 800 made by virtue of subsection (3)(b) (removal of restrictions in case of court-approved transfer).
(3)   Where shares are subject to the restriction in subsection (1)(c) or (d), an agreement to transfer any right to be issued with other shares in right of those shares, or to receive any payment on them (otherwise than in a liquidation), is void.
This does not apply to an agreement to transfer any such right on the making of an order under section 800 made by virtue of subsection (3)(b) (removal of restrictions in case of court-approved transfer).
(4)   The provisions of this section are subject—
  (a)   to any directions under section 794(2) or section 799(3) (directions for protection of third parties), and
  (b)   in the case of an interim order under section 794(3), to the terms of the order.

NOTES
Commencement: 20 January 2007.

[1.798]
798 Penalty for attempted evasion of restrictions
(1)   This section applies where shares are subject to restrictions by virtue of an order under section 794.
(2)   A person commits an offence if he—
  (a)   exercises or purports to exercise any right—
    (i)   to dispose of shares that to his knowledge, are for the time being subject to restrictions, or
    (ii)   to dispose of any right to be issued with any such shares, or
  (b)   votes in respect of any such shares (whether as holder or proxy), or appoints a proxy to vote in respect of them, or
  (c)   being the holder of any such shares, fails to notify of their being subject to those restrictions a person whom he does not know to be aware of that fact but does know to be entitled (apart from the restrictions) to vote in respect of those shares whether as holder or as proxy, or
  (d)   being the holder of any such shares, or being entitled to a right to be issued with other shares in right of them, or to receive any payment on them (otherwise than in a liquidation), enters into an agreement which is void under section 797(2) or (3).
(3)   If shares in a company are issued in contravention of the restrictions, an offence is committed by—
  (a)   the company, and
  (b)   every officer of the company who is in default.
(4)   A person guilty of an offence under this section is liable—
  (a)   on conviction on indictment, to a fine;
  (b)   on summary conviction, to a fine not exceeding the statutory maximum.
(5)   The provisions of this section are subject—
  (a)   to any directions under—
    section 794(2) (directions for protection of third parties), or
    section 799 or 800 (relaxation or removal of restrictions), and
  (b)   in the case of an interim order under section 794(3), to the terms of the order.

NOTES
  Commencement: 20 January 2007.

[1.799]
799 Relaxation of restrictions
(1)   An application may be made to the court on the ground that an order directing that shares shall be subject to restrictions unfairly affects the rights of third parties in respect of the shares.
(2)   An application for an order under this section may be made by the company or by any person aggrieved.
(3)   If the court is satisfied that the application is well-founded, it may, for the purpose of protecting the rights of third parties in respect of the shares, and subject to such terms as it thinks fit, direct that such acts by such persons or descriptions of persons and for such purposes as may be set out in the order do not constitute a breach of the restrictions.

NOTES
  Commencement: 20 January 2007.

[1.800]
800 Removal of restrictions
(1)   An application may be made to the court for an order directing that the shares shall cease to be subject to restrictions.
(2)   An application for an order under this section may be made by the company or by any person aggrieved.
(3)   The court must not make an order under this section unless—
  (a)   it is satisfied that the relevant facts about the shares have been disclosed to the company and no unfair advantage has accrued to any person as a result of the earlier failure to make that disclosure, or
  (b)   the shares are to be transferred for valuable consideration and the court approves the transfer.
(4)   An order under this section made by virtue of subsection (3)(b) may continue, in whole or in part, the restrictions mentioned in section 797(1)(c) and (d) (restrictions on issue of further shares or making of payments) so far as they relate to a right acquired or offer made before the transfer.
(5)   Where any restrictions continue in force under subsection (4)—
  (a)   an application may be made under this section for an order directing that the shares shall cease to be subject to those restrictions, and
  (b)   subsection (3) does not apply in relation to the making of such an order.

NOTES
Commencement: 20 January 2007.

[1.801]
801   Order for sale of shares
(1)   The court may order that the shares subject to restrictions be sold, subject to the court's approval as to the sale.
(2)   An application for an order under subsection (1) may only be made by the company.
(3)   Where the court has made an order under this section, it may make such further order relating to the sale or transfer of the shares as it thinks fit.
(4)   An application for an order under subsection (3) may be made—
   (a)   by the company,
   (b)   by the person appointed by or in pursuance of the order to effect the sale, or
   (c)   by any person interested in the shares.
(5)   On making an order under subsection (1) or (3) the court may order that the applicant's costs (in Scotland, expenses) be paid out of the proceeds of sale.

NOTES
Commencement: 20 January 2007.

[1.802]
802   Application of proceeds of sale under court order
(1)   Where shares are sold in pursuance of an order of the court under section 801, the proceeds of the sale, less the costs of the sale, must be paid into court for the benefit of the persons who are beneficially interested in the shares.
(2)   A person who is beneficially interested in the shares may apply to the court for the whole or part of those proceeds to be paid to him.
(3)   On such an application the court shall order the payment to the applicant of—
   (a)   the whole of the proceeds of sale together with any interest on them, or
   (b)   if another person had a beneficial interest in the shares at the time of their sale, such proportion of the proceeds and interest as the value of the applicant's interest in the shares bears to the total value of the shares.
   This is subject to the following qualification.
(4)   If the court has ordered under section 801(5) that the costs (in Scotland, expenses) of an applicant under that section are to be paid out of the proceeds of sale, the applicant is entitled to payment of his costs (or expenses) out of those proceeds before any person interested in the shares receives any part of those proceeds.

NOTES
Commencement: 20 January 2007.

Power of members to require company to act

[1.803]
803   Power of members to require company to act
(1)   The members of a company may require it to exercise its powers under section 793 (notice requiring information about interests in shares).
(2)   A company is required to do so once it has received requests (to the same effect) from members of the company holding at least 10% of such of the paid-up capital of the company as carries a right to vote at general meetings of the company (excluding any voting rights attached to any shares in the company held as treasury shares).
(3)   A request—
   (a)   may be in hard copy form or in electronic form,
   (b)   must—
      (i)   state that the company is requested to exercise its powers under section 793,
      (ii)   specify the manner in which the company is requested to act, and
      (iii) give reasonable grounds for requiring the company to exercise those powers in the manner specified, and
   (c)   must be authenticated by the person or persons making it.

NOTES
Commencement: 20 January 2007.

[1.804]
804   Duty of company to comply with requirement
(1)   A company that is required under section 803 to exercise its powers under section 793 (notice requiring information about interests in company's shares) must exercise those powers in the manner specified in the requests.

(2)   If default is made in complying with subsection (1) an offence is committed by every officer of the company who is in default.

(3)   A person guilty of an offence under this section is liable—

(a)   on conviction on indictment, to a fine;

(b)   on summary conviction, to a fine not exceeding the statutory maximum.

NOTES

Commencement: 20 January 2007.

[1.805]

805   Report to members on outcome of investigation

(1)   On the conclusion of an investigation carried out by a company in pursuance of a requirement under section 803 the company must cause a report of the information received in pursuance of the investigation to be prepared.

The report must be made available for inspection within a reasonable period (not more than 15 days) after the conclusion of the investigation.

(2)   Where—

(a)   a company undertakes an investigation in pursuance of a requirement under section 803, and

(b)   the investigation is not concluded within three months after the date on which the company became subject to the requirement,

the company must cause to be prepared in respect of that period, and in respect of each succeeding period of three months ending before the conclusion of the investigation, an interim report of the information received during that period in pursuance of the investigation.

(3)   Each such report must be made available for inspection within a reasonable period (not more than 15 days) after the end of the period to which it relates.

(4)   The reports must be retained by the company for at least six years from the date on which they are first made available for inspection and must be kept available for inspection during that time—

(a)   at the company's registered office, or

(b)   at a place specified in regulations under section 1136.

(5)   The company must give notice to the registrar—

(a)   of the place at which the reports are kept available for inspection, and

(b)   of any change in that place,

unless they have at all times been kept at the company's registered office.

(6)   The company must within three days of making any report prepared under this section available for inspection, notify the members who made the requests under section 803 where the report is so available.

(7)   For the purposes of this section an investigation carried out by a company in pursuance of a requirement under section 803 is concluded when—

(a)   the company has made all such inquiries as are necessary or expedient for the purposes of the requirement, and

(b)   in the case of each such inquiry—

(i)   a response has been received by the company, or

(ii)   the time allowed for a response has elapsed.

NOTES

Commencement: 20 January 2007.

[1.806]

806   Report to members: offences

(1)   If default is made for 14 days in complying with section 805(5) (notice to registrar of place at which reports made available for inspection) an offence is committed by—

(a)   the company, and

(b)   every officer of the company who is in default.

(2)   A person guilty of an offence under subsection (1) is liable on summary conviction to a fine not exceeding level 3 on the standard scale and, for continued contravention, a daily default fine not exceeding one-tenth of level 3 on the standard scale.

(3)   If default is made in complying with any other provision of section 805 (report to members on outcome of investigation), an offence is committed by every officer of the company who is in default.

(4)   A person guilty of an offence under subsection (3) is liable—

(a)   on conviction on indictment, to a fine;

(b)   on summary conviction, to a fine not exceeding the statutory maximum.

NOTES

Commencement: 20 January 2007.

[1.807]
807 Right to inspect and request copy of reports
(1) Any report prepared under section 805 must be open to inspection by any person without charge.

(2) Any person is entitled, on request and on payment of such fee as may be prescribed, to be provided with a copy of any such report or any part of it. The copy must be provided within ten days after the request is received by the company.

(3) If an inspection required under subsection (1) is refused, or default is made in complying with subsection (2), an offence is committed by—
   (a) the company, and
   (b) every officer of the company who is in default.

(4) A person guilty of an offence under this section is liable on summary conviction to a fine not exceeding level 3 on the standard scale and, for continued contravention, a daily default fine not exceeding one-tenth of level 3 on the standard scale.

(5) In the case of any such refusal or default the court may by order compel an immediate inspection or, as the case may be, direct that the copy required be sent to the person requiring it.

NOTES
Commencement: 20 January 2007.
Regulations: the Companies (Fees for Inspection and Copying of Company Records) Regulations 2007, SI 2007/2612 at **[4.12]**.

Register of interests disclosed

[1.808]
808 Register of interests disclosed
(1) The company must keep a register of information received by it in pursuance of a requirement imposed under section 793 (notice requiring information about interests in company's shares).

(2) A company which receives any such information must, within three days of the receipt, enter in the register—
   (a) the fact that the requirement was imposed and the date on which it was imposed, and
   (b) the information received in pursuance of the requirement.

(3) The information must be entered against the name of the present holder of the shares in question or, if there is no present holder or the present holder is not known, against the name of the person holding the interest.

(4) The register must be made up so that the entries against the names entered in it appear in chronological order.

(5) If default is made in complying with this section an offence is committed by—
   (a) the company, and
   (b) every officer of the company who is in default.

(6) A person guilty of an offence under this section is liable on summary conviction to a fine not exceeding level 3 on the standard scale and, for continued contravention, a daily default fine not exceeding one-tenth of level 3 on the standard scale.

(7) The company is not by virtue of anything done for the purposes of this section affected with notice of, or put upon inquiry as to, the rights of any person in relation to any shares.

NOTES
Commencement: 20 January 2007.
Commencement (transitional provisions): the Companies Act 2006 (Commencement No 1, Transitional Provisions and Savings) Order 2006, SI 2006/3428, Sch 5, Pt 2, para 2(3), (4) (at **[2.14]**) (as amended by the Companies Act 2006 (Commencement No 5, Transitional Provisions and Savings) Order 2007, SI 2007/3495, art 11, Sch 5, para 1, as from 14 January 2008) provide as follows—

"(3) On and after 20th January 2007 any separate part of a register kept by a company under section 213 of the 1985 Act or Article 221 of the 1986 Order (register of interests disclosed in response to requirement by company) shall continue to be kept by the company and shall be treated as a register kept under and for the purposes of section 808 of the Companies Act 2006.

(4) Until regulations under section 1136 of the Companies Act 2006 (regulations about where certain company records are to be kept available for inspection) [come into force] specifying a place for the purposes of section 809(1)(b) of that Act—
   (a) the register kept under section 808 of that Act (register of interests disclosed) may be kept by a company at any place where its register of members is kept; and
   (b) no notice need be given to the registrar of companies under section 809(2) of that Act.".

[1.809]
809 Register to be kept available for inspection
(1) The register kept under section 808 (register of interests disclosed) must be kept available for inspection—
   (a) at the company's registered office, or
   (b) at a place specified in regulations under section 1136.

(2) A company must give notice to the registrar of companies of the place where the register is kept available for inspection and of any change in that place.

(3)   No such notice is required if the register has at all times been kept available for inspection at the company's registered office.

(4)   If default is made in complying with subsection (1), or a company makes default for 14 days in complying with subsection (2), an offence is committed by—

  (a)   the company, and

  (b)   every officer of the company who is in default.

(5)   A person guilty of an offence under this section is liable on summary conviction to a fine not exceeding level 3 on the standard scale and, for continued contravention, a daily default fine not exceeding one-tenth of level 3 on the standard scale.

NOTES

Commencement: 20 January 2007.

Commencement (transitional provisions): see the note to s 808 at **[1.808]**.

[1.810]
810   Associated index

(1)   Unless the register kept under section 808 (register of interests disclosed) is kept in such a form as itself to constitute an index, the company must keep an index of the names entered in it.

(2)   The company must make any necessary entry or alteration in the index within ten days after the date on which any entry or alteration is made in the register.

(3)   The index must contain, in respect of each name, a sufficient indication to enable the information entered against it to be readily found.

(4)   The index must be at all times kept available for inspection at the same place as the register.

(5)   If default is made in complying with this section, an offence is committed by—

  (a)   the company, and

  (b)   every officer of the company who is in default.

(6)   A person guilty of an offence under this section is liable on summary conviction to a fine not exceeding level 3 on the standard scale and, for continued contravention, a daily default fine not exceeding one-tenth of level 3 on the standard scale.

NOTES

Commencement: 20 January 2007.

[1.811]
811   Rights to inspect and require copy of entries

(1)   The register required to be kept under section 808 (register of interests disclosed), and any associated index, must be open to inspection by any person without charge.

(2)   Any person is entitled, on request and on payment of such fee as may be prescribed, to be provided with a copy of any entry in the register.

(3)   A person seeking to exercise either of the rights conferred by this section must make a request to the company to that effect.

(4)   The request must contain the following information—

  (a)   in the case of an individual, his name and address;

  (b)   in the case of an organisation, the name and address of an individual responsible for making the request on behalf of the organisation;

  (c)   the purpose for which the information is to be used; and

  (d)   whether the information will be disclosed to any other person, and if so—

    (i)   where that person is an individual, his name and address,

    (ii)   where that person is an organisation, the name and address of an individual responsible for receiving the information on its behalf, and

    (iii) the purpose for which the information is to be used by that person.

NOTES

Commencement: 20 January 2007 (sub-ss (1)–(3)); 6 April 2008 (otherwise).

Commencement (transitional provisions): Sch 4, Pt 1, para 32 to the Companies Act 2006 (Commencement No 5, Transitional Provisions and Savings) Order 2007, SI 2007/3495 (at **[2.66]**) provides that sub-s (4) above and ss 812, 814 apply to requests under this section made on or after 6 April 2008.

Regulations: the Companies (Fees for Inspection and Copying of Company Records) Regulations 2007, SI 2007/2612 at **[4.12]**.

[1.812]
812   Court supervision of purpose for which rights may be exercised

(1)   Where a company receives a request under section 811 (register of interests disclosed: right to inspect and require copy), it must—

  (a)   comply with the request if it is satisfied that it is made for a proper purpose, and

  (b)   refuse the request if it is not so satisfied.

(2)   If the company refuses the request, it must inform the person making the request, stating the reason why it is not satisfied.

(3)   A person whose request is refused may apply to the court.

(4)   If an application is made to the court—

    (a)   the person who made the request must notify the company, and

    (b)   the company must use its best endeavours to notify any persons whose details would be disclosed if the company were required to comply with the request.

(5)   If the court is not satisfied that the inspection or copy is sought for a proper purpose, it shall direct the company not to comply with the request.

(6)   If the court makes such a direction and it appears to the court that the company is or may be subject to other requests made for a similar purpose (whether made by the same person or different persons), it may direct that the company is not to comply with any such request.

The order must contain such provision as appears to the court appropriate to identify the requests to which it applies.

(7)   If the court does not direct the company not to comply with the request, the company must comply with the request immediately upon the court giving its decision or, as the case may be, the proceedings being discontinued.

NOTES

Commencement: 6 April 2008.

Commencement (transitional provisions): see the note to s 811 at **[1.811]**.

[1.813]
813   Register of interests disclosed: refusal of inspection or default in providing copy

(1)   If an inspection required under section 811 (register of interests disclosed: right to inspect and require copy) is refused or default is made in providing a copy required under that section, otherwise than in accordance with an order of the court, an offence is committed by—

    (a)   the company, and

    (b)   every officer of the company who is in default.

(2)   A person guilty of an offence under this section is liable on summary conviction to a fine not exceeding level 3 on the standard scale and, for continued contravention, a daily default fine not exceeding one-tenth of level 3 on the standard scale.

(3)   In the case of any such refusal or default the court may by order compel an immediate inspection or, as the case may be, direct that the copy required be sent to the person requesting it.

NOTES

Commencement: 20 January 2007.

Commencement (transitional adaptations): the transitional adaptations of this section contained in the Companies Act 2006 (Commencement No 1, Transitional Provisions and Savings) Order 2006, SI 2006/3428, Sch 1, para 2 were revoked by the Companies Act 2006 (Commencement No 5, Transitional Provisions and Savings) Order 2007, SI 2007/3495, art 10(2), as from 1 October 2008. See **[2.9]**.

[1.814]
814   Register of interests disclosed: offences in connection with request for or disclosure of information

(1)   It is an offence for a person knowingly or recklessly to make in a request under section 811 (register of interests disclosed: right to inspect or require copy) a statement that is misleading, false or deceptive in a material particular.

(2)   It is an offence for a person in possession of information obtained by exercise of either of the rights conferred by that section—

    (a)   to do anything that results in the information being disclosed to another person, or

    (b)   to fail to do anything with the result that the information is disclosed to another person,

knowing, or having reason to suspect, that person may use the information for a purpose that is not a proper purpose.

(3)   A person guilty of an offence under this section is liable—

    (a)   on conviction on indictment, to imprisonment for a term not exceeding two years or a fine (or both);

    (b)   on summary conviction—

        (i)   in England and Wales, to imprisonment for a term not exceeding twelve months or to a fine not exceeding the statutory maximum (or both);

        (ii)   in Scotland or Northern Ireland, to imprisonment for a term not exceeding six months, or to a fine not exceeding the statutory maximum (or both).

NOTES

Commencement: 6 April 2008.

Commencement (transitional provisions): see the note to s 811 at **[1.811]**.

Offences under this section: see further s 1131 at **[1.1131]**.

[1.815]
815   Entries not to be removed from register

(1)   Entries in the register kept under section 808 (register of interests disclosed) must not be deleted except in accordance with—

    section 816 (old entries), or

    section 817 (incorrect entry relating to third party).

(2)   If an entry is deleted in contravention of subsection (1), the company must restore it as soon as reasonably practicable.

(3)   If default is made in complying with subsection (1) or (2), an offence is committed by—
  (a)   the company, and
  (b)   every officer of the company who is in default.

(4)   A person guilty of an offence under this section is liable on summary conviction to a fine not exceeding level 3 on the standard scale and, for continued contravention of subsection (2), a daily default fine not exceeding one-tenth of level 3 on the standard scale.

NOTES

Commencement: 20 January 2007.

[1.816]
816   Removal of entries from register: old entries
A company may remove an entry from the register kept under section 808 (register of interests disclosed) if more than six years have elapsed since the entry was made.

NOTES

Commencement: 20 January 2007.

[1.817]
817   Removal of entries from register: incorrect entry relating to third party
(1)   This section applies where in pursuance of an obligation imposed by a notice under section 793 (notice requiring information about interests in company's shares) a person gives to a company the name and address of another person as being interested in shares in the company.

(2)   That other person may apply to the company for the removal of the entry from the register.

(3)   If the company is satisfied that the information in pursuance of which the entry was made is incorrect, it shall remove the entry.

(4)   If an application under subsection (3) is refused, the applicant may apply to the court for an order directing the company to remove the entry in question from the register.

  The court may make such an order if it thinks fit.

NOTES

Commencement: 20 January 2007.

[1.818]
818   Adjustment of entry relating to share acquisition agreement
(1)   If a person who is identified in the register kept by a company under section 808 (register of interests disclosed) as being a party to an agreement to which section 824 applies (certain share acquisition agreements) ceases to be a party to the agreement, he may apply to the company for the inclusion of that information in the register.

(2)   If the company is satisfied that he has ceased to be a party to the agreement, it shall record that information (if not already recorded) in every place where his name appears in the register as a party to the agreement.

(3)   If an application under this section is refused (otherwise than on the ground that the information has already been recorded), the applicant may apply to the court for an order directing the company to include the information in question in the register.

  The court may make such an order if it thinks fit.

NOTES

Commencement: 20 January 2007.

[1.819]
819   Duty of company ceasing to be public company
(1)   If a company ceases to be a public company, it must continue to keep any register kept under section 808 (register of interests disclosed), and any associated index, until the end of the period of six years after it ceased to be such a company.

(2)   If default is made in complying with this section, an offence is committed by—
  (a)   the company, and
  (b)   every officer of the company who is in default.

(3)   A person guilty of an offence under this section is liable on summary conviction to a fine not exceeding level 3 on the standard scale and, for continued contravention, a daily default fine not exceeding one-tenth of level 3 on the standard scale.

NOTES

Commencement: 20 January 2007.

Meaning of interest in shares

[1.820]
820 Interest in shares: general
(1) This section applies to determine for the purposes of this Part whether a person has an interest in shares.
(2) In this Part—
 (a) a reference to an interest in shares includes an interest of any kind whatsoever in the shares, and
 (b) any restraints or restrictions to which the exercise of any right attached to the interest is or may be subject shall be disregarded.
(3) Where an interest in shares is comprised in property held on trust, every beneficiary of the trust is treated as having an interest in the shares.
(4) A person is treated as having an interest in shares if—
 (a) he enters into a contract to acquire them, or
 (b) not being the registered holder, he is entitled—
  (i) to exercise any right conferred by the holding of the shares, or
  (ii) to control the exercise of any such right.
(5) For the purposes of subsection (4)(b) a person is entitled to exercise or control the exercise of a right conferred by the holding of shares if he—
 (a) has a right (whether subject to conditions or not) the exercise of which would make him so entitled, or
 (b) is under an obligation (whether subject to conditions or not) the fulfilment of which would make him so entitled.
(6) A person is treated as having an interest in shares if—
 (a) he has a right to call for delivery of the shares to himself or to his order, or
 (b) he has a right to acquire an interest in shares or is under an obligation to take an interest in shares.
This applies whether the right or obligation is conditional or absolute.
(7) Persons having a joint interest are treated as each having that interest.
(8) It is immaterial that shares in which a person has an interest are unidentifiable.

NOTES
Commencement: 20 January 2007.

[1.821]
821 Interest in shares: right to subscribe for shares
(1) Section 793 (notice by company requiring information about interests in its shares) applies in relation to a person who has, or previously had, or is or was entitled to acquire, a right to subscribe for shares in the company as it applies in relation to a person who is or was interested in shares in that company.
(2) References in that section to an interest in shares shall be read accordingly.

NOTES
Commencement: 20 January 2007.

[1.822]
822 Interest in shares: family interests
(1) For the purposes of this Part a person is taken to be interested in shares in which—
 (a) his spouse or civil partner, or
 (b) any infant child or step-child of his,
is interested.
(2) In relation to Scotland "infant" means a person under the age of 18 years.

NOTES
Commencement: 20 January 2007.

[1.823]
823 Interest in shares: corporate interests
(1) For the purposes of this Part a person is taken to be interested in shares if a body corporate is interested in them and—
 (a) the body or its directors are accustomed to act in accordance with his directions or instructions, or
 (b) he is entitled to exercise or control the exercise of one-third or more of the voting power at general meetings of the body.
(2) For the purposes of this section a person is treated as entitled to exercise or control the exercise of voting power if—
 (a) another body corporate is entitled to exercise or control the exercise of that voting power, and

(b)   he is entitled to exercise or control the exercise of one-third or more of the voting power at general meetings of that body corporate.

(3)   For the purposes of this section a person is treated as entitled to exercise or control the exercise of voting power if—

(a)   he has a right (whether or not subject to conditions) the exercise of which would make him so entitled, or

(b)   he is under an obligation (whether or not subject to conditions) the fulfilment of which would make him so entitled.

NOTES
Commencement: 20 January 2007.

[1.824]
824   Interest in shares: agreement to acquire interests in a particular company

(1)   For the purposes of this Part an interest in shares may arise from an agreement between two or more persons that includes provision for the acquisition by any one or more of them of interests in shares of a particular public company (the "target company" for that agreement).

(2)   This section applies to such an agreement if—

(a)   the agreement includes provision imposing obligations or restrictions on any one or more of the parties to it with respect to their use, retention or disposal of their interests in the shares of the target company acquired in pursuance of the agreement (whether or not together with any other interests of theirs in the company's shares to which the agreement relates), and

(b)   an interest in the target company's shares is in fact acquired by any of the parties in pursuance of the agreement.

(3)   The reference in subsection (2) to the use of interests in shares in the target company is to the exercise of any rights or of any control or influence arising from those interests (including the right to enter into an agreement for the exercise, or for control of the exercise, of any of those rights by another person).

(4)   Once an interest in shares in the target company has been acquired in pursuance of the agreement, this section continues to apply to the agreement so long as the agreement continues to include provisions of any description mentioned in subsection (2).

This applies irrespective of—

(a)   whether or not any further acquisitions of interests in the company's shares take place in pursuance of the agreement;

(b)   any change in the persons who are for the time being parties to it;

(c)   any variation of the agreement.

References in this subsection to the agreement include any agreement having effect (whether directly or indirectly) in substitution for the original agreement.

(5)   In this section—

(a)   "agreement" includes any agreement or arrangement, and

(b)   references to provisions of an agreement include—

(i)   undertakings, expectations or understandings operative under an arrangement, and

(ii)   any provision whether express or implied and whether absolute or not.

References elsewhere in this Part to an agreement to which this section applies have a corresponding meaning.

(6)   This section does not apply—

(a)   to an agreement that is not legally binding unless it involves mutuality in the undertakings, expectations or understandings of the parties to it; or

(b)   to an agreement to underwrite or sub-underwrite an offer of shares in a company, provided the agreement is confined to that purpose and any matters incidental to it.

NOTES
Commencement: 20 January 2007.

[1.825]
825   Extent of obligation in case of share acquisition agreement

(1)   For the purposes of this Part each party to an agreement to which section 824 applies is treated as interested in all shares in the target company in which any other party to the agreement is interested apart from the agreement (whether or not the interest of the other party was acquired, or includes any interest that was acquired, in pursuance of the agreement).

(2)   For those purposes an interest of a party to such an agreement in shares in the target company is an interest apart from the agreement if he is interested in those shares otherwise than by virtue of the application of section 824 (and this section) in relation to the agreement.

(3)   Accordingly, any such interest of the person (apart from the agreement) includes for those purposes any interest treated as his under section 822 or 823 (family or corporate interests) or by the application of section 824 (and this section) in relation to any other agreement with respect to shares in the target company to which he is a party.

(4)   A notification with respect to his interest in shares in the target company made to the company under this Part by a person who is for the time being a party to an agreement to which section 824 applies must—

    (a)   state that the person making the notification is a party to such an agreement,

    (b)   include the names and (so far as known to him) the addresses of the other parties to the agreement, identifying them as such, and

    (c)   state whether or not any of the shares to which the notification relates are shares in which he is interested by virtue of section 824 (and this section) and, if so, the number of those shares.

NOTES

Commencement: 20 January 2007.

Other supplementary provisions

[1.826]

826   Information protected from wider disclosure

(1)   Information in respect of which a company is for the time being entitled to any exemption conferred by regulations under section 409(3) (information about related undertakings to be given in notes to accounts: exemption where disclosure harmful to company's business)—

    (a)   must not be included in a report under section 805 (report to members on outcome of investigation), and

    (b)   must not be made available under section 811 (right to inspect and request copy of entries).

(2)   Where any such information is omitted from a report under section 805, that fact must be stated in the report.

NOTES

Commencement: 20 January 2007.

Commencement (transitional adaptations): the transitional adaptations of this section contained in the Companies Act 2006 (Commencement No 1, Transitional Provisions and Savings) Order 2006, SI 2006/3428, Sch 1, para 3 were revoked by the Companies Act 2006 (Commencement No 5, Transitional Provisions and Savings) Order 2007, SI 2007/3495, art 10(1), (3), as from 6 April 2008 (subject to any transitional provisions and savings as apply, in accordance with Sch 4 to that Order, in relation to the repeal of any provision of the 1985 Act referred to in the adaptation). See **[2.9]**.

[1.827]

827   Reckoning of periods for fulfilling obligations

Where the period allowed by any provision of this Part for fulfilling an obligation is expressed as a number of days, any day that is not a working day shall be disregarded in reckoning that period.

NOTES

Commencement: 20 January 2007.

[1.828]

828   Power to make further provision by regulations

(1)   The Secretary of State may by regulations amend—

    (a)   the definition of shares to which this Part applies (section 792),

    (b)   the provisions as to notice by a company requiring information about interests in its shares (section 793), and

    (c)   the provisions as to what is taken to be an interest in shares (sections 820 and 821).

(2)   The regulations may amend, repeal or replace those provisions and make such other consequential amendments or repeals of provisions of this Part as appear to the Secretary of State to be appropriate.

(3)   Regulations under this section are subject to affirmative resolution procedure.

NOTES

Commencement: 20 January 2007.

PART 23
DISTRIBUTIONS

CHAPTER 1
RESTRICTIONS ON WHEN DISTRIBUTIONS MAY BE MADE

Introductory

[1.829]

829   Meaning of "distribution"

(1)   In this Part "distribution" means every description of distribution of a company's assets to its members, whether in cash or otherwise, subject to the following exceptions.

(2)   The following are not distributions for the purposes of this Part—

    (a)   an issue of shares as fully or partly paid bonus shares;

    (b)   the reduction of share capital—

      (i)   by extinguishing or reducing the liability of any of the members on any of the company's shares in respect of share capital not paid up, or

      (ii)   by repaying paid-up share capital;

   (c)   the redemption or purchase of any of the company's own shares out of capital (including the proceeds of any fresh issue of shares) or out of unrealised profits in accordance with Chapter 3, 4 or 5 of Part 18;

   (d)   a distribution of assets to members of the company on its winding up.

NOTES

Commencement: 6 April 2008.

Commencement (transitional provisions): Sch 4, Pt 1, paras 33–35 to the Companies Act 2006 (Commencement No 5, Transitional Provisions and Savings) Order 2007, SI 2007/3495 (at **[2.66]**) (as amended by the Companies Act 2006 (Commencement No 6, Saving and Commencement Nos 3 and 5 (Amendment)) Order 2008, SI 2008/674, art 5, Sch 3, para 6(1), (3), as from 6 April 2008) provide as follows—

"Distributions (ss 829 to 853)

33.—(1)   Sections 829 to 853 of the Companies Act 2006 (distributions) apply to distributions made on or after 6th April 2008.

(2)   Sections 263 to 281 of the 1985 Act or Articles 271 to 289 of the 1986 Order continue to apply to distributions made before that date.

34.   Until section 1068(1) of the Companies Act 2006 comes into force—

   (a)   the notice referred to in section 833(1)(a) (notice of intention to carry on business as investment company) must be in the form prescribed for the purposes of section 266(1) of the 1985 Act or Article 274(1) of the 1986 Order; and

   (b)   the notice referred to in section 833(4) (notice that company no longer wishes to be an investment company) must be in the form prescribed for the purposes of section 266(3) of the 1985 Act or Article 274(3) of the 1986 Order.

35.—(1)   The relevant accounts for the purposes of Chapter 2 of Part 23 of the Companies Act 2006 (justification of distribution by reference to accounts) may be accounts for financial years beginning before 6th April 2008 (to which the provisions of the 1985 Act or 1986 Order apply).

(2)   In that case the provisions of that Chapter and Chapter 3 of that Part (supplementary provisions) have effect with the following adaptations—

   (a)   in section 836(1)(b)(i), for "provisions of a kind specified for the purposes of this section by regulations under section 396" substitute "provisions of any of the kinds mentioned in paragraphs 88 and 89 of Schedule 4 to the Companies Act 1985 or paragraphs 87 and 88 of Schedule 4 to the Companies (Northern Ireland) Order 1986";

   (b)   in section 837—

      (i)   in subsection (1)(a), for "section 423" substitute "section 238 of the Companies Act 1985 or Article 246 of the Companies (Northern Ireland) Order 1986";

      (ii)   in subsection (1)(b), for "section 426" substitute "section 251 of the Companies Act 1985 or Article 259 of the Companies (Northern Ireland) Order 1986";

      (iii) in subsection (2), for "this Act" substitute "the Companies Act 1985 or the Companies (Northern Ireland) Order 1986";

      (iv) in subsection (4)(b)(i), for "section 423" substitute "section 238 of the Companies Act 1985 or Article 246 of the Companies (Northern Ireland) Order 1986";

   (c)   in section 838—

      (i)   in subsection (4), for "sections 395 to 397" substitute "sections 226 to 226B of the Companies Act 1985 or Articles 234 to 234B of the Companies (Northern Ireland) Order 1986";

      (ii)   in subsection (5), for "section 414" substitute "[section] 233 of the Companies Act 1985 or Article 241 of the Companies (Northern Ireland) Order 1986";

      (iii) in subsection (6), for "Part 35 of this Act" substitute "Part 24 of the Companies Act 1985 or Part 24 of the Companies (Northern Ireland) Order 1986";

   (d)   in section 839—

      (i)   in subsection (4), for "sections 395 to 397" substitute "sections 226 to 226B of the Companies Act 1985 or Articles 234 to 234B of the Companies (Northern Ireland) Order 1986";

      (ii)   in subsection (6)(b)(i), for "section 423" substitute "section 238 of the Companies Act 1985 or Article 246 of the Companies (Northern Ireland) Order 1986";

      (iii) in subsection (7), for "Part 35 of this Act" substitute "Part 24 of the Companies Act 1985 or Part 24 of the Companies (Northern Ireland) Order 1986";

   (e)   in section 841(2)(a), for "provisions of a kind specified for the purposes of this paragraph by regulations under section 396" to the end substitute "provisions of any kind mentioned in paragraphs 88 and 89 of Schedule 4 to the Companies Act 1985 or paragraphs 87 and 88 of Schedule 4 to the Companies (Northern Ireland) Order 1986";

   (f)   in section 844(3)(b)(i), for "the note required" to the end substitute "the note to the accounts required by paragraph 20 of Schedule 4 or paragraph 20 of Schedule 8 to the Companies Act 1985 or paragraph 20 of Schedule 4 or paragraph 20 of Schedule 8 to the Companies (Northern Ireland) Order 1986 (reasons for showing development costs as an asset)";

   (g)   in section 846(2)(b), for "any provision of regulations under section 396" to the end substitute "paragraphs 12(a) and 34(3)(a) of Schedule 4 or paragraphs 12(a) or 34(3)(a) of Schedule 8 to the Companies Act 1985 or paragraphs 12(a) and 34(3)(a) of Schedule 4 or paragraphs 12(a) or 34(3)(a) of Schedule 8 to the Companies (Northern Ireland) Order 1986 (only realised profits to be included in or transferred to the profit and loss account)".".

See also the Companies Act 2006 (Consequential Amendments etc) Order 2008, SI 2008/948, art 6(5) (at **[4.280]**) which provides that the provisions of the Companies Act 2006 (Commencement No 5, Transitional Provisions and Savings) Order 2007, SI 2007/3495, Sch 4, para 35 (as set out above) apply in any case where the effect of an amendment made by the

2008 Order is that the lawfulness of a distribution depends on Part 23 of the Companies Act 2006, or any provision of that Part, applying in relation to accounts for financial years beginning before 6 April 2008.

Commencement (transitional adaptations): art 6 of the Companies Act 2006 (Commencement No 5, Transitional Provisions and Savings) Order 2007, SI 2007/3495 provides that the provisions brought into force by arts 3 and 5 of that Order shall have effect subject to any transitional adaptations specified in Sch 1 to that Order. Schedule 1, Pt 1, para 14 to the Order (at **[2.62]**) provided for such transitional adaptations (note that this paragraph was revoked by the Companies Act 2006 (Commencement No 8, Transitional Provisions and Savings) Order 2008, SI 2008/2860, art 6, as from 1 October 2009 (subject to any relevant transitional provision or saving in Sch 2 to that Order)).

General rules

[1.830]
830   Distributions to be made only out of profits available for the purpose

(1)   A company may only make a distribution out of profits available for the purpose.

(2)   A company's profits available for distribution are its accumulated, realised profits, so far as not previously utilised by distribution or capitalisation, less its accumulated, realised losses, so far as not previously written off in a reduction or reorganisation of capital duly made.

(3)   Subsection (2) has effect subject to sections 832 and 835 (investment companies etc: distributions out of accumulated revenue profits).

NOTES
Commencement: 6 April 2008.
Commencement (transitional provisions): see the note to s 829 at **[1.829]**.

[1.831]
831   Net asset restriction on distributions by public companies

(1)   A public company may only make a distribution—
   (a)   if the amount of its net assets is not less than the aggregate of its called-up share capital and undistributable reserves, and
   (b)   if, and to the extent that, the distribution does not reduce the amount of those assets to less than that aggregate.

(2)   For this purpose a company's "net assets" means the aggregate of the company's assets less the aggregate of its liabilities.

(3)   "Liabilities" here includes—
   (a)   where the relevant accounts are Companies Act accounts, provisions of a kind specified for the purposes of this subsection by regulations under section 396;
   (b)   where the relevant accounts are IAS accounts, provisions of any kind.

(4)   A company's undistributable reserves are—
   (a)   its share premium account;
   (b)   its capital redemption reserve;
   (c)   the amount by which its accumulated, unrealised profits (so far as not previously utilised by capitalisation) exceed its accumulated, unrealised losses (so far as not previously written off in a reduction or reorganisation of capital duly made);
   (d)   any other reserve that the company is prohibited from distributing—
      (i)   by any enactment (other than one contained in this Part), or
      (ii)   by its articles.

The reference in paragraph (c) to capitalisation does not include a transfer of profits of the company to its capital redemption reserve.

(5)   A public company must not include any uncalled share capital as an asset in any accounts relevant for purposes of this section.

(6)   Subsection (1) has effect subject to sections 832 and 835 (investment companies etc: distributions out of accumulated revenue profits).

NOTES
Commencement: 6 April 2008.
Commencement (transitional provisions): see the note to s 829 at **[1.829]**.
Regulations under section 396: see the notes to that section at **[1.396]**. See also the Large and Medium-sized Companies and Groups (Accounts and Reports) Regulations 2008, SI 2008/410, reg 12 (at **[4.181]**) which provides that Sch 9 to those Regulations (at **[4.217]**, **[4.218]**) defines "provisions" for the purpose of those Regulations and for the purposes of sub-s (3)(a) above.

Distributions by investment companies

[1.832]
832   Distributions by investment companies out of accumulated revenue profits

(1)   An investment company may make a distribution out of its accumulated, realised revenue profits if the following conditions are met.

(2)   It may make such a distribution only if, and to the extent that, its accumulated, realised revenue profits, so far as not previously utilised by a distribution or capitalisation, exceed its accumulated revenue losses (whether realised or unrealised), so far as not previously written off in a reduction or reorganisation of capital duly made.

(3)   It may make such a distribution only—

(a) if the amount of its assets is at least equal to one and a half times the aggregate of its liabilities to creditors, and

(b) if, and to the extent that, the distribution does not reduce that amount to less than one and a half times that aggregate.

(4) For this purpose a company's liabilities to creditors include—

(a) in the case of Companies Act accounts, provisions of a kind specified for the purposes of this subsection by regulations under section 396;

(b) in the case of IAS accounts, provisions for liabilities to creditors.

(5) The following conditions must also be met—

(a) the company's shares must be listed on a recognised UK investment exchange;

(b) during the relevant period it must not have—

(i) distributed any capital profits otherwise than by way of the redemption or purchase of any of the company's own shares in accordance with Chapter 3 or 4 of Part 18, or

(ii) applied any unrealised profits or any capital profits (realised or unrealised) in paying up debentures or amounts unpaid on its issued shares;

(c) it must have given notice to the registrar under section 833(1) (notice of intention to carry on business as an investment company)—

(i) before the beginning of the relevant period, or

(ii) as soon as reasonably practicable after the date of its incorporation.

(6) For the purposes of this section—

(a) "recognised UK investment exchange" means a recognised investment exchange within the meaning of Part 18 of the Financial Services and Markets Act 2000 (c 8), other than an overseas investment exchange within the meaning of that Part; and

(b) the "relevant period" is the period beginning with—

(i) the first day of the accounting reference period immediately preceding that in which the proposed distribution is to be made, or

(ii) where the distribution is to be made in the company's first accounting reference period, the first day of that period,

and ending with the date of the distribution.

(7) The company must not include any uncalled share capital as an asset in any accounts relevant for purposes of this section.

NOTES

Commencement: 6 April 2008.

Commencement (transitional provisions): see the note to s 829 at [**1.829**].

Commencement (transitional adaptations): art 6 of the Companies Act 2006 (Commencement No 5, Transitional Provisions and Savings) Order 2007, SI 2007/3495 provides that the provisions brought into force by arts 3 and 5 of that Order shall have effect subject to any transitional adaptations specified in Sch 1 to that Order. Schedule 1, Pt 1, para 15 to the Order (at [**2.62**]) provided for such transitional adaptations (note that this paragraph was revoked by the Companies Act 2006 (Commencement No 8, Transitional Provisions and Savings) Order 2008, SI 2008/2860, art 6, as from 1 October 2009 (subject to any relevant transitional provision or saving in Sch 2 to that Order)).

Regulations under section 396: see the notes to that section at [**1.396**]. See also the Large and Medium-sized Companies and Groups (Accounts and Reports) Regulations 2008, SI 2008/410, reg 12 (at [**4.181**]) which provides that Sch 9 to those Regulations (at [**4.217**], [**4.218**]) defines "provisions" for the purpose of those Regulations and for the purposes of sub-s (4)(a) above.

[**1.833**]

833 Meaning of "investment company"

(1) In this Part an "investment company" means a public company that—

(a) has given notice (which has not been revoked) to the registrar of its intention to carry on business as an investment company, and

(b) since the date of that notice has complied with the following requirements.

(2) Those requirements are—

(a) that the business of the company consists of investing its funds mainly in securities, with the aim of spreading investment risk and giving members of the company the benefit of the results of the management of its funds;

(b) that the condition in section 834 is met as regards holdings in other companies;

(c) that distribution of the company's capital profits is prohibited by its articles;

(d) that the company has not retained, otherwise than in compliance with this Part, in respect of any accounting reference period more than 15% of the income it derives from securities.

(3) Subsection (2)(c) does not require an investment company to be prohibited by its articles from redeeming or purchasing its own shares in accordance with Chapter 3 or 4 of Part 18 out of its capital profits.

(4) Notice to the registrar under this section may be revoked at any time by the company on giving notice to the registrar that it no longer wishes to be an investment company within the meaning of this section.

(5) On giving such a notice, the company ceases to be such a company.

NOTES

Commencement: 6 April 2008.

Commencement (transitional provisions): see the note to s 829 at **[1.829]**.

Commencement (transitional adaptations): art 6 of the Companies Act 2006 (Commencement No 5, Transitional Provisions and Savings) Order 2007, SI 2007/3495 provides that the provisions brought into force by arts 3 and 5 of that Order shall have effect subject to any transitional adaptations specified in Sch 1 to that Order. Schedule 1, Pt 1, para 16 to the Order (at **[2.62]**) provided for such transitional adaptations (note that this paragraph was revoked by the Companies Act 2006 (Commencement No 8, Transitional Provisions and Savings) Order 2008, SI 2008/2860, art 6, as from 1 October 2009 (subject to any relevant transitional provision or saving in Sch 2 to that Order)).

[1.834]

834 Investment company: condition as to holdings in other companies

(1) The condition referred to in section 833(2)(b) (requirements to be complied with by investment company) is that none of the company's holdings in companies (other than those that are for the time being investment companies) represents more than 15% by value of the company's investments.

(2) For this purpose—

    (a) holdings in companies that—

        (i) are members of a group (whether or not including the investing company), and

        (ii) are not for the time being investment companies,

    are treated as holdings in a single company; and

    (b) where the investing company is a member of a group, money owed to it by another member of the group—

        (i) is treated as a security of the latter held by the investing company, and

        (ii) is accordingly treated as, or as part of, the holding of the investing company in the company owing the money.

(3) The condition does not apply—

    (a) to a holding in a company acquired before 6th April 1965 that on that date represented not more than 25% by value of the investing company's investments, or

    (b) to a holding in a company that, when it was acquired, represented not more than 15% by value of the investing company's investments,

so long as no addition is made to the holding.

(4) For the purposes of subsection (3)—

    (a) "holding" means the shares or securities (whether or one class or more than one class) held in any one company;

    (b) an addition is made to a holding whenever the investing company acquires shares or securities of that one company, otherwise than by being allotted shares or securities without becoming liable to give any consideration, and if an addition is made to a holding that holding is acquired when the addition or latest addition is made to the holding; and

    (c) where in connection with a scheme of reconstruction a company issues shares or securities to persons holding shares or securities in a second company in respect of and in proportion to (or as nearly as may be in proportion to) their holdings in the second company, without those persons becoming liable to give any consideration, a holding of the shares or securities in the second company and a corresponding holding of the shares or securities so issued shall be regarded as the same holding.

(5) In this section—

"company" and "shares" shall be construed in accordance with sections 99[, 103A] and 288 of the Taxation of Chargeable Gains Act 1992 (c 12);

"group" means a company and all companies that are its 51% subsidiaries (within the meaning of [Chapter 3 of Part 24 of the Corporation Tax Act 2010]); and

"scheme of reconstruction" has the same meaning as in section 136 of the Taxation of Chargeable Gains Act 1992.

NOTES

Commencement: 6 April 2008.

Commencement (transitional provisions): see the note to s 829 at **[1.829]**.

Sub-s (5): figure in square brackets in definitions "company" and "shares" inserted by the Finance Act 2009, s 44, Sch 22, Pt 2, para 11(4) (as to the commencement of this amendment, see the final note below); words in square brackets in definition "group" substituted by the Corporation Tax Act 2010, s 1177, Sch 1, Pt 2, paras 487, 489 (note that the 2010 Act came into force on 1 April 2010 and has effect, for corporation tax purposes for accounting periods ending on or after that day, and for income tax and capital gains tax purposes for the tax year 2010–11 and subsequent tax years; see s 1184(1) of the 2010 Act (and for transitional provisions and savings, see Sch 2 to that Act)).

Note: the Finance Act 2009, s 44, Sch 22, Pt 2, para 12–14 provide as follows—

"12   Commencement: general

(1) The amendments made by this Part of this Schedule have effect in relation to the acquisition, holding and disposal of rights in a relevant offshore fund on or after the commencement day, subject to paragraphs 13 and 15.

(2) In this paragraph and paragraphs 15 to 18, "the commencement day" means—

    (a) in relation to the acquisition, holding and disposal of rights by a person subject to the charge to capital gains tax, 1 December 2009, and

(b)   in relation to the acquisition, holding and disposal of rights by a person subject to the charge to corporation tax, such day as the Treasury may by order appoint.

13   Commencement: certain consequential amendments
(1)   *(Not relevant)*.
(2)   The amendments made by sub-paragraphs (2), (4) and (5) of paragraph 11 come into force in accordance with an order made by the Treasury.

14   Commencement orders
(1)   An order under paragraph 12(2)(b) or 13(2)—
    (a)   may make different provision for different cases or different purposes, and
    (b)   may include transitional provision and savings.
(2)   *(Not relevant)*.".

[1.835]
835   Power to extend provisions relating to investment companies
(1)   The Secretary of State may by regulations extend the provisions of sections 832 to 834 (distributions by investment companies out of accumulated profits), with or without modifications, to other companies whose principal business consists of investing their funds in securities, land or other assets with the aim of spreading investment risk and giving their members the benefit of the results of the management of the assets.
(2)   Regulations under this section are subject to affirmative resolution procedure.

NOTES
Commencement: 20 January 2007 (for the purpose of enabling the exercise of powers to make Orders or Regulations by statutory instrument); 6 April 2008 (otherwise).
Commencement (transitional provisions): see the note to s 829 at **[1.829]**.

CHAPTER 2
JUSTIFICATION OF DISTRIBUTION BY REFERENCE TO ACCOUNTS

Justification of distribution by reference to accounts

[1.836]
836   Justification of distribution by reference to relevant accounts
(1)   Whether a distribution may be made by a company without contravening this Part is determined by reference to the following items as stated in the relevant accounts—
    (a)   profits, losses, assets and liabilities;
    (b)   provisions of the following kinds—
        (i)   where the relevant accounts are Companies Act accounts, provisions of a kind specified for the purposes of this subsection by regulations under section 396;
        (ii)   where the relevant accounts are IAS accounts, provisions of any kind;
    (c)   share capital and reserves (including undistributable reserves).
(2)   The relevant accounts are the company's last annual accounts, except that—
    (a)   where the distribution would be found to contravene this Part by reference to the company's last annual accounts, it may be justified by reference to interim accounts, and
    (b)   where the distribution is proposed to be declared during the company's first accounting reference period, or before any accounts have been circulated in respect of that period, it may be justified by reference to initial accounts.
(3)   The requirements of—
    section 837 (as regards the company's last annual accounts),
    section 838 (as regards interim accounts), and
    section 839 (as regards initial accounts),
must be complied with, as and where applicable.
(4)   If any applicable requirement of those sections is not complied with, the accounts may not be relied on for the purposes of this Part and the distribution is accordingly treated as contravening this Part.

NOTES
Commencement: 6 April 2008.
Commencement (transitional provisions): see the note to s 829 at **[1.829]**.
Regulations under section 396: see the notes to that section at **[1.396]**. See also the Small Companies and Groups (Accounts and Directors' Report) Regulations 2008, SI 2008/409, reg 12 (at **[4.153]**), and the Large and Medium-sized Companies and Groups (Accounts and Reports) Regulations 2008, SI 2008/410, reg 12 (at **[4.181]**) which provide that Sch 7 to SI 2008/409 (at **[4.167]**, **[4.168]**) and Sch 9 to SI 2008/410 (at **[4.217]**, **[4.218]**) define "provisions" for the purpose of those Regulations and for the purposes of sub-s (1)(b)(i) above.

Requirements applicable in relation to relevant accounts

[1.837]
837   Requirements where last annual accounts used
(1)   The company's last annual accounts means the company's individual accounts—
    (a)   that were last circulated to members in accordance with section 423 (duty to circulate copies of annual accounts and reports), or

(b)   if in accordance with section 426 the company provided a summary financial statement instead, that formed the basis of that statement.

(2)   The accounts must have been properly prepared in accordance with this Act, or have been so prepared subject only to matters that are not material for determining (by reference to the items mentioned in section 836(1)) whether the distribution would contravene this Part.

(3)   Unless the company is exempt from audit and the directors take advantage of that exemption, the auditor must have made his report on the accounts.

(4)   If that report was qualified—

(a)   the auditor must have stated in writing (either at the time of his report or subsequently) whether in his opinion the matters in respect of which his report is qualified are material for determining whether a distribution would contravene this Part, and

(b)   a copy of that statement must—

(i)   in the case of a private company, have been circulated to members in accordance with section 423, or

(ii)   in the case of a public company, have been laid before the company in general meeting.

(5)   An auditor's statement is sufficient for the purposes of a distribution if it relates to distributions of a description that includes the distribution in question, even if at the time of the statement it had not been proposed.

NOTES

Commencement: 6 April 2008.

Commencement (transitional provisions): see the note to s 829 at **[1.829]**.

[1.838]
838   Requirements where interim accounts used

(1)   Interim accounts must be accounts that enable a reasonable judgment to be made as to the amounts of the items mentioned in section 836(1).

(2)   Where interim accounts are prepared for a proposed distribution by a public company, the following requirements apply.

(3)   The accounts must have been properly prepared, or have been so prepared subject to matters that are not material for determining (by reference to the items mentioned in section 836(1)) whether the distribution would contravene this Part.

(4)   "Properly prepared" means prepared in accordance with sections 395 to 397 (requirements for company individual accounts), applying those requirements with such modifications as are necessary because the accounts are prepared otherwise than in respect of an accounting reference period.

(5)   The balance sheet comprised in the accounts must have been signed in accordance with section 414.

(6)   A copy of the accounts must have been delivered to the registrar.

Any requirement of Part 35 of this Act as to the delivery of a certified translation into English of any document forming part of the accounts must also have been met.

NOTES

Commencement: 6 April 2008.

Commencement (transitional provisions): see the note to s 829 at **[1.829]**.

Commencement (transitional adaptations): art 6 of the Companies Act 2006 (Commencement No 5, Transitional Provisions and Savings) Order 2007, SI 2007/3495 provides that the provisions brought into force by arts 3 and 5 of that Order shall have effect subject to any transitional adaptations specified in Sch 1 to that Order. Schedule 1, Pt 1, para 17 to the Order (at **[2.62]**) provided for such transitional adaptations (note that this paragraph was revoked by the Companies Act 2006 (Commencement No 8, Transitional Provisions and Savings) Order 2008, SI 2008/2860, art 6, as from 1 October 2009 (subject to any relevant transitional provision or saving in Sch 2 to that Order)).

[1.839]
839   Requirements where initial accounts used

(1)   Initial accounts must be accounts that enable a reasonable judgment to be made as to the amounts of the items mentioned in section 836(1).

(2)   Where initial accounts are prepared for a proposed distribution by a public company, the following requirements apply.

(3)   The accounts must have been properly prepared, or have been so prepared subject to matters that are not material for determining (by reference to the items mentioned in section 836(1)) whether the distribution would contravene this Part.

(4)   "Properly prepared" means prepared in accordance with sections 395 to 397 (requirements for company individual accounts), applying those requirements with such modifications as are necessary because the accounts are prepared otherwise than in respect of an accounting reference period.

(5)   The company's auditor must have made a report stating whether, in his opinion, the accounts have been properly prepared.

(6)   If that report was qualified—

(a) the auditor must have stated in writing (either at the time of his report or subsequently) whether in his opinion the matters in respect of which his report is qualified are material for determining whether a distribution would contravene this Part, and

[(b) a copy of that statement must have been laid before the company in general meeting.]

(7) A copy of the accounts, of the auditor's report and of any auditor's statement must have been delivered to the registrar.

Any requirement of Part 35 of this Act as to the delivery of a certified translation into English of any of those documents must also have been met.

NOTES

Commencement: 6 April 2008.

Commencement (transitional provisions): see the note to s 829 at [**1.829**].

Commencement (transitional adaptations): art 6 of the Companies Act 2006 (Commencement No 5, Transitional Provisions and Savings) Order 2007, SI 2007/3495 provides that the provisions brought into force by arts 3 and 5 of that Order shall have effect subject to any transitional adaptations specified in Sch 1 to that Order. Schedule 1, Pt 1, para 18 to the Order (at [**2.62**]) provided for such transitional adaptations (note that this paragraph was revoked by the Companies Act 2006 (Commencement No 8, Transitional Provisions and Savings) Order 2008, SI 2008/2860, art 6, as from 1 October 2009 (subject to any relevant transitional provision or saving in Sch 2 to that Order)).

Sub-s (6): para (b) substituted by the Companies Act 2006 (Consequential Amendments, Transitional Provisions and Savings) Order 2009, SI 2009/1941, art 2(1), Sch 1, para 260(1), (4), as from 1 October 2009.

Application of provisions to successive distributions etc

[1.840]

840 Successive distributions etc by reference to the same accounts

(1) In determining whether a proposed distribution may be made by a company in a case where—
  (a) one or more previous distributions have been made in pursuance of a determination made by reference to the same relevant accounts, or
  (b) relevant financial assistance has been given, or other relevant payments have been made, since those accounts were prepared,

the provisions of this Part apply as if the amount of the proposed distribution was increased by the amount of the previous distributions, financial assistance and other payments.

(2) The financial assistance and other payments that are relevant for this purpose are—
  (a) financial assistance lawfully given by the company out of its distributable profits;
  (b) financial assistance given by the company in contravention of section 678 or 679 (prohibited financial assistance) in a case where the giving of that assistance reduces the company's net assets or increases its net liabilities;
  (c) payments made by the company in respect of the purchase by it of shares in the company, except a payment lawfully made otherwise than out of distributable profits;
  (d) payments of any description specified in section 705 (payments apart from purchase price of shares to be made out of distributable profits).

(3) In this section "financial assistance" has the same meaning as in Chapter 2 of Part 18 (see section 677).

(4) For the purpose of applying subsection (2)(b) in relation to any financial assistance—
  (a) "net assets" means the amount by which the aggregate amount of the company's assets exceeds the aggregate amount of its liabilities, and
  (b) "net liabilities" means the amount by which the aggregate amount of the company's liabilities exceeds the aggregate amount of its assets,

taking the amount of the assets and liabilities to be as stated in the company's accounting records immediately before the financial assistance is given.

(5) For this purpose a company's liabilities include any amount retained as reasonably necessary for the purposes of providing for any liability—
  (a) the nature of which is clearly defined, and
  (b) which is either likely to be incurred or certain to be incurred but uncertain as to amount or as to the date on which it will arise.

NOTES

Commencement: 6 April 2008.

Commencement (transitional provisions): see the note to s 829 at [**1.829**].

Commencement (transitional adaptations): art 6 of the Companies Act 2006 (Commencement No 5, Transitional Provisions and Savings) Order 2007, SI 2007/3495 provides that the provisions brought into force by arts 3 and 5 of that Order shall have effect subject to any transitional adaptations specified in Sch 1 to that Order. Schedule 1, Pt 1, para 19 to the Order (at [**2.62**]) provided for such transitional adaptations (note that this paragraph was revoked by the Companies Act 2006 (Commencement No 8, Transitional Provisions and Savings) Order 2008, SI 2008/2860, art 6, as from 1 October 2009 (subject to any relevant transitional provision or saving in Sch 2 to that Order)).

CHAPTER 3
SUPPLEMENTARY PROVISIONS

Accounting matters

[1.841]

841   Realised losses and profits and revaluation of fixed assets

(1)   The following provisions have effect for the purposes of this Part.

(2)   The following are treated as realised losses—

   (a)   in the case of Companies Act accounts, provisions of a kind specified for the purposes of this paragraph by regulations under section 396 (except revaluation provisions);

   (b)   in the case of IAS accounts, provisions of any kind (except revaluation provisions).

(3)   A "revaluation provision" means a provision in respect of a diminution in value of a fixed asset appearing on a revaluation of all the fixed assets of the company, or of all of its fixed assets other than goodwill.

(4)   For the purpose of subsections (2) and (3) any consideration by the directors of the value at a particular time of a fixed asset is treated as a revaluation provided—

   (a)   the directors are satisfied that the aggregate value at that time of the fixed assets of the company that have not actually been revalued is not less than the aggregate amount at which they are then stated in the company's accounts, and

   (b)   it is stated in a note to the accounts—

      (i)   that the directors have considered the value of some or all of the fixed assets of the company without actually revaluing them,

      (ii)   that they are satisfied that the aggregate value of those assets at the time of their consideration was not less than the aggregate amount at which they were then stated in the company's accounts, and

      (iii)   that accordingly, by virtue of this subsection, amounts are stated in the accounts on the basis that a revaluation of fixed assets of the company is treated as having taken place at that time.

(5)   Where—

   (a)   on the revaluation of a fixed asset, an unrealised profit is shown to have been made, and

   (b)   on or after the revaluation, a sum is written off or retained for depreciation of that asset over a period,

an amount equal to the amount by which that sum exceeds the sum which would have been so written off or retained for the depreciation of that asset over that period, if that profit had not been made, is treated as a realised profit made over that period.

NOTES

Commencement: 6 April 2008.

Commencement (transitional provisions): see the note to s 829 at **[1.829]**.

Regulations under section 396: see the notes to that section at **[1.396]**. See also the Small Companies and Groups (Accounts and Directors' Report) Regulations 2008, SI 2008/409, reg 12 (at **[4.153]**), and the Large and Medium-sized Companies and Groups (Accounts and Reports) Regulations 2008, SI 2008/410, reg 12 (at **[4.181]**) which provide that Sch 7 to SI 2008/409 (at **[4.167]**, **[4.168]**) and Sch 9 to SI 2008/410 (at **[4.217]**, **[4.218]**) define "provisions" for the purpose of those Regulations and for the purposes of sub-s (2)(a) above.

[1.842]

842   Determination of profit or loss in respect of asset where records incomplete

In determining for the purposes of this Part whether a company has made a profit or loss in respect of an asset where—

   (a)   there is no record of the original cost of the asset, or

   (b)   a record cannot be obtained without unreasonable expense or delay,

its cost is taken to be the value ascribed to it in the earliest available record of its value made on or after its acquisition by the company.

NOTES

Commencement: 6 April 2008.

Commencement (transitional provisions): see the note to s 829 at **[1.829]**.

[1.843]

843   Realised profits and losses of long-term insurance business

(1)   The provisions of this section have effect for the purposes of this Part as it applies in relation to an authorised insurance company[, other than an insurance special purpose vehicle,] carrying on long-term business.

(2)   An amount included in the relevant part of the company's balance sheet that—

   (a)   represents a surplus in the fund or funds maintained by it in respect of its long-term business, and

   (b)   has not been allocated to policy holders or, as the case may be, carried forward unappropriated in accordance with asset identification rules made under section 142(2) of the Financial Services and Markets Act 2000 (c 8),

is treated as a realised profit.

(3)   For the purposes of subsection (2)—

   (a)   the relevant part of the balance sheet is that part of the balance sheet that represents accumulated profit or loss;

   (b)   a surplus in the fund or funds maintained by the company in respect of its long-term business means an excess of the assets representing that fund or those funds over the liabilities of the company attributable to its long-term business, as shown by an actuarial investigation.

(4)   A deficit in the fund or funds maintained by the company in respect of its long-term business is treated as a realised loss.

For this purpose a deficit in any such fund or funds means an excess of the liabilities of the company attributable to its long-term business over the assets representing that fund or those funds, as shown by an actuarial investigation.

(5)   Subject to subsections (2) and (4), any profit or loss arising in the company's long-term business is to be left out of account.

(6)   For the purposes of this section an "actuarial investigation" means an investigation made into the financial condition of an authorised insurance company in respect of its long-term business—

   (a)   carried out once in every period of twelve months in accordance with rules made under Part 10 of the Financial Services and Markets Act 2000, or

   (b)   carried out in accordance with a requirement imposed under section 166 of that Act,

by an actuary appointed as actuary to the company.

(7)   In this section "long-term business" means business that consists of effecting or carrying out contracts of long-term insurance.

This definition must be read with section 22 of the Financial Services and Markets Act 2000, any relevant order under that section and Schedule 2 to that Act.

[(8)   In this section "insurance special purpose vehicle" means a special purpose vehicle within the meaning of Article 2.1(p) of Directive 2005/68/EC of the European Parliament and of the Council of 16 November 2005 on reinsurance and amending Council Directives 73/239/EEC, 92/49/EEC as well as Directives 98/78/EC and 2002/83/EC.]

NOTES

Commencement: 6 April 2008.

Commencement (transitional provisions): see the note to s 829 at **[1.829]**.

Sub-s (1): words in square brackets inserted by the Reinsurance Directive Regulations 2007, SI 2007/3253, reg 2(3), Sch 3, para 2(1)(a), as from 10 December 2007.

Sub-s (8): added by SI 2007/3253, reg 2(3), Sch 3, para 2(1)(b), as from 10 December 2007.

[1.844]
844   Treatment of development costs

(1)   Where development costs are shown or included as an asset in a company's accounts, any amount shown or included in respect of those costs is treated—

   (a)   for the purposes of section 830 (distributions to be made out of profits available for the purpose) as a realised loss, and

   (b)   for the purposes of section 832 (distributions by investment companies out of accumulated revenue profits) as a realised revenue loss.

This is subject to the following exceptions.

(2)   Subsection (1) does not apply to any part of that amount representing an unrealised profit made on revaluation of those costs.

(3)   Subsection (1) does not apply if—

   (a)   there are special circumstances in the company's case justifying the directors in deciding that the amount there mentioned is not to be treated as required by subsection (1),

   (b)   it is stated—

      (i)   in the case of Companies Act accounts, in the note required by regulations under section 396 as to the reasons for showing development costs as an asset, or

      (ii)   in the case of IAS accounts, in any note to the accounts,

      that the amount is not to be so treated, and

   (c)   the note explains the circumstances relied upon to justify the decision of the directors to that effect.

NOTES

Commencement: 6 April 2008.

Commencement (transitional provisions): see the note to s 829 at **[1.829]**.

Distributions in kind

[1.845]
845   Distributions in kind: determination of amount

(1)   This section applies for determining the amount of a distribution consisting of or including, or treated as arising in consequence of, the sale, transfer or other disposition by a company of a non-cash asset where—

   (a)   at the time of the distribution the company has profits available for distribution, and

(b)   if the amount of the distribution were to be determined in accordance with this section, the company could make the distribution without contravening this Part.

(2)   The amount of the distribution (or the relevant part of it) is taken to be—

   (a)   in a case where the amount or value of the consideration for the disposition is not less than the book value of the asset, zero;

   (b)   in any other case, the amount by which the book value of the asset exceeds the amount or value of any consideration for the disposition.

(3)   For the purposes of subsection (1)(a) the company's profits available for distribution are treated as increased by the amount (if any) by which the amount or value of any consideration for the disposition exceeds the book value of the asset.

(4)   In this section "book value", in relation to an asset, means—

   (a)   the amount at which the asset is stated in the relevant accounts, or

   (b)   where the asset is not stated in those accounts at any amount, zero.

(5)   The provisions of Chapter 2 (justification of distribution by reference to accounts) have effect subject to this section.

NOTES

Commencement: 6 April 2008.

Commencement (transitional provisions): see the note to s 829 at **[1.829]**.

[1.846]

846   Distributions in kind: treatment of unrealised profits

(1)   This section applies where—

   (a)   a company makes a distribution consisting of or including, or treated as arising in consequence of, the sale, transfer or other disposition by the company of a non-cash asset, and

   (b)   any part of the amount at which that asset is stated in the relevant accounts represents an unrealised profit.

(2)   That profit is treated as a realised profit—

   (a)   for the purpose of determining the lawfulness of the distribution in accordance with this Part (whether before or after the distribution takes place), and

   (b)   for the purpose of the application, in relation to anything done with a view to or in connection with the making of the distribution, of any provision of regulations under section 396 under which only realised profits are to be included in or transferred to the profit and loss account.

NOTES

Commencement: 6 April 2008.

Commencement (transitional provisions): see the note to s 829 at **[1.829]**.

Consequences of unlawful distribution

[1.847]

847   Consequences of unlawful distribution

(1)   This section applies where a distribution, or part of one, made by a company to one of its members is made in contravention of this Part.

(2)   If at the time of the distribution the member knows or has reasonable grounds for believing that it is so made, he is liable—

   (a)   to repay it (or that part of it, as the case may be) to the company, or

   (b)   in the case of a distribution made otherwise than in cash, to pay the company a sum equal to the value of the distribution (or part) at that time.

(3)   This is without prejudice to any obligation imposed apart from this section on a member of a company to repay a distribution unlawfully made to him.

(4)   This section does not apply in relation to—

   (a)   financial assistance given by a company in contravention of section 678 or 679, or

   (b)   any payment made by a company in respect of the redemption or purchase by the company of shares in itself.

NOTES

Commencement: 6 April 2008.

Commencement (transitional provisions): see the note to s 829 at **[1.829]**.

Commencement (transitional adaptations): art 6 of the Companies Act 2006 (Commencement No 5, Transitional Provisions and Savings) Order 2007, SI 2007/3495 provides that the provisions brought into force by arts 3 and 5 of that Order shall have effect subject to any transitional adaptations specified in Sch 1 to that Order. Schedule 1, Pt 1, para 20 to the Order (at **[2.62]**) provided for such transitional adaptations (note that this paragraph was revoked by the Companies Act 2006 (Commencement No 8, Transitional Provisions and Savings) Order 2008, SI 2008/2860, art 6, as from 1 October 2009 (subject to any relevant transitional provision or saving in Sch 2 to that Order)).

Other matters

[1.848]
848 Saving for certain older provisions in articles
(1) Where immediately before the relevant date a company was authorised by a provision of its articles to apply its unrealised profits in paying up in full or in part unissued shares to be allotted to members of the company as fully or partly paid bonus shares, that provision continues (subject to any alteration of the articles) as authority for those profits to be so applied after that date.
(2) For this purpose the relevant date is—
　(a)　for companies registered in Great Britain, 22nd December 1980;
　(b)　for companies registered in Northern Ireland, 1st July 1983.

NOTES
Commencement: 6 April 2008.
Commencement (transitional provisions): see the note to s 829 at **[1.829]**.

[1.849]
849 Restriction on application of unrealised profits
A company must not apply an unrealised profit in paying up debentures or any amounts unpaid on its issued shares.

NOTES
Commencement: 6 April 2008.
Commencement (transitional provisions): see the note to s 829 at **[1.829]**.

[1.850]
850 Treatment of certain older profits or losses
(1) Where the directors of a company are, after making all reasonable enquiries, unable to determine whether a particular profit made before the relevant date is realised or unrealised, they may treat the profit as realised.
(2) Where the directors of a company, after making all reasonable enquiries, are unable to determine whether a particular loss made before the relevant date is realised or unrealised, they may treat the loss as unrealised.
(3) For the purposes of this section the relevant date is—
　(a)　for companies registered in Great Britain, 22nd December 1980;
　(b)　for companies registered in Northern Ireland, 1st July 1983.

NOTES
Commencement: 6 April 2008.
Commencement (transitional provisions): see the note to s 829 at **[1.829]**.

[1.851]
851 Application of rules of law restricting distributions
(1) Except as provided in this section, the provisions of this Part are without prejudice to any rule of law restricting the sums out of which, or the cases in which, a distribution may be made.
(2) For the purposes of any rule of law requiring distributions to be paid out of profits or restricting the return of capital to members—
　(a)　section 845 (distributions in kind: determination of amount) applies to determine the amount of any distribution or return of capital consisting of or including, or treated as arising in consequence of the sale, transfer or other disposition by a company of a non-cash asset; and
　(b)　section 846 (distributions in kind: treatment of unrealised profits) applies as it applies for the purposes of this Part.
(3) In this section references to distributions are to amounts regarded as distributions for the purposes of any such rule of law as is referred to in subsection (1).

NOTES
Commencement: 6 April 2008.
Commencement (transitional provisions): see the note to s 829 at **[1.829]**.

[1.852]
852 Saving for other restrictions on distributions
The provisions of this Part are without prejudice to any enactment, or any provision of a company's articles, restricting the sums out of which, or the cases in which, a distribution may be made.

NOTES
Commencement: 6 April 2008.
Commencement (transitional provisions): see the note to s 829 at **[1.829]**.

[1.853]
853   Minor definitions
(1)   The following provisions apply for the purposes of this Part.
(2)   References to profit or losses of any description—
   (a)   are to profits or losses of that description made at any time, and
   (b)   except where the context otherwise requires, are to profits or losses of a revenue or capital character.
(3)   "Capitalisation", in relation to a company's profits, means any of the following operations (whenever carried out)—
   (a)   applying the profits in wholly or partly paying up unissued shares in the company to be allotted to members of the company as fully or partly paid bonus shares, or
   (b)   transferring the profits to capital redemption reserve.
(4)   References to "realised profits" and "realised losses", in relation to a company's accounts, are to such profits or losses of the company as fall to be treated as realised in accordance with principles generally accepted at the time when the accounts are prepared, with respect to the determination for accounting purposes of realised profits or losses.
(5)   Subsection (4) is without prejudice to—
   (a)   the construction of any other expression (where appropriate) by reference to accepted accounting principles or practice, or
   (b)   any specific provision for the treatment of profits or losses of any description as realised.
(6)   "Fixed assets" means assets of a company which are intended for use on a continuing basis in the company's activities.

NOTES
Commencement: 6 April 2008.
Commencement (transitional provisions): see the note to s 829 at **[1.829]**.

PART 24
A COMPANY'S ANNUAL RETURN

[1.854]
854   Duty to deliver annual returns
(1)   Every company must deliver to the registrar successive annual returns each of which is made up to a date not later than the date that is from time to time the company's return date.
(2)   The company's return date is—
   (a)   the anniversary of the company's incorporation, or
   (b)   if the company's last return delivered in accordance with this Part was made up to a different date, the anniversary of that date.
(3)   Each return must—
   (a)   contain the information required by or under the following provisions of this Part, and
   (b)   be delivered to the registrar within 28 days after the date to which it is made up.

NOTES
Commencement: 1 October 2009.
Commencement (transitional provisions): Sch 2, para 81 to the Companies Act 2006 (Commencement No 8, Transitional Provisions and Savings) Order 2008, SI 2008/2860 (at **[2.91]**) provides as follows—

"Annual returns (ss 854 to 859)
81.—(1)   Sections 854 to 859 of the Companies Act 2006 (a company's annual return) apply to annual returns made up to a date on or after 1st October 2009.
(2)   Sections 363 to 365 of the 1985 Act or Articles 371 to 373 of the 1986 Order continue to apply to annual returns made up to a date before 1st October 2009.
(3)   Any reference in the Companies Act 2006 to a company's last return, or to a return delivered in accordance with Part 24 of that Act, shall be read as including (so far as necessary to ensure the continuity of the law) a return made up to a date before 1st October 2009 or delivered in accordance with the 1985 Act or the 1986 Order."

[1.855]
855   Contents of annual return: general
(1)   Every annual return must state the date to which it is made up and contain the following information—
   (a)   the address of the company's registered office;
   (b)   the type of company it is and its principal business activities;
   (c)   [the required particulars (see section 855A)] of—
      (i)   the directors of the company, and
      (ii)   in the case of a private company with a secretary or a public company, the secretary or joint secretaries;
   [(d)   if any company records are (in accordance with regulations under section 1136) kept at a place other than the company's registered office, the address of that place and the records that are kept there;]
   [(f)   *whether the company was a traded company at any time during the return period.*]

(2)   The information as to the company's type must be given by reference to the classification scheme prescribed for the purposes of this section.

(3)   The information as to the company's principal business activities may be given by reference to one or more categories of any prescribed system of classifying business activities.

[(4)   In this Part—

["DTR5 issuer" means an issuer to which Chapter 5 of the Disclosure Rules and Transparency Rules sourcebook issued by the Financial Services Authority applies;

"relevant market" means any of the markets mentioned in article 4(1) of the Financial Services and Markets Act 2000 (Prescribed Markets and Qualifying Investments) Order 2001; and]

"return period", in relation to an annual return, means the period beginning immediately after the date to which the last return was made up (or, in the case of the first return, with the incorporation of the company) and ending with the date to which the return is made up; *and*

"traded company" means a company any of whose shares are shares admitted to trading on a regulated market (so that "non-traded company" means a company none of whose shares are shares admitted to trading on a regulated market).]

NOTES

Commencement: 20 January 2007 (for the purpose of enabling the exercise of powers to make Orders or Regulations by statutory instrument); 1 October 2009 (otherwise).

Commencement (transitional provisions): see the note to s 854 at **[1.854]**.

Sub-s (1) is amended as follows:

Words in square brackets in para (c) substituted by the Companies Act 2006 (Annual Return and Service Addresses) Regulations 2008, SI 2008/3000, reg 2(1), as from 1 October 2009 (in relation to annual returns made up to that date or a later date).

Para (d) substituted (for the original paras (d), (e)) by SI 2008/3000, reg 3, as from 1 October 2009 (in relation to annual returns made up to that date or a later date).

Para (f) inserted by SI 2008/3000, reg 4(1), as from 1 October 2009 (in relation to annual returns made up to that date or a later date), and is repealed by the Companies Act 2006 (Annual Returns) Regulations 2011, SI 2011/1487, reg 2(a), as from 1 October 2011 (in relation to annual returns made up to that date or a later date).

Sub-s (4): added by SI 2008/3000, reg 4(2), as from 1 October 2009 (in relation to annual returns made up to that date or a later date); the definitions in square brackets are inserted, and the words in italics are repealed, by SI 2011/1487, reg 2(b), as from 1 October 2011 (in relation to annual returns made up to that date or a later date).

Classification scheme prescribed for the purposes of sub-s (2) above: see the Companies Act 2006 (Annual Return and Service Addresses) Regulations 2008, SI 2008/3000, Sch 1 at **[4.316]**.

The Standard Industrial Classification 2003 is prescribed for the purposes of sub-s (3) above, with the addition of the following codes and designations, see the Companies Act 2006 (Annual Return and Service Addresses) Regulations 2008, SI 2008/3000, reg 6 and Sch 2 at **[4.314]**, **[4.317]** (and note that this is amended by SI 2011/1487, as from 1 October 2011):

*   7499 non-trading company
*   9800 residents' property management company.
*   9999 dormant company.

Regulations: the Companies Act 2006 (Annual Returns) Regulations 2011, SI 2011/1487.

[1.855A]

[855A   Required particulars of directors and secretaries

(1)   For the purposes of section 855(1)(c) the required particulars of a director are—

(a)   where the director is an individual, the particulars required by section 163 to be entered in the register of directors (subject to subsection (2) below); and

(b)   where the director is a body corporate or a firm that is a legal person under the law by which it is governed, the particulars required by section 164 to be entered in the register of directors.

(2)   The former name of a director who is an individual is a required particular in relation to an annual return only if the director was known by the name for business purposes during the return period.

(3)   For the purposes of section 855(1)(c)(ii) the required particulars of a secretary are—

(a)   where a secretary is an individual, the particulars required by section 277 to be entered in the register of secretaries (subject to subsection (4) below); and

(b)   where a secretary is a body corporate or a firm that is a legal person under the law by which it is governed, the particulars required by section 278(1) to be entered in the register of secretaries.

(4)   The former name of a secretary who is an individual is a required particular in relation to an annual return only if the secretary was known by the name for business purposes during the return period.

(5)   Where all the partners in a firm are joint secretaries, the required particulars are the particulars that would be required to be entered in the register of secretaries if the firm were a legal person and the firm had been appointed secretary.]

NOTES

Commencement: 1 October 2009.

Inserted by the Companies Act 2006 (Annual Return and Service Addresses) Regulations 2008, SI 2008/3000, reg 2(2), as from 1 October 2009 (in relation to annual returns made up to that date or a later date).

[1.856]

856   Contents of annual return: information about [shares and] share capital   . . .

(1)   The annual return of a company having a share capital must also contain [a statement of capital].

(2)   The statement of capital must state with respect to the company's share capital at the date to which the return is made up—

    (a)   the total number of shares of the company,

    (b)   the aggregate nominal value of those shares,

    (c)   for each class of shares—

       (i)   [the voting rights] attached to the shares,

       (ii)   the total number of shares of that class, and

       (iii)   the aggregate nominal value of shares of that class, and

    (d)   the amount paid up and the amount (if any) unpaid on each share (whether on account of the nominal value of the share or by way of premium).

[(2A)   The annual return must also state whether any of the company's shares were, at any time during the return period, shares admitted to trading on a relevant market or on any other market which is outside the United Kingdom.

(2B)   If any of the company's shares were shares admitted to trading as mentioned in subsection (2A), the annual return must also state whether both of the following conditions were satisfied throughout the return period—

    (a)   there were shares of the company which were shares admitted to trading on a relevant market;

    (b)   the company was a DTR5 issuer.]

(3)–(6)   . . .

NOTES

Commencement: 20 January 2007 (for the purpose of enabling the exercise of powers to make Orders or Regulations by statutory instrument); 1 October 2009 (otherwise).

Commencement (transitional provisions): see the note to s 854 at **[1.854]**.

Section heading: words omitted repealed by the Companies Act 2006 (Annual Return and Service Addresses) Regulations 2008, SI 2008/3000, reg 7(1)(a), as from 1 October 2009 (in relation to annual returns made up to that date or a later date); words in square brackets inserted by the Companies Act 2006 (Annual Returns) Regulations 2011, SI 2011/1487, reg 3(2), as from 1 October 2011 (in relation to annual returns made up to that date or a later date).

Sub-ss (1), (2): words in square brackets substituted by SI 2008/3000, reg 7(1)(b), (c), as from 1 October 2009 (in relation to annual returns made up to that date or a later date). Sub-s (1) subsequently substituted (by new sub-ss (1), (1A)) by SI 2011/1487, reg 3(1)(a), as from 1 October 2011 (in relation to annual returns made up to that date or a later date), as follows—

"(1)   The annual return of a company having a share capital must also contain the following information.

(1A)   The return must contain a statement of capital.".

Sub-ss (2A), (2B): inserted by SI 2011/1487, reg 3(1)(b), as from 1 October 2011 (in relation to annual returns made up to that date or a later date).

Sub-ss (3)–(6): repealed by SI 2008/3000, reg 7(1)(d), as from 1 October 2009 (in relation to annual returns made up to that date or a later date).

[1.856A]

[856A   Contents of annual return: information about shareholders: non-traded companies

(1)   The annual return of a company that was a non-traded company throughout the return period must also contain the following information.

(2)   The return must [also] contain the name (as it appears in the company's register of members) of every person who was a member of the company at any time during the return period.

    The return must conform to the following requirements for the purpose of enabling the entries relating to any given person to be easily found—

    (a)   the entries must be listed in alphabetical order by name; or

    (b)   the return must have annexed to it an index that is sufficient to enable the name of the person in question to be easily found.

(3)   The return must also state—

    (a)   the number of shares of each class held at the end of the date to which the return is made up by each person who was a member of the company at that time,

    (b)   the number of shares of each class transferred during the return period by or to each person who was a member of the company at any time during that period, and

    (c)   the dates of registration of those transfers.

(4)   If either of the two immediately preceding returns has given the full particulars required by subsections (2) and (3), the return need only give such particulars as relate—

    (a)   to persons who became, or ceased to be, members during the return period, and

    (b)   to shares transferred during that period.]

NOTES

Commencement: 1 October 2009

Inserted, together with s 856B, by the Companies Act 2006 (Annual Return and Service Addresses) Regulations 2008, SI 2008/3000, reg 7(2), as from 1 October 2009 (in relation to annual returns made up to that date or a later date).

Sub-s (1): substituted by the Companies Act 2006 (Annual Returns) Regulations 2011, SI 2011/1487, reg 4(1)(a), as from

1 October 2011 (in relation to annual returns made up to that date or a later date), as follows—

"(1)   This section applies to the annual return of a company none of whose shares were, at any time during the return period, shares admitted to trading on a relevant market or on any other market which is outside the United Kingdom.".

Sub-s (2): word in square brackets inserted by SI 2011/1487, reg 4(1)(b), as from 1 October 2011 (in relation to annual returns made up to that date or a later date).

[1.856B]
[856B   Contents of annual return: information about shareholders: traded companies
(1)   The annual return of a company that was a traded company at any time during the return period must also contain the following information.
(2)   The return must contain the name and address (as they appear in the company's register of members) of every person who held at least 5% of the issued shares of any class of the company at any time during the return period.
*   The return must conform to the following requirements for the purpose of enabling the entries relating to any given person to be easily found—*
(a)   the entries must be listed in alphabetical order by name; or
(b)   the return must have annexed to it an index that is sufficient to enable the name of the person in question to be easily found.
(3)   The return must also state—
(a)   the number of shares of each class held at the end of the date to which the return is made up by each person who held at least 5% of the issued shares of any class of the company at that time,
(b)   the number of shares of each class transferred during the return period by or to each person who held at least 5% of the issued shares of any class of the company at any time during that period, and
(c)   the dates of registration of those transfers.
(4)   If either of the two immediately preceding returns has given the full particulars required by subsections (2) and (3), the return need only give such particulars as relate—
(a)   to persons who came to hold, or ceased to hold, at least 5% of the issued shares of any class of the company during the return period, and
(b)   to shares transferred during that period.]

NOTES
Commencement: 1 October 2009
Inserted as noted to s 856A at **[1.856A]**.
Substituted by the Companies Act 2006 (Annual Returns) Regulations 2011, SI 2011/1487, reg 4(3), as from 1 October 2011 (in relation to annual returns made up to that date or a later date), as follows—

"856B   Contents of annual return: information about shareholders: certain traded companies
(1)   This section applies to the annual return of a company any of whose shares were, at any time during the return period, shares admitted to trading on a relevant market or on any other market which is outside the United Kingdom.
(2)   But this section does not apply to the annual return of a company if throughout the return period—
    (a)   there were shares of the company which were shares admitted to trading on a relevant market, and
    (b)   the company was a DTR5 issuer.
(3)   The annual return of a company to which this section applies must also state, in respect of each person who held at least 5% of the issued shares of any class of the company at the end of the date to which the return is made up—
    (a)   the person's name and address (as they appear in the company's register of members); and
    (b)   the number of shares of each class held by the person at that time.
(4)   The return must conform to the following requirements for the purpose of enabling entries relating to any given person to be easily found—
    (a)   the entries must be listed in alphabetical order by name; or
    (b)   the return must have annexed to it an index that is sufficient to enable the name of the person in question to be easily found.".

[1.857]
857   Contents of annual return: power to make further provision by regulations
(1)   The Secretary of State may by regulations make further provision as to the information to be given in a company's annual return.
(2)   The regulations may—
    (a)   amend or repeal the provisions of sections 855 and 856, and
    (b)   provide for exceptions from the requirements of those sections as they have effect from time to time.
(3)   Regulations under this section are subject to negative resolution procedure.

NOTES
Commencement: 20 January 2007 (for the purpose of enabling the exercise of powers to make Orders or Regulations by statutory instrument); 1 October 2009 (otherwise).
Commencement (transitional provisions): see the note to s 854 at **[1.854]**.
Regulations: the Companies Act 2006 (Annual Return and Service Addresses) Regulations 2008, SI 2008/3000 at **[4.312]**; the Companies Act 2006 (Annual Returns) Regulations 2011, SI 2011/1487.

[1.858]
858 Failure to deliver annual return
(1) If a company fails to deliver an annual return before the end of the period of 28 days after a return date, an offence is committed by—
  (a) the company,
  (b) subject to subsection (4)—
    (i) every director of the company, and
    (ii) in the case of a private company with a secretary or a public company, every secretary of the company, and
  (c) every other officer of the company who is in default.
  [For this purpose a shadow director is treated as a director.]
(2) A person guilty of an offence under subsection (1) is liable on summary conviction to a fine not exceeding level 5 on the standard scale and, for continued contravention, a daily default fine not exceeding one-tenth of level 5 on the standard scale.
(3) The contravention continues until such time as an annual return made up to that return date is delivered by the company to the registrar.
(4) It is a defence for a director or secretary charged with an offence under subsection (1)(b) to prove that he took all reasonable steps to avoid the commission or continuation of the offence.
(5) In the case of continued contravention, an offence is also committed by every officer of the company who did not commit an offence under subsection (1) in relation to the initial contravention but is in default in relation to the continued contravention.

A person guilty of an offence under this subsection is liable on summary conviction to a fine not exceeding one-tenth of level 5 on the standard scale for each day on which the contravention continues and he is in default.

NOTES
Commencement: 1 October 2009.
Commencement (transitional provisions): see the note to s 854 at **[1.854]**.
Sub-s (1): words in square brackets inserted by the Companies Act 2006 (Annual Return and Service Addresses) Regulations 2008, SI 2008/3000, reg 8(1), as from 1 October 2009 (in relation to annual returns made up to that date or a later date).

[1.859]
859 Application of provisions to shadow directors
(Repealed as noted below.)

NOTES
This section was due to come into force on 1 October 2009 but was repealed by the Companies Act 2006 (Annual Return and Service Addresses) Regulations 2008, SI 2008/3000, reg 8(2), as from that date.

PART 25
COMPANY CHARGES

NOTES
See further the Banking Act 2009, s 252 which provides as follows—

"252 Registration of charges
(1) Part 25 of the Companies Act 2006 (registration of charges) does not apply to a charge if the person interested in it is—
  (a) the Bank of England,
  (b) the central bank of a country or territory outside the United Kingdom, or
  (c) the European Central Bank.
(2) The reference in subsection (1) to Part 25 of the Companies Act 2006 includes a reference to—
  (a) Part 12 of the Companies Act 1985 (which has effect until the commencement of Part 25 of the 2006 Act),
  (b) Part 13 of the Companies (Northern Ireland) Order 1986 (which has effect until the commencement of Part 25 of the 2006 Act), and
  (c) any provision about registration of charges made under section 1052 of the Companies Act 2006 (overseas companies).".

CHAPTER 1
COMPANIES REGISTERED IN ENGLAND AND WALES OR IN NORTHERN IRELAND

Requirement to register company charges

[1.860]
860 Charges created by a company
(1) A company that creates a charge to which this section applies must deliver the prescribed particulars of the charge, together with the instrument (if any) by which the charge is created or evidenced, to the registrar for registration before the end of the period allowed for registration.
(2) Registration of a charge to which this section applies may instead be effected on the application of a person interested in it.

(3)   Where registration is effected on the application of some person other than the company, that person is entitled to recover from the company the amount of any fees properly paid by him to the registrar on registration.

(4)   If a company fails to comply with subsection (1), an offence is committed by—
   (a)   the company, and
   (b)   every officer of it who is in default.

(5)   A person guilty of an offence under this section is liable—
   (a)   on conviction on indictment, to a fine;
   (b)   on summary conviction, to a fine not exceeding the statutory maximum.

(6)   Subsection (4) does not apply if registration of the charge has been effected on the application of some other person.

(7)   This section applies to the following charges—
   (a)   a charge on land or any interest in land, other than a charge for any rent or other periodical sum issuing out of land,
   (b)   a charge created or evidenced by an instrument which, if executed by an individual, would require registration as a bill of sale,
   (c)   a charge for the purposes of securing any issue of debentures,
   (d)   a charge on uncalled share capital of the company,
   (e)   a charge on calls made but not paid,
   (f)   a charge on book debts of the company,
   (g)   a floating charge on the company's property or undertaking,
   (h)   a charge on a ship or aircraft, or any share in a ship,
   (i)   a charge on goodwill or on any intellectual property.

NOTES
Commencement: 20 January 2007 (for the purpose of enabling the exercise of powers to make Orders or Regulations by statutory instrument); 1 October 2009 (otherwise).

Commencement (transitional provisions): Sch 2, para 82 to the Companies Act 2006 (Commencement No 8, Transitional Provisions and Savings) Order 2008, SI 2008/2860 (at **[2.91]**) provides as follows—

"Company charges (ss 860 to 894)
82.—(1)   Sections 860 and 878 of the Companies Act 2006 (charges created by company) apply to charges created on or after 1st October 2009.
(2)   The corresponding provisions of the 1985 Act or the 1986 Order continue to apply to charges created before that date.".

Regulations: the Companies (Particulars of Company Charges) Regulations 2008, SI 2008/2996 at **[4.308]**.

[1.861]
861   Charges which have to be registered: supplementary
(1)   The holding of debentures entitling the holder to a charge on land is not, for the purposes of section 860(7)(a), an interest in the land.
(2)   It is immaterial for the purposes of this Chapter where land subject to a charge is situated.
(3)   The deposit by way of security of a negotiable instrument given to secure the payment of book debts is not, for the purposes of section 860(7)(f), a charge on those book debts.
(4)   For the purposes of section 860(7)(i), "intellectual property" means—
   (a)   any patent, trade mark, registered design, copyright or design right;
   (b)   any licence under or in respect of any such right.
(5)   In this Chapter—
   "charge" includes mortgage, and
   "company" means a company registered in England and Wales or in Northern Ireland.

NOTES
Commencement: 1 October 2009.

[1.862]
862   Charges existing on property acquired
(1)   This section applies where a company acquires property which is subject to a charge of a kind which would, if it had been created by the company after the acquisition of the property, have been required to be registered under this Chapter.
(2)   The company must deliver the prescribed particulars of the charge, together with a certified copy of the instrument (if any) by which the charge is created or evidenced, to the registrar for registration.
(3)   Subsection (2) must be complied with before the end of the period allowed for registration.
(4)   If default is made in complying with this section, an offence is committed by—
   (a)   the company, and
   (b)   every officer of it who is in default.
(5)   A person guilty of an offence under this section is liable—
   (a)   on conviction on indictment, to a fine;
   (b)   on summary conviction, to a fine not exceeding the statutory maximum.

NOTES

Commencement: 20 January 2007 (for the purpose of enabling the exercise of powers to make Orders or Regulations by statutory instrument); 1 October 2009 (otherwise).

Commencement (transitional provisions): Sch 2, para 83 to the Companies Act 2006 (Commencement No 8, Transitional Provisions and Savings) Order 2008, SI 2008/2860 (at **[2.91]**) provides that this section and s 880 apply to property acquired on or after 1 October 2009 (and that ss 400, 416 of the 1985 Act continue to apply to property acquired before that date).

Regulations: the Companies (Particulars of Company Charges) Regulations 2008, SI 2008/2996 at **[4.308]**.

Special rules about debentures

[1.863]

863   Charge in series of debentures

(1)   Where a series of debentures containing, or giving by reference to another instrument, any charge to the benefit of which debenture holders of that series are entitled *pari passu* is created by a company, it is for the purposes of section 860(1) sufficient if the required particulars, together with the deed containing the charge (or, if there is no such deed, one of the debentures of the series), are delivered to the registrar before the end of the period allowed for registration.

(2)   The following are the required particulars—

  (a)   the total amount secured by the whole series, and

  (b)   the dates of the resolutions authorising the issue of the series and the date of the covering deed (if any) by which the series is created or defined, and

  (c)   a general description of the property charged, and

  (d)   the names of the trustees (if any) for the debenture holders.

(3)   Particulars of the date and amount of each issue of debentures of a series of the kind mentioned in subsection (1) must be sent to the registrar for entry in the register of charges.

(4)   Failure to comply with subsection (3) does not affect the validity of the debentures issued.

(5)   Subsections (2) to (6) of section 860 apply for the purposes of this section as they apply for the purposes of that section, but as if references to the registration of a charge were references to the registration of a series of debentures.

NOTES

Commencement: 1 October 2009.

Commencement (transitional provisions): Sch 2, para 84 to the Companies Act 2006 (Commencement No 8, Transitional Provisions and Savings) Order 2008, SI 2008/2860 (at **[2.91]**) provides as follows—

"84.—(1)   Sections 863 and 882 of the Companies Act 2006 (charge in series of debentures) apply where the first debenture of the series is executed on or after 1st October 2009.

(2)   The corresponding provisions of the 1985 Act or the 1986 Order continue to apply where the first debenture of the series is executed before that date.".

[1.864]

864   Additional registration requirement for commission etc in relation to debentures

(1)   Where any commission, allowance or discount has been paid or made either directly or indirectly by a company to a person in consideration of his—

  (a)   subscribing or agreeing to subscribe, whether absolutely or conditionally, for debentures in a company, or

  (b)   procuring or agreeing to procure subscriptions, whether absolute or conditional, for such debentures,

the particulars required to be sent for registration under section 860 shall include particulars as to the amount or rate per cent. of the commission, discount or allowance so paid or made.

(2)   The deposit of debentures as security for a debt of the company is not, for the purposes of this section, treated as the issue of debentures at a discount.

(3)   Failure to comply with this section does not affect the validity of the debentures issued.

NOTES

Commencement: 1 October 2009.

[1.865]

865   Endorsement of certificate on debentures

(1)   The company shall cause a copy of every certificate of registration given under section 869 to be endorsed on every debenture or certificate of debenture stock which is issued by the company, and the payment of which is secured by the charge so registered.

(2)   But this does not require a company to cause a certificate of registration of any charge so given to be endorsed on any debenture or certificate of debenture stock issued by the company before the charge was created.

(3)   If a person knowingly and wilfully authorises or permits the delivery of a debenture or certificate of debenture stock which under this section is required to have endorsed on it a copy of a certificate of registration, without the copy being so endorsed upon it, he commits an offence.

(4)   A person guilty of an offence under this section is liable on summary conviction to a fine not exceeding level 3 on the standard scale.

NOTES
Commencement: 1 October 2009.

Charges in other jurisdictions

[1.866]
866 Charges created in, or over property in, jurisdictions outside the United Kingdom
(1) Where a charge is created outside the United Kingdom comprising property situated outside the United Kingdom, the delivery to the registrar of a verified copy of the instrument by which the charge is created or evidenced has the same effect for the purposes of this Chapter as the delivery of the instrument itself.
(2) Where a charge is created in the United Kingdom but comprises property outside the United Kingdom, the instrument creating or purporting to create the charge may be sent for registration under section 860 even if further proceedings may be necessary to make the charge valid or effectual according to the law of the country in which the property is situated.

NOTES
Commencement: 1 October 2009.

[1.867]
867 Charges created in, or over property in, another United Kingdom jurisdiction
(1) Subsection (2) applies where—
  (a) a charge comprises property situated in a part of the United Kingdom other than the part in which the company is registered, and
  (b) registration in that other part is necessary to make the charge valid or effectual under the law of that part of the United Kingdom.
(2) The delivery to the registrar of a verified copy of the instrument by which the charge is created or evidenced, together with a certificate stating that the charge was presented for registration in that other part of the United Kingdom on the date on which it was so presented has, for the purposes of this Chapter, the same effect as the delivery of the instrument itself.

NOTES
Commencement: 1 October 2009.

Orders charging land: Northern Ireland

[1.868]
868 Northern Ireland: registration of certain charges etc affecting land
(1) Where a charge imposed by an order under Article 46 of the 1981 Order or notice of such a charge is registered in the Land Registry against registered land or any estate in registered land of a company, the Registrar of Titles shall as soon as may be cause two copies of the order made under Article 46 of that Order or of any notice under Article 48 of that Order to be delivered to the registrar.
(2) Where a charge imposed by an order under Article 46 of the 1981 Order is registered in the Registry of Deeds against any unregistered land or estate in land of a company, the Registrar of Deeds shall as soon as may be cause two copies of the order to be delivered to the registrar.
(3) On delivery of copies under this section, the registrar shall—
  (a) register one of them in accordance with section 869, and
  (b) not later than 7 days from that date of delivery, cause the other copy together with a certificate of registration under section 869(5) to be sent to the company against which judgment was given.
(4) Where a charge to which subsection (1) or (2) applies is vacated, the Registrar of Titles or, as the case may be, the Registrar of Deeds shall cause a certified copy of the certificate of satisfaction lodged under Article 132(1) of the 1981 Order to be delivered to the registrar for entry of a memorandum of satisfaction in accordance with section 872.
(5) In this section—
  "the 1981 Order" means the Judgments Enforcement (Northern Ireland) Order 1981 (SI 1981/226 (NI 6));
  "the Registrar of Deeds" means the registrar appointed under the Registration of Deeds Act (Northern Ireland) 1970 (c 25);
  "Registry of Deeds" has the same meaning as in the Registration of Deeds Acts;
  "Registration of Deeds Acts" means the Registration of Deeds Act (Northern Ireland) 1970 and every statutory provision for the time being in force amending that Act or otherwise relating to the registry of deeds, or the registration of deeds, orders or other instruments or documents in such registry;
  "the Land Registry" and "the Registrar of Titles" are to be construed in accordance with section 1 of the Land Registration Act (Northern Ireland) 1970 (c 18);
  "registered land" and "unregistered land" have the same meaning as in Part 3 of the Land Registration Act (Northern Ireland) 1970.

Part 1　The Companies Act 2006

NOTES

Commencement: 1 October 2009.

Commencement (transitional provisions): the Companies Act 2006 (Commencement No 8, Transitional Provisions and Savings) Order 2008, SI 2008/2860, Sch 2, para 85 at **[2.91]** provides that this section applies where the date of registration of the charge in the Land Registry is on or after 1 October 2009 (and that Art 408 of the 1986 Order continues to apply where the date of registration of the charge in the Land Registry is before that date).

The register of charges

[1.869]
869　Register of charges to be kept by registrar

(1)　The registrar shall keep, with respect to each company, a register of all the charges requiring registration under this Chapter.

(2)　In the case of a charge to the benefit of which holders of a series of debentures are entitled, the registrar shall enter in the register the required particulars specified in section 863(2).

(3)　In the case of a charge imposed by the Enforcement of Judgments Office under Article 46 of the Judgments Enforcement (Northern Ireland) Order 1981, the registrar shall enter in the register the date on which the charge became effective.

(4)　In the case of any other charge, the registrar shall enter in the register the following particulars—

　(a)　if it is a charge created by a company, the date of its creation and, if it is a charge which was existing on property acquired by the company, the date of the acquisition,

　(b)　the amount secured by the charge,

　(c)　short particulars of the property charged, and

　(d)　the persons entitled to the charge.

(5)　The registrar shall give a certificate of the registration of any charge registered in pursuance of this Chapter, stating the amount secured by the charge.

(6)　The certificate—

　(a)　shall be signed by the registrar or authenticated by the registrar's official seal, and

　(b)　is conclusive evidence that the requirements of this Chapter as to registration have been satisfied.

(7)　The register kept in pursuance of this section shall be open to inspection by any person.

NOTES

Commencement: 1 October 2009.

[1.870]
870　The period allowed for registration

(1)　The period allowed for registration of a charge created by a company is—

　(a)　21 days beginning with the day after the day on which the charge is created, or

　(b)　if the charge is created outside the United Kingdom, 21 days beginning with the day after the day on which the instrument by which the charge is created or evidenced (or a copy of it) could, in due course of post (and if despatched with due diligence) have been received in the United Kingdom.

(2)　The period allowed for registration of a charge to which property acquired by a company is subject is—

　(a)　21 days beginning with the day after the day on which the acquisition is completed, or

　(b)　if the property is situated and the charge was created outside the United Kingdom, 21 days beginning with the day after the day on which the instrument by which the charge is created or evidenced (or a copy of it) could, in due course of post (and if despatched with due diligence) have been received in the United Kingdom.

(3)　The period allowed for registration of particulars of a series of debentures as a result of section 863 is—

　(a)　if there is a deed containing the charge mentioned in section 863(1), 21 days beginning with the day after the day on which that deed is executed, or

　(b)　if there is no such deed, 21 days beginning with the day after the day on which the first debenture of the series is executed.

NOTES

Commencement: 1 October 2009.

[1.871]
871　Registration of enforcement of security

(1)　If a person obtains an order for the appointment of a receiver or manager of a company's property, or appoints such a receiver or manager under powers contained in an instrument, he shall within 7 days of the order or of the appointment under those powers, give notice of the fact to the registrar.

(2)   Where a person appointed receiver or manager of a company's property under powers contained in an instrument ceases to act as such receiver or manager, he shall, on so ceasing, give the registrar notice to that effect.

(3)   The registrar must enter a fact of which he is given notice under this section in the register of charges.

(4)   A person who makes default in complying with the requirements of this section commits an offence.

(5)   A person guilty of an offence under this section is liable on summary conviction to a fine not exceeding level 3 on the standard scale and, for continued contravention, a daily default fine not exceeding one-tenth of level 3 on the standard scale.

NOTES
Commencement: 1 October 2009.
Commencement (transitional provisions): Sch 2, para 86 to the Companies Act 2006 (Commencement No 8, Transitional Provisions and Savings) Order 2008, SI 2008/2860 (at **[2.91]**) provides that this section applies where the order or appointment is made, or the receiver or manager ceases to act, on or after 1 October 2009 (and that s 405 of the 1985 Act continues to apply where the order or appointment is made, or the receiver or manager ceases to act, before that date).

[1.872]
872   Entries of satisfaction and release
(1)   Subsection (2) applies if a statement is delivered to the registrar verifying with respect to a registered charge—
   (a)   that the debt for which the charge was given has been paid or satisfied in whole or in part, or
   (b)   that part of the property or undertaking charged has been released from the charge or has ceased to form part of the company's property or undertaking.
(2)   The registrar may enter on the register a memorandum of satisfaction in whole or in part, or of the fact part of the property or undertaking has been released from the charge or has ceased to form part of the company's property or undertaking (as the case may be).
(3)   Where the registrar enters a memorandum of satisfaction in whole, the registrar shall if required send the company a copy of it.

NOTES
Commencement: 1 October 2009.
Commencement (transitional provisions): Sch 2, para 87 to the Companies Act 2006 (Commencement No 8, Transitional Provisions and Savings) Order 2008, SI 2008/2860 (at **[2.91]**) provides that this section and s 887 apply to statements delivered to the registrar on or after 1 October 2009 (and that ss 403 or 419 of the 1985 Act continue to apply where the relevant statutory declaration, statement or application and statutory declaration or statement is received by the registrar before that date).

[1.873]
873   Rectification of register of charges
(1)   Subsection (2) applies if the court is satisfied—
   (a)   that the failure to register a charge before the end of the period allowed for registration, or the omission or mis-statement of any particular with respect to any such charge or in a memorandum of satisfaction—
      (i)   was accidental or due to inadvertence or to some other sufficient cause, or
      (ii)   is not of a nature to prejudice the position of creditors or shareholders of the company, or
   (b)   that on other grounds it is just and equitable to grant relief.
(2)   The court may, on the application of the company or a person interested, and on such terms and conditions as seem to the court just and expedient, order that the period allowed for registration shall be extended or, as the case may be, that the omission or mis-statement shall be rectified.

NOTES
Commencement: 1 October 2009.

Avoidance of certain charges

[1.874]
874   Consequence of failure to register charges created by a company
(1)   If a company creates a charge to which section 860 applies, the charge is void (so far as any security on the company's property or undertaking is conferred by it) against—
   (a)   a liquidator of the company,
   (b)   an administrator of the company, and
   (c)   a creditor of the company,
unless that section is complied with.
(2)   Subsection (1) is subject to the provisions of this Chapter.
(3)   Subsection (1) is without prejudice to any contract or obligation for repayment of the money secured by the charge; and when a charge becomes void under this section, the money secured by it immediately becomes payable.

NOTES

Commencement: 1 October 2009.

Companies' records and registers

[1.875]

875 Companies to keep copies of instruments creating charges

(1) A company must keep available for inspection a copy of every instrument creating a charge requiring registration under this Chapter, including any document delivered to the company under section 868(3)(b) (Northern Ireland: orders imposing charges affecting land).

(2) In the case of a series of uniform debentures, a copy of one of the debentures of the series is sufficient.

NOTES

Commencement: 1 October 2009.

[1.876]

876 Company's register of charges

(1) Every limited company shall keep available for inspection a register of charges and enter in it—

    (a)   all charges specifically affecting property of the company, and

    (b)   all floating charges on the whole or part of the company's property or undertaking.

(2) The entry shall in each case give a short description of the property charged, the amount of the charge and, except in the cases of securities to bearer, the names of the persons entitled to it.

(3) If an officer of the company knowingly and wilfully authorises or permits the omission of an entry required to be made in pursuance of this section, he commits an offence.

(4) A person guilty of an offence under this section is liable—

    (a)   on conviction on indictment, to a fine;

    (b)   on summary conviction, to a fine not exceeding the statutory maximum.

NOTES

Commencement: 1 October 2009.

[1.877]

877 Instruments creating charges and register of charges to be available for inspection

(1) This section applies to—

    (a)   documents required to be kept available for inspection under section 875 (copies of instruments creating charges), and

    (b)   a company's register of charges kept in pursuance of section 876.

(2) The documents and register must be kept available for inspection—

    (a)   at the company's registered office, or

    (b)   at a place specified in regulations under section 1136.

(3) The company must give notice to the registrar—

    (a)   of the place at which the documents and register are kept available for inspection, and

    (b)   of any change in that place,

unless they have at all times been kept at the company's registered office.

(4) The documents and register shall be open to the inspection—

    (a)   of any creditor or member of the company without charge, and

    (b)   of any other person on payment of such fee as may be prescribed.

(5) If default is made for 14 days in complying with subsection (3) or an inspection required under subsection (4) is refused, an offence is committed by—

    (a)   the company, and

    (b)   every officer of the company who is in default.

(6) A person guilty of an offence under this section is liable on summary conviction to a fine not exceeding level 3 on the standard scale and, for continued contravention, a daily default fine not exceeding one-tenth of level 3 on the standard scale.

(7) If an inspection required under subsection (4) is refused the court may by order compel an immediate inspection.

NOTES

Commencement: 20 January 2007 (for the purpose of enabling the exercise of powers to make Orders or Regulations by statutory instrument); 1 October 2009 (otherwise).

Regulations: the Companies (Fees for Inspection of Company Records) Regulations 2008, SI 2008/3007 at **[4.327]**.

CHAPTER 2
COMPANIES REGISTERED IN SCOTLAND

Charges requiring registration

[1.878]
878 Charges created by a company

(1) A company that creates a charge to which this section applies must deliver the prescribed particulars of the charge, together with a copy certified as a correct copy of the instrument (if any) by which the charge is created or evidenced, to the registrar for registration before the end of the period allowed for registration.

(2) Registration of a charge to which this section applies may instead be effected on the application of a person interested in it.

(3) Where registration is effected on the application of some person other than the company, that person is entitled to recover from the company the amount of any fees properly paid by him to the registrar on the registration.

(4) If a company fails to comply with subsection (1), an offence is committed by—
  (a) the company, and
  (b) every officer of the company who is in default.

(5) A person guilty of an offence under this section is liable—
  (a) on conviction on indictment, to a fine;
  (b) on summary conviction, to a fine not exceeding the statutory maximum.

(6) Subsection (4) does not apply if registration of the charge has been effected on the application of some other person.

(7) This section applies to the following charges—
  (a) a charge on land or any interest in such land, other than a charge for any rent or other periodical sum payable in respect of the land,
  (b) a security over incorporeal moveable property of any of the following categories—
      (i) goodwill,
      (ii) a patent or a licence under a patent,
      (iii) a trademark,
      (iv) a copyright or a licence under a copyright,
      (v) a registered design or a licence in respect of such a design,
      (vi) a design right or a licence under a design right,
      (vii) the book debts (whether book debts of the company or assigned to it), and
      (viii) uncalled share capital of the company or calls made but not paid,
  (c) a security over a ship or aircraft or any share in a ship,
  (d) a floating charge.

NOTES
  Commencement: 20 January 2007 (for the purpose of enabling the exercise of powers to make Orders or Regulations by statutory instrument); 1 October 2009 (otherwise).
  Commencement (transitional provisions): see the note to s 860 at **[1.860]**.
  Regulations: the Companies (Particulars of Company Charges) Regulations 2008, SI 2008/2996 at **[4.308]**.

[1.879]
879 Charges which have to be registered: supplementary

(1) A charge on land, for the purposes of section 878(7)(a), includes a charge created by a heritable security within the meaning of section 9(8) of the Conveyancing and Feudal Reform (Scotland) Act 1970 (c 35).

(2) The holding of debentures entitling the holder to a charge on land is not, for the purposes of section 878(7)(a), deemed to be an interest in land.

(3) It is immaterial for the purposes of this Chapter where land subject to a charge is situated.

(4) The deposit by way of security of a negotiable instrument given to secure the payment of book debts is not, for the purposes of section 878(7)(b)(vii), to be treated as a charge on those book debts.

(5) References in this Chapter to the date of the creation of a charge are—
  (a) in the case of a floating charge, the date on which the instrument creating the floating charge was executed by the company creating the charge, and
  (b) in any other case, the date on which the right of the person entitled to the benefit of the charge was constituted as a real right.

(6) In this Chapter "company" means an incorporated company registered in Scotland.

NOTES
  Commencement: 1 October 2009.

[1.880]
880 Duty to register charges existing on property acquired

(1) Subsection (2) applies where a company acquires any property which is subject to a charge of any kind as would, if it had been created by the company after the acquisition of the property, have been required to be registered under this Chapter.

(2) The company must deliver the prescribed particulars of the charge, together with a copy (certified to be a correct copy) of the instrument (if any) by which the charge was created or is evidenced, to the registrar for registration before the end of the period allowed for registration.

(3) If default is made in complying with this section, an offence is committed by—

    (a) the company, and

    (b) every officer of it who is in default.

(4) A person guilty of an offence under this section is liable—

    (a) on conviction on indictment, to a fine;

    (b) on summary conviction, to a fine not exceeding the statutory maximum.

NOTES

Commencement: 20 January 2007 (for the purpose of enabling the exercise of powers to make Orders or Regulations by statutory instrument); 1 October 2009 (otherwise).

Commencement (transitional provisions): see the note to s 862 at **[1.862]**.

Regulations: the Companies (Particulars of Company Charges) Regulations 2008, SI 2008/2996 at **[4.308]**.

[1.881]
881   Charge by way of ex facie absolute disposition, etc

(1) For the avoidance of doubt, it is hereby declared that, in the case of a charge created by way of an *ex facie* absolute disposition or assignation qualified by a back letter or other agreement, or by a standard security qualified by an agreement, compliance with section 878(1) does not of itself render the charge unavailable as security for indebtedness incurred after the date of compliance.

(2) Where the amount secured by a charge so created is purported to be increased by a further back letter or agreement, a further charge is held to have been created by the *ex facie* absolute disposition or assignation or (as the case may be) by the standard security, as qualified by the further back letter or agreement.

(3) In that case, the provisions of this Chapter apply to the further charge as if—

    (a) references in this Chapter (other than in this section) to a charge were references to the further charge, and

    (b) references to the date of the creation of a charge were references to the date on which the further back letter or agreement was executed.

NOTES

Commencement: 1 October 2009.

Special rules about debentures

[1.882]
882   Charge in series of debentures

(1) Where a series of debentures containing, or giving by reference to any other instrument, any charge to the benefit of which the debenture-holders of that series are entitled *pari passu*, is created by a company, it is sufficient for purposes of section 878 if the required particulars, together with a copy of the deed containing the charge (or, if there is no such deed, of one of the debentures of the series) are delivered to the registrar before the end of the period allowed for registration.

(2) The following are the required particulars—

    (a) the total amount secured by the whole series,

    (b) the dates of the resolutions authorising the issue of the series and the date of the covering deed (if any) by which the security is created or defined,

    (c) a general description of the property charged,

    (d) the names of the trustees (if any) for the debenture-holders, and

    (e) in the case of a floating charge, a statement of any provisions of the charge and of any instrument relating to it which prohibit or restrict or regulate the power of the company to grant further securities ranking in priority to, or *pari passu* with, the floating charge, or which vary or otherwise regulate the order of ranking of the floating charge in relation to subsisting securities.

(3) Where more than one issue is made of debentures in the series, particulars of the date and amount of each issue of debentures of the series must be sent to the registrar for entry in the register of charges.

(4) Failure to comply with subsection (3) does not affect the validity of any of those debentures.

(5) Subsections (2) to (6) of section 878 apply for the purposes of this section as they apply for the purposes of that section but as if for the reference to the registration of the charge there was substituted a reference to the registration of the series of debentures.

NOTES

Commencement: 1 October 2009.

Commencement (transitional provisions): see the note to s 863 at **[1.863]**.

[1.883]
883   Additional registration requirement for commission etc in relation to debentures

(1) Where any commission, allowance or discount has been paid or made either directly or indirectly by a company to a person in consideration of his—

    (a)   subscribing or agreeing to subscribe, whether absolutely or conditionally, for debentures in a company, or

    (b)   procuring or agreeing to procure subscriptions, whether absolute or conditional, for such debentures,

the particulars required to be sent for registration under section 878 shall include particulars as to the amount or rate per cent. of the commission, discount or allowance so paid or made.

(2)   The deposit of debentures as security for a debt of the company is not, for the purposes of this section, treated as the issue of debentures at a discount.

(3)   Failure to comply with this section does not affect the validity of the debentures issued.

NOTES

Commencement: 1 October 2009.

Charges on property outside the United Kingdom

[1.884]

884   Charges on property outside United Kingdom

Where a charge is created in the United Kingdom but comprises property outside the United Kingdom, the copy of the instrument creating or purporting to create the charge may be sent for registration under section 878 even if further proceedings may be necessary to make the charge valid or effectual according to the law of the country in which the property is situated.

NOTES

Commencement: 1 October 2009.

The register of charges

[1.885]

885   Register of charges to be kept by registrar

(1)   The registrar shall keep, with respect to each company, a register of all the charges requiring registration under this Chapter.

(2)   In the case of a charge to the benefit of which holders of a series of debentures are entitled, the registrar shall enter in the register the required particulars specified in section 882(2).

(3)   In the case of any other charge, the registrar shall enter in the register the following particulars—

    (a)   if it is a charge created by a company, the date of its creation and, if it is a charge which was existing on property acquired by the company, the date of the acquisition,

    (b)   the amount secured by the charge,

    (c)   short particulars of the property charged,

    (d)   the persons entitled to the charge, and

    (e)   in the case of a floating charge, a statement of any of the provisions of the charge and of any instrument relating to it which prohibit or restrict or regulate the company's power to grant further securities ranking in

priority to, or *pari passu* with, the floating charge, or which vary or otherwise regulate the order of ranking of the floating charge in relation to subsisting securities.

(4)   The registrar shall give a certificate of the registration of any charge registered in pursuance of this Chapter, stating—

    (a)   the name of the company and the person first-named in the charge among those entitled to the benefit of the charge (or, in the case of a series of debentures, the name of the holder of the first such debenture issued), and

    (b)   the amount secured by the charge.

(5)   The certificate—

    (a)   shall be signed by the registrar or authenticated by the registrar's official seal, and

    (b)   is conclusive evidence that the requirements of this Chapter as to registration have been satisfied.

(6)   The register kept in pursuance of this section shall be open to inspection by any person.

NOTES

Commencement: 1 October 2009.

[1.886]

886   The period allowed for registration

(1)   The period allowed for registration of a charge created by a company is—

    (a)   21 days beginning with the day after the day on which the charge is created, or

    (b)   if the charge is created outside the United Kingdom, 21 days beginning with the day after the day on which a copy of the instrument by which the charge is created or evidenced could, in due course of post (and if despatched with due diligence) have been received in the United Kingdom.

(2)   The period allowed for registration of a charge to which property acquired by a company is subject is—

    (a)   21 days beginning with the day after the day on which the transaction is settled, or

(b)   if the property is situated and the charge was created outside the United Kingdom, 21 days beginning with the day after the day on which a copy of the instrument by which the charge is created or evidenced could, in due course of post (and if despatched with due diligence) have been received in the United Kingdom.

(3)   The period allowed for registration of particulars of a series of debentures as a result of section 882 is—

(a)   if there is a deed containing the charge mentioned in section 882(1), 21 days beginning with the day after the day on which that deed is executed, or

(b)   if there is no such deed, 21 days beginning with the day after the day on which the first debenture of the series is executed.

NOTES

Commencement: 1 October 2009.

[1.887]
887   Entries of satisfaction and relief
(1)   Subsection (2) applies if a statement is delivered to the registrar verifying with respect to any registered charge—

(a)   that the debt for which the charge was given has been paid or satisfied in whole or in part, or

(b)   that part of the property charged has been released from the charge or has ceased to form part of the company's property.

(2)   If the charge is a floating charge, the statement must be accompanied by either—

(a)   a statement by the creditor entitled to the benefit of the charge, or a person authorised by him for the purpose, verifying that the statement mentioned in subsection (1) is correct, or

(b)   a direction obtained from the court, on the ground that the statement by the creditor mentioned in paragraph (a) could not be readily obtained, dispensing with the need for that statement.

(3)   The registrar may enter on the register a memorandum of satisfaction (in whole or in part) regarding the fact contained in the statement mentioned in subsection (1).

(4)   Where the registrar enters a memorandum of satisfaction in whole, he shall, if required, furnish the company with a copy of the memorandum.

(5)   Nothing in this section requires the company to submit particulars with respect to the entry in the register of a memorandum of satisfaction where the company, having created a floating charge over all or any part of its property, disposes of part of the property subject to the floating charge.

NOTES

Commencement: 1 October 2009.
Commencement (transitional provisions): see the note to s 872 at **[1.872]**.

[1.888]
888   Rectification of register of charges
(1)   Subsection (2) applies if the court is satisfied—

(a)   that the failure to register a charge before the end of the period allowed for registration, or the omission or mis-statement of any particular with respect to any such charge or in a memorandum of satisfaction—

(i)   was accidental or due to inadvertence or to some other sufficient cause, or

(ii)   is not of a nature to prejudice the position of creditors or shareholders of the company, or

(b)   that on other grounds it is just and equitable to grant relief.

(2)   The court may, on the application of the company or a person interested, and on such terms and conditions as seem to the court just and expedient, order that the period allowed for registration shall be extended or, as the case may be, that the omission or mis-statement shall be rectified.

NOTES

Commencement: 1 October 2009.

Avoidance of certain charges

[1.889]
889   Charges void unless registered
(1)   If a company creates a charge to which section 878 applies, the charge is void (so far as any security on the company's property or any part of it is conferred by the charge) against—

(a)   the liquidator of the company,

(b)   an administrator of the company, and

(c)   any creditor of the company

unless that section is complied with.

(2)   Subsection (1) is without prejudice to any contract or obligation for repayment of the money secured by the charge; and when a charge becomes void under this section the money secured by it immediately becomes payable.

NOTES

Commencement: 1 October 2009.

Companies' records and registers

[1.890]

890 Copies of instruments creating charges to be kept by company

(1) Every company shall cause a copy of every instrument creating a charge requiring registration under this Chapter to be kept available for inspection.

(2) In the case of a series of uniform debentures, a copy of one debenture of the series is sufficient.

NOTES

Commencement: 1 October 2009.

[1.891]

891 Company's register of charges

(1) Every company shall keep available for inspection a register of charges and enter in it all charges specifically affecting property of the company, and all floating charges on any property of the company.

(2) There shall be given in each case a short description of the property charged, the amount of the charge and, except in the case of securities to bearer, the names of the persons entitled to it.

(3) If an officer of the company knowingly and wilfully authorises or permits the omission of an entry required to be made in pursuance of this section, he commits an offence.

(4) A person guilty of an offence under this section is liable—

   (a) on conviction on indictment, to a fine;

   (b) on summary conviction, to a fine not exceeding the statutory maximum.

NOTES

Commencement: 1 October 2009.

[1.892]

892 Instruments creating charges and register of charges to be available for inspection

(1) This section applies to—

   (a) documents required to be kept available for inspection under section 890 (copies of instruments creating charges), and

   (b) a company's register of charges kept in pursuance of section 891.

(2) The documents and register must be kept available for inspection—

   (a) at the company's registered office, or

   (b) at a place specified in regulations under section 1136.

(3) The company must give notice to the registrar—

   (a) of the place at which the documents and register are kept available for inspection, and

   (b) of any change in that place,

unless they have at all times been kept at the company's registered office.

(4) The documents and register shall be open to the inspection—

   (a) of any creditor or member of the company without charge, and

   (b) of any other person on payment of such fee as may be prescribed.

(5) If default is made for 14 days in complying with subsection (3) or an inspection required under subsection (4) is refused, an offence is committed by—

   (a) the company, and

   (b) every officer of the company who is in default.

(6) A person guilty of an offence under this section is liable on summary conviction to a fine not exceeding level 3 on the standard scale and, for continued contravention, a daily default fine not exceeding one-tenth of level 3 on the standard scale.

(7) If an inspection required under subsection (4) is refused the court may by order compel an immediate inspection.

NOTES

Commencement: 20 January 2007 (for the purpose of enabling the exercise of powers to make Orders or Regulations by statutory instrument); 1 October 2009 (otherwise).

Regulations: the Companies (Fees for Inspection of Company Records) Regulations 2008, SI 2008/3007 at **[4.327]**.

CHAPTER 3
POWERS OF THE SECRETARY OF STATE

[1.893]
893   Power to make provision for effect of registration in special register

(1)   In this section a "special register" means a register, other than the register of charges kept under this Part, in which a charge to which Chapter 1 or Chapter 2 applies is required or authorised to be registered.

(2)   The Secretary of State may by order make provision for facilitating the making of information-sharing arrangements between the person responsible for maintaining a special register ("the responsible person") and the registrar that meet the requirement in subsection (4).

"Information-sharing arrangements" are arrangements to share and make use of information held by the registrar or by the responsible person.

(3)   If the Secretary of State is satisfied that appropriate information-sharing arrangements have been made, he may by order provide that—

    (a)   the registrar is authorised not to register a charge of a specified description under Chapter 1 or Chapter 2,

    (b)   a charge of a specified description that is registered in the special register within a specified period is to be treated as if it had been registered (and certified by the registrar as registered) in accordance with the requirements of Chapter 1 or, as the case may be, Chapter 2, and

    (c)   the other provisions of Chapter 1 or, as the case may be, Chapter 2 apply to a charge so treated with specified modifications.

(4)   The information-sharing arrangements must ensure that persons inspecting the register of charges—

    (a)   are made aware, in a manner appropriate to the inspection, of the existence of charges in the special register which are treated in accordance with provision so made, and

    (b)   are able to obtain information from the special register about any such charge.

(5)   An order under this section may—

    (a)   modify any enactment or rule of law which would otherwise restrict or prevent the responsible person from entering into or giving effect to information-sharing arrangements,

    (b)   authorise the responsible person to require information to be provided to him for the purposes of the arrangements,

    (c)   make provision about—

        (i)   the charging by the responsible person of fees in connection with the arrangements and the destination of such fees (including provision modifying any enactment which would otherwise apply in relation to fees payable to the responsible person), and

        (ii)   the making of payments under the arrangements by the registrar to the responsible person,

    (d)   require the registrar to make copies of the arrangements available to the public (in hard copy or electronic form).

(6)   In this section "specified" means specified in an order under this section.

(7)   A description of charge may be specified, in particular, by reference to one or more of the following—

    (a)   the type of company by which it is created,

    (b)   the form of charge which it is,

    (c)   the description of assets over which it is granted,

    (d)   the length of the period between the date of its registration in the special register and the date of its creation.

(8)   Provision may be made under this section relating to registers maintained under the law of a country or territory outside the United Kingdom.

(9)   An order under this section is subject to negative resolution procedure.

NOTES

Commencement: 20 January 2007 (for the purpose of enabling the exercise of powers to make Orders or Regulations by statutory instrument); 1 October 2009 (otherwise).

[1.894]
894   General power to make amendments to this Part

(1)   The Secretary of State may by regulations under this section—

    (a)   amend this Part by altering, adding or repealing provisions,

    (b)   make consequential amendments or repeals in this Act or any other enactment (whether passed or made before or after this Act).

(2)   Regulations under this section are subject to affirmative resolution procedure.

NOTES

Commencement: 20 January 2007 (for the purpose of enabling the exercise of powers to make Orders or Regulations by statutory instrument); 1 October 2009 (otherwise).

PART 26
ARRANGEMENTS AND RECONSTRUCTIONS

Application of this Part

[1.895]
895 Application of this Part
(1) The provisions of this Part apply where a compromise or arrangement is proposed between a company and—
   (a)   its creditors, or any class of them, or
   (b)   its members, or any class of them.
(2) In this Part—
"arrangement" includes a reorganisation of the company's share capital by the consolidation of shares of different classes or by the division of shares into shares of different classes, or by both of those methods; and
"company"—
      (a)   in section 900 (powers of court to facilitate reconstruction or amalgamation) means a company within the meaning of this Act, and
      (b)   elsewhere in this Part means any company liable to be wound up under the Insolvency Act 1986 (c 45) or the Insolvency (Northern Ireland) Order 1989 (SI 1989/2405 (NI 19)).
(3) The provisions of this Part have effect subject to Part 27 (mergers and divisions of public companies) where that Part applies (see sections 902 and 903).

NOTES
Commencement: 6 April 2008.

Meeting of creditors or members

[1.896]
896 Court order for holding of meeting
(1) The court may, on an application under this section, order a meeting of the creditors or class of creditors, or of the members of the company or class of members (as the case may be), to be summoned in such manner as the court directs.
(2) An application under this section may be made by—
   (a)   the company,
   (b)   any creditor or member of the company,
   [(c)   if the company is being wound up, the liquidator, or
   (d)   if the company is in administration, the administrator.]
[(3) Section 323 (representation of corporations at meetings) applies to a meeting of creditors under this section as to a meeting of the company (references to a member of the company being read as references to a creditor).]

NOTES
Commencement: 6 April 2008.
Sub-s (2): paras (c), (d) substituted (for the original para (c) and the word "or" preceding it) by the Companies Act 2006 (Consequential Amendments etc) Order 2008, SI 2008/948, art 3(1), Sch 1, Pt 2, para 249(1), (2), as from 6 April 2008.
Sub-s (3): added by SI 2008/948, art 3(1), Sch 1, Pt 2, para 249(1), (3), as from 6 April 2008.

[1.897]
897 Statement to be circulated or made available
(1) Where a meeting is summoned under section 896—
   (a)   every notice summoning the meeting that is sent to a creditor or member must be accompanied by a statement complying with this section, and
   (b)   every notice summoning the meeting that is given by advertisement must either—
      (i)   include such a statement, or
      (ii)   state where and how creditors or members entitled to attend the meeting may obtain copies of such a statement.
(2) The statement must—
   (a)   explain the effect of the compromise or arrangement, and
   (b)   in particular, state—
      (i)   any material interests of the directors of the company (whether as directors or as members or as creditors of the company or otherwise), and
      (ii)   the effect on those interests of the compromise or arrangement, in so far as it is different from the effect on the like interests of other persons.
(3) Where the compromise or arrangement affects the rights of debenture holders of the company, the statement must give the like explanation as respects the trustees of any deed for securing the issue of the debentures as it is required to give as respects the company's directors.

(4)   Where a notice given by advertisement states that copies of an explanatory statement can be obtained by creditors or members entitled to attend the meeting, every such creditor or member is entitled, on making application in the manner indicated by the notice, to be provided by the company with a copy of the statement free of charge.

(5)   If a company makes default in complying with any requirement of this section, an offence is committed by—

  (a)   the company, and

  (b)   every officer of the company who is in default.

This is subject to subsection (7) below.

(6)   For this purpose the following are treated as officers of the company—

  (a)   a liquidator or administrator of the company, and

  (b)   a trustee of a deed for securing the issue of debentures of the company.

(7)   A person is not guilty of an offence under this section if he shows that the default was due to the refusal of a director or trustee for debenture holders to supply the necessary particulars of his interests.

(8)   A person guilty of an offence under this section is liable—

  (a)   on conviction on indictment, to a fine;

  (b)   on summary conviction, to a fine not exceeding the statutory maximum.

NOTES

Commencement: 6 April 2008.

[1.898]

898   Duty of directors and trustees to provide information

(1)   It is the duty of—

  (a)   any director of the company, and

  (b)   any trustee for its debenture holders,

to give notice to the company of such matters relating to himself as may be necessary for the purposes of section 897 (explanatory statement to be circulated or made available).

(2)   Any person who makes default in complying with this section commits an offence.

(3)   A person guilty of an offence under this section is liable on summary conviction to a fine not exceeding level 3 on the standard scale.

NOTES

Commencement: 6 April 2008.

Court sanction for compromise or arrangement

[1.899]

899   Court sanction for compromise or arrangement

(1)   If a majority in number representing 75% in value of the creditors or class of creditors or members or class of members (as the case may be), present and voting either in person or by proxy at the meeting summoned under section 896, agree a compromise or arrangement, the court may, on an application under this section, sanction the compromise or arrangement.

(2)   An application under this section may be made by—

  (a)   the company,

  (b)   any creditor or member of the company,

  [(c)   if the company is being wound up, the liquidator, or

  (d)   if the company is in administration, the administrator.]

(3)   A compromise or [arrangement] sanctioned by the court is binding on—

  (a)   all creditors or the class of creditors or on the members or class of members (as the case may be), and

  (b)   the company or, in the case of a company in the course of being wound up, the liquidator and contributories of the company.

(4)   The court's order has no effect until a copy of it has been delivered to the registrar.

[(5)   Section 323 (representation of corporations at meetings) applies to a meeting of creditors under this section as to a meeting of the company (references to a member of the company being read as references to a creditor).]

NOTES

Commencement: 6 April 2008.

Sub-s (2): paras (c), (d) substituted (for the original para (c) and the word "or" preceding it) by the Companies Act 2006 (Consequential Amendments etc) Order 2008, SI 2008/948, art 3(1), Sch 1, Pt 2, para 250(1), (2), as from 6 April 2008.

Sub-s (3): word in square brackets substituted by the Companies Act 2006 (Consequential Amendments and Transitional Provisions) Order 2011, SI 2011/1265, art 28(1), (3), as from 12 May 2011.

Sub-s (5): added by SI 2008/948, art 3(1), Sch 1, Pt 2, para 250(1), (3), as from 6 April 2008.

Reconstructions and amalgamations

[1.900]

900 Powers of court to facilitate reconstruction or amalgamation

(1) This section applies where application is made to the court under section 899 to sanction a compromise or arrangement and it is shown that—

(a) the compromise or arrangement is proposed for the purposes of, or in connection with, a scheme for the reconstruction of any company or companies, or the amalgamation of any two or more companies, and

(b) under the scheme the whole or any part of the undertaking or the property of any company concerned in the scheme ("a transferor company") is to be transferred to another company ("the transferee company").

(2) The court may, either by the order sanctioning the compromise or arrangement or by a subsequent order, make provision for all or any of the following matters—

(a) the transfer to the transferee company of the whole or any part of the undertaking and of the property or liabilities of any transferor company;

(b) the allotting or appropriation by the transferee company of any shares, debentures, policies or other like interests in that company which under the compromise or arrangement are to be allotted or appropriated by that company to or for any person;

(c) the continuation by or against the transferee company of any legal proceedings pending by or against any transferor company;

(d) the dissolution, without winding up, of any transferor company;

(e) the provision to be made for any persons who, within such time and in such manner as the court directs, dissent from the compromise or arrangement;

(f) such incidental, consequential and supplemental matters as are necessary to secure that the reconstruction or amalgamation is fully and effectively carried out.

(3) If an order under this section provides for the transfer of property or liabilities—

(a) the property is by virtue of the order transferred to, and vests in, the transferee company, and

(b) the liabilities are, by virtue of the order, transferred to and become liabilities of that company.

(4) The property (if the order so directs) vests freed from any charge that is by virtue of the compromise or arrangement to cease to have effect.

(5) In this section—

"property" includes property, rights and powers of every description; and

"liabilities" includes duties.

(6) Every company in relation to which an order is made under this section must cause a copy of the order to be delivered to the registrar within seven days after its making.

(7) If default is made in complying with subsection (6) an offence is committed by—

(a) the company, and

(b) every officer of the company who is in default.

(8) A person guilty of an offence under subsection (7) is liable on summary conviction to a fine not exceeding level 3 on the standard scale and, for continued contravention, a daily default fine not exceeding one-tenth of level 3 on the standard scale.

NOTES

Commencement: 6 April 2008.

Obligations of company with respect to articles etc

[1.901]

901 Obligations of company with respect to articles etc

(1) This section applies—

(a) to any order under section 899 (order sanctioning compromise or arrangement), and

(b) to any order under section 900 (order facilitating reconstruction or amalgamation) that alters the company's constitution.

(2) If the order amends—

(a) the company's articles, or

(b) any resolution or agreement to which Chapter 3 of Part 3 applies (resolution or agreement affecting a company's constitution),

the copy of the order delivered to the registrar by the company under section 899(4) or section 900(6) must be accompanied by a copy of the company's articles, or the resolution or agreement in question, as amended.

(3) Every copy of the company's articles issued by the company after the order is made must be accompanied by a copy of the order, unless the effect of the order has been incorporated into the articles by amendment.

(4) In this section—

(a) references to the effect of the order include the effect of the compromise or arrangement to which the order relates; and

(b)   in the case of a company not having articles, references to its articles shall be read as references to the instrument constituting the company or defining its constitution.

(5)   If a company makes default in complying with this section an offence is committed by—
(a)   the company, and
(b)   every officer of the company who is in default.

(6)   A person guilty of an offence under this section is liable on summary conviction to a fine not exceeding level 3 on the standard scale.

NOTES
Commencement: 6 April 2008.
Commencement (transitional provisions): Sch 4, Pt 1, para 36 to the Companies Act 2006 (Commencement No 5, Transitional Provisions and Savings) Order 2007, SI 2007/3495 (at **[2.66]**) provides as follows—

"**Arrangements and reconstructions (ss 896 to 901)**
36.—(1)   Section 901 of the Companies Act 2006 (obligations of company with respect to articles etc) applies to orders of the court made on or after 6th April 2008, including orders made under section 425(2) or 427 of the 1985 Act or 418(2) or 420 of the 1986 Order.
(2)   Section 425(3) and (4) of the 1985 Act or Article 418(3) and (4) of the 1986 Order continues to apply to orders made before that date.".

PART 27
MERGERS AND DIVISIONS OF PUBLIC COMPANIES

CHAPTER 1
INTRODUCTORY

[1.902]
902   Application of this Part
(1)   This Part applies where—
(a)   a compromise or arrangement is proposed between a public company and—
(i)   its creditors or any class of them, or
(ii)   its members or any class of them,
for the purposes of, or in connection with, a scheme for the reconstruction of any company or companies or the amalgamation of any two or more companies,
(b)   the scheme involves—
(i)   a merger (as defined in section 904), or
(ii)   a division (as defined in section 919), and
(c)   the consideration for the transfer (or each of the transfers) envisaged is to be shares in the transferee company (or one or more of the transferee companies) receivable by members of the transferor company (or transferor companies), with or without any cash payment to members.
(2)   In this Part—
(a)   a "new company" means a company formed for the purposes of, or in connection with, the scheme, and
(b)   an "existing company" means a company other than one formed for the purposes of, or in connection with, the scheme.
(3)   This Part does not apply where the company in respect of which the compromise or arrangement is proposed is being wound up.

NOTES
Commencement: 6 April 2008.

[1.903]
903   Relationship of this Part to Part 26
(1)   The court must not sanction the compromise or arrangement under Part 26 (arrangements and reconstructions) unless the relevant requirements of this Part have been complied with.
(2)   The requirements applicable to a merger are specified in sections 905 to 914. Certain of those requirements, and certain general requirements of Part 26, are modified or excluded by the provisions of sections 915 to *918*.
(3)   The requirements applicable to a division are specified in sections 920 to 930. Certain of those requirements, and certain general requirements of Part 26, are modified or excluded by the provisions of sections 931 to 934.

NOTES
Commencement: 6 April 2008.
Sub-s (2): for the number in italics there is substituted the number "918A" by the Companies (Reporting Requirements in Mergers and Divisions) Regulations 2011, SI 2011/1606, regs 3, 4, as from 1 August 2011 (except in relation to any merger or division the draft terms of which were adopted before that date).

CHAPTER 2
MERGER

Introductory

[1.904]
904 Mergers and merging companies
(1)   The scheme involves a merger where under the scheme—
  (a)   the undertaking, property and liabilities of one or more public companies, including the company in respect of which the compromise or arrangement is proposed, are to be transferred to another existing public company (a "merger by absorption"), or
  (b)   the undertaking, property and liabilities of two or more public companies, including the company in respect of which the compromise or arrangement is proposed, are to be transferred to a new company, whether or not a public company, (a "merger by formation of a new company").
(2)   References in this Part to "the merging companies" are—
  (a)   in relation to a merger by absorption, to the transferor and transferee companies;
  (b)   in relation to a merger by formation of a new company, to the transferor companies.

NOTES
Commencement: 6 April 2008.

Requirements applicable to merger

[1.905]
905 Draft terms of scheme (merger)
(1)   A draft of the proposed terms of the scheme must be drawn up and adopted by the directors of the merging companies.
(2)   The draft terms must give particulars of at least the following matters—
  (a)   in respect of each transferor company and the transferee company—
    (i)   its name,
    (ii)   the address of its registered office, and
    (iii) whether it is a company limited by shares or a company limited by guarantee and having a share capital;
  (b)   the number of shares in the transferee company to be allotted to members of a transferor company for a given number of their shares (the "share exchange ratio") and the amount of any cash payment;
  (c)   the terms relating to the allotment of shares in the transferee company;
  (d)   the date from which the holding of shares in the transferee company will entitle the holders to participate in profits, and any special conditions affecting that entitlement;
  (e)   the date from which the transactions of a transferor company are to be treated for accounting purposes as being those of the transferee company;
  (f)   any rights or restrictions attaching to shares or other securities in the transferee company to be allotted under the scheme to the holders of shares or other securities in a transferor company to which any special rights or restrictions attach, or the measures proposed concerning them;
  (g)   any amount of benefit paid or given or intended to be paid or given—
    (i)   to any of the experts referred to in section 909 (expert's report), or
    (ii)   to any director of a merging company,
    and the consideration for the payment of benefit.
(3)   The requirements in subsection (2)(b), (c) and (d) are subject to section 915 (circumstances in which certain particulars not required).

NOTES
Commencement: 6 April 2008.

[1.906]
906 Publication of draft terms [by registrar] (merger)
(1)   The directors of each of the merging companies must deliver a copy of the draft terms to the registrar.
(2)   The registrar must publish in the Gazette notice of receipt by him from that company of a copy of the draft terms.
(3)   That notice must be published at least one month before the date of any meeting of that company summoned for the purpose of approving the scheme.
[(4)   The requirements in this section are subject to section 906A (publication of draft terms on company website).]

NOTES
Commencement: 6 April 2008.

Part 1   The Companies Act 2006

The words in square brackets in the section heading were inserted, and sub-s (4) was added, by the Companies (Reporting Requirements in Mergers and Divisions) Regulations 2011, SI 2011/1606, regs 3, 5, as from 1 August 2011 (except in relation to any merger or division the draft terms of which were adopted before that date).

[1.906A]
[906A   Publication of draft terms on company website (merger)
(1)   Section 906 does not apply in respect of a company if the conditions in subsections (2) to (6) are met.
(2)   The first condition is that the draft terms are made available on a website which—
   (a)   is maintained by or on behalf of the company, and
   (b)   identifies the company.
(3)   The second condition is that neither access to the draft terms on the website nor the supply of a hard copy of them from the website is conditional on payment of a fee or otherwise restricted.
(4)   The third condition is that the directors of the company deliver to the registrar a notice giving details of the website.
(5)   The fourth condition is that the registrar publishes the notice in the Gazette at least one month before the date of any meeting of the company summoned for the purpose of approving the scheme.
(6)   The fifth condition is that the draft terms remain available on the website throughout the period beginning one month before, and ending on, the date of any such meeting.]

NOTES
  Commencement: 1 August 2011.
  Inserted by the Companies (Reporting Requirements in Mergers and Divisions) Regulations 2011, SI 2011/1606, regs 3, 6, as from 1 August 2011 (except in relation to any merger or division the draft terms of which were adopted before that date).

[1.907]
907   Approval of members of merging companies
(1)   The scheme must be approved by a majority in number, representing 75% in value, of each class of members of each of the merging companies, present and voting either in person or by proxy at a meeting.
(2)   This requirement is subject to sections 916, 917 and 918 (circumstances in which meetings of members not required).

NOTES
  Commencement: 6 April 2008.

[1.908]
908   Directors' explanatory report (merger)
(1)   The directors of each of the merging companies must draw up and adopt a report.
(2)   The report must consist of—
   (a)   the statement required by section 897 (statement explaining effect of compromise or arrangement), and
   (b)   insofar as that statement does not deal with the following matters, a further statement—
      (i)   setting out the legal and economic grounds for the draft terms, and in particular for the share exchange ratio, and
      (ii)   specifying any special valuation difficulties.
(3)   The requirement in this section is subject to section 915 (circumstances in which reports not required)[, section 915A (other circumstances in which reports and inspection not required) and section 918A (agreement to dispense with reports etc)].

NOTES
  Commencement: 6 April 2008.
  Sub-s (3): words in square brackets added by the Companies (Reporting Requirements in Mergers and Divisions) Regulations 2011, SI 2011/1606, regs 3, 7, as from 1 August 2011 (except in relation to any merger or division the draft terms of which were adopted before that date).

[1.909]
909   Expert's report (merger)
(1)   An expert's report must be drawn up on behalf of each of the merging companies.
(2)   The report required is a written report on the draft terms to the members of the company.
(3)   The court may on the joint application of all the merging companies approve the appointment of a joint expert to draw up a single report on behalf of all those companies.
  If no such appointment is made, there must be a separate expert's report to the members of each merging company drawn up by a separate expert appointed on behalf of that company.
(4)   The expert must be a person who—
   (a)   is eligible for appointment as a statutory auditor (see section 1212), and
   (b)   meets the independence requirement in section 936.
(5)   The expert's report must—
   (a)   indicate the method or methods used to arrive at the share exchange ratio;

(b) give an opinion as to whether the method or methods used are reasonable in all the circumstances of the case, indicate the values arrived at using each such method and (if there is more than one method) give an opinion on the relative importance attributed to such methods in arriving at the value decided on;

(c) describe any special valuation difficulties that have arisen;

(d) state whether in the expert's opinion the share exchange ratio is reasonable; and

(e) in the case of a valuation made by a person other than himself (see section 935), state that it appeared to him reasonable to arrange for it to be so made or to accept a valuation so made.

(6) The expert (or each of them) has—

(a) the right of access to all such documents of all the merging companies, and

(b) the right to require from the companies' officers all such information,

as he thinks necessary for the purposes of making his report.

(7) The requirement in this section is subject to section 915 (circumstances in which reports not required)[, section 915A (other circumstances in which reports and inspection not required)] [and section 918A (agreement to dispense with expert's report)].

NOTES

Commencement: 6 April 2008.

Sub-s (7): words in first pair of square brackets inserted by the Companies (Reporting Requirements in Mergers and Divisions) Regulations 2011, SI 2011/1606, regs 3, 8, as from 1 August 2011 (except in relation to any merger or division the draft terms of which were adopted before that date); words in second pair of square brackets inserted by the Companies (Mergers and Divisions of Public Companies) (Amendment) Regulations 2008, SI 2008/690, reg 2(1), as from 6 April 2008.

[1.910]

910 Supplementary accounting statement (merger)

(1) If the last annual accounts of any of the merging companies relate to a financial year ending more than seven months before the first meeting of the company summoned for the purposes of approving the scheme, the directors of that company must prepare a supplementary accounting statement.

(2) That statement must consist of—

(a) a balance sheet dealing with the state of affairs of the company as at a date not more than three months before the draft terms were adopted by the directors, and

(b) where the company would be required under section 399 to prepare group accounts if that date were the last day of a financial year, a consolidated balance sheet dealing with the state of affairs of the company and the undertakings that would be included in such a consolidation.

(3) The requirements of this Act (and where relevant Article 4 of the IAS Regulation) as to the balance sheet forming part of a company's annual accounts, and the matters to be included in notes to it, apply to the balance sheet required for an accounting statement under this section, with such modifications as are necessary by reason of its being prepared otherwise than as at the last day of a financial year.

(4) The provisions of section 414 as to the approval and signing of accounts apply to the balance sheet required for an accounting statement under this section.

[(5) In this section "half-yearly financial report" means a report of that description required to be made public by rules under section 89A of the Financial Services and Markets Act 2000 (transparency rules).

(6) The requirement in this section is subject to section 915A (other circumstances in which reports and inspection not required) and section 918A (agreement to dispense with reports etc).]

NOTES

Commencement: 6 April 2008.

Sub-s (1): substituted by the Companies (Reporting Requirements in Mergers and Divisions) Regulations 2011, SI 2011/1606, regs 3, 9(1), (2), as from 1 August 2011 (except in relation to any merger or division the draft terms of which were adopted before that date), as follows—

"(1) This section applies if the last annual accounts of any of the merging companies relate to a financial year ending before—

(a) the date seven months before the first meeting of the company summoned for the purposes of approving the scheme, or

(b) if no meeting of the company is required (by virtue of any of sections 916 to 918), the date six months before the directors of the company adopt the draft terms of the scheme.

(1A) If the company has not made public a half-yearly financial report relating to a period ending on or after the date mentioned in subsection (1), the directors of the company must prepare a supplementary accounting statement.".

Sub-ss (4), (5): added by SI 2011/1606, regs 3, 9(1), (3), as from 1 August 2011 (except in relation to any merger or division the draft terms of which were adopted before that date).

[1.911]

911 Inspection of documents (merger)

(1) The members of each of the merging companies must be able, during the period specified below—

(a) to inspect at the registered office of that company copies of the documents listed below relating to that company and every other merging company, and

(b) to obtain copies of those documents or any part of them on request free of charge.

(2) The period referred to above is the period—

(a) beginning one month before, and

(b) ending on the date of,

the first meeting of the members, or any class of members, of the company for the purposes of approving the scheme.

(3) The documents referred to above are—

(a) the draft terms;

(b) the directors' explanatory report;

(c) the expert's report;

(d) the company's annual accounts and reports for the last three financial years ending on or before the first meeting of the members, or any class of members, of the company summoned for the purposes of approving the scheme; *and*

(e) any supplementary accounting statement required by section 910[; and

(f) if no statement is required by section 910 because the company has made public a recent half-yearly financial report (see subsection (1A) of that section), that report].

[(3A) The requirement in subsection (1)(a) is subject to section 911A(1) (publication of documents on company website).]

(4) The requirements of subsection (3)(b) and (c) are subject to section 915 (circumstances in which reports not required) [and section 918A (agreement to dispense with reports etc)].

[(5) Section 1145 (right to hard copy) does not apply to a document sent or supplied in accordance with subsection (1)(b) to a member who has consented to information being sent or supplied by the company by electronic means and has not revoked that consent.

(6) Part 4 of Schedule 5 (communications by means of a website) does not apply for the purposes of subsection (1)(b) (but see section 911A(5)).

(7) The requirements in this section are subject to section 915A (other circumstances in which reports and inspection not required).]

NOTES

Commencement: 6 April 2008.

The word in italics in sub-s (3)(d) is repealed, sub-s (3)(f) (and the preceding word) is added, the words in square brackets in sub-s (4) are added, and sub-ss (3A), (5)–(7) are inserted and added respectively, by the Companies (Reporting Requirements in Mergers and Divisions) Regulations 2011, SI 2011/1606, regs 3, 10, as from 1 August 2011 (except in relation to any merger or division the draft terms of which were adopted before that date).

[1.911A]
[911A Publication of documents on company website (merger)

(1) Section 911(1)(a) does not apply to a document if the conditions in subsections (2) to (4) are met in relation to that document.

This is subject to subsection (6).

(2) The first condition is that the document is made available on a website which—

(a) is maintained by or on behalf of the company, and

(b) identifies the company.

(3) The second condition is that access to the document on the website is not conditional on payment of a fee or otherwise restricted.

(4) The third condition is that the document remains available on the website throughout the period beginning one month before, and ending on, the date of any meeting of the company summoned for the purpose of approving the scheme.

(5) A person is able to obtain a copy of a document as required by section 911(1)(b) if—

(a) the conditions in subsections (2) and (3) are met in relation to that document, and

(b) the person is able, throughout the period specified in subsection (4)—

(i) to retain a copy of the document as made available on the website, and

(ii) to produce a hard copy of it.

(6) Where members of a company are able to obtain copies of a document only as mentioned in subsection (5), section 911(1)(a) applies to that document even if the conditions in subsections (2) to (4) are met.]

NOTES

Commencement: 1 August 2011.

Inserted by the Companies (Reporting Requirements in Mergers and Divisions) Regulations 2011, SI 2011/1606, regs 3, 11, as from 1 August 2011 (except in relation to any merger or division the draft terms of which were adopted before that date).

[1.911B]
[911B Report on material changes of assets of merging companies

(1) The directors of each of the merging companies must report—

(a) to every meeting of the members, or any class of members, of that company summoned for the purpose of agreeing to the scheme, and

(b) to the directors of every other merging company,

any material changes in the property and liabilities of that company between the date when the draft terms were adopted and the date of the meeting in question.

(2)   The directors of each of the other merging companies must in turn—

(a)   report those matters to every meeting of the members, or any class of members, of that company summoned for the purpose of agreeing to the scheme, or

(b)   send a report of those matters to every member entitled to receive notice of such a meeting.

(3)   The requirement in this section is subject to section 915A (other circumstances in which reports and inspection not required) and section 918A (agreement to dispense with reports etc).]

NOTES

Commencement: 1 August 2011.

Inserted by the Companies (Reporting Requirements in Mergers and Divisions) Regulations 2011, SI 2011/1606, regs 3, 12, as from 1 August 2011 (except in relation to any merger or division the draft terms of which were adopted before that date).

[1.912]
912   Approval of articles of new transferee company (merger)
In the case of a merger by formation of a new company, the articles of the transferee company, or a draft of them, must be approved by ordinary resolution of *the transferor company or, as the case may be,* each of the transferor companies.

NOTES

Commencement: 6 April 2008.

Words in italics repealed by the Companies (Reporting Requirements in Mergers and Divisions) Regulations 2011, SI 2011/1606, regs 3, 13, as from 1 August 2011 (except in relation to any merger or division the draft terms of which were adopted before that date).

[1.913]
913   Protection of holders of securities to which special rights attached (merger)
(1)   The scheme must provide that where any securities of a transferor company (other than shares) to which special rights are attached are held by a person otherwise than as a member or creditor of the company, that person is to receive rights in the transferee company of equivalent value.

(2)   Subsection (1) does not apply if—

(a)   the holder has agreed otherwise, or

(b)   the holder is, or under the scheme is to be, entitled to have the securities purchased by the transferee company on terms that the court considers reasonable.

NOTES

Commencement: 6 April 2008.

[1.914]
[914   No allotment of shares to transferor company or transferee company (merger)
The scheme must not provide for any shares in the transferee company to be allotted to—

(a)   a transferor company (or its nominee) in respect of shares in the transferor company held by the transferor company itself (or its nominee); or

(b)   the transferee company (or its nominee) in respect of shares in a transferor company held by the transferee company (or its nominee).]

NOTES

Commencement: 6 April 2008.

Substituted by the Companies (Mergers and Divisions of Public Companies) (Amendment) Regulations 2008, SI 2008/690, reg 3, as from 6 April 2008. Note that the original s 914 was due to come into force on 6 April 2008 and was, therefore, substituted without ever coming into effect.

Exceptions where shares of transferor company held by transferee company

[1.915]
915   Circumstances in which certain particulars and reports not required (merger)
(1)   This section applies in the case of a merger by absorption where all of the relevant securities of the transferor company (or, if there is more than one transferor company, of each of them) are held by or on behalf of the transferee company.

(2)   The draft terms of the scheme need not give the particulars mentioned in section 905(2)(b), (c) or (d) (particulars relating to allotment of shares to members of transferor company).

(3)   Section 897 (explanatory statement to be circulated or made available) does not apply.

(4)   The requirements of the following sections do not apply—

section 908 (directors' explanatory report),

section 909 (expert's report).

(5)   The requirements of section 911 (inspection of documents) so far as relating to any document required to be drawn up under the provisions mentioned in [subsection (4)] above do not apply.

(6)   In this section "relevant securities", in relation to a company, means shares or other securities carrying the right to vote at general meetings of the company.

NOTES

Commencement: 6 April 2008.

Sub-s (5): words in square brackets substituted by the Companies Act 2006 (Consequential Amendments and Transitional Provisions) Order 2011, SI 2011/1265 art 28(1), (4), as from 12 May 2011. Note that this reference was previously changed (from the original reference to 'subsection (3)') by a correction slip issued in July 2010.

[1.915A]
[915A Other circumstances in which reports and inspection not required (merger)

(1)   This section applies in the case of a merger by absorption where 90% or more (but not all) of the relevant securities of the transferor company (or, if there is more than one transferor company, of each of them) are held by or on behalf of the transferee company.

(2)   If the conditions in subsections (3) and (4) are met, the requirements of the following sections do not apply—

   (a)   section 908 (directors' explanatory report),

   (b)   section 909 (expert's report),

   (c)   section 910 (supplementary accounting statement),

   (d)   section 911 (inspection of documents), and

   (e)   section 911B (report on material changes of assets of merging company).

(3)   The first condition is that the scheme provides that every other holder of relevant securities has the right to require the transferee company to acquire those securities.

(4)   The second condition is that, if a holder of securities exercises that right, the consideration to be given for those securities is fair and reasonable.

(5)   The powers of the court under section 900(2) (power to facilitate reconstruction or amalgamation) include the power to determine, or make provision for the determination of, the consideration to be given for securities acquired under this section.

(6)   In this section—

   "other holder" means a person who holds securities of the transferor company otherwise than on behalf of the transferee company (and does not include the transferee company itself);

   "relevant securities", in relation to a company, means shares or other securities carrying the right to vote at general meetings of the company.]

NOTES

Commencement: 1 August 2011.

Inserted by the Companies (Reporting Requirements in Mergers and Divisions) Regulations 2011, SI 2011/1606, regs 3, 14, as from 1 August 2011 (except in relation to any merger or division the draft terms of which were adopted before that date).

[1.916]
916 Circumstances in which meeting of members of transferee company not required (merger)

(1)   This section applies in the case of a merger by absorption where 90% or more (but not all) of the relevant securities of the transferor company (or, if there is more than one transferor company, of each of them) are held by or on behalf of the transferee company.

(2)   It is not necessary for the scheme to be approved at a meeting of the members, or any class of members, of the transferee company if the court is satisfied that the following conditions have been complied with.

(3)   The first condition is that publication of notice of receipt of the draft terms by the registrar took place in respect of the transferee company at least one month before the date of the first meeting of members, or any class of members, of the transferor company summoned for the purpose of agreeing to the scheme.

(4)   The second condition is that the members of the transferee company were able during the period beginning one month before, and ending on, that date—

   (a)   to inspect at the registered office of the transferee company copies of the documents listed in section 911(3)(a), (d) and (e) relating to that company and the transferor company (or, if there is more than one transferor company, each of them), and

   (b)   to obtain copies of those documents or any part of them on request free of charge.

(5)   The *third* condition is that—

   (a)   one or more members of the transferee company, who together held not less than 5% of the paid-up capital of the company which carried the right to vote at general meetings of the company (excluding any shares in the company held as treasury shares) would have been able, during that period, to require a meeting of each class of members to be called for the purpose of deciding whether or not to agree to the scheme, and

   (b)   no such requirement was made.

(6)   In this section "relevant securities", in relation to a company, means shares or other securities carrying the right to vote at general meetings of the company.

NOTES

Commencement: 6 April 2008.

Sub-s (3): substituted by the Companies (Reporting Requirements in Mergers and Divisions) Regulations 2011, SI 2011/1606, regs 3, 15(1), (2), as from 1 August 2011 (except in relation to any merger or division the draft terms of which were adopted before that date), as follows—

"(3)   The first condition is that either subsection (3A) or subsection (3B) is satisfied.
(3A)   This subsection is satisfied if publication of notice of receipt of the draft terms by the registrar took place in respect of the transferee company at least one month before the date of the first meeting of members, or any class of members, of the transferor company summoned for the purpose of agreeing to the scheme.
(3B)   This subsection is satisfied if—
   (a)   the conditions in section 906A(2) to (4) are met in respect of the transferee company,
   (b)   the registrar published the notice mentioned in subsection (4) of that section in the Gazette at least one month before the date of the first meeting of members, or any class of members, of the transferor company summoned for the purpose of agreeing to the scheme, and
   (c)   the draft terms remained available on the website throughout the period beginning one month before, and ending on, that date.".

Sub-s (4): substituted by SI 2011/1606, regs 3, 15(1), (3), as from 1 August 2011 (except in relation to any merger or division the draft terms of which were adopted before that date), as follows—

"(4)   The second condition is that subsection (4A) or (4B) is satisfied for each of the documents listed in the applicable paragraphs of section 911(3)(a) to (f) relating to the transferee company and the transferor company (or, if there is more than one transferor company, each of them).
(4A)   This subsection is satisfied for a document if the members of the transferee company were able during the period beginning one month before, and ending on, the date mentioned in subsection (3A) to inspect that document at the registered office of that company.
(4B)   This subsection is satisfied for a document if—
   (a)   the document is made available on a website which is maintained by or on behalf of the transferee company and identifies the company,
   (b)   access to the document on the website is not conditional on the payment of a fee or otherwise restricted, and
   (c)   the document remains available on the website throughout the period beginning one month before, and ending on, the date mentioned in subsection (3A).
(4C)   The third condition is that the members of the transferee company were able to obtain copies of the documents mentioned in subsection (4), or any part of those documents, on request and free of charge, throughout the period beginning one month before, and ending on, the date mentioned in subsection (3A).
(4D)   For the purposes of subsection (4C)—
   (a)   section 911A(5) applies as it applies for the purposes of section 911(1)(b), and
   (b)   Part 4 of Schedule 5 (communications by means of a website) does not apply.".

Sub-s (5): for the word in italics there is substituted the word "fourth" by SI 2011/1606, regs 3, 15(1), (4), as from 1 August 2011 (except in relation to any merger or division the draft terms of which were adopted before that date).

[1.917]
917   Circumstances in which no meetings required (merger)
(1)   This section applies in the case of a merger by absorption where all of the relevant securities of the transferor company (or, if there is more than one transferor company, of each of them) are held by or on behalf of the transferee company.
(2)   It is not necessary for the scheme to be approved at a meeting of the members, or any class of members, of any of the merging companies if the court is satisfied that the following conditions have been complied with.
(3)   The first condition is that publication of notice of receipt of the draft terms by the registrar took place in respect of all the merging companies at least one month before the date of the court's order.
(4)   The second condition is that the members of the transferee company were able during the period beginning one month before, and ending on, that date—
   (a)   to inspect at the registered office of that company copies of the documents listed in section 911(3) relating to that company and the transferor company (or, if there is more than one transferor company, each of them), and
   (b)   to obtain copies of those documents or any part of them on request free of charge.
(5)   The *third* condition is that—
   (a)   one or more members of the transferee company, who together held not less than 5% of the paid-up capital of the company which carried the right to vote at general meetings of the company (excluding any shares in the company held as treasury shares) would have been able, during that period, to require a meeting of each class of members to be called for the purpose of deciding whether or not to agree to the scheme, and
   (b)   no such requirement was made.
(6)   In this section "relevant securities", in relation to a company, means shares or other securities carrying the right to vote at general meetings of the company.

NOTES
Commencement: 6 April 2008.
Sub-s (3): substituted by the Companies (Reporting Requirements in Mergers and Divisions) Regulations 2011, SI 2011/1606, regs 3, 16(1), (2), as from 1 August 2011 (except in relation to any merger or division the draft terms of which were adopted before that date), as follows—

"(3)   The first condition is that either subsection (3A) or subsection (3B) is satisfied.
(3A)   This subsection is satisfied if publication of notice of receipt of the draft terms by the registrar took place in respect of all the merging companies at least one month before the date of the court's order.
(3B)   This subsection is satisfied if—

(a)   the conditions in section 906A(2) to (4) are met in respect of each of the merging companies,

(b)   in each case, the registrar published the notice mentioned in subsection (4) of that section in the Gazette at least one month before the date of the court's order, and

(c)   the draft terms remained available on the website throughout the period beginning one month before, and ending on, that date.".

Sub-s (4): substituted by SI 2011/1606, regs 3, 16(1), (3), as from 1 August 2011 (except in relation to any merger or division the draft terms of which were adopted before that date), as follows—

"(4)   The second condition is that subsection (4A) or (4B) is satisfied for each of the documents listed in the applicable paragraphs of section 911(3)(a) to (f) relating to the transferee company and the transferor company (or, if there is more than one transferor company, each of them).

(4A)   This subsection is satisfied for a document if the members of the transferee company were able during the period beginning one month before, and ending on, the date mentioned in subsection (3A) to inspect that document at the registered office of that company.

(4B)   This subsection is satisfied for a document if—

(a)   the document is made available on a website which is maintained by or on behalf of the transferee company and identifies the company,

(b)   access to the document on the website is not conditional on the payment of a fee or otherwise restricted, and

(c)   the document remains available on the website throughout the period beginning one month before, and ending on, the date mentioned in subsection (3A).

(4C)   The third condition is that the members of the transferee company were able to obtain copies of the documents mentioned in subsection (4), or any part of those documents, on request and free of charge, throughout the period beginning one month before, and ending on, the date mentioned in subsection (3A).

(4D)   For the purposes of subsection (4C)—

(a)   section 911A(5) applies as it applies for the purposes of section 911(1)(b), and

(b)   Part 4 of Schedule 5 (communications by means of a website) does not apply.".

Sub-s (5): for the word in italics there is substituted the word "fourth" by SI 2011/1606, regs 3, 16(1), (4), as from 1 August 2011 (except in relation to any merger or division the draft terms of which were adopted before that date).

Other exceptions

[1.918]

918   Other circumstances in which meeting of members of transferee company not required (merger)

(1)   In the case of any merger by absorption, it is not necessary for the scheme to be approved by the members of the transferee company if the court is satisfied that the following conditions have been complied with.

(2)   *The first condition is that publication of notice of receipt of the draft terms by the registrar took place in respect of that company at least one month before the date of the first meeting of members, or any class of members, of the transferor company (or, if there is more than one transferor company, any of them) summoned for the purposes of agreeing to the scheme.*

(3)   *The second condition is that the members of that company were able during the period beginning one month before, and ending on, the date of any such meeting—*

(a)   *to inspect at the registered office of that company copies of the documents specified in section 911(3) relating to that company and the transferor company (or, if there is more than one transferor company, each of them), and*

(b)   *to obtain copies of those documents or any part of them on request free of charge.*

(4)   The *third* condition is that—

(a)   one or more members of that company, who together held not less than 5% of the paid-up capital of the company which carried the right to vote at general meetings of the company (excluding any shares in the company held as treasury shares) would have been able, during that period, to require a meeting of each class of members to be called for the purpose of deciding whether or not to agree to the scheme, and

(b)   no such requirement was made.

NOTES

Commencement: 6 April 2008.

Sub-s (2): substituted by the Companies (Reporting Requirements in Mergers and Divisions) Regulations 2011, SI 2011/1606, regs 3, 17(1), (2), as from 1 August 2011 (except in relation to any merger or division the draft terms of which were adopted before that date), as follows—

"(2)   The first condition is that either subsection (2A) or subsection (2B) is satisfied.

(2A)   This subsection is satisfied if publication of notice of receipt of the draft terms by the registrar took place in respect of the transferee company at least one month before the date of the first meeting of members, or any class of members, of the transferor company (or, if there is more than one transferor company, any of them) summoned for the purposes of agreeing to the scheme.

(2B)   This subsection is satisfied if—

(a)   the conditions in section 906A(2) to (4) are met in respect of the transferee company,

(b)   the registrar published the notice mentioned in subsection (4) of that section in the Gazette at least one month before the date of the first meeting of members, or any class of members, of the transferor company (or, if there is more than one transferor company, any of them) summoned for the purposes of agreeing to the scheme, and

(c)   the draft terms remained available on the website throughout the period beginning one month before, and ending on, that date.".

Sub-s (3): substituted by SI 2011/1606, regs 3, 17(1), (3), as from 1 August 2011 (except in relation to any merger or division the draft terms of which were adopted before that date), as follows—

"(3)   The second condition is that subsection (3A) or (3B) is satisfied for each of the documents listed in the applicable paragraphs of section 911(3) relating to the transferee company and the transferor company (or, if there is more than one transferor company, each of them).

(3A)   This subsection is satisfied for a document if the members of the transferee company were able during the period beginning one month before, and ending on, the date of any such meeting as is mentioned in subsection (2A) to inspect that document at the registered office of that company.

(3B)   This subsection is satisfied for a document if—

(a)   the document is made available on a website which is maintained by or on behalf of the transferee company and identifies the company,

(b)   access to the document on the website is not conditional on the payment of a fee or otherwise restricted, and

(c)   the document remains available on the website throughout the period beginning one month before, and ending on, the date of any such meeting as is mentioned in subsection (2A).

(3C)   The third condition is that the members of the transferee company were able to obtain copies of the documents mentioned in subsection (3), or any part of those documents, on request and free of charge, throughout the period beginning one month before, and ending on, the date of any such meeting as is mentioned in subsection (2A).

(3D)   For the purposes of subsection (3C)—

(a)   section 911A(5) applies as it applies for the purposes of section 911(1)(b), and

(b)   Part 4 of Schedule 5 (communications by means of a website) does not apply.".

Sub-s (4): for the word in italics there is substituted the word "fourth" by SI 2011/1606, regs 3, 17(1), (4), as from 1 August 2011 (except in relation to any merger or division the draft terms of which were adopted before that date).

[1.918A]
[918A   Agreement to dispense with *expert's report* (merger)

(1)   If all members holding shares in, and all persons holding other securities of, the *companies involved in the merger*, being shares or securities that carry a right to vote in general meetings of the company in question, so agree, *the requirement of section 909 (expert's report) does not apply*.

[(1A)   The requirements that may be dispensed with under this section are—

(a)   the requirements of—

(i)   section 908 (directors' explanatory report),

(ii)   section 909 (expert's report),

(iii)   section 910 (supplementary accounting statement), and

(iv)   section 911B (report on material changes of assets of merging company); and

(b)   the requirements of section 911 (inspection of documents) so far as relating to any document required to be drawn up under sections 908, 909 or 910.]

(2)   For the purposes of this section—

(a)   the members, or holders of other securities, of a company, and

(b)   whether shares or other securities carry a right to vote in general meetings of the company, are determined as at the date of the application to the court under section 896.]

NOTES
Commencement: 6 April 2008.

Inserted by the Companies (Mergers and Divisions of Public Companies) (Amendment) Regulations 2008, SI 2008/690, reg 2(2), as from 6 April 2008.

Section heading: for the words in italics there are substituted the words "reports etc" by the Companies (Reporting Requirements in Mergers and Divisions) Regulations 2011, SI 2011/1606, regs 3, 18(1), (4), as from 1 August 2011 (except in relation to any merger or division the draft terms of which were adopted before that date).

Sub-s (1): for the first words in italics there are substituted the words "the merging companies", and for the second words in italics there are substituted the words "the following requirements do not apply", by SI 2011/1606, regs 3, 18(1), (2), as from 1 August 2011 (except in relation to any merger or division the draft terms of which were adopted before that date).

Sub-s (1A): inserted by SI 2011/1606, regs 3, 18(1), (3), as from 1 August 2011 (except in relation to any merger or division the draft terms of which were adopted before that date).

CHAPTER 3
DIVISION

Introductory

[1.919]
919   Divisions and companies involved in a division

(1)   The scheme involves a division where under the scheme the undertaking, property and liabilities of the company in respect of which the compromise or arrangement is proposed are to be divided among and transferred to two or more companies each of which is either—

(a)   an existing public company, or

(b)   a new company (whether or not a public company).

(2)   References in this Part to the companies involved in the division are to the transferor company and any existing transferee companies.

NOTES
Commencement: 6 April 2008.

Requirements to be complied with in case of division

[1.920]

920   Draft terms of scheme (division)

(1)   A draft of the proposed terms of the scheme must be drawn up and adopted by the directors of each of the companies involved in the division.

(2)   The draft terms must give particulars of at least the following matters—
  (a)   in respect of the transferor company and each transferee company—
    (i)   its name,
    (ii)   the address of its registered office, and
    (iii) whether it is a company limited by shares or a company limited by guarantee and having a share capital;
  (b)   the number of shares in a transferee company to be allotted to members of the transferor company for a given number of their shares (the "share exchange ratio") and the amount of any cash payment;
  (c)   the terms relating to the allotment of shares in a transferee company;
  (d)   the date from which the holding of shares in a transferee company will entitle the holders to participate in profits, and any special conditions affecting that entitlement;
  (e)   the date from which the transactions of the transferor company are to be treated for accounting purposes as being those of a transferee company;
  (f)   any rights or restrictions attaching to shares or other securities in a transferee company to be allotted under the scheme to the holders of shares or other securities in the transferor company to which any special rights or restrictions attach, or the measures proposed concerning them;
  (g)   any amount of benefit paid or given or intended to be paid or given—
    (i)   to any of the experts referred to in section 924 (expert's report), or
    (ii)   to any director of a company involved in the division,
    and the consideration for the payment of benefit.

(3)   The draft terms must also—
  (a)   give particulars of the property and liabilities to be transferred (to the extent that these are known to the transferor company) and their allocation among the transferee companies;
  (b)   make provision for the allocation among and transfer to the transferee companies of any other property and liabilities that the transferor company has acquired or may subsequently acquire; and
  (c)   specify the allocation to members of the transferor company of shares in the transferee companies and the criteria upon which that allocation is based.

NOTES

Commencement: 6 April 2008.

[1.921]

921   Publication of draft terms [by registrar] (division)

(1)   The directors of each company involved in the division must deliver a copy of the draft terms to the registrar.

(2)   The registrar must publish in the Gazette notice of receipt by him from that company of a copy of the draft terms.

(3)   That notice must be published at least one month before the date of any meeting of that company summoned for the purposes of approving the scheme.

(4)   The requirements in this section are subject to [section 921A (publication of draft terms on company website) and] section 934 (power of court to exclude certain requirements).

NOTES

Commencement: 6 April 2008.

Section heading, sub-s (4): words in square brackets inserted by the Companies (Reporting Requirements in Mergers and Divisions) Regulations 2011, SI 2011/1606, regs 3, 19, as from 1 August 2011 (except in relation to any merger or division the draft terms of which were adopted before that date).

[1.921A]

[921A   Publication of draft terms on company website (division)

(1)   Section 921 does not apply in respect of a company if the conditions in subsections (2) to (6) are met.

(2)   The first condition is that the draft terms are made available on a website which—
  (a)   is maintained by or on behalf of the company, and
  (b)   identifies the company.

(3)   The second condition is that neither access to the draft terms on the website nor the supply of a hard copy of them from the website is conditional on payment of a fee or otherwise restricted.

(4)   The third condition is that the directors of the company deliver to the registrar a notice giving details of the website.

(5)   The fourth condition is that the registrar publishes the notice in the Gazette at least one month before the date of any meeting of the company summoned for the purpose of approving the scheme.

(6) The fifth condition is that the draft terms remain available on the website throughout the period beginning one month before, and ending on, the date of any such meeting.]

NOTES

Commencement: 1 August 2011.

Inserted by the Companies (Reporting Requirements in Mergers and Divisions) Regulations 2011, SI 2011/1606, regs 3, 20, as from 1 August 2011 (except in relation to any merger or division the draft terms of which were adopted before that date).

[1.922]
922 Approval of members of companies involved in the division

(1) The compromise or arrangement must be approved by a majority in number, representing 75% in value, of each class of members of each of the companies involved in the division, present and voting either in person or by proxy at a meeting.

(2) This requirement is subject to sections 931 and 932 (circumstances in which meeting of members not required).

NOTES

Commencement: 6 April 2008.

[1.923]
923 Directors' explanatory report (division)

(1) The directors of the transferor and each existing transferee company must draw up and adopt a report.

(2) The report must consist of—
- (a) the statement required by section 897 (statement explaining effect of compromise or arrangement), and
- (b) insofar as that statement does not deal with the following matters, a further statement—
  - (i) setting out the legal and economic grounds for the draft terms, and in particular for the share exchange ratio and for the criteria on which the allocation to the members of the transferor company of shares in the transferee companies was based, and
  - (ii) specifying any special valuation difficulties.

(3) The report must also state—
- (a) whether a report has been made to any transferee company under section 593 (valuation of non-cash consideration for shares), and
- (b) if so, whether that report has been delivered to the registrar of companies.

(4) The requirement in this section is subject to section 933 (agreement to dispense with reports etc) [and section 933A (certain requirements excluded where shareholders given proportional rights)].

NOTES

Commencement: 6 April 2008.

Commencement (transitional adaptations): art 6 of the Companies Act 2006 (Commencement No 5, Transitional Provisions and Savings) Order 2007, SI 2007/3495 provides that the provisions brought into force by arts 3 and 5 of that Order shall have effect subject to any transitional adaptations specified in Sch 1 to that Order. Schedule 1, Pt 1, para 21 to the Order (at **[2.62]**) provided for such transitional adaptations (note that this paragraph was revoked by the Companies Act 2006 (Commencement No 8, Transitional Provisions and Savings) Order 2008, SI 2008/2860, art 6, as from 1 October 2009 (subject to any relevant transitional provision or saving in Sch 2 to that Order)).

Sub-s (4): words in square brackets inserted by the Companies (Reporting Requirements in Mergers and Divisions) Regulations 2011, SI 2011/1606, regs 3, 21, as from 1 August 2011 (except in relation to any merger or division the draft terms of which were adopted before that date).

[1.924]
924 Expert's report (division)

(1) An expert's report must be drawn up on behalf of each company involved in the division.

(2) The report required is a written report on the draft terms to the members of the company.

(3) The court may on the joint application of the companies involved in the division approve the appointment of a joint expert to draw up a single report on behalf of all those companies.

If no such appointment is made, there must be a separate expert's report to the members of each company involved in the division drawn up by a separate expert appointed on behalf of that company.

(4) The expert must be a person who—
- (a) is eligible for appointment as a statutory auditor (see section 1212), and
- (b) meets the independence requirement in section 936.

(5) The expert's report must—
- (a) indicate the method or methods used to arrive at the share exchange ratio;
- (b) give an opinion as to whether the method or methods used are reasonable in all the circumstances of the case, indicate the values arrived at using each such method and (if there is more than one method) give an opinion on the relative importance attributed to such methods in arriving at the value decided on;
- (c) describe any special valuation difficulties that have arisen;

(d)   state whether in the expert's opinion the share exchange ratio is reasonable; and

(e)   in the case of a valuation made by a person other than himself (see section 935), state that it appeared to him reasonable to arrange for it to be so made or to accept a valuation so made.

(6)   The expert (or each of them) has—

(a)   the right of access to all such documents of the companies involved in the division, and

(b)   the right to require from the companies' officers all such information,

as he thinks necessary for the purposes of making his report.

(7)   The requirement in this section is subject to section 933 (agreement to dispense with reports etc) [and section 933A (certain requirements excluded where shareholders given proportional rights)].

NOTES

Commencement: 6 April 2008.

Sub-s (7): words in square brackets inserted by the Companies (Reporting Requirements in Mergers and Divisions) Regulations 2011, SI 2011/1606, regs 3, 22, as from 1 August 2011 (except in relation to any merger or division the draft terms of which were adopted before that date).

[1.925]
925   Supplementary accounting statement (division)

(1)   If the last annual accounts of a company involved in the division relate to a financial year ending more than seven months before the first meeting of the company summoned for the purposes of approving the scheme, the directors of that company must prepare a supplementary accounting statement.

(2)   That statement must consist of—

(a)   a balance sheet dealing with the state of affairs of the company as at a date not more than three months before the draft terms were adopted by the directors, and

(b)   where the company would be required under section 399 to prepare group accounts if that date were the last day of a financial year, a consolidated balance sheet dealing with the state of affairs of the company and the undertakings that would be included in such a consolidation.

(3)   The requirements of this Act (and where relevant Article 4 of the IAS Regulation) as to the balance sheet forming part of a company's annual accounts, and the matters to be included in notes to it, apply to the balance sheet required for an accounting statement under this section, with such modifications as are necessary by reason of its being prepared otherwise than as at the last day of a financial year.

(4)   The provisions of section 414 as to the approval and signing of accounts apply to the balance sheet required for an accounting statement under this section.

[(4A)   In this section "half-yearly financial report" means a report of that description required to be made public by rules under section 89A of the Financial Services and Markets Act 2000 (transparency rules).]

(5)   The requirement in this section is subject to section 933 (agreement to dispense with reports etc) [and section 933A (certain requirements excluded where shareholders given proportional rights)].

NOTES

Commencement: 6 April 2008.

Sub-s (1): substituted by the Companies (Reporting Requirements in Mergers and Divisions) Regulations 2011, SI 2011/1606, regs 3, 23(1), (2), as from 1 August 2011 (except in relation to any merger or division the draft terms of which were adopted before that date), as follows—

"(1)   This section applies if the last annual accounts of a company involved in the division relate to a financial year ending before—

(a)   the date seven months before the first meeting of the company summoned for the purposes of approving the scheme, or

(b)   if no meeting of the company is required (by virtue of section 931 or 932), the date six months before the directors of the company adopt the draft terms of the scheme.

(1A)   If the company has not made public a half-yearly financial report relating to a period ending on or after the date mentioned in subsection (1), the directors of the company must prepare a supplementary accounting statement.".

Sub-s (4): inserted by SI 2011/1606, regs 3, 23(1), (3), as from 1 August 2011 (except in relation to any merger or division the draft terms of which were adopted before that date).

Sub-s (5): words in square brackets added by SI 2011/1606, regs 3, 23(1), (4), as from 1 August 2011 (except in relation to any merger or division the draft terms of which were adopted before that date).

[1.926]
926   Inspection of documents (division)

(1)   The members of each company involved in the division must be able, during the period specified below—

(a)   to inspect at the registered office of that company copies of the documents listed below relating to that company and every other company involved in the division, and

(b)   to obtain copies of those documents or any part of them on request free of charge.

(2)   The period referred to above is the period—
  (a)   beginning one month before, and
  (b)   ending on the date of,
the first meeting of the members, or any class of members, of the company for the purposes of approving the scheme.

(3)   The documents referred to above are—
  (a)   the draft terms;
  (b)   the directors' explanatory report;
  (c)   the expert's report;
  (d)   the company's annual accounts and reports for the last three financial years ending on or before the first meeting of the members, or any class of members, of the company summoned for the purposes of approving the scheme; *and*
  (e)   any supplementary accounting statement required by section 925[; and
  (f)   if no statement is required by section 925 because the company has made public a recent half-yearly financial report (see subsection (1A) of that section), that report].

[(3A)   The requirement in subsection (1)(a) is subject to section 926A(1) (publication of documents on company website).]

(4)   The requirements in subsection (3)(b), (c) and (e) are subject to section 933 (agreement to dispense with reports etc)[, section 933A (certain requirements excluded where shareholders given proportional rights)] and section 934 (power of court to exclude certain requirements).

[(5)   Section 1145 (right to hard copy) does not apply to a document sent or supplied in accordance with subsection (1)(b) to a member who has consented to information being sent or supplied by the company by electronic means and has not revoked that consent.

(6)   Part 4 of Schedule 5 (communications by means of a website) does not apply for the purposes of subsection (1)(b) (but see section 926A(5)).]

NOTES

Commencement: 6 April 2008.

The word in italics in sub-s (3)(d) is repealed, sub-s (3)(f) (and the preceding word) are added, the words in square brackets in sub-s (4) are inserted, and sub-ss (3A), (5), (6) are inserted and added respectively, by the Companies (Reporting Requirements in Mergers and Divisions) Regulations 2011, SI 2011/1606, regs 3, 24, as from 1 August 2011 (except in relation to any merger or division the draft terms of which were adopted before that date).

[1.926A]
[926A   Publication of documents on company website (division)
(1)   Section 926(1)(a) does not apply to a document if the conditions in subsections (2) to (4) are met in relation to that document.
This is subject to subsection (6).

(2)   The first condition is that the document is made available on a website which—
  (a)   is maintained by or on behalf of the company, and
  (b)   identifies the company.

(3)   The second condition is that access to the document on the website is not conditional on payment of a fee or otherwise restricted.

(4)   The third condition is that the document remains available on the website throughout the period beginning one month before, and ending on, the date of any meeting of the company summoned for the purpose of approving the scheme.

(5)   A person is able to obtain a copy of a document as required by section 926(1)(b) if—
  (a)   the conditions in subsections (2) and (3) are met in relation to that document, and
  (b)   the person is able, throughout the period specified in subsection (4)—
    (i)   to retain a copy of the document as made available on the website, and
    (ii)   to produce a hard copy of it.

(6)   Where members of a company are able to obtain copies of a document only as mentioned in subsection (5), section 926(1)(a) applies to that document even if the conditions in subsections (2) to (4) are met.]

NOTES

Commencement: 1 August 2011.

Inserted by the Companies (Reporting Requirements in Mergers and Divisions) Regulations 2011, SI 2011/1606, regs 3, 25, as from 1 August 2011 (except in relation to any merger or division the draft terms of which were adopted before that date).

[1.927]
927   Report on material changes of assets of transferor company (division)
(1)   The directors of the transferor company must report—
  (a)   to every meeting of the members, or any class of members, of that company summoned for the purpose of agreeing to the scheme, and
  (b)   to the directors of each existing transferee company,
any material changes in the property and liabilities of the transferor company between the date when the draft terms were adopted and the date of the meeting in question.

(2)   The directors of each existing transferee company must in turn—

(a)   report those matters to every meeting of the members, or any class of members, of that company summoned for the purpose of agreeing to the scheme, or

(b)   send a report of those matters to every member entitled to receive notice of such a meeting.

(3)   The requirement in this section is subject to section 933 (agreement to dispense with reports etc) [and section 933A (certain requirements excluded where shareholders given proportional rights)].

NOTES

Commencement: 6 April 2008.

Sub-s (3): words in square brackets added by the Companies (Reporting Requirements in Mergers and Divisions) Regulations 2011, SI 2011/1606, regs 3, 26, as from 1 August 2011 (except in relation to any merger or division the draft terms of which were adopted before that date).

[1.928]
928   Approval of articles of new transferee company (division)

The articles of every new transferee company, or a draft of them, must be approved by ordinary resolution of the transferor company.

NOTES

Commencement: 6 April 2008.

[1.929]
929   Protection of holders of securities to which special rights attached (division)

(1)   The scheme must provide that where any securities of the transferor company (other than shares) to which special rights are attached are held by a person otherwise than as a member or creditor of the company, that person is to receive rights in a transferee company of equivalent value.

(2)   Subsection (1) does not apply if—

(a)   the holder has agreed otherwise, or

(b)   the holder is, or under the scheme is to be, entitled to have the securities purchased by a transferee company on terms that the court considers reasonable.

NOTES

Commencement: 6 April 2008.

[1.930]
[930   No allotment of shares to transferor company or to transferee company (division)

The scheme must not provide for any shares in a transferee company to be allotted to—

(a)   the transferor company (or its nominee) in respect of shares in the transferor company held by the transferor company itself (or its nominee); or

(b)   a transferee company (or its nominee) in respect of shares in the transferor company held by the transferee company (or its nominee).]

NOTES

Commencement: 6 April 2008.

Substituted by the Companies (Mergers and Divisions of Public Companies) (Amendment) Regulations 2008, SI 2008/690, reg 4, as from 6 April 2008. Note that the original s 930 was due to come into force on 6 April 2008 and was, therefore, substituted without ever coming into effect.

Exceptions where shares of transferor company held by transferee company

[1.931]
931   Circumstances in which meeting of members of transferor company not required (division)

(1)   This section applies in the case of a division where all of the shares or other securities of the transferor company carrying the right to vote at general meetings of the company are held by or on behalf of one or more existing transferee companies.

(2)   It is not necessary for the scheme to be approved by a meeting of the members, or any class of members, of the transferor company if the court is satisfied that the following conditions have been complied with.

(3)   The first condition is that publication of notice of receipt of the draft terms by the registrar took place in respect of all the companies involved in the division at least one month before the date of the court's order.

(4)   The second condition is that the members of every company involved in the division were able during the period beginning one month before, and ending on, that date—

(a)   to inspect at the registered office of their company copies of the documents listed in section 926(3) relating to every company involved in the division, and

(b)   to obtain copies of those documents or any part of them on request free of charge.

(5)   The third condition is that—

    (a)   *one or more members of the transferor company, who together held not less than 5% of the paid-up capital of the company (excluding any shares in the company held as treasury shares) would have been able, during that period, to require a meeting of each class of members to be called for the purpose of deciding whether or not to agree to the scheme, and*

    (b)   *no such requirement was made.*

(6)   The fourth condition is that the directors of the transferor company have sent—

    (a)   to every member who would have been entitled to receive notice of a meeting to agree to the scheme (had any such meeting been called), and

    (b)   to the directors of every existing transferee company,

a report of any material change in the property and liabilities of the transferor company between the date when the terms were adopted by the directors and the date one month before the date of the court's order.

NOTES

Commencement: 6 April 2008.

Sub-s (3): substituted by the Companies (Reporting Requirements in Mergers and Divisions) Regulations 2011, SI 2011/1606, regs 3, 27(1), (2), as from 1 August 2011 (except in relation to any merger or division the draft terms of which were adopted before that date), as follows—

"(3)   The first condition is that either subsection (3A) or subsection (3B) is satisfied.

(3A)   This subsection is satisfied if publication of notice of receipt of the draft terms by the registrar took place in respect of all the companies involved in the division at least one month before the date of the court's order.

(3B)   This subsection is satisfied if—

    (a)   the conditions in section 921A(2) to (4) are met in respect of each of the companies involved in the division,

    (b)   in each case, the registrar published the notice mentioned in subsection (4) of that section in the Gazette at least one month before the date of the court's order, and

    (c)   the draft terms remained available on the website throughout the period beginning one month before, and ending on, that date.".

Sub-s (4): substituted by SI 2011/1606, regs 3, 27(1), (3), as from 1 August 2011 (except in relation to any merger or division the draft terms of which were adopted before that date), as follows—

"(4)   The second condition is that subsection (4A) or (4B) is satisfied for each of the documents listed in the applicable paragraphs of section 926(3) relating to every company involved in the division.

(4A)   This subsection is satisfied for a document if the members of every company involved in the division were able during the period beginning one month before, and ending on, the date of the court's order to inspect that document at the registered office of their company.

(4B)   This subsection is satisfied for a document if—

    (a)   the document is made available on a website which is maintained by or on behalf of the company to which it relates and identifies the company,

    (b)   access to the document on the website is not conditional on payment of a fee or otherwise restricted, and

    (c)   the document remains available on the website throughout the period beginning one month before and ending on, the date of the court's order.

(4C)   The third condition is that the members of every company involved in the division were able to obtain copies of the documents mentioned in subsection (4), or any part of those documents, on request and free of charge, throughout the period beginning one month before, and ending on, the date of the court's order.

(4D)   For the purposes of subsection (4C)—

    (a)   section 926A(5) applies as it applies for the purposes of section 926(1)(b), and

    (b)   Part 4 of Schedule 5 (communications by means of a website) does not apply.".

Sub-s (5): repealed by SI 2011/1606, regs 3, 27(1), (4), as from 1 August 2011 (except in relation to any merger or division the draft terms of which were adopted before that date).

Other exceptions

[1.932]

932   Circumstances in which meeting of members of transferee company not required (division)

(1)   In the case of a division, it is not necessary for the scheme to be approved by the members of a transferee company if the court is satisfied that the following conditions have been complied with in relation to that company.

(2)   *The first condition is that publication of notice of receipt of the draft terms by the registrar took place in respect of that company at least one month before the date of the first meeting of members of the transferor company summoned for the purposes of agreeing to the scheme.*

(3)   *The second condition is that the members of that company were able during the period beginning one month before, and ending on, that date—*

    (a)   *to inspect at the registered office of that company copies of the documents specified in section 926(3) relating to that company and every other company involved in the division, and*

    (b)   *to obtain copies of those documents or any part of them on request free of charge.*

(4)   The third condition is that—

    (a)   one or more members of that company, who together held not less than 5% of the paid-up capital of the company which carried the right to vote at general meetings of the company (excluding any shares in the company held as treasury shares) would have been able, during that period, to require a meeting of each class of members to be called for the purpose of deciding whether or not to agree to the scheme, and

(b)	no such requirement was made.

(5)	The first and second conditions above are subject to section 934 (power of court to exclude certain requirements).

NOTES

Commencement: 6 April 2008.

Sub-s (2): substituted by the Companies (Reporting Requirements in Mergers and Divisions) Regulations 2011, SI 2011/1606, regs 3, 28(1), (2), as from 1 August 2011 (except in relation to any merger or division the draft terms of which were adopted before that date), as follows—

"(2)	The first condition is that either subsection (2A) or subsection (2B) is satisfied.

(2A)	This subsection is satisfied if publication of notice of receipt of the draft terms by the registrar took place in respect of the transferee company at least one month before the date of the first meeting of members of the transferor company summoned for the purposes of agreeing to the scheme.

(2B)	This subsection is satisfied if—

(a)	the conditions in section 921A(2) to (4) are met in respect of the transferee company,

(b)	the registrar published the notice mentioned in subsection (4) of that section in the Gazette at least one month before the date of the first meeting of members of the transferor company summoned for the purposes of agreeing to the scheme, and

(c)	the draft terms remained available on the website throughout the period beginning one month before, and ending on, that date.".

Sub-s (3): substituted by SI 2011/1606, regs 3, 28(1), (3), as from 1 August 2011 (except in relation to any merger or division the draft terms of which were adopted before that date), as follows—

"(3)	The second condition is that subsection (3A) or (3B) is satisfied for each of the documents listed in the applicable paragraphs of section 926(3) relating to the transferee company and every other company involved in the division.

(3A)	This subsection is satisfied for a document if the members of the transferee company were able during the period beginning one month before, and ending on, the date mentioned in subsection (2A) to inspect that document at the registered office of that company.

(3B)	This subsection is satisfied for a document if—

(a)	the document is made available on a website which is maintained by or on behalf of the transferee company and identifies the company,

(b)	access to the document on the website is not conditional on payment of a fee or otherwise restricted, and

(c)	the document remains available on the website throughout the period beginning one month before, and ending on, the date mentioned in subsection (2A).

(3C)	The third condition is that the members of the transferee company were able to obtain copies of the documents mentioned in subsection (3), or any part of those documents, on request and free of charge, throughout the period beginning one month before, and ending on, the date mentioned in subsection (2A).

(3D)	For the purposes of subsection (3C)—

(a)	section 926A(5) applies as it applies for the purposes of section 926(1)(b), and

(b)	Part 4 of Schedule 5 (communications by means of a website) does not apply.".

Sub-s (4): for the word in italics there is substituted the word "fourth" by SI 2011/1606, regs 3, 28(1), (4), as from 1 August 2011 (except in relation to any merger or division the draft terms of which were adopted before that date).

Sub-s (5): for the words in italics there are substituted the words "first, second and third" by SI 2011/1606, regs 3, 28(1), (5), as from 1 August 2011 (except in relation to any merger or division the draft terms of which were adopted before that date).

[1.933]
### 933	Agreement to dispense with reports etc (division)

(1)	If all members holding shares in, and all persons holding other securities of, the companies involved in the division, being shares or securities that carry a right to vote in general meetings of the company in question, so agree, the following requirements do not apply.

(2)	The requirements that may be dispensed with under this section are—

(a)	the requirements of—

(i)	section 923 (directors' explanatory report),

(ii)	section 924 (expert's report),

(iii)	section 925 (supplementary accounting statement), and

(iv)	section 927 (report on material changes in assets of transferor company); and

(b)	the requirements of section 926 (inspection of documents) so far as relating to any document required to be drawn up under the provisions mentioned in paragraph (a)(i), (ii) or (iii) above.

(3)	For the purposes of this section—

(a)	the members, or holders of other securities, of a company, and

(b)	whether shares or other securities carry a right to vote in general meetings of the company, are determined as at the date of the application to the court under section 896.

NOTES

Commencement: 6 April 2008.

Part 1   The Companies Act 2006

[1.933A]
[933A Certain requirements excluded where shareholders given proportional rights (division)
(1)   This section applies in the case of a division where each of the transferee companies is a new company.
(2)   If all the shares in each of the transferee companies are to be allotted to the members of the transferor company in proportion to their rights in the allotted share capital of the transferor company, the following requirements do not apply.
(3)   The requirements which do not apply are—
  (a)   the requirements of—
    (i)   section 923 (directors' explanatory report),
    (ii)   section 924 (expert's report),
    (iii)   section 925 (supplementary accounting statement), and
    (iv)   section 927 (report on material changes in assets of transferor company); and
  (b)   the requirements of section 926 (inspection of documents) so far as relating to any document required to be drawn up under the provisions mentioned in paragraph (a)(i), (ii) or (iii) above.]

NOTES
Commencement: 1 August 2011.
Inserted by the Companies (Reporting Requirements in Mergers and Divisions) Regulations 2011, SI 2011/1606, regs 3, 29, as from 1 August 2011 (except in relation to any merger or division the draft terms of which were adopted before that date).

[1.934]
934   Power of court to exclude certain requirements (division)
(1)   In the case of a division, the court may by order direct that—
  (a)   in relation to any company involved in the division, the requirements of—
    (i)   section 921 (publication of draft terms), and
    (ii)   section 926 (inspection of documents),
    do not apply, and
  (b)   in relation to an existing transferee company, section 932 (circumstances in which meeting of members of transferee company not required) has effect with the omission of the *first and second* conditions specified in that section,
if the court is satisfied that the following conditions will be fulfilled in relation to that company.
(2)   The first condition is that the members of that company will have received, or will have been able to obtain free of charge, copies of the documents listed in section 926—
  (a)   in time to examine them before the date of the first meeting of the members, or any class of members, of that company summoned for the purposes of agreeing to the scheme, or
  (b)   in the case of an existing transferee company where in the circumstances described in section 932 no meeting is held, in time to require a meeting as mentioned in subsection (4) of that section.
(3)   The second condition is that the creditors of that company will have received or will have been able to obtain free of charge copies of the draft terms in time to examine them—
  (a)   before the date of the first meeting of the members, or any class of members, of the company summoned for the purposes of agreeing to the scheme, or
  (b)   in the circumstances mentioned in subsection (2)(b) above, at the same time as the members of the company.
(4)   The third condition is that no prejudice would be caused to the members or creditors of the transferor company or any transferee company by making the order in question.

NOTES
Commencement: 6 April 2008.
Sub-s (1): for the words in italics there are substituted the words "first, second and third" by the Companies (Reporting Requirements in Mergers and Divisions) Regulations 2011, SI 2011/1606, regs 3, 30, as from 1 August 2011 (except in relation to any merger or division the draft terms of which were adopted before that date).

CHAPTER 4
SUPPLEMENTARY PROVISIONS

Expert's report and related matters

[1.935]
935   Expert's report: valuation by another person
(1)   Where it appears to an expert—
  (a)   that a valuation is reasonably necessary to enable him to draw up his report, and
  (b)   that it is reasonable for that valuation, or part of it, to be made by (or for him to accept a valuation made by) another person who—
    (i)   appears to him to have the requisite knowledge and experience to make the valuation or that part of it, and
    (ii)   meets the independence requirement in section 936,

he may arrange for or accept such a valuation, together with a report which will enable him to make his own report under section 909 or 924.

(2)   Where any valuation is made by a person other than the expert himself, the latter's report must state that fact and must also—

    (a)   state the former's name and what knowledge and experience he has to carry out the valuation, and

    (b)   describe so much of the undertaking, property and liabilities as was valued by the other person, and the method used to value them, and specify the date of the valuation.

NOTES

Commencement: 6 April 2008.

[1.936]
936   Experts and valuers: independence requirement

(1)   A person meets the independence requirement for the purposes of section 909 or 924 (expert's report) or section 935 (valuation by another person) only if—

    (a)   he is not—

        (i)   an officer or employee of any of the companies concerned in the scheme, or

        (ii)   a partner or employee of such a person, or a partnership of which such a person is a partner;

    (b)   he is not—

        (i)   an officer or employee of an associated undertaking of any of the companies concerned in the scheme, or

        (ii)   a partner or employee of such a person, or a partnership of which such a person is a partner; and

    (c)   there does not exist between—

        (i)   the person or an associate of his, and

        (ii)   any of the companies concerned in the scheme or an associated undertaking of such a company,

    a connection of any such description as may be specified by regulations made by the Secretary of State.

(2)   An auditor of a company is not regarded as an officer or employee of the company for this purpose.

(3)   For the purposes of this section—

    (a)   the "companies concerned in the scheme" means every transferor and existing transferee company;

    (b)   "associated undertaking", in relation to a company, means—

        (i)   a parent undertaking or subsidiary undertaking of the company, or

        (ii)   a subsidiary undertaking of a parent undertaking of the company; and

    (c)   "associate" has the meaning given by section 937.

(4)   Regulations under this section are subject to negative resolution procedure.

NOTES

Commencement: 20 January 2007 (for the purpose of enabling the exercise of powers to make Orders or Regulations by statutory instrument); 6 April 2008 (otherwise).

[1.937]
937   Experts and valuers: meaning of "associate"

(1)   This section defines "associate" for the purposes of section 936 (experts and valuers: independence requirement).

(2)   In relation to an individual, "associate" means—

    (a)   that individual's spouse or civil partner or minor child or step-child,

    (b)   any body corporate of which that individual is a director, and

    (c)   any employee or partner of that individual.

(3)   In relation to a body corporate, "associate" means—

    (a)   any body corporate of which that body is a director,

    (b)   any body corporate in the same group as that body, and

    (c)   any employee or partner of that body or of any body corporate in the same group.

(4)   In relation to a partnership that is a legal person under the law by which it is governed, "associate" means—

    (a)   any body corporate of which that partnership is a director,

    (b)   any employee of or partner in that partnership, and

    (c)   any person who is an associate of a partner in that partnership.

(5)   In relation to a partnership that is not a legal person under the law by which it is governed, "associate" means any person who is an associate of any of the partners.

(6)   In this section, in relation to a limited liability partnership, for "director" read "member".

NOTES

Commencement: 6 April 2008.

Powers of the court

[1.938]
938 Power of court to summon meeting of members or creditors of existing transferee company

(1) The court may order a meeting of—
    (a) the members of an existing transferee company, or any class of them, or
    (b) the creditors of an existing transferee company, or any class of them, to be summoned in such manner as the court directs.

(2) An application for such an order may be made by—
    (a) the company concerned,
    (b) a member or creditor of the company, or
    [(c) if the company is being wound up, the liquidator, or
    (d) if the company is in administration, the administrator.]

[(3) Section 323 (representation of corporations at meetings) applies to a meeting of creditors under this section as to a meeting of the company (references to a member being read as references to a creditor).]

NOTES
Commencement: 6 April 2008.
Sub-s (2): paras (c), (d) substituted (for the original para (c)) by the Companies Act 2006 (Consequential Amendments, Transitional Provisions and Savings) Order 2009, SI 2009/1941, art 2(1), Sch 1, para 260(1), (5), as from 1 October 2009.
Sub-s (3): added by the Companies Act 2006 (Consequential Amendments etc) Order 2008, SI 2008/948, art 3(1), Sch 1, Pt 2, para 251, as from 6 April 2008.

[1.939]
939 Court to fix date for transfer of undertaking etc of transferor company

(1) Where the court sanctions the compromise or arrangement, it must—
    (a) in the order sanctioning the compromise or arrangement, or
    (b) in a subsequent order under section 900 (powers of court to facilitate reconstruction or amalgamation),
fix a date on which the transfer (or transfers) to the transferee company (or transferee companies) of the undertaking, property and liabilities of the transferor company is (or are) to take place.

(2) Any such order that provides for the dissolution of the transferor company must fix the same date for the dissolution.

(3) If it is necessary for the transferor company to take steps to ensure that the undertaking, property and liabilities are fully transferred, the court must fix a date, not later than six months after the date fixed under subsection (1), by which such steps must be taken.

(4) In that case, the court may postpone the dissolution of the transferor company until that date.

(5) The court may postpone or further postpone the date fixed under subsection (3) if it is satisfied that the steps mentioned cannot be completed by the date (or latest date) fixed under that subsection.

NOTES
Commencement: 6 April 2008.

Liability of transferee companies

[1.940]
940 Liability of transferee companies for each other's defaults

(1) In the case of a division, each transferee company is jointly and severally liable for any liability transferred to any other transferee company under the scheme to the extent that the other company has made default in satisfying that liability.
    This is subject to the following provisions.

(2) If a majority in number representing 75% in value of the creditors or any class of creditors of the transferor company, present and voting either in person or by proxy at a meeting summoned for the purposes of agreeing to the scheme, so agree, subsection (1) does not apply in relation to the liabilities owed to the creditors or that class of creditors.

(3) A transferee company is not liable under this section for an amount greater than the net value transferred to it under the scheme.
    The "net value transferred" is the value at the time of the transfer of the property transferred to it under the scheme less the amount at that date of the liabilities so transferred.

NOTES
Commencement: 6 April 2008.

[Disruption of websites

[1.940A]
940A Disregard of website failures beyond control of company

(1) A failure to make information or a document available on the website throughout a period specified in any of the provisions mentioned in subsection (2) is to be disregarded if—

    (a)   it is made available on the website for part of that period, and

    (b)   the failure to make it available throughout that period is wholly attributable to circumstances that it would not be reasonable to have expected the company to prevent or avoid.

(2)   The provisions referred to above are—

    (a)   section 906A(6),

    (b)   section 911A(4),

    (c)   section 916(3B) and (4B),

    (d)   section 917(3B) and (4B),

    (e)   section 918(2B) and (3B),

    (f)   section 921A(6),

    (g)   section 926A(4),

    (h)   section 931(3B) and (4B), and

    (i)   section 932(2B) and (3B).]

NOTES

Commencement: 1 August 2011.

Inserted, together with the preceding heading, by the Companies (Reporting Requirements in Mergers and Divisions) Regulations 2011, SI 2011/1606, regs 3, 31, as from 1 August 2011 (except in relation to any merger or division the draft terms of which were adopted before that date).

Interpretation

[1.941]
941 Meaning of "liabilities" and "property"
In this Part—

"liabilities" includes duties;

"property" includes property, rights and powers of every description.

NOTES

Commencement: 6 April 2008.

PART 28
TAKEOVERS ETC

NOTES

The Takeovers Directive (at **[11.360]**) had to be implemented by 20 May 2006 and, as this Act had not completed Parliamentary passage by that date, this was achieved by means of the Takeovers Directive (Interim Implementation) Regulations 2006, SI 2006/1183. The 2006 Regulations were revoked by the Companies Act 2006 (Commencement No 2, Consequential Amendments, Transitional Provisions and Savings) Order 2007, SI 2007/1093, art 7, Sch 5, as from 6 April 2007 (the same date as this Part came into force). The revocation of SI 2006/1183 is subject to certain savings contained in Sch 6, paras 2, 3 to the 2007 Order at **[2.30]**.

CHAPTER 1
THE TAKEOVER PANEL

NOTES

Application to the Isle of Man: see the Companies Act 2006 (Extension of Takeover Panel Provisions) (Isle of Man) Order 2008, SI 2008/3122 which extends (as from 1 March 2009) the provisions of Chapter 1 of Part 28 to the Isle of Man with the modifications set out in the Schedule. Its purpose is to place on a statutory footing the role of the Panel on Takeovers and Mergers in supervising relevant takeovers involving Isle of Man companies.

The Panel and its rules

[1.942]
942 The Panel
(1)   The body known as the Panel on Takeovers and Mergers ("the Panel") is to have the functions conferred on it by or under this Chapter.

(2)   The Panel may do anything that it considers necessary or expedient for the purposes of, or in connection with, its functions.

(3)   The Panel may make arrangements for any of its functions to be discharged by—

    (a)   a committee or sub-committee of the Panel, or

    (b)   an officer or member of staff of the Panel, or a person acting as such.

This is subject to section 943(4) and (5).

NOTES

Commencement: 6 April 2007.

[1.943]
943 Rules
(1)   The Panel must make rules giving effect to Articles 3.1, 4.2, 5, 6.1 to 6.3, 7 to 9 and 13 of the Takeovers Directive.

(2)   Rules made by the Panel may also make other provision—
  (a)   for or in connection with the regulation of—
    (i)   takeover bids,
    (ii)   merger transactions, and
    (iii) transactions (not falling within sub-paragraph (i) or (ii)) that have or may have, directly or indirectly, an effect on the ownership or control of companies;
  (b)   for or in connection with the regulation of things done in consequence of, or otherwise in relation to, any such bid or transaction;
  (c)   about cases where—
    (i)   any such bid or transaction is, or has been, contemplated or apprehended, or
    (ii)   an announcement is made denying that any such bid or transaction is intended.
(3)   The provision that may be made under subsection (2) includes, in particular, provision for a matter that is, or is similar to, a matter provided for by the Panel in the City Code on Takeovers and Mergers as it had effect immediately before the passing of this Act.
(4)   In relation to rules made by virtue of section 957 (fees and charges), functions under this section may be discharged either by the Panel itself or by a committee of the Panel (but not otherwise).
(5)   In relation to rules of any other description, the Panel must discharge its functions under this section by a committee of the Panel.
(6)   Section 1 (meaning of "company") does not apply for the purposes of this section.
(7)   In this section "takeover bid" includes a takeover bid within the meaning of the Takeovers Directive.
(8)   In this Chapter "the Takeovers Directive" means Directive 2004/25/EC of the European Parliament and of the Council.
(9)   A reference to rules in the following provisions of this Chapter is to rules under this section.

NOTES
Commencement: 6 April 2007.

Commencement (transitional adaptations): art 3 of the Companies Act 2006 (Commencement No 2, Consequential Amendments, Transitional Provisions and Savings) Order 2007, SI 2007/1093 provides that the provisions brought into force by art 2 of 2007 Order shall have effect subject to any transitional adaptations specified in Sch 1 to that Order. Schedule 1, para 2 to the Order (at [2.27]) provided for such transitional adaptations (note that this paragraph was revoked by the Companies Act 2006 (Commencement No 8, Transitional Provisions and Savings) Order 2008, SI 2008/2860, art 6, as from 1 October 2009 (subject to any relevant transitional provision or saving in Sch 2 to that Order)).

As to Rules made by the Takeover Panel under this section, see: http://www.thetakeoverpanel.org.uk/

[1.944]
944   Further provisions about rules
(1)   Rules may—
  (a)   make different provision for different purposes;
  (b)   make provision subject to exceptions or exemptions;
  (c)   contain incidental, supplemental, consequential or transitional provision;
  (d)   authorise the Panel to dispense with or modify the application of rules in particular cases and by reference to any circumstances.
  Rules made by virtue of paragraph (d) must require the Panel to give reasons for acting as mentioned in that paragraph.
(2)   Rules must be made by an instrument in writing.
(3)   Immediately after an instrument containing rules is made, the text must be made available to the public, with or without payment, in whatever way the Panel thinks appropriate.
(4)   A person is not to be taken to have contravened a rule if he shows that at the time of the alleged contravention the text of the rule had not been made available as required by subsection (3).
(5)   The production of a printed copy of an instrument purporting to be made by the Panel on which is endorsed a certificate signed by an officer of the Panel authorised by it for that purpose and stating—
  (a)   that the instrument was made by the Panel,
  (b)   that the copy is a true copy of the instrument, and
  (c)   that on a specified date the text of the instrument was made available to the public as required by subsection (3),
is evidence (or in Scotland sufficient evidence) of the facts stated in the certificate.
(6)   A certificate purporting to be signed as mentioned in subsection (5) is to be treated as having been properly signed unless the contrary is shown.
(7)   A person who wishes in any legal proceedings to rely on an instrument by which rules are made may require the Panel to endorse a copy of the instrument with a certificate of the kind mentioned in subsection (5).

NOTES
Commencement: 6 April 2007.

[1.945]
945 Rulings
(1) The Panel may give rulings on the interpretation, application or effect of rules.
(2) To the extent and in the circumstances specified in rules, and subject to any review or appeal, a ruling has binding effect.

NOTES
Commencement: 6 April 2007.

[1.946]
946 Directions
Rules may contain provision conferring power on the Panel to give any direction that appears to the Panel to be necessary in order—
    (a) to restrain a person from acting (or continuing to act) in breach of rules;
    (b) to restrain a person from doing (or continuing to do) a particular thing, pending determination of whether that or any other conduct of his is or would be a breach of rules;
    (c) otherwise to secure compliance with rules.

NOTES
Commencement: 6 April 2007.

Information

[1.947]
947 Power to require documents and information
(1) The Panel may by notice in writing require a person—
    (a) to produce any documents that are specified or described in the notice;
    (b) to provide, in the form and manner specified in the notice, such information as may be specified or described in the notice.
(2) A requirement under subsection (1) must be complied with—
    (a) at a place specified in the notice, and
    (b) before the end of such reasonable period as may be so specified.
(3) This section applies only to documents and information reasonably required in connection with the exercise by the Panel of its functions.
(4) The Panel may require—
    (a) any document produced to be authenticated, or
    (b) any information provided (whether in a document or otherwise) to be verified,
in such manner as it may reasonably require.
(5) The Panel may authorise a person to exercise any of its powers under this section.
(6) A person exercising a power by virtue of subsection (5) must, if required to do so, produce evidence of his authority to exercise the power.
(7) The production of a document in pursuance of this section does not affect any lien that a person has on the document.
(8) The Panel may take copies of or extracts from a document produced in pursuance of this section.
(9) A reference in this section to the production of a document includes a reference to the production of—
    (a) a hard copy of information recorded otherwise than in hard copy form, or
    (b) information in a form from which a hard copy can be readily obtained.
(10) A person is not required by this section to disclose documents or information in respect of which a claim to legal professional privilege (in Scotland, to confidentiality of communications) could be maintained in legal proceedings.

NOTES
Commencement: 6 April 2007.

[1.948]
948 Restrictions on disclosure
(1) This section applies to information (in whatever form)—
    (a) relating to the private affairs of an individual, or
    (b) relating to any particular business,
that is provided to the Panel in connection with the exercise of its functions.
(2) No such information may, during the lifetime of the individual or so long as the business continues to be carried on, be disclosed without the consent of that individual or (as the case may be) the person for the time being carrying on that business.
(3) Subsection (2) does not apply to any disclosure of information that—
    (a) is made for the purpose of facilitating the carrying out by the Panel of any of its functions,
    (b) is made to a person specified in Part 1 of Schedule 2,
    (c) is of a description specified in Part 2 of that Schedule, or
    (d) is made in accordance with Part 3 of that Schedule.

(4) The Secretary of State may amend Schedule 2 by order subject to negative resolution procedure.

(5) An order under subsection (4) must not—
  (a) amend Part 1 of Schedule 2 by specifying a person unless the person exercises functions of a public nature (whether or not he exercises any other function);
  (b) amend Part 2 of Schedule 2 by adding or modifying a description of disclosure unless the purpose for which the disclosure is permitted is likely to facilitate the exercise of a function of a public nature;
  (c) amend Part 3 of Schedule 2 so as to have the effect of permitting disclosures to be made to a body other than one that exercises functions of a public nature in a country or territory outside the United Kingdom.

(6) Subsection (2) does not apply to—
  (a) the disclosure by an authority within subsection (7) of information disclosed to it by the Panel in reliance on subsection (3);
  (b) the disclosure of such information by anyone who has obtained it directly or indirectly from an authority within subsection (7).

(7) The authorities within this subsection are—
  (a) the Financial Services Authority;
  (b) an authority designated as a supervisory authority for the purposes of Article 4.1 of the Takeovers Directive;
  (c) any other person or body that exercises functions of a public nature, under legislation in an EEA State other than the United Kingdom, that are similar to the Panel's functions or those of the Financial Services Authority.

(8) This section does not prohibit the disclosure of information if the information is or has been available to the public from any other source.

(9) Nothing in this section authorises the making of a disclosure in contravention of the Data Protection Act 1998 (c 29).

NOTES

Commencement: 20 January 2007 (for the purpose of enabling the exercise of powers to make Orders or Regulations by statutory instrument); 6 April 2007 (otherwise).

Orders: the Companies Act 2006 (Amendment of Schedule 2) (No 2) Order 2009, SI 2009/1208.

[1.949]
949 Offence of disclosure in contravention of section 948

(1) A person who discloses information in contravention of section 948 is guilty of an offence, unless—
  (a) he did not know, and had no reason to suspect, that the information had been provided as mentioned in section 948(1), or
  (b) he took all reasonable steps and exercised all due diligence to avoid the commission of the offence.

(2) A person guilty of an offence under this section is liable—
  (a) on conviction on indictment, to imprisonment for a term not exceeding two years or a fine (or both);
  (b) on summary conviction—
    (i) in England and Wales, to imprisonment for a term not exceeding twelve months or to a fine not exceeding the statutory maximum (or both);
    (ii) in Scotland or Northern Ireland, to imprisonment for a term not exceeding six months, or to a fine not exceeding the statutory maximum (or both).

(3) Where a company or other body corporate commits an offence under this section, an offence is also committed by every officer of the company or other body corporate who is in default.

NOTES

Commencement: 6 April 2007.

Offences under this section: see further s 1131 at **[1.1131]**.

Co-operation

[1.950]
950 Panel's duty of co-operation

(1) The Panel must take such steps as it considers appropriate to co-operate with—
  (a) the Financial Services Authority;
  (b) an authority designated as a supervisory authority for the purposes of Article 4.1 of the Takeovers Directive;
  (c) any other person or body that exercises functions of a public nature, under legislation in any country or territory outside the United Kingdom, that appear to the Panel to be similar to its own functions or those of the Financial Services Authority.

(2) Co-operation may include the sharing of information that the Panel is not prevented from disclosing.

NOTES
Commencement: 6 April 2007.

Hearings and appeals

[1.951]
951 Hearings and appeals
(1) Rules must provide for a decision of the Panel to be subject to review by a committee of the Panel (the "Hearings Committee") at the instance of such persons affected by the decision as are specified in the rules.
(2) Rules may also confer other functions on the Hearings Committee.
(3) Rules must provide for there to be a right of appeal against a decision of the Hearings Committee to an independent tribunal (the "Takeover Appeal Board") in such circumstances and subject to such conditions as are specified in the rules.
(4) Rules may contain—
  (a) provision as to matters of procedure in relation to proceedings before the Hearings Committee (including provision imposing time limits);
  (b) provision about evidence in such proceedings;
  (c) provision as to the powers of the Hearings Committee dealing with a matter referred to it;
  (d) provision about enforcement of decisions of the Hearings Committee and the Takeover Appeal Board.
(5) Rules must contain provision—
  (a) requiring the Panel, when acting in relation to any proceedings before the Hearings Committee or the Takeover Appeal Board, to do so by an officer or member of staff of the Panel (or a person acting as such);
  (b) preventing a person who is or has been a member of the committee mentioned in section 943(5) from being a member of the Hearings Committee or the Takeover Appeal Board;
  (c) preventing a person who is a member of the committee mentioned in section 943(5), of the Hearings Committee or of the Takeover Appeal Board from acting as mentioned in paragraph (a).

NOTES
Commencement: 6 April 2007.

Contravention of rules etc

[1.952]
952 Sanctions
(1) Rules may contain provision conferring power on the Panel to impose sanctions on a person who has—
  (a) acted in breach of rules, or
  (b) failed to comply with a direction given by virtue of section 946.
(2) Subsection (3) applies where rules made by virtue of subsection (1) confer power on the Panel to impose a sanction of a kind not provided for by the City Code on Takeovers and Mergers as it had effect immediately before the passing of this Act.
(3) The Panel must prepare a statement (a "policy statement") of its policy with respect to—
  (a) the imposition of the sanction in question, and
  (b) where the sanction is in the nature of a financial penalty, the amount of the penalty that may be imposed.
An element of the policy must be that, in making a decision about any such matter, the Panel has regard to the factors mentioned in subsection (4).
(4) The factors are—
  (a) the seriousness of the breach or failure in question in relation to the nature of the rule or direction contravened;
  (b) the extent to which the breach or failure was deliberate or reckless;
  (c) whether the person on whom the sanction is to be imposed is an individual.
(5) The Panel may at any time revise a policy statement.
(6) The Panel must prepare a draft of any proposed policy statement (or revised policy statement) and consult such persons about the draft as the Panel considers appropriate.
(7) The Panel must publish, in whatever way it considers appropriate, any policy statement (or revised policy statement) that it prepares.
(8) In exercising, or deciding whether to exercise, its power to impose a sanction within subsection (2) in the case of any particular breach or failure, the Panel must have regard to any relevant policy statement published and in force at the time when the breach or failure occurred.

NOTES
Commencement: 6 April 2007.

[1.953]
953 Failure to comply with rules about bid documentation

(1) This section applies where a takeover bid is made for a company that has securities carrying voting rights admitted to trading on a regulated market in the United Kingdom.

(2) Where an offer document published in respect of the bid does not comply with offer document rules, an offence is committed by—

(a) the person making the bid, and

(b) where the person making the bid is a body of persons, any director, officer or member of that body who caused the document to be published.

(3) A person commits an offence under subsection (2) only if—

(a) he knew that the offer document did not comply, or was reckless as to whether it complied, and

(b) he failed to take all reasonable steps to secure that it did comply.

(4) Where a response document published in respect of the bid does not comply with response document rules, an offence is committed by any director or other officer of the company referred to in subsection (1) who—

(a) knew that the response document did not comply, or was reckless as to whether it complied, and

(b) failed to take all reasonable steps to secure that it did comply.

(5) Where an offence is committed under subsection (2)(b) or (4) by a company or other body corporate ("the relevant body")—

(a) subsection (2)(b) has effect as if the reference to a director, officer or member of the person making the bid included a reference to a director, officer or member of the relevant body;

(b) subsection (4) has effect as if the reference to a director or other officer of the company referred to in subsection (1) included a reference to a director, officer or member of the relevant body.

(6) A person guilty of an offence under this section is liable—

(a) on conviction on indictment, to a fine;

(b) on summary conviction, to a fine not exceeding the statutory maximum.

(7) Nothing in this section affects any power of the Panel in relation to the enforcement of its rules.

(8) Section 1 (meaning of "company") does not apply for the purposes of this section.

(9) In this section—

"designated" means designated in rules;

"offer document" means a document required to be published by rules giving effect to Article 6.2 of the Takeovers Directive;

"offer document rules" means rules designated as rules that give effect to Article 6.3 of that Directive;

"response document" means a document required to be published by rules giving effect to Article 9.5 of that Directive;

"response document rules" means rules designated as rules that give effect to the first sentence of Article 9.5 of that Directive;

"securities" means shares or debentures;

"takeover bid" has the same meaning as in that Directive;

"voting rights" means rights to vote at general meetings of the company in question, including rights that arise only in certain circumstances.

NOTES
Commencement: 6 April 2007.

Commencement (transitional adaptations): art 3 of the Companies Act 2006 (Commencement No 2, Consequential Amendments, Transitional Provisions and Savings) Order 2007, SI 2007/1093 provides that the provisions brought into force by art 2 of 2007 Order shall have effect subject to any transitional adaptations specified in Sch 1 to that Order. Schedule 1, para 3 to the Order (at **[2.27]**) provided for such transitional adaptations (note that this paragraph was revoked by the Companies Act 2006 (Commencement No 8, Transitional Provisions and Savings) Order 2008, SI 2008/2860, art 6, as from 1 October 2009 (subject to any relevant transitional provision or saving in Sch 2 to that Order)).

[1.954]
954 Compensation

(1) Rules may confer power on the Panel to order a person to pay such compensation as it thinks just and reasonable if he is in breach of a rule the effect of which is to require the payment of money.

(2) Rules made by virtue of this section may include provision for the payment of interest (including compound interest).

NOTES
Commencement: 6 April 2007.

[1.955]
955 Enforcement by the court

(1) If, on the application of the Panel, the court is satisfied—

(a) that there is a reasonable likelihood that a person will contravene a rule-based requirement, or

(b) that a person has contravened a rule-based requirement or a disclosure requirement,

the court may make any order it thinks fit to secure compliance with the requirement.

(2) In subsection (1) "the court" means the High Court or, in Scotland, the Court of Session.

(3) Except as provided by subsection (1), no person—

(a) has a right to seek an injunction, or

(b) in Scotland, has title or interest to seek an interdict or an order for specific performance,

to prevent a person from contravening (or continuing to contravene) a rule-based requirement or a disclosure requirement.

(4) In this section—

"contravene" includes fail to comply;

"disclosure requirement" means a requirement imposed under section 947;

"rule-based requirement" means a requirement imposed by or under rules.

NOTES

Commencement: 6 April 2007.

[1.956]
956 No action for breach of statutory duty etc

(1) Contravention of a rule-based requirement or a disclosure requirement does not give rise to any right of action for breach of statutory duty.

(2) Contravention of a rule-based requirement does not make any transaction void or unenforceable or (subject to any provision made by rules) affect the validity of any other thing.

(3) In this section—

(a) "contravention" includes failure to comply;

(b) "disclosure requirement" and "rule-based requirement" have the same meaning as in section 955.

NOTES

Commencement: 6 April 2007.

Funding

[1.957]
957 Fees and charges

(1) Rules may provide for fees or charges to be payable to the Panel for the purpose of meeting any part of its expenses.

(2) A reference in this section or section 958 to expenses of the Panel is to any expenses that have been or are to be incurred by the Panel in, or in connection with, the discharge of its functions, including in particular—

(a) payments in respect of the expenses of the Takeover Appeal Board;

(b) the cost of repaying the principal of, and of paying any interest on, any money borrowed by the Panel;

(c) the cost of maintaining adequate reserves.

NOTES

Commencement: 6 April 2007.

[1.958]
958 Levy

(1) For the purpose of meeting any part of the expenses of the Panel, the Secretary of State may by regulations provide for a levy to be payable to the Panel—

(a) by specified persons or bodies, or persons or bodies of a specified description, or

(b) on transactions, of a specified description, in securities on specified markets.

In this subsection "specified" means specified in the regulations.

(2) The power to specify (or to specify descriptions of) persons or bodies must be exercised in such a way that the levy is payable only by persons or bodies that appear to the Secretary of State—

(a) to be capable of being directly affected by the exercise of any of the functions of the Panel, or

(b) otherwise to have a substantial interest in the exercise of any of those functions.

(3) Regulations under this section may in particular—

(a) specify the rate of the levy and the period in respect of which it is payable at that rate;

(b) make provision as to the times when, and the manner in which, payments are to be made in respect of the levy.

(4) In determining the rate of the levy payable in respect of a particular period, the Secretary of State—

(a) must take into account any other income received or expected by the Panel in respect of that period;

(b) may take into account estimated as well as actual expenses of the Panel in respect of that period.

(5) The Panel must—

(a) keep proper accounts in respect of any amounts of levy received by virtue of this section;

(b) prepare, in relation to each period in respect of which any such amounts are received, a statement of account relating to those amounts in such form and manner as is specified in the regulations.

Those accounts must be audited, and the statement certified, by persons appointed by the Secretary of State.

(6) Regulations under this section—

(a) are subject to affirmative resolution procedure if subsection (7) applies to them;

(b) otherwise, are subject to negative resolution procedure.

(7) This subsection applies to—

(a) the first regulations under this section;

(b) any other regulations under this section that would result in a change in the persons or bodies by whom, or the transactions on which, the levy is payable.

(8) If a draft of an instrument containing regulations under this section would, apart from this subsection, be treated for the purposes of the Standing Orders of either House of Parliament as a hybrid instrument, it is to proceed in that House as if it were not such an instrument.

NOTES

Commencement: 20 January 2007 (for the purpose of enabling the exercise of powers to make Orders or Regulations by statutory instrument); 6 April 2007 (otherwise).

[1.959]
959 Recovery of fees, charges or levy
An amount payable by any person or body by virtue of section 957 or 958 is a debt due from that person or body to the Panel, and is recoverable accordingly.

NOTES

Commencement: 6 April 2007.

Miscellaneous and supplementary

[1.960]
960 Panel as party to proceedings
The Panel is capable (despite being an unincorporated body) of—

(a) bringing proceedings under this Chapter in its own name;

(b) bringing or defending any other proceedings in its own name.

NOTES

Commencement: 6 April 2007.

[1.961]
961 Exemption from liability in damages
(1) Neither the Panel, nor any person within subsection (2), is to be liable in damages for anything done (or omitted to be done) in, or in connection with, the discharge or purported discharge of the Panel's functions.

(2) A person is within this subsection if—

(a) he is (or is acting as) a member, officer or member of staff of the Panel, or

(b) he is a person authorised under section 947(5).

(3) Subsection (1) does not apply—

(a) if the act or omission is shown to have been in bad faith, or

(b) so as to prevent an award of damages in respect of the act or omission on the ground that it was unlawful as a result of section 6(1) of the Human Rights Act 1998 (c 42) (acts of public authorities incompatible with Convention rights).

NOTES

Commencement: 6 April 2007.

[1.962]
962 Privilege against self-incrimination
(1) A statement made by a person in response to—

(a) a requirement under section 947(1), or

(b) an order made by the court under section 955 to secure compliance with such a requirement,

may not be used against him in criminal proceedings in which he is charged with an offence to which this subsection applies.

(2) Subsection (1) applies to any offence other than an offence under one of the following provisions (which concern false statements made otherwise than on oath)—

(a) section 5 of the Perjury Act 1911 (c 6);

(b)   section 44(2) of the Criminal Law (Consolidation) (Scotland) Act 1995 (c 39);
(c)   Article 10 of the Perjury (Northern Ireland) Order 1979 (SI 1979/1714 (NI 19)).

NOTES
Commencement: 6 April 2007.

[1.963]
963   Annual reports
(1)   After the end of each financial year the Panel must publish a report.
(2)   The report must—
   (a)   set out how the Panel's functions were discharged in the year in question;
   (b)   include the Panel's accounts for that year;
   (c)   mention any matters the Panel considers to be of relevance to the discharge of its functions.

NOTES
Commencement: 6 April 2007.

[1.964]
964   Amendments to Financial Services and Markets Act 2000
(Amends FSMA 2000, ss 144, 349, 354, 417, and repeals s 143 (power to make rules endorsing the
City Code on Takeovers and Mergers etc). The 2000 Act is at **[7.1]** *et seq.)*

NOTES
Commencement: 6 April 2007.

[1.965]
965   Power to extend to Isle of Man and Channel Islands
Her Majesty may by Order in Council direct that any of the provisions of this Chapter extend, with
such modifications as may be specified in the Order, to the Isle of Man or any of the Channel
Islands.

NOTES
Commencement: 20 January 2007 (for the purpose of enabling the exercise of powers to make Orders or Regulations by
statutory instrument); 6 April 2007 (otherwise).
Orders: the Companies Act 2006 (Extension of Takeover Panel Provisions) (Isle of Man) Order 2008, SI 2008/3122 at
[4.337]; the Companies Act 2006 (Extension of Takeover Panel Provisions) (Isle of Man) Order 2009, SI 2009/1378 at
[4.387].

CHAPTER 2
IMPEDIMENTS TO TAKEOVERS

Opting in and opting out

[1.966]
966   Opting in and opting out
(1)   A company may by special resolution (an "opting-in resolution") opt in for the purposes of
this Chapter if the following three conditions are met in relation to the company.
(2)   The first condition is that the company has voting shares admitted to trading on a regulated
market.
(3)   The second condition is that—
   (a)   the company's articles of association—
      (i)   do not contain any such restrictions as are mentioned in Article 11 of the Takeovers
         Directive, or
      (ii)   if they do contain any such restrictions, provide for the restrictions not to apply at a
         time when, or in circumstances in which, they would be disapplied by that Article,
     and
   (b)   those articles do not contain any other provision which would be incompatible with that
     Article.
(4)   The third condition is that—
   (a)   no shares conferring special rights in the company are held by—
      (i)   a minister,
      (ii)   a nominee of, or any other person acting on behalf of, a minister, or
      (iii)   a company directly or indirectly controlled by a minister,
     and
   (b)   no such rights are exercisable by or on behalf of a minister under any enactment.
(5)   A company may revoke an opting-in resolution by a further special resolution (an "opting-out
resolution").
(6)   For the purposes of subsection (3), a reference in Article 11 of the Takeovers Directive to
Article 7.1 or 9 of that Directive is to be read as referring to rules under section 943(1) giving effect
to the relevant Article.
(7)   In subsection (4) "minister" means—

(a) the holder of an office in Her Majesty's Government in the United Kingdom;
(b) the Scottish Ministers;
(c) a Minister within the meaning given by section 7(3) of the Northern Ireland Act 1998 (c 47);
[(d) the Welsh Ministers;]

and for the purposes of that subsection "minister" also includes the Treasury, the Board of Trade [and] the Defence Council . . .

(8) The Secretary of State may by order subject to negative resolution procedure provide that subsection (4) applies in relation to a specified person or body that exercises functions of a public nature as it applies in relation to a minister. "Specified" means specified in the order.

NOTES

Commencement: 20 January 2007 (for the purpose of enabling the exercise of powers to make Orders or Regulations by statutory instrument); 6 April 2007 (otherwise).

Sub-s (7): para (d) inserted, word in second pair of square brackets inserted, and words omitted repealed, by the Government of Wales Act 2006 (Consequential Modifications and Transitional Provisions) Order 2007, SI 2007/1388, art 3, Sch 1, para 142, as from 25 May 2007.

[1.967]
967 Further provision about opting-in and opting-out resolutions
(1) An opting-in resolution or an opting-out resolution must specify the date from which it is to have effect (the "effective date").
(2) The effective date of an opting-in resolution may not be earlier than the date on which the resolution is passed.
(3) The second and third conditions in section 966 must be met at the time when an opting-in resolution is passed, but the first one does not need to be met until the effective date.
(4) An opting-in resolution passed before the time when voting shares of the company are admitted to trading on a regulated market complies with the requirement in subsection (1) if, instead of specifying a particular date, it provides for the resolution to have effect from that time.
(5) An opting-in resolution passed before the commencement of this section complies with the requirement in subsection (1) if, instead of specifying a particular date, it provides for the resolution to have effect from that commencement.
(6) The effective date of an opting-out resolution may not be earlier than the first anniversary of the date on which a copy of the opting-in resolution was forwarded to the registrar.
(7) Where a company has passed an opting-in resolution, any alteration of its articles of association that would prevent the second condition in section 966 from being met is of no effect until the effective date of an opting-out resolution passed by the company.

NOTES

Commencement: 6 April 2007.

Consequences of opting in

[1.968]
968 Effect on contractual restrictions
(1) The following provisions have effect where a takeover bid is made for an opted-in company.
(2) An agreement to which this section applies is invalid in so far as it places any restriction—
    (a) on the transfer to the offeror, or at his direction to another person, of shares in the company during the offer period;
    (b) on the transfer to any person of shares in the company at a time during the offer period when the offeror holds shares amounting to not less than 75% in value of all the voting shares in the company;
    (c) on rights to vote at a general meeting of the company that decides whether to take any action which might result in the frustration of the bid;
    (d) on rights to vote at a general meeting of the company that—
        (i) is the first such meeting to be held after the end of the offer period, and
        (ii) is held at a time when the offeror holds shares amounting to not less than 75% in value of all the voting shares in the company.
(3) This section applies to an agreement—
    (a) entered into between a person holding shares in the company and another such person on or after 21st April 2004, or
    (b) entered into at any time between such a person and the company,
and it applies to such an agreement even if the law applicable to the agreement (apart from this section) is not the law of a part of the United Kingdom.
(4) The reference in subsection (2)(c) to rights to vote at a general meeting of the company that decides whether to take any action which might result in the frustration of the bid includes a reference to rights to vote on a written resolution concerned with that question.
(5) For the purposes of subsection (2)(c), action which might result in the frustration of a bid is any action of that kind specified in rules under section 943(1) giving effect to Article 9 of the Takeovers Directive.

(6)   If a person suffers loss as a result of any act or omission that would (but for this section) be a breach of an agreement to which this section applies, he is entitled to compensation, of such amount as the court considers just and equitable, from any person who would (but for this section) be liable to him for committing or inducing the breach.

(7)   In subsection (6) "the court" means the High Court or, in Scotland, the Court of Session.

(8)   A reference in this section to voting shares in the company does not include—
   (a)   debentures, or
   (b)   shares that, under the company's articles of association, do not normally carry rights to vote at its general meetings (for example, shares carrying rights to vote that, under those articles, arise only where specified pecuniary advantages are not provided).

NOTES

Commencement: 6 April 2007.

Commencement (transitional adaptations): the transitional adaptations of this section contained in the Companies Act 2006 (Commencement No 2, Consequential Amendments, Transitional Provisions and Savings) Order 2007, SI 2007/1093, Sch 1, para 4 were revoked by the Companies Act 2006 (Commencement No 3, Consequential Amendments, Transitional Provisions and Savings) Order 2007, SI 2007/2194, art 11(b), as from 1 October 2007. See **[2.27]**.

[1.969]
969   Power of offeror to require general meeting to be called

(1)   Where a takeover bid is made for an opted-in company, the offeror may by making a request to the directors of the company require them to call a general meeting of the company if, at the date at which the request is made, he holds shares amounting to not less than 75% in value of all the voting shares in the company.

(2)   The reference in subsection (1) to voting shares in the company does not include—
   (a)   debentures, or
   (b)   shares that, under the company's articles of association, do not normally carry rights to vote at its general meetings (for example, shares carrying rights to vote that, under those articles, arise only where specified pecuniary advantages are not provided).

(3)   Sections 303 to 305 (members' power to require general meetings to be called) apply as they would do if subsection (1) above were substituted for subsections (1) to (3) of section 303, and with any other necessary modifications.

NOTES

Commencement: 6 April 2007.

Supplementary

[1.970]
970   Communication of decisions

(1)   A company that has passed an opting-in resolution or an opting-out resolution must notify—
   (a)   the Panel, and
   (b)   where the company—
      (i)   has voting shares admitted to trading on a regulated market in an EEA State other than the United Kingdom, or
      (ii)   has requested such admission,
      the authority designated by that state as the supervisory authority for the purposes of Article 4.1 of the Takeovers Directive.

(2)   Notification must be given within 15 days after the resolution is passed and, if any admission or request such as is mentioned in subsection (1)(b) occurs at a later time, within 15 days after that time.

(3)   If a company fails to comply with this section, an offence is committed by—
   (a)   the company, and
   (b)   every officer of it who is in default.

(4)   A person guilty of an offence under this section is liable on summary conviction to a fine not exceeding level 3 on the standard scale and, for continued contravention, a daily default fine not exceeding one-tenth of level 3 on the standard scale.

NOTES

Commencement: 6 April 2007.

[1.971]
971   Interpretation of this Chapter

(1)   In this Chapter—
   "offeror" and "takeover bid" have the same meaning as in the Takeovers Directive;
   "offer period", in relation to a takeover bid, means the time allowed for acceptance of the bid by—
      (a)   rules under section 943(1) giving effect to Article 7.1 of the Takeovers Directive, or
      (b)   where the rules giving effect to that Article which apply to the bid are those of an EEA State other than the United Kingdom, those rules;
   "opted-in company" means a company in relation to which—

(a)　an opting-in resolution has effect, and

(b)　the conditions in section 966(2) and (4) continue to be met;

"opting-in resolution" has the meaning given by section 966(1);

"opting-out resolution" has the meaning given by section 966(5);

"the Takeovers Directive" means Directive 2004/25/EC of the European Parliament and of the Council;

"voting rights" means rights to vote at general meetings of the company in question, including rights that arise only in certain circumstances;

"voting shares" means shares carrying voting rights.

(2)　For the purposes of this Chapter—

(a)　securities of a company are treated as shares in the company if they are convertible into or entitle the holder to subscribe for such shares;

(b)　debentures issued by a company are treated as shares in the company if they carry voting rights.

NOTES

Commencement: 6 April 2007.

[1.972]
972　Transitory provision

(1)　Where a takeover bid is made for an opted-in company, section 368 of the Companies Act 1985 (c 6) (extraordinary general meeting on members' requisition) and section 378 of that Act (extraordinary and special resolutions) have effect as follows until their repeal by this Act.

(2)　Section 368 has effect as if a members' requisition included a requisition of a person who—

(a)　is the offeror in relation to the takeover bid, and

(b)　holds at the date of the deposit of the requisition shares amounting to not less than 75% in value of all the voting shares in the company.

(3)　In relation to a general meeting of the company that—

(a)　is the first such meeting to be held after the end of the offer period, and

(b)　is held at a time when the offeror holds shares amounting to not less than 75% in value of all the voting shares in the company,

section 378(2) (meaning of "special resolution") has effect as if "14 days' notice" were substituted for "21 days' notice".

(4)　A reference in this section to voting shares in the company does not include—

(a)　debentures, or

(b)　shares that, under the company's articles of association, do not normally carry rights to vote at its general meetings (for example, shares carrying rights to vote that, under those articles, arise only where specified pecuniary advantages are not provided).

NOTES

Commencement: 6 April 2007.

[1.973]
973　Power to extend to Isle of Man and Channel Islands

Her Majesty may by Order in Council direct that any of the provisions of this Chapter extend, with such modifications as may be specified in the Order, to the Isle of Man or any of the Channel Islands.

NOTES

Commencement: 20 January 2007 (for the purpose of enabling the exercise of powers to make Orders or Regulations by statutory instrument); 6 April 2007 (otherwise).

CHAPTER 3
"SQUEEZE-OUT" AND "SELL-OUT"

Takeover offers

[1.974]
974　Meaning of "takeover offer"

(1)　For the purposes of this Chapter an offer to acquire shares in a company is a "takeover offer" if the following two conditions are satisfied in relation to the offer.

(2)　The first condition is that it is an offer to acquire—

(a)　all the shares in a company, or

(b)　where there is more than one class of shares in a company, all the shares of one or more classes,

other than shares that at the date of the offer are already held by the offeror. Section 975 contains provision supplementing this subsection.

(3)　The second condition is that the terms of the offer are the same—

(a)　in relation to all the shares to which the offer relates, or

(b)   where the shares to which the offer relates include shares of different classes, in relation to all the shares of each class.

Section 976 contains provision treating this condition as satisfied in certain circumstances.

(4)   In subsections (1) to (3) "shares" means shares, other than relevant treasury shares, that have been allotted on the date of the offer (but see subsection (5)).

(5)   A takeover offer may include among the shares to which it relates—

(a)   all or any shares that are allotted after the date of the offer but before a specified date;

(b)   all or any relevant treasury shares that cease to be held as treasury shares before a specified date;

(c)   all or any other relevant treasury shares.

(6)   In this section—

"relevant treasury shares" means shares that—

(a)   are held by the company as treasury shares on the date of the offer, or

(b)   become shares held by the company as treasury shares after that date but before a specified date;

"specified date" means a date specified in or determined in accordance with the terms of the offer.

(7)   Where the terms of an offer make provision for their revision and for acceptances on the previous terms to be treated as acceptances on the revised terms, then, if the terms of the offer are revised in accordance with that provision—

(a)   the revision is not to be regarded for the purposes of this Chapter as the making of a fresh offer, and

(b)   references in this Chapter to the date of the offer are accordingly to be read as references to the date of the original offer.

NOTES

Commencement: 6 April 2007.

[1.975]
975   Shares already held by the offeror etc

(1)   The reference in section 974(2) to shares already held by the offeror includes a reference to shares that he has contracted to acquire, whether unconditionally or subject to conditions being met.

This is subject to subsection (2).

(2)   The reference in section 974(2) to shares already held by the offeror does not include a reference to shares that are the subject of a contract—

(a)   intended to secure that the holder of the shares will accept the offer when it is made, and

(b)   entered into—

(i)   by deed and for no consideration,

(ii)   for consideration of negligible value, or

(iii) for consideration consisting of a promise by the offeror to make the offer.

(3)   In relation to Scotland, this section applies as if the words "by deed and" in subsection (2)(b)(i) were omitted.

(4)   The condition in section 974(2) is treated as satisfied where—

(a)   the offer does not extend to shares that associates of the offeror hold or have contracted to acquire (whether unconditionally or subject to conditions being met), and

(b)   the condition would be satisfied if the offer did extend to those shares.

(For further provision about such shares, see section 977(2)).

NOTES

Commencement: 6 April 2007.

[1.976]
976   Cases where offer treated as being on same terms

(1)   The condition in section 974(3) (terms of offer to be the same for all shares or all shares of particular classes) is treated as satisfied where subsection (2) or (3) below applies.

(2)   This subsection applies where—

(a)   shares carry an entitlement to a particular dividend which other shares of the same class, by reason of being allotted later, do not carry,

(b)   there is a difference in the value of consideration offered for the shares allotted earlier as against that offered for those allotted later,

(c)   that difference merely reflects the difference in entitlement to the dividend, and

(d)   the condition in section 974(3) would be satisfied but for that difference.

(3)   This subsection applies where—

(a)   the law of a country or territory outside the United Kingdom—

(i)   precludes an offer of consideration in the form, or any of the forms, specified in the terms of the offer ("the specified form"), or

(ii)   precludes it except after compliance by the offeror with conditions with which he is unable to comply or which he regards as unduly onerous,

  (b)   the persons to whom an offer of consideration in the specified form is precluded are able to receive consideration in another form that is of substantially equivalent value, and

  (c)   the condition in section 974(3) would be satisfied but for the fact that an offer of consideration in the specified form to those persons is precluded.

NOTES

Commencement: 6 April 2007.

[1.977]
977   Shares to which an offer relates

(1)   Where a takeover offer is made and, during the period beginning with the date of the offer and ending when the offer can no longer be accepted, the offeror—

  (a)   acquires or unconditionally contracts to acquire any of the shares to which the offer relates, but

  (b)   does not do so by virtue of acceptances of the offer,

those shares are treated for the purposes of this Chapter as excluded from those to which the offer relates.

(2)   For the purposes of this Chapter shares that an associate of the offeror holds or has contracted to acquire, whether at the date of the offer or subsequently, are not treated as shares to which the offer relates, even if the offer extends to such shares.

In this subsection "contracted" means contracted unconditionally or subject to conditions being met.

(3)   This section is subject to section 979(8) and (9).

NOTES

Commencement: 6 April 2007.

[1.978]
978   Effect of impossibility etc of communicating or accepting offer

(1)   Where there are holders of shares in a company to whom an offer to acquire shares in the company is not communicated, that does not prevent the offer from being a takeover offer for the purposes of this Chapter if—

  (a)   those shareholders have no registered address in the United Kingdom,

  (b)   the offer was not communicated to those shareholders in order not to contravene the law of a country or territory outside the United Kingdom, and

  (c)   either—

      (i)   the offer is published in the Gazette, or

      (ii)   the offer can be inspected, or a copy of it obtained, at a place in an EEA State or on a website, and a notice is published in the Gazette specifying the address of that place or website.

(2)   Where an offer is made to acquire shares in a company and there are persons for whom, by reason of the law of a country or territory outside the United Kingdom, it is impossible to accept the offer, or more difficult to do so, that does not prevent the offer from being a takeover offer for the purposes of this Chapter.

(3)   It is not to be inferred—

  (a)   that an offer which is not communicated to every holder of shares in the company cannot be a takeover offer for the purposes of this Chapter unless the requirements of paragraphs (a) to (c) of subsection (1) are met, or

  (b)   that an offer which is impossible, or more difficult, for certain persons to accept cannot be a takeover offer for those purposes unless the reason for the impossibility or difficulty is the one mentioned in subsection (2).

NOTES

Commencement: 6 April 2007.

"Squeeze-out"

[1.979]
979   Right of offeror to buy out minority shareholder

(1)   Subsection (2) applies in a case where a takeover offer does not relate to shares of different classes.

(2)   If the offeror has, by virtue of acceptances of the offer, acquired or unconditionally contracted to acquire—

  (a)   not less than 90% in value of the shares to which the offer relates, and

  (b)   in a case where the shares to which the offer relates are voting shares, not less than 90% of the voting rights carried by those shares,

he may give notice to the holder of any shares to which the offer relates which the offeror has not acquired or unconditionally contracted to acquire that he desires to acquire those shares.

(3)   Subsection (4) applies in a case where a takeover offer relates to shares of different classes.

(4) If the offeror has, by virtue of acceptances of the offer, acquired or unconditionally contracted to acquire—

(a) not less than 90% in value of the shares of any class to which the offer relates, and

(b) in a case where the shares of that class are voting shares, not less than 90% of the voting rights carried by those shares,

he may give notice to the holder of any shares of that class to which the offer relates which the offeror has not acquired or unconditionally contracted to acquire that he desires to acquire those shares.

(5) In the case of a takeover offer which includes among the shares to which it relates—

(a) shares that are allotted after the date of the offer, or

(b) relevant treasury shares (within the meaning of section 974) that cease to be held as treasury shares after the date of the offer,

the offeror's entitlement to give a notice under subsection (2) or (4) on any particular date shall be determined as if the shares to which the offer relates did not include any allotted, or ceasing to be held as treasury shares, on or after that date.

(6) Subsection (7) applies where—

(a) the requirements for the giving of a notice under subsection (2) or (4) are satisfied, and

(b) there are shares in the company which the offeror, or an associate of his, has contracted to acquire subject to conditions being met, and in relation to which the contract has not become unconditional.

(7) The offeror's entitlement to give a notice under subsection (2) or (4) shall be determined as if—

(a) the shares to which the offer relates included shares falling within paragraph (b) of subsection (6), and

(b) in relation to shares falling within that paragraph, the words "by virtue of acceptances of the offer" in subsection (2) or (4) were omitted.

(8) Where—

(a) a takeover offer is made,

(b) during the period beginning with the date of the offer and ending when the offer can no longer be accepted, the offeror—

    (i) acquires or unconditionally contracts to acquire any of the shares to which the offer relates, but

    (ii) does not do so by virtue of acceptances of the offer, and

(c) subsection (10) applies,

then for the purposes of this section those shares are not excluded by section 977(1) from those to which the offer relates, and the offeror is treated as having acquired or contracted to acquire them by virtue of acceptances of the offer.

(9) Where—

(a) a takeover offer is made,

(b) during the period beginning with the date of the offer and ending when the offer can no longer be accepted, an associate of the offeror acquires or unconditionally contracts to acquire any of the shares to which the offer relates, and

(c) subsection (10) applies,

then for the purposes of this section those shares are not excluded by section 977(2) from those to which the offer relates.

(10) This subsection applies if—

(a) at the time the shares are acquired or contracted to be acquired as mentioned in subsection (8) or (9) (as the case may be), the value of the consideration for which they are acquired or contracted to be acquired ("the acquisition consideration") does not exceed the value of the consideration specified in the terms of the offer, or

(b) those terms are subsequently revised so that when the revision is announced the value of the acquisition consideration, at the time mentioned in paragraph (a), no longer exceeds the value of the consideration specified in those terms.

NOTES

Commencement: 6 April 2007.

[1.980]

980 Further provision about notices given under section 979

(1) A notice under section 979 must be given in the prescribed manner.

(2) No notice may be given under section 979(2) or (4) after the end of—

(a) the period of three months beginning with the day after the last day on which the offer can be accepted, or

(b) the period of six months beginning with the date of the offer, where that period ends earlier and the offer is one to which subsection (3) below applies.

(3) This subsection applies to an offer if the time allowed for acceptance of the offer is not governed by rules under section 943(1) that give effect to Article 7 of the Takeovers Directive.

In this subsection "the Takeovers Directive" has the same meaning as in section 943.

(4)   At the time when the offeror first gives a notice under section 979 in relation to an offer, he must send to the company—
  (a)   a copy of the notice, and
  (b)   a statutory declaration by him in the prescribed form, stating that the conditions for the giving of the notice are satisfied.
(5)   Where the offeror is a company (whether or not a company within the meaning of this Act) the statutory declaration must be signed by a director.
(6)   A person commits an offence if—
  (a)   he fails to send a copy of a notice or a statutory declaration as required by subsection (4), or
  (b)   he makes such a declaration for the purposes of that subsection knowing it to be false or without having reasonable grounds for believing it to be true.
(7)   It is a defence for a person charged with an offence for failing to send a copy of a notice as required by subsection (4) to prove that he took reasonable steps for securing compliance with that subsection.
(8)   A person guilty of an offence under this section is liable—
  (a)   on conviction on indictment, to imprisonment for a term not exceeding two years or a fine (or both);
  (b)   on summary conviction—
    (i)   in England and Wales, to imprisonment for a term not exceeding twelve months or to a fine not exceeding the statutory maximum (or both) and, for continued contravention, a daily default fine not exceeding one-fiftieth of the statutory maximum;
    (ii)   in Scotland or Northern Ireland, to imprisonment for a term not exceeding six months, or to a fine not exceeding the statutory maximum (or both) and, for continued contravention, a daily default fine not exceeding one-fiftieth of the statutory maximum.

NOTES

Commencement: 20 January 2007 (for the purpose of enabling the exercise of powers to make Orders or Regulations by statutory instrument); 6 April 2007 (otherwise).

Offences under this section: see further s 1131 at **[1.1131]**.

[1.981]
981   Effect of notice under section 979
(1)   Subject to section 986 (applications to the court), this section applies where the offeror gives a shareholder a notice under section 979.
(2)   The offeror is entitled and bound to acquire the shares to which the notice relates on the terms of the offer.
(3)   Where the terms of an offer are such as to give the shareholder a choice of consideration, the notice must give particulars of the choice and state—
  (a)   that the shareholder may, within six weeks from the date of the notice, indicate his choice by a written communication sent to the offeror at an address specified in the notice, and
  (b)   which consideration specified in the offer will apply if he does not indicate a choice.
  The reference in subsection (2) to the terms of the offer is to be read accordingly.
(4)   Subsection (3) applies whether or not any time-limit or other conditions applicable to the choice under the terms of the offer can still be complied with.
(5)   If the consideration offered to or (as the case may be) chosen by the shareholder—
  (a)   is not cash and the offeror is no longer able to provide it, or
  (b)   was to have been provided by a third party who is no longer bound or able to provide it,
the consideration is to be taken to consist of an amount of cash, payable by the offeror, which at the date of the notice is equivalent to the consideration offered or (as the case may be) chosen.
(6)   At the end of six weeks from the date of the notice the offeror must immediately—
  (a)   send a copy of the notice to the company, and
  (b)   pay or transfer to the company the consideration for the shares to which the notice relates.
  Where the consideration consists of shares or securities to be allotted by the offeror, the reference in paragraph (b) to the transfer of the consideration is to be read as a reference to the allotment of the shares or securities to the company.
(7)   If the shares to which the notice relates are registered, the copy of the notice sent to the company under subsection (6)(a) must be accompanied by an instrument of transfer executed on behalf of the holder of the shares by a person appointed by the offeror.
  On receipt of that instrument the company must register the offeror as the holder of those shares.
(8)   If the shares to which the notice relates are transferable by the delivery of warrants or other instruments, the copy of the notice sent to the company under subsection (6)(a) must be accompanied by a statement to that effect. On receipt of that statement the company must issue the offeror with warrants or other instruments in respect of the shares, and those already in issue in respect of the shares become void.

(9)   The company must hold any money or other consideration received by it under subsection (6)(b) on trust for the person who, before the offeror acquired them, was entitled to the shares in respect of which the money or other consideration was received.

Section 982 contains further provision about how the company should deal with such money or other consideration.

NOTES

Commencement: 6 April 2007.

[1.982]
982   Further provision about consideration held on trust under section 981(9)
(1)   This section applies where an offeror pays or transfers consideration to the company under section 981(6).
(2)   The company must pay into a separate bank account that complies with subsection (3)—
  (a)   any money it receives under paragraph (b) of section 981(6), and
  (b)   any dividend or other sum accruing from any other consideration it receives under that paragraph.
(3)   A bank account complies with this subsection if the balance on the account—
  (a)   bears interest at an appropriate rate, and
  (b)   can be withdrawn by such notice (if any) as is appropriate.
(4)   If—
  (a)   the person entitled to the consideration held on trust by virtue of section 981(9) cannot be found, and
  (b)   subsection (5) applies,
the consideration (together with any interest, dividend or other benefit that has accrued from it) must be paid into court.
(5)   This subsection applies where—
  (a)   reasonable enquiries have been made at reasonable intervals to find the person, and
  (b)   twelve years have elapsed since the consideration was received, or the company is wound up.
(6)   In relation to a company registered in Scotland, subsections (7) and (8) apply instead of subsection (4).
(7)   If the person entitled to the consideration held on trust by virtue of section 981(9) cannot be found and subsection (5) applies—
  (a)   the trust terminates,
  (b)   the company or (if the company is wound up) the liquidator must sell any consideration other than cash and any benefit other than cash that has accrued from the consideration, and
  (c)   a sum representing—
    (i)   the consideration so far as it is cash,
    (ii)   the proceeds of any sale under paragraph (b), and
    (iii) any interest, dividend or other benefit that has accrued from the consideration,
    must be deposited in the name of the Accountant of Court in a separate bank account complying with subsection (3) and the receipt for the deposit must be transmitted to the Accountant of Court.
(8)   Section 58 of the Bankruptcy (Scotland) Act 1985 (c 66) (so far as consistent with this Act) applies (with any necessary modifications) to sums deposited under subsection (7) as it applies to sums deposited under section 57(1)(a) of that Act.
(9)   The expenses of any such enquiries as are mentioned in subsection (5) may be paid out of the money or other property held on trust for the person to whom the enquiry relates.

NOTES

Commencement: 6 April 2007.

"Sell-out"

[1.983]
983   Right of minority shareholder to be bought out by offeror
(1)   Subsections (2) and (3) apply in a case where a takeover offer relates to all the shares in a company.
  For this purpose a takeover offer relates to all the shares in a company if it is an offer to acquire all the shares in the company within the meaning of section 974.
(2)   The holder of any voting shares to which the offer relates who has not accepted the offer may require the offeror to acquire those shares if, at any time before the end of the period within which the offer can be accepted—
  (a)   the offeror has by virtue of acceptances of the offer acquired or unconditionally contracted to acquire some (but not all) of the shares to which the offer relates, and
  (b)   those shares, with or without any other shares in the company which he has acquired or contracted to acquire (whether unconditionally or subject to conditions being met)—

    (i)   amount to not less than 90% in value of all the voting shares in the company (or would do so but for section 990(1)), and

    (ii)   carry not less than 90% of the voting rights in the company (or would do so but for section 990(1)).

(3)   The holder of any non-voting shares to which the offer relates who has not accepted the offer may require the offeror to acquire those shares if, at any time before the end of the period within which the offer can be accepted—

    (a)   the offeror has by virtue of acceptances of the offer acquired or unconditionally contracted to acquire some (but not all) of the shares to which the offer relates, and

    (b)   those shares, with or without any other shares in the company which he has acquired or contracted to acquire (whether unconditionally or subject to conditions being met), amount to not less than 90% in value of all the shares in the company (or would do so but for section 990(1)).

(4)   If a takeover offer relates to shares of one or more classes and at any time before the end of the period within which the offer can be accepted—

    (a)   the offeror has by virtue of acceptances of the offer acquired or unconditionally contracted to acquire some (but not all) of the shares of any class to which the offer relates, and

    (b)   those shares, with or without any other shares of that class which he has acquired or contracted to acquire (whether unconditionally or subject to conditions being met)—

        (i)   amount to not less than 90% in value of all the shares of that class, and

        (ii)   in a case where the shares of that class are voting shares, carry not less than 90% of the voting rights carried by the shares of that class,

the holder of any shares of that class to which the offer relates who has not accepted the offer may require the offeror to acquire those shares.

(5)   For the purposes of subsections (2) to (4), in calculating 90% of the value of any shares, shares held by the company as treasury shares are to be treated as having been acquired by the offeror.

(6)   Subsection (7) applies where—

    (a)   a shareholder exercises rights conferred on him by subsection (2), (3) or (4),

    (b)   at the time when he does so, there are shares in the company which the offeror has contracted to acquire subject to conditions being met, and in relation to which the contract has not become unconditional, and

    (c)   the requirement imposed by subsection (2)(b), (3)(b) or (4)(b) (as the case may be) would not be satisfied if those shares were not taken into account.

(7)   The shareholder is treated for the purposes of section 985 as not having exercised his rights under this section unless the requirement imposed by paragraph (b) of subsection (2), (3) or (4) (as the case may be) would be satisfied if—

    (a)   the reference in that paragraph to other shares in the company which the offeror has contracted to acquire unconditionally or subject to conditions being met were a reference to such shares which he has unconditionally contracted to acquire, and

    (b)   the reference in that subsection to the period within which the offer can be accepted were a reference to the period referred to in section 984(2).

(8)   A reference in subsection (2)(b), (3)(b), (4)(b), (6) or (7) to shares which the offeror has acquired or contracted to acquire includes a reference to shares which an associate of his has acquired or contracted to acquire.

NOTES

    Commencement: 6 April 2007.

[1.984]
984   Further provision about rights conferred by section 983

(1)   Rights conferred on a shareholder by subsection (2), (3) or (4) of section 983 are exercisable by a written communication addressed to the offeror.

(2)   Rights conferred on a shareholder by subsection (2), (3) or (4) of that section are not exercisable after the end of the period of three months from—

    (a)   the end of the period within which the offer can be accepted, or

    (b)   if later, the date of the notice that must be given under subsection (3) below.

(3)   Within one month of the time specified in subsection (2), (3) or (4) (as the case may be) of that section, the offeror must give any shareholder who has not accepted the offer notice in the prescribed manner of—

    (a)   the rights that are exercisable by the shareholder under that subsection, and

    (b)   the period within which the rights are exercisable.

    If the notice is given before the end of the period within which the offer can be accepted, it must state that the offer is still open for acceptance.

(4)   Subsection (3) does not apply if the offeror has given the shareholder a notice in respect of the shares in question under section 979.

(5)   An offeror who fails to comply with subsection (3) commits an offence.

    If the offeror is a company, every officer of that company who is in default or to whose neglect the failure is attributable also commits an offence.

(6)　If an offeror other than a company is charged with an offence for failing to comply with subsection (3), it is a defence for him to prove that he took all reasonable steps for securing compliance with that subsection.

(7)　A person guilty of an offence under this section is liable—

(a)　on conviction on indictment, to a fine;

(b)　on summary conviction, to a fine not exceeding the statutory maximum and, for continued contravention, a daily default fine not exceeding one-fiftieth of the statutory maximum.

NOTES

Commencement: 20 January 2007 (for the purpose of enabling the exercise of powers to make Orders or Regulations by statutory instrument); 6 April 2007 (otherwise).

[1.985]
985　Effect of requirement under section 983

(1)　Subject to section 986, this section applies where a shareholder exercises his rights under section 983 in respect of any shares held by him.

(2)　The offeror is entitled and bound to acquire those shares on the terms of the offer or on such other terms as may be agreed.

(3)　Where the terms of an offer are such as to give the shareholder a choice of consideration—

(a)　the shareholder may indicate his choice when requiring the offeror to acquire the shares, and

(b)　the notice given to the shareholder under section 984(3)—

(i)　must give particulars of the choice and of the rights conferred by this subsection, and

(ii)　may state which consideration specified in the offer will apply if he does not indicate a choice.

The reference in subsection (2) to the terms of the offer is to be read accordingly.

(4)　Subsection (3) applies whether or not any time-limit or other conditions applicable to the choice under the terms of the offer can still be complied with.

(5)　If the consideration offered to or (as the case may be) chosen by the shareholder—

(a)　is not cash and the offeror is no longer able to provide it, or

(b)　was to have been provided by a third party who is no longer bound or able to provide it,

the consideration is to be taken to consist of an amount of cash, payable by the offeror, which at the date when the shareholder requires the offeror to acquire the shares is equivalent to the consideration offered or (as the case may be) chosen.

NOTES

Commencement: 6 April 2007.

Supplementary

[1.986]
986　Applications to the court

(1)　Where a notice is given under section 979 to a shareholder the court may, on an application made by him, order—

(a)　that the offeror is not entitled and bound to acquire the shares to which the notice relates, or

(b)　that the terms on which the offeror is entitled and bound to acquire the shares shall be such as the court thinks fit.

(2)　An application under subsection (1) must be made within six weeks from the date on which the notice referred to in that subsection was given.

If an application to the court under subsection (1) is pending at the end of that period, section 981(6) does not have effect until the application has been disposed of.

(3)　Where a shareholder exercises his rights under section 983 in respect of any shares held by him, the court may, on an application made by him or the offeror, order that the terms on which the offeror is entitled and bound to acquire the shares shall be such as the court thinks fit.

(4)　On an application under subsection (1) or (3)—

(a)　the court may not require consideration of a higher value than that specified in the terms of the offer ("the offer value") to be given for the shares to which the application relates unless the holder of the shares shows that the offer value would be unfair;

(b)　the court may not require consideration of a lower value than the offer value to be given for the shares.

(5)　No order for costs or expenses may be made against a shareholder making an application under subsection (1) or (3) unless the court considers that—

(a)　the application was unnecessary, improper or vexatious,

(b)　there has been unreasonable delay in making the application, or

(c)　there has been unreasonable conduct on the shareholder's part in conducting the proceedings on the application.

(6)　A shareholder who has made an application under subsection (1) or (3) must give notice of the application to the offeror.

(7)   An offeror who is given notice of an application under subsection (1) or (3) must give a copy of the notice to—

   (a)   any person (other than the applicant) to whom a notice has been given under section 979;

   (b)   any person who has exercised his rights under section 983.

(8)   An offeror who makes an application under subsection (3) must give notice of the application to—

   (a)   any person to whom a notice has been given under section 979;

   (b)   any person who has exercised his rights under section 983.

(9)   Where a takeover offer has not been accepted to the extent necessary for entitling the offeror to give notices under subsection (2) or (4) of section 979 the court may, on an application made by him, make an order authorising him to give notices under that subsection if it is satisfied that—

   (a)   the offeror has after reasonable enquiry been unable to trace one or more of the persons holding shares to which the offer relates,

   (b)   the requirements of that subsection would have been met if the person, or all the persons, mentioned in paragraph (a) above had accepted the offer, and

   (c)   the consideration offered is fair and reasonable.

   This is subject to subsection (10).

(10)   The court may not make an order under subsection (9) unless it considers that it is just and equitable to do so having regard, in particular, to the number of shareholders who have been traced but who have not accepted the offer.

NOTES

Commencement: 6 April 2007.

[1.987]
987   Joint offers

(1)   In the case of a takeover offer made by two or more persons jointly, this Chapter has effect as follows.

(2)   The conditions for the exercise of the rights conferred by section 979 are satisfied—

   (a)   in the case of acquisitions by virtue of acceptances of the offer, by the joint offerors acquiring or unconditionally contracting to acquire the necessary shares jointly;

   (b)   in other cases, by the joint offerors acquiring or unconditionally contracting to acquire the necessary shares either jointly or separately.

(3)   The conditions for the exercise of the rights conferred by section 983 are satisfied—

   (a)   in the case of acquisitions by virtue of acceptances of the offer, by the joint offerors acquiring or unconditionally contracting to acquire the necessary shares jointly;

   (b)   in other cases, by the joint offerors acquiring or contracting (whether unconditionally or subject to conditions being met) to acquire the necessary shares either jointly or separately.

(4)   Subject to the following provisions, the rights and obligations of the offeror under sections 979 to 985 are respectively joint rights and joint and several obligations of the joint offerors.

(5)   A provision of sections 979 to 986 that requires or authorises a notice or other document to be given or sent by or to the joint offerors is complied with if the notice or document is given or sent by or to any of them (but see subsection (6)).

(6)   The statutory declaration required by section 980(4) must be made by all of the joint offerors and, where one or more of them is a company, signed by a director of that company.

(7)   In sections 974 to 977, 979(9), 981(6), 983(8) and 988 references to the offeror are to be read as references to the joint offerors or any of them.

(8)   In section 981(7) and (8) references to the offeror are to be read as references to the joint offerors or such of them as they may determine.

(9)   In sections 981(5)(a) and 985(5)(a) references to the offeror being no longer able to provide the relevant consideration are to be read as references to none of the joint offerors being able to do so.

(10)   In section 986 references to the offeror are to be read as references to the joint offerors, except that—

   (a)   an application under subsection (3) or (9) may be made by any of them, and

   (b)   the reference in subsection (9)(a) to the offeror having been unable to trace one or more of the persons holding shares is to be read as a reference to none of the offerors having been able to do so.

NOTES

Commencement: 6 April 2007.

Interpretation

[1.988]
988   Associates

(1)   In this Chapter "associate", in relation to an offeror, means—

   (a)   a nominee of the offeror,

(b)   a holding company, subsidiary or fellow subsidiary of the offeror or a nominee of such a holding company, subsidiary or fellow subsidiary,

(c)   a body corporate in which the offeror is substantially interested,

(d)   a person who is, or is a nominee of, a party to a share acquisition agreement with the offeror, or

(e)   (where the offeror is an individual) his spouse or civil partner and any minor child or step-child of his.

(2)   For the purposes of subsection (1)(b) a company is a fellow subsidiary of another body corporate if both are subsidiaries of the same body corporate but neither is a subsidiary of the other.

(3)   For the purposes of subsection (1)(c) an offeror has a substantial interest in a body corporate if—

(a)   the body or its directors are accustomed to act in accordance with his directions or instructions, or

(b)   he is entitled to exercise or control the exercise of one-third or more of the voting power at general meetings of the body.

Subsections (2) and (3) of section 823 (which contain provision about when a person is treated as entitled to exercise or control the exercise of voting power) apply for the purposes of this subsection as they apply for the purposes of that section.

(4)   For the purposes of subsection (1)(d) an agreement is a share acquisition agreement if—

(a)   it is an agreement for the acquisition of, or of an interest in, shares to which the offer relates,

(b)   it includes provisions imposing obligations or restrictions on any one or more of the parties to it with respect to their use, retention or disposal of such shares, or their interests in such shares, acquired in pursuance of the agreement (whether or not together with any other shares to which the offer relates or any other interests of theirs in such shares), and

(c)   it is not an excluded agreement (see subsection (5)).

(5)   An agreement is an "excluded agreement"—

(a)   if it is not legally binding, unless it involves mutuality in the undertakings, expectations or understandings of the parties to it, or

(b)   if it is an agreement to underwrite or sub-underwrite an offer of shares in a company, provided the agreement is confined to that purpose and any matters incidental to it.

(6)   The reference in subsection (4)(b) to the use of interests in shares is to the exercise of any rights or of any control or influence arising from those interests (including the right to enter into an agreement for the exercise, or for control of the exercise, of any of those rights by another person).

(7)   In this section—

(a)   "agreement" includes any agreement or arrangement;

(b)   references to provisions of an agreement include—

(i)   undertakings, expectations or understandings operative under an arrangement, and

(ii)   any provision whether express or implied and whether absolute or not.

NOTES

Commencement: 6 April 2007.

[1.989]
989   Convertible securities

(1)   For the purposes of this Chapter securities of a company are treated as shares in the company if they are convertible into or entitle the holder to subscribe for such shares.

References to the holder of shares or a shareholder are to be read accordingly.

(2)   Subsection (1) is not to be read as requiring any securities to be treated—

(a)   as shares of the same class as those into which they are convertible or for which the holder is entitled to subscribe, or

(b)   as shares of the same class as other securities by reason only that the shares into which they are convertible or for which the holder is entitled to subscribe are of the same class.

NOTES

Commencement: 6 April 2007.

[1.990]
990   Debentures carrying voting rights

(1)   For the purposes of this Chapter debentures issued by a company to which subsection (2) applies are treated as shares in the company if they carry voting rights.

(2)   This subsection applies to a company that has voting shares, or debentures carrying voting rights, which are admitted to trading on a regulated market.

(3)   In this Chapter, in relation to debentures treated as shares by virtue of subsection (1)—

(a)   references to the holder of shares or a shareholder are to be read accordingly;

(b)   references to shares being allotted are to be read as references to debentures being issued.

NOTES

Commencement: 6 April 2007.

[1.991]
991 Interpretation
(1)   In this Chapter—
"the company" means the company whose shares are the subject of a takeover offer;
"date of the offer" means—
  (a)   where the offer is published, the date of publication;
  (b)   where the offer is not published, or where any notices of the offer are given before
         the date of publication, the date when notices of the offer (or the first such notices)
         are given;
  and references to the date of the offer are to be read in accordance with section 974(7)
  (revision of offer terms) where that applies;
"non-voting shares" means shares that are not voting shares;
"offeror" means (subject to section 987) the person making a takeover offer;
"voting rights" means rights to vote at general meetings of the company, including rights that
  arise only in certain circumstances;
"voting shares" means shares carrying voting rights.
(2)   For the purposes of this Chapter a person contracts unconditionally to acquire shares if his
entitlement under the contract to acquire them is not (or is no longer) subject to conditions or if all
conditions to which it was subject have been met.
A reference to a contract becoming unconditional is to be read accordingly.

NOTES
Commencement: 6 April 2007.

CHAPTER 4
AMENDMENTS TO PART 7 OF THE COMPANIES ACT 1985

[1.992]
992 Matters to be dealt with in directors' report
(1)–(5)   *(Amend CA 1985, ss 234ZZA, 251 and add Sch 7, Pt 7 to that Act (all of which were
repealed with savings by this Act).)*
(6)   The amendments made by this section apply in relation to directors' reports for financial years
beginning on or after 20th May 2006.

NOTES
Commencement: 6 April 2007.
As to the application of this section to the Companies (Northern Ireland) Order 1986, see the Companies Act 2006
(Commencement No 2, Consequential Amendments, Transitional Provisions and Savings) Order 2007, SI 2007/1093, art 9 at
[2.24].

PART 29
FRAUDULENT TRADING

[1.993]
993 Offence of fraudulent trading
(1)   If any business of a company is carried on with intent to defraud creditors of the company or
creditors of any other person, or for any fraudulent purpose, every person who is knowingly a party
to the carrying on of the business in that manner commits an offence.
(2)   This applies whether or not the company has been, or is in the course of being, wound up.
(3)   A person guilty of an offence under this section is liable—
  (a)   on conviction on indictment, to imprisonment for a term not exceeding ten years or a fine
         (or both);
  (b)   on summary conviction—
    (i)   in England and Wales, to imprisonment for a term not exceeding twelve months or a
           fine not exceeding the statutory maximum (or both);
    (ii)   in Scotland or Northern Ireland, to imprisonment for a term not exceeding six
           months or a fine not exceeding the statutory maximum (or both).

NOTES
Commencement: 1 October 2007.
Commencement (transitional provisions): Sch 3, para 46 to the Companies Act 2006 (Commencement No 3, Consequential
Amendments, Transitional Provisions and Savings) Order 2007, SI 2007/2194 (at **[2.45]**) provides as follows—

"46   Fraudulent trading (s 993)
(1)   Section 458 of the 1985 Act or Article 451 of the 1986 Order (offences of fraudulent trading) continues to apply to
offences completed before 1st October 2007.
(2)   Where, in the case of an offence—
  (a)   a relevant event occurs before 1st October 2007, and
  (b)   another relevant event occurs on or after 1st October 2007,
the offence must be charged under section 993 of the Companies Act 2006 (and not under section 458 of the 1985 Act or
Article 451 of the 1986 Order).

(3)   If in the case of any such offence a relevant event occurred before 15th January 2007 section 993(3)(a) applies with the substitution of "seven years" for "ten years".

(4)   "Relevant event" means an act, omission or other event (including any result of one or more acts or omissions) proof of which is required for conviction of the offence.".

Offences under this section: see further s 1131 at **[1.1131]**.

PART 30
PROTECTION OF MEMBERS AGAINST UNFAIR PREJUDICE

NOTES

With regard to proceedings under this Part, see further the Companies (Authorised Minimum) Regulations 2008, SI 2008/729, reg 6 at **[4.273]** (Determination of exchange rates by the court in certain proceedings), and the Companies (Authorised Minimum) Regulations 2009, SI 2009/2425, reg 6 at **[4.591]** (Determination of exchange rates by the court in certain proceedings).

Main provisions

[1.994]
994   Petition by company member
(1)   A member of a company may apply to the court by petition for an order under this Part on the ground—
    (a)   that the company's affairs are being or have been conducted in a manner that is unfairly prejudicial to the interests of members generally or of some part of its members (including at least himself), or
    (b)   that an actual or proposed act or omission of the company (including an act or omission on its behalf) is or would be so prejudicial.
[(1A)   For the purposes of subsection (1)(a), a removal of the company's auditor from office—
    (a)   on grounds of divergence of opinions on accounting treatments or audit procedures, or
    (b)   on any other improper grounds,
shall be treated as being unfairly prejudicial to the interests of some part of the company's members.]
(2)   The provisions of this Part apply to a person who is not a member of a company but to whom shares in the company have been transferred or transmitted by operation of law as they apply to a member of a company.
(3)   In this section, and so far as applicable for the purposes of this section in the other provisions of this Part, "company" means—
    (a)   a company within the meaning of this Act, or
    (b)   a company that is not such a company but is a statutory water company within the meaning of the Statutory Water Companies Act 1991 (c 58).

NOTES

Commencement: 1 October 2007.

Commencement (transitional adaptations): art 6 of the Companies Act 2006 (Commencement No 3, Consequential Amendments, Transitional Provisions and Savings) Order 2007, SI 2007/2194 provides that the provisions brought into force by that Order shall have effect subject to any transitional adaptations specified in Sch 1 to that Order. Schedule 1, para 19 to the Order (at **[2.43]**) provided for such transitional adaptations (note that this paragraph was revoked by the Companies Act 2006 (Commencement No 8, Transitional Provisions and Savings) Order 2008, SI 2008/2860, art 6, as from 1 October 2009 (subject to any relevant transitional provision or saving in Sch 2 to that Order)).

Sub-s (1A): inserted by the Statutory Auditors and Third Country Auditors Regulations 2007, SI 2007/3494, reg 42, as from 6 April 2008, except in relation to auditors appointed for financial years beginning before that date.

[1.995]
995   Petition by Secretary of State
(1)   This section applies to a company in respect of which—
    (a)   the Secretary of State has received a report under section 437 of the Companies Act 1985 (c 6) (inspector's report);
    (b)   the Secretary of State has exercised his powers under section 447 or 448 of that Act (powers to require documents and information or to enter and search premises);
    (c)   the Secretary of State or the Financial Services Authority has exercised his or its powers under Part 11 of the Financial Services and Markets Act 2000 (c 8) (information gathering and investigations); or
    (d)   the Secretary of State has received a report from an investigator appointed by him or the Financial Services Authority under that Part.
(2)   If it appears to the Secretary of State that in the case of such a company—
    (a)   the company's affairs are being or have been conducted in a manner that is unfairly prejudicial to the interests of members generally or of some part of its members, or
    (b)   an actual or proposed act or omission of the company (including an act or omission on its behalf) is or would be so prejudicial,
he may apply to the court by petition for an order under this Part.
(3)   The Secretary of State may do this in addition to, or instead of, presenting a petition for the winding up of the company.

(4) In this section, and so far as applicable for the purposes of this section in the other provisions of this Part, "company" means any body corporate that is liable to be wound up under the Insolvency Act 1986 (c 45) or the Insolvency (Northern Ireland) Order 1989 (SI 1989/2405 (NI 19)).

NOTES

Commencement: 1 October 2007.

[1.996]
996 Powers of the court under this Part
(1) If the court is satisfied that a petition under this Part is well founded, it may make such order as it thinks fit for giving relief in respect of the matters complained of.
(2) Without prejudice to the generality of subsection (1), the court's order may—
    (a) regulate the conduct of the company's affairs in the future;
    (b) require the company—
       (i) to refrain from doing or continuing an act complained of, or
       (ii) to do an act that the petitioner has complained it has omitted to do;
    (c) authorise civil proceedings to be brought in the name and on behalf of the company by such person or persons and on such terms as the court may direct;
    (d) require the company not to make any, or any specified, alterations in its articles without the leave of the court;
    (e) provide for the purchase of the shares of any members of the company by other members or by the company itself and, in the case of a purchase by the company itself, the reduction of the company's capital accordingly.

NOTES

Commencement: 1 October 2007.

Supplementary provisions

[1.997]
997 Application of general rule-making powers
The power to make rules under section 411 of the Insolvency Act 1986 (c 45) or Article 359 of the Insolvency (Northern Ireland) Order 1989 (SI 1989/2405 (NI 19)), so far as relating to a winding-up petition, applies for the purposes of a petition under this Part.

NOTES

Commencement: 1 October 2007.

[1.998]
998 Copy of order affecting company's constitution to be delivered to registrar
(1) Where an order of the court under this Part—
    (a) alters the company's constitution, or
    (b) gives leave for the company to make any, or any specified, alterations to its constitution, the company must deliver a copy of the order to the registrar.
(2) It must do so within 14 days from the making of the order or such longer period as the court may allow.
(3) If a company makes default in complying with this section, an offence is committed by—
    (a) the company, and
    (b) every officer of the company who is in default.
(4) A person guilty of an offence under this section is liable on summary conviction to a fine not exceeding level 3 on the standard scale and, for continued contravention, a daily default fine not exceeding one-tenth of level 3 on the standard scale.

NOTES

Commencement: 1 October 2007.

[1.999]
999 Supplementary provisions where company's constitution altered
(1) This section applies where an order under this Part alters a company's constitution.
(2) If the order amends—
    (a) a company's articles, or
    (b) any resolution or agreement to which Chapter 3 of Part 3 applies (resolution or agreement affecting a company's constitution),
the copy of the order delivered to the registrar by the company under section 998 must be accompanied by a copy of the company's articles, or the resolution or agreement in question, as amended.
(3) Every copy of a company's articles issued by the company after the order is made must be accompanied by a copy of the order, unless the effect of the order has been incorporated into the articles by amendment.
(4) If a company makes default in complying with this section an offence is committed by—

(a)   the company, and

(b)   every officer of the company who is in default.

(5)   A person guilty of an offence under this section is liable on summary conviction to a fine not exceeding level 3 on the standard scale.

NOTES

Commencement: 1 October 2007.

Commencement (transitional provisions): Sch 3, para 47 to the Companies Act 2006 (Commencement No 3, Consequential Amendments, Transitional Provisions and Savings) Order 2007, SI 2007/2194 (at **[2.45]**) provides that this section does not apply (by virtue of s 1297 *post*) to an order of the court made before 1 October 2007.

PART 31
DISSOLUTION AND RESTORATION TO THE REGISTER

CHAPTER 1
STRIKING OFF

Registrar's power to strike off defunct company

[1.1000]

1000   Power to strike off company not carrying on business or in operation

(1)   If the registrar has reasonable cause to believe that a company is not carrying on business or in operation, the registrar may send to the company by post a letter inquiring whether the company is carrying on business or in operation.

(2)   If the registrar does not within one month of sending the letter receive any answer to it, the registrar must within 14 days after the expiration of that month send to the company by post a registered letter referring to the first letter, and stating—

(a)   that no answer to it has been received, and

(b)   that if an answer is not received to the second letter within one month from its date, a notice will be published in the Gazette with a view to striking the company's name off the register.

(3)   If the registrar—

(a)   receives an answer to the effect that the company is not carrying on business or in operation, or

(b)   does not within one month after sending the second letter receive any answer,

the registrar may publish in the Gazette, and send to the company by post, a notice that at the expiration of three months from the date of the notice the name of the company mentioned in it will, unless cause is shown to the contrary, be struck off the register and the company will be dissolved.

(4)   At the expiration of the time mentioned in the notice the registrar may, unless cause to the contrary is previously shown by the company, strike its name off the register.

(5)   The registrar must publish notice in the Gazette of the company's name having been struck off the register.

(6)   On the publication of the notice in the Gazette the company is dissolved.

(7)   However—

(a)   the liability (if any) of every director, managing officer and member of the company continues and may be enforced as if the company had not been dissolved, and

(b)   nothing in this section affects the power of the court to wind up a company the name of which has been struck off the register.

NOTES

Commencement: 1 October 2009.

[1.1001]

1001   Duty to act in case of company being wound up

(1)   If, in a case where a company is being wound up—

(a)   the registrar has reasonable cause to believe—

(i)   that no liquidator is acting, or

(ii)   that the affairs of the company are fully wound up, and

(b)   the returns required to be made by the liquidator have not been made for a period of six consecutive months,

the registrar must publish in the Gazette and send to the company or the liquidator (if any) a notice that at the expiration of three months from the date of the notice the name of the company mentioned in it will, unless cause is shown to the contrary, be struck off the register and the company will be dissolved.

(2)   At the expiration of the time mentioned in the notice the registrar may, unless cause to the contrary is previously shown by the company, strike its name off the register.

(3)   The registrar must publish notice in the Gazette of the company's name having been struck off the register.

(4)   On the publication of the notice in the Gazette the company is dissolved.

(5)   However—

(a) the liability (if any) of every director, managing officer and member of the company continues and may be enforced as if the company had not been dissolved, and

(b) nothing in this section affects the power of the court to wind up a company the name of which has been struck off the register.

NOTES

Commencement: 1 October 2009.

[1.1002]

1002 Supplementary provisions as to service of letter or notice

(1) A letter or notice to be sent under section 1000 or 1001 to a company may be addressed to the company at its registered office or, if no office has been registered, to the care of some officer of the company.

(2) If there is no officer of the company whose name and address are known to the registrar, the letter or notice may be sent to each of the persons who subscribed the memorandum (if their addresses are known to the registrar).

(3) A notice to be sent to a liquidator under section 1001 may be addressed to him at his last known place of business.

NOTES

Commencement: 1 October 2009.

Voluntary striking off

[1.1003]

1003 Striking off on application by company

(1) On application by a company, the registrar of companies may strike the company's name off the register.

(2) The application—

(a) must be made on the company's behalf by its directors or by a majority of them, and

(b) must contain the prescribed information.

(3) The registrar may not strike a company off under this section until after the expiration of three months from the publication by the registrar in the Gazette of a notice—

(a) stating that the registrar may exercise the power under this section in relation to the company, and

(b) inviting any person to show cause why that should not be done.

(4) The registrar must publish notice in the Gazette of the company's name having been struck off.

(5) On the publication of the notice in the Gazette the company is dissolved.

(6) However—

(a) the liability (if any) of every director, managing officer and member of the company continues and may be enforced as if the company had not been dissolved, and

(b) nothing in this section affects the power of the court to wind up a company the name of which has been struck off the register.

NOTES

Commencement: 20 January 2007 (for the purpose of enabling the exercise of powers to make Orders or Regulations by statutory instrument); 1 October 2009 (otherwise).

Regulations: the Registrar of Companies and Applications for Striking Off Regulations 2009, SI 2009/1803 at **[4.491]**.

[1.1004]

1004 Circumstances in which application not to be made: activities of company

(1) An application under section 1003 (application for voluntary striking off) on behalf of a company must not be made if, at any time in the previous three months, the company has—

(a) changed its name,

(b) traded or otherwise carried on business,

(c) made a disposal for value of property or rights that, immediately before ceasing to trade or otherwise carry on business, it held for the purpose of disposal for gain in the normal course of trading or otherwise carrying on business, or

(d) engaged in any other activity, except one which is—

(i) necessary or expedient for the purpose of making an application under that section, or deciding whether to do so,

(ii) necessary or expedient for the purpose of concluding the affairs of the company,

(iii) necessary or expedient for the purpose of complying with any statutory requirement, or

(iv) specified by the Secretary of State by order for the purposes of this sub-paragraph.

(2) For the purposes of this section, a company is not to be treated as trading or otherwise carrying on business by virtue only of the fact that it makes a payment in respect of a liability incurred in the course of trading or otherwise carrying on business.

(3)   The Secretary of State may by order amend subsection (1) for the purpose of altering the period in relation to which the doing of the things mentioned in paragraphs (a) to (d) of that subsection is relevant.

(4)   An order under this section is subject to negative resolution procedure.

(5)   It is an offence for a person to make an application in contravention of this section.

(6)   In proceedings for such an offence it is a defence for the accused to prove that he did not know, and could not reasonably have known, of the existence of the facts that led to the contravention.

(7)   A person guilty of an offence under this section is liable—

    (a)   on conviction on indictment, to a fine;

    (b)   on summary conviction, to a fine not exceeding the statutory maximum.

NOTES

Commencement: 20 January 2007 (for the purpose of enabling the exercise of powers to make Orders or Regulations by statutory instrument); 1 October 2009 (otherwise).

[1.1005]
1005   Circumstances in which application not to be made: other proceedings not concluded

(1)   An application under section 1003 (application for voluntary striking off) on behalf of a company must not be made at a time when—

    (a)   an application to the court under Part 26 has been made on behalf of the company for the sanctioning of a compromise or arrangement and the matter has not been finally concluded;

    (b)   a voluntary arrangement in relation to the company has been proposed under Part 1 of the Insolvency Act 1986 (c 45) or Part 2 of the Insolvency (Northern Ireland) Order 1989 (SI 1989/2405 (NI 19)) and the matter has not been finally concluded;

    (c)   the company is in administration under Part 2 of that Act or Part 3 of that Order;

    (d)   paragraph 44 of Schedule B1 to that Act or paragraph 45 of Schedule B1 to that Order applies (interim moratorium on proceedings where application to the court for an administration order has been made or notice of intention to appoint administrator has been filed);

    (e)   the company is being wound up under Part 4 of that Act or Part 5 of that Order, whether voluntarily or by the court, or a petition under that Part for winding up of the company by the court has been presented and not finally dealt with or withdrawn;

    (f)   there is a receiver or manager of the company's property;

    (g)   the company's estate is being administered by a judicial factor.

(2)   For the purposes of subsection (1)(a), the matter is finally concluded if—

    (a)   the application has been withdrawn,

    (b)   the application has been finally dealt with without a compromise or arrangement being sanctioned by the court, or

    (c)   a compromise or arrangement has been sanctioned by the court and has, together with anything required to be done under any provision made in relation to the matter by order of the court, been fully carried out.

(3)   For the purposes of subsection (1)(b), the matter is finally concluded if—

    (a)   no meetings are to be summoned under section 3 of the Insolvency Act 1986 (c 45) or Article 16 of the Insolvency (Northern Ireland) Order 1989,

    (b)   meetings summoned under that section or Article fail to approve the arrangement with no, or the same, modifications,

    (c)   an arrangement approved by meetings summoned under that section, or in consequence of a direction under section 6(4)(b) of that Act or Article 19(4)(b) of that Order, has been fully implemented, or

    (d)   the court makes an order under section 6(5) of that Act or Article 19(5) of that Order revoking approval given at previous meetings and, if the court gives any directions under section 6(6) of that Act or Article 19(6) of that Order, the company has done whatever it is required to do under those directions.

(4)   It is an offence for a person to make an application in contravention of this section.

(5)   In proceedings for such an offence it is a defence for the accused to prove that he did not know, and could not reasonably have known, of the existence of the facts that led to the contravention.

(6)   A person guilty of an offence under this section is liable—

    (a)   on conviction on indictment, to a fine;

    (b)   on summary conviction, to a fine not exceeding the statutory maximum.

NOTES

Commencement: 1 October 2009.

[1.1006]
1006 Copy of application to be given to members, employees, etc
(1) A person who makes an application under section 1003 (application for voluntary striking off) on behalf of a company must secure that, within seven days from the day on which the application is made, a copy of it is given to every person who at any time on that day is—
  (a) a member of the company,
  (b) an employee of the company,
  (c) a creditor of the company,
  (d) a director of the company,
  (e) a manager or trustee of any pension fund established for the benefit of employees of the company, or
  (f) a person of a description specified for the purposes of this paragraph by regulations made by the Secretary of State.
Regulations under paragraph (f) are subject to negative resolution procedure.
(2) Subsection (1) does not require a copy of the application to be given to a director who is a party to the application.
(3) The duty imposed by this section ceases to apply if the application is withdrawn before the end of the period for giving the copy application.
(4) A person who fails to perform the duty imposed on him by this section commits an offence.
  If he does so with the intention of concealing the making of the application from the person concerned, he commits an aggravated offence.
(5) In proceedings for an offence under this section it is a defence for the accused to prove that he took all reasonable steps to perform the duty.
(6) A person guilty of an offence under this section (other than an aggravated offence) is liable—
  (a) on conviction on indictment, to a fine;
  (b) on summary conviction, to a fine not exceeding the statutory maximum.
(7) A person guilty of an aggravated offence under this section is liable—
  (a) on conviction on indictment, to imprisonment for a term not exceeding seven years or a fine (or both);
  (b) on summary conviction—
     (i) in England and Wales, to imprisonment for a term not exceeding twelve months or to a fine not exceeding the statutory maximum (or both);
     (ii) in Scotland or Northern Ireland, to imprisonment for a term not exceeding six months, or to a fine not exceeding the statutory maximum (or both).

NOTES
  Commencement: 20 January 2007 (for the purpose of enabling the exercise of powers to make Orders or Regulations by statutory instrument); 1 October 2009 (otherwise).
  Offences under this section: see further s 1131 at **[1.1131]**.

[1.1007]
1007 Copy of application to be given to new members, employees, etc
(1) This section applies in relation to any time after the day on which a company makes an application under section 1003 (application for voluntary striking off) and before the day on which the application is finally dealt with or withdrawn.
(2) A person who is a director of the company at the end of a day on which a person (other than himself) becomes—
  (a) a member of the company,
  (b) an employee of the company,
  (c) a creditor of the company,
  (d) a director of the company,
  (e) a manager or trustee of any pension fund established for the benefit of employees of the company, or
  (f) a person of a description specified for the purposes of this paragraph by regulations made by the Secretary of State,
must secure that a copy of the application is given to that person within seven days from that day.
  Regulations under paragraph (f) are subject to negative resolution procedure.
(3) The duty imposed by this section ceases to apply if the application is finally dealt with or withdrawn before the end of the period for giving the copy application.
(4) A person who fails to perform the duty imposed on him by this section commits an offence.
  If he does so with the intention of concealing the making of the application from the person concerned, he commits an aggravated offence.
(5) In proceedings for an offence under this section it is a defence for the accused to prove—
  (a) that at the time of the failure he was not aware of the fact that the company had made an application under section 1003, or
  (b) that he took all reasonable steps to perform the duty.
(6) A person guilty of an offence under this section (other than an aggravated offence) is liable—
  (a) on conviction on indictment, to a fine;
  (b) on summary conviction, to a fine not exceeding the statutory maximum.

(7)   A person guilty of an aggravated offence under this section is liable—
  (a)   on conviction on indictment, to imprisonment for a term not exceeding seven years or a fine (or both);
  (b)   on summary conviction—
    (i)   in England and Wales, to imprisonment for a term not exceeding twelve months or to a fine not exceeding the statutory maximum (or both);
    (ii)   in Scotland or Northern Ireland, to imprisonment for a term not exceeding six months, or to a fine not exceeding the statutory maximum (or both).

NOTES

Commencement: 20 January 2007 (for the purpose of enabling the exercise of powers to make Orders or Regulations by statutory instrument); 1 October 2009 (otherwise).

Offences under this section: see further s 1131 at **[1.1131]**.

[1.1008]
1008   Copy of application: provisions as to service of documents
(1)   The following provisions have effect for the purposes of—
  section 1006 (copy of application to be given to members, employees, etc), and
  section 1007 (copy of application to be given to new members, employees, etc).
(2)   A document is treated as given to a person if it is—
  (a)   delivered to him, or
  (b)   left at his proper address, or
  (c)   sent by post to him at that address.
(3)   For the purposes of subsection (2) and section 7 of the Interpretation Act 1978 (c 30) (service of documents by post) as it applies in relation to that subsection, the proper address of a person is—
  (a)   in the case of a firm incorporated or formed in the United Kingdom, its registered or principal office;
  (b)   in the case of a firm incorporated or formed outside the United Kingdom—
    (i)   if it has a place of business in the United Kingdom, its principal office in the United Kingdom, or
    (ii)   if it does not have a place of business in the United Kingdom, its registered or principal office;
  (c)   in the case of an individual, his last known address.
(4)   In the case of a creditor of the company a document is treated as given to him if it is left or sent by post to him—
  (a)   at the place of business of his with which the company has had dealings by virtue of which he is a creditor of the company, or
  (b)   if there is more than one such place of business, at each of them.

NOTES

Commencement: 1 October 2009.

[1.1009]
1009   Circumstances in which application to be withdrawn
(1)   This section applies where, at any time on or after the day on which a company makes an application under section 1003 (application for voluntary striking off) and before the day on which the application is finally dealt with or withdrawn—
  (a)   the company—
    (i)   changes its name,
    (ii)   trades or otherwise carries on business,
    (iii)   makes a disposal for value of any property or rights other than those which it was necessary or expedient for it to hold for the purpose of making, or proceeding with, an application under that section, or
    (iv)   engages in any activity, except one to which subsection (4) applies;
  (b)   an application is made to the court under Part 26 on behalf of the company for the sanctioning of a compromise or arrangement;
  (c)   a voluntary arrangement in relation to the company is proposed under Part 1 of the Insolvency Act 1986 (c 45) or Part 2 of the Insolvency (Northern Ireland) Order 1989 (SI 1989/2405 (NI 19));
  (d)   an application to the court for an administration order in respect of the company is made under paragraph 12 of Schedule B1 to that Act or paragraph 13 of Schedule B1 to that Order;
  (e)   an administrator is appointed in respect of the company under paragraph 14 or 22 of Schedule B1 to that Act or paragraph 15 or 23 of Schedule B1 to that Order, or a copy of notice of intention to appoint an administrator of the company under any of those provisions is filed with the court;
  (f)   there arise any of the circumstances in which, under section 84(1) of that Act or Article 70 of that Order, the company may be voluntarily wound up;

(g)   a petition is presented for the winding up of the company by the court under Part 4 of that Act or Part 5 of that Order;

(h)   a receiver or manager of the company's property is appointed; or

(i)   a judicial factor is appointed to administer the company's estate.

(2)   A person who, at the end of a day on which any of the events mentioned in subsection (1) occurs, is a director of the company must secure that the company's application is withdrawn forthwith.

(3)   For the purposes of subsection (1)(a), a company is not treated as trading or otherwise carrying on business by virtue only of the fact that it makes a payment in respect of a liability incurred in the course of trading or otherwise carrying on business.

(4)   The excepted activities referred to in subsection (1)(a)(iv) are—

(a)   any activity necessary or expedient for the purposes of—

    (i)   making, or proceeding with, an application under section 1003 (application for voluntary striking off),

    (ii)   concluding affairs of the company that are outstanding because of what has been necessary or expedient for the purpose of making, or proceeding with, such an application, or

    (iii) complying with any statutory requirement;

(b)   any activity specified by the Secretary of State by order for the purposes of this subsection.

An order under paragraph (b) is subject to negative resolution procedure.

(5)   A person who fails to perform the duty imposed on him by this section commits an offence.

(6)   In proceedings for an offence under this section it is a defence for the accused to prove—

(a)   that at the time of the failure he was not aware of the fact that the company had made an application under section 1003, or

(b)   that he took all reasonable steps to perform the duty.

(7)   A person guilty of an offence under this section is liable—

(a)   on conviction on indictment, to a fine;

(b)   on summary conviction, to a fine not exceeding the statutory maximum.

NOTES

Commencement: 20 January 2007 (for the purpose of enabling the exercise of powers to make Orders or Regulations by statutory instrument); 1 October 2009 (otherwise).

[1.1010]
1010 Withdrawal of application
An application under section 1003 is withdrawn by notice to the registrar.

NOTES

Commencement: 1 October 2009.

[1.1011]
1011 Meaning of "creditor"
In this Chapter "creditor" includes a contingent or prospective creditor.

NOTES

Commencement: 1 October 2009.

CHAPTER 2
PROPERTY OF DISSOLVED COMPANY

Property vesting as bona vacantia

[1.1012]
1012 Property of dissolved company to be bona vacantia
(1)   When a company is dissolved, all property and rights whatsoever vested in or held on trust for the company immediately before its dissolution (including leasehold property, but not including property held by the company on trust for another person) are deemed to be *bona vacantia* and—

(a)   accordingly belong to the Crown, or to the Duchy of Lancaster or to the Duke of Cornwall for the time being (as the case may be), and

(b)   vest and may be dealt with in the same manner as other *bona vacantia* accruing to the Crown, to the Duchy of Lancaster or to the Duke of Cornwall.

(2)   Subsection (1) has effect subject to the possible restoration of the company to the register under Chapter 3 (see section 1034).

NOTES

Commencement: 1 October 2009.

Commencement (transitional provisions): Sch 2, paras 88, 88A to the Companies Act 2006 (Commencement No 8, Transitional Provisions and Savings) Order 2008, SI 2008/2860 (at **[2.91]**) provides as follows (note that paras 88, 88A were substituted for the original para 88 by the Companies Act 2006 and Limited Liability Partnerships (Transitional Provisions and Savings) (Amendment) Regulations 2009, SI 2009/2476, reg 2(1), (3), as from 1 October 2009)—

Part 1   The Companies Act 2006

"Property of dissolved company (ss 1012 to 1023)

88.—(1)   Sections 1012 to 1023 of the Companies Act 2006 (property of dissolved company) apply in relation to the property of a company dissolved on or after 1st October 2009.

(2)   Subject to paragraph 88A, the corresponding provisions of the 1985 Act or 1986 Order continue to apply in relation to the property of a company dissolved before that date.

88A.—(1)   Section 1013 of the Companies Act 2006 (Crown disclaimer of property vesting as bona vacantia) applies in relation to property of a company dissolved before 1st October 2009 if at that date—

    (a)   no period has begun to run in relation to the property under section 656(3)(a) or (b) of the 1985 Act or Article 607(3)(a) or (b) of the 1986 Order (period within which notice of disclaimer must be executed), and

    (b)   the right to disclaim has not ceased to be exercisable in relation to the property by virtue of section 656(2) of the 1985 Act or Article 607(2) of the 1986 Order (waiver of right to disclaim).

(2)   In section 1013 as it applies by virtue of this paragraph the references to property vesting under section 1012 shall be read as references to its vesting under section 654 of the 1985 Act or Article 605 of the 1986 Order (or corresponding earlier provisions).

(3)   Where section 1013 applies by virtue of this paragraph—

    (a)   the other provisions of sections 1012 to 1022 of the Companies Act 2006 apply accordingly, and

    (b)   the corresponding provisions of the 1985 Act or 1986 Order do not apply.".

[1.1013]

1013   Crown disclaimer of property vesting as bona vacantia

(1)   Where property vests in the Crown under section 1012, the Crown's title to it under that section may be disclaimed by a notice signed by the Crown representative, that is to say the Treasury Solicitor, or, in relation to property in Scotland, the Queen's and Lord Treasurer's Remembrancer.

(2)   The right to execute a notice of disclaimer under this section may be waived by or on behalf of the Crown either expressly or by taking possession.

(3)   A notice of disclaimer must be executed within three years after—

    (a)   the date on which the fact that the property may have vested in the Crown under section 1012 first comes to the notice of the Crown representative, or

    (b)   if ownership of the property is not established at that date, the end of the period reasonably necessary for the Crown representative to establish the ownership of the property.

(4)   If an application in writing is made to the Crown representative by a person interested in the property requiring him to decide whether he will or will not disclaim, any notice of disclaimer must be executed within twelve months after the making of the application or such further period as may be allowed by the court.

(5)   A notice of disclaimer under this section is of no effect if it is shown to have been executed after the end of the period specified by subsection (3) or (4).

(6)   A notice of disclaimer under this section must be delivered to the registrar and retained and registered by him.

(7)   Copies of it must be published in the Gazette and sent to any persons who have given the Crown representative notice that they claim to be interested in the property.

(8)   This section applies to property vested in the Duchy of Lancaster or the Duke of Cornwall under section 1012 as if for references to the Crown and the Crown representative there were respectively substituted references to the Duchy of Lancaster and to the Solicitor to that Duchy, or to the Duke of Cornwall and to the Solicitor to the Duchy of Cornwall, as the case may be.

NOTES

Commencement: 1 October 2009.

Commencement (transitional provisions): see the note to s 1012 at **[1.1012]**.

[1.1014]

1014   Effect of Crown disclaimer

(1)   Where notice of disclaimer is executed under section 1013 as respects any property, that property is deemed not to have vested in the Crown under section 1012.

(2)   The following sections contain provisions as to the effect of the Crown disclaimer—

    sections 1015 to 1019 apply in relation to property in England and Wales or Northern Ireland; sections 1020 to 1022 apply in relation to property in Scotland.

NOTES

Commencement: 1 October 2009.

Commencement (transitional provisions): see the note to s 1012 at **[1.1012]**.

Effect of Crown disclaimer: England and Wales and Northern Ireland

[1.1015]

1015   General effect of disclaimer

(1)   The Crown's disclaimer operates so as to terminate, as from the date of the disclaimer, the rights, interests and liabilities of the company in or in respect of the property disclaimed.

(2)   It does not, except so far as is necessary for the purpose of releasing the company from any liability, affect the rights or liabilities of any other person.

NOTES
Commencement: 1 October 2009.
Commencement (transitional provisions): see the note to s 1012 at [**1.1012**].

[1.1016]
1016 Disclaimer of leaseholds
(1) The disclaimer of any property of a leasehold character does not take effect unless a copy of the disclaimer has been served (so far as the Crown representative is aware of their addresses) on every person claiming under the company as underlessee or mortgagee, and either—
   (a) no application under section 1017 (power of court to make vesting order) is made with respect to that property before the end of the period of 14 days beginning with the day on which the last notice under this paragraph was served, or
   (b) where such an application has been made, the court directs that the disclaimer shall take effect.
(2) Where the court gives a direction under subsection (1)(b) it may also, instead of or in addition to any order it makes under section 1017, make such order as it thinks fit with respect to fixtures, tenant's improvements and other matters arising out of the lease.
(3) In this section the "Crown representative" means—
   (a) in relation to property vested in the Duchy of Lancaster, the Solicitor to that Duchy;
   (b) in relation to property vested in the Duke of Cornwall, the Solicitor to the Duchy of Cornwall;
   (c) in relation to property in Scotland, the Queen's and Lord Treasurer's Remembrancer;
   (d) in relation to other property, the Treasury Solicitor.

NOTES
Commencement: 1 October 2009.
Commencement (transitional provisions): see the note to s 1012 at [**1.1012**].

[1.1017]
1017 Power of court to make vesting order
(1) The court may on application by a person who—
   (a) claims an interest in the disclaimed property, or
   (b) is under a liability in respect of the disclaimed property that is not discharged by the disclaimer,
make an order under this section in respect of the property.
(2) An order under this section is an order for the vesting of the disclaimed property in, or its delivery to—
   (a) a person entitled to it (or a trustee for such a person), or
   (b) a person subject to such a liability as is mentioned in subsection (1)(b) (or a trustee for such a person).
(3) An order under subsection (2)(b) may only be made where it appears to the court that it would be just to do so for the purpose of compensating the person subject to the liability in respect of the disclaimer.
(4) An order under this section may be made on such terms as the court thinks fit.
(5) On a vesting order being made under this section, the property comprised in it vests in the person named in that behalf in the order without conveyance, assignment or transfer.

NOTES
Commencement: 1 October 2009.
Commencement (transitional provisions): see the note to s 1012 at [**1.1012**].

[1.1018]
1018 Protection of persons holding under a lease
(1) The court must not make an order under section 1017 vesting property of a leasehold nature in a person claiming under the company as underlessee or mortgagee except on terms making that person—
   (a) subject to the same liabilities and obligations as those to which the company was subject under the lease, or
   (b) if the court thinks fit, subject to the same liabilities and obligations as if the lease had been assigned to him.
(2) Where the order relates to only part of the property comprised in the lease, subsection (1) applies as if the lease had comprised only the property comprised in the vesting order.
(3) A person claiming under the company as underlessee or mortgagee who declines to accept a vesting order on such terms is excluded from all interest in the property.
(4) If there is no person claiming under the company who is willing to accept an order on such terms, the court has power to vest the company's estate and interest in the property in any person who is liable (whether personally or in a representative character, and whether alone or jointly with the company) to perform the lessee's covenants in the lease.

(5) The court may vest that estate and interest in such a person freed and discharged from all estates, incumbrances and interests created by the company.

NOTES
Commencement: 1 October 2009.
Commencement (transitional provisions): see the note to s 1012 at **[1.1012]**.

[1.1019]
1019 Land subject to rentcharge
Where in consequence of the disclaimer land that is subject to a rentcharge vests in any person, neither he nor his successors in title are subject to any personal liability in respect of sums becoming due under the rentcharge, except sums becoming due after he, or some person claiming under or through him, has taken possession or control of the land or has entered into occupation of it.

NOTES
Commencement: 1 October 2009.
Commencement (transitional provisions): see the note to s 1012 at **[1.1012]**.

Effect of Crown disclaimer: Scotland

[1.1020]
1020 General effect of disclaimer
(1) The Crown's disclaimer operates to determine, as from the date of the disclaimer, the rights, interests and liabilities of the company, and the property of the company, in or in respect of the property disclaimed.
(2) It does not (except so far as is necessary for the purpose of releasing the company and its property from liability) affect the rights or liabilities of any other person.

NOTES
Commencement: 1 October 2009.
Commencement (transitional provisions): see the note to s 1012 at **[1.1012]**.

[1.1021]
1021 Power of court to make vesting order
(1) The court may—
  (a) on application by a person who either claims an interest in disclaimed property or is under a liability not discharged by this Act in respect of disclaimed property, and
  (b) on hearing such persons as it thinks fit,
make an order for the vesting of the property in or its delivery to any persons entitled to it, or to whom it may seem just that the property should be delivered by way of compensation for such liability, or a trustee for him.
(2) The order may be made on such terms as the court thinks fit.
(3) On a vesting order being made under this section, the property comprised in it vests accordingly in the person named in that behalf in the order, without conveyance or assignation for that purpose.

NOTES
Commencement: 1 October 2009.
Commencement (transitional provisions): see the note to s 1012 at **[1.1012]**.

[1.1022]
1022 Protection of persons holding under a lease
(1) Where the property disclaimed is held under a lease the court must not make a vesting order in favour of a person claiming under the company, whether—
  (a) as sub-lessee, or
  (b) as creditor in a duly registered or (as the case may be) recorded heritable security over a lease,
except on the following terms.
(2) The person must by the order be made subject—
  (a) to the same liabilities and obligations as those to which the company was subject under the lease in respect of the property, or
  (b) if the court thinks fit, only to the same liabilities and obligations as if the lease had been assigned to him.
  In either event (if the case so requires) the liabilities and obligations must be as if the lease had comprised only the property comprised in the vesting order.
(3) A sub-lessee or creditor declining to accept a vesting order on such terms is excluded from all interest in and security over the property.

(4)   If there is no person claiming under the company who is willing to accept an order on such terms, the court has power to vest the company's estate and interest in the property in any person liable (either personally or in a representative character, and either alone or jointly with the company) to perform the lessee's obligations under the lease.

(5)   The court may vest that estate and interest in such a person freed and discharged from all interests, rights and obligations created by the company in the lease or in relation to the lease.

(6)   For the purposes of this section a heritable security—

(a)   is duly recorded if it is recorded in the Register of Sasines, and

(b)   is duly registered if registered in accordance with the Land Registration (Scotland) Act 1979 (c 33).

NOTES
Commencement: 1 October 2009.
Commencement (transitional provisions): see the note to s 1012 at **[1.1012]**.

Supplementary provisions

[1.1023]
1023   Liability for rentcharge on company's land after dissolution

(1)   This section applies where on the dissolution of a company land in England and Wales or Northern Ireland that is subject to a rentcharge vests by operation of law in the Crown or any other person ("the proprietor").

(2)   Neither the proprietor nor his successors in title are subject to any personal liability in respect of sums becoming due under the rentcharge, except sums becoming due after the proprietor, or some person claiming under or through him, has taken possession or control of the land or has entered into occupation of it.

(3)   In this section "company" includes any body corporate.

NOTES
Commencement: 1 October 2009.
Commencement (transitional provisions): see the note to s 1012 at **[1.1012]**.

CHAPTER 3
RESTORATION TO THE REGISTER

Administrative restoration to the register

[1.1024]
1024   Application for administrative restoration to the register

(1)   An application may be made to the registrar to restore to the register a company that has been struck off the register under section 1000 or 1001 (power of registrar to strike off defunct company).

(2)   An application under this section may be made whether or not the company has in consequence been dissolved.

(3)   An application under this section may only be made by a former director or former member of the company.

(4)   An application under this section may not be made after the end of the period of six years from the date of the dissolution of the company.

For this purpose an application is made when it is received by the registrar.

NOTES
Commencement: 1 October 2009.

[1.1025]
1025   Requirements for administrative restoration

(1)   On an application under section 1024 the registrar shall restore the company to the register if, and only if, the following conditions are met.

(2)   The first condition is that the company was carrying on business or in operation at the time of its striking off.

(3)   The second condition is that, if any property or right previously vested in or held on trust for the company has vested as *bona vacantia*, the Crown representative has signified to the registrar in writing consent to the company's restoration to the register.

(4)   It is the applicant's responsibility to obtain that consent and to pay any costs (in Scotland, expenses) of the Crown representative—

(a)   in dealing with the property during the period of dissolution, or

(b)   in connection with the proceedings on the application,

that may be demanded as a condition of giving consent.

(5)   The third condition is that the applicant has—

(a)   delivered to the registrar such documents relating to the company as are necessary to bring up to date the records kept by the registrar, and

(b)   paid any penalties under section 453 or corresponding earlier provisions (civil penalty for failure to deliver accounts) that were outstanding at the date of dissolution or striking off.

(6) In this section the "Crown representative" means—
  (a) in relation to property vested in the Duchy of Lancaster, the Solicitor to that Duchy;
  (b) in relation to property vested in the Duke of Cornwall, the Solicitor to the Duchy of Cornwall;
  (c) in relation to property in Scotland, the Queen's and Lord Treasurer's Remembrancer;
  (d) in relation to other property, the Treasury Solicitor.

NOTES
  Commencement: 1 October 2009.

[1.1026]
1026 Application to be accompanied by statement of compliance
(1) An application under section 1024 (application for administrative restoration to the register) must be accompanied by a statement of compliance.
(2) The statement of compliance required is a statement—
  (a) that the person making the application has standing to apply (see subsection (3) of that section), and
  (b) that the requirements for administrative restoration (see section 1025) are met.
(3) The registrar may accept the statement of compliance as sufficient evidence of those matters.

NOTES
  Commencement: 1 October 2009.

[1.1027]
1027 Registrar's decision on application for administrative restoration
(1) The registrar must give notice to the applicant of the decision on an application under section 1024 (application for administrative restoration to the register).
(2) If the decision is that the company should be restored to the register, the restoration takes effect as from the date that notice is sent.
(3) In the case of such a decision, the registrar must—
  (a) enter on the register a note of the date as from which the company's restoration to the register takes effect, and
  (b) cause notice of the restoration to be published in the Gazette.
(4) The notice under subsection (3)(b) must state—
  (a) the name of the company or, if the company is restored to the register under a different name (see section 1033), that name and its former name,
  (b) the company's registered number, and
  (c) the date as from which the restoration of the company to the register takes effect.

NOTES
  Commencement: 1 October 2009.

[1.1028]
1028 Effect of administrative restoration
(1) The general effect of administrative restoration to the register is that the company is deemed to have continued in existence as if it had not been dissolved or struck off the register.
(2) The company is not liable to a penalty under section 453 or any corresponding earlier provision (civil penalty for failure to deliver accounts) for a financial year in relation to which the period for filing accounts and reports ended—
  (a) after the date of dissolution or striking off, and
  (b) before the restoration of the company to the register.
(3) The court may give such directions and make such provision as seems just for placing the company and all other persons in the same position (as nearly as may be) as if the company had not been dissolved or struck off the register.
(4) An application to the court for such directions or provision may be made any time within three years after the date of restoration of the company to the register.

NOTES
  Commencement: 1 October 2009.

Restoration to the register by the court

[1.1029]
1029 Application to court for restoration to the register
(1) An application may be made to the court to restore to the register a company—
  (a) that has been dissolved under Chapter 9 of Part 4 of the Insolvency Act 1986 (c 45) or Chapter 9 of Part 5 of the Insolvency (Northern Ireland) Order 1989 (SI 1989/2405 (NI 19)) (dissolution of company after winding up),
  (b) that is deemed to have been dissolved under paragraph 84(6) of Schedule B1 to that Act or paragraph 85(6) of Schedule B1 to that Order (dissolution of company following administration), or

    (c)   that has been struck off the register—

        (i)   under section 1000 or 1001 (power of registrar to strike off defunct company), or

        (ii)   under section 1003 (voluntary striking off),

        whether or not the company has in consequence been dissolved.

(2)   An application under this section may be made by—

    (a)   the Secretary of State,

    (b)   any former director of the company,

    (c)   any person having an interest in land in which the company had a superior or derivative interest,

    (d)   any person having an interest in land or other property—

        (i)   that was subject to rights vested in the company, or

        (ii)   that was benefited by obligations owed by the company,

    (e)   any person who but for the company's dissolution would have been in a contractual relationship with it,

    (f)   any person with a potential legal claim against the company,

    (g)   any manager or trustee of a pension fund established for the benefit of employees of the company,

    (h)   any former member of the company (or the personal representatives of such a person),

    (i)   any person who was a creditor of the company at the time of its striking off or dissolution,

    (j)   any former liquidator of the company,

    (k)   where the company was struck off the register under section 1003 (voluntary striking off), any person of a description specified by regulations under section 1006(1)(f) or 1007(2)(f) (persons entitled to notice of application for voluntary striking off),

or by any other person appearing to the court to have an interest in the matter.

NOTES

Commencement: 1 October 2009.

Commencement (transitional provisions): Sch 2, paras 90, 91 to the Companies Act 2006 (Commencement No 8, Transitional Provisions and Savings) Order 2008, SI 2008/2860 (at **[2.91]**) provide as follows—

"Application to court for restoration to the register (ss 1029 to 1032)

90.   Sections 1029 to 1032 of the Companies Act 2006 (restoration to register by the court) apply whether the company was dissolved or struck off the register before, on or after 1st October 2009.

91.—(1)   The following provisions apply where the company was dissolved or struck off the register before 1st October 2009.

(2)   In section 1029 (application to court for restoration to register), the references in subsection (1) to enactments under which a company may have been dissolved or struck off include corresponding earlier enactments (and for this purpose sections 1000 and 1003 of that Act are regarded as corresponding to sections 652 and 652A of the 1985 Act and Articles 603 and 603A of the 1986 Order).

(3)   No application under section 1029 may be made if an application in respect of the same dissolution or striking off has been made under section 653 of the 1985 Act or Article 604 of the 1986 Order (objection to striking off by person aggrieved), and has not been withdrawn.

(4)   Section 1030(4) (general time limit of six years) does not enable an application to be made in respect of a company dissolved before 1st October 2007, subject to sub-paragraphs (5) and (6).

(5)   If the company was struck off under section 652 or 652A of the 1985 Act or Article 603 or 603A of the 1986 Order, section 1030(4) does not prevent an application being made at any time before—

    (a)   1st October 2015 (that is, six years after commencement), or

    (b)   the expiration of the period of 20 years from publication in the Gazette of notice under the relevant section or Article,

whichever occurs first.

(6)   Section 1030(5) (extension of period for application where application for administrative restoration refused) applies in relation to the time limit under sub-paragraph (5) above as in relation to the time limit in section 1030(4).".

[1.1030]
1030   When application to the court may be made

(1)   An application to the court for restoration of a company to the register may be made at any time for the purpose of bringing proceedings against the company for damages for personal injury.

(2)   No order shall be made on such an application if it appears to the court that the proceedings would fail by virtue of any enactment as to the time within which proceedings must be brought.

(3)   In making that decision the court must have regard to its power under section 1032(3) (power to give consequential directions etc) to direct that the period between the dissolution (or striking off) of the company and the making of the order is not to count for the purposes of any such enactment.

(4)   In any other case an application to the court for restoration of a company to the register may not be made after the end of the period of six years from the date of the dissolution of the company, subject as follows.

(5)   In a case where—

    (a)   the company has been struck off the register under section 1000 or 1001 (power of registrar to strike off defunct company),

    (b)   an application to the registrar has been made under section 1024 (application for administrative restoration to the register) within the time allowed for making such an application, and

    (c)   the registrar has refused the application,

an application to the court under this section may be made within 28 days of notice of the registrar's decision being issued by the registrar, even if the period of six years mentioned in subsection (4) above has expired.

(6)   For the purposes of this section—

    (a)   "personal injury" includes any disease and any impairment of a person's physical or mental condition; and

    (b)   references to damages for personal injury include—

        (i)   any sum claimed by virtue of section 1(2)(c) of the Law Reform (Miscellaneous Provisions) Act 1934 (c 41) or section 14(2)(c) of the Law Reform (Miscellaneous Provisions) Act (Northern Ireland) 1937 (1937 c 9 (NI)) (funeral expenses)), and

        (ii)   damages under the Fatal Accidents Act 1976 (c 30), the [Damages (Scotland) Act 2011 (asp 7)] or the Fatal Accidents (Northern Ireland) Order 1977 (SI 1977/1251 (NI 18)).

NOTES

Commencement: 1 October 2009.

Commencement (transitional provisions): see the note to s 1029 at **[1.1029]**.

Sub-s (6): words in square brackets substituted by the Damages (Scotland) Act 2011, s 15, Sch 1, para 9, as from 7 July 2011.

[1.1031]

1031   Decision on application for restoration by the court

(1)   On an application under section 1029 the court may order the restoration of the company to the register—

    (a)   if the company was struck off the register under section 1000 or 1001 (power of registrar to strike off defunct companies) and the company was, at the time of the striking off, carrying on business or in operation;

    (b)   if the company was struck off the register under section 1003 (voluntary striking off) and any of the requirements of sections 1004 to 1009 was not complied with;

    (c)   if in any other case the court considers it just to do so.

(2)   If the court orders restoration of the company to the register, the restoration takes effect on a copy of the court's order being delivered to the registrar.

(3)   The registrar must cause to be published in the Gazette notice of the restoration of the company to the register.

(4)   The notice must state—

    (a)   the name of the company or, if the company is restored to the register under a different name (see section 1033), that name and its former name,

    (b)   the company's registered number, and

    (c)   the date on which the restoration took effect.

NOTES

Commencement: 1 October 2009.

Commencement (transitional provisions): see the note to s 1029 at **[1.1029]**.

[1.1032]

1032   Effect of court order for restoration to the register

(1)   The general effect of an order by the court for restoration to the register is that the company is deemed to have continued in existence as if it had not been dissolved or struck off the register.

(2)   The company is not liable to a penalty under section 453 or any corresponding earlier provision (civil penalty for failure to deliver accounts) for a financial year in relation to which the period for filing accounts and reports ended—

    (a)   after the date of dissolution or striking off, and

    (b)   before the restoration of the company to the register.

(3)   The court may give such directions and make such provision as seems just for placing the company and all other persons in the same position (as nearly as may be) as if the company had not been dissolved or struck off the register.

(4)   The court may also give directions as to—

    (a)   the delivery to the registrar of such documents relating to the company as are necessary to bring up to date the records kept by the registrar,

    (b)   the payment of the costs (in Scotland, expenses) of the registrar in connection with the proceedings for the restoration of the company to the register,

    (c)   where any property or right previously vested in or held on trust for the company has vested as *bona vacantia*, the payment of the costs (in Scotland, expenses) of the Crown representative—

        (i)   in dealing with the property during the period of dissolution, or

        (ii)   in connection with the proceedings on the application.

(5)   In this section the "Crown representative" means—

   (a)   in relation to property vested in the Duchy of Lancaster, the Solicitor to that Duchy;
   (b)   in relation to property vested in the Duke of Cornwall, the Solicitor to the Duchy of Cornwall;
   (c)   in relation to property in Scotland, the Queen's and Lord Treasurer's Remembrancer;
   (d)   in relation to other property, the Treasury Solicitor.

NOTES
Commencement: 1 October 2009.
Commencement (transitional provisions): see the note to s 1029 at **[1.1029]**.

Supplementary provisions

[1.1033]
1033   Company's name on restoration
(1)   A company is restored to the register with the name it had before it was dissolved or struck off the register, subject to the following provisions.
(2)   If at the date of restoration the company could not be registered under its former name without contravening section 66 (name not to be the same as another in the registrar's index of company names), it must be restored to the register—

   (a)   under another name specified—
      (i)   in the case of administrative restoration, in the application to the registrar, or
      (ii)   in the case of restoration under a court order, in the court's order, or
   (b)   as if its registered number was also its name.

References to a company's being registered in a name, and to registration in that context, shall be read as including the company's being restored to the register.
(3)   If a company is restored to the register under a name specified in the application to the registrar, the provisions of—

   section 80 (change of name: registration and issue of new certificate of incorporation), and
   section 81 (change of name: effect),

apply as if the application to the registrar were notice of a change of name.
(4)   If a company is restored to the register under a name specified in the court's order, the provisions of—

   section 80 (change of name: registration and issue of new certificate of incorporation), and
   section 81 (change of name: effect),

apply as if the copy of the court order delivered to the registrar were notice of a change a name.
(5)   If the company is restored to the register as if its registered number was also its name—

   (a)   the company must change its name within 14 days after the date of the restoration,
   (b)   the change may be made by resolution of the directors (without prejudice to any other method of changing the company's name),
   (c)   the company must give notice to the registrar of the change, and
   (d)   sections 80 and 81 apply as regards the registration and effect of the change.

(6)   If the company fails to comply with subsection (5)(a) or (c) an offence is committed by—

   (a)   the company, and
   (b)   every officer of the company who is in default.

(7)   A person guilty of an offence under subsection (6) is liable on summary conviction to a fine not exceeding level 5 on the standard scale and, for continued contravention, a daily default fine not exceeding one-tenth of level 5 on the standard scale.

NOTES
Commencement: 1 October 2009.

[1.1034]
1034   Effect of restoration to the register where property has vested as bona vacantia
(1)   The person in whom any property or right is vested by section 1012 (property of dissolved company to be *bona vacantia*) may dispose of, or of an interest in, that property or right despite the fact that the company may be restored to the register under this Chapter.
(2)   If the company is restored to the register—

   (a)   the restoration does not affect the disposition (but without prejudice to its effect in relation to any other property or right previously vested in or held on trust for the company), and
   (b)   the Crown or, as the case may be, the Duke of Cornwall shall pay to the company an amount equal to—
      (i)   the amount of any consideration received for the property or right or, as the case may be, the interest in it, or
      (ii)   the value of any such consideration at the time of the disposition,

      or, if no consideration was received an amount equal to the value of the property, right or interest disposed of, as at the date of the disposition.

(3)   There may be deducted from the amount payable under subsection (2)(b) the reasonable costs of the Crown representative in connection with the disposition (to the extent that they have not been paid as a condition of administrative restoration or pursuant to a court order for restoration).

(4)   Where a liability accrues under subsection (2) in respect of any property or right which before the restoration of the company to the register had accrued as *bona vacantia* to the Duchy of Lancaster, the Attorney General of that Duchy shall represent Her Majesty in any proceedings arising in connection with that liability.

(5)   Where a liability accrues under subsection (2) in respect of any property or right which before the restoration of the company to the register had accrued as *bona vacantia* to the Duchy of Cornwall, such persons as the Duke of Cornwall (or other possessor for the time being of the Duchy) may appoint shall represent the Duke (or other possessor) in any proceedings arising out of that liability.

(6)   In this section the "Crown representative" means—

    (a)   in relation to property vested in the Duchy of Lancaster, the Solicitor to that Duchy;

    (b)   in relation to property vested in the Duke of Cornwall, the Solicitor to the Duchy of Cornwall;

    (c)   in relation to property in Scotland, the Queen's and Lord Treasurer's Remembrancer;

    (d)   in relation to other property, the Treasury Solicitor.

NOTES

Commencement: 1 October 2009.

Commencement (transitional provisions): Sch 2, para 92 to the Companies Act 2006 (Commencement No 8, Transitional Provisions and Savings) Order 2008, SI 2008/2860 (at **[2.91]**) provides as follows—

"Effect of restoration to the register where property has vested as bona vacantia (s 1034)

92.—(1)   Section 1034 of the Companies Act 2006 (effect of restoration to the register where property has vested as bona vacantia) applies whenever the company was dissolved.

(2)   The following provisions apply where the company was dissolved before 1st October 2009.

(3)   The reference in section 1034(1) to section 1012 (property of dissolved company to be bona vacantia) shall be read as a reference to section 654 of the 1985 Act or Article 605 of the 1986 Order (or corresponding earlier provisions).

(4)   No deduction is to be made under section 1034(3) (deduction of reasonable costs of Crown representative from amount payable to company) from consideration realised before 1st October 2009.".

PART 32
COMPANY INVESTIGATIONS: AMENDMENTS

[1.1035]
1035   Powers of Secretary of State to give directions to inspectors
(This section inserts CA 1985, ss 446A, 446B at **[5.13]**, **[5.14]** *and amends ss 431, 432, 437 and 442 at* **[5.2]**, **[5.3]**, **[5.6]** *and* **[5.9]**.*)*

NOTES

Commencement: 1 October 2007.

Commencement (transitional provisions): Sch 3, para 48 to the Companies Act 2006 (Commencement No 3, Consequential Amendments, Transitional Provisions and Savings) Order 2007, SI 2007/2194 (at **[2.45]**) (as amended by the Companies Act 2006 (Commencement No 6, Saving and Commencement Nos 3 and 5 (Amendment)) Order 2008, SI 2008/674, art 5, Sch 3, para 2(1), (3), as from 6 April 2008) provides as follows—

"48   Company investigations (ss 1035 to 1039)

Sections [1035 to 1037 and 1038(1)] of the Companies Act 2006 (company investigations: amendments) apply where an inspector is appointed under a provision of Part 14 of the 1985 Act on or after 1st October 2007.".

[1.1036]
1036   Resignation, removal and replacement of inspectors
(This section inserts CA 1985, ss 446C, 446D at **[5.15]**, **[5.16]**.*)*

NOTES

Commencement: 1 October 2007.

Commencement (transitional provisions): see the note to s 1035 at **[1.1035]**.

[1.1037]
1037   Power to obtain information from former inspectors etc
(This section inserts CA 1985, s 446E at **[5.17]** *and amends ss 451A and 452 at* **[5.25]** *and* **[5.26]**.*)*

NOTES

Commencement: 1 October 2007.

Commencement (transitional provisions): see the note to s 1035 at **[1.1035]**.

[1.1038]
1038   Power to require production of documents
(This section substitutes CA 1985, ss 434(6) and 447(9) at **[5.4]**, **[5.18]**.*)*

NOTES

Commencement: 1 October 2007.

Commencement (transitional provisions): see the note to s 1035 at **[1.1035]**.

[1.1039]
1039 Disqualification orders: consequential amendments
(This section amends the Company Directors Disqualification Act 1986, s 8(1A) at [5.56].)

NOTES
Commencement: 1 October 2007.

PART 33
UK COMPANIES NOT FORMED UNDER COMPANIES LEGISLATION

CHAPTER 1
COMPANIES NOT FORMED UNDER COMPANIES LEGISLATION BUT AUTHORISED TO REGISTER

[1.1040]
1040 Companies authorised to register under this Act
(1) This section applies to—
   (a) any company that was in existence on 2nd November 1862 (including any company registered under the Joint Stock Companies Acts), and
   (b) any company formed after that date (whether before or after the commencement of this Act)—
      (i) in pursuance of an Act of Parliament other than this Act or any of the former Companies Acts,
      (ii) in pursuance of letters patent, or
      (iii) that is otherwise duly constituted according to law.
(2) Any such company may on making application register under this Act.
(3) Subject to the following provisions, it may register as an unlimited company, as a company limited by shares or as a company limited by guarantee.
(4) A company having the liability of its members limited by Act of Parliament or letters patent—
   (a) may not register under this section unless it is a joint stock company, and
   (b) may not register under this section as an unlimited company or a company limited by guarantee.
(5) A company that is not a joint stock company may not register under this section as a company limited by shares.
(6) The registration of a company under this section is not invalid by reason that it has taken place with a view to the company's being wound up.

NOTES
Commencement: 1 October 2009.
Commencement (transitional provisions): Sch 2, para 93 to the Companies Act 2006 (Commencement No 8, Transitional Provisions and Savings) Order 2008, SI 2008/2860 (at **[2.91]**) provides as follows—

"Registration of companies not formed under companies legislation (ss 1040 to 1042)
93.—(1) The provisions of Chapter 1 of Part 33 of the Companies Act 2006 (registration of companies not formed under companies legislation) apply to applications for registration received by the registrar on or after 1st October 2009.
(2) Any application for registration under those provisions received by the registrar before that date shall not be entertained.
(3) The provisions of Chapter 2 of Part 22 of the 1985 Act or Chapter 2 of Part 22 of the 1986 Order continue to apply to an application for registration if—
   (a) it is received by the registrar, and
   (b) the requirements as to registration are met in relation to it,
before 1st October 2009.
(4) Any application for registration under that Act or Order in relation to which the requirements as to registration are not met before that date shall be treated as withdrawn.
(5) On an application to which sub-paragraph (1) above applies a resolution agreed to, or other thing done, before 1st October 2009 may be relied on for the purpose of meeting the requirements of the Companies Act 2006.
(6) For the purposes of section 1297(3) of the Companies Act 2006 (continuity of the law) as it applies to treat the registration of a company under Chapter 2 of Part 22 of the 1985 Act or Chapter 2 of Part 22 of the 1986 Order as if done under the corresponding provision of the Companies Act 2006, the registration of a company on an application to which sub-paragraph (3) above applies is to be regarded as in force and effective immediately before the commencement of Chapter 1 of Part 33 of the Companies Act 2006.".

Note: as to the registration of a company on an application under this section, see the Companies (Companies Authorised to Register) Regulations 2009, SI 2009/2437 at **[4.605]**.

[1.1041]
1041 Definition of "joint stock company"
(1) For the purposes of section 1040 (companies authorised to register under this Act) "joint stock company" means a company—
   (a) having a permanent paid-up or nominal share capital of fixed amount divided into shares, also of fixed amount, or held and transferable as stock, or divided and held partly in one way and partly in the other, and

(b)   formed on the principle of having for its members the holders of those shares or that stock, and no other persons.

(2)   Such a company when registered with limited liability under this Act is deemed a company limited by shares.

NOTES

Commencement: 1 October 2009.

Commencement (transitional provisions): see the note to s 1040 at **[1.1040]**.

[1.1042]
1042   Power to make provision by regulations

(1)   The Secretary of State may make provision by regulations—

(a)   for and in connection with registration under section 1040 (companies authorised to register under this Act), and

(b)   as to the application to companies so registered of the provisions of the Companies Acts.

(2)   Without prejudice to the generality of that power, regulations under this section may make provision corresponding to any provision formerly made by Chapter 2 of Part 22 of the Companies Act 1985 (c 6).

(3)   Regulations under this section are subject to negative resolution procedure.

NOTES

Commencement: 20 January 2007 (for the purpose of enabling the exercise of powers to make Orders or Regulations by statutory instrument); 1 October 2009 (otherwise).

Commencement (transitional provisions): see the note to s 1040 at **[1.1040]**.

Regulations: the Companies (Companies Authorised to Register) Regulations 2009, SI 2009/2437 at **[4.605]**.

CHAPTER 2
UNREGISTERED COMPANIES

[1.1043]
1043   Unregistered companies

(1)   This section applies to bodies corporate incorporated in and having a principal place of business in the United Kingdom, other than—

(a)   bodies incorporated by, or registered under, a public general Act of Parliament;

(b)   bodies not formed for the purpose of carrying on a business that has for its object the acquisition of gain by the body or its individual members;

(c)   bodies for the time being exempted from this section by direction of the Secretary of State;

(d)   open-ended investment companies.

(2)   The Secretary of State may make provision by regulations applying specified provisions of the Companies Acts to all, or any specified description of, the bodies to which this section applies.

(3)   The regulations may provide that the specified provisions of the Companies Acts apply subject to any specified limitations and to such adaptations and modifications (if any) as may be specified.

(4)   This section does not—

(a)   repeal or revoke in whole or in part any enactment, royal charter or other instrument constituting or regulating any body in relation to which provisions of the Companies Acts are applied by regulations under this section, or

(b)   restrict the power of Her Majesty to grant a charter in lieu or supplementary to any such charter.

But in relation to any such body the operation of any such enactment, charter or instrument is suspended in so far as it is inconsistent with any of those provisions as they apply for the time being to that body.

(5)   In this section "specified" means specified in the regulations.

(6)   Regulations under this section are subject to negative resolution procedure.

NOTES

Commencement: 20 January 2007 (for the purpose of enabling the exercise of powers to make Orders or Regulations by statutory instrument); 6 April 2007 (otherwise).

Regulations: the Unregistered Companies Regulations 2009, SI 2009/2436 at **[4.594]**.

PART 34
OVERSEAS COMPANIES

Introductory

[1.1044]
1044   Overseas companies

In the Companies Acts an "overseas company" means a company incorporated outside the United Kingdom.

NOTES

Commencement: 1 October 2009.

[1.1045]
1045 Company contracts and execution of documents by companies
(1) The Secretary of State may make provision by regulations applying sections 43 to 52 (formalities of doing business and other matters) to overseas companies, subject to such exceptions, adaptations or modifications as may be specified in the regulations.
(2) Regulations under this section are subject to negative resolution procedure.

NOTES

Commencement: 20 January 2007 (for the purpose of enabling the exercise of powers to make Orders or Regulations by statutory instrument); 1 October 2009 (otherwise).

Regulations: the Overseas Companies (Execution of Documents and Registration of Charges) Regulations 2009, SI 2009/1917 at **[4.500]**.

Registration of particulars

[1.1046]
1046 Duty to register particulars
(1) The Secretary of State may make provision by regulations requiring an overseas company—
    (a) to deliver to the registrar for registration a return containing specified particulars, and
    (b) to deliver to the registrar with the return specified documents.
(2) The regulations—
    (a) must, in the case of a company other than a Gibraltar company, require the company to register particulars if the company opens a branch in the United Kingdom, and
    (b) may, in the case of a Gibraltar company, require the company to register particulars if the company opens a branch in the United Kingdom, and
    (c) may, in any case, require the registration of particulars in such other circumstances as may be specified.
(3) In subsection (2)—
    "branch" means a branch within the meaning of the Eleventh Company Law Directive (89/666/EEC);
    "Gibraltar company" means a company incorporated in Gibraltar.
(4) The regulations may provide that where a company has registered particulars under this section and any alteration is made—
    (a) in the specified particulars, or
    (b) in any document delivered with the return,
the company must deliver to the registrar for registration a return containing specified particulars of the alteration.
(5) The regulations may make provision—
    (a) requiring the return under this section to be delivered for registration to the registrar for a specified part of the United Kingdom, and
    (b) requiring it to be so delivered before the end of a specified period.
(6) The regulations may make different provision according to—
    (a) the place where the company is incorporated, and
    (b) the activities carried on (or proposed to be carried on) by it.
This is without prejudice to the general power to make different provision for different cases.
(7) In this section "specified" means specified in the regulations.
(8) Regulations under this section are subject to affirmative resolution procedure.

NOTES

Commencement: 20 January 2007 (for the purpose of enabling the exercise of powers to make Orders or Regulations by statutory instrument); 1 October 2009 (otherwise).

Regulations: the Overseas Companies Regulations 2009, SI 2009/1801 at **[4.389]**.

[1.1047]
1047 Registered name of overseas company
(1) Regulations under section 1046 (duty to register particulars) must require an overseas company that is required to register particulars to register its name.
(2) This may be—
    (a) the company's corporate name (that is, its name under the law of the country or territory in which it is incorporated) or
    (b) an alternative name specified in accordance with section 1048.
(3) Subject only to subsection (5), an EEA company may always register its corporate name.
(4) In any other case, the following provisions of Part 5 (a company's name) apply in relation to the registration of the name of an overseas company—
    (a) section 53 (prohibited names);
    (b) sections 54 to 56 (sensitive words and expressions);
    (c) section 65 (inappropriate use of indications of company type or legal form);
    (d) sections 66 to 74 (similarity to other names);
    (e) section 75 (provision of misleading information etc);
    (f) section 76 (misleading indication of activities).
(5) The provisions of section 57 (permitted characters etc) apply in every case.

(6)   Any reference in the provisions mentioned in subsection (4) or (5) to a change of name shall be read as a reference to registration of a different name under section 1048.

NOTES
Commencement: 1 October 2009.
Regulations: the Overseas Companies Regulations 2009, SI 2009/1801 at **[4.389]**.

[1.1048]
1048   Registration under alternative name
(1)   An overseas company that is required to register particulars under section 1046 may at any time deliver to the registrar for registration a statement specifying a name, other than its corporate name, under which it proposes to carry on business in the United Kingdom.
(2)   An overseas company that has registered an alternative name may at any time deliver to the registrar of companies for registration a statement specifying a different name under which it proposes to carry on business in the United Kingdom (which may be its corporate name or a further alternative) in substitution for the name previously registered.
(3)   The alternative name for the time being registered under this section is treated for all purposes of the law applying in the United Kingdom as the company's corporate name.
(4)   This does not—
  (a)   affect the references in this section or section 1047 to the company's corporate name,
  (b)   affect any rights or obligation of the company, or
  (c)   render defective any legal proceedings by or against the company.
(5)   Any legal proceedings that might have been continued or commenced against the company by its corporate name, or any name previously registered under this section, may be continued or commenced against it by its name for the time being so registered.

NOTES
Commencement: 1 October 2009.

Other requirements

[1.1049]
1049   Accounts and reports: general
(1)   The Secretary of State may make provision by regulations requiring an overseas company that is required to register particulars under section 1046—
  (a)   to prepare the like accounts and directors' report, and
  (b)   to cause to be prepared such an auditor's report,
as would be required if the company were formed and registered under this Act.
(2)   The regulations may for this purpose apply, with or without modifications, all or any of the provisions of—
    Part 15 (accounts and reports), and
    Part 16 (audit).
(3)   The Secretary of State may make provision by regulations requiring an overseas company to deliver to the registrar copies of—
  (a)   the accounts and reports prepared in accordance with the regulations, or
  (b)   the accounts and reports that it is required to prepare and have audited under the law of the country in which it is incorporated.
(4)   Regulations under this section are subject to negative resolution procedure.

NOTES
Commencement: 20 January 2007 (for the purpose of enabling the exercise of powers to make Orders or Regulations by statutory instrument); 1 October 2009 (otherwise).
Regulations: the Overseas Companies Regulations 2009, SI 2009/1801 at **[4.389]**.

[1.1050]
1050   Accounts and reports: credit or financial institutions
(1)   This section applies to a credit or financial institution—
  (a)   that is incorporated or otherwise formed outside the United Kingdom and Gibraltar,
  (b)   whose head office is outside the United Kingdom and Gibraltar, and
  (c)   that has a branch in the United Kingdom.
(2)   In subsection (1) "branch" means a place of business that forms a legally dependent part of the institution and conducts directly all or some of the operations inherent in its business.
(3)   The Secretary of State may make provision by regulations requiring an institution to which this section applies—
  (a)   to prepare the like accounts and directors' report, and
  (b)   to cause to be prepared such an auditor's report,
as would be required if the institution were a company formed and registered under this Act.
(4)   The regulations may for this purpose apply, with or without modifications, all or any of the provisions of—
    Part 15 (accounts and reports), and
    Part 16 (audit).

(5)   The Secretary of State may make provision by regulations requiring an institution to which this section applies to deliver to the registrar copies of—
  (a)   accounts and reports prepared in accordance with the regulations, or
  (b)   accounts and reports that it is required to prepare and have audited under the law of the country in which the institution has its head office.
(6)   Regulations under this section are subject to negative resolution procedure.

NOTES
Commencement: 20 January 2007 (for the purpose of enabling the exercise of powers to make Orders or Regulations by statutory instrument); 1 October 2009 (otherwise).
Regulations: the Overseas Companies Regulations 2009, SI 2009/1801 at **[4.389]**.

[1.1051]
1051   Trading disclosures
(1)   The Secretary of State may by regulations make provision requiring overseas companies carrying on business in the United Kingdom—
  (a)   to display specified information in specified locations,
  (b)   to state specified information in specified descriptions of document or communication, and
  (c)   to provide specified information on request to those they deal with in the course of their business.
(2)   The regulations—
  (a)   shall in every case require a company that has registered particulars under section 1046 to disclose the name registered by it under section 1047, and
  (b)   may make provision as to the manner in which any specified information is to be displayed, stated or provided.
(3)   The regulations may make provision corresponding to that made by—
  section 83 (civil consequences of failure to make required disclosure), and
  section 84 (criminal consequences of failure to make required disclosure).
(4)   In this section "specified" means specified in the regulations.
(5)   Regulations under this section are subject to affirmative resolution procedure.

NOTES
Commencement: 20 January 2007 (for the purpose of enabling the exercise of powers to make Orders or Regulations by statutory instrument); 1 October 2009 (otherwise).
Regulations: the Overseas Companies Regulations 2009, SI 2009/1801 at **[4.389]**.

[1.1052]
1052   Company charges
(1)   The Secretary of State may by regulations make provision about the registration of specified charges over property in the United Kingdom of a registered overseas company.
(2)   The power in subsection (1) includes power to make provision about—
  (a)   a registered overseas company that—
    (i)   has particulars registered in more than one part of the United Kingdom;
    (ii)   has property in more than one part of the United Kingdom;
  (b)   the circumstances in which property is to be regarded, for the purposes of the regulations, as being, or not being, in the United Kingdom or in a particular part of the United Kingdom;
  (c)   the keeping by a registered overseas company of records and registers about specified charges and their inspection;
  (d)   the consequences of a failure to register a charge in accordance with the regulations;
  (e)   the circumstances in which a registered overseas company ceases to be subject to the regulations.
(3)   The regulations may for this purpose apply, with or without modifications, any of the provisions of Part 25 (company charges).
(4)   The regulations may modify any reference in an enactment to Part 25, or to a particular provision of that Part, so as to include a reference to the regulations or to a specified provision of the regulations.
(5)   Regulations under this section are subject to negative resolution procedure.
(6)   In this section—
  "registered overseas company" means an overseas company that has registered particulars under section 1046(1), and
  "specified" means specified in the regulations.

NOTES
Commencement: 20 January 2007 (for the purpose of enabling the exercise of powers to make Orders or Regulations by statutory instrument); 1 October 2009 (otherwise).
Regulations: the Overseas Companies (Execution of Documents and Registration of Charges) Regulations 2009, SI 2009/1917 at **[4.500]**.

[1.1053]
1053 Other returns etc

(1) This section applies to overseas companies that are required to register particulars under section 1046.

(2) The Secretary of State may make provision by regulations requiring the delivery to the registrar of returns—

    (a) by a company to which this section applies that—

        (i) is being wound up, or

        (ii) becomes or ceases to be subject to insolvency proceedings, or an arrangement or composition or any analogous proceedings;

    (b) by the liquidator of a company to which this section applies.

(3) The regulations may specify—

    (a) the circumstances in which a return is to be made,

    (b) the particulars to be given in it, and

    (c) the period within which it is to be made.

(4) The Secretary of State may make provision by regulations requiring notice to be given to the registrar of the appointment in relation to a company to which this section applies of a judicial factor (in Scotland).

(5) The regulations may include provision corresponding to any provision made by section 1154 of this Act (duty to notify registrar of certain appointments).

(6) Regulations under this section are subject to affirmative resolution procedure.

NOTES

Commencement: 20 January 2007 (for the purpose of enabling the exercise of powers to make Orders or Regulations by statutory instrument); 1 October 2009 (otherwise).

Regulations: the Overseas Companies Regulations 2009, SI 2009/1801 at **[4.389]**.

Supplementary

[1.1054]
1054 Offences

(1) Regulations under this Part may specify the person or persons responsible for complying with any specified requirement of the regulations.

(2) Regulations under this Part may make provision for offences, including provision as to—

    (a) the person or persons liable in the case of any specified contravention of the regulations, and

    (b) circumstances that are, or are not, to be a defence on a charge of such an offence.

(3) The regulations must not provide—

    (a) for imprisonment, or

    (b) for the imposition on summary conviction of a fine exceeding level 5 on the standard scale and, for continued contravention, a daily default fine not exceeding one-tenth of level 5 on the standard scale.

(4) In this section "specified" means specified in the regulations.

NOTES

Commencement: 20 January 2007 (for the purpose of enabling the exercise of powers to make Orders or Regulations by statutory instrument); 1 October 2009 (otherwise).

Regulations: the Overseas Companies Regulations 2009, SI 2009/1801 at **[4.389]**.

[1.1055]
1055 Disclosure of individual's residential address: protection from disclosure

Where regulations under section 1046 (overseas companies: duty to register particulars) require an overseas company to register particulars of an individual's usual residential address, they must contain provision corresponding to that made by Chapter 8 of Part 10 (directors' residential addresses: protection from disclosure).

NOTES

Commencement: 20 January 2007 (for the purpose of enabling the exercise of powers to make Orders or Regulations by statutory instrument); 1 October 2009 (otherwise).

Regulations under s 1046: see that section at **[1.1046]**.

[1.1056]
1056 Requirement to identify persons authorised to accept service of documents

Regulations under section 1046 (overseas companies: duty to register particulars) must require an overseas company to register—

    (a) particulars identifying every person resident in the United Kingdom authorised to accept service of documents on behalf of the company, or

    (b) a statement that there is no such person.

NOTES

Commencement: 20 January 2007 (for the purpose of enabling the exercise of powers to make Orders or Regulations by statutory instrument); 1 October 2009 (otherwise).

Regulations under s 1046: see that section at **[1.1046]**.

[1.1057]
1057 Registrar to whom returns, notices etc to be delivered

(1) This section applies to an overseas company that is required to register or has registered particulars under section 1046 in more than one part of the United Kingdom.

(2) The Secretary of State may provide by regulations that, in the case of such a company, anything authorised or required to be delivered to the registrar under this Part is to be delivered—

(a) to the registrar for each part of the United Kingdom in which the company is required to register or has registered particulars, or

(b) to the registrar for such part or parts of the United Kingdom as may be specified in or determined in accordance with the regulations.

(3) Regulations under this section are subject to negative resolution procedure.

NOTES

Commencement: 20 January 2007 (for the purpose of enabling the exercise of powers to make Orders or Regulations by statutory instrument); 1 October 2009 (otherwise).

[1.1058]
1058 Duty to give notice of ceasing to have registrable presence

(1) The Secretary of State may make provision by regulations requiring an overseas company—

(a) if it has registered particulars following the opening of a branch, in accordance with regulations under section 1046(2)(a) or (b), to give notice to the registrar if it closes that branch;

(b) if it has registered particulars in other circumstances, in accordance with regulations under section 1046(2)(c), to give notice to the registrar if the circumstances that gave rise to the obligation to register particulars cease to obtain.

(2) The regulations must provide for the notice to be given to the registrar for the part of the United Kingdom to which the original return of particulars was delivered.

(3) The regulations may specify the period within which notice must be given.

(4) Regulations under this section are subject to negative resolution procedure.

NOTES

Commencement: 20 January 2007 (for the purpose of enabling the exercise of powers to make Orders or Regulations by statutory instrument); 1 October 2009 (otherwise).

Regulations: the Overseas Companies Regulations 2009, SI 2009/1801 at **[4.389]**.

[1.1059]
1059 Application of provisions in case of relocation of branch

For the purposes of this Part—

(a) the relocation of a branch from one part of the United Kingdom to another counts as the closing of one branch and the opening of another;

(b) the relocation of a branch within the same part of the United Kingdom does not.

NOTES

Commencement: 1 October 2009.

PART 35
THE REGISTRAR OF COMPANIES

[Scheme of this Part]

[1.1059A]
1059A Scheme of this Part

(1) The scheme of this Part is as follows.

(2) The following provisions apply generally (to the registrar, to any functions of the registrar, or to documents delivered to or issued by the registrar under any enactment, as the case may be)—

sections 1060(1) and (2) and 1061 to 1063 (the registrar),

sections 1068 to 1071 (delivery of documents to the registrar),

sections 1072 to 1076 (requirements for proper delivery),

sections 1080(1), (4) and (5) and 1092 (keeping and production of records),

section 1083 (preservation of original documents),

sections 1108 to 1110 (language requirements: transliteration),

sections 1111 and 1114 to 1119 (supplementary provisions).

(3) The following provisions apply in relation to companies (to companies or for the purposes of the Companies Acts, as the case may be)—

section 1060(3) and (4) (references to the registrar in the Companies Acts),

sections 1064 and 1065 (certificates of incorporation),
section 1066 (companies' registered numbers),
sections 1077 to 1079 (public notice of receipt of certain documents),
sections 1080(2) and (3), 1081, 1082 and 1084 (the register),
sections 1085 to 1091 (inspection of the register),
sections 1093 to 1098 (correction or removal of material on the register),
section 1106 (voluntary filing of translations),
sections 1112 and 1113 (supplementary provisions).
(4)   The following provisions apply as indicated in the provisions concerned—
section 1067 (registered numbers of UK establishments of overseas companies),
sections 1099 to 1101 (the registrar's index of company names),
sections 1102 to 1105 and 1107 (language requirements: translation).
(5)   Unless the context otherwise requires, the provisions of this Part apply to an overseas company as they apply to a company as defined in section 1.]

NOTES
Commencement: 1 October 2009.
Inserted, together with the preceding heading, by the Companies Act 2006 (Part 35) (Consequential Amendments, Transitional Provisions and Savings) Order 2009, SI 2009/1802, arts 2, 3, as from 1 October 2009.

The registrar

[1.1060]
1060   The registrar
(1)   There shall continue to be—
   (a)   a registrar of companies for England and Wales,
   (b)   a registrar of companies for Scotland, and
   (c)   a registrar of companies for Northern Ireland.
(2)   The registrars shall be appointed by the Secretary of State.
(3)   In the Companies Acts "the registrar of companies" and "the registrar" mean the registrar of companies for England and Wales, Scotland or Northern Ireland, as the case may require.
(4)   References in the Companies Acts to registration in a particular part of the United Kingdom are to registration by the registrar for that part of the United Kingdom.

NOTES
Commencement: 6 April 2007 (certain purposes); 1 October 2009 (otherwise) (see the note below).
Commencement (note): the Companies Act 2006 (Commencement No 1, Transitional Provisions and Savings) Order 2006, SI 2006/3428, art 4(3) provides that this section shall come into force on 6 April 2007 so far as is necessary for the purposes of the provisions of this Act brought into force on that date by art 4(1), (2) of that Order (see **[2.4]**).

[1.1061]
1061   The registrar's functions
(1)   The registrar shall continue—
   [(a)   to perform the functions conferred on the registrar by or under the Companies Acts or any other enactment, and]
   (b)   to perform such functions on behalf of the Secretary of State, in relation to the registration of companies or other matters, as the Secretary of State may from time to time direct.
(2)   . . .
(3)   References in this Act to the functions of the registrar are to functions within subsection (1)(a) or (b).

NOTES
Commencement: 6 April 2007 (certain purposes); 1 October 2009 (otherwise) (see the note below).
Commencement (note): the Companies Act 2006 (Commencement No 1, Transitional Provisions and Savings) Order 2006, SI 2006/3428, art 4(3) provides that this section shall come into force on 6 April 2007 so far as is necessary for the purposes of the provisions of this Act brought into force on that date by art 4(1), (2) of that Order (see **[2.4]**).
Sub-s (1): para (a) substituted by the Companies Act 2006 (Part 35) (Consequential Amendments, Transitional Provisions and Savings) Order 2009, SI 2009/1802, arts 2, 4(a), as from 1 October 2009.
Sub-s (2): repealed by SI 2009/1802, arts 2, 4(b), as from 1 October 2009.

[1.1062]
1062   The registrar's official seal
The registrar shall have an official seal for the authentication of documents in connection with the performance of the registrar's functions.

NOTES
Commencement: 1 October 2009.

[1.1063]
1063   Fees payable to registrar
(1)   The Secretary of State may make provision by regulations requiring the payment to the registrar of fees in respect of—

(a)   the performance of any of the registrar's functions, or

(b)   the provision by the registrar of services or facilities for purposes incidental to, or otherwise connected with, the performance of any of the registrar's functions.

(2)   The matters for which fees may be charged include—

(a)   the performance of a duty imposed on the registrar or the Secretary of State,

(b)   the receipt of documents delivered to the registrar, and

(c)   the inspection, or provision of copies, of documents kept by the registrar.

(3)   The regulations may—

(a)   provide for the amount of the fees to be fixed by or determined under the regulations;

(b)   provide for different fees to be payable in respect of the same matter in different circumstances;

(c)   specify the person by whom any fee payable under the regulations is to be paid;

(d)   specify when and how fees are to be paid.

(4)   Regulations under this section are subject to negative resolution procedure.

(5)   In respect of the performance of functions or the provision of services or facilities—

(a)   for which fees are not provided for by regulations, or

(b)   in circumstances other than those for which fees are provided for by regulations,

the registrar may determine from time to time what fees (if any) are chargeable.

(6)   Fees received by the registrar are to be paid into the Consolidated Fund.

(7)   *(Amends the Limited Partnerships Act 1907, ss 16, 17 at* **[9.70]**, **[9.71]**.*)*

NOTES

Commencement: 20 January 2007 (for the purpose of enabling the exercise of powers to make Orders or Regulations by statutory instrument); 6 April 2007 (otherwise (except in relation to Northern Ireland)); 1 October 2009 (all remaining purposes).

Commencement (transitional provisions): the Companies Act 2006 (Commencement No 1, Transitional Provisions and Savings) Order 2006, SI 2006/3428, Sch 5, Pt 3, para 6(1), (2) at **[2.15]** (as amended by the Registrar of Companies (Fees) (Limited Partnerships and Newspaper Proprietors) Regulations 2009, SI 2009/2392, reg 7, as from 1 October 2009)) provides as follows—

"6   Saving for existing provisions relating to fees

(1)   The coming into force of section 1063 of the Companies Act 2006 (fees payable to the registrar) does not affect the continued operation of any other provision under which the payment of fees to the registrar of companies may be required until—

(a)   the coming into force of the repeal of the other provision; or

(b)   the exercise of the power in section 1063 in a manner inconsistent with its continued operation.

(2)   . . . "

Note that para 6(2) previously provided that notwithstanding the coming into force of the repeals in s 16 of the Limited Partnerships Act 1907 and the repeal of s 17(a) of that Act, the fees appointed under the said s 16 and having effect immediately before 6 April 2007 shall continue to be payable, and the rules in force under the said s 17(a) immediately before 6 April 2007 shall continue to have effect. This paragraph was revoked as noted above but subject to transitional provisions in reg 6 of the 2009 Regulations (See **[4.566]**).

Commencement (note): the commencement of this section on 6 April 2007 by SI 2006/3428 does not extend to Northern Ireland (see art 4(4) of that Order at **[2.4]**).

Transitional provisions (existing Regulations): the Companies Act 2006 (Commencement No 8, Transitional Provisions and Savings) Order 2008, SI 2008/2860, Sch 2, para 94 (fees payable to registrar) at **[2.91]** provides that any Regulations under s 708 of the 1985 Act (fees payable to registrar) that are in force immediately before 1 October 2009 have effect on or after that date as if made under this section (see the Open-Ended Investment Companies (Investment Companies with Variable Capital) (Fees) Regulations 1998, SI 1998/3087, and the Companies (Fees) Regulations 2004, SI 2004/2621). Note also that the Limited Liability Partnerships (Application of Companies Act 2006) Regulations 2009, SI 2009/1804, Sch 1, Pt 9, para 36 at **[10.1189]** provides that any Regulations made s 708 of the 1985 Act (as it applies to LLPs) that are in force immediately before that date also have effect, on or after that date, as if made under this section (see the Limited Liability Partnerships (Fees) Regulations 2004, SI 2004/2620).

Regulations: the Registrar of Companies (Fees) (Companies, Overseas Companies and Limited Liability Partnerships) Regulations 2009, SI 2009/2101 at **[4.543]**; the Registrar of Companies (Fees) (Limited Partnerships and Newspaper Proprietors) Regulations 2009, SI 2009/2392 at **[4.566]**; the Registrar of Companies (Fees) (European Economic Interest Grouping and European Public Limited-Liability Company) Regulations 2009, SI 2009/2403 at **[4.577]**; the Registrar of Companies (Fees) (Amendment) Regulations 2009, SI 2009/2439; the Registrar of Companies (Fees) (Companies, Overseas Companies and Limited Liability Partnerships) (Amendment) Regulations 2011, SI 2011/309; the Registrar of Companies (Fees) (Limited Partnerships) (Amendment) Regulations 2011, SI 2011/319; the Registrar of Companies (Fees) (European Economic Interest Grouping) (Amendment) Regulations 2011, SI 2011/324. See also the note above.

Certificates of incorporation

[1.1064]

1064   Public notice of issue of certificate of incorporation

(1)   The registrar must cause to be published—

(a)   in the Gazette, or

(b)   in accordance with section 1116 (alternative means of giving public notice),

notice of the issue by the registrar of any certificate of incorporation of a company.

(2)   The notice must state the name and registered number of the company and the date of issue of the certificate.

(3)   This section applies to a certificate of incorporation issued under—

(a)   section 80 (change of name),

(b)   section 88 (Welsh companies), or

(c)   any provision of Part 7 (re-registration),

as well as to the certificate issued on a company's formation.

NOTES

Commencement: 1 October 2009.

Commencement (transitional provisions): the Companies Act 2006 (Commencement No 8, Transitional Provisions and Savings) Order 2008, SI 2008/2860, Sch 2, para 95 (at **[2.91]**) provides that this section applies (a) to certificates of incorporation issued under this Act, and (b) to certificates of incorporation issued under the 1985 Act on or after 1 October 2009.

[1.1065]

1065   Right to certificate of incorporation

Any person may require the registrar to provide him with a copy of any certificate of incorporation of a company, signed by the registrar or authenticated by the registrar's seal.

NOTES

Commencement: 1 October 2009.

Commencement (transitional provisions): the Companies Act 2006 (Commencement No 8, Transitional Provisions and Savings) Order 2008, SI 2008/2860, Sch 2, para 96 (at **[2.91]**) provides that this section applies to certificates of incorporation whenever issued.

Registered numbers

[1.1066]

1066   Company's registered numbers

(1)   The registrar shall allocate to every company a number, which shall be known as the company's registered number.

(2)   Companies' registered numbers shall be in such form, consisting of one or more sequences of figures or letters, as the registrar may determine.

(3)   The registrar may on adopting a new form of registered number make such changes of existing registered numbers as appear necessary.

(4)   A change of a company's registered number has effect from the date on which the company is notified by the registrar of the change.

(5)   For a period of three years beginning with that date any requirement to disclose the company's registered number imposed by regulations under section 82 or section 1051 (trading disclosures) is satisfied by the use of either the old number or the new.

(6)   In this section "company" includes an overseas company whose particulars have been registered under section 1046, other than a company that appears to the registrar not to be required to register particulars under that section.

NOTES

Commencement: 1 October 2009.

[1.1067]

1067   Registered numbers of [UK establishments] of overseas company

(1)   The registrar shall allocate to every [UK establishment] of an overseas company whose particulars are registered under section 1046 a number, which shall be known as [the UK establishment's registered number].

(2)   [The registered numbers of UK establishments of overseas companies] shall be in such form, consisting of one or more sequences of figures or letters, as the registrar may determine.

(3)   The registrar may on adopting a new form of registered number make such changes of existing registered numbers as appear necessary.

(4)   A change of [the registered number of a UK establishment] has effect from the date on which the company is notified by the registrar of the change.

(5)   For a period of three years beginning with that date any requirement to disclose [the UK establishment's registered number] imposed by regulations under section 1051 (trading disclosures) is satisfied by the use of either the old number or the new.

[(6)   In this Part "establishment", in relation to an overseas company, means—

(a)   a branch within the meaning of the Eleventh Company Law Directive (89/666/EEC), or

(b)   a place of business that is not such a branch,

and "UK establishment" means an establishment in the United Kingdom.]

NOTES

Commencement: 1 October 2009.

Section heading, sub-ss (1), (2), (4), (5) words in square brackets substituted by the Companies Act 2006 (Part 35) (Consequential Amendments, Transitional Provisions and Savings) Order 2009, SI 2009/1802, arts 2, 5(a)–(e), as from 1 October 2009.

Sub-s (6): added by SI 2009/1802, arts 2, 5(f), as from 1 October 2009.

Delivery of documents to the registrar

[1.1068]

1068 Registrar's requirements as to form, authentication and manner of delivery

(1)   The registrar may impose requirements as to the form, authentication and manner of delivery of documents required or authorised to be delivered to the registrar under any enactment.

(2)   As regards the form of the document, the registrar may—

(a)   require the contents of the document to be in a standard form;

(b)   impose requirements for the purpose of enabling the document to be scanned or copied.

(3)   As regards authentication, the registrar may—

(a)   require the document to be authenticated by a particular person or a person of a particular description;

(b)   specify the means of authentication;

[(c)   require the document to contain or be accompanied by the name or registered number (or both) of the company (or other body) to which it relates.]

(4)   As regards the manner of delivery, the registrar may specify requirements as to—

(a)   the physical form of the document (for example, hard copy or electronic form);

(b)   the means to be used for delivering the document (for example, by post or electronic means);

(c)   the address to which the document is to be sent;

(d)   in the case of a document to be delivered by electronic means, the hardware and software to be used, and technical specifications (for example, matters relating to protocol, security, anti-virus protection or encryption).

(5)   The registrar must secure that as from 1st January 2007 all documents subject to the Directive disclosure requirements (see section 1078) may be delivered to the registrar by electronic means.

(6)   The power conferred by this section does not authorise the registrar to require documents to be delivered by electronic means (see section 1069).

(7)   Requirements imposed under this section must not be inconsistent with requirements imposed by any enactment with respect to the form, authentication or manner of delivery of the document concerned.

NOTES

Commencement: 1 January 2007 (sub-s (5), and sub-ss (1)–(4), (6), (7) for certain purposes); 15 December 2007 (sub-ss (1)–(4), (6), (7) for certain purposes); 1 October 2009 (otherwise) (see the notes below).

Commencement (transitional provisions): Sch 2, para 97 to the Companies Act 2006 (Commencement No 8, Transitional Provisions and Savings) Order 2008, SI 2008/2860 (at **[2.91]**) provides as follows. Note that the paragraph set out below is as it has effect following its substitution by the Companies Act 2006 (Part 35) (Consequential Amendments, Transitional Provisions and Savings) Order 2009, SI 2009/1802, art 18, Schedule, with effect from 1 October 2009—

"97.—(1)   Sections 1068 and 1069 of the Companies Act 2006 (registrar's requirements as to form, authentication and manner of delivery and power to require delivery by electronic means) apply to documents delivered to the registrar on or after 1st October 2009 other than those delivered in pursuance of an obligation arising before that date.

(2)   Where the obligation to deliver a document to the registrar arose before 1st October 2009, the provisions that would have applied if the document had been delivered before that date continue to apply.".

Commencement (transitional provisions): various transitional provisions contained in commencement orders made under s 1300 of this Act provide that until this section comes into force, the notice/form etc required for the purposes of this Act is the notice/form etc required for the purposes of the equivalent provision of the Companies Act 1985 or the Companies (Northern Ireland) Order 1986; see the Companies Act 2006 (Commencement No 3, Consequential Amendments, Transitional Provisions and Savings) Order 2007, SI 2007/2194, Sch 3 at **[2.45]**, and the Companies Act 2006 (Commencement No 5, Transitional Provisions and Savings) Order 2007, SI 2007/3495, art 9, Sch 4, Pt 1 at **[2.58]**, **[2.66]**.

Commencement (note): the Companies Act 2006 (Commencement No 1, Transitional Provisions and Savings) Order 2006, SI 2006/3428, art 2(2) provides that that sub-ss (1)–(4), (6), (7) shall come into force on 1 January 2007 so far as is necessary for the purposes of the provisions of this Act brought into force on that date by art 2(1) of that Order (see **[2.2]**).

Commencement (note): the Companies Act 2006 (Commencement No 3, Consequential Amendments, Transitional Provisions and Savings) Order 2007, SI 2007/2194, art 4(1) (as amended by the Companies (Cross-Border Mergers) Regulations 2007, SI 2007/2974, reg 4(5), as from 15 December 2007) provides that sub-ss (1)–(4), (6), (7) shall come into force on 15 December 2007 so far as necessary for the purposes of the Companies (Cross-Border Mergers) Regulations 2007 (see **[2.34]**).

Sub-s (3): para (c) substituted by the Companies Act 2006 (Part 35) (Consequential Amendments, Transitional Provisions and Savings) Order 2009, SI 2009/1802, arts 2, 6, as from 1 October 2009.

[1.1069]

1069 Power to require delivery by electronic means

(1)   The Secretary of State may make regulations requiring documents that are authorised or required to be delivered to the registrar to be delivered by electronic means.

(2)   Any such requirement to deliver documents by electronic means is effective only if registrar's rules have been published with respect to the detailed requirements for such delivery.

(3)   Regulations under this section are subject to affirmative resolution procedure.

NOTES

Commencement: 20 January 2007 (for the purpose of enabling the exercise of powers to make Orders or Regulations by statutory instrument); 1 October 2009 (otherwise).

Commencement (transitional provisions): see the note to s 1068 at **[1.1068]**.

[1.1070]
1070 Agreement for delivery by electronic means
(1) The registrar may agree with a company [(or other body)] that documents relating to the company [(or other body)] that are required or authorised to be delivered to the registrar—
  (a) will be delivered by electronic means, except as provided for in the agreement, and
  (b) will conform to such requirements as may be specified in the agreement or specified by the registrar in accordance with the agreement.
(2) An agreement under this section may relate to all or any description of documents to be delivered to the registrar.
(3) Documents in relation to which an agreement is in force under this section must be delivered in accordance with the agreement.

NOTES
Commencement: 1 October 2009.
Commencement (transitional provisions): the Companies Act 2006 (Commencement No 8, Transitional Provisions and Savings) Order 2008, SI 2008/2860, Sch 2, para 98 at **[2.91]** (as substituted by the Companies Act 2006 (Part 35) (Consequential Amendments, Transitional Provisions and Savings) Order 2009, SI 2009/1802, art 18, Schedule, with effect from 1 October 2009) provides that this section applies to all documents delivered to the registrar on or after 1 October 2009.
Sub-s (1): words in square brackets inserted by the Companies Act 2006 (Part 35) (Consequential Amendments, Transitional Provisions and Savings) Order 2009, SI 2009/1802, arts 2, 7, as from 1 October 2009.

[1.1071]
1071 Document not delivered until received
(1) A document is not delivered to the registrar until it is received by the registrar.
(2) Provision may be made by registrar's rules as to when a document is to be regarded as received.

NOTES
Commencement: 1 October 2009.
Commencement (transitional provisions): Sch 2, para 99 to the Companies Act 2006 (Commencement No 8, Transitional Provisions and Savings) Order 2008, SI 2008/2860 (at **[2.91]**) provides as follows. Note that the paragraph set out below is as it has effect following its substitution by the Companies Act 2006 (Part 35) (Consequential Amendments, Transitional Provisions and Savings) Order 2009, SI 2009/1802, art 18, Schedule, with effect from 1 October 2009—

"99.—(1) Section 1071 of the Companies Act 2006 (document not delivered until received) applies in relation to the delivery of documents to the registrar on or after 1st October 2009 other than those delivered in pursuance of an obligation arising before that date.
(2) Where the obligation to deliver a document to the registrar arose before 1st October 2009, the provisions that would have applied if the document had been delivered before that date continue to apply".

Requirements for proper delivery

[1.1072]
1072 Requirements for proper delivery
(1) A document delivered to the registrar is not properly delivered unless all the following requirements are met—
  (a) the requirements of the provision under which the document is to be delivered to the registrar as regards—
    (i) the contents of the document, and
    (ii) form, authentication and manner of delivery;
  (b) any applicable requirements under—
    section 1068 (registrar's requirements as to form, authentication and manner of delivery),
    section 1069 (power to require delivery by electronic means), or
    section 1070 (agreement for delivery by electronic means);
  (c) any requirements of this Part as to the language in which the document is drawn up and delivered or as to its being accompanied on delivery by a certified translation into English;
  (d) in so far as it consists of or includes names and addresses, any requirements of this Part as to permitted characters, letters or symbols or as to its being accompanied on delivery by a certificate as to the transliteration of any element;
  (e) any applicable requirements under section 1111 (registrar's requirements as to certification or verification);
  (f) any requirement of regulations under section 1082 (use of unique identifiers);
  (g) any requirements as regards payment of a fee in respect of its receipt by the registrar.
(2) A document that is not properly delivered is treated for the purposes of the provision requiring or authorising it to be delivered as not having been delivered, subject to the provisions of section 1073 (power to accept documents not meeting requirements for proper delivery).

NOTES
Commencement: 1 October 2009.
Commencement (transitional provisions): Sch 2, para 100 to the Companies Act 2006 (Commencement No 8, Transitional Provisions and Savings) Order 2008, SI 2008/2860 (at **[2.91]**) provides as follows. Note that the paragraph set out below is as it has effect following its substitution by the Companies Act 2006 (Part 35) (Consequential Amendments, Transitional Provisions and Savings) Order 2009, SI 2009/1802, art 18, Schedule, with effect from 1 October 2009—

"100.—(1)   Sections 1072 to 1074 of the Companies Act 2006 (requirements for proper delivery) apply to documents delivered to the registrar on or after 1st October 2009 other than those delivered in pursuance of an obligation arising before that date.

(2)   Where the obligation to deliver a document to the registrar arose before 1st October 2009, the provisions that would have applied if the document had been delivered before that date (and the registrar's former practice with respect to the requirements for proper delivery and documents containing unnecessary material) continue to apply.".

[1.1073]
1073   Power to accept documents not meeting requirements for proper delivery
(1)   The registrar may accept (and register) a document that does not comply with the requirements for proper delivery.
(2)   A document accepted by the registrar under this section is treated as received by the registrar for the purposes of section 1077 (public notice of receipt of certain documents).
(3)   No objection may be taken to the legal consequences of a document's being accepted (or registered) by the registrar under this section on the ground that the requirements for proper delivery were not met.
(4)   The acceptance of a document by the registrar under this section does not affect—
   (a)   the continuing obligation to comply with the requirements for proper delivery, or
   (b)   subject as follows, any liability for failure to comply with those requirements.
(5)   For the purposes of—
   (a)   section 453 (civil penalty for failure to file accounts and reports), and
   (b)   any enactment imposing a daily default fine for failure to deliver the document,
the period after the document is accepted does not count as a period during which there is default in complying with the requirements for proper delivery.
(6)   But if, subsequently—
   (a)   the registrar issues a notice under section 1094(4) in respect of the document (notice of administrative removal from the register), and
   (b)   the requirements for proper delivery are not complied with before the end of the period of 14 days after the issue of that notice,
any subsequent period of default does count for the purposes of those provisions.

NOTES
Commencement: 1 October 2009.
Commencement (transitional provisions): see the note to s 1072 at **[1.1072]**.

[1.1074]
1074   Documents containing unnecessary material
(1)   This section applies where a document delivered to the registrar contains unnecessary material.
(2)   "Unnecessary material" means material that—
   (a)   is not necessary in order to comply with an obligation under any enactment, and
   (b)   is not specifically authorised to be delivered to the registrar.
(3)   For this purpose an obligation to deliver a document of a particular description, or conforming to certain requirements, is regarded as not extending to anything that is not needed for a document of that description or, as the case may be, conforming to those requirements.
(4)   If the unnecessary material cannot readily be separated from the rest of the document, the document is treated as not meeting the requirements for proper delivery.
(5)   If the unnecessary material can readily be separated from the rest of the document, the registrar may register the document either—
   (a)   with the omission of the unnecessary material, or
   (b)   as delivered.

NOTES
Commencement: 1 October 2009.
Commencement (transitional provisions): see the note to s 1072 at **[1.1072]**.

[1.1075]
1075   Informal correction of document
(1)   A document delivered to the registrar may be corrected by the registrar if it appears to the registrar to be incomplete or internally inconsistent.
(2)   This power is exercisable only—
   (a)   on instructions, and
   (b)   if [the company (or other body) to which the document relates] has given (and has not withdrawn) its consent to instructions being given under this section.
(3)   The following requirements must be met as regards the instructions—
   (a)   the instructions must be given in response to an enquiry by the registrar;
   (b)   the registrar must be satisfied that the person giving the instructions is authorised to do so—
      (i)   by the person by whom the document was delivered, or
      (ii)   by the company [(or other body)] to which the document relates;

    (c)   the instructions must meet any requirements of registrar's rules as to—
        (i)   the form and manner in which they are given, and
        (ii)   authentication.
(4) [The consent of the company (or other body)] to instructions being given under this section (and any withdrawal of such consent)—
    (a)   may be in hard copy or electronic form, and
    (b)   must be notified to the registrar.
(5) This section applies in relation to documents delivered under Part 25 (company charges) by a person other than the company [(or other body)] as if the references to the company [(or other body)] were to the company [(or other body)] or the person by whom the document was delivered.
(6) A document that is corrected under this section is treated, for the purposes of any enactment relating to its delivery, as having been delivered when the correction is made.
(7) The power conferred by this section is not exercisable if the document has been registered under section 1073 (power to accept documents not meeting requirements for proper delivery).

NOTES
Commencement: 1 October 2009.
Commencement (transitional provisions): Sch 2, para 101 to the Companies Act 2006 (Commencement No 8, Transitional Provisions and Savings) Order 2008, SI 2008/2860 (at **[2.91]**) provides as follows. Note that the paragraph set out below is as it has effect following its substitution by the Companies Act 2006 (Part 35) (Consequential Amendments, Transitional Provisions and Savings) Order 2009, SI 2009/1802, art 18, Schedule, with effect from 1 October 2009—

    "101.—(1)   Section 1075 of the Companies Act 2006 (informal correction of document) applies to documents delivered to the registrar on or after 1st October 2009 other than those delivered in pursuance of an obligation arising before that date.
    (2)   Where the obligation to deliver a document to the registrar arose before 1st October 2009, the provisions that would have applied if the document had been delivered before that date (and the registrar's former practice with respect to documents requiring correction) continue to apply.".

All words in square brackets were either substituted or inserted by the Companies Act 2006 (Part 35) (Consequential Amendments, Transitional Provisions and Savings) Order 2009, SI 2009/1802, arts 2, 8, as from 1 October 2009.

[1.1076]
1076   Replacement of document not meeting requirements for proper delivery
(1) The registrar may accept a replacement for a document previously delivered that—
    (a)   did not comply with the requirements for proper delivery, or
    (b)   contained unnecessary material (within the meaning of section 1074).
(2) A replacement document must not be accepted unless the registrar is satisfied that it is delivered by—
    (a)   the person by whom the original document was delivered, or
    (b)   the company [(or other body)] to which the original document relates, and that it complies with the requirements for proper delivery.
(3) The power of the registrar to impose requirements as to the form and manner of delivery includes power to impose requirements as to the identification of the original document and the delivery of the replacement in a form and manner enabling it to be associated with the original.
(4) This section does not apply where the original document was delivered under Part 25 (company charges) (but see sections 873 and 888 (rectification of register of charges)).

NOTES
Commencement: 1 October 2009.
Commencement (transitional provisions): the Companies Act 2006 (Commencement No 8, Transitional Provisions and Savings) Order 2008, SI 2008/2860, Sch 2, para 102 at **[2.91]** (as substituted by the Companies Act 2006 (Part 35) (Consequential Amendments, Transitional Provisions and Savings) Order 2009, SI 2009/1802, art 18, Schedule, with effect from 1 October 2009) provides that this section applies to documents to which sections 1072–1074 of this Act apply.
Sub-s (2): words in square brackets inserted by the Companies Act 2006 (Part 35) (Consequential Amendments, Transitional Provisions and Savings) Order 2009, SI 2009/1802, arts 2, 9, as from 1 October 2009.

Public notice of receipt of certain documents

[1.1077]
1077   Public notice of receipt of certain documents
(1) The registrar must cause to be published—
    (a)   in the Gazette, or
    (b)   in accordance with section 1116 (alternative means of giving public notice),
notice of the receipt by the registrar of any document that, on receipt, is subject to the Directive disclosure requirements (see section 1078).
(2) The notice must state the name and registered number of the company, the description of document and the date of receipt.
(3) The registrar is not required to cause notice of the receipt of a document to be published before the date of incorporation of the company to which the document relates.

NOTES
Commencement: 1 January 2007.
Commencement (transitional adaptations): art 5 of the Companies Act 2006 (Commencement No 1, Transitional Provisions and Savings) Order 2006, SI 2006/3428 provides that the provisions brought into force by arts 2–4 of 2006 Order shall have

effect subject to any transitional adaptations specified in Sch 1 to that Order. Schedule 1, para 4 to the Order (at **[2.9]**) provided for such transitional adaptations (note that this paragraph was revoked by the Companies Act 2006 (Commencement No 8, Transitional Provisions and Savings) Order 2008, SI 2008/2860, art 6, as from 1 October 2009 (subject to any relevant transitional provision or saving in Sch 2 to that Order)).

[1.1078]
1078 Documents subject to Directive disclosure requirements
(1)   The documents subject to the "Directive disclosure requirements" are as follows.
  The requirements referred to are those of Article 3 of the First Company Law Directive (68/151/EEC), as amended, extended and applied.
(2)   In the case of every company—
  Constitutional documents
  1.   The company's memorandum and articles.
  2.   Any amendment of the company's articles (including every resolution or agreement required to be embodied in or annexed to copies of the company's articles issued by the company).
  3.   After any amendment of the company's articles, the text of the articles as amended.
  4.   Any notice of a change of the company's name.
  Directors
  1.   The statement of proposed officers required on formation of the company.
  2.   Notification of any change among the company's directors.
  3.   Notification of any change in the particulars of directors required to be delivered to the registrar.
  Accounts, reports and returns
  1.   All documents required to be delivered to the registrar under section 441 (annual accounts and reports).
  2.   The company's annual return.
  Registered office
  Notification of any change of the company's registered office.
  Winding up
  1.   Copy of any winding-up order in respect of the company.
  2.   Notice of the appointment of liquidators.
  3.   Order for the dissolution of a company on a winding up.
  4.   Return by a liquidator of the final meeting of a company on a winding up.
(3)   In the case of a public company—
  Share capital
  1.   Any statement of capital and initial shareholdings.
  2.   Any return of allotment and the statement of capital accompanying it.
  3.   Copy of any resolution under section 570 or 571 (disapplication of pre-emption rights).
  4.   Copy of any report under section 593 or 599 as to the value of a non-cash asset.
  5.   Statement of capital accompanying notice given under section 625 (notice by company of redenomination of shares).
  6.   Statement of capital accompanying notice given under section 627 (notice by company of reduction of capital in connection with redenomination of shares).
  7.   Notice delivered under section 636 (notice of new name of class of shares) or 637 (notice of variation of rights attached to shares).
  8.   Statement of capital accompanying order delivered under section 649 (order of court confirming reduction of capital).
  9.   Notification (under section 689) of the redemption of shares and the statement of capital accompanying it.
  10. Statement of capital accompanying return delivered under section 708 (notice of cancellation of shares on purchase of own shares) or 730 (notice of cancellation of shares held as treasury shares).
  11. Any statement of compliance delivered under section 762 (statement that company meets conditions for issue of trading certificate).
  Mergers and divisions
  1.   Copy of any draft of the terms of a scheme required to be delivered to the registrar under section 906 or 921.
  2.   Copy of any order under section 899 or 900 in respect of a compromise or arrangement to which Part 27 (mergers and divisions of public companies) applies.
(4)   Where a private company re-registers as a public company (see section 96)—
  (a)   the last statement of capital relating to the company received by the registrar under any provision of the Companies Acts becomes subject to the Directive disclosure requirements, and
  (b)   section 1077 (public notice of receipt of certain documents) applies as if the statement had been received by the registrar when the re-registration takes effect.
(5)   In the case of an overseas company, such particulars, returns and other documents required to be delivered under Part 34 as may be specified by the Secretary of State by regulations.

(6)   Regulations under subsection (5) are subject to negative resolution procedure.

NOTES

Commencement: 1 January 2007.

Commencement (transitional adaptations): art 5 of the Companies Act 2006 (Commencement No 1, Transitional Provisions and Savings) Order 2006, SI 2006/3428 provides that the provisions brought into force by arts 2–4 of 2006 Order shall have effect subject to any transitional adaptations specified in Sch 1 to that Order. Schedule 1, para 5 to the Order (at **[2.9]**) provided for such transitional adaptations. Note, however, that para 5(2)(b), (3)(a)(ix), (b) were revoked by the Companies Act 2006 (Commencement No 5, Transitional Provisions and Savings) Order 2007, SI 2007/3495, art 10(1), (3), as from 6 April 2008 (subject to any transitional provisions and savings as apply, in accordance with Sch 4 to that Order, in relation to the repeal of the provisions of the 1985 Act referred to in the adaptation; see art 10 at **[2.59]**). Note also that all of this paragraph was revoked by the Companies Act 2006 (Commencement No 8, Transitional Provisions and Savings) Order 2008, SI 2008/2860, art 6, as from 1 October 2009 (for transitional provisions see the note relating to Sch 2, para 103 of that Schedule below).

Transitional provisions: Sch 2, para 103 to the Companies Act 2006 (Commencement No 8, Transitional Provisions and Savings) Order 2008, SI 2008/2860 (at **[2.91]**) provides as follows. Note that the paragraph set out below is as it has effect following its substitution by the Companies Act 2006 (Part 35) (Consequential Amendments, Transitional Provisions and Savings) Order 2009, SI 2009/1802, art 18, Schedule, with effect from 1 October 2009—

"Documents subject to Directive disclosure requirements (s 1078)

103.—(1)   This paragraph has effect in relation to section 1078 of the Companies Act 2006 (documents subject to the Directive disclosure requirements) and the adaptations of that section made by paragraph 5 of Schedule 1 to the Companies Act 2006 (Commencement No 1, Transitional Provisions and Savings) Order 2006.

(2)   The adaptations continue to have effect in relation to documents delivered to the registrar on or after 1st October 2009 in pursuance of provisions of the 1985 Act or 1986 Order.

(3)   Documents subject to the Directive disclosure requirements by virtue of any such adaptation remain subject to the Directive disclosure requirements notwithstanding that the adaptation has ceased to have effect.".

Regulations: the Overseas Companies Regulations 2009, SI 2009/1801 at **[4.389]**.

[1.1079]
1079   Effect of failure to give public notice
(1)   A company is not entitled to rely against other persons on the happening of any event to which this section applies unless—
(a)   the event has been officially notified at the material time, or
(b)   the company shows that the person concerned knew of the event at the material time.
(2)   The events to which this section applies are—
(a)   an amendment of the company's articles,
(b)   a change among the company's directors,
(c)   (as regards service of any document on the company) a change of the company's registered office,
(d)   the making of a winding-up order in respect of the company, or
(e)   the appointment of a liquidator in a voluntary winding up of the company.
(3)   If the material time falls—
(a)   on or before the 15th day after the date of official notification, or
(b)   where the 15th day was not a working day, on or before the next day that was,
the company is not entitled to rely on the happening of the event as against a person who shows that he was unavoidably prevented from knowing of the event at that time.
(4)   "Official notification" means—
(a)   in relation to an amendment of the company's articles, notification in accordance with section 1077 (public notice of receipt by registrar of certain documents) of the amendment and the amended text of the articles;
(b)   in relation to anything else stated in a document subject to the Directive disclosure requirements, notification of that document in accordance with that section;
(c)   in relation to the appointment of a liquidator in a voluntary winding up, notification of that event in accordance with section 109 of the Insolvency Act 1986 (c 45) or Article 95 of the Insolvency (Northern Ireland) Order 1989 (SI 1989/2405 (NI 19)).

NOTES

Commencement: 1 January 2007.

Commencement (transitional adaptations): art 5 of the Companies Act 2006 (Commencement No 1, Transitional Provisions and Savings) Order 2006, SI 2006/3428 provides that the provisions brought into force by arts 2–4 of 2006 Order shall have effect subject to any transitional adaptations specified in Sch 1 to that Order. Schedule 1, para 6 to the Order (at **[2.9]**) provided for such transitional adaptations. Note, however, that this paragraph was revoked by the Companies Act 2006 (Commencement No 8, Transitional Provisions and Savings) Order 2008, SI 2008/2860, art 6, as from 1 October 2009 (see further the note relating to Sch 2, para 104 of that Schedule below).

Transitional provisions: Sch 2, para 104 to the Companies Act 2006 (Commencement No 8, Transitional Provisions and Savings) Order 2008, SI 2008/2860 (at **[2.91]**) provides as follows. Note that the paragraph set out below is as it has effect following its substitution by the Companies Act 2006 (Part 35) (Consequential Amendments, Transitional Provisions and Savings) Order 2009, SI 2009/1802, art 18, Schedule, with effect from 1 October 2009—

"Effect of failure to give public notice (s 1079)
104.   In section 1079 of the Companies Act 2006 (effect of failure to give public notice) the references to an amendment of the company's articles include an amendment before 1st October 2009 of the company's memorandum.".

The register

[1.1080]
1080 The register

(1)   The registrar shall continue to keep records of—
  (a)   the information contained in documents delivered to the registrar under any enactment, [and
  (b)   certificates issued by the registrar under any enactment].

(2)   The records relating to companies are referred to collectively in the Companies Acts as "the register".

(3)   Information deriving from documents subject to the Directive disclosure requirements (see section 1078) that are delivered to the registrar on or after 1st January 2007 must be kept by the registrar in electronic form.

(4)   Subject to that, information contained in documents delivered to the registrar may be recorded and kept in any form the registrar thinks fit, provided it is possible to inspect it and produce a copy of it.

  This is sufficient compliance with any duty of the registrar to keep, file or register the document or to record the information contained in it.

(5)   The records kept by the registrar must be such that information relating to a company [or other registered body] is associated with [that body], in such manner as the registrar may determine, so as to enable all the information relating to [the body] to be retrieved.

NOTES

Commencement: 1 January 2007.

Commencement (transitional adaptations): art 5 of the Companies Act 2006 (Commencement No 1, Transitional Provisions and Savings) Order 2006, SI 2006/3428 provides that the provisions brought into force by arts 2–4 of 2006 Order shall have effect subject to any transitional adaptations specified in Sch 1 to that Order. Schedule 1, para 7 to the Order (at **[2.9]**) provided for such transitional adaptations (note that this paragraph was revoked by the Companies Act 2006 (Commencement No 8, Transitional Provisions and Savings) Order 2008, SI 2008/2860, art 6, as from 1 October 2009 (subject to any relevant transitional provision or saving in Sch 2 to that Order)).

Sub-s (1): para (b) (and the word immediately preceding it) were substituted for the original paras (b), (c), by the Companies Act 2006 (Part 35) (Consequential Amendments, Transitional Provisions and Savings) Order 2009, SI 2009/1802, arts 2, 10(1), (2), as from 1 October 2009.

Sub-s (5): words in first pair of square brackets inserted, and other words in square brackets substituted, by SI 2009/1802, arts 2, 10(1), (3), as from 1 October 2009.

[1.1081]
1081 Annotation of the register

(1)   The registrar must place a note in the register recording—
  (a)   the date on which a document is delivered to the registrar;
  (b)   if a document is corrected under section 1075, the nature and date of the correction;
  (c)   if a document is replaced (whether or not material derived from it is removed), the fact that it has been replaced and the date of delivery of the replacement;
  (d)   if material is removed—
    (i)   what was removed (giving a general description of its contents),
    (ii)   under what power, and
    (iii)   the date on which that was done.

(2)   The Secretary of State may make provision by regulations—
  (a)   authorising or requiring the registrar to annotate the register in such other circumstances as may be specified in the regulations, and
  (b)   as to the contents of any such annotation.

(3)   No annotation is required in the case of a document that by virtue of section 1072(2) (documents not meeting requirements for proper delivery) is treated as not having been delivered.

(4)   A note may be removed if it no longer serves any useful purpose.

(5)   Any duty or power of the registrar with respect to annotation of the register is subject to the court's power under section 1097 (powers of court on ordering removal of material from the register) to direct—
  (a)   that a note be removed from the register, or
  (b)   that no note shall be made of the removal of material that is the subject of the court's order.

(6)   Notes placed in the register in accordance with subsection (1), or in pursuance of regulations under subsection (2), are part of the register for all purposes of the Companies Acts.

(7)   Regulations under this section are subject to negative resolution procedure.

NOTES

Commencement: 20 January 2007 (for the purpose of enabling the exercise of powers to make Orders or Regulations by statutory instrument); 1 October 2009 (otherwise).

Commencement (transitional provisions): Sch 2, para 105 to the Companies Act 2006 (Commencement No 8, Transitional Provisions and Savings) Order 2008, SI 2008/2860 (at **[2.91]**) provides as follows. Note that the paragraph set out below is as it has effect following its substitution by the Companies Act 2006 (Part 35) (Consequential Amendments, Transitional Provisions and Savings) Order 2009, SI 2009/1802, art 18, Schedule, with effect from 1 October 2009—

"Annotation of the register (s 1081)

105.—(1)   Section 1081 of the Companies Act 2006 (annotation of the register) applies in relation to—

(a)   documents delivered to the registrar on or after 1st October 2009 other than those delivered in pursuance of an obligation arising before that date, and

(b)   certificates issued by the registrar on or after 1st October 2009 other than those issued in response to a document delivered to the registrar before that date or in pursuance of an obligation arising before that date,

and in relation to the content of, and material derived from, such documents and certificates.

(2)   The provisions applicable before 1st October 2009 (and the registrar's former practice with respect to annotation of the register) continue to apply in relation to—

(a)   documents delivered to the registrar before that date, or in pursuance of an obligation arising before that date, and

(b)   certificates issued by the registrar before that date or in response to a document delivered to the registrar before that date or in pursuance of an obligation arising before that date,

and in relation to the content of, and material derived from, such documents and certificates.".

Regulations: the Registrar of Companies and Applications for Striking Off Regulations 2009, SI 2009/1803 at **[4.491]**.

[1.1082]
1082   Allocation of unique identifiers

(1)   The Secretary of State may make provision for the use, in connection with the register, of reference numbers ("unique identifiers") to identify each person who—

(a)   is a director of a company,

(b)   is secretary (or a joint secretary) of a company, or

(c)   in the case of an overseas company whose particulars are registered under section 1046, holds any such position as may be specified for the purposes of this section by regulations under that section.

(2)   The regulations may—

(a)   provide that a unique identifier may be in such form, consisting of one or more sequences of letters or numbers, as the registrar may from time to time determine;

(b)   make provision for the allocation of unique identifiers by the registrar;

(c)   require there to be included, in any specified description of documents delivered to the registrar, as well as a statement of the person's name—

(i)   a statement of the person's unique identifier, or

(ii)   a statement that the person has not been allocated a unique identifier;

(d)   enable the registrar to take steps where a person appears to have more than one unique identifier to discontinue the use of all but one of them.

(3)   The regulations may contain provision for the application of the scheme in relation to persons appointed, and documents registered, before the commencement of this Act.

(4)   The regulations may make different provision for different descriptions of person and different descriptions of document.

(5)   Regulations under this section are subject to affirmative resolution procedure.

NOTES

Commencement: 20 January 2007 (for the purpose of enabling the exercise of powers to make Orders or Regulations by statutory instrument); 1 October 2009 (otherwise).

[1.1083]
1083   Preservation of original documents

(1)   The originals of documents delivered to the registrar in hard copy form must be kept for three years after they are received by the registrar, after which they may be destroyed provided the information contained in them has been [recorded].

This is subject to section 1087(3) (extent of obligation to retain material not available for public inspection).

(2)   The registrar is under no obligation to keep the originals of documents delivered in electronic form, provided the information contained in them has been [recorded].

(3)   This section applies to documents held by the registrar when this section comes into force as well as to documents subsequently received.

NOTES

Commencement: 1 October 2009.

Sub-ss (1), (2): words in square brackets substituted by the Companies Act 2006 (Part 35) (Consequential Amendments, Transitional Provisions and Savings) Order 2009, SI 2009/1802, arts 2, 11, as from 1 October 2009.

[1.1084]
1084   Records relating to companies that have been dissolved etc

(1)   This section applies where—

(a)   a company is dissolved,

(b)   an overseas company ceases to have any connection with the United Kingdom by virtue of which it is required to register particulars under section 1046, or

(c)   a credit or financial institution ceases to be within section 1050 (overseas institutions required to file accounts with the registrar).

(2)   At any time after two years from the date on which it appears to the registrar that—

(a) the company has been dissolved,

(b) the overseas company has ceased to have any connection with the United Kingdom by virtue of which it is required to register particulars under section 1046, or

(c) the credit or financial institution has ceased to be within section 1050 (overseas institutions required to file accounts with the registrar),

the registrar may direct that records relating to the company or institution may be removed to the Public Record Office or, as the case may be, the Public Record Office of Northern Ireland.

(3) Records in respect of which such a direction is given shall be disposed of under the enactments relating to that Office and the rules made under them.

(4) In subsection (1)(a) "company" includes a company provisionally or completely registered under the Joint Stock Companies Act 1844 (c 110).

(5) This section does not extend to Scotland.

NOTES
Commencement: 1 October 2009.

Inspection etc of the register

[1.1085]
1085 Inspection of the register
(1) Any person may inspect the register.
(2) The right of inspection extends to the originals of documents delivered to the registrar in hard copy form if, and only if, the record kept by the registrar of the contents of the document is illegible or unavailable.

The period for which such originals are to be kept is limited by section 1083(1).
(3) This section has effect subject to section 1087 (material not available for public inspection).

NOTES
Commencement: 1 January 2007.
Commencement (transitional adaptations): art 5 of the Companies Act 2006 (Commencement No 1, Transitional Provisions and Savings) Order 2006, SI 2006/3428 provides that the provisions brought into force by arts 2–4 of 2006 Order shall have effect subject to any transitional adaptations specified in Sch 1 to that Order. Schedule 1, para 8 to the Order (at **[2.9]**) provided for such transitional adaptations (note that this paragraph was revoked by the Companies Act 2006 (Commencement No 8, Transitional Provisions and Savings) Order 2008, SI 2008/2860, art 6, as from 1 October 2009 (subject to any relevant transitional provision or saving in Sch 2 to that Order)).

[1.1086]
1086 Right to copy of material on the register
(1) Any person may require a copy of any material on the register.
(2) The fee for any such copy of material derived from a document subject to the Directive disclosure requirements (see section 1078), whether in hard copy or electronic form, must not exceed the administrative cost of providing it.
(3) This section has effect subject to section 1087 (material not available for public inspection).

NOTES
Commencement: 1 January 2007.

[1.1087]
1087 Material not available for public inspection
(1) The following material must not be made available by the registrar for public inspection—
(a) the contents of any document sent to the registrar containing views expressed pursuant to section 56 (comments on proposal by company to use certain words or expressions in company name);
(b) protected information within section 242(1) (directors' residential addresses: restriction on disclosure by registrar) or any corresponding provision of regulations under section 1046 (overseas companies);
[(ba) representations received by the registrar in response to a notice under—
    (i) section 245(2) (notice of proposal to put director's usual residential address on the public record), or
    (ii) any corresponding provision of regulations under section 1046 (overseas companies);]
(c) any application to the registrar under section 1024 (application for administrative restoration to the register) that has not yet been determined or was not successful;
(d) any document received by the registrar in connection with the giving or withdrawal of consent under section 1075 (informal correction of documents);
(e) any application or other document delivered to the registrar under section 1088 (application to make address unavailable for public inspection) and any address in respect of which such an application is successful;
(f) any application or other document delivered to the registrar under section 1095 (application for rectification of register);

(g) any court order under section 1096 (rectification of the register under court order) that the court has directed under section 1097 (powers of court on ordering removal of material from the register) is not to be made available for public inspection;

[(h) the contents of—
  (i) any instrument creating or evidencing a charge, or
  (ii) any certified or verified copy of an instrument creating or evidencing a charge,
  delivered to the registrar under Part 25 (company charges) or regulations under section 1052 (overseas companies);]

(i) any e-mail address, identification code or password deriving from a document delivered for the purpose of authorising or facilitating electronic filing procedures or providing information by telephone;

[(j) the contents of any documents held by the registrar pending a decision of the Regulator of Community Interest Companies under—
  (i) section 36A of the Companies (Audit, Investigations and Community Enterprise) Act 2004 (eligibility for registration as community interest company),
  (ii) section 38 of that Act (eligibility for conversion to community interest company), or
  (iii) section 55 of that Act (eligibility for conversion from community interest company to charity),
  and that the registrar is not later required to record;]

(k) any other material excluded from public inspection by or under any other enactment.

(2) A restriction applying by reference to material deriving from a particular description of document does not affect the availability for public inspection of the same information contained in material derived from another description of document in relation to which no such restriction applies.

(3) Material to which this section applies need not be retained by the registrar for longer than appears to the registrar reasonably necessary for the purposes for which the material was delivered to the registrar.

NOTES

Commencement: 1 January 2007.

Commencement (transitional adaptations): art 5 of the Companies Act 2006 (Commencement No 1, Transitional Provisions and Savings) Order 2006, SI 2006/3428 provides that the provisions brought into force by arts 2–4 of 2006 Order shall have effect subject to any transitional adaptations specified in Sch 1 to that Order. Schedule 1, para 9 to the Order (at **[2.9]**) provided for such transitional adaptations (note that this paragraph was revoked by the Companies Act 2006 (Commencement No 8, Transitional Provisions and Savings) Order 2008, SI 2008/2860, art 6, as from 1 October 2009 (subject to any relevant transitional provision or saving in Sch 2 to that Order)).

Sub-s (1): para (ba) inserted, and para (h) substituted, by the Companies Act 2006 (Part 35) (Consequential Amendments, Transitional Provisions and Savings) Order 2009, SI 2009/1802, arts 2, 12, as from 1 October 2009; para (j) substituted by the Companies Act 2006 (Consequential Amendments, Transitional Provisions and Savings) Order 2009, SI 2009/1941, art 2(1), Sch 1, para 260(1), (6), as from 1 October 2009.

[1.1088]
1088 Application to registrar to make address unavailable for public inspection

(1) The Secretary of State may make provision by regulations requiring the registrar, on application, to make an address on the register unavailable for public inspection.

(2) The regulations may make provision as to—
  (a) who may make an application,
  (b) the grounds on which an application may be made,
  (c) the information to be included in and documents to accompany an application,
  (d) the notice to be given of an application and of its outcome, and
  (e) how an application is to be determined.

(3) Provision under subsection (2)(e) may in particular—
  (a) confer a discretion on the registrar;
  (b) provide for a question to be referred to a person other than the registrar for the purposes of determining the application.

(4) An application must specify the address to be removed from the register and indicate where on the register it is.

(5) The regulations may provide—
  (a) that an address is not to be made unavailable for public inspection under this section unless replaced by a service address, and
  (b) that in such a case the application must specify a service address.

(6) Regulations under this section are subject to affirmative resolution procedure.

NOTES

Commencement: 1 January 2007.

Confidentiality orders under the Companies Act 1985: a director or secretary in relation to whom a confidentiality order under CA 1985, s 723B was in force immediately before 1 October 2009 is treated on and after that date as if (a) they had made an application under this section in respect of any address that immediately before that date was contained in "confidential records" as defined in s 723D(3) of the 1985 Act, and (b) that application had been determined by the registrar in their favour.

For general transitional provisions in connection with the continuation of protection afforded by confidentiality orders under the 1985 Act, see the Companies Act 2006 (Commencement No 8, Transitional Provisions and Savings) Order 2008, SI 2008/2860, Sch 2, paras 36–39 at **[2.91]**.

Regulations: the Companies (Disclosure of Address) Regulations 2009, SI 2009/214 at **[4.344]**.

Orders: the Companies Act 2006 (Consequential Amendments, Transitional Provisions and Savings) Order 2009, SI 2009/1941 at **[4.528]**.

[1.1089]
1089   Form of application for inspection or copy
(1)   The registrar may specify the form and manner in which application is to be made for—
  (a)   inspection under section 1085, or
  (b)   a copy under section 1086.
(2)   As from 1st January 2007, applications in respect of documents subject to the Directive disclosure requirements may be submitted to the registrar in hard copy or electronic form, as the applicant chooses.

This does not affect the registrar's power under subsection (1) above to impose requirements in respect of other matters.

NOTES

Commencement: 1 January 2007.

[1.1090]
1090   Form and manner in which copies to be provided
(1)   The following provisions apply as regards the form and manner in which copies are to be provided under section 1086.
(2)   As from 1st January 2007, copies of documents subject to the Directive disclosure requirements must be provided in hard copy or electronic form, as the applicant chooses.

This is subject to the following proviso.
(3)   The registrar is not obliged by subsection (2) to provide copies in electronic form of a document that was delivered to the registrar in hard copy form if—
  (a)   the document was delivered to the registrar on or before 31st December 1996, or
  (b)   the document was delivered to the registrar on or before 31st December 2006 and ten years or more elapsed between the date of delivery and the date of receipt of the first application for a copy on or after 1st January 2007.
(4)   Subject to the preceding provisions of this section, the registrar may determine the form and manner in which copies are to be provided.

NOTES

Commencement: 1 January 2007.

[1.1091]
1091   Certification of copies as accurate
(1)   Copies provided under section 1086 in hard copy form must be certified as true copies unless the applicant dispenses with such certification.
(2)   Copies so provided in electronic form must not be certified as true copies unless the applicant expressly requests such certification.
(3)   A copy provided under section 1086, certified by the registrar (whose official position it is unnecessary to prove) to be an accurate record of the contents of the original document, is in all legal proceedings admissible in evidence—
  (a)   as of equal validity with the original document, and
  (b)   as evidence (in Scotland, sufficient evidence) of any fact stated in the original document of which direct oral evidence would be admissible.
(4)   The Secretary of State may make provision by regulations as to the manner in which such a certificate is to be provided in a case where the copy is provided in electronic form.
(5)   Except in the case of documents that are subject to the Directive disclosure requirements (see section 1078), copies provided by the registrar may, instead of being certified in writing to be an accurate record, be sealed with the registrar's official seal.

NOTES

Commencement: 1 January 2007.

Regulations: the Companies (Registrar, Languages and Trading Disclosures) Regulations 2006, SI 2006/3429 at **[4.2]**.

[1.1092]
1092   Issue of process for production of records kept by the registrar
(1)   No process for compelling the production of a record kept by the registrar shall issue from any court except with the permission of the court.
(2)   Any such process shall bear on it a statement that it is issued with the permission of the court.

NOTES

Commencement: 1 January 2007.

Correction or removal of material on the register

[1.1093]
1093 Registrar's notice to resolve inconsistency on the register
(1) Where it appears to the registrar that the information contained in a document delivered to the registrar is inconsistent with other information on the register, the registrar may give notice to the company to which the document relates—
    (a) stating in what respects the information contained in it appears to be inconsistent with other information on the register, and
    (b) requiring the company to take steps to resolve the inconsistency.
(2) The notice must—
    (a) state the date on which it is issued, and
    (b) require the delivery to the registrar, within 14 days after that date, of such replacement or additional documents as may be required to resolve the inconsistency.
(3) If the necessary documents are not delivered within the period specified, an offence is committed by—
    (a) the company, and
    (b) every officer of the company who is in default.
(4) A person guilty of an offence under subsection (3) is liable on summary conviction to a fine not exceeding level 5 on the standard scale and, for continued contravention, a daily default fine not exceeding one-tenth of level 5 on the standard scale.

NOTES
Commencement: 1 October 2009.
Commencement (transitional provisions): Sch 2, para 106 to the Companies Act 2006 (Commencement No 8, Transitional Provisions and Savings) Order 2008, SI 2008/2860 (at **[2.91]**) provides as follows. Note that the paragraph set out below is as it has effect following its substitution by the Companies Act 2006 (Part 35) (Consequential Amendments, Transitional Provisions and Savings) Order 2009, SI 2009/1802, art 18, Schedule, with effect from 1 October 2009—

> **"Registrar's notice to resolve inconsistency on the register (s 1093)**
> 106.—(1) Section 1093 of the Companies Act 2006 (registrar's notice to resolve inconsistency on the register) applies where—
>   (a) a document is delivered to the registrar on or after 1st October 2009 otherwise than in pursuance of an obligation arising before that date, and
>   (b) it appears to the registrar that the information contained in the document is inconsistent with other information on the register.
> (2) The provisions applicable before 1st October 2009 (and the registrar's former practice with respect to inconsistencies on the register) continue to apply in relation to documents delivered to the registrar before that date or in pursuance of an obligation arising before that date.".

[1.1094]
1094 Administrative removal of material from the register
(1) The registrar may remove from the register anything that there was power, but no duty, to include.
(2) This power is exercisable, in particular, so as to remove—
    (a) unnecessary material within the meaning of section 1074, and
    (b) material derived from a document that has been replaced under—
        section 1076 (replacement of document not meeting requirements for proper delivery), or
        section 1093 (notice to remedy inconsistency on the register).
(3) This section does not authorise the removal from the register of—
    (a) anything whose registration has had legal consequences in relation to the company as regards—
        (i) its formation,
        (ii) a change of name,
        (iii) its re-registration,
        (iv) its becoming or ceasing to be a community interest company,
        (v) a reduction of capital,
        (vi) a change of registered office,
        (vii) the registration of a charge, or
        (viii) its dissolution;
    (b) an address that is a person's registered address for the purposes of section 1140 (service of documents on directors, secretaries and others).
(4) On or before removing any material under this section (otherwise than at the request of the company) the registrar must give notice—
    (a) to the person by whom the material was delivered (if the identity, and name and address of that person are known), or
    (b) to the company to which the material relates (if notice cannot be given under paragraph (a) and the identity of that company is known).
(5) The notice must—
    (a) state what material the registrar proposes to remove, or has removed, and on what grounds, and

(b)   state the date on which it is issued.

NOTES

Commencement: 1 October 2009.

Commencement (transitional provisions): Sch 2, para 107 to the Companies Act 2006 (Commencement No 8, Transitional Provisions and Savings) Order 2008, SI 2008/2860 (at **[2.91]**) provides as follows. Note that the paragraph set out below is as it has effect following its substitution by the Companies Act 2006 (Part 35) (Consequential Amendments, Transitional Provisions and Savings) Order 2009, SI 2009/1802, art 18, Schedule, with effect from 1 October 2009—

"Removal of material from the register (ss 1094 to 1098)
107.—(1)   This paragraph applies to—
   (a)   sections 1094 to 1097 of the Companies Act 2006 (removal of material from the register), and
   (b)   section 1098 of that Act (public notice of removal of certain material from the register).
(2)   Those provisions apply in relation to—
   (a)   documents delivered to the registrar on or after 1st October 2009 other than those delivered in pursuance of an obligation arising before that date, and
   (b)   certificates issued by the registrar on or after 1st October 2009, other than those issued in response to a document delivered to the registrar before that date or in pursuance of an obligation arising before that date,
and in relation to the content of, and material derived from, such documents and certificates.
(3)   The provisions applicable before 1st October 2009 (and the registrar's former practice with respect to removal of material from the register) continue to apply in relation to—
   (a)   documents delivered to the registrar before that date, or in pursuance of an obligation arising before that date, and
   (b)   certificates issued by the registrar before that date or in response to a document delivered to the registrar before that date or in pursuance of an obligation arising before that date,
and in relation to the content of, and material derived from, such documents or certificates.".

[1.1095]
1095   Rectification of register on application to registrar
(1)   The Secretary of State may make provision by regulations requiring the registrar, on application, to remove from the register material of a description specified in the regulations that—
   (a)   derives from anything invalid or ineffective or that was done without the authority of the company, or
   (b)   is factually inaccurate, or is derived from something that is factually inaccurate or forged.
(2)   The regulations may make provision as to—
   (a)   who may make an application,
   (b)   the information to be included in and documents to accompany an application,
   (c)   the notice to be given of an application and of its outcome,
   (d)   a period in which objections to an application may be made, and
   (e)   how an application is to be determined.
(3)   An application must—
   (a)   specify what is to be removed from the register and indicate where on the register it is, and
   (b)   be accompanied by a statement that the material specified in the application complies with this section and the regulations.
(4)   If no objections are made to the application, the registrar may accept the statement as sufficient evidence that the material specified in the application should be removed from the register.
(5)   Where anything is removed from the register under this section the registration of which had legal consequences as mentioned in section 1094(3), any person appearing to the court to have a sufficient interest may apply to the court for such consequential orders as appear just with respect to the legal effect (if any) to be accorded to the material by virtue of its having appeared on the register.
(6)   Regulations under this section are subject to affirmative resolution procedure.

NOTES

Commencement: 20 January 2007 (for the purpose of enabling the exercise of powers to make Orders or Regulations by statutory instrument); 1 October 2009 (otherwise).

Commencement (transitional provisions): see the note to s 1094 at **[1.1094]**.

Regulations: the Registrar of Companies and Applications for Striking Off Regulations 2009, SI 2009/1803 at **[4.491]**.

[1.1096]
1096   Rectification of the register under court order
(1)   The registrar shall remove from the register any material—
   (a)   that derives from anything that the court has declared to be invalid or ineffective, or to have been done without the authority of the company, or
   (b)   that a court declares to be factually inaccurate, or to be derived from something that is factually inaccurate, or forged,
and that the court directs should be removed from the register.
(2)   The court order must specify what is to be removed from the register and indicate where on the register it is.
(3)   The court must not make an order for the removal from the register of anything the registration of which had legal consequences as mentioned in section 1094(3) unless satisfied—

(a)   that the presence of the material on the register has caused, or may cause, damage to the company, and

(b)   that the company's interest in removing the material outweighs any interest of other persons in the material continuing to appear on the register.

(4)   Where in such a case the court does make an order for removal, it may make such consequential orders as appear just with respect to the legal effect (if any) to be accorded to the material by virtue of its having appeared on the register.

(5)   A copy of the court's order must be sent to the registrar for registration.

(6)   This section does not apply where the court has other, specific, powers to deal with the matter, for example under—

(a)   the provisions of Part 15 relating to the revision of defective accounts and reports, or

(b)   section 873 or 888 (rectification of the register of charges).

NOTES

Commencement: 1 October 2009.

Commencement (transitional provisions): see the note to s 1094 at **[1.1094]**.

[1.1097]
1097   Powers of court on ordering removal of material from the register

(1)   Where the court makes an order for the removal of anything from the register under section 1096 (rectification of the register), it may give directions under this section.

(2)   It may direct that any note on the register that is related to the material that is the subject of the court's order shall be removed from the register.

(3)   It may direct that its order shall not be available for public inspection as part of the register.

(4)   It may direct—

(a)   that no note shall be made on the register as a result of its order, or

(b)   that any such note shall be restricted to such matters as may be specified by the court.

(5)   The court shall not give any direction under this section unless it is satisfied—

(a)   that—

    (i)   the presence on the register of the note or, as the case may be, of an unrestricted note, or

    (ii)   the availability for public inspection of the court's order,

     may cause damage to the company, and

(b)   that the company's interest in non-disclosure outweighs any interest of other persons in disclosure.

NOTES

Commencement: 1 October 2009.

Commencement (transitional provisions): see the note to s 1094 at **[1.1094]**.

[1.1098]
1098   Public notice of removal of certain material from the register

(1)   The registrar must cause to be published—

(a)   in the Gazette, or

(b)   in accordance with section 1116 (alternative means of giving public notice),

notice of the removal from the register of any document subject to the Directive disclosure requirements (see section 1078) or of any material derived from such a document.

(2)   The notice must state the name and registered number of the company, the description of document and the date of receipt.

NOTES

Commencement: 1 October 2009.

Commencement (transitional provisions): see the note to s 1094 at **[1.1094]**.

The registrar's index of company names

[1.1099]
1099   The registrar's index of company names

(1)   The registrar of companies must keep an index of the names of the companies and other bodies to which this section applies.

This is "the registrar's index of company names".

(2)   This section applies to—

(a)   UK-registered companies;

(b)   any body to which any provision of the Companies Acts applies by virtue of regulations under section 1043 (unregistered companies); and

(c)   overseas companies that have registered particulars with the registrar under section 1046, other than companies that appear to the registrar not to be required to do so.

(3)   This section also applies to—

(a)   limited partnerships registered in the United Kingdom;

(b)   limited liability partnerships incorporated in the United Kingdom;

(c)   European Economic Interest Groupings registered in the United Kingdom;
(d)   open-ended investment companies authorised in the United Kingdom;
(e)   societies registered under the Industrial and Provident Societies Act 1965 (c 12) or the Industrial and Provident Societies Act (Northern Ireland) 1969 (c 24 (NI)).
(4)   The Secretary of State may by order amend subsection (3)—
(a)   by the addition of any description of body;
(b)   by the deletion of any description of body.
(5)   Any such order is subject to negative resolution procedure.

NOTES
Commencement: 20 January 2007 (for the purpose of enabling the exercise of powers to make Orders or Regulations by statutory instrument); 1 October 2009 (otherwise).
Industrial and Provident Societies Act 1965: see the Co-operative and Community Benefit Societies and Credit Unions Act 2010 which renames this Act as the Co-operative and Community Benefit Societies and Credit Unions Act 1965.

[1.1100]
1100   Right to inspect index
Any person may inspect the registrar's index of company names.

NOTES
Commencement: 1 October 2009.

[1.1101]
1101   Power to amend enactments relating to bodies other than companies
(1)   The Secretary of State may by regulations amend the enactments relating to any description of body for the time being within section 1099(3) (bodies other than companies whose names are to be entered in the registrar's index), so as to—
(a)   require the registrar to be provided with information as to the names of bodies registered, incorporated, authorised or otherwise regulated under those enactments, and
(b)   make provision in relation to such bodies corresponding to that made by—
section 66 (company name not to be the same as another in the index), and
sections 67 and 68 (power to direct change of company name in case of similarity to existing name).
(2)   Regulations under this section are subject to affirmative resolution procedure.

NOTES
Commencement: 20 January 2007 (for the purpose of enabling the exercise of powers to make Orders or Regulations by statutory instrument); 1 October 2009 (otherwise).
Regulations: the Limited Liability Partnerships (Application of Companies Act 2006) Regulations 2009, SI 2009/1804 at **[10.1097]**.

Language requirements: translation
[1.1102]
1102   Application of language requirements
(1)   The provisions listed below apply to all documents required to be delivered to the registrar under any provision of—
(a)   the Companies Acts, or
(b)   the Insolvency Act 1986 (c 45) or the Insolvency (Northern Ireland) Order 1989 (SI 1989/2405 (NI 19)).
(2)   The Secretary of State may make provision by regulations applying all or any of the listed provisions, with or without modifications, in relation to documents delivered to the registrar under any other enactment.
(3)   The provisions are—
section 1103 (documents to be drawn up and delivered in English),
section 1104 (documents relating to Welsh companies),
section 1105 (documents that may be drawn up and delivered in other languages),
section 1107 (certified translations).
(4)   Regulations under this section are subject to negative resolution procedure.

NOTES
Commencement: 1 January 2007.
Regulations: the Companies (Cross-Border Mergers) Regulations 2007, SI 2007/2974 at **[4.17]**; the European Public Limited-Liability Company (Amendment) Regulations 2009, SI 2009/2400.

[1.1103]
1103   Documents to be drawn up and delivered in English
(1)   The general rule is that all documents required to be delivered to the registrar must be drawn up and delivered in English.
(2)   This is subject to—
section 1104 (documents relating to Welsh companies) and

section 1105 (documents that may be drawn up and delivered in other languages).

NOTES

Commencement: 1 January 2007.

Commencement (transitional adaptations): the transitional adaptations of this section contained in the Companies Act 2006 (Commencement No 1, Transitional Provisions and Savings) Order 2006, SI 2006/3428, Sch 1, para 10 were revoked by the Companies Act 2006 (Commencement No 5, Transitional Provisions and Savings) Order 2007, SI 2007/3495, art 10(1), (3), as from 6 April 2008 (subject to any transitional provisions and savings as apply, in accordance with Sch 4 to that Order, in relation to the repeal of any provision of the 1985 Act referred to in the adaptation). See **[2.9]**.

[1.1104]
1104 Documents relating to Welsh companies

(1)   Documents relating to a Welsh company may be drawn up and delivered to the registrar in Welsh.

(2)   On delivery to the registrar any such document must be accompanied by a certified translation into English, unless it is—

(a)   of a description excepted from that requirement by regulations made by the Secretary of State, or

(b)   in a form prescribed in Welsh (or partly in Welsh and partly in English) by virtue of section 26 of the Welsh Language Act 1993 (c 38).

(3)   Where a document is properly delivered to the registrar in Welsh without a certified translation into English, the registrar must obtain such a translation if the document is to be available for public inspection.

The translation is treated as if delivered to the registrar in accordance with the same provision as the original.

(4)   A Welsh company may deliver to the registrar a certified translation into Welsh of any document in English that relates to the company and is or has been delivered to the registrar.

(5)   Section 1105 (which requires certified translations into English of documents delivered to the registrar in another language) does not apply to a document relating to a Welsh company that is drawn up and delivered in Welsh.

NOTES

Commencement: 1 January 2007.

Commencement (transitional adaptations): the transitional adaptations of this section contained in the Companies Act 2006 (Commencement No 1, Transitional Provisions and Savings) Order 2006, SI 2006/3428, Sch 1, para 11 were revoked by the Companies Act 2006 (Commencement No 5, Transitional Provisions and Savings) Order 2007, SI 2007/3495, art 10(1), (3), as from 6 April 2008 (subject to any transitional provisions and savings as apply, in accordance with Sch 4 to that Order, in relation to the repeal of any provision of the 1985 Act referred to in the adaptation). See **[2.9]**.

See also SI 2006/3428, Sch 5, Pt 1, para 1 which provides that regs 4 and 5 of the Companies (Welsh Language Forms and Documents) Regulations 1994, SI 1994/117 continue to have effect (notwithstanding the repeal of CA 1985, s 710B) as if reg 4 were made under sub-s (2) above, and reg 5 has effect as if the requirements imposed by it were requirements imposed by the registrar under CA 2006, s 1111 by means of rules under s 1117 of that Act. Note, however, that reg 4 was subsequently revoked (as from 1 October 2009) by the Registrar of Companies and Applications for Striking Off Regulations 2009, SI 2009/1803, reg 6(5).

Regulations: the Registrar of Companies and Applications for Striking Off Regulations 2009, SI 2009/1803 at **[4.491]**.

[1.1105]
1105 Documents that may be drawn up and delivered in other languages

(1)   Documents to which this section applies may be drawn up and delivered to the registrar in a language other than English, but when delivered to the registrar they must be accompanied by a certified translation into English.

(2)   This section applies to—

(a)   agreements required to be forwarded to the registrar under Chapter 3 of Part 3 (agreements affecting the company's constitution);

(b)   documents required to be delivered under section 400(2)(e) or section 401(2)(f) (company included in accounts of larger group: required to deliver copy of group accounts);

(c)   instruments or copy instruments required to be delivered under Part 25 (company charges);

(d)   documents of any other description specified in regulations made by the Secretary of State.

(3)   Regulations under this section are subject to negative resolution procedure.

NOTES

Commencement: 1 January 2007.

Commencement (transitional adaptations): art 5 of the Companies Act 2006 (Commencement No 1, Transitional Provisions and Savings) Order 2006, SI 2006/3428 provides that the provisions brought into force by arts 2–4 of 2006 Order shall have effect subject to any transitional adaptations specified in Sch 1 to that Order. Schedule 1, para 12 to the Order (at **[2.9]**) provided for such transitional adaptations. Note, however, that sub-para 12(2) was revoked by the Companies Act 2006 (Commencement No 3, Consequential Amendments, Transitional Provisions and Savings) Order 2007, SI 2007/2194, art 11(a), as from 1 October 2007, and that sub-para 12(3) was revoked by the Companies Act 2006 (Commencement No 5, Transitional Provisions and Savings) Order 2007, SI 2007/3495, art 10(1), (3), as from 6 April 2008 (subject to any transitional provisions and savings as apply, in accordance with Sch 4 to that Order, in relation to the repeal of the provisions of the 1985 Act referred to in the adaptation; see art 10 at **[2.59]**). All of this paragraph was revoked by the Companies Act 2006 (Commencement No 8, Transitional Provisions and Savings) Order 2008, SI 2008/2860, art 6, as from 1 October 2009 (subject to any relevant transitional provision or saving in Sch 2 to that Order).

Regulations: the Companies (Registrar, Languages and Trading Disclosures) Regulations 2006, SI 2006/3429 at **[4.2]**; the Companies (Cross-Border Mergers) Regulations 2007, SI 2007/2974 at **[4.17]**; the Overseas Companies Regulations 2009, SI 2009/1801 at **[4.389]**; the Registrar of Companies and Applications for Striking Off Regulations 2009, SI 2009/1803 at **[4.491]**; the Overseas Companies (Execution of Documents and Registration of Charges) Regulations 2009, SI 2009/1917 at **[4.500]**.

[1.1106]
1106 Voluntary filing of translations
(1)   A company may deliver to the registrar one or more certified translations of any document relating to the company that is or has been delivered to the registrar.
(2)   The Secretary of State may by regulations specify—
    (a)   the languages, and
    (b)   the descriptions of document,
in relation to which this facility is available.
(3)   The regulations must provide that it is available as from 1st January 2007—
    (a)   in relation to all the official languages of the European Union, and
    (b)   in relation to all documents subject to the Directive disclosure requirements (see section 1078).
(4)   The power of the registrar to impose requirements as to the form and manner of delivery includes power to impose requirements as to the identification of the original document and the delivery of the translation in a form and manner enabling it to be associated with the original.
(5)   Regulations under this section are subject to negative resolution procedure.
(6)   This section does not apply where the original document was delivered to the registrar before this section came into force.

NOTES
Commencement: 1 January 2007.
Regulations: the Companies (Registrar, Languages and Trading Disclosures) Regulations 2006, SI 2006/3429 at **[4.2]**; the Companies (Cross-Border Mergers) Regulations 2007, SI 2007/2974 at **[4.17]**.

[1.1107]
1107 Certified translations
(1)   In this Part a "certified translation" means a translation certified to be a correct translation.
(2)   In the case of any discrepancy between the original language version of a document and a certified translation—
    (a)   the company may not rely on the translation as against a third party, but
    (b)   a third party may rely on the translation unless the company shows that the third party had knowledge of the original.
(3)   A "third party" means a person other than the company or the registrar.

NOTES
Commencement: 1 January 2007.

Language requirements: transliteration
[1.1108]
1108 Transliteration of names and addresses: permitted characters
(1)   Names and addresses in a document delivered to the registrar must contain only letters, characters and symbols (including accents and other diacritical marks) that are permitted.
(2)   The Secretary of State may make provision by regulations—
    (a)   as to the letters, characters and symbols (including accents and other diacritical marks) that are permitted, and
    (b)   permitting or requiring the delivery of documents in which names and addresses have not been transliterated into a permitted form.
(3)   Regulations under this section are subject to negative resolution procedure.

NOTES
Commencement: 20 January 2007 (for the purpose of enabling the exercise of powers to make Orders or Regulations by statutory instrument); 1 October 2009 (otherwise).
Commencement (transitional provisions): the Companies Act 2006 (Commencement No 8, Transitional Provisions and Savings) Order 2008, SI 2008/2860, Sch 2, para 108 at **[2.91]** (as substituted by the Companies Act 2006 (Part 35) (Consequential Amendments, Transitional Provisions and Savings) Order 2009, SI 2009/1802, art 18, Schedule, with effect from 1 October 2009) provides that ss 1108–1110 of this Act apply in relation to all documents delivered to the registrar on or after 1 October 2009.
Regulations: the Registrar of Companies and Applications for Striking Off Regulations 2009, SI 2009/1803 at **[4.491]**; the European Economic Interest Grouping (Amendment) Regulations 2009, SI 2009/2399; the European Public Limited-Liability Company (Amendment) Regulations 2009, SI 2009/2400.

[1.1109]
1109 Transliteration of names and addresses: voluntary transliteration into Roman characters

(1) Where a name or address is or has been delivered to the registrar in a permitted form using other than Roman characters, [the company (or other body) to which the document relates] may deliver to the registrar a transliteration into Roman characters.

(2) The power of the registrar to impose requirements as to the form and manner of delivery includes power to impose requirements as to the identification of the original document and the delivery of the transliteration in a form and manner enabling it to be associated with the original.

NOTES
Commencement: 1 October 2009.
Commencement (transitional provisions): see the note to s 1108 at **[1.1108]**.
Sub-s (1): words in square brackets substituted by the Companies Act 2006 (Part 35) (Consequential Amendments, Transitional Provisions and Savings) Order 2009, SI 2009/1802, arts 2, 13, as from 1 October 2009.

[1.1110]
1110 Transliteration of names and addresses: certification

(1) The Secretary of State may make provision by regulations requiring the certification of transliterations and prescribing the form of certification.

(2) Different provision may be made for compulsory and voluntary transliterations.

(3) Regulations under this section are subject to negative resolution procedure.

NOTES
Commencement: 20 January 2007 (for the purpose of enabling the exercise of powers to make Orders or Regulations by statutory instrument); 1 October 2009 (otherwise).
Commencement (transitional provisions): see the note to s 1108 at **[1.1108]**.

Supplementary provisions

[1.1111]
1111 Registrar's requirements as to certification or verification

(1) Where a document required or authorised to be delivered to the registrar under any enactment is required—
    (a) to be certified as an accurate translation or transliteration, or
    (b) to be certified as a correct copy or verified,
the registrar may impose requirements as to the person, or description of person, by whom the certificate or verification is to be given.

(2) The power conferred by section 1068 (registrar's requirements as to form, authentication and manner of delivery) is exercisable in relation to the certificate or verification as if it were a separate document.

(3) Requirements imposed under this section must not be inconsistent with requirements imposed by any enactment with respect to the certification or verification of the document concerned.

NOTES
Commencement: 1 January 2007.
See also the penultimate note to s 1104 at **[1.1104]**.

[1.1112]
1112 General false statement offence

(1) It is an offence for a person knowingly or recklessly—
    (a) to deliver or cause to be delivered to the registrar, for any purpose of the Companies Acts, a document, or
    (b) to make to the registrar, for any such purpose, a statement,
that is misleading, false or deceptive in a material particular.

(2) A person guilty of an offence under this section is liable—
    (a) on conviction on indictment, to imprisonment for a term not exceeding two years or a fine (or both);
    (b) on summary conviction—
      (i) in England and Wales, to imprisonment for a term not exceeding twelve months or to a fine not exceeding the statutory maximum (or both);
      (ii) in Scotland or Northern Ireland, to imprisonment for a term not exceeding six months, or to a fine not exceeding the statutory maximum (or both).

NOTES
Commencement: 1 October 2009.
Commencement (transitional provisions): the Companies Act 2006 (Commencement No 8, Transitional Provisions and Savings) Order 2008, SI 2008/2860, Sch 2, para 109 at **[2.91]** (as substituted by the Companies Act 2006 (Part 35) (Consequential Amendments, Transitional Provisions and Savings) Order 2009, SI 2009/1802, art 18, Schedule, with effect from 1 October 2009) provides that this section applies to all documents delivered, and statements made, on or after 1 October 2009.
Offences under this section: see further s 1131 at **[1.1131]**.

[1.1113]

1113 Enforcement of company's filing obligations

(1) This section applies where a company has made default in complying with any obligation under the Companies Acts—

    (a)   to deliver a document to the registrar, or

    (b)   to give notice to the registrar of any matter.

(2) The registrar, or any member or creditor of the company, may give notice to the company requiring it to comply with the obligation.

(3) If the company fails to make good the default within 14 days after service of the notice, the registrar, or any member or creditor of the company, may apply to the court for an order directing the company, and any specified officer of it, to make good the default within a specified time.

(4) The court's order may provide that all costs (in Scotland, expenses) of or incidental to the application are to be borne by the company or by any officers of it responsible for the default.

(5) This section does not affect the operation of any enactment making it an offence, or imposing a civil penalty, for the default.

NOTES

Commencement: 1 October 2009.

[1.1114]

1114 Application of provisions about documents and delivery

(1) In this Part—

    (a)   "document" means information recorded in any form, and

    (b)   references to delivering a document include forwarding, lodging, registering, sending, producing or submitting it or (in the case of a notice) giving it.

(2) Except as otherwise provided, this Part applies in relation to the supply to the registrar of information otherwise than in documentary form as it applies in relation to the delivery of a document.

NOTES

Commencement: 1 January 2007 (certain purposes); 1 October 2009 (otherwise) (see the note below).

Commencement (note): the Companies Act 2006 (Commencement No 1, Transitional Provisions and Savings) Order 2006, SI 2006/3428, art 2(2) provides that this section shall come into force on 1 January 2007 so far as is necessary for the purposes of the provisions of this Act brought into force on that date by art 2(1) of that Order (see **[2.2]**).

[1.1115]

1115 Supplementary provisions relating to electronic communications

(1) Registrar's rules may require a company [(or other body)] to give any necessary consents to the use of electronic means for communications by the registrar to the company [(or other body)] as a condition of making use of any facility to deliver material to the registrar by electronic means.

(2) A document that is required to be signed by the registrar or authenticated by the registrar's seal shall, if sent by electronic means, be authenticated in such manner as may be specified by registrar's rules.

NOTES

Commencement: 1 October 2009.

Commencement (transitional provisions): Sch 2, para 111 to the Companies Act 2006 (Commencement No 8, Transitional Provisions and Savings) Order 2008, SI 2008/2860 (at **[2.91]**) provides as follows—

"Provision and authentication by registrar of documents sent by electronic means

111.—(1)   The repeal of section 710A of the 1985 Act or Article 659A of the 1986 Order (provision and authentication by registrar of documents in non-legible form) does not affect the application of those provisions on or after 1st October 2009 in relation to saved provisions of that Act or Order.

(2)   Section 1115(2) of the Companies Act 2006 (authentication in manner specified by registrar's rules) does not apply to a document in relation to which section 710A(2) of the 1985 Act or Article 659A(2) of the 1986 Order applies.".

Sub-s (1): words in square brackets inserted by the Companies Act 2006 (Part 35) (Consequential Amendments, Transitional Provisions and Savings) Order 2009, SI 2009/1802, arts 2, 14, as from 1 October 2009.

[1.1116]

1116 Alternative to publication in the Gazette

(1) Notices that would otherwise need to be published by the registrar in the Gazette may instead be published by such means as may from time to time be approved by the registrar in accordance with regulations made by the Secretary of State.

(2) The Secretary of State may make provision by regulations as to what alternative means may be approved.

(3) The regulations may, in particular—

    (a)   require the use of electronic means;

    (b)   require the same means to be used—

        (i)   for all notices or for all notices of specified descriptions, and

          (ii)   whether [the company (or other body) to which the notice relates] is registered in England and Wales, Scotland or Northern Ireland;

    (c)   impose conditions as to the manner in which access to the notices is to be made available.

(4)   Regulations under this section are subject to negative resolution procedure.

(5)   Before starting to publish notices by means approved under this section the registrar must publish at least one notice to that effect in the Gazette.

(6)   Nothing in this section prevents the registrar from giving public notice both in the Gazette and by means approved under this section.

    In that case, the requirement of public notice is met when notice is first given by either means.

NOTES

Commencement: 20 January 2007 (for the purpose of enabling the exercise of powers to make Orders or Regulations by statutory instrument); 1 October 2009 (otherwise).

Sub-s (3): words in square brackets substituted by the Companies Act 2006 (Part 35) (Consequential Amendments, Transitional Provisions and Savings) Order 2009, SI 2009/1802, arts 2, 15, as from 1 October 2009.

[1.1117]
1117   Registrar's rules
(1)   Where any provision of this Part enables the registrar to make provision, or impose requirements, as to any matter, the registrar may make such provision or impose such requirements by means of rules under this section.

    This is without prejudice to the making of such provision or the imposing of such requirements by other means.

(2)   Registrar's rules—

    (a)   may make different provision for different cases, and

    (b)   may allow the registrar to disapply or modify any of the rules.

(3)   The registrar must—

    (a)   publicise the rules in a manner appropriate to bring them to the notice of persons affected by them, and

    (b)   make copies of the rules available to the public (in hard copy or electronic form).

NOTES

Commencement: 1 January 2007 (certain purposes); 6 April 2008 (certain purposes); 1 October 2009 (otherwise) (see the notes below).

Commencement (note): the Companies Act 2006 (Commencement No 1, Transitional Provisions and Savings) Order 2006, SI 2006/3428, art 2(2) provides that this section shall come into force on 1 January 2007 so far as is necessary for the purposes of the provisions of this Act brought into force on that date by art 2(1) of that Order (see **[2.2]**).

Commencement (note): the Companies Act 2006 (Commencement No 5, Transitional Provisions and Savings) Order 2007, SI 2007/3495, art 3(2) provides (a) that sub-ss (1), (2) shall come into force on 6 April 2008 so far as may be necessary for the purpose of enabling rules to be made under this section before the date on which the section is brought generally into force, and (b) sub-s (3) has effect accordingly (see **[2.52]**).

See also the penultimate note to s 1104 at **[1.1104]**.

[1.1118]
1118   Payments into the Consolidated Fund
Nothing in the Companies Acts or any other enactment as to the payment of receipts into the Consolidated Fund shall be read as affecting the operation in relation to the registrar of section 3(1) of the Government Trading Funds Act 1973 (c 63).

NOTES

Commencement: 1 October 2009.

[1.1119]
1119   Contracting out of registrar's functions
(1)   Where by virtue of an order made under section 69 of the Deregulation and Contracting Out Act 1994 (c 40) a person is authorised by the registrar to accept delivery of any class of documents that are under any enactment to be delivered to the registrar, the registrar may direct that documents of that class shall be delivered to a specified address of the authorised person.

    Any such direction must be printed and made available to the public (with or without payment).

(2)   A document of that class that is delivered to an address other than the specified address is treated as not having been delivered.

(3)   Registrar's rules are not subordinate legislation for the purposes of section 71 of the Deregulation and Contracting Out Act 1994 (functions excluded from contracting out).

NOTES

Commencement: 1 October 2009.

[1.1120]
1120   Application of this Part to overseas companies
(Repealed as noted below.)

NOTES

This section came into force for certain purposes on 1 January 2007 (see SI 2006/3428, art 2(2)) and fully on 1 October 2009. It was repealed by the Companies Act 2006 (Part 35) (Consequential Amendments, Transitional Provisions and Savings) Order 2009, SI 2009/1802, arts 2, 16, as from 1 October 2009.

PART 36
OFFENCES UNDER THE COMPANIES ACTS

NOTES

Transitional provisions and savings in relation to offences: see the Companies Act 2006 (Commencement No 8, Transitional Provisions and Savings) Order 2008, SI 2008/2860, art 7 at **[2.88]** (prosecution of offences in transitional cases). In relation to offences under the Companies Act 1985, see also Sch 2, para 116 to that Order at **[2.91]** (savings for provisions relating to offences).

Liability of officer in default

[1.1121]
1121 Liability of officer in default
(1)   This section has effect for the purposes of any provision of the Companies Acts to the effect that, in the event of contravention of an enactment in relation to a company, an offence is committed by every officer of the company who is in default.
(2)   For this purpose "officer" includes—
   (a)   any director, manager or secretary, and
   (b)   any person who is to be treated as an officer of the company for the purposes of the provision in question.
(3)   An officer is "in default" for the purposes of the provision if he authorises or permits, participates in, or fails to take all reasonable steps to prevent, the contravention.

NOTES

Commencement: 20 January 2007 (certain purposes); 6 April 2007 (certain purposes); 1 October 2007 (certain purposes); 6 April 2008 (certain purposes); 1 October 2008 (certain purposes); 1 October 2009 (otherwise) (see the notes below).

Commencement (note): the Companies Act 2006 (Commencement No 1, Transitional Provisions and Savings) Order 2006, SI 2006/3428, art 3(2) provides that this section shall come into force on 20 January 2007 so far as is necessary for the purposes of the provisions of this Act brought into force on that date by art 3(1) of that Order (see **[2.3]**).

Commencement (note): the Companies Act 2006 (Commencement No 2, Consequential Amendments, Transitional Provisions and Savings) Order 2007, SI 2007/1093, art 2(2) provides that this section shall come into force on 6 April 2007 so far as is necessary for the purposes of the provisions of this Act brought into force on that date by art 2(1) of that Order (see **[2.17]**).

Commencement (note): the Companies Act 2006 (Commencement No 3, Consequential Amendments, Transitional Provisions and Savings) Order 2007, SI 2007/2194, art 2(1)(l) provides that this section shall come into force on 1 October 2007 in so far as it applies to offences under Parts XIV, XV of the Companies Act 1985 (see **[2.32]**).

Commencement (note): the Companies Act 2006 (Commencement No 3, Consequential Amendments, Transitional Provisions and Savings) Order 2007, SI 2007/2194, art 2(3) provides that this section shall come into force on 1 October 2007 so far as is necessary for the purposes of the provisions of this Act brought into force on that date by art 2(1), (2) of that Order (see **[2.32]**).

Commencement (note): the Companies Act 2006 (Commencement No 5, Transitional Provisions and Savings) Order 2007, SI 2007/3495, arts 3(3), 5(3), provide that this section shall come into force on 6 April 2008 and 1 October 2008 respectively so far as is necessary for the purposes of the provisions of this Act brought into force on those dates by arts 3(1)(a)–(t), (2), 5(1)(a)–(f) of that Order (see **[2.52]**, **[2.54]**).

Transitional provisions and savings in relation to offences: see the note at the start of this Part (preceding this section).

[1.1122]
1122 Liability of company as officer in default
(1)   Where a company is an officer of another company, it does not commit an offence as an officer in default unless one of its officers is in default.
(2)   Where any such offence is committed by a company the officer in question also commits the offence and is liable to be proceeded against and punished accordingly.
(3)   In this section "officer" and "in default" have the meanings given by section 1121.

NOTES

Commencement: 20 January 2007 (certain purposes); 6 April 2007 (certain purposes); 1 October 2007 (certain purposes); 6 April 2008 (certain purposes); 1 October 2008 (certain purposes); 1 October 2009 (otherwise) (see the notes below).

Commencement (note): the Companies Act 2006 (Commencement No 1, Transitional Provisions and Savings) Order 2006, SI 2006/3428, art 3(2) provides that this section shall come into force on 20 January 2007 so far as is necessary for the purposes of the provisions of this Act brought into force on that date by art 3(1) of that Order (see **[2.3]**).

Commencement (note): the Companies Act 2006 (Commencement No 2, Consequential Amendments, Transitional Provisions and Savings) Order 2007, SI 2007/1093, art 2(2) provides that this section shall come into force on 6 April 2007 so far as is necessary for the purposes of the provisions of this Act brought into force on that date by art 2(1) of that Order (see **[2.17]**).

Commencement (note): the Companies Act 2006 (Commencement No 3, Consequential Amendments, Transitional Provisions and Savings) Order 2007, SI 2007/2194, art 2(1)(l) provides that this section shall come into force on 1 October 2007 in so far as it applies to offences under Parts XIV, XV of the Companies Act 1985 (see **[2.32]**).

Commencement (note): the Companies Act 2006 (Commencement No 3, Consequential Amendments, Transitional Provisions and Savings) Order 2007, SI 2007/2194, art 2(3) provides that this section shall come into force on 1 October 2007 so far as is necessary for the purposes of the provisions of this Act brought into force on that date by art 2(1), (2) of that Order (see **[2.32]**).

Commencement (note): the Companies Act 2006 (Commencement No 5, Transitional Provisions and Savings) Order 2007, SI 2007/3495, arts 3(3), 5(3), provide that this section shall come into force on 6 April 2008 and 1 October 2008 respectively so far as is necessary for the purposes of the provisions of this Act brought into force on those dates by arts 3(1)(a)–(t), (2), 5(1)(a)–(f) of that Order (see **[2.52]**, **[2.54]**).

Transitional provisions and savings in relation to offences: see the note at the start of this Part (ie, preceding s 1121 at **[1.1121]**).

___

[1.1123]

1123 Application to bodies other than companies

(1) Section 1121 (liability of officers in default) applies to a body other than a company as it applies to a company.

(2) As it applies in relation to a body corporate other than a company—

    (a) the reference to a director of the company shall be read as referring—

        (i) where the body's affairs are managed by its members, to a member of the body,

        (ii) in any other case, to any corresponding officer of the body, and

    (b) the reference to a manager or secretary of the company shall be read as referring to any manager, secretary or similar officer of the body.

(3) As it applies in relation to a partnership—

    (a) the reference to a director of the company shall be read as referring to a member of the partnership, and

    (b) the reference to a manager or secretary of the company shall be read as referring to any manager, secretary or similar officer of the partnership.

(4) As it applies in relation to an unincorporated body other than a partnership—

    (a) the reference to a director of the company shall be read as referring—

        (i) where the body's affairs are managed by its members, to a member of the body,

        (ii) in any other case, to a member of the governing body, and

    (b) the reference to a manager or secretary of the company shall be read as referring to any manager, secretary or similar officer of the body.

___

NOTES

Commencement: 6 April 2007 (certain purposes); 1 October 2007 (certain purposes); 6 April 2008 (certain purposes); 1 October 2008 (certain purposes); 1 October 2009 (otherwise) (see the notes below).

Commencement (note): the Companies Act 2006 (Commencement No 2, Consequential Amendments, Transitional Provisions and Savings) Order 2007, SI 2007/1093, art 2(2) provides that this section shall come into force on 6 April 2007 so far as is necessary for the purposes of the provisions of this Act brought into force on that date by art 2(1) of that Order (see **[2.17]**).

Commencement (note): the Companies Act 2006 (Commencement No 3, Consequential Amendments, Transitional Provisions and Savings) Order 2007, SI 2007/2194, art 2(1)(l) provides that this section shall come into force on 1 October 2007 in so far as it applies to offences under Parts XIV, XV of the Companies Act 1985 (see **[2.32]**).

Commencement (note): the Companies Act 2006 (Commencement No 5, Transitional Provisions and Savings) Order 2007, SI 2007/3495, arts 3(3), 5(3), provide that this section shall come into force on 6 April 2008 and 1 October 2008 respectively so far as is necessary for the purposes of the provisions of this Act brought into force on those dates by arts 3(1)(a)–(t), (2), 5(1)(a)–(f) of that Order (see **[2.52]**, **[2.54]**).

Transitional provisions and savings in relation to offences: see the note at the start of this Part (ie, preceding s 1121 at **[1.1121]**).

___

Offences under the Companies Act 1985

[1.1124]

1124 Amendments of the Companies Act 1985

Schedule 3 contains amendments of the Companies Act 1985 (c 6) relating to offences.

___

NOTES

Commencement: 1 October 2007.

Transitional provisions and savings in relation to offences: see the note at the start of this Part (ie, preceding s 1121 at **[1.1121]**).

___

General provisions

[1.1125]

1125 Meaning of "daily default fine"

(1) This section defines what is meant in the Companies Acts where it is provided that a person guilty of an offence is liable on summary conviction to a fine not exceeding a specified amount "and, for continued contravention, a daily default fine" not exceeding a specified amount.

(2) This means that the person is liable on a second or subsequent summary conviction of the offence to a fine not exceeding the latter amount for each day on which the contravention is continued (instead of being liable to a fine not exceeding the former amount).

NOTES

Commencement: 20 January 2007 (certain purposes); 6 April 2007 (certain purposes); 1 October 2007 (certain purposes); 6 April 2008 (certain purposes); 1 October 2008 (certain purposes); 1 October 2009 (otherwise) (see the notes below).

Commencement (note): the Companies Act 2006 (Commencement No 1, Transitional Provisions and Savings) Order 2006, SI 2006/3428, art 3(2) provides that this section shall come into force on 20 January 2007 so far as is necessary for the purposes of the provisions of this Act brought into force on that date by art 3(1) of that Order (see **[2.3]**).

Commencement (note): the Companies Act 2006 (Commencement No 2, Consequential Amendments, Transitional Provisions and Savings) Order 2007, SI 2007/1093, art 2(2) provides that this section shall come into force on 6 April 2007 so far as is necessary for the purposes of the provisions of this Act brought into force on that date by art 2(1) of that Order (see **[2.17]**).

Commencement (note): the Companies Act 2006 (Commencement No 3, Consequential Amendments, Transitional Provisions and Savings) Order 2007, SI 2007/2194, art 2(1)(l) provides that this section shall come into force on 1 October 2007 in so far as it applies to offences under Parts XIV, XV of the Companies Act 1985 (see **[2.32]**).

Commencement (note): the Companies Act 2006 (Commencement No 3, Consequential Amendments, Transitional Provisions and Savings) Order 2007, SI 2007/2194, art 2(3) provides that this section shall come into force on 1 October 2007 so far as is necessary for the purposes of the provisions of this Act brought into force on that date by art 2(1), (2) of that Order (see **[2.32]**).

Commencement (note): the Companies Act 2006 (Commencement No 5, Transitional Provisions and Savings) Order 2007, SI 2007/3495, arts 3(3), 5(3), provide that this section shall come into force on 6 April 2008 and 1 October 2008 respectively so far as is necessary for the purposes of the provisions of this Act brought into force on those dates by arts 3(1)(a)–(t), (2), 5(1)(a)–(f) of that Order (see **[2.52]**, **[2.54]**).

Transitional provisions and savings in relation to offences: see the note at the start of this Part (ie, preceding s 1121 at **[1.1121]**).

[1.1126]
1126 Consents required for certain prosecutions
(1) This section applies to proceedings for an offence under any of the following provisions—
section 458, 460 or 949 of this Act (offences of unauthorised disclosure of information);
section 953 of this Act (failure to comply with rules about takeover bid documents);
section 448, 449, 450, 451 or 453A of the Companies Act 1985 (c 6) (offences in connection with company investigations);
section 798 of this Act or section 455 of the Companies Act 1985 (offence of attempting to evade restrictions on shares).
(2) No such proceedings are to be brought in England and Wales except by or with the consent of—
(a) in the case of an offence under—
(i) section 458, 460 or 949 of this Act,
(ii) section 953 of this Act, or
(iii) section 448, 449, 450, 451 or 453A of the Companies Act 1985,
the Secretary of State or the Director of Public Prosecutions;
(b) in the case of an offence under section 798 of this Act or section 455 of the Companies Act 1985, the Secretary of State.
(3) No such proceedings are to be brought in Northern Ireland except by or with the consent of—
(a) in the case of an offence under—
(i) section 458, 460 or 949 of this Act,
(ii) section 953 of this Act, or
(iii) section 448, 449, 450, 451 or 453A of the Companies Act 1985,
the Secretary of State or the Director of Public Prosecutions for Northern Ireland;
(b) in the case of an offence under section 798 of this Act or section 455 of the Companies Act 1985, the Secretary of State.

NOTES

Commencement: 20 January 2007 (certain purposes); 6 April 2007 (certain purposes); 1 October 2007 (certain purposes); 6 April 2008 (otherwise) (see the notes below).

Commencement (note): the Companies Act 2006 (Commencement No 1, Transitional Provisions and Savings) Order 2006, SI 2006/3428, art 3(2) provides that this section shall come into force on 20 January 2007 so far as is necessary for the purposes of the provisions of this Act brought into force on that date by art 3(1) of that Order (see **[2.3]**).

Commencement (note): the Companies Act 2006 (Commencement No 2, Consequential Amendments, Transitional Provisions and Savings) Order 2007, SI 2007/1093, art 2(2) provides that this section shall come into force on 6 April 2007 so far as is necessary for the purposes of the provisions of this Act brought into force on that date by art 2(1) of that Order (see **[2.17]**).

Commencement (note): the Companies Act 2006 (Commencement No 3, Consequential Amendments, Transitional Provisions and Savings) Order 2007, SI 2007/2194, art 2(1)(l) provides that this section shall come into force on 1 October 2007 in so far as it applies to offences under Parts XIV, XV of the Companies Act 1985 (see **[2.32]**).

Transitional provisions and savings in relation to offences: see the note at the start of this Part (ie, preceding s 1121 at **[1.1121]**).

[1.1127]
1127 Summary proceedings: venue
(1) Summary proceedings for any offence under the Companies Acts may be taken—
(a) against a body corporate, at any place at which the body has a place of business, and

   (b)   against any other person, at any place at which he is for the time being.

(2)   This is without prejudice to any jurisdiction exercisable apart from this section.

NOTES

Commencement: 20 January 2007 (certain purposes); 6 April 2007 (certain purposes); 1 October 2007 (certain purposes); 6 April 2008 (certain purposes); 1 October 2008 (certain purposes); 1 October 2009 (otherwise) (see the notes below).

Commencement (note): the Companies Act 2006 (Commencement No 1, Transitional Provisions and Savings) Order 2006, SI 2006/3428, art 3(2) provides that this section shall come into force on 20 January 2007 so far as is necessary for the purposes of the provisions of this Act brought into force on that date by art 3(1) of that Order (see **[2.3]**).

Commencement (note): the Companies Act 2006 (Commencement No 2, Consequential Amendments, Transitional Provisions and Savings) Order 2007, SI 2007/1093, art 2(2) provides that this section shall come into force on 6 April 2007 so far as is necessary for the purposes of the provisions of this Act brought into force on that date by art 2(1) of that Order (see **[2.17]**).

Commencement (note): the Companies Act 2006 (Commencement No 3, Consequential Amendments, Transitional Provisions and Savings) Order 2007, SI 2007/2194, art 2(1)(l) provides that this section shall come into force on 1 October 2007 in so far as it applies to offences under Parts XIV, XV of the Companies Act 1985 (see **[2.32]**).

Commencement (note): the Companies Act 2006 (Commencement No 3, Consequential Amendments, Transitional Provisions and Savings) Order 2007, SI 2007/2194, art 2(3) provides that this section shall come into force on 1 October 2007 so far as is necessary for the purposes of the provisions of this Act brought into force on that date by art 2(1), (2) of that Order (see **[2.32]**).

Commencement (note): the Companies Act 2006 (Commencement No 5, Transitional Provisions and Savings) Order 2007, SI 2007/3495, arts 3(3), 5(3), provide that this section shall come into force on 6 April 2008 and 1 October 2008 respectively so far as is necessary for the purposes of the provisions of this Act brought into force on those dates by arts 3(1)(a)–(t), (2), 5(1)(a)–(f) of that Order (see **[2.52]**, **[2.54]**).

Transitional provisions and savings in relation to offences: see the note at the start of this Part (ie, preceding s 1121 at **[1.1121]**).

[1.1128]

1128   Summary proceedings: time limit for proceedings

(1)   An information relating to an offence under the Companies Acts that is triable by a magistrates' court in England and Wales may be so tried if it is laid—

   (a)   at any time within three years after the commission of the offence, and

   (b)   within twelve months after the date on which evidence sufficient in the opinion of the Director of Public Prosecutions or the Secretary of State (as the case may be) to justify the proceedings comes to his knowledge.

(2)   Summary proceedings in Scotland for an offence under the Companies Acts—

   (a)   must not be commenced after the expiration of three years from the commission of the offence;

   (b)   subject to that, may be commenced at any time—

      (i)   within twelve months after the date on which evidence sufficient in the Lord Advocate's opinion to justify the proceedings came to his knowledge, or

      (ii)   where such evidence was reported to him by the Secretary of State, within twelve months after the date on which it came to the knowledge of the latter.

Section 136(3) of the Criminal Procedure (Scotland) Act 1995 (c 46) (date when proceedings deemed to be commenced) applies for the purposes of this subsection as for the purposes of that section.

(3)   A magistrates' court in Northern Ireland has jurisdiction to hear and determine a complaint charging the commission of a summary offence under the Companies Acts provided that the complaint is made—

   (a)   within three years from the time when the offence was committed, and

   (b)   within twelve months from the date on which evidence sufficient in the opinion of the Director of Public Prosecutions for Northern Ireland or the Secretary of State (as the case may be) to justify the proceedings comes to his knowledge.

(4)   For the purposes of this section a certificate of the Director of Public Prosecutions, the Lord Advocate, the Director of Public Prosecutions for Northern Ireland or the Secretary of State (as the case may be) as to the date on which such evidence as is referred to above came to his notice is conclusive evidence.

NOTES

Commencement: 20 January 2007 (certain purposes); 6 April 2007 (certain purposes); 1 October 2007 (certain purposes); 6 April 2008 (certain purposes); 1 October 2008 (certain purposes); 1 October 2009 (otherwise) (see the notes below).

Commencement (note): the Companies Act 2006 (Commencement No 1, Transitional Provisions and Savings) Order 2006, SI 2006/3428, art 3(2) provides that this section shall come into force on 20 January 2007 so far as is necessary for the purposes of the provisions of this Act brought into force on that date by art 3(1) of that Order (see **[2.3]**).

Commencement (note): the Companies Act 2006 (Commencement No 2, Consequential Amendments, Transitional Provisions and Savings) Order 2007, SI 2007/1093, art 2(2) provides that this section shall come into force on 6 April 2007 so far as is necessary for the purposes of the provisions of this Act brought into force on that date by art 2(1) of that Order (see **[2.17]**).

Commencement (note): the Companies Act 2006 (Commencement No 3, Consequential Amendments, Transitional Provisions and Savings) Order 2007, SI 2007/2194, art 2(1)(l) provides that this section shall come into force on 1 October 2007 in so far as it applies to offences under Parts XIV, XV of the Companies Act 1985 (see **[2.32]**).

Commencement (note): the Companies Act 2006 (Commencement No 3, Consequential Amendments, Transitional Provisions and Savings) Order 2007, SI 2007/2194, art 2(3) provides that this section shall come into force on 1 October 2007 so far as is necessary for the purposes of the provisions of this Act brought into force on that date by art 2(1), (2) of that Order (see **[2.32]**).

Commencement (note): the Companies Act 2006 (Commencement No 5, Transitional Provisions and Savings) Order 2007, SI 2007/3495, arts 3(3), 5(3), provide that this section shall come into force on 6 April 2008 and 1 October 2008 respectively so far as is necessary for the purposes of the provisions of this Act brought into force on those dates by arts 3(1)(a)–(t), (2), 5(1)(a)–(f) of that Order (see **[2.52]**, **[2.54]**).

Transitional provisions and savings in relation to offences: see the note at the start of this Part (ie, preceding s 1121 at **[1.1121]**).

[1.1129]
1129 Legal professional privilege

In proceedings against a person for an offence under the Companies Acts, nothing in those Acts is to be taken to require any person to disclose any information that he is entitled to refuse to disclose on grounds of legal professional privilege (in Scotland, confidentiality of communications).

NOTES

Commencement: 20 January 2007 (certain purposes); 6 April 2007 (certain purposes); 1 October 2007 (certain purposes); 6 April 2008 (certain purposes); 1 October 2008 (certain purposes); 1 October 2009 (otherwise) (see the notes below).

Commencement (note): the Companies Act 2006 (Commencement No 1, Transitional Provisions and Savings) Order 2006, SI 2006/3428, art 3(2) provides that this section shall come into force on 20 January 2007 so far as is necessary for the purposes of the provisions of this Act brought into force on that date by art 3(1) of that Order (see **[2.3]**).

Commencement (note): the Companies Act 2006 (Commencement No 2, Consequential Amendments, Transitional Provisions and Savings) Order 2007, SI 2007/1093, art 2(2) provides that this section shall come into force on 6 April 2007 so far as is necessary for the purposes of the provisions of this Act brought into force on that date by art 2(1) of that Order (see **[2.17]**).

Commencement (note): the Companies Act 2006 (Commencement No 3, Consequential Amendments, Transitional Provisions and Savings) Order 2007, SI 2007/2194, art 2(1)(l) provides that this section shall come into force on 1 October 2007 in so far as it applies to offences under Parts XIV, XV of the Companies Act 1985 (see **[2.32]**).

Commencement (note): the Companies Act 2006 (Commencement No 3, Consequential Amendments, Transitional Provisions and Savings) Order 2007, SI 2007/2194, art 2(3) provides that this section shall come into force on 1 October 2007 so far as is necessary for the purposes of the provisions of this Act brought into force on that date by art 2(1), (2) of that Order (see **[2.32]**).

Commencement (note): the Companies Act 2006 (Commencement No 5, Transitional Provisions and Savings) Order 2007, SI 2007/3495, arts 3(3), 5(3), provide that this section shall come into force on 6 April 2008 and 1 October 2008 respectively so far as is necessary for the purposes of the provisions of this Act brought into force on those dates by arts 3(1)(a)–(t), (2), 5(1)(a)–(f) of that Order (see **[2.52]**, **[2.54]**).

Transitional provisions and savings in relation to offences: see the note at the start of this Part (ie, preceding s 1121 at **[1.1121]**).

[1.1130]
1130 Proceedings against unincorporated bodies

(1) Proceedings for an offence under the Companies Acts alleged to have been committed by an unincorporated body must be brought in the name of the body (and not in that of any of its members).

(2) For the purposes of such proceedings—

    (a) any rules of court relating to the service of documents have effect as if the body were a body corporate, and

    (b) the following provisions apply as they apply in relation to a body corporate—

        (i) in England and Wales, section 33 of the Criminal Justice Act 1925 (c 86) and Schedule 3 to the Magistrates' Courts Act 1980 (c 43),

        (ii) in Scotland, sections 70 and 143 of the Criminal Procedure (Scotland) Act 1995 (c 46),

        (iii) in Northern Ireland, section 18 of the Criminal Justice Act (Northern Ireland) 1945 (c 15 (NI)) and Article 166 of and Schedule 4 to the Magistrates' Courts (Northern Ireland) Order 1981 (SI 1981/1675 (NI 26)).

(3) A fine imposed on an unincorporated body on its conviction of an offence under the Companies Acts must be paid out of the funds of the body.

NOTES

Commencement: 20 January 2007 (certain purposes); 6 April 2007 (certain purposes); 1 October 2007 (certain purposes); 6 April 2008 (certain purposes); 1 October 2008 (certain purposes); 1 October 2009 (otherwise) (see the notes below).

Commencement (note): the Companies Act 2006 (Commencement No 1, Transitional Provisions and Savings) Order 2006, SI 2006/3428, art 3(2) provides that this section shall come into force on 20 January 2007 so far as is necessary for the purposes of the provisions of this Act brought into force on that date by art 3(1) of that Order (see **[2.3]**).

Commencement (note): the Companies Act 2006 (Commencement No 2, Consequential Amendments, Transitional Provisions and Savings) Order 2007, SI 2007/1093, art 2(2) provides that this section shall come into force on 6 April 2007 so far as is necessary for the purposes of the provisions of this Act brought into force on that date by art 2(1) of that Order (see **[2.17]**).

Commencement (note): the Companies Act 2006 (Commencement No 3, Consequential Amendments, Transitional Provisions and Savings) Order 2007, SI 2007/2194, art 2(1)(l) provides that this section shall come into force on 1 October 2007 in so far as it applies to offences under Parts XIV, XV of the Companies Act 1985 (see **[2.32]**).

Commencement (note): the Companies Act 2006 (Commencement No 3, Consequential Amendments, Transitional Provisions and Savings) Order 2007, SI 2007/2194, art 2(3) provides that this section shall come into force on 1 October 2007 so far as is necessary for the purposes of the provisions of this Act brought into force on that date by art 2(1), (2) of that Order (see **[2.32]**).

Commencement (note): the Companies Act 2006 (Commencement No 5, Transitional Provisions and Savings) Order 2007, SI 2007/3495, arts 3(3), 5(3), provide that this section shall come into force on 6 April 2008 and 1 October 2008 respectively so far as is necessary for the purposes of the provisions of this Act brought into force on those dates by arts 3(1)(a)–(t), (2), 5(1)(a)–(f) of that Order (see **[2.52]**, **[2.54]**).

Transitional provisions and savings in relation to offences: see the note at the start of this Part (ie, preceding s 1121 at **[1.1121]**).

[1.1131]

1131 Imprisonment on summary conviction in England and Wales: transitory provision

(1) This section applies to any provision of the Companies Acts that provides that a person guilty of an offence is liable on summary conviction in England and Wales to imprisonment for a term not exceeding twelve months.

(2) In relation to an offence committed before the commencement of section 154(1) of the Criminal Justice Act 2003 (c 44), for "twelve months" substitute "six months".

NOTES

Commencement: 20 January 2007 (certain purposes); 6 April 2007 (certain purposes); 1 October 2007 (certain purposes); 6 April 2008 (certain purposes); 1 October 2008 (certain purposes); 1 October 2009 (otherwise) (see the notes below).

Commencement (note): the Companies Act 2006 (Commencement No 1, Transitional Provisions and Savings) Order 2006, SI 2006/3428, art 3(2) provides that this section shall come into force on 20 January 2007 so far as is necessary for the purposes of the provisions of this Act brought into force on that date by art 3(1) of that Order (see **[2.3]**).

Commencement (note): the Companies Act 2006 (Commencement No 2, Consequential Amendments, Transitional Provisions and Savings) Order 2007, SI 2007/1093, art 2(2) provides that this section shall come into force on 6 April 2007 so far as is necessary for the purposes of the provisions of this Act brought into force on that date by art 2(1) of that Order (see **[2.17]**).

Commencement (note): the Companies Act 2006 (Commencement No 3, Consequential Amendments, Transitional Provisions and Savings) Order 2007, SI 2007/2194, art 2(1)(l) provides that this section shall come into force on 1 October 2007 in so far as it applies to offences under Parts XIV, XV of the Companies Act 1985 (see **[2.32]**).

Commencement (note): the Companies Act 2006 (Commencement No 3, Consequential Amendments, Transitional Provisions and Savings) Order 2007, SI 2007/2194, art 2(3) provides that this section shall come into force on 1 October 2007 so far as is necessary for the purposes of the provisions of this Act brought into force on that date by art 2(1), (2) of that Order (see **[2.32]**).

Commencement (note): the Companies Act 2006 (Commencement No 5, Transitional Provisions and Savings) Order 2007, SI 2007/3495, arts 3(3), 5(3), provide that this section shall come into force on 6 April 2008 and 1 October 2008 respectively so far as is necessary for the purposes of the provisions of this Act brought into force on those dates by arts 3(1)(a)–(t), (2), 5(1)(a)–(f) of that Order (see **[2.52]**, **[2.54]**).

Transitional provisions and savings in relation to offences: see the note at the start of this Part (ie, preceding s 1121 at **[1.1121]**).

Note: as of 1 July 2011, s 154(1) of the Criminal Justice Act 2003 had not been brought into force.

Production and inspection of documents

[1.1132]

1132 Production and inspection of documents where offence suspected

(1) An application under this section may be made—

(a) in England and Wales, to a judge of the High Court by the Director of Public Prosecutions, the Secretary of State or a chief officer of police;

(b) in Scotland, to one of the Lords Commissioners of Justiciary by the Lord Advocate;

(c) in Northern Ireland, to the High Court by the Director of Public Prosecutions for Northern Ireland, the Department of Enterprise, Trade and Investment or a chief superintendent of the Police Service of Northern Ireland.

(2) If on an application under this section there is shown to be reasonable cause to believe—

(a) that any person has, while an officer of a company, committed an offence in connection with the management of the company's affairs, and

(b) that evidence of the commission of the offence is to be found in any documents in the possession or control of the company,

an order under this section may be made.

(3) The order may—

(a) authorise any person named in it to inspect the documents in question, or any of them, for the purpose of investigating and obtaining evidence of the offence, or

(b) require the secretary of the company, or such other officer of it as may be named in the order, to produce the documents (or any of them) to a person named in the order at a place so named.

(4) This section applies also in relation to documents in the possession or control of a person carrying on the business of banking, so far as they relate to the company's affairs, as it applies to documents in the possession or control of the company, except that no such order as is referred to in subsection (3)(b) may be made by virtue of this subsection.

(5) The decision under this section of a judge of the High Court, any of the Lords Commissioners of Justiciary or the High Court is not appealable.

(6) In this section "document" includes information recorded in any form.

NOTES

Commencement: 6 April 2007 (certain purposes); 1 October 2007 (certain purposes); 6 April 2008 (certain purposes); 1 October 2008 (certain purposes); 1 October 2009 (otherwise) (see the notes below).

Commencement (note): the Companies Act 2006 (Commencement No 2, Consequential Amendments, Transitional Provisions and Savings) Order 2007, SI 2007/1093, art 2(2) provides that this section shall come into force on 6 April 2007 so far as is necessary for the purposes of the provisions of this Act brought into force on that date by art 2(1) of that Order (see **[2.17]**).

Commencement (note): the Companies Act 2006 (Commencement No 3, Consequential Amendments, Transitional Provisions and Savings) Order 2007, SI 2007/2194, art 2(1)(l) provides that this section shall come into force on 1 October 2007 in so far as it applies to offences under Parts XIV, XV of the Companies Act 1985 (see **[2.32]**).

Commencement (note): the Companies Act 2006 (Commencement No 3, Consequential Amendments, Transitional Provisions and Savings) Order 2007, SI 2007/2194, art 2(3) provides that this section shall come into force on 1 October 2007 so far as is necessary for the purposes of the provisions of this Act brought into force on that date by art 2(1), (2) of that Order (see **[2.32]**).

Commencement (note): the Companies Act 2006 (Commencement No 5, Transitional Provisions and Savings) Order 2007, SI 2007/3495, arts 3(3), 5(3), provide that this section shall come into force on 6 April 2008 and 1 October 2008 respectively so far as is necessary for the purposes of the provisions of this Act brought into force on those dates by arts 3(1)(a)–(t), (2), 5(1)(a)–(f) of that Order (see **[2.52]**, **[2.54]**).

Transitional provisions and savings in relation to offences: see the note at the start of this Part (ie, preceding s 1121 at **[1.1121]**).

Supplementary

[1.1133]
1133 Transitional provision

The provisions of this Part except section 1132 do not apply to offences committed before the commencement of the relevant provision.

NOTES

Commencement: 20 January 2007 (certain purposes); 6 April 2007 (certain purposes); 1 October 2007 (certain purposes); 6 April 2008 (certain purposes); 1 October 2008 (certain purposes); 1 October 2009 (otherwise) (see the notes below).

Commencement (note): the Companies Act 2006 (Commencement No 1, Transitional Provisions and Savings) Order 2006, SI 2006/3428, art 3(2) provides that this section shall come into force on 20 January 2007 so far as is necessary for the purposes of the provisions of this Act brought into force on that date by art 3(1) of that Order (see **[2.3]**).

Commencement (note): the Companies Act 2006 (Commencement No 2, Consequential Amendments, Transitional Provisions and Savings) Order 2007, SI 2007/1093, art 2(2) provides that this section shall come into force on 6 April 2007 so far as is necessary for the purposes of the provisions of this Act brought into force on that date by art 2(1) of that Order (see **[2.17]**).

Commencement (note): the Companies Act 2006 (Commencement No 3, Consequential Amendments, Transitional Provisions and Savings) Order 2007, SI 2007/2194, art 2(1)(l) provides that this section shall come into force on 1 October 2007 in so far as it applies to offences under Parts XIV, XV of the Companies Act 1985 (see **[2.32]**).

Commencement (note): the Companies Act 2006 (Commencement No 3, Consequential Amendments, Transitional Provisions and Savings) Order 2007, SI 2007/2194, art 2(3) provides that this section shall come into force on 1 October 2007 so far as is necessary for the purposes of the provisions of this Act brought into force on that date by art 2(1), (2) of that Order (see **[2.32]**).

Commencement (note): the Companies Act 2006 (Commencement No 5, Transitional Provisions and Savings) Order 2007, SI 2007/3495, arts 3(3), 5(3), provide that this section shall come into force on 6 April 2008 and 1 October 2008 respectively so far as is necessary for the purposes of the provisions of this Act brought into force on those dates by arts 3(1)(a)–(t), (2), 5(1)(a)–(f) of that Order (see **[2.52]**, **[2.54]**).

Transitional provisions and savings in relation to offences: see the note at the start of this Part (ie, preceding s 1121 at **[1.1121]**).

PART 37
COMPANIES: SUPPLEMENTARY PROVISIONS

Company records

[1.1134]
1134 Meaning of "company records"

In this Part "company records" means—

(a) any register, index, accounting records, agreement, memorandum, minutes or other document required by the Companies Acts to be kept by a company, and

(b) any register kept by a company of its debenture holders.

NOTES

Commencement: 6 April 2007 (certain purposes); 1 October 2009 (otherwise) (see the note below).

Commencement (note): the Companies Act 2006 (Commencement No 2, Consequential Amendments, Transitional Provisions and Savings) Order 2007, SI 2007/1093, art 2(2) provides that this section shall come into force on 6 April 2007 so far as is necessary for the purposes of the provisions of this Act brought into force on that date by art 2(1) of that Order (see **[2.17]**).

[1.1135]
1135 Form of company records

(1) Company records—

(a)   may be kept in hard copy or electronic form, and

(b)   may be arranged in such manner as the directors of the company think fit,

provided the information in question is adequately recorded for future reference.

(2)   Where the records are kept in electronic form, they must be capable of being reproduced in hard copy form.

(3)   If a company fails to comply with this section, an offence is committed by every officer of the company who is in default.

(4)   A person guilty of an offence under this section is liable on summary conviction to a fine not exceeding level 3 on the standard scale and, for continued contravention, a daily default fine not exceeding one-tenth of level 3 on the standard scale.

(5)   Any provision of an instrument made by a company before 12th February 1979 that requires a register of holders of the company's debentures to be kept in hard copy form is to be read as requiring it to be kept in hard copy or electronic form.

NOTES

Commencement: 6 April 2007 (certain purposes); 1 October 2009 (otherwise) (see the note below).

Commencement (note): the Companies Act 2006 (Commencement No 2, Consequential Amendments, Transitional Provisions and Savings) Order 2007, SI 2007/1093, art 2(2) provides that this section shall come into force on 6 April 2007 so far as is necessary for the purposes of the provisions of this Act brought into force on that date by art 2(1) of that Order (see **[2.17]**).

[1.1136]

1136   Regulations about where certain company records to be kept available for inspection

(1)   The Secretary of State may make provision by regulations specifying places other than a company's registered office at which company records required to be kept available for inspection under a relevant provision may be so kept in compliance with that provision.

(2)   The "relevant provisions" are—

section 114 (register of members);

section 162 (register of directors);

section 228 (directors' service contracts);

section 237 (directors' indemnities);

section 275 (register of secretaries);

section 358 (records of resolutions etc);

section 702 (contracts relating to purchase of own shares);

section 720 (documents relating to redemption or purchase of own shares out of capital by private company);

section 743 (register of debenture holders);

section 805 (report to members of outcome of investigation by public company into interests in its shares);

section 809 (register of interests in shares disclosed to public company);

section 877 (instruments creating charges and register of charges: England and Wales);

section 892 (instruments creating charges and register of charges: Scotland).

(3)   The regulations may specify a place by reference to the company's principal place of business, the part of the United Kingdom in which the company is registered, the place at which the company keeps any other records available for inspection or in any other way.

(4)   The regulations may provide that a company does not comply with a relevant provision by keeping company records available for inspection at a place specified in the regulations unless conditions specified in the regulations are met.

(5)   The regulations—

(a)   need not specify a place in relation to each relevant provision;

(b)   may specify more than one place in relation to a relevant provision.

(6)   A requirement under a relevant provision to keep company records available for inspection is not complied with by keeping them available for inspection at a place specified in the regulations unless all the company's records subject to the requirement are kept there.

(7)   Regulations under this section are subject to negative resolution procedure.

NOTES

Commencement: 20 January 2007 (for the purpose of enabling the exercise of powers to make Orders or Regulations by statutory instrument); 1 October 2009 (otherwise).

Regulations: the Companies (Company Records) Regulations 2008, SI 2008/3006 at **[4.318]**.

[1.1137]

1137   Regulations about inspection of records and provision of copies

(1)   The Secretary of State may make provision by regulations as to the obligations of a company that is required by any provision of the Companies Acts—

(a)   to keep available for inspection any company records, or

(b)   to provide copies of any company records.

(2)   A company that fails to comply with the regulations is treated as having refused inspection or, as the case may be, having failed to provide a copy.

(3)   The regulations may—

(a)   make provision as to the time, duration and manner of inspection, including the circumstances in which and extent to which the copying of information is permitted in the course of inspection, and

(b)   define what may be required of the company as regards the nature, extent and manner of extracting or presenting any information for the purposes of inspection or the provision of copies.

(4)   Where there is power to charge a fee, the regulations may make provision as to the amount of the fee and the basis of its calculation.

(5)   Nothing in any provision of this Act or in the regulations shall be read as preventing a company—

(a)   from affording more extensive facilities than are required by the regulations, or

(b)   where a fee may be charged, from charging a lesser fee than that prescribed or none at all.

(6)   Regulations under this section are subject to negative resolution procedure.

NOTES

Commencement: 20 January 2007 (for the purpose of enabling the exercise of powers to make Orders or Regulations by statutory instrument); 30 September 2007 (sub-ss (1), (4), (5)(b), (6)); 1 October 2009 (otherwise).

Regulations: the Companies (Fees for Inspection and Copying of Company Records) Regulations 2007, SI 2007/2612 at **[4.12]**; the Companies (Fees for Inspection and Copying of Company Records) (No 2) Regulations 2007, SI 2007/3535 at **[4.95]**; the Companies (Company Records) Regulations 2008, SI 2008/3006 at **[4.318]**; the Companies (Fees for Inspection of Company Records) Regulations 2008, SI 2008/3007 at **[4.327]**.

[1.1138]
1138   Duty to take precautions against falsification

(1)   Where company records are kept otherwise than in bound books, adequate precautions must be taken—

(a)   to guard against falsification, and

(b)   to facilitate the discovery of falsification.

(2)   If a company fails to comply with this section, an offence is committed by every officer of the company who is in default.

(3)   A person guilty of an offence under this section is liable on summary conviction to a fine not exceeding level 3 on the standard scale and, for continued contravention, a daily default fine not exceeding one-tenth of level 3 on the standard scale.

(4)   This section does not apply to the documents required to be kept under—

(a)   section 228 (copy of director's service contract or memorandum of its terms); or

(b)   section 237 (qualifying indemnity provision).

NOTES

Commencement: 6 April 2007 (certain purposes); 1 October 2009 (otherwise) (see the note below).

Commencement (note): the Companies Act 2006 (Commencement No 2, Consequential Amendments, Transitional Provisions and Savings) Order 2007, SI 2007/1093, art 2(2) provides that this section shall come into force on 6 April 2007 so far as is necessary for the purposes of the provisions of this Act brought into force on that date by art 2(1) of that Order (see **[2.17]**).

Service addresses

[1.1139]
1139   Service of documents on company

(1)   A document may be served on a company registered under this Act by leaving it at, or sending it by post to, the company's registered office.

(2)   A document may be served on an overseas company whose particulars are registered under section 1046—

(a)   by leaving it at, or sending it by post to, the registered address of any person resident in the United Kingdom who is authorised to accept service of documents on the company's behalf, or

(b)   if there is no such person, or if any such person refuses service or service cannot for any other reason be effected, by leaving it at or sending by post to any place of business of the company in the United Kingdom.

(3)   For the purposes of this section a person's "registered address" means any address for the time being shown as a current address in relation to that person in the part of the register available for public inspection.

(4)   Where a company registered in Scotland or Northern Ireland carries on business in England and Wales, the process of any court in England and Wales may be served on the company by leaving it at, or sending it by post to, the company's principal place of business in England and Wales, addressed to the manager or other head officer in England and Wales of the company.

Where process is served on a company under this subsection, the person issuing out the process must send a copy of it by post to the company's registered office.

(5)   Further provision as to service and other matters is made in the company communications provisions (see section 1143).

Part 1 The Companies Act 2006

NOTES

Commencement: 6 April 2007 (certain purposes); 6 April 2008 (certain purposes); 1 October 2009 (otherwise) (see the notes below).

Commencement (transitional adaptations): art 3 of the Companies Act 2006 (Commencement No 2, Consequential Amendments, Transitional Provisions and Savings) Order 2007, SI 2007/1093 provides that the provisions brought into force by art 2 of 2007 Order shall have effect subject to any transitional adaptations specified in Sch 1 to that Order. Schedule 1, para 5 to the Order (at **[2.27]**) provided for such transitional adaptations (note that this paragraph was revoked by the Companies Act 2006 (Commencement No 8, Transitional Provisions and Savings) Order 2008, SI 2008/2860, art 6, as from 1 October 2009 (subject to any relevant transitional provision or saving in Sch 2 to that Order).

Commencement (note): the Companies Act 2006 (Commencement No 2, Consequential Amendments, Transitional Provisions and Savings) Order 2007, SI 2007/1093, art 2(2) provides that this section shall come into force on 6 April 2007 so far as is necessary for the purposes of the provisions of this Act brought into force on that date by art 2(1) of that Order (see **[2.17]**).

Commencement (note): the Companies Act 2006 (Commencement No 5, Transitional Provisions and Savings) Order 2007, SI 2007/3495, art 3(3) provides that this section shall come into force on 6 April 2008 so far as is necessary for the purposes of the provisions of this Act brought into force on that date by art 3(1)(a)–(t), (2) of that Order (see **[2.52]**).

[1.1140]
1140   Service of documents on directors, secretaries and others
(1)   A document may be served on a person to whom this section applies by leaving it at, or sending it by post to, the person's registered address.
(2)   This section applies to—
   (a)   a director or secretary of a company;
   (b)   in the case of an overseas company whose particulars are registered under section 1046, a person holding any such position as may be specified for the purposes of this section by regulations under that section;
   (c)   a person appointed in relation to a company as—
      (i)   a judicial factor (in Scotland),
      (ii)   [an interim manager] appointed under section 18 of the Charities Act 1993 (c 10), or
      (iii)   a manager appointed under section 47 of the Companies (Audit, Investigations and Community Enterprise) Act 2004 (c 27).
(3)   This section applies whatever the purpose of the document in question.
It is not restricted to service for purposes arising out of or in connection with the appointment or position mentioned in subsection (2) or in connection with the company concerned.
(4)   For the purposes of this section a person's "registered address" means any address for the time being shown as a current address in relation to that person in the part of the register available for public inspection.
(5)   If notice of a change of that address is given to the registrar, a person may validly serve a document at the address previously registered until the end of the period of 14 days beginning with the date on which notice of the change is registered.
(6)   Service may not be effected by virtue of this section at an address—
   (a)   if notice has been registered of the termination of the appointment in relation to which the address was registered and the address is not a registered address of the person concerned in relation to any other appointment;
   (b)   in the case of a person holding any such position as is mentioned in subsection (2)(b), if the overseas company has ceased to have any connection with the United Kingdom by virtue of which it is required to register particulars under section 1046.
(7)   Further provision as to service and other matters is made in the company communications provisions (see section 1143).
(8)   Nothing in this section shall be read as affecting any enactment or rule of law under which permission is required for service out of the jurisdiction.

NOTES

Commencement: 6 April 2007 (certain purposes); 6 April 2008 (certain purposes); 1 October 2009 (otherwise) (see the notes below).

Commencement (note): the Companies Act 2006 (Commencement No 2, Consequential Amendments, Transitional Provisions and Savings) Order 2007, SI 2007/1093, art 2(2) provides that this section shall come into force on 6 April 2007 so far as is necessary for the purposes of the provisions of this Act brought into force on that date by art 2(1) of that Order (see **[2.17]**).

Commencement (note): the Companies Act 2006 (Commencement No 5, Transitional Provisions and Savings) Order 2007, SI 2007/3495, art 3(3) provides that this section shall come into force on 6 April 2008 so far as is necessary for the purposes of the provisions of this Act brought into force on that date by art 3(1)(a)–(t), (2) of that Order (see **[2.52]**).

Sub-s (2): words in square brackets substituted by the Companies Act 2006 (Consequential Amendments, Transitional Provisions and Savings) Order 2009, SI 2009/1941, art 2(1), Sch 1, para 260(1), (7)(a), as from 1 October 2009.

Regulations: the Overseas Companies Regulations 2009, SI 2009/1801 at **[4.389]**.

[1.1141]
1141   Service addresses
(1)   In the Companies Acts a "service address", in relation to a person, means an address at which documents may be effectively served on that person.

(2)   The Secretary of State may by regulations specify conditions with which a service address must comply.

(3)   Regulations under this section are subject to negative resolution procedure.

NOTES
Commencement: 20 January 2007 (for the purpose of enabling the exercise of powers to make Orders or Regulations by statutory instrument); 1 October 2009 (otherwise).
Regulations: the Companies Act 2006 (Annual Return and Service Addresses) Regulations 2008, SI 2008/3000 at **[4.312]**.

[1.1142]
1142   Requirement to give service address
Any obligation under the Companies Acts to give a person's address is, unless otherwise expressly provided, to give a service address for that person.

NOTES
Commencement: 1 October 2009.

Sending or supplying documents or information

[1.1143]
1143   The company communications provisions
(1)   The provisions of sections 1144 to 1148 and Schedules 4 and 5 ("the company communications provisions") have effect for the purposes of any provision of the Companies Acts that authorises or requires documents or information to be sent or supplied by or to a company.
(2)   The company communications provisions have effect subject to any requirements imposed, or contrary provision made, by or under any enactment.
(3)   In particular, in their application in relation to documents or information to be sent or supplied to the registrar, they have effect subject to the provisions of Part 35.
(4)   For the purposes of subsection (2), provision is not to be regarded as contrary to the company communications provisions by reason only of the fact that it expressly authorises a document or information to be sent or supplied in hard copy form, in electronic form or by means of a website.

NOTES
Commencement: 20 January 2007.
Commencement (transitional adaptations): art 5 of the Companies Act 2006 (Commencement No 1, Transitional Provisions and Savings) Order 2006, SI 2006/3428 provides that the provisions brought into force by arts 2–4 of 2006 Order shall have effect subject to any transitional adaptations specified in Sch 1 to that Order. Schedule 1, para 14 to the Order (at **[2.9]**) provided for such transitional adaptations (note that this paragraph was revoked by the Companies Act 2006 (Commencement No 8, Transitional Provisions and Savings) Order 2008, SI 2008/2860, art 6, as from 1 October 2009 (subject to any relevant transitional provision or saving in Sch 2 to that Order)).

[1.1144]
1144   Sending or supplying documents or information
(1)   Documents or information to be sent or supplied to a company must be sent or supplied in accordance with the provisions of Schedule 4.
(2)   Documents or information to be sent or supplied by a company must be sent or supplied in accordance with the provisions of Schedule 5.
(3)   The provisions referred to in subsection (2) apply (and those referred to in subsection (1) do not apply) in relation to documents or information that are to be sent or supplied by one company to another.

NOTES
Commencement: 20 January 2007.

[1.1145]
1145   Right to hard copy version
(1)   Where a member of a company or a holder of a company's debentures has received a document or information from the company otherwise than in hard copy form, he is entitled to require the company to send him a version of the document or information in hard copy form.
(2)   The company must send the document or information in hard copy form within 21 days of receipt of the request from the member or debenture holder.
(3)   The company may not make a charge for providing the document or information in that form.
(4)   If a company fails to comply with this section, an offence is committed by the company and every officer of it who is in default.
(5)   A person guilty of an offence under this section is liable on summary conviction to a fine not exceeding level 3 on the standard scale and, for continued contravention, a daily default fine not exceeding one-tenth of level 3 on the standard scale.

NOTES
Commencement: 20 January 2007.

[1.1146]

1146 Requirement of authentication

(1) This section applies in relation to the authentication of a document or information sent or supplied by a person to a company.

(2) A document or information sent or supplied in hard copy form is sufficiently authenticated if it is signed by the person sending or supplying it.

(3) A document or information sent or supplied in electronic form is sufficiently authenticated—

    (a) if the identity of the sender is confirmed in a manner specified by the company, or

    (b) where no such manner has been specified by the company, if the communication contains or is accompanied by a statement of the identity of the sender and the company has no reason to doubt the truth of that statement.

(4) Where a document or information is sent or supplied by one person on behalf of another, nothing in this section affects any provision of the company's articles under which the company may require reasonable evidence of the authority of the former to act on behalf of the latter.

NOTES

Commencement: 20 January 2007.

[1.1147]

1147 Deemed delivery of documents and information

(1) This section applies in relation to documents and information sent or supplied by a company.

(2) Where—

    (a) the document or information is sent by post (whether in hard copy or electronic form) to an address in the United Kingdom, and

    (b) the company is able to show that it was properly addressed, prepaid and posted,

it is deemed to have been received by the intended recipient 48 hours after it was posted.

(3) Where—

    (a) the document or information is sent or supplied by electronic means, and

    (b) the company is able to show that it was properly addressed,

it is deemed to have been received by the intended recipient 48 hours after it was sent.

(4) Where the document or information is sent or supplied by means of a website, it is deemed to have been received by the intended recipient—

    (a) when the material was first made available on the website, or

    (b) if later, when the recipient received (or is deemed to have received) notice of the fact that the material was available on the website.

(5) In calculating a period of hours for the purposes of this section, no account shall be taken of any part of a day that is not a working day.

(6) This section has effect subject to—

    (a) in its application to documents or information sent or supplied by a company to its members, any contrary provision of the company's articles;

    (b) in its application to documents or information sent or supplied by a company to its debentures holders, any contrary provision in the instrument constituting the debentures;

    (c) in its application to documents or information sent or supplied by a company to a person otherwise than in his capacity as a member or debenture holder, any contrary provision in an agreement between the company and that person.

NOTES

Commencement: 20 January 2007.

[1.1148]

1148 Interpretation of company communications provisions

(1) In the company communications provisions—

    "address" includes a number or address used for the purposes of sending or receiving documents or information by electronic means;

    "company" includes any body corporate;

    "document" includes summons, notice, order or other legal process and registers.

(2) References in the company communications provisions to provisions of the Companies Acts authorising or requiring a document or information to be sent or supplied include all such provisions, whatever expression is used, and references to documents or information being sent or supplied shall be construed accordingly.

(3) References in the company communications provisions to documents or information being sent or supplied by or to a company include references to documents or information being sent or supplied by or to the directors of a company acting on behalf of the company.

NOTES

Commencement: 20 January 2007.

Requirements as to independent valuation

[1.1149]

1149 Application of valuation requirements

The provisions of sections 1150 to 1153 apply to the valuation and report required by—

section 93 (re-registration as public company: recent allotment of shares for non-cash consideration);

section 593 (allotment of shares of public company in consideration of non-cash asset);

section 599 (transfer of non-cash asset to public company).

NOTES

Commencement: 1 October 2009.

[1.1150]

1150 Valuation by qualified independent person

(1) The valuation and report must be made by a person ("the valuer") who—

(a) is eligible for appointment as a statutory auditor (see section 1212), and

(b) meets the independence requirement in section 1151.

(2) However, where it appears to the valuer to be reasonable for the valuation of the consideration, or part of it, to be made by (or for him to accept a valuation made by) another person who—

(a) appears to him to have the requisite knowledge and experience to value the consideration or that part of it, and

(b) is not an officer or employee of—

(i) the company, or

(ii) any other body corporate that is that company's subsidiary or holding company or a subsidiary of that company's holding company,

or a partner of or employed by any such officer or employee,

he may arrange for or accept such a valuation, together with a report which will enable him to make his own report under this section.

(3) The references in subsection (2)(b) to an officer or employee do not include an auditor.

(4) Where the consideration or part of it is valued by a person other than the valuer himself, the latter's report must state that fact and shall also—

(a) state the former's name and what knowledge and experience he has to carry out the valuation, and

(b) describe so much of the consideration as was valued by the other person, and the method used to value it, and specify the date of that valuation.

NOTES

Commencement: 1 October 2009.

[1.1151]

1151 The independence requirement

(1) A person meets the independence requirement for the purposes of section 1150 only if—

(a) he is not—

(i) an officer or employee of the company, or

(ii) a partner or employee of such a person, or a partnership of which such a person is a partner;

(b) he is not—

(i) an officer or employee of an associated undertaking of the company, or

(ii) a partner or employee of such a person, or a partnership of which such a person is a partner; and

(c) there does not exist between—

(i) the person or an associate of his, and

(ii) the company or an associated undertaking of the company,

a connection of any such description as may be specified by regulations made by the Secretary of State.

(2) An auditor of the company is not regarded as an officer or employee of the company for this purpose.

(3) In this section—

"associated undertaking" means—

(a) a parent undertaking or subsidiary undertaking of the company, or

(b) a subsidiary undertaking of a parent undertaking of the company; and

"associate" has the meaning given by section 1152.

(4) Regulations under this section are subject to negative resolution procedure.

NOTES

Commencement: 20 January 2007 (for the purpose of enabling the exercise of powers to make Orders or Regulations by statutory instrument); 1 October 2009 (otherwise).

[1.1152]
1152 Meaning of "associate"
(1) This section defines "associate" for the purposes of section 1151 (valuation: independence requirement).
(2) In relation to an individual, "associate" means—
   (a) that individual's spouse or civil partner or minor child or step-child,
   (b) any body corporate of which that individual is a director, and
   (c) any employee or partner of that individual.
(3) In relation to a body corporate, "associate" means—
   (a) any body corporate of which that body is a director,
   (b) any body corporate in the same group as that body, and
   (c) any employee or partner of that body or of any body corporate in the same group.
(4) In relation to a partnership that is a legal person under the law by which it is governed, "associate" means—
   (a) any body corporate of which that partnership is a director,
   (b) any employee of or partner in that partnership, and
   (c) any person who is an associate of a partner in that partnership.
(5) In relation to a partnership that is not a legal person under the law by which it is governed, "associate" means any person who is an associate of any of the partners.
(6) In this section, in relation to a limited liability partnership, for "director" read "member".

NOTES
Commencement: 1 October 2009.

[1.1153]
1153 Valuer entitled to full disclosure
(1) A person carrying out a valuation or making a report with respect to any consideration proposed to be accepted or given by a company, is entitled to require from the officers of the company such information and explanation as he thinks necessary to enable him to—
   (a) carry out the valuation or make the report, and
   (b) provide any note required by section 596(3) or 600(3) (note required where valuation carried out by another person).
(2) A person who knowingly or recklessly makes a statement to which this subsection applies that is misleading, false or deceptive in a material particular commits an offence.
(3) Subsection (2) applies to a statement—
   (a) made (whether orally or in writing) to a person carrying out a valuation or making a report, and
   (b) conveying or purporting to convey any information or explanation which that person requires, or is entitled to require, under subsection (1).
(4) A person guilty of an offence under subsection (2) is liable—
   (a) on conviction on indictment, to imprisonment for a term not exceeding two years or a fine (or both);
   (b) on summary conviction—
     (i) in England and Wales, to imprisonment for a term not exceeding twelve months or to a fine not exceeding the statutory maximum (or both);
     (ii) in Scotland or Northern Ireland, to imprisonment for a term not exceeding six months, or to a fine not exceeding the statutory maximum (or both).

NOTES
Commencement: 1 October 2009.
Offences under this section: see further s 1131 at **[1.1131]**.

Notice of appointment of certain officers

[1.1154]
1154 Duty to notify registrar of certain appointments etc
(1) Notice must be given to the registrar of the appointment in relation to a company of—
   (a) a judicial factor (in Scotland),
   (b) [an interim manager] appointed under section 18 of the Charities Act 1993 (c 10), or
   (c) a manager appointed under section 47 of the Companies (Audit, Investigations and Community Enterprise) Act 2004 (c 27).
(2) The notice must be given—
   (a) in the case of appointment of a judicial factor, by the judicial factor;
   (b) in the case of appointment of [an interim manager] under section 18 of the Charities Act 1993 (c 10), by the Charity Commission;
   (c) in the case of appointment of a manager under section 47 of the Companies (Audit, Investigations and Community Enterprise) Act 2004, by the Regulator of Community Interest Companies.
(3) The notice must specify an address at which service of documents (including legal process) may be effected on the person appointed.

Notice of a change in the address for service may be given to the registrar by the person appointed.

(4) Where notice has been given under this section of the appointment of a person, notice must also be given to the registrar of the termination of the appointment. This notice must be given by the person specified in subsection (2).

NOTES

Commencement: 1 October 2009.

Commencement (transitional provisions): the Companies Act 2006 (Commencement No 8, Transitional Provisions and Savings) Order 2008, SI 2008/2860, Sch 2, para 112 (at **[2.91]**) provides that ss 1154 and 1155 apply in relation to appointments made on or after 1 October 2009.

Sub-ss (1), (2): words in square brackets substituted by the Companies Act 2006 (Consequential Amendments, Transitional Provisions and Savings) Order 2009, SI 2009/1941, art 2(1), Sch 1, para 260(1), (7)(b), as from 1 October 2009.

[1.1155]

1155 Offence of failure to give notice

(1) If a judicial factor fails to give notice of his appointment in accordance with section 1154 within the period of 14 days after the appointment he commits an offence.

(2) A person guilty of an offence under this section is liable on summary conviction to a fine not exceeding level 5 on the standard scale and, for continued contravention, a daily default fine not exceeding one-tenth of level 5 on the standard scale.

NOTES

Commencement: 1 October 2009.

Commencement (transitional provisions): see the note to s 1154 at **[1.1154]**.

Courts and legal proceedings

[1.1156]

1156 Meaning of "the court"

(1) Except as otherwise provided, in the Companies Acts "the court" means—
  (a) in England and Wales, the High Court or (subject to subsection (3)) a county court;
  (b) in Scotland, the Court of Session or the sheriff court;
  (c) in Northern Ireland, the High Court.

(2) The provisions of the Companies Acts conferring jurisdiction on "the court" as defined above have effect subject to any enactment or rule of law relating to the allocation of jurisdiction or distribution of business between courts in any part of the United Kingdom.

(3) The Lord Chancellor may, with the concurrence of the Lord Chief Justice, by order—
  (a) exclude a county court from having jurisdiction under the Companies Acts, and
  (b) for the purposes of that jurisdiction attach that court's district, or any part of it, to another county court.

(4) The Lord Chief Justice may nominate a judicial office holder (as defined in section 109(4) of the Constitutional Reform Act 2005 (c 4)) to exercise his functions under subsection (3).

NOTES

Commencement: 20 January 2007 (for the purpose of enabling the exercise of powers to make Orders or Regulations by statutory instrument); 1 October 2009 (otherwise).

Orders: the Civil Courts (Amendment) Order 2009, SI 2009/2455.

[1.1157]

1157 Power of court to grant relief in certain cases

(1) If in proceedings for negligence, default, breach of duty or breach of trust against—
  (a) an officer of a company, or
  (b) a person employed by a company as auditor (whether he is or is not an officer of the company),

it appears to the court hearing the case that the officer or person is or may be liable but that he acted honestly and reasonably, and that having regard to all the circumstances of the case (including those connected with his appointment) he ought fairly to be excused, the court may relieve him, either wholly or in part, from his liability on such terms as it thinks fit.

(2) If any such officer or person has reason to apprehend that a claim will or might be made against him in respect of negligence, default, breach of duty or breach of trust—
  (a) he may apply to the court for relief, and
  (b) the court has the same power to relieve him as it would have had if it had been a court before which proceedings against him for negligence, default, breach of duty or breach of trust had been brought.

(3) Where a case to which subsection (1) applies is being tried by a judge with a jury, the judge, after hearing the evidence, may, if he is satisfied that the defendant (in Scotland, the defender) ought in pursuance of that subsection to be relieved either in whole or in part from the liability sought to be enforced against him, withdraw the case from the jury and forthwith direct judgment to be entered for the defendant (in Scotland, grant decree of absolvitor) on such terms as to costs (in Scotland, expenses) or otherwise as the judge may think proper.

NOTES
Commencement: 1 October 2008.

PART 38
COMPANIES: INTERPRETATION
Meaning of "UK-registered company"

[1.1158]
1158 Meaning of "UK-registered company"
In the Companies Acts "UK-registered company" means a company registered under this Act.

The expression does not include an overseas company that has registered particulars under section 1046.

NOTES
Commencement: 1 October 2007 (certain purposes); 1 November 2007 (certain purposes); 1 October 2009 (otherwise) (see the note below).

Commencement (transitional adaptations): art 6 of the Companies Act 2006 (Commencement No 3, Consequential Amendments, Transitional Provisions and Savings) Order 2007, SI 2007/2194 provides that the provisions brought into force by that Order shall have effect subject to any transitional adaptations specified in Sch 1 to that Order. Schedule 1, para 21 to the Order (at **[2.43]**) provided for such transitional adaptations (note that this paragraph was revoked by the Companies Act 2006 (Commencement No 8, Transitional Provisions and Savings) Order 2008, SI 2008/2860, art 6, as from 1 October 2009 (subject to any relevant transitional provision or saving in Sch 2 to that Order)).

Commencement (note): the Companies Act 2006 (Commencement No 3, Consequential Amendments, Transitional Provisions and Savings) Order 2007, SI 2007/2194, arts 2(3) and 3(2) provide that this section shall come into force on 1 October 2007 and 1 November 2007 so far as is necessary for the purposes of the provisions of this Act brought into force on those dates by arts 2(1), (2) and 3(2) of that Order respectively (see **[2.32]** and **[2.33]**).

Meaning of "subsidiary" and related expressions

[1.1159]
1159 Meaning of "subsidiary" etc
(1) A company is a "subsidiary" of another company, its "holding company", if that other company—
    (a) holds a majority of the voting rights in it, or
    (b) is a member of it and has the right to appoint or remove a majority of its board of directors, or
    (c) is a member of it and controls alone, pursuant to an agreement with other members, a majority of the voting rights in it,
or if it is a subsidiary of a company that is itself a subsidiary of that other company.
(2) A company is a "wholly-owned subsidiary" of another company if it has no members except that other and that other's wholly-owned subsidiaries or persons acting on behalf of that other or its wholly-owned subsidiaries.
(3) Schedule 6 contains provisions explaining expressions used in this section and otherwise supplementing this section.
(4) In this section and that Schedule "company" includes any body corporate.

NOTES
Commencement: 6 April 2008 (certain purposes); 1 October 2009 (otherwise) (see the note below).
Commencement (note): the Companies Act 2006 (Commencement No 5, Transitional Provisions and Savings) Order 2007, SI 2007/3495, art 3(4) provides that this section shall come into force on 6 April 2008 so far as is necessary for the purposes of the provisions of this Act brought into force on that date by art 3(1)(u) of that Order (see **[2.52]**).

[1.1160]
1160 Meaning of "subsidiary" etc: power to amend
(1) The Secretary of State may by regulations amend the provisions of section 1159 (meaning of "subsidiary" etc) and Schedule 6 (meaning of "subsidiary" etc: supplementary provisions) so as to alter the meaning of the expressions "subsidiary", "holding company" or "wholly-owned subsidiary".
(2) Regulations under this section are subject to negative resolution procedure.
(3) Any amendment made by regulations under this section does not apply for the purposes of enactments outside the Companies Acts unless the regulations so provide.
(4) So much of section 23(3) of the Interpretation Act 1978 (c 30) as applies section 17(2)(a) of that Act (effect of repeal and re-enactment) to deeds, instruments and documents other than enactments does not apply in relation to any repeal and re-enactment effected by regulations under this section.

NOTES
Commencement: 20 January 2007 (for the purpose of enabling the exercise of powers to make Orders or Regulations by statutory instrument); 6 April 2008 (certain purposes); 1 October 2009 (otherwise) (see the note below).

Commencement (note): the Companies Act 2006 (Commencement No 5, Transitional Provisions and Savings) Order 2007, SI 2007/3495, art 3(4) provides that this section shall come into force on 6 April 2008 so far as is necessary for the purposes of the provisions of this Act brought into force on that date by art 3(1)(u) of that Order (see **[2.52]**).

Meaning of "undertaking" and related expressions

[1.1161]

1161 Meaning of "undertaking" and related expressions

(1) In the Companies Acts "undertaking" means—

   (a) a body corporate or partnership, or

   (b) an unincorporated association carrying on a trade or business, with or without a view to profit.

(2) In the Companies Acts references to shares—

   (a) in relation to an undertaking with capital but no share capital, are to rights to share in the capital of the undertaking; and

   (b) in relation to an undertaking without capital, are to interests—

     (i) conferring any right to share in the profits or liability to contribute to the losses of the undertaking, or

     (ii) giving rise to an obligation to contribute to the debts or expenses of the undertaking in the event of a winding up.

(3) Other expressions appropriate to companies shall be construed, in relation to an undertaking which is not a company, as references to the corresponding persons, officers, documents or organs, as the case may be, appropriate to undertakings of that description.

This is subject to provision in any specific context providing for the translation of such expressions.

(4) References in the Companies Acts to "fellow subsidiary undertakings" are to undertakings which are subsidiary undertakings of the same parent undertaking but are not parent undertakings or subsidiary undertakings of each other.

(5) In the Companies Acts "group undertaking", in relation to an undertaking, means an undertaking which is—

   (a) a parent undertaking or subsidiary undertaking of that undertaking, or

   (b) a subsidiary undertaking of any parent undertaking of that undertaking.

NOTES

Commencement: 6 April 2008.

[1.1162]

1162 Parent and subsidiary undertakings

(1) This section (together with Schedule 7) defines "parent undertaking" and "subsidiary undertaking" for the purposes of the Companies Acts.

(2) An undertaking is a parent undertaking in relation to another undertaking, a subsidiary undertaking, if—

   (a) it holds a majority of the voting rights in the undertaking, or

   (b) it is a member of the undertaking and has the right to appoint or remove a majority of its board of directors, or

   (c) it has the right to exercise a dominant influence over the undertaking—

     (i) by virtue of provisions contained in the undertaking's articles, or

     (ii) by virtue of a control contract, or

   (d) it is a member of the undertaking and controls alone, pursuant to an agreement with other shareholders or members, a majority of the voting rights in the undertaking.

(3) For the purposes of subsection (2) an undertaking shall be treated as a member of another undertaking—

   (a) if any of its subsidiary undertakings is a member of that undertaking, or

   (b) if any shares in that other undertaking are held by a person acting on behalf of the undertaking or any of its subsidiary undertakings.

(4) An undertaking is also a parent undertaking in relation to another undertaking, a subsidiary undertaking, if—

   (a) it has the power to exercise, or actually exercises, dominant influence or control over it, or

   (b) it and the subsidiary undertaking are managed on a unified basis.

(5) A parent undertaking shall be treated as the parent undertaking of undertakings in relation to which any of its subsidiary undertakings are, or are to be treated as, parent undertakings; and references to its subsidiary undertakings shall be construed accordingly.

(6) Schedule 7 contains provisions explaining expressions used in this section and otherwise supplementing this section.

(7) In this section and that Schedule references to shares, in relation to an undertaking, are to allotted shares.

NOTES

Commencement: 6 April 2008.

Other definitions

[1.1163]
1163 "Non-cash asset"

(1) In the Companies Acts "non-cash asset" means any property or interest in property, other than cash.

For this purpose "cash" includes foreign currency.

(2) A reference to the transfer or acquisition of a non-cash asset includes—

    (a) the creation or extinction of an estate or interest in, or a right over, any property, and

    (b) the discharge of a liability of any person, other than a liability for a liquidated sum.

NOTES
Commencement: 1 October 2009.

[1.1164]
1164 Meaning of "banking company" and "banking group"

(1) This section defines "banking company" and "banking group" for the purposes of the Companies Acts.

(2) "Banking company" means a person who has permission under Part 4 of the Financial Services and Markets Act 2000 (c 8) to accept deposits, other than—

    (a) a person who is not a company, and

    (b) a person who has such permission only for the purpose of carrying on another regulated activity in accordance with permission under that Part.

(3) The definition in subsection (2) must be read with section 22 of that Act, any relevant order under that section and Schedule 2 to that Act.

(4) References to a banking group are to a group where the parent company is a banking company or where—

    (a) the parent company's principal subsidiary undertakings are wholly or mainly credit institutions, and

    (b) the parent company does not itself carry on any material business apart from the acquisition, management and disposal of interests in subsidiary undertakings.

"Group" here means a parent undertaking and its subsidiary undertakings.

(5) For the purposes of subsection (4)—

    (a) a parent company's principal subsidiary undertakings are the subsidiary undertakings of the company whose results or financial position would principally affect the figures shown in the group accounts, and

    (b) the management of interests in subsidiary undertakings includes the provision of services to such undertakings.

NOTES
Commencement: 6 April 2008.

[1.1165]
1165 Meaning of "insurance company" and related expressions

(1) This section defines "insurance company", "authorised insurance company", "insurance group" and "insurance market activity" for the purposes of the Companies Acts.

(2) An "authorised insurance company" means a person (whether incorporated or not) who has permission under Part 4 of the Financial Services and Markets Act 2000 (c 8) to effect or carry out contracts of insurance.

(3) An "insurance company" means—

    (a) an authorised insurance company, or

    (b) any other person (whether incorporated or not) who—

        (i) carries on insurance market activity, or

        (ii) may effect or carry out contracts of insurance under which the benefits provided by that person are exclusively or primarily benefits in kind in the event of accident to or breakdown of a vehicle.

(4) Neither expression includes a friendly society within the meaning of the Friendly Societies Act 1992 (c 40).

(5) References to an insurance group are to a group where the parent company is an insurance company or where—

    (a) the parent company's principal subsidiary undertakings are wholly or mainly insurance companies, and

    (b) the parent company does not itself carry on any material business apart from the acquisition, management and disposal of interests in subsidiary undertakings.

"Group" here means a parent undertaking and its subsidiary undertakings.

(6) For the purposes of subsection (5)—

    (a) a parent company's principal subsidiary undertakings are the subsidiary undertakings of the company whose results or financial position would principally affect the figures shown in the group accounts, and

(b) the management of interests in subsidiary undertakings includes the provision of services to such undertakings.

(7) "Insurance market activity" has the meaning given in section 316(3) of the Financial Services and Markets Act 2000.

(8) References in this section to contracts of insurance and to the effecting or carrying out of such contracts must be read with section 22 of that Act, any relevant order under that section and Schedule 2 to that Act.

NOTES

Commencement: 6 April 2008.

[1.1166]
1166 "Employees' share scheme"

For the purposes of the Companies Acts an employees' share scheme is a scheme for encouraging or facilitating the holding of shares in or debentures of a company by or for the benefit of—
(a) the bona fide employees or former employees of—
  (i) the company,
  (ii) any subsidiary of the company, or
  (iii) the company's holding company or any subsidiary of the company's holding company, or
(b) the spouses, civil partners, surviving spouses, surviving civil partners, or minor children or step-children of such employees or former employees.

NOTES

Commencement: 1 October 2009.

[1.1167]
1167 Meaning of "prescribed"

In the Companies Acts "prescribed" means prescribed (by order or by regulations) by the Secretary of State.

NOTES

Commencement: 20 January 2007 (for the purpose of enabling the exercise of powers to make Orders or Regulations by statutory instrument); 30 September 2007 (otherwise).

[1.1168]
1168 Hard copy and electronic form and related expressions

(1) The following provisions apply for the purposes of the Companies Acts.

(2) A document or information is sent or supplied in hard copy form if it is sent or supplied in a paper copy or similar form capable of being read.
References to hard copy have a corresponding meaning.

(3) A document or information is sent or supplied in electronic form if it is sent or supplied—
(a) by electronic means (for example, by e-mail or fax), or
(b) by any other means while in an electronic form (for example, sending a disk by post).
References to electronic copy have a corresponding meaning.

(4) A document or information is sent or supplied by electronic means if it is—
(a) sent initially and received at its destination by means of electronic equipment for the processing (which expression includes digital compression) or storage of data, and
(b) entirely transmitted, conveyed and received by wire, by radio, by optical means or by other electromagnetic means.
References to electronic means have a corresponding meaning.

(5) A document or information authorised or required to be sent or supplied in electronic form must be sent or supplied in a form, and by a means, that the sender or supplier reasonably considers will enable the recipient—
(a) to read it, and
(b) to retain a copy of it.

(6) For the purposes of this section, a document or information can be read only if—
(a) it can be read with the naked eye, or
(b) to the extent that it consists of images (for example photographs, pictures, maps, plans or drawings), it can be seen with the naked eye.

(7) The provisions of this section apply whether the provision of the Companies Acts in question uses the words "sent" or "supplied" or uses other words (such as "deliver", "provide", "produce" or, in the case of a notice, "give") to refer to the sending or supplying of a document or information.

NOTES

Commencement: 1 January 2007 (certain purposes); 20 January 2007 (certain purposes); 6 April 2007 (certain purposes); 1 October 2007 (certain purposes); 15 December 2007 (certain purposes); 6 April 2008 (certain purposes); 1 October 2008 (certain purposes); 1 October 2009 (otherwise) (see the notes below).

Commencement (note): the Companies Act 2006 (Commencement No 1, Transitional Provisions and Savings) Order 2006, SI 2006/3428, arts 2(2), 3(2) provide that this section shall come into force on 1 January 2007 and 20 January 2007 respectively so far as is necessary for the purposes of the provisions of this Act brought into force on those dates by arts 2(1), 3(1) of that Order (see **[2.2]**, **[2.3]**).

Commencement (note): the Companies Act 2006 (Commencement No 2, Consequential Amendments, Transitional Provisions and Savings) Order 2007, SI 2007/1093, art 2(2) provides that this section shall come into force on 6 April 2007 so far as is necessary for the purposes of the provisions of this Act brought into force on that date by art 2(1) of that Order (see **[2.17]**).

Commencement (note): the Companies Act 2006 (Commencement No 3, Consequential Amendments, Transitional Provisions and Savings) Order 2007, SI 2007/2194, art 2(3) provides that this section shall come into force on 1 October 2007 so far as is necessary for the purposes of the provisions of this Act brought into force on that date by art 2(1), (2) of that Order (see **[2.32]**).

Commencement (note): the Companies Act 2006 (Commencement No 3, Consequential Amendments, Transitional Provisions and Savings) Order 2007, SI 2007/2194, art 4(2) provides that this section shall come into force on 15 December 2007 so far as is necessary for the purposes of the provisions of this Act brought into force on that date by art 4(1) of that Order (see **[2.34]**).

Commencement (note): the Companies Act 2006 (Commencement No 5, Transitional Provisions and Savings) Order 2007, SI 2007/3495, arts 3(3), 5(3), provide that this section shall come into force on 6 April 2008 and 1 October 2008 respectively so far as is necessary for the purposes of the provisions of this Act brought into force on those dates by arts 3(1)(a)–(t), (2), 5(1)(a)–(f) of that Order (see **[2.52]**, **[2.54]**).

[1.1169]
1169 Dormant companies

(1) For the purposes of the Companies Acts a company is "dormant" during any period in which it has no significant accounting transaction.

(2) A "significant accounting transaction" means a transaction that is required by section 386 to be entered in the company's accounting records.

(3) In determining whether or when a company is dormant, there shall be disregarded—

   (a)   any transaction arising from the taking of shares in the company by a subscriber to the memorandum as a result of an undertaking of his in connection with the formation of the company;

   (b)   any transaction consisting of the payment of—

       (i)   a fee to the registrar on a change of the company's name,

       (ii)   a fee to the registrar on the re-registration of the company,

       (iii)   a penalty under section 453 (penalty for failure to file accounts), or

       (iv)   a fee to the registrar for the registration of an annual return.

(4) Any reference in the Companies Acts to a body corporate other than a company being dormant has a corresponding meaning.

NOTES

Commencement: 6 April 2008.

[1.1170]
1170 Meaning of "EEA State" and related expressions

In the Companies Acts—

   ["EEA State" has the meaning given by Schedule 1 to the Interpretation Act 1978;]

   "EEA company" and "EEA undertaking" mean a company or undertaking governed by the law of an EEA State.

NOTES

Commencement: 6 April 2007.

Definition "EEA State" substituted by the Companies (EEA State) Regulations 2007, SI 2007/732, reg 3, as from 9 March 2007.

[1.1170A]
[1170A Receiver or manager and certain related references

(1) Any reference in the Companies Acts to a receiver or manager of the property of a company, or to a receiver of it, includes a receiver or manager or (as the case may be) a receiver of part only of that property and a receiver only of the income arising from the property or from part of it.

(2) Any reference in the Companies Acts to the appointment of a receiver or manager under powers contained in an instrument includes an appointment made under powers that by virtue of an enactment are implied in and have effect as if contained in an instrument.]

NOTES

Commencement: 1 October 2009.

Inserted, together with s 1170B, by the Companies Act 2006 (Consequential Amendments, Transitional Provisions and Savings) Order 2009, SI 2009/1941, art 2(1), Sch 1, para 260(1), (8), as from 1 October 2009.

[1.1170B]
[1170B Meaning of "contributory"

(1) In the Companies Acts "contributory" means every person liable to contribute to the assets of a company in the event of its being wound up.

(2) For the purposes of all proceedings for determining, and all proceedings prior to the final determination of, the persons who are to be deemed contributories, the expression includes any person alleged to be a contributory.

(3) The reference in subsection (1) to persons liable to contribute to the assets does not include a person so liable by virtue of a declaration by the court under—

(a) section 213 of the Insolvency Act 1986 or Article 177 of the Insolvency (Northern Ireland) Order 1989 (fraudulent trading), or

(b) section 214 of that Act or Article 178 of that Order (wrongful trading).]

NOTES

Commencement: 1 October 2009.

Inserted as noted to s 1170A at **[1.1170A]**.

[1.1171]
1171 The former Companies Acts

In the Companies Acts—

"the former Companies Acts" means—

(a) the Joint Stock Companies Acts, the Companies Act 1862 (c 89), the Companies (Consolidation) Act 1908 (c 69), the Companies Act 1929 (c 23), the Companies Act (Northern Ireland) 1932 (c 7 (NI)), the Companies Acts 1948 to 1983, the Companies Act (Northern Ireland) 1960 (c 22 (NI)), the Companies (Northern Ireland) Order 1986 (SI 1986/1032 (NI 6)) and the Companies Consolidation (Consequential Provisions) (Northern Ireland) Order 1986 (SI 1986/1035 (NI 9)), and

(b) the provisions of the Companies Act 1985 (c 6) and the Companies Consolidation (Consequential Provisions) Act 1985 (c 9) that are no longer in force;

"the Joint Stock Companies Acts" means the Joint Stock Companies Act 1856 (c 47), the Joint Stock Companies Acts 1856, 1857 (20 & 21 Vict c 14), the Joint Stock Banking Companies Act 1857 (c 49), and the Act to enable Joint Stock Banking Companies to be formed on the principle of limited liability (1858 c 91), but does not include the Joint Stock Companies Act 1844 (c 110).

NOTES

Commencement: 1 October 2009.

General

[1.1172]
1172 References to requirements of this Act

References in the company law provisions of this Act to the requirements of this Act include the requirements of regulations and orders made under it.

NOTES

Commencement: 6 April 2008.

[1.1173]
1173 Minor definitions: general

(1) In the Companies Acts—

"body corporate" and "corporation" include a body incorporated outside the United Kingdom, but do not include—

(a) a corporation sole, or

(b) a partnership that, whether or not a legal person, is not regarded as a body corporate under the law by which it is governed;

"credit institution" means a credit institution as defined in [Article 4.1] of Directive 2006/48/EC of the European Parliament and of the Council relating to the taking up and pursuit of the business of credit institutions [as last amended by Directive 2009/111/EC];

"financial institution" means a financial institution within the meaning of Article 1.1 of the Council Directive on the obligations of branches established in a Member State of credit and financial institutions having their head offices outside that Member State regarding the publication of annual accounting documents (the Bank Branches Directive, 89/ 117/EEC);

"firm" means any entity, whether or not a legal person, that is not an individual and includes a body corporate, a corporation sole and a partnership or other unincorporated association;

"the Gazette" means—

(a) as respects companies registered in England and Wales, the London Gazette,

(b) as respects companies registered in Scotland, the Edinburgh Gazette, and

(c) as respects companies registered in Northern Ireland, the Belfast Gazette;

"hire-purchase agreement" has the same meaning as in the Consumer Credit Act 1974 (c 39);

"officer", in relation to a body corporate, includes a director, manager or secretary;

"parent company" means a company that is a parent undertaking (see section 1162 and Schedule 7);

"regulated activity" has the meaning given in section 22 of the Financial Services and Markets Act 2000 (c 8);

"regulated market" has the same meaning as in Directive 2004/39/EC of the European Parliament and of the Council on markets in financial instruments (see Article 4.1(14));

"working day", in relation to a company, means a day that is not a Saturday or Sunday, Christmas Day, Good Friday or any day that is a bank holiday under the Banking and Financial Dealings Act 1971 (c 80) in the part of the United Kingdom where the company is registered.

(2) In relation to an EEA State that has not implemented Directive 2004/39/EC of the European Parliament and of the Council on markets in financial instruments, the following definition of "regulated market" has effect in place of that in subsection (1)—

"regulated market" has the same meaning as it has in Council Directive 93/22/EEC on investment services in the securities field.

NOTES

Commencement: 1 January 2007 (certain purposes); 20 January 2007 (certain purposes); 6 April 2007 (certain purposes); 1 October 2007 (certain purposes); 1 November 2007 (certain purposes); 6 April 2008 (certain purposes); 1 October 2008 (certain purposes); 1 October 2009 (otherwise) (see the notes below).

Commencement (note): the Companies Act 2006 (Commencement No 1, Transitional Provisions and Savings) Order 2006, SI 2006/3428, art 2(2) provides that the definitions "the Gazette" and "working day" shall come into force on 1 January 2007 so far as is necessary for the purposes of the provisions of this Act brought into force on that date by art 2(1) of that Order (see **[2.2]**).

Commencement (note): the Companies Act 2006 (Commencement No 1, Transitional Provisions and Savings) Order 2006, SI 2006/3428, art 3(2) provides that the definition "working day" shall come into force on 20 January 2007 so far as is necessary for the purposes of the provisions of this Act brought into force on that date by art 3(1) of that Order (see **[2.3]**).

Commencement (note): the Companies Act 2006 (Commencement No 2, Consequential Amendments, Transitional Provisions and Savings) Order 2007, SI 2007/1093, art 2(2) provides that the definitions "body corporate", "the Gazette" and "regulated market" shall come into force on 6 April 2007 so far as is necessary for the purposes of the provisions of this Act brought into force on that date by art 2(1) of that Order (see **[2.17]**).

Commencement (note): the Companies Act 2006 (Commencement No 3, Consequential Amendments, Transitional Provisions and Savings) Order 2007, SI 2007/2194, art 2(3) provides that the definitions of "body corporate" (and "corporation"), "firm" and "working day" shall come into force on 1 October 2007 so far as is necessary for the purposes of the provisions of this Act brought into force on that date by art 2(1), (2) of that Order (see **[2.32]**).

Commencement (note): the Companies Act 2006 (Commencement No 3, Consequential Amendments, Transitional Provisions and Savings) Order 2007, SI 2007/2194, art 3(2) provides that the definition of "body corporate" shall come into force on 1 November 2007 so far as is necessary for the purposes of the provisions of this Act brought into force on that date by art 3(1) of that Order (see **[2.33]**).

Commencement (note): the Companies Act 2006 (Commencement No 5, Transitional Provisions and Savings) Order 2007, SI 2007/3495, art 3(1)(t) provides that the definitions of "credit institution" and "working day" shall come into force on 6 April 2008 (see **[2.52]**).

Commencement (note): the Companies Act 2006 (Commencement No 5, Transitional Provisions and Savings) Order 2007, SI 2007/3495, art 3(3) provides that the definitions of "body corporate" (and "corporation"), "firm", "the Gazette", "parent company" and "regulated market" shall come into force on 6 April 2008 so far as is necessary for the purposes of the provisions of this Act brought into force on that date by art 3(1)(a)–(t), (2) of that Order (see **[2.52]**). Article 5(3) of that Order further provides that the definitions of "body corporate" (and "corporation"), "firm" and "officer" shall come into force on 1 October 2008 so far as is necessary for the purposes of the provisions of this Act brought into force on that date by art 5(1)(a)–(f) of that Order (see **[2.54]**).

Sub-s (1): words in first pair of square brackets in the definition "credit institution" substituted, and words in second pair of square brackets added, by the Electronic Money Regulations 2011, SI 2011/99, reg 79, Sch 4, Pt 1, para 5(a), as from 30 April 2011.

[1.1174]
1174 Index of defined expressions

Schedule 8 contains an index of provisions defining or otherwise explaining expressions used in the Companies Acts.

NOTES

Commencement: 1 October 2009.

PART 39
COMPANIES: MINOR AMENDMENTS

[1.1175]
1175 Removal of special provisions about accounts and audit of charitable companies

(1) Part 7 of the Companies Act 1985 (c 6) and Part 8 of the Companies (Northern Ireland) Order 1986 (accounts and audit) are amended in accordance with Schedule 9 to this Act so as to remove the special provisions about companies that are charities.

(2) In that Schedule—

Part 1 contains repeals and consequential amendments of provisions of the Companies Act 1985;

Part 2 contains repeals and consequential amendments of provisions of the Companies (Northern Ireland) Order 1986.

NOTES

Commencement: 1 April 2008 (in so far as relating to the Companies Act 1985, Pt VII); to be appointed (otherwise).

Commencement (note): the government have announced that they do not intend to commence this section in so far as relating to Northern Ireland nor the associated Sch 9, Pt 2, and that they will be repealed in due course; see the written ministerial statements for 6 November 2008.

[1.1176]
1176 Power of Secretary of State to bring civil proceedings on company's behalf
(1)–(3) *(Repeal CA 1985, s 438, and amend ss 439, 453 of that Act at* **[5.7]**, **[5.27]**.)
(4) Nothing in this section affects proceedings brought under section 438 before the commencement of this section.

NOTES

Commencement: 6 April 2007.

[1.1177]
1177 Repeal of certain provisions about company directors
The following provisions of Part 10 of the Companies Act 1985 shall cease to have effect—
    section 311 (prohibition on tax-free payments to directors);
    sections 323 and 327 (prohibition on directors dealing in share options);
    sections 324 to 326 and 328 to 329, and Parts 2 to 4 of Schedule 13 (register of directors' interests);
    sections 343 and 344 (special procedure for disclosure by banks).

NOTES

Commencement: 6 April 2007.

[1.1178]
1178 Repeal of requirement that certain companies publish periodical statement
The following provisions shall cease to have effect—
    section 720 of the Companies Act 1985 (c 6) (certain companies to publish periodical statement), and
    Schedule 23 to that Act (form of statement under section 720).

NOTES

Commencement: 6 April 2007.

[1.1179]
1179 Repeal of requirement that Secretary of State prepare annual report
Section 729 of the Companies Act 1985 (annual report to Parliament by Secretary of State on matters within the Companies Acts) shall cease to have effect.

NOTES

Commencement: 6 April 2007.

[1.1180]
1180 Repeal of certain provisions about company charges
Part 4 of the Companies Act 1989 (c 40) (registration of company charges), which has not been brought into force, is repealed.

NOTES

Commencement: 1 October 2009.

[1.1181]
1181 Access to constitutional documents of RTE and RTM companies
(1) The Secretary of State may by order—
  (a) amend Chapter 1 of Part 1 of the Leasehold Reform, Housing and Urban Development Act 1993 (c 28) for the purpose of facilitating access to the provisions of the articles or any other constitutional document of RTE companies;
  (b) amend Chapter 1 of Part 2 of the Commonhold and Leasehold Reform Act 2002 (c 15) (leasehold reform) for the purpose of facilitating access to the provisions of the articles or any other constitutional document of RTM companies.
(2) References in subsection (1) to provisions of a company's articles or any other constitutional document include any provisions included in those documents by virtue of any enactment.
(3) An order under this section is subject to negative resolution procedure.
(4) In this section—

"RTE companies" has the same meaning as in Chapter 1 of Part 1 of the Leasehold Reform, Housing and Urban Development Act 1993;

"RTM companies" has the same meaning as in Chapter 1 of Part 2 of the Commonhold and Leasehold Reform Act 2002.

NOTES

Commencement: 20 January 2007 (for the purpose of enabling the exercise of powers to make Orders or Regulations by statutory instrument); 1 October 2009 (otherwise).

PART 40
COMPANY DIRECTORS: FOREIGN DISQUALIFICATION ETC

Introductory

[1.1182]
1182   Persons subject to foreign restrictions

(1)   This section defines what is meant by references in this Part to a person being subject to foreign restrictions.

(2)   A person is subject to foreign restrictions if under the law of a country or territory outside the United Kingdom—

(a)   he is, by reason of misconduct or unfitness, disqualified to any extent from acting in connection with the affairs of a company,

(b)   he is, by reason of misconduct or unfitness, required—

(i)   to obtain permission from a court or other authority, or

(ii)   to meet any other condition,

before acting in connection with the affairs of a company, or

(c)   he has, by reason of misconduct or unfitness, given undertakings to a court or other authority of a country or territory outside the United Kingdom—

(i)   not to act in connection with the affairs of a company, or

(ii)   restricting the extent to which, or the way in which, he may do so.

(3)   The references in subsection (2) to acting in connection with the affairs of a company are to doing any of the following—

(a)   being a director of a company,

(b)   acting as receiver of a company's property, or

(c)   being concerned or taking part in the promotion, formation or management of a company.

(4)   In this section—

(a)   "company" means a company incorporated or formed under the law of the country or territory in question, and

(b)   in relation to such a company—

"director" means the holder of an office corresponding to that of director of a UK company; and

"receiver" includes any corresponding officer under the law of that country or territory.

NOTES

Commencement: 1 October 2009.

[1.1183]
1183   Meaning of "the court" and "UK company"

In this Part—

"the court" means—

(a)   in England and Wales, the High Court or a county court;

(b)   in Scotland, the Court of Session or the sheriff court;

(c)   in Northern Ireland, the High Court;

"UK company" means a company registered under this Act.

NOTES

Commencement: 1 October 2009.

Power to disqualify

[1.1184]
1184   Disqualification of persons subject to foreign restrictions

(1)   The Secretary of State may make provision by regulations disqualifying a person subject to foreign restrictions from—

(a)   being a director of a UK company,

(b)   acting as receiver of a UK company's property, or

(c)   in any way, whether directly or indirectly, being concerned or taking part in the promotion, formation or management of a UK company.

(2)   The regulations may provide that a person subject to foreign restrictions—

(a)   is disqualified automatically by virtue of the regulations, or

(b)   may be disqualified by order of the court on the application of the Secretary of State.

(3) The regulations may provide that the Secretary of State may accept an undertaking (a "disqualification undertaking") from a person subject to foreign restrictions that he will not do anything which would be in breach of a disqualification under subsection (1).

(4) In this Part—

    (a) a "person disqualified under this Part" is a person—

        (i) disqualified as mentioned in subsection (2)(a) or (b), or

        (ii) who has given and is subject to a disqualification undertaking;

    (b) references to a breach of a disqualification include a breach of a disqualification undertaking.

(5) The regulations may provide for applications to the court by persons disqualified under this Part for permission to act in a way which would otherwise be in breach of the disqualification.

(6) The regulations must provide that a person ceases to be disqualified under this Part on his ceasing to be subject to foreign restrictions.

(7) Regulations under this section are subject to affirmative resolution procedure.

NOTES

Commencement: 20 January 2007 (for the purpose of enabling the exercise of powers to make Orders or Regulations by statutory instrument); 1 October 2009 (otherwise).

[1.1185]

1185 Disqualification regulations: supplementary

(1) Regulations under section 1184 may make different provision for different cases and may in particular distinguish between cases by reference to—

    (a) the conduct on the basis of which the person became subject to foreign restrictions;

    (b) the nature of the foreign restrictions;

    (c) the country or territory under whose law the foreign restrictions were imposed.

(2) Regulations under section 1184(2)(b) or (5) (provision for applications to the court)—

    (a) must specify the grounds on which an application may be made;

    (b) may specify factors to which the court shall have regard in determining an application.

(3) The regulations may, in particular, require the court to have regard to the following factors—

    (a) whether the conduct on the basis of which the person became subject to foreign restrictions would, if done in relation to a UK company, have led a court to make a disqualification order on an application under the Company Directors Disqualification Act 1986 (c 46) or the Company Directors Disqualification (Northern Ireland) Order 2002 (SI 2002/3150 (NI 4));

    (b) in a case in which the conduct on the basis of which the person became subject to foreign restrictions would not be unlawful if done in relation to a UK company, the fact that the person acted unlawfully under foreign law;

    (c) whether the person's activities in relation to UK companies began after he became subject to foreign restrictions;

    (d) whether the person's activities (or proposed activities) in relation to UK companies are undertaken (or are proposed to be undertaken) outside the United Kingdom.

(4) Regulations under section 1184(3) (provision as to undertakings given to the Secretary of State) may include provision allowing the Secretary of State, in determining whether to accept an undertaking, to take into account matters other than criminal convictions notwithstanding that the person may be criminally liable in respect of those matters.

(5) Regulations under section 1184(5) (provision for application to court for permission to act) may include provision—

    (a) entitling the Secretary of State to be represented at the hearing of the application, and

    (b) as to the giving of evidence or the calling of witnesses by the Secretary of State at the hearing of the application.

NOTES

Commencement: 20 January 2007 (for the purpose of enabling the exercise of powers to make Orders or Regulations by statutory instrument); 1 October 2009 (otherwise).

[1.1186]

1186 Offence of breach of disqualification

(1) Regulations under section 1184 may provide that a person disqualified under this Part who acts in breach of the disqualification commits an offence.

(2) The regulations may provide that a person guilty of such an offence is liable—

    (a) on conviction on indictment, to imprisonment for a term not exceeding two years or a fine (or both);

    (b) on summary conviction—

        (i) in England and Wales, to imprisonment for a term not exceeding twelve months or to a fine not exceeding the statutory maximum (or both);

        (ii) in Scotland or Northern Ireland, to imprisonment for a term not exceeding six months, or to a fine not exceeding the statutory maximum (or both).

(3)   In relation to an offence committed before the commencement of section 154(1) of the Criminal Justice Act 2003 (c 44), for "twelve months" in subsection (2)(b)(i) substitute "six months".

NOTES

Commencement: 20 January 2007 (for the purpose of enabling the exercise of powers to make Orders or Regulations by statutory instrument); 1 October 2009 (otherwise).

Power to make persons liable for company's debts

[1.1187]
1187   Personal liability for debts of company
(1)   The Secretary of State may provide by regulations that a person who, at a time when he is subject to foreign restrictions—
  (a)   is a director of a UK company, or
  (b)   is involved in the management of a UK company,
is personally responsible for all debts and other liabilities of the company incurred during that time.
(2)   A person who is personally responsible by virtue of this section for debts and other liabilities of a company is jointly and severally liable in respect of those debts and liabilities with—
  (a)   the company, and
  (b)   any other person who (whether by virtue of this section or otherwise) is so liable.
(3)   For the purposes of this section a person is involved in the management of a company if he is concerned, whether directly or indirectly, or takes part, in the management of the company.
(4)   The regulations may make different provision for different cases and may in particular distinguish between cases by reference to—
  (a)   the conduct on the basis of which the person became subject to foreign restrictions;
  (b)   the nature of the foreign restrictions;
  (c)   the country or territory under whose law the foreign restrictions were imposed.
(5)   Regulations under this section are subject to affirmative resolution procedure.

NOTES

Commencement: 20 January 2007 (for the purpose of enabling the exercise of powers to make Orders or Regulations by statutory instrument); 1 October 2009 (otherwise).

Power to require statements to be sent to the registrar of companies

[1.1188]
1188   Statements from persons subject to foreign restrictions
(1)   The Secretary of State may make provision by regulations requiring a person who—
  (a)   is subject to foreign restrictions, and
  (b)   is not disqualified under this Part,
to send a statement to the registrar if he does anything that, if done by a person disqualified under this Part, would be in breach of the disqualification.
(2)   The statement must include such information as may be specified in the regulations relating to—
  (a)   the person's activities in relation to UK companies, and
  (b)   the foreign restrictions to which the person is subject.
(3)   The statement must be sent to the registrar within such period as may be specified in the regulations.
(4)   The regulations may make different provision for different cases and may in particular distinguish between cases by reference to—
  (a)   the conduct on the basis of which the person became subject to foreign restrictions;
  (b)   the nature of the foreign restrictions;
  (c)   the country or territory under whose law the foreign restrictions were imposed.
(5)   Regulations under this section are subject to affirmative resolution procedure.

NOTES

Commencement: 20 January 2007 (for the purpose of enabling the exercise of powers to make Orders or Regulations by statutory instrument); 1 October 2009 (otherwise).

[1.1189]
1189   Statements from persons disqualified
(1)   The Secretary of State may make provision by regulations requiring a statement or notice sent to the registrar of companies under any of the provisions listed below that relates (wholly or partly) to a person who—
  (a)   is a person disqualified under this Part, or
  (b)   is subject to a disqualification order or disqualification undertaking under the Company Directors Disqualification Act 1986 (c 46) or the Company Directors Disqualification (Northern Ireland) Order 2002 (SI 2002/3150 (NI 4)),
to be accompanied by an additional statement.
(2)   The provisions referred to above are—
  (a)   section 12 (statement of a company's proposed officers),

   (b)   section 167(2) (notice of person having become director), and

   (c)   section 276 (notice of a person having become secretary or one of joint secretaries).

(3)   The additional statement is a statement that the person has obtained permission from a court, on an application under section 1184(5) or (as the case may be) for the purposes of section 1(1)(a) of the Company Directors Disqualification Act 1986 (c 46) or Article 3(1) of the Company Directors Disqualification (Northern Ireland) Order 2002 (SI 2002/3150 (NI 4)), to act in the capacity in question.

(4)   Regulations under this section are subject to affirmative resolution procedure.

NOTES

Commencement: 20 January 2007 (for the purpose of enabling the exercise of powers to make Orders or Regulations by statutory instrument); 1 October 2009 (otherwise).

[1.1190]
1190   Statements: whether to be made public

(1)   Regulations under section 1188 or 1189 (statements required to be sent to registrar) may provide that a statement sent to the registrar of companies under the regulations is to be treated as a record relating to a company for the purposes of section 1080 (the companies register).

(2)   The regulations may make provision as to the circumstances in which such a statement is to be, or may be—

   (a)   withheld from public inspection, or

   (b)   removed from the register.

(3)   The regulations may, in particular, provide that a statement is not to be withheld from public inspection or removed from the register unless the person to whom it relates provides such information, and satisfies such other conditions, as may be specified.

(4)   The regulations may provide that section 1081 (note of removal of material from the register) does not apply, or applies with such modifications as may be specified, in the case of material removed from the register under the regulations.

(5)   In this section "specified" means specified in the regulations.

NOTES

Commencement: 1 October 2009.

[1.1191]
1191   Offences

(1)   Regulations under section 1188 or 1189 may provide that it is an offence for a person—

   (a)   to fail to comply with a requirement under the regulations to send a statement to the registrar;

   (b)   knowingly or recklessly to send a statement under the regulations to the registrar that is misleading, false or deceptive in a material particular.

(2)   The regulations may provide that a person guilty of such an offence is liable—

   (a)   on conviction on indictment, to imprisonment for a term not exceeding two years or a fine (or both);

   (b)   on summary conviction—

      (i)   in England and Wales, to imprisonment for a term not exceeding twelve months or to a fine not exceeding the statutory maximum (or both);

      (ii)   in Scotland or Northern Ireland, to imprisonment for a term not exceeding six months, or to a fine not exceeding the statutory maximum (or both).

(3)   In relation to an offence committed before the commencement of section 154(1) of the Criminal Justice Act 2003 (c 44), for "twelve months" in subsection (2)(b)(i) substitute "six months".

NOTES

Commencement: 20 January 2007 (for the purpose of enabling the exercise of powers to make Orders or Regulations by statutory instrument); 1 October 2009 (otherwise).

PART 41
BUSINESS NAMES

CHAPTER 1
RESTRICTED OR PROHIBITED NAMES

Introductory

[1.1192]
1192   Application of this Chapter

(1)   This Chapter applies to any person carrying on business in the United Kingdom.

(2)   The provisions of this Chapter do not prevent—

   (a)   an individual carrying on business under a name consisting of his surname without any addition other than a permitted addition, or (b)　individuals carrying on business in partnership under a name consisting of the surnames of all the partners without any addition other than a permitted addition.

(3)　The following are the permitted additions—

  (a)　in the case of an individual, his forename or initial;

  (b)　in the case of a partnership—

    (i)　the forenames of individual partners or the initials of those forenames, or

    (ii)　where two or more individual partners have the same surname, the addition of "s" at the end of that surname;

  (c)　in either case, an addition merely indicating that the business is carried on in succession to a former owner of the business.

NOTES

Commencement: 1 October 2009.

Sensitive words or expressions

[1.1193]

1193　Name suggesting connection with government or public authority

(1)　A person must not, without the approval of the Secretary of State, carry on business in the United Kingdom under a name that would be likely to give the impression that the business is connected with—

  (a)　Her Majesty's Government, any part of the Scottish administration[, the Welsh Assembly Government] or Her Majesty's Government in Northern Ireland,

  (b)　any local authority, or

  (c)　any public authority specified for the purposes of this section by regulations made by the Secretary of State.

(2)　For the purposes of this section—

  "local authority" means—

    (a)　a local authority within the meaning of the Local Government Act 1972 (c 70), the Common Council of the City of London or the Council of the Isles of Scilly,

    (b)　a council constituted under section 2 of the Local Government etc (Scotland) Act 1994 (c 39), or

    (c)　a district council in Northern Ireland;

  "public authority" includes any person or body having functions of a public nature.

(3)　Regulations under this section are subject to affirmative resolution procedure.

(4)　A person who contravenes this section commits an offence.

(5)　Where an offence under this section is committed by a body corporate, an offence is also committed by every officer of the body who is in default.

(6)　A person guilty of an offence under this section is liable on summary conviction to a fine not exceeding level 3 on the standard scale and, for continued contravention, a daily default fine not exceeding one-tenth of level 3 on the standard scale.

NOTES

Commencement: 20 January 2007 (for the purpose of enabling the exercise of powers to make Orders or Regulations by statutory instrument); 1 October 2009 (otherwise).

Sub-s (1): words in square brackets inserted by the Government of Wales Act 2006 (Consequential Modifications, Transitional Provisions and Saving) Order 2009, SI 2009/2958, arts 8, 11, as from 6 November 2009.

Regulations: the Company, Limited Liability Partnership and Business Names (Public Authorities) Regulations 2009, SI 2009/2982 at **[4.641]**.

[1.1194]

1194　Other sensitive words or expressions

(1)　A person must not, without the approval of the Secretary of State, carry on business in the United Kingdom under a name that includes a word or expression for the time being specified in regulations made by the Secretary of State under this section.

(2)　Regulations under this section are subject to approval after being made.

(3)　A person who contravenes this section commits an offence.

(4)　Where an offence under this section is committed by a body corporate, an offence is also committed by every officer of the body who is in default.

(5)　A person guilty of an offence under this section is liable on summary conviction to a fine not exceeding level 3 on the standard scale and, for continued contravention, a daily default fine not exceeding one-tenth of level 3 on the standard scale.

NOTES

Commencement: 20 January 2007 (for the purpose of enabling the exercise of powers to make Orders or Regulations by statutory instrument); 1 October 2009 (otherwise).

Chamber of commerce: by the Company and Business Names (Chamber of Commerce, etc) Act 1999, s 1 (as amended), the Secretary of State is required to include the title "chamber of commerce" (and its Welsh equivalent) in the list of controlled titles maintained in accordance with regulations made under this section.

Regulations: the Company, Limited Liability Partnership and Business Names (Sensitive Words and Expressions) Regulations 2009, SI 2009/2615 at **[4.630]**.

[1.1195]
1195 Requirement to seek comments of government department or other relevant body
(1) The Secretary of State may by regulations under—
  (a)   section 1193 (name suggesting connection with government or public authority), or
  (b)   section 1194 (other sensitive words or expressions),
require that, in connection with an application for the approval of the Secretary of State under that section, the applicant must seek the view of a specified Government department or other body.
(2) Where such a requirement applies, the applicant must request the specified department or other body (in writing) to indicate whether (and if so why) it has any objections to the proposed name.
(3) He must submit to the Secretary of State a statement that such a request has been made and a copy of any response received from the specified body.
(4) If these requirements are not complied with, the Secretary of State may refuse to consider the application for approval.
(5) In this section "specified" means specified in the regulations.

NOTES
  Commencement: 20 January 2007 (for the purpose of enabling the exercise of powers to make Orders or Regulations by statutory instrument); 1 October 2009 (otherwise).
  Regulations: the Company, Limited Liability Partnership and Business Names (Sensitive Words and Expressions) Regulations 2009, SI 2009/2615 at **[4.630]**; the Company, Limited Liability Partnership and Business Names (Public Authorities) Regulations 2009, SI 2009/2982 at **[4.641]**.

[1.1196]
1196 Withdrawal of Secretary of State's approval
(1) This section applies to approval given for the purposes of—
    section 1193 (name suggesting connection with government or public authority), or
    section 1194 (other sensitive words or expressions).
(2) If it appears to the Secretary of State that there are overriding considerations of public policy that require such approval to be withdrawn, the approval may be withdrawn by notice in writing given to the person concerned.
(3) The notice must state the date as from which approval is withdrawn.

NOTES
  Commencement: 1 October 2009.

Misleading names
[1.1197]
1197 Name containing inappropriate indication of company type or legal form
(1) The Secretary of State may make provision by regulations prohibiting a person from carrying on business in the United Kingdom under a name consisting of or containing specified words, expressions or other indications—
  (a)   that are associated with a particular type of company or form of organisation, or
  (b)   that are similar to words, expressions or other indications associated with a particular type of company or form of organisation.
(2) The regulations may prohibit the use of words, expressions or other indications—
  (a)   in a specified part, or otherwise than in a specified part, of a name;
  (b)   in conjunction with, or otherwise than in conjunction with, such other words, expressions or indications as may be specified.
(3) In this section "specified" means specified in the regulations.
(4) Regulations under this section are subject to negative resolution procedure.
(5) A person who uses a name in contravention of regulations under this section commits an offence.
(6) Where an offence under this section is committed by a body corporate, an offence is also committed by every officer of the body who is in default.
(7) A person guilty of an offence under this section is liable on summary conviction to a fine not exceeding level 3 on the standard scale and, for continued contravention, a daily default fine not exceeding one-tenth of level 3 on the standard scale.

NOTES
  Commencement: 20 January 2007 (for the purpose of enabling the exercise of powers to make Orders or Regulations by statutory instrument); 1 October 2009 (otherwise).
  Regulations: the Company and Business Names (Miscellaneous Provisions) Regulations 2009, SI 2009/1085 at **[4.369]**; the Company, Limited Liability Partnership and Business Names (Miscellaneous Provisions) (Amendment) Regulations 2009, SI 2009/2404.

[1.1198]
1198　Name giving misleading indication of activities

(1)　A person must not carry on business in the United Kingdom under a name that gives so misleading an indication of the nature of the activities of the business as to be likely to cause harm to the public.

(2)　A person who uses a name in contravention of this section commits an offence.

(3)　Where an offence under this section is committed by a body corporate, an offence is also committed by every officer of the body who is in default.

(4)　A person guilty of an offence under this section is liable on summary conviction to a fine not exceeding level 3 on the standard scale and, for continued contravention, a daily default fine not exceeding one-tenth of level 3 on the standard scale.

NOTES
　Commencement: 1 October 2009.

Supplementary

[1.1199]
1199　Savings for existing lawful business names

(1)　This section has effect in relation to—
　　sections 1192 to 1196 (sensitive words or expressions), and
　　section 1197 (inappropriate indication of company type or legal form).

(2)　Those sections do not apply to the carrying on of a business by a person who—
　　(a)　carried on the business immediately before the date on which this Chapter came into force, and
　　(b)　continues to carry it on under the name that immediately before that date was its lawful business name.

(3)　Where—
　　(a)　a business is transferred to a person on or after the date on which this Chapter came into force, and
　　(b)　that person carries on the business under the name that was its lawful business name immediately before the transfer,

those sections do not apply in relation to the carrying on of the business under that name during the period of twelve months beginning with the date of the transfer.

(4)　In this section "lawful business name", in relation to a business, means a name under which the business was carried on without contravening—
　　(a)　section 2(1) of the Business Names Act 1985 (c 7) or Article 4(1) of the Business Names (Northern Ireland) Order 1986 (SI 1986/1033 NI 7)), or
　　(b)　after this Chapter has come into force, the provisions of this Chapter.

NOTES
　Commencement: 1 October 2009.

CHAPTER 2
DISCLOSURE REQUIRED IN CASE OF INDIVIDUAL OR PARTNERSHIP

Introductory

[1.1200]
1200　Application of this Chapter

(1)　This Chapter applies to an individual or partnership carrying on business in the United Kingdom under a business name.
　References in this Chapter to "a person to whom this Chapter applies" are to such an individual or partnership.

(2)　For the purposes of this Chapter a "business name" means a name other than—
　　(a)　in the case of an individual, his surname without any addition other than a permitted addition;
　　(b)　in the case of a partnership—
　　　(i)　the surnames of all partners who are individuals, and
　　　(ii)　the corporate names of all partners who are bodies corporate,
　　without any addition other than a permitted addition.

(3)　The following are the permitted additions—
　　(a)　in the case of an individual, his forename or initial;
　　(b)　in the case of a partnership—
　　　(i)　the forenames of individual partners or the initials of those forenames, or
　　　(ii)　where two or more individual partners have the same surname, the addition of "s" at the end of that surname;
　　(c)　in either case, an addition merely indicating that the business is carried on in succession to a former owner of the business.

NOTES
Commencement: 1 October 2009.

[1.1201]
[1201 Information required to be disclosed
(1)   The "information required by this Chapter" is—
  (a)   in the case of an individual, the individual's name;
  (b)   in the case of a partnership, the name of each member of the partnership;
and, in relation to each person so named, an address at which service of any document relating in any way to the business will be effective.
(2)   If the individual or partnership has a place of business in the United Kingdom, the address must be in the United Kingdom.
(3)   If the individual or partnership does not have a place of business in the United Kingdom, the address must be an address at which service of documents can be effected by physical delivery and the delivery of documents is capable of being recorded by the obtaining of an acknowledgement of delivery.]

NOTES
Commencement: 28 December 2009.
Substituted by the Companies Act 2006 (Substitution of Section 1201) Regulations 2009, SI 2009/3182, reg 2, as from 28 December 2009.

Disclosure requirements

[1.1202]
1202   Disclosure required: business documents etc
(1)   A person to whom this Chapter applies must state the information required by this Chapter, in legible characters, on all—
  (a)   business letters,
  (b)   written orders for goods or services to be supplied to the business,
  (c)   invoices and receipts issued in the course of the business, and
  (d)   written demands for payment of debts arising in the course of the business.
This subsection has effect subject to section 1203 (exemption for large partnerships if certain conditions met).
(2)   A person to whom this Chapter applies must secure that the information required by this Chapter is immediately given, by written notice, to any person with whom anything is done or discussed in the course of the business and who asks for that information.
(3)   The Secretary of State may by regulations require that such notices be given in a specified form.
(4)   Regulations under this section are subject to negative resolution procedure.

NOTES
Commencement: 20 January 2007 (for the purpose of enabling the exercise of powers to make Orders or Regulations by statutory instrument); 1 October 2009 (otherwise).

[1.1203]
1203   Exemption for large partnerships if certain conditions met
(1)   Section 1202(1) (disclosure required in business documents) does not apply in relation to a document issued by a partnership of more than 20 persons if the following conditions are met.
(2)   The conditions are that—
  (a)   the partnership maintains at its principal place of business a list of the names of all the partners,
  (b)   no partner's name appears in the document, except in the text or as a signatory, and
  (c)   the document states in legible characters the address of the partnership's principal place of business and that the list of the partners' names is open to inspection there.
(3)   Where a partnership maintains a list of the partners' names for the purposes of this section, any person may inspect the list during office hours.
(4)   Where an inspection required by a person in accordance with this section is refused, an offence is committed by any member of the partnership concerned who without reasonable excuse refused the inspection or permitted it to be refused.
(5)   A person guilty of an offence under subsection (4) is liable on summary conviction to a fine not exceeding level 3 on the standard scale and, for continued contravention, a daily default fine not exceeding one-tenth of level 3 on the standard scale.

NOTES
Commencement: 1 October 2009.

[1.1204]
1204   Disclosure required: business premises
(1)   A person to whom this Chapter applies must, in any premises—
    (a)   where the business is carried on, and
    (b)   to which customers of the business or suppliers of goods or services to the business have access,
display in a prominent position, so that it may easily be read by such customers or suppliers, a notice containing the information required by this Chapter.
(2)   The Secretary of State may by regulations require that such notices be displayed in a specified form.
(3)   Regulations under this section are subject to negative resolution procedure.

NOTES
Commencement: 20 January 2007 (for the purpose of enabling the exercise of powers to make Orders or Regulations by statutory instrument); 1 October 2009 (otherwise).

Consequences of failure to make required disclosure

[1.1205]
1205   Criminal consequences of failure to make required disclosure
(1)   A person who without reasonable excuse fails to comply with the requirements of—
    section 1202 (disclosure required: business documents etc), or
    section 1204 (disclosure required: business premises),
commits an offence.
(2)   Where an offence under this section is committed by a body corporate, an offence is also committed by every officer of the body who is in default.
(3)   A person guilty of an offence under this section is liable on summary conviction to a fine not exceeding level 3 on the standard scale and, for continued contravention, a daily default fine not exceeding one-tenth of level 3 on the standard scale.
(4)   References in this section to the requirements of section 1202 or 1204 include the requirements of regulations under that section.

NOTES
Commencement: 1 October 2009.

[1.1206]
1206   Civil consequences of failure to make required disclosure
(1)   This section applies to any legal proceedings brought by a person to whom this Chapter applies to enforce a right arising out of a contract made in the course of a business in respect of which he was, at the time the contract was made, in breach of section 1202(1) or (2) (disclosure in business documents etc) or section 1204(1) (disclosure at business premises).
(2)   The proceedings shall be dismissed if the defendant (in Scotland, the defender) to the proceedings shows—
    (a)   that he has a claim against the claimant (pursuer) arising out of the contract that he has been unable to pursue by reason of the latter's breach of the requirements of this Chapter, or
    (b)   that he has suffered some financial loss in connection with the contract by reason of the claimant's (pursuer's) breach of those requirements,
unless the court before which the proceedings are brought is satisfied that it is just and equitable to permit the proceedings to continue.
(3)   References in this section to the requirements of this Chapter include the requirements of regulations under this Chapter.
(4)   This section does not affect the right of any person to enforce such rights as he may have against another person in any proceedings brought by that person.

NOTES
Commencement: 1 October 2009.

CHAPTER 3
SUPPLEMENTARY

[1.1207]
1207   Application of general provisions about offences
The provisions of sections 1121 to 1123 (liability of officer in default) and 1125 to 1131 (general provisions about offences) apply in relation to offences under this Part as in relation to offences under the Companies Acts.

NOTES
Commencement: 1 October 2009.

[1.1208]
1208 Interpretation
In this Part—
"business" includes a profession;
"initial" includes any recognised abbreviation of a name;
"partnership" means—
  (a) a partnership within the Partnership Act 1890 (c 39), or
  (b) a limited partnership registered under the Limited Partnerships Act 1907 (c 24),
  or a firm or entity of a similar character formed under the law of a country or territory outside the United Kingdom;
"surname", in relation to a peer or person usually known by a British title different from his surname, means the title by which he is known.

NOTES
Commencement: 1 October 2009.

PART 42
STATUTORY AUDITORS

NOTES
Transfer of functions: as to the transfer of certain functions of the Secretary of State under this Part to the Professional Oversight Board, see the Statutory Auditors (Delegation of Functions etc) Order 2008, SI 2008/496, art 4 at **[4.243]**.

CHAPTER 1
INTRODUCTORY

[1.1209]
1209 Main purposes of Part
The main purposes of this Part are—
  (a) to secure that only persons who are properly supervised and appropriately qualified are appointed as statutory auditors, and
  (b) to secure that audits by persons so appointed are carried out properly, with integrity and with a proper degree of independence.

NOTES
Commencement: 6 April 2008.

[1.1210]
1210 Meaning of "statutory auditor" etc
(1) In this Part "statutory auditor" means—
  (a) a person appointed as auditor under Part 16 of this Act,
  (b) a person appointed as auditor under section 77 of or Schedule 11 to the Building Societies Act 1986 (c 53),
  (c) a person appointed as auditor of an insurer that is a friendly society under section 72 of or Schedule 14 to the Friendly Societies Act 1992 (c 40),
  (d) . . .
  [(e) a person appointed as auditor for the purposes of regulation 5 of the Insurance Accounts Directive (Lloyd's Syndicate and Aggregate Accounts) Regulations 2008 or appointed to report on the "aggregate accounts" within the meaning of those Regulations,]
  [(f) a person appointed as auditor of an insurance undertaking for the purposes of the Insurance Accounts Directive (Miscellaneous Insurance Undertakings) Regulations 2008,]
  [(g) a person appointed as auditor of a bank for the purposes of the Bank Accounts Directive (Miscellaneous Banks) Regulations 2008,]
  (h) a person appointed as auditor of a prescribed person under a prescribed enactment authorising or requiring the appointment;
and the expressions "statutory audit" and "statutory audit work" are to be construed accordingly.
(2) In this Part "audited person" means the person in respect of whom a statutory audit is conducted.
(3) In subsection (1)—
"bank" means a person who—
  (a) is a credit institution within the meaning given by [Article 4.1] of Directive 2006/48/EC of the European Parliament and of the Council relating to the taking up and pursuit of the business of credit institutions [as last amended by Directive 2009/111/EC], and
  (b) is a company or a firm as defined in Article 48 of the Treaty establishing the European Community;
"friendly society" means a friendly society within the meaning of the Friendly Societies Act 1992 (c 40);
. . .

"insurer" means a person who is an insurance undertaking within the meaning given by Article 2.1 of Council Directive 1991/674/EEC on the annual accounts and consolidated accounts of insurance undertakings;

"prescribed" means prescribed, or of a description prescribed, by order made by the Secretary of State for the purposes of subsection (1)(h).

(4) An order under this section is subject to negative resolution procedure.

NOTES

Commencement: 20 January 2007 (for the purpose of enabling the exercise of powers to make Orders or Regulations by statutory instrument); 6 April 2008 (otherwise).

Sub-s (1) is amended as follows:

Para (d) repealed, and para (f) substituted, by the Insurance Accounts Directive (Miscellaneous Insurance Undertakings) Regulations 2008, SI 2008/565, reg 15, as from 6 April 2008, in relation to insurance undertakings' financial years beginning on or after that date, and auditors appointed in respect of those financial years.

Para (e) substituted by the Insurance Accounts Directive (Lloyd's Syndicate and Aggregate Accounts) Regulations 2008, SI 2008/1950, reg 31, as from 15 August 2008, in relation to financial years beginning on or after 1 January 2009.

Para (g) substituted by the Bank Accounts Directive (Miscellaneous Banks) Regulations 2008, SI 2008/567, reg 14, as from 6 April 2008, in relation to qualifying banks' financial years beginning on or after that date, and auditors appointed in respect of those financial years.

Sub-s (3): definition "industrial and provident society" (omitted) repealed by SI 2008/565, reg 15, as from 6 April 2008, in relation to insurance undertakings' financial years beginning on or after that date, and auditors appointed in respect of those financial years; words in first pair of square brackets in the definition "bank" substituted, and words in second pair of square brackets added, by the Electronic Money Regulations 2011, SI 2011/99, reg 79, Sch 4, Pt 1, para 5(b), as from 30 April 2011.

Regulations: the Partnerships (Accounts) Regulations 2008, SI 2008/569 at **[10.984]** (reg 14 of which provides that for the purposes of sub-s (1)(h) a qualifying partnership is a prescribed person, and reg 4(1)(b) is a prescribed enactment); the Limited Liability Partnerships (Accounts and Audit) (Application of Companies Act 2006) Regulations 2008, SI 2008/1911 at **[10.1003]** (reg 48 of which provides that for the purposes of sub-s (1)(h) an LLP is a prescribed person, and Pt 16 of this Act (as applied to LLPs) is a prescribed enactment); the Unregistered Companies Regulations 2009, SI 2009/2436 at **[4.594]** (reg 6 of which provides that for the purposes of sub-s (1)(h) an unregistered company is a prescribed person, and Pt 16 of this Act (as applied to unregistered companies) is a prescribed enactment).

[1.1211]

1211 Eligibility for appointment as a statutory auditor: overview

A person is eligible for appointment as a statutory auditor only if the person is so eligible—

(a) by virtue of Chapter 2 (individuals and firms), or

(b) by virtue of Chapter 3 (Comptroller and Auditor General, etc).

NOTES

Commencement: 6 April 2008.

CHAPTER 2
INDIVIDUALS AND FIRMS
Eligibility for appointment

[1.1212]

1212 Individuals and firms: eligibility for appointment as a statutory auditor

(1) An individual or firm is eligible for appointment as a statutory auditor if the individual or firm—

(a) is a member of a recognised supervisory body, and

(b) is eligible for appointment under the rules of that body.

(2) In the cases to which section 1222 applies (individuals retaining only 1967 Act authorisation) a person's eligibility for appointment as a statutory auditor is restricted as mentioned in that section.

NOTES

Commencement: 6 April 2008.

Commencement (transitional provisions): Sch 4, Pt 1, para 37 to the Companies Act 2006 (Commencement No 5, Transitional Provisions and Savings) Order 2007, SI 2007/3495 (at **[2.66]**) provides that this section and ss 1213–1216 apply to the appointment of auditors for financial years beginning on or after 6 April 2008 (and that ss 25–28 of the Companies Act 1989 continue to apply to auditors appointed for financial years beginning before that date).

[1.1213]

1213 Effect of ineligibility

(1) No person may act as statutory auditor of an audited person if he is ineligible for appointment as a statutory auditor.

(2) If at any time during his term of office a statutory auditor becomes ineligible for appointment as a statutory auditor, he must immediately—

(a) resign his office (with immediate effect), and

(b) give notice in writing to the audited person that he has resigned by reason of his becoming ineligible for appointment.

(3) A person is guilty of an offence if—

(a) he acts as a statutory auditor in contravention of subsection (1), or

    (b) he fails to give the notice mentioned in paragraph (b) of subsection (2) in accordance with that subsection.

(4) A person guilty of an offence under subsection (3) is liable—
    (a) on conviction on indictment, to a fine;
    (b) on summary conviction, to a fine not exceeding the statutory maximum.

(5) A person is guilty of an offence if—
    (a) he has been convicted of an offence under subsection (3)(a) or this subsection, and
    (b) he continues to act as a statutory auditor in contravention of subsection (1) after the conviction.

(6) A person is guilty of an offence if—
    (a) he has been convicted of an offence under subsection (3)(b) or this subsection, and
    (b) he continues, after the conviction, to fail to give the notice mentioned in subsection (2)(b).

(7) A person guilty of an offence under subsection (5) or (6) is liable—
    (a) on conviction on indictment, to a fine;
    (b) on summary conviction, to a fine not exceeding one-tenth of the statutory maximum for each day on which the act or the failure continues.

(8) In proceedings against a person for an offence under this section it is a defence for him to show that he did not know and had no reason to believe that he was, or had become, ineligible for appointment as a statutory auditor.

NOTES

Commencement: 6 April 2008.

Commencement (transitional provisions): see the note to s 1212 at **[1.1212]**.

Independence requirement

[1.1214]
1214 Independence requirement

(1) A person may not act as statutory auditor of an audited person if one or more of subsections (2), (3) and (4) apply to him.

(2) This subsection applies if the person is—
    (a) an officer or employee of the audited person, or
    (b) a partner or employee of such a person, or a partnership of which such a person is a partner.

(3) This subsection applies if the person is—
    (a) an officer or employee of an associated undertaking of the audited person, or
    (b) a partner or employee of such a person, or a partnership of which such a person is a partner.

(4) This subsection applies if there exists, between—
    (a) the person or an associate of his, and
    (b) the audited person or an associated undertaking of the audited person,
a connection of any such description as may be specified by regulations made by the Secretary of State.

(5) An auditor of an audited person is not to be regarded as an officer or employee of the person for the purposes of subsections (2) and (3).

(6) In this section "associated undertaking", in relation to an audited person, means—
    (a) a parent undertaking or subsidiary undertaking of the audited person, or
    (b) a subsidiary undertaking of a parent undertaking of the audited person.

(7) Regulations under subsection (4) are subject to negative resolution procedure.

NOTES

Commencement: 20 January 2007 (for the purpose of enabling the exercise of powers to make Orders or Regulations by statutory instrument); 6 April 2008 (otherwise).

Commencement (transitional provisions): see the note to s 1212 at **[1.1212]**.

[1.1215]
1215 Effect of lack of independence

(1) If at any time during his term of office a statutory auditor becomes prohibited from acting by section 1214(1), he must immediately—
    (a) resign his office (with immediate effect), and
    (b) give notice in writing to the audited person that he has resigned by reason of his lack of independence.

(2) A person is guilty of an offence if—
    (a) he acts as a statutory auditor in contravention of section 1214(1), or
    (b) he fails to give the notice mentioned in paragraph (b) of subsection (1) in accordance with that subsection.

(3) A person guilty of an offence under subsection (2) is liable—
    (a) on conviction on indictment, to a fine;
    (b) on summary conviction, to a fine not exceeding the statutory maximum.

(4) A person is guilty of an offence if—
    (a) he has been convicted of an offence under subsection (2)(a) or this subsection, and

(b) he continues to act as a statutory auditor in contravention of section 1214(1) after the conviction.

(5) A person is guilty of an offence if—

(a) he has been convicted of an offence under subsection (2)(b) or this subsection, and

(b) after the conviction, he continues to fail to give the notice mentioned in subsection (1)(b).

(6) A person guilty of an offence under subsection (4) or (5) is liable—

(a) on conviction on indictment, to a fine;

(b) on summary conviction, to a fine not exceeding one-tenth of the statutory maximum for each day on which the act or the failure continues.

(7) In proceedings against a person for an offence under this section it is a defence for him to show that he did not know and had no reason to believe that he was, or had become, prohibited from acting as statutory auditor of the audited person by section 1214(1).

NOTES

Commencement: 6 April 2008.

Commencement (transitional provisions): see the note to s 1212 at **[1.1212]**.

Effect of appointment of a partnership

[1.1216]

1216 Effect of appointment of a partnership

(1) This section applies where a partnership constituted under the law of—

(a) England and Wales,

(b) Northern Ireland, or

(c) any other country or territory in which a partnership is not a legal person,

is by virtue of this Chapter appointed as statutory auditor of an audited person.

(2) Unless a contrary intention appears, the appointment is an appointment of the partnership as such and not of the partners.

(3) Where the partnership ceases, the appointment is to be treated as extending to—

(a) any appropriate partnership which succeeds to the practice of that partnership, or

(b) any other appropriate person who succeeds to that practice having previously carried it on in partnership.

(4) For the purposes of subsection (3)—

(a) a partnership is to be regarded as succeeding to the practice of another partnership only if the members of the successor partnership are substantially the same as those of the former partnership, and

(b) a partnership or other person is to be regarded as succeeding to the practice of a partnership only if it or he succeeds to the whole or substantially the whole of the business of the former partnership.

(5) Where the partnership ceases and the appointment is not treated under subsection (3) as extending to any partnership or other person, the appointment may with the consent of the audited person be treated as extending to an appropriate partnership, or other appropriate person, who succeeds to—

(a) the business of the former partnership, or

(b) such part of it as is agreed by the audited person is to be treated as comprising the appointment.

(6) For the purposes of this section, a partnership or other person is "appropriate" if it or he—

(a) is eligible for appointment as a statutory auditor by virtue of this Chapter, and

(b) is not prohibited by section 1214(1) from acting as statutory auditor of the audited person.

NOTES

Commencement: 6 April 2008.

Commencement (transitional provisions): see the note to s 1212 at **[1.1212]**.

See also the Companies Act 2006 (Consequential Amendments etc) Order 2008, SI 2008/948, art 5 (at **[4.279]**) which provides as follows—

"5 Eligibility for appointment as statutory auditor: effect of appointing partnership

(1) Section 1216 of the Companies Act 2006 (effect of appointing partnership) applies in relation to any statutory appointment where eligibility for the appointment depends on eligibility for appointment as a statutory auditor under Part 42 of that Act.

(2) In subsection (6)(b) of that section as it applies by virtue of this article, the reference to being prohibited by virtue of section 1214(1) of that Act from acting as statutory auditor shall be read as including a reference to being prohibited or disqualified from acting, or ineligible or disqualified for appointment, on the ground of lack of independence (of any description) by virtue of any other enactment applying in relation to the appointment.

(3) For the purposes of this article a "statutory appointment" means an appointment in pursuance of an enactment authorising or requiring the making of the appointment.

(4) This article applies only where that enactment was passed or made before 6th April 2008.".

Supervisory bodies

[1.1217]
1217 Supervisory bodies
(1) In this Part a "supervisory body" means a body established in the United Kingdom (whether a body corporate or an unincorporated association) which maintains and enforces rules as to—
  (a)   the eligibility of persons for appointment as a statutory auditor, and
  (b)   the conduct of statutory audit work,
which are binding on persons seeking appointment or acting as a statutory auditor . . . because they are members of that body . . .
[(1A)   The rules referred to in paragraphs 9(3)(b) (confidentiality of information) and 10C(3)(a) and (b) (bar on appointment as director or other officer) of Schedule 10 must also be binding on persons who—
  (a)   have sought appointment or acted as a statutory auditor, and
  (b)   have been members of the body at any time after the commencement of this Part.]
(2) In this Part references to the members of a supervisory body are to the persons who, whether or not members of the body, are subject to its rules in seeking appointment or acting as a statutory auditor.
(3) In this Part references to the rules of a supervisory body are to the rules (whether or not laid down by the body itself) which the body has power to enforce and which are relevant for the purposes of this Part.
  This includes rules relating to the admission or expulsion of members of the body, so far as relevant for the purposes of this Part.
(4) Schedule 10 has effect with respect to the recognition of supervisory bodies for the purposes of this Part.

NOTES
Commencement: 6 April 2008.
Commencement (transitional provisions): Sch 4, Pt 1, para 38 to the Companies Act 2006 (Commencement No 5, Transitional Provisions and Savings) Order 2007, SI 2007/3495 (at **[2.66]**) (as amended by the Companies Act 2006 (Commencement No 6, Saving and Commencement Nos 3 and 5 (Amendment)) Order 2008, SI 2008/674, art 5, Sch 3, para 6(1), (4), as from 6 April 2008) provides as follows—

  "38.—(1)   The following provisions of that Chapter apply in relation to the supervision and qualification of auditors appointed for financial years beginning on or after 6th April 2008—
    (a)   sections 1217 and 1218 and Schedule 10 (supervisory bodies);
    (b)   sections 1219 to 1222 and Schedule 11 (professional qualifications and qualifying bodies).
  (2)   Sections 30 to 34 and 48 of, and Schedules 11 and 12 to, the Companies Act 1989 or Articles 33 to 36 and 50 of, and Schedules 11 and 12 to, the Companies (Northern Ireland) Order 1990 continue to apply in relation to the supervision and qualification of auditors appointed for financial years beginning before that date.
  (3)   Any declaration by the Secretary of State in force under section 33 of the Companies Act 1989 or [by the Department of Enterprise, Trade and Investment in force under] Article 36 of the Companies (Northern Ireland) Order 1990 (approval of overseas qualifications) immediately before 6th April 2008 continues in force on and after that date as if made under section 1221 of the Companies Act 2006.".

Sub-s (1): words omitted repealed by the Statutory Auditors and Third Country Auditors Regulations 2007, SI 2007/3494, reg 4(1), (2), as from 6 April 2008.
Sub-s (1A): inserted by SI 2007/3494, reg 4(1), (3), as from 6 April 2008.

[1.1218]
1218 Exemption from liability for damages
(1)   No person within subsection (2) is to be liable in damages for anything done or omitted in the discharge or purported discharge of functions to which this subsection applies.
(2)   The persons within this subsection are—
  (a)   any recognised supervisory body,
  (b)   any officer or employee of a recognised supervisory body, and
  (c)   any member of the governing body of a recognised supervisory body.
(3)   Subsection (1) applies to the functions of a recognised supervisory body so far as relating to, or to matters arising out of, any of the following—
  (a)   rules, practices, powers and arrangements of the body to which the requirements of Part 2 of Schedule 10 apply;
  (b)   the obligations with which paragraph 20 of that Schedule requires the body to comply;
  (c)   any guidance issued by the body;
  (d)   the obligations imposed on the body by or by virtue of this Part.
(4)   The reference in subsection (3)(c) to guidance issued by a recognised supervisory body is a reference to any guidance or recommendation which is—
  (a)   issued or made by it to all or any class of its members or persons seeking to become members, and
  (b)   relevant for the purposes of this Part,
including any guidance or recommendation relating to the admission or expulsion of members of the body, so far as relevant for the purposes of this Part.
(5)   Subsection (1) does not apply—

(a) if the act or omission is shown to have been in bad faith, or

(b) so as to prevent an award of damages in respect of the act or omission on the ground that it was unlawful as a result of section 6(1) of the Human Rights Act 1998 (c 42) (acts of public authorities incompatible with Convention rights).

NOTES

Commencement: 6 April 2008.

Commencement (transitional provisions): see the note to s 1217 at **[1.1217]**.

Professional qualifications

[1.1219]

1219 Appropriate qualifications

(1) A person holds an appropriate qualification for the purposes of this Chapter if and only if—

(a) he holds a recognised professional qualification obtained in the United Kingdom,

(b) immediately before the commencement of this Chapter, he—

  (i) held an appropriate qualification for the purposes of Part 2 of the Companies Act 1989 (c 40) (eligibility for appointment as company auditor) by virtue of section 31(1)(a) or (c) of that Act, or

  (ii) was treated as holding an appropriate qualification for those purposes by virtue of section 31(2), (3) or (4) of that Act,

(c) immediately before the commencement of this Chapter, he—

  (i) held an appropriate qualification for the purposes of Part III of the Companies (Northern Ireland) Order 1990 (SI 1990/593 (NI 5)) by virtue of Article 34(1)(a) or (c) of that Order, or

  (ii) was treated as holding an appropriate qualification for those purposes by virtue of Article 34(2), (3) or (4) of that Order,

(d) he is within subsection (2), [or]

(e) . . .

(f) subject to any direction under section 1221(5), he is regarded for the purposes of this Chapter as holding an approved [third country] qualification.

(2) A person is within this subsection if—

(a) before 1st January 1990, he began a course of study or practical training leading to a professional qualification in accountancy offered by a body established in the United Kingdom,

(b) he obtained that qualification on or after 1st January 1990 and before 1st January 1996, and

(c) the Secretary of State approves his qualification as an appropriate qualification for the purposes of this Chapter.

(3) The Secretary of State may approve a qualification under subsection (2)(c) only if he is satisfied that, at the time the qualification was awarded, the body concerned had adequate arrangements to ensure that the qualification was awarded only to persons educated and trained to a standard equivalent to that required, at that time, in the case of a recognised professional qualification under Part 2 of the Companies Act 1989 (c 40) (eligibility for appointment as company auditor).

NOTES

Commencement: 6 April 2008.

Commencement (transitional provisions): see the note to s 1217 at **[1.1217]**.

Sub-s (1): word in square brackets in para (d) inserted, para (e) repealed, and words in square brackets in para (f) substituted, by the Statutory Auditors and Third Country Auditors Regulations 2007, SI 2007/3494, reg 5, as from 6 April 2008.

[1.1220]

1220 Qualifying bodies and recognised professional qualifications

(1) In this Part a "qualifying body" means a body established in the United Kingdom (whether a body corporate or an unincorporated association) which offers a professional qualification in accountancy.

(2) In this Part references to the rules of a qualifying body are to the rules (whether or not laid down by the body itself) which the body has power to enforce and which are relevant for the purposes of this Part.

This includes, so far as so relevant, rules relating to—

(a) admission to or expulsion from a course of study leading to a qualification,

(b) the award or deprivation of a qualification, or

(c) the approval of a person for the purposes of giving practical training or the withdrawal of such approval.

(3) Schedule 11 has effect with respect to the recognition for the purposes of this Part of a professional qualification offered by a qualifying body.

NOTES

Commencement: 6 April 2008.

Commencement (transitional provisions): see the note to s 1217 at **[1.1217]**.

[1.1221]
1221 Approval of [third country] qualifications

(1) The Secretary of State may declare that the following are to be regarded for the purposes of this Chapter as holding an approved [third country] qualification—

    (a) persons who are qualified to audit accounts under the law of a specified [third country], or

    (b) persons who hold a specified professional qualification in accountancy obtained in a specified [third country].

[(1A) A declaration under subsection (1)(a) or (b) must be expressed to be subject to the requirement that any person to whom the declaration relates must pass an aptitude test in accordance with subsection (7A), unless an aptitude test is not required (see subsection (7B)).]

(2) A declaration under subsection (1)(b) may be expressed to be subject to the satisfaction of any specified requirement or requirements.

(3) The Secretary of State may make a declaration under subsection (1) only if he is satisfied that—

    (a) in the case of a declaration under subsection (1)(a), the fact that the persons in question are qualified to audit accounts under the law of the specified [third country], or

    (b) in the case of a declaration under subsection (1)(b), the specified professional qualification taken with any requirement or requirements to be specified under subsection (2),

affords an assurance of professional competence equivalent to that afforded by a recognised professional qualification.

(4) The Secretary of State may make a declaration under subsection (1) only if he is satisfied that the treatment that the persons who are the subject of the declaration will receive as a result of it is comparable to the treatment which is, or is likely to be, afforded in the specified [third country] or a part of it to—

    (a) in the case of a declaration under subsection (1)(a), some or all persons who are eligible to be appointed as a statutory auditor, and

    (b) in the case of a declaration under subsection (1)(b), some or all persons who hold a corresponding recognised professional qualification.

(5) The Secretary of State may direct that persons holding an approved [third country] qualification are not to be treated as holding an appropriate qualification for the purposes of this Chapter unless they hold such additional educational qualifications as the Secretary of State may specify for the purpose of ensuring that such persons have an adequate knowledge of the law and practice in the United Kingdom relevant to the audit of accounts.

(6) The Secretary of State may give different directions in relation to different approved [third country] qualifications.

(7) The Secretary of State may, if he thinks fit, having regard to the considerations mentioned in subsections (3) and (4), withdraw a declaration under subsection (1) in relation to—

    (a) persons becoming qualified to audit accounts under the law of the specified [third country] after such date as he may specify, or

    (b) persons obtaining the specified professional qualification after such date as he may specify.

[(7A) An aptitude test required for the purposes of subsection (1A)—

    (a) must test the person's knowledge of subjects—

        (i) that are covered by a recognised professional qualification,

        (ii) that are not covered by the professional qualification already held by the person, and

        (iii) the knowledge of which is essential for the pursuit of the profession of statutory auditor;

    (b) may test the person's knowledge of rules of professional conduct;

    (c) must not test the person's knowledge of any other matters.

(7B) No aptitude test is required for the purposes of subsection (1A) if the subjects that are covered by a recognised professional qualification and the knowledge of which is essential for the pursuit of the profession of statutory auditor are covered by the professional qualification already held by the person.]

(8) The Secretary of State may, if he thinks fit, having regard to the considerations mentioned in subsections (3) and (4), vary or revoke a requirement specified under subsection (2) from such date as he may specify.

(9) . . .

NOTES

Commencement: 6 April 2008.

Commencement (transitional provisions): see the note to s 1217 at **[1.1217]**.

Section heading, sub-ss (1), (3)–(7): words in square brackets substituted by the Statutory Auditors and Third Country Auditors Regulations 2007, SI 2007/3494, reg 6(1)–(3), as from 6 April 2008.

Sub-ss (1A), (7A), (7B): inserted by SI 2007/3494, reg 6(1), (4), (5), as from 6 April 2008.

Sub-s (9): repealed by SI 2007/3494, reg 6(1), (6), as from 6 April 2008.

[1.1222]
1222   Eligibility of individuals retaining only 1967 Act authorisation

(1)   A person whose only appropriate qualification is based on his retention of an authorisation originally granted by the Board of Trade or the Secretary of State under section 13(1) of the Companies Act 1967 (c 81) is eligible only for appointment as auditor of an unquoted company.

(2)   A company is "unquoted" if, at the time of the person's appointment, neither the company, nor any parent undertaking of which it is a subsidiary undertaking, is a quoted company within the meaning of section 385(2).

(3)   References to a person eligible for appointment as a statutory auditor by virtue of this Part in enactments relating to eligibility for appointment as auditor of a person other than a company do not include a person to whom this section applies.

NOTES
Commencement: 6 April 2008.
Commencement (transitional provisions): see the note to s 1217 at **[1.1217]**.

Information

[1.1223]
1223   Matters to be notified to the Secretary of State

(1)   The Secretary of State may require a recognised supervisory body or a recognised qualifying body—
    (a)   to notify him immediately of the occurrence of such events as he may specify in writing and to give him such information in respect of those events as is so specified;
    (b)   to give him, at such times or in respect of such periods as he may specify in writing, such information as is so specified.

(2)   The notices and information required to be given must be such as the Secretary of State may reasonably require for the exercise of his functions under this Part.

(3)   The Secretary of State may require information given under this section to be given in a specified form or verified in a specified manner.

(4)   Any notice or information required to be given under this section must be given in writing unless the Secretary of State specifies or approves some other manner.

NOTES
Commencement: 6 April 2008.

[1.1223A]
[1223A   Notification of matters relevant to other EEA States

(1)   A recognised supervisory body must notify the Secretary of State of—
    (a)   any withdrawal of a notifiable person's eligibility for appointment as a statutory auditor; and
    (b)   the reasons for the withdrawal.

(2)   A recognised supervisory body must also notify the Secretary of State of any reasonable grounds it has for suspecting that—
    (a)   a person has contravened the law of the United Kingdom, or any other EEA State or part of an EEA State, implementing the Audit Directive, and
    (b)   the act or omission constituting that contravention took place on the territory of an EEA State other than the United Kingdom.

(3)   In this section "notifiable person" means a member of the recognised supervisory body in question—
    (a)   who is also an EEA auditor; and
    (b)   in respect of whom the EEA competent authority is not the recognised supervisory body itself.]

NOTES
Commencement: 6 April 2008.
Inserted by the Statutory Auditors and Third Country Auditors Regulations 2007, SI 2007/3494, reg 7, as from 6 April 2008.

[1.1224]
1224   The Secretary of State's power to call for information

(1)   The Secretary of State may by notice in writing require a person within subsection (2) to give him such information as he may reasonably require for the exercise of his functions under this Part.

(2)   The persons within this subsection are—
    (a)   any recognised supervisory body,
    (b)   any recognised qualifying body, and
    (c)   any person eligible for appointment as a statutory auditor by virtue of this Chapter.

(3)   The Secretary of State may require that any information which he requires under this section is to be given within such reasonable time and verified in such manner as he may specify.

NOTES
Commencement: 6 April 2008.

[1.1224A]
[1224A   Restrictions on disclosure
(1)   This section applies to information (in whatever form)—
  (a)   relating to the private affairs of an individual, or
  (b)   relating to any particular business,
that is provided to a body to which this section applies in connection with the exercise of its functions under this Part or sections 522 to 524 (notification to appropriate audit authority of resignation or removal of auditor).
(2)   This section applies to—
  (a)   a recognised supervisory body,
  (b)   a recognised qualifying body,
  (c)   a body performing functions for the purposes of arrangements within paragraph 23(1) (independent monitoring of certain audits) or paragraph 24(1) (independent investigation of public interest cases) of Schedule 10,
  (d)   the Independent Supervisor,
  (e)   the Secretary of State, and
  (f)   a body designated by the Secretary of State under section 1252 (delegation of the Secretary of State's functions).
(3)   No such information may, during the lifetime of the individual or so long as the business continues to be carried on, be disclosed without the consent of that individual or (as the case may be) the person for the time being carrying on that business.
(4)   Subsection (3) does not apply to any disclosure of information that—
  (a)   is made for the purpose of facilitating the carrying out by the body of any of its functions,
  (b)   is made to a person specified in Part 1 of Schedule 11A,
  (c)   is of a description specified in Part 2 of that Schedule, or
  (d)   is made in accordance with Part 3 of that Schedule.
(5)   Subsection (3) does not apply to—
  (a)   the disclosure by an EEA competent authority of information disclosed to it by the body in reliance on subsection (4);
  (b)   the disclosure of such information by anyone who has obtained it directly or indirectly from an EEA competent authority.
(6)   This section does not prohibit the disclosure of information if the information is or has been available to the public from any other source.
(7)   Nothing in this section authorises the making of a disclosure in contravention of the Data Protection Act 1998.]

NOTES
Commencement: 6 April 2008.
Inserted by the Statutory Auditors and Third Country Auditors Regulations 2007, SI 2007/3494, reg 8(1), (3), as from 6 April 2008, in relation to information that is provided to a body on or after that date.

[1.1224B]
[1224B   Offence of disclosure in contravention of section 1224A
(1)   A person who discloses information in contravention of section 1224A (restrictions on disclosure) is guilty of an offence, unless—
  (a)   he did not know, and had no reason to suspect, that the information had been provided as mentioned in section 1224A(1), or
  (b)   he took all reasonable steps and exercised all due diligence to avoid the commission of the offence.
(2)   A person guilty of an offence under this section is liable—
  (a)   on conviction on indictment, to imprisonment for a term not exceeding two years or a fine (or both);
  (b)   on summary conviction—
    (i)   in Scotland, to imprisonment for a term not exceeding 12 months or to a fine not exceeding the statutory maximum, or to both;
    (ii)   in England and Wales or Northern Ireland, to imprisonment for a term not exceeding three months or to a fine not exceeding the statutory maximum, or to both.]

NOTES
Commencement: 6 April 2008.
Inserted by the Statutory Auditors and Third Country Auditors Regulations 2007, SI 2007/3494, reg 8(1), as from 6 April 2008.

Enforcement

[1.1225]
1225 Compliance orders

(1) If at any time it appears to the Secretary of State—

    (a) in the case of a recognised supervisory body, that any requirement of Schedule 10 is not satisfied,

    (b) in the case of a recognised professional qualification, that any requirement of Schedule 11 is not satisfied, or

    (c) that a recognised supervisory body or a recognised qualifying body has failed to comply with an obligation to which it is subject under or by virtue of this Part,

he may, instead of revoking the relevant recognition order, make an application to the court under this section.

(2) If on an application under this section the court decides that the requirement in question is not satisfied or, as the case may be, that the body has failed to comply with the obligation in question, it may order the body to take such steps as the court directs for securing that the requirement is satisfied or that the obligation is complied with.

(3) In this section "the court" means the High Court or, in Scotland, the Court of Session.

NOTES

Commencement: 6 April 2008.

CHAPTER 3
AUDITORS GENERAL

Eligibility for appointment

[1.1226]
1226 Auditors General: eligibility for appointment as a statutory auditor

(1) In this Part "Auditor General" means—

    (a) the Comptroller and Auditor General,

    (b) the Auditor General for Scotland,

    (c) the Auditor General for Wales, or

    (d) the Comptroller and Auditor General for Northern Ireland.

(2) An Auditor General is eligible for appointment as a statutory auditor.

(3) Subsection (2) is subject to any suspension notice having effect under section 1234 (notices suspending eligibility for appointment as a statutory auditor).

NOTES

Commencement: 6 April 2008.

Commencement (transitional provisions): Sch 4, Pt 1, para 40 to the Companies Act 2006 (Commencement No 5, Transitional Provisions and Savings) Order 2007, SI 2007/3495 (at **[2.66]**) provides that sub-s (2) above applies to appointment as a statutory auditor for financial years beginning on or after 1 April 2008, and that ss 1229, 1230 apply accordingly.

Conduct of audits

[1.1227]
1227 Individuals responsible for audit work on behalf of Auditors General

An Auditor General must secure that each individual responsible for statutory audit work on behalf of that Auditor General is eligible for appointment as a statutory auditor by virtue of Chapter 2.

NOTES

Commencement: 6 April 2008.

The Independent Supervisor

[1.1228]
1228 Appointment of the Independent Supervisor

(1) The Secretary of State must appoint a body ("the Independent Supervisor") to discharge the function mentioned in section 1229(1) ("the supervision function").

(2) An appointment under this section must be made by order.

(3) The order has the effect of making the body appointed under subsection (1) designated under section 5 of the Freedom of Information Act 2000 (c 36) (further powers to designate public authorities).

(4) A body may be appointed under this section only if it is a body corporate or an unincorporated association which appears to the Secretary of State—

    (a) to be willing and able to discharge the supervision function, and

    (b) to have arrangements in place relating to the discharge of that function which are such as to be likely to ensure that the conditions in subsection (5) are met.

(5) The conditions are—

    (a) that the supervision function will be exercised effectively, and

(b)   where the order is to contain any requirements or other provisions specified under subsection (6), that that function will be exercised in accordance with any such requirements or provisions.

(6)   An order under this section may contain such requirements or other provisions relating to the exercise of the supervision function by the Independent Supervisor as appear to the Secretary of State to be appropriate.

(7)   An order under this section is subject to negative resolution procedure.

NOTES

Commencement: 20 January 2007 (for the purpose of enabling the exercise of powers to make Orders or Regulations by statutory instrument); 6 April 2008 (otherwise).

Orders: the Independent Supervisor Appointment Order 2007, SI 2007/3534 at **[4.88]** (this Order provides that the body known as the Professional Oversight Board, established under the articles of association of The Financial Reporting Council Limited, is appointed for the purposes of this section to discharge the supervision function (as from 6 April 2008)).

Supervision of Auditors General

[1.1229]
1229   Supervision of Auditors General by the Independent Supervisor
(1)   The Independent Supervisor must supervise the performance by each Auditor General of his functions as a statutory auditor.

[(2)   The Independent Supervisor must discharge that duty by—
    (a)   establishing supervision arrangements itself, or
    (b)   entering into supervision arrangements with one or more bodies.

(2A)   If the Independent Supervisor enters into supervision arrangements with one or more bodies, it must oversee the effective operation of those supervision arrangements.]

(3)   For this purpose "supervision arrangements" are arrangements [established by the Independent Supervisor or] entered into by the Independent Supervisor with a body, for the purposes of this section, in accordance with which [the Independent Supervisor or] the body does . . . the following—
    (a)   determines standards relating to professional integrity and independence which must be applied by an Auditor General in statutory audit work;
    (b)   determines technical standards which must be applied by an Auditor General in statutory audit work and the manner in which those standards are to be applied in practice;
    (c)   monitors the performance of statutory audits carried out by an Auditor General;
    (d)   investigates any matter arising from the performance by an Auditor General of a statutory audit;
    (e)   holds disciplinary hearings in respect of an Auditor General which appear to be desirable following the conclusion of such investigations;
    (f)   decides whether (and, if so, what) disciplinary action should be taken against an Auditor General to whom such a hearing related.

[(3A)   The requirements of paragraphs 9 to 10A and 12 to 15 of Schedule 10 (requirements for recognition of a supervisory body) apply in relation to supervision arrangements as they apply in relation to the rules, practices and arrangements of supervisory bodies.]

(4)   The Independent Supervisor may enter into supervision arrangements with a body despite any relationship that may exist between the Independent Supervisor and that body.

(5)   The Independent Supervisor must notify each Auditor General in writing of any supervision arrangements that it [establishes or] enters into under this section.

[(5A)   The Independent Supervisor must, at least once in every calendar year, deliver to the Secretary of State a summary of the results of any inspections conducted for the purposes of subsection (3)(c).]

(6)   Supervision arrangements within subsection (3)(f) may, in particular, provide for the payment by an Auditor General of a fine to any person.

(7)   Any fine received by the Independent Supervisor under supervision arrangements is to be paid into the Consolidated Fund.

NOTES

Commencement: 6 April 2008.

Commencement (transitional provisions): see the note to s 1226 at **[1.1226]**.

Sub-ss (2), (2A): substituted, for original sub-s (2), by the Statutory Auditors and Third Country Auditors Regulations 2007, SI 2007/3494, reg 9(1), (2), as from 6 April 2008.

Sub-s (3): words in square brackets inserted, and words omitted repealed, by SI 2007/3494, reg 9(1), (3), as from 6 April 2008.

Sub-ss (3A), (5A): inserted by SI 2007/3494, reg 9(1), (4), (6), as from 6 April 2008.

Sub-s (5): words in square brackets inserted by SI 2007/3494, reg 9(1), (5), as from 6 April 2008.

As to the duty of the Independent Supervisor to consult with the Auditors General (and such other persons as seem to it to be appropriate) before establishing or entering into a supervision arrangement for the purposes of this section, see the Independent Supervisor Appointment Order 2007, SI 2007/3534, art 6 at **[4.93]**.

[1.1230]
1230 Duties of Auditors General in relation to supervision arrangements

(1) Each Auditor General must—

   (a) comply with any standards of the kind mentioned in subsection (3)(a) or (b) of section 1229 determined under the supervision arrangements,

   (b) take such steps as may be reasonably required of that Auditor General to enable his performance of statutory audits to be monitored by means of inspections carried out under the supervision arrangements, and

   (c) comply with any decision of the kind mentioned in subsection (3)(f) of that section made under the supervision arrangements.

[(2) Each Auditor General must—

   (a) if the Independent Supervisor has established supervision arrangements, pay to the Independent Supervisor;

   (b) if the Independent Supervisor has entered into supervision arrangements with a body, pay to that body,

such proportion of the costs incurred by the Independent Supervisor or body for the purposes of the arrangements as the Independent Supervisor may notify to him in writing.]

(3) Expenditure under subsection (2) is—

   (a) in the case of expenditure of the Comptroller and Auditor General, to be regarded as expenditure of the National Audit Office for the purposes of section 4(1) of the National Audit Act 1983 (c 44);

   (b) in the case of expenditure of the Comptroller and Auditor General for Northern Ireland, to be regarded as expenditure of the Northern Ireland Audit Office for the purposes of Article 6(1) of the Audit (Northern Ireland) Order 1987 (SI 1987/460 (NI 5)).

(4) In this section "the supervision arrangements" means the arrangements [established or] entered into under section 1229.

NOTES

Commencement: 6 April 2008.

Commencement (transitional provisions): see the note to s 1226 at **[1.1226]**.

Sub-s (2): substituted by the Statutory Auditors and Third Country Auditors Regulations 2007, SI 2007/3494, reg 10(1), (2), as from 6 April 2008.

Sub-s (3): para (a) repealed by the Budget Responsibility and National Audit Act 2011, s 26, Sch 5, Pt 2, paras 29, 30, as from a day to be appointed.

Sub-s (4): words in square brackets inserted by SI 2007/3494, reg 10(1), (3), as from 6 April 2008.

Reporting requirement

[1.1231]
1231 Reports by the Independent Supervisor

(1) The Independent Supervisor must, at least once in each calendar year, prepare a report on the discharge of its functions.

(2) The Independent Supervisor must give a copy of each report prepared under subsection (1) to—

   (a) the Secretary of State;

   (b) the First Minister in Scotland;

   (c) the First Minister and the deputy First Minister in Northern Ireland;

   [(d) The First Minister for Wales].

(3) The Secretary of State must lay before each House of Parliament a copy of each report received by him under subsection (2)(a).

[(3A) The First Minister for Wales must lay before the National Assembly for Wales a copy of each report received by him under subsection (2)(d).]

(4) In relation to a calendar year during which an appointment of a body as the Independent Supervisor is made or revoked by an order under section 1228, this section applies with such modifications as may be specified in the order.

NOTES

Commencement: 20 January 2007 (for the purpose of enabling the exercise of powers to make Orders or Regulations by statutory instrument); 6 April 2008 (otherwise).

Sub-s (2): para (d) substituted by the Government of Wales Act 2006 (Consequential Modifications, Transitional Provisions and Saving) Order 2009, SI 2009/2958, arts 8, 12(1), (2), as from 6 November 2009.

Sub-s (3A): inserted by SI 2009/2958, arts 8, 12(1), (3), (4), as from 6 November 2009; but note that this amendment does not apply to calendar years before 2010.

As to the content of reports under this section, see the Independent Supervisor Appointment Order 2007, SI 2007/3534, art 4 at **[4.91]**.

Information

[1.1232]
1232 Matters to be notified to the Independent Supervisor

(1) The Independent Supervisor may require an Auditor General—

(a) to notify the Independent Supervisor immediately of the occurrence of such events as it may specify in writing and to give it such information in respect of those events as is so specified;

(b) to give the Independent Supervisor, at such times or in respect of such periods as it may specify in writing, such information as is so specified.

(2) The notices and information required to be given must be such as the Independent Supervisor may reasonably require for the exercise of the functions conferred on it by or by virtue of this Part.

(3) The Independent Supervisor may require information given under this section to be given in a specified form or verified in a specified manner.

(4) Any notice or information required to be given under this section must be given in writing unless the Independent Supervisor specifies or approves some other manner.

NOTES
Commencement: 6 April 2008.

[1.1233]
1233 The Independent Supervisor's power to call for information

(1) The Independent Supervisor may by notice in writing require an Auditor General to give it such information as it may reasonably require for the exercise of the functions conferred on it by or by virtue of this Part.

(2) The Independent Supervisor may require that any information which it requires under this section is to be given within such reasonable time and verified in such manner as it may specify.

NOTES
Commencement: 6 April 2008.

Enforcement

[1.1234]
1234 Suspension notices

(1) The Independent Supervisor may issue—
(a) a notice (a "suspension notice") suspending an Auditor General's eligibility for appointment as a statutory auditor in relation to all persons, or any specified person or persons, indefinitely or until a date specified in the notice;
(b) a notice amending or revoking a suspension notice previously issued to an Auditor General.

(2) In determining whether it is appropriate to issue a notice under subsection (1), the Independent Supervisor must have regard to—
(a) the Auditor General's performance of the obligations imposed on him by or by virtue of this Part, and
(b) the Auditor General's performance of his functions as a statutory auditor.

(3) A notice under subsection (1) must—
(a) be in writing, and
(b) state the date on which it takes effect (which must be after the period of three months beginning with the date on which it is issued).

(4) Before issuing a notice under subsection (1), the Independent Supervisor must—
(a) give written notice of its intention to do so to the Auditor General, and
(b) publish the notice mentioned in paragraph (a) in such manner as it thinks appropriate for bringing it to the attention of any other persons who are likely to be affected.

(5) A notice under subsection (4) must—
(a) state the reasons for which the Independent Supervisor proposes to act, and
(b) give particulars of the rights conferred by subsection (6).

(6) A person within subsection (7) may, within the period of three months beginning with the date of service or publication of the notice under subsection (4) or such longer period as the Independent Supervisor may allow, make written representations to the Independent Supervisor and, if desired, oral representations to a person appointed for that purpose by the Independent Supervisor.

(7) The persons within this subsection are—
(a) the Auditor General, and
(b) any other person who appears to the Independent Supervisor to be affected.

(8) The Independent Supervisor must have regard to any representations made in accordance with subsection (6) in determining—
(a) whether to issue a notice under subsection (1), and
(b) the terms of any such notice.

(9) If in any case the Independent Supervisor considers it appropriate to do so in the public interest it may issue a notice under subsection (1), without regard to the restriction in subsection (3)(b), even if—
(a) no notice has been given or published under subsection (4), or
(b) the period of time for making representations in pursuance of such a notice has not expired.

(10) On issuing a notice under subsection (1), the Independent Supervisor must—
(a) give a copy of the notice to the Auditor General, and

(b)   publish the notice in such manner as it thinks appropriate for bringing it to the attention of persons likely to be affected.

(11)   In this section "specified" means specified in, or of a description specified in, the suspension notice in question.

NOTES
Commencement: 6 April 2008.

[1.1235]
1235   Effect of suspension notices

(1)   An Auditor General must not act as a statutory auditor at any time when a suspension notice issued to him in respect of the audited person has effect.

(2)   If at any time during an Auditor General's term of office as a statutory auditor a suspension notice issued to him in respect of the audited person takes effect, he must immediately—

(a)   resign his office (with immediate effect), and

(b)   give notice in writing to the audited person that he has resigned by reason of his becoming ineligible for appointment.

(3)   A suspension notice does not make an Auditor General ineligible for appointment as a statutory auditor for the purposes of section 1213 (effect of ineligibility: criminal offences).

NOTES
Commencement: 6 April 2008.

[1.1236]
1236   Compliance orders

(1)   If at any time it appears to the Independent Supervisor that an Auditor General has failed to comply with an obligation imposed on him by or by virtue of this Part, the Independent Supervisor may make an application to the court under this section.

(2)   If on an application under this section the court decides that the Auditor General has failed to comply with the obligation in question, it may order the Auditor General to take such steps as the court directs for securing that the obligation is complied with.

(3)   In this section "the court" means the High Court or, in Scotland, the Court of Session.

NOTES
Commencement: 6 April 2008.

Proceedings

[1.1237]
1237   Proceedings involving the Independent Supervisor

(1)   If the Independent Supervisor is an unincorporated association, any relevant proceedings may be brought by or against it in the name of any body corporate whose constitution provides for the establishment of the body.

(2)   For this purpose "relevant proceedings" means proceedings brought in or in connection with the exercise of any function by the body as the Independent Supervisor.

(3)   Where an appointment under section 1228 is revoked, the revoking order may make such provision as the Secretary of State thinks fit with respect to pending proceedings.

NOTES
Commencement: 20 January 2007 (for the purpose of enabling the exercise of powers to make Orders or Regulations by statutory instrument); 6 April 2008 (otherwise).

Grants

[1.1238]
1238   Grants to the Independent Supervisor

(Inserts the Companies (Audit, Investigations and Community Enterprise) Act 2004, s 16(2)(ka) at **[5.171]**.)

NOTES
Commencement: 6 April 2008.

CHAPTER 4
THE REGISTER OF AUDITORS ETC

[1.1239]
1239   The register of auditors

(1)   The Secretary of State must make regulations requiring the keeping of a register of—

(a)   the persons eligible for appointment as a statutory auditor, and

(b)   third country auditors (see Chapter 5) who apply to be registered in the specified manner and in relation to whom specified requirements are met.

(2)   The regulations must require each person's entry in the register to contain—

(a) his name and address,

(b) in the case of an individual eligible for appointment as a statutory auditor, the specified information relating to any firm on whose behalf he is responsible for statutory audit work,

(c) in the case of a firm eligible for appointment as a statutory auditor, the specified information relating to the individuals responsible for statutory audit work on its behalf,

(d) in the case of an individual or firm eligible for appointment as a statutory auditor by virtue of Chapter 2, the name of the relevant supervisory body, . . .

(e) in the case of a firm eligible for appointment as a statutory auditor by virtue of Chapter 2 . . . , the information mentioned in subsection (3), [and

(f) in the case of a third country auditor which is a firm, the name and address of each person who is—

    (i) an owner or shareholder of the firm, or

    (ii) a member of the firm's administrative or management body],

and may require each person's entry to contain other specified information.

(3) The information referred to in subsection (2)(e) is—

(a) in relation to a body corporate, except where paragraph (b) applies, the name and address of each person who is a director of the body or holds any shares in it;

(b) in relation to a limited liability partnership, the name and address of each member of the partnership;

(c) in relation to a corporation sole, the name and address of the individual for the time being holding the office by the name of which he is the corporation sole;

(d) in relation to a partnership, the name and address of each partner.

(4) The regulations may provide that different parts of the register are to be kept by different persons.

(5) The regulations may impose such obligations as the Secretary of State thinks fit on—

(a) recognised supervisory bodies,

(b) any body designated by order under section 1252 (delegation of Secretary of State's functions),

(c) persons eligible for appointment as a statutory auditor,

(d) third country auditors,

(e) any person with whom arrangements are made by one or more recognised supervisory bodies, or by any body designated by order under section 1252, with respect to the keeping of the register, or

(f) the Independent Supervisor appointed under section 1228.

(6) The regulations may include—

(a) provision requiring that specified entries in the register be open to inspection at times and places specified or determined in accordance with the regulations;

(b) provision enabling a person to require a certified copy of specified entries in the register;

(c) provision authorising the charging of fees for inspection, or the provision of copies, of such reasonable amount as may be specified or determined in accordance with the regulations.

(7) The Secretary of State may direct in writing that the requirements imposed by the regulations . . . , or such of those requirements as are specified in the direction, are not to apply, in whole or in part, in relation to a particular registered third country auditor or class of registered third country auditors.

(8) The obligations imposed by regulations under this section on such persons as are mentioned in subsection (5)(b) or (e) are enforceable on the application of the Secretary of State by injunction or, in Scotland, by an order under section 45 of the Court of Session Act 1988 (c 36).

(9) In this section "specified" means specified by regulations under this section.

(10) Regulations under this section are subject to negative resolution procedure.

NOTES

Commencement: 20 January 2007 (for the purpose of enabling the exercise of powers to make Orders or Regulations by statutory instrument); 6 April 2008 (otherwise).

Sub-s (2): words omitted from paras (d), (e) repealed, and para (f) (and the word immediately preceding it) inserted, by the Statutory Auditors and Third Country Auditors Regulations 2007, SI 2007/3494, reg 30(1)–(4), as from 6 April 2008.

Sub-s (7): words omitted repealed by SI 2007/3494, reg 30(1), (5), as from 6 April 2008.

Regulations: the Statutory Auditors and Third Country Auditors Regulations 2007, SI 2007/3494 at **[4.79]**; the Statutory Auditors and Third Country Auditors (Amendment) Regulations 2008, SI 2008/499; the Statutory Auditors and Third Country Auditors (Amendment) (No 2) Regulations 2008, SI 2008/2639.

[1.1240]
1240 Information to be made available to public

(1) The Secretary of State may make regulations requiring a person eligible for appointment as a statutory auditor, or a member of a specified class of such persons, to keep and make available to the public specified information, including information regarding—

(a) the person's ownership and governance,

(b) the person's internal controls with respect to the quality and independence of its audit work,

(c) the person's turnover, and

(d) the audited persons of whom the person has acted as statutory auditor.

Part 1   The Companies Act 2006

(2) Regulations under this section may—

  (a) impose such obligations as the Secretary of State thinks fit on persons eligible for appointment as a statutory auditor;

  (b) require the information to be made available to the public in a specified manner.

(3) In this section "specified" means specified by regulations under this section.

(4) Regulations under this section are subject to negative resolution procedure.

NOTES

Commencement: 20 January 2007 (for the purpose of enabling the exercise of powers to make Orders or Regulations by statutory instrument); 6 April 2008 (otherwise).

CHAPTER 5
REGISTERED THIRD COUNTRY AUDITORS

Introductory

[1.1241]

1241 [Meaning of "registered third country auditor" and "UK-traded non-EEA company"]

(1) In this Part—

   . . .

"registered third country auditor" means a third country auditor who is entered in the register kept in accordance with regulations under section 1239(1).

(2) [In this Part "UK-traded non-EEA company" means a body corporate—]

  (a) which is incorporated or formed under the law of [a third country],

  (b) whose transferable securities are admitted to trading on a regulated market situated or operating in the United Kingdom, and

  (c) which has not been excluded, or is not of a description of bodies corporate which has been excluded, from this definition by an order made by the Secretary of State.

(3) For this purpose—

"regulated market" has the meaning given by Article 4.1(14) of Directive 2004/39/EC of the European Parliament and of the Council on markets in financial instruments;

"transferable securities" has the meaning given by Article 4.1(18) of that Directive.

(4) An order under this section is subject to negative resolution procedure.

NOTES

Commencement: 20 January 2007 (for the purpose of enabling the exercise of powers to make Orders or Regulations by statutory instrument); 6 April 2008 (otherwise).

Section heading: substituted by the Statutory Auditors and Third Country Auditors Regulations 2007, SI 2007/3494, reg 31(1), (2), as from 6 April 2008.

Sub-s (1): definition "third country auditor" (omitted) repealed by SI 2007/3494, reg 31(1), (3), as from 6 April 2008.

Sub-s (2): words in square brackets substituted by SI 2007/3494, reg 31(1), (4), as from 6 April 2008.

UK-traded non-EEA company: see further the Statutory Auditors and Third Country Auditors Regulations 2007, SI 2007/3494, reg 43 which provides as follows—

"**43 Exclusion of large debt securities issuer from definition of "UK-traded non-EEA company"**

(1) A large debt securities issuer is excluded from the definition of "UK-traded non-EEA company" for the purposes of Part 42 of the Companies Act 2006 (see section 1241(2)).

(2) In paragraph (1) "large debt securities issuer" means a body corporate whose only issued transferable securities admitted to trading on a regulated market are debt securities, the denomination per unit of which is not less than—

  (a) 50,000 euros, or

  (b) in the case of debt securities denominated in a currency other than euros, a sum equivalent at the date of issue to 50,000 euros.

(3) In paragraph (2)—

"debt securities" has the same meaning as in Article 2.1(b) of Directive 2004/109/EC of the European Parliament and of the Council on the harmonisation of transparency requirements in relation to information about issuers whose securities are admitted to trading on a regulated market and amending Directive 2001/34/EC(a);

"transferable securities" and "regulated market" have the same meaning as in section 1241(3) of the Companies Act 2006.".

Regulations: the Statutory Auditors and Third Country Auditors Regulations 2007, SI 2007/3494 at **[4.79]**.

Duties

[1.1242]

1242 Duties of registered third country auditors

(1) A registered third country auditor [who audits the accounts of a UK-traded non-EEA company] must participate in—

  (a) arrangements within paragraph 1 of Schedule 12 (arrangements for independent monitoring of audits . . .), and

  (b) arrangements within paragraph 2 of that Schedule (arrangements for independent investigation for disciplinary purposes of public interest cases).

(2) A registered third country auditor must—

(a) take such steps as may be reasonably required of it to enable its performance of [audits of accounts of UK-traded non-EEA companies] to be monitored by means of inspections carried out under the arrangements mentioned in subsection (1)(a), and

(b) comply with any decision as to disciplinary action to be taken against it made under the arrangements mentioned in subsection (1)(b).

(3) Schedule 12 makes further provision with respect to the arrangements in which registered third country auditors are required to participate.

(4) The Secretary of State may direct in writing that subsections (1) to (3) are not to apply, in whole or in part, in relation to a particular registered third country auditor or class of registered third country auditors.

NOTES

Commencement: 29 June 2008.

Commencement (transitional provisions): Sch 4, Pt 2, para 45 to the Companies Act 2006 (Commencement No 5, Transitional Provisions and Savings) Order 2007, SI 2007/3495 (at **[2.67]**) provides that ss 1242–1244 and Sch 12 apply to third country auditors appointed for financial years beginning on or after 29 June 2008.

Sub-s (1): words in square brackets inserted, and words omitted repealed, by the Statutory Auditors and Third Country Auditors Regulations 2007, SI 2007/3494, reg 32(1), (2), as from 29 June 2008.

Sub-s (2): words in square brackets substituted by SI 2007/3494, reg 32(1), (3), as from 29 June 2008.

Information

[1.1243]

1243 Matters to be notified to the Secretary of State

(1) The Secretary of State may require a registered third country auditor—

(a) to notify him immediately of the occurrence of such events as he may specify in writing and to give him such information in respect of those events as is so specified;

(b) to give him, at such times or in respect of such periods as he may specify in writing, such information as is so specified.

(2) The notices and information required to be given must be such as the Secretary of State may reasonably require for the exercise of his functions under this Part.

(3) The Secretary of State may require information given under this section to be given in a specified form or verified in a specified manner.

(4) Any notice or information required to be given under this section must be given in writing unless the Secretary of State specifies or approves some other manner.

NOTES

Commencement: 29 June 2008.

Commencement (transitional provisions): see the note to s 1242 at **[1.1242]**.

[1.1244]

1244 The Secretary of State's power to call for information

(1) The Secretary of State may by notice in writing require a registered third country auditor to give him such information as he may reasonably require for the exercise of his functions under this Part.

(2) The Secretary of State may require that any information which he requires under this section is to be given within such reasonable time and verified in such manner as he may specify.

NOTES

Commencement: 29 June 2008.

Commencement (transitional provisions): see the note to s 1242 at **[1.1242]**.

Enforcement

[1.1245]

1245 Compliance orders

(1) If at any time it appears to the Secretary of State that a registered third country auditor has failed to comply with an obligation imposed on him by or by virtue of this Part, the Secretary of State may make an application to the court under this section.

(2) If on an application under this section the court decides that the auditor has failed to comply with the obligation in question, it may order the auditor to take such steps as the court directs for securing that the obligation is complied with.

(3) In this section "the court" means the High Court or, in Scotland, the Court of Session.

NOTES

Commencement: 6 April 2008.

[1.1246]

1246 Removal of third country auditors from the register of auditors

(1) The Secretary of State may, by regulations, confer on the person keeping the register in accordance with regulations under section 1239(1) power to remove a third country auditor from the register.

(2) Regulations under this section must require the person keeping the register, in determining whether to remove a third country auditor from the register, to have regard to the auditor's compliance with obligations imposed on him by or by virtue of this Part.

(3) Where provision is made under section 1239(4) (different parts of the register to be kept by different persons), references in this section to the person keeping the register are to the person keeping that part of the register which relates to third country auditors.

(4) Regulations under this section are subject to negative resolution procedure.

NOTES

Commencement: 20 January 2007 (for the purpose of enabling the exercise of powers to make Orders or Regulations by statutory instrument); 6 April 2008 (otherwise).

Regulations: the Statutory Auditors and Third Country Auditors Regulations 2007, SI 2007/3494 at **[4.79]**; the Statutory Auditors and Third Country Auditors (Amendment) (No 2) Regulations 2008, SI 2008/2639.

[1.1247]
1247 Grants to bodies concerned with arrangements under Schedule 12
(Inserts the Companies (Audit, Investigations and Community Enterprise) Act 2004, s 16(2)(kb) at **[5.171].**)

NOTES
Commencement: 6 April 2008.

CHAPTER 6
SUPPLEMENTARY AND GENERAL
Power to require second company audit

[1.1248]
1248 Secretary of State's power to require second audit of a company
(1) This section applies where a person appointed as statutory auditor of a company was not an appropriate person for any part of the period during which the audit was conducted.

(2) The Secretary of State may direct the company concerned to retain an appropriate person—
  (a) to conduct a second audit of the relevant accounts, or
  (b) to review the first audit and to report (giving his reasons) whether a second audit is needed.

(3) For the purposes of subsections (1) and (2) a person is "appropriate" if he—
  (a) is eligible for appointment as a statutory auditor or, if the person is an Auditor General, for appointment as statutory auditor of the company, and
  (b) is not prohibited by section 1214(1) (independence requirement) from acting as statutory auditor of the company.

(4) The Secretary of State must send a copy of a direction under subsection (2) to the registrar of companies.

(5) The company is guilty of an offence if—
  (a) it fails to comply with a direction under subsection (2) within the period of 21 days beginning with the date on which it is given, or
  (b) it has been convicted of a previous offence under this subsection and the failure to comply with the direction which led to the conviction continues after the conviction.

(6) The company must—
  (a) send a copy of a report under subsection (2)(b) to the registrar of companies, and
  (b) if the report states that a second audit is needed, take such steps as are necessary for the carrying out of that audit.

(7) The company is guilty of an offence if—
  (a) it fails to send a copy of a report under subsection (2)(b) to the registrar within the period of 21 days beginning with the date on which it receives it,
  (b) in a case within subsection (6)(b), it fails to take the steps mentioned immediately it receives the report, or
  (c) it has been convicted of a previous offence under this subsection and the failure to send a copy of the report, or take the steps, which led to the conviction continues after the conviction.

(8) A company guilty of an offence under this section is liable on summary conviction—
  (a) in a case within subsection (5)(a) or (7)(a) or (b), to a fine not exceeding level 5 on the standard scale, and
  (b) in a case within subsection (5)(b) or (7)(c), to a fine not exceeding one-tenth of level 5 on the standard scale for each day on which the failure continues.

(9) In this section "registrar of companies" has the meaning given by section 1060.

NOTES
Commencement: 6 April 2008.
Commencement (transitional provisions): Sch 4, Pt 1, para 41 to the Companies Act 2006 (Commencement No 5, Transitional Provisions and Savings) Order 2007, SI 2007/3495 (at **[2.66]**) provides as follows—

"41.—(1) The following provisions of Chapter 6 of Part 42 of the Companies Act 2006 (statutory auditors: supplementary and general provisions) apply to auditors, supervisory bodies or qualifying bodies to whom Chapters 2 to 5 of that Part apply—

    (a)   sections 1248 and 1249 (second audits);

    (b)   section 1250 (false and misleading statements);

    (c)   section 1251 (fees);

    (d)   section 1254 (directions to comply with international obligations);

    (e)   sections 1255 to 1257 (general provisions about offences);

    (f)   sections 1258 and 1259 (notices etc).

(2) Sections 29, 40 to 45 and 49 of the Companies Act 1989 or Articles 32, 42 to 47 and 51 of the Companies (Northern Ireland) Order 1990 continue to apply to auditors, supervisory bodies or qualifying bodies to whom sections 25 to 28 and 30 to 39 of that Act or Articles 28 to 31 and 33 to 41 of that Order apply.

(3) The repeal of sections 52 to 54 of the Companies Act 1989 or Articles 54 to 56 of the Companies (Northern Ireland) Order 1990 (definitions) does not affect the operation of those provisions for the purposes of interpreting provisions of that Act or that Order that continue to apply on or after 6th April 2008.".

[1.1249]
1249 Supplementary provision about second audits

(1) If a person accepts an appointment, or continues to act, as statutory auditor of a company at a time when he knows he is not an appropriate person, the company may recover from him any costs incurred by it in complying with the requirements of section 1248.

For this purpose "appropriate" is to be construed in accordance with subsection (3) of that section.

(2) Where a second audit is carried out under section 1248, any statutory or other provision applying in relation to the first audit applies also, in so far as practicable, in relation to the second audit.

(3) A direction under section 1248(2) is, on the application of the Secretary of State, enforceable by injunction or, in Scotland, by an order under section 45 of the Court of Session Act 1988 (c 36).

NOTES

Commencement: 6 April 2008.

Commencement (transitional provisions): see the note to s 1248 at **[1.1248]**.

False and misleading statements

[1.1250]
1250 Misleading, false and deceptive statements

(1) A person is guilty of an offence if—

    (a)   for the purposes of or in connection with any application under this Part, or

    (b)   in purported compliance with any requirement imposed on him by or by virtue of this Part,

he knowingly or recklessly furnishes information which is misleading, false or deceptive in a material particular.

(2) It is an offence for a person whose name does not appear on the register of auditors kept under regulations under section 1239 in an entry made under subsection (1)(a) of that section to describe himself as a registered auditor or so to hold himself out as to indicate, or be reasonably understood to indicate, that he is a registered auditor.

(3) It is an offence for a person whose name does not appear on the register of auditors kept under regulations under that section in an entry made under subsection (1)(b) of that section to describe himself as a registered third country auditor or so to hold himself out as to indicate, or be reasonably understood to indicate, that he is a registered third country auditor.

(4) It is an offence for a body which is not a recognised supervisory body or a recognised qualifying body to describe itself as so recognised or so to describe itself or hold itself out as to indicate, or be reasonably understood to indicate, that it is so recognised.

(5) A person guilty of an offence under subsection (1) is liable—

    (a)   on conviction on indictment, to imprisonment for a term not exceeding two years or to a fine (or both);

    (b)   on summary conviction—

        (i)   in England and Wales, to imprisonment for a term not exceeding twelve months or to a fine not exceeding the statutory maximum (or both),

        (ii)   in Scotland or Northern Ireland, to imprisonment for a term not exceeding six months or to a fine not exceeding the statutory maximum (or both).

In relation to an offence committed before the commencement of section 154(1) of the Criminal Justice Act 2003 (c 44), for "twelve months" in paragraph (b)(i) substitute "six months".

(6) Subject to subsection (7), a person guilty of an offence under subsection (2), (3) or (4) is liable on summary conviction—

    (a)   in England and Wales, to imprisonment for a term not exceeding 51 weeks or to a fine not exceeding level 5 on the standard scale (or both),

    (b)   in Scotland or Northern Ireland, to imprisonment for a term not exceeding six months or to a fine not exceeding level 5 on the standard scale (or both).

In relation to an offence committed before the commencement of section 281(5) of the Criminal Justice Act 2003, for "51 weeks" in paragraph (a) substitute "six months".

(7)   Where a contravention of subsection (2), (3) or (4) involves a public display of the offending description, the maximum fine that may be imposed is an amount equal to level 5 on the standard scale multiplied by the number of days for which the display has continued.

(8)   It is a defence for a person charged with an offence under subsection (2), (3) or (4) to show that he took all reasonable precautions and exercised all due diligence to avoid the commission of the offence.

NOTES
Commencement: 6 April 2008.
Commencement (transitional provisions): see the note to s 1248 at **[1.1248]**.

Fees

[1.1251]
1251   Fees
(1)   An applicant for a recognition order under this Part must pay such fee in respect of his application as the Secretary of State may by regulations prescribe; and no application is to be regarded as duly made unless this subsection is complied with.
(2)   The Secretary of State may by regulations prescribe periodical fees to be paid by—
    (a)   every recognised supervisory body,
    (b)   every recognised qualifying body,
    (c)   every Auditor General, and
    (d)   every registered third country auditor.
(3)   Fees received by the Secretary of State by virtue of this Part are to be paid into the Consolidated Fund.
(4)   Regulations under this section are subject to negative resolution procedure.

NOTES
Commencement: 20 January 2007 (for the purpose of enabling the exercise of powers to make Orders or Regulations by statutory instrument); 6 April 2008 (otherwise).
Commencement (transitional provisions): see the note to s 1248 at **[1.1248]**.

[Duty of Secretary of State to Report on Inspections

[1.1251A]
1251A   Duty of the Secretary of State to report on inspections
The Secretary of State must, at least once in every calendar year, publish a report containing a summary of the results of inspections that are delivered to him—
    (a)   by the Independent Supervisor under section 1229(5A);
    (b)   by a recognised supervisory body under paragraph 13(9) of Schedule 10.]

NOTES
Commencement: 6 April 2008.
Inserted, together with the preceding heading, by the Statutory Auditors and Third Country Auditors Regulations 2007, SI 2007/3494, reg 11, as from 6 April 2008.

Delegation of Secretary of State's functions

[1.1252]
1252   Delegation of the Secretary of State's functions
(1)   The Secretary of State may make an order under this section (a "delegation order") for the purpose of enabling functions of the Secretary of State under this Part to be exercised by a body designated by the order.
(2)   The body designated by a delegation order may be either—
    (a)   a body corporate which is established by the order, or
    (b)   subject to section 1253, a body (whether a body corporate or an unincorporated association) which is already in existence ("an existing body").
(3)   A delegation order has the effect of making the body designated by the order designated under section 5 of the Freedom of Information Act 2000 (c 36) (further powers to designate public authorities).
(4)   A delegation order has the effect of transferring to the body designated by it all functions of the Secretary of State under this Part—
    (a)   subject to such exceptions and reservations as may be specified in the order, and
    (b)   except—
        (i)   his functions in relation to the body itself, and
        (ii)   his functions under section 1228 (appointment of Independent Supervisor).
(5)   A delegation order may confer on the body designated by it such other functions supplementary or incidental to those transferred as appear to the Secretary of State to be appropriate.
(6)   Any transfer of functions under the following provisions must be subject to the reservation that the functions remain exercisable concurrently by the Secretary of State—
    (a)   section 1224 (power to call for information from recognised bodies etc);
    (b)   section 1244 (power to call for information from registered third country auditors);

(c) section 1254 (directions to comply with international obligations).

(7) Any transfer of—

(a) the function of refusing to make a declaration under section 1221(1) (approval of [third country] qualifications) on the grounds referred to in section 1221(4) (lack of comparable treatment), or

(b) the function of withdrawing such a declaration under section 1221(7) on those grounds,

must be subject to the reservation that the function is exercisable only with the consent of the Secretary of State.

(8) A delegation order may be amended or, if it appears to the Secretary of State that it is no longer in the public interest that the order should remain in force, revoked by a further order under this section.

(9) Where functions are transferred or resumed, the Secretary of State may by order confer or, as the case may be, take away such other functions supplementary or incidental to those transferred or resumed as appear to him to be appropriate.

(10) Where a delegation order is made, Schedule 13 has effect with respect to—

(a) the status of the body designated by the order in exercising functions of the Secretary of State under this Part,

(b) the constitution and proceedings of the body where it is established by the order,

(c) the exercise by the body of certain functions transferred to it, and

(d) other supplementary matters.

(11) An order under this section which has the effect of transferring or resuming any functions is subject to affirmative resolution procedure.

(12) Any other order under this section is subject to negative resolution procedure.

NOTES

Commencement: 20 January 2007 (for the purpose of enabling the exercise of powers to make Orders or Regulations by statutory instrument); 6 April 2008 (otherwise).

Sub-s (7): words in square brackets substituted by the Statutory Auditors and Third Country Auditors Regulations 2007, SI 2007/3494, reg 12, as from 6 April 2008.

Orders: the Statutory Auditors (Delegation of Functions etc) Order 2008, SI 2008/496 at **[4.240]** (this Order transfers most of the functions of the Secretary of State under this Part to the Professional Oversight Board).

[1.1253]
1253 Delegation of functions to an existing body

(1) The Secretary of State's power to make a delegation order under section 1252 which designates an existing body is exercisable in accordance with this section.

(2) The Secretary of State may make such a delegation order if it appears to him that—

(a) the body is able and willing to exercise the functions that would be transferred by the order, and

(b) the body has arrangements in place relating to the exercise of those functions which are such as to be likely to ensure that the conditions in subsection (3) are met.

(3) The conditions are—

(a) that the functions in question will be exercised effectively, and

(b) where the delegation order is to contain any requirements or other provisions specified under subsection (4), that those functions will be exercised in accordance with any such requirements or provisions.

(4) The delegation order may contain such requirements or other provision relating to the exercise of the functions by the designated body as appear to the Secretary of State to be appropriate.

(5) An existing body—

(a) may be designated by a delegation order under section 1252, and

(b) may accordingly exercise functions of the Secretary of State in pursuance of the order, despite any involvement of the body in the exercise of any functions under arrangements within [paragraph 21 to 22B, 23(1) or 24(1) of Schedule 10] or paragraph 1 or 2 of Schedule 12.

NOTES

Commencement: 20 January 2007 (for the purpose of enabling the exercise of powers to make Orders or Regulations by statutory instrument); 6 April 2008 (otherwise).

Sub-s (5): words in square brackets substituted by the Statutory Auditors and Third Country Auditors Regulations 2007, SI 2007/3494, reg 13, as from 6 April 2008.

Orders: the Statutory Auditors (Delegation of Functions etc) Order 2008, SI 2008/496 at **[4.240]**.

[Cooperation with Foreign Competent Authorities

[1.1253A]
1253A Requests to foreign competent authorities

The Secretary of State may request from an EEA competent authority or a third country competent authority such assistance, information or investigation as he may reasonably require in connection with the exercise of his functions under this Part.]

NOTES

Commencement: 6 April 2008.

Inserted, together with the preceding heading and ss 1253B, 1253C, by the Statutory Auditors and Third Country Auditors Regulations 2007, SI 2007/3494, reg 14(1), as from 6 April 2008.

[1.1253B]
[1253B   Requests from EEA competent authorities
(1)   The Secretary of State must take all necessary steps to—
    (a)   ensure that an investigation is carried out, or
    (b)   provide any other assistance or information,
if requested to do so by an EEA competent authority in accordance with Article 36 of the Audit Directive (cooperation between Member State authorities).
(2)   Within 28 days following the date on which he receives the request, the Secretary of State must—
    (a)   provide the assistance or information required by the EEA competent authority under subsection (1)(b), or
    (b)   notify the EEA competent authority which made the request of the reasons why he has not done so.
(3)   But the Secretary of State need not take steps to comply with a request under subsection (1) if—
    (a)   he considers that complying with the request may prejudice the sovereignty, security or public order of the United Kingdom;
    (b)   legal proceedings have been brought in the United Kingdom (whether continuing or not) in relation to the persons and matters to which the request relates; or
    (c)   disciplinary action has been taken by a recognised supervisory body in relation to the persons and matters to which the request relates.]

NOTES
Commencement: 6 April 2008.
Inserted as noted to s 1253A at **[1.1253A]**. By virtue of reg 14(2) of the 2007 Regulations, this section applies only to investigations, assistance or information relating to auditors appointed for financial years beginning on or after 6 April 2008.

[1.1253C]
[1253C   Notification to competent authorities of other EEA States
(1)   The Secretary of State must notify the relevant EEA competent authority if he receives notice from a recognised supervisory body under section 1223A(1) (notification of withdrawal of eligibility for appointment) of the withdrawal of a person's eligibility for appointment as a statutory auditor.
(2)   In subsection (1) "the relevant EEA competent authority" means the EEA competent authority which has approved the person concerned in accordance with the Audit Directive to carry out audits of annual accounts or consolidated accounts required by Community law.
(3)   The notification under subsection (1) must include the name of the person concerned and the reasons for the withdrawal of his eligibility for appointment as statutory auditor.
(4)   The Secretary of State must notify the relevant EEA competent authority if he has reasonable grounds for suspecting that—
    (a)   a person has contravened the law of the United Kingdom, or any other EEA State or part of an EEA State, implementing the Audit Directive, and
    (b)   the act or omission constituting that contravention took place on the territory of an EEA State other than the United Kingdom.,
(5)   In subsection (4) "the relevant EEA competent authority" means the EEA competent authority for the EEA State in which the suspected contravention took place.
(6)   The notification under subsection (4) must include the name of the person concerned and the grounds for the Secretary of State's suspicion.]

NOTES
Commencement: 6 April 2008.
Inserted as noted to s 1253A at **[1.1253A]**.

[Transfer of Papers to Third Countries

[1.1253D]
[1253D   Restriction on transfer of audit working papers to third countries
(1)   Audit working papers must not be transferred to a third country competent authority except in accordance with—
    (a)   section 1253DA (transfer by Secretary of State),
    (b)   section 1253DB (transfer by statutory auditor with approval of Secretary of State), or
    (c)   section 1253DC (transfer by statutory auditor for purposes of investigation of auditor).
(2)   The following are approved third country competent authorities for the purposes of this Part—
    (a)   the Australian Securities and Investments Commission;
    (b)   the Canadian Public Accountability Board;
    (c)   the Certified Public Accountants and Auditing Oversight Board of Japan;
    (d)   the Financial Services Agency of Japan;

(e)   the Federal Audit Oversight Authority of Switzerland;

(f)   *the Public Company Accounting Oversight Board of the United States of America;*

(g)   *the Securities and Exchange Commission of the United States of America.*

(3)   Nothing in the sections referred to in subsection (1) authorises the making of a disclosure in contravention of the Data Protection Act 1998.]

NOTES

Commencement: 15 November 2010.

Sections 1253D, 1253DA–1253DE substituted for the original s 1253D (as inserted by the Statutory Auditors and Third Country Auditors Regulations 2007, SI 2007/3494, reg 15(1), as from 6 April 2008) by the Companies Act 2006 (Transfer of Audit Working Papers to Third Countries) Regulations 2010, SI 2010/2537, reg 2, as from 15 November 2010.

Sub-s (2): paras (f), (g) repealed by SI 2010/2537, reg 4(1), as from 31 July 2013.

[1.1253DA]

[1253DA   Transfer by Secretary of State

(1)   The Secretary of State may transfer audit working papers to an approved third country competent authority if the following conditions are met (but see also section 1253DD).

(2)   The first condition is that the authority has made a request to the Secretary of State for the transfer of the audit working papers.

(3)   The second condition is that the audit working papers relate to audits of companies that—

(a)   have issued securities in the third country in which the authority is established, or

(b)   form part of a group issuing statutory consolidated accounts in that third country.

(4)   The third condition is that the authority has entered into arrangements with the Secretary of State in accordance with section 1253E.]

NOTES

Commencement: 15 November 2010.

Substituted as noted to s 1253D at **[1.1253D]**.

[1.1253DB]

[1253DB   Transfer by statutory auditor with approval of Secretary of State

(1)   A statutory auditor may transfer audit working papers to an approved third country competent authority if the transfer is made—

(a)   with the prior approval of the Secretary of State, and

(b)   in accordance with rules of a recognised supervisory body meeting the requirements of paragraph 16AA of Schedule 10.

(2)   The Secretary of State must not approve a transfer of audit working papers to an approved third country competent authority for the purposes of this section unless the following conditions are met (see also section 1253DD).

(3)   The first condition is that the authority has made a request to the Secretary of State for the transfer of the audit working papers.

(4)   The second condition is that the audit working papers relate to audits of companies that—

(a)   have issued securities in the third country in which the authority is established, or

(b)   form part of a group issuing statutory consolidated accounts in that third country.

(5)   The third condition is that the authority has entered into arrangements with the Secretary of State in accordance with section 1253E.]

NOTES

Commencement: 15 November 2010.

Substituted as noted to s 1253D at **[1.1253D]**.

[1.1253DC]

[1253DC   Transfer by statutory auditor for purposes of investigation of auditor

A statutory auditor may transfer audit working papers to a third country competent authority if the transfer is made—

(a)   for the purposes of an investigation of an auditor or audit firm, and

(b)   in accordance with rules of a recognised supervisory body meeting the requirements of paragraph 16AB of Schedule 10.]

NOTES

Commencement: 15 November 2010.

Substituted as noted to s 1253D at **[1.1253D]**.

[1.1253DD]

[1253DD   Agreement of EEA competent authority

(1)   This section applies where—

(a)   an approved third country competent authority makes a request to the Secretary of State for the transfer of audit working papers which relate to the audit of the consolidated accounts of a group, and

(b)   the audit working papers that are the subject of the request—

     (i)   have been created by the auditor of a subsidiary that is located in another EEA State in relation to the audit of that subsidiary, and

     (ii)   are in the possession of a statutory auditor.

(2) In the case of a transfer by the Secretary of State under section 1253DA, the transfer must not take place unless the EEA competent authority responsible for the auditor of the subsidiary has given its express agreement to the transfer.

(3) In the case of a transfer by a statutory auditor under section 1253DB, the Secretary of State must not approve the transfer unless the EEA competent authority responsible for the auditor of the subsidiary has given its express agreement to the transfer.]

NOTES

Commencement: 15 November 2010.

Substituted as noted to s 1253D at **[1.1253D]**.

[1.1253DE]
[1253DE   Transfer by means of inspection

(1) This section applies in the case of a transfer of audit working papers if—

    (a)   it is a transfer to *an approved third country competent authority listed in section 1253D(2)(a), (f) or (g)*,

    (b)   it is a transfer under section 1253DA or 1253DB, and

    (c)   it is to take place by means of an inspection in the United Kingdom by *the authority*.

(2) The Secretary of State must participate in the inspection.

(3) The inspection must be under the leadership of the Secretary of State unless the Secretary of State otherwise permits.]

NOTES

Commencement: 15 November 2010.

Substituted as noted to s 1253D at **[1.1253D]**.

Sub-s (1): for the words in italics in para (a) there are substituted the words "the Australian Securities and Investments Commission" and for the words in italics in para (c) there are substituted the words "the Commission", by the Companies Act 2006 (Transfer of Audit Working Papers to Third Countries) Regulations 2010, SI 2010/2537, reg 4(2), as from 13 July 2013.

[1.1253E]
[1253E   Working arrangements for transfer of papers

(1) The Secretary of State may enter into arrangements with a third country competent authority relating to the transfer of audit working papers—

    (a)   from the third country competent authority or a third country auditor regulated by that authority to the Secretary of State, and

    (b)   from the Secretary of State or a statutory auditor to the third country competent authority.

(2) The arrangements must provide that a request by the Secretary of State or the third country competent authority for a transfer mentioned in subsection (1) must be accompanied by a statement explaining the reasons for the request.

(3) The arrangements must—

    (a)   provide that the Secretary of State may not use audit working papers obtained from the third country competent authority or a third country auditor regulated by that authority except in connection with one or more of the functions mentioned in subsection (4), and

    (b)   include comparable provision in relation to audit working papers obtained by the third country competent authority from the Secretary of State or a statutory auditor.

(4) Those functions are—

    (a)   quality assurance functions which meet requirements equivalent to those of Article 29 of the Audit Directive (quality assurance);

    (b)   investigation or disciplinary functions which meet requirements equivalent to those of Article 30 of the Audit Directive (investigations and penalties);

    (c)   public oversight functions which meet requirements equivalent to those of Article 32 of the Audit Directive (principles of public oversight).

(5) The arrangements must—

    (a)   provide that the Secretary of State, a person exercising the functions of the Secretary of State and persons employed or formerly employed in discharging those functions must be subject to obligations of confidentiality as to personal data, professional secrets and sensitive commercial information contained in audit working papers transferred to the Secretary of State, and

    (b)   provide that the third country competent authority and persons involved in exercising its functions are subject to comparable obligations in relation to audit working papers transferred to the authority.

(6) The arrangements must—

    (a)   provide that the Secretary of State may refuse, or direct a statutory auditor to refuse, a request from the third country competent authority for a transfer of audit working papers in a case mentioned in subsection (7)(a) or (b), and

(b)   provide that the third country competent authority has comparable rights in relation to a request from the Secretary of State.

(7)   Those cases are—

(a)   where the transfer of the papers would adversely affect the sovereignty, security or public order of the European Union or of the United Kingdom;

(b)   where legal proceedings have been brought in the United Kingdom (whether continuing or not) in relation to the persons and matters to which the request relates.

(8) Arrangements with *an approved third country competent authority listed in section 1253D(2)(a), (f) or (g)* must—

(a)   provide that any contact between a statutory auditor and *the authority* relating to a relevant transfer of audit working papers to *the authority* must take place via the Secretary of State, and

(b)   include comparable provision in relation to transfers of audit working papers to the Secretary of State.

(9) "Relevant transfer" means any transfer other than a transfer by a statutory auditor under section 1253DC.]

NOTES

Commencement: 15 November 2010.

Originally inserted by the Statutory Auditors and Third Country Auditors Regulations 2007, SI 2007/3494, reg 15(1), as from 6 April 2008.

Substituted by the Companies Act 2006 (Transfer of Audit Working Papers to Third Countries) Regulations 2010, SI 2010/2537, reg 3, as from 15 November 2010.

For the first words in italics in sub-s (8) there are substituted the words "the Australian Securities and Investments Commission", and for the second and third words in italics in that subsection there are substituted the words "the Commission", by SI 2010/2537, reg 4(3), as from 13 July 2013.

[1.1253F]
[1253F Publication of working arrangements
If the Secretary of State enters into working arrangements in accordance with section 1253E, he must publish on a website without undue delay—

(a)   the name of the third country competent authority with which he has entered into such arrangements, and

(b)   the country or territory in which it is established.]

NOTES

Commencement: 6 April 2008.

Inserted as noted to s 1253D at **[1.1253D]**.

International obligations

[1.1254]
1254 Directions to comply with international obligations
(1) If it appears to the Secretary of State—

(a)   that any action proposed to be taken by a recognised supervisory body or a recognised qualifying body, [the Independent Supervisor] or a body designated by order under section 1252, would be incompatible with Community obligations or any other international obligations of the United Kingdom, or

(b)   that any action which that body has power to take is required for the purpose of implementing any such obligations,

he may direct the body not to take or, as the case may be, to take the action in question.

(2) A direction may include such supplementary or incidental requirements as the Secretary of State thinks necessary or expedient.

(3) A direction under this section given to [the Independent Supervisor or] a body designated by order under section 1252 is enforceable on the application of the Secretary of State by injunction or, in Scotland, by an order under section 45 of the Court of Session Act 1988 (c 36).

NOTES

Commencement: 6 April 2008.

Commencement (transitional provisions): see the note to s 1248 at **[1.1248]**.

Sub-ss (1), (3): words in square brackets inserted by the Statutory Auditors and Third Country Auditors Regulations 2007, SI 2007/3494, reg 16, as from 6 April 2008.

General provision relating to offences

[1.1255]
1255 Offences by bodies corporate, partnerships and unincorporated associations
(1) Where an offence under this Part committed by a body corporate is proved to have been committed with the consent or connivance of, or to be attributable to any neglect on the part of, an officer of the body, or a person purporting to act in any such capacity, he as well as the body corporate is guilty of the offence and liable to be proceeded against and punished accordingly.

Part 1   The Companies Act 2006

(2)   Where an offence under this Part committed by a partnership is proved to have been committed with the consent or connivance of, or to be attributable to any neglect on the part of, a partner, he as well as the partnership is guilty of the offence and liable to be proceeded against and punished accordingly.

(3)   Where an offence under this Part committed by an unincorporated association (other than a partnership) is proved to have been committed with the consent or connivance of, or to be attributable to any neglect on the part of, any officer of the association or any member of its governing body, he as well as the association is guilty of the offence and liable to be proceeded against and punished accordingly.

NOTES

Commencement: 6 April 2008.

Commencement (transitional provisions): see the note to s 1248 at **[1.1248]**.

[1.1256]

1256   Time limits for prosecution of offences

(1)   An information relating to an offence under this Part which is triable by a magistrates' court in England and Wales may be so tried if it is laid at any time within the period of twelve months beginning with the date on which evidence sufficient in the opinion of the Director of Public Prosecutions or the Secretary of State to justify the proceedings comes to his knowledge.

(2)   Proceedings in Scotland for an offence under this Part may be commenced at any time within the period of twelve months beginning with the date on which evidence sufficient in the Lord Advocate's opinion to justify proceedings came to his knowledge or, where such evidence was reported to him by the Secretary of State, within the period of twelve months beginning with the date on which it came to the knowledge of the Secretary of State.

(3)   For the purposes of subsection (2) proceedings are to be deemed to be commenced on the date on which a warrant to apprehend or cite the accused is granted, if the warrant is executed without undue delay.

(4)   A complaint charging an offence under this Part which is triable by a magistrates' court in Northern Ireland may be so tried if it is made at any time within the period of twelve months beginning with the date on which evidence sufficient in the opinion of the Director of Public Prosecutions for Northern Ireland or the Secretary of State to justify the proceedings comes to his knowledge.

(5)   This section does not authorise—

   (a)   in the case of proceedings in England and Wales, the trial of an information laid,

   (b)   in the case of proceedings in Scotland, the commencement of proceedings, or

   (c)   in the case of proceedings in Northern Ireland, the trial of a complaint made,

more than three years after the commission of the offence.

(6)   For the purposes of this section a certificate of the Director of Public Prosecutions, the Lord Advocate, the Director of Public Prosecutions for Northern Ireland or the Secretary of State as to the date on which such evidence as is referred to above came to his knowledge is conclusive evidence.

(7)   Nothing in this section affects proceedings within the time limits prescribed by section 127(1) of the Magistrates' Courts Act 1980 (c 43), section 331 of the Criminal Procedure (Scotland) Act 1975 or Article 19 of the Magistrates' Courts (Northern Ireland) Order 1981 (SI 1981/1675 (NI 26)) (the usual time limits for criminal proceedings).

NOTES

Commencement: 6 April 2008.

Commencement (transitional provisions): see the note to s 1248 at **[1.1248]**.

Note: following the transfer of most of the Secretary of State's functions under this Part (see further the note at the beginning of this Part) the references in sub-ss (1), (2), (4) and (6) above to the Secretary of State have effect as references to the Secretary of State or the Professional Oversight Board; see the Statutory Auditors (Delegation of Functions etc) Order 2008, SI 2008/496, art 10 at **[4.249]**.

[1.1257]

1257   Jurisdiction and procedure in respect of offences

(1)   Summary proceedings for an offence under this Part may, without prejudice to any jurisdiction exercisable apart from this section, be taken—

   (a)   against a body corporate or unincorporated association at any place at which it has a place of business, and

   (b)   against an individual at any place where he is for the time being.

(2)   Proceedings for an offence alleged to have been committed under this Part by an unincorporated association must be brought in the name of the association (and not in that of any of its members), and for the purposes of any such proceedings any rules of court relating to the service of documents apply as in relation to a body corporate.

(3)   Section 33 of the Criminal Justice Act 1925 (c 86) and Schedule 3 to the Magistrates' Courts Act 1980 (c 43) (procedure on charge of offence against a corporation) apply in a case in which an unincorporated association is charged in England and Wales with an offence under this Part as they apply in the case of a corporation.

(4) Section 18 of the Criminal Justice Act (Northern Ireland) 1945 (c 15 (NI)) and Article 166 and Schedule 4 to the Magistrates' Courts (Northern Ireland) Order 1981 (SI 1981/1675 (NI 26)) (procedure on charge of offence against a corporation) apply in a case in which an unincorporated association is charged in Northern Ireland with an offence under this Part as they apply in the case of a corporation.

(5) In relation to proceedings on indictment in Scotland for an offence alleged to have been committed under this Part by an unincorporated association, section 70 of the Criminal Procedure (Scotland) Act 1995 (proceedings on indictment against bodies corporate) applies as if the association were a body corporate.

(6) A fine imposed on an unincorporated association on its conviction of such an offence must be paid out of the funds of the association.

NOTES
Commencement: 6 April 2008.
Commencement (transitional provisions): see the note to s 1248 at **[1.1248]**.

Notices etc

[1.1258]
1258 Service of notices
(1) This section has effect in relation to any notice, direction or other document required or authorised by or by virtue of this Part to be given to or served on any person other than the Secretary of State.
(2) Any such document may be given to or served on the person in question—
    (a) by delivering it to him,
    (b) by leaving it at his proper address, or
    (c) by sending it by post to him at that address.
(3) Any such document may—
    (a) in the case of a body corporate, be given to or served on an officer of that body;
    (b) in the case of a partnership, be given to or served on any partner;
    (c) in the case of an unincorporated association other than a partnership, be given to or served on any member of the governing body of that association.
(4) For the purposes of this section and section 7 of the Interpretation Act 1978 (c 30) (service of documents by post) in its application to this section, the proper address of any person is his last known address (whether of his residence or of a place where he carries on business or is employed) and also—
    (a) in the case of a person who is eligible under the rules of a recognised supervisory body for appointment as a statutory auditor and who does not have a place of business in the United Kingdom, the address of that body;
    (b) in the case of a body corporate or an officer of that body, the address of the registered or principal office of that body in the United Kingdom;
    (c) in the case of an unincorporated association other than a partnership or a member of its governing body, its principal office in the United Kingdom.

NOTES
Commencement: 6 April 2008.
Commencement (transitional provisions): see the note to s 1248 at **[1.1248]**.

[1.1259]
1259 Documents in electronic form
(1) This section applies where—
    (a) section 1258 authorises the giving or sending of a notice, direction or other document by its delivery to a particular person ("the recipient"), and
    (b) the notice, direction or other document is transmitted to the recipient—
        (i) by means of an electronic communications network, or
        (ii) by other means but in a form that requires the use of apparatus by the recipient to render it intelligible.
(2) The transmission has effect for the purposes of this Part as a delivery of the notice, direction or other document to the recipient, but only if the recipient has indicated to the person making the transmission his willingness to receive the notice, direction or other document in the form and manner used.
(3) An indication to a person for the purposes of subsection (2)—
    (a) must be given to the person in such manner as he may require,
    (b) may be a general indication or an indication that is limited to notices, directions or other documents of a particular description,
    (c) must state the address to be used,
    (d) must be accompanied by such other information as the person requires for the making of the transmission, and
    (e) may be modified or withdrawn at any time by a notice given to the person in such manner as he may require.

(4) In this section "electronic communications network" has the same meaning as in the Communications Act 2003 (c 21).

NOTES
Commencement: 6 April 2008.
Commencement (transitional provisions): see the note to s 1248 at **[1.1248]**.

Interpretation

[1.1260]
1260 Meaning of "associate"
(1) In this Part "associate", in relation to a person, is to be construed as follows.
(2) In relation to an individual, "associate" means—
    (a) that individual's spouse, civil partner or minor child or step-child,
    (b) any body corporate of which that individual is a director, and
    (c) any employee or partner of that individual.
(3) In relation to a body corporate, "associate" means—
    (a) any body corporate of which that body is a director,
    (b) any body corporate in the same group as that body, and
    (c) any employee or partner of that body or of any body corporate in the same group.
(4) In relation to a partnership constituted under the law of Scotland, or any other country or territory in which a partnership is a legal person, "associate" means—
    (a) any body corporate of which that partnership is a director,
    (b) any employee of or partner in that partnership, and
    (c) any person who is an associate of a partner in that partnership.
(5) In relation to a partnership constituted under the law of England and Wales or Northern Ireland, or the law of any other country or territory in which a partnership is not a legal person, "associate" means any person who is an associate of any of the partners.
(6) In subsections (2)(b), (3)(a) and (4)(a), in the case of a body corporate which is a limited liability partnership, "director" is to be read as "member".

NOTES
Commencement: 6 April 2008.

[1.1261]
1261 Minor definitions
(1) In this Part, unless a contrary intention appears—
"address" means—
        (a) in relation to an individual, his usual residential or business address;
        (b) in relation to a firm, its registered or principal office in the United Kingdom;
["the Audit Directive" means Directive 2006/43/EC of the European Parliament and of the Council on statutory audits of annual accounts and consolidated accounts, amending Council Directives 78/660/EEC and 83/349/EEC and repealing Council Directive 84/253/EEC, as amended at any time before 1st January 2009;]
["audit working papers" means any documents which—
        (a) are or have been held by a statutory auditor[, an EEA auditor] or a third country auditor, and
        (b) are related to the conduct of an audit conducted by that auditor;]
"company" means any company or other body the accounts of which must be audited in accordance with Part 16;
"director", in relation to a body corporate, includes any person occupying in relation to it the position of a director (by whatever name called) and any person in accordance with whose directions or instructions (not being advice given in a professional capacity) the directors of the body are accustomed to act;
["EEA auditor" means an individual or firm approved in accordance with the Audit Directive by an EEA competent authority to carry out audits of annual accounts or consolidated accounts required by European Union law;]
["EEA competent authority" means a competent authority within the meaning of Article 2.10 of the Audit Directive of an EEA State other than the United Kingdom;]
"firm" means any entity, whether or not a legal person, which is not an individual and includes a body corporate, a corporation sole and a partnership or other unincorporated association;
"group", in relation to a body corporate, means the body corporate, any other body corporate which is its holding company or subsidiary and any other body corporate which is a subsidiary of that holding company;
"holding company" and "subsidiary" are to be read in accordance with section 1159 and Schedule 6;
"officer", in relation to a body corporate, includes a director, a manager, a secretary or, where the affairs of the body are managed by its members, a member;
"parent undertaking" and "subsidiary undertaking" are to be read in accordance with section 1162 and Schedule 7;

["third country" means a country or territory that is not an EEA State or part of an EEA State;]

["third country auditor" means a person, other than a person eligible for appointment as a statutory auditor, who is eligible to conduct audits of the accounts of bodies corporate incorporated or formed under the law of a third country in accordance with the law of that country;]

["third country competent authority" means a body established in a third country exercising functions related to the regulation or oversight of auditors];

["transfer", in relation to audit working papers, includes physical and electronic transfer and allowing access to such papers].

(2) For the purposes of this Part a body is to be regarded as "established in the United Kingdom" if and only if—

(a) it is incorporated or formed under the law of the United Kingdom or a part of the United Kingdom, or

(b) its central management and control are exercised in the United Kingdom;

and any reference to a qualification "obtained in the United Kingdom" is to a qualification obtained from such a body.

[(2A) For the purposes of this Part, Gibraltar shall be treated as if it were an EEA State.]

(3) The Secretary of State may by regulations make such modifications of this Part as appear to him to be necessary or appropriate for the purposes of its application in relation to any firm, or description of firm, which is not a body corporate or a partnership.

(4) Regulations under subsection (3) are subject to negative resolution procedure.

NOTES

Commencement: 20 January 2007 (for the purpose of enabling the exercise of powers to make Orders or Regulations by statutory instrument); 6 April 2008 (otherwise).

Sub-s (1): words in square brackets in the definition of "audit working papers" inserted, definition of "EEA auditor" substituted, and definition "transfer" inserted, by the Companies Act 2006 (Transfer of Audit Working Papers to Third Countries) Regulations 2010, SI 2010/2537, reg 6(1)–(4), as from 15 November 2010; other definitions in square brackets inserted by the Statutory Auditors and Third Country Auditors Regulations 2007, SI 2007/3494, reg 1(1), (2), as from 6 April 2008.

Sub-s (2A): inserted by SI 2007/3494, reg 1(1), (3), as from 6 April 2008.

[1.1262]
1262 Index of defined expressions
The following Table shows provisions defining or otherwise explaining expressions used in this Part (other than provisions defining or explaining an expression used only in the same section)—

Expression	*Provision*
address	section 1261(1)
appropriate qualification	section 1219
[approved third country competent authority	Section 1253D(2)]
associate	section 1260
[Audit Directive	section 1261(1)]
audited person	section 1210(2)
Auditor General	section 1226(1)
[audit working papers	section 1261(1)]
company	section 1261(1)
delegation order	section 1252(1)
director (of a body corporate)	section 1261(1)
[EEA auditor	section 1261(1)]
[EEA competent authority	section 1261(1)]
enactment	section 1293
established in the United Kingdom	section 1261(2)
firm	section 1261(1)
group (in relation to a body corporate)	section 1261(1)
holding company	section 1261(1)
main purposes of this Part	section 1209
member (of a supervisory body)	section 1217(2)
obtained in the United Kingdom	section 1261(2)
officer	section 1261(1)
parent undertaking	section 1261(1)
qualifying body	section 1220(1)

Expression	Provision
recognised, in relation to a professional qualification	section 1220(3) and Schedule 11
recognised, in relation to a qualifying body	paragraph 1(2) of Schedule 11
recognised, in relation to a supervisory body	section 1217(4) and Schedule 10
registered third country auditor	section 1241(1)
rules of a qualifying body	section 1220(2)
rules of a supervisory body	section 1217(3)
statutory auditor, statutory audit and statutory audit work	section 1210(1)
subsidiary	section 1261(1)
supervisory body	section 1217(1)
subsidiary undertaking	section 1261(1)
[third country	section 1261(1)]
third country auditor . . .	[section 1261(1)]
[third country competent authority	section 1261(1)]
[transfer (in relation to audit working papers)	Section 1261(1)]
[UK traded non EEA company	section 1241(2)]

NOTES

Commencement: 6 April 2008.

Entries "approved third country competent authority" and "transfer (in relation to audit working papers)" inserted by the Companies Act 2006 (Transfer of Audit Working Papers to Third Countries) Regulations 2010, SI 2010/2537, reg 6(5), as from 15 November 2010.

Other entries in square brackets inserted by the Statutory Auditors and Third Country Auditors Regulations 2007, SI 2007/3494, reg 3(1), (2), as from 6 April 2008.

Words omitted from column 1 of the entry relating to "third country auditor" repealed, and words in square brackets in column 2 of that entry substituted, by SI 2007/3494, reg 3(1), (3), as from 6 April 2008.

Miscellaneous and general

[1.1263]
1263 Power to make provision in consequence of changes affecting accountancy bodies
(1) The Secretary of State may by regulations make such amendments of enactments as appear to him to be necessary or expedient in consequence of any change of name, merger or transfer of engagements affecting—
    (a) a recognised supervisory body or recognised qualifying body, or
    (b) a body of accountants referred to in, or approved, authorised or otherwise recognised for the purposes of, any other enactment.
(2) Regulations under this section are subject to negative resolution procedure.

NOTES

Commencement: 20 January 2007 (for the purpose of enabling the exercise of powers to make Orders or Regulations by statutory instrument); 6 April 2008 (otherwise).

[1.1264]
1264 Consequential amendments
Schedule 14 contains consequential amendments relating to this Part.

NOTES

Commencement: 6 April 2008.

PART 43
TRANSPARENCY OBLIGATIONS AND RELATED MATTERS
Introductory

[1.1265]
1265 The transparency obligations directive
(Amends FSMA 2000, s 103 at **[7.152]**.)

NOTES

Commencement: 8 November 2006.

Transparency obligations

[1.1266]

1266 Transparency rules

(1) *(Inserts FSMA 2000, ss 89A–89G at* **[7.115]** *et seq.)*

(2) The effectiveness for the purposes of section 155 of the Financial Services and Markets Act 2000 (c 8) (consultation on proposed rules) of things done by the Financial Services Authority before this section comes into force with a view to making transparency rules (as defined in the provisions to be inserted in that Act by subsection (1) above) is not affected by the fact that those provisions were not then in force.

NOTES

Commencement: 8 November 2006.

[1.1267]

1267 Competent authority's power to call for information

(Inserts FSMA 2000, ss 89H–89J at **[7.122]** *et seq.)*

NOTES

Commencement: 8 November 2006.

[1.1268]

1268 Powers exercisable in case of infringement of transparency obligation

(Inserts FSMA 2000, ss 89K–89N at **[7.125]** *et seq.)*

NOTES

Commencement: 8 November 2006.

Other matters

[1.1269]

1269 Corporate governance rules

(Inserts FSMA 2000, s 89O at **[7.129]**.)

NOTES

Commencement: 8 November 2006.

[1.1270]

1270 Liability for false or misleading statements in certain publications

(Inserts FSMA 2000, ss 90A, 90B at **[7.132]** *et seq.)*

NOTES

Commencement: 8 November 2006.

[1.1271]

1271 Exercise of powers where UK is host member State

(Inserts FSMA 2000, s 100A at **[7.146]**.)

NOTES

Commencement: 8 November 2006.

[1.1272]

1272 Transparency obligations and related matters: minor and consequential amendments

(1) Schedule 15 to this Act makes minor and consequential amendments in connection with the provision made by this Part.

(2) In that Schedule—

Part 1 contains amendments of the Financial Services and Markets Act 2000 (c 8);

Part 2 contains amendments of the Companies (Audit, Investigations and Community Enterprise) Act 2004 (c 27).

NOTES

Commencement: 8 November 2006 (except in so far as relating to the amendment in Sch 15, para 11(2) to this Act); 1 October 2008 (otherwise).

[1.1273]

1273 Corporate governance regulations

(1) The Secretary of State may make regulations—

(a) for the purpose of implementing, enabling the implementation of or dealing with matters arising out of or related to, any Community obligation relating to the corporate governance of issuers who have requested or approved admission of their securities to trading on a regulated market;

(b) about corporate governance in relation to such issuers for the purpose of implementing, or dealing with matters arising out of or related to, any Community obligation.

(2) "Corporate governance", in relation to an issuer, includes—
  (a) the nature, constitution or functions of the organs of the issuer;
  (b) the manner in which organs of the issuer conduct themselves;
  (c) the requirements imposed on organs of the issuer;
  (d) the relationship between different organs of the issuer;
  (e) the relationship between the organs of the issuer and the members of the issuer or holders of the issuer's securities.

(3) The regulations may—
  (a) make provision by reference to any specified code on corporate governance that may be issued from time to time by a specified body;
  (b) create new criminal offences (subject to subsection (4));
  (c) make provision excluding liability in damages in respect of things done or omitted for the purposes of, or in connection with, the carrying on, or purported carrying on, of any specified activities.
  "Specified" here means specified in the regulations.

(4) The regulations may not create a criminal offence punishable by a greater penalty than—
  (a) on indictment, a fine;
  (b) on summary conviction, a fine not exceeding the statutory maximum or (if calculated on a daily basis) £100 a day.

(5) Regulations under this section are subject to negative resolution procedure.

(6) In this section "issuer", "securities" and "regulated market" have the same meaning as in Part 6 of the Financial Services and Markets Act 2000 (c 8).

NOTES
Commencement: 8 November 2006.

PART 44
MISCELLANEOUS PROVISIONS
Regulation of actuaries etc

[1.1274]
1274 Grants to bodies concerned with actuarial standards etc
*(Substitutes the Companies (Audit, Investigations and Community Enterprise) Act 2004, s 16(2)(l)–(t) (for the original para (l)) and amends sub-s (5) at **[5.171]**.)*

NOTES
Commencement: 8 November 2006.

[1.1275]
1275 Levy to pay expenses of bodies concerned with actuarial standards etc
*(1)–(5) (Amend the Companies (Audit, Investigations and Community Enterprise) Act 2004, s 17 at **[5.172]**)*
(6) The above amendments have effect in relation to any exercise of the power to make regulations under section 17 of the Companies (Audit, Investigations and Community Enterprise) Act 2004 after this section comes into force, regardless of when the expenses to be met by the levy in respect of which the regulations are made were incurred.
(7) (Amends the Pensions Act 2004, Sch 3 (outside the scope of this work).)

NOTES
Commencement: 1 October 2009.

[1.1276]
1276 Application of provisions to Scotland and Northern Ireland
*(Amends the Companies (Audit, Investigations and Community Enterprise) Act 2004, ss 16, 66 at **[5.171]**, **[5.224]**.)*

NOTES
Commencement: 8 November 2006.

Information as to exercise of voting rights by institutional investors

[1.1277]
1277 Power to require information about exercise of voting rights
(1) The Treasury or the Secretary of State may make provision by regulations requiring institutions to which this section applies to provide information about the exercise of voting rights attached to shares to which this section applies.
(2) This power is exercisable in accordance with—
  section 1278 (institutions to which information provisions apply),

section 1279 (shares to which information provisions apply), and

section 1280 (obligations with respect to provision of information).

(3)　In this section and the sections mentioned above—

  (a)　references to a person acting on behalf of an institution include—

    (i)　any person to whom authority has been delegated by the institution to take decisions as to any matter relevant to the subject matter of the regulations, and

    (ii)　such other persons as may be specified; and

  (b)　"specified" means specified in the regulations.

(4)　The obligation imposed by regulations under this section is enforceable by civil proceedings brought by—

  (a)　any person to whom the information should have been provided, or

  (b)　a specified regulatory authority.

(5)　Regulations under this section may make different provision for different descriptions of institution, different descriptions of shares and for other different circumstances.

(6)　Regulations under this section are subject to affirmative resolution procedure.

NOTES

Commencement: 20 January 2007 (for the purpose of enabling the exercise of powers to make Orders or Regulations by statutory instrument); 1 October 2008 (otherwise).

[1.1278]

1278　Institutions to which information provisions apply

(1)　The institutions to which section 1277 applies are—

  (a)　unit trust schemes within the meaning of the Financial Services and Markets Act 2000 (c 8) in respect of which an order is in force under section 243 of that Act;

  (b)　open-ended investment companies incorporated by virtue of regulations under section 262 of that Act;

  (c)　companies approved for the purposes of [Chapter 4 of Part 24 of the Corporation Tax Act 2010] (investment trusts);

  (d)　pension schemes as defined in section 1(5) of the Pension Schemes Act 1993 (c 48) or the Pension Schemes (Northern Ireland) Act 1993 (c 49);

  (e)　undertakings authorised under the Financial Services and Markets Act 2000 to carry on long-term insurance business (that is, the activity of effecting or carrying out contracts of long-term insurance within the meaning of the Financial Services and Markets (Regulated Activities) Order 2001 (SI 2001/544);

  (f)　collective investment schemes that are recognised by virtue of section 270 of that Act (schemes authorised in designated countries or territories).

(2)　Regulations under that section may—

  (a)　provide that the section applies to other descriptions of institution;

  (b)　provide that the section does not apply to a specified description of institution.

(3)　The regulations must specify by whom, in the case of any description of institution, the duty imposed by the regulations is to be fulfilled.

NOTES

Commencement: 20 January 2007 (for the purpose of enabling the exercise of powers to make Orders or Regulations by statutory instrument); 1 October 2008 (otherwise).

Sub-s (1): words in square brackets in para (c) substituted by the Corporation Tax Act 2010, s 1177, Sch 1, Pt 2, paras 487, 490 (note that the 2010 Act comes into force on 1 April 2010 and has effect, for corporation tax purposes for accounting periods ending on or after that day, and for income tax and capital gains tax purposes for the tax year 2010–11 and subsequent tax years; see s 1184(1) of the 2010 Act (and for transitional provisions and savings, see Sch 2 to that Act)).

[1.1279]

1279　Shares to which information provisions apply

(1)　The shares to which section 1277 applies are shares—

  (a)　of a description traded on a specified market, and

  (b)　in which the institution has, or is taken to have, an interest.

Regulations under that section may provide that the section does not apply to shares of a specified description.

(2)　For this purpose an institution has an interest in shares if the shares, or a depositary certificate in respect of them, are held by it, or on its behalf.

A "depositary certificate" means an instrument conferring rights (other than options)—

  (a)　in respect of shares held by another person, and

  (b)　the transfer of which may be effected without the consent of that person.

(3)　Where an institution has an interest—

  (a)　in a specified description of collective investment scheme (within the meaning of the Financial Services and Markets Act 2000 (c 8)), or

  (b)　in any other specified description of scheme or collective investment vehicle,

it is taken to have an interest in any shares in which that scheme or vehicle has or is taken to have an interest.

(4) For this purpose a scheme or vehicle is taken to have an interest in shares if it would be regarded as having such an interest in accordance with subsection (2) if it was an institution to which section 1277 applied.

NOTES

Commencement: 20 January 2007 (for the purpose of enabling the exercise of powers to make Orders or Regulations by statutory instrument); 1 October 2008 (otherwise).

[1.1280]
1280 Obligations with respect to provision of information

(1) Regulations under section 1277 may require the provision of specified information about—
  (a) the exercise or non-exercise of voting rights by the institution or any person acting on its behalf,
  (b) any instructions given by the institution or any person acting on its behalf as to the exercise or non-exercise of voting rights, and
  (c) any delegation by the institution or any person acting on its behalf of any functions in relation to the exercise or non-exercise of voting rights or the giving of such instructions.

(2) The regulations may require information to be provided in respect of specified occasions or specified periods.

(3) Where instructions are given to act on the recommendations or advice of another person, the regulations may require the provision of information about what recommendations or advice were given.

(4) The regulations may require information to be provided—
  (a) in such manner as may be specified, and
  (b) to such persons as may be specified, or to the public, or both.

(5) The regulations may provide—
  (a) that an institution may discharge its obligations under the regulations by referring to information disclosed by a person acting on its behalf, and
  (b) that in such a case it is sufficient, where that other person acts on behalf of more than one institution, that the reference is to information given in aggregated form, that is—
    (i) relating to the exercise or non-exercise by that person of voting rights on behalf of more than one institution, or
    (ii) relating to the instructions given by that person in respect of the exercise or non-exercise of voting rights on behalf of more than one institution, or
    (iii) relating to the delegation by that person of functions in relation to the exercise or non-exercise of voting rights, or the giving of instructions in respect of the exercise or non-exercise of voting rights, on behalf of more than one institution.

(6) References in this section to instructions are to instructions of any description, whether general or specific, whether binding or not and whether or not acted upon.

NOTES

Commencement: 20 January 2007 (for the purpose of enabling the exercise of powers to make Orders or Regulations by statutory instrument); 1 October 2008 (otherwise).

Disclosure of information under the Enterprise Act 2002

[1.1281]
1281 Disclosure of information under the Enterprise Act 2002
(Inserts the Enterprise Act 2002, s 241A (outside the scope of this work).)

NOTES

Commencement: 6 April 2007.

Expenses of winding up

[1.1282]
1282 Payment of expenses of winding up
(Sub-s (1) inserts the Insolvency Act 1986, s 176ZA at **[9.269]***; sub-s (2) makes a corresponding amendment to the Insolvency (Northern Ireland) Order 1989, SI 1989/2405 (outside the scope of this work).)*

NOTES

Commencement: 6 April 2008.

Commencement (transitional provisions): Sch 4, Pt 1, para 43(1) to the Companies Act 2006 (Commencement No 5, Transitional Provisions and Savings) Order 2007, SI 2007/3495 (at **[2.66]**) (as substituted by the Companies Act 2006 (Commencement No 6, Saving and Commencement Nos 3 and 5 (Amendment)) Order 2008, SI 2008/674, art 5, Sch 3, para 6(1), (5), as from 6 April 2008) provides for transitional provisions in connection with the insertion of the Insolvency Act 1986, s 176ZA. See that section at **[9.269]**.

Commonhold associations

[1.1283]

1283 Amendment of memorandum or articles of commonhold association

(Amends the Commonhold and Leasehold Reform Act 2002, Sch 3 (outside the scope of this work).)

NOTES

Commencement: 1 October 2009.

Commencement (transitional provisions): the Companies Act 2006 (Commencement No 8, Transitional Provisions and Savings) Order 2008, SI 2008/2860, Sch 2, para 113 (Amendment of memorandum or articles of commonhold association (s 1283)) at **[2.91]** provides that this section applies to amendments made on or after 1 October 2009.

PART 45
NORTHERN IRELAND

[1.1284]

1284 Extension of Companies Acts to Northern Ireland

(1) The Companies Acts as defined by this Act (see section 2) extend to Northern Ireland.

(2) The Companies (Northern Ireland) Order 1986 (SI 1986/1032 (NI 6)), the Companies Consolidation (Consequential Provisions) (Northern Ireland) Order 1986 (SI 1986/1035 (NI 9)) and Part 3 of the Companies (Audit, Investigations and Community Enterprise) Order 2005 (SI 2005/1967 (NI 17)) shall cease to have effect accordingly.

NOTES

Commencement: 1 January 2007 (certain purposes); 20 January 2007 (certain purposes); 6 April 2007 (certain purposes); 1 October 2007 (certain purposes); 1 November 2007 (certain purposes); 15 December 2007 (certain purposes); 6 April 2008 (certain purposes); 1 October 2008 (certain purposes); 1 October 2009 (otherwise) (see the notes below).

Commencement (transitional provisions): Sch 2, para 114 to the Companies Act 2006 (Commencement No 8, Transitional Provisions and Savings) Order 2008, SI 2008/2860 (at **[2.91]**) provides as follows—

"Extension of provisions to Northern Ireland (s 1284)

114.—(1) The extension to Northern Ireland by section 1284 of the Companies Act 2006 of Parts 14 and 15 of the 1985 Act (company investigations) has effect to enable the exercise of the powers conferred by those Parts in relation to companies registered in Northern Ireland, and otherwise in relation to Northern Ireland, on and after 1st October 2009.

(2) Parts 15 and 16 of the 1986 Order, and any other provision of that Order having effect for the purposes of Part 15, continue to apply (subject to sub-paragraph (3) below)—

    (a) in relation to inspectors appointed under Part 15 before 1st October 2009 and matters arising in connection with or in consequence of any such appointment or any report of inspectors so appointed;

    (b) in relation to any exercise before 1st October 2009 of any power of the Department of Enterprise, Trade and Investment in Northern Ireland not within paragraph (a), and matters arising in connection with or in consequence of any such exercise.

(3) A direction in force immediately before 1st October 2009 under Article 438(1A) or 449(1A) of the 1986 Order (direction limiting or relaxing restrictions on shares) shall continue in force and have effect on and after that date as if made under the corresponding provision of Part 14 of the 1985 Act, and the provisions of Part 15 of that Act shall apply accordingly.".

Commencement (transitional adaptations): art 5 of the Companies Act 2006 (Commencement No 1, Transitional Provisions and Savings) Order 2006, SI 2006/3428 provides that the provisions brought into force by arts 2–4 of 2006 Order shall have effect subject to any transitional adaptations specified in Sch 1 to that Order. Schedule 1, para 15 to the Order (at **[2.9]**) provided for such transitional adaptations (note that this paragraph was revoked by the Companies Act 2006 (Commencement No 8, Transitional Provisions and Savings) Order 2008, SI 2008/2860, art 6, as from 1 October 2009 (subject to any relevant transitional provision or saving in Sch 2 to that Order)).

Commencement (note): the Companies Act 2006 (Commencement No 1, Transitional Provisions and Savings) Order 2006, SI 2006/3428, arts 2(2), 3(2), 4(3) provide that this section shall come into force on 1 January 2007, 20 January 2007, and 6 April 2007 respectively so far as is necessary for the purposes of the provisions of this Act brought into force on those dates by arts 2(1), 3(1), 4(1), (2) of that Order (see **[2.2], [2.3], [2.4]**).

Commencement (note): the Companies Act 2006 (Commencement No 2, Consequential Amendments, Transitional Provisions and Savings) Order 2007, SI 2007/1093, art 2(1)(e) provides that sub-s (1) shall come into force on 6 April 2007 so far as is necessary for the purposes of the provisions of this Act brought into force on that date by art 2(1)(a)–(c) of that Order, and so far as is necessary for the purposes of Part 2 of the Companies (Audit, Investigations and Community Enterprise) Act 2004 (see **[2.17]**). Article 5 of that Order (at **[2.20]**) further provides that sub-s (2) comes into force on 6 April 2007 in so far as relating to the repeals specified in Sch 2 to that Order.

Commencement (note): the Companies Act 2006 (Commencement No 3, Consequential Amendments, Transitional Provisions and Savings) Order 2007, SI 2007/2194, arts 2(4), 3(2), 4(2) and 5(2) provide that this section shall come into force on 1 October 2007, 1 November 2007, 15 December 2007 and 1 October 2008 respectively so far as is necessary for the purposes of the provisions of this Act brought into force on those dates by arts 2(1)(a)–(j), 3(1), 4(1) and 5(1) of that Order (see **[2.32]–[2.35]**). Article 8 of that Order further provides that sub-s (2) comes into force on 1 October 2007 in so far as relating to the repeals specified in Sch 2 to that Order.

Commencement (note): the Companies Act 2006 (Commencement No 4 and Commencement No 3 (Amendment)) Order 2007, SI 2007/2607, art 2(2) provides that this section shall come into force on 30 September 2007 so far as is necessary for the purposes of the provisions of this Act brought into force on that date by art 2(1) of that Order (see **[2.48]**).

Commencement (note): the Companies Act 2006 (Commencement No 5, Transitional Provisions and Savings) Order 2007, SI 2007/3495, arts 3(5), 5(4), provide that this section shall come into force on 6 April 2008 and 1 October 2008 respectively so far as is necessary for the purposes of the provisions of this Act brought into force on those dates by arts 3(1)(a)–(t), (2), (3), 5(1)–(3) of that Order (see **[2.52], [2.54]**).

Commencement (note): the Companies Act 2006 (Commencement No 7, Transitional Provisions and Savings) Order 2008, SI 2008/1886, art 2(d) provides that sub-s (1) shall come into force on 1 October 2008 so far as is necessary for the purposes of the provisions of this Act brought into force on that date by art 2(a)–(c) of that Order (see **[2.76]**).

[1.1285]
1285 Extension of GB enactments relating to SEs
(1) The enactments in force in Great Britain relating to SEs extend to Northern Ireland.
(2) The following enactments shall cease to have effect accordingly—
(a) the European Public Limited-Liability Company Regulations (Northern Ireland) 2004 (SR 2004/417), and
(b) the European Public Limited-Liability Company (Fees) Regulations (Northern Ireland) 2004 (SR 2004/418).

(3) In this section "SE" means a European Public Limited-Liability Company (or Societas Europaea) within the meaning of Council Regulation 2157/2001/EC of 8 October 2001 on the Statute for a European Company.

NOTES
Commencement: 1 October 2009.

[1.1286]
1286 Extension of GB enactments relating to certain other forms of business organisation
(1) The enactments in force in Great Britain relating to—
(a) limited liability partnerships,
(b) limited partnerships,
(c) open-ended investment companies, and
(d) European Economic Interest Groupings,
extend to Northern Ireland.
(2) The following enactments shall cease to have effect accordingly—
(a) the Limited Liability Partnerships Act (Northern Ireland) 2002 (c 12 (NI));
(b) the Limited Partnerships Act 1907 (c 24) as it formerly had effect in Northern Ireland;
(c) the Open-Ended Investment Companies Act (Northern Ireland) 2002 (c 13 (NI));
(d) the European Economic Interest Groupings Regulations (Northern Ireland) 1989 (SR 1989/216).

NOTES
Commencement: 1 October 2008 (certain purposes); 1 October 2009 (otherwise) (see the note below).
Commencement (note): the Companies Act 2006 (Commencement No 7, Transitional Provisions and Savings) Order 2008, SI 2008/1886, art 2(e) provides that sub-s (1)(a), (2)(a) shall come into force on 1 October 2008 so far as relating to the application to limited liability partnerships of the subject matter of Part 15 (accounts and reports), Part 16 (audit) and Part 42 (statutory auditors) (see **[2.76]**). Art 7(3) of the 2008 Order further provides that this has effect in relation to accounts and the audit of accounts for financial years beginning on or after that date (see **[2.81]**).

[1.1287]
1287 Extension of enactments relating to business names
(1) The provisions of Part 41 of this Act (business names) extend to Northern Ireland.
(2) The Business Names (Northern Ireland) Order 1986 (SI 1986/1033 (NI 7)) shall cease to have effect accordingly.

NOTES
Commencement: 1 October 2009.

PART 46
GENERAL SUPPLEMENTARY PROVISIONS
Regulations and orders

[1.1288]
1288 Regulations and orders: statutory instrument
Except as otherwise provided, regulations and orders under this Act shall be made by statutory instrument.

NOTES
Commencement: 8 November 2006.

[1.1289]
1289 Regulations and orders: negative resolution procedure
Where regulations or orders under this Act are subject to "negative resolution procedure" the statutory instrument containing the regulations or order shall be subject to annulment in pursuance of a resolution of either House of Parliament.

NOTES
Commencement: 8 November 2006.

[1.1290]
1290 Regulations and orders: affirmative resolution procedure
Where regulations or orders under this Act are subject to "affirmative resolution procedure" the regulations or order must not be made unless a draft of the statutory instrument containing them has been laid before Parliament and approved by a resolution of each House of Parliament.

NOTES
Commencement: 8 November 2006.

[1.1291]
1291 Regulations and orders: approval after being made
(1)   Regulations or orders under this Act that are subject to "approval after being made"—
   (a)   must be laid before Parliament after being made, and
   (b)   cease to have effect at the end of 28 days beginning with the day on which they were made unless during that period they are approved by resolution of each House.
(2)   In reckoning the period of 28 days no account shall be taken of any time during which Parliament is dissolved or prorogued or during which both Houses are adjourned for more than four days.
(3)   The regulations or order ceasing to have effect does not affect—
   (a)   anything previously done under them or it, or
   (b)   the making of new regulations or a new order.

NOTES
Commencement: 8 November 2006.

[1.1292]
1292 Regulations and orders: supplementary
(1)   Regulations or orders under this Act may—
   (a)   make different provision for different cases or circumstances,
   (b)   include supplementary, incidental and consequential provision, and
   (c)   make transitional provision and savings.
(2)   Any provision that may be made by regulations under this Act may be made by order; and any provision that may be made by order under this Act may be made by regulations.
(3)   Any provision that may be made by regulations or order under this Act for which no Parliamentary procedure is prescribed may be made by regulations or order subject to negative or affirmative resolution procedure.
(4)   Any provision that may be made by regulations or order under this Act subject to negative resolution procedure may be made by regulations or order subject to affirmative resolution procedure.

NOTES
Commencement: 8 November 2006.

Meaning of "enactment"

[1.1293]
1293 Meaning of "enactment"
In this Act, unless the context otherwise requires, "enactment" includes—
   (a)   an enactment contained in subordinate legislation within the meaning of the Interpretation Act 1978 (c 30),
   (b)   an enactment contained in, or in an instrument made under, an Act of the Scottish Parliament, and
   (c)   an enactment contained in, or in an instrument made under, Northern Ireland legislation within the meaning of the Interpretation Act 1978.

NOTES
Commencement: 8 November 2006.

Consequential and transitional provisions

[1.1294]
1294 Power to make consequential amendments etc
(1)   The Secretary of State or the Treasury may by order make such provision amending, repealing or revoking any enactment to which this section applies as they consider necessary or expedient in consequence of any provision made by or under this Act.
(2)   This section applies to—
   (a)   any enactment passed or made before the passing of this Act,

(b)   any enactment contained in this Act or in subordinate legislation made under it, and

(c)   any enactment passed or made before the end of the session after that in which this Act is passed.

(3)   Without prejudice to the generality of the power conferred by subsection (1), orders under this section may—

(a)   make provision extending to other forms of organisation any provision made by or under this Act in relation to companies, or

(b)   make provision corresponding to that made by or under this Act in relation to companies, in either case with such adaptations or other modifications as appear to the Secretary of State or the Treasury to be necessary or expedient.

(4)   The references in subsection (3) to provision made by this Act include provision conferring power to make provision by regulations, orders or other subordinate legislation.

(5)   Amendments and repeals made under this section are additional, and without prejudice, to those made by or under any other provision of this Act.

(6)   Orders under this section are subject to affirmative resolution procedure.

NOTES

Commencement: 8 November 2006.

Orders: the Companies Act 2006 (Commencement No 2, Consequential Amendments, Transitional Provisions and Savings) Order 2007, SI 2007/1093 at **[2.16]**; the Companies Act 2006 (Commencement No 3, Consequential Amendments, Transitional Provisions and Savings) Order 2007, SI 2007/2194 at **[2.31]**; the Companies Act 2006 (Consequential Amendments etc) Order 2008, SI 2008/948 at **[4.275]**; the Companies Act 2006 (Consequential Amendments) (Taxes and National Insurance) Order 2008, SI 2008/954; the Companies Act 2006 (Part 35) (Consequential Amendments, Transitional Provisions and Savings) Order 2009, SI 2009/1802 at **[4.490]**; the Companies Act 2006 (Consequential Amendments) (Uncertificated Securities) Order 2009, SI 2009/1889; the Companies Act 2006 (Consequential Amendments) (Taxes and National Insurance) Order 2009, SI 2009/1890; the Companies Act 2006 (Consequential Amendments, Transitional Provisions and Savings) Order 2009, SI 2009/1941 at **[4.528]**; the Companies Act 2006 (Consequential Amendments and Transitional Provisions) Order 2011, SI 2011/1265 at **[4.648]**.

Regulations: the Companies (Trading Disclosures) Regulations 2008, SI 2008/495 at **[4.230]**; the Overseas Companies Regulations 2009, SI 2009/1801 at **[4.389]**; the Limited Liability Partnerships (Application of Companies Act 2006) Regulations 2009, SI 2009/1804 at **[10.1097]**.

[1.1295]

1295   Repeals

The enactments specified in Schedule 16, which include enactments that are no longer of practical utility, are repealed to the extent specified.

NOTES

Commencement: see Sch 16 at **[1.1331]**.

[1.1296]

1296   Power to make transitional provision and savings

(1)   The Secretary of State or the Treasury may by order make such transitional provision and savings as they consider necessary or expedient in connection with the commencement of any provision made by or under this Act.

(2)   An order may, in particular, make such adaptations of provisions brought into force as appear to be necessary or expedient in consequence of other provisions of this Act not yet having come into force.

(3)   Transitional provision and savings made under this section are additional, and without prejudice, to those made by or under any other provision of this Act.

(4)   Orders under this section are subject to negative resolution procedure.

NOTES

Commencement: 8 November 2006.

Orders: the Companies Act 2006 (Commencement No 1, Transitional Provisions and Savings) Order 2006, SI 2006/3428 at **[2.1]**; the Companies Act 2006 (Commencement No 2, Consequential Amendments, Transitional Provisions and Savings) Order 2007, SI 2007/1093 at **[2.16]**; the Companies Act 2006 (Commencement No 3, Consequential Amendments, Transitional Provisions and Savings) Order 2007, SI 2007/2194 at **[2.31]**; the Companies Act 2006 (Commencement No 4 and Commencement No 3 (Amendment)) Order 2007, SI 2007/2607 at **[2.47]**; the Companies Act 2006 (Commencement No 5, Transitional Provisions and Savings) Order 2007, SI 2007/3495 at **[2.50]**; the Companies Act 2006 (Commencement No 6, Saving and Commencement Nos 3 and 5 (Amendment)) Order 2008, SI 2008/674 at **[2.69]**; the Companies Act 2006 (Consequential Amendments etc) Order 2008, SI 2008/948 at **[4.275]**; the Companies Act 2006 (Consequential Amendments) (Taxes and National Insurance) Order 2008, SI 2008/954; the Companies Act 2006 (Commencement No 7, Transitional Provisions and Savings) Order 2008, SI 2008/1886 at **[2.75]**; the Companies Act 2006 (Commencement No 8, Transitional Provisions and Savings) Order 2008, SI 2008/2860 at **[2.82]**; the Companies Act 2006 (Part 35) (Consequential Amendments, Transitional Provisions and Savings) Order 2009, SI 2009/1802 at **[4.490]**; the Limited Liability Partnerships (Application of Companies Act 2006) Regulations 2009, SI 2009/1804 at **[10.1097]**; the Companies Act 2006 (Consequential Amendments, Transitional Provisions and Savings) Order 2009, SI 2009/1941 at **[4.528]**; the Registrar of Companies (Fees) (Limited Partnerships and Newspaper Proprietors) Regulations 2009, SI 2009/2392 at **[4.566]**; the Companies Act 2006 and Limited Liability Partnerships (Transitional Provisions and Savings) (Amendment) Regulations 2009, SI 2009/2476 at **[4.629]**; the Companies Act 2006 (Consequential Amendments and Transitional Provisions) Order 2011, SI 2011/1265 at **[4.648]**.

[1.1297]
1297 Continuity of the law
(1)   This section applies where any provision of this Act re-enacts (with or without modification) an enactment repealed by this Act.
(2)   The repeal and re-enactment does not affect the continuity of the law.
(3)   Anything done (including subordinate legislation made), or having effect as if done, under or for the purposes of the repealed provision that could have been done under or for the purposes of the corresponding provision of this Act, if in force or effective immediately before the commencement of that corresponding provision, has effect thereafter as if done under or for the purposes of that corresponding provision.
(4)   Any reference (express or implied) in this Act or any other enactment, instrument or document to a provision of this Act shall be construed (so far as the context permits) as including, as respects times, circumstances or purposes in relation to which the corresponding repealed provision had effect, a reference to that corresponding provision.
(5)   Any reference (express or implied) in any enactment, instrument or document to a repealed provision shall be construed (so far as the context permits), as respects times, circumstances and purposes in relation to which the corresponding provision of this Act has effect, as being or (according to the context) including a reference to the corresponding provision of this Act.
(6)   This section has effect subject to any specific transitional provision or saving contained in this Act.
(7)   References in this section to this Act include subordinate legislation made under this Act.
(8)   In this section "subordinate legislation" has the same meaning as in the Interpretation Act 1978 (c 30).

NOTES
Commencement: 8 November 2006.
References to companies registered or re-registered under earlier legislation: see the Companies Act 2006 (Consequential Amendments, Transitional Provisions and Savings) Order 2009, SI 2009/1941, art 3, which provides as follows—

"3   References to companies registered or re-registered under earlier legislation
A reference in any enactment to—
(a)   a company formed and registered under the Companies Act 2006,
(b)   a company registered but not formed under that Act, or
(c)   a company re-registered under that Act,
includes a company treated as so formed and registered, registered or re-registered by virtue of section 1297(3) of that Act, including that provision as applied by paragraph 1(2) of Schedule 2 to the Companies Act 2006 (Commencement No. 8, Transitional Provisions and Savings) Order 2008.".

General saving for existing companies etc: the Companies Act 2006 (Commencement No 8, Transitional Provisions and Savings) Order 2008, SI 2008/2860, Sch 2, para 1(2), (3) (at **[2.91]**) provides as follows—

"(2)   Section 1297(3) of the Companies Act 2006 (continuity of the law: things done under old law to be treated as done under the corresponding provision of the new law) applies—
(a)   in relation to a company to which section 675(1) of the 1985 Act or Article 625(1) of the 1986 Order applied (application of Act or Order to companies formed and registered under earlier companies legislation) as if the company had been formed and registered under Part 1 of the 1985 Act or Part 2 of the 1986 Order;
(b)   in relation to a company to which section 676(1) of the 1985 Act or Article 626(1) of the 1986 Order applied (application of Act or Order to companies registered but not formed under earlier companies legislation) as if the company had been registered under Chapter 2 of Part 22 of the 1985 Act or Chapter 2 of Part 22 of the 1986 Order;
(c)   in relation to a company to which section 677(1) of the 1985 Act or Article 627(1) of the 1986 Order applied (application of Act or Order to companies re-registered under earlier companies legislation) as if the company had been re-registered under Part 2 of the 1985 Act or Part 3 of the 1986 Order.
(3)   Nothing in this paragraph or in section 1297(3) of the Companies Act 2006 shall be read as affecting any reference to the date on which a company was registered or re-registered.".

In relation to how sub-s (3) above applies to treat a company formed and registered under Part 1 of the 1985 Act or Part 2 of the 1986 Order as if formed and registered under the corresponding provisions of this Act, see further the transitional provisions note to s 7 of this Act (at **[1.7]**).
In relation to how sub-s (3) above applies to treat a company re-registered under the 1985 Act or the 1986 Order as re-registered under the corresponding provisions of this Act, see further the transitional provisions note to s 89 of this Act (at **[1.89]**).
In relation to how sub-s (3) above applies to treat the registration of a company under Chapter 2 of Part 22 of the 1985 Act or Chapter 2 of Part 22 of the 1986 Order as if done under the corresponding provisions of this Act, see further the transitional provisions note to s 1040 of this Act (at **[1.1040]**).
Note: the Companies Act 2006 (Commencement No 2, Consequential Amendments, Transitional Provisions and Savings) Order 2007, SI 2007/1093, art 10 at **[2.25]** provides as follows (note that by virtue of art 1(2) "the Interim Regulations" means the Takeovers Directive (Interim Implementation) Regulations 2006)—

"10.   Section 1297 of the Companies Act 2006 (continuity of the law) has effect as if, for the purpose of section 1297(1), the Interim Regulations were an enactment repealed and re-enacted by that Act.".

See also the Companies Act 2006 (Commencement No 3, Consequential Amendments, Transitional Provisions and Savings) Order 2007, SI 2007/2194, art 12(1) (at **[2.42]**), the Companies Act 2006 (Commencement No 5, Transitional Provisions and Savings) Order 2007, SI 2007/3495, art 12(2) (at **[2.61]**), the Companies Act 2006 (Commencement No 6, Saving and Commencement Nos 3 and 5 (Amendment)) Order 2008, SI 2008/674, art 6(2) (at **[2.72]**), the Companies Act 2006 (Consequential Amendments etc) Order 2008, SI 2008/948, art 12 (at **[4.286]**), and the Companies Act 2006 (Commencement

No 8, Transitional Provisions and Savings) Order 2008, SI 2008/2860, art 8 (at **[2.89]**) which provide that the amendments and repeals made by those Orders do not affect the operation of this section.

PART 47
FINAL PROVISIONS

[1.1298]
1298 Short title
The short title of this Act is the Companies Act 2006.

NOTES
Commencement: 8 November 2006.

[1.1299]
1299 Extent
Except as otherwise provided (or the context otherwise requires), the provisions of this Act extend to the whole of the United Kingdom.

NOTES
Commencement: 8 November 2006.

[1.1300]
1300 Commencement
(1) The following provisions come into force on the day this Act is passed—
  (a) Part 43 (transparency obligations and related matters), except the amendment in paragraph 11(2) of Schedule 15 of the definition of "regulated market" in Part 6 of the Financial Services and Markets Act 2000 (c 8),
  (b) in Part 44 (miscellaneous provisions)—
  section 1274 (grants to bodies concerned with actuarial standards etc), and
  section 1276 (application of provisions to Scotland and Northern Ireland),
  (c) Part 46 (general supplementary provisions), except section 1295 and Schedule 16 (repeals), and
  (d) this Part.
(2) The other provisions of this Act come into force on such day as may be appointed by order of the Secretary of State or the Treasury.

NOTES
Commencement: 8 November 2006.
Orders: the Companies Act 2006 (Commencement No 1, Transitional Provisions and Savings) Order 2006, SI 2006/3428 at **[2.1]**; the Companies Act 2006 (Commencement No 2, Consequential Amendments, Transitional Provisions and Savings) Order 2007, SI 2007/1093 at **[2.16]**; the Companies Act 2006 (Commencement No 3, Consequential Amendments, Transitional Provisions and Savings) Order 2007, SI 2007/2194 at **[2.31]**; the Companies Act 2006 (Commencement No 4 and Commencement No 3 (Amendment)) Order 2007, SI 2007/2607 at **[2.47]**; the Companies Act 2006 (Commencement No 5, Transitional Provisions and Savings) Order 2007, SI 2007/3495 at **[2.50]**; the Companies Act 2006 (Commencement No 6, Saving and Commencement Nos 3 and 5 (Amendment)) Order 2008, SI 2008/674 at **[2.69]**; the Companies Act 2006 (Commencement No 7, Transitional Provisions and Savings) Order 2008, SI 2008/1886 at **[2.75]**; the Companies Act 2006 (Commencement No 8, Transitional Provisions and Savings) Order 2008, SI 2008/2860 at **[2.82]**; the Companies Act 2006 (Consequential Amendments, Transitional Provisions and Savings) Order 2009, SI 2009/1941 at **[4.528]**; the Companies Act 2006 and Limited Liability Partnerships (Transitional Provisions and Savings) (Amendment) Regulations 2009, SI 2009/2476 at **[4.629]**.

SCHEDULES

SCHEDULE 1
CONNECTED PERSONS: REFERENCES TO AN INTEREST IN SHARES OR DEBENTURES
Sections 254 and 255

Introduction

[1.1301]
1. (1) The provisions of this Schedule have effect for the interpretation of references in sections 254 and 255 (directors connected with or controlling a body corporate) to an interest in shares or debentures.

(2) The provisions are expressed in relation to shares but apply to debentures as they apply to shares.

General provisions

2. (1) A reference to an interest in shares includes any interest of any kind whatsoever in shares.

(2) Any restraints or restrictions to which the exercise of any right attached to the interest is or may be subject shall be disregarded.

(3) It is immaterial that the shares in which a person has an interest are not identifiable.

(4) Persons having a joint interest in shares are deemed each of them to have that interest.

Rights to acquire shares

3. (1) A person is taken to have an interest in shares if he enters into a contract to acquire them.

(2) A person is taken to have an interest in shares if—
- (a) he has a right to call for delivery of the shares to himself or to his order, or
- (b) he has a right to acquire an interest in shares or is under an obligation to take an interest in shares,

whether the right or obligation is conditional or absolute.

(3) Rights or obligations to subscribe for shares are not to be taken for the purposes of sub-paragraph (2) to be rights to acquire or obligations to take an interest in shares.

(4) A person ceases to have an interest in shares by virtue of this paragraph—
- (a) on the shares being delivered to another person at his order—
  - (i) in fulfilment of a contract for their acquisition by him, or
  - (ii) in satisfaction of a right of his to call for their delivery;
- (b) on a failure to deliver the shares in accordance with the terms of such a contract or on which such a right falls to be satisfied;
- (c) on the lapse of his right to call for the delivery of shares.

Right to exercise or control exercise of rights

4. (1) A person is taken to have an interest in shares if, not being the registered holder, he is entitled—
- (a) to exercise any right conferred by the holding of the shares, or
- (b) to control the exercise of any such right.

(2) For this purpose a person is taken to be entitled to exercise or control the exercise of a right conferred by the holding of shares if he—
- (a) has a right (whether subject to conditions or not) the exercise of which would make him so entitled, or
- (b) is under an obligation (whether or not so subject) the fulfilment of which would make him so entitled.

(3) A person is not by virtue of this paragraph taken to be interested in shares by reason only that—
- (a) he has been appointed a proxy to exercise any of the rights attached to the shares, or
- (b) he has been appointed by a body corporate to act as its representative at any meeting of a company or of any class of its members.

Bodies corporate

5. (1) A person is taken to be interested in shares if a body corporate is interested in them and—
- (a) the body corporate or its directors are accustomed to act in accordance with his directions or instructions, or
- (b) he is entitled to exercise or control the exercise of more than one-half of the voting power at general meetings of the body corporate.

(2) For the purposes of sub-paragraph (1)(b) where—
- (a) a person is entitled to exercise or control the exercise of more than one-half of the voting power at general meetings of a body corporate, and
- (b) that body corporate is entitled to exercise or control the exercise of any of the voting power at general meetings of another body corporate,

the voting power mentioned in paragraph (b) above is taken to be exercisable by that person.

Trusts

6. (1) Where an interest in shares is comprised in property held on trust, every beneficiary of the trust is taken to have an interest in shares, subject as follows.

(2) So long as a person is entitled to receive, during the lifetime of himself or another, income from trust property comprising shares, an interest in the shares in reversion or remainder or (as regards Scotland) in fee shall be disregarded.

(3) A person is treated as not interested in shares if and so long as he holds them—
- (a) under the law in force in any part of the United Kingdom, as a bare trustee or as a custodian trustee, or
- (b) under the law in force in Scotland, as a simple trustee.

(4) There shall be disregarded any interest of a person subsisting by virtue of—
- (a) an authorised unit trust scheme (within the meaning of section 237 of the Financial Services and Markets Act 2000 (c 8));

(b)   a scheme made under section 22 or 22A of the Charities Act 1960 (c 58), section 25 of the Charities Act (Northern Ireland) 1964 (c 33 (NI)) or section 24 or 25 of the Charities Act 1993 (c 10), section 11 of the Trustee Investments Act 1961 (c 62) or section 42 of the Administration of Justice Act 1982 (c 53); or

(c)   the scheme set out in the Schedule to the Church Funds Investment Measure 1958 (1958 No 1).

(5)   There shall be disregarded any interest—

(a)   of the Church of Scotland General Trustees or of the Church of Scotland Trust in shares held by them;

(b)   of any other person in shares held by those Trustees or that Trust otherwise than as simple trustees.

"The Church of Scotland General Trustees" are the body incorporated by the order confirmed by the Church of Scotland (General Trustees) Order Confirmation Act 1921 (1921 c xxv), and "the Church of Scotland Trust" is the body incorporated by the order confirmed by the Church of Scotland Trust Order Confirmation Act 1932 (1932 c xxi).

NOTES

Commencement: 1 October 2007.

Commencement (note): the Companies Act 2006 (Commencement No 3, Consequential Amendments, Transitional Provisions and Savings) Order 2007, SI 2007/2194, art 2(1)(d) (at **[2.32]**) brings into force ss 254, 255 of this Act (the enabling sections for this Schedule) on 1 October 2007. Although not specifically mentioned in that commencement order, it is believed that the intention was also to bring Sch 1 into force on the same date.

SCHEDULE 2
SPECIFIED PERSONS, DESCRIPTIONS OF DISCLOSURES ETC FOR THE PURPOSES OF SECTION 948

Section 948

[PART 1
SPECIFIED PERSONS

(A)
UNITED KINGDOM

[1.1302]

1. The Secretary of State.

2. The Department of Enterprise, Trade and Investment for Northern Ireland.

3. The Treasury.

4. The Bank of England.

5. The Financial Services Authority.

6. The Commissioners for Her Majesty's Revenue and Customs.

7. The Lord Advocate.

8. The Director of Public Prosecutions.

9. The Director of Public Prosecutions for Northern Ireland.

10. A constable.

11. A procurator fiscal.

12. The Scottish Ministers.

(B)
JERSEY

1. The Minister for Economic Development.

2. The Minister for Treasury and Resources.

3. The Jersey Financial Services Commission.

4. The Comptroller of Income Tax.

5. The Agent of the Impôts.

6. Her Majesty's Attorney General for Jersey.

7. The Viscount.

8. A police officer (within the meaning of the Interpretation (Jersey) Law 1954: see Part 1 of the Schedule to that Law).

(C)
GUERNSEY

1. The Commerce and Employment Department.

2. The Treasury and Resources Department.

3. The Guernsey Financial Services Commission.

4. The Director of Income Tax.

5. The Chief Officer of Customs and Excise.

6. Her Majesty's Procureur.

7. A police officer (within the meaning of the Companies (Guernsey) Law 2008: see section 532 of that Law).

(D)
ISLE OF MAN

1. (1) The members and officers of each of the Departments constituted by section 1(1) of the Government Departments Act 1987 (an Act of Tynwald: c 13).

(2) In sub-paragraph (1) "member" has the same meaning as it has by virtue of section 7(1) of that Act.

2. The Treasury of the Isle of Man.

3. The Financial Supervision Commission of the Isle of Man.

4. Her Majesty's Attorney General of the Isle of Man.

5. A constable (within the meaning of the Interpretation Act 1976 (an Act of Tynwald: c 11): see section 3 of that Act).]

NOTES

Commencement: 1 July 2009.

Substituted by the Companies Act 2006 (Amendment of Schedule 2) (No 2) Order 2009, SI 2009/1208, art 2, Schedule, as from 1 July 2009.

Application to the Isle of Man: see the Companies Act 2006 (Extension of Takeover Panel Provisions) (Isle of Man) Order 2009, SI 2009/1378.

[PART 2
SPECIFIED DESCRIPTIONS OF DISCLOSURES

(A)
UNITED KINGDOM

[1.1303]
1. A disclosure for the purpose of enabling or assisting a person authorised under section 457 of this Act (revision of defective accounts: persons authorised to apply to court) to exercise their functions.

2. A disclosure for the purpose of enabling or assisting an inspector appointed under Part 14 of the Companies Act 1985 (c 6) (investigation of companies and their affairs, etc) to exercise their functions.

3. A disclosure for the purpose of enabling or assisting a person authorised under section 447 of the Companies Act 1985 (power to require production of documents) or section 84 of the Companies Act 1989 (c 40) (exercise of powers by officer etc) to exercise their functions.

4. A disclosure for the purpose of enabling or assisting a person appointed under section 167 of the Financial Services and Markets Act 2000 (c 8) (general investigations) to conduct an investigation to exercise their functions.

5. A disclosure for the purpose of enabling or assisting a person appointed under section 168 of the Financial Services and Markets Act 2000 (investigations in particular cases) to conduct an investigation to exercise their functions.

6. A disclosure for the purpose of enabling or assisting a person appointed under section 169(1)(b) of the Financial Services and Markets Act 2000 (investigation in support of overseas regulator) to conduct an investigation to exercise their functions.

7. A disclosure for the purpose of enabling or assisting the body corporate responsible for administering the scheme referred to in section 225 of the Financial Services and Markets Act 2000 (the ombudsman scheme) to exercise its functions.

8. A disclosure for the purpose of enabling or assisting a person appointed under paragraph 4 or 5 of Schedule 17 to the Financial Services and Markets Act 2000 (the panel of ombudsmen or the Chief Ombudsman) to exercise their functions.

9. A disclosure for the purpose of enabling or assisting a person appointed under regulations made under section 262(1) and (2)(k) of the Financial Services and Markets Act 2000 (investigations into open-ended investment companies) to conduct an investigation to exercise their functions.

10. A disclosure for the purpose of enabling or assisting a person appointed under section 284 of the Financial Services and Markets Act 2000 (investigations into affairs of certain collective investment schemes) to conduct an investigation to exercise their functions.

11. A disclosure for the purpose of enabling or assisting the investigator appointed under paragraph 7 of Schedule 1 to the Financial Services and Markets Act 2000 (arrangements for investigation of complaints) to exercise their functions.

12. A disclosure for the purpose of enabling or assisting a person appointed by the Treasury to hold an inquiry into matters relating to financial services (including an inquiry under section 15 of the Financial Services and Markets Act 2000) to exercise their functions.

13. A disclosure for the purpose of enabling or assisting the Secretary of State or the Treasury to exercise any of their functions under any of the following—
    (a)   the Companies Acts;
    (b)   the Insolvency Act 1986 (c 45);
    (c)   the Company Directors Disqualification Act 1986 (c 46);
    (d)   Part 3 (investigations and powers to obtain information) or 7 (financial markets and insolvency) of the Companies Act 1989 (c 40);
    (e)   Part 5 of the Criminal Justice Act 1993 (c 36) (insider dealing);
    (f)   the Financial Services and Markets Act 2000;
    (g)   Part 42 of this Act (statutory auditors).

14. A disclosure for the purpose of enabling or assisting the Scottish Ministers to exercise their functions under the enactments relating to insolvency.

15. A disclosure for the purpose of enabling or assisting the Department of Enterprise, Trade and Investment for Northern Ireland to exercise any powers conferred on it by the enactments relating to companies or insolvency.

16. A disclosure for the purpose of enabling or assisting a person appointed or authorised by the Department of Enterprise, Trade and Investment for Northern Ireland under the enactments relating to companies or insolvency to exercise their functions.

17. A disclosure for the purpose of enabling or assisting an official receiver (including the Accountant in Bankruptcy in Scotland and the Official Assignee in Northern Ireland) to exercise their functions under the enactments relating to insolvency.

18. A disclosure for the purpose of enabling or assisting the Insolvency Practitioners Tribunal to exercise its functions under the Insolvency Act 1986 (c 45).

19. A disclosure for the purpose of enabling or assisting a body that is for the time being a recognised professional body for the purposes of section 391 of the Insolvency Act 1986 (recognised professional bodies) to exercise its functions as such.

20. A disclosure for the purpose of enabling or assisting the Pensions Regulator to exercise the functions conferred on it by or by virtue of any of the following—
    (a)   the Pension Schemes Act 1993 (c 48);
    (b)   the Pensions Act 1995 (c 26);
    (c)   the Welfare Reform and Pensions Act 1999 (c 30);
    (d)   the Pensions Act 2004 (c 35);
    (e)   any enactment in force in Northern Ireland corresponding to any of those enactments.

21. A disclosure for the purpose of enabling or assisting the Board of the Pension Protection Fund to exercise the functions conferred on it by or by virtue of Part 2 of the Pensions Act 2004 or any enactment in force in Northern Ireland corresponding to that Part.

22. A disclosure for the purpose of enabling or assisting the Bank of England to exercise its functions.

23. A disclosure for the purpose of enabling or assisting the Commissioners for Her Majesty's Revenue and Customs to exercise their functions.

24. A disclosure for the purpose of enabling or assisting organs of the Society of Lloyd's (being organs constituted by or under the Lloyd's Act 1982 (c. xiv)) to exercise their functions under or by virtue of the Lloyd's Acts 1871 to 1982.

25. A disclosure for the purpose of enabling or assisting the Office of Fair Trading to exercise its functions under any of the following—
  (a)   the Fair Trading Act 1973 (c 41);
  (b)   the Consumer Credit Act 1974 (c 39);
  (c)   the Estate Agents Act 1979 (c 38);
  (d)   the Competition Act 1980 (c 21);
  (e)   the Competition Act 1998 (c 41);
  (f)   the Financial Services and Markets Act 2000 (c 8);
  (g)   the Enterprise Act 2002 (c 40);
  (h)   the Unfair Terms in Consumer Contracts Regulations 1999 (SI 1999/2083);
  (i)   the Business Protection from Misleading Marketing Regulations 2008 (SI 2008/1276);
  (j)   the Consumer Protection from Unfair Trading Regulations 2008 (SI 2008/1277).

26. A disclosure for the purpose of enabling or assisting the Competition Commission to exercise its functions under any of the following—
  (a)   the Fair Trading Act 1973;
  (b)   the Competition Act 1980;
  (c)   the Competition Act 1998;
  (d)   the Enterprise Act 2002.

27. A disclosure with a view to the institution of, or otherwise for the purposes of, proceedings before the Competition Appeal Tribunal.

28. A disclosure for the purpose of enabling or assisting an enforcer under Part 8 of the Enterprise Act 2002 (enforcement of consumer legislation) to exercise their functions under that Part.

29. A disclosure for the purpose of enabling or assisting the Charity Commission to exercise its functions.

30. A disclosure for the purpose of enabling or assisting the Attorney General to exercise their functions in connection with charities.

31. A disclosure for the purpose of enabling or assisting the National Lottery Commission to exercise its functions under sections 5 to 10 and 15 of the National Lottery etc Act 1993 (c 39) (licensing and power of Secretary of State to require information).

32. A disclosure by the National Lottery Commission to *the National Audit Office* for the purpose of enabling or assisting the Comptroller and Auditor General to carry out an examination under Part 2 of the National Audit Act 1983 (c 44) into the economy, effectiveness and efficiency with which the National Lottery Commission has used its resources in discharging its functions under sections 5 to 10 of the National Lottery etc Act 1993.

33. A disclosure for the purpose of enabling or assisting a qualifying body under the Unfair Terms in Consumer Contracts Regulations 1999 (SI 1999/2083) to exercise its functions under those Regulations.

34. A disclosure for the purpose of enabling or assisting an enforcement authority under the Consumer Protection (Distance Selling) Regulations 2000 (SI 2000/2334) to exercise its functions under those Regulations.

35. A disclosure for the purpose of enabling or assisting an enforcement authority under the Financial Services (Distance Marketing) Regulations 2004 (SI 2004/2095) to exercise its functions under those Regulations.

36. A disclosure for the purpose of enabling or assisting a local weights and measures authority in England and Wales to exercise its functions under section 230(2) of the Enterprise Act 2002 (c 40) (notice of intention to prosecute, etc).

37. A disclosure for the purpose of enabling or assisting the Financial Services Authority to exercise its functions under any of the following—
  (a)   the legislation relating to friendly societies or to industrial and provident societies;
  (b)   the Building Societies Act 1986 (c 53);
  (c)   Part 7 of the Companies Act 1989 (c 40) (financial markets and insolvency);
  (d)   the Financial Services and Markets Act 2000 (c 8).

38. A disclosure for the purpose of enabling or assisting the competent authority for the purposes of Part 6 of the Financial Services and Markets Act 2000 (official listing) to exercise its functions under that Part.

39. A disclosure for the purpose of enabling or assisting a body corporate established in accordance with section 212(1) of the Financial Services and Markets Act 2000 (compensation scheme manager) to exercise its functions.

40. (1) A disclosure for the purpose of enabling or assisting a recognised investment exchange or a recognised clearing house to exercise its functions as such.

(2) In sub-paragraph (1) "recognised investment exchange" and "recognised clearing house" have the same meaning as in section 285 of the Financial Services and Markets Act 2000.

41. A disclosure for the purpose of enabling or assisting a person approved under the Uncertificated Securities Regulations 2001 (SI 2001/3755) as an operator of a relevant system (within the meaning of those Regulations) to exercise their functions.

42. A disclosure for the purpose of enabling or assisting a body designated under section 326(1) of the Financial Services and Markets Act 2000 (designated professional bodies) to exercise its functions in its capacity as a body designated under that section.

43. A disclosure with a view to the institution of, or otherwise for the purposes of, civil proceedings arising under or by virtue of the Financial Services and Markets Act 2000.

44. A disclosure for the purpose of enabling or assisting a body designated by order under section 1252 of this Act (delegation of functions of Secretary of State) to exercise its functions under Part 42 of this Act (statutory auditors).

45. A disclosure for the purpose of enabling or assisting a recognised supervisory or qualifying body, within the meaning of Part 42 of this Act, to exercise its functions as such.

46. A disclosure for the purpose of enabling or assisting the Regulator of Community Interest Companies to exercise functions under the Companies (Audit, Investigations and Community Enterprise) Act 2004 (c 27).

47. A disclosure for the purpose of enabling or assisting a person authorised by the Secretary of State under Part 2, 3 or 4 of the Proceeds of Crime Act 2002 (c 29) to exercise their functions.

48. A disclosure with a view to the institution of, or otherwise for the purposes of, proceedings on an application under section 6, 7 or 8 of the Company Directors Disqualification Act 1986 (c 46) (disqualification for unfitness).

[49. A disclosure with a view to the institution of, or otherwise for the purposes of, proceedings before the Upper Tribunal in respect of—
    (a)   a decision of the Financial Services Authority;
    (b)   a decision of the Bank of England; or
    (c)   a decision of a person relating to the assessment of any compensation or consideration under the Banking (Special Provisions) Act 2008 or the Banking Act 2009.]

50. A disclosure for the purposes of proceedings before [a tribunal in relation to a decision of the Pensions Regulator].

51. A disclosure for the purpose of enabling or assisting a body appointed under section 14 of the Companies (Audit, Investigations and Community Enterprise) Act 2004 (supervision of periodic accounts and reports of issuers of listed securities) to exercise functions mentioned in subsection (2) of that section.

52. (1) A disclosure with a view to the institution of, or otherwise for the purposes of, disciplinary proceedings relating to the performance by a lawyer, auditor, accountant, valuer or actuary of their professional duties.

(2) In sub-paragraph (1) "lawyer" means—
    (a)   a person who for the purposes of the Legal Services Act 2007 (c 29) is an authorised person in relation to an activity that constitutes a reserved legal activity (within the meaning of that Act),
    (b)   a solicitor or barrister in Northern Ireland,
    (c)   a solicitor or advocate in Scotland, or
    (d)   a person who is a member, and entitled to practise as such, of a legal profession regulated in a jurisdiction outside the United Kingdom.

(3) Until the coming into force of section 18 of the Legal Services Act 2007, the following is substituted for paragraph (a) of sub-paragraph (2) above—

    "(a)   a solicitor or barrister in England and Wales,".

53. (1) A disclosure with a view to the institution of, or otherwise for the purposes of, disciplinary proceedings relating to the performance by a public servant of their duties.

(2) In sub-paragraph (1) "public servant" means—
    (a)   an officer or employee of the Crown, or

(b)   an officer or employee of any public or other authority for the time being designated for the purposes of this paragraph by the Secretary of State by order subject to negative resolution procedure.

(B)
JERSEY

1. A disclosure for the purpose of enabling or assisting an inspector appointed under Part 19 of the Companies (Jersey) Law 1991 to exercise their functions.

2. A disclosure for the purpose of enabling or assisting a person appointed under Article 33 of the Financial Services (Jersey) Law 1998 to exercise their functions.

3. A disclosure for the purpose of enabling or assisting an inspector appointed under Article 22 of the Collective Investment Funds (Jersey) Law 1988 to exercise their functions.

4. A disclosure for the purpose of enabling or assisting the Minister for Economic Development to exercise functions under any of the following—
(a)   the Bankruptcy Désastre (Jersey) Law 1990;
(b)   the Companies (Jersey) Law 1991;
(c)   the Financial Services (Jersey) Law 1998.

5. A disclosure for the purpose of enabling or assisting the Comptroller of Income Tax to exercise their functions.

6. A disclosure for the purpose of enabling or assisting the Agent of the Impôts to exercise their functions.

7. A disclosure for the purpose of enabling or assisting the Jersey Competition Regulatory Authority to exercise its functions.

8. A disclosure for the purpose of enabling or assisting Her Majesty's Attorney General for Jersey to exercise their functions in connection with charities.

9. A disclosure for the purpose of enabling or assisting Her Majesty's Attorney General for Jersey to exercise their functions under the Distance Selling (Jersey) Law 2007.

10. A disclosure for the purpose of enabling or assisting the Viscount to exercise their functions in relation to désastre or in relation to Part 2 of the Proceeds of Crime (Jersey) Law 1999.

11. A disclosure with a view to the institution of, or otherwise for the purposes of, proceedings on an application under Article 78 of the Companies (Jersey) Law 1991 (disqualification orders).

12. (1)   A disclosure with a view to the institution of, or otherwise for the purposes of, disciplinary proceedings relating to the performance by a solicitor, advocate, foreign lawyer, auditor, accountant, valuer or actuary of their professional duties.
(2)   In sub-paragraph (1)—
(a)   "solicitor" means a person who has been admitted as a solicitor under the Advocates and Solicitors (Jersey) Law 1997;
(b)   "advocate" means a person who has been admitted to the Bar under that Law; and
(c)   "foreign lawyer" means a person who has not been admitted as mentioned in paragraph (a) or (b) but is a member, and entitled to practise as such, of a legal profession regulated within a jurisdiction outside Jersey.

13. (1)   A disclosure with a view to the institution of, or otherwise for the purposes of, disciplinary proceedings relating to the performance by a public servant of their duties.
(2)   In sub-paragraph (1) "public servant" means—
(a)   an individual who holds office under, or is employed by, the Crown,
(b)   a member, officer or employee of the States of Jersey or an officer or employee in an administration of the States of Jersey,
(c)   a member, officer or employee of the Jersey Financial Services Commission, or
(d)   any person exercising public functions who is declared by Order of the Minister for Economic Development to be a public servant for the purposes of paragraph 25 of the Schedule to the Companies (Takeovers and Mergers Panel) (Jersey) Law 2009.

(C)
GUERNSEY

1. A disclosure for the purpose of enabling or assisting the Registrar of Companies appointed under the Companies (Guernsey) Law 2008 to exercise their functions under that Law.

2. A disclosure for the purpose of enabling or assisting a person appointed under—
(a)   section 27E or 41I of the Protection of Investors (Bailiwick of Guernsey) Law 1987,

(b)   section 27 of the Banking Supervision (Bailiwick of Guernsey) Law 1994,

(c)   section 10 of the Company Securities (Insider Dealing) (Bailiwick of Guernsey) Law 1996,

(d)   section 24 of the Regulation of Fiduciaries, Administration Businesses and Company Directors (Bailiwick of Guernsey) Law 2000,

(e)   section 69 of the Insurance Business (Bailiwick of Guernsey) Law 2002,

(f)   section 46 of the Insurance Managers and Insurance Intermediaries (Bailiwick of Guernsey) Law 2002,

(g)   section 19 of the Registration of Non-Regulated Financial Services Business (Bailiwick of Guernsey) Law 2008,

to exercise their functions.

3. A disclosure for the purpose of enabling or assisting Her Majesty's Procureur to exercise their functions in connection with charities.

4. A disclosure for the purpose of enabling or assisting the Guernsey Banking Deposit Compensation Scheme, established under section 46 of the Banking Supervision (Bailiwick of Guernsey) Law 1987 by the Banking Deposit Compensation Scheme (Bailiwick of Guernsey) Ordinance 2008, to exercise its functions.

5. A disclosure for the purpose of enabling or assisting any supervisory body or professional oversight body to exercise its functions under Part XVIA of the Companies (Guernsey) Law 2008 (regulation of auditors).

6. A disclosure with a view to the institution of, or otherwise for the purposes of, proceedings on an application under Part XXV of the Companies (Guernsey) Law 2008 (disqualification orders).

7. (1)   A disclosure with a view to the institution of, or otherwise for the purposes of, disciplinary proceedings relating to the performance by an Advocate of the Royal Court, foreign lawyer, auditor, accountant, valuer or actuary of their professional duties.

(2)   In sub-paragraph (1) "foreign lawyer" means a person who has not been admitted as an Advocate of the Royal Court, but is a member, and entitled to practise as such, of a legal profession regulated within a jurisdiction outside Guernsey.

8. (1)   A disclosure with a view to the institution of, or otherwise for the purposes of, disciplinary proceedings relating to the performance by a public servant of their duties.

(2)   In sub-paragraph (1) "public servant" means—

(a)   an officer or employee of the Crown,

(b)   a member, officer or employee of the States of Guernsey,

(c)   a member, officer or employee of the Guernsey Financial Services Commission, or

(d)   any person exercising public functions who is declared by regulations of the Commerce and Employment Department to be a public servant for the purposes of paragraph 17 of Schedule 6 to the Companies (Guernsey) Law 2008.

(D)
ISLE OF MAN

1. A disclosure for the purpose of enabling or assisting an inspector appointed by the High Court of the Isle of Man under the enactments of the Isle of Man relating to companies to discharge their functions.

2. A disclosure for the purpose of enabling or assisting a person conducting an investigation under—

(a)   section 16 of the Collective Investment Schemes Act 2008 (an Act of Tynwald: c 7);

(b)   Schedule 2 to the Financial Services Act 2008 (an Act of Tynwald: c 8); or

(c)   Schedule 5 to the Insurance Act 2008 (an Act of Tynwald: c 16),

to exercise their functions.

3. A disclosure for the purpose of enabling or assisting the Financial Supervision Commission of the Isle of Man to exercise any of its functions.

4. A disclosure for the purpose of enabling or assisting an auditor of a permitted person (within the meaning of the Financial Services Act 2008 (an Act of Tynwald)) to exercise their functions.

5. A disclosure for the purpose of enabling or assisting the Office of Fair Trading of the Isle of Man to exercise its functions under Schedule 4 to the Financial Services Act 2008 (an Act of Tynwald) in relation to a financial services dispute within the meaning of paragraph 1(1) of that Schedule.

6. A disclosure for the purpose of enabling or assisting an adjudicator appointed under paragraph 4 of Schedule 4 to the Financial Services Act 2008 (an Act of Tynwald) to exercise their functions.

7. A disclosure for the purpose of enabling or assisting the body administering a scheme under section 25 of the Financial Services Act 2008 (an Act of Tynwald) (compensation schemes) to exercise its functions under the scheme.

8. A disclosure with a view to the institution of, or otherwise for the purposes of, civil proceedings arising under or by virtue of the Financial Services Act 2008 (an Act of Tynwald).

9. A disclosure for the purpose of enabling or assisting—
  (a) the Insurance and Pensions Authority of the Isle of Man; or
  (b) the Retirement Benefits Schemes Supervisor of the Isle of Man,
to exercise its functions under the Retirement Benefits Schemes Act 2000 (an Act of Tynwald: c 14).

10. A disclosure for the purpose of enabling or assisting the Assessor of Income Tax to exercise their functions under enactments of the Isle of Man relating to income tax.

11. A disclosure for the purpose of enabling or assisting the Office of Fair Trading of the Isle of Man to exercise its functions under any of the following—
  (a) the Unsolicited Goods and Services (Isle of Man) Act 1974 (an Act of Tynwald: c 5);
  (b) the Moneylenders Act 1991 (an Act of Tynwald: c 6);
  (c) the Consumer Protection Act 1991 (an Act of Tynwald: c 11);
  (d) the Fair Trading Act 1996 (an Act of Tynwald: c 15).

12. A disclosure for the purpose of enabling or assisting the Department of Local Government and the Environment of the Isle of Man to exercise its functions under the Estate Agents Act 1975 (an Act of Tynwald: c 6) or the Estate Agents Act 1999 (an Act of Tynwald: c 7).

13. A disclosure for the purpose of enabling or assisting Her Majesty's Attorney General of the Isle of Man to exercise their functions in connection with charities.

14. A disclosure for the purpose of enabling or assisting the Treasury of the Isle of Man to exercise its functions under the enactments of the Isle of Man relating to companies, insurance companies or insolvency.

15. A disclosure for the purpose of enabling or assisting an official receiver appointed in the Isle of Man to exercise their functions under the enactments of the Isle of Man relating to insolvency.

16. (1) A disclosure with a view to the institution of, or otherwise for the purposes of, disciplinary proceedings relating to the performance by an advocate, registered legal practitioner, auditor, accountant, valuer or actuary of their professional duties.

(2) In sub-paragraph (1)—
  "advocate" means a person who is qualified to act as an advocate in any court in the Island in accordance with section 7 of the Advocates Act 1976 (an Act of Tynwald: c 27);
  "registered legal practitioner" means a legal practitioner within the meaning of section 10 of the Legal Practitioners Registration Act 1986 (an Act of Tynwald: c 15) who is registered within the meaning of that Act.

17. (1) A disclosure with a view to the institution of, or otherwise for the purposes of, disciplinary proceedings relating to the performance by a public servant of their duties.

(2) In sub-paragraph (1) "public servant" means—
  (a) an officer or employee of the Crown, or
  (b) an officer or employee of any public or other authority for the time being designated for the purposes of this paragraph by order made by the Council of Ministers of the Isle of Man.

(E)
GENERAL

1. A disclosure for the purpose of enabling or assisting—
  (a) the European Central Bank, or
  (b) the central bank of any country or territory outside the British Islands,
to exercise its functions.

2. (1) A disclosure for the purpose of enabling or assisting an overseas regulatory authority to exercise its regulatory functions.

(2) In sub-paragraph (1) "overseas regulatory authority" and "regulatory functions" have the same meaning as in section 82 of the Companies Act 1989 (assistance for overseas regulatory authorities).

3. A disclosure with a view to the institution of, or otherwise for the purposes of, criminal proceedings in the British Islands or elsewhere.

4. A disclosure for the purpose of the provision of a summary or collection of information framed in such a way as not to enable the identity of any person to whom the information relates to be ascertained.

5. A disclosure in pursuance of any Community obligation.]

NOTES

Commencement: 1 July 2009.

Substituted by the Companies Act 2006 (Amendment of Schedule 2) (No 2) Order 2009, SI 2009/1208, art 2, Schedule, as from 1 July 2009.

Part A, para 32: for the words in italics there are substituted the words "the Comptroller and Auditor General" by the Budget Responsibility and National Audit Act 2011, s 26, Sch 5, Pt 2, paras 29, 31, as from a day to be appointed.

Part A, para 49: substituted by the Transfer of Tribunal Functions Order 2010, SI 2010/22, art 5(1), Sch 2, paras 141, 142(a), as from 6 April 2010 (for transitional provisions and savings in relation to existing cases and appeals from the Financial Services and Markets Tribunal, see Sch 5 to that Order).

Part A, para 50: words in square brackets substituted by SI 2010/22, art 5(1), Sch 2, paras 141, 142(b), as from 6 April 2010 (for transitional provisions and savings in relation to existing cases and appeals from the Pensions Regulator Tribunal, see Sch 5 to that Order).

Application to the Isle of Man: see the Companies Act 2006 (Extension of Takeover Panel Provisions) (Isle of Man) Order 2009, SI 2009/1378.

[PART 3
OVERSEAS REGULATORY BODIES

[1.1304]

1. (1)   A disclosure is made in accordance with this Part of this Schedule if—
    (a)   it is made to a person or body exercising relevant functions under legislation in a country or territory outside the British Islands, and
    (b)   it is made for the purpose of enabling or assisting that person or body to exercise those functions.

(2)   "Relevant functions" for this purpose are functions of a public nature that appear to the Panel to be similar to its own functions or those of the Financial Services Authority.

2. In determining whether to disclose information to a person or body in accordance with this Part of this Schedule, the Panel must have regard to the following considerations—
    (a)   whether the use that the person or body is likely to make of the information is sufficiently important to justify making the disclosure;
    (b)   whether the person or body has adequate arrangements to prevent the information from being used or further disclosed, otherwise than—
        (i)   for the purposes of carrying out the functions mentioned in paragraph 1(1)(a), or
        (ii)   for other purposes substantially similar to those for which information disclosed to the Panel could be used or further disclosed.]

NOTES

Commencement: 1 July 2009.

Substituted by the Companies Act 2006 (Amendment of Schedule 2) (No 2) Order 2009, SI 2009/1208, art 2, Schedule, as from 1 July 2009.

Application to the Isle of Man: see the Companies Act 2006 (Extension of Takeover Panel Provisions) (Isle of Man) Order 2009, SI 2009/1378.

SCHEDULE 3
AMENDMENTS OF REMAINING PROVISIONS OF THE COMPANIES ACT 1985
RELATING TO OFFENCES

Section 1124

[1.1305]

(This Schedule amends CA 1985, ss 444, 448, 449, 450, 451, 453A and 455 at **[5.11]**, **[5.20]**, **[5.22]**, **[5.23]**, **[5.24]**, **[5.28]** *and* **[5.33]**.*)*

NOTES

Commencement: 1 October 2007.

Commencement (transitional adaptations): art 6 of the Companies Act 2006 (Commencement No 3, Consequential Amendments, Transitional Provisions and Savings) Order 2007, SI 2007/2194 provides that the provisions brought into force by that Order shall have effect subject to any transitional adaptations specified in Sch 1 to that Order. Schedule 1, para 20 to the Order provides for transitional adaptations of this Schedule (see that paragraph at **[2.43]**) and see the notes to the amended ss 444, 449, 450 and 451 of the 1985 Act (note that this paragraph was revoked by the Companies Act 2006 (Commencement No 8, Transitional Provisions and Savings) Order 2008, SI 2008/2860, art 6, as from 1 October 2009 (subject to any relevant transitional provision or saving in Sch 2 to that Order)).

SCHEDULE 4
DOCUMENTS AND INFORMATION SENT OR SUPPLIED TO A COMPANY
Section 1144(1)

PART 1
INTRODUCTION

Application of Schedule

[1.1306]

1. (1)   This Schedule applies to documents or information sent or supplied to a company.

(2)   It does not apply to documents or information sent or supplied by another company (see section 1144(3) and Schedule 5).

NOTES

Commencement: 20 January 2007.

PART 2
COMMUNICATIONS IN HARD COPY FORM

Introduction

[1.1307]

2. A document or information is validly sent or supplied to a company if it is sent or supplied in hard copy form in accordance with this Part of this Schedule.

Method of communication in hard copy form

3. (1)   A document or information in hard copy form may be sent or supplied by hand or by post to an address (in accordance with paragraph 4).

(2)   For the purposes of this Schedule, a person sends a document or information by post if he posts a prepaid envelope containing the document or information.

Address for communications in hard copy form

4. A document or information in hard copy form may be sent or supplied—

    (a)   to an address specified by the company for the purpose;

    (b)   to the company's registered office;

    (c)   to an address to which any provision of the Companies Acts authorises the document or information to be sent or supplied.

NOTES

Commencement: 20 January 2007.

PART 3
COMMUNICATIONS IN ELECTRONIC FORM

Introduction

[1.1308]

5. A document or information is validly sent or supplied to a company if it is sent or supplied in electronic form in accordance with this Part of this Schedule.

Conditions for use of communications in electronic form

6. A document or information may only be sent or supplied to a company in electronic form if—

    (a)   the company has agreed (generally or specifically) that the document or information may be sent or supplied in that form (and has not revoked that agreement), or

    (b)   the company is deemed to have so agreed by a provision in the Companies Acts.

Address for communications in electronic form

7. (1)   Where the document or information is sent or supplied by electronic means, it may only be sent or supplied to an address—

    (a)   specified for the purpose by the company (generally or specifically), or

    (b)   deemed by a provision in the Companies Acts to have been so specified.

(2)   Where the document or information is sent or supplied in electronic form by hand or by post, it must be sent or supplied to an address to which it could be validly sent if it were in hard copy form.

NOTES

Commencement: 20 January 2007.

PART 4
OTHER AGREED FORMS OF COMMUNICATION

[1.1309]

8. A document or information that is sent or supplied to a company otherwise than in hard copy form or electronic form is validly sent or supplied if it is sent or supplied in a form or manner that has been agreed by the company.

NOTES

Commencement: 20 January 2007.

SCHEDULE 5
COMMUNICATIONS BY A COMPANY

Section 1144(2)

PART 1
INTRODUCTION

Application of this Schedule

[1.1310]

1. This Schedule applies to documents or information sent or supplied by a company.

NOTES

Commencement: 20 January 2007.

PART 2
COMMUNICATIONS IN HARD COPY FORM

Introduction

[1.1311]

2. A document or information is validly sent or supplied by a company if it is sent or supplied in hard copy form in accordance with this Part of this Schedule.

Method of communication in hard copy form

3. (1)　A document or information in hard copy form must be—
(a)　handed to the intended recipient, or
(b)　sent or supplied by hand or by post to an address (in accordance with paragraph 4).

(2)　For the purposes of this Schedule, a person sends a document or information by post if he posts a prepaid envelope containing the document or information.

Address for communications in hard copy form

4. (1)　A document or information in hard copy form may be sent or supplied by the company—
(a)　to an address specified for the purpose by the intended recipient;
(b)　to a company at its registered office;
(c)　to a person in his capacity as a member of the company at his address as shown in the company's register of members;
(d)　to a person in his capacity as a director of the company at his address as shown in the company's register of directors;
(e)　to an address to which any provision of the Companies Acts authorises the document or information to be sent or supplied.

(2)　Where the company is unable to obtain an address falling within sub-paragraph (1), the document or information may be sent or supplied to the intended recipient's last address known to the company.

NOTES

Commencement: 20 January 2007.

PART 3
COMMUNICATIONS IN ELECTRONIC FORM

Introduction

[1.1312]

5. A document or information is validly sent or supplied by a company if it is sent in electronic form in accordance with this Part of this Schedule.

Agreement to communications in electronic form

6. A document or information may only be sent or supplied by a company in electronic form—
(a)　to a person who has agreed (generally or specifically) that the document or information may be sent or supplied in that form (and has not revoked that agreement), or

    (b)   to a company that is deemed to have so agreed by a provision in the Companies Acts.

Address for communications in electronic form

7. (1)   Where the document or information is sent or supplied by electronic means, it may only be sent or supplied to an address—
    (a)   specified for the purpose by the intended recipient (generally or specifically), or
    (b)   where the intended recipient is a company, deemed by a provision of the Companies Acts to have been so specified.

(2)   Where the document or information is sent or supplied in electronic form by hand or by post, it must be—
    (a)   handed to the intended recipient, or
    (b)   sent or supplied to an address to which it could be validly sent if it were in hard copy form.

NOTES

Commencement: 20 January 2007.

Commencement (transitional provisions): the Companies Act 2006 (Commencement No 1, Transitional Provisions and Savings) Order 2006, SI 2006/3428, Sch 5, Pt 2, para 4 (at **[2.14]**) provides as follows—

"4   **Existing agreements to communication by electronic means**

(1)   This paragraph applies where an address has been notified by a person to a company for the purposes of—
    (a)   section 238(4A) or 239(2A) of the 1985 Act or Article 246(4A) or 247(2A) of the 1986 Order (sending or supply of accounts and reports by means of electronic communications);
    (b)   section 251(2A) of the 1985 Act or Article 259(2A) of the 1986 Order (sending of summary financial statement by means of electronic communications); or
    (c)   section 369(4A) or 379A(2B) of the 1985 Act or Article 377(5) or 387A(2B) of the 1986 Order (notice of meeting given by means of electronic communications).

(2)   Any such notification that is in force immediately before 20th January 2007 shall have effect on and after that date, in relation to the matters to which it relates, as an agreement under paragraph 6(a) of Schedule 5 to the Companies Act 2006 (agreement to accept documents or information in electronic form) and as an address specified under paragraph 7(1) of Schedule 5 to that Act (address for communications in electronic form).".

PART 4
COMMUNICATIONS BY MEANS OF A WEBSITE

Use of website

[1.1313]

8.   A document or information is validly sent or supplied by a company if it is made available on a website in accordance with this Part of this Schedule.

Agreement to use of website

9.   A document or information may only be sent or supplied by the company to a person by being made available on a website if the person—
    (a)   has agreed (generally or specifically) that the document or information may be sent or supplied to him in that manner, or
    (b)   is taken to have so agreed under—
        (i)   paragraph 10 (members of the company etc), or
        (ii)   paragraph 11 (debenture holders),
and has not revoked that agreement.

Deemed agreement of members of company etc to use of website

10. (1)   This paragraph applies to a document or information to be sent or supplied to a person—
    (a)   as a member of the company, or
    (b)   as a person nominated by a member in accordance with the company's articles to enjoy or exercise all or any specified rights of the member in relation to the company, or
    (c)   as a person nominated by a member under section 146 to enjoy information rights.

(2)   To the extent that—
    (a)   the members of the company have resolved that the company may send or supply documents or information to members by making them available on a website, or
    (b)   the company's articles contain provision to that effect,
a person in relation to whom the following conditions are met is taken to have agreed that the company may send or supply documents or information to him in that manner.

(3)   The conditions are that—
    (a)   the person has been asked individually by the company to agree that the company may send or supply documents or information generally, or the documents or information in question, to him by means of a website, and
    (b)   the company has not received a response within the period of 28 days beginning with the date on which the company's request was sent.

(4)   A person is not taken to have so agreed if the company's request—
    (a)   did not state clearly what the effect of a failure to respond would be, or

(b)   was sent less than twelve months after a previous request made to him for the purposes of this paragraph in respect of the same or a similar class of documents or information.

(5)   Chapter 3 of Part 3 (resolutions affecting a company's constitution) applies to a resolution under this paragraph.

Deemed agreement of debenture holders to use of website

11. (1)   This paragraph applies to a document or information to be sent or supplied to a person as holder of a company's debentures.

(2)   To the extent that—
- (a)   the relevant debenture holders have duly resolved that the company may send or supply documents or information to them by making them available on a website, or
- (b)   the instrument creating the debenture in question contains provision to that effect,

a debenture holder in relation to whom the following conditions are met is taken to have agreed that the company may send or supply documents or information to him in that manner.

(3)   The conditions are that—
- (a)   the debenture holder has been asked individually by the company to agree that the company may send or supply documents or information generally, or the documents or information in question, to him by means of a website, and
- (b)   the company has not received a response within the period of 28 days beginning with the date on which the company's request was sent.

(4)   A person is not taken to have so agreed if the company's request—
- (a)   did not state clearly what the effect of a failure to respond would be, or
- (b)   was sent less than twelve months after a previous request made to him for the purposes of this paragraph in respect of the same or a similar class of documents or information.

(5)   For the purposes of this paragraph—
- (a)   the relevant debenture holders are the holders of debentures of the company ranking *pari passu* for all purposes with the intended recipient, and
- (b)   a resolution of the relevant debenture holders is duly passed if they agree in accordance with the provisions of the instruments creating the debentures.

Availability of document or information

12. (1)   A document or information authorised or required to be sent or supplied by means of a website must be made available in a form, and by a means, that the company reasonably considers will enable the recipient—
- (a)   to read it, and
- (b)   to retain a copy of it.

(2)   For this purpose a document or information can be read only if—
- (a)   it can be read with the naked eye, or
- (b)   to the extent that it consists of images (for example photographs, pictures, maps, plans or drawings), it can be seen with the naked eye.

Notification of availability

13. (1)   The company must notify the intended recipient of—
- (a)   the presence of the document or information on the website,
- (b)   the address of the website,
- (c)   the place on the website where it may be accessed, and
- (d)   how to access the document or information.

(2)   The document or information is taken to be sent—
- (a)   on the date on which the notification required by this paragraph is sent, or
- (b)   if later, the date on which the document or information first appears on the website after that notification is sent.

Period of availability on website

14. (1)   The company must make the document or information available on the website throughout—
- (a)   the period specified by any applicable provision of the Companies Acts, or
- (b)   if no such period is specified, the period of 28 days beginning with the date on which the notification required under paragraph 13 is sent to the person in question.

(2)   For the purposes of this paragraph, a failure to make a document or information available on a website throughout the period mentioned in sub-paragraph (1) shall be disregarded if—
- (a)   it is made available on the website for part of that period, and
- (b)   the failure to make it available throughout that period is wholly attributable to circumstances that it would not be reasonable to have expected the company to prevent or avoid.

NOTES

Commencement: 20 January 2007.

Commencement (transitional provisions): the Companies Act 2006 (Commencement No 1, Transitional Provisions and Savings) Order 2006, SI 2006/3428, Sch 5, Pt 2, para 5 (at **[2.14]**) provides as follows—

> "5.—(1)   This paragraph applies where an agreement between a person and a company has been entered into for the purposes of—
>
> (a)   section 238(4B) of the 1985 Act or Article 246(4B) of the 1986 Order (sending or supply of copies of accounts and reports by means of website);
>
> (b)   section 251(2B) of the 1985 Act or Article 259(2B) of the 1986 Order (sending of summary financial statement by means of website); or
>
> (c)   section 369(4B) or 379A(2C) of the 1985 Act or Article 377(6) or 387A(2C) of the 1986 Order (notice of meeting given by means of website).
>
> (2)   Any such agreement that is in force immediately before 20th January 2007 shall have effect on and after that date, in relation to the matters to which it relates, as an agreement under paragraph 9(a) of Schedule 5 to the Companies Act 2006 (agreement to accept documents or information by means of a website).".

Commencement (transitional adaptations): the transitional adaptations of this Part contained in the Companies Act 2006 (Commencement No 1, Transitional Provisions and Savings) Order 2006, SI 2006/3428, Sch 1, para 16 were revoked by the Companies Act 2006 (Commencement No 3, Consequential Amendments, Transitional Provisions and Savings) Order 2007, SI 2007/2194, art 11(a), as from 1 October 2007. See **[2.9]**.

PART 5
OTHER AGREED FORMS OF COMMUNICATION

[1.1314]

15.   A document or information that is sent or supplied otherwise than in hard copy or electronic form or by means of a website is validly sent or supplied if it is sent or supplied in a form or manner that has been agreed by the intended recipient.

NOTES

Commencement: 20 January 2007.

PART 6
SUPPLEMENTARY PROVISIONS

Joint holders of shares or debentures

[1.1315]

16.   (1)   This paragraph applies in relation to documents or information to be sent or supplied to joint holders of shares or debentures of a company.

(2)   Anything to be agreed or specified by the holder must be agreed or specified by all the joint holders.

(3)   Anything authorised or required to be sent or supplied to the holder may be sent or supplied either—

(a)   to each of the joint holders, or

(b)   to the holder whose name appears first in the register of members or the relevant register of debenture holders.

(4)   This paragraph has effect subject to anything in the company's articles.

Death or bankruptcy of holder of shares

17.   (1)   This paragraph has effect in the case of the death or bankruptcy of a holder of a company's shares.

(2)   Documents or information required or authorised to be sent or supplied to the member may be sent or supplied to the persons claiming to be entitled to the shares in consequence of the death or bankruptcy—

(a)   by name, or

(b)   by the title of representatives of the deceased, or trustee of the bankrupt, or by any like description,

at the address in the United Kingdom supplied for the purpose by those so claiming.

(3)   Until such an address has been so supplied, a document or information may be sent or supplied in any manner in which it might have been sent or supplied if the death or bankruptcy had not occurred.

(4)   This paragraph has effect subject to anything in the company's articles.

(5)   References in this paragraph to the bankruptcy of a person include—

(a)   the sequestration of the estate of a person;

(b)   a person's estate being the subject of a protected trust deed (within the meaning of the Bankruptcy (Scotland) Act 1985 (c 66)).

In such a case the reference in sub-paragraph (2)(b) to the trustee of the bankrupt is to be read as the permanent or interim trustee (within the meaning of that Act) on the sequestrated estate or, as the case may be, the trustee under the protected deed.

NOTES

Commencement: 20 January 2007.

SCHEDULE 6
MEANING OF "SUBSIDIARY" ETC: SUPPLEMENTARY PROVISIONS
Section 1159

Introduction

[1.1316]

1. The provisions of this Part of this Schedule explain expressions used in section 1159 (meaning of "subsidiary" etc) and otherwise supplement that section.

Voting rights in a company

2. In section 1159(1)(a) and (c) the references to the voting rights in a company are to the rights conferred on shareholders in respect of their shares or, in the case of a company not having a share capital, on members, to vote at general meetings of the company on all, or substantially all, matters.

Right to appoint or remove a majority of the directors

3. (1)　In section 1159(1)(b) the reference to the right to appoint or remove a majority of the board of directors is to the right to appoint or remove directors holding a majority of the voting rights at meetings of the board on all, or substantially all, matters.

(2)　A company shall be treated as having the right to appoint to a directorship if—

   (a)　a person's appointment to it follows necessarily from his appointment as director of the company, or

   (b)　the directorship is held by the company itself.

(3)　A right to appoint or remove which is exercisable only with the consent or concurrence of another person shall be left out of account unless no other person has a right to appoint or, as the case may be, remove in relation to that directorship.

Rights exercisable only in certain circumstances or temporarily incapable of exercise

4. (1)　Rights which are exercisable only in certain circumstances shall be taken into account only—

   (a)　when the circumstances have arisen, and for so long as they continue to obtain, or

   (b)　when the circumstances are within the control of the person having the rights.

(2)　Rights which are normally exercisable but are temporarily incapable of exercise shall continue to be taken into account.

Rights held by one person on behalf of another

5. Rights held by a person in a fiduciary capacity shall be treated as not held by him.

6. (1)　Rights held by a person as nominee for another shall be treated as held by the other.

(2)　Rights shall be regarded as held as nominee for another if they are exercisable only on his instructions or with his consent or concurrence.

Rights attached to shares held by way of security

7. Rights attached to shares held by way of security shall be treated as held by the person providing the security—

   (a)　where apart from the right to exercise them for the purpose of preserving the value of the security, or of realising it, the rights are exercisable only in accordance with his instructions, and

   (b)　where the shares are held in connection with the granting of loans as part of normal business activities and apart from the right to exercise them for the purpose of preserving the value of the security, or of realising it, the rights are exercisable only in his interests.

Rights attributed to holding company

8. (1)　Rights shall be treated as held by a holding company if they are held by any of its subsidiary companies.

(2)　Nothing in paragraph 6 or 7 shall be construed as requiring rights held by a holding company to be treated as held by any of its subsidiaries.

(3)　For the purposes of paragraph 7 rights shall be treated as being exercisable in accordance with the instructions or in the interests of a company if they are exercisable in accordance with the instructions of or, as the case may be, in the interests of—

   (a)　any subsidiary or holding company of that company, or

(b) any subsidiary of a holding company of that company.

Disregard of certain rights

9. The voting rights in a company shall be reduced by any rights held by the company itself.

Supplementary

10. References in any provision of paragraphs 5 to 9 to rights held by a person include rights falling to be treated as held by him by virtue of any other provision of those paragraphs but not rights which by virtue of any such provision are to be treated as not held by him.

NOTES

Commencement: 6 April 2008 (certain purposes); 1 October 2009 (otherwise) (see the note below).

Commencement (note): the Companies Act 2006 (Commencement No 5, Transitional Provisions and Savings) Order 2007, SI 2007/3495, art 3(4) provides that this section shall come into force on 6 April 2008 so far as is necessary for the purposes of the provisions of this Act brought into force on that date by art 3(1)(u) of that Order (see **[2.52]**).

SCHEDULE 7
PARENT AND SUBSIDIARY UNDERTAKINGS: SUPPLEMENTARY PROVISIONS
Section 1162

Introduction

[1.1317]
1. The provisions of this Schedule explain expressions used in section 1162 (parent and subsidiary undertakings) and otherwise supplement that section.

Voting rights in an undertaking

2. (1)   In section 1162(2)(a) and (d) the references to the voting rights in an undertaking are to the rights conferred on shareholders in respect of their shares or, in the case of an undertaking not having a share capital, on members, to vote at general meetings of the undertaking on all, or substantially all, matters.

(2)   In relation to an undertaking which does not have general meetings at which matters are decided by the exercise of voting rights the references to holding a majority of the voting rights in the undertaking shall be construed as references to having the right under the constitution of the undertaking to direct the overall policy of the undertaking or to alter the terms of its constitution.

Right to appoint or remove a majority of the directors

3. (1)   In section 1162(2)(b) the reference to the right to appoint or remove a majority of the board of directors is to the right to appoint or remove directors holding a majority of the voting rights at meetings of the board on all, or substantially all, matters.

(2)   An undertaking shall be treated as having the right to appoint to a directorship if—
   (a)   a person's appointment to it follows necessarily from his appointment as director of the undertaking, or
   (b)   the directorship is held by the undertaking itself.

(3)   A right to appoint or remove which is exercisable only with the consent or concurrence of another person shall be left out of account unless no other person has a right to appoint or, as the case may be, remove in relation to that directorship.

Right to exercise dominant influence

4. (1)   For the purposes of section 1162(2)(c) an undertaking shall not be regarded as having the right to exercise a dominant influence over another undertaking unless it has a right to give directions with respect to the operating and financial policies of that other undertaking which its directors are obliged to comply with whether or not they are for the benefit of that other undertaking.

(2)   A "control contract" means a contract in writing conferring such a right which—
   (a)   is of a kind authorised by the articles of the undertaking in relation to which the right is exercisable, and
   (b)   is permitted by the law under which that undertaking is established.

(3)   This paragraph shall not be read as affecting the construction of section 1162(4)(a).

Rights exercisable only in certain circumstances or temporarily incapable of exercise

5. (1)   Rights which are exercisable only in certain circumstances shall be taken into account only—
   (a)   when the circumstances have arisen, and for so long as they continue to obtain, or
   (b)   when the circumstances are within the control of the person having the rights.

(2)   Rights which are normally exercisable but are temporarily incapable of exercise shall continue to be taken into account.

Rights held by one person on behalf of another

6. Rights held by a person in a fiduciary capacity shall be treated as not held by him.

7. (1) Rights held by a person as nominee for another shall be treated as held by the other.

(2) Rights shall be regarded as held as nominee for another if they are exercisable only on his instructions or with his consent or concurrence.

Rights attached to shares held by way of security

8. Rights attached to shares held by way of security shall be treated as held by the person providing the security—

(a) where apart from the right to exercise them for the purpose of preserving the value of the security, or of realising it, the rights are exercisable only in accordance with his instructions, and

(b) where the shares are held in connection with the granting of loans as part of normal business activities and apart from the right to exercise them for the purpose of preserving the value of the security, or of realising it, the rights are exercisable only in his interests.

Rights attributed to parent undertaking

9. (1) Rights shall be treated as held by a parent undertaking if they are held by any of its subsidiary undertakings.

(2) Nothing in paragraph 7 or 8 shall be construed as requiring rights held by a parent undertaking to be treated as held by any of its subsidiary undertakings.

(3) For the purposes of paragraph 8 rights shall be treated as being exercisable in accordance with the instructions or in the interests of an undertaking if they are exercisable in accordance with the instructions of or, as the case may be, in the interests of any group undertaking.

Disregard of certain rights

10. The voting rights in an undertaking shall be reduced by any rights held by the undertaking itself.

Supplementary

11. References in any provision of paragraphs 6 to 10 to rights held by a person include rights falling to be treated as held by him by virtue of any other provision of those paragraphs but not rights which by virtue of any such provision are to be treated as not held by him.

NOTES

Commencement: 6 April 2008.

SCHEDULE 8
INDEX OF DEFINED EXPRESSIONS

Section 1174
[1.1318]

abbreviated accounts (in Part 15)	sections 444(4) and 445(3)
accounting reference date and accounting reference period	section 391
accounting standards (in Part 15)	section 464
accounts meeting	section 437(3)
acquisition, in relation to a non-cash asset	section 1163(2)
address	
— generally in the Companies Acts	section 1142
— in the company communications provisions	section 1148(1)
affirmative resolution procedure, in relation to regulations and orders	section 1290
allotment (time of)	section 558
allotment of equity securities (in Chapter 3 of Part 17)	[section 560(2) and (3)]
allotted share capital and allotted shares	section 546(1)(b) and (2)
annual accounts (in Part 15)	section 471
annual accounts and reports (in Part 15)	section 471
annual general meeting	section 336
annual return	section 854

appropriate audit authority (in sections 522, 523 and 524)	section 525(1)
appropriate rate of interest	
— in Chapter 5 of Part 17	section 592
— in Chapter 6 of Part 17	section 609
approval after being made, in relation to regulations and orders	section 1291
arrangement	
— in Chapter 7 of Part 17	section 616(1)
— in Part 26	section 895(2)
articles	section 18
associate (in Chapter 3 of Part 28)	section 988
associated bodies corporate and associated company (in Part 10)	section 256
authenticated, in relation to a document or information sent or supplied to a company	section 1146
authorised group, of members of a company (in Part 14)	section 370(3)
authorised insurance company	section 1165(2)
authorised minimum (in relation to share capital of public company)	section 763
available profits (in Chapter 5 of Part 18)	sections 711 and 712
banking company and banking group	section 1164
body corporate	section 1173(1)
called-up share capital	section 547
capital redemption reserve	section 733
capitalisation in relation to a company's profits (in Part 23)	section 853(3)
cash (in relation to paying up or allotting shares)	section 583
cause of action, in relation to derivative proceedings (in Chapter 2 of Part 11)	section 265(7)
certified translation (in Part 35)	section 1107
charge (in Chapter 1 of Part 25)	section 861(5)
circulation date, in relation to a written resolution (in Part 13)	section 290
class of shares	section 629
the Companies Acts	section 2
Companies Act accounts	sections 395(1)(a) and 403(2)(a)
Companies Act group accounts	section 403(2)(a)
Companies Act individual accounts	section 395(1)(a)
companies involved in the division (in Part 27)	section 919(2)
company	
— generally in the Companies Acts	section 1
— in Chapter 7 of Part 17	section 616(1)
— in Chapter 1 of Part 25	section 861(5)
— in Chapter 2 of Part 25	section 879(6)
— in Part 26	section 895(2)
— in Chapter 3 of Part 28	section 991(1)
— in the company communications provisions	section 1148(1)
the company communications provisions	section 1143
the company law provisions of this Act	section 2(2)
company records (in Part 37)	section 1134
connected with, in relation to a director (in Part 10)	sections 252 to 254
constitution, of a company	

equity securities (in Chapter 3 of Part 17)	section 560(1)
equity share capital	section 548
equity shares (in Chapter 7 of Part 17)	section 616(1)
[establishment of an overseas company (in Part 35)	section 1067(6)]
existing company (in Part 27)	section 902(2)
fellow subsidiary undertakings	section 1161(4)
financial assistance (in Chapter 2 of Part 18)	section 677
financial institution	section 1173(1)
financial year, of a company	section 390
firm	section 1173(1)
fixed assets (in Part 23)	section 853
the former Companies Acts	section 1171
the Gazette	section 1173(1)
group (in Part 15)	section 474(1)
group undertaking	section 1161(5)
hard copy form and hard copy	
— generally in the Companies Acts	section 1168(2)
— in relation to communications to a company	Part 2 of Schedule 4
— in relation to communications by a company	Part 2 of Schedule 5
hire-purchase agreement	section 1173(1)
holder of shares (in Chapter 3 of Part 17)	section 574
holding company	section 1159 (and see section 1160 and Schedule 6)
IAS accounts	sections 395(1)(b) and 403(1) and (2)(b)
IAS group accounts	section 403(1) and (2)(b)
IAS individual accounts	section 395(1)(b)
IAS Regulation (in Part 15)	section 474(1)
included in the consolidation, in relation to group accounts (in Part 15)	section 474(1)
individual accounts	section 394
information rights (in Part 9)	section 146(3)
insurance company	section 1165(3)
insurance group	section 1165(5)
insurance market activity	section 1165(7)
interest in shares (for the purposes of Part 22)	sections 820 to 825
international accounting standards (in Part 15)	section 474(1)
investment company (in Part 23)	section 833
. . .	. . .
issued share capital and issued shares	section 546(1)(a) and (2)
the issuing company (in Chapter 7 of Part 17)	section 610(6)
the Joint Stock Companies Acts	section 1171
liabilities (in Part 27)	section 941
liability, references to incurring, reducing or discharging (in Chapter 2 of Part 18)	section 683(2)
limited by guarantee	section 3(3)
limited by shares	section 3(2)
limited company	section 3
the main register (of members) (in Chapter 3 of Part 8)	section 131(1)
major audit (in sections 522 and 525)	section 525(2)
market purchase, by a company of its own shares (in Chapter 4 of Part 18)	section 693(4)
member, of a company	

— generally in the Companies Acts	section 112
— in Chapter 1 of Part 11	section 260(5)
— in Chapter 2 of Part 11	section 265(7)
memorandum of association	section 8
merger (in Part 27)	section 904
merging companies (in Part 27)	section 904(2)
merger by absorption (in Part 27)	section 904(1)(a)
merger by formation of a new company (in Part 27)	section 904(1)(b)
[MiFID investment firm	
— in Part 15	section 474(1)
— in Part 16	section 539]
negative resolution procedure, in relation to regulations and orders	section 1289
net assets (in Part 7)	section 92
new company (in Part 27)	section 902(2)
non-cash asset	section 1163
[*non-traded company (in Part 24)*	*section 855(4)*]
non-voting shares (in Chapter 3 of Part 28)	section 991(1)
number, in relation to shares	section 540(4)(b)
off-market purchase, by a company of its own shares (in Chapter 4 of Part 18)	section 693(2)
offer period (in Chapter 2 of Part 28)	section 971(1)
offer to the public (in Chapter 1 of Part 20)	section 756
offeror	
— in Chapter 2 of Part 28	section 971(1)
— in Chapter 3 of Part 28	section 991(1)
officer, in relation to a body corporate	section 1173(1)
officer in default	section 1121
official seal, of registrar	section 1062
opted-in company (in Chapter 2 of Part 28)	section 971(1)
opting-in resolution (in Chapter 2 of Part 28)	section 966(1)
opting-out resolution (in Chapter 2 of Part 28)	section 966(5)
ordinary resolution	section 282
ordinary shares (in Chapter 3 of Part 17)	section 560(1)
organisation (in Part 14)	section 379(1)
other relevant transactions or arrangements (in Chapter 4 of Part 10)	section 210
overseas company	section 1044
overseas branch register	section 129(1)
paid up	section 583
the Panel (in Part 28)	section 942
parent company	section 1173(1)
parent undertaking	section 1162 (and see Schedule 7)
payment for loss of office (in Chapter 4 of Part 10)	section 215
pension scheme (in Chapter 1 of Part 18)	section 675
period for appointing auditors, in relation to a private company	section 485(2)
period for filing, in relation to accounts and reports for a financial year	section 442
permissible capital payment (in Chapter 5 of Part 18)	section 710
political donation (in Part 14)	section 364

political expenditure (in Part 14)	section 365
political organisation (in Part 14)	section 363(2)
prescribed	section 1167
private company	section 4
profit and loss account (in Part 15)	section 474(1) and (2)
profits and losses (in Part 23)	section 853(2)
profits available for distribution (for the purposes of Part 23)	section 830(2)
property (in Part 27)	section 941
protected information (in Chapter 8 of Part 10)	section 240
provision for entrenchment, in relation to a company's articles	section 22
public company	section 4
publication, in relation to accounts and reports (in sections 433 to 435)	section 436
qualified, in relation to an auditor's report etc (in Part 16)	section 539
qualifying shares (in Chapter 6 of Part 18)	section 724(2)
qualifying third party indemnity provision (in Chapter 7 of Part 10)	section 234
qualifying pension scheme indemnity provision (in Chapter 7 of Part 10)	section 235
quasi-loan (in Chapter 4 of Part 10)	section 199
quoted company	
— in Part 13	section 361
— in Part 15	section 385
— in Chapter 5 of Part 16	section 531 (and section 385)
realised profits and losses (in Part 23)	section 853(4)
[receiver or manager (and certain related references)	section 1170A]
redeemable shares	section 684(1)
redenominate	section 622(1)
redenomination reserve	section 628
the register	section 1080
[registered number, of a company (or an overseas company)	section 1066 (and section 1059A(5))]
[registered number, of a UK establishment of an overseas company	section 1067]
register of charges, kept by registrar	
— in England and Wales and Northern Ireland	section 869
— in Scotland	section 885
register of directors	section 162
register of directors' residential addresses	section 165
register of members	section 113
register of secretaries	section 275
. . .	. . .
. . .	
registered office, of a company	section 86
registrar and registrar of companies	section 1060
registrar's index of company names	section 1099
registrar's rules	section 1117
registration in a particular part of the United Kingdom	section 1060(4)
regulated activity	
— generally in the Companies Acts	section 1173(1)

— in Part 15	section 474(1)
regulated market	section 1173(1)
relevant accounts (in Part 23)	section 836(2)
requirements for proper delivery (in Part 35)	section 1072 (and see section 1073)
requirements of this Act	section 1172
[return period (in Part 24)	section 855(4)]
securities (and related expressions)	
— in Chapter 1 of Part 20	section 755(5)
— in Chapter 2 of Part 21	section 783
senior statutory auditor	section 504
sent or supplied, in relation to documents or information (in the company communications provisions)	section 1148(2) and (3)
service address	section 1141
service contract, of a director (in Part 10)	section 227
shadow director	section 251
share	
— generally in the Companies Acts	section 540 (and see section 1161(2))
— in Part 22	section 792
— in section 1162 and Schedule 7	section 1162(7)
share capital, company having a	section 545
share exchange ratio	
— in Chapter 2 of Part 27	section 905(2)
— in Chapter 3 of Part 27	section 920(2)
share premium account	section 610(1)
share warrant	section 779(1)
[small companies exemption (in relation to directors' report)	section 415A]
small companies regime, [(for accounts)]	section 381
solvency statement (in sections 641 to 644)	section 643
special notice, in relation to a resolution	section 312
special resolution	section 283
statutory accounts	section 434(3)
subsidiary	section 1159 (and see section 1160 and Schedule 6)
subsidiary undertaking	section 1162 (and see Schedule 7)
summary financial statement	section 426
takeover bid (in Chapter 2 of Part 28)	section 971(1)
takeover offer (in Chapter 3 of Part 28)	section 974
the Takeovers Directive	
— in Chapter 1 of Part 28	section 943(8)
— in Chapter 2 of Part 28	section 971(1)
[traded company (in Part 13)	section 360C]
[*traded company (in Part 24)*	*section 855(4)*]
trading certificate	section 761(1)
transfer, in relation to a non-cash asset	section 1163(2)
treasury shares	section 724(5)
turnover	
— in Part 15	section 474(1)
— in Part 16	section 539
UCITS management company	
— in Part 15	section 474(1)
— in Part 16	section 539

[UK establishment of an overseas company (in Part 35)	section 1067(6)]
UK-registered company	section 1158
uncalled share capital	section 547
unconditional, in relation to a contract to acquire shares (in Chapter 3 of Part 28)	section 991(2)
undistributable reserves	section 831(4)
undertaking	section 1161(1)
unique identifier	section 1082
unlimited company	section 3
unquoted company (in Part 15)	section 385
voting rights	
— in Chapter 2 of Part 28	section 971(1)
— in Chapter 3 of Part 28	section 991(1)
— in section 1159 and Schedule 6	paragraph 2 of Schedule 6
— in section 1162 and Schedule 7	paragraph 2 of Schedule 7
voting shares	
— in Chapter 2 of Part 28	section 971(1)
— in Chapter 3 of Part 28	section 991(1)
website, communication by a company by means of	Part 4 of Schedule 5
Welsh company	section 88
wholly-owned subsidiary	section 1159(2) (and see section 1160 and Schedule 6)
working day, in relation to a company	section 1173(1)
written resolution	section 288

NOTES

Commencement: 1 October 2009.

Words in square brackets in entry "allotment of equity securities (in Chapter 3 of Part 17)" substituted by the Companies Act 2006 (Allotment of Shares and Right of Pre-emption) (Amendment) Regulations 2009, SI 2009/2561, reg 2(6), as from 1 October 2009.

Entries "contributory" and "receiver or manager (and certain related references)" inserted by the Companies Act 2006 (Consequential Amendments, Transitional Provisions and Savings) Order 2009, SI 2009/1941, art 2(1), Sch 1, para 260(1), (9), as from 1 October 2009.

Entry "corporate governance statement and separate corporate governance statement" inserted by the Companies Act 2006 (Accounts, Reports and Audit) Regulations 2009, SI 2009/1581, reg 9, as from 27 June 2009, in relation to financial years beginning on or after 29 June 2008 which have not ended before 27 June 2009.

Entries "establishment of an overseas company (in Part 35)", "registered number, of a company (or an overseas company)", "registered number, of a UK establishment of an overseas company" and "UK establishment of an overseas company (in Part 35)" inserted, and entries "registered number, of a branch of an overseas company" and "registered number, of a company" (omitted) repealed, by the Companies Act 2006 (Part 35) (Consequential Amendments, Transitional Provisions and Savings) Order 2009, SI 2009/1802, arts 2, 17, as from 1 October 2009.

Entry "ISD investment firm" (omitted) repealed, and entry "MiFID investment firm" inserted, by the Markets in Financial Instruments Directive (Consequential Amendments) Regulations 2007, SI 2007/2932, reg 3(8), as from 1 November 2007.

Entries "non-traded company (in Part 24)", "return period (in Part 24)", and "traded company (in Part 24)" inserted by the Companies Act 2006 (Annual Return and Service Addresses) Regulations 2008, SI 2008/3000, reg 9, as from 1 October 2009 (in relation to annual returns made up to that date or a later date).

Entries "non-traded company (in Part 24)" and "traded company (in Part 24)" repealed by the Companies Act 2006 (Annual Returns) Regulations 2011, SI 2011/1487, reg 5, as from 1 October 2011 (in relation to annual returns made up to that date or a later date).

Entry "small companies exemption (in relation to directors' report)" inserted by the Companies Act 2006 (Amendment) (Accounts and Reports) Regulations 2008, SI 2008/393, reg 6(11), as from 6 April 2008, in relation to financial years beginning on or after that date.

Words in square brackets in the entry "small companies regime" substituted by SI 2008/393, reg 6(12), as from 6 April 2008, in relation to financial years beginning on or after that date.

Entry "traded company (in Part 13)" inserted by the Companies (Shareholders' Rights) Regulations 2009, SI 2009/1632, reg 21(2), as from 3 August 2009, in relation to meetings of which notice is given, or first given, on or after that date.

SCHEDULE 9
REMOVAL OF SPECIAL PROVISIONS ABOUT ACCOUNTS AND AUDIT OF CHARITABLE COMPANIES

Section 1175

PART 1
THE COMPANIES ACT 1985 (C 6)

[1.1319]

(Amends CA 1985, ss 240, 245, 249A, 249B, 249E, 262A (all of which were repealed by this Act, as from 6 April 2008, except in relation to financial years beginning before that date), and repeals ss 249C, 249D of the 1985 Act.)

NOTES

Commencement: 1 April 2008.

PART 2
THE COMPANIES (NORTHERN IRELAND) ORDER 1986
(SI 1986/1032 (NI 6)

[1.1320]

(Contains amendments to the Companies (Northern Ireland) Order 1986, SI 1986/1032 (outside the scope of this work).)

NOTES

Commencement: to be appointed.

Commencement (note): the government have announced that they do not intend to commence this Part, and that it will be repealed in due course; see the written ministerial statements for 6 November 2008.

SCHEDULE 10
RECOGNISED SUPERVISORY BODIES

Section 1217

PART 1
GRANT AND REVOCATION OF RECOGNITION OF A SUPERVISORY BODY

Application for recognition of supervisory body

[1.1321]

1. (1)   A supervisory body may apply to the Secretary of State for an order declaring it to be a recognised supervisory body for the purposes of this Part of this Act ("a recognition order").

(2)   Any such application must be—

(a)   made in such manner as the Secretary of State may direct, and

(b)   accompanied by such information as the Secretary of State may reasonably require for the purpose of determining the application.

(3)   At any time after receiving an application and before determining it the Secretary of State may require the applicant to furnish additional information.

(4)   The directions and requirements given or imposed under sub-paragraphs (2) and (3) may differ as between different applications.

(5)   The Secretary of State may require any information to be furnished under this paragraph to be in such form or verified in such manner as he may specify.

(6)   Every application must be accompanied by—

(a)   a copy of the applicant's rules, and

(b)   a copy of any guidance issued by the applicant in writing.

(7)   The reference in sub-paragraph (6)(b) to guidance issued by the applicant is a reference to any guidance or recommendation—

(a)   issued or made by it to all or any class of its members or persons seeking to become members,

(b)   relevant for the purposes of this Part, and

(c)   intended to have continuing effect,

including any guidance or recommendation relating to the admission or expulsion of members of the body, so far as relevant for the purposes of this Part.

Grant and refusal of recognition

2. (1)   The Secretary of State may, on an application duly made in accordance with paragraph 1 and after being furnished with all such information as he may require under that paragraph, make or refuse to make a recognition order in respect of the applicant.

(2)   The Secretary of State may make a recognition order only if it appears to him, from the information furnished by the body and having regard to any other information in his possession, that the requirements of Part 2 of this Schedule are satisfied in the case of that body.

(3)   The Secretary of State may refuse to make a recognition order in respect of a body if he considers that its recognition is unnecessary having regard to the existence of one or more other bodies which—

    (a)   maintain and enforce rules as to the appointment and conduct of statutory auditors, and

    (b)   have been or are likely to be recognised.

(4)   Where the Secretary of State refuses an application for a recognition order he must give the applicant a written notice to that effect—

    (a)   specifying which requirements, in the opinion of the Secretary of State, are not satisfied, or

    (b)   stating that the application is refused on the ground mentioned in sub-paragraph (3).

(5)   A recognition order must state the date on which it takes effect.

Revocation of recognition

3. (1)   A recognition order may be revoked by a further order made by the Secretary of State if at any time it appears to him—

    (a)   that any requirement of Part 2 of this Schedule is not satisfied in the case of the body to which the recognition order relates ("the recognised body"),

    (b)   that the body has failed to comply with any obligation imposed on it by or by virtue of this Part of this Act, or

    (c)   that the continued recognition of the body is undesirable having regard to the existence of one or more other bodies which have been or are to be recognised.

(2)   An order revoking a recognition order must state the date on which it takes effect, which must be after the period of three months beginning with the date on which the revocation order is made.

(3)   Before revoking a recognition order the Secretary of State must—

    (a)   give written notice of his intention to do so to the recognised body,

    (b)   take such steps as he considers reasonably practicable for bringing the notice to the attention of the members of the body, and

    (c)   publish the notice in such manner as he thinks appropriate for bringing it to the attention of any other persons who are in his opinion likely to be affected.

(4)   A notice under sub-paragraph (3) must—

    (a)   state the reasons for which the Secretary of State proposes to act, and

    (b)   give particulars of the rights conferred by sub-paragraph (5).

(5)   A person within sub-paragraph (6) may, within the period of three months beginning with the date of service or publication of the notice under sub-paragraph (3) or such longer period as the Secretary of State may allow, make written representations to the Secretary of State and, if desired, oral representations to a person appointed for that purpose by the Secretary of State.

(6)   The persons within this sub-paragraph are—

    (a)   the recognised body on which a notice is served under sub-paragraph (3),

    (b)   any member of the body, and

    (c)   any other person who appears to the Secretary of State to be affected.

(7)   The Secretary of State must have regard to any representations made in accordance with sub-paragraph (5) in determining whether to revoke the recognition order.

(8)   If in any case the Secretary of State considers it essential to do so in the public interest he may revoke a recognition order without regard to the restriction imposed by sub-paragraph (2), even if—

    (a)   no notice has been given or published under sub-paragraph (3), or

    (b)   the period of time for making representations in pursuance of such a notice has not expired.

(9)   An order revoking a recognition order may contain such transitional provision as the Secretary of State thinks necessary or expedient.

(10)   A recognition order may be revoked at the request or with the consent of the recognised body and any such revocation is not subject to—

    (a)   the restrictions imposed by sub-paragraphs (1) and (2), or

    (b)   the requirements of sub-paragraphs (3) to (5) and (7).

(11)   On making an order revoking a recognition order in respect of a body the Secretary of State must—

    (a)   give written notice of the making of the order to the body,

    (b)   take such steps as he considers reasonably practicable for bringing the making of the order to the attention of the members of the body, and

    (c)   publish a notice of the making of the order in such manner as he thinks appropriate for bringing it to the attention of any other persons who are in his opinion likely to be affected.

Transitional provision

4. A recognition order made and not revoked under—

    (a)   paragraph 2(1) of Schedule 11 to the Companies Act 1989 (c 40), or

(b) paragraph 2(1) of Schedule 11 to the Companies (Northern Ireland) Order 1990 (SI 1990/593 (NI 5)),

before the commencement of this Chapter of this Part of this Act is to have effect after the commencement of this Chapter as a recognition order made under paragraph 2(1) of this Schedule.

Orders not statutory instruments

5. Orders under this Part of this Schedule shall not be made by statutory instrument.

NOTES
Commencement: 6 April 2008.
Commencement (transitional provisions): see the note to s 1217 at **[1.1217]**.
Transfer of functions: as to the transfer of the functions of the Secretary of State under Part 42 of this Act (which includes this Schedule) to the Professional Oversight Board, see the Statutory Auditors (Delegation of Functions etc) Order 2008, SI 2008/496, art 4.

PART 2
REQUIREMENTS FOR RECOGNITION OF A SUPERVISORY BODY

Holding of appropriate qualification

[1.1322]
6. (1) The body must have rules to the effect that a person is not eligible for appointment as a statutory auditor unless—
(a) in the case of an individual [other than an EEA auditor], he holds an appropriate qualification,
[(aa) in the case of an individual who is an EEA auditor—
  (i) he holds an appropriate qualification,
  (ii) he has been authorised on or before 5 April 2008 to practise the profession of company auditor pursuant to the European Communities (Recognition of Professional Qualifications) (First General System) Regulations 2005 (SI 2005/18) and has fulfilled any requirements imposed pursuant to regulation 6 of those Regulations, or
  (iii) he has passed an aptitude test in accordance with sub-paragraph (2), unless an aptitude test is not required (see sub-paragraph (2A)).]
(b) in the case of a firm—
  (i) each individual responsible for statutory audit work on behalf of the firm is eligible for appointment as a statutory auditor, and
  (ii) the firm is controlled by qualified persons (see paragraph 7 below).
[(2) The aptitude test—
(a) must test the person's knowledge of subjects—
  (i) that are covered by a recognised professional qualification,
  (ii) that are not covered by the professional qualification already held by the person, and
  (iii) the knowledge of which is essential for the pursuit of the profession of statutory auditor;
(b) may test the person's knowledge of rules of professional conduct;
(c) must not test the person's knowledge of any other matters.]
(2A) No aptitude test is required if the subjects that are covered by a recognised professional qualification and the knowledge of which is essential for the pursuit of the profession of statutory auditor are covered by the professional qualification already held by the person.]

(3) A firm which has ceased to comply with the conditions mentioned in sub-paragraph (1)(b) may be permitted to remain eligible for appointment as a statutory auditor for a period of not more than three months.

7. (1) This paragraph explains what is meant in paragraph 6(1)(b) by a firm being "controlled by qualified persons".
(2) In this paragraph references to a person being qualified are—
(a) in relation to an individual, to his holding—
  (i) an appropriate qualification, or
  (ii) a corresponding qualification to audit accounts under the law of [an EEA State], or part of [an EEA State], other than the United Kingdom;
(b) in relation to a firm, to its—
  (i) being eligible for appointment as a statutory auditor, or
  (ii) being eligible for a corresponding appointment as an auditor under the law of [an EEA State], or part of [an EEA State], other than the United Kingdom.
(3) A firm is to be treated as controlled by qualified persons if, and only if—
(a) a majority of the members of the firm are qualified persons, and
(b) where the firm's affairs are managed by a board of directors, committee or other management body, a majority of that body are qualified persons or, if the body consists of two persons only, at least one of them is a qualified person.

(4)   A majority of the members of a firm means—
  (a)   where under the firm's constitution matters are decided upon by the exercise of voting rights, members holding a majority of the rights to vote on all, or substantially all, matters;
  (b)   in any other case, members having such rights under the constitution of the firm as enable them to direct its overall policy or alter its constitution.

(5)   A majority of the members of the management body of a firm means—
  (a)   where matters are decided at meetings of the management body by the exercise of voting rights, members holding a majority of the rights to vote on all, or substantially all, matters at such meetings;
  (b)   in any other case, members having such rights under the constitution of the firm as enable them to direct its overall policy or alter its constitution.

(6)   Paragraphs 5 to 11 of Schedule 7 to this Act (rights to be taken into account and attribution of rights) apply for the purposes of this paragraph.

Auditors to be fit and proper persons

8. (1)   The body must have adequate rules and practices designed to ensure that the persons eligible under its rules for appointment as a statutory auditor are fit and proper persons to be so appointed.

(2)   The matters which the body may take into account for this purpose in relation to a person must include—
  (a)   any matter relating to any person who is or will be employed by or associated with him for the purposes of or in connection with statutory audit work;
  (b)   in the case of a body corporate, any matter relating to—
    (i)   any director or controller of the body,
    (ii)   any other body corporate in the same group, or
    (iii)   any director or controller of any such other body; and
  (c)   in the case of a partnership, any matter relating to—
    (i)   any of the partners,
    (ii)   any director or controller of any of the partners,
    (iii)   any body corporate in the same group as any of the partners, or
    (iv)   any director or controller of any such other body.

(3)   Where the person is a limited liability partnership, in sub-paragraph (2)(b) "director" is to be read as "member".

(4)   In sub-paragraph (2)(b) and (c) "controller", in relation to a body corporate, means a person who either alone or with an associate or associates is entitled to exercise or control the exercise of 15% or more of the rights to vote on all, or substantially all, matters at general meetings of the body or another body corporate of which it is a subsidiary.

Professional integrity and independence

9. (1)   The body must have adequate rules and practices designed to ensure that—
  (a)   statutory audit work is conducted properly and with integrity,
  (b)   persons are not appointed as statutory auditors in circumstances in which they have an interest likely to conflict with the proper conduct of the audit,
  [(c)   persons appointed as statutory auditors take steps to safeguard their independence from any significant threats to it,
  (d)   persons appointed as statutory auditors record any such threats and the steps taken to safeguard the proper conduct of the audit from them, and
  (e)   remuneration received or receivable by a statutory auditor in respect of statutory audit work is not—
    (i)   influenced or determined by the statutory auditor providing other services to the audited person, or
    (ii)   on a contingent fee basis.]

(2)   The body must participate in arrangements within paragraph 21, and the rules and practices mentioned in sub-paragraph (1) must include provision requiring compliance with any standards for the time being determined under such arrangements.

[(3)   The body must also have adequate rules and practices designed to ensure that—
  (a)   no firm is eligible under its rules for appointment as a statutory auditor unless the firm has arrangements to prevent any person from being able to exert any influence over the way in which a statutory audit is conducted in circumstances in which that influence would be likely to affect the independence or integrity of the audit;
  (b)   any rule of law relating to the confidentiality of information received in the course of statutory audit work by persons appointed as statutory auditors is complied with; and
  (c)   a person ceasing to hold office as a statutory auditor makes available to his successor in that office all relevant information which he holds in relation to that office.]

[(4)   The rules referred to in sub-paragraph (3)(b) (confidentiality of information) must apply to persons who are no longer members of the body as they apply to members and any fine imposed in the enforcement of those rules shall be recoverable by the body as a debt due to it from the person obliged to pay it.]

Technical standards

10. (1)   The body must have rules and practices as to—
  (a)   the technical standards to be applied in statutory audit work, and
  (b)   the manner in which those standards are to be applied in practice.
(2)   The body must participate in arrangements within paragraph 22, and the rules and practices mentioned in sub-paragraph (1) must include provision requiring compliance with any standards for the time being determined under such arrangements.

[Technical standards for group audits

10A. (1)   The body must have rules and practices as to technical standards ensuring that group auditors—
  (a)   review for the purposes of a group audit the audit work conducted by other persons, and
  (b)   record that review.
(2)   The body must participate in arrangements within paragraph 22, and the rules and practices mentioned in sub-paragraph (1) must include provision requiring compliance with any standards for the time being determined under such arrangements.
(3)   The body must also have rules and practices ensuring that group auditors—
  (a)   retain copies of any documents necessary for the purposes of the review that they have received from third country auditors who are not covered by working arrangements under section 1253E, or
  (b)   agree with those third country auditors proper and unrestricted access to those documents on request.
(4)   The body's rules and practices must ensure that group auditors make those documents available on request to—
  (a)   the body;
  (b)   any other body with which the body has entered into arrangements for the purposes of paragraph 23 or 24 (independent arrangements for monitoring and investigation);
  (c)   the Secretary of State.
(5)   The body may provide that the rules and practices referred to in sub-paragraphs (3) and (4) do not apply if, after taking all reasonable steps, a group auditor is unable to obtain the copies of the documents or the access to the documents necessary for the review.
(6)   If the body does so provide, its rules and practices must ensure that the group auditor records—
  (a)   the steps taken to obtain copies of or access to those documents,
  (b)   the reasons why the copies or access could not be obtained, and
  (c)   any evidence of those steps or those reasons.
(7)   In this paragraph—
    "group auditor" means a person appointed as statutory auditor to conduct an audit of group accounts;
    "group" has the same meaning as in Part 15 of this Act (see section 474).]

[Public interest entity reporting requirements

10B. (1)   The body must have adequate rules and practices designed to ensure that persons appointed as statutory auditors of public interest entities report to the entity's audit committee (if it has one) at least once in each calendar year at any time during which they hold the office of statutory auditor.
(2)   The report must include—
  (a)   a statement in writing confirming the person's independence from the public interest entity;
  (b)   a description of any services provided by the person to the public interest entity other than in his capacity as statutory auditor;
  (c)   a description of any significant threats to the person's independence;
  (d)   an explanation of the steps taken by the person to safeguard his independence from those threats;
  (e)   a description of any material weaknesses arising from the statutory audit in the public interest entity's internal control in relation to the preparation of accounts; and
  (f)   any other significant matters arising from the statutory audit.
(3)   The body must participate in arrangements within paragraph 22A (arrangements for setting standards), and the rules and practices mentioned in sub-paragraph (1) must include provision requiring compliance with any standards for the time being determined under such arrangements.
(4)   In this paragraph, "audit committee" means a body which performs the functions referred to in Article 41.2 of the Audit Directive or equivalent functions.

Public interest entity independence requirements

10C. (1)   The body must have adequate rules and practices designed to ensure that—
  (a)   an individual does not accept an appointment by a public interest entity as statutory auditor if—
    (i)   he has been the statutory auditor of the entity for a continuous period of more than seven years, and
    (ii)   less than two years have passed since he was last the statutory auditor of the entity;
  (b)   where a firm has been appointed by a public interest entity as statutory auditor, an individual may not be a key audit partner if—
    (i)   he has been a key audit partner in relation to audits of the entity for a continuous period of more than seven years, and
    (ii)   less than two years have passed since he was last the key audit partner in relation to an audit of the entity.

(2)   The body must participate in arrangements within paragraph 22B (arrangements for setting standards), and the rules and practices mentioned in sub-paragraph (1) must include provision requiring compliance with any standards for the time being determined under such arrangements.

(3)   The body must also have adequate rules and practices designed to ensure that—
  (a)   an individual who has been appointed by a public interest entity as statutory auditor may not be appointed as a director or other officer of the entity during a period of two years commencing on the date on which his appointment as statutory auditor ended;
  (b)   a key audit partner of a firm which has been appointed by a public interest entity as statutory auditor may not be appointed as a director or other officer of the entity during a period of two years commencing on the date on which his work as key audit partner ended.

(4)   The rules referred to in sub-paragraph (3) must apply to persons who are no longer members of the body as they apply to members and any fine imposed in the enforcement of those rules shall be recoverable by the body as a debt due to it from the person obliged to pay it.

(5)   An auditor of a public interest entity is not to be regarded as an officer of the entity for the purposes of sub-paragraph (3)(a) and (b).

(6)   For the purposes of this paragraph—
  (a)   a "key audit partner" is an individual identified by a firm appointed as statutory auditor as being primarily responsible for the statutory audit; and
  (b)   a key audit partner of a firm appointed as statutory auditor of a parent undertaking or a material subsidiary undertaking of a public interest entity is to be treated as if he were a key audit partner of the firm appointed as statutory auditor of the public interest entity.]

Procedures for maintaining competence

11.   The body must have rules and practices designed to ensure that persons eligible under its rules for appointment as a statutory auditor continue to maintain an appropriate level of competence in the conduct of statutory audits.

Monitoring and enforcement

12.   [(1)   The body must—
  (a)   have adequate resources for the effective monitoring and enforcement of compliance with its rules, and
  (b)   ensure that those resources may not be influenced improperly by the persons monitored.

(1A)   The body must—
  (a)   have adequate arrangements for the effective monitoring and enforcement of compliance with its rules, and
  (b)   ensure that those arrangements operate independently of the persons monitored.]

(2)   The arrangements for monitoring may make provision for that function to be performed on behalf of the body (and without affecting its responsibility) by any other body or person who is able and willing to perform it.

[(3)   The arrangements for enforcement must include provision for—
  (a)   sanctions which include—
    (i)   the withdrawal of eligibility for appointment as a statutory auditor; and
    (ii)   any other disciplinary measures necessary to ensure the effective enforcement of the body's rules; and
  (b)   the body making available to the public information relating to steps it has taken to ensure the effective enforcement of its rules.]

[Monitoring of audits

13.   (1)   The body must—
  (a)   in the case of members of the body who do not perform any statutory audit functions in respect of major audits, have adequate arrangements for enabling the performance by its members of statutory audit functions to be monitored by means of inspections;

(b)   in the case of members of the body who perform any statutory audit functions in respect of major audits, participate in arrangements within paragraph 23(1); and

(c)   have rules designed to ensure that members of the body take such steps as may reasonably be required of them to enable their performance of any statutory audit functions to be monitored by means of inspections.

(2) Any monitoring of members of the body under the arrangements within paragraph 23(1) is to be regarded (so far as their performance of statutory audit functions in respect of major audits is concerned) as monitoring of compliance with the body's rules for the purposes of paragraph 12(1) and (1A).

(3) The arrangements referred to in sub-paragraph (1)(a) must include an inspection which is conducted in relation to each person eligible for appointment as a statutory auditor at least once every six years.

(4) The inspection must be conducted by persons who—

    (a)   have an appropriate professional education;

    (b)   have experience of—

        (i)   statutory audit work, or

        (ii)   equivalent work on the audit of accounts under the law of an EEA State, or part of an EEA State, other than the United Kingdom;

    (c)   have received adequate training in the conduct of inspections;

    (d)   do not have any interests likely to conflict with the proper conduct of the inspection.

(5) The inspection must review one or more statutory audits in which the person to whom the inspection relates has participated.

(6) The inspection must include an assessment of—

    (a)   the person's compliance with the body's rules established for the purposes of paragraphs 9 (professional integrity and independence), 10 (technical standards), 10A (technical standards for group audits) and 10C (public interest entity independence requirements);

    (b)   the resources allocated by the person to statutory audit work;

    (c)   in the case of an inspection in relation to a firm, its internal quality control system;

    (d)   the remuneration received by the person in respect of statutory audit work.

(7) An inspection conducted in relation to a firm may be treated as an inspection of all individuals responsible for statutory audit work on behalf of that firm, if the firm has a common quality assurance policy with which each such individual is required to comply.

(8) The main conclusions of the inspection must be recorded in a report which is made available to—

    (a)   the person to whom the inspection relates, and

    (b)   the body.

(9) The body must, at least once in every calendar year, deliver to the Secretary of State a summary of the results of inspections conducted under this paragraph.

(10) In this paragraph—

    "major audit" means a statutory audit conducted in respect of—

        (a)   a public interest entity, or

        (b)   any other person in whose financial condition there is a major public interest;

    "statutory audit function" means any function performed as a statutory auditor.]

Membership, eligibility and discipline

14. The rules and practices of the body relating to—

    (a)   the admission and expulsion of members,

    (b)   the grant and withdrawal of eligibility for appointment as a statutory auditor, and

    (c)   the discipline it exercises over its members,

must be fair and reasonable and include adequate provision for appeals.

Investigation of complaints

15. (1) The body must have effective arrangements for the investigation of complaints against—

    (a)   persons who are eligible under its rules for appointment as a statutory auditor, and

    (b)   the body in respect of matters arising out of its functions as a supervisory body.

(2) The arrangements mentioned in sub-paragraph (1) may make provision for the whole or part of that function to be performed by and to be the responsibility of a body or person independent of the body itself.

Independent investigation for disciplinary purposes of public interest cases

16. (1) The body must—

    (a)   participate in arrangements within paragraph 24(1), and

    (b)   have rules and practices designed to ensure that, where the designated persons have decided that any particular disciplinary action should be taken against a member of the body following the conclusion of an investigation under such arrangements, that decision is to be treated as if it were a decision made by the body in disciplinary proceedings against the member.

(2) In sub-paragraph (1) "the designated persons" means the persons who, under the arrangements, have the function of deciding whether (and if so, what) disciplinary action should be taken against a member of the body in the light of an investigation carried out under the arrangements.

[Transfer of papers to third countries

16A. (1)   The body must have adequate rules and practices designed to ensure that a person eligible under its rules for appointment as a statutory auditor transfers audit working papers to a third country competent authority only in accordance with the requirements of—
(a)   paragraph 16AA (transfer to approved third country competent authority), or
(b)   paragraph 16AB (transfer for purposes of investigation).

(2)   The body must also have adequate rules and practices designed to ensure that a person eligible under its rules for appointment as a statutory auditor must refuse to transfer audit working papers to a third country competent authority if the Secretary of State directs under section 1253E(6) that such a transfer should not take place.

Transfer to approved third country competent authority

16AA. The requirements of this paragraph are that—
(a)   the transfer is to an approved third country competent authority, and
(b)   the Secretary of State has approved the transfer.

Transfer for purposes of investigation of auditor

16AB. (1)   The requirements of this paragraph are that—
(a)   the transfer to the third country competent authority is made for the purposes of an investigation of an auditor or audit firm, and
(b)   the following conditions are met.

(2)   The first condition is that the authority has requested the audit working papers for the purposes of an investigation which has been initiated by itself or another third country competent authority established in the same third country.

(3)   The second condition is that the audit working papers relate to audits of companies that—
(a)   have issued securities in that third country, or
(b)   form part of a group issuing statutory consolidated accounts in that third country.

(4)   The third condition is that, where the authority has made the request for the audit working papers directly to the statutory auditor, the authority has given the Secretary of State advance notice of the request, indicating the reasons for it.

(5)   The fourth condition is that the authority has entered into arrangements with the Secretary of State in accordance with section 1253E.]

Meeting of claims arising out of audit work

17. (1)   The body must have adequate rules or arrangements designed to ensure that persons eligible under its rules for appointment as a statutory auditor take such steps as may reasonably be expected of them to secure that they are able to meet claims against them arising out of statutory audit work.

(2)   This may be achieved by professional indemnity insurance or other appropriate arrangements.

Register of auditors and other information to be made available

18. The body must have rules requiring persons eligible under its rules for appointment as a statutory auditor to comply with any obligations imposed on them by—
(a)   requirements under section 1224 (Secretary of State's power to call for information);
(b)   regulations under section 1239 (the register of auditors);
(c)   regulations under section 1240 (information to be made available to the public).

Taking account of costs of compliance

19. The body must have satisfactory arrangements for taking account, in framing its rules, of the cost to those to whom the rules would apply of complying with those rules and any other controls to which they are subject.

Promotion and maintenance of standards

20. The body must be able and willing—
(a)   to promote and maintain high standards of integrity in the conduct of statutory audit work, and

(b) to co-operate, by the sharing of information and otherwise, with the Secretary of State and any other authority, body or person having responsibility in the United Kingdom for the qualification, supervision or regulation of auditors.

[Interpretation

20A. In this Part of this Schedule—
"public interest entity" means an issuer—
    (a) whose transferable securities are admitted to trading on a regulated market; and
    (b) the audit of which is a statutory audit (see section 1210(1));
"issuer" and "regulated market" have the same meaning as in Part 6 of the Financial Services and Markets Act 2000 (see sections 102A to 103); and
"transferable securities" means anything which is a transferable security for the purposes of Directive 2004/39/EC of the European Parliament and of the Council on markets in financial instruments.]

NOTES
Commencement: 6 April 2008.
Commencement (transitional provisions): see the note to s 1217 at **[1.1217]**.
Para 6: sub-para (1)(aa), and the words in square brackets in sub-para (1)(a) inserted, and sub-paras (2), (2A) substituted (for original sub-para (2)), by the Statutory Auditors and Third Country Auditors Regulations 2007, SI 2007/3494, reg 17, as from 6 April 2008.
Para 7: words in square brackets substituted by SI 2007/3494, reg 18, as from 6 April 2008.
Para 9: word omitted from sub-para (1)(a) repealed, sub-paras (1)(c)–(e) inserted, and sub-paras (3), (4) substituted, by SI 2007/3494, reg 19, as from 6 April 2008.
Paras 10A–10C, 20A: inserted by SI 2007/3494, regs 20, 21, 25, as from 6 April 2008.
Para 12: sub-paras (1), (1A) substituted (for original sub-para (1)), and sub-para (3) added, by SI 2007/3494, reg 22, as from 6 April 2008.
Para 13: substituted by SI 2007/3494, reg 23, as from 6 April 2008.
Para 16A: originally inserted by SI 2007/3494, regs 20, 24, as from 6 April 2008; subsequently substituted (by new paras 16A, 16AA, 16AB) by the Companies Act 2006 (Transfer of Audit Working Papers to Third Countries) Regulations 2010, SI 2010/2537, reg 5, as from 15 November 2010 (note that reg 8 of the 2010 Regulations provides that notwithstanding Sch 4, para 38 to the Companies Act 2006 (Commencement No 5, Transitional Provisions and Savings) Order 2007 (which limits the application of certain provisions of the Companies Act 2006, including this Schedule), paras 16A, 16AA, 16AB (as inserted by the 2010 Regulations) apply in relation to the supervision of auditors appointed for any financial year).
Transfer of functions: as to the transfer of the functions of the Secretary of State under Part 42 of this Act (which includes this Schedule) to the Professional Oversight Board, see the Statutory Auditors (Delegation of Functions etc) Order 2008, SI 2008/496, art 4.

PART 3
ARRANGEMENTS IN WHICH RECOGNISED SUPERVISORY BODIES ARE REQUIRED TO PARTICIPATE

Arrangements for setting standards relating to professional integrity and independence

[1.1323]
21. The arrangements referred to in paragraph 9(2) are appropriate arrangements—
    (a) for the determining of standards for the purposes of the rules and practices mentioned in paragraph 9(1), and
    (b) for ensuring that the determination of those standards is done independently of the body.

Arrangements for setting technical standards

22. The arrangements referred to in [paragraphs 10(2) and 10A(2)] are appropriate arrangements—
    (a) for the determining of standards for the purposes of the rules and practices mentioned in [paragraphs 10(1) and 10A(1) respectively], and
    (b) for ensuring that the determination of those standards is done independently of the body.

[Arrangements for setting standards relating to public interest entity reporting requirements

22A. The arrangements referred to in paragraph 10B(3) are appropriate arrangements—
    (a) for the determining of standards for the purposes of the rules and practices mentioned in paragraph 10B(1), and
    (b) for ensuring that the determination of those standards is done independently of the body.

Arrangements for setting standards relating to public interest entity independence requirements

22B. The arrangements referred to in paragraph 10C(2) are appropriate arrangements—
    (a) for the determining of standards for the purposes of the rules and practices mentioned in paragraph 10C(1), and
    (b) for ensuring that the determination of those standards is done independently of the body.]

Arrangements for independent monitoring of audits of listed companies and other major bodies

23. (1) The arrangements referred to in [paragraph 13(1)(b)] are appropriate arrangements—

(a) for enabling the performance by members of the body of statutory audit functions in respect of major audits to be monitored by means of inspections carried out under the arrangements, and

(b) for ensuring that the carrying out of such monitoring and inspections is done independently of the body.

[(1A) Subject to sub-paragraph (1C), the arrangements referred to in sub-paragraph (1) must include provision for an inspection conducted in relation to each person eligible for appointment as a statutory auditor at least once every three years.

(1B) Sub-paragraphs (4) to (9) of paragraph 13 apply in relation to inspections under sub-paragraph (1A) as they apply in relation to inspections under that paragraph.

(1C) The arrangements referred to in sub-paragraph (1) may provide that the body performing the inspections may decide that all or part of the inspection referred to in sub-paragraph (1A) is not required in the case of a member of a supervisory body who performs statutory audit functions in respect of ten or fewer major audits per year.

(1D) If—

(a) the arrangements make the provision referred to in sub-paragraph (1C), and

(b) the body performing the inspections decides that all of an inspection is not required in relation to a member,

the supervisory body must ensure that the arrangements referred to in paragraph 13(1)(a) apply in relation to that member, subject to the modification specified in sub-paragraph (1F).

(1E) If—

(a) the arrangements make the provision referred to in sub-paragraph (1C), and

(b) the body performing the inspections decides that part of an inspection is not required in relation to a member,

the supervisory body must ensure that the arrangements referred to in paragraph 13(1)(a) apply in relation to that part of the inspection of that member, subject to the modification specified in sub-paragraph (1F).

(1F) For the purposes of sub-paragraphs (1D) and (1E), paragraph 13(3) applies with the substitution of "three years" for "six years".]

(2) In this paragraph "major audit" and "statutory audit function" have the same meaning as in paragraph 13.

Arrangements for independent investigation for disciplinary purposes of public interest cases

24. (1) The arrangements referred to in paragraph 16(1) are appropriate arrangements—

(a) for the carrying out of investigations into public interest cases arising in connection with the performance of statutory audit functions by members of the body,

(b) for the holding of disciplinary hearings relating to members of the body which appear to be desirable following the conclusion of such investigations,

(c) for requiring such hearings to be held in public except where the interests of justice otherwise require,

(d) for the persons before whom such hearings have taken place to decide whether (and, if so, what) disciplinary action should be taken against the members to whom the hearings related, and

(e) for ensuring that the carrying out of those investigations, the holding of those hearings and the taking of those decisions are done independently of the body.

(2) In this paragraph—

"public interest cases" means matters which raise or appear to raise important issues affecting the public interest;

"statutory audit function" means any function performed as a statutory auditor.

Supplementary: arrangements to operate independently of body

25. (1) This paragraph applies for the purposes of—

(a) paragraph 21(b),

(b) paragraph 22(b),

(c) paragraph 23(1)(b), or

(d) paragraph 24(1)(e).

(2) Arrangements are not to be regarded as appropriate for the purpose of ensuring that a thing is done independently of the body unless they are designed to ensure that the body—

(a) will have no involvement in the appointment or selection of any of the persons who are to be responsible for doing that thing, and

(b) will not otherwise be involved in the doing of that thing.

(3) Sub-paragraph (2) imposes a minimum requirement and does not preclude the possibility that additional criteria may need to be satisfied in order for the arrangements to be regarded as appropriate for the purpose in question.

Supplementary: funding of arrangements

26. The body must pay any of the costs of maintaining any arrangements within paragraph 21, 22, 23 or 24 which the arrangements provide are to be paid by it.

Supplementary: scope of arrangement

27. Arrangements may qualify as arrangements within any of paragraphs 21, 22, 23 and 24 even though the matters for which they provide are more extensive in any respect than those mentioned in the applicable paragraph.

NOTES

Commencement: 6 April 2008.

Commencement (transitional provisions): see the note to s 1217 at **[1.1217]**.

Para 22: words in square brackets substituted by the Statutory Auditors and Third Country Auditors Regulations 2007, SI 2007/3494, reg 26, as from 6 April 2008.

Paras 22A, 22B: inserted by SI 2007/3494, reg 27, as from 6 April 2008.

Para 23: words in first pair of square brackets substituted, and sub-paras (1A)–(1F) inserted, by SI 2007/3494, reg 28, as from 6 April 2008.

SCHEDULE 11
RECOGNISED PROFESSIONAL QUALIFICATIONS

Section 1220

PART 1
GRANT AND REVOCATION OF RECOGNITION OF A PROFESSIONAL QUALIFICATION

Application for recognition of professional qualification

[1.1324]

1. (1) A qualifying body may apply to the Secretary of State for an order declaring a qualification offered by it to be a recognised professional qualification for the purposes of this Part of this Act ("a recognition order").

(2) In this Part of this Act "a recognised qualifying body" means a qualifying body offering a recognised professional qualification.

(3) Any application must be—

    (a)   made in such manner as the Secretary of State may direct, and

    (b)   accompanied by such information as the Secretary of State may reasonably require for the purpose of determining the application.

(4) At any time after receiving an application and before determining it the Secretary of State may require the applicant to furnish additional information.

(5) The directions and requirements given or imposed under sub-paragraphs (3) and (4) may differ as between different applications.

(6) The Secretary of State may require any information to be furnished under this paragraph to be in such form or verified in such manner as he may specify.

(7) In the case of examination standards, the verification required may include independent moderation of the examinations over such a period as the Secretary of State considers necessary.

(8) Every application must be accompanied by—

    (a)   a copy of the applicant's rules, and

    (b)   a copy of any guidance issued by the applicant in writing.

(9) The reference in sub-paragraph (8)(b) to guidance issued by the applicant is a reference to any guidance or recommendation—

    (a)   issued or made by it to all or any class of persons holding or seeking to hold a qualification, or approved or seeking to be approved by the body for the purposes of giving practical training,

    (b)   relevant for the purposes of this Part of this Act, and

    (c)   intended to have continuing effect,

including any guidance or recommendation relating to a matter within sub-paragraph (10).

(10) The matters within this sub-paragraph are—

    (a)   admission to or expulsion from a course of study leading to a qualification,

    (b)   the award or deprivation of a qualification, and

    (c)   the approval of a person for the purposes of giving practical training or the withdrawal of such an approval,

so far as relevant for the purposes of this Part of this Act.

Grant and refusal of recognition

2. (1)   The Secretary of State may, on an application duly made in accordance with paragraph 1 and after being furnished with all such information as he may require under that paragraph, make or refuse to make a recognition order in respect of the qualification in relation to which the application was made.

(2)   The Secretary of State may make a recognition order only if it appears to him, from the information furnished by the applicant and having regard to any other information in his possession, that the requirements of Part 2 of this Schedule are satisfied in relation to the qualification.

(3)   Where the Secretary of State refuses an application for a recognition order he must give the applicant a written notice to that effect specifying which requirements, in his opinion, are not satisfied.

(4)   A recognition order must state the date on which it takes effect.

Revocation of recognition

3. (1)   A recognition order may be revoked by a further order made by the Secretary of State if at any time it appears to him—

   (a)   that any requirement of Part 2 of this Schedule is not satisfied in relation to the qualification to which the recognition order relates, or

   (b)   that the qualifying body has failed to comply with any obligation imposed on it by or by virtue of this Part of this Act.

(2)   An order revoking a recognition order must state the date on which it takes effect, which must be after the period of three months beginning with the date on which the revocation order is made.

(3)   Before revoking a recognition order the Secretary of State must—

   (a)   give written notice of his intention to do so to the qualifying body,

   (b)   take such steps as he considers reasonably practicable for bringing the notice to the attention of persons holding the qualification or in the course of studying for it, and

   (c)   publish the notice in such manner as he thinks appropriate for bringing it to the attention of any other persons who are in his opinion likely to be affected.

(4)   A notice under sub-paragraph (3) must—

   (a)   state the reasons for which the Secretary of State proposes to act, and

   (b)   give particulars of the rights conferred by sub-paragraph (5).

(5)   A person within sub-paragraph (6) may, within the period of three months beginning with the date of service or publication or such longer period as the Secretary of State may allow, make written representations to the Secretary of State and, if desired, oral representations to a person appointed for that purpose by the Secretary of State.

(6)   The persons within this sub-paragraph are—

   (a)   the qualifying body on which a notice is served under sub-paragraph (3),

   (b)   any person holding the qualification or in the course of studying for it, and

   (c)   any other person who appears to the Secretary of State to be affected.

(7)   The Secretary of State must have regard to any representations made in accordance with sub-paragraph (5) in determining whether to revoke the recognition order.

(8)   If in any case the Secretary of State considers it essential to do so in the public interest he may revoke a recognition order without regard to the restriction imposed by sub-paragraph (2), even if—

   (a)   no notice has been given or published under sub-paragraph (3), or

   (b)   the period of time for making representations in pursuance of such a notice has not expired.

(9)   An order revoking a recognition order may contain such transitional provision as the Secretary of State thinks necessary or expedient.

(10)   A recognition order may be revoked at the request or with the consent of the qualifying body and any such revocation is not subject to—

   (a)   the restrictions imposed by sub-paragraphs (1) and (2), or

   (b)   the requirements of sub-paragraphs (3) to (5) and (7).

(11)   On making an order revoking a recognition order the Secretary of State must—

   (a)   give written notice of the making of the order to the qualifying body,

   (b)   take such steps as he considers reasonably practicable for bringing the making of the order to the attention of persons holding the qualification or in the course of studying for it, and

   (c)   publish a notice of the making of the order in such manner as he thinks appropriate for bringing it to the attention of any other persons who are in his opinion likely to be affected.

Transitional provision

4.   A recognition order made and not revoked under—

   (a)   paragraph 2(1) of Schedule 12 to the Companies Act 1989 (c 40), or

   (b)   paragraph 2(1) of Schedule 12 to the Companies (Northern Ireland) Order 1990 (SI 1990/593 (NI 5)), before the commencement of this Chapter of this Part of this Act is to have effect after the commencement of this Chapter as a recognition order made under paragraph 2(1) of this Schedule.

Orders not statutory instruments

5. Orders under this Part of this Schedule shall not be made by statutory instrument.

NOTES

Commencement: 20 January 2007 (for the purpose of enabling the exercise of powers to make Orders or Regulations by statutory instrument); 6 April 2008 (otherwise).

Commencement (transitional provisions): see the note to s 1217 at **[1.1217]**.

Transfer of functions: as to the transfer of the functions of the Secretary of State under Part 42 of this Act (which includes this Schedule) to the Professional Oversight Board, see the Statutory Auditors (Delegation of Functions etc) Order 2008, SI 2008/496, art 4.

PART 2
REQUIREMENTS FOR RECOGNITION OF A PROFESSIONAL QUALIFICATION

Entry requirements

[1.1325]

6. (1)　The qualification must only be open to persons who—
(a)　have attained university entrance level, or
(b)　have a sufficient period of professional experience.

(2)　In relation to a person who has not been admitted to a university or other similar establishment in the United Kingdom, "attaining university entrance level" means—
(a)　being educated to such a standard as would entitle him to be considered for such admission on the basis of—
(i)　academic or professional qualifications obtained in the United Kingdom and recognised by the Secretary of State to be of an appropriate standard, or
(ii)　academic or professional qualifications obtained outside the United Kingdom which the Secretary of State considers to be of an equivalent standard, or
(b)　being assessed, on the basis of written tests of a kind appearing to the Secretary of State to be adequate for the purpose (with or without oral examination), as of such a standard of ability as would entitle him to be considered for such admission.

(3)　The assessment, tests and oral examination referred to in sub-paragraph (2)(b) may be conducted by—
(a)　the qualifying body, or
(b)　some other body approved by the Secretary of State.

(4)　The reference in sub-paragraph (1)(b) to "a sufficient period of professional experience" is to not less than seven years' experience in a professional capacity in the fields of finance, law and accountancy.

Requirement for theoretical instruction or professional experience

7. (1)　The qualification must be restricted to persons who—
(a)　have completed a course of theoretical instruction in the subjects prescribed for the purposes of paragraph 8, or
(b)　have a sufficient period of professional experience.

(2)　The reference in sub-paragraph (1)(b) to "a sufficient period of professional experience" is to not less than seven years' experience in a professional capacity in the fields of finance, law and accountancy.

Examination

8. (1)　The qualification must be restricted to persons who have passed an examination (at least part of which is in writing) testing—
(a)　theoretical knowledge of the subjects prescribed for the purposes of this paragraph by regulations made by the Secretary of State, and
(b)　ability to apply that knowledge in practice,
and requiring a standard of attainment at least equivalent to that required to obtain a degree from a university or similar establishment in the United Kingdom.

(2)　The qualification may be awarded to a person without his theoretical knowledge of a subject being tested by examination if he has passed a university or other examination of equivalent standard in that subject or holds a university degree or equivalent qualification in it.

(3)　The qualification may be awarded to a person without his ability to apply his theoretical knowledge of a subject in practice being tested by examination if he has received practical training in that subject which is attested by an examination or diploma recognised by the Secretary of State for the purposes of this paragraph.

(4)　Regulations under this paragraph are subject to negative resolution procedure.

Practical training

9. (1)   The qualification must be restricted to persons who have completed at least three years' practical training of which—

    (a)   part was spent being trained in statutory audit work, and

    (b)   a substantial part was spent being trained in statutory audit work or other audit work of a description approved by the Secretary of State as being similar to statutory audit work.

(2)   For the purpose of sub-paragraph (1) "statutory audit work" includes the work of a person appointed as the auditor of a person under the law of a country or territory outside the United Kingdom where it appears to the Secretary of State that the law and practice with respect to the audit of accounts is similar to that in the United Kingdom.

(3)   The training must be given by persons approved by the body offering the qualification as persons whom the body is satisfied, in the light of undertakings given by them and the supervision to which they are subject (whether by the body itself or some other body or organisation), will provide adequate training.

(4)   At least two-thirds of the training must be given by a person—

    (a)   eligible for appointment as a statutory auditor, or

    (b)   eligible for a corresponding appointment as an auditor under the law of [an EEA State], or part of [an EEA State], other than the United Kingdom.

Supplementary provision with respect to a sufficient period of professional experience

10. (1)   Periods of theoretical instruction in the fields of finance, law and accountancy may be deducted from the required period of professional experience, provided the instruction—

    (a)   lasted at least one year, and

    (b)   is attested by an examination recognised by the Secretary of State for the purposes of this paragraph;

but the period of professional experience may not be so reduced by more than four years.

(2)   The period of professional experience together with the practical training required in the case of persons satisfying the requirement in paragraph 7 by virtue of having a sufficient period of professional experience must not be shorter than the course of theoretical instruction referred to in that paragraph and the practical training required in the case of persons satisfying the requirement of that paragraph by virtue of having completed such a course.

The body offering the qualification

11. (1)   The body offering the qualification must have—

    (a)   rules and arrangements adequate to ensure compliance with the requirements of paragraphs 6 to 10, and

    (b)   adequate arrangements for the effective monitoring of its continued compliance with those requirements.

(2)   The arrangements must include arrangements for monitoring—

    (a)   the standard of the body's examinations, and

    (b)   the adequacy of the practical training given by the persons approved by it for that purpose.

NOTES

Commencement: 20 January 2007 (for the purpose of enabling the exercise of powers to make Orders or Regulations by statutory instrument); 6 April 2008 (otherwise).

Commencement (transitional provisions): see the note to s 1217 at **[1.1217]**.

Para 9: words in square brackets in sub-para (4)(b) substituted by the Statutory Auditors and Third Country Auditors Regulations 2007, SI 2007/3494, reg 44, as from 6 April 2008.

Transfer of functions: as to the transfer of the functions of the Secretary of State under Part 42 of this Act (which includes this Schedule) to the Professional Oversight Board, see the Statutory Auditors (Delegation of Functions etc) Order 2008, SI 2008/496, art 4.

Regulations: the Statutory Auditors and Third Country Auditors Regulations 2007, SI 2007/3494 at **[4.79]**.

[SCHEDULE 11A
SPECIFIED PERSONS, DESCRIPTIONS, DISCLOSURES ETC FOR THE PURPOSES OF SECTION 1224A

PART 1
SPECIFIED PERSONS

[1.1325A]

1. The Secretary of State.

2. The Department of Enterprise, Trade and Investment for Northern Ireland.

3. The Treasury.

4. The Bank of England.

5. The Financial Services Authority.

6. The Commissioners for Her Majesty's Revenue and Customs.

7. The Lord Advocate.

8. The Director of Public Prosecutions.

9. The Director of Public Prosecutions for Northern Ireland.

10. A constable.

11. A procurator fiscal.

12. The Scottish Ministers.

13. A body designated by the Secretary of State under section 1252 (delegation of the Secretary of State's functions).

14. A recognised supervisory body.

15. A recognised qualifying body.

16. A body with which a recognised supervisory body is participating in arrangements for the purposes of paragraph 23 (independent monitoring of audits) or 24 (independent investigation for disciplinary purposes) of Schedule 10 to this Act.

17. The Independent Supervisor.]

NOTES

Commencement: 6 April 2008.

Inserted by the Statutory Auditors and Third Country Auditors Regulations 2007, SI 2007/3494, reg 10(2), Schedule, as from 6 April 2008.

Transfer of functions: as to the transfer of the functions of the Secretary of State under Part 42 of this Act (which includes this Schedule) to the Professional Oversight Board, see the Statutory Auditors (Delegation of Functions etc) Order 2008, SI 2008/496, art 4.

[**PART 2**
SPECIFIED DESCRIPTIONS OF DISCLOSURES

[1.1325B]
18. A disclosure for the purpose of enabling or assisting a person authorised under section 457 of this Act (persons authorised to apply to court) to exercise his functions.

19. A disclosure for the purpose of enabling or assisting an inspector appointed under Part 14 of the Companies Act 1985 (investigation of companies and their affairs, etc) to exercise his functions.

20. A disclosure for the purpose of enabling or assisting a person authorised under section 447 of the Companies Act 1985 (power to require production of documents) or section 84 of the Companies Act 1989 (c 40) (exercise of powers by officer etc) to exercise his functions.

21. A disclosure for the purpose of enabling or assisting a person appointed under section 167 of the Financial Services and Markets Act 2000 (c 8) (general investigations) to conduct an investigation to exercise his functions.

22. A disclosure for the purpose of enabling or assisting a person appointed under section 168 of the Financial Services and Markets Act 2000 (investigations in particular cases) to conduct an investigation to exercise his functions.

23. A disclosure for the purpose of enabling or assisting a person appointed under section 169(1)(b) of the Financial Services and Markets Act 2000 (investigation in support of overseas regulator) to conduct an investigation to exercise his functions.

24. A disclosure for the purpose of enabling or assisting the body corporate responsible for administering the scheme referred to in section 225 of the Financial Services and Markets Act 2000 (the ombudsman scheme) to exercise its functions.

25. A disclosure for the purpose of enabling or assisting a person appointed under paragraph 4 (the panel of ombudsmen) or 5 (the Chief Ombudsman) of Schedule 17 to the Financial Services and Markets Act 2000 to exercise his functions.

26. A disclosure for the purpose of enabling or assisting a person appointed under regulations made under section 262(1) and (2)(k) of the Financial Services and Markets Act 2000 (investigations into open-ended investment companies) to conduct an investigation to exercise his functions.

27. A disclosure for the purpose of enabling or assisting a person appointed under section 284 of the Financial Services and Markets Act 2000 (investigations into affairs of certain collective investment schemes) to conduct an investigation to exercise his functions.

28. A disclosure for the purpose of enabling or assisting the investigator appointed under paragraph 7 of Schedule 1 to the Financial Services and Markets Act 2000 (arrangements for investigation of complaints) to exercise his functions.

29. A disclosure for the purpose of enabling or assisting a person appointed by the Treasury to hold an inquiry into matters relating to financial services (including an inquiry under section 15 of the Financial Services and Markets Act 2000 (c 8)) to exercise his functions.

30. A disclosure for the purpose of enabling or assisting the Secretary of State or the Treasury to exercise any of their functions under any of the following—
   (a)   the Companies Acts;
   (b)   Part 5 of the Criminal Justice Act 1993 (c 36) (insider dealing);
   (c)   the Insolvency Act 1986 (c 45);
   (d)   the Company Directors Disqualification Act 1986 (c 46);
   (e)   Part 42 of this Act (statutory auditors)
   (f)   Part 3 (investigations and powers to obtain information) or 7 (financial markets and insolvency) of the Companies Act 1989 (c 40);
   (g)   the Financial Services and Markets Act 2000.

31. A disclosure for the purpose of enabling or assisting the Scottish Ministers to exercise their functions under the enactments relating to insolvency.

32. A disclosure for the purpose of enabling or assisting the Department of Enterprise, Trade and Investment for Northern Ireland to exercise any powers conferred on it by the enactments relating to companies or insolvency.

33. A disclosure for the purpose of enabling or assisting a person appointed or authorised by the Department of Enterprise, Trade and Investment for Northern Ireland under the enactments relating to companies or insolvency to exercise his functions.

34. A disclosure for the purpose of enabling or assisting the Pensions Regulator to exercise the functions conferred on it by or by virtue of any of the following—
   (a)   the Pension Schemes Act 1993 (c 48);
   (b)   the Pensions Act 1995 (c 26);
   (c)   the Welfare Reform and Pensions Act 1999 (c 30);
   (d)   the Pensions Act 2004 (c 35);
   (e)   any enactment in force in Northern Ireland corresponding to any of those enactments.

35. A disclosure for the purpose of enabling or assisting the Board of the Pension Protection Fund to exercise the functions conferred on it by or by virtue of Part 2 of the Pensions Act 2004 or any enactment in force in Northern Ireland corresponding to that Part.

36. A disclosure for the purpose of enabling or assisting—
   (a)   the Bank of England,
   (b)   the European Central Bank, or
   (c)   the central bank of any country or territory outside the United Kingdom, to exercise its functions.

37. A disclosure for the purpose of enabling or assisting the Commissioners for Her Majesty's Revenue and Customs to exercise their functions.

38. A disclosure for the purpose of enabling or assisting organs of the Society of Lloyd's (being organs constituted by or under the Lloyd's Act 1982 (c xiv)) to exercise their functions under or by virtue of the Lloyd's Acts 1871 to 1982.

39. A disclosure for the purpose of enabling or assisting the Office of Fair Trading to exercise its functions under any of the following—
   (a)   the Fair Trading Act 1973 (c 41);
   (b)   the Consumer Credit Act 1974 (c 39);
   (c)   the Estate Agents Act 1979 (c 38);
   (d)   the Competition Act 1980 (c 21);
   (e)   the Competition Act 1998 (c 41);
   (f)   the Financial Services and Markets Act 2000 (c 8);
   (g)   the Enterprise Act 2002 (c 40);
   (h)   the Control of Misleading Advertisements Regulations 1988 (SI 1988/915);
   (i)   the Unfair Terms in Consumer Contracts Regulations 1999 (SI 1999/2083).

40. A disclosure for the purpose of enabling or assisting the Competition Commission to exercise its functions under any of the following—

(a)   the Fair Trading Act 1973;
(b)   the Competition Act 1980;
(c)   the Competition Act 1998;
(d)   the Enterprise Act 2002.

41. A disclosure with a view to the institution of, or otherwise for the purposes of, proceedings before the Competition Appeal Tribunal.

42. A disclosure for the purpose of enabling or assisting an enforcer under Part 8 of the Enterprise Act 2002 (enforcement of consumer legislation) to exercise its functions under that Part.

43. A disclosure for the purpose of enabling or assisting the Takeover Panel to perform any of its functions under Part 28 of this Act (takeovers etc).

44. A disclosure for the purpose of enabling or assisting the Charity Commission to exercise its functions.

45. A disclosure for the purpose of enabling or assisting the Attorney General to exercise his functions in connection with charities.

46. A disclosure for the purpose of enabling or assisting the National Lottery Commission to exercise its functions under sections 5 to 10 (licensing) and 15 (power of Secretary of State to require information) of the National Lottery etc Act 1993 (c 39).

47. A disclosure by the National Lottery Commission to *the National Audit Office* for the purpose of enabling or assisting the Comptroller and Auditor General to carry out an examination under Part 2 of the National Audit Act 1983 (c 44) into the economy, effectiveness and efficiency with which the National Lottery Commission has used its resources in discharging its functions under sections 5 to 10 of the National Lottery etc Act 1993.

48. A disclosure for the purpose of enabling or assisting a qualifying body under the Unfair Terms in Consumer Contracts Regulations 1999 (SI 1999/2083) to exercise its functions under those Regulations.

49. A disclosure for the purpose of enabling or assisting an enforcement authority under the Consumer Protection (Distance Selling) Regulations 2000 (SI 2000/2334) to exercise its functions under those Regulations.

50. A disclosure for the purpose of enabling or assisting an enforcement authority under the Financial Services (Distance Marketing) Regulations 2004 (SI 2004/2095) to exercise its functions under those Regulations.

51. A disclosure for the purpose of enabling or assisting a local weights and measures authority in England and Wales to exercise its functions under section 230(2) of the Enterprise Act 2002 (c 40) (notice of intention to prosecute, etc).

52. A disclosure for the purpose of enabling or assisting the Financial Services Authority to exercise its functions under any of the following—
(a)   the legislation relating to friendly societies or to industrial and provident societies;
(b)   the Building Societies Act 1986 (c 53);
(c)   Part 7 of the Companies Act 1989 (c 40) (financial markets and insolvency);
(d)   the Financial Services and Markets Act 2000 (c 8).

53. A disclosure for the purpose of enabling or assisting the competent authority for the purposes of Part 6 of the Financial Services and Markets Act 2000 (official listing) to exercise its functions under that Part.

54. A disclosure for the purpose of enabling or assisting a body corporate established in accordance with section 212(1) of the Financial Services and Markets Act 2000 (compensation scheme manager) to exercise its functions.

55. A disclosure for the purpose of enabling or assisting a recognised investment exchange or a recognised clearing house to exercise its functions as such.
"Recognised investment exchange" and "recognised clearing house" have the same meaning as in section 285 of the Financial Services and Markets Act 2000.

56. A disclosure for the purpose of enabling or assisting a person approved under the Uncertificated Securities Regulations 2001 (SI 2001/3755) as an operator of a relevant system (within the meaning of those regulations) to exercise his functions.

57. A disclosure for the purpose of enabling or assisting a body designated under section 326(1) of the Financial Services and Markets Act 2000 (designated professional bodies) to exercise its functions in its capacity as a body designated under that section.

58. A disclosure with a view to the institution of, or otherwise for the purposes of, civil proceedings arising under or by virtue of the Financial Services and Markets Act 2000.

59. A disclosure for the purpose of enabling or assisting a body designated by order under section 1252 of this Act (delegation of functions of Secretary of State) to exercise its functions under Part 42 of this Act (statutory auditors).

60. A disclosure for the purpose of enabling or assisting a recognised supervisory or qualifying body, within the meaning of Part 42 of this Act, to exercise its functions as such.

61. A disclosure for the purpose of making available to an audited person information relating to a statutory audit of that person's accounts.

62. A disclosure for the purpose of making available to the public information relating to monitoring or inspections carried out under arrangements within paragraph 23(1) of Schedule 10 to this Act (arrangements for independent monitoring of audits of listed companies and other major bodies), provided such information does not identify any audited person.

63. A disclosure for the purpose of enabling or assisting an official receiver (including the Accountant in Bankruptcy in Scotland and the Official Assignee in Northern Ireland) to exercise his functions under the enactments relating to insolvency.

64. A disclosure for the purpose of enabling or assisting the Insolvency Practitioners Tribunal to exercise its functions under the Insolvency Act 1986 (c 45).

65. A disclosure for the purpose of enabling or assisting a body that is for the time being a recognised professional body for the purposes of section 391 of the Insolvency Act 1986 (recognised professional bodies) to exercise its functions as such.

66. A disclosure for the purpose of enabling or assisting an overseas regulatory authority to exercise its regulatory functions.
"Overseas regulatory authority" and "regulatory functions" have the same meaning as in section 82 of the Companies Act 1989.

67. A disclosure for the purpose of enabling or assisting the Regulator of Community Interest Companies to exercise functions under the Companies (Audit, Investigations and Community Enterprise) Act 2004 (c 27).

68. A disclosure with a view to the institution of, or otherwise for the purposes of, criminal proceedings.

69. A disclosure for the purpose of enabling or assisting a person authorised by the Secretary of State under Part 2, 3 or 4 of the Proceeds of Crime Act 2002 (c 29) to exercise his functions.

70. A disclosure with a view to the institution of, or otherwise for the purposes of, proceedings on an application under section 6, 7 or 8 of the Company Directors Disqualification Act 1986 (c 46) (disqualification for unfitness).

[**71.** A disclosure with a view to the institution of, or otherwise for the purposes of, proceedings before the Upper Tribunal in respect of—
- (a)   a decision of the Financial Services Authority;
- (b)   a decision of the Bank of England; or
- (c)   a decision of a person relating to the assessment of any compensation or consideration under the Banking (Special Provisions) Act 2008 or the Banking Act 2009.]

72. A disclosure for the purposes of proceedings before the Financial Services Tribunal by virtue of the Financial Services and Markets Act 2000 (Transitional Provisions) (Partly Completed Procedures) Order 2001 (SI 2001/3592).

73. A disclosure for the purposes of proceedings before [a tribunal in relation to a decision of the Pensions Regulator].

74. A disclosure for the purpose of enabling or assisting a body appointed under section 14 of the Companies (Audit, Investigations and Community Enterprise) Act 2004 (supervision of periodic accounts and reports of issuers of listed securities) to exercise functions mentioned in subsection (2) of that section.

75. A disclosure with a view to the institution of, or otherwise for the purposes of, disciplinary proceedings relating to the performance by a relevant lawyer, foreign lawyer, auditor, accountant, valuer or actuary of his professional duties.
In this paragraph—
"foreign lawyer" means a person (other than a relevant lawyer) who is a foreign lawyer within the meaning of section 89(9) of the Courts and Legal Services Act 1990;
"relevant lawyer" means—

(a)   a person who, for the purposes of the Legal Services Act 2007, is an authorised person in relation to an activity which constitutes a reserved legal activity (within the meaning of that Act),

(b)   a solicitor or barrister in Northern Ireland, or

(c)   a solicitor or advocate in Scotland.

76. A disclosure with a view to the institution of, or otherwise for the purposes of, disciplinary proceedings relating to the performance by a public servant of his duties.

"Public servant" means an officer or employee of the Crown.

77. A disclosure for the purpose of the provision of a summary or collection of information framed in such a way as not to enable the identity of any person to whom the information relates to be ascertained.

78. A disclosure in pursuance of any Community obligation.]

NOTES

Commencement: 6 April 2008.

Inserted by the Statutory Auditors and Third Country Auditors Regulations 2007, SI 2007/3494, reg 10(2), Schedule, as from 6 April 2008.

Para 47: for the words in italics there are substituted the words "the Comptroller and Auditor General" by the Budget Responsibility and National Audit Act 2011, s 26, Sch 5, Pt 2, paras 29, 31, as from a day to be appointed.

Para 71: substituted by the Transfer of Tribunal Functions Order 2010, SI 2010/22, art 5(1), Sch 2, paras 141, 143(a), as from 6 April 2010 (for transitional provisions and savings in relation to existing cases and appeals from the Financial Services and Markets Tribunal, see Sch 5 to that Order).

Para 73: words in square brackets substituted by SI 2010/22, art 5(1), Sch 2, paras 141, 143(b), as from 6 April 2010 (for transitional provisions and savings in relation to existing cases and appeals from the Pensions Regulator Tribunal, see Sch 5 to that Order).

Transfer of functions: as to the transfer of the functions of the Secretary of State under Part 42 of this Act (which includes this Schedule) to the Professional Oversight Board, see the Statutory Auditors (Delegation of Functions etc) Order 2008, SI 2008/496, art 4.

[PART 3
OVERSEAS REGULATORY BODIES

[1.1325C]

79. A disclosure is made in accordance with this Part of this Schedule if it is made to an EEA competent authority in accordance with section 1253B (requests from EEA competent authorities).

80. A disclosure is made in accordance with this Part of this Schedule if it is—

(a)   a transfer of audit working papers to a third country competent authority in accordance with rules imposed under paragraph 16A of Schedule 10 (transfer of papers to third countries), or

(b)   a disclosure other than a transfer of audit working papers made to a third country competent authority for the purpose of enabling or assisting the authority to exercise its functions.]

NOTES

Commencement: 6 April 2008.

Inserted by the Statutory Auditors and Third Country Auditors Regulations 2007, SI 2007/3494, reg 10(2), Schedule, as from 6 April 2008.

Transfer of functions: as to the transfer of the functions of the Secretary of State under Part 42 of this Act (which includes this Schedule) to the Professional Oversight Board, see the Statutory Auditors (Delegation of Functions etc) Order 2008, SI 2008/496, art 4.

SCHEDULE 12
ARRANGEMENTS IN WHICH REGISTERED THIRD COUNTRY AUDITORS ARE REQUIRED TO PARTICIPATE

Section 1242

Arrangements for independent monitoring of audits of [UK-traded non-EEA companies]

[1.1326]

1. (1)   The arrangements referred to in section 1242(1)(a) are appropriate arrangements—

(a)   for enabling the performance by the registered third country auditor of [functions related to the audit of UK-traded non-EEA companies] to be monitored by means of inspections carried out under the arrangements, and

(b)   for ensuring that the carrying out of such monitoring and inspections is done independently of the registered third country auditor.

(2)   . . .

Arrangements for independent investigations for disciplinary purposes

2. (1)   The arrangements referred to in section 1242(1)(b) are appropriate arrangements—

(a) for the carrying out of investigations into matters arising in connection with the performance of [functions related to the audit of UK-traded non-EEA companies] by the registered third country auditor,

(b) for the holding of disciplinary hearings relating to the registered third country auditor which appear to be desirable following the conclusion of such investigations,

(c) for requiring such hearings to be held in public except where the interests of justice otherwise require,

(d) for the persons before whom such hearings have taken place to decide whether (and, if so, what) disciplinary action should be taken against the registered third country auditor, and

(e) for ensuring that the carrying out of those investigations, the holding of those hearings and the taking of those decisions are done independently of the registered third country auditor.

(2) In this paragraph—

"disciplinary action" includes the imposition of a fine; and

. . .

Supplementary: arrangements to operate independently of third country auditor

3. (1) This paragraph applies for the purposes of—

(a) paragraph 1(1)(b), or

(b) paragraph 2(1)(e).

(2) Arrangements are not to be regarded as appropriate for the purpose of ensuring that a thing is done independently of the registered third country auditor unless they are designed to ensure that the registered third country auditor—

(a) will have no involvement in the appointment or selection of any of the persons who are to be responsible for doing that thing, and

(b) will not otherwise be involved in the doing of that thing.

(3) Sub-paragraph (2) imposes a minimum requirement and does not preclude the possibility that additional criteria may need to be satisfied in order for the arrangements to be regarded as appropriate for the purpose in question.

Supplementary: funding of arrangements

4. (1) The registered third country auditor must pay any of the costs of maintaining any relevant arrangements which the arrangements provide are to be paid by it.

(2) For this purpose "relevant arrangements" are arrangements within paragraph 1 or 2 in which the registered third country auditor is obliged to participate.

Supplementary: scope of arrangements

5. Arrangements may qualify as arrangements within either of paragraphs 1 and 2 even though the matters for which they provide are more extensive in any respect than those mentioned in the applicable paragraph.

Specification of particular arrangements by the Secretary of State

6. (1) If there exist two or more sets of arrangements within paragraph 1 or within paragraph 2, the obligation of a registered third country auditor under section 1242(1)(a) or (b), as the case may be, is to participate in such set of arrangements as the Secretary of State may by order specify.

(2) An order under sub-paragraph (1) is subject to negative resolution procedure.

NOTES

Commencement: 20 January 2007 (for the purpose of enabling the exercise of powers to make Orders or Regulations by statutory instrument); 29 June 2008 (otherwise).

Commencement (transitional provisions): see the note to s 1242 at **[1.1242]**.

Para 1: words in square brackets in sub-para (1)(a) and in the heading preceding this paragraph substituted, and sub-para (2) repealed, by the Statutory Auditors and Third Country Auditors Regulations 2007, SI 2007/3494, reg 33(1)–(3), as from 29 June 2008.

Para 2: words in square brackets in sub-para (1)(a) substituted, and definition omitted from sub-para (2) repealed, by SI 2007/3494, reg 33(1), (4), as from 29 June 2008.

Transfer of functions: as to the transfer of the functions of the Secretary of State under Part 42 of this Act (which includes this Schedule) to the Professional Oversight Board, see the Statutory Auditors (Delegation of Functions etc) Order 2008, SI 2008/496, art 4.

SCHEDULE 13
SUPPLEMENTARY PROVISIONS WITH RESPECT TO DELEGATION ORDER
Section 1252

Operation of this Schedule

[1.1327]

1. (1) This Schedule has effect in relation to a body designated by a delegation order under section 1252 as follows—

(a) paragraphs 2 to 12 have effect in relation to the body where it is established by the order;

(b)   paragraphs 2 and 6 to 11 have effect in relation to the body where it is an existing body;

(c)   paragraph 13 has effect in relation to the body where it is an existing body that is an unincorporated association.

(2)   In their operation in accordance with sub-paragraph (1)(b), paragraphs 2 and 6 apply only in relation to—

(a)   things done by or in relation to the body in or in connection with the exercise of functions transferred to it by the delegation order, and

(b)   functions of the body which are functions so transferred.

(3)   Any power conferred by this Schedule to make provision by order is a power to make provision by an order under section 1252.

Status

2. The body is not to be regarded as acting on behalf of the Crown and its members, officers and employees are not to be regarded as Crown servants.

Name, members and chairman

3. (1)   The body is to be known by such name as may be specified in the delegation order.

(2)   The body is to consist of such persons (not being less than eight) as the Secretary of State may appoint after such consultation as he thinks appropriate.

(3)   The chairman of the body is to be such person as the Secretary of State may appoint from among its members.

(4)   The Secretary of State may make provision by order as to—

(a)   the terms on which the members of the body are to hold and vacate office;

(b)   the terms on which a person appointed as chairman is to hold and vacate the office of chairman.

Financial provisions

4. (1)   The body must pay to its chairman and members such remuneration, and such allowances in respect of expenses properly incurred by them in the performance of their duties, as the Secretary of State may determine.

(2)   As regards any chairman or member in whose case the Secretary of State so determines, the body must pay or make provision for the payment of—

(a)   such pension, allowance or gratuity to or in respect of that person on his retirement or death, or

(b)   such contributions or other payment towards the provision of such a pension, allowance or gratuity,

as the Secretary of State may determine.

(3)   Where—

(a)   a person ceases to be a member of the body otherwise than on the expiry of his term of office, and

(b)   it appears to the Secretary of State that there are special circumstances which make it right for that person to receive compensation,

the body must make a payment to him by way of compensation of such amount as the Secretary of State may determine.

Proceedings

5. (1)   The delegation order may contain such provision as the Secretary of State considers appropriate with respect to the proceedings of the body.

(2)   The delegation order may, in particular—

(a)   authorise the body to discharge any functions by means of committees consisting wholly or partly of members of the body;

(b)   provide that the validity of proceedings of the body, or of any such committee, is not affected by any vacancy among the members or any defect in the appointment of any member.

Fees

6. (1)   The body may retain fees payable to it.

(2)   The fees must be applied for—

(a)   meeting the expenses of the body in discharging its functions, and

(b)   any purposes incidental to those functions.

(3)   Those expenses include any expenses incurred by the body on such staff, accommodation, services and other facilities as appear to it to be necessary or expedient for the proper performance of its functions.

(4) In prescribing the amount of fees in the exercise of the functions transferred to it the body must prescribe such fees as appear to it sufficient to defray those expenses, taking one year with another.

(5) Any exercise by the body of the power to prescribe fees requires the approval of the Secretary of State.

(6) The Secretary of State may, after consultation with the body, by order vary or revoke any regulations prescribing fees made by the body.

Legislative functions

7. (1) Regulations or an order made by the body in the exercise of the functions transferred to it must be made by instrument in writing, but not by statutory instrument.

(2) The instrument must specify the provision of this Part of this Act under which it is made.

(3) The Secretary of State may by order impose such requirements as he thinks necessary or expedient as to the circumstances and manner in which the body must consult on any regulations or order it proposes to make.

(4) Nothing in this Part applies to make regulations or an order made by the body subject to negative resolution procedure or affirmative resolution procedure.

8. (1) Immediately after an instrument is made it must be printed and made available to the public with or without payment.

(2) A person is not to be taken to have contravened any regulation or order if he shows that at the time of the alleged contravention the instrument containing the regulation or order had not been made available as required by this paragraph.

9. (1) The production of a printed copy of an instrument purporting to be made by the body on which is endorsed a certificate signed by an officer of the body authorised by it for the purpose and stating—
- (a) that the instrument was made by the body,
- (b) that the copy is a true copy of the instrument, and
- (c) that on a specified date the instrument was made available to the public as required by paragraph 8,

is evidence (or, in Scotland, sufficient evidence) of the facts stated in the certificate.

(2) A certificate purporting to be signed as mentioned in sub-paragraph (1) is to be deemed to have been duly signed unless the contrary is shown.

(3) Any person wishing in any legal proceedings to cite an instrument made by the body may require the body to cause a copy of it to be endorsed with such a certificate as is mentioned in this paragraph.

Report and accounts

10. (1) The body must, at least once in each calendar year for which the delegation order is in force, make a report to the Secretary of State on—
- (a) the discharge of the functions transferred to it, and
- (b) such other matters as the Secretary of State may by order require.

(2) The delegation order may modify sub-paragraph (1) as it has effect in relation to the calendar year in which the order comes into force or is revoked.

(3) The Secretary of State must lay before Parliament copies of each report received by him under this paragraph.

(4) The following provisions of this paragraph apply as follows—
- (a) sub-paragraphs (5) and (6) apply only where the body is established by the order, and
- (b) sub-paragraphs (7) and (8) apply only where the body is an existing body.

(5) The Secretary of State may, with the consent of the Treasury, give directions to the body with respect to its accounts and the audit of its accounts.

(6) A person may only be appointed as auditor of the body if he is eligible for appointment as a statutory auditor.

(7) Unless the body is a company to which section 394 (duty to prepare individual company accounts) applies, the Secretary of State may, with the consent of the Treasury, give directions to the body with respect to its accounts and the audit of its accounts.

(8) Whether or not the body is a company to which section 394 applies, the Secretary of State may direct that any provisions of this Act specified in the directions are to apply to the body, with or without any modifications so specified.

Other supplementary provisions

11. (1) The transfer of a function to a body designated by a delegation order does not affect anything previously done in the exercise of the function transferred; and the resumption of a function so transferred does not affect anything previously done in exercise of the function resumed.

(2) The Secretary of State may by order make such transitional and other supplementary provision as he thinks necessary or expedient in relation to the transfer or resumption of a function.

(3) The provision that may be made in connection with the transfer of a function includes, in particular, provision—

(a) for modifying or excluding any provision of this Part of this Act in its application to the function transferred;

(b) for applying to the body designated by the delegation order, in connection with the function transferred, any provision applying to the Secretary of State which is contained in or made under any other enactment;

(c) for the transfer of any property, rights or liabilities from the Secretary of State to that body;

(d) for the carrying on and completion by that body of anything in the process of being done by the Secretary of State when the order takes effect;

(e) for the substitution of that body for the Secretary of State in any instrument, contract or legal proceedings.

(4) The provision that may be made in connection with the resumption of a function includes, in particular, provision—

(a) for the transfer of any property, rights or liabilities from that body to the Secretary of State;

(b) for the carrying on and completion by the Secretary of State of anything in the process of being done by that body when the order takes effect;

(c) for the substitution of the Secretary of State for that body in any instrument, contract or legal proceedings.

12. Where a delegation order is revoked, the Secretary of State may by order make provision—

(a) for the payment of compensation to persons ceasing to be employed by the body established by the delegation order;

(b) as to the winding up and dissolution of the body.

13. (1) This paragraph applies where the body is an unincorporated association.

(2) Any relevant proceedings may be brought by or against the body in the name of any body corporate whose constitution provides for the establishment of the body.

(3) In sub-paragraph (2) "relevant proceedings" means proceedings brought in or in connection with the exercise of any transferred function.

(4) In relation to proceedings brought as mentioned in sub-paragraph (2), any reference in paragraph 11(3)(e) or (4)(c) to the body replacing or being replaced by the Secretary of State in any legal proceedings is to be read with the appropriate modifications.

NOTES

Commencement: 20 January 2007 (for the purpose of enabling the exercise of powers to make Orders or Regulations by statutory instrument); 6 April 2008 (otherwise).

Transfer of functions: as to the transfer of the functions of the Secretary of State under Part 42 of this Act (which includes this Schedule) to the Professional Oversight Board, see the Statutory Auditors (Delegation of Functions etc) Order 2008, SI 2008/496, art 4.

Orders: the Statutory Auditors (Delegation of Functions etc) Order 2008, SI 2008/496 at **[4.240]**.

SCHEDULE 14
STATUTORY AUDITORS: CONSEQUENTIAL AMENDMENTS

Section 1264

[1.1328]
(Amends the Companies (Audit, Investigations and Community Enterprise) Act 2004, s 16 at **[5.171].***)*

NOTES

Commencement: 6 April 2008.

SCHEDULE 15
TRANSPARENCY OBLIGATIONS AND RELATED MATTERS: MINOR AND CONSEQUENTIAL AMENDMENTS

Section 1272

PART 1
AMENDMENTS OF THE FINANCIAL SERVICES AND MARKETS ACT 2000

[1.1329]

(Amends FSMA 2000, ss 73, 73A, 90 (and the preceding heading), 91, 96B, 97, 99, 102A, 103, 429 (see **[7.1]** *et seq.)*

NOTES

Commencement: 8 November 2006 (except in so far as relating to the amendment in para 11(2) to the definition of "regulated market" in s 103 of the 2000 Act); 1 October 2008 (otherwise).

PART 2
AMENDMENTS OF THE COMPANIES (AUDIT, INVESTIGATIONS AND COMMUNITY ENTERPRISE) ACT 2004

[1.1330]

(Amends the Companies (Audit, Investigations and Community Enterprise) Act 2004, ss 14, 15 at **[5.164]**, **[5.165]**.)

NOTES

Commencement: 8 November 2006.

SCHEDULE 16
REPEALS

Section 1295

COMPANY LAW REPEALS (GREAT BRITAIN)

[1.1331]

Short title and chapter	Extent of repeal
Companies Act 1985 (c 6)	Sections 1 to 430F.
	In section 437—
	(a) in subsection (1), the second sentence, and
	(b) subsections (1B) and (1C).
	Section 438.
	In section 439—
	(a) in subsection (2), ", or is ordered to pay the whole or any part of the costs of proceedings brought under section 438",
	(b) subsections (3) and (7), and
	(c) in subsection (8), "; and any such liability imposed by subsection (2) is (subject as mentioned above) a liability also to indemnify all persons against liability under subsection (3)".
	Section 442(2).
	Section 446.
	In section 448(7), the words "and liable to a fine." to the end.
	Section 449(7).
	Section 450(4).
	Section 451(3).
	In section 453(1A)—
	(a) paragraph (b), and
	(b) paragraph (d) and the word "and" preceding it.
	Section 453A(6).
	Sections 458 to 461.
	Sections 651 to 746.
	Schedules 1 to 15B.

Short title and chapter	*Extent of repeal*
	Schedules 20 to 25.
Insolvency Act 1985 (c 65)	Schedule 6.
Insolvency Act 1986 (c 45)	In Schedule 13, in Part 1, the entries relating to the following provisions of the Companies Act 1985—
	(a) section 13(4),
	(b) section 44(7),
	(c) section 103(7),
	(d) section 131(7),
	(e) section 140(2),
	(f) section 156(3),
	(g) section 173(4),
	(h) section 196,
	(i) section 380(4),
	(j) section 461(6),
	(k) section 462(5),
	(l) section 463(2),
	(m) section 463(3),
	(n) section 464(6),
	(o) section 657(2),
	(p) section 658(1), and
	(q) section 711(2).
Building Societies Act 1986 (c 53)	Section 102C(5).
Finance Act 1988 (c 39)	In section 117(3), from the beginning to "that section";".
	In section 117(4), the words "and (3)".
Water Act 1989 (c 15)	In Schedule 25, paragraph 71(3).
Companies Act 1989 (c 40)	Sections 1 to 22.
	Section 56(5).
	Sections 57 and 58.
	Section 64(2).
	Section 66(3).
	Section 71.
	Sections 92 to 110.
	Sections 113 to 138.
	Section 139(1) to (3).
	Sections 141 to 143.
	Section 144(1) to (3) and (6).
	Section 207.
	Schedules 1 to 9.
	In Schedule 10, paragraphs 1 to 24.
	Schedules 15 to 17.
	In Schedule 18, paragraphs 32 to 38.
	In Schedule 19, paragraphs 1 to 9 and 11 to 21.
Age of Legal Capacity (Scotland) Act 1991 (c 50)	In Schedule 1, paragraph 39.
Water Consolidation (Consequential Provisions) Act 1991 (c 60)	In Schedule 1, paragraph 40(2).
Charities Act 1992 (c 41)	In Schedule 6, paragraph 11.
Charities Act 1993 (c 10)	In Schedule 6, paragraph 20.
Criminal Justice Act 1993 (c 36)	In Schedule 5, paragraph 4.
Welsh Language Act 1993 (c 38)	Section 30.
Pension Schemes Act 1993 (c 48)	In Schedule 8, paragraph 16.

Short title and chapter	Extent of repeal
Trade Marks Act 1994 (c 26)	In Schedule 4, in paragraph 1(2), the reference to the Companies Act 1985.
Deregulation and Contracting Out Act 1994 (c 40)	Section 13(1).
	Schedule 5.
	In Schedule 16, paragraphs 8 to 10.
Requirements of Writing (Scotland) Act 1995 (c 7)	In Schedule 4, paragraphs 51 to 56.
Criminal Procedure (Consequential Provisions) (Scotland) Act 1995 (c 40)	In Schedule 4, paragraph 56(3) and (4).
Disability Discrimination Act 1995 (c 50)	In Schedule 6, paragraph 4.
Financial Services and Markets Act 2000 (c 8)	Section 143.
	Section 263.
Limited Liability Partnerships Act 2000 (c 12)	In the Schedule, paragraph 1.
Political Parties, Elections and Referendums Act 2000 (c 41)	Sections 139 and 140.
	Schedule 19.
	In Schedule 23, paragraphs 12 and 13.
Criminal Justice and Police Act 2001 (c 16)	Section 45.
	In Schedule 2, paragraph 17.
Enterprise Act 2002 (c 40)	In Schedule 17, paragraphs 3 to 8.
Companies (Audit, Investigations and Community Enterprise) Act 2004 (c 27)	Sections 7 to 10.
	Section 11(1).
	Sections 12 and 13.
	Sections 19 and 20.
	Schedule 1.
	In Schedule 2, paragraphs 5 to 10, 22 to 24 and 26.
	In Schedule 6, paragraphs 1 to 9.
Civil Partnership Act 2004 (c 33)	In Schedule 27, paragraphs 99 to 105.
Constitutional Reform Act 2005 (c 4)	In Schedule 11, in paragraph 4(3), the reference to the Companies Act 1985.

REPEALS AND REVOCATIONS RELATING TO NORTHERN IRELAND

Short title and chapter	Extent of repeal or revocation
Companies (Northern Ireland) Order 1986 (SI 1986/1032 (NI 6))	The whole Order.
Companies Consolidation (Consequential Provisions) (Northern Ireland) Order 1986 (SI 1986/1035 (NI 9))	The whole Order.
Business Names (Northern Ireland) Order 1986 (SI 1986/1033 (NI 7))	The whole Order.
Industrial Relations (Northern Ireland) Order 1987 (SI 1987/936 NI 9))	Article 3.
Finance Act 1988 (c 39)	In section 117(3), the words from "and for" to the end.
Companies (Northern Ireland) Order 1989 (SI 1989/2404 (NI 18))	The whole Order.

Short title and chapter	Extent of repeal or revocation
Insolvency (Northern Ireland) Order 1989 (SI 1989/2405 (NI 19))	In Schedule 7, in the entry relating to Article 166(4), the word "office". In Schedule 9, Part I.
European Economic Interest Groupings Regulations (Northern Ireland) 1989 (SR 1989/216)	The whole Regulations.
Companies (Northern Ireland) Order 1990 (SI 1990/593 (NI 5))	The whole Order.
Companies (No 2) (Northern Ireland) Order 1990 (SI 1990/1504 (NI 10))	Parts II to IV.
	Part VI.
	Schedules 1 to 6.
Criminal Justice Act 1993 (c 36)	In Schedule 5, Part 2.
	Schedule 6.
Financial Provisions (Northern Ireland) Order 1993 (SI 1993/1252 (NI 5))	Article 15.
Deregulation and Contracting Out Act 1994 (c 40)	Section 13(2).
	Schedule 6.
Pensions (Northern Ireland) Order 1995 (SI 1995/3213 (NI 22))	In Schedule 3, paragraph 7.
Deregulation and Contracting Out (Northern Ireland) Order 1996 (SI 1996/1632 (NI 11))	Article 11.
	Schedule 2.
	In Schedule 5, paragraph 4.
Youth Justice and Criminal Evidence Act 1999 (c 23)	In Schedule 4, paragraph 18.
Limited Liability Partnerships Act (Northern Ireland) 2002 (c 12 (NI))	The whole Act.
Open-Ended Investment Companies Act (Northern Ireland) 2002 (c 13)	The whole Act.
Company Directors Disqualification (Northern Ireland) Order 2002 (SI 2002/3150 (NI 4))	In Schedule 3, paragraphs 3 to 5.
Companies (Audit, Investigations and Community Enterprise) Act 2004 (c 27)	Section 11(2). In Schedule 2, paragraphs 11 to 15.
Law Reform (Miscellaneous Provisions) (Northern Ireland) Order 2005 (SI 2005/1452 (NI 7))	Article 4(2).
Companies (Audit, Investigations and Community Enterprise) (Northern Ireland) Order 2005 (SI 2005/1967 (NI 17))	The whole Order.

OTHER REPEALS

Short title and chapter	Extent of repeal or revocation
Limited Partnerships Act 1907 (c 24)	In section 16(1)—
	(a) the words ", and there shall be paid for such inspection such fees as may be appointed by the Board of Trade, not exceeding 5p for each inspection", and
	(b) the words from "and there shall be paid for such certificate" to the end.
	In section 17—
	(a) the words "(but as to fees with the concurrence of the Treasury)", and

Short title and chapter	Extent of repeal or revocation
	(b) paragraph (a).
Business Names Act 1985 (c 7)	The whole Act.
Companies Act 1989 (c 40)	Sections 24 to 54.
	Schedules 11 to 13.
Criminal Procedure (Consequential Provisions) (Scotland) Act 1995 (c 40)	In Schedule 4, paragraph 74(2).
Companies (Audit, Investigations and Community Enterprise) Act 2004 (c 27)	Sections 1 to 6.
	In Schedule 2, Part 1.
Civil Partnership Act 2004 (c 33)	In Schedule 27, paragraph 128.

NOTES

Commencement: 1 January 2007 (in part); 20 January 2007 (in part); 6 April 2007 (in part); 1 October 2007 (in part); 1 April 2008 (in part); 6 April 2008 (in part); 1 October 2008 (in part); 1 October 2009 (otherwise) (see the notes below).

Commencement (note): the Companies Act 2006 (Commencement No 1, Transitional Provisions and Savings) Order 2006, SI 2006/3428, art 7(a)–(c) (at **[2.7]**) provide that this Schedule comes into force on 1 January 2007, 20 January 2007, and 6 April 2007 respectively, in so far as relating to the repeals specified in Schs 2–4 to that Order (at **[2.10]** et seq).

Commencement (note): the Companies Act 2006 (Commencement No 1, Transitional Provisions and Savings) Order 2006, SI 2006/3428, art 4(2) (at **[2.4]**) provides that this Schedule comes into force on 6 April 2007, in so far as relating to the repeals specified in sub-paras (a)–(c) of that paragraph.

Commencement (note): the Companies Act 2006 (Commencement No 2, Consequential Amendments, Transitional Provisions and Savings) Order 2007, SI 2007/1093, art 5 (at **[2.20]**) provides that this Schedule comes into force on 6 April 2007, in so far as relating to the repeals specified in Sch 2 to that Order (at **[2.28]**).

Commencement (note): the Companies Act 2006 (Commencement No 3, Consequential Amendments, Transitional Provisions and Savings) Order 2007, SI 2007/2194, art 8 (at **[2.38]**) provides that this Schedule comes into force on 1 October 2007 in so far as relating to the repeals specified in Sch 2 to that Order.

Commencement (note): the Companies Act 2006 (Commencement No 5, Transitional Provisions and Savings) Order 2007, SI 2007/3495, art 5(2) provides that this section shall come into force on 1 October 2008 in so far as relating to the repeal of the Companies Act 1985, ss 151–153, 155–158, and the Companies (Northern Ireland) Order 1986, arts 161–163, 165–168, as they apply to the giving of financial assistance by a private company for the purposes of the acquisition of shares in itself or another private company (see **[2.54]**). Article 8 of the 2007 Order further provides that this Schedule shall come into force on 6 April 2008 (in so far as relating to the repeals specified in Sch 2 to that Order), and on 1 October 2008 (in so far as relating to the repeals specified in Sch 3 to that Order) (see **[2.57]**).

Commencement (note): the Companies Act 2006 (Commencement No 6, Saving and Commencement Nos 3 and 5 (Amendment)) Order 2008, SI 2008/674, art 3(1)(c) (at **[2.71]**) provides that this Schedule comes into force on 1 April 2008 in so far as relating to the repeals specified in Sch 1 to that Order.

Commencement (note): the Companies Act 2006 (Commencement No 7, Transitional Provisions and Savings) Order 2008, SI 2008/1886, art 2(f) provides that this Schedule shall come into force on 1 October 2008 in so far as relating to the repeals of the second sentence of s 141(4) of the Companies Act 1989 and of the second sentence of Art 75(4) of the Companies (No 2) (Northern Ireland) Order 1990 (see **[2.76]**).

Commencement (note): the Companies Act 2006 (Commencement No 8, Transitional Provisions and Savings) Order 2008, SI 2008/2860, art 4 (at **[2.85]**) provides that this Schedule comes into force on 1 October 2009 in so far as relating to the repeals specified in Sch 1 to that Order.

General note: for any savings and transitional provisions associated with the repeal and revocation of the provisions listed in this Schedule, see the provision concerned.

PART 2
COMPANIES ACT 2006 COMMENCEMENT ORDERS, ETC

Part 2 CA 2006 commencement orders

COMPANIES ACT 2006 (COMMENCEMENT NO 1, TRANSITIONAL PROVISIONS AND SAVINGS) ORDER 2006

(SI 2006/3428)

NOTES

Made: 20 December 2006.

Authority: Companies Act 2006, s 1296(1), (2), 1300(2).

Commencement: 1 January 2007 (arts 1, 2, 5, 6, 7(a), 8, Sch 1, Sch 2, Sch 5, Pt 1); 20 January 2007 (arts 3, 7(b), Sch 3, Sch 5, Pt 2); 6 April 2007 (otherwise).

This Order is reproduced as amended by: the Companies Act 2006 (Commencement No 3, Consequential Amendments, Transitional Provisions and Savings) Order 2007, SI 2007/2194; the Companies Act 2006 (Commencement No 5, Transitional Provisions and Savings) Order 2007, SI 2007/3495; the Companies Act 2006 (Commencement No 8, Transitional Provisions and Savings) Order 2008, SI 2008/2860; the Registrar of Companies (Fees) (Limited Partnerships and Newspaper Proprietors) Regulations 2009, SI 2009/2392.

ARRANGEMENT OF ARTICLES

[2.1]
1   Citation, interpretation and coming into force

(1)   This Order may be cited as the Companies Act 2006 (Commencement No 1, Transitional Provisions and Savings) Order 2006.

(2)   In this Order—
   "the 1985 Act" means the Companies Act 1985; and
   "the 1986 Order" means the Companies (Northern Ireland) Order 1986.

(3)   Articles 1, 2, 5, 6, 7(a) and 8 and Schedules 1 and 2 and Part 1 of Schedule 5 come into force on 1st January 2007.

(4)   Articles 3 and 7(b) and Schedule 3 and Part 2 of Schedule 5 come into force on 20th January 2007.

(5)   Articles 4 and 7(c) and Schedule 4 and Part 3 of Schedule 5 come into force on 6th April 2007.

NOTES

Commencement: 1 January 2007.

[2.2]
2   Provisions coming into force on 1st January 2007

(1)   The following provisions of the Companies Act 2006 come into force on 1st January 2007—
   (a)   section 1068(5) (registrar's duty to accept delivery by electronic means of documents subject to Directive disclosure requirements);
   (b)   section 1077 (public notice of receipt of certain documents);
   (c)   section 1078 (documents subject to Directive disclosure requirements);
   (d)   section 1079 (effect of failure to give public notice);
   (e)   section 1080 (the register);
   (f)   sections 1085 to 1092 (inspection etc of the register);

(g) sections 1102 to 1107 (language requirements: translation); and
(h) section 1111 (registrar's requirements as to certification or verification).

(2) The following provisions of the Companies Act 2006 come into force on 1st January 2007 so far as necessary for the purposes of the provisions mentioned in paragraph (1)—
(a) section 2 (the Companies Acts);
(b) section 1068(1) to (4), (6) and (7) (registrar's requirements as to form, authentication and manner of delivery);
(c) section 1114 (application of provisions about documents and delivery);
(d) section 1117 (registrar's rules);
(e) section 1120 (application of provisions to overseas companies);
(f) section 1168 (hard copy and electronic form and related expressions);
(g) in section 1173 (minor definitions: general), the definitions of "Gazette" and "working day"; and
(h) section 1284 (extension of Companies Acts to Northern Ireland).

NOTES

Commencement: 1 January 2007.

[2.3]
3 Provisions coming into force on 20th January 2007

(1) The following provisions of the Companies Act 2006 come into force on 20th January 2007—
(a) sections 308 (manner in which notice to be given) and 309 (publication of notice of meeting on website);
(b) section 333 (sending documents relating to meetings etc in electronic form);
(c) section 463 (liability for false or misleading statements in reports);
(d) sections 791 to 810, 811(1) to (3), 813 and 815 to 828 (information about interests in a company's shares); and
(e) sections 1143 to 1148 and Schedules 4 and 5 (the company communications provisions).

(2) The following provisions of the Companies Act 2006 come into force on 20th January 2007 so far as necessary for the purposes of the provisions mentioned in paragraph (1)—
(a) section 2 (the Companies Acts);
(b) sections 1121, 1122, 1125 to 1131 and 1133 (provisions relating to offences);
(c) section 1168 (hard copy and electronic form and related expressions);
(d) in section 1173 (minor definitions: general), the definition of "working day"; and
(e) section 1284 (extension of Companies Acts to Northern Ireland).

(3) The provisions of the Companies Act 2006, so far as not brought into force by section 1300(1) of that Act or article 2 or the preceding provisions of this article, come into force on 20th January 2007 for the purpose of enabling the exercise of powers to make orders or regulations by statutory instrument.

NOTES

Commencement: 20 January 2007.

[2.4]
4 Provisions coming into force on 6th April 2007

(1) The following provisions of the Companies Act 2006 come into force on 6th April 2007—
(a) section 1063 (fees payable to registrar), so far as not in force by virtue of article 3(3);
(b) section 1176 (power of Secretary of State to bring civil proceedings on company's behalf);
(c) section 1177 (repeal of certain provisions about company directors);
(d) section 1178 (repeal of requirement that certain companies publish periodical statement);
(e) section 1179 (repeal of requirement that Secretary of State prepare annual report); and
(f) section 1281 (disclosure of information under the Enterprise Act 2002).

(2) Section 1295 of, and Schedule 16 to, the Companies Act 2006 (repeals) come into force on 6th April 2007 so far as relating to the repeal of—
(a) the provisions of the 1986 Order corresponding to the provisions of the 1985 Act repealed by the provisions mentioned in paragraph (1)(b) to (e);
(b) section 41 of the 1985 Act and Article 51 of the 1986 Order (authentication of documents on behalf of company); and
(c) sections 293 and 294 of the 1985 Act and Articles 301 and 302 of the 1986 Order (age limits for directors).

(3) The following provisions of the Companies Act 2006 come into force on 6th April 2007 so far as necessary for the purposes of the provisions mentioned in paragraphs (1) and (2)—
(a) section 1060 (the registrar of companies);
(b) section 1061 (the registrar's functions); and
(c) section 1284 (extension of Companies Acts to Northern Ireland).

(4) The coming into force of section 1063 by virtue of paragraph (1)(a) does not extend to Northern Ireland.

NOTES
Commencement: 6 April 2007.

[2.5]
5   Transitional adaptations of provisions brought into force
The provisions brought into force by articles 2, 3 and 4 have effect subject to any transitional adaptations specified in Schedule 1.

NOTES
Commencement: 1 January 2007.

[2.6]
6   Interpretation of provisions brought into force
Where an expression in a provision brought into force by this Order (or in an adaptation made by this Order of such a provision)—
    (a)   is defined in the 1985 Act or the 1986 Order ("the old definition"); and
    (b)   is defined in the Companies Act 2006 by another provision that is not yet in force for the purposes of the provision brought into force ("the new definition"),
the expression has, for the purposes of the provision brought into force (or the adaptation), the meaning given by the old definition until the new definition is brought into force for the purposes of that provision.

NOTES
Commencement: 1 January 2007.

[2.7]
7   Consequential repeals
Section 1295 of, and Schedule 16 to, the Companies Act 2006 (repeals) come into force—
    (a)   on 1st January 2007 so far as relating to the repeal of the provisions specified in Schedule 2;
    (b)   on 20th January 2007 so far as relating to the repeal of the provisions specified in Schedule 3; and
    (c)   on 6th April 2007 so far as relating to the repeal of the provisions specified in Schedule 4.

NOTES
Commencement: 1 January 2007 (para (a)); 20 January 2007 (para (b)); 6 April 2007 (para (c)).

[2.8]
8   Transitional provisions and savings
(1)   Schedule 5 contains transitional provisions and savings relating to the provisions (and repeals) brought into force by this Order.

(2)   Nothing in this Order affects the application of any provision of the 1985 Act or the 1986 Order as applied by the Limited Liability Partnerships Regulations 2001 or the Limited Liability Partnerships Regulations (Northern Ireland) 2004 to limited liability partnerships.

NOTES
Commencement: 1 January 2007.

SCHEDULES

SCHEDULE 1
TRANSITIONAL ADAPTATIONS OF PROVISIONS BROUGHT INTO FORCE
Article 5

The Companies Acts

[2.9]
1. (1)   Section 2 (the Companies Acts) has effect with the following adaptation.
(2)   For subsection (1)(c) substitute—

    "(c)   the provisions of the Companies Acts as defined in section 744 of the Companies Act 1985, and the Companies Orders as defined in Article 2(3) of the Companies (Northern Ireland) Order 1986, that remain in force.".

Information about interests in a company's shares

2. (1)   Section 813 (register of interests disclosed: refusal of inspection or default in providing copy) has effect with the following adaptation.
(2)   In subsection (1) omit ", otherwise than in accordance with an order of the court,".

3. *(1)   Section 826 (information about interests in a company's shares protected from wider disclosure) has effect with the following adaptation.*

(2)   In subsection (1) for "regulations under section 409(3)" substitute "section 231(3) of the Companies Act 1985 or Article 239(3) of the Companies (Northern Ireland) Order 1986".

Documents delivered to registrar of companies

4. *(1)   Section 1077 (public notice of receipt of certain documents) has effect with the following adaptation.*

(2)   Omit subsection (1)(b).

5. *(1)   Section 1078 (documents subject to Directive disclosure requirements) has effect with the following adaptations.*

(2)   In subsection (2) (documents relating to any company)—
- *(a)   under the heading "Constitutional documents"—*
  - *(i)   in item 2 for "Any amendment of the company's articles" substitute "Any amendment of the company's memorandum or articles";*
  - *(ii)   for item 3 substitute—*

    "3.   After any amendment of the company's memorandum or articles, the text of the document as amended.";

  - *(iii) omit item 4;*
- *(b)   under the heading "Accounts, reports and returns", in item 1 for "441" substitute "242 of the Companies Act 1985 or Article 250 of the Companies (Northern Ireland) Order 1986".*

(3)   In subsection (3) (documents relating to public company)—
- *(a)   under the heading "Share capital"—*
  - *(i)   in item 2 omit "and the statement of capital accompanying it";*
  - *(ii)   in item 3 for "section 570 or 571" substitute "section 95(1), (2) or (3) of the Companies Act 1985 or Article 105(1), (2) or (3) of the Companies (Northern Ireland) Order 1986";*
  - *(iii) in item 4 for "section 593 or 599" substitute "section 103 or 104 of the Companies Act 1985 or Article 113 or 114 of the Companies (Northern Ireland) Order 1986";*
  - *(iv)   omit items 5 and 6;*
  - *(v)   for item 7 substitute—*

    "7.   Statement or notice delivered under section 128 of the Companies Act 1985 or Article 138 of the Companies (Northern Ireland) Order 1986 (registration of particulars of special rights).";

  - *(vi)   omit item 8;*
  - *(vii) in item 9 for "section 689" substitute "section 122 of the Companies Act 1985 or Article 132 of the Companies (Northern Ireland) Order 1986" and omit "and the statement of capital accompanying it";*
  - *(viii) omit item 10;*
  - *(ix)   for item 11 substitute—"11. Any statutory declaration or statement delivered under section 117 of the Companies Act 1985 or Article 127 of the Companies (Northern Ireland) Order 1986 (public company share capital requirements).";*
- *(b)   under the heading "Mergers and divisions"—(i) in item 1 for "section 906 or 921" substitute "paragraph 2(1) of Schedule 15B to the Companies Act 1985 or paragraph 2(1) of Schedule 15B to the Companies (Northern Ireland) Order 1986";(ii) in item 2 for "section 899 or 900 in respect of a compromise or arrangement to which Part 27 (mergers and divisions of public companies) applies" substitute "section 425(2) or 427 of that Act in respect of a compromise or arrangement to which section 427A of that Act applies or under Article 418(2) or 420 of that Order in respect of a compromise or arrangement to which Article 420A of that Order applies".*

(4)   Omit subsection (4).

(5)   For subsections (5) and (6) (power to make provision for documents relating to overseas company) substitute—

> *"(5)   In the case of a company incorporated outside the United Kingdom or a credit or financial institution to which section 699A of the Companies Act 1985 or Article 648A of the Companies (Northern Ireland) Order 1986 applies—*
> - *1.   Any return delivered under paragraph 1, 7 or 8 of Schedule 21A to that Act or paragraph 1, 7 or 8 of Schedule 20A to that Order (branch registration).*
> - *2.   Any document delivered under paragraph 1 or 8 of Schedule 21A to that Act or under paragraph 1 or 8 of Schedule 20A to that Order.*
> - *3.   Any notice under section 695A(3) of that Act or Article 645A of that Order of the closure of a branch.*
> - *4.   Any document delivered under Schedule 21C to that Act or Schedule 20C to that Order (accounts and reports of foreign credit and financial institutions).*

5.   Any document delivered under Schedule 21D to that Act or Schedule 20D to that Order *(accounts and reports of companies subject to branch registration, other than credit and financial institutions).*

6.   Any return delivered under section 703P of that Act or Article 652O of that Order *(particulars on winding up).*".

6. *(1)   Section 1079 (effect of failure to give public notice) has effect with the following adaptations.*

(2)   In subsection (2)(a) and subsection (4)(a) for "amendment of the company's articles" substitute "amendment of the company's memorandum or articles".

7. *(1)   Section 1080 (the register) has effect with the following adaptation.*

(2)   In subsection (1)(c), for "section 869(5) or 885(4)" substitute "section 401(2) or 418 of the Companies Act 1985 or Article 409(3) of the Companies (Northern Ireland) Order 1986".

8. *(1)   Section 1085 (inspection of the register) has effect with the following adaptation.*

(2)   In subsection (2) for "section 1083(1)" substitute "section 707A(2) of the Companies Act 1985 or Article 656A(2) of the Companies (Northern Ireland) Order 1986".

9. *(1)   Section 1087 (material not available for public inspection) has effect with the following adaptations.*

(2)   In subsection (1)(a) for "views expressed pursuant to section 56" substitute "a statement that a request has been made pursuant to section 29(2) of the Companies Act 1985 or Article 39(2) of the Companies (Northern Ireland) Order 1986 or any response to such a request".

(3)   For subsection (1)(b) substitute—

"(b)   at any time when an order made under section 723B of the Companies Act 1985 is in force in relation to an individual, so much of any record kept by the registrar as contains information which is recorded as particulars of the individual's residential address that were contained in a document delivered to the registrar after the order came into force;".

(4)   Omit subsection (1)(c) to (g).

(5)   In subsection (1)(h)(i), for "section 860" substitute "section 395 of the Companies Act 1985 or Article 402 of the Companies (Northern Ireland) Order 1986".

(6)   In subsection (1)(h)(ii), for "section 878" substitute "section 410 of the Companies Act 1985".

10. *(1)   Section 1103 (documents to be drawn up and delivered in English) has effect with the following adaptation.*

(2)   After subsection (2) insert—

"(3)   This section does not affect the operation of the following provisions (under which documents may be delivered in a language other than English if a certified translation is delivered)—

(a)   section 228(2)(f) or 228A(2)(g) of the Companies Act 1985 or Article 236(2)(f) of the Companies (Northern Ireland) Order 1986 (conditions for exemption from duty to prepare group accounts: delivery of certain accounts and reports);

(b)   section 242(1) of that Act or Article 250(1) of that Order (main requirements as to accounts and reports);

(c)   section 272(5) of that Act or Article 280(5) of that Order (interim accounts prepared for a proposed distribution by a public company);

(d)   section 273(7) of that Act or Article 281(7) of that Order (initial accounts prepared for a proposed distribution by a public company);

(e)   paragraph 7(3) of Part 2 of Schedule 9 to that Act or paragraph 7(3) of Part 2 of Schedule 9 to that Order (information as to undertaking in which shares held as a result of financial assistance operation).".

11. *(1)   Section 1104 (documents relating to Welsh companies) has effect with the following adaptations.*

(2)   For subsection (5) substitute—

"(5)   None of the following provisions (which require certified translations into English of documents delivered to the registrar in another language) applies to a document relating to a Welsh company that is drawn up and delivered in Welsh—

(a)   section 228(2)(f) and section 228A(2)(g) of the Companies Act 1985;

(b)   section 242(1) of that Act;

(c)   section 272(5) of that Act;

(d)   section 273(7) of that Act;

(e)   paragraph 7(3) of Part 2 of Schedule 9 to that Act;

(f)   section 1105 of this Act.".

(3)   *After that subsection insert—*

"(6)   In this section, "a Welsh company" means a company whose memorandum states that its registered office is to be situated in Wales.".

12. (1)   *Section 1105 (documents that may be drawn up and delivered in other languages) has effect with the following adaptations.*

(2)   *In subsection (2)(a) for "Chapter 3 of Part 3" substitute "section 380 of the Companies Act 1985 or Article 388 of the Companies (Northern Ireland) Order 1986".*

(3)   *In subsection (2)(b) for "section 400(2)(e) or section 401(2)(f)" substitute "section 228(2)(e) or section 228A(2)(f) of the Companies Act 1985 or Article 236(2)(e) of the Companies (Northern Ireland) Order 1986".*

(4)   *In subsection (2)(c) for "Part 25" substitute "Part 12 of the Companies Act 1985 or Part 13 of the Companies (Northern Ireland) Order 1986".*

13. (1)   *Section 1120 (application of Part 35 to overseas companies) has effect with the following adaptations.*

(2)   *For "an overseas company" substitute "an oversea company (as defined in section 744 of the Companies Act 1985) or a Part 23 company (as defined in Article 640 of the Companies (Northern Ireland) Order 1986)".*

(3)   *For "a company as defined in section 1" substitute "a company as defined in section 735(1) of that Act or Article 3(1) of that Order".*

The company communications provisions

14. (1)   *Section 1143 (the company communications provisions) has effect with the following adaptation.*

(2)   *In subsection (3), after "Part 35" insert "and, to the extent that they remain in force, Part 24 of the Companies Act 1985 and Part 24 of the Companies (Northern Ireland) Order 1986".*

Extension of Companies Acts to Northern Ireland

15. (1)   *Section 1284 (extension of Companies Acts to Northern Ireland) has effect with the following adaptations.*

(2)   *In subsection (1) for "The Companies Acts as defined by this Act (see section 2)" substitute "The company law provisions of this Act that are for the time being in force".*

(3)   *For subsection (2) substitute—*

"(2)   The corresponding provisions of the Companies (Northern Ireland) Order 1986 shall cease to have effect accordingly.".

Communications by a company

16. (1)   *Schedule 5 (communications by a company) has effect with the following adaptation.*

(2)   *In paragraph 10(5), for "Chapter 3 of Part 3" substitute "section 380 of the Companies Act 1985 or Article 388 of the Companies (Northern Ireland) Order 1986".*

NOTES

Commencement: 1 January 2007.

This Schedule (in so far as it was still in force) was revoked by the Companies Act 2006 (Commencement No 8, Transitional Provisions and Savings) Order 2008, SI 2008/2860, art 6, as from 1 October 2009. For savings in relation to the application of para 5 above, see Sch 2, para 103 to the 2008 Order at **[2.91]** (as substituted).

This Schedule is reproduced here out of historical interest and because of the savings contained in the Companies Act 2006 (Commencement No 5, Transitional Provisions and Savings) Order 2007, SI 2007/3495, art 10(3) which provides that the revocation by that article of a spent transitional adaptation is subject to the same transitional provisions and savings as apply, in accordance with Sch 4 to that Order, in relation to the repeal of the provisions of the 1985 Act or 1986 Order referred to in the adaptation. As to prior revocations see the notes below.

Paras 2, 3, 5(2)(b), (3)(a)(ix), (b), 10, 11, 12(3) were revoked by the Companies Act 2006 (Commencement No 5, Transitional Provisions and Savings) Order 2007, SI 2007/3495, art 10(1)(a), (2)(a), as from 6 April 2008 (in the case of paras 3, 5(2)(b), (3)(a)(ix), (b), 10, 11, 12(3)), and as from 1 October 2008 (in the case of para 2).

Paras 12(2), 16 were revoked by the Companies Act 2006 (Commencement No 3, Consequential Amendments, Transitional Provisions and Savings) Order 2007, SI 2007/2194, art 11(a), as from 1 October 2007.

SCHEDULE 2
REPEALS BROUGHT INTO FORCE ON 1ST JANUARY 2007
Article 7(a)

PART 1
GREAT BRITAIN

[2.10]

Short title and chapter	Extent of repeal brought into force
Companies Act 1985 (c 6)	Section 29(4).
	Section 42.
	In sections 228(2)(f) and 228A(2)(g), the words from "subject to" to "without a translation)".
	In sections 242(1), 272(5) and 273(7), the words from "then, subject to" to "without a translation)".
	Section 707A(1).
	Section 709.
	Section 710B.
	Section 711.
	Section 723C(1)(a).
	In paragraph 7(3) of Part 2 of Schedule 9, the words from "then, subject to" to "without a translation)".
Insolvency Act 1986 (c 45)	In Schedule 13, in Part 1, the entry relating to section 711(2) of the Companies Act 1985.
Welsh Language Act 1993 (c 38)	Section 30.

NOTES

Commencement: 1 January 2007.

(Sch 2, Pt 2 (Northern Ireland) contains various repeals of provisions in the Companies (Northern Ireland) Order 1986, SI 1986/1032, the Insolvency (Northern Ireland) Order 1989, SI 1989/2405, and the Companies (Northern Ireland) Order 1990, SI 1990/593 (outside the scope of this work).)

SCHEDULE 3
REPEALS BROUGHT INTO FORCE ON 20TH JANUARY 2007
Article 7(b)

PART 1
GREAT BRITAIN

[2.11]

Short title and chapter	Extent of repeal brought into force
Companies Act 1985 (c 6)	Sections 198 to 220.
	Section 238(4A) to (4E).
	Section 239(2A) and (2B).
	Section 251(2A) to (2E).
	Section 253(2A).
	In section 262(1), the definition of "address".
	In section 262A, the entry for "address".
	Section 366A(3A) and (5A).
	Section 369(4A) to (4G).
	Section 372(2A), (2B) and (6A).
	Section 379A(2B) to (2F) and (5A).
Companies Act 1989 (c 40)	Section 134.
	Section 143(5).
	In Schedule 10, paragraphs 3, 6 and 14.
Criminal Justice and Police Act 2001 (c 16)	Section 45(4).

Part 2　CA 2006 commencement etc

Short title and chapter	Extent of repeal brought into force
Civil Partnership Act 2004 (c 33)	In Schedule 27, paragraph 99.

NOTES

Commencement: 20 January 2007.

(Sch 3, Pt 2 (Northern Ireland) contains various repeals of provisions in the Companies (Northern Ireland) Order 1986, SI 1986/1032, the Insolvency (Northern Ireland) Order 1989, SI 1990/593, and the Companies (No 2) (Northern Ireland) Order 1990, SI 1990/1504 (outside the scope of this work).)

SCHEDULE 4
REPEALS BROUGHT INTO FORCE ON 6TH APRIL 2007
Article 7(c)

PART 1
GREAT BRITAIN

[2.12]

Short title and chapter	Extent of repeal brought into force
Limited Partnerships Act 1907 (c 24)	In section 16(1)—
	(a) the words ", and there shall be paid for such inspection such fees as may be appointed by the Board of Trade, not exceeding 5p for each inspection"; and
	(b) the words from "and there shall be paid for each certificate" to the end.
	In section 17(1)—
	(a) the words "(but as to fees with the concurrence of the Treasury)"; and
	(b) paragraph (a).
Companies Act 1985 (c 6)	Section 311.
	Sections 323 to 329.
	Sections 343 and 344.
	Section 438.
	Section 439—
	(a) in subsection (2), the words ", or is ordered to pay the whole or any part of the costs of proceedings brought under section 438,";
	(b) subsections (3) and (7); and
	(c) in subsection (8), the words "; and any such liability imposed by subsection (2) is (subject as mentioned above) a liability also to indemnify all persons against liability under subsection (3)".
	Section 453(1A)(b).
	Section 708(5).
	Section 720.
	Section 729.
	Parts 2 to 4 of Schedule 13.
	Schedule 23.
Companies Act 1989 (c 40)	Section 58.
	Section 143(10).
	In Schedule 17, paragraph 4.
Age of Legal Capacity (Scotland) Act 1991 (c 50)	In Schedule 1, paragraph 39.
Civil Partnership Act 2004 (c 33)	In Schedule 27, paragraphs 100 and 101.

NOTES

Commencement: 6 April 2007.

(Sch 4, Pt 2 (Northern Ireland) contains various repeals of provisions in the Companies (Northern Ireland) Order 1986, SI 1986/1032, the Companies (Northern Ireland) Order 1990, SI 1990/593, and the Companies (No 2) (Northern Ireland) Order 1990, SI 1990/1504 (outside the scope of this work).)

SCHEDULE 5
TRANSITIONAL PROVISIONS AND SAVINGS

Article 8(1)

PART 1
PROVISIONS COMING INTO FORCE ON 1ST JANUARY 2007

[2.13]
1 Savings for certain provisions relating to Welsh companies

(1) Regulations 4 and 5 of the Companies (Welsh Language Forms and Documents) Regulations 1994 continue to have effect notwithstanding the repeal of section 710B of the 1985 Act.

(2) Regulation 4 (documents excepted from requirement to file certified translation into English) has effect as if made under section 1104(2) of the Companies Act 2006.

(3) As so continued in force, that regulation has effect with the following adaptations—
   (a) in paragraph (1) for "section 710B(3)(a)" substitute "section 1104(2)(a) of the Companies Act 2006"; and
   (b) in paragraph (3) for "such a company as is mentioned in section 710B(1)(b)" substitute "a Welsh company as defined in section 1104(6) of the Companies Act 2006".

(4) Regulation 5 (requirements as to person by whom a translation of a document into English is to be certified as correct) has effect as if the requirements imposed by it were requirements imposed by the registrar under section 1111 of the Companies Act 2006 by means of rules under section 1117 of that Act.

(5) As so continued in force, that regulation has effect with the following adaptations—
   (a) in the opening words for "section 710B(8)" substitute "section 1107 of the Companies Act 2006"; and
   (b) in paragraph (a)(iv) for "section 710(4)" substitute "section 1104(3) of the Companies Act 2006".

NOTES

Commencement: 1 January 2007.

PART 2
PROVISIONS COMING INTO FORCE ON 20TH JANUARY 2007

[2.14]
2 Information about interests in a company's shares

(1) The repeal of sections 198 to 210 and 220 of the 1985 Act or Articles 206 to 218 and 228 of the 1986 Order (obligation to disclose acquisitions and disposals of interests in shares) does not affect any obligation to which a person became subject under section 198 of that Act or Article 206 of that Order before 20th January 2007.

(2) The repeal of sections 212 to 220 of the 1985 Act or Articles 220 to 228 of the 1986 Order (power of public company to require disclosure of interests in shares) does not affect the operation of those provisions in relation to a notice issued by a company under section 212 of the 1985 Act or Article 220 of the 1986 Order before 20th January 2007.

(3) On and after 20th January 2007 any separate part of a register kept by a company under section 213 of the 1985 Act or Article 221 of the 1986 Order (register of interests disclosed in response to requirement by company) shall continue to be kept by the company and shall be treated as a register kept under and for the purposes of section 808 of the Companies Act 2006.

(4) Until regulations under section 1136 of the Companies Act 2006 (regulations about where certain company records are to be kept available for inspection) [come into force] specifying a place for the purposes of section 809(1)(b) of that Act—
   (a) the register kept under section 808 of that Act (register of interests disclosed) may be kept by a company at any place where its register of members is kept; and
   (b) no notice need be given to the registrar of companies under section 809(2) of that Act.

3 False or misleading statements in reports

Section 463 of the Companies Act 2006 (liability for false or misleading statements in reports) does not apply to a directors' report, directors' remuneration report or summary financial statement first sent to members and others under section 238 or 251 of the 1985 Act, or Article 246 or 259 of the 1986 Order, before 20th January 2007.

4 Existing agreements to communication by electronic means

(1)   This paragraph applies where an address has been notified by a person to a company for the purposes of—
- (a)   section 238(4A) or 239(2A) of the 1985 Act or Article 246(4A) or 247(2A) of the 1986 Order (sending or supply of accounts and reports by means of electronic communications);
- (b)   section 251(2A) of the 1985 Act or Article 259(2A) of the 1986 Order (sending of summary financial statement by means of electronic communications); or
- (c)   section 369(4A) or 379A(2B) of the 1985 Act or Article 377(5) or 387A(2B) of the 1986 Order (notice of meeting given by means of electronic communications).

(2)   Any such notification that is in force immediately before 20th January 2007 shall have effect on and after that date, in relation to the matters to which it relates, as an agreement under paragraph 6(a) of Schedule 5 to the Companies Act 2006 (agreement to accept documents or information in electronic form) and as an address specified under paragraph 7(1) of Schedule 5 to that Act (address for communications in electronic form).

5. (1)   This paragraph applies where an agreement between a person and a company has been entered into for the purposes of—
- (a)   section 238(4B) of the 1985 Act or Article 246(4B) of the 1986 Order (sending or supply of copies of accounts and reports by means of website);
- (b)   section 251(2B) of the 1985 Act or Article 259(2B) of the 1986 Order (sending of summary financial statement by means of website); or
- (c)   section 369(4B) or 379A(2C) of the 1985 Act or Article 377(6) or 387A(2C) of the 1986 Order (notice of meeting given by means of website).

(2)   Any such agreement that is in force immediately before 20th January 2007 shall have effect on and after that date, in relation to the matters to which it relates, as an agreement under paragraph 9(a) of Schedule 5 to the Companies Act 2006 (agreement to accept documents or information by means of a website).

NOTES
Commencement: 20 January 2007.
Para 2: words in square brackets in sub-para (4) substituted by the Companies Act 2006 (Commencement No 5, Transitional Provisions and Savings) Order 2007, SI 2007/3495, art 11, Sch 5, para 1, as from 14 January 2008.

PART 3
PROVISIONS COMING INTO FORCE ON 6TH APRIL 2007

[2.15]
6 Saving for existing provisions relating to fees

(1)   The coming into force of section 1063 of the Companies Act 2006 (fees payable to the registrar) does not affect the continued operation of any other provision under which the payment of fees to the registrar of companies may be required until—
- (a)   the coming into force of the repeal of the other provision; or
- (b)   the exercise of the power in section 1063 in a manner inconsistent with its continued operation.

(2)   . . .

(3)   The repeal of section 708(5) of the 1985 Act shall not prevent the registrar from continuing to charge fees thereunder of which notice had before the repeal been given to those to whom the services in question have been, are being or are to be provided (including notice by publication of a list of fees in respect of services provided to any person who seeks their provision).

7 Saving for certain acts done by a person as director

The repeal of section 293(3) of the 1985 Act or Article 301(3) of the 1986 Order (age limit for directors: validity of acts done before it is discovered appointment has terminated) does not affect the validity of acts done by a person acting as director to whom that section or Article applied.

8 Saving for civil proceedings brought by Department of Enterprise, Trade and Investment

The repeal of Article 431 of the 1986 Order (power of Department of Enterprise, Trade and Investment to bring civil proceedings on company's behalf) does not affect proceedings brought under that Article before 6th April 2007.

NOTES
Commencement: 6 April 2007.

Para 6: sub-para (2) revoked by the Registrar of Companies (Fees) (Limited Partnerships and Newspaper Proprietors) Regulations 2009, SI 2009/2392, reg 7, as from 1 October 2009, subject to transitional provisions in reg 6 which provides that where any application is made to the registrar on or before 30 September 2009 in respect of the inspection of, or the provision of copies of, material kept by the registrar, the fee prescribed in Sch 2 or determined by the registrar in the exercise of his powers under s 1063(5) of the Companies Act 2006 in respect of that application shall not apply and any fee payable under para 6(2) of Sch 5 to the Companies Act 2006 (Commencement No 1, Transitional Provisions and Savings) Order 2006 shall apply. This sub-para previously provided that notwithstanding the coming into force of the repeals in s 16 of the Limited Partnerships Act 1907 and the repeal of s 17(a) of that Act, the fees appointed under the said s 16 and having effect immediately before 6 April 2007 shall continue to be payable, and the rules in force under the said s 17(a) immediately before that date shall continue to have effect.

COMPANIES ACT 2006 (COMMENCEMENT NO 2, CONSEQUENTIAL AMENDMENTS, TRANSITIONAL PROVISIONS AND SAVINGS) ORDER 2007

(SI 2007/1093)

NOTES

Made: 29 March 2007.
Authority: Companies Act 2006, ss 1292(1), 1294(1), 1296(1), (2), 1300(2).
Commencement: 6 April 2007.
This Order (as reproduced here) is reproduced as amended by: the Companies Act 2006 (Commencement No 3, Consequential Amendments, Transitional Provisions and Savings) Order 2007, SI 2007/2194; the Companies Act 2006 (Commencement No 8, Transitional Provisions and Savings) Order 2008, SI 2008/2860.

ARRANGEMENT OF ARTICLES

[2.16]
1   Citation, interpretation and coming into force

(1)   This Order may be cited as the Companies Act 2006 (Commencement No 2, Consequential Amendments, Transitional Provisions and Savings) Order 2007.

(2)   In this Order—
"the 1985 Act" means the Companies Act 1985;
"the 1986 Order" means the Companies (Northern Ireland) Order 1986;
"the 2004 Act" means the Companies (Audit, Investigations and Community Enterprise) Act 2004;
"the 2005 Order" means the Companies (Audit, Investigations and Community Enterprise) (Northern Ireland) Order 2005;
"the 2005 Regulations" means the Community Interest Company Regulations 2005; and
"the Interim Regulations" means the Takeovers Directive (Interim Implementation) Regulations 2006.

(3)   This Order comes into force on 6th April 2007.

NOTES

Commencement: 6 April 2007.

[2.17]
2   Provisions coming into force on 6th April 2007

(1)   The following provisions of the Companies Act 2006 come into force on 6th April 2007—
(a)   section 2 (the Companies Acts);

   (b)   sections 942 to 992 and Schedule 2 (takeovers etc);

   (c)   section 1043 (unregistered companies);

   (d)   section 1170 (meaning of "EEA State" and related expressions); and

   (e)   section 1284(1) (extension of Companies Acts to Northern Ireland) so far as it relates to—

       (i)   the provisions mentioned in sub-paragraphs (a), (b) and (c) above, and

       (ii)   Part 2 of the 2004 Act (community interest companies).

(2)   The following provisions of the Companies Act 2006 come into force on 6th April 2007 so far as necessary for the purposes of the provisions mentioned in paragraph (1)—

   (a)   section 546 (issued and allotted share capital);

   (b)   section 558 (when shares are allotted);

   (c)   sections 1121 to 1123 and 1125 to 1133 (provisions relating to offences);

   (d)   sections 1134, 1135 and 1138 (company records);

   (e)   section 1139 (service of documents on a company);

   (f)   section 1140 (service of documents on directors, secretaries and others);

   (g)   section 1168 (hard copy and electronic form and related expressions); and

   (h)   in section 1173 (minor definitions: general), the definitions of "body corporate", "the Gazette" and "regulated market".

NOTES

Commencement: 6 April 2007.

[2.18]
3 Transitional adaptations of provisions brought into force

The provisions brought into force by article 2 have effect subject to any transitional adaptations specified in Schedule 1.

NOTES

Commencement: 6 April 2007.

[2.19]
4 Interpretation of provisions brought into force

Where an expression in a provision brought into force by this Order (or in an adaptation made by this Order of such a provision)—

   (a)   is defined in the 1985 Act or the 1986 Order ("the old definition"); and

   (b)   is defined in the Companies Act 2006 by another provision that is not yet in force for the purposes of the provision brought into force ("the new definition"),

the expression has, for the purposes of the provision brought into force (or the adaptation), the meaning given by the old definition until the new definition is brought into force for the purposes of that provision.

NOTES

Commencement: 6 April 2007.

[2.20]
5 Repeals

Sections 1284(2) and 1295 of, and Schedule 16 to, the Companies Act 2006 (repeals) come into force on 6th April 2007 so far as relating to the repeals specified in Schedule 2 to this Order.

NOTES

Commencement: 6 April 2007.

[2.21]
6 Consequential amendments

(1)   The amendments in Schedule 3 have effect in consequence of provision made by Part 28 of the Companies Act 2006 (takeovers etc).

(2)   The amendments in Schedule 4 have effect in consequence of the extension to Northern Ireland of Part 2 of the 2004 Act (community interest companies) and the revocation of Part 3 of the 2005 Order (which made corresponding provision for Northern Ireland).

(3)   In Schedule 4—

   (a)   Part 1 amends the 2004 Act,

   (b)   Part 2 amends the 2005 Regulations, and

   (c)   Part 3 makes amendments of other enactments.

NOTES

Commencement: 6 April 2007.

[2.22]
7   Consequential repeals and revocations
The repeals and revocations in Schedule 5 have effect in consequence of provision made by Part 28
of the Companies Act 2006 (takeovers etc).

NOTES
Commencement: 6 April 2007.

[2.23]
8   Transitional provisions and savings
Schedule 6 contains savings relating to the provisions (and repeals) brought into force by this Order.

NOTES
Commencement: 6 April 2007.

[2.24]
9
(1)   Section 992 of the Companies Act 2006 (matters to be dealt with in directors' report) applies
to the 1986 Order with the following modifications.
(2)   In subsection (1) for "Part 7 of the Companies Act 1985 (c 6)" substitute "Part 8 of
the Companies (Northern Ireland) Order 1986".
(3)   In subsection (3)—
  (a)   for "section 234ZZA" substitute "Article 242ZZA";
  (b)   for "subsection (4)" substitute "paragraph (4)".
(4)   In subsection (4) for "subsection" substitute "paragraph".
(5)   In subsection (5)—
  (a)   for "section 251" substitute "Article 259",
  (b)   for "subsection" substitute "paragraph",
  (c)   for "section 234ZZA(5)" substitute "Article 242ZZA(5)",
  (d)   for "paragraph" substitute "subparagraph",
  (e)   for "subsections (2A) to (2E)" substitute "paragraphs (2A) to (2E)".

NOTES
Commencement: 6 April 2007.

[2.25]
10
Section 1297 of the Companies Act 2006 (continuity of the law) has effect as if, for the purpose of
section 1297(1), the Interim Regulations were an enactment repealed and re-enacted by that Act.

NOTES
Commencement: 6 April 2007.

[2.26]
11
(1)   Nothing in this Order affects the application of any provision of the 1985 Act or the 1986
Order as applied by the Limited Liability Partnerships Regulations 2001 or the Limited Liability
Partnerships Regulations (Northern Ireland) 2004 to limited liability partnerships.
(2)   The repeal of section 723C(1)(a) of the 1985 Act by section 1295 of and Schedule 16 to
the Companies Act 2006, brought into force by article 7(a) of the Companies Act 2006
(Commencement No 1, Transitional Provisions and Savings) Order 2006, does not apply to the
application of the said section 723C(1)(a) to limited liability partnerships by the Limited Liability
Partnerships (No 2) Regulations 2002.

NOTES
Commencement: 6 April 2007.

SCHEDULES

SCHEDULE 1
TRANSITIONAL ADAPTATIONS OF PROVISIONS BROUGHT INTO FORCE
Article 3

The Companies Acts

[2.27]
1. *(1)   Section 2 (the Companies Acts) has effect with the following adaptation.*
(2)   For subsection (1)(c) substitute—

"(c)   the provisions of the Companies Acts as defined in section 744 of the Companies Act 1985, and the Companies Orders as defined in Article 2(3) of the Companies (Northern Ireland) Order 1986, that remain in force.".

Takeovers etc

2. (1)   Section 943 (power of Takeover Panel to make rules) has effect with the following adaptation.

(2)   For subsection (6) substitute—

"(6)   Section 735(1) of the Companies Act 1985 and Article 2(3) of the Companies (Northern Ireland) Order 1986 (meaning of "company") do not apply for the purposes of this section.".

3. (1)   Section 953 (failure to comply with rules about bid documentation) has effect with the following adaptation.

(2)   For subsection (8) substitute—

"(8)   Section 735(1) of the Companies Act 1985 and Article 2(3) of the Companies (Northern Ireland) Order 1986 (meaning of "company") do not apply for the purposes of this section.".

4. (1)   Section 968 (consequences of opting-in in relation to contractual restrictions on voting rights) has effect with the following adaptation.

(2)   In subsection (4), at the end add "A "written resolution" means a resolution in writing agreed to in accordance with sections 381A to 381C of the Companies Act 1985, or Articles 389A to 389C of the Companies (Northern Ireland) Order 1986, or in accordance with the company's articles.".

Service of documents on a company

5. (1)   Section 1139 has effect with the following adaptation.

(2)   In subsection (1) for "under this Act" substitute "under the Companies Act 1985 or the Companies (Northern Ireland) Order 1986".

NOTES

Commencement: 6 April 2007.

This Schedule (in so far as it was still in force) was revoked by the Companies Act 2006 (Commencement No 8, Transitional Provisions and Savings) Order 2008, SI 2008/2860, art 6(1), as from 1 October 2009. It is reproduced here out of historical interest and because of art 6(2) of the 2008 Order which provides that the revocations made by art 6(1) are subject to any relevant transitional provision or saving in Sch 2 to that Order (at **[2.91]**).

Prior to the revocation noted above, para 4 of this Schedule was revoked by the Companies Act 2006 (Commencement No 3, Consequential Amendments, Transitional Provisions and Savings) Order 2007, SI 2007/2194, art 11(b), as from 1 October 2007.

SCHEDULE 2
REPEALS BROUGHT INTO FORCE

Article 5

PART 1
GREAT BRITAIN

[2.28]

Short title and chapter	Extent of repeal brought into force
Companies Act 1985 (c 6)	Sections 428 to 430F.
	In section 744, the definition of "EEA State".
	Paragraphs 2, 2A and 2B of Schedule 7.

NOTES

Commencement: 6 April 2007.

SCHEDULE 2, PT 2, SCHEDULES 3 AND 4

(Sch 2, Pt 2 (Northern Ireland) contains various repeals in the Companies (Northern Ireland) Order 1986, SI 1986/1032, and the Companies (Audit, Investigations and Community Enterprise) (Northern Ireland) Order 2005, SI 2005/1967 (outside the scope of this work); Sch 3 (Amendments in Consequence of Provision made in Part 28 of the Companies Act 2006 (Takeovers etc)) amended the Companies Act 1985, s 162D (repealed with savings by CA 2006), the Income Tax (Earnings and Pensions) Act 2003, the Companies (Forms) (Amendment) Regulations 1987, SI 1987/752, the Financial Services and Markets Act 2000 (Regulated Activities) Order 2001, SI 2001/544 at **[8.1]** *et seq, the Uncertificated Securities Regulations 2001, SI 2001/3755 at* **[6.42]** *et seq, the Financial Services and Markets Act 2000 (Financial Promotion) Order 2005, SI 2005/1529 at* **[8.250]** *et seq, and contains various amendments to Northern Ireland legislation that is outside the scope of this*

work; *Sch 4 (Consequential Amendments) amends the Companies (Audit, Investigations and Community Enterprise) Act 2004 at* **[5.164]** *et seq, the Community Interest Company Regulations 2005, SI 2005/1788, and contains various amendments to Northern Ireland legislation that is outside the scope of this work*

SCHEDULE 5
CONSEQUENTIAL REPEALS AND REVOCATIONS

Article 7

[2.29]

Short title and chapter	Extent of repeal or revocation
Financial Services and Markets Act 2000 (c 8)	Section 349(8).
Companies (Forms) (Amendment) Regulations 1987 (SI 1987/752)	In regulation 5(4), the words "except to the extent specified in regulation 7 below".
	Regulation 7(2) and (3).
Companies (Acquisition of Own Shares) (Treasury Shares) No 2 Regulations 2003 (SI 2003/3031)	Regulations 5 to 7.
Companies (Acquisition of Own Shares) (Treasury Shares) Regulations (Northern Ireland) 2004 (SR No 275)	In the Schedule, paragraphs 27 and 28.
Takeovers Directive (Interim Implementation) Regulations 2006 (SI 2006/1183)	The whole Regulations.

NOTES

Commencement: 6 April 2007.

SCHEDULE 6
SAVINGS

Article 8

Savings for provisions relating to takeovers

[2.30]

1. The repeal of sections 428 to 430F of the 1985 Act and of Articles 421 to 423F of the 1986 Order (takeover offers) by article 5 does not affect the operation of those provisions in relation to a takeover offer where the date of the offer is before 6th April 2007.

The "date of the offer" for this purpose is the same as for the purposes of section 428(1) of the 1985 Act or Article 421(1) of the 1986 Order.

2. The revocation of the Interim Regulations by article 7 does not affect the operation of Part 5 of those Regulations (squeeze-out and sell-out) in relation to a takeover offer where the date of the offer is before 6th April 2007.

3. The revocation of the Interim Regulations by article 7, and the coming into force of section 949 of the Companies Act 2006 (offence of disclosure in contravention of section 948), and in particular of section 949(2)(b), by virtue of article 2, does not affect the continued operation of regulation 8(2)(b) of the Interim Regulations in respect of offences committed prior to 6th April 2007.

Saving for provisions relating to community interest companies

4. A community interest company in relation to which regulations 7 to 9 of the 2005 Regulations (matters to be included in memorandum and articles) were complied with immediately before the coming into force of this Order need not alter its memorandum or articles to take account of any amendment made by this Order.

Saving for provision relating to directors' report

5. The repeal by article 5 of paragraphs 2, 2A and 2B of Schedule 7 to the 1985 Act and of paragraphs 2, 2A and 2B of Schedule 7 to the 1986 Order (directors' interests) does not affect the operation of these provisions in relation to any directors' report referred to in section 234 of the 1985 Act or Article 242 of the 1986 Order that is approved before 6th April 2007.

NOTES

Commencement: 6 April 2007.

COMPANIES ACT 2006 (COMMENCEMENT NO 3, CONSEQUENTIAL AMENDMENTS, TRANSITIONAL PROVISIONS AND SAVINGS) ORDER 2007

(SI 2007/2194)

NOTES

Made: 25 July 2007.

Authority: Companies Act 2006, ss 1292, 1294, 1296, 1300(2).

Commencement: see art 1(3) (at **[2.32]**).

This Order is reproduced as amended by: the Companies Act 2006 (Commencement No 4 and Commencement No 3 (Amendment)) Order 2007, SI 2007/2607; the Companies (Cross-Border Mergers) Regulations 2007, SI 2007/2974; the Companies Act 2006 (Commencement No 5, Transitional Provisions and Savings) Order 2007, SI 2007/3495; the Companies Act 2006 (Commencement No 6, Saving and Commencement Nos 3 and 5 (Amendment)) Order 2008, SI 2008/674; the Companies Act 2006 (Commencement No 8, Transitional Provisions and Savings) Order 2008, SI 2008/2860; the Companies (Shareholders' Rights) Regulations 2009, SI 2009/1632.

ARRANGEMENT OF ARTICLES

[2.31]

1 Citation, interpretation and coming into force

(1) This Order may be cited as the Companies Act 2006 (Commencement No 3, Consequential Amendments, Transitional Provisions and Savings) Order 2007.

(2) In this Order—

"the 1985 Act" means the Companies Act 1985; and

"the 1986 Order" means the Companies (Northern Ireland) Order 1986.

(3) The provisions of this Order come into force as follows—

(a) articles 1, 2, 8, 10 and 11 and Schedules 2, 4 and 5 come into force on 1st October 2007;

(b) article 3 comes into force on 1st November 2007;

(c) article 4 comes into force on 15th December 2007;

(d) article 5 comes into force on 1st October 2008;

(e) other provisions of this Order come into force on the same date as the provisions (or repeals) in relation to which they apply.

NOTES

Commencement: 1 October 2007.

[2.32]

2 Provisions of the Companies Act 2006 coming into force on 1st October 2007

(1) The following provisions of the Companies Act 2006 come into force on 1st October 2007—

(a) sections 29 and 30 (resolutions and agreements affecting a company's constitution);

(b) sections 116 to 119 (inspection of register of members);

(c) sections 145 to 153 (exercise of members' rights);

(d) in Part 10 (a company's directors)—

section 154 (companies required to have directors);

section 160 (appointment of directors of public company to be voted on individually);

section 161 (validity of acts of directors);

sections 168 and 169 (removal of directors);

sections 170 to 181 (general duties of directors), except sections 175 to 177 (duty to avoid conflicts of interest, duty not to accept benefits from third parties and duty to declare interest in proposed transaction or arrangement);

sections 188 to 226 (transactions with directors requiring approval of members);

sections 227 to 230 (directors' service contracts);

section 231 (contract with sole member who is also a director);

sections 232 to 239 (directors' liabilities);

sections [248] to 259 (supplementary provisions);

(e) sections 260 to 269 (derivative claims and proceedings by members);

(f) in Part 13 (resolutions and meetings)—

sections 281 to 287 (general provisions about resolutions);

sections 288 to 300 (written resolutions);

sections 301 to 307, 310 to 326, 327(1), (2)(a) and (b) and (3), 328, 329, 330(1) to (5), (6)(a) and (b) and (7), 331, 332, 334 and 335 (resolutions at meetings);

sections 336 to 340 (public companies: additional requirements for AGMs);

sections 341 to 354 (additional requirements for quoted companies);

sections 355 to 359 (records of resolutions and meetings);

sections 360 and 361 (supplementary provisions);

(g) section 417 (contents of directors' report: business review);

(h) sections 485 to 488 (appointment of auditors of private companies);

(i) section 993 (fraudulent trading);

(j) sections 994 to 999 (protection of members against unfair prejudice);

(k) sections 1035 to 1039 and 1124 and Schedule 3 (company investigations: amendments);

(l) sections 1121 to 1123 and 1125 to 1133 (general supplementary provisions relating to offences), as they apply to offences under Part 14 or 15 of the 1985 Act.

(2) Sections 362 to 379 of the Companies Act 2006 (control of political donations and expenditure), with the exception of the provisions specified in article 5 of this Order (which relate to independent election candidates), come into force in Great Britain on 1st October 2007.

(3) The following provisions of the Companies Act 2006 come into force on 1st October 2007 so far as necessary for the purposes of the provisions mentioned in paragraphs (1) and (2)—

(a) section 17 (a company's constitution);

(b) section 385 (quoted and unquoted companies);

(c) section 540(1) and (4) (shares);

(d) section 545 (companies having a share capital);

(e) section 546 (issued and allotted share capital);

(f) section 548 (equity share capital);

(g) section 629 (classes of shares);

(h) sections 1121, 1122, 1125 and 1127 to 1133 (provisions relating to offences);

(i) section 1158 (meaning of "UK-registered company");

(j) section 1168 (hard copy and electronic form and related expressions); and

(k) in section 1173 (minor definitions: general), the definitions of "body corporate" (and "corporation"), "firm" and "working day".

(4) Section 1284 of the Companies Act 2006 (extension of Companies Acts to Northern Ireland) comes into force on 1st October 2007 so far as necessary for the purposes of the provisions mentioned in paragraph (1)(a) to (j).

NOTES

Commencement: 1 October 2007.

Para (1): number in square brackets in sub-para (d) substituted by the Companies Act 2006 (Commencement No 4 and Commencement No 3 (Amendment)) Order 2007, SI 2007/2607, art 4(1), as from 30 September 2007. The original number in this sub-para was '247' and this substitution (which came into force before this article came into force) had the effect of preventing s 247 of the 2006 Act coming into force on 1 October 2007.

[2.33]

3 Provisions of the Companies Act 2006 coming into force on 1st November 2007

(1) Sections 362 to 379 of the Companies Act 2006 (control of political donations and expenditure), with the exception of the provisions specified in article 5 of this Order (which relate to independent election candidates), come into force in Northern Ireland on 1st November 2007.

(2) The following provisions of the Companies Act 2006 come into force on 1st November 2007 so far as necessary for the purposes of the provisions mentioned in paragraph (1)—

(a) section 546 (issued and allotted share capital);

(b) section 1158 (meaning of "UK-registered company");

(c) in section 1173 (minor definitions: general), the definition of "body corporate"; and

(d) section 1284 (extension of Companies Acts to Northern Ireland).

NOTES

Commencement: 1 November 2007.

Part 2   CA 2006 commencement etc

[2.34]

4   Provisions of the Companies Act 2006 coming into force on 15th December 2007

(1)   Section 1068 of the Companies Act 2006 (registrar's requirements as to form, authentication and manner of delivery), other than subsection (5) (which is already wholly in force), comes into force on 15th December 2007 so far as necessary for the purposes of [the Companies (Cross-Border Mergers) Regulations 2007].

(2)   The following provisions of the Companies Act 2006 come into force on 15th December 2007 so far as necessary for the purposes of the provisions mentioned in paragraph (1)—
   (a)   section 1168 (hard copy and electronic form and related expressions); and
   (b)   section 1284 (extension of Companies Acts to Northern Ireland).

NOTES

Commencement: 15 December 2007.

Para (1): words in square brackets substituted the Companies (Cross-Border Mergers) Regulations 2007, SI 2007/2974, reg 4(5), as from 15 December 2007.

[2.35]

5   Provisions of the Companies Act 2006 coming into force on 1st October 2008

(1)   The following provisions of the Companies Act 2006 (which have the effect of applying the provisions about control of political donations and expenditure to independent election candidates) come into force on 1st October 2008—
   (a)   in section 362(a), the words "and to independent election candidates";
   (b)   in section 363(2)(a), the words "or an independent election candidate to whom";
   (c)   section 363(3);
   (d)   in section 363(4), the words "or independent election candidate" and "independent candidate";
   (e)   section 364(3);
   (f)   in section 365(1)(a) and (b)(i), the words "or an independent election candidate";
   (g)   in section 366(1)(a), the words "or to an independent election candidate";
   (h)   in section 367(3)(a), the words "or independent election candidates";
   (i)   in section 378(2), the words "or to an independent election candidate".

(2)   Section 1284 of the Companies Act 2006 (extension of Companies Acts to Northern Ireland) comes into force on 1st October 2008 so far as necessary for the purposes of the provisions mentioned in paragraph (1).

NOTES

Commencement: 1 October 2008.

[2.36]

6   Transitional adaptations of provisions brought into force

The provisions brought into force by this Order have effect subject to any transitional adaptations specified in Schedule 1 to this Order.

NOTES

Commencement: see art 1(3)(e) at **[2.31]**.

[2.37]

7   Interpretation of provisions brought into force

Where an expression in a provision brought into force by this Order (or in an adaptation made by this Order of such a provision)—
   (a)   is defined in the 1985 Act or the 1986 Order ("the old definition"); and
   (b)   is defined in the Companies Act 2006 by another provision that is not yet in force for the purposes of the provision brought into force ("the new definition"),
the expression has, for the purposes of the provision brought into force (or the adaptation), the meaning given by the old definition until the new definition is brought into force for the purposes of that provision.

NOTES

Commencement: see art 1(3)(e) at **[2.31]**.

[2.38]

8   Repeals

Sections 1284(2) and 1295 of, and Schedule 16 to, the Companies Act 2006 (repeals) come into force on 1st October 2007 so far as relating to the repeal of the provisions specified in Schedule 2 to this Order.

NOTES

Commencement: 1 October 2007.

[2.39]
9   Transitional provisions and savings

Schedule 3 to this Order contains transitional provisions and savings relating to the provisions (and repeals) brought into force by this Order.

NOTES
Commencement: see art 1(3)(e) at **[2.31]**.

[2.40]
10   Consequential amendments and repeals

(1)   The consequential amendments in Schedule 4 to this Order have effect.

(2)   In that Schedule—
Part 1 contains amendments of provisions of the 1985 Act,
Part 2 contains amendments of the 1986 Order, and
Part 3 contains amendments of other enactments and instruments.

(3)   The consequential repeals in Schedule 5 to this Order have effect.

NOTES
Commencement: 1 October 2007.

[2.41]
11   Revocation of spent transitional adaptations

The following provisions (which make transitional adaptations that are no longer needed as a result of this Order) are revoked—
   (a)   in Schedule 1 to the Companies Act 2006 (Commencement No 1, Transitional Provisions and Savings) Order 2006, paragraphs 12(2) and 16;
   (b)   in Schedule 1 to the Companies Act 2006 (Commencement No 2, Consequential Amendments, Transitional Provisions and Savings) Order 2007, paragraph 4.

NOTES
Commencement: 1 October 2007.

[2.42]
12   General savings

(1)   The amendments and repeals made by this Order do not affect the operation of section 1297 of the Companies Act 2006 (continuity of the law).

(2)   Nothing in this Order affects any provision of the 1985 Act or the 1986 Order as applied by the Limited Liability Partnerships Regulations 2001 or the Limited Liability Partnerships Regulations (Northern Ireland) 2004 to limited liability partnerships.

NOTES
Commencement: see art 1(3)(e) at **[2.31]**.

SCHEDULES

SCHEDULE 1
TRANSITIONAL ADAPTATIONS OF PROVISIONS BROUGHT INTO FORCE
Article 6

A company's constitution (s 17)

[2.43]
1. (1)   Section 17 (a company's constitution) has effect with the following adaptation.

(2)   Make the existing provision subsection (1).

(3)   After that subsection insert—

"(2)   Unless the context otherwise requires, references in this Act to a company's articles (including the reference in subsection (1) above) include the company's memorandum.".

Inspection of register of members (s 116)

2. (1)   Section 116 (rights to inspect and require copies of register and index of members' names) has effect with the following adaptation.

(2)   After subsection (1) (right of inspection) insert—

"(1A)   The right conferred by subsection (1) is not exercisable when the register is closed under section 358 of the Companies Act 1985 or Article 366 of the Companies (Northern Ireland) Order 1986.".

Exercise of members' rights (ss 145 to 153)

3. *(1)   Section 145 (effect of provision of articles as to enjoyment or exercise of members' rights) has effect with the following adaptation.*

(2)   In subsection (3)(h), for "section 423 (right to be sent a copy of annual accounts and reports)" substitute "section 238 of the Companies Act 1985 or Article 246 of the Companies (Northern Ireland) Order 1986 (persons entitled to receive copies of accounts and reports).".

4. *(1)   Section 146 (traded companies: nomination of persons to enjoy information rights) has effect with the following adaptations.*

(2)   In subsection (3)(b)(i), for "section 431 or 432 (right to require copies of accounts and reports)," substitute "section 239 of the Companies Act 1985 or Article 247 of the Companies (Northern Ireland) Order 1986 (right to demand copies of accounts and annual reports),".

(3)   For the second sentence of subsection (4) substitute "Section 251 of the Companies Act 1985 or Article 259 of the Companies (Northern Ireland) Order 1986 (summary financial statements) applies to copies of accounts and reports required to be sent out by virtue of this section to a person nominated to enjoy information rights as it applies to copies of accounts and reports required to be sent out to a member of the company in accordance with section 238 of that Act or Article 246 of that Order.".

5. *(1)   Section 153(1) (exercise of rights held on behalf of others: members' requests) has effect with the following adaptation.*

(2)   Omit paragraph (d).

General duties of directors (ss 170 to 181)

6. *(1)   Section 170 (scope and nature of general duties) has effect with the following adaptations.*

(2)   In subsection (1), for "177" substitute "174".

(3)   Omit subsection (2).

(4)   In subsection (3) after "The general duties" insert "in sections 171 to 174".

7. *(1)   Section 178 (civil consequences of breach of general duties) has effect with the following adaptation.*

(2)   In subsection (1), for "177" substitute "174".

8. *(1)   Section 180 (consent, approval or authorisation by members) has effect with the following adaptations.*

(2)   Omit subsection (1).

(3)   In subsection (2), omit the words from ", except that" to the end.

(4)   In subsection (4), omit paragraph (b).

9. *(1)   Section 181 (modification of provisions in relation to charitable companies) has effect with the following modifications.*

(2)   Omit subsections (2) and (3).

Transactions with directors requiring approval of members (ss 188 to 226)

10. *(1)   Section 191 (meaning of "substantial" non-cash asset) has effect with the following adaptations.*

(2)   In subsection (4)—
  (a)   for "Part 15" substitute "Part 7 of the Companies Act 1985 or Part 8 of the Companies (Northern Ireland) Order 1986", and
  (b)   for "section 424" substitute "section 238A of that Act or Article 246A of that Order".

11. *(1)   Section 205 (exception for expenditure on defending proceedings etc) has effect with the following adaptation.*

(2)   In subsection (5), for the words from "section 661(3)" to the end substitute—
  "section 144(3) or (4) of the Companies Act 1985 or Article 154(3) or (4) of the Companies (Northern Ireland) Order 1986 (acquisition of shares by innocent nominee), or
  section 727 of the Companies Act 1985 or Article 675 of the Companies (Northern Ireland) Order 1986 (general power to grant relief in case of honest and reasonable conduct).".

Directors' liabilities (ss 232 to 239)

12. *(1)   Section 234 (qualifying third party indemnity provision) has effect with the following adaptation.*

(2)   In subsection (6), for the words from "section 661(3)" to the end substitute—
  "section 144(3) or (4) of the Companies Act 1985 or Article 154(3) or (4) of the Companies (Northern Ireland) Order 1986 (acquisition of shares by innocent nominee), or

section 727 of the Companies Act 1985 or Article 675 of the Companies (Northern Ireland) Order 1986 (general power to grant relief in case of honest and reasonable conduct).".

Written resolutions (ss 288 to 300)

13.   (1)   Section 288 (written resolutions of private companies) has effect with the following adaptations.

(2)   In subsection (2) (resolutions that may not be passed as a written resolution)—

    (a)   in paragraph (b), for "a resolution under section 510" substitute "a resolution under section 391 of the Companies Act 1985 or Article 399 of the Companies (Northern Ireland) Order 1986";

    (b)   after that paragraph add—

        "(c)   a resolution under section 80A of the Companies Act 1985 or Article 90A of the Companies (Northern Ireland) Order 1986 revoking, varying or renewing the authority of the directors to allot securities.".

(3)   After subsection (5) add—

    "(6)   A written resolution under any of the provisions of the Companies Act 1985 or the Companies (Northern Ireland) Order 1986 mentioned in sections 300A to 300D is not effective unless the procedural requirements specified in those sections are complied with.".

(4)   After section 300 insert—

"*Transitional application of procedural requirements*

300A Disapplication of pre-emption rights

(1)   This section applies to a written resolution—

    (a)   under section 95(2) of the Companies Act 1985 or Article 105(2) of the Companies (Northern Ireland) Order 1986 (disapplication of pre-emption rights), or

    (b)   renewing a resolution under that provision.

(2)   The statement required by section 95(5) of that Act or Article 105(5) of that Order (statement by directors to be circulated with notice of meeting) must be sent or submitted to every eligible member at or before the time at which the resolution is sent or submitted to him.

(3)   Section 95(6) of that Act or Article 105(6) of that Order (offences) applies in relation to the inclusion in any such statement of matter that is misleading, false or deceptive in a material particular.

300B Financial assistance for purchase of company's own shares or those of holding company

(1)   This section applies to a written resolution under section 155(4) or (5) of the Companies Act 1985 or Article 165(4) or (5) of the Companies (Northern Ireland) Order 1986 (financial assistance for purchase of company's own shares or those of holding company).

(2)   The documents referred to in section 157(4)(a) of that Act or Article 167(4)(a) of that Order (documents to be available at meeting) must be sent or submitted to every eligible member at or before the time at which the resolution is sent or submitted to him.

300C Authority for off-market purchase or contingent purchase contract of company's own shares

(1)   This section applies to a written resolution—

    (a)   conferring authority to make an off-market purchase of the company's own shares under section 164(2) of the Companies Act 1985 or Article 174(2) of the Companies (Northern Ireland) Order 1986,

    (b)   conferring authority to vary a contract for an off-market purchase of the company's own shares under section 164(7) of that Act or Article 174(7) of that Order, or

    (c)   varying, revoking or renewing any such authority under section 164(3) of that Act or Article 174(3) of that Order.

(2)   Section 164(5) of that Act or Article 174(5) of that Order (resolution ineffective if passed by exercise of voting rights by member holding shares to which the resolution relates) does not apply.

    But for the purposes of section 289 of this Act (eligible members) a member holding shares to which the resolution relates shall not be regarded as a member who would be entitled to vote on the resolution.

(3)   The documents referred to in section 164(6) of that Act or Article 174(6) of that Order (documents to be available at company's registered office and at meeting), and, where that provision applies by virtue of section 164(7) of that Act or Article 174(7) of that Order, the further documents referred to in that provision, must be sent or submitted to every eligible member at or before the time at which the resolution is sent or submitted to him.

(4)   Subsections (2) and (3) above also have effect in relation to a written resolution in relation to which the provisions of section 164(3) to (7) of the Companies Act 1985 or Article 174(3) to (7) of the Companies (Northern Ireland) Order 1986 apply by virtue of—

    (a)   *section 165(2) of that Act or Article 175(2) of that Order (authority for contingent purchase contract), or*

    (b)   *section 167(2) of that Act or Article 177(2) of that Order (approval for release of rights under contracts approved under section 164 or 165 or Article 174 or 175).*

300D Approval for payment out of capital

(1) This section applies to a written resolution giving approval under section 173(2) of the Companies Act 1985 or Article 183(2) of the Companies (Northern Ireland) Order 1986 (redemption or purchase of company's own shares out of capital).

(2) Section 174(2) of that Act or Article 184(2) of that Order (resolution ineffective if passed by exercise of voting rights by member holding shares to which the resolution relates) does not apply.

    But for the purposes of section 289 of this Act (eligible members) a member holding shares to which the resolution relates shall not be regarded as a member who would be entitled to vote on the resolution.

(3) The documents referred to in section 174(4) of that Act or Article 184(4) of that Order (documents to be available at meeting) must be sent or submitted to every eligible member at or before the time at which the resolution is sent or submitted to him.".

Resolutions at meetings (ss 301 to 335)

14. *(1) Section 306 (power of court to order meeting) has effect with the following adaptation.*

(2) In subsection (1)(b) for "or this Act" substitute "this Act, the Companies Act 1985 or the Companies (Northern Ireland) Order 1986".

Public companies: additional requirements for AGMs (ss 336 to 340)

15. *(1) Section 336 (public companies: annual general meeting) has effect with the following adaptations.*

(2) In subsection (1), for "6 months" substitute "7 months".

(3) In subsection (2), for "notice under section 392 (alteration of accounting reference date)" substitute "notice under section 225 of the Companies Act 1985 or Article 233 of the Companies (Northern Ireland) Order 1986 (alteration of accounting reference date)".

Contents of directors' report: business review (s 417)

16. *(1) Section 417 (contents of directors' report: business review) has effect with the following adaptations.*

(2) For subsection (1) substitute—

    "(1) Unless the company is entitled to small companies exemption in relation to the directors' report, the report must contain a business review.

    (1A) A company is entitled to small companies exemption in relation to the directors' report for a financial year if it—

        (a)   *qualifies as small in relation to that year under Part 7 of the Companies Act 1985 or Part 8 of the Companies (Northern Ireland) Order 1986, and*

        (b)   *is not, and was not at any time within that year, an ineligible company as defined in section 247A(1B) of that Act or Article 255A(1B) of that Order.".*

(3) For subsection (7) substitute—

    "(7) Where a company—

        (a)   *qualifies as medium-sized in relation to a financial year under Part 7 of the Companies Act 1985 or Part 8 of the Companies (Northern Ireland) Order 1986, and*

        (b)   *is not, and was not at any time within that year, an ineligible company as defined in section 247A(1B) of that Act or Article 255A(1B) of that Order,*

    the directors' report for the year need not comply with the requirements of subsection (6) so far as they relate to non-financial information.".

Appointment of auditors of private company (ss 485 to 488)

17. *(1) Section 485 (appointment of auditors of private companies: general) has effect with the following adaptations.*

(2) For paragraph (a) of subsection (2) substitute—

    "(a) the end of the period allowed for delivering accounts and reports under section 244 of the Companies Act 1985 or Article 252 of the Companies (Northern Ireland) Order 1986, or".

(3) In paragraph (b) of subsection (2), for "section 423" substitute "section 238 of the Companies Act 1985 or Article 246 of the Companies (Northern Ireland) Order 1986".

18. *(1)   Section 487 (term of office of auditors of private company) has effect with the following adaptation.*

(2)   In subsection (3) for "the provisions of this Part" substitute "the provisions of Chapter 5 of Part 11 of the Companies Act 1985 or Chapter 5 of Part 12 of the Companies (Northern Ireland) Order 1986".

Protection of members against unfair prejudice (ss 994 to 999)

19. *(1)   Section 994(3) (meaning of "company") has effect with the following adaptation.*

(2)   For paragraph (a) substitute—

> *"(a)   a company within the meaning of the Companies Act 1985 or the Companies (Northern Ireland) Order 1986;".*

Company investigations: amendments relating to offences (s 1124 and Sch 3)

20. *(1)   Schedule 3 (amendments of remaining provisions of the 1985 Act relating to offences) has effect with the following adaptations.*

(2)   Omit the words "or Northern Ireland" in the following provisions inserted in the 1985 Act—
- *(a)   in the provision inserted by paragraph 1(2) as section 444(4)(b)(ii);*
- *(b)   in the provision inserted by paragraph 3(3) as section 449(6A)(b)(ii);*
- *(c)   in the provision inserted by paragraph 4(1) as section 450(3)(b)(ii);*
- *(d)   in the provision inserted by paragraph 5(1) as section 451(2)(b)(ii).*

Meaning of "UK-registered company" (s 1158)

21. *(1)   Section 1158 (meaning of "UK-registered company") has effect with the following adaptations.*

(2)   For "a company registered under this Act" substitute "a company within the meaning of the Companies Act 1985 or the Companies (Northern Ireland) Order 1986 or a company registered under section 680 of that Act or Article 629 of that Order.".

(3)   For "an overseas company that has registered particulars under section 1046" substitute "an oversea company within the meaning of that Act or a Part 23 company within the meaning of that Order".

NOTES

Commencement: see art 1(3)(e) at **[2.31]**.

This Schedule (in so far as it was still in force) was revoked by the Companies Act 2006 (Commencement No 8, Transitional Provisions and Savings) Order 2008, SI 2008/2860, art 6(1), as from 1 October 2009. It is reproduced here out of historical interest and because of art 6(2) of the 2008 Order which provides that the revocations made by art 6(1) are subject to any relevant transitional provision or saving in Sch 2 to that Order (at **[2.91]**). For other transitional provisions and savings, see the notes below.

Paras 3–5, 10, 15–18 were previously revoked by the Companies Act 2006 (Commencement No 5, Transitional Provisions and Savings) Order 2007, SI 2007/3495, art 10(1)(b), as from 6 April 2008. With regard to para 15(2) (transitional adaptation: period within which public company must hold AGM), note that the Companies Act 2006 (Commencement No 6, Saving and Commencement Nos 3 and 5 (Amendment)) Order 2008, SI 2008/674, art 5, Sch 3, para 4 provides that the revocation of that paragraph does not have effect in relation to a company until: (a) the directors of the company have complied with CA 1985, s 241 (or Art 249 of the Companies (Northern Ireland) Order 1986) in respect of the last financial year of the company beginning before 6 April 2008, or (b) the first financial year of the company beginning on or after that date comes to an end.

Paras 6–9, 11, 12 were previously revoked by SI 2007/3495, art 10(2)(b), as from 1 October 2008. Note that paras 11, 12 were also revoked by virtue of the Companies Act 2006 (Commencement No 6, Saving and Commencement Nos 3 and 5 (Amendment)) Order 2008, SI 2008/674, art 5, Sch 3, para 1(1)(a), as from 1 October 2008.

Para 13(2)(a) was previously revoked by SI 2007/3495, art 10(1)(b), as from 6 April 2008.

Savings: note that the Companies Act 2006 (Commencement No 5, Transitional Provisions and Savings) Order 2007, SI 2007/3495, art 10(3) provides as follows—

> *"(3)   The revocation by this article of a spent transitional adaptation is subject to the same transitional provisions and savings as apply, in accordance with Schedule 4 to this Order, in relation to the repeal of the provisions of the 1985 Act or 1986 Order referred to in the adaptation.".*

SCHEDULE 2
REPEALS

Article 8

[2.44]

NOTES

Only relevant entries of this Schedule are reproduced here; the entries omitted contain repeals to provisions in the following enactments: the Water Act 1989, the Political Parties, Elections and Referendums Act 2000, and the Civil Partnership Act 2004.

PART 1
GREAT BRITAIN

Short title and chapter	Extent of repeal brought into force
Companies Act 1985 (c 6)	Section 125(6).
	Section 234(1)(a).
	Section 234ZZB.
	Section 241, as it applies to private companies.
	In section 246(4)(a), the words "and 234ZZB (directors' report: business review)".
	Section 246A(2A).
	Sections 252 and 253.
	Section 282.
	Section 285.
	Section 292.
	Sections 303 and 304.
	Sections 309 to 309C.
	Sections 312 to 316.
	Sections 318 to 322.
	Section 322B.
	Sections 330 to 347.
	Sections 347A to 347K.
	Section 356.
	In section 357—
	(a) the words "section 356 (inspection)"; and
	(b) the words from "and the power of the court" to the end.
	Sections 366 to 379.
	Section 379A(1)(b) to (e).
	[380(4)(a) and (c) to (m)].
	Sections 381 to 383.
	Sections 384 and 385, as they apply to private companies.
	Sections 385A and 386.
	Sections 387 to 388A, as they apply to private companies.
	Section 393.
	In section 437—
	(a) in subsection (1), the second sentence; and
	(b) subsections (1B) and (1C).
	Section 442(2).
	Section 446.
	In section 448(7), the words from "and liable to a fine." to the end.
	Section 449(7).
	Section 450(4).
	Section 451(3).
	Section 453(1A)(d) and the word "and" preceding it.
	Section 453A(6).
	Sections 458 to 461.
	. . .
	Section 730(5).
	. . .
	Section 741.
	Part 1 of Schedule 13.
	Schedule 15A.

Short title and chapter	Extent of repeal brought into force
	In Schedule 24, the entries relating to—
	(a) sections 210(3), 211(10), 214(5), 215(8), 216(3), 217(7), 218(3) and 219(3),
	(b) section 241(2), as it applies to private companies,
	(c) sections 314(3), 318(8), 322B(4), 323(2), 324(7), 326(2), (3), (4) and (5), 328(6), 329(3), 342(1), (2) and (3), 343(8), 356(5), 366(4), 367(3) and (5), 372(4) and (6), 376(7), . . . 381B(2), 382(5), 382B(2) and 383(4),
	(d) section 387(2), as it applies to private companies, and
	(e) sections 429(6), 430A(6), 444(3), 448(7), 449(6), 450, 451, 453A(5), 455(1) and (2), 458, 461(5) and 720(4).
Insolvency Act 1986 (c 45)	In Schedule 13, in Part 1, the entries relating to the following provisions of the Companies Act 1985—
	(a) section 380(4), and
	(b) section 461(6).
Companies Act 1989 (c 40)	Section 16.
	Section 113.
	Section 114(1).
	Section 115(2) and (3).
	Section 138.
	Section 143(8) and (9).
	In Schedule 10, paragraph 10.
	In Schedule 18, paragraphs 34 to 36.
	In Schedule 19, paragraphs 8, 9, and 17.
Companies (Audit, Investigations and Community Enterprise) Act 2004 (c 27)	Section 19(1).
	Section 20.
	In Schedule 2, paragraphs 7 to 9, 22 and 23.

NOTES

Commencement: 1 October 2007.

Words in square brackets substituted, and first and final words omitted revoked, by the Companies Act 2006 (Commencement No 4 and Commencement No 3 (Amendment)) Order 2007, SI 2007/2607, art 4(2), as from 30 September 2007 (ie, before this Schedule came into force).

Entry relating to s 734(1) (ie, second words omitted) revoked by the Companies Act 2006 (Commencement No 5, Transitional Provisions and Savings) Order 2007, SI 2007/3495, art 11, Sch 5, para 2(1), (2), as from 14 January 2008 (as amended by the Companies Act 2006 (Commencement No 6, Saving and Commencement Nos 3 and 5 (Amendment)) Order 2008, SI 2008/674, art 5, Sch 3, para 7, as from 6 April 2008).

(*Sch 2, Pt 2 (Northern Ireland) contains various repeals to provisions in the Companies (Northern Ireland) Order 1986, the Companies (Northern Ireland) Order 1990, the Companies (No 2) (Northern Ireland) Order 1990, and the Companies (Audit, Investigations and Community Enterprises) (Northern Ireland) Order 2005 (outside the scope of this work).*)

SCHEDULE 3
TRANSITIONAL PROVISIONS AND SAVINGS

Article 9

Resolutions and agreements affecting a company's constitution (ss 29 and 30)

[2.45]

1. (1) Sections 29 and 30 of the Companies Act 2006 (resolutions and agreements affecting a company's constitution) apply to resolutions passed and agreements made on or after 1st October 2007.

(2) The provisions of section 380(1) and (5) of the 1985 Act or Article 388(1) and (5) of the 1986 Order continue to apply in relation to resolutions passed and agreements made, but not forwarded to the registrar, before that date.

This does not affect the operation of section 1297 of the Companies Act 2006 (continuity of the law) in relation to things done under those provisions.

Inspection of register of members (ss 116 to 119)

2. (1)   Sections 116 to 119 of the Companies Act 2006 (inspection of register of members) apply where—

  (a)   the request is made on or after 1st October 2007, and

  (b)   the company is not obliged to deliver an annual return under section 363 of the 1985 Act or Article 371 of the 1986 Order made up to a date before 1st October 2008.

(2)   Sections 356 and 357 of the 1985 Act or Articles 364 and 365 of the 1986 Order continue to apply to requests made before 1st October 2007 or after that date to a company that is so obliged.

Exercise of members' rights (ss 145 to 153)

3. (1)   Section 145 of the Companies Act 2006 (effect of provisions of articles as to enjoyment or exercise of members' rights) applies in relation to things required or authorised to be done as mentioned in subsection (2) of that section on or after 1st October 2007.

(2)   Nominations under section 146 of that Act (traded companies: nomination of persons to enjoy information rights) may be made at any time on or after 1st October 2007.

  A company is not required to act on a nomination before 1st January 2008; but if it does so, sections 147 to 150 apply.

(3)   Section 152 of that Act (exercise of rights where shares held on behalf of others: exercise in different ways) applies in relation to the exercise of rights on or after 1st October 2007.

(4)   A request may be made under section 153 of that Act (exercise of rights where shares held on behalf of others: members' requests) at any time on or after 1st October 2007.

Validity of acts of directors (s 161)

4. (1)   Section 161 of the Companies Act 2006 (validity of acts of directors) applies to acts done on or after 1st October 2007.

(2)   Section 285 of the 1985 Act (validity of acts of director or manager) or Article 293 of the 1986 Order (validity of acts of director) continues to apply to acts done before that date.

Removal of directors (ss 168 and 169)

5. (1)   Section 169(5) of the Companies Act 2006 (circumstances in which representations need not be sent out or read out at the meeting) applies where the representations are received by the company on or after 1st October 2007.

(2)   Section 304(4) of the 1985 Act or Article 312(4) of the 1986 Order continues to apply where the representations are received by the company before that date.

Transactions requiring members' approval: directors' long-term service contracts (ss 188 and 189)

6. (1)   Sections 188 and 189 of the Companies Act 2006 (directors' long-term service contracts: requirement of members' approval) apply to agreements made on or after 1st October 2007.

(2)   A resolution passed before that date approving the provision made by such an agreement is effective for the purposes of those sections if it complies with the requirements of those sections.

(3)   Section 188(4) (addition of unexpired period of earlier contract in determining guaranteed period under new contract) applies whether the original contract (within the meaning of that provision) was entered into before or after that date.

(4)   Section 319 of the 1985 Act or Article 327 of the 1986 Order continues to apply to agreements made before that date.

Transactions requiring members' approval: substantial property transactions (ss 190 to 196)

7. (1)   Sections 190 to 196 of the Companies Act 2006 (substantial property transactions: requirement of members' approval) apply to arrangements or transactions entered into on or after 1st October 2007.

(2)   A resolution passed before that date approving an arrangement or transaction is effective for the purposes of those sections if it complies with the requirements of those sections.

(3)   Sections 320 to 322 of the 1985 Act or Articles 328 to 330 of the 1986 Order continue to apply in relation to arrangements or transactions entered into before that date.

Transactions requiring members' approval: loans, quasi-loans and credit transactions (ss 197 to 214)

8. (1)   Sections 197 to 214 of the Companies Act 2006 (loans, quasi-loans and credit transactions: requirement of members' approval) apply to transactions or arrangements entered into on or after 1st October 2007.

(2)   A resolution passed before that date approving a transaction or arrangement is effective for the purposes of those sections if it complies with the requirements of those sections.

(3)   Sections 330 to 342 of the 1985 Act or Articles 338 to 350 of the 1986 Order continue to apply in relation to a contravention occurring before that date.

9. Approval is not required under section 197, 198, 200 or 201 of the Companies Act 2006 (requirement of members' approval for loans etc) for anything done by a company in pursuance of an agreement entered into before 1st October 2007 that, by virtue of section 337A of the 1985 Act or Article 345A of the 1986 Order (funding of director's expenditure on defending proceedings), would not have required approval if done before that date.

10.   (1)   This paragraph applies where before 1st October 2007 a company has done anything—
  (a)   pursuant to section 337(1) or (2) of the 1985 Act or Article 345(1) or (2) of the 1986 Order (funding of director's expenditure on duty to company), and
  (b)   on the condition mentioned in section 337(3)(b) of that Act or Article 345(3)(b) of that Order (condition requiring repayment of loan etc if approval of company in general meeting not given within six months).

(2)   If that condition has not been satisfied before that date, it continues to apply notwithstanding the repeal of that section or that Article, but subject as follows.

(3)   In the case of a private company that by reason of the repeal of section 366 of the 1985 Act or Article 374 of the 1986 Order with effect from that date ceases to be required to hold an annual general meeting, the condition shall be read as if it provided—
  (a)   that the approval of the company is required on or before the last date on which the company would have been required to hold an annual general meeting but for the repeal, and
  (b)   that the loan is to be repaid within six months from that date if such approval is not forthcoming.

11.   (1)   This paragraph applies where before 1st October 2007 a company has done anything—
  (a)   pursuant to section 337A(1) or (3) of the 1985 Act or Article 345A(1) or (3) of the 1986 Order (funding of director's expenditure on defending proceedings), and
  (b)   on the terms mentioned in section 337A(4) of that Act or Article 345A(4) of that Order (terms requiring repayment of loan etc if defendant convicted, has judgment given against him or refused relief).

(2)   If immediately before that date—
  (a)   it is not yet known whether repayment will be required, or
  (b)   repayment is required but had not been made,
those terms continue to apply notwithstanding the repeal of that section or that Article.

Transactions requiring members' approval: payments for loss of office (ss 215 to 222)

12.   (1)   Sections 215 to 222 of the Companies Act 2006 (payments for loss of office: requirement of members' approval) apply in relation to any such loss of office or employment as is mentioned in section 215(1)(a) or (b), or any such retirement as is mentioned in section 215(1)(c) or (d), occurring on or after 1st October 2007.

(2)   A resolution passed before that date approving a payment is effective for the purposes of those sections if it complies with the requirements of those sections.

(3)   Sections 312 to 316 of the 1985 Act or Articles 320 to 324 of the 1986 Order continue to apply in relation to loss of office or retirement within the meaning of those provisions occurring before that date.

(4)   For the purposes of this paragraph loss of office or retirement is regarded as occurring—
  (a)   in the case of a directorship, when the person ceases to be a director;
  (b)   in the case of any other office, when the person ceases to hold that office;
  (c)   in the case of employment, when the employment comes to an end.

Directors' service contracts (ss 227 to 230)

13.   (1)   Sections 228 to 230 of the Companies Act 2006 (directors' service contracts) apply to—
  (a)   contracts within section 227(1) of that Act entered into on or after 1st October 2007,
  (b)   appointments within section 227(2) of that Act made on or after that date, and
  (c)   contracts to which section 318(1) of the 1985 Act or Article 326(1) of the 1986 Order applied immediately before that date.

(2)   Until regulations under section 1136 of the Companies Act 2006 [come into force] specifying a place for the purposes of section 228(2)(b), the copies and memoranda referred to in section 228 may be kept by a company—
  (a)   at any place where its register of members is kept, or
  (b)   at its principal place of business,
provided that place is situated in the part of the United Kingdom in which the company is registered.

(3)   Until section 1068(1) of the Companies Act 2006 comes into force the notice referred to in section 228(4) must be given on the form prescribed for the purposes of section 318(4) of the 1985 Act or Article 326(4) of the 1986 Order.

(4) The provisions of section 318 of the 1985 Act or Article 326 of the 1986 Order continue to apply in relation to—

(a) any default before 1st October 2007 in complying with section 318(1) or (5) or Article 326(1) or (5);

(b) any request for inspection under section 318(7) or Article 326(7) made before that date;

(c) any duty to give notice under section 318(4) or Article 326(4) arising before that date.

Contracts with sole member who is a director (s 231)

14. (1) Section 231 of the Companies Act 2006 (contracts with sole member who is a director) applies to contracts entered into on or after 1st October 2007.

(2) Section 322B of the 1985 Act or Article 330B of the 1986 Order continues to apply to contracts entered into before that date.

Directors' liabilities (ss 232 to 239)

15. (1) Sections 232 to 236 of the Companies Act 2006 (restrictions on provision protecting directors from liability) apply to any provision made on or after 1st October 2007.

(2) Sections 309A, 309B and 309C(1) to (3) and (6) of the 1985 Act or Article 318 of the 1986 Order (so far as it relates to directors) continue to apply in relation to any provision to which they applied immediately before that date.

16. (1) Sections 237 and 238 of the Companies Act 2006 (copies of qualifying indemnity provision to be available for inspection etc) apply to—

(a) qualifying indemnity provision within the meaning of section 237 made on or after 1st October 2007, and

(b) qualifying third party indemnity provision within the meaning of section 309B(1) of the 1985 Act to which section 309C(4) and (5) of that Act applied immediately before that date.

(2) Until regulations under section 1136 of the Companies Act 2006 [come into force] specifying a place for the purposes of section 237(3)(b), the copies and memoranda referred to in section 237 may be kept by a company—

(a) at any place where its register of members is kept, or

(b) at its principal place of business,

provided that place is situated in the part of the United Kingdom in which the company is registered.

(3) Until section 1068(1) of the Companies Act 2006 comes into force the notice referred to in section 237(5) must be given on the form prescribed for the purposes of section 318(4) of the 1985 Act or Article 326(4) of the 1986 Order.

(4) The provisions of section 318 of the 1985 Act, as applied by section 309C(4) and (5), continue to apply in relation to—

(a) any default before 1st October 2007 in complying with section 318(1) or (5), as so applied;

(b) any request for inspection under section 318(7), as so applied, made before that date;

(c) any duty to give notice under section 318(4), as so applied, arising before that date.

17. (1) Section 239 of the Companies Act 2006 (ratification of acts of directors giving rise to liability) applies to conduct by a director on or after 1st October 2007.

(2) Conduct by a director before that date is subject to the law relating to ratification that applied immediately before that date.

18. . . .

Records of meetings of directors (ss 248 and 249)

19. (1) Sections 248 and 249 of the Companies Act 2006 (records of meetings of directors) apply to meetings held on or after 1st October 2007.

(2) Section 382 of the 1985 Act or Article 390 of the 1986 Order continues to apply to meetings of directors held before that date.

Derivative claims and proceedings by members (ss 260 to 269)

20. (1) On and after 1st October 2007 sections 260 to 264 of the Companies Act 2006 (derivative claims in England and Wales or Northern Ireland) apply to all derivative claims, subject to the following provisions.

(2) Those sections do not apply, and the law in force immediately before 1st October 2007 continues to apply, where the claimant (in Northern Ireland, the plaintiff) has applied for permission (in Northern Ireland, leave) to continue the claim before that date.

(3) If, or to the extent that, the claim arises from acts or omissions that occurred before 1st October 2007, the court must exercise its powers under those sections so as to secure that the claim is allowed to proceed as a derivative claim only if, or to the extent that, it would have been allowed to proceed as a derivative claim under the law in force immediately before that date.

21. (1) This paragraph applies where an application is made under section 266 or 267 (derivative proceedings in Scotland).

(2) If the cause of action arises, wholly or to any extent, from an act or omission that occurred before 1st October 2007, the court shall exercise its powers under those sections so as to secure that the proceedings in respect of that act or omission are allowed to proceed as derivative proceedings only to the extent that they could have been pursued by the applicant under the law in force immediately before that date.

General provisions about resolutions (ss 281 to 287)

22. (1) Sections 281 to 287 of the Companies Act 2006 (general provisions about resolutions), apply—

    (a)   to written resolutions to which sections 288 to 300 of that Act apply (see paragraph 24);

    (b)   to resolutions (other than written resolutions)—

        (i)   of which notice is given on or after 1st October 2007, or

        (ii) that are proposed at a meeting of which notice is given on or after 1st October 2007, other than a meeting convened in pursuance of a requisition made under section 368 or 376 of the 1985 Act or Article 376 or 384 of the 1986 Order made before that date.

(2) The provisions of the 1985 Act or 1986 Order continue to apply to resolutions (other than written resolutions)—

    (a)   of which notice is given before 1st October 2007, or

    (b)   that are proposed at a meeting—

        (i)   of which notice was given before 1st October 2007, or

        (ii) that is convened in pursuance of a requisition under section 368 or 376 of the 1985 Act or Article 376 or 384 of the 1986 Order made before that date.

(3) The provisions referred to in sub-paragraph (2) include—

    section 370(6) of the 1985 Act or Article 378(6) of the 1986 Order (voting entitlement of members); and

    section 378 of the 1985 Act or Article 386 of the 1986 Order (extraordinary and special resolutions).

(4) Where notice of a meeting is given over more than one day, it is treated for the purposes of this paragraph as given on the first of those days.

(5) Where copies of a requisition are deposited on more than one day, the references in this paragraph to the day on which the requisition is made shall be read as references to the first day on which the copies deposited are sufficient to require the company to act.

23. [(1)] Any reference to an extraordinary resolution in a provision—

    (a)   of a company's memorandum or articles, or

    (b)   of a contract,

continues to have effect and shall continue to be construed in accordance with section 378 of the 1985 Act or Article 386 of the 1986 Order as if that section or Article had not been repealed.

[(2) Chapter 3 of Part 3 of the Companies Act 2006 (resolutions affecting a company's constitution) applies to any such resolution.]

[23A. (1) This paragraph applies where, immediately before 1st October 2007, the articles of a company provided that in the event of equality of votes on an ordinary resolution, whether on a show of hands or on a poll, the chairman should have a casting vote in addition to any other vote that the chairman might have.

(2) If that provision has not been removed by a subsequent alteration of the articles, it continues to have effect notwithstanding sections 281(3) and 282.

(3) If that provision has been removed by a subsequent alteration of the articles, the company may at any time restore that provision, which shall have effect notwithstanding sections 281(3) and 282.

[(4) Nothing in this paragraph applies in relation to a traded company (as defined by section 360C of the Companies Act 2006).]]

Written resolutions (ss 288 to 300)

24. (1) Sections 288 to 300 of the Companies Act 2006 (written resolutions) apply to resolutions for which the circulation date (see section 290) is on or after 1st October 2007.

(2) Section 381A to 381C of, and Schedule 15A to, the 1985 Act or Article 389A to 389C of, and Schedule 15A to, the 1986 Order continue to apply to resolutions sent or circulated to any relevant member before that date.

    A "relevant member" means one whose signature is required by section 381A(1) or Article 389A(1).

Members' power to require directors to call meeting (ss 303 to 305)

25. (1)   Sections 303 to 305 of the Companies Act 2006 (meetings required by members) apply to requests made on or after 1st October 2007.

(2)   Section 368 of the 1985 Act or Article 376 of the 1986 Order continues to apply to requisitions made before that date.

(3)   Where requests are made or copies of a requisition are deposited on more than one day, the references in this paragraph to the day on which the request or requisition is made shall be read as references to the first day on which the requests made or copies deposited are sufficient to require the company to act.

Notice of meetings (ss 307, 310 and 311)

26. (1)   Sections 307, 310 and 311 of the Companies Act 2006 (notice of meetings) apply in relation to meetings of which notice is given on or after 1st October 2007.

(2)   The provisions of the 1985 Act or the 1986 Order continue to apply in relation to a meeting of which notice was given before that date.

(3)   The provisions referred to in sub-paragraph (2) include sections 369 and 370(2) of the 1985 Act or Articles 377 and 378(2) of the 1986 Order.

(4)   Where notice of a meeting is given over more than one day, it is treated for the purposes of this paragraph as given on the first of those days.

[**26A.** (1)   The following provisions have effect for the purposes of section 307(6)(a) of the Companies Act 2006 (private company: requisite percentage for calling general meeting at short notice).

(2)   If immediately before 1st October 2007 there was in force in relation to a company a resolution under section 369(4) of the 1985 Act or Article 377(4) of the 1986 Order—
   (a)   specifying 90%, or
   (b)   under which the company in general meeting had determined that the percentage should be 90%,
any provision of the company's articles specifying a higher percentage shall be disregarded.

(3)   If immediately before 1st October 2007 there was in force in relation to a company a resolution under section 369(4) of the 1985 Act or Article 377(4) of the 1986 Order—
   (a)   specifying a percentage greater than 90% but less than 95%, or
   (b)   under which the company in general meeting had determined a percentage greater than 90% but less than 95%,
any provision of the company's articles specifying a different percentage shall be disregarded.

(4)   Sub-paragraph (2) or (3) does not apply in relation to provisions of the company's articles adopted on or after 1st October 2007.]

Special notice (s 312)

27. (1)   Section 312 of the Companies Act 2006 (special notice) applies in relation to resolutions for which special notice is required where notice of the intention to move the resolution is given to the company on or after 1st October 2007.

(2)   Section 379 of the 1985 Act or Article 387 of the 1986 Order continues to apply to resolutions for which special notice is required where notice of the intention to move the resolution is given to the company before that date.

Accidental failure to give notice of resolution or meeting (s 313)

28. (1)   Section 313 of the Companies Act 2006 (accidental failure to give notice of resolution or meeting) applies to resolutions or meetings of which notice is given on or after 1st October 2007.

(2)   The reference in sub-paragraph (1) to cases in which notice is given on or after 1st October 2007 includes cases in which notice would be regarded as so given if section 313 applied.

Circulation of members' statements (ss 314 to 317)

29. (1)   Sections 314 to 317 of the Companies Act 2006 (circulation of members' statements) apply to requests made on or after 1st October 2007.

(2)   Sections 376 and 377 of the 1985 Act or Articles 384 and 385 of the 1986 Order continue to apply in relation to requisitions made before that date.

(3)   So long as such a requisition made to a private company under section 376(1)(b) or Article 384(1)(b) is not complied with, section 366 of the 1985 Act or Article 374 of the 1986 Order (duty to hold annual general meeting) continues to apply in relation to the company.

This does not apply if the company is not required to comply with the requisition (see section 377 of the 1985 Act or Article 385 of the 1986 Order).

(4)   Where requests are made or copies of a requisition are deposited on more than one day, the references in this paragraph to the day on which the request or requisition is made shall be read as references to the first day on which the requests made or copies deposited are sufficient to require the company to act.

Procedure at meetings and proxies (ss 318 to 331)

30. (1)   Sections 318 to 323 of the Companies Act 2006 (procedure at meetings) and sections 324 to 331 (proxies) apply to meetings of which notice is given on or after 1st October 2007.

(2)   The provisions of the 1985 Act or the 1986 Order continue to apply to meetings of which notice was given before that date.

(3)   The provisions referred to in sub-paragraph (2) include sections 370, 370A, 372 to 375 and 378(4) of the 1985 Act or Articles 378, 378A, 380 to 383 and 386(4) of the 1986 Order.

(4)   Where notice of a meeting is given over more than one day, it is treated for the purposes of this paragraph as given on the first of those days.

Application of provisions to class meetings (ss 334 and 335)

31. (1)   Sections 334 and 335 of the Companies Act 2006 (application of provisions of Chapter 3 to class meetings) apply to requests and meetings in relation to which the provisions applied by those sections have effect.

(2)   Section 125(6) of the 1985 Act or Article 135(6) of the 1986 Order continues to apply to meetings of which notice is given before 1st October 2007.

(3)   Where notice of a meeting is given over more than one day, it is treated for the purposes of sub-paragraph (2) as given on the first of those days.

Annual general meetings (ss 336 to 340)

32. (1)   The repeal of section 366 of the 1985 Act or Article 374 of the 1986 Order (duty to hold annual general meeting) does not affect any provision of a private company's memorandum or articles that expressly requires the company to hold an annual general meeting.

(2)   Any such provision continues to have such effect as it had immediately before 1st October 2007.

(3)   Provision specifying that one or more directors are to retire at an annual general meeting of the company is not provision expressly requiring the company to hold an annual general meeting.

[(4)   A company is not to be treated as one whose articles expressly require it to hold an annual general meeting if immediately before 1st October 2007 there was in force in relation to the company a resolution under section 366A of the 1985 Act or Article 374A of the 1986 Order (election to dispense with annual general meetings).]

33.   The repeal of section 367 of the 1985 Act (default power of Secretary of State to call AGM) has effect in relation to a private company as from 1st October 2007, even if an application under that section has been made, or the Secretary of State has called or directed the calling of a meeting under that section, before that date.

34. (1)   The repeal of sections 376 and 377 of the 1985 Act or Articles 384 and 385 of the 1986 Order does not affect their application in relation to a requisition under section 376(1)(a) or Article 384(1)(a) made to a private company before 1st October 2007.

(2)   So long as such a requisition has not been complied with, section 366 of the 1985 Act or Article 374 of the 1986 Order (duty to hold annual general meeting) continues to apply in relation to the company.

This does not apply if the company is not required to comply with the requisition (see section 377 of the 1985 Act or Article 385 of the 1986 Order).

(3)   Where copies of the requisition are deposited on more than one day, the reference in sub-paragraph (1) to the day on which the request or requisition is made shall be read as a reference to the first day on which the copies deposited are sufficient to require the company to act.

35. (1)   In the case of an existing public company—
  (a)   section 366 of the 1985 Act or section 374 of the 1986 Order (duty to hold annual general meeting) continues to apply to determine the date by which the company must hold its first annual general meeting after 30th September 2007, and
  (b)   section 336 of the Companies Act 2006 (public companies: annual general meeting) applies in relation to subsequent annual general meetings.

(2)   An "existing public company" means a company formed and registered before 1st October 2007 that is a public company immediately before that date.

36.   The repeal of section 367 of the 1985 Act (default power of Secretary of State to call AGM) does not affect the operation of that section in relation to a public company where an application under that section was made before 1st October 2007.

37. (1) Section 337 of the Companies Act 2006 (public companies: notice of AGM) applies to meetings of which notice is given on or after 1st October 2007.

(2) Section 369 of the 1985 Act or Article 377 of the 1986 Order continues to apply in relation to meetings of which notice is given before that date.

(3) Where notice of a meeting is given over more than one day, it is treated for the purposes of this paragraph as given on the first of those days.

38. (1) Sections 338 to 340 of the Companies Act 2006 (public companies: members' power to require circulation of resolutions for AGMs) apply to requests made on or after 1st October 2007.

(2) Sections 376 and 377 of the 1985 Act or Articles 384 and 385 of the 1986 Order continue to apply to requisitions made to a public company before that date.

(3) Where requests are made or copies of a requisition are deposited on more than one day, the references in this paragraph to the day on which the request or requisition is made shall be read as references to the first day on which the requests made or copies deposited are sufficient to require the company to act.

Additional requirements for quoted companies (ss 342 to 354)

39. (1) Sections 342 to 354 of the Companies Act 2006 apply to polls taken at meetings of which notice was given on or after 1st October 2007.

(2) Where notice of a meeting is given over more than one day, it is treated for the purposes of this paragraph as given on the first of those days.

Records of resolutions and meetings (ss 355 to 359)

40. (1) Sections 355 to 359 of the Companies Act 2006 (records of resolutions and meetings) apply to resolutions passed, meetings held or decisions taken on or after 1st October 2007.

(2) Sections 382, 382A, 382B and 383 of the 1985 Act or Articles 390, 390A, 390B and 391 of the 1986 Order continue to apply to resolutions passed, meetings held or decisions taken before that date.

Political donations and expenditure (ss 362 to 379)

41. (1) Sections 362 to 379 of the Companies Act 2006 (political donations and expenditure) apply to donations made or expenditure incurred on or after 1st October 2007.

Section 379(2) of that Act applies as to the time when a donation is regarded as made or expenditure as incurred, including where it is made or incurred in pursuance of a contract entered into before that date.

(2) Part 10A of the 1985 Act continues to apply to donations or expenditure in relation to which the relevant time, as defined in section 347A(10) of that Act, is before that date.

(3) The repeal of that Part does not affect paragraph 3(4) of Schedule 7 to the 1985 Act (matters to be dealt with in directors' report: expressions to have same meaning as in Part 10A).

42. An approval resolution passed in accordance with section 347C of the 1985 Act before 1st October 2007 is treated as complying with the requirements of section 367 of the Companies Act 2006 (form of authorising resolution) although it does not comply with the requirements of that section as to the heads under which donations and expenditure are to be stated.

Contents of directors' report: business review (s 417)

43. (1) Section 417 of the Companies Act 2006 (contents of directors' report: business review) applies to directors' reports for financial years beginning on or after 1st October 2007.

(2) Sections 234(1)(a), 234ZZB, 246(4)(a) and 246A(2A) of the 1985 Act or Articles 242(1), 242ZZB, 254(4)(a) and 254A(2A) of the 1986 Order continue to apply to directors' reports for financial years beginning before that date.

Appointment of auditors of private companies (ss 485 to 488)

44. (1) Sections 485 to 488 of the Companies Act 2006 (appointment of auditors of private companies) apply in relation to appointments for financial years beginning on or after 1st October 2007.

(2) Sections 384 to 388A of the 1985 Act or Articles 392 to 396A of the 1986 Order continue to apply in relation to appointments for financial years beginning before that date.

(3) Where—
    (a) a private company has elected under section 386 of the 1985 Act or Article 394 of the 1986 Order to dispense with the annual appointment of auditors, and
    (b) the election is in force immediately before 1st October 2007,
section 487(2)(a) of the Companies Act 2006 (no deemed reappointment of auditors appointed by directors) does not prevent the deemed reappointment under that subsection of auditors first appointed before 1st October 2007.

45. (1) This paragraph applies where immediately before 1st October 2007 a resolution of a private company under section 390A of the 1985 Act or Article 398A of the 1986 Order (remuneration of auditors) was in force and was expressed (in whatever terms) to continue to have effect so long as a resolution under section 386 of that Act or Article 394 of that Order (election to dispense with annual appointment of auditors) continued in force.

(2) The repeal of section 386 of the 1985 Act or Article 394 of the 1986 Order does not affect the continued operation of the resolution, which shall continue to have effect until—

    (a)   it is revoked or superseded by a further resolution,

    (b)   the auditors to which it applies cease to hold office, or

    (c)   it otherwise ceases to have effect in accordance with its terms.

Fraudulent trading (s 993)

46. (1) Section 458 of the 1985 Act or Article 451 of the 1986 Order (offences of fraudulent trading) continues to apply to offences completed before 1st October 2007.

(2) Where, in the case of an offence—

    (a)   a relevant event occurs before 1st October 2007, and

    (b)   another relevant event occurs on or after 1st October 2007,

the offence must be charged under section 993 of the Companies Act 2006 (and not under section 458 of the 1985 Act or Article 451 of the 1986 Order).

(3) If in the case of any such offence a relevant event occurred before 15th January 2007 section 993(3)(a) applies with the substitution of "seven years" for "ten years".

(4) "Relevant event" means an act, omission or other event (including any result of one or more acts or omissions) proof of which is required for conviction of the offence.

Protection of members against unfair prejudice (ss 994 to 999)

47. Section 999 of the Companies Act 2006 (provisions applying where court order alters a company's constitution) does not apply (by virtue of section 1297 of that Act) to an order of the court made before 1st October 2007.

Company investigations (ss 1035 to 1039)

48. Sections [1035 to 1037 and 1038(1)] of the Companies Act 2006 (company investigations: amendments) apply where an inspector is appointed under a provision of Part 14 of the 1985 Act on or after 1st October 2007.

Repeal of requirement for private companies to lay accounts and reports before general meeting

49. (1) The repeals of—

    (a)   section 241 of the 1985 Act or Article 264 of the 1986 Order (accounts and reports to be laid before company in general meeting) as it applies to private companies, and

    (b)   sections 252 and 253 of the 1985 Act or Articles 260 and 261 of the 1986 Order (election by private company to dispense with laying of accounts and report before general meeting),

have effect in relation to annual accounts and reports for financial years ending on or after 1st October 2007.

(2) Those provisions continue to have effect in relation to annual accounts for reports for financial years ending before that date.

Repeal of definition of "connected person"

50. The repeal of section 346 of and Schedule 13 to the 1985 Act or Article 354 of and Schedule 13 to the 1986 Order (meaning of "connected person") does not affect—

    (a)   section 317(3)(b) of the 1985 Act or Article 325(3)(b) of the 1986 Order (directors to disclose interest in contracts);

    (b)   section 7E and 7F(3) of the Industrial and Provident Societies Act 1965 or section 7D and 7E(3) of the Industrial and Provident Societies Act (Northern Ireland) 1969 (transactions with committee members: whether person "connected with" committee member or "associated with" society);

    (c)   *section 96B(2)(a) of the Financial Services and Markets Act 2000 (disclosure rules: responsibility for compliance: meaning of person connected with person having managerial responsibilities within an issuer).*

Provisions relating to trial and punishment of offences

51. Any saving in this Schedule for the effect of a provision of the 1985 Act or 1986 Order that creates an offence extends to the entry relating to that provision in Schedule 24 to that Act or Schedule 23 to that Order (punishment of offences).

[Requirements as to form, authentication and manner of delivery

52. Where any provision of this Schedule authorises or requires the use of a form prescribed under the 1985 Act or 1986 Order, the power to prescribe the form continues to be exercisable (so that the prescribed form may be amended or replaced) so long as the use of the form continues to be authorised or required.

53. Until section 1068(1) comes into force, the provisions of section 707B of 1985 Act or Article 656B of the 1986 Order (delivery using electronic communications) apply in relation to documents required or authorised to be delivered to the registrar under the provisions of the Companies Act 2006 brought into force by this Order.]

NOTES

Commencement: see art 1(3)(e) at **[2.31]**.

Paras 13, 16: words in square brackets in sub-para (2) substituted by the Companies Act 2006 (Commencement No 5, Transitional Provisions and Savings) Order 2007, SI 2007/3495, art 11, Sch 5, para 2(1), (3), as from 14 January 2008.

Para 18: revoked by the Companies Act 2006 (Commencement No 4 and Commencement No 3 (Amendment)) Order 2007, SI 2007/2607, art 4(4), as from 30 September 2007. Note that art 2 of this Order originally provided that s 247 of the 2006 Act would come into force on 1 October 2007, and that Sch 2 to this Order provided that the repeal of s 719 of the 1985 Act would come into force as from the same date. Art 2 and Sch 2 were amended by art 4(1), (2) of SI 2007/2607 (as noted *ante*) to prevent both of these things happening. This paragraph contained transitional provisions with regard to the commencement of s 247 of the 2006 Act and the repeal of s 719 of the 1985 Act and, therefore, became unnecessary following the amendments made by art 4(1), (2).

Para 23: sub-para (1) numbered as such, and sub-para (2) added, by SI 2007/3495, art 11, Sch 5, para 2(1), (4), as from 14 January 2008.

Paras 23A, 52, 53: inserted and added respectively by SI 2007/3495, art 11, Sch 5, para 2(1), (5), (7), as from 14 January 2008; para 23A(4) subsequently inserted by the Companies (Shareholders' Rights) Regulations 2009, SI 2009/1632, reg 22, as from 3 August 2009, in relation to meetings of which notice is given, or first given, on or after that date.

Para 26A: inserted by the Companies Act 2006 (Commencement No 6, Saving and Commencement Nos 3 and 5 (Amendment)) Order 2008, SI 2008/674, art 5, Sch 3, para 2(1), (2), as from 6 April 2008.

Para 32: sub-para (4) added by SI 2007/3495, art 11, Sch 5, para 2(1), (6), as from 31 December 2007.

Para 48: words in square brackets substituted by SI 2008/674, art 5, Sch 3, para 2(1), (3), as from 6 April 2008.

Para 50: the Financial Services and Markets Act 2000, s 96(2) was substituted by the Financial Services and Markets Act 2000 (Amendment) Regulations 2009, SI 2009/2461, reg 2(1), as from 1 October 2009. Those Regulations also added Sch 11B to the 2000 Act (Connected Persons). As a result of this amendment, para 50(c) is effectively spent.

Industrial and Provident Societies Act 1965: see the Co-operative and Community Benefit Societies and Credit Unions Act 2010 which renames this Act as the Co-operative and Community Benefit Societies and Credit Unions Act 1965.

SCHEDULE 4

(Sch 4 (Consequential Amendments): Sch 4, Pt 1 (Amendments of the 1985 Act) contains various amendments to the Companies Act 1985 and transitional provisions in relation to the application of those amendments. These have been taken in at the appropriate place and relevant transitional provisions are noted to the amendment concerned. Para 3(4) in Sch 4, Pt 1 also provides that references in any enactment or instrument to the period for laying and delivering accounts, and reports including those in CA 1985, s 244 (which defines that period), shall be read in relation to a private company as references to the period for delivering accounts and reports. Sch 4, Pt 2 (Amendments of the 1986 Order) contains various amendments to the Companies (Northern Ireland) Order 1986 (outside the scope of this work). Sch 4, Pt 3 (Amendments of other Enactments and Instruments) amends the Companies Consolidation (Consequential Provisions) Act 1985, the Insolvency Act 1986, the Company Directors Disqualification Act 1986, the Companies Act 1989, the Financial Services and Markets Act 2000, the Companies (Audit, Investigations and Community Enterprise) Act 2004, the Fraud Act 2006, and the Uncertificated Securities Regulations 2001 (SI 2001/3755) and contains transitional provisions in relation to the application of those amendments. They have been taken in at the appropriate place and relevant transitional provisions are noted to the amendment concerned. Sch 4, Pt 3 also amends various enactments that are outside the scope of this work.)

SCHEDULE 5
CONSEQUENTIAL REPEALS

Article 10(3)

[2.46]

NOTES

Only relevant entries of this Schedule are reproduced here; the entries omitted contain repeals to provisions in the following enactments: the Companies Consolidation (Consequential Provisions) (Northern Ireland) Order 1986, the Companies (Northern Ireland) Order 1989, the Insolvency (Northern Ireland) Order 1989, the Statutory Water Companies Act 1991, the Friendly Societies Act 1992, the Housing (Northern Ireland) Order 1992, the Coal Industry Act 1994, the Deregulation and Contracting Out (Northern Ireland) Order 1996, the Deregulation (Northern Ireland) Order 1997, the Postal Services Act 2000, the Enterprise Act 2002, and the Civil Partnership Act 2004.

Short title and chapter	Extent of repeal
Companies Act 1985 (c 5)	Section 455(3).
	In section 456—
	(a) in subsection (2), the words from "and if the order" to the end;
	(b) in subsection (3)(b), the words "210 or";
	(c) in subsection (4), in the second sentence, the words from "(unless" to "section 216)";
	(d) in subsection (5)(a), the words from "(unless" to "section 216)".
Companies Consolidation (Consequential Provisions) Act 1985 (c 9)	Sections 14 and 15.
	In Schedule 2, the entries relating to—
	(a) section 53(1) of the Industrial and Provident Societies Act 1965;
	(b) the Atomic Energy Authority Act 1971;
	(c) section 3 of the Industry Act 1980;
	(d) the Food Act 1984.
Insolvency Act 1986 (c 45)	Section 84(1)(c).
Companies (Audit, Investigations and Community Enterprise) Act 2004 (c 27)	In section 43(3), the words from "as in relation" to the end.
Fraud Act 2006 (c 35)	Section 9(4).

NOTES

Commencement: 1 October 2007.

Industrial and Provident Societies Act 1965: see the Co-operative and Community Benefit Societies and Credit Unions Act 2010 which renames this Act as the Co-operative and Community Benefit Societies and Credit Unions Act 1965.

COMPANIES ACT 2006 (COMMENCEMENT NO 4 AND COMMENCEMENT NO 3 (AMENDMENT)) ORDER 2007

(SI 2007/2607)

NOTES

Made: 6 September 2007.
Authority: Companies Act 2006, ss 1296(1), 1300(2).
Commencement: 30 September 2007.
Amendment: as of 1 July 2011 this Order had not been amended.

[2.47]
1   Citation and coming into force

This Order may be cited as the Companies Act 2006 (Commencement No 4 and Commencement No 3 (Amendment)) Order 2007 and comes into force on 30th September 2007.

NOTES

Commencement: 30 September 2007.

[2.48]
2   Provisions coming into force on 30th September 2007

(1)   Sections 1137(1), (4), (5)(b) and (6) (regulations about inspection of company records and provision of copies: fees) and 1167 (meaning of "prescribed") of the Companies Act 2006 come into force on 30th September 2007.

(2)   Section 1284 of the Companies Act 2006 (extension of Companies Acts to Northern Ireland) comes into force on 30th September 2007 so far as necessary for the purposes of the provisions mentioned in paragraph (1).

NOTES

Commencement: 30 September 2007.

[2.49]

3 Interpretation of provisions brought into force

Where an expression in a provision brought into force by this Order—

(a) is defined in the Companies Act 1985 or the Companies (Northern Ireland) Order 1986 ("the old definition"); and

(b) is defined in the Companies Act 2006 by another provision that is not yet in force for the purposes of the provision brought into force ("the new definition"),

the expression has, for the purposes of the provision brought into force, the meaning given by the old definition until the new definition is brought into force for the purposes of that provision.

NOTES

Commencement: 30 September 2007.

4 *(Amends the Companies Act 2006 (Commencement No 3, Consequential Amendments, Transitional Provisions and Savings) Order 2007, SI 2007/2194 at* **[2.31]** *et seq.)*

COMPANIES ACT 2006 (COMMENCEMENT NO 5, TRANSITIONAL PROVISIONS AND SAVINGS) ORDER 2007

(SI 2007/3495)

NOTES

Made: 17 December 2007.

Authority: Companies Act 2006, ss 1292, 1296, 1300(2).

Commencement: see art 2 at **[2.51]**.

This Order is reproduced as amended by: art 11(2)(c) (below); the Companies Act 2006 (Commencement No 6, Saving and Commencement Nos 3 and 5 (Amendment)) Order 2008, SI 2008/674; the Companies Act 2006 (Commencement No 7, Transitional Provisions and Savings) Order 2008, SI 2008/1886; the Companies Act 2006 (Commencement No 8, Transitional Provisions and Savings) Order 2008, SI 2008/2860.

ARRANGEMENT OF ARTICLES

[2.50]

1 Citation and interpretation

(1) This Order may be cited as the Companies Act 2006 (Commencement No 5, Transitional Provisions and Savings) Order 2007.

(2) In this Order—

"the 1985 Act" means the Companies Act 1985; and

"the 1986 Order" means the Companies (Northern Ireland) Order 1986.

NOTES

Commencement: 17 December 2007.

[2.51]

2   Coming into force

(1)   The provisions of this Order come into force as follows.

(2)   Articles 3, 7 and 10(1), Part 1 of Schedule 1, Schedule 2 and Part 1 of Schedule 4 come into force on 6th April 2008.

(3)   Article 4 and Part 2 of Schedule 4 come into force on 29th June 2008.

(4)   Articles 5 and 10(2), Part 2 of Schedule 1, Schedule 3 and Part 3 of Schedule 4 come into force on 1st October 2008.

(5)   Articles 6, 8, 9, 10(3) and 12 come into force—

   (a)   on 6th April 2008 so far as relating to provisions coming into force on that date;
   (b)   on 29th June 2008 so far as relating to provisions coming into force on that date;
   (c)   on 1st October 2008 so far as relating to provisions coming into force on that date.

(6)   Article 11 and Schedule 5 come into force—

   (a)   on 31st December 2007 so far as relating to the amendment made by paragraph 2(6) of that Schedule;
   (b)   on 14th January 2008 so far as relating to the other amendments made by that Schedule.

NOTES

Commencement: 17 December 2007.

[2.52]

3   Provisions of the Companies Act 2006 coming into force on 6th April 2008

(1)   The following provisions of the Companies Act 2006 come into force on 6th April 2008—

   (a)   section 44 (execution of documents);
   (b)   sections 121 and 128 (register of members: removal of entries and time limit for claims);
   (c)   sections 270 to 274 and 280 (company secretaries);
   (d)   sections 380 to 416, 418 to 462 and 464 to 474 (accounts and reports);
   (e)   sections 475 to 484 and 489 to 539 (audit);
   (f)   section 544 (transferability of shares);
   (g)   sections 738 to 754 (debentures);
   (h)   sections 755 to 767 (private and public companies);
   (i)   sections 768 to 790 (certification and transfer of securities);
   (j)   sections 811(4), 812 and 814 (exercise of right to inspect register of interests disclosed);
   (k)   sections 829 to 853 (distributions);
   (l)   sections 895 to 901 (arrangements and reconstructions);
   (m)   sections 902 to 941 (mergers and divisions of public companies);
   (n)   section 1126 (consents required for certain prosecutions);
   (o)   sections 1161 and 1162 and Schedule 7 (meaning of "undertaking" and related expressions);
   (p)   section 1164 (meaning of "banking company" and "banking group");
   (q)   section 1165 (meaning of "insurance company" and related expressions);
   (r)   section 1169 (dormant companies);
   (s)   section 1172 (references to requirements of this Act);
   (t)   in section 1173 (minor definitions: general), the definitions of "credit institution" and "working day";
   (u)   sections 1209 to 1241 and 1245 to 1264 and Schedules 10, 11, 13 and 14 (statutory auditors);
   (v)   section 1282 (payment of expenses of winding up).

(2)   In section 1117 of the Companies Act 2006 (registrar's rules)—

   (a)   subsections (1) and (2) come into force on 6th April 2008 so far as may be necessary for the purpose of enabling rules to be made under that section before the date on which the section is brought generally into force, and
   (b)   subsection (3) (duty to publicise and make available copies of rules made under that section) has effect accordingly.

(3)   The following provisions of the Companies Act 2006 come into force on 6th April 2008 so far as necessary for the purposes of the provisions mentioned in paragraphs (1)(a) to (t) and paragraph (2)—

   (a)   section 17 (a company's constitution);
   (b)   section 540(1) and (4) (shares);
   (c)   section 545 (companies having a share capital);
   (d)   section 546 (issued and allotted share capital);
   (e)   section 548 (equity share capital);
   (f)   section 629 (classes of shares);

(g)   sections 1121 to 1123, 1125 and 1127 to 1133 (provisions relating to offences);

(h)   sections 1139 and 1140 (service of documents);

(i)   section 1168 (hard copy and electronic form and related expressions);

(j)   in section 1173 (minor definitions: general), the definitions of "body corporate" (and "corporation"), "firm", "the Gazette", "parent company" and "regulated market".

(4)   Sections 1159 and 1160 of, and Schedule 6 to, the Companies Act 2006 (meaning of "subsidiary" etc) come into force on 6th April 2008 so far as necessary for the purposes of the provisions mentioned in paragraph (1)(u).

(5)   Section 1284 of the Companies Act 2006 (extension of Companies Acts to Northern Ireland) comes into force on 6th April 2008 so far as necessary for the purposes of the provisions mentioned in paragraphs (1)(a) to (t), (2) and (3).

NOTES

Commencement: 6 April 2008.

[2.53]

4   Provisions of the Companies Act 2006 coming into force on 29th June 2008

Sections 1242 to 1244 of, and Schedule 12 to, the Companies Act 2006 (duties of third country auditors: information to be supplied by third country auditors) come into force on 29th June 2008.

NOTES

Commencement: 29 June 2008.

[2.54]

5   Provisions of the Companies Act 2006 coming into force on 1st October 2008

(1)   The following provisions of the Companies Act 2006 come into force on 1st October 2008—

(a)   sections 69 to 74 (objections to company names);

(b)   sections 82 to 85 (trading disclosures);

(c)   sections 155 to 159 (appointment of directors);

(d)   sections 175 to 177 (general duties of directors);

(e)   sections 182 to 187 (duty of directors to declare interest in existing transaction or arrangement);

(f)   section 1157 (power of court to grant relief in certain cases);

(g)   sections 1277 to 1280 (information as to exercise of voting rights by institutional investors).

(2)   Section 1295 of, and Schedule 16 to, the Companies Act 2006 (repeals) come into force on 1st October 2008 so far as relating to the repeal of sections 151 to 153 and 155 to 158 of the 1985 Act and Articles 161 to 163 and 165 to 168 of the 1986 Order (financial assistance for acquisition of shares) as they apply to the giving of financial assistance by a private company for the purposes of the acquisition of shares in itself or another private company.

(3)   The following provisions of the Companies Act 2006 come into force on 1st October 2008 so far as necessary for the purposes of the provisions mentioned in paragraph (1)(a) to (f)—

(a)   sections 1121 to 1123, 1125 and 1127 to 1133 (provisions relating to offences);

(b)   section 1168 (hard copy and electronic form and related expressions);

(c)   in section 1173 (minor definitions: general), the definitions of "body corporate" (and "corporation"), "firm" and "officer".

(4)   Section 1284 of the Companies Act 2006 (extension of Companies Acts to Northern Ireland) comes into force on 1st October 2008 so far as necessary for the purposes of the provisions mentioned in paragraphs (1) to (3).

NOTES

Commencement: 1 October 2008.

[2.55]

6   Transitional adaptations of provisions brought into force

The provisions brought into force by articles 3 and 5 have effect subject to any transitional adaptations specified in Schedule 1 to this Order.

NOTES

Commencement: 6 April 2008 (certain purposes); 29 June 2008 (certain purposes); 1 October 2008 (otherwise).

[2.56]

7   Interpretation of company law provisions brought into force

(1)   Where an expression in a company law provision brought into force by this Order (or in an adaptation made by this Order of such a provision)—

(a)   is defined in the 1985 Act or the 1986 Order ("the old definition"); and

(b)   is defined in the Companies Act 2006 by another provision that is not yet in force for the purposes of the provision brought into force ("the new definition"), the expression has, for the purposes of the provision brought into force (or the adaptation), the meaning given by the old definition until the new definition is brought into force for the purposes of that provision.

(2) In paragraph (1) "company law provision" has the meaning given by section 2(2) of the Companies Act 2006.

NOTES

    Commencement: 6 April 2008.

[2.57]
8 Repeals

Sections 1284(2) and 1295 of, and Schedule 16 to, the Companies Act 2006 (repeals) come into force—

    (a)   on 6th April 2008 so far as relating to the repeal of the provisions specified in Schedule 2 to this Order;

    (b)   on 1st October 2008 so far as relating to the repeal of the provisions specified in Schedule 3 to this Order.

NOTES

    Commencement: 6 April 2008 (certain purposes); 29 June 2008 (certain purposes); 1 October 2008 (otherwise).

[2.58]
9 Transitional provisions and savings

(1) Schedule 4 to this Order contains transitional provisions and savings relating to the provisions (and repeals) brought into force by this Order.

(2) Any saving in that Schedule for the effect of a provision of the 1985 Act or 1986 Order that creates an offence extends to the entry relating to that provision in Schedule 24 to that Act or Schedule 23 to that Order (punishment of offences).

(3) Where any provision of that Schedule authorises or requires the use of a form prescribed under the 1985 Act or 1986 Order, the power to prescribe the form continues to be exercisable (so that the prescribed form may be amended or replaced) so long as the use of the form continues to be authorised or required.

(4) Until section 1068(1) comes into force, the provisions of section 707B of [the] 1985 Act or Article 656B of the 1986 Order (delivery using electronic communications) apply in relation to documents required or authorised to be delivered to the registrar under the provisions of the Companies Act 2006 brought into force by this Order.

NOTES

    Commencement: 6 April 2008 (certain purposes); 29 June 2008 (certain purposes); 1 October 2008 (otherwise).

    Para (4): word in square brackets inserted by the Companies Act 2006 (Commencement No 6, Saving and Commencement Nos 3 and 5 (Amendment)) Order 2008, SI 2008/674, art 5, Sch 3, para 3, as from 6 April 2008.

[2.59]
10 Revocation of spent transitional adaptations

(1) The following provisions (which make transitional adaptations that are no longer needed as a result of provisions brought into force by this Order on 6th April 2008) are revoked with effect from that date—

    (a)   in Schedule 1 to the Companies Act 2006 (Commencement No 1, Transitional Provisions and Savings) Order 2006, paragraphs 3, 5(2)(b), 5(3)(a)(ix), 5(3)(b), 10, 11 and 12(3);

    (b)   in Schedule 1 to the Companies Act 2006 (Commencement No 3, Consequential Amendments, Transitional Provisions and Savings) Order 2007, paragraphs 3 to 5, 10, 13(2)(a) and 15 to 18.

(2) The following provisions (which make transitional adaptations that are no longer needed as a result of provisions brought into force by this Order on 1st October 2008) are revoked with effect from that date—

    (a)   in Schedule 1 to the Companies Act 2006 (Commencement No 1, Transitional Provisions and Savings) Order 2006, paragraph 2;

    (b)   in Schedule 1 to the Companies Act 2006 (Commencement No 3, Consequential Amendments, Transitional Provisions and Savings) Order 2007, paragraphs 6 to 9, 11 and 12;

    (c)   paragraph 11 of Schedule 1 to this Order.

(3) The revocation by this article of a spent transitional adaptation is subject to the same transitional provisions and savings as apply, in accordance with Schedule 4 to this Order, in relation to the repeal of the provisions of the 1985 Act or 1986 Order referred to in the adaptation.

NOTES

    Commencement: 6 April 2008 (para (1), para (3) (certain purposes)); 29 June 2008 (para (3) (certain purposes)); 1 October 2008 (otherwise).

See further, the Companies Act 2006 (Commencement No 6, Saving and Commencement Nos 3 and 5 (Amendment)) Order 2008, SI 2008/674, Sch 3, para 4, which provides as follows—

"4. The revocation by article 10(1)(b) of the Companies Act 2006 (Commencement No 5, Transitional Provisions and Savings) Order 2007 of paragraph 15(2) of Schedule 1 to the Companies Act 2006 (Commencement No 3, Consequential Amendments, Transitional Provisions and Savings) Order 2007 (transitional adaptation: period within which public company must hold AGM) does not have effect in relation to a company until—

    (a) the directors of the company have complied with section 241 of the Companies Act 1985 or Article 249 of the Companies (Northern Ireland) Order 1986 in respect of the last financial year of the company beginning before 6th April 2008, or

    (b) the first financial year of the company beginning on or after that date comes to an end.".

[2.60]
11 Amendments of earlier Orders

Schedule 5 to this Order contains amendments of earlier commencement Orders.

NOTES

Commencement: 31 December 2007 (certain purposes); 14 January 2008 (otherwise).

[2.61]
12 Savings

(1) Nothing in this Order affects any provision of the 1985 Act or the 1986 Order as applied by the Limited Liability Partnerships Regulations 2001 or the Limited Liability Partnerships Regulations (Northern Ireland) 2004 to limited liability partnerships.

(2) The amendments and repeals made by this Order do not affect the operation of section 1297 of the Companies Act 2006 (continuity of the law).

NOTES

Commencement: 6 April 2008 (certain purposes); 29 June 2008 (certain purposes); 1 October 2008 (otherwise).

SCHEDULES

SCHEDULE 1
TRANSITIONAL ADAPTATIONS OF PROVISIONS BROUGHT INTO FORCE
Article 6

PART 1
PROVISIONS COMING INTO FORCE ON 6TH APRIL 2008

[2.62]
1, 2. . . .

Company secretaries (ss 270 to 274)

3. (1) Section 270(3) (private company without secretary: persons authorised to act) has effect with the following adaptation.

(2) Omit sub-paragraph (b)(ii).

4. (1) Section 272 (direction requiring public company to appoint secretary) has effect with the following adaptations.

(2) In subsections (4)(b) and (5) for "section 276" substitute "section 288(2) of the Companies Act 1985 or Article 296(2) of the Companies (Northern Ireland) Order 1986".

5. (1) Section 274 (discharge of functions where office vacant or secretary unable to act) has effect with the following adaptation.

(2) In paragraph (b) for "any person" substitute "any officer of the company".

Authentication of accounts and reports filed with registrar (ss 444 to 447 and 449)

6. (1) Section 444 (filing obligations of companies subject to the small companies regime) has effect with the following adaptations.

(2) For subsection (6) substitute—

    "(6) The copy of the balance sheet delivered to the registrar under this section must—

        (a) state the name of the person who signed it on behalf of the board under section 414, and

        (b) be signed on behalf of the board by a director of the company.

    (6A) The copy of the directors' report delivered to the registrar under this section must—

        (a) state the name of the person who signed it on behalf of the board under section 419, and

        (b) be signed on behalf of the board by a director or the secretary of the company.".

(3) For subsection (7) substitute—

> *"(7) The copy of the auditor's report delivered to the registrar under this section must—*
>
> > *(a) state the name of the auditor and (where the auditor is a firm) the name of the person who signed it as senior statutory auditor, and*
> >
> > *(b) be signed by the auditor or (where the auditor is a firm) in the name of the firm by a person authorised to sign on its behalf,*
>
> *or, if the conditions in section 506 (circumstances in which names may be omitted) are met, state that a resolution has been passed and notified to the Secretary of State in accordance with that section.".*

7. *(1) Section 445 (filing obligations of medium-sized companies) has effect with the following adaptations.*

(2) For subsection (5) substitute—

> *"(5) The copy of the balance sheet delivered to the registrar under this section must—*
>
> > *(a) state the name of the person who signed it on behalf of the board under section 414, and*
> >
> > *(b) be signed on behalf of the board by a director of the company.*
>
> *(5A) The copy of the directors' report delivered to the registrar under this section must—*
>
> > *(a) state the name of the person who signed it on behalf of the board under section 419, and*
> >
> > *(b) be signed on behalf of the board by a director or the secretary of the company.".*

(3) For subsection (6) substitute—

> *"(6) The copy of the auditor's report delivered to the registrar under this section must—*
>
> > *(a) state the name of the auditor and (where the auditor is a firm) the name of the person who signed it as senior statutory auditor, and*
> >
> > *(b) be signed by the auditor or (where the auditor is a firm) in the name of the firm by a person authorised to sign on its behalf,*
>
> *or, if the conditions in section 506 (circumstances in which names may be omitted) are met, state that a resolution has been passed and notified to the Secretary of State in accordance with that section.".*

8. *(1) Section 446 (filing obligations of unquoted companies) has effect with the following adaptations.*

(2) For subsection (3) substitute—

> *"(3) The copy of the balance sheet delivered to the registrar under this section must—*
>
> > *(a) state the name of the person who signed it on behalf of the board under section 414, and*
> >
> > *(b) be signed on behalf of the board by a director of the company.*
>
> *(3A) The copy of the directors' report delivered to the registrar under this section must—*
>
> > *(a) state the name of the person who signed it on behalf of the board under section 419, and*
> >
> > *(b) be signed on behalf of the board by a director or the secretary of the company.".*

(3) For subsection (4) substitute—

> *"(4) The copy of the auditor's report delivered to the registrar under this section must—*
>
> > *(a) state the name of the auditor and (where the auditor is a firm) the name of the person who signed it as senior statutory auditor, and*
> >
> > *(b) be signed by the auditor or (where the auditor is a firm) in the name of the firm by a person authorised to sign on its behalf,*
>
> *or, if the conditions in section 506 (circumstances in which names may be omitted) are met, state that a resolution has been passed and notified to the Secretary of State in accordance with that section.".*

9. *(1) Section 447 (filing obligations of quoted companies) has effect with the following adaptations.*

(2) For subsection (3) substitute—

> *"(3) The copy of the balance sheet delivered to the registrar under this section must—*
>
> > *(a) state the name of the person who signed it on behalf of the board under section 414, and*
> >
> > *(b) be signed on behalf of the board by a director of the company.*
>
> *(3A) The copy of the directors' remuneration report delivered to the registrar under this section must—*
>
> > *(a) state the name of the person who signed it on behalf of the board under section 422, and*
> >
> > *(b) be signed on behalf of the board by a director or the secretary of the company.*
>
> *(3B) The copy of the directors' report delivered to the registrar under this section must—*

> (a)   state the name of the person who signed it on behalf of the board under section 419, and
>
> (b)   be signed on behalf of the board by a director or the secretary of the company.".

(3)   For subsection (4) substitute—

> "(4)   The copy of the auditor's report delivered to the registrar under this section must—
>
> (a)   state the name of the auditor and (where the auditor is a firm) the name of the person who signed it as senior statutory auditor, and
>
> (b)   be signed by the auditor or (where the auditor is a firm) in the name of the firm by a person authorised to sign on its behalf,
>
> or, if the conditions in section 506 (circumstances in which names may be omitted) are met, state that a resolution has been passed and notified to the Secretary of State in accordance with that section.".

10.   (1)   Section 449 (special auditor's report where abbreviated accounts delivered) has effect with the following adaptation.

(2)   After subsection (4) insert—

> "(4A)   The copy of the special report delivered to the registrar under this section must—
>
> (a)   be signed by the auditor or (where the auditor is a firm) in the name of the firm by a person authorised to sign on its behalf, or
>
> (b)   if the conditions in section 506 (circumstances in which names may be omitted) are met, state that a resolution has been passed and notified to the Secretary of State in accordance with that section.".

Audit: indemnity for costs of successfully defending proceedings (s 533)

11.   (1)   Section 533 (indemnity for costs of successfully defending proceedings) has effect with the following adaptation.

(2)   In paragraph (b) for "section 1157" substitute "section 727 of the Companies Act 1985 or Article 675 of the Companies (Northern Ireland) Order 1986".

Authorised minimum: application of initial requirement (s 765)

12.   (1)   Section 765 (minimum share capital requirement for public companies: application of initial requirement) has effect with the following adaptation.

(2)   In subsection (1)(b) for "section 91(1)(a)" substitute "section 45(2)(a) of the Companies Act 1985 or Article 55(2)(a) of the Companies (Northern Ireland) Order 1986".

Authorised minimum: application where shares denominated in different currencies etc (s 766)

13.   (1)   Section 766 (authorised minimum: application where shares denominated in different currencies etc) has effect with the following adaptation.

(2)   In subsection (4) for "sections 664 to 667" substitute "sections 147 to 149 of the Companies Act 1985 or Articles 157 to 159 of the Companies (Northern Ireland) Order 1986".

Distributions (ss 829 to 853)

14.   (1)   Section 829 (meaning of "distribution") has effect with the following adaptation.

(2)   In subsection (2)(c) for "Chapter 3, 4 or 5 of Part 18" substitute "Chapter 7 of Part 5 of the Companies Act 1985 or Chapter 7 of Part 6 of the Companies (Northern Ireland) Order 1986".

15.   (1)   Section 832 (distributions by investment companies out of accumulated revenue profits) has effect with the following adaptation.

(2)   In subsection (5)(b)(i) for "Chapter 3 or 4 of Part 18" substitute "Chapter 7 of Part 5 of the Companies Act 1985 or Chapter 7 of Part 6 of the Companies (Northern Ireland) Order 1986".

16.   (1)   Section 833 (meaning of "investment company") has effect with the following adaptation.

(2)   In subsection (3) for "Chapter 3 or 4 of Part 18" substitute "Chapter 7 of Part 5 of the Companies Act 1985 or Chapter 7 of Part 6 of the Companies (Northern Ireland) Order 1986".

17.   (1)   Section 838 (requirements where interim accounts used) has effect with the following adaptations.

(2)   In subsection (6) after "copy of the accounts" insert ", complying with the requirements of subsection (7),".

(3)   After that subsection insert—

> "(7)   The requirements referred to in subsection (6) are that the balance sheet comprised in the copy of the accounts delivered to the registrar must—
>
> (a)   state the name of the person who signed it on behalf of the board, and
>
> (b)   be signed on behalf of the board by a director of the company.".

18. *(1)   Section 839 (requirements where initial accounts used) has effect with the following adaptations.*

(2)   In subsection (7) after "any auditor's statement" insert ", complying with the requirements of subsection (8),".

(3)   After that subsection insert—

> *"(8)   The requirements referred to in subsection (7) are—*
>> *(a)   as regards the accounts, that the balance sheet comprised in the copy delivered to the registrar must—*
>>> *(i)   state the name of the person who signed it on behalf of the board, and*
>>> *(ii)   be signed on behalf of the board by a director of the company;*
>> *(b)   as regards the auditor's report and any auditor's statement, that the report or statement must—*
>>> *(i)   state the name of the auditor and (where the auditor is a firm) the name of the person who signed it as senior statutory auditor, and*
>>> *(ii)   be signed by the auditor or (where the auditor is a firm) in the name of the firm by a person authorised to sign on its behalf,*
>
> *or, if the conditions in section 506 (circumstances in which names may be omitted) are met, state that a resolution has been passed and notified to the Secretary of State in accordance with that section.".*

19. *(1)   Section 840 (successive distributions etc by reference to the same accounts) has effect with the following adaptations.*

(2)   In subsection (2)(b) for "section 678 or 679" substitute "section 151 of the Companies Act 1985 or Article 161 of the Companies (Northern Ireland) Order 1986".

(3)   In subsection (2)(d) for "section 705" substitute "section 168 of the Companies Act 1985 or Article 178 of the Companies (Northern Ireland) Order 1986".

(4)   In subsection (3) for "the same meaning as in Chapter 2 of Part 18 (see section 677)" substitute "the meaning given by section 152(1)(a) of the Companies Act 1985 or Article 162(1)(a) of the Companies (Northern Ireland) Order 1986".

20. *(1)   Section 847 (consequences of unlawful distribution) has effect with the following adaptation.*

(2)   In subsection (4)(a) for "section 678 or 679" substitute "section 151 of the Companies Act 1985 or Article 161 of the Companies (Northern Ireland) Order 1986".

Mergers and divisions of public companies (s 923)

21. *(1)   Section 923 (mergers and divisions of public companies: report on valuation of non-cash consideration for shares) has effect with the following adaptation.*

(2)   In subsection (3)(a) for "section 593" substitute "section 103(1) of the Companies Act 1985 or Article 113(1) of the Companies (Northern Ireland) Order 1986".

NOTES

Commencement: 6 April 2008.

This Part of this Schedule (in so far as it was still in force) was revoked by the Companies Act 2006 (Commencement No 8, Transitional Provisions and Savings) Order 2008, SI 2008/2860, art 6(1), as from 1 October 2009. It is reproduced here out of historical interest and because of art 6(2) of the 2008 Order which provides that the revocations made by art 6(1) are subject to any relevant transitional provision or saving in Sch 2 to that Order (at **[2.91]**).

Paras 1, 2 were previously revoked by the Companies Act 2006 (Commencement No 6, Saving and Commencement Nos 3 and 5 (Amendment)) Order 2008, SI 2008/674, art 5, Sch 3, para 5, as from 6 April 2008 (ie, without ever coming into force). This revocation corrected an error in this Order.

Para 11 was previously revoked by art 10(2)(c) of this Order, as from 1 October 2008.

PART 2
PROVISIONS COMING INTO FORCE ON 1ST OCTOBER 2008

Order requiring name to be changed following objection (s 73)

[2.63]
22. *(1)   Section 73 (order requiring name to be changed) has effect with the following adaptations.*

(2)   In subsection (2)(a) for "section 67" substitute "section 28(2) of the Companies Act 1985 or Article 38(2) of the Companies (Northern Ireland) Order 1986".

(3)   In subsection (6) for "section 81(1)" substitute "section 28(6) of the Companies Act 1985 or Article 38(6) of the Companies (Northern Ireland) Order 1986".

Trading disclosures: minor variations in form of name (s 85)

23. *(1)   Section 85 (minor variations in form of name to be left out of account) has effect with the following adaptation.*

(2)   Omit subsections (1)(c) and (2).

Direction requiring company to appoint director (s 156)

24. (1)   Section 156 (direction requiring company to make appointment) has effect with the following adaptation.

(2)   In subsections (4)(b) and (5) for "section 167" substitute "section 288(2) of the Companies Act 1985 or Article 296(2) of the Companies (Northern Ireland) Order 1986".

NOTES

Commencement: 1 October 2008.

This Part of this Schedule was revoked by the Companies Act 2006 (Commencement No 8, Transitional Provisions and Savings) Order 2008, SI 2008/2860, art 6(1), as from 1 October 2009. It is reproduced here out of historical interest and because of art 6(2) of the 2008 Order which provides that the revocations made by art 6(1) are subject to any relevant transitional provision or saving in Sch 2 to that Order (at **[2.91]**).

SCHEDULE 2
REPEALS BROUGHT INTO FORCE ON 6TH APRIL 2008

Article 8(a)

PART 1
GREAT BRITAIN

[2.64]

Short title and chapter	Extent of repeal brought into force
Companies Act 1985 (c 6)	In section 36A—
	(a) subsection (2);
	(b) in subsection (3) the words from "however" to the end;
	(c) subsections (4) to (8).
	Section 58.
	Section 81.
	Sections 117 and 118.
	Section 182(1)(b).
	Sections 183 to 197.
	Sections 221 to 234ZZA.
	Sections 234ZA to 251.
	Sections 254 to 281.
	Sections 283, 284 and 286.
	Section 310.
	Section 352(6) and (7).
	Section 380(4)(b).
	Sections 384 and 385.
	Sections 387 to 388A.
	Sections 389A to 392A.
	Sections 394 and 394A.
	Sections 425 to 427A.
	Sections 732 to 734.
	Sections 742A to 742C
	In section 744, the definitions of "authorised minimum", "debenture", "insurance market activity", "prescribed" and "undistributable reserves".
	Schedules 4 to 11.
	Schedule 15B.

Short title and chapter	Extent of repeal brought into force
	In Schedule 24, the entries relating to sections 81(2), 117(7) and (7A),183(6), 185(5), 189(1) and (2), 191(4), 221(5) or 222(4), 222(6), 231(6), 232(4), 233(5) and (6), 234(5), 234ZA(7), 234A(4), 234AA(5), 234AB(4), 234B(3) and (6), 234C(4), 236(4), 238(5), 239(3), 240(6), 241(2) or 242(2), 241A(9) and (10), 245(1) and (2), 245E(3), 245G(7), 251(6), 255(5), 384(5), 387(2), 389B(1), (2) and (4), 390(7), 391(2), 392(3), 392A(5), 394A(1) and (4), 425(4), 426(6) and (7) and 427(5).
Insolvency Act 1985 (c 65)	In Schedule 6, paragraphs 11 and 12.
Insolvency Act 1986 (c 45)	In Schedule 13, the entry relating to section 196 of the Companies Act 1985.
Finance Act 1988 (c 39)	In section 117(3)—
	(a) in subsection (3), from the beginning to "that section";
	(b) in subsection (4), "and (3)".
Companies Act 1989 (c 40)	Sections 1 to 15 and 17 to 22.
	Sections 24 to 54.
	Section 114(2).
	Sections 118 to 122.
	Section 123(1) to (4).
	Section 137.
	Section 143(4).
	Section 207.
	Schedules 1 to 9.
	In Schedule 10, paragraphs 2, 4, 5, 7, 8 and 19 to 23.
	Schedules 11 to 13.
	In Schedule 17, paragraphs 5 and 6.
	In Schedule 19, paragraph 18.
Trade Marks Act 1994 (c 26)	In Schedule 4, in paragraph 1(2), the entries relating to Schedules 4 and 9 to the Companies Act 1985.
Requirements of Writing (Scotland) Act 1995 (c 7)	In Schedule 4, paragraphs 55 and 56.
Criminal Procedure (Consequential Provisions) (Scotland) Act 1995 (c 40)	In Schedule 4, paragraphs 56(4) and 74(2).
Disability Discrimination Act 1995 (c 50)	In Schedule 6, paragraph 4.
Political Parties, Elections and Referendums Act 2000 (c 41)	Section 139(2).
	Section 140.
	In Schedule 23, paragraph 13.
Enterprise Act 2002 (c 40)	In Schedule 17, paragraphs 4 to 6.
Companies (Audit, Investigations and Community Enterprise) Act 2004 (c 27)	Sections 1 to 10.
	Section 11(1).
	Sections 12 and 13.
	Section 19(2).
	Schedule 1.
	In Schedule 2, paragraphs 1 to 3, 5, 10 and 24.
Civil Partnership Act 2004 (c 33)	In Schedule 27, paragraphs 104, 105 and 128.

NOTES
Commencement: 6 April 2008.

(Sch 2, Pt 2 (Northern Ireland) contains various repeals to Northern Ireland legislation (outside the scope of this work).)

SCHEDULE 3
REPEALS BROUGHT INTO FORCE ON 1ST OCTOBER 2008
Article 8(b)

PART 1
GREAT BRITAIN

[2.65]

Short title and chapter	Extent of repeal brought into force
Companies Act 1985 (c 6)	Sections 151 to 153 and 155 to 158, to the extent specified in article 5(2) to this Order.
	Section 305.
	Section 317.
	Sections 348 and 349.
	Section 351.
	Section 727.
	In Schedule 24, the entries relating to sections 317(7), 348(2), 349(2), (3) and (4) and 351(5)(a) to (c).
Business Names Act 1985 (c 7)	Section 4, as it applies to companies.
Companies (Audit, Investigations and Community Enterprise) Act 2004 (c 27)	In Schedule 6, paragraph 8.

NOTES
Commencement: 1 October 2008.

(Sch 3, Pt 2 (Northern Ireland) contains various repeals to Northern Ireland legislation (outside the scope of this work).)

SCHEDULE 4
TRANSITIONAL PROVISIONS AND SAVINGS
Article 9

PART 1
PROVISIONS COMING INTO FORCE ON 6TH APRIL 2008

Execution of documents (s 44)

[2.66]

1. (1)   Section 44 of the Companies Act 2006 (execution of documents) applies in relation to the execution of documents on or after 6th April 2008.

(2)   Section 36A of the 1985 Act or Article 46A of the 1986 Order continues to apply in relation to documents executed before that date.

(3)   For the purposes of this paragraph a document signed by one authorised signatory before 6th April 2008 and by another on or after that date is treated as executed on or after 6th April 2008.

Register of members: removal of entries relating to former members (s 121)

2. (1)   The power conferred by section 121 of the Companies Act 2006 (removal after ten years of entries relating to former members) is exercisable on and after 6th April 2008, whenever the period of ten years referred to in that provision expired.

(2)   A copy of any details that were included in the register immediately before that date and that are removed from the register under that power must be retained by the company until 6th April [2018] or, if earlier, 20 years after the member concerned ceased to be a member.

Register of members: time limit for claims arising from entry (s 128)

3. (1)   Section 128 of the Companies Act 2006 (ten year time limit for claims arising from entry in register of members) applies to causes of action arising on or after 6th April 2008.

(2)   The time limit for causes of action arising before that date is—
(a)   ten years from 6th April 2008, or
(b)   20 years (as provided by section 352(7) of the 1985 Act or Article 360(7) of the 1986 Order) from when the cause of action arose,
whichever expires first.

(3)   This is without prejudice to any lesser period of limitation (and, in Scotland, to any rule that the obligation giving rise to the liability prescribes before the expiry of that period).

Company secretaries (ss 270 to 274 and 280)

4. (1)   A private company whose articles immediately before 6th April 2008 expressly required it to have a secretary is a company "with a secretary" for the purposes of section 270(2) until its articles are amended to remove the requirement.

(2)   For this purpose a provision—
(a)   requiring or authorising things to be done by or in relation to a secretary, or
(b)   as to the manner in which, or terms on which, a secretary is to be appointed or removed,
is not a provision expressly requiring the company to have a secretary.

5. (1)   Section 273 of the Companies Act 2006 (qualifications of secretaries of public companies) applies in relation to company secretaries appointed on or after 6th April 2008.

(2)   Section 286 of the 1985 Act or Article 294 of the 1986 Order continues to apply in relation to company secretaries appointed before that date.

Accounts and reports (ss 380 to 389, 393 to 416, 418 to 462 and 464 to 474)

6. (1)   Sections 380 to 389, 393 to 416, 418 to 462 and 464 to 474 of the Companies Act 2006 (accounts and reports) apply to accounts and reports for financial years beginning on or after 6th April 2008.

(2)   The corresponding provisions of the 1985 Act or the 1986 Order continue to apply to accounts and reports for financial years beginning before that date.

7. Any question whether—
(a)   for the purposes of section 382, 383, 384(3) or 467(3) of the Companies Act 2006 a company or group qualified as small in a financial year beginning before 6th April 2008, or
(b)   for the purposes of section 465 or 466 of that Act a company or group qualified as medium-sized in any such financial year,
is to be determined by reference to the corresponding provisions of the 1985 Act or the 1986 Order.

8. Until section 1068(1) of the Companies Act 2006 comes into force, the notice referred to in section 392 of that Act (notice of alteration of accounting reference date) must be given in the form prescribed for the purposes of section 225(1) of the 1985 Act or Article 233(1) of the 1986 Order.

Audit (ss 475 to 484 and 489 to 539)

9. (1)   In Chapter 1 of Part 16 of the Companies Act 2006 (requirement for audited accounts)—
(a)   sections 475 to 481 (general provisions) apply to accounts for financial years beginning on or after 6th April 2008;
(b)   sections 482 and 483 (companies subject to public sector audit) apply to accounts for financial years beginning on or after 1st April 2008;
(c)   section 484 (general power of amendment by regulations) applies accordingly.

(2)   Sections 235(1), 249A(1), (3) and (6) to (7), 249AA and 249B of the 1985 Act or Articles 243(1), 257A(1), (3) and (6) to (7), 257AA and 257B of the 1986 Order continue to apply to accounts for financial years beginning before 6th April 2008.

(3)   In section 482 of the Companies Act 2006 (non-profit-making companies subject to public sector audit) as it applies in relation to accounts for financial years beginning on or after 1st April 2008 and before 6th April 2008, the reference to the requirements of Part 16 of that Act shall be read as a reference to the requirements of Part 7 of the 1985 Act or Part 8 of the 1986 Order.

10. (1)   In Chapter 2 of Part 16 of that Act (appointment of auditors)—
(a)   sections 489 and 490 (appointment of auditors by public companies) apply to appointments for financial years beginning on or after 6th April 2008;
(b)   section 491 (term of office of auditors of public company) applies to auditors appointed for financial years beginning on or after that date.

(2)   Sections 384, 385, 387 and 388(1), (3) and (4) of the 1985 Act or Articles 392, 393, 395 and 396(1), (3) and (4) of the 1986 Order continue to apply to appointments by public companies for financial years beginning before that date.

11. (1)   In that Chapter, the following provisions apply to auditors appointed for financial years beginning on or after 6th April 2008—
    section 492 (fixing of auditor's remuneration),
    section 493 (disclosure of terms of audit appointment), and

Part 2   CA 2006 commencement etc

section 494 (disclosure of services provided by auditor or associated and related remuneration).

(2) Sections 390A and 390B of the 1985 Act or Articles 398A and 398B of the 1986 Order continue to apply to auditors appointed for financial years beginning before that date.

(3) The repeal of section 390A of the 1985 Act and Article 398A of the 1986 Order (remuneration of auditors) does not affect the operation of any such resolution as is mentioned in paragraph 45 of Schedule 3 to the Companies Act 2006 (Commencement No 3, Consequential Amendments, Transitional Provisions and Savings) Order 2007.

12. (1) In Chapter 3 of Part 16 of that Act (functions of auditor)—
  (a) sections 495 to 498 (auditor's report and duties of auditor) apply to auditors' reports on accounts or reports for financial years beginning on or after 6th April 2008;
  (b) sections 499 to 501 (rights of auditors) apply to auditors appointed for financial years beginning on or after that date;
  (c) sections 503 to 509 (signature of auditor's report and offences in connection with auditor's report) apply to auditors' reports on accounts or reports for financial years beginning on or after that date.

(2) Sections 235 to 237, 389A and 389B of the 1985 Act or Articles 243 to 245, 397A and 397B of the 1986 Order continue to apply as regards financial years beginning before that date.

(3) Section 502 of the Companies Act 2006 (auditor's rights in relation to resolutions and meetings) applies to auditors appointed on or after 6th April 2008.

(4) Section 390 of the 1985 Act or Article 398 of the 1986 Order continues to apply to auditors appointed before that date.

13. (1) In Chapter 4 of Part 16 of that Act (removal, resignation, etc of auditors), sections 510 to 513 (removal of auditor) apply where notice of the intended resolution is given to the company on or after 6th April 2008.

(2) Sections 391 and 391A of the 1985 Act or Articles 399 and 399A of the 1986 Order continue to apply where notice of the intended resolution is given to the company before that date.

(3) Until section 1068(1) of the Companies Act 2006 comes into force, the notice referred to in section 512(1) (notice to registrar of resolution removing auditor from office) must be in the form prescribed for the purposes of section 391(2) of the 1985 Act or Article 399(2) of the 1986 Order.

(4) In section 513 (rights of auditor removed from office) as it applies in relation to an auditor appointed before 6th April 2008, the reference to rights under section 502(2) shall be read as a reference to rights under section 390(1) of the 1985 Act or Article 398(1) of the 1986 Order.

14. (1) In that Chapter, sections 514 and 515 (failure to re-appoint auditor) apply to appointments for financial years beginning on or after 6th April 2008.

(2) Section 391A of the 1985 Act or Article 399A of the 1986 Order continues to apply to appointments for financial years beginning before that date.

15. (1) In that Chapter, sections 516 to 518 (resignation of auditor) apply to resignations occurring on or after 6th April 2008.

(2) Sections 392 and 392A of the 1985 Act or Articles 400 and 400A of the 1986 Order continue to apply to resignations occurring before that date.

[(3) In section 518 (rights of resigning auditor) as it applies in relation to an auditor appointed before 6th April 2008, the reference to rights under section 502(2) shall be read as a reference to rights under section 390(1) of the 1985 Act or Article 398(1) of the 1986 Order.]

16. (1) In that Chapter, sections 519 to 525 (statement by auditor ceasing to hold office) apply where the auditor ceases to hold office on or after 6th April 2008.

(2) Sections 394 and 394A of the 1985 Act or Articles 401A and 401B of the 1986 Order continue to apply where the auditor ceases to hold office before that date.

17. (1) In that Chapter, section 526 (effect of casual vacancies) applies where the vacancy occurs on or after 6th April 2008.

(2) Section 388(2) of the 1985 Act or Article 396(2) of the 1986 Order continues to apply where the vacancy occurred before that date.

18. In Chapter 5 of Part 16 of that Act (quoted companies: right of members to raise audit concerns at accounts meeting), in section 527 (members' powers to require website publication of audit concerns)—
  (a) subsection (1)(a) (matters relating to audit of company's accounts) applies to accounts for financial years beginning on or after 6th April 2008, and
  (b) subsection (1)(b) (matters relating to circumstances connected with an auditor of the company) applies to auditors appointed for financial years beginning on or after that date.

19. A resolution passed before 6th April 2008 authorising a liability limitation agreement is effective for the purposes of section 536 (authorisation of agreement by members of company) if it complies with the requirements of that section.

Debentures (ss 738 to 754)

20. Section 741 of the Companies Act 2006 (registration of allotment of debentures) applies to allotments of debentures made on or after 6th April 2008.

21. (1) Until regulations under section 1136 of the Companies Act 2006 come into force specifying a place for the purposes of section 743(1)(b), a company's register of debenture holders may be kept—

(a) at any office of the company at which the work of making it up is done, or

(b) if the company arranges with some other person for the making up of the register to be undertaken on its behalf by that other person, at the office of that other person at which the work is done,

provided that place is situated in the part of the United Kingdom in which the company is registered.

(2) Until section 1068(1) of the Companies Act 2006 comes into force, the notice referred to in section 743(2) (notice of place where register of debenture holders is kept) must be given in the form prescribed for the purposes of section 190(5) of the 1985 Act or Article 199(3) of the 1986 Order.

22. (1) Sections 744 to 747 (register of debenture holders: right to inspect or require copy) and section 749 (right of debenture holder to copy of deed) of the Companies Act 2006 apply where the request is made on or after 6th April 2008.

(2) Section 191(1) to (6) of the 1985 Act or Article 200(1) to (6) of the 1986 Order continue to apply to requests made before that date.

Prohibition of public offers by private companies (ss 755 to 759)

24. (1) Sections 755 and 756 of the Companies Act 2006 (prohibition of public offers by private companies) apply to offers made on or after 6th April 2008.

(2) Section 81 of the 1985 Act or Article 91 of the 1986 Order continues to apply to offers made before that date.

25. Sections 758 and 759 of the Companies Act 2006 (enforcement of prohibition: orders after contravention) apply to offers made on or after 6th April 2008.

Minimum share capital requirement for public companies (ss 761 to 767)

26. A certificate issued under section 117 of the 1985 Act or Article 127 of the 1986 Order (public company share capital requirements) has effect on and after 6th April 2008 as if issued under section 761 of the Companies Act 2006.

27. (1) Section 762 of the Companies Act 2006 (procedure for obtaining trading certificate) applies to applications made on or after 6th April 2008.

(2) Section 117(1) to (5) and (7A) of the 1985 Act or Article 127(1) to (5) and (7A) of the 1986 Order continue to apply to applications made before 6th April 2008.

(3) An application is treated as made before 6th April 2008 if—

(a) a statutory declaration is delivered to the registrar in accordance with section 117(2) of the 1985 Act or Article 127(2) of the 1986 Order, and

(b) the declaration was signed before that date.

28. (1) Until section 1068(1) of the Companies Act 2006 comes into force—

(a) an application under section 762 of that Act must be in the form prescribed for the purposes of section 117(2) of the 1985 Act or Article 127(2) of the 1986 Order;

(b) the statement and information required by section 762(1)(a) to (c) must be provided on the form prescribed for the statutory declaration required by section 117(3) of the 1985 Act or Article 127(3) of the 1986 Order (but not in the form of a statutory declaration and disregarding so much of the form as requires other information);

(c) a company seeking to satisfy the minimum share capital requirement in euros may adapt the form accordingly; and

(d) the form must be signed by a director or by the company secretary.

(2) A form completed in accordance with sub-paragraph (1) is treated as the statement of compliance required by section 762(1)(d) and (2).

(3) By adapting the form as mentioned in paragraph (1)(c) the applicant is treated as electing that euros shall be the currency by reference to which it is determined whether the requirement mentioned in section 765(1) is met.

(4) By not so adapting the form the applicant is treated as electing that sterling shall be that currency.

(5) Sub-paragraphs (1)(c), (3) and (4) above also apply in relation to the form prescribed for the purposes of section 43(3) of the 1985 Act or Article 53(3) of the 1986 Order (re-registration or private company as public) where a company seeks to satisfy the minimum share capital requirement in section 45(2)(a) of that Act or Article 55(2)(a) of that Order in euros.

29. (1) Section 767 of the Companies Act 2006 (consequences of doing business etc without a trading certificate) applies in relation to things done on or after 6th April 2008.

(2) Section 117(6), (7) and (8) of the 1985 Act or Article 127(6), (7) and (8) of the 1986 Order continue to apply in relation to things done before that date.

Certification and transfer of securities (ss 769 to 782)

30. Section 771 of the Companies Act 2006 (procedure on transfer being lodged) applies to transfers lodged with the company on or after 6th April 2008.

31. Section 780 of the Companies Act 2006 (duty of company as to issue of certificates on surrender of share warrant) applies to share warrants surrendered on or after 6th April 2008.

Request to inspect a company's register of interests disclosed (ss 811(4), 812 and 814)

32. Sections 811(4), 812 and 814 of the Companies Act 2006 (inspection of register of interests disclosed: further provision about requests) apply to requests under section 811 of that Act made on or after 6th April 2008.

Distributions (ss 829 to 853)

33. (1) Sections 829 to 853 of the Companies Act 2006 (distributions) apply to distributions made on or after 6th April 2008.

(2) Sections 263 to 281 of the 1985 Act or Articles 271 to 289 of the 1986 Order continue to apply to distributions made before that date.

34. Until section 1068(1) of the Companies Act 2006 comes into force—
  (a)   the notice referred to in section 833(1)(a) (notice of intention to carry on business as investment company) must be in the form prescribed for the purposes of section 266(1) of the 1985 Act or Article 274(1) of the 1986 Order; and
  (b)   the notice referred to in section 833(4) (notice that company no longer wishes to be an investment company) must be in the form prescribed for the purposes of section 266(3) of the 1985 Act or Article 274(3) of the 1986 Order.

35. (1) The relevant accounts for the purposes of Chapter 2 of Part 23 of the Companies Act 2006 (justification of distribution by reference to accounts) may be accounts for financial years beginning before 6th April 2008 (to which the provisions of the 1985 Act or 1986 Order apply).

(2) In that case the provisions of that Chapter and Chapter 3 of that Part (supplementary provisions) have effect with the following adaptations—
  (a)   in section 836(1)(b)(i), for "provisions of a kind specified for the purposes of this section by regulations under section 396" substitute "provisions of any of the kinds mentioned in paragraphs 88 and 89 of Schedule 4 to the Companies Act 1985 or paragraphs 87 and 88 of Schedule 4 to the Companies (Northern Ireland) Order 1986";
  (b)   in section 837—
    (i)   in subsection (1)(a), for "section 423" substitute "section 238 of the Companies Act 1985 or Article 246 of the Companies (Northern Ireland) Order 1986";
    (ii)   in subsection (1)(b), for "section 426" substitute "section 251 of the Companies Act 1985 or Article 259 of the Companies (Northern Ireland) Order 1986";
    (iii)   in subsection (2), for "this Act" substitute "the Companies Act 1985 or the Companies (Northern Ireland) Order 1986";
    (iv)   in subsection (4)(b)(i), for "section 423" substitute "section 238 of the Companies Act 1985 or Article 246 of the Companies (Northern Ireland) Order 1986";
  (c)   in section 838—
    (i)   in subsection (4), for "sections 395 to 397" substitute "sections 226 to 226B of the Companies Act 1985 or Articles 234 to 234B of the Companies (Northern Ireland) Order 1986";
    (ii)   in subsection (5), for "section 414" substitute "[section] 233 of the Companies Act 1985 or Article 241 of the Companies (Northern Ireland) Order 1986";
    (iii)   in subsection (6), for "Part 35 of this Act" substitute "Part 24 of the Companies Act 1985 or Part 24 of the Companies (Northern Ireland) Order 1986";
  (d)   in section 839—
    (i)   in subsection (4), for "sections 395 to 397" substitute "sections 226 to 226B of the Companies Act 1985 or Articles 234 to 234B of the Companies (Northern Ireland) Order 1986";
    (ii)   in subsection (6)(b)(i), for "section 423" substitute "section 238 of the Companies Act 1985 or Article 246 of the Companies (Northern Ireland) Order 1986";

      (iii) in subsection (7), for "Part 35 of this Act" substitute "Part 24 of the Companies Act 1985 or Part 24 of the Companies (Northern Ireland) Order 1986";

  (e) in section 841(2)(a), for "provisions of a kind specified for the purposes of this paragraph by regulations under section 396" to the end substitute "provisions of any kind mentioned in paragraphs 88 and 89 of Schedule 4 to the Companies Act 1985 or paragraphs 87 and 88 of Schedule 4 to the Companies (Northern Ireland) Order 1986";

  (f) in section 844(3)(b)(i), for "the note required" to the end substitute "the note to the accounts required by paragraph 20 of Schedule 4 or paragraph 20 of Schedule 8 to the Companies Act 1985 or paragraph 20 of Schedule 4 or paragraph 20 of Schedule 8 to the Companies (Northern Ireland) Order 1986 (reasons for showing development costs as an asset)";

  (g) in section 846(2)(b), for "any provision of regulations under section 396" to the end substitute "paragraphs 12(a) and 34(3)(a) of Schedule 4 or paragraphs 12(a) or 34(3)(a) of Schedule 8 to the Companies Act 1985 or paragraphs 12(a) and 34(3)(a) of Schedule 4 or paragraphs 12(a) or 34(3)(a) of Schedule 8 to the Companies (Northern Ireland) Order 1986 (only realised profits to be included in or transferred to the profit and loss account)".

Arrangements and reconstructions (ss 896 to 901)

36. (1) Section 901 of the Companies Act 2006 (obligations of company with respect to articles etc) applies to orders of the court made on or after 6th April 2008, including orders made under section 425(2) or 427 of the 1985 Act or 418(2) or 420 of the 1986 Order.

(2) Section 425(3) and (4) of the 1985 Act or Article 418(3) and (4) of the 1986 Order continues to apply to orders made before that date.

Statutory auditors (ss 1209 to 1241 and 1245 to 1264)

37. (1) The following provisions of Chapter 2 of Part 42 of the Companies Act 2006 (statutory auditors: individuals and firms) apply to the appointment of auditors for financial years beginning on or after 6th April 2008—

  (a) sections 1212 and 1213 (eligibility for appointment);

  (b) sections 1214 and 1215 (independence requirement);

  (c) section 1216 (effect of appointment of partnership).

(2) Sections 25 to 28 of the Companies Act 1989 or Articles 28 to 31 of the Companies (Northern Ireland) Order 1990 continue to apply to auditors appointed for financial years beginning before that date.

38. (1) The following provisions of that Chapter apply in relation to the supervision and qualification of auditors appointed for financial years beginning on or after 6th April 2008—

  (a) sections 1217 and 1218 and Schedule 10 (supervisory bodies);

  (b) sections 1219 to 1222 and Schedule 11 (professional qualifications and qualifying bodies).

(2) Sections 30 to 34 and 48 of, and Schedules 11 and 12 to, the Companies Act 1989 or Articles 33 to 36 and 50 of, and Schedules 11 and 12 to, the Companies (Northern Ireland) Order 1990 continue to apply in relation to the supervision and qualification of auditors appointed for financial years beginning before that date.

(3) Any declaration by the Secretary of State in force under section 33 of the Companies Act 1989 or [by the Department of Enterprise, Trade and Investment in force under] Article 36 of the Companies (Northern Ireland) Order 1990 (approval of overseas qualifications) immediately before 6th April 2008 continues in force on and after that date as if made under section 1221 of the Companies Act 2006.

39. The repeal of sections 37 and 38 of the Companies Act 1989 (information to be provided to the Secretary of State) or Articles 39 and 40 of the Companies (Northern Ireland) Order 1990 (information to be provided to the Department of Enterprise, Trade and Investment) does not affect the operation of those provisions in relation to functions exercised under Part 2 of that Act or Part 3 of that Order on or after 6th April 2008.

40. (1) Section 1226(2) of the Companies Act 2006 (eligibility of Auditor General for appointment as statutory auditor) applies to appointment as a statutory auditor for financial years beginning on or after 1st April 2008.

(2) Sections 1229 and 1230 (supervision of Auditors General by the Independent Supervisor) apply accordingly.

41. (1) The following provisions of Chapter 6 of Part 42 of the Companies Act 2006 (statutory auditors: supplementary and general provisions) apply to auditors, supervisory bodies or qualifying bodies to whom Chapters 2 to 5 of that Part apply—

  (a) sections 1248 and 1249 (second audits);

  (b) section 1250 (false and misleading statements);

  (c) section 1251 (fees);

(d)   section 1254 (directions to comply with international obligations);

(e)   sections 1255 to 1257 (general provisions about offences);

(f)   sections 1258 and 1259 (notices etc).

(2)   Sections 29, 40 to 45 and 49 of the Companies Act 1989 or Articles 32, 42 to 47 and 51 of the Companies (Northern Ireland) Order 1990 continue to apply to auditors, supervisory bodies or qualifying bodies to whom sections 25 to 28 and 30 to 39 of that Act or Articles 28 to 31 and 33 to 41 of that Order apply.

(3)   The repeal of sections 52 to 54 of the Companies Act 1989 or Articles 54 to 56 of the Companies (Northern Ireland) Order 1990 (definitions) does not affect the operation of those provisions for the purposes of interpreting provisions of that Act or that Order that continue to apply on or after 6th April 2008.

42. (1)   The repeal of sections 46 and 46A of, and Schedule 13 to, the Companies Act 1989 (delegation of functions of Secretary of State) does not affect the operation of those provisions in relation to functions exercised under Part 2 of that Act on or after 6th April 2008.

(2)   The repeal of Articles 48 and 48A of, and Schedule 13 to, the Companies (Northern Ireland) Order 1990 (delegation of functions of Department of Enterprise, Trade and Investment) does not affect the operation of those provisions in relation to functions exercised under Part 3 of that Order on or after 6th April 2008.

Expenses of winding up (s 1282)

[43. (1)   The amendment made to the Insolvency Act 1986 by section 1282(1) of the Companies Act 2006 (expenses of winding up) applies—

(a)   to a creditors' voluntary winding up—

(i)   for which the resolution is passed, or

(ii)   where commenced as a members' voluntary winding up, for which the conversion to a creditors' voluntary winding up under section 96 of the Insolvency Act 1986 takes effect, or

(iii)   in respect of which a notice is registered under paragraph 83 of Schedule B1 to the Insolvency Act 1986,

on or after 6th April 2008;

(b)   to a members' voluntary winding up for which the resolution is passed on or after 6th April 2008;

(c)   to the winding up of a company by the court where the winding-up order is made on or after 6th April 2008, except where the order is made following a resolution for voluntary winding up passed by the company before 6th April 2008.

(2)   The amendment made to the Insolvency (Northern Ireland) Order 1989 by section 1282(2) of the Companies Act 2006 (expenses of winding up) applies—

(a)   to a creditors' voluntary winding up—

(i)   in respect of which the resolution is passed, or

(ii)   where it commenced as a members' voluntary winding up, for which the conversion to a creditors' voluntary winding up under Article 82 of the Order takes effect, or

(iii)   in respect of which a notice is registered under paragraph 84 of Schedule B1 to the Order,

on or after 6th April 2008;

(b)   to a members' voluntary winding up for which the resolution is passed on or after 6th April 2008;

(c)   to the winding up of a company by the court where the winding-up order is made on or after 6th April 2008, except where the order is made following a resolution for voluntary winding up passed by the company before 6th April 2008.]

Repeal of provisions relating to prosecution of offences

44. The repeal of sections 732 to 734 of the 1985 Act or Articles 680 to 680B of the 1986 Order does not affect the operation of those provisions in relation to offences committed before 6th April 2008.

NOTES

Commencement: 6 April 2008.

Para 2: words in square brackets substituted by the Companies Act 2006 (Commencement No 6, Saving and Commencement Nos 3 and 5 (Amendment)) Order 2008, SI 2008/674, art 5, Sch 3, para 6(1), (2), (6), as from 6 April 2008.

Para 15: sub-para (3) added by the Companies Act 2006 (Commencement No 7, Transitional Provisions and Savings) Order 2008, SI 2008/1886, art 8, as from 11 August 2008.

Paras 35, 38: words in square brackets inserted by SI 2008/674, art 5, Sch 3, para 6(1), (3), (4), (6), as from 6 April 2008.

Para 43: substituted by SI 2008/674, art 5, Sch 3, para 6(1), (5), (6), as from 6 April 2008.

See also the Companies Act 2006 (Consequential Amendments etc) Order 2008, SI 2008/948, art 6(5) (at **[4.280]**) which provides that the provisions of para 35 above apply in any case where the effect of an amendment made by the 2008 Order is that the lawfulness of a distribution depends on Part 23 of the Companies Act 2006, or any provision of that Part, applying in relation to accounts for financial years beginning before 6 April 2008.

PART 2
PROVISIONS COMING INTO FORCE ON 29TH JUNE 2008

[2.67]

45. Sections 1242 to 1244 of, and Schedule 12 to, the Companies Act 2006 (duties of third country auditors: information to be supplied by third country auditors) apply to third country auditors appointed for financial years beginning on or after 29th June 2008.

NOTES

Commencement: 29 June 2008.

PART 3
PROVISIONS COMING INTO FORCE ON 1ST OCTOBER 2008

Requirement to have at least one director who is a natural person (s 155)

[2.68]

46. If on 8th November 2006—

    (a)   none of a company's directors were natural persons, and

    (b)   section 282 of the 1985 Act or Article 290 of the 1986 Order (requirement as to number of directors) was complied with in relation to the company,

section 155 of the Companies Act 2006 (companies required to have at least one director who is a natural person) does not apply to the company until 1st October 2010.

Duty of directors to avoid conflicts of interest (s 175)

47. (1)   Section 175 of the Companies Act 2006 (duty to avoid conflicts of interest) applies where the situation described in subsection (1) of that section arises on or after 1st October 2008.

(2)   The law that applied before that date continues to apply to such a situation that arose before that date.

(3)   Section 175(5)(a) of that Act (private companies: authorisation by directors) applies—

    (a)   to companies incorporated on or after 1st October 2008, and

    (b)   to companies incorporated before that date where the members of the company have resolved (before, on or after 1st October 2008) that authorisation may be given in accordance with that provision.

(4)   Chapter 3 of Part 3 of the Companies Act 2006 (resolutions and agreements affecting a company's constitution) applies to any such resolution.

(5)   For the purposes of section 30 of that Act (copies of resolutions to be forwarded to registrar) such a resolution passed before 1st October 2008 is treated as if passed on that date.

Declaration by directors of interest in proposed transaction or arrangement (s 177)

48. (1)   Section 177(1) of the Companies Act 2006 (duty of director to declare interest in proposed transaction or arrangement) applies where the duty to declare an interest arises on or after 1st October 2008.

(2)   Section 317 of the 1985 Act or Article 325 of the 1986 Order continues to apply in relation to a duty arising before that date.

(3)   For the purposes of section 177(3) of the Companies Act 2006 (previous declaration under that section proving or becoming inadequate), a declaration of interest in relation to a proposed transaction or arrangement made before 1st October 2008 under section 317 of the 1985 Act or Article 325 of the 1986 Order is treated on and after that date as if made under section 177 of the Companies Act 2006.

General duties of directors: approval by members (s 180(2))

49. The reference in section 180(2) of the Companies Act 2006 (exclusion of general duties where approval of members given) to approval given under Chapter 4 of Part 10 of that Act (transactions requiring approval of members) includes approval given by a resolution passed before 1st October 2007 that is effective by virtue of paragraph 6(2), 7(2), 8(2) or 12(2) of Schedule 3 to the Companies Act 2006 (Commencement No 3, Consequential Amendments, Transitional Provisions and Savings) Order 2007.

Declaration of interest in existing transaction or arrangement (ss 182 to 187)

50. (1)   Sections 182 to 187 of the Companies Act 2006 (declaration by director of interest in existing transaction or arrangement) apply in relation to transactions or arrangements entered into by a company on or after 1st October 2008.

(2)   Section 317 of the 1985 Act or Article 325 of the 1986 Order continues to apply in relation to transactions or arrangements entered into before that date.

Part 2   CA 2006 commencement etc

(3) For the purposes of section 182(1) of the Companies Act 2006 (declaration of interest in existing transaction not previously declared under section 177), a declaration of interest made before 1st October 2008 under section 317 of the 1985 Act or Article 325 of the 1986 Order is treated on and after that date as if made under section 177.

(4) For the purposes of section 182(3) of the Companies Act 2006 (previous declaration under that section proving or becoming inadequate), a declaration of interest made before 1st October 2008 under section 317 of the 1985 Act or Article 325 of the 1986 Order is treated on and after that date as if made under section 182.

Repeal of prohibition on private companies giving financial assistance for acquisition of shares

51. (1) The repeal by this Order of sections 151 to 153 and 155 to 158 of the Companies Act 1985 or Articles 161 to 163 and 165 to 168 of the Companies (Northern Ireland) Order 1986 (financial assistance for acquisition of shares), to the extent specified in article 5(2) of this Order, applies in relation to financial assistance given on or after 1st October 2008.

(2) This is so, in a case within section 151(2) or Article 161(2), even if the shares in question were acquired, and the liability in question incurred, before that date.

52. (1) This paragraph applies to anything that would have been unlawful by reason of any rule of law if that rule had not ceased to have effect, or been modified, as a consequence of the enactment of—

(a) any provision contained in section 151 to 153 or 155 to 158 of the 1985 Act or Article 161 to 163 or 165 to 168 of the 1986 Order (prohibition of financial assistance for acquisition of shares), or

(b) any former statutory provision substantially similar in effect to any such provision.

(2) The repeal by this Order of those sections or Articles shall not cause anything to which this paragraph applies to be rendered unlawful by reason of any rule of law that had so ceased to have effect or been modified.

NOTES

Commencement: 1 October 2008.

SCHEDULE 5

(Sch 5 (Amendments of Earlier Commencement Orders) (which is itself amended by the Companies Act 2006 (Commencement No 6, Saving and Commencement Nos 3 and 5 (Amendment)) Order 2008, SI 2008/674, art 5, Sch 3, para 7, as from 6 April 2008, to correct a drafting error) amends the Companies Act 2006 (Commencement No 1, Transitional Provisions and Savings) Order 2006, SI 2006/3428, Sch 5, Pt 2 at **[2.14]**, *and the Companies Act 2006 (Commencement No 3, Consequential Amendments, Transitional Provisions and Savings) Order 2007, SI 2007/2194, Sch 2, Pt 1, Sch 3 at* **[2.44]**, **[2.45]**.*)*

COMPANIES ACT 2006 (COMMENCEMENT NO 6, SAVING AND COMMENCEMENT NOS 3 AND 5 (AMENDMENT)) ORDER 2008

(SI 2008/674)

NOTES

Made: 7 March 2008.

Authority: Companies Act 2006, ss 1292(1)(b), 1296(1), (2), 1300(2).

Commencement: see art 2 at **[2.70]**.

This Order is reproduced as amended by: the Companies Act 2006 (Commencement No 8, Transitional Provisions and Savings) Order 2008, SI 2008/2860.

ARRANGEMENT OF ARTICLES

SCHEDULES

[2.69]
1 Citation

This Order may be cited as the Companies Act 2006 (Commencement No 6, Saving and Commencement Nos 3 and 5 (Amendment)) Order 2008.

NOTES

Commencement: 7 March 2008.

[2.70]
2 Coming into force

(1)   The provisions of this Order come into force as follows.

(2)   Article 3 and Schedule 1 come into force on 1st April 2008.

(3)   Subject to paragraph (4), articles 4 and 5 and Schedules 2 and 3 come into force on 6th April 2008.

(4)   Paragraph 1 of Schedule 3 comes into force on 1st October 2008.

(5)   Article 6 comes into force—
    (a)   on 1st April 2008 so far as relating to provisions coming into force on that date;
    (b)   on 6th April 2008 so far as relating to provisions coming into force on that date;
    (c)   on 1st October 2008 so far as relating to provisions coming into force on that date.

NOTES

Commencement: 7 March 2008.

[2.71]
3 Provisions of the Companies Act 2006 coming into force on 1st April 2008

(1)   The following provisions of the Companies Act 2006 come into force on 1st April 2008—
    (a)   section 1175 (removal of special provisions about accounts and audit of charitable companies: Great Britain), so far as it relates to Part 7 of the Companies Act 1985;
    (b)   Part 1 of Schedule 9;
    (c)   section 1295 and Schedule 16 (repeals), so far as relating to the repeals specified in Schedule 1 to this Order.

(2)   The provisions brought into force by paragraph (1) have effect in relation to accounts for financial years beginning on or after 1st April 2008.

(3)   Nothing in this article affects the operation of the repealed enactments—
    (a)   in relation to accounts for financial years beginning before 1st April 2008, or
    (b)   as applied by paragraph 16A of Schedule 1 to the Housing Act 1996 (registered social landlords).

NOTES

Commencement: 1 April 2008.

4, 5 *(Art 4 (Saving for small charitable companies in Northern Ireland) outside the scope of this work; art 5 introduces Sch 3 (Amendments of earlier commencement Orders).)*

[2.72]
6 Savings

(1)   Nothing in this Order affects any provision of the Companies Act 1985 or the Companies (Northern Ireland) Order 1986 as applied by the Limited Liability Partnerships Regulations 2001 or the Limited Liability Partnerships Regulations (Northern Ireland) 2004 to limited liability partnerships.

(2)   The amendments and repeals made by this Order do not affect the operation of section 1297 of the Companies Act 2006 (continuity of the law).

NOTES

Commencement: 1 April 2008 (certain purposes); 6 April 2008 (certain purposes); 1 October 2008 (otherwise).

SCHEDULES

SCHEDULE 1

Article 3(1)(c)

[2.73]

Short title and chapter	Extent of repeal brought into force
Companies Act 1985 (c 6)	In section 240—
	(a) in subsection (1), the words from "or, as the case may be," to "section 249A(2)";

Part 2 CA 2006 commencement etc

Short title and chapter	Extent of repeal brought into force
	(b) in subsection (3)(c), the words from "and, if no such report" to "any financial year";
	(c) subsection (3)(e) and the word "; and" preceding it;
	(d) in the closing words of subsection (3), the words from "or any report" to "section 249A(2)".
	In section 245(4)(b), the words "or reporting accountant".
	In section 249A—
	(a) subsections (2), (3A) and (4);
	(b) in subsection (6A), the words "or (2)";
	(c) in subsection (7), the definition of "gross income" and the word ", and" preceding it.
	In section 249B—
	(a) in the opening words of subsection (1), the words "or (2)";
	(b) in subsection (1C)(b), the words from "where the company referred to" to "is not a charity";
	(c) in subsection (3), the words "or (2)";
	(d) in subsection (4), in the opening words and in paragraph (a), the words "or (2)".
	Sections 249C and 249D.
	Section 249E(2).
	In section 262A, the entry for "reporting accountant".

NOTES

Commencement: 1 April 2008.

SCHEDULE 2

(Sch 2 (Saving for small charitable companies in Northern Ireland; consequential provision) outside the scope of this work.)

SCHEDULE 3
AMENDMENTS OF EARLIER COMMENCEMENT ORDERS
Article 5

Companies Act 2006 (Commencement No 3, Consequential Amendments, Transitional Provisions and Savings) Order 2007 (SI 2007/2194 (C 84))

[2.74]
1. (1) As from 1st October 2008—
  (a) the transitional adaptations of sections 205 and 234 of the Companies Act 2006 by paragraphs 11 and 12 of Schedule 1 to the Companies Act 2006 (Commencement No 3, Consequential Amendments, Transitional Provisions and Savings) Order 2007 cease to have effect, and
  (b) those sections have effect instead with the following adaptation.
(2) In section 205(5) and section 234(6), for the words from "section 661(3)" to "innocent nominee)" substitute "section 144(3) or (4) of the Companies Act 1985 or Article 154(3) or (4) of the Companies (Northern Ireland) Order 1986 (acquisition of shares by innocent nominee)".

2. *(Amends the Companies Act 2006 (Commencement No 3, Consequential Amendments, Transitional Provisions and Savings) Order 2007, SI 2007/2194, Sch 3 (at* **[2.45]***)).*

Companies Act 2006 (Commencement No 5, Transitional Provisions and Savings) Order 2007 (SI 2007/3495 (C 150))

3. *(Amends the Companies Act 2006 (Commencement No 5, Transitional Provisions and Savings) Order 2007, SI 2007/3495, art 9 (at* **[2.58]***)).*

4. The revocation by article 10(1)(b) of the Companies Act 2006 (Commencement No 5, Transitional Provisions and Savings) Order 2007 of paragraph 15(2) of Schedule 1 to the Companies Act 2006 (Commencement No 3, Consequential Amendments, Transitional Provisions and Savings) Order 2007 (transitional adaptation: period within which public company must hold AGM) does not have effect in relation to a company until—

    (a)   the directors of the company have complied with section 241 of the Companies Act 1985 or Article 249 of the Companies (Northern Ireland) Order 1986 in respect of the last financial year of the company beginning before 6th April 2008, or

    (b)   the first financial year of the company beginning on or after that date comes to an end.

5. In Schedule 1 to the Companies Act 2006 (Commencement No 5, Transitional Provisions and Savings) Order 2007 (transitional adaptations), omit paragraphs 1 and 2 (so that those paragraphs do not come into force on 6th April 2008).

6. *(Paras (1)–(5) amend the Companies Act 2006 (Commencement No 5, Transitional Provisions and Savings) Order 2007, SI 2007/3495, Sch 4, Pt 1 (at* **[2.66]***)).*

(6)   The amendments in this paragraph come into force at the same time as the provision amended.

7. *(Amends the Companies Act 2006 (Commencement No 5, Transitional Provisions and Savings) Order 2007, SI 2007/3495, Sch 5, para 2(2) to correct a drafting error in that paragraph.)*

NOTES

Commencement: 6 April 2008 (paras 2–7); 1 October 2008 (para 1).

Para 1: revoked by the Companies Act 2006 (Commencement No 8, Transitional Provisions and Savings) Order 2008, SI 2008/2860, art 6(1), as from 1 October 2009. This paragraph is reproduced here out of historical interest.

COMPANIES ACT 2006 (COMMENCEMENT NO 7, TRANSITIONAL PROVISIONS AND SAVINGS) ORDER 2008

(SI 2008/1886)

NOTES

Made: 16 July 2008.

Authority: Companies Act 2006, ss 1296(2), 1300(2).

Commencement: 11 August 2008 (art 8); 1 October 2008 (otherwise).

This Order is reproduced as amended by: the Companies Act 2006 (Commencement No 8, Transitional Provisions and Savings) Order 2008, SI 2008/2860.

ARRANGEMENT OF ARTICLES

[2.75]
1 Citation and commencement

(1)   This Order may be cited as the Companies Act 2006 (Commencement No 7, Transitional Provisions and Savings) Order 2008.

(2)   Article 8 of this Order comes into force on 11th August 2008.

(3)   The other provisions of this Order come into force on 1st October 2008.

NOTES

Commencement: 1 October 2008.

[2.76]
2 Provisions coming into force on 1st October 2008

The following provisions of the Companies Act 2006 come into force on 1st October 2008—

    (a)   sections 641(1)(a) and (2) to (6) and 642 to 644 (private companies: reduction of share capital supported by solvency statement);

    (b)   section 654 (treatment of reserve arising from reduction of capital);

    (c)   the following provisions—

        —   sections 610(2) to (4) (application to share premium account as if it were paid up share capital);

        —   652(1) and (3) (liability of members following reduction of capital);

        —   733(5) and (6) (application to capital redemption reserve as if it were paid up share capital), so far as relating to a reduction of capital under the provisions mentioned in sub-paragraph (a);

(d) section 1284(1) (extension of Companies Acts to Northern Ireland) so far as necessary for the purposes of the provisions mentioned in sub-paragraphs (a) to (c);

(e) section 1286(1)(a) and (2)(a) (extension to Northern Ireland of Great Britain enactments relating to limited liability partnerships), so far as relating to the application to limited liability partnerships of the subject matter of Part 15 (accounts and reports), Part 16 (audit) and Part 42 (statutory auditors);

(f) section 1295 and Schedule 16 (repeals), so far as relating to the repeals of the second sentence of section 141(4) of the Companies Act 1989 and of the second sentence of Article 75(4) of the Companies (No 2) (Northern Ireland) Order 1990;

(g) paragraph 11(2) of Schedule 15 (amendment of definition of "regulated market" in section 103(1) of the Financial Services and Markets Act 2000).

NOTES

Commencement: 1 October 2008.

Transitional adaptations

[2.77]

3

(1) Section 641 of the Companies Act 2006 (ways in which company may reduce its share capital) has effect with the following adaptations.

(2) After subsection (1) insert—

"(1A) Where a company reduces its share capital under subsection (1)(a), the special resolution under this section must make any necessary alterations of the company's memorandum by reducing the amount of its share capital and of its shares.".

(3) In subsection (3) for "this section" substitute "subsection (1)(a)".

(4) In subsection (6) for "the company's articles" substitute "the company's memorandum or articles".

NOTES

Commencement: 1 October 2008.

Revoked by the Companies Act 2006 (Commencement No 8, Transitional Provisions and Savings) Order 2008, SI 2008/2860, art 6(1), as from 1 October 2009. This regulation is reproduced here out of historical interest and because of art 6(2) of the 2008 Order which provides that the revocations made by art 6(1) are subject to any relevant transitional provision or saving in Sch 2 to that Order (at **[2.91]**).

[2.78]

4

(1) Section 644 of the Companies Act 2006 (reduction of capital supported by solvency statement: registration of resolution and supporting documents) has effect with the following adaptations.

(2) In subsection (1)(b), for "a statement of capital" substitute "a memorandum complying with subsection (2)".

(3) For subsection (2) substitute—

"(2) The memorandum must show with respect to the company's share capital as reduced by the resolution—

(a) the amount of the share capital,

(b) the number of shares into which it is to be divided, and the amount of each share, and

(c) the amount (if any) at the date of the registration deemed to be paid up on each share.".

NOTES

Commencement: 1 October 2008.

Revoked by the Companies Act 2006 (Commencement No 8, Transitional Provisions and Savings) Order 2008, SI 2008/2860, art 6(1), as from 1 October 2009. This regulation is reproduced here out of historical interest and because of art 6(2) of the 2008 Order which provides that the revocations made by art 6(1) are subject to any relevant transitional provision or saving in Sch 2 to that Order (at **[2.91]**).

[2.79]

5

(1) Section 652 of the Companies Act 2006 (liability of members following reduction of capital) has effect with the following adaptation.

(2) In subsection (1)(a), for "the statement of capital delivered under section 644 or 649" substitute "the memorandum delivered under section 644".

NOTES
Commencement: 1 October 2008.
Revoked by the Companies Act 2006 (Commencement No 8, Transitional Provisions and Savings) Order 2008, SI 2008/2860, art 6(1), as from 1 October 2009. This regulation is reproduced here out of historical interest and because of art 6(2) of the 2008 Order which provides that the revocations made by art 6(1) are subject to any relevant transitional provision or saving in Sch 2 to that Order (at [2.91]).

[2.80]

6 Interpretation of provisions brought into force

Where an expression in a provision brought into force by this Order—

   (a)   is defined in the Companies Act 1985 or in the Companies (Northern Ireland) Order 1986 ("the old definition"), and

   (b)   is defined in the Companies Act 2006 by another provision not yet in force for the purposes of the provision brought into force ("the new definition"),

the expression has, for the purposes of the provision brought into force the meaning given by the old definition until the new definition is brought into force for the purposes of that provision.

NOTES
Commencement: 1 October 2008.

[2.81]

7 Transitional provisions and savings

(1) Nothing in this Order affects the operation of section 140 of the Companies Act 1985 or Article 150 of the Companies (Northern Ireland) Order 1986 (liability of members on reduced shares) in relation to a reduction of capital under that Act or Order.

(2) Section 654 of the Companies Act 2006 (treatment of reserve arising from reduction of capital) and any order made under that section apply in relation to reserves arising from—

   (a)   a reduction of capital under Chapter 4 of Part 5 of the Companies Act 1985 or Chapter 4 of Part 6 of the Companies (Northern Ireland) Order 1986,

   (b)   a reduction of capital under the provisions of the Companies Act 2006 mentioned in article 2(a) above, or

   (c)   a reduction in the capital of an unlimited company not under those provisions,

irrespective of when the reduction occurred or the reserves arose.

(3) The provisions mentioned in article 2(e) have effect in relation to accounts and the audit of accounts for financial years beginning on or after 1st October 2008.

(4) Save as provided by article 2(e), nothing in this Order affects any provision of the Companies Act 1985 or the Companies (Northern Ireland) Order 1986 as applied by the Limited Liability Partnerships Regulations 2001 or the Limited Liability Partnerships Regulations (Northern Ireland) 2004 to limited liability partnerships.

NOTES
Commencement: 1 October 2008.

8 *(Amends the Companies Act 2006 (Commencement No 5, Transitional Provisions and Savings Order 2007, SI 2007/3495, Sch 4 at* **[2.66]**.*)*

COMPANIES ACT 2006 (COMMENCEMENT NO 8, TRANSITIONAL PROVISIONS AND SAVINGS) ORDER 2008

(SI 2008/2860)

NOTES
Made: 5 November 2008.
Authority: CA 2006, ss 1292(1), 1296(1), (2), 1300(2).
Commencement: 1 October 2009.
This Order is reproduced as amended by: the Companies Act 2006 (Part 35) (Consequential Amendments, Transitional Provisions and Savings) Order 2009, SI 2009/1802; the Companies Act 2006 (Consequential Amendments, Transitional Provisions and Savings) Order 2009, SI 2009/1941; the Companies Act 2006 and Limited Liability Partnerships (Transitional Provisions and Savings) (Amendment) Regulations 2009, SI 2009/2476; the Companies Act 2006 (Consequential Amendments and Transitional Provisions) Order 2011, SI 2011/1265.

ARRANGEMENT OF ARTICLES

SCHEDULES

[2.82]
1   Citation and commencement

(1)   This Order may be cited as the Companies Act 2006 (Commencement No 8, Transitional Provisions and Savings) Order 2008.

(2)   This Order comes into force on 1st October 2009.

NOTES
Commencement: 1 October 2009.

[2.83]
2   Interpretation

In this Order—
    "the 1985 Act" means the Companies Act 1985;
    "the 1986 Order" means the Companies (Northern Ireland) Order 1986;
    "existing company" means a company that immediately before 1st October 2009 was formed and
        registered under the 1985 Act or the 1986 Order or was an existing company for the
        purposes of that Act or Order;
    "transitional company" means a company that is formed and registered, or re-registered, under
        the 1985 Act or the 1986 Order on or after 1st October 2009 by virtue of paragraph 2(3) or
        22(3) of Schedule 2 to this Order.

NOTES
Commencement: 1 October 2009.

[2.84]
3   Provisions of the Companies Act 2006 coming into force on 1st October 2009

The following provisions of the Companies Act 2006 come into force on 1st October 2009—
    (a)   in Part 1 (general introductory provisions)—
          section 1 (companies);
          sections 3 to 6 (types of company);
    (b)   Part 2 (sections 7 to 16) (company formation);
    (c)   in Part 3 (a company's constitution)—
          section 17 (a company's constitution);
          [sections 18 to 21, 22(1), (3) and (4) and 23 to 28] (articles of association);
          sections 31 to 38 (other provisions relating to a company's constitution);
    (d)   in Part 4 (a company's capacity and related matters)—
          sections 39 to 42 (capacity of company and power of directors to bind it);
          sections 43 and 45 to 47 (formalities of doing business under the law of England and Wales
          or Northern Ireland);
          section 48 (formalities of doing business under the law of Scotland);
          sections 49 to 52 (other matters);
    (e)   in Part 5 (a company's name)—
          sections 53 to 57 (general requirements);
          sections 58 to 65 (indications of company type or legal form);
          sections 66 to 68 (similarity to other names);
          sections 75 and 76 (powers of Secretary of State in relation to company names);
          sections 77 to 81 (change of name);
    (f)   Part 6 (sections 86 to 88) (a company's registered office);
    (g)   Part 7 (sections 89 to 111) (re-registration as a means of altering a company's status);
    (h)   in Part 8 (a company's members)—
          section 112 (the members of a company);
          sections 113 to 115 and 120 and 122 to 127 (register of members);
          sections 129 to 135 (overseas branch registers);
          sections 136 to 144 (prohibition on subsidiary being member of its holding company);
    (i)   in Part 10 (a company's directors)—
          sections 162 to 167 (register of directors);
          sections 240 to 246 (directors' residential addresses: protection from disclosure);

section 247 (power to make provision for employees on cessation or transfer of business);

(j) in Part 12 (company secretaries), sections 275 to 279 (register of secretaries);

(k) in Part 17 (a company's share capital)—

sections 540 to 543 and 545 to 548 (shares and share capital);

sections 549 to 559 (allotment of shares: general provisions);

sections 560 to 577 (allotment of equity securities: shareholders' right of pre-emption);

sections 578 and 579 (public companies: allotment where issue not fully subscribed);

sections 580 to 592 (payment for shares);

sections 593 to 609 (public companies: independent valuation of non-cash consideration);

sections 610 to 616 (share premiums);

sections 617 to 628 (alteration of share capital);

sections 629 to 640 (classes of share and class rights);

sections 641(1)(b) and 645 to 653 (reduction of share capital confirmed by the court);

sections 655 to 657 (miscellaneous and supplementary provisions);

(l) Part 18 (sections 658 to 737) (acquisition by limited company of its own shares);

(m) Part 24 (sections 854 to 859) (a company's annual return);

(n) Part 25 (sections 860 to 894) (company charges);

(o) Part 31 (sections 1000 to 1034) (dissolution and restoration to the register);

(p) in Part 33 (UK companies not formed under companies legislation), sections 1040 to 1042 (companies not formed under companies legislation but authorised to register);

(q) Part 34 (sections 1044 to 1059) (overseas companies);

(r) in Part 35 (the registrar of companies)—

sections 1060 to 1062 (the registrar);

section 1063 (fees payable to registrar), so far as not already in force;

sections 1064 to 1067 (certificates of incorporation and registered numbers);

sections 1068(1) to (4), (6) and (7) and 1069 to 1071 (delivery of documents to the registrar);

sections 1072 to 1076 (requirements for proper delivery);

sections 1081 to 1084 (the register);

sections 1093 to 1098 (correction or removal of material on the register);

sections 1099 to 1101 (the registrar's index of company names);

sections 1108 to 1110 (language requirements: transliteration);

sections 1112 to 1120 (supplementary provisions);

(s) in Part 36 (offences under the Companies Acts)—

sections 1121 to 1123 (liability of officer in default);

section 1125 (meaning of "daily default fine");

sections 1127 to 1133 (other provisions);

(t) in Part 37 (companies: supplementary provisions)—

sections 1134 to 1136, 1137(2), (3) and (5)(a) and 1138 (company records);

sections 1139 to 1142 (service addresses);

sections 1149 to 1153 (requirements as to independent valuation);

sections 1154 and 1155 (notice of appointment of certain officers);

section 1156 (meaning of "the court");

(u) in Part 38 (companies: interpretation)—

section 1158 (meaning of "UK-registered company");

sections 1159 and 1160 and Schedule 6 (meaning of "subsidiary" and related expressions);

section 1163 (meaning of "non-cash asset");

section 1166 (meaning of "employees' share scheme");

sections 1168, 1171, 1173 (so far as not already in force) and 1174 and Schedule 8 (other definitions etc);

(v) in Part 39 (companies: minor amendments)—

section 1180 (repeal of certain provisions about company charges);

section 1181 (access to constitutional documents of RTE and RTM companies);

(w) Part 40 (sections 1182 to 1191) (company directors: foreign disqualification);

(x) Part 41 (sections 1192 to 1208) (business names);

(y) in Part 44 (miscellaneous provisions)—

section 1275 (levy to pay expenses of bodies concerned with actuarial standards etc);

section 1283 (commonhold associations);

(z) Part 45 (sections 1284 to 1287) (Northern Ireland).

NOTES

Commencement: 1 October 2009.

Words in square brackets in para (c) substituted by the Companies Act 2006 and Limited Liability Partnerships (Transitional Provisions and Savings) (Amendment) Regulations 2009, SI 2009/2476, reg 2(1), (2), as from 30 September 2009. Note that the original words were "sections 18 to 28" and that the purpose of this amendment is to prevent s 22(2) coming into force on 1 October 2009.

[2.85]
4 Repeals

Section 1295 of, and Schedule 16 to, the Companies Act 2006 (repeals) come into force on 1st October 2009 so far as relating to the repeal of the provisions specified in Schedule 1 to this Order.

NOTES
Commencement: 1 October 2009.

[2.86]
5 Transitional provisions and savings

Schedule 2 to this Order contains transitional provisions and savings relating to the provisions (and repeals) brought into force by this Order.

NOTES
Commencement: 1 October 2009.

[2.87]
6 Revocation of spent transitional adaptations

(1)   The following provisions (which make transitional adaptations that are no longer needed as a result of this Order) are revoked—

    (a)   Schedule 1 to the Companies Act 2006 (Commencement No 1, Transitional Provisions and Savings) Order 2006;

    (b)   Schedule 1 to the Companies Act 2006 (Commencement No 2, Consequential Amendments, Transitional Provisions and Savings) Order 2007;

    (c)   Schedule 1 to the Companies Act 2006 (Commencement No 3, Consequential Amendments, Transitional Provisions and Savings) Order 2007;

    (d)   Schedule 1 to the Companies Act 2006 (Commencement No 5, Transitional Provisions and Savings) Order 2007;

    (e)   paragraph 1 of Schedule 3 to the Companies Act 2006 (Commencement No 6, Saving and Commencement Nos 3 and 5 (Amendment)) Order 2008;

    (f)   articles 3 to 5 of the Companies Act 2006 (Commencement No 7, Transitional Provisions and Savings) Order 2008.

(2)   The revocations have effect subject to any relevant transitional provision or saving in Schedule 2 to this Order.

NOTES
Commencement: 1 October 2009.

[2.88]
7 Prosecution of offences in transitional cases

(1)   Where a provision creating an offence is repealed and re-enacted without modification by or under the Companies Act 2006—

    (a)   an offence committed before the commencement of the new law is to be charged under the old law,

    (b)   an offence committed after the commencement of the new law is to be charged under the new law, and

    (c)   an offence committed partly before and partly after the commencement of the new law is to be charged under the new law and not under the old.

(2)   For this purpose an offence is committed partly before and partly after the commencement of the new law if a relevant event occurs before commencement and another relevant event occurs after commencement.

(3)   A "relevant event" means an act, omission or other event (including any result of one or more acts or omissions) proof of which is required for conviction of the offence.

(4)   This article is without prejudice to section 1297(2) of the Companies Act 2006 (continuity of the law).

NOTES
Commencement: 1 October 2009.

[2.89]
8 General saving

The provisions of this Order do not affect the operation of section 1297 of the Companies Act 2006 (continuity of the law) except as expressly provided.

NOTES
Commencement: 1 October 2009.

SCHEDULES
SCHEDULE 1
REPEALS COMING INTO FORCE ON 1ST OCTOBER 2009

Article 4

PART 1
GREAT BRITAIN

[2.90]

Short title and chapter	Extent of repeal brought into force
Companies Act 1985 (c 6)	Sections 1 to 28.
	Section 29(1) to (3), (5) and (6).
	Sections 30 to 36.
	Section 36A(1) and (3).
	Sections 36AA to 40.
	Sections 43 to 55.
	Section 62 (so far as not previously repealed).
	Sections 80 and 80A.
	Sections 82 to 116.
	Sections 119 to 124.
	Section 125(1) to (5), (7) and (8).
	Sections 126 to 182.
	Sections 287 to 291.
	Sections 306 to 308.
	Section 322A.
	Section 350.
	Sections 352 to 355.
	Sections 357 to 365.
	Sections 379A and 380.
	Sections 395 to 424.
	Sections 651 to 706.
	Section 707A(2) to (4).
	Section 707B.
	Section 708(1) to (4).
	Sections 710 and 710A.
	Section 711A.
	Sections 713 and 714.
	Section 715A.
	Sections 718 and 719.
	[Sections 721 to 725 and 726(1)].
	Section 728.
	Section 730(1) to (4).
	Sections 730A and 731.
	Sections 735 to 740.
	Section 742.
	Sections 743 to 745.
	Schedules 1 and 2.
	Paragraph 2 of Schedule 3 (so far as not previously repealed).
	Schedule 14.
	Schedules 20 to 22.
	Schedule 24.
	Schedule 25.
Business Names Act 1985 (c 7)	The whole Act.
. . .	. . .

Short title and chapter	Extent of repeal brought into force
Insolvency Act 1985 (c 65)	In Schedule 6, paragraphs 10, 46 and 47.
Insolvency Act 1986 (c 45)	In Schedule 13, the entries relating to the following provisions of the Companies Act 1985—
	(a) section 13(4);
	(b) section 44(7);
	(c) section 103(7);
	(d) section 131(7);(e) section 140(2);
	(f) section 173(4);
	(g) section 657(2);
	(h) section 658(1).
Building Societies Act 1986 (c 53)	Section 102C(5).
Companies Act 1989 (c 40)	Sections 92 to 110.
	Section 115(1).
	Section 116(1) and (2).
	Section 117.
	Section 123(5).
	Section 125(1).
	Sections 126 to 129.
	Section 130(1) to (5) and (7).
	Sections 131 to 133.
	Section 136.
	Section 139(1) to (3).
	Sections 141 to 143.
	Section 144(1) and (3).
	In Schedule 10, paragraphs 1, 9 to 18 and 24.
	Schedules 15 to 17.
	In Schedule 18, paragraphs 32 to 38.
	In Schedule 19, paragraphs 1 to 7, 11 to 17 and 19 to 21.
Charities Act 1993 (c 10)	In Schedule 6, paragraph 20.
Criminal Justice Act 1993 (c 36)	In Schedule 5, paragraph 4.
Pension Schemes Act 1993 (c 48)	In Schedule 8, paragraph 16.
Trade Marks Act 1994 (c 26)	In Schedule 4, in paragraph 1(2), the entries relating to sections 392 and 410 of the Companies Act 1985.
Deregulation and Contracting Out Act 1994 (c 40)	Section 13(1).
	Schedule 5.
	In Schedule 16, paragraphs 8 to 10.
Requirements of Writing (Scotland) Act 1995 (c 7)	In Schedule 4, paragraphs 51 to 54.
Criminal Procedure (Consequential Provisions) (Scotland) Act 1995 (c 40)	In Schedule 4, paragraph 56(4).
Limited Liability Partnerships Act 2000 (c 12)	In the Schedule, paragraph 1.
Political Parties, Elections and Referendums Act 2000 (c 41)	Section 139(2).
Criminal Justice and Police Act 2001 (c 16)	Section 45.
	In Schedule 2, paragraph 17.
Enterprise Act 2002 (c 40)	In Schedule 17, paragraphs 3, 7 and 8.
Companies (Audit, Investigations and Community Enterprise) Act 2004 (c 27)	Sections 19(1) and 20.
	In Schedule 6, paragraphs 1 to 9.
Civil Partnership Act 2004 (c 33)	In Schedule 27, paragraph 104.

NOTES

Commencement: 1 October 2009.

In the entries relating to the Companies Act 1985, words "Sections 721 to 725 and 726(1)" in square brackets substituted by the Companies Act 2006 (Consequential Amendments, Transitional Provisions and Savings) Order 2009, SI 2009/1941, art 13(1)(a), as from 1 October 2009.

Entry relating to the Companies Consolidation (Consequential Provisions) Act 1985 (omitted) revoked by the Companies Act 2006 (Consequential Amendments and Transitional Provisions) Order 2011, SI 2011/1265, art 3, as from 12 May 2011 (see further the note below).

Note that this Part purported to bring into force the repeal of the Companies Consolidation (Consequential Provisions) Act 1985 on 1 October 2009 (that entry has now been omitted as noted above). However, the 1985 Act was not actually repealed by the Companies Act 2006 and, therefore, this was of no effect.

(Sch 1, Pt 2 (Repeals of Northern Ireland legislation) outside the scope of this work.)

SCHEDULE 2
TRANSITIONAL PROVISIONS AND SAVINGS

Article 5

General saving for existing companies etc

[2.91]

1. (1)   Nothing in the Companies Act 2006 affects—

(a)   the registration or re-registration of a company under the former Companies Acts, or the continued existence of a company by virtue of such registration or re-registration, or

(b)   the application in relation to an existing company of—

    (i)   Table B in the Joint Stock Companies Act 1856,

    (ii)   Table A in any of the former Companies Acts, or

    (iii)   the Companies (Tables A to F) Regulations 1985 or the Companies (Tables A to F) Regulations (Northern Ireland) 1986.

(2)   Section 1297(3) of the Companies Act 2006 (continuity of the law: things done under old law to be treated as done under the corresponding provision of the new law) applies—

(a)   in relation to a company to which section 675(1) of the 1985 Act or Article 625(1) of the 1986 Order applied (application of Act or Order to companies formed and registered under earlier companies legislation) as if the company had been formed and registered under Part 1 of the 1985 Act or Part 2 of the 1986 Order;

(b)   in relation to a company to which section 676(1) of the 1985 Act or Article 626(1) of the 1986 Order applied (application of Act or Order to companies registered but not formed under earlier companies legislation) as if the company had been registered under Chapter 2 of Part 22 of the 1985 Act or Chapter 2 of Part 22 of the 1986 Order;

(c)   in relation to a company to which section 677(1) of the 1985 Act or Article 627(1) of the 1986 Order applied (application of Act or Order to companies re-registered under earlier companies legislation) as if the company had been re-registered under Part 2 of the 1985 Act or Part 3 of the 1986 Order.

(3)   Nothing in this paragraph or in section 1297(3) of the Companies Act 2006 shall be read as affecting any reference to the date on which a company was registered or re-registered.

Company formation (ss 7 to 16)

2. (1)   Sections 7 to 16 of the Companies Act 2006 (company formation) apply to applications for registration received by the registrar on or after 1st October 2009.

(2)   Any application for registration under those provisions received by the registrar before that date shall not be entertained.

(3)   The corresponding provisions of the 1985 Act or 1986 Order continue to apply to an application for registration if—

(a)   it is received by the registrar, and

(b)   the requirements as to registration are met in relation to it,

before 1st October 2009.

(4)   Any application for registration under that Act or Order in relation to which the requirements as to registration are not met before that date shall be treated as withdrawn.

(5)   For the purposes of section 1297(3) of the Companies Act 2006 (continuity of the law) as it applies to treat a company formed and registered under Part 1 of the 1985 Act or Part 2 of the 1986 Order as if formed and registered under the corresponding provisions of the Companies Act 2006, the registration of a company on an application to which sub-paragraph (3) above applies is to be regarded as in force and effective immediately before the commencement of Part 1 of the Companies Act 2006.

(6)   In the definition of "company" in section 1 of the Companies Act 2006—

(a) the reference to a company formed and registered after the commencement of Part 1 of that Act shall be read as a reference to a company formed and registered on an application to which sub-paragraph (1) above applies, and

(b) the reference to a company formed and registered under the 1985 Act or 1986 Order immediately before the commencement of Part 1 of the Companies Act 2006 includes a company formed and registered on an application to which sub-paragraph (3) above applies.

Articles of association (ss 18 to 20)

3. (1)   Sections 7 and 8 of the 1985 Act or Articles 18 and 19 of the 1986 Order (articles of association) apply, and sections 18 to 20 of the Companies Act 2006 do not apply, to a company formed and registered under the 1985 Act or 1986 Order on an application to which paragraph 2(3) above applies.

(2)   Nothing in section 18(3) of the Companies Act 2006 (articles to be contained in single document divided into consecutively numbered paragraphs) is to be read as affecting the operation of section 28 of that Act (under which certain provisions are to be treated as part of a company's articles).

Amendment of provisions of articles (ss 21 and 22)

4. (1)   The power conferred by section 21(1) of the Companies Act 2006 (amendment of company's articles by special resolution) does not apply—

(a) to provisions of the articles of an existing company that were not capable of being so amended immediately before 1st October 2009; or

(b) to provisions of the articles of a transitional company that were not capable of being so amended under the company's constitution on its registration or re-registration (as the case may be).

(2)   The power conferred by section 22(3)(a) of that Act (amendment of entrenched provisions of articles by agreement of all the members of the company) does not apply—

(a) to provisions of the articles of an existing company that were not capable of being so amended immediately before 1st October 2009; or

(b) to provisions of the articles of a transitional company that were not capable of being so amended under the company's constitution on its registration or re-registration (as the case may be).

(3)   References in this paragraph to provisions of the articles of an existing or transitional company include provisions of the company's memorandum that are to be treated by virtue of section 28 of that Act as provisions of its articles.

(4)   A special resolution passed before 1st October 2009 removing or amending with effect from that date any provision that as from that date is treated by virtue of section 28 of that Act as a provision of the company's articles, has effect as if passed on that date.

Notice to registrar of existence of restrictions on amendment of articles (s 23)

5. Section 23(1)(a) of the Companies Act 2006 (notice to registrar of fact that company's articles on formation contain provision for entrenchment) does not apply to a transitional company.

Registrar to be sent copy of amended articles (s 26)

6. (1)   Section 26 of the Companies Act 2006 (registrar to be sent copy of amended articles) applies in relation to amendments taking effect on or after 1st October 2009.

(2)   Section 18(2) and (3) of the 1985 Act or Article 29(2) and (3) of the 1986 Order continue to apply in relation to amendments taking effect before that date.

Provisions of memorandum treated as provisions of articles (s 28)

7. (1)   Section 28 of the Companies Act 2006 (existing companies: provisions of memorandum treated as provisions of articles) applies not only to an existing company but also to a transitional company.

(2)   In its application to a transitional company the reference to provisions that were contained in the company's memorandum immediately before the commencement of Part 3 shall be read as a reference to provisions that are contained in the company's memorandum on its registration or re-registration (as the case may be).

(3)   Subject to sub-paragraphs (1) and (2), in subsection (1) of that section—

(a) "before the commencement of this Part" means before 1st October 2009, and

(b) "after the commencement of this Part" means on or after that date.

8. Nothing in section 28 of the Companies Act 2006 requires a company to give notice to the registrar of an alteration of its articles.

9. (1)   A company whose articles are deemed by virtue of section 28 of the Companies Act 2006 to contain provisions formerly in its memorandum may comply with any obligation to send a person a copy of its articles—

(a)　by appending to a copy of the other provisions of the articles a copy of the provisions of its old-style memorandum that are deemed to be provisions of the articles, or

(b)　by sending together with a copy of the other provisions of the articles a copy of its old-style memorandum indicating the provisions that are deemed to be provisions of the articles.

(2)　References in sub-paragraph (1) to a company's "old-style memorandum" are—

(a)　in the case of an existing company, to its memorandum of association as it stood immediately before 1st October 2009;

(b)　in the case of a transitional company, to its memorandum of association as it stood on its registration or re-registration (as the case may be) apart from the operation of section 28.

10.　Nothing in the Companies Act 2006 shall be read as enabling a company to amend or omit provisions of its articles that were formerly in its memorandum so as to change its status as a limited or unlimited company otherwise than in accordance with the relevant provisions of Part 7 of that Act (re-registration as a means of changing company's status).

Constitutional documents to be provided to members (s 32)

11.　(1)　Section 32 of the Companies Act 2006 (constitutional documents to be provided to members) applies where the request is received by the company on or after 1st October 2009.

(2)　Section 19 of the 1985 Act or Article 30 of the 1986 Order continues to apply where the request was received by the company before that date.

Notice to registrar where company's constitution altered by enactment (s 34)

12.　(1)　Section 34 of the Companies Act 2006 (notice to registrar where company's constitution altered by enactment) applies where the enactment in question comes into force on or after 1st October 2009.

(2)　Section 18(1) and (3) of the 1985 Act or Article 29(1) and (3) of the 1986 Order continue to apply in relation to alterations made by statutory provisions coming into force before that date.

Notice to registrar where company's constitution altered by order (s 35)

13.　Section 35 of the Companies Act 2006 (notice to registrar where company's constitution altered by order) applies in relation to orders made on or after 1st October 2009.

Documents to be incorporated in or accompany copies of articles issued by company (s 36)

14.　(1)　Section 36 of the Companies Act 2006 (documents to be incorporated in or accompany copies of articles issued by company) applies to copies of a company's articles issued on or after 1st October 2009.

(2)　Section 380(2), (6) and (7) of the 1985 Act or Article 388(2), (6) and (7) of the 1986 Order continue to apply to copies issued before that date.

A company's capacity (s 39)

15.　(1)　Section 39 of the Companies Act 2006 (a company's capacity) applies to acts of a company done on or after 1st October 2009.

(2)　Section 35 of the 1985 Act or Article 45 of the 1986 Order continues to apply to acts of a company done before that date.

Execution of deeds or other documents by attorney (s 47)

16.　(1)　Section 47 of the Companies Act 2006 (execution of deeds or other documents by attorney) applies where the instrument empowering a person to act as a company's attorney is executed on or after 1st October 2009.

(2)　Section 38 of the 1985 Act or Article 48 of the 1986 Order continue to have effect where the power to act as a company's attorney was conferred before that date (including in relation to instruments executed by the attorney on behalf of the company on or after that date).

A company's name (ss 53 to 81)

17.　(1)　The following provisions of the Companies Act 2006 do not affect the continued registration of a company by a name by which it was duly registered—

(a)　in the case of an existing company, immediately before 1st October 2009, or

(b)　in the case of a transitional company, on its registration or re-registration (as the case may be).

(2)　The provisions are—

(a)　section 54 (name suggesting connection with government or public authority);

(b)　section 55 (other sensitive words or expressions);

(c)　section 57 (permitted characters etc);

(d)　section 65 (inappropriate use of indications of company type or legal form);

(e)　section 66 (name not to be the same as another in registrar's index).

18.　(1)　Sections 54 to 56 of the Companies Act 2006 (sensitive words and expressions) apply to applications for approval received by the Secretary of State on or after 1st October 2009.

(2)   Section 29 of the 1985 Act or Article 39 of the 1986 Order continues to apply in relation to applications received by the Secretary of State or the Department of Enterprise, Trade and Investment in Northern Ireland before that date.

19. (1)   Sections 77(1)(a) and 78 of the Companies Act 2006 (change of name by special resolution), and sections 80 and 81 of that Act so far as relating to a change of name by special resolution, apply where—
  (a)   the resolution is passed on or after 1st October 2009, or
  (b)   the resolution is passed before that date but no copy of the resolution is received by the registrar under section 30 of that Act (resolution affecting a company's constitution) before that date.

(2)   Section 28(1), (6) and (7) of the 1985 Act or Article 38(1), (6) and (7) of the 1986 Order continue to apply to resolutions of which a copy is received by the registrar before that date.

20.   The provisions of section 31(2) to (4) and (6) of the 1985 Act or Article 41(2) to (4) and (6) of the 1986 Order (power to direct company to change its name so that it ends with "limited") continue to apply where a direction under section 31(2) or Article 41(2) was given before 1st October 2009.

21.   The provisions of section 32 of the 1985 Act or Article 42 of the 1986 Order (power to require company to abandon misleading name) continue to apply in relation to a direction under that section or Article given before 1st October 2009.

Re-registration as a means of altering a company's status (ss 89 to 108)
22. (1)   Sections 89 to 108 of the Companies Act 2006 (re-registration as a means of altering a company's status) apply to applications for re-registration received by the registrar on or after 1st October 2009.

(2)   Any application for re-registration under those provisions received by the registrar before that date shall not be entertained.

(3)   The corresponding provisions of the 1985 Act or 1986 Order continue to apply to an application for re-registration if—
  (a)   it is received by the registrar, and
  (b)   the requirements for re-registration are met in relation to it,
before 1st October 2009.

(4)   Any application for re-registration under that Act or Order in relation to which the requirements as to re-registration are not met before that date shall be treated as withdrawn.

(5)   On an application to which sub-paragraph (1) above applies a resolution agreed to, or other thing done, before 1st October 2009 may be relied on for the purpose of meeting the requirements of the Companies Act 2006.

(6)   For the purposes of section 1297(3) of the Companies Act 2006 (continuity of the law) as it applies to treat a company re-registered under the 1985 Act or the 1986 Order as if re-registered under the corresponding provisions of the Companies Act 2006, the re-registration of a company on an application to which sub-paragraph (3) above applies is to be regarded as in force and effective immediately before the commencement of Part 7 of the Companies Act 2006.

Register of members: information as to state of register and index (s 120)
23.   Section 120 of the Companies Act 2006 (information as to state of register or index) applies where a person—
  (a)   inspects a company's register of members or index of members' names on or after 1st October 2009, or
  (b)   is provided by a company on or after that date with a copy of the company's register of members or any part of it,
whether the person's request to inspect, or be provided with a copy, was made before, on or after that date.

Repeal of minimum membership requirement
24.   The repeal of section 24 of the 1985 Act or Article 34 of the 1986 Order (minimum membership for carrying on business) does not affect any liability under that section or Article for debts of the company contracted before 1st October 2009.

Registers of directors and secretaries (ss 162 and 275)
25.   On and after 1st October 2009 the register of directors and secretaries kept by a company under section 288(1) of the 1985 Act or Article 296(1) of the 1986 Order shall be treated as two separate registers—
  (a)   a register of directors kept under and for the purposes of section 162 of the Companies Act 2006, and
  (b)   a register of secretaries kept under and for the purposes of section 275 of that Act.

Particulars to be registered (ss 163, 164 and 166 and 277 to 279)

26. (1) Subject to the following provisions, an existing company need not comply with any provision of the Companies Act 2006 requiring the company's register of directors or secretaries to contain particulars additional to those required by the 1985 Act or the 1986 Order until the earlier of—

    (a)   the date to which the company makes up its first annual return made up to a date on or after 1st October 2009, and

    (b)   the last date to which the company should have made up that return.

(2) Sub-paragraph (1) does not apply in relation to a director or secretary of whom particulars are first registered on or after 1st October 2009 (whether the director or secretary was appointed before, on or after that date).

(3) Sub-paragraph (1) ceases to apply in relation to a director or secretary whose registered particulars fall to be altered on or after 1st October 2009 because they have changed (whether the change occurred before, on or after that date).

(4) This paragraph does not affect the particulars required to be included in the company's annual return.

27. (1) In the case of an existing company—

    (a)   the relevant existing address of a director or secretary is deemed, on and after 1st October 2009, to be a service address, and

    (b)   any entry in the company's register of directors or secretaries stating that address is treated, on and after that date, as complying with the obligation in section 163(1)(b) or 277(1)(b) of the Companies Act 2006 to state a service address.

(2) The relevant existing address is—

    (a)   the address that immediately before 1st October 2009 appeared in the company's register of directors and secretaries as having been notified to the company under section 289(1A) or 290(1A) of the 1985 Act (service address notified by individual applying for confidentiality order in respect of usual residential address), or

    (b)   if no such address appeared, the address that immediately before that date appeared in the company's register of directors and secretaries as the director's or secretary's usual residential address.

(3) Any notification of a change of a relevant existing address occurring before 1st October 2009 that is received by the company on or after that date is treated as being or, as the case may be, including notification of a change of service address.

(4) The operation of this paragraph does not give rise to any duty to notify the registrar under section 167 or 276 of the Companies Act 2006 (duty to notify registrar of changes in particulars contained in register).

28. (1) An existing company must remove from its register of directors on 1st October 2009 any entry relating to a shadow director.

(2) Section 167 of the Companies Act 2006 (duty to notify registrar of changes) applies as if the shadow director had ceased to be a director on that date.

29. The removal by an existing company from its register of directors or secretaries on or after 1st October 2009 of particulars required by the 1985 Act or the 1986 Order but not required by the Companies Act 2006 does not give rise to any duty to notify the registrar under section 167 or 276 of the Companies Act 2006 (duty to notify registrar of changes in particulars contained in register).

Register of directors' residential addresses (s 165)

30. (1) The duty of a company to keep a register of directors' residential addresses has effect on and after 1st October 2009.

(2) The entry on that register of information that immediately before that date was contained in the company's register of directors and secretaries does not give rise to any duty to notify the registrar under section 167 of the Companies Act 2006 (duty to notify registrar of changes in particulars contained in register).

Duty to notify registrar of changes (ss 167 and 276)

31. (1) Sections 167 and 276 of the Companies Act 2006 (duty to notify registrar of changes) apply in relation to—

    (a)   a change among a company's directors or in its secretaries, or

    (b)   a change in the particulars contained in the register,

occurring on or after 1st October 2009.

(2) Sections 288(2), (4) and (6), 289 and 290 of the 1985 Act or Articles 296(2), (4) and (6), 297 and 298 of the 1986 Order (notification to registrar of changes) continue to apply in relation to a change occurring before that date.

Directors and secretaries: entries on the register of companies

32. (1)   The registrar may make such entries in the register as appear to be appropriate having regard to paragraphs 26 to 30 and the information appearing on the register immediately before 1st October 2009 or notified to the registrar in accordance with paragraph 31(2).

(2)   In particular, the registrar may record as a service address—
   (a)   a relevant existing address (within the meaning of paragraph 27), or
   (b)   in the case of a company formed and registered on an application to which paragraph 2(3) applies, an address notified to the registrar in connection with that application as a director's or secretary's usual residential address.

(3)   Any notification of a change of a relevant existing address occurring before 1st October 2009 that is received by the registrar on or after that date is treated as being or, as the case may be, including notification of a change of service address.

Directors' residential addresses: protection from disclosure (ss 240 to 246)

33. Where a director's usual residential address appears as a service address—
   (a)   in the company's register of directors by virtue of paragraph 27, or
   (b)   in the register of companies by virtue of paragraph 32,
that address is not protected information for the purposes of Chapter 8 of Part 10 of the Companies Act 2006.

34. (1)   Section 242(1) of the Companies Act 2006 (duty of registrar to omit protected information from material available for inspection) does not apply—
   (a)   to material delivered to the registrar before 1st October 2009, or
   (b)   to material delivered to the registrar on or after 1st October 2009 by virtue of paragraph 31(2) (notification of change occurring before that date).

(2)   In section 242(2)(b) of the Companies Act 2006 (exclusion of material registered before commencement) the reference to things registered before Chapter 8 of Part 10 of that Act comes into force is treated as including anything registered as a result of a notification in accordance with paragraph 31(2) (notification on or after 1st October 2009 of change occurring before that date).

(3)   Sub-paragraphs (1) and (2) have effect subject to paragraph 36 below (which provides for the continued protection of information formerly protected by a confidentiality order).

35. In determining under section 245(1) of the Companies Act 2006 whether to put a director's usual residential address on the public record, the registrar may take into account only—
   (a)   communications sent by the registrar on or after 1st October 2009, and
   (b)   evidence as to the effectiveness of service coming to the registrar's attention on or after that date.

Continuation of protection afforded by confidentiality orders under the 1985 Act

36. (1)   A director or secretary in relation to whom a confidentiality order under section 723B of the 1985 Act was in force immediately before 1st October 2009 is treated on and after that date as if—
   (a)   they had made an application under section 1088 of the Companies Act 2006 (application to make address unavailable for public inspection) in respect of any address that immediately before that date was contained in "confidential records" as defined in section 723D(3) of the 1985 Act, and
   (b)   that application had been determined by the registrar in their favour.

(2)   The provisions of regulations under section 1088 relating to decisions of the registrar in favour of an applicant (in particular, as to the duration and revocation of such a decision) apply accordingly.

(3)   As those regulations apply in accordance with this paragraph any reference to an offence under section 1112 of the Companies Act 2006 (false statement) shall be read as a reference to an offence under regulations under section 723E(1)(a) of the 1985 Act in relation to the application for the confidentiality order.

37. (1)   A director in relation to whom a confidentiality order under section 723B of the 1985 Act was in force immediately before 1st October 2009 is treated on and after that date as if—
   (a)   they had made an application under section 243(4) of the Companies Act 2006 (application to prevent disclosure of protected information by registrar to credit reference agency), and
   (b)   that application had been determined by the registrar in their favour.

(2)   The provisions of regulations under section 243(4) relating to decisions of the registrar in favour of an applicant (in particular, as to the duration and revocation of such a decision) apply accordingly.

(3)   As those regulations apply in accordance with this paragraph any reference to an offence under section 1112 (false statement) shall be read as a reference to an offence under regulations under section 723E(1)(a) of the 1985 Act in relation to the application for the confidentiality order.

38. Where a confidentiality order under section 723B of the 1985 Act was in force immediately before 1st October 2009 in relation to a director or secretary of a company—

(a)   section 162(5) and (8) of the Companies Act 2006 (inspection of company's register of directors), or

(b)   section 275(5) and (8) of that Act (inspection of company's register of secretaries),

do not apply in relation to the part of the company's register containing particulars of the usual residential address of the individual that before that date were protected from disclosure by section 288(5A) of the 1985 Act.

Effect of pending application for confidentiality order

39. (1)   Section 723B(3) to (8) of the 1985 Act (application for confidentiality order) continue to apply in relation to an application for a confidentiality order made before 1st October 2009.

(2)   Paragraphs 36 to 38 (continuation of protection afforded by confidentiality orders) apply to a person in respect of whom such an application has been made, and has not been determined or withdrawn, as to a person in relation to whom a confidentiality order was in force immediately before that date.

(3)   If the application is dismissed or withdrawn, those paragraphs cease to apply.

(4)   If the application is successful those paragraphs continue to apply as in the case of an individual in relation to whom a confidentiality order was in force immediately before 1st October 2009.

Power to make provision for employees on cessation or transfer of business (s 247)

40. (1)   Section 247 of the Companies Act 2006 (power to make provision for employees on cessation or transfer of business) applies to provision made on or after 1st October 2009 (subject to sub-paragraph (2)(b)).

(2)   Section 719 of the 1985 Act or Article 668 of the 1986 Order continues to apply—

(a)   to provision made before that date, and

(b)   to anything sanctioned in accordance with subsection (3) of that section or paragraph (3) of that Article before that date.

Conversion of shares into stock (s 540(2) and (3))

41. (1)   Section 540(2) of the Companies Act 2006 (prohibition on conversion of shares into stock) does not affect the conversion of shares into stock in pursuance of a resolution of the company in general meeting passed, or a written resolution agreed to, before 1st October 2009.

(2)   The reference in section 540(3) (reconversion) to stock created before the commencement of Part 17 of that Act includes stock created in pursuance of such a resolution.

(3)   Section 122(1)(b) and (2) of the 1985 Act or Article 132(1)(b) and (2) of the 1986 Order (notice to registrar of conversion) continue to apply in relation to the conversion of shares into stock under such a resolution.

Saving for provisions as to amount of authorised share capital

42. (1)   This paragraph applies to any provision of a company's memorandum as to the amount of a company's authorised share capital that is in force immediately before 1st October 2009, as altered by anything done by virtue of section 121 of the 1985 Act or Article 131 of the 1986 Order (alteration of share capital) and in force immediately before that date.

(2)   Any such provision—

(a)   is treated on and after 1st October 2009 as a provision of the company's articles setting the maximum amount of shares that may be allotted by the company, and

(b)   may be amended or revoked by the company by ordinary resolution.

(3)   Chapter 3 of Part 3 of the Companies Act 2006 (resolutions and agreements affecting a company's constitution) applies to any such resolution.

(4)   Nothing in sub-paragraph (2) affects the power of a company by special resolution to adopt new articles, with effect from 1st October 2009 or any later date, that make no provision as to the maximum number of shares that may be allotted by the company.

(5)   Any such resolution as is mentioned in sub-paragraph (2) or (4) that is passed before 1st October 2009 is treated as passed on that date.

(6)   An amendment of a company's articles on or after 1st October 2009 authorising the directors to allot shares in excess of the amount allowed by any such provision as is mentioned in sub-paragraph (1) has effect although not expressed as amending or revoking it.

Power of directors to allot shares etc: private company with only one class of shares (s 550)

43. (1)   Section 550 of the Companies Act 2006 (power of directors to allot shares etc: private company with only one class of shares) applies to an existing or transitional company only if the members of the company have resolved that the directors should have the powers given by that section.

(2)   A resolution under this paragraph may be an ordinary resolution (even if it takes the form of an alteration of the company's articles).

(3)   Chapter 3 of Part 3 of the Companies Act 2006 (resolutions and agreements affecting a company's constitution) applies to any such resolution.

(4)   Any such resolution passed before 1st October 2009 is treated as if passed on that date.

(5)   Once the members of the company have resolved as mentioned in sub-paragraph (1), the application of section 550 in relation to the company is not affected by any subsequent resolution, except one altering the company's articles so as to prohibit (to any extent) exercise of the powers mentioned in the section.

44. For the purposes of section 550 of the Companies Act 2006 provisions of the articles of an existing or transitional company—

(a)   authorising the directors to allot shares in accordance with section 80 of the 1985 Act or Article 90 of the 1986 Order, or

(b)   added following an elective resolution under section 80A of the 1985 Act or Article 90A of the 1986 Order and authorising the directors to allot shares,

are not to be treated as provisions prohibiting the directors from exercising the powers conferred by section 550 in cases to which the authority does not extend.

Power of directors to allot shares etc: authorisation by company (s 551)

45. An authorisation in force immediately before 1st October 2009 under section 80 or 80A of the 1985 Act or Article 90 or 90A of the 1986 Order has effect on and after that date as if given under section 551 of the Companies Act 2006 (power of directors to allot shares etc: authorisation by company).

Registration of allotment (s 554)

46. Section 554 of the Companies Act 2006 (registration of allotment) applies to shares allotted on or after 1st October 2009.

Return of allotment (ss 555 to 557)

47. (1)   Section 555 of the Companies Act 2006 (return of allotment by limited company) applies to shares allotted on or after 1st October 2009.

(2)   Section 88 of the 1985 Act or Article 98 of the 1986 Order continues to apply to shares allotted before that date.

48. (1)   Section 556 of the Companies Act 2006 (return of allotment by unlimited company allotting new class of shares) applies to shares allotted on or after 1st October 2009.

(2)   Section 128(1), (2) and (5) of the 1985 Act or Article 138(1), (2) and (5) of the 1986 Order continue to apply to shares allotted before that date.

Existing shareholders' right of pre-emption (ss 561 to 577)

49. (1)   Section 561 of the Companies Act 2006 (prohibition on allotment unless offers made to existing shareholders) applies to the allotment of shares on or after 1st October 2009.

(2)   Where that section applies—

(a)   section 562 of that Act (communication of pre-emption offers to shareholders) applies to offers made on or after 1st October 2009, and

(b)   section 90 of the 1985 Act or Article 100 of the 1986 Order continues to apply to offers made before that date,

and the requirements of section 561 may be met by offers within paragraph (a) or (b) above.

(3)   Section 563 of the Companies Act 2006 (consequences of contravention) applies where section 561 applies and the reference to section 562 of that Act shall be read accordingly as including a reference to section 90 of the 1985 Act or Article 100 of the 1986 Order.

50. (1)   This paragraph applies where provision made by virtue of section 91 of the 1985 Act or Article 101 of the 1986 Order (exclusion of requirements by private company) excluding the requirements of section 89 or 90 or Article 99 or 100 is in force immediately before 1st October 2009.

(2)   That provision has effect on and after that date as if it was or, as the case may be, included provision made by virtue of section 567 of the Companies Act 2006 excluding the corresponding requirements of section 561 or 562 of that Act.

51. (1)   Section 568 of the Companies Act 2006 (exclusion of statutory pre-emption right where articles confer corresponding right) applies to the allotment of shares on or after 1st October 2009.

(2)   The reference in section 568(3) to section 562 of that Act (communication of pre-emption offers to shareholders) shall be read in relation to offers made before 1st October 2009 as a reference to section 90 of the 1985 Act or Article 100 of the 1986 Order.

(3)   Section 563 of the Companies Act 2006 (consequences of contravention) applies in relation to such an offer as if the reference to section 562 of that Act were a reference to section 90 of the 1985 Act or Article 100 of the 1986 Order.

52. (1)   This paragraph applies where provision excluding or modifying section 89(1) of the 1985 Act or Article 99(1) of the 1986 Order has been made by virtue of section 95(1) of the 1985 Act or Article 105(1) of the 1986 Order and is in force immediately before 1st October 2009.

(2) The provision has effect on and after that date as if it had been made by virtue of section 570 of the Companies Act 2006 (disapplication of pre-emption rights: directors acting under general authorisation) and excluded, or made corresponding modifications of, section 561 of that Act.

(3) The power conferred to allot equity securities may accordingly be renewed under section 570(3).

53. (1) This paragraph applies where a special resolution excluding or modifying section 89(1) of the 1985 Act or Article 99(1) of the 1986 Order has been passed by virtue of section 95(2) of the 1985 Act or Article 105(2) of the 1986 Order and is in force immediately before 1st October 2009.

(2) The resolution has effect on and after that date as if it had been passed by virtue of section 571 of the Companies Act 2006 (disapplication of pre-emption rights by special resolution) and excluded, or made corresponding modifications of, section 561 of that Act.

(3) The resolution may accordingly be renewed under section 571(3).

54. (1) It is immaterial whether the directors' statement required before a resolution can be proposed under section 571 of the Companies Act 2006 (disapplication of pre-emption rights by special resolution) is made, or is sent, submitted or circulated as required by subsection (7) of that section before, on or after 1st October 2009.

(2) Section 572 of that Act (criminal liability for false statement) applies to a directors' statement that is sent, submitted or circulated to a member on or after 1st October 2009.

(3) Section 95(6) of the 1985 Act or Article 105(6) of the 1986 Order applies to a directors' statement that is circulated or supplied to a member before that date.

55. (1) This paragraph applies where provision excluding or modifying section 89(1) of the 1985 Act or Article 99(1) of the 1986 Order has been made by virtue of section 95(2A) of the 1985 Act or Article 105(2A) of the 1986 Order and is in force immediately before 1st October 2009.

(2) The provision has effect on and after that date as if it had been made by virtue of section 573 of the Companies Act 2006 (disapplication of pre-emption rights: sale of treasury shares) and excluded, or made corresponding modifications of, section 561 of that Act.

(3) The power conferred to allot equity securities may accordingly be renewed under section 570(3) or, as the case may be, section 571(3).

Public companies: allotment where issue not fully subscribed (ss 578 and 579)
56. (1) Sections 578 and 579 of the Companies Act 2006 (public companies: allotment where issue not fully subscribed) apply where the offer is made on or after 1st October 2009, unless a prospectus has been issued before that date.

(2) Sections 84 and 85 of the 1985 Act or Articles 94 and 95 of the 1986 Order continue to apply where the offer was made, or a prospectus issued, before that date.

(3) In the case of an offer made or a prospectus issued on more than one day, the references in this paragraph to the date on which it is made or issued are to the first day on which it was made or issued.

(4) References in this paragraph to a prospectus being issued are to its being made available to the public in accordance with Part 6 of the Financial Services and Markets Act 2000.

Meaning of "cash consideration" for shares (ss 583 and 607)
57. (1) Section 583(3)(e) of the Companies Act 2006 (meaning of "cash consideration for shares": other means equivalent to payment in cash) applies only in relation to consideration received in pursuance of an obligation entered into on or after 1st October 2009.

(2) Section 607 of that Act (penalty for contravention of provisions about valuation of non-cash consideration) applies in relation to consideration received in pursuance of an obligation entered into on or after that date.

(3) Section 114 of the 1985 Act or Article 124 of the 1986 Order continues to apply in relation to consideration received in pursuance of an obligation entered into before that date.

Power of court to grant relief (ss 589 and 606)
58. In section 589(3) and (4) and section 606(2) and (3) of the Companies Act 2006 (power of court to grant relief from liabilities in connection with payment for shares: matters to be taken into account), the words from "having regard to" to the end of the subsection shall be omitted in relation to a decision whether to grant relief in respect of a liability for interest arising before 1st October 2009.

Sub-division or consolidation of shares (s 618)
59. The repeal of section 122(1)(a) and (d) and (2) of the 1985 Act or Article 132(1)(a) and (d) and (2) of the 1986 Order (notice to registrar of consolidation and division, or sub-division, of shares) does not affect the operation of those provisions in relation to a consolidation and division, or sub-division, of shares effected before 1st October 2009.

Reconversion of stock into shares (s 620)

60. The repeal of section 122(1)(c) and (2) of the 1985 Act or Article 132(1)(c) and (2) of the 1986 Order (notice to registrar of reconversion of stock into shares) does not affect the operation of those provisions in relation to a reconversion effected before 1st October 2009.

Variation of class rights: companies without a share capital (ss 631 and 634)

61. Nothing in section 631 or 634 of the Companies Act 2006 (variation of class rights by company without a share capital) affects a variation of class rights made (in accordance with provision in the company's memorandum or articles) before 1st October 2009.

Notice of name or other designation of class of shares (s 636)

62. (1) Section 636 of the Companies Act 2006 (notice of name or other designation of class of shares) applies where the new name or other designation is assigned on or after 1st October 2009.

(2) Section 128(4) and (5) of the 1985 Act or Article 138(4) and (5) of the 1986 Order continue to apply where the new name or other designation was assigned before that date.

Notice of particulars of variation of rights attached to shares (s 637)

63. (1) Section 637 of the Companies Act 2006 (notice of particulars of variation of rights attached to shares) applies where the variation is made on or after 1st October 2009.

(2) Section 128(3) and (5) of the 1985 Act or Article 138(3) and (5) of the 1986 Order continue to apply where the variation was made before that date.

Notice of new class of members (s 638)

64. (1) Section 638 of the Companies Act 2006 (notice of new class of members) applies where a new class of members is created on or after 1st October 2009.

(2) Section 129(1) and (4) of the 1985 Act or Article 139(1) and (4) of the 1986 Order continue to apply where a new class of members was created before that date.

Notice of name or other designation of class of members (s 639)

65. (1) Section 639 of the Companies Act 2006 (notice of name or other designation of class of members) applies where the name or other designation, or new name or other designation, is assigned on or after 1st October 2009.

(2) Section 129(3) and (4) of the 1985 Act or Article 139(3) and (4) of the 1986 Order continue to apply where the name or other designation, or new name or other designation, was assigned before that date.

Notice of particulars of variation of class rights (s 640)

66. (1) Section 640 of the Companies Act 2006 (notice of particulars of variation of class rights) applies where the variation is made on or after 1st October 2009.

(2) Section 129(2) and (4) of the 1985 Act or Article 139(2) and (4) of the 1986 Order continue to apply where the variation was made before that date.

Repeal of provisions about reserve liability and reserve capital

67. The repeal of—
    (a)   section 120 of the 1985 Act or Article 130 of the 1986 Order (reserve liability of limited company), or
    (b)   section 124 of the 1985 Act or Article 134 of the 1986 Order (reserve capital of unlimited company),
does not affect the validity of any resolution under those provisions that is in force immediately before 1st October 2009.

Reduction of capital confirmed by the court (ss 645 to 653)

68. (1) Sections 645 to 651 of the Companies Act 2006 (reduction of capital confirmed by the court) apply where an application to the court is made under section 645(1) on or after 1st October 2009.

(2) It is immaterial for the purposes of such an application whether the resolution for reducing share capital was agreed to before, on or after 1st October 2009.

(3) The corresponding provisions of the 1985 Act or the 1986 Order continue to apply where an application to the court has been made under section 136 of that Act or Article 146 of that Order before that date.

(4) For the purposes of an application under section 645(1) any amendments of a company's memorandum contained in a resolution agreed to before 1st October 2009 are treated as amendments of the company's articles.

69. (1) Nothing in section 652 of the Companies Act 2006 (liability of members following reduction of capital) as it applies in relation to a reduction of capital confirmed by the court, or in section 653 of that Act (liability to creditor in case of omission from list of creditors), applies in relation to a reduction of capital in pursuance of an application to the court made before 1st October 2009.

(2)   The provisions of section 140 of the 1985 Act or Article 150 of the 1986 Order continue to apply in relation to such a reduction.

Cancellation of shares in public company held by or for the company (ss 662 to 668)
70. (1)   Section 662 of the Companies Act 2006 (duty to cancel shares in public company held by or for the company) applies where an event mentioned in section 662(1) or 668(1)(a) to (d) occurs on or after 1st October 2009.

(2)   Section 662 also applies where an event mentioned in section 146(1) or 148(1)(a) to (d) of the 1985 Act or Article 156(1) or 158(1)(a) to (d) of the 1986 Order occurred before 1st October 2009, unless before that date—
   (a)   the company has complied with section 146(2) or Article 156(2), or
   (b)   the period for compliance specified in section 146(3) or Article 156(3) has expired.

(3)   The provisions of the 1985 Act or 1986 Order continue to apply in those cases where section 662 does not apply.

71. (1)   Section 663 of the Companies Act 2006 (notice of cancellation of shares in public company held by or for the company) applies where the shares referred to in subsection (1) of that section are cancelled on or after 1st October 2009.

(2)   Section 122(1)(f) and (2) of the 1985 Act or Article 132(1)(f) and (2) of the 1986 Order continue to apply where the shares referred to in section 122(1)(f) or Article 132(1)(f) are cancelled before that date.

72. (1)   Sections 664 to 667 of the Companies Act 2006 (re-registration as private company in consequence of cancellation) apply in any case where section 662 of that Act applies (see paragraph 70(1) and (2) above).

(2)   The corresponding provisions of the 1985 Act or 1986 Order continue to apply in any other case.

(3)   For the purposes of an application under section 664 made by virtue of paragraph 70(2) above a resolution agreed to before 1st October 2009 under section 147(2) of the 1985 Act or Article 157(2) of the 1986 Order may be treated as if agreed to under section 664(1) and (2) (and as if amendments of the company's memorandum were amendments of its articles).

Redeemable shares (ss 684 to 689)
73. (1)   Section 686(2) of the Companies Act 2006 (terms allowing for payment on date later than redemption date) applies—
   (a)   to shares issued on or after 1st October 2009, and
   (b)   to shares issued before that date where the terms of redemption have been amended on or after that date to allow for payment on a date later than the redemption date.

(2)   So much of section 159(3) of the 1985 Act or Article 169(3) of the 1986 Order as requires payment on redemption continues to apply in any other case.

74. (1)   Section 689 of the Companies Act 2006 (notice to registrar of redemption) applies where shares are redeemed on or after 1st October 2009.

(2)   Section 122(1)(e) and (2) of the 1985 Act or Article 132(1)(e) and (2) of the 1986 Order continue to apply where shares are redeemed before that date.

Purchase of own shares (ss 690 to 708)
75.   Where immediately before 1st October 2009 a resolution is in force having been passed under any provision of—
   (a)   section 164 of the 1985 Act or Article 174 of the 1986 Order (authority for off-market purchase),
   (b)   section 165 of the 1985 Act or Article 175 of the 1986 Order (authority for contingent purchase contract),
   (c)   section 166 of the 1985 Act or Article 176 of the 1986 Order (authority for market purchase), or
   (d)   section 167(2) of the 1985 Act or Article 177(2) of the 1986 Order (release of company's right to purchase own shares),
the resolution has effect on and after that date as if passed under the corresponding provision of the Companies Act 2006 and may be varied, revoked or renewed from time to time accordingly.

76. (1)   Sections 693(1)(a) and 694 of the Companies Act 2006 (purchase of own shares: authority for off-market purchase) apply—
   (a)   to contracts entered into on or after 1st October 2009, and
   (b)   to contracts entered into before that date that—
      (i)   provide that no shares may be purchased in pursuance of the contract until its terms have been authorised by a special resolution of the company, and
      (ii)   are authorised by a special resolution passed on or after that date.

(2)   Sections 164 and 165 of the 1985 Act or Articles 174 and 175 of the 1986 Order continue to apply to any other contract entered into before that date.

77. (1) Sections 707 and 708 of the Companies Act 2006 (return to registrar of purchase of own shares and notice of cancellation) apply in relation to shares delivered to the company on or after 1st October 2009.

(2) Section 169 of the 1985 Act or Article 179 of the 1986 Order continues to apply in relation to shares delivered to the company before that date.

Power of private company to redeem or purchase own shares out of capital (ss 709 to 723)
78. (1) Sections 709 to 723 of the Companies Act 2006 (redemption or purchase by private company out of capital) apply where the directors' statement referred to in section 714 is made on or after 1st October 2009.

(2) Sections 171 to 178 of the 1985 Act or Articles 181 to 188 of the 1986 Order continue to apply where the statutory declaration required by section 173(3) or Article 183(3) was made before that date.

Treasury shares: disposal (s 727)
79. (1) Section 727(1)(a) of the Companies Act 2006 (treasury shares: disposal) applies where the contract for the sale of the shares is entered into on or after 1st October 2009.

(2) Section 162D(1)(a) of the 1985 Act or Article 172D(1)(a) of the 1986 Order continues to apply where the contract for the sale of the shares was entered into before that date.

Treasury shares: notice of cancellation (s 730)
80. (1) Section 730 of the Companies Act 2006 (treasury shares: notice of cancellation) applies to shares cancelled on or after 1st October 2009.

(2) Section 169A of the 1985 Act or Article 179A of the 1986 Order continues to apply to shares cancelled before that date.

Annual returns (ss 854 to 859)
81. (1) Sections 854 to 859 of the Companies Act 2006 (a company's annual return) apply to annual returns made up to a date on or after 1st October 2009.

(2) Sections 363 to 365 of the 1985 Act or Articles 371 to 373 of the 1986 Order continue to apply to annual returns made up to a date before 1st October 2009.

(3) Any reference in the Companies Act 2006 to a company's last return, or to a return delivered in accordance with Part 24 of that Act, shall be read as including (so far as necessary to ensure the continuity of the law) a return made up to a date before 1st October 2009 or delivered in accordance with the 1985 Act or the 1986 Order.

Company charges (ss 860 to 894)
82. (1) Sections 860 and 878 of the Companies Act 2006 (charges created by company) apply to charges created on or after 1st October 2009.

(2) The corresponding provisions of the 1985 Act or the 1986 Order continue to apply to charges created before that date.

83. (1) Sections 862 and 880 of the Companies Act 2006 (charges existing on property acquired) apply to property acquired on or after 1st October 2009.

(2) Sections 400 and 416 of the 1985 Act or Article 407 of the 1986 Order continue to apply to property acquired before that date.

84. (1) Sections 863 and 882 of the Companies Act 2006 (charge in series of debentures) apply where the first debenture of the series is executed on or after 1st October 2009.

(2) The corresponding provisions of the 1985 Act or the 1986 Order continue to apply where the first debenture of the series is executed before that date.

85. (1) Section 868 of the Companies Act 2006 (Northern Ireland: registration of certain charges etc affecting land) applies where the date of registration of the charge in the Land Registry is on or after 1st October 2009.

(2) Article 408 of the 1986 Order continues to apply where the date of registration of the charge in the Land Registry is before that date.

86. (1) Section 871 of the Companies Act 2006 (notice to registrar of appointment of receiver or manager etc) applies where the order or appointment is made, or the receiver or manager ceases to act, on or after 1st October 2009.

(2) Section 405 of the 1985 Act or Article 413 of the 1986 Order continues to apply where the order or appointment is made, or the receiver or manager ceases to act, before that date.

87. (1) Sections 872 and 887 of the Companies Act 2006 (entries of satisfaction and release) apply to statements delivered to the registrar on or after 1st October 2009.

(2) Section 403 or 419 of the 1985 Act or Article 411 of the 1986 Order continues to apply where the relevant statutory declaration, statement or application and statutory declaration or statement is received by the registrar before that date.

[Property of dissolved company (ss 1012 to 1023)
88. (1)   Sections 1012 to 1023 of the Companies Act 2006 (property of dissolved company) apply in relation to the property of a company dissolved on or after 1st October 2009.

(2)   Subject to paragraph 88A, the corresponding provisions of the 1985 Act or 1986 Order continue to apply in relation to the property of a company dissolved before that date.

88A. (1)   Section 1013 of the Companies Act 2006 (Crown disclaimer of property vesting as bona vacantia) applies in relation to property of a company dissolved before 1st October 2009 if at that date—

(a)   no period has begun to run in relation to the property under section 656(3)(a) or (b) of the 1985 Act or Article 607(3)(a) or (b) of the 1986 Order (period within which notice of disclaimer must be executed), and

(b)   the right to disclaim has not ceased to be exercisable in relation to the property by virtue of section 656(2) of the 1985 Act or Article 607(2) of the 1986 Order (waiver of right to disclaim).

(2)   In section 1013 as it applies by virtue of this paragraph the references to property vesting under section 1012 shall be read as references to its vesting under section 654 of the 1985 Act or Article 605 of the 1986 Order (or corresponding earlier provisions).

(3)   Where section 1013 applies by virtue of this paragraph—

(a)   the other provisions of sections 1012 to 1022 of the Companies Act 2006 apply accordingly, and

(b)   the corresponding provisions of the 1985 Act or 1986 Order do not apply.]

Saving for applications to court made before 1st October 2009
89.   The repeal of—

(a)   section 651 of the 1985 Act or Article 602 of the 1986 Order (power of court to declare dissolution of company void), or

(b)   section 653 of the 1985 Act or Article 604 of the 1986 Order (objection to striking off by person aggrieved),

does not affect an application made under that section or Article before 1st October 2009.

Application to court for restoration to the register (ss 1029 to 1032)
90.   Sections 1029 to 1032 of the Companies Act 2006 (restoration to register by the court) apply whether the company was dissolved or struck off the register before, on or after 1st October 2009.

91. (1)   The following provisions apply where the company was dissolved or struck off the register before 1st October 2009.

(2)   In section 1029 (application to court for restoration to register), the references in subsection (1) to enactments under which a company may have been dissolved or struck off include corresponding earlier enactments (and for this purpose sections 1000 and 1003 of that Act are regarded as corresponding to sections 652 and 652A of the 1985 Act and Articles 603 and 603A of the 1986 Order).

(3)   No application under section 1029 may be made if an application in respect of the same dissolution or striking off has been made under section 653 of the 1985 Act or Article 604 of the 1986 Order (objection to striking off by person aggrieved), and has not been withdrawn.

(4)   Section 1030(4) (general time limit of six years) does not enable an application to be made in respect of a company dissolved before 1st October 2007, subject to sub-paragraphs (5) and (6).

(5)   If the company was struck off under section 652 or 652A of the 1985 Act or Article 603 or 603A of the 1986 Order, section 1030(4) does not prevent an application being made at any time before—

(a)   1st October 2015 (that is, six years after commencement), or

(b)   the expiration of the period of 20 years from publication in the Gazette of notice under the relevant section or Article,

whichever occurs first.

(6)   Section 1030(5) (extension of period for application where application for administrative restoration refused) applies in relation to the time limit under sub-paragraph (5) above as in relation to the time limit in section 1030(4).

Effect of restoration to the register where property has vested as bona vacantia (s 1034)
92. (1)   Section 1034 of the Companies Act 2006 (effect of restoration to the register where property has vested as *bona vacantia*) applies whenever the company was dissolved.

(2)   The following provisions apply where the company was dissolved before 1st October 2009.

(3)   The reference in section 1034(1) to section 1012 (property of dissolved company to be *bona vacantia*) shall be read as a reference to section 654 of the 1985 Act or Article 605 of the 1986 Order (or corresponding earlier provisions).

(4)   No deduction is to be made under section 1034(3) (deduction of reasonable costs of Crown representative from amount payable to company) from consideration realised before 1st October 2009.

Registration of companies not formed under companies legislation (ss 1040 to 1042)

93. (1)   The provisions of Chapter 1 of Part 33 of the Companies Act 2006 (registration of companies not formed under companies legislation) apply to applications for registration received by the registrar on or after 1st October 2009.

(2)   Any application for registration under those provisions received by the registrar before that date shall not be entertained.

(3)   The provisions of Chapter 2 of Part 22 of the 1985 Act or Chapter 2 of Part 22 of the 1986 Order continue to apply to an application for registration if—

    (a)   it is received by the registrar, and

    (b)   the requirements as to registration are met in relation to it,

before 1st October 2009.

(4)   Any application for registration under that Act or Order in relation to which the requirements as to registration are not met before that date shall be treated as withdrawn.

(5)   On an application to which sub-paragraph (1) above applies a resolution agreed to, or other thing done, before 1st October 2009 may be relied on for the purpose of meeting the requirements of the Companies Act 2006.

(6)   For the purposes of section 1297(3) of the Companies Act 2006 (continuity of the law) as it applies to treat the registration of a company under Chapter 2 of Part 22 of the 1985 Act or Chapter 2 of Part 22 of the 1986 Order as if done under the corresponding provision of the Companies Act 2006, the registration of a company on an application to which sub-paragraph (3) above applies is to be regarded as in force and effective immediately before the commencement of Chapter 1 of Part 33 of the Companies Act 2006.

Fees payable to registrar (s 1063)

94.   Any regulations under section 708 of the 1985 Act or Article 657 of the 1986 Order (fees payable to registrar) that are in force immediately before 1st October 2009 have effect on or after that date as if made under section 1063 of the Companies Act 2006.

Certificates of incorporation (ss 1064 and 1065)

95.   Section 1064 of the Companies Act 2006 (public notice of issue of certificate of incorporation) applies—

    (a)   to certificates of incorporation issued under that Act, and

    (b)   to certificates of incorporation issued under the 1985 Act or 1986 Order on or after 1st October 2009.

96.   Section 1065 of the Companies Act 2006 (right to be provided with copy of certificate of incorporation) applies to certificates of incorporation whenever issued.

[Delivery of documents to the registrar (ss 1068 to 1076)

97. (1)   Sections 1068 and 1069 of the Companies Act 2006 (registrar's requirements as to form, authentication and manner of delivery and power to require delivery by electronic means) apply to documents delivered to the registrar on or after 1st October 2009 other than those delivered in pursuance of an obligation arising before that date.

(2)   Where the obligation to deliver a document to the registrar arose before 1st October 2009, the provisions that would have applied if the document had been delivered before that date continue to apply.

98.   Section 1070 of the Companies Act 2006 (agreement for delivery by electronic means) applies to all documents delivered to the registrar on or after 1st October 2009.

99. (1)   Section 1071 of the Companies Act 2006 (document not delivered until received) applies in relation to the delivery of documents to the registrar on or after 1st October 2009 other than those delivered in pursuance of an obligation arising before that date.

(2)   Where the obligation to deliver a document to the registrar arose before 1st October 2009, the provisions that would have applied if the document had been delivered before that date continue to apply.

100. (1)   Sections 1072 to 1074 of the Companies Act 2006 (requirements for proper delivery) apply to documents delivered to the registrar on or after 1st October 2009 other than those delivered in pursuance of an obligation arising before that date.

(2)   Where the obligation to deliver a document to the registrar arose before 1st October 2009, the provisions that would have applied if the document had been delivered before that date (and the registrar's former practice with respect to the requirements for proper delivery and documents containing unnecessary material) continue to apply.

101. (1)   Section 1075 of the Companies Act 2006 (informal correction of document) applies to documents delivered to the registrar on or after 1st October 2009 other than those delivered in pursuance of an obligation arising before that date.

(2)   Where the obligation to deliver a document to the registrar arose before 1st October 2009, the provisions that would have applied if the document had been delivered before that date (and the registrar's former practice with respect to documents requiring correction) continue to apply.

102. Section 1076 of the Companies Act 2006 (replacement of document not meeting requirements for proper delivery) applies to documents to which sections 1072 to 1074 of that Act apply (see paragraph 100 above).

Documents subject to Directive disclosure requirements (s 1078)
103. (1)   This paragraph has effect in relation to section 1078 of the Companies Act 2006 (documents subject to the Directive disclosure requirements) and the adaptations of that section made by paragraph 5 of Schedule 1 to the Companies Act 2006 (Commencement No 1, Transitional Provisions and Savings) Order 2006.

(2)   The adaptations continue to have effect in relation to documents delivered to the registrar on or after 1st October 2009 in pursuance of provisions of the 1985 Act or 1986 Order.

(3)   Documents subject to the Directive disclosure requirements by virtue of any such adaptation remain subject to the Directive disclosure requirements notwithstanding that the adaptation has ceased to have effect.

Effect of failure to give public notice (s 1079)
104. In section 1079 of the Companies Act 2006 (effect of failure to give public notice) the references to an amendment of the company's articles include an amendment before 1st October 2009 of the company's memorandum.

Annotation of the register (s 1081)
105. (1)   Section 1081 of the Companies Act 2006 (annotation of the register) applies in relation to—
  (a)   documents delivered to the registrar on or after 1st October 2009 other than those delivered in pursuance of an obligation arising before that date, and
  (b)   certificates issued by the registrar on or after 1st October 2009 other than those issued in response to a document delivered to the registrar before that date or in pursuance of an obligation arising before that date,
and in relation to the content of, and material derived from, such documents and certificates.

(2)   The provisions applicable before 1st October 2009 (and the registrar's former practice with respect to annotation of the register) continue to apply in relation to—
  (a)   documents delivered to the registrar before that date, or in pursuance of an obligation arising before that date, and
  (b)   certificates issued by the registrar before that date or in response to a document delivered to the registrar before that date or in pursuance of an obligation arising before that date,
and in relation to the content of, and material derived from, such documents and certificates.".

Registrar's notice to resolve inconsistency on the register (s 1093)
106. (1)   Section 1093 of the Companies Act 2006 (registrar's notice to resolve inconsistency on the register) applies where—
  (a)   a document is delivered to the registrar on or after 1st October 2009 otherwise than in pursuance of an obligation arising before that date, and
  (b)   it appears to the registrar that the information contained in the document is inconsistent with other information on the register.

(2)   The provisions applicable before 1st October 2009 (and the registrar's former practice with respect to inconsistencies on the register) continue to apply in relation to documents delivered to the registrar before that date or in pursuance of an obligation arising before that date.".

Removal of material from the register (ss 1094 to 1098)
107. (1)   This paragraph applies to—
  (a)   sections 1094 to 1097 of the Companies Act 2006 (removal of material from the register), and
  (b)   section 1098 of that Act (public notice of removal of certain material from the register).

(2)   Those provisions apply in relation to—
  (a)   documents delivered to the registrar on or after 1st October 2009 other than those delivered in pursuance of an obligation arising before that date, and
  (b)   certificates issued by the registrar on or after 1st October 2009, other than those issued in response to a document delivered to the registrar before that date or in pursuance of an obligation arising before that date,
and in relation to the content of, and material derived from, such documents and certificates.

(3)   The provisions applicable before 1st October 2009 (and the registrar's former practice with respect to removal of material from the register) continue to apply in relation to—
  (a)   documents delivered to the registrar before that date, or in pursuance of an obligation arising before that date, and

(b)   certificates issued by the registrar before that date or in response to a document delivered to the registrar before that date or in pursuance of an obligation arising before that date, and in relation to the content of, and material derived from, such documents or certificates.".

Language requirements: transliteration (ss 1108 to 1110)
108. Sections 1108 to 1110 of the Companies Act 2006 (transliteration of names and addresses) apply in relation to all documents delivered to the registrar on or after 1st October 2009.

General false statement offence (s 1112)
109. Section 1112 of the Companies Act 2006 (general false statement offence) applies to all documents delivered, and statements made, on or after 1st October 2009.]

Resolution to alter company's objects agreed to before 1st October 2009
110. (1)   The repeal of sections 4 to 6 of the 1985 Act or Articles 15 to 17 of the 1986 Order (resolution to alter company's objects: procedure for objecting to alteration) does not affect the application of those provisions in relation to a resolution agreed to before 1st October 2009.

(2)   Where an application is made under section 5 of the 1985 Act or Article 16 of the 1986 Order (application to court for cancellation of alteration) and on or after 1st October 2009—
  (a)   the alteration is confirmed (either wholly or in part) by the court, or
  (b)   the court by order alters the company's memorandum under section 5(5) or Article 16(5) (alteration in consequence of provision for purchase by company of shares of members of the company),
the alteration has effect, in accordance with section 28 of the Companies Act 2006 (provisions of memorandum treated as provisions of articles), as an alteration of the company's articles of association.

Provision and authentication by registrar of documents sent by electronic means
111. (1)   The repeal of section 710A of the 1985 Act or Article 659A of the 1986 Order (provision and authentication by registrar of documents in non-legible form) does not affect the application of those provisions on or after 1st October 2009 in relation to saved provisions of that Act or Order.

(2)   Section 1115(2) of the Companies Act 2006 (authentication in manner specified by registrar's rules) does not apply to a document in relation to which section 710A(2) of the 1985 Act or Article 659A(2) of the 1986 Order applies.

Notice of appointment of certain officers (ss 1154 and 1155)
112. Sections 1154 and 1155 of the Companies Act 2006 (duty to notify registrar of certain appointments etc) apply in relation to appointments made on or after 1st October 2009.

Amendment of memorandum or articles of commonhold association (s 1283)
113. Section 1283 of the Companies Act 2006 (amendment of memorandum or articles of commonhold association) applies to amendments made on or after 1st October 2009.

Extension of provisions to Northern Ireland (s 1284)
114. (1)   The extension to Northern Ireland by section 1284 of the Companies Act 2006 of Parts 14 and 15 of the 1985 Act (company investigations) has effect to enable the exercise of the powers conferred by those Parts in relation to companies registered in Northern Ireland, and otherwise in relation to Northern Ireland, on and after 1st October 2009.

(2)   Parts 15 and 16 of the 1986 Order, and any other provision of that Order having effect for the purposes of Part 15, continue to apply (subject to sub-paragraph (3) below)—
  (a)   in relation to inspectors appointed under Part 15 before 1st October 2009 and matters arising in connection with or in consequence of any such appointment or any report of inspectors so appointed;
  (b)   in relation to any exercise before 1st October 2009 of any power of the Department of Enterprise, Trade and Investment in Northern Ireland not within paragraph (a), and matters arising in connection with or in consequence of any such exercise.

(3)   A direction in force immediately before 1st October 2009 under Article 438(1A) or 449(1A) of the 1986 Order (direction limiting or relaxing restrictions on shares) shall continue in force and have effect on and after that date as if made under the corresponding provision of Part 14 of the 1985 Act, and the provisions of Part 15 of that Act shall apply accordingly.

[Company or business name suggesting connection with Welsh Assembly Government
114A. (1)   The repeal of section 26(2)(a) of the 1985 Act or section 2(1)(a) of the Business Names Act 1985 does not affect the operation of that provision in relation to names suggesting a connection with the Welsh Assembly Government.

(2)   In section 26(2)(a) of the 1985 Act as it has effect by virtue of paragraph (1) above, the reference to registration under that Act shall be read as a reference to registration under the Companies Act 2006 in England and Wales or Scotland.

(3)   The other provisions of the Business Names Act 1985 continue to have effect for the purposes of section 2(1)(a) of that Act as it has effect by virtue of paragraph (1) above.

(4)   Paragraphs (1) to (3) above shall cease to have effect on the coming into force of amendments of the Companies Act 2006 having the effect of extending section 54(1)(a) (company names) or, as the case may be, section 1193(1)(a) (business names) of that Act to names suggesting a connection with the Welsh Assembly Government.]

Saving for provisions as to form or manner in which documents to be delivered

115. (1)   Any saving in this Schedule for the effect of a provision of the 1985 Act or 1986 Order requiring use of a prescribed form extends to the form and the power under which it is prescribed.

(2)   Any saving in this Schedule for the effect of a provision of the 1985 Act or 1986 Order requiring a document to be delivered to the registrar extends to section 707B of the 1985 Act or Article 656B of the 1986 Order (delivery to the registrar using electronic communications) so far as relating to the provision in question and the delivery of documents under it.

Savings for provisions relating to offences

116. (1)   The repeal of any provision of the 1985 Act or 1986 Order creating an offence does not affect the continued operation of that provision in relation to an offence committed before 1st October 2009.

(2)   Any saving in this Schedule for the effect of a provision of the 1985 Act or 1986 Order that creates an offence extends to the entry relating to that provision in Schedule 24 to that Act or Schedule 23 to that Order (punishment of offences).

(3)   References in this paragraph to provisions of the 1985 Act or 1986 Order include provisions of regulations or orders made under that Act or Order.

NOTES

Commencement: 1 October 2009.

Paras 88, 88A: substituted, for the original para 88, by the Companies Act 2006 and Limited Liability Partnerships (Transitional Provisions and Savings) (Amendment) Regulations 2009, SI 2009/2476, reg 2(1), (3), as from 1 October 2009.

Paras 97–109: substituted by the Companies Act 2006 (Part 35) (Consequential Amendments, Transitional Provisions and Savings) Order 2009, SI 2009/1802, art 18, Schedule, as from 1 October 2009.

Para 114A: inserted by SI 2009/2476, reg 2(1), (4), as from 1 October 2009.

TABLE OF COMMENCEMENTS FOR THE COMPANIES ACT 2006

[2.92]

NOTES

The commencement of the Companies Act 2006 is provided for by s 1300 (at **[1.1300]**). See also the Orders made under that section, ie: the Companies Act 2006 (Commencement No 1, Transitional Provisions and Savings) Order 2006, SI 2006/3428 (at **[2.1]**), the Companies Act 2006 (Commencement No 2, Consequential Amendments, Transitional Provisions and Savings) Order 2007, SI 2007/1093 (at **[2.16]**), the Companies Act 2006 (Commencement No 3, Consequential Amendments, Transitional Provisions and Savings) Order 2007, SI 2007/2194 (at **[2.31]**), the Companies Act 2006 (Commencement No 4 and Commencement No 3 (Amendment)) Order 2007, SI 2007/2607 (at **[2.47]**), the Companies Act 2006 (Commencement No 5, Transitional Provisions and Savings) Order 2007, SI 2007/3495 (at **[2.50]**), the Companies Act 2006 (Commencement No 6, Saving and Commencement Nos 3 and 5 (Amendment)) Order 2008, SI 2008/674 (at **[2.69]**), the Companies Act 2006 (Commencement No 7, Transitional Provisions and Savings) Order 2008, SI 2008/1886 (at **[2.75]**), and the Companies Act 2006 (Commencement No 8, Transitional Provisions and Savings) Order 2008, SI 2008/2860 (at **[2.82]**).

This table lists the commencement dates for each section of, and Schedule to, the 2006 Act (including those sections and Schedules subsequently added to the Act). An indication of the substitution of a whole section or Schedule is given in the footnotes, along with an indication of a change to the section name or other heading in this Act. The table does not, however, give details of amendments to the text of an individual section or Schedule.

Where a date has been appointed for a section or Schedule the number of the relevant commencement order is given in the same column – or the abbreviation 'RA' (Royal Assent) is used, as appropriate. Details of commencements for limited purposes, transitional adaptations, transitional provisions and savings, etc, are given in the footnotes to this table. Where transitional adaptations, transitional provisions and savings are subsequently amended or revoked, details are not given in the footnotes below but are noted on both the provision of the commencement order concerned and in the notes to the affected provision of the 2006 Act. See in particular the Companies Act 2006 (Commencement No 8, Transitional Provisions and Savings) Order 2008, SI 2008/2860, art 6 (Revocation of spent transitional adaptations) at **[2.87]**, which revokes many of the transitional adaptations in earlier Orders as from 1 October 2009.

Other abbreviations used in this table are as follows:

— CO No 1: the Companies Act 2006 (Commencement No 1, Transitional Provisions and Savings) Order 2006, SI 2006/3428.
— CO No 2: the Companies Act 2006 (Commencement No 2, Consequential Amendments, Transitional Provisions and Savings) Order 2007, SI 2007/1093.
— CO No 3: the Companies Act 2006 (Commencement No 3, Consequential Amendments, Transitional Provisions and Savings) Order 2007, SI 2007/2194.
— CO No 4: the Companies Act 2006 (Commencement No 4 and Commencement No 3 (Amendment)) Order 2007, SI 2007/2607.
— CO No 5: the Companies Act 2006 (Commencement No 5, Transitional Provisions and Savings) Order 2007, SI 2007/3495.
— CO No 6: the Companies Act 2006 (Commencement No 6, Saving and Commencement Nos 3 and 5 (Amendment)) Order 2008, SI 2008/674.
— CO No 7: the Companies Act 2006 (Commencement No 7, Transitional Provisions and Savings) Order 2008, SI 2008/1886.
— CO No 8: the Companies Act 2006 (Commencement No 8, Transitional Provisions and Savings) Order 2008, SI 2008/2860.
— GB: Great Britain.
— NI: Northern Ireland.

Provision of CA 2006	Commencement
Part 1: General Introductory Provisions	
1 Companies	1 Oct 2009 (CO No 8)
2 The Companies Acts	1 Jan 2007 (certain purposes) (CO No 1)[1]
	20 Jan 2007 (certain purposes) (CO No 1)[1]
	6 Apr 2007 (otherwise) (CO No 2)[2]
3 Limited and unlimited companies	1 Oct 2009 (CO No 8)
4 Private and public companies	1 Oct 2009 (CO No 8)
5 Companies limited by guarantee and having share capital	1 Oct 2009 (CO No 8)
6 Community interest companies	1 Oct 2009 (CO No 8)
Part 2: Company Formation	
7 Method of forming company	1 Oct 2009 (CO No 8)[129]
8 Memorandum of association	20 Jan 2007 (certain purposes) (CO No 1)[3]
	1 Oct 2009 (otherwise) (CO No 8)[129]
9 Registration documents	1 Oct 2009 (CO No 8)[129]
10 Statement of capital and initial shareholdings	20 Jan 2007 (certain purposes) (CO No 1)[3]

Provision of CA 2006	Commencement
	1 Oct 2009 (otherwise) (CO No 8)[129]
11 Statement of guarantee	20 Jan 2007 (certain purposes) (CO No 1)[3]
	1 Oct 2009 (otherwise) (CO No 8)[129]
12 Statement of proposed officers	1 Oct 2009 (CO No 8)[129]
13 Statement of compliance	1 Oct 2009 (CO No 8)[129]
14 Registration	1 Oct 2009 (CO No 8)[129]
15 Issue of certificate of incorporation	1 Oct 2009 (CO No 8)[129]
16 Effect of registration	1 Oct 2009 (CO No 8)[129]
Part 3: A Company's Constitution	
Chapter 1: Introductory	
17 A company's constitution	1 Oct 2007 (certain purposes) (CO No 3)[4]
	6 Apr 2008 (certain purposes) (CO No 5)[107]
	1 Oct 2009 (otherwise) (CO No 8)
Chapter 2: Articles of Association	
18 Articles of association	1 Oct 2009 (CO No 8)[130]
19 Power of Secretary of State to prescribe model articles	20 Jan 2007 (certain purposes) (CO No 1)[3]
	1 Oct 2009 (otherwise) (CO No 8)[130]
20 Default application of model articles	1 Oct 2009 (CO No 8)[130]
21 Amendment of articles	1 Oct 2009 (CO No 8)[131]
22 Entrenched provisions of the articles	1 Oct 2009 (sub-ss (1)–(3); to be appointed (otherwise) (CO No 8)[209]
23 Notice to registrar of existence of restriction on amendment of articles	1 Oct 2009 (CO No 8)[132]
24 Statement of compliance where amendment of articles restricted	1 Oct 2009 (CO No 8)
25 Effect of alteration of articles on company's members	1 Oct 2009 (CO No 8)
26 Registrar to be sent copy of amended articles	1 Oct 2009 (CO No 8)[133]
27 Registrar's notice to comply in case of failure with respect to amended articles	1 Oct 2009 (CO No 8)
28 Existing companies: provisions of memorandum treated as provisions of articles	1 Oct 2009 (CO No 8)[134]
Chapter 3: Resolutions and Agreements Affecting a Company's Constitution	
29 Resolutions and agreements affecting a company's constitution	1 Oct 2007 (CO No 3)[5]
30 Copies of resolutions or agreements to be forwarded to registrar	1 Oct 2007 (CO No 3)[5]
Chapter 4: Miscellaneous and Supplementary Provisions	
31 Statement of company's objects	1 Oct 2009 (CO No 8)
32 Constitutional documents to be provided to members	20 Jan 2007 (certain purposes) (CO No 1)[3]
	1 Oct 2009 (otherwise) (CO No 8)[135]
33 Effect of company's constitution	1 Oct 2009 (CO No 8)
34 Notice to registrar where company's constitution altered by enactment	1 Oct 2009 (CO No 8)[136]
35 Notice to registrar where company's constitution altered by order	1 Oct 2009 (CO No 8)[137]
36 Documents to be incorporated in or accompany copies of articles issued by company	1 Oct 2009 (CO No 8)[138]
37 Right to participate in profits otherwise than as member void	1 Oct 2009 (CO No 8)

Provision of CA 2006	Commencement
38 Application to single member companies of enactments and rules of law	1 Oct 2009 (CO No 8)
Part 4: A Company's Capacity and Related Matters	
39 A company's capacity	1 Oct 2009 (CO No 8)[139]
40 Power of directors to bind the company	1 Oct 2009 (CO No 8)
41 Constitutional limitations: transactions involving directors or their associates	1 Oct 2009 (CO No 8)
42 Constitutional limitations: companies that are charities	1 Oct 2009 (CO No 8)
43 Company contracts	1 Oct 2009 (CO No 8)
44 Execution of documents	6 Apr 2008 (CO No 5)[71]
45 Common seal	1 Oct 2009 (CO No 8)
46 Execution of deeds	1 Oct 2009 (CO No 8)
47 Execution of deeds or other documents by attorney	1 Oct 2009 (CO No 8)[140]
48 Execution of documents by companies	1 Oct 2009 (CO No 8)
49 Official seal for use abroad	1 Oct 2009 (CO No 8)
50 Official seal for share certificates etc	1 Oct 2009 (CO No 8)
51 Pre-incorporation contracts, deeds and obligations	1 Oct 2009 (CO No 8)
52 Bills of exchange and promissory notes	1 Oct 2009 (CO No 8)
Part 5: A Company's Name	
Chapter 1: General Requirements	
53 Prohibited names	1 Oct 2009 (CO No 8)
54 Names suggesting connection with government or public authority	20 Jan 2007 (certain purposes) (CO No 1)[3]
	1 Oct 2009 (otherwise) (CO No 8)[141]
55 Other sensitive words or expressions	20 Jan 2007 (certain purposes) (CO No 1)[3]
	1 Oct 2009 (otherwise) (CO No 8)[141]
56 Duty to seek comments of government department or other specified body	20 Jan 2007 (certain purposes) (CO No 1)[3]
	1 Oct 2009 (otherwise) (CO No 8)[141]
57 Permitted characters etc	20 Jan 2007 (certain purposes) (CO No 1)[3]
	1 Oct 2009 (otherwise) (CO No 8)[141]
Chapter 2: Indications of Company Type or Legal Form	
58 Public limited companies	1 Oct 2009 (CO No 8)
59 Private limited companies	1 Oct 2009 (CO No 8)
60 Exemption from requirement as to use of "limited"	20 Jan 2007 (certain purposes) (CO No 1)[3]
	1 Oct 2009 (otherwise) (CO No 8)
61 Continuation of existing exemption: companies limited by shares	1 Oct 2009 (CO No 8)
62 Continuation of existing exemption: companies limited by guarantee	1 Oct 2009 (CO No 8)
63 Exempt company: restriction on amendment of articles	1 Oct 2009 (CO No 8)
64 Power to direct change of name in case of company ceasing to be entitled to exemption	1 Oct 2009 (CO No 8)
65 Inappropriate use of indications of company type or legal form	20 Jan 2007 (certain purposes) (CO No 1)[3]
	1 Oct 2009 (otherwise) (CO No 8)[141]
Chapter 3: Similarity to Other Names	
66 Name not to be the same as another in the index	20 Jan 2007 (certain purposes) (CO No 1)[3]
	1 Oct 2009 (otherwise) (CO No 8)[141]

Provision of CA 2006	Commencement
67 Power to direct change of name in case of similarity to existing name	20 Jan 2007 (certain purposes) (CO No 1)[3]
	1 Oct 2009 (otherwise) (CO No 8)
68 Direction to change name: supplementary provisions	1 Oct 2009 (CO No 8)
69 Objection to company's registered name	1 Oct 2008 (CO No 5)
70 Company names adjudicators	1 Oct 2008 (CO No 5)
71 Procedural rules	1 Oct 2008 (CO No 5)
72 Decision of adjudicator to be made available to public	1 Oct 2008 (CO No 5)
73 Order requiring name to be changed	1 Oct 2008 (CO No 5)[111]
74 Appeal from adjudicator's decision	1 Oct 2008 (CO No 5)
Chapter 4: Other Powers of the Secretary of State	
75 Provision of misleading information etc	1 Oct 2009 (CO No 8)
76 Misleading indication of activities	1 Oct 2009 (CO No 8)
77 Change of name	1 Oct 2009 (CO No 8)[142]
78 Change of name by special resolution	1 Oct 2009 (CO No 8)[142]
79 Change of name by means provided for in company's articles	1 Oct 2009 (CO No 8)
80 Change of name: registration and issue of new certificate of incorporation	1 Oct 2009 (CO No 8)[142]
81 Change of name: effect	1 Oct 2009 (CO No 8)[142]
Chapter 6: Trading Disclosures	
82 Requirement to disclose company name etc	20 Jan 2007 (certain purposes) (CO No 1)[3]
	1 Oct 2008 (otherwise) (CO No 5)
83 Civil consequences of failure to make required disclosure	1 Oct 2008 (CO No 5)
84 Criminal consequences of failure to make required disclosures	20 Jan 2007 (certain purposes) (CO No 1)[3]
	1 Oct 2008 (otherwise) (CO No 5)
85 Minor variations in form of name to be left out of account	1 Oct 2008 (CO No 5)[112]
Part 6: A Company's Registered Office	
86 A company's registered office	1 Oct 2009 (CO No 8)
87 Change of address of registered office	1 Oct 2009 (CO No 8)
88 Welsh companies	1 Oct 2009 (CO No 8)
Part 7: Re-Registration as a Means of Altering a Company's Status	
89 Alteration of status by re-registration	1 Oct 2009 (CO No 8)[143]
90 Re-registration of private company as public	1 Oct 2009 (CO No 8)[143]
91 Requirements as to share capital	1 Oct 2009 (CO No 8)[143]
92 Requirements as to net assets	1 Oct 2009 (CO No 8)[143]
93 Recent allotment of shares for non-cash consideration	1 Oct 2009 (CO No 8)[143]
94 Application and accompanying documents	1 Oct 2009 (CO No 8)[143]
95 Statement of proposed secretary	1 Oct 2009 (CO No 8)[143]
96 Issue of certificate of incorporation on re-registration	1 Oct 2009 (CO No 8)[143]
97 Re-registration of public company as private limited company	1 Oct 2009 (CO No 8)[143]
98 Application to court to cancel resolution	1 Oct 2009 (CO No 8)[143]
99 Notice to registrar of court application or order	1 Oct 2009 (CO No 8)[143]

Provision of CA 2006	Commencement
100 Application and accompanying documents	1 Oct 2009 (CO No 8)[143]
101 Issue of certificate of incorporation on re-registration	1 Oct 2009 (CO No 8)[143]
102 Re-registration of private limited company as unlimited	1 Oct 2009 (CO No 8)[143]
103 Application and accompanying documents	20 Jan 2007 (certain purposes) (CO No 1)[3]
	1 Oct 2009 (otherwise) (CO No 8)[143]
104 Issue of certificate of incorporation on re-registration	1 Oct 2009 (CO No 8)[143]
105 Re-registration of unlimited company as limited	1 Oct 2009 (CO No 8)[143]
106 Application and accompanying documents	1 Oct 2009 (CO No 8)[143]
107 Issue of certificate of incorporation on re-registration	1 Oct 2009 (CO No 8)[143]
108 Statement of capital required where company already has share capital	20 Jan 2007 (certain purposes) (CO No 1)[3]
	1 Oct 2009 (otherwise) (CO No 8)[143]
109 Re-registration of public company as private and unlimited	1 Oct 2009 (CO No 8)
110 Application and accompanying documents	20 Jan 2007 (certain purposes) (CO No 1)[3]
	1 Oct 2009 (otherwise) (CO No 8)
111 Issue of certificate of incorporation on re-registration	1 Oct 2009 (CO No 8)
Part 8: A Company's Members	
Chapter 1: The Members of a Company	
112 The members of a company	1 Oct 2009 (CO No 8)
Chapter 2: Register of Members	
113 Register of members	1 Oct 2009 (CO No 8)
114 Register to be kept available for inspection	1 Oct 2009 (CO No 8)
115 Index of members	1 Oct 2009 (CO No 8)
116 Rights to inspect and require copies	20 Jan 2007 (certain purposes) (CO No 1)[3]
	1 Oct 2007 (otherwise) (CO No 3)[6]
117 Register of members: response to request for inspection or copy	1 Oct 2007 (CO No 3)[6]
118 Register of members: refusal of inspection or default in providing copy	1 Oct 2007 (CO No 3)[6]
119 Register of members: offences in connection with request for or disclosure of information	1 Oct 2007 (CO No 3)[6]
120 Information as to state of register and index	1 Oct 2009 (CO No 8)[144]
121 Removal of entries relating to former members	6 Apr 2008 (CO No 5)[72]
122 Share warrants	1 Oct 2009 (CO No 8)
123 Single member companies	1 Oct 2009 (CO No 8)
124 Company holding its own shares as treasury shares	1 Oct 2009 (CO No 8)
125 Power of court to rectify register	1 Oct 2009 (CO No 8)
126 Trusts not to be entered on register	1 Oct 2009 (CO No 8)
127 Register to be evidence	1 Oct 2009 (CO No 8)

Part 2   CA 2006 commencement etc

Provision of CA 2006	Commencement
128 Time limit for claims arising from entry in register	6 Apr 2008 (CO No 5)[73]
Chapter 3: Overseas Branch Registers	
129 Overseas branch registers	20 Jan 2007 (certain purposes) (CO No 1)[3]
	1 Oct 2009 (otherwise) (CO No 8)
130 Notice of opening of overseas branch register	1 Oct 2009 (CO No 8)
131 Keeping of overseas branch register	20 Jan 2007 (certain purposes) (CO No 1)[3]
	1 Oct 2009 (otherwise) (CO No 8)
132 Register or duplicate to be kept available for inspection in UK	1 Oct 2009 (CO No 8)
133 Transactions in shares registered in overseas branch register	1 Oct 2009 (CO No 8)
134 Jurisdiction of local courts	1 Oct 2009 (CO No 8)
135 Discontinuance of overseas branch register	1 Oct 2009 (CO No 8)
Chapter 4: Prohibition on Subsidiary being Member of its Holding Company	
136 Prohibition on subsidiary being a member of its holding company	1 Oct 2009 (CO No 8)
137 Shares acquired before prohibition became applicable	1 Oct 2009 (CO No 8)
138 Subsidiary acting as personal representative or trustee	1 Oct 2009 (CO No 8)
139 Interests to be disregarded: residual interest under pension scheme or employees' share scheme	1 Oct 2009 (CO No 8)
140 Interests to be disregarded: employer's rights of recovery under pension scheme or employees' share scheme	1 Oct 2009 (CO No 8)
141 Subsidiary acting as authorised dealer in securities	1 Oct 2009 (CO No 8)
142 Protection of third parties in other cases where subsidiary acting as dealer in securities	1 Oct 2009 (CO No 8)
143 Application of provisions to companies not limited by shares	1 Oct 2009 (CO No 8)
144 Application of provisions to nominees	1 Oct 2009 (CO No 8)
Part 9: Exercise of Members' Rights	
145 Effect of provisions of articles as to enjoyment or exercise of members' rights	1 Oct 2007 (CO No 3)[7]
146 Traded companies: nomination of persons to enjoy information rights	1 Oct 2007 (CO No 3)[7]
147 Information rights: form in which copies to be provided	1 Oct 2007 (CO No 3)[7]
148 Termination or suspension of nomination	1 Oct 2007 (CO No 3)[7]
149 Information as to possible rights in relation to voting	1 Oct 2007 (CO No 3)[7]
150 Information rights: status of rights	1 Oct 2007 (CO No 3)[7]
151 Information rights: power to amend	20 Jan 2007 (certain purposes) (CO No 1)[3]
	1 Oct 2007 (otherwise) (CO No 3)
152 Exercise of rights where shares held on behalf of others: exercise in different ways	1 Oct 2007 (CO No 3)[7]
153 Exercise of rights where shares held on behalf of others: members' requests	1 Oct 2007 (CO No 3)[7]
Part 10: A Company's Directors	
Chapter 1: Appointment and Removal of Directors	
154 Companies required to have directors	1 Oct 2007 (CO No 3)

Provision of CA 2006	Commencement
155 Companies required to have at least one director who is a natural person	1 Oct 2008 (CO No 5)[113]
156 Direction requiring company to make appointment	1 Oct 2008 (CO No 5)[114]
157 Minimum age for appointment as director	1 Oct 2008 (CO No 5)
158 Power to provide for exceptions from minimum age requirement	20 Jan 2007 (certain purposes) (CO No 1)[3]
	1 Oct 2008 (otherwise) (CO No 5)
159 Existing under-age directors	1 Oct 2008 (CO No 5)
160 Appointment of directors of public company to be voted on individually	1 Oct 2007 (CO No 3)
161 Validity of acts of directors	1 Oct 2007 (CO No 3)[8]
162 Register of directors	20 Jan 2007 (certain purposes) (CO No 1)[3]
	1 Oct 2009 (otherwise) (CO No 8)[145]
163 Particulars of directors to be registered: individuals	1 Oct 2009 (CO No 8)[145]
164 Particulars of directors to be registered: corporate directors and firms	1 Oct 2009 (CO No 8)[145]
165 Register of directors' residential addresses	1 Oct 2009 (CO No 8)[145]
166 Particulars of directors to be registered: power to make regulations	20 Jan 2007 (certain purposes) (CO No 1)[3]
	1 Oct 2009 (otherwise) (CO No 8)[145]
167 Duty to notify registrar of changes	1 Oct 2009 (CO No 8)[145]
168 Resolution to remove director	1 Oct 2007 (CO No 3)
169 Director's right to protest against removal	1 Oct 2007 (CO No 3)[9]
Chapter 2: General Duties of Directors	
170 Scope and nature of general duties	1 Oct 2007 (CO No 3)[10]
171 Duty to act within powers	1 Oct 2007 (CO No 3)
172 Duty to promote the success of the company	1 Oct 2007 (CO No 3)
173 Duty to exercise independent judgment	1 Oct 2007 (CO No 3)
174 Duty to exercise reasonable care, skill and diligence	1 Oct 2007 (CO No 3)
175 Duty to avoid conflicts of interest	1 Oct 2008 (CO No 5)[115]
176 Duty not to accept benefits from third parties	1 Oct 2008 (CO No 5)
177 Duty to declare interest in proposed transaction or arrangement	1 Oct 2008 (CO No 5)[116]
178 Civil consequences of breach of general duties	1 Oct 2007 (CO No 3)[10]
179 Cases within more than one of the general duties	1 Oct 2007 (CO No 3)
180 Consent, approval or authorisation by members	1 Oct 2007 (CO No 3)[10a]
181 Modification of provisions in relation to charitable companies	1 Oct 2007 (CO No 3)[10]
Chapter 3: Declaration of Interest in Existing Transaction or Arrangement	
182 Declaration of interest in existing transaction or arrangement	1 Oct 2008 (CO No 5)[117]
183 Offence of failure to declare interest	1 Oct 2008 (CO No 5)[117]
184 Declaration made by notice in writing	1 Oct 2008 (CO No 5)[117]
185 General notice treated as sufficient declaration	1 Oct 2008 (CO No 5)[117]

Provision of CA 2006	Commencement
186 Declaration of interest in case of company with sole director	1 Oct 2008 (CO No 5)[117]
187 Declaration of interest in existing transaction by shadow director	1 Oct 2008 (CO No 5)[117]
Chapter 4: Transactions with Directors Requiring Approval of Members	
188 Directors' long-term service contracts: requirement of members' approval	1 Oct 2007 (CO No 3)[11]
189 Directors' long-term service contracts: civil consequences of contravention	1 Oct 2007 (CO No 3)[11]
190 Substantial property transactions: requirement of members' approval	1 Oct 2007 (CO No 3)[12]
191 Meaning of "substantial"	1 Oct 2007 (CO No 3)[12]
192 Exception for transactions with members or other group companies	1 Oct 2007 (CO No 3)[12]
193 Exception in case of company in winding up or administration	1 Oct 2007 (CO No 3)[12]
194 Exception for transactions on recognised investment exchange	1 Oct 2007 (CO No 3)[12]
195 Property transactions: civil consequences of contravention	1 Oct 2007 (CO No 3)[12]
196 Property transactions: effect of subsequent affirmation	1 Oct 2007 (CO No 3)[12]
197 Loans to directors: requirement of members' approval	1 Oct 2007 (CO No 3)[13]
198 Quasi-loans to directors: requirement of members' approval	1 Oct 2007 (CO No 3)[13]
199 Meaning of "quasi-loan" and related expressions	1 Oct 2007 (CO No 3)[13]
200 Loans or quasi-loans to persons connected with directors: requirement of members' approval	1 Oct 2007 (CO No 3)[13]
201 Credit transactions: requirement of members' approval	1 Oct 2007 (CO No 3)[13]
202 Meaning of "credit transaction"	1 Oct 2007 (CO No 3)[13]
203 Related arrangements: requirement of members' approval	1 Oct 2007 (CO No 3)[13]
204 Exception for expenditure on company business	1 Oct 2007 (CO No 3)[13]
205 Exception for expenditure on defending proceedings etc	1 Oct 2007 (CO No 3)[13]
206 Exception for expenditure in connection with regulatory action or investigation	1 Oct 2007 (CO No 3)[13]
207 Exceptions for minor and business transactions	1 Oct 2007 (CO No 3)[13]
208 Exceptions for intra-group transactions	1 Oct 2007 (CO No 3)[13]
209 Exceptions for money-lending companies	1 Oct 2007 (CO No 3)[13]
210 Other relevant transactions or arrangements	1 Oct 2007 (CO No 3)[13]
211 The value of transactions and arrangements	1 Oct 2007 (CO No 3)[13]
212 The person for whom a transaction or arrangement is entered into	1 Oct 2007 (CO No 3)[13]
213 Loans etc: civil consequences of contravention	1 Oct 2007 (CO No 3)[13]
214 Loans etc: effect of subsequent affirmation	1 Oct 2007 (CO No 3)[13]
215 Payments for loss of office	1 Oct 2007 (CO No 3)[14]

Provision of CA 2006	Commencement
216 Amounts taken to be payments for loss of office	1 Oct 2007 (CO No 3)[14]
217 Payment by company: requirement of members' approval	1 Oct 2007 (CO No 3)[14]
218 Payment in connection with transfer of undertaking etc: requirement of members' approval	1 Oct 2007 (CO No 3)[14]
219 Payment in connection with share transfer: requirement of members' approval	1 Oct 2007 (CO No 3)[14]
220 Exception for payments in discharge of legal obligations etc	1 Oct 2007 (CO No 3)[14]
221 Exception for small payments	1 Oct 2007 (CO No 3)[14]
222 Payments made without approval: civil consequences	1 Oct 2007 (CO No 3)[14]
223 Transactions requiring members' approval: application of provisions to shadow directors	1 Oct 2007 (CO No 3)
224 Approval by written resolution: accidental failure to send memorandum	1 Oct 2007 (CO No 3)
225 Cases where approval is required under more than one provision	1 Oct 2007 (CO No 3)
226 Requirement of consent of Charity Commission: companies that are charities	1 Oct 2007 (CO No 3)
Chapter 5: Directors' Service Contracts	
227 Directors' service contracts	1 Oct 2007 (CO No 3)
228 Copy of contract or memorandum of terms to be available for inspection	1 Oct 2007 (CO No 3)[15]
229 Right of member to inspect and request copy	20 Jan 2007 (certain purposes) (CO No 1)[3]
	1 Oct 2007 (otherwise) (CO No 3)[15]
230 Directors' service contracts: application of provisions to shadow directors	1 Oct 2007 (CO No 3)[15]
Chapter 6: Contracts with Sole Members who are Directors	
231 Contract with sole member who is also a director	1 Oct 2007 (CO No 3)[16]
Chapter 7: Directors' Liabilities	
232 Provisions protecting directors from liability	1 Oct 2007 (CO No 3)[17]
233 Provision of insurance	1 Oct 2007 (CO No 3)[17]
234 Qualifying third party indemnity provision	1 Oct 2007 (CO No 3)[17]
235 Qualifying pension scheme indemnity provision	1 Oct 2007 (CO No 3)[17]
236 Qualifying indemnity provision to be disclosed in directors' report	1 Oct 2007 (CO No 3)[17]
237 Copy of qualifying indemnity provision to be available for inspection	1 Oct 2007 (CO No 3)[18]
238 Right of member to inspect and request copy	20 Jan 2007 (certain purposes) (CO No 1)[3]
	1 Oct 2007 (otherwise) (CO No 3)[18]
239 Ratification of acts of directors	1 Oct 2007 (CO No 3)[19]
Chapter 8: Directors' Residential Addresses: Protection From Disclosure	
240 Protected information	1 Oct 2009 (CO No 8)[145]
241 Protected information: restriction on use or disclosure by company	1 Oct 2009 (CO No 8)[145]
242 Protected information: restriction on use or disclosure by registrar	1 Oct 2009 (CO No 8)[145]

Part 2   CA 2006 commencement etc

Provision of CA 2006	Commencement
243 Permitted use or disclosure by the registrar	20 Jan 2007 (certain purposes) (CO No 1)[3]
	1 Oct 2009 (otherwise) (CO No 8)[145]
244 Disclosure under court order	1 Oct 2009 (CO No 8)[145]
245 Circumstances in which registrar may put address on the public record	1 Oct 2009 (CO No 8)[145]
246 Putting the address on the public record	1 Oct 2009 (CO No 8)[145]
Chapter 9: Supplementary Provisions	
247 Power to make provision for employees on cessation or transfer of business	1 Oct 2009 (CO No 8)[20]
248 Minutes of directors' meetings	1 Oct 2007 (CO No 3)[21]
249 Minutes as evidence	1 Oct 2007 (CO No 3)[21]
250 "Director"	1 Oct 2007 (CO No 3)
251 "Shadow director"	1 Oct 2007 (CO No 3)
252 Persons connected with a director	1 Oct 2007 (CO No 3)
253 Members of a director's family	1 Oct 2007 (CO No 3)
254 Director "connected with" a body corporate	1 Oct 2007 (CO No 3)
255 Director "controlling" a body corporate	1 Oct 2007 (CO No 3)
256 Associated bodies corporate	1 Oct 2007 (CO No 3)
257 References to company's constitution	1 Oct 2007 (CO No 3)
258 Power to increase financial limits	20 Jan 2007 (certain purposes) (CO No 1)[3]
	1 Oct 2007 (otherwise) (CO No 3)
259 Transactions under foreign law	1 Oct 2007 (CO No 3)
Part 11: Derivative Claims and Proceedings by Members	
Chapter 1: Derivative Claims in England and Wales or Northern Ireland	
260 Derivative claims	1 Oct 2007 (CO No 3)[22]
261 Application for permission to continue derivative claim	1 Oct 2007 (CO No 3)[22]
262 Application for permission to continue claim as a derivative claim	1 Oct 2007 (CO No 3)[22]
263 Whether permission to be given	20 Jan 2007 (certain purposes) (CO No 1)[3]
	1 Oct 2007 (otherwise) (CO No 3)[22]
264 Application for permission to continue derivative claim brought by another member	1 Oct 2007 (CO No 3)[22]
Chapter 2: Derivative Proceedings in Scotland	
265 Derivative proceedings	1 Oct 2007 (CO No 3)
266 Requirement for leave and notice	1 Oct 2007 (CO No 3)[22]
267 Application to continue proceedings as derivative proceedings	1 Oct 2007 (CO No 3)[22]
268 Granting of leave	20 Jan 2007 (certain purposes) (CO No 1)[3]
	1 Oct 2007 (otherwise) (CO No 3)
269 Application by member to be substituted for member pursuing derivative proceedings	1 Oct 2007 (CO No 3)
Part 12: Company Secretaries	
270 Private company not required to have secretary	6 Apr 2008 (CO No 5)[74]
271 Public company required to have secretary	6 Apr 2008 (CO No 5)
272 Direction requiring public company to appoint secretary	6 Apr 2008 (CO No 5)[75]
273 Qualifications of secretaries of public companies	6 Apr 2008 (CO No 5)[76]
274 Discharge of functions where office vacant or secretary unable to act	6 Apr 2008 (CO No 5)[75]

Provision of CA 2006	Commencement
275 Duty to keep register of secretaries	20 Jan 2007 (certain purposes) (CO No 1)[3]
	1 Oct 2009 (otherwise) (CO No 8)[145]
276 Duty to notify registrar of changes	1 Oct 2009 (CO No 8)[145]
277 Particulars of secretaries to be registered: individuals	1 Oct 2009 (CO No 8)[145]
278 Particulars of secretaries to be registered: corporate secretaries and firms	1 Oct 2009 (CO No 8)[145]
279 Particulars of secretaries to be registered: power to make regulations	20 Jan 2007 (certain purposes) (CO No 1)[3]
	1 Oct 2009 (otherwise) (CO No 8)[145]
280 Acts done by person in dual capacity	6 Apr 2008 (CO No 5)
Part 13: Resolutions and Meetings	
Chapter 1: General Provisions About Resolutions	
281 Resolutions	1 Oct 2007 (CO No 3)[23]
282 Ordinary resolutions	1 Oct 2007 (CO No 3)[23]
283 Special resolutions	1 Oct 2007 (CO No 3)[23]
284 Votes: general rules	1 Oct 2007 (CO No 3)[23]
285 Voting by proxy[204]	1 Oct 2007 (CO No 3)[23]
285A Voting rights on poll or written resolution[204]	3 Aug 2009
286 Votes of joint holders of shares	1 Oct 2007 (CO No 3)[23]
287 Saving for provisions of articles as to determination of entitlement to vote	1 Oct 2007 (CO No 3)[23]
Chapter 2: Written Resolutions	
288 Written resolutions of private companies	1 Oct 2007 (CO No 3)[24]
289 Eligible members	1 Oct 2007 (CO No 3)[24]
290 Circulation date	1 Oct 2007 (CO No 3)[24]
291 Circulation of written resolutions proposed by directors	1 Oct 2007 (CO No 3)[24]
292 Members' power to require circulation of written resolution	1 Oct 2007 (CO No 3)[24]
293 Circulation of written resolution proposed by members	1 Oct 2007 (CO No 3)[24]
294 Expenses of circulation	1 Oct 2007 (CO No 3)[24]
295 Application not to circulate members' statement	1 Oct 2007 (CO No 3)[24]
296 Procedure for signifying agreement to written resolution	1 Oct 2007 (CO No 3)[24]
297 Period for agreeing to written resolution	1 Oct 2007 (CO No 3)[24]
298 Sending documents relating to written resolutions by electronic means	1 Oct 2007 (CO No 3)[24]
299 Publication of written resolution on website	1 Oct 2007 (CO No 3)[24]
300 Relationship between this Chapter and provisions of company's articles	1 Oct 2007 (CO No 3)[24]
Chapter 3: Resolutions at Meetings	
301 Resolutions at general meetings	1 Oct 2007 (CO No 3)
302 Directors' power to call general meetings	1 Oct 2007 (CO No 3)
303 Members' power to require directors to call general meeting	1 Oct 2007 (CO No 3)[25]
304 Directors' duty to call meetings required by members	1 Oct 2007 (CO No 3)[25]
305 Power of members to call meeting at company's expense	1 Oct 2007 (CO No 3)[25]
306 Power of court to order meeting	1 Oct 2007 (CO No 3)[26]

Provision of CA 2006	Commencement
307 Notice required of general meeting	1 Oct 2007 (CO No 3)[27]
307A Notice required of general meeting: certain meetings of traded companies[205]	3 Aug 2009
308 Manner in which notice to be given	20 Jan 2007 (CO No 1)
309 Publication of notice of meeting on website	20 Jan 2007 (CO No 1)
310 Persons entitled to receive notice of meetings	1 Oct 2007 (CO No 3)[27]
311 Contents of notices of meetings	1 Oct 2007 (CO No 3)[27]
311A Traded companies: publication of information in advance of general meeting[205]	3 Aug 2009
312 Resolution requiring special notice	1 Oct 2007 (CO No 3)[28]
313 Accidental failure to give notice of resolution or meeting	1 Oct 2007 (CO No 3)[29]
314 Members' power to require circulation of statements	1 Oct 2007 (CO No 3)[30]
315 Company's duty to circulate members' statement	1 Oct 2007 (CO No 3)[30]
316 Expenses of circulating members' statement	1 Oct 2007 (CO No 3)[30]
317 Application not to circulate members' statement	1 Oct 2007 (CO No 3)[30]
318 Quorum at meetings	1 Oct 2007 (CO No 3)[31]
319 Chairman of meeting	1 Oct 2007 (CO No 3)[31]
319A Traded companies: questions at meetings[205]	3 Aug 2009
320 Declaration by chairman on a show of hands	1 Oct 2007 (CO No 3)[31]
321 Right to demand a poll	1 Oct 2007 (CO No 3)[31]
322 Voting on a poll	1 Oct 2007 (CO No 3)[31]
322A Voting on a poll: votes cast in advance[205]	1 Aug 2009
323 Representation of corporations at meetings	1 Oct 2007 (CO No 3)[31]
324 Rights to appoint proxies	1 Oct 2007 (CO No 3)[31]
324A Obligation of proxy to vote in accordance with instructions[205]	1 Aug 2009
325 Notice of meeting to contain statement of rights	1 Oct 2007 (CO No 3)[31]
326 Company-sponsored invitations to appoint proxies	1 Oct 2007 (CO No 3)[31]
327 Notice required of appointment of proxy etc	1 Oct 2007 (except sub-s (2)(c)) (CO No 3)[31] *Not in force* (otherwise)[200]
328 Chairing meetings	1 Oct 2007 (CO No 3)[31]
329 Right of proxy to demand a poll	1 Oct 2007 (CO No 3)[31]
330 Notice required of termination of proxy's authority	1 Oct 2007 (except sub-s (6)(c)) (CO No 3)[31] *Not in force* (otherwise)[200]
331 Saving for more extensive rights conferred by articles	1 Oct 2007 (CO No 3)[31]
332 Resolution passed at adjourned meeting	1 Oct 2007 (CO No 3)
333 Sending documents relating to meetings etc in electronic form	20 Jan 2007 (CO No 1)
333A Traded company: duty to provide electronic address for receipt of proxies etc[205]	1 Aug 2009

Provision of CA 2006	Commencement
334 Application to class meetings	1 Oct 2007 (CO No 3)[32]
335 Application to class meetings: companies without a share capital	1 Oct 2007 (CO No 3)[32]

Chapter 4: Public Companies and Traded Companies: Additional Requirements for AGMs[202]

336 Public companies and traded companies: annual general meeting[202]	1 Oct 2007 (CO No 3)[33]
337 Public companies and traded companies: notice of AGM[202]	1 Oct 2007 (CO No 3)[33]
338 Public companies: members' power to require circulation of resolutions for AGMs	1 Oct 2007 (CO No 3)[33]
338A Traded companies: members' power to include other matters in business dealt with at AGM[205]	1 Aug 2009
339 Public companies: company's duty to circulate members'resolutions for AGMs	1 Oct 2007 (CO No 3)[33]
340 Public companies: expenses of circulating members' resolutions for AGM	1 Oct 2007 (CO No 3)[33]
340A Traded companies: duty to circulate members' matters for AGM[205]	1 Aug 2009
340B Traded companies: expenses of circulating members' matters to be dealt with at AGM[205]	1 Aug 2009

Chapter 5: Additional Requirements for Quoted Companies and Traded Companies[202]

341 Results of poll to be made available on website	1 Oct 2007 (CO No 3)
342 Members' power to require independent report on poll	1 Oct 2007 (CO No 3)[34]
343 Appointment of independent assessor	1 Oct 2007 (CO No 3)[34]
344 Independence requirement	20 Jan 2007 (certain purposes) (CO No 1)[3] 1 Oct 2007 (otherwise) (CO No 3)[34]
345 Meaning of "associate"	1 Oct 2007 (CO No 3)[34]
346 Effect of appointment of a partnership	1 Oct 2007 (CO No 3)[34]
347 The independent assessor's report	1 Oct 2007 (CO No 3)[34]
348 Rights of independent assessor: right to attend meeting etc	1 Oct 2007 (CO No 3)[34]
349 Rights of independent assessor: right to information	1 Oct 2007 (CO No 3)[34]
350 Offences relating to provision of information	1 Oct 2007 (CO No 3)[34]
351 Information to be made available on website	1 Oct 2007 (CO No 3)[34]
352 Application of provisions to class meetings	1 Oct 2007 (CO No 3)[34]
353 Requirements as to website availability	1 Oct 2007 (CO No 3)[34]
354 Power to limit or extend the types of company to which provisions of this Chapter apply	20 Jan 2007 (certain purposes) (CO No 1)[3] 1 Oct 2007 (otherwise) (CO No 3)[34]

Chapter 6: Records of Resolutions and Meetings

355 Records of resolutions and meetings etc	1 Oct 2007 (CO No 3)[35]
356 Records as evidence of resolutions etc	1 Oct 2007 (CO No 3)[35]
357 Records of decisions by sole member	1 Oct 2007 (CO No 3)[35]
358 Inspection of records of resolutions and meetings	20 Jan 2007 (certain purposes) (CO No 1)[3] 1 Oct 2007 (otherwise) (CO No 3)[35]
359 Records of resolutions and meetings of class of members	1 Oct 2007 (CO No 3)[35]

Provision of CA 2006	Commencement
Chapter 7: Supplementary Provisions	
360 Computation of periods of notice etc: clear day rule	1 Oct 2007 (CO No 3)
360A Electronic meetings and voting[205]	3 Aug 2009
360B Traded companies: requirements for participating in and voting at general meetings[205]	3 Aug 2009
360C Meaning of "traded company"[205]	3 Aug 2009
361 Meaning of "quoted company"	1 Oct 2007 (CO No 3)
Part 14: Control of Political Donations and Expenditure	
362 Introductory	1 Oct 2007 (GB subject to an exception) (CO No 3)
	1 Nov 2007 (NI subject to an exception) (CO No 3)
	1 Oct 2008 (exception noted above) (CO No 3)[36]
363 Political parties, organisations etc to which this Part applies	1 Oct 2007 (GB subject to an exception) (CO No 3)
	1 Nov 2007 (NI subject to an exception) (CO No 3)
	1 Oct 2008 (exception noted above) (CO No 3)[36]
364 Meaning of "political donation"	1 Oct 2007 (GB subject to an exception) (CO No 3)
	1 Nov 2007 (NI subject to an exception) (CO No 3)
	1 Oct 2008 (exception noted above) (CO No 3)[36]
365 Meaning of "political expenditure"	1 Oct 2007 (GB subject to an exception) (CO No 3)
	1 Nov 2007 (NI subject to an exception) (CO No 3)
	1 Oct 2008 (exception noted above) (CO No 3)[36]
366 Authorisation required for donations or expenditure	1 Oct 2007 (GB subject to an exception) (CO No 3)
	1 Nov 2007 (NI subject to an exception) (CO No 3)
	1 Oct 2008 (exception noted above) (CO No 3)[36]
367 Form of authorising resolution	1 Oct 2007 (GB subject to an exception) (CO No 3)
	1 Nov 2007 (NI subject to an exception) (CO No 3)
	1 Oct 2008 (exception noted above) (CO No 3)[36]
368 Period for which resolution has effect	1 Oct 2007 (GB) (CO No 3)
	1 Nov 2007 (NI) (CO No 3)[36]
369 Liability of directors in case of unauthorised donation or expenditure	20 Jan 2007 (certain purposes) (CO No 1)[3]
	1 Oct 2007 (otherwise, GB) (CO No 3)
	1 Nov 2007 (otherwise, NI) (CO No 3)[36]
370 Enforcement of directors' liabilities by shareholder action	1 Oct 2007 (GB) (CO No 3)
	1 Nov 2007 (NI) (CO No 3)[36]
371 Enforcement of directors' liabilities by shareholder action: supplementary	1 Oct 2007 (GB) (CO No 3)

Provision of CA 2006	Commencement
	1 Nov 2007 (NI) (CO No 3)[36]
372 Costs of shareholder action	1 Oct 2007 (GB) (CO No 3)
	1 Nov 2007 (NI) (CO No 3)[36]
373 Information for purposes of shareholder action	1 Oct 2007 (GB) (CO No 3)
	1 Nov 2007 (NI) (CO No 3)[36]
374 Trade unions	1 Oct 2007 (GB) (CO No 3)
	1 Nov 2007 (NI) (CO No 3)[36]
375 Subscription for membership of trade association	1 Oct 2007 (GB) (CO No 3)
	1 Nov 2007 (NI) (CO No 3)[36]
376 All-party parliamentary groups	1 Oct 2007 (GB) (CO No 3)
	1 Nov 2007 (NI) (CO No 3)[36]
377 Political expenditure exempted by order	20 Jan 2007 (certain purposes) (CO No 1)[3]
	1 Oct 2007 (otherwise, GB) (CO No 3)
	1 Nov 2007 (otherwise, NI) (CO No 3)[36]
378 Donations not amounting to more than £5,000 in any twelve month period	1 Oct 2007 (GB subject to an exception) (CO No 3)
	1 Nov 2007 (NI subject to an exception) (CO No 3)
	1 Oct 2008 (exception noted above) (CO No 3)[36]
379 Minor definitions	1 Oct 2007 (GB) (CO No 3)
	1 Nov 2007 (NI) (CO No 3)[36]

Part 15: Accounts and Reports
Chapter 1: Introduction

380 Scheme of this Part	6 Apr 2008 (CO No 5)[77]
381 Companies subject to the small companies regime	6 Apr 2008 (CO No 5)[77]
382 Companies qualifying as small: general	6 Apr 2008 (CO No 5)[77]
383 Companies qualifying as small: parent companies	6 Apr 2008 (CO No 5)[77]
384 Companies excluded from the small companies regime	6 Apr 2008 (CO No 5)[77]
385 Quoted and unquoted companies	20 Jan 2007 (certain purposes) (CO No 1)[3]
	1 Oct 2007 (certain purposes) (CO No 3)[4]
	6 Apr 2008 (otherwise) (CO No 5)[77]

Chapter 2: Accounting Records

386 Duty to keep accounting records	6 Apr 2008 (CO No 5)[77]
387 Duty to keep accounting records: offence	6 Apr 2008 (CO No 5)[77]
388 Where and for how long records to be kept	6 Apr 2008 (CO No 5)[77]
389 Where and for how long records to be kept: offences	6 Apr 2008 (CO No 5)[77]

Chapter 3: A Company's Financial Year

390 A company's financial year	6 Apr 2008 (CO No 5)
391 Accounting reference periods and accounting reference date	6 Apr 2008 (CO No 5)
392 Alteration of accounting reference date	6 Apr 2008 (CO No 5)[77]

Chapter 4: Annual Accounts

393 Accounts to give true and fair view	6 Apr 2008 (CO No 5)[77]
394 Duty to prepare individual accounts	6 Apr 2008 (CO No 5)[77]
395 Individual accounts: applicable accounting framework	6 Apr 2008 (CO No 5)[77]

Part 2   CA 2006 commencement etc

Provision of CA 2006	Commencement
396 Companies Act individual accounts	20 Jan 2007 (certain purposes) (CO No 1)[3]
	6 Apr 2008 (otherwise) (CO No 5)[77]
397 IAS individual accounts	6 Apr 2008 (CO No 5)[77]
398 Option to prepare group accounts	6 Apr 2008 (CO No 5)[77]
399 Duty to prepare group accounts	6 Apr 2008 (CO No 5)[77]
400 Exemption for company included in EEA group accounts of larger group	6 Apr 2008 (CO No 5)[77]
401 Exemption for company included in non-EEA group accounts of larger group	6 Apr 2008 (CO No 5)[77]
402 Exemption if no subsidiary undertakings need be included in the consolidation	6 Apr 2008 (CO No 5)[77]
403 Group accounts: applicable accounting framework	6 Apr 2008 (CO No 5)[77]
404 Companies Act group accounts	20 Jan 2007 (certain purposes) (CO No 1)[3]
	6 Apr 2008 (otherwise) (CO No 5)[77]
405 Companies Act group accounts: subsidiary undertakings included in the consolidation	6 Apr 2008 (CO No 5)[77]
406 IAS group accounts	6 Apr 2008 (CO No 5)[77]
407 Consistency of financial reporting within group	6 Apr 2008 (CO No 5)[77]
408 Individual profit and loss account where group accounts prepared	6 Apr 2008 (CO No 5)[77]
409 Information about related undertakings	20 Jan 2007 (certain purposes) (CO No 1)[3]
	6 Apr 2008 (otherwise) (CO No 5)[77]
410 Information about related undertakings: alternative compliance	6 Apr 2008 (CO No 5)[77]
410A Information about off-balance sheet arrangements[122]	6 Apr 2008
411 Information about employee numbers and costs	6 Apr 2008 (CO No 5)[77]
412 Information about directors' benefits: remuneration	20 Jan 2007 (certain purposes) (CO No 1)[3]
	6 Apr 2008 (otherwise) (CO No 5)[77]
413 Information about directors' benefits: advances, credit and guarantees	6 Apr 2008 (CO No 5)[77]
414 Approval and signing of accounts	6 Apr 2008 (CO No 5)[77]
Chapter 5: Directors' Report	
415 Duty to prepare directors' report	6 Apr 2008 (CO No 5)[77]
415A Directors' report: small companies exemption[122]	6 Apr 2008
416 Contents of directors' report: general	20 Jan 2007 (certain purposes) (CO No 1)[3]
	6 Apr 2008 (otherwise) (CO No 5)[77]
417 Contents of directors' report: business review	1 Oct 2007 (CO No 3)[37]
418 Contents of directors' report: statement as to disclosure to auditors	6 Apr 2008 (CO No 5)[77]
419 Approval and signing of directors' report	6 Apr 2008 (CO No 5)[77]
419A Approval and signing of separate corporate governance statement[199]	27 Jun 2009
Chapter 6: Quoted Companies: Directors' Remuneration Report	
420 Duty to prepare directors' remuneration report	6 Apr 2008 (CO No 5)[77]
421 Contents of directors' remuneration report	20 Jan 2007 (certain purposes) (CO No 1)[3]
	6 Apr 2008 (otherwise) (CO No 5)[77]

Provision of CA 2006	Commencement
422 Approval and signing of directors' remuneration report	6 Apr 2008 (CO No 5)[77]
Chapter 7: Publication of Accounts and Reports	
423 Duty to circulate copies of annual accounts and reports	6 Apr 2008 (CO No 5)[77]
424 Time allowed for sending out copies of accounts and reports	6 Apr 2008 (CO No 5)[77]
425 Default in sending out copies of accounts and reports: offences	6 Apr 2008 (CO No 5)[77]
426 Option to provide summary financial statement	20 Jan 2007 (certain purposes) (CO No 1)[3] 6 Apr 2008 (otherwise) (CO No 5)[77]
427 Form and contents of summary financial statement: unquoted companies	20 Jan 2007 (certain purposes) (CO No 1)[3] 6 Apr 2008 (otherwise) (CO No 5)[77]
428 Form and contents of summary financial statement: quoted companies	20 Jan 2007 (certain purposes) (CO No 1)[3] 6 Apr 2008 (otherwise) (CO No 5)[77]
429 Summary financial statements: offences	6 Apr 2008 (CO No 5)[77]
430 Quoted companies: annual accounts and reports to be made available on website	6 Apr 2008 (CO No 5)[77]
431 Right of member or debenture holder to copies of accounts and reports: unquoted companies	6 Apr 2008 (CO No 5)[77]
432 Right of member or debenture holder to copies of accounts and reports: quoted companies	6 Apr 2008 (CO No 5)[77]
433 Name of signatory to be stated in published copies of accounts and reports	6 Apr 2008 (CO No 5)[77]
434 Requirements in connection with publication of statutory accounts	6 Apr 2008 (CO No 5)[77]
435 Requirements in connection with publication of non-statutory accounts	6 Apr 2008 (CO No 5)[77]
436 Meaning of "publication" in relation to accounts and reports	6 Apr 2008 (CO No 5)[77]
Chapter 8: Public Companies: Laying of Accounts and Reports Before General Meeting	
437 Public companies: laying of accounts and reports before general meeting	6 Apr 2008 (CO No 5)[77]
438 Public companies: offence of failure to lay accounts and reports	6 Apr 2008 (CO No 5)[77]
Chapter 9: Quoted Companies: Members' Approval of Directors' Remuneration Report	
439 Quoted companies: members' approval of directors' remuneration report	6 Apr 2008 (CO No 5)[77]
440 Quoted companies: offences in connection with procedure for approval	6 Apr 2008 (CO No 5)[77]
Chapter 10: Filing of Accounts and Reports	
441 Duty to file accounts and reports with the registrar	6 Apr 2008 (CO No 5)[77]
442 Period allowed for filing accounts	6 Apr 2008 (CO No 5)[77]
443 Calculation of period allowed	6 Apr 2008 (CO No 5)[77]
444 Filing obligations of companies subject to small companies regime	20 Jan 2007 (certain purposes) (CO No 1)[3] 6 Apr 2008 (otherwise) (CO No 5)[77]
444A Filing obligations of companies entitled to small companies exemption in relation to directors' report[122]	6 Apr 2008

Provision of CA 2006	Commencement
445 Filing obligations of medium-sized companies	20 Jan 2007 (certain purposes) (CO No 1)[3]
	6 Apr 2008 (otherwise) (CO No 5)[77]
446 Filing obligations of unquoted companies	6 Apr 2008 (CO No 5)[77]
447 Filing obligations of quoted companies	6 Apr 2008 (CO No 5)[77]
448 Unlimited companies exempt from obligation to file accounts	6 Apr 2008 (CO No 5)[77]
449 Special auditor's report where abbreviated accounts delivered	6 Apr 2008 (CO No 5)[77]
450 Approval and signing of abbreviated accounts	6 Apr 2008 (CO No 5)[77]
451 Default in filing accounts and reports: offences	6 Apr 2008 (CO No 5)[77]
452 Default in filing accounts and reports: court order	6 Apr 2008 (CO No 5)[77]
453 Civil penalty for failure to file accounts and reports	20 Jan 2007 (certain purposes) (CO No 1)[3]
	6 Apr 2008 (otherwise) (CO No 5)[77]
Chapter 11: Revision of Defective Accounts and Reports	
454 Voluntary revision of accounts etc	20 Jan 2007 (certain purposes) (CO No 1)[3]
	6 Apr 2008 (otherwise) (CO No 5)[77]
455 Secretary of State's notice in respect of accounts or reports	6 Apr 2008 (CO No 5)[77]
456 Application to court in respect of defective accounts or reports	6 Apr 2008 (CO No 5)[77]
457 Other persons authorised to apply to the court	20 Jan 2007 (certain purposes) (CO No 1)[3]
	6 Apr 2008 (otherwise) (CO No 5)[77]
458 Disclosure of information by tax authorities	6 Apr 2008 (CO No 5)[77]
459 Power of authorised person to require documents, information and explanations	6 Apr 2008 (CO No 5)[77]
460 Restrictions on disclosure of information obtained under compulsory powers	6 Apr 2008 (CO No 5)[77]
461 Permitted disclosure of information obtained under compulsory powers	6 Apr 2008 (CO No 5)[77]
462 Power to amend categories of permitted disclosure	20 Jan 2007 (certain purposes) (CO No 1)[3]
	6 Apr 2008 (otherwise) (CO No 5)[77]
Chapter 12: Supplementary Provisions	
463 Liability for false or misleading statements in reports	20 Jan 2007 (CO No 1)[38]
464 Accounting standards	20 Jan 2007 (certain purposes) (CO No 1)[3]
	6 Apr 2008 (otherwise) (CO No 5)[77]
465 Companies qualifying as medium-sized: general	6 Apr 2008 (CO No 5)[77]
466 Companies qualifying as medium-sized: parent companies	6 Apr 2008 (CO No 5)[77]
467 Companies excluded from being treated as medium-sized	6 Apr 2008 (CO No 5)[77]
468 General power to make further provision about accounts and reports	20 Jan 2007 (certain purposes) (CO No 1)[3]
	6 Apr 2008 (otherwise) (CO No 5)[77]
469 Preparation and filing of accounts in euros	6 Apr 2008 (CO No 5)[77]
470 Power to apply provisions to banking partnerships	20 Jan 2007 (certain purposes) (CO No 1)[3]

Provision of CA 2006	Commencement
	6 Apr 2008 (otherwise) (CO No 5)[77]
471 Meaning of "annual accounts" and related expressions	6 Apr 2008 (CO No 5)[77]
472 Notes to the accounts	6 Apr 2008 (CO No 5)[77]
472A Meaning of "corporate governance statement" etc[199]	27 Jun 2009
473 Parliamentary procedure for certain regulations under this Part	20 Jan 2007 (certain purposes) (CO No 1)[3]
	6 Apr 2008 (otherwise) (CO No 5)[77]
474 Minor definitions	6 Apr 2008 (CO No 5)[77]
Part 16: Audit	
Chapter 1: Requirement for Audited Accounts	
475 Requirement for audited accounts	6 Apr 2008 (CO No 5)[78]
476 Right of members to require audit	6 Apr 2008 (CO No 5)[78]
477 Small companies: conditions for exemption from audit	6 Apr 2008 (CO No 5)[78]
478 Companies excluded from small companies exemption	6 Apr 2008 (CO No 5)[78]
479 Availability of small companies exemption in case of group company	6 Apr 2008 (CO No 5)[78]
480 Dormant companies: conditions for exemption from audit	6 Apr 2008 (CO No 5)[78]
481 Companies excluded from dormant companies exemption	6 Apr 2008 (CO No 5)[78]
482 Non-profit-making companies subject to public sector audit	6 Apr 2008 (CO No 5)[78]
483 Scottish public sector companies: audit by Auditor General for Scotland	20 Jan 2007 (certain purposes) (CO No 1)[3]
	6 Apr 2008 (otherwise) (CO No 5)[78]
484 General power of amendment by regulations	20 Jan 2007 (certain purposes) (CO No 1)[3]
	6 Apr 2008 (otherwise) (CO No 5)[78]
Chapter 2: Appointment of Auditors	
485 Appointment of auditors of private company: general	1 Oct 2007 (CO No 3)[39]
486 Appointment of auditors of private company: default power of Secretary of State	1 Oct 2007 (CO No 3)[39]
487 Term of office of auditors of private company	1 Oct 2007 (CO No 3)[39]
488 Prevention by members of deemed reappointment of auditor	1 Oct 2007 (CO No 3)[39]
489 Appointment of auditors of public company: general	6 Apr 2008 (CO No 5)[79]
490 Appointment of auditors of public company: default power of Secretary of State	6 Apr 2008 (CO No 5)[79]
491 Term of office of auditors of public company	6 Apr 2008 (CO No 5)[79]
492 Fixing of auditor's remuneration	6 Apr 2008 (CO No 5)[79]
493 Disclosure of terms of audit appointment	20 Jan 2007 (certain purposes) (CO No 1)[3]
	6 Apr 2008 (otherwise) (CO No 5)[79]
494 Disclosure of services provided by auditor or associates and related remuneration	20 Jan 2007 (certain purposes) (CO No 1)[3]
	6 Apr 2008 (otherwise) (CO No 5)[79]
Chapter 3: Functions of Auditor	
495 Auditor's report on company's annual accounts	6 Apr 2008 (CO No 5)[80]
496 Auditor's report on directors' report	6 Apr 2008 (CO No 5)[80]

Provision of CA 2006	Commencement
497 Auditor's report on auditable part of directors' remuneration report	6 Apr 2008 (CO No 5)[80]
497A Auditor's report on separate corporate governance statement[199]	27 Jun 2009
498 Duties of auditor	6 Apr 2008 (CO No 5)[80]
498A Auditor's duties in relation to separate corporate governance statement[199]	27 Jun 2009
499 Auditor's general right to information	6 Apr 2008 (CO No 5)[80]
500 Auditor's right to information from overseas subsidiaries	6 Apr 2008 (CO No 5)[80]
501 Auditor's rights to information: offences	6 Apr 2008 (CO No 5)[80]
502 Auditor's rights in relation to resolutions and meetings	6 Apr 2008 (CO No 5)[80]
503 Signature of auditor's report	6 Apr 2008 (CO No 5)[80]
504 Senior statutory auditor	20 Jan 2007 (certain purposes) (CO No 1)[3] 6 Apr 2008 (otherwise) (CO No 5)[80]
505 Names to be stated in published copies of auditor's report	6 Apr 2008 (CO No 5)[80]
506 Circumstances in which names may be omitted	6 Apr 2008 (CO No 5)[80]
507 Offences in connection with auditor's report	6 Apr 2008 (CO No 5)[80]
508 Guidance for regulatory and prosecuting authorities: England, Wales and Northern Ireland	6 Apr 2008 (CO No 5)[80]
509 Guidance for regulatory authorities: Scotland	6 Apr 2008 (CO No 5)[80]
Chapter 4: Removal, Resignation, etc of Auditors	
510 Resolution removing auditor from office	6 Apr 2008 (CO No 5)[81]
511 Special notice required for resolution removing auditor from office	6 Apr 2008 (CO No 5)[81]
512 Notice to registrar of resolution removing auditor from office	6 Apr 2008 (CO No 5)[81]
513 Rights of auditor who has been removed from office	6 Apr 2008 (CO No 5)[81]
514 Failure to re-appoint auditor: special procedure required for written resolution	6 Apr 2008 (CO No 5)[81]
515 Failure to re-appoint auditor: special notice required for resolution at general meeting	6 Apr 2008 (CO No 5)[81]
516 Resignation of auditor	6 Apr 2008 (CO No 5)[81]
517 Notice to registrar of resignation of auditor	6 Apr 2008 (CO No 5)[81]
518 Rights of resigning auditor	6 Apr 2008 (CO No 5)[81]
519 Statement by auditor to be deposited with company	6 Apr 2008 (CO No 5)[81]
520 Company's duties in relation to statement	6 Apr 2008 (CO No 5)[81]
521 Copy of statement to be sent to registrar	6 Apr 2008 (CO No 5)[81]
522 Duty of auditor to notify appropriate audit authority	6 Apr 2008 (CO No 5)[81]
523 Duty of company to notify appropriate audit authority	6 Apr 2008 (CO No 5)[81]
524 Information to be given to accounting authorities	6 Apr 2008 (CO No 5)[81]
525 Meaning of "appropriate audit authority" and "major audit"	6 Apr 2008 (CO No 5)[81]
526 Effect of casual vacancies	6 Apr 2008 (CO No 5)[81]

Provision of CA 2006	Commencement
Chapter 5: Quoted Companies: Right of Members to Raise Audit Concerns at Accounts Meeting	
527 Members' power to require website publication of audit concerns	6 Apr 2008 (CO No 5)[82]
528 Requirements as to website availability	6 Apr 2008 (CO No 5)
529 Website publication: company's supplementary duties	6 Apr 2008 (CO No 5)
530 Website publication: offences	6 Apr 2008 (CO No 5)
531 Meaning of "quoted company"	6 Apr 2008 (CO No 5)
Chapter 6: Auditors' Liability	
532 Voidness of provisions protecting auditors from liability	6 Apr 2008 (CO No 5)
533 Indemnity for costs of successfully defending proceedings	6 Apr 2008 (CO No 5)[124]
534 Liability limitation agreements	6 Apr 2008 (CO No 5)
535 Terms of liability limitation agreement	20 Jan 2007 (certain purposes) (CO No 1)[3]
	6 Apr 2008 (otherwise) (CO No 5)
536 Authorisation of agreement by members of the company	6 Apr 2008 (CO No 5)[83]
537 Effect of liability limitation agreement	6 Apr 2008 (CO No 5)
538 Disclosure of agreement by company	20 Jan 2007 (certain purposes) (CO No 1)[3]
	6 Apr 2008 (otherwise) (CO No 5)
Chapter 7: Supplementary Provisions	
538A Meaning of "corporate governance statement" etc[199]	27 Jun 2009
539 Minor definitions	6 Apr 2008 (CO No 5)
Part 17: A Company's Share Capital	
Chapter 1: Shares and Share Capital of a Company	
540 Shares	1 Oct 2007 (sub-ss (1), (4)certain purposes) (CO No 3)[40]
	6 Apr 2008 (sub-ss (1), (4)certain purposes) (CO No 5)[107]
	1 Oct 2009 (otherwise) (CO No 8)[146]
541 Nature of shares	1 Oct 2009 (CO No 8)
542 Nominal value of shares	1 Oct 2009 (CO No 8)
543 Numbering of shares	1 Oct 2009 (CO No 8)
544 Transferability of shares	6 Apr 2008 (CO No 5)
545 Companies having a share capital	1 Oct 2007 (certain purposes) (CO No 3)[4]
	6 Apr 2008 (certain purposes) (CO No 5)[107]
	1 Oct 2009 (otherwise) (CO No 8)
546 Issued and allotted share capital	6 Apr 2007 (certain purposes) (CO No 2)[41]
	1 Oct 2007 (certain purposes) (CO No 3)[4]
	1 Nov 2007 (certain purposes) (CO No 3)[42]
	6 Apr 2008 (certain purposes) (CO No 5)[107]
	1 Oct 2009 (otherwise) (CO No 8)
547 Called-up share capital	1 Oct 2009 (CO No 8)
548 Equity share capital	1 Oct 2007 (certain purposes) (CO No 3)[4]
	6 Apr 2008 (certain purposes) (CO No 5)[107]
	1 Oct 2009 (otherwise) (CO No 8)
Chapter 2: Allotment of Shares: General Provisions	
549 Exercise by directors of power to allot shares etc	1 Oct 2009 (CO No 8)

Provision of CA 2006	Commencement
550 Power of directors to allot shares etc: private company with only one class of shares	1 Oct 2009 (CO No 8)[147]
551 Power of directors to allot shares etc: authorisation by company	1 Oct 2009 (CO No 8)[148]
552 General prohibition of commissions, discounts and allowances	1 Oct 2009 (CO No 8)
553 Permitted commission	1 Oct 2009 (CO No 8)
554 Registration of allotment	1 Oct 2009 (CO No 8)[149]
555 Return of allotment by limited company	20 Jan 2007 (certain purposes) (CO No 1)[3]
	1 Oct 2009 (otherwise) (CO No 8)
556 Return of allotment by unlimited company allotting new class of shares	20 Jan 2007 (certain purposes) (CO No 1)[3]
	1 Oct 2009 (otherwise) (CO No 8)
557 Offence of failure to make return	1 Oct 2009 (CO No 8)
558 When shares are allotted	6 Apr 2007 (certain purposes) (CO No 2)[41]
	1 Oct 2009 (otherwise) (CO No 8)
559 Provisions about allotment not applicable to shares taken on formation	1 Oct 2009 (CO No 8)
Chapter 3: Allotment of Equity Securities: Existing Shareholders': Right of Pre-emption	
560 Meaning of "equity securities" and related expressions	1 Oct 2009 (CO No 8)
561 Existing shareholders' right of pre-emption	1 Oct 2009 (CO No 8)[150]
562 Communication of pre-emption offers to shareholders	20 Jan 2007 (certain purposes) (CO No 1)[3]
	1 Oct 2009 (otherwise) (CO No 8)[150]
563 Liability of company and officers in case of contravention	1 Oct 2009 (CO No 8)[150]
564 Exception to pre-emption right: bonus shares	1 Oct 2009 (CO No 8)[150]
565 Exception to pre-emption right: issue for non-cash consideration	1 Oct 2009 (CO No 8)[150]
566 Exceptions to pre-emption right: employees' share schemes[201]	1 Oct 2009 (CO No 8)[150]
567 Exclusion of requirements by private companies	1 Oct 2009 (CO No 8)[150]
568 Exclusion of pre-emption right: articles conferring corresponding right	1 Oct 2009 (CO No 8)[150]
569 Disapplication of pre-emption rights: private company with only one class of shares	1 Oct 2009 (CO No 8)[150]
570 Disapplication of pre-emption rights: directors acting under general authorisation	1 Oct 2009 (CO No 8)[150]
571 Disapplication of pre-emption rights by special resolution	1 Oct 2009 (CO No 8)[150]
572 Liability for false statement in directors' statement	1 Oct 2009 (CO No 8)[150]
573 Disapplication of pre-emption rights: sale of treasury shares	1 Oct 2009 (CO No 8)[150]
574 References to holder of shares in relation to offer	1 Oct 2009 (CO No 8)[150]
575 Saving for other restrictions on offer or allotment	1 Oct 2009 (CO No 8)[150]
576 Saving for certain older pre-emption requirements	1 Oct 2009 (CO No 8)[150]

Provision of CA 2006	Commencement
577 Provisions about pre-emption not applicable to shares taken on formation	1 Oct 2009 (CO No 8)[150]

Chapter 4: Public Companies: Allotment Where Issue Not Fully Subscribed

578 Public companies: allotment where issue not fully subscribed	1 Oct 2009 (CO No 8)[151]
579 Public companies: effect of irregular allotment where issue not fully subscribed	1 Oct 2009 (CO No 8)[151]

Chapter 5: Payment for Shares

580 Shares not to be allotted at a discount	1 Oct 2009 (CO No 8)
581 Provision for different amounts to be paid on shares	1 Oct 2009 (CO No 8)
582 General rule as to means of payment	1 Oct 2009 (CO No 8)
583 Meaning of payment in cash	20 Jan 2007 (certain purposes) (CO No 1)[3]
	1 Oct 2009 (otherwise) (CO No 8)[152]
584 Public companies: shares taken by subscribers of memorandum	1 Oct 2009 (CO No 8)
585 Public companies: must not accept undertaking to do work or perform services	1 Oct 2009 (CO No 8)
586 Public companies: shares must be at least one-quarter paid up	1 Oct 2009 (CO No 8)
587 Public companies: payment by long-term undertaking	1 Oct 2009 (CO No 8)
588 Liability of subsequent holders of shares	1 Oct 2009 (CO No 8)
589 Power of court to grant relief	1 Oct 2009 (CO No 8)[153]
590 Penalty for contravention of this Chapter	1 Oct 2009 (CO No 8)
591 Enforceability of undertakings to do work etc	1 Oct 2009 (CO No 8)
592 The appropriate rate of interest	20 Jan 2007 (certain purposes) (CO No 1)[3]
	1 Oct 2009 (otherwise) (CO No 8)

Chapter 6: Public Companies: Independent Valuation of Non-Cash Consideration

593 Public company: valuation of non-cash consideration for shares	1 Oct 2009 (CO No 8)
594 Exception to valuation requirement: arrangement with another company	1 Oct 2009 (CO No 8)
595 Exception to valuation requirement: merger	1 Oct 2009 (CO No 8)
596 Non-cash consideration for shares: requirements as to valuation and report	1 Oct 2009 (CO No 8)
597 Copy of report to be delivered to registrar	1 Oct 2009 (CO No 8)
598 Public company: agreement for transfer of non-cash asset in initial period	1 Oct 2009 (CO No 8)
599 Agreement for transfer of non-cash asset: requirement of independent valuation	1 Oct 2009 (CO No 8)
600 Agreement for transfer of non-cash asset: requirements as to valuation and report	1 Oct 2009 (CO No 8)
601 Agreement for transfer of non-cash asset: requirement of approval by members	1 Oct 2009 (CO No 8)
602 Copy of resolution to be delivered to registrar	1 Oct 2009 (CO No 8)
603 Adaptation of provisions in relation to company re-registering as public	1 Oct 2009 (CO No 8)
604 Agreement for transfer of non-cash asset: effect of contravention	1 Oct 2009 (CO No 8)
605 Liability of subsequent holders of shares	1 Oct 2009 (CO No 8)
606 Power of court to grant relief	1 Oct 2009 (CO No 8)[153]

Part 2   CA 2006 commencement etc

Provision of CA 2006	Commencement
607 Penalty for contravention of this Chapter	1 Oct 2009 (CO No 8)[152]
608 Enforceability of undertakings to do work etc	1 Oct 2009 (CO No 8)
609 The appropriate rate of interest	20 Jan 2007 (certain purposes) (CO No 1)[3]
	1 Oct 2009 (otherwise) (CO No 8)
Chapter 7: Share Premiums	
610 Application of share premiums	1 Oct 2008 (certain purposes) (CO No 7)[127]
	1 Oct 2009 (otherwise) (CO No 8)
611 Group reconstruction relief	1 Oct 2009 (CO No 8)
612 Merger relief	1 Oct 2009 (CO No 8)
613 Merger relief: meaning of 90% equity holding	1 Oct 2009 (CO No 8)
614 Power to make further provision by regulations	20 Jan 2007 (certain purposes) (CO No 1)[3]
	1 Oct 2009 (otherwise) (CO No 8)
615 Relief may be reflected in company's balance sheet	1 Oct 2009 (CO No 8)
616 Interpretation of this Chapter	1 Oct 2009 (CO No 8)
Chapter 8: Alteration of Share Capital	
617 Alteration of share capital of limited company	1 Oct 2009 (CO No 8)
618 Sub-division or consolidation of shares	1 Oct 2009 (CO No 8)
619 Notice to registrar of sub-division or consolidation	20 Jan 2007 (certain purposes) (CO No 1)[3]
	1 Oct 2009 (otherwise) (CO No 8)
620 Reconversion of stock into shares	1 Oct 2009 (CO No 8)
621 Notice to registrar of reconversion of stock into shares	20 Jan 2007 (certain purposes) (CO No 1)[3]
	1 Oct 2009 (otherwise) (CO No 8)
622 Redenomination of share capital	1 Oct 2009 (CO No 8)
623 Calculation of new nominal values	1 Oct 2009 (CO No 8)
624 Effect of redenomination	1 Oct 2009 (CO No 8)
625 Notice to registrar of redenomination	20 Jan 2007 (certain purposes) (CO No 1)[3]
	1 Oct 2009 (otherwise) (CO No 8)
626 Reduction of capital in connection with redenomination	1 Oct 2009 (CO No 8)
627 Notice to registrar of reduction of capital in connection with redenomination	20 Jan 2007 (certain purposes) (CO No 1)[3]
	1 Oct 2009 (otherwise) (CO No 8)
628 Redenomination reserve	1 Oct 2009 (CO No 8)
Chapter 9: Classes of Share and Class Rights	
629 Classes of shares	1 Oct 2007 (certain purposes) (CO No 3)[4]
	6 Apr 2008 (certain purposes) (CO No 5)[107]
	1 Oct 2009 (otherwise) (CO No 8)
630 Variation of class rights: companies having a share capital	1 Oct 2009 (CO No 8)
631 Variation of class rights: companies without a share capital	1 Oct 2009 (CO No 8)[154]
632 Variation of class rights: saving for court's powers under other provisions	1 Oct 2009 (CO No 8)
633 Right to object to variation: companies having a share capital	1 Oct 2009 (CO No 8)
634 Right to object to variation: companies without a share capital	1 Oct 2009 (CO No 8)[154]

Provision of CA 2006	Commencement
635 Copy of court order to be forwarded to the registrar	1 Oct 2009 (CO No 8)
636 Notice of name or other designation of class of shares	1 Oct 2009 (CO No 8)[155]
637 Notice of particulars of variation of rights attached to shares	1 Oct 2009 (CO No 8)[156]
638 Notice of new class of members	1 Oct 2009 (CO No 8)[157]
639 Notice of name or other designation of class of members	1 Oct 2009 (CO No 8)[158]
640 Notice of particulars of variation of class rights	1 Oct 2009 (CO No 8)[159]
Chapter 10: Reduction of Share Capital	
641 Circumstances in which a company may reduce its share capital	1 Oct 2008 (sub-ss (1)(a), (2)–(6)) (CO No 7)[125]
	1 Oct 2009 (otherwise) (CO No 8)
642 Reduction of capital supported by solvency statement	1 Oct 2008 (CO No 7)
643 Solvency statement	20 Jan 2007 (certain purposes) (CO No 1)[3]
	1 Oct 2008 (otherwise) (CO No 7)
644 Registration of resolution and supporting documents	20 Jan 2007 (certain purposes) (CO No 1)[3]
	1 Oct 2008 (otherwise) (CO No 7)[125]
645 Application to court for order of confirmation	1 Oct 2009 (CO No 8)[160]
646 Creditors entitled to object to reduction	1 Oct 2009 (CO No 8)[160]
647 Offences in connection with list of creditors	1 Oct 2009 (CO No 8)[160]
648 Court order confirming reduction	1 Oct 2009 (CO No 8)[160]
649 Registration of order and statement of capital	20 Jan 2007 (certain purposes) (CO No 1)[3]
	1 Oct 2009 (otherwise) (CO No 8)[160]
650 Public company reducing capital below authorised minimum	1 Oct 2009 (CO No 8)[160]
651 Expedited procedure for re-registration as a private company	1 Oct 2009 (CO No 8)[160]
652 Liability of members following reduction of capital	1 Oct 2008 (certain purposes) (CO No 7)[127]
	1 Oct 2009 (otherwise) (CO No 8)[161]
653 Liability to creditor in case of omission from list of creditors	1 Oct 2009 (CO No 8)[161]
Chapter 11: Miscellaneous and Supplementary Provisions	
654 Treatment of reserve arising from reduction of capital	20 Jan 2007 (certain purposes) (CO No 1)[3]
	1 Oct 2008 (otherwise) (CO No 7)[126]
655 Shares no bar to damages against company	1 Oct 2009 (CO No 8)
656 Public companies: duty of directors to call meeting on serious loss of capital	1 Oct 2009 (CO No 8)
657 General power to make further provision by regulations	20 Jan 2007 (certain purposes) (CO No 1)[3]
	1 Oct 2009 (otherwise) (CO No 8)
Part 18: Acquisition by Limited Company of its Own Shares	
Chapter 1: General Provisions	
658 General rule against limited company acquiring its own shares	1 Oct 2009 (CO No 8)
659 Exceptions to general rule	1 Oct 2009 (CO No 8)

Provision of CA 2006	Commencement
660 Treatment of shares held by nominee	1 Oct 2009 (CO No 8)
661 Liability of others where nominee fails to make payment in respect of shares	1 Oct 2009 (CO No 8)
662 Duty to cancel shares in public company held by or for the company	1 Oct 2009 (CO No 8)[162]
663 Notice of cancellation of shares	20 Jan 2007 (certain purposes) (CO No 1)[3] 1 Oct 2009 (otherwise) (CO No 8)[162]
664 Re-registration as private company in consequence of cancellation	1 Oct 2009 (CO No 8)[162]
665 Issue of certificate of incorporation on re-registration	1 Oct 2009 (CO No 8)[162]
666 Effect of failure to re-register	1 Oct 2009 (CO No 8)[162]
667 Offence in case of failure to cancel shares or re-register	1 Oct 2009 (CO No 8)[162]
668 Application of provisions to company re-registering as public company	1 Oct 2009 (CO No 8)[162]
669 Transfer to reserve on acquisition of shares by public company or nominee	1 Oct 2009 (CO No 8)
670 Public companies: general rule against lien or charge on own shares	1 Oct 2009 (CO No 8)
671 Interests to be disregarded in determining whether company has beneficial interest	1 Oct 2009 (CO No 8)
672 Residual interest under pension scheme or employees' share scheme	1 Oct 2009 (CO No 8)
673 Employer's charges and other rights of recovery	1 Oct 2009 (CO No 8)
674 Rights as personal representative or trustee	1 Oct 2009 (CO No 8)
675 Meaning of "pension scheme"	1 Oct 2009 (CO No 8)
676 Application of provisions to directors	1 Oct 2009 (CO No 8)
Chapter 2: Financial Assistance for Purchase of Own Shares	
677 Meaning of "financial assistance"	1 Oct 2009 (CO No 8)
678 Assistance for acquisition of shares in public company	1 Oct 2009 (CO No 8)
679 Assistance by public company for acquisition of shares in its private holding company	1 Oct 2009 (CO No 8)
680 Prohibited financial assistance an offence	1 Oct 2009 (CO No 8)
681 Unconditional exceptions	1 Oct 2009 (CO No 8)
682 Conditional exceptions	1 Oct 2009 (CO No 8)
683 Definitions for this Chapter	1 Oct 2009 (CO No 8)
Chapter 3: Redeemable Shares	
684 Power of limited company to issue redeemable shares	1 Oct 2009 (CO No 8)
685 Terms and manner of redemption	1 Oct 2009 (CO No 8)
686 Payment for redeemable shares	1 Oct 2009 (CO No 8)[163]
687 Financing of redemption	1 Oct 2009 (CO No 8)
688 Redeemed shares treated as cancelled	1 Oct 2009 (CO No 8)
689 Notice to registrar of redemption	20 Jan 2007 (certain purposes) (CO No 1)[3] 1 Oct 2009 (otherwise) (CO No 8)[164]
Chapter 4: Purchase of Own Shares	
690 Power of limited company to purchase own shares	1 Oct 2009 (CO No 8)
691 Payment for purchase of own shares	1 Oct 2009 (CO No 8)
692 Financing of purchase of own shares	1 Oct 2009 (CO No 8)

Provision of CA 2006	Commencement
693 Authority for purchase of own shares	1 Oct 2009 (CO No 8)[165]
694 Authority for off-market purchase	1 Oct 2009 (CO No 8)[165]
695 Resolution authorising off-market purchase: exercise of voting rights	1 Oct 2009 (CO No 8)[165]
696 Resolution authorising off-market purchase: disclosure of details of contract	1 Oct 2009 (CO No 8)[165]
697 Variation of contract for off-market purchase	1 Oct 2009 (CO No 8)[165]
698 Resolution authorising variation: exercise of voting rights	1 Oct 2009 (CO No 8)[165]
699 Resolution authorising variation: disclosure of details of variation	1 Oct 2009 (CO No 8)[165]
700 Release of company's rights under contract for off-market purchase	1 Oct 2009 (CO No 8)[165]
701 Authority for market purchase	1 Oct 2009 (CO No 8)[165]
702 Copy of contract or memorandum to be available for inspection	1 Oct 2009 (CO No 8)
703 Enforcement of right to inspect copy or memorandum	1 Oct 2009 (CO No 8)
704 No assignment of company's right to purchase own shares	1 Oct 2009 (CO No 8)
705 Payments apart from purchase price to be made out of distributable profits	1 Oct 2009 (CO No 8)
706 Treatment of shares purchased	1 Oct 2009 (CO No 8)
707 Return to registrar of purchase of own shares	1 Oct 2009 (CO No 8)[166]
708 Notice to registrar of cancellation of shares	20 Jan 2007 (certain purposes) (CO No 1)[3]
	1 Oct 2009 (otherwise) (CO No 8)[166]

Chapter 5: Redemption or Purchase by Private Company Out of Capital

709 Power of private limited company to redeem or purchase own shares out of capital	1 Oct 2009 (CO No 8)[167]
710 The permissible capital payment	1 Oct 2009 (CO No 8)[167]
711 Available profits	1 Oct 2009 (CO No 8)[167]
712 Determination of available profits	1 Oct 2009 (CO No 8)[167]
713 Requirements for payment out of capital	1 Oct 2009 (CO No 8)[167]
714 Directors' statement and auditor's report	20 Jan 2007 (certain purposes) (CO No 1)[3]
	1 Oct 2009 (otherwise) (CO No 8)[167]
715 Directors' statement: offence if no reasonable grounds for opinion	1 Oct 2009 (CO No 8)[167]
716 Payment to be approved by special resolution	1 Oct 2009 (CO No 8)[167]
717 Resolution authorising payment: exercise of voting rights	1 Oct 2009 (CO No 8)[167]
718 Resolution authorising payment: disclosure of directors' statement and auditor's report	1 Oct 2009 (CO No 8)[167]
719 Public notice of proposed payment	1 Oct 2009 (CO No 8)[167]
720 Directors' statement and auditor's report to be available for inspection	1 Oct 2009 (CO No 8)[167]
721 Application to court to cancel resolution	1 Oct 2009 (CO No 8)[167]
722 Notice to registrar of court application or order	1 Oct 2009 (CO No 8)[167]
723 When payment out of capital to be made	1 Oct 2009 (CO No 8)[167]

Chapter 6: Treasury Shares

724 Treasury shares	1 Oct 2009 (CO No 8)

Provision of CA 2006	Commencement
725 *Treasury shares: maximum holdings*[208]	*1 Oct 2009 (CO No 8)*
726 Treasury shares: exercise of rights	1 Oct 2009 (CO No 8)
727 Treasury shares: disposal	20 Jan 2007 (certain purposes) (CO No 1)[3]
	1 Oct 2009 (otherwise) (CO No 8)[168]
728 Treasury shares: notice of disposal	1 Oct 2009 (CO No 8)
729 Treasury shares: cancellation	1 Oct 2009 (CO No 8)
730 Treasury shares: notice of cancellation	20 Jan 2007 (certain purposes) (CO No 1)[3]
	1 Oct 2009 (otherwise) (CO No 8)[169]
731 Treasury shares: treatment of proceeds of sale	1 Oct 2009 (CO No 8)
732 Treasury shares: offences	1 Oct 2009 (CO No 8)
Chapter 7: Supplementary Provisions	
733 The capital redemption reserve	1 Oct 2008 (certain purposes) (CO No 7)[127]
	1 Oct 2009 (otherwise) (CO No 8)
734 Accounting consequences of payment out of capital	1 Oct 2009 (CO No 8)
735 Effect of company's failure to redeem or purchase	1 Oct 2009 (CO No 8)
736 Meaning of "distributable profits"	1 Oct 2009 (CO No 8)
737 General power to make further provision by regulations	20 Jan 2007 (certain purposes) (CO No 1)[3]
	1 Oct 2009 (otherwise) (CO No 8)
Part 19: Debentures	
738 Meaning of "debenture"	6 Apr 2008 (CO No 5)
739 Perpetual debentures	6 Apr 2008 (CO No 5)
740 Enforcement of contract to subscribe for debentures	6 Apr 2008 (CO No 5)
741 Registration of allotment of debentures	6 Apr 2008 (CO No 5)[84]
742 Debentures to bearer (Scotland)	6 Apr 2008 (CO No 5)
743 Register of debenture holders	6 Apr 2008 (CO No 5)[85]
744 Register of debenture holders: right to inspect and require copy	20 Jan 2007 (certain purposes) (CO No 1)[3]
	6 Apr 2008 (otherwise) (CO No 5)[86]
745 Register of debenture holders: response to request for inspection or copy	6 Apr 2008 (CO No 5)[86]
746 Register of debenture holders: refusal of inspection or default in providing copy	6 Apr 2008 (CO No 5)[86]
747 Register of debenture holders: offences in connection with request for or disclosure of information	6 Apr 2008 (CO No 5)[86]
748 Time limit for claims arising from entry in register	6 Apr 2008 (CO No 5)[87]
749 Right of debenture holder to copy of deed	20 Jan 2007 (certain purposes) (CO No 1)[3]
	6 Apr 2008 (otherwise) (CO No 5)[86]
750 Liability of trustees of debentures	6 Apr 2008 (CO No 5)
751 Liability of trustees of debentures: saving for certain older provisions	6 Apr 2008 (CO No 5)
752 Power to re-issue redeemed debentures	6 Apr 2008 (CO No 5)
753 Deposit of debentures to secure advances	6 Apr 2008 (CO No 5)
754 Priorities where debentures secured by floating charge	6 Apr 2008 (CO No 5)

Provision of CA 2006	Commencement
Part 20: Private and Public Companies	
Chapter 1: Prohibition of Public Offers by Private Companies	
755 Prohibition of public offers by private company	6 Apr 2008 (CO No 5)[88]
756 Meaning of "offer to the public"	6 Apr 2008 (CO No 5)[88]
757 Enforcement of prohibition: order restraining proposed contravention	6 Apr 2008 (CO No 5)
758 Enforcement of prohibition: orders available to the court after contravention	6 Apr 2008 (CO No 5)[89]
759 Enforcement of prohibition: remedial order	6 Apr 2008 (CO No 5)[89]
760 Validity of allotment etc not affected	6 Apr 2008 (CO No 5)
Chapter 2: Minimum Share Capital Requirement for Public Companies	
761 Public company: requirement as to minimum share capital	6 Apr 2008 (CO No 5)[90]
762 Procedure for obtaining certificate	6 Apr 2008 (CO No 5)[91]
763 The authorised minimum	20 Jan 2007 (certain purposes) (CO No 1)[3]
	6 Apr 2008 (otherwise) (CO No 5)
764 Power to alter authorised minimum	20 Jan 2007 (certain purposes) (CO No 1)[3]
	6 Apr 2008 (otherwise) (CO No 5)
765 Authorised minimum: application of initial requirement	6 Apr 2008 (CO No 5)[92]
766 Authorised minimum: application where shares denominated in different currencies etc	20 Jan 2007 (certain purposes) (CO No 1)[3]
	6 Apr 2008 (otherwise) (CO No 5)[92]
767 Consequences of doing business etc without a trading certificate	6 Apr 2008 (CO No 5)[93]
Part 21: Certification and Transfer of Securities	
Chapter 1: Certification and Transfer of Securities: General	
768 Share certificate to be evidence of title	6 Apr 2008 (CO No 5)
769 Duty of company as to issue of certificates etc on allotment	6 Apr 2008 (CO No 5)
770 Registration of transfer	6 Apr 2008 (CO No 5)
771 Procedure on transfer being lodged	6 Apr 2008 (CO No 5)[94]
772 Transfer of shares on application of transferor	6 Apr 2008 (CO No 5)
773 Execution of share transfer by personal representative	6 Apr 2008 (CO No 5)
774 Evidence of grant of probate etc	6 Apr 2008 (CO No 5)
775 Certification of instrument of transfer	6 Apr 2008 (CO No 5)
776 Duty of company as to issue of certificates etc on transfer	6 Apr 2008 (CO No 5)
777 Issue of certificates etc: cases within the Stock Transfer Act 1982	6 Apr 2008 (CO No 5)
778 Issue of certificates etc: allotment or transfer to financial institution	6 Apr 2008 (CO No 5)
779 Issue and effect of share warrant to bearer	6 Apr 2008 (CO No 5)
780 Duty of company as to issue of certificates on surrender of share warrant	6 Apr 2008 (CO No 5)[95]
781 Offences in connection with share warrants (Scotland)	6 Apr 2008 (CO No 5)
782 Issue of certificates etc: court order to make good default	6 Apr 2008 (CO No 5)
Chapter 2: Evidencing and Transfer of Title to Securities Without Written Instrument	
783 Scope of this Chapter	6 Apr 2008 (CO No 5)

Provision of CA 2006	Commencement
784 Power to make regulations	20 Jan 2007 (certain purposes) (CO No 1)[3]
	6 Apr 2008 (otherwise) (CO No 5)
785 Provision enabling procedures for evidencing and transferring title	20 Jan 2007 (certain purposes) (CO No 1)[3]
	6 Apr 2008 (otherwise) (CO No 5)
786 Provision enabling or requiring arrangements to be adopted	20 Jan 2007 (certain purposes) (CO No 1)[3]
	6 Apr 2008 (otherwise) (CO No 5)
787 Provision enabling or requiring arrangements to be adopted: order-making powers	20 Jan 2007 (certain purposes) (CO No 1)[3]
	6 Apr 2008 (otherwise) (CO No 5)
788 Provision that may be included in regulations	20 Jan 2007 (certain purposes) (CO No 1)[3]
	6 Apr 2008 (otherwise) (CO No 5)
789 Duty to consult	20 Jan 2007 (certain purposes) (CO No 1)[3]
	6 Apr 2008 (otherwise) (CO No 5)
790 Resolutions to be forwarded to registrar	6 Apr 2008 (CO No 5)
Part 22: Information About Interests in a Company's Shares	
791 Companies to which this Part applies	20 Jan 2007 (CO No 1)
792 Shares to which this Part applies	20 Jan 2007 (CO No 1)
793 Notice by company requiring information about interests in its shares	20 Jan 2007 (CO No 1)
794 Notice requiring information: order imposing restrictions on shares	20 Jan 2007 (CO No 1)
795 Notice requiring information: offences	20 Jan 2007 (CO No 1)
796 Notice requiring information: persons exempted from obligation to comply	20 Jan 2007 (CO No 1)
797 Consequences of order imposing restrictions	20 Jan 2007 (CO No 1)
798 Penalty for attempted evasion of restrictions	20 Jan 2007 (CO No 1)
799 Relaxation of restrictions	20 Jan 2007 (CO No 1)
800 Removal of restrictions	20 Jan 2007 (CO No 1)
801 Order for sale of shares	20 Jan 2007 (CO No 1)
802 Application of proceeds of sale under court order	20 Jan 2007 (CO No 1)
803 Power of members to require company to act	20 Jan 2007 (CO No 1)
804 Duty of company to comply with requirement	20 Jan 2007 (CO No 1)
805 Report to members on outcome of investigation	20 Jan 2007 (CO No 1)
806 Report to members: offences	20 Jan 2007 (CO No 1)
807 Right to inspect and request copy of reports	20 Jan 2007 (CO No 1)
808 Register of interests disclosed	20 Jan 2007 (CO No 1)[70]
809 Register to be kept available for inspection	20 Jan 2007 (CO No 1)[70]
810 Associated index	20 Jan 2007 (CO No 1)
811 Rights to inspect and require copy of entries	20 Jan 2007 (sub-ss (1)–(3)) (CO No 1)
	6 Apr 2008 (otherwise) (CO No 5)[96]
812 Court supervision of purpose for which rights may be exercised	6 Apr 2008 (CO No 5)[96]
813 Register of interests disclosed: refusal of inspection or default in providing copy	20 Jan 2007 (CO No 1)[43]

Provision of CA 2006	Commencement
814 Register of interests disclosed: offences in connection with request for or disclosure of information	6 Apr 2008 (CO No 5)[96]
815 Entries not to be removed from register	20 Jan 2007 (CO No 1)
816 Removal of entries from register: old entries	20 Jan 2007 (CO No 1)
817 Removal of entries from register: incorrect entry relating to third party	20 Jan 2007 (CO No 1)
818 Adjustment of entry relating to share acquisition agreement	20 Jan 2007 (CO No 1)
819 Duty of company ceasing to be public company	20 Jan 2007 (CO No 1)
820 Interest in shares: general	20 Jan 2007 (CO No 1)
821 Interest in shares: right to subscribe for shares	20 Jan 2007 (CO No 1)
822 Interest in shares: family interests	20 Jan 2007 (CO No 1)
823 Interest in shares: corporate interests	20 Jan 2007 (CO No 1)
824 Interest in shares: agreement to acquire interests in a particular company	20 Jan 2007 (CO No 1)
825 Extent of obligation in case of share acquisition agreement	20 Jan 2007 (CO No 1)
826 Information protected from wider disclosure	20 Jan 2007 (CO No 1)[43]
827 Reckoning of periods for fulfilling obligations	20 Jan 2007 (CO No 1)
828 Power to make further provision by regulations	20 Jan 2007 (CO No 1)
Part 23: Distributions	
Chapter 1: Restrictions on When Distributions may be Made	
829 Meaning of "distribution"	6 Apr 2008 (CO No 5)[97]
830 Distributions to be made only out of profits available for the purpose	6 Apr 2008 (CO No 5)[97]
831 Net asset restriction on distributions by public companies	6 Apr 2008 (CO No 5)[97]
832 Distributions by investment companies out of accumulated revenue profits	6 Apr 2008 (CO No 5)[97]
833 Meaning of "investment company"	6 Apr 2008 (CO No 5)[97]
834 Investment company: condition as to holdings in other companies	6 Apr 2008 (CO No 5)[97]
835 Power to extend provisions relating to investment companies	20 Jan 2007 (certain purposes) (CO No 1)[3]
	6 Apr 2008 (otherwise) (CO No 5)[97]
Chapter 2: Justification of Distribution by Reference to Accounts	
836 Justification of distribution by reference to relevant accounts	6 Apr 2008 (CO No 5)[97]
837 Requirements where last annual accounts used	6 Apr 2008 (CO No 5)[97]
838 Requirements where interim accounts used	6 Apr 2008 (CO No 5)[97]
839 Requirements where initial accounts used	6 Apr 2008 (CO No 5)[97]
840 Successive distributions etc by reference to the same accounts	6 Apr 2008 (CO No 5)[97]
Chapter 3: Supplementary Provisions	
841 Realised losses and profits and revaluation of fixed assets	6 Apr 2008 (CO No 5)[97]
842 Determination of profit or loss in respect of asset where records incomplete	6 Apr 2008 (CO No 5)[97]

Part 2   CA 2006 commencement etc

Provision of CA 2006	Commencement
843 Realised profits and losses of long-term insurance business	6 Apr 2008 (CO No 5)[97]
844 Treatment of development costs	6 Apr 2008 (CO No 5)[97]
845 Distributions in kind: determination of amount	6 Apr 2008 (CO No 5)[97]
846 Distributions in kind: treatment of unrealised profits	6 Apr 2008 (CO No 5)[97]
847 Consequences of unlawful distribution	6 Apr 2008 (CO No 5)[97]
848 Saving for certain older provisions in articles	6 Apr 2008 (CO No 5)[97]
849 Restriction on application of unrealised profits	6 Apr 2008 (CO No 5)[97]
850 Treatment of certain older profits or losses	6 Apr 2008 (CO No 5)[97]
851 Application of rules of law restricting distributions	6 Apr 2008 (CO No 5)[97]
852 Saving for other restrictions on distributions	6 Apr 2008 (CO No 5)[97]
853 Minor definitions	6 Apr 2008 (CO No 5)[97]
Part 24: A Company's Annual Return	
854 Duty to deliver annual returns	1 Oct 2009 (CO No 8)[170]
855 Contents of annual return: general	20 Jan 2007 (certain purposes) (CO No 1)[3]
	1 Oct 2009 (otherwise) (CO No 8)[170]
855A Required particulars of directors and secretaries[198]	1 Oct 2009
856 Contents of annual return: information about share capital[202]	20 Jan 2007 (certain purposes) (CO No 1)[3]
	1 Oct 2009 (otherwise) (CO No 8)[170]
856A Contents of annual return: information about shareholders: non-traded companies[198]	1 Oct 2009
856B Contents of annual return: information about shareholders: traded companies[198]	1 Oct 2009
857 Contents of annual return: power to make further provision by regulations	20 Jan 2007 (certain purposes) (CO No 1)[3]
	1 Oct 2009 (otherwise) (CO No 8)[170]
858 Failure to deliver annual return	1 Oct 2009 (CO No 8)[170]
859 Application of provisions to shadow directors[203]	*1 Oct 2009 (CO No 8)*
Part 25: Company Charges	
Chapter 1: Companies Registered in England and Wales or in Northern Ireland	
860 Charges created by a company	20 Jan 2007 (certain purposes) (CO No 1)[3]
	1 Oct 2009 (otherwise) (CO No 8)[171]
861 Charges which have to be registered: supplementary	1 Oct 2009 (CO No 8)
862 Charges existing on property acquired	20 Jan 2007 (certain purposes) (CO No 1)[3]
	1 Oct 2009 (otherwise) (CO No 8)[172]
863 Charge in series of debentures	1 Oct 2009 (CO No 8)[173]
864 Additional registration requirement for commission etc in relation to debentures	1 Oct 2009 (CO No 8)
865 Endorsement of certificate on debentures	1 Oct 2009 (CO No 8)
866 Charges created in, or over property in, jurisdictions outside the United Kingdom	1 Oct 2009 (CO No 8)
867 Charges created in, or over property in, another United Kingdom jurisdiction	1 Oct 2009 (CO No 8)
868 Northern Ireland: registration of certain charges etc affecting land	1 Oct 2009 (CO No 8)[174]

Provision of CA 2006	Commencement
869 Register of charges to be kept by registrar	1 Oct 2009 (CO No 8)
870 The period allowed for registration	1 Oct 2009 (CO No 8)
871 Registration of enforcement of security	1 Oct 2009 (CO No 8)[175]
872 Entries of satisfaction and release	1 Oct 2009 (CO No 8)[176]
873 Rectification of register of charges	1 Oct 2009 (CO No 8)
874 Consequence of failure to register charges created by a company	1 Oct 2009 (CO No 8)
875 Companies to keep copies of instruments creating charges	1 Oct 2009 (CO No 8)
876 Company's register of charges	1 Oct 2009 (CO No 8)
877 Instruments creating charges and register of charges to be available for inspection	20 Jan 2007 (certain purposes) (CO No 1)[3]
	1 Oct 2009 (otherwise) (CO No 8)
Chapter 2: Companies Registered in Scotland	
878 Charges created by a company	20 Jan 2007 (certain purposes) (CO No 1)[3]
	1 Oct 2009 (otherwise) (CO No 8)[171]
879 Charges which have to be registered: supplementary	1 Oct 2009 (CO No 8)
880 Duty to register charges existing on property acquired	20 Jan 2007 (certain purposes) (CO No 1)[3]
	1 Oct 2009 (otherwise) (CO No 8)[172]
881 Charge by way of ex facie absolute disposition, etc	1 Oct 2009 (CO No 8)
882 Charge in series of debentures	1 Oct 2009 (CO No 8)[173]
883 Additional registration requirement for commission etc in relation to debentures	1 Oct 2009 (CO No 8)
884 Charges on property outside United Kingdom	1 Oct 2009 (CO No 8)
885 Register of charges to be kept by registrar	1 Oct 2009 (CO No 8)
886 The period allowed for registration	1 Oct 2009 (CO No 8)
887 Entries of satisfaction and relief	1 Oct 2009 (CO No 8)[176]
888 Rectification of register of charges	1 Oct 2009 (CO No 8)
889 Charges void unless registered	1 Oct 2009 (CO No 8)
890 Copies of instruments creating charges to be kept by company	1 Oct 2009 (CO No 8)
891 Company's register of charges	1 Oct 2009 (CO No 8)
892 Instruments creating charges and register of charges to be available for inspection	20 Jan 2007 (certain purposes) (CO No 1)[3]
	1 Oct 2009 (otherwise) (CO No 8)
Chapter 3: Powers of the Secretary of State	
893 Power to make provision for effect of registration in special register	20 Jan 2007 (certain purposes) (CO No 1)[3]
	1 Oct 2009 (otherwise) (CO No 8)
894 General power to make amendments to this Part	20 Jan 2007 (certain purposes) (CO No 1)[3]
	1 Oct 2009 (otherwise) (CO No 8)
Part 26: Arrangements and Reconstructions	
895 Application of this Part	6 Apr 2008 (CO No 5)
896 Court order for holding of meeting	6 Apr 2008 (CO No 5)
897 Statement to be circulated or made available	6 Apr 2008 (CO No 5)
898 Duty of directors and trustees to provide information	6 Apr 2008 (CO No 5)
899 Court sanction for compromise or arrangement	6 Apr 2008 (CO No 5)

Provision of CA 2006	Commencement
900 Powers of court to facilitate reconstruction or amalgamation	6 Apr 2008 (CO No 5)
901 Obligations of company with respect to articles etc	6 Apr 2008 (CO No 5)[98]

Part 27: Mergers and Divisions of Public Companies

Chapter 1: Introductory

902 Application of this Part	6 Apr 2008 (CO No 5)
903 Relationship of this Part to Part 26	6 Apr 2008 (CO No 5)

Chapter 2: Merger

904 Mergers and merging companies	6 Apr 2008 (CO No 5)
905 Draft terms of scheme (merger)	6 Apr 2008 (CO No 5)
906 Publication of draft terms (merger)	6 Apr 2008 (CO No 5)
907 Approval of members of merging companies	6 Apr 2008 (CO No 5)
908 Directors' explanatory report (merger)	6 Apr 2008 (CO No 5)
909 Expert's report (merger)	6 Apr 2008 (CO No 5)
910 Supplementary accounting statement (merger)	6 Apr 2008 (CO No 5)
911 Inspection of documents (merger)	6 Apr 2008 (CO No 5)
912 Approval of articles of new transferee company (merger)	6 Apr 2008 (CO No 5)
913 Protection of holders of securities to which special rights attached (merger)	6 Apr 2008 (CO No 5)
914 No allotment of shares to transferor company or transferee company (merger)[211]	6 Apr 2008 (CO No 5)
915 Circumstances in which certain particulars and reports not required (merger)	6 Apr 2008 (CO No 5)
916 Circumstances in which meeting of members of transferee company not required (merger)	6 Apr 2008 (CO No 5)
917 Circumstances in which no meetings required (merger)	6 Apr 2008 (CO No 5)
918 Other circumstances in which meeting of members of transferee company not required (merger)	6 Apr 2008 (CO No 5)
918A Agreement to dispense with expert's report (merger)[123]	6 Apr 2008

Chapter 3: Division

919 Divisions and companies involved in a division	6 Apr 2008 (CO No 5)
920 Draft terms of scheme (division)	6 Apr 2008 (CO No 5)
921 Publication of draft terms (division)	6 Apr 2008 (CO No 5)
922 Approval of members of companies involved in the division	6 Apr 2008 (CO No 5)
923 Directors' explanatory report (division)	6 Apr 2008 (CO No 5)[99]
924 Expert's report (division)	6 Apr 2008 (CO No 5)
925 Supplementary accounting statement (division)	6 Apr 2008 (CO No 5)
926 Inspection of documents (division)	6 Apr 2008 (CO No 5)
927 Report on material changes of assets of transferor company (division)	6 Apr 2008 (CO No 5)
928 Approval of articles of new transferee company (division)	6 Apr 2008 (CO No 5)
929 Protection of holders of securities to which special rights attached (division)	6 Apr 2008 (CO No 5)

Provision of CA 2006	Commencement
930 No allotment of shares to transferor company or to transferee company (division)[211]	6 Apr 2008 (CO No 5)
931 Circumstances in which meeting of members of transferor company not required (division)	6 Apr 2008 (CO No 5)
932 Circumstances in which meeting of members of transferee company not required (division)	6 Apr 2008 (CO No 5)
933 Agreement to dispense with reports etc (division)	6 Apr 2008 (CO No 5)
934 Power of court to exclude certain requirements (division)	6 Apr 2008 (CO No 5)
Chapter 4: Supplementary Provisions	
935 Expert's report: valuation by another person	6 Apr 2008 (CO No 5)
936 Experts and valuers: independence requirement	20 Jan 2007 (certain purposes) (CO No 1)[3]
	6 Apr 2008 (otherwise) (CO No 5)
937 Experts and valuers: meaning of "associate"	6 Apr 2008 (CO No 5)
938 Power of court to summon meeting of members or creditors of existing transferee company	6 Apr 2008 (CO No 5)
939 Court to fix date for transfer of undertaking etc of transferor company	6 Apr 2008 (CO No 5)
940 Liability of transferee companies for each other's defaults	6 Apr 2008 (CO No 5)
941 Meaning of "liabilities" and "property"	6 Apr 2008 (CO No 5)
Part 28: Takeovers etc	
Chapter 1: The Takeover Panel	
942 The Panel	6 Apr 2007 (CO No 2)
943 Rules	6 Apr 2007 (CO No 2)[44]
944 Further provisions about rules	6 Apr 2007 (CO No 2)
945 Rulings	6 Apr 2007 (CO No 2)
946 Directions	6 Apr 2007 (CO No 2)
947 Power to require documents and information	6 Apr 2007 (CO No 2)
948 Restrictions on disclosure	20 Jan 2007 (certain purposes) (CO No 1)[3]
	6 Apr 2007 (otherwise) (CO No 2)
949 Offence of disclosure in contravention of section 948	6 Apr 2007 (CO No 2)
950 Panel's duty of co-operation	6 Apr 2007 (CO No 2)
951 Hearings and appeals	6 Apr 2007 (CO No 2)
952 Sanctions	6 Apr 2007 (CO No 2)
953 Failure to comply with rules about bid documentation	6 Apr 2007 (CO No 2)[44]
954 Compensation	6 Apr 2007 (CO No 2)
955 Enforcement by the court	6 Apr 2007 (CO No 2)
956 No action for breach of statutory duty etc	6 Apr 2007 (CO No 2)
957 Fees and charges	6 Apr 2007 (CO No 2)
958 Levy	20 Jan 2007 (certain purposes) (CO No 1)[3]
	6 Apr 2007 (otherwise) (CO No 2)
959 Recovery of fees, charges or levy	6 Apr 2007 (CO No 2)
960 Panel as party to proceedings	6 Apr 2007 (CO No 2)
961 Exemption from liability in damages	6 Apr 2007 (CO No 2)

Provision of CA 2006	Commencement
962 Privilege against self-incrimination	6 Apr 2007 (CO No 2)
963 Annual reports	6 Apr 2007 (CO No 2)
964 Amendments to Financial Services and Markets Act 2000	6 Apr 2007 (CO No 2)
965 Power to extend to Isle of Man and Channel Islands	20 Jan 2007 (certain purposes) (CO No 1)[3]
	6 Apr 2007 (otherwise) (CO No 2)
Chapter 2: Impediments to Takeovers	
966 Opting in and opting out	20 Jan 2007 (certain purposes) (CO No 1)[3]
	6 Apr 2007 (otherwise) (CO No 2)
967 Further provision about opting-in and opting-out resolutions	6 Apr 2007 (CO No 2)
968 Effect on contractual restrictions	6 Apr 2007 (CO No 2)[45]
969 Power of offeror to require general meeting to be called	6 Apr 2007 (CO No 2)
970 Communication of decisions	6 Apr 2007 (CO No 2)
971 Interpretation of this Chapter	6 Apr 2007 (CO No 2)
972 Transitory provision	6 Apr 2007 (CO No 2)
973 Power to extend to Isle of Man and Channel Islands	20 Jan 2007 (certain purposes) (CO No 1)[3]
	6 Apr 2007 (otherwise) (CO No 2)
Chapter 3: "Squeeze-Out" and "Sell-Out"	
974 Meaning of "takeover offer"	6 Apr 2007 (CO No 2)
975 Shares already held by the offeror etc	6 Apr 2007 (CO No 2)
976 Cases where offer treated as being on same terms	6 Apr 2007 (CO No 2)
977 Shares to which an offer relates	6 Apr 2007 (CO No 2)
978 Effect of impossibility etc of communicating or accepting offer	6 Apr 2007 (CO No 2)
979 Right of offeror to buy out minority shareholder	6 Apr 2007 (CO No 2)
980 Further provision about notices given under section 979	20 Jan 2007 (certain purposes) (CO No 1)[3]
	6 Apr 2007 (otherwise) (CO No 2)
981 Effect of notice under section 979	6 Apr 2007 (CO No 2)
982 Further provision about consideration held on trust under section 981(9)	6 Apr 2007 (CO No 2)
983 Right of minority shareholder to be bought out by offeror	6 Apr 2007 (CO No 2)
984 Further provision about rights conferred by section 983	20 Jan 2007 (certain purposes) (CO No 1)[3]
	6 Apr 2007 (otherwise) (CO No 2)
985 Effect of requirement under section 983	6 Apr 2007 (CO No 2)
986 Applications to the court	6 Apr 2007 (CO No 2)
987 Joint offers	6 Apr 2007 (CO No 2)
988 Associates	6 Apr 2007 (CO No 2)
989 Convertible securities	6 Apr 2007 (CO No 2)
990 Debentures carrying voting rights	6 Apr 2007 (CO No 2)
991 Interpretation	6 Apr 2007 (CO No 2)
Chapter 4: Amendments to Part 7 of the Companies Act 1985	
992 Matters to be dealt with in directors' report	6 Apr 2007 (CO No 2)
Part 29: Fraudulent Trading	
993 Offence of fraudulent trading	1 Oct 2007 (CO No 3)[46]

Provision of CA 2006	Commencement
Part 30: Protection of Members Against Unfair Prejudice	
994 Petition by company member	1 Oct 2007 (CO No 3)[47]
995 Petition by Secretary of State	1 Oct 2007 (CO No 3)
996 Powers of the court under this Part	1 Oct 2007 (CO No 3)
997 Application of general rule-making powers	1 Oct 2007 (CO No 3)
998 Copy of order affecting company's constitution to be delivered to registrar	1 Oct 2007 (CO No 3)
999 Supplementary provisions where company's constitution altered	1 Oct 2007 (CO No 3)[48]
Part 31: Dissolution and Restoration to the Register	
Chapter 1: Striking Off	
1000 Power to strike off company not carrying on business or in operation	1 Oct 2009 (CO No 8)
1001 Duty to act in case of company being wound up	1 Oct 2009 (CO No 8)
1002 Supplementary provisions as to service of letter or notice	1 Oct 2009 (CO No 8)
1003 Striking off on application by company	20 Jan 2007 (certain purposes) (CO No 1)[3]
	1 Oct 2009 (otherwise) (CO No 8)
1004 Circumstances in which application not to be made: activities of company	20 Jan 2007 (certain purposes) (CO No 1)[3]
	1 Oct 2009 (otherwise) (CO No 8)
1005 Circumstances in which application not to be made: other proceedings not concluded	1 Oct 2009 (CO No 8)
1006 Copy of application to be given to members, employees, etc	20 Jan 2007 (certain purposes) (CO No 1)[3]
	1 Oct 2009 (otherwise) (CO No 8)
1007 Copy of application to be given to new members, employees, etc	20 Jan 2007 (certain purposes) (CO No 1)[3]
	1 Oct 2009 (otherwise) (CO No 8)
1008 Copy of application: provisions as to service of documents	1 Oct 2009 (CO No 8)
1009 Circumstances in which application to be withdrawn	20 Jan 2007 (certain purposes) (CO No 1)[3]
	1 Oct 2009 (otherwise) (CO No 8)
1010 Withdrawal of application	1 Oct 2009 (CO No 8)
1011 Meaning of "creditor"	1 Oct 2009 (CO No 8)
Chapter 2: Property of Dissolved Company	
1012 Property of dissolved company to be bona vacantia	1 Oct 2009 (CO No 8)[177]
1013 Crown disclaimer of property vesting as bona vacantia	1 Oct 2009 (CO No 8)[177]
1014 Effect of Crown disclaimer	1 Oct 2009 (CO No 8)[177]
1015 General effect of disclaimer	1 Oct 2009 (CO No 8)[177]
1016 Disclaimer of leaseholds	1 Oct 2009 (CO No 8)[177]
1017 Power of court to make vesting order	1 Oct 2009 (CO No 8)[177]
1018 Protection of persons holding under a lease	1 Oct 2009 (CO No 8)[177]
1019 Land subject to rentcharge	1 Oct 2009 (CO No 8)[177]
1020 General effect of disclaimer	1 Oct 2009 (CO No 8)[177]
1021 Power of court to make vesting order	1 Oct 2009 (CO No 8)[177]
1022 Protection of persons holding under a lease	1 Oct 2009 (CO No 8)[177]

Provision of CA 2006	Commencement
1023 Liability for rentcharge on company's land after dissolution	1 Oct 2009 (CO No 8)[177]
Chapter 3: Restoration to the Register	
1024 Application for administrative restoration to the register	1 Oct 2009 (CO No 8)
1025 Requirements for administrative restoration	1 Oct 2009 (CO No 8)
1026 Application to be accompanied by statement of compliance	1 Oct 2009 (CO No 8)
1027 Registrar's decision on application for administrative restoration	1 Oct 2009 (CO No 8)
1028 Effect of administrative restoration	1 Oct 2009 (CO No 8)
1029 Application to court for restoration to the register	1 Oct 2009 (CO No 8)[178]
1030 When application to the court may be made	1 Oct 2009 (CO No 8)[178]
1031 Decision on application for restoration by the court	1 Oct 2009 (CO No 8)[178]
1032 Effect of court order for restoration to the register	1 Oct 2009 (CO No 8)[178]
1033 Company's name on restoration	1 Oct 2009 (CO No 8)
1034 Effect of restoration to the register where property has vested as bona vacantia	1 Oct 2009 (CO No 8)[179]
Part 32: Company Investigations: Amendments	
1035 Powers of Secretary of State to give directions to inspectors	1 Oct 2007 (CO No 3)[49]
1036 Resignation, removal and replacement of inspectors	1 Oct 2007 (CO No 3)[49]
1037 Power to obtain information from former inspectors etc	1 Oct 2007 (CO No 3)[49]
1038 Power to require production of documents	1 Oct 2007 (CO No 3)[49]
1039 Disqualification orders: consequential amendments	1 Oct 2007 (CO No 3)[49]
Part 33: UK Companies Not Formed Under Companies Legislation	
Chapter 1: Companies Not Formed Under Companies Legislation but Authorised to Register	
1040 Companies authorised to register under this Act	1 Oct 2009 (CO No 8)[180]
1041 Definition of "joint stock company"	1 Oct 2009 (CO No 8)[180]
1042 Power to make provision by regulations	20 Jan 2007 (certain purposes) (CO No 1)[3]
	1 Oct 2009 (otherwise) (CO No 8)[180]
Chapter 2: Unregistered Companies	
1043 Unregistered companies	20 Jan 2007 (certain purposes) (CO No 1)[3]
	6 Apr 2007 (otherwise) (CO No 2)
Part 34: Overseas Companies	
1044 Overseas companies	1 Oct 2009 (CO No 8)
1045 Company contracts and execution of documents by companies	20 Jan 2007 (certain purposes) (CO No 1)[3]
	1 Oct 2009 (otherwise) (CO No 8)
1046 Duty to register particulars	20 Jan 2007 (certain purposes) (CO No 1)[3]
	1 Oct 2009 (otherwise) (CO No 8)
1047 Registered name of overseas company	1 Oct 2009 (CO No 8)
1048 Registration under alternative name	1 Oct 2009 (CO No 8)
1049 Accounts and reports: general	20 Jan 2007 (certain purposes) (CO No 1)[3]
	1 Oct 2009 (otherwise) (CO No 8)

Provision of CA 2006	Commencement
1050 Accounts and reports: credit or financial institutions	20 Jan 2007 (certain purposes) (CO No 1)[3]
	1 Oct 2009 (otherwise) (CO No 8)
1051 Trading disclosures	20 Jan 2007 (certain purposes) (CO No 1)[3]
	1 Oct 2009 (otherwise) (CO No 8)
1052 Company charges	20 Jan 2007 (certain purposes) (CO No 1)[3]
	1 Oct 2009 (otherwise) (CO No 8)
1053 Other returns etc	20 Jan 2007 (certain purposes) (CO No 1)[3]
	1 Oct 2009 (otherwise) (CO No 8)
1054 Offences	20 Jan 2007 (certain purposes) (CO No 1)[3]
	1 Oct 2009 (otherwise) (CO No 8)
1055 Disclosure of individual's residential address: protection from disclosure	20 Jan 2007 (certain purposes) (CO No 1)[3]
	1 Oct 2009 (otherwise) (CO No 8)
1056 Requirement to identify persons autho-rised to accept service of documents	20 Jan 2007 (certain purposes) (CO No 1)[3]
	1 Oct 2009 (otherwise) (CO No 8)
1057 Registrar to whom returns, notices etc to be delivered	20 Jan 2007 (certain purposes) (CO No 1)[3]
	1 Oct 2009 (otherwise) (CO No 8)
1058 Duty to give notice of ceasing to have registrable presence	20 Jan 2007 (certain purposes) (CO No 1)[3]
	1 Oct 2009 (otherwise) (CO No 8)
1059 Application of provisions in case of relocation of branch	1 Oct 2009 (CO No 8)
Part 35: The Registrar of Companies	
1059A Scheme of this Part[206]	1 Oct 2009
1060 The registrar	6 Apr 2007 (certain purposes) (CO No 1)[50]
	1 Oct 2009 (otherwise) (CO No 8)
1061 The registrar's functions	6 Apr 2007 (certain purposes) (CO No 1)[50]
	1 Oct 2009 (otherwise) (CO No 8)
1062 The registrar's official seal	1 Oct 2009 (CO No 8)
1063 Fees payable to registrar	20 Jan 2007 (certain purposes) (CO No 1)[3]
	6 Apr 2007 (GB otherwise) (CO No 1)[51]
	1 Oct 2009 (NI otherwise) (CO No 8)[181]
1064 Public notice of issue of certificate of incorporation	1 Oct 2009 (CO No 8)[182]
1065 Right to certificate of incorporation	1 Oct 2009 (CO No 8)[183]
1066 Company's registered numbers	1 Oct 2009 (CO No 8)
1067 Registered numbers of UK establish-ments of overseas company[202]	1 Oct 2009 (CO No 8)
1068 Registrar's requirements as to form, authentication and manner of delivery	1 Jan 2007 (sub-s (5), and sub-ss (1)–(4), (6), (7)for certain purposes) (CO No 1)[52]
	15 Dec 2007 (sub-ss (1)–(4), (6), (7)for certain purposes) (CO No 3)[53]
	1 Oct 2009 (otherwise) (CO No 8)[184]
1069 Power to require delivery by electronic means	20 Jan 2007 (certain purposes) (CO No 1)[3]
	1 Oct 2009 (otherwise) (CO No 8)[184]
1070 Agreement for delivery by electronic means	1 Oct 2009 (CO No 8)[185]
1071 Document not delivered until received	1 Oct 2009 (CO No 8)[186]
1072 Requirements for proper delivery	1 Oct 2009 (CO No 8)[187]

Provision of CA 2006	Commencement
1073 Power to accept documents not meeting requirements for proper delivery	1 Oct 2009 (CO No 8)[187]
1074 Documents containing unnecessary material	1 Oct 2009 (CO No 8)[187]
1075 Informal correction of document	1 Oct 2009 (CO No 8)[188]
1076 Replacement of document not meeting requirements for proper delivery	1 Oct 2009 (CO No 8)[189]
1077 Public notice of receipt of certain documents	1 Jan 2007 (CO No 1)[54]
1078 Documents subject to Directive disclosure requirements	1 Jan 2007 (CO No 1)[190]
1079 Effect of failure to give public notice	1 Jan 2007 (CO No 1)[190]
1080 The register	1 Jan 2007 (CO No 1)[54]
1081 Annotation of the register	20 Jan 2007 (certain purposes) (CO No 1)[3]
	1 Oct 2009 (otherwise) (CO No 8)[191]
1082 Allocation of unique identifiers	20 Jan 2007 (certain purposes) (CO No 1)[3]
	1 Oct 2009 (otherwise) (CO No 8)
1083 Preservation of original documents	1 Oct 2009 (CO No 8)
1084 Records relating to companies that have been dissolved etc	1 Oct 2009 (CO No 8)
1085 Inspection of the register	1 Jan 2007 (CO No 1)[54]
1086 Right to copy of material on the register	1 Jan 2007 (CO No 1)
1087 Material not available for public inspection	1 Jan 2007 (CO No 1)[54]
1088 Application to registrar to make address unavailable for public inspection	1 Jan 2007 (CO No 1)
1089 Form of application for inspection or copy	1 Jan 2007 (CO No 1)
1090 Form and manner in which copies to be provided	1 Jan 2007 (CO No 1)
1091 Certification of copies as accurate	1 Jan 2007 (CO No 1)
1092 Issue of process for production of records kept by the registrar	1 Jan 2007 (CO No 1)
1093 Registrar's notice to resolve inconsistency on the register	1 Oct 2009 (CO No 8)[192]
1094 Administrative removal of material from the register	1 Oct 2009 (CO No 8)[193]
1095 Rectification of register on application to registrar	20 Jan 2007 (certain purposes) (CO No 1)[3]
	1 Oct 2009 (otherwise) (CO No 8)[193]
1096 Rectification of the register under court order	1 Oct 2009 (CO No 8)[193]
1097 Powers of court on ordering removal of material from the register	1 Oct 2009 (CO No 8)[193]
1098 Public notice of removal of certain material from the register	1 Oct 2009 (CO No 8)[193]
1099 The registrar's index of company names	20 Jan 2007 (certain purposes) (CO No 1)[3]
	1 Oct 2009 (otherwise) (CO No 8)
1100 Right to inspect index	1 Oct 2009 (CO No 8)
1101 Power to amend enactments relating to bodies other than companies	20 Jan 2007 (certain purposes) (CO No 1)[3]
	1 Oct 2009 (otherwise) (CO No 8)
1102 Application of language requirements	1 Jan 2007 (CO No 1)
1103 Documents to be drawn up and delivered in English	1 Jan 2007 (CO No 1)[54]

Provision of CA 2006	Commencement
1104 Documents relating to Welsh companies	1 Jan 2007 (CO No 1)[54a]
1105 Documents that may be drawn up and delivered in other languages	1 Jan 2007 (CO No 1)[55]
1106 Voluntary filing of translations	1 Jan 2007 (CO No 1)
1107 Certified translations	1 Jan 2007 (CO No 1)
1108 Transliteration of names and addresses: permitted characters	20 Jan 2007 (certain purposes) (CO No 1)[3]
	1 Oct 2009 (otherwise) (CO No 8)[194]
1109 Transliteration of names and addresses: voluntary transliteration into Roman characters	1 Oct 2009 (CO No 8)[194]
1110 Transliteration of names and addresses: certification	20 Jan 2007 (certain purposes) (CO No 1)[3]
	1 Oct 2009 (otherwise) (CO No 8)[194]
1111 Registrar's requirements as to certification or verification	1 Jan 2007 (CO No 1)[54b]
1112 General false statement offence	1 Oct 2009 (CO No 8)[195]
1113 Enforcement of company's filing obligations	1 Oct 2009 (CO No 8)
1114 Application of provisions about documents and delivery	1 Jan 2007 (certain purposes) (CO No 1)[56]
	1 Oct 2009 (otherwise) (CO No 8)
1115 Supplementary provisions relating to electronic communications	1 Oct 2009 (CO No 8)
1116 Alternative to publication in the Gazette	20 Jan 2007 (certain purposes) (CO No 1)[3]
	1 Oct 2009 (otherwise) (CO No 8)
1117 Registrar's rules	1 Jan 2007 (certain purposes) (CO No 1)[56]
	6 Apr 2008 (certain purposes) (CO No 5)[106]
	1 Oct 2009 (otherwise) (CO No 8)
1118 Payments into the Consolidated Fund	1 Oct 2009 (CO No 8)
1119 Contracting out of registrar's functions	1 Oct 2009 (CO No 8)
1120 Application of this Part to overseas companies[207]	*1 Jan 2007 (certain purposes) (CO No 1)*[56]
	1 Oct 2009 (otherwise) (CO No 8)
Part 36: Offences Under the Companies Acts	
1121 Liability of officer in default	20 Jan 2007 (certain purposes) (CO No 1)[57]
	6 Apr 2007 (certain purposes) (CO No 2)[41]
	1 Oct 2007 (certain purposes) (CO No 3)[58]
	6 Apr 2008 (certain purposes) (CO No 5)[108]
	1 Oct 2008 (certain purposes) (CO No 5)[108]
	1 Oct 2009 (otherwise) (CO No 8)[196]
1122 Liability of company as officer in default	20 Jan 2007 (certain purposes) (CO No 1)[57]
	6 Apr 2007 (certain purposes) (CO No 2)[41]
	1 Oct 2007 (certain purposes) (CO No 3)[58]
	6 Apr 2008 (certain purposes) (CO No 5)[108]
	1 Oct 2008 (certain purposes) (CO No 5)[108]
	1 Oct 2009 (otherwise) (CO No 8)[196]
1123 Application to bodies other than companies	6 Apr 2007 (certain purposes) (CO No 2)[41]
	1 Oct 2007 (certain purposes) (CO No 3)[58]
	6 Apr 2008 (certain purposes) (CO No 5)[108]
	1 Oct 2008 (certain purposes) (CO No 5)[108]
	1 Oct 2009 (otherwise) (CO No 8)[196]

Part 2   CA 2006 commencement etc

Provision of CA 2006	Commencement
1124 Amendments of the Companies Act 1985	1 Oct 2007 (CO No 3)
1125 Meaning of "daily default fine"	20 Jan 2007 (certain purposes) (CO No 1)[57]
	6 Apr 2007 (certain purposes) (CO No 2)[41]
	1 Oct 2007 (certain purposes) (CO No 3)[58]
	6 Apr 2008 (certain purposes) (CO No 5)[108]
	1 Oct 2008 (certain purposes) (CO No 5)[108]
	1 Oct 2009 (otherwise) (CO No 8)[196]
1126 Consents required for certain prosecutions	20 Jan 2007 (certain purposes) (CO No 1)[57]
	6 Apr 2007 (certain purposes) (CO No 2)[41]
	1 Oct 2007 (certain purposes) (CO No 3)[58]
	6 Apr 2008 (otherwise) (CO No 5)
1127 Summary proceedings: venue	20 Jan 2007 (certain purposes) (CO No 1)[57]
	6 Apr 2007 (certain purposes) (CO No 2)[41]
	1 Oct 2007 (certain purposes) (CO No 3)[58]
	6 Apr 2008 (certain purposes) (CO No 5)[108]
	1 Oct 2008 (certain purposes) (CO No 5)[108]
	1 Oct 2009 (otherwise) (CO No 8)[196]
1128 Summary proceedings: time limit for proceedings	20 Jan 2007 (certain purposes) (CO No 1)[57]
	6 Apr 2007 (certain purposes) (CO No 2)[41]
	1 Oct 2007 (certain purposes) (CO No 3)[58]
	6 Apr 2008 (certain purposes) (CO No 5)[108]
	1 Oct 2008 (certain purposes) (CO No 5)[108]
	1 Oct 2009 (otherwise) (CO No 8)[196]
1129 Legal professional privilege	20 Jan 2007 (certain purposes) (CO No 1)[57]
	6 Apr 2007 (certain purposes) (CO No 2)[41]
	1 Oct 2007 (certain purposes) (CO No 3)[58]
	6 Apr 2008 (certain purposes) (CO No 5)[108]
	1 Oct 2008 (certain purposes) (CO No 5)[108]
	1 Oct 2009 (otherwise) (CO No 8)[196]
1130 Proceedings against unincorporated bodies	20 Jan 2007 (certain purposes) (CO No 1)[57]
	6 Apr 2007 (certain purposes) (CO No 2)[41]
	1 Oct 2007 (certain purposes) (CO No 3)[58]
	6 Apr 2008 (certain purposes) (CO No 5)[108]
	1 Oct 2008 (certain purposes) (CO No 5)[108]
	1 Oct 2009 (otherwise) (CO No 8)[196]
1131 Imprisonment on summary conviction in England and Wales: transitory provision	20 Jan 2007 (certain purposes) (CO No 1)[57]
	6 Apr 2007 (certain purposes) (CO No 2)[41]
	1 Oct 2007 (certain purposes) (CO No 3)[58]
	6 Apr 2008 (certain purposes) (CO No 5)[108]
	1 Oct 2008 (certain purposes) (CO No 5)[108]
	1 Oct 2009 (otherwise) (CO No 8)[196]
1132 Production and inspection of documents where offence suspected	6 Apr 2007 (certain purposes) (CO No 2)[41]
	1 Oct 2007 (certain purposes) (CO No 3)[58]
	6 Apr 2008 (certain purposes) (CO No 5)[108]
	1 Oct 2008 (certain purposes) (CO No 5)[108]
	1 Oct 2009 (otherwise) (CO No 8)[196]
1133 Transitional provision	20 Jan 2007 (certain purposes) (CO No 1)[57]

Provision of CA 2006	Commencement
	6 Apr 2007 (certain purposes) (CO No 2)[41]
	1 Oct 2007 (certain purposes) (CO No 3)[58]
	6 Apr 2008 (certain purposes) (CO No 5)[108]
	1 Oct 2008 (certain purposes) (CO No 5)[108]
	1 Oct 2009 (otherwise) (CO No 8)[196]
Part 37: Companies: Supplementary Provisions	
1134 Meaning of "company records"	6 Apr 2007 (certain purposes) (CO No 2)[41]
	1 Oct 2009 (otherwise) (CO No 8)
1135 Form of company records	6 Apr 2007 (certain purposes) (CO No 2)[41]
	1 Oct 2009 (otherwise) (CO No 8)
1136 Regulations about where certain company records to be kept available for inspection	20 Jan 2007 (certain purposes) (CO No 1)[3]
	1 Oct 2009 (otherwise) (CO No 8)
1137 Regulations about inspection of records and provision of copies	20 Jan 2007 (certain purposes) (CO No 1)[3]
	30 Sept 2007 (sub-ss (1), (4), (5)(b), (6)) (CO No 4)
	1 Oct 2009 (otherwise) (CO No 8)
1138 Duty to take precautions against falsification	6 Apr 2007 (certain purposes) (CO No 2)[41]
	1 Oct 2009 (otherwise) (CO No 8)
1139 Service of documents on company	6 Apr 2007 (certain purposes) (CO No 2)[41]
	6 Apr 2008 (certain purposes) (CO No 5)[107]
	1 Oct 2009 (otherwise) (CO No 8)
1140 Service of documents on directors, secretaries and others	6 Apr 2007 (certain purposes) (CO No 2)[41]
	6 Apr 2008 (certain purposes) (CO No 5)[107]
	1 Oct 2009 (otherwise) (CO No 8)
1141 Service addresses	20 Jan 2007 (certain purposes) (CO No 1)[3]
	1 Oct 2009 (otherwise) (CO No 8)
1142 Requirement to give service address	1 Oct 2009 (CO No 8)
1143 The company communications provisions	20 Jan 2007 (CO No 1)[43]
1144 Sending or supplying documents or information	20 Jan 2007 (CO No 1)
1145 Right to hard copy version	20 Jan 2007 (CO No 1)
1146 Requirement of authentication	20 Jan 2007 (CO No 1)
1147 Deemed delivery of documents and information	20 Jan 2007 (CO No 1)
1148 Interpretation of company communications provisions	20 Jan 2007 (CO No 1)
1149 Application of valuation requirements	1 Oct 2009 (CO No 8)
1150 Valuation by qualified independent person	1 Oct 2009 (CO No 8)
1151 The independence requirement	20 Jan 2007 (certain purposes) (CO No 1)[3]
	1 Oct 2009 (otherwise) (CO No 8)
1152 Meaning of "associate"	1 Oct 2009 (CO No 8)
1153 Valuer entitled to full disclosure	1 Oct 2009 (CO No 8)
1154 Duty to notify registrar of certain appointments etc	1 Oct 2009 (CO No 8)[197]
1155 Offence of failure to give notice	1 Oct 2009 (CO No 8)[197]
1156 Meaning of "the court"	20 Jan 2007 (certain purposes) (CO No 1)[3]
	1 Oct 2009 (otherwise) (CO No 8)

Provision of CA 2006	Commencement
1157 Power of court to grant relief in certain cases	1 Oct 2008 (CO No 5)
Part 38: Companies: Interpretation	
1158 Meaning of "UK-registered company"	1 Oct 2007 (certain purposes) (CO No 3)[4]
	1 Nov 2007 (certain purposes) (CO No 3)[42]
	1 Oct 2009 (otherwise) (CO No 8)
1159 Meaning of "subsidiary" etc	6 Apr 2008 (certain purposes) (CO No 5)[109]
	1 Oct 2009 (otherwise) (CO No 8)
1160 Meaning of "subsidiary" etc: power to amend	20 Jan 2007 (certain purposes) (CO No 1)[3]
	6 Apr 2008 (certain purposes) (CO No 5)[109]
	1 Oct 2009 (otherwise) (CO No 8)
1161 Meaning of "undertaking" and related expressions	6 Apr 2008 (CO No 5)
1162 Parent and subsidiary undertakings	6 Apr 2008 (CO No 5)
1163 "Non-cash asset"	1 Oct 2009 (CO No 8)
1164 Meaning of "banking company" and "banking group"	6 Apr 2008 (CO No 5)
1165 Meaning of "insurance company" and related expressions	6 Apr 2008 (CO No 5)
1166 "Employees' share scheme"	1 Oct 2009 (CO No 8)
1167 Meaning of "prescribed"	20 Jan 2007 (certain purposes) (CO No 1)[3]
	30 Sept 2007 (otherwise) (CO No 4)
1168 Hard copy and electronic form and related expressions	1 Jan 2007 (certain purposes) (CO No 1)[59]
	20 Jan 2007 (certain purposes) (CO No 1)[59]
	6 Apr 2007 (certain purposes) (CO No 2)[41]
	1 Oct 2007 (certain purposes) (CO No 3)[4]
	15 Dec 2007 (certain purposes) (CO No 3)[60]
	6 Apr 2008 (certain purposes) (CO No 5)[108]
	1 Oct 2008 (certain purposes) (CO No 5)[108]
	1 Oct 2009 (otherwise) (CO No 8)
1169 Dormant companies	6 Apr 2008 (CO No 5)
1170 Meaning of "EEA State" and related expressions	6 Apr 2007 (CO No 2)
1170A Receiver or manager and certain related references[210]	1 Oct 2009
1170B Meaning of "contributory"[210]	1 Oct 2009
1171 The former Companies Acts	1 Oct 2009 (CO No 8)
1172 References to requirements of this Act	6 Apr 2008 (CO No 5)
1173 Minor definitions: general	1 Jan 2007 (certain purposes) (CO No 1)[61]
	20 Jan 2007 (certain purposes) (CO No 1)[61]
	6 Apr 2007 (certain purposes) (CO No 2)[62]
	1 Oct 2007 (certain purposes) (CO No 3)[63]
	1 Nov 2007 (certain purposes) (CO No 3)[64]
	6 Apr 2008 (certain purposes) (CO No 5)[100]
	1 Oct 2008 (certain purposes) (CO No 3)[100]
	1 Oct 2009 (otherwise) (CO No 8)
1174 Index of defined expressions	1 Oct 2009 (CO No 8)
Part 39: Companies: Minor Amendments	
1175 Removal of special provisions about accounts and audit of charitable companies	1 Apr 2008 (certain purposes) (CO No 6)[120]
	Not in force (otherwise)[200]

Provision of CA 2006	Commencement
1176 Power of Secretary of State to bring civil proceedings on company's behalf	6 Apr 2007 (CO No 1)
1177 Repeal of certain provisions about company directors	6 Apr 2007 (CO No 1)
1178 Repeal of requirement that certain companies publish periodical statement	6 Apr 2007 (CO No 1)
1179 Repeal of requirement that Secretary of State prepare annual report	6 Apr 2007 (CO No 1)
1180 Repeal of certain provisions about company charges	1 Oct 2009 (CO No 8)
1181 Access to constitutional documents of RTE and RTM companies	20 Jan 2007 (certain purposes) (CO No 1)[3]
	1 Oct 2009 (otherwise) (CO No 8)

Part 40: Company Directors: Foreign Disqualification etc

1182 Persons subject to foreign restrictions	1 Oct 2009 (CO No 8)
1183 Meaning of "the court" and "UK company"	1 Oct 2009 (CO No 8)
1184 Disqualification of persons subject to foreign restrictions	20 Jan 2007 (certain purposes) (CO No 1)[3]
	1 Oct 2009 (otherwise) (CO No 8)
1185 Disqualification regulations: supplementary	20 Jan 2007 (certain purposes) (CO No 1)[3]
	1 Oct 2009 (otherwise) (CO No 8)
1186 Offence of breach of disqualification	20 Jan 2007 (certain purposes) (CO No 1)[3]
	1 Oct 2009 (otherwise) (CO No 8)
1187 Personal liability for debts of company	20 Jan 2007 (certain purposes) (CO No 1)[3]
	1 Oct 2009 (otherwise) (CO No 8)
1188 Statements from persons subject to foreign restrictions	20 Jan 2007 (certain purposes) (CO No 1)[3]
	1 Oct 2009 (otherwise) (CO No 8)
1189 Statements from persons disqualified	20 Jan 2007 (certain purposes) (CO No 1)[3]
	1 Oct 2009 (otherwise) (CO No 8)
1190 Statements: whether to be made public	1 Oct 2009 (CO No 8)
1191 Offences	20 Jan 2007 (certain purposes) (CO No 1)[3]
	1 Oct 2009 (otherwise) (CO No 8)

Part 41: Business Names
Chapter 1: Restricted or Prohibited Names

1192 Application of this Chapter	1 Oct 2009 (CO No 8)
1193 Name suggesting connection with government or public authority	20 Jan 2007 (certain purposes) (CO No 1)[3]
	1 Oct 2009 (otherwise) (CO No 8)
1194 Other sensitive words or expressions	20 Jan 2007 (certain purposes) (CO No 1)[3]
	1 Oct 2009 (otherwise) (CO No 8)
1195 Requirement to seek comments of government department or other relevant body	20 Jan 2007 (certain purposes) (CO No 1)[3]
	1 Oct 2009 (otherwise) (CO No 8)
1196 Withdrawal of Secretary of State's approval	1 Oct 2009 (CO No 8)
1197 Name containing inappropriate indication of company type or legal form	20 Jan 2007 (certain purposes) (CO No 1)[3]
	1 Oct 2009 (otherwise) (CO No 8)
1198 Name giving misleading indication of activities	1 Oct 2009 (CO No 8)
1199 Savings for existing lawful business names	1 Oct 2009 (CO No 8)

Provision of CA 2006	Commencement
Chapter 2: Disclosure Required in Case of Individual or Partnership	
1200 Application of this Chapter	1 Oct 2009 (CO No 8)
1201 Information required to be disclosed[212]	1 Oct 2009 (CO No 8)
1202 Disclosure required: business documents etc	20 Jan 2007 (certain purposes) (CO No 1)[3]
	1 Oct 2009 (otherwise) (CO No 8)
1203 Exemption for large partnerships if certain conditions met	1 Oct 2009 (CO No 8)
1204 Disclosure required: business premises	20 Jan 2007 (certain purposes) (CO No 1)[3]
	1 Oct 2009 (otherwise) (CO No 8)
1205 Criminal consequences of failure to make required disclosure	1 Oct 2009 (CO No 8)
1206 Civil consequences of failure to make required disclosure	1 Oct 2009 (CO No 8)
Chapter 3: Supplementary	
1207 Application of general provisions about offences	1 Oct 2009 (CO No 8)
1208 Interpretation	1 Oct 2009 (CO No 8)
Part 42: Statutory Auditors	
Chapter 1: Introductory	
1209 Main purposes of Part	6 Apr 2008 (CO No 5)
1210 Meaning of "statutory auditor" etc	20 Jan 2007 (certain purposes) (CO No 1)[3]
	6 Apr 2008 (otherwise) (CO No 5)
1211 Eligibility for appointment as a statutory auditor: overview	6 Apr 2008 (CO No 5)
Chapter 2: Individuals and Firms	
1212 Individuals and firms: eligibility for appointment as a statutory auditor	6 Apr 2008 (CO No 5)[101]
1213 Effect of ineligibility	6 Apr 2008 (CO No 5)[101]
1214 Independence requirement	20 Jan 2007 (certain purposes) (CO No 1)[3]
	6 Apr 2008 (otherwise) (CO No 5)[101]
1215 Effect of lack of independence	6 Apr 2008 (CO No 5)[101]
1216 Effect of appointment of a partnership	6 Apr 2008 (CO No 5)[101]
1217 Supervisory bodies	6 Apr 2008 (CO No 5)[102]
1218 Exemption from liability for damages	6 Apr 2008 (CO No 5)[102]
1219 Appropriate qualifications	6 Apr 2008 (CO No 5)[102]
1220 Qualifying bodies and recognised professional qualifications	6 Apr 2008 (CO No 5)[102]
1221 Approval of third country qualifications[202]	6 Apr 2008 (CO No 5)[102]
1222 Eligibility of individuals retaining only 1967 Act authorisation	6 Apr 2008 (CO No 5)[102]
1223 Matters to be notified to the Secretary of State	6 Apr 2008 (CO No 5)
1223A Notification of matters relevant to other EEA States[119]	6 Apr 2008
1224 The Secretary of State's power to call for information	6 Apr 2008 (CO No 5)
1224A Restrictions on disclosure[119]	6 Apr 2008
1224B Offence of disclosure in contravention of section 1224A[119]	6 Apr 2008
1225 Compliance orders	6 Apr 2008 (CO No 5)
Chapter 3: Auditors General	
1226 Auditors General: eligibility for appointment as a statutory auditor	6 Apr 2008 (CO No 5)[103]

Provision of CA 2006	Commencement
1227 Individuals responsible for audit work on behalf of Auditors General	6 Apr 2008 (CO No 5)
1228 Appointment of the Independent Supervisor	20 Jan 2007 (certain purposes) (CO No 1)[3]
	6 Apr 2008 (otherwise) (CO No 5)
1229 Supervision of Auditors General by the Independent Supervisor	6 Apr 2008 (CO No 5)[103]
1230 Duties of Auditors General in relation to supervision arrangements	6 Apr 2008 (CO No 5)[103]
1231 Reports by the Independent Supervisor	20 Jan 2007 (certain purposes) (CO No 1)[3]
	6 Apr 2008 (otherwise) (CO No 5)
1232 Matters to be notified to the Independent Supervisor	6 Apr 2008 (CO No 5)
1233 The Independent Supervisor's power to call for information	6 Apr 2008 (CO No 5)
1234 Suspension notices	6 Apr 2008 (CO No 5)
1235 Effect of suspension notices	6 Apr 2008 (CO No 5)
1236 Compliance orders	6 Apr 2008 (CO No 5)
1237 Proceedings involving the Independent Supervisor	20 Jan 2007 (certain purposes) (CO No 1)[3]
	6 Apr 2008 (otherwise) (CO No 5)
1238 Grants to the Independent Supervisor	6 Apr 2008 (CO No 5)
Chapter 4: The Register of Auditors etc	
1239 The register of auditors	20 Jan 2007 (certain purposes) (CO No 1)[3]
	6 Apr 2008 (otherwise) (CO No 5)
1240 Information to be made available to public	20 Jan 2007 (certain purposes) (CO No 1)[3]
	6 Apr 2008 (otherwise) (CO No 5)
Chapter 5: Registered Third Country Auditors	
1241 Meaning of "registered third country auditor" and "UK-traded non-EEA company"[202]	20 Jan 2007 (certain purposes) (CO No 1)[3]
	6 Apr 2008 (otherwise) (CO No 5)
1242 Duties of registered third country auditors	29 Jun 2008 (CO No 5)[110]
1243 Matters to be notified to the Secretary of State	29 Jun 2008 (CO No 5)[110]
1244 The Secretary of State's power to call for information	29 Jun 2008 (CO No 5)[110]
1245 Compliance orders	6 Apr 2008 (CO No 5)
1246 Removal of third country auditors from the register of auditors	20 Jan 2007 (certain purposes) (CO No 1)[3]
	6 Apr 2008 (otherwise) (CO No 5)
1247 Grants to bodies concerned with arrangements under Schedule 12	6 Apr 2008 (CO No 5)
Chapter 6: Supplementary and General	
1248 Secretary of State's power to require second audit of a company	6 Apr 2008 (CO No 5)[104]
1249 Supplementary provision about second audits	6 Apr 2008 (CO No 5)[104]
1250 Misleading, false and deceptive statements	6 Apr 2008 (CO No 5)[104]
1251 Fees	20 Jan 2007 (certain purposes) (CO No 1)[3]
	6 Apr 2008 (otherwise) (CO No 5)[104]
1251A Duty of the Secretary of State to report on inspections[119]	6 Apr 2008

Part 2   CA 2006 commencement etc

Provision of CA 2006	Commencement
1252 Delegation of the Secretary of State's functions	20 Jan 2007 (certain purposes) (CO No 1)[3]
	6 Apr 2008 (otherwise) (CO No 5)
1253 Delegation of functions to an existing body	20 Jan 2007 (certain purposes) (CO No 1)[3]
	6 Apr 2008 (otherwise) (CO No 5)
1253A Requests to foreign competent authorities[119]	6 Apr 2008
1253B Requests from EEA competent authorities[119]	6 Apr 2008
1253C Notification to competent authorities of other EEA States[119]	6 Apr 2008
1253D Restriction on transfer of audit working papers to third countries[214]	6 Apr 2008
1253DA Transfer by Secretary of State[214]	15 Nov 2010
1253DB Transfer by statutory auditor with approval of Secretary of State[214]	15 Nov 2010
1253DC Transfer by statutory auditor for purposes of investigation of auditor[214]	15 Nov 2010
1253DD Agreement of EEA competent authority[214]	15 Nov 2010
1253DE Transfer by means of inspection[214]	15 Nov 2010
1253E Working arrangements for transfer of papers[215]	6 Apr 2008
1253F Publication of working arrangements[119]	6 Apr 2008
1254 Directions to comply with international obligations	6 Apr 2008 (CO No 5)[104]
1255 Offences by bodies corporate, partnerships and unincorporated associations	6 Apr 2008 (CO No 5)[104]
1256 Time limits for prosecution of offences	6 Apr 2008 (CO No 5)[104]
1257 Jurisdiction and procedure in respect of offences	6 Apr 2008 (CO No 5)[104]
1258 Service of notices	6 Apr 2008 (CO No 5)[104]
1259 Documents in electronic form	6 Apr 2008 (CO No 5)[104]
1260 Meaning of "associate"	6 Apr 2008 (CO No 5)
1261 Minor definitions	20 Jan 2007 (certain purposes) (CO No 1)[3]
	6 Apr 2008 (otherwise) (CO No 5)
1262 Index of defined expressions	6 Apr 2008 (CO No 5)
1263 Power to make provision in consequence of changes affecting accountancy bodies	20 Jan 2007 (certain purposes) (CO No 1)[3]
	6 Apr 2008 (otherwise) (CO No 5)
1264 Consequential amendments	6 Apr 2008 (CO No 5)
Part 43: Transparency Obligations and Related Matters	
1265 The transparency obligations directive	8 Nov 2006 (RA)
1266 Transparency rules	8 Nov 2006 (RA)
1267 Competent authority's power to call for information	8 Nov 2006 (RA)
1268 Powers exercisable in case of infringement of transparency obligation	8 Nov 2006 (RA)
1269 Corporate governance rules	8 Nov 2006 (RA)
1270 Liability for false or misleading statements in certain publications	8 Nov 2006 (RA)
1271 Exercise of powers where UK is host member State	8 Nov 2006 (RA)

Provision of CA 2006	Commencement
1272 Transparency obligations and related matters: minor and consequential amendments	8 Nov 2006 (certain purposes) (RA)
	1 Oct 2008 (otherwise)[65]
1273 Corporate governance regulations	8 Nov 2006 (RA)
Part 44: Miscellaneous Provisions	
1274 Grants to bodies concerned with actuarial standards etc	8 Nov 2006 (RA)
1275 Levy to pay expenses of bodies concerned with actuarial standards etc	1 Oct 2009 (CO No 8)
1276 Application of provisions to Scotland and Northern Ireland	8 Nov 2006 (RA)
1277 Power to require information about exercise of voting rights	20 Jan 2007 (certain purposes) (CO No 1)[3]
	1 Oct 2008 (otherwise) (CO No 5)
1278 Institutions to which information provisions apply	20 Jan 2007 (certain purposes) (CO No 1)[3]
	1 Oct 2008 (otherwise) (CO No 5)
1279 Shares to which information provisions apply	20 Jan 2007 (certain purposes) (CO No 1)[3]
	1 Oct 2008 (otherwise) (CO No 5)
1280 Obligations with respect to provision of information	20 Jan 2007 (certain purposes) (CO No 1)[3]
	1 Oct 2008 (otherwise) (CO No 5)
1281 Disclosure of information under the Enterprise Act 2002	6 Apr 2007 (CO No 1)
1282 Payment of expenses of winding up	6 Apr 2008 (CO No 5)[105]
1283 Amendment of memorandum or articles of commonhold association	1 Oct 2009 (CO No 8)
Part 45: Northern Ireland	
1284 Extension of Companies Acts to Northern Ireland	1 Jan 2007 (certain purposes) (CO No 1)
	20 Jan 2007 (certain purposes) (CO No 1)
	6 Apr 2007 (certain purposes) (CO No 1 & CO No 2)
	30 Sept 2007 (certain purposes) (CO No 4)
	1 Oct 2007 (certain purposes) (CO No 3)
	1 Nov 2007 (certain purposes) (CO No 3)
	15 Dec 2007 (certain purposes) (CO No 3)
	6 Apr 2008 (certain purposes) (CO No 5)
	1 Oct 2008 (certain purposes) (CO No 3 & CO No 5 & CO No 7)
	1 Oct 2009 (otherwise) (CO No 8)[66]
1285 Extension of GB enactments relating to SEs	1 Oct 2009 (CO No 8)
1286 Extension of GB enactments relating to certain other forms of business organisation	1 Oct 2008 (certain purposes) (CO No 7)[128]
	1 Oct 2009 (otherwise) (CO No 8)
1287 Extension of enactments relating to business names	1 Oct 2009 (CO No 8)
Part 46: General Supplementary Provisions	
1288 Regulations and orders: statutory instrument	8 Nov 2006 (RA)
1289 Regulations and orders: negative resolution procedure	8 Nov 2006 (RA)

Provision of CA 2006	Commencement
1290 Regulations and orders: affirmative resolution procedure	8 Nov 2006 (RA)
1291 Regulations and orders: approval after being made	8 Nov 2006 (RA)
1292 Regulations and orders: supplementary	8 Nov 2006 (RA)
1293 Meaning of "enactment"	8 Nov 2006 (RA)
1294 Power to make consequential amendments etc	8 Nov 2006 (RA)
1295 Repeals	See Sch 16 below
1296 Power to make transitional provision and savings	8 Nov 2006 (RA)
1297 Continuity of the law	8 Nov 2006 (RA)
Part 47: Final Provisions	
1298 Short title	8 Nov 2006 (RA)
1299 Extent	8 Nov 2006 (RA)
1300 Commencement	8 Nov 2006 (RA)
Schedules	
Schedule 1—Connected Persons: References to an Interest in Shares or Debentures	1 Oct 2007 (CO No 3)[118]
Schedule 2—Specified Persons, Descriptions of Disclosures etc for the Purposes of Section 948[213]	
Part 1—Specified Persons	6 Apr 2007 (CO No 2)
Part 2—Specified Descriptions of Disclosures	20 Jan 2007 (certain purposes) (CO No 1)[3]
	6 Apr 2007 (otherwise) (CO No 2)
Part 3—Overseas Regulatory Bodies	6 Apr 2007 (CO No 2)
Schedule 3—Amendments of Remaining Provisions of the Companies Act 1985 Relating to Offences	1 Oct 2007 (CO No 3)[67]
Schedule 4—Documents and Information Sent or Supplied to a Company	
Part 1—Introduction	20 Jan 2007 (CO No 1)
Part 2—Communications in Hard Copy Form	20 Jan 2007 (CO No 1)
Part 3—Communications in Electronic Form	20 Jan 2007 (CO No 1)
Part 4—Other Agreed Forms of Communication	20 Jan 2007 (CO No 1)
Schedule 5—Communications by a Company	
Part 1—Introduction	20 Jan 2007 (CO No 1)
Part 2—Communications in Hard Copy Form	20 Jan 2007 (CO No 1)
Part 3—Communications in Electronic Form	20 Jan 2007 (CO No 1)[68]
Part 4—Communications by Means of a Website	20 Jan 2007 (CO No 1)[68]
Part 5—Other Agreed Forms of Communication	20 Jan 2007 (CO No 1)
Part 6—Supplementary Provisions	20 Jan 2007 (CO No 1)
Schedule 6—Meaning of "Subsidiary" etc: Supplementary Provisions	6 Apr 2008 (certain purposes) (CO No 5)[109]
	1 Oct 2009 (otherwise) (CO No 8)
Schedule 7—Parent and Subsidiary Undertakings: Supplementary Provisions	6 Apr 2008 (CO No 5)
Schedule 8—Index of Defined Expressions	1 Oct 2009 (CO No 8)

Provision of CA 2006	Commencement
Schedule 9—Removal of Special Provisions About Accounts and Audit of Charitable Companies	
Part 1—The Companies Act 1985 (c 6)	1 Apr 2008 (CO No 6)[121]
Part 2—The Companies (Northern Ireland) Order 1986 (SI 1986/1032 (NI 6)	*Not in force*[200]
Schedule 10—Recognised Supervisory Bodies	
Part 1—Grant and Revocation of Recognition of a Supervisory Body	6 Apr 2008 (CO No 5)[102]
Part 2—Requirements for Recognition of a Supervisory Body	6 Apr 2008 (CO No 5)[102]
Part 3—Arrangements in which Recognised Supervisory Bodies are Required to Participate	6 Apr 2008 (CO No 5)[102]
Schedule 11—Recognised Professional Qualifications	
Part 1—Grant and Revocation of Recognition of a Professional Qualification	6 Apr 2008 (CO No 5)[102]
Part 2—Requirements for Recognition of a Professional Qualification	20 Jan 2007 (certain purposes) (CO No 1)[3]
	6 Apr 2008 (otherwise) (CO No 5)[102]
Schedule 11A—Specified Persons, Descriptions, Disclosures etc for the Purposes of Section 1224A[119]	
Part 1—Specified Persons	6 Apr 2008
Part 2—Specified Descriptions of Disclosures	6 Apr 2008
Part 3—Overseas Regulatory Bodies	6 Apr 2008
Schedule 12—Arrangements in which Registered Third Country Auditors are Required to Participate	20 Jan 2007 (certain purposes) (CO No 1)[3]
	29 Jun 2008 (otherwise) (CO No 5)[110]
Schedule 13—Supplementary Provisions with Respect to Delegation Order	20 Jan 2007 (certain purposes) (CO No 1)[3]
	6 Apr 2008 (otherwise) (CO No 5)
Schedule 14—Statutory Auditors: Consequential Amendments	6 Apr 2008 (CO No 5)
Schedule 15—Transparency Obligations and Related Matters: Minor and Consequential Amendments	
Part 1—Amendments of the Financial Services and Markets Act 2000	8 Nov 2006 (certain purposes) (RA)
	1 Oct 2008 (otherwise)[65]
Part 2—Amendments of the Companies (Audit, Investigations and Community Enterprise) Act 2004	8 Nov 2006 (RA)
Schedule 16—Repeals	1 Jan 2007 (in part) (CO No 1)
	20 Jan 2007 (in part) (CO No 1)
	6 Apr 2007 (in part) (CO No 1 & CO No 2)
	1 Oct 2007 (in part) (CO No 3)
	1 Apr 2008 (in part) (CO No 5 & CO No 6)
	1 Oct 2008 (in part) (CO No 5 & CO No 7)
	1 Oct 2009 (in part) (CO No 8)[69]

Part 2   CA 2006 commencement etc

NOTES

1   CO No 1, arts 2(2), 3(2) provide that this section shall come into force on 1 Jan 2007 and 20 Jan 2007 respectively so far as is necessary for the purposes of the provisions of this Act brought into force on those dates by that Order (see **[2.2]**, **[2.3]**). For transitional adaptations of s 2, see CO No 1, Sch 1, para 1 (at **[2.9]**).

2   For transitional adaptations of s 2, see CO No 2, Sch 1, para 1 (at **[2.27]**).

3   CO No 1, art 3(3) provides that the provisions CA 2006, in so far as not brought into force by s 1300(1) of that Act, or arts 2, 3(1), (2) of that Order, come into force on 20 Jan 2007 for the purpose of enabling the exercise of powers to make Orders or Regulations by statutory instrument.

4   CO No 3, art 2(3) provides that this section shall come into force on 1 Oct 2007 so far as is necessary for the purposes of the provisions of this Act brought into force on that date by art 2(1), (2) of that Order (see **[2.32]**). For transitional adaptations of ss 17, 1158, see CO No 3, Sch 1, paras 1, 21.

5   For transitional provisions, see CO No 3, Sch 3, para 1 (at **[2.45]**).

6   For transitional provisions, see CO No 3, Sch 3, para 2 (at **[2.45]**). For transitional adaptations of s 116, see CO No 3, Sch 1, para 2 (at **[2.43]**).

7   For transitional provisions, see CO No 3, Sch 3, para 3 (at **[2.45]**). For transitional adaptations of ss 145, 146, 153, see CO No 3, Sch 1, paras 3–5 (at **[2.43]**).

8   For transitional provisions, see CO No 3, Sch 3, para 4 (at **[2.45]**).

9   For transitional provisions, see CO No 3, Sch 3, para 5 (at **[2.45]**).

10   For transitional adaptations of ss 170, 178, 181, see CO No 3, Sch 1, paras 6–9 (at **[2.43]**).

10a   For transitional adaptations of s 180, see CO No 3, Sch 1, para 8 (at **[2.43]**). For transitional provisions, see CO No 5, Sch 4, Pt 3, para 49 (at **[2.68]**).

11   For transitional provisions, see CO No 3, Sch 3, para 6 (at **[2.45]**).

12   For transitional provisions, see CO No 3, Sch 3, para 7 (at **[2.45]**). For transitional adaptations of s 191, see CO No 3, Sch 1, para 10 (at **[2.43]**).

13   For transitional provisions, see CO No 3, Sch 3, paras 8–11 (at **[2.45]**). For transitional adaptations of s 205, see CO No 3, Sch 1, para 11 (at **[2.43]**) and CO No 5, Sch 1, Pt 1, para 1 (at **[2.62]**).

14   For transitional provisions, see CO No 3, Sch 3, para 12 (at **[2.45]**).

15   For transitional provisions, see CO No 3, Sch 3, para 13 (at **[2.45]**).

16   For transitional provisions, see CO No 3, Sch 3, para 14 (at **[2.45]**).

17   For transitional provisions, see CO No 3, Sch 3, para 15 (at **[2.45]**). For transitional adaptations of s 234, see CO No 3, Sch 1, para 12 (at **[2.43]**) and CO No 5, Sch 1, Pt 1, para 2 (at **[2.62]**).

18   For transitional provisions, see CO No 3, Sch 3, para 16 (at **[2.45]**).

19   For transitional provisions, see CO No 3, Sch 3, para 17 (at **[2.45]**).

20   CO No 3, art 2(1)(d) originally provided that s 247 would come into force on 1 October 2007 (subject to transitional provisions in Sch 3, para 18 to that Order). Article 2(1)(d) was subsequently amended by CO No 4, art 4(1) (with effect from 30 September 2007) so that the commencement of this section on 1 October 2007 was reversed. The transitional provisions in Sch 3, para 18 were revoked at the same time. This section was subsequently commenced by CO No 8 (for transitional provisions see Sch 2, para 40 to that Order at **[2.91]**).

21   For transitional provisions, see CO No 3, Sch 3, para 19 (at **[2.45]**).

22   For transitional provisions, see CO No 3, Sch 3, paras 20, 21 (at **[2.45]**).

23   For transitional provisions, see CO No 3, Sch 3, paras 22, 23 (at **[2.45]**).

24   For transitional provisions, see CO No 3, Sch 3, para 24 (at **[2.45]**). For transitional adaptations of s 288 and the transitional insertion of ss 300A–300D, see CO No 3, Sch 1, para 13 (at **[2.43]**).

25   For transitional provisions, see CO No 3, Sch 3, para 25 (at **[2.45]**).

26   For transitional adaptations of s 306, see CO No 3, Sch 1, para 14 (at **[2.43]**).

27   For transitional provisions, see CO No 3, Sch 3, para 26 (at **[2.45]**).

28   For transitional provisions, see CO No 3, Sch 3, para 27 (at **[2.45]**).

29   For transitional provisions, see CO No 3, Sch 3, para 28 (at **[2.45]**).

30   For transitional provisions, see CO No 3, Sch 3, para 29 (at **[2.45]**).

31   For transitional provisions, see CO No 3, Sch 3, para 30 (at **[2.45]**).

32   For transitional provisions, see CO No 3, Sch 3, para 31 (at **[2.45]**).

33   For transitional provisions, see CO No 3, Sch 3, paras 32–38 (at **[2.45]**). For transitional adaptations of s 336, see CO No 3, Sch 1, para 15 (at **[2.43]**).

34   For transitional provisions, see CO No 3, Sch 3, para 39 (at **[2.45]**).

35   For transitional provisions, see CO No 3, Sch 3, para 40 (at **[2.45]**).

36   CO No 3, arts 2(2), 3(1) (at **[2.32]**, **[2.33]**) provide that Part 14 shall come into force on 1 Oct 2007 (in relation to Great Britain) and 1 Nov 2007 (in relation to Northern Ireland) except in so far as it relates to independent election candidates. Article 5 of that Order specifies certain words in ss 362–367, 378 which, accordingly, do not come into force until 1 Oct 2008. For transitional provisions in connection with the commencement of all of Part 14, see CO No 3, Sch 3, paras 41, 42.

37   For transitional provisions, see CO No 3, Sch 3, para 43 (at **[2.45]**). For transitional adaptations of s 417, see CO No 3, Sch 1, para 16.

³⁸   For transitional provisions, see CO No 1, Sch 5, Pt 2, para 3 (at **[2.14]**).

³⁹   For transitional provisions, see CO No 3, Sch 3, paras 44, 45 (at **[2.45]**). For transitional adaptations of ss 485, 487, see CO No 3, Sch 1, paras 17, 18 (at **[2.43]**).

⁴⁰   CO No 3, art 2(3) provides that sub-ss (1), (4) shall come into force on 1 Oct 2007 so far as is necessary for the purposes of the provisions of this Act brought into force on that date by art 2(1), (2) of that Order (see **[2.32]**).

⁴¹   CO No 2, art 2(2) provides that this section shall come into force on 6 Apr 2007 so far as is necessary for the purposes of the provisions of this Act brought into force on that date by that Order (see **[2.17]**). For transitional adaptations of s 1139, see CO No 2, Sch 1, para 5 (at **[2.27]**).

⁴²   CO No 3, art 3(2) provides that this section shall come into force on 1 Nov 2007 so far as is necessary for the purposes of the provisions of this Act brought into force on that date by art 3(1) of that Order (see **[2.33]**). For transitional adaptations of s 1158, see CO No 3, Sch 1, para 21.

⁴³   For transitional adaptations of ss 813, 826, 1143, see CO No 1, Sch 1, paras 2, 3 14, (at **[2.9]**).

⁴⁴   For transitional adaptations of ss 943, 953, see CO No 2, Sch 1, paras 2, 3 (at **[2.27]**).

⁴⁵   For transitional adaptations of s 968, see CO No 2, Sch 1, para 4 (at **[2.27]**).

⁴⁶   For transitional provisions, see CO No 3, Sch 3, para 46 (at **[2.45]**).

⁴⁷   For transitional adaptations of s 994, see CO No 3, Sch 1, para 19 (at **[2.43]**).

⁴⁸   For transitional provisions, see CO No 3, Sch 3, para 47 (at **[2.45]**).

⁴⁹   For transitional provisions, see CO No 3, Sch 3, para 48 (at **[2.45]**).

⁵⁰   CO No 1, art 4(3) provides that this section shall come into force on 6 Apr 2007 so far as is necessary for the purposes of the provisions of this Act brought into force on that date by that Order (see **[2.4]**).

⁵¹   For transitional provisions, see CO No 1, Sch 5, Pt 3, para 6 (at **[2.15]**). Note also that the commencement of this section on 6 Apr 2007 by CO No 1 does not extend to Northern Ireland (see art 4(4) of that Order at **[2.4]**).

⁵²   CO No 1, art 2(2) provides that sub-ss (1)–(4), (6), (7) shall come into force on 1 Jan 2007 so far as is necessary for the purposes of the provisions of this Act brought into force on that date by that Order (see **[2.2]**).

⁵³   CO No 3, art 4(1) (as amended by SI 2007/2974) provides that sub-ss (1)–(4), (6), (7) shall come into force on 15 Dec 2007 so far as necessary for the purposes of the Companies (Cross-Border Mergers) Regulations 2007 (see **[2.34]**).

⁵⁴   For transitional adaptations of ss 1077, 1080, 1085, 1087, 1103, see CO No 1, Sch 1, paras 4, 7–10 (at **[2.9]**).

^{54a}   For transitional adaptations of s 1104, see CO No 1, Sch 1, para 11 (at **[2.9]**). For savings in relation to the Companies (Welsh Language Forms and Documents) Regulations 1994, see CO No 1, Sch 5, para 1 (at **[2.13]**).

^{54b}   For savings in relation to the Companies (Welsh Language Forms and Documents) Regulations 1994, see CO No 1, Sch 5, para 1 (at **[2.13]**).

⁵⁵   For transitional adaptations of s 1105, see CO No 1, Sch 1, para 12 (at **[2.9]**).

⁵⁶   CO No 1, art 2(2) provides that this section shall come into force on 1 Jan 2007 so far as is necessary for the purposes of the provisions of this Act brought into force on that date by that Order (see **[2.2]**). For transitional adaptations of s 1120, see CO No 1, Sch 1, para 13 (at **[2.9]**).

⁵⁷   CO No 1, art 3(2) provides that this section shall come into force on 20 Jan 2007 so far as is necessary for the purposes of the provisions of this Act brought into force on that date by that Order (see **[2.3]**).

⁵⁸   CO No 3, art 2(1)(l) provides that ss 1121–1123, 1125–1133 shall come into force on 1 Oct 2007 in so far as applying to offences under CA 1985, Pts XIV, XV. Article 2(3)(h) of that Order further provides that ss 1121, 1122, 1125, 1127–1133 shall come into force on the same date so far as is necessary for the purposes of the provisions of this Act brought into force on that date by art 2(1), (2) of that Order (see **[2.32]**).

⁵⁹   CO No 1, arts 2(2), 3(2) provide that this section shall come into force on 1 Jan 2007 and 20 Jan 2007 respectively so far as is necessary for the purposes of the provisions of this Act brought into force on those dates by that Order (see **[2.2]**, **[2.3]**).

⁶⁰   CO No 3, art 4(2) provides that this section shall come into force on 15 Dec 2007 so far as is necessary for the purposes of the provisions of this Act brought into force on that date by art 4(1) of that Order (see **[2.34]**).

⁶¹   CO No 1, arts 2(2), 3(2) provide that specified definitions in this section shall come into force on 1 Jan 2007 and 20 Jan 2007 respectively so far as is necessary for the purposes of the provisions of this Act brought into force on those dates by that Order (see **[2.2]**, **[2.3]**).

⁶²   CO No 2, art 2(2) provides that specified definitions in this section shall come into force on 6 Apr 2007 so far as is necessary for the purposes of the provisions of this Act brought into force on that date by that Order (see **[2.17]**).

⁶³   CO No 3, art 2(3) provides that specified definitions in this section shall come into force on 1 Oct 2007 so far as is necessary for the purposes of the provisions of this Act brought into force on that date by art 2(1), (2) of that Order (see **[2.32]**).

⁶⁴   CO No 3, art 3(2) provides that specified definitions in this section shall come into force on 1 Nov 2007 so far as is necessary for the purposes of the provisions of this Act brought into force on that date by art 3(1) of that Order (see **[2.33]**).

⁶⁵   Part 43 (ss 1265–1273, Sch 15) came into force on Royal Assent except in so far as relating to the amendment in Sch 15, Pt 1, para 11(2) to this Act to the definition of "regulated market" in FSMA 2000, s 103; see s 1300 of this Act (at **[1.1300]**). Sch 15, Pt 1, para 11(2) (and s 1272 in so far as it introduces Sch 15) was brought into force on 1 Oct 2008 by CO No 7 (see **[2.76]**).

⁶⁶   CO No 1, arts 2(2), 3(2), 4(3) provide that this section shall come into force on 1 Jan 2007, 20 Jan 2007 and 6 Apr 2007 respectively so far as is necessary for the purposes of the provisions of this Act brought into force on those dates by that Order (see **[2.2]**–**[2.4]**). For transitional adaptations of s 1284, see CO No 1, Sch 1, para 15 (at **[2.9]**). CO No 2, art 2(1)(e) also provides that s 1284(1) comes into force on 6 Apr 2007 so far as relating to the provisions commenced

Part 2   CA 2006 commencement etc

by art 2(1)(a)–(c) of that Order and in so far as it relates to Part 2 of the Companies (Audit, Investigations and Community Enterprise) Act 2004. CO No 2, art 5 (at **[2.20]**) further provides that s 1284(2) comes into force on 6 Apr 2007 in so far as relating to the repeals specified in Sch 2 to that Order (at **[2.28]** et seq). CO No 3, arts 2(4), 3(2), 4(2) and 5(2) provide that this section shall come into force on 1 Oct 2007, 1 Nov 2007, 15 Dec 2007 and 1 Oct 2008 so far as is necessary for the purposes of the provisions of this Act brought into force on those dates by arts 2(1)(a)–(j), 3(1), 4(1) and 5(1) of that Order respectively (see **[2.32]**–**[2.35]**). CO No 3, art 8 (at **[2.38]**) further provides that s 1284(2) comes into force on 1 Oct 2007 in so far as relating to the repeals specified in Sch 2 to that Order. CO No 5, arts 3(5), 5(4) provide that this section shall come into force on 6 Apr 2008 and 1 Oct 2008 respectively so far as is necessary for the purposes of the provisions of this Act brought into force on those dates by arts 3(1)(a)–(t), (2), (3), 5(1)–(3) of that Order (see **[2.52]**, **[2.54]**). CO No 7, art 2(d) provides that sub-s (1) shall come into force on 1 Oct 2008 so far as is necessary for the purposes of the provisions of this Act brought into force on that date by art 2(a)–(c) of that Order (see **[2.76]**). CO No 8, art 3 brings this section into force in 1 Oct 2009 for all remaining purposes; for transitional provisions, see Sch 2, para 114 to that Order (at **[2.91]**).

67 For transitional adaptations of Sch 3, see CO No 3, Sch 1, para 20 (at **[2.43]**).

68 For transitional provisions, see CO No 1, Sch 5, Pt 2, paras 4, 5 (at **[2.14]**). For transitional adaptations of Sch 5, Pt 4, see CO No 1, Sch 1, para 16 (at **[2.9]**).

69 For details of the commencement of Sch 16 (Repeals) see that Schedule (at **[1.1331]**).

70 For transitional provisions, see CO No 1, Sch 5, Pt 2, para 2(3), (4) (at **[2.14]**).

71 For transitional provisions, see CO No 5, Sch 4, Pt 1, para 1 (at **[2.66]**).

72 For transitional provisions, see CO No 5, Sch 4, Pt 1, para 2 (at **[2.66]**).

73 For transitional provisions, see CO No 5, Sch 4, Pt 1, para 3 (at **[2.66]**).

74 For transitional provisions, see CO No 5, Sch 4, Pt 1, para 4 (at **[2.66]**). For transitional adaptations, see CO No 5, Sch 1, Pt 1, para 3 (at **[2.62]**).

75 For transitional adaptations, see CO No 5, Sch 1, Pt 1, paras 4, 5 (at **[2.62]**).

76 For transitional provisions, see CO No 5, Sch 4, Pt 1, para 5 (at **[2.66]**).

77 For transitional provisions, see CO No 5, Sch 4, Pt 1, paras 6–8 (at **[2.66]**). For transitional adaptations of ss 444–447, 449, see CO No 5, Sch 1, Pt 1, paras 6–10 (at **[2.62]**).

78 For transitional provisions, see CO No 5, Sch 4, Pt 1, para 9 (at **[2.66]**).

79 For transitional provisions, see CO No 5, Sch 4, Pt 1, paras 10, 11 (at **[2.66]**).

80 For transitional provisions, see CO No 5, Sch 4, Pt 1, para 12 (at **[2.66]**).

81 For transitional provisions, see CO No 5, Sch 4, Pt 1, paras 13–17 (at **[2.66]**).

82 For transitional provisions, see CO No 5, Sch 4, Pt 1, para 18 (at **[2.66]**).

83 For transitional provisions, see CO No 5, Sch 4, Pt 1, para 19 (at **[2.66]**).

84 For transitional provisions, see CO No 5, Sch 4, Pt 1, para 20 (at **[2.66]**).

85 For transitional provisions, see CO No 5, Sch 4, Pt 1, para 21 (at **[2.66]**).

86 For transitional provisions, see CO No 5, Sch 4, Pt 1, para 22 (at **[2.66]**).

87 For transitional provisions, see CO No 5, Sch 4, Pt 1, para 23 (at **[2.66]**).

88 For transitional provisions, see CO No 5, Sch 4, Pt 1, para 24 (at **[2.66]**).

89 For transitional provisions, see CO No 5, Sch 4, Pt 1, para 25 (at **[2.66]**).

90 For transitional provisions, see CO No 5, Sch 4, Pt 1, para 26 (at **[2.66]**).

91 For transitional provisions, see CO No 5, Sch 4, Pt 1, paras 27, 28 (at **[2.66]**).

92 For transitional adaptations, see CO No 5, Sch 1, Pt 1, paras 12, 13 (at **[2.62]**).

93 For transitional provisions, see CO No 5, Sch 4, Pt 1, para 29 (at **[2.66]**).

94 For transitional provisions, see CO No 5, Sch 4, Pt 1, para 30 (at **[2.66]**).

95 For transitional provisions, see CO No 5, Sch 4, Pt 1, para 31 (at **[2.66]**).

96 For transitional provisions, see CO No 5, Sch 4, Pt 1, para 32 (at **[2.66]**).

97 For transitional provisions, see CO No 5, Sch 4, Pt 1, paras 33–35 (at **[2.66]**). For transitional adaptations of ss 829, 832, 833, 838–840, 847, see CO No 5, Sch 1, Pt 1, paras 14–20 (at **[2.62]**).

98 For transitional provisions, see CO No 5, Sch 4, Pt 1, para 36 (at **[2.66]**).

99 For transitional adaptations, see CO No 5, Sch 1, Pt 1, para 21 (at **[2.62]**).

100 Certain specified definitions come into force on 6 Apr 2008 (see CO No 5, art 3(1)(t) at **[2.52]**). Also, arts 3(3)(j) and 5(3)(c) of that Order provide that specified definitions in this section shall come into force on 6 Apr 2008 and 1 Oct 2008 respectively so far as is necessary for the purposes of the provisions of this Act brought into force on those dates by arts 3(1)(a)–(t), (2), 5(1)(a)–(f) of that Order (see **[2.52]**, **[2.54]**).

101 For transitional provisions, see CO No 5, Sch 4, Pt 1, para 37 (at **[2.66]**).

102 For transitional provisions, see CO No 5, Sch 4, Pt 1, para 38 (at **[2.66]**).

103 For transitional provisions, see CO No 5, Sch 4, Pt 1, para 40 (at **[2.66]**).

104 For transitional provisions, see CO No 5, Sch 4, Pt 1, para 41 (at **[2.66]**).

105 For transitional provisions, see CO No 5, Sch 4, Pt 1, para 43 (at **[2.66]**).

106 CO No 5, art 3(2) (at **[2.52]**) provides that sub-ss (1), (2) come into force on 6 April 2008 so far as may be necessary for the purpose of enabling rules to be made under this section before the date on which the section is brought generally into force, and sub-s (3) has effect accordingly.

107   CO No 5, art 3(3)(a)–(f), (h) provides that this section shall come into force on 6 Apr 2008 so far as is necessary for the purposes of the provisions of this Act brought into force on that date by art 3(1)(a)–(t), (2) of that Order (see **[2.52]**).

108   CO No 5, arts 3(3)(g), (i), 5(3)(a), (b) provide that this section shall come into force on 6 Apr 2008 and 1 Oct 2008 respectively so far as is necessary for the purposes of the provisions of this Act brought into force on those dates by arts 3(1)(a)–(t), (2), 5(1)(a)–(f) of that Order (see **[2.52]**, **[2.54]**).

109   CO No 5, art 3(4) provides that ss 1159, 1160 and Sch 6 shall come into force on 6 Apr 2008 so far as is necessary for the purposes of the provisions of this Act brought into force on that date by art 3(1)(u) of that Order (see **[2.52]**).

110   For transitional provisions, see CO No 5, Sch 4, Pt 2, para 45 (at **[2.67]**).

111   For transitional adaptations, see CO No 5, Sch 1, Pt 2, para 22 (at **[2.63]**).

112   For transitional adaptations, see CO No 5, Sch 1, Pt 2, para 23 (at **[2.63]**).

113   For transitional provisions, see CO No 5, Sch 4, Pt 3, para 46 (at **[2.68]**).

114   For transitional adaptations, see CO No 5, Sch 1, Pt 2, para 24 (at **[2.63]**).

115   For transitional provisions, see CO No 5, Sch 4, Pt 3, para 47 (at **[2.68]**).

116   For transitional provisions, see CO No 5, Sch 4, Pt 3, para 48 (at **[2.68]**).

117   For transitional provisions, see CO No 5, Sch 4, Pt 3, paras 47(4), 50 (at **[2.68]**).

118   CO No 3, art 2(1)(d) (at **[2.32]**) brings into force ss 254, 255 of this Act (the enabling sections for this Schedule) on 1 Oct 2007. Although not specifically mentioned in that commencement order, it is believed that the intention was also to bring Sch 1 into force on the same date.

119   Inserted by SI 2007/3494 (subject, in certain cases, to transitional provisions contained in those Regulations).

120   CO No 6, art 3(1)(a) provides that this section shall come into force on 1 Apr 2008 in so far as it relates to CA 1985, Pt VII. For transitional provisions see art 3(2), (3) of that Order (at **[2.71]**).

121   For transitional provisions see CO No 6, art 3(2), (3) (at **[2.71]**).

122   Inserted by SI 2008/393, in relation to financial years beginning on or after 6 April 2008.

123   Inserted by SI 2008/690.

124   For transitional adaptations, see CO No 5, Sch 1, Pt 1, para 11 (at **[2.62]**).

125   For transitional adaptations, see CO No 7, arts 3, 4 (at **[2.77]**, **[2.78]**).

126   For transitional provisions see CO No 7, art 7(2) (at **[2.81]**).

127   CO No 7, art 2(c) provides that ss 610(2)–(4), 652(1), (3), 733(5), (6) shall come into force on 1 Oct 2008 in so far as relating to a reduction of capital under ss 641(1)(a), (2)–(6) and 642–644 (see **[2.76]**). For transitional adaptations of s 652, see art 5 of that Order (at **[2.79]**).

128   CO No 7, art 2(e) provides s 1286(1)(a), (2)(a) shall come into force on 1 Oct 2008 in so far as relating to the application to LLPs of the subject matter of Pt 15 (accounts and reports), Pt 16 (audit) and Pt 42 (statutory auditors) (see **[2.76]**). This applies in relation to accounts and the audit of accounts for financial years beginning on or after that date (see art 7(3) at **[2.81]**).

129   For transitional provisions, see CO No 8, Sch 2, para 2 (at **[2.91]**).

130   For transitional provisions, see CO No 8, Sch 2, para 3 (at **[2.91]**).

131   For transitional provisions, see CO No 8, Sch 2, para 4 (at **[2.91]**).

132   For transitional provisions, see CO No 8, Sch 2, para 5 (at **[2.91]**).

133   For transitional provisions, see CO No 8, Sch 2, para 6 (at **[2.91]**).

134   For transitional provisions, see CO No 8, Sch 2, paras 7–10 (at **[2.91]**).

135   For transitional provisions, see CO No 8, Sch 2, para 11 (at **[2.91]**).

136   For transitional provisions, see CO No 8, Sch 2, para 12 (at **[2.91]**).

137   For transitional provisions, see CO No 8, Sch 2, para 13 (at **[2.91]**).

138   For transitional provisions, see CO No 8, Sch 2, para 14 (at **[2.91]**).

139   For transitional provisions, see CO No 8, Sch 2, para 15 (at **[2.91]**).

140   For transitional provisions, see CO No 8, Sch 2, para 16 (at **[2.91]**).

141   For transitional provisions, see CO No 8, Sch 2, paras 17, 18 (at **[2.91]**).

142   For transitional provisions, see CO No 8, Sch 2, para 19 (at **[2.91]**).

143   For transitional provisions, see CO No 8, Sch 2, para 22 (at **[2.91]**).

144   For transitional provisions, see CO No 8, Sch 2, para 23 (at **[2.91]**).

145   For transitional provisions, see CO No 8, Sch 2, paras 25–39 (at **[2.91]**).

146   For transitional provisions, see CO No 8, Sch 2, para 41 (at **[2.91]**).

147   For transitional provisions, see CO No 8, Sch 2, paras 43, 44 (at **[2.91]**).

148   For transitional provisions, see CO No 8, Sch 2, para 45 (at **[2.91]**).

149   For transitional provisions, see CO No 8, Sch 2, para 46 (at **[2.91]**).

150   For transitional provisions, see CO No 8, Sch 2, paras 49–55 (at **[2.91]**).

151   For transitional provisions, see CO No 8, Sch 2, para 56 (at **[2.91]**).

152   For transitional provisions, see CO No 8, Sch 2, para 57 (at **[2.91]**).

153   For transitional provisions, see CO No 8, Sch 2, para 58 (at **[2.91]**).

154   For transitional provisions, see CO No 8, Sch 2, para 61 (at **[2.91]**).

Part 2   CA 2006 commencement etc

155 For transitional provisions, see CO No 8, Sch 2, para 62 (at **[2.91]**).

156 For transitional provisions, see CO No 8, Sch 2, para 63 (at **[2.91]**).

157 For transitional provisions, see CO No 8, Sch 2, para 64 (at **[2.91]**).

158 For transitional provisions, see CO No 8, Sch 2, para 65 (at **[2.91]**).

159 For transitional provisions, see CO No 8, Sch 2, para 66 (at **[2.91]**).

160 For transitional provisions, see CO No 8, Sch 2, para 68 (at **[2.91]**).

161 For transitional provisions, see CO No 8, Sch 2, para 69 (at **[2.91]**).

162 For transitional provisions, see CO No 8, Sch 2, paras 70–72 (at **[2.91]**).

163 For transitional provisions, see CO No 8, Sch 2, para 73 (at **[2.91]**).

164 For transitional provisions, see CO No 8, Sch 2, para 74 (at **[2.91]**).

165 For transitional provisions, see CO No 8, Sch 2, paras 75, 76 (at **[2.91]**).

166 For transitional provisions, see CO No 8, Sch 2, para 77 (at **[2.91]**).

167 For transitional provisions, see CO No 8, Sch 2, para 78 (at **[2.91]**).

168 For transitional provisions, see CO No 8, Sch 2, para 79 (at **[2.91]**).

169 For transitional provisions, see CO No 8, Sch 2, para 80 (at **[2.91]**).

170 For transitional provisions, see CO No 8, Sch 2, para 81 (at **[2.91]**).

171 For transitional provisions, see CO No 8, Sch 2, para 82 (at **[2.91]**).

172 For transitional provisions, see CO No 8, Sch 2, para 83 (at **[2.91]**).

173 For transitional provisions, see CO No 8, Sch 2, para 84 (at **[2.91]**).

174 For transitional provisions, see CO No 8, Sch 2, para 85 (at **[2.91]**).

175 For transitional provisions, see CO No 8, Sch 2, para 86 (at **[2.91]**).

176 For transitional provisions, see CO No 8, Sch 2, para 87 (at **[2.91]**).

177 For transitional provisions, see CO No 8, Sch 2, para 88 (at **[2.91]**).

178 For transitional provisions, see CO No 8, Sch 2, paras 90, 91 (at **[2.91]**).

179 For transitional provisions, see CO No 8, Sch 2, para 92 (at **[2.91]**).

180 For transitional provisions, see CO No 8, Sch 2, para 93 (at **[2.91]**).

181 For transitional provisions, see CO No 8, Sch 2, para 94 (at **[2.91]**).

182 For transitional provisions, see CO No 8, Sch 2, para 95 (at **[2.91]**).

183 For transitional provisions, see CO No 8, Sch 2, para 96 (at **[2.91]**).

184 For transitional provisions, see CO No 8, Sch 2, para 97 (at **[2.91]**).

185 For transitional provisions, see CO No 8, Sch 2, para 98 (at **[2.91]**).

186 For transitional provisions, see CO No 8, Sch 2, para 99 (at **[2.91]**).

187 For transitional provisions, see CO No 8, Sch 2, para 100 (at **[2.91]**).

188 For transitional provisions, see CO No 8, Sch 2, para 101 (at **[2.91]**).

189 For transitional provisions, see CO No 8, Sch 2, para 102 (at **[2.91]**).

190 For transitional adaptations of ss 1078, 1079, see CO No 1, Sch 1, paras 5, 6 (at **[2.9]**). For savings in relation to those transitional adaptations, see CO No 8, Sch 2, paras 103, 104 (at **[2.91]**).

191 For transitional provisions, see CO No 8, Sch 2, para 105 (at **[2.91]**).

192 For transitional provisions, see CO No 8, Sch 2, para 106 (at **[2.91]**).

193 For transitional provisions, see CO No 8, Sch 2, para 107 (at **[2.91]**).

194 For transitional provisions, see CO No 8, Sch 2, para 108 (at **[2.91]**).

195 For transitional provisions, see CO No 8, Sch 2, para 109 (at **[2.91]**).

196 For transitional provisions, see CO No 8, art 7 at **[2.88]**, and Sch 2, para 116 (at **[2.91]**).

197 For transitional provisions, see CO No 8, Sch 2, para 112 (at **[2.91]**).

198 Inserted by SI 2008/3000, in relation to annual returns made up to 1 Oct 2009 or a later date.

199 Inserted by SI 2009/1581, in relation to financial years beginning on or after 29 Jun 2008 which have not ended before the date of coming into force of the 2009 Regulations.

200 The government have announced that they do not intend to commence ss 327(2)(c), 330(6)(c), 1175 (in so far as relating to Northern Ireland) or Sch 9, Pt 2, and that they will be repealed in due course; see the written ministerial statements for 6 November 2008.

201 Section 566 was subsequently substituted by SI 2009/2561, as from 1 Oct 2009.

202 The section name (or, as the case may be, other heading) has subsequently been amended; for details, see the 2006 Act as set out in Part 1 of this Handbook.

203 Repealed by SI 2008/3000, as from 1 Oct 2009.

204 Sections 285, 285A were subsequently substituted (for the original s 285) by SI 2009/1632, as from 3 Aug 2009, in relation to meetings of which notice is given, or first given, on or after that date.

205 Inserted by SI 2009/1632, in relation to meetings of which notice is given, or first given, on or after 3 Aug 2009

206 Inserted by SI 2009/1802.

²⁰⁷   Repealed by SI 2009/1802, as from 1 Oct 2009.

²⁰⁸   Repealed by SI 2009/2022, as from 1 Oct 2009.

²⁰⁹   For transitional provisions, see CO No 8, Sch 2, para 4 (at **[2.91]**). Note also that sub-s (2) was originally scheduled to come into force on 1 Oct 2009. CO No 8 was amended by SI 2009/2476 (as from 30 Sept 2009) to stop this happening. See the note for those Regulations at **[4.629]**.

²¹⁰   Inserted by SI 2009/1941.

²¹¹   Sections 914, 930 were subsequently substituted by SI 2008/690, as from 6 Apr 2008.

²¹²   Section 1201 was subsequently substituted by SI 2009/3182, as from 28 Dec 2009.

²¹³   Sch 2 was subsequently substituted by SI 2009/1208, as from 1 Jul 2009.

²¹⁴   Sections 1253D, 1253DA–1253DE were subsequently substituted (for the original s 1253D) by SI 2010/2537, as from 15 Nov 2010. Section 1253D was originally inserted by SI 2007/3494.

²¹⁵   Section 1253E was subsequently substituted by SI 2010/2537, as from 15 Nov 2010. It was originally inserted by SI 2007/3494.

Part 2   CA 2006 commencement etc

PART 3
COMPANIES ACT 2006: SUPPORTING MATERIALS

COMPANIES ACT 2006
EXPLANATORY NOTES

NOTES

These Notes refer to the Companies Act 2006 (c 46) which received royal assent on 8 November 2006.

INTRODUCTION

[3.1]

1. These explanatory notes relate to the Companies Act 2006 (c 46) which received Royal Assent on 8 November 2006. They have been prepared by the Department of Trade and Industry (DTI) in order to assist the reader in understanding the Act. They do not form part of the Act and have not been endorsed by Parliament.

2. The notes need to be read in conjunction with the Act. They are not, and are not meant to be, a comprehensive description of the Act. So where a section or part of a section does not seem to require any explanation or comment, none is given. Further, where provisions in the Act restate what was in the Companies Act 1985 (the 1985 Act) an explanation is not always given, except to the extent required to explain changes to associated provisions.

Background

3. The UK was one of the first nations to establish rules for the operation of companies. Today our system of company law and corporate governance, setting out the legal basis on which companies are formed and run, is a vital part of the legal framework within which business is conducted. As the business environment evolves, there is a risk that the legal framework can become gradually divorced from the needs of companies, in particular the needs of smaller private businesses, creating obstacles to ways that companies want and need to operate.

4. In March 1998, the DTI commissioned a fundamental review of company law. An independent Steering Group led the "Company Law Review" (CLR) whose terms of reference required them to consider how core company law could be modernised in order to provide a simple, efficient and cost effective framework for British business in the twenty-first century. After extensive consultation with interested parties, the CLR presented its Final Report to the Secretary of State for Trade and Industry on 26 July 2001. The report contained a range of recommendations for substantive changes to many areas of company law, and a set of principles to guide the development of the law more generally, most notably that it should be as simple and as accessible as possible for smaller firms and their advisers and should avoid imposing unnecessary burdens on the ways companies operate.

5. Many of the provisions of the Act implement CLR recommendations. The Government set out and consulted on its intentions in this regard in the White Papers "Modernising Company Law" (July 2002) and "Company Law Reform" (March 2005). The 2005 White Paper included approximately 300 draft clauses and described in detail the policy intention for other areas. Further clauses were made publicly available for comment in July, September and October 2005. The Companies Bill, then titled the Company Law Reform Bill, was introduced to the House of Lords on 4 November 2005.

Overview Of The Structure Of The Act

6. The general arrangement of the Act is as follows:

PART	SUMMARY
Parts 1 to 7	The fundamentals of what a company is, how it can be formed and what it can be called.
Parts 8 to 12	The members (shareholders) and officers (management) of a company
Parts 13 and 14	How companies may take decisions
Parts 15 and 16	The safeguards for ensuring that the officers of a company are accountable to its members
Parts 17 to 25	Raising share capital, capital maintenance, annual returns, and company charges
Parts 26 to 28	Company reconstructions, mergers and takeovers
Parts 29 to 39	The regulatory framework, application to companies not formed under the Companies Acts and other company law provisions
Parts 40 to 42	Overseas disqualification of directors, business names and statutory auditors
Part 43	Transparency obligations
Parts 44 to 47	Miscellaneous and general

Summary Of Legislative Changes

7.   The company law provisions of the 2006 Act (Parts 1 to 39) restate almost all of the provisions of the 1985 Act, together with the company law provisions of the Companies Act 1989 (the 1989 Act) and the Companies (Audit, Investigations and Community Enterprise) Act 2004 (C(AICE) Act 2004). Paragraphs 9 and 10 below contain details of the provisions that remain in those Acts. The company law provisions also codify certain aspects of the case law.

8.   Tables of origins and destinations are available that show the origins of the company law provisions of the Act by reference to enactments in force on 8 November 2006. The tables identify where provisions of the existing law have been re-enacted with or without changes and where provisions of the new law have no predecessor or are fundamentally different from their predecessors.

9.   Of company law provisions in the Acts referred to in paragraph 7, the only ones that remain are those on investigations that go wider than companies (Part 14 of the 1985 Act) and the provisions on community interest companies in Part 2 of the C(AICE) Act 2004.

10.   The non-company law provisions in those Acts that remain are:
(a)   Part 18 of the 1985 Act (floating charges and receivers (Scotland)),
(b)   Part 3 of the 1989 Act (powers to require information and documents to assist overseas regulatory authorities),
(c)   Section 112 to 116 of the 1989 Act (provisions about Scottish incorporated charities)
(d)   Part 7 of the 1989 Act (provisions about financial markets and insolvency)
(e)   Schedule 18 of the 1989 Act (amendments and savings consequential upon changes in the law made by the 1989 Act)
(f)   Sections 14 and 15 of the C(AICE) Act 2004 (supervision of accounts and reports), and
(g)   Sections 16 and 17 of the C(AICE) Act 2004 (bodies concerned with accounting standards etc).

11.   In non-company law areas the Act makes amendments to other legislation, in particular the Financial Services and Markets Act 2000, and also makes new provision of various kinds. The main areas in which provision of this kind is made are:
•   overseas disqualification of company directors (Part 40),
•   business names (Part 41) – replacing the Business Names Act 1985,
•   statutory auditors (Part 42) – replacing Part 2 of the Companies Act 1989, and
•   transparency obligations (Part 43) – amending Part 6 of the Financial Services and Markets Act 2000.

Territorial Extent And Devolution

Northern Ireland

12.   Company law is a transferred matter. Currently, the provisions of GB company law are generally replicated, sometime later, in separate Northern Ireland legislation. The Act provides for a single company law regime applying to the whole of the UK, so that companies will be UK companies rather than GB companies or Northern Ireland companies as at present. This does not affect the legislative competence of Northern Ireland: company law remains a transferred matter, and the Act could be separately amended or repealed in Northern Ireland if that were so desired.

13.   Where a note describes a particular section as restating or replacing a provision in the 1985 Act, the 1989 Act or the C(AICE) Act 2004, this should be read as applying equally to the corresponding provision of the Companies (Northern Ireland) Order 1986, the Companies (Northern Ireland) Order 1990 or the Companies (Audit, Investigations and Community Enterprise) Order 2005.

Scotland

14.   Company law is a reserved matter and Companies Acts extend to the whole of Great Britain. However, there are several areas where, in legislating about companies, the Act deals with matters that are devolved:
•   changes (in Part 41) to the regulation of business names (a devolved matter) – these correspond to changes (in Part 5) to the regulation of company names (a reserved matter);
•   statutory guidance to prosecutors and other enforcement authorities in relation to a new offence of knowingly or recklessly causing an audit report to be misleading, false or deceptive – although the offence itself is a reserved matter, guidance is to be issued by the Lord Advocate in Scotland (see section 509);
•   changes relating to exemptions from audit requirements for companies that are charities (see section 1175);
•   conferral of a power on the Auditor General for Scotland to specify public bodies for his audit (see section 483).

These were the subject of a legislative consent motion agreed to by the Scottish Parliament on 16 March 2006.

Wales

15. Company law is not transferred to the Welsh Assembly. There are no provisions that impact on devolved competences.

Crown Dependencies

16. Part 28 of the Act (takeovers) contains provision enabling it to be extended by Order in Council to the Isle of Man or any of the Channel Islands. This reflects the existing jurisdiction of the Takeover Panel (as the takeover regulator) and has been agreed by the relevant Island authorities. If the power were to be exercised, there would be further consultation with the Island authorities beforehand.

PART 1: GENERAL INTRODUCTORY PROVISIONS

Section 1: Companies

[3.2]
17. This section restates section 735(1)(a) and (b) of the 1985 Act. It defines "company" and provides signposts to provisions in the Act which relate to companies that are registered but not formed under the Act or former Companies Acts, to unregistered companies and to overseas companies.

Section 2: The Companies Acts

18. This section replaces section 744 of the 1985 Act. The Act does not restate or replace all existing companies legislation and section 2 makes it clear that any reference to "Companies Acts" in the Act includes those provisions of the Acts listed in subsection (1)(c) that remain in force as well as the company law provisions of the Act and Part 2 of the C(AICE) Act 2004.

19. The CLR recommended that the law should provide for the formation of new companies of each of the types that are currently available (Final Report, paragraph 9.2). This recommendation is taken forward in the following group of sections, which retains all of the current forms of companies.

Section 3: Limited and unlimited companies

20. This section restates section 1(2) of the 1985 Act. It updates the Companies Acts definitions of "limited company" and "unlimited company" to reflect changes to what is to be included in a company's memorandum of association (see section 8). As now, a company may be limited by shares or by guarantee. Where there is no limit on the liability of the company's members, a company is an "unlimited company."

Section 4: Private and public companies

21. This section restates section 1(3) of the 1985 Act. It provides definitions of "private company" and "public company."

22. A "private company" is any company that is not a public company.

23. A "public company" is a company whose certificate of incorporation states that it is a public company. To obtain this certificate the company will need to comply with the provisions of the Act (or former Companies Acts) as regards registration or re-registration as a public company. There is a minimum share capital requirement (the "authorised minimum"), which is currently set at £50,000, and remains unchanged under the Act. In future the authorised minimum will however be capable of being satisfied in sterling or the euro equivalent to the prescribed sterling amount (see Chapter 2 of Part 20).

24. Section 4 also provides a signpost to Part 20 of the Act, which sets out key differences between public and private companies, for example, a private company may not offer shares to the public.

Section 5: Companies limited by guarantee and having share capital

25. This section restates section 1(4) and section 15(2) of the 1985 Act. It makes it clear that a company can no longer be formed (or re-register) as a company limited by guarantee and with a share capital. This provision has been in force in Great Britain since 22nd December 1980 and in Northern Ireland since 1st July 1983.

Section 6: Community interest companies

26. The C(AICE) Act 2004 came fully into force on 1 July 2005. Part 2 of that Act created a new company vehicle, the "community interest company" or "c.i.c.", which is designed for use by social enterprises.

27. This section provides a signpost to the provisions in the C(AICE) Act, which enable a company to be formed as or become a community interest company. Such companies are registered under the same legislation as other registered companies, but have to complete certain additional formalities and are subject to certain additional elements of regulation. Subsection (2) of this section highlights the fact that in some respects the requirements imposed on community interest companies are different from the requirements imposed on other registered companies.

PART 2: COMPANY FORMATION

[3.3]
28.   This Part of the Act is about how companies are formed. It replaces or, as the case may be, restates equivalent provisions in the 1985 Act.

Section 7: Method of forming company

29.   This section replaces sections 1(1) of the 1985 Act. It retains the current requirement that individuals who wish to form a company must subscribe their names to the memorandum of association ("memorandum"). Subsection (1) introduces the new provisions about forming a company. In line with the recommendations of the CLR, it is provided that a single person is able to form any sort of company (not just a private company) (Final Report, paragraph 9.2).

30.   Subsection (2) reproduces the existing requirement that a company may not be formed for an unlawful purpose.

Section 8: Memorandum of association

31.   This section replaces section 3(1) of the 1985 Act.

32.   Under the Act, the memorandum serves a more limited, but nonetheless important, purpose: it evidences the intention of the subscribers to the memorandum to form a company and become members of that company on formation. In the case of a company that is to be limited by shares, the memorandum will also provide evidence of the members' agreement to take at least one share each in the company.

33.   The memorandum of a company formed under the Act will, therefore, look very different from that of a company registered under the 1985 Act. In addition it will not be possible to amend or update the memorandum of a company formed under the Act.

34.   These changes to the memorandum are based on the CLR's recommendation that there should be a single constitution (Final Report, paragraph 9.4). In line with the principles behind this recommendation, in future key information regarding the internal allocation of powers between the directors and members of a company will be set out in one place: the articles of association ("articles").

35.   By virtue of section 28, provisions in the memoranda of existing companies will be treated as provisions in the articles if they are of a type that will not in be in the memoranda of companies formed under the Act. Existing companies will, therefore, not be required to amend their articles to reflect these changes, but they can do so if they wish. They will however be able to alter or update provisions in their constitution which are now set out in their memoranda by amending their articles, for example to reflect changes to the law made by the Act.

Section 9: Registration documents

36.   This section replaces various provisions in sections 2 and 10 of the 1985 Act. It prescribes the types of information or "documents" that must be delivered to the registrar when an application for registration is made and the registrar to whom the information must be delivered.

37.   The changes to the way in which certain information is delivered to the registrar are required as a result of the changes that have been made to the memorandum. In future, information which is currently set out in the memorandum will be provided to the registrar in accordance with the provisions of this section, which prescribes, amongst other things, the contents of the application for registration. In all cases this application must state:
- the company's proposed name;
- whether the company's registered office is to be situated in England and Wales (or Wales), in Scotland or in Northern Ireland;
- whether the liability of the company's members is to be limited and if so whether it is to be limited by shares or by guarantee;
- whether the company is to be a private or a public company.

38.   In the case of a company that is to have a share capital, the application must also contain a statement of capital and initial shareholdings (see section 10). In the case of a company that is to be limited by guarantee the application must also contain a statement of guarantee (see section 11).

39.   In all cases the application must also contain a statement of the company's proposed officers (see section 12) and a statement of the intended address of the company's registered office (that is, the postal address of the company's registered office as opposed to a statement confirming the jurisdiction in which the company's registered office is to be situated – which is also required).

40.   The application for registration must also contain a copy of any proposed articles (to the extent that the company does not intend to use the model articles (see sections 19 and 20) and must be accompanied by the memorandum (see subsection (1)) of this section and a statement of compliance (see section 13).

41.   In future it will be possible to form a company on-line and the various types of information referred to in the section are, therefore, capable of being delivered as a series of data entries as well as in paper or such other form as the registrar may permit or prescribe. The registrar has power under section 1068 to prescribe the form and manner in which documents are to be delivered to her.

Section 10: Statement of capital and initial shareholdings

42. This section is a new provision. It sets out the contents of the statement of capital and initial shareholdings.

43. Currently, in the case of a limited company with a share capital the memorandum is required to state the amount of the share capital with which the company proposes to be registered and the nominal amount of each of its shares. This is known as the "authorised share capital" and acts as a ceiling on the amount of capital which can be issued (although this limit can be increased by ordinary resolution). The CLR recommended that the requirement for a company to have an authorised share capital should be abolished (Final Report, paragraph 10.6).

44. The Act gives effect to this recommendation and in future, information about the shares subscribed for by the subscribers to the memorandum, which is currently set out in the memorandum itself, will be provided to the registrar in the statement of capital and initial shareholdings.

45. Like the statement of guarantee (see section 11), the statement of capital and initial shareholdings must contain such information as may be prescribed by the Secretary of State, in regulations made under the Act, for the purpose of identifying the subscribers to the memorandum (ie the founder members of the company).

46. The statement of capital and initial shareholdings is essentially a "snapshot" of a company's share capital at the point of registration. For public companies, this requirement is linked to the abolition of authorised share capital (see above). It implements (as far as public companies are concerned) Article 2 of the Second Company Law Directive (77/91/EC) (the "Second Directive") which states:

> "the statutes or instruments of incorporation of the company shall always give at least the following information . . . (c) when the company has no authorized capital, the amount of the subscribed capital . . . ".

47. The statement of capital and initial shareholdings must contain the following information:
- the total number of shares of the company to be taken on formation by the subscribers to the memorandum;
- the aggregate nominal value of those shares;
- for each class of shares: prescribed particulars of the rights attached to those shares, the total number of shares of that class and the aggregate nominal value of shares of that class; and
- the amount to be paid up and the amount (if any) to be unpaid on each share (whether on account of the nominal value of the shares or by way of premium).

48. The reference to "*prescribed particulars of the rights attached to the shares*" in this section (and elsewhere in the Act where a statement of capital is called for), refers to such particulars as may be prescribed by the Secretary of State by statutory instrument (see section 1167).

49. Whilst the Second Directive only applies to public companies it is important that the information on the public register is up-to-date for both public and private companies. A statement of capital will, therefore, be required where it is proposed that a company formed under the Act will have a share capital on formation and, with limited exceptions (in particular, where there has been a variation of class rights which does not affect the company's aggregate subscribed capital) whenever a limited company having a share capital makes an alteration to its share capital (and in certain cases where an unlimited company makes a return to the registrar).

Section 11: Statement of guarantee

50. This section replaces section 2(4) of the 1985 Act. It sets out the contents of the statement of guarantee that must accompany the application for registration where it is proposed that a company will be limited by guarantee on formation.

51. The statement of guarantee is essentially an undertaking, given by the founder members of the company, to contribute to the assets of the company up to a specified amount in the event of it being wound up. New members must also agree to make the same contribution.

52. A member of a company limited by guarantee is only liable to contribute to the assets of a company if it is wound up during the time that he is a member or within one year of him ceasing to be a member.

53. Like the statement of capital and initial shareholdings the statement of guarantee must contain such information as may be prescribed by the Secretary of State, in regulations made under the Act, for the purposes of identifying the subscribers to the memorandum (ie the founder members of the company).

Section 12: Statement of proposed officers

54. This section replaces section 10(2) and (3) of the 1985 Act and contains a new provision. Under section 10, details of the first director(s) and the secretary or joint secretaries must be given to the registrar at the time of application for registration. That requirement is carried forward but there are two changes:

- firstly, to the required particulars. These are specified in relation to directors in sections 163 to 166. The main change is that a service address must be provided for each director who is a natural person. This is in addition to the requirement for the usual residential address;
- secondly, as recommended by the CLR (Final Report, paragraph 4.7), there is no requirement for a private company to have a company secretary but it may do so if it wishes (see section 270(1)). As now, a company which proposes to be registered as a public company must have a company secretary (see section 271).

Section 13: Statement of compliance

55.   This section replaces section 12(3) and (3A) of the 1985 Act. At present, where an application for registration of a company is made in paper form, the application must be accompanied by a statutory declaration (made before a solicitor or commissioner of oaths) confirming that the requirements of the 1985 Act in respect of registration, and of matters precedent and incidental to it, have been complied with (see section 12(1) of that Act). This statutory declaration must be made by one of the persons whom it is proposed will be a founder director or secretary of the company (that is, on registration) or a solicitor engaged in the formation of the company.

56.   Where the application for registration is made in electronic form, in place of the statutory declaration required under section 12(3) of the 1985 Act, the same persons may, alternatively, deliver an "electronic statement" to the registrar. This statement must confirm that the requirements referred to in section 12(1) have been met.

57.   Based on the recommendations of the CLR (Final Report, paragraph 9.5), the current requirement for a statutory declaration or electronic statement, here and elsewhere in the Act, is replaced by a requirement to make a statement of compliance. This statement does not need to be witnessed and may be made in paper or electronic form. It will be for the registrar's rules under section 1068 to specify who may make this statement (and the form of it). As with all documents delivered to, or statements made to, the registrar, it is an offence to make a false statement of compliance – see section 1112.

Section 14: Registration

58.   This section restates section 12(1) and (2) of the 1985 Act. As now, where the registrar is satisfied that all of the requirements of the Act as to registration have been met she will register the documents delivered to her and issue a certificate of incorporation under section 15.

Section 15: Issue of certificate of incorporation

59.   This section restates section 13(1)(2) and (7)(a) of the 1985 Act and contains a new provision in subsection (2), which prescribes the contents of the certificate of incorporation issued by the registrar on registration of a company. The certificate of incorporation is conclusive evidence that the requirements of the Act as to registration have been met, that the company has been registered, and (where relevant) that the company has been registered as a limited company or a public company.

60.   There is one change to what the certificate of incorporation is required to state: in future this will include details of whether the company's registered office is situated in England and Wales (or in Wales), in Scotland or in Northern Ireland. The certificate will also state, where the company is limited, whether it is limited by shares or by guarantee.

Section 16: Effect of registration

61.   This section replaces section 13(3) to (5) of the 1985 Act. It provides, amongst other things, that the subscribers to the memorandum, together with such other persons as may from time to time become members of a company, are a body corporate by the name stated in the certificate of incorporation and, in the case of a company having a share capital, that the subscribers to the memorandum become holders of the shares specified in the statement of capital and initial shareholdings. This means that on registration a company becomes a legal person in its own right, which is distinct from the people who own it (the members) and the people who manage it (the directors).

PART 3: A COMPANY'S CONSTITUTION

[3.4]
62.   This Part deals with various matters relating to a company's constitution. It replaces similar provisions in the 1985 Act. It starts by defining (non-exhaustively) "*a company's constitution*" and then makes provision about the main constituent parts of a company's constitution (the articles of association and certain classes of members' resolutions and agreements), including their legal effects, how they are to be notified to the registrar and made available to members, and how changes to them are to be dealt with.

Chapter 1: Introductory

Section 17: A company's constitution

63.   This section is a new provision. It sets out a definition of "*a company's constitution*" which will apply throughout the Act, and the other "Companies Acts" (defined in section 2), unless the context requires a wider or more restricted meaning (see for example section 257, which expands the definition of a company's constitution for the purposes of Part 10). The concepts of a company's constitution and the rights and obligations arising under it are used both in this Part and elsewhere in the Act.

64. The definition is expressed to be non-exhaustive. In addition to the provisions of companies' articles and the resolutions and agreements to which Chapter 3 of this Part applies (described in section 29), the contents of certain other documents are clearly of constitutional relevance for certain purposes. For example the certificate of incorporation summarises key information pertaining to the company such as whether it is public or private limited – see section 15.

Chapter 2: Articles Of Association

65. A company's articles are rules, chosen by the company's members, which govern a company's internal affairs. They form a statutory contract between the company and its members, and between each of the members in their capacity as members, and are an integral part of a company's constitution. At present, companies may divide their constitutional rules between their memoranda and their articles, with the terms of their memoranda being capable of being altered after formation in some respects but not in others. In future, the memorandum will be a very simple document of purely historic significance, evidencing an intention to form a company, and all the company's key internal rules on matters such as the allocation of powers between the members of a company and its directors will be set out in the articles – see notes on sections 8 and 28.

Section 18: Articles of association

66. This section replaces section 7(1) and (3) and section 744 of the 1985 Act. It carries forward the requirement that all registered companies must have articles. The provisions of this section have been updated to reflect the changes made by section 19, which gives the Secretary of State the power to prescribe "default" model articles for different descriptions of companies. As a result of this change, some types of company that are currently required to register articles with the relevant registrar of companies (for example, private companies limited by guarantee) will have the option of not registering articles but relying on the "relevant model articles" for that description of company.

67. As now, the articles must be contained in a single document and must be divided into consecutively numbered paragraphs.

68. Generally speaking, companies formed under the 1985 Act have freedom to make such rules about their internal affairs as they see fit, subject to the qualification that if a company's articles contain anything that is contrary to the provisions of that Act, or against the general law, then it will have no effect. This principle will also apply to the articles of companies which are formed and registered under the Act.

Section 19: Power of Secretary of State to prescribe model articles
Section 20: Default application of model articles

69. Section 8 of the 1985 Act enables the Secretary of State to prescribe model forms of articles for companies registered under that Act (see the Companies (Tables A to F) Regulations 1985 (SI 1985/805)). Articles for certain special types of companies used in particular sectors, for example, commonhold associations, right to manage ("RTM") companies, and right to enfranchise ("RTE") companies are prescribed by regulations made under the Acts of Parliament that created these types of company.

70. Although sections 8 and 8A of the 1985 Act allow the Secretary of State to prescribe forms of articles (and memoranda) for a number of different types of company under section 8, he is only able to prescribe "default" model articles for companies limited by shares. "Default" model articles are model articles which apply to companies of a particular description where they have not registered any articles of their own, or have not made provision for a particular matter for which there is a corresponding model article. "Default" model articles apply to a company of the description for which they are prescribed only to the extent that it has not modified the default provision in question in its own registered articles or excluded it, or the model articles in their entirety, from the registered articles.

71. The rationale behind this is that the model articles should operate as a "safety net" which enables the members and directors of such companies to take decisions in circumstances where a company has failed to provide the appropriate authority in its registered articles (or failed to register articles at all).

72. These two sections replace section 8 of the 1985 Act. In line with the CLR's recommendations (Company Formation and Capital Maintenance, paragraph 2.22), the Secretary of State will have the power to prescribe model articles, including "default" model articles, for different descriptions of companies formed under the Act.

73. For existing companies, there will be no change. The principle is maintained that the version of the model articles that was in force at the time that a particular company was originally registered will continue to apply to that company. For the majority of companies limited by shares on the register at the date that the Act comes into force, the "default" model articles will continue to be the Companies Act 1985 Table A ("Table A").

74.   Existing companies will be free to adopt, wholly or in part, the model articles prescribed for companies of a particular description formed under the Act (see subsection (3) of section 19). For example, an existing private company limited by shares may prefer to adopt the new model articles for private companies limited by shares, or indeed the new model articles for public companies formed under the Act (with or without modification) in place of the current Table A articles, or previous articles of its own devising.

75.   As with Table A, the adoption of model articles by companies formed under the Act will be entirely a matter for individual companies. They will be able to incorporate (with or without amendment) provisions from the model articles, and/or add to those provisions, and/or exclude such provisions as they think fit.

76.   They will also be able to adopt the provisions of model articles by reference. This is a common practice, which enables a company that wishes to incorporate specific provisions of the model articles into its own registered articles to do this without having to copy out the provision in question. To take an example, a company's registered articles may say something to the following effect: "*the model articles apply except for articles x, y and z*", or "*the company's articles are A, B and C, plus model articles g, p and q. Model article n applies but is amended as follows: . . .*". Companies have found such techniques useful in the past and they will continue to be permitted.

Section 21: Amendment of articles

77.   Subsection (1) provides that, as now, a company's articles can in general be amended by special resolution. This restates section 9(1) of the 1985 Act.

78.   Subsections (2) and (3) make it clear that this general principle is subject to certain rules in charities legislation about the ability of companies which are charities to change their constitutions and the effects which such changes have. There are separate but broadly similar rules for English and Welsh, Scottish and Northern Irish charities.

Section 22: Entrenched provisions of the articles

79.   Section 22 is a new provision. It replaces the current practice (provided for in section 17(2)(b) of the 1985 Act), whereby companies are able to entrench certain elements of their constitution by putting them in their memoranda and providing that they cannot be altered.

80.   This section permits companies to provide in their articles that specified provisions may be amended or repealed only if conditions are met that are more restrictive than would apply in the case of a special resolution. Such a provision is referred to as a "provision for entrenchment". As a result of this section companies formed under the Act will not be permitted to provide in their articles that an entrenched provision can never be repealed or amended.

Section 23: Notice to registrar of existence of restriction on amendment of articles

81.   This is a new provision that requires a company to give notice to the registrar when an entrenching provision is included in its articles (whether on formation or subsequently) or where the company's articles are altered by order of a court or other authority so as to restrict or exclude the power of the company to amend its articles. There is a corresponding requirement as to notice where the company amends its articles so as to remove a provision for entrenchment or where the articles are altered by order of a court or other authority so as to remove a provision for entrenchment or any other restriction on, or any exclusion of, the power of the company to amend its articles.

Section 24: Statement of compliance where amendment of articles restricted

82.   This is a new provision. Where a company's articles contain provision for entrenchment or where the articles are subject to an order of a court or other authority restricting or excluding the company's power to amend its articles and the company subsequently amends its articles, it is required to send to the registrar the document making or evidencing the amendment. This document must be accompanied by a "statement of compliance" (see note on section 13).

83.   The statement of compliance must certify that the amendment to the articles has been made in accordance with the company's articles (including any provision for entrenchment) or, where relevant, in accordance with any order of the court or other authority that is in force at the time of the amendment.

84.   The purpose of the provisions in sections 23 and 24 is to ensure that the registrar, and any person searching the public register, is on notice that the articles contain entrenching provisions and that special rules therefore apply to the company's articles.

Section 25: Effect of alteration of articles on company's members

85.   This section restates section 16 of the 1985 Act. The only difference is that section 16 also applied to alterations of a company's memorandum. A company formed under the Act will not be able to (or need to) alter its memorandum.

86.   This section retains the principle that a member of a company is not bound by any alteration made to the articles subsequent to his becoming a member if the alteration has the effect of increasing his liability to the company or requires him to take more shares in the company. A member may however give his written consent to such an alteration and, where he does, he will be bound by it.

Section 26: Registrar to be sent copy of amended articles

87.   The First Company Law Directive (68/151/EEC) requires Member States to take such measures as are required to ensure that companies disclose certain constitutional information which will then be made available to the public in a central register. In particular, companies are to be required to disclose (i) their *"instrument of constitution, and the statutes if they are contained in a separate instrument"*; (ii) *any amendments to these instruments*; and (iii) *"after every [such] amendment . . . the complete text of the instrument or statutes as amended to date"*. For UK companies, the "instrument of constitution" equates to the memorandum and the "statutes" equate to the articles. The central registers are those kept by the registrars of companies for England and Wales, Scotland and Northern Ireland.

88.   This section replaces equivalent provisions in section 18(2) and (3) of the 1985 Act and Schedule 24 to that Act.

89.   Where a company fails to comply with the provisions of this section, the company and every officer of the company who is in default commits an offence. The penalty for this offence is set out in subsection (4).

Section 27: Registrar's notice to comply in case of failure with respect to amended articles

90.   This section is a new provision. It gives the registrar a means of ensuring that companies comply with the obligation set out in section 26 without having to resort to criminal proceedings. (However, the offence of failing to file amended articles is retained: see of section 26(3)).

91.   Where the registrar becomes aware of any default in complying with section 26 (or any similar provision of another enactment that was in force at the time of the default, for example, section 18(2) of the 1985 Act), she may give notice to the company requiring it to rectify the breach within 28 days. Where the company complies with the notice, the company will avoid prosecution for its initial failure to comply. If the company does not comply, it will be liable to a civil penalty of £200, recoverable by the registrar as a debt, in addition to any criminal penalty that may be imposed (see, for example, section 26(4)).

Section 28: Existing companies: provisions of memorandum treated as provisions of articles

92.   For companies formed under the Act, the memorandum will contain limited information evidencing the intention of the founder members to form a company. The memoranda of existing companies, on the other hand, will contain key constitutional information of a type which will in future be set out in the articles or provided to the registrar in another format (see Part 2). Subsection (1) of this section provides that such material is to be treated for the future as part of the company's articles.

93.   Subsection (2) of this section makes it clear that where the memorandum of an existing company contains a provision for entrenchment (see note on section 22) at the date that this part of the Act comes into force, this will be deemed, with effect from that date, to be a provision for entrenchment in the company's articles.

Chapter 3: Resolutions And Agreements Affecting A Company's Constitution

94.   This Chapter replaces equivalent provisions in the 1985 Act on the registration of resolutions and agreements and on making these available to members.

Section 29: Resolutions and agreements affecting a company's constitution

95.   This section replaces section 380(4) and (4A) of the 1985 Act. It lists the resolutions and agreements that must be forwarded to the registrar for registration (see section 30) and made available to members on request (see section 32).

Section 30: Copies of resolutions or agreements to be forwarded to registrar

96.   This section restates section 380 (1), (5) and (7) of the 1985 Act and Schedule 24 to that Act. Where a company passes a resolution or enters into an agreement of the type listed in section 29, it must forward a copy of the resolution or agreement to the registrar for registration within 15 days of the date on which the resolution was passed. If a company fails to do this, the company, and every officer of it who is in default, commits an offence. For the penalty, see subsection (3).

97.   Where a resolution or agreement which affects a company's constitution is not in writing, the company is required to provide the registrar with a written memorandum setting out the terms of the resolution or agreement in question.

Chapter 4: Miscellaneous and Supplementary Provisions

Section 31: Statement of company's objects

98. This section provides for a new approach to the question of a company's objects. Under the 1985 Act all companies are required to have objects and these objects are required to be specified in the memorandum. The 1985 Act also makes specific provision for where a company states its objects to be to carry on business as a general commercial company (see section 3A of the 1985 Act).

99. Based on a recommendation of the CLR (Final Report, paragraph 9.10), under the Act a different approach is taken. Instead of companies being required to specify their objects, companies will have unrestricted objects unless the objects are specifically restricted by the articles (see subsection (1)). This will mean that unless a company makes a deliberate choice to restrict its objects, the objects will have no bearing on what it can do. Some companies will continue to restrict their objects. Companies that are charities will need to restrict their objects (under charities legislation) and some community interest companies may also choose to do so.

100. Subsection (2) provides that where a company changes its articles to add, remove or alter a statement of the company's objects, it must give notice to the registrar. The registrar is to register that notice, and the alteration does not take effect until it has been so registered.

101. Subsection (3) ensures that such an amendment to the company's articles will not affect any rights or obligations of the company or render defective any legal proceedings by or against it.

102. For companies which are charities, the effect of this section is subject to section 64 of the Charities Act 1993 in England and Wales and in Northern Ireland subject to the Charities (Northern Ireland) Order 1987 (SI 1987/2048 (NI 19)) (subsection (4)).

103. Subsection (5) makes equivalent provision for Scotland. These provisions impose additional requirements in the case of companies which are charities when changing certain aspects of their constitutions, including their objects.

104. The directors of a company are under a duty to observe the company's constitution (see section 171) although restrictions in objects will, as now, have little effect outside of the internal workings of the company because of the effect of sections 39 and 40 (except in the case of charities where modified rules again apply – see section 42).

Section 32: Constitutional documents to be provided to members

105. This section replaces section 19 of the 1985 Act and Schedule 24 to that Act. It gives members the right to obtain from the company copies of the company's articles and certain other documents of constitutional importance (see subsection (1)).

106. The provision in the 1985 Act which enables a company to charge its members 5p for a copy of its articles and/or memorandum has been removed. This information must in future be provided to the members (on request) free of charge.

107. Where a company fails to comply with the provisions of this section, every officer of the company who is in default commits an offence. For the penalty for this offence, see subsection (4).

Section 33: Effect of company's constitution

108. Subsection (1) of this section replaces section 14(1) of the 1985 Act. Its effect is that the provisions of a company's constitution constitute a special kind of contract, whose terms bind the company and its members from time to time. Like section 14(1), the provisions of this section are excepted from the general principle set out in section 1 of the Contracts (Rights of Third Parties) Act 1999, so that provisions of a company's constitution will not confer any rights on persons other than the company and its members. Unlike section 14(1), section 34 refers to "*a company's constitution*", rather than its "*memorandum and articles*". This reflects the new division of formation and constitutional information between the memorandum, articles and other constitutional documents noted above.

109. The language in subsection (1) has been updated but there is no change to the law (the provision continues to reflect what the law has always been: in particular a company's constitution binds both the company and its members).

110. Subsection (2) replaces section 14(2) of the 1985 Act. It provides that amounts which a member of a company is obliged to pay to it under its constitution are debts due to the company. In England and Wales and Northern Ireland, such debts are ordinary contract debts.

Section 34: Notice to registrar where company's constitution altered by enactment

111. This section replaces section 18 of the 1985 Act and Schedule 24 to that Act.

112. The provisions of a company's constitution may be altered by legislation, rather than by a resolution or agreement of the company's members. Such legislation will either be of general relevance to all companies (for example, a new Companies Act provision that provisions of a certain type in any company's articles are void), or to all companies of a particular type (for example, new commonhold legislation changing the provisions prescribed for inclusion in the articles of all commonhold associations) or it will be relevant only to a particular company (for example, a private Act of Parliament amending the articles of a specific company established by an earlier Act).

113. In keeping with the principles underlying section 26, it is important that those searching the register of companies should be able to be made aware of the changes to companies' articles which legislation may effect. However, there is a balance to be struck between maintaining transparency on the one hand and inundating the registrar and searchers with mountains of paper which will be of little practical use to persons searching the public register (and whose contents are generally available in any event). The section therefore does not require companies to send copies of most public general Acts which alter their articles (such as Companies Acts or new commonhold legislation) to the registrar. It does however require "special enactments" (as defined in subsection (4)) to be sent to the registrar by companies whose articles are altered by the enactment in question.

114. Where an enactment to which this section applies alters a company's articles, or where such an enactment alters a resolution or agreement affecting the company's constitution, the company is obliged to send a copy of the articles, or the resolution or agreement in question, as altered, to the registrar.

115. The procedural rules for sending such legislation to the registrar, and the penalties for non-compliance with them, are as for section 26.

Section 35: Notice to registrar where company's constitution altered by order

116. This is a new provision which provides a mechanism for registering alterations which are made to a company's constitution by an order of the court or other authority (for example, the Charity Commission). It obliges companies to give notice of such alterations to the registrar, and to supply a copy of the articles, or the resolution or agreement in question, as altered, to the registrar.

Section 36: Documents to be incorporated in or accompany copies of articles issued by company

117. This section replaces section 380(2), (6) and (7) of the 1985 Act and Schedule 24 to that Act. It provides that every copy of a company's articles which it issues must be accompanied by various documents: in particular resolutions, agreements, enactments or orders which affect or evidence alterations to the company's constitution (see subsection (1)) unless the effect of the resolution, agreement, enactment or order has been incorporated into the company's articles or is no longer in force.

118. The intention behind this provision is that information provided on a request for a copy of the company's articles should be up-to-date but the company should not be obliged to provide the same information twice (ie in different forms).

Section 37: Right to participate in profits otherwise than as member void

119. This section restates section 15(1) of the 1985 Act. It provides that a company limited by guarantee without a share capital cannot, by means of a provision in its articles or a resolution of its members, confer on any person a right to participate in its divisible profits otherwise than as a member. As under the 1985 Act, there is no statutory restriction on the members of such companies participating in their profits, unless they have sought exemption from the use of the word "limited" in their names.

Section 38: Application to single member companies of enactments and rules of law

120. Under section 7 it will be possible for a single person to form any type of company. This section provides that in future any enactment or rule of law that is applicable to companies formed by two or more persons (or having two or more members) applies (with any necessary modifications) to companies formed with one member (or having only one person as a member). This is already the case in respect of private limited companies: see the Companies (Single Member Private Limited Companies) Regulations 1992 (SI 1992/1699).

PART 4: A COMPANY'S CAPACITY AND RELATED MATTERS

[3.5]
121. This Part replaces various provisions in the 1985 Act about a company's capacity and related matters, including in particular those in Chapter 3 of Part 1 of that Act.

Section 39: A company's capacity

122. This section provides that the validity of a company's acts is not to be questioned on the ground of lack of capacity because of anything in a company's constitution. It replaces the present section 35(1) and (4) of the 1985 Act, which made similar provision for restrictions of capacity contained in the memorandum.

123. The section does not contain provision corresponding to section 35(2) and (3) of the 1985 Act. It is considered that the combination of the fact that under the Act a company may have unrestricted objects (and where it has restricted objects the directors' powers are correspondingly restricted), and the fact that a specific duty on directors to abide by the company's constitution is provided for in section 171, makes these provisions unnecessary.

124.   Subsection (2) indicates that the section, like section 35 of the 1985 Act, is modified in its application to charities.

Section 40: Power of directors to bind the company

125.   This section provides safeguards for a person dealing with a company in good faith and restates section 35A and 35B of the 1985 Act. The power of the directors to bind the company, or authorise others to do so, is deemed not to be constrained by the company's constitution. This means that a third party dealing with a company in good faith need not concern itself about whether a company is acting within its constitution.

126.   Subsection (2)(b)(i) of the section replaces part of section 35B of the 1985 Act: an external party is not bound to enquire whether there are any limitations on the power of the directors. The first limb of section 35B (which refers to the memorandum) has not been carried forward. This is concerned with restrictions in a company's constitution that limit a company's ability to act and consequently the powers of the directors to bind the company (the so called "ultra vires rule"). Under the Act, the objects no longer affect the company's capacity to act and so this limb is not necessary.

Section 41: Constitutional limitations: transactions involving directors or their associates

127.   This section restates section 322A of the 1985 Act. It applies to a transaction if, or to the extent that, its validity depends on section 40 and provides that where the party to a transaction with a company is an "insider" (for example, a director of the company or person connected to such a director – see subsection (2)(b)(i) and (ii)), then the protection afforded by that section will not apply. Instead, the transaction will be voidable at the instance of the company.

128.   Irrespective of whether the transaction is avoided, the "insider" and any director who authorised the transaction is liable to account to the company for any gain he has made as a result of the transaction and to indemnify the company for any loss or damage that the company has incurred (see subsection (3)). However, where the "insider" is not a director of the company, it may be possible for him to avoid liability if he can show that at the time he entered into the transaction with the company he was unaware that the directors were exceeding their powers (see subsection (5)).

129.   As now, under subsection (4), a transaction will cease to be voidable in certain circumstances, for example, if restitution is no longer possible.

Section 42: Constitutional limitations: companies that are charities

130.   This section restates section 65 of the Charities Act 1993. It is a qualification of the rules in sections 39 and 40.

131.   It provides that the protection afforded to an external party by sections 39 and 40 will not apply where the company in question is a charity, unless:

- the external party was unaware (at the time that the act was done) that the company was a charity; or
- the company has received full consideration in respect of the act done, and the external party was unaware that the act in question was beyond the company's capacity or beyond the powers of the directors.

132.   Corresponding provisions for charities that are registered in Scotland can be found in section 112 of the Companies Act 1989 (see subsection (5)).

Section 43: Company contracts

133.   This section restates the provisions of section 36 of the 1985 Act.

Section 44: Execution of documents

134.   This section largely restates section 36A of the 1985 Act. It provides that a company may execute a document under the law of England and Wales or Northern Ireland by affixing the company seal or by signature by two directors or by one director and a secretary (or joint-secretary) or (for the first time) by a single director if that signature is witnessed and attested.

Section 45: Common seal

135.   This section replaces the provisions of sections 36A(3) and 350 of the 1985 Act. It permits but does not require a company to have a common seal. If a company has a common seal, it requires the seal to include the company's name: failure to do so is an offence.

Section 46: Execution of deeds

136.   This section restates section 36AA, inserted into the 1985 Act by the Regulatory Reform (Execution of Deeds and Documents) Order 2005 (SI 2005/1906). The only change is to extend the application for the purposes of the law of Northern Ireland.

Section 47: Execution of deeds and other documents by attorney

137. This section replaces section 38 of the 1985 Act. The 1985 Act does not require the appointment of the attorney to be by deed nor does it say anything about deeds executed on behalf of the company in the United Kingdom. This section provides that a company may appoint, under the law of England and Wales or Northern Ireland, attorneys to execute deeds or other documents on its behalf, and that documents executed in this manner, whether in the UK or abroad, have effect as if executed by the company. It also makes clear that the method for a company appointing an attorney is by instrument executed as a deed, which is the same method by which an individual appoints an attorney.

Section 48: Execution of documents by companies

138. This section restates section 36B of the 1985 Act. It makes clear that no seal is required regardless of any other statutory provision. The only change is the addition of subsection (1) which makes clear that this section forms part of the law of Scotland only.

Section 49: Official seal for use abroad

139. This section replaces section 39 of the 1985 Act. It sets out the circumstances and manner in which a company may use its common seal outside the UK.

Section 50: Official seal for share certificates etc

140. This section restates section 40(1) of the 1985 Act. It enables a company that has a common seal to have an official seal for sealing securities issued by the company and for sealing documents creating or evidencing securities so issued.

Section 51: Pre-incorporation contracts, deeds and obligations

141. This section restates section 36C of the 1985 Act. A company is not bound by a contract purportedly made on its behalf before it came into existence unless the obligations are novated, ie a new contract must come into existence after incorporation on the same terms as the old one. Novation may be express or implied.

Section 52: Bills of exchange and promissory notes

142. This section restates section 37 of the 1985 Act. A bill of exchange is an unconditional order in writing, addressed by one person to another, signed by the person giving it, requiring the person to whom it is addressed to pay on demand or at a fixed or determinable future time a sum certain in money to or to the order of a specified person, or to its bearer. A promissory note is an unconditional promise in writing made by one person to another, signed by the maker, engaging to pay, on demand or at a fixed or determinable future time, a sum certain in money to, or to the order of, a specified person or to its bearer. Where someone acting under a company's authority makes, accepts, or endorses such an instrument in the name of the company, or on its behalf, this section treats this as if these actions had been done by the company.

PART 5: A COMPANY'S NAME

[3.6]
143. This Part applies to the name under which a company is registered, sometimes called the "corporate name". This Part regulates the choice of name. The rules are primarily intended to ensure that third parties are not misled. There are no property rights in companies' registered names as such. While there is no requirement for a company to use its registered name in the course of business, this Part also requires a company to disclose its name in specified circumstances.

144. Sections 70 to 74 provide for the appointment of adjudicators in cases where there is dispute over the registering of a company name. Section 71 safeguards the independence of the adjudicators and section 74 provides a right of appeal to the court.

Chapter 1: General Requirements

Section 53: Prohibited names

145. This section replaces section 26(1)(d) and (e) of the 1985 Act. It retains the existing prohibition of companies registering names that cannot be used without commission of an offence and of those that are offensive.

Section 54: Names suggesting connection with government or public authority

146. This section replaces section 26(2)(a) of the 1985 Act. It prevents a name being registered without the Secretary of State's approval if it suggests a connection with Her Majesty's Government, a local authority or – which represents a change from the 1985 Act – any part of the Scottish administration, or Her Majesty's Government in Northern Ireland. A new power allows similar protection to be extended to other public authorities.

Section 55: Other sensitive words or expressions

147. This section replaces sections 26(2)(b), 29(1)(a) and 29(6) of the 1985 Act.

148. Subsection (1) requires prior approval for the adoption of a name that includes words or expressions specified in regulations. Subsection (2) provides for the procedure to be used for making the regulations. The words and expressions protected by the current Regulations (the Company and Business Names Regulations 1981, SI 1981/1685) include British, English, Scottish and Welsh; chamber of commerce, charity, Her Majesty, midwife, police, and university.

Section 56: Duty to seek comment of government department or other specified body

149. This section replaces section 29(1)(b) and (2) and (3) of the 1985 Act. It provides power for the Secretary of State to specify whose view must be sought when seeking approval for a name. For example, under the present Regulations, the approval of the General Dental Council is required for the use of either "dental" or "dentistry". Regulations under the new power would be able to replicate this. They could also require the approval of, say, the House Authorities for names suggesting a connection with Parliament.

150. When a request is made under section 56 in connection with the registration or the change of name of a company, the registrar must be sent a statement that a request has been made, and a copy of the response (see subsections (3) and (4)). But the registrar must not make the response available for public inspections (see section 1087(1)(a)).

Section 57: Permitted characters etc

151. This section is a new provision. It provides power for regulations to specify what letters, symbols, etc may be used in a company's registered name; the regulations may also specify a permitted format for a name (for example, to prevent the use of superscript or subscript).

Chapter 2: Indications Of Company Type Or Legal Form

Section 58: Public limited companies

152. This section replaces section 25(1) of the 1985 Act (and also section 27(4)(b) and (d) in its application to public limited companies). It brings together in a single provision all the alternative statutory indicators of legal status that must be used by a public company as part of its registered name, ie "public limited company" or the Welsh equivalent or the specified abbreviations. This section does not apply to community interest companies.

Section 59: Private limited companies

153. This section replaces section 25(2) of the 1985 Act (and also section 27(4)(a) and (c) in its application to private limited companies). It brings together in a single provision all the alternative statutory indicators of legal status that must be used by a private company as part of its registered name, ie "limited" or the Welsh equivalent or the specified abbreviations. Certain companies are exempt (see section 61). This section does not apply to community interest companies.

Sections 60 to 62: Exemption from requirement as to use of "limited"

154. These sections replace section 30 of the 1985 Act. Section 30 exempts certain companies from the requirement for their names to conclude with "limited". Exempt companies are also exempt under the 1985 Act from some of the requirements regarding publication of their name but they still have to disclose their limited status in correspondence. Those currently exempt are those with a licence granted under section 19 of the Companies Act 1948 which have delivered a statutory declaration to the Registrar that the company complies with the requirements for the exemption. These requirements are, in effect, that the company is non-profit-making and its objects are the promotion of commerce, art, science, education, religion, charity or any profession.

155. Section 60 continues the exemption for companies already exempt so long as they continue to meet the conditions and until they change their registered name. It also provides an exemption for charities and allows the Secretary of State to make regulations exempting other companies. Only private companies may be exempt

156. Sections 61 and 62, which replace section 30(2) and (3), specify the conditions that must be met for a company currently exempt to continue to qualify for the exemption: its objects must continue to satisfy the criteria for their exemption and its articles must both preclude distributions of dividends to its members and also, in the event of it being wound up, require its assets to be passed to a body with similar objects. For companies limited by shares benefiting from an exemption under the 1948 Act (or its Northern Irish equivalent), there is a new requirement that the articles prevent a distribution of capital. This is linked to the change in section 63(4) (see below).

Section 63: Exempt company: restriction on alteration of articles

157. This section replaces section 31(1) and (5). It prohibits a company benefiting from an exemption under the 1985 Act or the 1948 Act (or their Northern Irish equivalents) from changing its articles in such a way that it no longer meets the requirements for the exemption. It is an offence to change the company's articles in such a way. Many companies with an exemption under the 1948 Act (or its Northern Irish equivalent) were made to include a provision in their memoranda preventing an amendment to their memoranda or articles without the consent of the Board of Trade (there were a number of variations on this theme). Subsections (4) and (5) make provision to remove this administrative burden.

Section 64: Power to direct change of name in case of company ceasing to be entitled to exemption

158.   This section replaces section 31(2) to (6). It gives the Secretary of State power to withdraw a private company's exemption from the requirement for its name to conclude with "limited" and to direct it to change its name if it no longer meets the criteria that applied when it was granted the exemption.

Section 65: Inappropriate use of indications of company type or legal form

159.   This section replaces section 26(1)(a), (b), (bb) and (bbb) of the 1985 Act. These paragraphs restrict the use of various words, expressions and abbreviations that are indicators of legal status for various types of commercial entity, eg p.l.c., community interest company, open-ended investment company, etc. Some of the restrictions apply to the use of the particular indicator at the end of a company's name; some anywhere other than the end of the name; and some anywhere in a company's name.

160.   This section provides power to make regulations prohibiting the inclusion in a company's name of specified words, expressions and abbreviations. The only words etc that can be specified in the regulations are those associated with a particular type of company or form or organisation or those confusingly similar to such words and expressions. This section also provides power to require or prohibit the statutory indicators of legal status being used in conjunction with specified other words.

Chapter 3: Similarity To Other Names

Section 66: Name not to be the same as another in the index

161.   This section replaces section 26(1)(c) and (3) of the 1985 Act.

162.   Subsection (1) retains the present prohibition, in section 26(1)(c), on a company adopting a name that is already on the registrar's index of company names – which includes not only the names of Companies Act companies but various other business entities (see section 1099). Subsections (2) and (3) provide power for the Secretary of State to make regulations to replace the detailed rules presently contained in section 26(3) of the 1985 Act as to:

•   what is to be disregarded; and
•   what words, letters and symbols are to be taken as the same, or as not the same,

when comparing a proposed and an existing name. At present only "and" and "&" are taken as the same.

163.   The section provides power also to treat as the same:

•   currency symbols (eg £, $) and their respective English word equivalents;
•   "%" and "per cent";
•   "1", "2", "3" etc and "one", "two" "three".

164.   The prohibition of names that, under these rules, are the same as an existing name will not be discretionary. But in future, it will be possible for there to be exceptions: subsection (4) provides that the regulations may provide that names which would otherwise be prohibited as being the same may be permitted in specified circumstances, or with specified consent, and that a subsequent change of circumstances or withdrawal of consent will not affect the company's registration.

Section 67: Power to direct change of name in case of similarity to existing name

165.   This section replaces section 28(2) of the 1985 Act which provides power for the Secretary of State to direct a company to change its name if the name is the same as or too like a name already on the registrar's index of company names (or one which should have been there). The objective is to prevent the public being confused by the simultaneous appearance on the register of two very similar names when the similarity is such that the later name was not caught by the non-discretionary prohibition of adopting a name effectively the "same as" an existing name (see section 66).

166.   The section is intended to cover two circumstances. First, any delay in the entry on the index of company names of new names of entities that are not UK companies. Companies House enter all names immediately but there may be delays outside their control. If the name had already been taken by the other entity before the company adopted it, then the Secretary of State will direct the company to change its name. Second, the visual difference between the new name and an existing name being so small that third parties are likely to be confused by the simultaneous appearance of both names on the index of company names.

167.   Subsections (2) and (3) provide power to make regulations, corresponding to that provided by section 66, to replace the detailed rules presently contained in section 26(3) of the 1985 Act as to:

- what is to be disregarded; and
- what words, letters and symbols are to be taken as the same

when comparing a proposed and an existing name. As in section 67, subsection (4) provides for a power to make regulations permitting names that would otherwise be regarded as "too like" in certain circumstances or where consent is given.

Section 68: Direction to change name: supplementary provisions

168. This section replaces section 28(4) and (5) of the 1985 Act as they apply to section 28(2). It provides a deadline of 12 months for the Secretary of State to direct a change of name under section 67, and for the Secretary of State to specify a period for the company's compliance. It makes failure by the company to comply an offence.

Similarity to other name in which person has goodwill

169. Sections 69 to 74 are new provisions. They respond to the CLR recommendation (Final Report, paragraph 11.50) that there be provision so that a person can apply for a company to be directed to change its name if the applicant can show that the name was chosen with the principal intention of seeking money from him or preventing him registering the name where it is one in which he has previously acquired reputation or goodwill.

Section 69: Objection to company's registered name

170. This section provides for any person, not just a company, to object to a company names adjudicator if a company's name is similar to a name in which the objector has goodwill. There is list of circumstances raising a presumption that a name was adopted legitimately. The respondent must show that one of these applies, or otherwise that he acted in good faith or that the interests of the applicant are not significantly affected (for example, where the applicant has hardly used the name at all). The objection will be upheld if the respondent cannot do so, or if the objector can show that the name was registered either to obtain money from him or to prevent him using the name.

Section 70: Company names adjudicators

171. This section provides power for the Secretary of State to appoint company names adjudicators and their staff and to finance their activities. One of the adjudicators is to be appointed Chief Adjudicator.

Section 71: Procedural rules

172. This section provides the Secretary of State with power to make rules for the proceedings before a company names adjudicator. The list of matters which the rules may cover is not exhaustive. It also enables the rule to confer on the Chief Adjudicator power to determine any matter that could be the subject of the rules made under this power.

Section 72: Decision of adjudicator to be made available to public

173. This section requires the adjudicator to publish his decision and his reasons for it, possibly through a website. The publication must be within 90 days of the decision.

Section 73: Order requiring name to be changed

174. This section is a new provision. If an objection made under section 69 is upheld, then the adjudicator is to direct the company with the offending name to change its name to one that does not similarly offend. A deadline must be set for the change. If the offending name is not changed, then the adjudicator will determine a new name for the company.

Section 74: Appeal from adjudicator's decision

175. This section enables appeal to a court against the decision of the company names adjudicator. The court will either uphold or reverse the adjudicator's decision, and may make any order that the adjudicator might have made.

Chapter 4: Other Powers Of The Secretary Of State

Section 75: Provision of misleading information etc

176. This section replaces section 28(3) of the 1985 Act and, insofar as they support that subsection, section 28(4) and (5). It provides power for the Secretary of State to direct a company to change its name within a specified period in two circumstances. First, if misleading information was given to enable the adoption of the name. Second, if an undertaking or assurance given to enable the adoption of the name has not been fulfilled. The direction can only be made up to five years after the adoption of the name. It is an offence not to comply with the direction.

Section 76: Misleading indication of activities

177. This section replaces section 32 of the 1985 Act. It provides power for the Secretary of State to direct a company to change its name, regardless of how long the company has had the name, in the specified circumstances. The circumstances are that, in his opinion, not only does the name give a misleading indication of the nature of the company's activities but also that the public are likely to suffer harm as a result. The company may appeal to the court, who may either confirm the direction or set it aside. It is an offence not to comply with the direction.

178. The section also sets time limits for compliance with the direction (6 weeks) and the application to the court (3 weeks). If the court confirms the direction, it specifies the deadline for compliance.

Chapter 5: Change Of Name

Section 77: Change of name

179. This section replaces section 28(1) of the 1985 Act. Under the existing provision, companies can only change their names:
- by special resolution; or
- following a direction by the Secretary of State in the restricted circumstances provided by section 31 of the 1985 Act, which apply only to companies exempt from their name concluding in "limited."

180. This section also provides for the following means:
- whatever means are provided in the company's articles (this means that the company will be able to determine the procedures for changing its own name);
- by an order of the company names adjudicator if an objection under section 73 is upheld, or by a court following an appeal against the adjudicator's decision under section 74; and
- under section 1033 on the company's restoration to the register.

Section 78: Change of name by special resolution

181. This section is a new provision. It requires the company to notify the registrar of a change of name when it has been agreed by special resolution. This requirement is in addition to the obligation under Chapter 3 of Part 3 to forward a copy of the special resolution to the registrar. Subsections (2) and (3) address the particular situation where a company has passed a special resolution to change its name but the change is not to take place until some other event has occurred (eg a merger). The notice of change of name must say that the change is conditional and whether the event has occurred. If the event has not yet occurred, the registrar will not act on the notice to change the name until she has received a second notice stating that the specified event has occurred. The registrar may rely on that statement without further evidence.

Section 79: Change of name by means provided for in company's articles

182. This section is a new provision, supplementing the new provision (section 77(1)(b)) whereby a company may change its name by any means provided for in its articles. Subsection (1) requires the company to provide the registrar with both a notice of the name change and a statement that the change has been made in accordance with the company's articles. Subsection (2) ensures the registrar may rely on that statement without further evidence.

Section 80: Change of name: registration and issue of new certificate of incorporation

183. This section, which partly replaces sections 28(6) and 32(5) of the 1985 Act, provides for the procedures that the registrar must perform before a company's proposed new name is effective. Subsection (2) provides for the checks both that the name meets all the requirements for a company's name in this Part of the Act and that the necessary documents have been provided. Subsection (3) provides for the company to be issued with a certificate of incorporation with the new name.

Section 81: Change of name: effect

184. This section, which replaces sections 28(6) and 32(5) in part and, in total, section 28(7) of the 1985 Act, provides that the new name is effective as soon as the altered certificate of incorporation is issued. It also provides that the change of name does not affect the company's rights or obligations or legal proceedings by or against it in its previous name.

Chapter 6: Trading Disclosures

Section 82: Requirement to disclose company name etc

185. This section replaces sections 348(1), 349(1), and 351(1) and (2) of the 1985 Act and, insofar as it applies to companies, section 4(1) of the Business Names Act 1985. It provides power for the Secretary of State to make regulations requiring every company:
- to display a sign with its name and specified other information at specified locations;
- to include its name and specified other information in specified documents and communications;

- to provide its name and specified other information to those who request it in the course of business (this is a new provision insofar as it applies to companies doing business under their registered names).

Section 83: Civil consequences of failure to make required disclosure

186. This section replaces section 5 of the Business Names Act 1985, so far as it applies to companies. As recommended by the CLR (Final Report, paragraph 11.57), it follows the precedent of the Business Names Act as regards the civil consequences of failure to comply with the information requirements made in regulations under section 82: the provision for personal civil liability of officers in default in section 349(4) of the Companies Act 1985 is not included.

Section 84: Criminal consequences of failure to make required disclosures

187. This section replaces sections 348(2), 349(2) and (3) and 351(5) of the 1985 Act and, insofar as it applies to companies, part of section 7 of the Business Names Act 1985. It makes it an offence not to comply with the requirements, to be specified in regulations under section 82, for every company to disclose its name and specified other information.

Section 85: Minor variations in form of name to be left out of account

188. This section is a new provision. It means that the company's name as used to comply with the disclosure requirements need not be exactly the same as the registered name. The permitted differences are the case of the letters, the use of punctuation, accents, etc and formatting. However the differences must not result in there being a risk of confusion.

PART 6: A COMPANY'S REGISTERED OFFICE

Section 86: A company's registered office

[3.7]
189. This section restates section 287(1) of the 1985 Act. It requires every company to have a registered office and provides for that office to be an address to which communications and notices may be sent. Section 1139 provides that the service of a document on a company is effective if it is sent to its registered office.

Section 87: Change of address of registered office

190. This section restates section 287(3) to (6) of the provisions of the 1985 Act. It provides the means by which a company may change the address of its registered office.

Section 88: Welsh companies

191. This section provides a definition of a Welsh company. A company can be set up as a Welsh company by delivering to the registrar a statement on formation that its registered office is to be situated in Wales (see section 9(2)(b)). Subsection (2) restates section 2(2) of the 1985 Act whereby a company may become a Welsh company by passing a special resolution (so that the register states that its registered office is to be situated "in Wales"). As recommended by the CLR, subsection (3) provides a mechanism whereby a company can cease to be a Welsh company (ie so that the register states that its registered office is to be situated in "England and Wales"). This is new. At present, while a company may choose to restrict the address of its registered office to Wales on formation or subsequently by special resolution, it is not possible under the 1985 Act for a Welsh company to drop the restriction so that its registered office address can be changed to anywhere in England and Wales.

192. Welsh companies may deliver documents to the registrar in Welsh (see section 1104). Welsh companies may also end their company name with Welsh versions of the statutory indicators of legal status. For example, "cyfyngedig" in place of "limited" or "c.c.c." in place of "p.l.c." (see sections 58 and 59). When a company ceases to be a Welsh company using the procedure under this section, it may no longer take advantage of these provisions.

193. Where a company passes a special resolution under subsection (2) or (3) (and so becomes or ceases to be Welsh company) subsection (4) provides that the registrar will amend the register and issue the company with a new certificate of incorporation.

PART 7: RE-REGISTRATION AS A MEANS OF ALTERING A COMPANY'S STATUS

[3.8]
194. This Part of the Act is about the re-registration of companies. It replaces equivalent provisions in Part 2 of the 1985 Act. There are some substantive changes as well as amendments reflecting the new provisions of the Act about registration which are carried through to the re-registration provisions.

Introductory

Section 89: Alteration of status by re-registration

195. This section provides for various ways under the Act by which a company may alter its status. As recommended by the CLR (Final Report, paragraph 11.6) it retains the current possibilities for re-registration, but there is one significant change to the 1985 Act regime: in line with the recommendations of the CLR (Final Report, paragraph 11.11), in future a public company will be able to re-register as an unlimited private company without first having to re-register as private limited – see section 109.

Private company becoming public

Section 90: Re-registration of private company as public

196. This section restates section 43(1) and (2), and section 48 of the 1985 Act. It enables a private company (whether limited or unlimited) to re-register as a public company providing that certain conditions are met. These conditions are set out in subsections (2) to (4). They include a requirement for the company to make such alterations to its name and articles of association ("articles") as are necessary to reflect the fact that the company will be a public company. This will be particularly important for private companies formed under the Act who are using the model articles: in particular, the new model articles for private companies limited by shares formed under the Act will be written with such companies in mind and are unlikely to be suitable for use by a newly re-registered public company – see notes on sections 19 and 20.

197. As now (see section 48 of the 1985 Act), an unlimited private company with a share capital will be able to re-register as a public company and this is reflected in subsection (4) of this section.

198. Subsection (2)(e) retains the requirement that a private company may not re-register as a public company if it has previously re-registered as an unlimited company. The intention behind this provision is that a company should not be able to enjoy the benefits of limited liability or avoid the obligations that are attached to this, for example, the increased reporting requirements, by continually swapping from limited to unlimited status.

Section 91: Requirements as to share capital

199. This section restates sections 45, 47(3) and 48(5) to (7) of the 1985 Act. It sets out the requirements as to share capital of a company that it is proposing to re-register as a public company. These requirements carry forward the provisions of current companies legislation, for example, the company's share capital must not be less than the authorised minimum (defined in section 763) and each of the company's allotted shares must be paid up at least as to a quarter of the nominal value of that share and the whole of any premium on in.

200. Subsection (5) of this section replaces section 47(3) of the 1985 Act. It provides that the registrar must not issue a new certificate of incorporation on re-registration if the court has made an order confirming a reduction of capital which has the effect of bringing the company's allotted share capital below the authorised minimum (which remains at £50,000 but may be satisfied in sterling or euros – see section 763) or if the company has reduced its capital via the new solvency statement procedure for capital reductions (see section 642) or in connection with a redenomination of share capital (see section 626).

Section 92: Requirements as to net assets

201. This section restates section 43(3)(b), (c) and (e), and (4), and section 46 of the 1985 Act. The requirements as to net assets for a public company remain unchanged (as now, these are determined by reference to the company's most recent balance sheet).

Section 93: Recent allotment of shares for non-cash consideration

202. This section restates section 44 of the 1985 Act. As now, where there has been an allotment of shares for non-cash consideration between the date of the balance sheet required under section 92 and the date that the company passed the resolution to re-register as a public company, the registrar will not entertain an application for re-registration unless the consideration for the allotment has been valued in accordance with section 596.

Section 94: Application and accompanying documents

203. This section restates sections 43(3)(a) to (e) and 47(2) of the 1985 Act. It prescribes the contents of the application for re-registration where a private company is proposing to reregister as public. There is one important change, which is required as a result of the abolition of the current requirement for private companies to have a company secretary – see section 270. In future, where a private company is proposing to re-register as a public company the application for re-registration must include a statement of the company's proposed secretary where the company does not already have a secretary. The contents of this statement are prescribed in section 95.

204. The application for re-registration must be accompanied by a statement of compliance – see section 90(1)(c)(ii) – which replaces the present requirement for a statutory declaration (or its electronic equivalent), contained in subsections 43(3)(e) and (3A) of the 1985 Act, with a requirement to make this statement (see note on section 13).

Section 95: Statement of proposed secretary

205. This section is a new provision, which is required as a result of the abolition of the requirement for private companies to have a company secretary – see section 270. Where a private

Part 3   CA 2006 Supporting Materials

company is proposing to re-register as a public company and the company does not already have a company secretary, the application for re-registration must include details of the person or persons who will act as company secretary or joint secretaries on re-registration. The statement of proposed secretary must also contain a consent, given by the person or each of the persons named in the statement, to act as company secretary or joint secretaries. If all the partners in a firm are to be joint secretaries, one partner in the firm may give consent to act on behalf of all of the partners.

Section 96: Issue of certificate of incorporation on re-registration

206.   This section replaces section 47 of the 1985 Act. As now, where the registrar is satisfied that a company is entitled to be re-registered as a public company, she will issue a new certificate of incorporation (which must state that it is being issued on the re-registration of the company). On the issue of a new certificate of incorporation under this section: the company becomes a public company; the change to its name and any amendments that were made to the company's articles take effect; and the person (or persons) named as secretary (or joint secretaries) in the statement of proposed secretary (see section 95) is deemed to have been appointed as such.

207.   As now, the certificate of incorporation on re-registration is conclusive evidence that the company is now a public company and that the requirements of the Act as regards re-registration have been met.

Public company becoming private

Section 97: Re-registration of public company as private limited company

208.   This section replaces section 53 of the 1985 Act. It enables a public company to reregister as a private limited company if the conditions specified in subsection (2) are met. The conditions are the same as those which are presently set out in section 53 but there are two important changes:

- Consistent with the approach taken elsewhere in the Act, for example the sections on the re-registration of a private company as public, subsection (1)(c)(ii) of this section introduces a new requirement for a statement of compliance (see note on section 13).
- Subsection (2) introduces new provisions which enable the registrar to process an application for the re-registration of a company from public to private limited within the 28-day period during which dissenting members may apply to the court, under section 98, for an order cancelling the resolution for re-registration, providing that she is satisfied that such an application cannot be made. This change reflects the registrar's current practice.

209.   As now, the company must make such changes to its name and articles as are necessary in connection with it becoming a private company limited by shares or, as the case may be, a private company limited by guarantee.

Section 98: Application to court to cancel resolution

210.   This section restates section 54(1) to (3) and (5) to (6) of the 1985 Act. As now, where a public company has passed a special resolution to re-register as a private limited company, the requisite majority of the company's members (see subsection (1)) may apply to the court for the cancellation of this resolution. Such an application to the court must be made within 28 days of the resolution to re-register being passed and on hearing the application the court may confirm or cancel the resolution or make such other order as it thinks fit.

Section 99: Notice to registrar of court application or order

211.   This section replaces section 54(4) (7) and (10) of the 1985 Act. It makes it clear that, as now, where an application is made to the court under section 98 (that is, to cancel a resolution for re-registration as a private limited company), the company must immediately give notice to the registrar. Similarly, where the court has made an order in connection with such an application, the company must deliver a copy of that order to the registrar within 15 days of the order being made (or such longer time as the court may direct).

212.   Subsection (1) of this section is a new provision which requires the dissenting members, on making an application to court seeking to cancel the resolution for re-registration from public to private, to give notice direct to the registrar. This ensures that the registrar is aware of any applications which have been made under section 98 and therefore will enable the registrar to process the application for re-registration without further delay where she is satisfied that no application to court may be made – see note on section 97.

213.   Subsection (4) carries forward the offence in section 54(10) of the 1985 Act. Where the company fails to give notice to the registrar or fails to deliver a copy of the order made by the court under section 98 within the prescribed time limits (see subsections (2) and (3)), the company and every officer of the company who is in default commits an offence. The penalty for this offence is set out in subsection (5).

Section 100: Application and accompanying documents

214.   This section replaces section 53(1)(b) of the 1985 Act and contains new provisions. It prescribes the documents/information that must accompany the application for re-registration where a company is proposing to re-register from public to private limited. Consistent with the approach taken in the Act with other forms of re-registration, in future the application for re-registration as a private limited company must be accompanied by a statement of compliance – see note on section 13. (There is currently no requirement for a statutory declaration (or electronic equivalent) where a public company re-registers as a private limited company).

Section 101: Issue of certificate of incorporation on re-registration

215. This section restates section 55 of the 1985 Act. As now, where the registrar is satisfied that a company is entitled to be re-registered as a private limited company, she will issue a new certificate of incorporation (which must state that it is being issued on the re-registration of the company). On the issue of a new certificate of incorporation under this section, the company becomes a private limited company and the change to its name and any amendments that were required to be made to the articles take effect.

216. As now, the certificate of incorporation on re-registration issued under this section is conclusive evidence that the company is now a private limited company and that the requirements of the Act as regards re-registration have been met.

Private limited company becoming unlimited

Section 102: Re-registration of private limited company as unlimited

217. This section replaces section 49, of the 1985 Act. As now, this section permits a private company that is limited by shares or, as the case may be, by guarantee, to re-register as an unlimited private company, providing that certain conditions are met (see subsection (2)) and all of the members have given their assent to the company being so re-registered. In the case of a deceased member, assent may be given by the personal representative of the deceased member's estate. Where a member is bankrupt, assent may be given by his trustee in bankruptcy (to the exclusion of the member in question).

218. An "unlimited company" is a company not having any limit on the liability of its members.

219. As now, a company may not re-register as an unlimited company, if it has previously been re-registered as limited (having previously been unlimited) or as unlimited (having previously been limited).

220. The application for re-registration as an unlimited company must be accompanied by a statement of compliance (see note on section 13).

Section 103: Application and accompanying documents

221. This section replaces section 49(8) and (8A) of the 1985 Act. It prescribes the contents of the application for re-registration where a company is proposing to re-register from private limited to unlimited and the documents/information that must accompany this application. The current requirement for a statutory declaration made by the directors on application for re-registration as an unlimited company is replaced by a requirement for a statement of compliance. Unlike other statements of compliance made under the Act (see, for example, section 13) the statement of compliance made on application for re-registration as an unlimited company must contain a statement made by the directors confirming that:

- the persons by whom or on whose behalf the form of assent is authenticated constitute the whole membership of the company; and
- if any of the members have not authenticated that form themselves, that the directors have taken all reasonable steps to satisfy themselves that each person who authenticated it on behalf of a member was lawfully empowered to do so.

222. The contents of the directors' statement carry forward the provisions of section 49(8) of the 1985 Act.

Section 104: Issue of certificate of incorporation on re-registration

223. This section restates section 50 of the 1985 Act. As now, where the registrar is satisfied that a company is entitled to be re-registered as an unlimited company, she will issue a new certificate of incorporation (which must state that it is being issued on the re-registration of the company). On the issue of a new certificate of incorporation under this section, the company becomes an unlimited company and the change to its name and any amendments that were required to be made to the articles take effect.

224. As now, the certificate of incorporation on re-registration is conclusive evidence that the company is now an unlimited company and that the requirements of the Act as regards re-registration have been met.

Unlimited private company becoming limited

Section 105: Re-registration of unlimited company as limited

225. This section replaces section 51(1) to (3) of the 1985 Act. As now, this section permits an unlimited company to re-register as a private limited company if certain conditions are met (see

Part 3   CA 2006 Supporting Materials

subsection (2)). As now, a re-registration from unlimited to limited requires a special resolution of the company's members, (which must specify whether the company is to be limited by shares or limited by guarantee). The company must also make such changes to its name and articles as are required to reflect the change in the company's status. As is the case under section 51(6) of the 1985 Act, this section does not permit the re-registration of an unlimited company as a public company (this section provides for the re-registration of an unlimited company as a *private* limited company). There is a new requirement for a statement of compliance (see note on section 13).

Section 106: Application and accompanying documents

226. This section replaces section 51(5) of the 1985 Act and contains new provisions. It prescribes the contents of the application for re-registration where an unlimited private company is proposing to re-register as private limited and the documents/information that must accompany this application. Where the company is to be limited by guarantee, subsection (2)(b) requires the application for re-registration to be accompanied by a "statement of guarantee" (see note on section 11). It should be noted that there is no requirement for a statement of capital and initial shareholdings where the company is to be limited by shares. This is unnecessary because the company will be required to make a return of allotments to the registrar, under section 555 as soon as it allots shares subsequent to its registration and the return must be accompanied by a statement of capital.

Section 107: Issue of certificate of incorporation on re-registration

227. This section restates section 52 of the 1985 Act. As now, it provides that, where the registrar is satisfied that a company is entitled to be re-registered as a private company, she will issue a new certificate of incorporation (which must state that it is being issued on the re-registration of the company). On the issue of a new certificate of incorporation under this section, the company becomes a private limited company and the change to its name and any amendments that were required to be made to the articles take effect.

228. As now, the certificate of incorporation on re-registration issued under this section is conclusive evidence that the company is now a private limited company and that the requirements of the Act as regards re-registration have been met.

Section 108: Statement of capital required where company already has share capital

229. This section is a new provision which requires a company that has re-registered from unlimited having a share capital to private limited by shares to file a statement of capital with the registrar in certain circumstances. The statement must be delivered to the registrar within 15 days of the company's re-registration and, where the company fails to observe this requirement, the company and every officer of the company who is in default, commits an offence (see subsection (4)).

230. The provision is necessary because unlimited companies are required to provide a statement of capital to the registrar in a limited number of circumstances only: in particular, where the company has a share capital on formation (see section 10) or where an unlimited company having a share capital makes an annual return to the registrar under section 854. Consequently, where an unlimited company having a share capital re-registers as private limited by shares under section 107, in contrast to other companies that are limited by shares, the information on the public register pertaining to the company's subscribed capital may be out of date (in particular if the company has allotted further shares subsequent to its formation or, as the case may be, its last annual return).

231. The requirement for a statement of capital in this section puts companies which have re-registered as private limited by shares under section 107 on the same footing as other companies limited by shares on the register and ensures that the information on the public register is up-to-date. The company will, however, be exempted from the requirement to provide a statement of capital on re-registration where there has been no change to the company's total subscribed capital since it was first formed and registered or, as the case may be, since the company filed its most recent annual return (see subsection (2)).

Public company becoming private and unlimited

Section 109: Re-registration of public company as private and unlimited

232. This section is a new provision, which, as recommended by the CLR (Final Report, paragraph 11.11), enables a public company to re-register as a private unlimited company with a share capital without first having to re-register as a private limited company. The conditions specified in subsection (2) must be met and all of the members must give their assent to the company being so re-registered. In the case of a deceased member, assent may be given by the personal representative of the deceased member's estate. Where a member is bankrupt, assent may be given by his trustee in bankruptcy (to the exclusion of the member in question).

233. A public company may not re-register as an unlimited private company under this section if it has previously been re-registered as limited or as unlimited (see subsection (2)). The intention behind this subsection (which is based on the provision in subsection (2)(e) of section 90) is that a company should not be able to enjoy the benefits of limited liability or avoid the obligations that are attached to this, for example, the increased reporting requirements, by continually swapping from limited to unlimited status.

Section 110: Application and accompanying documents

234. This section is a new provision. It prescribes the contents of the application for re-registration where a company is proposing to re-register from public to unlimited private and the documents/information that must accompany this application. There is a requirement for a statement of compliance (see note on section 13) and, in contrast to the statements of compliance that are required elsewhere in the Act, the statement of compliance that is required here must contain a statement made by the directors confirming that:

- the persons by whom or on whose behalf the form of assent is authenticated constitute the whole membership of the company; and

- if any of the members have not authenticated that form themselves, that the directors have taken all reasonable steps to satisfy themselves that each person who authenticated it on behalf of a member was lawfully empowered to do so.

235. This mirrors the requirements of the directors' statement in section 103(4).

Section 111: Issue of certificate of incorporation on re-registration

236. This section is a new provision which requires the registrar to issue a new certificate of incorporation is she is satisfied that a public company is entitled to register as private and unlimited. On the issue of a new certificate of incorporation (which must state that it is being issued on the re-registration of the company), the company becomes a private unlimited company and the change to its name and any amendments that were made to the articles take effect.

237. The certificate of incorporation on re-registration is conclusive evidence that the company is now a private unlimited company and that the requirements of the Act as regards re-registration have been met.

PART 8: A COMPANY'S MEMBERS

[3.9]
238. This Part of the Act defines who are a company's members, provides rules relating to a company's register of members and overseas branch registers and, subject to certain exceptions, prohibits a company from being a member of its holding company.

Chapter 1: The Members Of A Company

Section 112: The members of a company

239. This section restates section 22 of the 1985 Act. There are additional words to make it clear that the subscribers to the memorandum become members on registration of the company, even if the company fails to enter their names in the register of members.

Chapter 2: Register Of Members

Section 113: Register of members

240. This section restates section 352(1) to (5) of the 1985 Act. The only new provision is subsection (5) which makes it clear that, for the purposes of this Chapter, joint holders of a share fall to be treated as a single member, so the register need only show a single address although all their names must be stated in the register.

Section 114: Register to be kept available for inspection

241. This section replaces section 353 of the 1985 Act. Currently, the register of members is required to be kept at the registered office of the company, except that if the company has appointed a third party to maintain or update the register, it may be kept at the office where that work is done, subject to that office being in the jurisdiction where the company is registered. Under the Act, it is immaterial where the work of compiling or updating the register is carried out. Subsection (1) provides that the register must be kept available for inspection either at the company's registered office or at a place permitted under regulations made under section 1136.

Section 115: Index of members

242. This section replaces section 354 of the 1985 Act. There is no change in the obligation of a company with more than 50 members to maintain an index of the names of the members (which the company is obliged to do unless the register itself is kept in such a form as to constitute an index).

Section 116: Rights to inspect and require copies

243. This section replaces section 356 of the 1985 Act. Under section 356, the obligation to make the register available for inspection is subject to an exception when the register is closed under section 358 of the 1985 Act. The power to close the register has not been carried forward in the Act and so the obligation in subsection (1) is absolute. The CLR recommended that information in a company's register of members should be made available only for certain specified purposes (Final

Part 3   CA 2006 Supporting Materials

Report, paragraph 11.44). This section follows this recommendation. It modifies the rights of inspection and to be provided with copies of the register of members and its index. (Section 1137 provides power for the Secretary of State to make regulations about the inspection of records and provision of copies and to set fees.) Subsections (3) and (4), which are new, require those seeking to inspect or to be provided with a copy of the register of members to provide their names and addresses, the purpose for which the information will be used, and, if the access is sought on behalf of others, similar information for them.

Section 117: Register of members: response to request for inspection or copy

244.   This is a new provision. This section provides a procedure by which the company can refer the matter to the court if it thinks that the request may not be for a proper purpose. It replaces the 10-day deadline for compliance with a request with a 5-day period within which the company must either comply with the request or apply to the court for relief from the obligation. If the company opts for the latter, then subsections (3), (4) and (5) apply. Under subsection (3), if the court is satisfied that the access to the register of members is not sought for a proper purpose, it will require the company of the obligation not to comply with the request and may require that the person who made the request pay the company's costs. Under subsection (4), the court may also require the company not to comply with other requests made requests for similar purposes. If the court does not make an order under subsection (3), or the proceedings are discontinued, then, under subsection (5), the company must immediately comply with the request.

Section 118: Register of members: refusal of inspection or default in providing copy

245.   This section replaces section 356(5) and (6) of and Schedule 24 to the 1985 Act. It retains the existing sanctions for the company's failure to comply with a request. They do not apply if the court has directed that the company need not comply with the request.

Section 119: Register of members: offences in connection with request for or disclosure of information.

246.   This is a new provision. It creates two offences. First, in relation to the new requirement in section 116 to provide information in a request for access, it is an offence knowingly or recklessly to make a statement that is misleading, false or deceptive in a material particular. Second, it is an offence for a person to disclose to another person information from a company's register of members obtained under section 116 knowing or having reason to suspect that the other person may use the information for a purpose that is not a proper purpose.

Section 120: Information as to state of register and index

247.   This is a new provision. It implements the CLR recommendation that companies be required to advise anyone exercising their right of inspection or right to demand a copy of the register or index whether the information is up-to-date and, if not, the date to which it has been made up (Final Report, paragraph 11.43). Failure to provide this information renders the company and any officer in default liable to a fine.

Section 121: Removal of entries relating to former members

248.   This section replaces section 352(6) of the 1985 Act. Based on a recommendation by the CLR (Final Report, paragraph 11.40), it reduces the period for which the entry of a past member must be kept on the register from 20 years to 10 years.

Section 122: Share warrants

249.   This section replaces section 355 of the 1985 Act and implements the CLR recommendation (Completing the Structure, paragraph 5.41) in making clear that shares need not first be issued in registered form, but can be issued directly in warrant to bearer form.

Section 123: Single member companies

250.   This section replaces section 352A of the 1985 Act, which implements the Twelfth Company Law Directive (89/667/EEC) on single member private limited liability companies. This section requires a statement to be entered in a company's register of members that it has only one member if that is the case on incorporation or at a later date – if the latter, the date on which it so became must also be entered. It also requires a statement that the company has ceased to have only one member together with the date of the increase. Section 352A of the 1985 Act applies to private companies alone, but this section applies to both private and public companies.

Section 124: Company holding its own shares as treasury shares

251.   This section replaces section 352(3A) as regards the entries required to be made in the register of members where a company holds treasury shares. The effect of that provision is unchanged.

Section 125: Power of court to rectify register
Section 126: Trusts not to be entered on register
Section 127: Register to be evidence

252. These sections restate sections 359, 360 and 361 of the 1985 Act.

Section 128: Time limit for claims arising from entry in register

253. This section replaces section 352(7) of the 1985 Act. Based on a recommendation by the CLR (Final Report, paragraph 11.40), it reduces the time limit for claims relating to entries in the register from 20 years to 10 years.

Chapter 3: Overseas Branch Registers

254. This Chapter restates the 1985 Act's provisions (section 362 and Parts I and II of Schedule 14) regarding overseas branch registers. It enables companies in specified circumstances to keep in a specified country or territory a register of those members resident in that country or territory. An overseas branch register is deemed to be part of the company's register of members. It differs from the provisions of the 1985 Act in two respects.

*   First, rather than providing for an Order in Council, section 129(3) provides the Secretary of State with power to make regulations as to the circumstances in which a company is to be regarded as keeping an overseas branch register.
*   Second, section 131 provides power to modify the provisions of Chapter 2 of this Part (relating to the company's register of members) in their application to overseas branch registers.

Chapter 4: Prohibition On Subsidiary Being Member Of Its Holding Company

255. This Chapter is a restatement of the provisions of section 23 of the 1985 Act and Schedule 2 to that Act as it applies for the purposes of that section. Unless in circumstances covered by an exception, a company cannot be a member of its own holding company. There is no change of substance to the provision in the 1985 Act.

PART 9: EXERCISE OF MEMBERS' RIGHTS

[3.10]
256. The CLR considered the rights of persons other than the registered shareholders, presenting their recommendations in Chapter 7 of the 'Final Report'. The new provisions in Part 9 have been developed with these recommendations in mind and are designed to make it easier for investors to exercise their governance rights fully and responsibly. Nowadays when investors, whether major institutional investors or retail investors, buy shares in a listed company they are increasingly likely to hold their shares through an intermediary or a chain of intermediaries. This means that it is an intermediary's name that appears on the company's register of members. As a result investors typically have to rely on contractual arrangements with the intermediaries both to obtain information from the company and also to give any instructions they wish about how shares should be voted.

257. This Part of the Act introduces new provisions dealing with the ability of indirect investors to exercise governance rights. The first section in the Part removes any doubts as to the ability of companies to make provision in their articles for others to enjoy and exercise membership rights and enables indirect investors to enjoy information rights via the registered member. The next group of sections provides that indirect investors in traded companies can be nominated by the registered member to receive company documents and information. It is up to the registered member, typically a broker, to decide whether to nominate or not. The last two sections in the Part make it easier for registered members to exercise rights in different ways to reflect the underlying holdings and allow indirect investors to participate in, for example, requests for resolutions at the AGM. The provisions of this Part should be looked at together with sections 324 to 331 on proxies in Part 13, which enable the registered member to appoint indirect investors as proxies to exercise voting rights.

258. An important principle to note is that the information rights and exercise of other rights where shares are held on behalf of others can be initiated and enforced with the company only by the registered member. This Part does not compel the registered member to confer such rights on third parties. It will be for indirect investors, such as shareholders holding through a nominee, to choose a nominee operator who offers such rights as part of their service.

Effect of provisions in company's articles

259. Section 145 protects arrangements through company articles to enfranchise indirect investors and provides that where a company makes provision, through its articles, to extend rights to those holding shares through intermediaries, the provision is legally effective in relation to various statutory requirements.

Section 145: Effect of provisions of articles as to enjoyment of exercise of members' rights

260. This section (subsection (1)) allows a company's articles to enable a member to identify another person or persons as entitled to enjoy or exercise all or any specified rights of a member. The

Part 3   CA 2006 Supporting Materials

articles may specify that this entitlement can apply only to certain rights or to all rights, except the right to transfer the shares. As subsection (4)(b) makes clear, the right to transfer shares must remain, as under the 1985 Act, with the member whose name is on the register.

261. Subsection (2) provides that where a company makes relevant provision in its articles, all the relevant references in the Companies Acts to 'member' should be read as if the reference to member was a reference to the person or persons nominated by the member. Subsection (3) provides a non-exhaustive list of the provisions in question.

262. Subsection (4)(a) makes clear that non-members do not have direct enforceable rights against the company. They should enforce their rights through the member whose name is on the register and who has the right to enforce the articles.

Information rights

263. Sections 146 to 150 introduce new provisions enabling indirect investors to be appointed by the registered member to receive information that is sent to members by the company. These provisions apply only to companies traded on a regulated market. The Secretary of State may extend or limit the classes of companies to which these provisions apply through the power provided under section 151.

Section 146: Traded companies: nomination of persons to enjoy information rights

264. Subsections (1) and (2) provide new rights for members of companies whose shares are traded on regulated markets to nominate those on whose behalf they hold shares to receive information that is sent to members direct from the company and to exercise certain rights.

265. Subsection (3) sets out what is meant by 'information rights', namely the right to receive all communications that the company sends to members, the right to require copies of accounts and reports (as in section 431 or 432), and the right to require hard copy versions of documents (section 1145).

266. Subsection (4) refers to section 426, which allows under certain circumstances for summary financial statements rather than full accounts to be sent out as part of the general information. These must also be sent to nominated persons.

267. Subsection (5) provides that the company does not need to respond to a nomination that specifies only certain information rights.

Section 147: Information rights: form in which copies to be provided

268. This section deals with the way in which information is to be provided to a nominated person. Subsection (2) explains that if a nominated person wants communications to be in hard copy, they must ask the member, providing a postal address, before the nomination is made. If the member then passes this on to the company, under subsection (3) the nominated person will have the right to receive hard copy communications.

Section 148: Termination or suspension of nomination

269. This section provides that a nomination will stop having effect on the request of the nominated person or the member (subsection (2)), or on the death, bankruptcy or winding up of the nominated person or the member (subsection (3)).

270. Subsection (5) explains that all nominations made by member will be suspended if there are more nominations that the total number of shares, and subsection (6) makes similar provision where there are different classes of shares.

Section 149: Information as to possible rights in relation to voting

271. This section requires the company, when sending a meeting notice to nominated persons, to include a statement that the nominated person may have voting rights that he can exercise through the person who nominated him.

Section 150: Information rights: status of rights

272. This section deals with the rights arising from a nomination under section 146, and in particular provides that it is the member, rather than the nominated person, who can enforce the rights against the company.

Section 151: Information rights: power to amend

273. This section gives a power for the Secretary of State to amend the provisions of sections 146 to 150. The power allows for changes in the companies covered, the circumstances in which nominations can be made and the rights conferred by nomination.

Effect of rights where shares held on behalf of others

274. Sections 152 and 153 enable indirect investors, via the registered member, to exercise voting and requisition rights by making it easier for registered members to exercise rights in different ways to reflect underlying holdings and by allowing those on whose behalf they hold shares to participate in requisitions. These two sections apply to all companies.

Section 152: Exercise of rights where shares held on behalf of others: exercise in different ways

275. This section provides that a member can choose to split his holding and exercise rights attached to shares in different ways. This is to accommodate members who hold shares on behalf of more than one person, each of whom may want to exercise rights attaching to their shares in different ways. So, for example, it enables votes to be cast in different ways. Subsection (4) provides that if the member does not make it clear to the company in what way he is exercising his rights the company can assume that all rights are being dealt with in the same way.

Section 153: Exercise of rights where shares held on behalf of others: members' requests

276. This section deals with four situations where the shareholder threshold required to trigger a right is 100 shareholders holding £100 each on average of paid-up capital. Indirect investors are able to count towards the total subject to certain conditions, intended to ensure that only genuine indirect investors are allowed to count towards the total, that the same shares cannot be used twice and that the indirect investor's contractual arrangements with the member allow the former to give voting instructions.

PART 10: COMPANY DIRECTORS

[3.11]

277. This Part replaces Part 10 of the 1985 Act (enforcement of fair dealing by directors), the provisions relating to directors in Part 9 of that Act and the provisions relating to confidentiality orders in Part 25 of that Act. It also introduces a statutory statement of directors' general duties to the company.

Who is a director?

278. Section 250 defines a director as including any person occupying the position of director, by whatever name called. This is the same as the definition contained in section 741(1) of the 1985 Act. The Act does not attempt a more detailed definition of a director because it is important to ensure that the term is applied to anybody who exercises real power within the company, particularly in relation to decision taking. The term "director" therefore includes:

- an executive director who has been properly appointed by the company;
- a non-executive director who has been properly appointed by the company;
- a de facto director (that is, a person who has assumed the status and functions of a company director even though he has not been properly appointed).

279. A "shadow director" is defined by section 251 as "a person in accordance with whose directions or instructions the directors of the company are accustomed to act". The section provides that a person is not to be regarded as a shadow director by reason only that the directors act on advice given by him in a professional capacity. This definition is the same as the definition contained in section 741(2) of the 1985 Act.

Powers of directors

280. This Part of the Act does not generally directly give powers to the directors, but, under the draft model articles of association for private companies limited by shares, the directors' functions are:

- to manage the company's business; and
- to exercise all the powers of the company.

Chapter 1: Appointment And Removal Of Directors

Section 154: Companies required to have directors

281. This section replaces section 282 of the 1985 Act. It distinguishes between private and public companies. It retains the requirement for a private company to have at least one director and requires all public companies to have at least two. There will no longer be an exception for public companies registered before 1st November 1929 (or before 1st January 1933 in Northern Ireland).

Section 155: Companies required to have at least one director who is a natural person

282. This section is a new provision. It introduces a requirement that every company have at least one director who is a natural person, ie an individual. Subject to this requirement being satisfied, any legal person, including one that is a company or a firm, can be a director but one company cannot be the sole director of another company. Subsection (2) provides that the requirement that the director be a natural person is met if the director is a corporation sole (for example, the Archbishop of Canterbury) or someone appointed on the basis of some other appointment that they hold.

Section 156: Direction requiring company to make appointment

283. This section is a new provision, enabling enforcement of the existing requirement for a private company to have at least one director and a public company to have at least two directors and of the new requirement for every company to have at least one director who is an individual. Where it appears to the Secretary of State that any of these requirements is not met, the Secretary of State will be able to direct the company to comply by issuing a notice. It will be an offence not to comply.

Section 157: Minimum age for appointment as director

284. This section is a new provision. It introduces a minimum age of 16 for a natural person to be a director. Subsection (2) provides that prohibition will not prevent the appointment of a younger person provided it is not to take effect until that person is 16. Subsection (3) provides that the age limit applies even if the director's appointment is a consequence of some other appointment. Subsection (5) provides that this prohibition on under-age directors does not provide protection from criminal prosecution or civil liability if he or she were to act as director, ie as a de facto director, or if the company's directors usually act on that young person's instructions.

Section 158: Power to provide for exceptions from minimum age requirement

285. This section is a new provision. It provides for an exception from the prohibition in section 157 on anyone under 16 being appointed a director of a company. It provides a power for the Secretary of State to make regulations specifying circumstances in which a younger person may be a director. The regulations may differ for different parts of the UK.

Section 159: Existing under-age directors

286. This section is a new transitional provision. Subsections (1) and (2) provide that where a person under 16 has been appointed as director (or holds the office of director by virtue of another office or is a corporation sole) prior to the prohibition on under age directors coming into force, that person will cease to be a director when the prohibition in section 157 comes into force. Subsection (3) makes it the company's responsibility to amend its register of directors accordingly but the company is not required to notify the registrar of the change. Subsection (4) gives the registrar power to amend the register without a notification by the company of the director's removal but rather on the basis of information already held (ie the date of birth as provided when the appointment was notified).

Section 160: Appointment of directors of public company to be voted on individually.

287. This restates section 292 of the 1985 Act: the appointment of each proposed director of a public company must be voted on individually unless there is unanimous agreement to a block resolution. Without such consent, any appointment of a director that is not voted on individually is void. This ensures that members can express their disapproval of any particular director without having to reject the entire board.

Section 161: Validity of acts of directors

288. This section, which replaces section 285 of the 1985 Act, provides that a director's actions are valid even if his or her appointment is subsequently found to have been defective or void.

Section 162: Register of directors

289. This section replaces part of section 288 of the 1985 Act. It imposes on every company a requirement to keep a register of its directors (secretaries are dealt with in Part 12). This register need not contain particulars of shadow directors.

290. This section requires the register to be kept available for inspection either at the company's registered office or at a place specified in regulations made under section 1136. It must be available for inspection by members (without charge) or the public (for a prescribed fee, set under powers provided under section 1137). Refusal to permit inspection is an offence for which every officer in default (including a shadow director) can be liable. In addition, the court may compel immediate inspection of the register if the company has refused.

Section 163: Particulars of directors to be registered: individuals

291. This section replaces section 289 of the 1985 Act so far as it applies to individuals. It specifies the particulars that must be entered in the register of directors for each director who is an individual (as opposed to a company or similar entity). The most significant change is the requirement for companies to provide a service address for a director rather than, as now, the director's usual residential address. A director may give the company's registered office as his or her service address; the service address may also be the same as the director's residential address – but this will not be apparent from the public record. In addition, in fulfilment of a Government commitment given in March 1998, the particulars no longer include details of other directorships held. There are also changes to the requirement to provide the director's name. The requirement is now to include any name by which the individual was formerly known for business purposes. As recommended by the CLR (Final Report, paragraph 11.38), there is no longer an exception for a married woman's former name. However the section retains a protective provision relating to the former names of peers.

Section 164: Particulars of directors to be registered: corporate directors and firms

292.   This section replaces section 289(1)(b) of the 1985 Act. It retains the requirement for the corporate or firm name and the registered or principal office to be recorded where the director is either a body corporate or a firm that is a legal person under the law by which it is governed. In addition, as recommended by the CLR (Final Report, paragraph 11.38), it requires for EEA companies the register where the company is registered and its registration number; for all others, particulars of the legal form of the company or firm, the law by which it is governed, and, if applicable, where it is registered and its registration number.

Section 165: Register of directors' residential addresses

293.   This section is a new provision. It requires companies to keep a register of the usual residential addresses of directors who are individuals. Provided that a director's service address is not the company's registered office, if his/her residential address is the same as his/her service address, then the register need only contain an entry making that clear. This register is not to be open to public inspection, but can be used in accordance with Chapter 8 of this Part.

Section 166: Particulars of directors to be registered: power to make regulations

294.   This section is a new provision. It provides power for the Secretary of State to make regulations that add or remove items from the particulars that have to be entered in a company's register of directors and register of directors' residential addresses.

Section 167: Duty to notify registrar of changes

295.   This section replaces section 288(2) of the 1985 Act insofar as it applies to directors. It retains the requirement that the appointment of a director, or a director's ceasing to hold office, and any change in an existing director's particulars, be notified to the registrar within 14 days. This requirement does not extend to shadow directors. Default is an offence. This section also requires a notice of appointment to be accompanied by the appointee's consent. This provision ensures that the public record is kept up to date. There is also a requirement to notify the registrar of changes to information in the register of directors' residential addresses (but this information is not to be open to public inspection at Companies House).

Section 168: Resolution to remove director

296.   This section replaces section 303 of the 1985 Act. Subsection (1) provides that an ordinary resolution is sufficient to remove a director, but requires that it be at a meeting so as to ensure the director's right to be heard.

Section 169: Director's right to protest removal

297.   This section replaces section 304 of the 1985 Act. The only change is to be found in subsection (5); the court need no longer be satisfied that the rights conferred by the section are being abused to secure needless publicity for defamatory matter, so long as it is satisfied that they are being abused

Chapter 2: General Duties Of Directors

Sections 170 to 181: General comments

298.   The general duties form a code of conduct, which sets out how directors are expected to behave; it does not tell them in terms what to do. More particularly, the duties address:
*   the possibility that a director may put his own or other interests ahead of those of the company;
*   the possibility that he may be negligent.

299.   The duties are derived from equitable and common law rules, and are not at the moment written down in statute.

300.   The Law Commission and the Scottish Law Commission recommended that there should be a statutory statement of a director's main fiduciary duties and his duty of care and skill in their joint report *Company Directors: Regulating Conflicts of Interests and Formulating a Statement of Duties*. The CLR's main recommendations in respect of directors' general duties are summarised in chapter 3 of the Final Report.

301.   The CLR recommended that there should be a statutory statement of directors' general duties, and that this should, with two exceptions, described in the next paragraph, be a codification of the current law. In particular they wanted:
*   to provide greater clarity on what is expected of directors and make the law more accessible. In particular, they sought to address the key question "in whose interests should companies be run?" in a way which reflects modern business needs and wider expectations of responsible business behaviour;
*   to make development of the law in this area more predictable (but without hindering development of the law by the courts);

Part 3   CA 2006 Supporting Materials

- to correct what the CLR saw as defects in the present duties relating to conflicts of interest.

The Government has accepted these recommendations.

302. There are two areas, both relating to the regulation of conflicts of interest, where the statutory statement departs from the current law:

- under section 175, transactions or arrangements with the company do not have to be authorised by either the members or by the board; instead interests in transactions or arrangements with the company must be declared under section 177 (in the case of proposed transactions) or under section 182 (in the case of existing transactions) unless an exception applies under those sections;

- section 175 also permits board authorisation of most conflicts of interest arising from third party dealings by the director (eg personal exploitation of corporate resources and opportunities). Such authorisation is effective only if the conflicted directors have not participated in the taking of the decision or if the decision would have been valid even without the participation of the conflicted directors. Board authorisation of conflicts of interest will be the default position for private companies, but public companies will need to make provision in their constitutions to permit this. Board authorisation is not permitted in respect of the acceptance of benefits from third parties (section 176).

303. Both reforms implement recommendations of the CLR, which noted that the basic principles in the current law relating to directors' conflicts of interest are very strict:

- they noted that in practice most companies permit a director to have an interest in a proposed transaction or arrangement with the company, provided that the interest is disclosed to his fellow directors. The statutory statement therefore reflects the current position in most companies;

- they also took the view that the current strict rule relating to conflicts of interest in respect of personal exploitation of corporate opportunities fettered entrepreneurial and business start-up activity by existing company directors. The statutory statement therefore provides for board authorisation of such conflicts.

304. These reforms are modified for charitable companies in England and Wales and Northern Ireland by section 181.

Codification of common law rules and equitable principles

305. Codification is not a matter of transposing wording taken from judgments into legislative propositions. Judgments are, of necessity, directed at particular cases. Even when they appear to state general principles, they will rarely be exhaustive. They will be the application of (perhaps unstated) general principles to particular facts. In the company law field, the principles being applied will frequently be taken from other areas, in particular trusts and agency. It is important that these connections are not lost and that company law may continue to reflect developments elsewhere. Frequently the courts may formulate the same idea in different ways. In contrast legislation is formal. It is not easy to reconcile these two approaches but the draft sections seek to balance precision against the need for continued flexibility and development. In particular:

- subsection (3) of section 170 provides that the statutory duties are based on, and have effect in place of, certain common law rules and equitable principles;

- subsection (4) of section 170 provides that the general duties should be interpreted and applied in the same way as common law rules and equitable principles. The courts should interpret and develop the general duties in a way that reflects the nature of the rules and principles they replace;

- subsection (4) of section 170 also provides when interpreting and applying the statutory duties, regard should be had to the common law rules and equitable principles which the general duties replace; thus developments in the law of trusts and agency should be reflected in the interpretation and application of the duties;

- section 178 provides that the civil consequences of breach (or threatened breach) of the statutory duties are the same as would apply if the corresponding common law rule or equitable principle applied. It also makes clear that the statutory duties are to be regarded as fiduciary, with the exception of the duty to exercise reasonable care skill and diligence which is not under the present law regarded as a fiduciary duty.

306. The statutory duties do not cover all the duties that a director may owe to the company. Many duties are imposed elsewhere in legislation, such as the duty to file accounts and reports with the registrar of companies (section 441). Other duties remain uncodified, such as any duty to consider the interests of creditors in times of threatened insolvency.

Duties owed to the company

307. Section 170(1) makes it clear that, as in the existing law, the general duties are owed by a director to the company. It follows that, as now, only the company can enforce them. Part 11 (derivative claims and actions by members) describes the mechanism whereby members may be able to enforce the duties on behalf of the company.

Who are the duties owed by?

308.   The duties are owed by every person who is a director of a company (as defined in section 250). They are therefore owed by a de facto director in the same way and to the same extent that they are owed by a properly appointed director.

309.   Certain aspects of the duty to avoid conflicts of interest and the duty not to accept benefits from third parties continue to apply even when a person ceases to be a director; this is necessary to ensure that a director cannot, for example, exploit an opportunity of which he became aware while managing the company's business without the necessary consent simply by resigning his position as director. The closing words of section 170(2) provide that these duties apply to a former director subject to any necessary adaptations. This is to reflect the fact that a former director is not in the same legal position as an actual director.

310.   The statutory duties apply to shadow directors where, and to the extent that, the common law rules or equitable principles which they replace so apply (section 170(5)). This means that where a common law rule or equitable principle applies to a shadow director, the statutory duty replacing that common law rule or equitable principle will apply to the shadow director (in place of that rule or principle). Where the rule or principle does not apply to a shadow director, the statutory duty replacing that rule or principle will not apply either.

The relationship between the duties

311.   Many of the general duties will frequently overlap. Taking a bribe from a third party would, for example, clearly fall within the duty not to accept benefits from third parties (section 176) but could also, depending on the facts, be characterised as a failure to promote the success of the company for the benefit of its members (section 172) or as an aspect of failing to exercise independent judgment (section 173).

312.   The effect of the duties is cumulative, so that it is necessary to comply with every duty that applies in any given case. This principle is stated in section 179. One exception relates to the duty to avoid conflicts of interest (section 175). This particular duty does not apply to a conflict of interest arising in relation to a transaction or arrangement with the company. In such cases the duty to declare interests in proposed transactions or arrangements (section 177) or the requirement to declare interests in existing transactions or arrangements (section 182) will apply instead. Section 181 modifies these provisions for charitable companies in England and Wales and Northern Ireland.

313.   The cumulative effect of the duties means that where more than one duty applies, the director must comply with each applicable duty, and the duties must be read in this context. So, for example, the duty to promote the success of the company will not authorise the director to breach his duty to act within his powers, even if he considers that it would be most likely to promote the success of the company.

314.   As well as complying with all the duties, the directors must continue to comply with all other applicable laws. The duties do not require or authorise a director to breach any other prohibition or requirement imposed on him by law.

Relationship between the duties and the company's constitution

315.   Under section 171 a director must act in accordance with the company's constitution.

316.   Companies may, through their articles, go further than the statutory duties by placing more onerous requirements on their directors (eg by requiring shareholder authorisation of the remuneration of the directors). The articles may not dilute the duties except to the extent that this is permitted by the following sections:

- section 173 provides that a director will not be in breach of the duty to exercise independent judgment if he has acted in a way that is authorised by the constitution;
- section 175 permits authorisation of some conflicts of interest by independent directors, subject to the constitution;
- subsection (4)(a) of section 180 preserves any rule of law enabling the company to give authority for anything that would otherwise be a breach of duty;
- subsection (4)(b) of section 180 provides that a director will not be in breach of duty if he acts in accordance with any provisions in the company's articles for dealing with conflicts of interest;
- section 232 places restrictions on the provisions that may be included in the company's articles. But nothing in that section prevents companies from including in their articles any such provisions as are currently lawful for dealing with conflicts of interest.

317.   The company's constitution may also set out the purposes of the company, especially in the case of an altruistic company which has purposes other than the benefit of the company's members. It is very important that directors understand the purposes of the company, so that they are able to comply with their duty to promote the success of the company in section 172.

Relationship between the duties and the detailed rules requiring member approval of conflicts of interest

318.   Under the provisions in Chapter 4 of this Part, the directors must sometimes obtain prior shareholder approval for the following types of transaction involving a director (or, in some cases,

Part 3   CA 2006 Supporting Materials

a person connected to a director): long-term service contracts; substantial property transactions; loans, quasi-loans and credit transactions; and payments for loss of office.

319.   Section 180 provides that:
* compliance with the general duties does not remove the need for member approval of such transactions (subsection (3));
* (subject to the exception set out in the bullet point below) the general duties apply even if the transaction also falls within Chapter 4 (because it is a long-term service contract, substantial property transaction, loan, quasi-loan, credit transaction or payment for loss of office). So, for example, the directors should only approve a loan to a director if they consider that it would promote the success of the company. This is so, even if the loan does not require the approval of members under Chapter 4 because it falls within a relevant exception, such as the exception for expenditure on company business in section 204;
* if the transaction falls within Chapter 4 (because it is a long-term service contract, substantial property transaction, loan, quasi-loan, credit transaction or payment for loss of office) and approval of the members is obtained to the transaction in accordance with that Chapter, or an exception applies, so that approval is not necessary under that Chapter, then the director does not need to comply with the duty to avoid conflicts of interest (section 175) or the duty not to accept benefits from third parties (section 176) in respect of that transaction. All other applicable duties will still apply. For example, a director would not be acting in breach of the duty to avoid conflicts of interests if he failed to obtain authorisation from the directors or the members for a loan from the company in respect of legal defence costs. Section 181 modifies this provision for charitable companies in England and Wales and Northern Ireland.

Relationship between the duties and the general law

320.   Section 180(5) provides that the general duties have effect notwithstanding any enactment or rule of law except where there is an express or implied exception to this rule. For example, section 247 provides that directors may make provision for employees on the cessation or transfer of a company's business even if this would otherwise constitute a breach of the general duty to promote the success of the company.

Consequences of breach

321.   Section 178 preserves the existing civil consequences of breach (or threatened breach) of any of the general duties. The remedies for breach of the general duties will be exactly the same as those that are currently available following a breach of the equitable principles and common law rules that the general duties replace.

322.   Subsection (2) of that section makes it clear that the duties are enforceable in the same way as any other fiduciary duty owed to a company by its directors (except for the duty to exercise reasonable care, skill and diligence, which is not considered to be a fiduciary duty). In the case of fiduciary duties the consequences of breach may include:
* damages or compensation where the company has suffered loss;
* restoration of the company's property;
* an account of profits made by the director; and
* rescission of a contract where the director failed to disclose an interest.

Commentary On Individual Duties

Section 171: Duty to act within powers

323.   This duty codifies the current principle of law under which a director should exercise his powers in accordance with the terms on which they were granted, and do so for a proper purpose. What constitutes a proper purpose must be ascertained in the context of the specific situation under consideration.

324.   This duty codifies the director's duty to comply with the company's constitution. The constitution is defined for the purpose of the general duties in section 257. As well as the company's articles of association it includes:
* decisions taken in accordance with the company's articles; and
* other decisions taken by the members (or a class of them) if they are to be treated by virtue of any enactment or rule of law as decisions of the company, for example a decision taken by informal unanimous consent of all the members.

Section 172: Duty to promote the success of the company

325.   This duty codifies the current law and enshrines in statute what is commonly referred to as the principle of "enlightened shareholder value". The duty requires a director to act in the way he or she considers, in good faith, would be most likely to promote the success of the company for the benefit of its members as a whole and, in doing so, have regard to the factors listed.

326.   This list is not exhaustive, but highlights areas of particular importance which reflect wider expectations of responsible business behaviour, such as the interests of the company's employees and the impact of the company's operations on the community and the environment.

327. The decision as to what will promote the success of the company, and what constitutes such success, is one for the director's good faith judgment. This ensures that business decisions on, for example, strategy and tactics are for the directors, and not subject to decision by the courts, subject to good faith.

328. In having regard to the factors listed, the duty to exercise reasonable care, skill and diligence (section 174) will apply. It will not be sufficient to pay lip service to the factors, and, in many cases the directors will need to take action to comply with this aspect of the duty. At the same time, the duty does not require a director to do more than good faith and the duty to exercise reasonable care, skill and diligence would require, nor would it be possible for a director acting in good faith to be held liable for a process failure which would not have affected his decision as to which course of action would best promote the success of the company.

329. In requiring directors to have regard to the interests of employees, this provision replaces section 309(1) of the 1985 Act.

330. Subsection (2) addresses the question of altruistic, or partly altruistic, companies. Examples of such companies include charitable companies and community interest companies, but it is possible for any company to have "unselfish" objectives which prevail over the "selfish" interests of members. Where the purpose of the company is something other than the benefit of its members, the directors must act in the way they consider, in good faith, would be most likely to achieve that purpose. It is a matter for the good faith judgment of the director as to what those purposes are, and, where the company is partially for the benefit of its members and partly for other purposes, the extent to which those other purposes apply in place of the benefit of the members.

331. Subsection (3) recognises that the duty to promote the success of the company is displaced when the company is insolvent. Section 214 of the Insolvency Act 1986 provides a mechanism under which the liquidator can require the directors to contribute towards the funds available to creditors in an insolvent winding up, where they ought to have recognised that the company had no reasonable prospect of avoiding insolvent liquidation and then failed to take all reasonable steps to minimise the loss to creditors.

332. It has been suggested that the duty to promote the success of the company may also be modified by an obligation to have regard to the interests of creditors as the company nears insolvency. Subsection (3) will leave the law to develop in this area.

Section 173: Duty to exercise independent judgment

333. This duty codifies the current principle of law under which directors must exercise their powers independently, without subordinating their powers to the will of others, whether by delegation or otherwise (unless authorised by or under the constitution to do so).

334. The section provides that directors must not fetter the future exercise of their discretion unless they are acting:
(a)   in accordance with an agreement which has been duly entered into by the company; or
(b)   in a way authorised by the company's constitution.

335. The duty does not confer a power on the directors to delegate, nor does it prevent a director from exercising a power to delegate conferred by the company's constitution provided that its exercise is in accordance with the company's constitution. Under the draft model articles of association for private companies limited by shares, the directors may delegate their functions in accordance with the articles.

Section 174: Duty to exercise reasonable care, skill and diligence

336. This duty codifies the director's duty to exercise reasonable, care, skill and diligence. Traditionally, the courts did not require directors to exhibit a greater degree of skill than may reasonably be expected from a person with their knowledge and experience (a subjective test). More recently, the courts have said that the common law standard now mirrors the tests laid down in section 214 of the Insolvency Act 1986, which includes an objective assessment of a director's conduct. This section is modelled on that section.

337. The section provides that a director owes a duty to his company to exercise the same standard of care, skill and diligence that would be exercised by a reasonably diligent person with:
(a)   the general knowledge, skill and experience that may reasonably be expected of a person carrying out the same functions as the director in relation to that company (an objective test); and
(b)   the general knowledge, skill and experience that the director actually has (a subjective test).

Section 175: Duty to avoid conflicts of interest

338. This duty replaces the no-conflict rule applying to directors. Under the current no-conflict rule, certain consequences flow if directors place themselves in a position where their personal interests or duties to other persons are liable to conflict with their duties to the company, unless the company gives its consent. A conflict of interest may, in particular, arise when a director makes personal use of information, property or opportunities belonging to the company or when a director enters into a contract with his company. Conflicts of interest may also arise whenever a director makes a profit in the course of being a director, in the matter of his directorship, without the knowledge and consent of his company.

339. This duty covers all conflicts, actual and potential, between the interests of the director and the interests of the company. This includes conflicts relating to the exploitation of the company's property, information or opportunity for personal purposes. The only conflicts not covered by this duty, are those relating to transactions or arrangements with the company (interests in transactions or arrangements with the company must be declared under section 177 in the case of proposed transactions or under section 182 in the case of existing transactions unless an exception applies under those sections).

340. Section 180(4) preserves any current ability of the members of a company to authorise conflicts that would otherwise be a breach of this duty.

341. Under subsections (4) to (6) the duty is also not infringed if:
- the situation cannot reasonably be regarded as likely to give rise to a conflict of interest;
- in the case of a private company, unless its constitution prevents this, authorisation has been given by directors who are genuinely independent (in the sense that they have no direct or indirect interest in the transaction);
- similarly, in the case of a public company, but only if its constitution expressly permits this, authorisation has been given by the independent directors.

342. The present law is that in all cases, conflicts of interest must be authorised by the members of the company, unless some alternative procedure is properly provided. The CLR were concerned that this strict requirement might stifle entrepreneurial activity; and therefore recommended that, in the case of a private company, it should be possible for conflicts to be authorised by independent directors unless the company's constitution prevents this.

343. Under subsection (6), board authorisation is effective only if the conflicted directors have not participated in the taking of the decision or if the decision would have been valid even without the participation of the conflicted directors: the votes of the conflicted directors in favour of the decision are ignored and the conflicted directors are not counted in the quorum.

Section 176: Duty not to accept benefits from third parties

344. This section codifies the rule prohibiting the exploitation of the position of director for personal benefit. This duty prohibits the acceptance of benefits (including bribes). The acceptance of a benefit giving rise to an actual or potential conflict of interest will fall within the duty to avoid conflicts of interest (section 175) as well as this duty. This specific duty dealing with benefits from third parties is not subject to any provision for board authorisation.

345. Any current ability of the members of a company to authorise the acceptance of benefits which would otherwise be a breach of this duty is preserved by section 180(4).

346. The duty is not infringed if the acceptance of the benefit cannot reasonably be regarded as likely to give rise to a conflict of interest. Benefits conferred by the company (and its holding company or subsidiaries) do not fall within this duty.

Section 177: Duty to declare interest in proposed transaction or arrangement

347. The equitable rule that directors may not have interests in transactions with the company unless the interest has been authorised by the members is replaced by this duty. This section requires a director to disclose any interest, direct or indirect, that he has in relation to a proposed transaction or arrangement with the company. The director does not need to be a party to the transaction for the duty to apply. An interest of another person in a contract with the company may require the director to make a disclosure under this duty, if that other person's interest amounts to a direct or indirect interest on the part of the director.

348. Under the current equitable rule, shareholder approval is required for transactions between a company and a director. Company articles often modify the equitable rule, requiring disclosure of the conflict instead. As proposed by the CLR, shareholder approval for the transaction is not a requirement of the statutory duty. The members of the company may however still impose requirements for shareholder approval in the articles.

349. The duty requires directors to disclose their interest in any transaction before the company enters into the transaction (subsection (4)). The duty does not impose any rules on how the disclosure of interest must be made, but subsection (2) allows the disclosure to be made by written notice, general notice or disclosure at a meeting of the directors.

350. Disclosure to the members is not sufficient. The director must declare the nature and extent of his interest to the other directors. It is not enough for the director to merely state that he has an interest.

351. If after he has disclosed his interest, he becomes aware that the facts have changed, or for some other reason the earlier disclosure is no longer accurate or complete, the director must make a further declaration, correcting the earlier one (subsection (3)). However, this is only necessary if the company has not yet entered into the transaction or arrangement at the time the director becomes aware of the inaccuracy or incompleteness of the earlier declaration (or ought reasonably to have become so aware).

352. As the duty requires disclosure to be made to the other directors, no disclosure is required where the company has only one director. There is no need to disclose anything the other directors already know about or ought reasonably to have known (subsection (6)(b)). A director will breach the duty if he fails to declare something he ought reasonably to have known, but the duty does not otherwise require a director to declare anything he does not know. Subsection (6)(c) makes special provision for service contracts that are considered by a meeting of the directors or a committee appointed for the purpose (such as a remuneration committee).

353. No declaration of interest is required if the director's interest in the transaction cannot reasonably be regarded as likely to give rise to a conflict of interest (subsection (6)(a)). Currently regulation 85 of Table A imposes a materiality test.

354. Conflicted directors may, subject to the company's articles of association, participate in decision-taking relating to such transactions with the company.

Section 181: Modification of provisions in relation to charitable companies

355. This section reverses certain relaxations made to the no-conflict rule as it applies to the directors of charitable companies in England and Wales and Northern Ireland.

356. Subsection (2)(a) replaces section 175(3) which excludes conflicts of interest arising out of transactions or arrangements with the company. The replacement excludes such conflicts of interest from the duty only if or to the extent that the charitable company's articles so allow. The articles must describe the transactions or arrangements which are to be so excluded from the duty.

357. Subsection (2)(b) replaces section 175(5) which allows authorisation for conflicts of interest to be given by the directors. The replacement only allows authorisation to be given by the directors where the charitable company's constitution expressly allows them to do so.

358. Subsection (3) restricts the application of section 180(2)(b) which disapplies sections 175 and 176 in relation to those matters excepted from the requirements for member approval under Chapter 4. Section 180(2)(b) is restricted so that it only applies if or to the extent that the charitable company's articles allow the duties in sections 175 and 176 to be disapplied. The articles must describe the transactions or arrangements which are to be so excluded from those duties.

359. Subsection (4) amends the Charities Act 1993 to give the Charity Commission the power to authorise acts that would otherwise be in breach of the general duties. This is necessary to preserve the current power of the Charity Commissioners to do so, in the light of the statutory statement of the general duties.

Chapter 3: Declaration Of Interest In Existing Transaction Or Arrangement

Section 182: Declaration of interest in existing transaction or arrangement

360. This section requires a director to declare the nature and extent of any direct or indirect interest that he has in any transaction or arrangement entered into by the company. It replaces the provision made by section 317 of the 1985 Act.

361. This chapter differs from the provisions of that section in a number of important respects. The main points are summarised below.

What should be declared?

362. Directors are required to declare any interest, direct or indirect, that they have in an existing transaction or arrangement entered into by the company. This section only applies to transactions or arrangements already entered into by the company. Section 177 (duty to declare interests) applies in the case of proposed transactions or arrangements with the company.

363. The director does not need to be a party to the transaction with the company in order for a declaration to be required under this section. For example, where the director's spouse enters into a transaction with the company that may (but need not necessarily) give rise to an indirect interest on the part of the director in that transaction.

364. The declaration must be of the nature and extent of the director's direct or indirect interest.

365. If the director has declared his interest in accordance with section 177 at the time the transaction was proposed, and before it was entered into by the company, the director does not need to repeat that declaration once the transaction becomes an existing transaction to which this section applies (subsection (1)).

366. Furthermore, a director need not declare any interest:
- that cannot reasonably be regarded as likely to give rise to a conflict of interest;
- that the other directors already know about, or ought reasonably to know about; or
- that concerns the terms of his service contract, considered (or to be considered) by a meeting of directors or by the relevant committee of directors.

367.   A director is regarded as failing to make the declarations required by this section if he fails to declare something that he ought reasonably to have known. But the director is not otherwise expected by this section to declare things he does not know (subsection (5)).

When should the declaration be made?

368.   The declaration should be made as soon as is reasonably practicable. But even if the declaration is not made as soon as it should have been, it must still be made (subsection (4)). If after a declaration has been made the director's interest in the transaction or arrangement changes, or the director realises that his interests were not as originally declared, the director must make another declaration of interest, correcting or updating the earlier one (subsection (3)).

How should the declaration be made?

369.   The declaration of interest must be made to the other directors using one of the following three methods:—

* at a meeting of the directors; or
* by notice in writing (in accordance with the requirements of section 184); or
* by general notice (in accordance with the requirements of section 185).

Section 183: Offence of failure to declare interest

370.   This section restates section 317(7) of the 1985 Act. A director who fails to comply with the requirements of section 182 commits an offence. On conviction on indictment the maximum liability is an unlimited fine. On summary conviction the fine must not exceed the statutory maximum (currently £5,000). This section does not affect the validity of the transaction or impose any other civil consequences for a failure to make the declarations of interest required by section 182.

Section 184: Declaration made by notice in writing

371.   This section provides a new written procedure for the declarations of interest required by section 182. A written notice declaring the nature and extent of the director's interest must be sent to all the other directors. It may be sent in hard copy form or, if the recipient agrees, in electronic form. It may be posted, delivered by hand or, if the recipient agrees, by electronic means. When this is done, the notice is treated as forming part of the proceedings of the next meeting of the directors, and so should form part of the minutes of that meeting (subsection (5)).

Section 185: General notice treated as sufficient declaration

372.   This section replaces section 317(3) and (4) of the 1985 Act. It enables a director to give a general notice of his interests. A general notice is a declaration that the director is interested in another body corporate or firm, or that the director is connected with another person. If the company enters into a contract with the body corporate, firm or other person named in the general notice, the director does not need to declare any direct or indirect interest that he has in that contract arising as a result of his interest in the body corporate or firm named in the general notice or arising as a result of his connection to the person named in the general notice.

373.   In order to be effective, the general notice must state the nature and extent of the director's interest in the body corporate or firm (for example, sole shareholder of the company) or the nature of his connection with the person (for example, spouse or other connected person as defined in section 253). The requirement to disclose the extent of the interest implements a recommendation of the Law Commissions.

Section 186: Declaration of interest in case of company with sole director

374.   This is a new provision. Where a company has only one director, it is not possible for the director to declare his interests to the other directors, because there are no other directors. Therefore, a sole director does not need to comply with section 182 (declaration of interest in existing transaction or arrangement).

375.   The section makes special provision where the company has only one director, when it should in fact have more than one director (for example, because it is a public company). In such a case, the sole director must record in writing the nature and extent of his interest in any transaction or arrangement that has been entered into by the company.

Section 187: Declaration of interest in existing transaction by shadow director

376.   This section replaces section 317(8) of the 1985 Act. It extends this Chapter to shadow directors, so that a shadow director must also declare the nature and extent of his interest in any transaction or arrangement that has been entered into by the company, in accordance with section 182. The declaration must be made by notice in writing (section 184) or by general notice (section 185).

377.   The declaration is not made at a meeting of the directors, as this is not appropriate in the case of a shadow director. If the shadow director makes the declaration by general notice, that notice must be given in accordance with the notice in writing procedure set out in section 184. This means that a general notice given by a shadow director must comply with both section 184 and the first three subsections of section 185.

378. Otherwise, apart from section 186 (declaration of interest in case of company with sole director), which is not relevant to a shadow director, all the other provisions of this chapter apply to a shadow director, including the exemptions in section 182.

General Introduction To Chapters 4 And 5

379. These Chapters contains several provisions designed to deal with particular situations in which a director has a conflict of interest. They replace provisions of Part 10 of the 1985 Act, but with a number of changes. The aim of the changes is:
- to improve accessibility and consistency. The Law Commissions commented that Part 10 of the 1985 Act "is widely perceived as being extremely detailed, fragmented, excessive, and in some respects, defective, regulation of directors"; and
- to implement various recommendations of the Law Commissions and the CLR (see in particular section B of the Law Commissions' joint report *Company Directors: Regulating Conflicts of Interests and Formulating a Statement of Duties*, annex C of *Developing the Framework*, chapter 4 of *Completing the Structure* and chapter 6 of the Final Report).

380. Provisions regulating directors' conflicts of interest fall into two main categories:
- requirements for disclosure to members;
- requirements for member approval.

381. The four types of transaction requiring the approval of members (long-term service contracts; substantial property transactions; loans, quasi-loans and credit transactions; and payments for loss of office) have been brought together within Chapter 4.

382. Provision for disclosure to members in respect of directors' service contracts is contained in Chapter 5.

383. On the other hand, the requirements in Part 10 of the 1985 Act to disclose, and maintain a register of, share dealings by directors and their families are repealed (see section 1177).

Chapter 4: Transactions With Directors Requiring Approval Of Members

Structure

384. This Chapter sets out requirements for member approval in relation to four different types of transaction by a company:
- long-term service contracts;
- substantial property transactions;
- loans, quasi-loans and credit transactions;
- payments for loss of office.

385. The rules relating to each type of transaction tend to adopt the following structure: they begin with the rule requiring member approval, followed by exceptions to that rule and finally the consequences of breaching that rule.

Alignment of provisions

386. The provisions of this Chapter have been aligned wherever appropriate so as to achieve greater consistency of approach. Particular examples of alignment are mentioned below.

Criminal penalties

387. This Chapter no longer imposes any criminal penalties for a failure to comply with its requirements.

Civil remedies

388. The civil consequences of a failure to comply with the requirements for member approval of substantial property transactions and loans, quasi-loans and credit transactions have been aligned.

Approval by holding company

389. This Chapter applies to long-term service contracts, substantial property transactions, loans etc and payments for loss of office entered into by a company and involving either a director of the company or a director of the company's holding company. In the latter case, the transaction must be approved by both the company and the holding company (unless an exception applies).

Transactions between a company and the director of a fellow subsidiary

390. This Chapter does not normally apply to transactions entered into by a company that is neither the company of which the person is a director nor a subsidiary of the company of which the person is a director. The two exceptions are section 218 (payment for loss of office in connection with transfer of undertaking) and section 219 (payment for loss of office in connection with share transfer), where member approval is required for such a payment by any person to a director.

Exception for wholly-owned subsidiary

391. Approval is never required under this Chapter on the part of the member of a wholly-owned subsidiary or on the part of the members of an overseas company.

Part 3   CA 2006 Supporting Materials

Shadow directors

392.   Section 223 applies all the requirements of this Chapter to shadow directors (with a small modification in the case of payments for loss of office).

Approval required

393.   Section 281(3) applies so that the member approval required is an ordinary resolution, but the company's articles may require a higher majority or even unanimity.

394.   Where approval for a transaction or arrangement is required under more than one set of rules in Chapter 4, all relevant sets of rules should apply, unless otherwise provided (section 225). For example, if the matter involves both a substantial property transaction and a loan, approval should be required under section 190 and under section 197 unless in each case a relevant exemption applies. Approval may be given for both purposes by a single resolution.

Memorandum with details of the transaction

395.   In the case of long-term service contracts, loans etc and payments for loss of office, a memorandum setting out certain particulars about the transaction requiring approval of the members must be made available to the members.

396.   If the approval is to be given by way of written resolution, the memorandum must be sent to the members able to vote on the written resolution no later than when the written resolution is sent to them. Section 224 provides that any accidental failure to send the memorandum to one or more members will not invalidate the approval given by the members, unless the company's articles state otherwise.

Requirement for Charity Commission consent for charitable companies

397.   Section 66 of the Charities Act 1993 renders prior authorisation by the members for certain transactions invalid unless the Charity Commissioners have given their prior written consent. This reflects concern that, in some cases, the members of a charitable company are not independent of the directors, and that requiring their approval would not provide sufficient protection for the charity. Section 226 inserts two new sections into the Charities Act 1993 in place of section 66 of that Act to reflect the changes made by this Chapter.

Commentary

Sections 188 and 189: Service contracts

398.   These sections replace section 319 of the 1985 Act and require member approval of long-term service contracts. In broad terms, these are contracts under which a director is guaranteed at least two years of employment with the company of which he is a director, or with any subsidiary of that company.

399.   A director's "service contract" is defined in section 227 to include a contract of service, a contract for services and a letter of appointment as director.

400.   Failure to obtain approval allows the company to terminate the service contract at any time by giving reasonable notice. The purpose of this section is to limit the duration of directors' service contracts, as a long-term contract can make it too expensive for the members to remove a director using the procedure in section 168 (ordinary resolution to remove director) while allowing the members to approve longer arrangements if they wish.

401.   The length of service contract for which member approval is required has been reduced from those longer than five years to those longer than two years.

Sections 190 to 196: Substantial property transactions

402.   These sections require member approval to substantial property transactions. These are transactions where the company buys or sells a non-cash asset (as defined in section 1163) to or from:

- a director of the company;
- a director of its holding company;
- a person connected with a director of the company; or
- a person connected with a director of its holding company.

Approval is only required where the value of the asset exceeds £100,000 or 10% of the company's net assets (based on its last set of annual accounts or called-up share capital if it has not yet produced any accounts). No approval is required if the value of the asset is less than £5,000.

403.   These sections replace sections 320 to 322 of the 1985 Act. The changes include:
- permitting a company to enter into a contract which is conditional on member approval (section 190(1)). This implements a recommendation of the Law Commissions. In cases where the approval of the members of the holding company is also required, the company may enter into arrangements conditional on approval being obtained from the members of the holding company (section 190(2)). The company is not to be liable under the contract if member approval is not forthcoming (section 190(3));

- providing for the aggregation of non-cash assets forming part of an arrangement or series of arrangements for the purpose of determining whether the financial thresholds have been exceeded so that member approval is required (section 190(5));
- excluding payments under directors' service contracts and payments for loss of office from the requirements of these sections (section 190(6)). This implements a recommendation of the Law Commissions;
- raising the minimum value of what may be regarded as a substantial non-cash asset from £2,000 to £5,000 (section 191);
- expanding the exception for transactions with members to include the acquisition of assets from a person in his character as a member of the company (section 192(a));
- providing an exception for transactions made by companies in administration (section 193). This implements a recommendation of the Law Commissions;
- not requiring approval on the part of the members of a company that is in administration or is being wound up (unless it is a members' voluntary winding up) (section 193).

Sections 197 to 214: Loans, quasi-loans and credit transactions

404. In the case of a private company which is not associated with a public company, section 197 requires member approval for loans and related guarantees or security made by a company for:
- a director of the company; or
- a director of its holding company.

405. In the case of a public company, or a private company associated with a public company, sections 197, 198, 200 and 201 require member approval for loans, quasi-loans (as defined in section 199), credit transactions (as defined in section 202) and related guarantees or security made by the company for:
- a director of the company; or
- a director of its holding company;
- a person connected with a director of the company; or
- a person connected with a director of its holding company.

406. Section 256 explains what is meant by references to associated companies. A holding company is associated with all its subsidiaries, and a subsidiary is associated with its holding company and all the other subsidiaries of its holding company.

407. Member approval is not required by these sections for:
- loans, quasi-loans, credit transactions and related guarantees or security to meet expenditure on company business. The total value of transactions under this exception made in respect of a director and any person connected to him must not exceed £50,000 (section 204);
- money lent to fund a director's defence costs for legal proceedings in connection with any alleged negligence, default, breach of duty or breach of trust by him in relation to the company or an associated company (section 205) or in connection with regulatory action or investigation under the same circumstances(section 206);
- small loans and quasi-loans, as long as the total value of such loans and quasi-loans made in respect of a director and any person connected to him does not exceed £10,000 (section 207(1));
- small credit transactions, as long as the total value of such credit transactions made in respect of a director and any person connected to him does not exceed £15,000 (section 207(2));
- credit transactions made in the ordinary course of the company's business (section 207(3));
- intra-group transactions (section 208); and
- loans and quasi-loans made by a money-lending company in the ordinary course of the company's business (as long as the requirements of section 209 are met).

408. These sections replace sections 330 to 341 of the 1985 Act. The changes include:
- abolishing the prohibition on loans, quasi-loans etc to directors and replacing it with a requirement for member approval. This implements a recommendation of the CLR;
- abolishing the criminal penalty for breach;
- replacing the concept of relevant company in section 331 of the 1985 Act with associated company, as defined in section 256;
- removing some of the requirements currently imposed by section 337 of the 1985 Act on the exception for expenditure on company business (section 204);
- widening the exception for expenditure on company business to include directors of the company's holding company and connected persons (section 204);
- creating a new exception specifically for expenditure in connection with regulatory action or investigations (section 206);
- restricting the exceptions for expenditure on defending legal or regulatory proceedings to proceedings in connection with any alleged negligence, default, breach of duty or breach of trust by the director in relation to the company or an associated company (sections 205 and 206);
- widening the exception for small loans to include small quasi-loans (section 207(1)) in place of the current exception for short-term small quasi-loans in section 332 of the 1985 Act;
- widening the exception for small loans and quasi-loans to include transactions with connected persons (section 207(1));

- widening the exception for "home loans" to include those connected persons who are employees (section 209(3));
- raising the maximum amounts permitted under the exception for expenditure on company business (section 204), the exception for small loans and small quasi-loans (section 207(1)) and the exception for small credit transactions (section 207(2));
- widening the exceptions for intra-group transactions (section 208);
- abolishing the maximum amounts permitted under the exception for money-lending companies (section 209); and
- allowing affirmation of loans, quasi-loans and credit transactions entered into by the company in line with the provision in respect of substantial property transactions (section 214).

Sections 215 to 222: Payments for loss of office

409. These sections require member approval for payments for loss of office. These are payments made to a director (or former director) to compensate them for ceasing to be a director, or for losing any other office or employment with the company or with a subsidiary of the company. They also include payments made in connection with retirement. In the case of loss of employment or retirement from employment, the employment must relate to the management of the affairs of the company.

410. Member approval is required under section 217 if a company wishes to make a payment for loss of office to:
- one of its directors;
- a director of its holding company.

411. Member approval is also required if any person (including the company or anyone else) wishes to make a payment for loss of office to a director of the company in connection with the transfer of the whole or any part of the undertaking or the property of the company or of a subsidiary of the company (section 218).

412. In the case of a payment for loss of office to a director in connection with the transfer of shares in the company or in a subsidiary of the company resulting from a takeover bid, approval is required of the holders of the shares to which the bid relates and of any other holders of shares of the same class (section 219).

413. These sections replace sections 312 to 316 of the 1985 Act. The changes include:
- extending the requirements to include payments to connected persons (section 215(3));
- extending the requirements to include payments to directors in respect of the loss of any office, or employment in connection with the management of the affairs of the company, and not merely loss of office as a director as such (section 215). This implements a recommendation of the Law Commissions;
- extending the requirements to include payments by a company to a director of its holding company (section 217(2));
- extending the requirements in connection with the transfer of the undertaking or property of the company to include transfers of the undertaking or property of a subsidiary (section 218(2));
- extending the requirements in connection with share transfers so as to include all transfers of shares in the company or in a subsidiary resulting from a takeover bid (section 219(1));
- excluding the persons making the offer for shares in the company and any associate of them from voting on any resolution to approve a payment for loss of office in connection with a share transfer (section 219(4)). This implements a recommendation of the Law Commissions;
- setting out the exception for payments in discharge of certain legal obligations (section 220);
- creating a new exception for small payments (section 221);
- clarifying the civil consequences of breach of these sections (section 222(1) to (3)); and
- resolving conflicts between the remedies where more than one requirement of these sections is breached (section 222(4) and (5)). For example, if the payment contravenes both section 217 and section 219 because it was a payment by a company to one of its directors and it was a payment in connection with a takeover bid, and none of the required member approvals have been obtained, then the payment is held on trust for the persons who have sold their shares as a result of the offer and not on trust for the company making the payment.

Chapter 5: Directors' Service Contracts

Section 227: Directors' service contracts

414. This section is a new provision. It defines what is meant in this Part by references to a director's service contract. The term is used in sections 177, 182, 188 and 190 and in this Chapter. It includes contracts of employment with the company, or with a subsidiary of the company. It also includes contracts for services and letters of appointment to the office of director. The contract may relate to services as a director or to any other services that a director undertakes personally to perform for the company or a subsidiary.

Section 228: Copy of contract or memorandum of terms to be available for inspection

415. This section requires a company to keep available for inspection copies of every director's service contract entered into by the company or by a subsidiary of the company. If the contract is not in writing, the company must keep available for inspection a written memorandum of its terms. This section, together with sections 229 and 230, replace section 318 of the 1985 Act.

416. Subsection (3) is new. It requires the service contracts to be retained and kept available for inspection by the company for at least one year after they have expired, but the subsection does not require the copies to be retained thereafter. As a result of the expanded definition of service contract in section 227, this section now applies to contracts for services and letters of appointment, as recommended by the Law Commissions.

417. As recommended by the Law Commissions, the exemption for contracts requiring a director to work outside the UK (section 318(5) of the 1985 Act) and the exemption for contracts with less than 12 months to run (section 318(11) of the 1985 Act) have not been retained.

418. Failure to comply with the requirements of this section is a criminal offence for which every officer of the company who is in default may be held liable on summary conviction to a fine not exceeding level 3 on the standard scale (currently £1,000) or in cases of continued contravention a daily default fine not exceeding one-tenth of that. In a change from the current position under section 318 of the 1985 Act, the company will no longer be liable under the criminal offence.

Section 229: Right of member to inspect and request copy

419. This section gives members a right to inspect without charge the copies of service contracts held by the company in accordance with section 228. Subsection (2) creates a new right for members to request a copy of the service contracts on payment of a fee set by regulations under section 1137.

Section 230: Directors' service contracts: application of provisions to shadow directors

420. This section applies the requirements of this Chapter to service contracts with shadow directors.

Chapter 6: Contracts With Sole Members Who Are Directors

Section 231: Contract with sole member who is also a director

421. Under this section, contracts entered into by a limited company with its only member must be recorded in writing if the sole member is also a director or shadow director of the company. This does not apply to contracts entered into in the ordinary course of the company's business. The purpose of this section is to ensure that records are kept in those cases where there is a high risk of the lines becoming blurred between where a person acts in his personal capacity and when he acts on behalf of the company. This may be of particular interest to a liquidator should the company become insolvent.

422. This section replaces section 322B of the 1985 Act, which implements article 5 of the 12th Company Law Directive (89/667/EEC). As the Act will permit public companies to have a single shareholder, this section applies to both private and public limited companies.

423. A failure to record the contract in writing will not affect the validity of the contract (subsection (6)) but other legislation or rules of law might (subsection (7)).

424. If there is a breach of this section, every officer of the company in default is liable on summary conviction to a fine not exceeding level 5 on the standard scale (currently £5,000). In a change from the current position under section 322B of the 1985 Act, the company will no longer be liable under the criminal offence.

Chapter 7: Directors' Liabilities

425. The sections in this Chapter (sections 232 to 239) deal with two matters:
- they restate sections 309A to 309C of the 1985 Act (provisions relating to directors' liability). The only substantive changes to those sections are a new provision permitting companies to indemnify the directors of companies acting as trustees of occupational pension schemes (section 235), the creation of a right for members to request a copy of a qualifying third party indemnity provision (section 238(2)), the removal of criminal liability on the part of the company for failures to comply with the requirements of section 237 (copy of qualifying indemnity provision to be available for inspection), provision for regulations to specify places in addition to the registered office where inspection may take place (section 237(3)) and a requirement for all qualifying indemnity provisions to be retained by a company for at least one year after they have expired (section 237(4));
- they introduce a substantive reform of the law on ratification of acts giving rise to liability on the part of a director (section 239).

Section 232: Provisions protecting directors from liability

426. This section prohibits a company from exempting a director from, or indemnifying him against, any liability in connection with any negligence, default, breach of duty or breach of trust by him in relation to the company. Subsection (2) prohibits indemnification by an associated company as well as by his own company. "Associated company" is defined in section 256 as, in effect, a company in the same group.

427. Any provision, whether in the company's articles, in a contract or otherwise, attempting to exempt or indemnify a director in breach of this section is void. But this does not apply to lawful provisions in the articles for dealing with conflicts of interest.

Section 233: Provision of insurance

428. This section permits a company to purchase and maintain insurance for its directors, or the directors of an associated company, against any liability attaching to them in connection with any negligence, default, breach of duty or breach of trust by them in relation to the company of which they are a director.

Section 234: Qualifying third party indemnity provision

429. This section permits (but does not require) companies to indemnify directors in respect of proceedings brought by third parties (such as class actions in the US). It also permits (but does not require) companies to indemnify directors in respect of applications for relief from liability made under section 1157 (general power of the court to grant relief in case of honest and reasonable conduct) or under section 661(3) or (4)(power of court to grant relief in case of acquisition of shares by innocent nominee).

430. The indemnity may cover liability incurred by the director to any person other than the company or an associated company. This may include both legal costs and the financial costs of an adverse judgement. But the indemnity must not cover liabilities to the company or to any associated company (subsection (2)).

431. Another condition is that the indemnity must not cover criminal fines, penalties imposed by regulatory bodies (such as the Financial Services Authority), the defence costs of criminal proceedings where the director is found guilty, the defence costs of civil proceedings successfully brought against the director by the company or an associated company and the costs of unsuccessful applications by the director for relief (subsection (3)).

432. Subsections (4) and (5) explain when legal proceedings will be considered to have concluded for the purpose of the conditions imposed by subsection (3).

433. An indemnity that complies with these conditions is described as a qualifying third party indemnity provision.

Section 235: Qualifying pension scheme indemnity provision

434. This section permits (but does not require) companies to indemnify a director of a company acting as a trustee of an occupational pension scheme against liability incurred in connection with the company's activities as trustee of the scheme. An indemnity that complies with the conditions set out in this section is described as a qualifying pension scheme indemnity provision.

Section 236: Qualifying indemnity provision to be disclosed in directors' report

435. If a qualifying indemnity provision is in force for the benefit of one or more directors or was in force during the previous year, this must be disclosed by the company in the directors' report (as to the directors' report, see Chapter 5 of Part 15). Where the director is of one company but the qualifying indemnity provision is provided by an associated company, then it must be disclosed in the directors' reports of both companies. Companies which choose not to indemnify directors will not have to make any disclosure.

Section 237: Copy of qualifying indemnity provision to be available for inspection

436. This section requires a company to keep available for inspection copies of all the qualifying indemnity provisions it has made for its own directors, and also copies of all those it has made for directors of associated companies.

437. Subsection (4) is a new provision. It requires all qualifying indemnity provisions to be retained and made available for inspection for a further year after they have expired or terminated. But the company is not required by this section to retain copies of the indemnity provision thereafter.

438. Subsection (6) makes a failure to comply with the requirements of this section a criminal offence. The maximum penalty that can be imposed on summary conviction is a fine not exceeding level 3 on the standard scale (currently £1,000) or in cases of continued contravention a daily default fine not exceeding one-tenth of that. In a change from the current position under section 309C of the 1985 Act, the company will no longer be liable under the criminal offence.

Section 238: Right of member to inspect and request copy

439. This section gives members a right to inspect without charge the copies of the qualifying indemnity provisions (or where they are not in writing, the written memorandum of their terms) held by the company in accordance with section 237.

440. This section also creates a new right for members on payment of a fee to request a copy of the copy or memorandum held by the company. The fee will be set by regulations made under section 1137.

Section 239: Ratification of acts of directors

441. This section preserves the current law on ratification of acts of directors, but with one significant change. Any decision by a company to ratify conduct by a director amounting to negligence, default, breach of duty or breach of trust in relation to the company must be taken by the members, and without reliance on the votes in favour by the director or any connected person. Section 252 defines what is meant by a person being connected with a director. For the purposes of this section it may also include fellow directors (subsection (5)(d)).

442. If the ratification decision is taken by way of a written resolution (see Chapter 2 of Part 13) the director and his connected persons may not take part in the written resolution procedure (subsection (3)). This means that the company does not need to send them a copy of the written resolution, and they are not counted when determining the number of votes required for the written resolution to be passed.

443. If the ratification decision is taken at a meeting, those members whose votes are to be disregarded may still attend the meeting, take part in the meeting and count towards the quorum for the meeting (if their membership gives them the right to do so).

444. Subsection (6) makes clear that nothing in this section changes the law on unanimous consent, so the restrictions imposed by this section as to who may vote on a ratification resolution will not apply when every member votes (informally or otherwise) in favour of the resolution. The subsection also makes clear that nothing in this section removes any powers of the directors that they may have to manage the affairs of the company.

445. Subsection (7) explains that the requirements imposed by this section are in addition to any other limitations or restrictions imposed by the law as to what may or may not be ratified and when.

Chapter 8: Directors' Residential Addresses: Protection From Disclosure

446. Under the 1985 Act (and previous Companies Acts), the usual residential address of every director must be entered on the public record held by:
*   the registrar; and
*   each company of which he is a director in its register of directors.

Access to the public record held by the registrar is made in a variety of ways, including daily bulk downloading by some subscribers. There is also a public right to inspect companies' registers of directors.

447. There is an exception for directors at serious risk of violence or intimidation, eg from political activists and terrorists. Under sections 723B – 723E of the 1985 Act, introduced by the Criminal Justice and Police Act 2001, they may apply for a "confidentiality order". A director with a confidentiality order provides a single service address in addition to his usual residential address. The service address is entered on the public record; the usual residential address is kept on a secure register to which access is restricted to specified enforcement authorities. The historic record is not affected by the confidentiality order. By October 2006, nearly 11,000 Confidentiality Orders had been issued of which, it is estimated that nearly 7,000 were to directors (certain other individuals, eg partners in Limited Liability Partnerships, are also eligible).

448. The CLR considered it essential that directors' residential addresses be filed with the central register, so that enforcement and regulatory bodies as well as liquidators and, in some circumstances, creditors and shareholders can discover the individual's residential address. However they were concerned that unrestricted public access to directors' residential addresses had been abused. They considered that there should not be any discretion as to whether particular addresses should or should not be placed on the public record. Therefore, while welcoming the introduction of the confidentiality order regime, they recommended all directors be given the option of:
*   either, as now, providing their residential address for the public record;
*   or, providing both a service address and their residential address, with the service address being on the public record and the residential address being on a separate secure register to which access would be restricted. Access to the restricted register would be available to certain public authorities. Other parties, such as members and creditors, should have a right to apply to the court for access to a director's residential address. (Final Report, paragraph 11.46)

449. This Chapter of the Act, together with the provisions on the register of directors' residential addresses in Chapter 1 of this Part, is based on this recommendation. These provisions, which are all new, replace the confidentiality order regime.

Section 240: Protected information

450. This section sets out the information about directors' usual residential addresses, recorded under Chapter 1 of this Part, that will be protected under the new provisions.

Part 3   CA 2006 Supporting Materials

Section 241: Protected information: restriction on use or disclosure by company

451.   This section provides for the protection that a company must give to the information covered by section 240. It prohibits the company from using or disclosing an individual director's home address without his consent except for communicating with him, or to comply with an obligation to send information to the registrar or when required by a court.

Section 242: Protected information: restriction on use or disclosure by the registrar

452.   This section provides for protection by the registrar of information that is covered by section 240. The registrar need only protect information where it is submitted on a form where directors' usual residential addresses are required and entered in the appropriate place. The registrar is not obliged to check all documents submitted to her to ensure that an address has not been inadvertently disclosed. The protection is not retrospective: it does not apply to information on the public record when these provisions come into force. The Act makes separate provision, in section 1088, for removal of addresses from the register in circumstances specified by regulations.

Section 243: Permitted use or disclosure by the registrar

453.   This section provides for certain kinds of permitted use or disclosure of protected information, ie directors' home addresses and whether a service address is a home address. Subsection (1) provides that the registrar may use the protected information for communicating with the director in question. Subsection (2) provides that the registrar may disclose protected information to a public authority or credit reference agency (the definition of the latter is drawn from the Consumer Credit Act 1974) but this should be read with subsections (3) and (4). Subsection (3) confers power on the Secretary of State to make regulations specifying conditions that must be met before the registrar may disclose protected information. The regulations may also provide for fees to be paid by the authority or agency seeking the address. Subsection (4) provides power to make regulations specifying the circumstances in which an application can be made for a director's address not to be revealed to a credit reference agency.

Section 244: Disclosure under court order

454.   This section provides for two circumstances in which the court may require the company to disclose protected information. The first circumstance is that the service address is not effective; the second is that the home address is needed for the enforcement of an order or decree of the court. If the company cannot provide the address, the court may require the registrar to reveal it. Subsection (3) provides that the application for the order may be made not only by a liquidator, creditor or member of the company but also by anyone with sufficient interest.

Section 245: Circumstances in which registrar may put address on the public record.

455.   This section provides that if a service address is not effective, then the home address can be put on the public record. It provides for the registrar to send a warning notice, with a specified period for representations before the intended action, both to the director and to every company of which he is a director. The registrar must take account of any representations made within the specified period in deciding whether to proceed as provided by the next section.

Section 246: Putting the address on the public record

456.   This section provides that, if the registrar is putting a director's home address on the public record under the previous section, then the registrar updates the public record as if she had been notified that the service address is the director's home address. She must also notify both the director and every company of which he/she is a director. The companies must each put the director's home address on its register of directors as his/her service address. And for the next five years, the director may not register a service address other than his usual residential address.

Chapter 9: Supplementary Provisions

Section 247: Power to make provision for employees on cessation or transfer of business

457.   This section confers a power on the directors to make provision for the benefit of employees (including former employees) of the company or its subsidiaries on the cessation or transfer of the whole or part of the undertaking of the company or the subsidiary (subsection (1)).

458.   The directors may exercise this power, even if it will not promote the success of the company. The directors' general duty under section 172 to act in the way they consider would be most likely to promote the success of the company for the benefit of its members as a whole, does not apply when the directors exercise this power to make provision for employees (subsection (2)).

459.   There are a number of conditions to the exercise of this power. It must be authorised by a resolution of the members or, if the articles of the company allow it, by the board of directors. The company's articles may also impose further conditions on its use (subsection (6)).

460.   Any payments made by the directors using the power conferred by this section must be made before the commencement of the winding up of the company and can only be made out of profits available for dividend. Section 187 of the Insolvency Act 1986 confers power to make provision for employees once the company has commenced winding up.

461.   This section replaces section 719 of the 1985 Act. In a change from that section, the directors can no longer use the power conferred by this section to make payments to themselves or to former directors or to shadow directors, unless the payments are authorised by the members. The CLR recommended that directors should be prevented from abusing the power by making excessive payments to themselves.

Section 248: Minutes of directors' meetings

462.   This section, together with section 249, replaces the provisions of section 382 of the 1985 Act relating to records of meetings of directors. The requirements of section 382 of the 1985 Act relating to records of meetings of managers have not been retained. This section requires a company to record minutes of all meetings of its directors.

463.   Subsection (2) is new. The minutes must be kept for at least ten years.

464.   Failure to make and keep minutes as required by this section is a criminal offence, applying to every officer of the company who is in default. In a change from section 382 of the 1985 Act, liability for the offence will no longer fall on the company.

465.   Part 37 of the Act makes provision as to the form in which company records (including minutes) may be kept and imposes a duty to take precautions against falsification.

Section 249: Minutes as evidence

466.   This section makes provision in respect of the evidential value of the minutes of directors' meetings.

Section 250: "Director"

467.   This section restates the definition of "director" in section 741(1) of the 1985 Act.

Section 251: "Shadow director"

468.   This section restates the definition of "shadow director" in section 741(2) of the 1985 Act.

Section 252: Persons connected with a director

469.   This section sets out the definition of "connected person" which is used in many of the sections in this Part in relation to the regulation of directors. The persons who are "connected" for this purpose with a director include:
*   certain family members (see section 253);
*   certain companies with which the director is connected (see section 254);
*   trustees of a trust under which the director or a relative mentioned in section 253 or a company with which the director is connected is a beneficiary (but not if the trust exists for the purposes of an employees' share scheme as defined in section 1166 or a pension scheme);
*   certain partners; and
*   certain firms with legal personality (such as a Scottish firm in which the director is a partner).

470.   This section, together with sections 253 to 255, replaces section 346 of the 1985 Act.

Section 253: Members of a director's family

471.   This section sets out those members of a director's family who fall within the definition of persons connected with the director. The list includes all those family members currently falling within the definition of connected person in section 346 of the 1985 Act, and in addition it covers:
*   the director's parents;
*   children or step-children of the director who are over 18 years old (those under 18 were already included under section 346 of the 1985 Act);
*   persons with whom the director lives as partner in an enduring family relationship; and
*   children or step-children of the director's unmarried partner if they live with the director and are under 18 years of age.

472.   This implements the Law Commissions' recommendation that the definition of connected person be extended so as to include cohabitants, infant children of the cohabitant if they live with the director, adult children of the director and the director's parents. The recommendation that the definition be extended to siblings has not been implemented.

Section 254: Director "connected with" a body corporate

473.   This section determines whether a company or other body corporate is a person connected with a director. Broadly speaking, the director, together with any other person connected with him, must be interested in 20% of the equity share capital, or control (directly or indirectly through another body corporate controlled by them) more than 20% of the voting power exercisable at any general meeting.

Part 3   CA 2006 Supporting Materials

474. Schedule 1 contains the rules for determining whether a person is "interested in shares" for this purpose.

Section 255: Director "controlling" a body corporate

475. This section defines the circumstances in which a director is deemed to control a body corporate for the purposes of section 254. These circumstances involve two cumulative hurdles. First, the director or any other person connected with him must be interested in the equity share capital or be entitled to control some part of the voting power exercisable at any general meeting. Secondly, the director, fellow directors and other persons connected with him must be interested in more than 50% of the equity share capital or be entitled to control more than 50% of the voting power exercisable at any general meeting.

476. Schedule 1 contains the rules for determining whether a person is "interested in shares" for this purpose.

Section 256: Associated bodies corporate

477. This section is a new provision. It explains what is meant by references in this Part to associated bodies corporate and associated companies. A holding company is associated with all its subsidiaries, and a subsidiary is associated with its holding company and all the other subsidiaries of its holding company.

Section 257: References to company's constitution

478. This section is new. It makes provision as to the meaning of references to a company's constitution in this Part.

479. The section is relevant to a number of provisions in this Part, including the duty to act within powers (section 171) and the duty to exercise independent judgment (section 173).

Section 258: Power to increase financial limits

480. This section confers power on the Secretary of State by order to increase financial limits in this Part of the Act. All the financial limits appear in Chapter 4 (provisions regulating transactions with directors requiring approval of members). This section restates section 345 of the 1985 Act.

Section 259: Transactions under foreign law

481. This section makes clear that the rules under this Part of the Act apply whether or not the proper law governing a transaction or arrangement is the law of the UK or a part of the UK.

482. This provision is necessary to prevent parties seeking to avoid the application of the rules relating to approval of long-term service contracts, substantial property transactions and loans and similar transactions by choosing a foreign law. This section restates section 347 of the 1985 Act.

PART 11: DERIVATIVE CLAIMS AND PROCEEDINGS BY MEMBERS

[3.12]
483. Section 170 provides that directors' general duties are owed to the company rather than to individual members (or third parties such as employees or pressure groups). It follows that, as now, only the company can enforce them. There are three main ways in which the company can take legal action against a director (or, more usually, a former director) for breach of duty:

* if the board of directors decides to commence proceedings;
* if the liquidator or administrator following the commencement of a formal insolvency procedure such as liquidation or administration decides to commence proceedings;
* through a derivative claim or action brought by one or more members to enforce a right which is vested not in himself but in the company.

This part of the Act is concerned with the third of these types of action.

Existing Law

England and Wales or Northern Ireland

484. In England and Wales, it is possible as a matter of common law for a member to bring an action, in certain circumstances, on behalf of the company of which he is a member. This is known as a derivative claim. As noted above, a member may bring such an action to enforce liability for a breach by one of the directors of his duties to the company.

485. The law relating to the ability of a member to bring proceedings on behalf of the company is not written down in statute. The general principle – commonly known as the rule in *Foss v Harbottle* – is that it is for the company itself to bring proceedings where a wrong has been done to the company. However, where there has been conduct amounting to a "fraud on the minority", an exception may be made to the rule, so that a minority shareholder may bring an action to enforce the company's rights (for example, where there has been an expropriation of company property or dishonest behaviour by a director, and the company is improperly prevented from bringing proceedings against the director by the majority shareholders, perhaps because the wrongdoing director controls the majority of votes).

486. Under the current law, if a wrong has been effectively ratified by the company, this will be a complete bar to a derivative claim. In addition, if a wrong is capable of being ratified, then even if there has been no formal ratification, it may not be possible for a minority shareholder to bring a derivative claim.

487. The law in Northern Ireland in this area is the same as that in England and Wales.

Scotland

488. Under Scots law, the member's right to raise an action is conferred by substantive law. Accordingly, a member has title as a matter of substantive law to raise proceedings in respect of a director's breach of duty to obtain a remedy for the company. The action is raised in the name of the member but the remedy is obtained for the company and the rights which the member can enforce against a director or third party are those of the company.

489. The member's right arises where the action complained of is fraudulent or *ultra vires* and so cannot be validated by a majority of the members of the company. This remedy is not available if the majority of members acting in good faith have validated or may validate the act complained of.

490. Two rules of substantive law apply to actions brought by the member to protect the company's interests (as well as to actions brought to protect the shareholder's personal interests such as enforcement of rights in the articles of association). First, the directors of a company owe duties to the company and not to the members. Second, the court will not interfere in matters of internal management which may be sanctioned by a majority of the members. The effect of these rules is similar to the first two legs of the rule in *Foss v Harbottle*.

Chapter 1: Derivative Claims In England And Wales Or Northern Ireland

491. The sections in this Part do not formulate a substantive rule to replace the rule in *Foss v Harbottle*, but instead reflect the recommendation of the Law Commission that there should be a "new derivative procedure with more modern, flexible and accessible criteria for determining whether a shareholder can pursue an action" (*Shareholder Remedies*, paragraph 6.15). In line with the recommendations of the Law Commission, the derivative claim will be available for breach of the duty to exercise reasonable care, skill and diligence, even if the director has not benefited personally, and it will not be necessary for the applicant to show that the wrongdoing directors control the majority of the company's shares.

492. The sections in Chapter 1 of this Part introduce a two-stage procedure for permission to continue a derivative claim. At the first stage the applicant will be required to make a *prima facie* case for permission to continue a derivative claim and the court will be required to consider the issue on the basis of the evidence filed by the applicant only, without requiring evidence from the defendant. The courts must dismiss the application if the applicant cannot establish a *prima facie* case. At the second stage – but before the substantive action begins – the court may require evidence to be provided by the company. The sections set out a list of the matters which the court must take into account in considering whether to give permission and the circumstances in which the court is bound to refuse permission.

493. The sections will be supplemented by amended Civil Procedure Rules.

Section 260: Derivative claims

494. This section sets out the key aspects of a derivative claim.
*   Subsection (1) defines what is meant by a derivative claim. There are three elements to this: the action is brought by a member of the company; the cause of action is vested in the company; and relief is sought on the company's behalf. (A "member" is defined in section 112. Subsection (5) provides that references to a member in this Chapter include a person who is not a member but to whom shares in the company have been transferred or transmitted by operation of law, for example where a trustee in bankruptcy or personal representative of a deceased member's estate acquires an interest in a share as a result of the bankruptcy or death of a member).
*   Subsection (2) provides that the claim may only be brought either under this Chapter or in pursuance of an order of the court in proceedings under section 994 (proceedings for protection of members against unfair prejudice).
*   Subsection (3) provides that a derivative claim "may be brought only in respect of a cause of action arising from an actual or proposed act or omission involving negligence, default, breach of duty or breach of trust by a director of the company". As such, a derivative claim may be brought in respect of an alleged breach of any of the general duties of directors in Chapter 2 of Part 10, including the duty to exercise reasonable care, skill and diligence (section 174).

Part 3   CA 2006 Supporting Materials

- Subsection (3) also provides that the cause of action may be against the director or against a third party, or both. Derivative claims against third parties would be permitted only in very narrow circumstances, where the damage suffered by the company arose from an act involving a breach of duty etc on the part of the director (eg for knowing receipt of money or property transferred in breach of trust or for knowing assistance in a breach of trust).
- Subsection (4) provides that a derivative claim may be brought by a member in respect of wrongs committed prior to his becoming a member. This reflects the fact that the rights being enforced are those of the company rather than those of the member and is the position at common law.
- Under subsection (5), the reference to a director in this Chapter includes a former director; and a shadow director is treated as a director.

Section 261: Application for permission to continue derivative claim

495. This clause provides that, once proceedings have been brought, the member is required to apply to the court for permission to continue the claim. This reflects the current procedure in England and Wales under the Civil Procedure Rules. The applicant is required to establish a *prima facie* case for the grant of permission, and the court will consider the issue on the basis of his evidence alone without requiring evidence to be filed by the defendant. The court must dismiss the application at this stage if what is filed does not show a *prima facie* case, and it may make any consequential order that it considers appropriate (for example, a costs order or a civil restraint order against the applicant). If the application is not dismissed, the court may direct the company to provide evidence and, on hearing the application, may grant permission, refuse permission and dismiss the claim, or adjourn the proceedings and give such directions as it thinks fit. This will enable the courts to dismiss unmeritorious claims at an early stage without involving the defendants or the company.

Section 262: Application for permission to continue claim as a derivative claim

496. This section addresses the possibility that, where a company has brought a claim and the cause of action on which the claim is based could be pursued by a member as a derivative action:
- the manner in which the company commenced or continued the claim may amount to an abuse of process (eg the company brought the claim with a view to preventing a member bringing a derivative claim);
- the company may fail to prosecute the claim diligently; and
- it may be appropriate for a member to continue the claim as a derivative claim;

497. The section provides that, in these circumstances, a member may apply to the court to continue the claim as a derivative action.

Section 263: Whether permission to be given

498. This section sets out the criteria which must be taken into account by the court in considering whether to give permission to continue a derivative claim.

499. Subsection (2) provides that the court must refuse leave to continue a derivative claim if it is satisfied that:
(a)   a person acting in accordance with the general duty of directors to promote the success of the company (section 172) would not seek to continue the claim; or
(b)   the act or omission giving rise to the cause of action has been authorised or ratified by the company. Section 180(4) preserves any rule of law enabling the company to give authority for anything that would otherwise be a breach of duty. Section 239 preserves the current law on ratification of acts of directors, but with one significant change. Any decision by a company to ratify conduct by a director amounting to negligence, default, breach of duty or breach of trust in relation to the company must be taken by the members, and without reliance on the votes in favour by the director or any connected person.)

500. Subsection (3) sets out the criteria which the court must, in particular, take into account in considering whether or not to grant permission for the derivative claim to be continued.

501. Subsection (4) provides that, in considering whether to give permission, the court must have particular regard to any evidence before it as to the views of independent members of the company ie members who have no personal interest, direct or indirect in the matter.

502. Subsection (5) confers on the Secretary of State a power to make regulations with regard to the criteria to which the court must have regard in determining whether to grant leave to continue a derivative claim and where leave of the court must be refused. Subsection (6) provides that, before making any such regulations, the Secretary of State must consult with such persons as he considers appropriate. The power reflects a recommendation by the Law Commission in its 1997 report on shareholder remedies in respect of analogous shareholder actions in Scotland. Under subsection (7), the regulations will be subject to the affirmative resolution procedure.

Section 264: Application for permission to continue derivative claim brought by another member

503. This section addresses the possibility that, where the court has already decided that there is an appropriate case for a derivative claim and a member has commenced or continued a claim:

- the manner in which the member commenced or continued the claim may amount to an abuse of the court (eg the member brought the claim with a view to preventing another member from bringing the claim);
- the member may fail to prosecute the claim diligently;
- it may be appropriate for another member to continue the claim (eg because the member who brought the claim has become very ill).

504. The section provides that, in these circumstances, another member may apply to the court to continue the claim as a derivative action.

Chapter 2: Derivative Proceedings In Scotland

505. Sections 265 to 269 seek to ensure maximum consistency between the position in England and Wales and Northern Ireland and the position in Scotland (although the clauses reflect the different procedural requirements which apply where proceedings are commenced in the Scottish courts, in particular the fact that the leave of court must be obtained before derivative proceedings may be raised). In view of this, they also put the rights of the member to raise actions on behalf of the company on a statutory footing.

506. Section 265 differs from section 260 in its approach in that it confers the right to bring the proceedings in the first place, and then, in the clauses which follow, regulate the proceedings. (By contrast, the sections relating to proceedings in England and Wales and Northern Ireland assume that there is already a right to bring such proceedings in England and Wales and Northern Ireland; they therefore regulate the proceedings rather than confer the right to bring them.)

507. Subsections (4) to (6) of section 268 confer on the Secretary of State a parallel power to that in section 263 to make regulations with regard to the criteria to which the court must have regard in determining whether to grant leave to continue a derivative claim and where leave of the court must be refused.

PART 12: COMPANY SECRETARIES

Section 270: Private company not required to have secretary

[3.13]
508. This section replaces section 283(1) of the 1985 Act insofar as it applies to private companies. It implements the CLR recommendation (Final Report, paragraph 4.7) that the requirement for a private company to have a secretary be abolished. It defines a private company "without a secretary" for the purposes of the Act as a company which has taken advantage of the exemption provided by subsection (1) as opposed to one which normally has a secretary but for some reason (for example the death of the office holder) is without a secretary at a given time. Subsection (3) makes provision for private companies without a secretary.

Section 271: Public company required to have secretary

509. This section replaces section 283(1) of the 1985 Act insofar as it applies to public companies. It retains the requirement that a public company must have a secretary. The secretary may also be one of the directors.

Section 272: Direction requiring public company to appoint secretary

510. This section is a new provision, enabling enforcement of the continuing requirement for a public company to have a secretary. It does not apply to private companies. Where it appears that a public company does not have a secretary, the Secretary of State may give a direction to the company. The company must comply with the direction (by making the appropriate appointment and giving notice of it) within the period specified in the direction. The section provides for an offence for failure to comply with a direction.

Section 273: Qualifications of secretaries of public companies

511. This section updates section 286 of the 1985 Act. It makes it the duty of the directors of a public company to ensure that the secretary has both the necessary knowledge and experience and one of the qualifications listed in subsection (2). The qualifications specified in this section are the same as in the 1985 Act except that:

- they do not include the qualification of having held the office of the company's secretary (or assistant or deputy secretary) on 22 December 1980;
- in subsection (3)(f), "Chartered Institute of Management Accountants" replaces "Institute of Cost and Management Accountants" as the Institute changed its name in 1986.

There is no requirement for the company secretary to be a natural person. (Compare the requirement in section 155 that a company must have at least one director who is a natural person.)

Section 274: Discharge of functions where office vacant or secretary unable to act

512. This section replaces section 283(3) of the 1985 Act. It provides for the situation where the office of secretary is vacant or there is no secretary capable of acting for any other reason. In these circumstances, if the company has an assistant or deputy secretary, then that person may fill the position of secretary; if not, any person authorised by the directors may do so. This section differs from section 283(3) of the 1985 Act by permitting the directors to authorise any person to act as secretary, rather than only an officer of the company.

Section 275: Duty to keep register of secretaries

513. This section replaces the requirement in section 288 of 1985 Act. It requires every company to keep a register of its secretaries containing specified details. Subsection (3) provides that the register must be kept available for inspection either at the company's registered office or at a place specified in regulations made under section 1136. Subsections (5) to (8) retain the public right of inspection, sanctions and means of enforcement of the right of inspection.

Section 276: Duty to notify registrar of changes

514. This section replaces the requirement in section 288(2) of the 1985 Act. It requires notification to the registrar within 14 days of any change in the company's secretary or any change in the particulars contained in the register of secretaries. The consent of the person having become a secretary or joint secretary of a company must accompany the notice. The section retains the existing sanction and ensures that the public record is kept up to date as regards the secretary of every company.

Section 277: Particulars of secretaries to be registered: individuals

515. This section replaces section 290 of the 1985 Act insofar as it applies to secretaries who are individuals. It requires a company to enter in its register of secretaries the name and address of any individual who is its secretary. The definition of name is the same as for directors (see section 163): in particular, the register must include any name used or in use for business purposes since the age of 16. The section retains an exception relating to the former names of peers but, as recommended by the CLR, not that for the former names of married women. The address to be registered is a service address: this implements the CLR recommendation (Final Report, paragraph 11.46) that the requirement for home addresses for company secretaries be abolished.

Section 278: Particulars of secretaries to be registered: corporate secretaries and firms

516. This section replaces section 290 of the 1985 Act insofar as it applies to secretaries who are not individuals. It sets out the details which must be registered where the secretary of a company is either a body corporate or a firm which is a legal person under the law by which it is governed. The requirements that apply in the case of an EEA company follow the recommendations of the CLR (Final Report, paragraph 11.39).

517. The section also makes provision about the details which must be registered where all the partners in a firm are joint secretaries.

Section 279: Particulars of secretaries to be registered: power to make regulations

518. This section is a new provision. It provides a power for the Secretary of State to make regulations that add or remove items from the particulars that have to be entered in a company's register of secretaries. A similar power is provided by section 166 for directors' particulars.

Section 280: Acts done by person in dual capacity

519. This section replaces section 284 of the 1985 Act. It provides that where a provision requires or authorises a thing to be done by or to both a director and a secretary of a company it will not be not be satisfied if done by the same person acting in both capacities.

PART 13: RESOLUTIONS AND MEETINGS

[3.14]

520. The provisions in this Part replace most of Chapter 4 of Part 11 of the 1985 Act on meetings and resolutions. The changes in the law derive principally from the CLR's consultation on "Company General Meetings and Shareholder Communications" and recommendations from Chapters 2, 6 and 7 of their "Final Report", together with two subsequent consultations; the Modernising Company Law White Paper of July 2002 and the Company Law Reform White Paper of March 2005.

521. In addition to implementing detailed policy changes, Part 13 implements two general changes.

- First, the law makes the current "elective" regime the default for private companies. This means, for instance, that private companies will no longer need to "elect" to dispense with the Annual General Meeting (AGM): they will not be required to hold an AGM in the first place.
- Second, the current law is drafted on the basis that the main way in which shareholder decisions are taken is in general meetings. The new provisions proceed on the basis that in future this will not be the case for many private companies. Private companies will not be required in future to hold general meetings; instead provision is made for new procedures for decisions to be taken by written resolution.

522. The law relating to decisions has been restated in a way that deals first with private companies. Additional layers of requirements for public and quoted companies holding general meetings follow in subsequent provisions. There are provisions at the end of the Part about record keeping. In general, where this Part imposes an obligation or confers a power, it will apply notwithstanding anything in the articles unless otherwise indicated.

Chapter 1: General Provisions About Resolutions

Section 281: Resolutions

523. This section provides that members' resolutions can only be passed in accordance with the provisions of this Part. There is no equivalent in the current legislation. Subsection (1) allows a private company to pass a resolution either as a written resolution or at a meeting of the members. Subsection (2) allows a public company to pass a resolution only at a meeting of the members. Subsection (3) ensures that where a resolution is required but the type of resolution is not specified, the default will be an ordinary resolution unless the articles require a higher majority. When a provision specifies that an ordinary resolution is required, the articles will not be able to specify a higher majority. Subsection (4) preserves the common law unanimous consent rule.

Section 282: Ordinary resolutions

524. This section provides a definition of an ordinary resolution, whether of the members generally or of a class of the members and whether as a written resolution or as a resolution passed at a meeting. A simple majority – that is, over 50% – is required.

Section 283: Special resolutions

525. This section provides a definition of a special resolution, whether of the members generally or of a class of the members and whether as a written resolution or as a resolution passed at a meeting. A 75% majority is required. If a resolution is proposed as a special resolution, there is a requirement to say so, either in the written resolution text or in the meeting notice. Where a resolution is proposed as a special resolution, it can only be passed as such. The main difference from the existing definition in section 378(2) of the 1985 Act is that there is no longer a requirement for 21 days' notice where a special resolution is to be passed at a meeting. The subject matter of section 378(3) of the 1985 Act is now dealt with in section 307(4) to (6) (notice required of general meeting), while the subject matter of section 378(4) and (6) is dealt with in sections 320 and 301 respectively.

Section 284: Votes: general rules

526. This section sets out the general rules on votes of members taken by written resolution, on a show of hands at a meeting or on a poll taken at a meeting. These are adapted from section 370 of the 1985 Act and the default regulations in Table A. Subsection (4) allows these general rules to be varied by the company's articles.

Section 285: Votes: specific requirements

527. This section sets out specific requirements on votes of members, which the company's articles may not override. Subsections (1) and (2) provide for entitlement to vote where proxies have been appointed and ensure that the articles do not disadvantage a member voting by proxy or proxies. Subsection (3) makes new provision for voting rights on written resolutions, reflecting the fact that they will no longer need to be passed unanimously. A member will have the same number of votes whether passing a resolution on a poll in general meeting or on a written resolution.

Section 286: Votes of joint holders of shares

528. This section puts on a statutory footing what was a default regulation under article 55 of Table A on votes of joint holders of shares. The person whose vote counts is the "senior" holder, the joint holder whose name appears first in the register of members

Section 287: Saving for provisions of articles as to determination of entitlement to vote

529. This section makes new provision to preserve the right for a company to require objections to votes to be made in accordance with procedures in their articles. If an objection is overruled, the decision will be final except in cases of fraud and certain other kinds of misconduct detailed in case law where a court may intervene. This provision preserves the current law. The provision ensures, on the one hand, certainty for company by enabling the chairman to settle matters relating to the admissibility of votes in accordance with the articles and, on the other hand, sufficient remedies for members to challenge a decision if they have suffered unfair prejudice.

Chapter 2: Written Resolutions

530. The provisions of this Chapter replace the present rules on written resolutions of private companies. A key change (apparent from sections 282 and 283) is that where the statutory procedure

Part 3   CA 2006 Supporting Materials

under the 1985 Act requires unanimity, the procedure in this Act does not. Consequently, the sections are more detailed than sections 381A to 381C of the 1985 Act and set out the procedures for decisions taken outside of a general meeting framework. The use of the expression "written resolution" does not mean that there is a requirement for "writing" in the sense of hard copy.

General provision about written resolutions

Section 288: Written resolutions of private companies

531.   This section introduces the written resolution provisions of this Chapter. They apply to private companies only. Subsection (2)(a) and (b) reproduce the two exceptions currently provided for in Part 1 of Schedule 15A to the 1985 Act: a resolution to remove a director or an auditor before the expiration of his term of office may not be passed as a written resolution. These are the only two exceptions to a private company's right to pass resolutions using the written resolution procedure.

Section 289: Eligible members

532.   The eligibility of members to vote on a written resolution is fixed on the day the resolution is circulated. Subsection (2) ensures that the same shares cannot be voted more than once on the same written resolution. If the person entitled to vote changes during the course of that day, the eligible member is the person entitled to vote at the time that the first copy of the resolution is sent or submitted to a member for his agreement.

Circulation of written resolutions

Section 290: Circulation date

533.   This section provides that the circulation date of a written resolution means the date on which copies are sent or submitted to members (or if copies are sent on different days, the first of those days.

Section 291: Circulation of written resolutions proposed by directors

534.   This section provides for the circulation of written resolutions by directors of the company. A company must circulate a written resolution either by sending it to all eligible members at the same time or, if it can be done without undue delay, submitting the same copy of the resolution to each eligible member in turn or a combination of these. The latter two options allow companies to pass round a document or email rather than sending out several copies.

Section 292: Members' power to require circulation of written resolution

535.   This section enables members to require a written resolution to be circulated. They may also require circulation of a statement about its subject matter. Like the members' right to require a resolution to be moved at an AGM, the percentage needed is 5% of the total voting rights (or lower if specified in the company's articles). Subsection (2) specifies some limits on the kind of resolution that may be circulated in this way, designed to stop the power being abused.

Section 293: Circulation of written resolution proposed by members

536.   This section specifies what a company has to do when it is required under section 292 to circulate a resolution and accompanying statement. It must circulate the resolution and statement by sending it to all eligible members at the same time or, if it can be done without undue delay, by submitting the same copy of the resolution and statement to each eligible member in turn or a combination of these. The latter two options would allow companies to pass round a document or email rather than sending out several copies. Subsection (3) requires that the members' written resolution be circulated within 21 days of the company being requested to do so by those members, except that if the written resolution is circulated to members on different days, then the first copy should be dispatched not more than 21 days after the request to circulate the resolution.

Section 294: Expenses of circulation

537.   This section provides that the expenses of complying with section 293 are to be paid by the members who requested the circulation of the resolution unless the company resolves otherwise. The company can require the deposit of a sum to meet its expenses before it circulates the resolution, again subject to any resolution to the contrary.

Section 295: Application not to circulate members' statement

538.   This section enables the court, on application by the company or other aggrieved person, to relieve the company of an obligation to circulate a members' statement under section 293 if in the court's view the right to require circulation is being abused. This mirrors section 317 in the context of general meetings.

Agreeing to written resolutions

Section 296: Procedure for signifying agreement to written resolution

539.   Under this section, a member may signify agreement to a written resolution in hard copy or electronic form, although if the company does not permit electronic form communications, or is not deemed to do so by virtue of section 298, the member will have to signify his consent in hard copy (see paragraph 6 (conditions for use of communications in electronic form) of Schedule 4 (documents and information sent or supplied to a company). Once a member has signified agreement to a written resolution, he cannot withdraw his agreement. This provides certainty for the company as to when the required majority of eligible members needed to agree the resolution has been reached.

Section 297: Period for agreeing to written resolution

540. This section puts a time limit of 28 days for passing a written resolution, unless the company's articles specify a different period. This means that there will be a definite point when the company can say that a resolution with insufficient support has not been passed.

Supplementary

Section 298: Sending documents relating to written resolutions by electronic means

541. This clause needs to be read together with the provisions about electronic communications to companies in Part 3 (communications in electronic form) of Schedule 4. Taken together, these provisions allow a member to communicate with the company by electronic means where the company has given an electronic address in a document containing or accompanying a proposed written resolution.

Section 299: Publication of written resolution on website

542. This section should be read in conjunction with the provisions about communications by means of a website by a company other than a traded company in Part 4 (communications by means of a website) of Schedule 5 (communications by a company). This clause, together with those provisions, allow a company, provided certain conditions are met, to publish a written resolution on a website rather than send it to a member individually.

Section 300: Relationship between this Chapter and provisions of company's articles

543. This section ensures that the company's articles cannot remove the ability of a private company and its members to propose and pass a statutory resolution using the statutory written resolutions procedures of this Chapter.

Chapter 3: Resolutions At Meetings

544. This Chapter replaces sections 368 to 377, 379 and 381 of the 1985 Act and makes provision about resolutions passed in general meeting. The provisions apply equally to private and public companies. The new provisions reflect the fact that private companies will no longer have to hold AGMs. For example, the provisions about circulation of statements in sections 376 and 377 of the 1985 Act have been separated from the provisions on circulation of resolutions prior to an AGM – which are in Chapter 4. The Act repeals section 367 of the 1985 Act which gives the Secretary of State a power to call a meeting where there is no AGM.

General provisions about resolutions at meetings

Section 301: Resolutions at general meetings

545. This is a general provision about the circumstances in which resolutions at meetings are validly passed. It extends to all resolutions the principle in section 378(6) of the 1985 Act relating to special resolutions: that passing a resolution in a meeting is not just a question of obtaining the right majority but of using the correct procedures. An important difference from the position under section 378(6) is that, under this section, a resolution must be passed in accordance with the relevant provisions of the Bill and any additional requirements imposed by the company's articles. So, where there are mandatory provisions in the Bill (like those about proxies' rights to vote) these cannot be avoided by making alternative provision in the articles; and where provision is made about meetings in a company's articles, these must also be complied with.

Calling meetings

Section 302: Directors' power to call general meetings

546. This section puts into statute part of the default regulation at article 37 of Table A which allows the directors to call a general meeting. The company's articles will set out how the directors act collectively.

Section 303: Members' power to require directors to call general meeting

547. This section, together with sections 304 and 305 make provision similar to that in section 368 of the 1985 Act requiring the directors to call a general meeting if requested by the members. There are three main changes.

548. First, there is a change in the threshold required for a meeting request. For public companies this remains members with voting rights holding at least 10% of the paid-up capital. For private

Part 3 CA 2006 Supporting Materials

companies the threshold is 5% or 10% of the paid-up capital (or, in a company with no share capital, 5% or 10% of the total voting rights) depending on when there was last a meeting in advance of which members had a right – equivalent to the right under this clause (see below) – to circulate resolutions. The threshold is lower if there has been no such meeting in the last twelve months. Second, as indicated above, subsection (4)(b) extends the provisions of the 1985 Act by enabling members to include the text of a resolution to be moved at the requested meeting. Subsection (5) defines what type of resolution may be properly moved. For example, if the resolution would have no effect, then it cannot be properly moved. Third, requests in electronic form are permitted.

Section 304: Directors' duty to call meetings required by members

549.   This section sets time limits within which the directors must call and hold a meeting required by members. Subsection (2) requires that if the members' request identifies a resolution to be moved at the meeting, notice of this resolution should be included in the notice of the meeting.

Section 305: Power of members to call meeting at company's expense

550.   This section enables the members to call a meeting at the company's expense in the event that the directors fail to call a meeting on the members' request. Subsections (6) and (7) provide for members to be reimbursed appropriately and that the directors are penalised directly by the reimbursement being taken out of the fees or other remuneration due to them.

Section 306: Power of court to order meeting

551.   This section reproduces the effect of section 371 of the 1985 Act and gives the court power to order a meeting of the company and to direct the manner in which that meeting is called, held and conducted.

Notice of meetings

Section 307: Notice required of general meeting

552.   This section replaces part of section 369 of the 1985 Act. It retains the current minimum notice period requirement of 21 days for public company AGMs, with 14 days' notice required for all other general meetings (whether public or private company general meetings). A general meeting may be called on shorter notice if the requisite majority of members agree. The key substantive change from the position under existing legislation is that the requisite majority required to agree a short notice period has been reduced for private companies from 95% to 90% of the voting rights, although the articles may specify up to 95% if the company wishes. For public companies, the majority required to agree a short notice period remains at 95% of the voting rights.

Section 308: Manner in which notice to be given

553.   This section should be read in conjunction with the general requirements for companies in sending and supplying information as set out in Part 37 and Schedule 5.

Section 309: Publication of notice of meeting on website

554.   This section contains some specific provisions on communications by means of a website and needs to be read with the general provisions on communications referred to above. The overall effect is similar to that of the website provisions in the current section 369 of the 1985 Act.

Section 310: Persons entitled to receive notice of meetings

555.   This section puts into statute part of article 38 of Table A. The new provision ensures that notice of meetings must be sent to all members, directors and any person entitled to a share as a consequence of the death or bankruptcy (or the equivalent in Scots insolvency law) of a member. The provision is subject to any enactment and to any provision in the articles. This means that a company may, for example, make provision in its articles to stop sending notice of meeting to members for whom the company no longer has a valid address.

Section 311: Contents of notices of meetings

556.   This section puts into statute another part of article 38 of Table A. The new provision ensures that the notice of meeting must include the time, date and place of the meeting and, subject to the articles, the general nature of the business to be conducted at the meeting.

Section 312: Resolution requiring special notice

557.   This section replaces section 379 of the 1985 Act setting out the requirements for special notice resolutions. It makes provision only in relation to resolutions passed at meetings. This is because the resolutions for which special notice is required are either resolutions that are not capable of being passed as written resolutions (in the case of sections 168 and 510) or in relation to which written resolutions have their own special procedure (see sections 514 and 515).

558.   There is no change from the existing law whereby at least 28 days' notice must be given to the company of the intention to move a resolution requiring special notice. Where it is not practicable for the company to give members notice of such a resolution at the same time as it gives notice of the meeting at which the resolution is to be moved, the company must in future give at least 14 days' notice either by newspaper advertisement or by any other manner allowed by the articles.

Section 313: Accidental failure to give notice of resolution or meeting

559. This section expands on article 39 of Table A. It contains the rule that an accidental failure to give notice of a resolution or a general meeting is generally disregarded. Under subsection (2), this rule can be altered by the articles in some but not all cases.

Members' statements

Section 314: Members' power to require circulation of statements

560. This section, together with section 315, replaces sections 376 and 377 of the 1985 Act and provides a right for members to require the company to circulate a statement of up to 1,000 words. The key policy change is that where the statement relates to a resolution or other matter to be dealt with at a public company's AGM and is received before the company's financial year-end, the shareholders are not required to cover the costs of circulating the statement. There are two other notable changes. The first is that the shares relied on to trigger the circulation of a statement must in each case carry rights to vote on the relevant resolution rather than just at the meeting. The second is that requests in electronic form are permitted.

Section 315: Company's duty to circulate members' statement

561. This section replaces the remainder of sections 376 and 377 of the 1985 Act and specifies what the company is to do when it is required to circulate a members' statement. The statement must be circulated in the same manner as notice of the meeting and at the same time, or as soon as reasonably practicable, after the company gives notice of the meeting. Where the company fails to comply with the provisions of this section an offence is committed by every officer of the company who is in default.

Section 316: Expenses of circulating members' statement

562. This section provides that the expenses of complying with section 315 need not be paid by the members if the meeting to which the request relates is a public company AGM and a sufficient number of requests are received before the company's year-end. Otherwise the company's expenses will have to be met by the members who requested the circulation of the statement unless the company resolves otherwise. In this case, the members requesting the statement must deposit a sum to cover the company's costs (unless the company has resolved otherwise).

Section 317: Application not to circulate members' statement

563. This section replaces section 377(3) of the 1985 Act. It enables the court on application to relieve the company of an obligation to circulate a members' statement if in its opinion the right to require circulation is being abused.

Procedure at meetings

Section 318: Quorum at meetings

564. This section replaces sections 370(4) and 370A of the 1985 Act. It sets a quorum for a meeting of one "qualifying person" in the case of a single member company and – as a default – two "qualifying persons" in any other case. Subsections (2) and (3) ensure that a member, corporate representative or proxy present at the meeting may all be "qualifying persons", but excludes the possibility of two or more corporate representatives or proxies of the same member comprising a quorum. Under these provisions, proxies and corporate representatives do not count towards a quorum in companies with more than one member.

Section 319: Chairman of meeting

565. This section reproduces the effect of section 370(5) of the 1985 Act and provides a default provision where the company's articles are silent, allowing any member to be elected as chairman of a general meeting by a resolution of the company passed at the meeting.

Section 320: Declaration by chairman on a show of hands

566. This section replaces section 378(4) of the 1985 Act and part of article 47 of Table A. This provision ensures that the chairman's declaration of a vote taken on a show of hands is conclusive evidence of the resolution being passed or lost without further proof being provided, unless a poll is demanded on the resolution. There are two main differences from section 378(4), both of which are drawn from Table A. First, if the demand for a poll is withdrawn, then the chairman's declaration will stand. Second, the minutes of the meeting also provide conclusive evidence of the chairman's declaration. This section is intended to provide certainty by preventing members from challenging a declaration of the chairman as to the votes cast on a resolution at a meeting otherwise than by calling a poll.

Part 3   CA 2006 Supporting Materials

Section 321: Right to demand a poll

567. This section replaces section 373 of the 1985 Act. It restricts companies' ability, through their articles, to exclude members' rights to call a poll. However, it allows articles to exclude the right to a poll on the election of the chairman of the meeting and the adjournment of the meeting. The section provides for three effective types of demands for a poll, including a demand made by at least 5 members with a right to vote on the resolution.

Section 322: Voting on a poll

568. This section replaces section 374 of the 1985 Act. This provision recognises that a member may hold shares on behalf of third parties and allows the member to cast votes in different ways according to instructions from his clients. The reference to class meetings in section 374 is dealt with by section 334.

Section 323: Representation of corporations at meetings

569. This section replaces section 375 of the 1985 Act. The section expressly provides for the appointment of multiple corporate representatives. This is possible under section 375 of the 1985 Act, although the effect of appointing multiple representatives under the existing law is in some cases unclear. The new section spells out the position. Any one of the corporate representatives will be entitled to vote and exercise other powers on behalf of the member at meetings, but in the event that representatives' votes or other powers conflict, the corporation is deemed to have abstained from exercising its vote or power. If a corporation wishes to appoint people with different voting intentions or with authority to vote different blocks of shares, they should appoint proxies.

Proxies

Section 324: Rights to appoint proxies

570. This section sets out new provisions for the appointment of proxies, expanding on the existing rights given under section 372 of the 1985 Act and Table A. It puts on a statutory footing certain rights that under the 1985 Act are subject to the articles. In future, members of both private and public companies will have the right to appoint more than one proxy. All proxies will be able to attend, to speak and to vote at a meeting. As to the voting rights of a proxy on a show of hands, see sections 284(2)(b) and 285. The effect of those sections is that the default position will be that, where a member appoints more than one proxy, each proxy will have a vote. The articles will be capable of restricting the number of votes of the proxies, provided that they still have at least one vote between them.

Section 325: Notice of meeting to contain statement of rights

571. This section replaces sections 372(3) and 372(4) of the 1985 Act with changes consequential on the extended rights to appoint proxies under section 324. The new provision requires every notice calling a meeting to contain a statement informing the member of his rights to appoint one or more proxies and any more extensive rights conferred by the company's articles. Failure to include such a statement will not invalidate the meeting, but is an offence attracting a fine for every officer of the company found in default.

Section 326: Company-sponsored invitations to appoint proxies

572. This section reproduces the effect of section 372(6) of the 1985 Act and requires a company to ensure that if it invites members to appoint a particular person or persons as proxy, such an invitation must be issued to all members entitled to vote at the meeting. Subsection (2) lists two exceptions to the requirement. Failure to comply attracts a fine for every officer in default.

Section 327: Notice required of appointment of proxy etc

573. This section replaces section 372(5) of the 1985 Act. There are two changes. The first relates to the timing required for a notice of proxy appointment. The new provision ensures that weekends, Christmas Day, Good Friday and any bank holiday are excluded from the time counting towards the minimum 48 hour notice required to appoint proxies. This means, for example, that for a meeting to be held at 3.00 pm on a Tuesday after a bank holiday Monday, the cut-off point for proxy appointment will be 3.00 pm the previous Thursday, not 3.00 pm on Sunday as under the 1985 Act. The second is that polls which are not taken immediately are covered by the rules as well as meetings and adjourned meetings.

Section 328: Chairing meetings

574. This section provides as a default rule, subject to the articles, that a proxy may be elected as chairman of a general meeting by resolution of the company passed at the meeting.

Section 329: Right of proxy to demand a poll

575. This section sets out the way in which a proxy may participate in a demand for a poll.

Section 330: Notice required of termination of proxy's authority

576.   This section provides a default regulation to replace article 63 of Table A. This ensures that, subject to the articles, an appointed proxy's actions at a meeting are valid unless notice of termination of the proxy's authority is given before the meeting starts. The company's articles may specify a longer advance notice period but this cannot be more than 48 hours in advance of the meeting (excluding weekends, Christmas Day, Good Friday and bank holidays).

Section 331: Saving for more extensive rights conferred by articles

577.   This section makes clear that the company's articles may confer more extensive rights than are provided for under the provisions of the Bill on members and their proxies.

Adjourned meetings

Section 332: Resolution passed at adjourned meeting

578.   This section reproduces the effect of part of section 381 of the 1985 Act as it applies to members' meetings. It ensures that a resolution of the members of the company passed at an adjourned meeting is treated as passed on that date and not on any earlier date. The reference to class meetings in section 381 is dealt with by section 334.

Electronic communications

Section 333: Sending documents relating to meetings etc in electronic form

579.   This section needs to be read together with the provisions about electronic communications to companies in Part 3 of Schedule 4. Taken together these provisions allow a member to communicate with the company by electronic means where the company has given an electronic address in a notice calling a meeting or in an instrument of proxy or proxy invitation.

Application to class meetings

Section 334: Application to class meetings

580.   This section applies the provisions of this Chapter with some modifications to meetings of holders of a class of shares in companies having a share capital.

Section 335: Application to class meetings: companies without a share capital

581.   This section applies the provisions of this Chapter with some modifications to meetings of classes of members of companies without a share capital.

Chapter 4: Public Companies: Additional Requirements For AGMs

582.   The requirements for public companies relating to annual general meetings are set out in this Chapter. The main substantive changes to the 1985 Act are, as the CLR recommended, that:
*   private companies will no longer be required to hold an AGM. The provisions of this Chapter therefore do not apply to private companies; and
*   public company AGMs must be held within six months of their financial year-end.

Section 336: Public companies: annual general meeting

583.   This section replaces section 366 of the 1985 Act but will apply only to public companies since private companies are no longer to be required to hold an AGM. Where section 366 required an AGM to be held each year and not more than 15 months after the previous AGM, a public company will now be required to hold an AGM within 6 months of its financial year-end. This new requirement is intended to ensure that shareholders have a more timely opportunity to hold the directors of a public company to account.

Section 337: Public companies: notice of AGM

584.   This section reproduces the effect of parts of section 369 of the 1985 Act relating to the AGM notice. The minimum notice period for calling a public company AGM is 21 days as set out in subsection (2) of section 307 or longer if provided for in the company's articles. An AGM may be called at shorter notice if all members of the company agree.

Section 338: Public companies: members' power to require circulation of resolutions for AGMs

585.   This section, with section 339, replaces sections 376 and 377 of the 1985 Act (to the extent that they relate to resolutions proposed by members to be moved at an AGM). Members holding at least 5% voting rights or at least 100 members holding on average £100 paid-up capital have the right to propose a resolution for the AGM agenda and to require the company to circulate details of the resolution to all members. A change from the existing legislation is that the shares must in each case carry rights to vote on the relevant resolution. The key policy change is that, if the members' request is received before the financial yearend, then the members are not required to cover the costs of circulation.

Part 3   CA 2006 Supporting Materials

Section 339: Public companies: company's duty to circulate members' resolutions for AGMs

586. This section replaces the remaining parts of sections 376 and 377 of the 1985 Act (to the extent that they relate to resolutions proposed by members to be moved at an AGM). It specifies what a company has to do when it is required to circulate a members' resolution for an AGM.

Section 340: Public companies: expenses of circulating members' resolutions for AGM

587. This section provides that the expenses of complying with section 339 need not be paid by the members who requested the circulation of the resolution if requests sufficient to require the company to circulate it are received before the company's year-end. Otherwise the company's expenses will have to be met by the members who requested the circulation of the resolution unless the company resolves otherwise. In this case, the members requesting the statement must deposit a sum to cover the company's costs (unless the company has resolved otherwise).

Chapter 5: Additional Requirements For Quoted Companies

588. This Chapter imposes new requirements on quoted companies relating to the disclosure on a website of the results of polls at general meetings, and an independent report on a poll if a sufficient number of members demand one. These two measures were recommended by the CLR (Final Report, paragraph 6.39(ii) and (iv)).

Website publication of poll results

Section 341: Results of poll to be made available on website

589. This section requires quoted companies to disclose on a website the results of all polls taken at a general meeting. Subsection (1) sets out the minimum information that must be disclosed. Companies may disclose additional information about the poll results if they wish. Subsection (4) imposes a penalty on every officer in default for non-compliance. Non-compliance however does not invalidate the poll, the resolution or other business to which the poll relates. Section 353 (requirements as to website availability) sets out the requirements relating to the website on which the poll results must be published.

Independent report on poll

Section 342: Members' power to require independent report on poll

590. This section gives members of a quoted company the right to require an independent report of any poll taken, or to be taken, at a general meeting. The minimum threshold required for the demand is the same as that for requiring the circulation of a resolution – that is members holding 5% of the voting rights or 100 members holding on average £100 of paid-up capital. The members' request must be made within one week of the meeting where the poll is taken. This allows members to decide after a poll is taken whether they wish to require an independent report, for example on a controversial resolution or where there appears to be a problem relating to voting procedures. Members may make their request in advance of the meeting if they wish, but unless the company's articles already require all votes to be taken on a poll, members may need to take steps to ensure that a poll is called.

Section 343: Appointment of independent assessor

591. The appointment of an independent assessor must be made within one week of the members' request. This means that the appointment could be made either before or after the meeting depending on when the members' request is made. The independent assessor must be independent (see section 344) and must not be someone already involved in the voting process for the company.

Section 344: Independence requirement

592. This section prevents a person acting as an independent assessor on a poll if he is too closely connected to the company or an associated undertaking of the company. The independence requirements are set out in subsection (1). They correspond to the independence requirements for a statutory auditor (see section 1214). Subsection (2) allows, but does not require, an auditor to be appointed as an assessor.

Section 345: Meaning of "associate"

593. This section defines "associate" for the purposes of the independence requirements in section 344.

Section 346: Effect of appointment of a partnership

594. This section provides for where a partnership that is not a legal person is appointed as an independent assessor on a poll.

Section 347: The independent assessor's report

595. This section sets out the minimum information the independent assessor's report must contain.

Section 348: Rights of independent assessor: right to attend meeting etc

596. This section gives the independent assessor rights to attend the meeting at which the poll or polls may be taken and to be provided with information relating to the meeting. He is to exercise these rights only to the extent he considers necessary for the preparation of his report.

Section 349: Rights of independent assessor: right to information

597. This section gives the independent assessor the right to access company records relating to any poll on which he is to report and to the meeting at which the poll or polls may be taken.

Section 350: Offences relating to provision of information

598. This section imposes a penalty on any person listed in subsection (2) of section 349 who fails to comply with the requirement to provide information or explanation relating to the poll on which the independent assessor is preparing a report.

Section 351: Information to be made available on website

599. This section requires the company to publish on a website the independent assessor's report of the poll or polls and sets out the minimum information relating to the assessor's appointment, his identity, the text of the resolution and the assessor's report that must be made available. Subsections (3) and (4) impose a penalty on every officer in default for non-compliance with this requirement. Failure to comply, however, does not invalidate the poll or the resolution or other business to which the poll relates. Section 353 sets out the requirements relating to the website on which the independent report must be published.

Supplementary

Section 352: Application of provisions to class meetings

600. This section applies the provisions of this Chapter to meetings of holders of a class of shares of a quoted company.

Section 353: Requirements as to website availability

601. This section sets out the minimum requirements that should apply to information to be published on a quoted company's website under section 341 and section 351. The website on which the information is made available must be maintained by or on behalf of the quoted company and must identify the company in question. This provides flexibility as to whether a website is the company's own or one operated by a website service provider. Information published on a website must be kept available for a minimum of two years. Subsection (5) provides a let-out when a company's failure to make the information available on a website for part of the period is wholly attributable to circumstances beyond the company's control.

Section 354: Power to limit or extend the types of company to which provisions of this Chapter apply

602. At present the provisions of this Chapter apply to quoted companies as defined in section 385, which replaces the definition of "quoted company" in section 262 of the 1985 Act. This section confers on the Secretary of State a power to make regulations to limit or extend the types of company to which the provisions of this Chapter apply. The Parliamentary procedure that will apply to such regulations depends on whether they extend or limit the application of the Chapter.

Chapter 6: Records Of Resolutions And Meetings

603. The following provisions replace sections 382, 382A, 382B and 383 of the 1985 Act relating to the records of company proceedings. They should be read in conjunction with the provisions on company records in Part 31. The main changes are the ten year minimum period for keeping records (the 1985 Act envisaged that records would be retained forever); that meetings of directors are dealt with elsewhere (in Part 10 of the Act); and that the new provisions apply to class meetings.

Section 355: Records of resolutions and meetings etc

604. This section requires all companies to maintain records comprising: copies of all resolutions passed otherwise than at general meetings (which would include all written resolutions), minutes of all proceedings of general meetings, and details of decisions of a sole member taken in accordance with section 357. All records must be kept for a minimum of 10 years. Subsections (3) and (4) impose a penalty on every officer in default for non-compliance.

Section 356: Records as evidence of resolutions etc

605. This section ensures that all records of resolutions or written resolutions and minutes of meetings, where signed off by a director or a company secretary or by the chairman in the case of a general meeting, are evidence of the passing of a resolution or the proceedings at the meeting. In legal proceedings, a litigant will have to accept that the records are accurate unless he can prove that they are not.

Part 3   CA 2006 Supporting Materials

Section 357: Records of decisions by sole member

606.   This section makes provision for the recording of decisions of a company with only one member.

Section 358: Inspection of records of resolutions and meetings

607.   This section requires every company to keep its records available for inspection by members for 10 years. Subsection (5) enables a member to seek a court order to compel the company to make the records available for inspection or to provide copies of the records.

Section 359: Records of resolutions and meetings of class of members

608.   This section applies the provisions of this Chapter to resolutions and meetings of holders of a class of shares in the case of a company with share capital or to classes of members in the case of a company without a share capital.

Chapter 7: Supplementary Provisions

Section 360: Computation of periods of notice etc: clear day rule

609.   This is a new provision to ensure clarity and consistency in the calculation of time periods in relation to meetings and resolutions under Part 13. The section provides that in calculating periods of notice, or periods before a meeting by which a request must be received or sum deposited or tendered, the following are to be excluded –

* the day of the meeting,
* the day on which notice is given,
* the day on which the request is received or the sum is deposited or tendered.

Section 361: Meaning of "quoted company"

610.   This section provides that the definition for "quoted company" is as stated in Part 15 (Accounts and reports) of the Act.

PART 14: CONTROL OF POLITICAL DONATIONS AND EXPENDITURE

Background and summary

[3.15]
611.   In October 1998 the Committee on Standards in Public Life presented to the Prime Minister its report on the funding of political parties in the UK. The Report recommended that any company intending to make a donation (whether in cash or in kind, and including any sponsorship, or loans or transactions at a favourable rate) to a political party or organisation should be required to have the prior authority of its shareholders. The Government accepted this recommendation, and implemented it through the Political Parties, Elections and Referendums Act 2000 ("the PPERA"). The new regime for control of political donations and expenditure is in Part 10A of the 1985 Act, as inserted by section 139 of and Schedule 19 to the PPERA.

612.   Part 14 of the Act restates the existing provisions in a style consistent with the other sections, but most of the key elements of the framework established by the PPERA remain. In particular:

* companies will continue to be prohibited from making a donation to a political party or other political organisation or from incurring political expenditure unless the donation or the expenditure has been authorised, in a typical case by the members of the company;
* a "political donation" will continue to be defined by reference to sections 50 to 52 of the PPERA, and for this purpose amendments made to the PPERA by the Electoral Adminis-tration Act 2006 (which remove from the definition of "donations" loans made otherwise than on commercial terms) will be disregarded;
* an approval resolution may authorise the making of donations and incurring of expenditure for a period of not more than four years commencing with the date of the passing of the resolution up to a value specified in the resolution;
* donations or expenditure by a subsidiary must, in general, be authorised by resolutions of the members of the subsidiary and of the holding company; and the directors of such a holding company will continue to be liable for unauthorised donations by the subsidiary company;
* a company need not seek prior shareholder consent for a donation to a political party or organisation unless the aggregate amount of the donation together with any other relevant donations made by the company and other companies in the group of which it is a member in the previous 12 months exceeds £5,000;
* there are no criminal sanctions in relation to the making of unauthorised donations or the incurring of unauthorised political expenditure;
* civil remedies are available to a company in the event of breach of the prohibitions and may be pursued in the normal manner by the company. There will continue to be available an action under which shareholders may enforce on behalf of the company any of the remedies available to a company.

613.   The main changes from Part 10A of the 1985 Act are that:
- in line with the general approach in the Act, references to the general meeting are removed to make it clearer that private companies can authorise donations and/or expenditure by written resolution;
- a holding company must authorise a donation or expenditure by a subsidiary company only if it is a "relevant holding company" (that is, the ultimate holding company or, where such a company is not a "UK-registered company", the holding company highest up the chain which is a "UK-registered company");
- a holding company is permitted to seek authorisation of donations and expenditure in respect of both the holding company itself and one or more subsidiaries (including wholly-owned subsidiaries) through a single approval resolution (section 367(1));
- companies are permitted to table separate approval resolutions in respect of donations to political parties and donations to other political organisations (section 367(3));
- companies are required to seek authorisation for donations to independent candidates at any election to public office held in the UK or other EU member state and for expenditure by the company relating to independent election candidates;
- the sections provide greater clarity for companies about the provision of facilities (for example, meeting rooms) for trade union officials by introducing a specific exemption for donations to trade unions (section 374). The Act does not introduce a specific exemption in relation to paid leave for local councillors because this does not constitute a political donation or political expenditure under Part 10A of the 1985 Act or this Act;
- there are important changes to the rules on ratification and liability in cases of unauthorised donations or expenditure;
- the special rules in respect of the parent company of a non-GB subsidiary undertaking (sections 347E and 347G of the 1985 Act) are not reproduced;
- The new provisions apply to Northern Ireland.

Commentary

Section 362: Introductory

614.   This section explains that this Part relates to political expenditure and to political donations made by companies to political parties, political organisations and independent election candidates.

Section 363: Political parties, organisations etc to which this Part applies

615.   This section establishes the general scope of the provisions of this Part and introduces the concepts of:
- political parties;
- political organisations other than political parties;
- independent election candidates at any election to public office.

Section 364: Meaning of "political donation"

616.   This section defines a "political donation" for the purposes of this Part by reference to sections 50 to 52 of the Political Parties, Elections and Referendums Act 2000. For this purpose, amendments made to the 2000 Act by the Electoral Administration Act 2006 (which remove from the definition of "donation" loans made otherwise than on commercial terms) are disregarded. This section reproduces the effect of section 347A(4) of the 1985 Act, except that it includes donations to independent election candidates.

Section 365: Meaning of "political expenditure"

617.   This section defines "political expenditure" for the purposes of this Part.

618.   It reproduces the effect of section 347A(5) of the 1985 Act, except that it extends the definition to expenditure incurred by the company in relation to independent election candidates.

Section 366: Authorisation required for donations or expenditure

619.   This section prohibits a company from making a donation or incurring political expenditure unless the transaction or the expenditure is authorised by a resolution of the members of the company. If the company is a subsidiary of another company, a resolution may instead, or in addition, be required from the members of the holding company. Sections 1159, 1160 and Schedule 6 provide the definition of "subsidiary". This section reproduces the effect of section 347C(1) and (6) and section 347D of the 1985 Act, except that:
- in line with the general approach in the Act, the section does not refer to the general meeting, to make it clear that private companies can authorise donations and/or expenditure by written resolution;
- a donation or expenditure by a subsidiary company must be authorised by the members of the company and by members of a "relevant holding company" (rather than by the members of each holding company within a group). A "relevant holding company" is the ultimate holding company or, where such a company is not a "UK-registered company", the holding company highest up the chain which is a "UK-registered company";

Part 3   CA 2006 Supporting Materials

- a resolution is not required on the part of a company that is a wholly-owned subsidiary of a "UK-registered company" (rather than of any holding company, as in section 347D of the 1985 Act);
- the section does not reproduce the prohibition (in section 347C(5) of the 1985 Act) on retrospective ratification of breaches of the rules.

Section 367: Form of authorising resolution

620. This section provides that an authorising resolution may identify the subsidiaries, the heads of donations or expenditure, and the amounts that it authorises. The section reproduces the effect of the 1985 Act, but with the following changes:
- under subsection (1) and (2), a holding company may seek authorisation of donations and expenditure in respect of both itself and one or more of its subsidiaries (including wholly-owned subsidiaries) in a single approval resolution. The subsidiaries do not need to be named in the resolution if it applies to all of a holding company's subsidiaries;
- under subsection (3), a company may pass separate approval resolutions in respect of donations to political parties and donations to other political organisations.

Section 368: Period for which resolution has effect

621. This section provides that an approval resolution may seek authorisation for the making of donations and incurring of expenditure having effect over a period of not more than four years. It reproduces the effect of the 1985 Act.

Section 369: Liability of directors in case of unauthorised donation or expenditure

622. This section imposes civil liability on directors where unauthorised donations are made or unauthorised political expenditure is incurred. The liabilities are owed to the company and may be pursued in the normal manner by the company; that is they may be pursued by the directors in the exercise of the management powers conferred by the articles of association. The directors will be subject to the general duties set out in Chapter 2 of Part 10 in the conduct of the company's business. In addition, section 370 provides for enforcement by shareholder action.

623. The section largely reproduces the effect of section 347F of the 1985 Act, but:
- only a director of the company and of a "relevant holding company" may be liable in respect of an unauthorised donation or unauthorised expenditure. This reflects the new rules relating to the authorisation of donations or expenditure by subsidiaries in section 366;
- directors of the "relevant holding company" will not be liable for an unauthorised political donation or unauthorised political expenditure by a subsidiary if they took "all reasonable steps to prevent the donation being made or the expenditure being incurred".

624. The conditions under which directors may be exempted from liability (currently set out in section 347H of the 1985 Act) are not reproduced in the new regime.

Section 370: Enforcement of directors' liabilities by shareholder action

625. This section provides a mechanism by which an authorised group of shareholders may enforce on behalf of the company any liability under section 369. In the case of a company limited by shares, an action may be brought by a group of shareholders if they are at least 50 in number, or hold at least 5% of the issued share capital. This section reproduces the effect of section 347I of the 1985 Act, except that, in a case where liability is owed by directors of a holding company in relation to a donation made by a subsidiary, the action may be brought by shareholders of the subsidiary or of the holding company.

Section 371: Enforcement of directors' liabilities by shareholder action: supplementary

626. This section makes further provision in relation to proceedings brought under section 370. It reproduces the effect of section 347I of the 1985 Act. The group of shareholders wanting to take action under section 370 must give written notice to the company at least 28 days in advance of bringing the proceedings. Any director of the company has the right to apply to the court within 28 days of when the notice was given to request that the proceedings not be brought.

627. This section also provides that if the liability is already being pursued with due diligence by the company, the court may direct that the proceedings brought by the group of shareholders are either discontinued or brought on such terms and conditions as the court sees fit.

Section 372: Costs of shareholder action

628. This section provides that the authorised group of members are not entitled as of right to have the cost of the shareholder action met from the funds of the company, but have the right to apply to the court for an indemnity out of the company's assets in respect of costs incurred or to be incurred in a shareholder action. The court would have full discretion to grant such an indemnity on such terms as it thinks fit. The section reproduces the effect of section 347J of the 1985 Act.

Section 373: Information for purposes of shareholder action

629. This section provides that the authorised group of members is entitled, once the action is commenced, to be provided by the company in whose name it is brought with all information possessed by the company, or in its control or obtainable by it, relating to the subject matter of the action. It reproduces the effect of section 347K of the 1985 Act.

Sections 374 to 378: Exemptions

630. These sections set out five exemptions from the requirement for prior shareholder authorisation:

* section 374 creates a new exemption in relation to donations to trade unions (including trade unions in countries other than the UK). The exemption covers donations such as the provision of company rooms for trade union meetings, the use of company vehicles by trade union officials and paid time off for trade union officials. However, a donation to a trade union's political fund is not covered by the exemption;
* section 375 restates the exemption in section 347B of the 1985 Act in respect of subscriptions paid to a trade association for membership of the association, except that it is not restricted to trade associations which carry out their activities mainly in the EU;
* section 376 restates the exemption in section 347B of the 1985 Act in respect of donations to all-party parliamentary groups;
* section 377 restates the exemption in section 347B of the 1985 Act for political expenditure that is exempt by virtue of an order by the Secretary of State. An order made by statutory instrument under this clause may confer an exemption on companies or expenditure of any description or category specified in the order. The parallel power in section 347B(8) to (11) of the 1985 Act was used in 2001 to exempt business activities such as the publication of newspapers which, by their very nature, involve the publication or dissemination of material which seeks to influence the views of members of the public;
* section 378 restates the exemption in section 347B of the 1985 Act under which authorisation for donations is not required unless the donation or aggregate amount of the donations by the company exceeds £5,000 in a 12 month period. Donations by other group companies (including subsidiaries) must be taken into account in calculating whether the £5,000 threshold has been exceeded.

Section 379: Minor definitions

631. This section contains minor definitions for this Part.

PART 15: ACCOUNTS AND REPORTS

[3.16]
632. The provisions of this Part replace the provisions of Part 7 of the 1985 Act relating to accounts and reports. The provisions of Part 7 of the 1985 Act relating to audit are replaced by provisions in Part 16 of the Act.

633. The provisions have been reordered and redrafted to make it easier for companies of whatever size to find the requirements relevant to them. In Part 7 of the 1985 Act the provisions applying to small companies are generally expressed as modifications of the provisions applying to large companies. These sections proceed on the opposite basis: where provisions do not apply to all kinds of company, provisions applying to small companies appear before the provisions applying to other companies.

634. A further change is to enable the Secretary of State to replace the detailed Schedules to Part 7 of the 1985 Act by regulations. This will give more flexibility to arrange the material currently in Schedules to make it easier to follow for different types of company. It is unnecessary and undesirable to have parallel and duplicative regimes on the detail for different types of company in primary legislation, but this could be done in parallel sets of regulations for different sizes and types of company.

635. The main substantive changes in this Part are:

* a reduction in the time limit for private companies to file their accounts from ten months to nine months after the year end (section 442);
* a reduction in the time limit for public companies to lay full financial statements before the company in general meeting and file them from 7 months to 6 months after the year end (section 442);
* new requirements for quoted companies to publish their annual accounts and reports on a website (section 430); and
* replacement of the general power of the Secretary of State to alter accounting requirements in section 257 of the 1985 Act by a general power of amendment by regulations (section 468) and more specific powers in relation to specific sections.

Chapter 1: Introduction

Section 380: Scheme of this Part

636. This introductory section indicates the main way in which the structure of this Part differs from that of Part 7 of the 1985 Act: provisions relating to small companies are set out before

Part 3   CA 2006 Supporting Materials

provisions relating to larger companies; provisions applying to private companies appear before those applying to public companies; and provisions applying to quoted companies appear after those applying to other companies.

Companies subject to the small companies regime

Section 381: Companies subject to the small companies regime
Section 382: Companies qualifying as small: general
Section 383: Companies qualifying as small: parent companies
Section 384: Companies excluded from the small companies regime

637.   These sections set out which companies, parent companies or groups fall within the small companies regime – that is, those that qualify as small companies or groups and are not excluded from the regime for one of the reasons set out in section 384. With two small changes, the conditions for qualification as a small company are unchanged from the current regime (sections 247, 247A and 249 of the 1985 Act). Firstly, section 382(5) now contains a generalised definition of balance sheet total for both Companies Act and IAS individual accounts. Secondly, whereas section 247A(2) of the 1985 Act provides that a group is ineligible if any of its members is a body corporate having power to offer its shares or debentures to the public, the reference in section 384(2)(b) is now to a body corporate whose securities are admitted to trading on a regulated market in an EEA state. The definition of "regulated market" is to be found in section 1173. This reflects changes made by the Accounts Modernisation Directive (2003/51/EEC).

Section 385: Quoted and unquoted companies

638.   The definitions of quoted and unquoted company in this section are equivalent to the definition of "quoted company" in section 262 of the 1985 Act. A power is conferred to amend the definition of "quoted company" by regulations. If the regulations extend the application of this Part then they will be subject to affirmative resolution procedure. Otherwise they are subject to negative resolution procedure.

Chapter 2: Accounting Records

Sections 386 to 389: Accounting records

639.   These sections set out the general duty to keep accounting records and specify where and for how long records are to be kept. They replace equivalent provisions in sections 221 and 222 of the 1985 Act. Their purpose is to ensure that businesses record transactions to enable them to show the company's financial position and to prepare accounts which comply with the Companies Act and, where relevant, with International Accounting Standards. "Accounting records" is a broad term and there is no specific definition as the records may differ depending on the nature and complexity of the business. For a simple business these may include, for example, bank statements, purchase orders, sales and purchase invoices, whilst a more sophisticated business may have integrated records, which it holds electronically.

640.   Section 387 creates a criminal offence for every officer of a company who is in default, where the company has failed to keep adequate accounting records under section 386. The section replicates the existing penalties under section 221(5) and (6) of the 1985 Act (imprisonment or a fine).

641.   Section 389 makes similar provision in relation to failure to comply with section 388, replacing section 222(4) and (6) of the 1985 Act.

Chapter 3: A Company's Financial Year

Section 390: A company's financial year

642.   This section replaces section 223 of the 1985 Act. A company's financial year is the period for which its accounts and reports must be prepared. A company's financial year is the same as its accounting reference period (see section 391), subject to the directors' decision to alter the last day of the period by plus or minus seven days.

Section 391: Accounting reference periods and accounting reference date
Section 392: Alteration of accounting reference date

643.   These sections replace sections 224 and 225 of the 1985 Act.

644.   Section 391(2) and (3) preserve the accounting reference dates of companies incorporated before 1st April 1996 (in the case of GB companies), and before 22nd August 1997 (in the case of Northern Irish companies). Otherwise, a company's accounting reference date is the last day of the month in which the anniversary of its incorporation falls. Its first accounting reference period is a period of more than six months but not more than eighteen months beginning with the date of incorporation and ending with the accounting reference date unless the company changes its accounting reference date (the date on which the accounting reference period ends), in accordance with section 392. Subsequent accounting reference periods (financial years) are successive periods of 12 months, again subject to any alteration of the accounting reference date.

645.　Section 392(4) provides that a company cannot change its accounting reference date if the period allowed for delivering accounts and reports to the registrar for that period has already expired. Under the corresponding provision in the 1985 Act, the company cannot change the date "if the period allowed for laying and delivering accounts and reports in relation to that period has already expired." Under the Act only public companies are obliged to lay their accounts at a general meeting (section 437).

Chapter 4: Annual Accounts

Section 393: Accounts to give true and fair view

646.　Subsection (1) introduces an overarching obligation on directors (the preparers of accounts) not to approve accounts unless they give a true and fair view of the financial position of the company and, in the case of group accounts, the group. This provision reflects the underlying legal duty already expressed in Community law.

647.　Subsection (2) in addition places a requirement on auditors to take this overarching duty to give a true and fair view into consideration when giving an opinion on the accounts. This requirement supplements the functions of an auditor set out in section 485.

Individual accounts

648.　Sections 394 to 397, which replace sections 226, 226A and 226B of the 1985 Act, concern the duty of the directors to prepare individual accounts. The individual accounts may either be prepared under the Act (Companies Act individual accounts) or (unless the company is a charity) in accordance with international accounting standards adopted under the IAS Regulation (IAS individual accounts). The terms "IAS Regulation" and "international accounting standards" are defined in section 474. Once a company has switched to IAS individual accounts all subsequent individual accounts must be prepared in accordance with IAS unless there is a relevant change of circumstance (see section 395(3) to (5)). The provisions concerning the form and content of Companies Act accounts to be found in the Schedules to Part 7 of the 1985 Act will in future be contained in regulations to be made by the Secretary of State (section 396(3)). The Parliamentary procedure for such regulations is set out in section 473.

Group accounts: small companies

Section 398: Option to prepare group accounts

649.　This section provides that a company that is subject to the small companies regime and is a parent company is not obliged to prepare group accounts in addition to its individual accounts, (restating section 248 of the 1985 Act), but it may opt to do so. The current exemption in section 248 of the 1985 Act from preparation of group accounts by parent companies heading medium sized groups has been abolished, following the substantial increase in the financial thresholds for medium sized groups in 2004.

Group accounts: other companies

Sections 399 to 402: group accounts: other companies

650.　The sections relating to group accounts have been reorganised to make them easier to follow.

651.　Sections 399 to 402 re-enact sections 227(1) and (8), 228, 228A and 229(5) of the 1985 Act. Section 399 concerns the requirements and exemptions from requirements in relation to group accounts. Parent companies not subject to the small companies regime have the duty to prepare consolidated accounts unless exempt from having to do so under sections 400 to 402. Section 400 provides an exemption from preparing group accounts for companies included in EEA group accounts of a larger group. Section 401 provides such an exemption for companies included in non-EEA group accounts of a larger group, and section 402 provides an exemption when all the company's subsidiary undertakings could be excluded from consolidation in Companies Act group accounts (see section 405).

Group accounts: general

Section 403: Group accounts: applicable accounting framework

652.　This section replaces section 227(2) to (7) of the 1985 Act. Parent companies whose securities are publicly traded must prepare group accounts in accordance with the IAS Regulation. Other parent companies (with the exception of charitable companies) have the choice whether to prepare group accounts under the Companies Act (Companies Act group accounts) or in accordance with adopted international accounting standards (IAS group accounts). Once a company has switched to IAS group accounts all subsequent group accounts must be prepared in accordance with IAS unless there is a relevant change of circumstance (see subsections (4) to (6)).

Section 404: Companies Act group accounts

653.   For companies preparing Companies Act group accounts, this section gives the Secretary of State power to make provision by regulations as to the form and content of the consolidated balance sheet and consolidated profit and loss account and additional information to be provided by way of notes to the accounts. The regulations will replace the current requirements contained in Schedule 4A to the 1985 Act. These regulations are subject to the Parliamentary procedure in section 473.

Section 405: Companies Act group accounts: subsidiary undertakings included in the consolidation

654.   This section replaces section 229 of the 1985 Act. It requires all subsidiary undertakings to be included in the consolidated accounts subject to certain permitted exclusions.

Section 406: IAS group accounts

655.   This section re-enacts section 227B of the 1985 Act. A company may opt or may be required to prepare group accounts in accordance with international accounting standards. This section provides that where it does so, this must be stated in the notes to the accounts.

Section 407: Consistency of financial reporting within group

656.   This section re-enacts section 227C of the 1985 Act. If the parent company prepares both consolidated and individual accounts under IAS, it is not required to ensure that all its subsidiary undertakings also use IAS. However, it must otherwise ensure that its individual accounts and those of all its subsidiary undertakings use the same financial reporting framework, unless there are good reasons for not doing so.

Section 408: Individual profit and loss account where group accounts prepared

657.   This section replaces section 230 of the 1985 Act. A parent company that prepares group accounts and that meets the criteria in subsection (1)(a) and (b) may, subject to the profit and loss account being approved by the directors, dispense with the inclusion of a profit and loss account in the company's accounts, for example when delivered to the registrar. The profit and loss account may also omit the information on employee numbers and costs required by section 411. The exemption currently provided for in section 230(2) of the 1985 Act for certain information required by provisions of Schedule 4 to the 1985 Act, will be provided for in regulations under section 396.

Information to be given in notes to the accounts

Section 409: Information about related undertakings

658.   This section replaces section 231(1) to (4) of the 1985 Act. The requirement to disclose information about related undertakings in the notes to a company's annual accounts applies whether or not the company has to produce group accounts but there are different disclosure requirements in each case. This section gives the Secretary of State a new power to make regulations requiring information about related undertakings to be given in notes to a company's annual accounts. These regulations are subject to the Parliamentary procedure in section 473. The regulations will replace the provisions of Schedule 5 to the 1985 Act.

659.   Subsection (3) enables regulations under the section to make provision corresponding to section 231(3) of the 1985 Act authorising the omission from the notes to the accounts of information in respect of undertakings established outside the UK, or carrying on business outside the UK where the directors consider that disclosure would be seriously prejudicial to the business of that undertaking, or to the business of the company or any of its subsidiary undertakings. The Secretary of State must agree to the omission. This exemption is sought by a very small number of companies each year.

Section 410: Information about related undertakings: alternative compliance

660.   This section replaces section 231(5) to (7) of the 1985 Act. Where there are numerous related undertakings and the directors believe that full disclosure would result in information of excessive length in the notes to the accounts, they may give more limited information. As a minimum this must include information in subsection (2)(a) and (b). Subsection (3) provides that the full information on the related undertakings must be submitted with the next annual return.

Section 411: Information about employee numbers and costs

661.   This section replaces section 231A of the 1985 Act concerning particulars of staff. Section 231A was inserted by the 1985 Act (International Accounting Standards and Other Accounting Amendments) Regulations 2004 (SI. 2004/2947) re-enacting provisions previously in the Schedules to Part 7 of the 1985 Act so that they continued to apply both to companies preparing Companies Act accounts and to those preparing IAS accounts.

Section 412: Information about directors' benefits: remuneration

662.   This section, together with section 413, replaces section 232 of the 1985 Act. Section 232 of the 1985 Act, with Schedules 6 and 7A, provides for disclosure of specified information on directors' remuneration in notes to a company's annual accounts. Section 412 of the 2006 Act instead gives the Secretary of State a new power to make provision by regulations requiring information about directors' remuneration to be given in notes to a company's annual accounts. Regulations under this section are subject to the Parliamentary procedure in section 473.

Section 413: Information about directors' benefits: advances, credit and guarantees

663. This section replaces section 232 of the 1985 Act as regards the disclosure of advances, credit and guarantees. Under section 232 of the 1985 Act, information on the following areas must be given in notes to a company's annual accounts:

* details of loans, quasi-loans, credit transactions and related guarantees and security between a company and its directors or persons connected with its directors;
* details of any other transactions or arrangements in which a director, indirectly or directly, has a material interest.

This can be seen as an extension of the internal disclosure of directors' interests required by section 317 of the 1985 Act.

664. Section 413 sets out the new disclosure requirements in respect of (a) advances and credits granted by the company to its directors, and (b) guarantees of any kind entered into by the company on behalf of its directors. The wording of section 413 is much closer to that of articles 43(1)(13) and 34(13) of the Fourth (78/660/EEC) and Seventh (83/349/EEC) Company Law Directives.

665. The powers under section 396(3)(b) (Companies Act individual accounts) and section 404(3)(b) (Companies Act group accounts) will be used to require the disclosure of information about certain related party transactions in the notes to Companies Act accounts. Companies will no longer be required to disclose transactions made between the company and officers other than directors.

666. Under section 413(8) banks and the holding companies of credit institutions need only state (a) the amount of an advance or credit, and (b) in relation to a guarantee, the amount of the maximum liability that may be incurred by the company (or its subsidiary). In the light of the simplified disclosure regime for advances, credit and guarantees, sections 343 and 344 of the 1985 Act, which make special provision for financial institutions, are repealed.

Section 414: Approval and signing of accounts

667. This section replaces section 233 of the 1985 Act. It provides that a company's annual accounts (its individual accounts and any group accounts) must be approved by the board of directors and the balance sheet must be signed. Subsection (3), which requires the balance sheet of accounts prepared in accordance with the small companies regime to carry a statement to that effect, re-enacts section 246(8) of the 1985 Act. Subsections (4) and (5) re-enact the criminal offence in section 233 of the 1985 Act for approval of accounts that do not comply with the requirements of the Companies Act or, where applicable, of Article 4 of the IAS Regulation. Section 233 (4) of the 1985 Act, which required that a director of the company should sign the copy of the balance sheet delivered to the registrar, has not been reproduced. This requirement would have hampered developments in the electronic delivery of accounts.

Chapter 5: Directors' Report

Sections 415 to 419: Directors' report

668. These sections concern the duty to prepare a directors' report, its content, approval and signature. They replace sections 234, 234ZZA, 234ZZB, 234ZA, 234A, 246(4)(a) and 246A(2A) and 246(8) of the 1985 Act.

669. Section 416(4) gives the Secretary of State power to make provisions by regulations as to other matters that must be disclosed in the directors' report. These regulations replace the provision formerly made by Schedule 7 to the 1985 Act. The regulations are subject to the Parliamentary procedure in section 473.

670. Section 417 provides for what must be contained in the business review element of the directors' report. All companies, other than small companies, will need to produce a business review, as required by the EU Accounts Modernisation Directive (2003/51/EEC). Subsection (2) sets out the purpose of the review, that is, to inform members of the company and help them assess how the directors have performed their duty under section 172 (duty to promote the success of the company). Subsections (3), (4), (6) and (8) specify the content of the review. Subsection (5) specifies information that quoted companies in particular must include in their review where necessary for an understanding of the company's business. Where directors of quoted companies have nothing to report on environmental, employee, social and community matters or essential contractual or other arrangements, their review must say so. Subsection (7) exempts medium-sized companies from reporting non-financial key performance indicators – an exemption allowed by the EU directive. Subsection (9) provides that where the directors' report is a group report, all references in section 417 to the company are to be read as references to the company and its consolidated subsidiary undertakings. Subsection (10) enables directors to omit from the business review

Part 3   CA 2006 Supporting Materials

information about impending developments or matters in the course of negotiation where in their opinion disclosure would be seriously prejudicial to the interests of the company. Subsection (11) enables directors to omit from the business review information about a third party otherwise required by subsection (5)(c) (essential contractual or other arrangements) where in the directors' opinion it would be seriously prejudicial to that third party and contrary to the public interest.

Chapter 6: Quoted Companies: Directors' Remuneration Report

Sections 420 to 422: Quoted companies: directors' remuneration report

671. These sections replace sections 234B and 234C of the 1985 Act. Those sections, which were inserted into the Act by the Directors' Remuneration Report Regulations 2002 (SI 2002/1986), require quoted companies to:

* publish a report on directors' remuneration as part of the company's annual reporting cycle; and
* disclose within the report details of individual directors' remuneration packages, the company's remuneration policy, and the role of the board and remuneration committee in this area.

672. Section 421 gives the Secretary of State power to make provision by regulations as to the information that must be contained in a directors' remuneration report and how it should be set out. These matters are currently set out in Schedule 7A to the 1985 Act, and regulations made under section 421 will replace the provisions in Schedule 7A. The regulations will also specify the extent to which the directors' remuneration report should be subject to audit. Regulations under section 421 are subject to the Parliamentary procedure in section 473.

Chapter 7: Publication Of Accounts And Reports

Section 423: Duty to circulate copies of annual accounts and reports

673. This section replaces section 238 of the 1985 Act. Subsection (1) provides that a company must send a copy of its annual accounts and reports (as defined in section 471 and including any relevant auditor's report) to specified persons. Subsection (2) restricts the general obligation of companies to send copies of accounts and reports. The obligation will in future be to send the accounts and reports only to persons for whom the company has a current address. This is to avoid companies having to send copies of the annual accounts and reports to addresses from which correspondence has previously been returned marked not known at this address (or its electronic equivalent). General provisions about how to supply copies to joint holders are in Part 6 of Schedule 5 (Communications by a company).

Section 424: Time allowed for sending out copies of accounts and reports

674. This section makes changes to the time for distributing accounts and reports for both private and public companies. Private companies (unless they opted out of the requirement) were previously required to lay their accounts at a general meeting and to send their accounts and reports to members 21 days before that meeting. They are no longer required to hold any general meeting and the requirement now is to send out their accounts and reports no later than the earlier of the date of actual delivery to the registrar or the deadline for delivery (see section 442 for the time limits for filing). Public companies must still send the annual accounts and reports out at least 21 days before the general meeting at which the accounts and reports are to be laid (defined as the "relevant accounts meeting").

Section 425: Default in sending out copies of accounts and reports: offences

675. There is no change to these offences (in section 238(5) of the 1985 Act).

Sections 426 to 429: Option to provide summary financial statement

676. These sections restate section 251 of the 1985 Act. All companies have the option under section 426 to provide summary financial statements instead of copies of the full accounts and reports. This section reproduces the existing power for the Secretary of State to make provision by regulations:

* as to the circumstances in which a company may send out summary financial statements; and
* as to the manner in which it is to be ascertained whether a person wishes to receive a copy of the (full) accounts and reports.

It also makes new provision for persons nominated to enjoy information rights under section 146 (indirect investors) to be able to be provided with summary financial statements rather than the full accounts and reports.

677. Section 427 sets out the form and content requirements for summary financial statements prepared by unquoted companies, whilst section 428 sets out the form and content requirements for summary financial statements prepared by quoted companies. In both cases, the Secretary of State may make regulations as to the form and content of summary financial statements. There is also a new power for regulations to provide that any specified material be sent separately at the same time as the summary financial statement instead of being included in it. This is to cover the requirements of the Takeovers Directive as to necessary explanatory material (see section 992). As in the 1985 Act, these powers are subject to the negative resolution procedure. Section 429 restates the existing offences in section 251(6) of the 1985 Act.

Section 430: Quoted companies: requirements as to website publication

678. This section introduces a new requirement on quoted companies (as defined in section 385) to put the full annual accounts and reports on a website. A quoted company will still have to send the full accounts and reports to its members under section 423.

679. The annual accounts and reports must be made available as soon as is reasonably practicable on a website that is maintained by or on behalf of the company, and that identifies the company in question. Access to the website must be available to all members of the public and not just to members, and there must be continuous access to the website without charge. Access to the information on the website and the ability to obtain a hard copy of the information from the website, may be restricted by the company where necessary to comply with any statutory or regulatory requirement (eg of an overseas regulator).

680. The annual accounts and reports for a financial year must remain available until the accounts and reports for the next financial year are published on the website. Right of member or debenture holder to demand copies of accounts and reports

Sections 431 and 432: Right of member or debenture holder to demand copies of accounts and reports

681. These sections re-enact section 239 of the 1985 Act and entitle a member or debenture holder to demand a copy of the company's last annual accounts and reports without charge. Section 431 lists the documents to which members or debenture holders of unquoted companies are entitled, while section 432 lists those to which members or debenture holders of quoted companies are entitled. The company must comply with a demand within seven days of receipt of the request by the company.

Sections 433 to 436: Requirements in connection with publication of accounts and reports

682. Section 433 brings together provisions scattered throughout Part 7 of the 1985 Act (in sections 233(3) and (6)(a), 234A(2) and (4)(a) and 234C(2) and (4)(a)) concerning statements of the name of the signatory in published accounts and reports. In the case of unquoted companies, every copy of the balance sheet and directors' report that is published by or on behalf of the company must state the name of the director who signed it on behalf of the board. For quoted companies this applies to copies of the balance sheet, directors' remuneration report and directors' report.

683. Sections 434 and 435 re-enact section 240 of the 1985 Act concerning requirements in connection with the publication of statutory or non-statutory accounts.

684. "Publication" is defined in section 436.

Chapter 8: Public Companies: Laying Of Accounts And Reports Before General Meeting

Section 437: Public companies: laying of accounts and reports before general meeting
Section 438: Public companies: offence of failure to lay accounts and reports

685. These sections re-enact section 241 of the 1985 Act on the laying of accounts and reports before the company in general meeting, but restrict its application to public companies. Under the Act, private companies are under no statutory obligation to hold an AGM or to lay accounts and reports in general meetings. There is therefore no statutory link for them between the accounts and AGMs (although such a link might be provided for in the company's articles). Any AGM that a private company may hold pursuant to its articles will not be a statutory meeting. Public companies will still be required to hold AGMs and they must now hold them within 6 months of the end of the accounting reference period.

Chapter 9: Quoted Companies: Members' Approval Of Directors' Remuneration Report

Section 439: Quoted companies: members' approval of directors' remuneration report
Section 440: Quoted companies: offences in connection with procedure for approval

686. These sections restate the requirement under section 241A of the 1985 Act that a quoted company circulate a resolution approving the directors' remuneration report for the preceding financial year to its shareholders prior to its annual general meeting. The vote is advisory: as such, it does not require directors to amend contractual entitlements, nor to amend their remuneration policy, but the result of the vote will send a very strong signal to directors about the level of support among shareholders for the board's remuneration policy. In practice, directors will wish to take notice of the views of the company's members, and to respond appropriately. All "existing directors" (that is, every person who, immediately before the general meeting, is a director of the company) have a responsibility to ensure that the resolution is put to the vote of the meeting. As such, the requirement does not apply to past directors (even if they served on the board or as members of the remuneration committee in the current financial year), but it does apply to "existing directors" who were, for whatever reason, not present at the general meeting.

Chapter 10: Filing Of Accounts And Reports

Sections 441 to 443: Duty to file accounts and reports

687. These sections cover the general duty to file accounts and reports with the registrar of companies and the period allowed for filing accounts.

688. Section 442 reduces the period for filing accounts from ten months to nine months for private companies and from seven months to six months for public companies. These periods are calculated from the end of the relevant accounting reference period. The timetable for delivering accounts to the registrar was last amended in 1976. The periods have been reduced to reflect improvements in technology and the increased rate at which information becomes out of date. Filing timescales in other countries are generally less generous than in the UK. Under subsection (6), whether a company is private or public for the purpose of its filing obligations is determined by its status immediately before the end of the relevant accounting reference period.

689. Section 443 is a new provision defining how to calculate the periods allowed for filing accounts and reports. In general this is the same date the relevant number of months later. So, for example, if the end of the accounting reference period is 5th June, 6 months from then is 5th December. However, as months are of unequal length, there can be confusion as to whether 6 months from say 30th June is 30th December (exactly 6 months later) or 31st December (the end of the sixth month). Under the rule laid down in this section, 6 months from 30th June will be 31st December. This reverses the "corresponding date rule" laid down by the House of Lords in *Dodds v Walker* [1981] 1 WLR 1027.

Sections 444 to 448: Filing obligations of different descriptions of company

690. These sections concern the filing obligations of different sizes of company. They restructure the provisions in sections 242, 246, 246A and 254 of the 1985 Act to make clearer what companies have to do.

691. Section 444 concerns the filing obligations of companies subject to the small companies regime. Such companies may file abbreviated accounts and this section gives the Secretary of State the power to make regulations concerning abbreviated accounts for such companies. Under subsection (5), small companies filing a full balance sheet with the registrar (whether prepared in accordance with international accounting standards or under the Act), but omitting a copy of the profit and loss account and/or the directors' report, must include a statement on the balance sheet that they are delivered in accordance with the small companies regime. Subsection (7) requires the filed copy of the audit report to state the name of the auditor and, if there is one, of the senior statutory auditor, unless they are taking advantage of the exemption in section 506, in which case they must state that they are doing so.

692. Section 445 restates provisions in section 246A of the 1985 Act permitting medium-sized companies (as defined in section 465) to file abbreviated accounts and gives the Secretary of State the power to make regulations concerning abbreviated accounts for such companies.

693. Section 446 concerns the filing obligations of unquoted companies.

694. Section 447 concerns the filing obligations of quoted companies. This is a restatement of section 242 of the 1985 Act. Subsection (3) provides for the copies of the filed documents including the balance sheet to state the name of the person who signed the documents.

695. Section 448 replaces section 254 of the 1985 Act. It exempts unlimited companies from the obligation to file accounts. There are limitations on the exemption set out in subsections (2) and (3).

Sections 449 and 450: Requirements where abbreviated accounts delivered

696. Section 449 replaces the provision in section 247B of the 1985 Act. It requires a special auditor's report in place of the auditor's report required by section 495 where a company delivers abbreviated accounts to the registrar of companies. There is no requirement for the special auditor's report where the company is entitled to exemption from audit and has taken advantage of that exemption.

697. Section 450 replaces sections 246(7) and (8) and 246A(4) of the 1985 Act concerning the approval and signing of abbreviated accounts.

Sections 451 to 453: Failure to file accounts and reports

698. Sections 451 and 452 re-enact sanctions in section 242(2) to (5) of the 1985 Act for failing to file accounts and reports within the required periods.

699.   Section 453, which provides a civil penalty for failure to file accounts, restates section 242A of the 1985 Act with one change. Rather than setting out the table of penalties in the legislation, subsection (2) provides for the Secretary of State to make regulations specifying both the relevant periods and the amounts of the penalties. Regulations that have the effect of increasing the penalty will be subject to the affirmative resolution procedure. Otherwise, they will be subject to the negative resolution procedure.

Chapter 11: Revision Of Defective Accounts And Reports

Section 454: Voluntary revision of accounts etc

700.   This section restates section 245 of the 1985 Act providing for the voluntary revision of defective accounts and reports and summary financial statements. It replicates the existing power for the Secretary of State to make provision in regulations as to the application of the provisions of this Act to revised annual accounts and reports and summary financial statements. Regulations under this section are subject to the negative resolution procedure, which is consistent with the existing powers.

Section 455: Secretary of State's notice in respect of accounts or reports

701.   This section re-enacts section 245A of the 1985 Act. It concerns the Secretary of State's giving notice to the directors of a company if there is or may be a question as to whether the annual accounts or directors' report comply with the requirements of the Act or the IAS Regulation (Regulation (EC) 1606/2002 on the application of international accounting standards).

Sections 456 to 458: Application to court

702.   Sections 456 and 457 concern applications to the court in respect of defective accounts or reports. They re-enact sections 245B and 245C of the 1985 Act. Section 457 gives the Secretary of State the power to authorise a person for the purposes of section 456 to apply to the courts to require the directors of companies to prepare revised accounts and reports where the original accounts or reports were defective. Authorisation is subject to the negative resolution procedure, which corresponds to the existing provision. The Financial Reporting Review Panel (FRRP) is the only authorised person under this provision to date (the Companies (Defective Accounts) (Authorised Person) Order 2005: SI 2005/699).

703.   Section 458 re-enacts sections 245D and 245E of the 1985 Act. It provides for the disclosure of information by the Commissioners for Her Majesty's Revenue and Customs to a person authorised under section 457 (currently the FRRP) to apply to the court in respect of defective accounts and reports. The provision contains important limitations, including criminal offences for use or disclosure of the information other than for permitted purposes. Section 458(5)(b)(ii) increases the term of imprisonment from three months to six months for a person convicted on summary conviction in Scotland or Northern Ireland for an offence of unlawful disclosure. Subsection (2) provides that personal data may not be disclosed in contravention of the Data Protection Act 1998.

Section 459: Power of authorised person to require documents, information and explanations

704.   This section re-enacts section 245F of the 1985 Act. Subsections (1) to (3) provide the FRRP (as the person authorised under section 457) with a statutory power to require a company and its officers, employees and auditors to provide documents and information. Where a person refuses to provide information or documents to the FRRP, the FRRP may apply to the court for an order. The court may make an order requiring disclosure. Failure to comply with such an order would be contempt of court.

Section 460: Restrictions on disclosure of information obtained under compulsory powers

705.   This section re-enacts section 245G of the 1985 Act. It ensures that information obtained by the FRRP under the powers in section 459 is subject to restrictions on onward disclosure. Information relating to the private affairs of an individual or to any particular business may not be disclosed by the FRRP without the consent of the individual or business in question, except for the purposes of carrying out the FRRP's functions, or unless it is disclosed to specified persons or for specified purposes set out in section 461.

Section 461: Permitted disclosure of information obtained under compulsory powers

706.   This section restates section 245G(3) of, and Schedule 7B to, the 1985 Act with modifications. It sets out the disclosures of information obtained by the authorised person under section 459 that are permitted. Subsection (3) lists the specified persons to whom disclosures are permitted and subsection (4) lists the specified purposes for which disclosure may be made. Subsections (5) and (6) set out the circumstances in which a disclosure to an overseas regulatory authority is permitted. Subsection (7) provides that nothing in the section authorises a disclosure in contravention of the Data Protection Act 1998.

Section 462: Power to amend categories of permitted disclosure

707.   This section re-enacts section 245G(4) to (6) of the 1985 Act. It gives the Secretary of State power to amend the disclosure provisions relating to information obtained by the authorised person. As under the current law, an order under the section is subject to the negative resolution procedure.

Chapter 12: Supplementary Provisions

Section 463: Liability for false or misleading statements in reports

708.   This section is concerned with the extent of directors' liability in relation to the statutory narrative reporting requirements under this Part of the Act (accounts and reports). Subsection (1) specifies that the liability provision applies to statements made in the directors' report (which includes the business review under section 417), the directors' remuneration report (under section 420) or summary financial statements derived from them. Subsection (2) limits the directors' liability to the company only in respect of loss suffered by it as a result of any untrue or misleading statement in a report, or the omission from a report of anything required to be included. Subsection (3) specifies that a director will only be liable in certain circumstances – that is, if an untrue or misleading statement is made deliberately or recklessly, or an omission amounts to dishonest concealment of a material fact. Subsection (4) ensures that third parties, such as auditors, will remain liable only to the company for negligence in preparing their own report. Subsection (6) ensures that these liability provisions do not affect any liability for a civil penalty or for a criminal offence.

Section 464: Accounting standards

709.   This section re-enacts section 256 of the 1985 Act.

Sections 465 to 467: Companies qualifying as medium-sized

710.   Medium-sized companies benefit from certain limited accounting and reporting exemptions. For example, section 417(7) exempts medium-sized companies from disclosing certain non-financial information in their directors' reports.

711.   Sections 465 to 467 set out which companies or parent companies qualify as medium-sized. The conditions for qualification as a medium sized company have been separated from those relating to small companies to make them easier to follow but are otherwise unchanged from the current regime (sections 247, 247A and 249 of the 1985 Act), save that, as in the case of the definition of small companies, the definition of balance sheet total in section 465(5) has been generalised.

Section 468: General power to make further provision about accounts and reports

712.   This section gives the Secretary of State a general power to amend Part 15 by regulations in the areas specified in subsection (1)(a) to (d). This power, together with a number of specific powers in Part 15 to enable the form and contents of accounts and reports to be prescribed by regulations, replaces the wider general power in section 257 of the 1985 Act. Subsection (3) provides that the general power may not be used to amend the provisions of section 393 (accounts to give true and fair view) or Chapter 11 (revision of defective accounts and reports) other than consequentially. Subsections (4) and (5) enable regulations under the section to create criminal offences or provide for civil penalties in circumstances corresponding to those in Part 15. The regulations are subject to the Parliamentary procedure in section 473.

Section 469: Preparation and filing of accounts in euros

713.   This section re-enacts section 242B of the 1985 Act, replacing references to ECUs with references to euros. It enables companies to show the amounts in their annual accounts additionally in euros, and to deliver to the registrar an additional copy of their accounts translated into euros.

Section 470: Power to apply provisions to banking partnerships

714.   This section re-enacts section 255D of the 1985 Act. It gives the Secretary of State the power to apply the accounting and reporting provisions of this Act that apply to banking companies to banking partnerships. As under the current law, the regulations are subject to the affirmative resolution procedure.

Section 471: Meaning of "annual accounts" and related expressions

715.   This section provides definitions of the terms "annual accounts" and "annual accounts and reports" for the purpose of this Part, the meaning being different for unquoted and quoted companies.

Section 472: Notes to the accounts

716.   This section re-enacts section 261 of the 1985 Act. It concerns the notes to a company's accounts.

Section 473: Parliamentary procedure for certain regulations under this Part

717.   This section specifies the Parliamentary procedure that must be followed in connection with regulations made under the various provisions of this Part which replace the requirements as to the form and content of accounts and reports currently contained in Schedules to Part 7 of the 1985 Act, and in relation to the general regulation-making power in section 468. This section follows section 257 of the 1985 Act in requiring affirmative resolution procedure for regulations which add to the documents required to be prepared by companies, restrict the exemptions available to particular classes or types of company, add to the information to be included in any particular document or otherwise make the requirements more onerous. Other regulations are subject to negative resolution procedure.

Section 474: Minor definitions

718.   This section contains other definitions for the purposes of this Part.

PART 16: AUDIT

[3.17]
719.   This Part brings together various provisions on the audit of companies from the 1985 Act. It also introduces a number of significant changes to the law on auditing. Much of the law in this area reflects EU Company Law Directives, including parts of the Fourth (78/660/EEC), Seventh (83/349/EEC) and Eighth (84/253/EEC) Company Law Directives, and of the new Audit Directive (2006/43/EC), which will replace the Eighth.

Chapter 1: Requirement For Audited Accounts

720.   This Chapter restates the existing requirement for company accounts to be audited, currently in section 235 of the 1985 Act, and the existing exemptions (except for the special provisions about charities).

721.   The only changes from the existing law in this Chapter are the removal of special rules for the audit of the accounts of small charitable companies (see note on section 1175), and new provisions disapplying the requirement for audit in relation to certain companies in the public sector audited by public sector auditors.

Section 475: Requirement for audited accounts

722.   This section restates the basic requirement for accounts to be audited, unless they are exempt. The obligation is now expressed as a duty on the company to have its accounts audited, whereas section 235 of the 1985 Act expressed it as a duty on the auditor to audit the accounts.

723.   Directors must state in the balance sheet if they are taking advantage of an exemption. Unless the company is subject to a public sector audit, the statement must say that the members have not required an audit, and that the directors take responsibility for producing compliant accounts.

Section 476: Right of members to require audit

724.   This section restates the right of members to require an audit, even if the company qualifies for one of the audit exemptions.

Sections 477 to 479: Exemption from audit: small companies

725.   These sections restate the exemption from audit for small companies. Section 477 provides that a company must not only meet the general small company criteria in section 382, but its turnover and balance sheet totals must also fall below £5.6 million and £2.8 million respectively.

726.   Section 478 excludes from the exemption various categories of company including public companies and some financial services companies. Section 479 sets out the conditions for qualification for the small company exemption of a company which is in a group.

Sections 480 and 481: Exemption from audit: dormant companies

727.   These two sections restate the exemption from audit available to dormant companies. "Dormant" is defined in section 1169. Certain financial services companies are excluded from using the exemption even if they are dormant.

Sections 482 and 483: Companies subject to public sector audit

728.   These two sections, the only wholly new provisions in this Chapter, are intended to ensure that certain non-commercial, public sector bodies constituted as companies that are audited by a public sector auditor are not required to be audited under the Act.

729.   Section 482 exempts from Companies Act audit any non-departmental public body that is a company and is non-profit-making, if it is subject to public sector audit.

730.   A UK body may be subject to public sector audit by virtue of an order under the Government Resources and Accounts Act 2000 The body in question will then be audited by the National Audit

Part 3   CA 2006 Supporting Materials

Office on behalf of the UK Comptroller and Auditor General. Under the Audit and Accountability (Northern Ireland) Order 2003, an order can make a body subject to audit by the Comptroller and Auditor General for Northern Ireland. Alternatively, a body may be subject to audit by the Auditor General for Wales under section 96 of the Government of Wales Act 1998, or an order under section 144 of that Act.

731.   Some Scottish bodies are subject to public sector audit by the Auditor General for Scotland (AGS) under the Public Finance and Accountability (Scotland) Act 2000.

732.   The companies exempted by this section are not subject to the Fourth Company Law Directive: the Directive is based on Article 44(2)(g) of the EC Treaty (formerly 54(3)(g) of the EEC Treaty), and Article 48 of the Treaty excludes from the scope of Article 44 undertakings that are non-profit-making. That is why subsection (3) gives "non-profit-making" the same meaning as in the Treaty.

733.   Subsection (2) provides that a group company can benefit from this exemption only if every company in the group is non-profit-making. The effect of subsection (4) is that the exemption is not available unless the balance sheet contains a statement that the company is entitled to it.

734.   Section 483 confers a new power on Scottish Ministers to provide that a company should have its accounts audited by the Auditor General for Scotland (AGS). This is available for companies depending on their functions or their funding. The Scottish Ministers can designate a company under this power if its functions are public functions that are all covered by the Scottish Parliament's responsibilities, or if the company receives all or most of its funding from a public body already audited by the AGS. In the latter case, the funding body may be audited by the AGS because it is covered by the Public Finance and Accountability (Scotland) Act 2000, or because it is itself a company that Scottish Ministers have made auditable by the AGS by a previous order under this section.

735.   If an order is made under this section providing that a company should have a public sector audit by the AGS, and if that company is non-profit-making, then it will benefit from the exemption from audit in the preceding section.

Section 484: General power of amendment by regulations

736.   This section provides a power for the Secretary of State to amend the provisions of this Chapter. Taken together with section 468, it broadly restates the power in section 257 of the 1985 Act. Subsection (2) enables the regulations to make consequential changes to other legislation. The power is subject to affirmative resolution if it is extending the requirement for audit, or otherwise making requirements more onerous; and to negative resolution otherwise.

Chapter 2: Appointment Of Auditors

737.   This Chapter broadly restates the existing law in sections 384 to 388A of the 1985 Act on the way in which shareholders appoint a company's auditors, with some minor changes (as explained below). The provisions are reorganised to deal with private and public companies separately. The Chapter also restates the rules in sections 390A and 390B of the 1985 Act on auditors' remuneration and the disclosure required of services provided by auditors and introduces a new power for the Secretary of State to require disclosure of the terms of audit appointments.

Private companies

738.   Sections 485 to 488 restate the law on appointment of auditors of private companies, providing that auditors are generally to be appointed by shareholders by ordinary resolution. For any financial year other than the first, this will generally be done within 28 days of the circulation to a company's shareholders of the accounts for the previous year.

739.   There are two changes: firstly, an auditor's term of office will typically run from the end of the 28 day period following circulation of the accounts until the end of the corresponding period the following year. This will apply even if the auditor is appointed at a meeting where the company's accounts are laid. The second change is that an auditor is now deemed to be re-appointed unless the company decides otherwise.

Section 485: Appointment of auditors of private company: general

740.   This section provides for a private company's obligation to appoint an auditor, unless it is taking advantage of an exemption from audit. The appointment is to be made by the shareholders by ordinary resolution, except that the directors can appoint the company's first auditor (or the first after a period of audit exemption), and can fill a casual vacancy.

Section 486: Appointment of auditors of private company: default power of Secretary of State

741.   This section requires a company to inform the Secretary of State if it has failed to appoint an auditor within 28 days of circulation of its accounts. The Secretary of State has power to appoint an auditor in those circumstances.

Section 487: Term of office of auditors of private company

742.   This section provides that the end of the term of office of the auditor of a private company is to be the end of the next period for appointing auditors. At the end of his term an auditor will automatically be deemed to be re-appointed except in five cases:
- if he was appointed by the directors;
- if the company's articles require actual re-appointment;
- if enough members have given notice to the company under section 488;
- if there has been a resolution that the auditor should not be reappointed; or
- if the directors decide that they do not need auditors for the following year.

743.   When there is a change of auditor the term of office of the incoming auditor does not begin before the end of the previous auditor's term. This means that a new auditor's term will typically begin immediately after the end of the 28-day period for appointing auditors.

Section 488: Prevention by members of deemed re-appointment of auditor

744.   This section enables members with at least 5% of the voting rights in a private company to prevent an auditor being automatically re-appointed by giving notice to the company. The company's articles can enable members to do this with less than 5% of the voting rights, but cannot increase the required percentage.

745.   Subsection (3) provides that the deadline for a notice preventing the deemed reappointment of an auditor is the end of the financial year for the accounts he is auditing.

Public companies

746.   Sections 489 to 491 restate the law on appointment of auditors of public companies, providing that auditors are generally to be appointed by shareholders by ordinary resolution in the general meeting before which the company's accounts are laid.

Section 489: Appointment of auditors of public company: general

747.   This section restates a public company's obligation to appoint auditors, unless it is taking advantage of exemption from audit. This is to be done by the shareholders by ordinary resolution, normally at the general meeting at which the accounts are laid. The directors can appoint the company's first auditors (or the first after a period of audit exemption), and can fill a casual vacancy.

Section 490: Appointment of auditors of public company: default power of Secretary of State

748.   This section restates the obligation of a company to inform the Secretary of State if it has failed to appoint an auditor at the general meeting that considers the previous year's accounts. The Secretary of State has power to appoint an auditor in those circumstances.

Section 491: Term of office of auditors of public company

749.   This section restates the rule that an auditor of a public company holds office until the end of the meeting at which the accounts are laid, unless re-appointed. Where there is a change of auditor, the term of office of the incoming auditor does not begin before the end of the previous auditor's term. This means that a new auditor's term will typically begin immediately after the end of the accounts meeting.

General provisions

750.   These sections apply to both private and public companies.

Section 492: Fixing of auditor's remuneration

751.   This section restates the rule that it is the members of a company, by ordinary resolution, who determine the auditor's remuneration, or decide the method by which it should be determined. If the auditor was appointed by someone other than the members, then it will be the directors or the Secretary of State as appropriate who will determine his remuneration.

Section 493: Disclosure of terms of audit appointment

752.   This section creates a new power for the Secretary of State to require companies to disclose information about the terms on which they engage their auditors. Subsection (2) provides some examples of the detailed requirements that the Secretary of State could specify in regulations. Subsection (3) provides that regulations can require disclosure of changes in terms as well as the terms at the time of appointment. Subsection (4) specifies that the regulations are to be made by affirmative resolution procedure.

Section 494: Disclosure of services provided by auditor or associates and related remuneration

753.   This section restates the existing power of the Secretary of State, in section 390B of the 1985 Act, to require disclosure of details of all the services supplied to a company by its auditor, and the remuneration involved. Subsections (2) to (4) give the detailed requirements that the Secretary of State can specify in regulations: subsection (2) relates to the level of disaggregation of different

Part 3   CA 2006 Supporting Materials

services and remunerations, and between the auditor and his associates; subsection (3) makes provision for some of the definitional issues that can be covered in regulations; and subsection (4) provides for where the information should be disclosed.

754.   Under subsection (4), the regulations might require disclosure in a document compiled by the company rather than the auditor. Subsection (5) provides that, if so, the regulations can require the auditor to supply the directors with the information to be disclosed eg about the auditor's associates. Subsection (6) specifies that the regulations are to be made by negative resolution procedure.

Chapter 3: Functions Of Auditors

Sections 495 to 497: Auditor's report

755.   These sections restate, with modifications, the provisions of section 235 of the 1985 Act as to what the auditor should include in his report on the accounts.

756.   Section 495 imposes the basic duty to produce an audit report and requires that it should set out the way the auditor has approached the audit. Subsection (3) requires the auditor in his report to state his opinion on three matters: (i) whether the accounts provide a true and fair view, (ii) whether they comply with the appropriate reporting framework, and (iii) whether the accounts comply with the requirements in Part 15 of the Act (and, where applicable, with article 4 of the IAS Regulation (Regulation (EC) 1606/2002 on the application of international accounting standards)). Subsection (4) requires the audit report to be either qualified or unqualified, though it is open to the auditor to draw attention to aspects of his audit without qualifying the report.

757.   Sections 496 and 497 restate the law on what the auditor should include in relation to the directors' report and the directors' remuneration report.

Sections 498 to 502: Duties and rights of auditors

758.   These sections bring together and restate the existing law on the auditor's duties (currently in section 237 of the 1985 Act) in investigating, forming an opinion, and making his report; and on the auditor's rights (sections 389A to 390 of that Act) to be provided with appropriate information.

759.   Section 498 lists areas where an auditor must investigate and report on any problems: the company's accounting records, and whether there is consistency between these and (i) the accounts and (ii) – where there is one – the appropriate part of the directors' remuneration report. The auditor is also to report if he has not been able to get all the information he needs. If possible, he is to make good any gaps in the information relating to payments to directors. And he is to report if he believes that the company is taking advantage of the small companies accounts regime without being entitled to do so.

760.   Section 499 restates the auditor's rights to obtain information and explanations from the company and its UK subsidiaries, and from appropriate associated individuals. Section 500 sets out the corresponding right to require the company to obtain information or explanations from any subsidiaries that are not incorporated in the UK.

761.   Section 501 sets out offences for those who supply inaccurate information to auditors or fail to respond to auditors' requests for information without delay.

762.   Section 502 requires a private company to send to its auditor all the information about any written resolutions that it sends to its shareholders. It also gives the auditor of any company – public or private – the right to attend any general meetings it may have, and to be allowed to speak on anything relevant to the audit. The auditor must also receive all communications relating to general meetings.

Section 503: Signature of auditor's report

763.   This section specifies who must sign the audit report submitted to a company by its auditor. The report must state the name of the audit firm, or if an individual has been appointed as auditor, his name. This is as currently required by section 236 of the 1985 Act.

764.   For cases where the auditor is a firm, the section makes a change from the 1985 Act by requiring the senior statutory auditor, as defined in section 504, to sign the report in his own name on behalf of the firm. This implements a requirement of the Audit Directive (2006/43/EC). If the auditor is an individual, he must sign as under the 1985 Act.

Section 504: Senior statutory auditor

765.   This section defines a new term – "the senior statutory auditor" – for the individual who will be asked to sign his name to an audit report carried out by a firm. The firm will identify this individual according to standards to be issued by the European Commission, or if there are no standards, to guidance issued either by the Secretary of State or by a body appointed by him by order subject to negative resolution. Subsection (2) specifies that to be identified as a senior statutory auditor of a company, an individual must be eligible himself to be appointed as auditor of the company. Subsection (3) ensures that for an individual to be nominated as senior statutory auditor will not affect his exposure to liability in any way.

Section 505: Names to be stated in published copies of auditor's report

766.   This section requires a company to ensure that the copies of its auditor's report it sends out include the name of the auditor and of the senior statutory auditor if there is one, or to say that it is taking advantage of the exemption in the following section. Subsection (2) provides that this includes copies circulated to shareholders, as well as any others that would be expected to be seen by members of the public. It does not, however, cover copies sent to the registrar: these are dealt with by sections 444(7), 445(6), 446(4) and 447(4). Subsections (3) and (4) restate the offence, currently in section 236 of the 1985 Act, of not including the auditor's name – and now also the senior statutory auditor's name – as required.

Section 506: Circumstances in which names may be omitted

767.   This section provides an exemption from the requirements to include the names of the auditor in both the published and filed copies of the audit report. This is available if the company passes a resolution not to reveal the names because it considers on reasonable grounds that revealing them would lead to a serious risk of violence or intimidation. It is also a condition of using the exemption that the company must inform the Secretary of State, giving details of the name of the auditor, and of the senior statutory auditor if there is one.

Section 507: Offences in connection with auditors' report

768.   This section creates a new criminal offence in relation to inaccurate auditors' reports. The offence consists of knowingly or recklessly causing a report to include anything that is misleading, false or deceptive, or omitting a required statement of a problem with the accounts or audit.

769.   Subsection (1) sets out the offence of commission, and subsection (2) that of omission. The items whose omission can be an offence are listed in paragraphs (a) to (c) of subsection (2): statements about accounting records not being properly reflected in the accounts, about the auditor having been unable to obtain all necessary information and explanations, and about the directors wrongly claiming the company is exempt from the requirement for group accounts.

770.   Subsection (3) defines the individuals potentially caught by the offence as the auditor, if a sole practitioner, and his employees and agents; and the directors, members, employees and agents of an audit firm. But the offence only applies to such an individual if he is an accountant who would be qualified to act as auditor of the company in his own right. Subsection (4) sets out the maximum penalty as an unlimited fine.

Section 508: Guidance for regulatory and prosecuting authorities: England, Wales and Northern Ireland

771.   This section enables the Secretary of State to issue guidance about handling matters where the same behaviour by an auditor could give rise both to disciplinary proceedings by a regulatory body, and to prosecution for the new offence. Subsection (2) requires the Secretary of State to obtain the Attorney's General agreement to any guidance. Subsection (3) lists the regulatory and prosecuting authorities the guidance would be intended to help. The list comprises the accountancy supervisory bodies, recipients of grants under section 16 of the Companies (Audit, Investigations and Community Enterprise) Act 2004) (currently the Financial Reporting Council and its subsidiaries), the Director of the Serious Fraud Office and the Director of Public Prosecutions, as well as the Secretary of State himself. Under subsection (4), the Secretary of State's guidance is limited to England, Wales and Northern Ireland.

772.   It is likely that one of the most important aspects of the guidance would be to enable prosecutors to decide not to prosecute in a particular case that would be better handled through disciplinary proceedings.

Section 509: Guidance for regulatory authorities: Scotland

773.   This section enables the Lord Advocate to issue guidance about handling matters in Scotland where the same auditor's report could give rise both to disciplinary proceedings by a regulatory body, and to prosecution for the new offence. Subsection (2) requires the Lord Advocate to consult the Secretary of State before issuing guidance. Subsection (3) lists the regulatory bodies the guidance is intended to help. The list comprises the accountancy supervisory bodies, recipients of grants under section 16 of the C(AICE) Act 2004) (currently the Financial Reporting Council and its subsidiaries) and the Secretary of State.

Chapter 4: Removal, Resignation, Etc Of Auditors

774.   This Chapter restates the law on the ways in which auditors can cease to hold office. The current provisions are in section 388 and sections 391 to 394A of the 1985 Act. There are some changes to the existing law resulting from the changes elsewhere in the Act relating to written resolutions of private companies. There are also changes in the requirements when auditors leave office: increasing the range of cases in which there is a requirement for a statement explaining why they are leaving, and for copies of any statement to be sent to shareholders and to appropriate regulators.

Section 510: Resolution removing auditor from office

775.   This section restates the rule that the shareholders in a company always have the right to dismiss its auditor by ordinary resolution. As at present, to remove the auditor before the end of his term of office, even a private company will need to hold a general meeting to pass such a resolution.

776.   Subsection (2) requires special notice of the resolution (see note on section 511). Subsection (3) provides that shareholders' right provided by this section does not prevent the auditor being entitled to being compensated for termination of his appointment. Subsection (4) specifies that the resolution described here is the only way in which an auditor can be removed before the end of his term of office.

Section 511: Special notice required for resolution removing auditor from office

777.   This section restates the requirement that a resolution to dismiss an auditor needs special notice (ie 28 days before the general meeting, as provided in section 312). The company must send a copy to the auditor it is proposed to dismiss, and he has the right to make a statement of his case. The company then has to circulate his statement to the shareholders (or if time does not allow, the statement can be read out at the meeting).

778.   Subsection (6) provides protection if the auditor it is proposed to dismiss is using the provision to have a statement circulated to secure needless publicity for defamatory material. It enables the company, or anyone else who is aggrieved by the statement, to apply to the court, and the court can then determine whether the auditor is using the provision in that way, in which case the company is not obliged to circulate the statement. The court can order the auditor to pay some or all of the costs of the proceedings.

Section 512: Notice to registrar of resolution removing auditor from office

779.   This section restates the obligation on a company that has decided to dismiss its auditor to inform the registrar within 14 days.

Section 513: Rights of auditor who has been removed from office

780.   This section restates the right of a dismissed auditor to attend certain meetings, namely, any meeting at which his term of office would have expired (ie a public company's accounts meeting) and any meeting at which it is proposed to replace him.

Section 514: Failure to re-appoint auditor: special procedure required for written resolution

781.   This section sets out the procedure for changing auditor from one financial year to the next by written resolution (a procedure only available to private companies). This may be done (i) during the term of office of the outgoing auditor, or (ii) afterwards, if no replacement has been appointed. But case (ii) will arise only if there is no automatic deemed reappointment for one of the five reasons in section 487(2).

782.   Subsection (3) provides that the company must send a copy of the proposed resolution both to the outgoing auditor and to his proposed replacement; and subsection (4) provides that the former then has 14 days to make a statement setting out his views. Subsection (5) then provides that the company must send, to its shareholders, the resolution together with any statement from the outgoing auditor. Subsection (6) specifies how the general rules on written resolutions are to apply in this case.

783.   Subsection (7) provides protection if the outgoing auditor is using the provision to have a statement circulated to secure needless publicity for defamatory material. It enables the company, or anyone else who is aggrieved by the statement, to apply to the court, and the court can then determine whether the auditor is using the provision in that way, in which case the company is not obliged to circulate the auditor's representations. The court can order the auditor to pay some or all of the costs of the proceedings.

784.   Subsection (8) provides that failure to comply with the rules in this section will make the resolution ineffective.

Section 515: Failure to re-appoint auditor: special notice required for resolution at general meeting

785.   This section sets out the procedure for changing auditor between one financial year and the next at a general meeting. This may be done by resolution at the meeting, but special notice is required if no deadline for appointing auditors has passed since the outgoing auditor left, or if the deadline has passed when an auditor should have been appointed without one being appointed. So, for example, if a public company intends not to re-appoint an auditor at its accounts meeting, it would need to give special notice of the meeting to be able to appoint replacement auditors.

786.   Subsection (3) provides that immediately it receives a proposed resolution for changing auditor, the company should send a copy of it both to the outgoing auditor and to his proposed replacement; and subsection (4) provides that the former may then send the company a written statement setting out his views. Subsections (5) and (6) provide that the company must send its shareholders any statement from the outgoing auditor, and that if it is received too late for this it should be read out at the meeting.

787. Subsection (7) provides protection if the outgoing auditor is using the provision to have a statement circulated to secure needless publicity for defamatory material. It enables the company, or anyone else who is aggrieved by the statement, to apply to the court, and the court can then determine whether the auditor is using the provision in that way, in which case the company is not obliged to circulate the auditor's representations, nor need they be read out at the meeting. The court can order the auditor to pay some or all of the costs of the proceedings.

Section 516: Resignation of auditor

788. This section restates the right of an auditor to resign by written notice to the company. His resignation is effective from the date it is delivered to the company's registered office, or from a later date specified in it. To be effective it must be accompanied by the statement required by section 519.

Section 517: Notice to registrar of resignation of auditor

789. This section restates the obligation on a company whose auditor resigns to inform the registrar. Default in complying is an offence.

Section 518: Rights of resigning auditor

790. This section restates the right of an auditor who resigns to require the directors to convene a general meeting of the company so that it can consider his explanation of the circumstances that led to his decision to resign. The auditor can ask the company to send out a written explanation either in advance of that meeting if he has requested one, or before the next appropriate general meeting. The directors have 21 days to send out a notice convening a meeting once a resigning auditor has asked for it, and it must then be held within 28 days of the notice.

791. Subsection (9) provides protection if the resigning auditor is using the provision to have a statement circulated to secure needless publicity for defamatory material. It enables the company, or anyone else who is aggrieved by the statement, to apply to the court, and the court can then determine whether the auditor is using the provision in that way, in which case the company is not obliged to circulate the statement. The court can order the auditor to pay some or all of the costs of the proceedings.

Section 519: Statement by auditor to be deposited with company

792. This section requires a departing auditor to make a statement when he stops being the auditor of a company and to deposit it with the company. For quoted companies, this statement should explain the circumstances surrounding his departure. For other public companies and all private companies, it should explain the circumstances unless the auditor thinks that there is no need for them to be brought to the attention of the shareholders or creditors. In that case, the statement should state that there are no such circumstances.

793. This changes the position under section 394 of the 1985 Act, where auditors were only required to make a statement if they considered there were relevant circumstances: auditors leaving quoted companies will now always be required to make a statement of the circumstances; and auditors leaving other companies must make a statement unless they think that there are no relevant circumstances.

794. Subsection (4) sets out the deadline for depositing such a statement with the company, namely:

- if the auditor is resigning, the statement should accompany the resignation letter;
- if the auditor is deciding not to seek re-appointment, the statement should be deposited at least 14 days before the end of the time allowed for appointing the next auditor; or
- in any other case, no more than 14 days after the date on which he stops being the auditor.

Section 520: Company's duties in relation to statement

795. Unless the departing auditor's statement says that there are no circumstances to be brought to the attention of shareholders and creditors, this section obliges the company to circulate the statement to everyone to whom it needs to send the annual accounts. The company must do this within 14 days of receiving it.

796. If the company does not want to circulate the statement, it can apply to the court, and if the court decides that the departing auditor is trying to secure needless publicity for defamatory material, then the company need not circulate the statement, but instead must send an account of the court decision to those to whom it would have sent the statement. In the event of a successful application, the court can order the auditor to pay some or all of the costs. In the event of an unsuccessful application, the company must circulate the statement within 14 days of the end of the court proceedings.

Section 521: Copy of statement to be sent to registrar

797. This section provides that the departing auditor must send a copy of his statement to the registrar, unless within 21 days of depositing it he hears that the company has applied to the court. If he does not hear of an application to the court within that time, he must send the statement to the

Part 3　CA 2006 Supporting Materials

registrar within the next seven days; and if an application is made and the company lets him know that it was unsuccessful, he must send the statement to the registrar within seven days of being told.

Section 522: Duty of auditor to notify appropriate audit authority

798.   This section introduces a new obligation on departing auditors to send copies of their leaving statements to an appropriate audit authority as defined in section 525. It contains different rules depending on whether the company the auditor is leaving is classified as a "major audit" as defined in section 525.

799.   In relation to major audits, the departing auditor should always send a copy of his statement to the appropriate audit authority. He should do this as the same time as he deposits his statement with the company under section 519. In relation to other audits, the departing auditor is required to send his statement to the appropriate audit authority only if he is leaving before the end of his term of office, meaning only if he has resigned or has been dismissed; and he must do so at the time required by the authority.

800.   Subsection (3) provides that where the auditor's statement to the company said that there were no circumstances that needed to be brought to the attention of shareholders or creditors, that statement must have attached to it a statement of the auditor's reasons for leaving when sending it to the audit authority.

801.   Subsections (5) to (8) set out the offence of failure to comply with these requirements, and the maximum penalties.

Section 523: Duty of company to notify appropriate audit authority

802.   This section introduces a new duty on a company to notify the appropriate audit authority whenever an auditor leaves office before the end of his term, that is when he has resigned or is dismissed. The company has the choice of sending in the statement of circumstances made by the auditor under section 519, or of sending in its own statement of the reasons. Subsection (3) sets the deadline for notification as 14 days after the auditor has deposited his statement with the company. Subsections (4) to (6) set out the offence of failure to comply with this requirement, and the maximum penalties.

Section 524: Information to be given to accounting authorities

803.   This section sets out the duty of the audit authorities to give the accounting authorities information about auditors' departure, and the power, if they think it right to do so, to pass on the statements which they receive from departing auditors under the section 522 or from companies under section 523. The accounting authorities are the Secretary of State and anyone the Secretary of State has authorised under Part 15 to apply to the court in respect of the revision of defective accounts. At present this is the Financial Reporting Review Panel, part of the Financial Reporting Council organisation.

804.   Subsection (3) deals with the situation where the same body is both an audit authority and an accounting authority. If an accounting authority receives a statement that the court has determined need not be circulated to members, then subsection (4) provides that it must treat the statement as confidential, in the same way that authorities have to treat information obtained under compulsory powers under Part 15.

Section 525: Meaning of "appropriate audit authority" and "major audit"

805.   This section defines two terms used in connection with the duty to inform the audit authority when an auditor leaves office, namely *appropriate audit authority* and *major audit*. The former means the Secretary of State, or the body to whom he has delegated functions in relation to the supervision of statutory auditors under Part 42, currently the Professional Oversight Board, part of the Financial Reporting Council organisation.

806.   A major audit is defined as meaning the audit of a listed company, or of any other company where there is a major public interest. Whether there is a major public interest is to be determined by reference to guidance issued by any of the audit authorities. In practice, this will generally be guidance issued by the Financial Reporting Council.

Section 526: Effect of casual vacancies

807.   This section applies when one out of two or more joint auditors ceases to be an auditor of the company. It enables the remaining auditors to continue in office. It restates section 388(2) of the 1985 Act.

Chapter 5: Quoted Companies: Right Of Members To Raise Audit Concerns At Accounts Meeting

808.   This Chapter introduces a new right for members of a quoted company to raise questions about the work of the auditors (all shareholders in a company limited by shares are members).

Section 527: Members' power to require website publication of audit concerns

809. This section creates a new right for members of a quoted company – if they have a large enough holding in the company, or there are enough of them – to ask the company to publish on a website a statement raising questions about the accounts, or about the departure of an auditor, that they propose to bring up at the next meeting where the accounts are to be discussed.

810. Subsection (2) specifies the thresholds the members have to meet, which are the same as for shareholders who want to ask a company to circulate a statement under section 314: they must either have 5% of the total voting rights, or there must be at least 100 of them, holding shares on which there has been paid up an average sum per member of at least £100. Subsection (4) sets out the mechanics of transmitting the request to the company: it may be in hard copy or electronic.

811. Subsection (5) protects the company if members abuse the new right, eg by requesting a defamatory statement to be published. It enables the company, or someone else such as the auditor or a director, to apply to the court, and the court can then determine whether the right is being abused, in which case the company is not obliged to publish the statement. Subsection (6) provides that the court can order the shareholders who requested publication to pay some or all of the costs of the proceedings.

Section 528: Requirements as to website availability

812. This section sets out the requirements which the company must meet in making the shareholders' statements available on a website, in the same way as section 353. Subsection (4) requires the company to get the statement onto a website within three days of receiving it, and to keep it available at least until after the meeting to which it relates.

Section 529: Website publication: company's supplementary duties

813. This section requires quoted companies to draw attention to the possibility of a website statement in the notice of the accounts meeting. It also specifies the costs of publication are to be borne by the company. Subsection (3) requires the company to forward the statement to the auditor at the same time as it puts it on a website. Subsection (4) provides that a statement under this chapter can be dealt with at the accounts meeting.

Section 530: Website publication: offences

814. This section provides for offences when a company fails to comply with either of the preceding two sections, with maximum penalties of an unlimited fine.

Section 531: Meaning of "quoted company"

815. This section defines the phrase "quoted company" for the purposes of Chapter 5 of Part 16 as being the same as the definition in section 385 in Part 15, and that the power in Part 15 to amend the definition also applies in this Chapter.

Chapter 6: Auditors' Liability

816. This Chapter makes it possible for auditors to limit their liability by agreement with a company, but the agreement will be effective only to the extent that it is fair and reasonable.

817. It achieves this by defining a "liability limitation agreement" – a contractual limitation of an auditor's liability to a company, requiring member agreement – as a new exception to the general prohibition, restated here, on a company indemnifying its auditor. The court will be able to substitute its own limitation if the agreement purports to limit liability to an amount that is not fair and reasonable in all the circumstances.

Section 532: Voidness of provisions protecting auditors from liability

818. This section restates the existing general prohibition, currently in section 310 of the 1985 Act, against a company indemnifying its auditor against claims by the company in the case of negligence or other default. Any such indemnities are void and unenforceable except where permitted by sections 533 to 536.

Section 533: Indemnity for costs of successfully defending proceedings

819. This section contains the current exception from the prohibition in section 532 allowing the company to indemnify the auditor against the costs of successfully defending himself against a claim, though it does not repeat the current exception that allows the company to buy insurance for its auditor.

Section 534: Liability limitation agreements

820. This section defines a "liability limitation agreement" as an agreement that seeks to limit the liability of an auditor to a company whose accounts he audits. The agreement can cover liability for negligence, default, breach of duty or breach of trust by the auditor.

821. Subsection (2) provides that such an agreement is excepted from the general voidness of such agreements under section 532, provided that the agreement complies with the rules in section 535, and that it has been authorised by the members of the company in the way specified in section 536. Subsection (3) provides that the agreement's effect is limited by section 537, which contains the test of fairness and reasonableness, and that certain provisions of the Unfair Contracts Terms Act 1977 do not apply.

Section 535: Terms of liability limitation agreement

822. This section contains rules about the terms of a liability limitation agreement. An agreement must relate to the audit of a specified financial year, and the limitation may be expressed in any terms, not necessarily as a fixed financial amount or a formula.

823. Subsection (2) confers on the Secretary of State a power to make regulations (subject to negative resolution) prescribing or proscribing specified provisions or descriptions of provisions; and subsection (3) provides that the power may be used to prevent adverse effects on competition.

Section 536: Authorisation of agreement by members of the company

824. This section specifies the way in which members of a company are to give their approval to a liability limitation agreement, without which approval the agreement will not be effective. The members of a private company can pass a resolution waiving the need for approval. The members in a private or a public company can pass a resolution before an agreement is signed approving its principal terms, or can approve the agreement after it is signed. The resolution may be an ordinary resolution, unless a higher threshold is set in the company's articles.

825. Subsection (5) specifies what the principal terms of a liability limitation agreement are for this purpose, namely the terms that specify, or enable one to determine, (i) the sorts of faults by the auditor that are covered, (ii) the financial year in relation to which those faults are covered, and (iii) the limit on the auditor's liability.

826. Subsection (6) provides that members, by passing an ordinary resolution, can withdraw their approval of a liability limitation agreement at any time before the agreement is entered into. If the company has already entered into the agreement, approval can be withdrawn, by ordinary resolution, only before the start of the financial year to which the agreement relates.

Section 537: Effect of liability limitation agreement

827. This section provides that a liability limitation agreement will not be effective to limit an auditor's liability if the limitation would result in the company recovering an amount that was less than what was fair and reasonable, in all the circumstances of the case, having regard in particular to the auditor's responsibilities, the auditor's contractual obligations, and the standards expected of the auditor. If a court decides that a liability limitation agreement would limit the auditor's liability to an excessive degree, the agreement will have effect as if it limited liability to the amount that the court determines is fair and reasonable.

828. Subsection (3) provides that in assessing what is fair and reasonable, the court should not take into account circumstances arising after the loss or damage in question has been incurred. Nor should it take into account the chances of the company successfully claiming compensation from any other people responsible for the loss or damage.

Section 538: Disclosure of agreement by company

829. This section requires companies to disclose any liability limitation agreement they have made with their auditor in accordance with any regulations made by the Secretary of State subject to negative resolution. Subsection (2) provides that the regulations may require this disclosure to be in a company's annual accounts (or in any other manner in the case of group accounts), or in the directors' report.

Chapter 7: Supplementary Provisions

Section 539: Minor definitions

830. This section defines a number of terms used in this Part.

PART 17: A COMPANY'S SHARE CAPITAL

[3.18]
831. This Part of the Act deals with various matters relating to a company's share capital. It replaces Part 4 and (in part) Part 5 of the 1985 Act and contains a mixture of new sections which replace corresponding provisions in the 1985 Act and sections which restate corresponding provisions in that Act. Sections 541, 543 to 544, 547 to 548, 552 to 553, 558, 561, 563 to 568, 570 to 572, 574 to 577, 579 to 582, 584 to 588, 590 to 605, 607 to 609, 611 to 616, 645 to 648 and 655 to 656 restate various provisions in the 1985 Act but do not make any changes to those provisions.

Chapter 1: Shares And Share Capital Of A Company

Section 540: Shares

832. As now, generally speaking, references to a "share" in the Companies Acts (defined in section 2) includes stock. However, as recommended by the CLR, in future it will no longer be possible for a company to convert its shares into stock (see subsection (2)) but a company that has stock at the date that this provision comes into force will be able to reconvert its stock back into shares (see note on section 620).

Section 542: Nominal value of shares

833. This is a new provision, which is required as a result of the changes to the requirements with respect to the memorandum (see note on section 8).

834. Currently, section 2(5)(a) of the 1985 Act (requirements with respect to memorandum) requires that, in the case of a company having a share capital, the memorandum of a limited company must state the amount of the share capital with which the company proposes to be registered and the division of that share capital into shares of a fixed amount. This capital figure as stated in the memorandum (known as the "authorised share capital") acts as a ceiling on the amount of shares that a company may issue. Such authorised share capital may, however, be increased by ordinary resolution under section 121 of that Act. The CLR recommended that the requirement for a company to have an authorised share capital should be abolished (Final Report, paragraph 10.6), and so the Act does not require a company to state in its memorandum the amount of its authorised share capital.

835. This section is required as a consequence of the repeal of this requirement. It does two key things:

*   it makes it clear that the shares in a limited company having a share capital must have a fixed nominal value, eg 1p, £1, $1 or 1 euro and therefore prevents a company from issuing shares of no par value (thereby implementing for public companies, Article 8 of the Second Company Law Directive (77/91/EEC)); and
*   it places in statute the common law rule that shares may be denominated in any currency and that different classes of shares may be denominated in different currencies. However, this is subject to the requirement in section 765 that a public company may only satisfy its initial authorised minimum share capital requirement if its shares are denominated in either sterling or euros.

836. Where a company purports to allot shares without a fixed nominal value, every officer of the company who is in default commits an offence and is liable to a fine (see subsections (4) and (5)). Moreover, such a purported allotment is void (see subsection (2)).

837. This section needs to be read alongside section 9, which requires the application for registration of a company that is to be formed with a share capital to include a "statement of capital and initial shareholdings". The contents of this statement are prescribed in section 10 and this includes a requirement to set out the total number of shares and the aggregate nominal value of the shares which are to be taken by the subscribers to the memorandum on formation.

Section 545: Companies having a share capital

838. Section 545 is a new provision which makes it clear that references in the Companies Acts (defined in section 2) to a company having a share capital are to company that has power under its constitution to issue shares.

Section 546: Issued and allotted share capital

839. Section 546 is a new provision which makes it clear that references in the Companies Acts (defined in section 2) to issued or allotted shares include the shares taken by the subscribers to the memorandum on the formation of a company.

Chapter 2: Allotment Of Shares: General Provisions

840. Generally speaking, the directors of a company may currently only allot shares (or grant rights to subscribe for shares or to convert any security into shares) if they are authorised to do so by ordinary resolution of the company's members or by the articles.

841. Such an authority may be general or specific (that is, it may, for example, be restricted to a specified allotment, an allotment of shares up to a specified value, or an allotment of shares of a particular class). In either case, the authority must state the "maximum amount of relevant securities that may be allotted under it" and the date when the authority will expire, (which must not be more than five years from the date on which the authority is given). The authority may be renewed for further periods not exceeding five years.

842. There is a relaxation for private companies from the requirement to state the date on which the authority will expire and so such companies may, by elective resolution under section 379A of the 1985 Act, give such authority either for an indefinite period or a fixed period of the company's choice.

Part 3   CA 2006 Supporting Materials

843.   The Act removes for private companies the requirement for prior authorisation in certain circumstances (described in section 550). It also abolishes the concept of authorised share capital (see note on section 542) and a company's constitution will therefore no longer have to contain a ceiling on the number of shares that the directors are authorised to allot.

Section 549: Exercise by directors of power to allot shares etc

844.   This section replaces section 80(1), (2), (9) and (10) of the 1985 Act. It provides that the directors may not allot shares (or grant rights to subscribe for shares or to convert any security into shares) except in accordance with one of the following two sections.

845.   Subsection (2) of this section provides that directors may allot shares in pursuance of an employees' share scheme without having to comply with one of the following two sections. This mirrors the current position (see section 80(2) of the 1985 Act).

846.   Similarly, where a right to subscribe for, or to convert any security into, shares already exists, then the directors may allot shares pursuant to that right without having to comply with one of the following two sections (see subsection 3).

847.   A director who knowingly allots shares in contravention of the requirements imposed by this section commits an offence. Such an allotment is not, however, invalid.

Section 550: Power of directors to allot shares etc: private company with only one class of shares

848.   In line with the recommendations of the CLR (Final Report, paragraph 4.5), this is a new provision which empowers the directors to allot shares (or to grant rights to subscribe for or convert any security into shares) where the company is a private company which will have only one class of shares after the proposed allotment and removes the current requirement, contained in section 80 of the 1985 Act, for the directors to have prior authority from the company's members for such an allotment of shares. In addition, it provides that the members may, if they wish, restrict or prohibit this power through the articles. The definition of "class of shares" is contained in section 629.

Section 551: Power of directors to allot shares etc: authorisation by company

849.   This section replaces section 80(1) and (3) to (8) of the 1985 Act and applies both to private companies which will have more than one class of shares after a proposed allotment and to public companies. It provides that the directors may only allot shares (or grant rights to subscribe for shares or to convert any security into shares) if they have been given prior authorisation for the proposed allotment by ordinary resolution of the company's members or by the articles.

850.   Subsections (2) to (5) set out details of the way in which prior authorisation (or a renewal of such authorisation) may be given and, in particular, provides that the authority may not be given for a period of more than five years. An authority given to the directors under this section, and any resolution of the company renewing such an authority, must state "the maximum amount of shares" to be allotted pursuant to the authority. This mirrors the formulation of words used in section 80 of the 1985 Act and enables the members to limit the authority to a specific number of shares or shares up to a given maximum nominal value.

851.   Subsection (8) makes it clear that an ordinary resolution of the company's members will suffice for the purposes of giving authority to the directors, even where the effect of the resolution is to alter the company's articles of association (which would normally require a special resolution of the company's members).

Section 554: Registration of allotment

852.   This is a new provision which requires the directors to register an allotment of shares as soon as practicable (but in any event within two months of the date of allotment). Whereas the 1985 Act imposes a duty on the company to issue certificates within two months after the allotment of its shares it does not stipulate a timescale relating to the step which is anterior to this, namely the registration of the allotment.

853.   Subsection (2) makes it clear that the requirement to register an allotment of shares does not apply if the company has issued a share warrant in respect of the shares in question (see section 779).

854.   Where a company fails to comply with this section, the company and every officer of the company who is in default commits an offence. The penalty for this offence is set out in subsection (4).

Section 555: Return of allotment by limited company

855.   This section replaces section 88 of the 1985 Act. As now, within one month of an allotment of new shares in a limited company, the company is required to make a return of allotments to the registrar. This return must contain "*prescribed information*" relating to the allotment (that is, prescribed by the Secretary of State by order or by regulations made under the Act).

856.   A return of allotments made under this section must be accompanied by a statement of capital. A statement of capital is in essence a "snapshot" of a company's total subscribed capital at a particular point in time (in this context, the date to which the return of allotments is made up).

857.   The requirement for a statement of capital when an allotment of new shares is made is new. It is based on a recommendation by the CLR (Final Report, paragraph 7.30) and for public companies, this implements a requirement in the Second Company Law Directive (77/91/EEC) which states:

> "the statutes or instruments of incorporation of the company shall always give at least the following information . . . (c) when the company has no authorized capital, the amount of the subscribed capital . . . ".

"Statutes" and "instruments of incorporation" equate to the articles and memorandum and the need to disclose information pertaining to the aggregate of a company's subscribed capital flows from the abolition of the requirement for a company to have an authorised share capital (see note on section 542).

858.   Whilst this Directive only applies to public companies, the requirement to provide a statement of capital, here and elsewhere in the Act, has been extended to private companies limited by shares (and in certain cases to unlimited companies having a share capital, for example, where such companies make their annual return to the registrar). This will mean that the public register will contain up-to-date information on a company's share capital (the requirement for a statement of capital supplements existing provisions which require a company to give notice to the registrar when it amends its share capital in any way).

859.   The information which will in future be set out in the statement of capital includes prescribed particulars of the rights attached to each class of shares. Again this information will be prescribed in regulations or by order made under the Act. Such information is currently required to be filed under either section 123 of the 1985 Act (which relates to increases in authorised share capital) or section 128(1) and (2) of that Act (which relates to allotments of a new class of shares).

860.   Currently, if shares are allotted as fully or partly paid up otherwise than in cash, the company must deliver the contract that it has with the allottee (or details of this contract if it is not in writing) to the registrar. Such a contract may contain commercially sensitive information which the company would not normally want to disclose. This section does not reproduce this requirement. It should be noted, however, that, in prescribing the information which must be included in the return of allotments, the Secretary of State may require details of any consideration received in respect of shares which are allotted as fully or partly paid up otherwise than in cash.

Section 556: Return of allotment by unlimited company allotting new class of shares

861.   This section requires unlimited companies to make a return of allotments to the registrar where the directors allot a new class of shares. This carries forward the provisions of section 128(1) and (2) of the 1985 Act as they apply to unlimited companies. The return must contain "prescribed particulars of the rights attached to the shares", that is such information as may be prescribed by the Secretary of State in regulations or by order made under the Act.

Section 557: Offence of failure to make return

862.   This section replaces section 88(5) and (insofar as it relates to a requirement for an unlimited company to register particulars of an allotment of a new class of shares) section 128(5) of the 1985 Act. Where a company fails to comply with the requirements to make a return of allotments to the registrar, every officer of the company who is in default commits an offence.

863.   As now under section 88(6), where there is a default in making a return of allotments within the specified time (one month after the allotment) a person who is liable for the default may apply to the court for relief (see subsection (3) which extends the right to apply for relief to a person liable under section 556).

Section 559: Provisions about allotment not applicable to shares taken on formation

864.   This provision replicates the effect of section 80(2)(a) of the 1985 act and provides that the allotment provisions in Chapter 2 of this Part do not apply to the shares taken by the subscribers to the memorandum on the formation of a company. Such persons become members of the company in respect of the shares that are taken by them on formation by virtue of section 16 and the provisions of the Act on share allotments do not apply to them.

Chapter 3: Allotment Of Equity Securities: Existing Shareholders' Right Of Pre-Emption

Section 560: Meaning of "equity securities" and related expressions

865.   This section sets out a definition of "equity securities" for the purposes of Chapter 3 of this Part (which is concerned with the allotment of equity securities and existing shareholders' right of pre-emption). It partially restates section 94(2), (3), (3A) and (5) of the 1985 Act. The exception for shares taken by a subscriber to the memorandum and for bonus shares provided in section 94(2) of the 1985 Act is contained in sections 577 and 564. The exclusion of the allotment of shares pursuant to the grant of a right to subscribe for such shares contained in section 93(3) of the 1985 Act is contained in section 561(3).

Section 561: Existing shareholders' right of pre-emption

866. Subject to some exceptions, under section 89(1) of the 1985 Act, a company that is proposing to allot equity securities (defined in section 560) must offer them to existing shareholders first (that is, on a pre-emptive basis). The basic principle (which is unchanged by the Act) is that a shareholder should be able to protect his proportion of the total equity of a company by having the opportunity to subscribe for any new issue of equity securities. This is subject to various exceptions and subsection (5) provides a pointer to these exceptions.

Section 562: Communication of pre-emption offers to shareholders

867. This section replaces section 90(1), (5) and (6) of the 1985 Act. Section 90(6) of the 1985 Act provides that where a company communicates a pre-emption offer to its existing shareholders the offer must state a period of not less than 21 days during which it may be accepted and it may not be withdrawn before the end of that period. This section contains a new provision which gives the Secretary of State the power to vary, in regulations made under the Act, the period of 21 days (but not so as to reduce it to fewer than 14 days) – see subsection (6).

868. It also updates the 1985 Act provision to ensure that the communications of pre-emption offers to shareholders continue to be compatible with EU law: in particular, in future companies will be required to give individual notice (which may be in hard copy or electronic form) to all shareholders who have a registered address in the EEA or who have given an address for service of notices in the EEA (under the 1985 Act, a company is only required to give individual notice to shareholders who have given a service address in the UK). As now, where no relevant address for service has been provided, the company may discharge its obligation by causing notice of the offer to be published in the London, Edinburgh or Belfast Gazette as appropriate.

Sections 569 to 573: Disapplication of pre-emption rights

869. This group of sections deals with the circumstances in which the statutory pre-emption requirements may be disapplied or modified by a power under the articles or by special resolution in accordance with the detailed rules in these sections. The rules replace or restate equivalent provisions in section 95 of the 1985 Act.

870. Section 569 is a new provision which sets out how members of a private company with only one class of shares may authorise the directors to allot shares without complying with the statutory pre-emption provisions.

871. Section 573 is concerned with the disapplication of pre-emption rights in connection with a sale of treasury shares. Generally speaking, where a company buys back its own shares, it is normally required to cancel those shares (see section 706(b)). Certain companies (principally those which are listed or those whose shares are traded on the Alternative Investment Market and equivalent companies in the EEA) may however elect not to cancel shares which have been bought back but may hold the shares "in treasury". A share which is held in treasury may be sold at a future point in time and this facility enables such companies to raise capital more quickly than they would otherwise be able to do, as the directors do not have to obtain prior authority from the company's members before selling treasury shares. However, the provisions of section 561 do apply to sales of treasury shares as they apply to allotments of shares (see section 560(2)(b)).

872. This section applies to a sale of shares which have been held in treasury by the company. It replaces section 95(2A) of the 1985 Act and reproduces the effect of that section by enabling a company's members to give a general power to the directors (through the company's articles or by special resolution of the company's members) to sell such shares as if statutory pre-emption rights did not apply, or applied with modifications.

873. This section also permits the members to confer upon the directors (by special resolution) a specific power which enables them to sell treasury shares as if statutory pre-emption rights did not apply to a specified sale, or applied with modifications.

Chapter 4: Public Companies: Allotment Where Issue Not Fully Subscribed

Section 578: Public companies: allotment where issue not fully subscribed

874. The provisions of this section restate section 84 of the 1985 Act and relate to the allotment of shares by public companies, and apply where not all the shares offered are taken up. A public company must not allot shares following an offer to subscribe for shares unless all the shares offered are taken up or the offer is made on the basis that it will go ahead even if all the shares offered are not taken up or if other conditions specified in the offer are met. It is not possible for the terms of the offer to override the requirements of this section (subsection 6)).

875. The purpose of this rule is to protect persons who apply for shares, by ensuring that if the increase in capital is not fully subscribed, the capital will be increased by the amount of the subscriptions received only if the conditions of the issue so provide (Article 28 of the Second Company Law Directive (77/91/EEC)).

876. If 40 days after first making the offer, the offer is unsuccessful because not enough shares have been applied for under the offer, any money or other consideration received from those that did apply for shares under the offer must be repaid or returned (subsection (2)). Interest becomes payable after the expiration of the 48th day after the offer was first made (subsection (3)). The rate of interest will be as specified at the time under section 17 of the Judgments Act 1838 (currently 8%). This is a change from section 84(3) of the 1985 Act which sets the interest rate at 5% per annum.

877.   The 40 day and 48 day time limits imposed by subsections (2) and (3) now run from the making of the offer rather than from the issue of any prospectus (as was the case under section 84 of the 1985 Act) given that the requirement or otherwise for a prospectus is a matter of securities law.

878.   The regulation of public offers, especially requirements relating to prospectuses, is generally a matter of securities law. Sections 82 and 83 of the 1985 Act are, therefore, not restated in this Act.

Section 583: Meaning of payment in cash

879.   This section replaces section 738(2) to (4) of the 1985 Act. It provides a definition of "payment in cash" for the purposes of the Companies Acts and is relevant to a number of provisions (for example section 593 requires public companies to obtain an independent valuation of any non-cash consideration where it allots shares otherwise than for cash).

880.   Subsection (3) provides a definition of "cash consideration" which lists the items currently contained in section 738(2) of the 1985 Act. It is generally accepted that certain forms of payment, in addition to those listed in subsection (3), constitute "payment in cash" where shares in a company are deemed to be paid up or allotted for cash, for example an assured payment obligation under the CREST assured payment system, but this matter is not beyond doubt. (An assured payment obligation is the creation of an obligation to make payment to or for the account of the company in accordance with the rules and practices of the operator of a relevant system as defined by regulation 2(1) of the Uncertificated Securities Regulations 2001). The power contained in subsection (4) will enable the Secretary of State to make provision for other forms of payment to be regarded as falling within the definition of "payment in cash". This will eradicate the uncertainty which currently surrounds certain forms of payment and will also "future proof" the current definition should other settlement systems be developed in the future (or should other settlement systems within the EU be identified).

Section 589: Power of court to grant relief

881.   Section 589 restates section 113(1) to (7) of the 1985 Act. It enables the court to grant relief, to the applicant, from a liability to the company which has arisen as a result of a contravention of section 585, 587(2) or (4) or 588. There is a minor change in the restatement insofar as the matters to which the court must have regard in applying the just and equitable test in subsection (3) also apply where the liability relates to the payment of interest (under section 113(2)(b)) of the 1985 Act the court is not required to have regard to those matters in applying the just and equitable test).

Section 606: Power of court to grant relief

882.   Section 606 restates section 113(1) to (8) of the 1985 Act. It enables the court to grant relief, to the applicant, from a liability to the company which has arisen (under any provision of Chapter 6) in relation to payment in respect of shares in a company or an undertaking given to the company in, or in connection with, payment for any shares in it. There is a minor change in the restatement insofar as the matters to which the court must have regard in applying the just and equitable test in subsection (2) also apply where the liability relates to the payment of interest (under section 113(2)(b)) of the 1985 Act the court is not required to have regard to those matters in applying the just and equitable test).

Chapter 7: Share Premiums

883.   Under section 130 of the 1985 Act, where shares in a company are issued at a premium, (that is, at a price which is greater than their nominal value), an amount equal to the premium paid on those shares must be transferred to a non-distributable reserve: the share premium account. This account can only be used in a limited number of circumstances described in section 130.

Section 610: Application of share premiums

884.   In line with the recommendations of the CLR (Completing the Structure, paragraph 7.8), this section further restricts the application of the share premium account and in the future, companies will not be able to use the share premium account to write off preliminary expenses (that is, expenses incurred in connection with the company's formation). Companies will continue to be able to use the share premium account to write off any expenses incurred, or commission paid, in connection with an issue of shares but the application of the share premium account in these circumstances will be limited so that the company will only be able to use the share premium account arising on a particular issue of shares to write off expenses incurred or commission paid in respect of that issue. As now, companies will also be able to use the share premium account to pay up new shares to be allotted to existing members as fully paid bonus shares.

885.   A further change is that in future companies will not be able to use the share premium account to write off any expenses incurred, commission paid or discount allowed in respect of an issue of debentures or in providing for the premium payable on a redemption of debentures.

Part 3   CA 2006 Supporting Materials

Chapter 8: Alteration Of Share Capital

Section 617: Alteration of share capital of limited company

886. This section prohibits a limited company from altering its share capital except in the ways permitted under the Act. It includes a signpost to a new provision which will enable companies limited by shares easily to convert (or "redenominate") their share capital from one currency to another (see section 622).

Section 618: Sub-division or consolidation of shares

887. Consolidation of a company's share capital involves combining a number of shares into a new share of commensurate nominal value: for example, ten £1 shares may be combined to make one £10 share. Sub-division of a company's share capital involves dividing a share into a number of new shares with a smaller nominal value: for example, a £10 share may be sub-divided into ten £1 shares.

888. Section 618 replaces section 121(2)(b) and (d) of the 1985 Act. It sets out the circumstances and manner in which a limited company may consolidate or sub-divide its share capital. Where shares in a company are sub-divided or consolidated, the proportion between the amount paid and the amount unpaid (if any) on the original share(s) must remain the same in relation to the share(s) resulting from the sub-division or consolidation. If, for example, £2 is unpaid on a £10 share that is subsequently sub-divided into ten £1 shares, there will now be 20p unpaid on each of those ten shares.

889. A company may exercise a power conferred on it under this section only if the members have passed a resolution authorising it to do so, which may be an ordinary resolution or a resolution requiring a higher majority (as the articles may require). Such a resolution may authorise a company to exercise more than one of the powers conferred on it under this section, for example, the resolution may authorise a sub-division of one class of the company's shares and a consolidation of another. It may also authorise the company to exercise a power conferred on it under this section on more than one occasion or at a specified time or in specified circumstances. This avoids the directors having to obtain authorisation from the company's members on each and every occasion that a company alters its share capital under this section (which may be inconvenient to the directors and members alike or impractical due to timing constraints).

890. The flexibility to pass a conditional resolution (that is, a resolution that will only take effect if certain conditions are met) given in subsection (4)(c) is necessary as a sub-division or consolidation of share capital (or any class of it) may form part of a wider re-organisation of a company's share capital, for example, a reduction of share capital following a redenomination of share capital. It may, therefore, not be appropriate, or necessary, for a company's share capital to be altered in this way if the reorganisation of share capital that the sub-division or consolidation is linked to does not go ahead.

891. Under the 1985 Act a company may only sub-divide or consolidate its share capital if it is authorised to do so by the company's articles (see section 121 of that Act). This restriction has not been retained.

Section 619: Notice to registrar of sub-division or consolidation

892. The section replaces a similar requirement to notify the registrar contained in section 122(1)(a) and (d) of the 1985 Act. Where a company sub-divides or consolidates its share capital under section 618, it will continue to be required to give notice of this alteration to its share capital to the registrar within one month. However, there is a new requirement to file a statement of capital (see subsections (2) and (3)), which is in essence a "snap-shot" of the company's total share capital at a particular point in time: in this case following the consolidation/sub-division.

893. For public companies, the requirement for a statement of capital is linked to the abolition of authorised share capital: it implements Article 2 of the Second Company Law Directive (77/91/EEC) which states:

> "the statutes or instruments of incorporation of the company shall always give at least the following information . . .   (c) when the company has no authorized capital, the amount of the subscribed capital . . . ".

894. The statement of capital will require the following information to be provided:
- the total number of shares of the company,
- the aggregate nominal value of those shares,
- for each class of shares, prescribed particulars of the rights attached to the shares, the total number of shares of that class and the aggregate nominal value of shares of that class, and
- the amount paid up and the amount (if any) unpaid on each share (whether on account of the nominal value of the share or by way of premium).

895. Whilst this Directive applies only to public companies it is important that the information on the public register is up-to-date. A statement of capital will, therefore, be required where it is proposed that a company formed under the Act will have a share capital on formation and, with limited exceptions (in particular, where there has been a variation of class rights which does not affect the company's aggregate subscribed capital) whenever a limited company makes an alteration to its share capital. A statement of capital is also called for in certain circumstances where an unlimited company having a share capital makes a return to the registrar (see, section 856).

896. In making a statement of capital, a company is required to provide "prescribed particulars of the rights attached to the shares". Here, and elsewhere in the Act where a statement of capital is called for, "prescribed" means prescribed by the Secretary of State in regulations or by order made under the Act.

897. The power conferred on the Secretary of State under this section enables the Secretary of State to specify the particular detail of the information which he requires to be filed with the registrar by a company. A statutory instrument made pursuant to this power will not be subject to any form of Parliamentary scrutiny.

898. Criminal liability for any failure to comply with the procedural requirements as to notice is retained (see subsection (4)). The penalty for this offence is set out in subsection (5).

Section 620: Re-conversion of stock into shares

899. Stock cannot be issued directly by a company but arises from a conversion of fully paid up shares into stock under section 121(2)(c) of the 1985 Act. This ability to convert shares into stock has not been retained. A company that currently has stock may, however, wish to re-convert this stock back into fully paid shares, and this is permitted by the following section.

900. Section 620 replaces section 121(2)(c) of the 1985 Act. It retains the ability to reconvert stock back into fully paid shares but removes the requirement for prior authorisation in the articles (currently a company may only re-convert stock back into shares if provision for this is made in its articles).

901. A re-conversion of stock into shares will require an ordinary resolution of the company's members. Such a resolution may give the directors power to convert stock into fully paid shares on more than one occasion; at a specified time; or only if certain conditions are met (see subsection (3)). The flexibility to pass a conditional resolution (that is, a resolution that will only take effect if certain conditions are met) is necessary as a re-conversion of stock into shares may form part of a wider re-organisation of a company's share capital.

Section 621: Notice to registrar of reconversion of stock into shares

902. Where a company re-converts stock into shares it must give notice of the alteration to its share capital to the registrar under the provisions in section 621. This requirement replaces a similar provision in section 122(1)(c) of the 1985 Act.

903. A statement of capital is required (see note on section 619).

904. Criminal liability for any failure to comply with the procedural requirements as to notice is retained (see subsection (4)). The penalty for this offence is set out in subsection (5).

Section 622: Redenomination of share capital

905. Where a public company applies for a trading certificate under section 117 of the 1985 Act it must satisfy a minimum share capital requirement (known as the "authorised minimum"). There is a similar requirement where a private company re-registers as a public company under section 43 of that Act. The authorised minimum is currently set at £50,000 and must be expressed in sterling. This implements Article 6 of the Second Company Law Directive (77/91/EEC) which requires that, in order that a company may be incorporated or obtain authorisation to commence business, a minimum capital shall be subscribed the amount of which shall be not less than 25000 ECU (expressed in the domestic currency of the Member State). Under section 763, in future the authorised minimum will be capable of being satisfied in sterling (£50,000) or the euro equivalent to the sterling amount. Subject to this change, the Act retains the effect of the 1985 Act provisions on the authorised minimum (see, for example, section 91, section 650 and section 761).

906. Subject to the above qualification (and any restriction in a company's articles) a company is free to allot shares in any currency that it wishes (see section 542(3)). It may also have its share capital made up of shares of a mixture of denominations, for example, one class of a company's shares may be denominated in sterling, whereas another class may be denominated in dollars, euros or some other currency of the company's choosing. What a company cannot currently do is easily redenominate its share capital (or any class of it) from one currency to another, for example, from dollars to sterling or vice versa. The current procedure involves cancelling existing shares under the court approved procedure for capital reductions set out in section 135 of the 1985 Act or, in the case of private companies only, buying back or redeeming shares out of capital under section 171 of that Act, and then issuing new shares in the desired currency.

907. Section 622 introduces a new procedure that will allow a company limited by shares to redenominate its share capital easily. This requires a resolution of the company's members. (Unlimited companies having a share capital are already free to redenominate their share capital as they see fit and no change to the legislation is required in respect of such companies).

908. Subsection (2) of this section provides that the spot rate used when converting a company's share capital from one currency to another must be specified in the resolution to redenominate the company's share capital. There is a choice of spot rates and this is set out in subsection (3).

909. A company is free to pass a conditional resolution under this section (see subsection (4)). A resolution will, however, lapse if the redenomination of share capital has not taken effect within 28 days of the date on which the resolution is passed (see subsection (6)). Where a resolution lapses, the company will not be able to redenominate its capital unless it passes a new resolution and the redenomination is effected in accordance with the new resolution.

910. Subsection (7) makes it clear that, if it wishes, a company may restrict or prohibit a redenomination of its share capital by incorporating a provision to this effect in the company's articles.

911. It should be noted that this section does not make provision for the authorised minimum to continue to be denominated in sterling (or the euro equivalent). This means that once a public company has obtained a trading certificate under section 761 (or previously under section 117 of the 1985 Act) or where a private company has re-registered as a public company, such a company is free, if it wishes, to redenominate all of its share capital, including the authorised minimum into any currency of its choosing.

Section 623: Calculation of new nominal values

912. This section explains how the new nominal value of a share which has been redenominated from one currency to another should be calculated.

Section 624: Effect of redenomination

913. This section makes it clear that a redenomination of a company's share capital (or any class of it) does not affect any rights or obligations that the members may have under the company's constitution or any restrictions affecting members under the company's constitution. In particular, it does not affect entitlement to dividends, voting rights or any liability in respect of amounts unpaid on shares. If, for example, a dividend of 20p was declared on a £1 share prior to a redenomination of that share, and that £1 share is subsequently converted into a $1.5 share, the member who now owns a $1.5 share in the company will still be entitled to a 20p dividend (albeit that the company and the member in question may agree that the 20p dividend can be paid in cents – or indeed in some other currency). Similarly, where a company has issued partly paid shares, the member's liability to the company will remain in the currency in which the share was originally denominated.

Section 625: Notice to registrar of redenomination

914. This section sets out the requirements as to notice where a company redenominates its share capital (or any class of it). Notice must be given to the registrar in accordance with subsections (1) and (2) of this section and there is a requirement for a statement of capital (see note on section 619).

915. A copy of the resolution to redenominate the company's share capital must be forwarded to the registrar within 15 days after it is passed notwithstanding that it may be an ordinary resolution (see section 622(8) which provides that Chapter 3 of Part 3 applies to the resolution and in particular section 30)

916. If a company fails to comply with the procedural requirements as to notice the company and every officer of the company commits an offence. The penalty for this offence is set out in subsection (5).

Section 626: Reduction of capital in connection with redenomination

917. Following a redenomination of a company's share capital, it is likely that the company will be left with shares expressed in awkward fractions of the new currency, for example, 0.997 dollars or 1.01 euros. The company may therefore wish to renominalise the value of the shares affected (that is, alter the nominal value of these shares) to obtain share values in whole units of the new currency. It can do this in one of two ways: if the company has distributable reserves it may capitalise those reserves to increase the nominal value of the shares affected; alternatively, it may reduce its share capital using the procedure set out in section 626.

918. This section enables a company to renominalise the value of its shares by cancelling part of its share capital. A special resolution of the company's members is required but there is no need for the directors to make a solvency statement or for the company to go to court (as required where a company reduces its share capital under Chapter 10 of this Part).

919. Under subsection (3), a resolution to reduce capital in connection with a redenomination must be passed within 3 months of the resolution to redenominate the company's share capital.

920. Subsection (4) provides that the amount by which a company can reduce its share capital using this new provision is capped at 10% of the nominal value of the company's share capital immediately after the reduction. This 10% cap is required by the Second Company Law Directive (77/91/EEC) and applies to any reduction of capital in a public company which is not approved by the court.

921. Where a company reduces its share capital under this section, the amount by which the company's share capital is reduced must be transferred to a new non-distributable reserve (see section 628).

Section 627: Notice to registrar of reduction of capital in connection with redenomination

922.   This section sets out the requirements as to notice where a company reduces its share capital in connection with a redenomination of its share capital (that is, to renominalise the value of its shares). Notice must be given to the registrar in accordance with subsection (1) of this section. This notice must be accompanied by a statement of capital (see note on section 619).

923.   The resolution to reduce the share capital must be filed with the registrar in accordance with section 30.

924.   The reduction of capital will not take effect until the documents that are required to be delivered to the registrar under subsections (1) and (2) are registered by the registrar (see subsection (5)).

925.   In addition to delivering the above documents to the registrar, within 15 days of the date that a resolution to reduce capital in connection with a redenomination is passed, under subsection (6) the company must also deliver to the registrar a statement made by the directors confirming that the reduction of share capital was made in accordance with subsection (4) of section 626.

926.   If a company fails to comply with the procedural requirements as to notice the company and every officer of the company commits an offence. The penalty for this offence is set out in subsection (8). In addition, where the statement made by the directors under subsection (6) is misleading, false or deceptive in a material particular, the directors are liable to an offence under section 1112.

Section 628: Redenomination reserve

927.   Where a company reduces its share capital under section 626 it must transfer an amount equal to the value of the reduction to a non-distributable reserve known as the redenomination reserve.

928.   This section provides that amounts transferred to the redenomination reserve may be used by the company in paying up shares to be allotted to existing members as fully paid bonus shares. Subject to this, the provisions of the Companies Acts relating to the reduction of a company's share capital, apply to the redenomination reserve as if it were paid-up share capital. These provisions mirror those contained in section 733 (which restates section 170 of the 1985 Act).

Chapter 9: Classes Of Shares And Class Rights

929.   "Classes of shares" (or "class rights") is not defined in the 1985 Act but at common law this term is normally used where the rights that attach to a particular share relate to matters such as voting rights, a right to dividends and a right to a return of capital when a company is wound-up. Rights attach to a particular class of shares if the holders of shares in that class enjoy rights that are not enjoyed by the holders of shares in another class.

Section 629: Classes of shares

930.   This section provides that for the purposes of the Act, shares are of one class if the rights attached to them are in all respects uniform. It reproduces the provision in section 128(2) of the 1985 Act. It is particularly relevant to the provisions of section 550 and section 569. This definition of "classes of shares" also applies in determining the extent to which shares constitute different classes for the purposes of the statement of capital required to be filed under various provisions of the Bill (see note on section 619).

Section 630: Variation of class rights: companies having a share capital

931.   On variation of class rights the CLR recommended (Final Report, paragraph 7.28) that the current provisions should be retained with some simplification, and extended to companies without a share capital (see section 631).

932.   Section 630 replaces section 125 of the 1985 Act. It is concerned with the manner in which rights attached to a class of shares may be varied. Class rights typically cover matters such as voting rights, rights to dividends and rights to a return of capital on a winding up.

933.   Currently class rights may be set out in the memorandum or articles or elsewhere, and provision may or may not be made for their alteration. Under the Act it will not be possible for class rights to be set out in the memorandum (see section 8) and where class rights attaching to shares in an existing company are specified in the memorandum these will be deemed, by virtue of section 28, to be a provision in the company's articles.

934.   Class rights are "attached to a class of shares" (see subsection (1)). Where all the shares in a company fall within the one class, there are no class rights, only shareholder rights. What amounts to a class is not defined either in the current law or the Act (other than in section 629) and remains a matter for case law.

935.   The current requirement for an extraordinary resolution where a company is proposing to vary the rights attached to a class of its shares is replaced with a requirement for a special resolution (see subsection (4)(b)). The Act abolishes the concept of an extraordinary resolution. Special resolution is defined in section 283.

Part 3   CA 2006 Supporting Materials

936.   Subsections (2) and (4) provide that rights may be varied in accordance with the company's articles or, where the articles make no provision for a variation of class rights, if the holders of at least three-quarters in nominal value of the issued shares of that class consent in writing or a special resolution passed by the holders of that class sanctions the variation. This means that the articles may specify a less demanding procedure for a variation of class rights than the statutory scheme (for example, that the holders of 51% by nominal value of the class consent in writing), or may permit a simple majority of the class at a class meeting.

937.   The provisions of section 630 are expressed to be without prejudice to any other restriction on the variation of rights (see subsection (3)). This has two important effects. First, if and to the extent that the company has adopted a more onerous regime in its articles for the variation of class rights, for example requiring a higher percentage than the statutory minimum, the company must comply with the more onerous regime. Second, if and to the extent that the company has protected class rights by making provision for the entrenchment of those rights in its articles (see section 22), that protection cannot be circumvented by changing the rights attached to a class of shares under this section.

Section 631: Variation of class rights: companies without a share capital

938.   This section extends the statutory provisions on variation of class rights to companies without a share capital. Companies limited by guarantee (which since December 1980 cannot be formed with a share capital) may, for example, have different classes of members with different voting rights.

939.   At present the question of how members' rights may be varied will depend to a large extent on whether provision has been made, either in the memorandum or articles, for their variation. Under the Act class rights may also be varied in accordance with this section, which contains new provisions, comparable to those for companies with a share capital. Thus there is a minimum requirement that class rights may be varied if three-quarters of that class consent in writing or a special resolution of those members sanctions the variation, unless the company has made provision for a less onerous regime to apply in its articles. Again, a company may also make provision, in its articles, for a more onerous regime to apply than that provided in this section and where they do the company must comply with the regime set out in the articles.

Section 632: Variation of class rights: saving for court's power under other provisions

940.   This section preserves the court's powers under various other provisions of the Act and substantially restates section 126 of the 1985 Act.

Sections 633 and 634: Right to object to variation

941.   Section 633 replaces section 127 (which confers a right on shareholders to object to a variation of class rights). It sets out the procedure that must be followed where there is an objection to a variation of the rights attached to a class of a company's shares and enables shareholders holding not less in aggregate than 15% of the issued shares of the class in question (being persons who did not consent to or vote in favour of the resolution approving the variation) to apply to the court for the variation to be cancelled.

942.   Section 634 makes similar provision in respect of a variation of class rights in companies not having a share capital. This is a new provision which enables members, amounting to not less than 15% of the members of the class affected (being persons who did not consent to or vote in favour of the resolution approving the variation), to apply to the court to have the variation cancelled and gives the court the power to confirm the variation, or disallow it if the court is satisfied that it would unfairly prejudice the members in that class.

Section 635: Copy of court order to be forwarded to the registrar

943.   Section 635 sets out the procedural requirements as to notice where the court has made an order on an application under section 633 or 634. Where the court has made an order on application under these sections, the company must forward a copy of that order to the registrar within 15 days of the date on which the order is made. Where a company fails to comply with the provisions of this section, the company, and every officer of the company who is in default, commits an offence (see subsections (2) and (3)).

Section 636 to 640: Matters to be notified to the registrar

944.   These sections replace various provisions in sections 128 and 129 of the 1985 Act which are concerned with notification to the registrar of the creation of, and variations to, rights attached to a class of a company's shares (section 128 of the 1985 Act) or class rights of members (section 129 of that Act).

945.   Under the Act, where a limited company creates a new class of shares, it will be required to provide details of the rights attached to the shares in the return of allotment and statement of capital required under section 555. There is a similar requirement in section 556 where an unlimited company allots a new class of share. Those provisions replace section 128(1) and (2) of the 1985 Act.

946.   In addition, where a company varies the rights attached to any of its shares (or assigns a name or other designation, or a new name or other designation to any class or description of its shares) it will in future be required to register particulars of the rights affected under section 637 (or 636) irrespective of how the variation in rights was achieved. Currently companies are not required to provide this information if the rights attached to a particular share or class of shares are varied by an amendment to the company's memorandum or articles or by special resolution or agreement of the company's members which is required to be filed under section 380 of the 1985 Act. Sections 638 to 640 make similar changes to the disclosure requirements which apply to companies limited by guarantee not having a share capital and unlimited companies not having a share capital which may, nevertheless, have different classes of members.

947. It should be noted, that, in contrast to other alterations to a company's share capital, there is no requirement in section 637 for a statement of capital (see note on section 619). Such a requirement would be superfluous, as a variation of class rights will not result in a change to the aggregate amount of a company's subscribed capital.

Chapter 10: Reduction Of Share Capital

948. Section 135 of the 1985 Act lays down a statutory procedure under which a limited company may, if authorised by its articles, reduce its share capital. This requires a special resolution of the company's members and the reduction must be confirmed by the court. Companies limited by shares may also reduce their share capital under section 171 (private company redemption or purchase of own shares out of capital) and sections 146 to 147 of the 1985 Act (which require a public company which acquires shares in any of the specified ways, for example, through forfeiture for failure to pay up, to cancel those shares within a specified period), the provisions of both of which are carried forward by the Act. A reduction of capital may also occur as a result of the court making an order for the purchase by a company of its members' shares.

949. A company may wish to reduce its share capital for a variety of reasons, for example, where its capital is in excess of the company's wants or where the value of the company's net assets has fallen below the amount of its capital (as stated in the company's accounts) and the position is likely to be permanent.

Section 641: Circumstances in which a company may reduce its share capital

950. This section replaces section 135(1) and (2) of the 1985 Act. It sets out the circumstances and manner in which a company limited by shares may reduce its share capital. As recommended by the CLR (Final Report, paragraph 10.6), in future a private company limited by shares will be able to reduce its share capital using a new solvency statement procedure for capital reductions (see section 642).

951. A company may only reduce its share capital under section 135 of the 1985 Act if it is authorised to do so by its articles. In line with the recommendations of the CLR (Completing the Structure, paragraph 2.15), the requirement for prior authorisation in the articles has not been retained but, if it wishes, a company may restrict or prohibit a reduction of capital by making provision to this effect in its articles (see subsection (6)).

952. Subsection (1)(a) contains a signpost to a new provision, which will enable a private company limited by shares to reduce its share capital using the new solvency statement procedure (see above). In addition, private companies and public companies alike will continue to be able to use the current court approved procedure for capital reductions – which is retained in subsection (1)(b).

953. In the case of a private company limited by shares which is proposing to use the new solvency statement procedure to effect a reduction of capital, the company may only reduce its share capital under subsection (1)(a) if it will have at least one member remaining after the proposed reduction (see subsection (2)). That member need only hold one share in the company but that share must not be a redeemable share. The principle behind this requirement is that a private company limited by shares should not be capable of reducing its share capital to zero unless the reduction of capital is sanctioned by the court. This mirrors the existing equivalent provision in section 162(3) of the 1985 Act – which applies to a purchase of own shares.

954. Both the solvency statement procedure for capital reductions and the court-approved procedure require a special resolution of the company's members. Under subsection (5) a special resolution to reduce a company's share capital may not provide for the proposed reduction to take effect on a date later than the date on which the resolution to reduce capital takes effect. Under the solvency statement procedure a resolution to reduce capital will take effect when the documents referred to in section 644 have been registered by the registrar (see section 644(4)). This would operate to prevent a company passing a resolution on, say, 1st January stating that the reduction is to take effect on 1st October. Under the court approved procedure, the resolution will take effect on the registration of the court order and statement of capital or, in the context of a reduction forming part of a compromise or arrangement under Part 26, on delivery of those documents to the registrar (unless the court orders otherwise) (see section 649).

Section 642: Reduction of capital supported by solvency statement

955. This section sets out the conditions that must be satisfied in order for a private company limited by shares to reduce its share capital using the new solvency statement procedure.

Part 3   CA 2006 Supporting Materials

956. The procedural requirements that the directors must follow when they propose a capital reduction using the solvency statement route are set out in subsections (1) to (3) which provides that the solvency statement made in connection with a reduction of capital by a private company cannot be made more than 15 days before the date on which the resolution to reduce capital is passed. It also provides that both the resolution and the solvency statement must be filed with the registrar in accordance with the provisions of section 644.

957. The solvency statement must also be made available to the company's members when they vote on the resolution to reduce capital and the procedure for providing a copy of the solvency statement to the members varies according to whether the resolution to reduce capital is proposed as a written resolution or at a meeting of the company's members (see subsections (2) and (3)). Whilst a failure to observe these procedural requirements will not affect the validity of the resolution to reduce capital, if a solvency statement which has not been provided to the company's members in accordance with the provision of this section is subsequently filed with the registrar, every officer of the company who is in default commits an offence (see section 644).

Section 643: Solvency statement

958. A solvency statement made under section 643 must be made by all of the directors. If one or more of the directors is unable or unwilling to make this statement, the company will not be able to use the solvency statement procedure to effect a reduction of capital unless the dissenting director or directors resign (in which case the solvency statement must be made by all of the remaining directors).

959. The solvency statement must be in the "prescribed form" and "prescribed" in this context means prescribed by the Secretary of State in regulations or by order made under the Act.

960. The solvency statement must state the date on which it is made and the name of each director of the company but there is no requirement that the directors must all be in the same location when they make this statement. The registrar will be able to make rules under section 1068 as to the form of the solvency statement.

961. In forming their opinions, the directors must take account of all the company's liabilities including contingent and prospective liabilities (see subsection (2)). So, in circumstances where a company holds redeemable preference shares which, for the purposes of the accounting standards that applied to the company on the date that the directors made the solvency statement, are treated as liabilities, a proposed redemption or purchase of these shares in the relevant period should be treated as a contingent or prospective liability.

962. If the directors make a solvency statement without having reasonable grounds for the opinions expressed in it, and that statement is subsequently delivered to the registrar, every director who is in default commits an offence (see subsection (4)). The penalty for this offence is set out in subsection (5).

Registration of resolution and supporting documents

963. This section sets out the requirements as to delivery of the solvency statement and other key documents to the registrar. The resolution to reduce capital itself must be filed with the registrar within the same time period as currently applies – that is, within 15 days of the date that it is passed (see section 30) and it will not take effect until the solvency statement and statement of capital (see subsections (1) and (2)) are registered by the registrar. As with all circumstances where the company makes an alteration to its subscribed capital, the company is required to deliver a statement of capital to the registrar (see note on section 619).

964. In addition to making a solvency statement in accordance with section 643, the directors must also make a statement confirming that the solvency statement was made not more than 15 days before the date on which the resolution to reduce capital was passed and that this statement was provided to the company's members in accordance with section 642 – see subsection (5).

965. In addition to the new offences which are set out in sections 643(4) (directors making solvency statement without reasonable grounds for the opinion expressed in it) and subsection (7) (company delivering solvency statement that was not provided to members to registrar), where a company fails to comply with any of the filing requirements under section 644, an offence is committed by the company and every officer of the company who is in default (see subsection (8)). The penalty for this offence is set out subsection (9).

Sections 645 to 649: Reduction of capital confirmed by the court

966. These sections replace or restate various provisions in the 1985 Act that are concerned with reductions of capital confirmed by order of the court.

967. Sections 645 and 646 restate section 136 of the 1985 Act which is concerned with the procedure for making an application to court to confirm a reduction of capital (including the creditors' right to object). If, on such an application, an officer of the company intentionally or recklessly conceals a creditor or misrepresents the nature or amount of a debt owed by the company, or is knowingly concerned in any such concealment or misrepresentation he commits an offence (see section 647). As now the court may make an order confirming the reduction of capital on such terms and conditions as it thinks fit (see section 648 which restates section 137 of the 1985 Act).

968.   Section 649 replaces section 138(1) to (4) of the 1985 Act. Under section 138 of that Act, a resolution to reduce capital using the existing court approved scheme takes effect when the court order confirming the reduction and minute of the reduction are registered by the registrar. The minute (which must be approved by the court) sets out key information regarding the company's share capital immediately after the reduction. Section 649 updates the 1985 Act provisions by replacing the current requirement for a minute of the reduction with a statement of capital (see note on section 619). Like the minute confirming the reduction, this statement must be approved by the court.

969.   In line with the CLR's recommendations (Final Report, paragraph 13.11), subsection (3)(a)(i) of this section provides that a reduction of capital that forms part of a compromise or arrangement under Part 26 of the Act will take effect at the same time as other aspects of that compromise or arrangement: namely on delivery of the court order confirming the reduction (and statement of capital approved by the court) to the registrar (unless the court orders that it should take effect on the registration of these documents) (see new subsection (3)(a)(ii)).

970.   In all other cases, that is, where the reduction of capital does not form part of a compromise or scheme of arrangement under Part 26, where a company reduces its share capital using the court approved procedure the reduction will, as now, take effect on registration of the court order confirming the reduction (and statement of capital) by the registrar. Subsection (5) requires the registrar to certify the registration of the order and statement of capital. Subsection (6) restates section 138(4) of the 1985 Act in relation to such certificate.

Section 651: Expedited procedure for re-registration as a private company

971.   This section, together with section 650, substantially restates section 139 of the 1985 Act and provides for the consequences where the court confirms the reduction by a public company of its share capital below the authorised minimum (defined in section 763): in particular they facilitate the re-registration of the company as private.

972.   Subsection (3) replaces section 139(4) of the 1985 Act. It introduces a requirement to send a copy of the court's order (that is, the order authorising the company to be so reregistered without its having passed a special resolution) to the registrar, together with an application for re-registration. The current requirement for the application to be signed by a director (or secretary) has not been retained.

Sections 652 and 653: Effect of reduction of capital

973.   These sections restate section 140 of the 1985 Act (with the exception of references to the "minute" being replaced with references to the statement of capital) which is concerned with the liability of a company's members in respect of any amounts unpaid on its shares following a reduction of capital. As now, there are special rules where a creditor was omitted from the list of creditors settled by the court.

Chapter 11: Miscellaneous And Supplementary Provisions

Section 654: Treatment of reserve arising from reduction of capital

974.   This is a new provision which enables the Secretary of State, by order, to specify the circumstances in which a reserve arising from a reduction of capital will be distributable.

975.   Whilst there is no requirement in the Act (or indeed the 1985 Act) to create a statutory reserve following such a reduction, we understand that it is usual for companies to create an accounting reserve in these circumstances to "balance the books" (that is, the section relates to reserves that arise as a result of generally accepted accounting treatments). Currently, the question whether a reserve arising from a reduction of capital (which, for a limited company, may currently only be made pursuant to a court order) may be treated as a realised profit for the purposes of computing whether a company has sufficient distributable profits to make a distribution, is the subject of technical guidance issued by the Institutes of Chartered Accountants. The Act introduces a new procedure which enables private companies to reduce their share capital without going to court (see section 641) which is not on all fours with the court approved route (in particular there is no requirement to settle a list of creditors or to provide security for the company's debts) and in the circumstances it is desirable to deal with the question of when amounts credited to such a reserve should be treated as a realised profit in statute. Owing to the technical nature of the rules that will need to be made this issue will be dealt with in secondary legislation. An order made under section 654 will however be subject to the affirmative resolution procedure – that is, the regulations will need to be approved by both Houses of Parliament.

Section 656: Public companies: duty of directors to call meeting on serious loss of capital

976.   Section 656 restates section 142(1) and (3) of the 1985 Act. It sets out the procedure that must be followed where the net assets of a public company fall below half (or less) of the company's called up share capital. Subsection (4) imposes liability on any director who knowingly authorised or permitted a failure to call a meeting as required by this section.

Section 657: General power to make further provision by regulations

977.   This is a new provision which enables the Secretary of State, in regulations made under the Act, to modify various provisions in Part 17 of the Act (see subsection (1)).

978.   Regulations made under this section may amend or repeal any of the specified provisions or make such other provision as appears to the Secretary of State appropriate in place of those provisions. This will enable the Secretary of State to future-proof the specified provisions in this Part of the Act.

979.   Regulations made pursuant to the power in this section are subject to the affirmative resolution procedure.

PART 18: ACQUISITION BY LIMITED COMPANY OF ITS OWN SHARES

[3.19]
980.   This Part replaces various provisions in Chapters 6 and 7 of Part 5 of the 1985 Act and makes substantive changes to some of those provisions. Sections 658 to 659, 662, 666 to 677, 680 to 683, 687, 691, 693, 695 to 701, 704 to 706, 710 to 713, 716 to 719, 721 to 726, 728 to 729, 731 and 733 to 736 restate various provisions in the 1985 Act but do not make any changes to those provisions.

Chapter 1: General Provisions

Sections 660 and 661: Shares held by company's nominee

981.   These sections restate sections 144 and 145(1) and (2) of the 1985 Act, but with the clarification that they apply to shares taken by a subscriber to the memorandum as nominee of the company.

Section 663: Notice of cancellation of shares

982.   This section restates section 122(1)(f) and (2) of the 1985 Act and Schedule 24 to that Act. Subsections (2) and (3) update the current notice requirements to require a company that has cancelled shares in order to comply with section 662 to provide the registrar with a statement of capital (see note on section 619) at the time of giving notice of the cancellation.

Section 664: Re-registration as private company in consequence of cancellation

983.   This section replaces section 147(2) and (3) of the 1985 Act. These provisions have been updated to reflect the fact that in future it will not be possible to alter the memorandum and that key information of a type which was previously in the memorandum will now be in the articles (see note on section 8). The resolution to re-register as a private company in consequence of a duty to cancel shares will however still need to be filed with the registrar under Chapter 3 of Part 3 of the Act.

984.   There is also a new requirement, in subsection (3), for the application for re-registration to be accompanied by a statement of the company's proposed name on re-registration, Subsections (5) and (6) are also new. Consistent with the approach taken where a company is formed as a private company under the Act (see section 9), where a public company applies to re-register as private under this section the application for re-registration must be accompanied by a statement of compliance (see note on section 13).

Section 665: Issue of certificate of incorporation on re-registration

985.   This section replaces section 147(4)(a) of the 1985 Act and restates section 147(4) and (4)(b) of that Act. As with the previous section, the provision has been updated to reflect the fact that in future companies will not be capable of, and will not need to, alter their memoranda. Subsection (3) is new. Consistent with the approach taken in Part 7 of the Act, a certificate of incorporation issued on the re-registration of a company under section 664 will need to specify that it is being issued on the re-registration of the company and the date on which it is issued.

Chapter 2: Financial Assistance For Purchase Of Own Shares

986.   The following sections replace Chapter 6 of Part 5 of the 1985 Act which contains a prohibition on the giving of financial assistance (broadly defined) by a company or any of its subsidiaries for the purpose of the acquisition of shares in itself. There are exceptions which apply to all companies, contained in section 153 of the 1985 Act, and a relaxation of the general rule for private companies in sections 155 to 158 of that Act.

987.   As recommended by the CLR (Final Report, paragraph 10.6), the Act abolishes the prohibition on private companies giving financial assistance for a purchase of own shares and, as a consequence, the relaxation for private companies (sometimes referred to as the "whitewash" procedure) is no longer required. The provisions in sections 155 to 158 have therefore been repealed and are not carried forward in the Act.

Section 678: Assistance for acquisition of shares in public company

988.   This section replaces section 151(1) and (2) of the 1985 Act and restates section 153(1) and (2) of that Act. The key change is that the prohibition on private companies providing financial assistance for a purchase of own shares is not carried forward.

989.   The general prohibition on the giving of financial assistance by a public company is required by the Second Company Law Directive (77/91/EEC) and this prohibition is retained in subsection (1). As under the current law, the prohibition extends to post-acquisition assistance (see subsection (3)).

990.   The prohibition on the giving of post-acquisition assistance only applies if the company in which the shares were acquired is a public company at the time that the assistance is given (see subsection (3)). It follows that where a company has re-registered as a private company since the shares were acquired and is a private company at the time the post-acquisition assistance is given, the prohibition in this section will not apply. However, if at the time the shares were acquired the company was a private company, but at the time the post-acquisition assistance is given it has re-registered as a public company, the prohibition will apply.

991.   The provisions of section 153(1) and (2) of the 1985 Act are retained in subsections (2) and (4) which carry forward the current exemption from the prohibition on the giving of financial assistance: namely, that such assistance is not prohibited if the principal purpose of the assistance is not to give it for the purpose of an acquisition of shares, or where this assistance is incidental to some other larger purpose of the company and (in either case) where the assistance is given in good faith in the interests of the company. As now, in these circumstances no offence is committed by the company or its officers (see section 680). The changes introduced by section 678 also give statutory effect to the decision in *Arab Bank plc v Mercantile Holdings Ltd* [1994] 2 All ER 74: namely, that the statutory prohibition on a company giving financial assistance for the purpose of acquiring its own shares or shares in its holding company does not apply to the giving of assistance by a subsidiary incorporated in an overseas jurisdiction.

992.   In the Arab Bank case, Millett J considered the geographical scope of section 151 of the 1985 Act and concluded that this had inadvertently been altered during the consolidation of UK companies legislation in 1985. In particular, the 1985 Act appears to go further than the 1980 Act and, in interpreting the current provision, Millett J applied the presumption that, in the absence of a contrary intention, section 151 could not have extra-territorial effect. The difficulty with the 1985 Act provision arises as a result of how the prohibition is framed: in particular, the prohibition applies "*to the company or any of its subsidiaries*" and "subsidiary", as defined in section 736 of the 1985 Act, includes foreign companies. The prohibition in the Act is restricted to UK public companies and their UK subsidiaries as a result of the definition of "company" in section 1. Subsection (1) of that section makes it clear that, unless the context otherwise requires, "company" means a company which is formed and registered under the Act or a former UK Companies Act.

Section 679: Assistance by public company for acquisition of shares in its private holding company

993.   This section replaces sections 151(1) and (2) and 153(1) and (2) of the 1985 Act.

994.   Like section 678 this section does not carry forward the prohibition on private companies providing financial assistance for a purchase of own shares, but the current prohibition on the giving of financial assistance by a public company subsidiary for the purpose of an acquisition of shares in its private holding company is retained. Section 679 also retains the prohibition on the giving of post-acquisition assistance by a public company subsidiary.

Chapter 3: Redeemable Shares

995.   Under section 159 of the 1985 Act a company that is limited by shares, or limited by guarantee and having a share capital, may, if authorised to do so by its articles, issue shares which may be redeemed at a future point in time at the option of the company or the shareholder. The provisions of section 159 are carried forward in the following sections but there are changes to the ways in which companies may issue redeemable shares and redeem such shares (see below).

Section 684: Power of limited company to issue redeemable shares

996.   This section replaces section 159(1) of the 1985 Act and restates section 159(2) of that Act.

997.   For private companies only, it removes the requirement for prior authorisation in the company's articles for a proposed allotment of redeemable shares. If they wish, the members may, however, restrict or prohibit the authority given to a company by this section, by including a provision to this effect in the company's articles (see subsection (2)).

Section 685: Terms and manner of redemption

998.   This replaces section 160(3) of the 1985 Act (which provides that the terms and manner of redemption must be set out in the company's articles) and existing section 159A (also entitled "terms and manner of redemption"), which was inserted into the 1985 Act by section 133 of the Companies Act 1989 and remains uncommenced.

999.   As recommended by the CLR (Final Report, paragraph 4.5), this section enables the directors of both private and public companies alike to determine the terms, conditions and manner of a redemption of redeemable shares. The power conferred on the directors by this section requires prior authorisation by the company's members, either by resolution of the company or through the articles (see subsection (1)). As recommended by the CLR (Final Report, paragraph 7.30) the terms and conditions of redemption will have to be stated in the statement of capital required to be filed under section 555. If the directors are not authorised to set the terms of the redemption, then they must be set out in the company's articles (see subsection (4)).

1000.   Where the directors exercise this power they must do so before the shares in question are allotted (see subsection (3)).

Section 686: Payment for redeemable shares

1001.   This section replaces section 159(3) of the 1985 Act (which requires that where a company issues redeemable shares, the terms of redemption must provide for payment on redemption). It removes the current requirement, in section 159(3), that the terms of redemption must provide for payment on redemption. This means that the terms of redemption may provide for the company and the holder of the shares to agree that payment may be made on a date later than the redemption date.

Section 688: Redeemed shares treated as cancelled

1002.   This section restates section 160(4) of the 1985 Act but with the exception of the reference to the impact of the redemption on the authorised share capital of the company – the concept of which is not replicated under the Act.

Section 689: Notice to registrar of redemption

1003.   This section restates section 122(1)(e) and 122(2) of the 1985 Act and Schedule 24 to that Act but there is a new requirement for a statement of capital where a company gives notice to the registrar of a redemption of redeemable shares (see subsections (2) and (3) and the note on section 619).

Chapter 4: Purchase Of Own Shares

1004.   Section 162 of the 1985 Act enables a company limited by shares or limited by guarantee and having a share capital to purchase its own shares, provided it is authorised to do so by the articles. It is common for the members to give authority for such a purchase of own shares through the articles, see, for example, regulation 35 of the Companies Act 1985, Table A.

Section 690: Power of limited company to purchase own shares

1005.   This section replaces section 162(1) of the 1985 Act and restates section 162(3) of that Act.

1006.   In line with the recommendations of the CLR (Completing the Structure, paragraph 2.15), section 690 removes the requirement for prior authorisation in a company's articles for a purchase of own shares (including any redeemable shares) by the company but makes it clear that, if they wish, the members may restrict or prohibit a purchase of own shares by including a provision to this effect in the company's articles.

Section 692: Financing of purchase of own shares

1007.   This section restates, the provisions of section 160(1) and (2) and 162(2) of the 1985 Act on a redemption of own shares which are applicable to a purchase of own shares, and makes such adaptations to those provisions as are necessary to ensure that the restated provisions work in this context.

Section 694: Authority for off-market purchase

1008.   This section replaces sections 164(2) and 165(2) of the 1985 Act and restates sections 164(1), (3) and (4) and 165(1) of that Act.

1009.   Under the 1985 Act a company may only enter into a contract for an off-market purchase of shares if the shareholders approve the contract by special resolution before the contract is entered into. An off-market purchase of shares is a purchase that is not conducted through a recognised investment exchange (for example, the London Stock Market).

1010.   Section 694 enables a company to enter into a contract for an off-market purchase of its own shares conditional on the contract being approved by the shareholders. This will save companies valuable time as it will be possible for the directors to negotiate and agree the terms of a contract for an off-market purchase of shares ahead of seeking shareholder approval. If, however, the shareholders do not subsequently pass a special resolution approving the contract, the company may not purchase the shares in question and the contract will lapse.

Section 702: Copy of contract or memorandum to be available for inspection

1011.   This section replaces section 169(4) and (9) of the 1985 Act. Under the 1985 Act, where a company enters into a contract for a purchase of own shares it must make available for inspection a copy of the relevant contract or a memorandum of its terms at the company's registered office for a period of 10 years. Subsection (4) alters the current requirements by providing that the contract may, alternatively, be kept available for inspection at a place specified in regulations made under section 1136. If the company is a private company, the contract must be available for inspection by any of its members; otherwise it must be open to inspection by anyone. If default is made an offence is committed by the company and every officer in default.

1012. Subsection (5) is a new provision which requires companies to give notice to the registrar of the place where the contract is kept available for inspection. This is consequential on the choice conferred on companies under subsection (4) as to where such documents are kept.

Section 703: Enforcement of right to inspect copy or memorandum

1013. This section replaces section 169(7) of the 1985 Act and Schedule 24 to that Act. It retains the existing offences for failing to keep available/allow inspection of the contract/memorandum as required under section 702, but with the addition of a new offence for failure to notify the registrar of the place where such documentation is kept. It also restates section 169(8) of the 1985 Act.

Section 707: Return to registrar of purchase of own shares

1014. This section replaces section 169(1), (1A) and (1B) and restates section 169(2), (3) and (6) of the 1985 Act and Schedule 24 to that Act. It requires a company to make a return to the registrar within 28 days of a purchase of own shares stating, amongst other things, the number and nominal value of the shares purchased. The return must indicate whether the shares are of a type which could be held in treasury (see section 724), and, if so, whether the shares were cancelled forthwith or whether they are being held in treasury.

Section 708: Notice to registrar of cancellation of shares

1015. This section replaces sections 169(1), (1A) and (1B) and restates 169(6) of the 1985 Act and Schedule 24 to that Act. It updates the notice requirements so as to require that where shares are cancelled forthwith following a purchase (either in circumstances where the shares are treated as automatically cancelled or where treasury shares are cancelled) the company has to notify the registrar of such cancellation and provide the registrar with a statement of capital (see note on section 619).

1016. As now, where a company fails to comply with the procedural requirements as to notice, the company, and every officer of the company who is in default, commits an offence (see subsection (4)).

Chapter 5: Redemption Or Purchase By Private Company Out Of Capital

1017. Sections 171 to 177 of the 1985 Act provide a statutory scheme for the redemption or purchase of own shares out of capital. This scheme is available to private companies only and the facility to redeem or purchase shares out of capital is carried forward in the following sections.

Section 709: Power of private limited company to redeem or purchase own shares out of capital

1018. This section replaces section 171(1) of the 1985 Act and restates section 171(2) of that Act. It removes the current requirement for prior authorisation in the articles where a private company makes a payment out of capital in respect of a redemption or purchase of its own shares. If they wish, the members may, however, restrict or prohibit such a payment by including a provision to this effect in the company's articles.

Section 714: Directors' statement and auditor's report

1019. This section replaces section 173(3) to (5) of the 1985 Act.

1020. Currently, before a private company may make a payment out of capital in respect of a purchase of own shares, the directors must have made a full enquiry into the affairs and prospects of the company and are required, under section 173, to make a statutory declaration confirming that: as regards the company's situation immediately after the date on which the payment out of capital is made, there will be no grounds on which the company could then be found unable to pay its debts; and as regards the company's prospects for the year immediately following that date, the company will be able to continue to carry on business as a going concern and be able to pay its debts as they fall due in the year immediately following the date on which the payment out of capital is made. In forming their opinion on the company's solvency and prospects, the directors must take into account the same liabilities (including contingent and prospective liabilities) as would be relevant under section 122 of the Insolvency Act 1986 (winding up by the court) to the question whether a company is unable to pay its debts.

1021. Consistent with the approach taken in respect of reductions of capital using the new solvency statement procedure (see sections 642 and 643 and in particular subsection (2) of section 643), this section requires a private company limited by shares that wishes to use this statutory scheme for a purchase or redemption of shares to take account of all contingent and prospective liabilities, not just those that are relevant for the purposes of section 122 of the Insolvency Act 1986 (see subsection (4)).

Part 3   CA 2006 Supporting Materials

1022.   Again, to achieve consistency with the approach taken elsewhere in the Act, the current requirement for a statutory declaration is replaced with a requirement for a simple statement. In contrast to a statutory declaration, the directors' statement does not need to be sworn before a solicitor or Commissioner of Oaths.

Section 715: Directors' statement: offence if no reasonable grounds for opinion

1023.   This section restates section 173(6) of the 1985 Act and Schedule 24 to that Act (but substitutes the reference to "declaration" with "statement"). The offence that is currently contained in subsection (6) of section 173 (offence of making declaration without reasonable grounds) is replaced with an offence of making a statement under section 714 without having reasonable grounds for the opinion expressed in it. As now, the offence is committed by every director of the company who is in default.

Section 720: Directors' statement and auditor's report to be available for inspection

1024.   This section replaces section 175(6)(a) and (7) and restates section 175(4), (6)(b), and (8) of the 1985 Act and Schedule 24 to that Act. Subsection (2) alters the current requirement, contained in section 175(6)(a), by providing that the directors' statement and auditor's report may, alternatively, be kept available for inspection at a place specified in regulations made under section 1136. There is a new requirement (in subsection (3)) for the company to give notice to the registrar of the place where the statement and report are kept available for inspection and of any change to that place. This change is consequential on the change introduced by subsection (2).

1025.   Subsection (5) provides that if the company fails to give such notice to the registrar within 14 days or an inspection of the statement and report are refused, the company and every officer in default commit an offence.

Chapter 6: Treasury Shares

1026.   Where a company buys back its own shares, it is normally required to cancel those shares. Certain companies (principally those which are listed or those which are traded on the Alternative Investment Market and equivalent companies in the EEA) may elect not to cancel shares which have been bought back but may hold the shares "in treasury". A share which is held in treasury may be sold at a future point in time and this facility enables such companies to raise capital more quickly than they would otherwise be able to, as the directors do not have to obtain prior authority from the company's members before selling treasury shares.

Section 727: Treasury shares: disposal

1027.   This section replaces section 162D(2) of the 1985 Act and restates section 162D(1)(a) and (b) and 162D(3) of that Act. It defines (in subsection (2)) what is meant by "cash consideration" where treasury shares are sold and this mirrors, in part, the definition in section 583 (which restates section 738(2) to (4) of the 1985 Act and defines when a share is deemed to be paid up or allotted for cash).

1028.   Subsections (2)(e), (3) and (5) are new. They enable the Secretary of State to specify, by order, what, in addition to the items specifically referred to in subsection (2), constitutes "cash consideration" for the purposes of subsection (1)(a).

1029.   The power to make further provision in respect of what constitutes "cash consideration" for the purposes of a sale of treasury shares (that is, in addition to those already specified in subsection (2)) is intended to remove uncertainties surrounding other methods of settlement, for example, the CREST settlement system (see note on section 583) and will also act as a future proofing mechanism in the event that new methods of settlement are developed or identified.

Section 730: Treasury shares: notice of cancellation

1030.   This section restates sections 169A(1)(b)(i), (2) to (4) of the 1985 Act and Schedule 24 to that Act. As now, where a company cancels shares which it has held in treasury it is required to give notice of this to the registrar within 28 days of the cancellation. The provision has, however, been updated to require companies to file a statement of capital in these circumstances (see note on section 619).

Section 732: Treasury shares: offences

1031.   This section replaces section 162G of the 1985 Act. It renders both the company and every officer in default liable to an offence for any contravention of the provisions of this Chapter.

Section 737: General power to make further provision by regulations

1032.   This section is a new provision which enables the Secretary of State, by regulations, to modify the provisions of Part 18 (see subsection (1)).

1033.   Regulations made under this section may amend or repeal any of the provisions in this Part or make such other provision as appears to the Secretary of State appropriate in place of those provisions.

1034. The power to make regulations in this section will enable the Secretary of State to "future-proof" the provisions in Part 18 – which are primarily concerned with the maintenance of capital. This is desirable as many of these provisions are derived from EU law and may require amendment in the relatively near future (subject in part to the outcome of a fundamental study into alternatives to the current capital maintenance regime which is being carried out at EU level).

1035. Regulations made pursuant to the power in this section are subject to the affirmative resolution procedure, which means that they must be approved by both Houses of Parliament.

PART 19: DEBENTURES

[3.20]

1036. This part restates the provisions of the 1985 Act relating to debentures. Sections 738–740, 742 and 749–754 make no change to the law.

Section 741: Registration of allotment of debentures

1037. This is a new section which obliges a company to register an allotment of debentures as soon as practicable, but in any event within two months after their allotment. It completes the picture as regards the existing requirement in section 185(1) of the 1985 Act (which is restated in section 769(1)) which obliges a company to complete and deliver certificates for debentures within two months after their allotment.

Section 743: Register of debenture holders

1038. This section replaces section 190 of the 1985 Act. There is no requirement for a company to keep a register of debenture holders but if such a register is kept, then it (or any duplicate) must be kept available for inspection at either the company's registered office or a place permitted under regulations made under section 1136. (This is the same as for the obligatory registers of members, see section 114.)

Section 744: Register of debenture holders: right to inspect and require copy

1039. This section replaces part of section 191 of the 1985 Act. It modifies the existing right of public access to any register of debenture holders kept by a company. The changes mirror similar requirements in Part 8 relating to the register of members. Subsections (3) and (4) require those seeking to inspect or to be provided with a copy of the register to provide their names and addresses, the purpose for which the information will be used, and, if the access is sought on behalf of others, similar information for them.

Section 745: Register of debenture holders: response to request for inspection or copy

1040. This is a new provision. It provides a procedure by which the company can refer the matter to the court if it considers the request is not for a proper purpose. It specifies a 5-day period within which the company must either comply with the request or apply to the court for relief from the obligation. If the company opts for the latter, then subsections (3), (4) and (5) apply. Under subsection (3), if the court is satisfied that the access to the register of debenture holders is not sought for a proper purpose, it will require the company not to comply with the obligation to meet the request and may require that the person who made the request pay the company's costs. Under subsection (4), the court may also require the company not to comply with other requests made for similar purposes. If the court does not make an order under subsection (3), or the proceedings are discontinued, then, under subsection (5), the company must immediately comply with the request.

Section 746: Register of debenture holders: refusal of inspection or default in providing copy

1041. This section retains the existing sanctions under section 191 of the 1985 Act for failure to comply with a request. They do not apply if the court has directed that the company need not comply with the request.

Section 747: Register of debenture holders: offences in connection with request for or disclosure of information

1042. This is a new provision. It creates two offences. First, in relation to the new requirement in section 744 to provide information in a request for access, it is an offence knowingly or recklessly to make a statement that is misleading, false or deceptive in a material particular. Second, it is an offence for a person having obtained information pursuant to an exercise of the rights in section 744 to do anything or fail to do anything which results in that information being disclosed to another person knowing or having reason to suspect that the other person may use the information for a purpose that is not a proper purpose.

Section 748: Time limit for claims arising from entry in register

1043. This section replaces section 191(7) of the 1985 Act. It amends the existing time limit for claims arising from errors in the register from twenty years to ten years. This mirrors equivalent provisions applicable to the register of members (see section 128).

PART 20: PRIVATE AND PUBLIC COMPANIES

[3.21]

1044. The provisions of this Part set out the two major differences between public and private companies.

1045. Chapter 1 replaces sections 58(3), 81 and 742A of the 1985 Act which provide that private companies are not allowed to offer their shares to the public.

1046. Chapter 2 replaces sections 117 and 118 of the 1985 Act which deal with the minimum share capital requirement for public companies (known as the "authorised minimum"). It contains new provisions that enable this requirement to be satisfied in euros as well as sterling. To facilitate this change it has been necessary to seek two new powers:—

(a)   a power to prescribe the amount in euros that is to be treated as equivalent to the sterling amount of the authorised minimum (see section 763); and

(b)   a power to prescribe how references to the authorised minimum in the Act are to be applied where a public company has shares denominated in more than one currency or redenominates its share capital (that is, converts its share capital from one currency to another) and to require that a company must re-register as a private company where the effect of redenomination is to bring the value of the company's share capital below the authorised minimum (see section 766).

1047. The authorised minimum is relevant to all public companies, not just those that are incorporated as such, see for example, section 91.

Chapter 1: Prohibition Of Public Offers By Private Companies

1048. The CLR considered the prohibition on private companies offering their shares to the public in paragraph 4.160 of Developing the Framework and then examined the dividing line between public and private companies in Chapter 2 of Completing the Structure. The CLR presented their conclusions in paragraphs 4.54 to 4.62 of the Final Report.

Section 755: Prohibition of public offers by private company

1049. Subsection (1) of this section continues the prohibition in section 81(1) of the 1985 Act on private companies offering their shares or debentures to the public, though the consequences of breaching the prohibition are changed. The prohibition applies only to private companies limited by shares or limited by guarantee and having a share capital. The prohibition does not apply to unlimited companies or to companies limited by guarantee and not having a share capital.

1050. Private companies are also prohibited from allotting their shares or debentures with the intention that they are offered to the public by someone else. Subsection (2) creates a presumption as to when shares or debentures have been allotted in this way. Similar provision was made in section 58(3) of the 1985 Act which this subsection replaces.

1051. A private company will no longer commit an offence if it offers its securities to the public. Instead, if a private company does breach the prohibition it will be compelled to reregister as a public company, unless it appears to the court that the company does not meet the requirements for re-registration and that it is impractical or undesirable to require it to take steps to do so, in which case the court may make a remedial order and/or an order for the compulsory winding up of the company.

1052. Subsection (3) contains an exemption to the prohibition on public offers. Where a private company intends to become a public company it will be able to make an offer before it has completed the formalities of re-registration as a public company. Acts done in good faith before allotment in anticipation of re-registration will not be treated as breaching the prohibition on offers to the public, even if the re-registration arrangements do not ultimately succeed. The exemption also applies if, as part of the terms of the offer, the company undertakes to re-register as a public company and then complies with that undertaking not later than 6 months after the day on which the offer is first made to the public.

Section 756: Meaning of "offer to the public"

1053. This section explains what is meant by "offer to the public" for the purposes of the prohibition on public offers contained in section 755. This section also sets out certain circumstances where an offer is not to be regarded as an offer to the public. It replaces section 742A of the 1985 Act.

1054. An offer will not be an offer to the public if it is not calculated to result in shares or debentures of the company becoming available to anyone other than those receiving the offer. An example would be where shares are offered to a particular person, with the intention that no one other than that particular person may take up the offer or acquire the shares as a result. Nor will an offer be an offer to the public if the offer is otherwise a private concern of the person receiving it and the person making it.

1055. Subsection (4) creates two further exemptions for offers to persons already connected with the company (as defined in subsection (5)) and for offers in respect of securities to be held under an employees' share scheme (as defined in section 1166). Such offers are presumed to be the private concern of those involved and so not an offer to the public if the conditions set out in subsection (4) are met.

1056.   The range of persons already connected with the company for the purposes of subsection (4) has been expanded slightly from the current provision in section 742A of the 1985 Act. Subsection (5) now includes a trustee of a trust where the principal beneficiary is an existing debenture holder of the company or the widow or widower, or surviving civil partner of a person who was a member or employee of the company.

1057.   Subsection (6) explains what is meant by a member of a person's family for the purposes of subsection (5).

Section 757: Enforcement of prohibition: order restraining proposed contravention

1058.   This section enables members, creditors or the Secretary of State to apply to the court for an order restraining a private company from carrying out any proposed contravention of the prohibition on offering shares or debentures to the public. This is a new procedure which will enable the member, the creditor or the Secretary of State to prevent by civil action any further activity by the company towards making an offer in contravention of the public offer prohibition. The court must also make such an order if, in proceedings brought by a member under section 994 or by the Secretary of State under section 995, it appears to the court that the company is proposing to breach the public offer prohibition.

Section 758: Enforcement of prohibition: orders available to the court after contravention

1059.   This section applies where a private company breaches the prohibition on offering securities to the public. It introduces a new enforcement procedure for breaches; it replaces the criminal offence currently imposed in section 81 of the 1985 Act with a civil enforcement procedure.

1060.   If a company breaches the prohibition, certain members, certain creditors or the Secretary of State may apply to the court. In order to have standing to bring the application, the member or creditor must have been a member or a creditor at the time the offer was made in contravention of the public offer prohibition; in addition anyone who became a member as a result of the offer to the public may bring an application.

1061.   On such an application, if the court decides the company has acted in contravention of the public offer prohibition then it must order the re-registration of the company as a public company, unless it appears to the court that the company does not meet the requirements for re-registration as a public company (see Part 7 of the Act), and it is impracticable or undesirable to require it to take steps to do so. If the court is unable to order re-registration for these reasons, it may instead make a remedial order or an order for the compulsory winding up of the company (see Chapter 6 of Part 4 of the Insolvency Act 1986). The court has discretion as to whether or not to make these orders. This might be appropriate for example where the company has breached the prohibition but has not allotted shares, and has withdrawn the offer and undertaken not to do it again.

Section 759: Enforcement of prohibition: remedial order

1062.   A remedial order is an order for the purpose of putting anyone affected by the breach of the public offer prohibition back in the position they would have been in if the breach had not occurred. It may require any person knowingly concerned in the contravention, whether or not an officer of the company, to offer to purchase the shares or debentures that were the subject of the offer on such terms as the court thinks fit. The remedial order will override the terms of the company's constitution, but no one holding the securities will be obliged to accept the offer made to purchase them. It may be made whether or not the holder of the securities subject to the order is the person to whom the company allotted or agreed to allot them.

Section 760: Validity of allotment etc not affected

1063.   This section makes clear that any allotment or sale of securities or any agreement to allot or sell securities is not made void simply because there has been a breach of the prohibition on offers to the public. Equivalent provision was made in section 81(3) of the 1985 Act.

Chapter 2: Minimum Share Capital Requirement For Public Companies

1064.   Under the 1985 Act, a public company which is incorporated as such may not do business without first obtaining a trading certificate from the registrar. There is a minimum allotted share capital requirement, known as the "authorised minimum", which is currently set at £50,000 and which must be denominated in sterling. The same minimum share capital requirement applies where a private company re-registers as a public company under Part 7 of the Act.

1065.   If a public company reduces its share capital below the authorised minimum it will no longer meet the minimum share capital requirement for a public company and must reregister as a private company.

1066.   The requirement for public companies to have a minimum share capital is derived from EU law. Article 6 of the Second Company Law Directive (77/91/EEC) provides that:

"The laws of member states shall require that in order that a company may be incorporated or obtain authorisation to commence business, a minimum share capital shall be subscribed the amount of which shall not be less than 25,000 euros."

1067. The Department's interpretation of this Directive is that it permits the authorised minimum to be denominated in euros, or the national currency of the Member State, but not in other currencies (so for example, the authorised minimum could not be satisfied in dollars).

1068. When this requirement was implemented in the Companies Act 1980 the amount of the authorised minimum was set at £50,000 (a figure considerably higher than the minimum required under the Directive). The CLR considered whether the authorised minimum should be maintained, increased or reduced. Their recommendation was to maintain it at £50,000.

Section 761: Public company: requirement as to minimum share capital

1069. This section replaces section 117(2) of the 1985 Act and restates section 117(1), (4) and (6) of that Act. Like the provisions of the 1985 Act, it only applies to public companies that are formed as such on their original incorporation (as opposed to companies that reregister from private limited to public under the provisions of Part 7 of the Act).

1070. The current requirement for a statutory declaration to be filed with an application for a trading certificate, contained in section 117(2) of the 1985 Act, has not been carried forward. This is replaced by a requirement for a statement of compliance (see section 762 and the note on section 13).

1071. As now, the registrar will only issue a trading certificate if she is satisfied that certain conditions are met: in particular the company must satisfy the minimum share capital requirement for public companies – known as the "authorised minimum" (see subsection (2)).

1072. A trading certificate has effect from the date that it is issued and is conclusive evidence that the company is entitled to do business as a public company.

Section 762: Procedure for obtaining certificate

1073. This section replaces section 117(3) of the 1985 Act. It prescribes the contents of the application for a trading certificate (see subsection (1)), which, amongst other things, must include a statement that the nominal value of the company's share capital is not less than the authorised minimum.

1074. The current requirement for a statutory declaration (or "electronic statement") when an application is made for a trading certificate is replaced by a requirement to make a statement of compliance. This statement does not need to be witnessed and may be made in paper or electronic form. It will be for the registrar's rules to specify who may make this statement (and the form of it).

Section 763: The authorised minimum

1075. This section replaces section 118(1) of the 1985 Act. Under section 118 the authorised minimum is £50,000. This implements Article 6 of the Second Company Law Directive which requires that in order that a public company may be incorporated or obtain authorisation to commence business, a minimum capital shall be subscribed (see above). As recommended by the CLR (Completing the Structure, paragraph 7.6), this section retains the authorised minimum at £50,000. In contrast to the 1985 Act provisions, the section also enables the minimum share capital requirement for public companies to be satisfied in sterling or the prescribed euro equivalent (see subsection (1)).

1076. Once a company has obtained a trading certificate under section 762 or section 117 of the 1985 Act (in the case of companies that obtain a trading certificate before these provisions of the Act come into force), there is no requirement for the authorised minimum to remain denominated in sterling or euro, and if it wishes a public company may subsequently redenominate all of its share capital (including the authorised minimum) under the provisions of Chapter 8 of Part 17 of the Act (which contains new provisions which permit companies easily to redenominate or convert their share capital from one currency to another).

1077. Subsection (2) of section 763 contains a new power which enables the Secretary of State, in regulations made under the Act, to prescribe the amount in euros that is for the time being to be treated as equivalent to the sterling amount of the authorised minimum. This is required in order to achieve parity between the prescribed sterling and euro amounts (which may become necessary due to exchange rate fluctuations). The amount prescribed will be determined by applying an appropriate spot rate of exchange to the prescribed sterling amount and rounding to the nearest 100 euros (see subsection (4)).

1078. The power to alter the authorised minimum, contained in section 118 of the 1985 Act, is carried forward in section 764.

Section 764: Power to alter authorised minimum

1079. This section replaces section 118(1) of the 1985 Act and restates section 118(2) and (3) of that Act. The power to alter the authorised minimum, contained in section 118, is carried forward but this has been updated to reflect the fact that in future companies will be able to satisfy the authorised minimum in sterling or the prescribed euro equivalent of the sterling amount (see section 763).

1080. Section 764 also contains a new provision which enables the Secretary of State, in regulations made under the Act, to alter both the sterling amount of the authorised minimum and to make a corresponding alteration to the prescribed euro equivalent (which is to be determined by applying an appropriate spot rate of exchange to the sterling amount and rounding up to the nearest 100 euros – see subsection (2)).

1081. As now, the power in this section will enable the Secretary of State to alter the sterling amount of the authorised minimum, for example from £50,000 to £60,000, (and the prescribed euro equivalent) should it become necessary to do so (for example, because of changes to the prescribed minimum capital requirement for public companies at EU level) or desirable (for example, if it was considered appropriate for business reasons to raise or lower the minimum share capital requirement for public companies within the limits permitted by the Second Company Law Directive).

Section 765: Authorised minimum: application of initial requirement

1082. This section is a new provision which prescribes how the authorised minimum is to be met. Subsection (1) makes it clear that the authorised minimum may be satisfied by reference to allotted share capital denominated in sterling or euros (but not a combination of both).

1083. Where a company has allotted sterling and euro shares, the question of whether the authorised minimum has been satisfied will be determined firstly by reference to the total sterling amount of the company's allotted share capital and then by reference to the company's euros shares (see subsection (2)). To take an example, if a company has allotted sterling shares to the total value of £25,000 and euro shares to the equivalent of £60,000, the authorised minimum will have been satisfied in euros. If the same company had allotted sterling shares to the total value of £10,000 and euro shares to the equivalent of £40,000 it would not have satisfied the minimum share capital requirement for a public company as the authorised minimum may be satisfied in sterling or euro but not partly in sterling and partly in euro.

Section 766: Authorised minimum: application where shares denominated in different currencies etc

1084. This section is a new provision which enables the Secretary of State to prescribe, in regulations made under the Act, how references to the authorised minimum are to be applied where a public company has its share capital denominated in more than one currency, or where it redenominates (converts) its share capital from one currency to another (see section 622).

1085. There are various provisions in the Act (for example where a public company applies to court to reduce its share capital) which provide that a company must re-register as a private company where the nominal value of its allotted share capital falls below the authorised minimum. It is therefore necessary to make provision for how references to the authorised minimum in the Act are to be applied where a public company has its shares denominated in different currencies, or currencies other than those in which the authorised minimum may be satisfied, and to require that a company must re-register as a private company where the effect of a redenomination of its share capital is to bring the value of the company's share capital below the authorised minimum.

1086. To take an extreme example, the type of scenario that the power in this section is intended for is the situation where a public company incorporates with a share capital of £50,000 (expressed in sterling), allots additional dollar shares, subsequently redenominates part of its share capital into euros and then applies to the court to reduce its share capital. It will be necessary in such circumstances to determine what test should be applied to ascertain whether the company's allotted share capital has fallen below the authorised minimum (in other words what exchange rates must be applied, as at what date they should be applied and as between what currencies). Regulations made pursuant to this section will need to deal with this type of issue. They will be subject to the negative resolution procedure due to their highly technical nature.

Section 767: Consequences of doing business etc without a trading certificate

1087. This section restates section 117 (7) and (8) of and Schedule 24 to the 1985 Act.

1088. As now, where a public company which is required to have a trading certificate enters into a transaction without first obtaining such a certificate, the directors are jointly and severally liable for any loss or damage caused to the other party to the transaction as a result of the company failing to meet its obligations. A director will only be jointly and severally liable with the company if he was a director at the time that the transaction was entered into and if the company has failed to meet its obligations under the transaction in question within 21 days of being called on to do so (see subsection (3)).

1089. Notwithstanding the fact that the company should not have entered into the transaction, the transaction itself is valid.

1090. Where a public company that is formed under this section, or under section 117 of the 1985 Act, has not obtained a trading certificate within a year of its incorporation, it may be wound up by the court (see section 122(1)(b) of the Insolvency Act 1986).

PART 21: CERTIFICATION AND TRANSFER OF SECURITIES

Chapter 1: Certification And Transfer Of Securities: General

[3.22]

1091. Sections 768 to 770, 772 to 779 and 781 to 782 in this Chapter restate the provisions in Part 5 of the 1985 Act (sections 183 to 189) relating to the certification and transfer of shares and other securities.

Section 771: Procedure on transfer being lodged

1092. Under section 183(5) of the 1985 Act, if a company refuses to register a transfer of shares (or debentures), it must, within two months of receipt of the transfer, send to the transferee notice of its refusal to register the transfer of shares. Such a refusal will not affect the transferee's beneficial interest in a share, for example, he will still be entitled to any dividend declared on that share, and a return of capital on winding-up, but the transferee will not be able to exercise all of the rights of a member of the company, for example, he may not vote at meetings, until such time as the transfer is registered and his name is entered in the register of members.

1093. Section 771 is a new provision which amends the law on the registration of transfers. As recommended by the CLR, it requires the directors to either register a transfer of shares or debentures or provide the transferee with reasons for their refusal to register (see Final Report, paragraphs 7.44 and 7.45).

1094. In either case, this must be done as soon as practicable, but in any event within two months of the transfer being lodged with the company.

1095. Under subsection (2), where the directors refuse to register the transfer of a share, the transferee is entitled to receive such information as he may reasonably require regarding the reasons for the directors' refusal to register the transfer. Such information does not extend to minutes of meetings of the directors.

1096. Where a company fails to comply with this section, the company and every officer of the company who is in default commits an offence (see subsection (3)).

1097. Subsection (5) makes it clear that this section does not apply to a transfer of shares if the company has issued a share warrant in respect of the shares under section 779 or in relation to a transmission of shares by operation of the law (for example, where a bankrupt member's trustee in bankruptcy or a deceased member's personal representative becomes entitled to shares).

Section 780: Duty of company as to issue of certificates on surrender of share warrant

1098. This provision is new and makes it clear that a company must issue a share certificate where a share warrant is subsequently surrendered for cancellation. It gives a company two months from the date of surrender to complete and have ready for delivery a certificate of the shares specified in the warrant and failure to do so is a criminal offence (see subsection (3)). This requirement is subject to any contrary provisions in the company's articles, which may give the company more or less time to deliver such certificates to the transferee (see subsection (2)).

Chapter 2: Evidencing And Transfer Of Title To Securities Without Written Instrument

1099. This Chapter replaces the existing power under section 207 of the 1989 Act relating to transfer of securities without a written instrument but goes beyond it in that it can be used to require, as well as to permit, the paper-free holding and transfer of shares or other securities. The provisions that make changes to the power are in sections 784, 786, 787 and 789.

Section 784: Power to make regulations

1100. This section provides for the power to make regulations about the transfer of title to securities without written instrument to be exercisable by the Secretary of State or the Treasury. Responsibility for section 207 of the 1989 Act and the regulations made under it passed from the Department of Trade and Industry to HM Treasury by virtue of article 2(1) of the Transfer of Functions (Financial Services) Order 1992 (SI 1992/1315) as part of a general transfer of responsibility for financial services matters. Dual responsibility is considered more appropriate for the making of regulations under the new power as the extension of paperless holding and transfer to new classes of shares or other securities involve matters which are part of company law. Exercise of the power will continue to be subject to the affirmative procedure.

Section 786: Provision enabling or requiring arrangements to be adopted

1101. This section provides that regulations under this Chapter may require, as well as permit, the paper-free holding and transfer of securities. The effect of subsections (1) and (2) is that regulations made under section 207 may:

- enable members of companies, or of designated classes of company, by ordinary resolution, to adopt a new form of paperless holding and transfer of shares and abandon paper-based forms of holding and transfer in relation to all existing and new securities of that company, or to specified types of securities; or

- make the adoption of a form of paperless transfer and the abandonment of paper-based forms of transfer mandatory for all securities, or specified types of securities, issued by companies generally or by designated classes of company.

1102.   Regulations do not need to make it obligatory both to hold and to transfer securities in a paper-free way: the new arrangements could relate just to holding or just to transfer.

1103.   Subsection (3) is designed to protect the right of individual investors to continue to hold shares in their own names rather than through nominees. It ensures that the new arrangements prescribed in the regulations will not mean that:

- people who would have been entitled to have their names entered in the company's register of members will lose that entitlement; or
- people who are entitled to exercise rights in respect of securities will lose that right.

1104.   Subsection (4) provides that the regulations will be able to:

- prohibit the issue of share certificates or certificates for other types of security. Holders of securities to which any such prohibition applies will lose the option of continuing to hold certificates and transfer their shares by paper-based methods;
- ensure that such holders of securities are sent periodic statements of their holdings;
- make provision about the evidential value of certificates or statements.

Section 787: Provision enabling or requiring arrangements to be adopted: order-making powers

1105.   This section provides additional flexibility by enabling Ministers to designate, by order (subject to negative resolution procedure), companies or classes of company to which the regulations are to apply, or to modify the effect of the regulations (or disapply them) in relation to a designated class of companies or specified companies.

Section 789: Duty to consult

1106.   Ministers will be obliged to consult such persons as they consider appropriate before making regulations or designating a class of companies by order under the new powers. This obligation reflects the breadth of the proposed new powers, as well as the technical nature of some of the regulations which could be made under it.

PART 22: INFORMATION ABOUT INTERESTS IN COMPANY'S SHARES

Background

[3.23]
1107.   The provisions of this Part concern a public company's right to investigate who has an interest in its shares. They replace equivalent provisions in Part 6 of the 1985 Act. These are purely domestic provisions, and are not required by European Community Law.

1108.   The automatic disclosure obligations currently contained in sections 198 to 211 of Part 6 of the 1985 Act will be replaced by regulations under the Financial Services and Markets Act 2000, as amended by Part 43 of this Act, in implementation of the Transparency Obligations Directive. In the regulations, a different concept of "interest in voting rights" will be adopted in order to implement the Transparency Obligations Directive.

1109.   This Part re-enacts, with certain modifications, the disclosure obligations pursuant to a notice issued by the company contained in sections 212 to 219 of the 1985 Act. There is no change to the definition of "interest in shares" for this purpose.

1110.   The main changes to section 212 of the 1985 Act and related provisions are:

- making clear that notices are not required to be in hard copy, and therefore can be given in electronic form (section 793 read in conjunction with the provisions in Part 37 on the sending or supplying of documents or information);
- providing for how information is to be entered on the register of interests disclosed when the name of the present holder of the shares is not known or there is no present holder (section 808);
- removing the requirement on the company to verify third party information supplied in response to a section 793 notice before putting it on the register (section 817);
- requiring a company to refuse a request to inspect the register if it is not satisfied that the request is made for a proper purpose (section 812);
- removing the requirement for a company to keep information on the register in relation to entries made more than six years previously (section 816).

Section 791: Companies to which this Part applies

1111.   This section provides that this Part only applies to public companies (as section 212 of the 1985 Act provides currently).

Section 792: Shares to which this Part applies

1112.   This section re-enacts in part the definition in section 198(2) of the 1985 Act of the type of shares concerning which a section 793 notice may be issued, namely shares carrying rights to vote in all circumstances at general meetings. However, shares held by a company "in treasury" following a purchase of its own shares (as an alternative to cancelling such shares on purchase) are now included in the definition.

Section 793: Notice by company requiring information about interests in its shares

1113. This section re-enacts section 212(1) to (4) of the 1985 Act. It allows a public company to issue a notice requiring a person it knows, or has reasonable cause to believe, has an interest in its shares (or to have had an interest in the previous three years) to confirm or deny the fact, and, if the former, to disclose certain information about the interest, including information about any other person with an interest in the shares.

1114. Subsections (3) and (4) enable the company to require details to be given of a person's past or present interests and to provide details of any other interest subsisting in the shares of which he is aware. This provision allows the company to pursue information through a chain of nominees by requiring each in the chain to disclose the person for whom they are acting. Under subsection (6), where the addressee's interest is a past one, a company can ask for information concerning any person by whom the interest was acquired immediately subsequent to their interest. Particulars may also be required of any share acquisition agreements, or any agreement or arrangement as to how the rights attaching to those shares should be exercised (sections 824 and 825).

1115. This section serves a different purpose to the automatic disclosure obligations currently contained in sections 198 to 211 of Part 6 of the 1985 Act. It enables companies to discover the identity of those with voting rights (direct or indirect) that fall below the thresholds for automatic disclosure, and it also enables companies (and members of the company) to ascertain the underlying beneficial owners of shares.

1116. The notice is not required to be in hard copy (see the general provisions on sending or supplying documents or information in Part 37 of the Bill). Notices, and responses thereto, may be given in electronic form. A response must be given in a reasonable time. What is reasonable has not been defined so as to allow flexibility according to the circumstances, but if the time given is not reasonable, the company will not have served a valid notice.

Sections 794 and 795: Notice requiring information: order imposing restrictions on shares and offences

1117. These sections re-enact section 216(1) to (4) of the 1985 Act. They specify the penalties for failure to provide information within the specified time when served with a notice under section 793. There are criminal penalties (although a person does not commit an offence if he can show that the requirement to give information was frivolous or vexatious).

1118. Additionally, application may be made to the court for a direction that the shares in question are to be subject to the restrictions specified in section 797.

Section 796: Notice requiring information: persons exempted from obligation to comply

1119. This section re-enacts section 216(5) of the 1985 Act. It provides that the Secretary of State may exempt a person from complying with a notice. The Secretary of State must consult the Governor of the Bank of England, and must be satisfied that there are special reasons for exempting the person (taking account of any undertaking given).

Sections 797 to 802: Orders imposing restrictions on shares

1120. These sections restate Part 15 of the 1985 Act without substantive change in so far as its provisions apply in relation to Part 22 of this Act. They set out the effect of a court order made under section 794 imposing restrictions on shares, and the penalties for attempted evasion of the restrictions. They also make provision for the relaxation or removal of restrictions, or for an order for the sale of shares.

Section 803: Power of members to require company to act

1121. This section re-enacts section 214(1) and (2) of the 1985 Act. It requires a company to exercise its powers under section 793 on the request of members holding at least 10% of such of the paid up capital of the company as carries the right to vote at general meetings (other than voting rights attached to shares held in treasury). This provision, which has rarely been used under the 1985 Act, recognises that members of a company may have a legitimate reason for wanting the company to exercise its statutory powers to demand information even if the management does not want to. For example, the members might want to act where they suspect that the directors are involved in building a holding from behind the shelter of nominees.

1122. Provision is made as to the form and the procedure in relation to requests. In contrast to section 214, the 10% threshold may be met by a series of requests from members that the company act, rather than one collective request. Those making a request must not only specify the manner in which they require the powers to be exercised, but must also give reasonable grounds for requiring the company to exercise the powers in the manner specified (subsection (3)(b)(ii) and (iii)).

Section 804: Duty of company to comply with requirement

1123. This section re-enacts section 214(4) and (5) of the 1985 Act. It specifies the criminal penalties arising if the company fails to act as required. In contrast to section 214, every officer in default is liable to a fine, but the company itself is not.

Section 805: Report to members on outcome of investigation

1124. This section re-enacts section 215 of the 1985 Act. It specifies that on the conclusion of an investigation required by members it is the duty of the company to prepare a report of the information received. The report must be available within a reasonable period (not exceeding 15 days) after the conclusion of the investigation. Where the company's investigation exceeds three months, it must make interim reports available at three monthly intervals. Those making the request must be notified of reports being available. In contrast to section 215, the report may be kept at the company's registered office or at a place specified in regulations made under section 1136.

Section 806: Report to members: offences

1125. This section re-enacts section 215(8) of the 1985 Act. It specifies the criminal penalties arising if the company fails to report as required on the outcome of the investigation or to keep the report under section 805. Unlike section 215, every officer in default is liable to a fine for a failure to report, but the company itself is not.

Section 807: Right to inspect and request copy of reports

1126. This section re-enacts provisions in section 219 of the 1985 Act. It requires the company to allow reports to members to be inspected by anyone without charge. Any person can request a copy of a report, on payment of the prescribed fee. Subsections (3) to (5) specify the criminal penalties arising if the company fails to disclose a report as required and make provision for the courts to compel disclosure.

Section 808: Register of interests disclosed

1127. The register required to be kept by section 211 of the 1985 Act covers all interests notified, whether under the automatic disclosure rules or in response to a notice served under section 212 of that Act (company investigations). The latter are kept as a separate part of the register of interests in shares. In future it will be for regulations made under the Financial Services and Markets Act 2000 (as amended by Part 43 of this Act) to make provision as to how interests notified under the automatic disclosure rules will be made public.

1128. This section provides that if, as a result of a section 793 investigation, the company receives information relating to interests held by any person in relevant shares, it must within three days enter in a register of interests disclosed:
- the fact that the requirement (to disclose information under the notice) was imposed and the date on which it was imposed; and
- the information received in response to the notice under section 793.

1129. The section provides that the information must be entered either against the name of the present holder of the shares in question (as under the 1985 Act), or if the present holder is not known or there is no present holder, then against the name of the person holding the interest. Subsections (5) and (6) provide for criminal penalties for any default in complying with this section. Subsection (7) makes clear that information that a company receives under this Part does not mean that the company needs to be concerned with the existence of any trust over the shares.

Sections 809 and 810: Register to be kept available for inspection; and associated index

1130. These sections re-enact section 211(6) and (8) (as applied by section 213(3)) of the 1985 Act. Section 809 provides that the register of interests disclosed must be kept available for inspection at the company's registered office or at a place specified in regulations made under section 1136. The company must advise the registrar where the register is kept (unless it has always been kept at the registered office). Subsections (4) and (5) provide for criminal penalties for any default in complying with this section.

1131. Section 810 provides that the register should have an index unless it is in a form that itself constitutes an index (for example a searchable database).

Section 811: Right to inspect and require copy of entries

1132. This section re-enacts section 219 of the 1985 Act. It provides that the register and index must be open to inspection by any person without charge. For a prescribed fee, any person is entitled to a copy of any entry on the register. A person seeking access to the register under this section must provide the information specified in subsection (4), including his name and address and the purpose for which the information is to be used.

Section 812: Court supervision of purpose for which rights may be exercised

1133. This section provides that the company must only allow the inspection of the register or provide the copy requested if satisfied that it is for a proper purpose. If it refuses, the person concerned may apply to the court for it to allow the inspection or require the copy to be provided. If an application to the court is made, the person must notify the company, and the company must use its best endeavours to notify any persons whose details might be disclosed.

Section 813: Register of interests disclosed: refusal of inspection or default in providing copy

1134.   This section provides for court enforcement and criminal penalties for any default in complying with section 811.

Section 814: Register of interests disclosed: offences in connection with request for or disclosure of information

1135.   This section provides for criminal penalties for misleading, false or deceptive statements given when making a request under section 811. It also makes it a criminal offence for the person who receives information under section 811 to disclose it to another person, if he knows or has reason to suspect that it may be used for an improper purpose.

Section 815: Entries not to be removed from register

1136.   This section re-enacts section 218 of the 1985 Act. It provides that entries can only be removed from the register in accordance with sections 816 and 817, and if wrongly deleted must be restored as soon as reasonably practicable. Subsections (3) and (4) provide for criminal penalties for any default in complying with this section.

Section 816: Removal of entries from register: old entries

1137.   Section 217(1) of the 1985 Act provides that a company may remove an entry against a person's name from the register of interests in shares if more than six years have elapsed since the date of the entry being made, and either:
* the entry recorded the fact that the person in question had ceased to have an interest notifiable under Part 6 in the company's relevant share capital (in which case the person's name may also be removed from the register); or
* the entry has been superseded by a later entry against the same person's name.

1138.   By contrast, this section simply provides that a company is not required to keep information on the register if more than six years have elapsed since the entry was made.

Section 817: Removal of entries from register: incorrect entry relating to third party

1139.   This section re-enacts in part section 217 of the 1985 Act but does not include the requirement for the company to verify information relating to third parties supplied in response to a section 793 notice. However, the third party retains the right to apply to have his name removed from the register if the information is incorrect. Subsection (4) provides for the courts to enforce removal of incorrect information.

Section 818: Adjustment of entry relating to share acquisition agreement

1140.   This section re-enacts section 217(4) and (5) of the 1985 Act. It provides that a person identified in the register as being party to a section 824 share acquisition agreement (this may include a concert party agreement) may when he ceases to be party to the agreement, request that the register should be amended to record that information. Such entries may appear in several places on the register, as each member of the concert party is required in their individual notification to identify the other members of the concert party. If the company refuses an application, the court may order the company to comply if it thinks fit.

Section 819: Duty of company ceasing to be public company

1141.   This section re-enacts provisions in section 211(7) and (10) (as applied by section 213(3)) of the 1985 Act. It provides that a company ceasing to be a public company must continue to keep any register it has kept under section 808 and any associated index for six years after it ceases to be a public company.

Section 820: Interest in shares: general

1142.   This section re-enacts the definition of "interest in shares" in section 208 (as applied by section 212(5)) of the 1985 Act for the purposes of Part 22 of this Act. An "interest in shares" is widely defined as an interest of any kind whatsoever in the shares, and includes beneficial ownership as well as direct ownership. The courts have described this wide definition as being designed "to counter the limitless ingenuity of persons who prefer to conceal their interests behind trusts and corporate entities" (*re TR Technology Investment Trust plc* [1988] BCLC 256 at 261).

Section 821: Interest in shares: right to subscribe for shares

1143.   This section re-enacts section 212(6) of the 1985 Act. It provides that a notice under section 793 applies in relation to rights to subscribe for shares.

Sections 822 and 823: Interest in shares: family and corporate interests

1144.   These sections re-enact section 203 (as applied by section 212(5)) of the 1985 Act. They provides for certain family interests to be attributed to persons for the purpose of disclosure, as well as certain interests held indirectly through a corporate body.

Sections 824: Interest in shares: agreement to acquire interests in a particular company

1145.   This section re-enacts section 204 (as applied by section 212(5)) of the 1985 Act concerning the obligation to give details of certain share acquisition arrangements in response to a notice under section 793. It covers any agreement or arrangement, whether or not legally binding, which involves undertakings, expectations or understandings that interests in shares will be acquired and that they will be subject to relevant restrictions while the agreement subsists. This may include groups of persons acting in concert to prepare the way for a takeover offer for the company or to support a pending takeover offer.

Section 825: Extent of obligation in case of share acquisition agreement

1146.   This section re-enacts section 205 (as applied by section 212(5)) of the 1985 Act. It attributes interests in shares held by a party to a section 824 agreement to the other parties to the agreement.

Section 826: Information protected from wider disclosure

1147.   This section re-enacts provisions in section 211(9) (as applied by section 213(3)) and 215(4) of the 1985 Act. Under section 409 the Secretary of State may make regulations exempting a company from the need to disclose information relating to related undertakings in notes to its accounts in certain circumstances. The Secretary of State must agree that the information need not be disclosed. Where advantage is taken of this exemption, the fact must be stated in the company's annual accounts. This section provides that this same information must not be included in a section 805 report, (though its omission must be noted in the report), and must not be available for inspection under section 811.

Section 827: Reckoning of periods for fulfilling obligations

1148.   This provision re-enacts the provision of section 220(2) of the 1985 Act concerning the calculation of periods in the Part expressed as a number of working days (as defined in section 1173). In contrast to section 220(2), the definition of "working days" excludes bank holidays only in the part of the UK where the company is registered.

Section 828: Power to make further provision by regulations

1149.   This section re-enacts section 210A of the 1985 Act. It confers power on the Secretary of State to make regulations to amend the definition of shares to which this Part applies (subsection (1)(a) re-enacting section 210A(1)(a)). Power is also conferred to amend the provisions in section 793 as to notice by a company requiring information about interests in its shares, (subsection (1)(b) re-enacting section 210A(1)(e)), and the provisions as to what is to be taken to be an interest in shares, (subsection (1)(c) re-enacting section 210A(1)(d)).

PART 23: DISTRIBUTIONS

[3.24]
1150.   This Part restates the provisions on distributions in Part 8 of the 1985 Act. The only substantive change is to the rules on distributions in kind, and the new provisions are in sections 845, 846 and 851.

Sections 845 and 846: Distributions in kind

1151.   In Capital Maintenance: Other Issues (paragraphs 24 to 43) the CLR explored the difficulties created by the decision in *Aveling Barford Ltd v Perion Ltd* [1989] BCLC 626 and made a number of suggestions as to how these difficulties might be overcome. Section 845 is a new provision which removes doubts to which the decision in this case has given rise: in particular when a transfer of an asset to a member amounts to a distribution. The concern behind this section is that, following the decision in the *Aveling Barford* case, it is unclear when intra-group transfers of assets can be conducted by reference to the asset's book value rather than its market value (which will frequently be higher than the book value).

1152.   The decision in *Aveling Barford* concerned the sale of a property by a company (which had no distributable profits) at a considerable undervalue to another company controlled by the company's ultimate sole beneficial shareholder. The transaction was held to be void as an unauthorised return of capital. Whilst this case decided nothing about the situation where a company that has distributable profits makes an intra-group transfer of assets at book value, there was a concern that, as such a transfer of an asset at book value may have an element of undervalue, the transaction would constitute a distribution thereby requiring the company to have distributable profits sufficient to cover the difference in value. The result has been that companies are often required either to abandon a transfer or to structure it in a more complex way, for example, having the assets revalued and then sold (or distributed under section 276 of the 1985 Act) so that the distributable reserves are increased by the "realised profit" arising on the sale/distribution followed by a capital contribution of the asset to the relevant group member.

1153.   Section 845 does not disturb the position in the *Aveling Barford* case such that where a company which does not have distributable profits makes a distribution by way of a transfer of assets at an undervalue, this will be an unlawful distribution contrary to Part 23 of the Act.

1154.   It clarifies, however, the position where a company does have distributable profits and provides that where the conditions referred to in subsection (1)(a) and (b) are met, the amount of any distribution consisting of or arising from the sale, transfer or other disposition by a company of a non-cash asset to a member of the company should be calculated by reference to the value at which that asset is included in the company's accounts, that is, its "book value". Thus, if an asset is transferred for a consideration not less than its book value, the amount of the distribution is zero, but if the asset is transferred for a consideration less than its book value, the amount of the distribution is equal to that shortfall (which will therefore need to be covered by distributable profits) – see subsection (2)(a) and (b). This avoids the potential need for many companies to carry out asset revaluations requiring professional advice and incurring fees to advisors prior to making a distribution of a non-cash asset.

1155.   The conditions that must be satisfied for subsection (2)(a) and (b) to apply are that at the time of the disposition of the asset, the company must have profits available for distribution and that if the amount of such a distribution were to be determined in accordance with this section, it could be made without contravening any of the provisions of this Part (for example, section 830 and section 831).

1156.   Under subsection (3), in determining whether it has profits available for distribution (as defined in section 830), a company may treat any profit that would arise on the proposed disposition of the non-cash asset (that is, the amount (if any) by which the consideration received exceeds the book value of the asset) as increasing its distributable profits.

1157.   Section 846 replaces section 276 of the 1985 Act which applies where a company "*makes a distribution of or including a non-cash asset*" and allows a company which has revalued assets showing an unrealised profit in the accounts, to treat that profit as a realised profit where the distribution is one of, or including, a non-cash asset. Section 846 tracks the drafting of section 845 so that it applies not only where the company makes a distribution consisting of or including a non-cash asset, but also where a company makes a distribution arising from the sale, transfer or other disposition by it of a non-cash asset, in other words in the same circumstances that are described in section 845.

Section 851: Application of rules of law restricting distributions

1158.   This section is a new provision which preserves the existing common law rules on unlawful distributions (see subsection (1)) – which continue to be an essential component in determining what amounts to an unlawful distribution.

1159.   Subsection (2) makes an exception to this: in particular, it provides that the lawfulness and amount of distributions in kind are established by the statutory rules in sections 845 and 846 and not by any applicable common law rules.

PART 24: A COMPANY'S ANNUAL RETURN

[3.25]
1160.   This Part restates Chapter 3 of Part 11 of the 1985 Act. It requires every company to deliver to Companies House an Annual Return with the specified information. The only significant difference from the 1985 provisions is that section 857 confers power on the Secretary of State not only to amend or repeal sections 855 and 856 but also, in subsection (2)(b), to make exceptions from the requirements of those sections. (The comparable power in the 1985 Act is only to amend or repeal.)

PART 25: COMPANY CHARGES

Chapters 1 And 2: Companies Registered In England And Wales Or In Northern Ireland; And Companies Registered In Scotland

[3.26]
1161.   This Part of the Act provides a scheme for the registration of charges created by a company. Part 12 of the 1985 Act was prospectively repealed and replaced by the 1989 Act, but these amendments and repeals were never brought into force, and they are now themselves being repealed (see Schedule 16).

1162.   Chapters 1 and 2 of Part 25 restate Part 12 of the 1985 Act, with a few changes. The principal differences between the restated provisions and those of the 1985 Act are described below.
*   Changes have been made to provisions in this Part as a result of other provisions in the Act. So, for example, references to a statutory declaration in sections 403 and 419 of the 1985 Act are replaced by references to a statement in sections 872 and 887. Additionally changes have

been made to sections 408 and 423 of the 1985 Act (now sections 877 and 892 respectively) to enable a company to keep its instruments creating charges and its register of charges in a place other than its registered office, bringing these provisions into line with provisions elsewhere in the Act relating to availability of documents for inspection.

- The provisions relating to charges created by an overseas company in sections 409 and 424 of the 1985 Act have not been restated. Instead section 1052 provides a new regulation-making power for the Secretary of State to make provision about the registration of charges over property in the United Kingdom of an overseas company that has registered its particulars with the registrar under section 1046.

- There are no longer to be daily default fines for the offences under this Part of failure to register a new charge under section 860 or 878 (compare sections 399 and 415 of the 1985 Act) and failure to register an existing charge over acquired property under section 862 or 880 (compare sections 400 and 416).

Chapter 3: Powers Of The Secretary Of State

Section 893: Power to make provision for effect of registration in special register

1163. This is a new provision, which provides power for the Secretary of State to make an order providing that, if a charge is registered in another register (for example, the register of floating charges to be established under the Bankruptcy and Diligence etc (Scotland) Bill), then the registrar may not register it, but it will be treated as if it had been registered in accordance with the requirements of Part 25. The power may only be exercised if appropriate information-sharing arrangements have been made between the registrar and the person responsible for the other register. This is to ensure that a person searching of the register will have access to information about charges registered in that other register.

Section 894: General power to make amendments to this Part

1164. This is a new provision providing the Secretary of State with a power to amend the provisions of Part 25.

PART 26: ARRANGEMENTS AND RECONSTRUCTIONS

[3.27]
1165. The provisions of this Part enable companies to apply to the court for an order sanctioning an arrangement or reconstruction agreed with a majority of members or creditors. They restate sections 425 to 427 of the 1985 Act. In addition to drafting changes resulting from the re-arrangement of the provisions, there are two changes of substance.

1166. Section 899(2) makes clear that the persons who may apply for a court order sanctioning a compromise or arrangement are the same as those who may apply to the court for an order for a meeting (under section 896(2));

1167. Section 901 requires a company to deliver to the registrar a court order that alters the company's constitution. It also requires that every copy of the company's articles subsequently issued must be accompanied by a copy of the order, unless the effect of the order has been incorporated into the articles by amendment. These changes are included for consistency with other provisions in the Act concerning such orders.

PART 27: MERGERS AND DIVISIONS OF PUBLIC COMPANIES

[3.28]
1168. The provisions of this Part enable a public company – under certain conditions – to apply to the court for an order under Part 26 sanctioning an arrangement or reconstruction which concerns the merger or division of a public company. They implement the Third Council Directive 78/855/EEC concerning mergers of public limited liability companies and the Sixth Council Directive 82/891/EEC concerning the division of public limited liability companies.

1169. The provisions of this Part restate section 427A and Schedule 15B to the 1985 Act. The opportunity has been taken to put the provisions in a form more closely corresponding to that of the Directives. Chapters 2 and 3 deal separately with mergers and divisions and the provisions within those Chapters broadly follow the order of the provisions of the relevant Directive.

1170. The independence requirements for experts and valuers in sections 936 and 937 are new and correspond to the new independence requirements for a statutory auditor (see section 1214). They include a new power for the Secretary of State to define a disallowed connection for the purposes of determining whether a person is sufficiently independent to be an expert or valuer under this Part. This is consistent with the approach taken in sections 344 and 1151 of the Act.

PART 28: TAKEOVERS ETC

Introduction

[3.29]
1171. This Part implements the European Directive on Takeover Bids (2004/25/EC, the "Take-

Part 3   CA 2006 Supporting Materials

overs Directive") which was adopted on 21 April 2004 and had to be implemented by 20 May 2006. It also contains a few minor amendments to the existing law not required by the Directive.

Summary and background

1172. With the exception of Chapter 3 which restates, with amendments, Part 13A of the 1985 Act, the provisions in Part 28 are new. The principal body of provisions emerged from the consultation document, "Company Law – Implementation of the European Directive on Takeover Bids" published by the DTI in January 2005. Additionally, the CLR considered issues related to "squeeze-out" and "sell-out" (concerning the problems of, and for, residual minority shareholders following a successful takeover bid) in Chapter 11 and Annex B of "Completing the Structure" and presented their conclusions in Chapter 13 of the Final Report. Certain provisions in this Part have been developed in the light of these conclusions.

Overview of the Part

1173. The Part is divided into 4 Chapters:
- Chapter 1 deals with matters related to the Takeover Panel and its takeover regulatory functions;
- Chapter 2 concerns matters related to barriers to takeovers;
- Chapter 3 contains provisions relating to "squeeze-out" and "sell-out" (concepts designed to address the problems of, and for, residual minority shareholders following a successful takeover bid); and
- Chapter 4 amends the provisions in Part 7 of the 1985 Act about the content of annual reports of companies traded on a regulated market.

Note: It is intended that certain provisions of Part 28 will be extended to unregistered companies with shares traded on a regulated market. This will be achieved by the regulation-making power at section 1043 of the Act. It is necessary to ensure compliance with the Takeovers Directive.

Chapter 1: The Takeover Panel

Summary And Background

1174. Since 1968, takeover regulation in the UK has been overseen by the Panel on Takeovers and Mergers ("the Panel") which administered rules and principles contained in the non-statutory City Code on Takeovers and Mergers. In order to bring UK takeover regulation within the requirements laid down in the Takeovers Directive, Chapter 1 places it within a statutory framework.

1175. The Panel will supervise takeover activity and similar types of transactions. The Panel will retain considerable autonomy to provide for its own constitution and appointment procedures. However, a minimum constitutional structure is laid down, providing for the Panel to make arrangements for carrying out its functions and, in particular, to function through committees, sub-committees, officers and members of staff. It is envisaged that the Panel will continue to carry out its day-to-day activities through its Executive. Provisions underpinning the funding of the Panel's regulatory activities are also included.

1176. Principally, the Panel is placed under an obligation to make statutory rules giving effect to certain Articles of the Directive. It is also given a statutory rule-making power to make rules in relation to takeover activity and similar types of transactions, reflecting the current field of activity over which the existing Code lays down rules.

1177. Sections 945, 951, 955, 956 and 961 of the Act are intended to limit litigation by: (a) channelling parties to seek decisions of the Panel (including the Panel's Hearings Committee and the independent Takeover Appeal Board) before having recourse to the courts; (b) excluding new rights of action for breach of statutory duty; (c) protecting concluded transactions from challenge for breach of the Panel's rules; and (d) exempting the Panel and its individual members, officers and staff from liability in damages for things done in, or in connection with, the discharge of the regulatory functions of the Panel.

1178. The Bill does not affect the availability of judicial review by the courts. In the takeovers field, in the Datafin case (*R v Panel on Takeovers, ex parte Datafin plc* [1987] QB 815) the Court of Appeal concluded that generally the courts should limit themselves only to reviewing the Panel's decision-making processes after the bid has been concluded.

1179. The Bill confers on the Panel powers to make rulings and directions and to enforce these through the courts, to obtain information and documents from those involved in regulated activities and to impose sanctions on those who transgress its rules.

The Panel and its rules

Section 942: The Panel

1180. This section confers on the Panel the takeover regulatory functions set out in Chapter 1. The Panel is empowered to do anything that it considers necessary or expedient in relation to its prescribed functions and it may also make arrangements for such functions to be carried out on its behalf by a committee or sub-committee of the Panel or an officer or member of staff of the Panel or a person acting as such.

1181. This Chapter does not confer on the Panel the status of a statutory body. The Panel will remain an unincorporated body, as constituted from time to time, and, as such, having rights and obligations under the common law. Those rights and obligations will be supplemented by the specific provisions set out in the Bill.

Sections 943 and 944: Rules; Further provisions about rules

1182. The Panel is given the power to make rules in relation to takeover regulation. The rule-making power is broadly drawn to ensure that the Panel can continue to make rules on the range of matters presently regulated by the City Code on Takeovers and Mergers. The following provisions are included:

(a)   The Panel is placed under an obligation to make rules as required by specified Articles of the Takeovers Directive. These are the general principles (Article 3.1 of the Directive), jurisdictional rules (Article 4.2), matters related to the protection of minority shareholders, mandatory bid and equitable price (Article 5), contents of the bid documentation (Article 6.1 to 6.3), time allowed for acceptance of a bid and publication of a bid (Articles 7 and 8), obligations of the management of the target company (Article 9) and other rules applicable to the conduct of bids (Article 13). In making rules in relation to these Articles, the Panel will be entitled to exercise Member State options where these are provided for in the Directive. The Panel's rules will not, however, deal with certain matters contained in the Directive such as barriers to takeovers (Article 11), squeeze-out and sell-out (Articles 15 and 16), and information to be published by companies in their annual reports (Article 10) which are more appropriately dealt with in company legislation (and are the subject of further provision at Chapters 2, 3 and 4 of this Part).

(b)   The Panel is permitted to make rules on takeover bids (including, but not limited to, those which are the subject of the Directive), mergers and other transactions affecting the ownership or control of companies. The power is designed to be broad enough to cover the existing scope of the Code and sufficiently flexible to take account of future market developments. Types of matters currently covered by the Code but not covered by the Directive include the takeovers of companies not traded on a regulated market and transactions involving a change of control of a like nature to takeovers.

1183. When making rules under this section, the Panel must do so by a committee of the Panel, except in the case of rules for fees and charges under section 957 which must be made either by a committee of the Panel or by the Panel itself.

1184. The further provisions about rules that may be made by the Panel under section 944 include the power to grant derogations and waivers, which by virtue of section 943(1) must respect the general principles laid down in Article 3.1 of the Directive.

1185. Section 944(2) to (7) makes provision as to the form, public availability and verification of rules made by the Panel.

Section 945: Rulings

1186. This section enables the Panel, including (by virtue of section 942(3)) its Executive, to make rulings on the interpretation, application or effect of the rules made by the Panel.

1187. To the extent and in the circumstances specified in the rules, a ruling of the Panel has binding effect unless reviewed by the Hearings Committee or successfully appealed to the Takeover Appeal Board in accordance with rules made under section 951. It is envisaged that rules made under sections 943 and 944 will address matters such as notice to parties and right of representation of persons who might be bound by a Panel ruling.

Section 946: Directions

1188. This section allows the Panel to make provision in its rules for it to give a direction preventing a person from breaching the rules (including a direction operating on an interim basis whilst a matter is awaiting determination by the Panel) or otherwise to ensure compliance with the rules.

Information

Section 947: Power to require documents and information

1189. The Panel has historically had no formal power to require those involved in takeover activity to provide it with the information the Panel requires to carry out its functions. Persons authorised under the Financial Services and Markets Act 2000 are required by the rules of the Financial Services Authority to provide information and assistance to the Panel. In relation to others, the Panel has relied on the voluntary co-operation of market participants to provide explanations and documents which are not publicly available.

1190. This section enables the Panel to require the production of such documents and information as it may reasonably require in the exercise of its functions. The Panel may also authorise a person to exercise the powers under the section on its behalf, for example, if the Panel were to appoint a law or accountancy firm to help it collect and analyse documents.

Part 3   CA 2006 Supporting Materials

1191. Subsection (7) provides that a lien on a document is not affected by the production of that document in compliance with a requirement imposed by the Panel or someone authorised on its behalf. A lien is a legal right to keep possession of a document belonging to someone else until a claim is satisfied – for example, a claim for payment of professional fees. This subsection does not entitle a professional to refuse to hand over a document to the Panel but preserves his rights over those documents.

1192. The section provides that the Panel may require the production of information in hard copy where it is held in some other form (for instance, electronically on a floppy disk).

1193. The Panel may not compel the production of documents which would be protected from disclosure in legal proceedings on the grounds of legal professional privilege or confidentiality of communications.

Sections 948 and 949: Restrictions on disclosure; Offence of disclosure in contravention of section 948

1194. These sections provide that information obtained by the Panel in the course of exercising its functions will be subject to restrictions on onward disclosure. Aside from the desirability of such provisions, so that those providing information to the Panel can do so knowing that it will not be subject to improper further disclosure, these provisions also meet a requirement under Article 4.3 of the Directive that Member States shall ensure that information provided to those employed, or formerly employed, by takeover supervisory authorities shall not be further divulged: "*to any person or authority except under provisions laid down by law.*" Section 948, accordingly, prescribes the conditions under which such information can be released.

1195. Information concerning the private affairs of an individual or a business provided to the Panel in connection with its functions may not be disclosed during the individual's lifetime or while the business is carried on without the consent of the individual or business in question except for the purposes of carrying out the Panel's functions or unless it is disclosed to a person or for a purpose set out in Schedule 2.

1196. Schedule 2 sets out the "gateways" for disclosure of information obtained by the Panel in the exercise of its functions which are permitted under section 948, including the circumstances in which a disclosure to an overseas regulatory authority is permitted. Under section 948(4) and (5), the Secretary of State has the power to amend the Schedule, but only to specify persons exercising functions of a public nature or descriptions of disclosure where the purpose for which the disclosure is permitted is likely to assist in the exercise of a function of a public nature.

1197. Section 948(6)(a) provides that certain authorities mentioned in subsection (7) are not bound by the restrictions on disclosure imposed by subsection (2). These bodies are those other takeover supervisory authorities and financial services regulators with which the Panel has a duty to co-operate. Subsection (6)(b) provides that persons or bodies obtaining information from those authorities (whether directly or indirectly) are also not bound by the restrictions on disclosure imposed by subsection (2). These provisions are necessary to implement fully Article 4.4 of the Directive. Those bodies mentioned in subsection (7), and persons and bodies receiving information from them, will themselves be subject to restrictions on disclosure that will mirror those imposed by section 948, and so information originating from the Panel will still be protected from improper further disclosure.

1198. Section 949 makes it an offence to disclose information in contravention of section 948. A person guilty of such an offence is liable on conviction on indictment to two years' imprisonment or a fine or both; and on summary conviction to twelve months' imprisonment (six months in Scotland and Northern Ireland) or a fine or both. Section 949(1) provides a person with a defence if he can prove that he did not know, and had no reason to suspect, that the information in question had been provided to the Panel in the exercise of its functions; or that he took reasonable steps to prevent wrongful disclosure.

Co-operation

Section 950: Panel's duty of co-operation

1199. Article 4.4 of the Directive requires that takeover supervisory authorities and financial services regulators provide reasonable assistance to other such authorities within the EEA for the purposes of the Directive. This section is designed to give effect to this requirement by obliging the Panel to co-operate with overseas takeover and financial services regulatory authorities.

1200. The form and manner of co-operation will be as the Panel considers appropriate in the light of the circumstances (in particular, its power to require documents and information may be exercised to support such an authority) and may include sharing information which the Panel is not prevented from disclosing. The section mirrors similar co-operation obligations imposed on the Financial Services Authority by section 354 of the Financial Services and Markets Act 2000.

Hearings and Appeals

Section 951: Hearings and Appeals

1201. This section ensures that proper procedures for review of and appeal against decisions taken by the Panel in connection with its regulatory functions are provided. Section 951(1) requires that the rules made by the Panel provide for a decision of the Panel to be subject to review by a "Hearings Committee" when requested by affected persons specified in the rules. Section 951(3) provides that the rules must give a right of appeal to an independent tribunal (the "Takeover Appeal Board") against a decision of the Hearings Committee. The rules may make provision in relation to the Hearings Committee as to procedural matters, evidence and the powers of the Committee. Further, rules may contain provisions related to enforcement of decisions of the Hearings Committee and the Takeover Appeal Board.

1202. The section also requires the rules to provide that:

(a)   when appearing before the Hearings Committee or the Takeover Appeal Board, the Panel must act through an officer or member of staff of the Panel (who must not be a member of the rule-making committee referred to in section 943(5), the Hearings Committee or the Appeal Board); and

(b)   no person who is, or has been, a member of the rule-making committee can be a member of the Hearings Committee or the Takeover Appeal Board.

1203. The general rules of natural justice will preclude a person who had taken part in a decision from later considering a review or appeal in relation to that decision.

1204. This approach is designed to ensure a clear and transparent division of responsibilities between the various organs of the Panel in its executive, judicial and rule-making roles.

Contravention of rules, etc

Section 952: Sanctions

1205. This section confers on the Panel the power to make rules for imposing sanctions for breach of its rules or directions given under section 946. The Panel's current sanctions regime, which is set out in the Introduction to the City Code on Takeovers and Mergers and which it is envisaged will remain in place under the Act, provides for private and public statements of censure of persons in breach of the Code.

1206. Particularly flagrant breaches may lead to the Panel publishing a statement indicating that the offender is someone who is not likely to comply. The rules of the Financial Services Authority and certain professional organisations contain provisions obliging their members, in certain circumstances, not to act for a person named in such a statement. This is referred to as "cold-shouldering". The provisions in question cover transactions that are subject to the City Code on Takeovers and Mergers, such as transactions in relevant securities requiring disclosure under rule 8 of the Code. Under section 952, it will continue to be possible, in the case of transactions that are subject to the Panel rules, for the Panel to issue "cold-shouldering" statements in appropriate cases. (The Panel will also be able to pass information concerning breaches of rules to other regulatory authorities and professional bodies by virtue of the statutory "gateways" set out at section 948 and Schedule 2.)

1207. Should future rules made by the Panel confer a power on the Panel to impose a sanction of a kind not contained in the City Code on Takeovers and Mergers as it has effect immediately before the passing of the Act, the Panel must prepare a policy statement in respect of the sanction. The policy statement must set out the policy of the Panel with regard to imposition of the sanction and, for financial penalties, the penalty that may be imposed. An element of the policy must be that the Panel, in making a decision about any such matter, have regard to the seriousness of the breach or failure, the extent to which the breach or failure was deliberate or reckless and whether the person on whom the sanction is to be imposed is an individual.

Section 953: Failure to comply with rules about bid documentation

1208. This section creates new offences in relation to takeover bid documentation (ie offer documents prepared by the bidder and documents in response to the bid prepared by the board of the target company). Provisions related to bid documentation are laid down in particular by Articles 6.3 and 9.5 of the Directive which are to be implemented by rules which the Panel are obliged to make under section 943. Consequently, in each case an offence will be committed where the document in question does not comply with rules designated by the Panel as giving effect to those provisions. The offence relating to offer documents may be committed by the bidder and any of its directors, officers or members who caused the offer document to be published. The offence relating to response documents may be committed by directors or other officers of the target company. Where either offence is committed by a corporate body (for instance, a corporate director), provisions are also included dealing with liability of directors, officers or members of that body. In each case, an offence will be committed only where the relevant person knew that the document did not comply (or was reckless as to whether it did so) and failed to take all reasonable steps to ensure that it did comply.

1209. A person guilty of an offence under this provision is liable on conviction to a fine (on summary conviction limited to the statutory maximum).

Section 954: Compensation

1210. This section confers on the Panel the power to make rules providing for financial redress (together with interest (including compound interest)) in consequence of a breach of rules which

Part 3   CA 2006 Supporting Materials

require monetary payments to be made (for instance, a payment by the bidder to shareholders of any difference between the price actually paid and any higher price for shares that the bidder should have paid under the rules).

Section 955: Enforcement by the court

1211. This section provides a mechanism by which the Panel may, if necessary, apply to the court in order to enforce Panel rule-based requirements as well as requests for documents and information under section 947. The Panel may apply to the court either where there is reasonable likelihood that a person will contravene a requirement imposed by or under the rules or where a person has failed to comply with such a requirement or with a requirement imposed under section 947.

1212. It is expected that in accordance with usual practice, the court will not, in exercising its jurisdiction under this section, rehear substantively the matter or examine the issues giving rise to the ruling or, as the case may be, the request for documents or information except on "judicial review principles", where there has been an error of law or procedure.

1213. The court is given a broad discretion as to the order it may make to secure compliance with the requirement; but aside from the power granted to the Panel by this section, there is no right to seek an injunction (or interdict) to prevent a person contravening, or continuing to contravene, a rule-based requirement or disclosure requirement.

Section 956: No action for breach of statutory duty etc

1214. Compliance with the rules made by the Panel is a matter solely for the Panel. This section does two things:
(a)   it excludes new rights of action for breach of statutory duty for contraventions of requirements imposed by or under rules or a requirement imposed under section 947; and
(b)   in order to ensure certainty, it provides that a contravention of a rule based requirement does not make a transaction void or unenforceable and (subject to any provision of the rules) does not affect the validity of any other thing. As currently, transactions will be capable of being set aside or unravelled in cases of, for example, misrepresentation or fraud.

Funding

Section 957: Fees and charges

1215. This section enables the Panel to make rules for the payment of fees or charges to the Panel for the purposes of meeting the Panel's expenses incurred in exercising its functions. Such fees and charges may be imposed to meet expenses of the Takeover Appeal Board; the cost of repaying capital and paying interest on loans; and the cost of maintaining adequate reserves. The rules under this section must be made by the Panel itself or by a committee of the Panel (section 943(4)).

Section 958: Levy

1216. This section gives the Secretary of State the power to make regulations imposing a levy for meeting the costs of the Panel. In determining the appropriate rate of the levy, the Secretary of State must take account of other income received, or expected to be received, by the Panel (which would include fees and charges under section 957) and may take account of estimated as well as actual costs of the Panel.

1217. It is anticipated that a levy would only be imposed if the existing voluntary levy funding arrangements (contributions collected by member firms of the London Stock Exchange and Ofex currently set at a flat rate charge of £1 on contract notes on all chargeable transactions with a consideration in excess of £10,000) were no longer viable. The categories of persons or bodies to which the levy would apply may include only those capable of being directly affected by the exercise of the Panel's functions or otherwise having a substantial interest in the exercise of those functions.

1218. The first regulations made in respect of the levy power – and any further regulations which change the persons or bodies by whom, or the transactions on which, the levy is payable – will be subject to the affirmative resolution procedure in both Houses of Parliament. A draft of an instrument containing such regulations will not be treated as being hybrid even if otherwise it would be. Any other subsequent regulations will be subject to the negative resolution procedure.

Section 959: Recovery of fees, charges or levy

1219. This section provides that an amount payable by a person as a consequence of fees and charges imposed by the Panel under section 957 or as a result of any levy fixed by the Secretary of State under section 958 will constitute a debt owed by that person to the Panel and be recoverable by the Panel as a debt.

Miscellaneous and supplementary

Section 960: Panel as party to proceedings

1220. This section provides that, notwithstanding its unincorporated status, the Panel may in its own name bring proceedings under this Chapter and bring or defend other proceedings.

Section 961: Exemption from liability in damages

1221. This section confers limited immunity on the Panel and those involved in carrying out its regulatory activities. The immunity provisions are consistent with those recently extended to the Financial Services Authority and the Financial Reporting Council in the exercise of their duties under financial services and companies legislation.

1222. The section exempts the Panel, its members, officers and staff (which would include secondees), and persons authorised under section 947(5) by the Panel to exercise its powers in relation to requiring documents and information, from liability in damages for things done or omitted in relation to the Panel's regulatory activities. (The Takeover Appeal Board benefits from a common law immunity on account of its exercise of judicial functions.)

1223. Section 961(3) sets out the circumstances where the exemption will not apply – that is to say, where the act or omission was in bad faith or where it was unlawful under section 6(1) of the Human Rights Act 1998.

Section 962: Privilege against self-incrimination

1224. This section provides that a statement made by a person to the Panel, or a person authorised on its behalf, in compliance with a requirement to provide information under section 947 (or a court order made to secure compliance with such a requirement under section 955) cannot be used against that person in most types of criminal proceedings. Such statements can, however, be used in proceedings for offences of making false statements otherwise than on oath under section 5 of the Perjury Act 1911 and its Scottish and Northern Irish equivalents. These offences exist to deter and punish the making of false statements and it would not be possible to prosecute such offences if the false statements themselves could not be used in evidence against those by whom they were made.

Section 963: Annual reports

1225. As is the Panel's existing practice, the Panel will be required to publish an annual report containing annual accounts, setting out how the Panel's functions were discharged and including other matters considered by the Panel to be of relevance. Annual reports published by the Panel are available on the Panel's website.

Section 964: Amendments to Financial Services and Markets Act 2000

1226. This section repeals section 143 of the Financial Services and Markets Act 2000 ("FSMA") which, by endorsing the City Code on Takeovers and Mergers, presently provides a mechanism for the Financial Services Authority to bring disciplinary and enforcement action against authorised persons for misconduct in relation to the Code. Given that the Code will be replaced by rules which have legal force as a consequence of the Act, it is considered that there is no longer a need to maintain section 143.

1227. This will not, however, preclude the Panel from reporting breaches of the Code by authorised persons in relation to takeover bids to the Financial Services Authority, as at present, and any such breaches will still be taken into account by the FSA, for example, in assessing whether such persons are fit and proper to be authorised for business of that kind or have otherwise complied with their regulatory obligations (for example, whether they are meeting proper standards of market conduct).

1228. A consequential amendment is made by section 964(3) to preserve the definition of "consultation procedures" currently contained at section 143(7) for the purposes of the provisions in section 144 of FSMA relating to price stabilising rules. Additionally, to ensure consistency with the requirements of Article 4.4 of the Directive as regards the duties of takeover regulatory and financial services authorities within the EU to co-operate with each other, the existing disclosure and regulatory co-operation obligations of the Financial Services Authority under sections 349 and 354 of FSMA are amended to include cooperation with relevant authorities referred to by the Directive and to remove restrictions on disclosure to such authorities. These duties reflect the disclosure and co-operation provisions in sections 948 and 950 (including provisions related to the rules on disclosure that apply where information is passed to other takeover supervisory authorities and financial services regulators described in relation to section 948(6)).

Sections 965 and 973: Power to extend to Isle of Man and Channel Islands

1229. These sections allow any provisions of Chapters 1 and 2 to be extended to the Isle of Man or any of the Channel Islands by Order in Council, with any specified modifications.

Chapter 2: Impediments To Takeovers

Summary and background

1230. Article 11 of the Takeovers Directive seeks to override, in certain circumstances relating to a takeover, a number of defensive devices that may be adopted by companies prior to the bid, such as: differential share structures under which minority shareholders may exercise disproportionate voting rights; restrictions on transfer of shares in the company articles or in contractual agreements; and limitations on share ownership.

1231. There are currently no restrictions on the way that UK companies which are admitted to trading on a regulated market can structure their share capital and control. However, market pressure brought to bear, in particular, by institutional investors has ensured that there are now few UK listed companies with differential voting structures.

1232. As permitted by Article 12 of the Directive, it has been decided not to apply the provisions of Article 11 in all cases but instead to include in the Act (sections 966 to 972) provision for companies with voting shares traded on a regulated market to opt in to its provisions should they choose to do so.

Sections 966, 967 and 970: Opting in and opting out; Further provision about opting-in and opting-out resolutions; Communication of decisions

1233. A company may pass a special resolution opting in to Article 11 (an "opting-in resolution") provided that three conditions are met:

(a)   it has voting shares admitted to trading on a regulated market (it is not considered necessary to extend this provision to other types of companies which are not covered by the Directive);

(b)   the company's articles of association do not contain restrictions of the kind mentioned in Article 11 (or other provisions which would be incompatible with Article 11) or, if they do contain such restrictions, the restrictions will not apply in circumstances related to a takeover bid as described by Article 11. Article 11 relates to both the takeover bid period and the time following the bid when the bidder has acquired 75% or more of the company's capital carrying voting rights. It provides that restrictions both on the rights to transfer shares and on voting rights that are contained in the articles of the company should not apply. It also provides that, in certain circumstances, shares carrying multiple voting rights shall only have one vote and extraordinary rights of shareholders concerning the appointment or removal of board members should be disapplied; and

(c)   no shares are held by a Minister conferring special rights in the company and no such special rights are provided for in law. The Directive expressly provides that Article 11 does not apply to shares held by Member States conferring special rights on the Member State which are compatible with the Treaty, or to special rights provided for in national law which are compatible with the Treaty. The UK Government holds a number of so-called "golden shares" in formerly publicly-owned businesses which have been privatised to ensure that essential public interest considerations are protected. This provision will exclude all such companies where the Government holds the beneficial ownership of a golden share (since holdings by nominees and subsidiaries are also covered). The concept of Minister is broadly defined in section 966(7) of the Act to include Scottish Ministers and Northern Ireland Ministers under section 7(3) of the Northern Ireland Act 1998. (As a result of the Government of Wales Act 2006, the definition of Minister will be changed to include Welsh Ministers). Under section 966(8), a power is provided to the Secretary of State by the negative resolution procedure to apply the provision in section 966(4) (Minister holding golden shares) to persons or bodies exercising functions of a public nature as it applies in relation to a Minister.

1234. Section 966(5) enables a company to revoke an opting-in resolution by means of a further special resolution (an "opting-out resolution").

1235. Section 967 sets down provisions relating to the date on which the opting-in and opting-out resolutions will take effect. Generally, this will be the date stated in the resolution.

1236. Section 970 requires companies, within 15 days of an opting-in or opting-out resolution being passed, to notify the Panel and any other takeover supervisory authority in a Member State in which the company has shares admitted to trading on a regulated market or has requested such admission. Where a company fails to comply with this requirement, the company and every officer in default will be guilty of an offence and be liable on summary conviction to a fine not exceeding level 3 on the standard scale (and to a daily default fine for continued contravention).

Section 968: Effect on contractual restrictions

1237. This section provides that agreements entered into between shareholders in the company on or after 21 April 2004 (the date on which the Takeovers Directive was adopted), and agreements entered into between a shareholder and the company before as well as on or after that date, are invalid in so far as they impose any of the restrictions set out in subsection (2).

1238. Those restrictions relate both to the bid period and to the time following a takeover bid when the bidder holds 75% or more in value of all the voting shares in the company. Types of restrictions overridden are those imposing restrictions on the transfer of shares and on rights to vote at general meetings of the company to decide on action to frustrate the bid and at the first meeting to be held after the end of the offer period. For the purposes of determining when the bidder holds 75% or more in value of all the voting shares in the company, both debentures and shares which do not normally carry rights to vote at a general meeting (such as preference shares) held by the bidder are to be disregarded (see subsection (8)).

1239. The provisions related to the types of contractual agreements to which the override will apply (including the date at which such contracts were entered into) and the restrictions which are made invalid are designed to replicate the provisions of Article 11 of the Directive.

1240. Section 968(6) provides that a person who suffers loss as a result of a contractual agreement being overridden can apply to the court for compensation. It is expected that, in the first instance, such compensation will be offered by the bidder in making the takeover offer. Where, however, the compensation offered by the bidder is not acceptable to the person whose rights are being overridden, there is a right to apply to the court. The court will award compensation to the person who suffers loss on a just and equitable basis to be paid by any person (which could include the bidder or the other party to the contract which has been overridden) who would have been liable to him for committing or inducing the breach of contract which would have been committed had the restriction in question not been made invalid by this section.

Sections 969 and 972: Power of offeror to require general meeting to be called; Transitory provision

1241. Section 969 provides the bidder with the special right to require the directors of an opted-in company to call a general meeting of the company when he holds 75% in value of all the voting shares in the company (excluding debentures and shares that do not normally carry rights to vote at a general meeting (such as preference shares)). Section 969(3) applies sections 303 to 305 of the Act, which deal with the calling of meetings, to such a request (with the necessary modifications). But as those sections may not be in force at the time when section 969 comes into force, section 972 makes the same sort of adaptations in relation to the equivalent provisions of the 1985 Act. In particular, section 972(3) alters the application of section 378(2) so that a special resolution may still be passed at a general meeting called at only 14 days' notice (normally at least 21 days' notice would have to be given of the meeting for it to be able to pass a special resolution).

Chapter 3: "squeeze-out" and "sell-out"

Summary and background

1242. The concepts of "squeeze-out" and "sell-out" are designed to address the problems of, and for, residual minority shareholders following a successful takeover bid. Squeeze-out rights enable a successful bidder to compulsorily purchase the shares of remaining minority shareholders who have not accepted the bid. Sell-out rights enable minority shareholders, in the wake of such a bid, to require the majority shareholder to purchase their shares. Because they involve the compulsory purchase or acquisition of shares against the will of the holder of the shares or the acquirer, high thresholds apply to the exercising of such rights and there are protective rules on the price that must be paid for the shares concerned.

1243. Squeeze-out and sell-out provisions have been a feature of national company law for many years (and were previously contained in Part 13A (Takeover Offers) of the 1985 Act). Articles 15 and 16 of the Takeovers Directive, however, introduce EU-wide rules requiring all Member States to put appropriate provisions in place for the first time. The provisions at sections 974 to 991 of the Act restate Part 13A of the 1985 Act in a clearer form. However, in doing so they also make important changes to reflect the need to ensure compliance with the Directive and the decision to accept some recommendations of the CLR. These are described below.

Detail of changes made to the operation of provisions previously contained in Part 13A of the 1985 Act

1244. The rules laid down in the Directive in relation to squeeze-out and sell-out are broadly consistent with provisions of Part 13A (sections 428 to 430F) of the 1985 Act. The restated and amended provisions will apply equally to all companies and all bids within the ambit of Part 13A of the 1985 Act, regardless of whether or not the Directive is required to be applied to such companies and bids.

1245. The following changes are made in implementation of the Directive:

- Calculation of Squeeze-out Threshold (section 979) – there is a dual test imposed: in order to acquire the minority shareholder's shares, the bidder must have acquired both 90% of the shares to which the offer relates, and 90% of the voting rights carried by those shares. Where the offer relates to shares of different classes, then, in order to acquire the remaining shares in a class, the bidder must have acquired 90% of the shares of that class to which the offer relates, and 90% of the voting rights carried by those shares. Under section 429 of the 1985 Act, in each case only the first limb of that test applied.
- Calculation of Sell-out Threshold (section 983) – mirroring the change to be made in relation to the squeeze-out threshold, a dual test is similarly imposed in relation to the sell-out threshold, so that a minority shareholder may force a bidder to acquire his shares (i) when the bidder holds 90% of the shares in the company, and 90% of the voting rights attached to those shares, or (ii) when the bidder holds 90% of the shares in the class to which the minority shareholder's shares belong, and 90% of the voting rights attached to those shares. Under section 430A of the 1985 Act, the test was that the bidder should have acquired 90% of all shares in the company (or in the class concerned).
- Revised Period during which Squeeze-Out and Sell-Out Rights may be Exercised (section 980(2)) – the Directive provides (Articles 15.4 and 16.3) that squeeze-out and sell-out rights must be exercisable within a three month period following the time allowed for acceptance of the bid. Section 429(3) of the 1985 Act provided that squeeze-out could be exercised within a period of four months beginning with the date of the offer and had to be

Part 3   CA 2006 Supporting Materials

exercised within two months of reaching the 90% threshold. Accordingly, the rule provided by the Directive is substituted for the rule in the 1985 Act. An exception to this rule is provided where takeover bids are not subject to the Directive, for instance takeovers of most private companies. In these cases, the squeeze-out notices must be given within six months of the date of the offer if this is earlier than the period ending three months after the end of the offer. This is intended to prevent offerors in such circumstances continually extending the offer period. A change is also made as regards the period during which sell-out may be exercisable so that this period is to be either three months from the end of the offer or, if later, three months from the notice given to the shareholder of his right to exercise sell-out rights (section 984(2)). An extended period during which the sell-out right can be exercised where notice of such a right is only given after the end of the offer period is consistent with provisions of the Directive allowing more stringent provisions to be put in place (in this case to ensure the proper protection of minority shareholders).

- The court will no longer be able to reduce the consideration in relation to squeeze-out or sell-out following a takeover bid to below the consideration offered in the bid (which the Takeovers Directive presumes to be fair in all cases). Again utilising provisions of the Directive which allow more stringent provisions to be included to protect minority shareholders, minority shareholders will continue to be able to apply to the court to request that consideration higher than that offered in the bid be paid in exceptional circumstances (section 986(4)).

1246.   In most instances, it is considered that the first and second changes above will make no practical difference as the percentage of total capital carrying voting rights in a company (or class of shares) and the percentage of voting rights will normally be the same. The provisions about voting rights will not apply where the shares being squeezed out or sold out are non-voting shares.

1247.   The CLR also considered the issue of squeeze-out and sell-out and the scope for improving the provisions in the 1985 Act. Its Final Report (chapter 13, pages 282 – 300), made a number of recommendations in relation to the reform of the squeeze-out and sell-out regime. Some of these recommendations are closely related to implementation of the Takeovers Directive. For instance, the CLR questioned whether, in calculating the relevant squeeze-out and sell-out thresholds, only shares that had been unconditionally acquired should be taken into account or whether shares acquired subject to contract should also be included.

1248.   In implementing the Takeovers Directive, the opportunity is being taken to adopt recommendations of the CLR, whether or not related to implementation of the Directive, except to the extent that they are not consistent with Articles 15 and 16 of the Directive or are no longer appropriate as a consequence of the Directive. The recommendations made by the CLR implemented by Chapter 3 of Part 28 are set out below:

Meaning of takeover offer and entitlement to dividends (sections 974 and 976)

1249.   In order to be a takeover offer for the purposes of Part 13A of the 1985 Act, an offer to acquire shares had to be on terms which were the same in relation to all the shares to which the offer related. One problem with the 1985 legislation was how to treat any variations in value between shares of the same class that were attributable to the fact that some of the shares, because they were allotted later, do not yet carry a dividend. Section 976(2) rectifies this problem by providing that, even if the offeror offers to pay more for shares that carry a dividend than for those in the same class which do not, the offer will be treated as being made on the same terms in relation to those shares.

Meaning of a takeover offer and communication of that offer (sections 974 and 978)

1250.   To deal with issues arising from an increasingly globalised market in shares and different legislative regimes outside the EEA, it is made clear that an offer is not prevented from being a takeover offer for the purposes of Chapter 3 of Part 28 merely because there are some offerees who will be unable to accept it (for instance, where the offeree cannot accept the offer because of restrictions on the cross-border transfer of cash or securities in the country in which the offeree resides). It is also provided that an offer can still be a takeover offer for the purposes of the squeeze-out and sell-out provisions if a shareholder has no registered address in the UK and the offer is not communicated to him to avoid contravening the law of another country as long as either the offer itself is published in the Gazette or a notice is published in the Gazette stating that a copy of the offer document can be obtained from a place in the EEA or on a website.

Shares that the offeror has "contracted to acquire" (section 975)

1251.   Clarificatory amendments are made on this issue. Section 428(5) of the 1985 Act dealt with the offeror's position at the start of the bid, for the purpose of determining which shares could not be counted towards the achievement of the 90% threshold (at which point shares may be compulsorily purchased). It was unclear as to whether the phrase "contracted to acquire" in section 428(5) covered conditional as well as unconditional contracts. It is, therefore, clarified that, in ascertaining the offeror's position at the start of the bid, the shares he has conditionally contracted to acquire (other than those subject to irrevocable undertakings (see below), as under the 1985 Act) should be treated as being shares already held by the offeror. This means that only shares that the offeror has either acquired or unconditionally contracted to acquire will count towards the 90% total needed to exercise squeeze-out. Consequential changes are also made to the provisions on joint offers and associates of the offeror to bring these into line with the above.

1252.   Under the 1985 Act, the registered holder of shares could give an irrevocable undertaking to accept a takeover bid, and if he did this for no consideration or only in exchange for a promise to make the bid, his shares were still treated for the purposes of squeeze-out as included within the offer. This is extended to include undertakings given for only negligible consideration and undertakings the effect of which is to require the registered holder to accept the offer (where the undertaking is given by a person who is not the registered holder of the shares but can contract to bind the registered holder, such as the manager of shares held by a bare nominee). ("Irrevocable undertakings" are contractual agreements entered into by a bidder usually with major shareholder(s) of a proposed target company. Such agreements aim to give the bidder certainty – he will know that support for the offer can be guaranteed from shareholders party to the contract – so that his bid has a greater prospect of success. Such undertakings would normally prevent the giver of the undertaking from selling their shares or exercising voting rights to prevent the takeover from becoming successful.)

Date of the offer (section 991(1))

1253.   The "date of the offer" is defined to mean either the date of publication, or if the offer is not published or notice of the offer is sent out earlier, the date on which the offeror first sends notice of the offer to the offerees.

Right of offeror to buy out minority shareholders: treatment of options etc (section 979(5))

1254.   Where an offeror makes an offer for all the target company's allotted shares and all or any shares subsequently allotted, it is provided that (a) in deciding whether the offeror has reached the 90% threshold for the purposes of section 979, the offeror need only bring into the calculation shares which are actually in issue (ie allotted) at the relevant time; (b) if the offeror serves squeeze-out notices and more shares are subsequently allotted which take the percentage of acceptances then received below 90%, that will not invalidate squeeze-out notices already served; and (c) if the offeror wishes to serve further squeeze-out notices, he must have at least 90% acceptances of shares (or shares in a class) then in issue and subject to the offer at the time he sends the notices out.

Consideration not exclusively in cash (section 981(5))

1255.   It is clarified that where an offer of shares, or a mixture of shares and cash, is made, and it is no longer possible when the offeror exercises his right of squeeze-out to give the consideration in shares, the offeror should pay the cash equivalent irrespective of whether the shareholders had previously been offered a choice (ie whether the offer was "mix and match" or not). Parallel changes are made as regards sell-out (section 985(5)).

Shares that the offeror has "contracted to acquire" (section 983)

1256.   It is clarified that, in addition to shares acquired by the offeror, shares subject to both conditional and unconditional contracts of acquisition are included in calculating whether the sell-out threshold has been reached. As a result of this change, there might be circumstances where the 90% threshold required for sell-out to be exercised was reached only because of shares which the offeror had conditionally contracted to acquire. However, if the conditions of such contracts were not fulfilled, the offeror could in fact find that he was being required to buy a minority shareholder's shares even though the offeror had not actually acquired 90% of the shares. So section 983 also provides that, if that is the case at the time when the minority shareholder exercises his right of sell-out, the offeror does not have to purchase the shares unless he has acquired or unconditionally contracted to acquire 90% or more of the shares by the time the period referred to in section 984(2) (the period within which shareholders can exercise sell-out rights) ends. (A corresponding change is made in section 979(6) and (7) to prevent minority shareholders in this situation who have to wait to see if they can exercise sell-out from being squeezed out in the meantime.)

Applications to the Court (section 986)

1257.   This section provides that a shareholder receiving a squeeze-out notice may make an application to the court (within six weeks of receiving the notice) seeking to overturn an offeror's intention to purchase his shares compulsorily (or the terms of that purchase). A requirement that the offeror be promptly notified of such an application is now included (this was not previously required by section 430C of the 1985 Act). As a consequence of this requirement, it is also required that the offeror is obliged, at the earliest opportunity, to notify shareholders who are being squeezed out or who are exercising their rights of sell-out, and are not party to a section 986 application, that proceedings have been initiated.

Chapter 4: Amendments To Part 7 Of The Companies Act 1985

Section 992: Matters to be dealt with in directors' report

1258.   This section implements Article 10 of the Takeovers Directive. Article 10.1 and 10.2 require companies admitted to trading on a regulated market to provide in their annual reports detailed information relating to matters such as the control and share structures of the company. It is, therefore, provided by amendment to Part 7 of the 1985 Act that the information required by the Directive must be set out in the directors' report.

1259.   Additionally, Article 10.3 of the Directive requires boards of companies to present an explanatory report to shareholders on the issues referred to in Article 10.1 and 10.2 at the company's annual general meeting. This section requires this additional explanatory material to be contained in the directors' report submitted to the annual meeting of shareholders.

1260.   Section 992(5) amends section 251 of the 1985 Act on summary financial statements. It provides for the explanatory material required by Article 10.3 of the Takeovers Directive either to be included in the summary financial statement or to accompany it.

1261.   Failure to include either the information concerning control and share structures or explanatory material in the annual report will attract existing criminal sanctions under section 234(5) of the 1985 Act (directors responsible for the failure to comply with provisions related to the directors' report are to be liable to a fine).

1262.   Section 992(6) provides that these new provisions will apply in relation to directors' reports for financial years beginning on or after 20 May 2006 (the date by which the Directive had to be implemented).

1263.   These are general requirements designed to bring greater transparency to the market and apply to all relevant companies whether or not they are involved in a takeover. Accordingly, the requirements will apply to all companies registered in the UK which have voting shares traded on a regulated market, whether or not that includes an official listing on the London Stock Exchange.

Under Part 15 of the Act (section 416), the Secretary of State may in future make regulations as to the contents of the directors' report and those regulations will be able to incorporate the provisions introduced by section 992(2) to (4). Regulations under sections 427 and 428 will be able to make provision for the additional explanatory material when a summary financial statement is sent out rather than the full accounts and report.

PART 29: FRAUDULENT TRADING

Section 993: Offence of fraudulent trading

[3.30]
1264.   This section restates section 458 of the 1985 Act, but in doing so increases the maximum sentence for the offence from seven years' imprisonment to ten years.

PART 30: PROTECTION OF MEMBERS AGAINST UNFAIR PREJUDICE

[3.31]
1265.   Sections 994–998 restate sections 459, 460 and 461 of the 1985 Act, which provide a remedy where a company's affairs are being conducted in a manner which is unfairly prejudicial to the interests of its members.

Section 999: Supplementary provisions where company's constitution altered

1266.   Section 999 is a new section which ensures that, if the court makes an order under Part 30 amending the company's articles, updated articles are registered and a copy of the court order is supplied with any copies of the articles that are issued by the company, unless they already incorporate the amendments.

PART 31: DISSOLUTION AND RESTORATION TO THE REGISTER

Chapters 1 And 2: Striking Off And Property Of Dissolved Company

[3.32]
1267.   These Chapters restate sections 652 to 654 and sections 656 to 658 of the 1985 Act with no changes of effect, except as described below for sections 1003 and 1013.

Section 1003: Striking off on applications by company

1268.   Section 652A of the 1985 Act currently provides that, in certain circumstances, a company may apply to the registrar to be struck off the register. The provision is limited to private companies. This section, in restating that provision, no longer includes the limitation, with the effect that public companies too may now apply for voluntary strike-off.

Section 1013: Crown disclaimer of property vesting as bona vacantia

1269.   Where a company is dissolved while still holding property, that property passes to the Crown. Section 656 of the 1985 Act provides that the Crown's title to the property may be disclaimed by means of a notice signed by the Crown representative.

1270.   At present this disclaimer must generally be executed within 12 months of the date on which vesting of the property came to the notice of the Crown representative or within three years of the Crown representative receiving an application from an interested party. This section, in restating the relevant provisions, extends the 12-month period to three years, and provides that, if the ownership of the property is not established when the Crown representative first has notice that the property may have vested, that period runs from the end of the period reasonably necessary for the Crown representative to establish ownership.

1271.   Section 656 of the 1985 Act also provides that a disclaimer may be made within three years of the Crown representative receiving an application from an interested party. This section changes this to 12 months.

Chapter 3: Restoration To The Register

1272.   Under the 1985 Act, where a company has been struck off the register, mechanisms are available (sections 651 and 653) by which the company may be restored to the register following a court order. The CLR (Final Report, pages 227 to 229) recommended that an alternative, administrative restoration procedure should be available in certain circumstances. Sections 1024 to 1028 make provision implementing that recommendation.

Section 1024: Application for administrative restoration to the register

1273.   This section provides that an application may be made to restore a company that has been struck off under sections 1000 or 1001; that it can be made whether or not the company has also been dissolved; that the application must be made by a former director or former member of the company, and that it must be made within six years of the date of dissolution.

Section 1025: Requirements for administrative restoration

1274.   This section sets out the requirements for restoration, including the conditions that the company was carrying on business or in operation at the time of its striking off; that the Crown representative has given any consent that may be necessary; and that the applicant has delivered any documents necessary to bring the registrar's records up to date and has paid any penalties due at the date of dissolution or striking off.

Section 1026: Application to be accompanied by statement of compliance

1275.   This section provides that an application for restoration must be accompanied by a statement that the applicant has the necessary standing to make the application and that the requirements for administrative restoration have been met. The registrar may accept the statement of compliance as sufficient evidence of the matters stated in it.

Section 1027: Registrar's decision on application for administrative restoration

1276.   This section provides that the registrar must give notice of her decision, and that (if the decision is that the company is restored) the restoration takes effect from the date that notice is sent. The section also sets out the consequential actions the registrar must take.

Section 1028: Effect of administrative restoration

1277.   This section provides that the effect of restoration is that the company is deemed to have continued in existence as if it had not been struck off, and that application may be made to the court within three years of restoration for the court to make such directions as may be needed to place the company itself, and other persons, in the same position as they would have been had the company not been struck off.

Restoration to the register by the court

1278.   These sections bring together what are currently two separate procedures for a company to be restored to the register by court order (under sections 651 and 653 of the 1985 Act). The CLR recommended (Final report pages 227 to 229) that the two separate procedures be replaced by a single new procedure, which should largely be based on the precedent of the procedure under section 653 of the 1985 Act.

Section 1029: Application to court for restoration to the register

1279.   The section sets out that an application may be made for the restoration of companies which have been dissolved, are deemed to be dissolved, or have been struck off under the various provisions set out in subsection (1). Subsection (2) sets out the persons who may make such an application.

Section 1030: When application to the court may be made

1280. At the moment, applications to the court under section 651 of the 1985 Act must be made within two years, and under section 653 within twenty years. This new section provides that the time limit for the new single procedure will generally be six years, although special provision is made (subsection (5)) for situations where an application for administrative restoration has been made and refused.

1281. Subsection (1) makes clear that there is no time limit where the application is for the purpose of bringing proceedings against the company for damages for personal injury.

Section 1031: Decision on application for restoration by the court

1282. This section sets out the circumstances in which the court may order restoration (including any case in which the court considers it just to do so) and provides that restoration takes effect when the court's order is delivered to the registrar. It also requires the registrar to give appropriate public notice of the restoration.

Section 1032: Effect of court order for restoration to the register

1283. This section provides that the effect of restoration is that the company is deemed to have continued in existence as if it had not been struck off, and that the court may make such directions as are needed to place the company itself, and other persons, in the same position as they would have been had the company not been struck off. The court may also make directions as to the issues set out in subsection (4) to do with the company's file at Companies House and costs.

Restoration to the register: supplementary provisions

Section 1033: Company's name on restoration

1284. This section establishes the fundamental position that a company is restored to the register with the name it had before it was struck off, but also makes new provision for circumstances where restoration of a company would have the effect that two companies with the same or very similar names would appear in the registrar's index. There is a procedure for the restored company to change its name.

Section 1034: Effect of restoration to the register where property has vested a bona vacantia

1285. This section replaces section 655 of the 1985 Act with little change of substance. However, it makes new provision (subsection (3)) that, where a company's property has passed to the Crown and been disposed of, the Crown, in reimbursing the newly restored company, may deduct the reasonable costs of sale which were incurred.

PART 32: COMPANY INVESTIGATIONS: AMENDMENTS

Powers to appoint inspectors

[3.33]

1286. The 1985 Act gives the Secretary of State the power to appoint competent inspectors to carry out inspections, and report the result to him, in a number of circumstances. There are three categories of inspections at present:
- investigations into the affairs of companies;
- investigations into the membership or control of companies; and
- investigations of dealings in share options by company directors and their families and failure to disclose interests in shares.

1287. Investigations by inspectors into the affairs of companies and certain other bodies corporate can be initiated under sections 431 and 432. Such inspections can be launched on the application of a company or a proportion of its members, or on the Secretary of State's own initiative, and must be carried out where the court orders it.

1288. Investigations by inspectors into the membership or control of companies can be initiated under section 442. The Secretary of State can launch such an inspection on his own initiative under section 442(1), and is obliged to do so where the requisite number of members of a company apply.

1289. Inspections in the third category, under section 446, relate to suspected contraventions of certain provisions of Part 10 of the 1985 Act. The 2006 Act repeals the relevant provisions of Part 10 (see section 1177) and section 446 is repealed in consequence.

1290. Two inspectors are generally appointed to carry out an inspection – usually a QC and a partner in one of the leading accountancy firms.

1291. Inspectors are appointed to investigate and to report the results of their investigations to the Secretary of State. At the end of an inspection, the inspectors generally have a duty to make a final report to the Secretary of State. The inspectors may also make interim reports during the course of the inspection, and the Secretary of State can direct them to do so.

1292. Unless the appointment was made under section 432 of the 1985 Act on terms that any report is not for publication (section 432(2A)) interim and final reports are publishable; the Secretary of State has discretion to publish an interim or final report under section 437(3). The availability of a published report is a crucial aspect of the inspection system.

Changes brought in by the 2006 Act

1293. The 2006 Act confers new powers on the Secretary of State to bring to an end an investigation when it is no longer in the public interest to continue with it, to revoke the appointment of an inspector and to issue directions about the scope of an investigation, its duration and certain other matters.

1294. The main purpose of these sections is to give the Secretary of State power to take appropriate action where an investigation appears to be taking too long. The sections also provide for situations not currently explicitly provided for, such as the resignation or death of inspectors, and the ability to appoint replacement inspectors.

1295. The details of these changes and the circumstances in which the changes will apply are set out below.

Section 1035: Powers of Secretary of State to give directions to inspectors

1296. Subsection (1) inserts new sections 446A and 446B into the 1985 Act, which provide new powers for the Secretary of State to give directions to inspectors with which they are obliged to comply (new sections 446A(1) and 446B(5)).

1297. The power in new section 446A(2) is exercisable by the Secretary of State in relation to inspectors appointed under sections 431, 432(2) and 442(1). Directions under new section 446A(2) can either relate to the investigation itself or the inspectors' reports of the results of their investigations. Regarding the former, such directions can take two forms:
- a direction as to the subject matter of an investigation (whether by reference to a specified area of a company's operation, a specified transaction, a period of time or otherwise); or
- a direction which requires an inspector to take or not to take a specified step in his investigation.

1298. As regards inspectors' reports the Secretary of State will have a power to secure that any report (new section 446A(3)):
- includes the inspector's views on a specified matter;
- does not include any reference to a specified matter;
- is made in a specified form or manner; or
- is made by a specified date.

1299. New section 446A(4) enables directions by the Secretary of State to be capable of being given on an inspector's appointment. It also provides that directions may vary or revoke a direction previously given and may be given at the request of an inspector.

1300. New section 446A(5) confirms that the scope of the term "investigation" will include any investigation undertaken under section 433(1) into the affairs of the company's holding company or subsidiary (or a subsidiary of its holding company or a holding company of its subsidiary).

1301. New section 446B(1) will give the Secretary of State power to direct an inspector to take no further steps in an investigation, and the inspector shall comply with any direction given to him under this section (new section 446B(5)). However, if the appointment of inspectors is one that the Secretary of State is obliged to make (either because a court orders that a company's affairs ought to be so investigated or because the requisite number of its members has applied for an investigation into its ownership), such a direction can only be given if matters have come to light in the course of the investigation which suggest that a criminal offence has been committed and those matters have been referred to the appropriate prosecuting authority (new section 446B(2)).

1302. Under new section 446B(3), any direction given to the inspector under section 437(1) to produce an interim report, and any direction under new section 446A(3) in relation such a report, shall cease to have effect.

1303. If the Secretary of State directs an inspector to take no further steps in an investigation then the inspector shall not make a final report to him unless:
- the requisite number of a company's members has applied for an investigation into its ownership, matters have come to light in the course of the investigation which suggest that a criminal offence has been committed, those matters have been referred to the appropriate prosecuting authority and the Secretary of State directs the inspectors to make a final report; or
- the inspector was appointed following a court order that a company's affairs ought to be investigated (new section 446B(4)).

1304. New section 446B(6) confirms that the scope of the term "investigation" will include any investigation undertaken under section 433(1) into the affairs of the company's holding company or subsidiary (or a subsidiary of its holding company or a holding company of its subsidiary).

1305. Subsections (2) to (5) concern consequential changes to other sections within the 1985 Act.

Section 1036: Resignation, removal and replacement of inspectors

1306. This section inserts new sections 446C and 446D which provide for the resignation or revocation of an inspector's appointment and the provision to replace an inspector.

1307.   New section 446C(1) and (2) provides not only that an inspector may resign but also that the Secretary of State has the power to revoke his appointment.

1308.   New section 446D(1) provides that, if an inspector resigns, dies or has his appointment revoked, the Secretary of State has the power to appoint a replacement inspector to continue the investigation. Any appointment which takes place under new subsection (1) will be treated as though it were made under the provision under which the former inspector were appointed (new section 446D(2)).

1309.   The Secretary of State is obliged to ensure that at least one inspector continues the investigation (new section 446D(3)) unless such a step would be pointless because he could direct the termination of the investigation in circumstances which would result in a final report not being made (new section 446D(4)).

1310.   New section 446D(5) confirms that the scope of the term "investigation" will include any investigation undertaken under section 433(1) into the affairs of the company's holding company or subsidiary (or a subsidiary of its holding company or a holding company of its subsidiary).

Section 1037: Power to obtain information from former inspectors etc

1311.   Subsection (1) inserts new section 446E into the 1985 Act.

1312.   New section 446E(1) provides that, where an inspector resigns or has his appointment revoked or is given a direction under section 446B (termination of an investigation) (new section 446E(2)), the Secretary of State can direct him to hand over documents that he has obtained or generated during the course of his investigation, either to the Secretary of State or to another inspector appointed under this Part (new section 446E(3)).

1313.   A requirement under new subsection (3) includes the power to ensure that the production of a copy of the document is made in hard copy or in a form from which a hard copy can be obtained (new section 446E(4)). A document includes information recorded in any form (new section 446E(7)(b)). New section 446E(5) enables the Secretary of State to direct any person to whom this section applies to inform him of any matters that came to that person's attention as a result of the investigation. New section 446E(6) confirms that a person shall comply with any direction given to him under this section.

1314.   New section 446E(7)(a) confirms that the scope of the term "investigation" will include any investigation undertaken under section 433(1) into the affairs of the company's holding company or subsidiary (or a subsidiary of its holding company or a holding company of its subsidiary).

1315.   Subsections (2) and (3) concern consequential changes to other sections within the 1985 Act.

Section 1038: Power to require production of documents

1316.   The 2006 Act introduces a new definition for documents in hard copy form, (see section 1135). This section ensures that there is a consistent approach in existing investigation provisions where there is a requirement to produce documents.

Section 1039: Disqualification orders: consequential amendments

1317.   Subsections (a) and (b) extend the Company Directors Disqualification Act 1986 so that decisions on whether to take action to disqualify directors can be taken on the basis of information that was obtained or generated by an inspector (or came to his knowledge) as a result of his investigation, notwithstanding whether such information is or will be included in any formal report. In some cases this may speed up the ability to seek to disqualify directors.

PART 33: UK COMPANIES NOT FORMED UNDER COMPANIES LEGISLATION

[3.34]
1318.   The CLR considered the position of unregistered companies in Chapter 9 of *Completing the Structure* and presented their recommendations in paragraphs 11.34 to 11.37 of the Final Report. The provisions in this Part have been developed with these recommendations in mind.

Chapter 1: Companies Not Formed Under Companies Legislation But Authorised To Register

Section 1040: Companies authorised to register under this Act

1319.   This section replaces section 680 of the 1985 Act. It applies to companies incorporated within the UK but not formed under the Companies Acts (or certain earlier companies legislation). It enables such companies to register under the Act. The types of company that can take advantage of this provision are listed in subsection (1). They include companies formed before 2 November 1862; companies formed by private Act of Parliament and companies incorporated by royal charter.

1320.   The company may apply to register as a company limited by shares, a company limited by guarantee or as an unlimited company. Subsections (4) and (5) impose restrictions on this choice. So, a company with limited liability may not register as an unlimited company, and only a company with share capital may register as a company limited by shares.

1321. A company may wish to apply to register under the Act in order to take advantage of legislation applying to companies registered under the Companies Acts. Subsection (6) makes clear that a company may register even if it is in order to take advantage of certain provisions of the Insolvency Act 1986 not available to unregistered companies. For example, under section 221(4) of the Insolvency Act 1986, unregistered companies may not be wound up under that Act voluntarily (except in accordance with the EC regulation on insolvency proceedings).

Section 1041: Definition of "joint stock company"

1322. This section restates section 683 of the 1985 Act. It defines the joint stock companies that may register under section 1040.

Section 1042: Power to make provision by regulations

1323. This section is a new provision. It confers power on the Secretary of State to make regulations in connection with the registration of a company following an application under section 1040 (application by UK company not formed under the Companies Acts to register under the Companies Acts). Regulations made under this section will replace the provisions made by sections 681 to 682, 684 to 690 and Schedule 21 of the 1985 Act. The regulations will cover the procedural requirements for registration, the conditions to be satisfied before registration and the documents to be supplied on an application for registration. The regulations will also set out the consequences of registration, including the status of the company following registration and the application of the Companies Acts to such companies following registration. The regulations are subject to the negative resolution procedure.

Chapter 2: Unregistered Companies

Section 1043: Unregistered companies

1324. This section replaces section 718 of the 1985 Act. The section confers a power on the Secretary of State to apply provisions of the Companies Acts to certain unregistered companies. These are companies incorporated in the UK, and having their principal place of business in the UK, but not formed or registered under the Companies Acts or any other public general Act of Parliament. Examples include companies formed by letters patent or by private Act of Parliament. Subsection (1) exempts certain other companies from regulations under this section, including those exempted by direction of the Secretary of State.

1325. Regulations under this section will replace the provision made by Schedule 22 to the 1985 Act. The regulations may apply specified provisions of the Companies Acts to specified descriptions of unregistered company, and may make limitations, adaptations and modifications to the application of the Companies Acts to unregistered companies. The regulations are subject to the negative resolution procedure.

PART 34: OVERSEAS COMPANIES

[3.35]
1326. This Part applies to companies incorporated outside the UK ("overseas companies"). It enables various registration, reporting and disclosure requirements to be imposed on overseas companies.

1327. This Part, together with the regulations to be made under it, will replace the provisions made by Part 23 (including Schedules 21A to D) of the 1985 Act. Regulations made under this Part will continue to implement the requirements of the Eleventh Company Law Directive (89/666/EEC), which imposes disclosure requirements on overseas companies that set up branches in the UK.

1328. As originally enacted, Part 23 of the 1985 Act applied to companies incorporated outside Great Britain that established a place of business in Great Britain. Subsequently, the Eleventh Company Law Directive imposed a different set of disclosure requirements on those overseas companies with branches in the UK. The branch disclosure requirements also differ depending on whether or not the overseas company is incorporated within another EEA State. The result is that there are at present effectively two parallel regimes that apply to overseas companies.

1329. The CLR set out their initial analysis of the rules for regulating companies formed abroad in Chapter 5.6 of the Strategic Framework and then put forward their provisional detailed conclusions in their consultation document of October 1999 entitled "Reforming the law concerning overseas companies." The CLR presented their conclusions in paragraphs 11.21 to 11.33 of the Final Report.

Section 1044: Overseas companies

1330. This section explains that for the purposes of the Companies Acts an "overseas company" means a company incorporated outside the UK. This is wider than the definition of "oversea company" in section 744 of the 1985 Act which it replaces. The definition in section 744 refers to companies incorporated outside Great Britain that establish a place of business in Great Britain. Under the Act the regulations will be able to specify the connection with the UK that gives rise to the various disclosure obligations imposed under this Part.

Section 1045: Company contracts and execution of documents by companies

1331.   This section restates section 130(6) of the Companies Act 1989 (company contracts and execution of documents by companies).

Section 1046: Duty to register particulars

1332.   This section confers on the Secretary of State a new power to make regulations to require overseas companies to register with the registrar of companies. The regulations may require particular information to be included in the registration. For example, an address for the company and details of its directors. The regulations may also require particular documents to be sent to the registrar, such as a copy of the company's constitution. Subsection (2) ensures that the regulations implement the requirements of the Eleventh Company Law Directive (89/666/EEC), under which an overseas company must register if the company opens a branch in the UK.

1333.   Regulations may require the overseas company to inform the registrar of companies of any changes in the details or documents it has registered (subsection (4)). The regulations may set deadlines for sending the information to the registrar of companies. They may also determine whether the overseas company should register with the registrar for England and Wales, the registrar for Scotland or the registrar for Northern Ireland. For example, an overseas company that opens a branch in Scotland may be required to register with the registrar of companies for Scotland.

1334.   The Eleventh Company Law Directive imposes different disclosure requirements depending on where the overseas company setting up the branch is incorporated. Different reporting requirements are imposed on credit and financial institutions. Therefore regulations under this section may make different provision according to the place where the company is incorporated and the activities carried on by it.

1335.   Regulations made under this section will be subject to the affirmative resolution procedure.

Section 1047: Registered name of overseas company

1336.   This section applies to overseas companies required to register with the registrar of companies by regulations made under section 1046 (duty to register particulars). Overseas companies registered under that section must be required to provide a name for registration. The name will be entered on the index of company names (see section 1099).

1337.   The company may register its corporate name (by which is meant its registered or legal name in its place of incorporation) or another name. All companies are free to choose whether to register their corporate name or another name, subject to the restrictions imposed by subsections (4) and (5). A name other than the corporate name can be registered only if it complies with the requirements imposed on the names of companies formed and registered under the Act. Likewise, unless the overseas company is incorporated in an EEA State, its corporate name can only be registered if it complies with these requirements. The only requirements of Chapters 1 to 4 of Part 5 (a company's name) that do not apply are the requirements for the names of certain types of company to end with certain words (sections 58 and 59). These rules are not appropriate for overseas companies as they are specific to the types of company formed under the Companies Acts.

1338.   Where the overseas company is incorporated in an EEA State (defined in section 1170), it may always register its corporate name, even if it does not comply with the requirements imposed on the names of companies formed under the Act provided that it complies with the requirement relating to permitted characters (contained in section 57). This section, together with section 1048 (registration under alternative name) replaces section 694 of the 1985 Act.

Section 1048: Registration under alternative name

1339.   This section enables an overseas company to be registered under a name other than its corporate name. It also enables an overseas company to change the name by which it is registered. To do so it must deliver a statement to the registrar of companies with its proposed new name for registration. As long as the proposed name complies with the requirements for registration (see section 1047) the registrar of companies will enter it on the index of company names in place of the name previously registered.

1340.   The section also provides that whatever name an overseas company is registered under, whether its corporate name or another, it is treated as being its corporate name for the purposes of the law in the UK. The change of name will not affect any legal proceedings that are continued or commenced by or against the company.

Section 1049: Accounts and reports: general

1341.   This section confers on the Secretary of State a power to make regulations requiring overseas companies to prepare accounts and directors' reports, and to obtain an auditor's report. The requirements must be like those imposed on companies formed and registered under the Act. The accounts, directors' report and auditor's report requirements applying to companies formed and registered under the Act appear in Part 15 (accounts and reports) and Part 16 (audit).

1342. Regulations under this section may require the overseas company to deliver to the registrar of companies copies of the accounts and reports prepared in accordance with the regulations; alternatively the overseas company may be required to deliver to the registrar a copy of the accounts and reports that it prepared and had audited in accordance with the law of the country in which it is incorporated. The registrar will place the accounts and reports on the public register.

1343. Regulations under this section will replace sections 699AA to 703 of, and Schedule 21D to, the 1985 Act. The regulations will be subject to the negative resolution procedure.

Section 1050: Accounts and reports: credit or financial institutions

1344. This section applies only to credit or financial institutions incorporated or formed outside the UK and Gibraltar, with their head office outside the UK and Gibraltar but having a branch in the UK (subsection (1)). This section confers on the Secretary of State a power to make regulations specifically in respect of accounts and directors' reports by these credit or financial institutions.

1345. Credit institution and financial institution are both defined in section 1173.

1346. Regulations under this section will implement requirements of the Bank Branches Directive 89/117/EEC of the Council of 13 February 1989. The definition of "branch" for the purposes of this section (subsection (2)) is based on Article 1.3 of Directive 2000/12/EC of the European Parliament and of the Council of 20 March 2000 relating to the taking up and pursuit of the business of credit institutions. The power to make regulations under this section is similar to that in under section 1049 (accounts and reports: general).

1347. The regulations will replace section 699A of, and Schedule 21C to, the 1985 Act. The regulations will be subject to the negative resolution procedure.

Section 1051: Trading disclosures

1348. This section confers on the Secretary of State a power to make regulations as to the information that overseas companies must display in specified locations, include in specified documents or communications, or provide to those who make a request in the course of business. Regulations made under this section will replace the provision made by section 693 of the 1985 Act. This section complements the similar power under section 82 to make regulations imposing trading disclosure obligations on companies formed and registered under the Companies Acts. Regulations under this section may require an overseas company carrying on business in the UK:

- to display particular information in particular places. For example, a sign with its name outside every branch;
- to include particular information in certain documents. For example, its name and country of incorporation on every invoice;
- to provide certain information, such as its name, to those who request it when doing business with the overseas company.

1349. They may also make provision, corresponding to that made in sections 83 and 84, in respect of a failure by a company formed and registered under the Companies Acts to comply with the trading disclosure requirements imposed on them by regulations under section 82.

1350. Regulations under this section, like those under section 82, are subject to the affirmative resolution procedure.

Section 1052: Company charges

1351. This section applies to overseas companies that are required to register particulars under section 1046. It confers on the Secretary of State a power to make regulations about the registration by those companies of charges they grant over property in the United Kingdom. Subsection (2) lists some of the matters that may be dealt with in such regulations, and subsections (3) and (4) enable the regime for overseas companies to mirror specified provisions in Part 25, with modifications. This section replaces sections 409 (charges on property in England and Wales created by an overseas company) and 424 (extension of Chapter 2) of the 1985 Act.

Section 1053: Other returns etc

1352. This section applies to overseas companies that are required to register particulars under section 1046. It confers on the Secretary of State a power to make regulations requiring those companies to deliver returns to the registrar if they are being wound up or subjected to insolvency proceedings. The regulations may also require the liquidator of such a company to deliver returns to the registrar. They may specify the circumstances in which a return is to be made to the registrar. For example, on termination of the winding-up. The regulations may specify the information to be included in the return and set deadlines for sending it to the registrar (subsection (3)). They may require notice to be given to the registrar of certain appointments (subsections (4) and (5)).

1353. The regulations will replace sections 703P and 703Q of the 1985 Act. The regulations will be subject to the affirmative resolution procedure.

Part 3   CA 2006 Supporting Materials

Section 1054: Offences

1354.   This section ensures that the regulations will be able to specify the person or persons who would be responsible for complying with any specified requirement of the regulations. It allows regulations to provide for offences, including who would be liable in the event of any contravention and what might be considered a defence should a charge be brought. The maximum level of penalty permissible under the regulations on indictment is an unlimited fine and on summary conviction a fine not exceeding level 5 on the standard scale, or for continued contravention, a daily default fine not exceeding one-tenth of that.

Section 1055: Disclosure of individual's residential address: protection from disclosure

1355.   If the regulations under section 1046 require an overseas company to register an individual's usual residential address, then the regulations must also provide for its protection on the same basis as is provided for directors' residential addresses in Chapter 8 of Part 10.

Section 1056: Requirement to identify persons authorised to accept service of documents

1356.   Every overseas company required by regulations under section 1046 to register with the registrar of companies must register particulars identifying every person resident in the UK who is authorised to accept service of documents on the company's behalf or make a statement that there is no such person.

1357.   As to how a document may be served on a registered overseas company, see section 1139(2) and the company communications provisions (sections 1144 to 1148 and Schedules 4 and 5).

1358.   This section replaces the provision made by section 691(1)(b)(ii) and paragraph 3(e) of Schedule 21A to the 1985 Act.

Section 1057: Registrar to whom returns, notices etc to be delivered

1359.   This section makes provision for regulations in respect of overseas companies that are required to register, or have registered, particulars under section 1046 in more than one part of the United Kingdom. The regulations may set out what should happen, for example, if the overseas company has registered branches in Scotland and in Northern Ireland; the regulations may require the returns or notices to be delivered to each registrar with whom the company is registered, or to the registrar for such part or parts of the United Kingdom as the regulations may specify.

1360.   Regulations made under this section will be subject to the negative resolution procedure.

Section 1058: Duty to give notice of ceasing to have registrable presence

1361.   Where an overseas company has registered particulars with the registrar following the opening of a branch in the United Kingdom, this section will enable regulations to require the overseas company to give notice to the registrar if it subsequently closes that branch. In addition, an overseas company that has registered particulars in other circumstances specified by regulations under section 1046 may be required by regulations to give notice to the registrar if those circumstances cease to obtain.

1362.   The regulations will require the notice to be delivered to the registrar for the part of the United Kingdom in which the overseas company was registered and may set deadlines for sending the information to the registrar.

1363.   Regulations made under this section will be subject to negative resolution procedure.

Section 1059: Application of provisions in case of relocation of branch

1364.   This section provides that the relocation of a branch from one part of the UK to another is to be treated as the closing of the branch in one part and the opening in another. For example, if an overseas company moves a branch from Scotland to Wales, it must tell the registrar for Scotland that it is closing the branch. It must also tell the registrar for England and Wales that it is opening a branch in Wales. This section replaces the provision made by section 695A(4) of the 1985 Act.

PART 35: THE REGISTRAR OF COMPANIES

[3.36]
1365.   This Part largely replaces Part 24 of the 1985 Act, and sets out the basic functions of the registrar of companies (these functions are currently carried out by Companies House for England and Wales and in Scotland and by the equivalent registry in Northern Ireland). The new sections implement a number of recommendations of the CLR.

Sections 1060 and 1061: The registrar and the registrar's functions

1366.   Section 1060 carries forward the approach of section 704 of the 1985 Act as to the appointment and status of the registrar of companies but omits some of the more antiquated parts of that provision. It specifies that there shall continue to be a registrar for England and Wales, for Scotland and for Northern Ireland.

1367.   Section 1061 the registrar continues to have the functions conferred by the Companies Acts and in other legislation as specified in the section. The Secretary of State also has power to confer functions on the registrar, in relation to the registration of companies or other matters.

Section 1062: The registrar's official seal

1368.   This section, replacing section 704(4) of the 1985 Act, provides that the registrar must have an official seal for the authentication of documents.

Section 1063: Fees payable to the registrar

1369.   This section gives the Secretary of State a power to set fees by regulations in relation to any function of the registrar and in relation to the provision of services and facilities incidental to the registrar's functions. It replaces section 708 of the 1985 Act, but is more specific about the types of things for which fees may be charged, although this list is not exhaustive.

1370.   As now, fees relating to the normal statutory obligations of companies under companies legislation are to be set by regulations made by the Secretary of State. It is also possible for fees to be charged for any ad hoc or bespoke services that Companies House provides. The 1985 Act (section 708(5)) provides that the registrar determines fees for services for which there is no direct legal obligation. Subsection (6) of this section replaces this with a more general power for the registrar to determine fees where no fee has been set in regulations by the Secretary of State. Such fees might relate for example to the introduction of new services (eg those made possible by new technologies) which could not have been anticipated when the Secretary of State last made fees regulations; or for services such as seminars and road shows which Companies House arranges.

Section 1064 to 1065: Certificates of incorporation

1371.   Section 1064 replaces section 711(1)(a) of the 1985 Act and provides for notice of the issue of certificates of incorporation to be published in the Gazette. The publication must include the company's registered number as well as its name. Section 1065 replaces section 710 of that Act and allows any person to obtain a certificate of incorporation of a company. These sections cover all certificates of incorporation (including, for example, certificates of incorporation on change of name).

Section 1066 and 1067: Registered numbers

1372.   Section 1066 replaces section 705 of the 1985 Act on companies' registered numbers, without change of substance. Section 1067 replaces the provisions of section 705A of that Act relating to registered numbers of branches of overseas companies.

Delivery of documents to the registrar

Section 1068: Registrar's requirements

1373.   This section gives the registrar power to make rules about form, authentication and manner of delivery of documents, including the physical form and means of communication, the format, and the address to which they are to be sent, and where appropriate, technical specification. The power conferred by this section does not authorise the registrar to require documents to be delivered in electronic form.

Section 1069: Power to require delivery by electronic means

1374.   This section provides that the Secretary of State (not the registrar) has a new power to provide for electronic-only delivery of classes of document. The Secretary of State may only exercise this power in respect of classes of document which are authorised or required to be delivered and for which the registrar has published rules relating to electronic delivery (in other words where it is clear precisely what mechanism is to be used for the electronic communication).

Section 1070: Agreement for delivery by electronic means

1375.   This section sets out the power of the registrar to make agreements with companies to deliver information only electronically. The agreements could cover all documents (to the extent that electronic means of filing are available) or just selected documents. It is envisaged that the agreements will be in a standard form and contain detailed provisions for communications between the registrar and the company (including possible use of codes and encryption). The agreements need not be available to be entered into by everyone in the same form or at all.

Section 1071: Document not delivered until received

1376.   This section provides that "delivery" obligations go beyond an obligation simply to send or post information to the registrar, and that the registrar may make rules governing what it means for a document to be "received" (which might include, for example, setting out which offices of the registrar should receive a document).

Requirements for proper delivery

Section 1072: Requirements for proper delivery

1377. This section provides that, in order for a document to be properly delivered to the registrar, various conditions (specified in subsection (1)(a) to (g)) must be met. Where those conditions are not satisfied, and the document is therefore not "properly" delivered, it is not to be treated as having been delivered for the purposes of the underlying provision which authorises or requires it.

Section 1073: Power to accept documents not meeting requirements for proper delivery

1378. The registrar may still accept (and register) a document that does not comply with the requirements for proper delivery, although such acceptance does not (subsection (4)) exempt the filer from any consequence attaching to failure to comply with the original requirements for delivery.

Section 1074: Documents containing unnecessary material

1379. Documents are sometimes delivered to the registrar which contain "unnecessary" material, ie material for which there was no legal requirement or authorisation. Where the unnecessary material cannot readily be separated from the necessary material, then the document as a whole is treated as not properly delivered. Where it is separable, the registrar has the option of either registering the entire document as delivered, or excising the unnecessary material and registering the remainder.

Section 1075: Informal correction of document

1380. This is a new provision, giving the registrar power to correct information in a document by informal means (for example, by taking revisions or supplementary information from the company over the telephone) but only in very limited circumstances. It can be used as an alternative to rejecting or removing information:

* on the grounds that it is incomplete (eg empty fields within the document);
* on the grounds that it is internally inconsistent (eg the company number does not correspond to the company name);

1381. This ability to make informal corrections only applies where companies have informed the registrar that it should apply. The registrar needs to initiate the correction and be satisfied that the person is authorised to give the information sought. In order to be satisfied as to the authority of the person she is telephoning, the registrar may provide for identification numbers or other checks on identity.

Section 1076: Replacement of document not meeting requirements for proper delivery

1382. This section sets out how the registrar may accept a replacement document that was not properly delivered in the first place. In essence, the registrar must be satisfied that the replacement document is delivered by the original filer, or by the company to which the original document relates, and that the replacement is "properly delivered" (as defined in section 1072)). It also allows the registrar to impose requirements to ensure that the replacement can clearly be associated with a particular original.

Sections 1077 and 1078: Public notice of receipt of documents subject to Directive disclosure requirements

1383. These sections replace section 711 of the 1985 Act, which provides that certain notices must be published in the Gazette, and lists the documents to which that requirement relates. This list derives from Community legislation, principally the First Company Law Directive (68/151/EEC) as amended by Directive 2003/58/EC.

1384. Section 1077 provides that notice of receipt of these documents must be published either in the Gazette, or by some other means (as may be specified under section 1116). Section 1078 lists the documents subject to Directive disclosure requirements.

Section 1079: Effect of failure to give public notice

1385. This section effectively replaces section 42 of the 1985 Act. It sets out how a company, in its dealings with third parties, may not rely on the consequences of certain events (those which are set out in subsection (2)) unless notice of the event has duly appeared in the Gazette or been published in some other way provided for in section 1116.

The register

Section 1080: The register

1386. This section imposes an obligation on the registrar to keep a record of the material received. It gives a discretion as to the form in which the record is kept. Subsection (3) provides that this discretion is subject to the terms of the amended First Company Law Directive (68/151/EEC), Article 3.2 of which requires any documents and particulars it covers which are delivered on after 1 January 2007 to be retained in electronic form. The documents covered by this obligation are those set out in section 1078.

Section 1081: Annotation of the register

1387. It is important that the register is as useful and transparent a source of information as possible for users. Hence, this section sets out certain circumstances in which the registrar is obliged to annotate the information on the register to gloss it or provide supplementary information. Annotations must for example be provided to show the date of delivery of information; and the fact that information has been replaced, corrected or removed. This section responds to a recommendation of the CLR (summarised in their Final Report at paragraph 11.48). Subsection (5) provides that the court can dispense with the need for annotation in certain circumstances.

1388. The Secretary of State has power to make provision by regulations extending the circumstances where the registrar can or should make annotations.

Section 1082: Allocation of unique identifiers

1389. This section is a new provision. It gives the Secretary of State a power to make regulations so that unique identifiers can be allocated to company officers such as directors. This provision supports those that provide for the home addresses of directors no longer to be kept on the public record. The unique identifier enables searchers to distinguish between different persons of the same name.

Sections 1083 and 1084: Preservation of original documents and records relating to companies that have been dissolved etc

1390. Section 1083 replaces section 707A(2) of the 1985 Act. However, the obligation on the registrar to keep the originals of documents received now only applies for three years (as opposed to ten in the existing provision). This section also provides that the obligation to retain originals does not extend to an original document provided electronically (provided that the information itself has been placed on the register).

1391. Section 1084 replaces sections 707(3) and (4) of the 1985 Act, and provides that records may be transferred to the Public Records Office two years after a company has been dissolved. It also makes equivalent provision for certain overseas companies which, for example, by ceasing to have any connection with the UK, are no longer caught by UK regulatory requirements.

Inspection etc of the register

Section 1085: Inspection of the register

1392. This section provides that any person may inspect the register. Searchers however have a right to inspect the original of a hard copy document only where the registrar still retains it and where the public record kept by the registrar and derived from it is illegible or unavailable.

Section 1086: Right to copy of material on the register

1393. This section provides that any person is entitled to a copy of material on the register. Consistent with the provisions of the amended First Company Law Directive (68/151/EEC), subsection (2) provides that the fee for a copy may not exceed the administrative cost of providing the service.

Section 1087: Material not available for public inspection

1394. This section sets out a number of exceptions to the above rights to inspect and copy material on the register. These are listed in subsection (1)(a) to (k) and include, for example, "protected information", ie information about directors' home addresses. Subsection (2) provides that the fact that certain material (for example, an address), which has been placed on the register as a result of the filing of two or more different types of document, is confidential in one of those contexts, does not mean that it cannot be made public in its other context.

Section 1088: Application to registrar to make address unavailable for public inspection

1395. This section is a new provision. It confers power on the Secretary of State to make regulations providing for applications to remove addresses from the public record held by Companies House. The regulations may set out the details of who can apply and on what grounds and the procedure involved. They are subject to the affirmative resolution procedure.

Sections 1089 to 1091: Provision of copies of material on the register

1396. These sections enable the registrar to specify the form and manner in which applications for inspection of the register, or for copies of material on it, must be made, and to determine the form and manner in which copies are provided. They are subject to important exceptions, arising from the amended First Company Law Directive (68/151/EEC), in respect of the documents listed at section 1078.

1397. Section 1089 provides that applications must be capable of being submitted in hard copy or in electronic form, as the applicant chooses. Section 1090 similarly provides that the applicant is entitled to insist on receiving the copies themselves in hard copy or in electronic form (subject to an exception in respect of documents delivered before 1 January 2007).

1398. Section 1091, again responding to provisions of the amended First Company Law Directive (68/151/EEC), provides that, unless the applicant chooses otherwise, copies of information provided in hard copy must be certified as true copies but electronic copies must not be so certified. Subsection (3) provides for the evidential status of certified hard copies in legal proceedings. The Secretary of State has power to prescribe by regulations methods of certification for copies provided by electronic means.

Section 1092: Issue of process for production of records kept by the registrar

1399. This section restates section 709(5) of the 1985 Act and provides that no-one can take proceedings against the registrar for production of records without first obtaining the permission of the court.

Correction or removal of material on the register

Section 1093: Registrar's notice to resolve inconsistency on the register

1400. This section enables the registrar to notify a company of an apparent inconsistency in the information on the register. An example might be where a document is received notifying the removal of a director where there is no record of his appointment. In such circumstances, the registrar may give notice to the company requiring them to resolve the inconsistency within 14 days by providing additional or replacement documents. Failure to do so on the company's part is an offence (subsection (3)).

Section 1094: Administrative removal of material from the register

1401. The registrar has a power to remove from the register information that there was a power but no duty to enter. Under subsection (4), the registrar will need to send a notice to the presenter of the information in question, or to the company to which the material relates, on or before removing the material.

1402. The registrar may not however remove information from the register where registration has had legal consequences for the company as regards certain key events, as set out in subsection (3), including for example its formation or a change of registered office.

Section 1095: Rectification of register on application to registrar

1403. This section gives the Secretary of State a power to make regulations under which, following a successful application, the registrar may be required to remove certain kinds of material from the register. The procedure may only cover certain types of document. It may operate in respect of material that derives from something that is invalid or ineffective or from something that was done without the authority of the company (this would cover forms filed without authority); and material that is factually inaccurate or forged or derives from something that is factually inaccurate or forged.

1404. The registrar may only act as a result of an application, and regulations may provide for matters such as who may make the application and what information will need to be provided with it. Where the material removed is of a kind whose registration has had legal consequences, subsection (5) provides that interested parties have the right to go to court to obtain an order as to the material's legal effect.

Section 1096: Rectification of the register under court order

1405. The registrar is also required to remove material from the register where there is a court order to that effect. The court's rectification power operates in the same circumstances as the registrar's power following regulations made under section 1094. However, the court's power is of general application. For example, there is no limit on the types of document covered. The court may make an order to remove material from the register where its presence on the register has caused damage or may cause damage to the company and the company's interests in removing the material outweigh the interests of others in it continuing to be on the register. The court may make such consequential orders as appear just regarding the period that the information was on the register and the effect of the information being on the register during that period. The court's rectification power does not operate where the court has other rectification powers (eg in relation to accounts or charges).

Section 1097: Powers of court on ordering removal of material from the register

1406. This section provides that where a court decides that certain information should be removed from the public register, the court may also make directions as to annotations (removing notes that are already there or directing that now new notes appear as a result of its order – or that notes appear in a restricted form) and as to whether its own order should be available for public inspection.

Section 1098: Public notice of removal of certain material from the register

1407. Section 1077 provides for the registrar to give public notice that she has received certain documents relating to a company in the Gazette or through some other form of publication. This section creates a corresponding obligation for her to give notice where she removes such material.

Section 1099: The registrar's index of company names

1408. This section replaces section 714 of the 1985 Act with changes. It provides for the registrar of companies to keep an index of the names not only of companies incorporated under Companies Acts but also of business entities formed under other legislation and of overseas companies with a UK branch.

1409. The section provides power for regulations to update the categories of business entities that are included in the index. This power is subject to negative resolution procedure.

Section 1100: Right to inspect index

1410. This section retains the public right to inspect the index. (It can be searched online, without charge, at http://www.companieshouse.gov.uk.) The index of company names is important not only as the means of access to the information on the public record of companies incorporated in the United Kingdom but also as the list of names with which a proposed new name is compared to ensure that a new entity is not registered in a name that is the same or similar to that of an existing entity.

Section 1101: Power to amend enactments relating to bodies other than companies

1411. This section provides power for the Secretary of State to amend the rules for the names that can be adopted by other business entities on the index of company names. This power is subject to affirmative resolution procedure.

1412. Each category of business entity is subject to its own rules which include various safeguards to minimise the risk of public confusion. These rules differ from those that apply to companies in particular as regards the adoption of a name the same or similar to one already on the index. This lack of reciprocity is a weakness of the existing system which this section provides power to address.

Section 1102: Application of language requirements
Section 1103: Documents to be drawn up and delivered in English

1413. These sections set out language requirements. Section 1103 sets out the general rule that all documents must be in English (subject to the exceptions in the following sections). Section 1102 provides that this general rule, and its exceptions, apply automatically to documents required under the Companies Acts and Insolvency Act 1986 (and its Northern Ireland equivalent).

1414. There are however a variety of other pieces of legislation which may require companies in certain circumstances to supply material to the registrar. Depending on the nature of the particular requirement and its origin (for example, whether it responds to European Community law), it may or may not be appropriate to apply the language provisions of this Act unchanged to such material. Subsection (2) of section 1102 therefore enables the Secretary of State to make regulations to apply specified requirements to documents filed under other legislation.

Section 1104: Documents relating to Welsh companies

1415. This section provides an exception to the general rule in section 1103: documents relating to Welsh companies may be drawn up and filed in Welsh (and sometimes only in Welsh). It replaces, without any substantive change, section 710B of the 1985 Act.

Section 1105: Documents that may be drawn up and delivered in other languages

1416. This section sets out the circumstances in which documents may be drawn up and filed in other languages, but requires them to be accompanied by a certified translation into English. These documents are listed in subsection (2): agreements affecting the company's constitution, documents relating to group accounts for companies in a group, and instruments relating to company charges. For some companies, documents of these sorts may well originate in languages other than English, and there may be an interest in ensuring that the original version is registered with the registrar. Subsection (2)(d) also allows the Secretary of State to extend the categories of documents to which this section applies.

Section 1106: Voluntary filing of translations

1417. The main purpose of this section is to implement aspects of the amended First Company Law Directive (68/151/EEC). It provides that companies may send the registrar certified translations of documents relating to the company. Subsection (2) enables the Secretary of State to set out in regulations the languages and documents in relation to which this facility is available. Subsection (3) provides that these regulations must as a minimum specify the official languages of the EU, and the documents covered by the amended First Company Law Directive (68/151/EEC) (see section 1078), to ensure compliance with that Directive. However, other languages (and categories of document) may be covered by the regulations.

Section 1107: Certified translations

1418. This section provides that a "certified translation" is one that has been certified in a manner prescribed by the registrar. It also provides that, where there is a discrepancy between an original and

Part 3   CA 2006 Supporting Materials

a translation, the company may not rely on the translation as against a third party, but the third party may rely on the translation (unless the company can show that the third party had knowledge of the original). This implements article 3a.4 of the amended First Company Law Directive (68/151/EEC).

Section 1108: Transliteration of names and addresses: permitted characters

1419. This section is a new provision. It deals with the possibility that the name and address of a director or of an overseas company may use a character set (for example, that of Urdu or Japanese) which is different from those with which the bulk of Companies House's users are familiar. This section restricts the characters that are permitted for names and addresses in a document delivered to the registrar to those specified in regulations. The regulations, which are subject to negative resolution procedure, may also provide for names and addresses to be delivered in their original form.

Section 1109: Transliteration of names and addresses: voluntary transliteration into Roman characters

1420. This section is a new provision. It provides for the possibility that the Regulations made under section 1108 may permit letters and characters that are not drawn from the Roman alphabet, for example Greek letters. This section permits these names to be transliterated provided that certain requirements are met.

Section 1110: Transliteration of names and addresses: certification

1421. This section is a new provision. It confers power on the Secretary of State to make regulations relating to the certification of the transliteration of names and addresses. The regulations, which are subject to negative resolution procedure, may distinguish between compulsory transliteration under section 1108 and voluntary transliteration under section 1109.

Section 1111: Registrar's requirements as to certification or verification

1422. Documents delivered to the registrar are sometimes required to be certified or verified in some way, for example to the effect that they are an accurate translation. This section allows the registrar to impose requirements as who must provide the relevant certification or verification. Subsection (2) provides that the registrar's general powers to specify requirements in relation to documents submitted to her (section 1068) extends to the certification or verification as if it were a separate document.

Section 1112: General false statement offence

1423. This section provides a new offence of knowingly or recklessly delivering to the registrar information which is misleading, false or deceptive in a material particular. It responds to a recommendation of the CLR (Final Report, paragraph 11.48). This new general offence makes it unnecessary to reproduce specific offences covering false information or false statements in respect of specific legislative requirements that were a feature of the 1985 Act.

Section 1113: Enforcement of company's filing obligations

1424. This section, which restates section 713 of the 1985 Act, provides the mechanism for ensuring that companies can be compelled to comply with their obligations to file documents or give notices to the registrar. Where a company has defaulted on an obligation, the registrar herself, any member of the company, or any creditor, may serve a notice on the company requiring it to file. If the company continues the breach after 14 days, the applicant may apply to the court for an order requiring the company, or any specified officer of it, to make good the default. The court may order that the costs of the proceedings are borne by the company or its officers. Subsection (5) provides that this process does not affect any offence or civil penalty arising from the company's failure to comply with the original requirement.

Section 1114: Application of provisions about documents and delivery

1425. This section, which replaces section 715A of the 1985 Act, provides that "document" means information recorded in any form, and that "delivering" a document includes forwarding, lodging, registering, producing or submitting it, or giving a notice. It also provides that requirements relating to documents also apply (unless otherwise provided for) to information passed to the registrar in some other way. This caters for the possibility that information may not be in documentary form, for example when it is sent via a link to a website.

Section 1115: Supplementary provisions relating to electronic communications

1426. This section, which replaces section 710A of the 1985 Act, allows the registrar to require those who choose to file electronically to accept electronic communications from the registrar. It also provides that, where a document is required to be signed by the registrar, or authenticated by seal, she may determine by rules how it is to be authenticated when it is sent by electronic means.

Section 1116: Alternative to publication in the Gazette

1427. The registrar is required under the 1985 Act to publish certain statutory notices in the Gazette. The objective of that requirement is to ensure that such notices are well-publicised and made available to all those who might wish to take notice of them. The Gazette is a long-established and well-understood mechanism for ensuring such publicity. However, it is possible that developments, in particular in electronic publishing, will mean over time that alternative mechanisms are equally or more appropriate as ways of meeting the underlying policy objective. The CLR envisaged that the registrar should be able to make use of such mechanisms (Final Report, paragraph 11.48). This section therefore provides a power for the Secretary of State to specify alternative means which the registrar may then approve for use. To ensure that any such change is itself well-publicised in advance, subsection (5) provides that the change must itself be announced in the Gazette.

Section 1117: Registrar's rules

1428. Other provisions in this Part enable the registrar to impose requirements in relation to certain matters. For example, section 1068 enables the registrar to specify the form, authentication and manner of delivery of documents to her; and section 1075 similarly enables her to determine the form and manner of any company instructions as to informal correction of the register. This section provides that the registrar may set out these requirements in registrar's rules. The rules can make different provision for different cases, and may allow the registrar to modify or disapply the rules. The registrar must publicise any rules in a way designed to make sure that those who will need to know about them get to hear of them (which might in practice, for example, be by using the Companies House website); and must make copies of the rules publicly available.

Section 1118: Payments into the Consolidated Fund

1429. This section ensures that nothing in this or other companies legislation affects the continued operation in relation to the registrar of the Government Trading Funds Act 1973. (Companies House is and remains a Trading Fund.)

Section 1119: Contracting out of registrar's functions

1430. This section largely restates subsections (7) and (8) of section 704 of the 1985 Act. The Deregulation and Contracting Out Act 1994 envisages that some of the registrar's functions may be contracted out. This section provides for this possibility by saying that where a contractor is processing documents the registrar can provide for them to be sent directly to the contractor.

1431. The Deregulation and Contracting Out Act 1994 does not permit the function of making subordinate legislation to be delegated. Subsection (3) provides that registrar's rules are not regarded as subordinate legislation for this purpose, permitting the contractor to make rules about form and manner of delivery, for example.

Section 1120: Application of Part to overseas companies

1432. This section provides that, except where the context otherwise requires, the provisions of this Part of the Act apply equally to overseas companies.

PART 36: OFFENCES UNDER THE COMPANIES ACTS

[3.37]
1433. The CLR sought to draw out the basis on which criminal liability for a breach of Companies Act requirements is allocated under existing legislation to companies and to officers of companies. It stated in its final report that a reformed Companies Act must be underpinned by effective and proportionate sanctions and enforcement.

1434. The key changes in the Act are:
*   refinements to the "officer in default" provisions to make it clearer which individuals in which circumstances may be liable for a breach; and
*   removal of criminal liability from the company itself in certain circumstances.

1435. The general principle adopted as to whether a company should be liable for a breach of requirements of the Companies Acts is that where the only victims of the offence are the company or its members, the company should not be liable for the offence. On the other hand, where other persons may be victims of the offence, then the company should be potentially liable for a breach, whether or not the offence may also harm the company or its members.

Section 1121: Liability of officer in default

1436. This section specifies which persons may be liable as an officer of a company for an offence committed by the company under the Act (or the other Companies Acts). It only applies where another provision expressly states that an offence is committed by every officer of a company who is in default.

1437. An "officer" of a company is defined as including a director, manager or (company) secretary, and any person who is to be treated as an officer of the company for the purposes of the

(vertical text, right margin) Part 3   CA 2006 Supporting Materials

provisions in question. An officer is liable for an offence when he is "in default", meaning he authorises or permits, participates in, or fails to take all reasonable steps to prevent the offence being committed.

Section 1122: Liability of company as officer in default

1438. Under this provision, where a company is an officer of another company, liability for an offence can be fixed upon the company as an officer in default only if one of its officers is in default.

Section 1123: Application to bodies other than companies

1439. This clause provides that section 1121 applies to persons in bodies other than companies where their role is equivalent to that of an officer of a company. It makes specific provision for bodies corporate, partnerships and unincorporated bodies.

Section 1124: Amendments of the Companies Act 1985
Schedule 3: Amendments of remaining provisions of the Companies Act 1985 relating to offences

1440. Section 1124 introduces Schedule 3, which contains amendments to certain provisions relating to offences which remain in Parts 14 and 15 of the 1985 Act.

1441. Many of these amendments are necessary due to the repeal by the Act of Schedule 24 to the 1985 Act. Schedule 24 set out the level of punishment for offences under the 1985 Act. The provisions in Parts 14 and 15 are amended so that the applicable punishments are now included alongside the description of the offence instead of in Schedule 24.

1442. Schedule 3 also makes amendments to the offences provisions remaining in Parts 14 and 15 of the 1985 Act to reflect the (non-textual) changes made to that Act by the Criminal Justice Act 2003. Section 282 of the Criminal Justice Act increases from 6 months to 12 months the maximum term of imprisonment to which a person is liable on summary conviction of an offence triable either way, and section 154(1) of that Act gives power to magistrates to impose a 12 month term of imprisonment. The increased penalties only apply in England and Wales; in Scotland and Northern Ireland the maximum term of imprisonment that may be imposed on summary conviction remains 6 months. When the Act received Royal Assent, neither section 282 nor section 154(1) of the Criminal Justice Act 2003 had come into force (which is the reason for the transitory provision in section 1131).

1443. A number of the amendments make reference to "the statutory maximum fine". This was set at £5,000 at the time the Act received Royal Assent.

1444. Schedule 3 makes only one substantive change to the offence provisions in Parts 14 and 15. This is to include a daily default fine, of one-fiftieth of the statutory maximum, for continued contravention of section 444(3) (failure to provide information about interests in shares).

Section 1125: Meaning of "daily default fine"

1445. This section defines "daily default fine". It replaces provision currently in section 730(4) of the 1985 Act.

Section 1126: Consents required for certain prosecutions

1446. This section provides that certain proceedings can only be brought with the consent of specified persons. It replaces section 732(1) and (2) of the 1985 Act.

Section 1127: Summary proceedings: venue

1447. This section restates section 731(1) of the 1985 Act. It specifies the possible venues for summary proceedings for any breach of Companies Acts requirements. For a body corporate the venue may be any place at which the body corporate has a place of business, and for any other person, it may be at any place that the person is.

Section 1128: Summary proceedings: time limit for proceedings

1448. This section restates section 731(2) to (4) of the 1985 Act. It sets out time limits for summary proceedings. The prosecution must be commenced within three years of the offence being committed, and within one year of the prosecuting authorities receiving sufficient evidence to justify the prosecution.

Section 1129: Legal professional privilege

1449. This section restates section 732(3) of the 1985 Act and applies its provisions to all offences prosecuted under the Companies Acts, rather than just those instituted by the Director of Public Prosecutions or the Secretary of State. It provides that the Companies Acts provisions on offences are not to be read as requiring any person to disclose information that is protected by legal professional privilege.

Section 1130: Proceedings against unincorporated bodies

1450.   This section restates section 734(1) to (4) of the 1985 Act. It provides for proceedings for offences under the Companies Acts committed by unincorporated bodies to be brought against such bodies as if they were corporate bodies.

Section 1131: Imprisonment on summary conviction in England and Wales: transitory provision

1451.   This section provides for the period before the commencement of section 154(1) of the Criminal Justice Act 2003, which makes new provision about the powers of magistrates' courts in England and Wales to impose sentences of imprisonment on summary conviction. For offences committed before section 154(1) is brought into force, the maximum term of imprisonment in England and Wales for a person guilty of an offence on summary conviction under the Companies Acts is to be 6 months (as it is at present) instead of 12 months.

Section 1132: Production and inspection of documents where offence suspected

1452.   This section restates section 721 of the 1985. It makes provision about orders for the production of documents where there is reasonable cause to believe that an offence has been committed.

Section 1133: Transitional provision

1453.   This section provides that this Part of the Act (with the exception of section 1132) does not apply to offences committed before the commencement of the provision relevant to the offence.

PART 37: COMPANIES: SUPPLEMENTARY PROVISIONS

Sections 1134 and 1135: Company records

[3.38]
1454.   These sections replace sections 722(1) and 723(1) and (2) of the 1985 Act and enable a company to use electronic storage or paper for its records provided that there can be paper printouts of electronic records. Section 1135(1) also enables the contents to be arranged as the directors see fit provided that it is adequately recorded. Section 1138 (duty to take precautions against falsification) also applies if the records are not kept in bound books.

Section 1136: Regulations about where certain company records to be kept available for inspection

1455.   This section is a new provision. It provides power for the Secretary of State to make regulations to provide an alternative to the company's registered office as the location for inspection of specified records. The regulations are subject to negative resolution procedure.

Section 1137: Regulations about inspection of records and provision of copies

1456.   This section replaces section 723A of the 1985 Act. It allows the Secretary of State to make regulations about the inspection and provision of copies of company records.

Section 1138: Duty to take precautions against falsification

1457.   This section replaces section 722(2) and (3) of the 1985 Act. It makes it an offence not to take measures that protect records from falsification or help trace any falsification. This provision applies to records that are not kept in bound books, whether or not they are kept electronically, but does not apply either to companies' copies of the directors' service contracts or to copies of any qualifying third party indemnity provisions benefiting a director.

Section 1139: Service of documents on company

1458.   This section replaces section 725 of the 1985 Act. It ensures that there is a place at which a document may be served on companies registered under the Act. It also applies to overseas companies registered in accordance with regulations made under section 1046. Subsection (4) enables court service on a company registered in Scotland or Northern Ireland at the company's principal place of business in England and Wales. (Since this is a provision about court service, the rules on companies registered in England and Wales carrying on business elsewhere in the UK will be found in the relevant legislation in those parts of the UK.) Subsection (5) makes clear that this section is supplemented by the "company communications provisions" referenced by section 1143.

Section 1140: Service of documents on directors, secretaries and others

1459.   This section is a new provision. It ensures that the address on the public record for any director or secretary is effective for the service of documents on that person. Subsection (3) provides that the address is effective even if the document has no bearing on the person's responsibilities as director or secretary. This provision also applies to the address on the public record of various other persons for whom the Act requires an address on the public record. Subsection (7) similarly makes clear that this section is supplemented by the "company communications provisions" referenced by section 1143.

Section 1141: Service addresses

1460.   This section defines "service address" for the purposes of the Companies Acts as an address at which documents may be effectively served and provides a power for regulations to specify conditions with which a service address must comply.

Section 1142: Requirement to give service address

1461.   This section is a new provision. It qualifies requirements elsewhere to give an "address". Unless the requirement is for a particular kind of address (say, the usual residential address), the section makes clear that a service address (as defined in the previous Section) is what is required.

Section 1143: The company communications provisions

1462.   Section 1143 introduces sections 1144 to 1148 and Schedules 4 and 5. These make new provision for communications with or from companies, typically with their members but also with debenture-holders and others.

1463.   The Companies Act 1985 (Electronic Communications) Order 2000 facilitated the use of electronic and website communications in certain contexts, but there has been uncertainty as to whether other provisions under the 1985 Act for information to be communicated 'in writing' required the use of paper or could be satisfied by electronic communications. The Act makes new general provision about communications, including electronic and website communications for the Companies Acts as a whole.

1464.   The general principle behind the company communications provisions is that companies should be able to use hard copy or electronic communications in all cases. However, these provisions are subject to anything in or under any other enactment, and, as regards communications between companies and Companies House, they are also subject to the provisions of Part 35 of the Act.

Section 1144: Sending or supplying documents or information

1465.   This section introduces two Schedules, which apply irrespective of the company's articles:
* Schedule 4 deals with documents and information sent or supplied to a company;
* Schedule 5 deals with communications by a company and between companies

1466.   Sections 1146 (requirement of authentication), 1148 (interpretation of company communications provisions) and 1168 (hard copy and electronic form and related expressions) contain provisions necessary for the interpretation of Schedules 4 and 5.

Schedule 4: Documents and information sent or supplied to a company

1467.   This Schedule brings together the rules on communications to a company. In some cases a company will have other companies as members, debenture holders etc, and paragraph 1(2) of the Schedule makes clear that communications by such members etc is governed by Schedule 5.

1468.   Part 2 of the Schedule sets out the position for communications sent or supplied in hard copy form. These are very similar to the present position. Part 3 sets out rules for communications in electronic form. Part 4 is a more general provision and means that unless the Companies Acts specify a means of communication, for example under section 291(3)(a) (circulation of written resolutions proposed by directors), then a communication to the company can be sent or supplied in any way agreed by the company.

Schedule 5: Communications by a company

1469.   This Schedule sets out provisions on how companies are to communicate with their members, debenture holders etc. These rules are subject to, for example, additional rules which the FSA may require of companies traded on a regulated market.

1470.   Part 2 of the Schedule sets out standard rules for communications in hard copy. Paragraph 4 lists the addresses to which the company may send or supply documents or information. Where the company has no address for the intended recipient, the company may use the recipient's last known address. By virtue of section 310(4), this provision does not prevent a company making provision in its articles not to send notice of a general meeting to members for whom the company no longer has a valid address. Section 423(2) makes similar provision for the annual report and accounts.

1471.   Part 3 of the Schedule relates to communications by Email or other electronic methods. Paragraph 6 allows a company to send a document or information in electronic form to a person who has agreed (either generally for all communications or specifically for a particular document or piece of information) and where such person has not revoked that agreement.

1472.   Part 4 deals with publication of documents or information on a website. Paragraph 10 allows a company to pass a members' resolution or make provision in its articles about website communication. If it has done so, members (or their nominees) are taken to have agreed to receiving information from the company via a website if they have also been asked individually for their acceptance and have either agreed or not responded within 28 days of the company's request. Where a member has not agreed to communications in this way, the company may not ask the member again within a period of twelve months. In addition, section 1145 (right to hard copy version) gives a member the right to request a hard copy of the communication. Paragraph 11 and section 1145 make equivalent provision for debenture holders. Paragraph 13 requires companies to notify intended recipients each time material is published on a website. Paragraph 15 enables the company and a member to agree alternative methods of communication, for example other than website communication where a company has defaulted to website communications.

Section 1145: Right to hard copy version

1473. This section provides individual members or debenture holders the right to require information to be sent in paper copy form. A company is required to send a paper copy of the document or information within 21 days of receiving a member's request at no charge to the member. Subsections (4) and (5) impose a penalty on every officer in default if the company fails to comply.

Section 1146: Requirement of authentication

1474. This section operates where provisions of the Companies Acts require information sent or supplied to a company to be authenticated. This is chiefly the case in the context of written resolutions and requests (formerly requisitions) for meetings, etc. The rule is that a signature on a document in hard copy form by the person sending it is always sufficient authentication. The company can make its own rules in respect of documents in electronic form (but there is a default where no such rules exist). Subsection (4) makes it clear that, where someone purports to authenticate a document on another's behalf, the company can require proof of the former's authority to do so.

Section 1147: Deemed delivery of documents and information

1475. This section sets out when communications from the company are deemed to have been delivered, but it can be excluded by contrary provision elsewhere (for example, in other legislation, in contracts or in the articles). Subsection (5) provides that the 48-hour period for deemed delivery is counted during normal working days only. For example, a document posted on a Friday at 3.00 pm is deemed to have been delivered the following Tuesday at 3.00 pm, unless it is a bank holiday weekend, in which case deemed delivery is the Wednesday at 3.00 pm.

Section 1148: Interpretation of company communications provisions

1476. This section sets out defined terms used in the company communications provisions and, in particular, makes clear that references in the Companies Acts to "sending" and "supplying" documents or information include all such similar expressions.

Sections 1149 to 1153: Requirements as to independent valuation

1477. These sections restate the requirements in sections 108 and 110 of the 1985 Act for the independent valuation of non-cash assets accepted by a public company. The independence requirements in sections 1151 and 1152 correspond to the independence requirements for a statutory auditor (see section 1214). They include a new specific power for the Secretary of State to define a disallowed connection for the purposes of determining whether a person is sufficiently independent to be a valuer. This is consistent with the approach taken in sections 344 and 936 of the Act.

Sections 1154 and 1155: Duty to notify registrar of certain appointments etc and failure to give such notice

1478. These sections are new provisions. The requirement to give notice of the appointment of a judicial factor (in Scotland) gives effect to a recommendation by the CLR (Final Report, paragraph 11.39). The section also requires the Charity Commissioners to notify their appointment of a receiver and manager and the regulator of community interest companies to give notice of the appointment of a manager. These officers displace directors. Section 1155 makes failure by a judicial factor to give notice an offence.

Section 1156: Meaning of "the court"

1479. This section defines the term "the court" for the purposes of the Companies Acts. The effect of this definition is that, except where an enactment or rule of law provides otherwise, cases under the Companies Acts can be heard either in the High Court or the county court in England and Wales, in the Court of Session or the sheriff court in Scotland, and, in Northern Ireland, in the High Court of Northern Ireland.

1480. The allocation of cases between the county court (or sheriff court) and the High Court (or Court of Session) will be determined partly by the courts' general powers and partly by subordinate legislation. The allocation of cases between county courts will, as now, be determined by orders made by the Lord Chancellor (see subsection (3)).

Section 1157: Power of court to grant relief in certain cases

1481. Under this section, which restates section 727 of the 1985 Act without substantive amendment, an officer of a company (such as a director) or a person employed by a company as auditor may apply to the court for relief from liability for negligence, default, breach of duty or breach of trust. A court may grant relief if it appears to the court that:

- the director (or other officer or auditor) has acted honestly and reasonably; and
- having regard to all the circumstances, he ought fairly to be excused.

PART 38: COMPANIES: INTERPRETATION

[3.39]

1482. This Part gives an interpretation of definitions used throughout the Act. Most are based on corresponding definitions in the 1985 Act. Those that are changed or new are described below.

Section 1158: Meaning of "UK-registered company"

1483. The expression "UK-registered company" is used as a drafting device to refer to any company registered under this Act. The expression includes companies treated as so registered (for instance, by virtue of having been registered under earlier legislation). It does not include an overseas company that is not itself registered in the UK but has registered particulars in the UK under section 1046.

Section 1168: Hard copy and electronic form and related expressions

1484. Subsections (2) to (4) of this section contain new definitions of the terms "hard copy", "electronic form" and related expressions for all purposes of the Companies Acts. Subsection (5) requires that documents or information be sent in electronic form must be in a form that is capable of being read and retained for future reference.

Section 1171: The former Companies Acts

1485. This section defines "former Companies Acts". The list includes the companies legislation listed in section 735 of the 1985 Act and the later enactments repealed by the Act.

Section 1172: References to requirements of this Act

1486. This section provides that requirements to be imposed under the Act (by regulations or orders to be made under a power contained in the Act) are included in references in the company law provisions of the Act to "the requirements of this Act".

Section 1173: Minor definitions: general

1487. The definitions in subsection (1) that are new or changed are as follows.

1488. The definitions of "body corporate" and "corporation", and of "firm", are new in part. They clarify the position of corporations sole and of partnerships that are legal persons but are not regarded as bodies corporate (as under Scots law).

1489. The definitions of "credit institution" and "regulated market" are changed to follow the definitions in more recent EU Directives. Subsection (2) makes provision to deal with the postponement of the Directive on markets in financial instruments and the fact that it may be implemented in different member States on different dates.

1490. The definition of "working day" is new. This expression replaces a variety of expressions in the existing legislation; there is no change of substance.

Section 1174 and Schedule 8: Index of defined expressions

1491. Section 1174 introduces Schedule 8 to the Act, which provides an index setting out where the definitions of terms used in the Companies Acts are to be found.

PART 39: COMPANIES: MINOR AMENDMENTS

Section 1175 and Schedule 9: Removal of special provisions about accounts and audit of charitable companies

[3.40]

1492. This section and Schedule remove from company law special rules about the audit of companies that are charities. Under section 249A of the 1985 Act, certain companies are subject to audit, or to an accountant's report, because they are charities, when they would be exempt as small companies if they were not charities.

1493. This section is part of achieving the objective of changing the treatment of small charitable companies so that, as far as their accounts scrutiny is concerned, they will be required to comply with the requirements of charity law rather than those of company law. The Charities Act 2006 introduced a power (section 77 of that Act) to enable the Office of the Third Sector to bring forward regulations, subject to the affirmative resolution procedure, applying charity law rules about scrutiny of financial records to charitable companies.

Section 1176: Power of Secretary of State to bring civil proceedings on company's behalf

1494. This section repeals the power of the Secretary of State, under section 438 of the 1985 Act, to bring civil proceedings on behalf of a company. Subsections (2) and (3) are consequential amendments to sections 439 and 453 of the 1985 Act respectively. This repeal does not affect any proceedings begun before this section comes into force.

Section 1177: Repeal of certain provisions about company directors

1495.   This section repeals various provisions of Part 10 of the 1985 Act.

1496.   Section 311 of the 1985 Act prohibits a company from paying director remuneration free of income tax. The Law Commissions recommended its repeal as the tax which the company agreed to pay is itself taxed as part of the emoluments of a director, and as the company is required to disclose in its annual accounts an estimate of the tax which it has undertaken to pay.

1497.   Section 323 of the 1985 Act prohibits directors (including shadow directors) from buying "put" and "call" options in listed shares or debentures in the company or another in the same group. This prohibition is extended to spouses and minor children of directors by section 327 of the 1985 Act. The Law Commissions recommended its repeal.

1498.   Sections 324 to 326 and 328 to 329 of, and Parts 2 to 4 of Schedule 13 to, the 1985 Act deal with the duty of a director to notify interests in shareholdings to his company and impose an obligation on the company to record those interests in a register and to disclose them to the relevant exchanges. They are repealed.

1499.   Sections 343 and 344 of the 1985 Act make special provision for banking companies and the holding companies of credit institutions, allowing them to disclose in their annual accounts abbreviated particulars of loans, quasi-loans and credit transactions with directors or their connected persons. Section 413 of the Act, which replaces the annual accounts disclosure requirements of the 1985 Act in respect of loans, quasi-loans and credit transactions, makes its own special provision in subsection (8) of that section for banking companies and the holding companies of credit institutions.

Section 1178: Repeal of requirement that certain companies publish periodical statement

1500.   This section repeals section 720 of, and the related Schedule 23 to, the 1985 Act. Section 720 requires certain insurers and deposit, provident or benefit societies to publish a periodical statement in the form set out in the Schedule. The statement contains basic information about certain liabilities and assets and, in the case of a company with shares, basic information about its share capital and issued shares. This general disclosure requirement has been superseded by specialised regulatory developments in particular fields of financial services. The application of the section is now very limited as it does not apply to any UK insurance company which is regulated by the FSA under FSMA and which complies with its rules as to the publication of annual accounts and balance sheet. Nor does it apply to any insurer authorised in any other EEA State carrying on business in the UK if it complies with equivalent rules of its home State.

Section 1179: Repeal of requirement that Secretary of State prepare annual report

1501.   This section repeals the requirement, under section 729 of the 1985 Act, for the Secretary of State to cause a "general annual report on matters within the Companies Acts" to be prepared and laid before both Houses of Parliament.

Section 1180: Repeal of certain provisions about company charges

1502.   This section repeals the provisions in Part 4 of the 1989 Act relating to company charges. These provisions have not been brought into force.

Section 1181: Access to constitutional documents of RTE and RTM companies

1503.   This section enables the Secretary of State to make an order amending certain provisions of the Commonhold and Leasehold Reform Act 2002 and the Leasehold Reform, Housing and Urban Development Act 1993 so as to make it easier to ascertain the contents of the articles and other constitutional documents of Right To Manage ("RTM") and Right to Enfranchise ("RTE") companies (two new types of company provided for in the 2002 Act – in the case of RTE companies, by amendment to the 1993 Act).

1504.   Under the Commonhold and Leasehold Reform Act 2002 and the Leasehold Reform, Housing and Urban Development Act 1993 as amended by it, the Secretary of State may make regulations prescribing model memoranda and articles of association for RTM and RTE companies, and the provisions of the model memoranda and articles so prescribed may have effect notwithstanding contrary provision in the memoranda and articles of such companies as registered at Companies House. As the legislation stands currently, a person consulting the Companies House record of an RTM or RTE company's memorandum or articles may not be aware of the company's RTM or RTE status, and therefore may also be unaware that its registered memorandum and articles have to be read in the light of any relevant regulations prescribing model memoranda and articles for RTM or RTE companies. Since the prescribed memoranda and articles may invalidate provisions of the registered documents and apply in place of them, this may cause problems.

1505.   The RTM and RTE legislation is likely to be adjusted to reflect the new status of the memorandum under sections 8 and 28 in particular. Reference is made to "other constitutional

Part 3   CA 2006 Supporting Materials

documents" because it is possible that under the new constitutional arrangements, the RTM and RTE legislation should make provision about the contents of constitutional documents other than articles.

PART 40: COMPANY DIRECTORS: FOREIGN DISQUALIFICATION ETC

[3.41]

1506. Part 40 addresses a gap in the present law. Persons who have been disqualified from being a director, or from holding an equivalent position, or engaging in the management of a company in another State, are currently able to form a company in the UK, to appoint themselves a director of that company and then operate that company either in the UK or in the State where they have been disqualified. The provisions in this Part give the Secretary of State a power to close the gap by making regulations to disqualify from being a director of a UK company, persons who have been disqualified in another State.

1507. Part 40 is the first Part which is outside the company law provisions of the Act. It does not, therefore, form part of the Companies Acts. This is due to the fact that the provisions in this Part are linked with those of the Company Directors' Disqualification Act 1986. That Act is not part of the Companies Acts because it has implications beyond companies to other bodies (such as NHS foundation trusts) and extends beyond persons covered by the Companies Acts to persons such as insolvency practitioners. The fact that Part 40 is not part of the Companies Acts has the consequence that the definitions in the earlier Parts of the Act do not apply – hence the need to define the term "the court" in section 1183. Similarly, the definitions for Part 40 are not listed in Schedule 8 to the Act.

Section 1182: Persons subject to foreign restrictions

1508. Section 1182 defines what is meant by "a person being subject to foreign restrictions." Only persons falling into this category may be disqualified by regulations made under this Part. This category is intended to include those who have been disqualified under (or otherwise fallen foul of) a foreign law equivalent to that in the Company Directors' Disqualification Act 1986.

Section 1183: Meaning of "the court" and "UK company"

1509. Section 1183 sets out the meaning of "the court" and "UK company" for the purposes of this Part.

Section 1184: Disqualification of persons subject to foreign restrictions

1510. Section 1184 provides a power for the Secretary of State to make regulations disqualifying a person subject to foreign restrictions from being the director of a UK company, acting as a receiver of a UK company's property, or, in any way, taking part in the promotion, formation or management of a UK company.

1511. The power is subject to affirmative resolution procedure.

Section 1185: Disqualification regulations: supplementary

1512. Section 1185 states that the regulations under section 1184 may make different provision for different types of case, and sets out some examples. If the regulations provide for application to the court (either by the Secretary of State for a disqualification order under section 1184(2)(b), or by a disqualified person seeking relief under section 1184(5)), the section requires the regulations to specify the grounds on which an application to the court may be made. It also allows the regulations to set out matters to which the court should have regard when considering an application.

Section 1186: Offence of breach of disqualification

1513. Section 1186 provides that regulations made under section 1184 may provide that a person disqualified under this Part who acts in breach of the disqualification commits an offence.

Section 1187: Personal liability for debts of company

1514. Section 1187 provides for the Secretary of State to make regulations to the effect that a person disqualified under this part who acts as a director of a UK company, or is involved in the management of a UK company is personally responsible for all debts and liabilities of the company incurred during the time that he or she is subject to foreign restrictions.

Section 1188: Statements from persons subject to foreign restrictions

1515. Section 1188 provides a power for the Secretary of State to make regulations providing that a person not disqualified under this Part but subject to foreign restrictions must send a statement to the registrar if he or she does anything that, if done by a person disqualified under this Part, would be a breach of the disqualification.

1516. The power is subject to affirmative resolution procedure.

Section 1189: Statements from persons disqualified

1517. Section 1189 provides a power for the Secretary of State to make provisions by regulation that would require a disqualified director to provide an additional statement where he or she has received approval from the court to act in a capacity that would otherwise be in breach of the disqualification.

1518. The power is subject to affirmative resolution procedure.

Section 1190: Statements: whether to be made public

1519. Section 1190 provides for regulations under sections 1188 and 1189 to state whether statements made under those regulations shall be on the public register, and the circumstances in which they may withheld from public inspection or removed from the register.

Section 1191: Offences

1520. Section 1191 provides for regulations to apply criminal sanctions for a failure to comply with any requirements on statements under sections 1188 and 1189.

PART 41: BUSINESS NAMES

[3.42]
1521. The provisions of this Part replace the Business Names Act 1985.

Chapter 1: Restricted Or Prohibited Names

Section 1192: Application of this Chapter

1522. This section partly replaces section 1 of the Business Names Act 1985. It ensures that the restrictions on the use of names in the course of business apply to all persons carrying on business in the UK, other than certain individuals or partnerships (see below). In particular, the restrictions:
* apply to all companies (and not as in the Business Names Act, just to any company capable of being wound up under the Insolvency Act 1986 which trades under a name other than that under which it is registered); and
* apply to any partnership whose members include a company (and not, as in the Business Names Act, only if the name under which such a partnership does business includes names for the corporate partners other than those under which they are registered).

1523. As in the Business Names Act, the restrictions do not apply to individuals if they trade either alone or in partnership under their surnames augmented only by their forenames and/or initials. Sole traders and individuals carrying on business in partnership are also excluded from the scope of the Chapter if the only addition to their name shows the business's previous ownership.

1524. The main effect of the wider coverage is that controls apply to all overseas companies carrying on business in the UK. It also removes any uncertainty as to whether the controls apply to business entities other than companies incorporated under the Companies Acts.

Section 1193 to 1196: Sensitive words or expressions

1525. Sections 1193 to 1195 replace sections 2, 3, 6 and 7 of the Business Names Act 1985. Section 1199 (see below) contains savings equivalent to those currently in section 2(2) of the Business Names Act.

1526. These sections require prior approval for the use of any name for carrying on business for which a company would require approval before it could be registered under it. (Sections 54 to 56, replacing sections 26(2) and 29 of the 1985 Act, apply corresponding restrictions to company names.) The differences between the requirements under these sections and the requirements under the Business Names Act are:
* Section 1193(1)(a) requires prior approval for names likely to give the impression that the business is connected with Her Majesty's Government in Northern Ireland;
* Section 1193(1)(c) provides a power for the Secretary of State to specify in regulations the public authorities such that prior approval will be required for names likely to give the impression that the business is connected with it;
* The definition of local authority in section 1193(2) is brought up to date for Scotland and includes a district council in Northern Ireland;
* Section 1195(4) provides that the Secretary of State may refuse to consider an application for approval that is not compliant with the statutory requirements.

1527. Section 1196 provides that approval for the use of a name may be withdrawn in appropriate circumstances.

Section 1197: Name containing inappropriate indication of company type or legal form

1528. This section replaces sections 33, 34 and 34A of the 1985 Act. Rather than making it an offence on the face of the Act to use prohibited words, this section provides that the Secretary of State may by regulations make it an offence to carry on business under names using indicators of particular legal status, or similar words, unless entitled to do so. It complements sections 58 and 59, which control the use of statutory indicators of legal status (eg "Ltd" and "p.l.c.") in companies' registered names.

Section 1198: Name giving misleading indication of activities

1529. This section makes it an offence to use a business name that gives so misleading an indication of the nature of the activities of the business as to be likely to cause harm to the public. This section complements section 76 which gives the Secretary of State power to direct a company to change its registered name in these circumstances.

Section 1199: Savings for existing lawful business names

1530. This section provides exemptions for those continuing to use a name that was lawful before the Act comes into force. The exemption is both from the requirement for prior approval and from using names that include a protected indicator of company status. It also retains the existing provision for when a business is transferred: providing the name was previously lawful, the business may continue under that name for 12 months even if otherwise it would not be lawful for whoever is now carrying on the business (see subsection (3)).

Chapter 2: Disclosure Required In Case Of Individual Or Partnership

1531. This Chapter re-enacts for individuals and partnerships the Business Names Act provisions relating to information which must be displayed at places of business and in correspondence. These sections ensure that a business's suppliers and customers can discover the legal identity of the person with whom they are doing business and can serve documents upon it. Section 1203 makes special provision for large partnerships so that not all the partners' names are required in all business documents, provided certain conditions are met.

Section 1200: Application of this Chapter

1532. This section partly replaces section 1 of the Business Names Act 1985. It provides that Chapter 2 applies to:

- sole traders if they trade under any name other than their true surnames augmented only by their forenames and/or initials. (Section 1208 defines initial to include any recognised abbreviation of a name);
- partnerships unless their name is the surnames of all its human partners (augmented only by their forenames and/or initials) and the registered names of its other partners.

1533. It also excludes sole traders and partnerships if the only addition to their name shows the business's previous ownership.

1534. This section ensures that the coverage of this Chapter is the same as the Business Names Act except that, unlike that Act, it does not apply to any companies. The comparable requirements for companies are in Part 5, Chapter 6.

Section 1201: Information required to be disclosed

1535. This section replaces section 4(1)(a)(i), (ii) and (iv) of the Business Names Act 1985. It specifies the information that is to be the subject of disclosure under this Chapter (ie names and addresses for service).

Sections 1202 to 1204: Disclosure requirements

1536. Sections 1202 and 1203 replace section 4(1)(a) and (2) to (7) of the Business Names Act 1985. They are designed to ensure that customers and suppliers:

- of sole traders know the true identity of the person with whom they are dealing and have an address for him/her which is effective for the service of documents relating to the business;
- of partnerships with 20 or fewer partners know the identity of every partner and the address which is effective for the service of documents relating to the business;
- of larger partnerships know the address which is effective for the service of documents relating to the business and either the identity of every partner or the address at which they can discover the identity of every partner.

1537. Large partnerships are not permitted to choose which partners' names are included in documents: they must either include the names of all the partners or none (except in the text or as a signatory) (see subsection (2)(b)).

1538. Section 1202 also provides power for regulations relating to the form of a notice giving the trader's or partners' name(s) and address in response to any person who asks for the information in the course of business. For companies' registered names, equivalent provision may be made in regulations under section 82.

1539. Section 1204 replaces section 4(1)(b) of the Business Names Act 1985 so far as it applies to sole traders and partnerships. It makes provision to enable customers and suppliers to discover the name(s) and the address for service of documents when visiting any business premises of the trader or partners.

Section 1205: Criminal consequences of failure to make required disclosure

1540. This section provides that certain provisions in Part 36 (offences under the Companies Acts) also apply to offences under this Part. It replaces and expands upon section 7 of the Business Names Act 1985 so far as it applies to sole traders and partnerships. It retains the existing offences of failure to comply with the requirements relating to disclosure of name and address in documents and notices.

Section 1206: Civil consequences of failure to make required disclosure

1541. This section replaces section 5 of the Business Names Act 1985 so far as it applies to sole traders and partnerships. It provides legal rights to anyone who has sustained losses as a result of failure to comply with this Chapter's requirements by a sole trader or partnership.

Chapter 3: Supplementary

Section 1207: Application of general provisions about offences

1542. This section replaces section 7(6) of the Business Names Act 1985.

Section 1208: Interpretation

1543. This section replaces section 8 of the Business Names Act 1985. In particular, the definition of "initial" means that the restrictions on names in Chapter 1 not only would not apply to James Alexander Scotland if he were to trade as "James Alexander Scotland" or "J. A. Scotland" but also if he were to trade as "Jimmy Scotland" or "Jim A. Scotland". However, the restrictions would apply if he were to trade as "Scotland Bakers" or "John Scotland".

PART 42: STATUTORY AUDITORS

[3.43]
1544. The provisions of this Part concern the regulation of auditors. The effects of this Part are:
*   To replace Part 2 of the 1989 Act and equivalent Northern Ireland provisions, by restating those provisions with some modifications.
*   To extend the category of auditors that are subject to regulation and to make provision for the registration and regulation of auditors (whether based in the UK or not) who audit companies which are incorporated outside the EU but listed in the UK;
*   To provide that the Comptroller and Auditor General and the regional Auditors General are eligible to be appointed to perform statutory audits and provide a mechanism for the regulation and supervision of their functions as statutory auditor.

1545. Many of the provisions in this Part implement obligations contained in the Updated Eighth Company Law Directive on Audit (2006/43/EC) that was published on 9 June 2006. The provisions relating to Auditors General implement recommendations contained in Lord Sharman's report, "Holding to Account, The Review of Audit and Accountability for Central Government", published in 2001.

Chapter 1: Introductory

Sections 1209 to 1211: Introductory

1546. Part 2 of the 1989 Act regulates only the auditors of companies. Section 1210(1) defines the meaning of statutory auditor more broadly. Persons within subsection (1)(a) to (g) are 'statutory auditors'. This list includes those persons who audit companies (as required under Part 16 of the Act) and those who audit building societies, insurers and banks. In addition, the Secretary of State has a power to add auditors of other persons to this list. Section 1211 cross-refers the eligibility for appointment as a statutory auditor to the requirements contained in Chapter 2 or Chapter 3 of this Part of the Act.

Chapter 2: Individuals And Firms

Sections 1212 and 1213: Eligibility for appointment

1547. These sections are restatements of sections 25 and 28 of the 1989 Act adapted so as to apply in relation to statutory auditors. The sections provide that for a person or firm (defined in section 1261) to be eligible for appointment as a statutory auditor, the person must be a member of a recognised supervisory body and be eligible for appointment under the rules of that body. Section 1217(2) clarifies that references to such members include references to persons who are not members but who are subject to the body's rules. (Section 1217 and Schedule 10 address the recognition of supervisory bodies, and lay down the requirements they must meet to be recognised.)
1548. Section 1213 provides that no person may act as a statutory auditor if he is ineligible. It specifies that, on becoming ineligible, the auditor must resign his office and give notice in writing.

Failure to comply with this requirement is an offence, conviction of which can result in a fine (subsections (3) and (4)). If the auditor continues to act as a statutory auditor after conviction (subsection (5)), or continues to fail to give notice that he is ineligible for appointment as a statutory auditor (subsection (6)), he commits a further offence for which a daily fine may be imposed after conviction (subsection (7)). Subsection (8) provides a defence if the person did not know or had no reason to believe that he was, or had become, ineligible.

Section 1214: Independence requirement

1549. This section restates section 27 of the 1989 Act and indicates circumstances where a person may not act as a statutory auditor on grounds of lack of independence. Under subsection (2) this includes persons who are officers or employees of the audited entity, or the partner or employee of such a person. Under subsection (3), this includes where the person is an officer or employee of a subsidiary of the audited entity. Subsection (4) allows the Secretary of State to make regulations regarding other connections between the audited entity and the statutory auditor by virtue of which a person will be regarded as lacking independence.

Section 1215: Effect of lack of independence

1550. This section sets out the consequences of the prohibition from acting as a statutory auditor on grounds of lack of independence, as defined in section 1214. They replicate the effect of ineligibility as explained for section 1213.

Section 1216: Effect of appointment of a partnership

1551. This section is a restatement of section 26 of the 1989 Act. The effect of the section is to ensure that when a partnership constituted in England and Wales, Northern Ireland, or any other country or territory in which a partnership is not a legal person, is appointed as a statutory auditor under this Part, the appointment may continue even if a partner leaves the partnership. For a partnership or other person to be considered as appropriate for the appointment to continue, they must be eligible for appointment as a statutory auditor and not be prohibited (as indicated in section 1214(1)). Without this provision, the appointment would cease every time the membership of the partnership changed.

Section 1217: Supervisory bodies

1552. This section restates section 30 of the 1989 Act and defines a supervisory body as a body established in the UK which maintains and enforces rules regarding the eligibility of persons appointed as statutory auditors and the conduct of statutory audit work. Subsection (4) introduces Schedule 10, which specifies the requirements supervisory bodies must meet in order to be recognised, and the process for doing so.

Schedule 10: Recognised supervisory bodies

Part 1: Grant and Revocation of recognition of a Supervisory Body

1553. This Schedule restates provisions in Schedule 11 to the 1989 Act. Paragraph 1 identifies the steps a body is required to take to become recognised by the Secretary of State. Paragraph 3 specifies the steps that the Secretary of State is required to take if the recognition of the body is revoked. Paragraph 5 provides that recognition (and revocation) orders are not statutory instruments. Paragraph 4 is a transitional provision that allows bodies recognised under the 1989 Act or the Companies (Northern Ireland) Order 1990 to continue to be recognised.

Part 2: Requirements for recognition of a supervisory body

1554. Paragraphs 6 and 7 require a recognised supervisory body to ensure that persons eligible for appointment as a statutory auditor hold appropriate qualifications (as defined in section 1219). They require a firm that is a statutory auditor to be controlled by qualified persons. Paragraphs 8 to 11 require the bodies to have rules and practices which ensure that auditors are fit and proper persons, that professional integrity and independence is maintained, that technical standards for audits are assured and that there are procedures for maintaining appropriate levels of competence. Paragraphs 12 to 16 specify the requirements for monitoring, enforcement, discipline and investigation of complaints.

Part 3: Arrangements in which recognised supervisory bodies are required to participate

1555. Paragraphs 21 to 27 specify the arrangements with independent bodies that recognised supervisory bodies must enter into in order to meet the requirements of this Schedule described above.

Section 1218: Exemption from liability for damages

1556. This section is a restatement of section 48 of the 1989 Act. It sets out those bodies and individuals that are exempt from liability for damages arising from the discharge or claimed discharge of supervisory functions as specified in this Part of the Act (these include the effects of rules, practices, powers and arrangements of the body). It applies to recognised supervisory bodies (see sections 1217 and Schedule 10) and their officers, employees and members of their governing bodies. The exemption does not apply if they have acted in bad faith, or if it would prevent an award of damages because the act was unlawful under the Human Rights Act.

Section 1219: Appropriate qualifications

1557. This section restates section 31 of the 1989 Act. It provides that a person holds an appropriate audit qualification if he holds a professional qualification obtained in the UK which is recognised in accordance with section 1220 and Schedule 11. Qualifications recognised under Part 2 of the 1989 Act or the Companies (Northern Ireland) Order 1990 will continue to be recognised.

1558. Persons whose qualifications from other EU Member States are recognised under the European Communities (Recognition of Professional Qualifications) (First General System) Regulations 2005 to practise as statutory auditors are also considered to hold an appropriate qualification. So too are overseas qualifications from non-EU countries if approved under section 1221. Subsection (2) restates a transitional provision from the 1989 Act for those persons who began a course of study in accountancy before 1 January 1990 and obtained a qualification between 1 January 1990 and 1 January 1996, enabling them to apply to the Secretary of State for approval of their qualification. The transitional provisions contained in section 31(2) and (3) of the 1989 Act have not been restated.

Section 1220: Qualifying bodies and recognised professional qualifications

1559. This section is a restatement of section 32 of the 1989 Act. It defines the term "qualifying body" as a body that offers a professional qualification in accountancy and introduces Schedule 11 which sets out the requirements that qualifying bodies must impose. Only a qualification recognised in accordance with these provisions can be considered a recognised professional qualification within the meaning of section 1219(1)(a).

Schedule 11: Recognised Professional Qualifications

Part 1: Grant and revocation of recognition of a professional qualification

Paragraph 1: Application for recognition of professional qualification

1560. This Schedule restates provisions in Schedule 12 to the 1989 Act. Paragraph 1 identifies the steps a body is required to take for a qualification it offers to be recognised by the Secretary of State. Paragraph 3 specifies the steps that the Secretary of State is required to take if the recognition is revoked. Paragraph 5 provides that recognition (and revocation) orders are not statutory instruments. Paragraph 4 is a transitional provision that allows qualifications recognised under the 1989 Act or the Companies (Northern Ireland) Order 1990 to continue to be recognised.

Part 2: Requirements for recognition of a professional qualification

1561. Paragraph 6 sets the minimum academic standards that a person must have attained before he can attempt to gain the professional qualification. Paragraph 7 requires that the qualification is restricted to persons who have either completed a relevant academic course or have seven years' professional experience. Paragraph 8 requires that an examination must be passed (part of which has to be in writing) for the person to achieve the qualification. This examination must be in subjects of theoretical knowledge prescribed by the Secretary of State; or a university or equivalent level examination; or by practical demonstration of knowledge to examination or diploma level that is recognised by the Secretary of State. Paragraph 9 requires persons to carry out at least three years' practical training.

Section 1221: Approval of overseas qualifications

1562. This section restates section 33 of the 1989 Act as regards the approval of overseas qualifications from non-EU countries. It sets out the conditions that will need to be satisfied, relating to the assurance of professional competence. The section provides for approval of all those in a specified country who are qualified to audit accounts, or only those who hold specified qualifications in that country. In the case of the latter, the Secretary of State may specify any additional requirements to be satisfied. The section allows the Secretary of State to recognise an overseas qualification only if there is comparability of treatment of UK qualifications in the country in question.

Section 1222: Eligibility of individuals retaining only 1967 Act authorisation

1563. This section restates section 34 of the 1989 Act. Prior to 1967 auditors of an unquoted company were exempt from the statutory qualification requirements placed on other company auditors. The Companies Act 1967 abolished this exemption but allowed an auditor with sufficient practical experience to apply to the Secretary of State for authorisation to practise. Past authorisations will continue to be valid by virtue of the transitional provision in section 1219(1)(b). Section 1222 provides that auditors authorised under the 1967 Act may not be treated as statutory auditors for any purpose other than to perform the statutory audit of an unquoted company (as defined in section 385(2)).

Part 3   CA 2006 Supporting Materials

Section 1223: Matters to be notified to the Secretary of State

1564.   This section is a restatement of section 37 of the 1989 Act and allows the Secretary of State to identify events that must be notified to him if they occur. It requires that recognised supervisory and qualifying bodies must provide information, either in writing or some other specified manner, that is reasonably required for the Secretary of State to carry out his functions – this might include annual reports, or notification of rule or bye-law changes. This information might relate to specific time periods or specific occurrences.

Section 1224: The Secretary of State's power to call for information

1565.   This section restates section 38 of the 1989 Act. It provides the Secretary of State with the power to require information from a recognised supervisory body, a recognised qualifying body or an individual statutory auditor. For example, as a result of a report provided under section 1223, the Secretary of State may request further information on a specific point to clarify if a recognised supervisory body is complying with the requirements in Schedule 10. The Secretary of State can specify the time period in which this information has to be provided.

Section 1225: Compliance orders

1566.   This section is a restatement of section 39 of the 1989 Act. If a recognised supervisory or qualifying body fails to meet the requirements in Schedule 10 or 11, or it fails to comply with another requirement contained in this Part of the Act, then the Secretary of State may apply to the court for an order to make the body comply. The ultimate sanction for non-compliance by a body would be revocation of its status as a recognised body under Schedule 10 or 11.

Chapter 3: Auditors General

Section 1226: Auditors General: eligibility for appointment as a statutory auditor

1567.   Subsection (1) defines an "Auditor General" for the purposes of this Part as the Comptroller and Auditor General, the Auditor General for Scotland, the Auditor General for Wales or the Comptroller and Auditor General for Northern Ireland. Subsections (2) and (3) explain that an Auditor General is eligible for appointment as a statutory auditor, unless his eligibility has been suspended by the Independent Supervisor under section 1234.

Section 1227: Individuals responsible for audit work on behalf of Auditors General

1568.   This section provides that an Auditor General must ensure that the individuals within his charge, who are carrying out statutory audits on the Auditor General's behalf, are, in their own right, eligible for appointment as a statutory auditor by virtue of the qualifications and requirements that are set out in Chapter 2.

Section 1228: Appointment of the Independent Supervisor

1569.   Subsections (1) and (2) provide that the Secretary of State must appoint a body to be the Independent Supervisor of Auditors General in respect of the exercise of statutory audit functions. Subsection (3) provides for the appointment of the Independent Supervisor to have the effect of making it subject to the obligations of the Freedom of Information Act 2000. Subsections (4), (5) and (6) provide that a body may be appointed as Independent Supervisor of an Auditor General if it is a corporate body or unincorporated association that is willing to carry out the function, that has arrangements in place that will ensure the supervision is carried out effectively, and that will exercise such functions and requirements that may be laid down in the Secretary of State's order appointing it. The appointed Independent Supervisor must perform its function on a UK-wide basis for all four Auditors General in accordance with section 1229(1).

Section 1229: Supervision of Auditors General by the Independent Supervisor

1570.   This section sets the framework for the supervision arrangements to be carried out by the Independent Supervisor. Subsection (2) provides that the Independent Supervisor must establish arrangements with one or more third parties to carry out aspects of the supervisory function. Subsection (3) provides that the arrangements with a third party cover standards on professional integrity and independence, as well as the technical standards for statutory audit work; monitoring performance; investigating matters arising from that performance; and as necessary holding disciplinary hearings and deciding whether any disciplinary action should be taken. Subsections (6) and (7) make provisions relating to the payment of fines under the disciplinary arrangements.

Section 1230: Duties of Auditors General in relation to supervision arrangements

1571.   Subsection (1) makes it a duty for each Auditor General to comply with the standards set by, as well as the monitoring arrangements and decisions of, the independent supervision arrangements. It also provides in subsection (2) for each Auditor General to pay the proportion of the costs of the independent supervisory arrangements that may be notified to the Auditor General in writing. Subsection (3) provides that the payment of such costs is to be regarded as expenditure of the

National Audit Office in the case of the Comptroller and Auditor General, and as expenditure of the Northern Ireland Audit Office in the case of the Comptroller and Auditor General for Northern Ireland. In the case of the Auditor General for Scotland, under section 13 of the Public Finance and Accountability (Scotland) Act 2000 (asp 1) the expenses of the Auditor General are paid by Audit Scotland. In the case of the Auditor General for Wales, under section 93 of the Government of Wales Act 1998 the expenses of the Auditor General are met by the Assembly.

Section 1231: Reports by the Independent Supervisor

1572. This section provides that the Independent Supervisor must provide at least one report each calendar year to the Secretary of State and to the First Minister in Scotland, The First Minister and the Deputy First Minister in Northern Ireland and the Assembly First Minister in Wales. The Secretary of State must then lay the report before each House of Parliament.

Section 1232: Matters to be notified to the Independent Supervisor

1573. This section makes it a legal requirement for an Auditor General to notify the Independent Supervisor in writing of events that the Independent Supervisor may specify and is consistent with the requirement for other statutory auditors as contained in section 1223.

Section 1233: The Independent Supervisor's power to call for information

1574. This section makes provision enabling the Independent Supervisor to require an Auditor General to provide information. It enables the Independent Supervisor to specify the period within which the information must be provided and how the information must be verified. This section is consistent with the requirement for other statutory auditors as contained in section 1224.

Section 1234: Suspension notices

1575. This section provides the Independent Supervisor with the power to suspend an Auditor General's eligibility for appointment as a statutory auditor if, for example, he falls short of the standards laid down for performance of statutory audit work. It also sets out the provisions as to how the suspension will be effected, and the considerations pertaining to the decision to suspend. It provides for a process leading up to the issuing of a suspension notice, including the hearing of representations from the Auditor General in question.

Section 1235: Effect of suspension notices

1576. This section provides that an Auditor General must not act as a statutory auditor of a particular person if he is suspended in relation to that person. If the suspension starts during his term of office, the Auditor General must resign as a statutory auditor immediately, and tell the audited person that he has resigned. Subsection (3) makes it clear that the criminal offences in section 1213 (ineligibility for appointment as a statutory auditor) do not apply to an Auditor General who is ineligible by virtue of a suspension notice.

Section 1236: Compliance orders

1577. This section provides the power for the Independent Supervisor to take an Auditor General to court if he fails to comply with any obligation imposed by or by virtue of this Part of the Act. The court may direct the Auditor General to take such steps as it thinks fit to ensure compliance.

Section 1237: Proceedings involving the Independent Supervisor

1578. This section provides that where the Independent Supervisor is an unincorporated association it may take proceedings in the name of the body corporate under which it is constituted.

Section 1238: Grants to the Independent Supervisor

1579. This section amends section 16(2) of the C(AICE) Act 2004. The effect of the amendment is that the body that carries out the functions of the Independent Supervisor is eligible for grants from the Secretary of State under section 16 of that Act to meet the expenditure of the body and any subsidiary. It also means that the body may be exempt from liability in damages under section 18 of the Act.

Chapter 4: The Register Of Auditors Etc

Section 1239: The register of auditors

1580. This section restates section 35 of the 1989 Act but extends the provision to cover other statutory auditors (as defined in section 1210) and third country auditors (as defined in section 1241). It requires the Secretary of State to make regulations that require the keeping of a register of those persons eligible to be a statutory auditor and third country auditors. Subsection (2) sets out the information that must be included on the register and includes the person's name and address and the name of the relevant supervisory body for the person. If an individual statutory auditor works for a firm that is a statutory auditor, both must be entered separately on the register and cross-referenced.

In subsection (3) additional information, namely the name and address of directors, members or partners, is required from bodies corporate (including limited liability partnerships), corporations sole and partnerships. The section allows for certain parts of the register to be kept by different persons, for example an oversight body may keep the information regarding third country auditors, whilst the recognised supervisory bodies may keep information regarding other statutory auditors. Subsection (6) confers a power to provide that information in the register, or a certified copy of it, is to be made available to the public upon request. A charge for access to this information is permitted. Subsection (7) allows the Secretary of State to disapply some or all of the requirements of subsections (2)(e) and (3) in relation to third country auditors (for example, if they are already subject to equivalent supervision in their home country).

Section 1240: Information to be made available to public

1581. This new provision gives the Secretary of State the power to make regulations placing an obligation on statutory auditors to make information regarding their ownership, governance, internal controls with respect to quality and independence of audit work, turnover and names of persons for whom the person has acted as statutory auditor, available to the public. Any such obligations are additional to those referred to in section 1239.

Chapter 5: Registered Third Country Auditors

Section 1241: Meaning of "third country auditor", "registered third country auditor" etc

1582. This is a new provision that sets out the definition of a third country auditor and a registered third country auditor. The section provides that a third country auditor is an auditor (whether based in the UK or not) of the accounts of a company incorporated or formed in a non-EU country, whose shares are admitted for trading on a UK market such as the London Stock Exchange.

Section 1242: Duties of registered third country auditors

1583. Subsections (1) to (3) require registered third country auditors to be subject to systems of independent monitoring and discipline in the UK in accordance with Schedule 12. These provisions are similar to supervision arrangements for statutory auditors contained in section 1212(1) (membership of a Recognised Supervisory Body) and section 1217 (Supervisory Bodies) and Schedule 10. Subsection (4) empowers the Secretary of State to disapply the requirements in subsections (1) to (3). For example, he may disapply the requirements if satisfied that the third country auditor is already subject to equivalent supervision arrangements in his home country.

Schedule 12: Arrangements in which registered third country auditors are required to participate

1584. The requirements in this Schedule are new. They describe the independent monitoring and investigation arrangements which third country auditors must participate in.

Sections 1243 and 1244: Information

1585. These sections replicate for registered third country auditors the requirements in section 1223 and 1224 for the notification of information to the Secretary of State. Third country auditors may be required to provide any information that might reasonably be required for the Secretary of State to carry out his functions.

Sections 1245 and 1246: Enforcement

1586. The provisions in section 1245 enable the Secretary of State to apply to the court for an order to make a registered third country auditor comply with its obligations under the Part. The provisions in section 1246 empower the Secretary of State to make provision as to the removal of the third country auditors from the register of auditors in certain circumstances. In doing so, regard must be had to whether the third country auditor has complied with his obligations under this Part.

Section 1247: Grants to bodies concerned with arrangements under Schedule 12

1587. This section amends section 16(2) of the C(AICE) Act 2004. The effect of the amendment is that the body that carries out the monitoring and investigation functions in relation to third country auditors is eligible for grants from the Secretary of State under section 16 of that Act. It also means that the body may be exempt from liability in damages under section 18 of the Act.

Chapter 6: Supplementary And General

Sections 1248 and 1249: Power to require second company audit

1588. These sections restate section 29 of the 1989 Act empowering the Secretary of State to require a second audit of a company in circumstances where the person appointed as statutory auditor was not eligible for appointment or was not independent of the company audited. Subsection (2) permits the Secretary of State to direct either that a second audit is performed or that a review of the first audit is carried out (which will inform whether a second audit is required).

Subsections (5) to (8) set out the criminal sanctions on the company should it fail to comply with that order. Section 1249 allows the audited person to recover the costs of the second audit from the first auditor, if the first auditor knew when he acted that he was not eligible or not independent.

Section 1250: Misleading, false and deceptive statements

1589. This section is a restatement of the offences in section 41 of the 1989 Act but also extends these offences to third country auditors. Subsection (1) sets out offences in respect of persons who provide information that they know to be misleading, false or deceptive. Subsection (2) makes it an offence for a person to hold himself out as a registered auditor where he is not registered as such in accordance with section 1239. Subsection (3) makes a similar provision for third country auditors. Subsection (4) makes it an offence for either a supervisory or qualifying body to hold itself out as recognised when it is not so recognised. Subsection (8) provides a defence if the person took all reasonable precautions and exercised due diligence to avoid committing the offence.

Section 1251: Fees

1590. This provision is based on section 45 of the 1989 Act and extends the powers of the Secretary of State to make regulations to prescribe periodical fees which must be paid by the Auditors General and registered third country auditors as well as recognised supervisory bodies and recognised qualifying bodies.

Section 1252 and 1253: Delegation of Secretary of State's functions

1591. These provisions replace sections 46 and 46A of the 1989 Act and empower the Secretary of State to establish a body, or appoint an existing body, to exercise his functions relating to statutory auditors and the recognition of bodies that supervise auditors and/or provide professional qualifications. To do so, the Secretary of State must make a delegation order that is in accordance with Schedule 13. However, subsection (6) provides that some delegated functions must remain exercisable concurrently by the Secretary of State: namely the power to call for information (sections 1224 and 1244) and the power to issue directions to comply with international obligations (section 1254). Subsection (7) also provides that certain delegated functions concerning the approval of overseas qualifications (section 1221) can be exercised only with the consent of the Secretary of State. Subsection (3) provides for the delegation of the body to have the effect of making it subject to the obligations of the Freedom of Information Act 2000. The Professional Oversight Board is currently appointed under section 46 of the 1989 Act to exercise the Secretary of State's functions.

1592. Section 1253 specifies the conditions for delegating functions to an existing body. It ensures that an existing body is not precluded from exercising any delegated function on the basis of its involvement with the monitoring, investigation or disciplinary arrangements that are set out in Schedule 10.

Schedule 13: Supplementary provisions with respect to delegation order

1593. This Schedule restates the provisions of Schedule 13 to the 1989 Act. Paragraph 2 provides that the delegated body is not to be regarded as acting on behalf of the Crown. Paragraphs 7 to 9 provide for the delegated body to exercise any legislative functions by instrument in writing and not by statutory instrument. Instruments must be made available to the public and the Secretary of State may require the body to consult prior to the making of regulations. Paragraph 10 requires the delegated body to report annually to the Secretary of State on the performance of its functions.

Section 1254: Directions to comply with international obligations

1594. This provision restates section 40 of the 1989 Act and empowers the Secretary of State to direct recognised supervisory or qualifying bodies, or any body delegated under section 1252, to comply with Community or other international obligations. If the body fails to comply with a direction, the Secretary of State can apply to the court for his direction to be enforced.

Section 1255: Offences by bodies corporate, partnerships and unincorporated associations

1595. This provision restates section 42 of the 1989 Act and deals with offences committed by bodies corporate, partnerships and other unincorporated associations. Where an offence committed by such a body is committed with the consent or connivance of, or is attributable to the neglect of, an officer (in the case of a body corporate), a partner (in the case of a partnership) or an officer or member (in the case of an unincorporated association), that officer, partner or member is also guilty of the offence.

Section 1256: Time limits for prosecution of offences

1596. This provision restates section 43 of the 1989 Act and sets a twelve-month time limit for the prosecution of offences within each of the jurisdictions. Subsections (1) to (4) identify that the date on which knowledge of sufficient evidence of the offence to justify prosecuting becomes known to either the Secretary of State or Director of Public Prosecutions (for England and Wales), the Lord Advocate (for Scotland) or Director of Public Prosecutions for Northern Ireland is taken as the date from which the twelve month time limit commences. In any event, the prosecution may not be commenced if three years have passed since the date on which the offence was committed.

Section 1257: Jurisdiction and procedure in respect of offences

1597. This provision restates section 44 of the 1989 Act and deals with the jurisdiction and procedure in respect of offences. It specifies that the jurisdiction is that in which a body corporate or unincorporated association has its place of business or, in the case of an individual, where he is located. It also provides for an unincorporated association to be treated in the same way as a body corporate.

Section 1258: Service of notices

1598. This provision restates section 49 of the 1989 Act and states how notices and other documents may be served under this Part of the Act on any person other than the Secretary of State. The three permitted methods of service are: delivery to the person, leaving the document at the person's address, or sending it by post to the person's address.

Section 1259: Documents in electronic form

1599. This is a new provision to allow delivery of notices, directions or other documents in electronic form. It allows the use of e-communications where existing provisions in this Part impose requirements on the giving or sending of notices, directions or other documents, provided the recipient indicates he is prepared to accept this form of delivery.

Section 1260: Meaning of "associate"

1600. This provision restates section 52 of the 1989 Act and defines the meaning of "associate". This definition is particularly relevant for the independence requirement for statutory auditors set out in section 1214.

Section 1261: Minor definitions

1601. This provision is a restatement of section 53 of the 1989 Act with certain extra definitions. Subsection (3) empowers the Secretary of State, by regulations, to make amendments to this Part which are needed in relation to the application of the Part to a "firm" (as defined by subsection (1)) which is not a partnership or body corporate.

Section 1262: Index of defined expressions

1602. This provision contains an index to the defined terms used in the Part.

Section 1263: Power to make provision in consequence of changes affecting accountancy bodies

1603. This provision restates section 51 of the 1989 Act. The provision empowers the Secretary of State to amend by regulation legislation (including this Act) that refers to accountancy bodies in the event of a name change, merger or transfer of engagements affecting the bodies.

Section 1264 and Schedule 14: Consequential amendments

1604. Section 1264 introduces Schedule 14, which contains amendments consequential on this Part to the C(AICE) Act 2004.

PART 43: TRANSPARENCY OBLIGATIONS AND RELATED MATTERS

Section 1265: The transparency obligations directive

[3.44]
1605. Section 1265 inserts a definition of the "transparency obligations directive" at the appropriate place in Part 6 of the Financial Services and Markets Act 2000 ("FSMA").

Section 1266: Transparency rules

1606. Section 1266 inserts seven new sections into Part 6 of FSMA: sections 89A, 89B, 89C, 89D, 89E, 89F and 89G. Part 6 of FSMA deals with certain aspects of the regulation of securities that are traded on regulated markets in the UK. These new sections make provision about rules that may be made by the "competent authority" (which is the Financial Services Authority ("the Authority")) for the purposes of the Transparency Directive (2004/109/EC)"transparency rules".

New Section 89A: Transparency rules

1607. Subsection (1) of new section 89A of FSMA enables the Authority to make transparency rules to implement the Transparency Directive in the UK. Subsection (2) enables the rules to include provision for any matter arising out of or related to the Directive provisions.

1608. The Transparency Directive itself covers issuers whose securities are traded on regulated markets and people who hold voting rights attached to shares in such issuers. The scope of the rule-making power allows the rules to address other matters arising from the Directive's implementation, for example, to ensure that secondary legislation adopted by the Commission can be incorporated into the transparency rules, and that optional aspects of the Directive can be implemented, where the Authority considers this appropriate.

1609. It is expected that rules made under section 89A(1) will implement the Transparency Directive by—

- requiring holders of votes attached to shares in issuers to make disclosure about their holdings at certain thresholds (see new section 89B);
- requiring issuers to make public their annual accounts and reports, prepared in accordance with the EU International Accounts Standards Regulation (Regulation (EC) 1606/2002), and, where appropriate, half-yearly and interim management statements about their business(see new section 89C);
- requiring issuers to make notification about voting rights held by themselves in respect of their own voting shares (see new section 89D);
- requiring issuers to notify the Authority and the market of any proposed change to their constitution (see new section 89E).

1610. Subsection (3)(a) enables the Authority to make rules about disclosures of voteholdings to UK markets that are not regulated markets (within the meaning of section 103(1) of FSMA) (such as the AIM). Subsection (3)(b) enables the Authority to make rules about disclosure in relation to certain comparable instruments in respect of voting shares. These are instruments that give the holder a level of economic, as opposed to legal, control over votes attached to shares. An example of the type of instrument that the rules could extend to cover is a contract for difference, known as a "CFD".

1611. Subsection (4) specifies further matters that the rules may cover. These include: how the proportion of voting rights held by an issuer is to be determined; when voting rights held by one person may be regarded as being held by another; the nature, form, timing and presentation of any notification; and the circumstances in which any of the requirements of section 89A may not apply.

New Section 89B: Provision of voteholder information

1612. New section 89B sets out provisions for notifications by voteholders under transparency rules. Subsection (1) specifies that notification can be required to be made to the issuer or to the public or to both. Under subsection (2), rules may provide for such information to be notified at the same time to the Authority.

1613. Subsection (5) sets out the circumstances in which voteholders may be required to notify of a change in the proportion of voting rights (ie when a proportion crosses above or below, or reaches, a proportion designated in the rules).

New Section 89C: Provision of information by issuers of transferable securities

1614. New section 89C sets out provisions for issuers of transferable securities to provide information under transparency rules. Subsection (1) clarifies that information can be required to be given to the public or the Authority or both.

1615. The rules cover annual financial reports (both financial statements and management reports) and, for certain issuers, half-yearly financial reports and interim management statements, as required by the Transparency Directive. The rules can also require issuers to disclose certain other information relating to voteholder information, information about the different classes of share they have issued and the total number of voting rights attached to each class, their own voteholdings, their capital, and information about new loan issues.

New Section 89D: Notification of voting rights held by issuer

1616. New section 89D enables the rules to provide for issuers to make notification of the proportion of voting rights they hold in respect of their own voting shares. Subsection (1)(a) permits rules to set the initial notification period in accordance with the requirements of the Transparency Directive at Article 30.2. Subsections (1)(b), (2) and (3) set out the circumstances under which issuers of transferable securities must notify of a change in the proportion of voting rights (ie when a proportion crosses above or below, or reaches, a proportion designated in the rules).

New Section 89E: Notification of proposed amendment of issuer's constitution

1617. New section 89E enables the rules to provide that an issuer of transferable securities admitted to trading on a regulated market must notify a proposed amendment to its constitution to the Authority and the market.

New Section 89F: Transparency rules: interpretation etc

1618. New section 89F defines a number of terms used in the sections 89A to 89G.

New Section 89G: Transparency rules: other supplementary provisions

1619. New section 89G sets out further supplementary provisions relating to the transparency rules. Subsection (1) enables the Authority to make rules imposing the same obligations on a person who has applied for the admission of transferable securities to trading on a regulated market without the issuer's consent as they impose on an issuer of transferable securities. Subsection (2) enables the Authority to make rules to allow it to make public information that voteholders or issuers are

Part 3   CA 2006 Supporting Materials

required to make public, where they fail to do so themselves. Subsection (3) will enable the Authority to make public information notified to it in accordance with transparency rules.

1620. There is some overlap between notifications required by the Panel on Takeovers and Mergers in the rules made under Part 28, and notifications required by the Transparency Directive. Subsection (4) enables transparency rules to cross-refer to rules made by the Panel under Part 28, which will enable greater alignment between the two sets of rules.

Section 1267: Competent Authority's power to call for information

1621. Section 1267 inserts three new sections into Part 6 of FSMA: sections 89H to 89J.

1622. New section 89H permits the Authority to call for information from specified persons, set out in subsection (2), including issuers of shares and their auditors and directors, and voteholders and their auditors, directors and persons controlling or controlled by voteholders.

1623. Subsection (3) limits the Authority to requesting information and documents reasonably required in connection with the transparency rules. Subsection (4) enables the Authority to determine the timeframe for production and provision of information, and the location for the information to be provided. Subsection (5) makes it clear that the production of the material as required by this section does not affect any lien on a document.

1624. New section 89I sets outs the requirements connected with the Authority's power to call for information. The Authority will be empowered to specify the form of the information or documents it calls for under section 89H (1), and may require its authentication or verification (subsection (2)). The Authority is permitted, under subsection (3), to take copies of and extracts from the documentation provided, and may also require the persons providing the information, or any "relevant person" within the meaning of subsection (4) (which includes directors, auditors, actuaries, accountants, lawyers and employees), to submit an explanation of any documentation produced.

1625. If a person fails to comply with the requirement to produce a document, the Authority is permitted under subsection (5) to require a person to state where the document is.

1626. New section 89J sets out the supplementary provisions in relation to the competent authority's power to call for information in sections 89H and 89I.

Section 1268: Powers exercisable in case of infringement of transparency obligation

1627. Section 1268 inserts four new sections into Part 6 of FSMA: sections 89K to 89N.

1628. The four new sections set out the Authority's powers in case of infringement of transparency obligations. Section 89K enables the Authority to make a public statement if an issuer is failing or has failed to comply with its obligations. It may only do so after it has issued a warning notice to the issuer (subsection (2)), and after any representations from the issuer, it has provided the issuer with a decision notice (subsection (3)). Subsection (4) requires the Authority to provide the issuer with notice that it has a right to refer the matter to the Tribunal.

1629. New section 89L gives the Authority the power, in certain circumstances, to suspend or prohibit trading of securities admitted to trading on a regulated market, or to request the market operator to suspend or prohibit such trading. The powers are to be used where the Authority suspects (subsections (2) and (3)) or finds (subsection 4) applicable breaches of transparency obligations. The Authority's powers to request a market operator to prohibit trading could be used where and issuer whose home member State is the UK is listed in another EEA State.

1630. Section 89M sets out the procedures relating to the suspension and prohibition powers of the Authority set out in section 89L.

1631. New section 89N sets out the right for those who receive a decision notice or a notice under section 89M to refer matters to the Tribunal.

Section 1269: Corporate governance rules

1632. Section 1269 inserts new section 89O into FSMA which gives the Authority a power (under Part 6 of FSMA) to make rules implementing, enabling the implementation of or dealing with matters arising out of Community obligations on corporate governance of issuers on a regulated market.

1633. This rule-making power will enable the Authority to make corporate governance rules to cover issuers for whom the UK is the home member State, and whose securities are traded on a regulated market in the UK or elsewhere in the EEA.

1634. Subsection (2) sets out the type of corporate governance provision covered by this rule making power. These include:
- the nature, constitution or functions of the organs of issuers;
- the manner in which organs of the issuer conduct themselves;
- the requirements imposed on organs of the issuer;
- the relationship between the different organs of the issuer;
- the relationship between the organs of the issuer and the members of the issuer (or holders of the issuer's securities).

1635.   Subsection (3) provides that greater burdens must not be imposed by corporate governance rules on issuers whose securities are traded outside the UK than those imposed by corporate governance rules or listing rules on issuers with securities on UK markets.

Section 1270: Liability for false or misleading statements in certain publications

1636.   Section 1270 inserts sections 90A and 90B into FSMA and establishes a regime for civil liability to third parties by issuers admitted to trading on a regulated market in respect of disclosures made public in response to provisions implementing obligations imposed by the Transparency Directive.

1637.   Although no issuer has been found liable in damages under English law in respect of statements made in narrative reports or financial statements, the law relating to financial markets and to the obligations of issuers to investors on those markets has been developing, in the light of increased regulation of both domestic and European origin. The Transparency Directive has continued that process and increased the level of uncertainty as to whether any actionable duty is owed by an issuer and its directors to investors.

1638.   The Transparency Directive sets out the periodic financial disclosures that must be made by issuers admitted to trading on a regulated market. Articles 4 and 5 of the Transparency Directive provide for annual and half-yearly reports, including management statements, to be made public, and requires statements made by persons responsible within the issuer for these disclosures (the directors in the case of a public company) that these give a true and fair view, and that the management report includes a fair review of certain matters. Article 6 requires the disclosure of interim management statements.

1639.   The Transparency Directive also sets out the minimum requirements for a liability regime that must be adopted by the UK at Article 7, and recital (17) states "Member States should remain free to determine the extent of the liability".

1640.   These provisions give considerable flexibility to Member States in the liability regime they choose to adopt in respect of disclosures under the Directive. The Government has established an exhaustive regime in relation to ensuring the delivery and accuracy of these reports including criminal offences, administrative penalties and actions for civil damages. The provisions in this section relate only to the position in respect of the civil liability of issuers on regulated markets to investors in their securities. The liability regime does not cover issuers on exchange-regulated markets. Their position remains unchanged by implementation of the Transparency Directive.

1641.   While it is intended that there be no additional liability under the Directive in respect of the disclosures to which it relates, the regime leaves undisturbed any other liability owed by directors to the issuer and to members of the company under UK and other national law, and any liability under other FSA rules. It also leaves undisturbed any liability of the issuer in respect of any loss or damage arising otherwise than as a result of acquiring securities in reliance on the relevant statement or report.

1642.   The primary liability of directors and issuers for the accuracy of the required disclosures comprises criminal offences and administrative penalties under the provisions of Part 15 of this Act and Part 6 of FSMA. The provisions in Part 6 require compliance with FSA rules giving effect to the obligations in the Directive and provide for penalties in respect of failure to comply with the rules. In addition, restitution can potentially be ordered by the court, on application of the Authority or Secretary of State, under section 382 of FSMA or by the Authority directly under section 384 of FSMA.

1643.   The Government's intention in developing a civil liability regime has been to provide certainty in an uncertain area and to ensure that the potential scope of liability is reasonable, in relation both to expectations and the likely state of the law after the implementation of the Transparency Directive. In particular, the Government was anxious not to extend unnecessarily the scope of any duties which might be owed to investors or wider classes of third parties, in order to protect the interests of company members, employees and creditors. However, as the state of the law after the implementation of the Transparency Directive is not certain, the Government has taken a power, at new section 90B, that will enable the provision introduced by section 1270 to be added to or amended if a wider or narrower civil liability regime is deemed appropriate.

New section 90A: Compensation for statements in certain publications

1644.   Subsection (1)(a) of new section 90A provides that the civil liability regime set out in that section applies to those reports and statements required by provisions implementing Articles 4 to 6 of the Transparency Directive. Depending on transparency rules, we would expect this to include annual and half yearly financial statements and management reports, the sign-off by directors or other responsible parties, as well as interim management statements.

1645.   Subsection (1)(b) adds to the scope of the regime the information included in preliminary announcements of results made in advance of the reports and statements required by provision implementing Article 4 of the Transparency Directive, but only to the extent that it is intended that the information will appear in the final report or statement and be presented in substantially the same form as that in which it is presented in the preliminary announcement.

1646.   Subsection (2) sets the scope of the civil liability regime to cover securities of all issuers for which the UK is the home Member State (whether the regulated market on which they are traded is situated in or outside the UK), as well as to cover those issuers whose securities are traded on a regulated market situated in the UK and for whom the UK is the host Member State. UK holders of securities of other issuers (ie those for whom the UK is neither a host nor a home State) will not be able to rely on the rights of action set out.

1647.   Subsection (3) provides that issuers of such securities are liable to pay compensation to a person who has acquired those securities and has suffered loss in respect of them as a result of any untrue or misleading statement in a publication to which this section applies, or an omission of a required statement from such a statement. Subsection (4) however limits the liability of the issuer to circumstances where a "person discharging managerial responsibilities" in relation to the publication within the issuer (see subsection (9)) knows the statement to be untrue or misleading, or is reckless as to whether the statement is untrue or misleading, or, in the case of omissions, where it is known to be a dishonest concealment of a material fact.

1648.   Subsection (5) provides that loss will not be regarded as having been suffered for the purposes of subsection (3) unless the person suffering it acquired the relevant securities in reliance on the information in the publication and at a time when and in circumstances where it was reasonable to rely on that publication.

1649.   Subsection (6) limits the liability with regard to untrue or misleading statements, or omissions, in documents to which the section applies. It sets out that issuers are not liable for any liability other than that provided for by the section and that any person who is not the issuer is not liable, other than to the issuer.

1650.   Subsection (8) clarifies that the section does not affect Part 6 of FSMA conferring liability for a civil penalty, liability for a criminal offence or the right to seek restitution.

1651.   Subsection (9) sets out the persons who are to be considered as discharging managerial responsibilities for the purposes of the section. This is any director of the issuer, or where the issuer's affairs are managed by the members, a member of the issuer. In the case where the issuer does not have directors, or members, any senior executive with responsibilities in relation to the publication is considered as discharging managerial responsibilities.

New section 90B: Power to make further provision about liability for published information

1652.   Subsection (1) of new section 90B establishes a power to make further provision about liability for published information. The new section allows the Treasury by regulations to amend any primary or subordinate legislation relating to the liability of issuers and others in respect of information, including the regime set out in new section 90A of FSMA. The exercise of the proposed power could, for example, result in that regime or some other appropriate regime applying to other classes of information, such as information that is required to be disclosed by issuers to shareholders or markets under the Market Abuse Directive (MAD).

1653.   Regulations made under the section would be made using the affirmative procedure (see the amendment to section 429(2) of FSMA made by paragraph 12 of Schedule 15).

Section 1271: exercise of powers where UK is host member State

1654.   Section 1271 inserts a new section into Part 6 of FSMA: section 100A.

1655.   New section 100A sets out the Authority's ability to exercise powers in relation to infringements of prospectus rules and transparency rules or related provisions where issuers' home State is not the UK. Subsection (2) clarifies that the enforcement powers extend only to cover infringements required by the relevant directive. Subsection (3) sets out the process by which the Authority must engage with the home State competent authority when it finds there has been an infringement. Subsection (4) sets out limitations on the Authority's ability to act in those circumstances, but subsection (5) provides that, in the appropriate circumstances, it must take all appropriate measures to protect investors.

1656.   Subsection (6) imposes an obligation on the Authority to inform the Commission where it takes action to protect investors.

Section 1272 and Schedule 15: Transparency obligations and related matters: minor and consequential amendments

1657.   Section 1272 introduces Schedule 15, which makes minor and consequential amendments to FSMA related to the provision in sections 1265 to 1271. The Schedule also makes amendments to the C(AICE)Act 2004.

Part 1: Amendments of the Financial Services and Markets Act 2000

1658.   Part 1 of Schedule 15 makes minor and consequential amendments to FSMA.

1659.   Paragraph 2 amends section 73 of FSMA to extend, for the purposes of the transparency rules (which can apply to non-regulated UK markets), the factors to which the Authority must have regard when making rules under Part 6 of FSMA, so that these extend to effects on markets other than regulated markets.

1660. Paragraph 3 amends section 73A of FSMA to provide that transparency rules and corporate governance rules are "Part 6 rules" for the purposes of Part 6 of FSMA. But paragraph 3 also makes clear that these rules are distinct and separate from other Part 6 rules, such as the listing rules, disclosure rules, and prospectus rules. These different kinds of rules impose different, and sometimes overlapping, obligations on different groups of issuers.

1661. Paragraph 6 amends the penalty regime for breaches of Part 6 rules in section 91 of FSMA, so that it applies also to non-compliance with transparency rules, provisions made under the Transparency Directive, and corporate governance rules.

1662. Paragraph 8 amends section 97 of FSMA to enable the Authority to appoint a person to carry out investigations into breaches of the transparency rules or related provisions or the corporate governance rules.

1663. Paragraph 9 amends section 99 of FSMA, which relates to fees, so as to enable the Authority to levy fees under the transparency rules.

1664. Paragraphs 10 and 11 amend two definitions in Part 6 of FSMA ("transferable securities" in section 102A and "regulated market" in section 103) to refer to the up-to-date Community legislation (ie the Markets in Financial Instruments Directive (2004/39)). These paragraphs also add definitions for the purposes of the provisions on transparency rules.

1665. Paragraph 12 adds regulations made under new section 90B of FSMA to the list of statutory instruments subject to the affirmative procedure in section 429(2) of FSMA.

Part 2: Amendments of Companies (Audit, Investigations and Community Enterprise) Act 2004

1666. Paragraphs 14 and 15 amend section 14 and 15 of the C(AICE) Act 2004. The amendments mean that periodic accounts and reports of issuers required under corporate governance rules or transparency rules may be examined by the FRRP.

Section 1273: Corporate governance regulations

1667. Section 1273 provides the Secretary of State with a regulation-making power similar to the power given to the Authority in new section 89O of FSMA inserted by section 1269.

1668. The Secretary of State may make regulations for the purposes of implementing, enabling the implementation of or dealing with matters arising out of Community obligations on corporate governance for UK companies whose securities are traded on a regulated market in the UK or elsewhere in the EEA.

1669. Subsection (3)(a) allows for regulations to be made by reference to any code regulating corporate governance. This could include, for example, the Combined Code on Corporate Governance (issued by the Financial Reporting Council).

1670. Subsection (4) specifies that any criminal offence created by the regulations may not impose a greater penalty than an unlimited fine.

1671. Subsection (5) provides for regulations to be made by way of negative resolution. However, by virtue of section 1292(4), it will also be possible to make regulations under this power by affirmative procedure.

PART 44: MISCELLANEOUS PROVISIONS

Regulation of actuaries etc

[3.45]

1672. These provisions are the first step in implementing the central recommendation of the Morris Review of the Actuarial Profession: that the Financial Reporting Council (the "FRC") take on a similar role in relation to the oversight of the actuarial profession to the one it currently exercises in relation to accountancy and the auditors' profession.

1673. The Government announced in Budget 2005 its intention to legislate in due course to put the oversight regime onto a full statutory footing. It has not been possible to develop such a regime in time for inclusion in this Act. It was therefore agreed with the FRC and the Institute and Faculty of Actuaries that, pending the introduction of a full statutory regime, the FRC would begin voluntary oversight of the actuarial profession at the earliest possible opportunity. The FRC assumed this responsibility for actuarial standards and oversight of the profession in April 2006.

1674. The aim of these provisions is to provide the minimum necessary statutory underpinning for a voluntary regime. They amend the C(AICE) Act 2004 in two ways:
- they extend the statutory immunity conferred on the FRC and its companion bodies so that it covers acts or omissions relating to oversight of the actuarial profession;
- they allow the Secretary of State, if necessary, to make regulations to require beneficiaries of the actuarial oversight to contribute towards the funding costs of the proposed regime.

1675. This latter is a reserve power. It is proposed, as is currently the case with accountancy and the auditors' professions, to fund this activity on a non-statutory basis by agreement with the insurance and pensions industries and the actuarial profession. The FRC published its final funding proposals in March 2006.

Section 1274: Grants to bodies concerned with actuarial standards etc

1676.   This section amends section 16(2) of the C(AICE) Act 2004 so as to include in the list of matters carried on by bodies eligible for grants activities concerned with the setting of actuarial standards, compliance with those standards, oversight of the actuarial profession and related matters.

1677.   A body to which a grant has been paid under section 16 is protected by section 18 of that Act from certain liabilities in connection with its section 16(2) activities.

Section 1275: Levy to pay expenses of bodies concerned with actuarial standards etc

1678.   This section amends section 17 of the C(AICE) Act 2004 so as to include amongst those by whom a levy may be payable—

• the administrators of a public service pension scheme, and
• the trustees and managers of an occupational or personal pension scheme.

1679.   The effect of the amendments is to enable the Secretary of State to make regulations specifying such persons as liable to pay a levy if he considers that the oversight activities of the FRC are relevant to them to a significant extent.

1680.   Subsection (4) enables regulations under section 17 to make different provision for different cases so that, for example, they can provide for different rates of levy to be payable by different kinds of bodies or persons.

1681.   Subsection (5) prevents the first regulations under section 17, and any other regulations under that section that would result in any change in the bodies or persons by whom the levy is payable, from being treated as hybrid instruments for the purposes of the standing orders of either House of Parliament. The effect is that such regulations are not subject to the special procedures in the House of Lords that apply to such instruments.

1682.   Subsection (7) amends Schedule 3 to the Pensions Act 2004 to enable the Pensions Regulator to disclose restricted information to the Secretary of State to enable or assist him in the exercise of his functions under section 17 of the C(AICE) Act 2004.

Section 1276: Application of provisions to Scotland and Northern Ireland

1683.   This section amends the C(AICE) Act 2004 as regards the application of certain provisions to Scotland and Northern Ireland.

1684.   Subsection (2) amends section 16 of that Act so that paragraphs (a) to (t) of subsection (2) of that section, which list matters carried on by bodies eligible for grants, only apply to Scotland insofar as they relate to matters for which provision would be outside the legislative competence of the Scottish Parliament. This is necessary because, whilst section 16 and the provisions of this Act amending it extend to Scotland, some of the matters listed in paragraphs (a) to (t) are not reserved matters for the purposes of section 30 of the Scotland Act 1998 and are therefore within the legislative competence of the Scottish Parliament.

1685.   Subsections (3) to (5) amend section 16(2) and (5) and section 66(2) of the C(AICE) Act 2004 so that sections 16 and 18, as well as section 17, of that Act extend to Northern Ireland.

Exercise of voting rights by institutional investors

1686.   Institutional investors own and manage assets on behalf of and for the benefit of clients or members and have an obligation to manage those assets in their interests. In some cases there is a trustee-beneficiary relationship between the institution and the client, and in all cases there are contractual and regulatory requirements imposing duties of asset management on the institution. Voting is central to the exercise of ownership control. However, the ability of ultimate beneficiaries (eg members of a pension fund) to monitor the way in which institutional investors exercise voting rights is limited in practice.

1687.   The CLR (Final Report, paragraph 6.39) concluded that disclosure of voting by institutional shareholders was a desirable objective. There has been a growing trend internationally to require disclosure. There has also been an increasing trend by UK fund managers towards voluntary disclosure.

Section 1277: Power to require information about exercise of voting rights

1688.   This section confers a power on the Secretary of State and the Treasury to make regulations requiring certain categories of institutional investor to provide information about the exercise of their voting rights. The power is drawn intentionally widely to enable any mandatory disclosure regime to respond to varied corporate governance arrangements and to capture a range of institutions investing in different markets. Exercise of the power is subject to affirmative resolution procedure.

1689.   Subsection (4) provides that the obligation imposed by regulations under this section is enforceable by civil proceedings brought either by the person to whom the information should have been provided or by a regulatory authority specified in the regulations (which could, for example, be the FSA).

Section 1278: Institutions to which information provisions apply

1690. This section lists the categories of institutions in relation to which the power conferred by section 1277 is exercisable. Subsection (2) enables the Treasury or Secretary of State to add to or amend the categories. Subsection (3) requires that the regulations specify by whom the duty imposed by the regulations is to be fulfilled.

Section 1279: Shares to which the information provisions apply

1691. This section confers power to specify by regulations the descriptions of shares in relation to which the information provisions apply. They will apply wherever a listed institution has an interest in such shares. Subsections (2) to (4) provide that an institution is taken to have an interest in shares in certain cases.

Section 1280: Obligations with respect to provision of information

1692. This section specifies the information that can be required. This covers the exercise or non-exercise of voting rights, instructions given by the institution and any delegation of a function related to the exercise or non-exercise of voting rights.

1693. Subsection (1) contains a power to require institutional investors to procure disclosure of voting or of any instructions given by any person acting on the institution's behalf. Institutional investors would need to make sure that their investment contracts required such information to be passed on to them or disclosed on their behalf.

1694. Under subsection (4), the regulations may specify how and to whom the disclosure is to be made. This would allow the regulations to both specify the manner of disclosure and require disclosure to (for example) clients and members only, or to the public generally.

Disclosure of information under the Enterprise Act 2002

1695. Part 9 of the Enterprise Act applies to information which public authorities receive in connection with competition and consumer functions under certain Parts of the Enterprise Act 2002 and under other specified competition and consumer protection legislation. Information relating to the affairs of an individual or business must be kept confidential unless Part 9 permits its disclosure.

1696. This provision amends Part 9 so as to enable public authorities to disclose information for the purposes of civil proceedings or otherwise for the purpose of establishing, enforcing or defending legal rights.

Section 1281: Disclosure of information under the Enterprise Act 2002

1697. The new section 241A allows a public authority to disclose prescribed information to any person for the purposes of prescribed civil proceedings in the United Kingdom or elsewhere. Prescribed means prescribed by the Secretary of State by order. The new provision extends to prospective proceedings, taking legal advice about proceedings and other ways of establishing, enforcing or defending legal rights (such as alternative dispute resolution schemes).

1698. Information obtained by a public authority in connection with competition functions is excluded from the new provision.

Expenses of winding up

1699. The House of Lords decided in *Buchler and another v Talbot and others, in re Leyland Daf* [2004] UKHL 9 that property subject to a floating charge is not available to fund the general expenses of winding up. This provision is intended to reverse that decision.

Section 1282: Payment of expenses of winding up (England and Wales)

1700. Subsection (1) inserts a new section 176ZA in the Insolvency Act 1986 under which property subject to a floating charge may, where necessary, be used to fund the general expenses of winding up in priority to the floating charge holder and to any preferential creditors entitled to be paid out of that property. There is power to make provision by rules requiring the authorisation or approval of the floating charge holder, or any preferential creditors, or the court, in certain circumstances.

1701. Subsection (2) makes a corresponding amendment of the Insolvency (Northern Ireland) Order 1989 (SI 1989/2405 (NI 19)).

Commonhold associations

1702. Commonhold associations are a new form of company limited by guarantee established under the Commonhold and Leasehold Reform Act 2002. Commonhold associations must register their memorandum and articles of association both with Companies House (on formation) and with HM Land Registry (on registration of the commonhold).

1703. At present paragraph 3(1) of Schedule 3 to the Commonhold and Leasehold Reform Act 2002 provides that an alteration of a commonhold association's memorandum or articles is of no effect if it is not registered with the Land Registry. The purpose of the provision is to ensure that the version of those documents held by the Land Registry is up to date. An unintended consequence of it, however, is that it effectively prohibits any change of an association's memorandum or articles before the land which the commonhold association is established to manage is registered as commonhold land or after it has stopped being commonhold land.

Section 1283: Amendment of memorandum or articles of commonhold association

1704. This section amends paragraph 3(1) of Schedule 3 to the Commonhold and Leasehold Reform Act 2002 so as to limit the application of the provision to alterations made at a time when the land the association is established to manage is commonhold land.

PART 45: NORTHERN IRELAND

[3.46]
1705. Companies Acts since 1929 have extended to Great Britain only. But Northern Ireland companies legislation has followed changes in GB companies legislation very closely. The principal piece of current Northern Irish companies legislation, the Companies (Northern Ireland) Order 1986, is effectively a copy of the 1985 Act, with only very minor modifications to fit the Northern Irish context.

1706. Following public consultation, it was decided that the new Act should extend directly to Northern Ireland, along with certain other closely related areas of law. Company law would remain in formal terms a transferred matter, and a future Northern Ireland Assembly could for example decide to enact separate Northern Ireland companies legislation if it considered it desirable. In the meantime, companies in Northern Ireland would experience the regulatory effects of new companies legislation at the same time as their GB counterparts. The Act gives effect to these arrangements.

Section 1284: Extension of Companies Acts to Northern Ireland

1707. This section provides that the Companies Acts extend Northern Ireland. The Companies Acts are defined in section 2 of the Act: in essence, they include the company law provisions of this Act, the remaining provisions of the 1985 Act, and Part 2 of the C(AICE) Act 2004 (which relates to community interest companies). Section 1284 also repeals the principal pieces of separate Northern Ireland companies legislation The other (non-company law) provisions of this Act extend to Northern Ireland by virtue of section 1299.

Sections 1285 to 1287: Extension of certain other GB enactments to Northern Ireland

1708. These sections similarly extend to Northern Ireland other GB legislation in various areas related to company law, and repeal the separate Northern Ireland legislation in these areas. This is the case in relation to:
* SEs (European Public Limited-Liability Companies);
* certain other forms of business organisation where the law is partly modelled on, and closely relates to, company law; namely limited liability partnerships, limited partnerships, open-ended investment companies, and European Economic Interest Groupings; and
* business names.

PART 46: GENERAL SUPPLEMENTARY PROVISIONS

Sections 1288 to 1292: Regulations and orders

[3.47]
1709. These sections provide how regulations and orders made under the Act are to be made.

1710. Section 1288 provides that, unless the provision in the Act creating the power states otherwise, all regulations and orders are to be made by statutory instrument.

1711. Most of the powers to make regulations or orders are exercisable by the Secretary of State and are to be made by statutory instrument. The Act also confers powers on the registrar of companies to make rules, which are not required to be made by statutory instrument (section 1117(3) requires appropriate publicity). Other non-statutory instrument powers are conferred on the Takeover Panel (see Part 28) and the Financial Services Authority (see Part 43, which inserts new sections into the FSMA).

1712. Virtually all the provisions of the Act conferring power to make regulations or orders by statutory instrument specify one or other of the following three types of Parliamentary procedure:
* negative resolution procedure (defined in section 1289): the statutory instrument containing the regulations or order is laid before Parliament and must be revoked if either House passes a resolution against it within 40 Parliamentary days. An instrument subject to the negative procedure is normally laid at least 21 days before it is to come into effect to ensure scrutiny of the instrument before its provisions come into force;
* affirmative resolution procedure (defined in section 1290): the statutory instrument containing the regulations or order is laid before Parliament in draft and can only be made when approved by affirmative resolution in each House. This means that they are always subject to debate in each House;

- approval after being made (defined in section 1291): the statutory instrument containing the regulations or order is laid before Parliament after being made. It ceases to have effect after 28 Parliamentary days unless it is approved by resolution of each House during the 28 day period. Should the regulations or order cease to have effect at the end of the 28 days, anything done under them during the period remains effective and new regulations or a new order may be made.

1713. Section 1292(1) provides that regulations or orders may make different provision for different cases or circumstances, may include supplementary, incidental and consequential provision, and may make transitional provision and savings.

1714. Subsections (2) to (4) of section 1292 enable orders or regulations to be made combining provisions in relation to which different procedural requirements apply. A power to make regulations can be exercised by making an order, and a power to make an order can be exercised by making regulations. Provisions subject to the affirmative resolution procedure, provisions subject to the negative resolution procedure and provisions subject to no Parliamentary procedure at all may be included in a single instrument, and subsections (3) and (4) clarify which procedure applies when powers are combined.

Section 1293: Meaning of "enactment"

1715. This clause explains what the term "enactment" includes, when used in the Act, to make it clear that it goes beyond the definition in the Interpretation Act 1978 (c.30). Unless the context in which it is used dictates otherwise, "enactment" includes:

- an enactment contained in subordinate legislation within the meaning of the Interpretation Act 1978 (c.30);
- an enactment contained in, or in an instrument made under, an Act of the Scottish Parliament;
- an enactment contained in, or in an instrument made under, Northern Ireland legislation within the meaning of the Interpretation Act 1978.

Section 1294: Power to make consequential amendments etc

1716. This section confers on the Secretary of State, and on the Treasury, order-making powers to amend enactments in consequence of any provision in the Act. Such amendments and repeals are additional to those made by any other provision of the Act. Orders under this section are subject to the affirmative resolution procedure.

1717. Orders may be made to amend, repeal or revoke any enactment that is:

- passed or made before the passing of the Act;
- contained in the Act or in subordinate legislation made under it;
- passed or made before the end of Parliamentary session 2006–7.

1718. In particular, orders may make provision corresponding to that made in the Act in relation to companies, and may extend provision to other forms of organisation. The provisions of the Act may be applied with any adaptations or other modifications that appear to be necessary or expedient.

Section 1295: Repeals

1719. This section introduces Schedule 16, the repeal Schedule. The repeals include, in addition to purely consequential repeals, repeals of the restated provisions of the 1985 Act and repeals of enactments that are no longer of practical utility.

1720. Schedule 16 repeals a number of Parts and/or sections of a number of pieces of legislation, including most of the 1985 Act, most of the Companies Act 1989 and the whole of the Business Names Act 1985.

Section 1296: Power to make transitional provision and savings

1721. This section gives the Secretary of State and the Treasury order-making powers to make transitional provision and savings in connection with the commencement of any provision made in the Act. Orders are subject to the negative resolution procedure.

Section 1297: Continuity of the law

1722. This section provides that things done under the provisions in the 1985 Act that are repealed and replaced by the Act will continue to be legally effective. Similarly, references to the repealed provisions in enactments, instruments or documents are to be construed as including references to the corresponding new provision.

1723. Articles of association, company resolutions and contracts are all likely to refer to provisions of the Companies Acts or to rely for their effect on the way in which those provisions work. Except where a change is intended, those articles, resolutions and contracts should continue to have effect, not only with old references converted into new but also with their legal effect capable of continuing despite verbal differences between the old and the new.

1724. The section applies automatically in all cases in which it is capable of applying. It is in addition to any more specific transitional provisions, which may be included in commencement orders by use of the power in section 1296.

PART 47: FINAL PROVISIONS

Section 1298: Short title

[3.48]

1725.   This section sets out the short title of the Act.

Section 1299: Extent

1726.   This section provides that, except where otherwise provided for or the context requires otherwise, the Act extends to the whole of the United Kingdom (in other words, including Northern Ireland, as provided for in Part 45 and discussed in the notes to that Part).

Section 1300: Commencement

1727.   Subsection (1) provides for commencement on Royal Assent of Part 43 (except for a definition not yet in force) and of sections 1274 and 1276, so that the provisions on transparency obligations and related matters, those conferring a statutory immunity from liability in damages in relation to the oversight of the actuarial profession and those relating to the extension of provisions of the C(AICE) Act 2004 to Scotland and Northern Ireland came into force on that date (8 November 2006). It also provides for Parts 46 (general supplementary provisions) and this Part to come into force on Royal Assent, except for the repeals Schedule.

1728.   Subsection (2) provides for the Secretary of State or the Treasury to appoint by order the timing of commencement of the other provisions of the Act.

Commencement

1729.   As explained in the note on section 1300 immediately above, certain provisions came into force on the day of Royal Assent. The other provisions will be the subject of commencement orders, and the Government has announced its intention to commence all parts of the Act by October 2008.

PARLIAMENTARY HISTORY

[3.49]

1730.   The following table sets out the dates and Hansard references for each stage of this Act's passage through Parliament.

Stage	Date	Hansard reference
House of Lords		
First Reading	1 November 2005, HL Bill 34	Vol. 675, Col. 127
Second Reading	11 January 2006	Vol. 677, Cols. 180–249
Grand Committee	30 January, 1, 6, 9, 27 February, 1, 7, 14, 15, 20, 28, 30 March, 25 April 2006, reprinted HL Bill 98	Vol. 678, Cols. GC1–GC64, GC119–GC176, GC237–GC296, GC 321–GC382, Vol. 679, Cols. GC1–GC62, GC121–GC188, GC263–GC324, GC395–GC466, GC467–GC532, Vol. 680, Cols. GC1–GC70, GC285–GC356, GC357–GC440, Vol. 681, Cols. GC61–GC100
Report	9, 10, 16 May 2006, reprinted HL Bill 108	Vol. 681, Cols. 777–898, 912–1034, Vol. 682, Cols. 141–253
Third Reading	23 May 2006	Vol. 682, Cols. 709–797
House of Commons		
First Reading	24 May 2006, reprinted Bill 190	Votes and proceedings
Second Reading	6 June 2006	Vol. 447, Cols. 122–223
Committee	15, 20, 22, 27, 29 June, 4, 6, 11, 13, 18, 20 July 2006, reprinted Bill 218	Hansard Standing Committee D
Report and Third Reading	17, 18, 19 October 2006	Vol. 450, Cols. 743–838, 881–980, 1030–1108
House of Lords		
Consideration of Commons Amendments	3 November 2006, HL Bill 155	Vol. 686, Cols. 428–510

Stage	Date	Hansard reference
House of Commons		
Lords Reasons for insisting on certain of their amendments to which the Commons have disagreed, considered	6 November 2006, Bill 245	Vol. 451, Cols. 667–676

Royal Assent – 8 November 2006

House of Lords Hansard Vol 686 Col 750

House of Commons Hansard Vol 451 Col 825

ANNEX A: TRANSPOSITION NOTES

Part 28: Takeovers, etc – Directive on Takeovers Bids (2004/25/EC)

The Takeovers Directive

[3.50]
1731. Part 28 of the Act implements Directive 2004/25 EC of the European Parliament and of the Council of 21 April 2004 on Takeover Bids (OJ L142, 30 April 2004).

1732. The Takeovers Directive lays down, for the first time, minimum EU rules concerning the regulation of takeovers of companies whose shares are traded on a regulated market. The Directive was one of the measures adopted under the EU Financial Services Action Plan and aims to strengthen the Single Market in financial services by facilitating cross-border restructuring and enhancing minority shareholder protection.

1733. The Takeovers Directive contains general principles that Member States must adhere to in regulating takeover activity and a framework relating to the functions and jurisdiction of takeover regulatory authorities. It also lays down provisions relating to the mandatory bid (a requirement whereby a party gaining control of a company must make an offer to all shareholders at an equitable price), takeover bid documentation, time allowed for acceptance of the bid, the obligations of the board of the offeree company and other matters related to the bid.

1734. Additionally, the Takeovers Directive has provisions addressing barriers to takeovers (such as action that might be taken by a company or its board before or during a bid to prevent a takeover), requiring disclosure of certain information by companies traded on a regulated market and dealing with the problems of, and for, residual minority shareholders following a successful takeover bid (so-called 'squeeze-out' and 'sell-out' provisions).

The Takeovers Directive (Interim Implementation) Regulations 2006

1735. In view of the fact that the Takeovers Directive was required to be implemented by 20 May 2006, by which date the Act had not completed Parliamentary passage and received Royal Assent, interim implementation provisions were introduced under section 2(2) of the European Communities Act 1972 (ECA 1972). These provisions are contained in The Takeovers Directive (Interim Implementation) Regulations 2006 (SI 2006/1183). A copy of those Regulations together with the accompanying Explanatory Memorandum, Regulatory Impact Assessment and Transposition Notes is available on the website of the Office of Public Sector Information (http://www.opsi.gov.uk/stat.htm). The Regulations will be repealed and replaced on commencement of Part 28 of the Act.

Part 28 – Takeovers etc

1736. Since 1968, takeover regulation in the UK has been overseen by the Takeover Panel administering rules and principles contained in the "City Code on Takeovers and Mergers". In order to bring UK takeover regulation within the requirements laid down in the Directive, Part 28 of the Act is designed to place it within a complete and coherent statutory framework.

1737. The detailed rules relating to takeover regulation in compliance with the Directive will be prescribed by the Panel in its Takeover Code, under a statutory rule-making obligation imposed upon the Panel by the Act (section 943(1)). The Takeover Code has already been revised with effect from 20 May 2006, on an interim basis under the 2006 Regulations, to make it wholly consistent with the requirements of the Takeovers Directive.

1738. 'Squeeze-out' and 'sell-out' provisions were previously prescribed by Part 13A of the 1985 Act. Chapter 3 of Part 28 of the Act replaces those provisions in their entirety with certain amendments which ensure they are wholly consistent with the Takeovers Directive requirements.

1739. Provisions related to disclosures by companies are contained in Part 7 of the 1985 Act and amendments to that Part are made in Chapter 4 of Part 28 to give effect to the additional disclosure requirements imposed by the Takeovers Directive on companies traded on a regulated market.

1740. Responsibility for the measures, described in this transposition note, taken to implement the Takeovers Directive lies with the Secretary of State for Trade and Industry.

1741. The table below describes the substantive provisions implementing the Takeovers Directive.

Part 24: Takeovers etc: Transposition Measures		
Article	**Objective**	**Implementation**
1	Defines the scope of Directive in terms of transactions and types of company to which it applies ("takeover bids for the securities of companies governed by the laws of Member States, where all or some of those securities are admitted to trading on a regulated market").	No specific implementing provision necessary.
2	Contains key definitions for the purposes of the Directive (such as, "takeover bid", "offeree company", and "securities").	No specific implementing provision necessary.
3.1	Lays down general principles which Member States shall ensure are adhered to for the purpose of implementing the Directive.	Section 943(1) requires that the Panel give effect to the general principles set out at Article 3.1 of the Directive in the exercise of their statutory rule-making duty.
3.2	Provides that Member States may, in ensuring that the minimum requirements laid down by the Directive are adhered to, lay down additional conditions and provisions more stringent than those of the Directive.	No specific implementing provision necessary.
4.1	Requires Member States to designate supervisory authorities (which must act independently of parties to a bid).	This will be achieved by administrative designation of the Takeover Panel as supervisory authority for the purposes of the Directive.
4.2	Lays down jurisdictional rules in relation to takeover regulation	Section 943(1) requires that the Panel give effect to the jurisdictional provisions of the Directive in the exercise of their statutory rule-making duty.
4.3	Requires Member States to ensure that persons employed or formerly employed by takeover regulatory authorities are bound by professional secrecy (information covered by this obligation should not be disclosed other than under conditions laid down by national law).	Section 949 makes it a criminal offence to disclose information provided to the Takeover Panel other than under the circumstances and gateways laid down in section 948 and Schedule 2.
4.4	Lays down cooperation obligations in relation to EU takeover and financial markets supervisory authorities.	Section 950 requires the Takeover Panel to cooperate with EU takeover and financial services regulators. The existing cooperation duties of the Financial Services Authority under section 354 of the Financial Services and Markets Act 2000 are extended to include relevant authorities (section 964).
4.5	Requires that takeover supervisory authorities be provided with all powers necessary for carrying out their duties and provides that Member States may, provided that the general principles are respected, permit derogation from the rules of the Directive in certain circumstances and grant supervisory authorities the power to grant waivers.	In addition to the rule-making duty at section 943(1) and rule-making powers at section 943(2), the following powers are provided to the Takeover Panel: Section 945 – power to make rulings Section 946 – power to give directions Section 947 – power to require documents and information Section 952 – power to set down sanctions by rules Section 954 – power to order compensation in certain circumstances

Part 24: Takeovers etc: Transposition Measures		
Article	**Objective**	**Implementation**
		Section 955 – power to apply to the court for enforcement
		Section 960 – power to bring and defend proceedings.
		Section 944(1) authorises the Takeover Panel to provide for derogations and waivers in certain circumstances from rules made under section 943.
4.6	Makes provision for certain Member States' powers to be unaffected by the Directive (for instance, designation of judicial or other authorities responsible for dealing with disputes, the circumstances in which parties may bring administrative or judicial proceedings, any capacity of the courts to decline to hear legal proceedings and the liability of supervisory authorities).	Section 945(2) provides that a ruling of the Takeover Panel is to have binding effect (subject to provisions in the Panel's rules and any review or appeal). Section 951 provides for matters relating to reviews of and appeals from Takeover Panel decisions to be contained in the rules made by the Panel. Section 956 provides that there shall be no action for breach of statutory duty, or any voidness or unenforceability of transactions, as a result of breach of rules made by the Panel. Section 961 provides for exemption of the Takeover Panel (and those involved in its functions) from liability in damages in certain circumstances related to the regulatory activities of the Panel.
5	Requires that a "mandatory bid rule" is introduced requiring a person acquiring "control" of a company to make a bid to all holders of securities at an equitable price Contains rules related to the calculation of the equitable price.	Section 943(1) requires that the Panel give effect to the "mandatory bid" and "equitable price" provisions in the exercise of their statutory rule-making duty.
6	Requires that the decision to make a takeover bid is made public. Contains detailed provision related to the contents of the takeover offer document. Requires that the parties to a bid are obliged to provide supervisory authorities with information related to the bid.	Section 943(1) requires that the Panel give effect to the "bid" disclosure and documentation provisions in the exercise of its statutory rule-making duty. Section 947 provides the Takeover Panel with power to require documents and information.
7	Lays down rules related to the time allowed for acceptance of the takeover bid.	Section 943(1) requires that the Panel give effect to the offer "acceptance" period provision in the exercise of its statutory rule-making duty.
8	Requires that takeover bids are made public so as to ensure market transparency. It also provides for the disclosure of bid documentation to shareholders and employees' representatives (or, where there are no such representatives, the employees directly).	Section 943(1) requires that the Panel give effect to the bid disclosure provisions in the exercise of their statutory rule-making duty.

Part 3   CA 2006 Supporting Materials

Part 24: Takeovers etc: Transposition Measures		
Article	**Objective**	**Implementation**
9	Imposes obligations on the board of the offeree company, including the obligation not to take action to frustrate the bid without the approval of shareholders at the time of the bid and to draw up and make public a statement containing their views on the effects of implementation of the bid.	Section 943(1) requires that the Panel give effect to the provisions relating to the obligations of the board of the offeree company in the exercise of their statutory rule-making duty.
10	Requires that companies shall publish detailed information on their share and control structures, etc in their annual report and present an explanatory report on such matters to the annual general meeting of shareholders.	Section 992 (amending Part 7 of the 1985 Act) requires that the relevant information, including necessary explanatory material, is set out in the annual report of companies.
11	"Breakthrough" – This provision overrides, in certain circumstances connected with a takeover, provisions in the articles of companies and contractual arrangements related to restrictions on transfer and voting rights of shares, etc. It does not apply to special shares held by Member States or to cooperatives. This provision may be made optional by Member States for companies under the provisions of article 12.	The right to make these provisions optional for companies is exercised in the implementing provisions. Sections 966 and 967 define the types of companies, circumstances and mechanisms by which a company may opt-in to "breakthrough". Section 968 lays down the effect on contractual restrictions overridden by "breakthrough".
12.1	Provides that Member States may make optional the provisions of articles 9(2) and (3) and/or Article 11.	Exercise of this option has been taken only in relation to the provisions of Article 11 (the relevant implementing provisions of which are described above).
12.2 (and 12.4)	Requires, where optional arrangements are in place, that companies have the right to voluntarily opt-in to the provisions of the relevant articles. Such a decision must be communicated to the supervisory authorities and be disclosed.	Section 970 requires that any opting-in decision be communicated to the Takeover Panel without delay. The opting-in resolution passed by the company must be filed with the Registrar of Companies under section 30.
12.3 (and 12.5)	Permits Member States to provide that the effects of Articles 9(2) and (3) and/or Article 11 only apply on a "reciprocal" basis, ie where the takeover bid is made by a company also subject to the effects of the relevant articles. Such restrictions on the application of Articles 9(2) and (3) and Article 11 shall be subject to the authorisation of the general meeting of shareholders of the offeree company.	The Member State option to provide for "reciprocity" has not been exercised.
13	Requires that rules relating to the lapsing or revision of bids, competing bids, disclosure of results of bids and irrevocability of bids be put in place.	Section 943(1) requires that the Panel give effect to the requirement that such rules be put in place in the exercise of its statutory rule-making duty.
14	Provides that the Directive shall be without prejudice to various provisions relating to information and consultation of employees and their representatives.	No specific implementing provision necessary.
15	Requires Member States to put in place rules enabling a bidder to compulsorily purchase the shares of minority shareholders following a successful takeover bid ("squeeze-out" rights). The circumstances in which such a right must apply (including time periods and relevant thresholds) and relating to the price that must be paid are set out.	"Squeeze-out" rights were previously contained in the 1985 Act (Part 13A (sections 428–430F)). These have been replaced by Chapter 3 of Part 28 of the Act (necessary amendments to ensure these provisions are consistent with Article 15 have been made).

Part 24: Takeovers etc: Transposition Measures		
Article	**Objective**	**Implementation**
16	Requires Member States to put in place rules enabling minority shareholders to require a bidder to compulsorily purchase their shares following a successful takeover bid ("sell-out" rights).	"Sell-out" rights were previously contained in the 1985 Act (Part 13A).
	The circumstances in which such a rule must apply (including time periods and relevant thresholds) and relating to the price that must be paid are set out.	These have been replaced by Chapter 3 of Part 28 of the Act (necessary amendments to ensure these provisions are consistent with article 16 have been made).
17	Requires that effective, proportionate and dissuasive sanctions be put in place.	Sections 952 and 954 provide that the rules made by the Takeover Panel may confer power on the Panel to impose sanctions on those who transgress its rules or order compensation in certain circumstances.
		Section 949 makes it an offence to contravene the provisions of section 948 (relating to the restrictions on disclosure of information provided to the Takeover Panel).
		Section 953 provides an offence where takeover bid documentation does not comply with Panel rules giving effect to Articles 6.3 and 9.5 of the Directive.
		Misconduct in relation to takeover activity also needs to be viewed in the wider context of the overall regulatory framework and the protections available to shareholders and others.
		A robust market regulatory regime and company law framework is in place in the UK to investigate and pursue misconduct in relation to takeover activity (for instance, sanctions with stringent sanctions are already in place to deter fraudulent misrepresentation or market abuse).
18	Lays down a Committee procedure whereby the Commission may adopt rules related to the application of Article 6.3 (contents of takeover bid documentation).	No implementing provision necessary (no such rules have been adopted).
19	Requires the EU Commission to establish a Contact Committee to facilitate the harmonised application of the Directive and advise the Commission, if necessary, on any additions or amendments to the Directive.	No implementing provision necessary.
20	Provides for the review of the Directive by the EU Commission five years after its entry into force.	No implementing provision necessary.
	Requires that Member States provide the Commission annually with certain information related to takeover bids.	Such information will be provided to the EU Commission as an administrative process.
21	Requires that the relevant provisions of the Directive be transposed no later than 20 May 2006. Details of transposition measures shall be communicated to the Commission.	No specific implementing provision necessary (NB paragraph 5 above regarding the Takeovers Directive (Interim Implementation) Regulations 2006 which came into force on 20th May 2006). Details of the transposition measures will be communicated to the EU Commission by administrative process.

Part 24: Takeovers etc: Transposition Measures		
Article	**Objective**	**Implementation**
22	Provides that the Directive enters into force on 20 May 2004	No implementing provision necessary.
23	Addresses the Directive to the Member States.	No implementing provision necessary.

Part 35: The Registrar of Companies – Directive 2003/58/EC (which amends Council Directive 68/151/EEC as regards disclosure requirements in respect of certain types of companies)

1742. Various provisions within Part 35 of the Act serve to implement Directive 2003/58/EEC, which amends section I of the First Company Law Directive (68/151/EEC), primarily to enable companies to register certain documents electronically and searchers to access them electronically.

1743. Section I of the First Company Law Directive requires that basic company documents be disclosed via filing with a company registry, and by publication in the national gazette either of the full or partial text of the document or by reference to the document deposited in the company registry. It also requires that those documents be available for inspection. In addition, the First Company Law Directive specifies minimum information that companies must include on their letters and order forms. The First Company Law Directive assumes the use of paper documents. The amended directive reflects the use of information technology and electronic communications.

1744. In practice, the 1985 Act already allows the Registrar to accept electronic filing of all documents covered by the First Company Law Directive, although specific directions as to the form and manner of filing any particular document electronically have to be given by the Registrar. At present, the Registrar has mechanisms for the electronic filing of many of those documents.

1745. The 1985 Act also already allows the Registrar to keep documents in electronic form, and to provide for inspection by electronic means. Legislation is however necessary to impose formal obligations on the Registrar in relation to electronic filing, so as to transpose the amending Directive properly.

1746. Responsibility for the transposition of the amending Directive lies with the Secretary of State for Trade and Industry. The table below describes the substantive provisions in the Act which implement it.

Part 35: The Registrar of Companies		
Article	**Objective**	**Implementation**
2	(Which amends Article 2.1(f) of the First Company Law Directive) requires certain accounting documents to be filed.	Part 35 of the Act contains the relevant filing requirements (which are restated from the current legislation).
3	(So far as it amends Article 3.2.) Company Registries must allow companies to file electronically all basic documents (those specified in Article 2 of the First Company Law Directive, and those to which Article 3 of the First Company Law Directive is applied by other legislation).	Section 1078 lists the documents which are now subject to the Directive disclosure requirements under Article 2 of the First Company Law Directive as amended. Section 1068(5) provides that all such documents may be delivered to the Registrar in electronic form.
3	(So far as it also amends Article 3.2.) Company Registries must allow requests for inspection of such documents to be made electronically.	Section 1089(2) provides that applications in respect of such documents may be submitted electronically.
3	(So far as it also amends Article 3.2.) Company Registries must offer electronic copies of such documents to those inspecting the register (subject to a permitted derogation in respect of documents filed before 1 January 2007).	Section 1090(2) provides that copies of such documents must be provided in electronic form if the applicant so chooses (subject to section 1090(3) which takes advantage of the permitted derogation).
3.	(So far as it also amends Article 3.2.) Company Registries must keep all such documents (whether submitted electronically or in hard copy) in electronic form.	Section 1080(3) provides that information from such documents must be kept in electronic form.

Part 35: The Registrar of Companies		
Article	**Objective**	**Implementation**
3	(So far as it amends Article 3.3) In the case of electronic copies, Company Registries need only provide certified copies if they are asked to do so. Member States need to take measures to ensure the authenticity of electronic certified copies.	Section 1091 contains provision about certifying copies and allows the Secretary of State to make regulations about how electronic copies are certified.
3	(So far as it amends Article 3.4.) The option is provided to Members States of using an alternative to publication in the National Gazette as a means of publicising information received.	Section 1077 specifies that notices must be published either in the Gazette, or in accordance with section 1116. The latter section enables the Secretary of State to make regulations specifying alternative means of publication.
4	(Which inserts a new Article 3a.) This provides that, while documents must be submitted in a language permitted by the language rules of the member state in question, voluntary translations in other Community languages must also be accepted.	Sections 1106 and 1107 provide that companies may deliver certified translations of documents. The languages and types of document in respect of which this facility is available will be specified in regulations made by the Secretary of State, but subsection (3) of section 1106 provides that these regulations must as a minimum cover the documents subject to the directive disclosure requirements and the official languages of the EU.
5	(Which replaces the previous Article 4). This provides that certain information (already currently required on hard copy letters and order forms) must be stated in documents in any form and displayed on websites.	This will be implemented by regulations under section 82.
6	This provides that that there must be appropriate penalties for breach of new Articles 2(1)(f) and 4 of the First Company Law Directive.	See entries for new Articles 2(1)(f) and 4 above.

Part 43: Transparency obligations and related matters – Transparency Directive (2004/109/EC)

1747. Sections 1265, 1266, 1267, 1268, 1270, 1271, and 1272 in Part 43 (Transparency obligations and related matters) of the Act implement Directive 2004/109/EC on the harmonisation of transparency requirements in relation to information about issuers whose securities are admitted to trading on a regulated market and amending Directive 2001/34/EC. Section 1266 inserts seven new sections into Part 6 of the Financial Services and Markets Act 2000; sections 89A, 89B, 89C, 89D, 89E, 89F and 89G. The new sections give power to the competent authority (at present the Financial Services Authority ("FSA")) to make rules for the purposes of the Transparency Directive (2004/109/EC) ("Transparency Directive") and connected regulatory purposes. Sections 1267 and 1268 insert three and four sections, respectively, into Part 6 of FSMA (89H to 89N) setting out the regulatory powers of the FSA in connection with the Directive. Section 1270 inserts new sections 90A and 90B into FSMA, which set out the issuers' liability in damages for disclosures required under the Transparency Directive, and section 1271 inserts a new section 100A into FSMA setting out provisions in relation to the exercise of the FSA's powers where the UK is a host member state.

1748. The Transparency Directive imposes minimum harmonisation requirements on the information to be provided to the public about issuers whose securities are traded on a regulated market and the control of votes attached to shares in those issuers. It permits Home Member States to impose more stringent requirements on entities that they regulate but Host Member States, ie those states in which the issuers securities are traded on a regulated market but whose competent authority are not responsible for primary oversight of that issuer, are not permitted to impose any requirements more stringent than those contained in the Transparency Directive.

1749. There are three main categories of obligation that are imposed under the Transparency Directive and that the FSA's transparency rules will implement in respect of UK markets and issuers:

(a)   requirements for issuers to make public, at regular intervals, information about their financial position and the progress and management of the business of the issuer;

(b)   requirements for holders of votes attached to shares of issuers to notify the issuers when the number of votes they control reaches specified proportions of the total votes available; and

(c)   requirements for issuers to treat the holders of the same securities equally.

1750. The detailed and technical provisions about the required notifications, disclosures and treatment of security-holders will be prescribed in rules made by the FSA under the new rulemaking power at section 89A of the Financial Services and Markets Act 2000. The FSA is required by that Act to carry out consultation and a cost benefit analysis when making any rules under this power.

1751. Having the power to make these rules will promote the harmonisation of practice with other EU jurisdictions, and help enhance investor confidence through increased transparency of the financial markets.

1752. Responsibility for the transposition of the Transparency Directive lies both with HM Treasury and with the FSA. The measures in the Companies Act that implement the Transparency Directive are the responsibility of HM Treasury.

1753. The table below describes the substantive provisions in the Act implementing the Transparency Directive.

Part 43: Transparency obligations and related matters		
Article	**Objective**	**Implementation**
1	Sets out scope of the Directive and two derogations from the requirements of the Directive. The Member States may apply the derogations in respect of securities issued by the government, local government or a state's national central bank.	Part 43 of the Act inserts new provisions into the Financial Services and Markets Act 2000 ("FSMA") to give the Financial Services Authority power to make Transparency Rules. Most provisions in the Transparency Directive will be implemented by the FSA's Transparency Rules. Other provisions in the Act or in FSMA implement the other requirements. If the derogations are to be implemented, the FSA's Transparency Rules will do this.
2	Provides various definitions used in the Directive.	These will be applied in Transparency Rules, or apply in relation to the implementation of the Article to which they relate.
3	Limits the circumstances in which Member States may impose more stringent requirements than those contained in the Directive on issuers of securities and holders of interests in those issuers' shares.	Transparency Rules and new FSMA section 100A(2) introduced by section 1271 of the Act.
4	Requires issuers of securities which are traded on regulated markets to make public its annual financial report consisting of its audited financial statements and the management report.	Transparency Rules: see in particular new sections 89A and 89C of FSMA, inserted by section 1266 of the Act.
5	Requires issuers of shares or debt securities which are traded on a regulated market to make public a half-yearly financial report.	Transparency Rules: see in particular new sections 89A and 89C of FSMA, inserted by section 1266 of the Act.
6	Requires issuers whose shares are traded on a regulated market to make public an interim quarterly statement.	Transparency Rules: see in particular new sections 89A and 89C of FSMA, inserted by section 1266 of the Act.
7	Requires Member States to ensure that responsibility for the information to be drawn up and made public in accordance with Articles 4, 5, 6 and 16 lies at least with the issuer or its administrative, management or supervisory bodies and to ensure that their laws, regulations and administrative provisions on liability apply to the issuers, the bodies referred to in this article or the persons responsible within the issuers.	Provisions relating to liability inserted into FSMA as new sections 90A and 90B by section 1270 of the Act.
8	Provides various exemptions from the requirements of articles 4, 5 and 6 including to optional exemptions.	Transparency Rules.

Part 43: Transparency obligations and related matters		
Article	Objective	Implementation
9	Provides that where a shareholder with a significant level of holding acquires or disposes of shares of an issuer whose shares are admitted to trading on a regulated market and to which voting rights are attached, such shareholder notifies the issuer of the proportion of voting rights in the issuer held by the shareholder as a result of the acquisition or disposal where that proportion reaches, exceeds or falls below the thresholds of 5%, 10%, 15%, 20%, 25%, 30%, 50% and 75%.	Transparency Rules: see in particular new sections 89A and 89B of FSMA, inserted by section 1266 of the Act.
10	The notification requirements in Article 9 shall also apply to a natural person or legal entity to the extent it is entitled to acquire, to dispose of, or to exercise voting rights in any of the cases set out in the Article or a combination of them. (Voting rights acquired through agreement or interest).	Transparency Rules.
11	Exempts shares provided to or by the members of the ESCB in certain circumstances from the notification requirements imposed by Articles 9 and 10.	Transparency Rules.
12	Sets out the information that must be included in the notification under Articles 9 and 10 and includes provision on the timing of the notification and when aggregation of holdings required. Paragraph (6) requires the issuer to make public all information contained within a notification within 3 days.	Transparency Rules.
13	Requires the holders of financial instruments, which are to be specified by the Commission, to notify the issuer of their control of votes in accordance with the requirements in Article 9.	Transparency Rules.
14	Requires an issuer of shares admitted to trading on a regulated market to make public the proportion of its own shares that it holds when those proportions reach, exceed or fall below the thresholds of 5% or 10%.	Transparency Rules: see in particular new sections 89A and 89C of FSMA, inserted by section 1266 of the Act.
15	Requires the Member State to ensure that an issuer of shares traded on a regulated market, makes public the total number of voting rights and capital at the end of each month during which the number changes.	Transparency Rules.
16	Requires issuers of securities to make public information about any changes in the rights attached to their securities and any new loan issues and any guarantee or security in respect of such loans.	Transparency Rules: see in particular new sections 89A and 89C of FSMA, inserted by section 1266 of the Act.
17	Requires issuers of shares admitted to trading on a regulated market to treat their shareholders, who are in the same position, equally. It provides for information to be distributed in particular ways and for shareholders to be able to exercise their rights in specified ways.	Transparency Rules.

Part 3   CA 2006 Supporting Materials

Part 43: Transparency obligations and related matters

Article	Objective	Implementation
18	Makes similar provision as that contained in Article 17 but in respect of issuers whose debt securities are admitted to trading on a regulated market.	Transparency Rules.
19	Requires issuers to file information that they are required to make public under the Directive, with the FSA and permits the FSA to publish that information itself. It also requires issuers to inform the FSA and the regulated market to which its securities are admitted of any proposed change to its instrument of incorporation.	Transparency Rules.
20	Sets out the rules for determining which language the issuer must use to disclose regulated information in various circumstances.	Transparency Rules.
21	Requires issuers to disclose regulated information in a manner ensuring fast access to such information on a non-discriminatory basis. Also requires each Member State to have an officially appointed mechanism for the central storage of regulated information.	Transparency Rules.
22	Requires the competent authorities of the Member States (for the UK it is the FSA) to draw up guidelines to create an electronic network at national level to share information between the various competent authorities, operators of regulated markets and national company registers. Such guidelines must aim to further facilitate public access to be disclosed under this Directive, Directive 2003/6/EC (the Market Abuse Directive) and Directive 2003/71/EC (Prospectus Directive).	The FSA will draw up guidelines in accordance with the obligations under this Article.
23	Enables the FSA to exempt issuers based in third countries from certain disclosure requirements if there are equivalent provisions in the third country. Requires the FSA to ensure that where a third country issuer is regulated in the UK for EU purposes, any information which may be important to the public in the Community is disclosed in accordance with Articles 20 and 21.	Transparency Rules.
24	Requires each Member State to designate a central competent authority responsible for ensuring that the Directive is applied and to give that competent authority specified powers which are necessary for the performance of its functions.	The central competent authority in the UK will be the FSA, by virtue of the amendments being inserted into Part 6 of FSMA.
	Permits each Member State to designate a competent authority for examining that information is drawn up in accordance with the relevant reporting framework.	The FSA already has various powers under FSMA. Other powers for the FSA to perform its functions are contained in new FSMA sections 89H to 89N inserted by sections 1267 and 1268 of the Act.

Part 43: Transparency obligations and related matters		
Article	**Objective**	**Implementation**
		The Act provides power to designate a competent authority for reporting framework purposes by amending the Companies (Audit, Investigations and Community Enterprise) Act 2004. See Schedule 15 (Part 2) of the Act.
25	Imposes a requirement for professional secrecy on those who work for the competent authority and requires cooperation between the competent authorities of the various Member States.	FSMA already contains provisions relating to professional secrecy for those who work for the FSA and the Companies (Audit, Investigations and Community Enterprise) Act 2004 also contains provisions in relation to authorities appointed under that Act.
26	Provides for host Member States to take action in relation to infringements where an issuer or security holder continues to infringe the requirements of the Directive.	New section 100A of FSMA introduced by section 1271 of the Act.
27	Sets out the committee procedure for the Commission to make implementing measures required by the Directive.	No implementing provision required.
28	Requires, without prejudice to the right of Member States to impose criminal penalties, Member States to ensure, in conformity with their national law that at least the appropriate administrative measure may be taken or civil and/or administrative penalties imposed in respect of the persons responsible.	Schedule 15 (Part 1) of the Act amends section 91 of FSMA to enable the FSA to impose financial penalties for breach of the Transparency Rules.
29	Requires a right of appeal to the courts to be in place.	No further implementation is required. FSMA already makes provision for appeals of FSA decisions to the Financial Services and Markets Tribunal and to the Court of Appeal.
30–35	These articles contain transitional and final provisions, including the date by which the Directive must be transposed – 20 January 2007.	No specific implementation is required for most of these provisions. New sections 89B(4) and 89D(1) introduced by section 1266 of the Act make provision for transitional arrangements.

ANNEX B: GLOSSARY

[3.51]

1985 Act	The Companies Act 1985
AGM	Annual General Meeting
BCLC	Butterworths Company Law Cases
C(AICE) Act 2004	Companies (Audit, Investigations and Community Enterprise) Act 2004
CFD	Contract for Difference
c.i.c.	Community Interest Company
CLR	Company Law Review
DTI	Department of Trade and Industry
EC	European Community
ECU	European Currency Unit
EEA	European Economic Area
EEC	European Economic Community
ESCB	European System of Central Banks
EU	European Union
FRC	Financial Reporting Council
FRRP	Financial Reporting Review Panel
FSA	Financial Services Authority
FSMA	Financial Services and Markets Act 2000
GB	Great Britain
IAS	International Accounting Standards
NI	Northern Ireland
PPERA	Political Parties, Elections and Referendums Act 2000
PSM	Professional Securities Market
QC	Queen's Counsel
RTE	Right to Enfranchise
RTM	Right to Manage
SE	Societas Europaea (European Public Limited-Liability Company)
SI	Statutory Instrument
UK	United Kingdom
UKHL	UK House of Lords

TABLE OF ORIGINS FOR THE COMPANIES ACT 2006

[3.52]

NOTES

(1) This table shows the origin of the company law provisions of the Companies Act 2006 by reference to the enactments in force on the date that Act received Royal assent (subject to the note to the origins for Part 28). The Act received Royal Assent on 8 November 2006. Where an enactment had been amended before that date, the reference is to the text at that date; the table does not show the source of such amendments. [Editorial note: the "company law provisions of the Companies Act 2006" is defined by s 2 of the 2006 Act at **[1.2]**, ie, "(a) the provisions of Parts 1 to 39 of this Act, and (b) the provisions of Parts 45 to 47 of this Act so far as they apply for the purposes of those Parts"].

(2) The origin of a provision of the Companies Act 2006 in the Companies (Northern Ireland) Order 1986 is acknowledged where it makes significantly different provision in relation to Northern Ireland than in relation to England and Wales or, as the case may be, Great Britain.

(3) In the table—
    "1985" means the Companies Act 1985 (c 6);
    "IA 1986" means the Insolvency Act 1986 (c 45);
    "1986" means the Companies (Northern Ireland) Order 1986, SI 1096/1032 (NI 6);
    "ICTA" means the Income and Corporation Taxes Act 1988 (c 1);
    "1989" means the Companies Act 1989 (c 40).

(4) The entry "drafting" indicates a new provision of a mechanical or editorial nature – for example, a provision defining an expression to avoid repetition or indicating where other relevant provisions are to be found.

(5) A reference followed by "(changed)" means that the provision referred to has been re-enacted with one or more changes. In general, a change is noted only in the primary context affected and not in every provision where a consequential change results The table does not show changes in the maximum penalties for offences.

(6) The entry "new" indicates a provision which has no predecessor in the repealed legislation or which is fundamentally different from its predecessor.

(7) The entries in the table are intended only as a general indication of what has changed and what is new. They should not be read as expressing any view as to the application or otherwise of any provision relating to enactments repealed and re-enacted.

CA 2006	Origin
PART 1 GENERAL INTRODUCTORY PROVISIONS	
1(1)	1985, s 735(1)(a), (b)
(2), (3)	drafting
2(1), (2)	1985, s 744 (changed)
3(1)–(4)	1985, s 1(2)
4(1), (2)	1985, s 1(3)
(3)	1985, s 1(3), 1986 art 12(3)
(4)	drafting
5(1)	1985, s 1(4)
(2)	1985, s 1(4), 1986 art 12(4)
(3)	1985, s 15(2)
6(1), (2)	drafting
PART 2 COMPANY FORMATION	
7(1), (2)	1985, s 1(1) (changed)
8(1)	new
(2)	1985, s 3(1)
9(1)	1985, s 10(1) (changed)
(2)	1985, s 2(1)(a), (b), (2), (3) (changed)
(3)	1985, s 10(4)
(4)	new
(5)	1985, s 10(1), (6)
(6)	1985, s 10(1)
10(1)–(5)	new
11(1)	drafting
(2)	new
(3)	1985, s 2(4) (changed)
12(1)	1985, s 10(2) (changed)
(2)	new
(3), first sentence	1985, s 10(3)
(3), second sentence	new

CA 2006	Origin
13(1), (2)	1985, s 12(3), (3A) (changed)
14	1985, s 12(1), (2)
15(1)	1985, s 13(1)
(2)	new
(3)	1985, s 13(2)
(4)	1985, s 13(7)(a)
16(1)	drafting
(2)	1985, s 13(3) (changed)
(3)	1985, s 13(4)
(4)	new
(5)	new
(6)	1985, s 13(5)
PART 3 A COMPANY'S CONSTITUTION	
Chapter 1 Introductory	
17	new
Chapter 2 Articles of association	
18(1)	new
(2)	1985, s 7(1) (changed)
(3)	1985, s 7(3) (changed)
(4)	1985, s 744
19(1)–(3)	1985, s 8(1), (4) (changed)
(4)	1985, s 8(3)
(5)	1985, s 8(5)
20(1), (2)	1985, s 8(2) (changed)
21(1)	1985, s 9(1)
(2), (3)	drafting
22(1)–(3)	new
23(1), (2)	new
24(1)–(4)	new
25(1)	1985, s 16(1)

CA 2006	Origin
(2)	1985, s 16(2)
26(1)	1985, s 18(2) (changed)
(2)	new
(3), (4)	1985, s 18(3) and Sch 24
27(1)–(5)	new
28(1)–(3)	new

Chapter 3 Resolutions and agreements affecting a company's constitution

CA 2006	Origin
29(1)	1985, s 380(4) (changed)
(2)	1985, s 380(4A)
30(1)	1985, s 380(1)
(2), (3)	1985, s 380(5) and Sch 24
(4)	1985, s 380(7)

Chapter 4 Miscellaneous and supplementary provisions

CA 2006	Origin
31(1)–(5)	new
32(1)	1985, s 19(1) (changed)
(2)	new
(3), (4)	1985, s 19(2) (changed) and Sch 24
33(1)	1985, s 14(1) (changed)
(2)	1985, s 14(2) (changed)
34(1)	drafting
(2)	1985, s 18(1) (changed)
(3)	1985, s 18(2) (changed)
(4)	new
(5), (6)	1985, s 18(3) and Sch 24
35(1)–(5)	new
36(1), (2)	1985, s 380(2) (changed)
(3), (4)	1985, s 380(6) (changed) and Sch 24
(5)	1985, s 380(7)
37	1985, s 15(1)
38	Companies (Single Member Private Limited Companies) Regulations 1992 (SI 1992/1699) (changed)

PART 4 A COMPANY'S CAPACITY AND RELATED MATTERS

CA 2006	Origin
39(1)	1985, s 35(1) (changed)
(2)	1985, s 35(4)
40(1)	1985, s 35A(1)
(2)	1985, s 35A(2) and 35B
(3)	1985, s 35A(3)
(4)	1985, s 35A(4)
(5)	1985, s 35A(5)
(6)	1985, s 35A(6)
41(1)	1985, s 322A(1), (4)
(2)	1985, s 322A(1), (2)
(3)	1985, s 322A(3)
(4)	1985, s 322A(5)
(5)	1985, s 322A(6)
(6)	1985, s 322A(7)
(7)	1985, s 322A(8)
42(1)	Charities Act 1993, s 65(1)
(2)	Charities Act 1993, s 65(2)
(3)	Charities Act 1993, s 65(3)

CA 2006	Origin
(4)	Charities Act 1993, s 65(4)
(5)	drafting
43(1), (2)	1985, s 36
44(1)	1985, s 36A(1)–(3)
(2)(a), (3), (4)	1985, s 36A(4)
(2)(b)	new
(5)	1985, s 36A(6) (changed)
(6)	1985, s 36A(4A)
(7)	1985, s 36A(8)
(8)	1985, s 36A(7)
45(1)	1985, s 36A(3)
(2)	1985, s 350(1)
(3)	1985, s 350(1) (changed)
(4), (5)	1985, s 350(2) and Sch 24
(6)	drafting
46(1)	1985, s 36AA(1)
(2)	1985, s 36AA(2)
47(1)	1985, s 38(1) (changed), (3)
(2)	1985, s 38(2) (changed)
48(1)	Requirements of Writing (Scotland) Act 1995 (c 7), s 15(3)
(2)	1985, s 36B(1)
(3)	1985, s 36B(2)
49(1)	1985, s 39(1) (changed)
(2)	1985, s 39(1)
(3)	1985, s 39(2), (2A)
(4)	1985, s 39(3)
(5)	1985, s 39(4)
(6)	1985, s 39(5)
50(1), (2)	1985, s 40(1)
51(1)	1985, s 36C(1)
(2)	1985, s 36C(2)
52	1985, s 37

PART 5 A COMPANY'S NAME

Chapter 1 General requirements

CA 2006	Origin
53	1985, s 26(1)(d), (e)
54(1)–(3)	1985, s 26(2)(a) and second sentence (changed)
55(1)	1985, s 26(2)(b) and 29(1)(a)
(2)	1985, s 29(6)
56(1)	1985, s 29(1)(b) (changed)
(2)	1985, s 29(2)
(3), (4)	1985, s 29(3) (changed)
(5)	drafting
57(1)–(5)	new

Chapter 2 Indications of company type or legal form

CA 2006	Origin
58(1)	1985, s 25(1) and 27(4)(b)
(2)	1985, s 25(1) and 27(4)(d)
(3)	drafting
59(1)	1985, s 25(2) (opening words) and 27(4)(a)
(2)	1985, s 25(2)(b) and 27(4)(c)

CA 2006	Origin
(3)	1985, s 25(2)(a)
(4)	drafting
60(1)(a), (b)	new
(1)(c)	drafting
(2)	1985, s 30(5B)
(3)	1985, s 30(4)
(4)	new
61(1)	1985, s 30(2), 1986 art 40(2)
(2)–(4)	1985, s 30(2), (3) (changed)
62(1)–(3)	1985, s 30(2), (3) (changed)
63(1)	1985, s 31(1)
(2), (3)	1985, s 31(5) and Sch 24
(4), (5)	new
64(1)–(3)	1985, s 31(2) first sentence
(4)	1985, s 31(2) second sentence (changed)
(5), (6)	1985, s 31(6) and Sch 24
(7)	1985, s 31(3)
65(1)–(5)	1985, s 26(1)(a), (b), (bb), (bbb) (changed)

Chapter 3 Similarity to other names

CA 2006	Origin
66(1)	1985, s 26(1)(c)
(2), (3)	1985, s 26(3) (changed)
(4)–(6)	new
67(1)	1985, s 28(2)
(2)–(6)	new
68(1)	drafting
(2)	1985, s 28(2) full out
(3)	1985, s 28(4)
(4)	1985, s 28(2) full out and (4)
(5), (6)	1985, s 28(5) and Sch 24
69(1)–(7)	new
70(1)–(6)	new
71(1)–(4)	new
72(1), (2)	new
73(1)–(6)	new
74(1)–(5)	new

Chapter 4 Other powers of the Secretary of State

CA 2006	Origin
75(1), (2)	1985, s 28(3)
(3)	1985, s 28(4)
(4)	1985, s 28(3)
(5), (6)	1985, s 28(5) and Sch 24
76(1)	1985, s 32(1)
(2)	new
(3)	1985, s 32(2)
(4), (5)	1985, s 32(3)
(6), (7)	1985, s 32(4) (changed) and Sch 24

Chapter 5 Change of name

CA 2006	Origin
77(1)(a)	1985, s 28(1)
(1)(b)	new
(2)	drafting
78(1)–(3)	new

CA 2006	Origin
79(1), (2)	new
80(1), (2)	1985, s 28(6) and 32(5) (changed)
(3)	1985, s 28(6) and 32(5)
81(1)	1985, s 28(6) and 32(5)
(2), (3)	1985, s 28(7) and 32(6)

Chapter 6 Trading disclosures

CA 2006	Origin
82(1), (2)	1985, ss 348(1), 349(1), 351(1), (2), Business Names Act 1985, s 4(1) (changed)
(3)–(5)	new
83(1), (2)	Business Names Act 1985, s 5(1)
(3)	Business Names Act 1985, s 5(2)
84(1), (2)	1985, ss 348(2), 349(2), (3), 351(5), Business Names Act 1985, s 7 (changed)
(3)	new
85(1), (2)	new

PART 6 A COMPANY'S REGISTERED OFFICE

CA 2006	Origin
86	1985, s 287(1)
87(1)	1985, s 287(3)
(2)	1985, s 287(4)
(3)	1985, s 287(5)
(4)	1985, s 287(6)
88(1)	drafting
(2)	1985, s 2(2)
(3), (4)	new

PART 7 RE-REGISTRATION AS A MEANS OF ALTERING A COMPANY'S STATUS

CA 2006	Origin
89	drafting
90(1)	1985, s 43(1) (changed)
(2)	1985, s 43(1); drafting
(3)	1985, s 43(2)
(4)	1985, s 48(1), (2)
91(1)	1985, s 45(1)–(4)
(2)	1985, s 45(5), 1986 art 55(5)
(3)	1985, s 45(6)
(4)	1985, s 45(7)
(5)	1985, s 47(3) (changed)
92(1)	1985, s 43(3)(b), (c), (4)
(2)	1985, s 43(e)(ii)
(3), (4)	1985, s 46(2), (3)
(5), (6)	1985, s 46(4)
93(1)	1985, s 44(1)
(2)	1985, s 44(2), drafting
(3)–(5)	1985, s 44(4), (5)
(6)	1985, s 44(6), (7)(b)
(7)	1985, s 44(2), (7)(a)
94(1)	new
(2)	1985, s 43(3)(a)–(d)
(3)	1985, s 43(e)(i)
(4)	1985, s 47(2)
95(1)–(3)	new

Part 3 CA 2006 Supporting Materials

CA 2006	Origin
96(1), (2)	1985, s 47(1)
(3)	new
(4), (5)	1985, s 47(4), (5)
97(1)	1985, s 53(1) (changed)
(2)	new
(3)	1985, s 53(2)
98(1)	1985, s 54(1), (2)
(2)	1985, s 54(3)
(3), (4)	1985, s 54(5)
(5)	1985, s 54(6)
(6)	1985, s 54(8)
99(1), (2)	1985, s 54(4) (changed)
(3)	1985, s 54(7)
(4), (5)	1985, s 54(10), Sch 24
100(1)	new
(2)	1985, s 53(1)(b) (changed)
(3), (4)	new
101(1), (2)	1985, s 55(1)
(3)	new
(4), (5)	1985, s 55(2), (3)
102(1)	1985, s 49(1), (4), (8)(a) (changed)
(2)	1985, s 49(2)
(3)	1985, s 49(5)–(7) (changed)
(4)	1985, s 49(9)
(5)	new
103(1)	new
(2)	1985, s 49(8)(a), (c), (d)
(3), (4)	1985, s 49(8)(b), (8A) (changed)
(5)	new
104(1), (2)	1985, s 50(1)(b)
(3)	new
(4), (5)	1985, s 50(2), (3)
105(1)	1985, s 51(1) (changed)
(2)	1985, s 51(2)
(3), (4)	1985, s 51(3)
106(1)	new
(2)	1985, s 51(5) (changed)
(3)–(5)	new
107(1), (2)	1985, s 52(1)
(3)	new
(4), (5)	1985, s 52(2), (3)
108(1)–(5)	new
109(1)–(5)	new
110(1)–(5)	new
111(1)–(5)	new

PART 8 A COMPANY'S MEMBERS

Chapter 1 The members of a company

CA 2006	Origin
112(1)	1985, s 22(1) (changed)
(2)	1985, s 22(2)

Chapter 2 Register of members

CA 2006	Origin
113(1), (2)	1985, s 352(1), (2)
(3), (4)	1985, s 352(3)

CA 2006	Origin
(5)	new
(6)	1985, s 352(4)
(7), (8)	1985, s 352(5), Sch 24
114(1)	1985, s 353(1) (changed)
(2)	1985, s 353(2)
(3)	1985, s 353(3)
(4)	1985, s 353(3), 1986 art 361(3)
(5), (6)	1985, s 353(4), Sch 24
115(1), (2)	1985, s 354(1)
(3)	1985, s 354(2)
(4)	1985, s 354(3) (changed)
(5), (6)	1985, s 354(4), Sch 24
116(1)	1985, s 356(1) (changed)
(2)	1985, s 356(3) first branch
(3), (4)	new
117(1)–(5)	new
118(1), (2)	1985, s 356(5), Sch 24 (changed)
(3)	1985, s 356(6)
119(1)–(3)	new
120(1)–(4)	new
121	1985, s 352(6) (changed)
122(1)	1985, s 355(1) (changed)
(2)	1985, s 355(4)
(3)	1985, s 355(5)
(4), (5)	1985, s 355(2), (3)
(6)	1985, s 355(4)
123(1)	new
(2), (3)	1985, s 352A(1), (2) (changed)
(4), (5)	1985, s 352A(3), Sch 24
124(1), (2)	1985, s 352(3A)
125(1)–(4)	1985, s 359(1)–(4)
126	1985, s 360
127	1985, s 361
128(1), (2)	1985, s 352(7)

Chapter 3 Overseas branch registers

CA 2006	Origin
129(1)	1985, s 362(1), (2) opening words
(2)	1985, Sch 14, Pt 1
(3), (4)	new
(5)	1985, s 362(2)(b), (c)
130(1)	1985, s 362(3), Sch 14, Pt 2, para 1(1), (2)
(2), (3)	1985, s 362(3), Sch 14, Pt 2, para 1(3), Sch 24
131(1)	1985, s 362(3), Sch 14, Pt 2, para 2(1)
(2), (3)	new
(4)	1985, s 362(3), Sch 14, Pt 2, para 7
132(1), (2)	1985, s 362(3), Sch 14, Pt 2, para 4(1) (changed)
(3), (4)	1985, s 362(3), Sch 14, Pt 2, para 4(2), Sch 24

CA 2006	Origin
133(1), (2)	1985, s 362(3), Sch 14, Pt 2, para 5
(3)	1985, s 362(3), Sch 14, Pt 2, para 8
134(1), (2)	1985, s 362(3), Sch 14, Pt 2, para 3(1) (changed)
(3)	1985, s 362(3), Sch 14, Pt 2, para 3(2)
135(1), (2)	1985, s 362(3), Sch 14, Pt 2, para 6
(3)	1985, s 362(3), Sch 14, Pt 2, para 1(1), (2)
(4), (5)	1985, s 362(3), Sch 14, Pt 2, para 1(3), Sch 24
Chapter 4 Prohibition on subsidiary being member of its holding company	
136(1)	1985, s 23(1)
(2)	drafting
137(1)	1985, s 23(4), (5)
(2)	1985, s 23(4), 1986 art 33(4)
(3), (4)	1985, s 23(6)
138(1), (2)	1985, s 23(2), Sch 2, para 4(1), (2); drafting
139(1)–(4)	1985, Sch 2, para 1(1)–(4)
(5)	1985, Sch 2, para 5(2)
(6)	1985, Sch 2, para 5(2), (3)
140(1), (2)	1985, Sch 2, para 3(1), (2)
(3), (4)	1985, Sch 2, para 5(2), (3)
141(1), (2)	1985, s 23(3)
141(3), (4)	1985, s 23(3A), (3B)
(5)	1985, s 23(3BA)
142(1), (2)	1985, s 23(3C)
143	1985, s 23(8)
144	1985, s 23(7)
PART 9 EXERCISE OF MEMBERS' RIGHTS	
145(1)–(4)	new
146(1)–(5)	new
147(1)–(6)	new
148(1)–(8)	new
149(1)–(3)	new
150(1)–(7)	new
151(1)–(3)	new
152(1)–(4)	new
153(1), (2)	new
PART 10 A COMPANY'S DIRECTORS	
Chapter 1 Appointment and removal of directors	
154(1)	1985, s 282(3)
(2)	1985, s 282(1) (changed)
155(1), (2)	new
156(1)–(7)	new
157(1)–(6)	new
158(1)–(5)	new
159(1)–(4)	new
160(1)–(4)	1985, s 292(1)–(4)
161(1), (2)	1985, s 285 (changed)
162(1)–(3)	1985, s 288(1) (changed)

CA 2006	Origin
(4)	new
(5)	1985, s 288(3)
(6)	1985, s 288(4), (6)
(7)	1985, s 288(4), Sch 24
(8)	1985, s 288(5)
163(1)	1985, s 289(1)(a) (changed)
(2)	1985, s 289(2)(a)
(3)	new
(4)	1985, s 289(2)(b) (changed)
(5)	new
164	1985, s 289(1)(b) (changed)
165(1)–(6)	new
166(1), (2)	new
167(1), (2)	1985, s 288(2) (changed)
(3)	new
(4)	1985, s 288(4), (6)
(5)	1985, s 288(4), Sch 24
168(1)	1985, s 303(1) (changed)
(2)–(5)	1985, s 303(2)–(5)
169(1), (2)	1985, s 304(1)
(3), (4)	1985, s 304(2), (3)
(5)	1985, s 304(4) (changed)
(6)	1985, s 304(5)
Chapter 2 General duties of directors	
170(1)–(5)	new
171	new
172(1)	1985, s 309(1) (changed)
(2), (3)	new
173(1), (2)	new
174(1), (2)	new
175(1)–(7)	new
176(1)–(5)	new
177(1)–(6)	new
178(1), (2)	new
179	new
180(1)–(5)	new
181(1)–(5)	new
Chapter 3 Declaration of interest in existing transaction or arrangement	
182(1)	1985, s 317(1), (5) (changed)
(2)	1985, s 317(2) (changed)
(3)–(6)	new
183(1)	1985, s 317(7)
(2)	1985, s 317(7), Sch 24
184(1)–(5)	new
185(1), (2)	1985, s 317(3) (changed)
(3)	new
(4)	1985, s 317(4)
186(1), (2)	new
187(1)–(4)	1985, s 317(8) (changed)
Chapter 4 Transactions with directors requiring approval of members	
188(1)	1985, s 319(1) (changed)
(2)	1985, s 319(3) (changed)

CA 2006	Origin
(3)	1985, s 319(1) (changed)
(4)	1985, s 319(2) (changed)
(5)	1985, s 319(5), para 7 of Sch 15A (changed)
(6)	1985, s 319(4)
(7)	1985, s 319(7)(a)
189	1985, s 319(6)
190(1), (2)	1985, s 320(1) (changed)
(3)	new
(4)	1985, s 321(1)
(5), (6)	new
191(1)–(5)	1985, s 320(2) (changed)
192	1985, s 321(2)(a), (3) (changed)
193(1), (2)	1985, s 321(2)(b) (changed)
194(1), (2)	1985, s 321(4)
195(1)	1985, s 322(1), (3)
(2)	1985, s 322(1), (2)(a), (b)
(3)	1985, s 322(3), (4)
(4)	1985, s 322(3)
(5)	1985, s 322(4)
(6)	1985, s 322(5)
(7)	1985, s 322(6)
(8)	1985, s 322(4)
196	1985, s 322(2)(c)
197(1)	1985, s 330(2) (changed)
(2)–(5)	new
198(1)	1985, s 330(3), s 331(6)
(2)	1985, s 330(3)(a), (c) (changed)
(3)–(6)	new
199(1)	1985, s 331(3)
(2), (3)	1985, s 331(4)
200(1)	1985, s 330(3), s 331(6)
(2)	1985, s 330(3)(b), (c) (changed)
(3)–(6)	new
201(1)	1985, s 330(4), s 331(6)
(2)	1985, s 330(4) (changed)
(3)–(6)	new
202(1)	1985, s 331(7)
(2)	1985, s 331(9)(b)
(3)	1985, s 331(8), (10)
203(1)	1985, s 330(6), (7) (changed)
(2)–(5)	new
(6)	1985, s 330(6)
204(1)	1985, s 337(1), (2) (changed)
(2)	1985, s 337(3), s 339(1), (2) (changed)
205(1)	1985, s 337A(1), (3) (changed)
(2)	1985, s 337A(4)
(3)	1985, s 337A(5)
(4)	1985, s 337A(6)
(5)	1985, s 337A(2)

CA 2006	Origin
206	new
207(1)	1985, s 334, s 339(1), (2) (changed)
(2)	1985, s 335(1), s 339(1), (2) (changed)
(3)	1985, s 335(2)
208(1)	1985, s 333, s 336(a) (changed)
(2)	1985, s 336(b) (changed)
209(1)	1985, s 338(1), (3)
(2)	1985, s 338(2)
(3), (4)	1985, s 338(6) (changed)
210(1)	1985, s 339(1)
(2)	1985, s 339(2)
(3)	1985, s 339(2), (3)
(4)	1985, s 339(2), (3)
(5)	1985, s 339(5)
211(1)	1985, s 339(6) and, s 340(1)
(2)	1985, s 340(2)
(3)	1985, s 340(3)
(4)	1985, s 340(6)
(5)	1985, s 340(4)
(6)	1985, s 340(5)
(7)	1985, s 340(7) (changed)
212	1985, s 331(9)(a)–(d)
213(1), (2)	1985, s 341(1)
(3), (4)	1985, s 341(2)
(5)	1985, s 341(3)
(6)	1985, s 341(4)
(7)	1985, s 341(5)
(8)	1985, s 341(3)
214	new
215(1)	1985, s 312, s 313(1), s 314(1) (changed)
(2)–(4)	new
216(1), (2)	1985, s 316(2) (changed)
217(1)	1985, s 312
(2)	new
(3)	1985, s 312 (changed)
(4)	new
218(1)	1985, s 313(1)
(2)	new
(3)	1985, s 313(1) (changed)
(4)	new
(5)	1985, s 316(1)
219(1)	1985, s 314(1), s 315(1)(b) (changed)
(2)	1985, s 315(1)(b)
(3), (4)	new
(5)	1985, s 315(3)
(6)	new
(7)	1985, s 316(1)
220(1)	1985, s 316(3) (changed)
(2)–(5)	new
221(1)–(4)	new
222(1)	new

CA 2006	Origin
(2)	1985, s 313(2)
(3)	1985, s 315(1)
(4), (5)	new
223(1)	1985, s 319(6), 320(3), 330(5)
(2)	new
224(1) and (2)	new
225(1)–(3)	new
226	new
Chapter 5 Directors' service contracts	
227	new
228(1)	1985, s 318(1)
(2)	1985, s 318(2), (3) (changed)
(3)	new
(4)	1985, s 318(4)
(5)	1985, s 318(8) (changed)
(6)	1985, s 318(8), Sch 24
(7)	1985, s 318(10)
229(1)	1985, s 318(7)
(2)	new
(3)	1985, s 318(8) (changed)
(4)	1985, s 318(8), Sch 24
(5)	1985, s 318(9) (changed)
230	1985, s 318(6)
Chapter 6 Contracts with sole members who are directors	
231(1)	1985, s 322B(1), (2) (changed)
(2)	1985, s 322B(1)
(3)	1985, s 322B(4) (changed)
(4)	1985, s 322B(4), Sch 24
(5)	1985, s 322B(3)
(6)	1985, s 322B(6)
(7)	1985, s 322B(5)
Chapter 7 Directors' liabilities	
232(1)	1985, s 309A(1), (2)
(2)	1985, s 309A(1), (3) (changed)
(3)	1985, s 309A(6)
(4)	new
233	1985, s 309A(5)
234(1)	1985, s 309A(4)
(2)	1985, s 309B(1), (2)
(3)	1985, s 309B(3), (4)
(4)	1985, s 309B(5)
(5)	1985, s 309B(6), (7)
(6)	1985, s 309B(4)(c)
235(1)–(6)	new
236(1)	1985, s 309C(1) (changed)
(2), (3)	1985, s 309C(2)
(4), (5)	1985, s 309C(3)
237(1)	1985, s 309C(4), (5)
(2)	1985, s 309C(5), s 318(1)
(3)	1985, s 309C(5), s 318(2), (3) (changed)

CA 2006	Origin
(4)	new
(5)	1985, s 309C(5), s 318(4)
(6)	1985, s 309C(5), s 318(8) (changed).
(7)	1985, s 309C(5), s 318(8), Sch 24
(8)	1985, s 309C(5), s 318(10)
(9)	new
238(1)	1985, s 309C(5), s 318(7)
(2)	new
(3)	1985, s 309C(5), s 318(8) (changed)
(4)	1985, s 309C(5), 1985, s 318(8), Sch 24
(5)	1985, s 309C(5), s 318(9) (changed)
239(1)–(7)	new
Chapter 8 Directors' residential addresses: protection from disclosure	
240(1)–(3)	new
241(1), (2)	new
242(1)–(3)	new
243(1)–(8)	new
244(1)–(4)	new
245(1)–(6)	new
246(1)–(7)	new
Chapter 9 Supplementary provisions	
247(1)	1985, s 719(1)
(2)	1985, s 719(2) (changed)
(3)	new
(4)	1985, s 719(3)
(5)	1985, s 719(3) (changed)
(6)	1985, s 719(3)
(7)	1985, s 719(4) (changed)
248(1)	1985, s 382(1)
(2)	new
(3)	1985, s 382(5) (changed)
(4)	1985, s 382(5), Sch 24
249(1)	1985, s 382(2)
(2)	1985, s 382(4)
250	1985, s 741(1)
251(1), (2)	1985, s 741(2)
(3)	1985, s 741(3)
252(1)	1985, s 346(1)
(2)	1985, s 346(2), (3) (changed)
(3)	1985, s 346(2)
253(1)	drafting
(2)	1985, s 346(2), (3) (changed)
(3)	new
254(1)	1985, s 346(1)
(2)	1985, s 346(4)
(3)	1985, s 346(7)
(4)	1985, s 346(8)
(5)	1985, s 346(4)

CA 2006	Origin
(6)	1985, s 346(6)
255(1)	1985, s 346(1)
(2)	1985, s 346(5)
(3)	1985, s 346(7)
(4)	1985, s 346(8)
(5)	1985, s 346(5)
(6)	1985, s 346(6)
256	new
257(1), (2)	new
258(1)	1985, s 345(1)
(2)	1985, s 345(2)
(3)	1985, s 345(3)
259	1985, s 347
PART 11 DERIVATIVE CLAIMS AND PRO-CEEDINGS BY MEMBERS	
Chapter 1 Derivative claims in England and Wales or Northern Ireland	
260(1)–(5)	new
261(1)–(4)	new
262(1)–(5)	new
263(1)–(7)	new
264(1)–(5)	new
Chapter 2 Derivative proceedings in Scotland	
265(1)–(7)	new
266(1)–(5)	new
267(1)–(5)	new
268(1)–(6)	new
269(1)–(5)	new
PART 12 COMPANY SECRETARIES	
270(1), (2)	new
(3)	1985, s 283(3) (changed)
271	1985, s 283(1) (changed)
272(1)–(7)	new
273(1), (2)	1985, s 286(1) (changed)
(3)	1985, s 286(2)
274	1985, s 283(3) (changed)
275(1)–(3)	1985, s 288(1) (changed)
(4)	new
(5)	1985, s 288(3)
(6)	1985, s 288(4), (6)
(7)	1985, s 288(4), Sch 24
(8)	1985, s 288(5)
276(1), (2)	1985, s 288(2)
(3)	1985, s 288(4), (6) (changed)
(4)	1985, s 288(4), Sch 24
277(1)	1985, s 290(1)(a) (changed)
(2)	1985, s 289(2)(a), s 290(3)
(3)	new
(4)	1985, s 289(2)(b), s 290(3) (changed)
(5)	new
278(1)	1985, s 290(1)(b) (changed)
(2)	1985, s 290(2)
279(1), (2)	new
280	1985, s 284

CA 2006	Origin
PART 13 RESOLUTIONS AND MEETINGS	
Chapter 1 General provisions about resolutions	
281(1)–(4)	new
282(1)–(5)	new
283(1)	1985, s 378(1), (2) (changed)
(2), (3)	new
(4)	1985, s 378(1), (2) (changed)
(5)	1985, s 378(1), (2), (5) (changed)
(6)	1985, s 378(2) (changed)
284(1)	1985, s 370(6)
(2)	Table A, para 54 (changed)
(3)	1985, s 370(6), Table A, para 54 (changed)
(4)	1985, s 370(1), Table A, para 54
285(1)–(3)	new
286(1)–(3)	Table A, para 55
287	new
Chapter 2 Written resolutions	
288(1)	new
(2)	1985, s 381A(7), Sch 15A, para 1
(3)	new
(4)	1985, s 381A(1) (changed)
(5)	1985, s 381A(4)
289(1)	1985, s 381A(1) (changed)
(2)	new
290	new
291(1)–(7)	new
292(1)–(6)	new
293(1)–(7)	new
294(1), (2)	new
295(1), (2)	new
296(1)	1985, s 381A(2) (changed)
(2)–(4)	new
297(1), (2)	new
298(1), (2)	new
299(1), (2)	new
300	1985, s 381C(1)
Chapter 3 Resolutions at meetings	
301	1985, s 378(6) (changed)
302	Table A, para 37
303(1)	1985, s 368(1)
(2)	1985, s 368(1), (2), (2A)
(3)	1985, s 368(2) (changed)
(4)	1985, s 368(3) (changed)
(5)	new
(6)	1985, s 368(3) (changed)
304(1)	1985, s 368(4), (8)
(2), (3)	new
(4)	1985, s 368(7)
305(1)	1985, s 368(4)
(2)	new

CA 2006	Origin
(3)	1985, s 368(4)
(4)	1985, s 368(5)
(5)	new
(6), (7)	1985, s 368(6)
306(1), (2)	1985, s 371(1)
(3), (4)	1985, s 371(2)
(5)	1985, s 371(3)
307(1)	new
(2)	1985, s 369(1), (2) (changed)
(3)	1985, s 369(1), (2)
(4)	1985, s 369(3) (changed)
(5), (6)	1985, s 369(4) (changed)
(7)	drafting
308	1985, s 369(4A), (4B) (changed)
309(1)	1985, s 369(4B)
(2)	1985, s 369(4C) (changed)
(3)	1985, s 369(4B)(d)
310(1)	1985, s 370(2), Table A, para 38 (changed)
(2)	Table A, para 38 (changed)
(3)	new
(4)	1985, s 370(1), Table A, para 38
311(1), (2)	Table A, para 38
312(1)	1985, s 379(1)
(2)	1985, s 379(2)
(3)	1985, s 379(2) (changed)
(4)	1985, s 379(3)
313(1), (2)	1985 Table A, para 39 (changed)
314(1)	1985, s 376(1)(b)
(2), (3)	1985, s 376(2) (changed)
(4)	1985, s 376(1), s 377(1)(a) (changed)
315(1)	1985, s 376(3), (5)
(2)	1985, s 376(1)
(3)	1985, s 376(7)
(4)	1985, s 376(7), Sch 24
316(1)	new
(2)	1985, s 376(1), s 377(1)(b) (changed)
317(1)	1985, s 377(3) (changed)
(2)	1985, s 377(3)
318(1)	1985, s 370A
(2)	1985, s 370(1), (4) (changed)
(3)	1985, s 370A (changed)
319(1)	1985, s 370(5)
(2)	1985, s 370(1)
320(1)	1985, s 378(4), Table A, para 47
(2)	Table A, para 47
(3)	1985, s 378(4), Table A, paras 47 and 48 (changed)
321(1)	1985, s 373(1)(a)
(2)	1985, s 373(1)(b) (changed)

CA 2006	Origin
322	1985, s 374
323(1)	1985, s 375(1)(a)
(2), (3)	1985, s 375(2) (changed)
(4)	new
324(1)	1985, s 372(1) (changed)
(2)	1985, s 372(2)(b) (changed)
325(1)	1985, s 372(3) (changed)
(2)	new
(3)	1985, s 372(4)
(4)	1985, s 372(4), Sch 24
326(1), (2)	1985, s 372(6)
(3)	1985, s 372(6) (changed)
(4)	1985, s 372(6), Sch 24
327(1)	1985, s 372(5)
(2)	1985, s 372(5) (changed)
(3)	new
328(1), (2)	new
329(1)	1985, s 373(2)
(2)	1985, s 373(2) (changed)
330(1)–(7)	Table A, para 63 (changed)
331	new
332	1985, s 381
333(1)–(4)	new
334(1)–(3)	1985, s 125(6) (changed)
(4)	1985, s 125(6)(a)
(5)	new
(6)	1985, s 125(6)(b)
(7)	1985, s 125(7), (8)
335(1)–(6)	new

Chapter 4 Public companies: additional requirements for AGMs

CA 2006	Origin
336(1)	1985, s 366(1) (changed)
(2)	new
(3)	1985, s 366(4) (changed)
(4)	1985, s 366(4), Sch 24
337(1)	1985, s 366(1)
(2)	1985, s 369(3)(a)
338(1)	1985, s 376(1)(b)
(2)	new
(3)	1985, s 376(2) (changed)
(4)	1985, s 376(1), s 377(1)(a), (2) (changed)
339(1)	1985, s 376(3), (5)
(2)	1985, s 376(1)
(3)	1985, s 376(6)
(4)	1985, s 376(7)
(5)	1985, s 376(7), Sch 24
340(1)	new
(2)	1985, s 376(1), s 377(1)(b) (changed)

Chapter 5 Additional requirements for quoted companies

CA 2006	Origin
341(1)–(6)	new
342(1)–(4)	new
343(1)–(6)	new
344(1)–(4)	new

Part 3 CA 2006 Supporting Materials

CA 2006	Origin
345(1)–(6)	new
346(1)–(5)	new
347(1)–(4)	new
348(1)–(4)	new
349(1)–(5)	new
350(1)–(5)	new
351(1)–(5)	new
352(1), (2)	new
353(1)–(5)	new
354(1)–(4)	new
Chapter 6 Records of resolutions and meetings	
355(1)	1985, s 382(1), s 382A(1) (changed)
(2)	new
(3)	1985, s 382(5) (changed)
(4)	1985, s 382(5), Sch 24
356(1)	drafting
(2), (3)	1985, s 382A(2)
(4)	1985, s 382(2)
(5)	1985, s 382(4)
357(1), (2)	1985, s 382B(1)
(3)	1985, s 382B(2)
(4)	1985, s 382B(2), Sch 24
(5)	1985, s 382B(3)
358(1)	1985, s 383(1) (changed)
(2)	new
(3)	1985, s 383(1)
(4)	1985, s 383(3) (changed)
(5)	1985, s 383(4) (changed)
(6)	1985, s 383(4), Sch 24
(7)	1985, s 383(5)
359	new
Chapter 7 Supplementary provisions	
360(1), (2)	new
361	new
PART 14 CONTROL OF POLITICAL DONATIONS AND EXPENDITURE	
362	1985, s 347A(1) (changed)
363(1)	1985, s 347A(6), (7)(a), (9)
(2)	1985, s 347A(6)(b), (7)(b), (c) (changed)
(3)	new
(4)	drafting
364(1)	drafting
(2)	1985, s 347A(4)
(3)	new
(4)	new
365(1)	1985, s 347A(5) (changed)
(2)	new
366(1)	1985, s 347C(1) (changed)
(2)	1985, s 347C(1), 347D(1), (2), (3) (changed)
(3)	1985, s 347D(3) (changed)
(4)	new
(5)	1985, s 347A(10), s 347C(1), s 347D(2), (3)

CA 2006	Origin
(6)	1985, s 347C(6), s 347D(9)
367(1), (2)	new
(3)	1985, s 347C(2), s 347D(4) (changed)
(4)	new
(5)	1985, s 347C(4), s 347D(6)
(6)	1985, s 347C(2), s 347D(4) (changed)
(7)	new
368(1)	1985, s 347C(3)(b), s 347D(5)
(2)	1985, s 347C(3), s 347D(5)
369(1)	1985, s 347F(1)
(2)	1985, s 347F(2), (3), (4)
(3)	1985, s 347F(2), (6) (changed)
(4)	new
(5)	1985, s 347F(3)
(6)	1985, s 347F(5)
370(1)	1985, s 347I(1) (changed)
(2)	1985, s 347I(1)
(3)	1985, s 54(2), s 347I(2) (changed)
(4)	1985, s 347I(3)
(5)	new
371(1)	1985, s 347I(3)
(2)	1985, s 347I(4), (5)
(3)	1985, s 347I(6)
(4)	1985, s 347I(7)
(5)	1985, s 347I(8)
372(1)	1985, s 347J(1)
(2)	1985, s 347J(2)
(3)	1985, s 347J(3)
(4)	1985, s 347J(4), (5)
(5)	1985, s 347J(6)
373(1)	1985, s 347K(1)
(2)	1985, s 347K(2)
374(1)–(3)	new
375(1)	1985, s 347B(1)
(2)	1985, s 347B(2) (changed)
376(1), (2)	1985, s 347B(3)
377(1)	1985, s 347B(8)
(2)	1985, s 347B(10)
(3)	1985, s 347B(9)
(4)	1985, s 347B(11)
378(1)	1985, ss 347B(4), (6), (7) (changed)
(2)	new
(3)	1985, s 347B(5)
379(1)	1985, s 347A(3), (8)
(2)	1985, s 347A(10)
PART 15 ACCOUNTS AND REPORTS	
Chapter 1 Introduction	
380(1)–(4)	drafting
381	drafting
382(1)	1985, s 247(1)(a)

CA 2006	Origin
(2)	1985, s 247(1)(b), (2)
(3), (4)	1985, s 247(3), (4)
(5)	1985, s 247(5) (changed)
(6)	1985, s 247(6), Sch 4, para 56(2), (3)
(7)	drafting
383(1)	1985, s 247A(3)
(2)	1985, s 249(1)(a)
(3)	1985, s 249(1)(b), (2)
(4)	1985, s 249(3)
(5), (6)	1985, s 249(4)
(7)	1985, s 249(5), (6)
384(1)	1985, s 247A(1)–(1B)
(2)	1985, s 247A(2) (changed)
(3)	1985, s 247A(2A)
385(1)	new
(2)	1985, s 262(1) "quoted company"
(3)	drafting
(4)–(6)	new
Chapter 2 Accounting records	
386(1), (2)	1985, s 221(1)
(3)–(5)	1985, s 221(2)–(4)
387(1), (2)	1985, s 221(5)
(3)	1985, s 221(6), Sch 24
388(1)–(3)	1985, s 222(1)–(3)
(4), (5)	1985, s 222(5)
389(1), (2)	1985, s 222(4)
(3)	1985, s 222(6)
(4)	1985, s 222(4), (6), Sch 24
Chapter 3 A company's financial year	
390(1)–(5)	1985, s 223(1)–(5)
391(1)	1985, s 224(1)
(2)	1985, s 224(2), (3)
(3)	1986 art 232(2), (3)
(4)	1985, s 224(3A), 1986 art 232(3A)
(5)–(7)	1985, s 224(4)–(6)
392(1)	1985, s 225(1)
(2)–(6)	1985, s 225(3)–(7)
Chapter 4 Annual accounts	
393(1), (2)	new
394	1985, s 226(1)
395(1)–(5)	1985, s 226(2)–(6)
396(1), (2)	1985, s 226A(1), (2)
(3)	1985, s 226A(3) (changed)
(4)	1985, s 226A(4)
(5)	1985, s 226A(5), (6)
397	1985, s 226B
398	1985, ss 227(8), 248(1) (changed)
399(1), (2)	1985, ss 227(1), (8), 248(1), (2) (changed)
(3)	1985, s 227(8)
(4)	new
400(1), (2)	1985, s 228(1), (2)

CA 2006	Origin
(3)	1985, s 228(5)
(4)	1985, s 228(3)
(5)	1985, s 228(4)
(6)	1985, s 228(6)
401(1), (2)	1985, s 228A(1), (2)
(3)	1985, s 228A(5)
(4)	1985, s 228A(3)
(5)	1985, s 228A(4)
(6)	1985, s 228A(6)
402	1985, s 229(5)
403(1)–(6)	1985, s 227(2)–(7)
404(1), (2)	1985, s 227A(1), (2)
(3)	1985, s 227A(3) (changed)
(4)	1985, s 227A(4)
(5)	1985, s 227A(5), (6)
405(1), (2)	1985, s 229(1), (2)
(3), (4)	1985, s 229(3)
406	1985, s 227B
407(1)–(5)	1985, s 227C(1)–(5)
408(1)	1985, s 230(1) (changed)
(2)	1985, s 230(2) (changed)
(3), (4)	1985, s 230(3), (4)
409(1), (2)	1985, s 231(1), (2) (changed)
(3), (4)	1985, s 231(3) (changed)
(5)	1985, s 231(4)
410(1), (2)	1985, s 231(5)
(3)	1985, s 231(6)
(4), (5)	1985, s 231(7), Sch 24
411(1)	1985, ss 231A(1), 246(3)(b)(ai)
(2)	1985, s 231A(5)
(3)–(5)	1985, s 231A(2)–(4)
(6)	1985, s 231A(7), Sch 4, para 94(1), (2)
(7)	1985, s 231A(6)
412(1)–(4)	new
(5)	1985, s 232(3)
(6)	1985, s 232(4), Sch 24
413(1)–(8)	new
414(1), (2)	1985, s 233(1), (2)
(3)	1985, s 246(8)
(4), (5)	1985, s 233(5) (changed), Sch 24
Chapter 5 Directors' report	
415(1)	1985, s 234(1)
(2), (3)	1985, s 234(2), (3)
(4), (5)	1985, s 234(5), Sch 24
416(1)	1985, s 234ZZA(1)(a), (b)
(2)	1985, s 234ZZA(2)
(3)	1985, ss 234ZZA(1)(c), 246(4)(a)
(4)	1985, s 234ZZA(3), (4) (changed)
417(1)	1985, ss 234(1)(a), 246(4)(a)
(2)	new

CA 2006	Origin
(3), (4)	1985, s 234ZZB(1), (2)
(5)	new
(6)	1985, s 234ZZB(3), (5)
(7)	1985, s 246A(2A)
(8)	1985, s 234ZZB(4)
(9)	1985, s 234ZZB(6)
(10), (11)	new
418(1)	1985, s 234ZA(1)
(2)	1985, ss 234(1)(b), 234ZA(2)
(3), (4)	1985, s 234ZA(3), (4)
(5), (6)	1985, s 234ZA(6), Sch 24
419(1)	1985, s 234A(1)
(2)	1985, s 246(8)(b)
(3), (4)	1985, ss 234(5), 234A(4) (changed), Sch 24

Chapter 6 Quoted companies: directors' remuneration report

CA 2006	Origin
420(1)	1985, s 421(1)
(2)	1985, s 234B(3), (4) (changed)
(3)	1985, s 234B(3), Sch 24
421(1), (2)	1985, s 234B(1), (2) (changed)
(3)	1985, s 234B(5), (6)
(4)	1985, s 234B(6), Sch 24
422(1)	1985, s 234C(1)
(2), (3)	1985, s 234C(4) (changed), Sch 24

Chapter 7 Publication of accounts and reports

CA 2006	Origin
423(1)	1985, s 238(1), (1A)
(2), (3)	new
(4)	1985, s 238(3)
(5)	1985, s 238(6)
(6)	drafting
424(1)–(3)	1985, s 238(1) (changed)
(4)	1985, s 238(4) (changed)
(5)	new
(6)	drafting
425(1), (2)	1985, s 238(5), Sch 24
426(1)	1985, s 251(1)
(2), (3)	1985, s 251(2)
(4)	drafting
(5)	new
(6)	1985, s 251(5)
427(1)	1985, s 251(1) "summary financial statement"
(2)	1985, s 251(3)
(3)	1985, s 251(3A)
(4)	1985, s 251(4)
(5)	new
(6)	1985, s 251(5)
428(1)	1985, s 251(1) "summary financial statement"
(2)	1985, s 251(3)
(3)	1985, s 251(3A)

CA 2006	Origin
(4)	1985, s 251(4)
(5)	new
(6)	1985, s 251(5)
429(1), (2)	1985, s 251(6), Sch 24
430(1)–(7)	new
431(1), (2)	1985, s 239(1), (2)
(3), (4)	1985, s 239(3), Sch 24
432(1), (2)	1985, s 239(1), (2)
(3), (4)	1985, s 239(3), Sch 24
433(1)–(3)	1985, ss 233(3), 234A(2) and 234C(2)
(4), (5)	1985, ss 233(6)(a), 234A(4)(a) and 234C(4)(a), Sch 24
434(1)	1985, s 240(1) (changed)
(2)	1985, s 240(2) (changed)
(3)	1985, s 240(5)
(4), (5)	1985, s 240(6), Sch 24
(6)	1985, s 251(7)
435(1), (2)	1985, s 240(3) (changed)
(3)	1985, s 240(5) (changed)
(4)	new
(5), (6)	1985, s 240(6), Sch 24
(7)	1985, s 251(7)
436(1), (2)	1985, ss 233(3), 234A(2), 234C(2), 240(4) (changed)

Chapter 8 Public companies: laying of accounts and reports before general meeting

CA 2006	Origin
437(1)	1985, s 241(1) (changed)
(2)	1985, s 241(2)
(3)	drafting
438(1)–(3)	1985, s 241(2)–(4)
(4)	1985, s 241(2), Sch 24

Chapter 9 Quoted companies: members' approval of directors' remuneration report

CA 2006	Origin
439(1)	1985, s 241A(1), (3)
(2)	1985, s 241A(4)
(3)	1985, s 241A(5), (7)
(4)	1985, s 241A(6)
(5)	1985, s 241A(8)
(6)	1985, s 241A(2), (12)
440(1)	1985, s 241A(9)
(2), (3)	1985, s 241A(10), (11)
(4)	1985, s 241A(9), (10), Sch 24
(5)	1985, s 241A(2), (12)

Chapter 10 Filing of accounts and reports

CA 2006	Origin
441(1)	1985, s 242(1)
(2)	drafting
442(1)	drafting
(2), (3)	1985, s 244(1), (2) (changed)
(4), (5)	1985, s 244(4), (5)
(6)	new
(7)	1985, s 244(6)
443(1)–(5)	new

CA 2006	Origin
444(1)	1985, ss 242(1)(a), (b), 246(5)
(2)	1985, ss 242(1)(d), 249E(1)(b) (changed)
(3)	1985, s 246(5), (6) (changed)
(4)	1985, s 247B(2)
(5)	1985, s 246(8)
(6)	1985, ss 233(4), 234A(3), 246(7)
(7)	1985, s 236(3)
445(1)	1985, ss 242(1)(a), (b), 246A(1)
(2)	1985, ss 242(1)(d), 249E(1)(b) (changed)
(3)	1985, s 246A(2), (3) (changed)
(4)	1985, s 247B(2)
(5)	1985, ss 233(4), 234A(3) (changed)
(6)	new
(7)	drafting
446(1)	1985, s 242(1)(a), (b)
(2)	1985, ss 242(1)(d), 249E(1)(b)
(3)	1985, ss 233(4), 234A(3) (changed)
(4)	new
(5)	drafting
447(1)	1985, s 242(1)(a), (b), (c)
(2)	1985, ss 242(1)(d)
(3)	1985, ss 233(4), 234A(3), 234C(3) (changed)
(4)	new
448(1)–(3)	1985, s 254(1)–(3)
(4)	1985, s 254(4)
(5)	1985, s 244(6)
449(1)–(5)	1985, s 247B(1)–(5)
450(1), (2)	1985, ss 233(1), (2), 246(7)
(3)	1985, s 246(8), 246A(4)
(4), (5)	1985, s 233(5), Sch 24
451(1)	1985, s 242(2)
(2), (3)	1985, s 242(4), (5)
(4)	1985, s 242(2), Sch 24
452(1), (2)	1985, s 242(3)
453(1)	1985, s 242A(1)
(2)	1985, s 242A(2) (changed)
(3), (4)	1985, s 242A(3), (4)
(5)	new
Chapter 11 Revision of defective accounts and reports	
454(1)–(3)	1985, s 245(1)–(3)
(4)	1985, s 245(4) (changed)
(5)	1985, s 245(5)
455(1), (2)	1985, s 245A(1)
(3)–(5)	1985, s 245A(2)–(4)
456(1)–(3)	1985, s 245B(1)–(3)
(4)	1985, s 245B(3A)

CA 2006	Origin
(5)–(8)	1985, s 245B(4)–(7)
457(1)	1985, s 245C(1)
(2), (3)	1985, s 245C(2), (3)
(4)	1985, s 245C(4B)
(5)	1985, s 245C(1A), (4A)
(6)	1985, s 245C(5)
(7)	1985, s 245C(4)
458(1)	1985, s 245D(1), (3)
(2)	1985, s 245D(2)
(3)	1985, s 245E(1), (2)
(4)	1985, s 245E(3), (4) (changed)
(5)	1985, s 245E(3), Sch 24
459(1)–(8)	1985, s 245F(1)–(8)
460(1), (2)	1985, s 245G(1), (2)
(3)	drafting; 1985, s 245G(3), (10)
(4)	1985, s 245G(7)(a), (8)
(5)	1985, s 245G(7)(b), Sch 24
461(1)	1985, s 245G(3)
(2)	1985, s 245G(3)(a)
(3)	1985, s 245G(3)(b), Sch 7B, Pt 1
(4)	1985, s 245G(3)(c), Sch 7B, Pt 2
(5), (6)	1985, s 245G(3)(d), Sch 7B, Pt 3
(7)	1985, s 245G(11)
462(1)–(3)	1985, s 245G(4)–(6)
Chapter 12 Supplementary provisions	
463(1)–(6)	new
464(1), (2)	1985, s 256(1), (2)
(3)	1985, s 256(4)
465(1)	1985, s 247(1)(a)
(2)	1985, s 247(1)(b), (2)
(3), (4)	1985, s 247(3), (4)
(5)	1985, s 247(5) (changed)
(6)	1985, s 247(6), Sch 4, para 56(2), (3)
(7)	drafting
466(1)	1985, s 247A(3)
(2)	1985, s 249(1)(a)
(3)	1985, s 249(1)(b), (2)
(4)	1985, s 249(3)
(5), (6)	1985, s 249(4)
(7)	1985, s 249(5), (6)
467(1)	1985, s 247A(1)–(1B)
(2)	1985, s 247A(2)
(3)	1985, s 247A(2A)
468(1)–(5)	new
469(1)–(4)	1985, s 242B(1)–(4) (changed)
470(1)	1985, s 255D(1)
(2)	1985, s 255D(2), (2A)
(3)	1985, s 255D(5)
(4)	1985, s 255D(4)

CA 2006	Origin
471(1)	1985, s 262(1) "annual accounts"
(2), (3)	1985, s 238(1A); drafting
472(1), (2)	1985, s 261(1), (2)
473(1)–(4)	1985, s 257(2), (3) (changed)
474(1)	1985, ss 262(1), 744 "regulated activity"
(2)	1985, s 262(2)
PART 16 AUDIT	
Chapter 1 Requirement for audited accounts	
475(1)	1985, s 235(1) (changed)
(2), (3)	1985, s 249B(4)
(4)	1985, s 249B(5)
476(1)–(3)	1985, s 249B(2)
477(1)	1985, s 249A(1)
(2)	1985, s 249A(3)
(3)	1985, s 249A(6)
(4)	1985, s 249A(3)(a), (7)
(5)	drafting
478	1985, s 249B(1)(a)–(e)
479(1)–(3)	1985, s 249B(1)(f), (1A)–(1C)
(4)	drafting
(5), (6)	1985, s 249B(1)(C)
480(1), (2)	1985, s 249AA(1), (2)
(3)	drafting
481	1985, s 249AA(3)
482(1)–(4)	new
483(1)–(5)	new
484(1)	1985, s 257(1)
484(2)	1985, s 257(4)(c)
484(3)	1985, s 257 (2)(b), (d)
484(4)	1985, s 257 (3)
Chapter 2 Appointment of auditors	
485(1)	1985, s 384(1)
(2)–(5)	new
486(1), (2)	1985, s 387(1), (2)
(3), (4)	1985, s 387(2), Sch 24
487(1)–(4)	new
488(1)–(3)	new
489(1)	1985, s 384(1) (changed)
(2)	1985, ss 384(2), 385(2)
(3)	1985, ss 385(3), 388(1) (changed)
(4)	1985, s 385(2), (4) (changed)
(5)	drafting
490(1), (2)	1985, s 387(1), (2)
(3), (4)	1985, s 387(2), Sch 24
491(1)	1985, s 385(2) (changed)
(2)	drafting
492(1)	1985, s 390A(1)
(2), (3)	1985, s 390A(2)
(4), (5)	1985, s 390A(4), (5)
493(1)–(4)	new

CA 2006	Origin
494(1)	1985, s 390B(1), (8)
(2)–(4)	1985, s 390B(2)–(4)
(5)	1985, s 390B(5)(a)
(6)	1985, s 390B(9)
Chapter 3 Functions of auditor	
495(1)	1985, s 235(1); drafting
(2)	1985, s 235(1A)
(3)	1985, s 235(1B), (2)
(4)	1985, s 235(2A)
496	1985, s 235(3)
497(1), (2)	1985, s 235(4), (5)
498(1)–(4)	1985, s 237(1)–(4)
(5)	1985, s 237(4A)
499(1), (2)	1985, s 389A(1), (2)
(3)	1985, s 389A(6)
(4)	1985, s 389A(7)
500(1)–(3)	1985, s 389A(3)–(5)
(4)	1985, s 389A(6)
(5)	1985, s 389A(7)
501(1)	1985, s 389B(1)
(2)	1985, s 389B(1), Sch 24
(3)	1985, s 389B(2), (3) (changed)
(4)	1985, s 389B(4)
(5)	1985, s 389B(4), Sch 24
(6)	1985, s 389B(5)
502(1)	1985, s 390(2)
(2)	1985, s 390(1)
(3)	1985, s 390(3)
503(1), (2)	1985, s 236(1)
(3)	new
504(1)–(4)	new
505(1), (2)	1985, s 236(2) (changed)
(3), (4)	1985, s 236(4), Sch 24
506(1), (2)	new
507(1)–(4)	new
508(1)–(4)	new
509(1)–(4)	new
Chapter 4 Removal, resignation, etc of auditors	
510(1), (2)	1985, s 391(1); drafting
(3)	1985, s 391(3)
(4)	drafting
511(1)	1985, s 391A(1)(a)
(2)–(6)	1985, s 391A(2)–(6)
512(1)	1985, s 391(2)
(2), (3)	1985, s 391(2), Sch 24
513(1), (2)	1985, s 391(4)
514(1)–(8)	new
515(1)	1985, s 391A(1)(b)
(2)	1985, s 391A(1) opening words (changed)
(3)–(7)	1985, s 391A(2)–(6)
516(1), (2)	1985, s 392(1)
(3)	1985, s 392(2)

CA 2006	Origin
517(1)	1985, s 392(3)
(2), (3)	1985, s 392(3), Sch 24
518(1)–(4)	1985, s 392A(1)–(4)
(5)	1985, s 392A(5)
(6), (7)	1985, s 392(5), Sch 24
(8)–(10)	1985, s 392A(6)–(8)
519(1)–(3)	1985, s 394(1) (changed)
(4)	1985, s 394(2) (changed)
(5), (6)	1985, s 394A(1), (2)
(7)	1985, s 394(1), Sch 24
520(1)	drafting
(2), (3)	1985, s 394(3), (4)
(4)	1985, s 394(6)
(5)	1985, s 394(7) (changed)
(6)	1985, s 394A(4)
(7)	new
(8)	1985, s 394A(4), Sch 24 (changed)
521(1)	1985, s 394(5)
(2)	1985, s 394(7)
(3), (4)	1985, s 394A(1), (2)
(5)	1985, s 394A(1), Sch 24
522(1)–(8)	new
523(1)–(6)	new
524(1)–(4)	new
525(1)–(3)	new
526	1985, s 388(2)

Chapter 5 Quoted companies: right of members to raise audit concerns at accounts meeting

CA 2006	Origin
527(1)–(6)	new
528(1)–(5)	new
529(1)–(4)	new
530(1), (2)	new
531(1), (2)	new

Chapter 6 Auditors' liability

CA 2006	Origin
532(1)	1985, s 310(1) (changed)
(2)	1985, s 310(2), drafting
(3)	1985, s 310(1)
(4)	new
533	1985, s 310(3)(b)
534(1)–(3)	new
535(1)–(5)	new
536(1)–(5)	new
537(1)–(3)	new
538(1)–(3)	new

Chapter 7 Supplementary provisions

CA 2006	Origin
539	1985, ss 262(1)

PART 17 A COMPANY'S SHARE CAPITAL

Chapter 1 Shares and share capital of a company

CA 2006	Origin
540(1)	1985, s 744 ("share")
(2), (3)	new
(4)	1985, s 744 ("share"), drafting
541	1985, s 182(1)(a)
542(1)–(5)	new

CA 2006	Origin
543(1), (2)	1985, s 182(2)
544(1), (2)	1985, s 182(1)(b)
(3)	drafting
545	new
546(1), (2)	new
547	1985, s 737(1), (2)
548	1985, s 744 ("equity share capital")

Chapter 2 Allotment of shares: general provisions

CA 2006	Origin
549(1)	1985, s 80(1), (2) (changed)
(2), (3)	1985, s 80(2)
(4)	1985, s 80(9)
(5)	1985, s 80(9), Sch 24
(6)	1985, s 80(10) (changed)
550	new
551(1)	1985, s 80(1), (2)
(2)	1985, s 80(3)
(3)	1985, s 80(4)
(4)	1985, s 80(4), (5)
(5)	1985, s 80(5)
(6)	1985, s 80(6)
(7)	1985, s 80(7)
(8)	1985, s 80(8)
(9)	drafting
552(1)	1985, s 98(1)
(2)	1985, s 98(2)
(3)	1985, s 98(3)
553(1)	1985, s 97(1)
(2)	1985, s 97(2)(a)
(3)	1985, s 98(4)
554(1)–(5)	new
555(1)	1985, s 88(1)
(2)	1985, s 88(2) (changed)
(3), (4)	new
556(1)	1985, s 128(1), (2) (changed)
(2), (3)	1985, s 128(1)
(4)	1985, s 128(2)
557(1)	1985, s 88(5), 128(5) (changed)
(2)	1985, s 88(5), s 128(5), Sch 24
(3)	1985, s 88(6) (changed)
558	1985, s 738(1)
559	1985, s 80(2)(a)

Chapter 3 Allotment of equity securities: existing shareholders' right of pre-emption

CA 2006	Origin
560(1)	1985, s 94(2), (5)
(2)	1985, s 94(3), (3A)
561(1)	1985, s 89(1)
(2)	1985, s 89(4)
(3)	1985, s 94(3)
(4)	1985, s 89(6)
(5)	drafting
562(1)	1985, s 90(1)

CA 2006	Origin
(2)	new
(3)	1985, s 90(5) (changed)
(4)	1985, s 90(6)
(5)	1985, s 90(6) (changed)
(6), (7)	new
563(1), (2)	1985, s 92(1)
(3)	1985, s 92(2)
564	1985, s 94(2)
565	1985, s 89(4)
566	1985, s 89(5)
567(1), (2)	1985, s 91(1)
(3), (4)	1985, s 91(2)
568(1)	1985, s 89(2), (3)
(2)	1985, s 89(3)
(3)	1985, s 90(1)
(4)	1985, s 92(1)
(5)	1985, s 92(2)
569(1), (2)	new
570(1), (2)	1985, s 95(1)
(3)	1985, s 95(3)
(4)	1985, s 95(4)
571(1), (2)	1985, s 95(2)
(3)	1985, s 95(3)
(4)	1985, s 95(4)
(5), (6)	1985, s 95(5)
(7)	1985, s 95(5), Sch 15A, para 3(1), (2)
572(1), (2)	1985, s 95(6)
(3)	1985, s 95(6), Sch 24
573(1)	1985, s 95(2A)
(2)	1985, s 95(1), (2A)
(3)	1985, s 95(1), (2A), (4)
(4)	1985, s 95(2), (2A)
(5)	1985, s 95(1), (2A), (4), (5), Sch 15A, para 3(1), (2)
574(1), (2)	1985, s 94(7)
575(1)	1985, s 93(1)
(2)	1985, s 93(2)
576(1)	1985, s 96(1), (2)
(2)	1985, s 96(3)
(3)	1985, s 96(4)
577	1985, s 94(2)

Chapter 4 Public companies: allotment where issue not fully subscribed

CA 2006	Origin
578(1)	1985, s 84(1)
(2)	1985, s 84(2)
(3)	1985, s 84(3) (changed)
(4)	1985, s 84(4)
(5)	1985, s 84(4), (5)
(6)	1985, s 84(6)
579(1), (2)	1985, s 85(1)
(3)	1985, s 85(2)
(4)	1985, s 85(3)

Chapter 5 Payment for shares

CA 2006	Origin
580(1)	1985, s 100(1)
(2)	1985, s 100(2)

CA 2006	Origin
581	1985, s 119
582(1)	1985, s 99(1)
(2)	1985, s 99(4)
(3)	1985, s 99(1)
583(1)	drafting
(2)–(3)(d)	1985, s 738(2)
(3)(e), (4)	new
(4)	new
(5)	1985, s 738(3)
(6)	1985, s 738(4)
(7)	new
584	1985, s 106
585(1)	1985, s 99(2)
(2)	1985, s 99(3)
(3)	1985, s 99(5)
586(1)	1985, s 101(1)
(2)	1985, s 101(2)
(3)	1985, s 101(3), (4)
(4)	1985, s 101(5)
587(1)	1985, s 102(1)
(2)	1985, s 102(2)
(3)	1985, s 102(3), (4)
(4)	1985, s 102(5), (6)
(5)	1985, s 102(7)
588(1)	1985, s 112(1), (5)(a)
(2)	1985, s 112(3)
(3)	1985, s 112(4)
(4)	1985, s 112(5)(b)
589(1), (2)	1985, s 113(1)
(3)	1985, s 113(2), (3) (changed)
(4)	1985, s 113(4)
(5)	1985, s 113(5)
(6)	1985, s 113(6), (7)
590(1)	1985, s 114
(2)	1985, s 114., Sch 24
591(1), (2)	1985, s 115(1)
592(1), (2)	1985, s 107

Chapter 6 Public companies: independent valuation of non-cash consideration

CA 2006	Origin
593(1)	1985, s 103(1)
(2)	1985, s 103(2)
(3)	1985, s 103(6)
(4)	drafting
594(1)–(3)	1985, s 103(3)
(4), (5)	1985, s 103(4)
(6)	1985, s 103(7)
595(1), (2)	1985, s 103(5)
(3)	1985, s 103(7)(b)
596(1)	drafting
(2)	1985, s 108(4)
(3)	1985, s 108(6)
(4), (5)	1985, s 108(7)
597(1), (2)	1985, s 111(1)
(3), (4)	1985, s 111(3), Sch 24

CA 2006	Origin
(5), (6)	1985, ss 88(6), 111(3)
598(1)	1985, s 104(1)
(2)	1985, s 104(2)
(3)	drafting
(4)	1985, s 104(6)(a)
(5)	1985, s 104(6)(b)
599(1)	1985, s 104(4)(a), (b), (d)
(2)	1985, s 104(5)(a)
(3)	1985, s 104(4)(d)
(4)	1985, s 104(5)(b)
600(1)	drafting
(2)	1985, s 109(2)(a), (b)
(3)	1985, s 108(6)(a), (b), (c), 109(2)(c), (d)
(4), (5)	1985, s 109(3)
601(1), (2)	1985, s 104(4)(c), (d)
(3)	1985, s 104(4)(c) (changed)
602(1)	1985, s 111(2)
(2), (3)	1985, s 111(4), Sch 24
603	1985, s 104(3)
604(1)	1985, s 105(1)
(2)	1985, s 105(2)
(3)	1985, s 105(3)
605(1)	1985, s 112(1)
(2)	1985, s 112(2)
(3)	1985, s 112(3)
(4)	1985, s 112(4)
606(1)	1985, s 113(1)
(2)	1985, s 113(2), (3) (changed)
(3)	1985, s 113(4)
(4)	1985, s 113(5)
(5)	1986, s 113(6), (7)
(6)	1986, s 113(8)
607(1)	drafting
(2)	1985, s 114
(3)	1985, s 114, Sch 24
608(1), (2)	1985, s 115(1)
609(1), (2)	1985, s 107
Chapter 7 Share premiums	
610(1)	1985, s 130(1)
(2), (3)	1985, s 130(2) (changed)
(4)	1985, s 130(3)
(5), (6)	1985, s 130(4)
611(1)	1985, s 132(1)
(2)	1985, s 132(2)
(3)	1985, s 132(3)
(4)	1985, s 132(4)
(5)	1985, s 132(5)
612(1)	1985, s 131(1)
(2)	1985, s 131(2)
(3)	1985, s 131(3)
(4)	1985, s 131(1), 132(8)
613(1)	drafting
(2), (3)	1985, s 131(4)

CA 2006	Origin
(4)	1985, s 131(5)
(5)	1985, s 131(6)
614(1)	1985, s 134(1)
(2)	1985, s 134(3)
615	1985, s 133(1)
616(1)	1985, s 131(7), 133(4)
(2)	1985, s 133(2)
(3)	1985, s 133(3)
Chapter 8 Alteration of share capital	
617(1)	1985, s 121(1) (changed)
(2)	1985, s 121(2)(a) (changed)
(3)	1985, s 121(2)(b), (c), (d) (changed)
(4), (5)	new
618(1)	1985, s 121(2)(b), (d)
(2)	1985, s 121(3) (changed)
(3)	1985, s 121(4) (changed)
(4), (5)	new
619(1)	1985, s 122(1)(a), (d)
(2), (3)	1985, s 122(1) (changed)
(4)	1985, s 122(2)
(5)	1985, s 122(2), Sch 24
620(1)	1985, s 121(2)(c) (changed)
(2)	1985, s 121(4) (changed)
(3)	new
621(1)	1985, s 122(1)(c)
(2), (3)	new
(4)	1985, s 122(2)
(5)	1985, s 122(2), Sch 24
622(1)–(8)	new
623	new
624(1)–(3)	new
625(1)–(5)	new
626(1)–(6)	new
627(1)–(8)	new
628(1)–(3)	new
Chapter 9 Classes of share and class rights	
629(1)	new
(2)	1985, s 128(2)
630(1)	1985, s 125(1)
(2)–(4)	1985, s 125(2) (changed)
(5)	1985, s 125(7)
(6)	1985, s 125(8)
631(1)–(6)	new
632	1985, s 126 (changed)
633(1)	1985, s 127(1)(b)
(2)	1985, s 127(2), (2A)
(3)	1985, s 127(2)
(4)	1985, s 127(3)
(5)	1985, s 127(4)
(6)	1985, s 127(6)
634(1)–(6)	new
635(1)–(3)	1985, s 127(5)
636(1)	1985, s 128(4) (changed)

Part 3 CA 2006 Supporting Materials

CA 2006	Origin
(2)	1985, s 128(5)
(3)	1985, s 128(5), Sch 24
637(1)	1985, s 128(3) (changed)
(2)	1985, s 128(5)
(3)	1985, s 128(5), Sch 24
638(1)	1985, s 129(1) (changed)
(2)	1985, s 129(4)
(3)	1985, s 129(4), Sch 24
639(1)	1985, s 129(3) (changed)
(2)	1985, s 129(4)
(3)	1985, s 129(4), Sch 24
640(1)	1985, s 129(2) (changed)
(2)	1985, s 129(4)
(3)	1985, s 129(4), Sch 24
Chapter 10 Reduction of share capital	
641(1)–(3)	1985, s 135(1) (changed)
(4)	1985, s 135(2)
(5), (6)	new
642(1)–(4)	new
643(1)–(5)	new
644(1)–(9)	new
645(1)	1985, s 136(1)
(2)	1985, s 136(2), (6)
(3)	1985, s 136(6)
(4)	1985, s 136(2)
646(1)	1985, s 136(3)
(2), (3)	1985, s 136(4)
(4), (5)	1985, s 136(5)
647(1)	1985, s 141 (changed)
(2)	1985, s 141, Sch 24
648(1), (2)	1985, s 137(1)
(3)	1985, s 137(2)(b)
(4)	1985, s 137(2)(a), (3)
649(1)	1985, s 138(1) (changed)
(2)	new
(3)	1985, s 138(2) (changed)
(4)	1985, s 138(3) (changed)
(5)	1985, s 138(4) (changed)
(6)	1985, s 138(4)
650(1)	1985, s 139(1)
(2)	1985, s 139(2)
(3)	drafting
651(1), (2)	1985, s 139(3)
(3)	1985, s 139(4) (changed)
(4)	1985, s 139(5)
(5)	new
(6)	1985, s 139(5)(a)
(7)	1985, s 139(5)(b)
652(1)	1985, s 140(1) (changed)
(2)	drafting
(3)	1985, s 140(5)
653(1)	1985, s 140(2)
(2)	1985, s 140(3)
(3)	1985, s 140(4)
(4)	drafting

CA 2006	Origin
Chapter 11 Miscellaneous and supplementary provisions	
654(1)–(3)	new
655	1985, s 111A
656(1)–(3)	1985, s 142(1)
(4)	1985, s 142(2) (changed)
(5)	1985, s 142(2), Sch 24
(6)	1985, s 142(3)
657(1)–(4)	new
PART 18 ACQUISITION BY LIMITED COMPANY OF ITS OWN SHARES	
Chapter 1 General provisions	
658(1)	1985, s 143(1)
(2)	1985, s 143(2)
(3)	1985, s 143(2), Sch 24
659(1), (2)	1985, s 143(3)
660(1), (2)	1985, s 144(1) (changed)
(3)	1985, s 145(1), (2)(a)
661(1), (2)	1985, s 144(2) (changed)
(3)	1985, s 144(3)
(4)	1985, s 144(4)
(5)	1985, s 145(2)(a)
662(1)	1985, s 146(1)
(2)	1985, s 146(2)
(3)	1985, s 146(2), (3)
(4)	1985, s 147(1)
(5), (6)	1985, s 146(4)
663(1)	1985, s 122(1)(f)
(2), (3)	new
(4)	1985, s 122(2)
(5)	1985, s 122(2), Sch 24
664(1), (2)	1985, s 147(2) (changed)
(3)	new
(4)	1985, s 147(3) (changed)
(5), (6)	new
665(1), (2)	1985, s 147(4)
(3)	new
(4)	1985, s 147(4)(a) (changed)
(5)	1985, s 147(4)(b)
666(1), (2)	1985, s 149(1)
667(1), (2)	1985, s 149(2)
(3)	1985, s 149(2), Sch 24
668(1), (2)	1985, s 148(1)
(3)	1985, s 148(2)
669(1), (2)	1985, s 148(4)
670(1)	1985, s 150(1)
(2)	1985, s 150(2)
(3)	1985, s 150(3)
(4)	1985, s 150(4)
671	1985, s 145(3), s 146(1), s 148(3)
672(1)	1985, Sch 2, para 1(1)
(2)	1985, Sch 2, para 1(2)
(3)	1985, Sch 2, para 1(3)
(4)	1985, Sch 2, para 1(4)

CA 2006	Origin
(5)	1985, Sch 2, para 2(3)
(6)	1985, Sch 2, para 2(4)
673(1)	1985, Sch 2, para 3(1)(a), (2)
(2)	1985, Sch 2, para 3(1)(b), (2)(a)
674	1985, Sch 2, para 4(1), (3)
675(1), (2)	1985, Sch 2, para 5(1), (2)
676	1985, Sch 2, para 5(1), (3)
Chapter 2 Financial assistance for purchase of own shares	
677(1)	1985, s 152(1)(a)
(2), (3)	1985, s 152(2)
678(1)	1985, s 151(1) (changed)
(2)	1985, s 153(1)
(3)	1985, s 151(2) (changed)
(4)	1985, s 153(2)
(5)	drafting
679(1)	1985, s 151(1) (changed)
(2)	1985, s 153(1) (changed)
(3)	1985, s 151(2) (changed)
(4)	1985, s 153(2) (changed)
(5)	drafting
680(1)	1985, s 151(3)
(2)	1985, s 151(3), Sch 24
681(1), (2)	1985, s 153(3)
682(1)	1985, s 153(4), s 154(1)
(2)	1985, s 153(4)
(3), (4)	1985, s 154(2)
(5)	1985, s 153(5)
683(1)	1985, s 152(1)(b), (c)
(2)	1985, s 152(3)
Chapter 3 Redeemable shares	
684(1)	1985, s 159(1) (changed)
(2)	new
(3)	1985, s 159(1) (changed)
(4)	1985, s 159(2)
685(1)–(4)	new
686(1)–(3)	1985, s 159(3) (changed)
687(1)–(3)	1985, s 160(1)
(4), (5)	1985, s 160(2)
(6)	1985, s 160(1)
688	1985, s 160(4) (changed)
689(1)	1985, s 122(1)(e)
(2), (3)	new
(4)	1985, s 122(2)
(5)	1985, s 122(2), Sch 24
Chapter 4 Purchase of own shares	
690(1)	1985, s 162(1) (changed)
(2)	1985, s 162(3)
691(1), (2)	1985, s 159(3), s 162(2)
692(1), (2)	1985, s 160(1), s 162(2)
(3), (4)	1985, s 160(2), s 162(2)
(5)	1985, s 160(1), s 162(2)
693(1)	1985, s 164(1), s 166(1)

CA 2006	Origin
(2)	1985, s 163(1)
(3)	1985, s 163(2)
(4)	1985, s 163(3)
(5)	1985, s 163(4), (5)
694(1)	1985, s 164(1)
(2)	1985, s 164(2), s 165(2) (changed)
(3)	1985, s 165(1)
(4)	1985, s 164(3), 165(2)
(5)	1985, s 164(4), 165(2)
(6)	drafting
695(1)	1985, s 164(5), 165(2)
(2)	1985, Sch 15A, para 5(1), (2)
(3), (4)	1985, s 164(5), s 165(2)
696(1)	1985, s 164(6), s 165(2)
(2)	1985, s 164(6), s 165(2), Sch 15A, para 5(3), (4)
(3)–(5)	1985, s 164(6), s 165(2)
697(1), (2)	1985, s 164(7)
(3)	1985, s 164(3), (7)
(4)	1985, s 164(4), (7)
(5)	drafting
698(1)	1985, s 164(5), (7)
(2)	1985, Sch 15A, para 5(1), (2)
(3), (4)	1985, s 164(5), (7)
699(1)	1985, s 164(6), (7)
(2)	1985, s 164(6), (7), Sch 15A, para 5(3)
(3)–(6)	1985, s 164(6), (7)
700(1), (2)	1985, s 167(2)
(3)	1985, s 164(3), (7), s 167(2)
(4)	1985, s 164(4), (7), s 167(2)
(5)	1985, s 164(5), (6), (7), s 167(2)
701(1)	1985, s 166(1)
(2)	1985, s 166(2)
(3)	1985, s 166(3)(a), (b)
(4)	1985, s 166(4)
(5)	1985, s 166(3)(c), (4)
(6)	1985, s 166(5)
(7)	1985, s 166(6)
(8)	1985, s 166(7)
702(1)–(4)	1985, s 169(4) (changed)
(5)	new
(6)	1985, s 169(5)
(7)	1985, s 169(9)
703(1)	1985, s 169(7) (changed)
(2)	1985, s 169(7), Sch 24
(3)	1985, s 169(8)
704	1985, s 167(1)
705(1)	1985, s 168(1)
(2)	1985, s 168(2)
706	1985, s 160(4), s 162(2), (2B)

CA 2006	Origin
707(1)–(3)	1985, s 169(1), (1A), (1B) (changed)
(4)	1985, s 169(2)
(5)	1985, s 169(3)
(6)	1985, s 169(6)
(7)	1985, s 169(6), Sch 24
708(1)	1985, s 169(1), (1A), (1B) (changed)
(2), (3)	new
(4)	1985, s 169(6)
(5)	1985, s 169(6), Sch 24

Chapter 5 Redemption or purchase by private company out of capital

CA 2006	Origin
709(1)	1985, s 171(1) (changed)
(2)	1985, s 171(2)
710(1), (2)	1985, s 171(3)
711(1), (2)	1985, s 172(1)
712(1)	drafting
(2)	1985, s 172(2)
(3)	1985, s 172(4)
(4)	1985, s 172(5)
(5)	drafting
(6)	1985, s 172(3)
(7)	1985, s 172(6)
713(1), (2)	1985, s 173(1)
714(1)–(3)	1985, s 173(3) (changed)
(4)	1985, s 173(4) (changed)
(5), (6)	1985, s 173(5) (changed)
715(1)	1985, s 173(6)
(2)	1985, s 173(6), Sch 24
716(1)	1985, s 173(2)
(2)	1985, s 174(1)
(3)	drafting
717(1)	drafting
(2)	1985, Sch 15A, para 6(1), (2)
(3)	1985, s 174(2)
(4)	1985, s 174(3), (5)
718(1)	drafting
(2)	1985, s 174(4), Sch 15A, para 6(1), (3)
(3)	1985, s 174(4)
719(1)	1985, s 175(1)
(2)	1985, s 175(2)
(3)	1985, s 175(3)
(4)	1985, s 175(4), (5)
720(1)	1985, s 175(4), (6)(a)
(2)	1985, s 175(6)(a) (changed)
(3)	new
(4)	1985, s 175(6)(b)
(5)	1985, s 175(7) (changed)
(6)	1985, s 175(7), Sch 24
(7)	1985, s 175(8)
721(1)	1985, s 176(1)
(2)	1985, s 176(1), (2)
(3)	1985, s 177(1)

CA 2006	Origin
(4), (5)	1985, s 177(2)
(6)	1985, s 177(3)
(7)	1985, s 177(4)
722(1)	new
(2)	1985, s 176(3)(a)
(3)	1985, s 176(3)(b)
(4)	1985, s 176(4)
(5)	1985, s 176(4), Sch 24
723(1)	1985, s 174(1)
(2)	drafting

Chapter 6 Treasury shares

CA 2006	Origin
724(1)	1985, s 162(2B)
(2)	1985, s 162(4)
(3)	1985, s 162A(1)
(4)	1985, s 162A(2)
(5)	1985, s 162A(3)
725(1)	1985, s 162B(1)
(2)	1985, s 162B(2)
(3)	1985, s 162B(3)
(4)	1985, s 143(2A)
726(1)	1985, s 162C(1)
(2)	1985, s 162C(2), (3)
(3)	1985, s 162C(4)
(4)	1985, s 162C(5)
(5)	1985, s 162C(6)
727(1)	1985, s 162D(1)(a), (b)
(2)	1985, s 162D(2) (changed)
(3)	1985, s 162D(3)
(4), (5)	new
728(1)	1985, s 169A(1)(b)(ii), (2)
(2)	1985, s 169A(2)
(3)	1985, s 169A(3)
(4)	1985, s 169A(4)
(5)	1985, s 169A(4), Sch 24
729(1)	1985, s 162D(1)(c)
(2)	1985, s 162E(1)
(3)	1985, s 162E(2)
(4)	1985, s 162D(4)
(5)	1985, s 162D(5)
730(1)	1985, s 169A(1)(b)(i), (2)
(2)	1985, s 169A(2)
(3)	1985, s 169A(3)
(4), (5)	new
(6)	1985, s 169A(4)
(7)	1985, s 169A(4), Sch 24
731(1)	1985, s 162F(1)
(2)	1985, s 162F(2)
(3)	1985, s 162F(3)
(4)	1985, s 162F(4), (5)
732(1)	1985, s 162G (changed)
(2)	1985, s 162G

Chapter 7 Supplementary provisions

CA 2006	Origin
733(1), (2)	1985, s 170(1)
(3)	1985, s 170(2), (3)

CA 2006	Origin
(4)	1985, s 170(1)
(5), (6)	1985, s 170(4)
734(1)	drafting
(2)	1985, s 171(4)
(3)	1985, s 171(5)
(4)	1985, s 171(6)
735(1)	1985, s 178(1)
(2)	1985, s 178(2), (3)
(3)	1985, s 178(3)
(4)	1985, s 178(4)
(5)	1985, s 178(5)
(6)	1985, s 178(6)
736	1985, s 181(a)
737(1)–(4)	new

PART 19 DEBENTURES

CA 2006	Origin
738	1985, s 744 ("debenture")
739(1), (2)	1985, s 193
740	1985, s 195
741(1)–(4)	new
742	1985, s 197
743(1)	new
(2)	1985, s 190(5) (changed)
(3)	1985, s 190(6)
(4), (5)	new
(6)	1985, s 190(1), (5)
744(1)	1985, s 191(1)
(2)	1985, s 191(2)
(3), (4)	new
(5)	1985, s 191(6)
(6)	new
745(1)–(5)	new
746(1)	1985, s 191(4) (changed)
(2)	1985, s 191(4), Sch 24
(3)	1985, s 191(5)
747(1)–(3)	new
748(1)	1985, s 191(7) (changed)
(2)	1985, s 191(7)
749(1)	1985, s 191(3)
(2)	1985, s 191(4)
(3)	1985, s 191(4), Sch 24
(4)	1985, s 191(5)
750(1)	1985, s 192(1)
(2)	1985, s 192(2)
(3)	1985, s 192(1)
751(1)	1985, s 192(3)
(2)	1985, s 192(3), 1986 art 201(3)
(3), (4)	1985, s 192(4)
752(1)	1985, s 194(1)
(2)	1985, s 194(2)
(3)	1985, s 194(4)
(4)	1985, s 194(5)
753	1985, s 194(3)
754(1)	1985, s 196(1)
(2)	1985, s 196(2)

CA 2006	Origin
(3)	1985, s 196(3)
(4)	1985, s 196(4)

PART 20 PUBLIC AND PRIVATE COMPANIES

Chapter 1 Prohibition of public offers by private companies

CA 2006	Origin
755(1)	1985, s 81(1) (changed)
(2)	1985, s 58(3)
(3), (4)	new
(5)	drafting
756(1), (2)	1985, s 742A(1)
(3)	1985, s 742A(2)
(4)	1985, s 742A(3), (4), and (5)
(5)	1985, s 742A(3)(a), (6)(b) (changed)
(6)	1985, s 742A(6)(a)
757(1)–(3)	new
758(1)–(4)	new
759(1)–(5)	new
760	1985, s 81(3)

Chapter 2 Minimum share capital requirement for public companies

CA 2006	Origin
761(1)	1985, s 117(1)
(2)	1985, s 117(2) (changed)
(3)	1985, s 117(4)
(4)	1985, s 117(6) (changed)
762(1)	1985, s 117(3) (changed)
(2)	new
(3)	1985, s 117(5)
763(1)	1985, s 118(1) (changed)
(2)–(6)	new
764(1)	1985, s 118(1) (changed)
(2)	new
(3)	1985, s 118(2)
(4)	1985, s 118(3)
765(1)–(4)	new
766(1)–(6)	new
767(1)	1985, s 117(7)
(2)	1985, s 117(7), Sch 24
(3)	1985, s 117(8)
(4)	new

PART 21 CERTIFICATION AND TRANSFER OF SECURITIES

Chapter 1 Certification and transfer of securities: general

CA 2006	Origin
768(1)	1985, s 186(1)(a)
(2)	1985, s 186(1)(b), (2)
769(1)	1985, s 185(1)(a)
(2)	1985, s 185(1), (4)(a), (b)
(3)	1985, s 185(5)
(4)	1985, s 185(5), Sch 24
770(1)	1985, s 183(1)
(2)	1985, s 183(2)
771(1)–(6)	new
772	1985, s 183(4)

Part 3   CA 2006 Supporting Materials

CA 2006	Origin
773	1985, s 183(3)
774	1985, s 187
775(1), (2)	1985, s 184(1)
(3)	1985, s 184(2)
(4)	1985, s 184(3)
776(1)	1985, s 185(1)(b)
(2)	1985, s 185(2)
(3)	1985, s 185(1), (4)(c)
(4)	drafting
(5)	1985, s 185(5)
(6)	1985, s 185(5), Sch 24
777(1), (2)	1985, s 185(3)
778(1)	1985, s 185(4), (4A)
(2)	1985, s 185(4B), (4C)
(3)	1985, s 185(4D)
779(1)	1985, s 188(1)
(2)	1985, s 188(2)
(3)	1985, s 188(3)
780(1)–(4)	new
781(1)	1985, s 189(1)
(2)	1985, s 189(2)
(3)	1985, s 189(1), Sch 24
(4)	1985, s 189(2), Sch 24
782(1)	1985, s 185(6)
(2), (3)	1985, s 185(7)

Chapter 2 Evidencing and transfer of title to securities without written instrument

CA 2006	Origin
783	1989, s 207(1), (10)
784(1), (2)	new
(3)	1989, s 207(9)
785(1)	1989, s 207(1)
(2)	1989, s 207(2)
(3)	1989, s 207(3)
(4)	1989, s 207(4)
(5)	1989, s 207(5)
(6)	1989, s 207(6)
786(1)–(5)	new
787(1)–(3)	new
788	1989, s 207(7)
789	new
790	new

PART 22 INFORMATION ABOUT INTERESTS IN A COMPANY'S SHARES

CA 2006	Origin
791	new
792(1)	1985, s 198(2) (changed)
(2)	1985, s 198(2)(b)
793(1), (2)	1985, s 212(1) (changed)
(3)	1985, s 212(2)(a)
(4)	1985, s 212(2)(b)
(5)	1985, s 212(3)
(6)	1985, s 212(2)(c)
(7)	1985, s 212(4)
794(1)	1985, s 216(1)
(2)	1985, s 216(1B)
(3)	1985, s 216(1A)

CA 2006	Origin
(4)	drafting
795(1)	1985, s 216(3)
(2)	1985, s 216(4)
(3)	1985, s 216(3), Sch 24
796(1), (2)	1985, s 216(5)
797(1)	1985, s 454(1)
(2)	1985, s 454(2)
(3)	1985, s 454(3)
(4)	1985, s 454(2), (3)
798(1), (2)	1985, s 455(1)
(3)	1985, s 455(2)
(4)	1985, s 455(2), Sch 24
(5)	1985, s 455(1), (2)
799(1)	1985, s 456(1A)
(2)	1985, s 456(2)
(3)	1985, s 456(1A)
800(1)	1985, s 456(1)
(2)	1985, s 456(2)
(3)	1985, s 456(3)
(4)	1985, s 456(6)
(5)	1985, s 456(7)
801(1), (2)	1985, s 456(4)
(3), (4)	1985, s 456(5)
(5)	1985, s 457(3)
802(1), (2)	1985, s 457(1)
(3)	1985, s 457(2)
(4)	1985, s 457(3)
803(1), (2)	1985, s 214(1) (changed)
(3)	1985, s 214(2) (changed)
804(1)	1985, s 214(4)
(2)	1985, s 214(5) (changed)
(3)	1985, s 214(5), Sch 24
805(1)	1985, s 215(1), (3)
(2)	1985, s 215(2)
(3)	1985, s 215(2), (3)
(4)	1985, s 215(7) (changed)
(5)	new
(6)	1985, s 215(5)
(7)	1985, s 215(6)
806(1), (2)	new
(3)	1985, s 215(8) (changed)
(4)	1985, s 215(8), Sch 24
807(1)	1985, s 215(7)(b), s 219(1)
(2)	1985, s 215(7)(b), s 219(2)
(3)	1985, s 215(7)(b), s 219(3)
(4)	1985, s 215(7)(b), s 219(3), Sch 24
(5)	1985, s 215(7)(b), s 219(4)
808(1)	1985, s 213(1)
(2)	1985, s 211(3), s 213(1), (3)
(3)	1985, s 213(1) (changed)
(4)	1985, s 211(5), s 213(3)
(5)	1985, s 211(10), s 213(3)
(6)	1985, s 211(10), s 213(3), Sch 24

CA 2006	Origin
(7)	1985, s 211(4), s 213(3)
809(1)	1985, s 211(8), s 213(3) (changed)
(2), (3)	1985, s 211(8), s 213(3), s 325(5), Sch 13, para 27
(4), (5)	new
810(1)–(3)	1985, s 211(6), s 213(3)
(4)	1985, s 211(8), s 213(3)
(5), (6)	new
811(1)	1985, s 211(8)(b), s 213(3), s 219(1)
(2)	1985, s 211(8)(b), s 213(3), s 219(2) (changed)
(3)	new
(4)	new
812(1)–(7)	new
813(1)	1985, s 211(8)(b), s 213(3), s 219(3) (changed)
(2)	1985, s 211(8)(b), s 213(3), s 219(3), Sch 24
(3)	1985, s 211(8)(b), s 213(3), s 219(4)
814(1)–(3)	new
815(1)	1985, s 218(1)
(2)	1985, s 218(2)
(3)	1985, s 218(3)
(4)	1985, s 218(3), Sch 24
816	1985, s 217(1) (changed)
817(1)	1985, s 217(2) (changed)
(2), (3)	1985, s 217(3)
(4)	1985, s 217(5)
818(1), (2)	1985, s 217(4)
(3)	1985, s 217(5)
819(1)	1985, s 211(7), s 213(3)
(2)	1985, s 211(10), s 213(3)
(3)	1985, s 211(10), s 213(3), Sch 24
820(1)	1985, s 208(1), s 212(5)
(2)	1985, s 208(2), s 212(5)
(3)	1985, s 208(3), s 212(5)
(4)	1985, s 208(4), s 212(5)
(5)	1985, s 208(6), s 212(5)
(6)	1985, s 208(5), s 212(5)
(7)	1985, s 208(7), s 212(5)
(8)	1985, s 208(8), s 212(5)
821(1), (2)	1985, s 212(6)
822(1), (2)	1985, s 203(1), s 212(5)
823(1)	1985, s 203(2), s 212(5)
(2)	1985, s 203(3), s 212(5)
(3)	1985, s 203(4), s 212(5)
824(1)	1985, s 204(1), (2), s 212(5)
(2)	1985, s 204(2), s 212(5)
(3)	1985, s 204(3), s 212(5)
(4)	1985, s 204(4), s 212(5)
(5)	1985, s 204(5), s 212(5)
(6)	1985, s 204(6), s 212(5)
825(1)	1985, s 205(1), s 212(5)

CA 2006	Origin
(2)	1985, s 205(2), s 212(5)
(3)	1985, s 205(3), s 212(5)
(4)	1985, s 205(4), s 212(5)
826(1)	1985, s 211(9), s 213(3), s 215(4)
(2)	1985, s 215(4)
827	1985, s 220(2) (changed)
828(1), (2)	1985, s 210A(1)
(3)	1985, s 210A(5)

PART 23 DISTRIBUTIONS

Chapter 1 Restrictions on when distributions may be made

829(1), (2)	1985, s 263(2)
830(1)	1985, s 263(1)
(2), (3)	1985, s 263(3)
831(1)	1985, s 264(1)
(2), (3)	1985, s 264(2)
(4)	1985, s 264(3)
(5)	1985, s 264(4)
(6)	1985, s 264(1)
832(1)–(3)	1985, s 265(1)
(4)	1985, s 265(2)
(5)	1985, s 265(4), (6)
(6)	1985, s 265(4A), (5)
(7)	1985, s 265(3)
833(1)	1985, s 266(1)
(2)	1985, s 266(2)
(3)	1985, s 266(2A)
(4), (5)	1985, s 266(3)
834(1)	1985, s 266(2)(b)
(2)	1985, s 266(4), ICTA, s 842(1A)
(3)	1985, s 266(4), ICTA, s 842(2)
(4)	1985, s 266(4), ICTA, s 842(3)
(5)	1985, s 266(4), ICTA, s 838, s 842(1A), (4)
835(1)	1985, s 267(1)
(2)	1985, s 267(2)(b)

Chapter 2 Justification of distribution by reference to accounts

836(1)	1985, s 270(1), (2)
(2)	1985, s 270(3), (4)
(3), (4)	1985, s 270(5)
837(1)	1985, s 270(3)
(2)	1985, s 271(2)
(3)	1985, s 271(3)
(4)	1985, s 271(3), (4)
(5)	1985, s 271(5)
838(1)	1985, s 270(4)
(2)	1985, s 272(1)
(3)	1985, s 272(2)
(4), (5)	1985, s 272(3)
(6)	1985, s 272(4), (5)
839(1)	1985, s 270(4)

CA 2006	Origin
(2)	1985, s 273(1)
(3)	1985, s 273(2)
(4)	1985, s 272(3), s 273(3)
(5)	1985, s 273(4)
(6)	1985, s 273(4), (5)
(7)	1985, s 273(6), (7)
840(1)	1985, s 274(1), (2)
(2)	1985, s 274(2)
(3)	1985, s 274(3) ("financial assistance")
(4)	1985, s 154(2)(a), s 274(3) ("net assets" and "net liabilities")
(5)	1985, s 154(2)(b), s 274(3) ("net liabilities")

Chapter 3 Supplementary provisions

CA 2006	Origin
841(1), (2)	1985, s 275(1)
(3)	1985, s 275(1A)
(4)	1985, s 275(4), (5), (6)
(5)	1985, s 275(2)
842	1985, s 275(3)
843(1)	1985, s 268(1)
(2)	1985, s 268(1)(a)
(3)	1985, s 268(2)(aa), (a)
(4)	1985, s 268(1)(b), (2)(b)
(5)	1985, s 268(1)
(6)	1985, s 268(3)(a)
(7)	1985, s 268(3)(b), (4)
844(1)	1985, s 269(1)
(2), (3)	1985, s 269(2)
845(1)–(5)	new
846(1), (2)	1985, s 276 (changed)
847(1), (2)	1985, s 277(1)
(3), (4)	1985, s 277(2)
848(1)	1985, s 278
(2)	1985, s 278, 1986 art 286
849	1985, s 263(4)
850(1), (2)	1985, s 263(5)
(3)	1985, s 263(5), 1986 art 271(5)
851(1)	1985, s 281 (changed)
(2), (3)	new
852	1985, s 281
853(1)	1985, s 280(1)
(2)	1985, s 280(3)
(3)	1985, s 280(2)
(4), (5)	1985, s 262(3), s 742(2)
(6)	1985, s 262(1), s 742(1)

PART 24 A COMPANY'S ANNUAL RETURN

CA 2006	Origin
854(1), (2)	1985, s 363(1)
(3)	1985, s 363(2) (changed)
855(1)	1985, s 364(1) (changed)
(2)	1985, s 364(2)
(3)	1985, s 364(3)
856(1)	1985, s 364A(1)

CA 2006	Origin
(2)	1985, s 364A(2), (3) (changed)
(3)	1985, s 364A(4) (changed)
(4)	1985, s 364A(5)
(5)	1985, s 364A(6)
(6)	1985, s 364A(8)
857(1), (2)	1985, s 365(1)
(3)	1985, s 365(2)
858(1)	1985, s 363(3), (4) (changed)
(2)	1985, s 363(3), (4), Sch 24
(3)	1985, s 363(3)
(4)	1985, s 363(4)
(5)	new
859	1985, s 365(3)

PART 25 COMPANY CHARGES

Chapter 1 Companies registered in England and Wales or in Northern Ireland

CA 2006	Origin
860(1)	1985, ss 395(1), 399(1)
(2)	1985, s 399(1)
(3)	1985, s 399(2)
(4)–(6)	1985, s 399(3), Sch 24 (changed)
(7)	1985, s 396(1)
861(1)	1985, s 396(3)
(2)	1985, s 396(1)(d)
(3)	1985, s 396(2)
(4)	1985, s 396(3A)
(5)	1985, ss 395(1) ("company"), 396(4) ("charge"), 400(1) ("company")
862(1)	1985, s 400(1)
(2), (3)	1985, s 400(2)
(4), (5)	1985, s 400(4), Sch 24 (changed)
863(1)–(4)	1985, s 397(1)
(5)	1985, s 399(1)–(3)
864(1)	1985, s 397(2)
(2)	1985, s 397(3)
(3)	1985, s 397(2)
865(1)	1985, s 402(1)
(2)	1985, s 402(2)
(3), (4)	1985, s 402(3), Sch 24
866(1)	1985, s 398(1)
(2)	1985, s 398(3)
867(1), (2)	1985, s 398(4)
868(1), (2)	1986 art 408(1)
(3)	1986 art 408(2)
(4)	1986 art 408(3)
(5)	Drafting
869(1)	1985, s 401(1) (opening words)
(2)	1985, s 401(1)(a)
(3)	1986 art 409(2)(b)
(4)	1985, s 401(1)(b)

CA 2006	Origin
(5), (6)	1985, s 401(2)
(7)	1985, s 401(3)
870(1)	1985, ss 395(1), 398(2)
(2)	1985, s 400(2), (3)
(3)	1985, s 397(1)
871(1)	1985, s 405(1)
(2)	1985, s 405(2)
(3)	1985, s 405(1), (2)
(4), (5)	1985, s 405(4), Sch 24
872(1), (2)	1985, s 403(1) (changed)
(3)	1985, s 403(2)
873(1)	1985, s 404(1)
(2)	1985, s 404(2)
874(1), (2)	1985, s 395(1)
(3)	1985, s 395(2)
875(1)	1985, s 406(1), 1986 art 414(1)
(2)	1985, s 406(2)
876(1)	1985, s 407(1)
(2)	1985, s 407(2)
(3), (4)	1985, s 407(3), Sch 24
877(1)	1985, s 408(1)
(2)	1985, ss 406(1), 407(1), 408(1) (changed)
(3)	new
(4)	1985, s 408(1), (2) (changed)
(5), (6)	1985, s 408(3), Sch 24 (changed)
(7)	1985, s 408(4)
Chapter 2 Companies registered in Scotland	
878(1)	1985, ss 410(2), 415(1)
(2)	1985, s 415(1)
(3)	1985, s 415(2)
(4)–(6)	1985, s 415(3), Sch 24 (changed)
(7)	1985, s 410(4)
879(1)	1985, s 410(4)(a)
(2)	1985, s 413(1)
(3)	1985, s 410(4)(a)
(4)	1985, s 412
(5)	1985, s 410(5)
(6)	1985, s 410(5) ("company")
880(1), (2)	1985, s 416(1)
(3), (4)	1985, s 416(3), Sch 24 (changed)
881(1)	1985, s 414(1)
(2), (3)	1985, s 414(2)
882(1)–(4)	1985, s 413(2)
(5)	1985, s 415(1)–(3)
883(1)–(3)	1985, s 413(3)
884	1985, s 411(2)
885(1)	1985, s 417(1)
(2)	1985, s 417(2)
(3)	1985, s 417(3)
(4)	1985, s 418(1), (2)(b)

CA 2006	Origin
(5)	1985, s 418(2)(a), (c)
(6)	1985, s 417(4)
886(1)	1985, ss 410(2), 411(1)
(2)	1985, s 416(1), (2)
(3)	1985, s 413(2)
887(1)	1985, s 419(1) (changed)
(2)	1985, s 419(1B)(a), (c), (3) (changed)
(3)	1985, s 419(1)
(4)	1985, s 419(2)
(5)	1985, s 419(4)
888(1), (2)	1985, s 420
889(1)	1985, s 410(2)
(2)	1985, s 410(3)
890(1)	1985, s 421(1)
(2)	1985, s 421(2)
891(1)	1985, s 422(1)
(2)	1985, s 422(2)
(3), (4)	1985, s 422(3), Sch 24
892(1)	1985, s 423(1)
(2)	1985, ss 421(1), 422(1), 423(1) (changed)
(3)	new
(4)	1985, s 423(1), (2) (changed)
(5), (6)	1985, s 423(3), Sch 24 (changed)
(7)	1985, s 423(4)
Chapter 3 Powers of the Secretary of State	
893(1)–(9)	new
894(1), (2)	new
PART 26 ARRANGEMENTS AND RECON-STRUCTIONS	
895(1)	1985, s 425(1)
(2)	1985, ss 425(6), 427(6)
(3)	drafting
896(1), (2)	1985, s 425(1)
897(1)	1985, s 426(1), (2), (3)
(2)	1985, s 426(2)
(3)	1985, s 426(4)
(4)	1985, s 426(5)
(5)–(8)	1985, s 426(6), Sch 24
898(1)–(3)	1985, s 426(7), Sch 24
899(1)	1985, s 425(2)
(2)	new
(3)	1985, s 425(2)
(4)	1985, s 425(3)
900(1)	1985, s 427(1), (2)
(2)	1985, s 427(2), (3)
(3), (4)	1985, s 427(4)
(5)	1985, s 427(6)
(6)–(8)	1985, s 427(5), Sch 24
901(1), (2)	new
(3), (4)	1985, s 425(3) (changed)
(5), (6)	1985, s 425(4), Sch 24

CA 2006	Origin
PART 27 MERGERS AND DIVISIONS OF PUBLIC COMPANIES	
Chapter 1 Introductory	
902(1)	1985, s 427A(1)
(2)	drafting
(3)	1985, s 427A(4)
903(1)	1985, s 427A(1)
(2), (3)	drafting
Chapter 2 Merger	
904(1)	1985, s 427A(2) Cases 1 and 2
(2)	drafting
905(1)	1985, Sch 15B, para 2(1)(a)
(2), (3)	1985, Sch 15B, para 2(2)
906(1), (2)	1985, Sch 15B, para 2(1)(b)
(3)	1985, Sch 15B, para 2(1)(c)
907(1)	1985, s 425(2), Sch 15B, para 1
(2)	1985, s 427A(1) closing words, Sch 15B, para 1 opening words
908(1)	1985, Sch 15B, para 3(a)
(2)	1985, Sch 15B, para 4(1)
(3)	1985, Sch 15B, para 3 opening words
909(1)	1985, Sch 15B, para 3(d)
(2)	1985, Sch 15B, para 5(1)
(3)	1985, Sch 15B, para 5(1), (2)
(4)	1985, Sch 15B, para 5(3)
(5)	1985, Sch 15B, para 5(7)
(6)	1985, Sch 15B, para 5(8)
(7)	1985, Sch 15B, para 3 opening words
910(1)	1985, Sch 15B, para 6(1)(e)
(2)	1985, Sch 15B, para 6(2)
(3)	1985, Sch 15B, para 6(3) (changed)
(4)	1985, Sch 15B, para 6(4)
911(1), (2)	1985, Sch 15B, para 3(e)
(3)	1985, Sch 15B, para 6(1)
(4)	1985, Sch 15B, para 3 opening words
912	1985, Sch 15B, para 3(f)
913(1)	1985, Sch 15B, para 8(1)
(2)	1985, Sch 15B, para 8(2)
914	1985, Sch 15B, para 7
915(1)	1985, Sch 15B, para 12(1)
(2)	1985, Sch 15B, para 12(2)
(3)–(5)	1985, Sch 15B, para 12(3)
(6)	1985, Sch 15B, para 12(1)(a), (b)
916(1)	1985, Sch 15B, para 14(1)
(2)	1985, Sch 15B, para 14(2)
(3)–(5)	1985, Sch 15B paras 10(2), 14(3)
(6)	1985, Sch 15B para14(1)(a), (b)

CA 2006	Origin
917(1)	1985, Sch 15B, para 12(1)
(2)	1985, Sch 15B, para 12(4)
(3)–(5)	1985, Sch 15B, para 12(5)
(6)	1985, Sch 15B, para 12(1)(a), (b)
918(1)	1985, Sch 15B, para 10(1)
(2)–(4)	1985, Sch 15B, para 10(2)
Chapter 3 Division	
919(1)	1985, s 427A(2) Case 3
(2)	drafting
920(1)	1985, Sch 15B, para 2(1)(a)
(2)	1985, Sch 15B, para 2(2)
(3)	1985, Sch 15B, para 2(3)
921(1), (2)	1985, Sch 15B, para 2(1)(b)
(3)	1985, Sch 15B, para 2(1)(c)
(4)	1985, Sch 15B, para 2(1)(b), (c) opening words
922(1)	1985, s 425(2), Sch 15B, para 1
(2)	1985, s 427A(1) closing words, Sch 15B, para 1 opening words
923(1)	1985, Sch 15B, para 3(a)
(2)	1985, Sch 15B, para 4(1)
(3)	1985, Sch 15B, para 4(2)
(4)	1985, Sch 15B, para 3 opening words
924(1)	1985, Sch 15B, para 3(d)
(2)	1985, Sch 15B, para 5(1)
(3)	1985, Sch 15B, para 5(1), (2)
(4)	1985, Sch 15B, para 5(3)
(5)	1985, Sch 15B, para 5(7)
(6)	1985, Sch 15B, para 5(8)
(7)	1985, Sch 15B, para 3 opening words
925(1)	1985, Sch 15B, para 6(1)(e)
(2)	1985, Sch 15B, para 6(2)
(3)	1985, Sch 15B, para 6(3) (changed)
(4)	1985, Sch 15B, para 6(4)
(5)	1985, Sch 15B, para 3 opening words
926(1), (2)	1985, Sch 15B, para 3(e)
(3)	1985, Sch 15B, para 6(1)
(4)	1985, Sch 15B, para 3 opening words
927(1)	1985, Sch 15B, para 3(b)
(2)	1985, Sch 15B, para 3(c)
(3)	1985, Sch 15B, para 3 opening words
928	1985, Sch 15B, para 3(f)
929(1)	1985, Sch 15B, para 8(1)
(2)	1985, Sch 15B, para 8(2)
930	1985, Sch 15B, para 7
931(1)	1985, Sch 15B, para 13(1)
(2)	1985, Sch 15B, para 13(2)

CA 2006	Origin
(3)	1985, Sch 15B paras 12(5)(a), 13(3)(a)
(4)	1985, Sch 15B, para 13(3)(b)
(5)	1985, Sch 15B paras 12(5)(c), 13(3)(a)
(6)	1985, Sch 15B, para 13(3)(c)
932(1)	1985, Sch 15B, para 10(1)
(2)–(4)	1985, Sch 15B, para 10(2)
(5)	1985, Sch 15B, para 10(2) opening words
933(1)–(3)	1985, Sch 15B, para 11(1), (2)
934(1)	1985, Sch 15B, para 11(1), (3)
(2)	1985, Sch 15B, para 11(4)(a), (b)
(3)	1985, Sch 15B, para 11(4)(c)
(4)	1985, Sch 15B, para 11(4)(d)

Chapter 4 Supplementary provisions

CA 2006	Origin
935(1)	1985, Sch 15B, para 5(4) (changed)
(2)	1985, Sch 15B, para 5(6)
936(1)–(4)	new
937(1)–(6)	new
938(1), (2)	1985, s 427A(3)
939(1)	1985, Sch 15B, para 9(1), (2)
(2)	1985, Sch 15B, para 9(2)
(3), (4)	1985, Sch 15B, para 9(3)
(5)	1985, Sch 15B, para 9(4)
940(1)	1985, Sch 15B, para 15(1)
(2)	1985, Sch 15B, para 15(2)
(3)	1985, Sch 15B, para 15(1)
941	1985, ss 427(6), 427A(8)

PART 28 TAKEOVERS ETC

[Note: The Takeovers Directive (Interim Implementation) Regulations 2006, SI 2006/1183 are based on the provisions of this Part. So although the regulations came into force on 20 May 2006 and so before the date of Royal assent to the Companies Act 2006, they are not cited as origins for those provisions].

Chapter 1 The Takeover Panel

CA 2006	Origin
942(1)–(3)	new
943(1)–(9)	new
944(1)–(7)	new
945(1), (2)	new
946	new
947(1)–(10)	new
948(1)–(9)	new
949(1)–(3)	new
950(1), (2)	new
951(1)–(5)	new
952(1)–(8)	new
953(1)–(9)	new
954(1), (2)	new

CA 2006	Origin
955(1)–(4)	new
956(1)–(3)	new
957(1), (2)	new
958(1)–(8)	new
959	new
960	new
961(1)–(3)	new
962(1), (2)	new
963(1), (2)	new
964(1)–(6)	new
965	new

Chapter 2 Impediments to takeovers

CA 2006	Origin
966(1)–(8)	new
967(1)–(7)	new
968(1)–(8)	new
969(1)–(3)	new
970(1)–(4)	new
971(1), (2)	new
972(1)–(4)	new
973	new

Chapter 3 "Squeeze-out" and "sell-out"

CA 2006	Origin
974(1)–(3)	1985, s 428(1), drafting
(4), (5)	1985, s 428(2)
(6)	1985, s 428(2A)
(7)	1985, s 428(7)
975(1), (2)	1985, s 428(5) (changed)
(3)	1985, s 428(6) (changed)
(4)	1985, s 430E(1)
976(1)	1985, s 428(3)
(2)	new
(3)	1985, s 428(4)
977(1)	1985, s 429(8) (changed)
(2)	1985, s 430E(1) (changed)
(3)	drafting
978(1)–(3)	new
979(1), (2)	1985, s 429(1) (changed)
(3), (4)	1985, s 429(2) (changed)
(5)–(7)	new
(8)	1985, s 429(8) (changed)
(9)	1985, ss 429(8), 430E(2) (changed)
(10)	1985, s 429(8) (changed)
980(1)	1985, s 429(4)
(2)	1985, s 429(3) (changed)
(3)	new
(4)	1985, s 429(4)
(5)	1985, s 429(5)
(6)	1985, s 429(6)
(7)	1985, s 429(7)
(8)	1985, s 429(6), Sch 24
981(1)	1985, s 430(1)
(2)	1985, s 430(2)
(3)	1985, s 430(3)
(4)	1985, s 430(4)
(5)	1985, s 430(4) (changed)

CA 2006	Origin
(6)	1985, s 430(5), (8)
(7)	1985, s 430(6)
(8)	1985, s 430(7)
(9)	1985, s 430(9), drafting
982(1)	drafting
(2), (3)	1985, s 430(10)
(4), (5)	1985, s 430(11)
(6)	1985, s 430(12)
(7)	1985, s 430(13)
(8)	1985, s 430(14)
(9)	1985, s 430(15)
983(1)	1985, s 430A(1), (1A)
(2), (3)	1985, s 430A(1) (changed)
(4)	1985, s 430A(2) (changed)
(5)	1985, s 430A(2A)
(6), (7)	new
(8)	1985, s 430E(3)
984(1)	1985, s 430A(1)
(2)	1985, s 430A(4) (changed)
(3)	1985, s 430A(3)
(4)	1985, s 430A(5)
(5)	1985, s 430A(6)
(6)	1985, s 430A(7)
(7)	1985, s 430A(6), Sch 24
985(1)	1985, s 430B(1)
(2)	1985, s 430B(2)
(3)	1985, s 430B(3)
(4)	1985, s 430B(4)
(5)	1985, s 430B(4) (changed)
986(1)	1985, s 430C(1)
(2)	1985, s 430C(1), (2)
(3)	1985, s 430C(3)
(4)	new
(5)	1985, s 430C(4)
(6)–(8)	new
(9), (10)	1985, s 430C(5)
987(1)	1985, s 430D(1)
(2), (3)	1985, s 430D(2) (changed)
(4)	1985, s 430D(4) (changed)
(5), (6)	1985, s 430D(3)
(7)	1985, s 430D(4)
(8)	1985, s 430D(5)
(9)	1985, s 430D(6)
(10)	1985, s 430D(7)
988(1)	1985, s 430E(4), (8)
(2)	1985, s 430E(5)
(3)	1985, s 430E(6), (7)
(4)	1985, ss 204(2)(a), 430E(4)(d)
(5)	1985, ss 204(6), 430E(7)
(6)	1985, s 204(3)
(7)	1985, ss 204(5), 430E(7)
989(1)	1985, s 430F(1)
(2)	1985, s 430F(2)
990(1)–(3)	new

CA 2006	Origin
991(1)	1985, s 428(8) ("the company" and "the offeror"), new ("date of the offer", "non-voting shares", "voting rights" and "voting shares")
(2)	new
Chapter 4 Amendments to Part 7 of the Companies Act 1985	
992(1)–(6)	new (amends 1985 Pt 7)
PART 29 FRAUDULENT TRADING	
993(1)–(3)	1985, s 458, Sch 24
PART 30 PROTECTION OF MEMBERS AGAINST UNFAIR PREJUDICE	
994(1)	1985, s 459(1)
(2)	1985, s 459(2)
(3)	1985, s 459(3)
995(1)	1985, s 460(1A)
(2), (3)	1985, s 460(1)
(4)	1985, s 460(2)
996(1)	1985, s 461(1)
(2)	1985, s 461(2), (3)
997	1985, s 461(6)
998(1)–(4)	1985, s 461(5)
999(1)–(5)	new
PART 31 DISSOLUTION AND RESTORATION TO THE REGISTER	
Chapter 1 Striking off	
1000(1)	1985, s 652(1)
(2)	1985, s 652(2)
(3)	1985, s 652(3)
(4)–(6)	1985, s 652(5)
(7)	1985, s 652(6)
1001(1)	1985, s 652(4)
(2)–(4)	1985, s 652(5)
(5)	1985, s 652(6)
1002(1)–(3)	1985, s 652(7)
1003(1)	1985, s 652A(1) (changed)
(2)	1985, s 652A(2) (changed)
(3)	1985, s 652A(3)
(4)	1985, s 652A(4)
(5)	1985, s 652A(5)
(6)	1985, s 652A(6), (7)
1004(1)	1985, s 652B(1)
(2)	1985, s 652B(2)
(3)	1985, s 652B(9)
(4)	1985, s 652D(5)(c)
(5)	1985, s 652E(1)
(6)	1985, s 652E(3)
(7)	1985, s 652E(1), Sch 24
1005(1)	1985, s 652B(3)
(2)	1985, s 652B(4)
(3)	1985, s 652B(5)
(4)	1985, s 652E(1)
(5)	1985, s 652E(3)
(6)	1985, s 652E(1), Sch 24
1006(1)	1985, ss 652B(6), 652D(5)(c)

CA 2006	Origin		CA 2006	Origin
(2)	1985, s 652B(7)		(3)	1985, s 657(2), IA 1986, s 182(4)
(3)	1985, s 652B(8)			
(4)	1985, s 652E(1), (2)		(4), (5)	1985, s 657(2), IA 1986, s 182(3)
(5)	1985, s 652E(4)			
(6)	1985, s 652E(1), Sch 24		1019	1985, s 657(2), IA 1986, s 180(1), (2)
(7)	1985, s 652E(2), Sch 24			
1007(1)	1985, s 652C(1)		1020(1), (2)	1985, s 657(4)
(2)	1985, ss 652C(2), 652D(5)(c)		1021(1), (2)	1985, s 657(5)
			(3)	1985, s 657(6)
(3)	1985, s 652C(3)		1022(1)	1985, Sch 20, para 5
(4)	1985, s 652E(1), (2)		(2)	1985, Sch 20, para 6
(5)	1985, s 652E(5)		(3)	1985, Sch 20, para 7
(6)	1985, s 652E(1), Sch 24		(4), (5)	1985, Sch 20, para 8
(7)	1985, s 652E(2), Sch 24		(6)	1985, Sch 20, para 9
1008(1), (2)	1985, s 652D(1)		1023(1)	1985, s 658(1), IA, s 180(1)
(3)	1985, s 652D(2), (3)		(2)	1985, s 658(1), IA, s 180(2)
(4)	1985, s 652D(4)		(3)	1985, s 658(2)
1009(1)	1985, s 652C(4)		**Chapter 3 Restoration to the register**	
(2)	1985, s 652C(5)		1024(1)–(4)	new
(3)	1985, s 652C(7)		1025(1)–(6)	new
(4)	1985, ss 652C(6), 652D(5)(c)		1026(1)–(3)	new
			1027(1)–(4)	new
(5)	1985, s 652E(1)		1028(1)–(4)	new
(6)	1985, s 652E(5)		1029(1), (2)	new
(7)	1985, s 652E(1), Sch 24		1030(1)–(6)	new
1010	1985, s 652D(6)		1031(1)–(4)	new
1011	1985, s 652D(8)		1032(1)–(5)	new
Chapter 2 Property of dissolved company			1033(1)–(7)	new
1012(1)	1985, s 654(1)		1034(1)	1985, s 655(1)
(2)	1985, s 654(2)		(2)	1985, s 655(2)
1013(1)	1985, s 656(1)		(3)	new
(2)	1985, s 656(2) (changed)		(4)	1985, s 655(3)
(3)–(5)	1985, s 656(3) (changed)		(5)	1985, s 655(4)
(6), (7)	1985, s 656(5)		(6)	drafting
(8)	1985, s 656(6)		**PART 32 COMPANY INVESTIGATIONS: AMENDMENTS**	
1014(1)	1985, s 657(1)			
(2)	drafting		1035(1)–(5)	new (inserts 1985, ss 446A and 446B; amends 1985 s, s 431, 432, 437 and 442)
1015(1), (2)	1985, s 657(2), IA 1986, s 178(4)			
1016(1)	1985, s 657(2), IA 1986, s 179(1)		1036	new (inserts 1985, ss 446C and 446D)
(2)	1985, s 657(2), IA 1986, s 179(2)		1037(1)–(3)	new (inserts 1985, s 446E; amends 1985, ss 451A and 452)
(3)	drafting			
1017(1)	1985, s 657(2), IA 1986, s 181(2), (3)		1038(1), (2)	new (amends 1985, ss 434 and 447)
(2)	1985, s 657(2), IA 1986, s 181(3)		1039	new (amends Company Directors Disqualification Act 1986, s 8)
(3)	1985, s 657(2), IA 1986, s 181(4)		**PART 33 UK COMPANIES NOT FORMED UNDER THE COMPANIES LEGISLATION**	
(4)	1985, s 657(2), IA 1986, s 181(3)		**Chapter 1 Companies not formed under companies legislation but authorised to register**	
(5)	1985, s 657(2), IA 1986, s 181(6)		1040(1)	1985, s 680(1)(a), (b), (1A), (2)
1018(1)	1985, s 657(2), IA 1986, s 182(1)		(2), (3)	1985, s 680(1) (closing words)
(2)	1985, s 657(2), IA 1986, s 182(2)		(4)	1985, s 680(3), (4)
			(5)	1985, s 680(5)

CA 2006	Origin	CA 2006	Origin
(6)	1985, s 680(1) (closing words)	1069(1)–(3)	new
1041(1)	1985, s 683(1)	1070(1)–(3)	new
(2)	1985, s 683(2)	1071(1), (2)	new
1042(1)–(3)	new	1072(1), (2)	new
Chapter 2 Unregistered companies		1073(1)–(6)	new
1043(1)	1985, s 718(1), (2)	1074(1)–(5)	new
(2)	1985, s 718(3) (changed)	1075(1)–(7)	new
(3)	1985, s 718(1) (changed)	1076(1)–(4)	new
(4)	1985, s 718(5)	1077(1)	1985, s 711(1) opening words
(5)	1985, s 718(1), (3)	(2), (3)	new
(6)	1985, s 718(6)	1078(1)	drafting
PART 34 OVERSEAS COMPANIES		(2), (3)	1985, s 711(1) (changed)
1044	1985, s 744 ("overseas company") (changed)	(4)	new
		(5), (6)	new
1045(1), (2)	1989, s 130(6)	1079(1)–(3)	1985, s 42(1)
1046(1)–(8)	new	(4)	1985, s 711(2) (changed)
1047(1)–(6)	new	1080(1), (2)	drafting
1048(1), (2)	1985, s 694(4) (changed)	(3)	new
(3)–(5)	1985, s 694(5)	(4)	1985, s 707A(1)
1049(1)–(4)	new	(5)	new
1050(1)–(6)	new	1081(1)–(7)	new
1051(1)–(5)	new	1082(1)–(5)	new
1052(1)–(6)	new	1083(1)	1985, s 707A(2) (changed)
1053(1)–(6)	new	(2), (3)	new
1054(1)–(4)	new	1084(1)–(3)	1985, s 707A(3) (changed)
1055	new	(4)	1985, s 707A(4)
1056	new	(5)	1985, s 707A(3)
1057(1)–(3)	new	1085(1)	1985, s 709(1) opening words
1058(1)–(4)	new	(2)	1985, s 709(2) (changed)
1059	1985, s 695A(4)	(3)	drafting
PART 35 THE REGISTRAR OF COMPANIES		1086(1)	1985, s 709(1)(a), (b)
1060(1), (2)	1985, s 704(2)	(2)	new
(3)	1985, s 744 ("the registrar of companies" and "the registrar")	(3)	drafting
		1087(1)–(3)	new
		1088(1)–(6)	new
(4)	drafting	1089(1), (2)	new
1061(1)–(3)	drafting	1090(1)–(4)	new
1062	1985, s 704(4) (changed)	1091(1), (2)	new
1063(1)–(3)	1985, s 708(1) (changed)	(3)	1985, s 709(3)
(4)	1985, s 708(2), (3) (changed)	(4)	new
(5)	1985, s 708(5) (changed)	(5)	1985, s 709(4)
(6)	1985, s 708(4)	1092(1), (2)	1985, s 709(5)
(7)	new	1093(1)–(4)	new
1064(1)–(3)	1985, s 711(1)(a) (changed)	1094(1)–(5)	new
1065	1985, s 710	1095(1)–(6)	new
1066(1)–(3)	1985, s 705(1)–(3)	1096(1)–(6)	new
(4), (5)	1985, s 705(4)	1097(1)–(5)	new
(6)	1985, s 705(5)(za)	1098(1), (2)	new
1067(1)	1985, s 705A(1), (2) (changed)	1099(1)–(3)	1985, s 714(1) (changed)
		(4), (5)	1985, s 714(2)
(2)	1985, s 705A(3)	1100	1985, s 709(1) opening words
(3)	1985, s 705A(4)		
(4), (5)	1985, s 705A(5)		
1068(1)–(7)	new	1101(1), (2)	new

CA 2006	Origin
1102(1)–(4)	new
1103(1), (2)	new
1104(1), (2)	1985, s 710B(1)–(3)
(3)	1985, s 710B(4)
(4)	1985, s 710B(5)
(5)	drafting
1105(1)–(3)	new
1106(1)–(6)	new
1107(1)	drafting
1107(2), (3)	new
1108(1)–(3)	new
1109(1), (2)	new
1110(1)–(3)	new
1111(1)–(3)	new
1112(1), (2)	new
1113(1)–(3)	1985, s 713(1)
(4), (5)	1985, s 713(2), (3)
1114(1)	1985, s 715A(1) "document", (2)
(2)	new
1115(1)	new
(2)	1985, s 710A(2)
1116(1)–(6)	new
1117(1)–(3)	new
1118	drafting
1119(1), (2)	1985, s 704(7), (8)
(3)	new
1120	new

PART 36 OFFENCES UNDER THE COMPANIES ACTS

1121(1)	1985, s 730(5)
(2)	1985, s 744 "officer"
(3)	1985, s 730(5) (changed)
1122(1)–(3)	new
1123(1)–(4)	new
1124 and Sch 3	new (amend 1985 Act)
1125(1)	drafting
(2)	1985, s 730(4)
1126(1)	1985, s 732(1)
(2)	1985, s 732(2) (changed)
(3)	1986 art 680(2) (changed)
1127(1), (2)	1985, s 731(1)
1128(1)	1985, s 731(2)
(2)	1985, s 731(3)
(3)	1986 art 679(2)
(4)	1985, s 731(4), 1986 art 679(3)
1129	1985, s 732(3) (changed)
1130(1)	1985, s 734(1) (changed)
(2)	1985, s 734(1), (3), (4)
(3)	1985, s 734(2)
1131(1), (2)	new
1132(1), (2)	1985, s 721(1)
(3)–(5)	1985, s 721(2)–(4)
(6)	drafting
1133	new

CA 2006	Origin
PART 37 COMPANIES: SUPPLEMENTARY PROVISIONS	
1134	1985, s 722(1) (changed)
1135(1)	1985, ss 722(1), 723(1) (changed)
(2)	new
(3), (4)	new
(5)	1985, s 723(2)
1136(1)–(7)	new
1137(1), (2)	1985, s 723A(1)
(3)	1985, s 723A(2), (3)
(4)	1985, s 723A(4)
(5), (6)	1985, s 723A(6), (7)
1138(1)	1985, s 722(2)
(2), (3)	1985, s 722(3), Sch 24
(4)	new
1139(1)	1985, s 725(1)
(2)	1985, s 695(1), (2) (changed)
(3)	new
(4)	1985, s 725(2), (3)
(5)	drafting
1140(1)–(8)	new
1141(1)	drafting
(2), (3)	new
1142	new
1143(1)–(4), Schs 4 and 5	new
1144(1)–(3)	new
1145(1)–(5)	new
1146(1)–(4)	new
1147(1)–(6)	new
1148(1)–(3)	new
1149	drafting
1150(1)	1985, s 108(1) (changed)
(2), (3)	1985, s 108(2), (3)
(4)	1985, s 108(5)
1151(1)–(4)	new
1152(1)–(6)	new
1153(1)	1985, s 110(1)
(2), (3)	1985, s 110(2), (3)
(4)	1985, s 110(2), Sch 24
1154(1)–(4)	new
1155(1), (2)	new
1156(1)–(3)	1985, s 744 "the court", IA 1986, s 117 (changed)
1157(1)–(3)	1985, s 727(1)–(3)
PART 38 COMPANIES: INTERPRETATION	
1158	drafting
1159(1), (2)	1985, s 736(1), (2)
(3) and Sch 6	1985, s 736A(1)–(11)
(4)	1985, ss 736(3), 736A(12)
1160(1)	1985, s 736B(1)
(2)–(4)	1985, s 736B(3)–(5)
1161(1)–(5)	1985, s 259(1)–(5)
1162(1)–(5)	1985, s 258(1)–(5)

CA 2006	Origin
(6) and Sch 7	1985, s 258(6) and Sch 10A
1163(1), (2)	1985, s 739(1), (2)
1164(1)–(3)	1985, s 742B(1)–(3)
(4)	1985, s 255A(4)
(5)	1985, s 255A(5A)
1165(1)	drafting
(2)–(4)	1985, s 742C(1)–(4)
(5)	1985, s 255A(5)
(6)	1985, s 255A(5A)
(7)	1985, s 744 "insurance market activity"
(8)	1985, s 742C(5)
1166	1985, s 743
1167	1985, s 744 "prescribed"
1168(1)–(7)	new
1169(1)	1985, s 249AA(4)
(2), (3)	1985, s 249AA(5)–(7)
(4)	drafting
1170	1985, s 744 "EEA State", drafting
1171 "the former Companies Acts"	1985, s 735(1)(c) (changed)
"the Joint Stock Companies Acts"	1985, s 735(3)
1172	drafting
1173(1) "body corporate" and "corporation"	new
"credit institution"	1985, s 262 "credit institution" (changed)

CA 2006	Origin
"financial institution"	1985, s 699A(3) "financial institution"
"firm"	new
"the Gazette"	1985, s 744 "the Gazette"
"hire-purchase agreement"	1985, s 744 "hire purchase agreement"
"officer"	1985, s 744 "officer"
"parent company"	1985, ss 258(1) and 742(1)
"regulated activity"	1985, s 744 "regulated activity"
"regulated market"	1985 passim (changed)
"working day"	drafting
(2)	drafting
1174 and Sch 8	drafting

PART 39 COMPANIES: MINOR AMENDMENTS

CA 2006	Origin
1175(1), (2), Sch 9	new (amend 1985, Pt 7 and 1986, Pt 8)
1176(1)–(3)	new (repeals 1985, s 438, amends 1985, ss 439 and 453)
1177	new (repeals 1985, ss 311, 323 and 327, 324–326, 328, 329, Pts 2–4 of Sch 13 and ss 343 and 344)
1178	new (repeals 1985, s 720 and Sch 23)
1179	new (repeals 1985, s 729)
1180	new (repeals 1985, Pt 4)
1181(1)–(4)	new (power to amend)

TABLES OF DESTINATIONS
(COMPANIES ACTS 1985 AND 1989)

[3.53]

NOTES

(1)   The table identifies the provisions of the Companies Act 1985 (c 6) that are repealed and re-enacted (with or without changes) by the Companies Act 2006 and identifies the corresponding provisions in that Act.

(2)   The table is based on the table of origins. So it only shows a provision of the Companies Act 2006 as a destination of a provision of the Companies Act 1985 if the latter is cited in that table as an origin for the new provision.

(3)   A repealed provision of the Companies Act 1985 may not be listed in this table because the provision is spent or it is otherwise unnecessary to re-enact it, because the new provision is fundamentally different from the existing provision or because as a matter of policy it has been decided to repeal the existing provision without replacing it.

(4)   There is no entry for Schedule 24 to the Companies Act 1985 (punishment of offences) in the table. This is cited in the table of origins as the origin for a large number of provisions in the Companies Act 2006.

(5)   A section at the end of the table identifies the substantive provisions of the Companies Act 1989 (c 40) that are repealed and re-enacted by the Companies Act 2006.

COMPANIES ACT 1985

CA 1985	CA 2006	CA 1985	CA 2006
1 Mode of forming incorporated company		**14 Effect of memorandum and articles**	
(1)	s 7(1), (2) (changed)	(1)	s 33(1) (changed)
(2)	s 3(1)–(4)	(2)	s 33(2) (changed)
(3)	s 4(1)–(3)	**15 Memorandum and articles of company limited by guarantee**	
(4)	s 5(1), (2)		
2 Requirements with respect to memorandum		(1)	s 37
(1)	s 9(2)	(2)	s 5(3)
(2)	ss 9(2), 88(2)	**16 Effect of alteration on company's members**	
(3)	s 9(2) (changed)	(1)	s 25(1)
(4)	s 11(3) (changed)	(2)	s 25(2)
3 Forms of memorandum		**18 Amendments of memorandum or articles to be registered**	
(1)	s 8(2)		
7 Articles prescribing regulations for companies		(1)	s 34(2) (changed)
(1)	s 18(2) (changed)	(2)	ss 26(1), 34(3) (changed)
(3)	s 18(3) (changed)	(3)	ss 26(3), (4), 34(5), (6)
8 Tables A, C, D and E		**19 Copies of memorandum and articles to be given to members**	
(1)	s 19(1)–(3) (changed)		
(2)	s 20(1), (2) (changed)	(1)	s 32(1) (changed)
(3)	s 19(4)	(2)	s 32(3), (4) (changed)
(4)	s 19(1)–(3) (changed)	**22 Definition of "member"**	
(5)	s 19(5)	(1)	s 112(1) (changed)
9 Alteration of articles by special resolution		(2)	s 112(2)
(1), (2)	s 21(1)	**23 Membership of holding company**	
10 Documents to be sent to registrar		(1)	s 136(1)
(1)	s 9(1), (5), (6) (changed)	(2)	s 138(1), (2)
(2)	s 12(1) (changed)	(3)	s 141(1), (2)
(3)	s 12(3)	(3A)	s 141(3)
(4)	s 9(3)	(3B)	s 141(4)
(6)	s 9(5)	(3BA)	s 141(5)
12 Duty of registrar		(3C)	s 142(1), (2)
(1), (2)	s 14	(4), (5)	s 137(1), (2)
(3), (3A)	s 13(1), (2) (changed)	(6)	s 137(3), (4)
13 Effect of registration		(7)	s 144
(1)	s 15(1)	(8)	s 143
(2)	s 15(3)	**25 Name as stated in memorandum**	
(3)	s 16(2) (changed)	(1)	s 58(1), (2)
(4)	s 16(3)	(2)	s 59(1), (2), (3)
(5)	s 16(6)	**26 Prohibition on registration of certain names**	
(7)	s 15(4)	(1)	ss 53, 65(1)–(5), 66(1) (changed)

Part 3   CA 2006 Supporting Materials

CA 1985	CA 2006
(2)	ss 54(1)–(3) and 55(1) (changed)
(3)	s 66(2), (3) (changed)
27 Alternatives of statutory designations	
(4)	ss 58(1), (2), 59(1), (2)
28 Change of name	
(1)	s 77(1)
(2)	ss 67(1), 68(2), (3)
(3)	s 75(1), (2), (4)
(4)	ss 68(3), 75(3)
(5)	ss 68(5), (6), 75(5), (6)
(6)	ss 80(1)–(3), 81(1)
(7)	s 81(2), (3)
29 Regulations about names	
(1)	ss 55(1), 56(1)
(2)	s 56(2)
(3)	s 56(3), (4) (changed)
(6)	s 55(2)
30 Exemption from requirement of "limited" as part of the name	
(2), (3)	ss 61(1)–(4), 62(1)–(3) (changed)
(4)	s 60(3)
(5B)	s 60(2)
31 Provisions applying to company exempt under s 30	
(1)	s 63(1)
(2)	s 64(1)–(4) (changed)
(3)	s 64(7)
(5)	s 63(2), (3)
(6)	s 64(5), (6)
32 Power to require company to abandon misleading name	
(1)	s 76(1)
(2)	s 76(3)
(3)	s 76(4), (5)
(4)	s 76(6), (7) (changed)
(5)	ss 80(1)–(3), 81(1)
(6)	s 81(2), (3)
35 A company's capacity not limited by its memorandum	
(1)	s 39(1) (changed)
(4)	s 39(2)
35A Power of directors to bind the company	
(1)	s 40(1)
(2)	s 40(2)
(3)	s 40(3)
(4)	s 40(4)
(5)	s 40(5)
(6)	s 40(6)
35B No duty to enquire as to capacity of company or authority of directors	
	s 40(2)
36 Company contracts: England and Wales	
(1), (2)	s 43(1), (2)
36A Execution of documents: England and Wales	

CA 1985	CA 2006
(2)	ss 44(1)
(3)	s 45(1)
(4)	s 44(2), (3), (4)
(4A)	s 44(6)
(6)	s 44(5)
(7)	s 44(8)
(8)	s 44(7)
36AA Execution of deeds: England and Wales	
(1)	s 46(1)
(2)	s 46(2)
36B Execution of documents by companies	
(1)	s 48(2)
(2)	s 48(3)
36C Pre-incorporation contracts, deeds and obligations	
(1)	s 51(1)
(2)	s 51(2)
37 Bills of exchange and promissory notes	
	s 52
38 Execution of deeds abroad	
(1)	s 47(1) (changed)
(2)	s 47(2)
(3)	s 47(1)
39 Power of company to have official seal for use abroad	
(1)	s 49(1), (2) (changed)
(2), (2A)	s 49(3)
(3)	s 49(4)
(4)	s 49(5)
(5)	s 49(6)
40 Official seal for share certificates, etc	
(1)	s 50(1), (2)
42 Events affecting a company's status	
(1)	s 1079(1)–(3)
43 Re-registration of private company as public	
(1)	s 90(1), (2) (changed)
(2)	s 90(3)
(3)	ss 92(1), (2), 94(2), (3)
(4)	s 92(1)
44 Consideration for shares recently allotted to be valued	
(1)	s 93(1)
(2)	s 93(2), (7)
(4), (5)	s 93(3)–(5)
(6)	s 93(6)
(7)	s 93(6), (7)
45 Additional requirements relating to share capital	
(1)–(4)	s 91(1)
46 Meaning of "unqualified report" in s 43(3)	
(2)	s 92(3)
(3)	s 92(4)
(4)	s 92(5), (6)
47 Certificate of re-registration under s 43	
(1)	s 96(1), (2)

CA 1985	CA 2006
(2)	s 94(4)
(3)	s 91(5) (changed)
(4)	s 96(4)
(5)	s 96(5)
48 Modification for unlimited company re-registering	
(1), (2)	s 90(4)
(5)	s 91(2)
(6)	s 91(3)
(7)	s 91(4)
49 Re-registration of limited company as unlimited	
(1)	s 102(1)
(2)	s 102(2)
(4)	s 102(1)
(5)–(7)	s 102(3)
(8)	ss 102(1), 103(2)–(4) (changed)
(8A)	s 103(3), (4) (changed)
(9)	s 102(4)
50 Certificate of re-registration under s 49	
(1)	s 104(1), (2)
(2)	s 104(4)
(3)	s 104(5)
51 Re-registration of unlimited company as limited	
(1)	s 105(1) (changed)
(2)	s 105(2)
(3)	s 105(3), (4)
(5)	s 106(2)
52 Certificate of re-registration under s 51	
(1)	s 107(1), (2)
(2)	s 107(4)
(3)	s 107(5)
53 Re-registration of public company as private	
(1)	ss 97(1), 100(2) (changed)
(2)	s 97(3)
54 Litigated objection to resolution under s 53	
(1)	s 98(1)
(2)	ss 98(1), 370(3) (changed)
(3)	s 98(2)
(4)	s 99(1), (2) (changed)
(5)	s 98(3), (4)
(6)	s 98(5), (6)
(7)	s 99(3)
(8)	s 98(6)
(10)	s 99(4), (5)
55 Certificate of re-registration under s 53	
(1)	s 101(1), (2)
(2)	s 101(4)
(3)	s 101(5)
58 Document offering shares etc for sale deemed a prospectus	
(3)	s 755(2)
80 Authority of company required for certain allotments	

CA 1985	CA 2006
(1)	s 549(1),s 551(1) (changed)
(2)	ss 549(1)–(3), 551(1), 559
(3)	s 551(2)
(4)	s 551(3), (4)
(5)	s 551(5)
(6)	s 551(6)
(7)	s 551(7)
(8)	s 551(8)
(9)	s 549(4), (5)
(10)	s 549(6) (changed)
81 Restriction on public offers by private company	
(1)	s 755(1)
(3)	s 760
84 Allotment where issue not fully subscribed	
(1)	s 578(1)
(2)	s 578(2)
(3)	s 578(3) (changed)
(4)	s 578(4), (5)
(5)	s 578(5)
(6)	s 578(6)
85 Effect of irregular allotment	
(1)	s 579(1), (2)
(2)	s 579(3)
(3)	s 579(4)
88 Return as to allotments, etc	
(1)	s 555(1)
(2)	s 555(2) (changed)
(5)	s 557(1), (2)
(6)	ss 557(3), 597(5), (6)
89 Offers to shareholders to be on pre-emptive basis	
(1)	s 561(1)
(2)	s 568(1)
(3)	s 568(1), (2)
(4)	ss 561(2), 565
(5)	s 566
(6)	s 561(4)
90 Communication of pre-emption offers to shareholders	
(1)	s 562(1)
(2)	s 568(3)
(5)	s 562(3) (changed)
(6)	s 562(4), (5) (changed)
91 Exclusion of ss 89, 90 by private company	
(1)	s 567(1), (2)
(2)	s 567(3), (4)
92 Consequences of contravening ss 89, 90	
(1)	ss 563(1), (2), 568(4)
(2)	ss 563(3), 568(5)
93 Saving for other restrictions as to offers	
(1)	s 575(1)
(2)	s 575(2)
94 Definitions for ss 89–96	
(2)	ss 560(1), 564, 577

CA 1985	CA 2006
(3)	ss 560(2), 561(3)
(3A)	s 560(2)
(5)	s 560(1)
(7)	s 574(1), (2)
95 Disapplication of pre-emption rights	
(1)	ss 570(1), (2), 573(2), (3), (5)
(2)	ss 571(1), (2), 573(4)
(2A)	s 573(1)–(5l)
(3)	ss 570(3), 571(3)
(4)	ss 570(4), 571(4), 573(3), (5)
(5)	ss 571(5)–(7), 573(5) (changed)
(6)	s 572(1)–(3)
96 Saving for company's pre-emption procedure operative before 1982	
(1), (2)	s 576(1)
(3)	s 576(2)
(4)	s 576(3)
97 Power of company to pay commissions	
(1)	s 553(1)
(2)	s 553(2)
98 Apart from s 97, commissions and discounts barred	
(1)	s 552(1)
(2)	s 552(2)
(3)	s 552(3)
(4)	s 553(3)
99 General rules as to payment for shares on allotment	
(1)	s 582(1), (3)
(2)	s 585(1)
(3)	s 585(2)
(4)	s 582(2)
(5)	s 585(3)
100 Prohibition on allotment of shares at a discount	
(1)	s 580(1)
(2)	s 580(2)
101 Shares to be allotted as at least one-quarter paid-up	
(1)	s 586(1)
(2)	s 586(2)
(3), (4)	s 586(3)
(5)	s 586(4)
102 Restriction on payment by long-term undertaking	
(1)	s 587(1)
(2)	s 587(2)
(3), (4)	s 587(3)
(5), (6)	s 587(4)
(7)	s 587(5)
103 Non-cash consideration to be valued before allotment	
(1)	s 593(1)
(2)	s 593(2)
(3)	s 594(1)–(3)

CA 1985	CA 2006
(4)	s 594(4), (5)
(5)	s 595(1), (2)
(6)	s 593(3)
(7)	ss 594(6), 595(3)
104 Transfer to public company of non-cash asset in initial period	
(1)	s 598(1)
(2)	s 598(2)
(3)	s 603
(4)	ss 599(1), (3), 601(1)–(3) (changed)
(5)	s 599(2), (4)
(6)	s 598(4), (5)
105 Agreements contravening s 104	
(1)	s 604(1)
(2)	s 604(2)
(3)	s 604(3)
106 Shares issued to subscribers of memorandum	
	s 584
107 Meaning of "the appropriate rate"	
	ss 592(1), (2), 609(1), (2)
108 Valuation and report (s 103)	
(1)	s 1150(1) (changed)
(2)	s 1150(2)
(3)	s 1150(3)
(4)	s 596(2)
(5)	s 1150(4)
(6)	ss 596(3), 600(3)
(7)	s 596(4), (5)
109 Valuation and report (s 104)	
(2)	s 600(2), (3)
(3)	s 600(4), (5)
110 Entitlement of valuer to full disclosure	
(1)	s 1153(1)
(2)	s 1153(2), (4)
(3)	s 1153(3)
111 Matters to be communicated to registrar	
(1)	s 597(1), (2)
(2)	s 602(1)
(3)	s 597(3)–(6)
(4)	s 602(2), (3)
111A Right to damages, &c not affected	
	s 655
112 Liability of subsequent holders of shares allotted	
(1)	ss 588(1), 605(1)
(2)	s 605(2)
(3)	ss 588(2), 605(3)
(4)	ss 588(3), 605(4)
(5)	s 588(1), (4)
113 Relief in respect of certain liabilities under ss 99 ff	
(1)	ss 589(1), (2), 606(1)
(2)	ss 589(3), 606(2) (changed)
(3)	ss 589(3), 606(2)

CA 1985	CA 2006
(4)	ss 589(4), 606(3)
(5)	ss 589(5), 606(4)
(6), (7)	ss 589(6), 606(5)
(8)	s 606(6)
114 Penalty for contravention	
	ss 590(1), (2), 607(2), (3)
115 Undertakings to do work, etc	
(1)	ss 591(1), (2), 608(1), (2)
117 Public company share capital requirements	
(1)	s 761(1)
(2)	s 761(2) (changed)
(3)	s 762(1) (changed)
(4)	s 761(3)
(5)	s 762(3)
(6)	s 761(4) (changed)
(7)	s 767(1), (2)
(8)	s 767(3)
118 The authorised minimum	
(1)	ss 763(1), 764(1) (changed)
(2)	s 764(3)
(3)	s 764(4)
119 Provision for different amounts to be paid on shares	
	s 581
121 Alteration of share capital (limited companies)	
(1)	s 617(1) (changed)
(2)	ss 617(2), (3), 618(1), 620(1) (changed)
(3)	s 618(2)
(4)	ss 618(3), 620(2) (changed)
122 Notice to registrar of alteration	
(1)	ss 619(1)–(3), 621(1), 663(1), 689(1) (changed)
(2)	ss 619(4), (5), 621(4), (5), 663(4), (5), 689(4), (5)
125 Variation of class rights	
(1)	s 630(1)
(2)	s 630(2)–(4) (changed)
(6)	s 334(1)–(4), (6) (changed)
(7)	ss 334(7), 630(5)
(8)	s 630(6)
126 Saving for court's powers under other provisions	
	s 632
127 Shareholders' right to object to variation	
(1)	s 633(1)
(2)	s 633(2), (3)
(2A)	s 633(2)
(3)	s 633(4)
(4)	s 633(5)
(5)	s 635(1)–(3)
(6)	s 633(6)
128 Registration of particulars of special rights	
(1)	s 556(1)–(3) (changed)
(2)	ss 556(1), (4), 629(2)

CA 1985	CA 2006
(3)	s 637(1) (changed)
(4)	s 636(1) (changed)
(5)	ss 557(1), (2), 636(2), (3), 637(2), (3) (changed)
129 Registration of newly created class rights	
(1)	s 638(1) (changed)
(2)	s 640(1) (changed)
(3)	s 639(1) (changed)
(4)	ss 638(2), (3), 639(2), (3), 640(2), (3)
130 Application of share premiums	
(1)	s 610(1)
(2)	s 610(2), (2) (changed)
(3)	s 610(4)
(4)	s 610(5), (6)
131 Merger relief	
(1)	s 612(1), (4)
(2)	s 612(2)
(3)	s 612(3)
(4)	s 613(2), (3)
(5)	s 613(4)
(6)	s 613(5)
(7)	s 616(1)
132 Relief in respect of group reconstructions	
(1)	s 611(1)
(2)	s 611(2)
(3)	s 611(3)
(4)	s 611(4)
(5)	s 611(5)
(8)	s 612(4)
133 Provisions supplementing ss 131, 132	
(1)	s 615
(2)	s 616(2)
(3)	s 616(3)
(4)	s 616(1)
134 Provision for extending or restricting relief from s 130	
(1)	s 614(1)
(3)	s 614(2)
135 Special resolution for reduction of share capital	
(1)	s 641(1)–(3) (changed)
(2)	s 641(4)
136 Application to court for order of confirmation	
(1)	s 645(1)
(2)	ss 645(2), (4), 646(4)
(3)	s 646(1)
(4)	s 646(2), (3)
(5)	s 646(4), (5)
(6)	s 645(2), (3)
137 Court order confirming reduction	
(1)	s 648(1), (2)
(2)	s 648(3), (4)
(3)	s 648(4)

CA 1985	CA 2006
138 Registration of order and minute of reduction	
(1)	s 649(1) (changed)
(2)	s 649(3) (changed)
(3)	s 649(4) (changed)
(4)	s 649(5), (6) (changed)
139 Public company reducing capital below authorised minimum	
(1)	s 650(1)
(2)	s 650(2)
(3)	s 651(1), (2)
(4)	s 651(3) (changed)
(5)	s 651(4), (6), (7)
140 Liability of members on reduced shares	
(1)	s 652(1) (changed)
(2)	s 653(1)
(3)	s 653(2)
(4)	s 653(3)
(5)	s 653(3)
141 Penalty for concealing name of creditor, etc	
	s 647(1), (2) (changed)
142 Duty of directors on serious loss of capital	
(1)	s 656(1)–(3)
(2)	s 656(4), (5) (changed)
(3)	s 656(6)
143 General rule against company acquiring own shares	
(1)	s 658(1)
(2)	s 658(2), (3)
(2A)	s 725(4)
(3)	s 659(1), (2)
144 Acquisition of shares by company's nominee	
(1)	s 660(1), (2) (changed)
(2)	s 661(1), (2) (changed)
(3)	s 661(3)
(4)	s 661(4)
145 Exceptions from s 144	
(1)	s 660(3)
(2)	ss 660(3), 661(5)
(3)	s 671
146 Treatment of shares held by or for public company	
(1)	ss 662(1), 671
(2)	s 662(2), (3)
(3)	s 662(3)
(4)	s 662(5), (6)
147 Matters arising out of compliance with s 146(2)	
(2)	s 664(1), (2)
(3)	s 664(4) (changed)
(4)	s 665(1), (2), (4), (5) (changed)
148 Further provisions supplementing ss 146, 147	
(1)	s 668(1), (2)
(2)	s 668(3)

CA 1985	CA 2006
(3)	s 671
(4)	s 669(1), (2)
149 Sanctions for non-compliance	
(1)	s 666(1), (2)
(2)	s 667(1)–(3)
150 Charges of public companies on own shares	
(1)	s 670(1)
(2)	s 670(2)
(3)	s 670(3)
(4)	s 670(4)
151 Financial assistance generally prohibited	
(1)	ss 678(1), 679(1) (changed)
(2)	ss 678(3), 679(3) (changed)
(3)	s 680(1), (2)
152 Definitions for this Chapter	
(1)	ss 677(1), 683(1)
(2)	s 677(2), (3)
(3)	s 683(2)
153 Transactions not prohibited by s 151	
(1)	ss 678(2), 679(2) (changed)
(2)	ss 678(4), 679(4)
(3)	s 681(1), (2)
(4)	s 682(1), (2)
(5)	s 682(5)
154 Special restriction for public companies	
(1)	s 682(1)
(2)	ss 682(3), (4), 840(4), (5)
159 Power to issue redeemable shares	
(1)	s 684(1), (3) (changed)
(2)	s 684(4)
(3)	ss 686(1)–(3) (changed), 691(1), (2)
160 Financing etc of redemption	
(1)	ss 687(1)–(3), (6), 692(1), (2), (5)
(2)	ss 687(4), (5), 692(3), (4)
(4)	ss 688, 706 (changed)
162 Power of company to purchase own shares	
(1)	s 690(1) (changed)
(2)	ss 691(1), (2), 692(1)–(5)
(2A)	s 706
(2B)	ss 706, 724(1)
(3)	s 690(2)
(4)	s 724(2)
162A Treasury shares	
(1)	s 724(3)
(2)	s 724(4)
(3)	s 724(5)
162B Treasury shares: maximum holdings	
(1)	s 725(1)
(2)	s 725(2)
(3)	s 725(4)
162C Treasury shares: voting and other rights	
(1)	s 726(1)
(2), (3)	s 726(2)

CA 1985	CA 2006
(4)	s 726(3)
(5)	s 726(4)
(6)	s 726(5)
162D Treasury shares: disposal and cancellation	
(1)	ss 727(1), 729(1)
(2)	s 727(2) (changed)
(3)	s 727(3)
(4)	s 729(4)
(5)	s 729(5)
162E Treasury shares: mandatory cancellation	
(1)	s 729(2)
(2)	s 729(3)
162F Treasury shares: proceeds of sale	
(1)	s 731(1)
(2)	s 731(2)
(3)	s 731(3)
(4), (5)	s 731(4)
162G Treasury shares: penalty for contravention	
	s 732(1), (2) (changed)
163 Definitions of "off-market" and "market" purchase	
(1)	s 693(2)
(2)	s 693(3)
(3)	s 693(4)
(4), (5)	s 693(5)
164 Authority for off-market purchase	
(1)	ss 693(1), 694(1)
(2)	s 694(2) (changed)
(3)	ss 694(4), 697(3), 700(3)
(4)	ss 694(5), 697(4), 700(4)
(5)	ss 694(1), (3), (4), 698(1), (3), (4), 700(5)
(6)	ss 696(1)–(5), 699(1)–(6), 700(5) (changed)
(7)	ss 697(1)–(4), 698(1), (3), (4), 699(1)–(6), 700(3)–(5)
165 Authority for contingent purchase contract	
(1)	s 694(3)
(2)	ss 694(2), (4), (5), 695(1), (3), (5), 696(1)–(5)
166 Authority for market purchase	
(1)	ss 693(1), 701(1)
(2)	s 701(2)
(3)	s 701(3), (5)
(4)	s 701(4), (5)
(5)	s 701(6)
(6)	s 701(7)
(7)	s 701(8)
167 Assignment or release of company's right to purchase own shares	
(1)	s 704
(2)	s 700(1)–(5)
168 Payments apart from purchase price to be made out of distributable profits	
(1)	s 705(1)
(2)	s 705(2)

CA 1985	CA 2006
169 Disclosure by company of purchase of own shares	
(1)	ss 707(1)–(3), 708(1) (changed)
(1A)	ss 707(1)–(3), 708(1) (changed)
(1B)	ss 707(1)–(3), 708(1) (changed)
(2)	s 707(4)
(3)	s 707(5)
(4)	s 702(1)–(4) (changed)
(5)	s 702(6)
(6)	ss 707(6), (7), 708(4), (5)
(7)	s 703(1), (2) (changed)
(8)	s 703(3)
(9)	s 702(7)
169A Disclosure by company of cancellation or disposal of treasury shares	
(1)	ss 728(1), 730(1)
(2)	ss 728(2), 730(2)
(3)	ss 728(3), 730(3)
(4)	ss 728(4), (5), 730(6), (7)
170 The capital redemption reserve	
(1)	s 733(1), (2), (4)
(2), (3)	s 733(3)
(4)	s 733(5), (6)
171 Power of private companies to redeem or purchase own shares out of capital	
(1)	s 709(1) (changed)
(2)	s 709(2)
(3)	s 710(1), (2)
(4)	s 734(2)
(5)	s 734(3)
(6)	s 734(4)
172 Availability of profits for purposes of s 171	
(1)	s 711(1), (2)
(2)	s 712(2)
(3)	s 712(6)
(4)	s 712(3)
(5)	s 712(4)
(6)	s 712(7)
173 Conditions for payment out of capital	
(1)	s 713(1), (2)
(2)	s 716(1)
(3)	s 714(1)–(3)
(4)	s 714(4) (changed)
(5)	s 714(5), (6) (changed)
(6)	s 715(1), (2)
174 Procedure for special resolution under s 173	
(1)	ss 716(2), 723(1)
(2)	s 717(3)
(3)	s 717(4)
(4)	s 718(2), (3) (changed)
(5)	s 717(5)

Part 3   CA 2006 Supporting Materials

CA 1985	CA 2006
175 Publicity for proposed payment out of capital	
(1)	s 719(1)
(2)	s 719(2)
(3)	s 719(3)
(4)	ss 719(4), 720(1)
(5)	s 719(4)
(6)	s 720(1), (2), (4) (changed)
(7)	s 720(5), (6)
(8)	s 720(7)
176 Objections by company's members or creditors	
(1)	s 721(1), (2)
(2)	s 721(2)
(3)	s 722(2), (3)
(4)	s 722(4), (5)
177 Powers of court on application under s 176	
(1)	s 721(3)
(2)	s 721(4), (5)
(3)	s 721(6)
(4)	s 721(7)
178 Effect of company's failure to redeem or purchase	
(1)	s 735(1)
(2)	s 735(2)
(3)	s 735(2), (3)
(4)	s 735(4)
(5)	s 735(5)
(6)	s 735(6)
181 Definitions for Chapter VII	
	s 736
182 Nature, transfer and numbering of shares	
(1)	ss 541, 544(1), (2)
(2)	s 543(1), (2)
183 Transfer and registration	
(1)	s 770(1)
(2)	s 770(2)
(3)	s 773
(4)	s 772
184 Certification of transfers	
(1)	s 775(1), (2)
(2)	s 775(3)
(3)	s 775(4)
185 Duty of company as to issue of certificates	
(1)	ss 769(1), (2), 776(1), (3)
(2)	s 776(2)
(3)	s 777(1), (2)
(4)	ss 769(2), 776(3), 778(1)
(4A)	s 778(1)
(4B), (4C)	s 778(2)
(4D)	s 778(3)
(5)	ss 769(3), (4), 776(5), (6)
(6)	s 782(1)
(7)	s 782(2), (3)
186 Certificate to be evidence of title	
(1)	s 768(1), (2)

CA 1985	CA 2006
(2)	s 768(2)
187 Evidence of grant of probate or confirmation as executor	
	s 774
188 Issue and effect of share warrant to bearer	
(1)	s 779(1)
(2)	s 779(2)
(3)	s 779(3)
189 Offences in connections with share warrants (Scotland)	
(1)	s 781(1), (3)
(2)	s 781(2), (4)
190 Register of debenture holders	
(1)	s 743(6)
(5)	s 743(2), (6) (changed)
(6)	s 743(3)
191 Right to inspect register	
(1)	s 744(1)
(2)	s 744(2)
(3)	s 749(1)
(4)	ss 746(1), (2), 749(2), (3)
(5)	ss 746(3), 749(4)
(6)	s 744(5)
(7)	s 748(1), (2) (changed)
192 Liability of trustees of debentures	
(1)	s 750(1), (3)
(2)	s 750(2)
(3)	s 751(1), (2)
(4)	s 751(3), (4)
193 Perpetual debentures	
	s 739(1), (2)
194 Power to re-issue redeemed debentures	
(1)	s 752(1)
(2)	s 752(2)
(3)	s 753
(4)	s 752(3)
(5)	s 752(4)
195 Contract to subscribe for debentures	
	s 740
196 Payment of debts out of assets subject to floating charge (England and Wales)	
(1)	s 754(1)
(2)	s 754(2)
(3)	s 754(3)
(4)	s 754(4)
197 Debentures to bearer (Scotland)	
	s 742
198 Obligation of disclosure: the cases in which it may arise and "the relevant time"	
(2)	s 792(1), (2) (changed)
203 Notification of family and corporate interests	
(1)	s 822(1), (2)
(2)	s 823(1)
(3)	s 832(2)
(4)	s 823(3)

CA 1985	CA 2006
204 Agreement to acquire interests in a particular company	
(1)	s 824(1)
(2)	ss 824(1), (2), 988(4)
(3)	ss 824(3), 988(6)
(4)	s 824(4)
(5)	ss 824(5), 988(7)
(6)	ss 824(6), 988(5)
205 Obligation of disclosure arising under s 204	
(1)	s 825(1)
(2)	s 825(2)
(3)	s 825(3)
(4)	s 825(4)
207 Interests in shares by attribution	
(1)	ss 783, 785(1)
(2)	s 785(2)
(3)	s 785(3)
(4)	s 785(4)
(5)	s 785(5)
(6)	s 785(6)
(7)	s 788
(9)	s 784(3)
(10)	s 783
208 Interests in shares which are to be notified	
(1)	s 820(1)
(2)	s 820(2)
(3)	s 820(3)
(4)	s 820(4)
(5)	s 820(6)
(6)	s 820(5)
(7)	s 820(7)
(8)	s 820(8)
210A Power to make further provision by regulations	
(1)	s 828(1), (2)
(5)	s 828(3)
211 Register of interests in shares	
(3)	s 808(2)
(4)	s 808(7)
(5)	s 808(4)
(6)	s 810(1)–(3)
(7)	s 819(1)
(8)	ss 809(1), 810(4), 811(1), (2), 813(1)–(3) (changed)
(9)	s 826(1)
(10)	ss 808(5), (6), 819(2), (3)
212 Company investigations	
(1)	s 793(1), (2) (changed)
(2)	s 793(3), (4), (6)
(3)	s 793(5)
(4)	s 793(7)
(5)	ss 820(1)–(8), 822(1), (2), 823(1)–(3), 824(1)–(6), 825(1)–(4)
(6)	s 821(1), (2)

CA 1985	CA 2006
213 Registration of interests disclosed under s 212	
(1)	s 808(1)–(3) (changed)
(3)	ss 808(2), (4)–(7), 809(1), 810(1)–(4), 811(1), (2), 813(1)–(3), 819(1)–(3), 826(1)
214 Company investigation on requisition by members	
(1)	s 803(1), (2) (changed)
(2)	s 803(3) (changed)
(4)	s 804(1)
(5)	s 804(2), (3) (changed)
215 Company report to members	
(1)	s 805(1)
(2)	s 805(2), (3)
(3)	s 805(1), (3)
(4)	s 826(1), (2)
(5)	s 805(6)
(6)	s 805(7)
(7)	ss 805(4), 807(1)–(5)
(8)	s 806(3), (4)
216 Penalty for failure to provide information	
(1)	s 794(1)
(1A)	s 794(3)
(1B)	s 794(2)
(3)	s 795(1), (3)
(4)	s 795(2)
(5)	s 796(1), (2)
217 Removal of entries from register	
(1)	s 816 (changed)
(2)	s 817(1) (changed)
(3)	s 817(2), (3)
(4)	s 818(1), (2)
(5)	ss 817(4), 818(3)
218 Otherwise, entries not to be removed	
(1)	s 815(1)
(2)	s 815(2)
(3)	s 815(3), (4)
219 Inspection of register and reports	
(1)	s 807(1), 811(1)
(2)	s 807(2), 811(2)
(3)	ss 807(3), (4), 813(1), (2) (changed)
(4)	ss 807(5), 813(3)
220 Definitions for Part VI	
(2)	s 827
221 Duty to keep accounting records	
(1)	s 386(1), (2)
(2)–(4)	s 386(3)–(5)
(5)	s 387(1), (2)
(6)	s 387(3)
222 Where and for how long records to be kept	
(1)–(3)	s 388(1)–(3)
(4)	s 389(1), (2), (4)

CA 1985	CA 2006
(5)	s 388(4), (5)
(6)	s 389(3), (4)
223 A company's financial year	
(1)–(5)	s 390(1)–(5)
224 Accounting reference periods and accounting reference date	
(1)	s 391(1)
(2), (3)	s 391(2)
(3A)	s 391(4)
(4)–(6)	s 391(5)–(7)
225 Alteration of accounting reference date	
(1)	s 392(1)
(3)–(7)	s 392(2)–(6)
226 Duty to prepare individual accounts	
(1)	s 394
(2)–(6)	s 395(1)–(5)
226A Companies Act individual accounts	
(1), (2)	s 396(1), (2)
(3)	s 396(3) (changed)
(4)	s 396(4)
(5), (6)	s 396(5)
226B IAS individual accounts	
	s 397
227 Duty to prepare group accounts	
(1)	s 399(2)
(2)–(7)	s 403(1)–(6)
(8)	s 399(2), (3)
227A Companies Act group accounts	
(1), (2)	s 404(1), (2)
(3)	s 404(3) (changed)
(4)	s 404(4)
(5), (6)	s 404(5)
227B IAS group accounts	
	s 406
227C Consistency of accounts	
(1)–(5)	s 407(1)–(5)
228 Exemption for parent companies included in accounts of larger group	
(1), (2)	s 400(1), (2)
(3)	s 400(4)
(4)	s 400(5)
(5)	s 400(3)
(6)	s 400(6)
228A Exemption for parent companies included in non-EEA group accounts	
(1), (2)	s 401(1), (2)
(3)	s 401(4)
(4)	s 401(5)
(5)	s 401(3)
(6)	s 401(6)
229 Subsidiary undertakings included in the consolidation	
(1), (2)	s 405(1), (2)
(3)	s 405(3), (4)
(5)	s 402

CA 1985	CA 2006
230 Treatment of individual profit and loss account where group accounts prepared	
(1)	s 408(1) (changed)
(2)	s 408(2) (changed)
(3), (40	s 408(3), (4)
231 Disclosure required in notes to accounts: related undertakings	
(1), (2)	s 409(1), (2) (changed)
(3)	s 409(3), (4) (changed)
(4)	s 409(5)
(5)	s 410(1), (2)
(6)	s 410(3)
(7)	s 410(4), (5)
231A Disclosure required in notes to annual accounts: particulars of staff	
(1)	s 411(1)
(2)–(4)	s 411(3)–(5)
(5)	s 411(2)
(6)	s 411(7)
(7)	s 411(6)
232 Disclosure required in notes to accounts: emoluments and other benefits of directors and others	
(3)	s 412(5)
(4)	s 412(6)
233 Approval and signing of accounts	
(1), (2)	ss 414(1), (2), 450(1), (2)
(3)	ss 433(1)–(3), 436(1), (2),
(4)	ss 444(6), 445(5), 446(3), 447(3) (changed)
(5)	s 414(4), (5) (changed)
(6)(a)	s 433(4), (5),
234 Duty to prepare directors' report	
(1)	ss 415(1), 417(1), 418(2)
(2), (3)	s 415(2), (3)
(5)	ss 415(4), (5), 419(3), (4)
234ZZA Directors' report: general requirements	
(1)	s 416(1), (3)
(2)	s 416(2)
(3), (4)	s 416(4) (changed)
234ZZB Directors' report: business review	
(1), (2)	s 417(3), (4)
(3)	s 417(6)
(4)	s 417(8)
(5)	s 417(6)
(6)	s 417(9)
234ZA Statement as to disclosure of information to auditors	
(1)–(4)	s 418(1)–(4)
(6)	s 418(5), (6)
234A Approval and signing of directors' report	
(1)	s 419(1)
(2)	ss 433(1)–(3), 436(1), (2)
(3)	ss 444(6), 445(5), 446(3), 447(3)
(4)	ss 419(3), (4), 433(4), (5)

CA 1985	CA 2006
234B Duty to prepare directors' remuneration report	
(1)	ss 420(1), 421(1), (2)
(2)	s 421(1), (2)
(3), (4)	s 420(2), (3)
(5), (6)	s 421(3), (4)
234C Approval and signing of directors' remuneration report	
(1)	s 422(1)
(2)	ss 433(1)–(3), 436(1), (2)
(3)	s 447(3)
(4)	s 422(2), (3)
235 Auditors' report	
(1)	ss 475(1), 495(1)
(1A)	s 495(2)
(1B), (2)	s 495(3)
(2A)	s 495(4)
(3)	s 496
(4), (5)	s 497(1), (2)
236 Signature of auditors' report	
(1)	s 503(1), (2)
(2)	s 505(1), (2) (changed)
(3)	s 444(7) (changed)
(4)	s 505(3), (4)
237 Duties of auditors	
(1)–(4)	s 498(1)–(4)
(4A)	s 498(5)
238 Persons entitled to receive copies of accounts and reports	
(1), (1A)	ss 423(1), 424(1)–(3) (changed)
(3)	s 423(4)
(4)	s 424(4) (changed)
(5)	s 425(1), (2)
(6)	s 423(5)
239 Right to demand copies of accounts and reports	
(1), (2)	ss 431(1), (2), 432(1), (2)
(3)	ss 431(3), (4), 432(3), (4)
240 Requirements in connection with publication of accounts	
(1)	s 434(1) (changed)
(2)	s 434(2) (changed)
(3)	s 435(1), (2) (changed)
(4)	s 436(1), (2) (changed)
(5)	ss 434(3), 435(3) (changed)
(6)	s 435(5), (6)
241 Accounts and reports to be laid before company in general meeting	
(1)	s 437(1) (changed)
(2)	ss 437(2), 438(1), (4)
(3), (4)	s 438(2), (3)
241A Members' approval of directors' remuneration report	
(1), (3)	s 439(1)
(4)	s 439(2)
(5)	s 439(3)

CA 1985	CA 2006
(6)	s 439(4)
(7)	s 439(3)
(8)	s 439(5)
(9)	s 440(1), (4)
(10)	s 440(2)–(4)
(11)	s 440(2), (3)
(12)	s 439(6)
242 Accounts and reports to be delivered to the registrar	
(1)	ss 441(1), 444(1), (2), 445(1), (2), 446(1), (2), 447(1), (2) (changed)
(2)	s 451(1)
(3)	s 452(1), (2)
(4), (5)	s 451(2), (3)
242A Civil penalty for failure to deliver accounts	
(1)	s 453(1)
(2)	s 453(2) (changed)
(3), (4)	s 453(3), (4)
242B Delivery and publication of accounts in ECUs	
(1)–(4)	s 469(1)–(4)
244 Period allowed for laying and delivering accounts and reports	
(1), (2)	s 442(2), (3) (changed)
(4), (5)	s 442(4), (5)
(6)	s 442(7)
245 Voluntary revision of annual accounts or directors' report	
(1)–(3)	s 454(1)–(3)
(4)	s 454(4) (changed)
(5)	s 454(5)
245A Secretary of State's notice in respect of annual accounts	
(1)	s 455(1), (2)
(2)–(4)	s 455(3)–(5)
245B Application to court in respect of defective accounts	
(1)–(3)	s 456(1)–(3)
(3A)	s 456(4)
(4)–(7)	s 456(5)–(8)
245C Other persons authorised to apply to court	
(1)	s 457(1)
(1A)	s 457(5)
(2), (3)	s 457(2), (3)
(4)	s 457(7)
(4A)	s 457(5)
(4B)	s 457(4)
(5)	s 457(6)
245D Disclosure of information held by Inland Revenue to persons authorised to apply to court	
(1)	s 458(1)
(2)	s 458(2)
(3)	s 458(1)

Part 3   CA 2006 Supporting Materials

CA 1985	CA 2006
245E Restrictions on use and further disclosure of information disclosed under section 245D	
(1), (2)	s 458(3)
(3)	s 458(4), (5)
(4)	s 458(4) (changed)
(5)	ss 1126, 1130
245F Power of authorised persons to require documents, information and explanations	
(1)–(8)	s 459(1)–(8)
245G Restrictions on further disclosure of information obtained under section 245F	
(1), (2)	s 460(1), (2)
(3)	ss 460(3), 461(1)–(6)
(4)–(6)	s 462(1)–(3)
(7)	s 460(4), (5)
(8)	s 460(4)
(9)	ss 1126, 1130
(10)	s 460(3)
(11)	s 461(7)
246 Special provisions for small companies	
(3)	s 411(1)
(4)	ss 416(3), 417(1)
(5)	s 444(1), (3) (changed)
(6)	s 444(3) (changed)
(7)	ss 444(6), 450(1), (2)
(8)	ss 414(3), 419(2), 444(5), 450(3)
246A Special provisions for medium-sized companies	
(1)	s 445(1)
(2)	s 445(3) (changed)
(2A)	s 417(7)
(3)	s 445(3) (changed)
(4)	s 450(3)
247 Qualification of company as small or medium-sized	
(1)(a)	ss 382(1), 465(1)
(1)(b), (2)	ss 382(2), 465(2)
(3), (4)	ss 382(3), (4), 465(3), (4)
(5)	ss 382(5), 465(5) (changed)
(6)	ss 382(6), 465(6)
247A Cases in which special provisions do not apply	
(1)–(1B)	ss 384(1), 467(1)
(2)	ss 384(2), 467(2) (changed)
(2A)	ss 384(3), 467(3)
(3)	ss 383(1), 466(1)
247B Special auditors' report	
(1)	s 449(1)
(2)	ss 444(4), 445(4), 449(2)
(3)–(5)	s 449(3)–(5)
248 Exemption for small and medium-sized groups	
(1), (2)	ss 398, 399(1), (2) (changed)
249 Qualification of group as small or medium-sized	
(1)(a)	s 466(2)

CA 1985	CA 2006
(1)(b), (2)	s 466(3)
(3)	s 466(4)
(4)	s 466(5), (6)
(5), (6)	s 466(7)
249A Exemptions from audit	
(1)	s 477(1)
(3)	s 477(2), (4)
(6)	s 477(3)
(7)	s 477(4)
249AA Dormant companies	
(1), (2)	s 480(1), (2)
(3)	s 481
(4)	s 1169(1)
(5)–(7)	s 1169(2), (3)
249B Cases where exemptions not available	
(1)	ss 478, 479(1)–(3)
(1A)	s 479(3)
(1B)	s 479(1)–(3)
(1C)	s 479(2), (5), (6)
(2), (3)	s 476(1)–(3)
(4)	s 475(2), (3)
(5)	s 475(4)
249E Effect of exemptions	
(1)(b)	ss 444(2), 445(2), 446(2) (changed)
251 Provision of summary financial statement to shareholders	
(1)	ss 426(1), 427(1)
(2)	s 426(2), (3)
(3)	ss 427(2), 428(2)
(3A)	ss 427(3), 428(3)
(4)	ss 427(4), 428(4)
(5)	ss 427(6), 428(6)
(6)	s 429(1), (2)
(7)	ss 434(6), 435(7)
254 Exemption from requirement to deliver accounts and reports	
(1)–(3)	s 448(1)–(3)
(4)	s 448(4)
255A Special provisions for banking and insurance groups	
(4)	s 1164(5)
(5)	s 1165(5)
(5A)	ss 1164(5), 1165(6)
255D Power to apply provisions to banking partnerships	
(1)	s 470(1)
(2), (2A)	s 470(2)
(4)	s 470(4)
(5)	s 470(3)
256 Accounting standards	
(1), (2)	s 464(1), (2)
(4)	s 464(3)
257 Power of Secretary of State to alter accounting requirements	
(1)	s 484(1)

CA 1985	CA 2006
(2)	ss 473(1)–(4) (changed), 484(3)
(3)	s 484(4)
(4)(c)	s 484(2)

258 Parent and subsidiary undertakings

CA 1985	CA 2006
(1)–(6)	s 1162(1)–(6)

259 Meaning of "undertaking" and related expressions

CA 1985	CA 2006
(1)	ss 1161(1), 1173 "parent company"
(2)–(5)	s 1161(2)–(5)

261 Notes to the accounts

CA 1985	CA 2006
(1), (2)	s 472(1), (2)

262 Minor definitions

CA 1985	CA 2006
(1)	ss 474(1), 539, 835(6), 1173 "credit institution" (changed)
(2)	s 474(2)
(3)	s 853(4), (5)

263 Certain distributions prohibited

CA 1985	CA 2006
(1)	s 830(1)
(2)	s 829(1), (2)
(3)	s 830(2), (3)
(4)	s 849
(5)	s 850(1)–(3)

264 Restriction on distribution of assets

CA 1985	CA 2006
(1)	s 831(1), (6)
(2)	s 831(2), (3)
(3)	s 831(4)
(4)	s 831(5)

265 Other distributions by investment companies

CA 1985	CA 2006
(1)	s 832(1)–(3)
(2)	s 832(4)
(3)	s 832(7)
(4)	s 832(5)
(4A)	s 832(6)
(5)	s 832(6)
(6)	s 832(5)

266 Meaning of "investment company"

CA 1985	CA 2006
(1)	s 833(1)
(2)	ss 833(2), 834(1)
(2A)	s 833(3)
(3)	s 833(4), (5)
(4)	s 834(2)–(5)

267 Extension of ss 265, 266 to other companies

CA 1985	CA 2006
(1)	s 835(1)
(2)	s 835(2)

268 Realised profits of insurance company with long term business

CA 1985	CA 2006
(1)	s 843(1), (2), (4), (5)
(2)	s 843(3), (4)
(3)	s 843(6), (7)
(4)	s 843(7)

269 Treatment of development costs

CA 1985	CA 2006
(1)	s 844(1)
(2)	s 844(2), (3)

270 Distribution to be justified by reference to company's accounts

CA 1985	CA 2006
(1), (2)	s 836(1)
(3)	ss 836(2), 837(1)
(4)	ss 836(2), 838(1), 839(1)
(5)	s 836(3), (4)

271 Requirements for last annual accounts

CA 1985	CA 2006
(2)	s 837(2)
(3)	s 837(3), (4)
(4)	s 837(4)
(5)	s 837(5)

272 Requirements for interim accounts

CA 1985	CA 2006
(1)	s 838(2)
(2)	s 838(3)
(3)	ss 838(4), (5), 839(4)
(4), (5)	s 838(6)

273 Requirements for initial accounts

CA 1985	CA 2006
(1)	s 839(2)
(2)	s 839(3)
(3)	s 839(4)
(4)	s 839(5), (6)
(5)	s 839(6)
(6), (7)	s 839(7)

274 Method of applying s 270 to successive distributions

CA 1985	CA 2006
(1)	s 840(1)
(2)	s 840(1), (2)
(3)	s 840(3)–(5)

275 Treatment of assets in the relevant accounts

CA 1985	CA 2006
(1)	s 841(1), (2)
(1A)	s 841(3)
(2)	s 841(5)
(3)	s 842
(4)–(6)	s 841(4)

276 Distributions in kind

CA 1985	CA 2006
	s 846(1), (2) (changed)

277 Consequences of unlawful distribution

CA 1985	CA 2006
(1)	s 847(1), (2)
(2)	s 847(3), (4)

278 Saving for provision in articles operative before Act of 1980

CA 1985	CA 2006
	s 848(1), (2)

280 Definitions for Part VIII

CA 1985	CA 2006
(1)	s 853(1)
(2)	s 853(2)
(3)	s 853(3)

281 Saving for other restraints on distribution

CA 1985	CA 2006
	ss 851, 852 (changed)
282 Directors	
(1)	s 154(2) (changed)
(3)	s 154(1)
283 Secretary	
(1)	s 271 (changed)
(3)	ss 270(3), 274 (changed)

CA 1985	CA 2006
284 Acts done by person in dual capacity	
	s 280
285 Validity of acts of directors	
	s 161(1), (2) (changed)
286 Qualifications of company secretaries	
(1)	s 273(1), (2) (changed)
(2)	s 273(3)
287 Registered office	
(1)	s 86
(3)	s 87(1)
(4)	s 87(2)
(5)	s 87(3)
(6)	s 87(4)
288 Register of directors and secretaries	
(1)	ss 162(1)–(3), 275(1)–(3) (changed)
(2)	ss 167(1), (2), 276(1), (2)
(3)	ss 162(5), 275(5)
(4)	ss 162(6), (7), 167(4), (5), 275(6), (7), 276(3), (4)
(5)	ss 162(8), 275(8)
(6)	ss 162(6), 167(4), 275(6), 276(3)
289 Particulars of directors to be registered under s 288	
(1)	ss 163(1), 164 (changed)
(2)	ss 163(2), (4), 277(2), (4) (changed)
290 Particulars of secretaries to be registered under s 288	
(1)	ss 277(1), 278(1) (changed)
(2)	s 278(2)
(3)	s 277(2), (4)
292 Appointment of directors to be voted on individually	
(1)	s 160(1)
(2)	s 160(2)
(3)	s 160(3)
(4)	s 160(4)
303 Resolution to remove director	
(1)	s 168(1) (changed)
(2)	s 168(2)
(3)	s 168(3)
(4)	s 168(4)
(5)	s 168(5)
304 Director's right to protest removal	
(1)	s 169(1), (2)
(2)	s 169(3)
(3)	s 169(4)
(4)	s 169(5)
(5)	s 169(6)
309 Directors to have regard to interests of employees	
(1)	s 172(1)
309A Provisions protecting directors from liability	
(1)	s 232(1), (2)

CA 1985	CA 2006
(2)	s 232(1)
(3)	s 232(2)
(4)	s 234(1)
(5)	s 233
(6)	s 232(3)
309B Qualifying third party indemnity provisions	
(1), (2)	s 234(2)
(3)	s 234(3)
(4)	s 234(3), (6)
(5)	s 234(4)
(6), (7)	s 234(5)
309C Disclosure of qualifying third party indemnity provisions	
(1)	s 236(1) (changed)
(2)	s 236(2), (3)
(3)	s 236(4), (5) (changed)
(4)	s 237(1)
(5)	ss 237(1)–(3), (5)–(8), 238(1), (3)–(5)
310 Provisions protecting auditors from liability	
(1)	s 532(1), (3) (changed)
(2)	s 532(2)
(3)	s 533
312 Payment to director for loss of office, etc	
	ss 215(1), 217(1), (3) (changed)
313 Company approval for property transfer	
(1)	ss 215(1), 218(1), (3) (changed)
(2)	s 222(2)
314 Director's duty of disclosure on takeover, etc	
(1)	ss 215(1), 219(1) (changed)
315 Consequences of non-compliance with s 314	
(1)	ss 219(1), (2), 222(3) (changed)
(3)	s 219(5)
316 Provisions supplementing ss 312 to 315	
(1)	ss 218(5), 219(7)
(2)	s 216(1), (2) (changed)
(3)	s 220(1)
317 Directors to disclose interest in contracts	
(1)	s 182(1) (changed)
(2)	s 182(2) (changed)
(3)	s 185(1), (2) (changed)
(4)	s 185(4)
(5)	s 185(1) (changed)
(7)	s 183(1), (2)
(8)	s 187(1)–(4)
318 Director's service contracts to be open to inspection	
(1)	ss 228(1), 237(2)
(2), (3)	ss 228(2), 237(3) (changed)
(4)	ss 228(4), 237(5)
(6)	s 230

CA 1985	CA 2006
(7)	ss 229(1), 238(1)
(8)	ss 228(5), (6), 229(3), (4), 237(6), (7), 238(3), (4) (changed)
(9)	ss 229(5), 238(5) (changed)
(10)	ss 228(7), 237(8)
319 Director's contract of employment for more than 5 years	
(1)	s 188(1), (3) (changed)
(2)	s 188(4) (changed)
(3)	s 188(2) (changed)
(4)	s 188(6)
(5)	s 188(5)
(6)	s 189
(7)	ss 188(7), 223(1)
320 Substantial property transactions involving directors, etc	
(1)	s 190(1), (2) (changed)
(2)	s 191(1)–(5) (changed)
(3)	s 223(1)
321 Exceptions from s 320	
(1)	s 190(4)
(2)	ss 192, 193(1), (2) (changed)
(3)	s 192
(4)	s 194(1), (2)
322 Liabilities arising from contravention of s 320	
(1)	s 195(1), (2)
(2)	ss 195(2) and 196
(3)	s 195(1), (3), (4)
(4)	s 195(3), (5), (8)
(5)	s 195(6)
(6)	s 195(7)
322A Invalidity of certain transactions involving directors, etc	
(1)	s 41(1), (2)
(2)	s 41(2)
(3)	s 41(3)
(4)	s 41(1)
(5)	s 41(4)
(6)	s 41(5)
(7)	s 41(6)
(8)	s 41(7)
322B Contracts with sole members who are directors	
(1)	s 231(1), (2) (changed)
(2)	s 231(1)
(3)	s 231(5)
(4)	s 231(3), (4) (changed)
(5)	s 231(7)
(6)	s 231(6)
325 Register of directors' interests notified under s 324	
(5)	s 809(2), (3)
330 General restriction on loans etc to directors and persons connected with them	
(2)	s 197(1) (changed)

CA 1985	CA 2006
(3)	ss 198(1), (2) (changed), 200(1), (2)
(4)	s 201(1), (2) (changed)
(5)	s 223(1)
(6)	s 203(1), (6) (changed)
(7)	s 203(1) (changed)
331 Definitions for ss 330 ff	
(3)	s 199(1)
(4)	s 199(2), (3)
(6)	ss 198(1), 200(1), 201(1)
(7)	s 202(1)
(8)	s 202(3)
(9)	ss 202(2), 212
(10)	s 202(3)
333 Inter-company loans in same group	
	s 208(1) (changed)
334 Loans of small amounts	
	s 207(1) (changed)
335 Minor and business transactions	
(1)	s 207(2) (changed)
(2)	s 207(3)
336 Transactions at behest of holding company	
	208(1), (2) (changed)
337 Funding of director's expenditure on duty to company	
(1), (2)	s 204(1) (changed)
(3)	s 204(2) (changed)
337A Funding of director's expenditure on defending proceedings	
(1)	s 205(1) (changed)
(2)	s 205(5)
(3)	s 205(1) (changed)
(4)	s 205(2)
(5)	s 205(3)
(6)	s 205(4)
338 Loan or quasi-loan by money-lending company	
(1)	s 209(1)
(2)	s 209(2)
(3)	s 209(1)
(6)	s 209(3), (4)
339 "Relevant amounts" for purposes of ss 334 ff	
(1)	ss 204(2), 207(1), (2), 210(1)
(2)	ss 204(2), 207(1), (2), 210(2)–(4)
(3)	s 210(3), (4)
(5)	s 210(5)
(6)	s 211(1)
340 "Value" of transactions and arrangements	
(2)	s 211(2)
(3)	s 211(3)
(4)	s 211(5)
(5)	s 211(6)
(6)	s 211(4)
(7)	s 211(7) (changed)

Part 3   CA 2006 Supporting Materials

CA 1985	CA 2006
341 Civil remedies for breach of s 330	
(1)	s 213(1), (2)
(2)	s 213(3), (4)
(3)	s 213(5), (8)
(4)	s 213(6)
(5)	s 213(7)
345 Power to increase financial limits	
(1)	s 258(1)
(2)	s 258(2)
(3)	s 258(3)
346 "Connected persons", etc	
(1)	ss 252(1), 254(1), 255(1)
(2), (3)	ss 252(2), (3), 253(2) (changed)
(4)	s 254(2), (5)
(5)	s 255(2), (5)
(6)	ss 254(6), 255(6)
(7)	ss 254(3), 255(3)
(8)	ss 254(4), 255(4)
347 Transactions under foreign law	
	s 259
347A Introductory provisions	
(1)	s 362 (changed)
(3)	s 379(1)
(4)	s 364(2)
(5)	s 365(1) (changed)
(6)	s 363(1), (2)
(7)	s 363(1), (2) (changed)
(8)	s 379(1)
(9)	s 363(1)
(10)	ss 366(5), 379(2)
347B Exemptions	
(1)	s 375(1)
(2)	s 375(2) (changed)
(3)	s 376(1), (2)
(4)	s 378(1) (changed)
(5)	s 378(3)
(6), (7)	s 378(1) (changed)
(8)	s 377(1)
(9)	s 377(3)
(10)	s 377(2)
(11)	s 377(4)
347C Prohibition on donations and political expenditure by companies	
(1)	s 366(1), (2), (5) (changed)
(2)	s 367(3), (6) (changed)
(3)	s 368(1), (2)
(4)	s 367(5)
(6)	s 366(6)
347D Special rules for subsidiaries	
(1)	s 366(2)
(2)	s 366(2), (5) (changed)
(3)	s 366(2), (3), (5) (changed)
(4)	s 367(3), (6) (changed)
(5)	s 368(1), (2)

CA 1985	CA 2006
(6)	s 367(5)
(9)	s 366(6)
347F Remedies for breach of prohibitions on company donations etc	
(1)	s 369(1)
(2)	s 369(2), (3) (changed)
(3)	s 369(2), (5)
(4)	s 369(2)
(5)	s 369(6)
(6)	s 369(3) (changed)
347I Enforcement of directors' liabilities by shareholder action	
(1)	s 370(1), (2) (changed)
(2)	s 370(3)
(3)	ss 370(4), 371(1)
(4), (5)	s 371(2)
(6)	s 371(3)
(7)	s 371(4)
(8)	s 371(5)
347J Costs of shareholder action	
(1)	s 372(1)
(2)	s 372(2)
(3)	s 372(3)
(4), (5)	s 372(4)
(6)	s 372(5)
347K Information for purposes of shareholder action	
(1)	s 373(1)
(2)	s 373(2)
348 Company name to appear outside place of business	
(1)	s 82(1), (2)
(2)	s 84(1), (2)
349 Company's name to appear in its correspondence, etc	
(1)	s 82(1), (2)
(2), (3)	s 84(1), (2)
350 Company seal	
(1)	s 45(2), (3) (changed)
(2)	s 45(4), (5)
351 Particulars in correspondence etc	
(1), (2)	s 82(1), (2)
(5)	s 84(1), (2)
352 Obligation to keep and enter up register	
(1)	s 113(1)
(2)	s 113(2)
(3)	s 113(3), (4)
(4)	s 113(6)
(5)	s 113(7), (8)
(6)	s 121 (changed)
(7)	s 128(1), (2)
352A Statement that company has only one member	
(1)	s 123(2) (changed)
(2)	s 123(3) (changed)
(3)	s 123(4), (5)

CA 1985	CA 2006
(3A)	s 124(1), (2)
353 Location of register	
(1)	s 114(1) (changed)
(2)	s 114(2)
(3)	s 114(3), (4)
(4)	s 114(5), (6)
354 Index of members	
(1)	s 115(1), (2)
(2)	s 115(3)
(3)	s 115(4) (changed)
(4)	s 115(5), (6)
355 Entries in register in relation to share warrants	
(1)	s 122(1) (changed)
(2)	s 122(4)
(3)	s 122(5)
(4)	s 122(2), (6)
(5)	s 122(3)
356 Inspection of register and index	
(1)	s 116(1) (changed)
(3)	s 116(2)
(5)	s 118(1), (2) (changed)
(6)	s 118(3)
359 Power of court to rectify register	
(1)	s 125(1)
(2)	s 125(2)
(3)	s 125(3)
(4)	s 125(4)
360 Trusts not to be entered on register in England and Wales	
	s 126
361 Register to be evidence	
	s 127
362 Overseas branch registers	
(1)	s 129(1)
(2)	s 129(1), (5)
(3)	ss 130(1)–(3), 131(1), (4), 132(1)–(4), 133(1)–(3), 134(1)–(3), 135(1)–(5)
363 Duty to deliver annual returns	
(1)	s 854(1), (2)
(2)	s 854(3) (changed)
(3)	s 858(1)–(3)
(4)	s 858(1), (2), (4) (changed)
364 Contents of annual return: general	
(1)	s 855(1) (changed)
(2)	s 855(2)
(3)	s 855(3)
364A Contents of annual return: particulars of share capital and shareholders	
(1)	s 856(1)
(2)	s 856(2)
(3)	s 856(2) (changed)
(4)	s 856(3)
(5)	s 856(4)
(6)	s 856(5)

CA 1985	CA 2006
(8)	s 856(6)
365 Supplementary provisions: regulations and interpretation	
(1)	s 857(1), (2)
(2)	s 857(3)
(3)	s 859
366 Annual general meeting	
(1)	ss 336(1), 337(1)
(4)	s 336(3), (4)
368 Extraordinary general meeting on members' requisition	
(1)	s 303(1), (2)
(2)	s 303(2), (3) (changed)
(2A)	s 303(2)
(3)	s 303(4), (6) (changed)
(4)	ss 304(1), 305(1), (3)
(5)	s 305(4)
(6)	s 305(6), (7)
(7)	s 304(4)
(8)	s 304(1)
369 Length of notice for calling meetings	
(1), (2)	s 307(2), (3) (changed)
(3)	ss 307(4), 337(2) (changed)
(4)	s 307(5), (6) (changed)
(4A)	s 308 (changed)
(4B)	ss 308, 309(1), (3) (changed)
(4C)	s 309(2)
370 General provisions as to meetings and votes	
(1)	ss 284(4), 310(4), 318(2), 319(2)
(2)	s 310(1)
(4)	s 318(2) (changed)
(5)	s 319(1)
(6)	s 284(1), (3)
370A Quorum at meetings of the sole member	
	s 318(1), (3) (changed)
371 Power of court to order meeting	
(1)	s 306(1), (2)
(2)	s 306(3), (4)
(3)	s 306(5)
372 Proxies	
(1)	s 324(1)
(2)	s 324(2) (changed)
(3)	s 325(1) (changed)
(4)	s 325(3), (4)
(5)	s 327(1), (2) (changed)
(6)	s 326(1)–(4) (changed)
373 Right to demand a poll	
(1)	s 321(1), (2) (changed)
(2)	s 329(1), (2) (changed)
374 Voting on a poll	
	s 322
375 Representation of corporations at meetings	
(1)	s 323(1)

Part 3   CA 2006 Supporting Materials

CA 1985	CA 2006
(2)	s 323(2), (3) (changed)
376 Circulation of members' resolutions	
(1)	ss 314(1), (4), 315(2), 316(2), 338(1), (4), 339(2), 340(2)
(2)	ss 314(2), (3), 338(3)
(3)	ss 315(1), 339(1)
(5)	ss 315(1), 339(1)
(6)	s 339(3)
(7)	ss 315(3), (4), 339(4), (5)
377 In certain cases, compliance with s 376 not required	
(1)	ss 314(4), 316(2), 338(4), 340(2) (changed)
(3)	s 317(1), (2) (changed)
378 Extraordinary and special resolutions	
(1)	s 283(1), (4), (5) (changed)
(2)	s 283(1), (4)–(6) (changed)
(4)	s 320(1), (3)
(5)	s 283(5) (changed)
(6)	s 301 (changed)
379 Resolution requiring special notice	
(1)	s 312(1)
(2)	s 312(2), (3) (changed)
(3)	s 312(4)
380 Registration, etc of resolutions and agreements	
(1)	s 30(1)
(2)	s 36(1), (2) (changed)
(4)	s 29(1) (changed)
(4A)	s 29(2)
(5)	s 30(2), (3)
(6)	s 36(3), (4) (changed)
(7)	ss 30(4), 36(5)
381 Resolution passed at adjourned meeting	
	s 332
381A Written resolutions of private companies	
(1)	ss 288(1), 289(1) (changed)
(2)	s 296(1) (changed)
(4)	s 288(5)
(7)	s 288(2)
381C Written resolutions: supplementary provisions	
(1)	s 300
382 Minutes of meetings	
(1)	ss 248(1), 355(1)
(2)	ss 249(1), 356(4)
(4)	ss 249(2), 356(5)
(5)	ss 248(3), (4), 355(3), (4) (changed)
382A Recording of written resolutions	
(1)	s 355(1) (changed)
(2)	s 356(2), (3)
382B Recording of decisions by the sole member	
(1)	s 357(1), (2)

CA 1985	CA 2006
(2)	s 357(3), (4)
(3)	s 357(5)
383 Inspection of minute books	
(1)	s 358(1), (3) (changed)
(3)	s 358(4) (changed)
(4)	s 358(5), (6) (changed)
(5)	s 358(7)
384 Duty to appoint auditors	
(1)	ss 485(1), 489(1) (changed)
(2)	s 489(2)
385 Appointment at general meeting at which accounts laid	
(2)	ss 489(2), (4), 491(1) (changed)
(3)	s 489(3) (changed)
(4)	s 489(4) (changed)
387 Appointment by Secretary of State in default of appointment by company	
(1)	ss 486(1), 490(1)
(2)	ss 486(2)–(4), 490(2)–(4)
388 Filling of casual vacancies	
(1)	ss 489(3), 526
389A Rights to information	
(1)	s 499(1)
(2)	s 499(2)
(3)	s 500(1)
(4)	s 500(2)
(5)	s 500(3)
(6)	ss 499(3), 500(4)
(7)	ss 499(4) 500(5)
389B Offences relating to the provision of information to auditors	
(1)	s 501(1), (2)
(2)	s 501(3)
(3)	s 501(3) (changed)
(4)	s 501(4), (5)
(5)	s 501(6)
390 Right to attend company meetings, &c	
(1)	s 502(2)
(2)	s 502(1)
(3)	s 502(2)
390A Remuneration of auditors	
(1)	s 492(1)
(2)	s 492(2), (3)
(4)	s 492(4)
(5)	s 492(5)
390B Disclosure of services provided by auditors or associates and related remuneration	
(1)	ss 494(1), 501(1), (2)
(2)	s 494(2)
(3)	s 494(3)
(4)	s 494(4)
(5)	s 494(5)
(8)	s 494(1)
(9)	s 494(6)

CA 1985	CA 2006
391 Removal of auditors	
(1)	s 510(1), (2)
(2)	s 512(1)–(3)
(3)	s 510(3)
(4)	s 513(1), (2)
391A Rights of auditors who are removed or not re-appointed	
(1)	ss 511(1), 515(1), (2) (changed)
(2)	ss 511(2), 515(3)
(3)	ss 511(3), 515(4)
(4)	ss 511(4), 515(5)
(5)	ss 511(5), 515(6)
(6)	ss 511(6), 515(7)
392 Resignation of auditors	
(1)	s 516(1), (2)
(2)	s 516(3)
(3)	s 517(1)–(3)
392A Rights of resigning auditors	
(1)	s 518(1)
(2)	s 518(2)
(3)	s 518(3)
(4)	s 518(4)
(5)	s 518(5)–(7)
(6)	s 518(8)
(7)	s 518(9)
(8)	s 518(10)
394 Statement by person ceasing to hold office as auditor	
(1)	s 519(1)–(3), (7) (changed)
(2)	s 519(4) (changed)
(3)	s 520(2)
(4)	s 520(3)
(5)	s 521(1)
(6)	s 520(4)
(7)	ss 520(5), 521(2) (changed)
394A Offences of failing to comply with s 394	
(1)	ss 519(5), 521(3)–(5)
(2)	ss 519(6), 521(4)
(4)	s 520(6), (8) (changed)
395 Certain charges void if not registered	
(1)	ss 860(1), 861(5), 870(1), 874(1), (2)
(2)	s 874(3)
396 Charges which have to be registered	
(1)	ss 860(7), 861(2)
(2)	s 861(3)
(3)	s 861(1)
(3A)	s 861(4)
(4)	s 861(5)
397 Formalities of registration (debentures)	
(1)	ss 863(1)–(4), 870(3)
(2)	s 864(1), (3)
(3)	s 864(2)

CA 1985	CA 2006
398 Verification of charge on property outside United Kingdom	
(1)	s 866(1)
(2)	s 870(1)
(3)	s 866(2)
(4)	s 867(1), (2)
399 Company's duty to register charges it creates	
(1)	ss 860(1), (2), 863(5)
(2)	ss 860(3), 863(5)
(3)	ss 860(4)–(6), 863(5)
400 Charges existing on property acquired	
(1)	ss 861(5), 862(1)
(2)	ss 862(2), (3), 870(2)
(3)	s 870(2)
(4)	s 862(4), (5) (changed)
401 Register of charges to be kept by registrar of companies	
(1)	s 869(1), (2), (4)
(2)	s 869(5), (6)
(3)	s 869(7)
402 Endorsement of certificate on debentures	
(1)	s 865(1)
(2)	s 865(2)
(3)	s 865(3), (4)
403 Entries of satisfaction and release	
(1)	s 872(1), (2) (changed)
(2)	s 872(3)
404 Rectification of register of charges	
(1)	s 873(1)
(2)	s 873(2)
405 Registration of enforcement of security	
(1)	s 871(1), (3)
(2)	s 871(2), (3)
(4)	s 871(4), (5)
406 Companies to keep copies of instrument creating charges	
(1)	ss 875(1), 877(2) (changed)
(2)	s 875(2)
407 Company's register of charges	
(1)	ss 876(1), 877(2) (changed)
(2)	s 876(2)
(3)	s 876(3), (4)
408 Right to inspect instruments which create charges, etc	
(1)	s 877(1), (2), (4) (changed)
(2)	s 877(2) (changed)
(3)	s 877(5), (6)
(4)	s 877(7)
410 Charges void unless registered	
(1)	s 878(1)
(2)	ss 886(1), 889(1)
(3)	s 889(2)
(4)	ss 878(7), 879(1), (3)
(5)	s 879(5), (6)

CA 1985	CA 2006
411 Charges on property outside United Kingdom	
(1)	s 886(1)
(2)	s 884
412 Negotiable instrument to secure book debts	
	s 879(4)
413 Charges associated with debentures	
(1)	s 879(2)
(2)	ss 882(1)–(4), 886(3)
(3)	s 883(1)–(3)
414 Charge by way of ex facie absolute disposition, etc	
(1)	s 881(1)
(2)	s 881(2), (3)
415 Company's duty to register charges created by it	
(1)	ss 878(1), (2), 882(5)
(2)	s 878(3), 882(5)
(3)	s 878(4)–(6), 882(5)
416 Duty to register charges existing on property acquired	
(1)	ss 880(1), (2), 886(2)
(2)	s 886(2)
(3)	s 880(3), (4) (changed)
417 Register of charges to be kept by registrar of companies	
(1)	s 885(1)
(2)	s 885(2)
(3)	s 885(3)
(4)	s 886(6)
418 Certificate of registration to be issued	
(1)	s 885(4)
(2)	s 885(4), (5)
419 Entries of satisfaction and release	
(1)	s 887(1), (3) (changed)
(1B)	s 887(2)
(2)	s 887(4)
(3)	s 887(2) (changed)
(4)	s 887(5)
420 Rectification of register	
	s 888(1), (2)
421 Copies of instruments creating charges to be kept by company	
(1)	ss 890(1), 892(2) (changed)
(2)	s 890(2)
422 Company's register of charges	
(1)	ss 891(1), 892(2) (changed)
(2)	s 891(2)
(3)	s 891(3), (4)
423 Right to inspect copies of instruments, and company's register	
(1)	s 892(1), (2), (4) (changed)
(2)	s 892(4) (changed)
(3)	s 892(5), (6)
(4)	s 892(7)
425 Power of company to compromise with creditors and members	

CA 1985	CA 2006
(1)	ss 895(1), 896(1), (2)
(2)	ss 899(1), (3), 907(1), 922(1)
(3)	s 899(4), 901(3), (4) (changed)
(4)	s 901(5) and (6)
(6)	s 895(2)
426 Information as to compromise to be circulated	
(1)	s 897(1)
(2)	s 897(1), (2)
(3)	s 897(1)
(4)	s 897(3)
(5)	s 897(4)
(6)	ss 895(1), 897(5)–(8)
(7)	s 898(1)–(3)
427 Provisions for facilitating company reconstruction or amalgamation	
(1)	s 900(1)
(2)	s 900(1), (2)
(3)	s 900(2)
(4)	s 900(3), (4)
(5)	s 900(6)–(8)
(6)	ss 900(5), 941
427A Application of ss 425–427 to mergers and divisions of public companies	
(1)	ss 902(1), 903(1), 907(2), 922(2)
(2)	ss 904(1), 919(1)
(3)	s 938(1), (2)
(4)	s 902(3)
(8)	s 941
428 Takeover offers	
(1)	s 974(1)–(3)
(2)	s 974(4), (5)
(2A)	s 974(6)
(3)	s 976(1)
(4)	s 976(3)
(5)	s 975(1), (2) (changed)
(6)	s 975(3) (changed)
(7)	s 974(7)
(8)	s 991(1)
429 Right of offeror to buy out minority shareholders	
(1)	s 979(1), (2) (changed)
(2)	s 979(3), (4) (changed)
(3)	s 980(2) (changed)
(4)	s 980(1), (4)
(5)	s 980(5)
(6)	s 980(6), (8)
(7)	s 980(7)
(8)	ss 977(1), 979(8)–(10) (changed)
430 Effect of notice under s 429	
(1)	s 981(1)
(2)	s 981(2)
(3)	s 981(3)

CA 1985	CA 2006
(4)	s 981(4), (5) (changed)
(5)	s 981(6)
(6)	s 981(7)
(7)	s 981(8)
(8)	s 981(6)
(9)	s 981(9)
(10)	s 982(2), (3)
(11)	s 982(4), (5)
(12)	s 982(6)
(13)	s 982(7)
(14)	s 982(8)
(15)	s 982(9)
430A Right of minority shareholder to be bought out by offeror	
(1)	ss 983(1)–(3), 984(1)
(1A)	s 983(1)
(2)	s 983(4)
(2A)	s 983(5)
(3)	s 984(3)
(4)	s 984(2)
(5)	s 984(4)
(6)	s 984(5), (7)
(7)	s 984(6)
430B Effect of requirement under s 430A	
(1)	s 985(1)
(2)	s 985(2)
(3)	s 985(3)
(4)	s 985(4), (5) (changed)
430C Applications to the court	
(1)	s 986(1), (2)
(2)	s 986(2)
(3)	s 986(3)
(4)	s 986(5)
(5)	s 986(9), (10)
430D Joint offers	
(1)	s 987(1)
(2)	s 987(2), (3) (changed)
(3)	s 987(5), (6)
(4)	s 987(4), (7)
(5)	s 987(8)
(6)	s 987(9)
(7)	s 987(10)
430E Associates	
(1)	ss 975(4), 977(2) (changed)
(2)	s 979(9)
(3)	s 983(8)
(4)	s 988(1), (4)
(5)	s 988(2)
(6)	s 988(3)
(7)	s 988(3), (5), (7)
(8)	s 988(1)
430F Convertible securities	
(1)	s 989(1)
(2)	s 989(2)

CA 1985	CA 2006
458 Punishment for fraudulent trading	
	s 993(1)–(3)
459 Order on application of company member	
(1)	s 994(1)
(2)	s 994(2)
(3)	s 994(3)
460 Order on application of Secretary of State	
(1)	s 995(2), (3)
(1A)	s 995(1)
(2)	s 995(4)
461 Provisions as to petitions and orders under this Part	
(1)	s 996(1)
(2)	s 996(2)
(3)	s 996(2)
(5)	s 998(1)–(4)
(6)	s 997
652 Registrar may strike defunct company off register	
(1)	s 1000(1)
(2)	s 1000(2)
(3)	s 1000(3)
(4)	s 1001(1)
(5)	ss 1000(4)–(6), 1001(2)–(4)
(6)	ss 1000(7), 1001(5)
(7)	s 1002(1)–(3)
652A Registrar may strike private company off register on application	
(1)	s 1003(1) (changed)
(2)	s 1003(2) (changed)
(3)	s 1003(3)
(4)	s 1003(4)
(5)	s 1003(5)
(6)	s 1003(6)
(7)	s 1003(6)
652B Duties in connection with making application under section 652A	
(1)	s 1004(1)
(2)	s 1004(2)
(3)	s 1005(1)
(4)	s 1005(2)
(5)	s 1005(3)
(6)	s 1006(1)
(7)	s 1006(2)
(8)	s 1006(3)
(9)	s 1004(3)
652C Directors' duties following application under section 652A	
(1)	s 1007(1)
(2)	s 1007(2)
(3)	s 1007(3)
(4)	s 1009(1)
(5)	s 1009(2)
(6)	s 1009(4)
(7)	s 1009(3)

CA 1985	CA 2006
652D Sections 652B and 652C: supplementary provisions	
(1)	ss 1008(1), (2)
(2)	s 1008(3)
(3)	s 1008(3)
(4)	s 1008(4)
(5)(c)	ss 1004(4), 1006(1), 1007(2), 1009(4)
(6)	s 1010
(8)	s 1011
652E Sections 652B and 652C: enforcement	
(1)	ss 1004(5), (7), 1005(4), (6), 1006(4), (6), 1007(4), (6), 1009(5), (7)
(2)	ss 1006(4), (7), 1007(4), (7)
(3)	ss 1004(6), 1005(5)
(4)	s 1006(5)
(5)	ss 1007(5), 1009(6)
654 Property of dissolved company to be bona vacantia	
(1)	s 1012(1)
(2)	s 1012(2)
655 Effect on s 654 of company's revival after dissolution	
(1)	s 1034(1)
(2)	s 1034(2)
(3)	s 1034(4)
(4)	s 1034(5)
656 Crown disclaimer of property vesting as bona vacantia	
(1)	s 1013(1)
(2)	s 1013(2) (changed)
(3)	s 1013(3)–(5) (changed)
(5)	s 1013(6), (7)
(6)	s 1013(8)
657 Effect of Crown disclaimer under s 656	
(1)	s 1014(1)
(2)	ss 1015(1), (2), 1016(1), (2), 1017(1)–(5), 1018(1)–(5), 1019
(4)	s 1020(1), (2)
(5)	s 1021(1), (2)
(6)	s 1021(3)
658 Liability for rentcharge on company's land after dissolution	
(1)	s 1023(1), (2)
(2)	s 1023(3)
680 Companies capable of being registered under this Chapter	
(1)(a), (b)	s 1040(1)
(1) (closing words)	s 1040(2), (3), (6)
(1A)	s 1040(1)
(2)	s 1040(1)
(3)	s 1040(4)
(4)	s 1040(4)
(5)	s 1040(5)
683 Definition of "joint stock company"	
(1)	s 1041(1)

CA 1985	CA 2006
(2)	s 1041(2)
694 Regulation of oversea companies in respect of their names	
(4)	s 1048(1), (2) (changed)
(5)	s 1048(3)–(5)
695 Service of documents on oversea company	
(1), (2)	s 1139(2) (changed)
695A Registrar to whom documents to be delivered: companies to which section 690A applies	
(4)	s 1059
699A Credit and financial institutions to which the Bank Branches Directive (89/117/EEC) applies	
(3) ("financial institution")	s 1173(1)
704 Registration offices	
(2)	s 1060(1), (2)
(4)	s 1062 (changed)
(7), (8)	s 1119(1), (2)
705 Companies' registered numbers	
(1)–(3)	s 1066(1)–(3)
(4)	s 1066(4), (5)
(5)(za)	s 1066(6)
705A Registration of branches of oversea companies	
(1)	s 1067(1) (changed)
(2)	s 1067(1)
(3)	s 1067(2)
(4)	s 1067(3)
(5)	s 1067(4), (5)
707A The keeping of company records by the registrar	
(1)	s 1080(4)
(2)	s 1083(1) (changed)
(3)	s 1084(1)–(3) (changed), (5)
(4)	s 1084(4)
708 Fees payable to registrar	
(1)	s 1063(1)–(3) (changed)
(2), (3)	s 1063(4) (changed)
(4)	s 1063(6)
(5)	s 1063(5) (changed)
709 Inspection, &c. of records kept by the registrar	
(1) opening words	s 1085(1) ands 1100
(1)(a), (b)	s 1086(1)
(2)	s 1085(2) (changed)
(3)	s 1091(3)
(4)	s 1091(5)
(5)	s 1092(1), (2)
710 Certificate of incorporation	
	s 1065
710A Provision and authentication by registrar of documents in non-legible form	
(2)	s 1115(2)
710B Documents relating to Welsh companies	
(1)–(3)	s 1104(1), (2)
(4)	s 1104(3)

CA 1985	CA 2006
(5)	s 1104(4)
711 Public notice by registrar of receipt and issue of certain documents	
(1)	ss 1064(1)–(3), 1077(1)–(3), 1078(2), (3) (changed)
(2)	s 1079(4) (changed)
713 Enforcement of company's duty to make returns	
(1)	s 1113(1)–(3)
(2), (3)	s 1113(4), (5)
714 Registrar's index of company and corporate names	
(1)	s 1099(1)–(3) (changed)
(2)	s 1099(4), (5)
715A Interpretation	
(1) ("document"), (2)	s 1114(1)
718 Unregistered companies	
(1)	s 1043(1), (3), (5) (changed)
(2)	s 1043(1)
(3)	s 1043(2), (5) (changed)
(5)	s 1043(4)
(6)	s 1043(6)
719 Power of company to provide for employees on cessation or transfer of business	
(1)	s 247(1)
(2)	s 247(2) (changed)
(3)	s 247(4)–(6) (changed)
(4)	s 247(7) (changed)
721 Production and inspection of books where offence suspected	
(1)	s 1132(1), (2)
(2)–(4)	s 1132(3)–(5)
722 Form of company registers, etc	
(1)	ss 1134 and 1135(1) (changed)
(2)	s 1138(1)
(3)	s 1138(2), (3)
723 Use of computers for company records	
(1)	s 1135(1) (changed)
(2)	s 1135(5)
723A Obligations of company as to inspections of registers, &c.	
(1)	s 1137(1), (2)
(2)	s 1137(3)
(3)	s 1137(3)
(4)	s 1137(4)
(6), (7)	s 1137(5), (6)
725 Service of documents	
(1)	s 1139(1)
(2)	s 1139(4)
(3)	s 1139(4)
727 Power of court to grant relief in certain cases	
(1)–(3)	s 1157(1)–(3)
730 Punishment of offences	
(4)	s 1125(2)
(5)	s 1121(1), (3) (changed)

CA 1985	CA 2006
731 Summary proceedings	
(1)	s 1127(1), (2)
(2)	s 1128(1)
(3)	s 1128(2)
(4)	s 1128(4)
732 Prosecution by public authorities	
(1)	s 1126(1)
(2)	s 1126(2) (changed)
(3)	s 1129 (changed)
734 Criminal proceedings against unincorporated bodies	
(1)	s 1130(1), (2) (changed)
(2)	s 1130(3)
(3)	s 1130(2)
(4)	s 1130(2)
735 "Company", etc	
(1)(a), (b)	s 1(1)
(1)(c)	s 1171 (changed)
(3)	s 1171
736 "Subsidiary"; "holding company" and "wholly-owned subsidiary"	
(1), (2)	s 1159(1), (2)
(3)	s 1159(4)
736A Provisions supplementing s 736	
(1)–(11)	s 1159(3), Sch 6
736B Power to amend ss 736 and 736A	
(1)	s 1160(1)
(3)–(5)	s 1160(2)–(4)
737 "Called-up share capital"	
(1), (2)	s 547
738 "Allotment" and "paid up"	
(1)	s 558
(2)	s 583(2)–(3)(d)
(3)	s 583(5)
(4)	s 583(6)
739 "Non-cash asset"	
(1), (2)	s 1163(1), (2)
741 "Director" and "shadow director"	
(1)	s 250
(2)	s 251(1), (2)
(3)	s 251(3)
742 Expressions used in connection with accounts	
(1) ("fixed assets")	s 853(6)
(1) ("parent company")	s 1173(1)
(2)	s 853(4), (5)
742A Meaning of "offer to the public"	
(1)	s 756(1), (2)
(2)	s 756(3)
(3)	s 756(4), (5)(a)–(d) (changed)
(4)	s 756(4)
(5)	s 756(4)
(6)	s 756(5)(e), (6)
742B Meaning of "banking company"	

CA 1985	CA 2006
(1)–(3)	s 1164(1)–(3)
742C Meaning of "insurance company" and "authorised insurance company"	
(1)–(4)	s 1165(2)–(4)
(5)	s 1165(8)
743 "Employees' share scheme"	
	s 1166
744 Expressions used generally in this Act	
"articles"	s 18(4)
"the Companies Acts"	s 2(1), (2) (changed)
"the court"	s 1156(1)–(3) (changed)
"debenture"	s 738
"EEA State"	s 1170
"equity share capital"	s 548
"the Gazette"	s 1173(1)
"hire-purchase agreement"	s 1173(1)
"insurance market activity"	s 1165(7)
"officer"	ss 1121(2), 1173(1)
"oversea company"	s 1044 (changed)
"prescribed"	s 1167
"the registrar of companies" and "the registrar"	s 1060(3)
"regulated activity"	s 1173(1)
"share"	s 540(1), (4)
744A Index of defined expressions	
	Sch 8
Sch 2 Interpretation of references to "beneficial interest"	
Part 1 References in sections 23, 145, 146 and 148	
para 1(1)	ss 139(1), 672(1)
para 1(2)	ss 139(2), 672(2)
para 1(3)	ss 139(3), 672(3)
para 1(4)	ss 139(4), 672(4)
para 2(3)	s 672(5)
para 2(4)	s 672(6)
para 3(1), (2)	ss 140(1), (2), 673(1), (2)
para 4(1)	ss 138(1), (2), 674
para 4(2)	s 138(1)
para 4(3)	s 674
para 5(1)	ss 675(1), (2), 676
para 5(2)	ss 139(5), (6), 140(3), 675(1), (2)
para 5(3)	ss 139(6), 140(4), 676
Sch 4 Form and content of company accounts	
Part 3 Notes to the accounts	
para 56(2), (3)	ss 382(6), 465(6)
Part 7 Interpretation of Schedule	
para 94(1), (2)	s 411(6)
Sch 7B Specified persons, descriptions of disclosures etc for the purposes of section 245G	
Part 1 Specified persons	
	s 461(1)

CA 1985	CA 2006
Part 2 Specified descriptions of disclosures	
	s 461(4)
Part 3 Overseas regulatory bodies	
	s 461(5), (6)
Sch 10A Parent and subsidiary undertakings: supplementary provisions	
para 1	Sch 7, para 1
para 2(1)	Sch 7, para 2(1)
para 2(2)	Sch 7, para 2(2)
para 3(1)	Sch 7, para 3(1)
para 3(2)	Sch 7, para 3(2)
para 3(2)	Sch 7, para 3(3)
para 4(1)	Sch 7, para 4(1)
para 4(2)	Sch 7, para 4(2)
para 4(3)	Sch 7, para 4(3)
para 5(1)	Sch 7, para 5(1)
para 5(2)	Sch 7, para 5(2)
para 6	Sch 7, para 6
para 7(1)	Sch 7, para 7(1)
para 7(2)	Sch 7, para 7(2)
para 8	Sch 7, para 8
para 9(1)	Sch 7, para 9(1)
para 9(2)	Sch 7, para 9(2)
para 9(3)	Sch 7, para 9(3)
para 10	Sch 7, para 10
para 11	Sch 7, para 11
Sch 13 Provisions supplementing and interpreting sections 324 to 328	
Part 4 Provisions with respect to register of directors' interests to be kept under section 325	
para 27	s 809(2), (3)
Sch 14 Overseas branch registers	
Part 1 Countries and territories in which overseas branch register may be kept	
	s 129(1)
Part 2 General provisions with respect to overseas branch registers	
para 1(1), (2)	ss 130(1), 135(3)
para 1(3)	ss 130(2), (3), 135(4), (5)
para 2(1)	s 131(1)
para 3(1)	s 134(1), (2) (changed)
para 3(2)	s 134(3)
para 4(1)	s 132(1), (2) (changed)
para 4(2)	s 132(3), (4)
para 5	s 133(1), (2)
para 6	s 135(1), (2)
para 7	s 131(4)
Sch 15A Written resolutions of private companies	
Part 1 Exceptions	
para 1	s 288(2)
Part 2 Adaptation of procedural requirements	
para 3(1), (2)	ss 571(7), 573(5)
para 5(1), (2)	ss 695(2), 698(2)
para 5(3), (4)	ss 696(2), 699(2)
para 6(1)	ss 717(2), 718(2)

CA 1985	CA 2006
para 6(2)	s 717(2)
para 6(3)	s 718(2)
para 7	s 188(5)
Sch 15B Provisions subject to which ss 425–427 have effect in their application to mergers and divisions of public companies	
para 1	ss 907(1), (2), 922(1), (2)
para 2(1)	ss 905(1), 906(1)–(3), 920(1), 921(1)–(4)
para 2(2)	ss 905(2), (3), 920(2)
para 2(3)	s 920(3)
para 3	ss 908(1), (3), 909(1), (7), 911(1), (2), (4), 912, 923(1), (4), 924(1), (7), 925(5), 926(1), (2), (4), 927(1)–(3), 928
para 4(1)	ss 908(2), 923(2)
para 4(2)	s 923(3)
para 5(1)	ss 909(2), (3), 924(2), (3)
para 5(2)	ss 909(3), 924(3)
para 5(3)	ss 909(4), 924(4)
para 5(4)	s 935(1) (changed)
para 5(6)	s 935(2)
para 5(7)	ss 909(5), 924(5)
para 5(8)	ss 909(6), 924(6)
para 6(1)	ss 910(1), 911(3), 925(1), 926(3)
para 6(2)	ss 910(2), 925(2)
para 6(3)	ss 910(3), 925(3) (changed)
para 6(4)	ss 910(4), 925(4),
para 7	ss 914, 930
para 8(1)	ss 913(1), 929(1)
para 8(2)	ss 913(2), 929(2)
para 9(1)	s 939(1)
para 9(2)	s 939(1), (2)

CA 1985	CA 2006
para 9(3)	s 939(3), (4)
para 9(4)	s 939(5)
para 10(1)	ss 918(1), 932(1)
para 10(2)	ss 916(3)–(5), 918(2)–(4), 932(2)–(5)
para 11(1)	s 933(1)–(3), 934(1)
para 11(2)	s 933(1)–(3)
para 11(3)	s 934(1)
para 11(4)	s 934(2)–(4)
para 12(1)	ss 915(1), (6), 917(1), (6)
para 12(2)	s 915(2)
para 12(3)	s 915(3)–(5)
para 12(4)	s 917(2)
para 12(5)	ss 917(3)–(5), 931(3), (5)
para 13(1)	s 931(1)
para 13(2)	s 931(2)
para 13(3)	s 931(3), (4), (6)
para 14(1)	s 916(1)
para 14(2)	s 916(2)
para 14(3)	s 916(3)–(5)
para 15(1)	s 940(1)
para 15(2)	s 940(2)
para 15(3)	s 940(3)
Sch 20 Vesting of disclaimed property; protection of third parties	
Part 2 Crown disclaimer under section 656 (Scotland only)	
para 5	s 1022(1)
para 6	s 1022(2)
para 7	s 1022(3)
para 8	s 1022(4), (5)
para 9	s 1022(6)

COMPANIES ACT 1989

(1) Section 130(6) of the Companies Act 1989 (power by regulations to apply provisions relating to company contracts and execution of documents by companies to overseas companies) is re-enacted in section 1045 of the Companies Act 2006.

(2) Section 207 of the Companies Act 1989 (transfer of securities) is re-enacted in sections 783, 784(3), 785 and 788 of the Companies Act 2006.

MINISTERIAL STATEMENTS ON DUTIES OF DIRECTORS

COMPANIES ACT 2006
DUTIES OF COMPANY DIRECTORS
MINISTERIAL STATEMENTS
DTI
JUNE 2007

Introduction

Rt Hon Margaret Hodge MP MBE (Minister of State for Industry and the Regions)

[3.54]

I know that the new statutory duties of directors set out in Part 10 of the Companies Act 2006 were keenly debated while the Bill was going through Parliament, and I am sure they will continue to be seen as one of the most significant parts of the Act.

During those debates, I and the other Ministers were questioned about the meaning of the provisions. Some of our responses and statements may be helpful to people interested in what the provisions mean, and I am pleased to be publishing this structured collection of what we believe are the most useful of them.

There are two ways of looking at the statutory statement of directors' duties: on the one the hand it simply codifies the existing common law obligations of company directors; on the other – especially in section 172: the duty to act in the interests of the company – it marks a radical departure in articulating the connection between what is good for a company and what is good for society at large.

Continuity

The statutory expression of the duties is essentially the same as the existing duties established by case law, the only major exception being the new procedures for dealing with conflicts of interest.

The simple high-level guidance for directors in the box on the following page illustrates the way in which the codification maintains continuity with the existing law: this advice on how a director has to live up to his position of trust is applicable to the pre-existing common law as well as to the new codification. For most directors, who are working hard and put the interests of their company before their own, there will be no need to change their behaviour.

Guidance for company directors—

(1) Act in the company's best interests, taking everything you think relevant into account.
(2) Obey the company's constitution and decisions taken under it.
(3) Be honest, and remember that the company's property belongs to it and not to you or to its shareholders.
(4) Be diligent, careful and well informed about the company's affairs. If you have any special skills or experience, use them.
(5) Make sure the company keeps records of your decisions.
(6) Remember that you remain responsible for the work you give to others.
(7) Avoid situations where your interests conflict with those of the company. When in doubt disclose potential conflicts quickly.
(8) Seek external advice where necessary, particularly if the company is in financial difficulty.

Change

But compared with most text-book definitions of the common law duties of directors, the new statutory statement captures a cultural change in the way in which companies conduct their business. There was a time when business success in the interests of shareholders was thought to be in conflict with society's aspirations for people who work in the company or in supply chain companies, for the long-term well-being of the community and for the protection of the environment. The law is now based on a new approach. Pursuing the interests of shareholders and embracing wider responsibilities are complementary purposes, not contradictory ones.

I strongly believe that businesses perform better, and are more sustainable in the long term, when they have regard to a wider group of issues in pursuing success. That is a common-sense approach that reflects a modern view of the way in which businesses operate in their community: they interact with customers and suppliers; they make sure that employees are motivated and properly rewarded; and they think about their impact on communities and the environment. They do so at least partly because it makes good business sense.

The new expression of the duties is part of the wider recognition and encouragement of change in the Act. The enhanced business review, which for quoted companies must now include information on environmental, employee, social and community issues, is another key example that builds on the growing consensus that it is good business sense for companies to embrace wider social responsibilities.

Part 3   CA 2006 Supporting Materials

I am sure that directors' duties will continue to evolve as times change and as societal norms are transformed. Corporate social responsibility has developed and evolved over time. The relationship between business interests and the wider world is changing all the time. The best way of achieving lasting cultural change is to go with the tide and the broad consensus of opinion.

Margaret Hodge

Notes on the ministerial statements

The quotations should be read in conjunction with the Act itself (available in hard copy at http://www. tsoshop.co.uk or online at http://www.opsi.gov.uk) and should not be regarded as a substitute for reading that Act or seeking legal advice. Full explanatory notes on the provisions of the Act are also available at http://www.tsoshop.co.uk and at http://www.opsi.gov.uk together with tables of origins and destinations for the Act's provisions.

It should be noted that on occasion the Parliamentary quotes have been edited in order to make it easier to read them. References to Hansard have been given so the full discussion can be seen if so desired.

Companies Act 2006 – Duties of directors

Collated Hansard extracts from debates on Companies Bill (originally Company Law Reform Bill)

Background

"The law commissions and the Company Law Review concluded that a statutory statement of duties would be helpful . . . it is important that . . . flexibility and ability to note changing circumstances are not lost".

Lord Goldsmith, Lords Grand Committee, 6 February 2006, column 242

"First . . . .the origins of the general duties [is] . . . that they are based in certain common law rules and equitable principles . . . the statutory statement replaces the common rule equitable principle . . . once the Act is passed, one will go to the statutory statement of duties to identify the duties to identify the duty the director owed".

Lord Goldsmith, Lords Grand Committee, 6 February 2006, column 243

" . . . the main purpose in codifying the general duties of directors is to make what is expected of directors clearer and to make the law more accessible to them and to others".

Lord Goldsmith, Lords Grand Committee, 6 February 2006, column 254

"We should remind ourselves that being a company director is a wonderful thing for the person who is a company director. But it is a position of great responsibility which involves running the affairs of a company for the benefit of other people. It is a heavy responsibility we should not water down".

Lord Goldsmith, Lords Grand Committee, 6 February 2006, column 291

Interpretation by the courts

"The courts should be left to interpret the words Parliament passes".

Lord Goldsmith, Lords Grand Committee, 6 February 2006, column 243

"Although the duties in relation to directors have developed in a distinctive way, they are often manifestations of more general principles . . . [it] is intended to enable the courts to continue to have regard to development in the common law rules and equitable principles applying to these other types of fiduciary relationships. The advantage of that is it will enable the statutory duties to develop in line with relevant developments in the law as it applies elsewhere."

Lord Goldsmith, Lords Grand Committee, 6 February 2006, column 244

Effect of codification

"One proposition [is] that the result of this codification will be increased litigation. That is not how we see it . . . as in existing law, the general duties are owed by the director to the company. It follows that, as now, only the company can enforce them. Directors are liable to the company for loss to the company, and not more widely. It is quite rare for companies to sue their directors for breach of duty. That may well continue to be the position."

Lord Goldsmith, Lords Grand Committee, 6 February 2006, column 242

Effect of the provision of new duties

"[On] the provision of new duties, we do not see why that should lead to increased litigation either. For example . . . the need to have regard to the interests of employees as part of the main duty to promote the success of the company . . . was part of case law before becoming statute. It is an important principle, and plays a crucial part in business decisions . . . however . . . there is not evidence of which we are aware that it has led to legalistic decision making by companies, or people turning away from bringing their talent to the world of enterprise. We have no reason to expect that there will be a greater degree of litigation on those duties than there is now".

Lord Goldsmith, Lords Grand Committee, 6 February 2006, column 243

Statement of general duties

"The statement of general duties . . . is not intended to be an exhaustive list of all the duties owed by a director to his company. The directors may owe a wide range of duties to their companies in addition to the general duties listed. Those are general, basic duties which it is seen as right and important to set out in this way. The statement that these are the general duties does not allow a director to escape any other obligation he has, including obligations under the Insolvency Act 1986."

Lord Goldsmith, Lords Grand Committee, 6 February 2006, column 249

Enlightened shareholder value

"The Company Law Review considered and consulted on two main options. The first was "enlightened shareholder value", under which a director must first act in the way that he or she considers, in good faith, would be most likely to promote the success of the company for its members . . . The Government agrees this is the right approach. It resolves any confusion in the mind of directors as to what that the interests of the company are, and prevents any inclination to identify those interests with their own. It also prevents confusion between the interests of those who depend on the company and those of the members".

Lord Goldsmith, Lords Grand Committee, 6 February 2006, column 255

"For the first time, the Bill includes a statutory statement of directors' general duties. It provides a code of conduct that sets out how directors are expected to behave. That enshrines in statue what the law review called "enlightened shareholder value". It recognises that directors will be more likely to achieve long term sustainable success for the benefit of their shareholders if their companies pay attention to a wider range of matters . . . Directors will be required to promote the success of the company in the collective best interest of the shareholders, but in doing so they will have to have regard to a wider range of factors, including the interests of employees and the environment".

Alistair Darling, Commons Second Reading, 6 June 2006, column 125

Duty to promote the success of the company

"What is success? The starting point is that it is essentially for the members of the company to define the objective they wish to achieve. Success means what the members collectively want the company to achieve. For a commercial company, success will usually mean long-term increase in value. For certain companies, such as charities and community interest companies, it will mean the attainment of the objectives for which the company has been established".

Lord Goldsmith, Lords Grand Committee, 6 February 2006, column 255

" . . . for a commercial company, success will normally mean long-term increase in value, but the company's constitution and decisions made under it may also lay down the appropriate success model for the company. . . . it is essentially for the members of a company to define the objectives they wish to achieve. The normal way for that to be done—the traditional way—is that the members do it at the time the company is established. In the old style, it would have been set down in the company's memorandum. That is changing . . . but the principle does not change that those who establish the company will start off by setting out what they hope to achieve. For most people who invest in companies, there is never any doubt about it—money. That is what they want. They want a long-term increase in the company. It is not a snap poll to be taken at any point in time."

Lord Goldsmith, Lords Grand Committee, 6 February 2006, column 258

" . . . it is for the directors, by reference to those things we are talking about – the objective of the company – to judge and form a good faith judgment about what is to be regarded as success for the members as a whole . . . .they will need to look at the company's constitution, shareholder decisions and anything else that they consider relevant in helping them to reach that judge-ment . . . the duty is to promote the success for the benefit of the members as a whole – that is, for the members as a collective body – not only to benefit the majority shareholders, or any particular shareholder or section of shareholders, still less the interests of directors who might happen to be shareholders themselves. That is an important statement of the way in which directors need to look at this judgement they have to make".

Lord Goldsmith, Lords Grand Committee, 6 February 2006, column 256

" . . . we have included the words "amongst other matters". We want to be clear that the list of factors [for a director to have regard to] is not exhaustive".

Lord Goldsmith, Lords Grand Committee, 9 May 2006, column 846

"The clause does not impose a requirement on directors to keep records, as some people have suggested, in any circumstances in which they would not have to do so now."

Margaret Hodge, Commons Committee, 11 July 2006, column 592

"The Government believe that our enlightened shareholder value approach will be mutually beneficial to business and society. We do not, however, claim that the interests of the company and of its employees will always be identical; regrettably, it will sometimes be necessary, for example, to lay off staff. The drafting   . . .   must therefore clearly point directors towards their overarching objective. We have made it clear that [the clause] will make a difference, and a very important difference. The words "have regard to" mean "think about"; they are absolutely not about just ticking boxes. If "thinking about" leads to the conclusion, as we believe it will in many cases, that the proper course is to act positively to achieve the objectives in the clause, that will be what the director's duty is. In other words "have regard to" means "give proper consideration to"   . . .   Consideration of the factors will be an integral part of the duty to promote the success of the company for the benefit of its members as a whole. The clause makes it clear that a director is to have regard to the factors in fulfilling that duty. The decisions taken by a director and the weight given to the factors will continue to be a matter for his good faith judgment.".

Margaret Hodge, Commons Report, 17 October 2006, column 789

Duty to exercise independent judgement

"   . . .   the clause does not mean that a director has to form his judgement totally independently from anyone or anything. It does not actually mean that the director has to be independent himself. He can have an interest in the matter   . . .   It is the exercise of the judgement of a director that must be independent in the sense of it being his own judgement   . . .   The duty does not prevent a director from relying on the advice or work of others, but the final judgement must be his responsibility. He clearly cannot be expected to do everything himself. Indeed, in certain circumstances directors may be in breach of duty if they fail to take appropriate advice – for example, legal advice. As with all advice, slavish reliance is not acceptable, and the obtaining of outside advice does not absolve directors from exercising their judgement on the basis of such advice".

Lord Goldsmith, Lords Grand Committee, 6 February 2006, column 282

Standard of care owed by a director

"   . . .   the standard of care which a director owes is enormously important   . . .   it is now accepted that the duty of care   . . .   is accurately stated in Section 214(4) of the Insolvency Act 1986   . . . . .   Under the clause you take account both of the general knowledge, skills and experience that may be reasonably expected of a person carrying out those functions and the general knowledge, skills and experience that that director has. It is a cumulative requirement   . . .   I want to emphasise the point that it is not making a change from what is already the common law".

Lord Goldsmith, Lords Grand Committee, 6 February 2006, column 284

Duty to avoid conflicts of interest

"   . . .   the law already recognises that potential conflicts in certain circumstances are to be avoided   . . .   there is currently no absolute rule prohibiting directors from holding multiple directorships or even from engaging in business that competes with the company of which they are a director, but obviously a tension results from that degree of tolerance and the fiduciary duties which the director owes. The solution to it is   . . .   there is no prohibition of a conflict or potential conflict as long as it is has been authorised by the directors in accordance with the requirements set out in [the Act]".

Lord Goldsmith, Lords Grand Committee, 6 February 2006, column 288

"   . . .   we do not say that this should happen just because in the mind of a director it is all right; there should be a process for the company, through its members or directors, to make that decision, and that is what these new regulations permit".

Lord Goldsmith, Lords Grand Committee, 6 February 2006, column 289

"Following consultation, the Government have already adjusted the provision   . . .   to use instead the expression "if the situation cannot reasonably be regarded as likely to give rise to a conflict of interest". This introduces the concept of reasonableness which makes the situation easier from the point of view of a director and avoids a very harsh test, although it is still a heavy duty and intended to be so."

Lord Goldsmith, Lords Grand Committee, 6 February 2006, column 293

"So far as private companies are concerned, the default position is that the directors may authorise the matter unless there is a provision in the company's constitution saying otherwise. In the case of a public company   . . .   [d]irectors may authorise the matter only if the company's constitution includes provisions saying they can do so. It must follow that if the constitution does not do so, steps will have to be taken to amend it to that effect and the members of the company will be able to take a view about whether they think that is a good move".

Lord Goldsmith, Lords Grand Committee, 6 February 2006, column 294

" . . . the authorisation has to be given without relying on the votes of directors seeking the authorisation or any other director with an interest in it . . . . Those directors cannot count towards the quorum either . . . .[and] any requirements under the common law for what is necessary for a valid authorisation remain in force . . . Finally, in general terms, the directors who are giving the authorisation will need to comply with the general duties imposed on them. Those will include, specifically, the general duty . . . to act in such a way that in good faith they consider that authorisation is the course of action most likely to promote the success of the company".

Lord Goldsmith, Lords Grand Committee, 9 February 2006, column 327

" . . . the duty does not apply if the situation cannot reasonably be regarded as being likely to give rise to a conflict of interest. If the matter falls outside the ambit of the company's business, a real conflict of interest is unlikely".

Lord Goldsmith, Lords Grand Committee, 9 May 2006, column 864

" . . . the company's articles may contain provisions for dealing with conflicts of interests, and directors will not be in breach of duty if they act in accordance with those provisions. Examples might include arrangements whereby the directors withdraw from any board meeting at which the matters relating to conflicts of interest are discussed . . . our amendments will allow all the normal, perfectly acceptable, lawful ways in which companies and their directors deal with conflicts of interest to continue."

Lord Sainsbury of Turville, Lords Report, 23 May 2006, column 722

Duty not to accept benefits from third parties

" . . . the purpose of the clause . . . is to impose on a director a duty not to accept benefits from third parties. It applies only to benefits conferred because the director is a director of the company or because of something that the director does or doesn't do as director. The word "benefit" . . . includes benefits of any description, including non-financial benefits. The clause codifies . . . [the] long-standing rule, prohibiting the exploitation of the position of director for personal benefit. It does not apply to benefits that the director receives from the company, or from any associated company, or from any person acting on behalf of any of those companies . . . . I . . . draw attention to the fact that benefits are prohibited by the duty only if their acceptance is likely to give rise to a conflict of interest".

Lord Goldsmith, Lords Grand Committee, 9 February 2006, column 330

Duty to declare interest in proposed transaction or arrangement

"[This] clause . . . is deliberately intended to apply only to proposed transactions . . . if a company is told that a director has an interest in a proposed transaction, it can decide whether to enter into the transaction, on what terms and with what safeguards. [As for] "a director is treated as being aware of matters he ought reasonably to be aware" . . . I believe that the test is objective – that is, one judges objectively whether this is a matter of which the director ought to be aware reasonably".

Lord Goldsmith, Lords Grand Committee, 9 February 2006, column 334

Civil consequences of breach of general duties

" . . . we take the view that the "duty to exercise reasonable care, skill and diligence" is not a fiduciary duty. It may be owed by someone who is a fiduciary. But that is not the same thing. ..It is important to keep to the principle that these are enforceable in the same way as any other fiduciary duty owed to the company by its directors."

Lord Goldsmith, Lords Grand Committee, 9 February 2006, column 336

Consent, approval or authorisation by members

"[The Bill] permitted director authorisation of what would otherwise be impermissible conflicts of interests [and] . . . required declarations of interest in proposed company transactions. In both those cases, the general duty no longer requires the consent of the members. The common law rules or principles that refer to the failure to have had a conflict of interest approved by the member of a company under certain circumstances need to be set aside . . . . However . . . the company's constitution can reverse the change and can insist on certain steps being taken requiring the consent of the members in certain circumstances".

Lord Goldsmith, Lords Grand Committee, 9 February 2006, column 337

Indemnifying directors

" . . . the starting point for our reform package was a principle . . . that companies should be prohibited from exempting directors from, or indemnifying them against, liability for negligence, default, breach of duty or breach of trust in relation to the company. However the reform package also recognised that companies should be permitted to indemnify directors in respect of third-party claims in most circumstances . . . There are four main possible exceptions to indemnification: criminal penalties; penalties imposed by regulatory bodies: costs incurred by the director in defending criminal proceedings in which he is convicted; and costs incurred by the director in defending civil proceedings brought by the company in which final judgement is given against him".

Lord Goldsmith, Lords Grand Committee, 9 February 2006, column 364

"[The Companies (Audit, Investigations and Community Enterprise) Act 2004] . . . closed an important loophole concerning the indemnification of directors by third parties. It used to be the practice in some groups that one group company would indemnify the director of another group company . . . in effect to circumvent the rule that the company could not indemnify its own directors. We take the view that . . . continu[ing] to make directors properly accountable for what they do in relation to the company . . . should stand".

Lord Goldsmith, Lords Grand Committee, 9 February 2006, column 366

"It is also important to remember that at the same time as the loophole was closed, important reforms were introduced that permit all companies to indemnify directors against third-party claims, subject to . . . [certain] requirements. Although we agree that indemnification by a parent company of the directors is less likely to result in attempts at circumvention of the prohibition than indemnification by a wholly owned subsidiary company of the director of a holding company, we still believe there is scope for mischief. We cannot . . . accept [any] amendment".

Lord Sainsbury of Turville, Lords Report, 23 May 2006, column 724

Shadow directors

"The law is still developing. It would not be right for the general duties not to apply at all to a shadow directors, but the law may develop in such a way that some do and some don't. It is right to leave those areas, as now, to the courts . . . "

Lord Goldsmith, Lords Grand Committee, 9 May 2006, column 828

PART 4
COMPANIES ACT 2006 STATUTORY INSTRUMENTS

[4.1]

INTRODUCTION: STATUTORY INSTRUMENTS MADE UNDER THE COMPANIES ACT 2006

The following is a complete chronological list of all statutory instruments made under, or partly under, the Companies Act 2006. The majority of the statutory instruments listed below are set out in this Part of the Handbook. Note, however, that where the substantive authority for a statutory instrument is an Act other than the Companies Act 2006 (and the 2006 Act authority is merely ancillary) the statutory instrument will be elsewhere in this Handbook.

2006 STATUTORY INSTRUMENTS

SI 2006/3428: Companies Act 2006 (Commencement No 1, Transitional Provisions and Savings) Order 2006

Authority: CA 2006, ss 1296(1), (2), 1300(2)

This Order brings into force certain provisions of CA 2006 on various dates and contains transitional provisions and savings. See **[2.1]** et seq.

SI 2006/3429: Companies (Registrar, Languages and Trading Disclosures) Regulations 2006

Authority: CA 2006, ss 1091(4), 1105(2)(d), 1106(2); European Communities Act 1972, s 2(2); Limited Liability Partnerships Act 2000, ss 15, 17

These Regulations implement provisions of European Parliament and Council Directive 2003/58/EC amending Council Directive 68/151/EEC, as regards disclosure requirements in respect of certain types of companies. They amend CA 1985 and the Companies (Northern Ireland) Order 1986, and supplement provisions of CA 2006 brought into force on the same date as these Regulations come into force. See **[4.2]** et seq.

2007 STATUTORY INSTRUMENTS

SI 2007/318: Companies Acts (Unregistered Companies) Regulations 2007

Authority: CA 2006, s 1043

These Regulations applied Part 28 of CA 2006 (takeovers etc), and certain ancillary provisions, to unregistered companies. They further implemented Directive 2004/25/EC of the European Parliament and of the Council on Takeover Bids. See **[4.2]** *et seq. These Regulations were revoked by the Unregistered Companies Regulations 2009, SI 2009/2436, reg 8, as from 1 October 2009, subject to transitional provisions and savings in Sch 2 to those Regulations at* **[4.604]**.

SI 2007/1093: Companies Act 2006 (Commencement No 2, Consequential Amendments, Transitional Provisions and Savings) Order 2007

Authority: CA 2006, ss 1292(1), 1294(1), 1296(1), (2), 1300(2)

This Order brings into force certain provisions of CA 2006 on various dates and contains transitional provisions and savings. See **[2.16]** et seq.

SI 2007/2081: Companies (Political Expenditure Exemption) Order 2007

Authority: CA 2006, ss 377, 1292(1)(c)

This Order exempts certain political expenditure incurred by news companies from the need for authorisation by the company's members under Part 14 of CA 2006. It replaces the Companies (EU Political Expenditure) Exemption Order 2001 (SI 2001/445), which was made under CA 1985, s 347B. That section was repealed by CA 2006 (subject to transitional provisions and savings) as from 1 October 2007. See **[4.7]** et seq.

SI 2007/2194: Companies Act 2006 (Commencement No 3, Consequential Amendments, Transitional Provisions and Savings) Order 2007

Authority: CA 2006, ss 1292, 1294, 1296, 1300(2)

This Order brings into force certain provisions of CA 2006 on various dates and contains transitional provisions and savings. See **[2.31]** et seq.

SI 2007/2242: Companies (Interest Rate for Unauthorised Political Donation or Expenditure) Regulations 2007

Authority: CA 2006, ss 369(5)(b), 1167

Where a company has made a political donation or incurred political expenditure without the authorisation required by CA 2006 the directors are liable to make good to the company the amount of the unauthorised donation or expenditure with interest. These Regulations set the rate of interest to be applied at 8% per annum. See the note to CA 2006, s 369 at **[1.369]**.

SI 2007/2607: Companies Act 2006 (Commencement No 4 and Commencement No 3 (Amendment)) Order 2007

Authority: CA 2006, ss 1296(1), 1300(2)

This Order brings into force the power to make Regulations about fees charged by companies for inspection of company records and provision of copies. It also amends the third commencement Order (SI 2007/2194) in order to reverse the repeal of certain provisions of CA 1985. See **[2.47]** et seq.

SI 2007/2612: Companies (Fees for Inspection and Copying of Company Records) Regulations 2007

Authority: CA 2006, ss 116(1)(b), (2), 229(2), 238(2), 358(4), 807(2), 811(2), 1137(1), (4), 1167, 1292(1)(a), (c)

These Regulations prescribe the fees payable by a person who wishes to exercise a right under CA 2006 to inspect a company record or to receive a copy of a company record. They replace fees prescribed in the Companies (Inspection and Copying of Registers, Indices and Documents) Regulations 1991 (SI 1991/1998) subject to transitional savings. See **[4.12]**.

SI 2007/2974: Companies (Cross-Border Mergers) Regulations 2007

Authority: CA 2006, ss 1102(2), 1105(2)(d), 1106(2); European Communities Act 1972, s 2(2)

These Regulations implement Directive 2005/56/EC on cross-border mergers of limited liability companies. See **[4.17]** et seq.

SI 2007/3494: Statutory Auditors and Third Country Auditors Regulations 2007

Authority: CA 2006, ss 1239, 1241(2)(c), 1246, 1292(1)(a), (b), (2), Sch 11, para 8(1)(a); European Communities Act 1972, s 2(2)

These Regulations implement, in part, Directive 2006/43/EC of the European Parliament and of the Council on statutory audits of annual accounts and consolidated accounts, amending Council Directives 78/660/EEC and 83/349/EEC and repealing Council Directive 84/253/EEC. They make various amendments to Pt 42 of CA 2006 (at **[1.1209]** et seq) and the substantive parts of these Regulations are set out at **[4.79]** et seq.

SI 2007/3495: Companies Act 2006 (Commencement No 5, Transitional Provisions and Savings) Order 2007

Authority: CA 2006, ss 1292, 1296, 1300(2)

This Order brings into force certain provisions of CA 2006 on various dates and contains transitional provisions and savings. See **[2.50]** et seq.

SI 2007/3534: Independent Supervisor Appointment Order 2007

Authority: CA 2006, s 1228

This Order appoints the Professional Oversight Board as Independent Supervisor of the Auditors General when they carry out the functions of statutory auditors (see **[4.88]** et seq).

SI 2007/3535: Companies (Fees for Inspection and Copying of Company Records) (No 2) Regulations 2007

Authority: CA 2006, ss 744(1)(b), (2), 749(1), 1137(1), (4), 1167, 1292(1)(a), (c)

These Regulations prescribe the fees payable by a person who wishes to exercise a right under CA 2006 to inspect the register of debenture holders of a company or to receive a copy of that register or a copy of a debenture trust deed. These Regulations replace fees prescribed in the Companies (Inspection and Copying of Registers, Indices and Documents) Regulations 1991, SI 1991/1998 (and the Companies (Inspection and Copying of Registers, Indices and Documents) Regulations 1993 (Northern Ireland)) subject to transitional savings. See **[4.95]**.

2008 STATUTORY INSTRUMENTS

SSI 2008/144: Companies Act 2006 (Scottish public sector companies to be audited by the Auditor General for Scotland) Order 2008

Authority: CA 2006, s 483(1)–(3)

This Order provides that certain companies with registered offices in Scotland are to have their accounts audited by the Auditor General for Scotland. This means that in terms of s 475 of the 2006 Act, these companies will be exempt from the auditing of company accounts requirements of Part 16. The companies subject to this Order are non-profit making public sector companies, which appear to Scottish Ministers to carry out functions of a public nature or are funded by bodies audited by the Auditor General for Scotland.

SI 2008/373: Companies (Revision of Defective Accounts and Reports) Regulations 2008

Authority: CA 2006, ss 454(3), (4), 1292(1)(a), (c)

These Regulations set out how the provisions of CA 2006 are to apply to revised annual accounts, directors' reports, directors' remuneration reports and summary financial statements prepared under this section. They come into force on 6 April 2008 and apply in relation to companies' financial years beginning on or after that date. They revoke and replace (subject to transitional provisions) the Companies (Revision of Defective Accounts and Report) Regulations 1990, SI 1990/2570 which were made under the Companies Act 1985, and the Companies (Revision of Defective Accounts and Report) Regulations (Northern Ireland) 1991, SR 1991/268. See **[4.100]** et seq.

SI 2008/374: Companies (Summary Financial Statement) Regulations 2008

Authority: CA 2006, ss 426(1), (3), 427(2), (5), 428(2), (5), 1292(1)

These Regulations concern the summary financial statements which companies may send out in place of their full accounts and reports under ss 426–428 of CA 2006. They come into force on 6 April 2008 and apply in relation to companies' financial years beginning on or after that date. They revoke and replace the Companies (Summary Financial Statement) Regulations 1995, SI 1995/2092 (which were made under the corresponding provisions of CA 1985), and the Companies (Summary Financial Statement) Regulations (Northern Ireland) 1996, SR 1996/179. See **[4.120]** et seq.

SI 2008/393: Companies Act 2006 (Amendment) (Accounts and Reports) Regulations 2008

Authority: CA 2006, ss 468(1), (2), 473(2), 484, 1292(1)(a), (c)

These Regulations amend various provisions in Parts 15 and 16 of CA 2006. They come into force on 6 April 2008 and apply in relation to financial years beginning on or after that date. See **[4.140]** et seq.

SI 2008/409: Small Companies and Groups (Accounts and Directors' Report) Regulations 2008

Authority: CA 2006, ss 396(3), 404(3), 409(1), (3), 412(1), (3), 416(4), 444(3)(a), (b), 677(3)(a), 712(2)(b)(i), 836(1)(b)(i), 1292(1)(a), (c)

These Regulations specify the form and content of the accounts and directors' report of companies subject to the small companies regime under Part 15 of CA 2006. The Regulations replace provisions previously contained in the Schedules to Part VII of CA 1985, and in the Schedules to Part VIII of the Companies (Northern Ireland) Order 1986 (SI 1986/1032). The Regulations come into force on 6 April 2008, and apply in relation to financial years beginning on or after that date. The corresponding provisions of the 1985 Act or the 1986 Order continue to apply to accounts and directors' reports for financial years beginning before that date. See **[4.142]** et seq.

SI 2008/410: Large and Medium-sized Companies and Groups (Accounts and Reports) Regulations 2008

Authority: CA 2006, ss 396(3), 404(3), 409(1)–(3), 412(1)–(3), 416(4), 421(1), (2), 445(3)(a), (b), 677(3)(a), 712(2)(b)(i), 831(3)(a), 832(4)(a), 836(1)(b)(i), 1292(1)(a), (c)

These Regulations specify the form and content of the accounts and reports of companies under Part 15 of this Act (other than those subject to the small companies regime). The Regulations replace provisions previously contained in the Schedules to Part VII of the Companies Act 1985, and in the Schedules to Part VIII of the Companies (Northern Ireland) Order 1986 (SI 1986/1032). The Regulations come into force on 6 April 2008 and, with one exception, apply to financial years beginning on or after that date. The corresponding provisions of the 1985 Act or the 1986 Order continue to apply to accounts and reports for financial years beginning before that date. The new disclosure required by Sch 8, para 4 to the Regulations applies in relation to financial years beginning on or after 6 April 2009. See **[4.170]** et seq.

SI 2008/489: Companies (Disclosure of Auditor Remuneration and Liability Limitation Agreements) Regulations 2008

Authority: CA 2006, ss 494, 538, 1292(1)(a); European Communities Act 1972, s 2(2)

These Regulations provide for companies to disclose fees receivable by their auditors and their auditors' associates' (in relation to the accounts of a company for any financial year beginning on or after 6 April 2008), and also to disclose liability limitation agreements that they make with their auditors (as from 6 April 2008). Disclosure must be in a note to the company's annual accounts. See **[4.220]** et seq.

SI 2008/495: Companies (Trading Disclosures) Regulations 2008

Authority: CA 2006, ss 82, 84, 1292(1)(a), 1294.

These Regulations deal with trading disclosures to be made by a company. See **[4.230]** et seq.

SI 2008/496: Statutory Auditors (Delegation of Functions etc) Order 2008

Authority: CA 1989, s 46(4); CA 2006, ss 504(1)(b)(ii), 1252(1), (4)(a), (5), (8), 1253(4), Sch 13, paras 7(3), 11(2), (3)(a)

This Order transfers most of the functions of the Secretary of State under CA 2006, Pt 42 to the Professional Oversight Board. It revokes and replaces the Companies Act 1989 (Delegation) Order 2005, SI 2005/2337, as from 6 April 2008, except in relation to functions relating to appointments of company auditors for any financial year beginning before that date. See **[4.240]** et seq.

SI 2008/497: Companies (Late Filing Penalties) and Limited Liability Partnerships (Filing Periods and Late Filing Penalties) Regulations 2008

Authority: CA 1985, s 257(1), (4)(a), (d); Limited Liability Partnerships Act 2000, s 15(a); CA 2006, ss 453, 1292(1)(a), (c)

These Regulations determine the penalties which companies must pay to the registrar of companies if they file their annual accounts and reports late, and which limited liability partnerships must pay if they deliver their accounts and auditors' reports late. See **[4.252]** et seq.

SI 2008/499: Statutory Auditors and Third Country Auditors (Amendment) Regulations 2008

Authority: CA 2006, s 1239; European Communities Act 1972, s 2(2)

These Regulations correct errors in the Statutory Auditors and Third Country Auditors Regulations 2007, SI 2007/3494 at **[4.79]**. Regulation 1(3) of the 2007 Regulations purports to bring reg 38(2)(b)–(d) into force on 29 June 2008. There is no para (2)(b)–(d) of reg 38, and it is para (2)(b)–(d) of reg 40 that should have been brought into force on that date. Regulation 7(2) of the 2007 Regulations provides that the new s 1223A of the Companies Act 2006 (as inserted by reg 7(1) of the 2007 Regulations) applies only to "EEA auditors" (ie, auditors qualified elsewhere in the European Economic Area) appointed as statutory auditors for financial years beginning on or after 6 April 2008. These Regulations revoke reg 7(2) so that s 1223A also applies to EEA auditors who have not been appointed as statutory auditors at all. Regulation 15(1) of the 2007 Regulations inserts three new sections into the Companies Act 2006, about the transfer of audit working papers to countries outside the European Economic Area. Regulation 15(2) provides that one of those new sections (ie, s 1253E) applies only to working papers for audits for financial years beginning on or after 6 April 2008. These Regulations provide that another of those new sections (s 1253D) also applies only to working papers for audits for financial years beginning on or after that date. These Regulations also correct drafting errors in regs 34 and 36 of the 2007 Regulations.

SI 2008/569: Partnerships (Accounts) Regulations 2008

Authority: CA 2006, ss 1210(1)(h), 1292(2); European Communities Act 1972, s 2(2)

These Regulations replace the provisions of the Partnerships and Unlimited Companies (Accounts) Regulations 1993 (SI 1993/1820), and of the Partnerships and Unlimited Companies (Accounts) Regulations (Northern Ireland) 1994 (SR 1994/133). They continue the implementation of Council Directive 90/605/EEC amending Directive 78/660/EEC on annual accounts, and Directive 83/349/EEC on consolidated accounts. They also implement, in part, Directive 2006/43/EC on statutory audits of annual accounts and consolidated accounts. The Regulations come into force on 6 April 2008 and apply to financial years of qualifying partnerships beginning on or after that date, and auditors appointed in respect of those financial years. See **[10.984]** et seq.

SI 2008/623: Companies (Defective Accounts and Directors' Reports) (Authorised Person) and Supervision of Accounts and Reports (Prescribed Body) Order 2008

Authority: Companies (Audit, Investigations and Community Enterprise) Act 2004, s 14(1), (5), (8); CA 2006, s 457(1), (2), (5), (6)

This Order authorises the Financial Reporting Review Panel established under the articles of association of the Financial Reporting Council Limited for the purposes of CA 2006, s 456 (application to court in respect of defective accounts or directors' reports). It replaces the Companies (Defective Accounts) (Authorised Person) Order 2005 (SI 2005/699) and the Companies (Defective Accounts) (Authorised Person) Order (Northern Ireland) 1991 under which the Financial Reporting Review Panel as established under the articles of association of the Financial Reporting Review Panel Limited was authorised for the purposes of s 245B of CA 1985 and Article 253B of the Companies (Northern Ireland) Order 1986. It also appoints the FRRP to exercise the functions mentioned in s 14(2) of the Companies (Audit, Investigations and Community Enterprise) Act 2004. These functions are the keeping under review of periodic accounts and reports that are produced by issuers of transferable securities and are required to comply with any accounting requirements imposed by Part 6 rules made under FSMA 2000, and informing the FSA of any conclusions the Panel reaches if it thinks fit. It replaces the Supervision of Accounts and Reports (Prescribed Body) Order 2007 (SI 2007/2583) and continues the implementation of the Transparency Directive (Directive 2004/109/EC). The appointment is limited to issuers of transferable securities admitted to trading on a regulated market which are bodies corporate and of which the UK is the home Member State for the purposes of the Directive. It is also limited to annual and half-yearly financial reports. See **[4.258]** et seq.

SI 2008/651: Accounting Standards (Prescribed Body) Regulations 2008

Authority: CA 2006, s 464(1), (3)

These Regulations prescribe the Accounting Standards Board established under the articles of association of The Financial Reporting Council Limited for the purposes of CA 2006, s 464. They also revoke (as from 6 April 2008) the Accounting Standards (Prescribed Body) Regulations 2005 (SI 2005/697), and the Accounting Standards (Prescribed Body) Regulations (Northern Ireland) 1990, under which the Accounting Standards Board as established under the articles of association of the Accounting Standards Board Limited was prescribed for the purposes of CA 1985, s 256 and the Companies (Northern Ireland) Order 1986, art 264. They also contain transitional provisions. See **[4.265]** et seq.

SI 2008/674: Companies Act 2006 (Commencement No 6, Saving and Commencement Nos 3 and 5 (Amendment)) Order 2008

Authority: CA 2006, ss 1292(1)(b), 1296(1), (2), 1300(2)

This Order brings into force certain provisions of CA 2006 on various dates and contains savings provisions. See **[2.69]** et seq.

SI 2008/729: Companies (Authorised Minimum) Regulations 2008

Authority: CA 2006, ss 763(2), 766(1)(a), (2), 1292(1)(a), (b)

These Regulations relate to provisions of CA 1985, the Companies (Northern Ireland) Order 1986, and CA 2006 which refer to the "authorised minimum" share capital requirement for public companies. Reg 2 prescribes, for the purposes of s 763 of the 2006 Act, the amount in euros which is to be treated as equivalent to the sterling amount of the authorised minimum (ie, €65,600). Regulations 3 and 4 provide for the application of the authorised minimum requirement for the purposes of particular provisions of the 1985 Act and the 1986 Order which refer to it. Regulation 5 deals with registration by the registrar of companies of court orders confirming the reduction of public companies' share capital and with re-registration of public companies as private companies where a mandatory cancellation of shares has the effect of bringing the nominal value of the company's allotted share capital below the authorised minimum. Regulation 6 enables the courts, in specified proceedings, to make a determination in certain circumstances about the exchange rates to be applied in working out whether a public company satisfies the authorised minimum requirement. Regulation 7 prevents anyone from being liable as a result of reliance, for the purposes of these Regulations, on an exchange rate published by the Financial Times. It also prevents liability arising if an erroneous exchange rate published by the Financial Times is relied on for the purposes of the Regulations. Finally, it excludes liability for acts or omissions leading to the Financial Times not publishing an exchange rate capable of being relied on for the purposes of the Regulations. See **[4.269]** et seq.

SI 2008/948: Companies Act 2006 (Consequential Amendments etc) Order 2008

Authority: CA 2006, ss 1292, 1294, 1296

This Order makes a variety of amendments to legislation consequential on the coming into force, on 6 April 2008, of various provisions of the 2006 Act. It also contains savings provisions. See **[4.275]** et seq.

SI 2008/954: Companies Act 2006 (Consequential Amendments) (Taxes and National Insurance) Order 2008
Authority: CA 2006, ss 1292, 1294, 1296
This Order makes consequential amendments to the legislation for which Her Majesty's Revenue and Customs are responsible to take account of the provisions of the Companies Act 2006 which came into force on 6 April 2008. All of the enactments amended relate to taxation and national insurance, and none of them are included in this work.

SI 2008/1659: Companies Act 1985 (Annual Return) and Companies (Principal Business Activities) (Amendment) Regulations 2008
Authority: CA 1985, ss 364(3), 365(1); CA 2006, s 1167
These Regulations concerned the information to be provided about share capital and shareholders in the annual return of a company under CA 1985. The type of information to be supplied depended on whether or not any of the company's shares were shares admitted to trading on a regulated market during the period to which the return related. These Regulations amended various provisions in Chapter III of Part XI of the 1985 Act (Company Administration and Procedure) and in the Companies (Forms Amendment No 2 and Company's Type and Principal Business Activities) Regulations 1990 (SI 1990/1766). Section 1167 of the Companies Act 2006 merely defines the term "prescribed" for the purposes of the 2006 Act and, therefore, these Regulations effectively lapsed on the repeal of ss 364(3), 365(1) of the 1985 Act on 1 October 2009.

SI 2008/1738: Company Names Adjudicator Rules 2008
Authority: CA 2006, s 71
These Rules regulate the proceedings before a company names adjudicator under s 69 of the 2006 Act in cases where an application has been made objecting to a company's registered name because of its similarity to another name in which the objector has goodwill. See **[4.287]** et seq.

SI 2008/1861: Companies (Forms) (Amendment) Regulations 2008
Authority: CA 1985, s 363(2); CA 2006, s 1167
These Regulations prescribed amended form 363a for the purposes of s 363(2) of CA 1985, with effect from 1 October 2008. The Regulations also revoked the existing forms 363a and 363s (prescribed by the Companies (Forms) (Amendment) Regulations 2002) and form 363a and 363s (prescribed by Companies (Forms) (Amendment) Regulations 1999 and retained as alternatives to the forms prescribed by the 2002 Regulations). However, continued use of those revoked forms was permitted for returns made up to a date before 1 October 2008. Form 363a was amended to reflect amendments to the shareholder information provided. The amendments were made by the Companies Act 1985 (Annual Return) Regulations 2008 (SI 2008/1659) applying to annual returns made up to a date on or after 1 October 2008. See also the Companies (Welsh Language Forms) (Amendment) Regulations 2008, SI 2008/1861 (made under the same sections as extended by the Welsh language Act 1993) for the Welsh equivalents. Section 1167 of the Companies Act 2006 merely defines the term "prescribed" for the purposes of the 2006 Act and, therefore, these Regulations effectively lapsed on the repeal of s 363(2) of the 1985 Act on 1 October 2009.

SI 2008/1886: Companies Act 2006 (Commencement No 7, Transitional Provisions and Savings) Order 2008
Authority: CA 2006, ss 1296(2), 1300(2)
This Order brings into force certain provisions of CA 2006 on various dates and contains transitional provisions and savings provisions. See **[2.75]** et seq.

SI 2008/1911: Limited Liability Partnerships (Accounts and Audit) (Application of Companies Act 2006) Regulations 2008
Authority: Limited Liability Partnerships Act 2000, ss 15, 17; CA 2006, ss 1210(1)(h), 1292(2)
These Regulations replace provisions of the Limited Liability Partnerships Regulations 2001, SI 2001/1090 and the Limited Liability Partnerships Regulations (Northern Ireland) 2004 which apply provisions of the Companies Act 1985 and the Companies (Northern Ireland) Order 1986 relating to accounts and audit to LLPs. They apply to LLPs, with modifications, provisions on the accounts and audit of companies contained in the Companies Act 2006 and extend to the UK (reflecting the extent of the 2006 Act). See **[10.1003]** et seq.

SI 2008/1915: Companies (Reduction of Share Capital) Order 2008
Authority: CA 2006, ss 643(3), 654, 1167
This Order prescribes the form in which a solvency statement must be made when a private company proposes to reduce its share capital in reliance on the statement without getting a court order. The Order also provides that when a company reduces its share capital, the prohibition on distribution in s 654(1) of the 2006 Act does not apply unless, where the reduction is confirmed by court order, the court orders that it is not distributable. That, however, does not affect the operation of anything to the contrary in (i) an order of, or undertaking to, the court, (ii) the resolution for, or any other resolution relevant to, the reduction, or (iii) the company's memorandum or articles. See **[4.303]** et seq.

SI 2008/2639: Statutory Auditors and Third Country Auditors (Amendment) (No 2) Regulations 2008
Authority: CA 2006, ss 1239(1)(b), (2), (5)(d), 1246(1), 1292(1)(c)
These Regulations amend the Statutory Auditors and Third Country Auditors Regulations 2007, SI 2007/3494. They make provision in respect of "exempt third country auditors" and give effect to Commission Decision 2008/627/EC of 29 July 2008 concerning a transitional period for audit activities of certain third country auditors and audit entities (OJ L202,31.7.2008, p 70). See **[4.306]** and note that the 2007 Regulations are at **[4.79]** et seq.

SI 2008/2860: Companies Act 2006 (Commencement No 8, Transitional Provisions and Savings) Order 2008
Authority: CA 2006, ss 1292(1), 1296(1), (2), 1300(2)
This Order brings into force certain provisions of CA 2006 on various dates and contains transitional provisions and savings provisions. See **[2.82]** et seq.

SI 2008/2996: Companies (Particulars of Company Charges) Regulations 2008
Authority: CA 2006, ss 860, 862, 878, 880, 1167
These Regulations deal with the information to be provided to the Registrar of Companies on the registration of a company charge under Part 25 of the Companies Act 2006. Regulation 2 sets out the information that is to be provided when a company registered in England and Wales or Northern Ireland creates a charge of a kind specified in s 860(7) of the Act. Regulation 3 makes the same provision but for companies registered in Scotland which create a charge of the kind specified in s 878(7) of the Act. Regulation 4 sets out the information that is to be provided when a company registered in England and Wales, Northern Ireland or Scotland acquires property which is already subject to a charge which, if it had been created by the company after the acquisition of the property, would have been required to be registered under Part 25 of the Act. See **[4.308]** et seq.

SI 2008/3000: Companies Act 2006 (Annual Return and Service Addresses) Regulations 2008
Authority: CA 2006, ss 857, 1141, 1167, 1292(1)
These Regulations (which come into force on 1 October 2009) deal with the information to be provided in the annual return of a company under the Companies Act 2006. They also prescribe conditions to be met by a service address for the purposes of the Companies Acts. See **[4.312]** et seq.

SI 2008/3006: Companies (Company Records) Regulations 2008
Authority: CA 2006, ss 1136, 1137, 1292(1)
These Regulations (which come into force on 1 October 2009) relate to the inspection and provision of copies of company records. They revoke and replace the Companies (Inspection and Copying of Registers, Indices and Documents) Regulations 1991, SI 1991/1998 (subject to savings in relation to any request made before that date to be provided with a copy of a company record). See **[4.318]** et seq.

SI 2008/3007: Companies (Fees for Inspection of Company Records) Regulations 2008
Authority: CA 2006, ss 162(5)(b), 275(5)(b), 877(4)(b), 892(4)(b), 1137(4), 1167, 1292(1)(c)
These Regulations (which come into force on 1 October 2009) prescribe the fees payable by a person who wishes to exercise a right under the Companies Act 2006 to inspect, in relation to a company, its register of directors, its register of secretaries or its register of charges and instruments creating those charges. See **[4.327]**.

SI 2008/3014: Companies (Registration) Regulations 2008
Authority: CA 2006, ss 8(2), 10(3), 11(2), 103(2)(a), 110(2)(a), 1167, 1292(1)(a)
The Companies Act 2006 makes changes to the form of a company's constitutional documents. The Companies Act 1985 and the Companies (Northern Ireland) Order 1986 (SI 1986/1032) both require a company to include a substantial amount of information in its memorandum of association and allow a company's constitutional rules to be divided between its memorandum and articles of association. Under the 2006 Act, all the constitutional rules will be contained in the articles of association; the memorandum of association will, therefore, be a much shorter document. Regulation 2 prescribes the form of the memorandum of association required under the 2006 Act. The forms in Schs 1 and 2 serve the limited purpose of providing evidence of the intention of each subscriber to form a company and become a member of that company and, in the case of a company that is to have a share capital on formation, to take at least one share. Regulations 3 and 4 prescribe the information required to be contained in the statement of capital and the statement of guarantee to identify each subscriber to the memorandum of association. This is the name and address of each subscriber. Regulations 5 and 6 prescribe the forms of assent for re-registration of a private limited company as an unlimited company and re-registration of a public company as a private and unlimited company. These forms are set out in Schs 3 and 4. These Regulations come into force on 1 October 2009. See **[4.329]** et seq.

SI 2008/3122: Companies Act 2006 (Extension of Takeover Panel Provisions) (Isle of Man) Order 2008
Authority: CA 2006, s 965
This Order extends the provisions of Chapter 1 of Part 28 of the 2006 Act to the Isle of Man with certain modifications. Its purpose is to place on a statutory footing the role of the Panel on Takeovers and Mergers ("the Takeovers Panel") in supervising relevant takeovers involving Isle of Man companies. The modifications in the Schedule reflect differences in the legal system and governmental and regulatory structures of the Isle of Man, and make necessary consequential amendments to the Financial Services Act 2008 (an Act of Tynwald). Among other things, the modifications impose a duty on the Island's Financial Supervision Commission to co-operate with the Takeover Panel. The modifications also provide for the exchange of information about takeovers (subject to appropriate safeguards) between: (i) the Takeover Panel and those with regulatory, registry, prosecution and disciplinary functions on the Isle of Man in relation to companies and their officers; and (ii) those Manx authorities and corresponding bodies elsewhere. See **[4.337]**.

SI 2008/3229: Companies (Model Articles) Regulations 2008
Authority: CA 2006, s 19
These Regulations prescribe model forms of articles of association for: (i) private companies limited by shares (reg 2 and Sch 1), (ii) private companies limited by guarantee (reg 3 and Sch 2), and (iii) public companies (reg 4 and Sch 3). These model articles will automatically form the articles of association for companies formed under the Companies Act 2006 which, on their formation, either do not register their own articles of association with the registrar of companies under that Act, or, if they do so, do not exclude the model articles in whole or in part (s 20 of the 2006 Act). Other companies are free to adopt the model articles in whole or in part.. See **[4.340]**.

2009 STATUTORY INSTRUMENTS

SI 2009/202: Companies Act 2006 (Amendment of Schedule 2) Order 2009
Authority: CA 2006, s 948(4)
This Order amended CA 2006, Sch 2 in consequence of the enactment of the Companies Act 2006 (Extension of Takeover Panel Provisions) (Isle of Man) Order 2008 (SI 2008/3122). That Order applied the Takeover Panel provisions of Part 28 of, and Sch 2 to, CA 2006 in the Isle of Man. It was revoked by the Companies Act 2006 (Amendment of Schedule 2) (No 2) Order 2009, SI 2008/1208, as from 1 July 2009 and the amendments made by this instrument were re-enacted in the substituted Schedule contained in the No 2 Order.

SI 2009/214: Companies (Disclosure of Address) Regulations 2009
Authority: CA 2006, ss 243(2)–(6), 1088(1)–(3), (5), 1292(1), (4)
These Regulations specify the conditions for disclosure of directors' usual residential addresses to public authorities and credit reference agencies under CA 2006, s 243, make provision for applications to the registrar of companies under that section to refrain from disclosing a director's usual residential address to a credit reference agency, and make provision for applications to the registrar of companies under s 1088 of the 2006 Act for addresses on the register to be made unavailable for public inspection. They come into force on 1 October 2009. See **[4.344]**.

SI 2009/218: Companies (Trading Disclosures) (Amendment) Regulations 2009
Authority: CA 2006, ss 82, 1292(1)(a)
These Regulations deal with trading disclosures to be made by a company. They amend the Companies (Trading Disclosures) Regulations 2008 (SI 2008/495) to provide two further exceptions from the obligation on a company to display its registered name at business premises. See the amendments to regs 3 and 4 of the 2008 Regulations at **[4.232]** and **[4.233]**.

SI 2009/388: Companies (Shares and Share Capital) Order 2009
Authority: CA 2006, ss 10(2)(c)(i), 32(2)(c)(i), 108(3)(c)(i), 555(3)(a), (4)(c)(i), 556(3), 583(4), 619(3)(c)(i), 621(3)(c)(i), 625(3)(c)(i), 627(3)(c)(i), 644(2)(c)(i), 649(2)(c)(i), 663(3)(c)(i), 689(3)(c)(i), 708(3)(c)(i), 714(5), 727(3), 730(5)(c)(i), 1167
This Order makes provision in relation to shares and share capital for the purposes of various provisions of the Companies Act 2006. The Act requires companies, in various circumstances, to deliver a statement of capital to the registrar of companies. It also requires a company to send a current statement of capital to any member of the company on request. A statement of

capital must state, for each class of the company's shares, such particulars of the rights attached to shares as are prescribed by order or regulations. This Order prescribes these particulars. It comes into force on 1 October 2009 and is at **[4.364]** et seq.

SI 2009/1085: Company and Business Names (Miscellaneous Provisions) Regulations 2009
Authority: CA 2006, ss 57(1)(a), (2), (5), 60(1), 65, 66, 1197, 1292(1)
These Regulations deal with restrictions relating to the registered name of a company and to business names. See **[4.369]** et seq.

SI 2009/1208: Companies Act 2006 (Amendment of Schedule 2) (No 2) Order 2009
Authority: CA 2006, ss 948(4), 1292(1)(c)
This Order substitutes Sch 2 to the Companies Act 2006 and revokes the Companies Act 2006 (Amendment of Schedule 2) Order 2009, SI 2009/202. Under s 948 of the 2006 Act, information received by the Takeover Panel in connection with the exercise of its statutory functions may not be disclosed without the consent of the individual (where it concerns a person's private affairs) or business to which it relates except as permitted by that section. Schedule 2 specifies for the purposes of s 948(3) of the Act the persons to whom disclosure may be made and the descriptions of disclosures which are exempt from the prohibition in s 948(2). Schedule 2 is amended by this Order to include specified persons exercising functions of a public nature in the Isle of Man, Jersey and Guernsey, and to add descriptions of disclosures the purpose of which is to facilitate the exercise of functions of a public nature in the Isle of Man, Jersey and Guernsey.

SI 2009/1378: Companies Act 2006 (Extension of Takeover Panel Provisions) (Isle of Man) Order 2009
Authority: CA 2006, s 965
This Order applies Sch 2 to the Companies Act 2006 (as substituted by the Companies Act 2006 (Amendment of Schedule 2) (No 2) Order 2009, SI 2008/1208) to the Isle of Man. See the Note at **[4.387]**.

SI 2009/1581: Companies Act 2006 (Accounts, Reports and Audit) Regulations 2009
Authority: CA 2006, ss 468(1), (2), 1292(1); European Communities Act 1972, s 2(2)
These Regulations implement, in part, Directive 2006/46 of the European Parliament and the Council amending Council Directives 78/660/EEC on the annual accounts of certain types of companies, 83/349/EEC on consolidated accounts, 86/635/EEC on the annual accounts and consolidated accounts of banks and other financial institutions and 91/674/EEC on the annual accounts and consolidated accounts of insurance undertakings. Annex C of the Disclosure Rules and Transparency Rules Sourcebook (Corporate Governance Rules) Instrument 2008 made by the Financial Services Authority on 26 June 2008 (FSA 2008/32) requires certain publicly traded companies to prepare a corporate governance statement in implementation of Articles 1.7 and 2.2 of Directive 2006/46. Part 2 of the Regulations implements the Directive's requirements that where the corporate governance statement is a separate statement and not part of the directors' report, it must be filed with the registrar of companies and the auditor must give an opinion as to whether the information required to be shown in the statement as to internal control and risk management systems in relation to the financial reporting process and certain disclosures required by the Takeovers Directive (Directive 2004/25/EEC) is consistent with the annual accounts for the year in question. For the remaining information in the corporate governance statement, the auditor must check that the statement has been produced. Part 3 of the Regulations amends Part 15 of CA 2006 (accounts and reports) and Regulations made under that Part (ie, the Small Companies and Groups (Accounts and Directors' Report) Regulations 2008, SI 2008/409 and the Large and Medium-sized Companies and Groups (Accounts and Reports) Regulations 2008, SI 2008/410). See **[4.388]**.

SI 2009/1801: Overseas Companies Regulations 2009
Authority: CA 2006, ss 1046(1), (2), (4)–(6), 1047(1), 1049(1)–(3), 1050(3)–(5), 1051(1)–(3), 1053(2)–(5), 1054(1), (2), 1055, 1056, 1058(1)–(3), 1078(5), 1105(1), (2), 1140(2), 1292(1), (4), 1294
These Regulations, which come into force on 1 October 2009, impose various registration and filing requirements on companies incorporated outside the UK ("overseas companies") that open an establishment, whether a place of business or a branch, in the UK (a "UK establishment"). They replace Part 23 of, and Schedules 21A–21D to, the Companies Act 1985 (and the equivalent Northern Ireland provisions). See **[4.389]** et seq.

SI 2009/1802: Companies Act 2006 (Part 35) (Consequential Amendments, Transitional Provisions and Savings) Order 2009
Authority: CA 2006, ss 1290, 1292(4), 1294(6); European Communities Act 1972, s 2(2)
This Order, which comes into force on 1 October 2009, amends Part 35 of the 2006 Act (at **[1.1059A]** et seq) and the Companies Act 2006 (Commencement No 8, Transitional Provisions and Savings) Order 2008, SI 2008/2860, Sch 2 (at **[2.91]**). See the note at **[4.490]**.

SI 2009/1803: Registrar of Companies and Applications for Striking Off Regulations 2009
Authority: CA 2006, ss 1003(2)(b), 1081(2), 1095(1), (2), 1104(2)(a), 1105(2)(d), 1108(2), 1167, 1292(1), (3), (4)
These Regulations, which come into force on 1 October 2009, make provision relating to the functions of the registrar of companies under Part 35 of the Companies Act 2006 and the delivery of documents to the registrar under the Act and under other enactments. They also make provision relating to applications for striking a company's name off the register under Part 31 of the Act. See **[4.491]** et seq.

SI 2009/1804: Limited Liability Partnerships (Application of Companies Act 2006) Regulations 2009
Authority: CA 2006, ss 1101, 1292, 1294 and 1296; Limited Liability Partnerships Act 2000, ss 15, 17
These Regulations replace provisions of the Limited Liability Partnerships Regulations 2001 (SI 2001/1090) and the Limited Liability Partnerships Regulations (Northern Ireland) 2004 (SR 2004/307) which apply to LLPs provisions of the Companies Act 1985 and the Companies (Northern Ireland) Order 1986 (with modifications). They apply instead provisions of the Companies Act 2006 to LLPs (with modifications). Separate regulations (ie, the Limited Liability Partnerships (Accounts and Audit) (Application of Companies Act 2006) Regulations 2008 (SI 2008/1911), the Small Limited Liability Partnerships (Accounts) Regulations 2008 (SI 2008/1912), and the Large and Medium-sized Limited Liability Partnerships (Accounts) Regulations 2008 (SI 2008/1913)) have previously applied to LLPs provisions on accounts and audit contained in the 2006 Act and Regulations made under that Act. See **[10.1097]**.

SI 2009/1889: Companies Act 2006 (Consequential Amendments) (Uncertificated Securities) Order 2009
Authority: CA 2006, ss 784, 785, 788, 1292, 1294
This Order makes consequential amendments to the Uncertificated Securities Regulations 2001, SI 2001/3755 at **[6.42]** et seq to take account of provisions of the Companies Act 2006 which enter into force on 1 October 2009.

SI 2009/1890: Companies Act 2006 (Consequential Amendments) (Taxes and National Insurance) Order 2009
Authority: CA 2006, s 1294
This Order makes consequential amendments to tax and national insurance legislation to take account of provisions of the Companies Act 2006 (and related secondary legislation) which are in force, or enter into force on 1 October 2009. None of the enactments amended by this Order appear in this Handbook.

SI 2009/1917: Overseas Companies (Execution of Documents and Registration of Charges) Regulations 2009
Authority: CA 2006, ss 1045, 1052, 1105, 1292(1)
These Regulations, which come into force on 1 October 2009, apply to companies incorporated outside the UK as defined in the Companies Act 2006, s 1044. Part 2 of the Regulations makes provision in respect of overseas companies for the application (with modifications) of provisions of the 2006 Act relating to company contracts and the formalities of doing business under the law of England and Wales, Northern Ireland and Scotland. Part 3 of the Regulations makes provision for the registration of charges created by those overseas companies which have registered particulars with the registrar of companies under s 1046 of the 2006 Act. The Regulations revoke the Foreign Companies (Execution of Documents) Regulations 1994, SI 1994/950 and also provide for transitional provisions and savings in relation to the previous law. See **[4.500]**.

SI 2009/1941: Companies Act 2006 (Consequential Amendments, Transitional Provisions and Savings) Order 2009
Authority: CA 2006, ss 657, 1088, 1292, 1294, 1296(1), 1300(2); European Communities Act 1972, s 2(2)
This Order makes consequential amendments, repeals and revocations in connection with the coming into force of various provisions of CA 2006 on 1 October 2009. It also contains some further transitional provisions and savings. See **[4.528]**.

SI 2009/2022: Companies (Share Capital and Acquisition by Company of its Own Shares) Regulations 2009
Authority: CA 2006, ss 562(6)(a), 657, 737, 1292(1)(c)
These Regulations change 3 elements of the Companies Act 2006 to: (i) reduce the minimum pre-emption rights issue subscription period set out in s 562(5) of the 2006 Act from 21 days to 14 days (this amendment will align UK and EU Company law (Directive 77/91/EEC) in this area); (ii) introduce a requirement in s 646 of the 2006 Act so that, when creditors object to a reduction in a company's capital, they should demonstrate that their claim is at risk and that the company has not provided adequate safeguards; (iii) repeal s 725 of the 2006 Act to remove the 10% limit on companies holding shares in treasury. The Regulations also amend ss 694, 697, 700 and 701 of the 2006 Act to extend the period for which authorisation may be given for the purchase by a company of its own shares from 18 months to 5 years. An option arising from Directive 2006/68/EC. See **[4.542]**.

SI 2009/2101: Registrar of Companies (Fees) (Companies, Overseas Companies and Limited Liability Partnerships) Regulations 2009
Authority: CA 2006, ss 243(3), 1063(1)–(3), 1292(1)
These Regulations were made on 30 July 2009 and come into force on 1 October 2009. They provide for the fees to be payable to the registrar of companies in respect of his functions relating to the registration of documents, the inspection or provision of copies of documents kept by him and the disclosure of information protected under the CA 2006 relating to companies, overseas companies and LLPs. The Regulations extend to the whole of the UK. They replace the Companies (Fees) Regulations (Northern Ireland) 1995 (SR 1995/312), the Companies (Fees) Regulations 2004 (SI 2004/2621), the Limited Liability Partnerships (Fees) Regulations 2004 (SI 2004/2620), the Limited Liability Partnerships (Fees) Regulations (Northern Ireland) 2004 (SR 2004/396), the Companies (Competent Authority) (Fees) Regulations 2002 (SI 2002/502), the Limited Liability Partnerships (Competent Authority) (Fees) Regulations 2002 (SI 2002/503) and the Limited Liability Partnerships (Records Inspection) (Fee) Regulations (Northern Ireland) 2004 (SR 2004/397), subject to the transitional provisions contained in regs 6–8 and Sch 5 to the Regulations. See **[4.543]**.

SI 2009/2392: Registrar of Companies (Fees) (Limited Partnerships and Newspaper Proprietors) Regulations 2009
Authority: CA 2006, ss 1063(1)–(3), 1292(1), (2), 1296
These Regulations were made on 28 August 2009. They provide for the fees to be payable to the registrar of companies in respect of his functions relating to the registration of documents relating to limited partnerships and the register of the proprietors of newspapers, and the inspection or provision of copies of documents kept by him relating to limited partnerships. See **[4.566]**.

SI 2009/2399: European Economic Interest Grouping (Amendment) Regulations 2009
Authority: CA 2006, s 1108(2)(b); European Communities Act 1972, s 2(2)
These Regulations come into force on 1 October 2009 and amend the European Economic Interest Grouping Regulations 1989 (SI 1989/638) at **[10.696]** et seq. Some of the amendments are consequential on the extension of the 1989 Regulations to Northern Ireland, and the revocation of the equivalent Northern Ireland Regulations by s 1286 of CA 2006. Other amendments replace references to provisions of CA 1985 with references to the equivalent provisions of the 2006 Act. Other amendments are consequential on changes to UK company law and reflect changes made to company law by CA 2006. The Regulations also prescribe new forms for EEIGs which replace those currently contained in the 1989 Regulations.

SI 2009/2400: European Public Limited-Liability Company (Amendment) Regulations 2009
Authority: CA 2006, ss 1102(2), (3), 1108(2)(b); European Communities Act 1972, s 2(2)
These Regulations, which come into force on 1 October 2009, amend the European Public Limited-Liability Company Regulations 2004 (SI 2004/2326). Some of the amendments are consequential on the extension of the 2004 Regulations to Northern Ireland, and the revocation of the equivalent Northern Ireland Regulations by s 1285 of CA 2006. Other amendments replace references to provisions of CA 1985 with references to the equivalent provisions of the 2006 Act. Other amendments are consequential on changes to UK company law and reflect changes made to company law by CA 2006. These Regulations also prescribe new forms for SEs which replace those currently contained in the 2004 Regulations. In addition, Part 3 of the 2004 Regulations, which relates to the involvement of employees in relation to the running of an SE, is omitted and is re-enacted with modifications in the European Public Limited-Liability Company (Employee Involvement) (Great Britain) Regulations 2009 (SI 2009/2401). The 2004 Regulations are at **[10.851]** et seq.

SI 2009/2403: Registrar of Companies (Fees) (European Economic Interest Grouping and European Public Limited-Liability Company) Regulations 2009
Authority: CA 2006, ss 1063(1)–(3), 1292(1)
These Regulations provide for the fees to be payable to the registrar of companies in respect of his functions relating to the registration of documents relating to European Economic Interest Groupings ("EEIGs") and European Public Limited-Liability Companies ("SEs"), and the inspection or provision of copies of documents kept by him relating to EEIGs. The Regulations come into force on 1 October 2009 and extend to the UK. See **[4.577]**.

SI 2009/2404: Company, Limited Liability Partnership and Business Names (Miscellaneous Provisions) (Amendment) Regulations 2009
Authority: CA 2006, ss 65, 66, 1197, 1292(1); Limited Liability Partnerships Act 2000, ss 15, 17
These Regulations correct errors in the Company and Business Names (Miscellaneous Provisions) Regulations 2009, SI 2009/1085. Regulation 2(1), (2) amends SI 2009/1085, reg 13. That regulation permits certain bodies corporate to carry on business under a name that includes the word "limited" (or its Welsh equivalent, "cyfyngedig") even though they are not companies incorporated under the Companies Act 2006 or earlier companies legislation. Regulation 2(1), (2) of these Regulations adds two further categories to those corporate bodies. See **[4.381]**. Regulation 2(1), (3) corrects an abbreviation in SI 2009/1085, Sch 2 and adds "industrial and provident society" to the list of specified expressions. See **[4.385]**.

SI 2009/2425: Companies (Authorised Minimum) Regulations 2009
Authority: CA 2006, ss 763(2)–(4), 766(1)(a), (2), 1292(1), (2)

These Regulations relate to provisions of the Companies Act 2006 which refer to the "authorised minimum" share capital requirement for public companies. There is a definition of "the authorised minimum" in s 763(1) of the 2006 Act, ie, £50,000 or the prescribed euro equivalent. Regulation 2 prescribes, for the purposes of this definition, the amount in euros which is to be treated as equivalent to the sterling amount of the authorised minimum (€57,100). Regulations 3 and 4 provide for the application of the authorised minimum requirement for the purposes of certain provisions of the 2006 Act. The provisions in question have the effect of requiring a public company to re-register as a private company where certain events cause the nominal value of its allotted share capital to fall below the authorised minimum. The events are a reduction of share capital confirmed by court order or the mandatory cancellation of shares in particular circumstances. Regulation 5 deals with registration by the registrar of companies of court orders confirming the reduction of public companies' share capital. It enables the registrar to assume, in certain circumstances, that the authorised minimum requirement is no longer satisfied by the company. Regulation 6 enables the courts, in specified proceedings, to make a determination in certain circumstances about the exchange rates to be applied in working out whether a public company satisfies the authorised minimum requirement. Regulation 7 prevents anyone from being liable as a result of reliance, for the purposes of these Regulations, on an exchange rate published by the Financial Times. It also prevents liability arising if an erroneous exchange rate published by the Financial Times is relied on for the purposes of the Regulations. Finally, it excludes liability for acts or omissions leading to the Financial Times not publishing an exchange rate capable of being relied on for the purposes of the Regulations. Regulation 8 revokes regulation 2 of the Companies (Authorised Minimum) Regulations 2008 (SI 2008/729); and regulation 9 makes transitional provisions and savings. Those transitional provisions and savings take account of transitional provisions and savings in Schedule 2 to the Companies Act 2006 (Commencement No 8, Transitional Provisions and Savings) Order 2008 (SI 2008/2860). See **[4.586]** et seq.

SI 2009/2436: Unregistered Companies Regulations 2009
Authority: CA 2006, ss 1043, 1210(1)(h), 1292(2)

These Regulations apply specified provisions of the 2006 Act (and also provisions of the Companies Act 1985) to unregistered companies. Regulation 3 applies the provisions of the 1985 Act and the 2006 Act that are specified in Schedule 1 (with specified modifications). Regulations 4 and 5 contain adaptations of general effect. Regulation 6 provides for a person appointed as auditor of an unregistered company to be a statutory auditor for the purposes of Part 42 of the Act. Regulation 7 revokes specified regulations (including those applying to Northern Ireland) which apply provisions of the 1985 Act and the Act to unregistered companies. Provisions in those Regulations are reproduced in these Regulations. Transitional and saving provisions are set out in Schedule 2 to the Regulations. See **[4.594]** et seq.

SI 2009/2437: Companies (Companies Authorised to Register) Regulations 2009
Authority: European Communities Act 1972, s 2(2); CA 2006, ss 1042, 1292(1)

These Regulations make provision in connection with the registration of a company on an application under s 1040 of the Companies Act 2006 (ie, a company not formed under the Companies Acts but authorised to register). These Regulations replace the provisions made by sections 681–682, and 684–690 of, and Sch 21 to, the Companies Act 1985 (and the equivalent provisions of the Companies (Northern Ireland) Order 1986, SI 1986/1032). See **[4.605]** et seq.

SI 2009/2439: Registrar of Companies (Fees) (Amendment) Regulations 2009
Authority: CA 2006, s 1063(1)–(3)

These Regulations amend the Registrar of Companies (Fees) (Companies, Overseas Companies and Limited Liability Partnerships) Regulations 2009, SI 2009/2101 at **[4.543]**. These amendments have two main purposes: (i) to extend their application to companies within the Companies Act 2006, s 1040 (ie, a company not formed under the Companies Acts but authorised to register), and unregistered companies under s 1043 of the 2006 Act; (ii) to disapply the subscription fee payable for Companies House Direct, Extranet and XML, which provide inspection, or provision of copies, of documents kept by the registrar, where the subscription fee is paid under Regulations relating to European Economic Interest Groupings and limited partnerships.

SI 2009/2455: Civil Courts (Amendment) Order 2009
Authority: CA 2006, s 1156(3)

This Order amends the Civil Courts Order 1983 (SI 1983/713) as a consequence of the Companies Act 2006 and Regulations made under the Limited Liability Partnerships Act 2000 which apply and modify provisions of the 2006 Act in relation to LLPs. The 2006 Act and the Regulations give the power to exclude a county court from having jurisdiction to deal with matters under that Act (including as applied to LLP) and, for the purposes of those jurisdictions, assign the district of that court to another county court. A new art 10A of the Order sets out the provision to exclude specified county courts from having the jurisdiction to deal with matters under the 2006 Act and the Regulations, and assigns the district of each excluded court to another county court. A sixth column is inserted in Schedule 3 of the Order to set out those courts to which are attached the district of the county courts excluded from having jurisdiction under the 2006 Act and the Regulations.

SI 2009/2476: Companies Act 2006 and Limited Liability Partnerships (Transitional Provisions and Savings) (Amendment) Regulations 2009
Authority: CA 2006, ss 1292(2), 1296(1), 1300(2); Limited Liability Partnerships Act 2000, ss 15, 17

These Regulations amend the 8th Companies Act 2006 commencement order in order to prevent s 22(2) of the 2006 Act coming into force on 1 October 2009. They also (i) amend the transitional provisions in connection with the commencement of ss 1012–1023 of the 2006 Act; (ii) make corresponding amendments in relation the application of those sections to LLPs; (iii) provide for new savings in relation to the repeal of CA 1985, s 26(2) and the Business Names Act 1985 (ie, in relation to names likely to give an impression of a connection with the Welsh Assembly Government). See the note at **[4.629]**.

SI 2009/2615: Company, Limited Liability Partnership and Business Names (Sensitive Words and Expressions) Regulations 2009
Authority: CA 2006, ss 55(1), 56(1)(b), 1194(1), 1195(1)(b), 1292(1)

Under ss 55(1) and 1194(1) of the Companies Act 2006 (including s 55(1) as applied to LLPs by the Limited Liability Partnerships (Application of Companies Act 2006) Regulations 2009, SI 2009/1804, reg 8), a person must obtain the approval of the Secretary of State to register a company or LLP by a name, or carry on business in the UK under a name, that includes a word or expression that is specified in regulations made by the Secretary of State. These Regulations also provide that the view of a specified Government department or other body must be obtained in relation to certain other specified words. They also provide that the specified words and expressions are specified in all their plural, possessive and (where relevant) feminine forms, and, in the case of Gaelic and Welsh words, in their grammatically mutated forms. See **[4.630]**.

SI 2009/2982: Company, Limited Liability Partnership and Business Names (Public Authorities) Regulations 2009
Authority: CA 2006, ss 54(1)(c), 56(1)(a), 1193(1)(c), 1195(1)(a), 1292(1)

Under ss 54(1)(c) and 1193(1)(c) of CA 2006 a person is required to obtain the approval of the Secretary of State to register a company by a name, or carry on business in the UK under a name, that would be likely to give the impression that the company or business is connected with a public authority specified by the Secretary of State. These Regulations (i) specify the public authorities for these purposes; (ii) sets out the relevant government department or other body whose view an applicant must seek in connection with an application for approval of the Secretary of State for use of a name under section 54(1)(c) or 1193(1)(c) of the Act. The Regulations make the same provision for limited liability partnerships. See **[4.641]** et seq.

SI 2009/3022: Companies Act 2006 (Amendment of Section 413) Regulations 2009
Authority: CA 2006, s 468(1), (2)

These Regulations amend s 413(8) of the 2006 Act (at **[1.413]**) so that banking companies and the holding companies of credit institutions are only required to make aggregate disclosures of the amounts specified in s 413(5)(a) and (c) (correcting an incorrect cross-reference). This is in implementation of the Member State option in Article 40(7) of Council Directive 86/635/EEC on the annual accounts and consolidated accounts of banks and other financial institutions.

2010 STATUTORY INSTRUMENTS

SI 2010/2156: Companies (Disclosure of Address) (Amendment) Regulations 2010
Authority: CA 2006, s 243(2), (3)

These Regulations amend the Companies (Disclosure of Address) Regulations 2009 by including the Marine Management Organisation in Sch 1 to those Regulations (see at **[4.360]**). Schedule 1 to those Regulations specifies the public authorities to whom the registrar may disclose protected information in accordance with s 243 of the Companies Act 2006. For this purpose "protected information" is defined by s 240(1) of the 2006 Act.

2011 STATUTORY INSTRUMENTS

SI 2011/309: Registrar of Companies (Fees) (Companies, Overseas Companies and Limited Liability Partnerships) (Amendment) Regulations 2011
Authority: CA 2006, ss 243(3), 1063(1)–(3)

These Regulations amend the Registrar of Companies (Fees) (Companies, Overseas Companies and Limited Liability Partnerships) Regulations 2009, SI 2009/2101, as from 6 April 2011. See the 2009 Regulations at **[4.543]**.

SI 2011/319: Registrar of Companies (Fees) (Limited Partnerships) (Amendment) Regulations 2011
Authority: CA 2006, s 1063(1)–(3)

These Regulations amend the Registrar of Companies (Fees) (Limited Partnerships and Newspaper Proprietors) Regulations 2009, SI 2009/2392, as from 6 April 2011. See the 2009 Regulations at **[4.566]**.

SI 2011/324: Registrar of Companies (Fees) (European Economic Interest Grouping) (Amendment) Regulations 2011
Authority: CA 2006, s 1063(1)–(3)

These Regulations amend the Registrar of Companies (Fees) (European Economic Interest Grouping and European Public Limited-Liability Company) Regulations 2009, SI 2009/2403, as from 6 April 2011. See the 2009 Regulations at **[4.577]**.

SI 2011/1265: Companies Act 2006 (Consequential Amendments and Transitional Provisions) Order 2011
Authority: CA 2006, ss 1292, 1294, 1296

This Order makes amendments to primary and secondary legislation that are consequential on certain provisions of the Companies Act 2006 having been brought into force, including the replacement of references to various provisions of the Companies Act 1985 with references to the appropriate, superseding provisions of the Companies Act 2006. It also repeals the Companies Consolidation (Consequential Provisions) Act 1985 subject to savings and transitional provisions. See **[4.648]** et seq.

SI 2011/1487: Companies Act 2006 (Annual Returns) Regulations 2011
Authority: CA 2006, ss 855(3), 857, 1167, 1292(1)

These Regulations are concerned with the information which must be included in a company's annual return under Part 24 of the Companies Act 2006. They amend ss 855, 856, and 856A of the 2006 Act and substitute s 856B (see **[1.855]** et seq). They also make consequential amendments to Sch 8 to the 2006 Act, and amend the Companies Act 2006 (Annual Return and Service Addresses) Regulations 2008, SI 2008/3000) at **[4.312]**.

COMPANIES (REGISTRAR, LANGUAGES AND TRADING DISCLOSURES) REGULATIONS 2006

(SI 2006/3429)

NOTES
Made: 20 December 2006.
Authority: European Communities Act 1972, s 2(2); Limited Liability Partnerships Act 2000, ss 15, 17; Companies Act 2006, ss 1091(4), 1105(2)(d), 1106(2).
Commencement: 1 January 2007.
These Regulations are reproduced as amended by: the Companies (Trading Disclosures) Regulations 2008, SI 2008/495.

[4.2]

1 Citation, commencement and interpretation

(1) These Regulations may be cited as the Companies (Registrar, Languages and Trading Disclosures) Regulations 2006 and shall come into force on 1st January 2007.

(2) In these Regulations—
"the 1985 Act" means the Companies Act 1985,
"the 1986 Order" means the Companies (Northern Ireland) Order 1986, and
"the 2006 Act" means the Companies Act 2006.

NOTES
Commencement: 1 January 2007.

[4.3]

2 Certification of electronic copies by registrar

(1) Where—
(a)   a person requires a copy of material on the register under section 1086 of the 2006 Act,
(b)   that person expressly requests that the copy be certified as a true copy, and
(c)   the registrar provides the copy in electronic form,
the registrar's certificate that the copy is an accurate record of the contents of the original document must be provided in accordance with the following provisions.

(2) The certificate must be authenticated by means of an electronic signature that—
(a)   is uniquely linked to the registrar,
(b)   indicates that the registrar has caused it to be applied,
(c)   is created using means that the registrar can maintain under his sole control, and
(d)   is linked—
(i)   to the certificate, and
(ii)   to the copy provided under section 1086 of the 2006 Act
in such a manner that any subsequent change of the data comprised in either is detectable.

(3) For the purposes of this regulation, an "electronic signature" means data in electronic form which are attached to or logically associated with other electronic data and which serve as a method of authentication.

NOTES
Commencement: 1 January 2007.

[4.4]

3 Provisions requiring office copies to be delivered to the registrar

(1) In the following provisions (which require an office copy of certain orders to be delivered to the registrar) for "an office copy" substitute "a copy"—
(a)   section 54(7) of the 1985 Act and article 64(7) of the 1986 Order (order on litigated objection to resolution that public company be re-registered as private),
(b)   section 425(3) of the 1985 Act and article 418(3) of the 1986 Order (order sanctioning compromise or arrangement),
(c)   section 427(5) of the 1985 Act and article 420(5) of the 1986 Order (order sanctioning compromise or arrangement),
(d)   section 201(4) of the Insolvency Act 1986 and article 166(4) of the Insolvency (Northern Ireland) Order 1989 (order deferring date at which dissolution of company after winding up is to take effect).

(2) In—
(a)   Form 139, in Schedule 3 to the Companies (Forms) Regulations 1985 and
(b)   Form 149, in Schedule 3 to the Companies (Forms) Regulations (Northern Ireland) 1986, for "Office copy" substitute "Copy".

(3)   For the purposes of their application to limited liability partnerships by the Limited Liability Partnerships Regulations 2001 or the Limited Liability Partnerships Regulations (Northern Ireland) 2004, the provisions specified in paragraph (1)(b), (c) and (d) have effect as if not amended by this regulation.

NOTES
Commencement: 1 January 2007.

[4.5]
4   Language requirements: contracts relating to allotments of shares

Section 1105 of the 2006 Act (documents that may be drawn up and delivered in languages other than English) applies to contracts required to be delivered to the registrar under section 88(2)(b)(i) of the 1985 Act or article 98(2)(b)(i) of the 1986 Order.

NOTES
Commencement: 1 January 2007.

[4.6]
5   Voluntary filing of translations

The facility described in section 1106 of the 2006 Act (voluntary filing of translations) is available in relation to—

  (a)   all the official languages of the European Union, and
  (b)   all documents subject to the Directive disclosure requirements.

NOTES
Commencement: 1 January 2007.

6, 7   (*Reg 6 introduced Schs 1 and 2 to these Regulations (amendments to the Companies Act 1985 and the Companies (Northern Ireland) Order 1986), and was revoked by the Companies (Trading Disclosures) Regulations 2008, SI 2008/495, reg 11, as from 1 October 2008; reg 7 amends the Insolvency Act 1986, s 188 at* **[9.282]**, *and the Insolvency (Northern Ireland) Order 1989.*)

SCHEDULES 1 AND 2

(*Sch 1 amended the Companies Act 1985, ss 349, 351, 705, Sch 24, and was revoked by the Companies (Trading Disclosures) Regulations 2008, SI 2008/495, reg 11, as from 1 October 2008; Sch 2 amended the Companies (Northern Ireland) Order 1986, and was also revoked by SI 2008/495, reg 11, as from 1 October 2008.*)

COMPANIES (POLITICAL EXPENDITURE EXEMPTION) ORDER 2007

(SI 2007/2081)

NOTES
Made: 18 July 2007.
Authority: Companies Act 2006, ss 377, 1292(1)(c).
Commencement: 1 October 2007 (in relation to Great Britain); 1 November 2007 (in relation to Northern Ireland).
Amendment: as of 1 July 2011 this Order had not been amended.

[4.7]
1   Citation, commencement and interpretation

(1)   This Order may be cited as the Companies (Political Expenditure Exemption) Order 2007 and shall come into force—

  (a)   for the purposes of its application to Great Britain, on 1st October 2007;
  (b)   for the purposes of its application to Northern Ireland, on 1st November 2007.

(2)   In this Order, "news material" means material relating to—

  (a)   news,
  (b)   public and political affairs,
  (c)   public and political events, or
  (d)   views, opinion or comment on such news, affairs or events.

NOTES
Commencement: 1 October 2007 (in relation to Great Britain); 1 November 2007 (in relation to Northern Ireland).

[4.8]
2 Exemption from authorisation

Political expenditure is exempt from the need for authorisation under Part 14 of the Companies Act 2006 if it is—

(a) political expenditure to which article 3 applies, and

(b) incurred by a company to which article 4 applies.

NOTES
Commencement: 1 October 2007 (in relation to Great Britain); 1 November 2007 (in relation to Northern Ireland).

[4.9]
3 Description of political expenditure

(1) This article applies to political expenditure incurred in respect of the preparation, publication or dissemination of news material, where that material contains matter which would render that preparation, publication or dissemination on the part of the company an activity on the part of the company that is capable of being reasonably regarded as intended—

(a) to affect public support for a political party or other political organisation, or an independent election candidate, or

(b) to influence voters in relation to any national or regional referendum held under the law of a member State.

(2) Until 1st October 2008, paragraph (1)(a) has effect as if the words "or an independent election candidate" were omitted.

NOTES
Commencement: 1 October 2007 (in relation to Great Britain); 1 November 2007 (in relation to Northern Ireland).

[4.10]
4 Description of company

(1) This article applies to any company whose ordinary course of business includes, or is proposed to include, the publication or dissemination to the public, or any part of the public, of news material, or the preparation of such material for publication or dissemination to the public, or any part of the public.

(2) For the purposes of paragraph (1), it is to be irrelevant—

(a) by which means or modes the news material is to be prepared, published or disseminated; or

(b) where the public, or any part of the public, to which such material is published or disseminated is located or the identity or description of the public or any part of it.

NOTES
Commencement: 1 October 2007 (in relation to Great Britain); 1 November 2007 (in relation to Northern Ireland).

COMPANIES (INTEREST RATE FOR UNAUTHORISED POLITICAL DONATION OR EXPENDITURE) REGULATIONS 2007 (NOTE)

(SI 2007/2242)

[4.11]

NOTES
These Regulations were made on 25 July 2007 under the Companies Act 2006, ss 369(5)(b) and 1167 and came into force on 1 October 2007 (for the purpose of their application to Great Britain) and on 1 November 2007 (for the purpose of their application to Northern Ireland). Under the Companies Act 2006, s 369, where a company has made a political donation or incurred political expenditure without the authorisation required by CA 2006 the directors are liable to make good to the company the amount of the unauthorised donation or expenditure with interest. These Regulations set the rate of interest to be applied at 8% per annum.

COMPANIES (FEES FOR INSPECTION AND COPYING OF COMPANY RECORDS) REGULATIONS 2007

(SI 2007/2612)

NOTES
Made: 6 September 2007.
Authority: CA 2006, ss 116(1)(b), (2), 229(2), 238(2), 358(4), 807(2), 811(2), 1137(1), (4), 1167, 1292(1)(a), (c).
Commencement: 1 October 2007.
As of 1 July 2011, these Regulations had not been amended.

[4.12]
1 Citation, commencement and interpretation

(1) These Regulations may be cited as the Companies (Fees for Inspection and Copying of Company Records) Regulations 2007 and shall come into force on 1st October 2007.

(2) In these Regulations—
"the Act" means the Companies Act 2006; and
"the Commencement Order" means the Companies Act 2006 (Commencement No 3, Consequential Amendments, Transitional Provisions and Savings) Order 2007.

NOTES
Commencement: 1 October 2007.

[4.13]
2 Fee for inspection of registers

For the purpose of section 116(1)(b) of the Act (inspection of register and index of members' names) the fee prescribed is £3.50 for each hour or part thereof during which the right of inspection is exercised.

NOTES
Commencement: 1 October 2007.

[4.14]
3 Fee for copy of registers

(1) For the purposes of the following sections of the Act—
  (a) section 116(2) (copy of company's register of members); and
  (b) section 811(2) (copy of entries in register of interests in shares disclosed),
the fee prescribed is—
  (i) the amount per number of entries copied by the company as set out in paragraph (2); and
  (ii) the reasonable costs incurred by the company in delivering the copy of the entries to the person entitled to be provided with that copy.

(2) The amounts per number of entries copied are—
  (a) £1 for each of the first 5 entries;
  (b) £30 for the next 95 entries or part thereof;
  (c) £30 for the next 900 entries or part thereof;
  (d) £30 for the next 99,000 entries or part thereof; and
  (e) £30 for the remainder of the entries in the register or part thereof.

NOTES
Commencement: 1 October 2007.

[4.15]
4 Fee for copy of company records

For the purposes of the following sections of the Act—
  (a) section 229(2) (copy of director's service contract or memorandum setting out the terms of that contract);
  (b) section 238(2) (copy of director's qualifying indemnity provision);
  (c) section 358(4) (copy of records of resolutions and meetings); and
  (d) section 807(2) (copy of report under section 805 of the Act),
the fee prescribed is—
  (i) 10 pence per 500 words or part thereof copied; and
  (ii) the reasonable costs incurred by the company in delivering the copy of the company record to the person entitled to be provided with that copy.

NOTES
Commencement: 1 October 2007.

[4.16]
5 Revocation and savings: Great Britain

(1) *(Revokes the Companies (Inspection and Copying of Registers, Indices and Documents) Regulations 1991, SI 1991/1998, Sch 2, paras 1(d), 2(b), (d), 3(b), subject to the savings in paras (2), (3) below.)*

(2) The fees prescribed in the following paragraphs of Schedule 2 to the 1991 Regulations—
  (a) paragraph 1(d) (fee for inspection of register of members and index); and
  (b) paragraph 2(d) (fee for copies of entries in the register of members),
shall continue to apply in respect of requests relating to the register of members or the index of members' names of a company which are subject to section 356 of the Companies Act 1985 by virtue of paragraph 2(2) of Schedule 3 to the Commencement Order.

(3)   The fee prescribed in paragraph 3(b) of Schedule 2 to the 1991 Regulations shall continue to apply in respect of requests relating to minutes of general meetings which are subject to section 383 of the Companies Act 1985 by virtue of paragraph 40(2) of Schedule 3 to the Commencement Order.

NOTES
Commencement: 1 October 2007.

6   *((Revocation and savings: Northern Ireland) outside the scope of this work.)*

COMPANIES (CROSS-BORDER MERGERS) REGULATIONS 2007

(SI 2007/2974)

NOTES
Made: 15 October 2007.
Authority: European Communities Act 1972, s 2(2); Companies Act 2006, ss 1102(2), 1105(2)(d), 1106(2).
Commencement: 15 December 2007.
These Regulations are reproduced as amended by: the Companies (Cross-Border Mergers) (Amendment) Regulations 2008, SI 2008/583; the Legal Services Act 2007 (Consequential Amendments) Order 2009, SI 2009/3348; the Agency Workers Regulations 2010, SI 2010/93; the Companies (Reporting Requirements in Mergers and Divisions) Regulations 2011, SI 2011/1606.
References to the "European Community", "Community", etc: see the Treaty of Lisbon (Changes in Terminology) Order 2011, SI 2011/1043, which provides (with effect from 22 April 2011): (1) that for references to the "European Communities" or to the "European Community" (including references to "the Communities", "the Community", "the EC" or "the EEC") substitute references to the European Union; and (2) that "EU" should be substituted for the word "Community" (subject to certain exceptions) in references to "Community treaties", "Community customs duty", "Community institution", "Community instrument", "Community obligation", "enforceable Community right", "Community law", "Community legislation", and "Community provision". Also, where such a term is preceded by the word "a", for "a" substitute "an".
Application to limited liability partnerships: as to the application of Parts 1–3, 5 of these Regulations to LLPs, see the Limited Liability Partnerships (Application of Companies Act 2006) Regulations 2009, SI 2009/1804, reg 46 at **[10.1142]**.
Application to bank insolvency and administration: as to the application of these Regulations to bank insolvency and administration, see the Banking Act 2009 (Parts 2 and 3 Consequential Amendments) Order 2009, SI 2009/317.

ARRANGEMENT OF REGULATIONS

PART 4
EMPLOYEE PARTICIPATION

CHAPTER 1
APPLICATION OF THIS PART

CHAPTER 2
MERGING COMPANIES AND THE SPECIAL NEGOTIATING BODY

CHAPTER 3
NEGOTIATION OF THE EMPLOYEE PARTICIPATION AGREEMENT

CHAPTER 4
ELECTION OF UNITED KINGDOM MEMBERS OF THE SPECIAL NEGOTIATING BODY

CHAPTER 5
STANDARD RULES OF EMPLOYEE PARTICIPATION IN A UK TRANSFEREE COMPANY

CHAPTER 6
CONFIDENTIAL INFORMATION

CHAPTER 7
PROTECTION FOR EMPLOYEES AND MEMBERS OF SPECIAL NEGOTIATING BODY, ETC

CHAPTER 8
COMPLIANCE AND ENFORCEMENT

CHAPTER 9
MISCELLANEOUS

SCHEDULES

PART 1
GENERAL

[4.17]
1 Citation and commencement

These Regulations may be cited as the Companies (Cross-Border Mergers) Regulations 2007 and come into force on 15th December 2007.

NOTES
Commencement: 15 December 2007.

[4.18]
2 Meaning of "cross-border merger"

(1) In these Regulations "cross-border merger" means a merger by absorption, a merger by absorption of a wholly-owned subsidiary, or a merger by formation of a new company.

(2) In these Regulations "merger by absorption" means an operation in which—
- (a)   there are one or more transferor companies;
- (b)   there is an existing transferee company;
- (c)   at least one of those companies is a UK company;
- (d)   at least one of those companies is an EEA company;
- (e)   every transferor company is dissolved without going into liquidation, and on its dissolution transfers all its assets and liabilities to the transferee company; and
- (f)   the consideration for the transfer is—
    - (i)   shares or other securities representing the capital of the transferee company, and
    - (ii)   if so agreed, a cash payment,
    receivable by members of the transferor company.

(3) In these Regulations "merger by absorption of a wholly-owned subsidiary" means an operation in which—
- (a)   there is one transferor company, of which all the shares or other securities representing its capital are held by an existing transferee company;
- (b)   either the transferor company or the transferee company is a UK company;
- (c)   either the transferor company or the transferee company is an EEA company; and
- (d)   the transferor company is dissolved without going into liquidation, and on its dissolution transfers all its assets and liabilities to the transferee company.

(4) In these Regulations "merger by formation of a new company" means an operation in which—
- (a)   there are two or more transferor companies, at least two of which are each governed by the law of a different EEA State;
- (b)   every transferor company is dissolved without going into liquidation, and on its dissolution transfers all its assets and liabilities to a transferee company formed for the purposes of, or in connection with, the operation;
- (c)   the consideration for the transfer is—
    - (i)   shares or other securities representing the capital of the transferee company, and
    - (ii)   if so agreed, a cash payment,
    receivable by members of the transferor company;
- (d)   at least one of the transferor companies or the transferee company is a UK company.

NOTES
Commencement: 15 December 2007.

[4.19]
3 Interpretation

(1) In these Regulations—
"the 1996 Act" means the Employment Rights Act 1996;
["agency worker" has the same meaning as in regulation 3 of the Agency Workers Regulations 2010;]
"the Appeal Tribunal" means the Employment Appeal Tribunal;
["assignment" has the same meaning as in regulation 2 of the Agency Workers Regulations 2010;]
"the CAC" means the Central Arbitration Committee;
"the Companies Acts" has the same meaning as in section 2 of the Companies Act 2006;

"competent authority of another EEA State" means a court or other authority designated in accordance with the law of an EEA State other than the United Kingdom as competent for the purposes of Article 8 (appointment of independent expert), Article 10 (issue of pre-merger certificate) or Article 11 (scrutiny of completion of merger) of the Directive;

"the court" means—

    (a)   in England and Wales, the High Court,

    (b)   in Scotland, the Court of Session, or

    (c)   in Northern Ireland, the High Court;

"the Directive" means Directive 2005/56/EC on cross-border mergers of limited liability companies;

"director" has the same meaning as in the Companies Acts (see section 250 of the Companies Act 2006);

"directors' report" means a report prepared and adopted in accordance with regulation 8 (directors' report), and includes any opinion of the employee representatives which must accompany it in accordance with regulation 8(6);

"dismissed" and "dismissal", in relation to an employee, shall be construed in accordance with Part 10 of the 1996 Act;

"draft terms of merger" means a draft of the proposed terms of a cross-border merger drawn up and adopted in accordance with regulation 7 (draft terms of merger);

"EEA company" means a body corporate governed by the law of an EEA State other than the United Kingdom;

"employee" means an individual who has entered into or works under a contract of employment and includes, where the employment has ceased, an individual who worked under a contract of employment;

"employee participation" means the influence of the employees and/or the employee representatives in the transferee company or a merging company by way of the right to—

    (a)   elect or appoint some of the members of the transferee company's or the merging company's supervisory or administrative organ; or

    (b)   recommend and/or oppose the appointment of some or all of the members of the transferee's or the merging company's supervisory or administrative organ;

"employee representatives" means—

    (a)   if the employees are of a description in respect of which an independent trade union is recognised by their employer for the purpose of collective bargaining, representatives of the trade union who normally take part as negotiators in the collective bargaining process, and

    (b)   any other employees of their employer who are elected or appointed as employee representatives to positions in which they are expected to receive, on behalf of the employees, information—

        (i)   which is relevant to the terms and conditions of employment of the employees, or

        (ii)   about the activities of the undertaking which may significantly affect the interests of the employees,

but excluding representatives who are expected to receive information relevant only to a specific aspect of the terms and conditions or interests of the employees, such as health and safety, collective redundancies, or pension schemes;

"existing transferee company" means a transferee company other than one formed for the purposes of, or in connection with, a cross-border merger;

"First Company Law Directive" means First Council Directive on co-ordination of safeguards which, for the protection of the interests of members and others, are required by Member States of companies within the meaning of the second paragraph of Article 58 of the Treaty, with a view to making such safeguards equivalent throughout the Community (68/151/EEC);

"the Gazette" means—

    (a)   as respects UK companies registered in England and Wales, the London Gazette,

    (b)   as respects UK companies registered in Scotland, the Edinburgh Gazette, and

    (c)   as respects UK companies registered in Northern Ireland, the Belfast Gazette;

["hirer" has the same meaning as in regulation 2 of the Agency Workers Regulations 2010;]

"independent expert's report" means a report prepared in accordance with regulation 9 (independent expert's report);

"liabilities" includes duties;

"member" in relation to a UK company has the same meaning as in the Companies Acts (see section 112 of the Companies Act 2006);

"registrar of companies" has the same meaning as in the Companies Acts (see section 1060 of the Companies Act 2006);

"share exchange ratio" means the number of shares or other securities in any transferee company that the draft terms of merger provide to be allotted to members of any transferor company for a given number of their shares or other securities;

"standard rules of employee participation" means the rules in regulation 38;

["suitable information relating to the use of agency workers" means—
    (a)   the number of agency workers working temporarily for and under the supervision and direction of a merging company or the transferee company (as the case may be);
    (b)   the parts of the undertaking in which those agency workers are working; and
    (c)   the type of work those agency workers are carrying out;]
["temporary work agency" has the same meaning as in regulation 4 of the Agency Workers Regulations 2010;]
"transferee company" means a UK company or an EEA company to which assets and liabilities are to be transferred by way of a cross-border merger;
"transferor company" means a UK company or an EEA company whose assets and liabilities are to be transferred by way of a cross-border merger;
"treasury shares" has the same meaning as in the Companies Acts (see section 724 of the Companies Act 2006);
"UK company" means a company within the meaning of the Companies Acts (see section 1 of the Companies Act 2006) other than—
    (a)   a company limited by guarantee without a share capital (see section 5 of the Companies Act 2006), or
    (b)   a company being wound up;
"UK employee" means an employee who has entered into or works under a contract of employment with a UK company;
"UK members of the special negotiating body" means members of the special negotiating body, established pursuant to regulation 25, elected or appointed by UK employees; and
"the UK register" means the register within the meaning of the Companies Acts (see section 1080 of the Companies Act 2006).

(2)   References in these Regulations to "the merging companies" are—
    (a)   in relation to a merger by absorption or a merger by absorption of a wholly-owned subsidiary, to the transferor company or companies and the existing transferee company;
    (b)   in relation to a merger by formation of a new company, to the transferor companies.

(3)   References in these Regulations to—
    (a)   "a UK merging company" are to a merging company which is a UK company;
    (b)   "a UK transferee company" are to a transferee company which is a UK company;
    (c)   "a UK transferor company" are to a transferor company which is a UK company.

NOTES
Commencement: 15 December 2007.
Para (1): definitions in square brackets inserted by the Agency Workers Regulations 2010, SI 2010/93, reg 25, Sch 2, Pt 2, paras 39, 40, as from 1 October 2011.

[4.20]
4   The Companies Act 2006
(1)   The following provisions of the Companies Act 2006 apply for the purposes of these Regulations as they apply for the purposes of the Companies Acts—
    (a)   section 1081 (annotation of the register);
    (b)   sections 1102 to 1104 and 1107 (language requirements for documents delivered to registrar);
    (c)   section 1112 (offence of false statement to registrar);
    (d)   section 1113 (enforcement of company's filing obligations);
    (e)   sections 1121 to 1123 (liability of officer in default);
    (f)   section 1125 (meaning of "daily default fine");
    (g)   sections 1127 and 1128 (summary proceedings);
    (h)   section 1129 (legal professional privilege);
    (i)   section 1130 (proceedings against unincorporated bodies).

(2)   Section 1063 of the Companies Act 2006 (fees payable to registrar) applies to the functions conferred on the registrar of companies by these Regulations as it applies to the functions conferred on the registrar of companies by the Companies Acts.

(3)   Section 1105 of the Companies Act 2006 (documents that may be drawn up and delivered in other languages) applies to the documents required to be delivered to the registrar of companies under—
    (a)   regulation 12(1)(b) (draft terms of merger), and
    (b)   regulation 19(3) (order of competent authority of another EEA State).

(4)   The facility described in section 1106 of the Companies Act 2006 (voluntary filing of translations) is available in relation to—
    (a)   all official languages of EEA States, and
    (b)   all documents required to be delivered to the registrar of companies under these Regulations.

(5)   . . .

(6) Schedule 1 makes transitional modifications to provisions of these Regulations that refer to provisions of the Companies Act 2006 that are not yet in force.

NOTES

Commencement: 15 December 2007.

Para (5): amends the Companies Act 2006 (Commencement No 3, Consequential Amendments, Transitional Provisions and Savings) Order 2007, SI 2007/2194, art 4 at **[2.34]**.

[4.21]

5 Unregistered companies

(1) These Regulations apply to an unregistered company as they apply to a UK company.

(2) In the application of these Regulations to an unregistered company any reference to—

(a) a UK company's registered office shall be read as a reference to the unregistered company's principal office in the United Kingdom;

(b) a part of the United Kingdom in which a UK company is registered shall be read as a reference to the part of the United Kingdom in which the unregistered company's principal office is situated and "Gazette" and "registrar of companies" shall be construed accordingly (see regulation 3(1)).

(3) In the application of these Regulations to an unregistered company, regulation 12(1)(c) applies with the omission of item (iv) (duty to state company's registered number).

(4) In this regulation "unregistered company" means a body to which section 1043 of the Companies Act 2006 (unregistered companies) applies.

NOTES

Commencement: 15 December 2007.

PART 2
PRE-MERGER REQUIREMENTS

[4.22]

6 Court approval of pre-merger requirements

(1) A UK merging company may apply to the court for an order certifying for the purposes of Article 10.2 of the Directive (issue of pre-merger certificate) that the company has completed properly the pre-merger acts and formalities for the cross-border merger.

(2) The court must not make such an order unless the requirements of regulations 7 to 10 and 12 to 15 (pre-merger requirements) have been complied with.

[(3) In a case falling within regulation 9A (circumstances in which independent expert's report not required), the court may determine, or make provision for the determination of, the consideration to be given for securities acquired under that regulation.]

NOTES

Commencement: 15 December 2007.

Para (3): added by the Companies (Reporting Requirements in Mergers and Divisions) Regulations 2011, SI 2011/1606, regs 32, 33, as from 1 August 2011 (except in relation to any merger or division the draft terms of which were adopted before that date).

[4.23]

7 Draft terms of merger

(1) The directors of the UK merging company must draw up and adopt a draft of the proposed terms of the cross-border merger.

(2) The draft must give particulars of at least the following matters—

(a) in relation to each transferor company and transferee company—

    (i) its name,

    (ii) its registered office, and

    (iii) its legal form and the law by which it is governed;

(b) the share exchange ratio and the amount of any cash payment;

(c) the terms relating to the allotment of shares or other securities in the transferee company;

(d) the likely effects of the cross-border merger for employees of each merging company;

(e) the date from which the holding of shares or other securities in the transferee company will entitle the holders to participate in profits, and any special conditions affecting that entitlement;

(f) the date from which the transactions of the transferor companies are to be treated for accounting purposes as being those of the transferee company;

(g) any rights or restrictions attaching to shares or other securities in the transferee company to be allotted under the cross-border merger to the holders of shares or other securities in a transferor company to which any special rights or restrictions attach, or the measures proposed concerning them;

(h)   any amount or benefit paid or given or intended to be paid or given to the independent expert referred to in regulation 9 (independent expert's report) or to any director of a merging company, and the consideration for the payment of benefit;

(i)   the transferee company's articles of association, or if it does not have articles, the instrument constituting the company or defining its constitution;

(j)   information on the procedures by which any employee participation rights are to be determined in accordance with Part 4 of these Regulations (employee participation);

(k)   information on the evaluation of the assets and liabilities to be transferred to the transferee company; and

(l)   the dates of the accounts of every merging company which were used for the purpose of preparing the draft terms of merger.

(3)   Particulars of the matters referred to in sub-paragraphs (b), (c) and (e) of paragraph (2) may be omitted in the case of a merger by absorption of a wholly-owned subsidiary.

(4)   The draft—

(a)   must not provide for any shares in the transferee company to be allotted to—

(i)   a transferor company (or its nominee) in respect of shares in the transferor company held by the transferor company itself (or its nominee); or

(ii)   the transferee company (or its nominee) in respect of shares in the transferor company held by the transferee company (or its nominee); and

(b)   must provide that where any securities of a UK transferor company (other than shares) to which special rights are attached are held by a person other than as a member or creditor of the company, that person is to receive rights in the transferee company of equivalent value, unless—

(i)   the holder has agreed otherwise; or

(ii)   the holder is, or under the draft is to be, entitled to have the securities purchased by the transferee company on terms which the court considers reasonable.

NOTES

Commencement: 15 December 2007.

[4.24]

8   Directors' report

(1)   The directors of the UK merging company must draw up and adopt a report.

(2)   The report must—

(a)   explain the effect of the cross-border merger for members, creditors and employees of the company; and

(b)   state—

(i)   the legal and economic grounds for the draft terms;

(ii)   any material interests of the directors (whether as directors or as members or as creditors or otherwise);

(iii)   the effect on those interests of the cross-border merger, in so far as it is different from the effect on the like interests of other persons.

[(2A)   Where information to be provided under paragraph (2)(a) relates to the employment situation, it must include suitable information relating to the use of agency workers.]

(3)   Where the cross-border merger affects the rights of debenture holders of the company, the report must state—

(a)   any material interests of the trustees of any deed for securing the issue of the debentures (whether as trustees or as members or as creditors or otherwise);

(b)   the effect on those interests of the cross-border merger, in so far as it is different from the effect on the like interests of other persons.

(4)   It is the duty of any trustee for the company's debenture holders to give notice to the company's directors of such matters relating to himself as may be necessary for the purposes of paragraph (3).

(5)   The directors of the UK merging company must deliver copies of the report to its employee representatives (or if there are no such representatives, the employees) not less than 2 months before the date of the first meeting of the members, or any class of members, of the company (see regulation 13).

(6)   If the employee representatives deliver an opinion on the report to the company's registered office not less than 1 month before the date of the first meeting of the members, or any class of members, of the company, every copy of the report issued after the date on which the opinion was delivered must be accompanied by the opinion.

(7)   Any person who makes default in complying with paragraph (4) commits an offence.

(8)   A person guilty of an offence under this regulation is liable on summary conviction to a fine not exceeding level 3 on the standard scale.

NOTES

Commencement: 15 December 2007.

Para (2A): inserted by the Agency Workers Regulations 2010, SI 2010/93, reg 25, Sch 2, Pt 2, paras 39, 41, as from 1 October 2011.

[4.25]
9   Independent expert's report
(1)   A report must be drawn up in accordance with this regulation, unless—
   (a)   the cross-border merger is a merger by absorption of a wholly-owned subsidiary;
   (b)   *the cross-border merger is a merger by absorption where 90% or more (but not all) of the relevant securities of the transferor company (or, if there is more than one transferor company, of each of them) are held by or on behalf of the transferee company; or*
   (c)   every member of every merging company agrees that such a report is not required.
(2)   The report must be prepared by—
   (a)   an independent expert who has been appointed for the UK merging company by its directors;
   (b)   an independent expert who has been appointed for all the merging companies by the court in accordance with paragraph (3); or
   (c)   a person who has been appointed for all the merging companies for the purposes of Article 8 (independent expert's report) of the Directive by a competent authority of another EEA State.
(3)   The court may, on the joint application of all the merging companies, order the appointment of an independent expert to prepare a report for those companies in accordance with this regulation.
(4)   Where it appears to an independent expert that a valuation is reasonably necessary to enable him to draw up the report, and it appears to him to be reasonable for that valuation, or part of it, to be made by another person who—
   (a)   appears to him to have the requisite knowledge and experience to make the valuation or that part of it, and
   (b)   is independent,
he may arrange for such a valuation (or accept one which has already been made), together with a report which will enable him to prepare his own report in accordance with this regulation.
(5)   In the report the independent expert must—
   (a)   indicate—
      (i)   the methods used to arrive at the share exchange ratio; and
      (ii)   the values arrived at using each such method;
   (b)   describe any special valuation difficulties which have arisen;
   (c)   give an opinion—
      (i)   as to whether the methods used are reasonable in all the circumstances of the case;
      (ii)   if there is more than one method, on the relative importance attributed to each method in arriving at the value decided on; and
      (iii)   as to whether the share exchange ratio is reasonable;
   (d)   in the case of a valuation made by another person in accordance with paragraph (4)—
      (i)   state that fact and the date of the valuation;
      (ii)   state the person's name and what knowledge and experience he has to carry out the valuation;
      (iii)   describe so much of the assets and liabilities as was valued by the other person, and the method used to value them; and
      (iv)   state that it appeared to himself reasonable to arrange for the valuation to be so made or to accept a valuation so made.
(6)   The independent expert has the right—
   (a)   of access to all such documents of every merging company; and
   (b)   to require from the companies' officers all such information,
as he thinks necessary for the purpose of making his report.
(7)   In this regulation, "independent expert" means a person who—
   (a)   is eligible for appointment as a statutory auditor in accordance with section 1212 of the Companies Act 2006 (eligibility for appointment as statutory auditor), and
   (b)   is independent.
(8)   For the purposes of this regulation—
   (a)   a person is not independent if, by virtue of section 1214 of the Companies Act 2006 (independence requirement for statutory auditor), he would not be able to act as statutory auditor of all the merging companies; and
   (b)   section 1214 of the Companies Act 2006 applies in relation to all the merging companies as if they were companies in respect of which a person must be appointed as auditor under Part 16 of that Act (audit of companies).
(9)   In this regulation "relevant securities", in relation to a transferor company, means shares or other securities carrying the right to vote at general meetings of the company.

NOTES
Commencement: 15 December 2007.

Para (1): sub-para (b) substituted by the Companies (Reporting Requirements in Mergers and Divisions) Regulations 2011, SI 2011/1606, regs 32, 34, as from 1 August 2011 (except in relation to any merger or division the draft terms of which were adopted before that date), as follows—

"(b)   the conditions in regulation 9A are met; or".

[4.26]
[9A Circumstances in which independent expert's report not required

(1)   The requirement to draw up a report in accordance with regulation 9 does not apply if the conditions in paragraphs (2) to (4) are met.

(2)   The first condition is that the cross-border merger is a merger by absorption where 90% or more (but not all) of the relevant securities of the transferor company (or, if there is more than one transferor company, of each of them) are held by or on behalf of the transferee company.

(3)   The second condition is that the draft terms of merger provide that every other holder of relevant securities has the right to require the transferee company to acquire those securities.

(4)   The third condition is that, if a holder of securities exercises that right, the consideration to be given for those securities is fair and reasonable.

(5)   In this regulation—
"other holder" means a person who holds securities of the transferor company otherwise than on behalf of the transferee company (and does not include the transferee company itself);
"relevant securities", in relation to a company, means shares or other securities carrying the right to vote at general meetings of the company.]

NOTES
Commencement: 1 August 2011.

Inserted by the Companies (Reporting Requirements in Mergers and Divisions) Regulations 2011, SI 2011/1606, regs 32, 35, as from 1 August 2011 (except in relation to any merger or division the draft terms of which were adopted before that date).

[4.27]
10 Inspection of documents

(1)   The members of the UK merging company and its employee representatives (or if there are no such representatives, the employees) must be able, during the period specified in paragraph (2)—
- (a)   to inspect at the registered office of the company copies of the documents listed in paragraph (3);
- (b)   to obtain copies of those documents or any part of them on request free of charge.

(2)   The period referred to above is the period—
- (a)   beginning one month before, and
- (b)   ending on the date of,
the first meeting of the members, or any class of members, of the company (see regulation 13).

(3)   The documents referred to above are—
- (a)   the draft terms of merger;
- (b)   the directors' report;
- (c)   the independent expert's report, if such a report is required by regulation 9 (independent expert's report).

NOTES
Commencement: 15 December 2007.

[4.28]
11 Power of court to summon meeting of members or creditors

(1)   The court may, on an application under this regulation, order a meeting of—
- (a)   members or a class of members, for the purposes of regulation 13 (approval of members in meeting);
- (b)   creditors or a class of creditors, for the purposes of regulation 14 (approval of creditors in meeting);
to be summoned in such manner as the court directs.

(2)   An application under this regulation may be made by—
- (a)   the UK merging company,
- (b)   any member of the UK merging company in the case of a meeting of members or a class of members,
- (c)   any creditor of the UK merging company in the case of a meeting of creditors or a class of creditors, or
- (d)   in the case of a UK merging company in administration, the administrator.

(3)   Section 323 of the Companies Act 2006 (representation of corporations at meetings) applies to a meeting of the creditors summoned under this regulation as to a meeting of the company (the references in that section to a member of the company being read as references to a creditor).

NOTES
Commencement: 15 December 2007.

[4.29]
12 Public notice of receipt of registered documents

(1) The directors of the UK merging company must deliver to the registrar of companies particulars of the date, time and place of every meeting summoned under regulation 11 (power of court to summon meeting of members or creditors) together with—

   (a) a copy of the order made under that regulation;

   (b) a copy of the draft terms of merger; and

   (c) documents giving the following particulars in relation to each merging company—

      (i) its name;

      (ii) its registered office;

      (iii) its legal form and the law by which it is governed;

      (iv) in the case of a UK company, its registered number;

      (v) in the case of an EEA company to which the First Company Law Directive applies, particulars of the register in which the company file mentioned in Article 3 of that Directive (file for each registered company to be kept in national register) is kept (including details of the relevant State) and its registration number in that register;

      (vi) in the case of any other EEA company, particulars, if any, of the register in which it is entered (including details of the relevant State) and its registration number in that register.

(2) The directors must deliver these documents to the registrar not less than two months before the date of the first meeting of the members, or any class of members, of the company (see regulation 13).

(3) If the documents are delivered to the registrar in accordance with paragraphs (1) and (2), he must publish—

   (a) in the Gazette, or

   (b) if regulations have been made under section 1116 of the Companies Act 2006 (alternative to publication in the Gazette), in accordance with those regulations,

notice of his receipt of the documents.

(4) The notice must be published by the registrar at least one month before the date of the first meeting of the members, or any class of members, of the company (see regulation 13).

(5) The notice must include—

   (a) the date of receipt of the documents;

   (b) the particulars referred to in paragraph (1)(c);

   (c) in relation to each UK merging company, a statement that information related to the company is kept in the UK register;

   (d) a statement that regulation 10 (inspection of documents) requires copies of the draft terms of merger, the directors' report and (if there is one) the independent expert's report to be kept available for inspection;

   (e) the date, time and place of every meeting summoned under regulation 11 (power of court to summon meeting of members or creditors).

(6) The following provisions of the Companies Act 2006 apply to the documents delivered to the registrar in accordance with paragraph (1) in the same way as they apply to documents subject to the Directive disclosure requirements (as defined in section 1078(1) of that Act)—

   (a) section 1068 (registrar's requirements as to form, authentication and manner of delivery);

   (b) section 1080 (the register);

   (c) section 1086 (right to copy of material on the register);

   (d) section 1089 (form of application for inspection or copy);

   (e) section 1090 (form and manner in which copies to be provided);

   (f) section 1091 (certification of copies as accurate); and

   (g) section 1098 (public notice of removal of certain material from register).

[(7) The requirements in paragraphs (1) to (4), so far as they relate to the draft terms of the merger, are subject to regulation 12A.]

NOTES
Commencement: 15 December 2007.
Para (7): added by the Companies (Reporting Requirements in Mergers and Divisions) Regulations 2011, SI 2011/1606, regs 32, 36, as from 1 August 2011 (except in relation to any merger or division the draft terms of which were adopted before that date).

[4.30]
[12A Publication of draft terms of merger on company website

(1) The following requirements of regulation 12 do not apply where the conditions in paragraphs (2) to (6) are met—

Part 4   CA 2006 SIs

(a) the requirement in paragraph (1)(b) (directors to deliver copy of draft terms of merger to registrar), and

(b) the requirement in paragraph (3), so far as it relates to the draft terms of merger (registrar to publish notice of receipt in the Gazette etc).

(2) The first condition is that the draft terms of merger are made available on a website which—

(a) is maintained by or on behalf of the UK merging company, and

(b) identifies the company.

(3) The second condition is that neither access to the draft terms of merger on the website nor the supply of a hard copy of them from the website is conditional on payment of a fee or otherwise restricted.

(4) The third condition is that the directors of the company deliver to the registrar a notice giving details of the website.

(5) The fourth condition is that the registrar publishes the notice in the Gazette at least one month before the date of the first meeting of the members, or any class of members, of the company (see regulation 13).

(6) The fifth condition is that the draft terms of merger remain available on the website throughout the period beginning one month before, and ending on, the date of any such meeting.

(7) A failure to make the draft terms available on the website throughout the period specified in paragraph (6) is to be disregarded if—

(a) they are made available on the website for part of that period, and

(b) the failure to make them available throughout that period is wholly attributable to circumstances that it would not be reasonable to have expected the company to prevent or avoid.]

NOTES

Commencement: 1 August 2011.

Inserted by the Companies (Reporting Requirements in Mergers and Divisions) Regulations 2011, SI 2011/1606, regs 32, 37, as from 1 August 2011 (except in relation to any merger or division the draft terms of which were adopted before that date).

[4.31]
13 Approval of members in meeting

(1) Except as provided in paragraphs (3) and (4), the draft terms of merger must be approved by a majority in number, representing 75% in value, of each class of members of the UK merging company, present and voting either in person or by proxy at a meeting summoned under regulation 11 (power of court to summon meeting of members or creditors).

(2) The approval of the members may be made subject to—

(a) ratification of any arrangements adopted for employee participation in the transferee company in accordance with Part 4 of these Regulations (employee participation);

(b) an order of a competent authority of another EEA State which amends the share exchange ratio in accordance with Article 10.3 of the Directive (national procedure for amendment of share exchange ratio).

(3) The approval of the members is not required in the case of a transferor company concerned in a merger by absorption of a wholly-owned subsidiary.

(4) The approval of the members is not required in the case of an existing transferee company if—

(a) the publication of the notice required by regulation 12 (public notice of receipt of registered documents) [or 12A (public notice of draft terms of merger on company website)] took place in respect of the company at least one month before the date of the first meeting of members of the transferor companies;

(b) *the members of the transferee company were able during a period beginning one month before, and ending on, the date of the first such meeting—*

(i) *to inspect at the registered office of the transferee company copies of the documents listed in regulation 10(3) (inspection of documents) in relation to all the merging companies, and*

(ii) *to obtain copies of those documents or any part of them on request; and*

(c)

(i) one or more members of the transferee company, who together held not less than 5% of the paid-up capital of the company which carried the right to vote at general meetings of the company (excluding any shares held as treasury shares), would have been able, during that period, to require a meeting of each class of members to be called for the purpose of deciding whether or not to agree to the scheme, and

(ii) no such requirement was made.

[(5) This paragraph is satisfied for a document if the members of the transferee company were able during the period beginning one month before, and ending on, the date of the first meeting of members of the transferor companies—

(a) to inspect at the registered office of the transferee company a copy of the document and

(b) to obtain copies of it or any part of it on request.

(6)   This paragraph is satisfied for a document if—
- (a)   the document is made available on a website which is maintained by or on behalf of the transferee company and identifies the company,
- (b)   access to it on the website is not conditional on the payment of a fee or otherwise restricted,
- (c)   it remains available on the website throughout the period beginning one month before, and ending on, the date of the first meeting of members of the transferor company, and
- (d)   members of the transferee company were able, during that period, to obtain copies of it or any part of it on request.

(7)   A failure to make a document available on the website throughout the period specified in paragraph (6)(c) is to be disregarded if—
- (a)   the document is made available on the website for part of that period, and
- (b)   the failure to make it available throughout that period is wholly attributable to circumstances that it would not be reasonable to have expected the company to prevent or avoid.]

NOTES

Commencement: 15 December 2007.

Para (4): the words in square brackets in sub-para (a) are inserted, and sub-para (b) is substituted, by the Companies (Reporting Requirements in Mergers and Divisions) Regulations 2011, SI 2011/1606, regs 32, 38(1)–(3), as from 1 August 2011 (except in relation to any merger or division the draft terms of which were adopted before that date), as follows—

"(b)   paragraph (5) or (6) is satisfied for each of the documents listed in regulation 10(3) (inspection of documents) in relation to all the merging companies; and".

Paras (5)–(7): added by SI 2011/1606, regs 32, 38(1), (4), as from 1 August 2011 (except in relation to any merger or division the draft terms of which were adopted before that date).

[4.32]
14   Approval of creditors in meeting

If a meeting of creditors or a class of creditors is summoned under regulation 11 (power of court to summon meeting of members or creditors), the draft terms of merger must be approved by a majority in number, representing 75% in value, of the creditors or class of creditors (as the case may be), present and voting either in person or by proxy at the meeting.

NOTES

Commencement: 15 December 2007.

[4.33]
15   Documents to be circulated or made available

(1)   Where a meeting is summoned under regulation 11 (power of court to summon meeting of members or creditors)—
- (a)   every notice summoning the meeting that is sent to a member or creditor must include copies of the documents referred to in regulation 10(3) (inspection of documents), and
- (b)   every notice summoning the meeting that is given by advertisement must—
  - (i)   include copies of those documents, or
  - (ii)   state where and how members or creditors may obtain copies of those documents.

(2)   Where a notice given by advertisement states that copies of the documents referred to in regulation 10(3) (inspection of documents) can be obtained by members or creditors entitled to attend the meeting, every such member or creditor is entitled, on making application in the manner indicated by the notice, to be provided by the company with a copy of the documents free of charge.

NOTES

Commencement: 15 December 2007.

PART 3
COURT APPROVAL OF CROSS-BORDER MERGER

[4.34]
16   Court approval of cross-border merger

(1)   The court may, on the joint application of all the merging companies, make an order approving the completion of the cross-border merger for the purposes of Article 11 of the Directive (scrutiny of completion of merger) if—
- (a)   the transferee company is a UK company;
- (b)   an order has been made under regulation 6 (court approval of pre-merger requirements) in relation to each UK merging company;
- (c)   an order has been made by a competent authority of another EEA State for the purposes of Article 10.2 of the Directive (issue of pre-merger certificate) in relation to each merging company which is an EEA company;

(d)   the application is made to the court on a date not more than 6 months after the making of any order referred to in sub-paragraph (b) or (c);

(e)   the draft terms of merger approved by every order referred to in sub-paragraphs (b) and (c) are the same; and

(f)   where appropriate, any arrangements for employee participation in the transferee company have been determined in accordance with Part 4 of these Regulations (employee participation).

(2)   Where the court makes such an order—

(a)   it must in the order fix a date on which the consequences of the cross-border merger (see regulation 17) are to have effect; and

(b)   that date must be not less than 21 days after the date on which the order is made.

(3)   After the consequences of the cross-border merger have taken effect (see regulation 17), an order made under this regulation is conclusive evidence that—

(a)   the conditions set out in paragraph (1) have been satisfied; and

(b)   the requirements of regulations 7 to 10 and 12 to 15 (pre-merger requirements) have been complied with.

NOTES

Commencement: 15 December 2007.

[4.35]

17   Consequences of a cross-border merger

(1)   The consequences of a cross-border merger are that—

(a)   the assets and liabilities of the transferor companies are transferred to the transferee company;

(b)   the rights and obligations arising from the contracts of employment of the transferor companies are transferred to the transferee company;

(c)   the transferor companies are dissolved; and

(d)   in the case of a merger by absorption or a merger by formation of a new company, the members of the transferor companies except the transferee company (if it is a member of a transferor company) become members of the transferee company.

(2)   The consequences take effect—

(a)   where an order has been made under regulation 16 (court approval of merger), on the date fixed in that order; or

(b)   where an order has been made by a competent authority of another EEA State for the purposes of Article 11 of the Directive (scrutiny of completion of merger), on the date fixed in accordance with the law of that State.

(3)   The transferee company must take such steps as are required by law (including by the law of another EEA State) for the transfer of the assets and liabilities of the transferor companies to be effective in relation to other persons.

NOTES

Commencement: 15 December 2007.

[4.36]

18   Copy of order to be provided to members

(1)   Where an order is made under regulation 16 (court approval of merger) approving the completion of a cross-border merger, the UK transferee company must, on request by any member, send to him a copy of the order.

(2)   If a company makes default in complying with this regulation, an offence is committed by every officer of the company who is in default.

(3)   A person guilty of an offence under this regulation is liable on summary conviction to a fine not exceeding level 3 on the standard scale.

NOTES

Commencement: 15 December 2007.

[4.37]

19   Copy of order to be delivered to the registrar of companies

(1)   Where an order is made under regulation 16 (court approval of merger)—

(a)   the UK transferee company, and

(b)   every UK transferor company,

must deliver the documents and particulars specified in paragraph (2) to the registrar of companies for registration not more than 7 days after the date on which it was made.

(2)   The documents and particulars referred to in paragraph (1) are—

(a)   a copy of the order made under regulation 16 (court approval of merger);

(b) in the case of a transferor company which is an EEA company to which the First Company Law Directive applies, particulars of the register in which the company file mentioned in Article 3 of that Directive (file for each registered company to be kept in national register) is kept (including details of the relevant State) and its registration number in that register;

(c) in the case of any other transferor company which is a EEA company, particulars, if any, of the register in which it is entered (including details of the relevant State) and its registration number in that register.

(3) Where an order is made by a competent authority of another EEA State approving the completion of a cross-border merger for the purposes of Article 11 of the Directive (scrutiny of completion of merger), every transferor company which is a UK company must deliver a copy of the order to the registrar of companies for registration not more than 14 days after the date on which it was made.

(4) The following provisions of the Companies Act 2006 apply to an order delivered to the registrar in accordance with paragraph (1) or (2) in the same way as they apply to documents subject to the Directive disclosure requirements (as defined in section 1078(1) of that Act)—

(a) section 1068 (registrar's requirements as to form, authentication and manner of delivery);
(b) section 1077 (public notice of receipt of certain documents);
(c) section 1079 (effect of failure to give public notice);
(d) section 1080 (the register);
(e) section 1086 (right to copy of material on the register);
(f) section 1089 (form of application for inspection or copy);
(g) section 1090 (form and manner in which copies to be provided);
(h) section 1091 (certification of copies as accurate); and
(i) section 1098 (public notice of removal of certain material from register).

(5) If a UK merging company makes default in complying with [paragraph (1) or (3)], an offence is committed by—

(a) the company, and
(b) every officer of the company who is in default.

(6) A person guilty of an offence under this regulation is liable on summary conviction to a fine not exceeding level 3 on the standard scale and, for continued contravention, a daily default fine not exceeding one-tenth of level 3 on the standard scale.

NOTES
Commencement: 15 December 2007.
Para (5): words in square brackets substituted by the Companies (Cross-Border Mergers) (Amendment) Regulations 2008, SI 2008/583, reg 2, as from 6 April 2008.

[4.38]
20 Obligations of transferee company with respect to articles etc

(1) If an order made under regulation 16 (court approval of merger) amends—
(a) the articles of association of the UK transferee company, or
(b) any resolution or agreement in relation to the UK transferee company to which Chapter 3 of Part 3 of the Companies Act 2006 (resolutions and agreements affecting a company's constitution) applies,

the copy of the order delivered to the registrar of companies by the UK transferee company under regulation 19 (copy of order to be delivered to the registrar of companies) must be accompanied by a copy of the company's articles, or the resolution or agreement in question, as amended.

(2) Every copy of the company's articles issued by the company after the order is made must be accompanied by a copy of the order, unless the effect of the order has been incorporated into the articles by amendment.

(3) In this regulation—
(a) references to the effect of the order include the effect of the cross-border merger to which the order relates; and
(b) in the case of a company not having articles, references to its articles shall be read as references to the instrument constituting the company or defining its constitution.

(4) If a UK transferee company makes default in complying with this regulation, an offence is committed by—
(a) the company, and
(b) every officer of the company who is in default.

(5) A person guilty of an offence under this regulation is liable on summary conviction to a fine not exceeding level 3 on the standard scale.

NOTES
Commencement: 15 December 2007.

[4.39]
21 Notification of registration

(1) Where the registrar of companies receives a copy of an order made under regulation 16 (court approval of merger) approving the completion of a cross-border merger, he must—

(a) without undue delay, in relation to each transferor company which is an EEA company to which the First Company Law Directive applies, give notice of that order to the register in which the company file mentioned in Article 3 of the First Company Law Directive (file for each registered company to be kept in national register) is kept;

(b) without undue delay, in relation to any other transferor company which is a EEA company, give notice of the order to the register, if any, in which it is entered; and

(c) on or without undue delay after the date fixed in the order for the purposes of regulation 16(2) (court approval of merger), take the steps specified in paragraph (3) in relation to every UK transferor company.

(2) Where the registrar of companies receives from the registry of another EEA State notice for the purposes of Article 13 of the Directive (notification of registries in other Member States) of an order approving the completion of a cross-border merger, he must on or without undue delay after the date fixed for the purposes of Article 12 of the Directive (entry into effect of the cross-border merger) take the steps specified in paragraph (3) in relation to every UK transferor company.

(3) The steps referred to in paragraphs (1)(c) and (2) are—

(a) striking the name of the UK transferor company from the UK register, and

(b) placing a note in the register stating that as from the date on which the consequences of the cross-border merger had effect (see regulation 16(2) and Article 12 of the Directive), the assets and liabilities of the UK transferor company were transferred to the transferee company.

NOTES
Commencement: 15 December 2007.

PART 4
EMPLOYEE PARTICIPATION

CHAPTER 1
APPLICATION OF THIS PART

[4.40]
22 Application of this Part

(1) Subject to paragraph (2), this Part shall apply where the transferee company is a UK company and where—

(a) a merging company has, in the six months before the publication of the draft terms of merger, an average number of employees that exceeds 500 and has a system of employee participation, or

(b) a UK merging company has a proportion of employee representatives amongst the directors, or

(c) a merging company has employee representatives amongst members of the administrative or supervisory organ or their committees or of the management group which covers the profit units of the company.

[(1A) For the purposes of paragraph (1)(a), agency workers whose contract within regulation 3(1)(b) of the Agency Workers Regulations 2010 was not a contract of employment with one or more temporary work agencies that were merging companies at the relevant time are to be treated as having been employed by such a temporary work agency or agencies for the duration of their assignment with a hirer.]

(2) Chapters 4 and 6 to 9 shall apply to a UK merging company, its employees or their representatives, regardless of whether the transferee company is a UK company.

(3) This Part applies to Northern Ireland with the modifications contained in Schedule 2.

NOTES
Commencement: 15 December 2007.
Para (1A): inserted by the Agency Workers Regulations 2010, SI 2010/93, reg 25, Sch 2, Pt 2, paras 39, 42, as from 1 October 2011.

CHAPTER 2
MERGING COMPANIES AND THE SPECIAL NEGOTIATING BODY

[4.41]
23 Duty on merging company to provide information

(1) As soon as possible after adopting the draft terms of merger (see regulation 7), each merging company shall provide information to the employee representatives of that company or, if no such representatives exist, the employees themselves.

(2)   The information referred to in paragraph (1) must include, as a minimum, information—

    (a)   identifying the merging companies,

    (b)   of any decision taken pursuant to regulation 36 (merging companies may select standard rules of employee participation), and

    (c)   giving the number of employees employed by each merging company.

(3)   When a special negotiating body has been formed in accordance with regulation 25, each merging company must provide that body with such information as is necessary to keep it informed of the plan and progress of establishing the UK transferee company until the date upon which the consequences of the cross-border merger take effect (see regulation 17).

[(4)   Where under the provisions of this regulation a merging company is to provide information, such information must include suitable information relating to the use of agency workers (if any) in that company.]

NOTES

   Commencement: 15 December 2007.

   Para (4): added by the Agency Workers Regulations 2010, SI 2010/93, reg 25, Sch 2, Pt 2, paras 39, 43, as from 1 October 2011.

[4.42]
24 Complaint of failure to provide information

(1)   An employee representative or, where no such representative exists, any employee may present a complaint to the CAC that—

    (a)   a merging company has failed to provide information as required by regulation 23; or

    (b)   the information is false or incomplete in a material particular.

(2)   Where the CAC finds the complaint well-founded it shall make an order requiring the company to disclose information to the complainant specifying—

    (a)   the information in respect of which the CAC finds that the complaint is well-founded and which is to be disclosed to the complainant; and

    (b)   a date (not being less than one week from the date of the order) by which the company must disclose the information specified in the order.

NOTES

   Commencement: 15 December 2007.

[4.43]
25 The special negotiating body

(1)   Subject to regulation 36 (merging companies may select standard rules of employee participation), each merging company shall make arrangements for the establishment of a special negotiating body.

(2)   The task of the special negotiating body shall be to reach an employee participation agreement with the merging companies (see Chapter 3).

(3)   The special negotiating body shall be constituted in accordance with regulation 26.

NOTES

   Commencement: 15 December 2007.

[4.44]
26 Composition of the special negotiating body

(1)   Employees of merging companies registered in each EEA State (including the UK) shall be given an entitlement to elect one member of the special negotiating body, in accordance with these Regulations, for each 10% or fraction thereof which employees of merging companies registered in that State represent of the total workforce of the merging companies. These members shall be the "constituent members".

(2)   If, following an election under paragraph (1), the members elected to the special negotiating body do not include at least one constituent member in respect of each merging company, the employees of any merging company in respect of which there is no constituent member shall be given an entitlement, subject to paragraph (3), to elect an additional member to the special negotiating body.

(3)   The number of additional members which the employees of the merging companies are entitled to elect under paragraph (2) shall not exceed 20% of the number of constituent members elected under paragraph (1) and if the number of additional members under paragraph (2) would exceed that percentage the employees who are entitled to elect the additional members shall be—

    (a)   if one additional member is to be elected, those employed by the merging company not represented under paragraph (1) having the highest number of employees; and

    (b)   if more than one additional member is to be elected, those employed by the merging companies registered in each EEA State that are not represented under paragraph (1) having the highest number of employees in descending order, starting with the company with the highest number, followed by those employed by the companies registered in each EEA State that are not so represented having the second highest number of employees in descending order, starting with the company (among those companies) with the highest number.

(4)   Each merging company shall, as soon as reasonably practicable and in any event no later than one month after the establishment of the special negotiating body, inform their employees of the outcome of any elections held under this regulation.

(5)   If, following the election of members to the special negotiating body under this regulation—
  (a)   changes to the merging companies result in the number of members which employees would be entitled to elect under this regulation either increasing or decreasing, the original election of members of the special negotiating body shall cease to have effect and the employees of the merging companies shall be entitled to elect the new number of members in accordance with the provisions of these Regulations; and
  (b)   a member of the special negotiating body is no longer willing or able to continue serving as such a member, the employees whom he represents shall be entitled to elect a new member in his place.

NOTES
Commencement: 15 December 2007.

[4.45]
27   Complaint about establishment of special negotiating body
(1)   An application may be presented to the CAC for a declaration that the special negotiating body has not been established at all or has not been established properly in accordance with regulation 25 or 26.

(2)   Where it is alleged that the failure is attributable to the conduct of the merging company, an application may be presented under this regulation by—
  (a)   a person elected under regulation 26 to be a member of the special negotiating body; or
  (b)   an employee representative or, where no such representative exists in respect of the company, an employee of the company.

(3)   Where it is alleged that the failure is attributable to the conduct of the employees or the employee representatives, an application may be presented under this regulation by the merging company.

(4)   The CAC shall only consider an application made under this regulation if it is made within a period of one month from the date or, if more than one, the last date on which the merging companies complied or should have complied with the obligation to inform their employees under regulation 26(4).

(5)   Where the CAC finds an application made under paragraph (2) well-founded it shall make a declaration that the special negotiating body has not been established at all or has not been established properly and the merging companies continue to be under the obligation in regulation 25.

(6)   Where the CAC finds an application made under paragraph (3) well-founded it shall make a declaration that the special negotiating body has not been established at all or has not been established properly and the merging companies no longer continue to be under the obligation in regulation 25.

NOTES
Commencement: 15 December 2007.

CHAPTER 3
NEGOTIATION OF THE EMPLOYEE PARTICIPATION AGREEMENT

[4.46]
28   Negotiations to reach an employee participation agreement
(1)   In Chapters 3 and 5 the merging companies and the special negotiating body are referred to as "the parties".

(2)   Subject to regulations 31 (decision not to open or to terminate negotiations) and 36 (merging companies may select standard rules of employee participation), the parties are under a duty to negotiate in a spirit of cooperation with a view to reaching an employee participation agreement.

(3)   The duty referred to in paragraph (2) commences one month after the date or, if more than one, the last date on which the members of the special negotiating body were elected or appointed and applies—
  (a)   for the period of six months starting with the day on which the duty commenced or, where an employee participation agreement is successfully negotiated within that period, until the completion of the negotiations;

(b)   where the parties agree before the end of that six month period that it is to be extended, for the period of twelve months starting with the day on which the duty commenced or, where an employee participation agreement is successfully negotiated within the twelve month period, until the completion of the negotiations.

NOTES
Commencement: 15 December 2007.

[4.47]
29   The employee participation agreement

(1)   The employee participation agreement must be in writing.

(2)   Without prejudice to the autonomy of the parties, the employee participation agreement shall specify—

(a)   the scope of the agreement;

(b)   if, during negotiations, the parties decide to establish arrangements for employee participation, the substance of those arrangements including (if applicable) the number of directors of the UK transferee company which the employees will be entitled to elect, appoint, recommend or oppose, the procedures as to how these directors may be elected, appointed, recommended or opposed by the employees, and their rights; and

(c)   the date of entry into force of the agreement, its duration, the circumstances, if any in which the agreement is required to be re-negotiated and the procedure for its re-negotiation.

[(2A)   Where under the employee participation agreement the transferee company is to provide information on the employment situation in that company, such information must include suitable information relating to the use of agency workers (if any) in that company.]

(3)   The employee participation agreement shall not be subject to the standard rules of employee participation (see regulation 38), unless it contains a provision to the contrary.

NOTES
Commencement: 15 December 2007.
Para (2A): inserted by the Agency Workers Regulations 2010, SI 2010/93, reg 25, Sch 2, Pt 2, paras 39, 44, as from 1 October 2011.

[4.48]
30   Decisions of the special negotiating body

(1)   Each member of the special negotiating body shall have one vote.

(2)   Subject to paragraph (3) and regulation 31 (decision not to open or to terminate negotiations), the special negotiating body shall take decisions by an absolute majority vote.

(3)   Where at least 25% of the employees of the merging companies have participation rights, any decision which would result in a reduction of participation rights must be taken by a two thirds majority vote.

(4)   In paragraph (3), reduction of participation rights means that the proportion of directors of the UK transferee company who may be elected or appointed (or whose appointment may be recommended or opposed) by virtue of employee participation is lower than the proportion of such directors or members in the merging company which had the highest proportion of such directors or members.

(5)   The special negotiating body must publish the details of any decision taken under this regulation or under regulation 31 (decision not to open or to terminate negotiations) in such a manner as to bring the decision, so far as reasonably practicable, to the attention of the employees whom they represent and such publication shall take place as soon as reasonably practicable and, in any event no later than 14 days after the decision has been taken.

(6)   For the purpose of negotiations, the special negotiating body may be assisted by experts of its choice.

(7)   The merging companies shall pay for any reasonable expenses of the functioning of the special negotiating body and any reasonable expenses relating to the negotiations that are necessary to enable the special negotiating body to carry out its functions in an appropriate manner; but where the special negotiating body is assisted by more than one expert the merging companies are not required to pay such expenses in respect of more than one of them.

NOTES
Commencement: 15 December 2007.

[4.49]
31 Decision not to open or to terminate negotiations

(1)   The special negotiating body may decide, by a majority vote of two thirds of its members, representing at least two thirds of the employees of the merging companies, including the votes of members representing employees in at least two different EEA States, not to open negotiations pursuant to regulation 28 (negotiations to reach an employee participation agreement) or to terminate negotiations already opened.

(2)   Following any decision made under paragraph (1), the duty of the parties set out in regulation 28 to negotiate with a view to establishing an employee participation agreement shall cease as from the date of the decision.

NOTES
Commencement: 15 December 2007.

[4.50]
32 Complaint about decisions of special negotiating body

(1)   A member of the special negotiating body, an employee representative, or where there is no such representative in respect of an employee, that employee may present a complaint to the CAC if he believes that the special negotiating body has taken a decision referred to in regulation 30 or 31 and—

- (a)   that the decision was not taken by the majority required by regulation 30 or 31; or
- (b)   that the special negotiating body failed to publish the decision in accordance with regulation 30(5).

(2)   The complaint must be presented to the CAC—

- (a)   in the case of a complaint under paragraph (1)(a) (required majority), within 21 days of publication of the decision of the special negotiating body;
- (b)   in the case of a complaint under paragraph (1)(b) (failure to publish decision), within 21 days of the date by which the decision should have been published.

(3)   Where the CAC finds the complaint well-founded it shall make a declaration that the decision was not taken properly and that it shall have no effect.

NOTES
Commencement: 15 December 2007.

CHAPTER 4
ELECTION OF UNITED KINGDOM MEMBERS OF THE SPECIAL NEGOTIATING BODY

[4.51]
33 Ballot arrangements

(1)   The UK members of the special negotiating body shall be elected by balloting the UK employees.

(2)   The UK merging company must arrange for the holding of a ballot of those employees in accordance with the requirements of paragraph (3).

(3)   The requirements referred to in paragraph (2) are—

- (a)   in relation to the election of constituent members of the special negotiating body under regulation 26(1), that—
  - (i)   if the number of members which UK employees are entitled to elect to the special negotiating body is equal to the number of UK merging companies, there shall be separate ballots of the UK employees in each UK merging company;
  - (ii)   if the number of members which the UK employees are entitled to elect to the special negotiating body is greater than the number of UK merging companies, there shall be separate ballots of the UK employees in each UK merging company and the directors shall ensure, as far as practicable, that at least one member representing each such merging company is elected to the special negotiating body and that the number of members representing each UK company is proportionate to the number of employees in that company;
  - (iii) if the number of members which the UK employees are entitled to elect to the special negotiating body is smaller than the number of UK merging companies—
    - (aa)   the number of ballots held shall be equivalent to the number of members to be elected;
    - (bb)   a separate ballot shall be held in respect of each of the merging companies with the higher or highest number of employees; and
    - (cc)   it shall be ensured that any employees of a merging company in respect of which a ballot does not have to be held are entitled to vote in a ballot held in respect of one of the other merging companies;

(b)   that in relation to the election of additional members under regulation 26(2) the directors shall hold a separate ballot in respect of each UK merging company entitled to elect an additional member;

(c)   that in a ballot in respect of a particular UK merging company, all UK employees employed by that merging company are entitled to vote;

(d)   that in a ballot in respect of a particular UK merging company, any person who is immediately before the latest time at which a person may become a candidate—

    (i)   a UK employee employed by that company; or

    (ii)   if the directors of that company so permit, a representative of a trade union who is not an employee of that company,

is entitled to stand as a candidate for election as a member of the special negotiating body in that ballot;

(e)   that the directors must, in accordance with paragraph (7), appoint an independent ballot supervisor to supervise the conduct of the ballot of UK employees but may instead, where there is to be more than one ballot, appoint more than one independent ballot supervisor in accordance with that paragraph, each of whom is to supervise such of the separate ballots as the directors may determine, provided that each separate ballot is supervised by a supervisor;

(f)   that after the directors have formulated proposals as to the arrangements for the ballot of UK employees and before they have published the final arrangements under sub-paragraph (g) they must, so far as reasonably practicable, consult with the employee representatives on the proposed arrangements for the ballot of UK employees; and

(g)   that the directors must publish, as soon as reasonably practicable, the final arrangements for the ballot of UK employees in such manner as to bring them to the attention of, so far as reasonably practicable, all UK employees and the employee representatives.

(4)   Any UK employee or employee representative who believes that the arrangements for the ballot of the UK employees do not comply with the requirements of paragraph (3)(a) to (e) or that there has been a failure to satisfy the requirements of sub-paragraph (f) or (g) may, within a period of 21 days beginning on the date on which the directors published, or should have published, the final arrangements under sub-paragraph (g), present a complaint to the CAC.

(5)   Where the CAC finds the complaint well-founded it shall make a declaration to that effect and may make an order requiring the directors to modify the arrangements they have made for the ballot of UK employees or to satisfy the requirements in sub-paragraph (f) or (g) of paragraph (3).

(6)   An order under paragraph (5) shall specify the modifications to the arrangements which the directors are required to make and the requirements they must satisfy.

(7)   A person is an independent ballot supervisor for the purposes of paragraph (3)(e) if the directors reasonably believe that he will carry out any functions conferred on him in relation to the ballot competently and have no reasonable grounds for believing that his independence in relation to the ballot might reasonably be called into question.

NOTES

Commencement: 15 December 2007.

[4.52]
34 Conduct of the ballot

(1)   The directors must—

    (a)   ensure that a ballot supervisor appointed under regulation 33(3)(e) carries out his functions under this regulation and that there is no interference with his carrying out of those functions from the directors; and

    (b)   comply with all reasonable requests made by a ballot supervisor for the purposes of, or in connection with, the carrying out of those functions.

(2)   A ballot supervisor's appointment shall require that he—

    (a)   supervises the conduct of the ballot, or the separate ballots he is being appointed to supervise, in accordance with the arrangements for the ballot of UK employees published by the directors under regulation 33(3)(g) or, where appropriate, in accordance with the arrangements as required to be modified by an order made as a result of a complaint presented under regulation 33(4);

    (b)   does not conduct the ballot or any of the separate ballots before the directors have satisfied the requirement specified in regulation 33(3)(g) (publication of final arrangements for ballot) and—

        (i)   where no complaint has been presented under regulation 33(4), before the expiry of a period of 21 days beginning on the date on which the directors published the arrangements under regulation 33(3)(g); or

        (ii)   where a complaint has been presented under regulation 33(4), before the complaint has been determined and, where appropriate, the arrangements have been modified as required by an order made as a result of that complaint;

    (c)   conducts the ballot, or each separate ballot so as to secure that—

    (i)   so far as reasonably practicable, those entitled to vote are given the opportunity to vote;

    (ii)   so far as reasonably practicable, those entitled to stand as candidates are given the opportunity to stand;

    (iii) so far as reasonably practicable, those voting are able to do so in secret; and

    (iv) the votes given in the ballot are fairly and accurately counted.

(3)   As soon as reasonably practicable after the holding of the ballot, the ballot supervisor must publish the results of the ballot in such manner as to make them available to the directors and, so far as reasonably practicable, the UK employees entitled to vote in the ballot and the persons who stood as candidates.

(4)   A ballot supervisor shall publish a report ("an ineffective ballot report") where he considers (whether on the basis of representations made to him by another person or otherwise) that—

    (a)   any of the requirements referred to in paragraph (2) was not satisfied with the result that the outcome of the ballot would have been different; or

    (b)   there was interference with the carrying out of his functions or a failure by the directors to comply with all reasonable requests made by him with the result that he was unable to form a proper judgement as to whether each of the requirements referred to in paragraph (2) was satisfied in the ballot.

(5)   Where a ballot supervisor publishes an ineffective ballot report the report must be published within a period of one month commencing on the date on which the ballot supervisor publishes the results of the ballot under paragraph (3).

(6)   A ballot supervisor shall publish an ineffective ballot report in such manner as to make it available to the directors and, so far as reasonably practicable, the UK employees entitled to vote in the ballot and the persons who stood as candidates in the ballot.

(7)   Where a ballot supervisor publishes an ineffective ballot report then—

    (a)   if there has been a single ballot or an ineffective ballot report has been published in respect of every separate ballot, the outcome of the ballot or ballots shall have no effect and the directors shall again be under the obligation in regulation 33(2) (directors to hold ballot for election of special negotiating body);

    (b)   if there have been separate ballots and sub-paragraph (a) does not apply—

       (i)   the directors shall arrange for the separate ballot or ballots in respect of which an ineffective ballot report was published to be re-held in accordance with regulation 33 and this regulation; and

       (ii) no such ballot shall have effect until it has been re-held and no ineffective ballot report has been published in respect of it.

(8)   All costs relating to the holding of a ballot of UK employees, including payments made to a ballot supervisor for supervising the conduct of the ballot, shall be borne by the UK merging company (whether or not an ineffective ballot report has been published).

NOTES

Commencement: 15 December 2007.

[4.53]
35 Representation of employees

(1)   Subject to paragraph (2), a member elected in accordance with regulation 26(1), shall be treated as representing the employees for the time being of the merging company whose employees were entitled to vote in the ballot in which he was elected.

(2)   If an additional member is elected in accordance with regulation 26(2) and (3), he, and not any member elected in accordance with regulation 26(1), shall be treated as representing the employees for the time being of the merging company whose employees were entitled to vote in the ballot in which he was elected.

NOTES

Commencement: 15 December 2007.

CHAPTER 5
STANDARD RULES OF EMPLOYEE PARTICIPATION IN A UK TRANSFEREE COMPANY

[4.54]
36 Merging Companies may select standard rules of employee participation

The merging companies may choose, without negotiating with the special negotiating body, the employee representatives or the employees, that a UK transferee company shall be subject to the standard rules of employee participation in regulation 38 (the standard rules of employee participation) from the date upon which the consequences of the cross-border merger take effect (see regulation 17).

NOTES
   Commencement: 15 December 2007.

[4.55]
37   Application of the standard rules

(1)   Notwithstanding regulation 36 (merging companies may select standard rules of employee participation), the standard rules of employee participation shall apply to a UK transferee company in circumstances where paragraph (2) applies and where—

   (a)   the parties agree that they should; or

   (b)   the period specified in regulation 28(3) (duty to negotiate employee participation agreement) has expired without the parties reaching an employee participation agreement and—

    (i)   the merging companies agree that they should; and

    (ii)   the special negotiating body has not taken any decision under regulation 31 either not to open or to terminate the negotiations referred to in that regulation.

(2)   This paragraph applies where before registration of the UK transferee company, one or more forms of employee participation existed in at least one of the merging companies and either—

   (a)   that participation applied to at least one third of the total number of employees of the merging companies, or

   (b)   that participation applied to less than one third of the total number of employees of the merging companies but the special negotiating body has decided that the standard rules of employee participation should apply.

[(2A)   For the purposes of paragraph (2), agency workers whose contract within regulation 3(1)(b) of the Agency Workers Regulations 2010 was not a contract of employment with one or more temporary work agencies that were merging companies at the relevant time, are to be treated as having been employed by such a temporary work agency or agencies for the duration of their assignment with a hirer.]

(3)   Where the standard rules of employee participation apply and more than one form of employee participation existed in the merging companies, the special negotiating body shall decide which of the existing forms of participation shall apply in the UK transferee company and shall inform the merging companies accordingly.

(4)   In circumstances where—

   (a)   the standard rules of employee participation apply, more than one form of employee participation existed in the merging companies and the special negotiating body has failed to make a decision in accordance with paragraph (3); or

   (b)   one or more form of employee participation existed in the merging companies and the merging companies have chosen, without any prior negotiation, to be directly subject to the standard rules of employee participation,

the merging companies shall be responsible for determining the form of employee participation in the UK transferee company.

NOTES
   Commencement: 15 December 2007.
   Para (2A): inserted by the Agency Workers Regulations 2010, SI 2010/93, reg 25, Sch 2, Pt 2, paras 39, 45, as from 1 October 2011.

[4.56]
38   The standard rules of employee participation

(1)   The employee representatives of the UK transferee company, or if there are no such representatives, the employees, shall have the right to elect, appoint, recommend or oppose the appointment of a number of directors of the transferee company, such number to be equal to the number in the merging company which had the highest proportion of directors (or their EEA equivalent) so elected or appointed (subject to regulation 39).

(2)   Subject to paragraph (3), the employee representatives, or if there are no such representatives, the employees, shall, taking into account the proportion of employees of the transferee company formerly employed in each merging company, decide on the allocation of directorships, or on the means by which the transferee's employees may recommend or oppose the appointment of directors.

(3)   In making the decision set out in paragraph (2), if the employees of one or more merging company are not covered by the proportional criterion set out in paragraph (2), the employee representatives, or if there are no such representatives, the employees, shall appoint a member from one of those merging companies including one from the United Kingdom, if appropriate.

(4)   Every director of the transferee company who has been elected, appointed or recommended by the employee representatives or the employees, shall be a full director with the same rights and obligations as the directors representing shareholders, including the right to vote.

[(5)   Where under the standard rules of employee participation the transferee company is to provide information on the employment situation in that company, such information must include suitable information relating to the use of agency workers (if any) in that company.]

NOTES

Commencement: 15 December 2007.

Para (5): added by the Agency Workers Regulations 2010, SI 2010/93, reg 25, Sch 2, Pt 2, paras 39, 46, as from 1 October 2011.

[4.57]
39   Limit on level of employee participation

Where, following prior negotiation, the standard rules of employee participation apply, the UK transferee company may limit the proportion of directors elected, appointed, recommended or opposed through employee participation to a level which is the lesser of—
(a)   the highest proportion in force in the merging companies prior to registration, and
(b)   one third of the directors.

NOTES

Commencement: 15 December 2007.

[4.58]
40   Subsequent domestic mergers

(1)   A transferee company resulting from a cross-border merger that operates under an employee participation system shall ensure that employees' rights to employee participation shall not be affected before the end of the period of three years commencing on the date on which the consequences of the cross-border merger have effect (see regulation 17) by any order made by the court under section 899 of the Companies Act 2006 (court sanction for compromise or arrangement) for the purposes of—
(a)   a reconstruction of the company or the amalgamation of the company with another company (see section 900 of that Act (reconstruction or amalgamation of company)), or
(b)   a merger involving a public company (see sections 902 and 903 and Chapter 2 of Part 27 of that Act).

(2)   For the purposes of this regulation, any subsequent order made by the court under section 900(2) of the Companies Act 2006 has effect as if it were an order made under section 899 of that Act.

NOTES

Commencement: 15 December 2007.

CHAPTER 6
CONFIDENTIAL INFORMATION

[4.59]
41   Duty of confidentiality

(1)   Where a transferee company or merging company entrusts a person, pursuant to the provisions of this Part, with any information or document on terms requiring it to be held in confidence, the person shall not disclose that information or document except in accordance with the terms on which it was disclosed to him.

(2)   In this regulation a person referred to in paragraph (1) to whom information or a document is entrusted is referred to as a "recipient".

(3)   The obligation to comply with paragraph (1) is a duty owed to the company that disclosed the information or document to the recipient and a breach of the duty is actionable accordingly (subject to the defences and other incidents applying to actions for breach of statutory duty).

(4)   Paragraph (3) does not affect any legal liability which any person may incur by disclosing the information or document, or any right which any person may have in relation to such disclosure otherwise than under this regulation.

(5)   No action shall lie under paragraph (3) where the recipient reasonably believed the disclosure to be a protected disclosure within the meaning given to that expression by section 43A of the 1996 Act.

(6)   A recipient may apply to the CAC for a declaration as to whether it was reasonable for the company to require the recipient to hold the information or document in confidence.

(7)   If the CAC considers that the disclosure of the information or document by the recipient would not, or would not be likely to, harm the legitimate interests of the undertaking, it shall make a declaration that it was not reasonable for the company to require the recipient to hold the information or document in confidence.

(8)   If a declaration is made under paragraph (7), the information or document shall not at any time thereafter be regarded as having been entrusted to any recipient on terms requiring it to be held in confidence.

NOTES
Commencement: 15 December 2007.

[4.60]
42   Withholding of information by the transferee or merging company

(1)   Neither a transferee company nor a merging company is required to disclose any information or document to a person for the purposes of this Part where the nature of the information or document is such that, according to objective criteria, the disclosure of the information or document would seriously harm the functioning of, or would be prejudicial to the transferee company or merging company.

(2)   Where there is a dispute between the transferee company or merging company and—
    (a)   where a special negotiating body has been appointed or elected, a member of that body; or
    (b)   where no special negotiating body has been elected or appointed, an employee,
as to whether the nature of any information or document is such as is described in paragraph (1), the transferee company or merging company or a person referred to in sub-paragraph (a) or (b) may apply to the CAC for a declaration as to whether the information or document is of such a nature.

(3)   If the CAC makes a declaration that the disclosure of the information or document in question would not, according to objective criteria, be seriously harmful or prejudicial as mentioned in paragraph (1), the CAC shall order the transferee company or merging company to disclose the information or document.

(4)   An order under paragraph (3) shall specify—
    (a)   the information or document to be disclosed;
    (b)   the person or persons to whom the information or document is to be disclosed;
    (c)   any terms on which the information or document is to be disclosed; and
    (d)   the date before which the information or document is to be disclosed.

NOTES
Commencement: 15 December 2007.

CHAPTER 7
PROTECTION FOR EMPLOYEES AND MEMBERS OF
SPECIAL NEGOTIATING BODY, ETC

[4.61]
43   Right to time off for members of special negotiating body, etc

(1)   An employee who is—
    (a)   a member of a special negotiating body;
    (b)   a director of a transferee company; or
    (c)   a candidate in an election in which any person elected will, on being elected, be such a director or member,
is entitled to be permitted by his employer to take reasonable time off during the employee's working hours in order to perform his functions as such a member, director or candidate.

(2)   For the purpose of this regulation the working hours of an employee shall be taken to be any time when, in accordance with his contract of employment, the employee is required to be at work.

NOTES
Commencement: 15 December 2007.

[4.62]
44   Right to remuneration for time off under regulation 43

(1)   An employee who is permitted to take time off under regulation 43 is entitled to be paid remuneration by his employer for the time taken off at the appropriate hourly rate.

(2)   Chapter 2 of Part 14 of the 1996 Act (a week's pay) shall apply in relation to this regulation as it applies in relation to section 62 of the 1996 Act.

(3)   The appropriate hourly rate, in relation to an employee, is the amount of one week's pay divided by the number of normal working hours in a week for that employee when employed under the contract of employment in force on the day when the time is taken.

(4)   But where the number of normal working hours differs from week to week or over a longer period, the amount of one week's pay shall be divided instead by—
    (a)   the average number of normal working hours calculated by dividing by twelve the total number of the employee's normal working hours during the period of twelve weeks ending with the last complete week before the day on which the time off is taken; or

(b)   where the employee has not been employed for a sufficient period to enable the calculation to be made under sub-paragraph (a), a number which fairly represents the number of normal working hours in a week having regard to such of the considerations specified in paragraph (5) as are appropriate in the circumstances.

(5)   The considerations referred to in paragraph (4)(b) are—
   (a)   the average number of normal working hours in a week which the employee could expect in accordance with the terms of his contract; and
   (b)   the average number of normal working hours of other employees engaged in relevant comparable employment with the same employer.

(6)   A right to any amount under paragraph (1) does not affect any right of an employee in relation to remuneration under his contract of employment.

(7)   Any contractual remuneration paid to an employee in respect of a period of time off under regulation 43 goes towards discharging any liability of the employer to pay remuneration under paragraph (1) in respect of that period, and conversely, any payment of remuneration under paragraph (1) in respect of a period goes towards discharging any liability of the employer to pay contractual remuneration in respect of that period.

NOTES
   Commencement: 15 December 2007.

[4.63]
45   Right to time off: complaints to employment tribunals

(1)   An employee may present a complaint to an employment tribunal that his employer—
   (a)   has unreasonably refused to permit him to take time off as required under regulation 43; or
   (b)   has failed to pay the whole or any part of any amount to which the employee is entitled under regulation 44.

(2)   An employment tribunal shall not consider a complaint under this regulation unless it is presented—
   (a)   before the end of the period of three months beginning with the day on which the time off was taken or on which it is alleged the time off should have been permitted; or
   (b)   within such further period as the tribunal considers reasonable in a case where it is satisfied that it was not reasonably practicable for the complaint to be presented before the end of that period of three months.

(3)   Where an employment tribunal finds a complaint under this regulation well-founded, the tribunal shall make a declaration to that effect.

(4)   If the complaint is that the employer has unreasonably refused to permit the employee to take time off, the tribunal shall also order the employer to pay to the employee an amount equal to the remuneration to which he would have been entitled under regulation 44 if the employer had not refused.

(5)   If the complaint is that the employer has failed to pay the employee the whole or part of any amount to which he is entitled under regulation 44, the tribunal shall also order him to pay to the employee the amount which it finds is due to him.

NOTES
   Commencement: 15 December 2007.

[4.64]
46   Unfair dismissal of employee

(1)   An employee who is dismissed shall be regarded as unfairly dismissed for the purposes of Part 10 of the 1996 Act if the reason (or, if more than one, the principal reason) for the dismissal is one specified in paragraph (2).

(2)   The reasons are that the employee—
   (a)   took, or proposed to take, any proceedings before an employment tribunal to enforce any right conferred on him by these Regulations;
   (b)   exercised, or proposed to exercise, any entitlement to apply or complain to the CAC or the Appeal Tribunal conferred by these Regulations or exercised or proposed to exercise the right to appeal in connection with any rights conferred by these Regulations;
   (c)   acted with a view to securing that a special negotiating body did or did not come into existence;
   (d)   indicated that he did or did not support the coming into existence of a special negotiating body;
   (e)   stood as a candidate in an election in which any person elected would, on being elected, be a member of a special negotiating body or a director of a UK transferee company;
   (f)   influenced or sought to influence by lawful means the way in which votes were to be cast by other employees in a ballot arranged under these Regulations;
   (g)   voted in such a ballot;

(h)   expressed doubts, whether to a ballot supervisor or otherwise, as to whether such a ballot had been properly conducted; or

(i)   proposed to do, failed to do, or proposed to decline to do, any of the things mentioned in sub-paragraphs (e) to (h).

(3)   Paragraph (1) does not apply where the reason (or principal reason) for the dismissal is that in the performance, or purported performance, of the employee's functions or activities he has disclosed any information or document in breach of the duty in regulation 41 (duty of confidentiality), unless the employee reasonably believed the disclosure to be a protected disclosure within the meaning given to that expression by section 43A of the 1996 Act.

(4)   For the purposes of paragraph (2)(a) it is immaterial—

(a)   whether or not the employee has the right or entitlement; or

(b)   whether or not the right has been infringed,

but for that sub-paragraph to apply, the claim to the right and, if applicable, the claim that it has been infringed must be made in good faith.

NOTES

Commencement: 15 December 2007.

[4.65]

47   Unfair dismissal of member of special negotiating body, etc

(1)   An employee who is—

(a)   a member of a special negotiating body;

(b)   a director of a transferee company; or

(c)   a candidate in an election in which any person elected will, on being elected, be such a director or member,

who is dismissed shall be regarded as unfairly dismissed for the purposes of Part 10 of the 1996 Act if the reason (or, if more than one, the principal reason) for the dismissal is one specified in paragraph (2).

(2)   The reasons are that—

(a)   the employee performed or proposed to perform any functions or activities as such a member, director or candidate; or

(b)   the employee or a person acting on his behalf made or proposed to make a request to exercise an entitlement conferred on the employee by regulation 43 (right to time off work) or 44 (right to remuneration for time off work).

(3)   Paragraph (1) does not apply in the circumstances set out in paragraph (2)(a) where the reason (or principal reason) for the dismissal is that in the performance, or purported performance, of the employee's functions or activities he has disclosed any information or document in breach of the duty in regulation 41 (duty of confidentiality), unless the employee reasonably believed the disclosure to be a protected disclosure within the meaning given to that expression by section 43A of the 1996 Act.

NOTES

Commencement: 15 December 2007.

48   (*Amends the Employment Rights Act 1996, ss 105, 108.*)

[4.66]

49   Detriment

(1)   An employee has the right not to be subjected to any detriment by any act, or deliberate failure to act, by his employer, done on a ground specified in paragraph (2).

(2)   The grounds are that the employee—

(a)   took, or proposed to take, any proceedings before an employment tribunal to enforce any right conferred on him by these Regulations;

(b)   exercised, or proposed to exercise, any entitlement to apply or complain to the CAC or the Appeal Tribunal conferred by these Regulations or exercised or proposed to exercise the right to appeal in connection with any rights conferred by these Regulations;

(c)   acted with a view to securing that a special negotiating body did or did not come into existence;

(d)   indicated that he did or did not support the coming into existence of a special negotiating body;

(e)   stood as a candidate in an election in which any person elected would, on being elected, be a member of a special negotiating body or a director of a UK transferee company;

(f)   influenced or sought to influence by lawful means the way in which votes were to be cast by other employees in a ballot arranged under these Regulations;

(g)   voted in such a ballot;

(h)   expressed doubts, whether to a ballot supervisor or otherwise, as to whether such a ballot had been properly conducted; or

(i) proposed to do, failed to do, or proposed to decline to do, any of the things mentioned in sub-paragraphs (d) to (h).

(3) It is immaterial for the purposes of paragraph (2)(a)—

(a) whether or not the employee has the right or entitlement; or

(b) whether or not the right has been infringed,

but for that sub-paragraph to apply, the claim to the right and, if applicable, the claim that has been infringed must be made in good faith.

(4) This regulation does not apply where the detriment in question amounts to dismissal.

NOTES

Commencement: 15 December 2007.

[4.67]

50 Detriment for member of special negotiating body, etc

(1) An employee who is—

(a) a member of a special negotiating body;

(b) a director of a transferee company; or

(c) a candidate in an election in which any person elected will, on being elected, be such a director or member,

has the right not to be subjected to any detriment by any act, or deliberate failure to act, by his employer, done on a ground specified in paragraph (2).

(2) The ground is that—

(a) the employee performed or proposed to perform any functions or activities as such a director, member or candidate; or

(b) the employee or person acting on his behalf made or proposed to make a request to exercise an entitlement conferred on the employee by regulation 43 (right to time off work) or 44 (right to remuneration for time off work).

(3) Paragraph (1) does not apply in the circumstances set out in paragraph (2)(a) where the ground for the subjection to detriment is that in the performance, or purported performance, of the employee's functions or activities he has disclosed any information or document in breach of the duty in regulation 41 (duty of confidentiality), unless the employee reasonably believed the disclosure to be a protected disclosure within the meaning given to that expression by section 43A of the 1996 Act.

(4) This regulation does not apply where the detriment in question amounts to a dismissal.

NOTES

Commencement: 15 December 2007.

[4.68]

51 Detriment: enforcement and subsidiary provisions

(1) An employee may present a complaint to an employment tribunal that he has been subjected to a detriment in contravention of regulation 49 or 50.

(2) The provisions of section 49(1) to (5) of the 1996 Act shall apply in relation to a complaint under this regulation.

NOTES

Commencement: 15 December 2007.

52 (*Amends the Employment Tribunals Act 1996, s 18.*)

CHAPTER 8
COMPLIANCE AND ENFORCEMENT

[4.69]

53 Disputes about operation of an employee participation agreement or the standard rules of employee participation

(1) Where—

(a) an employee participation agreement has been agreed; or

(b) the standard rules of employee participation apply,

a complaint may be presented to the CAC by a relevant applicant who considers that the transferee company has failed to comply with the terms of the employee participation agreement or, where applicable, the standard rules of employee participation.

(2) A complaint brought under paragraph (1) must be brought within a period of 3 months commencing with the date of the alleged failure, or where the failure takes place over a period, the last day of that period.

(3) In this regulation—

"failure" includes failure by means of an act or omission,

"relevant applicant" means—

    (a)   a special negotiating body; or

    (b)   in a case where no special negotiating body has been elected or appointed, or has been dissolved, an employee representative or employee of the transferee company.

(4)   Where the CAC finds the complaint well-founded it shall make a declaration to that effect and may make an order requiring the transferee company to take such steps as are necessary to comply with the terms of the employee participation agreement or, where applicable, the standard rules of employee participation.

(5)   An order made under paragraph (4) shall specify—

    (a)   the steps which the transferee company is required to take;

    (b)   the date of the failure; and

    (c)   the period within which the order must be complied with.

(6)   If the CAC makes a declaration under paragraph (4), the relevant applicant may, within the period of three months beginning with the day on which the decision is made, make an application to the Appeal Tribunal for a penalty notice to be issued.

(7)   Where such an application is made, the Appeal Tribunal shall issue a written penalty notice to the transferee company requiring it to pay a penalty to the Secretary of State in respect of the failure unless satisfied, on hearing representations from the transferee company, that the failure resulted from a reason beyond its control or that it has some other reasonable excuse for its failure.

(8)   Regulation 55 (penalties) shall apply in respect of a penalty notice issued under this regulation.

(9)   No order of the CAC under this regulation shall have the effect of suspending or altering the effect of any act done or of any agreement made by the transferee company or merging company.

NOTES

Commencement: 15 December 2007.

[4.70]
54   Misuse of procedures

(1)   If an employee representative, or where there is no such representative in relation to an employee, an employee, believes that a transferee company or merging company is misusing or intending to misuse the transferee company or the powers in these Regulations for the purpose of—

    (a)   depriving the employees of that merging company or the transferee company of their rights to employee participation; or

    (b)   withholding such rights from any of the people referred to in sub-paragraph (a), he may make a complaint to the CAC.

(2)   A complaint must be made to the CAC under paragraph (1) before the date upon which the consequences of the cross-border merger take effect (see regulation 17) or within a period of 12 months after that date.

(3)   The CAC shall uphold the complaint unless the respondent proves that it did not misuse or intend to misuse the transferee company or the powers in these Regulations for either of the purposes set out in sub-paragraph (a) or (b) of paragraph (1).

(4)   If the CAC finds the complaint to be well-founded it shall make a declaration to that effect and may make an order requiring the transferee company or merging company to take such action as is specified in the order to ensure that the employees referred to in paragraph (1)(a) are not deprived of their rights to employee participation or that such rights are not withheld from them; and

(5)   If the CAC makes a declaration under paragraph (4), the complainant under paragraph (1) may, within the period of three months beginning with the day on which the decision is made, make an application to the Appeal Tribunal for a penalty notice to be issued.

(6)   Where such an application is made, the Appeal Tribunal shall issue a written penalty notice to the transferee company or merging company requiring it to pay a penalty to the Secretary of State in respect of the failure unless satisfied, on hearing representations from the transferee company or merging company, that the failure resulted from a reason beyond its control or that it has some other reasonable excuse for its failure.

(7)   The provisions in regulations 53(8) to (9) and 55 shall apply to the complaint.

NOTES

Commencement: 15 December 2007.

[4.71]
55   Penalties

(1)   A penalty notice issued under regulation 53 (disputes) or 54 (misuse of procedures) shall specify—

    (a)   the amount of the penalty which is payable;

    (b)   the date before which the penalty must be paid; and

    (c)   the failure and period to which the penalty relates.

(2)   No penalty set by the Appeal Tribunal under this regulation may exceed £75,000.

(3)　When setting the amount of the penalty, the Appeal Tribunal shall take into account—

   (a)　the gravity of the failure;

   (b)　the period of time over which the failure occurred;

   (c)　the reason for the failure;

   (d)　the number of employees affected by the failure; and

   (e)　the number of employees employed by the undertaking.

(4)　The date specified under paragraph (1)(b) above must not be earlier than the end of the period within which an appeal against a decision or order made by the CAC under regulation 53 or 54 may be made.

(5)　If the specified date in a penalty notice has passed and—

   (a)　the period during which an appeal may be made has expired without an appeal having been made; or

   (b)　such an appeal has been made and determined,

the Secretary of State may recover from the transferee company or merging company, as a civil debt due to him, any amount payable under the penalty notice which remains outstanding.

(6)　The making of an appeal suspends the effect of the penalty notice.

(7)　Any sums received by the Secretary of State under regulation 53, 54 or this regulation shall be paid into the Consolidated Fund.

NOTES

   Commencement: 15 December 2007.

[4.72]
56　Exclusivity of remedy

Where these Regulations provide for a remedy of infringement of any right by way of application or complaint to the CAC, and provide for no other remedy, no other remedy is available for infringement of that right.

NOTES

   Commencement: 15 December 2007.

CHAPTER 9
MISCELLANEOUS

[4.73]
57　CAC proceedings

(1)　Where under these Regulations a person presents a complaint or makes an application to the CAC the complaint or application must be in writing and in such form as the CAC may require.

(2)　In its consideration of a complaint or application under these Regulations, the CAC shall make such enquiries as it sees fit and give any person whom it considers has a proper interest in the complaint or application an opportunity to be heard.

(3)　Where a transferee company or merging company has its registered office in England and Wales—

   (a)　a declaration made by the CAC under these Regulations may be relied on as if it were a declaration or order made by the High Court in England and Wales; and

   (b)　an order made by the CAC under these Regulations may be enforced in the same way as an order of the High Court in England and Wales.

(4)　Where a transferee company or merging company has its registered office in Scotland—

   (a)　a declaration or order made by the CAC under these Regulations may be relied on as if it were a declaration or order made by the Court of Session; and

   (b)　an order made by the CAC under these Regulations may be enforced in the same way as an order of the Court of Session.

(5)　A declaration or order made by the CAC under these Regulations must be in writing and state the reasons for the CAC's findings.

(6)　An appeal lies to the Appeal Tribunal on any question of law arising from any declaration or order of, or arising in any proceedings before, the CAC under these Regulations.

NOTES

   Commencement: 15 December 2007.

[4.74]
58　Appeal Tribunal: location of certain proceedings under these Regulations

(1)　Any proceedings before the Appeal Tribunal under these Regulations, other than appeals under paragraph (u) of section 21(1) of the Employment Tribunals Act 1996 (appeals from employment tribunals on questions of law), shall—

   (a)　where the registered office of the transferee company or merging company is situated in England and Wales, be held in England and Wales; and (b)	where the registered office of the transferee company or merging company is situated in Scotland, be held in Scotland.

(2)	. . .

NOTES

Commencement: 15 December 2007.

Para (2): amends the Employment Tribunals Act 1996, s 20.

59	(*Amends the Employment Tribunals Act 1996, s 21.*)

[4.75]
**60	ACAS**

(1)	If on receipt of an application or complaint under these Regulations the CAC is of the opinion that it is reasonably likely to be settled by conciliation, it shall refer the application or complaint to the Advisory, Conciliation and Arbitration Service ("ACAS") and shall notify the applicant or complainant and any persons whom it considers have a proper interest in the application or complaint accordingly, whereupon ACAS shall seek to promote a settlement of the matter.

(2)	If an application or complaint so referred is not settled or withdrawn and ACAS is of the opinion that further attempts at conciliation are unlikely to result in a settlement, it shall inform the CAC of its opinion.

(3)	If—
(a)	the application or complaint is not referred to ACAS; or
(b)	ACAS informs the CAC of its opinion that further attempts at conciliation are unlikely to result in a settlement,
the CAC shall proceed to hear and determine the application or complaint.

NOTES

Commencement: 15 December 2007.

[4.76]
**61	Restrictions on contracting out: general**

(1)	Any provision in any agreement (whether an employee's contract or not) is void in so far as it purports—
(a)	to exclude or limit the operation of any provision of this Part of these Regulations other than a provision of Chapter 7 (protection for employees and members of special negotiating body) (but see regulation 62); or
(b)	to preclude a person from bringing any proceedings before the CAC, under any provision of this Part (other than a provision of that Chapter).

(2)	Paragraph (1) does not apply to any agreement to refrain from continuing any proceedings referred to in sub-paragraph (b) of that paragraph made after the proceedings have been instituted.

NOTES

Commencement: 15 December 2007.

[4.77]
**62	Restrictions on contracting out: Chapter 7 of this Part**

(1)	Any provision in any agreement (whether an employee's contract or not) is void in so far as it purports—
(a)	to exclude or limit the operation of any provision of Chapter 7 of this Part of these Regulations; or
(b)	to preclude a person from bringing any proceedings before an employment tribunal under that Chapter.

(2)	Paragraph (1) does not apply to any agreement to refrain from instituting or continuing proceedings before an employment tribunal where a conciliation officer has taken action under section 18 of the Employment Tribunals Act 1996 (conciliation).

(3)	Paragraph (1) does not apply to any agreement to refrain from instituting or continuing before an employment tribunal proceedings within section 18(1) of the Employment Tribunals Act 1996 if the conditions regulating compromise agreements under these Regulations are satisfied in relation to the agreement.

(4)	For the purposes of paragraph (3) the conditions regulating compromise agreements are that—
(a)	the agreement must be in writing;
(b)	the agreement must relate to the particular proceedings;
(c)	the employee must have received advice from a relevant independent adviser as to the terms and effect of the proposed agreement and, in particular, its effect on his ability to pursue his rights before an employment tribunal;
(d)	there must be in force, when the adviser gives the advice, a contract of insurance, or an indemnity provided for members of a profession or professional body, covering the risk of a claim by the employee in respect of loss arising in consequence of the advice;

(e)   the agreement must identify the adviser; and

(f)   the agreement must state that the conditions in sub-paragraphs (a) to (e) are satisfied.

(5)   A person is a relevant independent adviser for the purposes of paragraph (4)(c)—

(a)   if he is a qualified lawyer;

(b)   if he is an officer, official, employee or member of an independent trade union who has been certified in writing by the trade union as competent to give advice and authorised to do so on behalf of the trade union; or

(c)   if he works at an advice centre (whether as an employee or as a volunteer) and has been certified in writing by the centre as competent to give advice and authorised to do so on behalf of the centre.

(6)   But a person is not a relevant independent adviser for the purposes of paragraph (4)(c) in relation to the employee—

(a)   if he is, is employed by or is acting in the matter for the employer or an associated employer; or

(b)   in the case of a person within paragraph (5)(b) or (c), if the trade union or advice centre is the employer or an associated employer.

(7)   In paragraph (5)(a), a "qualified lawyer" means—

(a)   as respects England and Wales, [a person who, for the purposes of the Legal Services Act 2007), is an authorised person in relation to an activity which constitutes the exercise of a right of audience or the conduct of litigation (within the meaning of that Act)]; and

(b)   as respects Scotland, an advocate (whether in practice as such or employed to give legal advice) or a solicitor who holds a practising certificate.

(8)   A person shall be treated as being a qualified lawyer within paragraph (7)(a) if he is a Fellow of the Institute of Legal Executives [practising in a solicitor's practice (including a body recognised under section 9 of the Administration of Justice Act 1985)].

(9)   For the purposes of paragraph (6) any two employers shall be treated as associated if—

(a)   one is a company of which the other (directly or indirectly) has control; or

(b)   both are companies of which a third person (directly or indirectly) has control, and "associated employer" shall be construed accordingly.

NOTES

Commencement: 15 December 2007.

Paras (7), (8): words in square brackets substituted by the Legal Services Act 2007 (Consequential Amendments) Order 2009, SI 2009/3348, arts 22, 23, Schs 1, 2, as from 1 January 2010 (in the case of the para (7) amendment), and as from 16 December 2009 (in the case of the para (8) amendment).

63–66   (*Reg 63 amends the Employment Act 2002; reg 64 contains various amendments to the Employment Appeal Tribunal Rules 1993, SI 2003/2854; reg 65 amends the Insolvency Act 1986, Sch B1 at* **[9.412]***; reg 66 amends the Insolvency (Northern Ireland) Order 1989.*)

SCHEDULES

SCHEDULE 1
TRANSITIONAL MODIFICATIONS WHERE PROVISIONS OF COMPANIES ACT 2006 NOT IN FORCE

Regulation 4(6)

[4.78]
1   Regulation 3(1)

(1)   Regulation 3(1) is modified as follows.

(2)   In the definition of "member", until the entry into force of section 112 of the Companies Act 2006 for "section 112 of the Companies Act 2006" substitute "section 22 of the Companies Act 1985 or Article 32 of the Companies (Northern Ireland) Order 1986".

(3)   In the definition of "registrar of companies", until the entry into force of section 1060 of the 2006 Act for "section 1060 of the Companies Act 2006" substitute "section 744 of the Companies Act 1985 or Article 2 of the Companies (Northern Ireland) Order 1986".

(4)   In the definition of "treasury shares", until the entry into force of section 724 of the Companies Act 2006 for "section 724 of the Companies Act 2006" substitute "section 162A of the Companies Act 1985 or Article 172A of the Companies (Northern Ireland) Order 1986".

(5)   In the definition of "UK company", until the entry into force of section 1 of the Companies Act 2006 for "section 1 of the Companies Act 2006" substitute "section 735 of the Companies Act 1985 or Article 3 of the Companies (Northern Ireland) Order 1986".

2   Regulation 4

(1)   Regulation 4 is modified as follows.

(2)   Until the entry into force of section 1081 of the Companies Act 2006 (annotation of the register), omit paragraph (1)(a).

(3) Until the entry into force of section 1112 of the Companies Act 2006 (offence of false statement to registrar), omit paragraph (1)(c).

(4) Until the entry into force of section 1113 of the Companies Act 2006 (enforcement of a company's filing obligations)—

    (a) omit paragraph (1)(d); and

    (b) after paragraph (4) insert—

> "(4A) Section 713 of the Companies Act 1985 or Article 662 of the Companies (Northern Ireland) Order 1986 (enforcement of company's duty to make returns) applies for the purposes of these Regulations as it applies for the purposes of the Companies Acts.".

(5) Until the entry into force of sections 1121 to 1123 of the Companies Act 2006 (liability of officer in default)—

    (a) omit paragraph (1)(e); and

    (b) after paragraph (4A) insert—

> "(4B) Section 730A of the Companies Act 1985 or Article 678(5) of the Companies (Northern Ireland) Order 1986 (meaning of "officer in default") applies to offences under these Regulations as it applies to offences under that Act or that Order.".

(6) Until the entry into force of section 1125 of the Companies Act 2006 (meaning of "daily default fine")—

    (a) omit paragraph (1)(f); and

    (b) after paragraph (4B) insert—

> "(4C) Section 730(4) of the Companies Act 1985 or Article 678(4) of the Companies (Northern Ireland) Order 1986 (meaning of daily default fine) applies for the purposes of these Regulations as it applies for the purposes of Schedule 24 to that Act or Schedule 23 to that Order.".

(7) Until the entry into force of sections 1127 and 1128 of the Companies Act 2006 (summary proceedings)—

    (a) omit paragraph (1)(g); and

    (b) after paragraph (4C) insert—

> "(4D) Section 731 of the Companies Act 1985 or Article 679 of the Companies (Northern Ireland) Order 1986 (summary proceedings) applies to offences under these Regulations as it applies to offences under that Act or that Order.".

(8) Until the entry into force of section 1129 of the Companies Act 2006 (legal professional privilege)—

    (a) omit paragraph (1)(h); and

    (b) after paragraph (4D) insert—

> "(4E) Section 732(3) of the Companies Act 1985 or Article 680(3) of the Companies (Northern Ireland) Order 1986 (legal professional privilege) applies to proceedings for an offence under these Regulations as it applies to proceedings instituted under the Companies Acts by the Director of Public Prosecutions or by or on behalf of the Secretary of State or the Lord Advocate, or proceedings instituted under the 1986 Order by the Director of Public Prosecutions for Northern Ireland or by or on behalf of the Department of Economic Development.".

(9) Until the entry into force of section 1130 of the Companies Act 2006 (proceedings against unincorporated bodies)—

    (a) omit paragraph (1)(i); and

    (b) after paragraph (4E) insert—

> "(4F) Section 734 of the Companies Act 1985 or Article 680B of the Companies (Northern Ireland) Order 1986 (summary proceedings) applies to offences under these Regulations as it applies to offences under that Act or that Order.".

3   Regulations 7 and 20

Until the entry into force of Chapter 2 of Part 3 of the Companies Act 2006 (a company's articles of association), the references in regulations 7 and 20 to a company's articles include the company's memorandum of association.

4   Regulation 9

(1) Until the entry into force of Part 42 of the Companies Act 2006 (statutory auditors), regulation 9 is modified as follows.

(2) For paragraph (7)(a) substitute—

>   "(a) is eligible for appointment as a company auditor in accordance with section 25 of the Companies Act 1989 or Article 28 of the Companies (Northern Ireland) Order 1990;".

(3) For paragraph (8)(a) and (b) substitute—

"(a) a person is not independent if, by virtue of section 27 of the Companies Act 1989 or Article 30 of the Companies (Northern Ireland) Order 1990, he would not be able to act as company auditor of all the merging companies; and

(b) section 27 of the Companies Act 1989 or Article 30 of the Companies (Northern Ireland) Order 1990 applies in relation to all the merging companies as if they were companies within the meaning of Part 2 of that Act or Part 3 of that Order.".

5 Regulations 12 and 19

Until the entry into force of section 1098 of the Companies Act 2006 (public notice of removal of certain material from register)), omit regulation 12(6)(g) and regulation 19(4)(i).

6 Regulation 40

(1) Until the entry into force of Part 26 (arrangements and reconstructions) and Part 27 (mergers and divisions of public companies) of the Companies Act 2006, regulation 40 is modified as follows.

(2) In paragraph (1)—

(a) in the opening words, for "section 899 of the Companies Act 2006" substitute "section 425(2) of the Companies Act 1985 or Article 418(2) of the Companies (Northern Ireland) Order 1986";

(b) in sub-paragraph (a), for "section 900 of that Act" substitute "section 427 of that Act or Article 420 of that Order";

(c) in sub-paragraph (b), for "sections 902 and 903 and Chapter 2 of Part 27 of that Act" substitute "section 427A(1) and Cases 1 and 2 in section 427A(2) of that Act or Article 420A(1) and Cases 1 and 2 in Article 420A(2) of that Order".

(3) In paragraph (2)—

(a) for "section 900(2) of the Companies Act 2006" substitute "section 427(2) of the Companies Act 1985 or Article 420(2) of the Companies (Northern Ireland) Order 1986";

(b) for "section 899 of that Act" substitute "section 425(2) of that Act or Article 418(2) of that Order".

NOTES
Commencement: 15 December 2007.

SCHEDULE 2

(Sch 2 (Application of the Regulations in Relation to Northern Ireland) outside the scope of this work.)

STATUTORY AUDITORS AND THIRD COUNTRY AUDITORS REGULATIONS 2007

(SI 2007/3494)

NOTES
Made: 17 December 2007.
Authority: Companies Act 2006, ss 1239, 1241(2)(c), 1246, 1292(1)(a), (b), (2), Sch 11, para 8(1)(a); European Communities Act 1972, s 2(2).
Commencement: 6 April 2008 (all provisions except regs 32, 33 and 40(2)(b)–(d)); 29 June 2008 (otherwise).
These Regulations are reproduced as amended by: the Statutory Auditors and Third Country Auditors (Amendment) Regulations 2008, SI 2008/499 (note that SI 2008/499 corrects drafting errors in these Regulations and, therefore, the amendments made by that SI come into force before these Regulations come into force); the Statutory Auditors and Third Country Auditors (Amendment) (No 2) Regulations 2008, SI 2008/2639; the Statutory Auditors and Third Country Auditors (Amendment) Regulations 2009, SI 2009/2798.

ARRANGEMENT OF REGULATIONS

PART 1
CITATION, COMMENCEMENT AND INTERPRETATION

PART 5
REGISTRATION OF THIRD COUNTRY AUDITORS

PART 1
CITATION, COMMENCEMENT AND INTERPRETATION

[4.79]
1   Citation and commencement

(1)   These Regulations may be cited as the Statutory Auditors and Third Country Auditors Regulations 2007.

(2)   These Regulations, except for the provisions referred to in paragraph (3), come into force on 6th April 2008.

[(3)   Regulations 32, 33 and 40(2)(b) to (d) come into force on 29th June 2008.]

NOTES

Commencement: 6 April 2008.

Para (3): substituted by the Statutory Auditors and Third Country Auditors (Amendment) Regulations 2008, SI 2008/499, reg 2(1), (2), as from 5 April 2008.

2–28   *(Regs, 2, 3 amend the Companies Act 2006, ss 1261, 1262 at* **[1.1261]**, **[1.1262]**; *regs 4–6 (Pt 2) amend CA 2006, ss 1217, 1219, 1221 at* **[1.1217]**, **[1.1219]**, **[1.1221]**; *regs 7–16 (Pt 3) insert CA 2006, ss 1223A, 1224A, 1224B, 1251A, 1253A–1253F (see* **[1.1223A]** *et seq) and contain various other amendments to provisions in Pat 42 of the 2006 Act (at* **[1.1209]** *et seq); regs 17–28 (Pt 4) amend CA 2006, Sch 10 at* **[1.1321]***. Note that regs 7, 15 are amended by the Statutory Auditors and Third Country Auditors (Amendment) Regulations 2008, SI 2008/499, reg 2(1), (3), (4), as from 5 April 2008 (see further the introductory notes to these Regulations). Note also that reg 15(2) (transitional provisions in connection with ss 1253D, 1253E of the 2006 Act) was revoked by the Statutory Auditors and Third Country Auditors (Amendment) Regulations 2009, SI 2009/2798, reg 2, as from 21 October 2009.)*

PART 5
REGISTRATION OF THIRD COUNTRY AUDITORS

[4.80]
[29   Interpretation

In this Part of these Regulations—

"the Commission Decision" means Commission Decision 2008/627/EC of 29 July 2008 concerning a transitional period for audit activities of certain third country auditors and audit entities;

"the designated body" means the body known as the Professional Oversight Board established under the articles of association of The Financial Reporting Council Limited;

"exempt third country auditor" means a third country auditor—

    (a)   who is—

        (i)   overseen or regulated by a third country competent authority established in a specified third country, and

        (ii)   eligible to conduct audits of the accounts of bodies corporate incorporated or formed under the law of that specified third country; and

    (b)   in relation to whom the designated body has, for the purposes of the Commission Decision, directed under section 1239(7) of the Companies Act 2006 that requirements imposed by this Part specified in the direction are not to apply;

"specified third country" means any of the Channel Islands, the Isle of Man and the following countries and territories—

    Argentina, Australia, The Bahamas, Bermuda, Brazil, Canada, Cayman Islands, Chile, China, Croatia, Hong Kong, India, Indonesia, Israel, Japan, Kazakhstan, Malaysia, Mauritius, Mexico, Morocco, New Zealand, Pakistan, Russia, Singapore, South Africa, South Korea, Switzerland, Taiwan, Thailand, Turkey, Ukraine, United Arab Emirates, United States of America.]

NOTES

Commencement: 31 October 2008.

Substituted by the Statutory Auditors and Third Country Auditors (Amendment) (No 2) Regulations 2008, SI 2008/2639, reg 2(1), (2), as from 31 October 2008.

30–33   *(Amend the Companies Act 2006, ss 1239, 1241, 1242, Sch 12 at* **[1.1239]**, **[1.1241]**, **[1.1242]**, **[1.1326]**.*)*

[4.81]

34 Register of third country auditors

(1) The designated body must keep the register of third country auditors (see section 1239 of the Companies Act 2006).

(2) The register must contain the following information [in relation to each registered third country auditor] who is an individual—

(a) his name and address;

(b) his registered number;

(c) an indication that he is a third country auditor;

(d) if he is responsible for audit work on behalf of a third country auditor which is a firm, the firm's name, address, registered number and, if it has a website, its address;

(e) in the case of a third country auditor who has registered with an EEA competent authority—

   (i)   the name and address of that authority, and

   (ii) the registration number which that authority has allocated to it;

(f) the name and address of any body which has authorised the third country auditor to conduct audits in accordance with the law of a third country; and

(g) if he has entered into arrangements with a body for the purposes of section 1242(1) of the Companies Act 2006 (duties of registered third country auditors), the name and address of that body.

(3) The register must contain the following information [in relation to each registered third country auditor] which is a firm—

(a) its name and address;

(b) the address of each of its offices in which it carries out third country audit work;

(c) its registered number;

(d) an indication that it is a third country auditor;

(e) its contact information and, if it has a website, its address;

(f) its legal form;

(g) the name and address of each person who is—

   (i)   an owner or shareholder of the firm, or

   (ii) a member of the firm's administrative or management body;

(h) the name, address and registered number of each individual who performs third country audits on behalf of the firm;

(i) in the case of a third country auditor which is a member of a network—

   (i)   a list of the names and addresses of the other members of that network, or

   (ii) an indication of where that information is available to the public;

(j) in the case of a third country auditor which has registered with an EEA competent authority—

   (i)   the name and address of that authority, and

   (ii) the registration number which that authority has allocated to it;

(k) the name and address of any body which has authorised the third country auditor to conduct audits in accordance with the law of a third country; and

(l) if it has entered into arrangements with a body for the purposes of section 1242(1) of the Companies Act 2006 (duties of registered third country auditors), the name and address of that body.

(4) The register of third country auditors must be kept in electronic form.

(5) The information on the register must be kept available for inspection by any person by electronic means, unless it is excluded in accordance with paragraph (6).

(6) Information on the register relating to an individual may be excluded from being made available for inspection if making the information so available would create or be likely to create a serious risk that the individual, or any other person, would be subject to violence or intimidation.

(7) In this regulation "network" means an association of persons cooperating in audit work by way of—

(a) profit sharing,

(b) cost sharing,

(c) common ownership, control or management,

(d) common quality control policies and procedures,

(e) common business strategy, or

(f) use of a common brand name.

(8) For the purposes of this regulation—

(a) a network is not a firm, and

(b) an association of individuals which is a firm is not a network.

NOTES

Commencement: 6 April 2008.

Paras (2), (3): words in square brackets substituted by the Statutory Auditors and Third Country Auditors (Amendment) Regulations 2008, SI 2008/499, reg 2(1), (5), as from 5 April 2008.

[4.82]

35 Application for registration of third country auditor

(1)   A third country auditor may apply to the designated body for registration in accordance with this regulation.

(2)   An application for registration must be in writing.

(3)   An application for registration of a third country auditor must include—
  (a)   the information required for his entry in the register (see regulation 34), other than—
    (i)   his registered number, and
    (ii)   the name and address of any body with which he has entered into arrangements for the purposes of section 1242(1) of the Companies Act 2006 (duties of registered third country auditors);
  (b)   the statement required by regulation 36 (application statement); and
  (c)   evidence demonstrating that the matters included in the statement required by regulation 36 (application statement) are correct.

[(3A)   An application for registration of an exempt third country auditor must include—
  (a)   a statement of the auditing standards and independence requirements applied to the audit or audits in respect of which the application is made,
  (b)   a description of the auditor's internal quality control system,
  (c)   a statement of whether and (if so) when a quality assurance review has been carried out in respect of the auditor,
  (d)   information required by the designated body about the outcome of a quality assurance review.]

(4)   For the purposes of paragraph (3)(c) a statement by the third country competent authority which oversees or regulates the third country auditor to the effect that the third country auditor is a fit and proper person to conduct audits in that third country may be treated as evidence demonstrating that the statement required by regulation 36(c) is correct.

(5)   An application for registration must—
  (a)   in the case of a third country auditor who is an individual, be signed by the third country auditor;
  (b)   in the case of a third country auditor which is a firm, be signed by a person authorised by the firm to sign on its behalf.

(6)   An application may be delivered to the designated body by electronic means, if the designated body so agrees.

NOTES

Commencement: 6 April 2008.
  Para (3A): inserted by the Statutory Auditors and Third Country Auditors (Amendment) (No 2) Regulations 2008, SI 2008/2639, reg 2(1), (3), as from 31 October 2008, subject to transitional provisions relating to applications for registration made before that date (see reg 3 of the 2008 Regulations at **[4.307]**).

[4.83]

36 Application statement

(1)   A third country auditor must make a statement for the purposes of his [application under regulation 35] (application for registration of third country auditor) to the effect that—
  (a)   in the case of a third country auditor who is an individual, he holds a qualification which meets requirements equivalent to those which apply to an appropriate qualification for the purposes of section 1219 of the Companies Act 2006;
  (b)   in the case of a third country auditor which is a firm—
    (i)   a majority of the members of the firm's administrative or management body hold qualifications which meet requirements equivalent to those which apply to an appropriate qualification for the purposes of that section, and
    (ii)   each individual who conducts audits of UK-traded non-EEA companies (within the meaning of Part 42 of the Companies Act 2006) on behalf of that firm holds a qualification which meets requirements equivalent to those which apply to an appropriate qualification for the purposes of that section;
  (c)   he is a fit and proper person to conduct audits of UK-traded non-EEA companies;
  (d)   he conducts such audits in accordance with standards equivalent to those required by Articles 22, 24 and 25 of the Audit Directive (independence, objectivity and audit fees);
  (e)   he conducts such audits in accordance with standards equivalent to those determined under arrangements within paragraph 22 of Schedule 10 to the Companies Act 2006 (independent determination of technical standards); and
  (f)   he publishes on a website an annual transparency report equivalent to that required for auditors of public interest entities by Article 40 of the Audit Directive (transparency report).

NOTES

Commencement: 6 April 2008.

Words in square brackets substituted by the Statutory Auditors and Third Country Auditors (Amendment) Regulations 2008, SI 2008/499, reg 2(1), (6), as from 5 April 2008.

Reproduced as per the original version, ie, there is no paragraph (2).

[4.84]
37 Acceptance and refusal of application for registration

(1)   The designated body may register a third country auditor if he has made an application in accordance with regulation 35 (application for registration of third country auditor).

(2)   The designated body may not register a third country auditor if it considers that the statement required by regulation 36 (application statement) made by him is not correct.

(3)   If the designated body refuses to register a third country auditor, it must give him written notice to that effect stating the reason for the refusal.

NOTES
Commencement: 6 April 2008.

[4.85]
38 Allocation of registered number

The designated body must allocate a number to each third country auditor which it registers, which shall be known as the third country auditor's registered number.

NOTES
Commencement: 6 April 2008.

[4.86]
39 Duty to provide updated information

(1)   A registered third country auditor must take all reasonable steps to notify the designated body without undue delay of—

   (a)   the name and address of any body he has entered into arrangements with for the purposes of section 1242(1) of the Companies Act 2006 (arrangements for monitoring of audits of UK-traded non-EEA companies);

   (b)   any information or event which may lead the designated body to consider that the statement required by regulation 36 (application statement) made by the third country auditor is not correct;

   (c)   any information necessary to ensure that the information in the register relating to him is correct.

[(2)   An exempt third country auditor who for the purpose of registration has provided to the designated body information falling within subparagraphs (a) to (d) and the first sentence of subparagraph (e) of Article 1.1 of the Commission Decision must take all reasonable steps to notify the designated body without undue delay of any change or addition to that information.]

NOTES
Commencement: 6 April 2008.
Para (2): added by the Statutory Auditors and Third Country Auditors (Amendment) (No 2) Regulations 2008, SI 2008/2639, reg 2(1), (4), as from 31 October 2008.

[4.87]
40 Removal of third country auditor from the register

(1)   If the designated body considers that the statement required by regulation 36 (application statement) made by the third country auditor is no longer correct, it must—

   (a)   notify the third country auditor of the steps he must take to ensure that the statement is correct, and

   (b)   if the third country auditor has not taken those steps on or before the date three months after the notification, remove him from the register.

(2)   The designated body may remove a third country auditor from the register if it considers that the third country auditor has failed to comply with his obligations under—

   (a)   [regulation 39(1)] (duty to provide updated information),

   (b)   section 1242 of the Companies Act 2006(a) (duties of registered third country auditors),

   (c)   section 1243 of that Act (matters to be notified to the Secretary of State), or

   (d)   section 1244 of that Act (Secretary of State's power to call for information).

[(3)   The designated body may remove an exempt third country auditor from the register if—

   (a)   it considers that the auditor—

      (i)   has failed—

         (aa)   to comply with the obligations of the auditor under regulation 39(2) (duty of exempt third country auditor to provide updated information), or

         (bb)   to apply the auditing standards and independence requirements set out in the statement provided for in regulation 35(3A)(a), or

      (ii)   is not a fit and proper person to conduct audits of the accounts of UK-traded non-EEA companies, or

  (b) it appears to the designated body that a third country competent authority which oversees or regulates the auditor considers that the auditor is not—

      (i)   a fit and proper person to conduct audits in the specified third country in which the authority is established, or

      (ii)   eligible to conduct audits of the accounts of bodies corporate incorporated or formed under the law of that country.]

NOTES

Commencement: 6 April 2008 (paras (1), (2)(a)); 29 June 2008 (otherwise).

Para (2): words in square brackets in sub-para (a) substituted by the Statutory Auditors and Third Country Auditors (Amendment) (No 2) Regulations 2008, SI 2008/2639, reg 2(1), (5)(a), as from 31 October 2008.

Para (3): added by SI 2008/2639, reg 2(1), (5)(b), as from 31 October 2008.

41–45 *((Pt 6): Regs 41, 42 amend the Companies Act 2006, ss 525, 994 at* **[1.525]**, **[1.994]***; reg 43 (Exclusion of large debt securities issuer from definition of "UK-traded non-EEA company") modifies s 1241 of the 2006 Act (see the notes to that section at* **[1.1241]***); reg 44 amends Sch 11, Pt 2 to the 2006 Act at* **[1.1325]***; reg 45 revokes the Company Auditors (Examinations) Regulations 1990, SI 1990/1146, the Company Auditors (Examinations) Regulations (Northern Ireland) 1990, SR 1990/1309, the Companies Act 1989 (Register of Auditors and Information About Audit Firms) Regulations 1991, SI 1991/1566, the Companies (1990 Order) (Register of Auditors and Information About Audit Firms) Regulations (Northern Ireland) 1991, SR 1991/500, and the European Communities (Recognition of Professional Qualifications) (First General System) Regulations 2005, SI 2005/18 (for the purposes of their application to the profession of company auditor, except for the purposes of their application in relation to auditors appointed for financial years beginning before 6 April 2008).)*

SCHEDULE

(Schedule: inserts the Companies Act 2006, Sch 11A at **[1.1325A]** *et seq).*

INDEPENDENT SUPERVISOR APPOINTMENT ORDER 2007

(SI 2007/3534)

NOTES

Made: 17 December 2007.

Authority: Companies Act 2006, s 1228.

Commencement: 6 April 2008.

Amendment: as of 1 July 2011, this Order had not been amended.

[4.88]

1 Citation and commencement

This Order may be cited as the Independent Supervisor Appointment Order 2007 and comes into force on 6th April 2008.

NOTES

Commencement: 6 April 2008.

[4.89]

2 Interpretation

In this Order "the Act" means the Companies Act 2006.

NOTES

Commencement: 6 April 2008.

[4.90]

3 Appointment of Independent Supervisor

The body known as the Professional Oversight Board, established under the articles of association of The Financial Reporting Council Limited, is appointed for the purposes of section 1228 of the Act (appointment of the Independent Supervisor) to discharge the supervision function.

NOTES

Commencement: 6 April 2008.

[4.91]
4 Requirements and provisions concerning the exercise of the supervision function

The report which is required under section 1231 of the Act (reports by the Independent Supervisor) must include—

    (a)   an account of how the Independent Supervisor has discharged the supervision function, including why it considers that this function has been discharged effectively;

    (b)   an account of the extent to which each Auditor General has complied with its duties under the Act;

    (c)   an account of any matters notified to the Independent Supervisor under section 1232 of the Act (matters to be notified to the Independent Supervisor);

    (d)   an account of the Independent Supervisor's enforcement activity, including the issue of any suspension notices and any applications for compliance orders; and

    (e)   an account of the activities carried out by the Independent Supervisor as a consequence of its status as a public authority for the purpose of the Freedom of Information Act 2000.

NOTES
Commencement: 6 April 2008.

[4.92]
5

(1)   The Independent Supervisor must, at least once in each calendar year, prepare and publish in such manner as it sees fit financial statements of its expenditure.

(2)   The financial statements shall be audited by a person other than an Auditor General who is eligible for appointment as a statutory auditor.

NOTES
Commencement: 6 April 2008.

[4.93]
6

(1)   The Independent Supervisor must consult with the Auditors General and such other persons as seem to it to be appropriate before establishing or entering into a supervision arrangement for the purposes of section 1229 of the Act (supervision of Auditors General by the Independent Supervisor).

(2)   Any consultation carried out for this purpose before the date on which this Order comes into force, including by the Public Oversight Board established under the articles of association of The Public Oversight Board Limited, shall be treated as if it had been carried out under this article.

NOTES
Commencement: 6 April 2008.

[4.94]
7

The Independent Supervisor shall have satisfactory arrangements for recording decisions made in the exercise of the supervision function and for the safekeeping of those records which ought to be preserved.

NOTES
Commencement: 6 April 2008.

COMPANIES (FEES FOR INSPECTION AND COPYING OF COMPANY RECORDS) (NO 2) REGULATIONS 2007

(SI 2007/3535)

NOTES
Made: 17 December 2007.
Authority: CA 2006, ss 744(1)(b), (2), 749(1), 1137(1), (4), 1167, 1292(1)(a), (c).
Commencement: 6 April 2008.
As of 1 July 2011, these Regulations had not been amended.

[4.95]
1 Citation, commencement and interpretation

(1)   These Regulations may be cited as the Companies (Fees for Inspection and Copying of Company Records) (No 2) Regulations 2007 and come into force on 6th April 2008.

(2)   In these Regulations—

(a)   "the Act" means the Companies Act 2006; and

(b)   "the Commencement Order" means the Companies Act 2006 (Commencement No 5, Transitional Provisions and Savings) Order 2007.

NOTES
> Commencement: 6 April 2008.

[4.96]
2   Fee for inspection of register of debenture holders

For the purpose of section 744(1)(b) of the Act (inspection of register of debenture holders) the fee prescribed is £3.50 for each hour or part thereof during which the right of inspection is exercised.

NOTES
> Commencement: 6 April 2008.

[4.97]
3   Fee for copy of register of debenture holders

(1)   The fee prescribed for the purpose of section 744(2) of the Act (copy of entries in register of debenture holders) is—

   (a)   the amount per number of entries copied by the company as set out in paragraph (2); and

   (b)   the reasonable costs incurred by the company in delivering the copy of the entries to the person entitled to be provided with that copy.

(2)   The amounts per number of entries copied are—

   (a)   £1 for each of the first 5 entries;

   (b)   £30 for the next 95 entries or part thereof;

   (c)   £30 for the next 900 entries or part thereof;

   (d)   £30 for the next 99,000 entries or part thereof; and

   (e)   £30 for the remainder of the entries in the register or part thereof.

NOTES
> Commencement: 6 April 2008.

[4.98]
4   Fee for copy of debenture trust deed

The fee prescribed for the purpose of section 749(1) of the Act (right of debenture holder to copy of debenture trust deed) is—

   (a)   10 pence per 500 words or part thereof copied; and

   (b)   the reasonable costs incurred by the company in delivering the copy of the debenture trust deed or part thereof to the person entitled to be provided with it.

NOTES
> Commencement: 6 April 2008.

[4.99]
5   Revocation and savings: Great Britain

(1)   (*Revokes the Companies (Inspection and Copying of Registers, Indices and Documents) Regulations 1991, SI 1991/1998, Sch 2, paras 1(a), 2(a), 3(a), subject to the savings in para (2) below.*)

(2)   The fees prescribed in paragraphs 1(a), 2(a) and 3(a) of Schedule 2 to the 1991 Regulations shall continue to apply in respect of requests relating to the register of debenture holders or a debenture trust deed of a company which are subject to section 191(1) to (6) of the Companies Act 1985 by virtue of paragraph 22(2) of Schedule 4 to the Commencement Order.

NOTES
> Commencement: 6 April 2008.

6   (*(Revocation and savings: Northern Ireland) outside the scope of this work.*)

COMPANIES (REVISION OF DEFECTIVE ACCOUNTS AND REPORTS) REGULATIONS 2008

(SI 2008/373)

NOTES
> Made: 19 February 2008.
> Authority: Companies Act 2006, ss 454(3), (4), 1292(1)(a), (c).
> Commencement: 6 April 2008.
> **Amendment:** as of 1 July 2011 these Regulations had not been amended.

Part 4   CA 2006 SIs

PART 1
INTRODUCTION

[4.100]
1   Citation, commencement and application
(1)   These Regulations may be cited as the Companies (Revision of Defective Accounts and Reports) Regulations 2008.
(2)   These Regulations come into force on 6th April 2008 and apply in relation to companies' financial years beginning on or after that date.

NOTES
    Commencement: 6 April 2008.

[4.101]
2   Interpretation
(1)   In these Regulations—
    "the 2006 Act" means the Companies Act 2006;
    "date of the original annual accounts" means the date on which the original annual accounts were
        approved by the board of directors under section 414 of the 2006 Act (approval and signing
        of accounts);
    "date of the original directors' remuneration report" means the date on which the original
        directors' remuneration report was approved by the board of directors under section 422 of
        the 2006 Act (approval and signing of directors' remuneration report);

"date of the original directors' report" means the date on which the original directors' report was approved by the board of directors under section 419 of the 2006 Act (approval and signing of directors' report);

"date of revision" means the date on which revised accounts are approved by the board of directors under regulation 4 or (as the case may be) a revised directors' report or directors' remuneration report is approved by them under regulation 5 or 6;

"original", in relation to annual accounts, or a directors' report or directors' remuneration report, means the annual accounts or (as the case may be) directors' report or directors' remuneration report which are the subject of revision by, respectively, revised accounts or a revised report and, in relation to abbreviated accounts or a summary financial statement, means abbreviated accounts or a summary financial statement based on the original annual accounts or directors' report or directors' remuneration report;

"revised accounts" mean revised annual accounts of a company prepared by the directors under section 454 of the 2006 Act (voluntary revision of accounts etc), either through revision by replacement or revision by supplementary note; in the latter case the revised accounts comprise the original annual accounts together with the supplementary note;

"revised report" means a revised directors' report or directors' remuneration report prepared by the directors under section 454 of the 2006 Act, either through revision by replacement or revision by supplementary note; in the latter case the revised report comprises the original directors' report or directors' remuneration report together with the supplementary note;

"revision by replacement" means revision by the preparation of a replacement set of accounts, directors' report or directors' remuneration report, in substitution for the original annual accounts, directors' report or directors' remuneration report; and

"revision by supplementary note" means revision by the preparation of a note indicating corrections to be made to the original annual accounts, directors' report or directors' remuneration report.

(2)   References in these Regulations to a member or members of a company include a reference to a person nominated to enjoy information rights under section 146 of the 2006 Act (traded companies: nomination of persons to enjoy information rights).

(3)   References in these Regulations to provisions or requirements of the 2006 Act as to matters to be included in annual accounts and reports include relevant provisions of the Small Companies and Groups (Accounts and Directors' Report) Regulations 2008 and the Large and Medium-sized Companies and Groups (Accounts and Reports) Regulations 2008.

NOTES

Commencement: 6 April 2008.

PART 2
REVISED ACCOUNTS AND REPORTS

[4.102]
3   Content of revised accounts or revised report

(1)   Subject to regulation 19(1), the provisions of the 2006 Act and, where applicable, Article 4 of the IAS Regulation as to the matters to be included in the annual accounts of a company apply to revised accounts as if the revised accounts were prepared and approved by the directors as at the date of the original annual accounts.

(2)   In particular—
   (a)   in the case of Companies Act accounts—
       (i)   section 393 of the 2006 Act (accounts to give true and fair view),
       (ii)   section 396(2) of that Act (Companies Act individual accounts: true and fair view), and
       (iii) section 404(2) of that Act (Companies Act group accounts: true and fair view), and
   (b)   in the case of IAS accounts, section 393 of the 2006 Act and international accounting standards,
apply so as to require a true and fair view to be shown in the revised accounts of the matters referred to in those accounts, viewed as at the date of the original annual accounts.

(3)   In the case of Companies Act accounts, paragraph 13(b) of Schedule 1 to the Small Companies and Groups (Accounts and Directors' Report) Regulations 2008 or (where applicable) paragraph 13(b) of Schedule 1 to the Large and Medium-sized Companies and Groups (Accounts and Reports) Regulations 2008 apply to revised accounts as if the reference in those paragraphs to the date on which the accounts were signed was to the date of the original annual accounts.

(4)   The provisions of the 2006 Act as to the matters to be included in a directors' report or directors' remuneration report apply to a revised report as if the revised report was prepared and approved by the directors of the company as at the date of the original directors' report or directors' remuneration report.

NOTES
Commencement: 6 April 2008.

[4.103]
4　Approval and signature of revised accounts

(1)　Section 414 of the 2006 Act applies to revised accounts, save that in the case of revision by supplementary note, it applies as if it required a signature on the supplementary note instead of on the company's balance sheet.

(2)　Where copies of the original annual accounts have been sent out to members under section 423(1) of the 2006 Act (duty to circulate copies of annual accounts and reports), laid before the company in general meeting under section 437(1) of that Act (public companies: laying of accounts and reports before general meeting) in the case of a public company, or delivered to the registrar under section 441(1) of that Act (duty to file accounts and reports with the registrar), the directors must before approving the revised accounts under section 414, cause statements as to the following matters to be made in a prominent position in the revised accounts (in the case of a revision by supplementary note, in that note)—

  (a)　in the case of a revision by replacement—
     (i)　that the revised accounts replace the original annual accounts for the financial year (specifying it),
     (ii)　that they are now the statutory accounts of the company for that financial year,
     (iii)　that they have been prepared as at the date of the original annual accounts and not as at the date of revision and accordingly do not deal with events between those dates,
     (iv)　the respects in which the original annual accounts did not comply with the requirements of the 2006 Act, and
     (v)　any significant amendments made consequential upon the remedying of those defects,
  (b)　in the case of a revision by supplementary note—
     (i)　that the note revises in certain respects the original annual accounts of the company and is to be treated as forming part of those accounts, and
     (ii)　that the annual accounts have been revised as at the date of the original annual accounts and not as at the date of revision and accordingly do not deal with events between those dates,

and must, when approving the revised accounts, cause the date on which the approval is given to be stated in them (in the case of revision by supplementary note, in that note); section 414(4) and (5) apply with respect to a failure to comply with this paragraph as if the requirements of this paragraph were requirements of Part 15 of that Act.

NOTES
Commencement: 6 April 2008.

[4.104]
5　Approval and signature of revised directors' report

(1)　Section 419 of the 2006 Act applies to a revised directors' report, save that in the case of revision by supplementary note, it applies as if it required the signature to be on the supplementary note.

(2)　Where copies of the original directors' report have been sent out to members under section 423(1) of the 2006 Act, laid before the company in general meeting under section 437(1) of that Act in the case of a public company, or delivered to the registrar under section 441(1), the directors must, before approving the revised report under section 419, cause statements as to the following matters to be made in a prominent position in the revised report (in the case of a revision by supplementary note, in that note)—

  (a)　in the case of a revision by replacement—
     (i)　that the revised report replaces the original report for the financial year (specifying it),
     (ii)　that it has been prepared as at the date of the original directors' report and not as at the date of revision and accordingly does not deal with any events between those dates,
     (iii)　the respects in which the original directors' report did not comply with the requirements of the 2006 Act, and
     (iv)　any significant amendments made consequential upon the remedying of those defects,
  (b)　in the case of a revision by supplementary note—
     (i)　that the note revises in certain respects the original directors' report of the company and is to be treated as forming part of that report, and
     (ii)　that the directors' report has been revised as at the date of the original directors' report and not as at the date of the revision and accordingly does not deal with events between those dates,

and must, when approving the revised report, cause the date on which the approval is given to be stated in them (in the case of a revision by supplementary note, in that note); section 419(3) and (4) of the 2006 Act apply with respect to a failure to comply with this paragraph as if the requirements of this paragraph were requirements of Part 15 of that Act.

NOTES
    Commencement: 6 April 2008.

[4.105]
6   Approval and signature of revised directors' remuneration report

(1)   Section 422 of the 2006 Act applies to a revised directors' remuneration report, save that in the case of revision by supplementary note, it applies as if it required the signature to be on the supplementary note.

(2)   Where copies of the original directors' remuneration report have been sent out to members under section 423(1) of the 2006 Act, laid before the company in general meeting under section 437(1) of that Act in the case of a public company, or delivered to the registrar under section 441(1) of that Act, the directors must, before approving the revised report under section 422, cause statements as to the following matters to be made in a prominent position in the revised report (in the case of a revision by supplementary note, in that note)—

(a)   in the case of a revision by replacement—
   (i)   that the revised report replaces the original report for the financial year (specifying it),
   (ii)   that it has been prepared as at the date of the original directors' remuneration report and not as at the date of revision and accordingly does not deal with any events between those dates,
   (iii)   the respects in which the original directors' remuneration report did not comply with the requirements of the 2006 Act, and
   (iv)   any significant amendments made consequential upon the remedying of those defects,
(b)   in the case of a revision by supplementary note—
   (i)   that the note revises in certain respects the original directors' remuneration report of the company and is to be treated as forming part of that report, and
   (ii)   that the directors' remuneration report has been revised as at the date of the original directors' remuneration report and not as at the date of the revision and accordingly does not deal with events between those dates,

and must, when approving the revised report, cause the date on which the approval is given to be stated in it (in the case of a revision by supplementary note, in that note); section 422(2) and (3) of the 2006 Act apply with respect to a failure to comply with this paragraph as if the requirements of this paragraph were requirements of Part 15 of that Act.

NOTES
    Commencement: 6 April 2008.

PART 3
AUDITOR'S REPORTS

[4.106]
7   Auditor's report on revised accounts and revised report

(1)   Subject to paragraph (2), a company's current auditor shall make a report or (as the case may be) further report under section 495 of the 2006 Act (auditor's report on company's annual accounts), to the company's members under this regulation on any revised accounts prepared under section 454 of that Act and—

(a)   section 498 of that Act (duties of auditor) applies with any necessary modifications, and
(b)   section 495(1) does not apply with respect to the revised accounts.

(2)   Where the auditor's report on the original annual accounts was not made by the company's current auditor, the directors of the company may resolve that the report required by paragraph (1) is to be made by the person or persons who made that report, provided that that person or those persons agree to do so and would be qualified for appointment as auditor of the company.

(3)   Subject to regulation 19(1), an auditor's report under this regulation must state whether in the auditor's opinion the revised accounts have been properly prepared in accordance with the provisions of the 2006 Act and, where applicable, Article 4 of the IAS Regulation as they have effect under these Regulations, and in particular whether a true and fair view, seen as at the date the original annual accounts were approved, is given by the revised accounts with respect to the matters set out in section 495(3)(a) to (c) of that Act.

The report must also state whether in the auditor's opinion the original annual accounts failed to comply with the requirements of the 2006 Act and, where applicable, Article 4 of the IAS

Regulation in the respects identified by the directors (in the case of a revision by replacement) in the statement required by regulation 4(2)(a)(iv) or (in the case of a revision by supplementary note) in the supplementary note.

(4)   The auditor must also state whether the information contained in the directors' report for the financial year for which the annual accounts are prepared (which is, if the report has been revised under these Regulations, that revised report) is consistent with those accounts.

(5)   Sections 503 to 506 of the 2006 Act (signature of auditor's report) apply to an auditor's report under this regulation as they apply to an auditor's report under section 495(1) of that Act, with any necessary modifications.

(6)   An auditor's report under this regulation shall, upon being signed under section 503 of the 2006 Act as so applied, be, as from the date of signature, the auditor's report on the annual accounts of the company in place of the report on the original annual accounts.

NOTES
Commencement: 6 April 2008.

[4.107]
8   Auditor's report where company ceases to be exempt from audit

(1)   Where as a result of the revisions to the accounts, the company is no longer entitled to exemption from audit under Chapter 1 of Part 16 of the 2006 Act, the company shall cause an auditor's report on the revised accounts to be prepared.

(2)   The auditor's report must be delivered to the registrar within 28 days after the date of revision of the accounts.

(3)   Sections 451 (default in filing accounts and reports: offences) and 452 (default in filing accounts: court order) of the 2006 Act apply with respect to a failure to comply with the requirements of this regulation as they apply with respect to a failure to comply with the requirements of section 441 of that Act but as if—

   (a)   the references in section 451(1) and in section 452(1)(a) to "the period for filing those accounts and reports" were references to the period of 28 days referred to in paragraph (2); the reference in section 451(1) and (2) to "that period" are to be construed accordingly, and

   (b)   the references in section 451(3) to "the documents in question" and "this Part" were, respectively, a reference to the auditor's report referred to in paragraph (2) and the provisions of Part 16 of the 2006 Act as applied by these Regulations.

NOTES
Commencement: 6 April 2008.

[4.108]
9   Auditor's report on revised report alone

(1)   Subject to paragraph (2), a company's current auditor shall make a report or (as the case may be) further report under section 496 or 497 of the 2006 Act (as the case may be) to the company's members under this regulation on any revised report prepared under section 454 of that Act if the relevant annual accounts have not been revised at the same time.

(2)   Where the auditor's report on the annual accounts for the financial year covered by the revised report was not made by the company's current auditor, the directors of the company may resolve that the report required by paragraph (1) is to be made by the person or persons who made that report, provided that that person or those persons agree to do so and would be qualified for appointment as auditor of the company.

(3)   Where a revised directors' report is prepared under section 454 of the 2006 Act, the auditor's report must state whether in his opinion the information given in that revised report is consistent with the annual accounts for the relevant year (specifying it).

(4)   Where a revised directors' remuneration report is prepared under section 454 of the 2006 Act, the auditor's report must state whether in his opinion any auditable part of that revised report has been properly prepared ("auditable part" being a part containing information required by Part 3 of Schedule 8 to the Large and Medium-sized Companies and Groups (Accounts and Reports) Regulations 2008).

(5)   Sections 503 to 506 of the 2006 Act apply to an auditor's report under this regulation as they apply to an auditor's report under section 495 of that Act, with any necessary modifications.

NOTES
Commencement: 6 April 2008.

PART 4
EFFECT OF REVISION

[4.109]
10   Effect of revision of accounts

(1)   Upon the directors approving revised accounts under regulation 4, the provisions of the 2006 Act have effect as if the revised accounts were, as from the date of their approval, the annual accounts of the company in place of the original annual accounts.

(2)   In particular, the revised accounts shall as from that date be the company's annual accounts for the relevant financial year for the purposes of the following provisions of the 2006 Act—

(a)   section 431 (right of member or debenture holder to copies of accounts and reports: unquoted companies),

(b)   section 432 (right of member or debenture holder to copies of accounts and reports: quoted companies),

(c)   section 434(3) (requirements in connection with publication of statutory accounts), and

(d)   sections 423 (duty to circulate copies of annual accounts and reports), 437 (public companies; laying of accounts and reports before general meeting) and 441 (duty to file accounts and reports with the registrar), if the requirements of those sections have not been complied with prior to the date of revision.

NOTES
Commencement: 6 April 2008.

[4.110]
11   Effect of revision of report

(1)   Subject to the following provisions of these Regulations, upon the directors approving a revised report under regulation 5 or 6 the provisions of the 2006 Act have effect as if the revised report was, as from the date of its approval, the directors' report or the directors' remuneration report (as the case may be) in place of the original directors' report or directors' remuneration report (as the case may be).

(2)   In particular, the revised report shall as from that date be the directors' report or the directors' remuneration report for the relevant financial year for the purposes of—

(a)   sections 431 and 432 of the 2006 Act, and

(b)   sections 423, 437 and 441 of that Act if the requirements of those sections have not been complied with prior to the date of revision.

NOTES
Commencement: 6 April 2008.

PART 5
PUBLICATION, LAYING AND DELIVERY OF REVISED ACCOUNTS ETC

[4.111]
12   Publication of revised accounts and reports

(1)   This regulation has effect where the directors have prepared revised accounts or a revised report under section 454 of the 2006 Act and copies of the original annual accounts or report have been sent to any person under section 423 or 146 of that Act.

(2)   The directors must send to any such person—

(a)   in the case of a revision by replacement, a copy of the revised accounts, or (as the case may be) the revised report, together with a copy of the auditor's report on those accounts, or (as the case may be) on that report, or

(b)   in the case of a revision by supplementary note, a copy of that note together with a copy of the auditor's report on the revised accounts, or (as the case may be) on the revised report,

not more than 28 days after the date of revision.

(3)   The directors must also, not more than 28 days after the revision, send a copy of the revised accounts or (as the case may be) revised report, together with a copy of the auditor's report on those accounts or (as the case may be) on that report, to any person who is not a person entitled to receive a copy under paragraph (2) but who is, as at the date of revision—

(a)   a member of the company,

(b)   a holder of the company's debentures, or

(c)   a person who is entitled to receive notice of general meetings,

unless the company would be entitled at that date to send to that person a summary financial statement under section 426 of the 2006 Act (option to provide summary financial statement). Section 423(2) to (4) of that Act apply to this paragraph as they apply to section 423(1).

(4)   Section 425 of the 2006 Act (default in sending out copies of accounts and reports: offences) applies to a default in complying with this regulation as if the provisions of this regulation were provisions of section 423 and as if the references in that section to "the company" and "every officer of the company who is in default" were a reference to each of the directors who approved the revised accounts under regulation 4 or revised report under regulation 5 or 6.

(5)   Where, prior to the date of revision of the original annual accounts, the company had completed sending out copies of those accounts under section 423 of the 2006 Act, references in that Act to the day on which accounts are sent out under section 423 are to be construed as referring to the day on which the original accounts were sent out (applying section 423(5) as necessary) notwithstanding that those accounts have been revised; where the company had not completed, prior to the date of revision, the sending out of copies of those accounts under that section, such references are to the day, or the last day, on which the revised accounts are sent out.

NOTES
Commencement: 6 April 2008.

[4.112]
13   Laying of revised accounts or a revised report

(1)   This regulation has effect where the directors of a public company have prepared revised accounts or a revised report under section 454 of the 2006 Act and copies of the original annual accounts or report have been laid before a general meeting under section 437 of that Act.

(2)   A copy of the revised accounts or (as the case may be) the revised report, together with a copy of the auditor's report on those accounts, or (as the case may be) on that report, must be laid before the next general meeting of the company held after the date of revision at which any annual accounts for a financial year are laid, unless the revised accounts, or (as the case may be) the revised report, have already been laid before an earlier general meeting.

(3)   Section 438 of the 2006 Act (public companies: offence of failure to lay accounts and reports) applies with respect to a failure to comply with the requirements of this regulation as it has effect with respect to a failure to comply with the requirements of section 437 of that Act but as if—

   (a)   the reference in section 438(1) to "the period allowed" was a reference to the period between the date of revision of the revised accounts or (as the case may be) the revised report and the date of the next general meeting of the company held after the date of revision at which any annual accounts for a financial year are laid; references in section 438(1) and (2) to "that period" are to be construed accordingly; and

   (b)   the references in section 438(3) to "the documents in question" and "this Part" were, respectively, a reference to the documents referred to in paragraph (2) and the provisions of Part 15 of the 2006 Act as applied by these Regulations.

NOTES
Commencement: 6 April 2008.

[4.113]
14   Delivery of revised accounts or a revised report

(1)   This regulation has effect where the directors have prepared revised accounts or a revised report under section 454 of the 2006 Act and a copy of the original annual accounts or report has been delivered to the registrar under section 441(1) of that Act.

(2)   The directors of the company must, within 28 days of the date of revision, deliver to the registrar—

   (a)   in the case of a revision by replacement, a copy of the revised accounts or (as the case may be) the revised report, together with a copy of the auditor's report on those accounts or (as the case may be) on that report, or

   (b)   in the case of a revision by supplementary note, a copy of that note, together with a copy of the auditor's report on the revised accounts or (as the case may be) on the revised report.

(3)   Sections 451 (default in filing accounts and reports: offences) and 452 (default in filing accounts: court order) of the 2006 Act apply with respect to a failure to comply with the requirements of this regulation as they apply with respect to a failure to comply with the requirements of section 441 of that Act but as if—

   (a)   the references in section 451(1) and in section 452(1)(a) to "the period for filing those accounts and reports" were references to the period of 28 days referred to in paragraph (2); the references in section 451(1) and (2) to "that period" are to be construed accordingly, and

   (b)   the references in section 451(3) to "the documents in question" and "this Part" were, respectively, a reference to the documents referred to in paragraph (2) and the provisions of Part 15 of the 2006 Act as applied by these Regulations.

NOTES
Commencement: 6 April 2008.

PART 6
ABBREVIATED ACCOUNTS AND SUMMARY FINANCIAL STATEMENTS

[4.114]
15   Small and medium sized companies

(1)   This regulation has effect (subject to regulation 19(2)) where the directors have prepared revised accounts under section 454 of the 2006 Act and the company has, prior to the date of revision, delivered to the registrar accounts which are abbreviated accounts within the meaning of section 444(3) and (4) (filing obligations of companies subject to small companies regime) or 445(3) and (4) (filing obligations of medium-sized companies) of that Act.

(2)   Where the abbreviated accounts so delivered to the registrar would, if they had been prepared by reference to the revised accounts, not comply with the provisions of the 2006 Act (whether because the company would not have qualified as a small or (as the case may be) medium-sized company in the light of the revised accounts or because the accounts have been revised in a manner which affects the content of the abbreviated accounts), the directors of the company shall cause the company either—

    (a)   to deliver to the registrar a copy of the revised accounts, together with a copy of the directors' report and the auditor's report on the revised accounts, or

    (b)   (if on the basis of the revised accounts they would be entitled under the 2006 Act to do so) to prepare further abbreviated accounts drawn up in accordance with the provisions of that Act and deliver them to the registrar together with a statement as to the effect of the revisions made.

(3)   Where the abbreviated accounts would, if they had been prepared by reference to the revised accounts, comply with the requirements of the 2006 Act, the directors of the company shall cause the company to deliver to the registrar—

    (a)   a note stating that the annual accounts of the company for the relevant financial year (specifying it) have been revised in a respect which has no bearing on the abbreviated accounts delivered for that year, together with

    (b)   a copy of any auditor's report on the revised accounts.

(4)   Revised abbreviated accounts or a note under this regulation must be delivered to the registrar within 28 days after the date of revision of the revised accounts.

(5)   Sections 451 (default in filing accounts and reports: offences) and 452 (default in filing accounts: court order) of the 2006 Act apply with respect to a failure to comply with the requirements of this regulation as they apply with respect to a failure to comply with the requirements of section 441 of that Act but as if—

    (a)   the references in section 451(1) and in section 452(1)(a) to "the period for filing those accounts and reports" were references to the period of 28 days referred to in paragraph (4); the references in section 451(1) and (2) to "that period" are to be construed accordingly, and

    (b)   the references in section 451(3) to "the documents in question" and "this Part" were, respectively, a reference to the documents referred to in paragraph (4) and the provisions of Part 15 of the 2006 Act as applied by these Regulations.

NOTES

Commencement: 6 April 2008.

[4.115]
16

(1)   This regulation has effect (subject to regulation 19(2)) where the directors have delivered to the registrar abbreviated accounts which do not comply with the provisions of the 2006 Act for reasons other than those specified in regulation 15(2).

(2)   The directors of the company shall cause the company—

    (a)   to prepare further abbreviated accounts in accordance with the provisions of section 444(3) and (4) or 445(3) and (4) of the 2006 Act (as the case may be), and

    (b)   to deliver those accounts to the registrar within 28 days after the date of revision together with a statement as to the effect of the revisions made.

(3)   Sections 451 and 452 of the 2006 Act apply with respect to a failure to comply with the requirements of this regulation as they apply with respect to a failure to comply with the requirements of section 441 of that Act but as if—

    (a)   the references in section 451(1) and in section 452(1)(a) to "the period for filing those accounts and reports" were references to the period of 28 days referred to in paragraph (2); the references in section 451(1) and (2) to "that period" are to be construed accordingly, and

    (b)   the references in section 451(3) to "the documents in question" and "this Part" were, respectively, a reference to the documents referred to in paragraph (2) and the provisions of Part 15 of the 2006 Act as applied by these Regulations.

NOTES
Commencement: 6 April 2008.

[4.116]
17 Summary financial statements

(1) This regulation has effect subject to regulation 19(3) where a summary financial statement has been sent to any person specified in regulation 3 of the Companies (Summary Financial Statement) Regulations 2008.

(2) Where the summary financial statement does not comply with the requirements of section 426 of the 2006 Act or the Companies (Summary Financial Statement) Regulations 2008, or if it had been prepared by reference to revised accounts or a revised report would not have complied with those requirements, the directors of the company shall, subject to paragraphs (4) and (5), cause the company to prepare a further summary financial statement under section 426 of that Act and to send that statement to—

   (a)   any person who received a copy of the original summary financial statement, and

   (b)   any person to whom the company would be entitled, as at the date the revised summary financial statement is prepared, to send a summary financial statement for the current financial year,

and sections 426(1) to (4), 434(6) and 435(7) of that Act (requirements in connection with the publication of statutory accounts and of non-statutory accounts) respectively apply with necessary modifications to a summary financial statement under this regulation.

(3) A summary financial statement prepared under paragraph (2) must contain a short statement of the revisions made and their effect.

(4) The directors of the company may, instead of causing the company to prepare a further summary financial statement under paragraph (2), cause the company to prepare and send to the persons mentioned in that paragraph a supplementary note indicating the corrections to the original summary financial statement, and sections 426(1) and (2), 434(6) and 435(7) of the 2006 Act apply with necessary modifications to such a supplementary note.

(5) A supplementary note prepared under the last paragraph must contain a statement that it revises the original summary financial statement in certain respects and is to be treated as forming part of that statement.

(6) Where the summary financial statement would, if it had been prepared by reference to the revised accounts or revised report, comply with the requirements of section 426 of the 2006 Act and the Companies (Summary Financial Statement) Regulations 2008, the directors of the company shall cause the company to send to the persons referred to in paragraph (2) a note stating that the annual accounts of the company for the relevant financial year (specifying it) or (as the case may be) the directors' report or directors' remuneration report for that year have or has been revised in a respect which has no bearing on the summary financial statement for that year.

If the auditor's report under regulation 7, 8 or 9 on the revised accounts or revised report is qualified, a copy of that report must be attached to the note sent out under this paragraph.

(7) A summary financial statement revised, or a note prepared, under this regulation must be sent to the persons referred to in paragraph (2) within 28 days after the date of revision of the revised accounts or revised report.

(8) Section 429 of the 2006 Act (summary financial statements: offences) applies with respect to a failure to comply with the requirements of this regulation as if the provisions of this regulation were provisions of that section and as if the reference in that section to "the company", and "every officer of the company who is in default" were references to each of the directors of the company who approved the revised accounts under regulation 4, the revised directors' report under regulation 5 or the revised directors' remuneration report under regulation 6.

NOTES
Commencement: 6 April 2008.

PART 7
COMPANIES EXEMPT FROM AUDIT

[4.117]
18 Companies exempt from audit under section 477 or 480

Where, in respect of any financial year, a company is exempt under section 477 (small companies: conditions for exemption from audit) or 480 (dormant companies: conditions for exemption from audit) of the 2006 Act from the requirements of that Act relating to the audit of accounts, these Regulations apply as if they omitted any reference to an auditor's report, or to the making of such a report.

NOTES
Commencement: 6 April 2008.

PART 8
FINAL PROVISIONS

[4.118]
19 Modifications of the 2006 Act

(1) Where the provisions of the 2006 Act as to the matters to be included in the annual accounts of a company or (as the case may be) in a directors' report or directors' remuneration report have been amended after the date of the original annual accounts or (as the case may be) directors' report or directors' remuneration report but prior to the date of revision, references in regulations 3 and 7(3) to the provisions of that Act are to be construed as references to the provisions of that Act as in force at the date of the original annual accounts or (as the case may be) directors' report or directors' remuneration report.

(2) Where the provisions of sections 444(3) and (4) and 445(3) and (4) of the 2006 Act as to the matters to be included in abbreviated accounts have been amended after the date of delivery of the original abbreviated accounts but prior to the date of revision of the revised accounts or report, references in regulations 15 and 16 to the provisions of the 2006 Act or to any particular provisions of that Act are to be construed as references to the provisions of that Act, or to the particular provision, as in force at the date of the delivery of the original abbreviated accounts.

(3) Where the provisions of section 426 of the 2006 Act or of the Companies (Summary Financial Statement) Regulations 2008 as to the matters to be included in a summary financial statement have been amended after the date of the sending out of the original summary financial statement but prior to the date of revision of the revised accounts or report, references in regulation 17 to section 426 or to those Regulations are to be construed as references to that section or those Regulations as in force at the date of the sending out of the original summary financial statements.

NOTES
Commencement: 6 April 2008.

[4.119]
20 Revocations etc

(1) The Companies (Revision of Defective Accounts and Report) Regulations 1990 and the Companies (Revision of Defective Accounts and Report) Regulations (Northern Ireland) 1991 are revoked.

(2) Notwithstanding the revocation of the regulations specified in paragraph (1), the provisions of those regulations continue to apply in relation to financial years of a company beginning before 6th April 2008.

NOTES
Commencement: 6 April 2008.

COMPANIES (SUMMARY FINANCIAL STATEMENT) REGULATIONS 2008

(SI 2008/374)

NOTES
Made: 19 February 2008.
Authority: Companies Act 2006, ss 426(1), (3), 427(2), (5), 428(2), (5), 1292(1).
Commencement: 6 April 2008.
Amendment: as of 1 July 2011 these Regulations had not been amended.

ARRANGEMENT OF REGULATIONS

PART 1
INTRODUCTION

PART 2
CONDITIONS FOR SENDING OUT SUMMARY FINANCIAL STATEMENT

PART 3
FORM AND CONTENT OF SUMMARY FINANCIAL STATEMENT

PART 4
SUPPLEMENTARY PROVISIONS

SCHEDULES

PART 1
INTRODUCTION

[4.120]
1   Citation, commencement and application

(1)   These Regulations may be cited as the Companies (Summary Financial Statement) Regulations 2008.

(2)   These Regulations come into force on 6th April 2008 and apply in relation to companies' financial years beginning on or after that date.

NOTES
Commencement: 6 April 2008.

[4.121]
2   Interpretation

In these Regulations, unless otherwise stated—
   "the 2006 Act" means the Companies Act 2006;
   "the Large and Medium-sized Companies Accounts Regulations" means the Large and Medium-sized Companies and Groups (Accounts and Reports) Regulations 2008;
   "the Small Companies Accounts Regulations" means the Small Companies (Accounts and Directors' Report) Regulations 2008;
   "full accounts and reports" means, in relation to a company, the annual accounts and reports, copies of which the company is required to send to the persons specified in section 423(1) of the 2006 Act, and "full" in relation to any balance sheet, profit and loss account, group accounts, directors' report or directors' remuneration report means any such document contained in the full accounts and reports.

NOTES
Commencement: 6 April 2008.

[4.122]
3   Persons to whom a company may send a summary financial statement

Subject to these Regulations, a company may send a summary financial statement instead of a copy of its full accounts and reports to—
   (a)   a person specified in section 423(1) of the 2006 Act (duty to circulate copies of annual accounts and reports); and
   (b)   a person nominated to enjoy information rights under section 146 of the 2006 Act (traded companies: nomination of persons to enjoy information rights).

NOTES
Commencement: 6 April 2008.

PART 2
CONDITIONS FOR SENDING OUT SUMMARY FINANCIAL STATEMENT

[4.123]
4 Cases in which sending of summary financial statement prohibited

(1) In the following cases a company may not send a summary financial statement to a person specified in regulation 3—

    (a) in the case of any such person, where it is prohibited from doing so by any relevant provision of its constitution, and

    (b) in the case of any such person who is the holder of a debenture, where it is prohibited from doing so by a relevant provision in any instrument constituting or otherwise governing any of the company's debentures of which that person is a holder.

(2) In the following cases a company may not send a summary financial statement to any person specified in regulation 3 in relation to any financial year—

    (a) where, in relation to that year, no auditor's report has been made in respect of the annual accounts of the company, or the directors' report, or the auditable part of the directors' remuneration report, where relevant, under sections 495 (auditor's report on company's annual accounts), 496 (auditor's report on directors' report) and 497 (auditor's report on auditable part of directors' remuneration report) of the 2006 Act respectively;

    (b) where the period for filing accounts and reports for that year under section 442 of the 2006 Act (period for filing accounts) has expired;

    (c) where the summary financial statement in respect of that financial year has not been approved by the board of directors and the original statement has not been signed on behalf of the board by a director of the company.

(3) For the purposes of paragraph (1) any provision (however expressed) which requires copies of the full accounts and reports to be sent to a person specified in regulation 3, or which forbids the sending of summary financial statements under section 426 of the 2006 Act (option to provide summary financial statement), is a relevant provision.

NOTES
Commencement: 6 April 2008.

[4.124]
5 Ascertainment of the wishes of a person specified in regulation 3

(1) A company may not send a summary financial statement to a person specified in regulation 3 unless the company has ascertained that the person does not wish to receive copies of its full accounts and reports, and paragraphs (2) and (3) apply for the ascertainment of whether or not such a person wishes to receive copies of the full accounts and reports for a financial year.

(2) Where a person specified in regulation 3 has expressly notified the company either that he wishes to receive copies of the full accounts and reports or that he wishes, instead of copies of those documents, to receive summary financial statements, the company must send copies of the full accounts and reports or summary financial statement, as appropriate, to that person in respect of the financial years to which the notification applies.

(3) Where there has been no such express notification to the company by such a person, that person may be taken to have elected to receive summary financial statements if he fails to respond to an opportunity to elect to receive copies of the full accounts and reports given to him either—

    (a) by a consultation notice under regulation 6, or

    (b) as part of a relevant consultation of his wishes by the company under regulation 7.

(4) For the purposes of paragraph (2) a notification has effect in relation to a financial year if it relates to that year (whether or not it has been given at the invitation of the company) and if it has been received by the company not later than 28 days before the first date on which copies of the full accounts and reports for that year are sent to the persons specified in regulation 3 in accordance with section 423 of the 2006 Act.

NOTES
Commencement: 6 April 2008.

[4.125]
6 Consultation by notice

(1) A consultation notice under this regulation is notice given by a company to a person specified in regulation 3 which—

(a) states that for the future, so long as he is a person so specified, he will be sent a summary financial statement for each financial year instead of a copy of the company's full accounts and reports, unless he notifies the company that he wishes to receive full accounts and reports,

(b) states that the summary financial statement for a financial year will contain a summary of the company's or group's profit and loss account, balance sheet and, in the case of a quoted company, directors' remuneration report for that year, and may contain additional information derived from the directors' report,

(c) states that the card or form accompanying the notice in accordance with regulation 8(3) must be returned by a date specified in the notice, being a date at least 21 days after service of the notice and not less than 28 days before the first date on which copies of the full accounts and reports for the next financial year for which that person is entitled to receive them are sent out to persons specified in regulation 3 in accordance with section 423 of the 2006 Act,

(d) includes a statement in a prominent position to the effect that a summary financial statement will not contain sufficient information to allow as full an understanding of the results and state of affairs of the company or group as would be provided by the full annual accounts and reports and that persons specified in regulation 3 requiring more detailed information have the right to obtain, free of charge, a copy of the company's last full accounts and reports.

(2) In the case of an unquoted company the notice must also state that the summary financial statement will—

(a) contain a statement by the company's auditor of his opinion as to whether the summary financial statement—

    (i) is consistent with the company's annual accounts and, where information derived from the directors' report is included in the statement, with that report, and

    (ii) complies with the requirements of section 427 of the 2006 Act (form and contents of summary financial statement: unquoted companies) and of these Regulations;

(b) state whether the auditor's report on the annual accounts was unqualified or qualified.

(3) In the case of a quoted company the notice must also state that the summary financial statement will—

(a) contain a statement by the company's auditor of his opinion as to whether the summary financial statement—

    (i) is consistent with the company's annual accounts and the directors' remuneration report and, where information derived from the directors' report is included in the statement, with that report, and

    (ii) complies with the requirements of section 428 of the 2006 Act (form and contents of summary financial statement: quoted companies) and of these Regulations;

(b) state whether the auditor's report on the annual accounts was unqualified or qualified.

NOTES
Commencement: 6 April 2008.

[4.126]
7 Relevant consultation

(1) A company may conduct a relevant consultation to ascertain the wishes of a person specified in regulation 3.

(2) For the purposes of this regulation, a relevant consultation of the wishes of such a person is a notice given to that person which—

(a) states that for the future, so long as he is a person specified in regulation 3, he will be sent a summary financial statement instead of the full accounts and reports of the company, unless he notifies the company that he wishes to continue to receive full accounts and reports;

(b) accompanies a copy of the full accounts and reports; and

(c) accompanies a copy of a summary financial statement, prepared in accordance with section 426 of the 2006 Act, and sections 427 and 428 of that Act, as appropriate, and these Regulations, with respect to the financial year covered by those full accounts and reports and which is identified in the notice as an example of the document which that person will receive for the future, so long as he is a person specified in regulation 3, unless he notifies the company to the contrary.

NOTES
Commencement: 6 April 2008.

[4.127]
8   Supplementary provisions for Part 2

(1)   Subject to any requirement or contrary provision of this Part the company communications provisions of the 2006 Act apply to any notice or other communication required or authorised to be sent to or by the company by any provision in this Part.

(2)   This regulation and regulations 5, 6 and 7 apply to a person who is entitled, whether conditionally or unconditionally, to become a person specified in section 423(1) of the 2006 Act in relation to the company, but who has not yet become such a person, as they apply to a person specified in regulation 3.

(3)   Subject to paragraph (4), a notice given under regulation 6 or 7 must be accompanied by a card or form—

    (a)   in respect of which, in the case of a card or form sent by post, any postage necessary for its return to the company has been, or will be, paid by the company, and

    (b)   which is so worded as to enable a person specified in regulation 3, by marking a box and returning the card or form, to notify the company that he wishes to receive full accounts and reports for the next financial year for which he is entitled to receive them as such a person and for all future financial years after that.

(4)   The company need not pay the postage in respect of the return of the card or form in the following circumstances—

    (a)   if the address of a member to which notices are sent in accordance with the company's constitution is not within an EEA State,

    (b)   if the address of a debenture holder to which notices are sent in accordance with the terms of any instrument constituting or otherwise governing the debentures of which he is a holder is not within an EEA State, or

    (c)   if the address of a person to whom paragraph (2) applies to which notices are sent, in accordance with the contractual provisions under which he has a right (conditionally or unconditionally) to become a person specified in section 423(1) of the 2006 Act, is not within an EEA State.

NOTES

Commencement: 6 April 2008.

PART 3
FORM AND CONTENT OF SUMMARY FINANCIAL STATEMENT

[4.128]
9   Provisions applying to all companies and groups

(1)   Every summary financial statement issued by a company in place of the full accounts and reports must comply with this regulation.

(2)   The summary financial statement must state the name of the person who signed it on behalf of the board.

(3)   The summary financial statement of a company the directors of which do not prepare group accounts under Part 15 of the 2006 Act must include a statement in a prominent position to the effect that the summary financial statement does not contain sufficient information to allow as full an understanding of the results and state of affairs of the company, and of its policies and arrangements concerning directors' remuneration (where appropriate) as would be provided by the full annual accounts and reports, and that persons specified in regulation 3 requiring more detailed information have the right to obtain, free of charge, a copy of the company's last full accounts and reports.

(4)   The summary financial statement of a company the directors of which prepare group accounts under Part 15 of the 2006 Act must include a statement in a prominent position to the effect that the summary financial statement does not contain sufficient information to allow as full an understanding of the results of the group and state of affairs of the company or of the group, and of their policies and arrangements concerning directors' remuneration (where appropriate) as would be provided by the full annual accounts and reports, and that persons specified in regulation 3 requiring more detailed information have the right to obtain, free of charge, a copy of the company's last full accounts and reports.

(5)   The summary financial statement must contain a clear, conspicuous statement—

    (a)   of how persons specified in regulation 3 can obtain, free of charge, a copy of the company's last full accounts and reports, and

    (b)   of how such persons may elect to receive full accounts and reports in place of summary financial statements for all future financial years.

(6)   The summary financial statement must contain the whole of, or a summary of, that portion of the notes to the accounts for the financial year in question which sets out the information required by paragraph 1 of Schedule 3 to the Small Companies Accounts Regulations or paragraph 1 of Schedule 5 to the Large and Medium-sized Companies Accounts Regulations, as the case may be (total amount of directors' remuneration etc).

(7) The summary financial statement must contain the information prescribed in relation to the company by the provisions of this Part of the Regulations which apply to the company in such order, and under such headings, as the directors consider appropriate.

(8) The summary financial statement must contain any other information necessary to ensure that the statement is consistent with the full accounts and reports for the financial year in question.

NOTES
Commencement: 6 April 2008.

[4.129]
10 Provisions applying only to certain types of company

(1) The summary financial statement of a company having certain securities publicly traded as specified in paragraph 13 of Schedule 7 to the Large and Medium-sized Companies Accounts Regulations (disclosure required by certain publicly-traded companies) must—
    (a)   include in the statement the explanatory material required to be included in the directors' report by paragraph 14 of that Schedule, or
    (b)   send that material to the person receiving the summary financial statement at the same time as it sends the statement.

(2) The summary financial statement of a quoted company must contain the whole of, or a summary of, those portions of the directors' remuneration report for the financial year in question which set out the matters required by paragraphs 3 (statement of company's policy on directors' remuneration) and 5 (performance graph) of Schedule 8 to the Large and Medium-sized Companies Accounts Regulations.

NOTES
Commencement: 6 April 2008.

[4.130]
11 Contents of summary financial statements

(1) Subject to regulations 9 and 10, the summary financial statement of a company must be in such form, and contain such information, as is prescribed in relation to that company in the following paragraphs of this regulation so far as applicable to that company.

(2) The summary financial statement of a company (other than a banking or insurance company) the directors of which—
    (a)   do not prepare group accounts under Part 15 of the 2006 Act, and
    (b)   prepare Companies Act individual accounts under section 396 of the 2006 Act,
must comply with Schedule 1 to these Regulations.

(3) The summary financial statement of a banking company the directors of which—
    (a)   do not prepare group accounts under Part 15 of the 2006 Act, and
    (b)   prepare Companies Act individual accounts under section 396 of the 2006 Act,
must comply with Schedule 2 to these Regulations.

(4) The summary financial statement of an insurance company the directors of which—
    (a)   do not prepare group accounts under Part 15 of the 2006 Act, and
    (b)   prepare Companies Act individual accounts under section 396 of the 2006 Act,
must comply with Schedule 3 to these Regulations.

(5) The summary financial statement of a parent company (other than the parent company of a banking or insurance group) the directors of which prepare Companies Act group accounts under section 403 of the 2006 Act (group accounts: applicable accounting framework), must comply with Schedule 4 to these Regulations.

(6) The summary financial statement of the parent company of a banking group the directors of which prepare Companies Act group accounts under section 403 of the 2006 Act, must comply with Schedule 5 to these Regulations.

(7) The summary financial statement of the parent company of an insurance group the directors of which prepare Companies Act group accounts under section 403 of the 2006 Act, must comply with Schedule 6 to these Regulations.

(8) Where the directors of a company do not prepare group accounts but prepare IAS individual accounts, the provisions of Schedule 7 to these Regulations apply to the company's summary financial statement.

(9) Where the directors of a company prepare IAS group accounts the provisions of Schedule 8 to these Regulations apply to the company's summary financial statement.

NOTES
Commencement: 6 April 2008.

PART 4
SUPPLEMENTARY PROVISIONS

[4.131]
12   Revocation, transitionals and saving

(1)   Subject to paragraph (2), the Companies (Summary Financial Statement) Regulations 1995 and the Companies (Summary Financial Statement) Regulations (Northern Ireland) 1996 are revoked.

(2)   The Companies (Summary Financial Statement) Regulations 1995 and the Companies (Summary Financial Statement) Regulations (Northern Ireland) 1996 continue to apply in relation to financial years beginning before 6th April 2008.

(3)   Paragraph (4) has effect in relation to the ascertainment of the wishes of any person for the purposes of section 426 of the 2006 Act and these Regulations.

(4)   So far as anything done under or for the purposes of any provision of either the Companies (Summary Financial Statement) Regulations 1995 or the Companies (Summary Financial Statement) Regulations (Northern Ireland) 1996 could have been done under or for the purposes of the corresponding provision of these Regulations, it is not invalidated by the revocation of that provision but has effect as if done under or for the purposes of the corresponding provision.

NOTES
Commencement: 6 April 2008.

SCHEDULES

SCHEDULE 1
FORM AND CONTENT OF SUMMARY FINANCIAL STATEMENT OF COMPANY PREPARING COMPANIES ACT INDIVIDUAL ACCOUNTS (OTHER THAN A BANKING OR INSURANCE COMPANY)
Regulation 11(2)

[4.132]
1   Summary profit and loss account

(1)   The summary financial statement must contain a summary profit and loss account showing, in so far as they may be derived from the full profit and loss account, the items, or combinations of items, listed in sub-paragraph (3), in the order set out in that sub-paragraph.

(2)   The items or combinations of items listed in sub-paragraph (3) may appear under such headings as the directors consider appropriate.

(3)   The items, or combinations of items, referred to in sub-paragraph (1) are—
  (a) turnover—
    (i)   format 1, item 1
    (ii)   format 2, item 1
    (iii) format 3, item B1
    (iv) format 4, item B1;
  (b) income from shares in group undertakings and participating interests; the combination of the following two items—
    (i)   format 1, items 7 and 8
    (ii)   format 2, items 9 and 10
    (iii) format 3, items B3 and B4
    (iv) format 4, items B5 and B6;
  (c) other interest receivable and similar income and interest payable and similar charges; the net figure resulting from the combination of the following two items—
    (i)   format 1, items 10 and 12
    (ii)   format 2, items 12 and 14
    (iii) format 3, items B6 and A5
    (iv) format 4, items B8 and A7;
  (d) the profit or loss on ordinary activities before taxation;
  (e) tax on profit or loss on ordinary activities—
    (i)   format 1, item 13
    (ii)   format 2, item 15
    (iii) format 3, item A6
    (iv) format 4, item A8;
  (f) profit or loss on ordinary activities after taxation—
    (i)   format 1, item 14
    (ii)   format 2, item 16
    (iii) format 3, item A7 or B7
    (iv) format 4, item A9 or B9;
  (g) extraordinary income and charges after tax; the net figure resulting from the combination of the following items—

      (i)   format 1, items 17 and 18
      (ii)   format 2, items 19 and 20
      (iii) format 3, items A8, A9 and B8
      (iv) format 4, items A10, A11 and B10; and
  (h) profit or loss for the financial year—
      (i)   format 1, item 20
      (ii)   format 2, item 22
      (iii) format 3, item A11 or B9
      (iv) format 4, item A13 or B11.

2 Dividends

The summary financial statement must also contain the information concerning recognized and proposed dividends included in the full accounts and reports.

3 Summary balance sheet

(1) The summary financial statement must contain a summary balance sheet.

(2) Subject to sub-paragraphs (3) and (4), the summary balance sheet must show, in so far as it can be derived from the full balance sheet and under such heading as the directors consider appropriate, a single amount for each of the headings to which letters are assigned in the balance sheet format which has been used for the full balance sheet (where necessary by the combination of the items to which Roman and Arabic numbers are assigned under those headings) in the order set out in the full balance sheet.

(3) Where an alternative position is permitted for any item in the balance sheet format used, the summary balance sheet must use the position used by the full balance sheet.

(4) Where the full balance sheet used is format 2 in Schedule 1 to the Small Companies Accounts Regulations or format 2 in Schedule 1 to the Large and Medium-sized Companies Accounts Regulations, then in the case of heading C under "Liabilities" two figures must be shown, one figure for amounts falling due within one year and one for amounts falling due after one year.

4 Corresponding amounts

(1) In respect of every item shown in the summary profit and loss account, or in the summary balance sheet, the corresponding amount must be shown for the immediately preceding financial year.

(2) For the purposes of sub-paragraph (1), "the corresponding amount" is the amount shown in the summary financial statement for that year or which would have been so shown had such a statement been prepared for that year, taking account of any adjustments to corresponding amounts made in the full accounts and reports.

NOTES

  Commencement: 6 April 2008.

SCHEDULE 2
FORM AND CONTENT OF SUMMARY FINANCIAL STATEMENT OF
BANKING COMPANY PREPARING COMPANIES ACT INDIVIDUAL ACCOUNTS

Regulation 11(3)

[4.133]
1 Summary profit and loss account

(1) The summary financial statement must contain a summary profit and loss account showing, in so far as they may be derived from the full profit and loss account, the items, or combinations of items, listed in sub-paragraph (3), in the order set out in that sub-paragraph.

(2) The items or combinations of items listed in sub-paragraph (3) may appear under such headings as the directors consider appropriate.

(3) The items, or combinations of items, referred to in sub-paragraph (1) are—
  (a) interest receivable and payable; the net figure resulting from the combination of the following two items—
      (i)   format 1, items 1 and 2
      (ii)   format 2, items A1 and B1;
  (b) dividend income, fees and commissions receivable and payable, dealing profits or losses and other operating income; the net figure resulting from the combination of the following items—
      (i)   format 1, items 3, 4, 5, 6 and 7
      (ii)   format 2, items A2, A3, B2, B3, B4 and B7;
  (c) administrative expenses, depreciation and amortisation, other operating charges, amounts written off, and adjustments to amounts written off, fixed asset investments; the net figure resulting from the combination of the following items—
      (i)   format 1, items 8, 9, 10, 13 and 14
      (ii)   format 2, items A4, A5, A6, A8 and B6;

(d) provisions and adjustments to provisions; the net figure resulting from the combination of the following two items—
    (i)   format 1, items 11 and 12
    (ii)   format 2, items A7 and B5;

(e) profit or loss on ordinary activities before tax—
    (i)   format 1, item 15
    (ii)   format 2, item A9 or B8;

(f) tax on profit or loss on ordinary activities—
    (i)   format 1, item 16
    (ii)   format 2, item A10;

(g) profit or loss on ordinary activities after tax—
    (i)   format 1, item 17
    (ii)   format 2, item A11 or B9;

(h) extraordinary profit or loss after tax—
    (i)   format 1, item 22
    (ii)   the net figure resulting from the combination of format 2, items A14 and B11;

(i) other taxes not shown under the preceding items—
    (i)   format 1, item 23
    (ii)   format 2, item A15; and

(j) profit or loss for the financial year—
    (i)   format 1, item 24
    (ii)   format 2, item A16 or B12.

2   Dividends

The summary financial statement must also contain the information concerning recognised and proposed dividends included in the full accounts and reports.

3   Summary balance sheet

(1) The summary financial statement must contain a summary balance sheet which must show, in so far as they may be derived from the full balance sheet, the items, or combinations of items, set out in sub-paragraph (2), in the order set out in that sub-paragraph and under such headings as the directors consider appropriate.

(2) The items, or combinations of items, referred to in sub-paragraph (1) are as follows—

(a) cash and balances at central [or post office] banks, treasury bills and other eligible bills— the aggregate of items 1 and 2 under the heading "ASSETS";

(b) loans and advances to banks— item 3 under the heading "ASSETS";

(c) loans and advances to customers— item 4 under the heading "ASSETS";

(d) debt securities [and other fixed income securities], equity shares [and other variable-yield securities], participating interests and shares in group undertakings— the aggregate of items 5, 6, 7 and 8 under the heading "ASSETS";

(e) intangible and tangible fixed assets— the aggregate of items 9 and 10 under the heading "ASSETS";

(f) called up capital not paid, own shares, other assets, prepayments and accrued income— the aggregate of items 11 (or 14), 12, 13 and 15 under the heading "ASSETS";

(g) total assets under the heading "ASSETS";

(h) deposits by banks— item 1 under the heading "LIABILITIES";

(i) customer accounts— item 2 under the heading "LIABILITIES";

(j) debt securities in issue— item 3 under the heading "LIABILITIES";

(k) other liabilities, accruals and deferred income and provisions for liabilities and charges— the aggregate of items 4, 5 and 6 under the heading "LIABILITIES";

(l) subordinated liabilities— item 7 under the heading "LIABILITIES";

(m) called up share capital, share premium account, reserves, revaluation reserve and profit and loss account— the aggregate of items 8, 9, 10, 11 and 12 under the heading "LIABILITIES";

(n) total liabilities under the heading "LIABILITIES";

(o) contingent liabilities— item 1 under the heading "MEMORANDUM ITEMS", and

(p) commitments— item 2 under the heading "MEMORANDUM ITEMS".

4 Corresponding amounts

(1) In respect of every item shown in the summary profit and loss account, or in the summary balance sheet, the corresponding amount must be shown for the immediately preceding financial year.

(2) For the purposes of sub-paragraph (1), "the corresponding amount" is the amount shown in the summary financial statement for that year or which would have been so shown had such a statement been prepared for that year, taking account of any adjustments to corresponding amounts made in the full account and reports.

NOTES

Commencement: 6 April 2008.

SCHEDULE 3
FORM AND CONTENT OF SUMMARY FINANCIAL STATEMENT OF INSURANCE COMPANY PREPARING COMPANIES ACT INDIVIDUAL ACCOUNTS
Regulation 11(4)

[4.134]
1 Summary profit and loss account

(1) The summary financial statement must contain a summary profit and loss account showing, in so far as they may be derived from the full profit and loss account, the items, or combinations of items, listed in sub-paragraph (3), in the order set out in that sub-paragraph.

(2) The items or combinations of items listed in sub-paragraph (3) may appear under such headings as the directors consider appropriate.

(3) The items, or combinations of items referred to in sub-paragraph (1) are—
- (a) gross premiums written-general business— item I 1(a);
- (b) gross premiums written-long term business— item II 1(a);
- (c) balance on the technical account for general business— item I 10;
- (d) balance on the technical account for long term business— item II 13;
- (e) other income and charges; the net figure resulting from the combination of the following items—
  - (i) item III 3
  - (ii) item III 3a
  - (iii) item III 4
  - (iv) item III 5
  - (v) item III 5a
  - (vi) item III 6
  - (vii) item III 7
  - (viii) item III 8;
- (f) the profit or loss on ordinary activities before tax— item III 8a;
- (g) tax on profit or loss on ordinary activities— item III 9;
- (h) profit or loss on ordinary activities after tax— item III 10;
- (i) extraordinary profit or loss after tax— the net figure resulting from the combination of items III 13 and 14;
- (j) other taxes— item III 15; and
- (k) profit or loss for the financial year— item III 16.

2 Dividends

The summary financial statement must also contain the information concerning recognized and proposed dividends included in the full accounts and reports.

3 Summary balance sheet

(1) The summary financial statement must contain a summary balance sheet which must show, in so far as they may be derived from the full balance sheet, the items, or combinations of items, set out in sub-paragraph (2) in the order of that sub-paragraph and under such headings as the directors consider appropriate.

(2) The items, or combinations of items, referred to in sub-paragraph (1) are—
- (a) investments— the aggregate of items C and D under the heading "ASSETS";

(b)   reinsurers' share of technical provisions—
        item Da under the heading "ASSETS";

(c)   other assets—
        the aggregate of items A or E(IV), B, E(I) to (III), F and G under the heading "ASSETS";

(d)   total assets under the heading "ASSETS";

(e)   capital and reserves—
        item A under the heading "LIABILITIES";

(f)   subordinated liabilities—
        item B under the heading "LIABILITIES";

(g)   fund for future appropriations—
        item Ba under the heading "LIABILITIES";

(h)   gross technical provisions—
        the aggregate of items C1(a), C2(a), C3(a), C4(a), C5, C6(a) and D(a) under the heading "LIABILITIES";

(i)   technical provisions-reinsurance amounts—
        the aggregate of items C1(b), C2(b), C3(b), C4(b), C6(b) and D(b) under the heading "LIABILITIES";

(j)   other liabilities—
        the aggregate of items E, F, G and H under the heading "LIABILITIES"; and

(k)   total liabilities under the heading "LIABILITIES".

4 Corresponding amounts

(1)   In respect of every item shown in the summary profit and loss account, or in the summary balance sheet, the corresponding amount must be shown for the immediately preceding financial year.

(2)   For the purposes of sub-paragraph (1), "the corresponding amount" is the amount shown in the summary financial statement for that year or which would have been so shown had such a statement been prepared for that year, taking account of any adjustments to corresponding amounts made in the full accounts and reports.

NOTES

Commencement: 6 April 2008.

SCHEDULE 4
FORM AND CONTENT OF SUMMARY FINANCIAL STATEMENT OF PARENT COMPANY PREPARING COMPANIES ACT GROUP ACCOUNTS (OTHER THAN BANKING OR INSURANCE GROUP ACCOUNTS)

Regulation 11(5)

[4.135]
1 Summary profit and loss account

(1)   The summary financial statement must contain a summary consolidated profit and loss account showing the items or combinations of items required by paragraph 1 of Schedule 1 to these Regulations in the order required by that paragraph and under such headings as the directors consider appropriate, but with the modifications specified in sub-paragraph (3).

(2)   The summary financial statement must also contain the information required by paragraph 2 of Schedule 1 to these Regulations.

(3)   The modifications referred to in sub-paragraph (1) are as follows—

(a)   in place of the information required by paragraph 1(3)(b) of Schedule 1 to these Regulations, there must be shown, under such heading as the directors consider appropriate, the item "Income from interests in associated undertakings" required to be shown—

    (i)   in the profit and loss account formats in Part 1 of Schedule 1 to the Small Companies Accounts Regulations by paragraph 1(3) of Schedule 6 to those Regulations (Companies Act: group accounts), or

    (ii) in the profit and loss account formats in Part 1 of Schedule 1 to the Large and Medium-sized Companies Accounts Regulations, by paragraph 20(3) of Schedule 6 to those Regulations (Companies Act: group accounts);

(b)   between the information required by paragraph 1(3)(f) and that required by paragraph 1(3)(g) of Schedule 1 to these Regulations there must in addition be shown, under such heading as the directors consider appropriate, the item required to be shown—

    (i)   in the profit and loss account formats in Part 1 of Schedule 1 to the Small Companies Accounts Regulations by paragraph 17(3)(a) of Schedule 6 to those Regulations (minority interests), or

    (ii) in the profit and loss account formats in Part 1 of Schedule 1 to the Large and Medium-sized Companies Accounts Regulations, by paragraph 17(3)(a) of Schedule 6 to those Regulations (minority interests); and

(c) the figure required by paragraph 1(3)(g) of Schedule 1 to these Regulations must be shown after the deduction or the addition (as the case may be) of the item required to be shown—

    (i) in the profit and loss account formats in Part 1 of Schedule 1 to the Small Companies Accounts Regulations by paragraph 17(3)(b) of Schedule 6 to those Regulations (minority interests), or

    (ii) in the profit and loss account formats in Part 1 of Schedule 1 to the Large and Medium-sized Companies Accounts Regulations, by paragraph 17(3)(b) of Schedule 6 to those Regulations (minority interests).

2 Summary balance sheet

The summary financial statement must contain a summary consolidated balance sheet showing the items required by paragraph 3 of Schedule 1 to these Regulations in the order required by that paragraph and under such headings as the directors consider appropriate, but with the addition of the item required to be inserted—

(a) by paragraph 17(2) of Schedule 6 to the Small Companies Accounts Regulations (minority interests), or

(b) by paragraph 17(2) of Schedule 6 to the Large and Medium-sized Companies Accounts Regulations (minority interests).

3 Corresponding amounts

(1) In respect of every item shown in the summary consolidated profit and loss account, or in the summary consolidated balance sheet, the corresponding amount must be shown for the immediately preceding financial year.

(2) For the purposes of sub-paragraph (1), "the corresponding amount" is the amount shown in the summary financial statement for that year or which would have been so shown had such a statement been prepared for that year, taking account of any adjustments to corresponding amounts made in the full accounts and reports.

NOTES

Commencement: 6 April 2008.

SCHEDULE 5
FORM AND CONTENT OF SUMMARY FINANCIAL STATEMENT OF PARENT COMPANY OF BANKING GROUP PREPARING COMPANIES ACT GROUP ACCOUNTS

Regulation 11(6)

[4.136]
1 Summary profit and loss account

(1) The summary financial statement must contain a summary consolidated profit and loss account showing the items, or combinations of items, required by paragraph 1 of Schedule 2 to these Regulations, in the order required by that paragraph and under such headings as the directors consider appropriate, but with the modifications specified in sub-paragraph (3).

(2) The summary financial statement must also contain the information required by paragraph 2 of Schedule 2 to these Regulations.

(3) The modifications referred to in sub-paragraph (1) are as follows—

(a) between the information required by paragraph 1(3)(d) and that required by paragraph 1(3)(e) of Schedule 2 to these Regulations there must in addition be shown, under such heading as the directors consider appropriate, the item "Income from associated undertakings" required to be shown in the profit and loss account formats in Schedule 2 to the Large and Medium-sized Companies Accounts Regulations (banking companies: Companies Act individual accounts) by paragraph 25(4)(ii) of Schedule 6 to those Regulations;

(b) between the information required by paragraph 1(3)(g) and that required by paragraph 1(3)(h) of Schedule 2 to these Regulations there must in addition be shown, under such heading as the directors consider appropriate, the item required to be shown in the formats in Schedule 2 to the Large and Medium-sized Companies Accounts Regulations by paragraph 17(3)(a) of Schedule 6 to those Regulations (minority interests) as applied by paragraph 25 of Schedule 6 to those Regulations; and

(c) the figures required by paragraph 1(3)(h) and (i) of Schedule 2 to these Regulations must each be shown after the deduction or the addition (as the case may be) of the item required to be shown in the formats in Schedule 2 to the Large and Medium-sized Companies Accounts Regulations by paragraph 17(3)(b) of Schedule 6 to those Regulations (minority interests) as applied by paragraph 25 of Schedule 6 to those Regulations.

2   Summary balance sheet

(1)   The summary financial statement must contain a summary consolidated balance sheet showing the items required by paragraph 3 of Schedule 2 to these Regulations, in the order required by that paragraph and under such headings as the directors consider appropriate, but with the addition specified in sub-paragraph (2).

(2)   Between the items required by paragraph 3(2)(1) and (m) or after the item required by paragraph 3(2)(m) (whichever is the position adopted for the full accounts), there must in addition be shown under an appropriate heading the item required to be shown in the balance sheet format in Schedule 2 to the Large and Medium-sized Companies Accounts Regulations by paragraph 17(2) of Schedule 6 to those Regulations (minority interests) as applied by paragraph 25 in Part 2 of Schedule 6 to those Regulations.

3   Corresponding amounts

(1)   In respect of every item shown in the summary consolidated profit and loss account, or in the summary consolidated balance sheet, the corresponding amount must be shown for the immediately preceding financial year.

(2)   For the purposes of sub-paragraph (1), "the corresponding amount" is the amount shown in the summary financial statement for that year or which would have been so shown had such a statement been prepared for that year, taking account of any adjustments to corresponding accounts made in the full accounts and reports.

NOTES

Commencement: 6 April 2008.

SCHEDULE 6

FORM AND CONTENT OF SUMMARY FINANCIAL STATEMENT OF PARENT COMPANY OF INSURANCE GROUP PREPARING COMPANIES ACT GROUP ACCOUNTS

Regulation 11(7)

[4.137]

1   Summary profit and loss account

(1)   The summary financial statement must contain a summary consolidated profit and loss account showing the items, or combinations of items, required by paragraph 1 of Schedule 3 to these Regulations, in the order required by that paragraph and under such headings as the directors consider appropriate, but with the modifications specified in sub-paragraph (3).

(2)   The summary financial statement must also contain the information required by paragraph 2 of that Schedule.

(3)   The modifications referred to in sub-paragraph (1) are as follows—

    (a)   between the information required by paragraph 1(3)(e) and that required by paragraph 1(3)(f) of Schedule 3 to these Regulations there must in addition be shown, under such heading as the directors consider appropriate, the item "Income from associated undertakings" required to be shown in the profit and loss account formats in Schedule 3 to the Large and Medium-sized Companies Accounts Regulations (insurance companies: Companies Act individual accounts) by paragraph 20(3)(b) of Schedule 6 to those Regulations as substituted by paragraph 37 of Schedule 6 to those Regulations;

    (b)   between the information required by paragraph 1(3)(h) and that required by paragraph 1(3)(i) of Schedule 3 to these Regulations there must in addition be shown, under such heading as the directors consider appropriate, the item required to be shown in the profit and loss account formats in Schedule 3 to the Large and Medium-sized Companies Accounts Regulations by paragraph 17(3)(a) of Schedule 6 to those Regulations (minority interests) as applied by paragraph 36 of Schedule 6 to those Regulations; and

    (c)   the figures required by paragraph 1(3)(i) and (j) of Schedule 3 to these Regulations must each be shown after the deduction or the addition (as the case may be) of the item required to be shown in the profit and loss account formats in Schedule 3 to the Large and Medium-sized Companies Accounts Regulations by paragraph 17(3)(b) of Schedule 6 to those Regulations (minority interests) as applied by paragraph 36 of Schedule 6 to those Regulations.

2   Summary balance sheet

(1)   The summary financial statement must contain a summary consolidated balance sheet showing the items required by paragraph 3 of Schedule 3 to these Regulations, in the order required by that paragraph and under such headings as the directors consider appropriate, but with the addition of the item specified in sub-paragraph (2).

(2) Between the items required by paragraph 3(2)(d) and (e) of Schedule 3 to these Regulations, there must in addition be shown under an appropriate heading the item required to be shown in the balance sheet format in Schedule 3 to the Large and Medium-sized Companies Accounts Regulations by paragraph 17(2) of Schedule 6 to those Regulations (minority interests), as applied by paragraph 36 of Schedule 6 to those Regulations.

3 Corresponding amounts

(1) In respect of every item shown in the summary consolidated profit and loss account, or in the summary consolidated balance sheet, the corresponding amount must be shown for the immediately preceding financial year.

(2) For the purposes of sub-paragraph (1), "the corresponding amount" is the amount shown in the summary financial statement for that year or which would have been so shown had such a statement been prepared for that year, taking account of any adjustments to corresponding amounts made in the full accounts and reports.

NOTES

Commencement: 6 April 2008.

SCHEDULE 7
FORM AND CONTENT OF SUMMARY FINANCIAL STATEMENT OF COMPANY PREPARING IAS INDIVIDUAL ACCOUNTS

Regulation 11(8)

[4.138]
1 Summary profit and loss account

(1) The summary financial statement must contain a summary profit and loss account showing either—

    (a)   each of the headings and sub-totals included in the full profit and loss account in accordance with international accounting standards, or

    (b)   where the directors consider it appropriate, a combination of such headings and sub-totals where they are of a similar nature.

(2) The summary financial statement must also contain the information concerning recognised and proposed dividends included in the full accounts and reports.

(3) In this paragraph and in paragraph 2, the expressions "headings" and "subtotals" have the same meaning as in international accounting standard 1 on the presentation of financial statements.

2 Summary balance sheet

The summary financial statement must contain a summary balance sheet showing either—

    (a)   each of the headings and sub-totals included in the full balance sheet in accordance with international accounting standards, or

    (b)   where the directors consider it appropriate, a combination of such headings and sub-totals where they are of a similar nature.

3 Corresponding amounts

(1) In respect of every item shown in the summary profit and loss account, or in the summary balance sheet, the corresponding amount must be shown for the immediately preceding financial year.

(2) For the purposes of sub-paragraph (1), "the corresponding amount" is the amount shown in the summary financial statement for that year or which would have been so shown had such a statement been prepared for that year, taking account of any adjustments to corresponding amounts made in the full accounts and reports.

NOTES

Commencement: 6 April 2008.

SCHEDULE 8
FORM AND CONTENT OF SUMMARY FINANCIAL STATEMENT OF COMPANY PREPARING IAS GROUP ACCOUNTS

Regulation 11(9)

[4.139]
1 Summary profit and loss account

(1) The summary financial statement must contain a summary consolidated profit and loss account showing either—

    (a)   each of the headings and sub-totals included in the full consolidated profit and loss account in accordance with international accounting standards, or

    (b)   where the directors consider it appropriate, a combination of such headings and sub-totals where they are of a similar nature.

(2)   The summary financial statement must also contain the information concerning recognised and proposed dividends included in the full accounts and reports.

(3)   In this paragraph and in paragraph 2, the expressions "headings" and "subtotals" have the same meaning as in international accounting standard 1 on the presentation of financial statements.

2   Summary balance sheet

The summary financial statement must contain a summary consolidated balance sheet showing either—

(a)   each of the headings and sub-totals included in the full consolidated balance sheet in accordance with international accounting standards, or

(b)   where the directors consider it appropriate, a combination of such headings and sub-totals where they are of a similar nature.

3   Corresponding amounts

(1)   In respect of every item shown in the summary consolidated profit and loss account, or in the summary consolidated balance sheet, the corresponding amount must be shown for the immediately preceding financial year.

(2)   For the purposes of sub-paragraph (1), "the corresponding amount" is the amount shown in the summary financial statement for that year or which would have been so shown had such a statement been prepared for that year, taking account of any adjustments to corresponding amounts made in the full accounts and reports.

NOTES
Commencement: 6 April 2008.

COMPANIES ACT 2006 (AMENDMENT) (ACCOUNTS AND REPORTS) REGULATIONS 2008

(SI 2008/393)

NOTES
Made: 19 February 2008.
Authority: Companies Act 2006, ss 468(1), (2), 473(2), 484, 1292(1)(a), (c).
Commencement: 6 April 2008.
Amendment: as of 1 July 2011 these Regulations had not been amended.

PART 1
INTRODUCTION

[4.140]
1   Citation and interpretation

(1)   These Regulations may be cited as the Companies Act 2006 (Amendment) (Accounts and Reports) Regulations 2008.

(2)   In these Regulations "the 2006 Act" means the Companies Act 2006.

NOTES
Commencement: 6 April 2008.

[4.141]
2   Commencement and application

(1)   These Regulations come into force on 6th April 2008.

(2)   They apply in relation to financial years beginning on or after 6th April 2008.

(3)   In determining whether a company or group qualifies as small or medium-sized under section 382(2), 383(3), 465(2) or 466(3) of the 2006 Act (qualification in relation to subsequent financial year by reference to circumstances in preceding financial years) in relation to a financial year ending on or after 6th April 2008, the company or group shall be treated as having qualified as small or medium-sized (as the case may be) in any previous financial year in which it would have so qualified if amendments to the same effect as those made by these Regulations had been in force.

NOTES
Commencement: 6 April 2008.

3–13   *((Pts 2–4) contain various amendments to Pts 15 and 16 of the Companies Act 2006 (at* **[1.380]** *and* **[1.475]** *respectively).)*

SMALL COMPANIES AND GROUPS (ACCOUNTS AND DIRECTORS' REPORT) REGULATIONS 2008

(SI 2008/409)

NOTES

Made: 19 February 2008.

Authority: Companies Act 2006, ss 396(3), 404(3), 409(1), (3), 412(1), (3), 416(4), 444(3)(a), (b), 677(3)(a), 712(2)(b)(i), 836(1)(b)(i), 1292(1)(a), (c).

Commencement: 6 April 2008.

These Regulations are reproduced as amended by: the Partnerships (Accounts) Regulations 2008, SI 2008/569; the Companies Act 2006 (Accounts, Reports and Audit) Regulations 2009, SI 2009/1581.

Application to limited liability partnerships: see the Limited Liability Partnerships (Accounts and Audit) (Application of Companies Act 2006) Regulations 2008, SI 2008/1911 at **[10.1003]**, and the Small Limited Liability Partnerships (Accounts) Regulations 2008, SI 2008/1912 at **[10.1061]**.

Application to partnerships: see the Partnerships (Accounts) Regulations 2008, SI 2008/569 at **[10.984]**.

ARRANGEMENT OF REGULATIONS

PART 1
INTRODUCTION

[4.142]
1   Citation and interpretation

(1)   These Regulations may be cited as the Small Companies and Groups (Accounts and Directors' Report) Regulations 2008.

(2)   In these Regulations "the 2006 Act" means the Companies Act 2006.

NOTES
Commencement: 6 April 2008.

[4.143]
2   Commencement and application

(1)   These Regulations come into force on 6th April 2008.

(2)   They apply in relation to financial years beginning on or after 6th April 2008.

(3)   They apply to companies which are subject to the small companies regime under Part 15 of the 2006 Act (see section 381 of that Act).

NOTES
Commencement: 6 April 2008.

PART 2
FORM AND CONTENT OF INDIVIDUAL ACCOUNTS

[4.144]
3   Companies Act individual accounts

(1)   Companies Act individual accounts under section 396 of the 2006 Act (Companies Act: individual accounts) must comply with the provisions of Schedule 1 to these Regulations as to the form and content of the balance sheet and profit and loss account, and additional information to be provided by way of notes to the accounts.

(2)   The profit and loss account of a company that falls within section 408 of the 2006 Act (individual profit and loss account where group accounts prepared) need not contain the information specified in paragraphs 59 to 61 of Schedule 1 to these Regulations (information supplementing the profit and loss account).

(3)   Accounts are treated as having complied with any provision of Schedule 1 to these Regulations if they comply instead with the corresponding provision of Schedule 1 to the Large and Medium-Sized Companies and Groups (Accounts and Reports) Regulations 2008.

NOTES
Commencement: 6 April 2008.

[4.145]
4   Information about related undertakings (Companies Act or IAS individual accounts)

(1)   Companies Act or IAS individual accounts must comply with the provisions of Schedule 2 to these Regulations as to information about related undertakings to be given in notes to the company's accounts.

(2)   Information otherwise required to be given by Schedule 2 to these Regulations need not be disclosed with respect to an undertaking that—
    (a)   is established under the law of a country outside the United Kingdom, or
    (b)   carries on business outside the United Kingdom,
if the conditions specified in section 409(4) of the 2006 Act are met (see section 409(5) of the 2006 Act for disclosure required where advantage taken of this exemption).
    This paragraph does not apply in relation to the information required by paragraphs 4 and 8 of Schedule 2 to these Regulations.

NOTES
Commencement: 6 April 2008.

[4.146]
5   Information about directors' benefits: remuneration (Companies Act or IAS individual accounts)

Companies Act or IAS individual accounts must comply with the provisions of Schedule 3 to these Regulations as to information about directors' remuneration to be given in notes to the company's accounts.

NOTES
Commencement: 6 April 2008.

[4.147]
6   Accounts for delivery to registrar of companies (Companies Act individual accounts)

(1)   The directors of a company for which they are preparing Companies Act individual accounts may deliver to the registrar of companies under section 444 of the 2006 Act (filing obligations of companies subject to small companies regime) a copy of a balance sheet which complies with Schedule 4 to these Regulations rather than Schedule 1.

(2)   Companies Act individual accounts delivered to the registrar need not give the information required by—
    (a)   paragraph 4 of Schedule 2 to these Regulations (shares of company held by subsidiary undertakings), or
    (b)   Schedule 3 to these Regulations (directors' benefits).

NOTES
Commencement: 6 April 2008.

PART 3
DIRECTORS' REPORT

[4.148]
7   Directors' report

The report which the directors of a company are required to prepare under section 415 of the 2006 Act (duty to prepare directors' report) must disclose the matters specified in Schedule 5 to these Regulations.

NOTES
Commencement: 6 April 2008.

PART 4
FORM AND CONTENT OF GROUP ACCOUNTS

[4.149]
8   Companies Act group accounts

(1)   Where the directors of a parent company which—
    (a)   is subject to the small companies regime, and
    (b)   has prepared Companies Act individual accounts in accordance with regulation 3,
prepare Companies Act group accounts under section 398 of the 2006 Act (option to prepare group accounts), those accounts must comply with the provisions of Part 1 of Schedule 6 to these Regulations as to the form and content of the consolidated balance sheet and consolidated profit and loss account, and additional information to be provided by way of notes to the accounts.

(2)   Accounts are treated as having complied with any provision of Part 1 of Schedule 6 if they comply instead with the corresponding provision of Schedule 6 to the Large and Medium-Sized Companies and Groups (Accounts and Reports) Regulations 2008.

NOTES
Commencement: 6 April 2008.

[4.150]
9   Information about directors' benefits: remuneration (Companies Act or IAS group accounts)

Companies Act or IAS group accounts must comply with the provisions of Schedule 3 to these Regulations as to information about directors' remuneration to be given in notes to the company's accounts.

NOTES
Commencement: 6 April 2008.

[4.151]
10   Information about related undertakings (Companies Act or IAS group accounts)

(1)   Companies Act or IAS group accounts must comply with the provisions of Part 2 of Schedule 6 to these Regulations as to information about related undertakings to be given in notes to the company's accounts.

(2)   Information otherwise required to be given by Part 2 of Schedule 6 need not be disclosed with respect to an undertaking that—
    (a)   is established under the law of a country outside the United Kingdom, or

(b)   carries on business outside the United Kingdom,

if the conditions specified in section 409(4) of the 2006 Act are met (see section 409(5) of the 2006 Act for disclosure required where advantage taken of this exemption).

This paragraph does not apply in relation to the information required by paragraphs 26 and 35 of Schedule 6 to these Regulations.

NOTES
Commencement: 6 April 2008.

[4.152]
11   Accounts for delivery to registrar of companies (Companies Act group accounts)

Companies Act group accounts delivered to the registrar of companies under section 444 of the 2006 Act need not give the information required by—
(a)   Schedule 3 to these Regulations (directors' benefits), or
(b)   paragraph 25 of Schedule 6 to these Regulations (shares of company held by subsidiary undertakings).

NOTES
Commencement: 6 April 2008.

PART 5
INTERPRETATION

[4.153]
12   Definition of "provisions"

Schedule 7 to these Regulations defines "provisions" for the purpose of these Regulations and for the purposes of—
(a)   section 677(3)(a) (Companies Act accounts: relevant provisions for purposes of financial assistance) in Part 18 of the 2006 Act,
(b)   section 712(2)(b)(i) (Companies Act accounts: relevant provisions to determine available profits for redemption or purchase by private company out of capital) in that Part, . . .
(c)   section 836(1)(b)(i) (Companies Act accounts: relevant provisions for distribution purposes) in Part 23 of that Act[, and
(d)   section 841(2)(a) (Companies Act accounts: provisions to be treated as realised losses) in that Part].

NOTES
Commencement: 6 April 2008.
The word "and" at the end of para (b) was revoked, and para (d) (and the word immediately preceding it) was added, by the Companies Act 2006 (Accounts, Reports and Audit) Regulations 2009, SI 2009/1581, reg 11(1), (2), as from 27 June 2009, in relation to financial years beginning on or after 6 April 2008 which have not ended before 27 June 2009.

[4.154]
13   General interpretation

Schedule 8 to these Regulations contains general definitions for the purposes of these Regulations.

NOTES
Commencement: 6 April 2008.

SCHEDULES

SCHEDULE 1
COMPANIES ACT INDIVIDUAL ACCOUNTS

Regulation 3(1)

PART 1
GENERAL RULES AND FORMATS

SECTION A
GENERAL RULES

[4.155]
1. (1)   Subject to the following provisions of this Schedule—
(a)   every balance sheet of a company must show the items listed in either of the balance sheet formats in Section B of this Part, and
(b)   every profit and loss account must show the items listed in any one of the profit and loss account formats in Section B.

(2)   References in this Schedule to the items listed in any of the formats in Section B are to those items read together with any of the notes following the formats which apply to those items.

(3)   The items must be shown in the order and under the headings and sub-headings given in the particular format used, but—

(a)   the notes to the formats may permit alternative positions for any particular items, and

(b)   the heading or sub-heading for any item does not have to be distinguished by any letter or number assigned to that item in the format used.

2. (1)   Where in accordance with paragraph 1 a company's balance sheet or profit and loss account for any financial year has been prepared by reference to one of the formats in Section B, the company's directors must use the same format in preparing Companies Act individual accounts for subsequent financial years, unless in their opinion there are special reasons for a change.

(2)   Particulars of any such change must be given in a note to the accounts in which the new format is first used, and the reasons for the change must be explained.

3. (1)   Any item required to be shown in a company's balance sheet or profit and loss account may be shown in greater detail than required by the particular format used.

(2)   The balance sheet or profit and loss account may include an item representing or covering the amount of any asset or liability, income or expenditure not otherwise covered by any of the items listed in the format used, save that none of the following may be treated as assets in any balance sheet—

(a)   preliminary expenses,

(b)   expenses of, and commission on, any issue of shares or debentures,

(c)   costs of research.

4. (1)   Where the special nature of the company's business requires it, the company's directors must adapt the arrangement, headings and sub-headings otherwise required in respect of items given an Arabic number in the balance sheet or profit and loss account format used.

(2)   The directors may combine items to which Arabic numbers are given in any of the formats set out in Section B if—

(a)   their individual amounts are not material to assessing the state of affairs or profit or loss of the company for the financial year in question, or

(b)   the combination facilitates that assessment.

(3)   Where sub-paragraph (2)(b) applies, the individual amounts of any items which have been combined must be disclosed in a note to the accounts.

5. (1)   Subject to sub-paragraph (2), the directors must not include a heading or sub-heading corresponding to an item in the balance sheet or profit and loss account format used if there is no amount to be shown for that item for the financial year to which the balance sheet or profit and loss account relates.

(2)   Where an amount can be shown for the item in question for the immediately preceding financial year that amount must be shown under the heading or sub-heading required by the format for that item.

6. Every profit and loss account must show the amount of a company's profit or loss on ordinary activities before taxation.

7. (1)   For every item shown in the balance sheet or profit and loss account the corresponding amount for the immediately preceding financial year must also be shown.

(2)   Where that corresponding amount is not comparable with the amount to be shown for the item in question in respect of the financial year to which the balance sheet or profit and loss account relates, the former amount may be adjusted, and particulars of the non-comparability and of any adjustment must be disclosed in a note to the accounts.

8. Amounts in respect of items representing assets or income may not be set off against amounts in respect of items representing liabilities or expenditure (as the case may be), or vice versa.

9. The company's directors must, in determining how amounts are presented within items in the profit and loss account and balance sheet, have regard to the substance of the reported transaction or arrangement, in accordance with generally accepted accounting principles or practice.

SECTION B
THE REQUIRED FORMATS FOR ACCOUNTS

Balance sheet formats

Format 1

A   Called up share capital not paid [(1)]

B   Fixed assets

  I   Intangible assets

        1   Goodwill [2]
        2   Other intangible assets [3]
   II   Tangible assets
        1   Land and buildings
        2   Plant and machinery etc
   III Investments
        1   Shares in group undertakings and participating interests
        2   Loans to group undertakings and undertakings in which the company has a participating interest
        3   Other investments other than loans
        4   Other investments [4]

C Current assets
   I   Stocks
        1   Stocks
        2   Payments on account
   II   Debtors [5]
        1   Trade debtors
        2   Amounts owed by group undertakings and undertakings in which the company has a participating interest
        3   Other debtors [1]
   III Investments
        1   Shares in group undertakings
        2   Other investments [4]
   IV Cash at bank and in hand

D Prepayments and accrued income [6]

E Creditors: amounts falling due within one year
   1   Bank loans and overdrafts
   2   Trade creditors
   3   Amounts owed to group undertakings and undertakings in which the company has a participating interest
   4   Other creditors [7]

F Net current assets (liabilities) [8]

G Total assets less current liabilities

H Creditors: amounts falling due after more than one year
   1   Bank loans and overdrafts
   2   Trade creditors
   3   Amounts owed to group undertakings and undertakings in which the company has a participating interest
   4   Other creditors [7]

I Provisions for liabilities

J Accruals and deferred income [7]

K Capital and reserves
   I   Called up share capital [9]
   II   Share premium account
   III Revaluation reserve
   IV Other reserves
   V   Profit and loss account

Balance sheet formats

Format 2

ASSETS

A Called up share capital not paid [1]

B Fixed assets
   I   Intangible assets
        1   Goodwill [2]
        2   Other intangible assets [3]
   II   Tangible assets
        1   Land and buildings
        2   Plant and machinery etc

III   Investments
    1   Shares in group undertakings and participating interests
    2   Loans to group undertakings and undertakings in which the company has a participating interest
    3   Other investments other than loans
    4   Other investments [(4)]

C   Current assets
  I   Stocks
    1   Stocks
    2   Payments on account
  II   Debtors [(5)]
    1   Trade debtors
    2   Amounts owed by group undertakings and undertakings in which the company has a participating interest
    3   Other debtors [(1)]
  III   Investments
    1   Shares in group undertakings
    2   Other investments [(4)]
  IV   Cash at bank and in hand

D   Prepayments and accrued income [(6)]

LIABILITIES

A   Capital and reserves
  I   Called up share capital [(9)]
  II   Share premium account
  III   Revaluation reserve
  IV   Other reserves
  V   Profit and loss account

B   Provisions for liabilities

C   Creditors [(10)]
  1   Bank loans and overdrafts
  2   Trade creditors
  3   Amounts owed to group undertakings and undertakings in which the company has a participating interest
  4   Other creditors [(7)]

D   Accruals and deferred income [(7)]

Notes on the balance sheet formats

(1)   Called up share capital not paid

(Formats 1 and 2, items A and C II 3)

This item may either be shown at item A or included under item C II 3 in Format 1 or 2.

(2)   Goodwill

(Formats 1 and 2, item B I 1)

Amounts representing goodwill must only be included to the extent that the goodwill was acquired for valuable consideration.

(3)   Other intangible assets

(Formats 1 and 2, item B I 2)

Amounts in respect of concessions, patents, licences, trade marks and similar rights and assets must only be included in a company's balance sheet under this item if either—
  (a)   the assets were acquired for valuable consideration and are not required to be shown under goodwill, or
  (b)   the assets in question were created by the company itself.

(4)   Others: Other investments

(Formats 1 and 2, items B III 4 and C III 2)

Where amounts in respect of own shares held are included under either of these items, the nominal value of such shares must be shown separately.

(5)   Debtors

(Formats 1 and 2, items C II 1 to 3)

The amount falling due after more than one year must be shown separately for each item included under debtors unless the aggregate amount of debtors falling due after more than one year is disclosed in the notes to the accounts.

(6)   Prepayments and accrued income

(Formats 1 and 2, item D.)

This item may alternatively be included under item C II 3 in Format 1 or 2.

(7)   Other creditors

(Format 1, items E 4, H 4 and J and Format 2, items C 4 and D.)

There must be shown separately—

    (a)   the amount of any convertible loans, and

    (b)   the amount for creditors in respect of taxation and social security.

Payments received on account of orders must be included in so far as they are not shown as deductions from stocks.

In Format 1, accruals and deferred income may be shown under item J or included under item E 4 or H 4, or both (as the case may require). In Format 2, accruals and deferred income may be shown under item D or within item C 4 under Liabilities.

(8)   Net current assets (liabilities)

(Format 1, item F)

In determining the amount to be shown under this item any prepayments and accrued income must be taken into account wherever shown.

(9)   Called up share capital

(Format 1, item K I and Format 2, Liabilities item A I)

The amount of allotted share capital and the amount of called up share capital which has been paid up must be shown separately.

(10)   Creditors

(Format 2, Liabilities items C 1 to 4)

Amounts falling due within one year and after one year must be shown separately for each of these items and for the aggregate of all of these items unless the aggregate amount of creditors falling due within one year and the aggregate amount of creditors falling due after more than one year is disclosed in the notes to the accounts.

Profit and loss account formats

Format 1
(see note (14) below)

1   Turnover

2   Cost of sales[11]

3   Gross profit or loss

4   Distribution costs[11]

5   Administrative expenses[11]

6   Other operating income

7   Income from shares in group undertakings

8   Income from participating interests

9   Income from other fixed asset investments[12]

10   Other interest receivable and similar income[12]

11   Amounts written off investments

12   Interest payable and similar charges[13]

13   Tax on profit or loss on ordinary activities

14   Profit or loss on ordinary activities after taxation

15   Extraordinary income

16   Extraordinary charges

17   Extraordinary profit or loss

18   Tax on extraordinary profit or loss

19   Other taxes not shown under the above items

20   Profit or loss for the financial year

Profit and loss account formats

Format 2

1 Turnover

2 Change in stocks of finished goods and in work in progress

3 Own work capitalised

4 Other operating income

5
(a) Raw materials and consumables
(b) Other external charges

6 Staff costs
(a) wages and salaries
(b) social security costs
(c) other pension costs

7
(a) Depreciation and other amounts written off tangible and intangible fixed assets
(b) Exceptional amounts written off current assets

8 Other operating charges

9 Income from shares in group undertakings

10 Income from participating interests

11 Income from other fixed asset investments[12]

12 Other interest receivable and similar income[12]

13 Amounts written off investments

14 Interest payable and similar charges[13]

15 Tax on profit or loss on ordinary activities

16 Profit or loss on ordinary activities after taxation

17 Extraordinary income

18 Extraordinary charges

19 Extraordinary profit or loss

20 Tax on extraordinary profit or loss

21 Other taxes not shown under the above items

22 Profit or loss for the financial year

Profit and loss account formats

Format 3
(see note (14) below)

A Charges
1 Cost of sales[11]
2 Distribution costs[11]
3 Administrative expenses[11]
4 Amounts written off investments
5 Interest payable and similar charges[13]
6 Tax on profit or loss on ordinary activities
7 Profit or loss on ordinary activities after taxation
8 Extraordinary charges
9 Tax on extraordinary profit or loss
10 Other taxes not shown under the above items
11 Profit or loss for the financial year

B Income
1 Turnover
2 Other operating income

3   Income from shares in group undertakings
4   Income from participating interests
5   Income from other fixed asset investments[12]
6   Other interest receivable and similar income[12]
7   Profit or loss on ordinary activities after taxation
8   Extraordinary income
9   Profit or loss for the financial year

Profit and loss account formats

Format 4

A   Charges
1   Reduction in stocks of finished goods and in work in progress
2
    (a)   Raw materials and consumables
    (b)   Other external charges
3   Staff costs
    (a)   wages and salaries
    (b)   social security costs
    (c)   other pension costs
4
    (a)   Depreciation and other amounts written off tangible and intangible fixed assets
    (b)   Exceptional amounts written off current assets
5   Other operating charges
6   Amounts written off investments
7   Interest payable and similar charges[13]
8   Tax on profit or loss on ordinary activities
9   Profit or loss on ordinary activities after taxation
10   Extraordinary charges
11   Tax on extraordinary profit or loss
12   Other taxes not shown under the above items
13   Profit or loss for the financial year

B   Income
1   Turnover
2   Increase in stocks of finished goods and in work in progress
3   Own work capitalised
4   Other operating income
5   Income from shares in group undertakings
6   Income from participating interests
7   Income from other fixed asset investments[12]
8   Other interest receivable and similar income[12]
9   Profit or loss on ordinary activities after taxation
10   Extraordinary income
11   Profit or loss for the financial year

Notes on the profit and loss account formats

(11)   Cost of sales: distribution costs: administrative expenses

(Format 1, items 2, 4 and 5 and Format 3, items A 1, 2 and 3)

These items must be stated after taking into account any necessary provisions for depreciation or diminution in value of assets.

(12)   Income from other fixed asset investments: other interest receivable and similar income

(Format 1, items 9 and 10; Format 2, items 11 and 12; Format 3, items B 5 and 6 and Format 4, items B 7 and 8)

Income and interest derived from group undertakings must be shown separately from income and interest derived from other sources.

(13)   Interest payable and similar charges

(Format 1, item 12; Format 2, item 14; Format 3, item A 5 and Format 4, item A 7)

The amount payable to group undertakings must be shown separately.

(14)   Formats 1 and 3

The amount of any provisions for depreciation and diminution in value of tangible and intangible fixed assets falling to be shown under items 7(a) and A 4(a) respectively in Formats 2 and 4 must be disclosed in a note to the accounts in any case where the profit and loss account is prepared using Format 1 or Format 3.

NOTES

Commencement: 6 April 2008.

PART 2
ACCOUNTING PRINCIPLES AND RULES

SECTION A
ACCOUNTING PRINCIPLES

Preliminary

[4.156]

10. (1) The amounts to be included in respect of all items shown in a company's accounts must be determined in accordance with the principles set out in this Section.

(2) But if it appears to the company's directors that there are special reasons for departing from any of those principles in preparing the company's accounts in respect of any financial year they may do so, in which case particulars of the departure, the reasons for it and its effect must be given in a note to the accounts.

Accounting principles

11. The company is presumed to be carrying on business as a going concern.

12. Accounting policies must be applied consistently within the same accounts and from one financial year to the next.

13. The amount of any item must be determined on a prudent basis, and in particular—
- (a) only profits realised at the balance sheet date must be included in the profit and loss account, and
- (b) all liabilities which have arisen in respect of the financial year to which the accounts relate or a previous financial year must be taken into account, including those which only become apparent between the balance sheet date and the date on which it is signed on behalf of the board of directors in accordance with section 414 of the 2006 Act (approval and signing of accounts).

14. All income and charges relating to the financial year to which the accounts relate must be taken into account, without regard to the date of receipt or payment.

15. In determining the aggregate amount of any item, the amount of each individual asset or liability that falls to be taken into account must be determined separately.

SECTION B
HISTORICAL COST ACCOUNTING RULES

Preliminary

16. Subject to Sections C and D of this Part of this Schedule, the amounts to be included in respect of all items shown in a company's accounts must be determined in accordance with the rules set out in this Section.

Fixed Assets

General rules

17. (1) The amount to be included in respect of any fixed asset must be its purchase price or production cost.

(2) This is subject to any provision for depreciation or diminution in value made in accordance with paragraphs 18 to 20.

Rules for depreciation and diminution in value

18. In the case of any fixed asset which has a limited useful economic life, the amount of—
- (a) its purchase price or production cost, or
- (b) where it is estimated that any such asset will have a residual value at the end of the period of its useful economic life, its purchase price or production cost less that estimated residual value,

must be reduced by provisions for depreciation calculated to write off that amount systematically over the period of the asset's useful economic life.

19. (1) Where a fixed asset investment of a description falling to be included under item B.III of either of the balance sheet formats set out in Part 1 of this Schedule has diminished in value, provisions for diminution in value may be made in respect of it and the amount to be included in respect of it may be reduced accordingly.

(2)   Provisions for diminution in value must be made in respect of any fixed asset which has diminished in value if the reduction in its value is expected to be permanent (whether its useful economic life is limited or not), and the amount to be included in respect of it must be reduced accordingly.

(3)   Any provisions made under sub-paragraph (1) or (2) which are not shown in the profit and loss account must be disclosed (either separately or in aggregate) in a note to the accounts.

20. (1)   Where the reasons for which any provision was made in accordance with paragraph 19 have ceased to apply to any extent, that provision must be written back to the extent that it is no longer necessary.

(2)   Any amounts written back in accordance with sub-paragraph (1) which are not shown in the profit and loss account must be disclosed (either separately or in aggregate) in a note to the accounts.

Development costs

21. (1)   Notwithstanding that an item in respect of "development costs" is included under "fixed assets" in the balance sheet formats set out in Part 1 of this Schedule, an amount may only be included in a company's balance sheet in respect of development costs in special circumstances.

(2)   If any amount is included in a company's balance sheet in respect of development costs the following information must be given in a note to the accounts—
- (a)   the period over which the amount of those costs originally capitalised is being or is to be written off, and
- (b)   the reasons for capitalising the development costs in question.

Goodwill

22. (1)   The application of paragraphs 17 to 20 in relation to goodwill (in any case where goodwill is treated as an asset) is subject to the following.

(2)   Subject to sub-paragraph (3), the amount of the consideration for any goodwill acquired by a company must be reduced by provisions for depreciation calculated to write off that amount systematically over a period chosen by the directors of the company.

(3)   The period chosen must not exceed the useful economic life of the goodwill in question.

(4)   In any case where any goodwill acquired by a company is shown or included as an asset in the company's balance sheet there must be disclosed in a note to the accounts—
- (a)   the period chosen for writing off the consideration for that goodwill, and
- (b)   the reasons for choosing that period.

Current assets

23.   Subject to paragraph 24, the amount to be included in respect of any current asset must be its purchase price or production cost.

24. (1)   If the net realisable value of any current asset is lower than its purchase price or production cost, the amount to be included in respect of that asset must be the net realisable value.

(2)   Where the reasons for which any provision for diminution in value was made in accordance with sub-paragraph (1) have ceased to apply to any extent, that provision must be written back to the extent that it is no longer necessary.

Miscellaneous and Supplementary Provisions

Excess of money owed over value received as an asset item

25. (1)   Where the amount repayable on any debt owed by a company is greater than the value of the consideration received in the transaction giving rise to the debt, the amount of the difference may be treated as an asset.

(2)   Where any such amount is so treated—
- (a)   it must be written off by reasonable amounts each year and must be completely written off before repayment of the debt, and
- (b)   if the current amount is not shown as a separate item in the company's balance sheet, it must be disclosed in a note to the accounts.

Assets included at a fixed amount

26. (1)   Subject to sub-paragraph (2), assets which fall to be included—
- (a)   amongst the fixed assets of a company under the item "tangible assets", or
- (b)   amongst the current assets of a company under the item "raw materials and consumables", may be included at a fixed quantity and value.

(2)   Sub-paragraph (1) applies to assets of a kind which are constantly being replaced where—
- (a)   their overall value is not material to assessing the company's state of affairs, and
- (b)   their quantity, value and composition are not subject to material variation.

Determination of purchase price or production cost

27. (1)   The purchase price of an asset is to be determined by adding to the actual price paid any expenses incidental to its acquisition.

(2)   The production cost of an asset is to be determined by adding to the purchase price of the raw materials and consumables used the amount of the costs incurred by the company which are directly attributable to the production of that asset.

(3)   In addition, there may be included in the production cost of an asset—
- (a)   a reasonable proportion of the costs incurred by the company which are only indirectly attributable to the production of that asset, but only to the extent that they relate to the period of production, and
- (b)   interest on capital borrowed to finance the production of that asset, to the extent that it accrues in respect of the period of production,

provided, however, in a case within paragraph (b), that the inclusion of the interest in determining the cost of that asset and the amount of the interest so included is disclosed in a note to the accounts.

(4)   In the case of current assets distribution costs may not be included in production costs.

28. (1)   The purchase price or production cost of—
- (a)   any assets which fall to be included under any item shown in a company's balance sheet under the general item "stocks", and
- (b)   any assets which are fungible assets (including investments),

may be determined by the application of any of the methods mentioned in sub-paragraph (2) in relation to any such assets of the same class, provided that the method chosen is one which appears to the directors to be appropriate in the circumstances of the company.

(2)   Those methods are—
- (a)   the method known as "first in, first out" (FIFO),
- (b)   the method known as "last in, first out" (LIFO),
- (c)   a weighted average price, and
- (d)   any other method similar to any of the methods mentioned above.

(3)   For the purposes of this paragraph, assets of any description must be regarded as fungible if assets of that description are substantially indistinguishable one from another.

Substitution of original stated amount where price or cost unknown

29. (1)   This paragraph applies where—
- (a)   there is no record of the purchase price or production cost of any asset of a company or of any price, expenses or costs relevant for determining its purchase price or production cost in accordance with paragraph 27, or
- (b)   any such record cannot be obtained without unreasonable expense or delay.

(2)   In such a case, the purchase price or production cost of the asset must be taken, for the purposes of paragraphs 17 to 24, to be the value ascribed to it in the earliest available record of its value made on or after its acquisition or production by the company.

SECTION C
ALTERNATIVE ACCOUNTING RULES

Preliminary

30. (1)   The rules set out in Section B are referred to below in this Schedule as the historical cost accounting rules.

(2)   Those rules, with the omission of paragraphs 16, 22 and 26 to 29, are referred to below in this Part of this Schedule as the depreciation rules; and references below in this Schedule to the historical cost accounting rules do not include the depreciation rules as they apply by virtue of paragraph 33.

31.   Subject to paragraphs 33 to 35, the amounts to be included in respect of assets of any description mentioned in paragraph 32 may be determined on any basis so mentioned.

Alternative accounting rules

32. (1)   Intangible fixed assets, other than goodwill, may be included at their current cost.

(2)   Tangible fixed assets may be included at a market value determined as at the date of their last valuation or at their current cost.

(3)   Investments of any description falling to be included under item B III of either of the balance sheet formats set out Part 1 of this Schedule may be included either—
- (a)   at a market value determined as at the date of their last valuation, or
- (b)   at a value determined on any basis which appears to the directors to be appropriate in the circumstances of the company.

But in the latter case particulars of the method of valuation adopted and of the reasons for adopting it must be disclosed in a note to the accounts.

(4)   Investments of any description falling to be included under item C III of either of the balance sheet formats set out in Part 1 of this Schedule may be included at their current cost.

(5)   Stocks may be included at their current cost.

Application of the depreciation rules

33. (1)   Where the value of any asset of a company is determined on any basis mentioned in paragraph 32, that value must be, or (as the case may require) be the starting point for determining, the amount to be included in respect of that asset in the company's accounts, instead of its purchase price or production cost or any value previously so determined for that asset.

The depreciation rules apply accordingly in relation to any such asset with the substitution for any reference to its purchase price or production cost of a reference to the value most recently determined for that asset on any basis mentioned in paragraph 32.

(2)   The amount of any provision for depreciation required in the case of any fixed asset by paragraphs 18 to 20 as they apply by virtue of sub-paragraph (1) is referred to below in this paragraph as the adjusted amount, and the amount of any provision which would be required by any of those paragraphs in the case of that asset according to the historical cost accounting rules is referred to as the historical cost amount.

(3)   Where sub-paragraph (1) applies in the case of any fixed asset the amount of any provision for depreciation in respect of that asset—

  (a)   included in any item shown in the profit and loss account in respect of amounts written off assets of the description in question, or

  (b)   taken into account in stating any item so shown which is required by note *(11)* of the notes on the profit and loss account formats set out in Part 1 of this Schedule to be stated after taking into account any necessary provision for depreciation or diminution in value of assets included under it,

may be the historical cost amount instead of the adjusted amount, provided that the amount of any difference between the two is shown separately in the profit and loss account or in a note to the accounts.

Additional information to be provided in case of departure from historical cost accounting rules

34. (1)   This paragraph applies where the amounts to be included in respect of assets covered by any items shown in a company's accounts have been determined on any basis mentioned in paragraph 32.

(2)   The items affected and the basis of valuation adopted in determining the amounts of the assets in question in the case of each such item must be disclosed in a note to the accounts.

(3)   In the case of each balance sheet item affected (except stocks) either—

  (a)   the comparable amounts determined according to the historical cost accounting rules, or

  (b)   the differences between those amounts and the corresponding amounts actually shown in the balance sheet in respect of that item,

must be shown separately in the balance sheet or in a note to the accounts.

(4)   In sub-paragraph (3), references in relation to any item to the comparable amounts determined as there mentioned are references to—

  (a)   the aggregate amount which would be required to be shown in respect of that item if the amounts to be included in respect of all the assets covered by that item were determined according to the historical cost accounting rules, and

  (b)   the aggregate amount of the cumulative provisions for depreciation or diminution in value which would be permitted or required in determining those amounts according to those rules.

Revaluation reserve

35. (1)   With respect to any determination of the value of an asset of a company on any basis mentioned in paragraph 32, the amount of any profit or loss arising from that determination (after allowing, where appropriate, for any provisions for depreciation or diminution in value made otherwise than by reference to the value so determined and any adjustments of any such provisions made in the light of that determination) must be credited or (as the case may be) debited to a separate reserve ("the revaluation reserve").

(2)   The amount of the revaluation reserve must be shown in the company's balance sheet under a separate sub-heading in the position given for the item "revaluation reserve" in Format 1 or 2 of the balance sheet formats set out in Part 1 of this Schedule, but need not be shown under that name.

(3)   An amount may be transferred—

  (a)   from the revaluation reserve—

    (i)   to the profit and loss account, if the amount was previously charged to that account or represents realised profit, or

    (ii)   on capitalisation,

(b) to or from the revaluation reserve in respect of the taxation relating to any profit or loss credited or debited to the reserve.

The revaluation reserve must be reduced to the extent that the amounts transferred to it are no longer necessary for the purposes of the valuation method used.

(4) In sub-paragraph (3)(a)(ii) "capitalisation", in relation to an amount standing to the credit of the revaluation reserve, means applying it in wholly or partly paying up unissued shares in the company to be allotted to members of the company as fully or partly paid shares.

(5) The revaluation reserve must not be reduced except as mentioned in this paragraph.

(6) The treatment for taxation purposes of amounts credited or debited to the revaluation reserve must be disclosed in a note to the accounts.

SECTION D
FAIR VALUE ACCOUNTING
Inclusion of financial instruments at fair value

36. (1) Subject to sub-paragraphs (2) to (5), financial instruments (including derivatives) may be included at fair value.

(2) Sub-paragraph (1) does not apply to financial instruments that constitute liabilities unless—
(a) they are held as part of a trading portfolio,
(b) they are derivatives, or
(c) they are financial instruments falling within sub-paragraph (4).

(3) Unless they are financial instruments falling within sub-paragraph (4), sub-paragraph (1) does not apply to—
(a) financial instruments (other than derivatives) held to maturity,
(b) loans and receivables originated by the company and not held for trading purposes,
(c) interests in subsidiary undertakings, associated undertakings and joint ventures,
(d) equity instruments issued by the company,
(e) contracts for contingent consideration in a business combination, or
(f) other financial instruments with such special characteristics that the instruments, according to generally accepted accounting principles or practice, should be accounted for differently from other financial instruments.

(4) Financial instruments that, under international accounting standards adopted by the European Commission on or before 5th September 2006 in accordance with the IAS Regulation, may be included in accounts at fair value, may be so included, provided that the disclosures required by such accounting standards are made.

(5) If the fair value of a financial instrument cannot be determined reliably in accordance with paragraph 37, sub-paragraph (1) does not apply to that financial instrument.

(6) In this paragraph—
"associated undertaking" has the meaning given by paragraph 19 of Schedule 6 to these Regulations;
"joint venture" has the meaning given by paragraph 18 of that Schedule.

Determination of fair value

37. (1) The fair value of a financial instrument is its value determined in accordance with this paragraph.

(2) If a reliable market can readily be identified for the financial instrument, its fair value is to be determined by reference to its market value.

(3) If a reliable market cannot readily be identified for the financial instrument but can be identified for its components or for a similar instrument, its fair value is determined by reference to the market value of its components or of the similar instrument.

(4) If neither sub-paragraph (2) nor (3) applies, the fair value of the financial instrument is a value resulting from generally accepted valuation models and techniques.

(5) Any valuation models and techniques used for the purposes of sub-paragraph (4) must ensure a reasonable approximation of the market value.

Hedged items

38. A company may include any assets and liabilities, or identified portions of such assets or liabilities, that qualify as hedged items under a fair value hedge accounting system at the amount required under that system.

Other assets that may be included at fair value

39. (1) This paragraph applies to—
(a) investment property, and
(b) living animals and plants,
that, under international accounting standards, may be included in accounts at fair value.

(2) Such investment property and such living animals and plants may be included at fair value, provided that all such investment property or, as the case may be, all such living animals and plants are so included where their fair value can reliably be determined.

(3) In this paragraph, "fair value" means fair value determined in accordance with relevant international accounting standards.

Accounting for changes in value

40. (1) This paragraph applies where a financial instrument is valued in accordance with paragraph 36 or 38 or an asset is valued in accordance with paragraph 39.

(2) Notwithstanding paragraph 13 in this Part of this Schedule, and subject to sub-paragraphs (3) and (4), a change in the value of the financial instrument or of the investment property or living animal or plant must be included in the profit and loss account.

(3) Where—
- (a) the financial instrument accounted for is a hedging instrument under a hedge accounting system that allows some or all of the change in value not to be shown in the profit and loss account, or
- (b) the change in value relates to an exchange difference arising on a monetary item that forms part of a company's net investment in a foreign entity,

the amount of the change in value must be credited to or (as the case may be) debited from a separate reserve ("the fair value reserve").

(4) Where the instrument accounted for—
- (a) is an available for sale financial asset, and
- (b) is not a derivative,

the change in value may be credited to or (as the case may be) debited from the fair value reserve.

The fair value reserve

41. (1) The fair value reserve must be adjusted to the extent that the amounts shown in it are no longer necessary for the purposes of paragraph 40(3) or (4).

(2) The treatment for taxation purposes of amounts credited or debited to the fair value reserve must be disclosed in a note to the accounts.

NOTES

Commencement: 6 April 2008.

PART 3
NOTES TO THE ACCOUNTS

Preliminary

[4.157]
42. Any information required in the case of any company by the following provisions of this Part of this Schedule must (if not given in the company's accounts) be given by way of a note to those accounts.

Reserves and dividends

43. There must be stated—
- (a) any amount set aside or proposed to be set aside to, or withdrawn or proposed to be withdrawn from, reserves,
- (b) the aggregate amount of dividends paid in the financial year (other than those for which a liability existed at the immediately preceding balance sheet date),
- (c) the aggregate amount of dividends that the company is liable to pay at the balance sheet date, and
- (d) the aggregate amount of dividends that are proposed before the date of approval of the accounts, and not otherwise disclosed under paragraph (b) or (c).

Disclosure of accounting policies

44. The accounting policies adopted by the company in determining the amounts to be included in respect of items shown in the balance sheet and in determining the profit or loss of the company must be stated (including such policies with respect to the depreciation and diminution in value of assets).

Information Supplementing the Balance Sheet

45. Paragraphs 46 to 58 require information which either supplements the information given with respect to any particular items shown in the balance sheet or is otherwise relevant to assessing the company's state of affairs in the light of the information so given.

Part 4   CA 2006 SIs

Share capital

46. (1) Where shares of more than one class have been allotted, the number and aggregate nominal value of shares of each class allotted must be given.

(2) In the case of any part of the allotted share capital that consists of redeemable shares, the following information must be given—

- (a) the earliest and latest dates on which the company has power to redeem those shares,
- (b) whether those shares must be redeemed in any event or are liable to be redeemed at the option of the company or of the shareholder, and
- (c) whether any (and, if so, what) premium is payable on redemption.

47. If the company has allotted any shares during the financial year, the following information must be given—

- (a) the classes of shares allotted, and
- (b) as respects each class of shares, the number allotted, their aggregate nominal value, and the consideration received by the company for the allotment.

Fixed assets

48. (1) In respect of each item which is or would but for paragraph 4(2)(b) be shown under the general item "fixed assets" in the company's balance sheet the following information must be given—

- (a) the appropriate amounts in respect of that item as at the date of the beginning of the financial year and as at the balance sheet date respectively,
- (b) the effect on any amount shown in the balance sheet in respect of that item of—
  - (i) any revision of the amount in respect of any assets included under that item made during that year on any basis mentioned in paragraph 32,
  - (ii) acquisitions during that year of any assets,
  - (iii) disposals during that year of any assets, and
  - (iv) any transfers of assets of the company to and from that item during that year.

(2) The reference in sub-paragraph (1)(a) to the appropriate amounts in respect of any item as at any date there mentioned is a reference to amounts representing the aggregate amounts determined, as at that date, in respect of assets falling to be included under that item on either of the following bases, that is to say—

- (a) on the basis of purchase price or production cost (determined in accordance with paragraphs 27 and 28), or
- (b) on any basis mentioned in paragraph 32,

(leaving out of account in either case any provisions for depreciation or diminution in value).

(3) In respect of each item within sub-paragraph (1) there must also be stated—

- (a) the cumulative amount of provisions for depreciation or diminution in value of assets included under that item as at each date mentioned in sub-paragraph (1)(a),
- (b) the amount of any such provisions made in respect of the financial year,
- (c) the amount of any adjustments made in respect of any such provisions during that year in consequence of the disposal of any assets, and
- (d) the amount of any other adjustments made in respect of any such provisions during that year.

49. Where any fixed assets of the company (other than listed investments) are included under any item shown in the company's balance sheet at an amount determined on any basis mentioned in paragraph 32, the following information must be given—

- (a) the years (so far as they are known to the directors) in which the assets were severally valued and the several values, and
- (b) in the case of assets that have been valued during the financial year, the names of the persons who valued them or particulars of their qualifications for doing so and (whichever is stated) the bases of valuation used by them.

Investments

50. (1) In respect of the amount of each item which is or would but for paragraph 4(2)(b) be shown in the company's balance sheet under the general item "investments" (whether as fixed assets or as current assets) there must be stated how much of that amount is ascribable to listed investments.

(2) Where the amount of any listed investments is stated for any item in accordance with sub-paragraph (1), the following amounts must also be stated—

- (a) the aggregate market value of those investments where it differs from the amount so stated, and
- (b) both the market value and the stock exchange value of any investments of which the former value is, for the purposes of the accounts, taken as being higher than the latter.

Information about fair value of assets and liabilities

51. (1)   This paragraph applies where financial instruments have been valued in accordance with paragraph 36 or 38.

(2)   There must be stated—

    (a)   the significant assumptions underlying the valuation models and techniques used where the fair value of the instruments has been determined in accordance with paragraph 37(4),

    (b)   for each category of financial instrument, the fair value of the instruments in that category and the changes in value—

        (i)   included in the profit and loss account, or

        (ii)   credited to or (as the case may be) debited from the fair value reserve,

    in respect of those instruments, and

    (c)   for each class of derivatives, the extent and nature of the instruments, including significant terms and conditions that may affect the amount, timing and certainty of future cash flows.

(3)   Where any amount is transferred to or from the fair value reserve during the financial year, there must be stated in tabular form—

    (a)   the amount of the reserve as at the date of the beginning of the financial year and as at the balance sheet date respectively,

    (b)   the amount transferred to or from the reserve during that year, and

    (c)   the source and application respectively of the amounts so transferred.

52. (1)   This paragraph applies if—

    (a)   the company has financial fixed assets that could be included at fair value by virtue of paragraph 36,

    (b)   the amount at which those items are included under any item in the company's accounts is in excess of their fair value, and

    (c)   the company has not made provision for diminution in value of those assets in accordance with paragraph 19(1) of this Schedule.

(2)   There must be stated—

    (a)   the amount at which either the individual assets or appropriate groupings of those individual assets are included in the company's accounts,

    (b)   the fair value of those assets or groupings, and

    (c)   the reasons for not making a provision for diminution in value of those assets, including the nature of the evidence that provides the basis for the belief that the amount at which they are stated in the accounts will be recovered.

Information where investment property and living animals and plants included at fair value

53. (1)   This paragraph applies where the amounts to be included in a company's accounts in respect of investment property or living animals and plants have been determined in accordance with paragraph 39.

(2)   The balance sheet items affected and the basis of valuation adopted in determining the amounts of the assets in question in the case of each such item must be disclosed in a note to the accounts.

(3)   In the case of investment property, for each balance sheet item affected there must be shown, either separately in the balance sheet or in a note to the accounts—

    (a)   the comparable amounts determined according to the historical cost accounting rules, or

    (b)   the differences between those amounts and the corresponding amounts actually shown in the balance sheet in respect of that item.

(4)   In sub-paragraph (3), references in relation to any item to the comparable amounts determined in accordance with that sub-paragraph are to—

    (a)   the aggregate amount which would be required to be shown in respect of that item if the amounts to be included in respect of all the assets covered by that item were determined according to the historical cost accounting rules, and

    (b)   the aggregate amount of the cumulative provisions for depreciation or diminution in value which would be permitted or required in determining those amounts according to those rules.

Reserves and provisions

54. (1)   This paragraph applies where any amount is transferred—

    (a)   to or from any reserves, or

    (b)   to any provisions for liabilities, or

    (c)   from any provision for liabilities otherwise than for the purpose for which the provision was established,

and the reserves or provisions are or would but for paragraph 4(2)(b) be shown as separate items in the company's balance sheet.

(2)   The following information must be given in respect of the aggregate of reserves or provisions included in the same item—

(a) the amount of the reserves or provisions as at the date of the beginning of the financial year and as at the balance sheet date respectively,

(b) any amounts transferred to or from the reserves or provisions during that year, and

(c) the source and application respectively of any amounts so transferred.

(3) Particulars must be given of each provision included in the item "other provisions" in the company's balance sheet in any case where the amount of that provision is material.

Details of indebtedness

55. (1) For the aggregate of all items shown under "creditors" in the company's balance sheet there must be stated the aggregate of the following amounts—

(a) the amount of any debts included under "creditors" which are payable or repayable otherwise than by instalments and fall due for payment or repayment after the end of the period of five years beginning with the day next following the end of the financial year, and

(b) in the case of any debts so included which are payable or repayable by instalments, the amount of any instalments which fall due for payment after the end of that period.

(2) In respect of each item shown under "creditors" in the company's balance sheet there must be stated the aggregate amount of any debts included under that item in respect of which any security has been given by the company.

(3) References above in this paragraph to an item shown under "creditors" in the company's balance sheet include references, where amounts falling due to creditors within one year and after more than one year are distinguished in the balance sheet—

(a) in a case within sub-paragraph (1), to an item shown under the latter of those categories,

(b) in a case within sub-paragraph (2), to an item shown under either of those categories.

References to items shown under "creditors" include references to items which would but for paragraph 4(2)(b) be shown under that heading.

56. If any fixed cumulative dividends on the company's shares are in arrear, there must be stated—

(a) the amount of the arrears, and

(b) the period for which the dividends or, if there is more than one class, each class of them are in arrear.

Guarantees and other financial commitments

57. (1) Particulars must be given of any charge on the assets of the company to secure the liabilities of any other person, including, where practicable, the amount secured.

(2) The following information must be given with respect to any other contingent liability not provided for—

(a) the amount or estimated amount of that liability,

(b) its legal nature, and

(c) whether any valuable security has been provided by the company in connection with that liability and if so, what.

(3) There must be stated, where practicable, the aggregate amount or estimated amount of contracts for capital expenditure, so far as not provided for.

(4) Particulars must be given of—

(a) any pension commitments included under any provision shown in the company's balance sheet, and

(b) any such commitments for which no provision has been made,

and where any such commitment relates wholly or partly to pensions payable to past directors of the company separate particulars must be given of that commitment so far as it relates to such pensions.

(5) Particulars must also be given of any other financial commitments that—

(a) have not been provided for, and

(b) are relevant to assessing the company's state of affairs.

(6) Commitments within any of sub-paragraphs (1) to (5) which are undertaken on behalf of or for the benefit of—

(a) any parent undertaking or fellow subsidiary undertaking, or

(b) any subsidiary undertaking of the company,

must be stated separately from the other commitments within that sub-paragraph, and commitments within paragraph (a) must also be stated separately from those within paragraph (b).

Miscellaneous matters

58. Particulars must be given of any case where the purchase price or production cost of any asset is for the first time determined under paragraph 29.

Information supplementing the profit and loss account

59. Paragraphs 60 and 61 require information which either supplements the information given with respect to any particular items shown in the profit and loss account or otherwise provides particulars of income or expenditure of the company or of circumstances affecting the items shown in the profit and loss account (see regulation 3(2) for exemption for companies falling within section 408 of the 2006 Act).

Particulars of turnover

60. (1)   If the company has supplied geographical markets outside the United Kingdom during the financial year in question, there must be stated the percentage of its turnover that, in the opinion of the directors, is attributable to those markets.

(2)   In analysing for the purposes of this paragraph the source of turnover, the directors of the company must have regard to the manner in which the company's activities are organised.

Miscellaneous matters

61. (1)   Where any amount relating to any preceding financial year is included in any item in the profit and loss account, the effect must be stated.

(2)   Particulars must be given of any extraordinary income or charges arising in the financial year.

(3)   The effect must be stated of any transactions that are exceptional by virtue of size or incidence though they fall within the ordinary activities of the company.

Sums denominated in foreign currencies

62. Where sums originally denominated in foreign currencies have been brought into account under any items shown in the balance sheet or profit and loss account, the basis on which those sums have been translated into sterling (or the currency in which the accounts are drawn up) must be stated.

Dormant companies acting as agents

63. Where the directors of a company take advantage of the exemption conferred by section 480 of the 2006 Act (dormant companies: exemption from audit), and the company has during the financial year in question acted as an agent for any person, the fact that it has so acted must be stated.

NOTES
Commencement: 6 April 2008.

SCHEDULE 2
INFORMATION ABOUT RELATED UNDERTAKINGS WHERE COMPANY NOT PREPARING GROUP ACCOUNTS (COMPANIES ACT OR IAS INDIVIDUAL ACCOUNTS)
Regulation 4

PART 1
REQUIRED DISCLOSURES

Subsidiary undertakings

[4.158]
1. (1)   The following information must be given where at the end of the financial year the company has subsidiary undertakings.

(2)   The name of each subsidiary undertaking must be stated.

(3)   There must be stated with respect to each subsidiary undertaking—
   (a)   if it is incorporated outside the United Kingdom, the country in which it is incorporated,
   (b)   if it is unincorporated, the address of its principal place of business.

Holdings in subsidiary undertakings

2. (1)   There must be stated in relation to shares of each class held by the company in a subsidiary undertaking—
   (a)   the identity of the class, and
   (b)   the proportion of the nominal value of the shares of that class represented by those shares.

(2)   The shares held by or on behalf of the company itself must be distinguished from those attributed to the company which are held by or on behalf of a subsidiary undertaking.

Financial information about subsidiary undertakings

3. (1)   There must be disclosed with respect to each subsidiary undertaking—
   (a)   the aggregate amount of its capital and reserves as at the end of its relevant financial year, and

(b)   its profit or loss for that year.

(2)   That information need not be given if the company would (if it were not subject to the small companies regime) be exempt by virtue of section 400 or 401 of the 2006 Act (parent company included in accounts of larger group) from the requirement to prepare group accounts.

(3)   That information need not be given if the company's investment in the subsidiary undertaking is included in the company's accounts by way of the equity method of valuation.

(4)   That information need not be given if—
(a)   the subsidiary undertaking is not required by any provision of the 2006 Act to deliver a copy of its balance sheet for its relevant financial year and does not otherwise publish that balance sheet in the United Kingdom or elsewhere, and
(b)   the company's holding is less than 50% of the nominal value of the shares in the undertaking.

(5)   Information otherwise required by this paragraph need not be given if it is not material.

(6)   For the purposes of this paragraph the "relevant financial year" of a subsidiary undertaking is—
(a)   if its financial year ends with that of the company, that year, and
(b)   if not, its financial year ending last before the end of the company's financial year.

Shares of company held by subsidiary undertakings

4. (1)   The number, description and amount of the shares in the company held by or on behalf of its subsidiary undertakings must be disclosed.

(2)   Sub-paragraph (1) does not apply in relation to shares in the case of which the subsidiary undertaking is concerned as personal representative or, subject as follows, as trustee.

(3)   The exception for shares in relation to which the subsidiary undertaking is concerned as trustee does not apply if the company, or any subsidiary undertaking of the company, is beneficially interested under the trust, otherwise than by way of security only for the purposes of a transaction entered into by it in the ordinary course of a business which includes the lending of money.

(4)   Part 2 of this Schedule has effect for the interpretation of the reference in sub-paragraph (3) to a beneficial interest under a trust.

Significant holdings in undertakings other than subsidiary undertakings

5. (1)   The information required by paragraphs 6 and 7 must be given where at the end of the financial year the company has a significant holding in an undertaking which is not a subsidiary undertaking of the company.

(2)   A holding is significant for this purpose if—
(a)   it amounts to 20% or more of the nominal value of any class of shares in the undertaking, or
(b)   the amount of the holding (as stated or included in the company's accounts) exceeds 20% of the amount (as so stated) of the company's assets.

6. (1)   The name of the undertaking must be stated.

(2)   There must be stated—
(a)   if the undertaking is incorporated outside the United Kingdom, the country in which it is incorporated,
(b)   if it is unincorporated, the address of its principal place of business.

(3)   There must also be stated—
(a)   the identity of each class of shares in the undertaking held by the company, and
(b)   the proportion of the nominal value of the shares of that class represented by those shares.

7. (1)   There must also be stated—
(a)   the aggregate amount of the capital and reserves of the undertaking as at the end of its relevant financial year, and
(b)   its profit or loss for that year.

(2)   That information need not be given if—
(a)   the company would (if it were not subject to the small companies regime) be exempt by virtue of section 400 or 401 of the 2006 Act (parent company included in accounts of larger group) from the requirement to prepare group accounts, and
(b)   the investment of the company in all undertakings in which it has such a holding as is mentioned in sub-paragraph (1) is shown, in aggregate, in the notes to the accounts by way of the equity method of valuation.

(3)   That information need not be given in respect of an undertaking if—
(a)   the undertaking is not required by any provision of the 2006 Act to deliver to the registrar a copy of its balance sheet for its relevant financial year and does not otherwise publish that balance sheet in the United Kingdom or elsewhere, and
(b)   the company's holding is less than 50% of the nominal value of the shares in the undertaking.

(4) Information otherwise required by this paragraph need not be given if it is not material.

(5) For the purposes of this paragraph the "relevant financial year" of an undertaking is—

  (a) if its financial year ends with that of the company, that year, and

  (b) if not, its financial year ending last before the end of the company's financial year.

Membership of certain undertakings

8. (1) The information required by this paragraph must be given where at the end of the financial year the company is a member of a qualifying undertaking.

(2) There must be stated—

  (a) the name and legal form of the undertaking, and

  (b) the address of the undertaking's registered office (whether in or outside the United Kingdom) or, if it does not have such an office, its head office (whether in or outside the United Kingdom).

(3) Where the undertaking is a qualifying partnership there must also be stated either—

  (a) that a copy of the latest accounts of the undertaking has been or is to be appended to the copy of the company's accounts sent to the registrar under section 444 of the 2006 Act, or

  (b) the name of at least one body corporate (which may be the company) in whose group accounts the undertaking has been or is to be dealt with on a consolidated basis.

(4) Information otherwise required by sub-paragraph (2) need not be given if it is not material.

(5) Information otherwise required by sub-paragraph (3)(b) need not be given if the notes to the company's accounts disclose that advantage has been taken of the exemption conferred by regulation 7 of the [Partnerships (Accounts) Regulations 2008].

(6) In this paragraph—

  "dealt with on a consolidated basis", "member" and "qualifying partnership" have the same meanings as in the [Partnerships (Accounts) Regulations 2008];

  "qualifying undertaking" means—

  (a) a qualifying partnership, or

  (b) an unlimited company each of whose members is—

   (i) a limited company,

   (ii) another unlimited company each of whose members is a limited company, or

   (iii) a Scottish partnership each of whose members is a limited company,

   and references in this paragraph to a limited company, another unlimited company or a Scottish partnership include a comparable undertaking incorporated in or formed under the law of a country or territory outside the United Kingdom.

Parent undertaking drawing up accounts for larger group

9. (1) Where the company is a subsidiary undertaking, the following information must be given with respect to the parent undertaking of—

  (a) the largest group of undertakings for which group accounts are drawn up and of which the company is a member, and

  (b) the smallest such group of undertakings.

(2) The name of the parent undertaking must be stated.

(3) There must be stated—

  (a) if the undertaking is incorporated outside the United Kingdom, the country in which it is incorporated,

  (b) if it is unincorporated, the address of its principal place of business.

(4) If copies of the group accounts referred to in sub-paragraph (1) are available to the public, there must also be stated the addresses from which copies of the accounts can be obtained.

Identification of ultimate parent company

10. (1) Where the company is a subsidiary undertaking, the following information must be given with respect to the company (if any) regarded by the directors as being the company's ultimate parent company.

(2) The name of that company must be stated.

(3) If that company is incorporated outside the United Kingdom, the country in which it is incorporated must be stated (if known to the directors).

(4) In this paragraph "company" includes any body corporate.

Construction of references to shares held by company

11. (1) References in this Part of this Schedule to shares held by a company are to be construed as follows.

(2) For the purposes of paragraphs 2 and 3 (information about subsidiary undertakings)—

  (a) there must be attributed to the company any shares held by a subsidiary undertaking, or by a person acting on behalf of the company or a subsidiary undertaking; but

(b) there must be treated as not held by the company any shares held on behalf of a person other than the company or a subsidiary undertaking.

(3) For the purposes of paragraphs 5 to 7 (information about undertakings other than subsidiary undertakings)—

(a) there must be attributed to the company shares held on its behalf by any person; but

(b) there must be treated as not held by a company shares held on behalf of a person other than the company.

(4) For the purposes of any of those provisions, shares held by way of security must be treated as held by the person providing the security—

(a) where apart from the right to exercise them for the purpose of preserving the value of the security, or of realising it, the rights attached to the shares are exercisable only in accordance with his instructions, and

(b) where the shares are held in connection with the granting of loans as part of normal business activities and apart from the right to exercise them for the purpose of preserving the value of the security, or of realising it, the rights attached to the shares are exercisable only in his interests.

NOTES

Commencement: 6 April 2008.

Para 8: words in square brackets in sub-paras (5), (6) substituted by the Partnerships (Accounts) Regulations 2008, SI 2008/569, reg 17(1)(a), as from 6 April 2008, in relation to qualifying partnerships' financial years beginning on or after that date, and auditors appointed in respect of those financial years.

PART 2
INTERPRETATION OF REFERENCES TO "BENEFICIAL INTEREST"

Introduction

[4.159]

12. (1) References in this Schedule to a beneficial interest are to be interpreted in accordance with the following provisions.

(2) This Part of this Schedule applies in relation to debentures as it applies in relation to shares.

Residual interests under pension and employees' share schemes

13. (1) Where shares in an undertaking are held on trust for the purposes of a pension scheme or an employees' share scheme, there must be disregarded any residual interest of the undertaking or any of its subsidiary undertakings (the "residual beneficiary") that has not vested in possession.

(2) A "residual interest" means a right to receive any of the trust property in the event of—

(a) all the liabilities arising under the scheme having been satisfied or provided for, or

(b) the residual beneficiary ceasing to participate in the scheme, or

(c) the trust property at any time exceeding what is necessary for satisfying the liabilities arising or expected to arise under the scheme.

(3) In sub-paragraph (2)—

(a) references to a right include a right dependent on the exercise of a discretion vested by the scheme in the trustee or any other person, and

(b) references to liabilities arising under a scheme include liabilities that have resulted or may result from the exercise of any such discretion.

(4) For the purposes of this paragraph a residual interest vests in possession—

(a) in a case within sub-paragraph (2)(a), on the occurrence of the event there mentioned, whether or not the amount of the property receivable pursuant to the right mentioned in that sub-paragraph is then ascertained,

(b) in a case within sub-paragraph (2)(b) or (c), when the residual beneficiary becomes entitled to require the trustee to transfer to it any of the property receivable pursuant to that right.

Employer's charges and other rights of recovery

14. (1) Where shares in an undertaking are held on trust there must be disregarded—

(a) if the trust is for the purposes of a pension scheme, any such rights as are mentioned in sub-paragraph (2),

(b) if the trust is for the purposes of an employees' share scheme, any such rights as are mentioned in paragraph (a) of that sub-paragraph,

being rights of the undertaking or any of its subsidiary undertakings.

(2) The rights referred to are—

(a) any charge or lien on, or set-off against, any benefit or other right or interest under the scheme for the purpose of enabling the employer or former employer of a member of the scheme to obtain the discharge of a monetary obligation due to him from the member,

(b) any right to receive from the trustee of the scheme, or as trustee of the scheme to retain, an amount that can be recovered or retained under section 61 of the Pension Schemes Act 1993 or section 57 of the Pension Schemes (Northern Ireland) Act 1993 (deduction of contributions equivalent premium from refund of scheme contributions) or otherwise, as reimbursement or partial reimbursement for any contributions equivalent premium paid in connection with the scheme under Chapter 3 of Part 3 of that Act.

Trustee's right to expenses, remuneration, indemnity etc

15. (1)   Where an undertaking is a trustee, there must be disregarded any rights which the undertaking has in its capacity as trustee.

(2)   This includes in particular—
  (a)   any right to recover its expenses or be remunerated out of the trust property, and
  (b)   any right to be indemnified out of that property for any liability incurred by reason of any act or omission of the undertaking in the performance of its duties as trustee.

Meaning of "pension scheme"

16. (1)   In this Part of this Schedule "pension scheme" means any scheme for the provision of benefits consisting of or including relevant benefits for or in respect of employees or former employees.

(2)   For this purpose "relevant benefits" means any pension, lump sum, gratuity or other like benefit given or to be given on retirement or on death or in anticipation of retirement or, in connection with past service, after retirement or death.

Application of provisions to directors

17.   In paragraphs 14(2) and 16, "employee" and "employer" are to be read as if a director of an undertaking were employed by it.

NOTES
  Commencement: 6 April 2008.

SCHEDULE 3
INFORMATION ABOUT DIRECTORS' BENEFITS: REMUNERATION (COMPANIES ACT OR IAS ACCOUNTS)
Regulations 5 and 9

PART 1
INFORMATION REQUIRED TO BE DISCLOSED
Total amount of directors' remuneration etc

[4.160]
1. (1)   There must be shown the overall total of the following amounts—
  (a)   the amount of remuneration paid to or receivable by directors in respect of qualifying services;
  (b)   the amount of money paid to or receivable by directors, and the net value of assets (other than money, share options or shares) received or receivable by directors, under long term incentive schemes in respect of qualifying services; and
  (c)   the value of any company contributions—
    (i)   paid, or treated as paid, to a pension scheme in respect of directors' qualifying services, and
    (ii)   by reference to which the rate or amount of any money purchase benefits that may become payable will be calculated.

(2)   There must be shown the number of directors (if any) to whom retirement benefits are accruing in respect of qualifying services—
  (a)   under money purchase schemes, and
  (b)   under defined benefit schemes.

Compensation to directors for loss of office

2. (1)   There must be shown the aggregate amount of any payments made to directors or past directors for loss of office.

(2)   "Payment for loss of office" has the same meaning as in section 215 of the 2006 Act.

Sums paid to third parties in respect of directors' services

3. (1)   There must be shown the aggregate amount of any consideration paid to or receivable by third parties for making available the services of any person—
  (a)   as a director of the company, or
  (b)   while director of the company—
    (i)   as director of any of its subsidiary undertakings, or
    (ii)   otherwise in connection with the management of the affairs of the company or any of its subsidiary undertakings.

(2)   In sub-paragraph (1)—

(a) the reference to consideration includes benefits otherwise than in cash, and

(b) in relation to such consideration the reference to its amount is to the estimated money value of the benefit.

The nature of any such consideration must be disclosed.

(3) For the purposes of this paragraph a "third party" means a person other than—

(a) the director himself or a person connected with him or body corporate controlled by him, or

(b) the company or any of its subsidiary undertakings.

NOTES

Commencement: 6 April 2008.

PART 2
SUPPLEMENTARY PROVISIONS

General nature of obligations

[4.161]

4. (1) This Schedule requires information to be given only so far as it is contained in the company's books and papers or the company has the right to obtain it from the persons concerned.

(2) For the purposes of this Schedule any information is treated as shown if it is capable of being readily ascertained from other information which is shown.

Provisions as to amounts to be shown

5. (1) The following provisions apply with respect to the amounts to be shown under this Schedule.

(2) The amount in each case includes all relevant sums, whether paid by or receivable from the company, any of the company's subsidiary undertakings or any other person.

(3) References to amounts paid to or receivable by a person include amounts paid to or receivable by a person connected with him or a body corporate controlled by him (but not so as to require an amount to be counted twice).

(4) Except as otherwise provided, the amounts to be shown for any financial year are—

(a) the sums receivable in respect of that year (whenever paid) or,

(b) in the case of sums not receivable in respect of a period, the sums paid during that year.

(5) Sums paid by way of expenses allowance that are charged to United Kingdom income tax after the end of the relevant financial year must be shown in a note to the first accounts in which it is practicable to show them and must be distinguished from the amounts to be shown apart from this provision.

(6) Where it is necessary to do so for the purpose of making any distinction required in complying with this Schedule, the directors may apportion payments between the matters in respect of which they have been paid or are receivable in such manner as they think appropriate.

Exclusion of sums liable to be accounted for to company etc

6. (1) The amounts to be shown under this Schedule do not include any sums that are to be accounted for—

(a) to the company or any of its subsidiary undertakings, or

(b) by virtue of sections 219 and 222(3) of the 2006 Act (payments in connection with share transfers: duty to account), to persons who sold their shares as a result of the offer made.

(2) Where—

(a) any such sums are not shown in a note to the accounts for the relevant financial year on the ground that the person receiving them is liable to account for them, and

(b) the liability is afterwards wholly or partly released or is not enforced within a period of two years,

those sums, to the extent to which the liability is released or not enforced, must be shown in a note to the first accounts in which it is practicable to show them and must be distinguished from the amounts to be shown apart from this provision.

Meaning of "remuneration"

7. (1) In this Schedule "remuneration" of a director includes—

(a) salary, fees and bonuses, sums paid by way of expenses allowance (so far as they are chargeable to United Kingdom income tax), and

(b) subject to sub-paragraph (2), the estimated money value of any other benefits received by him otherwise than in cash.

(2) The expression does not include—

(a) the value of any share options granted to a director or the amount of any gains made on the exercise of any such options,

(b)   any company contributions paid, or treated as paid, in respect of him under any pension scheme or any benefits to which he is entitled under any such scheme, or

(c)   any money or other assets paid to or received or receivable by him under any long term incentive scheme.

Meaning of "long term incentive scheme"

8. (1)   In this Schedule "long term incentive scheme" means an agreement or arrangement—

(a)   under which money or other assets may become receivable by a director, and

(b)   which includes one or more qualifying conditions with respect to service or performance which cannot be fulfilled within a single financial year.

(2)   For this purpose the following must be disregarded—

(a)   bonuses the amount of which falls to be determined by reference to service or performance within a single financial year;

(b)   compensation for loss of office, payments for breach of contract and other termination payments; and

(c)   retirement benefits.

Meaning of "shares" and "share option" and related expressions

9. In this Schedule—

(a)   "shares" means shares (whether allotted or not) in the company, or any undertaking which is a group undertaking in relation to the company, and includes a share warrant as defined by section 779(1) of the 2006 Act; and

(b)   "share option" means a right to acquire shares.

Meaning of "pension scheme" and related expressions

10. (1)   In this Schedule—

"pension scheme" means a retirement benefits scheme as defined by section 611 of the Income and Corporation Taxes Act 1988; and

"retirement benefits" has the meaning given by section 612(1) of that Act.

(2)   In this Schedule, "company contributions", in relation to a pension scheme and a director, means any payments (including insurance premiums) made, or treated as made, to the scheme in respect of the director by a person other than the director.

(3)   In this Schedule, in relation to a director—

"defined benefits" means retirement benefits payable under a pension scheme that are not money purchase benefits;

"defined benefit scheme" means a pension scheme that is not a money purchase scheme;

"money purchase benefits" means retirement benefits payable under a pension scheme the rate or amount of which is calculated by reference to payments made, or treated as made, by the director or by any other person in respect of the director and which are not average salary benefits; and

"money purchase scheme" means a pension scheme under which all of the benefits that may become payable to or in respect of the director are money purchase benefits.

(4)   Where a pension scheme provides for any benefits that may become payable to or in respect of any director to be whichever are the greater of—

(a)   money purchase benefits as determined by or under the scheme; and

(b)   defined benefits as so determined,

the company may assume for the purposes of this paragraph that those benefits will be money purchase benefits, or defined benefits, according to whichever appears more likely at the end of the financial year.

(5)   For the purpose of determining whether a pension scheme is a money purchase or defined benefit scheme, any death in service benefits provided for by the scheme are to be disregarded.

References to subsidiary undertakings

11. (1)   Any reference in this Schedule to a subsidiary undertaking of the company, in relation to a person who is or was, while a director of the company, a director also, by virtue of the company's nomination (direct or indirect) of any other undertaking, includes that undertaking, whether or not it is or was in fact a subsidiary undertaking of the company.

(2)   Any reference to a subsidiary undertaking of the company—

(a)   for the purposes of paragraph 1 (remuneration etc) is to an undertaking which is a subsidiary undertaking at the time the services were rendered, and

(b)   for the purposes of paragraph 2 (compensation for loss of office) is to a subsidiary undertaking immediately before the loss of office as director.

Other minor definitions

12. (1) In this Schedule—

"net value", in relation to any assets received or receivable by a director, means value after deducting any money paid or other value given by the director in respect of those assets;

"qualifying services", in relation to any person, means his services as a director of the company, and his services while director of the company—

(a) as director of any of its subsidiary undertakings; or

(b) otherwise in connection with the management of the affairs of the company or any of its subsidiary undertakings.

(2) For the purposes of this Schedule, remuneration paid or receivable or share options granted in respect of a person's accepting office as a director are treated as emoluments paid or receivable or share options granted in respect of his services as a director.

NOTES

Commencement: 6 April 2008.

SCHEDULE 4
COMPANIES ACT ABBREVIATED ACCOUNTS FOR DELIVERY TO REGISTRAR OF COMPANIES

Regulation 6(1)

PART 1
THE REQUIRED BALANCE SHEET FORMATS

[4.162]

1. (1) A company may deliver to the registrar a copy of the balance sheet showing the items listed in either of the balance sheet formats set out below, in the order and under the headings and sub-headings given in the format adopted, but in other respects corresponding to the full balance sheet.

(2) The copy balance sheet must contain in a prominent position a statement that it has been prepared in accordance with the provisions applicable to companies subject to the small companies regime.

Balance sheet formats

Format 1

A   Called up share capital not paid

B   Fixed assets
   I   Intangible assets
   II   Tangible assets
   III   Investments

C   Current assets
   I   Stocks
   II   Debtors [(1)]
   III   Investments
   IV   Cash at bank and in hand

D   Prepayments and accrued income

E   Creditors: amounts falling due within one year

F   Net current assets (liabilities)

G   Total assets less current liabilities

H   Creditors: amounts falling due after more than one year

I   Provisions for liabilities

J   Accruals and deferred income

K   Capital and reserves
   I   Called up share capital
   II   Share premium account
   III   Revaluation reserve
   IV   Other reserves
   V   Profit and loss account

Balance sheet formats

Format 2

ASSETS

A   Called up share capital not paid

B   Fixed assets
  I   Intangible assets
  II   Tangible assets
  III   Investments

C   Current assets
  I   Stocks
  II   Debtors [1]
  III   Investments
  IV   Cash at bank and in hand

D   Prepayments and accrued income

LIABILITIES

A   Capital and reserves
  I   Called up share capital
  II   Share premium account
  III   Revaluation reserve
  IV   Other reserves
  V   Profit and loss account

B   Provisions for liabilities

C   Creditors [2]

D   Accruals and deferred income

Notes on the balance sheet formats

(1)   Debtors

(Formats 1 and 2, items C II)

The aggregate amount of debtors falling due after more than one year must be shown separately, unless it is disclosed in the notes to the accounts.

(2)   Creditors

(Format 2, Liabilities item C)

The aggregate amount of creditors falling due within one year and of creditors falling due after more than one year must be shown separately, unless it is disclosed in the notes to the accounts.

NOTES

Commencement: 6 April 2008.

PART 2
NOTES TO THE ACCOUNTS

Preliminary

[4.163]

2. Any information required in the case of any company by the following provisions of this Part of this Schedule must (if not given in the company's accounts) be given by way of a note to those accounts.

Disclosure of accounting policies

3. The accounting policies adopted by the company in determining the amounts to be included in respect of items shown in the balance sheet and in determining the profit or loss of the company must be stated (including such policies with respect to the depreciation and diminution in value of assets).

Information Supplementing the Balance Sheet

Share capital and debentures

4. (1)   Where shares of more than one class have been allotted, the number and aggregate nominal value of shares of each class allotted must be given.

(2)   In the case of any part of the allotted share capital that consists of redeemable shares, the following information must be given—
- (a)   the earliest and latest dates on which the company has power to redeem those shares,
- (b)   whether those shares must be redeemed in any event or are liable to be redeemed at the option of the company or of the shareholder, and
- (c)   whether any (and, if so, what) premium is payable on redemption.

5. If the company has allotted any shares during the financial year, the following information must be given—
- (a)   the classes of shares allotted, and
- (b)   as respects each class of shares, the number allotted, their aggregate nominal value, and the consideration received by the company for the allotment.

Fixed assets

6. (1)   In respect of each item to which a letter or Roman number is assigned under the general item "fixed assets" in the company's balance sheet the following information must be given—
- (a)   the appropriate amounts in respect of that item as at the date of the beginning of the financial year and as at the balance sheet date respectively,
- (b)   the effect on any amount shown in the balance sheet in respect of that item of—
  - (i)   any revision of the amount in respect of any assets included under that item made during that year on any basis mentioned in paragraph 32 of Schedule 1 to these Regulations,
  - (ii)   acquisitions during that year of any assets,
  - (iii)   disposals during that year of any assets, and
  - (iv)   any transfers of assets of the company to and from that item during that year.

(2)   The reference in sub-paragraph (1)(a) to the appropriate amounts in respect of any item as at any date there mentioned is a reference to amounts representing the aggregate amounts determined, as at that date, in respect of assets falling to be included under that item on either of the following bases, that is to say—
- (a)   on the basis of purchase price or production cost (determined in accordance with paragraphs 27 and 28 of Schedule 1 to these Regulations), or
- (b)   on any basis mentioned in paragraph 32 of that Schedule, (leaving out of account in either case any provisions for depreciation or diminution in value).

(3)   In respect of each item within sub-paragraph (1) there must also be stated—
- (a)   the cumulative amount of provisions for depreciation or diminution in value of assets included under that item as at each date mentioned in sub-paragraph (1)(a),
- (b)   the amount of any such provisions made in respect of the financial year,
- (c)   the amount of any adjustments made in respect of any such provisions during that year in consequence of the disposal of any assets, and
- (d)   the amount of any other adjustments made in respect of any such provisions during that year.

Financial fixed assets

7. (1)   This paragraph applies if—
- (a)   the company has financial fixed assets that could be included at fair value by virtue of paragraph 36 of Schedule 1 to these Regulations,
- (b)   the amount at which those items are included under any item in the company's accounts is in excess of their fair value, and
- (c)   the company has not made provision for diminution in value of those assets in accordance with paragraph 19(1) of that Schedule.

(2)   There must be stated—
- (a)   the amount at which either the individual assets or appropriate groupings of those individual assets are included in the company's accounts,
- (b)   the fair value of those assets or groupings, and
- (c)   the reasons for not making a provision for diminution in value of those assets, including the nature of the evidence that provides the basis for the belief that the amount at which they are stated in the accounts will be recovered.

Details of indebtedness

8. (1)   For the aggregate of all items shown under "creditors" in the company's balance sheet there must be stated the aggregate of the following amounts—
- (a)   the amount of any debts included under "creditors" which are payable or repayable otherwise than by instalments and fall due for payment or repayment after the end of the period of five years beginning with the day next following the end of the financial year, and
- (b)   in the case of any debts so included which are payable or repayable by instalments, the amount of any instalments which fall due for payment after the end of that period.

(2)   In respect of each item shown under "creditors" in the company's balance sheet there must be stated the aggregate amount of any debts included under that item in respect of which any security has been given by the company.

Sums denominated in foreign currencies

9.   Where sums originally denominated in foreign currencies have been brought into account under any items shown in the balance sheet or profit and loss account, the basis on which those sums have been translated into sterling (or the currency in which the accounts are drawn up) must be stated.

Dormant companies acting as agents

10.   Where the directors of a company take advantage of the exemption conferred by section 480 of the 2006 Act (dormant companies: exemption from audit), and the company has during the financial year in question acted as an agent for any person, the fact that it has so acted must be stated.

NOTES

Commencement: 6 April 2008.

SCHEDULE 5
MATTERS TO BE DEALT WITH IN DIRECTORS' REPORT
Regulation 7

Introduction

[4.164]
1.   In addition to the information required by section 416 of the 2006 Act, the directors' report must contain the following information.

Political donations and expenditure

2. (1)   If—
  (a)   the company (not being the wholly-owned subsidiary of a company incorporated in the United Kingdom) has in the financial year—
       (i)   made any political donation to any political party or other political organisation,
       (ii)   made any political donation to any independent election candidate, or
       (iii) incurred any political expenditure, and
  (b)   the amount of the donation or expenditure, or (as the case may be) the aggregate amount of all donations and expenditure falling within paragraph (a), exceeded £2000,
the directors' report for the year must contain the following particulars.

(2)   Those particulars are—
  (a)   as respects donations falling within sub-paragraph (1)(a)(i) or (ii)—
       (i)   the name of each political party, other political organisation or independent election candidate to whom any such donation has been made, and
       (ii)   the total amount given to that party, organisation or candidate by way of such donations in the financial year; and
  (b)   as respects expenditure falling within sub-paragraph (1)(a)(iii), the total amount incurred by way of such expenditure in the financial year.

(3)   If—
  (a)   at the end of the financial year the company has subsidiaries which have, in that year, made any donations or incurred any such expenditure as is mentioned in sub-paragraph (1)(a), and
  (b)   it is not itself the wholly-owned subsidiary of a company incorporated in the United Kingdom,
the directors' report for the year is not, by virtue of sub-paragraph (1), required to contain the particulars specified in sub-paragraph (2).
  But, if the total amount of any such donations or expenditure (or both) made or incurred in that year by the company and the subsidiaries between them exceeds £2000, the directors' report for the year must contain those particulars in relation to each body by whom any such donation or expenditure has been made or incurred.

(4)   Any expression used in this paragraph which is also used in Part 14 of the 2006 Act (control of political donations and expenditure) has the same meaning as in that Part.

3. (1)   If the company (not being the wholly-owned subsidiary of a company incorporated in the United Kingdom) has in the financial year made any contribution to a non-EU political party, the directors' report for the year must contain—
  (a)   a statement of the amount of the contribution, or
  (b)   (if it has made two or more such contributions in the year) a statement of the total amount of the contributions.

(2)   If—

(a) at the end of the financial year the company has subsidiaries which have, in that year, made any such contributions as are mentioned in sub-paragraph (1), and

(b) it is not itself the wholly-owned subsidiary of a company incorporated in the United Kingdom,

the directors' report for the year is not, by virtue of sub-paragraph (1), required to contain any such statement as is there mentioned, but it must instead contain a statement of the total amount of the contributions made in the year by the company and the subsidiaries between them.

(3) In this paragraph, "contribution", in relation to an organisation, means—

(a) any gift of money to the organisation (whether made directly or indirectly);

(b) any subscription or other fee paid for affiliation to, or membership of, the organisation; or

(c) any money spent (otherwise than by the organisation or a person acting on its behalf) in paying any expenses incurred directly or indirectly by the organisation.

(4) In this paragraph, "non-EU political party" means any political party which carries on, or proposes to carry on, its activities wholly outside the member States.

Charitable donations

4. (1) If—

(a) the company (not being the wholly-owned subsidiary of a company incorporated in the United Kingdom) has in the financial year given money for charitable purposes, and

(b) the money given exceeded £2000 in amount,

the directors' report for the year must contain, in the case of each of the purposes for which money has been given, a statement of the amount of money given for that purpose.

(2) If—

(a) at the end of the financial year the company has subsidiaries which have, in that year, given money for charitable purposes, and

(b) it is not itself the wholly owned subsidiary of a company incorporated in the United Kingdom, sub-paragraph (1) does not apply to the company.

But, if the amount given in that year for charitable purposes by the company and the subsidiaries between them exceeds £2000, the directors' report for the year must contain, in the case of each of the purposes for which money has been given by the company and the subsidiaries between them, a statement of the amount of money given for that purpose.

(3) Money given for charitable purposes to a person who, when it was given, was ordinarily resident outside the United Kingdom is to be left out of account for the purposes of this paragraph.

(4) For the purposes of this paragraph, "charitable purposes" means purposes which are exclusively charitable, and as respects Scotland a purpose is charitable if it is listed in section 7(2) of the Charities and Trustee Investment (Scotland) Act 2005.

Disclosure concerning employment etc of disabled persons

5. (1) This paragraph applies to the directors' report where the average number of persons employed by the company in each week during the financial year exceeded 250.

(2) That average number is the quotient derived by dividing, by the number of weeks in the financial year, the number derived by ascertaining, in relation to each of those weeks, the number of persons who, under contracts of service, were employed in the week (whether throughout it or not) by the company, and adding up the numbers ascertained.

(3) The directors' report must in that case contain a statement describing such policy as the company has applied during the financial year—

(a) for giving full and fair consideration to applications for employment by the company made by disabled persons, having regard to their particular aptitudes and abilities,

(b) for continuing the employment of, and for arranging appropriate training for, employees of the company who have become disabled persons during the period when they were employed by the company, and

(c) otherwise for the training, career development and promotion of disabled persons employed by the company.

(4) In this paragraph—

(a) "employment" means employment other than employment to work wholly or mainly outside the United Kingdom, and "employed" and "employee" are to be construed accordingly; and

(b) "disabled person" means the same as in the Disability Discrimination Act 1995.

Disclosure required by company acquiring its own shares etc

6. (1) This paragraph applies where shares in a company—

(a) are purchased by the company or are acquired by it by forfeiture or surrender in lieu of forfeiture, or in pursuance of any of the following provisions (acquisition of own shares by company limited by shares)—

(i) section 143(3) of the Companies Act 1985,

(ii) Article 153(3) of the Companies (Northern Ireland) Order 1986, or

(iii)   section 659 of the 2006 Act, or

(b)   are acquired by another person in circumstances where paragraph (c) or (d) of any of the following provisions applies (acquisition by company's nominee, or by another with company financial assistance, the company having a beneficial interest)—

(i)   section 146(1) of the Companies Act 1985,

(ii)   Article 156(1) of the Companies (Northern Ireland) Order 1986, or

(iii)   section 662(1) of the 2006 Act, or

(c)   are made subject to a lien or other charge taken (whether expressly or otherwise) by the company and permitted by any of the following provisions (exceptions from general rule against a company having a lien or charge on its own shares)—

(i)   section 150(2) or (4) of the Companies Act 1985,

(ii)   Article 160(2) or (4) of the Companies (Northern Ireland) Order 1986, or

(iii)   section 670(2) or (4) of the 2006 Act.

(2)   The directors' report for a financial year must state—

(a)   the number and nominal value of the shares so purchased, the aggregate amount of the consideration paid by the company for such shares and the reasons for their purchase;

(b)   the number and nominal value of the shares so acquired by the company, acquired by another person in such circumstances and so charged respectively during the financial year;

(c)   the maximum number and nominal value of shares which, having been so acquired by the company, acquired by another person in such circumstances or so charged (whether or not during that year) are held at any time by the company or that other person during that year;

(d)   the number and nominal value of the shares so acquired by the company, acquired by another person in such circumstances or so charged (whether or not during that year) which are disposed of by the company or that other person or cancelled by the company during that year;

(e)   where the number and nominal value of the shares of any particular description are stated in pursuance of any of the preceding sub-paragraphs, the percentage of the called-up share capital which shares of that description represent;

(f)   where any of the shares have been so charged the amount of the charge in each case; and

(g)   where any of the shares have been disposed of by the company or the person who acquired them in such circumstances for money or money's worth the amount or value of the consideration in each case.

NOTES

Commencement: 6 April 2008.

SCHEDULE 6
GROUP ACCOUNTS

Regulations 8(1) and 10

PART 1
FORM AND CONTENT OF COMPANIES ACT GROUP ACCOUNTS

General rules

[4.165]

1. (1)   Subject to sub-paragraphs (1) and (2), group accounts must comply so far as practicable with the provisions of Schedule 1 to these Regulations (Companies Act individual accounts) as if the undertakings included in the consolidation ("the group") were a single company.

(2)   For item B III in each balance sheet format set out in that Schedule substitute—

"B III   Investments

1   Shares in group undertakings

2   Interests in associated undertakings

3   Other participating interests

4   Loans to group undertakings and undertakings in which a participating interest is held

5   Other investments other than loans

6   Others".

(3)   In the profit and loss account formats replace the items headed "Income from participating interests", that is—

(a)   in Format 1, item 8,

(b)   in Format 2, item 10,

(c)   in Format 3, item B 4, and

(d)   in Format 4, item B 6,

by two items: "Income from interests in associated undertakings" and "Income from other participating interests".

2. (1)   The consolidated balance sheet and profit and loss account must incorporate in full the information contained in the individual accounts of the undertakings included in the consolidation, subject to the adjustments authorised or required by the following provisions of this Schedule and to such other adjustments (if any) as may be appropriate in accordance with generally accepted accounting principles or practice.

(2)   If the financial year of a subsidiary undertaking included in the consolidation does not end with that of the parent company, the group accounts must be made up—

(a)   from the accounts of the subsidiary undertaking for its financial year last ending before the end of the parent company's financial year, provided that year ended no more than three months before that of the parent company, or

(b)   from interim accounts prepared by the subsidiary undertaking as at the end of the parent company's financial year.

3. (1)   Where assets and liabilities to be included in the group accounts have been valued or otherwise determined by undertakings according to accounting rules differing from those used for the group accounts, the values or amounts must be adjusted so as to accord with the rules used for the group accounts.

(2)   If it appears to the directors of the parent company that there are special reasons for departing from sub-paragraph (1) they may do so, but particulars of any such departure, the reasons for it and its effect must be given in a note to the accounts.

(3)   The adjustments referred to in this paragraph need not be made if they are not material for the purpose of giving a true and fair view.

4. Any differences of accounting rules as between a parent company's individual accounts for a financial year and its group accounts must be disclosed in a note to the latter accounts and the reasons for the difference given.

5. Amounts that in the particular context of any provision of this Schedule are not material may be disregarded for the purposes of that provision.

Elimination of group transactions

6. (1)   Debts and claims between undertakings included in the consolidation, and income and expenditure relating to transactions between such undertakings, must be eliminated in preparing the group accounts.

(2)   Where profits and losses resulting from transactions between undertakings included in the consolidation are included in the book value of assets, they must be eliminated in preparing the group accounts.

(3)   The elimination required by sub-paragraph (2) may be effected in proportion to the group's interest in the shares of the undertakings.

(4)   Sub-paragraphs (1) and (2) need not be complied with if the amounts concerned are not material for the purpose of giving a true and fair view.

Acquisition and merger accounting

7. (1)   The following provisions apply where an undertaking becomes a subsidiary undertaking of the parent company.

(2)   That event is referred to in those provisions as an "acquisition", and references to the "undertaking acquired" are to be construed accordingly.

8. An acquisition must be accounted for by the acquisition method of accounting unless the conditions for accounting for it as a merger are met and the merger method of accounting is adopted.

9. (1)   The acquisition method of accounting is as follows.

(2)   The identifiable assets and liabilities of the undertaking acquired must be included in the consolidated balance sheet at their fair values as at the date of acquisition.

(3)   The income and expenditure of the undertaking acquired must be brought into the group accounts only as from the date of the acquisition.

(4)   There must be set off against the acquisition cost of the interest in the shares of the undertaking held by the parent company and its subsidiary undertakings the interest of the parent company and its subsidiary undertakings in the adjusted capital and reserves of the undertaking acquired.

(5)   The resulting amount if positive must be treated as goodwill, and if negative as a negative consolidation difference.

10. (1)   The conditions for accounting for an acquisition as a merger are—

(a)   that at least 90% of the nominal value of the relevant shares in the undertaking acquired (excluding any shares in the undertaking held as treasury shares) is held by or on behalf of the parent company and its subsidiary undertakings,

   (b)   that the proportion referred to in paragraph (a) was attained pursuant to an arrangement providing for the issue of equity shares by the parent company or one or more of its subsidiary undertakings,

   (c)   that the fair value of any consideration other than the issue of equity shares given pursuant to the arrangement by the parent company and its subsidiary undertakings did not exceed 10% of the nominal value of the equity shares issued, and

   (d)   that adoption of the merger method of accounting accords with generally accepted accounting principles or practice.

(2)   The reference in sub-paragraph (1)(a) to the "relevant shares" in an undertaking acquired is to those carrying unrestricted rights to participate both in distributions and in the assets of the undertaking upon liquidation.

11. (1)   The merger method of accounting is as follows.

(2)   The assets and liabilities of the undertaking acquired must be brought into the group accounts at the figures at which they stand in the undertaking's accounts, subject to any adjustment authorised or required by this Schedule.

(3)   The income and expenditure of the undertaking acquired must be included in the group accounts for the entire financial year, including the period before the acquisition.

(4)   The group accounts must show corresponding amounts relating to the previous financial year as if the undertaking acquired had been included in the consolidation throughout that year.

(5)   There must be set off against the aggregate of—

   (a)   the appropriate amount in respect of qualifying shares issued by the parent company or its subsidiary undertakings in consideration for the acquisition of shares in the undertaking acquired, and

   (b)   the fair value of any other consideration for the acquisition of shares in the undertaking acquired, determined as at the date when those shares were acquired,

the nominal value of the issued share capital of the undertaking acquired held by the parent company and its subsidiary undertakings.

(6)   The resulting amount must be shown as an adjustment to the consolidated reserves.

(7)   In sub-paragraph (5)(a) "qualifying shares" means—

   (a)   shares in relation to which any of the following provisions applies (merger relief), and in respect of which the appropriate amount is the nominal value—

      (i)   section 131 of the Companies Act 1985,

     (ii)   Article 141 of the Companies (Northern Ireland) Order 1986, or

    (iii)   section 612 of the 2006 Act, or

   (b)   shares in relation to which any of the following provisions applies (group reconstruction relief), and in respect of which the appropriate amount is the nominal value together with any minimum premium value within the meaning of that section—

      (i)   section 132 of the Companies Act 1985,

     (ii)   Article 142 of the Companies (Northern Ireland) Order 1986, or

    (iii)   section 611 of the 2006 Act.

12. (1)   Where a group is acquired, paragraphs 9 to 11 apply with the following adaptations.

(2)   References to shares of the undertaking acquired are to be construed as references to shares of the parent undertaking of the group.

(3)   Other references to the undertaking acquired are to be construed as references to the group; and references to the assets and liabilities, income and expenditure and capital and reserves of the undertaking acquired must be construed as references to the assets and liabilities, income and expenditure and capital and reserves of the group after making the set-offs and other adjustments required by this Schedule in the case of group accounts.

13. (1)   The following information with respect to acquisitions taking place in the financial year must be given in a note to the accounts.

(2)   There must be stated—

   (a)   the name of the undertaking acquired or, where a group was acquired, the name of the parent undertaking of that group, and

   (b)   whether the acquisition has been accounted for by the acquisition or the merger method of accounting;

and in relation to an acquisition which significantly affects the figures shown in the group accounts, the following further information must be given.

(3)   The composition and fair value of the consideration for the acquisition given by the parent company and its subsidiary undertakings must be stated.

(4)   Where the acquisition method of accounting has been adopted, the book values immediately prior to the acquisition, and the fair values at the date of acquisition, of each class of assets and liabilities of the undertaking or group acquired must be stated in tabular form, including a statement of the amount of any goodwill or negative consolidation difference arising on the acquisition, together with an explanation of any significant adjustments made.

(5)   In ascertaining for the purposes of sub-paragraph (4) the profit or loss of a group, the book values and fair values of assets and liabilities of a group or the amount of the assets and liabilities of a group, the set-offs and other adjustments required by this Schedule in the case of group accounts must be made.

14. (1)   There must also be stated in a note to the accounts the cumulative amount of goodwill resulting from acquisitions in that and earlier financial years which has been written off otherwise than in the consolidated profit and loss account for that or any earlier financial year.

(2)   That figure must be shown net of any goodwill attributable to subsidiary undertakings or businesses disposed of prior to the balance sheet date.

15.   Where during the financial year there has been a disposal of an undertaking or group which significantly affects the figure shown in the group accounts, there must be stated in a note to the accounts—

    (a)   the name of that undertaking or, as the case may be, of the parent undertaking of that group, and

    (b)   the extent to which the profit or loss shown in the group accounts is attributable to profit or loss of that undertaking or group.

16.   The information required by paragraph 13, 14 or 15 need not be disclosed with respect to an undertaking which—

    (a)   is established under the law of a country outside the United Kingdom, or

    (b)   carries on business outside the United Kingdom,

if in the opinion of the directors of the parent company the disclosure would be seriously prejudicial to the business of that undertaking or to the business of the parent company or any of its subsidiary undertakings and the Secretary of State agrees that the information should not be disclosed.

Minority interests

17. (1)   The formats set out in Schedule 1 to these Regulations have effect in relation to group accounts with the following additions.

(2)   In the Balance Sheet Formats there must be shown, as a separate item and under an appropriate heading, the amount of capital and reserves attributable to shares in subsidiary undertakings included in the consolidation held by or on behalf of persons other than the parent company and its subsidiary undertakings.

(3)   In the Profit and Loss Account Formats there must be shown, as a separate item and under an appropriate heading—

    (a)   the amount of any profit or loss on ordinary activities, and

    (b)   the amount of any profit or loss on extraordinary activities,

attributable to shares in subsidiary undertakings included in the consolidation held by or on behalf of persons other than the parent company and its subsidiary undertakings.

(4)   For the purposes of paragraph 4 of Schedule 1 (power to adapt or combine items)—

    (a)   the additional item required by sub-paragraph (2) is treated as one to which a letter is assigned, and

    (b)   the additional items required by sub-paragraph (3)(a) and (b) are treated as ones to which an Arabic number is assigned.

Joint ventures

18. (1)   Where an undertaking included in the consolidation manages another undertaking jointly with one or more undertakings not included in the consolidation, that other undertaking ("the joint venture") may, if it is not—

    (a)   a body corporate, or

    (b)   a subsidiary undertaking of the parent company,

be dealt with in the group accounts by the method of proportional consolidation.

(2)   The provisions of this Schedule relating to the preparation of consolidated accounts apply, with any necessary modifications, to proportional consolidation under this paragraph.

Associated undertakings

19. (1)   An "associated undertaking" means an undertaking in which an undertaking included in the consolidation has a participating interest and over whose operating and financial policy it exercises a significant influence, and which is not—

    (a)   a subsidiary undertaking of the parent company, or

    (b)   a joint venture dealt with in accordance with paragraph 18.

(2)   Where an undertaking holds 20% or more of the voting rights in another undertaking, it is presumed to exercise such an influence over it unless the contrary is shown.

(3)   The voting rights in an undertaking means the rights conferred on shareholders in respect of their shares or, in the case of an undertaking not having a share capital, on members, to vote at general meetings of the undertaking on all, or substantially all, matters.

(4)   The provisions of paragraphs 5 to 11 of Schedule 7 to the 2006 Act (parent and subsidiary undertakings: rights to be taken into account and attribution of rights) apply in determining for the purposes of this paragraph whether an undertaking holds 20% or more of the voting rights in another undertaking.

20.   (1)   The interest of an undertaking in an associated undertaking, and the amount of profit or loss attributable to such an interest, must be shown by the equity method of accounting (including dealing with any goodwill arising in accordance with paragraphs 17 to 20 and 22 of Schedule 1 to these Regulations).

(2)   Where the associated undertaking is itself a parent undertaking, the net assets and profits or losses to be taken into account are those of the parent and its subsidiary undertakings (after making any consolidation adjustments).

(3)   The equity method of accounting need not be applied if the amounts in question are not material for the purpose of giving a true and fair view.

NOTES
Commencement: 6 April 2008.

PART 2
INFORMATION ABOUT RELATED UNDERTAKINGS WHERE COMPANY PREPARING GROUP ACCOUNTS (COMPANIES ACT OR IAS GROUP ACCOUNTS)
Introduction and interpretation
[4.166]
21.   In this Part of this Schedule "the group" means the group consisting of the parent company and its subsidiary undertakings.

Subsidiary undertakings
22.   (1)   The following information must be given with respect to the undertakings that are subsidiary undertakings of the parent company at the end of the financial year.

(2)   The name of each undertaking must be stated.

(3)   There must be stated—
  (a)   if the undertaking is incorporated outside the United Kingdom, the country in which it is incorporated,
  (b)   if it is unincorporated, the address of its principal place of business.

(4)   It must also be stated whether the subsidiary undertaking is included in the consolidation and, if it is not, the reasons for excluding it from consolidation must be given.

(5)   It must be stated with respect to each subsidiary undertaking by virtue of which of the conditions specified in section 1162(2) or (4) of the 2006 Act it is a subsidiary undertaking of its immediate parent undertaking.

That information need not be given if the relevant condition is that specified in subsection (2)(a) of that section (holding of a majority of the voting rights) and the immediate parent undertaking holds the same proportion of the shares in the undertaking as it holds voting rights.

Holdings in subsidiary undertakings

23.   (1)   The following information must be given with respect to the shares of a subsidiary undertaking held—
  (a)   by the parent company, and
  (b)   by the group,
and the information under paragraphs (a) and (b) must (if different) be shown separately.

(2)   There must be stated—
  (a)   the identity of each class of shares held, and
  (b)   the proportion of the nominal value of the shares of that class represented by those shares.

Financial information about subsidiary undertakings not included in the consolidation

24.   (1)   There must be shown with respect to each subsidiary undertaking not included in the consolidation—
  (a)   the aggregate amount of its capital and reserves as at the end of its relevant financial year, and
  (b)   its profit or loss for that year.

(2)   That information need not be given if the group's investment in the undertaking is included in the accounts by way of the equity method of valuation or if—
  (a)   the undertaking is not required by any provision of the 2006 Act to deliver a copy of its balance sheet for its relevant financial year and does not otherwise publish that balance sheet in the United Kingdom or elsewhere, and
  (b)   the holding of the group is less than 50% of the nominal value of the shares in the undertaking.

(3) Information otherwise required by this paragraph need not be given if it is not material.

(4) For the purposes of this paragraph the "relevant financial year" of a subsidiary undertaking is—

(a) if its financial year ends with that of the company, that year, and

(b) if not, its financial year ending last before the end of the company's financial year.

Shares of company held by subsidiary undertakings

25. (1) The number, description and amount of the shares in the company held by or on behalf of its subsidiary undertakings must be disclosed.

(2) Sub-paragraph (1) does not apply in relation to shares in the case of which the subsidiary undertaking is concerned as personal representative or, subject as follows, as trustee.

(3) The exception for shares in relation to which the subsidiary undertaking is concerned as trustee does not apply if the company or any of its subsidiary undertakings is beneficially interested under the trust, otherwise than by way of security only for the purposes of a transaction entered into by it in the ordinary course of a business which includes the lending of money.

(4) Part 2 of Schedule 2 to these Regulations has effect for the interpretation of the reference in sub-paragraph (3) to a beneficial interest under a trust.

Joint ventures

26. (1) The following information must be given where an undertaking is dealt with in the consolidated accounts by the method of proportional consolidation in accordance with paragraph 18 of this Schedule (joint ventures)—

(a) the name of the undertaking,

(b) the address of the principal place of business of the undertaking,

(c) the factors on which joint management of the undertaking is based, and

(d) the proportion of the capital of the undertaking held by undertakings included in the consolidation.

(2) Where the financial year of the undertaking did not end with that of the company, there must be stated the date on which a financial year of the undertaking last ended before that date.

Associated undertakings

27. (1) The following information must be given where an undertaking included in the consolidation has an interest in an associated undertaking.

(2) The name of the associated undertaking must be stated.

(3) There must be stated—

(a) if the undertaking is incorporated outside the United Kingdom, the country in which it is incorporated,

(b) if it is unincorporated, the address of its principal place of business.

(4) The following information must be given with respect to the shares of the undertaking held—

(a) by the parent company, and

(b) by the group,

and the information under paragraphs (a) and (b) must be shown separately.

(5) There must be stated—

(a) the identity of each class of shares held, and

(b) the proportion of the nominal value of the shares of that class represented by those shares.

(6) In this paragraph "associated undertaking" has the meaning given by paragraph 19 of this Schedule; and the information required by this paragraph must be given notwithstanding that paragraph 20(3) of this Schedule (materiality) applies in relation to the accounts themselves.

Other significant holdings of parent company or group

28. (1) The information required by paragraphs 29 and 30 must be given where at the end of the financial year the parent company has a significant holding in an undertaking which is not one of its subsidiary undertakings and does not fall within paragraph 26 (joint ventures) or paragraph 27 (associated undertakings).

(2) A holding is significant for this purpose if—

(a) it amounts to 20% or more of the nominal value of any class of shares in the undertaking, or

(b) the amount of the holding (as stated or included in the company's individual accounts) exceeds 20% of the amount of its assets (as so stated).

29. (1) The name of the undertaking must be stated.

(2) There must be stated—

(a) if the undertaking is incorporated outside the United Kingdom, the country in which it is incorporated,

(b) if it is unincorporated, the address of its principal place of business.

(3)   The following information must be given with respect to the shares of the undertaking held by the parent company.

(4)   There must be stated—
    (a)   the identity of each class of shares held, and
    (b)   the proportion of the nominal value of the shares of that class represented by those shares.

30. (1)   There must also be stated—
    (a)   the aggregate amount of the capital and reserves of the undertaking as at the end of its relevant financial year, and
    (b)   its profit or loss for that year.

(2)   That information need not be given in respect of an undertaking if—
    (a)   the undertaking is not required by any provision of the 2006 Act to deliver a copy of its balance sheet for its relevant financial year and does not otherwise publish that balance sheet in the United Kingdom or elsewhere, and
    (b)   the company's holding is less than 50% of the nominal value of the shares in the undertaking.

(3)   Information otherwise required by this paragraph need not be given if it is not material.

(4)   For the purposes of this paragraph the "relevant financial year" of an undertaking is—
    (a)   if its financial year ends with that of the company, that year, and
    (b)   if not, its financial year ending last before the end of the company's financial year.

31. (1)   The information required by paragraphs 32 and 33 must be given where at the end of the financial year the group has a significant holding in an undertaking which is not a subsidiary undertaking of the parent company and does not fall within paragraph 26 (joint ventures) or paragraph 27 (associated undertakings).

(2)   A holding is significant for this purpose if—
    (a)   it amounts to 20% or more of the nominal value of any class of shares in the undertaking, or
    (b)   the amount of the holding (as stated or included in the group accounts) exceeds 20% of the amount of the group's assets (as so stated).

32. (1)   The name of the undertaking must be stated.

(2)   There must be stated—
    (a)   if the undertaking is incorporated outside the United Kingdom, the country in which it is incorporated,
    (b)   if it is unincorporated, the address of its principal place of business.

(3)   The following information must be given with respect to the shares of the undertaking held by the group.

(4)   There must be stated—
    (a)   the identity of each class of shares held, and
    (b)   the proportion of the nominal value of the shares of that class represented by those shares.

33. (1)   There must also be stated—
    (a)   the aggregate amount of the capital and reserves of the undertaking as at the end of its relevant financial year, and
    (b)   its profit or loss for that year.

(2)   That information need not be given if—
    (a)   the undertaking is not required by any provision of the 2006 Act to deliver a copy of its balance sheet for its relevant financial year and does not otherwise publish that balance sheet in the United Kingdom or elsewhere, and
    (b)   the holding of the group is less than 50% of the nominal value of the shares in the undertaking.

(3)   Information otherwise required by this paragraph need not be given if it is not material.

(4)   For the purposes of this paragraph the "relevant financial year" of an outside undertaking is—
    (a)   if its financial year ends with that of the parent company, that year, and
    (b)   if not, its financial year ending last before the end of the parent company's financial year.

Parent company's or group's membership of certain undertakings

34. (1)   The information required by this paragraph must be given where at the end of the financial year the parent company or group is a member of a qualifying undertaking.

(2)   There must be stated—
    (a)   the name and legal form of the undertaking, and
    (b)   the address of the undertaking's registered office (whether in or outside the United Kingdom) or, if it does not have such an office, its head office (whether in or outside the United Kingdom).

(3)   Where the undertaking is a qualifying partnership there must also be stated either—

- (a) that a copy of the latest accounts of the undertaking has been or is to be appended to the copy of the company's accounts sent to the registrar under section 444 of the 2006 Act, or
- (b) the name of at least one body corporate (which may be the company) in whose group accounts the undertaking has been or is to be dealt with on a consolidated basis.

(4) Information otherwise required by sub-paragraph (2) need not be given if it is not material.

(5) Information otherwise required by sub-paragraph (3)(b) need not be given if the notes to the company's accounts disclose that advantage has been taken of the exemption conferred by regulation 7 of the [Partnerships (Accounts) Regulations 2008].

(6) In this paragraph—
"dealt with on a consolidated basis", "member" and "qualifying partnership" have the same meanings as in the [Partnerships (Accounts) Regulations 2008];
"qualifying undertaking" means—
- (a) a qualifying partnership, or
- (b) an unlimited company each of whose members is—
  - (i) a limited company,
  - (ii) another unlimited company each of whose members is a limited company, or
  - (iii) a Scottish partnership each of whose members is a limited company,
  and references in this paragraph to a limited company, another unlimited company or a Scottish partnership include a comparable undertaking incorporated in or formed under the law of a country or territory outside the United Kingdom.

Parent undertaking drawing up accounts for larger group

35. (1) Where the parent company is itself a subsidiary undertaking, the following information must be given with respect to that parent undertaking of the company which heads—
- (a) the largest group of undertakings for which group accounts are drawn up and of which that company is a member, and
- (b) the smallest such group of undertakings.

(2) The name of the parent undertaking must be stated.

(3) There must be stated—
- (a) if the undertaking is incorporated outside the United Kingdom, the country in which it is incorporated,
- (b) if it is unincorporated, the address of its principal place of business.

(4) If copies of the group accounts referred to in sub-paragraph (1) are available to the public, there must also be stated the addresses from which copies of the accounts can be obtained.

Identification of ultimate parent company

36. (1) Where the parent company is itself a subsidiary undertaking, the following information must be given with respect to the company (if any) regarded by the directors as being that company's ultimate parent company.

(2) The name of that company must be stated.

(3) If that company is incorporated outside the United Kingdom, the country in which it is incorporated must be stated (if known to the directors).

(4) In this paragraph "company" includes any body corporate.

Construction of references to shares held by parent company or group

37. (1) References in this Part of this Schedule to shares held by the parent company or the group are to be construed as follows.

(2) For the purposes of paragraphs 23, 27(4) and (5) and 28 to 30 (information about holdings in subsidiary and other undertakings)—
- (a) there must be attributed to the parent company shares held on its behalf by any person; but
- (b) there must be treated as not held by the parent company shares held on behalf of a person other than the company.

(3) References to shares held by the group are to any shares held by or on behalf of the parent company or any of its subsidiary undertakings; but any shares held on behalf of a person other than the parent company or any of its subsidiary undertakings are not to be treated as held by the group.

(4) Shares held by way of security must be treated as held by the person providing the security—
- (a) where apart from the right to exercise them for the purpose of preserving the value of the security, or of realising it, the rights attached to the shares are exercisable only in accordance with his instructions, and
- (b) where the shares are held in connection with the granting of loans as part of normal business activities and apart from the right to exercise them for the purpose of preserving the value of the security, or of realising it, the rights attached to the shares are exercisable only in his interests.

NOTES

Commencement: 6 April 2008.

Para 34: words in square brackets in sub-paras (5), (6) substituted by the Partnerships (Accounts) Regulations 2008, SI 2008/569, reg 17(1)(b), as from 6 April 2008, in relation to qualifying partnerships' financial years beginning on or after that date, and auditors appointed in respect of those financial years.

SCHEDULE 7
INTERPRETATION OF TERM "PROVISIONS"

Regulation 12

PART 1
MEANING FOR PURPOSES OF THESE REGULATIONS

Definition of "Provisions"

[4.167]

1. (1)   In these Regulations, references to provisions for depreciation or diminution in value of assets are to any amount written off by way of providing for depreciation or diminution in value of assets.

(2)   Any reference in the profit and loss account formats set out in Part 1 of Schedule 1 to these Regulations to the depreciation of, or amounts written off, assets of any description is to any provision for depreciation or diminution in value of assets of that description.

2. References in these Regulations to provisions for liabilities are to any amount retained as reasonably necessary for the purpose of providing for any liability the nature of which is clearly defined and which is either likely to be incurred, or certain to be incurred but uncertain as to amount or as to the date on which it will arise.

NOTES

Commencement: 6 April 2008.

PART 2
MEANING FOR PURPOSES OF PARTS 18 AND 23 OF THE 2006 ACT

Financial assistance for purchase of own shares

[4.168]

3. The specified provisions for the purposes of section 677(3)(a) of the 2006 Act (Companies Act accounts: relevant provisions for purposes of financial assistance) are provisions for liabilities within paragraph 2 of this Schedule.

Redemption or purchase by private company out of capital

4. The specified provisions for the purposes of section 712(2)(b)(i) of the 2006 Act (Companies Act accounts: relevant provisions to determine available profits for redemption or purchase out of capital) are provisions of any of the kinds mentioned in paragraphs 1 and 2 of this Schedule.

Justification of distribution by references to accounts

5. The specified provisions for the purposes of section 836(1)(b)(i) of the 2006 Act (Companies Act accounts: relevant provisions for distribution purposes) are provisions of any of the kinds mentioned in paragraphs 1 and 2 of this Schedule.

[Realised losses

6. The specified provisions for the purposes of section 841(2)(a) of the 2006 Act (Companies Act accounts: treatment of provisions as realised losses) are provisions of any of the kinds mentioned in paragraphs 1 and 2 of this Schedule.]

NOTES

Commencement: 6 April 2008.

Para 6: added by the Companies Act 2006 (Accounts, Reports and Audit) Regulations 2009, SI 2009/1581, reg 11(1), (3), as from 27 June 2009, in relation to financial years beginning on or after 6 April 2008 which have not ended before 27 June 2009.

SCHEDULE 8
GENERAL INTERPRETATION

Regulation 13

Financial instruments

[4.169]

1. References to "derivatives" include commodity-based contracts that give either contracting party the right to settle in cash or in some other financial instrument, except where such contracts—

(a) were entered into for the purpose of, and continue to meet, the company's expected purchase, sale or usage requirements,

(b) were designated for such purpose at their inception, and

(c) are expected to be settled by delivery of the commodity.

2. (1) The expressions listed in sub-paragraph (2) have the same meaning as they have in Council Directive 78/660/EEC on the annual accounts of certain types of companies.

(2) Those expressions are "available for sale financial asset", "business combination", "commodity-based contracts", "derivative", "equity instrument", "exchange difference", "fair value hedge accounting system", "financial fixed asset", "financial instrument", "foreign entity", "hedge accounting", "hedge accounting system", "hedged items", "hedging instrument", "held for trading purposes", "held to maturity", "monetary item", "receivables", "reliable market" and "trading portfolio".

Fixed and current assets

3. "Fixed assets" means assets of a company which are intended for use on a continuing basis in the company's activities, and "current assets" means assets not intended for such use.

Historical cost accounting rules

4. References to the historical cost accounting rules are to be read in accordance with paragraph 30 of Schedule 1 to these Regulations.

Listed investments

5. (1) "Listed investment" means an investment as respects which there has been granted a listing on—

(a) a recognised investment exchange other than an overseas investment exchange, or

(b) a stock exchange of repute outside the United Kingdom.

(2) "Recognised investment exchange" and "overseas investment exchange" have the meaning given in Part 18 of the Financial Services and Markets Act 2000.

Loans

6. A loan is treated as falling due for repayment, and an instalment of a loan is treated as falling due for payment, on the earliest date on which the lender could require repayment or (as the case may be) payment, if he exercised all options and rights available to him.

Materiality

7. Amounts which in the particular context of any provision of Schedule 1 to these Regulations are not material may be disregarded for the purposes of that provision.

Participating interests

8. (1) A "participating interest" means an interest held by an undertaking in the shares of another undertaking which it holds on a long-term basis for the purpose of securing a contribution to its activities by the exercise of control or influence arising from or related to that interest.

(2) A holding of 20% or more of the shares of the undertaking is to be presumed to be a participating interest unless the contrary is shown.

(3) The reference in sub-paragraph (1) to an interest in shares includes—

(a) an interest which is convertible into an interest in shares, and

(b) an option to acquire shares or any such interest,

and an interest or option falls within paragraph (a) or (b) notwithstanding that the shares to which it relates are, until the conversion or the exercise of the option, unissued.

(4) For the purposes of this paragraph an interest held on behalf of an undertaking is to be treated as held by it.

(5) In the balance sheet and profit and loss formats set out in Part 1 of Schedule 1 and Part 1 of Schedule 4 to these Regulations, "participating interest" does not include an interest in a group undertaking.

(6) For the purpose of this paragraph as it applies in relation to the expression "participating interest"—

(a) in those formats as they apply in relation to group accounts, and

(b) in paragraph 19 of Schedule 6 (group accounts: undertakings to be accounted for as associated undertakings),

the references in sub-paragraphs (1) to (4) to the interest held by, and the purposes and activities of, the undertaking concerned are to be construed as references to the interest held by, and the purposes and activities of, the group (within the meaning of paragraph 1 of that Schedule).

Purchase price

9. "Purchase price", in relation to an asset of a company or any raw materials or consumables used in the production of such an asset, includes any consideration (whether in cash or otherwise) given by the company in respect of that asset or those materials or consumables, as the case may be.

Realised profits and losses

10. "Realised profits" and "realised losses" have the same meaning as in section 853(4) and (5) of the 2006 Act.

Staff costs

11. (1) "Social security costs" means any contributions by the company to any state social security or pension scheme, fund or arrangement.

(2) "Pension costs" includes—
  (a) any costs incurred by the company in respect of any pension scheme established for the purpose of providing pensions for persons currently or formerly employed by the company,
  (b) any sums set aside for the future payment of pensions directly by the company to current or former employees, and
  (c) any pensions paid directly to such persons without having first been set aside.

(3) Any amount stated in respect of the item "social security costs" or in respect of the item "wages and salaries" in the company's profit and loss account must be determined by reference to payments made or costs incurred in respect of all persons employed by the company during the financial year under contracts of service.

NOTES

Commencement: 6 April 2008.

LARGE AND MEDIUM-SIZED COMPANIES AND GROUPS (ACCOUNTS AND REPORTS) REGULATIONS 2008

(SI 2008/410)

NOTES

Made: 19 February 2008.

Authority: Companies Act 2006, ss 396(3), 404(3), 409(1)–(3), 412(1)–(3), 416(4), 421(1), (2), 445(3)(a), (b), 677(3)(a), 712(2)(b)(i), 831(3)(a), 832(4)(a), 836(1)(b)(i), 1292(1)(a), (c).

Commencement: 6 April 2008.

These Regulations are reproduced as amended by: the Partnerships (Accounts) Regulations 2008, SI 2008/569; the Companies Act 2006 (Accounts, Reports and Audit) Regulations 2009, SI 2009/1581.

Application to limited liability partnerships: see the Limited Liability Partnerships (Accounts and Audit) (Application of Companies Act 2006) Regulations 2008, SI 2008/1911 at **[10.1003]**, and Large and Medium-sized Limited Liability Partnerships (Accounts) Regulations 2008, SI 2008/1913 at **[10.1078]**.

Application to partnerships: see the Partnerships (Accounts) Regulations 2008, SI 2008/569 at **[10.984]**.

Application to banks: see the Bank Accounts Directive (Miscellaneous Banks) Regulations 2008, SI 2008/567 (see the note at **[10.983]**).

Application to insurance undertakings: see the Insurance Accounts Directive (Miscellaneous Insurance Undertakings) Regulations 2008, SI 2008/565 (see the note at **[10.982]**).

ARRANGEMENT OF REGULATIONS

PART 1
INTRODUCTION

Part 4   CA 2006 SIs

PART 1
INTRODUCTION

[4.170]

1 Citation and interpretation

(1) These Regulations may be cited as the Large and Medium-sized Companies and Groups (Accounts and Reports) Regulations 2008.

(2) In these Regulations "the 2006 Act" means the Companies Act 2006.

NOTES
Commencement: 6 April 2008.

[4.171]
2   Commencement and application

(1)   These Regulations come into force on 6th April 2008.

(2)   Subject to paragraph (3), they apply in relation to financial years beginning on or after 6th April 2008.

(3)   The requirement for disclosure in paragraph 4 of Schedule 8 to these Regulations (directors' remuneration report: disclosure relating to consideration of conditions in company and group) applies in relation to financial years beginning on or after 6th April 2009.

(4)   These Regulations apply to companies other than those which are subject to the small companies regime under Part 15 of the 2006 Act.

NOTES
Commencement: 6 April 2008.

PART 2
FORM AND CONTENT OF ACCOUNTS

[4.172]
3   Companies Act individual accounts (companies other than banking and insurance companies)

(1)   Subject to regulation 4, the directors of a company—
    (a)   for which they are preparing Companies Act individual accounts under section 396 of the 2006 Act (Companies Act: individual accounts), and
    (b)   which is not a banking company or an insurance company,
must comply with the provisions of Schedule 1 to these Regulations as to the form and content of the balance sheet and profit and loss account, and additional information to be provided by way of notes to the accounts.

(2)   The profit and loss account of a company that falls within section 408 of the 2006 Act (individual profit and loss account where group accounts prepared) need not contain the information specified in paragraphs 65 to 69 of Schedule 1 to these Regulations (information supplementing the profit and loss account).

NOTES
Commencement: 6 April 2008.

[4.173]
4   Medium-sized companies: exemptions for Companies Act individual accounts

(1)   This regulation applies to a company—
    (a)   which qualifies as medium-sized in relation to a financial year under section 465 of the 2006 Act, and
    (b)   the directors of which are preparing Companies Act individual accounts under section 396 of that Act for that year.

(2)   The individual accounts for the year need not comply with the following provisions of Schedule 1 to these Regulations—
    (a)   paragraph 45 (disclosure with respect to compliance with accounting standards), and
    (b)   paragraph 72 (related party transactions).

(3)   The directors of the company may deliver to the registrar of companies a copy of the accounts for the year—
    (a)   which includes a profit and loss account in which the following items listed in the profit and loss account formats set out in Schedule 1 are combined as one item—
        items 2, 3 and 6 in format 1;
        items 2 to 5 in format 2;
        items A.1 and B.2 in format 3;
        items A.1, A.2 and B.2 to B.4 in format 4;
    (b)   which does not contain the information required by paragraph 68 of Schedule 1 (particulars of turnover).

NOTES
Commencement: 6 April 2008.

[4.174]
5   Companies Act individual accounts: banking companies

(1)   The directors of a company—

(a)   for which they are preparing Companies Act individual accounts under section 396 of the 2006 Act, and

(b)   which is a banking company,

must comply with the provisions of Schedule 2 to these Regulations as to the form and content of the balance sheet and profit and loss account, and additional information to be provided by way of notes to the accounts.

(2)   The profit and loss account of a banking company that falls within section 408 of the 2006 Act (individual profit and loss account where group accounts prepared) need not contain the information specified in paragraphs 85 to 91 of Schedule 2 to these Regulations (information supplementing the profit and loss account).

(3)   Accounts prepared in accordance with this regulation must contain a statement that they are prepared in accordance with the provisions of these Regulations relating to banking companies.

NOTES

Commencement: 6 April 2008.

[4.175]
6   Companies Act individual accounts: insurance companies

(1)   The directors of a company—
(a)   for which they are preparing Companies Act individual accounts under section 396 of the 2006 Act, and
(b)   which is an insurance company,

must comply with the provisions of Schedule 3 to these Regulations as to the form and content of the balance sheet and profit and loss account, and additional information to be provided by way of notes to the accounts.

(2)   The profit and loss account of a company that falls within section 408 of the 2006 Act (individual profit and loss account where group accounts prepared) need not contain the information specified in paragraphs 83 to 89 of Schedule 3 to these Regulations (information supplementing the profit and loss account).

(3)   Accounts prepared in accordance with this regulation must contain a statement that they are prepared in accordance with the provisions of these Regulations relating to insurance companies.

NOTES

Commencement: 6 April 2008.

[4.176]
7   Information about related undertakings (Companies Act or IAS individual or group accounts)

(1)   Companies Act or IAS individual or group accounts must comply with the provisions of Schedule 4 to these Regulations as to information about related undertakings to be given in notes to the company's accounts.

(2)   In Schedule 4—
Part 1 contains provisions applying to all companies
Part 2 contains provisions applying only to companies not required to prepare group accounts
Part 3 contains provisions applying only to companies required to prepare group accounts
Part 4 contains additional disclosures for banking companies and groups
Part 5 contains interpretative provisions.

(3)   Information otherwise required to be given by Schedule 4 need not be disclosed with respect to an undertaking that—
(a)   is established under the law of a country outside the United Kingdom, or
(b)   carries on business outside the United Kingdom,
if the conditions specified in section 409(4) of the 2006 Act are met (see section 409(5) of the 2006 Act for disclosure required where advantage taken of this exemption).

This paragraph does not apply in relation to the information otherwise required by paragraph 3, 7 or 21 of Schedule 4.

NOTES

Commencement: 6 April 2008.

[4.177]
8   Information about directors' benefits: remuneration (Companies Act or IAS individual or group accounts: quoted and unquoted companies)

(1)   Companies Act or IAS individual or group accounts must comply with the provisions of Schedule 5 to these Regulations as to information about directors' remuneration to be given in notes to the company's accounts.

(2)   In Schedule 5—
Part 1 contains provisions applying to quoted and unquoted companies,

Part 2 contains provisions applying only to unquoted companies, and
Part 3 contains supplementary provisions.

NOTES
Commencement: 6 April 2008.

[4.178]
9　Companies Act group accounts
(1)　Subject to paragraphs (2) and (3), where the directors of a parent company prepare Companies Act group accounts under section 403 of the 2006 Act (group accounts: applicable accounting framework), those accounts must comply with the provisions of Part 1 of Schedule 6 to these Regulations as to the form and content of the consolidated balance sheet and consolidated profit and loss account, and additional information to be provided by way of notes to the accounts.

(2)　The directors of the parent company of a banking group preparing Companies Act group accounts must do so in accordance with the provisions of Part 1 of Schedule 6 as modified by Part 2 of that Schedule.

(3)　The directors of the parent company of an insurance group preparing Companies Act group accounts must do so in accordance with the provisions of Part 1 of Schedule 6 as modified by Part 3 of that Schedule.

(4)　Accounts prepared in accordance with paragraph (2) or (3) must contain a statement that they are prepared in accordance with the provisions of these Regulations relating to banking groups or to insurance groups, as the case may be.

NOTES
Commencement: 6 April 2008.

PART 3
DIRECTORS' REPORT

[4.179]
10　Directors' report
(1)　The report which the directors of a company are required to prepare under section 415 of the 2006 Act (duty to prepare directors' report) must disclose the matters specified in Schedule 7 to these Regulations.

(2)　In Schedule 7—
　　Part 1 relates to matters of a general nature, including changes in asset values and contributions for political and charitable purposes,
　　Part 2 relates to the acquisition by a company of its own shares or a charge on them,
　　Part 3 relates to the employment, training and advancement of disabled persons,
　　Part 4 relates to the involvement of employees in the affairs, policy and performance of the company, and
　　Part 5 relates to the company's policy and practice on the payment of creditors.

NOTES
Commencement: 6 April 2008.

PART 4
DIRECTORS' REMUNERATION REPORT

[4.180]
11　Directors' remuneration report (quoted companies)
(1)　The remuneration report which the directors of a quoted company are required to prepare under section 420 of the 2006 Act (duty to prepare directors' remuneration report) must contain the information specified in Schedule 8 to these Regulations, and must comply with any requirement of that Schedule as to how information is to be set out in the report.

(2)　In Schedule 8—
　　Part 1 is introductory,
　　Part 2 relates to information about remuneration committees, performance related remuneration, consideration of conditions elsewhere in company and group and liabilities in respect of directors' contracts,
　　Part 3 relates to detailed information about directors' remuneration (information included under Part 3 is required to be reported on by the auditor (see subsection (3)), and
　　Part 4 contains interpretative and supplementary provisions.

(3)　For the purposes of section 497 in Part 16 of the 2006 Act (auditor's report on auditable part of directors' remuneration report), "the auditable part" of a directors' remuneration report is the part containing the information required by Part 3 of Schedule 8 to these Regulations.

NOTES
Commencement: 6 April 2008.

PART 5
INTERPRETATION

[4.181]
12 Definition of "provisions"

Schedule 9 to these Regulations defines "provisions" for the purposes of these Regulations and for the purposes of—

(a) section 677(3)(a) (Companies Act accounts: relevant provisions for purposes of financial assistance) in Part 18 of the 2006 Act,

(b) section 712(2)(b)(i) (Companies Act accounts: relevant provisions to determine available profits for redemption or purchase by private company out of capital) in that Part, . . .

(c) sections 831(3)(a) (Companies Act accounts: net asset restriction on public company distributions), 832(4)(a) (Companies Act accounts: investment companies distributions) and 836(1)(b)(i) (Companies Act accounts: relevant provisions for distribution purposes) in Part 23 of that Act[, and

(d) section 841(2)(a) (Companies Act accounts: provisions to be treated as realised losses) in that Part].

NOTES
Commencement: 6 April 2008.
The word "and" omitted from the end of para (b) was revoked, and para (d) (and the word immediately preceding it) was added, by the Companies Act 2006 (Accounts, Reports and Audit) Regulations 2009, SI 2009/1581, reg 12(1), (2), as from 27 June 2009, in relation to financial years beginning on or after 6 April 2008 which have not ended before 27 June 2009.

[4.182]
13 General interpretation

Schedule 10 to these Regulations contains general definitions for the purposes of these Regulations.

NOTES
Commencement: 6 April 2008.

SCHEDULES

SCHEDULE 1
COMPANIES ACT INDIVIDUAL ACCOUNTS: COMPANIES WHICH ARE NOT BANKING OR INSURANCE COMPANIES

Regulation 3(1)

PART 1
GENERAL RULES AND FORMATS

SECTION A
GENERAL RULES

[4.183]
1. (1) Subject to the following provisions of this Schedule—

(a) every balance sheet of a company must show the items listed in either of the balance sheet formats in Section B of this Part, and

(b) every profit and loss account must show the items listed in any one of the profit and loss account formats in Section B.

(2) References in this Schedule to the items listed in any of the formats in Section B are to those items read together with any of the notes following the formats which apply to those items.

(3) The items must be shown in the order and under the headings and sub-headings given in the particular format used, but—

(a) the notes to the formats may permit alternative positions for any particular items, and

(b) the heading or sub-heading for any item does not have to be distinguished by any letter or number assigned to that item in the format used.

2. (1) Where in accordance with paragraph 1 a company's balance sheet or profit and loss account for any financial year has been prepared by reference to one of the formats in Section B, the company's directors must use the same format in preparing Companies Act individual accounts for subsequent financial years, unless in their opinion there are special reasons for a change.

(2) Particulars of any such change must be given in a note to the accounts in which the new format is first used, and the reasons for the change must be explained.

3. (1)   Any item required to be shown in a company's balance sheet or profit and loss account may be shown in greater detail than required by the particular format used.

(2)   The balance sheet or profit and loss account may include an item representing or covering the amount of any asset or liability, income or expenditure not otherwise covered by any of the items listed in the format used, save that none of the following may be treated as assets in any balance sheet—
  (a)   preliminary expenses,
  (b)   expenses of, and commission on, any issue of shares or debentures, and
  (c)   costs of research.

4. (1)   Where the special nature of the company's business requires it, the company's directors must adapt the arrangement, headings and sub-headings otherwise required in respect of items given an Arabic number in the balance sheet or profit and loss account format used.

(2)   The directors may combine items to which Arabic numbers are given in any of the formats in Section B if—
  (a)   their individual amounts are not material to assessing the state of affairs or profit or loss of the company for the financial year in question, or
  (b)   the combination facilitates that assessment.

(3)   Where sub-paragraph (2)(b) applies, the individual amounts of any items which have been combined must be disclosed in a note to the accounts.

5. (1)   Subject to sub-paragraph (2), the directors must not include a heading or sub-heading corresponding to an item in the balance sheet or profit and loss account format used if there is no amount to be shown for that item for the financial year to which the balance sheet or profit and loss account relates.

(2)   Where an amount can be shown for the item in question for the immediately preceding financial year that amount must be shown under the heading or sub-heading required by the format for that item.

6. Every profit and loss account must show the amount of a company's profit or loss on ordinary activities before taxation.

7. (1)   For every item shown in the balance sheet or profit and loss account the corresponding amount for the immediately preceding financial year must also be shown.

(2)   Where that corresponding amount is not comparable with the amount to be shown for the item in question in respect of the financial year to which the balance sheet or profit and loss account relates, the former amount may be adjusted, and particulars of the non-comparability and of any adjustment must be disclosed in a note to the accounts.

8. Amounts in respect of items representing assets or income may not be set off against amounts in respect of items representing liabilities or expenditure (as the case may be), or vice versa.

9. The company's directors must, in determining how amounts are presented within items in the profit and loss account and balance sheet, have regard to the substance of the reported transaction or arrangement, in accordance with generally accepted accounting principles or practice.

SECTION B
THE REQUIRED FORMATS FOR ACCOUNTS

Balance sheet formats

Format 1

A   Called up share capital not paid [1]

B   Fixed assets
  I   Intangible assets
      1   Development costs
      2   Concessions, patents, licences, trade marks and similar rights and assets [2]
      3   Goodwill [3]
      4   Payments on account
  II   Tangible assets
      1   Land and buildings
      2   Plant and machinery
      3   Fixtures, fittings, tools and equipment
      4   Payments on account and assets in course of construction
  III   Investments
      1   Shares in group undertakings
      2   Loans to group undertakings
      3   Participating interests

4   Loans to undertakings in which the company has a participating interest
5   Other investments other than loans
6   Other loans
7   Own shares [(4)]

C   Current assets
  I   Stocks
    1   Raw materials and consumables
    2   Work in progress
    3   Finished goods and goods for resale
    4   Payments on account
  II   Debtors [(5)]
    1   Trade debtors
    2   Amounts owed by group undertakings
    3   Amounts owed by undertakings in which the company has a participating interest
    4   Other debtors
    5   Called up share capital not paid [(1)]
    6   repayments and accrued income [(6)]
  III Investments
    1   Shares in group undertakings
    2   Own shares [(4)]
    3   Other investments
  IV   Cash at bank and in hand

D   Prepayments and accrued income [(6)]

E   Creditors: amounts falling due within one year
    1   Debenture loans [(7)]
    2   Bank loans and overdrafts
    3   Payments received on account [(8)]
    4   Trade creditors
    5   Bills of exchange payable
    6   Amounts owed to group undertakings
    7   Amounts owed to undertakings in which the company has a participating interest
    8   Other creditors including taxation and social security [(9)]
    9   Accruals and deferred income [(10)]

F   Net current assets (liabilities) [(11)]

G   Total assets less current liabilities

H   Creditors: amounts falling due after more than one year
    1   Debenture loans [(7)]
    2   Bank loans and overdrafts
    3   Payments received on account [(8)]
    4   Trade creditors
    5   Bills of exchange payable
    6   Amounts owed to group undertakings
    7   Amounts owed to undertakings in which the company has a participating interest
    8   Other creditors including taxation and social security [(9)]
    9   Accruals and deferred income [(10)]

I   Provisions for liabilities
    1   Pensions and similar obligations
    2   Taxation, including deferred taxation
    3   Other provisions

J   Accruals and deferred income [(10)]

K   Capital and reserves
  I   Called up share capital [(12)]
  II   Share premium account
  III Revaluation reserve
  IV   Other reserves
    1   Capital redemption reserve
    2   Reserve for own shares
    3   Reserves provided for by the articles of association
    4   Other reserves
  V   Profit and loss account

Balance sheet formats

Format 2

ASSETS

A   Called up share capital not paid [(1)]

B   Fixed assets
   I   Intangible assets
      1   Development costs
      2   Concessions, patents, licences, trade marks and similar rights and assets [(2)]
      3   Goodwill [(3)]
      4   Payments on account
   II   Tangible assets
      1   Land and buildings
      2   Plant and machinery
      3   Fixtures, fittings, tools and equipment
      4   Payments on account and assets in course of construction
   III   Investments
      1   Shares in group undertakings
      2   Loans to group undertakings
      3   participating interests
      4   Loans to undertakings in which the company has a participating interest
      5   Other investments other than loans
      6   Other loans
      7   Own shares [(4)]

C   Current assets
   I   Stocks
      1   Raw materials and consumables
      2   Work in progress
      3   Finished goods and goods for resale
      4   Payments on account
   II   Debtors [(5)]
      1   Trade debtors
      2   Amounts owed by group undertakings
      3   Amounts owed by undertakings in which the company has a participating interest
      4   Other debtors
      5   Called up share capital not paid [(1)]
      6   Prepayments and accrued income [(6)]
   III   Investments
      1   Shares in group undertakings
      2   Own shares [(4)]
      3   Other investments
   IV   Cash at bank and in hand

D   Prepayments and accrued income [(6)]

LIABILITIES

A   Capital and reserves
   I   Called up share capital [(12)]
   II   Share premium account
   III   Revaluation reserve
   IV   Other reserves
      1   Capital redemption reserve
      2   Reserve for own shares
      3   Reserves provided for by the articles of association
      4   Other reserves
   V   Profit and loss account

B   Provisions for liabilities
      1   Pensions and similar obligations
      2   Taxation, including deferred taxation
      3   Other provisions

C   Creditors [(13)]
      1   Debenture loans [(7)]
      2   Bank loans and overdrafts
      3   Payments received on account [(8)]

4   Trade creditors
5   Bills of exchange payable
6   Amounts owed to group undertakings
7   Amounts owed to undertakings in which the company has a participating interest
8   Other creditors including taxation and social security [9]
9   Accruals and deferred income [10]

D   Accruals and deferred income [10]

Notes on the balance sheet formats

(1)   Called up share capital not paid

(Formats 1 and 2, items A and CII.5.)

This item may be shown in either of the two positions given in formats 1 and 2.

(2)   Concessions, patents, licences, trade marks and similar rights and assets

(Formats 1 and 2, item B.I.2.)

Amounts in respect of assets are only to be included in a company's balance sheet under this item if either—

(a)   the assets were acquired for valuable consideration and are not required to be shown under goodwill, or

(b)   the assets in question were created by the company itself.

(3)   Goodwill

(Formats 1 and 2, item B.I.3.)

Amounts representing goodwill are only to be included to the extent that the goodwill was acquired for valuable consideration.

(4)   Own shares

(Formats 1 and 2, items B.III.7 and CIII.2.)

The nominal value of the shares held must be shown separately.

(5)   Debtors

(Formats 1 and 2, items CII.1 to 6.)

The amount falling due after more than one year must be shown separately for each item included under debtors.

(6)   Prepayments and accrued income

(Formats 1 and 2, items CII.6 and D.)

This item may be shown in either of the two positions given in formats 1 and 2.

(7)   Debenture loans

(Format 1, items E.1 and H.1 and format 2, item C1.)

The amount of any convertible loans must be shown separately.

(8)   Payments received on account

(Format 1, items E.3 and H.3 and format 2, item C3.)

Payments received on account of orders must be shown for each of these items in so far as they are not shown as deductions from stocks.

(9)   Other creditors including taxation and social security

(Format 1, items E.8 and H.8 and format 2, item C8.)

The amount for creditors in respect of taxation and social security must be shown separately from the amount for other creditors.

(10)   Accruals and deferred income

(Format 1, items E.9, H.9 and J and format 2, items C9 and D.)

The two positions given for this item in format 1 at E.9 and H.9 are an alternative to the position at J, but if the item is not shown in a position corresponding to that at J it may be shown in either or both of the other two positions (as the case may require).

The two positions given for this item in format 2 are alternatives.

(11)   Net current assets (liabilities)

(Format 1, item F.)

In determining the amount to be shown for this item any amounts shown under "prepayments and accrued income" must be taken into account wherever shown.

(12)   Called up share capital

(Format 1, item K.I and format 2, item A.I.)

The amount of allotted share capital and the amount of called up share capital which has been paid up must be shown separately.

(13)   Creditors

(Format 2, items C1 to 9.)

Amounts falling due within one year and after one year must be shown separately for each of these items and for the aggregate of all of these items.

Profit and loss account formats

Format 1
(see note [14] below)

1   Turnover

2   Cost of sales [14]

3   Gross profit or loss

4   Distribution costs [14]

5   Administrative expenses [14]

6   Other operating income

7   Income from shares in group undertakings

8   Income from participating interests

9   Income from other fixed asset investments [15]

10   Other interest receivable and similar income [15]

11   Amounts written off investments

12   Interest payable and similar charges [16]

13   Tax on profit or loss on ordinary activities

14   Profit or loss on ordinary activities after taxation

15   Extraordinary income

16   Extraordinary charges

17   Extraordinary profit or loss

18   Tax on extraordinary profit or loss

19   Other taxes not shown under the above items

20   Profit or loss for the financial year

Profit and loss account formats

Format 2

1   Turnover

2   Change in stocks of finished goods and in work in progress

3   Own work capitalised

4   Other operating income

5
   (a)   Raw materials and consumables
   (b)   Other external charges

6   Staff costs
   (a)   wages and salaries
   (b)   social security costs
   (c)   other pension costs

7
   (a)   Depreciation and other amounts written off tangible and intangible fixed assets
   (b)   Exceptional amounts written off current assets

8   Other operating charges

9   Income from shares in group undertakings

10   Income from participating interests

11 Income from other fixed asset investments [15]

12 Other interest receivable and similar income [15]

13 Amounts written off investments

14 Interest payable and similar charges [16]

15 Tax on profit or loss on ordinary activities

16 Profit or loss on ordinary activities after taxation

17 Extraordinary income

18 Extraordinary charges

19 Extraordinary profit or loss

20 Tax on extraordinary profit or loss

21 Other taxes not shown under the above items

22 Profit or loss for the financial year

Profit and loss account formats

Format 3
(see note [14] below)

A Charges
1   Cost of sales [14]
2   Distribution costs [14]
3   Administrative expenses [14]
4   Amounts written off investments
5   Interest payable and similar charges [16]
6   Tax on profit or loss on ordinary activities
7   Profit or loss on ordinary activities after taxation
8   Extraordinary charges
9   Tax on extraordinary profit or loss
10   Other taxes not shown under the above items
11   Profit or loss for the financial year

B Income
1   Turnover
2   Other operating income
3   Income from shares in group undertakings
4   Income from participating interests
5   Income from other fixed asset investments [15]
6   Other interest receivable and similar income [15]
7   Profit or loss on ordinary activities after taxation
8   Extraordinary income
9   Profit or loss for the financial year

Profit and loss account formats

Format 4

A Charges
1   Reduction in stocks of finished goods and in work in progress
2
       (a)   Raw materials and consumables
       (b)   Other external charges
3   Staff costs
       (a)   wages and salaries
       (b)   social security costs
       (c)   other pension costs
4
       (a)   Depreciation and other amounts written off tangible and intangible fixed assets
       (b)   Exceptional amounts written off current assets
5   Other operating charges
6   Amounts written off investments
7   Interest payable and similar charges [16]
8   Tax on profit or loss on ordinary activities

9   Profit or loss on ordinary activities after taxation
10   Extraordinary charges
11   Tax on extraordinary profit or loss
12   Other taxes not shown under the above items
13   Profit or loss for the financial year

B Income
1   Turnover
2   Increase in stocks of finished goods and in work in progress
3   Own work capitalised
4   Other operating income
5   Income from shares in group undertakings
6   Income from participating interests
7   Income from other fixed asset investments [(15)]
8   Other interest receivable and similar income [(15)]
9   Profit or loss on ordinary activities after taxation
10   Extraordinary income
11   Profit or loss for the financial year

Notes on the profit and loss account formats

(14) Cost of sales: distribution costs: administrative expenses

(Format 1, items 2, 4 and 5 and format 3, items A.1, 2 and 3.)

These items must be stated after taking into account any necessary provisions for depreciation or diminution in value of assets.

(15) Income from other fixed asset investments: other interest receivable and similar income

(Format 1, items 9 and 10; format 2, items 11 and 12; format 3, items B.5 and 6 and format 4, items B.7 and 8.)

Income and interest derived from group undertakings must be shown separately from income and interest derived from other sources.

(16) Interest payable and similar charges

(Format 1, item 12; format 2, item 14; format 3, item A.5 and format 4, item A.7.)

The amount payable to group undertakings must be shown separately.

(17) Formats 1 and 3

The amount of any provisions for depreciation and diminution in value of tangible and intangible fixed assets falling to be shown under items 7(a) and A.4(a) respectively in formats 2 and 4 must be disclosed in a note to the accounts in any case where the profit and loss account is prepared using format 1 or format 3.

NOTES
Commencement: 6 April 2008.

PART 2
ACCOUNTING PRINCIPLES AND RULES

SECTION A
ACCOUNTING PRINCIPLES

Preliminary

[4.184]
10. (1) The amounts to be included in respect of all items shown in a company's accounts must be determined in accordance with the principles set out in this Section.

(2) But if it appears to the company's directors that there are special reasons for departing from any of those principles in preparing the company's accounts in respect of any financial year they may do so, in which case particulars of the departure, the reasons for it and its effect must be given in a note to the accounts.

Accounting principles

11. The company is presumed to be carrying on business as a going concern.

12. Accounting policies must be applied consistently within the same accounts and from one financial year to the next.

13. The amount of any item must be determined on a prudent basis, and in particular—
   (a)   only profits realised at the balance sheet date are to be included in the profit and loss account, and

(b)   all liabilities which have arisen in respect of the financial year to which the accounts relate or a previous financial year must be taken into account, including those which only become apparent between the balance sheet date and the date on which it is signed on behalf of the board of directors in accordance with section 414 of the 2006 Act (approval and signing of accounts).

14. All income and charges relating to the financial year to which the accounts relate must be taken into account, without regard to the date of receipt or payment.

15. In determining the aggregate amount of any item, the amount of each individual asset or liability that falls to be taken into account must be determined separately.

SECTION B
HISTORICAL COST ACCOUNTING RULES
Preliminary

16. Subject to Sections C and D of this Part of this Schedule, the amounts to be included in respect of all items shown in a company's accounts must be determined in accordance with the rules set out in this Section.

Fixed assets
General rules

17. (1)   The amount to be included in respect of any fixed asset must be its purchase price or production cost.

(2)   This is subject to any provision for depreciation or diminution in value made in accordance with paragraphs 18 to 20.

Rules for depreciation and diminution in value

18. In the case of any fixed asset which has a limited useful economic life, the amount of—
   (a)   its purchase price or production cost, or
   (b)   where it is estimated that any such asset will have a residual value at the end of the period of its useful economic life, its purchase price or production cost less that estimated residual value,
must be reduced by provisions for depreciation calculated to write off that amount systematically over the period of the asset's useful economic life.

19. (1)   Where a fixed asset investment falling to be included under item B.III of either of the balance sheet formats set out in Part 1 of this Schedule has diminished in value, provisions for diminution in value may be made in respect of it and the amount to be included in respect of it may be reduced accordingly.

(2)   Provisions for diminution in value must be made in respect of any fixed asset which has diminished in value if the reduction in its value is expected to be permanent (whether its useful economic life is limited or not), and the amount to be included in respect of it must be reduced accordingly.

(3)   Any provisions made under sub-paragraph (1) or (2) which are not shown in the profit and loss account must be disclosed (either separately or in aggregate) in a note to the accounts.

20. (1)   Where the reasons for which any provision was made in accordance with paragraph 19 have ceased to apply to any extent, that provision must be written back to the extent that it is no longer necessary.

(2)   Any amounts written back in accordance with sub-paragraph (1) which are not shown in the profit and loss account must be disclosed (either separately or in aggregate) in a note to the accounts.

Development costs

21. (1)   Notwithstanding that an item in respect of "development costs" is included under "fixed assets" in the balance sheet formats set out in Part 1 of this Schedule, an amount may only be included in a company's balance sheet in respect of development costs in special circumstances.

(2)   If any amount is included in a company's balance sheet in respect of development costs the following information must be given in a note to the accounts—
   (a)   the period over which the amount of those costs originally capitalised is being or is to be written off, and
   (b)   the reasons for capitalising the development costs in question.

Goodwill

22. (1)   The application of paragraphs 17 to 20 in relation to goodwill (in any case where goodwill is treated as an asset) is subject to the following.

(2)   Subject to sub-paragraph (3), the amount of the consideration for any goodwill acquired by a company must be reduced by provisions for depreciation calculated to write off that amount systematically over a period chosen by the directors of the company.

(3)   The period chosen must not exceed the useful economic life of the goodwill in question.

(4)   In any case where any goodwill acquired by a company is shown or included as an asset in the company's balance sheet there must be disclosed in a note to the accounts—
- (a)   the period chosen for writing off the consideration for that goodwill, and
- (b)   the reasons for choosing that period.

Current assets

23.   Subject to paragraph 24, the amount to be included in respect of any current asset must be its purchase price or production cost.

24.   (1)   If the net realisable value of any current asset is lower than its purchase price or production cost, the amount to be included in respect of that asset must be the net realisable value.

(2)   Where the reasons for which any provision for diminution in value was made in accordance with sub-paragraph (1) have ceased to apply to any extent, that provision must be written back to the extent that it is no longer necessary.

Miscellaneous and supplementary provisions

Excess of money owed over value received as an asset item

25.   (1)   Where the amount repayable on any debt owed by a company is greater than the value of the consideration received in the transaction giving rise to the debt, the amount of the difference may be treated as an asset.

(2)   Where any such amount is so treated—
- (a)   it must be written off by reasonable amounts each year and must be completely written off before repayment of the debt, and
- (b)   if the current amount is not shown as a separate item in the company's balance sheet, it must be disclosed in a note to the accounts.

Assets included at a fixed amount

26.   (1)   Subject to sub-paragraph (2), assets which fall to be included—
- (a)   amongst the fixed assets of a company under the item "tangible assets", or
- (b)   amongst the current assets of a company under the item "raw materials and consumables",

may be included at a fixed quantity and value.

(2)   Sub-paragraph (1) applies to assets of a kind which are constantly being replaced where—
- (a)   their overall value is not material to assessing the company's state of affairs, and
- (b)   their quantity, value and composition are not subject to material variation.

Determination of purchase price or production cost

27.   (1)   The purchase price of an asset is to be determined by adding to the actual price paid any expenses incidental to its acquisition.

(2)   The production cost of an asset is to be determined by adding to the purchase price of the raw materials and consumables used the amount of the costs incurred by the company which are directly attributable to the production of that asset.

(3)   In addition, there may be included in the production cost of an asset—
- (a)   a reasonable proportion of the costs incurred by the company which are only indirectly attributable to the production of that asset, but only to the extent that they relate to the period of production, and
- (b)   interest on capital borrowed to finance the production of that asset, to the extent that it accrues in respect of the period of production,

provided, however, in a case within paragraph (b), that the inclusion of the interest in determining the cost of that asset and the amount of the interest so included is disclosed in a note to the accounts.

(4)   In the case of current assets distribution costs may not be included in production costs.

28.   (1)   The purchase price or production cost of—
- (a)   any assets which fall to be included under any item shown in a company's balance sheet under the general item "stocks", and
- (b)   any assets which are fungible assets (including investments),

may be determined by the application of any of the methods mentioned in sub-paragraph (2) in relation to any such assets of the same class, provided that the method chosen is one which appears to the directors to be appropriate in the circumstances of the company.

(2)   Those methods are—
- (a)   the method known as "first in, first out" (FIFO),
- (b)   the method known as "last in, first out" (LIFO),

    (c)   a weighted average price, and

    (d)   any other method similar to any of the methods mentioned above.

(3)   Where in the case of any company—

    (a)   the purchase price or production cost of assets falling to be included under any item shown in the company's balance sheet has been determined by the application of any method permitted by this paragraph, and

    (b)   the amount shown in respect of that item differs materially from the relevant alternative amount given below in this paragraph,

the amount of that difference must be disclosed in a note to the accounts.

(4)   Subject to sub-paragraph (5), for the purposes of sub-paragraph (3)(b), the relevant alternative amount, in relation to any item shown in a company's balance sheet, is the amount which would have been shown in respect of that item if assets of any class included under that item at an amount determined by any method permitted by this paragraph had instead been included at their replacement cost as at the balance sheet date.

(5)   The relevant alternative amount may be determined by reference to the most recent actual purchase price or production cost before the balance sheet date of assets of any class included under the item in question instead of by reference to their replacement cost as at that date, but only if the former appears to the directors of the company to constitute the more appropriate standard of comparison in the case of assets of that class.

Substitution of original stated amount where price or cost unknown

29. (1)   This paragraph applies where—

    (a)   there is no record of the purchase price or production cost of any asset of a company or of any price, expenses or costs relevant for determining its purchase price or production cost in accordance with paragraph 27, or

    (b)   any such record cannot be obtained without unreasonable expense or delay.

(2)   In such a case, the purchase price or production cost of the asset must be taken, for the purposes of paragraphs 17 to 24, to be the value ascribed to it in the earliest available record of its value made on or after its acquisition or production by the company.

SECTION C
ALTERNATIVE ACCOUNTING RULES

Preliminary

30. (1)   The rules set out in Section B are referred to below in this Schedule as the historical cost accounting rules.

(2)   Those rules, with the omission of paragraphs 16, 22 and 26 to 29, are referred to below in this Part of this Schedule as the depreciation rules; and references below in this Schedule to the historical cost accounting rules do not include the depreciation rules as they apply by virtue of paragraph 33.

31.   Subject to paragraphs 33 to 35, the amounts to be included in respect of assets of any description mentioned in paragraph 32 may be determined on any basis so mentioned.

Alternative accounting rules

32. (1)   Intangible fixed assets, other than goodwill, may be included at their current cost.

(2)   Tangible fixed assets may be included at a market value determined as at the date of their last valuation or at their current cost.

(3)   Investments of any description falling to be included under item B III of either of the balance sheet formats set out in Part 1 of this Schedule may be included either—

    (a)   at a market value determined as at the date of their last valuation, or

    (b)   at a value determined on any basis which appears to the directors to be appropriate in the circumstances of the company.

But in the latter case particulars of the method of valuation adopted and of the reasons for adopting it must be disclosed in a note to the accounts.

(4)   Investments of any description falling to be included under item C III of either of the balance sheet formats set out in Part 1 of this Schedule may be included at their current cost.

(5)   Stocks may be included at their current cost.

Application of the depreciation rules

33. (1)   Where the value of any asset of a company is determined on any basis mentioned in paragraph 32, that value must be, or (as the case may require) be the starting point for determining, the amount to be included in respect of that asset in the company's accounts, instead of its purchase price or production cost or any value previously so determined for that asset.

The depreciation rules apply accordingly in relation to any such asset with the substitution for any reference to its purchase price or production cost of a reference to the value most recently determined for that asset on any basis mentioned in paragraph 32.

(2) The amount of any provision for depreciation required in the case of any fixed asset by paragraphs 18 to 20 as they apply by virtue of sub-paragraph (1) is referred to below in this paragraph as the adjusted amount, and the amount of any provision which would be required by any of those paragraphs in the case of that asset according to the historical cost accounting rules is referred to as the historical cost amount.

(3) Where sub-paragraph (1) applies in the case of any fixed asset the amount of any provision for depreciation in respect of that asset—

(a) included in any item shown in the profit and loss account in respect of amounts written off assets of the description in question, or

(b) taken into account in stating any item so shown which is required by note (14) of the notes on the profit and loss account formats set out in Part 1 of this Schedule to be stated after taking into account any necessary provision for depreciation or diminution in value of assets included under it,

may be the historical cost amount instead of the adjusted amount, provided that the amount of any difference between the two is shown separately in the profit and loss account or in a note to the accounts.

Additional information to be provided in case of departure from historical cost accounting rules

34. (1) This paragraph applies where the amounts to be included in respect of assets covered by any items shown in a company's accounts have been determined on any basis mentioned in paragraph 32.

(2) The items affected and the basis of valuation adopted in determining the amounts of the assets in question in the case of each such item must be disclosed in a note to the accounts.

(3) In the case of each balance sheet item affected (except stocks) either—

(a) the comparable amounts determined according to the historical cost accounting rules, or

(b) the differences between those amounts and the corresponding amounts actually shown in the balance sheet in respect of that item,

must be shown separately in the balance sheet or in a note to the accounts.

(4) In sub-paragraph (3), references in relation to any item to the comparable amounts determined as there mentioned are references to—

(a) the aggregate amount which would be required to be shown in respect of that item if the amounts to be included in respect of all the assets covered by that item were determined according to the historical cost accounting rules, and

(b) the aggregate amount of the cumulative provisions for depreciation or diminution in value which would be permitted or required in determining those amounts according to those rules.

Revaluation reserve

35. (1) With respect to any determination of the value of an asset of a company on any basis mentioned in paragraph 32, the amount of any profit or loss arising from that determination (after allowing, where appropriate, for any provisions for depreciation or diminution in value made otherwise than by reference to the value so determined and any adjustments of any such provisions made in the light of that determination) must be credited or (as the case may be) debited to a separate reserve ("the revaluation reserve").

(2) The amount of the revaluation reserve must be shown in the company's balance sheet under a separate sub-heading in the position given for the item "revaluation reserve" in format 1 or 2 of the balance sheet formats set out in Part 1 of this Schedule, but need not be shown under that name.

(3) An amount may be transferred—

(a) from the revaluation reserve—

(i) to the profit and loss account, if the amount was previously charged to that account or represents realised profit, or

(ii) on capitalisation,

(b) to or from the revaluation reserve in respect of the taxation relating to any profit or loss credited or debited to the reserve.

The revaluation reserve must be reduced to the extent that the amounts transferred to it are no longer necessary for the purposes of the valuation method used.

(4) In sub-paragraph (3)(a)(ii) "capitalisation", in relation to an amount standing to the credit of the revaluation reserve, means applying it in wholly or partly paying up unissued shares in the company to be allotted to members of the company as fully or partly paid shares.

(5) The revaluation reserve must not be reduced except as mentioned in this paragraph.

(6) The treatment for taxation purposes of amounts credited or debited to the revaluation reserve must be disclosed in a note to the accounts.

SECTION D
FAIR VALUE ACCOUNTING

Inclusion of financial instruments at fair value

36. (1)   Subject to sub-paragraphs (2) to (5), financial instruments (including derivatives) may be included at fair value.

(2)   Sub-paragraph (1) does not apply to financial instruments that constitute liabilities unless—
    (a)   they are held as part of a trading portfolio,
    (b)   they are derivatives, or
    (c)   they are financial instruments falling within sub-paragraph (4).

(3)   Unless they are financial instruments falling within sub-paragraph (4), sub-paragraph (1) does not apply to—
    (a)   financial instruments (other than derivatives) held to maturity,
    (b)   loans and receivables originated by the company and not held for trading purposes,
    (c)   interests in subsidiary undertakings, associated undertakings and joint ventures,
    (d)   equity instruments issued by the company,
    (e)   contracts for contingent consideration in a business combination, or
    (f)   other financial instruments with such special characteristics that the instruments, according to generally accepted accounting principles or practice, should be accounted for differently from other financial instruments.

(4)   Financial instruments that, under international accounting standards adopted by the European Commission on or before 5th September 2006 in accordance with the IAS Regulation, may be included in accounts at fair value, may be so included, provided that the disclosures required by such accounting standards are made.

(5)   If the fair value of a financial instrument cannot be determined reliably in accordance with paragraph 37, sub-paragraph (1) does not apply to that financial instrument.

(6)   In this paragraph—
    "associated undertaking" has the meaning given by paragraph 19 of Schedule 6 to these Regulations;
    "joint venture" has the meaning given by paragraph 18 of that Schedule.

Determination of fair value

37. (1)   The fair value of a financial instrument is its value determined in accordance with this paragraph.

(2)   If a reliable market can readily be identified for the financial instrument, its fair value is determined by reference to its market value.

(3)   If a reliable market cannot readily be identified for the financial instrument but can be identified for its components or for a similar instrument, its fair value is determined by reference to the market value of its components or of the similar instrument.

(4)   If neither sub-paragraph (2) nor (3) applies, the fair value of the financial instrument is a value resulting from generally accepted valuation models and techniques.

(5)   Any valuation models and techniques used for the purposes of sub-paragraph (4) must ensure a reasonable approximation of the market value.

Hedged items

38. A company may include any assets and liabilities, or identified portions of such assets or liabilities, that qualify as hedged items under a fair value hedge accounting system at the amount required under that system.

Other assets that may be included at fair value

39. (1)   This paragraph applies to—
    (a)   investment property, and
    (b)   living animals and plants,
that, under international accounting standards, may be included in accounts at fair value.

(2)   Such investment property and such living animals and plants may be included at fair value, provided that all such investment property or, as the case may be, all such living animals and plants are so included where their fair value can reliably be determined.

(3)   In this paragraph, "fair value" means fair value determined in accordance with relevant international accounting standards.

Accounting for changes in value

40. (1)   This paragraph applies where a financial instrument is valued in accordance with paragraph 36 or 38 or an asset is valued in accordance with paragraph 39.

(2)   Notwithstanding paragraph 13 in this Part of this Schedule, and subject to sub-paragraphs (3) and (4), a change in the value of the financial instrument or of the investment property or living animal or plant must be included in the profit and loss account.

(3)   Where—
- (a)   the financial instrument accounted for is a hedging instrument under a hedge accounting system that allows some or all of the change in value not to be shown in the profit and loss account, or
- (b)   the change in value relates to an exchange difference arising on a monetary item that forms part of a company's net investment in a foreign entity,

the amount of the change in value must be credited to or (as the case may be) debited from a separate reserve ("the fair value reserve").

(4)   Where the instrument accounted for—
- (a)   is an available for sale financial asset, and
- (b)   is not a derivative,

the change in value may be credited to or (as the case may be) debited from the fair value reserve.

The fair value reserve

41.   (1)   The fair value reserve must be adjusted to the extent that the amounts shown in it are no longer necessary for the purposes of paragraph 40(3) or (4).

(2)   The treatment for taxation purposes of amounts credited or debited to the fair value reserve must be disclosed in a note to the accounts.

NOTES

Commencement: 6 April 2008.

PART 3
NOTES TO THE ACCOUNTS

Preliminary

[4.185]

42.   Any information required in the case of any company by the following provisions of this Part of this Schedule must (if not given in the company's accounts) be given by way of a note to the accounts.

General

Reserves and dividends

43.   There must be stated—
- (a)   any amount set aside or proposed to be set aside to, or withdrawn or proposed to be withdrawn from, reserves,
- (b)   the aggregate amount of dividends paid in the financial year (other than those for which a liability existed at the immediately preceding balance sheet date),
- (c)   the aggregate amount of dividends that the company is liable to pay at the balance sheet date, and
- (d)   the aggregate amount of dividends that are proposed before the date of approval of the accounts, and not otherwise disclosed under sub-paragraph (b) or (c).

Disclosure of accounting policies

44.   The accounting policies adopted by the company in determining the amounts to be included in respect of items shown in the balance sheet and in determining the profit or loss of the company must be stated (including such policies with respect to the depreciation and diminution in value of assets).

45.   It must be stated whether the accounts have been prepared in accordance with applicable accounting standards and particulars of any material departure from those standards and the reasons for it must be given (see regulation 4(2) for exemption for medium-sized companies).

Information supplementing the balance sheet

46.   Paragraphs 47 to 64 require information which either supplements the information given with respect to any particular items shown in the balance sheet or is otherwise relevant to assessing the company's state of affairs in the light of the information so given.

Share capital and debentures

47.   (1)   The following information must be given with respect to the company's share capital—
- (a)   where shares of more than one class have been allotted, the number and aggregate nominal value of shares of each class allotted, and

(b)   where shares are held as treasury shares, the number and aggregate nominal value of the treasury shares and, where shares of more than one class have been allotted, the number and aggregate nominal value of the shares of each class held as treasury shares.

(2)   In the case of any part of the allotted share capital that consists of redeemable shares, the following information must be given—

(a)   the earliest and latest dates on which the company has power to redeem those shares,

(b)   whether those shares must be redeemed in any event or are liable to be redeemed at the option of the company or of the shareholder, and

(c)   whether any (and, if so, what) premium is payable on redemption.

48.   If the company has allotted any shares during the financial year, the following information must be given—

(a)   the classes of shares allotted, and

(b)   as respects each class of shares, the number allotted, their aggregate nominal value, and the consideration received by the company for the allotment.

49. (1)   With respect to any contingent right to the allotment of shares in the company the following particulars must be given—

(a)   the number, description and amount of the shares in relation to which the right is exercisable,

(b)   the period during which it is exercisable, and

(c)   the price to be paid for the shares allotted.

(2)   In sub-paragraph (1) "contingent right to the allotment of shares" means any option to subscribe for shares and any other right to require the allotment of shares to any person whether arising on the conversion into shares of securities of any other description or otherwise.

50. (1)   If the company has issued any debentures during the financial year to which the accounts relate, the following information must be given—

(a)   the classes of debentures issued, and

(b)   as respects each class of debentures, the amount issued and the consideration received by the company for the issue.

(2)   Where any of the company's debentures are held by a nominee of or trustee for the company, the nominal amount of the debentures and the amount at which they are stated in the accounting records kept by the company in accordance with section 386 of the 2006 Act (duty to keep accounting records) must be stated.

Fixed assets

51. (1)   In respect of each item which is or would but for paragraph 4(2)(b) be shown under the general item "fixed assets" in the company's balance sheet the following information must be given—

(a)   the appropriate amounts in respect of that item as at the date of the beginning of the financial year and as at the balance sheet date respectively,

(b)   the effect on any amount shown in the balance sheet in respect of that item of—

(i)   any revision of the amount in respect of any assets included under that item made during that year on any basis mentioned in paragraph 32,

(ii)   acquisitions during that year of any assets,

(iii) disposals during that year of any assets, and

(iv) any transfers of assets of the company to and from that item during that year.

(2)   The reference in sub-paragraph (1)(a) to the appropriate amounts in respect of any item as at any date there mentioned is a reference to amounts representing the aggregate amounts determined, as at that date, in respect of assets falling to be included under that item on either of the following bases, that is to say—

(a)   on the basis of purchase price or production cost (determined in accordance with paragraphs 27 and 28), or

(b)   on any basis mentioned in paragraph 32,

(leaving out of account in either case any provisions for depreciation or diminution in value).

(3)   In respect of each item within sub-paragraph (1) there must also be stated—

(a)   the cumulative amount of provisions for depreciation or diminution in value of assets included under that item as at each date mentioned in sub-paragraph (1)(a),

(b)   the amount of any such provisions made in respect of the financial year,

(c)   the amount of any adjustments made in respect of any such provisions during that year in consequence of the disposal of any assets, and

(d)   the amount of any other adjustments made in respect of any such provisions during that year.

52.   Where any fixed assets of the company (other than listed investments) are included under any item shown in the company's balance sheet at an amount determined on any basis mentioned in paragraph 32, the following information must be given—

(a)   the years (so far as they are known to the directors) in which the assets were severally valued and the several values, and

(b)   in the case of assets that have been valued during the financial year, the names of the persons who valued them or particulars of their qualifications for doing so and (whichever is stated) the bases of valuation used by them.

53. In relation to any amount which is or would but for paragraph 4(2)(b) be shown in respect of the item "land and buildings" in the company's balance sheet there must be stated—

(a)   how much of that amount is ascribable to land of freehold tenure and how much to land of leasehold tenure, and

(b)   how much of the amount ascribable to land of leasehold tenure is ascribable to land held on long lease and how much to land held on short lease.

Investments

54. (1)   In respect of the amount of each item which is or would but for paragraph 4(2)(b) be shown in the company's balance sheet under the general item "investments" (whether as fixed assets or as current assets) there must be stated how much of that amount is ascribable to listed investments.

(2)   Where the amount of any listed investments is stated for any item in accordance with sub-paragraph (1), the following amounts must also be stated—

(a)   the aggregate market value of those investments where it differs from the amount so stated, and

(b)   both the market value and the stock exchange value of any investments of which the former value is, for the purposes of the accounts, taken as being higher than the latter.

Information about fair value of assets and liabilities

55. (1)   This paragraph applies where financial instruments have been valued in accordance with paragraph 36 or 38.

(2)   There must be stated—

(a)   the significant assumptions underlying the valuation models and techniques used where the fair value of the instruments has been determined in accordance with paragraph 37(4),

(b)   for each category of financial instrument, the fair value of the instruments in that category and the changes in value—

(i)   included in the profit and loss account, or

(ii)   credited to or (as the case may be) debited from the fair value reserve,

in respect of those instruments, and

(c)   for each class of derivatives, the extent and nature of the instruments, including significant terms and conditions that may affect the amount, timing and certainty of future cash flows.

(3)   Where any amount is transferred to or from the fair value reserve during the financial year, there must be stated in tabular form—

(a)   the amount of the reserve as at the date of the beginning of the financial year and as at the balance sheet date respectively,

(b)   the amount transferred to or from the reserve during that year, and

(c)   the source and application respectively of the amounts so transferred.

56. Where the company has derivatives that it has not included at fair value, there must be stated for each class of such derivatives—

(a)   the fair value of the derivatives in that class, if such a value can be determined in accordance with paragraph 37, and

(b)   the extent and nature of the derivatives.

57. (1)   This paragraph applies if—

(a)   the company has financial fixed assets that could be included at fair value by virtue of paragraph 36,

(b)   the amount at which those items are included under any item in the company's accounts is in excess of their fair value, and

(c)   the company has not made provision for diminution in value of those assets in accordance with paragraph 19(1) of this Schedule.

(2)   There must be stated—

(a)   the amount at which either the individual assets or appropriate groupings of those individual assets are included in the company's accounts,

(b)   the fair value of those assets or groupings, and

(c)   the reasons for not making a provision for diminution in value of those assets, including the nature of the evidence that provides the basis for the belief that the amount at which they are stated in the accounts will be recovered.

Information where investment property and living animals and plants included at fair value

58. (1)   This paragraph applies where the amounts to be included in a company's accounts in respect of investment property or living animals and plants have been determined in accordance with paragraph 39.

(2)   The balance sheet items affected and the basis of valuation adopted in determining the amounts of the assets in question in the case of each such item must be disclosed in a note to the accounts.

(3)   In the case of investment property, for each balance sheet item affected there must be shown, either separately in the balance sheet or in a note to the accounts—
- (a)   the comparable amounts determined according to the historical cost accounting rules, or
- (b)   the differences between those amounts and the corresponding amounts actually shown in the balance sheet in respect of that item.

(4)   In sub-paragraph (3), references in relation to any item to the comparable amounts determined in accordance with that sub-paragraph are to—
- (a)   the aggregate amount which would be required to be shown in respect of that item if the amounts to be included in respect of all the assets covered by that item were determined according to the historical cost accounting rules, and
- (b)   the aggregate amount of the cumulative provisions for depreciation or diminution in value which would be permitted or required in determining those amounts according to those rules.

Reserves and provisions

59. (1)   This paragraph applies where any amount is transferred—
- (a)   to or from any reserves, or
- (b)   to any provision for liabilities, or
- (c)   from any provision for liabilities otherwise than for the purpose for which the provision was established,

and the reserves or provisions are or would but for paragraph 4(2)(b) be shown as separate items in the company's balance sheet.

(2)   The following information must be given in respect of the aggregate of reserves or provisions included in the same item—
- (a)   the amount of the reserves or provisions as at the date of the beginning of the financial year and as at the balance sheet date respectively,
- (b)   any amounts transferred to or from the reserves or provisions during that year, and
- (c)   the source and application respectively of any amounts so transferred.

(3)   Particulars must be given of each provision included in the item "other provisions" in the company's balance sheet in any case where the amount of that provision is material.

Provision for taxation

60.   The amount of any provision for deferred taxation must be stated separately from the amount of any provision for other taxation.

Details of indebtedness

61. (1)   For the aggregate of all items shown under "creditors" in the company's balance sheet there must be stated the aggregate of the following amounts—
- (a)   the amount of any debts included under "creditors" which are payable or repayable otherwise than by instalments and fall due for payment or repayment after the end of the period of five years beginning with the day next following the end of the financial year, and
- (b)   in the case of any debts so included which are payable or repayable by instalments, the amount of any instalments which fall due for payment after the end of that period.

(2)   Subject to sub-paragraph (3), in relation to each debt falling to be taken into account under sub-paragraph (1), the terms of payment or repayment and the rate of any interest payable on the debt must be stated.

(3)   If the number of debts is such that, in the opinion of the directors, compliance with sub-paragraph (2) would result in a statement of excessive length, it is sufficient to give a general indication of the terms of payment or repayment and the rates of any interest payable on the debts.

(4)   In respect of each item shown under "creditors" in the company's balance sheet there must be stated—
- (a)   the aggregate amount of any debts included under that item in respect of which any security has been given by the company, and
- (b)   an indication of the nature of the securities so given.

(5)   References above in this paragraph to an item shown under "creditors" in the company's balance sheet include references, where amounts falling due to creditors within one year and after more than one year are distinguished in the balance sheet—

(a) in a case within sub-paragraph (1), to an item shown under the latter of those categories, and

(b) in a case within sub-paragraph (4), to an item shown under either of those categories.

References to items shown under "creditors" include references to items which would but for paragraph 4(2)(b) be shown under that heading.

62. If any fixed cumulative dividends on the company's shares are in arrear, there must be stated—

(a) the amount of the arrears, and

(b) the period for which the dividends or, if there is more than one class, each class of them are in arrear.

Guarantees and other financial commitments

63. (1) Particulars must be given of any charge on the assets of the company to secure the liabilities of any other person, including, where practicable, the amount secured.

(2) The following information must be given with respect to any other contingent liability not provided for—

(a) the amount or estimated amount of that liability,

(b) its legal nature, and

(c) whether any valuable security has been provided by the company in connection with that liability and if so, what.

(3) There must be stated, where practicable, the aggregate amount or estimated amount of contracts for capital expenditure, so far as not provided for.

(4) Particulars must be given of—

(a) any pension commitments included under any provision shown in the company's balance sheet, and

(b) any such commitments for which no provision has been made,

and where any such commitment relates wholly or partly to pensions payable to past directors of the company separate particulars must be given of that commitment so far as it relates to such pensions.

(5) Particulars must also be given of any other financial commitments that—

(a) have not been provided for, and

(b) are relevant to assessing the company's state of affairs.

Miscellaneous matters

64. (1) Particulars must be given of any case where the purchase price or production cost of any asset is for the first time determined under paragraph 29.

(2) Where any outstanding loans made under the authority of section 682(2)(b), (c) or (d) of the 2006 Act (various cases of financial assistance by a company for purchase of its own shares) are included under any item shown in the company's balance sheet, the aggregate amount of those loans must be disclosed for each item in question.

Information supplementing the profit and loss account

65. Paragraphs 66 to 69 require information which either supplements the information given with respect to any particular items shown in the profit and loss account or otherwise provides particulars of income or expenditure of the company or of circumstances affecting the items shown in the profit and loss account (see regulation 3(2) for exemption for companies falling within section 408 of the 2006 Act (individual profit and loss account where group accounts prepared)).

Separate statement of certain items of income and expenditure

66. (1) Subject to sub-paragraph (2), there must be stated the amount of the interest on or any similar charges in respect of bank loans and overdrafts, and loans of any other kind made to the company.

(2) Sub-paragraph (1) does not apply to interest or charges on loans to the company from group undertakings, but, with that exception, it applies to interest or charges on all loans, whether made on the security of debentures or not.

Particulars of tax

67. (1) Particulars must be given of any special circumstances which affect liability in respect of taxation of profits, income or capital gains for the financial year or liability in respect of taxation of profits, income or capital gains for succeeding financial years.

(2) The following amounts must be stated—

(a) the amount of the charge for United Kingdom corporation tax,

(b) if that amount would have been greater but for relief from double taxation, the amount which it would have been but for such relief,

(c) the amount of the charge for United Kingdom income tax, and

(d) the amount of the charge for taxation imposed outside the United Kingdom of profits, income and (so far as charged to revenue) capital gains.

These amounts must be stated separately in respect of each of the amounts which is or would but for paragraph 4(2)(b) be shown under the items "tax on profit or loss on ordinary activities" and "tax on extraordinary profit or loss" in the profit and loss account.

Particulars of turnover

68. (1) If in the course of the financial year the company has carried on business of two or more classes that, in the opinion of the directors, differ substantially from each other, the amount of the turnover attributable to each class must be stated and the class described (see regulation 4(3)(b) for exemption for medium-sized companies in accounts delivered to registrar).

(2) If in the course of the financial year the company has supplied markets that, in the opinion of the directors, differ substantially from each other, the amount of the turnover attributable to each such market must also be stated.

In this paragraph "market" means a market delimited by geographical bounds.

(3) In analysing for the purposes of this paragraph the source (in terms of business or in terms of market) of turnover, the directors of the company must have regard to the manner in which the company's activities are organised.

(4) For the purposes of this paragraph—
   (a)   classes of business which, in the opinion of the directors, do not differ substantially from each other must be treated as one class, and
   (b)   markets which, in the opinion of the directors, do not differ substantially from each other must be treated as one market,

and any amounts properly attributable to one class of business or (as the case may be) to one market which are not material may be included in the amount stated in respect of another.

(5) Where in the opinion of the directors the disclosure of any information required by this paragraph would be seriously prejudicial to the interests of the company, that information need not be disclosed, but the fact that any such information has not been disclosed must be stated.

Miscellaneous matters

69. (1) Where any amount relating to any preceding financial year is included in any item in the profit and loss account, the effect must be stated.

(2) Particulars must be given of any extraordinary income or charges arising in the financial year.

(3) The effect must be stated of any transactions that are exceptional by virtue of size or incidence though they fall within the ordinary activities of the company.

Sums denominated in foreign currencies

70. Where any sums originally denominated in foreign currencies have been brought into account under any items shown in the balance sheet format or profit and loss account formats, the basis on which those sums have been translated into sterling (or the currency in which the accounts are drawn up) must be stated.

Dormant companies acting as agents

71. Where the directors of a company take advantage of the exemption conferred by section 480 of the 2006 Act (dormant companies: exemption from audit), and the company has during the financial year in question acted as an agent for any person, the fact that it has so acted must be stated.

Related party transactions

72. (1) Particulars may be given of transactions which the company has entered into with related parties, and must be given if such transactions are material and have not been concluded under normal market conditions (see regulation 4(2) for exemption for medium-sized companies).

(2) The particulars of transactions required to be disclosed by sub-paragraph (1) must include—
   (a)   the amount of such transactions,
   (b)   the nature of the related party relationship, and
   (c)   other information about the transactions necessary for an understanding of the financial position of the company.

(3) Information about individual transactions may be aggregated according to their nature, except where separate information is necessary for an understanding of the effects of related party transactions on the financial position of the company.

(4) Particulars need not be given of transactions entered into between two or more members of a group, provided that any subsidiary undertaking which is a party to the transaction is wholly-owned by such a member.

(5) In this paragraph, "related party" has the same meaning as in international accounting standards.

NOTES

Commencement: 6 April 2008.

PART 4

SPECIAL PROVISION WHERE COMPANY IS A PARENT COMPANY OR SUBSIDIARY UNDERTAKING

Company's own accounts: guarantees and other financial commitments in favour of group undertakings

[4.186]

73. Commitments within any of sub-paragraphs (1) to (5) of paragraph 63 (guarantees and other financial commitments) which are undertaken on behalf of or for the benefit of—

   (a)   any parent undertaking or fellow subsidiary undertaking, or

   (b)   any subsidiary undertaking of the company,

must be stated separately from the other commitments within that paragraph, and commitments within paragraph (a) must also be stated separately from those within paragraph (b).

NOTES

Commencement: 6 April 2008.

PART 5

SPECIAL PROVISIONS WHERE THE COMPANY IS AN INVESTMENT COMPANY

[4.187]

74. (1) Paragraph 35 does not apply to the amount of any profit or loss arising from a determination of the value of any investments of an investment company on any basis mentioned in paragraph 32(3).

(2) Any provisions made by virtue of paragraph 19(1) or (2) in the case of an investment company in respect of any fixed asset investments need not be charged to the company's profit and loss account provided they are either—

   (a)   charged against any reserve account to which any amount excluded by sub-paragraph (1) from the requirements of paragraph 35 has been credited, or

   (b)   shown as a separate item in the company's balance sheet under the sub-heading "other reserves".

(3) For the purposes of this paragraph, as it applies in relation to any company, "fixed asset investment" means any asset falling to be included under any item shown in the company's balance sheet under the subdivision "investments" under the general item "fixed assets".

75. (1) Any distribution made by an investment company which reduces the amount of its net assets to less than the aggregate of its called-up share capital and undistributable reserves shall be disclosed in a note to the company's accounts.

(2) For purposes of this paragraph, a company's net assets are the aggregate of its assets less the aggregate of its liabilities (including any provision for liabilities within paragraph 2 of Schedule 9 to these Regulations that is made in Companies Act accounts and any provision that is made in IAS accounts); and "undistributable reserves" has the meaning given by section 831(4) of the 2006 Act.

(3) A company shall be treated as an investment company for the purposes of this Part of this Schedule in relation to any financial year of the company if—

   (a)   during the whole of that year it was an investment company as defined by section 833 of the 2006 Act, and

   (b)   it was not at any time during that year prohibited from making a distribution by virtue of section 832 of the 2006 Act due to either or both of the conditions specified in section 832(5)(a) or (b) (no distribution where capital profits have been distributed etc) not being met.

NOTES

Commencement: 6 April 2008.

SCHEDULE 2
BANKING COMPANIES: COMPANIES ACT INDIVIDUAL ACCOUNTS
Regulation 5(1)

PART 1
GENERAL RULES AND FORMATS

SECTION A
GENERAL RULES

[4.188]

1. Subject to the following provisions of this Part of this Schedule—
    (a) every balance sheet of a company must show the items listed in the balance sheet format set out in Section B of this Part, and
    (b) every profit and loss account must show the items listed in either of the profit and loss account formats in Section B.

2. (1) References in this Part of this Schedule to the items listed in any of the formats set out in Section B, are to those items read together with any of the notes following the formats which apply to those items.

(2) The items must be shown in the order and under the headings and sub-headings given in the particular format used, but—
    (a) the notes to the formats may permit alternative positions for any particular items,
    (b) the heading or sub-heading for any item does not have to be distinguished by any letter or number assigned to that item in the format used, and
    (c) where the heading of an item in the format used contains any wording in square brackets, that wording may be omitted if not applicable to the company.

3. (1) Where in accordance with paragraph 1 a company's profit and loss account for any financial year has been prepared by reference to one of the formats in Section B, the company's directors must use the same format in preparing the profit and loss account for subsequent financial years, unless in their opinion there are special reasons for a change.

(2) Particulars of any change must be given in a note to the accounts in which the new format is first used, and the reasons for the change must be explained.

4. (1) Any item required to be shown in a company's balance sheet or profit and loss account may be shown in greater detail than required by the particular format used.

(2) The balance sheet or profit and loss account may include an item representing or covering the amount of any asset or liability, income or expenditure not specifically covered by any of the items listed in the format used, save that none of the following may be treated as assets in any balance sheet—
    (a) preliminary expenses,
    (b) expenses of, and commission on, any issue of shares or debentures, and
    (c) costs of research.

5. (1) Items to which lower case letters are assigned in any of the formats in Section B may be combined in a company's accounts for any financial year if—
    (a) their individual amounts are not material for the purpose of giving a true and fair view, or
    (b) the combination facilitates the assessment of the state of affairs or profit or loss of the company for that year.

(2) Where sub-paragraph (1)(b) applies, the individual amounts of any items so combined must be disclosed in a note to the accounts and any notes required by this Schedule to the items so combined must, notwithstanding the combination, be given.

6. (1) Subject to sub-paragraph (2), the directors must not include a heading or sub-heading corresponding to an item in the balance sheet or profit and loss account format used if there is no amount to be shown for that item for the financial year to which the balance sheet or profit and loss account relates.

(2) Where an amount can be shown for the item in question for the immediately preceding financial year, that amount must be shown under the heading or sub-heading required by the format for that item.

7. (1) For every item shown in the balance sheet or profit and loss account the corresponding amount for the immediately preceding financial year must also be shown.

(2) Where that corresponding amount is not comparable with the amount to be shown for the item in question in respect of the financial year to which the balance sheet or profit and loss account relates, the former amount may be adjusted, and particulars of the non-comparability and of any adjustment must be disclosed in a note to the accounts.

8. (1)   Subject to the following provisions of this paragraph and without prejudice to note (6) to the balance sheet format, amounts in respect of items representing assets or income may not be set off against amounts in respect of items representing liabilities or expenditure (as the case may be), or vice versa.

(2)   Charges required to be included in profit and loss account format 1, items 11(a) and 11(b) or format 2, items A7(a) and A7(b) may be set off against income required to be included in format 1, items 12(a) and 12(b) or format 2, items B5(a) and B5(b) and the resulting figure shown as a single item (in format 2 at position A7 if negative and at position B5 if positive).

(3)   Charges required to be included in profit and loss account format 1, item 13 or format 2, item A8 may also be set off against income required to be included in format 1, item 14 or format 2, item B6 and the resulting figure shown as a single item (in format 2 at position A8 if negative and at position B6 if positive).

9. (1)   Assets must be shown under the relevant balance sheet headings even where the company has pledged them as security for its own liabilities or for those of third parties or has otherwise assigned them as security to third parties.

(2)   A company may not include in its balance sheet assets pledged or otherwise assigned to it as security unless such assets are in the form of cash in the hands of the company.

(3)   Assets acquired in the name of and on behalf of third parties must not be shown in the balance sheet.

10.   The company's directors must, in determining how amounts are presented within items in the profit and loss account and balance sheet, have regard to the substance of the reported transaction or arrangement, in accordance with generally accepted accounting principles or practice.

SECTION B
THE REQUIRED FORMATS

Balance sheet format

ASSETS

1   Cash and balances at central [or post office] banks [1]

2   Treasury bills and other eligible bills [20]
   (a)   Treasury bills and similar securities [2]
   (b)   Other eligible bills [3]

3   Loans and advances to banks [4] [20]
   (a)   Repayable on demand
   (b)   Other loans and advances

4   Loans and advances to customers [5] [20]

5   Debt securities [and other fixed-income securities] [6] [20]
   (a)   Issued by public bodies
   (b)   Issued by other issuers

6   Equity shares [and other variable-yield securities]

7   Participating interests

8   Shares in group undertakings

9   Intangible fixed assets [7]

10   Tangible fixed assets [8]

11   Called up capital not paid [9]

12   Own shares [10]

13   Other assets

14   Called up capital not paid [9]

15   Prepayments and accrued income

Total assets

LIABILITIES

1   Deposits by banks [11] [20]
   (a)   Repayable on demand
   (b)   With agreed maturity dates or periods of notice

2　Customer accounts [12] [20]
 (a)　Repayable on demand
 (b)　With agreed maturity dates or periods of notice

3　Debt securities in issue [13] [20]
 (a)　Bonds and medium term notes
 (b)　Others

4　Other liabilities

5　Accruals and deferred income

6　Provisions for liabilities
 (a)　Provisions for pensions and similar obligations
 (b)　Provisions for tax
 (c)　Other provisions

7　Subordinated liabilities [14] [20]

8　Called up share capital [15]

9　Share premium account

10　Reserves
 (a)　Capital redemption reserve
 (b)　Reserve for own shares
 (c)　Reserves provided for by the articles of association
 (d)　Other reserves

11　Revaluation reserve

12　Profit and loss account

Total liabilities

MEMORANDUM ITEMS

1　Contingent liabilities [16]
 (1)　Acceptances and endorsements
 (2)　Guarantees and assets pledged as collateral security [17]
 (3)　Other contingent liabilities

2　Commitments [18]

(1)　Commitments arising out of sale and option to resell transactions [19]

(2)　Other commitments

Notes on the balance sheet format and memorandum items
(1)　Cash and balances at central [or post office] banks
(Assets item 1.)
Cash is to comprise all currency including foreign notes and coins.

Only those balances which may be withdrawn without notice and which are deposited with central or post office banks of the country or countries in which the company is established may be included in this item. All other claims on central or post office banks must be shown under assets items 3 or 4.

(2)　Treasury bills and other eligible bills: Treasury bills and similar securities
(Assets item 2.(a).)
Treasury bills and similar securities are to comprise treasury bills and similar debt instruments issued by public bodies which are eligible for refinancing with central banks of the country or countries in which the company is established. Any treasury bills or similar debt instruments not so eligible must be included under assets item 5(a).

(3)　Treasury bills and other eligible bills: Other eligible bills
(Assets item 2.(b).)
Other eligible bills are to comprise all bills purchased to the extent that they are eligible, under national law, for refinancing with the central banks of the country or countries in which the company is established.

(4)　Loans and advances to banks
(Assets item 3.)
Loans and advances to banks are to comprise all loans and advances to domestic or foreign credit institutions made by the company arising out of banking transactions. However loans and advances

to credit institutions represented by debt securities or other fixed-income securities must be included under assets item 5 and not this item.

(5)   Loans and advances to customers

(Assets item 4.)

Loans and advances to customers are to comprise all types of assets in the form of claims on domestic and foreign customers other than credit institutions. However loans and advances represented by debt securities or other fixed-income securities must be included under assets item 5 and not this item.

(6)   Debt securities [and other fixed-income securities]

(Assets item 5.)

This item is to comprise transferable debt securities and any other transferable fixed-income securities issued by credit institutions, other undertakings or public bodies. Debt securities and other fixed-income securities issued by public bodies are, however, only to be included in this item if they may not be shown under assets item 2.

Where a company holds its own debt securities these must not be included under this item but must be deducted from liabilities item 3.(a) or (b), as appropriate.

Securities bearing interest rates that vary in accordance with specific factors, for example the interest rate on the inter-bank market or on the Euromarket, are also to be regarded as fixed- income securities to be included under this item.

(7)   Intangible fixed assets

(Assets item 9.)

This item is to comprise—
  (a)   development costs,
  (b)   concessions, patents, licences, trade marks and similar rights and assets,
  (c)   goodwill, and
  (d)   payments on account.

Amounts are, however, to be included in respect of (b) only if the assets were acquired for valuable consideration or the assets in question were created by the company itself.

Amounts representing goodwill are only to be included to the extent that the goodwill was acquired for valuable consideration.

The amount of any goodwill included in this item must be disclosed in a note to the accounts.

(8)   Tangible fixed assets

(Assets item 10.)

This item is to comprise—
  (a)   land and buildings,
  (b)   plant and machinery,
  (c)   fixtures and fittings, tools and equipment, and
  (d)   payments on account and assets in the course of construction.

The amount included in this item with respect to land and buildings occupied by the company for its own activities must be disclosed in a note to the accounts.

(9)   Called up capital not paid

(Assets items 11 and 14.)

The two positions shown for this item are alternatives.

(10)   Own shares

(Assets item 12.)

The nominal value of the shares held must be shown separately under this item.

(11)   Deposits by banks

(Liabilities item 1.)

Deposits by banks are to comprise all amounts arising out of banking transactions owed to other domestic or foreign credit institutions by the company. However liabilities in the form of debt securities and any liabilities for which transferable certificates have been issued must be included under liabilities item 3 and not this item.

(12)   Customer accounts

(Liabilities item 2.)

This item is to comprise all amounts owed to creditors that are not credit institutions. However liabilities in the form of debt securities and any liabilities for which transferable certificates have been issued must be shown under liabilities item 3 and not this item.

(13)   Debt securities in issue

(Liabilities item 3.)

This item is to include both debt securities and debts for which transferable certificates have been issued, including liabilities arising out of own acceptances and promissory notes. (Only acceptances which a company has issued for its own refinancing and in respect of which it is the first party liable are to be treated as own acceptances.)

(14)   Subordinated liabilities

(Liabilities item 7.)

This item is to comprise all liabilities in respect of which there is a contractual obligation that, in the event of winding up or bankruptcy, they are to be repaid only after the claims of other creditors have been met.

This item must include all subordinated liabilities, whether or not a ranking has been agreed between the subordinated creditors concerned.

(15)   Called up share capital

(Liabilities item 8.)

The amount of allotted share capital and the amount of called up share capital which has been paid up must be shown separately.

(16)   Contingent liabilities

(Memorandum item 1.)

This item is to include all transactions whereby the company has underwritten the obligations of a third party.

Liabilities arising out of the endorsement of rediscounted bills must be included in this item. Acceptances other than own acceptances must also be included.

(17)   Contingent liabilities: Guarantees and assets pledged as collateral security

(Memorandum item 1(2).)

This item is to include all guarantee obligations incurred and assets pledged as collateral security on behalf of third parties, particularly in respect of sureties and irrevocable letters of credit.

(18)   Commitments

(Memorandum item 2.)

This item is to include every irrevocable commitment which could give rise to a credit risk.

(19)   Commitments: Commitments arising out of sale and option to resell transactions

(Memorandum item 2(1).)

This item is to comprise commitments entered into by the company in the context of sale and option to resell transactions.

(20)   Claims on, and liabilities to, undertakings in which a participating interest is held or group undertakings

(Assets items 2 to 5, liabilities items 1 to 3 and 7.)

The following information must be given either by way of subdivision of the relevant items or by way of notes to the accounts.

The amount of the following must be shown for each of assets items 2 to 5—

(a)   claims on group undertakings included therein, and

(b)   claims on undertakings in which the company has a participating interest included therein.

The amount of the following must be shown for each of liabilities items 1, 2, 3 and 7—

(i)   liabilities to group undertakings included therein, and

(ii)   liabilities to undertakings in which the company has a participating interest included therein.

Special rules

11   Subordinated assets

(1)   The amount of any assets that are subordinated must be shown either as a subdivision of any relevant asset item or in the notes to the accounts; in the latter case disclosure must be by reference to the relevant asset item or items in which the assets are included.

(2)   In the case of assets items 2 to 5 in the balance sheet format, the amounts required to be shown by note (20) to the format as sub-items of those items must be further subdivided so as to show the amount of any claims included therein that are subordinated.

(3)   For this purpose, assets are subordinated if there is a contractual obligation to the effect that, in the event of winding up or bankruptcy, they are to be repaid only after the claims of other creditors have been met, whether or not a ranking has been agreed between the subordinated creditors concerned.

12   Syndicated loans

(1)   Where a company is a party to a syndicated loan transaction the company must include only that part of the total loan which it itself has funded.

(2) Where a company is a party to a syndicated loan transaction and has agreed to reimburse (in whole or in part) any other party to the syndicate any funds advanced by that party or any interest thereon upon the occurrence of any event, including the default of the borrower, any additional liability by reason of such a guarantee must be included as a contingent liability in Memorandum item 1(2).

13 Sale and repurchase transactions

(1) The following rules apply where a company is a party to a sale and repurchase transaction.

(2) Where the company is the transferor of the assets under the transaction—
  (a) the assets transferred must, notwithstanding the transfer, be included in its balance sheet,
  (b) the purchase price received by it must be included in its balance sheet as an amount owed to the transferee, and
  (c) the value of the assets transferred must be disclosed in a note to its accounts.

(3) Where the company is the transferee of the assets under the transaction, it must not include the assets transferred in its balance sheet but the purchase price paid by it to the transferor must be so included as an amount owed by the transferor.

14 Sale and option to resell transactions

(1) The following rules apply where a company is a party to a sale and option to resell transaction.

(2) Where the company is the transferor of the assets under the transaction, it must not include in its balance sheet the assets transferred but it must enter under Memorandum item 2 an amount equal to the price agreed in the event of repurchase.

(3) Where the company is the transferee of the assets under the transaction it must include those assets in its balance sheet.

15 Managed funds

(1) For the purposes of this paragraph, "managed funds" are funds which the company administers in its own name but on behalf of others and to which it has legal title.

(2) The company must, in any case where claims and obligations arising in respect of managed funds fall to be treated as claims and obligations of the company, adopt the following accounting treatment.

(3) Claims and obligations representing managed funds are to be included in the company's balance sheet, with the notes to the accounts disclosing the total amount included with respect to such assets and liabilities in the balance sheet and showing the amount included under each relevant balance sheet item in respect of such assets or (as the case may be) liabilities.

Profit and loss account formats

Format 1

Vertical layout

1 Interest receivable [1]
  (1) Interest receivable and similar income arising from debt securities [and other fixed-income securities]
  (2) Other interest receivable and similar income

2 Interest payable [2]

3 Dividend income
  (a) Income from equity shares [and other variable-yield securities]
  (b) Income from participating interests
  (c) Income from shares in group undertakings

4 Fees and commissions receivable [3]

5 Fees and commissions payable [4]

6 Dealing [profits] [losses] [5]

7 Other operating income

8 Administrative expenses
  (a) Staff costs
    (i)   Wages and salaries
    (ii) Social security costs
    (iii) Other pension costs
  (b) Other administrative expenses

9 Depreciation and amortisation [6]

10   Other operating charges

11   Provisions
   (a)   Provisions for bad and doubtful debts [7]
   (b)   Provisions for contingent liabilities and commitments [8]

12   Adjustments to provisions
   (a)   Adjustments to provisions for bad and doubtful debts [9]
   (b)   Adjustments to provisions for contingent liabilities and commitments [10]

13   Amounts written off fixed asset investments [11]

14   Adjustments to amounts written off fixed asset investments [12]

15   [Profit] [loss] on ordinary activities before tax

16   Tax on [profit] [loss] on ordinary activities

17   [Profit] [loss] on ordinary activities after tax

18   Extraordinary income

19   Extraordinary charges

20   Extraordinary [profit] [loss]

21   Tax on extraordinary [profit] [loss]

22   Extraordinary [profit] [loss] after tax

23   Other taxes not shown under the preceding items

24   [Profit] [loss] for the financial year

Profit and loss account formats

Format 2

Horizontal layout

A   Charges
  1   Interest payable [2]
  2   Fees and commissions payable [4]
  3   Dealing losses [5]
  4   Administrative expenses
     (a)   Staff costs
         (i)   Wages and salaries
         (ii)   Social security costs
         (iii) Other pension costs
     (b)   Other administrative expenses
  5   Depreciation and amortisation [6]
  6   Other operating charges
  7   Provisions
     (a)   Provisions for bad and doubtful debts [7]
     (b)   Provisions for contingent liabilities and commitments [8]
  8   Amounts written off fixed asset investments [11]
  9   Profit on ordinary activities before tax
 10   Tax on [profit] [loss] on ordinary activities
 11   Profit on ordinary activities after tax
 12   Extraordinary charges
 13   Tax on extraordinary [profit] [loss]
 14   Extraordinary loss after tax
 15   Other taxes not shown under the preceding items
 16   Profit for the financial year

B   Income
  1   Interest receivable [1]
     (1)   Interest receivable and similar income arising from debt securities [and other fixed-income securities]
     (2)   Other interest receivable and similar income
  2   Dividend income
     (a)   Income from equity shares [and other variable-yield securities]
     (b)   Income from participating interests
     (c)   Income from shares in group undertakings

3 Fees and commissions receivable [(3)]
4 Dealing profits [(5)]
5 Adjustments to provisions
   (a) Adjustments to provisions for bad and doubtful debts [(9)]
   (b) Adjustments to provisions for contingent liabilities and commitments [(10)]
6 Adjustments to amounts written off fixed asset investments [(12)]
7 Other operating income
8 Loss on ordinary activities before tax
9 Loss on ordinary activities after tax
10 Extraordinary income
11 Extraordinary profit after tax
12 Loss for the financial year

Notes on the profit and loss account formats

(1) Interest receivable

(Format 1, item 1; format 2, item B1.)

   This item is to include all income arising out of banking activities, including—
   (a) income from assets included in assets items 1 to 5 in the balance sheet format, however calculated,
   (b) income resulting from covered forward contracts spread over the actual duration of the contract and similar in nature to interest, and
   (c) fees and commissions receivable similar in nature to interest and calculated on a time basis or by reference to the amount of the claim (but not other fees and commissions receivable).

(2) Interest payable

(Format 1, item 2; format 2, item A1.)

   This item is to include all expenditure arising out of banking activities, including—
   (a) charges arising out of liabilities included in liabilities items 1, 2, 3 and 7 in the balance sheet format, however calculated,
   (b) charges resulting from covered forward contracts, spread over the actual duration of the contract and similar in nature to interest, and
   (c) fees and commissions payable similar in nature to interest and calculated on a time basis or by reference to the amount of the liability (but not other fees and commissions payable).

(3) Fees and commissions receivable

(Format 1, item 4; format 2, item B3.)

   Fees and commissions receivable are to comprise income in respect of all services supplied by the company to third parties, but not fees or commissions required to be included under interest receivable (format 1, item 1; format 2, item B1).

   In particular the following fees and commissions receivable must be included (unless required to be included under interest receivable)—
   (a) fees and commissions for guarantees, loan administration on behalf of other lenders and securities transactions,
   (b) fees, commissions and other income in respect of payment transactions, account administration charges and commissions for the safe custody and administration of securities,
   (c) fees and commissions for foreign currency transactions and for the sale and purchase of coin and precious metals, and
   (d) fees and commissions charged for brokerage services in connection with savings and insurance contracts and loans.

(4) Fees and commissions payable

(Format 1, item 5; format 2, item A2.)

   Fees and commissions payable are to comprise charges for all services rendered to the company by third parties but not fees or commissions required to be included under interest payable (format 1, item 2; format 2, item A1).

   In particular the following fees and commissions payable must be included (unless required to be included under interest payable)—
   (a) fees and commissions for guarantees, loan administration and securities transactions;
   (b) fees, commissions and other charges in respect of payment transactions, account administration charges and commissions for the safe custody and administration of securities;
   (c) fees and commissions for foreign currency transactions and for the sale and purchase of coin and precious metals; and
   (d) fees and commissions for brokerage services in connection with savings and insurance contracts and loans.

(5) Dealing [profits] [losses]

(Format 1, item 6; format 2, items B4 and A3.)

   This item is to comprise—

(a) the net profit or net loss on transactions in securities which are not held as financial fixed assets together with amounts written off or written back with respect to such securities, including amounts written off or written back as a result of the application of paragraph 33(1),

(b) the net profit or loss on exchange activities, save in so far as the profit or loss is included in interest receivable or interest payable (format 1, items 1 or 2; format 2, items B1 or A1), and

(c) the net profits and losses on other dealing operations involving financial instruments, including precious metals.

(6) Depreciation and amortisation

(Format 1, item 9; format 2, item A5.)

This item is to comprise depreciation and other amounts written off in respect of balance sheet assets items 9 and 10.

(7) Provisions: Provisions for bad and doubtful debts

(Format 1, item 11(a); format 2, item A7(a).)

Provisions for bad and doubtful debts are to comprise charges for amounts written off and for provisions made in respect of loans and advances shown under balance sheet assets items 3 and 4.

(8) Provisions: Provisions for contingent liabilities and commitments

(Format 1, item 11(b); format 2, item A7(b).)

This item is to comprise charges for provisions for contingent liabilities and commitments of a type which would, if not provided for, be shown under Memorandum items 1 and 2.

(9) Adjustments to provisions: Adjustments to provisions for bad and doubtful debts

(Format 1, item 12(a); format 2, item B5(a).)

This item is to include credits from the recovery of loans that have been written off, from other advances written back following earlier write offs and from the reduction of provisions previously made with respect to loans and advances.

(10) Adjustments to provisions: Adjustments to provisions for contingent liabilities and commitments

(Format 1, item 12(b); format 2, item B5(b).)

This item comprises credits from the reduction of provisions previously made with respect to contingent liabilities and commitments.

(11) Amounts written off fixed asset investments

(Format 1, item 13; format 2, item A8.)

Amounts written off fixed asset investments are to comprise amounts written off in respect of assets which are transferable securities held as financial fixed assets, participating interests and shares in group undertakings and which are included in assets items 5 to 8 in the balance sheet format.

(12) Adjustments to amounts written off fixed asset investments

(Format 1, item 14; format 2, item B6.)

Adjustments to amounts written off fixed asset investments are to include amounts written back following earlier write offs and provisions in respect of assets which are transferable securities held as financial fixed assets, participating interests and group undertakings and which are included in assets items 5 to 8 in the balance sheet format.

NOTES

Commencement: 6 April 2008.

PART 2
ACCOUNTING PRINCIPLES AND RULES

SECTION A
ACCOUNTING PRINCIPLES

Preliminary

[4.189]

16. (1) The amounts to be included in respect of all items shown in a company's accounts must be determined in accordance with the principles set out in this Section.

(2) But if it appears to the company's directors that there are special reasons for departing from any of those principles in preparing the company's accounts in respect of any financial year they may do so, in which case particulars of the departure, the reasons for it and its effect must be given in a note to the accounts.

Accounting principles

17. The company is presumed to be carrying on business as a going concern.

18. Accounting policies must be applied consistently within the same accounts and from one financial year to the next.

19. The amount of any item must be determined on a prudent basis, and in particular—
 (a) only profits realised at the balance sheet date are to be included in the profit and loss account, and
 (b) all liabilities which have arisen in respect of the financial year to which the accounts relate or a previous financial year must be taken into account, including those which only become apparent between the balance sheet date and the date on which it is signed on behalf of the board of directors in accordance with section 414 of the 2006 Act (approval and signing of accounts).

20. All income and charges relating to the financial year to which the accounts relate must be taken into account, without regard to the date of receipt or payment.

21. In determining the aggregate amount of any item, the amount of each individual asset or liability that falls to be taken into account must be determined separately.

SECTION B
HISTORICAL COST ACCOUNTING RULES

Preliminary

22. Subject to Sections C and D of this Part of this Schedule, the amounts to be included in respect of all items shown in a company's accounts must be determined in accordance with the rules set out in this Section.

Fixed assets

General rules

23. (1) The amount to be included in respect of any fixed asset is its cost.

(2) This is subject to any provision for depreciation or diminution in value made in accordance with paragraphs 24 to 26.

Rules for depreciation and diminution in value

24. In the case of any fixed asset which has a limited useful economic life, the amount of—
 (a) its cost, or
 (b) where it is estimated that any such asset will have a residual value at the end of the period of its useful economic life, its cost less that estimated residual value,
must be reduced by provisions for depreciation calculated to write off that amount systematically over the period of the asset's useful economic life.

25. (1) Where a fixed asset investment to which sub-paragraph (2) applies has diminished in value, provisions for diminution in value may be made in respect of it and the amount to be included in respect of it may be reduced accordingly.

(2) This sub-paragraph applies to fixed asset investments of a description falling to be included under assets item 7 (participating interests) or 8 (shares in group undertakings) in the balance sheet format, or any other holding of securities held as a financial fixed asset.

(3) Provisions for diminution in value must be made in respect of any fixed asset which has diminished in value if the reduction in its value is expected to be permanent (whether its useful economic life is limited or not), and the amount to be included in respect of it must be reduced accordingly.

(4) Any provisions made under this paragraph which are not shown in the profit and loss account must be disclosed (either separately or in aggregate) in a note to the accounts.

26. (1) Where the reasons for which any provision was made in accordance with paragraph 25 have ceased to apply to any extent, that provision must be written back to the extent that it is no longer necessary.

(2) Any amounts written back in accordance with sub-paragraph (1) which are not shown in the profit and loss account must be disclosed (either separately or in aggregate) in a note to the accounts.

Development costs

27. (1) Notwithstanding that amounts representing "development costs" may be included under assets item 9 in the balance sheet format, an amount may only be included in a company's balance sheet in respect of development costs in special circumstances.

(2) If any amount is included in a company's balance sheet in respect of development costs the following information must be given in a note to the accounts—
 (a) the period over which the amount of those costs originally capitalised is being or is to be written off, and

(b)   the reasons for capitalising the development costs in question.

Goodwill

28. (1)   The application of paragraphs 23 to 26 in relation to goodwill (in any case where goodwill is treated as an asset) is subject to the following.

(2)   Subject to sub-paragraph (3), the amount of the consideration for any goodwill acquired by a company must be reduced by provisions for depreciation calculated to write off that amount systematically over a period chosen by the directors of the company.

(3)   The period chosen must not exceed the useful economic life of the goodwill in question.

(4)   In any case where any goodwill acquired by a company is included as an asset in the company's balance sheet there must be disclosed in a note to the accounts—
   (a)   the period chosen for writing off the consideration for that goodwill, and
   (b)   the reasons for choosing that period.

Treatment of fixed assets

29. (1)   Assets included in assets items 9 (intangible fixed assets) and 10 (tangible fixed assets) in the balance sheet format must be valued as fixed assets.

(2)   Other assets falling to be included in the balance sheet must be valued as fixed assets where they are intended for use on a continuing basis in the company's activities.

Financial fixed assets

30. (1)   Debt securities, including fixed-income securities, held as financial fixed assets must be included in the balance sheet at an amount equal to their maturity value plus any premium, or less any discount, on their purchase, subject to the following provisions of this paragraph.

(2)   The amount included in the balance sheet with respect to such securities purchased at a premium must be reduced each financial year on a systematic basis so as to write the premium off over the period to the maturity date of the security and the amounts so written off must be charged to the profit and loss account for the relevant financial years.

(3)   The amount included in the balance sheet with respect to such securities purchased at a discount must be increased each financial year on a systematic basis so as to extinguish the discount over the period to the maturity date of the security and the amounts by which the amount is increased must be credited to the profit and loss account for the relevant years.

(4)   The notes to the accounts must disclose the amount of any unamortized premium or discount not extinguished which is included in the balance sheet by virtue of sub-paragraph (1).

(5)   For the purposes of this paragraph "premium" means any excess of the amount paid for a security over its maturity value and "discount" means any deficit of the amount paid for a security over its maturity value.

Current assets

31.   The amount to be included in respect of loans and advances, debt or other fixed-income securities and equity shares or other variable yield securities not held as financial fixed assets must be their cost, subject to paragraphs 32 and 33.

32. (1)   If the net realisable value of any asset referred to in paragraph 31 is lower than its cost, the amount to be included in respect of that asset is the net realisable value.

(2)   Where the reasons for which any provision for diminution in value was made in accordance with sub-paragraph (1) have ceased to apply to any extent, that provision must be written back to the extent that it is no longer necessary.

33. (1)   Subject to paragraph 32, the amount to be included in the balance sheet in respect of transferable securities not held as financial fixed assets may be the higher of their cost or their market value at the balance sheet date.

(2)   The difference between the cost of any securities included in the balance sheet at a valuation under sub-paragraph (1) and their market value must be shown (in aggregate) in the notes to the accounts.

Miscellaneous and supplementary provisions

Excess of money owed over value received as an asset item

34. (1)   Where the amount repayable on any debt owed by a company is greater than the value of the consideration received in the transaction giving rise to the debt, the amount of the difference may be treated as an asset.

(2)   Where any such amount is so treated—
   (a)   it must be written off by reasonable amounts each year and must be completely written off before repayment of the debt, and

(b)   if the current amount is not shown as a separate item in the company's balance sheet, it must be disclosed in a note to the accounts.

Determination of cost

35. (1)   The cost of an asset that has been acquired by the company is to be determined by adding to the actual price paid any expenses incidental to its acquisition.

(2)   The cost of an asset constructed by the company is to be determined by adding to the purchase price of the raw materials and consumables used the amount of the costs incurred by the company which are directly attributable to the construction of that asset.

(3)   In addition, there may be included in the cost of an asset constructed by the company—
  (a)   a reasonable proportion of the costs incurred by the company which are only indirectly attributable to the construction of that asset, but only to the extent that they relate to the period of construction, and
  (b)   interest on capital borrowed to finance the construction of that asset, to the extent that it accrues in respect of the period of construction,

provided, however, in a case within paragraph (b), that the inclusion of the interest in determining the cost of that asset and the amount of the interest so included is disclosed in a note to the accounts.

36. (1)   The cost of any assets which are fungible assets (including investments), may be determined by the application of any of the methods mentioned in sub-paragraph (2) in relation to any such assets of the same class, provided that the method chosen is one which appears to the directors to be appropriate in the circumstances of the company.

(2)   Those methods are—
  (a)   the method known as "first in, first out" (FIFO),
  (b)   the method known as "last in, first out" (LIFO),
  (c)   a weighted average price, and
  (d)   any other method similar to any of the methods mentioned above.

(3)   Where in the case of any company—
  (a)   the cost of assets falling to be included under any item shown in the company's balance sheet has been determined by the application of any method permitted by this paragraph, and
  (b)   the amount shown in respect of that item differs materially from the relevant alternative amount given below in this paragraph,

the amount of that difference must be disclosed in a note to the accounts.

(4)   Subject to sub-paragraph (5), for the purposes of sub-paragraph (3)(b), the relevant alternative amount, in relation to any item shown in a company's balance sheet, is the amount which would have been shown in respect of that item if assets of any class included under that item at an amount determined by any method permitted by this paragraph had instead been included at their replacement cost as at the balance sheet date.

(5)   The relevant alternative amount may be determined by reference to the most recent actual purchase price before the balance sheet date of assets of any class included under the item in question instead of by reference to their replacement cost as at that date, but only if the former appears to the directors of the company to constitute the more appropriate standard of comparison in the case of assets of that class.

Substitution of original stated amount where price or cost unknown

37. (1)   This paragraph applies where—
  (a)   there is no record of the purchase price of any asset acquired by a company or of any price, expenses or costs relevant for determining its cost in accordance with paragraph 35, or
  (b)   any such record cannot be obtained without unreasonable expense or delay.

(2)   In such a case, its cost is to be taken, for the purposes of paragraphs 23 to 33, to be the value ascribed to it in the earliest available record of its value made on or after its acquisition by the company.

SECTION C
ALTERNATIVE ACCOUNTING RULES

Preliminary

38. (1)   The rules set out in Section B are referred to below in this Schedule as the historical cost accounting rules.

(2)   Paragraphs 23 to 26 and 30 to 34 are referred to below in this Section as the depreciation rules; and references below in this Schedule to the historical cost accounting rules do not include the depreciation rules as they apply by virtue of paragraph 41.

39. Subject to paragraphs 41 to 43, the amounts to be included in respect of assets of any description mentioned in paragraph 40 may be determined on any basis so mentioned.

Alternative accounting rules

40. (1) Intangible fixed assets, other than goodwill, may be included at their current cost.

(2) Tangible fixed assets may be included at a market value determined as at the date of their last valuation or at their current cost.

(3) Investments of any description falling to be included under assets items 7 (participating interests) or 8 (shares in group undertakings) of the balance sheet format and any other securities held as financial fixed assets may be included either—

    (a)   at a market value determined as at the date of their last valuation, or

    (b)   at a value determined on any basis which appears to the directors to be appropriate in the circumstances of the company.

But in the latter case particulars of the method of valuation adopted and of the reasons for adopting it must be disclosed in a note to the accounts.

(4) Securities of any description not held as financial fixed assets (if not valued in accordance with paragraph 33) may be included at their current cost.

Application of the depreciation rules

41. (1) Where the value of any asset of a company is determined in accordance with paragraph 40, that value must be, or (as the case may require) be the starting point for determining, the amount to be included in respect of that asset in the company's accounts, instead of its cost or any value previously so determined for that asset.

The depreciation rules apply accordingly in relation to any such asset with the substitution for any reference to its cost of a reference to the value most recently determined for that asset in accordance with paragraph 40.

(2) The amount of any provision for depreciation required in the case of any fixed asset by paragraphs 24 to 26 as they apply by virtue of sub-paragraph (1) is referred to below in this paragraph as the adjusted amount, and the amount of any provision which would be required by any of those paragraphs in the case of that asset according to the historical cost accounting rules is referred to as the historical cost amount.

(3) Where sub-paragraph (1) applies in the case of any fixed asset the amount of any provision for depreciation in respect of that asset included in any item shown in the profit and loss account in respect of amounts written off assets of the description in question may be the historical cost amount instead of the adjusted amount, provided that the amount of any difference between the two is shown separately in the profit and loss account or in a note to the accounts.

Additional information to be provided in case of departure from historical cost accounting rules

42. (1) This paragraph applies where the amounts to be included in respect of assets covered by any items shown in a company's accounts have been determined in accordance with paragraph 40.

(2) The items affected and the basis of valuation adopted in determining the amounts of the assets in question in the case of each such item must be disclosed in a note to the accounts.

(3) In the case of each balance sheet item affected either—

    (a)   the comparable amounts determined according to the historical cost accounting rules, or

    (b)   the differences between those amounts and the corresponding amounts actually shown in the balance sheet in respect of that item,

must be shown separately in the balance sheet or in a note to the accounts.

(4) In sub-paragraph (3), references in relation to any item to the comparable amounts determined as there mentioned are references to—

    (a)   the aggregate amount which would be required to be shown in respect of that item if the amounts to be included in respect of all the assets covered by that item were determined according to the historical cost accounting rules, and

    (b)   the aggregate amount of the cumulative provisions for depreciation or diminution in value which would be permitted or required in determining those amounts according to those rules.

Revaluation reserve

43. (1) With respect to any determination of the value of an asset of a company in accordance with paragraph 40, the amount of any profit or loss arising from that determination (after allowing, where appropriate, for any provisions for depreciation or diminution in value made otherwise than by reference to the value so determined and any adjustments of any such provisions made in the light of that determination) must be credited or (as the case may be) debited to a separate reserve ("the revaluation reserve").

(2) The amount of the revaluation reserve must be shown in the company's balance sheet under liabilities item 11 in the balance sheet format, but need not be shown under that name.

(3) An amount may be transferred—

    (a)   from the revaluation reserve—

      (i)   to the profit and loss account, if the amount was previously charged to that account or represents realised profit, or

      (ii) on capitalisation,

  (b)   to or from the revaluation reserve in respect of the taxation relating to any profit or loss credited or debited to the reserve.

The revaluation reserve must be reduced to the extent that the amounts transferred to it are no longer necessary for the purposes of the valuation method used.

(4)   In sub-paragraph (3)(a)(ii) "capitalisation", in relation to an amount standing to the credit of the revaluation reserve, means applying it in wholly or partly paying up unissued shares in the company to be allotted to members of the company as fully or partly paid shares.

(5)   The revaluation reserve must not be reduced except as mentioned in this paragraph.

(6)   The treatment for taxation purposes of amounts credited or debited to the revaluation reserve must be disclosed in a note to the accounts.

SECTION D
FAIR VALUE ACCOUNTING

Inclusion of financial instruments at fair value

44. (1)   Subject to sub-paragraphs (2) to (5), financial instruments (including derivatives) may be included at fair value.

(2)   Sub-paragraph (1) does not apply to financial instruments that constitute liabilities unless—

  (a)   they are held as part of a trading portfolio,

  (b)   they are derivatives, or

  (c)   they are financial instruments falling within sub-paragraph (4).

(3)   Unless they are financial instruments falling within sub-paragraph (4), sub-paragraph (1) does not apply to—

  (a)   financial instruments (other than derivatives) held to maturity,

  (b)   loans and receivables originated by the company and not held for trading purposes,

  (c)   interests in subsidiary undertakings, associated undertakings and joint ventures,

  (d)   equity instruments issued by the company,

  (e)   contracts for contingent consideration in a business combination, or

  (f)   other financial instruments with such special characteristics that the instruments, according to generally accepted accounting principles or practice, should be accounted for differently from other financial instruments.

(4)   Financial instruments that, under international accounting standards adopted by the European Commission on or before 5th September 2006 in accordance with the IAS Regulation, may be included in accounts at fair value, may be so included, provided that the disclosures required by such accounting standards are made.

(5)   If the fair value of a financial instrument cannot be determined reliably in accordance with paragraph 45, sub-paragraph (1) does not apply to that financial instrument.

(6)   In this paragraph—

"associated undertaking" has the meaning given by paragraph 19 of Schedule 6 to these Regulations;

"joint venture" has the meaning given by paragraph 18 of that Schedule.

Determination of fair value

45. (1)   The fair value of a financial instrument is its value determined in accordance with this paragraph.

(2)   If a reliable market can readily be identified for the financial instrument, its fair value is determined by reference to its market value.

(3)   If a reliable market cannot readily be identified for the financial instrument but can be identified for its components or for a similar instrument, its fair value is determined by reference to the market value of its components or of the similar instrument.

(4)   If neither sub-paragraph (2) nor (3) applies, the fair value of the financial instrument is a value resulting from generally accepted valuation models and techniques.

(5)   Any valuation models and techniques used for the purposes of sub-paragraph (4) must ensure a reasonable approximation of the market value.

Hedged items

46. A company may include any assets and liabilities, or identified portions of such assets or liabilities, that qualify as hedged items under a fair value hedge accounting system at the amount required under that system.

Other assets that may be included at fair value

47. (1)   This paragraph applies to—

(a) investment property, and

(b) living animals and plants,

that, under international accounting standards, may be included in accounts at fair value.

(2) Such investment property and such living animals and plants may be included at fair value, provided that all such investment property or, as the case may be, all such living animals and plants are so included where their fair value can reliably be determined.

(3) In this paragraph, "fair value" means fair value determined in accordance with relevant international accounting standards.

Accounting for changes in value

48. (1) This paragraph applies where a financial instrument is valued in accordance with paragraph 44 or 46 or an asset is valued in accordance with paragraph 47.

(2) Notwithstanding paragraph 19 in this Part of this Schedule, and subject to sub-paragraphs (3) and (4), a change in the value of the financial instrument or of the investment property or living animal or plant must be included in the profit and loss account.

(3) Where—

(a) the financial instrument accounted for is a hedging instrument under a hedge accounting system that allows some or all of the change in value not to be shown in the profit and loss account, or

(b) the change in value relates to an exchange difference arising on a monetary item that forms part of a company's net investment in a foreign entity,

the amount of the change in value must be credited to or (as the case may be) debited from a separate reserve ("the fair value reserve").

(4) Where the instrument accounted for—

(a) is an available for sale financial asset, and

(b) is not a derivative,

the change in value may be credited to or (as the case may be) debited from the fair value reserve.

The fair value reserve

49. (1) The fair value reserve must be adjusted to the extent that the amounts shown in it are no longer necessary for the purposes of paragraph 48(3) or (4).

(2) The treatment for taxation purposes of amounts credited or debited to the fair value reserve must be disclosed in a note to the accounts.

Assets and liabilities denominated in foreign currencies

50. (1) Subject to the following sub-paragraphs, amounts to be included in respect of assets and liabilities denominated in foreign currencies must be in sterling (or the currency in which the accounts are drawn up) after translation at an appropriate spot rate of exchange prevailing at the balance sheet date.

(2) An appropriate rate of exchange prevailing on the date of purchase may however be used for assets held as financial fixed assets and assets to be included under assets items 9 (intangible fixed assets) and 10 (tangible fixed assets) in the balance sheet format, if they are not covered or not specifically covered in either the spot or forward currency markets.

(3) An appropriate spot rate of exchange prevailing at the balance sheet date must be used for translating uncompleted spot exchange transactions.

(4) An appropriate forward rate of exchange prevailing at the balance sheet date must be used for translating uncompleted forward exchange transactions.

(5) This paragraph does not apply to any assets or liabilities held, or any transactions entered into, for hedging purposes or to any assets or liabilities which are themselves hedged.

51. (1) Subject to sub-paragraph (2), any difference between the amount to be included in respect of an asset or liability under paragraph 50 and the book value, after translation into sterling (or the currency in which the accounts are drawn up) at an appropriate rate, of that asset or liability must be credited or, as the case may be, debited to the profit and loss account.

(2) In the case, however, of assets held as financial fixed assets, of assets to be included under assets items 9 (intangible fixed assets) and 10 (tangible fixed assets) in the balance sheet format and of transactions undertaken to cover such assets, any such difference may be deducted from or credited to any non-distributable reserve available for the purpose.

NOTES

Commencement: 6 April 2008.

PART 3
NOTES TO THE ACCOUNTS
Preliminary

[4.190]

52. Any information required in the case of any company by the following provisions of this Part of this Schedule must (if not given in the company's accounts) be given by way of a note to the accounts.

General

Disclosure of accounting policies

53. The accounting policies adopted by the company in determining the amounts to be included in respect of items shown in the balance sheet and in determining the profit or loss of the company must be stated (including such policies with respect to the depreciation and diminution in value of assets).

54. It must be stated whether the accounts have been prepared in accordance with applicable accounting standards and particulars of any material departure from those standards and the reasons for it must be given.

Sums denominated in foreign currencies

55. Where any sums originally denominated in foreign currencies have been brought into account under any items shown in the balance sheet format or profit and loss account formats, the basis on which those sums have been translated into sterling (or the currency in which the accounts are drawn up) must be stated.

Reserves and dividends

56. There must be stated—
- (a) any amount set aside or proposed to be set aside to, or withdrawn or proposed to be withdrawn from, reserves,
- (b) the aggregate amount of dividends paid in the financial year (other than those for which a liability existed at the immediately preceding balance sheet date),
- (c) the aggregate amount of dividends that the company is liable to pay at the balance sheet date, and
- (d) the aggregate amount of dividends that are proposed before the date of approval of the accounts, and not otherwise disclosed under sub-paragraph (b) or (c).

Information supplementing the balance sheet

57. Paragraphs 58 to 84 require information which either supplements the information given with respect to any particular items shown in the balance sheet or is otherwise relevant to assessing the company's state of affairs in the light of the information so given.

Share capital and debentures

58. (1) Where shares of more than one class have been allotted, the number and aggregate nominal value of shares of each class allotted must be given.

(2) In the case of any part of the allotted share capital that consists of redeemable shares, the following information must be given—
- (a) the earliest and latest dates on which the company has power to redeem those shares,
- (b) whether those shares must be redeemed in any event or are liable to be redeemed at the option of the company or of the shareholder, and
- (c) whether any (and, if so, what) premium is payable on redemption.

59. If the company has allotted any shares during the financial year, the following information must be given—
- (a) the classes of shares allotted, and
- (b) as respects each class of shares, the number allotted, their aggregate nominal value and the consideration received by the company for the allotment.

60. (1) With respect to any contingent right to the allotment of shares in the company the following particulars must be given—
- (a) the number, description and amount of the shares in relation to which the right is exercisable,
- (b) the period during which it is exercisable, and
- (c) the price to be paid for the shares allotted.

(2) In sub-paragraph (1) "contingent right to the allotment of shares" means any option to subscribe for shares and any other right to require the allotment of shares to any person whether arising on the conversion into shares of securities of any other description or otherwise.

61. (1)   If the company has issued any debentures during the financial year to which the accounts relate, the following information must be given—
- (a)   the classes of debentures issued, and
- (b)   as respects each class of debentures, the amount issued and the consideration received by the company for the issue.

(2)   Where any of the company's debentures are held by a nominee of or trustee for the company, the nominal amount of the debentures and the amount at which they are stated in the accounting records kept by the company in accordance with section 386 of the 2006 Act (duty to keep accounting records) must be stated.

Fixed assets

62. (1)   In respect of any fixed assets of the company included in any assets item in the company's balance sheet the following information must be given by reference to each such item—
- (a)   the appropriate amounts in respect of those assets included in the item as at the date of the beginning of the financial year and as at the balance sheet date respectively,
- (b)   the effect on any amount shown included in the item in respect of those assets of—
  - (i)   any determination during that year of the value to be ascribed to any of those assets in accordance with paragraph 40,
  - (ii)   acquisitions during that year of any fixed assets,
  - (iii)   disposals during that year of any fixed assets, and
  - (iv)   any transfers of fixed assets of the company to and from that item during that year.

(2)   The reference in sub-paragraph (1)(a) to the appropriate amounts in respect of any fixed assets (included in an assets item) as at any date there mentioned is a reference to amounts representing the aggregate amounts determined, as at that date, in respect of fixed assets falling to be included under the item on either of the following bases—
- (a)   on the basis of cost (determined in accordance with paragraphs 35 and 36), or
- (b)   on any basis permitted by paragraph 40,

(leaving out of account in either case any provisions for depreciation or diminution in value).

(3)   In addition, in respect of any fixed assets of the company included in any assets item in the company's balance sheet, there must be stated (by reference to each such item)—
- (a)   the cumulative amount of provisions for depreciation or diminution in value of those assets included under that item as at each date mentioned in sub-paragraph (1)(a),
- (b)   the amount of any such provisions made in respect of the financial year,
- (c)   the amount of any adjustments made in respect of any such provisions during that year in consequence of the disposal of any of those assets, and
- (d)   the amount of any other adjustments made in respect of any such provisions during that year.

(4)   The requirements of this paragraph need not be complied with to the extent that a company takes advantage of the option of setting off charges and income afforded by paragraph 8(3) in Part 1 of this Schedule.

63.   Where any fixed assets of the company (other than listed investments) are included under any item shown in the company's balance sheet at an amount determined in accordance with paragraph 40, the following information must be given—
- (a)   the years (so far as they are known to the directors) in which the assets were severally valued and the several values, and
- (b)   in the case of assets that have been valued during the financial year, the names of the persons who valued them or particulars of their qualifications for doing so and (whichever is stated) the bases of valuation used by them.

64.   In relation to any amount which is included under assets item 10 in the balance sheet format (tangible fixed assets) with respect to land and buildings there must be stated—
- (a)   how much of that amount is ascribable to land of freehold tenure and how much to land of leasehold tenure, and
- (b)   how much of the amount ascribable to land of leasehold tenure is ascribable to land held on long lease and how much to land held on short lease.

65.   There must be disclosed separately the amount of—
- (a)   any participating interests, and
- (b)   any shares in group undertakings that are held in credit institutions.

Information about fair value of assets and liabilities

66. (1)   This paragraph applies where financial instruments have been valued in accordance with paragraph 44 or 46.

(2)   There must be stated—
- (a)   the significant assumptions underlying the valuation models and techniques used where the fair value of the instruments has been determined in accordance with paragraph 45(4),

(b) for each category of financial instrument, the fair value of the instruments in that category and the changes in value—
   (i)   included in the profit and loss account, or
   (ii)   credited to or (as the case may be) debited from the fair value reserve,
   in respect of those instruments, and
(c) for each class of derivatives, the extent and nature of the instruments, including significant terms and conditions that may affect the amount, timing and certainty of future cash flows.

(3) Where any amount is transferred to or from the fair value reserve during the financial year, there must be stated in tabular form—
   (a) the amount of the reserve as at the date of the beginning of the financial year and as at the balance sheet date respectively,
   (b) the amount transferred to or from the reserve during that year, and
   (c) the source and application respectively of the amounts so transferred.

67. Where the company has derivatives that it has not included at fair value, there must be stated for each class of such derivatives—
   (a) the fair value of the derivatives in that class, if such a value can be determined in accordance with paragraph 45, and
   (b) the extent and nature of the derivatives.

68. (1) This paragraph applies if—
   (a) the company has financial fixed assets that could be included at fair value by virtue of paragraph 44,
   (b) the amount at which those items are included under any item in the company's accounts is in excess of their fair value, and
   (c) the company has not made provision for diminution in value of those assets in accordance with paragraph 25(1) in Part 2 of this Schedule.

(2) There must be stated—
   (a) the amount at which either the individual assets or appropriate groupings of those individual assets are included in the company's accounts,
   (b) the fair value of those assets or groupings, and
   (c) the reasons for not making a provision for diminution in value of those assets, including the nature of the evidence that provides the basis for the belief that the amount at which they are stated in the accounts will be recovered.

Information where investment property and living animals and plants included at fair value

69. (1) This paragraph applies where the amounts to be included in a company's accounts in respect of investment property or living animals and plants have been determined in accordance with paragraph 47.

(2) The balance sheet items affected and the basis of valuation adopted in determining the amounts of the assets in question in the case of each such item must be disclosed in a note to the accounts.

(3) In the case of investment property, for each balance sheet item affected there must be shown, either separately in the balance sheet or in a note to the accounts—
   (a) the comparable amounts determined according to the historical cost accounting rules, or
   (b) the differences between those amounts and the corresponding amounts actually shown in the balance sheet in respect of that item.

(4) In sub-paragraph (3), references in relation to any item to the comparable amounts determined in accordance with that sub-paragraph are to—
   (a) the aggregate amount which would be required to be shown in respect of that item if the amounts to be included in respect of all the assets covered by that item were determined according to the historical cost accounting rules, and
   (b) the aggregate amount of the cumulative provisions for depreciation or diminution in value which would be permitted or required in determining those amounts according to those rules.

Reserves and provisions

70. (1) This paragraph applies where any amount is transferred—
   (a) to or from any reserves, or
   (b) to any provision for liabilities, or
   (c) from any provision for liabilities otherwise than for the purpose for which the provision was established,
and the reserves or provisions are or would but for paragraph 5(1) in Part 1 of this Schedule be shown as separate items in the company's balance sheet.

(2) The following information must be given in respect of the aggregate of reserves or provisions included in the same item—
   (a) the amount of the reserves or provisions as at the date of the beginning of the financial year and as at the balance sheet date respectively,

(b)   any amounts transferred to or from the reserves or provisions during that year, and

(c)   the source and application respectively of any amounts so transferred.

(3) Particulars must be given of each provision included in liabilities item 6.(c) (other provisions) in the company's balance sheet in any case where the amount of that provision is material.

Provision for taxation

71. The amount of any provision for deferred taxation must be stated separately from the amount of any provision for other taxation.

Maturity analysis

72. (1) A company must disclose separately for each of assets items 3.(b) and 4 and liabilities items 1.(b), 2.(b) and 3.(b) the aggregate amount of the loans and advances and liabilities included in those items broken down into the following categories—

(a)   those repayable in not more than three months,

(b)   those repayable in more than three months but not more than one year,

(c)   those repayable in more than one year but not more than five years,

(d)   those repayable in more than five years,

from the balance sheet date.

(2) A company must also disclose the aggregate amounts of all loans and advances falling within assets item 4 (loans and advances to customers) which are—

(a)   repayable on demand, or

(b)   are for an indeterminate period, being repayable upon short notice.

(3) For the purposes of sub-paragraph (1), where a loan or advance or liability is repayable by instalments, each such instalment is to be treated as a separate loan or advance or liability.

Debt and other fixed-income securities

73. A company must disclose the amount of debt and fixed-income securities included in assets item 5 (debt securities [and other fixed-income securities]) and the amount of such securities included in liabilities item 3.(a) (bonds and medium term notes) that (in each case) will become due within one year of the balance sheet date.

Subordinated liabilities

74. (1) The following information must be disclosed in relation to any borrowing included in liabilities item 7 (subordinated liabilities) that exceeds 10% of the total for that item—

(a)   its amount,

(b)   the currency in which it is denominated,

(c)   the rate of interest and the maturity date (or the fact that it is perpetual),

(d)   the circumstances in which early repayment may be demanded,

(e)   the terms of the subordination, and

(f)   the existence of any provisions whereby it may be converted into capital or some other form of liability and the terms of any such provisions.

(2) The general terms of any other borrowings included in liabilities item 7 must also be stated.

Fixed cumulative dividends

75. If any fixed cumulative dividends on the company's shares are in arrear, there must be stated—

(a)   the amount of the arrears, and

(b)   the period for which the dividends or, if there is more than one class, each class of them are in arrear.

Details of assets charged

76. (1) There must be disclosed, in relation to each liabilities and memorandum item of the balance sheet format—

(a)   the aggregate amount of any assets of the company which have been charged to secure any liability or potential liability included under that item,

(b)   the aggregate amount of the liabilities or potential liabilities so secured, and

(c)   an indication of the nature of the security given.

(2) Particulars must also be given of any other charge on the assets of the company to secure the liabilities of any other person, including, where practicable, the amount secured.

Guarantees and other financial commitments

77. (1) There must be stated, where practicable, the aggregate amount or estimated amount of contracts for capital expenditure, so far as not provided for.

(2) Particulars must be given of—

(a)   any pension commitments included under any provision shown in the company's balance sheet, and

(b)   any such commitments for which no provision has been made, and where any such commitment relates wholly or partly to pensions payable to past directors of the company separate particulars must be given of that commitment so far as it relates to such pensions.

(3) Particulars must also be given of any other financial commitments, including any contingent liabilities, that—

(a) have not been provided for,

(b) have not been included in the memorandum items in the balance sheet format, and

(c) are relevant to assessing the company's state of affairs.

(4) Commitments within any of the preceding sub-paragraphs undertaken on behalf of or for the benefit of—

(a) any parent company or fellow subsidiary undertaking of the company, or

(b) any subsidiary undertaking of the company,

must be stated separately from the other commitments within that sub-paragraph (and commitments within paragraph (a) must be stated separately from those within paragraph (b)).

(5) There must be disclosed the nature and amount of any contingent liabilities and commitments included in Memorandum items 1 and 2 which are material in relation to the company's activities.

Memorandum items: Group undertakings

78. (1) With respect to contingent liabilities required to be included under Memorandum item 1 in the balance sheet format, there must be stated in a note to the accounts the amount of such contingent liabilities incurred on behalf of or for the benefit of—

(a) any parent undertaking or fellow subsidiary undertaking, or

(b) any subsidiary undertaking,

of the company; in addition the amount incurred in respect of the undertakings referred to in paragraph (a) must be stated separately from the amount incurred in respect of the undertakings referred to in paragraph (b).

(2) With respect to commitments required to be included under Memorandum item 2 in the balance sheet format, there must be stated in a note to the accounts the amount of such commitments undertaken on behalf of or for the benefit of—

(a) any parent undertaking or fellow subsidiary undertaking, or

(b) any subsidiary undertaking,

of the company; in addition the amount incurred in respect of the undertakings referred to in paragraph (a) must be stated separately from the amount incurred in respect of the undertakings referred to in paragraph (b).

Transferable securities

79. (1) There must be disclosed for each of assets items 5 to 8 in the balance sheet format the amount of transferable securities included under those items that are listed and the amount of those that are unlisted.

(2) In the case of each amount shown in respect of listed securities under sub-paragraph (1), there must also be disclosed the aggregate market value of those securities, if different from the amount shown.

(3) There must also be disclosed for each of assets items 5 and 6 the amount of transferable securities included under those items that are held as financial fixed assets and the amount of those that are not so held, together with the criterion used by the directors to distinguish those held as financial fixed assets.

Leasing transactions

80. The aggregate amount of all property (other than land) leased by the company to other persons must be disclosed, broken down so as to show the aggregate amount included in each relevant balance sheet item.

Assets and liabilities denominated in a currency other than sterling (or the currency in which the accounts are drawn up)

81. (1) The aggregate amount, in sterling (or the currency in which the accounts are drawn up), of all assets denominated in a currency other than sterling (or the currency used) together with the aggregate amount, in sterling (or the currency used), of all liabilities so denominated, is to be disclosed.

(2) For the purposes of this paragraph an appropriate rate of exchange prevailing at the balance sheet date must be used to determine the amounts concerned.

Sundry assets and liabilities

82. Where any amount shown under either of the following items is material, particulars must be given of each type of asset or liability included in that item, including an explanation of the nature of the asset or liability and the amount included with respect to assets or liabilities of that type—

(a) assets item 13 (other assets),

(b) liabilities item 4 (other liabilities).

Unmatured forward transactions

83. (1)   The following must be disclosed with respect to unmatured forward transactions outstanding at the balance sheet date—
(a)   the categories of such transactions, by reference to an appropriate system of classification,
(b)   whether, in the case of each such category, they have been made, to any material extent, for the purpose of hedging the effects of fluctuations in interest rates, exchange rates and market prices or whether they have been made, to any material extent, for dealing purposes.

(2)   Transactions falling within sub-paragraph (1) must include all those in relation to which income or expenditure is to be included in—
(a)   format 1, item 6 or format 2, items B4 or A3 (dealing [profits][losses]),
(b)   format 1, items 1 or 2, or format 2, items B1 or A1, by virtue of notes (1)(b) and (2)(b) to the profit and loss account formats (forward contracts, spread over the actual duration of the contract and similar in nature to interest).

Miscellaneous matters

84. (1)   Particulars must be given of any case where the cost of any asset is for the first time determined under paragraph 37 in Part 2 of this Schedule.

(2)   Where any outstanding loans made under the authority of section 682(2)(b), (c) or (d) of the 2006 Act (various cases of financial assistance by a company for purchase of its own shares) are included under any item shown in the company's balance sheet, the aggregate amount of those loans must be disclosed for each item in question.

Information supplementing the profit and loss account

85.   Paragraphs 86 to 91 require information which either supplements the information given with respect to any particular items shown in the profit and loss account or otherwise provides particulars of income or expenditure of the company or of circumstances affecting the items shown in the profit and loss account (see regulation 5(2) for exemption for companies falling within section 408 of the 2006 Act (individual profit and loss account where group accounts prepared)).

Particulars of tax

86. (1)   Particulars must be given of any special circumstances which affect liability in respect of taxation of profits, income or capital gains for the financial year or liability in respect of taxation of profits, income or capital gains for succeeding financial years.

(2)   The following amounts must be stated—
(a)   the amount of the charge for United Kingdom corporation tax,
(b)   if that amount would have been greater but for relief from double taxation, the amount which it would have been but for such relief,
(c)   the amount of the charge for United Kingdom income tax, and
(d)   the amount of the charge for taxation imposed outside the United Kingdom of profits, income and (so far as charged to revenue) capital gains.
These amounts must be stated separately in respect of each of the amounts which is shown under the following items in the profit and loss account, that is to say format 1 item 16, format 2 item A10 (tax on [profit][loss] on ordinary activities) and format 1 item 21, format 2 item A13 (tax on extraordinary [profit][loss]).

Particulars of income

87. (1)   A company must disclose, with respect to income included in the following items in the profit and loss account formats, the amount of that income attributable to each of the geographical markets in which the company has operated during the financial year—
(a)   format 1 item 1, format 2 item B1 (interest receivable),
(b)   format 1 item 3, format 2 item B2 (dividend income),
(c)   format 1 item 4, format 2 item B3 (fees and commissions receivable),
(d)   format 1 item 6, format 2 item B4 (dealing profits), and
(e)   format 1 item 7, format 2 item B7 (other operating income).

(2)   In analysing for the purposes of this paragraph the source of any income, the directors must have regard to the manner in which the company's activities are organised.

(3)   For the purposes of this paragraph, markets which do not differ substantially from each other shall be treated as one market.

(4)   Where in the opinion of the directors the disclosure of any information required by this paragraph would be seriously prejudicial to the interests of the company, that information need not be disclosed, but the fact that any such information has not been disclosed must be stated.

Management and agency services

88.   A company providing any management and agency services to customers must disclose that fact, if the scale of such services provided is material in the context of its business as a whole.

Subordinated liabilities

89. Any amounts charged to the profit and loss account representing charges incurred during the year with respect to subordinated liabilities must be disclosed.

Sundry income and charges

90. Where any amount to be included in any of the following items is material, particulars must be given of each individual component of the figure, including an explanation of their nature and amount—
- (a)   in format 1—
  - (i)   items 7 and 10 (other operating income and charges),
  - (ii)   items 18 and 19 (extraordinary income and charges);
- (b)   in format 2—
  - (i)   items A6 and B7 (other operating charges and income),
  - (ii)   items A12 and B10 (extraordinary charges and income).

Miscellaneous matters

91. (1)   Where any amount relating to any preceding financial year is included in any item in the profit and loss account, the effect must be stated.

(2)   The effect must be stated of any transactions that are exceptional by virtue of size or incidence though they fall within the ordinary activities of the company.

Related party transactions

92. (1)   Particulars may be given of transactions which the company has entered into with related parties, and must be given if such transactions are material and have not been concluded under normal market conditions.

(2)   The particulars of transactions required to be disclosed by sub-paragraph (1) must include—
- (a)   the amount of such transactions,
- (b)   the nature of the related party relationship, and
- (c)   other information about the transactions necessary for an understanding of the financial position of the company.

(3)   Information about individual transactions may be aggregated according to their nature, except where separate information is necessary for an understanding of the effects of related party transactions on the financial position of the company.

(4)   Particulars need not be given of transactions entered into between two or more members of a group, provided that any subsidiary undertaking which is a party to the transaction is wholly-owned by such a member.

(5)   In this paragraph, "related party" has the same meaning as in international accounting standards.

NOTES

Commencement: 6 April 2008.

PART 4
INTERPRETATION OF THIS SCHEDULE

Definitions for this Schedule

[4.191]
93. The following definitions apply for the purposes of this Schedule.

Financial fixed assets

94. "Financial fixed assets" means loans and advances and securities held as fixed assets; participating interests and shareholdings in group undertakings are to be regarded as financial fixed assets.

Financial instruments

95. For the purposes of this Schedule, references to "derivatives" include commodity-based contracts that give either contracting party the right to settle in cash or in some other financial instrument, except when such contracts—
- (a)   were entered into for the purpose of, and continue to meet, the company's expected purchase, sale or usage requirements,
- (b)   were designated for such purpose at their inception, and
- (c)   are expected to be settled by delivery of the commodity.

96. (1)   The expressions listed in sub-paragraph (2) have the same meaning in paragraphs 44 to 49, 66 to 68 and 95 of this Schedule as they have in Council Directives 78/660/EEC on the annual accounts of certain types of companies and 86/635/EEC on the annual accounts and consolidated accounts of banks and other financial institutions.

(2)   Those expressions are "available for sale financial asset", "business combination", "commodity-based contracts", "derivative", "equity instrument", "exchange difference", "fair value hedge accounting system", "financial fixed asset", "financial instrument", "foreign entity", "hedge accounting", "hedge accounting system", "hedged items", "hedging instrument", "held for trading purposes", "held to maturity", "monetary item", "receivables", "reliable market" and "trading portfolio".

Repayable on demand

97.   "Repayable on demand", in connection with deposits, loans or advances, means that they can at any time be withdrawn or demanded without notice or that a maturity or period of notice of not more than 24 hours or one working day has been agreed for them.

Sale and repurchase transaction

98. (1)   "Sale and repurchase transaction" means a transaction which involves the transfer by a credit institution or customer ("the transferor") to another credit institution or customer ("the transferee") of assets subject to an agreement that the same assets, or (in the case of fungible assets) equivalent assets, will subsequently be transferred back to the transferor at a specified price on a date specified or to be specified by the transferor.

(2)   The following are not to be regarded as sale and repurchase transactions for the purposes of sub-paragraph (1)—
   (a)   forward exchange transactions,
   (b)   options,
   (c)   transactions involving the issue of debt securities with a commitment to repurchase all or part of the issue before maturity, or
   (d)   any similar transactions.

Sale and option to resell transaction

99.   "Sale and option to resell transaction" means a transaction which involves the transfer by a credit institution or customer ("the transferor") to another credit institution or customer ("the transferee") of assets subject to an agreement that the transferee is entitled to require the subsequent transfer of the same assets, or (in the case of fungible assets) equivalent assets, back to the transferor at the purchase price or another price agreed in advance on a date specified or to be specified.

NOTES
Commencement: 6 April 2008.

SCHEDULE 3
INSURANCE COMPANIES: COMPANIES ACT INDIVIDUAL ACCOUNTS
Regulation 6(1)

PART 1
GENERAL RULES AND FORMATS

SECTION A
GENERAL RULES

[4.192]
1. (1)   Subject to the following provisions of this Schedule—
   (a)   every balance sheet of a company must show the items listed in the balance sheet format in Section B of this Part, and
   (b)   every profit and loss account must show the items listed in the profit and loss account format in Section B.

(2)   References in this Schedule to the items listed in any of the formats in Section B are to those items read together with any of the notes following the formats which apply to those items.

(3)   The items must be shown in the order and under the headings and sub-headings given in the particular format, but—
   (a)   the notes to the formats may permit alternative positions for any particular items, and
   (b)   the heading or sub-heading for any item does not have to be distinguished by any letter or number assigned to that item in the format used.

2. (1)   Any item required to be shown in a company's balance sheet or profit and loss account may be shown in greater detail than required by the particular format.

(2)   The balance sheet or profit and loss account may include an item representing or covering the amount of any asset or liability, income or expenditure not specifically covered by any of the items listed in the formats set out in Section B, save that none of the following may be treated as assets in any balance sheet—
  (a)   preliminary expenses,
  (b)   expenses of, and commission on, any issue of shares or debentures, and
  (c)   costs of research.

3.   (1)   The directors may combine items to which Arabic numbers are given in the balance sheet format set out in Section B (except for items concerning technical provisions and the reinsurers' share of technical provisions), and items to which lower case letters in parentheses are given in the profit and loss account format so set out (except for items within items I.1 and 4 and II.1, 5 and 6) if—
  (a)   their individual amounts are not material for the purpose of giving a true and fair view, or
  (b)   the combination facilitates the assessment of the state of affairs or profit or loss of the company for the financial year in question.

(2)   Where sub-paragraph (1)(b) applies—
  (a)   the individual amounts of any items which have been combined must be disclosed in a note to the accounts, and
  (b)   any notes required by this Schedule to the items so combined must, notwithstanding the combination, be given.

4.   (1)   Subject to sub-paragraph (2), the directors must not include a heading or sub-heading corresponding to an item in the balance sheet or profit and loss account format used if there is no amount to be shown for that item for the financial year to which the balance sheet or profit and loss account relates.

(2)   Where an amount can be shown for the item in question for the immediately preceding financial year that amount must be shown under the heading or sub-heading required by the format for that item.

5.   (1)   For every item shown in the balance sheet or profit and loss account the corresponding amount for the immediately preceding financial year must also be shown.

(2)   Where that corresponding amount is not comparable with the amount to be shown for the item in question in respect of the financial year to which the balance sheet or profit and loss account relates, the former amount may be adjusted, and particulars of the non-comparability and of any adjustment must be disclosed in a note to the accounts.

6.   Subject to the provisions of this Schedule, amounts in respect of items representing assets or income may not be set off against amounts in respect of items representing liabilities or expenditure (as the case may be), or vice versa.

7.   (1)   The provisions of this Schedule which relate to long-term business apply, with necessary modifications, to business which consists of effecting or carrying out relevant contracts of general insurance which—
  (a)   is transacted exclusively or principally according to the technical principles of long-term business, and
  (b)   is a significant amount of the business of the company.

(2)   For the purposes of paragraph (1), a contract of general insurance is a relevant contract if the risk insured against relates to—
  (a)   accident, or
  (b)   sickness.

(3)   Sub-paragraph (2) must be read with—
  (a)   section 22 of the Financial Services and Markets Act 2000,
  (b)   the Financial Services and Markets Act 2000 (Regulated Activities) Order 2001, and
  (c)   Schedule 2 to that Act.

8.   The company's directors must, in determining how amounts are presented within items in the profit and loss account and balance sheet, have regard to the substance of the reported transaction or arrangement, in accordance with generally accepted accounting principles or practice.

SECTION B
THE REQUIRED FORMATS

9.   (1)   Where in respect of any item to which an Arabic number is assigned in the balance sheet or profit and loss account format, the gross amount and reinsurance amount or reinsurers' share are required to be shown, a sub-total of those amounts must also be given.

(2)   Where in respect of any item to which an Arabic number is assigned in the profit and loss account format, separate items are required to be shown, then a separate sub-total of those items must also be given in addition to any sub-total required by sub-paragraph (1).

10. (1)   In the profit and loss account format set out below—

(a)   the heading "Technical account—General business" is for business which consists of effecting or carrying out contracts of general business; and

(b)   the heading "Technical account—Long-term business" is for business which consists of effecting or carrying out contracts of long-term insurance.

(2)   In sub-paragraph (1), references to—

(a)   contracts of general or long-term insurance, and

(b)   the effecting or carrying out of such contracts,

must be read with section 22 of the Financial Services and Markets Act 2000, the Financial Services and Markets Act 2000 (Regulated Activities) Order 2001, and Schedule 2 to that Act.

Balance sheet format

ASSETS

A   Called up share capital not paid [1]

B   Intangible assets
1   Development costs
2   Concessions, patents, licences, trade marks and similar rights and assets [2]
3   Goodwill [3]
4   Payments on account

C   Investments
I   Land and buildings [4]
II   Investments in group undertakings and participating interests
1   Shares in group undertakings
2   Debt securities issued by, and loans to, group undertakings
3   Participating interests
4   Debt securities issued by, and loans to, undertakings in which the company has a participating interest
III   Other financial investments
1   Shares and other variable-yield securities and units in unit trusts
2   Debt securities and other fixed-income securities [5]
3   Participation in investment pools [6]
4   Loans secured by mortgages [7]
5   Other loans [7]
6   Deposits with credit institutions [8]
7   Other [9]
IV   Deposits with ceding undertakings [10]

D   Assets held to cover linked liabilities [11]

Da   Reinsurers' share of technical provisions [12]
1   Provision for unearned premiums
2   Long-term business provision
3   Claims outstanding
4   Provisions for bonuses and rebates
5   Other technical provisions
6   Technical provisions for unit-linked liabilities

E   Debtors [13]
I   Debtors arising out of direct insurance operations
1   Policyholders
2   Intermediaries
II   Debtors arising out of reinsurance operations
III   Other debtors
IV   Called up share capital not paid [1]

F   Other assets
I   Tangible assets
1   Plant and machinery
2   Fixtures, fittings, tools and equipment
3   Payments on account (other than deposits paid on land and buildings) and assets (other than buildings) in course of construction
II   Stocks
1   Raw materials and consumables
2   Work in progress
3   Finished goods and goods for resale
4   Payments on account
III   Cash at bank and in hand

IV   Own shares [14]
V   Other [15]

G   Prepayments and accrued income
    I   Accrued interest and rent [16]
    II   Deferred acquisition costs [17]
    III   Other prepayments and accrued income

LIABILITIES

A   Capital and reserves
    I   Called up share capital or equivalent funds
    II   Share premium account
    III   Revaluation reserve
    IV   Reserves
         1   Capital redemption reserve
         2   Reserve for own shares
         3   Reserves provided for by the articles of association
         4   Other reserves
    V   Profit and loss account

B   Subordinated liabilities [18]

Ba   Fund for future appropriations [19]

C   Technical provisions
    1   Provision for unearned premiums [20]
        (a)   gross amount
        (b)   reinsurance amount [12]
    2   Long-term business provision [20] [21] [26]
        (a)   gross amount
        (b)   reinsurance amount [12]
    3   Claims outstanding [22]
        (a)   gross amount
        (b)   reinsurance amount [12]
    4   Provision for bonuses and rebates [23]
        (a)   gross amount
        (b)   reinsurance amount [12]
    5   Equalisation provision [24]
    6   Other technical provisions [25]
        (a)   gross amount
        (b)   reinsurance amount [12]

D   Technical provisions for linked liabilities [26]
    (a)   gross amount
    (b)   reinsurance amount [12]

E   Provisions for other risks
    1   Provisions for pensions and similar obligations
    2   Provisions for taxation
    3   Other provisions

F   Deposits received from reinsurers [27]

G   Creditors [28]
    I   Creditors arising out of direct insurance operations
    II   Creditors arising out of reinsurance operations
    III   Debenture loans [29]
    IV   Amounts owed to credit institutions
    V   Other creditors including taxation and social security

H   Accruals and deferred income

Notes on the balance sheet format

(1)   Called up share capital not paid

(Assets items A and E.IV.)

    This item may be shown in either of the positions given in the format.

(2)   Concessions, patents, licences, trade marks and similar rights and assets

(Assets item B.2.)

    Amounts in respect of assets are only to be included in a company's balance sheet under this item if either—

(a) the assets were acquired for valuable consideration and are not required to be shown under goodwill, or

(b) the assets in question were created by the company itself.

(3) Goodwill

(Assets item B.3.)

Amounts representing goodwill are only to be included to the extent that the goodwill was acquired for valuable consideration.

(4) Land and buildings

(Assets item CI.)

The amount of any land and buildings occupied by the company for its own activities must be shown separately in the notes to the accounts.

(5) Debt securities and other fixed-income securities

(Assets item CIII.2.)

This item is to comprise transferable debt securities and any other transferable fixed-income securities issued by credit institutions, other undertakings or public bodies, in so far as they are not covered by assets item CII.2 or CII.4.

Securities bearing interest rates that vary in accordance with specific factors, for example the interest rate on the inter-bank market or on the Euromarket, are also to be regarded as debt securities and other fixed-income securities and so be included under this item.

(6) Participation in investment pools

(Assets item CIII.3.)

This item is to comprise shares held by the company in joint investments constituted by several undertakings or pension funds, the management of which has been entrusted to one of those undertakings or to one of those pension funds.

(7) Loans secured by mortgages and other loans

(Assets items CIII.4 and CIII.5.)

Loans to policyholders for which the policy is the main security are to be included under "Other loans" and their amount must be disclosed in the notes to the accounts. Loans secured by mortgage are to be shown as such even where they are also secured by insurance policies. Where the amount of "Other loans" not secured by policies is material, an appropriate breakdown must be given in the notes to the accounts.

(8) Deposits with credit institutions

(Assets item CIII.6.)

This item is to comprise sums the withdrawal of which is subject to a time restriction. Sums deposited with no such restriction must be shown under assets item F.III even if they bear interest.

(9) Other

(Assets item CIII.7.)

This item is to comprise those investments which are not covered by assets items CIII.1 to 6. Where the amount of such investments is significant, they must be disclosed in the notes to the accounts.

(10) Deposits with ceding undertakings

(Assets item CIV.)

Where the company accepts reinsurance this item is to comprise amounts, owed by the ceding undertakings and corresponding to guarantees, which are deposited with those ceding undertakings or with third parties or which are retained by those undertakings.

These amounts may not be combined with other amounts owed by the ceding insurer to the reinsurer or set off against amounts owed by the reinsurer to the ceding insurer.

Securities deposited with ceding undertakings or third parties which remain the property of the company must be entered in the company's accounts as an investment, under the appropriate item.

(11) Assets held to cover linked liabilities

(Assets item D)

In respect of long-term business, this item is to comprise investments made pursuant to long-term policies under which the benefits payable to the policyholder are wholly or partly to be determined by reference to the value of, or the income from, property of any description (whether or not specified in the contract) or by reference to fluctuations in, or in an index of, the value of property of any description (whether or not so specified).

This item is also to comprise investments which are held on behalf of the members of a tontine and are intended for distribution among them.

(12) Reinsurance amounts

(Assets item Da: liabilities items C1.(b), 2.(b), 3.(b), 4.(b) and 6.(b) and D.(b).)

The reinsurance amounts may be shown either under assets item Da or under liabilities items C1.(b), 2.(b), 3.(b), 4.(b) and 6.(b) and D.(b).

The reinsurance amounts are to comprise the actual or estimated amounts which, under contractual reinsurance arrangements, are deducted from the gross amounts of technical provisions.

As regards the provision for unearned premiums, the reinsurance amounts must be calculated according to the methods referred to in paragraph 50 below or in accordance with the terms of the reinsurance policy.

(13) Debtors

(Assets item E.)

Amounts owed by group undertakings and undertakings in which the company has a participating interest must be shown separately as sub-items of assets items E.I, II and III.

(14) Own shares

(Assets item F.IV.)

The nominal value of the shares must be shown separately under this item.

(15) Other

(Assets item F.V.)

This item is to comprise those assets which are not covered by assets items F.I to IV. Where such assets are material they must be disclosed in the notes to the accounts.

(16) Accrued interest and rent

(Assets item G.I.)

This item is to comprise those items that represent interest and rent that have been earned up to the balance-sheet date but have not yet become receivable.

(17) Deferred acquisition costs

(Assets item G.II.)

This item is to comprise the costs of acquiring insurance policies which are incurred during a financial year but relate to a subsequent financial year ("deferred acquisition costs"), except in so far as—

    (a)   allowance has been made in the computation of the long-term business provision made under paragraph 52 below and shown under liabilities item C2 or D in the balance sheet, for—

        (i)   the explicit recognition of such costs, or

        (ii)   the implicit recognition of such costs by virtue of the anticipation of future income from which such costs may prudently be expected to be recovered, or

    (b)   allowance has been made for such costs in respect of general business policies by a deduction from the provision for unearned premiums made under paragraph 50 below and shown under liabilities item CI in the balance sheet.

Deferred acquisition costs arising in general business must be distinguished from those arising in long-term business.

In the case of general business, the amount of any deferred acquisition costs must be established on a basis compatible with that used for unearned premiums.

There must be disclosed in the notes to the accounts—

    (c)   how the deferral of acquisition costs has been treated (unless otherwise expressly stated in the accounts), and

    (d)   where such costs are included as a deduction from the provisions at liabilities item CI, the amount of such deduction, or

    (e)   where the actuarial method used in the calculation of the provisions at liabilities item C2 or D has made allowance for the explicit recognition of such costs, the amount of the costs so recognised.

(18) Subordinated liabilities

(Liabilities item B.)

This item is to comprise all liabilities in respect of which there is a contractual obligation that, in the event of winding up or of bankruptcy, they are to be repaid only after the claims of all other creditors have been met (whether or not they are represented by certificates).

(19) Fund for future appropriations

(Liabilities item Ba.)

This item is to comprise all funds the allocation of which either to policyholders or to shareholders has not been determined by the end of the financial year.

Transfers to and from this item must be shown in item II.12a in the profit and loss account.

(20) Provision for unearned premiums

(Liabilities item C1.)

In the case of long-term business the provision for unearned premiums may be included in liabilities item C2 rather than in this item.

The provision for unearned premiums is to comprise the amount representing that part of gross premiums written which is estimated to be earned in the following financial year or to subsequent financial years.

(21) Long-term business provision

(Liabilities item C2.)

This item is to comprise the actuarially estimated value of the company's liabilities (excluding technical provisions included in liabilities item D), including bonuses already declared and after deducting the actuarial value of future premiums.

This item is also to comprise claims incurred but not reported, plus the estimated costs of settling such claims.

(22) Claims outstanding

(Liabilities item C3.)

This item is to comprise the total estimated ultimate cost to the company of settling all claims arising from events which have occurred up to the end of the financial year (including, in the case of general business, claims incurred but not reported) less amounts already paid in respect of such claims.

(23) Provision for bonuses and rebates

(Liabilities item C4.)

This item is to comprise amounts intended for policyholders or contract beneficiaries by way of bonuses and rebates as defined in Note *(5)* on the profit and loss account format to the extent that such amounts have not been credited to policyholders or contract beneficiaries or included in liabilities item Ba or in liabilities item C2.

(24) Equalisation provision

(Liabilities item C5.)

This item is to comprise the amount of any equalisation reserve maintained in respect of general business by the company, in accordance with the rules in section 1.4 of the Prudential Sourcebook for Insurers made by the Financial Services Authority under Part 10 of the Financial Services and Markets Act 2000.

This item is also to comprise any amounts which, in accordance with Council Directive 87/343/EEC of 22nd June 1987, are required to be set aside by a company to equalise fluctuations in loss ratios in future years or to provide for special risks.

A company which otherwise constitutes reserves to equalise fluctuations in loss ratios in future years or to provide for special risks must disclose that fact in the notes to the accounts.

(25) Other technical provisions

(Liabilities item C6.)

This item is to comprise, inter alia, the provision for unexpired risks as defined in paragraph 91 below. Where the amount of the provision for unexpired risks is significant, it must be disclosed separately either in the balance sheet or in the notes to the accounts.

(26) Technical provisions for linked liabilities

(Liabilities item D.)

This item is to comprise technical provisions constituted to cover liabilities relating to investment in the context of long-term policies under which the benefits payable to policyholders are wholly or partly to be determined by reference to the value of, or the income from, property of any description (whether or not specified in the contract) or by reference to fluctuations in, or in an index of, the value of property of any description (whether or not so specified).

Any additional technical provisions constituted to cover death risks, operating expenses or other risks (such as benefits payable at the maturity date or guaranteed surrender values) must be included under liabilities item C2.

This item must also comprise technical provisions representing the obligations of a tontine's organiser in relation to its members.

(27) Deposits received from reinsurers

(Liabilities item F.)

Where the company cedes reinsurance, this item is to comprise amounts deposited by or withheld from other insurance undertakings under reinsurance contracts. These amounts may not be merged with other amounts owed to or by those other undertakings.

Where the company cedes reinsurance and has received as a deposit securities which have been transferred to its ownership, this item is to comprise the amount owed by the company by virtue of the deposit.

(28) Creditors

(Liabilities item G.)

Amounts owed to group undertakings and undertakings in which the company has a participating interest must be shown separately as sub-items.

(29) Debenture loans

(Liabilities item G.III.)

> *The amount of any convertible loans must be shown separately.*

11   Additional items

(1)   Every balance sheet of a company which carries on long-term business must show separately as an additional item the aggregate of any amounts included in liabilities item A (capital and reserves) which are required not to be treated as realised profits under section 843 of the 2006 Act.

(2)   A company which carries on long-term business must show separately, in the balance sheet or in the notes to the accounts, the total amount of assets representing the long-term fund valued in accordance with the provisions of this Schedule.

12   Managed funds

(1)   For the purposes of this paragraph "managed funds" are funds of a group pension fund—
   (a)   the management of which constitutes long-term insurance business, and
   (b)   which the company administers in its own name but on behalf of others, and
   (c)   to which it has legal title.

(2)   The company must, in any case where assets and liabilities arising in respect of managed funds fall to be treated as assets and liabilities of the company, adopt the following accounting treatment: assets and liabilities representing managed funds are to be included in the company's balance sheet, with the notes to the accounts disclosing the total amount included with respect to such assets and liabilities in the balance sheet and showing the amount included under each relevant balance sheet item in respect of such assets or (as the case may be) liabilities.

13   Deferred acquisition costs

The costs of acquiring insurance policies which are incurred during a financial year but which relate to a subsequent financial year must be deferred in a manner specified in Note *(17)* on the balance sheet format.

Profit and loss account format

I   Technical account—General business
   1   Earned premiums, net of reinsurance
      (a)   gross premiums written [1]
      (b)   outward reinsurance premiums [2]
      (c)   change in the gross provision for unearned premiums
      (d)   change in the provision for unearned premiums, reinsurers' share
   2   Allocated investment return transferred from the non-technical account (item III.6) [10]
   2a   Investment income [8] [10]
      (a)   income from participating interests, with a separate indication of that derived from group undertakings
      (b)   income from other investments, with a separate indication of that derived from group undertakings
         (aa)   income from land and buildings
         (bb)   income from other investments
      (c)   value re-adjustments on investments
      (d)   gains on the realisation of investments
   3   Other technical income, net of reinsurance
   4   Claims incurred, net of reinsurance [4]
      (a)   claims paid
         (aa)   gross amount
         (bb)   reinsurers' share
      (b)   change in the provision for claims
         (aa)   gross amount
         (bb)   reinsurers' share
   5   Changes in other technical provisions, net of reinsurance, not shown under other headings
   6   Bonuses and rebates, net of reinsurance [5]
   7   Net operating expenses
      (a)   acquisition costs [6]
      (b)   change in deferred acquisition costs
      (c)   administrative expenses [7]
      (d)   reinsurance commissions and profit participation
   8   Other technical charges, net of reinsurance
   8a   Investment expenses and charges [8]
      (a)   investment management expenses, including interest

      (b)   value adjustments on investments
      (c)   losses on the realisation of investments
  9   Change in the equalisation provision
  10   Sub-total (balance on the technical account for general business) (item III.1)

II   Technical account—Long-term business
  1   Earned premiums, net of reinsurance
      (a)   gross premiums written [1]
      (b)   outward reinsurance premiums [2]
      (c)   change in the provision for unearned premiums, net of reinsurance [3]
  2   Investment income [8] [10]
      (a)   income from participating interests, with a separate indication of that derived from group undertakings
      (b)   income from other investments, with a separate indication of that derived from group undertakings
          (aa)   income from land and buildings
          (bb)   income from other investments
      (c)   value re-adjustments on investments
      (d)   gains on the realisation of investments
  3   Unrealised gains on investments [9]
  4   Other technical income, net of reinsurance
  5   Claims incurred, net of reinsurance [4]
      (a)   claims paid
          (aa)   gross amount
          (bb)   reinsurers' share
      (b)   change in the provision for claims
          (aa)   gross amount
          (bb)   reinsurers' share
  6   Change in other technical provisions, net of reinsurance, not shown under other headings
      (a)   Long-term business provision, net of reinsurance [3]
          (aa)   gross amount
          (bb)   reinsurers' share
      (b)   other technical provisions, net of reinsurance
  7   Bonuses and rebates, net of reinsurance [5]
  8   Net operating expenses
      (a)   acquisition costs [6]
      (b)   change in deferred acquisition costs
      (c)   administrative expenses [7]
      (d)   reinsurance commissions and profit participation
  9   Investment expenses and charges [8]
      (a)   investment management expenses, including interest
      (b)   value adjustments on investments
      (c)   losses on the realisation of investments
  10   Unrealised losses on investments [9]
  11   Other technical charges, net of reinsurance
  11a   Tax attributable to the long-term business
  12   Allocated investment return transferred to the non-technical account (item III.4)
  12a   Transfers to or from the fund for future appropriations
  13   Sub-total (balance on the technical account—long-term business) (item III.2)

III Non-technical account
  1   Balance on the general business technical account (item I.10)
  2   Balance on the long-term business technical account (item II.13)
  2a   Tax credit attributable to balance on the long-term business technical account
  3   Investment income [8]
      (a)   income from participating interests, with a separate indication of that derived from group undertakings
      (b)   income from other investments, with a separate indication of that derived from group undertakings
          (aa)   income from land and buildings
          (bb)   income from other investments
      (c)   value re-adjustments on investments
      (d)   gains on the realisation of investments
  3a   Unrealised gains on investments [9]
  4   Allocated investment return transferred from the long-term business technical account (item II.12) [10]
  5   Investment expenses and charges [8]
      (a)   investment management expenses, including interest

    (b)   value adjustments on investments

    (c)   losses on the realisation of investments

5a   Unrealised losses on investments [9]

6   Allocated investment return transferred to the general business technical account (item I.2) [10]

7   Other income

8   Other charges, including value adjustments

8a   Profit or loss on ordinary activities before tax

9   Tax on profit or loss on ordinary activities

10   Profit or loss on ordinary activities after tax

11   Extraordinary income

12   Extraordinary charges

13   Extraordinary profit or loss

14   Tax on extraordinary profit or loss

15   Other taxes not shown under the preceding items

16   Profit or loss for the financial year

Notes on the profit and loss account format

(1) Gross premiums written

(General business technical account: item I.1.(a).

Long-term business technical account: item II.1.(a).)

This item is to comprise all amounts due during the financial year in respect of insurance contracts entered into regardless of the fact that such amounts may relate in whole or in part to a later financial year, and must include inter alia—

    (i)   premiums yet to be determined, where the premium calculation can be done only at the end of the year;

    (ii)   single premiums, including annuity premiums, and, in long-term business, single premiums resulting from bonus and rebate provisions in so far as they must be considered as premiums under the terms of the contract;

    (iii)   additional premiums in the case of half-yearly, quarterly or monthly payments and additional payments from policyholders for expenses borne by the company;

    (iv)   in the case of co-insurance, the company's portion of total premiums;

    (v)   reinsurance premiums due from ceding and retroceding insurance undertakings, including portfolio entries,

after deduction of cancellations and portfolio withdrawals credited to ceding and retroceding insurance undertakings.

The above amounts must not include the amounts of taxes or duties levied with premiums.

(2) Outward reinsurance premiums

(General business technical account: item I.1.(b).

Long-term business technical account: item II.1.(b).)

This item is to comprise all premiums paid or payable in respect of outward reinsurance contracts entered into by the company. Portfolio entries payable on the conclusion or amendment of outward reinsurance contracts must be added; portfolio withdrawals receivable must be deducted.

(3) Change in the provision for unearned premiums, net of reinsurance

(Long-term business technical account: items II.1.(c) and II.6.(a).)

In the case of long-term business, the change in unearned premiums may be included either in item II.1.(c) or in item II.6.(a) of the long-term business technical account.

(4) Claims incurred, net of reinsurance

(General business technical account: item I.4.

Long-term business technical account: item II.5.)

This item is to comprise all payments made in respect of the financial year with the addition of the provision for claims (but after deducting the provision for claims for the preceding financial year).

These amounts must include annuities, surrenders, entries and withdrawals of loss provisions to and from ceding insurance undertakings and reinsurers and external and internal claims management costs and charges for claims incurred but not reported such as are referred to in paragraphs 53(2) and 55 below.

Sums recoverable on the basis of subrogation and salvage (within the meaning of paragraph 53 below) must be deducted.

Where the difference between—

    (a)   the loss provision made at the beginning of the year for outstanding claims incurred in previous years, and

    (b)   the payments made during the year on account of claims incurred in previous years and the loss provision shown at the end of the year for such outstanding claims,

is material, it must be shown in the notes to the accounts, broken down by category and amount.

(5) Bonuses and rebates, net of reinsurance

(General business technical account: item I.6.

Long-term business technical account: item II.7.)

Bonuses are to comprise all amounts chargeable for the financial year which are paid or payable to policyholders and other insured parties or provided for their benefit, including amounts used to increase technical provisions or applied to the reduction of future premiums, to the extent that such amounts represent an allocation of surplus or profit arising on business as a whole or a section of business, after deduction of amounts provided in previous years which are no longer required.

Rebates are to comprise such amounts to the extent that they represent a partial refund of premiums resulting from the experience of individual contracts.

Where material, the amount charged for bonuses and that charged for rebates must be disclosed separately in the notes to the accounts.

(6) Acquisition costs

(General business technical account: item I.7.(a).

Long-term business technical account: item II.8.(a).)

This item is to comprise the costs arising from the conclusion of insurance contracts. They must cover both direct costs, such as acquisition commissions or the cost of drawing up the insurance document or including the insurance contract in the portfolio, and indirect costs, such as advertising costs or the administrative expenses connected with the processing of proposals and the issuing of policies.

In the case of long-term business, policy renewal commissions must be included under item II.8.(c) in the long-term business technical account.

(7) Administrative expenses

(General business technical account: item I.7.(c).

Long-term business technical account: item II.8.(c).)

This item must include the costs arising from premium collection, portfolio administration, handling of bonuses and rebates, and inward and outward reinsurance. They must in particular include staff costs and depreciation provisions in respect of office furniture and equipment in so far as these need not be shown under acquisition costs, claims incurred or investment charges.

Item II.8.(c) must also include policy renewal commissions.

(8) Investment income, expenses and charges

(General business technical account: items I.2a and 8a.

Long-term business technical account: items II.2 and 9.

Non-technical account: items III.3 and 5.)

Investment income, expenses and charges must, to the extent that they arise in the long-term fund, be disclosed in the long-term business technical account. Other investment income, expenses and charges must either be disclosed in the non-technical account or attributed between the appropriate technical and non-technical accounts. Where the company makes such an attribution it must disclose the basis for it in the notes to the accounts.

(9) Unrealised gains and losses on investments

(Long-term business technical account: items II.3 and 10.

Non-technical account: items III.3a and 5a.)

In the case of investments attributed to the long-term fund, the difference between the valuation of the investments and their purchase price or, if they have previously been valued, their valuation as at the last balance sheet date, may be disclosed (in whole or in part) in item II.3 or II.10 (as the case may be) of the long-term business technical account, and in the case of investments shown as assets under assets item D (assets held to cover linked liabilities) must be so disclosed.

In the case of other investments, the difference between the valuation of the investments and their purchase price or, if they have previously been valued, their valuation as at the last balance sheet date, may be disclosed (in whole or in part) in item III.3a or III.5a (as the case may require) of the non-technical account.

(10) Allocated investment return

(General business technical account: item I.2.

Long-term business technical account: item II.2.

Non-technical account: items III.4 and 6.)

The allocated return may be transferred from one part of the profit and loss account to another.

Where part of the investment return is transferred to the general business technical account, the transfer from the non-technical account must be deducted from item III.6 and added to item I.2.

Where part of the investment return disclosed in the long-term business technical account is transferred to the non-technical account, the transfer to the non-technical account shall be deducted from item II.12 and added to item III.4.

The reasons for such transfers (which may consist of a reference to any relevant statutory requirement) and the bases on which they are made must be disclosed in the notes to the accounts.

NOTES

Commencement: 6 April 2008.

PART 2
ACCOUNTING PRINCIPLES AND RULES

SECTION A
ACCOUNTING PRINCIPLES

Preliminary

[4.193]

14. The amounts to be included in respect of all items shown in a company's accounts must be determined in accordance with the principles set out in this Section.

15. But if it appears to the company's directors that there are special reasons for departing from any of those principles in preparing the company's accounts in respect of any financial year they may do so, in which case particulars of the departure, the reasons for it and its effect must be given in a note to the accounts.

Accounting principles

16. The company is presumed to be carrying on business as a going concern.

17. Accounting policies must be applied consistently within the same accounts and from one financial year to the next.

18. The amount of any item must be determined on a prudent basis, and in particular—

(a) subject to note (9) on the profit and loss account format, only profits realised at the balance sheet date are to be included in the profit and loss account, and

(b) all liabilities which have arisen in respect of the financial year to which the accounts relate or a previous financial year must be taken into account, including those which only become apparent between the balance sheet date and the date on which it is signed on behalf of the board of directors in accordance with section 414 of the 2006 Act (approval and signing of accounts).

19. All income and charges relating to the financial year to which the accounts relate are to be taken into account, without regard to the date of receipt or payment.

20. In determining the aggregate amount of any item, the amount of each individual asset or liability that falls to be taken into account must be determined separately.

Valuation

21. (1) The amounts to be included in respect of assets of any description mentioned in paragraph 22 (valuation of assets: general) must be determined either—

(a) in accordance with that paragraph and paragraph 24 (but subject to paragraphs 27 to 29), or

(b) so far as applicable to an asset of that description, in accordance with Section C (valuation at fair value).

(2) The amounts to be included in respect of assets of any description mentioned in paragraph 24 (alternative valuation of fixed-income securities) may be determined—

(a) in accordance with that paragraph (but subject to paragraphs 27 to 29), or

(b) so far as applicable to an asset of that description, in accordance with Section C

(3) The amounts to be included in respect of assets which—

(a) are not assets of a description mentioned in paragraph 22 or 23, but

(b) are assets of a description to which Section C is applicable,

may be determined in accordance with that Section.

(4) Subject to sub-paragraphs (1) to (3), the amounts to be included in respect of all items shown in a company's accounts are determined in accordance with Section C

SECTION B
CURRENT VALUE ACCOUNTING RULES

Valuation of assets: general

22. (1) Subject to paragraph 24, investments falling to be included under assets item C (investments) must be included at their current value calculated in accordance with paragraphs 25 and 26.

(2) Investments falling to be included under assets item D (assets held to cover linked liabilities) must be shown at their current value calculated in accordance with paragraphs 25 and 26.

23. (1)   Intangible assets other than goodwill may be shown at their current cost.

(2)   Assets falling to be included under assets items F.I (tangible assets) and F.IV (own shares) in the balance sheet format may be shown at their current value calculated in accordance with paragraphs 25 and 26 or at their current cost.

(3)   Assets falling to be included under assets item F.II (stocks) may be shown at current cost.

Alternative valuation of fixed-income securities

24. (1)   This paragraph applies to debt securities and other fixed-income securities shown as assets under assets items CII (investments in group undertakings and participating interests) and CIII (other financial investments).

(2)   Securities to which this paragraph applies may either be valued in accordance with paragraph 22 or their amortised value may be shown in the balance sheet, in which case the provisions of this paragraph apply.

(3)   Subject to sub-paragraph (4), where the purchase price of securities to which this paragraph applies exceeds the amount repayable at maturity, the amount of the difference—

  (a)   must be charged to the profit and loss account, and

  (b)   must be shown separately in the balance sheet or in the notes to the accounts.

(4)   The amount of the difference referred to in sub-paragraph (3) may be written off in instalments so that it is completely written off when the securities are repaid, in which case there must be shown separately in the balance sheet or in the notes to the accounts the difference between the purchase price (less the aggregate amount written off) and the amount repayable at maturity.

(5)   Where the purchase price of securities to which this paragraph applies is less than the amount repayable at maturity, the amount of the difference must be released to income in instalments over the period remaining until repayment, in which case there must be shown separately in the balance sheet or in the notes to the accounts the difference between the purchase price (plus the aggregate amount released to income) and the amount repayable at maturity.

(6)   Both the purchase price and the current value of securities valued in accordance with this paragraph must be disclosed in the notes to the accounts.

(7)   Where securities to which this paragraph applies which are not valued in accordance with paragraph 22 are sold before maturity, and the proceeds are used to purchase other securities to which this paragraph applies, the difference between the proceeds of sale and their book value may be spread uniformly over the period remaining until the maturity of the original investment.

Meaning of "current value"

25. (1)   Subject to sub-paragraph (5), in the case of investments other than land and buildings, current value means market value determined in accordance with this paragraph.

(2)   In the case of listed investments, market value means the value on the balance sheet date or, when the balance sheet date is not a stock exchange trading day, on the last stock exchange trading day before that date.

(3)   Where a market exists for unlisted investments, market value means the average price at which such investments were traded on the balance sheet date or, when the balance sheet date is not a trading day, on the last trading day before that date.

(4)   Where, on the date on which the accounts are drawn up, listed or unlisted investments have been sold or are to be sold within the short term, the market value must be reduced by the actual or estimated realisation costs.

(5)   Except where the equity method of accounting is applied, all investments other than those referred to in sub-paragraphs (2) and (3) must be valued on a basis which has prudent regard to the likely realisable value.

26. (1)   In the case of land and buildings, current value means the market value on the date of valuation, where relevant reduced as provided in sub-paragraphs (4) and (5).

(2)   Market value means the price at which land and buildings could be sold under private contract between a willing seller and an arm's length buyer on the date of valuation, it being assumed that the property is publicly exposed to the market, that market conditions permit orderly disposal and that a normal period, having regard to the nature of the property, is available for the negotiation of the sale.

(3)   The market value must be determined through the separate valuation of each land and buildings item, carried out at least every five years in accordance with generally recognised methods of valuation.

(4)   Where the value of any land and buildings item has diminished since the preceding valuation under sub-paragraph (3), an appropriate value adjustment must be made.

(5)   The lower value arrived at under sub-paragraph (4) must not be increased in subsequent balance sheets unless such increase results from a new determination of market value arrived at in accordance with sub-paragraphs (2) and (3).

(6)   Where, on the date on which the accounts are drawn up, land and buildings have been sold or are to be sold within the short term, the value arrived at in accordance with sub-paragraphs (2) and (4) must be reduced by the actual or estimated realisation costs.

(7)   Where it is impossible to determine the market value of a land and buildings item, the value arrived at on the basis of the principle of purchase price or production cost is deemed to be its current value.

Application of the depreciation rules

27. (1)   Where—

- (a)   the value of any asset of a company is determined in accordance with paragraph 22 or 23, and
- (b)   in the case of a determination under paragraph 22, the asset falls to be included under assets item CI,

that value must be, or (as the case may require) must be the starting point for determining, the amount to be included in respect of that asset in the company's accounts, instead of its cost or any value previously so determined for that asset.

Paragraphs 36 to 41 and 43 apply accordingly in relation to any such asset with the substitution for any reference to its cost of a reference to the value most recently determined for that asset in accordance with paragraph 22 or 23 (as the case may be).

(2)   The amount of any provision for depreciation required in the case of any asset by paragraph 37 or 38 as it applies by virtue of sub-paragraph (1) is referred to below in this paragraph as the adjusted amount, and the amount of any provision which would be required by that paragraph in the case of that asset according to the historical cost accounting rules is referred to as the historical cost amount.

(3)   Where sub-paragraph (1) applies in the case of any asset the amount of any provision for depreciation in respect of that asset included in any item shown in the profit and loss account in respect of amounts written off assets of the description in question may be the historical cost amount instead of the adjusted amount, provided that the amount of any difference between the two is shown separately in the profit and loss account or in a note to the accounts.

Additional information to be provided

28. (1)   This paragraph applies where the amounts to be included in respect of assets covered by any items shown in a company's accounts have been determined in accordance with paragraph 22 or 23.

(2)   The items affected and the basis of valuation adopted in determining the amounts of the assets in question in the case of each such item must be disclosed in a note to the accounts.

(3)   The purchase price of investments valued in accordance with paragraph 22 must be disclosed in the notes to the accounts.

(4)   In the case of each balance sheet item valued in accordance with paragraph 23 either—

- (a)   the comparable amounts determined according to the historical cost accounting rules (without any provision for depreciation or diminution in value), or
- (b)   the differences between those amounts and the corresponding amounts actually shown in the balance sheet in respect of that item,

must be shown separately in the balance sheet or in a note to the accounts.

(5)   In sub-paragraph (4), references in relation to any item to the comparable amounts determined as there mentioned are references to—

- (a)   the aggregate amount which would be required to be shown in respect of that item if the amounts to be included in respect of all the assets covered by that item were determined according to the historical cost accounting rules, and
- (b)   the aggregate amount of the cumulative provisions for depreciation or diminution in value which would be permitted or required in determining those amounts according to those rules.

Revaluation reserve

29. (1)   Subject to sub-paragraph (7), with respect to any determination of the value of an asset of a company in accordance with paragraph 22 or 23, the amount of any profit or loss arising from that determination (after allowing, where appropriate, for any provisions for depreciation or diminution in value made otherwise than by reference to the value so determined and any adjustments of any such provisions made in the light of that determination) must be credited or (as the case may be) debited to a separate reserve ("the revaluation reserve").

(2)   The amount of the revaluation reserve must be shown in the company's balance sheet under liabilities item A.III, but need not be shown under the name "revaluation reserve".

(3)   An amount may be transferred—

- (a)   from the revaluation reserve—
  - (i)   to the profit and loss account, if the amount was previously charged to that account or represents realised profit, or

(ii) on capitalisation,

(b) to or from the revaluation reserve in respect of the taxation relating to any profit or loss credited or debited to the reserve.

The revaluation reserve must be reduced to the extent that the amounts transferred to it are no longer necessary for the purposes of the valuation method used.

(4) In sub-paragraph (3)(a)(ii) "capitalisation", in relation to an amount standing to the credit of the revaluation reserve, means applying it in wholly or partly paying up unissued shares in the company to be allotted to members of the company as fully or partly paid shares.

(5) The revaluation reserve must not be reduced except as mentioned in this paragraph.

(6) The treatment for taxation purposes of amounts credited or debited to the revaluation reserve must be disclosed in a note to the accounts.

(7) This paragraph does not apply to the difference between the valuation of investments and their purchase price or previous valuation shown in the long-term business technical account or the non-technical account in accordance with note (9) on the profit and loss account format.

SECTION C
VALUATION AT FAIR VALUE

Inclusion of financial instruments at fair value

30. (1) Subject to sub-paragraphs (2) to (5), financial instruments (including derivatives) may be included at fair value.

(2) Sub-paragraph (1) does not apply to financial instruments that constitute liabilities unless—
   (a) they are held as part of a trading portfolio,
   (b) they are derivatives, or
   (c) they are financial instruments falling within paragraph (4).

(3) Except where they fall within paragraph (4), or fall to be included under assets item D (assets held to cover linked liabilities), sub-paragraph (1) does not apply to—
   (a) financial instruments (other than derivatives) held to maturity,
   (b) loans and receivables originated by the company and not held for trading purposes,
   (c) interests in subsidiary undertakings, associated undertakings and joint ventures,
   (d) equity instruments issued by the company,
   (e) contracts for contingent consideration in a business combination, or
   (f) other financial instruments with such special characteristics that the instruments, according to generally accepted accounting principles or practice, should be accounted for differently from other financial instruments.

(4) Financial instruments that, under international accounting standards adopted by the European Commission on or before 5th September 2006 in accordance with the IAS Regulation, may be included in accounts at fair value, may be so included, provided that the disclosures required by such accounting standards are made.

(5) If the fair value of a financial instrument cannot be determined reliably in accordance with paragraph 31, sub-paragraph (1) does not apply to that financial instrument.

(6) In this paragraph—
   "associated undertaking" has the meaning given by paragraph 19 of Schedule 6 to these Regulations; and
   "joint venture" has the meaning given by paragraph 18 of that Schedule.

Determination of fair value

31. (1) The fair value of a financial instrument is its value determined in accordance with this paragraph.

(2) If a reliable market can readily be identified for the financial instrument, its fair value is determined by reference to its market value.

(3) If a reliable market cannot readily be identified for the financial instrument but can be identified for its components or for a similar instrument, its fair value is determined by reference to the market value of its components or of the similar instrument.

(4) If neither sub-paragraph (2) nor (3) applies, the fair value of the financial instrument is a value resulting from generally accepted valuation models and techniques.

(5) Any valuation models and techniques used for the purposes of sub-paragraph (4) must ensure a reasonable approximation of the market value.

Hedged items

32. A company may include any assets and liabilities, or identified portions of such assets or liabilities, that qualify as hedged items under a fair value hedge accounting system at the amount required under that system.

Other assets that may be included at fair value

33. (1) This paragraph applies to—
  (a) investment property, and
  (b) living animals and plants,
that, under international accounting standards, may be included in accounts at fair value.

(2) Such investment property and such living animals and plants may be included at fair value, provided that all such investment property or, as the case may be, all such living animals and plants are so included where their fair value can reliably be determined.

(3) In this paragraph, "fair value" means fair value determined in accordance with relevant international accounting standards.

Accounting for changes in value

34. (1) This paragraph applies where a financial instrument is valued in accordance with paragraph 30 or 32 or an asset is valued in accordance with paragraph 33.

(2) Notwithstanding paragraph 18 in this Part of this Schedule, and subject to sub-paragraphs (3) and (4), a change in the value of the financial instrument or of the investment property or living animal or plant must be included in the profit and loss account.

(3) Where—
  (a) the financial instrument accounted for is a hedging instrument under a hedge accounting system that allows some or all of the change in value not to be shown in the profit and loss account, or
  (b) the change in value relates to an exchange difference arising on a monetary item that forms part of a company's net investment in a foreign entity,
the amount of the change in value must be credited to or (as the case may be) debited from a separate reserve ("the fair value reserve").

(4) Where the instrument accounted for—
  (a) is an available for sale financial asset, and
  (b) is not a derivative,
the change in value may be credited to or (as the case may be) debited from the fair value reserve.

The fair value reserve

35. (1) The fair value reserve must be adjusted to the extent that the amounts shown in it are no longer necessary for the purposes of paragraph 34(3) or (4).

(2) The treatment for taxation purposes of amounts credited or debited to the fair value reserve must be disclosed in a note to the accounts.

SECTION D
HISTORICAL COST ACCOUNTING RULES

Valuation of assets

General rules

36. (1) The rules in this Section are "the historical cost accounting rules".

(2) Subject to any provision for depreciation or diminution in value made in accordance with paragraph 37 or 38, the amount to be included in respect of any asset in the balance sheet format is its cost.

37. In the case of any asset included under assets item B (intangible assets), CI (land and buildings), F.I (tangible assets) or F.II (stocks) which has a limited useful economic life, the amount of—
  (a) its cost, or
  (b) where it is estimated that any such asset will have a residual value at the end of the period of its useful economic life, its cost less that estimated residual value,
must be reduced by provisions for depreciation calculated to write off that amount systematically over the period of the asset's useful economic life.

38. (1) This paragraph applies to any asset included under assets item B (intangible assets), C (investments), F.I (tangible assets) or F.IV (own shares).

(2) Where an asset to which this paragraph applies has diminished in value, provisions for diminution in value may be made in respect of it and the amount to be included in respect of it may be reduced accordingly.

(3) Provisions for diminution in value must be made in respect of any asset to which this paragraph applies if the reduction in its value is expected to be permanent (whether its useful economic life is limited or not), and the amount to be included in respect of it must be reduced accordingly.

(4)   Any provisions made under sub-paragraph (2) or (3) which are not shown in the profit and loss account must be disclosed (either separately or in aggregate) in a note to the accounts.

39.   (1)   Where the reasons for which any provision was made in accordance with paragraph 38 have ceased to apply to any extent, that provision must be written back to the extent that it is no longer necessary.

(2)   Any amounts written back in accordance with sub-paragraph (1) which are not shown in the profit and loss account must be disclosed (either separately or in aggregate) in a note to the accounts.

40.   (1)   This paragraph applies to assets included under assets items E.I, II and III (debtors) and F.III (cash at bank and in hand) in the balance sheet.

(2)   If the net realisable value of an asset to which this paragraph applies is lower than its cost the amount to be included in respect of that asset is the net realisable value.

(3)   Where the reasons for which any provision for diminution in value was made in accordance with sub-paragraph (2) have ceased to apply to any extent, that provision must be written back to the extent that it is no longer necessary.

Development costs

41.   (1)   Notwithstanding that amounts representing "development costs" may be included under assets item B (intangible assets) in the balance sheet format, an amount may only be included in a company's balance sheet in respect of development costs in special circumstances.

(2)   If any amount is included in a company's balance sheet in respect of development costs the following information must be given in a note to the accounts—
- (a)   the period over which the amount of those costs originally capitalised is being or is to be written off, and
- (b)   the reasons for capitalising the development costs in question.

Goodwill

42.   (1)   The application of paragraphs 36 to 39 in relation to goodwill (in any case where goodwill is treated as an asset) is subject to the following.

(2)   Subject to sub-paragraph (3), the amount of the consideration for any goodwill acquired by a company must be reduced by provisions for depreciation calculated to write off that amount systematically over a period chosen by the directors of the company.

(3)   The period chosen must not exceed the useful economic life of the goodwill in question.

(4)   In any case where any goodwill acquired by a company is included as an asset in the company's balance sheet, there must be disclosed in a note to the accounts—
- (a)   the period chosen for writing off the consideration for that goodwill, and
- (b)   the reasons for choosing that period.

Miscellaneous and supplementary provisions

Excess of money owed over value received as an asset item

43.   (1)   Where the amount repayable on any debt owed by a company is greater than the value of the consideration received in the transaction giving rise to the debt, the amount of the difference may be treated as an asset.

(2)   Where any such amount is so treated—
- (a)   it must be written off by reasonable amounts each year and must be completely written off before repayment of the debt, and
- (b)   if the current amount is not shown as a separate item in the company's balance sheet, it must be disclosed in a note to the accounts.

Assets included at a fixed amount

44.   (1)   Subject to sub-paragraph (2), assets which fall to be included under assets item F.I (tangible assets) in the balance sheet format may be included at a fixed quantity and value.

(2)   Sub-paragraph (1) applies to assets of a kind which are constantly being replaced where—
- (a)   their overall value is not material to assessing the company's state of affairs, and
- (b)   their quantity, value and composition are not subject to material variation.

Determination of cost

45.   (1)   The cost of an asset that has been acquired by the company is to be determined by adding to the actual price paid any expenses incidental to its acquisition.

(2)   The cost of an asset constructed by the company is to be determined by adding to the purchase price of the raw materials and consumables used the amount of the costs incurred by the company which are directly attributable to the construction of that asset.

(3)   In addition, there may be included in the cost of an asset constructed by the company—

    (a)   a reasonable proportion of the costs incurred by the company which are only indirectly attributable to the construction of that asset, but only to the extent that they relate to the period of construction, and

    (b)   interest on capital borrowed to finance the construction of that asset, to the extent that it accrues in respect of the period of construction,

provided, however, in a case within paragraph (b), that the inclusion of the interest in determining the cost of that asset and the amount of the interest so included is disclosed in a note to the accounts.

46. (1) The cost of any assets which are fungible assets may be determined by the application of any of the methods mentioned in sub-paragraph (2) in relation to any such assets of the same class, provided that the method chosen is one which appears to the directors to be appropriate in the circumstances of the company.

(2) Those methods are—

    (a)   the method known as "first in, first out" (FIFO),

    (b)   the method known as "last in, first out" (LIFO),

    (c)   a weighted average price, and

    (d)   any other method similar to any of the methods mentioned above.

(3) Where in the case of any company—

    (a)   the cost of assets falling to be included under any item shown in the company's balance sheet has been determined by the application of any method permitted by this paragraph, and

    (b)   the amount shown in respect of that item differs materially from the relevant alternative amount given below in this paragraph,

the amount of that difference must be disclosed in a note to the accounts.

(4) Subject to sub-paragraph (5), for the purposes of sub-paragraph (3)(b), the relevant alternative amount, in relation to any item shown in a company's balance sheet, is the amount which would have been shown in respect of that item if assets of any class included under that item at an amount determined by any method permitted by this paragraph had instead been included at their replacement cost as at the balance sheet date.

(5) The relevant alternative amount may be determined by reference to the most recent actual purchase price before the balance sheet date of assets of any class included under the item in question instead of by reference to their replacement cost as at that date, but only if the former appears to the directors of the company to constitute the more appropriate standard of comparison in the case of assets of that class.

Substitution of original amount where price or cost unknown

47. (1) This paragraph applies where—

    (a)   there is no record of the purchase price of any asset acquired by a company or of any price, expenses or costs relevant for determining its cost in accordance with paragraph 45, or

    (b)   any such record cannot be obtained without unreasonable expense or delay.

(2) In such a case, the cost of the asset must be taken, for the purposes of paragraphs 36 to 42, to be the value ascribed to it in the earliest available record of its value made on or after its acquisition by the company.

SECTION E
RULES FOR DETERMINING PROVISIONS

Preliminary

48. Provisions which are to be shown in a company's accounts are to be determined in accordance with this Section.

Technical provisions

49. The amount of technical provisions must at all times be sufficient to cover any liabilities arising out of insurance contracts as far as can reasonably be foreseen.

Provision for unearned premiums

50. (1) The provision for unearned premiums must in principle be computed separately for each insurance contract, save that statistical methods (and in particular proportional and flat rate methods) may be used where they may be expected to give approximately the same results as individual calculations.

(2) Where the pattern of risk varies over the life of a contract, this must be taken into account in the calculation methods.

Provision for unexpired risks

51. The provision for unexpired risks (as defined in paragraph 91) must be computed on the basis of claims and administrative expenses likely to arise after the end of the financial year from contracts concluded before that date, in so far as their estimated value exceeds the provision for unearned premiums and any premiums receivable under those contracts.

Long-term business provision

52. (1)   The long-term business provision must in principle be computed separately for each long-term contract, save that statistical or mathematical methods may be used where they may be expected to give approximately the same results as individual calculations.

(2)   A summary of the principal assumptions in making the provision under sub-paragraph (1) must be given in the notes to the accounts.

(3)   The computation must be made annually by a Fellow of the Institute or Faculty of Actuaries on the basis of recognised actuarial methods, with due regard to the actuarial principles laid down in Directive 2002/83/EC of the European Parliament and of the Council of 5th November 2002 concerning life assurance.

Provisions for claims outstanding

General business

53. (1)   A provision must in principle be computed separately for each claim on the basis of the costs still expected to arise, save that statistical methods may be used if they result in an adequate provision having regard to the nature of the risks.

(2)   This provision must also allow for claims incurred but not reported by the balance sheet date, the amount of the allowance being determined having regard to past experience as to the number and magnitude of claims reported after previous balance sheet dates.

(3)   All claims settlement costs (whether direct or indirect) must be included in the calculation of the provision.

(4)   Recoverable amounts arising out of subrogation or salvage must be estimated on a prudent basis and either deducted from the provision for claims outstanding (in which case if the amounts are material they must be shown in the notes to the accounts) or shown as assets.

(5)   In sub-paragraph (4), "subrogation" means the acquisition of the rights of policy holders with respect to third parties, and "salvage" means the acquisition of the legal ownership of insured property.

(6)   Where benefits resulting from a claim must be paid in the form of annuity, the amounts to be set aside for that purpose must be calculated by recognised actuarial methods, and paragraph 54 does not apply to such calculations.

(7)   Implicit discounting or deductions, whether resulting from the placing of a current value on a provision for an outstanding claim which is expected to be settled later at a higher figure or otherwise effected, is prohibited.

54. (1)   Explicit discounting or deductions to take account of investment income is permitted, subject to the following conditions—
   (a)   the expected average interval between the date for the settlement of claims being discounted and the accounting date must be at least four years;
   (b)   the discounting or deductions must be effected on a recognised prudential basis;
   (c)   when calculating the total cost of settling claims, the company must take account of all factors that could cause increases in that cost;
   (d)   the company must have adequate data at its disposal to construct a reliable model of the rate of claims settlements;
   (e)   the rate of interest used for the calculation of present values must not exceed a rate prudently estimated to be earned by assets of the company which are appropriate in magnitude and nature to cover the provisions for claims being discounted during the period necessary for the payment of such claims, and must not exceed either—
      (i)   a rate justified by the performance of such assets over the preceding five years, or
      (ii)   a rate justified by the performance of such assets during the year preceding the balance sheet date.

(2)   When discounting or effecting deductions, the company must, in the notes to the accounts, disclose—
   (a)   the total amount of provisions before discounting or deductions,
   (b)   the categories of claims which are discounted or from which deductions have been made,
   (c)   for each category of claims, the methods used, in particular the rates used for the estimates referred to in sub-paragraph (1)(d) and (e), and the criteria adopted for estimating the period that will elapse before the claims are settled.

Long-term business

55. The amount of the provision for claims must be equal to the sums due to beneficiaries, plus the costs of settling claims.

Equalisation reserves

56. The amount of any equalisation reserve maintained in respect of general business by the company, in accordance with the rules in section 1.4 of the Prudential Sourcebook for Insurers made by the Financial Services Authority under Part 10 of the Financial Services and Markets Act 2000, must be determined in accordance with such rules.

Accounting on a non-annual basis

57. (1) Either of the methods described in paragraphs 58 and 59 may be applied where, because of the nature of the class or type of insurance in question, information about premiums receivable or claims payable (or both) for the underwriting years is insufficient when the accounts are drawn up for reliable estimates to be made.

(2) The use of either of the methods referred to in sub-paragraph (1) must be disclosed in the notes to the accounts together with the reasons for adopting it.

(3) Where one of the methods referred to in sub-paragraph (1) is adopted, it must be applied systematically in successive years unless circumstances justify a change.

(4) In the event of a change in the method applied, the effect on the assets, liabilities, financial position and profit or loss must be stated in the notes to the accounts.

(5) For the purposes of this paragraph and paragraph 58, "underwriting year" means the financial year in which the insurance contracts in the class or type of insurance in question commenced.

58. (1) The excess of the premiums written over the claims and expenses paid in respect of contracts commencing in the underwriting year shall form a technical provision included in the technical provision for claims outstanding shown in the balance sheet under liabilities item C3.

(2) The provision may also be computed on the basis of a given percentage of the premiums written where such a method is appropriate for the type of risk insured.

(3) If necessary, the amount of this technical provision must be increased to make it sufficient to meet present and future obligations.

(4) The technical provision constituted under this paragraph must be replaced by a provision for claims outstanding estimated in accordance with paragraph 53 as soon as sufficient information has been gathered and not later than the end of the third year following the underwriting year.

(5) The length of time that elapses before a provision for claims outstanding is constituted in accordance with sub-paragraph (4) must be disclosed in the notes to the accounts.

59. (1) The figures shown in the technical account or in certain items within it must relate to a year which wholly or partly precedes the financial year (but by no more than 12 months).

(2) The amounts of the technical provisions shown in the accounts must if necessary be increased to make them sufficient to meet present and future obligations.

(3) The length of time by which the earlier year to which the figures relate precedes the financial year and the magnitude of the transactions concerned must be disclosed in the notes to the accounts.

NOTES

Commencement: 6 April 2008.

PART 3
NOTES TO THE ACCOUNTS

Preliminary

[4.194]
60. Any information required in the case of any company by the following provisions of this Part of this Schedule must (if not given in the company's accounts) be given by way of a note to the accounts.

General

Disclosure of accounting policies

61. The accounting policies adopted by the company in determining the amounts to be included in respect of items shown in the balance sheet and in determining the profit or loss of the company must be stated (including such policies with respect to the depreciation and diminution in value of assets).

62. It must be stated whether the accounts have been prepared in accordance with applicable accounting standards and particulars of any material departure from those standards and the reasons for it must be given.

Sums denominated in foreign currencies

63. Where any sums originally denominated in foreign currencies have been brought into account under any items shown in the balance sheet or profit and loss account format, the basis on which those sums have been translated into sterling (or the currency in which the accounts are drawn up) must be stated.

Reserves and dividends

64. There must be stated—
- (a) any amount set aside or proposed to be set aside to, or withdrawn or proposed to be withdrawn from, reserves,
- (b) the aggregate amount of dividends paid in the financial year (other than those for which a liability existed at the immediately preceding balance sheet date),
- (c) the aggregate amount of dividends that the company is liable to pay at the balance sheet date, and
- (d) the aggregate amount of dividends that are proposed before the date of approval of the accounts, and not otherwise disclosed under sub-paragraph (b) or (c).

Information Supplementing the Balance Sheet

Share capital and debentures

65. (1) Where shares of more than one class have been allotted, the number and aggregate nominal value of shares of each class allotted must be given.

(2) In the case of any part of the allotted share capital that consists of redeemable shares, the following information must be given—
- (a) the earliest and latest dates on which the company has power to redeem those shares,
- (b) whether those shares must be redeemed in any event or are liable to be redeemed at the option of the company or of the shareholder, and
- (c) whether any (and, if so, what) premium is payable on redemption.

66. If the company has allotted any shares during the financial year, the following information must be given—
- (a) the classes of shares allotted, and
- (b) as respects each class of shares, the number allotted, their aggregate nominal value and the consideration received by the company for the allotment.

67. (1) With respect to any contingent right to the allotment of shares in the company the following particulars must be given—
- (a) the number, description and amount of the shares in relation to which the right is exercisable,
- (b) the period during which it is exercisable, and
- (c) the price to be paid for the shares allotted.

(2) In sub-paragraph (1) "contingent right to the allotment of shares" means any option to subscribe for shares and any other right to require the allotment of shares to any person whether arising on the conversion into shares of securities of any other description or otherwise.

68. (1) If the company has issued any debentures during the financial year to which the accounts relate, the following information must be given—
- (a) the classes of debentures issued, and
- (b) as respects each class of debentures, the amount issued and the consideration received by the company for the issue.

(2) Where any of the company's debentures are held by a nominee of or trustee for the company, the nominal amount of the debentures and the amount at which they are stated in the accounting records kept by the company in accordance with section 386 of the 2006 Act (duty to keep accounting records) must be stated.

Assets

69. (1) In respect of any assets of the company included in assets items B (intangible assets), CI (land and buildings) and CII (investments in group undertakings and participating interests) in the company's balance sheet the following information must be given by reference to each such item—
- (a) the appropriate amounts in respect of those assets included in the item as at the date of the beginning of the financial year and as at the balance sheet date respectively,
- (b) the effect on any amount included in assets item B in respect of those assets of—
  - (i) any determination during that year of the value to be ascribed to any of those assets in accordance with paragraph 23,
  - (ii) acquisitions during that year of any assets,
  - (iii) disposals during that year of any assets, and
  - (iv) any transfers of assets of the company to and from the item during that year.

(2)   The reference in sub-paragraph (1)(a) to the appropriate amounts in respect of any assets (included in an assets item) as at any date there mentioned is a reference to amounts representing the aggregate amounts determined, as at that date, in respect of assets falling to be included under the item on either of the following bases—

(a)   on the basis of cost (determined in accordance with paragraphs 45 and 46), or

(b)   on any basis permitted by paragraph 22 or 23,

(leaving out of account in either case any provisions for depreciation or diminution in value).

(3)   In addition, in respect of any assets of the company included in any assets item in the company's balance sheet, there must be stated (by reference to each such item)—

(a)   the cumulative amount of provisions for depreciation or diminution in value of those assets included under the item as at each date mentioned in sub-paragraph (1)(a),

(b)   the amount of any such provisions made in respect of the financial year,

(c)   the amount of any adjustments made in respect of any such provisions during that year in consequence of the disposal of any of those assets, and

(d)   the amount of any other adjustments made in respect of any such provisions during that year.

70. Where any assets of the company (other than listed investments) are included under any item shown in the company's balance sheet at an amount determined on any basis mentioned in paragraph 22 or 23, the following information must be given—

(a)   the years (so far as they are known to the directors) in which the assets were severally valued and the several values, and

(b)   in the case of assets that have been valued during the financial year, the names of the persons who valued them or particulars of their qualifications for doing so and (whichever is stated) the bases of valuation used by them.

71. In relation to any amount which is included under assets item CI (land and buildings) there must be stated—

(a)   how much of that amount is ascribable to land of freehold tenure and how much to land of leasehold tenure, and

(b)   how much of the amount ascribable to land of leasehold tenure is ascribable to land held on long lease and how much to land held on short lease.

Investments

72. In respect of the amount of each item which is shown in the company's balance sheet under assets item C (investments) there must be stated how much of that amount is ascribable to listed investments.

Information about fair value of assets and liabilities

73. (1)   This paragraph applies where financial instruments have been valued in accordance with paragraph 30 or 32.

(2)   The items affected and the basis of valuation adopted in determining the amounts of the financial instruments must be disclosed.

(3)   The purchase price of the financial instruments must be disclosed.

(4)   There must be stated—

(a)   the significant assumptions underlying the valuation models and techniques used, where the fair value of the instruments has been determined in accordance with paragraph 31(4),

(b)   for each category of financial instrument, the fair value of the instruments in that category and the changes in value—

(i)   included in the profit and loss account, or

(ii)   credited to or (as the case may be) debited from the fair value reserve,

in respect of those instruments, and

(c)   for each class of derivatives, the extent and nature of the instruments, including significant terms and conditions that may affect the amount, timing and certainty of future cash flows.

(5)   Where any amount is transferred to or from the fair value reserve during the financial year, there must be stated in tabular form—

(a)   the amount of the reserve as at the date of the beginning of the financial year and as at the balance sheet date respectively,

(b)   the amount transferred to or from the reserve during that year, and

(c)   the source and application respectively of the amounts so transferred.

74. Where the company has derivatives that it has not included at fair value, there must be stated for each class of such derivatives—

(a)   the fair value of the derivatives in that class, if such a value can be determined in accordance with paragraph 31, and

(b)   the extent and nature of the derivatives.

75. (1)   This paragraph applies if—

    (a)   the company has financial fixed assets that could be included at fair value by virtue of paragraph 30,

    (b)   the amount at which those assets are included under any item in the company's accounts is in excess of their fair value, and

    (c)   the company has not made provision for diminution in value of those assets in accordance with paragraph 38(2) of this Schedule.

(2)   There must be stated—

    (a)   the amount at which either the individual assets or appropriate groupings of those individual assets are included in the company's accounts,

    (b)   the fair value of those assets or groupings, and

    (c)   the reasons for not making a provision for diminution in value of those assets, including the nature of the evidence that provides the basis for the belief that the amount at which they are stated in the accounts will be recovered.

Information where investment property and living animals and plants included at fair value

76. (1) This paragraph applies where the amounts to be included in a company's accounts in respect of investment property or living animals and plants have been determined in accordance with paragraph 33.

(2) The balance sheet items affected and the basis of valuation adopted in determining the amounts of the assets in question in the case of each such item must be disclosed in a note to the accounts.

(3) In the case of investment property, for each balance sheet item affected there must be shown, either separately in the balance sheet or in a note to the accounts—

    (a)   the comparable amounts determined according to the historical cost accounting rules, or

    (b)   the differences between those amounts and the corresponding amounts actually shown in the balance sheet in respect of that item.

(4) In sub-paragraph (3), references in relation to any item to the comparable amounts determined in accordance with that sub-paragraph are to—

    (a)   the aggregate amount which would be required to be shown in respect of that item if the amounts to be included in respect of all the assets covered by that item were determined according to the historical cost accounting rules, and

    (b)   the aggregate amount of the cumulative provisions for depreciation or diminution in value which would be permitted or required in determining those amounts according to those rules.

Reserves and provisions

77. (1) This paragraph applies where any amount is transferred—

    (a)   to or from any reserves,

    (b)   to any provisions for other risks, or

    (c)   from any provisions for other risks otherwise than for the purpose for which the provision was established,

and the reserves or provisions are or would but for paragraph 3(1) be shown as separate items in the company's balance sheet.

(2) The following information must be given in respect of the aggregate of reserves or provisions included in the same item—

    (a)   the amount of the reserves or provisions as at the date of the beginning of the financial year and as at the balance sheet date respectively,

    (b)   any amounts transferred to or from the reserves or provisions during that year, and

    (c)   the source and application respectively of any amounts so transferred.

(3) Particulars must be given of each provision included in liabilities item E.3 (other provisions) in the company's balance sheet in any case where the amount of that provision is material.

Provision for taxation

78. The amount of any provision for deferred taxation must be stated separately from the amount of any provision for other taxation.

Details of indebtedness

79. (1) In respect of each item shown under "creditors" in the company's balance sheet there must be stated the aggregate of the following amounts—

    (a)   the amount of any debts included under that item which are payable or repayable otherwise than by instalments and fall due for payment or repayment after the end of the period of five years beginning with the day next following the end of the financial year, and

    (b)   in the case of any debts so included which are payable or repayable by instalments, the amount of any instalments which fall due for payment after the end of that period.

(2)   Subject to sub-paragraph (3), in relation to each debt falling to be taken into account under sub-paragraph (1), the terms of payment or repayment and the rate of any interest payable on the debt must be stated.

(3)   If the number of debts is such that, in the opinion of the directors, compliance with sub-paragraph (2) would result in a statement of excessive length, it is sufficient to give a general indication of the terms of payment or repayment and the rates of any interest payable on the debts.

(4)   In respect of each item shown under "creditors" in the company's balance sheet there must be stated—
   (a)   the aggregate amount of any debts included under that item in respect of which any security has been given by the company, and
   (b)   an indication of the nature of the securities so given.

(5)   References above in this paragraph to an item shown under "creditors" in the company's balance sheet include references, where amounts falling due to creditors within one year and after more than one year are distinguished in the balance sheet—
   (a)   in a case within sub-paragraph (1), to an item shown under the latter of those categories, and
   (b)   in a case within sub-paragraph (4), to an item shown under either of those categories.
References to items shown under "creditors" include references to items which would but for paragraph 3(1)(b) be shown under that heading.

80.   If any fixed cumulative dividends on the company's shares are in arrear, there must be stated—
   (a)   the amount of the arrears, and
   (b)   the period for which the dividends or, if there is more than one class, each class of them are in arrear.

Guarantees and other financial commitments

81.   (1)   Particulars must be given of any charge on the assets of the company to secure the liabilities of any other person, including, where practicable, the amount secured.

(2)   The following information must be given with respect to any other contingent liability not provided for (other than a contingent liability arising out of an insurance contract)—
   (a)   the amount or estimated amount of that liability,
   (b)   its legal nature, and
   (c)   whether any valuable security has been provided by the company in connection with that liability and if so, what.

(3)   There must be stated, where practicable, the aggregate amount or estimated amount of contracts for capital expenditure, so far as not provided for.

(4)   Particulars must be given of—
   (a)   any pension commitments included under any provision shown in the company's balance sheet, and
   (b)   any such commitments for which no provision has been made,
and where any such commitment relates wholly or partly to pensions payable to past directors of the company separate particulars must be given of that commitment so far as it relates to such pensions.

(5)   Particulars must also be given of any other financial commitments, other than commitments arising out of insurance contracts, that—
   (a)   have not been provided for, and
   (b)   are relevant to assessing the company's state of affairs.

(6)   Commitments within any of the preceding sub-paragraphs undertaken on behalf of or for the benefit of—
   (a)   any parent undertaking or fellow subsidiary undertaking, or
   (b)   any subsidiary undertaking of the company,
must be stated separately from the other commitments within that sub-paragraph, and commitments within paragraph (a) must also be stated separately from those within paragraph (b).

Miscellaneous matters

82.   (1)   Particulars must be given of any case where the cost of any asset is for the first time determined under paragraph 47.

(2)   Where any outstanding loans made under the authority of section 682(2)(b), (c) or (d) of the 2006 Act (various cases of financial assistance by a company for purchase of its own shares) are included under any item shown in the company's balance sheet, the aggregate amount of those loans must be disclosed for each item in question.

Information supplementing the profit and loss account

Separate statement of certain items of income and expenditure

83.   (1)   Subject to sub-paragraph (2), there must be stated the amount of the interest on or any similar charges in respect of—
   (a)   bank loans and overdrafts, and

(b)   loans of any other kind made to the company.

(2)   Sub-paragraph (1) does not apply to interest or charges on loans to the company from group undertakings, but, with that exception, it applies to interest or charges on all loans, whether made on the security of debentures or not.

Particulars of tax

84. (1)   Particulars must be given of any special circumstances which affect liability in respect of taxation of profits, income or capital gains for the financial year or liability in respect of taxation of profits, income or capital gains for succeeding financial years.

(2)   The following amounts must be stated—
    (a)   the amount of the charge for United Kingdom corporation tax,
    (b)   if that amount would have been greater but for relief from double taxation, the amount which it would have been but for such relief,
    (c)   the amount of the charge for United Kingdom income tax, and
    (d)   the amount of the charge for taxation imposed outside the United Kingdom of profits, income and (so far as charged to revenue) capital gains.

Those amounts must be stated separately in respect of each of the amounts which is shown under the following items in the profit and loss account, that is to say item III.9 (tax on profit or loss on ordinary activities) and item III.14 (tax on extraordinary profit or loss).

Particulars of business

85. (1)   As regards general business a company must disclose—
    (a)   gross premiums written,
    (b)   gross premiums earned,
    (c)   gross claims incurred,
    (d)   gross operating expenses, and
    (e)   the reinsurance balance.

(2)   The amounts required to be disclosed by sub-paragraph (1) must be broken down between direct insurance and reinsurance acceptances, if reinsurance acceptances amount to 10 per cent or more of gross premiums written.

(3)   Subject to sub-paragraph (4), the amounts required to be disclosed by sub-paragraphs (1) and (2) with respect to direct insurance must be further broken down into the following groups of classes—
    (a)   accident and health,
    (b)   motor (third party liability),
    (c)   motor (other classes),
    (d)   marine, aviation and transport,
    (e)   fire and other damage to property,
    (f)   third-party liability,
    (g)   credit and suretyship,
    (h)   legal expenses,
    (i)   assistance, and
    (j)   miscellaneous,
where the amount of the gross premiums written in direct insurance for each such group exceeds 10 million Euros.

(4)   The company must in any event disclose the amounts relating to the three largest groups of classes in its business.

86. (1)   As regards long-term business, the company must disclose—
    (a)   gross premiums written, and
    (b)   the reinsurance balance.

(2)   Subject to sub-paragraph (3)—
    (a)   gross premiums written must be broken down between those written by way of direct insurance and those written by way of reinsurance, and
    (b)   gross premiums written by way of direct insurance must be broken down—
        (i)   between individual premiums and premiums under group contracts,
        (ii)   between periodic premiums and single premiums, and
        (iii)   between premiums from non-participating contracts, premiums from participating contracts and premiums from contracts where the investment risk is borne by policyholders.

(3)   Disclosure of any amount referred to in sub-paragraph (2)(a) or (2)(b)(i), (ii) or (iii) is not required if it does not exceed 10 per cent of the gross premiums written or (as the case may be) of the gross premiums written by way of direct insurance.

87. (1)   Subject to sub-paragraph (2), there must be disclosed as regards both general and long-term business the total gross direct insurance premiums resulting from contracts concluded by the company—

(a)   in the member State of its head office,

(b)   in the other member States, and

(c)   in other countries.

(2)   Disclosure of any amount referred to in sub-paragraph (1) is not required if it does not exceed 5 per cent of total gross premiums.

Commissions

88. There must be disclosed the total amount of commissions for direct insurance business accounted for in the financial year, including acquisition, renewal, collection and portfolio management commissions.

Miscellaneous matters

89. (1)   Where any amount relating to any preceding financial year is included in any item in the profit and loss account, the effect must be stated.

(2)   Particulars must be given of any extraordinary income or charges arising in the financial year.

(3)   The effect must be stated of any transactions that are exceptional by virtue of size or incidence though they fall within the ordinary activities of the company.

Related party transactions

90. (1)   Particulars may be given of transactions which the company has entered into with related parties, and must be given if such transactions are material and have not been concluded under normal market conditions.

(2)   The particulars of transactions required to be disclosed by sub-paragraph (1) must include—

(a)   the amount of such transactions,

(b)   the nature of the related party relationship, and

(c)   other information about the transactions necessary for an understanding of the financial position of the company.

(3)   Information about individual transactions may be aggregated according to their nature, except where separate information is necessary for an understanding of the effects of related party transactions on the financial position of the company.

(4)   Particulars need not be given of transactions entered into between two or more members of a group, provided that any subsidiary undertaking which is a party to the transaction is wholly-owned by such a member.

(5)   In this paragraph, "related party" has the same meaning as in international accounting standards.

NOTES

Commencement: 6 April 2008.

PART 4
INTERPRETATION OF THIS SCHEDULE

Definitions for this Schedule

[4.195]

91. The following definitions apply for the purposes of this Schedule and its interpretation—

"general business" means business which consists of effecting or carrying out contracts of general insurance;

"long-term business" means business which consists of effecting or carrying out contracts of long-term insurance;

"long-term fund" means the fund or funds maintained by a company in respect of its long-term business in accordance with rule 1.5.22 in the Prudential Sourcebook for Insurers made by the Financial Services Authority under Part 10 of the Financial Services and Markets Act 2000;

"policyholder" has the meaning given by article 3 of the Financial Services and Markets Act 2000 (Meaning of "Policy" and "Policyholder") Order 2001;

"provision for unexpired risks" means the amount set aside in addition to unearned premiums in respect of risks to be borne by the company after the end of the financial year, in order to provide for all claims and expenses in connection with insurance contracts in force in excess of the related unearned premiums and any premiums receivable on those contracts.

NOTES

Commencement: 6 April 2008.

SCHEDULE 4
INFORMATION ON RELATED UNDERTAKINGS REQUIRED WHETHER PREPARING COMPANIES ACT OR IAS ACCOUNTS
Regulation 7

PART 1
PROVISIONS APPLYING TO ALL COMPANIES

Subsidiary undertakings

[4.196]

1. (1) The following information must be given where at the end of the financial year the company has subsidiary undertakings.

(2) The name of each subsidiary undertaking must be stated.

(3) There must be stated with respect to each subsidiary undertaking—
  (a) if it is incorporated outside the United Kingdom, the country in which it is incorporated,
  (b) if it is unincorporated, the address of its principal place of business.

Financial information about subsidiary undertakings

2. (1) There must be disclosed with respect to each subsidiary undertaking not included in consolidated accounts by the company—
  (a) the aggregate amount of its capital and reserves as at the end of its relevant financial year, and
  (b) its profit or loss for that year.

(2) That information need not be given if the company is exempt by virtue of section 400 or 401 of the 2006 Act from the requirement to prepare group accounts (parent company included in accounts of larger group).

(3) That information need not be given if the company's investment in the subsidiary undertaking is included in the company's accounts by way of the equity method of valuation.

(4) That information need not be given if—
  (a) the subsidiary undertaking is not required by any provision of the 2006 Act to deliver a copy of its balance sheet for its relevant financial year and does not otherwise publish that balance sheet in the United Kingdom or elsewhere, and
  (b) the company's holding is less than 50% of the nominal value of the shares in the undertaking.

(5) Information otherwise required by this paragraph need not be given if it is not material.

(6) For the purposes of this paragraph the "relevant financial year" of a subsidiary undertaking is—
  (a) if its financial year ends with that of the company, that year, and
  (b) if not, its financial year ending last before the end of the company's financial year.

Shares and debentures of company held by subsidiary undertakings

3. (1) The number, description and amount of the shares in the company held by or on behalf of its subsidiary undertakings must be disclosed.

(2) Sub-paragraph (1) does not apply in relation to shares in the case of which the subsidiary undertaking is concerned as personal representative or, subject as follows, as trustee.

(3) The exception for shares in relation to which the subsidiary undertaking is concerned as trustee does not apply if the company, or any of its subsidiary undertakings, is beneficially interested under the trust, otherwise than by way of security only for the purposes of a transaction entered into by it in the ordinary course of a business which includes the lending of money.

(4) Part 5 of this Schedule has effect for the interpretation of the reference in sub-paragraph (3) to a beneficial interest under a trust.

Significant holdings in undertakings other than subsidiary undertakings

4. (1) The information required by paragraphs 5 and 6 must be given where at the end of the financial year the company has a significant holding in an undertaking which is not a subsidiary undertaking of the company, and which does not fall within paragraph 18 (joint ventures) or 19 (associated undertakings).

(2) A holding is significant for this purpose if—
  (a) it amounts to 20% or more of the nominal value of any class of shares in the undertaking, or
  (b) the amount of the holding (as stated or included in the company's individual accounts) exceeds one-fifth of the amount (as so stated) of the company's assets.

5. (1) The name of the undertaking must be stated.

(2) There must be stated—

(a)   if the undertaking is incorporated outside the United Kingdom, the country in which it is incorporated,

(b)   if it is unincorporated, the address of its principal place of business.

(3)   There must also be stated—

(a)   the identity of each class of shares in the undertaking held by the company, and

(b)   the proportion of the nominal value of the shares of that class represented by those shares.

6. (1)   Subject to paragraph 14, there must also be stated—

(a)   the aggregate amount of the capital and reserves of the undertaking as at the end of its relevant financial year, and

(b)   its profit or loss for that year.

(2)   That information need not be given in respect of an undertaking if—

(a)   the undertaking is not required by any provision of the 2006 Act to deliver a copy of its balance sheet for its relevant financial year and does not otherwise publish that balance sheet in the United Kingdom or elsewhere, and

(b)   the company's holding is less than 50% of the nominal value of the shares in the undertaking.

(3)   Information otherwise required by this paragraph need not be given if it is not material.

(4)   For the purposes of this paragraph the "relevant financial year" of an undertaking is—

(a)   if its financial year ends with that of the company, that year, and

(b)   if not, its financial year ending last before the end of the company's financial year.

Membership of certain undertakings

7. (1)   The information required by this paragraph must be given where at the end of the financial year the company is a member of a qualifying undertaking.

(2)   There must be stated—

(a)   the name and legal form of the undertaking, and

(b)   the address of the undertaking's registered office (whether in or outside the United Kingdom) or, if it does not have such an office, its head office (whether in or outside the United Kingdom).

(3)   Where the undertaking is a qualifying partnership there must also be stated either—

(a)   that a copy of the latest accounts of the undertaking has been or is to be appended to the copy of the company's accounts sent to the registrar under section 444 of the 2006 Act, or

(b)   the name of at least one body corporate (which may be the company) in whose group accounts the undertaking has been or is to be dealt with on a consolidated basis.

(4)   Information otherwise required by sub-paragraph (2) need not be given if it is not material.

(5)   Information otherwise required by sub-paragraph (3)(b) need not be given if the notes to the company's accounts disclose that advantage has been taken of the exemption conferred by regulation 7 of the [Partnerships (Accounts) Regulations 2008].

(6)   In this paragraph—

"dealt with on a consolidated basis", "member" and "qualifying partnership" have the same meanings as in the [Partnerships (Accounts) Regulations 2008];

"qualifying undertaking" means—

(a)   a qualifying partnership, or

(b)   an unlimited company each of whose members is—

(i)   a limited company,

(ii)   another unlimited company each of whose members is a limited company, or

(iii)   a Scottish partnership each of whose members is a limited company,

and references in this paragraph to a limited company, another unlimited company or a Scottish partnership include a comparable undertaking incorporated in or formed under the law of a country or territory outside the United Kingdom.

Parent undertaking drawing up accounts for larger group

8. (1)   Where the company is a subsidiary undertaking, the following information must be given with respect to the parent undertaking of—

(a)   the largest group of undertakings for which group accounts are drawn up and of which the company is a member, and

(b)   the smallest such group of undertakings.

(2)   The name of the parent undertaking must be stated.

(3)   There must be stated—

(a)   if the undertaking is incorporated outside the United Kingdom, the country in which it is incorporated,

(b)   if it is unincorporated, the address of its principal place of business.

(4)   If copies of the group accounts referred to in sub-paragraph (1) are available to the public, there must also be stated the addresses from which copies of the accounts can be obtained.

Identification of ultimate parent company

9. (1)   Where the company is a subsidiary undertaking, the following information must be given with respect to the company (if any) regarded by the directors as being the company's ultimate parent company.

(2)   The name of that company must be stated.

(3)   If that company is incorporated outside the United Kingdom, the country in which it is incorporated must be stated (if known to the directors).

(4)   In this paragraph "company" includes any body corporate.

NOTES

Commencement: 6 April 2008.

Para 7: words in square brackets in sub-paras (5), (6) substituted by the Partnerships (Accounts) Regulations 2008, SI 2008/569, reg 17(2), as from 6 April 2008, in relation to qualifying partnerships' financial years beginning on or after that date, and auditors appointed in respect of those financial years.

PART 2
COMPANIES NOT REQUIRED TO PREPARE GROUP ACCOUNTS

Reason for not preparing group accounts

[4.197]

10. (1)   The reason why the company is not required to prepare group accounts must be stated.

(2)   If the reason is that all the subsidiary undertakings of the company fall within the exclusions provided for in section 405 of the 2006 Act (Companies Act group accounts: subsidiary undertakings included in the consolidation), it must be stated with respect to each subsidiary undertaking which of those exclusions applies.

Holdings in subsidiary undertakings

11. (1)   There must be stated in relation to shares of each class held by the company in a subsidiary undertaking—
  (a)   the identity of the class, and
  (b)   the proportion of the nominal value of the shares of that class represented by those shares.

(2)   The shares held by or on behalf of the company itself must be distinguished from those attributed to the company which are held by or on behalf of a subsidiary undertaking.

Financial years of subsidiary undertakings

12. Where—
  (a)   disclosure is made under paragraph 2(1) with respect to a subsidiary undertaking, and
  (b)   that undertaking's financial year does not end with that of the company,
there must be stated in relation to that undertaking the date on which its last financial year ended (last before the end of the company's financial year).

Exemption from giving information about significant holdings in non-subsidiary undertakings

13. (1)   The information otherwise required by paragraph 6 (significant holdings in undertakings other than subsidiary undertaking) need not be given if—
  (a)   the company is exempt by virtue of section 400 or 401 of the 2006 Act from the requirement to prepare group accounts (parent company included in accounts of larger group), and
  (b)   the investment of the company in all undertakings in which it has such a holding as is mentioned in sub-paragraph (1) is shown, in aggregate, in the notes to the accounts by way of the equity method of valuation.

Construction of references to shares held by company

14. (1)   References in Parts 1 and 2 of this Schedule to shares held by a company are to be construed as follows.

(2)   For the purposes of paragraphs 2, 11 and 12 (information about subsidiary undertakings)—
  (a)   there must be attributed to the company any shares held by a subsidiary undertaking, or by a person acting on behalf of the company or a subsidiary undertaking; but
  (b)   there must be treated as not held by the company any shares held on behalf of a person other than the company or a subsidiary undertaking.

(3)   For the purposes of paragraphs 4 to 6 (information about undertakings other than subsidiary undertakings)—
  (a)   there must be attributed to the company shares held on its behalf by any person; but
  (b)   there must be treated as not held by a company shares held on behalf of a person other than the company.

(4)   For the purposes of any of those provisions, shares held by way of security must be treated as held by the person providing the security—

(a) where apart from the right to exercise them for the purpose of preserving the value of the security, or of realising it, the rights attached to the shares are exercisable only in accordance with that person's instructions, and

(b) where the shares are held in connection with the granting of loans as part of normal business activities and apart from the right to exercise them for the purpose of preserving the value of the security, or of realising it, the rights attached to the shares are exercisable only in that person's interests.

NOTES

Commencement: 6 April 2008.

PART 3
COMPANIES REQUIRED TO PREPARE GROUP ACCOUNTS

Introductory

[4.198]

15. In this Part of this Schedule "the group" means the group consisting of the parent company and its subsidiary undertakings.

Subsidiary undertakings

16. (1) In addition to the information required by paragraph 2, the following information must also be given with respect to the undertakings which are subsidiary undertakings of the parent company at the end of the financial year.

(2) It must be stated whether the subsidiary undertaking is included in the consolidation and, if it is not, the reasons for excluding it from consolidation must be given.

(3) It must be stated with respect to each subsidiary undertaking by virtue of which of the conditions specified in section 1162(2) or (4) of the 2006 Act it is a subsidiary undertaking of its immediate parent undertaking.

That information need not be given if the relevant condition is that specified in subsection (2)(a) of that section (holding of a majority of the voting rights) and the immediate parent undertaking holds the same proportion of the shares in the undertaking as it holds voting rights.

Holdings in subsidiary undertakings

17. (1) The following information must be given with respect to the shares of a subsidiary undertaking held—

(a) by the parent company, and

(b) by the group,

and the information under paragraphs (a) and (b) must (if different) be shown separately.

(2) There must be stated—

(a) the identity of each class of shares held, and

(b) the proportion of the nominal value of the shares of that class represented by those shares.

Joint ventures

18. (1) The following information must be given where an undertaking is dealt with in the consolidated accounts by the method of proportional consolidation in accordance with paragraph 18 of Schedule 6 to these Regulations (joint ventures)—

(a) the name of the undertaking,

(b) the address of the principal place of business of the undertaking,

(c) the factors on which joint management of the undertaking is based, and

(d) the proportion of the capital of the undertaking held by undertakings included in the consolidation.

(2) Where the financial year of the undertaking did not end with that of the company, there must be stated the date on which a financial year of the undertaking last ended before that date.

Associated undertakings

19. (1) The following information must be given where an undertaking included in the consolidation has an interest in an associated undertaking.

(2) The name of the associated undertaking must be stated.

(3) There must be stated—

(a) if the undertaking is incorporated outside the United Kingdom, the country in which it is incorporated,

(b) if it is unincorporated, the address of its principal place of business.

(4) The following information must be given with respect to the shares of the undertaking held—

(a) by the parent company, and

(b) by the group,

and the information under paragraphs (a) and (b) must be shown separately.

(5) There must be stated—
  (a) the identity of each class of shares held, and
  (b) the proportion of the nominal value of the shares of that class represented by those shares.

(6) In this paragraph "associated undertaking" has the meaning given by paragraph 19 of Schedule 6 to these Regulations; and the information required by this paragraph must be given notwithstanding that paragraph 21(3) of that Schedule (materiality) applies in relation to the accounts themselves.

Requirement to give information about other significant holdings of parent company or group

20. (1) The information required by paragraphs 5 and 6 must also be given where at the end of the financial year the group has a significant holding in an undertaking which is not a subsidiary undertaking of the parent company and does not fall within paragraph 18 (joint ventures) or 19 (associated undertakings), as though the references to the company in those paragraphs were a reference to the group.

(2) A holding is significant for this purpose if—
  (a) it amounts to 20% or more of the nominal value of any class of shares in the undertaking, or
  (b) the amount of the holding (as stated or included in the group accounts) exceeds one-fifth of the amount of the group's assets (as so stated).

(3) For the purposes of those paragraphs as applied to a group the "relevant financial year" of an outside undertaking is—
  (a) if its financial year ends with that of the parent company, that year, and
  (b) if not, its financial year ending last before the end of the parent company's financial year.

Group's membership of certain undertakings

21. The information required by paragraph 7 must also be given where at the end of the financial year the group is a member of a qualifying undertaking.

Construction of references to shares held by parent company or group

22. (1) References in Parts 1 and 3 of this Schedule to shares held by that parent company or group are to be construed as follows.

(2) For the purposes of paragraphs 4 to 6, 17, 19(4) and (5) and 12 (information about holdings in subsidiary and other undertakings)—
  (a) there must be attributed to the parent company shares held on its behalf by any person; but
  (b) there must be treated as not held by the parent company shares held on behalf of a person other than the company.

(3) References to shares held by the group are to any shares held by or on behalf of the parent company or any of its subsidiary undertakings; but any shares held on behalf of a person other than the parent company or any of its subsidiary undertakings are not to be treated as held by the group.

(4) Shares held by way of security must be treated as held by the person providing the security—
  (a) where apart from the right to exercise them for the purpose of preserving the value of the security, or of realising it, the rights attached to the shares are exercisable only in accordance with his instructions, and
  (b) where the shares are held in connection with the granting of loans as part of normal business activities and apart from the right to exercise them for the purpose of preserving the value of the security, or of realising it, the rights attached to the shares are exercisable only in his interests.

NOTES
Commencement: 6 April 2008.

PART 4
ADDITIONAL DISCLOSURES FOR BANKING COMPANIES AND GROUPS
[4.199]
23. (1) This paragraph applies where accounts are prepared in accordance with the special provisions of Schedules 2 and 6 relating to banking companies or groups.

(2) The information required by paragraph 5 of this Schedule, modified where applicable by paragraph 20 (information about significant holdings of the company or group in undertakings other than subsidiary undertakings) need only be given in respect of undertakings (otherwise falling within the class of undertakings in respect of which disclosure is required) in which the company or group has a significant holding amounting to 20 % or more of the nominal value of the shares in the undertaking.

In addition any information required by those paragraphs may be omitted if it is not material.

(3) Paragraphs 14(3) and (4) and 22(3) and (4) of this Schedule apply with necessary modifications for the purposes of this paragraph.

NOTES
Commencement: 6 April 2008.

PART 5
INTERPRETATION OF REFERENCES TO "BENEFICIAL INTEREST"

Residual interests under pension and employees' share schemes

[4.200]

24. (1) Where shares in an undertaking are held on trust for the purposes of a pension scheme or an employees' share scheme, there must be disregarded any residual interest which has not vested in possession, being an interest of the undertaking or any of its subsidiary undertakings.

(2) In this paragraph a "residual interest" means a right of the undertaking in question (the "residual beneficiary") to receive any of the trust property in the event of—

    (a)   all the liabilities arising under the scheme having been satisfied or provided for, or

    (b)   the residual beneficiary ceasing to participate in the scheme, or

    (c)   the trust property at any time exceeding what is necessary for satisfying the liabilities arising or expected to arise under the scheme.

(3) In sub-paragraph (2) references to a right include a right dependent on the exercise of a discretion vested by the scheme in the trustee or any other person; and references to liabilities arising under a scheme include liabilities that have resulted or may result from the exercise of any such discretion.

(4) For the purposes of this paragraph a residual interest vests in possession—

    (a)   in a case within sub-paragraph (2)(a), on the occurrence of the event there mentioned, whether or not the amount of the property receivable pursuant to the right mentioned in that sub-paragraph is then ascertained,

    (b)   in a case within sub-paragraph (2)(b) or (c), when the residual beneficiary becomes entitled to require the trustee to transfer to that beneficiary any of the property receivable pursuant to that right.

Employer's charges and other rights of recovery

25. (1) Where shares in an undertaking are held on trust there must be disregarded—

    (a)   if the trust is for the purposes of a pension scheme, any such rights as are mentioned in sub-paragraph (2),

    (b)   if the trust is for the purposes of an employees' share scheme, any such rights as are mentioned in paragraph (a) of that sub-paragraph,

being rights of the undertaking or any of its subsidiary undertakings.

(2) The rights referred to are—

    (a)   any charge or lien on, or set-off against, any benefit or other right or interest under the scheme for the purpose of enabling the employer or former employer of a member of the scheme to obtain the discharge of a monetary obligation due to him from the member, and

    (b)   any right to receive from the trustee of the scheme, or as trustee of the scheme to retain, an amount that can be recovered or retained under section 61 of the Pension Schemes Act 1993 or section 57 of the Pension Schemes (Northern Ireland) Act 1993 (deduction of contributions equivalent premium from refund of scheme contributions) or otherwise as reimbursement or partial reimbursement for any contributions equivalent premium paid in connection with the scheme under Chapter 3 of Part 3 of that Act.

Trustee's right to expenses, remuneration, indemnity etc

26. Where an undertaking is a trustee, there must be disregarded any rights which the undertaking has in its capacity as trustee including, in particular, any right to recover its expenses or be remunerated out of the trust property and any right to be indemnified out of that property for any liability incurred by reason of any act or omission of the undertaking in the performance of its duties as trustee.

Supplementary

27. (1) This Schedule applies in relation to debentures as it applies in relation to shares.

(2) "Pension scheme" means any scheme for the provision of benefits consisting of or including relevant benefits for or in respect of employees or former employees; and "relevant benefits" means any pension, lump sum, gratuity or other like benefit given or to be given on retirement or on death or in anticipation of retirement or, in connection with past service, after retirement or death.

(3) In sub-paragraph (2) of this paragraph and in paragraph 25(2) "employee" and "employer" are to be read as if a director of an undertaking were employed by it.

NOTES
Commencement: 6 April 2008.

SCHEDULE 5
INFORMATION ABOUT BENEFITS OF DIRECTORS
Regulation 8

PART 1
PROVISIONS APPLYING TO QUOTED AND UNQUOTED COMPANIES
Total amount of directors' remuneration etc

[4.201]

1. (1) There must be shown—
   (a) the aggregate amount of remuneration paid to or receivable by directors in respect of qualifying services;
   (b) the aggregate of the amount of gains made by directors on the exercise of share options;
   (c) the aggregate of the amount of money paid to or receivable by directors, and the net value of assets (other than money and share options) received or receivable by directors, under long term incentive schemes in respect of qualifying services; and
   (d) the aggregate value of any company contributions—
      (i) paid, or treated as paid, to a pension scheme in respect of directors' qualifying services, and
      (ii) by reference to which the rate or amount of any money purchase benefits that may become payable will be calculated.

(2) There must be shown the number of directors (if any) to whom retirement benefits are accruing in respect of qualifying services—
   (a) under money purchase schemes, and
   (b) under defined benefit schemes.

(3) In the case of a company which is not a quoted company and whose equity share capital is not listed on the market known as AIM—
   (a) sub-paragraph (1) has effect as if paragraph (b) were omitted and, in paragraph (c), "assets" did not include shares; and
   (b) the number of each of the following (if any) must be shown, namely—
      (i) the directors who exercised share options, and
      (ii) the directors in respect of whose qualifying services shares were received or receivable under long term incentive schemes.

NOTES

Commencement: 6 April 2008.

PART 2
PROVISIONS APPLYING ONLY TO UNQUOTED COMPANIES
Details of highest paid director's emoluments etc

[4.202]

2. (1) Where the aggregates shown under paragraph 1(1)(a), (b) and (c) total £200,000 or more, there must be shown—
   (a) so much of the total of those aggregates as is attributable to the highest paid director, and
   (b) so much of the aggregate mentioned in paragraph 1(1)(d) as is so attributable.

(2) Where sub-paragraph (1) applies and the highest paid director has performed qualifying services during the financial year by reference to which the rate or amount of any defined benefits that may become payable will be calculated, there must also be shown—
   (a) the amount at the end of the year of his accrued pension, and
   (b) where applicable, the amount at the end of the year of his accrued lump sum.

(3) Subject to sub-paragraph (4), where sub-paragraph (1) applies in the case of a company which is not a listed company, there must also be shown—
   (a) whether the highest paid director exercised any share options, and
   (b) whether any shares were received or receivable by that director in respect of qualifying services under a long term incentive scheme.

(4) Where the highest paid director has not been involved in any of the transactions specified in sub-paragraph (3), that fact need not be stated.

Excess retirement benefits of directors and past directors

3. (1) Subject to sub-paragraph (2), there must be shown the aggregate amount of—
   (a) so much of retirement benefits paid to or receivable by directors under pension schemes, and
   (b) so much of retirement benefits paid to or receivable by past directors under such schemes,
as (in each case) is in excess of the retirement benefits to which they were respectively entitled on the date on which the benefits first became payable or 31st March 1997, whichever is the later.

(2)   Amounts paid or receivable under a pension scheme need not be included in the aggregate amount if—

    (a)   the funding of the scheme was such that the amounts were or, as the case may be, could have been paid without recourse to additional contributions, and

    (b)   amounts were paid to or receivable by all pensioner members of the scheme on the same basis.

(3)   In sub-paragraph (2), "pensioner member", in relation to a pension scheme, means any person who is entitled to the present payment of retirement benefits under the scheme.

(4)   In this paragraph—

    (a)   references to retirement benefits include benefits otherwise than in cash, and

    (b)   in relation to so much of retirement benefits as consists of a benefit otherwise than in cash, references to their amount are to the estimated money value of the benefit,

and the nature of any such benefit must also be disclosed.

Compensation to directors for loss of office

4. (1)   There must be shown the aggregate amount of any compensation to directors or past directors in respect of loss of office.

(2)   This includes compensation received or receivable by a director or past director—

    (a)   for loss of office as director of the company, or

    (b)   for loss, while director of the company or on or in connection with his ceasing to be a director of it, of—

        (i)   any other office in connection with the management of the company's affairs, or

        (ii)   any office as director or otherwise in connection with the management of the affairs of any subsidiary undertaking of the company.

(3)   In this paragraph references to compensation for loss of office include—

    (a)   compensation in consideration for, or in connection with, a person's retirement from office, and

    (b)   where such a retirement is occasioned by a breach of the person's contract with the company or with a subsidiary undertaking of the company—

        (i)   payments made by way of damages for the breach, or

        (ii)   payments made by way of settlement or compromise of any claim in respect of the breach.

(4)   In this paragraph—

    (a)   references to compensation include benefits otherwise than in cash, and

    (b)   in relation to such compensation references to its amount are to the estimated money value of the benefit.

The nature of any such compensation must be disclosed.

Sums paid to third parties in respect of directors' services

5. (1)   There must be shown the aggregate amount of any consideration paid to or receivable by third parties for making available the services of any person—

    (a)   as a director of the company, or

    (b)   while director of the company—

        (i)   as director of any of its subsidiary undertakings, or

        (ii)   otherwise in connection with the management of the affairs of the company or any of its subsidiary undertakings.

(2)   In sub-paragraph (1)—

    (a)   the reference to consideration includes benefits otherwise than in cash, and

    (b)   in relation to such consideration the reference to its amount is to the estimated money value of the benefit.

The nature of any such consideration must be disclosed.

(3)   For the purposes of this paragraph a "third party" means a person other than—

    (a)   the director himself or a person connected with him or a body corporate controlled by him, or

    (b)   the company or any of its subsidiary undertakings.

NOTES

Commencement: 6 April 2008.

PART 3
SUPPLEMENTARY PROVISIONS

General nature of obligations

[4.203]

6. (1)   This Schedule requires information to be given only so far as it is contained in the company's books and papers or the company has the right to obtain it from the persons concerned.

(2)   For the purposes of this Schedule any information is treated as shown if it is capable of being readily ascertained from other information which is shown.

Provisions as to amounts to be shown

7. (1)   The following provisions apply with respect to the amounts to be shown under this Schedule.

(2)   The amount in each case includes all relevant sums, whether paid by or receivable from the company, any of the company's subsidiary undertakings or any other person.

(3)   References to amounts paid to or receivable by a person include amounts paid to or receivable by a person connected with him or a body corporate controlled by him (but not so as to require an amount to be counted twice).

(4)   Except as otherwise provided, the amounts to be shown for any financial year are—
  (a)   the sums receivable in respect of that year (whenever paid), or
  (b)   in the case of sums not receivable in respect of a period, the sums paid during that year.

(5)   Sums paid by way of expenses allowance that are charged to United Kingdom income tax after the end of the relevant financial year must be shown in a note to the first accounts in which it is practicable to show them and must be distinguished from the amounts to be shown apart from this provision.

(6)   Where it is necessary to do so for the purpose of making any distinction required in complying with this Schedule, the directors may apportion payments between the matters in respect of which they have been paid or are receivable in such manner as they think appropriate.

Exclusion of sums liable to be accounted for to company etc

8. (1)   The amounts to be shown under this Schedule do not include any sums that are to be accounted for—
  (a)   to the company or any of its subsidiary undertakings, or
  (b)   by virtue of sections 219 and 222(3) of the 2006 Act (payments in connection with share transfers: duty to account) to persons who sold their shares as a result of the offer made.

(2)   Where—
  (a)   any such sums are not shown in a note to the accounts for the relevant financial year on the ground that the person receiving them is liable to account for them, and
  (b)   the liability is afterwards wholly or partly released or is not enforced within a period of two years,
those sums, to the extent to which the liability is released or not enforced, must be shown in a note to the first accounts in which it is practicable to show them and must be distinguished from the amounts to be shown apart from this provision.

Meaning of "remuneration"

9. (1)   In this Schedule "remuneration" of a director includes—
  (a)   salary, fees and bonuses, sums paid by way of expenses allowance (so far as they are chargeable to United Kingdom income tax), and
  (b)   subject to sub-paragraph (2), the estimated money value of any other benefits received by the director otherwise than in cash.

(2)   The expression does not include—
  (a)   the value of any share options granted to the director or the amount of any gains made on the exercise of any such options,
  (b)   any company contributions paid, or treated as paid, under any pension scheme or any benefits to which the director is entitled under any such scheme, or
  (c)   any money or other assets paid to or received or receivable by the director under any long term incentive scheme.

Meaning of "highest paid director"

10.   In this Schedule, "the highest paid director" means the director to whom is attributable the greatest part of the total of the aggregates shown under paragraph 1(1)(a), (b) and (c).

Meaning of "long term incentive scheme"

11. (1)   In this Schedule "long term incentive scheme" means an agreement or arrangement—
  (a)   under which money or other assets may become receivable by a director, and
  (b)   which includes one or more qualifying conditions with respect to service or performance which cannot be fulfilled within a single financial year.

(2)   For this purpose the following must be disregarded—
  (a)   bonuses the amount of which falls to be determined by reference to service or performance within a single financial year;
  (b)   compensation for loss of office, payments for breach of contract and other termination payments; and
  (c)   retirement benefits.

Meaning of "shares" and "share option" and related expressions

12. In this Schedule—
  (a) "shares" means shares (whether allotted or not) in the company, or any undertaking which is a group undertaking in relation to the company, and includes a share warrant as defined by section 779(1) of the 2006 Act; and
  (b) "share option" means a right to acquire shares.

Meaning of "pension scheme" and related expressions

13. (1) In this Schedule—
  "pension scheme" means a retirement benefits scheme as defined by section 611 of the Income and Corporation Taxes Act 1988; and
  "retirement benefits" has the meaning given by section 612(1) of that Act.

(2) In this Schedule "accrued pension" and "accrued lump sum", in relation to any pension scheme and any director, mean respectively the amount of the annual pension, and the amount of the lump sum, which would be payable under the scheme on his attaining normal pension age if—
  (a) he had left the company's service at the end of the financial year,
  (b) there was no increase in the general level of prices in the United Kingdom during the period beginning with the end of that year and ending with his attaining that age,
  (c) no question arose of any commutation of the pension or inverse commutation of the lump sum, and
  (d) any amounts attributable to voluntary contributions paid by the director to the scheme, and any money purchase benefits which would be payable under the scheme, were disregarded.

(3) In this Schedule, "company contributions", in relation to a pension scheme and a director, means any payments (including insurance premiums) made, or treated as made, to the scheme in respect of the director by a person other than the director.

(4) In this Schedule, in relation to a director—
  "defined benefits" means retirement benefits payable under a pension scheme that are not money purchase benefits;
  "defined benefit scheme" means a pension scheme that is not a money purchase scheme;
  "money purchase benefits" means retirement benefits payable under a pension scheme the rate or amount of which is calculated by reference to payments made, or treated as made, by the director or by any other person in respect of the director and which are not average salary benefits; and
  "money purchase scheme" means a pension scheme under which all of the benefits that may become payable to or in respect of the director are money purchase benefits.

(5) In this Schedule, "normal pension age", in relation to any pension scheme and any director, means the age at which the director will first become entitled to receive a full pension on retirement of an amount determined without reduction to take account of its payment before a later age (but disregarding any entitlement to pension upon retirement in the event of illness, incapacity or redundancy).

(6) Where a pension scheme provides for any benefits that may become payable to or in respect of any director to be whichever are the greater of—
  (a) money purchase benefits as determined by or under the scheme; and
  (b) defined benefits as so determined,
the company may assume for the purposes of this paragraph that those benefits will be money purchase benefits, or defined benefits, according to whichever appears more likely at the end of the financial year.

(7) For the purpose of determining whether a pension scheme is a money purchase or defined benefit scheme, any death in service benefits provided for by the scheme are to be disregarded.

References to subsidiary undertakings

14. (1) Any reference in this Schedule to a subsidiary undertaking of the company, in relation to a person who is or was, while a director of the company, a director also, by virtue of the company's nomination (direct or indirect) of any other undertaking, includes that undertaking, whether or not it is or was in fact a subsidiary undertaking of the company.

(2) Any reference to a subsidiary undertaking of the company—
  (a) for the purposes of paragraph 1 (remuneration etc) is to an undertaking which is a subsidiary undertaking at the time the services were rendered, and
  (b) for the purposes of paragraph 4 (compensation for loss of office) is to a subsidiary undertaking immediately before the loss of office as director.

Other minor definitions

15. (1) In this Schedule—
  "net value", in relation to any assets received or receivable by a director, means value after deducting any money paid or other value given by the director in respect of those assets;

"qualifying services", in relation to any person, means his services as a director of the company, and his services while director of the company—

(a)   as director of any of its subsidiary undertakings; or

(b)   otherwise in connection with the management of the affairs of the company or any of its subsidiary undertakings.

(2)   References in this Schedule to a person being "connected" with a director, and to a director "controlling" a body corporate, are to be construed in accordance with sections 252 to 255 of the 2006 Act.

(3)   For the purposes of this Schedule, remuneration paid or receivable or share options granted in respect of a person's accepting office as a director are treated as emoluments paid or receivable or share options granted in respect of his services as a director.

NOTES

Commencement: 6 April 2008.

SCHEDULE 6
COMPANIES ACT GROUP ACCOUNTS

Regulation 9

PART 1
GENERAL RULES

General rules

[4.204]

1. (1)   Group accounts must comply so far as practicable with the provisions of Schedule 1 to these Regulations as if the undertakings included in the consolidation ("the group") were a single company (see Parts 2 and 3 of this Schedule for modifications for banking and insurance groups).

(2)   Where the parent company is treated as an investment company for the purposes of Part 5 of Schedule 1 (special provisions for investment companies) the group must be similarly treated.

2. (1)   The consolidated balance sheet and profit and loss account must incorporate in full the information contained in the individual accounts of the undertakings included in the consolidation, subject to the adjustments authorised or required by the following provisions of this Schedule and to such other adjustments (if any) as may be appropriate in accordance with generally accepted accounting principles or practice.

(2)   If the financial year of a subsidiary undertaking included in the consolidation does not end with that of the parent company, the group accounts must be made up—

(a)   from the accounts of the subsidiary undertaking for its financial year last ending before the end of the parent company's financial year, provided that year ended no more than three months before that of the parent company, or

(b)   from interim accounts prepared by the subsidiary undertaking as at the end of the parent company's financial year.

3. (1)   Where assets and liabilities to be included in the group accounts have been valued or otherwise determined by undertakings according to accounting rules differing from those used for the group accounts, the values or amounts must be adjusted so as to accord with the rules used for the group accounts.

(2)   If it appears to the directors of the parent company that there are special reasons for departing from sub-paragraph (1) they may do so, but particulars of any such departure, the reasons for it and its effect must be given in a note to the accounts.

(3)   The adjustments referred to in this paragraph need not be made if they are not material for the purpose of giving a true and fair view.

4.   Any differences of accounting rules as between a parent company's individual accounts for a financial year and its group accounts must be disclosed in a note to the latter accounts and the reasons for the difference given.

5.   Amounts that in the particular context of any provision of this Schedule are not material may be disregarded for the purposes of that provision.

Elimination of group transactions

6. (1)   Debts and claims between undertakings included in the consolidation, and income and expenditure relating to transactions between such undertakings, must be eliminated in preparing the group accounts.

(2)   Where profits and losses resulting from transactions between undertakings included in the consolidation are included in the book value of assets, they must be eliminated in preparing the group accounts.

(3) The elimination required by sub-paragraph (2) may be effected in proportion to the group's interest in the shares of the undertakings.

(4) Sub-paragraphs (1) and (2) need not be complied with if the amounts concerned are not material for the purpose of giving a true and fair view.

Acquisition and merger accounting

7. (1) The following provisions apply where an undertaking becomes a subsidiary undertaking of the parent company.

(2) That event is referred to in those provisions as an "acquisition", and references to the "undertaking acquired" are to be construed accordingly.

8. An acquisition must be accounted for by the acquisition method of accounting unless the conditions for accounting for it as a merger are met and the merger method of accounting is adopted.

9. (1) The acquisition method of accounting is as follows.

(2) The identifiable assets and liabilities of the undertaking acquired must be included in the consolidated balance sheet at their fair values as at the date of acquisition.

(3) The income and expenditure of the undertaking acquired must be brought into the group accounts only as from the date of the acquisition.

(4) There must be set off against the acquisition cost of the interest in the shares of the undertaking held by the parent company and its subsidiary undertakings the interest of the parent company and its subsidiary undertakings in the adjusted capital and reserves of the undertaking acquired.

(5) The resulting amount if positive must be treated as goodwill, and if negative as a negative consolidation difference.

10. (1) The conditions for accounting for an acquisition as a merger are—
   (a) that at least 90% of the nominal value of the relevant shares in the undertaking acquired (excluding any shares in the undertaking held as treasury shares) is held by or on behalf of the parent company and its subsidiary undertakings,
   (b) that the proportion referred to in paragraph (a) was attained pursuant to an arrangement providing for the issue of equity shares by the parent company or one or more of its subsidiary undertakings,
   (c) that the fair value of any consideration other than the issue of equity shares given pursuant to the arrangement by the parent company and its subsidiary undertakings did not exceed 10% of the nominal value of the equity shares issued, and
   (d) that adoption of the merger method of accounting accords with generally accepted accounting principles or practice.

(2) The reference in sub-paragraph (1)(a) to the "relevant shares" in an undertaking acquired is to those carrying unrestricted rights to participate both in distributions and in the assets of the undertaking upon liquidation.

11. (1) The merger method of accounting is as follows.

(2) The assets and liabilities of the undertaking acquired must be brought into the group accounts at the figures at which they stand in the undertaking's accounts, subject to any adjustment authorised or required by this Schedule.

(3) The income and expenditure of the undertaking acquired must be included in the group accounts for the entire financial year, including the period before the acquisition.

(4) The group accounts must show corresponding amounts relating to the previous financial year as if the undertaking acquired had been included in the consolidation throughout that year.

(5) There must be set off against the aggregate of—
   (a) the appropriate amount in respect of qualifying shares issued by the parent company or its subsidiary undertakings in consideration for the acquisition of shares in the undertaking acquired, and
   (b) the fair value of any other consideration for the acquisition of shares in the undertaking acquired, determined as at the date when those shares were acquired,
the nominal value of the issued share capital of the undertaking acquired held by the parent company and its subsidiary undertakings.

(6) The resulting amount must be shown as an adjustment to the consolidated reserves.

(7) In sub-paragraph (5)(a) "qualifying shares" means—
   (a) shares in relation to which any of the following provisions applies (merger relief), and in respect of which the appropriate amount is the nominal value—
      (i) section 131 of the Companies Act 1985,
      (ii) Article 141 of the Companies (Northern Ireland) Order 1986, or
      (iii) section 612 of the 2006 Act, or

(b)   shares in relation to which any of the following provisions applies (group reconstruction relief), and in respect of which the appropriate amount is the nominal value together with any minimum premium value within the meaning of that section—
   (i)   section 132 of the Companies Act 1985,
   (ii)   Article 142 of the Companies (Northern Ireland) Order 1986, or
   (iii)   section 611 of the 2006 Act.

12.   (1)   Where a group is acquired, paragraphs 9 to 11 apply with the following adaptations.

(2)   References to shares of the undertaking acquired are to be construed as references to shares of the parent undertaking of the group.

(3)   Other references to the undertaking acquired are to be construed as references to the group; and references to the assets and liabilities, income and expenditure and capital and reserves of the undertaking acquired must be construed as references to the assets and liabilities, income and expenditure and capital and reserves of the group after making the set-offs and other adjustments required by this Schedule in the case of group accounts.

13.   (1)   The following information with respect to acquisitions taking place in the financial year must be given in a note to the accounts.

(2)   There must be stated—
   (a)   the name of the undertaking acquired or, where a group was acquired, the name of the parent undertaking of that group, and
   (b)   whether the acquisition has been accounted for by the acquisition or the merger method of accounting;
and in relation to an acquisition which significantly affects the figures shown in the group accounts, the following further information must be given.

(3)   The composition and fair value of the consideration for the acquisition given by the parent company and its subsidiary undertakings must be stated.

(4)   Where the acquisition method of accounting has been adopted, the book values immediately prior to the acquisition, and the fair values at the date of acquisition, of each class of assets and liabilities of the undertaking or group acquired must be stated in tabular form, including a statement of the amount of any goodwill or negative consolidation difference arising on the acquisition, together with an explanation of any significant adjustments made.

(5)   In ascertaining for the purposes of sub-paragraph (4) the profit or loss of a group, the book values and fair values of assets and liabilities of a group or the amount of the assets and liabilities of a group, the set-offs and other adjustments required by this Schedule in the case of group accounts must be made.

14.   (1)   There must also be stated in a note to the accounts the cumulative amount of goodwill resulting from acquisitions in that and earlier financial years which has been written off otherwise than in the consolidated profit and loss account for that or any earlier financial year.

(2)   That figure must be shown net of any goodwill attributable to subsidiary undertakings or businesses disposed of prior to the balance sheet date.

15.   Where during the financial year there has been a disposal of an undertaking or group which significantly affects the figure shown in the group accounts, there must be stated in a note to the accounts—
   (a)   the name of that undertaking or, as the case may be, of the parent undertaking of that group, and
   (b)   the extent to which the profit or loss shown in the group accounts is attributable to profit or loss of that undertaking or group.

16.   The information required by paragraph 13, 14 or 15 need not be disclosed with respect to an undertaking which—
   (a)   is established under the law of a country outside the United Kingdom, or
   (b)   carries on business outside the United Kingdom,
if in the opinion of the directors of the parent company the disclosure would be seriously prejudicial to the business of that undertaking or to the business of the parent company or any of its subsidiary undertakings and the Secretary of State agrees that the information should not be disclosed.

Minority interests

17.   (1)   The formats set out in Schedule 1 to these Regulations have effect in relation to group accounts with the following additions.

(2)   In the balance sheet formats there must be shown, as a separate item and under an appropriate heading, the amount of capital and reserves attributable to shares in subsidiary undertakings included in the consolidation held by or on behalf of persons other than the parent company and its subsidiary undertakings.

(3)   In the profit and loss account formats there must be shown, as a separate item and under an appropriate heading—

(a)   the amount of any profit or loss on ordinary activities, and

(b)   the amount of any profit or loss on extraordinary activities,

attributable to shares in subsidiary undertakings included in the consolidation held by or on behalf of persons other than the parent company and its subsidiary undertakings.

(4)   For the purposes of paragraph 4(1) and (2) of Schedule 1 (power to adapt or combine items)—

(a)   the additional item required by sub-paragraph (2) above is treated as one to which a letter is assigned, and

(b)   the additional items required by sub-paragraph (3)(a) and (b) above are treated as ones to which an Arabic number is assigned.

Joint ventures

18. (1)   Where an undertaking included in the consolidation manages another undertaking jointly with one or more undertakings not included in the consolidation, that other undertaking ("the joint venture") may, if it is not—

(a)   a body corporate, or

(b)   a subsidiary undertaking of the parent company,

be dealt with in the group accounts by the method of proportional consolidation.

(2)   The provisions of this Schedule relating to the preparation of consolidated accounts apply, with any necessary modifications, to proportional consolidation under this paragraph.

Associated undertakings

19. (1)   An "associated undertaking" means an undertaking in which an undertaking included in the consolidation has a participating interest and over whose operating and financial policy it exercises a significant influence, and which is not—

(a)   a subsidiary undertaking of the parent company, or

(b)   a joint venture dealt with in accordance with paragraph 18.

(2)   Where an undertaking holds 20% or more of the voting rights in another undertaking, it is presumed to exercise such an influence over it unless the contrary is shown.

(3)   The voting rights in an undertaking means the rights conferred on shareholders in respect of their shares or, in the case of an undertaking not having a share capital, on members, to vote at general meetings of the undertaking on all, or substantially all, matters.

(4)   The provisions of paragraphs 5 to 11 of Schedule 7 to the 2006 Act (parent and subsidiary undertakings: rights to be taken into account and attribution of rights) apply in determining for the purposes of this paragraph whether an undertaking holds 20% or more of the voting rights in another undertaking.

20. (1)   The formats set out in Schedule 1 to these Regulations have effect in relation to group accounts with the following modifications.

(2)   In the balance sheet formats replace the items headed "Participating interests", that is—

(a)   in format 1, item B.III.3, and

(b)   in format 2, item B.III.3 under the heading "ASSETS",

by two items: "Interests in associated undertakings" and "Other participating interests".

(3)   In the profit and loss account formats replace the items headed "Income from participating interests", that is—

(a)   in format 1, item 8,

(b)   in format 2, item 10,

(c)   in format 3, item B.4, and

(d)   in format 4, item B.6,

by two items: "Income from interests in associated undertakings" and "Income from other participating interests".

21. (1)   The interest of an undertaking in an associated undertaking, and the amount of profit or loss attributable to such an interest, must be shown by the equity method of accounting (including dealing with any goodwill arising in accordance with paragraphs 17 to 20 and 22 of Schedule 1 to these Regulations).

(2)   Where the associated undertaking is itself a parent undertaking, the net assets and profits or losses to be taken into account are those of the parent and its subsidiary undertakings (after making any consolidation adjustments).

(3)   The equity method of accounting need not be applied if the amounts in question are not material for the purpose of giving a true and fair view.

Related party transactions

22. Paragraph 72 of Schedule 1 to these Regulations applies to transactions which the parent company, or other undertakings included in the consolidation, have entered into with related parties, unless they are intra group transactions.

NOTES

Commencement: 6 April 2008.

PART 2
MODIFICATIONS FOR BANKING GROUPS

General application of provisions applicable to individual accounts

[4.205]

23. In its application to banking groups, Part 1 of this Schedule has effect with the following modifications.

24. In paragraph 1 of this Schedule—
- (a) the reference in sub-paragraph (1) to the provisions of Schedule 1 to these Regulations is to be construed as a reference to the provisions of Schedule 2 to these Regulations, and
- (b) sub-paragraph (2) is to be omitted.

Minority interests and associated undertakings

25. (1) This paragraph adapts paragraphs 17 and 20 (which require items in respect of "Minority interests" and associated undertakings to be added to the formats set out in Schedule 1 to these Regulations) to the formats prescribed by Schedule 2 to these Regulations.

(2) In paragraph 17—
- (a) in sub-paragraph (1), for the reference to Schedule 1 to these Regulations, substitute a reference to Schedule 2, and
- (b) paragraph 17(4) is not to apply, but for the purposes of paragraph 5(1) of Part I of Schedule 2 to these Regulations (power to combine items) the additional items required by the foregoing provisions of this paragraph are to be treated as items to which a letter is assigned.

(3) Paragraph 20(2) is to apply with respect to a balance sheet prepared under Schedule 2 to these Regulations as if it required assets item 7 (participating interests) in the balance sheet format to be replaced by the two replacement items referred to in that paragraph.

(4) Paragraph 20(3) is not to apply, but the following items in the profit and loss account formats—
- (a) format 1 item 3(b) (income from participating interests),
- (b) format 2 item B2(b) (income from participating interests),

are replaced by the following—
- (i) "Income from participating interests other than associated undertakings", to be shown at position 3(b) in format 1 and position B2(b) in format 2, and
- (ii) "Income from associated undertakings", to be shown at an appropriate position.

26. In paragraph 21(1) of this Schedule, for the references to paragraphs 17 to 20 and 22 of Schedule 1 to these Regulations substitute references to paragraphs 23 to 26 and 28 of Schedule 2 to these Regulations.

Related party transactions

27. In paragraph 22 of this Schedule, for the reference to paragraph 72 of Schedule 1 to these Regulations substitute a reference to paragraph 92 of Schedule 2 to these Regulations.

Foreign currency translation

28. Any difference between—
- (a) the amount included in the consolidated accounts for the previous financial year with respect to any undertaking included in the consolidation or the group's interest in any associated undertaking, together with the amount of any transactions undertaken to cover any such interest, and
- (b) the opening amount for the financial year in respect of those undertakings and in respect of any such transactions,

arising as a result of the application of paragraph 50 of Schedule 2 to these Regulations may be credited to (where (a) is less than (b)), or deducted from (where (a) is greater than (b)), (as the case may be) consolidated reserves.

29. Any income and expenditure of undertakings included in the consolidation and associated undertakings in a foreign currency may be translated for the purposes of the consolidated accounts at the average rates of exchange prevailing during the financial year.

Information as to undertaking in which shares held as a result of financial assistance operation

30. (1) The following provisions apply where the parent company of a banking group has a subsidiary undertaking which—

(a)   is a credit institution of which shares are held as a result of a financial assistance operation with a view to its reorganisation or rescue, and

(b)   is excluded from consolidation under section 405(3)(c) of the 2006 Act (interest held with a view to resale).

(2)   Information as to the nature and terms of the operations must be given in a note to the group accounts, and there must be appended to the copy of the group accounts delivered to the registrar in accordance with section 441 of the 2006 Act a copy of the undertaking's latest individual accounts and, if it is a parent undertaking, its latest group accounts.

If the accounts appended are required by law to be audited, a copy of the auditor's report must also be appended.

(3)   Any requirement of Part 35 of the 2006 Act as to the delivery to the registrar of a certified translation into English must be met in relation to any document required to be appended by sub-paragraph (2).

(4)   The above requirements are subject to the following qualifications—

(a)   an undertaking is not required to prepare for the purposes of this paragraph accounts which would not otherwise be prepared, and if no accounts satisfying the above requirements are prepared none need be appended;

(b)   the accounts of an undertaking need not be appended if they would not otherwise be required to be published, or made available for public inspection, anywhere in the world, but in that case the reason for not appending the accounts must be stated in a note to the consolidated accounts.

(5)   Where a copy of an undertaking's accounts is required to be appended to the copy of the group accounts delivered to the registrar, that fact must be stated in a note to the group accounts.

NOTES

Commencement: 6 April 2008.

PART 3
MODIFICATIONS FOR INSURANCE GROUPS

General application of provisions applicable to individual accounts

[4.206]
31.   In its application to insurance groups, Part 1 of this Schedule has effect with the following modifications.

32.   In paragraph 1 of this Schedule—

(a)   the reference in sub-paragraph (1) to the provisions of Schedule 1 to these Regulations is to be construed as a reference to the provisions of Schedule 3 to these Regulations, and

(b)   sub-paragraph (2) is to be omitted.

Financial years of subsidiary undertakings

33.   In paragraph 2(2)(a), for "three months" substitute "six months".

Assets and liabilities to be included in group accounts

34.   In paragraph 3, after sub-paragraph (1) insert—

"(1A)   Sub-paragraph (1) is not to apply to those liabilities items the valuation of which by the undertakings included in a consolidation is based on the application of provisions applying only to insurance undertakings, nor to those assets items changes in the values of which also affect or establish policyholders' rights.

(1B)   Where sub-paragraph (1A) applies, that fact must be disclosed in the notes to the consolidated accounts.".

Elimination of group transactions

35.   For sub-paragraph (4) of paragraph 6 substitute—

"(4)   Sub-paragraphs (1) and (2) need not be complied with—

(a)   where a transaction has been concluded according to normal market conditions and a policyholder has rights in respect of the transaction, or

(b)   if the amounts concerned are not material for the purpose of giving a true and fair view.

(5)   Where advantage is taken of sub-paragraph (4)(a) that fact must be disclosed in the notes to the accounts, and where the transaction in question has a material effect on the assets, liabilities, financial position and profit or loss of all the undertakings included in the consolidation that fact must also be so disclosed.".

Minority interests

36.   In paragraph 17—

(a) in sub-paragraph (1), for the reference to Schedule 1 to these Regulations, substitute a reference to Schedule 3, and

(b) for sub-paragraph (4) substitute—

"(4) Paragraph 3(1) of Schedule 3 to these Regulations (power to combine items) does not apply in relation to the additional items required by the above provisions of this paragraph.".

Associated undertakings

37. In paragraph 20—

(a) in sub-paragraph (1), for the reference to Schedule 1 to these Regulations substitute a reference to Schedule 3 to these Regulations, and

(b) for sub-paragraphs (2) and (3) substitute—

"(2) In the balance sheet format, replace asset item CII.3 (participating interests) with two items, "Interests in associated undertakings" and "Other participating interests".

(3) In the profit and loss account format, replace items II.2.(a) and III.3.(a) (income from participating interests, with a separate indication of that derived from group undertakings) with—

(a) "Income from participating interests other than associated undertakings, with a separate indication of that derived from group undertakings", to be shown as items II.2.(a) and III.3.(a), and

(b) "Income from associated undertakings", to be shown as items II.2.(aa) and III.3.(aa).".

38. In paragraph 21(1) of this Schedule, for the references to paragraphs 17 to 20 and 22 of Schedule 1 to these Regulations, substitute references to paragraphs 36 to 39 and 42 of Schedule 3 to these Regulations.

Related party transactions

39. In paragraph 22 of this Schedule, for the reference to paragraph 72 of Schedule 1 to these Regulations substitute a reference to paragraph 90 of Schedule 3 to these Regulations.

Modifications of Schedule 3 to these Regulations for purposes of paragraph 31

40. (1) For the purposes of paragraph 31 of this Schedule, Schedule 3 to these Regulations is to be modified as follows.

(2) The information required by paragraph 11 (additional items) need not be given.

(3) In the case of general business, investment income, expenses and charges may be disclosed in the non-technical account rather than in the technical account.

(4) In the case of subsidiary undertakings which are not authorised to carry on long-term business in the United Kingdom, notes (8) and (9) to the profit and loss account format have effect as if references to investment income, expenses and charges arising in the long-term fund or to investments attributed to the long-term fund were references to investment income, expenses and charges or (as the case may be) investments relating to long-term business.

(5) In the case of subsidiary undertakings which do not have a head office in the United Kingdom, the computation required by paragraph 52 must be made annually by an actuary or other specialist in the field on the basis of recognised actuarial methods.

(6) The information required by paragraphs 85 to 88 need not be shown.

NOTES

Commencement: 6 April 2008.

SCHEDULE 7
MATTERS TO BE DEALT WITH IN DIRECTORS' REPORT

Regulation 10

PART 1
MATTERS OF A GENERAL NATURE

Introduction

[4.207]

1. In addition to the information required by section 416 of the 2006 Act, the directors' report must contain the following information.

Asset values

2. (1) If, in the case of such of the fixed assets of the company as consist in interests in land, their market value (as at the end of the financial year) differs substantially from the amount at which they are included in the balance sheet, and the difference is, in the directors' opinion, of such significance as to require that the attention of members of the company or of holders of its debentures should be drawn to it, the report must indicate the difference with such degree of precision as is practicable.

(2)   In relation to a group directors' report sub-paragraph (1) has effect as if the reference to the fixed assets of the company was a reference to the fixed assets of the company and of its subsidiary undertakings included in the consolidation.

Political donations and expenditure

3. (1)   If—
  (a)   the company (not being the wholly-owned subsidiary of a company incorporated in the United Kingdom) has in the financial year—
    (i)   made any political donation to any political party or other political organisation,
    (ii)   made any political donation to any independent election candidate, or
    (iii)   incurred any political expenditure, and
  (b)   the amount of the donation or expenditure, or (as the case may be) the aggregate amount of all donations and expenditure falling within paragraph (a), exceeded £2000,
the directors' report for the year must contain the following particulars.

(2)   Those particulars are—
  (a)   as respects donations falling within sub-paragraph (1)(a)(i) or (ii)—
    (i)   the name of each political party, other political organisation or independent election candidate to whom any such donation has been made, and
    (ii)   the total amount given to that party, organisation or candidate by way of such donations in the financial year; and
  (b)   as respects expenditure falling within sub-paragraph (1)(a)(iii), the total amount incurred by way of such expenditure in the financial year.

(3)   If—
  (a)   at the end of the financial year the company has subsidiaries which have, in that year, made any donations or incurred any such expenditure as is mentioned in sub-paragraph (1)(a), and
  (b)   it is not itself the wholly-owned subsidiary of a company incorporated in the United Kingdom,
the directors' report for the year is not, by virtue of sub-paragraph (1), required to contain the particulars specified in sub-paragraph (2).
  But, if the total amount of any such donations or expenditure (or both) made or incurred in that year by the company and the subsidiaries between them exceeds £2000, the directors' report for the year must contain those particulars in relation to each body by whom any such donation or expenditure has been made or incurred.

(4)   Any expression used in this paragraph which is also used in Part 14 of the 2006 Act (control of political donations and expenditure) has the same meaning as in that Part.

4. (1)   If the company (not being the wholly-owned subsidiary of a company incorporated in the United Kingdom) has in the financial year made any contribution to a non-EU political party, the directors' report for the year must contain—
  (a)   a statement of the amount of the contribution, or
  (b)   (if it has made two or more such contributions in the year) a statement of the total amount of the contributions.

(2)   If—
  (a)   at the end of the financial year the company has subsidiaries which have, in that year, made any such contributions as are mentioned in sub-paragraph (1), and
  (b)   it is not itself the wholly-owned subsidiary of a company incorporated in the United Kingdom,
the directors' report for the year is not, by virtue of sub-paragraph (1), required to contain any such statement as is there mentioned, but it must instead contain a statement of the total amount of the contributions made in the year by the company and the subsidiaries between them.

(3)   In this paragraph, "contribution", in relation to an organisation, means—
  (a)   any gift of money to the organisation (whether made directly or indirectly);
  (b)   any subscription or other fee paid for affiliation to, or membership of, the organisation; or
  (c)   any money spent (otherwise than by the organisation or a person acting on its behalf) in paying any expenses incurred directly or indirectly by the organisation.

(4)   In this paragraph, "non-EU political party" means any political party which carries on, or proposes to carry on, its activities wholly outside the member States.

Charitable donations

5. (1)   If—
  (a)   the company (not being the wholly-owned subsidiary of a company incorporated in the United Kingdom) has in the financial year given money for charitable purposes, and
  (b)   the money given exceeded £2000 in amount,

the directors' report for the year must contain, in the case of each of the purposes for which money has been given, a statement of the amount of money given for that purpose.

(2) If—

(a)   at the end of the financial year the company has subsidiaries which have, in that year, given money for charitable purposes, and

(b)   it is not itself the wholly owned subsidiary of a company incorporated in the United Kingdom,

sub-paragraph (1) does not apply to the company.

But, if the amount given in that year for charitable purposes by the company and the subsidiaries between them exceeds £2000, the directors' report for the year must contain, in the case of each of the purposes for which money has been given by the company and the subsidiaries between them, a statement of the amount of money given for that purpose.

(3)   Money given for charitable purposes to a person who, when it was given, was ordinarily resident outside the United Kingdom is to be left out of account for the purposes of this paragraph.

(4)   For the purposes of this paragraph, "charitable purposes" means purposes which are exclusively charitable, and as respects Scotland a purpose is charitable if it is listed in section 7(2) of the Charities and Trustee Investment (Scotland) Act 2005.

Financial instruments

6. (1) In relation to the use of financial instruments by a company, the directors' report must contain an indication of—

(a)   the financial risk management objectives and policies of the company, including the policy for hedging each major type of forecasted transaction for which hedge accounting is used, and

(b)   the exposure of the company to price risk, credit risk, liquidity risk and cash flow risk, unless such information is not material for the assessment of the assets, liabilities, financial position and profit or loss of the company.

(2)   In relation to a group directors' report sub-paragraph (1) has effect as if the references to the company were references to the company and its subsidiary undertakings included in the consolidation.

(3)   In sub-paragraph (1) the expressions "hedge accounting", "price risk", "credit risk", "liquidity risk" and "cash flow risk" have the same meaning as they have in Council Directive 78/660/EEC on the annual accounts of certain types of companies, and in Council Directive 83/349/EEC on consolidated accounts.

Miscellaneous

7. (1) The directors' report must contain—

(a)   particulars of any important events affecting the company which have occurred since the end of the financial year,

(b)   an indication of likely future developments in the business of the company,

(c)   an indication of the activities (if any) of the company in the field of research and development, and

(d)   (unless the company is an unlimited company) an indication of the existence of branches (as defined in section 1046(3) of the 2006 Act) of the company outside the United Kingdom.

(2)   In relation to a group directors' report paragraphs (a), (b) and (c) of sub-paragraph (1) have effect as if the references to the company were references to the company and its subsidiary undertakings included in the consolidation.

NOTES

Commencement: 6 April 2008.

PART 2
DISCLOSURE REQUIRED BY COMPANY ACQUIRING ITS OWN SHARES ETC

[4.208]

8. This Part of this Schedule applies where shares in a company—

(a)   are purchased by the company or are acquired by it by forfeiture or surrender in lieu of forfeiture, or in pursuance of any of the following provisions (acquisition of own shares by company limited by shares)—

(i)   section 143(3) of the Companies Act 1985,

(ii)   Article 153(3) of the Companies (Northern Ireland) Order 1986, or

(iii)   section 659 of the 2006 Act, or

(b)   are acquired by another person in circumstances where paragraph (c) or (d) of any of the following provisions applies (acquisition by company's nominee, or by another with company financial assistance, the company having a beneficial interest)—

(i)   section 146(1) of the Companies Act 1985,

    (ii)   Article 156(1) of the Companies (Northern Ireland) Order 1986, or

    (iii)   section 662(1) of the 2006 Act applies, or

  (c) are made subject to a lien or other charge taken (whether expressly or otherwise) by the company and permitted by any of the following provisions (exceptions from general rule against a company having a lien or charge on its own shares)—

    (i)   section 150(2) or (4) of the Companies Act 1985,

    (ii)   Article 160(2) or (4) of the Companies (Northern Ireland) Order 1986, or

    (iii)   section 670(2) or (4) of the 2006 Act.

9. The directors' report for a financial year must state—

  (a) the number and nominal value of the shares so purchased, the aggregate amount of the consideration paid by the company for such shares and the reasons for their purchase;

  (b) the number and nominal value of the shares so acquired by the company, acquired by another person in such circumstances and so charged respectively during the financial year;

  (c) the maximum number and nominal value of shares which, having been so acquired by the company, acquired by another person in such circumstances or so charged (whether or not during that year) are held at any time by the company or that other person during that year;

  (d) the number and nominal value of the shares so acquired by the company, acquired by another person in such circumstances or so charged (whether or not during that year) which are disposed of by the company or that other person or cancelled by the company during that year;

  (e) where the number and nominal value of the shares of any particular description are stated in pursuance of any of the preceding sub-paragraphs, the percentage of the called-up share capital which shares of that description represent;

  (f) where any of the shares have been so charged the amount of the charge in each case; and

  (g) where any of the shares have been disposed of by the company or the person who acquired them in such circumstances for money or money's worth the amount or value of the consideration in each case.

NOTES

Commencement: 6 April 2008.

PART 3
DISCLOSURE CONCERNING EMPLOYMENT ETC OF DISABLED PERSONS

[4.209]

10. (1) This Part of this Schedule applies to the directors' report where the average number of persons employed by the company in each week during the financial year exceeded 250.

(2) That average number is the quotient derived by dividing, by the number of weeks in the financial year, the number derived by ascertaining, in relation to each of those weeks, the number of persons who, under contracts of service, were employed in the week (whether throughout it or not) by the company, and adding up the numbers ascertained.

(3) The directors' report must in that case contain a statement describing such policy as the company has applied during the financial year—

  (a) for giving full and fair consideration to applications for employment by the company made by disabled persons, having regard to their particular aptitudes and abilities,

  (b) for continuing the employment of, and for arranging appropriate training for, employees of the company who have become disabled persons during the period when they were employed by the company, and

  (c) otherwise for the training, career development and promotion of disabled persons employed by the company.

(4) In this Part—

  (a) "employment" means employment other than employment to work wholly or mainly outside the United Kingdom, and "employed" and "employee" are to be construed accordingly; and

  (b) "disabled person" means the same as in the Disability Discrimination Act 1995.

NOTES

Commencement: 6 April 2008.

PART 4
EMPLOYEE INVOLVEMENT

[4.210]

11. (1) This Part of this Schedule applies to the directors' report where the average number of persons employed by the company in each week during the financial year exceeded 250.

(2)   That average number is the quotient derived by dividing, by the number of weeks in the financial year, the number derived by ascertaining, in relation to each of those weeks, the number of persons who, under contracts of service, were employed in the week (whether throughout it or not) by the company, and adding up the numbers ascertained.

(3)   The directors' report must in that case contain a statement describing the action that has been taken during the financial year to introduce, maintain or develop arrangements aimed at—
- (a)   providing employees systematically with information on matters of concern to them as employees,
- (b)   consulting employees or their representatives on a regular basis so that the views of employees can be taken into account in making decisions which are likely to affect their interests,
- (c)   encouraging the involvement of employees in the company's performance through an employees' share scheme or by some other means,
- (d)   achieving a common awareness on the part of all employees of the financial and economic factors affecting the performance of the company.

(4)   In sub-paragraph (3) "employee" does not include a person employed to work wholly or mainly outside the United Kingdom; and for the purposes of sub-paragraph (2) no regard is to be had to such a person.

NOTES

Commencement: 6 April 2008.

PART 5
POLICY AND PRACTICE ON PAYMENT OF CREDITORS

[4.211]
12.   (1)   This Part of this Schedule applies to the directors' report for a financial year if—
- (a)   the company was at any time within the year a public company, or
- (b)   the company did not qualify as small or medium-sized in relation to the year by virtue of section 382 or 465 of the 2006 Act and was at any time within the year a member of a group of which the parent company was a public company.

(2)   The report must state, with respect to the next following financial year—
- (a)   whether in respect of some or all of its suppliers it is the company's policy to follow any code or standard on payment practice and, if so, the name of the code or standard and the place where information about, and copies of, the code or standard can be obtained,
- (b)   whether in respect of some or all of its suppliers it is the company's policy—
  - (i)   to settle the terms of payment with those suppliers when agreeing the terms of each transaction,
  - (ii)   to ensure that those suppliers are made aware of the terms of payment, and
  - (iii) to abide by the terms of payment,
- (c)   where the company's policy is not as mentioned in paragraph (a) or (b) in respect of some or all of its suppliers, what its policy is with respect to the payment of those suppliers;

and if the company's policy is different for different suppliers or classes of suppliers, the report must identify the suppliers to which the different policies apply.

In this sub-paragraph references to the company's suppliers are references to persons who are or may become its suppliers.

(3)   The report must also state the number of days which bears to the number of days in the financial year the same proportion as X bears to Y where—

X = the aggregate of the amounts which were owed to trade creditors at the end of the year; and

Y = the aggregate of the amounts in which the company was invoiced by suppliers during the year.

(4)   For the purposes of sub-paragraphs (2) and (3) a person is a supplier of the company at any time if—
- (a)   at that time, he is owed an amount in respect of goods or services supplied, and
- (b)   that amount would be included under the heading corresponding to item E.4 (trade creditors) in format 1 if—
  - (i)   the company's accounts fell to be prepared as at that time,
  - (ii)   those accounts were prepared in accordance with Schedule 1 to these Regulations, and
  - (iii) that format were adopted.

(5)   For the purpose of sub-paragraph (3), the aggregate of the amounts which at the end of the financial year were owed to trade creditors is taken to be—
- (a)   where in the company's accounts format 1 of the balance sheet formats set out in Part 1 of Schedule 1 to these Regulations is adopted, the amount shown under the heading corresponding to item E.4 (trade creditors) in that format,

(b)   where format 2 is adopted, the amount which, under the heading corresponding to item C4 (trade creditors) in that format, is shown as falling due within one year, and

(c)   where the company's accounts are prepared in accordance with Schedule 2 or 3 to these Regulations or the company's accounts are IAS accounts, the amount which would be shown under the heading corresponding to item E.4 (trade creditors) in format 1 if the company's accounts were prepared in accordance with Schedule 1 and that format were adopted.

NOTES

Commencement: 6 April 2008.

PART 6
DISCLOSURE REQUIRED BY CERTAIN PUBLICLY-TRADED COMPANIES

[4.212]

13. (1)   This Part of this Schedule applies to the directors' report for a financial year if the company had securities carrying voting rights admitted to trading on a regulated market at the end of that year.

(2)   The report must contain detailed information, by reference to the end of that year, on the following matters—

(a)   the structure of the company's capital, including in particular—
  (i)   the rights and obligations attaching to the shares or, as the case may be, to each class of shares in the company, and
  (ii)   where there are two or more such classes, the percentage of the total share capital represented by each class;

(b)   any restrictions on the transfer of securities in the company, including in particular—
  (i)   limitations on the holding of securities, and
  (ii)   requirements to obtain the approval of the company, or of other holders of securities in the company, for a transfer of securities;

(c)   in the case of each person with a significant direct or indirect holding of securities in the company, such details as are known to the company of—
  (i)   the identity of the person,
  (ii)   the size of the holding, and
  (iii)   the nature of the holding;

(d)   in the case of each person who holds securities carrying special rights with regard to control of the company—
  (i)   the identity of the person, and
  (ii)   the nature of the rights;

(e)   where—
  (i)   the company has an employees' share scheme, and
  (ii)   shares to which the scheme relates have rights with regard to control of the company that are not exercisable directly by the employees,
  how those rights are exercisable;

(f)   any restrictions on voting rights, including in particular—
  (i)   limitations on voting rights of holders of a given percentage or number of votes,
  (ii)   deadlines for exercising voting rights, and
  (iii)   arrangements by which, with the company's co-operation, financial rights carried by securities are held by a person other than the holder of the securities;

(g)   any agreements between holders of securities that are known to the company and may result in restrictions on the transfer of securities or on voting rights;

(h)   any rules that the company has about—
  (i)   appointment and replacement of directors, or
  (ii)   amendment of the company's articles of association;

(i)   the powers of the company's directors, including in particular any powers in relation to the issuing or buying back by the company of its shares;

(j)   any significant agreements to which the company is a party that take effect, alter or terminate upon a change of control of the company following a takeover bid, and the effects of any such agreements;

(k)   any agreements between the company and its directors or employees providing for compensation for loss of office or employment (whether through resignation, purported redundancy or otherwise) that occurs because of a takeover bid.

(3)   For the purposes of sub-paragraph (2)(a) a company's capital includes any securities in the company that are not admitted to trading on a regulated market.

(4)   For the purposes of sub-paragraph (2)(c) a person has an indirect holding of securities if—
  (a)   they are held on his behalf, or
  (b)   he is able to secure that rights carried by the securities are exercised in accordance with his wishes.

(5)   Sub-paragraph (2)(j) does not apply to an agreement if—

(a)   disclosure of the agreement would be seriously prejudicial to the company, and

(b)   the company is not under any other obligation to disclose it.

(6)   In this paragraph—

"securities" means shares or debentures;

"takeover bid" has the same meaning as in the Takeovers Directive;

"the Takeovers Directive" means Directive 2004/25/EC of the European Parliament and of the Council;

"voting rights" means rights to vote at general meetings of the company in question, including rights that arise only in certain circumstances.

14.   The directors' report must also contain any necessary explanatory material with regard to information that is required to be included in the report by this Part.

NOTES
Commencement: 6 April 2008.

SCHEDULE 8
QUOTED COMPANIES: DIRECTORS' REMUNERATION REPORT
Regulation 11

PART 1
INTRODUCTORY

[4.213]
1. (1)   In the directors' remuneration report for a financial year ("the relevant financial year") there must be shown the information specified in Parts 2 and 3.

(2)   Information required to be shown in the report for or in respect of a particular person must be shown in the report in a manner that links the information to that person identified by name.

NOTES
Commencement: 6 April 2008.

PART 2
INFORMATION NOT SUBJECT TO AUDIT

Consideration by the directors of matters relating to directors' remuneration

[4.214]
2. (1)   If a committee of the company's directors has considered matters relating to the directors' remuneration for the relevant financial year, the directors' remuneration report must—

(a)   name each director who was a member of the committee at any time when the committee was considering any such matter;

(b)   name any person who provided to the committee advice, or services, that materially assisted the committee in their consideration of any such matter;

(c)   in the case of any person named under paragraph (b), who is not a director of the company, state—

(i)   the nature of any other services that that person has provided to the company during the relevant financial year; and

(ii)   whether that person was appointed by the committee.

(2)   In sub-paragraph (1)(b) "person" includes (in particular) any director of the company who does not fall within sub-paragraph (1)(a).

Statement of company's policy on directors' remuneration

3. (1)   The directors' remuneration report must contain a statement of the company's policy on directors' remuneration for the following financial year and for financial years subsequent to that.

(2)   The policy statement must include—

(a)   for each director, a detailed summary of any performance conditions to which any entitlement of the director—

(i)   to share options, or

(ii)   under a long term incentive scheme,

is subject;

(b)   an explanation as to why any such performance conditions were chosen;

(c)   a summary of the methods to be used in assessing whether any such performance conditions are met and an explanation as to why those methods were chosen;

(d)   if any such performance condition involves any comparison with factors external to the company—

(i)   a summary of the factors to be used in making each such comparison, and

(ii)   if any of the factors relates to the performance of another company, of two or more other companies or of an index on which the securities of a company or companies are listed, the identity of that company, of each of those companies or of the index;

(e)   a description of, and an explanation for, any significant amendment proposed to be made to the terms and conditions of any entitlement of a director to share options or under a long term incentive scheme; and

(f)   if any entitlement of a director to share options, or under a long term incentive scheme, is not subject to performance conditions, an explanation as to why that is the case.

(3)   The policy statement must, in respect of each director's terms and conditions relating to remuneration, explain the relative importance of those elements which are, and those which are not, related to performance.

(4)   The policy statement must summarise, and explain, the company's policy on—

   (a)   the duration of contracts with directors, and

   (b)   notice periods, and termination payments, under such contracts.

(5)   In sub-paragraphs (2) and (3), references to a director are to any person who serves as a director of the company at any time in the period beginning with the end of the relevant financial year and ending with the date on which the directors' remuneration report is laid before the company in general meeting.

Statement of consideration of conditions elsewhere in company and group

4. The directors' remuneration report must contain a statement of how pay and employment conditions of employees of the company and of other undertakings within the same group as the company were taken into account when determining directors' remuneration for the relevant financial year.

Performance graph

5. (1) The directors' remuneration report must—

   (a)   contain a line graph that shows for each of—

      (i)   a holding of shares of that class of the company's equity share capital whose listing, or admission to dealing, has resulted in the company falling within the definition of "quoted company", and

      (ii) a hypothetical holding of shares made up of shares of the same kinds and number as those by reference to which a broad equity market index is calculated,

      a line drawn by joining up points plotted to represent, for each of the financial years in the relevant period, the total shareholder return on that holding; and

   (b)   state the name of the index selected for the purposes of the graph and set out the reasons for selecting that index.

(2)   For the purposes of sub-paragraphs (1) and (4), "relevant period" means the five financial years of which the last is the relevant financial year.

(3)   Where the relevant financial year—

   (a)   is the company's second, third or fourth financial year, sub-paragraph (2) has effect with the substitution of "two", "three" or "four" (as the case may be) for "five"; and

   (b)   is the company's first financial year, "relevant period", for the purposes of sub-paragraphs (1) and (4), means the relevant financial year.

(4)   For the purposes of sub-paragraph (1), the "total shareholder return" for a relevant period on a holding of shares must be calculated using a fair method that—

   (a)   takes as its starting point the percentage change over the period in the market price of the holding;

   (b)   involves making—

      (i)   the assumptions specified in sub-paragraph (5) as to reinvestment of income, and

      (ii) the assumption specified in sub-paragraph (7) as to the funding of liabilities, and

   (c)   makes provision for any replacement of shares in the holding by shares of a different description;

and the same method must be used for each of the holdings mentioned in sub-paragraph (1).

(5)   The assumptions as to reinvestment of income are—

   (a)   that any benefit in the form of shares of the same kind as those in the holding is added to the holding at the time the benefit becomes receivable; and

   (b)   that any benefit in cash, and an amount equal to the value of any benefit not in cash and not falling within paragraph (a), is applied at the time the benefit becomes receivable in the purchase at their market price of shares of the same kind as those in the holding and that the shares purchased are added to the holding at that time.

(6)   In sub-paragraph (5) "benefit" means any benefit (including, in particular, any dividend) receivable in respect of any shares in the holding by the holder from the company of whose share capital the shares form part.

(7)   The assumption as to the funding of liabilities is that, where the holder has a liability to the company of whose capital the shares in the holding form part, shares are sold from the holding—

   (a)   immediately before the time by which the liability is due to be satisfied, and

   (b)   in such numbers that, at the time of the sale, the market price of the shares sold equals the amount of the liability in respect of the shares in the holding that are not being sold.

(8)   In sub-paragraph (7) "liability" means a liability arising in respect of any shares in the holding or from the exercise of a right attached to any of those shares.

Service contracts

6. (1)   The directors' remuneration report must contain, in respect of the contract of service or contract for services of each person who has served as a director of the company at any time during the relevant financial year, the following information—

    (a)   the date of the contract, the unexpired term and the details of any notice periods;

    (b)   any provision for compensation payable upon early termination of the contract; and

    (c)   such details of other provisions in the contract as are necessary to enable members of the company to estimate the liability of the company in the event of early termination of the contract.

(2)   The directors' remuneration report must contain an explanation for any significant award made to a person in the circumstances described in paragraph 15.

NOTES

    Commencement: 6 April 2008. Note that requirement for disclosure in para 4 of this Schedule applies in relation to financial years beginning on or after 6 April 2009 (see reg 2(3) *ante*).

PART 3
INFORMATION SUBJECT TO AUDIT

Amount of each director's emoluments and compensation in the relevant financial year

[4.215]

7. (1)   The directors' remuneration report must for the relevant financial year show, for each person who has served as a director of the company at any time during that year, each of the following—

    (a)   the total amount of salary and fees paid to or receivable by the person in respect of qualifying services;

    (b)   the total amount of bonuses so paid or receivable;

    (c)   the total amount of sums paid by way of expenses allowance that are—

        (i)   chargeable to United Kingdom income tax (or would be if the person were an individual), and

        (ii)   paid to or receivable by the person in respect of qualifying services;

    (d)   the total amount of—

        (i)   any compensation for loss of office paid to or receivable by the person, and

        (ii)   any other payments paid to or receivable by the person in connection with the termination of qualifying services;

    (e)   the total estimated value of any benefits received by the person otherwise than in cash that—

        (i)   do not fall within any of paragraphs (a) to (d) or paragraphs 8 to 12,

        (ii)   are emoluments of the person, and

        (iii)   are received by the person in respect of qualifying services; and

    (f)   the amount that is the total of the sums mentioned in paragraphs (a) to (e).

(2)   The directors' remuneration report must show, for each person who has served as a director of the company at any time during the relevant financial year, the amount that for the financial year preceding the relevant financial year is the total of the sums mentioned in paragraphs (a) to (e) of sub-paragraph (1).

(3)   The directors' remuneration report must also state the nature of any element of a remuneration package which is not cash.

(4)   The information required by sub-paragraphs (1) and (2) must be presented in tabular form.

Share options

8. (1)   The directors' remuneration report must contain, in respect of each person who has served as a director of the company at any time in the relevant financial year, the information specified in paragraph 9.

(2)   Sub-paragraph (1) is subject to paragraph 10 (aggregation of information to avoid excessively lengthy reports).

(3)   The information specified in sub-paragraphs (a) to (c) of paragraph 9 must be presented in tabular form in the report.

(4)   In paragraph 9 "share option", in relation to a person, means a share option granted in respect of qualifying services of the person.

9. The information required by sub-paragraph (1) of paragraph 8 in respect of such a person as is mentioned in that sub-paragraph is—

    (a)   the number of shares that are subject to a share option—

(i)   at the beginning of the relevant financial year or, if later, on the date of the appointment of the person as a director of the company, and

(ii)   at the end of the relevant financial year or, if earlier, on the cessation of the person's appointment as a director of the company,

in each case differentiating between share options having different terms and conditions;

(b)   information identifying those share options that have been awarded in the relevant financial year, those that have been exercised in that year, those that in that year have expired unexercised and those whose terms and conditions have been varied in that year;

(c)   for each share option that is unexpired at any time in the relevant financial year—

(i)   the price paid, if any, for its award,

(ii)   the exercise price,

(iii) the date from which the option may be exercised, and

(iv) the date on which the option expires;

(d)   a description of any variation made in the relevant financial year in the terms and conditions of a share option;

(e)   a summary of any performance criteria upon which the award or exercise of a share option is conditional, including a description of any variation made in such performance criteria during the relevant financial year;

(f)   for each share option that has been exercised during the relevant financial year, the market price of the shares, in relation to which it is exercised, at the time of exercise; and

(g)   for each share option that is unexpired at the end of the relevant financial year—

(i)   the market price at the end of that year, and

(ii)   the highest and lowest market prices during that year,

of each share that is subject to the option.

10. (1) If, in the opinion of the directors of the company, disclosure in accordance with paragraphs 8 and 9 would result in a disclosure of excessive length then, (subject to sub-paragraphs (2) and (3))—

(a)   information disclosed for a person under paragraph 9(a) need not differentiate between share options having different terms and conditions;

(b)   for the purposes of disclosure in respect of a person under paragraph 9(c)(i) and (ii) and (g), share options may be aggregated and (instead of disclosing prices for each share option) disclosure may be made of weighted average prices of aggregations of share options;

(c)   for the purposes of disclosure in respect of a person under paragraph 9(c)(iii) and (iv), share options may be aggregated and (instead of disclosing dates for each share option) disclosure may be made of ranges of dates for aggregation of share options.

(2) Sub-paragraph (1)(b) and (c) does not permit the aggregation of—

(a)   share options in respect of shares whose market price at the end of the relevant financial year is below the option exercise price, with

(b)   share options in respect of shares whose market price at the end of the relevant financial year is equal to, or exceeds, the option exercise price.

(3) Sub-paragraph (1) does not apply (and accordingly, full disclosure must be made in accordance with paragraphs 8 and 9) in respect of share options that during the relevant financial year have been awarded or exercised or had their terms and conditions varied.

Long term incentive schemes

11. (1) The directors' remuneration report must contain, in respect of each person who has served as a director of the company at any time in the relevant financial year, the information specified in paragraph 12.

(2) Sub-paragraph (1) does not require the report to contain share option details that are contained in the report in compliance with paragraphs 8 to 10.

(3) The information specified in paragraph 12 must be presented in tabular form in the report.

(4) For the purposes of paragraph 12—

(a)   "scheme interest", in relation to a person, means an interest under a long term incentive scheme that is an interest in respect of which assets may become receivable under the scheme in respect of qualifying services of the person; and

(b)   such an interest "vests" at the earliest time when—

(i)   it has been ascertained that the qualifying conditions have been fulfilled, and

(ii)   the nature and quantity of the assets receivable under the scheme in respect of the interest have been ascertained.

(5) In this Schedule "long term incentive scheme" means any agreement or arrangement under which money or other assets may become receivable by a person and which includes one or more qualifying conditions with respect to service or performance that cannot be fulfilled within a single financial year, and for this purpose the following must be disregarded, namely—

(a)   any bonus the amount of which falls to be determined by reference to service or performance within a single financial year;

(b)   compensation in respect of loss of office, payments for breach of contract and other termination payments; and

(c)   retirement benefits.

12. (1)   The information required by sub-paragraph (1) of paragraph 11 in respect of such a person as is mentioned in that sub-paragraph is—

(a)   details of the scheme interests that the person has at the beginning of the relevant financial year or if later on the date of the appointment of the person as a director of the company;

(b)   details of the scheme interests awarded to the person during the relevant financial year;

(c)   details of the scheme interests that the person has at the end of the relevant financial year or if earlier on the cessation of the person's appointment as a director of the company;

(d)   for each scheme interest within paragraphs (a) to (c)—

    (i)   the end of the period over which the qualifying conditions for that interest have to be fulfilled (or if there are different periods for different conditions, the end of whichever of those periods ends last); and

    (ii)   a description of any variation made in the terms and conditions of the scheme interests during the relevant financial year; and

(e)   for each scheme interest that has vested in the relevant financial year—

    (i)   the relevant details (see sub-paragraph (3)) of any shares,

    (ii)   the amount of any money, and

    (iii)   the value of any other assets,

that have become receivable in respect of the interest.

(2)   The details that sub-paragraph (1)(b) requires of a scheme interest awarded during the relevant financial year include, if shares may become receivable in respect of the interest, the following—

(a)   the number of those shares;

(b)   the market price of each of those shares when the scheme interest was awarded; and

(c)   details of qualifying conditions that are conditions with respect to performance.

(3)   In sub-paragraph (1)(e)(i) "the relevant details", in relation to any shares that have become receivable in respect of a scheme interest, means—

(a)   the number of those shares;

(b)   the date on which the scheme interest was awarded;

(c)   the market price of each of those shares when the scheme interest was awarded;

(d)   the market price of each of those shares when the scheme interest vested; and

(e)   details of qualifying conditions that were conditions with respect to performance.

Pensions

13. (1)   The directors' remuneration report must, for each person who has served as a director of the company at any time during the relevant financial year, contain the information in respect of pensions that is specified in sub-paragraphs (2) and (3).

(2)   Where the person has rights under a pension scheme that is a defined benefit scheme in relation to the person and any of those rights are rights to which he has become entitled in respect of qualifying services of his—

(a)   details—

    (i)   of any changes during the relevant financial year in the person's accrued benefits under the scheme, and

    (ii)   of the person's accrued benefits under the scheme as at the end of that year;

[(b)   the transfer value, calculated in accordance with regulations 7 to 7E of the Occupational Pension Schemes (Transfer Values) Regulations 1996, of the person's accrued benefits under the scheme at the end of the relevant financial year;]

(c)   the transfer value of the person's accrued benefits under the scheme that in compliance with paragraph (b) was contained in the directors' remuneration report for the previous financial year or, if there was no such report or no such value was contained in that report, the transfer value, calculated in such a manner as is mentioned in paragraph (b), of the person's accrued benefits under the scheme at the beginning of the relevant financial year;

(d)   the amount obtained by subtracting—

    (i)   the transfer value of the person's accrued benefits under the scheme that is required to be contained in the report by paragraph (c), from

    (ii)   the transfer value of those benefits that is required to be contained in the report by paragraph (b),

and then subtracting from the result of that calculation the amount of any contributions made to the scheme by the person in the relevant financial year.

(3)   Where—

(a)   the person has rights under a pension scheme that is a money purchase scheme in relation to the person, and

(b)   any of those rights are rights to which he has become entitled in respect of qualifying services of his, details of any contribution to the scheme in respect of the person that is paid or payable by the company for the relevant financial year or paid by the company in that year for another financial year.

Excess retirement benefits of directors and past directors

14. (1) Subject to sub-paragraph (3), the directors' remuneration report must show in respect of each person who has served as a director of the company—

(a) at any time during the relevant financial year, or

(b) at any time before the beginning of that year,

the amount of so much of retirement benefits paid to or receivable by the person under pension schemes as is in excess of the retirement benefits to which he was entitled on the date on which the benefits first became payable or 31st March 1997, whichever is the later.

(2) In subsection (1) "retirement benefits" means retirement benefits to which the person became entitled in respect of qualifying services of his.

(3) Amounts paid or receivable under a pension scheme need not be included in an amount required to be shown under sub-paragraph (1) if—

(a) the funding of the scheme was such that the amounts were or, as the case may be, could have been paid without recourse to additional contributions; and

(b) amounts were paid to or receivable by all pensioner members of the scheme on the same basis;

and in this sub-paragraph "pensioner member", in relation to a pension scheme, means any person who is entitled to the present payment of retirement benefits under the scheme.

(4) In this paragraph—

(a) references to retirement benefits include benefits otherwise than in cash; and

(b) in relation to so much of retirement benefits as consists of a benefit otherwise than in cash, references to their amount are to the estimated money value of the benefit,

and the nature of any such benefit must also be shown in the report.

Compensation for past directors

15. The directors' remuneration report must contain details of any significant award made in the relevant financial year to any person who was not a director of the company at the time the award was made but had previously been a director of the company, including (in particular) compensation in respect of loss of office and pensions but excluding any sums which have already been shown in the report under paragraph 7(1)(d).

Sums paid to third parties in respect of a director's services

16. (1) The directors' remuneration report must show, in respect of each person who served as a director of the company at any time during the relevant financial year, the aggregate amount of any consideration paid to or receivable by third parties for making available the services of the person—

(a) as a director of the company, or

(b) while director of the company—

(i) as director of any of its subsidiary undertakings, or

(ii) as director of any other undertaking of which he was (while director of the company) a director by virtue of the company's nomination (direct or indirect), or

(iii) otherwise in connection with the management of the affairs of the company or any such other undertaking.

(2) The reference to consideration includes benefits otherwise than in cash; and in relation to such consideration the reference to its amount is to the estimated money value of the benefit.

The nature of any such consideration must be shown in the report.

(3) The reference to third parties is to persons other than—

(a) the person himself or a person connected with him or a body corporate controlled by him, and

(b) the company or any such other undertaking as is mentioned in sub-paragraph (1)(b)(ii).

NOTES

Commencement: 6 April 2008.

Para 13: sub-para (2)(b) substituted by the Companies Act 2006 (Accounts, Reports and Audit) Regulations 2009, SI 2009/1581, reg 12(1), (3), as from 27 June 2009, in relation to financial years beginning on or after 6 April 2008 which have not ended before 27 June 2009.

PART 4
INTERPRETATION AND SUPPLEMENTARY

[4.216]

17. (1) In this Schedule—

"amount", in relation to a gain made on the exercise of a share option, means the difference between—

(a) the market price of the shares on the day on which the option was exercised; and

(b)   the price actually paid for the shares;

"company contributions", in relation to a pension scheme and a person, means any payments (including insurance premiums) made, or treated as made, to the scheme in respect of the person by anyone other than the person;

"defined benefit scheme", in relation to a person, means a pension scheme which is not a money purchase scheme in relation to the person;

"emoluments" of a person—

   (a)   includes salary, fees and bonuses, sums paid by way of expenses allowance (so far as they are chargeable to United Kingdom income tax or would be if the person were an individual), but

   (b)   does not include any of the following, namely—

      (i)   the value of any share options granted to him or the amount of any gains made on the exercise of any such options;

      (ii)   any company contributions paid, or treated as paid, in respect of him under any pension scheme or any benefits to which he is entitled under any such scheme; or

      (iii)   any money or other assets paid to or received or receivable by him under any long term incentive scheme;

"long term incentive scheme" has the meaning given by paragraph 11(5);

"money purchase benefits", in relation to a person, means retirement benefits the rate or amount of which is calculated by reference to payments made, or treated as made, by the person or by any other person in respect of that person and which are not average salary benefits;

"money purchase scheme", in relation to a person, means a pension scheme under which all of the benefits that may become payable to or in respect of the person are money purchase benefits in relation to the person;

"pension scheme" means a retirement benefits scheme within the meaning given by section 611 of the Income and Corporation Taxes Act 1988;

"qualifying services", in relation to any person, means his services as a director of the company, and his services at any time while he is a director of the company—

   (a)   as a director of an undertaking that is a subsidiary undertaking of the company at that time;

   (b)   as a director of any other undertaking of which he is a director by virtue of the company's nomination (direct or indirect); or

   (c)   otherwise in connection with the management of the affairs of the company or any such subsidiary undertaking or any such other undertaking;

"retirement benefits" means relevant benefits within the meaning given by section 612(1) of the Income and Corporation Taxes Act 1988;

"shares" means shares (whether allotted or not) in the company, or any undertaking which is a group undertaking in relation to the company, and includes a share warrant as defined by section 779(1) of the 2006 Act;

"share option" means a right to acquire shares;

"value", in relation to shares received or receivable on any day by a person who is or has been a director of the company, means the market price of the shares on that day.

(2)   In this Schedule "compensation in respect of loss of office" includes compensation received or receivable by a person for—

   (a)   loss of office as director of the company, or

   (b)   loss, while director of the company or on or in connection with his ceasing to be a director of it, of—

      (i)   any other office in connection with the management of the company's affairs, or

      (ii)   any office as director or otherwise in connection with the management of the affairs of any undertaking that, immediately before the loss, is a subsidiary undertaking of the company or an undertaking of which he is a director by virtue of the company's nomination (direct or indirect);

   (c)   compensation in consideration for, or in connection with, a person's retirement from office; and

   (d)   where such a retirement is occasioned by a breach of the person's contract with the company or with an undertaking that, immediately before the breach, is a subsidiary undertaking of the company or an undertaking of which he is a director by virtue of the company's nomination (direct or indirect)—

      (i)   payments made by way of damages for the breach; or

      (ii)   payments made by way of settlement or compromise of any claim in respect of the breach.

(3)   References in this Schedule to compensation include benefits otherwise than in cash; and in relation to such compensation references in this Schedule to its amounts are to the estimated money value of the benefit.

(4)   References in this Schedule to a person being "connected" with a director, and to a director "controlling" a body corporate, are to be construed in accordance with sections 252 to 255 of the 2006 Act.

18. (1) For the purposes of this Schedule emoluments paid or receivable or share options granted in respect of a person's accepting office as a director are to be treated as emoluments paid or receivable or share options granted in respect of his services as a director.

(2) Where a pension scheme provides for any benefits that may become payable to or in respect of a person to be whichever are the greater of—

(a) such benefits determined by or under the scheme as are money purchase benefits in relation to the person; and

(b) such retirement benefits determined by or under the scheme to be payable to or in respect of the person as are not money purchase benefits in relation to the person,

the company may assume for the purposes of this Schedule that those benefits will be money purchase benefits in relation to the person, or not, according to whichever appears more likely at the end of the relevant financial year.

(3) In determining for the purposes of this Schedule whether a pension scheme is a money purchase scheme in relation to a person or a defined benefit scheme in relation to a person, any death in service benefits provided for by the scheme are to be disregarded.

19. (1) The following applies with respect to the amounts to be shown under this Schedule.

(2) The amount in each case includes all relevant sums paid by or receivable from—

(a) the company; and

(b) the company's subsidiary undertakings; and

(c) any other person,

except sums to be accounted for to the company or any of its subsidiary undertakings or any other undertaking of which any person has been a director while director of the company, by virtue of section 219 of the 2006 Act (payment in connection with share transfer: requirement of members' approval), to past or present members of the company or any of its subsidiaries or any class of those members.

(3) Reference to amounts paid to or receivable by a person include amounts paid to or receivable by a person connected with him or a body corporate controlled by him (but not so as to require an amount to be counted twice).

20. (1) The amounts to be shown for any financial year under Part 3 of this Schedule are the sums receivable in respect of that year (whenever paid) or, in the case of sums not receivable in respect of a period, the sums paid during that year.

(2) But where—

(a) any sums are not shown in the directors' remuneration report for the relevant financial year on the ground that the person receiving them is liable to account for them as mentioned in paragraph 19(2), but the liability is thereafter wholly or partly released or is not enforced within a period of 2 years; or

(b) any sums paid by way of expenses allowance are charged to United Kingdom income tax after the end of the relevant financial year or, in the case of any such sums paid otherwise than to an individual, it does not become clear until the end of the relevant financial year that those sums would be charged to such tax were the person an individual,

those sums must, to the extent to which the liability is released or not enforced or they are charged as mentioned above (as the case may be), be shown in the first directors' remuneration report in which it is practicable to show them and must be distinguished from the amounts to be shown apart from this provision.

21. Where it is necessary to do so for the purpose of making any distinction required by the preceding paragraphs in an amount to be shown in compliance with this Part of this Schedule, the directors may apportion any payments between the matters in respect of which these have been paid or are receivable in such manner as they think appropriate.

22. The Schedule requires information to be given only so far as it is contained in the company's books and papers, available to members of the public or the company has the right to obtain it.

NOTES

Commencement: 6 April 2008.

SCHEDULE 9
INTERPRETATION OF TERM "PROVISIONS"
Regulation 12

PART 1
MEANING FOR PURPOSES OF THESE REGULATIONS
Definition of "Provisions"
[4.217]
1. (1) In these Regulations, references to provisions for depreciation or diminution in value of assets are to any amount written off by way of providing for depreciation or diminution in value of assets.

(2) Any reference in the profit and loss account formats or the notes to them set out in Schedule 1, 2 or 3 to these Regulations to the depreciation of, or amounts written off, assets of any description is to any provision for depreciation or diminution in value of assets of that description.

2. References in these Regulations to provisions for liabilities or, in the case of insurance companies, to provisions for other risks are to any amount retained as reasonably necessary for the purpose of providing for any liability the nature of which is clearly defined and which is either likely to be incurred, or certain to be incurred but uncertain as to amount or as to the date on which it will arise.

NOTES
Commencement: 6 April 2008.

PART 2
MEANING FOR PURPOSES OF PARTS 18 AND 23 OF THE 2006 ACT
Financial assistance for purchase of own shares
[4.218]
3. The specified provisions for the purposes of section 677(3)(a) of the 2006 Act (Companies Act accounts: relevant provisions for purposes of financial assistance) are provisions within paragraph 2 of this Schedule.

Redemption or purchase by private company out of capital
4. The specified provisions for the purposes of section 712(2)(b)(i) of the 2006 Act (Companies Act accounts: relevant provisions to determine available profits for redemption or purchase out of capital) are provisions of any of the kinds mentioned in paragraphs 1 and 2 of this Schedule.

Net asset restriction on public companies distributions
5. The specified provisions for the purposes of section 831(3)(a) of the 2006 Act (Companies Act accounts: net asset restriction on public company distributions) are—
(a) provisions within paragraph 2 of this Schedule, and
(b) in the case of an insurance company, any amount included under liabilities items Ba (fund for future appropriations), C (technical provisions) and D (technical provisions for linked liabilities) in a balance sheet drawn up in accordance with Schedule 3 to these Regulations.

Distributions by investment companies
6. The specified provisions for the purposes of section 832(4)(a) of the 2006 Act (Companies Act accounts: investment companies distributions) are provisions within paragraph 2 of this Schedule.

Justification of distribution by references to accounts
7. The specified provisions for the purposes of section 836(1)(b)(i) of the 2006 Act (Companies Act accounts: relevant provisions for distribution purposes)—
(a) are provisions of any of the kinds mentioned in paragraphs 1 and 2 of this Schedule, and
(b) in the case of an insurance company, any amount included under liabilities items Ba (fund for future appropriations), C (technical provisions) and D (technical provisions for linked liabilities) in a balance sheet drawn up in accordance with Schedule 3 to these Regulations.

[Realised losses
8 The specified provisions for the purposes of section 841(2)(a) of the 2006 Act (Companies Act accounts: treatment of provisions as realised losses) are provisions of any of the kinds mentioned in paragraphs 1 and 2 of this Schedule.]

NOTES
Commencement: 6 April 2008.
Para 8: added by the Companies Act 2006 (Accounts, Reports and Audit) Regulations 2009, SI 2009/1581, reg 12(1), (4), as from 27 June 2009, in relation to financial years beginning on or after 6 April 2008 which have not ended before 27 June 2009.

SCHEDULE 10
GENERAL INTERPRETATION

Regulation 13

Capitalisation

[4.219]

1. "Capitalisation", in relation to work or costs, means treating that work or those costs as a fixed asset.

Financial instruments

2. Save in Schedule 2 to these Regulations, references to "derivatives" include commodity-based contracts that give either contracting party the right to settle in cash or in some other financial instrument, except where such contracts—

(a)　were entered into for the purpose of, and continue to meet, the company's expected purchase, sale or usage requirements,

(b)　were designated for such purpose at their inception, and

(c)　are expected to be settled by delivery of the commodity (for banking companies, see the definition in paragraph 94 of Schedule 2 to these Regulations).

3. (1)　Save in Schedule 2 to these Regulations, the expressions listed in sub-paragraph (2) have the same meaning as they have in Council Directive 78/660/EEC on the annual accounts of certain types of companies and 91/674/EEC on the annual accounts and consolidated accounts of insurance undertakings (for banking companies, see the definition in paragraph 96 of Schedule 2 to these Regulations).

(2)　Those expressions are "available for sale financial asset", "business combination", "commodity-based contracts", "derivative", "equity instrument", "exchange difference", "fair value hedge accounting system", "financial fixed asset", "financial instrument", "foreign entity", "hedge accounting", "hedge accounting system", "hedged items", "hedging instrument", "held for trading purposes", "held to maturity", "monetary item", "receivables", "reliable market" and "trading portfolio".

Fixed and current assets

4. "Fixed assets" means assets of a company which are intended for use on a continuing basis in the company's activities, and "current assets" means assets not intended for such use.

Fungible assets

5. "Fungible assets" means assets of any description which are substantially indistinguishable one from another.

Historical cost accounting rules

6. References to the historical cost accounting rules are to be read in accordance with paragraph 30 of Schedule 1, paragraph 38 of Schedule 2 and paragraph 36(1) of Schedule 3 to these Regulations.

Leases

7. (1)　"Long lease" means a lease in the case of which the portion of the term for which it was granted remaining unexpired at the end of the financial year is not less than 50 years.

(2)　"Short lease" means a lease which is not a long lease.

(3)　"Lease" includes an agreement for a lease.

Listed investments

8. (1)　"Listed investment" means an investment as respects which there has been granted a listing on—

(a)　a recognised investment exchange other than an overseas investment exchange, or

(b)　a stock exchange of repute outside the United Kingdom.

(2)　"Recognised investment exchange" and "overseas investment exchange" have the meaning given in Part 18 of the Financial Services and Markets Act 2000.

Loans

9. A loan or advance (including a liability comprising a loan or advance) is treated as falling due for repayment, and an instalment of a loan or advance is treated as falling due for payment, on the earliest date on which the lender could require repayment or (as the case may be) payment, if he exercised all options and rights available to him.

Materiality

10. Amounts which in the particular context of any provision of Schedules 1, 2 or 3 to these Regulations are not material may be disregarded for the purposes of that provision.

Participating interests

11. (1)   A "participating interest" means an interest held by an undertaking in the shares of another undertaking which it holds on a long-term basis for the purpose of securing a contribution to its activities by the exercise of control or influence arising from or related to that interest.

(2)   A holding of 20% or more of the shares of the undertaking is to be presumed to be a participating interest unless the contrary is shown.

(3)   The reference in sub-paragraph (1) to an interest in shares includes—
   (a)   an interest which is convertible into an interest in shares, and
   (b)   an option to acquire shares or any such interest,
and an interest or option falls within paragraph (a) or (b) notwithstanding that the shares to which it relates are, until the conversion or the exercise of the option, unissued.

(4)   For the purposes of this regulation an interest held on behalf of an undertaking is to be treated as held by it.

(5)   In the balance sheet and profit and loss formats set out in Schedules 1, 2 and 3 to these Regulations, "participating interest" does not include an interest in a group undertaking.

(6)   For the purpose of this regulation as it applies in relation to the expression "participating interest"—
   (a)   in those formats as they apply in relation to group accounts, and
   (b)   in paragraph 19 of Schedule 6 (group accounts: undertakings to be accounted for as associated undertakings),
the references in sub-paragraphs (1) to (4) to the interest held by, and the purposes and activities of, the undertaking concerned are to be construed as references to the interest held by, and the purposes and activities of, the group (within the meaning of paragraph 1 of that Schedule).

Purchase price

12.   "Purchase price", in relation to an asset of a company or any raw materials or consumables used in the production of such an asset, includes any consideration (whether in cash or otherwise) given by the company in respect of that asset or those materials or consumables, as the case may be.

Realised profits and realised losses

13.   "Realised profits" and "realised losses" have the same meaning as in section 853(4) and (5) of the 2006 Act.

Staff costs

14. (1)   "Social security costs" means any contributions by the company to any state social security or pension scheme, fund or arrangement.

(2)   "Pension costs" includes—
   (a)   any costs incurred by the company in respect of any pension scheme established for the purpose of providing pensions for persons currently or formerly employed by the company,
   (b)   any sums set aside for the future payment of pensions directly by the company to current or former employees, and
   (c)   any pensions paid directly to such persons without having first been set aside.

(3)   Any amount stated in respect of the item "social security costs" or in respect of the item "wages and salaries" in the company's profit and loss account must be determined by reference to payments made or costs incurred in respect of all persons employed by the company during the financial year under contracts of service.

Scots land tenure

15.   In the application of these Regulations to Scotland, "land of freehold tenure" means land in respect of which the company is the owner; "land of leasehold tenure" means land of which the company is the tenant under a lease.

NOTES
   Commencement: 6 April 2008.

COMPANIES (DISCLOSURE OF AUDITOR REMUNERATION AND LIABILITY LIMITATION AGREEMENTS) REGULATIONS 2008

(SI 2008/489)

NOTES
   Made: 23 February 2008.
   Authority: Companies Act 2006, ss 494, 538, 1292(1)(a); European Communities Act 1972, s 2(2).
   Commencement: 6 April 2008.
   Amendment: as of 1 July 2011 these Regulations had not been amended.
   Application to partnerships: see the Partnerships (Accounts) Regulations 2008, SI 2008/569 at **[10.984]**.

Application to banks: see the Bank Accounts Directive (Miscellaneous Banks) Regulations 2008, SI 2008/567 (see the note at **[10.983]**).

Application to insurance undertakings: see the Insurance Accounts Directive (Miscellaneous Insurance Undertakings) Regulations 2008, SI 2008/565 (see the note at **[10.982]**).

ARRANGEMENT OF REGULATIONS

PART 1
INTRODUCTORY

PART 2
DISCLOSURE OF REMUNERATION

PART 3
LIABILITY LIMITATION AGREEMENTS

SCHEDULES

PART 1
INTRODUCTORY

[4.220]
1　Citation and commencement

These Regulations may be cited as the Companies (Disclosure of Auditor Remuneration and Liability Limitation Agreements) Regulations 2008 and come into force on 6th April 2008.

NOTES
　Commencement: 6 April 2008.

[4.221]
2　Application and revocation

(1)　Regulations 3 to 7 do not apply to the accounts of a company for any financial year beginning before 6th April 2008.

(2)　The Companies (Disclosure of Auditor Remuneration) Regulations 2005 continue to apply to the accounts of a company for any financial year beginning before 6th April 2008.

(3)　Subject to paragraph (2), the Companies (Disclosure of Auditor Remuneration) Regulations 2005 are revoked.

NOTES
　Commencement: 6 April 2008.

[4.222]
3　Interpretation

(1)　In these Regulations—
　　"the Act" means the Companies Act 2006;
　　"associated pension scheme" means, in relation to a company, a scheme for the provision of benefits for or in respect of directors or employees (or former directors or employees) of the company or any subsidiary of the company where—
　　　(a)　the benefits consist of or include any pension, lump sum, gratuity or other like benefit given or to be given on retirement or on death or in anticipation of retirement or, in connection with past service, after retirement or death; and
　　　(b)　either—
　　　　(i)　a majority of the trustees are appointed by, or by a person acting on behalf of, the company or a subsidiary of the company; or
　　　　(ii)　the company, or a subsidiary of the company, exercises a dominant influence over the appointment of the auditor (if any) of the scheme;

"parent" means a parent undertaking (as defined in section 1162 of the Act) which is a body corporate, and "parent company" is a parent which is a company;

"principal terms" has the meaning in section 536(4) of the Act;

"remuneration" includes payments in respect of expenses and benefits in kind;

"subsidiary" means a subsidiary undertaking (as defined in section 1162 of the Act) which is a body corporate, and "subsidiary company" is a subsidiary which is a company.

(2) For the purposes of these Regulations—

(a) a company is small in relation to a financial year if the small companies regime as defined in section 381 of the Act applies to it for that year;

(b) a company is medium-sized in relation to a financial year if—

(i) it qualifies as medium-sized in relation to that year under section 465 of the Act; and

(ii) it is not excluded from being medium-sized under section 467(1) of the Act;

(c) references to an associate of a company are references to—

(i) any subsidiary of that company, other than a subsidiary in respect of which severe long-term restrictions substantially hinder the exercise of the rights of the company over the assets or management of that subsidiary; and

(ii) any scheme which is an associated pension scheme in relation to that company; and

(d) a person is an associate, or a distant associate, of a company's auditor if that person is specified as such by Schedule 1 to these Regulations.

NOTES

Commencement: 6 April 2008.

PART 2
DISCLOSURE OF REMUNERATION

[4.223]
4 Disclosure of remuneration: small and medium-sized companies

(1) A note to the annual accounts of a small or medium-sized company must disclose the amount of any remuneration receivable by the company's auditor for the auditing of those accounts.

(2) Where the remuneration includes benefits in kind, the nature and estimated money-value of those benefits must also be disclosed in a note.

(3) Where more than one person has been appointed as a company's auditor in respect of the period to which the accounts relate, separate disclosure is required in respect of the remuneration of each such person.

(4) For the purposes of section 1224 of the Act, the functions of the Secretary of State under Part 42 of the Act include (without prejudice to the generality of that section) consideration of the total remuneration receivable by the auditor of a medium-sized company for the supply by the auditor to the company of each of the following types of service where that remuneration is not disclosed in a note to the company's annual accounts—

(a) assurance services other than the auditing of the company's accounts;

(b) tax advisory services;

(c) other services.

NOTES

Commencement: 6 April 2008.

[4.224]
5 Disclosure of remuneration: other companies

(1) A note to the annual accounts of a company which is not a small or medium-sized company must disclose the amount of—

(a) any remuneration receivable by the company's auditor for the auditing of those accounts; and

(b) subject to paragraph (6) and regulation 6(2), any remuneration receivable in respect of the period to which the accounts relate by—

(i) the company's auditor; or

(ii) any person who was, at any time during the period to which the accounts relate, an associate of the company's auditor,

for the supply of other services to the company or any associate of the company.

(2) Where the remuneration includes benefits in kind, the nature and estimated money-value of those benefits must also be disclosed in a note.

(3) Separate disclosure is required in respect of the auditing of the accounts in question and of each type of service specified in Schedule 2, but not in respect of each service falling within a type of service.

(4) Separate disclosure is required in respect of services supplied to the company and its subsidiaries on the one hand and to associated pension schemes on the other.

(5)   Where more than one person has been appointed as a company's auditor in respect of the period to which the accounts relate, separate disclosure is required in respect of the remuneration of each such person and his associates.

(6)   Disclosure is not required of remuneration receivable for the supply of services falling within paragraph 10 of Schedule 2 supplied by a distant associate of the company's auditor where the total remuneration receivable for all of those services supplied by that associate does not exceed either—
    (a)   £10,000, or
    (b)   1% of the total audit remuneration received by the company's auditor in the most recent financial year of the auditor which ended no later than the end of the financial year of the company to which the accounts relate.

(7)   In paragraph (6)(b)—
    (a)   "financial year of the auditor" means—
        (i)   the period of not more than 18 months in respect of which the auditor's profit and loss account is required to be made up (whether by law or by or in accordance with the auditor's constitution (if any)), or
        (ii)   failing any such requirement, the period of 12 months beginning with 1st April;
    (b)   "total audit remuneration received" means the total remuneration received for the auditing pursuant to legislation (including that of countries and territories outside the United Kingdom) of any accounts of any person.

NOTES
Commencement: 6 April 2008.

[4.225]
6   Group Accounts

(1)   Group accounts must comply with regulation 5(1)(b) as if the undertakings included in the consolidation were a single company except where the group—
    (a)   qualifies as small or medium-sized under section 383 or 466 of the Act; and
    (b)   is not an ineligible group under section 384(2) or 467(2) of the Act.

(2)   A note to the individual accounts of—
    (a)   a parent company which is required to prepare and does prepare group accounts in accordance with the Act; and
    (b)   a subsidiary company where its parent is required to prepare and does prepare group accounts in accordance with the Act and the company is included in the consolidation;
does not have to disclose the information required by regulation 5(1)(b) if the conditions in paragraph (3) are satisfied.

(3)   Those conditions are that—
    (a)   the group accounts are required to comply with paragraph (1); and
    (b)   the individual accounts state that the group accounts are so required.

NOTES
Commencement: 6 April 2008.

[4.226]
7   Duty of auditor to supply information
The auditor of a company must supply the directors of the company with such information as is necessary to enable the disclosure required by regulation 5(1)(b) or 6(1) to be made.

NOTES
Commencement: 6 April 2008.

PART 3
LIABILITY LIMITATION AGREEMENTS

[4.227]
8   Disclosure of liability limitation agreements
(1)   A company which has entered into a liability limitation agreement must disclose—
    (a)   its principal terms; and
    (b)   the date of the resolution approving the agreement or the agreement's principal terms or, in the case of a private company, the date of the resolution waiving the need for such approval,
in a note to the company's annual accounts.

(2)   The annual accounts in which the disclosure required by paragraph (1) must be made shall be those for the financial year to which the agreement relates unless the agreement was entered into too late for it to be reasonably practicable for the disclosure to be made in those accounts.

(3)   If the agreement was entered into too late for it to be reasonably practicable for the disclosure required by paragraph (1) to be made in the accounts for the financial year to which the agreement relates, the disclosure shall be made in a note to the company's next following annual accounts.

NOTES
Commencement: 6 April 2008.

SCHEDULES

SCHEDULE 1
ASSOCIATES OF A COMPANY'S AUDITOR

Regulation 3(2)(d)

[4.228]

1. Each of the following shall be regarded as an associate of a company's auditor—
   (a) any person controlled by the company's auditor or by any associate of the company's auditor (whether alone or through two or more persons acting together to secure or exercise control), but only if that control does not arise solely by virtue of the company's auditor or any associate of the company's auditor acting—
      (i) as an insolvency practitioner in relation to any person;
      (ii) in the capacity of a receiver, or a receiver or manager, of the property of a company or other body corporate; or
      (iii) as a judicial factor on the estate of any person;
   (b) any person who, or group of persons acting together which, has control of the company's auditor;
   (c) any person using a trading name which is the same as or similar to a trading name used by the company's auditor, but only if the company's auditor uses that trading name with the intention of creating the impression of a connection between the auditor and that other person;
   (d) any person who is a party to an arrangement with the company's auditor, with or without any other person, under which costs, profits, quality control, business strategy or significant professional resources are shared.

2. Where a company's auditor is a partnership, each of the following shall also be regarded as an associate of the auditor—
   (a) any other partnership which has a partner in common with the company's auditor;
   (b) any partner in the company's auditor;
   (c) any body corporate which is in the same group as a body corporate which is a partner in the company's auditor;
   (d) any body corporate which is in the same group as a body corporate which is a partner in a partnership which has a partner in common with the company's auditor;
   (e) any body corporate of which a partner in the company's auditor is a director.

3. Where a company's auditor is a body corporate (other than one which is also a partnership as defined in paragraph 5(c)), each of the following shall also be regarded as an associate of the auditor—
   (a) any other body corporate which has a director in common with the company's auditor;
   (b) any director of the company's auditor;
   (c) any body corporate which is in the same group as a body corporate which is a director of the company's auditor;
   (d) any body corporate which is in the same group as a body corporate which has a director in common with the company's auditor;
   (e) any partnership in which a director of the company's auditor is a partner;
   (f) any body corporate which is in the same group as the company's auditor;
   (g) any partnership in which any body corporate which is in the same group as the company's auditor is a partner.

4. A distant associate of a company's auditor is a person who is an associate of that auditor by reason only that that person is an associate within one or more of—
   (a) paragraph 1(a) where the person in question is controlled by a distant associate of the company's auditor but not by the auditor or by an associate who is not a distant associate;
   (b) paragraph 2(a), (d) or (e);
   (c) paragraph 3(a), (d) or (e).

5. In this Schedule—
   (a) "acting as an insolvency practitioner" shall be construed in accordance with section 388 of the Insolvency Act 1986 or Article 3 of the Insolvency (Northern Ireland) Order 1989;
   (b) "partner" includes a member of a limited liability partnership;
   (c) "partnership" includes a limited liability partnership and a partnership constituted under the law of a country or a territory outside the United Kingdom;
   (d) a reference to "a receiver, or a receiver or manager, of the property of a company or other body corporate" includes a receiver, or (as the case may be) a receiver or manager, of part only of that property;

(e)   a person able, directly or indirectly to control or materially to influence the operating and financial policy of another person shall be treated as having control of that other person; and

(f)   a body corporate is in the same group as another body corporate if it is a parent or subsidiary of that body corporate, or a subsidiary of a parent of that body corporate.

NOTES

Commencement: 6 April 2008.

SCHEDULE 2
TYPE OF SERVICE IN RESPECT OF WHICH DISCLOSURE IS TO BE MADE

Regulation 5(3)

[4.229]

1. The auditing of accounts of associates of the company pursuant to legislation (including that of countries and territories outside the United Kingdom).

2. Other services supplied pursuant to such legislation.

3. Other services relating to taxation.

4. Services relating to information technology.

5. Internal audit services.

6. Valuation and actuarial services.

7. Services relating to litigation.

8. Services relating to recruitment and remuneration.

9. Services relating to corporate finance transactions entered into or proposed to be entered into on behalf of the company or any of its associates.

10. All other services.

NOTES

Commencement: 6 April 2008.

COMPANIES (TRADING DISCLOSURES) REGULATIONS 2008

(SI 2008/495)

NOTES

Made: 23 February 2008.
Authority: Companies Act 2006, ss 82, 84, 1292(1)(a), 1294.
Commencement: 1 October 2008.
These Regulations are reproduced as amended by: the Companies (Trading Disclosures) (Amendment) Regulations 2009, SI 2009/218.

ARRANGEMENT OF REGULATIONS

[4.230]
1   Citation, commencement and interpretation

(1)   These Regulations may be cited as the Companies (Trading Disclosures) Regulations 2008 and come into force on 1st October 2008.

(2)   In these Regulations—

    (a)   "the Act" means the Companies Act 2006;

    (b)   "company record" means—

  (i)   any register, index, accounting records, agreement, memorandum, minutes or other
        document required by the Companies Acts to be kept by a company; and
  (ii) any register kept by a company of its debenture holders;
  (c) "inspection place" means any location, other than a company's registered office, at which
       a company keeps available for inspection any company record which it is required under
       the Companies Acts to keep available for inspection;
  (d) a reference to any type of document is a reference to a document of that type in hard copy,
       electronic or any other form; and
  (e) in relation to a company, a reference to "its websites" includes a reference to any part of a
       website relating to that company which that company has caused or authorised to appear.

NOTES
Commencement: 1 October 2008.

[4.231]
2   Legibility of displays and disclosures
Any display or disclosure of information required by these Regulations must be in characters that
can be read with the naked eye.

NOTES
Commencement: 1 October 2008.

[4.232]
3   Requirement to display registered name at registered office and inspection place
(1)   A company shall display its registered name at—
  (a)   its registered office; and
  (b)   any inspection place.
(2)   But paragraph (1) does not apply to any company which has at all times since its incorporation
been dormant.
[(3)   Paragraph (1) shall also not apply to the registered office or an inspection place of a company
where—
  (a)   in respect of that company, a liquidator, administrator or administrative receiver has been
        appointed; and
  (b)   the registered office or inspection place is also a place of business of that liquidator,
        administrator or administrative receiver.]

NOTES
Commencement: 1 October 2008.
Para (3): added by the Companies (Trading Disclosures) (Amendment) Regulations 2009, SI 2009/218, reg 2, as from
1 October 2009.

[4.233]
4   Requirement to display registered name at other business locations
(1)   This regulation applies to a location other than a company's registered office or any inspection
place.
(2)   A company shall display its registered name at any such location at which it carries on
business.
(3)   But paragraph (2) shall not apply to a location which is primarily used for living
accommodation.
[(4)   Paragraph (2) shall also not apply to any location at which business is carried on by a
company where—
  (a)   in respect of that company, a liquidator, administrator or administrative receiver has been
        appointed; and
  (b)   the location is also a place of business of that liquidator, administrator or administrative
        receiver.
(5)   Paragraph (2) shall also not apply to any location at which business is carried on by a
company of which every director who is an individual is a relevant director.
(6)   In this regulation—
  (a)   "administrative receiver" has the meaning given—
    (i)   in England and Wales or Scotland, by section 251 of the Insolvency Act 1986, and
    (ii) in Northern Ireland, by Article 5 of the Insolvency (Northern Ireland) Order 1989;
  (b)   "credit reference agency" has the meaning given in section 243(7) of the Act;
  (c)   "protected information" has the meaning given in section 240 of the Act; and
  (d)   "relevant director" means an individual in respect of whom the registrar is required by
        regulations made pursuant to section 243(4) of the Act to refrain from disclosing protected
        information to a credit reference agency.]

NOTES

Commencement: 1 October 2008.

Paras (4)–(6): added by the Companies (Trading Disclosures) (Amendment) Regulations 2009, SI 2009/218, reg 3, as from 1 October 2009.

[4.234]
5 Manner of display of registered name

(1) This regulation applies where a company is required to display its registered name at any office, place or location.

(2) The registered name shall be so positioned that it may be easily seen by any visitor to that office, place or location.

(3) The registered name shall be displayed continuously but where any such office, place or location is shared by six or more companies, each such company is only required to display its registered name for at least fifteen continuous seconds at least once in every three minutes.

NOTES

Commencement: 1 October 2008.

[4.235]
6 Registered name to appear in communications

(1) Every company shall disclose its registered name on—
- (a) its business letters, notices and other official publications;
- (b) its bills of exchange, promissory notes, endorsements and order forms;
- (c) cheques purporting to be signed by or on behalf of the company;
- (d) orders for money, goods or services purporting to be signed by or on behalf of the company;
- (e) its bills of parcels, invoices and other demands for payment, receipts and letters of credit;
- (f) its applications for licences to carry on a trade or activity; and
- (g) all other forms of its business correspondence and documentation.

(2) Every company shall disclose its registered name on its websites.

NOTES

Commencement: 1 October 2008.

[4.236]
7 Further particulars to appear in business letters, order forms and websites

(1) Every company shall disclose the particulars set out in paragraph (2) on—
- (a) its business letters;
- (b) its order forms; and
- (c) its websites.

(2) The particulars are—
- (a) the part of the United Kingdom in which the company is registered;
- (b) the company's registered number;
- (c) the address of the company's registered office;
- (d) in the case of a limited company exempt from the obligation to use the word "limited" as part of its registered name under [section 60 of the Act], the fact that it is a limited company;
- (e) in the case of a community interest company which is not a public company, the fact that it is a limited company; and
- (f) in the case of an investment company within the meaning of section 833 of the Act, the fact that it is such a company.

(3) If, in the case of a company having a share capital, there is a disclosure as to the amount of share capital on—
- (a) its business letters;
- (b) its order forms; or
- (c) its websites,

that disclosure must be to paid up share capital.

NOTES

Commencement: 1 October 2008.

Para (2): words in square brackets in sub-para (d) substituted by the Companies (Trading Disclosures) (Amendment) Regulations 2009, SI 2009/218, reg 4, as from 1 October 2009.

Part 4   CA 2006 SIs

[4.237]
8 Disclosure of names of directors

(1)   Where a company's business letter includes the name of any director of that company, other than in the text or as a signatory, the letter must disclose the name of every director of that company.

(2)   In paragraph (1), "name" has the following meanings—
  (a)   in the case of a director who is an individual, "name" has the meaning given in section 163(2) of the Act; and
  (b)   in the case of a director who is a body corporate or a firm that is a legal person under the law by which it is governed, "name" means corporate name or firm name.

NOTES
Commencement: 1 October 2008.

[4.238]
9 Disclosures relating to registered office and inspection place

(1)   A company shall disclose—
  (a)   the address of its registered office;
  (b)   any inspection place; and
  (c)   the type of company records which are kept at that office or place,
to any person it deals with in the course of business who makes a written request to the company for that information.

(2)   The company shall send a written response to that person within five working days of the receipt of that request.

NOTES
Commencement: 1 October 2008.

[4.239]
10 Offence

(1)   Where a company fails, without reasonable excuse, to comply with any requirement in regulations 2 to 9, an offence is committed by—
  (a)   the company; and
  (b)   every officer of the company who is in default.

(2)   A person guilty of an offence under paragraph (1) is liable on summary conviction to—
  (a)   a fine not exceeding level 3 on the standard scale; and
  (b)   for continued contravention, a daily default fine not exceeding one-tenth of level 3 on the standard scale.

(3)   For the purposes of this regulation a shadow director is to be treated as an officer of the company.

NOTES
Commencement: 1 October 2008.

11   *(Revokes the Companies (Registrar, Languages and Trading Disclosures) Regulations 2006, SI 2006/3429, reg 6, Schs 1, 2, as from 1 October 2008.)*

STATUTORY AUDITORS (DELEGATION OF FUNCTIONS ETC) ORDER 2008

(SI 2008/496)

NOTES
Made: 23 February 2008.
Authority: Companies Act 1989, s 46(4); Companies Act 2006, ss 504(1)(b)(ii), 1252(1), (4)(a), (5), (8), 1253(4), Sch 13, paras 7(3), 11(2), (3)(a). Note that s 46(4) of the 1989 At was repealed by the Companies Act 2006, s 1295, Sch 16, as from 6 April 2008 (except in so far as it related to the operation of that section with regard to functions exercised under Part II of the 1989 Act).
Commencement: see art 1 at **[4.240]**.
This Order is reproduced as amended by: the Companies Act 2006 (Transfer of Audit Working Papers to Third Countries) Regulations 2010, SI 2010/2537.

ARRANGEMENT OF ARTICLES

[4.240]
1   Citation and commencement
(1)   This Order may be cited as the Statutory Auditors (Delegation of Functions etc) Order 2008.

(2)   This article and article 2 come into force on 1st March 2008.

(3)   Articles 3, 6 and 8 come into force on 1st March 2008 for the purposes of functions in relation to appointments of auditors for financial years beginning on or after 6th April 2008.

(4)   Subject to paragraph (6), articles 4, 5, 7 and 9 to 11 come into force on 6th April 2008 for the purposes of functions in relation to appointments of auditors for financial years beginning on or after 6th April 2008.

(5)   Article 12 comes into force on 6th April 2008.

(6)   Articles 4 and 9 come into force on 29th June 2008 for the purpose of transferring the functions under sections 1242, 1243 and 1244 of, and Schedule 12 to, the Act (registered third country auditors) in relation to appointments of registered third country auditors for financial years beginning on or after 29th June 2008.

NOTES
Commencement: 1 March 2008.

[4.241]
2   Interpretation
In this Order—
"the Act" means the Companies Act 2006;
"the first designated body" means the body known as the Professional Oversight Board established under the articles of association of The Professional Oversight Board Limited;
"the second designated body" means the body known as the Professional Oversight Board established under the articles of association of The Financial Reporting Council Limited.

NOTES
Commencement: 1 March 2008.

[4.242]
3   Transfer of certain functions conferring a power to make regulations
(1)   The functions of the Secretary of State conferring a power to make regulations under—
  (a)   section 1239 of the Act (register of auditors) except for the function under subsection (1)(b) of that section,
  (b)   section 1240 of the Act (information to be made available to public), and
  (c)   paragraph 8(1)(a) of Schedule 11 to the Act (prescription of examination subjects),
are transferred to the first designated body, subject to the reservation specified in paragraph (2).

(2)   The transfer of the functions conferring a power to make regulations referred to in paragraph (1) is subject to the reservations that such regulations—
  (a)   must not come into force before 6th April 2008; and
  (b)   must not apply in relation to appointments of auditors for financial years beginning before 6th April 2008.

(3)   The transfer of the functions referred to in paragraph (1) ceases to have effect on 6th April 2008.

NOTES
Commencement: 1 March 2008 (for effect see art 1 at **[4.240]**).

[4.243]
4   Transfer of functions
(1)   All the functions of the Secretary of State under Part 42 of the Act (statutory auditors) are transferred to the second designated body, subject to—
  (a)   the exceptions specified in section 1252(4)(b) of the Act (functions not transferred by the Order);
  (b)   the exceptions specified in paragraph (2); and
  (c)   the reservations specified in paragraphs (3) and (4).

(2) The functions of the Secretary of State under—
  (a)   section 1210 of the Act (meaning of "statutory auditor"),
  (b)   section 1214 of the Act (power to specify connection between persons for purposes of independence requirement),
  (c)   section 1231 of the Act (laying report by independent supervisor of auditors general before each House of Parliament),
  (d)   section 1237(3) of the Act (provision for pending proceedings in order revoking appointment of independent supervisor),
  (e)   section 1239(1)(b) of the Act (making regulations for register of third country auditors),
  (f)   section 1241(2)(c) of the Act (exclusion of bodies corporate from definition of "traded non-Community company"),
  (g)   section 1246 of the Act (removal of third country auditors from the register of auditors),
  (h)   section 1261(3) of the Act (power to modify Part 42 of the Act (statutory auditors) for purposes of application to certain bodies), and
  (i)   section 1263 of the Act (power to amend enactments in consequence of changes affecting accountancy bodies),
are not transferred by this Order.

(3) The transfer of the functions of the Secretary of State under—
  (a)   section 1224 of the Act (power to call for information from recognised bodies etc),
  (b)   section 1239(8) of the Act (obligations relating to register enforceable by injunction etc),
  (c)   section 1244 of the Act (power to call for information from registered third country auditors),
  (d)   section 1253A of the Act (requests to EEA competent authorities), and
  (e)   section 1254 of the Act (directions to comply with international obligations),
is subject to the reservation that the functions remain exercisable concurrently by the Secretary of State.

(4) The transfer of the functions of the Secretary of State of—
  (a)   refusing to make a declaration under section 1221(1) of the Act (approval of overseas qualification) on the grounds referred to in section 1221(4) (lack of comparable treatment),
  (b)   withdrawing such a declaration under section 1221(7) of the Act on those grounds,
  (c)   refusing to comply with a request under section 1253B(1) of the Act (requests from EEA competent authorities) on the grounds referred to in section 1253B(3)(a) (prejudice to sovereignty, security or public order), and
  [(d)   refusing a request, or directing a statutory auditor to refuse a request, from a third country competent authority in a case referred to in section 1253E(7)(a) (prejudice to sovereignty, security or public order)],
is subject to the reservation that the functions are exercisable only with the consent of the Secretary of State.

NOTES

Commencement: 6 April 2008 (certain purposes); 29 June 2008 (otherwise) (for purposes and effect see art 1 at **[4.240]**).

Para (4): sub-para (d) substituted by the Companies Act 2006 (Transfer of Audit Working Papers to Third Countries) Regulations 2010, SI 2010/2537, reg 7(1), (3), as from 15 November 2010.

Note that the Companies Act 2006 (Transfer of Audit Working Papers to Third Countries) Regulations 2010, SI 2010/2537, reg 7(2) provides that the reference to the functions of the Secretary of State in para(1) above includes the functions conferred on the Secretary of State by the amendments made by those Regulations.

[4.244]
5 Appropriate audit authority
The functions of the second designated body include the receipt of notices under sections 522 and 523 of the Act (notice of auditor ceasing to hold office) (and accordingly the second designated body is the appropriate authority under section 525(1)(a)(ii) of the Act (notices concerning auditors ceasing to hold office)).

NOTES

Commencement: 6 April 2008 (for effect see art 1 at **[4.240]**).

[4.245]
6 Consultation requirement
(1) Before the first designated body or the second designated body makes any regulations in exercise of the functions transferred to it by this Order, it must, unless paragraph (2) applies—
  (a)   publish the proposed regulations in such manner as appears to the body to be best calculated to bring them to the attention of persons who may be affected by the proposed regulations;
  (b)   publish at the same time a statement that representations in respect of the proposals may be made to the body within a specified period which must not be less than 12 weeks following the date of publication of the proposed regulations; and
  (c)   have regard to any representations duly made in accordance with the statement before making the regulations.

(2) Paragraph (1) does not apply in any case in which the body considers that the delay involved in complying with that paragraph would be prejudicial to the public interest.

(3) Documents published by the first designated body or the second designated body before the date on which this article comes into force shall be treated as meeting the requirements of paragraph (1)(a) and (b) if documents published in the same way after that date would have met those requirements.

(4) For the purposes of this article, on or after 6th April 2008 any document published by the first designated body before that date shall be treated as if it had been published by the second designated body.

NOTES

Commencement: 1 March 2008 (for effect see art 1 at **[4.240]**).

[4.246]
7 Annual work programme

The second designated body must publish a work programme at least once in every calendar year.

NOTES

Commencement: 6 April 2008 (for effect see art 1 at **[4.240]**).

[4.247]
8 Requirements for recording decisions

The first designated body and the second designated body must have satisfactory arrangements for—

   (a) recording decisions made in the exercise of the functions transferred by this Order; and

   (b) the safekeeping of those records.

NOTES

Commencement: 1 March 2008 (for effect see art 1 at **[4.240]**).

[4.248]
9 Matters notified to the designated body

(1) If the second designated body requires a notification or the provision of information for the purposes of section 1223(1) or 1243(1), it must notify the Secretary of State of the requirement without undue delay.

(2) If the Secretary of State so requests, the second designated body must send to him a copy of any such notification or information received pursuant to the requirement.

NOTES

Commencement: 6 April 2008 (certain purposes); 29 June 2008 (otherwise) (for purposes and effect see art 1 at **[4.240]**).

[4.249]
10 Time limits for prosecution of offences

Section 1256(1), (2), (4) and (6) of the Act (time limits for prosecution of offences) has effect as if the references to the Secretary of State were references to the Secretary of State or the second designated body.

NOTES

Commencement: 6 April 2008 (for effect see art 1 at **[4.240]**).

[4.250]
11 Appointment of body to issue guidance on senior statutory auditors

The body known as the Auditing Practices Board established under the articles of association of The Financial Reporting Council Limited is appointed for the purposes of section 504(1)(b)(ii) of the Act (body to issue guidance on meaning of senior statutory auditor).

NOTES

Commencement: 6 April 2008 (for effect see art 1 at **[4.240]**).

[4.251]
12 Companies Act 1989 (Delegation) Order 2005

(1) . . .

(2) The Companies Act 1989 (Delegation) Order 2005 continues to apply in relation to functions relating to appointments of company auditors for any financial year beginning before 6th April 2008.

(3) Subject to paragraph (2), the Companies Act 1989 (Delegation) Order 2005 is revoked.

NOTES
Commencement: 6 April 2008.
Para (1): substitutes the Companies Act 1989 (Delegation) Order 2005, SI 2005/2337, art 2(2).

COMPANIES (LATE FILING PENALTIES) AND LIMITED LIABILITY PARTNERSHIPS (FILING PERIODS AND LATE FILING PENALTIES) REGULATIONS 2008

(SI 2008/497)

NOTES
Made: 23 February 2008.
Authority: Companies Act 1985, s 247(1), (4)(a), (d); Limited Liability Partnerships Act 2000, s 15(a); Companies Act 2006, ss 453, 1292(1)(a), (c). Note that s 247 of the 1985 Act was repealed by CA 2006, as from 6 April 2008, subject to savings in relation to financial years beginning before that date.
Commencement: 6 April 2008.
These Regulations are reproduced as amended by: the Limited Liability Partnerships (Accounts and Audit) (Application of Companies Act 2006) Regulations 2008, SI 2008/1911.

[4.252]
1 Citation, coming into force and interpretation
(1) These Regulations may be cited as the Companies (Late Filing Penalties) and Limited Liability Partnerships (Filing Periods and Late Filing Penalties) Regulations 2008.

(2) These Regulations come into force on 6th April 2008.

(3) References in these Regulations to late filing, or to a failure to comply with filing requirements, are to a failure to comply with the requirements of section 441 of the Companies Act 2006 (which apply in relation to financial years beginning on or after 6th April 2008) in relation to a company's accounts and reports before the end of the period for filing those accounts and reports.

(4) For the purposes of regulations 2 and 4, whether a company is a public company or a private company depends upon its status at the end of the financial year in question.

NOTES
Commencement: 6 April 2008.

[4.253]
2 Late filing penalties under the Companies Act 2006 as from 6th April 2008
(1) This regulation applies where the requirements of section 441 of the Companies Act 2006 are complied with before 1st February 2009.

(2) The amount of the civil penalty to which a company is liable under section 453 of the Companies Act 2006 in a case of late filing is that shown in the following table:

Length of period	Public company	Private company
Not more than 3 months	£500	£100
More than 3 months but not more than 6 months	£1,000	£250
More than 6 months	£2,000	£500

(3) The first column of the table ("length of period") refers to the length of the period between the end of the period for filing the accounts and reports in question and the day on which the requirements of section 441 are complied with.

NOTES
Commencement: 6 April 2008.

3 *(This regulation inserts the Companies Act 1985, s 242A(2A), and applies where the require-ments of s 242(1) of that Act are complied with on or after 6 April 2008. Note that s 242 of the 1985 Act was repealed by CA 2006, as from 6 April 2008, subject to savings in relation to financial years beginning before that date.)*

[4.254]
4 Late filing penalties under the Companies Act 2006 as from 1st February 2009
(1) This regulation applies where the requirements of section 441 of the Companies Act 2006 are complied with on or after 1st February 2009.

(2)   The amount of the civil penalty to which a company is liable under section 453 of the Companies Act 2006 in a case of late filing is that shown in the following table or, if there was a failure to comply with filing requirements in relation to the previous financial year of the company and that previous financial year had begun on or after 6th April 2008, double that shown in the table:

Length of period	Public company	Private company
Not more than 1 month	£750	£150
More than 1 month but not more than 3 months	£1,500	£375
More than 3 months but not more than 6 months	£3,000	£750
More than 6 months	£7,500	£1,500

(3)   The first column of the table ("length of period") refers to the length of the period between the end of the period for filing the accounts and reports in question and the day on which the requirements of section 441 are complied with.

NOTES

Commencement: 6 April 2008.

5   *(This regulation substitutes the table in sub-s (2) of the Companies Act 1985, s 242A, and applies where the requirements of s 242(1) of that Act (which continue to apply in relation to financial years beginning before 6 April 2008 and, in the case of LLPs, in relation to financial years beginning on or after that date) are complied with on or after 1 February 2009. Note that s 242A of the 1985 Act was repealed by CA 2006, as from 6 April 2008, subject to savings in relation to financial years beginning before that date.)*

[4.255]
6   Limited liability partnerships: filing periods and late filing penalties

(1)   Section 443 of the Companies Act 2006 (calculation of period allowed for filing accounts and reports) applies to limited liability partnerships with the modification in Part 1 of the Schedule to these Regulations.

(2)   Schedule 1 to the Limited Liability Partnership Regulations 2001 is amended as provided in Part 2 of the Schedule to these Regulations.

(3)   This regulation applies to accounts and auditors' reports for financial years beginning on or after 6th April 2008[, but paragraph (1) does not apply to accounts or reports for financial years beginning on or after 1st October 2008].

NOTES

Commencement: 6 April 2008.
Para (3): words in square brackets added by the Limited Liability Partnerships (Accounts and Audit) (Application of Companies Act 2006) Regulations 2008, SI 2008/1911, reg 22(2), as from 1 October 2008.

SCHEDULE
Regulation 6

PART 1
MODIFICATION OF SECTION 443 OF THE COMPANIES ACT 2006 IN ITS APPLICATION TO LIMITED LIABILITY PARTNERSHIPS

[4.256]
In subsection (1), for the words "the period for filing a company's reports and accounts" substitute "the period allowed for delivering the accounts and the auditor's report".

NOTES

Commencement: 6 April 2008.

(Part 2 of the Schedule amended the Limited Liability Partnerships Regulations 2001, SI 2001/1090, Sch 1 (which was revoked by the Limited Liability Partnerships (Accounts and Audit) (Application of Companies Act 2006) Regulations 2008, SI 2008/1911, reg 58(1)(a), as from 1 October 2008, except in relation to accounts for, and otherwise as regards, financial years beginning before that date).)

STATUTORY AUDITORS AND THIRD COUNTRY AUDITORS (AMENDMENT) REGULATIONS 2008 (NOTE)

(SI 2008/499)

[4.257]

NOTES

These Regulations were made on 26 February 2008 under the powers conferred by the European Communities Act 1972, s 2(2) and the Companies Act 2006, s 1239.

These Regulations correct errors in the Statutory Auditors and Third Country Auditors Regulations 2007, SI 2007/3494 at **[4.79]**. They come into force on 5 April 2008, ie, before the 2007 Regulations come into force.

Regulation 1(3) of the 2007 Regulations purports to bring reg 38(2)(b)–(d) into force on 29 June 2008. There is no paragraph (2)(b)–(d) of reg 38, and it is para (2)(b)–(d) of reg 40 that should have been brought into force on that date.

Regulation 7(2) of the 2007 Regulations provides that the new s 1223A of the Companies Act 2006 (as inserted by reg 7(1) of the 2007 Regulations) applies only to "EEA auditors" (ie, auditors qualified elsewhere in the European Economic Area) appointed as statutory auditors for financial years beginning on or after 6 April 2008. These Regulations revoke reg 7(2) so that s 1223A also applies to EEA auditors who have not been appointed as statutory auditors at all.

Regulation 15(1) of the 2007 Regulations inserts three new sections into the Companies Act 2006, concerning the transfer of audit working papers to countries outside the European Economic Area. Regulation 15(2) provides that one of those new sections (s 1253E) applies only to working papers for audits for financial years beginning on or after 6 April 2008. These Regulations provide that another of those new sections (s 1253D) also applies only to working papers for audits for financial years beginning on or after that date.

The opening words of reg 34(2) and (3) of the 2007 Regulations are expressed so as to make provision for information in relation to third country auditors. These Regulations limit that provision to information in relation to registered third country auditors (ie, third country auditors registered under reg 34 of the 2007 Regulations).

Regulation 36 of the 2007 Regulations incorrectly refers to application for registration as a third country auditor under reg 33. The reference should have been to application under reg 35. The error is corrected by these Regulations.

COMPANIES (DEFECTIVE ACCOUNTS AND DIRECTORS' REPORTS) (AUTHORISED PERSON) AND SUPERVISION OF ACCOUNTS AND REPORTS (PRESCRIBED BODY) ORDER 2008

(SI 2008/623)

NOTES

Made: 5 March 2008.

Authority: Companies (Audit, Investigations and Community Enterprise) Act 2004, s 14(1), (5), (8); Companies Act 2006, s 457(1), (2), (5), (6).

Commencement: 6 April 2008.

Amendment: as of 1 July 2011 this Order had not been amended.

ARRANGEMENT OF ARTICLES

[4.258]
1   Citation, commencement and interpretation

(1)   This Order may be cited as the Companies (Defective Accounts and Directors' Reports) (Authorised Person) and Supervision of Accounts and Reports (Prescribed Body) Order 2008 and comes into force on 6th April 2008.

(2)   In this Order—

"the FRRP" means the body known as the Financial Reporting Review Panel established under the articles of association of The Financial Reporting Council Limited;

"regulated market" has the meaning given by Article 4(1)(14) of Directive 2004/39/EC of the European Parliament and of the Council on markets in financial instruments;

"the transparency obligations directive" means Directive 2004/109/EC of the European Parliament and of the Council relating to the harmonisation of transparency requirements in relation to information about issuers whose securities are admitted to trading on a regulated market.

NOTES

Commencement: 6 April 2008.

[4.259]
2   Authorisation

The FRRP is hereby authorised for the purposes of section 456 of the Companies Act 2006 (application to court in respect of defective accounts or reports).

NOTES
Commencement: 6 April 2008.

[4.260]
3   Appointment in relation to issuers

(1)   The FRRP is appointed to exercise the functions mentioned in section 14(2) of the Companies (Audit, Investigations and Community Enterprise) Act 2004 in respect of any issuer of transferable securities admitted to trading on a regulated market which is—

    (a)   a body corporate incorporated or otherwise formed under the law of, or of a part of, the United Kingdom of which the United Kingdom is the home Member State for the purposes of the transparency obligations directive;

    (b)   a body corporate incorporated or otherwise formed under the law of a place outside the United Kingdom of which the United Kingdom is the home Member State for the purposes of the transparency obligations directive.

(2)   In paragraph (1), "issuer" does not include a person which is not required to comply with the reporting requirements of provisions implementing Articles 4 and 5 of the transparency obligations directive (annual financial reports and half-yearly financial reports) by virtue of—

    (a)   provisions implementing Article 8(1) of that Directive (exemptions), or

    (b)   the Transparency Obligations Directive (Disclosure and Transparency Rules) Instrument 2006 made by the Financial Services Authority under the Financial Services and Markets Act 2000 on 21st December 2006.

NOTES
Commencement: 6 April 2008.

[4.261]
4   Appointment in relation to accounts

The FRRP is appointed to exercise the functions mentioned in section 14(2) of the Companies (Audit, Investigations and Community Enterprise) Act 2004 only in respect of the periodic accounts and reports required to be produced under Articles 4 and 5 of the transparency obligations directive.

NOTES
Commencement: 6 April 2008.

[4.262]
5   Decision recording requirements

The FRRP must have satisfactory arrangements for recording decisions made in the exercise of the functions it exercises by virtue of its authorisation or appointment and for the safekeeping of those records which ought to be preserved.

NOTES
Commencement: 6 April 2008.

[4.263]
6   Revocations and transitional provisions

(1)   Subject to paragraph (2), the Companies (Defective Accounts) (Authorised Person) Order (Northern Ireland) 1991 and the Companies (Defective Accounts) (Authorised Person) Order 2005 are hereby revoked.

(2)   Any proceedings by the former body known as the Financial Reporting Review Panel under section 245B of the Companies Act 1985 or Article 253B of the Companies (Northern Ireland) Order 1986 which are pending immediately before 6th April 2008 are to continue as proceedings by the FRRP.

NOTES
Commencement: 6 April 2008.

[4.264]
7.

(1)   Articles 3 and 4 of this Order apply in respect of periodic accounts and reports relating to financial years beginning on or after 6th April 2008.

(2)   Subject to paragraphs (3) and (4), the Supervision of Accounts and Reports (Prescribed Body) Order 2007 is hereby revoked.

(3)   The Supervision of Accounts and Reports (Prescribed Body) Order 2005, which continues in operation by virtue of article 2 of the Supervision of Accounts and Reports (Prescribed Body) Order 2007, shall continue to apply in respect of periodic accounts and reports—

(a)   to which section 14(2)(a) of the Act as amended by the Companies Act 2006 applies; and

(b)   which relate to financial years beginning before 20th January 2007,

and the FRRP shall exercise the functions for the exercise of which the prescribed body had been appointed by the Supervision of Accounts and Reports (Prescribed Body) Order 2005.

(4)   The Supervision of Accounts and Reports (Prescribed Body) Order 2007 shall continue to apply in respect of periodic accounts and reports which relate to financial years beginning on or after 20th January 2007, and the FRRP shall exercise the functions for the exercise of which the prescribed body had been appointed by the Supervision of Accounts and Reports (Prescribed Body) Order 2007.

NOTES
Commencement: 6 April 2008.

ACCOUNTING STANDARDS (PRESCRIBED BODY) REGULATIONS 2008

(SI 2008/651)

NOTES
Made: 5 March 2008.
Authority: Companies Act 2006, s 464(1), (3).
Commencement: 6 April 2008.
Amendment: as of 1 July 2011 these Regulations had not been amended.

[4.265]
1   Citation and commencement

These Regulations may be cited as the Accounting Standards (Prescribed Body) Regulations 2008 and come into force on 6th April 2008.

NOTES
Commencement: 6 April 2008.

[4.266]
2   Prescribed body

The body known as the Accounting Standards Board established under the articles of association of The Financial Reporting Council Limited is hereby prescribed for the purposes of section 464 of the Companies Act 2006.

NOTES
Commencement: 6 April 2008.

[4.267]
3   Revocation

The Accounting Standards (Prescribed Body) Regulations (Northern Ireland) 1990 and the Accounting Standards (Prescribed Body) Regulations 2005 are hereby revoked.

NOTES
Commencement: 6 April 2008.

[4.268]
4   Transitional Provision

Statements of standard accounting practice which immediately before 6th April 2008 have been issued and not withdrawn by the former body known as the Accounting Standards Board for the purposes of section 256 of the Companies Act 1985 or Article 264 of the Companies (Northern Ireland) Order 1986 shall be treated on and after that date as statements of standard accounting practice issued by the Accounting Standards Board for the purposes of section 464 of the Companies Act 2006.

NOTES
Commencement: 6 April 2008.

COMPANIES (AUTHORISED MINIMUM) REGULATIONS 2008

(SI 2008/729)

NOTES
Made: 12 March 2008.
Authority: Companies Act 2006, ss 763(2), 766(1)(a), (2), 1292(1)(a), (b).
Commencement: 6 April 2008.
These Regulations are reproduced as amended by: the Companies (Authorised Minimum) Regulations 2009,
SI 2009/2425.

ARRANGEMENT OF REGULATIONS

[4.269]
1   Citation, commencement and interpretation

(1) These Regulations may be cited as the Companies (Authorised Minimum) Regulations 2008
and shall come into force on 6th April 2008.

(2) In these Regulations—
    "the 1985 Act" means the Companies Act 1985;
    "the 1986 Order" means the Companies (Northern Ireland) Order 1986;
    "the 2006 Act" means the Companies Act 2006;
    "the appropriate spot rate of exchange" is to be interpreted in accordance with regulation 4(1);
    "the certified spot rate" has the meaning given in regulation 4(3);
    "published spot rate" has the meaning given in regulation 4(2);
    "reference date" is to be interpreted in accordance with regulation 4(7) and (8);
    "relevant day" is to be interpreted in accordance with regulation 4(5) and (6); and
    "working day" means a day which is not a Saturday or Sunday, Christmas Day, Good Friday or
         any day that is a bank holiday under the Banking and Financial Dealings Act 1971 in
         England and Wales.

NOTES
Commencement: 6 April 2008.

2 *(Revoked by the Companies (Authorised Minimum) Regulations 2009, SI 2009/2425, reg 8, as
from 1 October 2009. Note that prior to its revocation, this regulation provided that for the purposes
of the definition of "the authorised minimum" in s 763(1) of the 2006 Act, the amount in euros that
is to be treated as equivalent to the sterling amount is €65,600. For transitional provisions in
relation to the revocation of this regulation, see reg 9 of the 2009 Regulations at* **[4.593]**.*)*

[4.270]
3   Application of the authorised minimum where a public company has shares denominated in more than one currency

(1) This regulation applies for either of the purposes in paragraphs (2) and (3).

(2) The first purpose is to determine whether, for the purposes of section 139 of the 1985 Act or
Article 149 of the 1986 Order, a court order under section 137 of the 1985 Act or Article 147 of the
1986 Order has the effect of bringing the nominal value of a public company's allotted share capital
below the authorised minimum.

(3) The second purpose is to determine whether, for the purposes of section 146(2)(b) of the
1985 Act or Article 156(2)(b) of the 1986 Order, the cancellation of a public company's shares
under that section or that Article will have the effect of bringing the nominal value of the
company's allotted share capital below the authorised minimum.

(4) This regulation applies only where the company has or will have allotted share capital
denominated in more than one currency, taking account (where the purpose is that in paragraph (2))
of the effect of the court order or (where the purpose is that in paragraph (3)) of the cancellation of
the shares.

(5) The nominal value of a public company's allotted share capital is to be treated as being below
the authorised minimum if—
    (a)   the sterling value is less than £50,000; and

(b)　the euro value is less than €65,600.

(6)　The "sterling value" is the sum in sterling of—
(a)　the nominal value of the company's allotted share capital denominated in sterling;
(b)　the nominal value of the company's allotted share capital denominated in euros if it were to be converted into sterling at the appropriate spot rate of exchange; and
(c)　the nominal value of the company's allotted share capital denominated in a currency other than sterling or euros if it were to be converted into sterling at the appropriate spot rate of exchange.

(7)　The "euro value" is the sum in euros of—
(a)　the nominal value of the company's allotted share capital denominated in euros;
(b)　the nominal value of the company's allotted share capital denominated in sterling if it were to be converted into euros at the appropriate spot rate of exchange; and
(c)　the nominal value of the company's allotted share capital denominated in a currency other than sterling or euros if it were to be converted into euros at the appropriate spot rate of exchange.

(8)　Regulation 4 applies to determine the appropriate spot rate of exchange.

NOTES
Commencement: 6 April 2008.

[4.271]
4　The appropriate spot rate of exchange
(1)　The appropriate spot rate of exchange for a currency conversion referred to in regulation 3(6) and (7) is the published spot rate relevant to the currency conversion in question or, where the circumstances in paragraph (4) exist, the certified spot rate relevant to that currency conversion.

(2)　The published spot rate is the middle spot exchange rate prevailing on the foreign exchange market at 4pm on the relevant day as published in respect of that day by the Financial Times.

(3)　The certified spot rate is the middle spot exchange rate prevailing on the foreign exchange market at 4pm on the relevant day and stated in a certificate obtained by the company from—
(a)　a person, nominated by the company, who under Part 4 of the Financial Services and Markets Act 2000 has permission to accept deposits; or
(b)　a firm, nominated by the company, which has permission to carry on the activity of accepting deposits in the United Kingdom by virtue of Schedule 3 to that Act.

(4)　The circumstances in this paragraph exist where—
(a)　the Financial Times has not, on or before the reference date, published an exchange rate referred to in paragraph (2) relevant to the currency conversion in question; or
(b)　the Financial Times has, on or before the reference date, published what appears to be an exchange rate referred to in paragraph (2) relevant to the currency conversion in question but the company can show that there was a publication error; or
(c)　there is no evidence of what (if any) was the rate referred to in paragraph (2) relevant to the currency conversion in question as published on or before the reference date by the Financial Times.

(5)　Where the currency conversion is relevant to the calculation of the sterling value or the euro value for the purpose in regulation 3(2), the "relevant day" is the working day which immediately preceded the working day immediately preceding the date of the court order under section 137 of the 1985 Act or Article 147 of the 1986 Order.

(6)　Where the currency conversion is relevant to the calculation of the sterling value or the euro value for the purpose in regulation 3(3), the "relevant day" is—
(a)　in a case within section 146(1)(a) or (aa) of the 1985 Act or Article 156(1)(a) or (aa) of the 1986 Order, the working day immediately preceding the date of the forfeiture or surrender; and
(b)　in a case within section 146(1)(b), (c) or (d) of the 1985 Act or Article 156(1)(b), (c) or (d) of the 1986 Order, the working day immediately preceding the date of the acquisition.

(7)　Where the currency calculation is relevant to the calculation of the sterling value or the euro value for the purpose in regulation 3(2), the "reference date" is the date of the court order under section 137 of the 1985 Act or Article 147 of the 1986 Order.

(8)　Where the currency conversion is relevant to the calculation of the sterling value or the euro value for the purpose in regulation 3(3), the "reference date" is—
(a)　in the case within section 146(1)(a) or (aa) of the 1985 Act or Article 156(1)(a) or (aa) of the 1986 Order, the fifth working day following the date of the forfeiture or surrender; and
(b)　in the case within section 146(1)(b), (c) or (d) of the 1985 Act or Article 156(1)(b), (c) or (d) of the 1986 Order, the fifth working day following the date of the acquisition.

NOTES
Commencement: 6 April 2008.

[4.272]
5   Registration of a court order confirming a capital reduction and applications by public companies for re-registration: assumptions which may be made by the registrar

(1)   This regulation applies where—
   (a)   a public company delivers to the registrar under section 138 of the 1985 Act or Article 148 of the 1986 Order a copy of an order of the court confirming a reduction of its share capital and the court has not directed the order to be registered; or
   (b)   an application is made to the registrar under section 147(3) of the 1985 Act or Article 157(3) of the 1986 Order for re-registration of a public company as a private company.

(2)   Where the circumstances in paragraph (3), (4) or (5) exist, the registrar may make (in a case within paragraph (1)(a)) the assumption in paragraph (6) or (in a case within paragraph (1)(b)) the assumption in paragraph (7).

(3)   The circumstances in this paragraph are that—
   (a)   the company has or will have (taking account, where the case is within paragraph (1)(a), of the effect of the court order or, where the case is within paragraph (1)(b), of the effect of the cancellation of shares under section 146(2)(a) of the 1985 Act or Article 156(2)(a) of the 1986 Order) allotted share capital denominated in more than one currency;
   (b)   either the Financial Times did not publish, on or before the reference date, an exchange rate referred to in regulation 4(2) relevant to converting into sterling a currency in which the company's allotted share capital is denominated or it did not publish, on or before that date, such a rate relevant to converting such a currency into euros; and
   (c)   the company has not delivered to the registrar, in respect of every such currency for which the Financial Times did not publish such an exchange rate on or before the reference date, a copy of a certificate referred to in regulation 4(3).

(4)   The circumstances in this paragraph are that—
   (a)   the company has or will have (taking account, where the case is within paragraph (1)(a), of the effect of the court order or, where the case is within paragraph (1)(b), of the effect of the cancellation of shares under section 146(2)(a) of the 1985 Act or Article 156(2)(a) of the 1986 Order) allotted share capital denominated in more than one currency;
   (b)   the Financial Times published, on or before the reference date, what appears to be an exchange rate referred to in regulation 4(2) relevant to converting into sterling or euros a currency in which the company's allotted share capital is denominated but the company can show that there was a publication error; and
   (c)   the company has not delivered to the registrar, for every currency in respect of which the company can show such a publication error, a copy of a certificate referred to in regulation 4(3).

(5)   The circumstances in this paragraph are that—
   (a)   the company has or will have (taking account, where the case is within paragraph (1)(a), of the effect of the court order or, where the case is within paragraph (1)(b), of the effect of the cancellation of shares under section 146(2)(a) of the 1985 Act or Article 156(2)(a) of the 1986 Order) allotted share capital denominated in more than one currency;
   (b)   in respect of one or more of the exchange rates referred to in regulation 4(2) relevant to converting into sterling or euros the currencies in which the company's allotted share capital is denominated there is no evidence of what (if any) was the rate published on or before the reference date by the Financial Times; and
   (c)   the company has not delivered to the registrar, for every such currency in respect of which there is no such evidence, a copy of a certificate referred to in regulation 4(3).

(6)   The registrar may (but is not required to) assume for the purposes of sections 138(1) and 139(2) of the 1985 Act or Articles 148(1) and 149(2) of the 1986 Order that the court order has the effect of bringing the nominal value of the company's allotted share capital below the authorised minimum.

(7)   The registrar may (but is not required to) assume for the purposes of section 147(4) of the 1985 Act or Article 157(4) of the 1986 Order that the effect of the cancellation of shares under section 146(2)(a) of the 1985 Act or Article 156(2)(a) of the 1986 Order is or will be that the nominal value of the company's allotted share capital is brought below the authorised minimum.

NOTES
Commencement: 6 April 2008.

[4.273]
6   Determination of exchange rates by the court in certain proceedings

(1)   This regulation applies to—
   (a)   proceedings against a public company or any officer of a public company for an offence under section 149(2) of the 1985 Act or Article 159(2) of the 1986 Order; and
   (b)   proceedings under section 757 or 758 or Part 30 of the 2006 Act.

(2) Where the circumstances in paragraph (3) exist, the court may make a determination referred to in paragraph (4) in the proceedings.

(3) The circumstances are that—

(a) in proceedings referred to in paragraph (1)(a) it is alleged that, or in proceedings referred to in paragraph (1)(b) the question arises whether, the effect of a cancellation of the company's shares under section 146(2)(a) of the 1985 Act or Article 156(2)(a) of the 1986 Order was or will be that the nominal value of the company's allotted share capital was or is brought below the authorised minimum; and

(b) as a result of that cancellation the company had (or continued to have) allotted share capital denominated in more than one currency.

(4) The court may make such determination as it thinks fit as to the exchange rate to be applied to a currency conversion referred to in regulation 3(6) and (7) where—

(a) the Financial Times did not publish, on or before the reference date, an exchange rate referred to in regulation 4(2) relevant to that currency conversion; or

(b) the Financial Times published, on or before the reference date, what appears to be an exchange rate referred to in regulation 4(2) relevant to that currency conversion but the company or officer of the company (as the case may be) can show that there was a publication error; or

(c) there is no evidence of what (if any) was the exchange rate referred to in regulation 4(2) as published on or before the reference date by the Financial Times relevant to that currency conversion,

and there has not been produced to the court in the proceedings a copy of a certificate referred to in regulation 4(3) in respect of that currency conversion.

(5) In this regulation, "the court" in relation to proceedings referred to in paragraph (1)(a) means the court of criminal jurisdiction in which the proceedings are brought.

NOTES
Commencement: 6 April 2008.

[4.274]
7 Exclusion of liability in respect of publication of spot rate
No person shall be liable to any other person as a result of—

(a) that or any other person having placed reliance for the purposes of these Regulations upon a rate published by the Financial Times; or

(b) any error in a rate published by the Financial Times which is relied upon for the purposes of these Regulations; or

(c) any act or omission as a result of which the Financial Times did not publish a rate capable of being relied upon for the purposes of these Regulations.

NOTES
Commencement: 6 April 2008.

COMPANIES ACT 2006 (CONSEQUENTIAL AMENDMENTS ETC) ORDER 2008

(SI 2008/948)

NOTES
Made: 1 April 2008.
Authority: Companies Act 2006, ss 1292, 1294, 1296.
Commencement: see art 1 at **[4.275]**.
Amendment: as of 1 July 2011 this Order (as reproduced here) had not been amended.

ARRANGEMENT OF ARTICLES

[4.275]
1 Citation
This Order may be cited as the Companies Act 2006 (Consequential Amendments etc) Order 2008.

NOTES
Commencement: 6 April 2008.

[4.276]
2 Coming into force
(1) The provisions of this Order come into force as follows.

(2) Articles 1 to 3 and 5 to 12 and Schedules 1 and 2 come into force on 6th April 2008.

(3) Article 4 and Schedules 3 and 4 come into force on 1st October 2008.

NOTES
Commencement: 6 April 2008.

[4.277]
3 Consequential amendments, repeals and revocations: 6th April 2008
(1) Schedule 1 to this Order contains amendments coming into force on 6th April 2008—
   (a) Part 1 contains amendments about eligibility for appointment as auditor and related matters;
   (b) Part 2 contains other amendments.

(2) Schedule 2 to this Order contains repeals and revocations coming into force on that date.

NOTES
Commencement: 6 April 2008.

[4.278]
4 Consequential amendments, repeals and revocations: 1st October 2008
(1) Schedule 3 to this Order contains amendments coming into force on 1st October 2008.

(2) Schedule 4 to this Order contains repeals and revocations coming into force on that date.

NOTES
Commencement: 1 October 2008.

[4.279]
5 Eligibility for appointment as statutory auditor: effect of appointing partnership
(1) Section 1216 of the Companies Act 2006 (effect of appointing partnership) applies in relation to any statutory appointment where eligibility for the appointment depends on eligibility for appointment as a statutory auditor under Part 42 of that Act.

(2) In subsection (6)(b) of that section as it applies by virtue of this article, the reference to being prohibited by virtue of section 1214(1) of that Act from acting as statutory auditor shall be read as including a reference to being prohibited or disqualified from acting, or ineligible or disqualified for appointment, on the ground of lack of independence (of any description) by virtue of any other enactment applying in relation to the appointment.

(3) For the purposes of this article a "statutory appointment" means an appointment in pursuance of an enactment authorising or requiring the making of the appointment.

(4) This article applies only where that enactment was passed or made before 6th April 2008.

NOTES
Commencement: 6 April 2008.

[4.280]
6 Provisions referred to in amendments
(1) The following provisions have effect in relation to any amendment made by this Order.

(2) Any reference to the Companies Act 2006, the provisions of that Act or any particular provision of that Act includes any provision made under that Act or, as the case may be, the provision referred to.

(3) Any provision of the Companies Act 2006 referred to in the amendment has effect for the purposes of the amendment although not yet brought into force generally.

(4) Where by virtue of any transitional provision a provision of the Companies Act 2006 has effect only—
   (a) on or after a specified date, or
   (b) in relation to matters occurring or arising on or after a specified date,
any amendment substituting or inserting a reference to that provision has effect correspondingly.

(5) Without prejudice to the generality of paragraph (4), the provisions of paragraph 35 of Schedule 4 to the Companies Act 2006 (Commencement No 5, Transitional Provisions and Savings) Order 2007 apply in any case where the effect of an amendment made by this Order is that the lawfulness of a distribution depends on Part 23 of the Companies Act 2006, or any provision of that Part, applying in relation to accounts for financial years beginning before 6th April 2008.

NOTES

Commencement: 6 April 2008.

[4.281]
7 Savings for provisions relating to execution of documents

(1) The repeal of provisions of section 36A of the Companies Act 1985 (execution of documents) does not affect the operation of that section as applied by the Foreign Companies (Execution of Documents) Regulations 1994.

(2) That section as so applied does not apply to companies registered in Northern Ireland to which section 44 of the Companies Act 2006 applies.

NOTES

Commencement: 6 April 2008.

[4.282]
8

(1) The repeal of provisions of Article 46A of the Companies (Northern Ireland) Order 1986 (execution of documents) does not affect the operation of that Article—
  (a)   in relation to a liquidator of a company, or
  (b)   as applied by the Foreign Companies (Execution of Documents) Regulations (Northern Ireland) 2003.

(2) That Article as so applied does not apply to companies registered in Great Britain to which section 44 of the Companies Act 2006 applies.

NOTES

Commencement: 6 April 2008.

[4.283]
9 Saving for accounting definitions

(1) The repeal of paragraphs 88 and 89 of Schedule 4 to the Companies Act 1985 (accounting definitions) does not affect the operation of those provisions for the purposes of section 152(2) or 172(2)(b)(i) of that Act.

(2) The repeal of paragraphs 87 and 88 of Schedule 4 to the Companies (Northern Ireland) Order 1986 (accounting definitions) does not affect the operation of those provisions for the purposes of Article 162(2) or 182(2)(b)(i) of that Order.

NOTES

Commencement: 6 April 2008.

[4.284]
10 Saving for earlier consequential amendments

The repeal of section 50 of the Companies Act 1989 or Article 52 of the Companies (Northern Ireland) Order 1990 (appointment etc of auditors: power to make consequential amendments) does not affect any amendments made by regulations under that section or Article that are in force immediately before 6th April 2008.

NOTES

Commencement: 6 April 2008.

[4.285]
11 Saving for limited liability partnerships

Nothing in this Order affects any provision of the Companies Act 1985 or the Companies (Northern Ireland) Order 1986 as applied by the Limited Liability Partnerships Regulations 2001 or the Limited Liability Partnerships Regulations (Northern Ireland) 2004 to limited liability partnerships.

NOTES

Commencement: 6 April 2008.

[4.286]
12 General saving

The amendments, revocations and repeals made by this Order do not affect the operation of section 1297 of the Companies Act 2006 (continuity of the law).

NOTES
Commencement: 6 April 2008.

SCHEDULES 1–4

(Sch 1 (Amendments Coming Into Force on 6th April 2008), Sch 2 (Repeals and Revocations Coming into Force on 6th April 2008), Sch 3 (Amendments Coming into Force on 1st October 2008), and Sch 4 (Repeals and Revocations Coming into Force on 1st October 2008) contain various amendments, repeals and revocations which, where relevant, have been incorporated at the appropriate place.)

COMPANY NAMES ADJUDICATOR RULES 2008

(SI 2008/1738)

NOTES
Made: 1 July 2008.
Authority: Companies Act 2006, s 71.
Commencement: 1 October 2008.
Amendment: as of 1 July 2011 these Regulations had not been amended.

ARRANGEMENT OF REGULATIONS

Introductory

[4.287]
1 Citation, commencement and interpretation

(1)　These Rules may be cited as the Company Names Adjudicator Rules 2008 and come into force on 1st October 2008.

(2)　In these Rules—

"the Act" means the Companies Act 2006 and references to a "section" are to a section of the Act;

"the appropriate form" means the form determined by the Chief Adjudicator in relation to a particular matter; and

"the Office" means the office of the company names adjudicator at the Intellectual Property Office, Concept House, Cardiff Road, Newport, South Wales, NP10 8QQ.

(3)　In these Rules references to the filing of any application or other document are to be construed as references to its being delivered to the adjudicator at the Office.

NOTES
Commencement: 1 October 2008.

[4.288]
2 Forms and fees

(1)   The Chief Adjudicator shall have the power to determine the form and content of any form required to be used by these Rules.

(2)   Where a form is required to be used by these Rules that form shall be accompanied by the fee, if any, specified in the Schedule in respect of that matter.

NOTES
Commencement: 1 October 2008.

Proceedings before the adjudicator

[4.289]
3 Procedure for objecting to a company's registered name

(1)   An application under section 69(2) shall—
  (a)   be made on the appropriate form;
  (b)   include a concise statement of the grounds on which the application is made;
  (c)   include an address for service in the United Kingdom; and
  (d)   be filed at the Office.

(2)   The adjudicator shall send a copy of the appropriate form to the primary respondent.

(3)   The adjudicator shall specify a period within which the primary respondent must file its defence.

(4)   The primary respondent, before the end of that period, shall file a counter-statement on the appropriate form, otherwise the adjudicator may treat it as not opposing the application and may make an order under section 73(1).

(5)   In its counter-statement the primary respondent shall—
  (a)   include an address for service in the United Kingdom;
  (b)   include a concise statement of the grounds on which it relies;
  (c)   state which of the allegations in the statement of grounds of the applicant it admits and which it denies; and
  (d)   state which of the allegations it is unable to admit or deny, but which it requires the applicant to prove.

(6)   Any member or director of the primary respondent who is joined as a respondent to the application must be joined before the end of a period specified by the adjudicator.

(7)   The adjudicator shall send a copy of the appropriate form referred to in paragraph (4) to the applicant.

NOTES
Commencement: 1 October 2008.

[4.290]
4 Evidence rounds

(1)   When the period specified under rule 3(3) has expired, the adjudicator shall specify the periods within which evidence may be filed by the parties.

(2)   All evidence must be—
  (a)   accompanied by the appropriate form, and
  (b)   copied to all other parties in the proceedings.

NOTES
Commencement: 1 October 2008.

[4.291]
5 Decision of adjudicator and hearings

(1)   Where the applicant files no evidence in support of its application the adjudicator may treat it as having withdrawn its application.

(2)   The adjudicator may strike out the application or any defence in whole or in part if it is vexatious, has no reasonable prospect of success or is otherwise misconceived.

(3)   Any party may, by filing the appropriate form, request to be heard in person before a decision is made by the adjudicator under the Act or these Rules.

(4)   Following a request under rule 5(3) the adjudicator shall decide whether a decision can be made without an oral hearing in circumstances where—
  (a)   the primary respondent files no evidence; or
  (b)   the applicant files no evidence in reply to the respondent's evidence; or

(c)   the decision will not terminate the proceedings.

(5)   Where the adjudicator decides that a decision can be made without an oral hearing the adjudicator will specify a period for the parties to submit written submissions before making a decision.

(6)   Where the adjudicator decides that a hearing is necessary he shall require the parties or their legal representatives to attend a hearing and shall give the parties at least 14 days' notice of the hearing.

(7)   When the adjudicator has made a decision on the application under section 69(2) he shall send to the parties written notice of it, stating the reasons for his decision.

(8)   The date on which the decision was sent to the parties shall be taken to be the date of the decision for the purposes of any appeal.

NOTES

Commencement: 1 October 2008.

[4.292]
6 General powers of adjudicator in relation to proceedings before him

(1)   At any stage of proceedings before him, the adjudicator may direct that the parties to the proceedings attend a case management conference or pre-hearing review.

(2)   The adjudicator may give such directions as to the management of the proceedings as he thinks fit, and in particular he may—

    (a)   direct a document to be filed or to be copied to a party to proceedings within a specified period;

    (b)   allow for the electronic filing and sending of documents;

    (c)   direct how documents filed or sent electronically are to be authenticated;

    (d)   direct that a document shall not be available for public inspection;

    (e)   require a translation of any document;

    (f)   direct that a witness be cross-examined;

    (g)   consolidate proceedings;

    (h)   direct that proceedings are to be heard by more than one adjudicator;

    (i)   direct that part of any proceedings be dealt with as separate proceedings; or

    (j)   suspend or stay proceedings.

(3)   The adjudicator may control the evidence by giving directions as to—

    (a)   the issues on which he requires evidence;

    (b)   the nature of the evidence which he requires to decide those issues; and

    (c)   the way in which the evidence is to be placed before him,

and the adjudicator may use his power under this paragraph to exclude evidence which would otherwise be admissible.

NOTES

Commencement: 1 October 2008.

[4.293]
7 Requests for extensions of time

(1)   The adjudicator may extend (or further extend) any period which has been specified under any provision of these Rules even if the period has expired.

(2)   Any party can request an extension of any time period specified under any provision of these Rules.

(3)   Any request for a retrospective extension must be filed before the end of the period of 2 months beginning with the date the time period in question expired.

(4)   Any request made under paragraph (2) shall be made on the appropriate form and shall include reasons why the extra time is required. A request for a retrospective extension shall also include reasons why the request is being made out of time.

NOTES

Commencement: 1 October 2008.

[4.294]
8 Public proceedings

(1)   Subject to paragraphs (3) and (4), any hearing before the adjudicator of proceedings relating to an application under section 69(2) shall be held in public.

(2)   Any party to the proceedings may apply to the adjudicator for the hearing to be held in private.

(3)   The adjudicator shall only grant an application under paragraph (2) where—

    (a)   it is in the interests of justice for the hearing to be in held in private; and

    (b)   all the parties to the proceedings have had an opportunity to be heard on the matter,

and where the application is granted the hearing shall be held in private.

(4) Any hearing of an application under paragraph (2) shall be held in private.

(5) In this rule a reference to a hearing includes any part of a hearing.

(6) Nothing in this rule shall prevent a member of the Administrative Justice and Tribunals Council or of its Scottish Committee from attending a hearing.

(7) All documents connected to proceedings shall be available for public inspection unless the adjudicator directs otherwise.

NOTES
Commencement: 1 October 2008.

[4.295]
9 Evidence in proceedings before the adjudicator

(1) Subject to rule 6(3), evidence filed under these Rules may be given—
  (a) by witness statement, affidavit or statutory declaration; or
  (b) in any other form which would be admissible as evidence in proceedings before the court,
and a witness statement may only be given in evidence if it includes a statement of truth.

(2) For the purposes of these Rules, a statement of truth—
  (a) means a statement that the person making the statement believes that the facts stated in a particular document are true; and
  (b) shall be dated and signed by the maker of the statement.

(3) In these Rules, a witness statement is a written statement signed by a person that contains the evidence which that person would be allowed to give orally.

NOTES
Commencement: 1 October 2008.

[4.296]
10 Correction of irregularities of procedure

(1) Any irregularity in procedure may be rectified on such terms as the adjudicator may direct.

(2) Where rectification includes the amendment of a document by the adjudicator the parties will be given notice of this amendment.

NOTES
Commencement: 1 October 2008.

Costs or expenses

[4.297]
11 Costs or expenses of proceedings

The adjudicator may, at any stage in any proceedings before him under the Act, award to any party by order such costs (in Scotland, expenses) as he considers reasonable, and direct how and by what parties they are to be paid.

NOTES
Commencement: 1 October 2008.

[4.298]
12 Security for costs or expenses

An application for security for costs (in Scotland, caution for expenses) shall be made on the appropriate form. The adjudicator may require a person to give security for costs (in Scotland, caution for expenses) if he is satisfied, having regard to all the circumstances of the case, that it is just to require such security or caution.

NOTES
Commencement: 1 October 2008.

Address for service

[4.299]
13 Address for service

(1) Where a person has provided an address for service in the United Kingdom under rule 3 he may substitute a new address for service in the United Kingdom by notifying the adjudicator on the appropriate form.

(2) Where the primary respondent has a registered office in the United Kingdom the adjudicator may treat this as the address for service in the United Kingdom unless and until an alternative address is provided.

NOTES
Commencement: 1 October 2008.

Miscellaneous

[4.300]
14 Hours of business

(1)   For the transaction of relevant business by the public under the Act the Office shall be open—
  (a)   on Monday to Friday between 9.00 am and midnight; and
  (b)   on Saturday between 9.00 am and 1.00 pm,
unless the day is an excluded day (see rule 15).

(2)   For the transaction of all other business by the public under the Act the Office shall be open on Monday to Friday between 9.00 am and 5.00 pm unless the day is an excluded day (see rule 15).

(3)   In this rule and in rule 15 "relevant business" means the filing of any application or other document.

NOTES
Commencement: 1 October 2008.

[4.301]
15 Excluded days

(1)   The following shall be excluded days for the transaction of any business by the public under the Act—
  (a)   a Sunday;
  (b)   Good Friday;
  (c)   Christmas Day;
  (d)   a day which is specified or proclaimed to be a bank holiday by or under section 1 of the Banking and Financial Dealings Act 1971; or
  (e)   a Saturday where the previous Friday and the following Monday are both excluded days.

(2)   Any application or document received on an excluded day shall be treated as having been filed on the next day on which the Office is open for relevant business.

(3)   Where any period for filing any document ends on an excluded day that period shall be extended to the next day on which the Office is open for relevant business.

NOTES
Commencement: 1 October 2008.

SCHEDULE
FEES

[4.302]

Form	Fee (£)
Form required by rule 3(1)	400
Form required by rule 3(4)	150
Form required by rule 4(2)	150
Form required by rule 5(3)	100
Form required by rule 7(4)	100
Form required by rule 12	150

NOTES
Commencement: 1 October 2008.

COMPANIES (REDUCTION OF SHARE CAPITAL) ORDER 2008

(SI 2008/1915)

NOTES
Made: 17 July 2008.
Authority: Companies Act 2006, ss 643(3), 654, 1167.
Commencement: 1 October 2008.
Amendment: as of 1 July 2011, this Order had not been amended.

[4.303]
1

(1)   This Order may be cited as the Companies (Reduction of Share Capital) Order 2008 and comes into force on 1st October 2008.

(2)   In this Order, "the Act" means the Companies Act 2006.

NOTES
Commencement: 1 October 2008.

[4.304]

2

A solvency statement under section 643 of the Act must—
- (a)   be in writing,
- (b)   indicate that it is a solvency statement for the purposes of section 642 of the Act, and
- (c)   be signed by each of the directors.

NOTES
Commencement: 1 October 2008.

[4.305]

3

(1)   If an unlimited company reduces its share capital—
- (a)   the prohibition in section 654(1) of the Act does not apply, and
- (b)   a reserve arising from the reduction is to be treated for the purposes of Part 23 of the Act as a realised profit.

(2)   If a private company limited by shares reduces its share capital and the reduction is supported by a solvency statement but has not been the subject of an application to the court for an order confirming it—
- (a)   the prohibition in section 654(1) of the Act does not apply, and
- (b)   a reserve arising from the reduction is to be treated for the purposes of Part 23 of the Act as a realised profit.

(3)   If a limited company having a share capital reduces its share capital and the reduction is confirmed by order of the court—
- (a)   the prohibition in section 654(1) of the Act does not apply, and
- (b)   a reserve arising from the reduction is to be treated for the purposes of Part 23 of the Act as a realised profit unless the court orders otherwise under section 648(1) of the Act.

(4)   This article is without prejudice to any contrary provision of—
- (a)   an order of, or undertaking given to, the court,
- (b)   the resolution for, or any other resolution relevant to, the reduction of share capital, or
- (c)   the company's memorandum or articles of association.

NOTES
Commencement: 1 October 2008.

STATUTORY AUDITORS AND THIRD COUNTRY AUDITORS (AMENDMENT) (NO 2) REGULATIONS 2008

(SI 2008/2639)

NOTES
Made: 6 October 2008.
Authority: Companies Act 2006, ss 1239(1)(b), (2), (5)(d), 1246(1), 1292(1)(c).
Commencement: 31 October 2008 (see reg 1 at **[4.306]**).
Amendment: as of 1 July 2011, these Regulations had not been amended.

[4.306]

1

These Regulations may be cited as the Statutory Auditors and Third Country Auditors (Amendment) (No 2) Regulations 2008 and come into force on 31st October 2008.

NOTES
Commencement: 31 October 2008.

2   *(Substitutes the Statutory Auditors and Third Country Auditors Regulations 2007, SI 2007/3494, reg 29 at* **[4.80]***, and amends regs 35, 39, 40 of those Regulations at* **[4.82]**, **[4.86]**, **[4.87]**.*)*

[4.307]

3

If—
- (a)   before 31st October 2008 an exempt third country auditor, with a view to being registered in accordance with Article 1.2 of Commission Decision 2008/627/EC of 29 July 2008

concerning a transitional period for audit activities of certain third country auditors and audit entities, has provided to the designated body information falling within subparagraphs (a) to (d) and the first sentence of subparagraph (e) of Article 1.1 of that Decision, and

(b)   that information satisfies the requirements of regulation 35 of the Statutory Auditors and Third Country Auditors Regulations 2007 as it applies to that auditor,

the designated body may register the auditor under regulation 37 of those Regulations as if the auditor had made an application in accordance with regulation 35.".

NOTES
Commencement: 31 October 2008.

COMPANIES (PARTICULARS OF COMPANY CHARGES) REGULATIONS 2008

(SI 2008/2996)

NOTES
Made: 17 November 2008.
Authority: Companies Act 2006, ss 860, 862, 878, 880, 1167.
Commencement: 1 October 2009.
Amendment: as of 1 July 2011, these Regulations had not been amended.

[4.308]
1   Citation, commencement and interpretation
(1) These Regulations may be cited as the Companies (Particulars of Company Charges) Regulations 2008 and come into force on 1st October 2009.

(2) In these Regulations "the Act" means the Companies Act 2006.

NOTES
Commencement: 1 October 2009.

[4.309]
2   Prescribed particulars of charges created by a company
The prescribed particulars for the purposes of section 860(1) of the Act are—
(a)   the date of the creation of the charge;
(b)   a description of the instrument (if any) creating or evidencing the charge;
(c)   the amount secured by the charge;
(d)   the name and address of the person entitled to the charge; and
(e)   short particulars of the property charged.

NOTES
Commencement: 1 October 2009.

[4.310]
3
The prescribed particulars for the purposes of section 878(1) of the Act are—
(a)   the particulars prescribed by regulation 2; and
(b)   in the case of a floating charge, a statement as to any provisions of the charge and of any instrument relating to it which prohibit or restrict or regulate the power of the company to grant further securities ranking in priority to, or pari passu with, the floating charge, or which vary or otherwise regulate the order of ranking of the floating charge in relation to subsisting securities.

NOTES
Commencement: 1 October 2009.

[4.311]
4   Prescribed particulars of charges existing on property acquired
The prescribed particulars for the purposes of sections 862(2) and 880(2) of the Act are—
(a)   the particulars prescribed by regulation 2; and
(b)   the date of the acquisition of the property which is subject to the charge.

NOTES
Commencement: 1 October 2009.

COMPANIES ACT 2006 (ANNUAL RETURN AND SERVICE ADDRESSES) REGULATIONS 2008

(SI 2008/3000)

NOTES
Made: 18 November 2008.
Authority: Companies Act 2006, ss 857, 1141, 1167, 1292(1).
Commencement: 1 October 2009.
These Regulations are reproduced as amended by: the Companies Act 2006 (Annual Returns) Regulations 2011, SI 2011/1487.

ARRANGEMENT OF REGULATIONS

PART 1
INTRODUCTION

[4.312]
1   Citation, commencement and application

(1)   These Regulations may be cited as the Companies Act 2006 (Annual Return and Service Addresses) Regulations 2008 and come into force on 1st October 2009.

(2)   Part 2 applies in relation to annual returns made up to 1st October 2009 or a later date.

NOTES
Commencement: 1 October 2009.

2–4   *(Reg 2 amends the Companies Act 2006, s 855(1) at* **[1.855]** *and inserts s 855A at* **[1.855A]**; *regs 3 and 4 also amend s 855 of the 2006 Act.)*

[4.313]
5   Classification scheme for company type

(1)   The classification scheme set out in the table in Schedule 1 is prescribed for the purposes of section 855(2) of the Companies Act 2006.

(2)   The annual return must indicate the type of company to which the return relates as set out in column 1 of that table by reference to the code opposite that type in column 2.

NOTES
Commencement: 1 October 2009.

[4.314]
6   Classification system for company's principal business activities

(1)   The Standard Industrial Classification *2003* is prescribed for the purposes of section 855(3) of the Companies Act 2006, with the addition of the codes and designations in the table in Schedule 2, where the code set out in column 1 of the table represents the designation opposite it in column 2 of the table.

(2)   *In paragraph (1), "Standard Industrial Classification 2003" means the UK Standard Industrial Classification of Economic Activities 2003, prepared by the Office for National Statistics and published by The Stationery Office with ISBN number 0116216417.*

NOTES
Commencement: 1 October 2009.

For the number in italics in para (1) there is substituted the number "2007", and para (2) is substituted (as follows) by the Companies Act 2006 (Annual Returns) Regulations 2011, SI 2011/1487, reg 6(1), as from 1 October 2011 (in relation to annual returns made up to that date or a later date)—

"(2)   In paragraph (1), "Standard Industrial Classification 2007" means the UK Standard Industrial Classification of Economic Activities 2007, prepared by the Office for National Statistics and published by Palgrave Macmillan with the permission of the Office of Public Sector Information (OPSI) with ISBN number 978-0-230-21012-7.".

7–9   *(Reg 7 amends the Companies Act 2006, s 856 at* **[1.856]**, *and inserts ss 856A, 856B of the 2006 Act at* **[1.856A]**, **[1.856B]**; *reg 8 amends s 858 of the 2006 Act at* **[1.858]**, *and repeals s 859; reg 9 amends Sch 8 to the 2006 Act at* **[1.1318]**.*)*

PART 3
SERVICE ADDRESSES

[4.315]
10   Service addresses

For the purposes of section 1141 of the Companies Act 2006 (conditions with which a service address must comply) the conditions are that the service address must be a place where—

  (a)   the service of documents can be effected by physical delivery; and

  (b)   the delivery of documents is capable of being recorded by the obtaining of an acknowledgement of delivery.

NOTES

Commencement: 1 October 2009.

SCHEDULES

SCHEDULE 1
CLASSIFICATION SCHEME FOR TYPE OF COMPANY

Regulation 5
[4.316]

Column 1: Type of company	Column 2: Code
Public limited company	T1
Private company limited by shares	T2
Private company limited by guarantee	T3
Private company limited by shares exempt under section 60 of the Companies Act 2006	T4
Private company limited by guarantee exempt under section 60 of the Companies Act 2006	T5
Private unlimited company with share capital	T6
Private unlimited company without share capital	T7

NOTES

Commencement: 1 October 2009.

SCHEDULE 2
ADDITIONAL CODES AND DESIGNATIONS

Regulation 6
[4.317]

Column 1: Codes	Column 2: Designations
7499	Non-trading company
9800	Residents' property management company
9999	Dormant company

NOTES

Commencement: 1 October 2009.

For the numbers in italics in Column 1 there are substituted the numbers "74990", "98000", and "99999" respectively by the Companies Act 2006 (Annual Returns) Regulations 2011, SI 2011/1487, reg 6(2), as from 1 October 2011 (in relation to annual returns made up to that date or a later date).

COMPANIES (COMPANY RECORDS) REGULATIONS 2008

(SI 2008/3006)

NOTES
Made: 19 November 2008.
Authority: Companies Act 2006, ss 1136, 1137, 1292(1).
Commencement: 1 October 2009.
Amendment: as of 1 July 2011, these Regulations had not been amended.

ARRANGEMENT OF REGULATIONS

PART 1
INTRODUCTORY

[4.318]
1   Citation, commencement, application and interpretation

(1)   These Regulations may be cited as the Companies (Company Records) Regulations 2008 and come into force on 1st October 2009.

(2)   Part 4 applies to any request made on or after 1st October 2009 to be provided with a copy of a company record.

(3)   In these Regulations "the Act" means the Companies Act 2006.

NOTES
Commencement: 1 October 2009.

[4.319]
2   Revocations and saving

(1)   The following Regulations are revoked subject to paragraph (2)—
   (a)   the Companies (Inspection and Copying of Registers, Indices and Documents) Regulations 1991 ("the 1991 Regulations"); and
   (b)   the Companies (Inspection and Copying of Registers, Indices and Documents) Regulations (Northern Ireland) 1993 ("the 1993 Regulations").

(2)   The 1991 Regulations and the 1993 Regulations continue to apply to any request made before 1st October 2009 to be provided with a copy of a company record.

NOTES
Commencement: 1 October 2009.

PART 2
ALTERNATIVE INSPECTION LOCATION

[4.320]
3   Single alternative inspection location

The specified place in respect of the relevant provisions listed in section 1136(2) of the Act—
   (a)   is a place that is situated in the part of the United Kingdom in which the company is registered;

(b)   must be the same place for all the relevant provisions; and

(c)   must have been notified to the registrar as being the company's alternative inspection location.

NOTES
Commencement: 1 October 2009.

PART 3
INSPECTION OF COMPANY RECORDS

[4.321]
4   Inspection: private company

(1)   A private company shall make its company records available for inspection by a person on a day which has been specified by that person ("the specified day") provided that—

(a)   the specified day is a working day; and

(b)   that person gives the company the required notice of the specified day.

(2)   The required notice is at least 2 working days' notice of the specified day if the notice is given—

(a)   during the period of notice for a general meeting or a class meeting; or

(b)   where the company circulates a written resolution, during the period provided for in section 297(1) of the Act,

provided that the notice given both begins and ends during the period referred to in sub-paragraph (a) or (b) (as the case may be).

(3)   In all other cases the required notice is at least 10 working days' notice of the specified day.

(4)   When the person gives notice of the specified day he shall also give notice of the time on that day at which he wishes to start the inspection (which shall be any time between 9 am and 3 pm) and the company shall make its company records available for inspection by that person for a period of at least 2 hours beginning with that time.

NOTES
Commencement: 1 October 2009.

[4.322]
5   Inspection: public company

A public company shall make its company records available for inspection for at least 2 hours between 9 am and 5 pm on each working day.

NOTES
Commencement: 1 October 2009.

[4.323]
6   Inspection: general

(1)   A company is not required for the purposes of inspection of a company record to present information in that record in a different order, structure or form from that set out in that record.

(2)   A company shall permit a person to make a copy of the whole or any part of a company record in the course of inspection at—

(a)   the location at which the record is made available for inspection; and

(b)   any time during which the record is made available for inspection,

but a company is not required to assist that person in making his copy of that record.

NOTES
Commencement: 1 October 2009.

PART 4
PROVISION OF COPIES OF COMPANY RECORDS

[4.324]
7   Right to hard copy

Where a company is requested to provide a copy of a company record in hard copy form, the company shall provide that copy in hard copy form.

NOTES
Commencement: 1 October 2009.

[4.325]
8   Copy in electronic form

(1)   Where a person requests a company to provide a copy of a company record in electronic form, the company shall provide that copy in such electronic form as the company shall decide.

(2)   But where a company keeps a company record in hard copy form only, it is not required to provide a copy of that record in electronic form.

(3)   Where a company provides a copy of a company record in electronic form to a member of the company or to a holder of the company's debentures, the company is not required to provide a hard copy of that record in accordance with section 1145 of the Act.

NOTES
   Commencement: 1 October 2009.

[4.326]
9   Re-ordering of information in copy of record
A company is not required to present information in a copy of a company record that it provides in a different order, structure or form from that set out in the record.

NOTES
   Commencement: 1 October 2009.

COMPANIES (FEES FOR INSPECTION OF COMPANY RECORDS) REGULATIONS 2008

(SI 2008/3007)

NOTES
   Made: 19 November 2008.
   Authority: CA 2006, ss 162(5)(b), 275(5)(b), 877(4)(b), 892(4)(b), 1137(4), 1167, 1292(1)(c).
   Commencement: 1 October 2009.
   As of 1 July 2011, these Regulations had not been amended.

[4.327]
1   Citation, commencement and application
(1)   These Regulations may be cited as the Companies (Fees for Inspection of Company Records) Regulations 2008 and come into force on 1st October 2009.

(2)   These Regulations apply where a person inspects a register or instrument referred to in regulation 2 on or after 1st October 2009 regardless of the date on which the request to inspect that register or instrument was made.

NOTES
   Commencement: 1 October 2009.

[4.328]
2   Fee for inspection of company records
For the purposes of the following provisions of the Companies Act 2006—
   (a)   section 162(5)(b) (register of directors);
   (b)   section 275(5)(b) (register of secretaries);
   (c)   section 877(4)(b) (instruments creating charges and register of charges: England and Wales and Northern Ireland); and
   (d)   section 892(4)(b) (instruments creating charges and register of charges: Scotland),
the fee prescribed is £3.50 for each hour or part thereof during which the right of inspection is exercised.

NOTES
   Commencement: 1 October 2009.

COMPANIES (REGISTRATION) REGULATIONS 2008

(SI 2008/3014)

NOTES
   Made: 20 November 2008.
   Authority: Companies Act 2006, ss 8(2), 10(3), 11(2), 103(2)(a), 110(2)(a), 1167, 1292(1)(a).
   Commencement: 1 October 2009.
   Amendment: as of 1 July 2011, these Regulations had not been amended.

ARRANGEMENT OF REGULATIONS

[4.329]
1   Citation, commencement and interpretation

(1)   These Regulations may be cited as the Companies (Registration) Regulations 2008 and come into force on 1st October 2009.

(2)   In these Regulations "the Act" means the Companies Act 2006.

NOTES

Commencement: 1 October 2009.

[4.330]
2   Memorandum of association

For the purposes of section 8 of the Act—

(a)   the memorandum of association of a company having a share capital shall be in the form set out in Schedule 1; and

(b)   the memorandum of association of a company not having a share capital shall be in the form set out in Schedule 2.

NOTES

Commencement: 1 October 2009.

[4.331]
3   Statement of capital and initial shareholdings

For the purposes of section 10(3) of the Act, the statement of capital and initial shareholdings shall contain the name and address of each subscriber to the memorandum of association.

NOTES

Commencement: 1 October 2009.

[4.332]
4   Statement of guarantee

For the purposes of section 11(2) of the Act, the statement of guarantee shall contain the name and address of each subscriber to the memorandum of association.

NOTES

Commencement: 1 October 2009.

[4.333]
5   Form of assent for re-registration of private limited company as unlimited

The form set out in Schedule 3 is the form prescribed for the purposes of section 103(2)(a) of the Act.

NOTES

Commencement: 1 October 2009.

[4.334]
6   Form of assent for re-registration of public company as private and unlimited

The form set out in Schedule 4 is the form prescribed for the purposes of section 110(2)(a) of the Act.

NOTES

Commencement: 1 October 2009.

SCHEDULES

SCHEDULE 1
COMPANY HAVING A SHARE CAPITAL

Regulation 2(a)

[4.335]

Memorandum of association of [*insert name of company*]	
Each subscriber to this memorandum of association wishes to form a company under the Companies Act 2006 and agrees to become a member of the company and to take at least one share.	
Name of each subscriber	*Authentication by each subscriber*
Dated	

NOTES

Commencement: 1 October 2009.

SCHEDULE 2
COMPANY NOT HAVING A SHARE CAPITAL

Regulation 2(b)

[4.336]

Memorandum of association of [*insert name of company*]	
Each subscriber to this memorandum of association wishes to form a company under the Companies Act 2006 and agrees to become a member of the company.	
Name of each subscriber	*Authentication by each subscriber*
Dated	

NOTES

Commencement: 1 October 2009.

SCHEDULES 3 AND 4

(Sch 3 (as introduced by reg 5) sets out the form of assent for re-registration of private limited company as unlimited; Sch 4 (as introduced by reg 6) sets out the form of assent for re-registration of public company as private and unlimited; neither form is reproduced in this work but both are available at: http://www.legislation.gov.uk/.*)*

COMPANIES ACT 2006 (EXTENSION OF TAKEOVER PANEL PROVISIONS) (ISLE OF MAN) ORDER 2008

(SI 2008/3122)

NOTES

Made: 10 December 2008.

Authority: Companies Act 2006, s 965.

Commencement: 1 March 2009.

This Order is reproduced as amended by: the Companies Act 2006 (Extension of Takeover Panel Provisions) (Isle of Man) Order 2009, SI 2009/1378.

References to the "European Community", "Community", etc: see the Treaty of Lisbon (Changes in Terminology) Order 2011, SI 2011/1043, which provides (with effect from 22 April 2011): (1) that for references to the "European Communities" or to the "European Community" (including references to "the Communities", "the Community", "the EC" or "the EEC") substitute references to the European Union; and (2) that "EU" should be substituted for the word "Community" (subject to certain exceptions) in references to "Community treaties", "Community customs duty", "Community institution", "Community instrument", "Community obligation", "enforceable Community right", "Community law", "Community legislation", and "Community provision". Also, where such a term is preceded by the word "a", for "a" substitute "an".

[4.337]
1 Citation and commencement

This Order may be cited as the Companies Act 2006 (Extension of Takeover Panel Provisions) (Isle of Man) Order 2008 and shall come into force on 1st March 2009.

NOTES
Commencement: 1 March 2009.

[4.338]
2 Extension of Takeover Panel provisions to the Isle of Man

Chapter 1 of Part 28 of the Companies Act 2006 (takeovers etc: the Takeover Panel) shall extend to the Isle of Man with the modifications set out in the Schedule to this Order.

NOTES
Commencement: 1 March 2009.

SCHEDULE
MODIFICATIONS WITH WHICH CHAPTER 1 OF PART 28 OF THE COMPANIES ACT 2006 EXTENDS TO THE ISLE OF MAN

Article 2

[4.339]
1. In section 948 (restrictions on disclosure)—
   (a)   omit subsections (4) and (5);
   (b)   in subsection (7) after paragraph (a) insert—

   "(aa) the Financial Supervision Commission of the Isle of Man;"; and

   (c)   in subsection (9) for "the Data Protection Act 1998 (c 29)" substitute "the Data Protection Act 2002 (an Act of Tynwald: c 2)".

2. In section 949(2) (punishment of disclosure in contravention of section 948)—
   (a)   in paragraph (a) for "on indictment, to imprisonment" substitute "on information, to custody"; and
   (b)   for paragraph (b) substitute—

   "(b)   on summary conviction, to custody for a term not exceeding six months or to a fine not exceeding £5,000 (or both).".

3. In section 950(1) (Panel's duty of co-operation) after paragraph (a) insert—

   "(aa) the Financial Supervision Commission of the Isle of Man;".

4. In section 953(6) (punishment for failure to comply with rules about bid documentation)—
   (a)   in paragraph (a) for "indictment" substitute "information"; and
   (b)   in paragraph (b) for "the statutory maximum" substitute "£5,000".

5. In section 955 (enforcement by the court)—
   (a)   in subsection (2) for "the High Court or, in Scotland, the Court of Session" substitute "the High Court of the Isle of Man"; and
   (b)   in subsection (3) omit paragraph (b) and the word "or" preceding it.

6. In section 961(3) (extent of exemption from liability in damages) for "section 6(1) of the Human Rights Act 1998 (c 42)" substitute "section 6(1) of the Human Rights Act 2001 (an Act of Tynwald: c 1)".

7. In section 962(2) (exceptions to the privilege against self-incrimination) for "one of the following provisions" to the end substitute "section 5 of the Perjury Act 1952 (an Act of Tynwald: Volume XVIII of the Isle of Man Statutes, p 86).".

8. For section 964 (amendments to Financial Services and Markets Act 2000) substitute—

   "964 Amendments to the Financial Services Act 2008 (an Act of Tynwald)
   (1)   The Financial Services 2008 (an Act of Tynwald: c 8) is amended as follows.
   (2)   In section 48 (interpretation)—
      (a)   in subsection (1) insert at the appropriate places—
      ""the Panel on Takeovers and Mergers" means the body referred to in section 942(1) of the Companies Act 2006 (an Act of Parliament: c 46);" and
      ""the Takeovers Directive" means Directive 2004/25/EC of the European Parliament and the Council of the European Communities;
      (b)   after subsection (4) insert—
   "(4A)   In this Act—
   "public functions" includes—

(a)   functions conferred by or in accordance with any provision contained in any enactment or subordinate legislation;

(b)   functions conferred by or in accordance with any provisions contained in the Community Treaties within the meaning of the European Communities (Isle of Man) Act 1973 (c 14);

(c)   similar functions conferred on persons by or under provisions having effect as part of the law of—

    (i)   a part of the British Islands outside the Island; or

    (ii)   a country or territory outside the British Islands;

(d)   functions in relation to disciplinary proceedings of a description prescribed by regulations made by the Treasury.

(3)   In paragraph 2 of Schedule 1 (functions of the Financial Supervision Commission)—

(a)   in sub-paragraph (1) after paragraph (e) insert—

"(ea)   the duty to take such steps as it considers appropriate to co-operate with the bodies specified in sub-paragraph (1A);"; and

(b)   after sub-paragraph (1) insert—

"(1A)   The bodies referred to in sub-paragraph (1)(ea) are—

(a)   the Panel on Takeovers and Mergers;

(b)   an authority designated as a supervisory authority for the purposes of Article 4.1 of the Takeovers Directive; and

(c)   any other person or body which exercises functions of a public nature, under legislation, in any country or territory outside the British Islands, that appear to the Commission to be similar to those of the Panel on Takeovers and Mergers.".

(4)   In paragraph 2 of Schedule 5 (exceptions from restrictions on disclosure) after sub-paragraph (4) insert—

"(4A)   Paragraph 1 shall not preclude—

(a)   the disclosure by a recipient to which sub-paragraph (4B) applies of confidential information disclosed to it by the Commission if the Commission's disclosure was made for the purpose of facilitating the carrying out of a public function;

(b)   the disclosure of such information by a person obtaining it directly or indirectly from a recipient to which subsection (4B) applies.

(4B)   This sub-paragraph applies to—

(a)   the Panel on Takeovers and Mergers;

(b)   an authority designated as a supervisory authority for the purposes of Article 4.1 of the Takeovers Directive;

(c)   any other person or body that exercises public functions, under legislation in an EEA State other than the United Kingdom, that are similar to the Commission's functions or those of the Panel on Takeovers and Mergers.".".

9, 10.   . . .

NOTES

Commencement: 1 March 2009.
Paras 9, 10: revoked by the Companies Act 2006 (Extension of Takeover Panel Provisions) (Isle of Man) Order 2009, SI 2009/1378, art 3, as from 1 July 2009.

COMPANIES (MODEL ARTICLES) REGULATIONS 2008

(SI 2008/3229)

NOTES

Made: 16 December 2008.
Authority: Companies Act 2006, s 19.
Commencement: 1 October 2009.
Amendment: as of 1 July 2011, these Regulations had not been amended.

ARRANGEMENT OF REGULATIONS

[4.340]
1   Citation and Commencement

These Regulations may be cited as the Companies (Model Articles) Regulations 2008 and come into force on 1st October 2009.

NOTES
Commencement: 1 October 2009.

[4.341]
2 Model articles for private companies limited by shares

Schedule 1 to these Regulations prescribes the model articles of association for private companies limited by shares.

NOTES
Commencement: 1 October 2009.

[4.342]
3 Model articles for private companies limited by guarantee

Schedule 2 to these Regulations prescribes the model articles of association for private companies limited by guarantee.

NOTES
Commencement: 1 October 2009.

[4.343]
4 Model articles for public companies

Schedule 3 to these Regulations prescribes the model articles of association for public companies.

NOTES
Commencement: 1 October 2009.

SCHEDULES

SCHEDULES 1–3

(Sch 1 (Model Articles for Private Companies Limited by Shares), Sch 2 (Model Articles for Private Companies Limited by Guarantee), and Sch 3 (Model Articles for Public Companies) are reproduced in Appendix 1 at **[A1.1]**, **[A1.2]**, *and* **[A1.3]** *respectively.)*

COMPANIES (DISCLOSURE OF ADDRESS) REGULATIONS 2009

(SI 2009/214)

NOTES
Made: 1 February 2009.
Authority: Companies Act 2006, ss 243(2)–(6), 1088(1)–(3), (5), 1292(1), (4).
Commencement: 1 October 2009.
These Regulations are reproduced as amended by: the Companies Act 2006 (Consequential Amendments, Transitional Provisions and Savings) Order 2009, SI 2009/1941; the European Public Limited-Liability Company (Amendment) Regulations 2009, SI 2009/2400; the Companies (Disclosure of Address) (Amendment) Regulations 2010, SI 2010/2156.
References to the "European Community", "Community", etc: see the Treaty of Lisbon (Changes in Terminology) Order 2011, SI 2011/1043, which provides (with effect from 22 April 2011): (1) that for references to the "European Communities" or to the "European Community" (including references to "the Communities", "the Community", "the EC" or "the EEC") substitute references to the European Union; and (2) that "EU" should be substituted for the word "Community" (subject to certain exceptions) in references to "Community treaties", "Community customs duty", "Community institution", "Community instrument", "Community obligation", "enforceable Community right", "Community law", "Community legislation", and "Community provision". Also, where such a term is preceded by the word "a", for "a" substitute "an".
Limited liability partnerships: as to the application of these Regulations to limited liability partnerships, see the Limited Liability Partnerships (Application of Companies Act 2006) Regulations 2009, SI 2009/1804 at **[10.1097]**.

ARRANGEMENT OF REGULATIONS

PART 1

PART 2
DISCLOSURE OF PROTECTED INFORMATION

PART 3
APPLICATION TO MAKE AN ADDRESS UNAVAILABLE FOR PUBLIC INSPECTION UNDER SECTION 1088

PART 4
MATTERS RELATING TO APPLICATIONS UNDER SECTION 243 AND UNDER SECTION 1088

SCHEDULES

PART 1

[4.344]
1   Citation, commencement and interpretation

(1)   These Regulations may be cited as the Companies (Disclosure of Address) Regulations 2009 and come into force on 1st October 2009.

(2)   In these Regulations—
"the Act" means the Companies Act 2006 and, unless the context otherwise requires, any reference to a numbered section is to a section so numbered in that Act;

"the 1985 Act" means the Companies Act 1985;

"the 1986 Order" means the Companies (Northern Ireland) Order 1986;

"confidentiality order" means an order under section 723B of the 1985 Act (confidentiality orders);

"former name" means a name by which an individual was formerly known and which has been notified to the registrar under section 10 (documents to be sent to the registrar) or section 288 (register of directors and secretaries) of the 1985 Act, or Article 21 or 296 of the 1986 Order, [or regulation 80C of the SEs Regulations, or regulation 79 of the old SEs Regulations, or regulation 77 of the Northern Ireland SEs Regulations,] or section 12 (statement of proposed officers) or section 167 (duty to notify registrar of changes) of the Act;

"limited liability partnership" means a limited liability partnership incorporated under the Limited Liability Partnerships Act 2000 or Limited Liability Partnerships Act (Northern Ireland) 2002;

"name" means a person's Christian name (or other forename) and surname, except that in the case of—
    (a)   a peer; or
    (b)   an individual usually known by a title,
the title may be stated instead of his Christian name (or other forename) and surname or in addition to either or both of them;

["the Northern Ireland SEs Regulations" means the European Public Limited-Liability Company Regulations (Northern Ireland) 2004;]

["the old SEs Regulations" means the SEs Regulations, disregarding the amendments made by the European Public Limited-Liability Company (Amendment) Regulations 2009;]

"permanent representative" means an individual who was a permanent representative for the purposes of sections 723B and 723C (effect of confidentiality orders) of the 1985 Act;

"police force" means a police force within the meaning of section 101(1) of the Police Act 1996 (interpretation), section 50 of the Police (Scotland) Act 1967 (meaning of police area, etc) or section 1 of the Police (Northern Ireland) Act 2000 (name of the police in Northern Ireland);

"relevant body" means any police force and any other person whom the registrar considers may be able to assist in answering a question referred to that person by the registrar under these Regulations;

"relevant organisation" means the Government Communications Headquarters, the Secret Intelligence Service, the Security Service or a police force;

["the SEs Regulations" means the European Public Limited-Liability Company Regulations 2004;]

"section 243 applicant" means an individual by whom or in respect of whom a section 243 application has been made but in respect of which application the registrar either has not made a determination, or has made a determination, not being a section 243 decision, and any appeal to the court in respect of that application under regulation 14 has not been determined by the court;

"section 243 application" means an application under section 243(4) (permitted use or disclosure by the registrar) for the purpose of requiring the registrar to refrain from disclosing protected information relating to a director to a credit reference agency;

"section 243 beneficiary" means—

(a)   an individual who has made a section 243 application in respect of which a section 243 decision has been made; or

(b)   an individual on whose behalf a company or a subscriber to a memorandum of association has made a section 243 application in respect of which a section 243 decision has been made; or

(c)   an individual in relation to whom a confidentiality order was in force immediately before 1st October 2009 and who, by paragraph 37 of Schedule 2 to the Companies Act 2006 (Commencement No 8, Transitional Provisions and Savings) Order 2008 is treated as having made a section 243 application in respect of which a section 243 decision has been made;

"section 243 decision" means a determination by the registrar on a section 243 application in favour of the applicant;

"section 1088 application" means an application under section 1088 (application to registrar to make address unavailable for public inspection) for the purpose of requiring the registrar to make an address on the register unavailable for public inspection;

"section 1088 beneficiary" means a person who has made a section 1088 application in respect of which a section 1088 decision has been made;

"section 1088 decision" means a determination by the registrar on a section 1088 application in favour of the applicant;

"specified public authority" means any public authority specified in Schedule 1 to these Regulations; and

"working day" means a day that is not a Saturday or Sunday, Christmas Day, Good Friday or any day that is a bank holiday under the Banking and Financial Dealings Act 1971 in England and Wales.

NOTES

Commencement: 1 October 2009.

Para (2): words in square brackets in definition "former name" inserted, and definitions "the Northern Ireland SEs Regulations", "the old SEs Regulations" and "the SEs Regulations" inserted, by the European Public Limited-Liability Company (Amendment) Regulations 2009, SI 2009/2400, reg 42(1), (2), as from 1 October 2009.

PART 2
DISCLOSURE OF PROTECTED INFORMATION

[4.345]
2   Permitted disclosure by the registrar to specified public authorities

(1)   The registrar may disclose protected information to a specified public authority where the conditions specified in paragraphs 2 and 3 of Schedule 2 are satisfied.

(2)   A specified public authority shall deliver to the registrar such information or evidence as he may direct for the purpose of enabling him to determine in accordance with these Regulations whether to disclose protected information.

(3)   The registrar may require such information or evidence to be verified in such manner as he may direct.

(4)   The specified public authority must inform the registrar immediately of any change in respect of any statement delivered to the registrar pursuant to Schedule 2 or information or evidence provided for the purpose of enabling the registrar to determine whether to disclose protected information.

(5)   The public authorities specified for the purposes of section 243(2) are set out in Schedule 1 to these Regulations.

NOTES
Commencement: 1 October 2009.

[4.346]

3 Permitted disclosure by the registrar to credit reference agencies

(1) Subject to regulation 4, the registrar may disclose protected information to a credit reference agency where the conditions specified in paragraphs 6 to 10 of Schedule 2 are satisfied.

(2) The registrar may rely on a statement delivered to him by a credit reference agency under paragraph 10 of Schedule 2 as sufficient evidence of the matters stated in it.

(3) Notwithstanding paragraph (2), a credit reference agency shall deliver to the registrar such information or evidence in addition to the statement required by paragraph 10 of Schedule 2 as he may direct for the purpose of enabling him to determine in accordance with these Regulations whether to disclose protected information.

(4) The registrar may require such information or evidence to be verified in such manner as he may direct.

(5) The credit reference agency must inform the registrar immediately of any change in respect of any statement delivered to the registrar pursuant to Schedule 2 or information or evidence provided for the purpose of enabling the registrar to determine whether to disclose protected information.

NOTES

Commencement: 1 October 2009.

[4.347]

4 Registrar to refrain from disclosure of protected information

The registrar shall refrain from disclosing protected information to a credit reference agency if such information relates to a section 243 beneficiary or a section 243 applicant.

NOTES

Commencement: 1 October 2009.

[4.348]

5 Application under section 243 by an individual

(1) A section 243 application may be made to the registrar by an individual who is, or proposes to become, a director.

(2) The grounds on which an application under paragraph (1) may be made are that the individual making the application—
- (a) considers that there is a serious risk that he, or a person who lives with him, will be subjected to violence or intimidation as a result of the activities of at least one of—
  - (i) the companies of which he is, or proposes to become, a director;
  - (ii) the companies of which he was a director;
  - (iii) the overseas companies of which he is or has been a director, secretary or permanent representative; or,
  - (iv) the limited liability partnerships of which he is or has been a member; or
- (b) is or has been employed by a relevant organisation.

(3) The application shall—
- (a) contain—
  - (i) a statement of the grounds on which the application is made;
  - (ii) the name and any former name of the applicant;
  - (iii) the date of birth of the applicant;
  - (iv) the usual residential address of the applicant;
  - (v) where the registrar has allocated a unique identifier to the applicant, that unique identifier;
  - (vi) the name and registered number of each company of which the applicant is, or proposes to become, a director;
  - (vii) where the grounds of the application are those described in paragraph (2)(a)(ii), (iii) or (iv), the name and registered number of the company, overseas company or limited liability partnership; and
- (b) be accompanied by evidence which—
  - (i) where the grounds of the application are those described in paragraph (2)(a) supports the applicant's statement of the grounds of the application; or,
  - (ii) where the grounds of the application are those described in paragraph (2)(b), establishes that the applicant is or has been employed by a relevant organisation.

(4) The registrar may refer to a relevant body any question relating to an assessment of—
- (a) where the grounds of the application are those described in paragraph (2)(a), the nature and extent of any risk of violence or intimidation considered by the applicant to arise in relation to himself, or to a person who lives with him; or
- (b) where the grounds of the application are those described in paragraph (2)(b), whether the applicant is or has been employed by a relevant organisation.

(5) The registrar shall determine the application and send the applicant to his usual residential address, as stated in his application, notice of his determination on the section 243 application within five working days of that determination being made.

NOTES
  Commencement: 1 October 2009.

[4.349]
6   Application under section 243 by a company

(1) A section 243 application may be made to the registrar by a company on behalf of any of its directors who are individuals.

(2) The grounds on which an application under paragraph (1) may be made are that the company making the application considers that there is a serious risk that the director on behalf of whom the application is made, or a person who lives with that director, will be subjected to violence or intimidation as a result of the activities of the company making the application.

(3) The application shall—
    (a) contain—
        (i)   a statement of the grounds on which the application is made;
        (ii)   the name and registered number of the applicant;
        (iii) the name and any former name of each director on behalf of whom the application is made;
        (iv) the date of birth of each such director;
        (v)   the usual residential address of each such director;
        (vi) where the registrar has allocated a unique identifier to any such director, that unique identifier;
        (vii) the name and registered number of each company of which each such director is a director; and
    (b) be accompanied by evidence which supports the applicant's statement of the grounds of the application.

(4) The registrar may refer to a relevant body any question relating to an assessment of the nature and extent of any risk of violence or intimidation considered by the applicant to arise in relation to its directors on behalf of whom the application is made or to persons who live with those directors as a result of any of its activities.

(5) The registrar shall determine the application and send—
    (a) the applicant, to its registered office; and
    (b) each director on behalf of whom the application was made, to his usual residential address as stated in the application,
notice of his determination on the section 243 application within five working days of that determination being made.

NOTES
  Commencement: 1 October 2009.

[4.350]
7   Application under section 243 by a subscriber to a memorandum of association

(1) A section 243 application may be made to the registrar by a subscriber to a memorandum of association on behalf of any of the proposed directors of a proposed company who are individuals.

(2) The grounds on which an application under paragraph (1) may be made are that the subscriber making the application considers that there is a serious risk that the proposed directors of the proposed company on behalf of whom the application is made, or persons who live with them, will be subjected to violence or intimidation as a result of the proposed activities of that proposed company.

(3) The application shall—
    (a) contain—
        (i)   a statement of the grounds on which the application is made;
        (ii)   the name of the applicant;
        (iii) the address of the applicant;
        (iv) the name of the proposed company;
        (v)   the name and any former name of each of the proposed directors on behalf of whom the application is made;
        (vi) the date of birth of each such proposed director;
        (vii) the usual residential address of each such proposed director;
        (viii) the name and registered number of each company of which each such proposed director is a director; and
    (b) be accompanied by evidence which supports the applicant's statement of the grounds of the application.

(4)   The registrar may refer to a relevant body any question relating to an assessment of the nature and extent of any risk of violence or intimidation considered by the applicant to arise in relation to its proposed directors on behalf of whom the application is made or to persons who live with those proposed directors as a result of any of the proposed activities of the proposed company.

(5)   The registrar shall determine the application and send—
  (a)   the applicant, to the address stated in the application, and
  (b)   each of the proposed directors on behalf of whom the application was made, to their usual residential address as stated in the application,
notice of his determination on the section 243 application within five working days of that determination being made.

NOTES
Commencement: 1 October 2009.

[4.351]
8   Matters relating to a section 243 application

(1)   For the purpose of regulations 5, 6 and 7 the registrar may direct that additional information or evidence should be delivered to him, what such information or evidence should be and how it should be verified.

(2)   The registrar shall not make available for public inspection—
  (a)   any section 243 application; or
  (b)   any documents provided in support of that application.

(3)   For the purpose of determining any section 243 application the registrar may accept any answer to a question referred in accordance with regulation 5(4), 6(4) or 7(4) as providing sufficient evidence of—
  (a)   the nature and extent of any risk relevant to—
    (i)   where the grounds of the application are those described in regulation 5(2)(a), the applicant;
    (ii)   where the grounds of the application are those described in regulation 6(2), the directors on behalf of whom the application is made;
    (iii) where the grounds of the application are those described in regulation 7(2), the proposed directors on behalf of whom the application is made,
    or to persons who live with any of the above individuals, or
  (b)   whether an applicant is or has been employed by a relevant organisation.

NOTES
Commencement: 1 October 2009.

PART 3
APPLICATION TO MAKE AN ADDRESS UNAVAILABLE FOR PUBLIC INSPECTION UNDER SECTION 1088

[4.352]
9   Application under section 1088 to make an address unavailable for public inspection by an individual

(1)   A section 1088 application may be made to the registrar by an individual whose usual residential address was placed on the register either—
  (a)   under section 10 (documents to be sent to registrar), 288 (register of directors and secretaries), 363 (duty to deliver annual returns), 691 (documents to be delivered to registrar) or 692 (registration of altered particulars) of or paragraph 2 of Schedule 21A to the 1985 Act;
  (b)   under Article 21, 296, 371, 641 or 642 of the 1986 Order;   . . .
  [(ba) as a service address under regulation 80C of the SEs Regulations (duty to notify registrar of changes of particulars of members of an SE's supervisory organ),
  (bb)   under regulation 79 of the old SEs Regulations or regulation 77 of the Northern Ireland SEs Regulations, or]
  (c)   as a service address under section 12 (statement of proposed officers), 167 (duty to notify registrar of changes of director's particulars) or 855 (contents of annual return) of the Act [or under regulations made under section 1046],
in respect of that usual residential address where it was placed on the register on or after 1st January 2003.

(2)   The grounds on which an application under paragraph (1) may be made are that the individual making the application—
  (a)   considers that there is a serious risk that he, or a person who lives with him, will be subjected to violence or intimidation as a result of the activities of at least one of the companies of which—
    (i)   he is, or proposes to become, a director; or

(ii)   he is not a director but of which he has been at any time a director, secretary or permanent representative;

(b)   he is or has been employed by a relevant organisation;

(c)   is a section 243 beneficiary.

(3)   The application shall—

    (a)   contain—

        (i)   a statement of the grounds on which the application is made;

        (ii)   the name and any former name of the applicant;

        (iii)   the usual residential address of the applicant that is to be made unavailable for public inspection;

        (iv)   an address for correspondence in respect of the application;

        (v)   the name and registered number of each company of which the applicant is or has been at any time since 1st January 2003 a director, secretary or permanent representative;

        (vi)   the service address which is to replace that usual residential address on the register;

        (vii)   subject to paragraph (4)—

            (aa)   the date of birth of the applicant;

            (bb)   the name of each company of which the applicant proposes to become a director; and

            (cc)   where the registrar has allotted a unique identifier to the applicant, that unique identifier; and

    (b)   be accompanied by evidence which—

        (i)   where the grounds of the application are those described in paragraph (2)(a), supports the applicant's assertion that his application falls within the grounds stated in his application;

        (ii)   where the grounds of the application are those described in paragraph (2)(b), establishes that the applicant is or has been employed by a relevant organisation;

        (iii)   where the grounds of the application are those described in paragraph (2)(c), establishes that he is a section 243 beneficiary.

(4)   The application need not contain the information described at paragraph (3)(a)(vii) where the application is delivered to the registrar on the same day as the applicant delivers a section 243 application.

(5)   The registrar may refer to a relevant body any question relating to an assessment of—

    (a)   the nature and extent of any risk of violence or intimidation considered by the applicant to arise in relation to himself, or a person who lives with him, as a result of the activities of any company of which he is or proposes to become a director or has been at any time a director, secretary or permanent representative; or

    (b)   whether the applicant is or has been employed by a relevant organisation.

(6)   The registrar shall determine the application and send the applicant to the address for correspondence stated in his application, notice of his determination on the section 1088 application within five working days of that determination being made.

NOTES

Commencement: 1 October 2009.

Para (1): word omitted from sub-para (b) revoked, and sub-paras (ba), (bb) inserted, by the European Public Limited-Liability Company (Amendment) Regulations 2009, SI 2009/2400, reg 42(1), (3), as from 1 October 2009; words in square brackets in sub-para (c) inserted by the Companies Act 2006 (Consequential Amendments, Transitional Provisions and Savings) Order 2009, SI 2009/1941, art 2(1), Sch 1, para 270(1), (2), as from 1 October 2009.

[4.353]
10   Application under section 1088 to make an address unavailable for public inspection by a company

(1)   A section 1088 application may be made to the registrar by a company in respect of the addresses of—

    (a)   all of its members and former members whose addresses were contained in—

        (i)   an annual return; or

        (ii)   a return of allotment of shares,

        delivered to the registrar on or after 1st January 2003; or

    (b)   the subscribers to its memorandum of association where that memorandum was delivered to the registrar on or after 1st January 2003.

(2)   The grounds on which an application under paragraph (1) may be made are that the company making the application considers that, as a result of its activities, the availability to members of the public of the addresses described in paragraph (1) creates a serious risk that its members or former members or subscribers, or persons who live at those addresses, will be subjected to violence or intimidation.

(3)   The application shall—

    (a)   contain—

> (i)   the name of the applicant and its registered number; and
> (ii)   a statement of the grounds on which the application is made; and
>
> (b) be accompanied by evidence—
> > (i)   which supports the applicant's assertion that its application falls within the grounds stated in its application; or
> > (ii)   where the court has made an order under section 117(3) (register of members: response to request for inspection or copy) directing the applicant not to comply with a request under section 116 (rights to inspect and require copies), a copy of that order.

(4)   The registrar may refer to a relevant body any question relating to the assessment of the nature and extent of any risk of violence or intimidation considered by the applicant to arise in relation to any of its members or former members or subscribers, or persons who live at the addresses described in paragraph (1), as a result of its activities by virtue of the availability to members of the public of particulars of the addresses of such members or former members or subscribers.

(5)   The registrar shall determine the application and send the applicant to its registered office notice of his determination on the section 1088 application within five working days of that determination being made.

NOTES

Commencement: 1 October 2009.

[4.354]
11   Application under section 1088 to make an address unavailable for public inspection by a person who registers a charge

(1)   A section 1088 application may be made to the registrar by a person who—
> (a)
> > (i)   on or after 1st January 2003, registered a charge under Part 12 of the 1985 Act (registration of charges) or Part 13 of the 1986 Order; or
> > (ii)   has registered a charge under Part 25 of the Act (company charges) [or under regulations made under section 1052]; and
> (b) is not the company which created the charge or acquired the property subject to a charge,
in respect of his address delivered to the registrar for the purposes of that registration.

(2)   The grounds on which an application under paragraph (1) may be made are that the person making the application considers that there is a serious risk that he, or if applicable his employees, or persons who live with him or his employees, will be subjected to violence or intimidation as a result of the activities of the company which is, or was, subject to the charge.

(3)   The application shall—
> (a) contain—
> > (i)   a statement of the grounds on which the application is made;
> > (ii)   the name of the applicant, and where the applicant is a company, its registered number;
> > (iii) the address of the applicant that is to be made unavailable for public inspection;
> > (iv) the name and registered number of the company which is or was subject to the charge;
> > (v)   an address for correspondence with the registrar in respect of the application;
> > (vi) where the applicant is the chargee, the service address which is to replace the address of the applicant on the register; and
> (b) be accompanied by evidence which supports the applicant's assertion that there is a serious risk that he or, if applicable, his employees, or persons who live with him or his employees, will be subjected to violence or intimidation as a result of the activities of the company which is or was subject to the charge.

(4)   The registrar may refer to a relevant body any question relating to the assessment of the nature and extent of any risk of violence or intimidation considered by the applicant to arise in relation to himself or, if applicable, his employees, or persons who live with him or his employees, as a result of the activities of the company which is or was subject to the charge.

(5)   The registrar shall determine the application and send the applicant to the address stated in the application in accordance with paragraph (3)(a)(v) notice of his determination on the section 1088 application within five working days of that determination being made.

NOTES

Commencement: 1 October 2009.

Para (1): words in square brackets in sub-para (a)(ii) inserted by the Companies Act 2006 (Consequential Amendments, Transitional Provisions and Savings) Order 2009, SI 2009/1941, art 2(1), Sch 1, para 270(1), (3), as from 1 October 2009.

[4.355]

12   Matters relevant to section 1088 applications

(1)   For the purpose of regulations 9, 10 and 11 the registrar may direct that additional information or evidence should be delivered to him, what such information or evidence should be and how it should be verified.

(2)   For the purpose of determining any section 1088 application the registrar may accept any answer to a question referred in accordance with regulation 9(5), 10(4) or 11(4) as providing sufficient evidence of—

    (a)   the nature and extent of any risk relevant to—

        (i)   where the grounds of the application are those described in regulation 9(2)(a), the applicant;

        (ii)   where the grounds of the application are those described in regulation 10(2), the subscribers or members or former members of an applicant; or

        (iii)   where the grounds of the application are those described in regulation 11(2), where the applicant is an individual, the applicant, or any employees of an applicant,

        or to persons who live with any of the above individuals or, in the case of members, former members or subscribers, to persons who live at their addresses, or

    (b)   whether an applicant is or has been employed by a relevant organisation.

NOTES

Commencement: 1 October 2009.

[4.356]

13   Effect of a successful section 1088 application

(1)   Where a section 1088 application has been determined in favour of the applicant the registrar shall—

    (a)   in the case of an application made under regulation 9(1) or 11(1) make the specified address unavailable for public inspection;

    (b)   in the case of an application under regulation 10(1) make all of the members', former members' or subscribers' addresses unavailable for public inspection;

    (c)   in the case of a person to whom paragraph 36 of Schedule 2 to the Companies Act 2006 (Commencement No 8, Transitional Provisions and Savings) Order 2008 applies, make unavailable for public inspection the address referred to in sub-paragraph (1)(a) of that paragraph.

(2)   In this regulation "specified address" means the address specified in the application as being the one to be made unavailable for public inspection.

NOTES

Commencement: 1 October 2009.

PART 4

MATTERS RELATING TO APPLICATIONS UNDER SECTION 243

AND UNDER SECTION 1088

[4.357]

14   Appeals

(1)   An applicant who has received notice under regulation 5(5), 6(5), 7(5), 9(6), 10(5) or 11(5) that his application has been unsuccessful may appeal to the High Court or, in Scotland, the Court of Session on the grounds that the decision—

    (a)   is unlawful;

    (b)   is irrational or unreasonable;

    (c)   has been made on the basis of a procedural impropriety or otherwise contravenes the rules of natural justice.

(2)   No appeal under this regulation may be brought unless the leave of the court has been obtained.

(3)   An applicant must bring an appeal within 21 days of the date of the notice or, with the court's permission, after the end of such period, but only if the court is satisfied—

    (a)   where permission is sought before the end of that period, that there is good reason for the applicant being unable to bring the appeal in time; or

    (b)   where permission is sought after that time, that there was a good reason for the applicant's failure to bring the appeal in time and for any delay in applying for permission.

(4)   The court determining an appeal may—

    (a)   dismiss the appeal; or

    (b)   quash the decision,

and where the court quashes a decision it may refer the matter to the registrar with a direction to reconsider it and make a determination in accordance with the findings of the court.

NOTES
Commencement: 1 October 2009.

[4.358]
15 Duration of a section 243 decision or a section 1088 decision

(1)   A section 243 decision shall continue to have effect until—
  (a)   either—
    (i)   the section 243 beneficiary, or
    (ii)   his personal representative,
    has notified the registrar in writing that he wishes the section 243 decision to cease to apply; or
  (b)   the registrar has made a revocation decision in relation to that beneficiary,
whichever first occurs.

(2)   A section 1088 decision shall continue to have effect until the registrar has made a revocation decision in relation to the section 1088 beneficiary.

(3)   In this regulation—
  "personal representative" means the executor, original or by representation, or administrator for the time being of a deceased person; and
  "revocation decision" in relation to a section 243 decision or a section 1088 decision means a determination by the registrar to revoke that decision in accordance with regulation 16.

NOTES
Commencement: 1 October 2009.

[4.359]
16 Revocation of a section 243 decision or a section 1088 decision

(1)   The registrar may revoke a section 243 decision or a section 1088 decision at any time if he is satisfied that the section 243 beneficiary or section 1088 beneficiary, as the case may be, or any other person, in purported compliance with any provision of these Regulations, is found guilty of an offence under section 1112 (general false statement offence) ("a revocation decision").

(2)   If the registrar proposes to make a revocation decision he shall send the beneficiary notice of his intention.

(3)   The notice must—
  (a)   inform the beneficiary that he may, within the period of 28 days beginning with the date of the notice, deliver representations in writing to the registrar; and
  (b)   state that if representations are not received by the registrar within that period, the revocation decision will be made at the expiry of that period.

(4)   If within the period specified in paragraph (3) the beneficiary delivers representations as to why the revocation decision should not be made, the registrar shall have regard to the representations in determining whether to make the revocation decision, and shall, within five working days of making his decision, send notice of it to the beneficiary.

(5)   Any communication by the registrar in respect of a revocation decision or proposed revocation decision shall be sent to the beneficiary—
  (a)   in the case of an individual, to his usual residential address;
  (b)   in the case of a company, to its registered office; or
  (c)   in the case of a partnership, to the address specified in its section 1088 application.

(6)   In this regulation—
  "partnership" includes a limited liability partnership;
  "section 243 beneficiary" includes where the section 243 decision was made following an application under regulation 6 or 7, the applicant.

NOTES
Commencement: 1 October 2009.

SCHEDULES

SCHEDULE 1
SPECIFIED PUBLIC AUTHORITIES

Regulation 2

[4.360]
The Secretary of State;

any Northern Ireland Department;

the Scottish Ministers;

the Welsh Ministers;

the Treasury;

the Commissioners for Her Majesty's Revenue and Customs;

the Bank of England;

the Director of Public Prosecutions;

the Director of Public Prosecutions for Northern Ireland;

the Serious Fraud Office;

the Secret Intelligence Service;

the Security Service;

the Government Communications Headquarters;

the Financial Services Authority;

the Competition Commission;

the Pensions Regulator;

the Panel on Takeovers and Mergers;

the Regulator of Community Interest Companies;

the Registrar of Credit Unions for Northern Ireland;

the Office of Fair Trading;

the Office of the Information Commissioner;

the Charity Commission;

the Charity Commission for Northern Ireland;

the Office of the Scottish Charity Regulator;

the Postal Services Commission;

the Gas and Electricity Markets Authority;

the Northern Ireland Authority for Utility Regulation;

the Gambling Commission;

the Serious Organised Crime Agency;

the Health and Safety Executive;

the Health and Safety Executive for Northern Ireland;

the Food Standards Agency;

the Gangmasters Licensing Authority;

the Security Industry Authority;

a local authority within the meaning of section 54(2) of the Act;

an official receiver appointed under section 399 of the Insolvency Act 1986 (appointment, etc, of official receivers);

the Official Receiver for Northern Ireland;

the Crown Office and Procurator Fiscal Services;

[the Marine Management Organisation;]

a person acting as an insolvency practitioner within the meaning of section 388 of the Insolvency Act 1986 (meaning of "act as an insolvency practitioner") or Article 3 of the Insolvency (Northern Ireland) Order 1989 ("act as an insolvency practitioner");

an inspector appointed under Part 14 of the 1985 Act (investigation of companies and their affairs: requisition of documents) or Part 15 of the 1986 Order or a person appointed under regulation 30 of the Open-Ended Investment Companies Regulations 2001 (power to investigate) or regulation 22 of the Open-Ended Investment Companies Regulations (Northern Ireland) 2004;

any person authorised to exercise powers under section 447 of the 1985 Act (power to require documents and information), or section 84 of the Companies Act 1989 (exercise of powers by officers, etc) or Article 440 of the 1986 Order;

any person exercising functions conferred by Part 6 of the Financial Services and Markets Act 2000 (official listing) or the competent authority under that Part;

a person appointed to make a report under section 166 (reports by skilled persons) of the Financial Services and Markets Act 2000;

a person appointed to conduct an investigation under section 167 (appointment of persons to carry out general investigations) or 168(3) or (5) (appointment of persons to carry out investigations in particular cases) of the Financial Services and Markets Act 2000;

an inspector appointed under section 284 (power to investigate) of the Financial Services and Markets Act 2000;

an overseas regulatory authority within the meaning of section 82 of the Companies Act 1989 (request for assistance by overseas regulatory authority);

a police force.

NOTES

Commencement: 1 October 2009.

Entry "the Marine Management Organisation" inserted by the Companies (Disclosure of Address) (Amendment) Regulations 2010, SI 2010/2156, reg 2, as from 1 October 2010.

SCHEDULE 2
CONDITIONS FOR PERMITTED DISCLOSURE

Regulations 2 and 3

PART 1
DISCLOSURE TO SPECIFIED PUBLIC AUTHORITIES

[4.361]

1. Paragraphs 2 and 3 set out the conditions specified for the disclosure of protected information by the registrar to a specified public authority.

2. The specified public authority has delivered to the registrar a statement that it intends to use the protected information only for the purpose of facilitating the carrying out by that specified public authority of a public function ("the permitted purpose").

3. Subject to paragraph 4, the specified public authority ("the authority") has delivered to the registrar a statement that it will, where it supplies a copy of the protected information to a processor for the purpose of processing the information for use in respect of the permitted purpose—
  (a)　ensure that the processor is one who carries on business in the European Economic Area;
  (b)　require that the information is not transmitted outside the European Economic Area by the processor; and
  (c)　require that the processor does not disclose the information except to the authority or an employee of the authority.

4. Paragraph 3 does not apply where the specified public authority is the Secret Intelligence Service, Security Service or Government Communications Headquarters.

NOTES

Commencement: 1 October 2009.

PART 2
DISCLOSURE TO A CREDIT REFERENCE AGENCY

[4.362]

5. Paragraphs 6 to 10 set out the conditions specified for the disclosure of protected information by the registrar to a credit reference agency.

6. The credit reference agency—
  (a)　is carrying on in the United Kingdom or in another EEA State a business comprising the furnishing of information relevant to the financial standing of individuals, being information collected by the agency for that purpose;
  (b)　maintains appropriate procedures—
    (i)　to ensure that an independent person can investigate and audit the measures maintained by the agency for the purposes of ensuring the security of any protected information disclosed to that agency; and

(ii) for the purposes of ensuring that it complies with its obligations under the Data Protection Act 1998, or, where the agency carries on business in a EEA State other than the United Kingdom, with its obligations under legislation implementing Directive 95/46/EC of the European Parliament and of the Council of 24 October 1995 on the protection of individuals with regard to the processing of personal data and on the free movement of such data;

(c) has not been found guilty of an offence under—

(i) section 1112 (general false statement offence) of the Act or section 2 of the Fraud Act 2006 (fraud by false representation); or

(ii) section 47 (failure to comply with enforcement notice) of the Data Protection Act 1998 in circumstances where it has used the protected information for purposes other than those described in sub-paragraphs (a) to (e) of paragraph 7 below.

7. The credit reference agency has delivered to the registrar a statement that it intends to use the protected information only for the purposes of—

(a) providing an assessment of the financial standing of a person;

(b) meeting any obligations contained in the Money Laundering Regulations 2007 or any rules made pursuant to section 146 of the Financial Services and Markets Act 2000 (money laundering rules), or in any legislation of another EEA State implementing Directive 2005/60/EC of the European Parliament and of the Council of 26 October 2005 on the prevention of the use of the financial system for the purpose of money laundering and terrorist financing;

(c) conducting conflict of interest checks required or made necessary by any enactment;

(d) the provision of protected information to—

(i) a public authority specified in Schedule 1 which has satisfied the requirements of paragraphs 2 and 3 of this Schedule; or

(ii) a credit reference agency which has satisfied the requirements of this Part of this Schedule; or

(e) conducting checks for the prevention and detection of crime and fraud.

8. The credit reference agency has delivered to the registrar a statement that it intends to take delivery of and to use the protected information only in the United Kingdom or in another EEA State.

9. The credit reference agency has delivered to the registrar a statement that it will, where it supplies a copy of the protected information to a processor for the purpose of processing the information for use in respect of the purposes referred to in paragraph 7—

(a) ensure that the processor is one who carries on business in the European Economic Area;

(b) require that the information is not transmitted outside the European Economic Area by the processor; and

(c) require that the processor does not disclose the information except to the credit reference agency or an employee of the credit reference agency.

10. The credit reference agency has delivered to the registrar a statement that it meets the conditions in paragraph 6 above.

NOTES

Commencement: 1 October 2009.

PART 3
INTERPRETATION OF THIS SCHEDULE

[4.363]

11. (1) In this Schedule—

"processor" means any person who provides a service which consists of putting information into data form or processing information in data form and any reference to a processor includes a reference to his employees; and

"public function" includes—

(a) any function conferred by or in accordance with any provision contained in any enactment;

(b) any function conferred by or in accordance with any provision contained in the Community Treaties or any Community instrument;

(c) any similar function conferred on persons by or under provisions having effect as part of the law of a country or territory outside the United Kingdom; and

(d) any function exercisable in relation to the investigation of any criminal offence or for the purpose of any criminal proceedings.

(2) In this Schedule any reference to—

(a) an employee of any person who has access to protected information shall be deemed to include any person working or providing services for the purposes of that person or employed by or on behalf of, or working for, any person who is so working or who is supplying such a service; and

(b) the disclosure for the purpose of facilitating the carrying out of a public function includes disclosure in relation to, and for the purpose of, any proceedings whether civil, criminal or disciplinary in which the specified public authority engages while carrying out its public functions.

NOTES
Commencement: 1 October 2009.

COMPANIES (SHARES AND SHARE CAPITAL) ORDER 2009

(SI 2009/388)

NOTES
Made: 26 February 2009.
Authority: Companies Act 2006, ss 10(2)(c)(i), 32(2)(c)(i), 108(3)(c)(i), 555(3)(a), (4)(c)(i), 556(3), 583(4), 619(3)(c)(i), 621(3)(c)(i), 625(3)(c)(i), 627(3)(c)(i), 644(2)(c)(i), 649(2)(c)(i), 663(3)(c)(i), 689(3)(c)(i), 708(3)(c)(i), 714(5), 727(3), 730(5)(c)(i), 1167.
Commencement: 1 October 2009.
Amendment: as of 1 July 2011, this Order had not been amended.

[4.364]
1   Citation, commencement and interpretation

(1)   This Order may be cited as the Companies (Shares and Share Capital) Order 2009 and shall come into force on 1st October 2009.

(2)   In this Order, a reference to a section is a reference to a section of the Companies Act 2006.

NOTES
Commencement: 1 October 2009.

[4.365]
2   Statements of capital, and returns of allotment by unlimited companies: prescribed particulars of the rights attached to shares

(1)   The particulars in paragraph (3) are prescribed for the purposes of the provisions in paragraph (2).

(2)   The provisions are—
  (a)   section 10(2)(c)(i);
  (b)   section 32(2)(c)(i);
  (c)   section 108(3)(c)(i);
  (d)   section 555(4)(c)(i);
  (e)   section 556(3);
  (f)   section 619(3)(c)(i);
  (g)   section 621(3)(c)(i);
  (h)   section 625(3)(c)(i);
  (i)   section 627(3)(c)(i);
  (j)   section 644(2)(c)(i);
  (k)   section 649(2)(c)(i);
  (l)   section 663(3)(c)(i);
  (m)   section 689(3)(c)(i);
  (n)   section 708(3)(c)(i); and
  (o)   section 730(5)(c)(i).

(3)   The particulars are—
  (a)   particulars of any voting rights attached to the shares, including rights that arise only in certain circumstances;
  (b)   particulars of any rights attached to the shares, as respects dividends, to participate in a distribution;
  (c)   particulars of any rights attached to the shares, as respects capital, to participate in a distribution (including on winding up); and
  (d)   whether the shares are to be redeemed or are liable to be redeemed at the option of the company or the shareholder.

NOTES
Commencement: 1 October 2009.

[4.366]

3 Prescribed information for a return of an allotment by a limited company

(1) The information in paragraph (2) is prescribed for the purposes of section 555(3)(a) (information to be contained in a return of an allotment by a limited company).

(2) The information is—

  (a) the number of shares allotted;

  (b) the amount paid up and the amount (if any) unpaid on each allotted share (whether on account of the nominal value of the share or by way of premium); and

  (c) where the shares are allotted as fully or partly paid up (as to their nominal value or any premium on them) otherwise than in cash, the consideration for the allotment.

NOTES

Commencement: 1 October 2009.

[4.367]

4 Shares deemed paid up in or allotted for cash, and sale of treasury shares for a cash consideration: meaning of cash consideration

(1) The creation of an obligation on the part of a settlement bank to make a relevant payment in respect of the allotment of a share to a system-member by means of a relevant system is to be regarded as a means of payment falling within section 583(3)(e).

(2) The creation of an obligation on the part of a settlement bank to make a relevant payment in respect of the payment up of a share by a system-member by means of a relevant system is to be regarded as a means of payment falling within section 583(3)(e).

(3) The creation of an obligation on the part of a settlement bank to make a relevant payment in respect of the transfer by a company to a system-member, by means of a relevant system, of a share held by the company as a treasury share is to be regarded as a means of payment falling within section 727(2)(e).

(4) In this article—

  (a) the expressions "Operator", "relevant system", "rules", "settlement bank", "system-member" and "uncertificated" have the meanings given in the Uncertificated Securities Regulations 2001; and

  (b) "relevant payment" means a payment in accordance with the rules and practices of an Operator of a relevant system.

NOTES

Commencement: 1 October 2009.

[4.368]

5 Redemption or purchase of own shares out of capital by a private company: prescribed form of, and information with respect to the nature of the company's business to be contained in, a directors' statement

(1) The directors' statement required by section 714 (directors' statement to be made where a private company makes a payment out of capital for the redemption or purchase of its own shares) must—

  (a) be in writing;

  (b) indicate that it is a directors' statement made under that section; and

  (c) be signed by each of the company's directors.

(2) The statement must state—

  (a) whether the company's business includes that of a banking company; and

  (b) whether its business includes that of an insurance company.

NOTES

Commencement: 1 October 2009.

COMPANY AND BUSINESS NAMES (MISCELLANEOUS PROVISIONS) REGULATIONS 2009

(SI 2009/1085)

NOTES

Made: 24 April 2009.

Authority: Companies Act 2006, ss 57(1)(a), (2), (5), 60(1), 65, 66, 1197, 1292(1).

Commencement: 1 October 2009.

These Regulations are reproduced as amended by: the Company, Limited Liability Partnership and Business Names (Miscellaneous Provisions) (Amendment) Regulations 2009, SI 2009/2404.

ARRANGEMENT OF REGULATIONS

PART 1
INTRODUCTORY

[4.369]
1   Citation, commencement and interpretation

(1)   These Regulations may be cited as the Company and Business Names (Miscellaneous Provisions) Regulations 2009 and come into force on 1st October 2009.

(2)   In these Regulations—
    "the Act" means the Companies Act 2006;
    "expression or abbreviation specified as similar" has the meaning given in paragraph 4 of
        Schedule 2 and "abbreviation specified as similar" has the meaning that would be given to
        it in that paragraph if that paragraph made no reference to "expressions";
    "permitted characters" has the meaning given in regulation 2(1);
    "word or abbreviation specified as similar" has the meaning given in paragraph 2 of Schedule 2;
        and
    "word specified as similar" has the meaning given in paragraph 2 of Schedule 2.

(3)   For the purposes of computing the number of permitted characters in regulation 2(4) and paragraph 7 of Schedule 3 (but not in regulation 2(3)), any blank space between one permitted character and another in the name shall be counted as though it was a permitted character.

NOTES
    Commencement: 1 October 2009.

PART 2
COMPANY NAMES

[4.370]
2   Permitted characters

(1)   This regulation sets out the characters, signs, symbols and punctuation that may be used in the name of a company registered under the Act ("the permitted characters").

(2)   The following permitted characters may be used in any part of the name—

   (a)   any character, sign or symbol set out in table 1 in Schedule 1;
   (b)   0, 1, 2, 3, 4, 5, 6, 7, 8 or 9;
   (c)   full stop, comma, colon, semi-colon or hyphen; and
   (d)   any other punctuation referred to in column 1 of table 2 in Schedule 1 but only in one of the forms set out opposite that punctuation in column 2 of that table.

(3)   The signs and symbols set out in table 3 in Schedule 1 are permitted characters that may be used but not as one of the first three permitted characters of the name.

(4)   The name must not consist of more than 160 permitted characters.

NOTES
   Commencement: 1 October 2009.

[4.371]
3   Exemption from requirement as to use of "limited"

(1)   A private company limited by guarantee is exempt from the requirement of section 59 of the Act (requirement to have name ending with "limited" or permitted alternative) so long as it meets the following two conditions.

(2)   The first condition is that the objects of that company are the promotion or regulation of commerce, art, science, education, religion, charity or any profession, and anything incidental or conducive to any of those objects.

(3)   The second condition is that the company's articles—
   (a)   require its income to be applied in promoting its objects;
   (b)   prohibit the payment of dividends, or any return of capital, to its members; and
   (c)   require all the assets that would otherwise be available to its members generally to be transferred on its winding up either—
      (i)   to another body with objects similar to its own; or
      (ii)   to another body the objects of which are the promotion of charity and anything incidental or conducive thereto,
   (whether or not the body is a member of the company).

NOTES
   Commencement: 1 October 2009.

[4.372]
4   Inappropriate indication of company type or legal form: generally applicable provisions

(1)   A company must not be registered under the Act by a name that includes, otherwise than at the end of the name, an expression or abbreviation specified in inverted commas in paragraph 3(a) to (f) of Schedule 2 (or any expression or abbreviation specified as similar).

(2)   A company must not be registered under the Act by a name that includes in any part of the name an expression or abbreviation specified in inverted commas in paragraph 3(g) or (h) of Schedule 2 (or any expression or abbreviation specified as similar) unless that company is a RTE company within the meaning of section 4A of the Leasehold Reform, Housing and Urban Development Act 1993.

(3)   A company must not be registered under the Act by a name that includes in any part of the name an expression or abbreviation specified in inverted commas in paragraph 3(i) or (j) of Schedule 2 (or any expression or abbreviation specified as similar) unless that company is a RTM company within the meaning of section 73 of the Commonhold and Leasehold Reform Act 2002.

(4)   A company must not be registered under the Act by a name that includes in any part of the name an expression or abbreviation specified in inverted commas in paragraph 3(k) to (u) of Schedule 2 (or any expression or abbreviation specified as similar).

(5)   A company must not be registered under the Act by a name that includes immediately before an expression or abbreviation specified in inverted commas in paragraph 3(a) to (j) of Schedule 2 an abbreviation specified in inverted commas in paragraph 3(v) of that Schedule (or any abbreviation specified as similar).

(6)   Paragraph (1) is subject to regulations 5(b) and 6(b).

NOTES
   Commencement: 1 October 2009.

[4.373]
5   Inappropriate indication of company type or legal form: company exempt from requirement to have name ending in "limited"

A company which is exempt from the requirement of section 59 of the Act (requirement to have name ending with "limited" or permitted alternative) under section 60 of the Act must not be registered under the Act by a name that concludes with—
   (a)   a word specified in inverted commas in paragraph 1(c) or (d) of Schedule 2 (or any word specified as similar); or

(b)   an expression or abbreviation specified in inverted commas in paragraph 3(a) to (f) or (v) of Schedule 2 (or any expression or abbreviation specified as similar).

NOTES
Commencement: 1 October 2009.

[4.374]
6   Inappropriate indication of company type or legal form: unlimited company
An unlimited company must not be registered under the Act by a name that concludes with—
(a)   a word or abbreviation specified in inverted commas in paragraph 1(a) or (b) of Schedule 2 (or any word or abbreviation specified as similar); or
(b)   an expression or abbreviation specified in inverted commas in paragraph 3(a) to (f) or (v) of Schedule 2 (or any expression or abbreviation specified as similar).

NOTES
Commencement: 1 October 2009.

[4.375]
7   Name not to be the same as another in the registrar's index of company names
For the purposes of section 66 of the Act (determining whether a name to be registered under the Act is the same as another name appearing in the registrar's index of company names) Schedule 3 has effect for setting out—
(a)   the matters that are to be disregarded; and
(b)   the words, expressions, signs and symbols that are to be regarded as the same.

NOTES
Commencement: 1 October 2009.

[4.376]
8   Consent to registration of a name which is the same as another in the registrar's index of company names
(1)   A company may be registered under the Act by a proposed same name if the conditions in paragraph (2) are met.
(2)   The conditions are—
(a)   the company or other body whose name already appears in the registrar's index of company names ("Body X") consents to the proposed same name being the name of a company ("Company Y");
(b)   Company Y forms, or is to form, part of the same group as Body X; and
(c)   Company Y provides to the registrar a copy of a statement made by Body X indicating—
(i)   the consent of Body X as referred to in sub-paragraph (a); and
(ii)   that Company Y forms, or is to form, part of the same group as Body X.
(3)   If the proposed same name is to be taken by a company which has not yet been incorporated, the copy of such statement must be provided to the registrar instead by the person who delivers to the registrar the application for registration of the company (and the reference in paragraph (1) to the conditions in paragraph (2) shall be read accordingly).
(4)   The registrar may accept the statement referred to in paragraph (2)(c) as sufficient evidence that the conditions referred to in paragraph (2)(a) and (b) have been met.
(5)   If the consent referred to in paragraph (2)(a) is given by Body X, a subsequent withdrawal of that consent does not affect the registration of Company Y by that proposed same name.
(6)   In this regulation—
(a)   "group" has the meaning given in section 474(1) of the Act; and
(b)   "proposed same name" means a name which is, due to the application of regulation 7 and Schedule 3, considered the same as a name appearing in the registrar's index of company names and differs from that name appearing in the index only by one of the matters set out in inverted commas in paragraph 4 of Schedule 3.

NOTES
Commencement: 1 October 2009.

PART 3
OVERSEAS COMPANY NAMES

[4.377]
9   Interpretation and permitted characters
Regulations 1(2) and (3) and 2 apply to the name of an overseas company which is registered by that company under Part 34 of the Act (overseas companies) as they apply to the name of a company formed and registered under the Act.

NOTES
Commencement: 1 October 2009.

[4.378]
10   Inappropriate indication of company type or legal form

(1)   An overseas company must not be registered under the Act by a name that concludes with a word or abbreviation specified in inverted commas in paragraph 1(a) or (b) of Schedule 2 (or any word or abbreviation specified as similar) unless the liability of the members of the company is limited by its constitution.

(2)   An overseas company must not be registered under the Act by a name that concludes with a word specified in inverted commas in paragraph 1(c) or (d) of Schedule 2 (or any word specified as similar) unless the liability of the members of the company is not limited by its constitution.

(3)   An overseas company must not be registered under the Act by a name that includes in any part of the name an expression or abbreviation specified in inverted commas in paragraph 3 of Schedule 2 (or any expression or abbreviation specified as similar).

NOTES
Commencement: 1 October 2009.

[4.379]
11   Name not to be the same as another in the registrar's index of company names

Regulation 7 applies to the name of an overseas company which is registered by that company under Part 34 of the Act as it applies to the name of a company formed and registered under the Act.

NOTES
Commencement: 1 October 2009.

[4.380]
12   Consent to registration of a name which is the same as another in the registrar's index of company names

(1)   Regulation 8 applies to the proposed same name of an overseas company as it applies to the proposed same name of a company formed and registered under the Act.

(2)   In this regulation "proposed same name" has the same meaning as in regulation 8.

NOTES
Commencement: 1 October 2009.

PART 4
BUSINESS NAMES

[4.381]
13   "Limited" and permitted alternatives

(1)   A person must not carry on business in the United Kingdom under a name that concludes with any word or abbreviation set out in inverted commas in paragraph 1(a) or (b) of Schedule 2 unless that person is—

(a)   a company or an overseas company registered in the United Kingdom by that name;

(b)   an overseas company incorporated with that name; . . .

(c)   a society registered under the Industrial and Provident Societies Act 1965 or the Industrial and Provident Societies Act (Northern Ireland) 1969 by that name;

[(d)   an incorporated friendly society (as defined in section 116 of the Friendly Societies Act 1992) which has that name; or

(e)   a company to which section 1040 of the Companies Act 2006 (companies authorised to register under the Companies Act 2006) applies which has that name.]

(2)   A person must not carry on business in the United Kingdom under a name that concludes with any word or abbreviation specified as similar to any word or abbreviation set out in inverted commas in paragraph 1(a) or (b) of Schedule 2.

NOTES
Commencement: 1 October 2009.
Para (1): word omitted from sub-para (b) revoked, and sub-paras (d), (e) added, by the Company, Limited Liability Partnership and Business Names (Miscellaneous Provisions) (Amendment) Regulations 2009, SI 2009/2404, reg 2(1), (2), as from 1 October 2009.
Industrial and Provident Societies Act 1965: see the Co-operative and Community Benefit Societies and Credit Unions Act 2010 which renames this Act as the Co-operative and Community Benefit Societies and Credit Unions Act 1965.

Part 4   CA 2006 SIs

[4.382]
14　Other indications of legal form

(1)　A person must not carry on business in the United Kingdom under a name that includes any expression or abbreviation set out in inverted commas in paragraph 3 of Schedule 2 unless that person is such a company, partnership, grouping or organisation as is indicated in that expression or abbreviation.

(2)　A person must not carry on business in the United Kingdom under a name that includes any expression or abbreviation specified as similar to any expression or abbreviation set out in inverted commas in paragraph 3 of Schedule 2.

NOTES
Commencement: 1 October 2009.

[4.383]
15　Transitional provisions

(1)　Regulation 14 does not apply to the carrying on of a business under a name by a person who—
  (a)　carried on that business under that name immediately before these Regulations came into force; and
  (b)　continues to carry it on under that name,
if it was lawful for the business to be carried on under that name immediately before these Regulations came into force.

(2)　Regulation 14 does not apply to the carrying on of a business under a name by a person to whom the business is transferred on or after the date on which these Regulations came into force—
  (a)　where that person continues to carry on the business under that name; and
  (b)　where it was lawful for the business to be carried on under that name immediately before the transfer,
during the period of 12 months beginning with the date of the transfer.

NOTES
Commencement: 1 October 2009.

SCHEDULES

SCHEDULE 1
CHARACTERS, SIGNS, SYMBOLS AND PUNCTUATION

Regulation 2
[4.384]

Table 1: Characters, signs and symbols				
A	B	C	D	E
F	G	H	I	J
K	L	M	N	O
P	Q	R	S	T
U	V	W	X	Y
Z	&	@	£	$
€	¥			

Table 2	
Type of punctuation	*Punctuation mark*
Apostrophe	'
	'
	'
Bracket	(
	)
	[
	]
	{
	}
	<
	>
Exclamation mark	!

Table 2	
Guillemet	«
	»
Inverted comma	"
	"
	"
Question mark	?
Solidus	\
	/

Table 3: Signs and symbols
*
=
#
%
+

NOTES

Commencement: 1 October 2009.

SCHEDULE 2
SPECIFIED WORDS, EXPRESSIONS AND ABBREVIATIONS
Regulations 1, 4 to 6, 10, 13 and 14

[4.385]

1. The words and abbreviations specified are—
- (a) "LIMITED" or (with or without full stops) the abbreviation "LTD";
- (b) "CYFYNGEDIG" or (with or without full stops) the abbreviation "CYF";
- (c) "UNLIMITED"; and
- (d) "ANGHYFYNGEDIG".

2. The words and abbreviations specified as similar to the words and abbreviations set out in inverted commas in paragraph 1(a) and (b) and the words specified as similar to the words set out in inverted commas in paragraph 1(c) and (d) are any in which—
- (a) one or more characters has been omitted;
- (b) one or more characters, signs, symbols or punctuation has been added; or
- (c) each of one or more characters has been substituted by one or more other characters, signs, symbols or punctuation,

in such a way as to be likely to mislead the public as to the legal form of a company or business if included in the registered name of the company or in a business name.

3. The expressions and abbreviations specified are—
- (a) "PUBLIC LIMITED COMPANY" or (with or without full stops) the abbreviation "PLC";
- (b) "CWMNI CYFYNGEDIG CYHOEDDUS" or (with or without full stops) the abbreviation "CCC";
- (c) "COMMUNITY INTEREST COMPANY" or (with or without full stops) the abbreviation "CIC";
- (d) "CWMNI BUDDIANT CYMUNEDOL" or (with or without full stops) the abbreviation "CBC";
- (e) "COMMUNITY INTEREST PUBLIC LIMITED COMPANY" or (with or without full stops) the abbreviation "COMMUNITY INTEREST PLC";
- (f) "CWMNI BUDDIANT CYMUNEDOL CYHOEDDUS CYFYNGEDIG" or (with or without full stops) the abbreviation "[CWMNI BUDDIANT CYMUNEDOL CCC]";
- (g) "RIGHT TO ENFRANCHISEMENT" or (with or without full stops) the abbreviation "RTE";
- (h) "HAWL I RYDDFREINIAD";
- (i) "RIGHT TO MANAGE" or (with or without full stops) the abbreviation "RTM";
- (j) "CWMNI RTM CYFYNGEDIG";
- (k) "EUROPEAN ECONOMIC INTEREST GROUPING" or (with or without full stops) the abbreviation "EEIG";
- (l) "INVESTMENT COMPANY WITH VARIABLE CAPITAL";
- (m) "CWMNI BUDDSODDI A CHYFALAF NEWIDIOL";
- (n) "LIMITED PARTNERSHIP";
- (o) "PARTNERIAETH CYFYNGEDIG";

(p) "LIMITED LIABILITY PARTNERSHIP";
(q) "PARTNERIAETH ATEBOLRWYDD CYFYNGEDIG";
(r) "OPEN-ENDED INVESTMENT COMPANY";
(s) "CWMNI BUDDSODDIANT PENAGORED";
(t) "CHARITABLE INCORPORATED ORGANISATION";
(u) "SEFDYDLIAD ELUSENNOL CORFFOREDIG"; . . .
[(ua) "INDUSTRIAL AND PROVIDENT SOCIETY"; and]
(v) the following abbreviations (with or without full stops) of the expressions specified in sub-paragraphs (n), (o), (p), (q), (t) and (u) respectively, namely "LP", "PC", "LLP", "PAC", "CIO" and "SEC".

4. The expressions and abbreviations specified as similar to the expressions and abbreviations set out in inverted commas in paragraph 3 are any in which—
(a) one or more characters has been omitted;
(b) one or more characters, signs, symbols or punctuation has been added; or
(c) each of one or more characters has been substituted by one or more other characters, signs, symbols or punctuation,
in such a way as to be likely to mislead the public as to the legal form of a company or business if included in the registered name of the company or in a business name.

NOTES
Commencement: 1 October 2009.
Para 3: words in square brackets in sub-para (f) substituted, word omitted from sub-para (u) revoked, and sub-para (ua) inserted, by the Company, Limited Liability Partnership and Business Names (Miscellaneous Provisions) (Amendment) Regulations 2009, SI 2009/2404, reg 2(1), as from 1 October 2009. Note that reg 2(3) of the 2009 Regulations provides that this amendment also applies to this Schedule as it is applied to limited liability partnerships by Limited Liability Partnerships (Application of Companies Act 2006) Regulations 2009, SI 2009/1804, reg 10.

SCHEDULE 3
NAME SAME AS ANOTHER IN THE REGISTRAR'S INDEX OF COMPANY NAMES
Regulations 7 and 8

[4.386]
1. In determining whether a name is the same as another name appearing in the registrar's index of company names the provisions in this Schedule are to be applied in the order set out in the Schedule.

2. Disregard any word, expression or abbreviation set out in inverted commas in Schedule 2 where it appears at the end of the name.

3. (1) Taking the name remaining after the application of paragraph 2, regard each of the words, expressions, signs and symbols set out in inverted commas in any of the paragraphs of sub-paragraph (2) ("relevant matters") as the same as the other relevant matters set out in that paragraph where each relevant matter—
(a) is preceded by and followed by a blank space; or
(b) where the relevant matter is at the beginning of the name, where it is followed by a blank space.

(2) The words, expressions, signs and symbols are—
(a) "AND" and "&";
(b) "PLUS" and "+";
(c) "0", "ZERO" and "O";
(d) "1" and "ONE";
(e) "2", "TWO", "TO" and "TOO";
(f) "3" and "THREE";
(g) "4", "FOUR" and "FOR";
(h) "5" and "FIVE";
(i) "6" and "SIX";
(j) "7" and "SEVEN";
(k) "8" and "EIGHT";
(l) "9" and "NINE";
(m) "£" and "POUND";
(n) "€" and "EURO";
(o) "$" and "DOLLAR";
(p) "¥" and "YEN";
(q) "%", "PER CENT", "PERCENT", "PER CENTUM" and "PERCENTUM"; and
(r) "@" and "AT".

4. (1) Taking the name remaining after the application of paragraphs 2 and 3, disregard at the end of the name the matters set out in inverted commas in sub-paragraph (2) (or any combination of such matters) where the matter (or combination) is preceded by the following punctuation or symbol in inverted commas—

    (a)   a blank space;
    (b)   a full stop; or
    (c)   "@".
(2)   The matters are—
    (a)   "BIZ";
    (b)   "CO";
    (c)   "CO UK";
    (d)   "CO.UK";
    (e)   "COM";
    (f)   "COMPANY";
    (g)   "EU";
    (h)   "EXPORTS";
    (i)   "GB";
    (j)   "GREAT BRITAIN";
    (k)   "GROUP";
    (l)   "HOLDINGS";
    (m)   "IMPORTS";
    (n)   "INTERNATIONAL";
    (o)   "NET";
    (p)   "NI";
    (q)   "NORTHERN IRELAND";
    (r)   "ORG";
    (s)   "ORG UK";
    (t)   "ORG.UK";
    (u)   "SERVICES";
    (v)   "UK";
    (w)   "UNITED KINGDOM";
    (x)   "WALES";
    (y)   "ALLFORION";
    (z)   "CWMNI";
    (aa)   "CYM";
    (bb)   "CYMRU";
    (cc)   "CYNHEILIAID";
    (dd)   "CYRDDAU";
    (ee)   "DALIADAU";
    (ff)   "DU";
    (gg)   "GRWP";
    (hh)   "GWASANAETHAU";
    (ii)   "MEWNFORION";
    (jj)   "PF";
    (kk)   "PRYDAIN FAWR";
    (ll)   "RHYNGWLADOL";
    (mm) "RYNGWLADOL"; and
    (nn)   "Y DEYRNAS UNEDIG".

5. Taking the name remaining after the application of paragraphs 2 to 4, disregard the following matters in any part of the name—
    (a)   any punctuation set out in regulation 2(2)(c) or in column 2 of table 2 in Schedule 1; and
    (b)   the following symbols set out in inverted commas—
        (i)   "*";
        (ii) "="; and
        (iii) "#".

6. Taking the name remaining after the application of paragraphs 2 to 5, disregard the letter "S" at the end of the name.

7. Taking the name remaining after the application of paragraphs 2 to 6, disregard any permitted character after the first 60 permitted characters of the name.

8. Taking the name remaining after the application of paragraphs 2 to 7, disregard the following matters or any combination of the following matters set out in inverted commas where they appear at the beginning of the name—
    (a)   "@";
    (b)   "THE" (but only where followed by a blank space); and
    (c)   "WWW".

9. Taking the name remaining after the application of paragraphs 2 to 8, disregard blank spaces between permitted characters.

NOTES
Commencement: 1 October 2009.

COMPANIES ACT 2006 (EXTENSION OF TAKEOVER PANEL PROVISIONS) (ISLE OF MAN) ORDER 2009 (NOTE)

(SI 2009/1378)

[4.387]

NOTES
This Order was made on 10 June 2009 under the powers conferred by the Companies Act 2006, s 965. It came into force on 1 July 2009.

This Order applies Sch 2 to CA 2006 (as substituted by the Companies Act 2006 (Amendment of Schedule 2) (No 2) Order 2009) to the Isle of Man. The substituted Schedule forms part of Chapter 1 of Part 28 of the 2006 Act, which was extended to the Isle of Man by the Companies Act 2006 (Extension of Takeover Panel Provisions) (Isle of Man) Order 2008, SI 2008/3122, and which deals with disclosures of information arising from the exercise by the Takeover Panel of its powers and duties. Article 1 of this Order provides for citation and commencement. Article 2 provides for the extension of the substituted Schedule to the Isle of Man. Article 3 contains revocations of spent provisions of the 2008 Order, namely Schedule, paras 9, 10.

COMPANIES ACT 2006 (ACCOUNTS, REPORTS AND AUDIT) REGULATIONS 2009 (NOTE)

(SI 2009/1581)

[4.388]

NOTES
These Regulations were made on 26 June 2009 under the powers conferred by the European Communities Act 1972, s 2(2), and the Companies Act 2006, ss 468(1), (2), 1292(1). Regs 1–9, 11, 12 came into force on 27 June 2009, and reg 10 comes into force on 1 October 2009.

Reg 1(3) provides that Part 2 of these Regulations (corporate governance statements) applies in relation to financial years beginning on or after 29 June 2008 which have not ended before the date of coming into force of these Regulations. Reg 1(4) provides that regs 11 and 12 in Part 3 of the Regulations (accounts amendments) apply in relation to financial years beginning on or after 6 April 2008 which have not ended before the date of coming into force of these Regulations.

Regs 2–9 (Part 2: Corporate Governance Statements) provide as follows. Reg 2 inserts the Companies Act 2006, s 419A at **[1.419A]**. Regs 3, 4 amend ss 446, 447 of the 2006 Act (including providing for further transitional adaptations of those sections (for details see **[1.446]**, **[1.447]**)). Reg 5 inserts CA 2006, s 472A at **[1.472A]**. Reg 6 inserts CA 2006, s 497A at **[1.497A]**. Reg 7 inserts CA 2006, s 498A at **[1.498A]**. Reg 8 inserts CA 2006, s 538A at **[1.538A]**. Reg 9 amends CA 2006, Sch 8 at **[1.538A]**.

Regs 10–12 (Part 3: Accounts Amendments) provide as follows. Reg 10 substitutes CA 2006, s 444A(4) at **[1.444A]**. Reg 11 amends the Small Companies and Groups (Accounts and Directors' Report) Regulations 2008, SI 2009/409, reg 12, Sch 7 (see those Regulations at **[4.142]** et seq). Reg 12 amends the Large and Medium-sized Companies and Groups (Accounts and Reports) Regulations 2008, SI 2008/410, reg 12, Schs 8, 9 (see those Regulations at **[4.170]** et seq).

OVERSEAS COMPANIES REGULATIONS 2009

(SI 2009/1801)

NOTES
Made: 8 July 2009.

Authority: Companies Act 2006, ss 1046(1), (2), (4)–(6), 1047(1), 1049(1)–(3), 1050(3)–(5), 1051(1)–(3), 1053(2)–(5), 1054(1), (2), 1055, 1056, 1058(1)–(3), 1078(5), 1105(1), (2), 1140(2), 1292(1), (4), 1294.

Commencement: 1 October 2009.

Amendment: as of 1 July 2011, these Regulations had not been amended.

References to the "European Community", "Community", etc: see the Treaty of Lisbon (Changes in Terminology) Order 2011, SI 2011/1043, which provides (with effect from 22 April 2011): (1) that for references to the "European Communities" or to the "European Community" (including references to "the Communities", "the Community", "the EC" or "the EEC") substitute references to the European Union; and (2) that "EU" should be substituted for the word "Community" (subject to certain exceptions) in references to "Community treaties", "Community customs duty", "Community institution", "Community instrument", "Community obligation", "enforceable Community right", "Community law", "Community legislation", and "Community provision". Also, where such a term is preceded by the word "a", for "a" substitute "an".

ARRANGEMENT OF REGULATIONS

PART 1
INTRODUCTION

PART 1
INTRODUCTION

[4.389]
1   Citation and commencement

(1)   These Regulations may be cited as the Overseas Companies Regulations 2009.

(2)   These Regulations come into force on 1st October 2009.

NOTES
Commencement: 1 October 2009.

[4.390]
2   Interpretation

In these Regulations—
   "accounting documents"—
      (a)   in relation to an overseas company to which Chapter 2 of Part 5 applies (companies required to prepare and disclose accounts under parent law), has the meaning given by regulation 31(2), and
      (b)   in relation to a credit or financial institution to which Chapter 2 of Part 6 applies (institutions required to prepare accounts under parent law), has the meaning given by regulation 44(2);
   "certified copy" means a copy certified as a correct copy;
   "constitution", in relation to an overseas company, means the charter, statutes, memorandum and articles of association or other instrument constituting or defining the company's constitution;
   "credit or financial institution" means a credit or financial institution to which section 1050 of the Companies Act 2006 applies;
   "disclosure", in relation to a credit or financial institution to which Chapter 2 of Part 6 applies, has the meaning given by regulation 44(2);
   "establishment" means—
      (a)   a branch within the meaning of the Eleventh Company Law Directive (89/666/EEC), or
      (b)   a place of business that is not such a branch,
   and "UK establishment" means an establishment in the United Kingdom;
   "financial period"—
      (a)   in relation to an overseas company to which Chapter 2 of Part 5 applies (companies required to prepare and disclose accounts under parent law), has the meaning given by regulation 31(2), and
      (b)   in relation to a credit or financial institution to which Chapter 2 of Part 6 applies (institutions required to prepare accounts under parent law), has the meaning given by regulation 44(2);
   "First Company Law Directive" means the First Council Directive on co-ordination of safeguards which, for the protection of the interests of members and others, are required by Member States of companies within the meaning of the second paragraph of Article 58 of the Treaty, with a view to making such safeguards equivalent throughout the Community (68/151/EEC);
   "former name", in the case of an individual, means a name by which the individual was formerly known for business purposes;
   "name", in the case of an individual, means the person's Christian name (or other forename) and surname, except that in the case of—
      (a)   a peer, or
      (b)   an individual usually known by a title,
   the title may be stated instead of the individual's Christian name (or other forename) and surname or in addition to either or both of them; and

"parent law"—

    (a)   in relation to an overseas company to which Chapter 2 of Part 5 applies (companies required to prepare and disclose accounts under parent law), has the meaning given by regulation 31(2), and

    (b)   in relation to a credit or financial institution to which Chapter 2 of Part 6 applies (institutions required to prepare accounts under parent law), has the meaning given by regulation 44(2).

NOTES

Commencement: 1 October 2009.

PART 2
INITIAL REGISTRATION OF PARTICULARS

[4.391]
3 Application and interpretation of Part

(1)   This Part applies to an overseas company that opens a UK establishment.

(2)   In this Part—

"director" includes shadow director; and

"secretary" includes any person occupying the position of secretary by whatever name called.

NOTES

Commencement: 1 October 2009.

[4.392]
4 Duty to deliver return and documents

(1)   The company must within one month of having opened a UK establishment—

    (a)   deliver to the registrar a return complying with the requirements of this Part, and

    (b)   deliver with the return the documents required by this Part.

(2)   These requirements apply each time a company opens an establishment in the United Kingdom.

NOTES

Commencement: 1 October 2009.

[4.393]
5 Particulars to be included in return

(1)   The return must contain—

    (a)   the particulars specified in regulation 6 (particulars of the company), and

    (b)   the particulars specified in regulation 7 (particulars of the establishment).

(2)   If at the time the return is delivered the company—

    (a)   has another UK establishment,

    (b)   has delivered a return in respect of that establishment containing the particulars specified in regulation 6, and

    (c)   has no outstanding obligation under Part 3 in respect of an alteration to those particulars,

the company may instead state in the return that those particulars are included in the particulars delivered in respect of another UK establishment (giving the registered number of that establishment).

NOTES

Commencement: 1 October 2009.

[4.394]
6 Particulars of the company

(1)   The particulars of the company to be included in the return are—

    (a)   the company's name,

    (b)   the company's legal form,

    (c)   if it is registered in the country of its incorporation, the identity of the register in which it is registered and the number with which it is so registered,

    (d)   a list of its directors and secretary, containing—

        (i)   with respect to each director, the particulars specified in paragraph (3), and

        (ii)   with respect to the secretary (or where there are joint secretaries, with respect to each of them) the particulars specified in paragraph (4),

    (e)   the extent of the powers of the directors or secretary to represent the company in dealings with third parties and in legal proceedings, together with a statement as to whether they may act alone or must act jointly and, if jointly, the name of any other person concerned, and

    (f)   whether the company is a credit or financial institution.

(2) In the case of a company that is not incorporated in an EEA State, the particulars of the company to be included in the return must also include—

   (a)   the law under which the company is incorporated,

   (b)   in the case of a company to which Chapter 2 of Part 5 or Chapter 2 of Part 6 applies (requirement to prepare and disclose accounts under parent law), the period for which the company is required by its parent law to prepare accounts, together with the period allowed for the preparation and public disclosure (if any) of accounts for such a period,

   (c)   unless disclosed by the company's constitution (see regulation 8)—

       (i)   the address of its principal place of business in its country of incorporation or, if applicable, its registered office,

      (ii)   its objects, and

     (iii)   the amount of its issued share capital.

(3) The particulars referred to in paragraph (1)(d)(i) (directors) are—

   (a)   in the case of an individual—

       (i)   name,

      (ii)   any former name,

     (iii)   a service address,

     (iv)   usual residential address,

      (v)   the country or state in which the individual is usually resident,

     (vi)   nationality,

    (vii)   business occupation (if any), and

    (viii)   date of birth;

   (b)   in the case of a body corporate, or a firm that is a legal person under the law by which it is governed—

       (i)   corporate or firm name,

      (ii)   registered or principal office,

     (iii)   in the case of an EEA company to which the First Company Law Directive applies, particulars of—

          (aa)   the register in which the company file mentioned in Article 3 of that Directive is kept (including details of the relevant state), and

          (bb)   the registration number in that register,

     (iv)   in any other case, particulars of—

          (aa)   the legal form of the company or firm and the law by which it is governed, and

          (bb)   if applicable, the register in which it is entered (including details of the state) and its registration number in that register.

(4) The particulars referred to in paragraph (1)(d)(ii) (secretary) are—

   (a)   in the case of an individual—

       (i)   name,

      (ii)   any former name, and

     (iii)   a service address;

   (b)   in the case of a body corporate, or a firm that is a legal person under the law by which it is governed—

       (i)   corporate or firm name,

      (ii)   registered or principal office,

     (iii)   in the case of an EEA company to which the First Company Law Directive applies, particulars of—

          (aa)   the register in which the company file mentioned in Article 3 of that Directive is kept (including details of the relevant state), and

          (bb)   the registration number in that register,

     (iv)   in any other case, particulars of—

          (aa)   the legal form of the company or firm and the law by which it is governed, and

          (bb)   if applicable, the register in which it is entered (including details of the state) and its registration number in that register.

But if all the partners in a firm are joint secretaries of the company it is sufficient to state the particulars that would be required if the firm were a legal person and the firm had been appointed secretary.

(5) For the purposes of paragraphs (3)(a)(ii) and (4)(a)(ii), where a person is or was formerly known by more than one former name, each of them must be stated.

(6) It is not necessary to include in the return particulars of a former name in the following cases—

   (a)   in the case of a peer or an individual normally known by a title, where the name is one by which the person was known previous to the adoption of or succession to the title,

   (b)   in the case of any person, where the former name—

       (i)   was changed or disused before the person attained the age of 16 years, or

      (ii)   has been changed or disused for 20 years or more.

(7)   For the purposes of paragraph (3)(a)(iv) if the person's usual residential address is the same as the person's service address the return need only contain a statement to that effect.

NOTES
Commencement: 1 October 2009.

[4.395]
7   Particulars of the establishment
(1)   The particulars of the establishment to be included in the return are—
  (a)   address of the establishment,
  (b)   date on which it was opened,
  (c)   business carried on at it,
  (d)   name of the establishment if different from the name of the company,
  (e)   name and service address of every person resident in the United Kingdom authorised to accept service of documents on behalf of the company in respect of the establishment, or a statement that there is no such person,
  (f)   a list of every person authorised to represent the company as a permanent representative of the company in respect of the establishment, containing the following particulars with respect to each such person—
    (i)   name,
    (ii)   any former name,
    (iii)   service address, and
    (iv)   usual residential address,
  (g)   extent of the authority of any person falling within sub-paragraph (f), including whether that person is authorised to act alone or jointly, and
  (h)   if a person falling within sub-paragraph (f) is not authorised to act alone, the name of any person with whom they are authorised to act.
(2)   For the purpose of paragraph (1)(f)(iv) if the person's usual residential address is the same as the person's service address the return need only contain a statement to that effect.

NOTES
Commencement: 1 October 2009.

[4.396]
8   Documents to be delivered with the return: copy of company's constitution
(1)   A certified copy of the company's constitution must be delivered to the registrar with the return.
(2)   If at the time the return is delivered the company—
  (a)   has another UK establishment,
  (b)   has delivered a certified copy of the company's constitution with a return relating to that establishment, and
  (c)   has no outstanding obligation under Part 3 in respect of an alteration to its constitution,
the company may instead state in the return that a certified copy of the company's constitution has been delivered in respect of another UK establishment (giving the registered number of that establishment).

NOTES
Commencement: 1 October 2009.

[4.397]
9   Documents to be delivered with the return: copies of accounting documents
(1)   If the company is one to which Chapter 2 of Part 5 applies (companies required to prepare and disclose accounts under parent law), copies of the company's latest accounting documents must be delivered to the registrar with the return.
(2)   The company's latest accounting documents means the accounting documents, prepared for a financial period of the company, last disclosed in accordance with its parent law before the end of the period allowed for delivery of the return or, if earlier, the date on which the company delivers the return.
(3)   If at the time the return is delivered the company—
  (a)   has another UK establishment, and
  (b)   has delivered the documents required by paragraph (1) in connection with a return relating to that establishment,
the company may instead state in the return that the documents are included in the material delivered in respect of another UK establishment (giving the registered number of that establishment).

NOTES
Commencement: 1 October 2009.

[4.398]
10 Statement as to future manner of compliance with accounting requirements

(1) If the company is one to which Part 5 applies (delivery of accounting documents: general), the return must state—

 (a) in the case of a company to which Chapter 2 of that Part applies (companies required to file copies of accounting documents disclosed under parent law), whether it is intended to file copies of accounting documents in accordance with the provisions of that Chapter in respect of the establishment to which the return relates or in respect of another UK establishment;

 (b) in the case of a company to which Chapter 3 of that Part applies (companies required to file accounts under UK law), whether it is intended to file accounts in accordance with the provisions of that Chapter in respect of the establishment to which the return relates or in respect of another UK establishment.

(2) If the return states that it is intended to file copies of accounting documents, or accounts, in respect of another UK establishment, it must give the registered number of that establishment.

NOTES
Commencement: 1 October 2009.

[4.399]
11 Penalty for non-compliance

(1) If a company fails to comply with any of the requirements of this Part, an offence is committed by—

 (a) the company, and

 (b) every officer or agent of the company who knowingly and wilfully authorises or permits the default.

(2) A person guilty of an offence under paragraph (1) is liable on summary conviction to—

 (a) a fine not exceeding level 3 on the standard scale, and

 (b) for continued contravention, a daily default fine not exceeding one-tenth of level 3 on the standard scale.

NOTES
Commencement: 1 October 2009.

PART 3
ALTERATION IN REGISTERED PARTICULARS

[4.400]
12 Application of Part

This Part applies to an overseas company that—

 (a) has complied with Part 2 (initial registration of particulars) in respect of one or more UK establishments, and

 (b) has not subsequently given notice under regulation 77 (notice of closure of UK establishment) in respect of all those establishments.

NOTES
Commencement: 1 October 2009.

[4.401]
13 Return of alteration in registered particulars

(1) If an alteration is made in any of the particulars delivered under—

 (a) regulation 6 (particulars of the company), or

 (b) regulation 7 (particulars of the establishment),

the company must deliver to the registrar a return containing details of the alteration.

(2) Where a company has more than one UK establishment a return is required in respect of each UK establishment to which the alteration relates; but a return giving the registered numbers of more than one UK establishment is treated as a return in respect of each of them.

(3) An alteration in any of the particulars specified in regulation 6 (particulars of the company) is treated as relating to every UK establishment of the company.

(4) The details required of the alteration are—

 (a) the particular that has been altered,

 (b) details of the particular as altered, and

 (c) the date on which the alteration was made.

(5) The return must also state—

 (a) the company's name,

 (b) the company's registered number, and

   (c)   the name (if different from the company's name) and registered number of each UK establishment to which the return relates.

(6)   The period allowed for delivery of the return is—

   (a)   in the case of an alteration of any of the particulars specified in regulation 6 (particulars of the company), 21 days after the date on which notice of the alteration in question could have been received in the United Kingdom in due course of post (if despatched with due diligence);

   (b)   in the case of an alteration of any of the particulars specified in regulation 7 (particulars of the establishment), 21 days after the alteration is made.

NOTES

Commencement: 1 October 2009.

[4.402]

14 Return of alteration in company's constitution

(1)   If any alteration is made in the company's constitution the company must deliver to the registrar a return stating—

   (a)   that an alteration has been made to the company's constitution, and

   (b)   the date on which the alteration was made.

(2)   The return must be accompanied by a certified copy of the constitution as altered.

(3)   Where a company has more than one UK establishment a return is required in respect of each UK establishment to which the alteration relates; but a return giving the registered numbers of more than one UK establishment is treated as a return in respect of each of them.

(4)   An alteration in the company's constitution is treated as relating to a UK establishment only if a copy of the constitution is included in the material registered in respect of that establishment.

(5)   The return must also state—

   (a)   the company's name,

   (b)   the company's registered number, and

   (c)   the name (if different from the company's name) and registered number of each UK establishment to which the return relates.

(6)   The period allowed for delivery of the return is 21 days after the date on which notice of the alteration in question could have been received in the United Kingdom in due course of post (if despatched with due diligence).

NOTES

Commencement: 1 October 2009.

[4.403]

15 Return of alteration as regards filing of certified copy of constitution

(1)   This regulation applies where—

   (a)   the company's return under Part 2 in respect of an establishment states that a certified copy of the company's constitution has been delivered in respect of another UK establishment, and

   (b)   that statement ceases to be true.

(2)   The company must deliver to the registrar a further return in respect of the first-mentioned establishment—

   (a)   stating that the previous statement has ceased to be true, and

   (b)   either—

      (i)   accompanied by a certified copy of the company's constitution, or

      (ii)   stating that a copy of the company's constitution is included in the material delivered in respect of another UK establishment (giving the registered number of that establishment).

(3)   Where the company has more than one UK establishment a return giving the registered numbers of more than one UK establishment is treated as a return in respect of each of them.

(4)   The return must also state—

   (a)   the company's name,

   (b)   the company's registered number, and

   (c)   the name (if different from the company's name) and registered number of each UK establishment to which the return relates.

(5)   The period allowed for delivery of the return is 21 days after the date on which notice of the fact that the statement in the earlier return has ceased to be true could have been received in the United Kingdom in due course of post (if despatched with due diligence).

(6)   Where, after a company has made a return under this regulation, the statement mentioned in paragraph (2)(b)(ii) ceases to be true, paragraphs (2) to (5) (and this paragraph) apply again.

NOTES
Commencement: 1 October 2009.

[4.404]

16 Return of alteration of manner of compliance with accounting requirements

(1) This regulation applies where—

    (a) the company's return under Part 2 in respect of a UK establishment states an intention as to whether accounting documents, or accounts, are to be filed in accordance with the provisions of that Part in respect of that establishment or in respect of another UK establishment, and

    (b) that intention changes.

(2) The company must deliver to the registrar a further return in respect of the first-mentioned establishment stating—

    (a) that the intention has changed, and

    (b) either—

        (i) that it is intended to file accounting documents, or accounts, in respect of the establishment to which the return relates, or

        (ii) that it is intended to file accounting documents, or accounts, in respect of another UK establishment (giving the registered number of that establishment).

(3) Where the company has more than one UK establishment a return giving the registered numbers of more than one UK establishment is treated as a return in respect of each of them.

(4) The return must also state—

    (a) the company's name,

    (b) the company's registered number, and

    (c) the name (if different from the company's name) and registered number of each UK establishment to which the return relates.

(5) The period allowed for delivery of the return is 21 days after the date on which notice of the fact that the intention stated in the earlier return has changed could have been received in the United Kingdom in due course of post (if despatched with due diligence).

(6) Where, after a company has made a return under this regulation, the intention stated in accordance with paragraph (2)(b)(i) or (ii) changes again, paragraphs (2) to (5) (and this paragraph) apply again.

NOTES
Commencement: 1 October 2009.

[4.405]

17 Penalty for non-compliance

(1) If a company fails to comply with any of the requirements of this Part within the period allowed, an offence is committed by—

    (a) the company, and

    (b) every officer or agent of the company who knowingly and wilfully authorises or permits the default.

(2) A person guilty of an offence under paragraph (1) is liable on summary conviction to—

    (a) a fine not exceeding level 3 on the standard scale, and

    (b) for continued contravention, a daily default fine not exceeding one-tenth of level 3 on the standard scale.

NOTES
Commencement: 1 October 2009.

PART 4
USUAL RESIDENTIAL ADDRESSES: PROTECTION FROM DISCLOSURE

[4.406]

18 Application and interpretation of Part

(1) This Part applies to an overseas company that has one or more UK establishments in respect of which it has registered particulars under Part 2.

(2) In this Part—

    "credit reference agency" means a person carrying on a business comprising the furnishing of information relevant to the financial standing of individuals, being information collected by the agency for that purpose;

    "director" means a director of a company who is an individual and whose particulars have been delivered to the registrar under regulation 6(1)(d)(i);

"limited liability partnership" means a limited liability partnership incorporated under the Limited Liability Partnerships Act 2000 or Limited Liability Partnerships Act (Northern Ireland) 2002;

"permanent representative" means a permanent representative of a company whose particulars have been delivered to the registrar under regulation 7(1)(f);

"police force" means a police force within the meaning of section 101(1) of the Police Act 1996 (interpretation), section 50 of the Police (Scotland) Act 1967 (meaning of police area, etc) or section 1 of the Police (Northern Ireland) Act 2000 (name of the police in Northern Ireland); and

"specified public authority" means a public authority specified in Schedule 1.

NOTES
Commencement: 1 October 2009.

[4.407]
19   Protected information

(1)   This Part makes provision for protecting, in the case of a director or permanent representative of a company to which this Part applies—
(a)   information as to their usual residential address;
(b)   the information that their service address is their usual residential address.

(2)   That information is referred to in this Part as "protected information".

(3)   Information does not cease to be protected information on the person ceasing to be a director or permanent representative and references in this Part to a director or permanent representative include, to that extent, a person who was formerly a director or permanent representative.

NOTES
Commencement: 1 October 2009.

[4.408]
20   Protected information: restriction on use or disclosure by company

(1)   A company to which this Part applies must not use or disclose protected information about a director or permanent representative, except—
(a)   for communicating with the individual concerned,
(b)   in order to comply with any requirement in these Regulations as to particulars to be sent to the registrar, or
(c)   in accordance with regulation 26 (disclosure under court order).

(2)   Paragraph (1) does not prohibit the use or disclosure of protected information with the consent of the director or permanent representative.

NOTES
Commencement: 1 October 2009.

[4.409]
21   Protected information: restriction on use or disclosure by registrar

(1)   The registrar must omit protected information from the material on the register that is available for inspection where—
(a)   it is contained in a document delivered to the registrar in which such information is required to be stated, and
(b)   in the case of a document having more than one part, it is contained in a part of the document in which such information is required to be stated.

(2)   The registrar is not obliged—
(a)   to check other documents or (as the case may be) other parts of the document to ensure the absence of protected information, or
(b)   to omit from the material that is available for public inspection anything registered before 1st October 2009.

(3)   The registrar must not use or disclose protected information except—
(a)   as permitted by regulations 22 to 24 (permitted use or disclosure by registrar), or
(b)   in accordance with regulation 26 (disclosure under court order).

NOTES
Commencement: 1 October 2009.

[4.410]
22   Permitted use of protected information by the registrar: communication

The registrar may use protected information for communicating with the director or permanent representative.

NOTES

Commencement: 1 October 2009.

[4.411]
23 Permitted disclosure by the registrar: disclosure to specified public authority

(1) The registrar may disclose protected information to a specified public authority where the conditions set out in Part 1 of Schedule 2 are satisfied.

(2) A specified public authority must deliver to the registrar such information or evidence as the registrar may direct for the purpose of enabling the registrar to determine in accordance with these Regulations whether to disclose protected information.

(3) The registrar may require such information or evidence to be verified in such manner as the registrar may direct.

(4) The specified public authority must inform the registrar immediately of any change in respect of any statement delivered to the registrar pursuant to Schedule 2 or information or evidence provided for the purpose of enabling the registrar to determine whether to disclose protected information.

NOTES

Commencement: 1 October 2009.

[4.412]
24 Permitted disclosure by the registrar: disclosure to credit reference agency

(1) Subject to regulation 25, the registrar may disclose protected information to a credit reference agency where the conditions set out in Part 2 of Schedule 2 are satisfied.

(2) The registrar may rely on a statement delivered by a credit reference agency under paragraph 10 of Schedule 2 as sufficient evidence of the matters stated in it.

(3) Notwithstanding paragraph (2), a credit reference agency shall deliver to the registrar such information or evidence in addition to the statement required by paragraph 10 of Schedule 2 as the registrar may direct for the purpose of enabling the registrar to determine in accordance with these Regulations whether to disclose protected information.

(4) The registrar may require such information or evidence to be verified in such manner as the registrar may direct.

(5) The credit reference agency must inform the registrar immediately of any change in respect of any statement delivered to the registrar pursuant to Schedule 2 or information or evidence provided for the purpose of enabling the registrar to determine whether to disclose protected information.

NOTES

Commencement: 1 October 2009.

[4.413]
25 Application to prevent disclosure to credit reference agency

(1) An application may be made to the registrar to prevent the disclosure to a credit reference agency of protected information relating to a director or permanent representative (an "application for higher protection").

(2) An application for higher protection shall be made and determined in accordance with the provisions of Schedule 3.

(3) The registrar shall refrain from disclosing to a credit reference agency protected information relating to—
  (a) an individual in respect of whom a successful application for higher protection has been made, or
  (b) an individual in respect of whom an application for higher protection has been made where—
    (i) the registrar has not made a determination, or
    (ii) the registrar has made a determination rejecting the application and an appeal against that determination has been brought but has not been determined;
  (c) an individual in relation to whom an order was in force under section 723B of the Companies Act 1985 (confidentiality orders) immediately before 1st October 2009 and who, by virtue of paragraph 21 of Schedule 8 (transitional provisions and savings: individuals with a confidentiality order) is to be treated as having made a successful application for higher protection.

NOTES

Commencement: 1 October 2009.

[4.414]
26 Disclosure under court order

(1) The court may make an order for the disclosure of protected information by the company or by the registrar if—

  (a) there is evidence that service of documents at a service address other than the director or permanent representative's usual residential address is not effective to bring them to the notice of that individual, or

  (b) it is necessary or expedient for the information to be provided in connection with the enforcement of an order or decree of the court,

and the court is otherwise satisfied that it is appropriate to make the order.

(2) An order for disclosure by the registrar is to be made only if the company—

  (a) does not have the director or permanent representative's usual residential address,

  (b) no longer has a UK establishment and has given notice of that fact under regulation 77, or

  (c) has been dissolved.

(3) The order may be made on the application of a liquidator, creditor or member of the company, or any other person appearing to the court to have a sufficient interest.

(4) The order must specify the persons to whom, and purposes for which, disclosure is authorised.

NOTES
Commencement: 1 October 2009.

[4.415]
27 Circumstances in which registrar may put address on the public record

(1) The registrar may put a director's or permanent representative's usual residential address on the public record if—

  (a) communications sent by the registrar to that individual and requiring a response within a specified period of time remain unanswered, or

  (b) there is evidence that service of documents at a service address provided in place of their usual residential address is not effective to bring them to the notice of the director or permanent representative.

(2) The registrar must give notice of the proposal—

  (a) to the director or permanent representative, and

  (b) to the company.

(3) The notice must—

  (a) state the grounds on which it is proposed to put the director's or permanent representative's usual residential address on the public record, and

  (b) specify a period within which representations may be made before that is done.

(4) The notice must be sent to the director or permanent representative at their usual residential address, unless it appears to the registrar that service at that address may be ineffective to bring it to their notice, in which case it may be sent to any service address provided in place of that address.

(5) The registrar must take account of any representations received within the specified period.

(6) What is meant by putting the address on the public record is explained in regulation 28.

NOTES
Commencement: 1 October 2009.

[4.416]
28 Putting the address on the public record

(1) The registrar, on deciding in accordance with regulation 27 that a director's or permanent representative's usual residential address is to be put on the public record, shall proceed as if a return containing altered particulars had been given under Part 3—

  (a) stating that address as the director's or permanent representative's service address, and

  (b) stating that their usual residential address is the same as their service address.

(2) The registrar must give notice of having done so—

  (a) to the director or permanent representative, and

  (b) to the company.

(3) If the company has been notified by the director or permanent representative of a more recent address as their usual residential address, it must notify the registrar in accordance with regulation 13 (return of alteration in registered particulars).

(4) A director or permanent representative whose usual residential address has been put on the public record by the registrar under this regulation may not register a service address other than their usual residential address for a period of five years from the date of the registrar's decision.

NOTES
Commencement: 1 October 2009.

[4.417]

29 Penalty for non-compliance

(1)   If a company fails to comply with regulation 28(3) an offence is committed by—

     (a)   the company, and

     (b)   every officer of the company who is in default.

(2)   A person guilty of an offence under paragraph (1) is liable on summary conviction to—

     (a)   a fine not exceeding level 5 on the standard scale, and

     (b)   for continued contravention, a daily default fine not exceeding one tenth of level 5 on the standard scale.

NOTES

Commencement: 1 October 2009.

PART 5
DELIVERY OF ACCOUNTING DOCUMENTS: GENERAL

CHAPTER 1
INTRODUCTORY PROVISIONS

[4.418]

30 Application of Part

This Part applies to every overseas company that has an establishment in the United Kingdom and is not—

     (a)   a credit or financial institution (as to which, see Part 6), or

     (b)   a company whose constitution does not limit the liability of its members.

NOTES

Commencement: 1 October 2009.

CHAPTER 2
COMPANIES REQUIRED TO PREPARE AND DISCLOSE ACCOUNTS UNDER PARENT LAW

[4.419]

31 Application and interpretation of Chapter

(1)   This Chapter applies to an overseas company to which this Part applies that—

     (a)   is required by its parent law to prepare, have audited and disclose accounts, or

     (b)   is incorporated in an EEA State and is required by its parent law to prepare and disclose accounts, but is not required by its parent law to have its accounts audited or deliver its accounts.

(2)   In relation to a company to which this Chapter applies—

"accounting documents", in relation to a financial period of the company, means—

         (a)   the accounts of the company for the period, including if it has one or more subsidiaries, any consolidated accounts of the group,

         (b)   any annual report of the directors for the period,

         (c)   any report of the auditors on the accounts mentioned in sub-paragraph (a), and

         (d)   any report of the auditors on the report mentioned in sub-paragraph (b),

and for this purpose "subsidiaries" and "consolidated group accounts" have the meaning given to them by the company's parent law;

"financial period" means a period for which the company is required or permitted by its parent law to prepare accounts;

"parent law", in relation to a company, means the law of the country in which the company is incorporated;

and references to disclose or disclosure are to public disclosure.

NOTES

Commencement: 1 October 2009.

[4.420]

32 Duty to file copies of accounting documents disclosed under parent law

(1)   The directors of a company to which this Chapter applies must deliver to the registrar a copy of all the accounting documents prepared in relation to a financial period of the company that are disclosed in accordance with its parent law.

(2)   Where the company's parent law permits it to discharge its obligation with respect to the disclosure of accounting documents by disclosing documents in a modified form, the directors may discharge their obligation under paragraph (1) by delivering a copy of documents modified as permitted by that law.

(3)   Where the company is incorporated in an EEA State—

(a)   the directors are not required to deliver copies of accounting documents under paragraph (1) if the company's parent law does not require it to deliver accounting documents, and

(b)   the directors may discharge their obligation under paragraph (1) by delivering the accounting documents without an auditor's report if the company's parent law does not require it to have its accounts audited.

(4)   This regulation does not apply in relation to copies of accounting documents disclosed under the company's parent law before—

(a)   the date on which the company first delivered a return under Part 2 (initial registration of particulars) in respect of a UK establishment, or

(b)   if earlier, the last day of the period allowed for delivery of a return under that Part in respect of its first UK establishment.

(5)   The directors required by this regulation to deliver copies of accounting documents must deliver them in respect of each UK establishment that the company has at the end of the financial period to which the documents relate, subject as follows.

(6)   Paragraph (5) does not require the delivery of copies of accounting documents in respect of an establishment if—

(a)   a return in respect of that establishment has stated the intention to file copies of accounting documents in respect of another UK establishment (giving the registered number of that establishment), and

(b)   copies of the accounting documents are delivered in respect of that establishment before the end of the period allowed for doing so.

NOTES

Commencement: 1 October 2009.

[4.421]
33   Statement of details of parent law and other information

(1)   The accounting documents delivered to the registrar under regulation 32 must be accompanied by a statement containing the following information.

(2)   The information required is—

(a)   the legislation under which the accounts have been prepared and, if applicable, audited,

(b)   whether those accounts have been prepared in accordance with a set of generally accepted accounting principles and, if so, the name of the organisation or other body which issued those principles,

(c)   whether the accounts have been audited,

(d)   if they have been audited—

(i)   whether they have been audited in accordance with a set of generally accepted auditing standards, and

(ii)   if so, the name of the organisation or other body which issued those standards, and

(e)   if they have not been audited, whether the company is not required to have its accounts audited.

NOTES

Commencement: 1 October 2009.

[4.422]
34   Period allowed for filing copies of accounting documents

The period allowed for delivery, in relation to a copy of a document required to be delivered under regulation 32, is three months from the date on which the document is required to be disclosed in accordance with the company's parent law.

NOTES

Commencement: 1 October 2009.

[4.423]
35   Penalty for non-compliance

(1)   If any of the requirements of this Chapter (other than that in regulation 33) are not complied with in relation to a company's accounting documents before the end of the period allowed for delivering copies of those documents, every person who immediately before the end of that period was a director of the company commits an offence.

(2)   It is a defence for a person charged with such an offence to prove that they took all reasonable steps for securing that those requirements would be complied with before the end of that period.

(3)   A person guilty of an offence under paragraph (1) is liable on summary conviction to a fine not exceeding level 5 on the standard scale and, for continued contravention, a daily default fine not exceeding one-tenth of level 5 on the standard scale.

NOTES
Commencement: 1 October 2009.

CHAPTER 3
COMPANIES NOT REQUIRED TO PREPARE AND DISCLOSE ACCOUNTS
UNDER PARENT LAW

[4.424]
36 Application of Chapter

This Chapter applies to an overseas company to which this Part applies that is not a company to which Chapter 2 of this Part applies.

NOTES
Commencement: 1 October 2009.

[4.425]
37 A company's financial year

Sections 390 to 392 of the Companies Act 2006 apply in relation to a company to which this Chapter applies, modified so that they read as follows—

"390 A company's financial year

(1) A company's financial year is determined as follows.

(2) Its first financial year—
- (a) begins with the first day of its first accounting reference period, and
- (b) ends with the last day of that period or such other date, not more than seven days before or after the end of that period, as the directors may determine.

(3) Subsequent financial years—
- (a) begin with the day immediately following the end of the company's previous financial year, and
- (b) end with the last day of its next accounting reference period or such other date, not more than seven days before or after the end of that period, as the directors may determine.

391 Accounting reference periods and accounting reference date

(1) A company's accounting reference periods are determined according to its accounting reference date in each calendar year.

(2) The accounting reference date of a company is the last day of the month in which the anniversary of its becoming a relevant overseas company falls.

(3) A company's first accounting reference period is the period of more than six months, but not more than eighteen months, beginning with the date of its becoming a relevant overseas company and ending with its accounting reference date.

(4) Its subsequent accounting reference periods are successive periods of twelve months beginning immediately after the end of the previous accounting reference period and ending with its accounting reference date.

(5) This section has effect subject to the provisions of section 392.

392 Alteration of accounting reference date

(1) A company may by notice given to the registrar specify a new accounting reference date having effect in relation to—
- (a) the company's current accounting reference period and subsequent periods, or
- (b) the company's previous accounting reference period and subsequent periods.

A company's "previous accounting reference period" means the one immediately preceding its current accounting reference period.

(2) The notice must state whether the current or previous accounting reference period—
- (a) is to be shortened, so as to come to an end on the first occasion on which the new accounting reference date falls or fell after the beginning of the period, or
- (b) is to be extended, so as to come to an end on the second occasion on which that date falls or fell after the beginning of the period.

(3) A notice under this section may not be given in respect of a previous accounting reference period if the period for filing accounts for the financial year determined by reference to that accounting reference period has already expired.

(4) An accounting reference period may not be extended so as to exceed eighteen months and a notice under this section is ineffective if the current or previous accounting reference period as extended in accordance with the notice would exceed that limit.

This does not apply where the company is in administration under Part 2 of the Insolvency Act 1986 (c 45) or Part 3 of the Insolvency (Northern Ireland) Order 1989 (SI 1989/2405 (NI 19)).".

NOTES
Commencement: 1 October 2009.

[4.426]
38 Duty to prepare accounts

Sections 394 to 397, 399, and 402 to 406 of the Companies Act 2006 apply in relation to a company to which this Chapter applies, modified so that they read as follows—

"394 Duty to prepare individual accounts

Subject to section 399 (duty to prepare group accounts), the directors of a company must prepare accounts for the company for each of its financial years.

Those accounts are referred to as the company's "individual accounts".

395 Individual accounts: applicable accounting framework

(1)   A company's annual accounts may be prepared in accordance with—
- (a)   its parent law ("parent law individual accounts"),
- (b)   international accounting standards ("IAS individual accounts"), or
- (c)   section 396 ("overseas companies individual accounts").

(2)   A company may only prepare parent law individual accounts if the content of such accounts includes that required by section 396.

396 Overseas companies individual accounts

(1)   Overseas companies individual accounts must comprise—
- (a)   a balance sheet as at the last day of the financial year, and
- (b)   a profit and loss account.

(2)   The accounts must comply with the provisions in Schedule 4 to the Overseas Companies Regulations as to—
- (a)   the content of the balance sheet and the profit and loss account, and
- (b)   additional information to be provided by way of notes to the accounts.

397 IAS individual accounts, parent law individual accounts and overseas company individual accounts

(1)   Where the directors of a company prepare IAS individual accounts they must state in the notes—
- (a)   that the accounts have been prepared in accordance with international accounting standards,
- (b)   whether the accounts have been audited, and
- (c)   if they have been audited—
  - (i)   whether they have been audited in accordance with a set of generally accepted auditing standards, and
  - (ii)   if so, the name of the organisation or other body which issued those standards.

(2)   Where the directors of a company prepare parent law individual accounts they must state in the notes—
- (a)   that the accounts have been prepared in accordance with the company's parent law,
- (b)   the legislation under which the accounts have been prepared,
- (c)   whether the accounts have been prepared in accordance with a set of generally accepted accounting principles, and if so, the name of the organisation or other body which issued those principles,
- (d)   whether the accounts have been audited, and
- (e)   if they have been audited—
  - (i)   whether they have been audited in accordance with a set of generally accepted auditing standards, and
  - (ii)   if so, the name of the organisation or other body which issued those standards.

(3)   Where the directors of a company prepare overseas company individual accounts they must state in the notes—
- (a)   that the accounts have been prepared in accordance with section 396,
- (b)   whether the accounts have been prepared in accordance with a set of generally accepted accounting principles, and if so, the name of the organisation or other body which issued those principles,
- (c)   whether the accounts have been audited, and
- (d)   if they have been audited—
  - (i)   whether they have been audited in accordance with a set of generally accepted auditing standards, and
  - (ii)   if so, the name of the organisation or other body which issued those standards.

399 Duty to prepare group accounts

If at the end of a financial year a company is a parent company the directors must, instead of preparing individual accounts for the year, prepare group accounts for the year.

402 Exemption from duty to prepare group accounts

A parent company is exempt from the requirement to prepare group accounts where—

   (a)   it has prepared accounts under section 395(1)(a) and its parent law does not require consolidated accounts;

   (b)   it has prepared accounts under section 395(1)(b) and in accordance with the international accounting standards it is not required to prepare consolidated accounts;

   (c)   it has prepared accounts under section 395(1)(c) and if under section 405 all of the company's subsidiary undertakings could be excluded from the consolidation.

402A Holding company accounts to be regarded as group accounts

Where a company, being a parent company, is required by section 399 to prepare group accounts, and that company is itself the subsidiary of another company ("the holding company"), the group accounts of the holding company are deemed to satisfy the requirements of section 399 to prepare group accounts.

403 Group accounts: applicable accounting framework

(1)   The group accounts of an overseas company may be prepared in accordance with—

   (a)   its parent law ("parent law group accounts"),

   (b)   international accounting standards ("IAS group accounts"), or

   (c)   section 404 ("overseas companies group accounts").

(2)   A company may only prepare parent law group accounts if the content of such accounts includes that required by section 404.

404 Overseas companies group accounts

(1)   Overseas companies group accounts must comprise—

   (a)   a consolidated balance sheet dealing with the state of affairs of the parent company and its subsidiary undertakings, and

   (b)   a consolidated profit and loss account dealing with the profit or loss of the parent company and its subsidiary undertakings.

(2)   The accounts must comply with the provisions of Schedule 5 to the Overseas Companies Regulations as to—

   (a)   the content of the consolidated balance sheet and consolidated profit and loss account, and

   (b)   additional information to be provided by way of notes to the accounts.

405 Overseas companies group accounts: subsidiary undertakings included in the consolidation

(1)   Where a parent company prepares overseas companies group accounts, all the subsidiary undertakings of the company must be included in the consolidation, subject to the following exceptions.

(2)   A subsidiary undertaking may be excluded from the consolidation if its inclusion is not material (but two or more undertakings may be excluded only if they are not material taken together).

(3)   A subsidiary undertaking may be excluded from consolidation where—

   (a)   severe long-term restrictions substantially hinder the exercise of the rights of the parent company over the assets or management of that undertaking, or

   (b)   the information necessary for the preparation of group accounts cannot be obtained without disproportionate expense or undue delay, or

   (c)   the interest of the parent company is held exclusively with a view to subsequent resale.

(4)   The reference in subsection (3)(a) to the rights of the parent company and the reference in subsection (3)(c) to the interest of the parent company are, respectively, to rights and interests held by or attributed to the company for the purposes of the definition of "parent undertaking" (see section 1162) in the absence of which it would not be the parent company.

406 IAS group accounts, parent law group accounts and overseas company group accounts

(1)   Where the directors of a company prepare IAS group accounts they must state in the notes—

   (a)   that the accounts have been prepared in accordance with international accounting standards,

   (b)   whether the accounts have been audited, and

   (c)   if they have been audited—

      (i)   whether they have been audited in accordance with a set of generally accepted auditing standards, and

      (ii)   if so, the name of the organisation or other body which issued those standards.

(2)   Where the directors of a company prepare parent law group accounts they must state in the notes—

   (a)   that the accounts have been prepared in accordance with the company's parent law,

   (b)   the legislation under which the accounts have been prepared,

    (c)   whether the accounts have been prepared in accordance with a set of generally accepted accounting principles, and if so, the name of the organisation or other body which issued those principles,

    (d)   whether the accounts have been audited, and

    (e)   if they have been audited—

        (i)   whether they have been audited in accordance with a set of generally accepted auditing standards, and

        (ii)   if so, the name of the organisation or other body which issued those standards.

(3)   Where the directors of a company prepare overseas company group accounts they must state in the notes—

    (a)   that the accounts have been prepared in accordance with section 404,

    (b)   whether the accounts have been prepared in accordance with a set of generally accepted accounting principles, and if so, the name of the organisation or other body which issued those principles,

    (c)   whether the accounts have been audited, and

    (d)   if they have been audited—

        (i)   whether they have been audited in accordance with a set of generally accepted auditing standards, and

        (ii)   if so, the name of the organisation or other body which issued those standards.".

NOTES

Commencement: 1 October 2009.

[4.427]

39 Approval and signing of accounts

Section 414 of the Companies Act 2006 applies in relation to a company to which this Chapter applies, modified so that it reads as follows—

"414 Approval and signing of accounts

(1)   A company's annual accounts must be approved by the board of directors and signed on behalf of the board by a director of the company.

(2)   The signature must be on the company's balance sheet.

(3)   If annual accounts are approved that do not comply with the requirements of Part 15 as applied (with modifications) by Part 5 of the Overseas Companies Regulations, every director of the company who—

    (a)   knew that they did not comply, or was reckless as to whether they complied, and

    (b)   failed to take reasonable steps to secure compliance with those requirements or, as the case may be, to prevent the accounts from being approved,

commits an offence.

(4)   A person guilty of an offence under this section is liable—

    (a)   on conviction on indictment, to a fine;

    (b)   on summary conviction, to a fine not exceeding the statutory maximum.".

NOTES

Commencement: 1 October 2009.

[4.428]

40 Duty to file accounts

Sections 441 and 442 of the Companies Act 2006 apply in relation to a company to which this Chapter applies, modified so that they read as follows—

"441 Duty to file accounts with the registrar

(1)   The directors of a company must deliver to the registrar for each financial year a copy of the company's annual accounts and such other reports as are required to be prepared.

(2)   The copy of the balance sheet delivered to the registrar under this section must state the name of the person who signed it on behalf of the board.

(3)   The directors required by this section to deliver accounts must deliver them in respect of each UK establishment that it has at the end of that year, subject as follows.

(4)   Subsection (3) does not require the delivery of accounts in respect of an establishment if—

    (a)   a return under the Overseas Companies Regulations in respect of that establishment has stated the intention to file accounts in respect of another UK establishment (giving the registered number of that establishment), and

    (b)   the accounts are delivered in respect of that establishment before the end of the period allowed for doing so.

442 Period allowed for filing accounts

(1)   This section specifies the period allowed for directors of a company to comply with their obligation under section 441 to deliver accounts for a financial year to the registrar.

This is referred to in sections 392 and 451 as the "period for filing" those accounts.

(2)   The period is thirteen months after the end of the relevant accounting reference period. This is subject to the following provisions of this section.

(3)   If the relevant accounting reference period is the company's first and is a period of more than twelve months, the period allowed is thirteen months from the first anniversary of the company becoming a relevant overseas company.

(4)   If the relevant accounting reference period is treated as shortened by virtue of a notice given under section 392, the period is—

(a)   that applicable in accordance with the above provisions, or

(b)   three months from the date of the notice under that section,

whichever last expires.

(5)   If for any special reason the Secretary of State thinks fit he may, on an application made before the expiry of the period otherwise allowed, by notice in writing to a company extend that period by such further period as may be specified in the notice.

(6)   In this section "the relevant accounting reference period" means the accounting reference period by reference to which the financial year for the accounts in question was determined.".

NOTES

Commencement: 1 October 2009.

[4.429]
41   Penalty for non-compliance
Section 451 of the Companies Act 2006 applies in relation to a company to which this Chapter applies, modified so that it reads as follows—

"451   Default in filing accounts: offences
(1)   If the requirements of section 441 (duty to file accounts) are not complied with in relation to a company's accounts for a financial year before the end of the period for filing those accounts, every person who immediately before the end of that period was a director of the company commits an offence.

(2)   It is a defence for a person charged with such an offence to prove that he took all reasonable steps for securing that those requirements would be complied with before the end of that period.

(3)   It is not a defence to prove that the documents in question were not in fact prepared as required by this Part.

(4)   A person guilty of an offence under this section is liable on summary conviction to a fine not exceeding level 5 on the standard scale and, for continued contravention, a daily default fine not exceeding one-tenth of level 5 on the standard scale.".

NOTES

Commencement: 1 October 2009.

[4.430]
42   Supplementary provisions
Sections 471, 472 and 474 of the Companies Act 2006 apply in relation to a company to which this Chapter applies, modified so that they read as follows—

"471   Meaning of "annual accounts"
In this Part a company's "annual accounts", in relation to a financial year, means the company's individual accounts for that year (see section 394) or, if applicable, the company's group accounts for that year (see section 399).

472   Notes to the accounts
(1)   Information required by this Part to be given in notes to a company's annual accounts may be contained in the accounts or in a separate document annexed to the accounts.

(2)   References in this Part to a company's annual accounts, or to a balance sheet or profit and loss account, include notes to the accounts.

474   Minor definitions
In this Part—
"balance sheet" includes a statement of financial position or other equivalent financial statement;
"group" means a parent undertaking and its subsidiary undertakings;
"IAS Regulation" means EC Regulation No 1606/2002 of the European Parliament and of the Council of 19th July 2002 on the application of international accounting standards;
"international accounting standards" means the international accounting standards, within the meaning of Article 2 of the IAS Regulation;

"Overseas Companies Regulations" means the Overseas Companies Regulations 2009 (SI 2009/1801);

"profit and loss account" includes an income statement or other equivalent financial statement;

"relevant overseas company" means a company to which Chapter 3 of Part 5 of the Overseas Companies Regulations applies,

and references to "this Part" are to be read as references to those sections of Part 15 of the Companies Act 2006 as applied (with modification) by the Overseas Companies Regulations and include Schedules 4 and 5 to those Regulations.".

NOTES

Commencement: 1 October 2009.

PART 6
DELIVERY OF ACCOUNTING DOCUMENTS: CREDIT OR FINANCIAL INSTITUTIONS

CHAPTER 1
INTRODUCTORY PROVISIONS

[4.431]
43   Application and interpretation of Part

(1)   This Part applies to every credit or financial institution that has a branch in the United Kingdom.

(2)   In this Part "branch" means a place of business that forms a legally dependent part of the institution and conducts directly all or some of the operations inherent in its business.

NOTES

Commencement: 1 October 2009.

CHAPTER 2
INSTITUTIONS REQUIRED TO PREPARE ACCOUNTS UNDER PARENT LAW

[4.432]
44   Application and interpretation of Chapter

(1)   This Chapter applies to a credit or financial institution to which this Part applies that—
   (a)   is required by its parent law to prepare and have audited accounts; or
   (b)   is incorporated in an EEA State, and is required by its parent law to prepare and disclose accounts, but is not required by its parent law to have its accounts audited or deliver its accounts.

(2)   In relation to an institution to which this Chapter applies—
   "accounting documents" in relation to a financial period of the institution, means—
      (a)   the accounts of the institution for the period, including, if it has one or more subsidiaries, any consolidated accounts of its group,
      (b)   any annual report of the directors for the period,
      (c)   any report of the auditors on the accounts mentioned in sub-paragraph (a),
      (d)   any report of the auditors on the report mentioned in sub-paragraph (b),
      and for this purpose "subsidiaries" and "consolidated group accounts" have the meaning given to them by the institution's parent law;
   "director", in the case of an institution which does not have directors, means persons occupying equivalent offices;
   "disclosure" means public disclosure, except where an institution is not required under its parent law, any enactment having effect for the United Kingdom or its constitution to publicly disclose its accounts, in which case it means disclosure of the accounts to the persons for whose information they have been prepared;
   "financial period" means a period for which the institution is required or permitted by its parent law to prepare accounts;
   "parent law" means the law of the country in which the institution has its head office; and in the case of an institution which does not have directors, references to "directors" shall include the persons occupying equivalent offices.

NOTES

Commencement: 1 October 2009.

[4.433]
45   Initial filing of copies of accounting documents

A credit or financial institution must within one month of becoming an institution to which this Chapter applies deliver to the registrar copies of the latest accounting documents of the institution prepared in accordance with its parent law to have been disclosed before the end of the period allowed for compliance with this regulation, or, if earlier, the date of compliance with it.

NOTES
Commencement: 1 October 2009.

[4.434]
46   Filing of copies of subsequent accounting documents
(1)   A credit or financial institution to which this Chapter applies must deliver to the registrar copies of all the accounting documents of the institution prepared in accordance with its parent law that are disclosed on or after the end of the period allowed for compliance with regulation 45, or, if earlier, the date on which it complies with that paragraph.

(2)   The period allowed for delivery, in relation to a copy of a document required to be delivered under paragraph (1), is three months from the date on which the document is required to be disclosed in accordance with the institution's parent law.

NOTES
Commencement: 1 October 2009.

[4.435]
47   Statement of details of parent law and other information
(1)   The copies of accounting documents delivered to the registrar under regulation 45 or 46 must be accompanied by a statement containing the following information.

(2)   The information required is—
  (a)   the legislation under which the accounts have been prepared and, if applicable, audited,
  (b)   whether those accounts have been prepared in accordance with a set of generally accepted accounting principles, and if so, the name of the organisation or other body which issued those principles,
  (c)   whether the accounts have been audited,
  (d)   if they have been audited—
      (i)   whether they have been audited in accordance with a set of generally accepted auditing standards, and
      (ii)   if so, the name of the organisation or other body which issued those standards, and
  (e)   if they have not been audited, whether the institution is not required to have its accounts audited.

NOTES
Commencement: 1 October 2009.

[4.436]
48   Supplementary provisions as to obligation to file copies of accounting documents
(1)   The following provisions apply in relation to the obligations imposed by regulation 45 or 46.

(2)   Where the institution is incorporated or otherwise formed in an EEA State—
  (a)   it is not required to deliver copies of accounting documents if its parent law does not require it to deliver accounting documents, and
  (b)   it may discharge its obligation by delivering accounting documents without an auditor's report if its parent law does not require it to have its accounts audited.

(3)   Where the institution's parent law permits it to discharge an obligation with respect to the disclosure of accounting documents by disclosing documents in a modified form, it may discharge its obligation under regulations 45 and 46 by delivering copies of documents modified as permitted by that law.

NOTES
Commencement: 1 October 2009.

[4.437]
49   Exception where documents available for inspection
(1)   Neither regulation 45 nor regulation 46 requires an institution to deliver copies of accounting documents if at the end of the period allowed for compliance with those regulations—
  (a)   it is not required by its parent law to register them,
  (b)   they are made available for inspection at each branch of the institution in the United Kingdom, and
  (c)   copies of them are available on request at a cost not exceeding the cost of supplying them.

(2)   Where—
  (a)   by virtue of paragraph (1) an institution is not required to deliver documents under regulation 45 or 46, and
  (b)   any of the conditions specified in paragraph (1) ceases to be met,

the institution must deliver the documents to the registrar for registration within seven days of the condition ceasing to be met.

NOTES
Commencement: 1 October 2009.

[4.438]
50 Penalty for non-compliance
(1) If any of the requirements of this Chapter are not complied with before the end of the period allowed for delivery of copies of accounting documents, an offence is committed by every person who immediately before the end of that period was a director of the institution.

(2) It is a defence for a person charged with such an offence to prove that they took all reasonable steps for securing that those requirements would be complied with before the end of that period.

(3) A person guilty of an offence under paragraph (1) is liable on summary conviction to a fine not exceeding level 5 on the standard scale and, for continued contravention, a daily default fine not exceeding one-tenth of level 5 on the standard scale.

NOTES
Commencement: 1 October 2009.

CHAPTER 3
INSTITUTIONS NOT REQUIRED TO PREPARE ACCOUNTS UNDER PARENT LAW

[4.439]
51 Application of Chapter
This Chapter applies to a credit or financial institution to which this Part applies that is not one to which Chapter 2 of this Part applies.

NOTES
Commencement: 1 October 2009.

[4.440]
52 An institution's financial year
Sections 390 to 392 of the Companies Act 2006 apply in relation to an institution to which this Chapter applies, modified so that they read as follows—

"390 An institution's financial year
(1) An institution's financial year is determined as follows.
(2) Its first financial year—
    (a) begins with the first day of its first accounting reference period, and
    (b) ends with the last day of that period or such other date, not more than seven days before or after the end of that period, as the directors may determine.
(3) Subsequent financial years—
    (a) begin with the day immediately following the end of the institution's previous financial year, and
    (b) end with the last day of its next accounting reference period or such other date, not more than seven days before or after the end of that period, as the directors may determine.

391 Accounting reference periods and accounting reference date
(1) An institution's accounting reference periods are determined according to its accounting reference date in each calendar year.
(2) The accounting reference date of an institution is the last day of the month in which the anniversary of its becoming a relevant overseas institution falls.
(3) An institution's first accounting reference period is the period of more than six months, but not more than eighteen months, beginning with the date of its becoming a relevant overseas institution and ending with its accounting reference date.
(4) Its subsequent accounting reference periods are successive periods of twelve months beginning immediately after the end of the previous accounting reference period and ending with its accounting reference date.
(5) This section has effect subject to the provisions of section 392.

392 Alteration of accounting reference date
(1) An institution may by notice given to the registrar specify a new accounting reference date having effect in relation to—
    (a) the institution's current accounting reference period and subsequent periods, or
    (b) the institution's previous accounting reference period and subsequent periods.
An institution's "previous accounting reference period" means the one immediately preceding its current accounting reference period.
(2) The notice must state whether the current or previous accounting reference period—

    (a)   is to be shortened, so as to come to an end on the first occasion on which the new accounting reference date falls or fell after the beginning of the period, or

    (b)   is to be extended, so as to come to an end on the second occasion on which that date falls or fell after the beginning of the period.

(3)   A notice under this section may not be given in respect of a previous accounting reference period if the period for filing accounts for the financial year determined by reference to that accounting reference period has already expired.

(4)   An accounting reference period may not be extended so as to exceed eighteen months and a notice under this section is ineffective if the current or previous accounting reference period as extended in accordance with the notice would exceed that limit.

This does not apply where the institution is in administration under Part 2 of the Insolvency Act 1986 (c 45) or Part 3 of the Insolvency (Northern Ireland) Order 1989 (SI 1989/2405 (NI 19)).".

NOTES

Commencement: 1 October 2009.

[4.441]

53 Duty to prepare accounts

Sections 394 to 397, 399, and 402 to 406 of the Companies Act 2006 apply in relation to an institution to which this Chapter applies, modified so that they read as follows—

"394 Duty to prepare individual accounts

Subject to section 399 (duty to prepare group accounts) the directors of an institution must prepare accounts for the institution for each of its financial years.

Those accounts are referred to as the institution's "individual accounts".

395 Individual accounts: applicable accounting framework

(1)   An institution's annual accounts may be prepared in accordance with—

    (a)   its parent law ("parent law individual accounts"),

    (b)   international accounting standards ("IAS individual accounts"), or

    (c)   section 396 ("overseas institutions individual accounts").

(2)   An institution may only prepare parent law individual accounts if the content of such accounts includes that required by section 396.

396 Overseas institutions individual accounts

(1)   Overseas institutions individual accounts must comprise—

    (a)   a balance sheet as at the last day of the financial year, and

    (b)   a profit and loss account.

(2)   The accounts must comply with the provisions in Schedule 6 to the Overseas Companies Regulations as to—

    (a)   the content of the balance sheet and the profit and loss account, and

    (b)   additional information to be provided by way of notes to the accounts.

397 IAS individual accounts, parent law individual accounts and overseas institutions individual accounts

(1)   Where the directors of an institution prepare IAS individual accounts they must state in the notes—

    (a)   that the accounts have been prepared in accordance with international accounting standards,

    (b)   whether the accounts have been audited, and

    (c)   if they have been audited—

        (i)   whether they have been audited in accordance with a set of generally accepted auditing standards, and

        (ii)   if so, the name of the organisation or other body which issued those standards.

(2)   Where the directors of an institution prepare parent law individual accounts they must state in the notes—

    (a)   that the accounts have been prepared in accordance with the institution's parent law,

    (b)   the legislation under which the accounts have been prepared,

    (c)   whether the accounts have been prepared in accordance with a set of generally accepted accounting principles, and if so, the name of the organisation or other body which issued those principles,

    (d)   whether the accounts have been audited, and

    (e)   if they have been audited—

        (i)   whether they have been audited in accordance with a set of generally accepted auditing standards, and

        (ii)   if so, the name of the organisation or other body which issued those standards.

(3)   Where the directors of an institution prepare overseas institutions individual accounts they must state in the notes—

    (a)   that the accounts have been prepared in accordance with section 396,

(b) whether the accounts have been prepared in accordance with a set of generally accepted accounting principles, and if so, the name of the organisation or other body which issued those principles,

(c) whether the accounts have been audited, and

(d) if they have been audited—

    (i) whether they have been audited in accordance with a set of generally accepted auditing standards, and

    (ii) if so, the name of the organisation or other body which issued those standards.

399 Duty to prepare group accounts

If at the end of a financial year an institution is a parent institution the directors must, instead of preparing individual accounts for the year, prepare group accounts for the year.

402 Exemption from duty to prepare group accounts

A parent institution is exempt from the requirement to prepare group accounts where—

(a) it has prepared accounts under section 395(1)(a) and its parent law does not require consolidated accounts;

(b) it has prepared accounts under section 395(1)(b) and in accordance with the international accounting standards it is not required to prepare consolidated accounts;

(c) it has prepared accounts under section 395(1)(c) and if under section 405 all of the institution's subsidiary undertakings could be excluded from consolidation.

402A Holding institution accounts to be regarded as group accounts

Where an institution, being a parent institution, is required by section 399 to prepare group accounts, and that institution is itself the subsidiary of another institution ("the holding institution"), the group accounts of the holding institution may be deemed to satisfy the requirements of section 399 to prepare group accounts.

403 Group accounts: applicable accounting framework

(1) The group accounts of an institution may be prepared in accordance with—

(a) its parent law ("parent law group accounts"),

(b) international accounting standards ("IAS group accounts"), or

(c) section 404 ("overseas institutions group accounts").

(2) An institution may only prepare parent law group accounts if the content of such accounts includes that required by section 404.

404 Overseas institutions group accounts

(1) Overseas institutions group accounts must comprise—

(a) a consolidated balance sheet dealing with the state of affairs of the parent institution and its subsidiary undertakings, and

(b) a consolidated profit and loss account dealing with the profit or loss of the parent institution and its subsidiary undertakings.

(2) The accounts must comply with the provisions of Schedule 7 to the Overseas Companies Regulations as to—

(a) the content of the consolidated balance sheet and consolidated profit and loss account, and

(b) additional information to be provided by way of notes to the accounts.

405 Overseas institutions group accounts: subsidiary undertakings included in the consolidation

(1) Where a parent institution prepares overseas institutions group accounts, all the subsidiary undertakings of the institution must be included in the consolidation, subject to the following exceptions.

(2) A subsidiary undertaking may be excluded from the consolidation if its inclusion is not material (but two or more undertakings may be excluded only if they are not material taken together).

(3) A subsidiary undertaking may be excluded from consolidation where—

(a) severe long-term restrictions substantially hinder the exercise of the rights of the parent institution over the assets or management of that undertaking, or

(b) the information necessary for the preparation of group accounts cannot be obtained without disproportionate expense or undue delay, or

(c) the interest of the parent institution is held exclusively with a view to subsequent resale.

(4) The reference in subsection (3)(a) to the rights of the parent institution and the reference in subsection (3)(c) to the interest of the parent institution are, respectively, to rights and interests held by or attributed to the institution for the purposes of the definition of "parent undertaking" (see section 1162) in the absence of which it would not be the parent institution.

406 IAS group accounts, parent law group accounts and overseas institutions group accounts

(1)   Where the directors of an institution prepare IAS group accounts they must state in the notes—

    (a)   that the accounts have been prepared in accordance with international accounting standards,

    (b)   whether the accounts have been audited, and

    (c)   if they have been audited—

        (i)   whether they have been audited in accordance with a set of generally accepted auditing standards, and

        (ii)   if so, the name of the organisation or other body which issued those standards.

(2)   Where the directors of an institution prepare parent law group accounts they must state in the notes—

    (a)   that the accounts have been prepared in accordance with the institution's parent law,

    (b)   the legislation under which the accounts have been prepared,

    (c)   whether the accounts have been prepared in accordance with a set of generally accepted accounting principles, and if so, the name of the organisation or other body which issued those principles,

    (d)   whether the accounts have been audited, and

    (e)   if they have been audited—

        (i)   whether they have been audited in accordance with a set of generally accepted auditing standards, and

        (ii)   if so, the name of the organisation or other body which issued those standards.

(3)   Where the directors of an institution prepare overseas institutions group accounts they must state in the notes—

    (a)   that the accounts have been prepared in accordance with section 404,

    (b)   whether the accounts have been prepared in accordance with a set of generally accepted accounting principles, and if so, the name of the organisation or other body which issued those principles,

    (c)   whether the accounts have been audited, and

    (d)   if they have been audited—

        (i)   whether they have been audited in accordance with a set of generally accepted auditing standards, and

        (ii)   if so, the name of the organisation or other body which issued those standards.".

NOTES

  Commencement: 1 October 2009.

[4.442]

54   Approval and signing of accounts

Section 414 of the Companies Act 2006 applies in relation to an institution to which this Chapter applies, modified so that it reads as follows—

  "414   Approval and signing of accounts

  (1)   An institution's annual accounts must be approved by the board of directors and signed on behalf of the board by a director of the institution.

  (2)   The signature must be on the institution's balance sheet.

  (3)   If annual accounts are approved that do not comply with the requirements of Part 15 as applied (with modifications) by Part 6 of the Overseas Companies Regulations, every director of the institution who—

    (a)   knew that they did not comply, or was reckless as to whether they complied, and

    (b)   failed to take reasonable steps to secure compliance with those requirements or, as the case may be, to prevent the accounts from being approved,

  commits an offence.

  (4)   A person guilty of an offence under this section is liable—

    (a)   on conviction on indictment, to a fine;

    (b)   on summary conviction, to a fine not exceeding the statutory maximum.".

NOTES

  Commencement: 1 October 2009.

[4.443]

55   Duty to file accounts

Sections 441 and 442 of the Companies Act 2006 apply in relation to an institution to which this Chapter applies, modified so that they read as follows—

  "441   Duty to file accounts with the registrar

  (1)   The directors of an institution must deliver to the registrar for each financial year a copy

of the institution's annual accounts and such other reports as are required to be prepared.

(2)   The copy of the balance sheet delivered to the registrar under this section must state the name of the person who signed it on behalf of the board.

442 Period allowed for filing accounts

(1)   This section specifies the period allowed for directors of an institution to comply with their obligation under section 441 to deliver accounts for a financial year to the registrar.

This is referred to in sections 392 and 451 as the "period for filing" those accounts.

(2)   The period is thirteen months after the end of the relevant accounting reference period.

This is subject to the following provisions of this section.

(3)   If the relevant accounting reference period is the institution's first and is a period of more than twelve months, the period allowed is thirteen months from the first anniversary of the institution becoming a relevant overseas institution.

(4)   If the relevant accounting reference period is treated as shortened by virtue of a notice given under section 392, the period is—

    (a)   that applicable in accordance with the above provisions, or

    (b)   three months from the date of the notice under that section,

whichever last expires.

(5)   If for any special reason the Secretary of State thinks fit he may, on an application made before the expiry of the period otherwise allowed, by notice in writing to an institution extend that period by such further period as may be specified in the notice.

(6)   In this section "the relevant accounting reference period" means the accounting reference period by reference to which the financial year for the accounts in question was determined.".

NOTES

Commencement: 1 October 2009.

[4.444]
56   Penalty for non-compliance

Section 451 of the Companies Act 2006 applies in relation to an institution to which this Chapter applies, modified so that it reads as follows—

"451   Default in filing accounts: offences

(1)   If the requirements of section 441 (duty to file accounts) are not complied with in relation to an institution's accounts for a financial year before the end of the period for filing those accounts, every person who immediately before the end of that period was a director of the institution commits an offence.

(2)   It is a defence for a person charged with such an offence to prove that he took all reasonable steps for securing that those requirements would be complied with before the end of that period.

(3)   It is not a defence to prove that the documents in question were not in fact prepared as required by this Part.

(4)   A person guilty of an offence under this section is liable on summary conviction to a fine not exceeding level 5 on the standard scale and, for continued contravention, a daily default fine not exceeding one-tenth of level 5 on the standard scale.".

NOTES

Commencement: 1 October 2009.

[4.445]
57   Supplementary provisions

Sections 471, 472 and 474 of the Companies Act 2006 apply in relation to an institution to which this Chapter applies, modified so that they read as follows—

"471   Meaning of "annual accounts"

In this Part an institution's "annual accounts", in relation to a financial year, means the institution's individual accounts for that year (see section 394) or, if applicable, the institution's group accounts for that year (see section 399).

472   Notes to the accounts

(1)   Information required by this Part to be given in notes to an institution's annual accounts may be contained in the accounts or in a separate document annexed to the accounts.

(2)   References in this Part to an institution's annual accounts, or to a balance sheet or profit and loss account, include notes to the accounts.

474   Minor definitions

In this Part—

    "balance sheet" includes a statement of financial position or other equivalent financial statement;

"directors", in the case of an institution which does not have directors, means persons occupying equivalent offices;

"group" means a parent institution and its subsidiary undertakings;

"IAS Regulation" means EC Regulation No 1606/2002 of the European Parliament and of the Council of 19th July 2002 on the application of international accounting standards;

"international accounting standards" means the international accounting standards, within the meaning of Article 2 of the IAS Regulation;

"Overseas Companies Regulations" means the Overseas Companies Regulations 2009 (SI 2009/1801);

"parent institution" means an institution that is a parent undertaking (see section 1162 of and Schedule 7 to the Companies Act 2006);

"profit and loss account" includes an income statement or other equivalent financial statement;

"relevant overseas institution" means an institution to which Chapter 3 of Part 6 of the Overseas Companies Regulations applies;

and references to "this Part" are references to those sections of Part 15 of the Companies Act 2006 as applied (with or without modification) by the Overseas Companies Regulations and include Schedules 6 and 7 to those Regulations.".

NOTES
Commencement: 1 October 2009.

PART 7
TRADING DISCLOSURES

[4.446]
58 Application and interpretation of Part

(1) This Part applies to an overseas company that carries on business in the United Kingdom.

(2) In this Part—
  (a) a reference to any type of document is a reference to a document of that type in hard copy, electronic or any other form;
  (b) in relation to a company, a reference to "its websites" includes a reference to any part of a website relating to that company which that company has caused or authorised to appear.

NOTES
Commencement: 1 October 2009.

[4.447]
59 Legibility of displays and disclosures

Any display or disclosure of information required by this Part must be in characters that can be read with the naked eye.

NOTES
Commencement: 1 October 2009.

[4.448]
60 Requirement to display name etc at business location

(1) A company to which this Part applies must display the company's name and country of incorporation—
  (a) at every location in the United Kingdom at which it carries on business, and
  (b) at the service address of every person resident in the United Kingdom authorised to accept service of documents on behalf of the company.

(2) Paragraph (1)(a) does not apply to a location—
  (a) that is primarily used for living accommodation;
  (b) at which business is carried on by a company of which every director or permanent representative who is an individual is entitled to higher protection from disclosure of their residential address; or
  (c) at which business is carried on by a company in respect of which a liquidator, administrator or administrative receiver has been appointed if the location is also a place of business of the liquidator, administrator or administrative receiver.

(3) The reference in paragraph (2)(b) to an individual who is entitled to higher protection from disclosure of their residential address is to an individual in respect of whom the registrar is prohibited from disclosing protected information to a credit reference agency.

NOTES
Commencement: 1 October 2009.

[4.449]

61 Manner of display of name etc

(1)   The following requirements apply where a company is required by regulation 60 to display its name and country of incorporation at a location in the United Kingdom.

(2)   A company must display its name and country of incorporation in such a way so that they may be easily seen by any visitor to the location.

(3)   The company's name and country of incorporation must be displayed continuously.

But, if the place of business is shared by six or more companies, this requirement is treated as met if the company's name and country of incorporation are displayed for at least fifteen continuous seconds at least once in every three minutes.

NOTES

Commencement: 1 October 2009.

[4.450]

62 Company's name to appear on communications

A company to which this Part applies must state the company's name on all—
  (a)   its business letters, notices and other official publications;
  (b)   its bills of exchange, promissory notes, endorsements and order forms;
  (c)   cheques purporting to be signed by or on behalf of the company;
  (d)   orders for money, goods or services purporting to be signed by or on behalf of the company;
  (e)   its bills of parcels, invoices and other demands for payments, receipts, and letters of credit;
  (f)   its applications for licences to carry on a trade or activity;
  (g)   other forms of its business correspondence and documentation; and
  (h)   its websites,
that are used in carrying on the activities of its business in the United Kingdom.

NOTES

Commencement: 1 October 2009.

[4.451]

63 Particulars to appear in business letters, order forms and websites

(1)   An overseas company that has a UK establishment in respect of which it has registered particulars under Part 2 must state the particulars required by paragraph (2) on all—
  (a)   its business letters,
  (b)   its order forms, and
  (c)   its websites,
that are used in carrying on the activities of a UK establishment of the company.

(2)   The particulars are—
  (a)   where the establishment is registered, and
  (b)   its registered number.

(3)   An overseas company which is not incorporated in an EEA State must state the particulars required by paragraph (4) on all—
  (a)   its business letters,
  (b)   its order forms, and
  (c)   its websites,
that are used in carrying on business in the United Kingdom.

(4)   The particulars are—
  (a)   the company's country of incorporation,
  (b)   the identity of the registry, if any, in which the company is registered in its country of incorporation,
  (c)   if applicable, the number with which the company is registered in that registry,
  (d)   the location of its head office,
  (e)   the legal form of the company,
  (f)   if the liability of the members of the company is limited, the fact that it is a limited company, and
  (g)   if applicable, the fact that the company is being wound up, or is subject to other insolvency proceedings or an arrangement or composition or any analogous proceedings.

(5)   If, in the case of an overseas company which is not incorporated in an EEA State having a share capital, there is reference to the amount of share capital on—
  (a)   its business letters,
  (b)   its order forms, or
  (c)   its websites,
the reference must be to paid up share capital.

(6)   Paragraph (4)(g) does not apply to a company required to make disclosures under—

  (a)   section 39(1) or 188(a) of, or paragraph 16(1) of Schedule A1 or paragraph 45 of Schedule B1 to, the Insolvency Act 1986, or

  (b)   Article 49(1) or 159(1) of, or paragraph 27(1) of Schedule A1 or paragraph 46 of Schedule B1 to, the Insolvency (Northern Ireland) Order 1989.

NOTES

Commencement: 1 October 2009.

[4.452]
64   Disclosure of names of directors

(1)   Where a business letter of a company to which this Part applies includes the name of any director of the company, other than in the text or as a signatory, the letter must disclose the name of every director of the company.

(2)   In the case of a body corporate, or a firm that is a legal person under the law by which it is governed, its corporate or firm name must be given.

NOTES

Commencement: 1 October 2009.

[4.453]
65   Disclosures relating to address for service

(1)   A company shall disclose the address of any person resident in the United Kingdom authorised to accept service of documents on behalf of the company to any person it deals with in the course of business who makes a written request to the company for that information.

(2)   The company shall send a written response to that person within five working days of the receipt of that request.

NOTES

Commencement: 1 October 2009.

[4.454]
66   Civil consequences of failure to make a required disclosure

(1)   This regulation applies to any legal proceedings brought by a company to which this Part applies to enforce a right arising out of a contract made in the course of a business in respect of which, at the time the contract was made, there was a failure to comply with the requirements of this Part.

(2)   The proceedings must be dismissed if it is shown that the defendant (in Scotland, the defender)—

  (a)   has a claim against the claimant (pursuer) arising out of the contract and has been unable to pursue that claim by reason of the latter's failure to comply with the requirements of this Part, or

  (b)   has suffered some financial loss in connection with the contract by reason of the claimant's (pursuer's) failure to comply with those requirements,

unless the court before which the proceedings are brought is satisfied that it is just and equitable to permit the proceedings to continue.

(3)   This regulation does not affect the right of any person to enforce such rights as the person may have against another in any proceedings brought by the other.

NOTES

Commencement: 1 October 2009.

[4.455]
67   Penalty for non-compliance

(1)   Where a company fails, without reasonable excuse, to comply with any requirement of this Part, an offence is committed by—

  (a)   the company, and

  (b)   every officer of the company who is in default.

(2)   A person guilty of an offence under paragraph (1) is liable on summary conviction to—

  (a)   a fine not exceeding level 3 on the standard scale, and

  (b)   for continued contravention, a daily default fine not exceeding one-tenth of level 3 on the standard scale.

(3)   For the purposes of this regulation a shadow director is to be treated as an officer of the company.

NOTES

Commencement: 1 October 2009.

PART 8
RETURNS IN CASE OF WINDING UP ETC

[4.456]
68   Application of Part

This Part applies to an overseas company that has one or more UK establishments.

NOTES
Commencement: 1 October 2009.

[4.457]
69   Return in case of winding up

(1)   Where a company to which this Part applies is being wound up, it must deliver to the registrar a return containing the following particulars—
- (a)   the company's name;
- (b)   whether the company is being wound up by an order of a court and if so, the name and address of the court and the date of the order;
- (c)   if the company is not being so wound up, as a result of what action the winding up has commenced;
- (d)   whether the winding up has been instigated by—
  - (i)   the company's members,
  - (ii)   the company's creditors, or
  - (iii)   some other person (stating the person's identity); and
- (e)   the date on which the winding up became or will become effective.

(2)   The return must be delivered not later than—
- (a)   if the winding up began before the company had a UK establishment, one month after the company first opens a UK establishment;
- (b)   if the winding up begins when the company has a UK establishment, 14 days after the date on which the winding up begins.

(3)   Where the company has more than one UK establishment the obligation to deliver a return under this regulation applies in respect of each of them, but a return giving the registered numbers of more than one UK establishment is regarded as a return in respect of each establishment whose number is given.

(4)   No return is required under this regulation in respect of winding up under the Insolvency Act 1986 or the Insolvency (Northern Ireland) Order 1989.

NOTES
Commencement: 1 October 2009.

[4.458]
70   Returns to be made by liquidator

(1)   A person appointed to be the liquidator of a company to which this Part applies must deliver to the registrar a return containing the following particulars—
- (a)   their name and address,
- (b)   date of the appointment, and
- (c)   a description of such of the person's powers, if any, as are derived otherwise than from the general law or the company's constitution.

(2)   The period allowed for delivery of the return required by paragraph (1) is—
- (a)   if the liquidator was appointed before the company had a UK establishment (and continues in office at the date of the opening), one month after the company first opens a UK establishment;
- (b)   if the liquidator is appointed when the company has a UK establishment, 14 days after the date of the appointment.

(3)   The liquidator of a company to which this Part applies must—
- (a)   on the termination of the winding up of the company, deliver a return to the registrar stating the name of the company and the date on which the winding up terminated;
- (b)   on the company ceasing to be registered in circumstances where ceasing to be registered is an event of legal significance, deliver a return to the registrar stating the name of the company and the date on which it ceased to be registered.

(4)   The period allowed for delivery of the return required by paragraph (3)(a) or (b) is 14 days from the date of the event.

(5)   Where the company has more than one UK establishment the obligation to deliver a return under this regulation applies in respect of each of them, but a return giving the registered numbers of more than one UK establishment is regarded as a return in respect of each establishment whose number is given.

(6)   No return is required under this regulation in respect of a liquidator appointed under the Insolvency Act 1986 or the Insolvency (Northern Ireland) Order 1989.

NOTES
Commencement: 1 October 2009.

[4.459]
71   Return in case of insolvency proceedings etc (other than winding up)

(1)   Where a company to which this Part applies becomes subject to insolvency proceedings or an arrangement or composition or any analogous proceedings (other than proceedings for winding up of the company), it must deliver to the registrar a return containing the following particulars—
     (a)   the company's name;
     (b)   whether the proceedings are by an order of a court and if so, the name and address of the court and the date of the order;
     (c)   if the proceedings are not by an order of a court, as a result of what action the proceedings have been commenced;
     (d)   whether the proceedings have been commenced by—
         (i)   the company's members,
         (ii)   the company's creditors, or
         (iii)   some other person (giving the person's identity);
     (e)   the date on which the proceedings became or will become effective.

(2)   The period allowed for delivery of the return required by paragraph (1) is—
     (a)   if the company became subject to the proceedings before it had a UK establishment, one month after the company first opens a UK establishment;
     (b)   if the company becomes subject to the proceedings when it has a UK establishment, 14 days from the date on which it becomes subject to the proceedings.

(3)   Where a company to which this Part applies ceases to be subject to any of the proceedings referred to in paragraph (1) it must deliver to the registrar a return stating—
     (a)   the company's name, and
     (b)   the date on which it ceased to be subject to the proceedings.

(4)   The period allowed for delivery of the return required by paragraph (3) is 14 days from the date on which it ceases to be subject to the proceedings.

(5)   Where the company has more than one UK establishment the obligation to deliver a return under this regulation applies in respect of each of them, but a return giving the registered numbers of more than one UK establishment is regarded as a return in respect of each establishment whose number is given.

(6)   No return is required under this regulation in respect of—
     (a)   a company's becoming or ceasing to be subject to a voluntary arrangement under Part 1 of the Insolvency Act 1986 or Part 2 of the Insolvency (Northern Ireland) Order 1989, or
     (b)   a company's entering administration under Part 2 and Schedule B1 of that Act or becoming or ceasing to be subject to an administration order under Part 3 of that Order.

NOTES
Commencement: 1 October 2009.

[4.460]
72   Penalties for non-compliance

(1)   If a company fails to comply with regulation 69(1) or 71(1) or (3) within the period allowed for compliance, an offence is committed by—
     (a)   the company, and
     (b)   every person who immediately before the end of that period was a director of the company.

(2)   A liquidator who fails to comply with regulation 70(1) or (3)(a) or (b) within the period allowed for compliance commits an offence.

(3)   A person who takes all reasonable steps to secure compliance with the requirements concerned does not commit an offence under this regulation.

(4)   A person guilty of an offence under this regulation is liable—
     (a)   on conviction on indictment, to a fine;
     (b)   on summary conviction to a fine not exceeding the statutory maximum and, for continued contravention, a daily default fine not exceeding one-fiftieth of the statutory maximum.

NOTES
Commencement: 1 October 2009.

[4.461]
73   Notice of appointment of judicial factor

(1)   Notice must be given to the registrar of the appointment in relation to a company to which this Part applies of a judicial factor (in Scotland).

(2)   The notice must be given by the judicial factor.

(3)   The notice must specify an address at which service of documents (including legal process) may be effected on the judicial factor.

(4)   Notice of a change in the address for service may be given to the registrar by the judicial factor.

(5)   A judicial factor who has notified the registrar of the appointment must also notify the registrar of the termination of the appointment.

NOTES

Commencement: 1 October 2009.

[4.462]
74   Offence of failure to give notice

(1)   A judicial factor who fails to give notice of the appointment in accordance with regulation 73 within the period of 14 days after the appointment commits an offence.

(2)   A person guilty of an offence under this regulation is liable on summary conviction to—
   (a)   a fine not exceeding level 5 on the standard scale, and
   (b)   for continued contravention, a daily default fine not exceeding one-tenth of level 5 on the standard scale.

NOTES

Commencement: 1 October 2009.

PART 9
MISCELLANEOUS PROVISIONS

[4.463]
75   Service of documents on director, secretary or permanent representative

The positions specified for the purposes of section 1140(2)(b) of the Companies Act 2006 (overseas companies that have registered particulars: persons on whom document may be served at registered address) are—
   (a)   director,
   (b)   secretary, and
   (c)   permanent representative.

NOTES

Commencement: 1 October 2009.

[4.464]
76   Documents subject to Directive disclosure requirements

The particulars, returns and other documents specified for the purposes of section 1078(5) of the Companies Act 2006 (overseas companies: documents subject to Directive disclosure requirements) are—
   (a)   any return or document delivered under Part 2 (initial registration of particulars);
   (b)   any return or document delivered under Part 3 (alterations in registered particulars);
   (c)   any document delivered under Part 5 (delivery of accounting documents: general);
   (d)   any document delivered under Part 6 (delivery of accounting documents: credit or financial institutions);
   (e)   any return delivered under regulation 69 (return in case of winding up) or 70 (returns to be made by liquidator);
   (f)   any notice under regulation 77 (duty to give notice of closure of UK establishment).

NOTES

Commencement: 1 October 2009.

[4.465]
77   Duty to give notice of closure of UK establishment

(1)   If an overseas company closes a UK establishment in respect of which it has registered particulars under Part 2, it must forthwith give notice of that fact to the registrar.

(2)   From the date on which notice is given under paragraph (1) the company is no longer obliged to deliver documents to the registrar in respect of that establishment.

(3)   If a company fails to comply with paragraph (1) an offence is committed by—
   (a)   the company, and
   (b)   every officer or agent of the company who knowingly and willingly authorises or permits the default.

(4)   A person guilty of an offence under this regulation is liable on summary conviction to—
   (a)   a fine not exceeding level 3 on the standard scale, and

(b)   for continued contravention, a daily default fine not exceeding one-tenth of level 3 on the standard scale.

NOTES

Commencement: 1 October 2009.

PART 10
SUPPLEMENTARY PROVISIONS

[4.466]
78   Documents that may be drawn up and delivered in a language other than English

(1)   The following documents are specified for the purposes of section 1105(2)(d) of the Companies Act 2006 as documents that may be drawn up and delivered to the registrar in a language other than English, but which must, when delivered to the registrar, be accompanied by a certified translation into English.

(2)   The documents are—
   (a)   a certified copy of the constitution required to be delivered under regulation 8, 14 or 15 of these Regulations;
   (b)   copies of accounting documents required to be delivered under regulation 9, 32, 45 or 46;
   (c)   copies of accounts required to be delivered under section 441 as modified by regulations 40 and 55.

NOTES

Commencement: 1 October 2009.

[4.467]
79   Revocations

The following Regulations are revoked—
   (a)   the Oversea Companies and Credit and Financial Institutions (Branch Disclosure) Regulations 1992,
   (b)   the Part XXIII Companies and Credit and Financial Institutions (Branch Disclosure) Regulations (Northern Ireland) 1993.

NOTES

Commencement: 1 October 2009.

[4.468]
80   Transitional provisions and savings

Schedule 8 contains transitional provisions and savings.

NOTES

Commencement: 1 October 2009.

SCHEDULES

SCHEDULE 1
SPECIFIED PUBLIC AUTHORITIES

Regulation 18

[4.469]
The Secretary of State;

any Northern Ireland Department;

the Scottish Ministers;

the Welsh Ministers;

the Treasury;

the Commissioners for Her Majesty's Revenue and Customs;

the Bank of England;

the Director of Public Prosecutions;

the Director of Public Prosecutions for Northern Ireland;

the Serious Fraud Office;

the Secret Intelligence Service;

the Security Service;

the Government Communications Headquarters;

the Financial Services Authority;

the Competition Commission;

the Pensions Regulator;

the Panel on Takeovers and Mergers;

the Regulator of Community Interest Companies;

the Registrar of Credit Unions for Northern Ireland;

the Office of Fair Trading;

the Office of the Information Commissioner;

the Charity Commission;

the Charity Commission for Northern Ireland;

the Office of the Scottish Charity Regulator;

the Postal Services Commission;

the Gas and Electricity Markets Authority;

the Northern Ireland Authority for Utility Regulation;

the Gambling Commission;

the Serious Organised Crime Agency;

the Health and Safety Executive;

the Health and Safety Executive for Northern Ireland;

the Food Standards Agency;

the Gangmasters Licensing Authority;

the Security Industry Authority;

a local authority within the meaning of section 54(2) of the Companies Act 2006;

an official receiver appointed under section 399 of the Insolvency Act 1986 (appointment, etc, of official receivers);

the Official Receiver for Northern Ireland;

the Crown Office and Procurator Fiscal Services;

a person acting as an insolvency practitioner within the meaning of section 388 of the Insolvency Act 1986 (meaning of "act as an insolvency practitioner") or Article 3 of the Insolvency (Northern Ireland) Order 1989 ("act as an insolvency practitioner");

an inspector appointed under Part 14 of the Companies Act 1985 (investigation of companies and their affairs: requisition of documents) or Part 15 of the Companies (Northern Ireland) Order 1986 or a person appointed under regulation 30 of the Open-Ended Investment Companies Regulations 2001 (power to investigate) or regulation 22 of the Open-Ended Investment Companies Regulations (Northern Ireland) 2004;

any person authorised to exercise powers under section 447 of the Companies Act 1985 (power to require documents and information), or section 84 of the Companies Act 1989 (exercise of powers by officers, etc) or Article 440 of the Companies (Northern Ireland) Order;

any person exercising functions conferred by Part 6 of the Financial Services and Markets Act 2000 (official listing) or the competent authority under that Part;

a person appointed to make a report under section 166 (reports by skilled persons) of the Financial Services and Markets Act 2000;

a person appointed to conduct an investigation under section 167 (appointment of persons to carry out general investigations) or 168(3) or (5) (appointment of persons to carry out investigations in particular cases) of the Financial Services and Markets Act 2000;

an inspector appointed under section 284 (power to investigate) of the Financial Services and Markets Act 2000;

an overseas regulatory authority within the meaning of section 82 of the Companies Act 1989 (request for assistance by overseas regulatory authority);

a police force.

NOTES
Commencement: 1 October 2009.

SCHEDULE 2
CONDITIONS FOR PERMITTED DISCLOSURE
Regulations 23 and 24

PART 1
DISCLOSURE TO SPECIFIED PUBLIC AUTHORITY

[4.470]
1. Paragraphs 2 and 3 set out the conditions specified for the disclosure of protected information by the registrar to a specified public authority.

2. The specified public authority has delivered to the registrar a statement that it intends to use the protected information only for the purpose of facilitating the carrying out by that specified public authority of a public function ("the permitted purpose").

3. Subject to paragraph 4, the specified public authority ("the authority") has delivered to the registrar a statement that it will, where it supplies a copy of the protected information to a processor for the purpose of processing the information for use in respect of the permitted purpose—
   (a)   ensure that the processor is one who carries on business in the European Economic Area;
   (b)   require that the information is not transmitted outside the European Economic Area by the processor; and
   (c)   require that the processor does not disclose the information except to the authority or an employee of the authority.

4. Paragraph 3 does not apply where the specified public authority is the Secret Intelligence Service, Security Service or Government Communications Headquarters.

NOTES
Commencement: 1 October 2009.

PART 2
DISCLOSURE TO CREDIT REFERENCE AGENCY

[4.471]
5. Paragraphs 6 to 10 set out the conditions specified for the disclosure of protected information by the registrar to a credit reference agency.

6. The credit reference agency—
   (a)   is carrying on in the United Kingdom or in another EEA State a business comprising the furnishing of information relevant to the financial standing of individuals, being information collected by the agency for that purpose;
   (b)   maintains appropriate procedures—
       (i)   to ensure that an independent person can investigate and audit the measures maintained by the agency for the purposes of ensuring the security of any protected information disclosed to that agency; and
       (ii)   for the purposes of ensuring that it complies with its obligations under the Data Protection Act 1998, or, where the agency carries on business in a EEA State other than the United Kingdom, with its obligations under legislation implementing Directive 95/46/EC of the European Parliament and of the Council of 24 October 1995 on the protection of individuals with regard to the processing of personal data and on the free movement of such data;
   (c)   has not been found guilty of an offence under—
       (i)   section 1112 (general false statement offence) of the Companies Act 2006 or section 2 of the Fraud Act 2006 (fraud by false representation); or
       (ii)   section 47 (failure to comply with enforcement notice) of the Data Protection Act 1998 in circumstances where it has used the protected information for purposes other than those described in sub-paragraphs (a) to (e) of paragraph 7 below.

7. The credit reference agency has delivered to the registrar a statement that it intends to use that protected information only for the purposes of—
   (a)   providing an assessment of the financial standing of a person;
   (b)   meeting any obligations contained in the Money Laundering Regulations 2007 or any rules made pursuant to section 146 of the Financial Services and Markets Act 2000 (money

laundering rules), or in any legislation of another EEA State implementing Directive 2005/60/EC of the European Parliament and of the Council of 26 October 2005 on the prevention of the use of the financial system for the purpose of money laundering and terrorist financing;

(c) conducting conflict of interest checks required or made necessary by any enactment;

(d) the provision of protected information to—

    (i) a public authority specified in Schedule 1 which has satisfied the requirements of paragraphs 2 and 3 of this Schedule; or

    (ii) a credit reference agency which has satisfied the requirements of this Part of this Schedule; or

(e) conducting checks for the prevention and detection of crime and fraud.

8. The credit reference agency has delivered to the registrar a statement that it intends to take delivery of and to use the protected information only in the United Kingdom or in another EEA State.

9. The credit reference agency has delivered to the registrar a statement that it will, where it supplies a copy of the protected information to a processor for the purpose of processing the information for use in respect of the purposes referred to in paragraph 7—

    (a) ensure that the processor is one who carries on business in the European Economic Area;

    (b) require that the information is not transmitted outside the European Economic Area by the processor; and

    (c) require that the processor does not disclose the information except to the credit reference agency or an employee of the credit reference agency.

10. The credit reference agency has delivered to the registrar a statement that it meets the conditions in paragraph 6 above.

NOTES

Commencement: 1 October 2009.

PART 3
INTERPRETATION OF THIS SCHEDULE

[4.472]

11. (1) In this Schedule—

"processor" means any person who provides a service which consists of putting information into data form or processing information in data form, and any reference to a processor includes a reference to the processor's employees; and

"public function" includes—

    (a) any function conferred by or in accordance with any provision contained in any enactment;

    (b) any function conferred by or in accordance with any provision contained in the Community Treaties or any Community instrument;

    (c) any similar function conferred on persons by or under provisions having effect as part of the law of a country or territory outside the United Kingdom; and

    (d) any function exercisable in relation to the investigation of any criminal offence or for the purpose of any criminal proceedings.

(2) In this Schedule any reference to—

    (a) an employee of any person who has access to protected information shall be deemed to include any person working or providing services for the purposes of that person or employed by or on behalf of, or working for, any person who is so working or who is supplying such a service; and

    (b) the disclosure for the purpose of facilitating the carrying out of a public function includes disclosure in relation to, and for the purpose of, any proceedings whether civil, criminal or disciplinary in which the specified public authority engages while carrying out its public functions.

NOTES

Commencement: 1 October 2009.

SCHEDULE 3
APPLICATION TO PREVENT DISCLOSURE OF ADDRESS TO CREDIT REFERENCE AGENCY

Regulation 25

[4.473]

1 Introductory

In this Schedule "application for higher protection" has the meaning given by regulation 25(1).

2 Application by the individual concerned

(1) An application for higher protection may be made to the registrar by an individual who is, or proposes to become, a director or permanent representative of a company to which Part 4 applies.

(2) The grounds on which an application may be made under this paragraph are that the applicant considers that there is a serious risk that the applicant, or a person who lives with the applicant, will be subjected to violence or intimidation as a result of the activities of at least one of—

    (a) the overseas companies of which the applicant is, or proposes to become, a director or permanent representative;

    (b) the overseas companies of which the applicant was a director or permanent representative or secretary;

    (c) the companies of which the applicant is or has been a director; or

    (d) the limited liability partnerships of which the applicant is or has been a member.

(3) The application must contain—

    (a) a statement of the grounds on which the application is made;

    (b) the name and any former name of the applicant;

    (c) the date of birth of the applicant;

    (d) the usual residential address of the applicant;

    (e) where the registrar has allocated a unique identifier to the applicant, that unique identifier;

    (f) the name and registered number of each overseas company of which the applicant is, or proposes to become, a director or permanent representative; and

    (g) where the grounds of the application are those described in sub-paragraph (2)(b), (c) or (d), the name and registered number of the overseas company, company or limited liability partnership.

(4) The application must be accompanied by evidence which supports the applicant's statement of the grounds of the application.

(5) The registrar may refer to—

    (a) a police force, or

    (b) any other person whom the registrar considers may be able to assist in answering the question,

any question relating to an assessment of the nature and extent of any risk of violence or intimidation.

(6) The registrar shall—

    (a) determine the application, and

    (b) send notice of the determination to the applicant (to the applicant's usual residential address as stated in the application) within five working days of the determination's being made.

3 Application by company

(1) An application for higher protection may be made to the registrar by a company to which Part 4 applies on behalf of any of its directors or permanent representatives.

(2) The grounds on which an application under sub-paragraph (1) may be made are that the company considers that there is a serious risk that the director or permanent representative on behalf of whom the application is made, or a person who lives with that director or permanent representative, will be subjected to violence or intimidation as a result of the company's activities.

(3) The application must contain—

    (a) a statement of the grounds on which the application is made;

    (b) the name and registered number of the applicant;

    (c) the name and any former name of each director or permanent representative on behalf of whom the application is made;

    (d) the date of birth of each such director or permanent representative;

    (e) the usual residential address of each such director or permanent representative;

    (f) where the registrar has allocated a unique identifier to any such director or permanent representative, that unique identifier;

    (g) the name and registered number of each UK-registered company or overseas company to which Part 4 applies of which each such director or permanent representative is a director or permanent representative.

(4) The application must be accompanied by evidence which supports the applicant's statement of the grounds of the application.

(5) The registrar may refer to—

    (a) a police force, or

    (b) any other person whom the registrar considers may be able to assist in answering the question,

any question relating to an assessment of the nature and extent of any risk of violence or intimidation.

(6) The registrar shall—

    (a) determine the application, and

(b)   send notice of the determination within five working days of its being made—

    (i)   to the applicant (to its registered office or, if it is not registered, to the address of its principal place of business in its country of incorporation), and

    (ii)   to each director or permanent representative on behalf of whom the application was made (to the usual residential address of the director or permanent representative as stated in the application).

4 Supplementary provisions relating to applications

(1)   For the purpose of paragraphs 2(4) and 3(4) the registrar may direct that additional information or evidence should be delivered to him, what such information or evidence should be and how it should be verified.

(2)   The registrar shall not make available for public inspection—

(a)   any application for higher protection; or

(b)   any documents provided in support of that application; or

(c)   any representations received in connection with the revocation of a decision under paragraph 7.

(3)   For the purpose of determining an application for higher protection the registrar may accept any answer to a question referred in accordance with paragraph 2(5) or 3(5) as providing sufficient evidence of the nature and extent of any risk of violence or intimidation.

(4)   In paragraphs 2 and 3 "former name" means a name that has been notified to the registrar under regulation 6(3)(a)(ii) or 7(1)(f)(ii) and the definition in regulation 2 shall not apply.

5 Appeals

(1)   An applicant who has received notice under paragraph 2 or 3 that the application has been unsuccessful may appeal to the High Court or, in Scotland, the Court of Session on the grounds that the decision—

(a)   is unlawful;

(b)   is irrational or unreasonable;

(c)   has been made on the basis of a procedural impropriety or otherwise contravenes the rules of natural justice.

(2)   No appeal under this paragraph may be brought unless the leave of the court has been obtained.

(3)   An applicant must bring an appeal within 35 days of the date of the notice or, with the court's permission, after the end of such period, but only if the court is satisfied—

(a)   where permission is sought before the end of that period, that there is good reason for the applicant being unable to bring the appeal in time; or

(b)   where permission is sought after that time, that there was a good reason for the applicant's failure to bring the appeal in time and for any delay in applying for permission.

(4)   The court determining an appeal may—

(a)   dismiss the appeal, or

(b)   quash the decision,

and where the court quashes a decision it may refer the matter to the registrar with a direction to reconsider it and make a determination in accordance with the findings of the court.

6 Duration of favourable decision on application

A decision of the registrar in favour of the applicant on an application for higher protection continues to have effect until—

(a)   the registrar is notified by the individual in respect of whom the application was made (or their personal representative) of the wish that the decision should cease to apply, or

(b)   the registrar revokes the decision in accordance with paragraph 7.

7 Revocation of favourable decision on application

(1)   The registrar may revoke a decision in favour of the applicant on an application for higher protection if the individual in respect of whom the application was made, or any other person, is found guilty of an offence under section 1112 of the Companies Act 2006 (general false statement offence) committed in purporting to comply with any provision of this Schedule.

(2)   The registrar must send to the individual notice of any proposal to revoke a decision under this paragraph.

(3)   The notice must—

(a)   inform the individual that they may, within the period of 28 days beginning with the date of the notice, deliver representations to the registrar, and

(b)   state that if representations are not received by the registrar within that period, the decision will be revoked at the expiry of that period.

(4)   If within the period specified in sub-paragraph (3) the individual delivers representations as to why the decision should not be revoked, the registrar must—

(a)   have regard to the representations in determining whether to revoke the decision, and

(b)   send notice of the determination to the individual within five working days of its being made.

(5)   Any communication by the registrar under this paragraph in respect of a proposal or determination must be sent to the individual's usual residential address.

NOTES
Commencement: 1 October 2009.

SCHEDULE 4
OVERSEAS COMPANIES INDIVIDUAL ACCOUNTS

Regulation 38

PART 1
GENERAL RULES

[4.474]
1. Subject to the following provisions of this Schedule—
   (a)   every balance sheet must show each of the line items required to be included in a balance sheet in accordance with international accounting standards;
   (b)   every profit and loss account must show each of the line items required to be included in a profit and loss account in accordance with international accounting standards;
   (c)   every balance sheet and profit and loss account must clearly indicate in what currency it is prepared.

2. (1)   The company's directors must use the same line items in preparing overseas companies individual accounts for each financial year, unless in their opinion there are special reasons for a change.

(2)   Particulars of any such change must be given in a note to the accounts in which the new line item is first used, and the reasons for the change must be explained.

3. Where the company's directors consider it appropriate, the balance sheet or the profit and loss account may show a combination of line items where they are of a similar nature.

4. (1)   Items that are not of a similar nature or function shall be presented separately unless they are not material.

(2)   For the purpose of this paragraph an item is "material" if it either supplements the information given with respect to any particular item shown in the balance sheet and profit and loss account or is otherwise relevant to assessing the company's state of affairs.

(3)   Amounts which in the particular context of any provision of this Schedule are not material may be disregarded for the purposes of that provision.

5. (1)   Where the nature of the company's business requires it, the company's directors must adapt the line items in the balance sheet or profit and loss account.

(2)   The directors may combine items if—
   (a)   their individual amounts are not material to assessing the state of affairs or profit and loss of the company for the financial year in question, or
   (b)   the combination facilitates that assessment.

(3)   Where sub-paragraph (2)(b) applies, the individual amounts of any items which have been combined must be disclosed in a note to the accounts.

6. (1)   Subject to sub-paragraph (2), the directors may exclude an item in the balance sheet or profit and loss account if there is no amount to be shown for that item for the financial year to which the balance sheet or the profit and loss account relates.

(2)   Where an amount can be shown for the item in question for the immediately preceding financial year that amount must be shown under the line item for that item.

7. (1)   For every item shown in the balance sheet or profit and loss account the corresponding amount for the immediately preceding financial year must also be shown.

(2)   Where that corresponding amount is not comparable with the amount to be shown for the item in question in respect of the financial year to which the balance sheet or profit and loss account relates, the former amount may be adjusted and particulars of the non-comparability and of any adjustment must be disclosed in a note to the accounts.

8. Amounts in respect of items representing assets or income may not be set off against amounts in respect of items representing liabilities or expenditure (as the case may be), or vice versa.

9. The company's directors must, in determining how amounts are presented within items in the profit and loss account and balance sheet, have regard to the substance of the reported transaction or arrangement, in accordance with generally accepted accounting principles or practice.

PART 2
ACCOUNTING PRINCIPLES AND RULES

Preliminary

[4.475]
10. (1)   The amounts to be included in respect of all items shown in a company's accounts must be determined in accordance with the principles set out in this Part.

(2)   But if it appears to the company's directors that there are special reasons for departing from any of those principles in preparing the company's accounts in respect of any financial year they may do so, in which case particulars of the departure, the reasons for it and its effect must be given in a note to the accounts.

Accounting principles
11. (1)   The company is presumed to be carrying on business as a going concern.

(2)   If the accounts are not prepared on a going concern basis, that fact shall be disclosed, together with the basis on which the accounts are prepared and the reason why the company is not a going concern.

12. Accounting policies must be applied consistently within the same accounts and from one financial year to the next.

13. All income and charges relating to the financial year to which the accounts relate must be taken into account, without regard to the date of receipt or payment.

14. In determining the aggregate amount of any item, the amount of each individual asset or liability that falls to be taken into account must be determined separately.

PART 3
NOTES TO THE ACCOUNTS

[4.476]
15. Any information required in the case of any company by the following provisions of this Part of this Schedule must (if not given in the company's accounts) be given by way of a note to the accounts.

16. The accounting policies adopted by the company in determining the amounts to be included in respect of items shown in the balance sheet and in determining the profit or loss of the company must be stated (including such policies with respect to the depreciation and diminution in value of assets).

17. It must be stated whether the accounts have been prepared in accordance with the applied accounting standards and particulars of any material departure from those standards and the reasons for it must be given.

18. The company must include in the statement of accounting policies—
   (a)   the measurement basis (or bases) used in preparing the accounts; and
   (b)   any other accounting policies used that are relevant to an understanding of the accounts.

19. (1)   The company must provide information which is relevant to assessing the company's state of affairs.

(2)   As a minimum that information must relate, where applicable, to—
   (a)   property, plant and equipment;
   (b)   investment property;
   (c)   intangible assets;
   (d)   financial assets;
   (e)   biological assets;
   (f)   inventories;
   (g)   trade and other receivables (and the amount falling due after more than one year must be shown separately for each item included under receivables);
   (h)   trade and other payables (and the amount falling due after more than one year must be shown separately for each item included under payables);
   (i)   provisions;
   (j)   financial liabilities;

(k)   issued capital and reserves;

(l)   finance costs;

(m)   finance income;

(n)   expenses and interest paid to group undertakings (this must be shown separately from expenses and interest paid to other entities);

(o)   income and interest derived from group undertakings (this must be shown separately from income and interest derived from other sources);

(p)   transactions with related parties;

(q)   dividends;

(r)   items described as other, sundry, miscellaneous or equivalent;

(s)   guarantees;

(t)   contingent liabilities;

(u)   commitments;

(v)   other off-balance sheet arrangements;

(w)   financial instruments.

20. In this Schedule the expression "line item" has the same meaning as in international accounting standard 1 on the presentation of financial statements and includes "items", "layout items" and other equivalent terms.

NOTES

Commencement: 1 October 2009.

SCHEDULE 5
OVERSEAS COMPANIES GROUP ACCOUNTS

Regulation 38

General rules

[4.477]

1. (1)   Overseas companies group accounts must comply so far as practicable with the provisions of Schedule 4 as if the undertakings included in the consolidation ("the group") were a single company.

(2)   In the case of overseas companies group accounts the minimum information listed in paragraph 19(2) of Schedule 4 must also relate to—

(a)   investments accounted for using the equity method;

(b)   minority interests, presented within equity.

2. The consolidated balance sheet and profit and loss account must incorporate in full the information contained in the individual accounts of the undertakings included in the consolidation, subject to the adjustments authorised or required by the following provisions of this Schedule and to such other adjustments (if any) as may be appropriate in accordance with generally accepted accounting principles or practice.

3. (1)   Where assets and liabilities to be included in the group accounts have been valued or otherwise determined by undertakings according to accounting rules differing from those used for the group accounts, the values or amounts must be adjusted so as to accord with the rules used for the group accounts.

(2)   If it appears to the directors of the parent company that there are special reasons for departing from sub-paragraph (1) they may do so, but particulars of any such departure, the reasons for it and its effect must be given in a note to the accounts.

(3)   The adjustments referred to in this paragraph need not be made if they are not material.

4. Amounts that in the particular context of any provision of this Schedule are not material may be disregarded for the purposes of that provision.

Elimination of group transactions

5. (1)   Debts and claims between undertakings included in the consolidation, and income and expenditure relating to transactions between such undertakings, must be eliminated in preparing the group accounts.

(2)   Where profits and losses resulting from transactions between undertakings included in the consolidation are included in the book value of assets, they must be eliminated in preparing the group accounts.

(3)   The elimination required by sub-paragraph (2) may be effected in proportion to the group's interest in the shares of the undertakings.

(4)   Sub-paragraphs (1) and (2) need not be complied with if the amounts concerned are not material.

6. (1)   The following provisions apply where an undertaking becomes a subsidiary undertaking of the parent company.

(2) That event is referred to in those provisions as an "acquisition", and references to the "undertaking acquired" are to be construed accordingly.

7. (1) An acquisition must be accounted for—
  (a) by the acquisition method of accounting, or
  (b) if the generally accepted accounting principles under which the accounts have been prepared allow it to be accounted for by another method, by that method.

(2) If an acquisition is accounted for in accordance with sub-paragraph (1)(b), the method used must be disclosed in the notes to the accounts.

Minority interests

8. (1) In the balance sheet there must be shown, as a separate item and under an appropriate line item, the amount of capital and reserves attributable to shares in subsidiary undertakings included in the consolidation held by or on behalf of persons other than the parent company and its subsidiary undertakings.

(2) In the profit and loss account formats there must be shown, as a separate item and under an appropriate line item—
  (a) the amount of any profit or loss on ordinary activities, and
  (b) the amount of any profit or loss on extraordinary activities,
attributable to shares in subsidiary undertakings included in the consolidation held by or on behalf of persons other than the parent company and its subsidiary undertakings.

Joint ventures

9. (1) Where an undertaking included in the consolidation manages another undertaking jointly with one or more undertakings not included in the consolidation, that other undertaking ("the joint venture") may, if it is not—
  (a) a body corporate, or
  (b) a subsidiary undertaking of the parent company,
be dealt with in the group accounts by the method of proportional consolidation.

(2) The provisions of this Schedule relating to the preparation of consolidated accounts apply, with any necessary modifications, to proportional consolidation under this paragraph.

Associated undertakings

10. An "associated undertaking" means an undertaking in which an undertaking included in the consolidation has a participating interest and over whose operating and financial policy it exercises a significant influence, and which is not—
  (a) a subsidiary undertaking of the parent company, or
  (b) a joint venture dealt with in accordance with paragraph 9.

11. (1) The interest of an undertaking in an associated undertaking, and the amount of profit or loss attributable to such an interest, shall be shown—
  (a) by the equity method of accounting, or
  (b) if the generally accepted accounting principles under which the accounts have been prepared allow it to be accounted for by another method, by that method.

(2) If an interest is accounted for in accordance with sub-paragraph (1)(b), the method used must be disclosed in the notes to the accounts.

(3) Where the associated undertaking is itself a parent undertaking, the net assets and profits or losses to be taken into account are those of the parent and its subsidiary undertakings (after making any consolidation adjustments).

NOTES

Commencement: 1 October 2009.

SCHEDULE 6
CREDIT AND FINANCIAL INSTITUTIONS INDIVIDUAL ACCOUNTS
Regulation 53

PART 1
GENERAL RULES

[4.478]
1. Subject to the following provisions of this Schedule—
  (a) every balance sheet must show each of the line items required to be included in a balance sheet in accordance with international accounting standards;
  (b) every profit and loss account must show each of the line items required to be included in a profit and loss account in accordance with international accounting standards;
  (c) every balance sheet and profit and loss account must clearly indicate in what currency it is prepared.

2. (1) The institution's directors must use the same line items in preparing overseas institutions individual accounts for each financial year, unless in their opinion there are special reasons for a change.

(2) Particulars of any such change must be given in a note to the accounts in which the new line item is first used, and the reasons for the change must be explained.

3. Where the institution's directors consider it appropriate, the balance sheet or the profit and loss account may show a combination of line items where they are of a similar nature.

4. (1) Items that are not of a similar nature or function shall be presented separately unless they are not material.

(2) For the purpose of this paragraph an item is "material" if it either supplements the information given with respect to any particular item shown in the balance sheet and profit and loss account or is otherwise relevant to assessing the institution's state of affairs.

(3) Amounts which in the particular context of any provision of this Schedule are not material may be disregarded for the purposes of that provision.

5. (1) Where the nature of the institution's business requires it, the directors must adapt the line items in the balance sheet or profit and loss account.

(2) The directors may combine items if—
   (a) their individual amounts are not material to assessing the state of affairs or profit or loss of the institution for the financial year in question, or
   (b) the combination facilitates that assessment.

(3) Where sub-paragraph (2)(b) applies, the individual amounts of any items which have been combined must be disclosed in a note to the accounts.

6. (1) Subject to sub-paragraph (2), the directors may exclude an item in the balance sheet or profit and loss account if there is no amount to be shown for that item for the financial year to which the balance sheet or the profit and loss account relates.

(2) Where an amount can be shown for the item in question for the immediately preceding financial year that amount must be shown under the line item for that item.

7. (1) For every item shown in the balance sheet or profit and loss account the corresponding amount for the immediately preceding financial year must also be shown.

(2) Where that corresponding amount is not comparable with the amount to be shown for the item in question in respect of the financial year to which the balance sheet or profit and loss account relates, the former amount may be adjusted and particulars of the non-comparability and of any adjustment must be disclosed in a note to the accounts.

8. Amounts in respect of items representing assets or income may not be set off against amounts in respect of items representing liabilities or expenditure (as the case may be), or vice versa.

9. The institution's directors must, in determining how amounts are presented within items in the profit and loss account and balance sheet, have regard to the substance of the reported transaction or arrangement, in accordance with generally accepted accounting principles or practice.

NOTES
Commencement: 1 October 2009.

PART 2
ACCOUNTING PRINCIPLES AND RULES

[4.479]
10. (1) The amounts to be included in respect of all items shown in an institution's accounts must be determined in accordance with the principles set out in this Part.

(2) But if it appears to the directors that there are special reasons for departing from any of those principles in preparing the accounts in respect of any financial year they may do so, in which case particulars of the departure, the reasons for it and its effect must be given in a note to the accounts.

11. (1) The institution is presumed to be carrying on business as a going concern.

(2) If the accounts are not prepared on a going concern basis, that fact shall be disclosed, together with the basis on which the accounts are prepared and the reason why the institution is not a going concern.

12. Accounting policies must be applied consistently within the same accounts and from one financial year to the next.

13. All income and charges relating to the financial year to which the accounts relate must be taken into account, without regard to the date of receipt or payment.

14. In determining the aggregate amount of any item, the amount of each individual asset or liability that falls to be taken into account must be determined separately.

NOTES

Commencement: 1 October 2009.

PART 3
NOTES TO THE ACCOUNTS

[4.480]
15. Any information required in the case of any institution by the following provisions of this Part of this Schedule must (if not given in the accounts) be given by way of a note to the accounts.

16. The accounting policies adopted by the institution in determining the amounts to be included in respect of items shown in the balance sheet and in determining the profit or loss of the institution must be stated (including such policies with respect to the depreciation and diminution in value of assets).

17. It must be stated whether the accounts have been prepared in accordance with the applied accounting standards and particulars of any material departure from those standards and the reasons for it must be given.

18. The institution must include in the statement of accounting policies—
   (a) the measurement basis (or bases) used in preparing the accounts; and
   (b) any other accounting policies used that are relevant to an understanding of the accounts.

19. (1) The institution must provide information which is relevant to assessing the institution's state of affairs.

(2) As a minimum that information must relate, where applicable, to—
   (a) property, plant and equipment;
   (b) investment property;
   (c) intangible assets;
   (d) financial assets;
   (e) biological assets;
   (f) inventories;
   (g) trade and other receivables (and the amount falling due after more than one year must be shown separately for each item included under receivables);
   (h) trade and other payables (and the amount falling due after more than one year must be shown separately for each item included under payables);
   (i) provisions;
   (j) financial liabilities;
   (k) issued capital and reserves;
   (l) finance costs;
   (m) finance income;
   (n) expenses and interest paid to group undertakings (this must be shown separately from expenses and interest paid to other entities);
   (o) income and interest derived from group undertakings (this must be shown separately from income and interest derived from other sources);
   (p) transactions with related parties;
   (q) dividends;
   (r) items described as other, sundry, miscellaneous or equivalent;
   (s) guarantees;
   (t) contingent liabilities;
   (u) commitments;
   (v) other off balance sheet arrangements;
   (w) financial instruments.

20. In this Schedule the expression "line item" has the same meaning as in international accounting standard 1 on the presentation of financial statements and includes "items", "layout items" and other equivalent terms.

NOTES

Commencement: 1 October 2009.

SCHEDULE 7
CREDIT AND FINANCIAL INSTITUTIONS GROUP ACCOUNTS

Regulation 53

General rules

[4.481]

1. (1) Overseas institutions group accounts must comply so far as practicable with the provisions of Schedule 6 as if the undertakings included in the consolidation ("the group") were a single institution.

(2) In the case of group accounts the minimum information listed in paragraph 19(2) of Schedule 6 must also relate to—

    (a) investments accounted for using the equity method;

    (b) minority interests, presented within equity.

2. The consolidated balance sheet and profit and loss account must incorporate in full the information contained in the individual accounts of the undertakings included in the consolidation, subject to the adjustments authorised or required by the following provisions of this Schedule and to such other adjustments (if any) as may be appropriate in accordance with generally accepted accounting principles or practice.

3. (1) Where assets and liabilities to be included in the group accounts have been valued or otherwise determined by undertakings according to accounting rules differing from those used for the group accounts, the values or amounts must be adjusted so as to accord with the rules used for the group accounts.

(2) If it appears to the directors of the parent institution that there are special reasons for departing from sub-paragraph (1) they may do so, but particulars of any such departure, the reasons for it and its effect must be given in a note to the accounts.

(3) The adjustments referred to in this paragraph need not be made if they are not material.

4. Amounts that in the particular context of any provision of this Schedule are not material may be disregarded for the purposes of that provision.

Elimination of group transactions

5. (1) Debts and claims between undertakings included in the consolidation, and income and expenditure relating to transactions between such undertakings, must be eliminated in preparing the group accounts.

(2) Where profits and losses resulting from transactions between undertakings included in the consolidation are included in the book value of assets, they must be eliminated in preparing the group accounts.

(3) The elimination required by sub-paragraph (2) may be effected in proportion to the group's interest in the shares of the undertakings.

(4) Sub-paragraphs (1) and (2) need not be complied with if the amounts concerned are not material.

6. (1) The following provisions apply where an undertaking becomes a subsidiary undertaking of the parent institution.

(2) That event is referred to in those provisions as an "acquisition", and references to the "undertaking acquired" are to be construed accordingly.

7. (1) An acquisition must be accounted for—

    (a) by the acquisition method of accounting, or

    (b) if the generally accepted accounting principles under which the accounts have been prepared allow it to be accounted for by another method, by that method.

(2) If an acquisition is accounted for in accordance with sub-paragraph (1)(b), the method used must be disclosed in the notes to the accounts.

Minority interests

8. (1) In the balance sheet there must be shown, as a separate item and under an appropriate line item, the amount of capital and reserves attributable to shares in subsidiary undertakings included in the consolidation held by or on behalf of persons other than the parent institution and its subsidiary undertakings.

(2) In the profit and loss account formats there must be shown, as a separate item and under an appropriate line item—

    (a) the amount of any profit or loss on ordinary activities, and

    (b) the amount of any profit or loss on extraordinary activities,

attributable to shares in subsidiary undertakings included in the consolidation held by or on behalf of persons other than the parent institution and its subsidiary undertakings.

Joint ventures
9. (1)   Where an undertaking included in the consolidation manages another undertaking jointly with one or more undertakings not included in the consolidation, that other undertaking ("the joint venture") may, if it is not—
(a)   a body corporate, or
(b)   a subsidiary undertaking of the parent institution,
be dealt with in the group accounts by the method of proportional consolidation.

(2)   The provisions of this Schedule relating to the preparation of consolidated accounts apply, with any necessary modifications, to proportional consolidation under this paragraph.

Associated undertakings
10.   An "associated undertaking" means an undertaking in which an undertaking included in the consolidation has a participating interest and over whose operating and financial policy it exercises a significant influence, and which is not—
(a)   a subsidiary undertaking of the parent institution, or
(b)   a joint venture dealt with in accordance with paragraph 9.

11. (1)   The interest of an undertaking in an associated undertaking, and the amount of profit or loss attributable to such an interest, shall be shown—
(a)   by the equity method of accounting, or
(b)   if the generally accepted accounting principles under which the accounts have been prepared allow it to be accounted for by another method, by that method.

(2)   If an interest is accounted for in accordance with sub-paragraph (1)(b), the method used must be disclosed in the notes to the accounts.

(3)   Where the associated undertaking is itself a parent undertaking, the net assets and profits or losses to be taken into account are those of the parent and its subsidiary undertakings (after making any consolidation adjustments).

NOTES
Commencement: 1 October 2009.

SCHEDULE 8
TRANSITIONAL PROVISIONS AND SAVINGS

Regulation 80

PART 1
INTRODUCTION

Interpretation

[4.482]
1.   In this Schedule—
"the 1985 Act" means the Companies Act 1985;
"the 1986 Order" means the Companies (Northern Ireland) Order 1986;
"the register" means the records kept by the registrar relating to overseas companies;
"the registrar" means the registrar of companies for England and Wales, Scotland or Northern Ireland.

Registration of returns and documents delivered before 1st October 2009
2. (1)   The provisions of Chapter 1 of Part 23 of the 1985 Act or Chapter 1 of Part 23 of the 1986 Order (oversea companies: registration etc) continue to have effect on and after 1st October 2009 so far as necessary for the purposes of the registration of returns or other documents delivered to the registrar before that date.

(2)   References in this Schedule to matters appearing on the register, or to documents held by the registrar, immediately before 1st October 2009 include any such return or other document that is subsequently registered.

NOTES
Commencement: 1 October 2009.

PART 2
INITIAL REGISTRATION OF PARTICULARS

Company with existing registered branch

[4.483]
3. (1)   An overseas company that immediately before 1st October 2009—
(a)   had a branch in the United Kingdom, and
(b)   had complied in respect of that branch with the requirements of paragraph 1(1) to (3) of Schedule 21A to the 1985 Act or paragraph 1(1) to (3) of Schedule 20A to the 1986 Order,

is treated as having complied in respect of that branch with the requirements of Part 2 of these Regulations (initial registration of particulars).

(2)   Paragraphs 4 to 8 supplement sub-paragraph (1) and provide for particular things done under the 1985 Act or 1986 Order to be treated as if done under the corresponding provision of these Regulations.

4. (1)   The following particulars about the company, as they appeared on the register immediately before 1st October 2009, are treated as if delivered and registered under regulation 6(1)—
  (a)   the company's name;
  (b)   the company's legal form;
  (c)   if it is registered in the country of its incorporation, the identity of the register in which it is registered and the number with which it is so registered;
  (d)   the list of its directors and secretaries, together with—
      (i)   with respect to each director, the particulars specified in sub-paragraph (3), and
      (ii)   with respect to each secretary, the particulars specified in sub-paragraph (4);
  (e)   the extent of the powers of the directors to represent the company in dealings with third parties and in legal proceedings, together with a statement as to whether they may act alone or must act jointly and, if jointly, the name of any other person concerned;
  (f)   whether the company is a credit or financial institution.

(2)   In the case of a company that is not incorporated in an EEA State, the following particulars about the company, as they appeared on the register immediately before 1st October 2009, are treated as delivered and registered under regulation 6(2)—
  (a)   the law under which the company is incorporated;
  (b)   in the case of—
      (i)   a company to which Chapter 2 of Part 5 of these Regulations applies (companies required to prepare and disclose accounts under parent law), or
      (ii)   a company to which Chapter 2 of Part 6 of these Regulations applies (institutions required to prepare accounts under parent law),
      the period for which the company is required by its parent law to prepare accounts, together with the period allowed for the preparation and public disclosure (if any) of accounts for such a period;
  (c)   unless disclosed by the company's constitution (see paragraph 6)—
      (i)   the address of its principal place of business in its country of incorporation or, if applicable, its registered office,
      (ii)   its objects, and
      (iii) the amount of its issued share capital.

(3)   The particulars referred to in sub-paragraph (1)(d)(i) (directors) are—
  (a)   in the case of an individual—
      (i)   name,
      (ii)   any former name,
      (iii) service address,
      (iv)   usual residential address,
      (v)   nationality,
      (vi)   business occupation (if any), and
      (vii) date of birth;
  (b)   in the case of a body corporate, or a firm that is a legal person under the law by which it is governed—
      (i)   corporate or firm name, and
      (ii)   registered or principal office.

(4)   The particulars referred to in sub-paragraph (1)(d)(ii)) (secretaries) are—
  (a)   in the case of an individual—
      (i)   name,
      (ii)   any former name, and
      (iii) service address;
  (b)   in the case of a body corporate, or a firm that is a legal person under the law by which it is governed—
      (i)   corporate or firm name, and
      (ii)   registered or principal office.

(5)   For the purposes of sub-paragraph (1)(f) the statement whether the company is an institution to which section 699A of the 1985 Act or Article 648A of the 1986 Order applies is treated as a statement whether the company is a credit or financial institution as defined for the purposes of these Regulations.

(6)   For the purposes of sub-paragraphs (3)(a)(iii) and (4)(a)(iii) the individual's usual residential address as registered immediately before 1st October 2009 is treated as a service address.

5. (1)   The following particulars about the branch, as they appeared on the register immediately before 1st October 2009, are treated as if delivered and registered under regulation 7—
  (a)   the address of the branch,

(b)   the date on which it was opened,
(c)   the business carried on at it,
(d)   the name of the branch (if different from the company's name),
(e)   the name and service address of every person resident in the United Kingdom authorised to accept service of documents on behalf of the company in respect of the branch, or a statement that there is no such person,
(f)   the list of persons authorised to represent the company as a permanent representative of the company in respect of the branch, together with the following particulars of each such person—
    (i)   name,
    (ii)   any former name,
    (iii)   service address, and
    (iv)   usual residential address,
(g)   the extent of the authority of any person falling within paragraph (f), including whether that person is authorised to act alone or jointly, and
(h)   if a person falling within paragraph (f) is not authorised to act alone, the name of any person with whom they are authorised to act.

(2)   For the purposes of sub-paragraph (1)(e) and (f)(iii), the individual's usual residential address as registered immediately before 1st October 2009 is treated as a service address.

6. (1)   The certified copy of the company's constitution delivered under paragraph 5(a) of Schedule 21A to the 1985 Act or paragraph 5(a) of Schedule 20A to the 1986 Order, as held by the registrar immediately before 1st October 2009, is treated as if delivered and registered under regulation 8(1).

(2)   Any certified translation delivered under paragraph 5(b) of Schedule 21A to that Act or paragraph 5(b) of Schedule 20A to that Order, as held by the registrar immediately before 1st October 2009, is treated as if delivered under regulation 8(1) in accordance with regulation 78 of these Regulations.

(3)   The following, as they appeared on the register immediately before 1st October 2009, are treated as if delivered and registered under regulation 8(2)—
(a)   any statement under paragraph 1(3)(b) of Schedule 21A to the 1985 Act or paragraph 1(3)(b) of Schedule 20A to the 1986 Order to the effect that a copy of the company's constitution is included in the material delivered in respect of another branch;
(b)   the registered number of that other branch.

7. (1)   Copies of accounting documents delivered under paragraph 6(1)(a) of Schedule 21A to the 1985 Act or paragraph 6(1)(a) of Schedule 20A to the 1986 Order, if not superseded by the delivery of copies of accounting documents for a subsequent financial period, are treated as if delivered and registered under regulation 9(1).

(2)   A certified translation of any such document delivered under paragraph 6(1)(b) of Schedule 21A to that Act or paragraph 6(1)(b) of Schedule 20A to that Order is treated as if delivered under regulation 9(1) in accordance with regulation 78.

(3)   The following, as they appeared on the register immediately before 1st October 2009, are treated as if delivered and registered under regulation 9(2)—
(a)   any statement under paragraph 1(3)(b) of Schedule 21A to the 1985 Act or paragraph 1(3)(b) of Schedule 20A to the 1986 Order to the effect that copies of accounting documents are included in the material registered in respect of another branch;
(b)   the registered number of that other branch.

8. (1)   If the company is one to which Chapter 2 of Part 5 of these Regulations applies (companies required to prepare and disclose accounts under parent law), the following, as they appeared on the register immediately before 1st October 2009, are treated as if delivered and registered under regulation 10—
(a)   the statement in the return in respect of a branch whether it is intended to file copies of accounting documents in respect of that branch or in respect of another branch;
(b)   if the return states that it is intended to file copies of accounting documents in respect of another branch, the registered number of that branch.

(2)   The statement of intention with respect to the registration of documents under paragraph 2(2) or 10(1) of Schedule 21D to the 1985 Act or paragraph 2(2) or 10(1) of Schedule 20D to the 1986 Order shall be read as a statement of intention with respect to the filing of copies of accounting documents under Chapter 2 of Part 5 of these Regulations.

Company with existing registered place of business
9. (1)   An overseas company that immediately before 1st October 2009—
(a)   had a place of business (other than a branch) in the United Kingdom, and
(b)   had delivered to the registrar in respect of that place of business the documents required by section 691(1) of the 1985 Act of Article 641(1) of the 1986 Order,
is treated as having complied in respect of that place of business with the requirements of Part 2 of these Regulations (initial registration of particulars).

(2) Paragraphs 10 to 12 below supplement sub-paragraph (1) and provide for particular things done under the 1985 Act or 1986 Order to be treated as if done under the corresponding provision of these Regulations.

10. (1) The following particulars about the company, as they appeared on the register immediately before 1st October 2009, are treated as if delivered and registered under regulation 6(1)—

    (a) the company's name;

    (b) the list of the company's directors and secretaries together with—

        (i) with respect to each director, the particulars specified in sub-paragraph (2), and

        (ii) with respect to each secretary, the particulars specified in sub-paragraph (3).

(2) The particulars referred to in sub-paragraph (1)(b)(i) (directors) are—

    (a) in the case of an individual—

        (i) name,

        (ii) any former name,

        (iii) service address,

        (iv) usual residential address,

        (v) nationality,

        (vi) business occupation (if any), and

        (vii) date of birth;

    (b) in the case of a body corporate or a firm that is a legal person under the law by which it is governed—

        (i) its corporate or firm name, and

        (ii) its registered or principal office.

(3) The particulars referred to in sub-paragraph (2)(b)(ii) (secretaries) are—

    (a) in the case of an individual—

        (i) name,

        (ii) any former name, and

        (iii) service address;

    (b) in the case of a body corporate or a firm that is a legal person under the law by which it is governed—

        (i) its corporate or firm name, and

        (ii) its registered or principal office.

(4) For the purposes of sub-paragraph (1)(a) the company's name is treated as registered immediately before 1st October 2009 if it then appeared in the index maintained under section 714 of the 1985 Act or Article 663 of the 1986 Order (the registrar's index of company and corporate names).

(5) For the purposes of sub-paragraphs (2)(a)(iii) and (3)(a)(iii), the individual's usual residential address as registered immediately before 1st October 2009 is treated as a service address.

11. (1) The following particulars about the place of business, as they appeared on the register immediately before 1st October 2009, are treated as registered under regulation 7—

    (a) the date on which the place of business was opened, and

    (b) the name and service address of one or more persons resident in the United Kingdom authorised to accept service of documents on behalf of the company.

(2) For the purposes of sub-paragraph (1)(b) an individual's usual residential address as registered immediately before 1st October 2009 is treated as a service address.

12. (1) The certified copy of the company's constitution delivered under section 691(1)(a) of the 1985 Act or Article 641(1)(a) of the 1986 Order, as held by the registrar immediately before 1st October 2009, is treated as if delivered and registered under regulation 8(1).

(2) Any certified translation delivered under section 691(1)(a) of the 1985 Act or Article 641(1)(a) of the 1986 Order, as held by the registrar immediately before 1st October 2009, is treated as if delivered under regulation 8(1) in accordance with regulation 78.

Duty to deliver transitional return

13. (1) Where paragraph 3 or 9 applies in relation to an establishment, the company must deliver to the registrar not later than 31st March 2010 a transitional return in respect of the establishment.

(2) The return must contain such of the particulars specified in regulation 6 (particulars of the company) as are not treated as registered in respect of the establishment by virtue of paragraph 3 or 9.

Regulation 5(2) (reference to particulars included in those delivered in respect of another UK establishment) applies in relation to the return required by this paragraph as in relation to a return under Part 2 of these Regulations.

(3) The return must contain such of the particulars specified in regulation 7 (particulars of the establishment) as are not treated as registered by virtue of paragraph 5 or 11.

(4) If the company is one to which Part 5 of these Regulations applies (delivery of accounting documents: general), the return must—

(a)   make any statement required by regulation 10 (statement as to future manner of compliance with accounting requirements) that is not treated as made by virtue of paragraph 8, and

(b)   if the company states that it intends to file copies of accounting documents, or accounts, in respect of another UK establishment, give the registered number of that establishment.

(5)   If the company is one to which Chapter 2 of Part 5 of these Regulations applies (companies required to prepare and disclose accounts under parent law), the return must, as regards any document specified in regulation 9(1) (copies of accounting documents) that is not treated as delivered by virtue of paragraph 7, either—

(a)   be accompanied by the document, or

(b)   make the statement specified in regulation 9(3) (statement that document included in those delivered in respect of another UK establishment).

(6)   Sub-paragraph (5) does not apply if the company is required by its parent law to prepare and disclose accounts made up to a date before 1st October 2010.

Company with existing unregistered branch or place of business

14. (1) An overseas company that immediately before 1st October 2009—

(a)   had a branch in the United Kingdom in respect of which it had not complied with paragraph 1(1) to (3) of Schedule 21A to the 1985 Act or paragraph 1(1) to (3) of Schedule 20A to the 1986 Order,

(b)   had a place of business (other than a branch) in the United Kingdom in respect of which it had not complied with section 691 of the 1985 Act or Article 641 of the 1986 Order,

is treated for the purposes of these Regulations as if it had opened that establishment on 1st October 2009.

(2)   This does not affect any liability under section 697(1) or (3) of the 1985 Act or Article 647(1) or (3) of the 1986 Order (penalties for non-compliance) in respect of failure to comply with the provisions mentioned in sub-paragraph (1)(a) or (b) before 1st October 2009.

NOTES

Commencement: 1 October 2009.

PART 3
ALTERATIONS TO REGISTERED PARTICULARS

Alteration to registered particulars

[4.484]

15. (1) The provisions of the 1985 Act or 1986 Order relating to alterations of registered particulars continue to apply in relation to an alteration made before 1st October 2009.

(2)   Those provisions are—

(a)   in the case of a company subject to section 690A of the 1985 Act or Article 640A of the 1986 Order (branch registration under the 11th Company Law Directive), paragraph 7(1)(b) of Schedule 21A to that Act or paragraph 7(1)(b) of Schedule 20A to that Order;

(b)   in the case of a company to which section 691 of the 1985 Act or Article 641 of the 1986 Order (registration of place of business other than branch) applies, section 692(1)(b) and (c) and (2) of that Act or Article 642(1)(b) and (c) and (2) of that Order.

(3)   If a return giving the particulars of the alteration required by the 1985 Act or 1986 Order is duly delivered on or after 1st October 2009, Part 2 of this Schedule (initial registration of particulars) applies as if it had been delivered and registered immediately before that date.

(4)   Regulation 13 (return of alteration in registered particulars) applies to alterations made on or after 1st October 2009.

Alteration in company's constitution

16. (1) The provisions of the 1985 Act or 1986 Order relating to alterations of the company's constitution continue to apply in relation to an alteration made before 1st October 2009.

(2)   Those provisions are—

(a)   in the case of a company subject to section 690A of the 1985 Act or Article 640A of the 1986 Order (branch registration under the 11th Company Law Directive), paragraph 7(1)(a) of Schedule 21A to that Act or paragraph 7(1)(a) of Schedule 20A to that Order;

(b)   in the case of a company to which section 691 of the 1985 Act or Article 641 of the 1986 Order (registration of place of business other than branch) applies, section 692(1)(a) of that Act or Article 642(1)(a) of that Order.

(3)   If the following are duly delivered on or after 1st October 2009—

(a)   a return giving the particulars of the alteration required by the 1985 Act or 1986 Order,

(b)   a certified copy of the company's constitution as altered, and

(c)   any certified translation required by the 1985 Act or 1986 Order,

Part 2 of this Schedule (initial registration of particulars) applies as if they had been delivered and registered immediately before that date.

(4) Regulation 14 (return of alteration in company's constitution) applies to alterations made on or after 1st October 2009.

Alteration as regards filing of certified copy of constitution

17. (1) The provisions of paragraph 8 of Schedule 21A to the 1985 Act or paragraph 8 of Schedule 20A to the 1986 Order (statement that certified copy of company's constitution included in the material registered in respect of another UK branch ceasing to be true) continue to apply where that statement ceased to be true before 1st October 2009.

(2) If there is duly delivered on or after 1st October 2009—

    (a) a certified copy of the company's constitution and any certified translation required by the 1985 Act or 1986 Order, or

    (b) a return stating that those documents are included in the material registered in respect of another UK branch (giving the registered number of that other branch),

Part 2 of this Schedule (initial registration of particulars) applies as if they had been delivered and registered immediately before that date.

(3) Regulation 15 (return of alteration as regards filing of certified copy of constitution) applies where that statement ceases to be true on or after 1st October 2009.

NOTES

Commencement: 1 October 2009.

PART 4
RESIDENTIAL ADDRESSES: PROTECTION FROM DISCLOSURE

Existing registered residential address treated as service address

[4.485]

18. (1) This paragraph applies where an address that immediately before 1st October 2009 appeared on the register as the usual residential address of a director, secretary or permanent representative of an overseas company is to be treated, on and after that date, as a service address.

(2) Any return of an alteration in any such residential address of a director, secretary or permanent representative of an overseas company occurring before 1st October 2009 that is received by the registrar on or after that date is treated as being or, as the case may be, including notification of a change of service address.

(3) The registrar may make such entries in the register as appear to be appropriate having regard to any provision to the effect mentioned in sub-paragraph (1) and to sub-paragraph (2).

(4) Where a residential address appears in the register as a service address by virtue of this paragraph, that address is not protected information for the purposes of Part 4 of these Regulations.

Residential addresses: protection from disclosure

19. (1) Regulation 21 (duty of registrar to omit protected information from material available for inspection) does not apply—

    (a) to material delivered to the registrar before 1st October 2009, or

    (b) to material delivered to the registrar on or after 1st October 2009 by virtue of paragraph 18 (return of alteration occurring before that date).

(2) In regulation 21(2)(b) (exclusion of material registered before commencement) the reference to things registered before 1st October 2009 is treated as including anything registered as a result of a return in accordance with paragraph 18(2) (return on or after 1st October 2009 of alteration occurring before that date).

(3) Sub-paragraphs (1) and (2) have effect subject to paragraph 21 below (which provides for the continued protection of information formerly protected by a confidentiality order).

20. In determining under regulation 27 whether to put a director or permanent representative's usual residential address on the public record, the registrar may take into account only—

    (a) communications sent by the registrar on or after 1st October 2009, and

    (b) evidence as to the effectiveness of service coming to the registrar's attention on or after that date.

Continuation of protection afforded by confidentiality orders under the 1985 Act

21. (1) A director or permanent representative of an overseas company in relation to whom a confidentiality order under section 723B of the 1985 Act was in force immediately before 1st October 2009 is treated on and after that date as if—

    (a) they had made an application under regulation 25 (application to prevent disclosure of protected information by registrar to credit reference agency), and

    (b) that application had been determined by the registrar in their favour.

(2)   The provisions of Schedule 3 to these Regulations relating to decisions of the registrar in favour of an applicant (in particular, as to the duration and revocation of such a decision) apply accordingly.

(3)   As those provisions apply in accordance with this paragraph any reference to an offence under section 1112 of the Companies Act 2006 (general false statement offence) shall be read as a reference to an offence under regulations under section 723E(1)(a) of the 1985 Act in relation to the application for the confidentiality order.

Effect of pending application for confidentiality order

22.   (1)   Section 723B(3) to (8) of the 1985 Act (application for confidentiality order) continue to apply in relation to an application for a confidentiality order made before 1st October 2009.

(2)   Paragraph 21 (continuation of protection afforded by confidentiality orders) applies to an individual in respect of whom such an application has been made, and has not been determined or withdrawn, as to an individual in relation to whom a confidentiality order was in force immediately before that date.

(3)   If the application is dismissed or withdrawn, that paragraph ceases to apply.

(4)   If the application is successful that paragraph continues to apply as in the case of an individual in relation to whom a confidentiality order was in force immediately before 1st October 2009.

NOTES

Commencement: 1 October 2009.

PART 5
DELIVERY OF ACCOUNTING DOCUMENTS: GENERAL

Companies required to prepare and disclose accounts under parent law

[4.486]

23.   (1)   This paragraph applies to companies to which Chapter 2 of Part 5 of these Regulations applies (companies required to prepare and disclose accounts under parent law).

(2)   The provisions of that Chapter apply in relation to accounting documents first disclosed in accordance with the company's parent law on or after 1st October 2009.

(3)   In the case of a company to which section 699AA of the 1985 Act or Article 648AA of the 1986 Order applied (company to which 11th Company Law Directive applies), the provisions of Part 1 of Schedule 21D to that Act or Part 1 of Schedule 20D to that Order continue to apply in relation to accounting documents first disclosed in accordance with the company's parent law before 1st October 2009.

(4)   In the case of a company to which section 700 of the 1985 Act or Article 649 of the 1986 Order applied (company with place of business but not branch in UK), the relevant provisions of that Act or Order continue to apply in relation to the period between—

   (a)   the end of the last financial year of the company beginning before 1st October 2009, and
   (b)   the beginning of the first financial period of the company in respect of which accounting documents are first disclosed in accordance with the company's parent law on or after that date,

and that period shall be treated as a financial year of the company (if it would otherwise not be) for the purposes of those provisions.

(5)   For the purposes of sub-paragraph (4)—

   (a)   the relevant provisions of the 1985 Act are sections 700 to 703 and the provisions applied by those sections;
   (b)   the relevant provisions of the 1986 Order are Articles 649 to 652 and the provisions applied by those Articles.

Companies not required to prepare and disclose accounts under parent law

24.   (1)   This paragraph applies to companies to which Chapter 3 of Part 5 of these Regulations applies (companies not required to prepare and disclose accounts under parent law).

(2)   The provisions of that Chapter apply in relation to accounting documents for financial years of the company beginning on or after 1st October 2009.

(3)   The provisions of—

   (a)   Part 2 of Schedule 21D to the 1985 Act or Part 2 of Schedule 20D to the 1986 Order (companies to which the 11th Company Law Directive applies), or
   (b)   sections 700 to 702 of that Act or Articles 649 to 652 of that Order (companies with place of business but not branch in the UK),

continue to apply in relation to accounting documents for financial years beginning before that date.

NOTES

Commencement: 1 October 2009.

PART 6
DELIVERY OF ACCOUNTING DOCUMENTS: CREDIT OR
FINANCIAL INSTITUTIONS

Institutions required to prepare accounts under parent law

[4.487]
25. (1) This paragraph applies to credit or financial institutions to which Chapter 2 of Part 6 of these Regulations applies (institutions required to prepare accounts under parent law).

(2) An institution that immediately before 1st October 2009—
  (a) had a branch in the United Kingdom, and
  (b) had complied with the requirements of paragraph 2 of Schedule 21C to the 1985 Act or paragraph 2 of Schedule 20C to the 1986 Order,
is treated as having complied with the requirements of regulation 45 (initial filing of copies of accounting documents).

(3) Regulation 46 (filing of copies of subsequent accounting documents) applies in relation to accounting documents first disclosed in accordance with the company's parent law on or after 1st October 2009.

(4) Paragraph 3 of Schedule 21C to the 1985 Act or paragraph 3 of Schedule 20D to the 1986 Order continues to apply in relation to accounting documents first disclosed in accordance with the company's parent law before 1st October 2009.

Institutions not require to prepare accounts under parent law
26. (1) This paragraph applies to credit or financial institutions to which Chapter 3 of Part 6 of these Regulations applies (institutions not required to prepare accounts under parent law).

(2) The provisions of that Chapter apply in relation to accounting documents for financial years of the institution beginning on or after 1st October 2009.

(3) The provisions of Part 2 of Schedule 21C to the 1985 Act or Part 2 of Schedule 20C to the 1986 Order continue to apply in relation to accounting documents for financial years beginning before that date.

NOTES
Commencement: 1 October 2009.

PART 7
RETURNS IN CASE OF WINDING UP ETC

Return in case of winding up

[4.488]
27. (1) Regulation 69 (return in case of winding up) applies in relation to a winding up beginning on or after 1st October 2009.

(2) Section 703P(1) of the 1985 Act or Article 652P(1) of the 1986 Order (particulars to be delivered: winding up) continues to apply in relation to a winding up beginning before that date.

Returns to be made by liquidator
28. (1) Regulation 70(1) (return of appointment of liquidator) applies in relation to an appointment made on or after 1st October 2009.

(2) Section 703P(3) of the 1985 Act or Article 652P(3) of the 1986 Order continues to apply in relation to an appointment made before that date.

(3) Regulation 70(3) (return by liquidator where winding up terminates or company ceases to be registered) applies where the event concerned occurs on or after 1st October 2009.

(4) Section 703P(5) of the 1985 Act or Article 652P(5) of the 1986 Order continues to apply where the event occurred before that date.

Return in case of insolvency proceedings etc (other than winding up)
29. (1) Regulation 71 (return of insolvency proceedings etc) applies where the proceedings in question begin on or after 1st October 2009.

(2) Section 703Q of the 1985 Act or Article 652Q of the 1986 Order continues to apply where the proceedings began before that date.

Notice of appointment of judicial factor
30. Regulation 73 (notice of appointment of judicial factor) applies in relation to appointments made on or after 1st October 2009.

NOTES
Commencement: 1 October 2009.

PART 8
SUPPLEMENTARY PROVISIONS

Saving for provisions as to form or manner in which documents to be delivered

[4.489]
31. (1)   Any saving in this Schedule for the effect of a provision of the 1985 Act or 1986 Order requiring the use of a prescribed form extends to the form and the power under which it is prescribed.

(2)   Any saving in this Schedule for the effect of a provision of the 1985 Act or 1986 Order requiring a document to be delivered to the registrar extends to section 707B of the 1985 Act or Article 656B of the 1986 Order (delivery to the registrar using electronic communications) so far as relating to the provision in question and the delivery of documents under it.

NOTES
Commencement: 1 October 2009.

COMPANIES ACT 2006 (PART 35) (CONSEQUENTIAL AMENDMENTS, TRANSITIONAL PROVISIONS AND SAVINGS) ORDER 2009 (NOTE)

(SI 2009/1802)

[4.490]

NOTES
This Order was made on 8 July 2009 under the powers conferred by the European Communities Act 1972, s 2(2) and the Companies Act 2006, ss 1290, 1292(4) and 1294(6).

Article 1 of the Order provides for citation and commencement; art 2 introduces the amendments that follow.

Articles 4, 6–11 and 13–16 make consequential amendments to Part 35 of the 2006 Act at **[1.1059A]** et seq. The effect of these is to extend certain provisions of Part 35 to documents or, as the case may be, functions of the registrar relating to bodies other than companies or overseas companies. Article 3 adds to Part 35 a new section indicating how the provisions of Part 35, as amended by the Order, apply.

Article 5 makes consequential amendments to s 1067 in Part 35 of the 2006 Act. These relate to overseas companies and are made in consequence of provision made by the Overseas Companies Regulations 2009 (SI 2009/1801). References to "branches" of overseas companies in s 1067 are replaced by references to the "UK establishments" of overseas companies. Article 17 makes incidental amendments to Schedule 8 to the 2006 Act (Index of defined terms).

Article 12 amends s 1087 to expand the list in that section of material which the registrar must not make available for public inspection.

Article 18 and the Schedule replace a number of the transitional provisions and savings relating to Part 35 of the 2006 Act which are contained in Schedule 2 to the Companies Act 2006 (Commencement No 8, Transitional Provisions and Savings) Order 2008, SI 2008/2860 (at **[2.91]**).

REGISTRAR OF COMPANIES AND APPLICATIONS FOR STRIKING OFF REGULATIONS 2009

(SI 2009/1803)

NOTES
Made: 8 July 2009.

Authority: Companies Act 2006, ss 1003(2)(b), 1081(2), 1095(1), (2), 1104(2)(a), 1105(2)(d), 1108(2), 1167, 1292(1), (3), (4).

Commencement: 1 October 2009.

These Regulations are reproduced as amended by: the European Economic Interest Grouping (Amendment) Regulations 2009, SI 2009/2399; the European Public Limited-Liability Company (Amendment) Regulations 2009, SI 2009/2400.

ARRANGEMENT OF REGULATIONS

Schedule—Permitted Characters and Symbols. . . . .[4.499]

[4.491]
1 Citation, commencement and interpretation

(1)   These Regulations may be cited as the Registrar of Companies and Applications for Striking Off Regulations 2009 and come into force on 1st October 2009.

(2)   In these Regulations—
- (a)   "relevant company form" has the meaning given in regulation 4(3);
- (b)   "relevant material" has the meaning given in regulation 4(2);
- (c)   "relevant overseas company form" has the meaning given in regulation 4(4); and
- (d)   "valid objection" has the meaning given in regulation 4(8).

NOTES
  Commencement: 1 October 2009.

[4.492]
2 Voluntary striking off: contents of an application

(1)   An application under section 1003 of the Companies Act 2006 (application for voluntary striking off) must contain a declaration that neither section 1004 nor section 1005 of that Act prevents the application from being made.

(2)   The declaration must be made by the directors who are making the application on behalf of the company.

NOTES
  Commencement: 1 October 2009.

[4.493]
3 Annotation of the register

Where it appears to the registrar that material on the register is misleading or confusing, the registrar may place a note in the register containing such information as appears to the registrar to be necessary to remedy, as far as possible, the misleading or confusing nature of the material.

NOTES
  Commencement: 1 October 2009.

[4.494]
4 Rectification of the register on application

(1)   On application under this regulation (but not if there is a valid objection to the application) the registrar must remove from the register any relevant material that—
- (a)   derives from anything invalid or ineffective or that was done without the authority of the company or overseas company to which the material relates, or
- (b)   is factually inaccurate, or is derived from something that is factually inaccurate or forged.

(2)   "Relevant material" means material on the register that was included in, or is derived from material that was included in, a relevant company form or a relevant overseas company form delivered to the registrar by any person.

(3)   A "relevant company form" is—
- (a)   a standard form required for giving notice under section 87 (change of address of registered office), section 167 (changes relating to directors) or section 276 (changes relating to secretaries) of the Companies Act 2006; or
- (b)   so much of a standard form required for delivering an application under section 9 of that Act (application for registration of a company) as is required for the statement of a company's proposed officers referred to in section 9(4)(c).

(4)   A "relevant overseas company form" is—
- (a)   so much of a standard form required for delivering a return under regulation 4 of the Overseas Companies Regulations 2009 as is required for—
  - (i)   the list referred to in regulation 6(1)(d) of those Regulations (list of directors and secretary of an overseas company);
  - (ii)   the names and service addresses referred to in regulation 7(1)(e) of those Regulations (names and service addresses of persons authorised to accept service of documents on behalf of an overseas company in respect of a UK establishment); or
  - (iii)   the list referred to in regulation 7(1)(f) of those Regulations (list of permanent representatives of an overseas company in respect of a UK establishment); or
- (b)   so much of a standard form required for delivering a return under regulation 13 of those Regulations as is required for details of the alteration of particulars delivered under—
  - (i)   regulation 6(1)(d) of those Regulations (directors and secretary);
  - (ii)   regulation 7(1)(a) of those Regulations (address of UK establishment);

      (iii)   regulation 7(1)(e) of those Regulations (names and service addresses of persons authorised to accept service); or

      (iv)   regulation 7(1)(f) of those Regulations (list of permanent representatives).

(5)   An application to the registrar for the removal from the register (on the grounds in paragraph (1)) of material that was included in a standard form required for giving notice under section 87 of the Companies Act 2006 (change of address of registered office), or of material that is derived from material that was included in such a form, may be made by (and only by) the company to which the material relates.

(6)   An application to the registrar for the removal from the register (on the grounds in paragraph (1)) of material that was included in, or is derived from material that was included in, so much of a standard form required for delivering a return under regulation 13 of the Overseas Companies Regulations 2009 as is required for details of the alteration of particulars delivered under regulation 7(1)(a) of those Regulations (address of UK establishment) may be made by (and only by) the overseas company to which the material relates.

(7)   An application to the registrar for the removal from the register on the grounds in paragraph (1) of relevant material other than material referred to in paragraph (5) or (6) may be made by (and only by)—

    (a)   the person by whom the relevant company form or relevant overseas company form (as the case may be) was delivered to the registrar;

    (b)   the company or overseas company to which the material relates; or

    (c)   any other person to whom the material relates.

(8)   A "valid objection" is—

    (a)   an objection made in accordance with regulation 5(10) and (11) by a person to whom notice of the application was given under regulation 5(2), (3), (4) or (5), or

    (b)   an objection made in accordance with regulation 5(10) by any other person which is not an objection that the registrar is prevented from taking into account under regulation 5(12).

(9)   In this regulation "required" means required by rules made by the registrar under section 1117 of the Companies Act 2006.

NOTES

Commencement: 1 October 2009.

[4.495]

5   Applications to rectify: further requirements, objections and notices to be issued by the registrar

(1)   An application to the registrar under regulation 4 must, in addition to satisfying the requirements of section 1095(3) of the Companies Act 2006—

    (a)   state the applicant's name and address;

    (b)   where the application is an application referred to in regulation 4(5) or (6), confirm that the applicant is the company or (as the case may be) the overseas company to which the relevant material which is the subject of the application relates;

    (c)   in any other case, state whether the applicant is a person mentioned in regulation 4(7)(a), a person mentioned in regulation 4(7)(b) or a person mentioned in regulation 4(7)(c); and

    (d)   state whether the relevant material which is the subject of the application—

      (i)   derives from anything invalid or ineffective;

      (ii)   derives from anything that was done without the authority of the company or overseas company to which the material relates;

      (iii)   is factually inaccurate or is derived from something that is factually inaccurate; or

      (iv)   is derived from something that is forged.

(2)   Where the application is an application referred to in regulation 4(5), the registrar must give notice of the application to—

    (a)   the person who delivered the standard form mentioned in that regulation to the registrar (but only if the registrar knows the identity and name and address of that person);

    (b)   every person who (to the registrar's knowledge) was a director or secretary of the company at the time when the application was delivered to the registrar; and

    (c)   the company at the address of its registered office.

(3)   Where the material which is the subject of the application relates to a company (rather than an overseas company), but the application is not an application referred to in regulation 4(5), the registrar must give notice of the application to—

    (a)   every person mentioned in regulation 4(7) whose identity and name and address the registrar knows (other than the applicant); and

    (b)   every person who (to the registrar's knowledge) was a director or secretary of the company at the time when the application was delivered to the registrar.

(4)   Where the application is an application referred to in regulation 4(6), the registrar must give notice of the application to—

    (a)   the person who delivered the standard form mentioned in that regulation to the registrar (but only if the registrar knows the identity and name and address of that person);

(b)   every person registered under regulation 4 or 13 of the Overseas Companies Regulations 2009, at the time when the application was delivered to the registrar, as a director or secretary of the overseas company;

(c)   the persons mentioned in paragraph (6); and

(d)   the overseas company.

(5)   Where the material which is the subject of the application relates to an overseas company, but the application is not an application referred to in regulation 4(6), the registrar must give notice of the application to—

(a)   every person mentioned in regulation 4(7) whose identity and name and address the registrar knows (other than the applicant);

(b)   every person registered under regulation 4 or 13 of the Overseas Companies Regulations 2009, at the time when the application was delivered to the registrar, as a director or secretary of the overseas company; and

(c)   the persons mentioned in paragraph (6).

(6)   The persons are—

(a)   every person registered under regulation 4 or 13 of the Overseas Companies Regulations 2009, at the time when the application was delivered to the registrar, as a person authorised to accept service of documents on behalf of the overseas company in respect of a UK establishment of the company; and

(b)   every person registered under regulation 4 or 13 of those Regulations, at the time when the application was delivered to the registrar, as a permanent representative of the overseas company in respect of a UK establishment of the company.

(7)   Where the material which is the subject of the application is material that was included in, or is derived from material that was included in, a relevant overseas company form described in regulation 4(4)(a)(ii) or (iii) or regulation 4(4)(b)(ii), (iii) or (iv), the notice which the registrar is required by paragraph (4) or (5) to give to the overseas company must be given to the company at the address which was, at the time when the application was delivered to the registrar, registered under regulation 4 or 13 of the Overseas Companies Regulations 2009 as the address of the company's UK establishment to which the material relates (and notice need not be given to the company at any other address).

(8)   The notice given by the registrar under paragraph (2), (3), (4) or (5) must—

(a)   where the material which is the subject of the application relates to a company (rather than an overseas company), state the name and registered number of the company to which the material relates;

(b)   where the material which is the subject of the application relates to an overseas company, state the overseas company's name registered under regulation 4 or 13 of the Overseas Companies Regulations 2009 or section 1048 of the Companies Act 2006 and its registered number allocated under section 1066 of that Act;

(c)   where the material which is the subject of the application is material that was included in, or is derived from material that was included in, a relevant overseas company form described in regulation 4(4)(a)(ii) or (iii) or regulation 4(4)(b)(ii), (iii) or (iv), state the registered number allocated under section 1067 of the Companies Act 2006 to the UK establishment to which the material relates;

(d)   specify what is to be removed from the register and indicate where on the register it is;

(e)   state the information provided to the registrar under paragraph (1)(d);

(f)   state the date on which the notice is issued;

(g)   give particulars of the recipient's right to object to the application and the requirements applying to that right under paragraphs (10) and (11);

(h)   explain the effect of paragraph (13); and

(i)   explain the effect of regulation 4(1) and of section 1095(4) of the Companies Act 2006.

(9)   An objection to an application under regulation 4 may be made to the registrar by any person.

(10)   An objection must be made by giving notice in writing to the registrar, and the notice must state the name and address of the person making the objection and identify the application to which the objection relates.

(11)   A person to whom notice of an application was given under paragraph (2), (3), (4) or (5) and who wishes to object to the application must do so before the end of the period of 28 days beginning with the date on which that notice was issued (as stated in the notice).

(12)   The registrar must not take account of an objection made by any other person after the end of the period of 28 days beginning with the date on which the notices under paragraph (2), (3), (4) or (5) were issued.

(13)   If a valid objection is made to the application, the registrar must reject the application.

(14)   When a valid objection is made, the registrar must also—

(a)   send an acknowledgment of receipt to the person who made the objection;

(b)   notify the applicant of the fact that an objection has been made; and

(c)   notify every other person to whom the registrar gave notice under paragraph (2), (3), (4) or (5) (but not the person who made the objection or any other person who has made an objection).

(15)   If no valid objection is made, the registrar must notify the applicant of that fact.

(16)   In this regulation "UK establishment" has the meaning given in section 1067(6) of the Companies Act 2006.

NOTES
Commencement: 1 October 2009.

[4.496]
6   Documents relating to Welsh companies: exceptions to the requirement for a certified translation, and revocation of previous exceptions

(1)   The documents in paragraph (2) are excepted from the requirement in section 1104(2) of the Companies Act 2006 that a document relating to a Welsh company must, on delivery to the registrar in Welsh, be accompanied by a certified translation into English.

(2)   The documents are—
(a)   a non-traded company's memorandum of association;
(b)   a non-traded company's articles;
(c)   a community interest company report prepared for a non-traded company under section 34 of the Companies (Audit, Investigations and Community Enterprise) Act 2004;
(d)   a resolution or agreement which was agreed to by members of a non-traded company and to which Chapter 3 of Part 3 of the Companies Act 2006 applies, except for a resolution or agreement listed in paragraph (3);
(e)   annual accounts and reports of a non-traded company required to be delivered to the registrar under Part 15 of the Companies Act 2006;
(f)   a declaration referred to in regulation 11(1)(b) or regulation 12(1)(b) or (c) of the Community Interest Company Regulations 2005 which relates to a non-traded company;
(g)   revised accounts and any revised report of a non-traded company, and any auditor's report on such revised accounts and reports, required to be delivered to the registrar by the Companies (Revision of Defective Accounts and Reports) Regulations 2008;
(h)   a document required to be appended to the group accounts of a non-traded company by paragraph 30(2) of Schedule 6 to the Large and Medium-sized Companies and Groups (Accounts and Reports) Regulations 2008 (banking groups: information as to undertaking in which shares held as a result of financial assistance operation).

(3)   The following is the list of resolutions and agreements referred to in paragraph (2)(d)—
(a)   a special resolution that—
(i)   a private company should be re-registered as a public company;
(ii)   a public company should be re-registered as a private limited company;
(iii)   a private limited company should be re-registered as an unlimited company; or
(iv)   an unlimited company should be re-registered as a limited company;
(b)   a special resolution agreeing to the change of a company's name;
(c)   a special resolution required by section 37 of the Companies (Audit, Investigations and Community Enterprise) Act 2004 (requirements for an existing company to become a community interest company);
(d)   a resolution or agreement as altered by an enactment other than an enactment amending the general law, required to be delivered to the registrar under section 34 of the Companies Act 2006;
(e)   a resolution or agreement as altered by an order of a court or other authority, required to be delivered to the registrar under section 35 or 999 of that Act;
(f)   a special resolution under section 88(2) of that Act requiring the register to be amended so that it states that a company's registered office is to be situated in Wales;
(g)   a special resolution under section 626 of that Act (reduction of capital in connection with redenomination);
(h)   a special resolution under section 641(1)(a) of that Act (resolution for reducing the share capital of a private limited company supported by solvency statement);
(i)   a resolution under section 664(1) of that Act that a public company should be re-registered as a private company to comply with section 662.

(4)   For the purposes of paragraph (2)(g), "revised accounts" and "revised report" have the meanings given in regulation 2 of the Companies (Revision of Defective Accounts and Reports) Regulations 2008.

(5)   *(Revokes the Companies (Welsh Language Forms and Documents) Regulations 1994, SI 1994/117, reg 4.)*

NOTES
Commencement: 1 October 2009.

[4.497]
7 Documents that may be delivered under the Companies Acts in a language other than English

(1)   The documents listed in paragraph (2) are specified for the purposes of section 1105(2)(d) of the Companies Act 2006 as documents which may be drawn up and delivered to the registrar under the Companies Acts in a language other than English but which must, when delivered to the registrar, be accompanied by a certified translation into English.

(2)   The documents are—
   (a)   a memorandum of association;
   (b)   a company's articles;
   (c)   a valuation report required to be delivered to the registrar under section 94(2)(d) of the Companies Act 2006;
   (d)   any order made by a competent court in the United Kingdom or elsewhere.

NOTES
Commencement: 1 October 2009.

[4.498]
8 Permitted characters and symbols for names and addresses in documents delivered to the registrar

(1)   The characters and symbols specified in paragraph (3) are permitted for the purposes of section 1108(1) of the Companies Act 2006 (and names and addresses in documents delivered to the registrar must therefore contain only those characters and symbols).

(2)   But the requirement in section 1108(1) does not apply to the following documents—
   (a)   a memorandum of association;
   (b)   a company's articles;
   (c)   an order made by a competent court in the United Kingdom or elsewhere;
   (d)   an agreement required to be forwarded to the registrar under Chapter 3 of Part 3 of the Companies Act 2006 (agreements affecting a company's constitution);
   (e)   a valuation report required to be delivered to the registrar under section 94(2)(d) of that Act;
   (f)   a document required to be delivered to the registrar under section 400(2)(e) or section 401(2)(f) of that Act (company included in accounts of larger group: required to deliver copy of group accounts);
   (g)   an instrument or copy instrument required to be delivered to the registrar under Part 25 of that Act (company charges);
   (h)   a certified copy of the constitution of an overseas company required to be delivered to the registrar under regulation 8, 14 or 15 of the Overseas Companies Regulations 2009;
   (i)   a copy of accounting documents of an overseas company required to be delivered to the registrar under regulation 9, 32, 45 or 46 of those Regulations;
   (j)   a copy of the annual accounts of an overseas company, or of a credit or financial institution to which Chapter 2 of Part 6 of the Overseas Companies Regulations 2009 applies, required to be delivered to the registrar under section 441 of the Companies Act 2006;
   [(k)   a contract for the formation of a European Economic Interest Grouping;
   (l)   an amendment to such a contract;]
   [(m)   documents specified in respect of any of the Forms mentioned in regulations 5 to 11 of the European Public Limited-Liability Company Regulations 2004 (provisions relating to registration etc);
   (n)   copies of transfer proposals required to be delivered under regulation 68(1)(a) of those Regulations (publication of terms of transfer);
   (o)   copies of draft terms required to be delivered under regulation 68(2)(a) or (3)(a) of those Regulations (publication of terms for formation of holding SE or conversion of company into SE);
   (p)   copies of amendments to statutes required to be delivered under regulation 82(1)(a) of those Regulations (notification of amendments to statutes);
   (q)   documents required to be delivered with Form SE CV01 under regulation 85 of those Regulations (registration of a public company by conversion of SE);
   (r)   copies of draft terms required to be delivered under regulation 86 of those Regulations (publication of draft terms of conversion).]

(3)   The characters and symbols specified in this paragraph are—
   (a)   those in the Schedule;
   (b)   full stops, commas, colons, semi-colons and hyphens;
   (c)   the numerals 0, 1, 2, 3, 4, 5, 6, 7, 8 and 9.

(4)   In this regulation the expressions "accounting documents", "certified copy" and "constitution" have the meanings given in the Overseas Companies Regulations 2009.

NOTES
Commencement: 1 October 2009.

Para (2): sub-paras (k), (l) added by the European Economic Interest Grouping (Amendment) Regulations 2009, SI 2009/2399, reg 24, as from 1 October 2009; sub-paras (m)–(r) added by the European Public Limited-Liability Company (Amendment) Regulations 2009, SI 2009/2400, reg 43, as from 1 October 2009.

SCHEDULE
PERMITTED CHARACTERS AND SYMBOLS

Regulation 8(3)

[4.499]

Characters and symbols referred to in regulation 8(3)					
A	a	B	b	C	
c	D	d	E	e	
F	f	G	g	H	
h	I	i	J	j	
K	k	L	l	M	
m	N	n	O	o	
P	p	Q	q	R	
r	S	s	T	t	
U	u	V	v	W	
w	X	x	Y	y	
Z	z	&	@	£	
$	€	¥	*	=	
#	%	+	'	'	
'	(	)	[	]	
{	}	<	>	!	
«	»	?	"	"	
"	\	/			

NOTES

Commencement: 1 October 2009.

OVERSEAS COMPANIES (EXECUTION OF DOCUMENTS AND REGISTRATION OF CHARGES) REGULATIONS 2009

(SI 2009/1917)

NOTES

Made: 16 July 2009.

Authority: Companies Act 2006, ss 1045, 1052, 1105, 1292(1).

Commencement: 1 October 2009.

Amendment: as of 1 July 2011 these Regulations had not been amended.

ARRANGEMENT OF REGULATIONS

PART 1
INTRODUCTION

PART 2
EXECUTION OF DOCUMENTS ETC

PART 3
REGISTRATION OF CHARGES

Introduction

PART 1
INTRODUCTION

[4.500]
1 Citation and commencement

(1) These Regulations may be cited as the Overseas Companies (Execution of Documents and Registration of Charges) Regulations 2009.

(2) These Regulations come into force on 1st October 2009.

NOTES
Commencement: 1 October 2009.

[4.501]
2 Interpretation

In these Regulations—
    "certified copy" means a copy certified as a correct copy;
    "establishment" means—
        (a)   a branch within the meaning of the Eleventh Company Law Directive (89/666/EEC),
           or
        (b)   a place of business that is not such a branch, and
    "UK establishment" means an establishment in the United Kingdom.

NOTES
Commencement: 1 October 2009.

PART 2
EXECUTION OF DOCUMENTS ETC

[4.502]
3 Application of Part

This Part applies to all overseas companies.

NOTES
Commencement: 1 October 2009.

[4.503]

4 Formalities of doing business under the law of England and Wales and Northern Ireland

Sections 43, 44 and 46 of the Companies Act 2006 apply to overseas companies, modified so that they read as follows—

"43 Company contracts

(1)   Under the law of England and Wales or Northern Ireland a contract may be made—

  (a)   by an overseas company, by writing under its common seal or in any manner permitted by the laws of the territory in which the company is incorporated for the execution of documents by such a company, and

  (b)   on behalf of an overseas company, by any person who, in accordance with the laws of the territory in which the company is incorporated, is acting under the authority (express or implied) of that company.

(2)   Any formalities required by law in the case of a contract made by an individual also apply, unless a contrary intention appears, to a contract made by or on behalf of an overseas company.

44 Execution of documents

(1)   Under the law of England and Wales or Northern Ireland a document is executed by an overseas company—

  (a)   by the affixing of its common seal, or

  (b)   if it is executed in any manner permitted by the laws of the territory in which the company is incorporated for the execution of documents by such a company.

(2)   A document which—

  (a)   is signed by a person who, in accordance with the laws of the territory in which an overseas company is incorporated, is acting under the authority (express or implied) of the company, and

  (b)   is expressed (in whatever form of words) to be executed by the company,

has the same effect in relation to that company as it would have in relation to a company incorporated in England and Wales or Northern Ireland if executed under the common seal of a company so incorporated.

(3)   In favour of a purchaser a document is deemed to have been duly executed by an overseas company if it purports to be signed in accordance with subsection (2).

A "purchaser" means a purchaser in good faith for valuable consideration and includes a lessee, mortgagee or other person who for valuable consideration acquires an interest in property.

(4)   Where a document is to be signed by a person on behalf of more than one overseas company, it is not duly signed by that person for the purposes of this section unless he signs it separately in each capacity.

(5)   References in this section to a document being (or purporting to be) signed by a person who, in accordance with the laws of the territory in which an overseas company is incorporated, is acting under the authority (express or implied) of the company are to be read, in a case where that person is a firm, as references to its being (or purporting to be) signed by an individual authorised by the firm to sign on its behalf.

(6)   This section applies to a document that is (or purports to be) executed by an overseas company in the name of or on behalf of another person whether or not that person is also an overseas company.

46 Execution of deeds

(1)   A document is validly executed by an overseas company as a deed for the purposes of section 1(2)(b) of the Law of Property (Miscellaneous Provisions) Act 1989 (c 34) and for the purposes of the law of Northern Ireland if, and only if—

  (a)   it is duly executed by the company, and

  (b)   it is delivered as a deed.

(2)   For the purposes of subsection (1)(b) a document is presumed to be delivered upon its being executed, unless a contrary intention is proved.".

NOTES

Commencement: 1 October 2009.

[4.504]

5 Formalities of doing business under the law of Scotland

Section 48 of the Companies Act 2006 applies to overseas companies, modified so that it reads as follows—

"48 Execution of documents by overseas companies

(1)   The following provision forms part of the law of Scotland only.

(2)   For the purposes of any enactment—

  (a)   providing for a document to be executed by a company by affixing its common seal, or

(b)   referring (in whatever terms) to a document so executed,

a document signed or subscribed by or on behalf of an overseas company in accordance with the provisions of the Requirements of Writing (Scotland) Act 1995 (c 7) has effect as if so executed.".

NOTES
Commencement: 1 October 2009.

[4.505]
6   Other matters

Section 51 of the Companies Act 2006 applies to overseas companies, modified so that it reads as follows—

> ### "51   Pre-incorporation contracts, deeds and obligations
>
> (1)   A contract that purports to be made by or on behalf of an overseas company at a time when the company has not been formed has effect, subject to any agreement to the contrary, as one made with the person purporting to act for the company or as agent for it, and he is personally liable on the contract accordingly.
>
> (2)   Subsection (1) applies—
>
> (a)   to the making of a deed under the law of England and Wales or Northern Ireland, and
>
> (b)   to the undertaking of an obligation under the law of Scotland,
>
> as it applies to the making of a contract.".

NOTES
Commencement: 1 October 2009.

---

7   *(Revokes the Foreign Companies (Execution of Documents) Regulations 1994, SI 1994/950 and the Foreign Companies (Execution of Documents) Regulations (Northern Ireland) 2003, SR 2003/5.)*

PART 3
REGISTRATION OF CHARGES
Introduction
[4.506]
8   Application and interpretation of Part

(1)   This Part applies to an overseas company that is registered (as defined below).

(2)   For the purposes of this Part—

(a)   an overseas company becomes registered when it complies with Part 2 (initial registration of particulars) of the Overseas Companies Regulations 2009 in respect of one or more UK establishments and those particulars are registered, and

(b)   an overseas company ceases to be registered when it gives notice under regulation 77 (notice of closure of UK establishment) of those regulations in respect of all its UK establishments and that notice is registered.

(3)   For the purposes of this Part the particulars and notice referred to in paragraph (2) are not treated as registered unless and until they are on the register and accordingly available for public inspection.

(4)   In this Part "charge"—

(a)   in England and Wales and Northern Ireland, includes a mortgage;

(b)   in Scotland, includes any right in security.

(5)   In relation to a charge created under the law of Scotland, references in this Part to the date of creation of the charge are to—

(a)   in the case of a floating charge, the date on which the instrument creating the floating charge was executed by the company creating the charge;

(b)   in any other case, the date on which the right of the person entitled to the benefit of the charge was constituted as a real right.

NOTES
Commencement: 1 October 2009.

Charges requiring registration
[4.507]
9   Charges requiring registration

(1)   A charge requires registration under this Part if—

(a)   it is created by a company to which this Part applies,

(b)   the property subject to the charge is situated in the United Kingdom, and

(c)   the charge is of a type requiring registration.

(2)   Whether the conditions in paragraph (1)(a) and (b) are met is determined when the charge is created.

(3)   The types of charge requiring registration are—
  (a)   a charge on land or any interest in land, other than a charge for rent or any other periodical sum issuing out of (in Scotland, payable in respect of) land;
  (b)   a charge created or evidenced by an instrument that, if executed by an individual, would require registration as a bill of sale;
  (c)   a charge for the purposes of securing any issue of debentures;
  (d)   a charge on uncalled share capital of the company;
  (e)   a charge on calls made but not paid;
  (f)   a charge on book debts of the company;
  (g)   a floating charge on the company's property or undertaking;
  (h)   a charge on a ship or aircraft, or any share in a ship;
  (i)   a charge on goodwill or on any intellectual property.

(4)   For the purposes of paragraph (3)(a)—
  (a)   a charge on land includes a charge created by a heritable security within the meaning of section 9(8) of the Conveyancing and Feudal Reform (Scotland) Act 1970; and
  (b)   the holding of debentures entitling the holder to a charge on land is not an interest in the land.

(5)   For the purposes of paragraph (3)(f) the deposit by way of security of a negotiable instrument given to secure the payment of book debts is not a charge on those book debts.

(6)   For the purposes of paragraph (3)(i), "intellectual property" means—
  (a)   any patent, trade mark, registered design, copyright or design right; or
  (b)   any licence under or in respect of any such right.

NOTES
Commencement: 1 October 2009.

[4.508]
10   Duty to deliver particulars of charge etc for registration

(1)   A company to which this Part applies that creates a charge requiring registration must deliver the required particulars of the charge, together with a certified copy of the instrument (if any) by which the charge is created or evidenced, to the registrar before the end of the period allowed for registration.

(2)   Registration of the charge may instead be effected on the application of a person interested in it.

(3)   Where registration is effected on the application of some person other than the company, that person is entitled to recover from the company the amount of any fees properly paid by him to the registrar on registration.

(4)   Paragraph (1) does not apply if the property subject to the charge is, at the end of the period allowed for registration, no longer situated in the United Kingdom.

NOTES
Commencement: 1 October 2009.

[4.509]
11   The required particulars

(1)   The required particulars are—
  (a)   the date of the creation of the charge,
  (b)   a description of the instrument (if any) creating or evidencing the charge,
  (c)   the amount secured by the charge,
  (d)   the name and address of the person entitled to the charge, and
  (e)   short particulars of the property charged.

(2)   In the case of a floating charge created under the law of Scotland, the required particulars include a statement as to any provisions of the charge and of any instrument relating to it—
  (a)   which prohibit or restrict or regulate the power of the company to grant further securities ranking in priority to, or pari passu with, the floating charge, or
  (b)   which vary or otherwise regulate the order of ranking of the floating charge in relation to subsisting securities.

NOTES
Commencement: 1 October 2009.

[4.510]
12   The period allowed for registration

The period allowed for registration of the charge is—
  (a)   21 days, beginning with the day after the day on which the charge is created, or

(b)   if the charge is created outside the United Kingdom, 21 days beginning with the day after the day on which the instrument by which the charge is created or evidenced (or a copy of it) could, in due course of post (and if despatched with due diligence) have been received in the United Kingdom.

NOTES
Commencement: 1 October 2009.

[4.511]
13   Charge by way of ex facie absolute disposition

(1)   For the avoidance of doubt, it is hereby declared that, in the case of a charge created under the law of Scotland by way of an *ex facie* absolute disposition or assignation qualified by a back letter or other agreement, or by a standard security qualified by an agreement, compliance with regulation 10(1) does not of itself render the charge unavailable as security for indebtedness incurred after the date of compliance.

(2)   Where the amount secured by a charge so created is purported to be increased by a further back letter or agreement, a further charge is held to have been created by the *ex facie* absolute disposition or assignation or (as the case may be) by the standard security, as qualified by the further back letter or agreement.

(3)   In that case, the provisions of this Part apply to the further charge as if—
   (a)   references in this Part (other than in this regulation) to a charge were references to the further charge, and
   (b)   references to the date of creation of a charge were references to the date on which the further back letter or agreement was executed.

NOTES
Commencement: 1 October 2009.

Special rules for debentures

[4.512]
14   Special rules about debentures: charge in series of debentures

(1)   Where a series of debentures containing, or giving by reference to another instrument, any charge to the benefit of which debenture holders of that series are entitled *pari passu* is created by a company, it is for the purposes of regulation 10 sufficient if the following particulars, together with a certified copy of the instrument containing the charge (or, if there is no such instrument, a certified copy of one of the debentures of the series), are delivered to the registrar before the end of the period allowed for registration.

(2)   The required particulars are—
   (a)   the total amount secured by the whole series,
   (b)   the dates of the resolutions authorising the issue of the series and the date of the covering instrument (if any) by which the series is created or defined,
   (c)   a general description of the property charged, and
   (d)   the names of the trustees (if any) for the debenture holders.

(3)   In the case of a floating charge created under the law of Scotland, the required particulars include a statement as to any provisions of the charge and of any instrument relating to it—
   (a)   which prohibit or restrict or regulate the power of the company to grant further securities ranking in priority to, or pari passu with, the floating charge, or
   (b)   which vary or otherwise regulate the order of ranking of the floating charge in relation to subsisting securities.

(4)   Where more than one issue is made of debentures in the series, particulars of the date and amount of each issue of debentures of the series must be sent to the registrar for entry in the register of charges.

NOTES
Commencement: 1 October 2009.

[4.513]
15   Special rules about debentures: additional registration requirement for commission etc

(1)   Where any commission, allowance or discount has been paid or made either directly or indirectly by a company to a person in consideration of their—
   (a)   subscribing or agreeing to subscribe, whether absolutely or conditionally, for debentures in a company, or
   (b)   procuring or agreeing to procure subscriptions, whether absolute or conditional, for such debentures,
the particulars required to be sent for registration under regulation 10 include particulars as to the amount or rate per cent. of the commission, discount or allowance so paid or made.

(2)   The deposit of debentures as security for a debt of the company is not, for the purposes of this regulation, treated as the issue of debentures at a discount.

NOTES
Commencement: 1 October 2009.

[4.514]
16   Special rules about debentures: period allowed for registration
The period allowed for registration of particulars of a series of debentures as a result of regulation 14 is—
(a)   if there is an instrument containing the charge mentioned in paragraph (1) of that regulation, 21 days beginning with the day after the date on which that instrument is executed;
(b)   if there is no such instrument, 21 days beginning with the day after the day on which the first debenture of the series is executed.

NOTES
Commencement: 1 October 2009.

[4.515]
17   Special rules about debentures: endorsement of certificate on debentures
(1)   The company shall cause a copy of every certificate of registration given under regulation 18(4) to be endorsed on every debenture or certificate of debenture stock which is issued by the company, and the payment of which is secured by the charge so registered.
(2)   This does not require a company to cause a certificate of registration of any charge so given to be endorsed on any debenture or certificate of debenture stock issued by the company before the charge was created.
(3)   A person commits an offence who knowingly and wilfully authorises or permits the delivery of a debenture or certificate of debenture stock which under this regulation is required to have endorsed on it a copy of a certificate of registration, without the copy being so endorsed upon it.
(4)   A person guilty of an offence under this regulation is liable on summary conviction to a fine not exceeding level 3 on the standard scale.

NOTES
Commencement: 1 October 2009.

The register of charges

[4.516]
18   The register of charges
(1)   The registrar shall keep for each company to which this Part applies a register of all the charges requiring registration under this Part.
(2)   The registrar shall enter in the register the particulars required to be delivered to the registrar under this Part.
(3)   In the case of a charge imposed by the Enforcement of Judgments Office under Article 46 of the Judgments Enforcement (Northern Ireland) Order 1981, the registrar shall enter in the register the date on which the charge became effective.
(4)   The registrar shall give a certificate of the registration of any charge registered in pursuance of this Part, stating the name of the company and the amount secured by the charge
(5)   The certificate—
(a)   shall be signed by the registrar or authenticated by the registrar's official seal, and
(b)   is conclusive evidence that the requirements of this Part as to registration have been satisfied.
(6)   The register kept in pursuance of this regulation shall be open to inspection by any person.

NOTES
Commencement: 1 October 2009.

[4.517]
19   Consequences of failure to register
(1)   If a company creates a charge requiring registration under this Part, the charge is void (so far as any security on the company's property or undertaking is conferred by it) against—
(a)   a liquidator of the company,
(b)   an administrator of the company, and
(c)   a creditor of the company,
if regulation 10 (duty to deliver particulars of charge etc for registration) is not complied with.
(2)   Failure to comply with—

    (a)   regulation 14(4) (special rules for debentures: duty to send particulars of each issue of debentures), or

    (b)   regulation 15 (special rules for debentures: additional registration requirement for commission etc),

does not affect the validity of the debentures issued.

(3)   Paragraph (1) is without prejudice to any contract or obligation for repayment of the money secured by the charge; and when a charge becomes void under this regulation, the money secured by it immediately becomes payable.

NOTES
Commencement: 1 October 2009.

[4.518]
20   Registration of enforcement of security

(1)   A person who—

    (a)   obtains an order for the appointment of a receiver or manager of property of a company to which this Part applies, or

    (b)   appoints such a receiver or manager under powers contained in an instrument,

must give notice of the fact to the registrar within seven days of the order or of the appointment under those powers.

(2)   A person appointed receiver or manager of a company's property under powers contained in an instrument who ceases to act as such receiver or manager must, on so ceasing, give the registrar notice to that effect.

(3)   The registrar must enter a fact of which notice is given under this regulation in the register of charges.

(4)   A person who makes default in complying with the requirements of paragraph (1) or (2) commits an offence.

(5)   A person guilty of an offence under this regulation is liable on summary conviction to a fine not exceeding level 3 on the standard scale and, for continued contravention, a daily default fine not exceeding one-tenth of level 3 on the standard scale.

(6)   This regulation does not apply in relation to the appointment of a receiver under section 51(1) or (2) of the Insolvency Act 1986 (appointment under law of Scotland by holder of floating charge or by court on application of holder), as respects which section 53(1) or 54(3) of that Act requires the delivery to the registrar of a copy of the instrument or interlocutor making the appointment.

NOTES
Commencement: 1 October 2009.

[4.519]
21   Entries of satisfaction and release

(1)   This regulation applies if a statement is delivered to the registrar verifying with respect to a registered charge—

    (a)   that the debt for which the charge was given has been paid or satisfied in whole or in part, or

    (b)   that part of the property or undertaking charged has been released from the charge or has ceased to form part of the company's property or undertaking.

(2)   If the charge is a floating charge created under the law of Scotland, the statement must be accompanied by either—

    (a)   a statement by the creditor entitled to the benefit of the charge, or a person authorised by the creditor for that purpose, verifying that the statement mentioned in paragraph (1) is correct, or

    (b)   a direction obtained from the court, on the ground that the statement by the creditor mentioned in sub-paragraph (a) could not be readily obtained, dispensing with the need for that statement.

(3)   The registrar may enter on the register a memorandum of satisfaction in whole or in part, or of the fact that part of the property or undertaking has been released from the charge or has ceased to form part of the company's property or undertaking (as the case may be).

(4)   Where the registrar enters a memorandum of satisfaction in whole, the registrar must if required send the company a copy of it.

(5)   Nothing in this regulation requires the company to submit particulars with respect to the entry in the register of a memorandum of satisfaction where the company, having created a floating charge under the law of Scotland over all or any part of its property, disposes of part of the property subject to the floating charge.

NOTES
Commencement: 1 October 2009.

[4.520]
22 Rectification of register of charges

If the court is satisfied—
- (a) that the failure to register a charge before the end of the period allowed for registration, or the omission or mis-statement of any particular with respect to any such charge or in a memorandum of satisfaction—
  - (i) was accidental or due to inadvertence or to some other sufficient cause, or
  - (ii) is not of a nature to prejudice the position of creditors or shareholders of the company, or
- (b) that on other grounds it is just and equitable to grant relief,

the court may, on the application of the company or a person interested, and on such terms and conditions as seem to the court just and expedient, order that the period allowed for registration shall be extended or, as the case may be, that the omission or mis-statement shall be rectified.

NOTES
Commencement: 1 October 2009.

Companies' records and register

[4.521]
23 Companies to keep available for inspection copies of instruments creating charges

(1) A company to which this Part applies must keep available for inspection a copy of every instrument creating a charge requiring registration under this Part.

(2) In the case of a series of uniform debentures, a copy of one of the debentures of the series is sufficient.

NOTES
Commencement: 1 October 2009.

[4.522]
24 Company's register of charges

(1) Every company to which this Part applies must keep available for inspection a register of charges and must enter in it—
- (a) all charges specifically affecting property of the company situated in the United Kingdom, and
- (b) all floating charges on the whole or part of the company's property or undertaking situated in the United Kingdom.

(2) The entry must in each case give a short description of the property charged, the amount of the charge and, except in the cases of securities to bearer, the names of the persons entitled to it.

(3) An officer of the company who knowingly and wilfully authorises or permits the omission of an entry required to be made in pursuance of this regulation commits an offence.

(4) A person guilty of an offence under this regulation is liable—
- (a) on conviction on indictment, to a fine;
- (b) on summary conviction, to a fine not exceeding the statutory maximum.

NOTES
Commencement: 1 October 2009.

[4.523]
25 Copies of instruments and company's register of charges to be available for inspection

(1) This regulation applies to—
- (a) documents required to be kept available for inspection under regulation 23 (copies of instruments creating charges), and
- (b) a company's register of charges kept in pursuance of regulation 24.

(2) The documents and register must be kept available for inspection at a location in the United Kingdom at which the company carries on business notified to the registrar in accordance with paragraph (3).

(3) The company must give notice to the registrar—
- (a) of the place at which the documents and register are kept available for inspection, within 14 days of the first registration of a charge under this Part, and
- (b) of any change in that place, within 14 days of any such change.

(4) The documents and register shall be open to the inspection—
- (a) of any creditor or member of the company without charge, and
- (b) of any other person on payment of £3.50 for each hour or part of an hour during which the right of inspection is exercised.

(5) If default is made in complying with paragraph (3) or an inspection required under paragraph (4) is refused, an offence is committed by—
- (a) the company, and

(b)   every officer of the company who is in default.

(6)   A person guilty of an offence under this regulation is liable on summary conviction to a fine not exceeding level 3 on the standard scale and, for continued contravention, a daily default fine not exceeding one-tenth of level 3 on the standard scale.

(7)   If an inspection required under paragraph (4) is refused the court may by order compel an immediate inspection.

NOTES

    Commencement: 1 October 2009.

[4.524]
26   Exercise of right of inspection

(1)   A company to which this Part applies shall make the documents and register referred to in regulation 25 available for inspection by a person on a day which has been specified by that person ("the specified day") provided that—

   (a)   the specified day is a working day; and

   (b)   that person gives the company the required notice of the specified day.

(2)   The required notice is at least 10 working days' notice of the specified day.

(3)   When a person gives notice of the specified day he shall also give notice of the time on that day at which he wishes to start the inspection (which shall be any time between 9 am and 3 pm) and the company shall make its company records available for inspection by that person for a period of at least 2 hours beginning with that time.

(4)   A company that fails to comply with this regulation is treated as having refused inspection.

NOTES

    Commencement: 1 October 2009.

Supplementary provisions

[4.525]
27   Delivery of documents in language other than English

(1)   The following documents are specified for the purposes of section 1105(2)(d) of the Companies Act 2006 as documents that may be drawn up and delivered to the registrar in a language other than English, but which must, when delivered to the registrar, be accompanied by a certified translation into English.

(2)   The documents are a certified copy of a debenture or other instrument creating or evidencing a charge over the property of an overseas company to which this Part applies.

NOTES

    Commencement: 1 October 2009.

[4.526]
28   Transitional provisions and savings

The Schedule to these Regulations contains transitional provisions and savings.

NOTES

    Commencement: 1 October 2009.

SCHEDULE
REGISTRATION OF CHARGES: TRANSITIONAL PROVISIONS AND SAVINGS
Regulation 28

[4.527]
1   Introduction

In this Schedule—

    "the 1985 Act" means the Companies Act 1985; and

    "the 1986 Order" means the Companies (Northern Ireland) Order 1986.

2   Charge created by company

(1)   The provisions of Part 12 of the 1985 Act relating to charges created by companies incorporated outside Great Britain continue to apply in relation to charges created before 1st October 2009.

(2)   The provisions of Part 13 of the 1986 Order relating to charges created by companies incorporated outside Northern Ireland continue to apply in relation to charges created before 1st October 2009.

(3)   The provisions of Part 3 of these Regulations apply to charges created on or after that date.

3 Charge in series of debentures

(1)   The provisions of Part 12 of the 1985 Act relating to the registration of a series of debentures of a company incorporated outside Great Britain continue to apply where the first debenture of the series was executed before 1st October 2009.

(2)   The provisions of Part 13 of the 1986 Order relating to the registration of a series of debentures of a company incorporated outside Northern Ireland continue to apply where the first debenture of the series was executed before 1st October 2009.

(3)   The provisions of Part 3 of these Regulations apply where the first debenture of the series is executed on or after that date.

4 Charge on property acquired by company

(1)   The provisions of Part 12 of the 1985 Act relating to charges existing on property acquired by a company incorporated outside Great Britain continue to apply to property acquired before 1st October 2009.

(2)   The provisions of Part 13 of the 1986 Order relating to charges existing on property acquired by a company incorporated outside Northern Ireland continue to apply to property acquired before 1st October 2009.

5 Northern Ireland: registration of certain charges etc affecting land

Article 408 of the 1986 Order (Northern Ireland: registration of certain charges etc affecting land) continues to apply in relation to a charge against land, or an estate in land, of a company incorporated outside Northern Ireland imposed by an order under Article 46 of the Judgments Enforcement (Northern Ireland) Order 1981 made before 1st October 2009.

6 Registration of enforcement of security

(1)   Section 405 of the 1985 Act or Article 413 of the 1986 Order (registration of enforcement of security) continues to apply where the order or appointment is made, or the receiver or manager ceases to act, before 1st October 2009.

(2)   Regulation 20 applies where the order or appointment is made, or the receiver or manager ceases to act, on or after that date.

7 Entries of satisfaction and release

(1)   Section 403 or 419 of the 1985 Act or Article 411 of the 1986 Order (entries of satisfaction and release) continues to apply where the relevant statutory declaration, statement or application and statutory declaration or statement is received by the registrar before 1st October 2009.

(2)   Regulation 21 applies to statements delivered to the registrar on or after 1st October 2009.

NOTES
Commencement: 1 October 2009.

COMPANIES ACT 2006 (CONSEQUENTIAL AMENDMENTS, TRANSITIONAL PROVISIONS AND SAVINGS) ORDER 2009

(SI 2009/1941)

NOTES
Made: 21 July 2008.
Authority: European Communities Act 1972, s 2(2); Companies Act 2006, ss 657, 1088, 1292, 1294, 1296(1), 1300(2); Charities Act 2006, s 75(4), (5).
Commencement: 1 October 2009.
This Order is reproduced as amended by: the Companies Act 2006 (Consequential Amendments and Transitional Provisions) Order 2011, SI 2011/1265.

ARRANGEMENT OF ARTICLES

Introductory

[4.528]
1   Citation and commencement

(1)   This Order may be cited as the Companies Act 2006 (Consequential Amendments, Transitional Provisions and Savings) Order 2009.

(2)   The provisions of this Order come into force on 1st October 2009.

NOTES
Commencement: 1 October 2009.

Consequential amendments

[4.529]
2   Consequential amendments, repeals and revocations

(1)   Schedule 1 to this Order contains consequential amendments.

(2)   Schedule 2 to this Order contains other consequential repeals and revocations.

NOTES
Commencement: 1 October 2009.

[4.530]
3   References to companies registered or re-registered under earlier legislation

A reference in any enactment to—
    (a)   a company formed and registered under the Companies Act 2006,
    (b)   a company registered but not formed under that Act, or
    (c)   a company re-registered under that Act,
includes a company treated as so formed and registered, registered or re-registered by virtue of section 1297(3) of that Act, including that provision as applied by paragraph 1(2) of Schedule 2 to the Companies Act 2006 (Commencement No 8, Transitional Provisions and Savings) Order 2008.

NOTES
Commencement: 1 October 2009.

[4.531]
4   References to Northern Ireland directors disqualification orders

A reference in any enactment to a disqualification order under the Company Directors Disqualification (Northern Ireland) Order 2002 includes a disqualification order made under Part 2 of the Companies (Northern Ireland) Order 1989 that by virtue of section 29(3)(a) of the Interpretation Act (Northern Ireland) 1954 has effect as if made under the 2002 Order.

NOTES
Commencement: 1 October 2009.

Transitional provisions

[4.532]
5   Change of name by existing or transitional company

(1)   This article applies where, in the case of an existing or transitional company—
    (a)   the company's articles are deemed to contain a statement of its name by virtue of section 28 of the Companies Act 2006 (provisions of memorandum treated as provisions of articles), and
    (b)   the company changes its name (by any means) on or after 1st October 2009.

(2)   The company is not required to amend its articles in order to effect the change of name.

(3)   The deemed statement in the company's articles ceases to have effect when the change of name takes effect.

(4)   The company is not required to send a copy of its articles to the registrar in accordance with section 26 of the Companies Act 2006.

(5)   Where the company, in complying with any obligation to send a person a copy of its articles, relies on paragraph 9(1)(a) or (b) of Schedule 2 to the Companies Act 2006 (Commencement No 8, Transitional Provisions and Savings) Order 2008, it must—

    (a)   if it relies on paragraph 9(1)(a) (provisions of old-style memorandum appended to other provisions of articles), omit the provision stating the company's former name;

    (b)   if it relies on paragraph 9(1)(b) (copy of old-style memorandum with indication of provisions deemed to be provisions of the articles), indicate that the provision stating the company's former name is no longer effective.

(6)   In this article—

"existing company" and "transitional company" have the same meaning as in the Companies Act 2006 (Commencement No 8, Transitional Provisions and Savings) Order 2008 (see article 2 of that Order); and

"old-style memorandum" has the same meaning as in paragraph 9(1) of Schedule 2 to that Order (see sub-paragraph (2) of that paragraph).

NOTES

    Commencement: 1 October 2009.

[4.533]
6   Companies that are charities: requirement of consent for affirmation of certain transactions

(1)   Section 42(4) of the Companies Act 2006 (companies that are charities: requirement of consent for affirmation of certain transactions with directors or their associates) applies where the request for consent is received on or after 1st October 2009.

(2)   Any request for consent under section 65(4) of the Charities Act 1993 or Article 9A(4) of the Charities (Northern Ireland) Order 1987 received but not determined before that date is treated as if made under section 42(4) of the Companies Act 2006.

(3)   In relation to a decision under section 65(4) of the Charities Act 1993 made before 1st October 2009 the provisions of that Act as to appeals continue to have effect without the amendments made by this Order.

NOTES

    Commencement: 1 October 2009.

[4.534]
7   Functions of registrar of companies for Northern Ireland: contracting out

(1)   On the coming into force in relation to the registrar of companies for Northern Ireland of an order under Part 2 of the Deregulation and Contracting Out Act 1994, as amended by this Order, the provisions of the Deregulation and Contracting Out (Northern Ireland) Order 1996 relating to that registrar shall cease to have effect.

(2)   Those provisions are—

    (a)   in Article 2(2), the definition of "registrar of companies";

    (b)   Article 11; and

    (c)   Part 1 of Schedule 2.

NOTES

    Commencement: 1 October 2009.

[4.535]
8   Amendments of insolvency legislation

(1)   The amendments by this Order of the Insolvency Act 1986 ("the 1986 Act") and the Insolvency (Northern Ireland) Order 1989 ("the 1989 Order") apply as follows.

(2)   They apply where, in a company voluntary arrangement, a moratorium comes into force in relation to a company on or after 1st October 2009.

(3)   They apply where a company enters administration on or after 1st October 2009, except where—

    (a)   it enters administration by virtue of an administration order under paragraph 10 of Schedule B1 to the 1986 Act (or paragraph 11 of Schedule B1 to the 1989 Order) on an application made before 1st October 2009,

    (b)   the administration is immediately preceded by a voluntary liquidation in respect of which the resolution to wind up was passed before 1st October 2009, or

    (c)   the administration is immediately preceded by a liquidation on the making of a winding-up order on a petition which was presented before 1st October 2009.

(4)   They apply where, in a receivership, a receiver or manager is appointed in respect of a company on or after 1st October 2009.

(5) They apply where a company goes into liquidation upon the passing on or after 1st October 2009 of a resolution to wind up.

(6) They apply where a company goes into voluntary liquidation under paragraph 83 of Schedule B1 to the 1986 Act (or paragraph 84 of Schedule B1 to the 1989 Order), except where the preceding administration—

   (a) commenced before 1st October 2009, or

   (b) is an administration which commenced by virtue of an administration order under paragraph 10 of Schedule B1 to the 1986 Act (or paragraph 11 of Schedule B1 to the 1989 Order) on an application which was made before 1st October 2009.

(7) They apply where a company goes into liquidation on the making of a winding-up order on a petition presented on or after 1st October 2009, except where the liquidation is immediately preceded by—

   (a) an administration under paragraph 10 of Schedule B1 to the 1986 Act (or paragraph 11 of Schedule B1 to the 1989 Order) where the administration order was made on an application made before 1st October 2009,

   (b) an administration in respect of which the appointment of an administrator under paragraph 14 or 22 of Schedule B1 to the 1986 Act (or paragraph 15 or 23 of Schedule B1 to the 1989 Order) took effect before 1st October 2009, or

   (c) a voluntary liquidation in respect of which the resolution to wind up was passed before 1st October 2009.

NOTES
Commencement: 1 October 2009.

Savings

[4.536]
9   Saving for unlimited liabilities of directors etc

The repeal of the provisions relating to unlimited liability of directors and others, that is—

   (a) sections 306 and 307 of the Companies Act 1985 and section 75 of the Insolvency Act 1986, or

   (b) Articles 314 and 315 of the Companies (Northern Ireland) Order 1986 and Article 62 of the Insolvency (Northern Ireland) Order 1989,

does not affect the operation of those provisions in relation to liabilities arising before 1st October 2009 or in connection with the holding of an office to which a person was appointed before that date on the understanding that their liability would be unlimited.

NOTES
Commencement: 1 October 2009.

[4.537]
10   Saving for information obtained or report made under repealed NI provisions

(1) The operation of any provision about the disclosure of information—

   (a) obtained under a repealed NI provision, or

   (b) contained in a report made under a repealed NI provision,

is not affected by the repeal of that provision (or the repeal of the NI provision).

(2) So far as may be necessary for continuing the operation of any such provision—

   (a) information obtained as mentioned in paragraph (1)(a) is to be treated in the same way as information obtained under the corresponding GB provision, and

   (b) information contained in any such report as is mentioned in paragraph (1)(b) is to be treated in the same way as information contained in a report made under the corresponding GB provision.

(3) In this article—

"repealed NI provision" means a provision of Northern Ireland legislation that is repealed in consequence of the extension to Northern Ireland, by any provision of Part 45 of the Companies Act 2006, of provisions applying in Great Britain; and

"corresponding GB provision" means the corresponding provision so applied.

NOTES
Commencement: 1 October 2009.

[4.538]
11   Saving for provisions relating to nature of liability of member or contributory

(1) The new provisions as to the nature of a member's or contributory's liability apply to liabilities arising on or after 1st October 2009 and the old provisions continue to apply to liabilities arising before that date.

(2) The new provisions are section 33(2) of the Companies Act 2006 and (in England and Wales) section 80 of the Insolvency Act 1986 as amended by this Order.

(3)   The old provisions are—
  (a)   in England and Wales, section 14(2) of the Companies Act 1985 and section 80 of the Insolvency Act 1986 as it has effect before that amendment;
  (b)   in Northern Ireland, Articles 4(d)(ii) and 15(c) of the Limitation (Northern Ireland) Order 1989.

(4)   For the purposes of this article a liability is treated as arising when the limitation period starts to run for the purposes of the Limitation Act 1980 or the Limitation (Northern Ireland) Order 1989.

NOTES
Commencement: 1 October 2009.

[4.539]
12   Saving for earlier consequential amendments, transitional provisions and savings
(1)   Schedule 3 to this Order contains provisions preserving the effect of the provisions of . . . the Companies Consolidation (Consequential Provisions) (Northern Ireland) Order 1986 relating to old public companies.

(2)   The repeal of the other provisions of that . . .   Order does not affect the operation of—
  (a)   any provision amending an enactment that remains in force;
  (b)   any transitional provision that remains capable of having effect in relation to the corresponding provision of the Companies Act 2006;
  (c)   any saving that remains capable of having effect in relation to the repeal of an enactment by that . . .   Order.

NOTES
Commencement: 1 October 2009.
Words omitted revoked by the Companies Act 2006 (Consequential Amendments and Transitional Provisions) Order 2011, SI 2011/1265, art 4(1), (2), as from 12 May 2011.
Note that the words omitted from this article were references to the Companies Consolidation (Consequential Provisions) Act 1985. That Act was repealed by the Companies Act 2006 (Consequential Amendments and Transitional Provisions) Order 2011, SI 2011/1265, art 2, as from 12 May 2011. For provision relating to old public companies within the meaning of the 1985 Act, see now Sch 1 to the 2011 Order at **[4.651]**.

[4.540]
13   Saving of power to order caution for expenses (in Scotland) or security for costs (in Northern Ireland)
(1)   Schedule 1 to the Companies Act 2006 (Commencement No 8, Transitional Provisions and Savings) Order 2008 (repeals coming into force on 1st October 2009) is amended as follows—
  (a)   in Part 1 (Great Britain repeals), in the list of provisions of the Companies Act 1985, for "Sections 721 to 726" substitute "Sections 721 to 725 and 726(1)";
  (b)   in Part 2 (Northern Ireland repeals), in the list of provisions of the Companies (Northern Ireland) Order 1986, for "Articles 670 to 674" substitute "Articles 670 to 673".

(2)   In Article 674 of the Companies (Northern Ireland) Order 1986 (power to order security for costs in Northern Ireland) the expression "limited company" has the same meaning as in the Companies Acts (see section 3 of the Companies Act 2006).

(3)   That Article and section 726(2) of the Companies Act 1985 (power to order caution for expenses in Scotland) apply to a limited liability partnership registered under the Limited Liability Partnerships Act 2000 as they apply to a limited company.

NOTES
Commencement: 1 October 2009.

SCHEDULES

SCHEDULES 1 AND 2

(Sch 1 contains 270 paragraphs of consequential amendments which, in so far as relevant to this work, have been incorporated at the appropriate place; Sch 2 provides for other consequential repeals and revocations which, in so far as relevant to this work, have been incorporated at the appropriate place.)

SCHEDULE 3
PROVISIONS RELATING TO OLD PUBLIC COMPANIES

Article 12(1)

[4.541]
1 Meaning of "old public company"

[For the purposes of this Schedule an "old public company" is a company limited by shares, or a company limited by guarantee and having a share capital, in respect of which the following conditions are met—

   (a)   the company either existed on 1st July 1983 or was incorporated after that date pursuant to an application made before that date,

   (b)   on that date or, if later, on the day of the company's incorporation, the company was not or (as the case may be) would not have been a private company within the meaning of section 28 of the Companies Act (Northern Ireland) 1960, and

   (c)   the company has not since that date or the day of the company's incorporation (as the case may be) either been re-registered as a public company within the meaning of Article 12(3) of the Companies (Northern Ireland) Order or section 4(2) of the Companies Act 2006 or become a private company within the meaning of Article 12(3) of the Companies (Northern Ireland) Order or section 4(1) of the Companies Act 2006.]

2 Application of Companies Acts to old public companies

(1)   References in the Companies Acts to—

   (a)   a public company, or

   (b)   a company other than a private company,

are to be read (unless the context otherwise requires) as including an old public company.

(2)   References in the Companies Acts to a private company are to be read accordingly.

(3)   Sub-paragraphs (1) and (2)—

   (a)   do not apply in relation to—

      (i)   Part 7 of the Companies Act 2006 (re-registration as a means of altering a company's status), and

      (ii)   sections 662 to 669 of that Act (treatment of shares held by or for public company) (see paragraph 7(1) and (2) below), and

   (b)   do not restrict the power to make provision by regulations under section 65 of that Act (inappropriate use of indications of company type or legal form).

3 Old public company re-registering as a public company

(1)   Sections 90 to 96 of the Companies Act 2006 (re-registration as public company limited by shares) apply to an old public company.

(2)   As they so apply—

   (a)   references to a private company shall be read as references to an old public company, and

   (b)   references to a special resolution of the company shall be read as references to a resolution of the directors.

(3)   Chapter 3 of Part 3 of that Act (resolutions affecting a company's constitution) applies to any such resolution.

(4)   References in this Schedule to re-registration as a public company, in relation to an old public company, are to re-registration by virtue of this paragraph.

4 Old public company becoming private: special resolution

(1)   An old public company may pass a special resolution not to be re-registered as a public company.

(2)   Sections 98 and 99 of the Companies Act 2006 (application to court to cancel resolution; notice to registrar of court application or order) apply to such a resolution as they would apply to a special resolution by a public company to be re-registered as private.

(3)   If either—

   (a)   28 days from the passing of the resolution elapse without an application being made under section 98 of the Companies Act 2006 (as applied), or

   (b)   such an application is made and proceedings are concluded on the application without the court making an order for the cancellation of the resolution,

the registrar of companies shall issue the company with a certificate stating that it is a private company.

(4)   The company then becomes a private company by virtue of the issue of the certificate.

(5)   For the purposes of sub-paragraph (3)(b), proceedings on the application are concluded—

   (a)   except in a case within the following paragraph, when the period mentioned in section 99(3) of the Companies Act 2006 (as applied) for delivering a copy of the court's order on the application to the registrar has expired, or

   (b)   when the company has been notified that the application has been withdrawn.

(6)   A certificate issued to a company under sub-paragraph (3) is conclusive evidence that the requirements of this paragraph have been complied with and that the company is a private company.

5   Old public company becoming private: statutory declaration

(1)   If an old public company delivers to the registrar a statutory declaration by a director or secretary of the company that the company does not at the time of the declaration satisfy the conditions for the company to be re-registered as public, the registrar shall issue the company with a certificate stating that it is a private company.

(2)   The company then becomes a private company by virtue of the issue of the certificate.

(3)   A certificate issued to a company under sub-paragraph (1) is conclusive evidence that the requirements of this paragraph have been complied with and that the company is a private company.

6   Failure by old public company to obtain new classification

(1)   If at any time a company which is an old public company has not delivered to the registrar of companies a declaration under paragraph 5, the company and any officer of it who is in default is guilty of an offence unless at the time the company—
   (a)   has applied to be re-registered as a public company, and the application has not been refused or withdrawn, or
   (b)   has passed a special resolution not to be re-registered as a public company, and the resolution has not been revoked, and has not been cancelled under section 98 of the Companies Act 2006 as applied by paragraph 4.

(2)   A person guilty of an offence under this paragraph is liable on summary conviction to a fine not exceeding level 3 on the standard scale and, for continued contravention, a daily default fine not exceeding one-tenth of level 3 on the standard scale.

7   Old public company holding, or having charge on, own shares

(1)   In sections 662 to 669 of the Companies Act 2006 (treatment of shares held by or for public company) references to a public company do not include an old public company.

(2)   Section 668 of that Act (application of sections 662 to 667 to private company re-registering as public company) applies to an old public company as to a private company.

(3)   In the case of a company that—
   (a)   after [30th September 1984] remained an old public company, and
   (b)   did not before that date apply to be re-registered as a public company,
any charge on its own shares which was in existence on or immediately before that date is a permitted charge and not void under section 670 of the Companies Act 2006.

(4)   . . .

8   Old public companies: trading under misleading name

(1)   An old public company commits an offence if it carries on a trade, profession or business under a name that includes, as its last part, the words "public limited company" or "cwmni cyfyngedig cyhoeddus".

(2)   Where an offence under this paragraph is committed by a company, an offence is also committed by every officer of the company who is in default.

(3)   A person guilty of an offence under this paragraph is liable on summary conviction to a fine not exceeding level 3 on the standard scale and, for continued contravention, a daily default fine not exceeding one-tenth of level 3 on the standard scale.

9   Old public companies: payment for share capital

Sections 584 to 587 of the Companies Act 2006 (payment for shares: additional rules for public companies) apply to an old public company whose directors have passed and not revoked a resolution to be re-registered as a public company, as those sections apply to a public company.

NOTES

Commencement: 1 October 2009.

Para 1 substituted, words in square brackets in para 7(3) substituted, and para 7(4) revoked, by the Companies Act 2006 (Consequential Amendments and Transitional Provisions) Order 2011, SI 2011/1265, art 4(1), (3), as from 12 May 2011.

COMPANIES (SHARE CAPITAL AND ACQUISITION BY COMPANY OF ITS OWN SHARES) REGULATIONS 2009 (NOTE)

(SI 2009/2022)

[4.542]

NOTES

These Regulations were made on 21 July 2009 under the powers conferred by the Companies Act 2006, ss 562(6)(a), 657, 737, 1292(1)(c). They come into force on 1 October 2009.

- Reg 1 of the Regulations provides for citation and commencement.
- Reg 2 amends CA 2006, s 562 at **[1.562]** so that the minimum period for which rights issues must be kept open for acceptance is reduced from 21 days to 14 days.
- Regulation 3 implements, in respect of CA 2006, the amendment made to Article 32(1) of Council Directive 77/91/EEC by Directive 2006/68/EC of the European Parliament and of the Council. That Directive was implemented in respect of CA 1985 by the Companies (Reduction of Capital) (Creditor Protection) Regulations 2008 (SI 2008/719)). The latter Directive amended the former as regards the formation of public companies and the maintenance and alteration of their capital. Regulation 3 also makes corresponding amendments to the law as it relates to private companies. Regulation 3 amends CA 2006, s 646 at **[1.646]**. Under s 645 of the 2006 Act a company may reduce its share capital by special resolution subject to confirmation by the court. Section 646 provides a procedure for identifying and producing a list of creditors entitled to object to a proposed capital reduction. Under s 648, before the court may confirm a reduction it must be satisfied that the consent of the listed creditors has been obtained or their claims have been discharged or have determined or have been secured by the company. Regulation 3 amends s 646 to exclude from the list of creditors those who cannot show that there is a real likelihood that the proposed capital reduction would result in the company being unable to discharge their debts or claims when they fell due.
- Regulation 4(1) amends ss 694(5), 697(4) and 700(4) of the 2006 Act at **[1.694]**, **[1.697]**, **[1.700]**. It increases from 18 months to five years the amount of time for which a public company may be authorised by special resolution of its members to make off-market purchases of its own shares, vary a contract for off-market purchase of its own shares or release its rights under a contract for off-market purchase of its own shares. Regulation 4(2) amends s 701(5) of the 2006 Act at **[1.701]**. It increases from 18 months to five years the amount of time for which a public or private company may be authorised by ordinary resolution of its members to make market purchases of its own shares.
- Regulation 5 removes from companies the restriction that the maximum amount of their own shares which they may hold as treasury shares is limited to 10% of the nominal value of their issued share capital (or of the class of issued share capital in question). It repeals s 725 of the 2006 Act at **[1.725]**, subject to transitional provisions, as follows—

"(2) Any outstanding obligation to dispose of or cancel excess shares arising under section 725(3) of that Act (duty to dispose of excess shares) shall cease to exist on 1st October 2009, whether or not the period mentioned in that provision has expired, but this is subject to paragraph (3).

(3) This amendment does not affect any liability under section 732 of that Act (treasury shares: offences) in respect of a failure to comply with section 725(3) where the period mentioned in that provision expired before 1st October 2009.".

REGISTRAR OF COMPANIES (FEES) (COMPANIES, OVERSEAS COMPANIES AND LIMITED LIABILITY PARTNERSHIPS) REGULATIONS 2009

(SI 2009/2101)

NOTES

Made: 30 July 2009.

Authority: CA 2006, ss 243(3), 1063(1)–(3), 1292(1).

Commencement: 1 October 2009.

These Regulations are reproduced as amended by: the Registrar of Companies (Fees) (Amendment) Regulations 2009, SI 2009/2439; the Registrar of Companies (Fees) (Companies, Overseas Companies and Limited Liability Partnerships) (Amendment) Regulations 2011, SI 2011/309.

ARRANGEMENT OF REGULATIONS

SCHEDULES

[4.543]
1 Citation and commencement

These Regulations may be cited as the Registrar of Companies (Fees) (Companies, Overseas Companies and Limited Liability Partnerships) Regulations 2009 and come into force on 1st October 2009.

NOTES
Commencement: 1 October 2009.

[4.544]
2 Interpretation

In these Regulations—
   "the 2006 Act" means the Companies Act 2006;
   "revoked provisions" means those regulations listed in Schedule 5 to these Regulations; and
      "continuing provisions" means the provisions of those regulations excepted from revocation in that Schedule.

NOTES
Commencement: 1 October 2009.

[4.545]
[2A

In these Regulations any reference to a "company" includes, where appropriate, a reference to a company to which section 1040 or 1043 of the 2006 Act applies.]

NOTES
Commencement: 1 October 2009.
Inserted by the Registrar of Companies (Fees) (Amendment) Regulations 2009, SI 2009/2439, reg 3, as from 1 October 2009.

[4.546]
3 Fees payable in respect of functions relating to the registration of documents by the registrar

Schedule 1 to these Regulations makes provision for the fees that are payable to the registrar in respect of the receipt of documents relating to companies, overseas companies and limited liability partnerships by the registrar and their registration.

NOTES
Commencement: 1 October 2009.

[4.547]
4 Fees payable in respect of the inspection or provision of copies of documents kept by the registrar

Schedule 2 to these Regulations makes provision for the fees that are payable to the registrar in respect of the inspection, or provision of copies, of documents kept by the registrar relating to companies, overseas companies and limited liability partnerships.

NOTES
Commencement: 1 October 2009.

[4.548]

[4A

The fees prescribed in relation to paragraphs 7(a), 8(a) and 10(a) of Schedule 2 to these Regulations are not payable in respect of any month for which the applicant pays a fee to the registrar for subscription to Companies House Direct, Extranet or XML (those terms are defined in paragraph 1 of Schedule 2) under regulations providing for the payment of fees in respect of the functions of the registrar in relation to the inspection, or provision of copies, of documents kept by the registrar relating to European Economic Interest Groupings and limited partnerships.]

NOTES

Commencement: 1 October 2009.

Inserted by the Registrar of Companies (Fees) (Amendment) Regulations 2009, SI 2009/2439, reg 4, as from 1 October 2009.

[4.549]

5   Fees payable in respect of the disclosure of protected information

Schedule 3 to these Regulations makes provision for the fees that are payable to the registrar in respect of the disclosure of protected information relating to directors of companies, directors and permanent representatives of overseas companies and members of limited liability partnerships.

NOTES

Commencement: 1 October 2009.

[4.550]

6   Transitional provisions

Where any document delivered to the registrar on or before 30th September 2009 is registered on or after 1st October 2009 the fee prescribed in Schedule 1 to these Regulations in respect of that document shall not apply and any fee payable in respect of that document by virtue of the revoked provisions shall apply.

NOTES

Commencement: 1 October 2009.

[4.551]

7

Where any document is delivered to the registrar on or after 1st October 2009 under a provision specified in Schedule 4 to these Regulations in the circumstances specified there the fee prescribed in Schedule 1 to these Regulations shall not apply and any fee payable in respect of that document by virtue of the continuing provisions shall apply.

NOTES

Commencement: 1 October 2009.

[4.552]

8

Where any application is made to the registrar on or before 30th September 2009 in respect of the inspection of, or the provision of copies of, material kept by the registrar, the fee prescribed in Schedule 2 to these Regulations or determined by the registrar in the exercise of his power under section 1063(5) of the 2006 Act in respect of that application shall not apply and any fee payable under the revoked provisions shall apply.

NOTES

Commencement: 1 October 2009.

[4.553]

9   Revocation

The regulations listed in Schedule 5 to these Regulations are revoked to the extent specified.

NOTES

Commencement: 1 October 2009.

SCHEDULES

SCHEDULE 1
THE PERFORMANCE OF FUNCTIONS RELATING TO THE RECEIPT OF DOCUMENTS BY THE REGISTRAR AND THEIR REGISTRATION
Regulation 3

PART 1
INTERPRETATION

Enactments and legal entities

[4.554]

1. (1)   In this Schedule the following meanings are given to the enactments referred to and, where relevant, to the legal entities created under them—

the "2000 Act" means the Limited Liability Partnerships Act 2000 and "limited liability partnership" means a body corporate incorporated under that Act,

the "LLP Regulations" means the Limited Liability Partnerships (Application of Companies Act 2006) Regulations 2009,

the "OC Regulations" means the Overseas Companies Regulations 2009,

the "OC Charges Regulations" means the Overseas Companies (Execution of Documents and Registration of Charges) Regulations 2009.

(2)   In paragraph 10(e) in Part 2 of this Schedule, a reference to an "overseas company" includes a reference to any credit or financial institution to which section 1050 of the 2006 Act applies.

(3)   Words and expressions used in the enactments set out in sub-paragraph (1) have the same meaning when used in this Schedule as they have in those enactments.

[Means of electronic delivery to the registrar

1A. In this Schedule—

"Web Incorporation Service" means a service by which the documents required to be delivered under section 9 of the 2006 Act are delivered to the registrar by electronic means using a website of the registrar;

"Software Incorporation Service" means a service by which the documents required to be delivered under section 9 of the 2006 Act are delivered to the registrar by electronic means other than using a website of the registrar.]

Meaning of "relevant documents"

2. (1)   For the purposes of paragraphs 7(e), 9(b) and 10(e) a "relevant document" is any document required or authorised to be delivered to the registrar in respect of a company, limited liability partnership or overseas company, as the case may be, by or under any provision of—

(a)   the 2006 Act, or

(b)   the 2000 Act, or

(c)   the OC Regulations, or

(d)   the LLP Regulations,

other than a document specified in sub-paragraph (2) below.

(2)   A document is not a relevant document if—

(a)   a fee is specified in this Schedule in relation to the registration of a document, or the performance by the registrar of a function, under any particular provision of the enactments listed in sub-paragraph (1) above; or

(b)   that document is required or authorised to be delivered to the registrar by or under an excluded provision; and, for these purposes, an excluded provision is any provision of the enactments listed in sub-paragraph (1) above which is specified in Part 3 of this Schedule.

Meaning of "relevant period"

3. (1)   In this Schedule in relation to a company or a limited liability partnership a "relevant period" means one of the following periods—

(a)   the period beginning with its incorporation and ending immediately after the delivery to the registrar of its first annual return; or

(b)   a period beginning immediately after the delivery to the registrar of an annual return and ending immediately after the delivery to the registrar of the next annual return.

(2)   In this Schedule in relation to an overseas company a "relevant period" means one of the following periods—

(a)   the period beginning with the registration of the documents required to be delivered to the registrar under Part 2 of the OC Regulations in respect of the opening of an establishment in the United Kingdom and ending immediately after the first delivery to the registrar of its accounting documents or, as the case may be, its annual accounts; or

(b)   a period beginning immediately after a delivery of accounting documents or annual accounts to the registrar and ending immediately after delivery to the registrar of the next accounting documents or annual accounts.

Meaning of "same day registration"

4. For the purposes of this Schedule documents are delivered for "same day registration" if—

(a) a request for same day registration and all documents required to be delivered to the registrar in connection with that registration are received by the registrar before 3.00 pm on the day in question; and

(b) the registration is completed on that day.

General

5. Where, in relation to any matter in respect of which a fee is payable under this Schedule, the means of delivery to the registrar of the documents required to be delivered in relation to that matter, or the form of those documents are not specified, that fee is payable only in respect of documents that are delivered in hard copy form.

6. Where, in relation to any matter in respect of which a fee is payable under this Schedule, no provision is made for same day registration of the documents required to be delivered to the registrar in relation to that matter, that fee is only payable in respect of the delivery of documents other than for same day registration.

NOTES

Commencement: 1 October 2009.

Para 1A: inserted by the Registrar of Companies (Fees) (Companies, Overseas Companies and Limited Liability Partnerships) (Amendment) Regulations 2011, SI 2011/309, reg 2(1), (2), as from 6 April 2011.

PART 2
FEES PAYABLE

Companies

[4.555]

7. Subject to paragraph 8, in respect of the performance by the registrar of his functions in relation to the registration of documents delivered to him in respect of companies, the fee specified in relation to each matter below is payable on the registration of the documents so delivered relating to that matter except as provided in sub-paragraphs (e) and (h)—

Matter in relation to which fee is payable	Amount of fee
[(a) for the registration of a company under section 14 of the 2006 Act—	
(i) where the required documents are delivered by means of the Web Incorporation Service,	£18.00
(ii) where the required documents are delivered by means of the Software Incorporation Service for same day registration,	£30.00
(iii) where the required documents are delivered by means of the Software Incorporation Service other than for same day registration,	£14.00
(iv) where the required documents are delivered in hard copy form for same day registration,	£100.00
(v) where the required documents are delivered in hard copy form other than for same day registration except as provided in Paragraphs (vi) to (viii),	£40.00
(vi) where the required documents are delivered in respect of a Welsh company in Welsh in hard copy form other than for same day registration,	£20.00
(vii) where the required documents are delivered in respect of a community interest company within the meaning of section 26 of the Companies (Audit, Investigations and Community Enterprise) Act 2004 in hard copy form other than for same day registration,	£20.00
(viii) where the required documents are delivered in respect of an unlimited company in hard copy form other than for same day registration;	£20.00]
[(aa) for the registration of a company under Chapter 1 of Part 33 of the 2006 Act;	£20.00]
(b) for the re-registration of a company under Part 7 of the 2006 Act—	
(i) where the required documents are delivered for same day registration,	£50.00
(ii) where the required documents are delivered other than for same day registration;	£20.00
(c) for the re-registration of a company as a private company under section 651 of the 2006 Act—	

Matter in relation to which fee is payable	Amount of fee
(i) where the required documents are delivered for same day registration,	£50.00
(ii) where the required documents are delivered other than for same day registration;	£20.00
(d) for the re-registration of a company as a private company under section 665 of the 2006 Act—	
(i) where the required documents are delivered for same day registration,	£50.00
(ii) where the required documents are delivered other than for same day registration;	£20.00
(e) for the registration of all relevant documents in respect of a company delivered during a relevant period payable at the end of that period on the registration of the annual return of the company under section 854 of the 2006 Act—	
(i) where the annual return is delivered in hard copy form,	[£40.00]
(ii) where the annual return is delivered by electronic means,	[£14.00]
(iii) where the annual return of a company is delivered in hard copy form with the exception of a list of members of that company exceeding 49 pages, and that list is delivered in electronic form other than by electronic means;	[£40.00]
(f) for the registration of a change of name of a company under section 80 of the 2006 Act (other than a change made in response to a direction of the Secretary of State under section 64 or 67 of the 2006 Act, a determination by a company names adjudicator or a court under section 73(5) or 74(5) of that Act or on the restoration of the company to the register under section 1033(2)(a)(i) of that Act)—	
(i) where the required documents are delivered [in hard copy form] for same day registration,	£50.00
(ii) where the required documents are delivered [in hard copy form] other than for same day registration;	£10.00
[(iii) where the required documents are delivered by electronic means for same day registration,	£30.00
(iv) where the required documents are delivered by electronic means other than for same day registration;	£8.00
(g) for the registration of a charge under Part 25 of the 2006 Act;	£13.00
(h) for the striking off the register of a company's name payable on an application under section 1003 of the 2006 Act.	£10.00
[(i) for the registration of the reduction of share capital of a company under section 644 of the 2006 Act—	
(i) where the required documents are delivered for same day registration,	£50.00
(ii) where the required documents are delivered other than for same day registration;	£10.00
(j) for the registration of the reduction of share capital of a company under section 649 of the 2006 Act—	
(i) where the required documents are delivered for same day registration,	£50.00
(ii) where the required documents are delivered other than for same day registration.	£10.00

8. (1)   The fee specified in paragraph 7(f) is not payable where the change of name relates solely to the indication of the particular type of company that the company whose name is changed becomes on its re-registration under Part 7 of the 2006 Act.

(2)   Where a change of name is conditional on the occurrence of an event and that event occurs on or after 1st October 2009 the giving of notice of the event to the registrar, under section 78(3)(b) of the 2006 Act, is the required document for the registration of the change of name for the purposes of this Schedule.

Limited liability partnerships

9. In respect of the performance by the registrar of his functions in relation to the registration of documents delivered to him in respect of limited liability partnerships the fee specified in relation to each matter set out below is payable on the registration of the documents so delivered relating to that matter except as provided in sub-paragraphs (b) and (e)—

Matter in relation to which fee is payable	Amount of fee
[(a) for the registration of a limited liability partnership under section 3 of the 2000 Act—	
(i) where the required documents are delivered by electronic means for same day registration,	£30.00
(ii) where the required documents are delivered by electronic means other than for same day registration,	£14.00
(iii) where the required documents are delivered in hard copy form for same day registration,	£100.00
(iv) where the required documents are delivered in hard copy form other than for same day registration except as provided in Paragraph (v),	£40.00
(v) where the required documents are delivered in respect of a Welsh limited liability partnership in Welsh in hard copy form other than for same day registration;	£20.00]
(b) for the registration of all relevant documents in respect of a limited liability partnership delivered during a relevant period payable at the end of that period on the registration of the annual return of the limited liability partnership under section 854 of the 2006 Act as applied to limited liability partnerships by regulation 30 of the LLP Regulations;	. . .
(i) where the annual return is delivered in hard copy form,	£40.00
(ii) where the annual return is delivered by electronic means;	£14.00]
(c) for the registration of a change of name of a limited liability partnership under paragraph 5 of the Schedule to the 2000 Act (other than a change made in response to a direction of the Secretary of State under section 67 of the 2006 Act as applied by regulation 11 of the LLP Regulations, a determination by a company names adjudicator or a court under section 73(5) or 74(5) of the 2006 Act as applied by regulation 12 of the LLP Regulations or on the restoration of the limited liability partnership to the register under section 1033(2)(a)(i) of the 2006 Act as applied by regulation 58 of the LLP Regulations)—	
(i) where the required documents are delivered [in hard copy form] for same day registration,	£50.00
(ii) where the required documents are delivered [in hard copy form] other than for same day registration;	£10.00
[(iii) where the required documents are delivered by electronic means for same day registration,	£30.00
(iv) where the required documents are delivered by electronic means other than for same day registration;	£8.00]
(d) for the registration of a charge under Part 25 of the 2006 Act as applied to limited liability partnerships by Part 9 of the LLP Regulations;	£13.00
(e) for the striking off the register of a limited liability partnership's name payable on an application under section 1003 of the 2006 Act as applied to limited liability partnerships by regulation 51 of the LLP Regulations.	£10.00

Overseas companies

10. In respect of the performance by the registrar of his functions in relation to the registration of documents delivered to him in respect of overseas companies the fee specified in relation to each matter set out below is payable on the registration of the documents so delivered relating to that matter except as provided in sub-paragraph (e)—

Matter in relation to which fee is payable	Amount of fee
(a) for the registration of documents required to be delivered to the registrar under Part 2 of the OC Regulations in respect of the opening of an establishment in the United Kingdom—	
(i) where the required documents are delivered for same day registration,	[£100.00]

Matter in relation to which fee is payable	Amount of fee
(ii) where the required documents are delivered other than for same day registration;	£20.00
(b) for the registration of an alteration to the registered particulars of an overseas company under Part 3 of the OC Regulations where the alteration is a change of the name of the overseas company—	
(i) where the required documents are delivered for same day registration,	£50.00
(ii) where the required documents are delivered other than for same day registration;	£10.00
(c) for the registration of an alternative name specified in accordance with section 1048 of the 2006 Act—	
(i) where the required documents are delivered for same day registration,	£50.00
(ii) where the required documents are delivered other than for same day registration;	£10.00
(d) for the registration of a charge under Part 3 of the OC Charges Regulations;	£13.00
(e) for the registration of all relevant documents in respect of an overseas company delivered during a relevant period payable at the end of that period on registration of the accounting documents or, as the case may be, the annual accounts of the overseas company required to be delivered to the registrar under Parts 5 and 6 of the OC Regulations.	[£20.00]

NOTES

Commencement: 1 October 2009.

Para 7 is amended as follows:

Sub-para (a) substituted by the Registrar of Companies (Fees) (Companies, Overseas Companies and Limited Liability Partnerships) (Amendment) Regulations 2011, SI 2011/309, reg 2(3), as from 6 April 2011 (see further the final note below).

Sub-para (aa) inserted by the Registrar of Companies (Fees) (Amendment) Regulations 2009, SI 2009/2439, reg 5, as from 1 October 2009.

The fees in the second column in sub-paras (e)(i), (ii), (iii) were substituted by SI 2011/309, reg 2(4), (5), (6) respectively, as from 6 April 2011 (see further the final note below).

The words in square brackets in sub-paras (f)(i), (ii) were inserted by SI 2011/309, reg 2(7), (8) respectively, as from 6 April 2011 (see further the final note below).

Sub-paras (f)(iii), (iv) were inserted by SI 2011/309, reg 2(9), as from 6 April 2011 (see further the final note below).

Sub-paras (i), (j) were inserted by SI 2011/309, reg 2(10), as from 6 April 2011 (see further the final note below).

Para 9 is amended as follows:

Sub-para (a) substituted by SI 2011/309, reg 2(11), as from 6 April 2011 (see further the final note below).

Sum omitted from sub-para (b) revoked, and paras (i), (ii) added, by SI 2011/309, reg 2(12), as from 6 April 2011 (see further the final note below).

The words in square brackets in sub-paras (c)(i), (ii) were inserted by SI 2011/309, reg 2(13), (14) respectively, as from 6 April 2011 (see further the final note below).

Sub-paras (c)(iii), (iv) were inserted by SI 2011/309, reg 2(15), as from 6 April 2011 (see further the final note below).

Para 10: the fees in the second column in sub-paras (a)(i), (e) were substituted by SI 2011/309, reg 2(16), (17) respectively, as from 6 April 2011 (see further the final note below).

Regulation 5(1) of the Registrar of Companies (Fees) (Companies, Overseas Companies and Limited Liability Partnerships) (Amendment) Regulations 2011, SI 2011/309 provides that the fees prescribed by reg 2 of those Regulations (ie, the amendments noted above) apply: (a) in relation to paragraphs (4), (5), (6) and (12) to the registration of an annual return delivered to the registrar on or after 6 April 2011; and (b) in relation to the other paragraphs to any registration in respect of which every document necessary for the registrar to effect such an act is delivered to the registrar on or after that date.

PART 3
PROVISIONS REFERRED TO IN PARAGRAPH 2(2)(B)

Excluded provisions

[4.556]
11. For the purposes of paragraph 2(2)(b) of this Schedule, the excluded provisions are—
  (a) in relation to a company, sections 108, . . . 1024, 1088, 1094 and 1095 of the 2006 Act;
  (b) in relation to a limited liability partnership, sections 1024, 1088, 1094 and 1095 of the 2006 Act as applied by regulations 56, 66 and 67 of the LLP Regulations; and
  (c) in relation to an overseas company, sections 1088, 1094 and 1095 of the 2006 Act.

NOTES

Commencement: 1 October 2009.

Para 11: figures omitted revoked by the Registrar of Companies (Fees) (Companies, Overseas Companies and Limited Liability Partnerships) (Amendment) Regulations 2011, SI 2011/309, reg 2(1), (18), as from 6 April 2011.

SCHEDULE 2
THE PERFORMANCE OF FUNCTIONS RELATING TO THE INSPECTION OR PROVISION OF COPIES OF DOCUMENTS KEPT BY THE REGISTRAR
Regulation 4

PART 1
INTERPRETATION

Means by which the register may be inspected and copies provided

[4.557]
1. In this Schedule—

"Companies House Contact Centre" and "CHCC" mean a contact centre maintained by or on behalf of the registrar through which a facility is provided for applying by telephone, fax and email for copies of material on the register;

"Companies House Direct" and "CHD" mean the service by which information is accessed by the applicant in Hyper Text Markup Language using a website of the registrar by delivering a non-encrypted access code;

"Companies House Information Centre" and "CHIC" mean an office of the registrar where facilities are made available for applicants to inspect the register and to obtain copies of material on the register and "searchroom terminal" means a computer terminal operated by an applicant at a CHIC;

"Extranet" means the service by which information is accessed by means of the access codes of the applicant in Hyper Text Markup Language using a website of the registrar;

"WebCHeck" means the service by which information is accessed by the applicant in Hypertext Markup Language using a website of the registrar with no requirement for the applicant to deliver an access code;

"XML Gateway" and "XML" mean the service by which information is accessed by the applicant in Extensible Markup Language by means of a partially encrypted access code.

Company and limited liability partnership reports

2. In this Schedule—

"company report" means a report containing the information relating to a company set out in Part 3 of this Schedule in so far as recorded by the registrar in records kept by the registrar for the purposes of the 2006 Act;

"limited liability partnership report" means a report containing the information relating to a limited liability partnership set out in Part 4 of this Schedule in so far as recorded by the registrar in records kept by the registrar for the purposes of the 2006 Act as applied to limited liability partnerships, by the LLP Regulations and the Limited Liability Partnerships (Accounts and Audit) (Application of Companies Act 2006) Regulations 2008.

Document packages

3. In this Schedule—

a "document package" means in relation to a company, one of the sets of copies of documents relating to a company (in so far as such documents are delivered to the registrar in respect of the company) as described in one of the paragraphs in Part 5 of this Schedule and with the maximum number of documents in each package being as specified in Part 2 of this Schedule, with the documents in the package being primarily determinable in reverse order of the dates of delivery to the registrar; and

a "document package" means in relation to a limited liability partnership, one of the sets of copies of documents relating to a limited liability partnership (in so far as such documents are delivered to the registrar in respect of the limited liability partnership) as described in one of the paragraphs in Part 6 of this Schedule and with the maximum number of documents in each package being as specified in Part 2 of this Schedule, with the documents in the package being primarily determinable in reverse order of the dates of delivery to the registrar.

Meaning of "same day delivery" and "same day collection"

4. For the purposes of this Schedule certificates and certified copies are provided for "same day delivery" or "same day collection" if—

(a)   a request for same day delivery or same day collection is received by the registrar before 2.00 pm on the day in question; and

(b)   the appropriate certificate or certified copy is issued to the applicant on that day.

Long list of members

5. Except where expressly provided to the contrary any references in this Schedule to a "document" or to "information" does not include a reference to a "long list of members" and, for the purposes of this Schedule, a "long list of members" has the meaning given to it in paragraph 12.

Part 4   CA 2006 SIs

Enactments and legal entities

6. (1)   Paragraph 1 of Schedule 1 to these Regulations applies to this Schedule as it does to that Schedule.

(2)   References to a company in this Schedule include a reference to an overseas company except where express provision is made to the contrary.

NOTES

Commencement: 1 October 2009.

PART 2
FEES PAYABLE

Companies House Direct

[4.558]

7. In respect of the performance of the registrar's functions in relation to the inspection of the register and the provision of copies of material on the register, where an application for inspection or a copy is made by means of CHD, the following fees are payable—

Matter in relation to which fee is payable	Amount of fee
(a) for subscribing to CHD, for each calendar month payable in arrears at the end of that month;	[£4.00]
(b) for the inspection by means of CHD of particulars of—	
(i) the directors and secretary of a company,	£1.00
(ii) directorships held by a named person,	£1.00
(iii) the members of a limited liability partnership,	£1.00
(iv) memberships of limited liability partnerships held by a named person;	£1.00
(c) for a copy provided by means of CHD of a company report or a limited liability partnership report;	£1.00
(d) for the inspection by means of CHD of a statement of particulars of a charge registered in respect of a company or a limited liability partnership;	£1.00
(e) for a copy provided by means of CHD (without prior inspection) of a document in respect of a company or a limited liability partnership;	£1.00
(f) for the inspection and provision of a copy of a document, by means of CHD, in respect of a company or a limited liability partnership;	£4.00
(g) for the delivery by post in hard copy form of any document specified in sub-paragraphs (c), (e) and (f) above applied for by means of CHD;	£3.00
(h) for the delivery by post in hard copy form of a document package of up to 50 documents applied for by means of CHD;	£20.00
(i) for the provision by means of CHD of a document package of up to 50 documents;	£4.00
(j) for a copy of a document or extract from a document in hard copy form, certified under section 1091 of the 2006 Act in relation to companies, and under that provision as applied to limited liability partnerships by regulation 66 of the LLP Regulations, applied for by means of CHD—	
(i) where that copy is delivered by post by same day delivery,	[£60.00]
(ii) where that copy is delivered by post other than by same day delivery,	[£20.00]
(iii) where that copy is made available for collection at a CHIC other than same day collection,	[£20.00]
(iv) where that copy is made available for collection at a CHIC for same day collection;	[£60.00]
[(k) for a copy certificate of incorporation in hard copy form under section 1065 of the 2006 Act, in relation to companies other than overseas companies, and under that provision as applied to limited liability partnerships by regulation 61 of the LLP Regulations, applied for by means of CHD—	
(i) where that certificate is delivered by post other than by same day delivery and it is the first certificate relating to that body corporate provided to an applicant on any one occasion,	£20.00

Matter in relation to which fee is payable	Amount of fee
(ii) where that certificate is delivered by post by same day delivery and it is the first certificate relating to that body corporate provided to an applicant on any one occasion,	£60.00
(iii) where it is an additional certificate delivered by post (by same day delivery or not) relating to the same body corporate provided to the same applicant on the same occasion;	£10.00]
[(l) for a copy certificate of incorporation of the type referred to in sub-paragraph (k) above applied for by means of CHD and made available for collection at a CHIC—	
(i) where that certificate is made available other than for same day collection and it is the first certificate relating to that body corporate provided to an applicant on any one occasion,	£20.00
(ii) where that certificate is made available for same day collection and it is the first certificate relating to that body corporate provided to an applicant on any one occasion,	£60.00
(iii) where it is an additional certificate made available for collection (for same day collection or not) relating to the same body corporate provided to the same applicant on the same occasion.	£10.00]

Extranet

8. In respect of the performance of the registrar's functions in relation to the inspection of the register and the provision of copies of material on the register, where the application for inspection or a copy is made by means of Extranet, the following fees are payable—

Matter in relation to which fee is payable	Amount of fee
(a) for subscribing to Extranet, for each calendar month payable in arrears at the end of that month;	[£4.70]
(b) for the inspection by means of Extranet of particulars of—	
(i) the directors and secretary of a company,	£1.00
(ii) directorships held by a named person,	£1.00
(iii) the members of a limited liability partnership,	£1.00
(iv) memberships of limited liability partnerships held by a named person;	£1.00
(c) for a copy provided by means of Extranet of a company report or a limited liability partnership report;	£1.00
(d) for the inspection by means of Extranet of a statement of particulars of a charge registered in respect of a company, or a limited liability partnership;	£1.00
(e) for a copy provided by means of Extranet (without prior inspection) of a document in respect of a company or a limited liability partnership;	£1.00
(f) for the inspection and provision of a copy of a document by means of Extranet in respect of a company or a limited liability partnership;	£4.00
(g) for the provision by means of Extranet of a document package of up to 50 documents.	£4.00

WebCHeck

9. In respect of the performance of the registrar's functions in relation to the provision of copies of material on the register, where the application for a copy is made by means of WebCHeck, the following fees are payable—

Matter in relation to which fee is payable	Amount of fee
(a) for a copy provided by means of WebCHeck (without prior inspection) of a document in respect of a company or a limited liability partnership;	£1.00
(b) for a copy provided by means of WebCHeck of a company report or a limited liability partnership report.	£1.00

XML

10. In respect of the performance of the registrar's functions in relation to the inspection of the register and the provision of copies of material on the register, where the application for inspection or a copy is made by means of XML, the following fees are payable—

Matter in relation to which fee is payable	Amount of fee
(a) for subscribing to XML, for each calendar month payable in arrears at the end of that month;	[£4.70]
(b) for the inspection by means of XML of particulars of—	
(i) the directors and secretary of a company,	£1.00
(ii) directorships held by a named person,	£1.00
(iii) the members of a limited liability partnership,	£1.00
(iv) memberships of limited liability partnerships held by a named person;	£1.00
(c) for a copy provided by means of XML (without prior inspection) of a document in respect of a company or a limited liability partnership.	£1.00

Companies House Information Centre

11. In respect of the performance of the registrar's functions in relation to the inspection of the register and the provision of copies of material on the register, where the application for inspection or a copy is made at a CHIC, the following fees are payable—

Matter in relation to which fee is payable	Amount of fee
(a) for the inspection by means of a search room terminal of particulars of—	
(i) the directors and secretary of a company,	£1.00
(ii) directorships held by a named person,	£1.00
(iii) the members of a limited liability partnership,	£1.00
(iv) memberships of a limited liability partnership held by a named person;	£1.00
(b) for the inspection by means of a searchroom terminal of a statement of particulars of a charge registered in respect of a company or a limited liability partnership;	£1.00
(c) for the inspection by means of a searchroom terminal of a company report or a limited liability partnership report;	£1.00
(d) for the provision of a document package of up to 25 documents applied for at a CHIC or by means of a searchroom terminal and made available for collection in hard copy form at a CHIC;	£7.00
(e) for the inspection of a document, by means of a searchroom terminal, in respect of a company or a limited liability partnership;	£2.00
(f) for a copy, in hard copy form, provided by means of a searchroom terminal, (without prior inspection) of a document in respect of a company or a limited liability partnership and made available for collection at a CHIC;	£1.00
(g) for a copy of any document specified in sub-paragraphs (a) to (c) and (e) above applied for at a CHIC and made available for collection at a CHIC;	£3.00
(h) for the inspection, at a CHIC, of an original document delivered to the registrar in hard copy form in respect of a company or a limited liability partnership when the record of the contents kept by the registrar is illegible or unavailable;	£6.00
(i) for the inspection and for a copy in hard copy form of a document of the type specified in sub-paragraph (h) above;	£9.00
(j) for a copy in hard copy form of a screen of information in respect of a company or a limited liability partnership displayed on a searchroom terminal and made available for collection at a CHIC;	£0.10
(k) for a copy in hard copy form of a document or extract from a document certified under section 1091 of the 2006 Act in relation to companies, and under that provision as applied to limited liability partnerships by regulation 66 of the LLP Regulations, applied for at a CHIC and delivered to the applicant by post—	

Matter in relation to which fee is payable	Amount of fee
(i) where the copy consists of up to 10 pages (including the tenth page),	[£20.00]
(ii) for each subsequent page of the copy,	£1.00
(iii) where any copy is delivered by same day delivery;	[£60.00]
(l) for a copy in hard copy form of a document or extract from a document certified under section 1091 of the 2006 Act in relation to companies, and under that provision as applied to limited liability partnerships by regulation 66 of the LLP Regulations, applied for at a CHIC and made available for collection at a CHIC—	
(i) where the copy consists of up to 10 pages (including the tenth page),	[£20.00]
(ii) for each subsequent page of the copy,	£1.00
(iii) where the copy is made available for same day collection;	[£60.00]
[(m) for a copy certificate of incorporation in hard copy form under section 1065 of the 2006 Act, in relation to companies other than overseas companies, and under that provision as applied to limited liability partnerships by regulation 61 of the LLP Regulations, applied for at a CHIC—	
(i) where that certificate is delivered by post other than by same day delivery and it is the first certificate relating to that body corporate provided to an applicant on any one occasion,	£20.00
(ii) where that certificate is delivered by post by same day delivery and it is the first certificate relating to that body corporate provided to an applicant on any one occasion,	£60.00
(iii) where it is an additional certificate delivered by post (by same day delivery or not) relating to the same body corporate provided to the same applicant on the same occasion;	£10.00]
[(n) for a copy certificate of incorporation, in hard copy form, of the type referred to in sub-paragraph (m) above applied for at a CHIC and made available for collection at a CHIC—	
(i) where that certificate is made available other than for same day collection and it is the first certificate relating to that body corporate provided to an applicant on any one occasion,	£20.00
(ii) where that certificate is made available for same day collection and it is the first certificate relating to that body corporate provided to an applicant on any one occasion,	£60.00
(iii) where it is an additional certificate made available for collection (for same day collection or not) relating to the same body corporate provided to the same applicant on the same occasion.	£10.00]

Companies House Contact Centre

12. In respect of the performance of the registrar's functions in relation to provision of copies of material on the register, where the application for a copy is made by means of a CHCC, the following fees are payable—

Matter in relation to which fee is payable	Amount of fee
(a) for a copy, provided on an application to a CHCC, of a page of the registrar's index of company names kept under section 1099 of the 2006 Act delivered by post;	£2.00
(b) for a copy of the type specified in sub-paragraph (a) above, provided on an application to a CHCC, delivered by email;	£2.00
(c) for a copy, in hard copy form, provided on an application to a CHCC, of the particulars of the directors and secretary of a company or the members of a limited liability partnership delivered by post;	£3.00
(d) for a copy, provided on an application to a CHCC, of the particulars of the directors and secretary of a company or the members of a limited liability partnership delivered by email;	£3.00
(e) for a copy, provided on an application to a CHCC, of a statement of particulars of a charge registered in respect of a company or a limited liability partnership delivered by post;	£3.00

Matter in relation to which fee is payable	Amount of fee
(f) for a copy, provided on an application to a CHCC, of a statement of particulars of a charge registered in respect of a company or a limited liability partnership delivered by email;	£3.00
(g) for a copy, in hard copy form, provided on an application to a CHCC, of a company report or a limited liability partnership report delivered by post;	£3.00
(h) for a copy, provided on an application to a CHCC, of a company report or a limited liability partnership report delivered by email;	£3.00
(i) for a copy, in hard copy form, provided on an application to a CHCC, of a document in respect of a company or a limited liability partnership delivered by post;	£3.00
(j) for a copy, provided on an application to a CHCC, of a document in respect of a company or a limited liability partnership delivered by email;	£3.00
(k) for a copy, provided on an application to a CHCC, of an original document delivered to the register before 1st January 1978 and kept by the registrar in hard copy form, in respect of a company and delivered by post;	£9.00
(l) for a copy, in hard copy form, of a long list of members of a company, other than an overseas company, provided on an application to a CHCC, delivered by post—	
(i) for the first 50 pages of the copy,	£12.50
(ii) for each additional page of the copy;	£0.20
(m) for a copy, in hard copy form, provided on an application to a CHCC, of a document or extract from a document, certified under section 1091 of the 2006 Act in relation to companies, and under that provision as applied to limited liability partnerships by regulation 66 of the LLP Regulations—	
(i) where that copy is delivered by post other than by same day delivery,	[£20.00]
(ii) where that copy is delivered by same day delivery;	[£60.00]
(n) for a copy, in hard copy form, provided on an application to a CHCC of a document or extract from a document of the type specified in sub-paragraph (m) above and made available for collection at a CHIC—	
(i) where that copy is made available for collection other than by same day collection,	[£20.00]
(ii) where that copy is made available for same day collection;	[£60.00]
[(o) for a copy certificate of incorporation provided on an application to a CHCC, in hard copy form, under section 1065 of the 2006 Act, in relation to companies other than overseas companies, and under that provision as applied to limited liability partnerships by regulation 61 of the LLP Regulations—	
(i) where that certificate is delivered by post other than by same day delivery and it is the first certificate relating to that body corporate provided to an applicant on any one occasion,	£20.00
(ii) where that certificate is delivered by post by same day delivery and it is the first certificate relating to that body corporate provided to an applicant on any one occasion,	£60.00
(iii) where it is an additional certificate delivered by post (by same day delivery or not) relating to the same body corporate provided to the same applicant on the same occasion;	£10.00]
[(p) for a copy certificate of incorporation of the type referred to in sub-paragraph (o) above, provided on an application to a CHCC, and made available for collection at a CHIC—	
(i) where that certificate is made available other than for same day collection and it is the first certificate relating to that body corporate provided to an applicant on any one occasion,	£20.00
(ii) where that certificate is made available for same day collection and it is the first certificate relating to that body corporate provided to an applicant on any one occasion,	£60.00
(iii) where it is an additional certificate made available for collection (for same day collection or not) relating to the same body corporate provided to the same applicant on the same occasion.	£10.00]

and, for the purposes of this paragraph a "long list of members" means a list of members delivered to the registrar under section 856A or 856B of the 2006 Act in relation to companies which exceeds 49 pages and which is delivered in hard copy form.

NOTES

Commencement: 1 October 2009.

Para 7 is amended as follows:

The fees in the second column in sub-paras (a), (j)(i), (ii), (iii), (iv) were substituted by the Registrar of Companies (Fees) (Companies, Overseas Companies and Limited Liability Partnerships) (Amendment) Regulations 2011, SI 2011/309, reg 3(1)(a), (b), (c), (d), (e) respectively, as from 6 April 2011 (see further the final note below).

Sub-paras (k), (l) were substituted by SI 2011/309, reg 3(1)(f), (g) respectively, as from 6 April 2011 (see further the final note below).

Para 8: the fee in the second column in para (a) was substituted by SI 2011/309, reg 3(2), as from 6 April 2011 (see further the final note below).

Para 10: the fee in the second column in para (a) was substituted by SI 2011/309, reg 3(3), as from 6 April 2011 (see further the final note below).

Para 11 is amended as follows:

The fees in the second column in sub-paras (k)(i), (iii), (l)(i), (iii) were substituted by SI 2011/309, reg 3(4)(a), (b), (c), (d) respectively, as from 6 April 2011 (see further the final note below).

Sub-paras (m), (n) were substituted by SI 2011/309, reg 3(1)(e), (f) respectively, as from 6 April 2011 (see further the final note below).

Para 12 is amended as follows:

The fees in the second column in sub-paras (m)(i), (ii), (n)(i), (ii) were substituted by SI 2011/309, reg 3(5)(a), (b), (c), (d) respectively, as from 6 April 2011 (see further the final note below).

Sub-paras (o), (p) were substituted by SI 2011/309, reg 3(1)(e), (f) respectively, as from 6 April 2011 (see further the final note below).

Regulation 5(2) of the Registrar of Companies (Fees) (Companies, Overseas Companies and Limited Liability Partnerships) (Amendment) Regulations 2011, SI 2011/309 provides that the fees prescribed by reg 3 of those Regulations (ie, the amendments noted above) apply: (a) in relation to paragraphs (1)(a), (2) and (3) in respect of a subscription payable on or after 6 April 2011; and (b) in relation to the other paragraphs in that regulation in respect of an application received by the registrar on or after that date.

PART 3
CONTENTS OF COMPANY REPORT

Companies register information

[4.559]

13. Information relating to the company including its registered number, its date of incorporation, its name and the number of registered charges.

14. Any previous names of the company during the period of 20 years prior to the date to which the company report is made up.

15. A list of dates including those relating to latest annual accounts and annual returns and dates for the next such documents to be delivered to the registrar.

Appointments and charges

16. At the option of the applicant, either or both of the following sets of particulars—
   (a)   particulars of the directors and secretary of the company;
   (b)   particulars of charges registered in respect of the company;
except that an applicant using WebCHeck can not elect to have only the particulars under sub-paragraph (b).

Recent filing history

17. List of documents delivered to the registrar during the previous 18 months up to a maximum of 100 documents listed in the reverse order of the dates of delivery excluding returns of allotments unless requested by the applicant.

NOTES

Commencement: 1 October 2009.

PART 4
CONTENTS OF LIMITED LIABILITY PARTNERSHIP REPORT

Limited liability partnership register information

[4.560]

18. Information relating to a limited liability partnership including its registered number, its date of incorporation, its name and the number of registered charges.

19. Any previous names of a limited liability partnership.

Part 4   CA 2006 SIs

20. A list of dates including those relating to latest annual accounts and annual returns and dates for the next such documents to be delivered to the registrar.

Appointments and charges

21. At the option of the applicant, either or both of the following sets of particulars—
  (a) particulars of the members of a limited liability partnership;
  (b) particulars of charges registered in respect of a limited liability partnership;
except that an applicant using WebCHeck can not elect to have only the particulars under sub-paragraph (b).

Recent filing history

22. List of documents delivered to the registrar during the previous 18 months up to a maximum of 100 documents listed in the reverse order of the dates of delivery.

NOTES
Commencement: 1 October 2009.

PART 5
DOCUMENT PACKAGES FOR COMPANIES

[4.561]
Listed below are the document packages and the documents included in each package:

General package

23. Incorporation documents and name change documents.

Resolutions and memorandum and articles of association.

Any documents relating to strike-off.

Latest annual accounts or, as the case may be, accounting documents and notices specifying accounting reference date or extending the period allowed for laying and delivering accounts and reports.

Latest annual return.

Notification of change among directors or in secretary or their particulars and changes in registered office in each case since the date to which the latest annual return was made up.

(at the option of the applicant) Returns of allotments of shares delivered to the registrar since the date to which the latest annual return giving full particulars of the members is made up.

(long list of members not available).

Current package

24. Latest annual accounts or, as the case may be, accounting documents and notices specifying accounting reference date or extending the period allowed for laying and delivering accounts and reports.

Latest annual return.

Notification of change among directors or in secretary or their particulars and changes in registered office in each case since the date to which the latest annual return was made up.

Any documents relating to strike-off.

(at the option of the applicant) Returns of allotments of shares delivered to the registrar since the date to which the latest annual return giving full particulars of the members is made up.

(long list of members not available).

Charges package

25. Charge related documents since incorporation.

The company report containing the particulars in paragraph 16(b) above but not the particulars in paragraph 16(a).

Insolvency package

26. Company voluntary arrangements, administration, receivership, winding up, dissolution and strike-off related documents delivered to the registrar since April 1995.

Accounts package

27. Annual accounts, or as the case may be, accounting documents and notices specifying accounting reference date or extending the period allowed for laying and delivering accounts and reports delivered to the registrar over the previous 5 years.

The company report.

Constitution package

28. The most recently delivered to the registrar of any of the documents specified below—

The certificate of incorporation where issued on incorporation, a change of name or re-registration.

The articles of association, or in the case of an existing company, the memorandum and articles of association.

Any resolutions and agreements affecting a company's constitution.

The statement of capital contained in the most recent annual return, or, where no annual return has been delivered, the statement of capital required by section 10 of the 2006 Act.

Any statement of capital delivered to the registrar under any of the following provisions of the 2006 Act—

Sections 108, 555, 619, 621, 625, 627, 644, 649, 663, 689, 708 and 730.

For the purposes of this paragraph an "existing company" is a company to which section 28 of the 2006 Act applies and a "statement of capital" is one delivered to the registrar under any of the provisions listed in respect of statements of capital above.

Package of documents delivered in a calendar year selected by the applicant

29. Documents delivered to the registrar by the company in a calendar year selected by the applicant (not available for years prior to 2003).

NOTES

Commencement: 1 October 2009.

PART 6
DOCUMENT PACKAGES FOR LIMITED LIABILITY PARTNERSHIPS

[4.562]

Listed below are the document packages and the documents included in each package:

General package

30. Incorporation document and name change documents.

Any documents relating to strike-off.

Latest annual accounts and notices specifying accounting reference date or extending the period allowed for delivering the accounts and the auditor's report.

Latest annual return.

Notification of change among members or their particulars and changes in registered office in each case since the date to which the latest annual return was made up.

Current package

31. Latest annual accounts and notices specifying accounting reference date or extending the period allowed for delivering the accounts and the auditor's report.

Latest annual return.

Notification of change among members or their particulars and changes in registered office in each case since the date to which the latest annual return was made up.

Any documents relating to strike-off.

Charges package

32. Charge related documents since incorporation.

The limited liability partnership report containing the particulars in paragraph 21(b) above but not the particulars in paragraph 21(a).

Insolvency package

33. Limited liability partnership voluntary arrangements, administration, receivership, winding up, dissolution and strike-off related documents delivered to the registrar since April 2001.

Accounts package

34. Annual accounts and notices specifying accounting reference date or extending the period allowed for delivering the accounts and the auditor's report delivered to the registrar over the previous 5 years.

The limited liability partnership report.

Package of documents delivered in a calendar year selected by the applicant

35. Documents delivered to the registrar of companies by the limited liability partnership in a calendar year selected by the applicant (not available for years prior to 2003).

NOTES
Commencement: 1 October 2009.

SCHEDULE 3
THE PERFORMANCE OF FUNCTIONS RELATING TO THE DISCLOSURE OF PROTECTED INFORMATION

Regulation 5

[4.563]

1. In respect of the performance of the registrar's functions in relation to the inspection of the register and the provision of copies of material on the register, where that material is protected information to which section 242(1) of the 2006 Act or that section as applied to limited liability partnerships by regulation 19 of the LLP Regulations or regulation 21(1) of the OC Regulations apply, the following fees are payable—

Matters in relation to which a fee is payable	Amount of fee
(a) for an application by a specified public authority or a credit reference agency under regulations 2 and 3 of the CDA Regulations or those regulations as applied to limited liability partnerships by regulation 19 of the LLP Regulations or regulations 23 and 24 of the OC Regulations for the registrar to determine whether to disclose protected information to that authority or agency;	£140.00
(b) for an application by a specified public authority or a credit reference agency for the provision by encrypted electronic data transfer of the directors' snapshot package;	[£3,600.00]
(c) for a specified public authority or credit reference agency subscribing to the provision by encrypted electronic data transfer of the directors' daily update package for the period of one calendar year;	[£43,000.00]
(d) for the provision by means of an encrypted email of the particulars of the usual residential address of a specified director on the request of a specified public authority or a credit reference agency.	£5.00

Interpretation

2. In this Schedule—
a "directors' snapshot package" means a set of documents containing particulars of the usual residential address of all directors and related information contained in material on the register on the date on which the request for that set of documents is fulfilled by the registrar;
a "directors' daily update package" means a set of documents containing those particulars of the usual residential address of all directors and related information which are contained in material on the register on a particular day and which are sent to the subscriber on the following day or, where the particulars are delivered on a Saturday or Sunday, on the following Tuesday;
"particulars of the usual residential address of all directors" or "particulars of the usual residential address of a specified director" means the following information—
the house name or number,
the street,
the area,
the post town,
the region,
the country and
the postcode;
"related information" means the following information in relation to a director—
the name of the director,
the date of birth of the director,
the registered number or numbers of the company or companies, and
if appropriate a statement that the usual residential address is the same as a service address;
"the CDA Regulations" mean the Companies (Disclosure of Address) Regulations 2009 and "the OC Regulations" have the same meaning given to them in paragraph 1 of Schedule 1 to these Regulations.

3. In this Schedule—
(a) any reference to a director is also a reference to a member of a limited liability partnership; and
(b) any such reference in respect of an overseas company is also a reference to a permanent representative of that company as that expression is used in the OC Regulations.

NOTES
Commencement: 1 October 2009.
Para 1: sums in square brackets in para (b) and (c) of column 2 substituted by the Registrar of Companies (Fees) (Companies, Overseas Companies and Limited Liability Partnerships) (Amendment) Regulations 2011, SI 2011/309, reg 4(a), (b) respectively, as from 6 April 2011. Note that reg 5(3) of the 2011 Regulations provides that the fees prescribed by reg 4 apply: (a) in relation to the first-mentioned amendment to an application received by the registrar on or after 6 April 2011; and (b) in relation to the second-mentioned amendment in respect of a subscription payable on or after that date.

SCHEDULE 4
APPLICATION OF CONTINUING PROVISIONS

Regulation 7

[4.564]

1. Listed below are the circumstances when a fee required by the continuing provisions is payable—

(a) where an annual return of a company or a limited liability partnership made up to a date on or before 30th September 2009 is delivered to the registrar under section 363 of the Companies Act 1985 or that provision as applied to limited liability partnerships by the Limited Liability Partnerships Regulations 2001;

(b) where any resolution of a company, or other notification, confirming the satisfaction of conditions for a change of name of the company on or before 30th September 2009 is delivered to the registrar on or after 1st October 2009;

(c) where the documents required for the registration of a charge by a company, an oversea company or a limited liability partnership under Part 12 of the Companies Act 1985 (including that Part as applied to limited liability partnerships) are delivered to the registrar on or after 1st October 2009 and the charge was created, the property subject to the charge acquired, or the first debenture of the series was executed on or before the 30th September 2009;

(d) where the documents required for the registration of a charge of the type described in sub-paragraph (c) above are not delivered within the time specified for their delivery and the documents are subsequently delivered pursuant to an order of the court under the enactments specified in that sub-paragraph;

(e) where the documents required for the registration of a charge by a company, a company incorporated outside Northern Ireland or a limited liability partnership under Part 13 of the Companies (Northern Ireland) Order 1986 (including that Part as applied to limited liability partnerships by the Limited Liability Partnerships Regulations (Northern Ireland) 2004) are delivered to the registrar on or after 1st October 2009 and the charge was created, the property subject to the charge acquired, or the first debenture of the series was executed on or before 30th September 2009;

(f) where the documents required for the registration of a charge of the type described in sub-paragraph (e) above are not delivered within the time specified for their delivery and the documents are subsequently delivered pursuant to an order of the court under the enactments specified in that sub-paragraph;

(g) where an annual return made up to a date on or before 30th September 2009 is delivered to the registrar by a company or a limited liability partnership under article 371 of the Companies (Northern Ireland) Order 1986 or that provision as applied to limited liability partnerships;

(h) where an oversea company delivers accounts to the registrar under Part 23 of the Companies Act 1985 on or after 1st October 2009 in respect of a period or financial year specified in paragraphs 23, 24, 25 and 26 of Schedule 8 to the OC Regulations ending on or before 30th September 2009;

(i) where a company incorporated outside Northern Ireland delivers copies of accounts and reports to the registrar under Chapter 2 of Part 23 of the Companies (Northern Ireland) Order 1986 on or after 1st October 2009 in respect of a period or financial year specified in paragraphs 23, 24, 25 and 26 of the OC Regulations ending on or before 30 September 2009.

2. In this Schedule—

(a) words and expressions defined in Part 1 of Schedule 1 to these Regulations have the same meaning when used in this Schedule; and

(b) words and expressions defined or used in the Companies Act 1985 or the Companies (Northern Ireland) Order 1986, have the same meaning when so used.

NOTES
Commencement: 1 October 2009.

SCHEDULE 5

Regulation 9

[4.565]

Regulation	Extent of Revocation
The Companies (Fees) Regulations (Northern Ireland) 1995	The whole Regulations with the exception of Fees Nos 4 and 8 in the Schedule
The Companies (Competent Authority) (Fees) Regulations 2002	The whole Regulations
The Limited Liability Partnerships (Competent Authority) (Fees) Regulations 2002	The whole Regulations
The Companies (Fees) Regulations 2004	The whole Regulations with the exception of Fees Nos 5 (5(a) and 5(b)), 6, and 9 in Schedule 4
The Limited Liability Partnerships (Fees) Regulations 2004	The whole Regulations with the exception of Fees Nos 2 and 4 in Schedule 3
The Limited Liability Partnerships (Fees) Regulations (Northern Ireland) 2004	The whole Regulations with the exception of Fees Nos 2 and 5 in the Schedule
The Limited Liability Partnerships (Records Inspection) (Fee) Regulations (Northern Ireland) 2004	The whole Regulations

NOTES

Commencement: 1 October 2009.

REGISTRAR OF COMPANIES (FEES) (LIMITED PARTNERSHIPS AND NEWSPAPER PROPRIETORS) REGULATIONS 2009

(SI 2009/2392)

NOTES

Made: 28 August 2009.
Authority: CA 2006, ss 243(3), 1063(1)–(3), 1292(1).
Commencement: 1 October 2009.
These Regulations are reproduced as amended by: the Registrar of Companies (Fees) (Limited Partnerships) (Amendment) Regulations 2011, SI 2011/319.

ARRANGEMENT OF REGULATIONS

[4.566]
1 Citation and commencement

These Regulations may be cited as the Registrar of Companies (Fees) (Limited Partnerships and Newspaper Proprietors) Regulations 2009 and come into force on 1st October 2009.

NOTES
Commencement: 1 October 2009.

[4.567]
2 Interpretation

In these Regulations—
  "Companies House Direct" and "CHD" mean the service by which information is accessed by the applicant in Hyper Text Markup Language using a website of the registrar by delivering a non-encrypted access code;
  "European Economic Interest Grouping" means a grouping formed in pursuance of article 1 of Council Regulation (EEC) No 2137/85 of 25th July 1985;
  "limited liability partnership" means a body corporate incorporated under the Limited Liability Partnerships Act 2000;
  "limited partnership" means a partnership registered under the Limited Partnerships Act 1907; and
  "the register of the proprietors of newspapers" means the register established under section 8 of the Newspaper Libel and Registration Act 1881.

NOTES
Commencement: 1 October 2009.

[4.568]
3 Fees payable in respect of functions relating to the registration of documents by the registrar

Schedule 1 makes provision for the fees that are payable to the registrar in respect of the registration of documents relating to limited partnerships and the register of the proprietors of newspapers by the registrar.

NOTES
Commencement: 1 October 2009.

[4.569]
4 Fees payable in respect of the inspection or provision of copies of documents kept by the registrar relating to limited partnerships

(1) Schedule 2 makes provision for the fees that are payable to the registrar in respect of the inspection, or provision of copies, of documents kept by the registrar relating to limited partnerships.

(2) The fees prescribed in relation to paragraph 4(a) of Schedule 2 are not payable in respect of any month for which the applicant pays a fee to the registrar for subscription to Companies House Direct under regulations providing for the payment of fees in respect of the functions of the registrar in relation to the inspection, or provision of copies, of documents kept by the registrar relating to companies, overseas companies, limited liability partnerships and European Economic Interest Groupings.

NOTES
Commencement: 1 October 2009.

[4.570]
5 Transitional provisions

Where any document is delivered to the registrar on or before 30th September 2009 to which any fee set under section 14 of the Newspaper Libel and Registration Act 1881 would have applied if registered on or before that date, and that document is registered on or after 1st October 2009, the fee prescribed in Schedule 1 in respect of that document shall not apply and any fee set under section 14 of the Newspaper Libel and Registrations Act 1881 shall apply.

NOTES
Commencement: 1 October 2009.

[4.571]
6

Where any application is made to the registrar on or before 30th September 2009 in respect of the inspection of, or the provision of copies of, material kept by the registrar, the fee prescribed in Schedule 2 or determined by the registrar in the exercise of his powers under section 1063(5) of the Companies Act 2006 in respect of that application shall not apply and any fee payable under paragraph 6(2) of Schedule 5 to the Companies Act 2006 (Commencement No 1, Transitional Provisions and Savings) Order 2006 shall apply.

NOTES
Commencement: 1 October 2009.

[4.572]
7 Revocation
Subject to Regulation 6, paragraph 6(2) of Schedule 5 to the Companies Act 2006 (Commencement No 1, Transitional Provisions and Savings) Order 2006 is revoked.

NOTES
Commencement: 1 October 2009.

SCHEDULES

SCHEDULE 1
THE PERFORMANCE OF FUNCTIONS RELATING TO THE REGISTRATION OF DOCUMENTS BY THE REGISTRAR
Regulation 3

PART 1
INTERPRETATION

Meaning of "the 1881 Act" and "the LP Act" and words and expressions used in those Acts

[4.573]
1. (1) In this Schedule—
"the 1881 Act" means the Newspaper Libel and Registration Act 1881;
"the LP Act" means the Limited Partnerships Act 1907.

(2) Words and expressions used in the enactments set out in sub-paragraph (1) have the same meaning when used in this Schedule as they have in those enactments.

Meaning of "same day registration"
2. For the purposes of this Schedule a document is delivered for "same day registration" if—
   (a) a request for same day registration and the document required to be delivered to the registrar in connection with that registration is received by the registrar by 3.00 pm on the day in question; and
   (b) the registration is completed on that day.

General
3. Where, in relation to any matter in respect of which a fee is payable under this Schedule, the means of delivery to the registrar of the documents required to be delivered in relation to that matter, or the form of those documents, are not specified that fee is payable only in respect of documents that are delivered in hard copy form.

4. Where, in relation to any matter in respect of which a fee is payable under this Schedule, no provision is made for same day registration of the documents required to be delivered to the registrar in relation to that matter, that fee is only payable in respect of the delivery of documents other than for same day registration.

NOTES
Commencement: 1 October 2009.

PART 2
FEES PAYABLE

Limited partnerships

[4.574]
5. In respect of the performance by the registrar of his functions in relation to the registration of documents delivered to him in respect of limited partnerships, the fee specified in relation to the matter below is payable on the registration of the documents so delivered relating to that matter—

Matter in relation to which the fee is payable	Amount of fee
(a) for the registration of a limited partnership under section 8 of the LP Act—	
(i) where the application is delivered for same day registration,	[£100.00]
(ii) where the application is delivered other than for same day registration.	£20.00

Newspaper proprietors

6 In respect of the performance by the registrar of his functions in relation to the register of the proprietors of newspapers, the fee specified in relation to the matter below is payable on the registration of the documents so delivered relating to that matter—

Matter in relation to which the fee is payable	Amount of fee
For the making of a return under section 9 of the 1881 Act;	£10.00

NOTES

Commencement: 1 October 2009.

Para 5: sum in square brackets substituted by the Registrar of Companies (Fees) (Limited Partnerships) (Amendment) Regulations 2011, SI 2011/319, reg 2, as from 6 April 2011. Note that reg 4(1) of the 2011 Regulations provides that the fee prescribed by reg 2 of those Regulations applies to any registration in respect of which the document necessary for the registrar to effect such an act is delivered to the registrar on or after 6 April 2011.

SCHEDULE 2
THE PERFORMANCE OF FUNCTIONS RELATING TO THE INSPECTION OR PROVISION OF COPIES OF DOCUMENTS KEPT BY THE REGISTRAR IN RELATION TO LIMITED PARTNERSHIPS

Regulation 4

PART 1
INTERPRETATION

[4.575]
1 Means by which material kept by the registrar may be inspected and copies provided

In this Schedule—

"Companies House Contact Centre" and "CHCC" mean a contact centre maintained by or on behalf of the registrar through which a facility is provided for applying by telephone, fax or email for copies of material kept by the registrar;

"Companies House Information Centre" and "CHIC" mean an office of the registrar where facilities are made available for applicants to inspect and to obtain copies of material kept by the registrar.

2 Meaning of "same day delivery" and "same day collection"

For the purposes of this Schedule certificates and certified copies are provided for "same day delivery" or "same day collection" if—

(a) a request for same day delivery or same day collection is received by the registrar before 2.00pm on the day in question; and

(b) the appropriate certificate or certified copy is issued to the applicant on that day.

3 Meaning of "the LP Act" and words and expressions used in that Act

In this Schedule "the LP Act" means the Limited Partnerships Act 1907; and words and expressions used in that Act have the same meaning when used in this Schedule as they have in that Act.

NOTES

Commencement: 1 October 2009.

PART 2
FEES PAYABLE

[4.576]
4 Companies House Direct

In respect of the performance of the registrar's functions in relation to the provision of certificates of registration in respect of limited partnerships, where an application for a certificate is made by means of CHD, the following fees are payable—

Matter in relation to which the fee is payable	Amount of fee
(a) for subscribing to CHD, for each calendar month payable in arrears at the end of that month;	[£4.00]
[(b) for a certificate of registration of a limited partnership, in hard copy form, under section 16 of the LP Act, applied for by means of CHD—	
(i) where that certificate is delivered by post other than by same day delivery and it is the first certificate relating to that limited partnership provided to an applicant on any one occasion,	£20.00

Matter in relation to which the fee is payable	Amount of fee
(ii) where that certificate is delivered by post by same delivery and it is the first certificate relating to that limited partnership provided to an applicant on any one occasion,	£60.00
(iii) where it is an additional certificate delivered by post (by same day delivery or not) relating to the same limited partnership provided to the same applicant on the same occasion;	£10.00]
[(c) for a certificate of registration of the type referred to in sub-paragraph (b) above applied for by means of CHD and made available for collection at a CHIC—	
(i) where that certificate is made available other than for same day collection and it is the first certificate relating to that limited partnership provided to an applicant on any one occasion,	£20.00
(ii) where that certificate is made available for same day collection and it is the first certificate relating to that limited partnership provided to an applicant on any one occasion,	£60.00
(iii) where it is an additional certificate made available for collection (for same day collection or not) relating to the same limited partnership provided to the same applicant on the same occasion.	£10.00]

5 Companies House Information Centre

In respect of the performance of the registrar's functions in relation to the inspection of material kept by the registrar and the provision of copies of material kept by the registrar in respect of limited partnerships, where an application for inspection or a copy is made at a CHIC, the following fees are payable—

Matter in relation to which the fee is payable	Amount of fee
(a) for the inspection, at a CHIC, of an original statement or application delivered to the registrar in hard copy form;	£6.00
(b) for the inspection and for a copy in hard copy form, of a statement or application of the type specified in sub-paragraph (a) above;	£9.00
(c) for a copy (without prior inspection), in hard copy form, of an original statement or application kept by the registrar in hard copy form applied for at a CHIC and delivered by post;	£3.00
(d) for a copy (without prior inspection), in hard copy form, of an original statement or application kept by the registrar in hard copy form applied for at a CHIC and made available for collection at a CHIC;	£3.00
(e) for a copy of or extract from, in hard copy form, a statement or application certified under section 16 of the LP Act, applied for at a CHIC and delivered to the applicant by post—	
(i) where the copy or extract consists of up to 10 pages (including the tenth page),	[£20.00]
(ii) for each subsequent page of the copy or extract,	£1.00
(iii) where any copy or extract is delivered by same day delivery;	[£60.00]
(f) for a copy of or extract from, in hard copy form, a statement or application certified under section 16 of the LP Act, applied for at a CHIC and made available for collection at a CHIC—	
(i) where the copy or extract consists of up to 10 pages (including the tenth page),	[£20.00]
(ii) for each subsequent page of the copy or extract,	£1.00
(iii) where any copy or extract is made available for same day collection;	[£60.00]
[(g) for a certificate of registration of a limited partnership, in hard copy form, under section 16 of the LP Act, applied for at a CHIC—	
(i) where that certificate is delivered by post other than by same day delivery and it is the first certificate relating to that limited partnership provided to an applicant on any one occasion,	£20.00
(ii) where that certificate is delivered by post by same day delivery and it is the first certificate relating to that limited partnership provided to an applicant on any one occasion,	£60.00

Matter in relation to which the fee is payable	Amount of fee
(iii) where it is an additional certificate delivered by post (by same day delivery or not) relating to the same limited partnership provided to the same applicant on the same occasion;	£10.00]
[(h) for a certificate of registration of the type referred to in sub-paragraph (g) above and applied for at a CHIC and made available for collection at a CHIC—	
(i) where that certificate is made available other than for same day collection and it is the first certificate relating to that limited partnership provided to an applicant on any one occasion,	£20.00
(ii) where that certificate is made available for same day collection and it is the first certificate relating to that limited partnership provided to an applicant on any one occasion,	£60.00
(iii) where it is an additional certificate made available for collection (for same day collection or not) relating to the same limited partnership provided to the same applicant on the same occasion.	£10.00]

Companies House Contact Centre

6 In respect of the performance of the registrar's functions in relation to the provision of copies of material kept by the registrar in respect of limited partnerships, where the application for a copy is made by means of a CHCC, the following fees are payable—

Matter in relation to which the fee is payable	Amount of fee
(a) for a copy, in hard copy form, provided on an application to a CHCC, of an original statement or application in relation to a limited partnership kept by the registrar in hard copy form and delivered by post;	£3.00
(b) for a copy, in hard copy form, provided on an application to a CHCC, of an original statement or application in relation to a limited partnership kept by the registrar in hard copy form and made available for collection at a CHIC;	£3.00
(c) for a copy of or extract from, in hard copy form, a statement or application certified under section 16 of the LP Act applied for at a CHCC—	
(i) where that copy or extract is delivered by post other than by same day delivery,	[£20.00]
(ii) where that copy or extract is delivered by post by same day delivery;	[£60.00]
(d) for a copy of or extract from, in hard copy form, a statement or application certified under section 16 of the LP Act, applied for at a CHCC and made available for collection at a CHIC—	
(i) where that copy or extract is made available for collection other than by same day collection,	[£20.00]
(ii) where that copy or extract is made available for same day collection;	[£60.00]
[(e) for a certificate of registration of a limited partnership, provided on application to a CHCC, in hard copy form, under section 16 of the LP Act—	
(i) where that certificate is delivered by post other than by same day delivery and it is the first certificate relating to that limited partnership provided to an applicant on any one occasion,	£20.00
(ii) where that certificate is delivered by post by same day delivery and it is the first certificate relating to that limited partnership provided to an applicant on any one occasion,	£60.00
(iii) where it is an additional certificate delivered by post (by same day delivery or not) relating to the same limited partnership provided to the same applicant on the same occasion;	£10.00]
[(f) for a certificate of registration of a limited partnership, provided on application to a CHCC, in hard copy form, under section 16 of the LP Act and made available for collection at a CHIC—	
(i) where that certificate is made available other than for same day collection and it is the first certificate relating to that limited partnership provided to an applicant on any one occasion,	£20.00

Matter in relation to which the fee is payable	Amount of fee
(ii) where that certificate is made available for same day collection and it is the first certificate relating to that limited partnership provided to an applicant on any one occasion,	£60.00
(iii) where it is an additional certificate made available for collection (for same day collection or not) relating to the same limited partnership provided to the same applicant on the same occasion.	£10.00]

NOTES

Para 4 is amended as follows:

The fee in the second column in sub-para (a) was substituted by Registrar of Companies (Fees) (Limited Partnerships) (Amendment) Regulations 2011, SI 2011/319, reg 3(a), as from 6 April 2011 (see further the final note below).

Sub-paras (b), (c) substituted by SI 2011/319, reg 3(b), (c) respectively, as from 6 April 2011 (see further the final note below).

Para 5 is amended as follows:

The fees in the second column in sub-paras (e)(i), (iii), (f)(i), (iii) were substituted by SI 2011/319, reg 3(d), (e), (f), (g) respectively, as from 6 April 2011 (see further the final note below).

Sub-paras (g), (h) substituted by SI 2011/319, reg 3(h), (i) respectively, as from 6 April 2011 (see further the final note below).

Para 6 is amended as follows:

The fees in the second column in sub-paras (c)(i), (ii), (d)(i), (ii) were substituted by SI 2011/319, reg 3(j), (k), (l), (m) respectively, as from 6 April 2011 (see further the final note below).

Sub-paras (e), (f) substituted by SI 2011/319, reg 3(n), (o) respectively, as from 6 April 2011 (see further the final note below).

Regulation 4(2) of the Registrar of Companies (Fees) (Limited Partnerships) (Amendment) Regulations 2011, SI 2011/319 provides that the fees prescribed by reg 3 of those Regulations (ie, the amendments noted above) apply: (a) in relation to paragraph (a) in respect of a subscription payable on or after 6 April 2011; and (b) in relation to the other paragraphs in that regulation in respect of an application received by the registrar on or after that date.

REGISTRAR OF COMPANIES (FEES) (EUROPEAN ECONOMIC INTEREST GROUPING AND EUROPEAN PUBLIC LIMITED-LIABILITY COMPANY) REGULATIONS 2009

(SI 2009/2403)

NOTES

Made: 8 September 2009.

Authority: CA 2006, ss 1063(1)–(3), 1292(1).

Commencement: 1 October 2009.

These Regulations are reproduced as amended by: the Registrar of Companies (Fees) (European Economic Interest Grouping) (Amendment) Regulations 2011, SI 2011/324.

ARRANGEMENT OF REGULATIONS

[4.577]

1   Citation and commencement

These Regulations may be cited as the Registrar of Companies (Fees) (European Economic Interest Grouping and European Public Limited-Liability Company) Regulations 2009 and come into force on 1st October 2009.

NOTES
Commencement: 1 October 2009.

[4.578]
2   Interpretation

In these Regulations—

"the 2006 Act" means the Companies Act 2006;

"Companies House Direct" and "CHD" mean the service by which information is accessed by the applicant in Hyper Text Markup Language using a website of the registrar by delivering a non-encrypted access code;

"EEIG" means a European Economic Interest Grouping formed under Council Regulation (EEC) No 2137/85 of 25th July 1985 on the European Economic Interest Grouping;

"Extranet" means the service by which information is accessed by means of the access codes of the applicant in Hyper Text Markup Language using a website of the registrar;

"limited liability partnership" means a body corporate incorporated under the Limited Liability Partnerships Act 2000;

"limited partnership" means a partnership registered under the Limited Partnerships Act 1907;

"SE" means a European Public Limited-Liability Company within the meaning of Council Regulation 2157/2001/EC of 8 October 2001 on the Statute for a European Company;

"XML Gateway" and "XML" mean the service by which information is accessed by the applicant in Extensible Markup Language by means of a partially encrypted access code.

NOTES
Commencement: 1 October 2009.

[4.579]
3   Fees payable in respect of functions relating to the registration of documents by the registrar

Schedule 1 makes provision for the fees that are payable to the registrar in respect of the registration of documents relating to EEIGs and SEs by the registrar.

NOTES
Commencement: 1 October 2009.

[4.580]
4   Fees payable in respect of the inspection or provision of copies of documents kept by the registrar relating to EEIGs

(1)   Schedule 2 makes provision for the fees that are payable to the registrar in respect of the inspection, or provision of copies, of documents kept by the registrar relating to EEIGs.

(2)   The fees prescribed in relation to paragraphs 3(a), 4(a) and 6(a) of Schedule 2 are not payable in respect of any month for which the applicant pays a fee to the registrar for subscription to Companies House Direct, Extranet or XML under regulations providing for the payment of fees in respect of the functions of the registrar in relation to the inspection, or provision of copies, of documents kept by the registrar relating to companies, overseas companies, limited liability partnerships and limited partnerships

NOTES
Commencement: 1 October 2009.

[4.581]
5   Transitional provisions

Where any document is delivered to the registrar on or before 30th September 2009 to which the European Public Limited-Liability Company (Fees) Regulations (Northern Ireland) 2004 ("the Repealed Regulations") would have applied, if registered on or before that date, and that document is registered on or after 1st October 2009, the fee prescribed in Schedule 1 shall not apply and any fee payable in respect of that document by virtue of the Repealed Regulations shall apply.

NOTES
Commencement: 1 October 2009.

SCHEDULES

SCHEDULE 1
THE PERFORMANCE OF FUNCTIONS RELATING TO THE REGISTRATION OF DOCUMENTS BY THE REGISTRAR

Regulation 3

PART 1
INTERPRETATION

Meaning of "the EC Regulation" and "the EEIG Regulations" and words and expressions used in those Regulations

[4.582]
1. (1)   In this Schedule—
the "EC Regulation" means Council Regulation 2157/2001/EC of 8 October 2001 on the Statute
for a European Company;
the "EEIG Regulations" mean the European Economic Interest Grouping Regulations 1989.

(2)   Words and expressions used in the enactments set out in sub-paragraph (1) have the same meaning when used in this Schedule as they have in those enactments.

Meaning of "same day registration"
2. For the purposes of this Schedule documents are delivered for "same day registration" if—
    (a)   a request for same day registration and all documents required to be delivered to the registrar in connection with that registration are received by the registrar by 3.00 pm on the day in question; and
    (b)   the registration is completed on that day.

General
3. Where, in relation to any matter in respect of which a fee is payable under this Schedule, the means of delivery to the registrar of the documents required to be delivered in relation to that matter, or the form of those documents are not specified, that fee is payable only in respect of documents that are delivered in hard copy form.

4. Where, in relation to any matter in respect of which a fee is payable under this Schedule, no provision is made for same day registration of the documents required to be delivered to the registrar in relation to that matter, that fee is only payable in respect of the delivery of documents other than for same day registration.

NOTES
    Commencement: 1 October 2009.

PART 2
FEES PAYABLE

European Economic Interest Groupings

[4.583]
5. In respect of the performance by the registrar of his functions in relation to the registration of documents delivered to him in respect of EEIGs, the fee specified in relation to each matter below is payable on the registration of the documents so delivered relating to that matter—

Matter in relation to which the fee is payable	Amount of fee
(a) for the registration under regulation 9 of the EEIG Regulations of an EEIG;	£20.00
(b) for the registration under regulation 12 of the EEIG Regulations of an EEIG that is situating an establishment in the United Kingdom but whose official address is outside the United Kingdom;	£20.00
(c) for the registration of a change of name of an EEIG under regulation 11 of the EEIG Regulations;	£10.00
(d) for the registration of a charge under paragraph 26 of Schedule 4 to the EEIG Regulations.	£13.00

European Public Limited-Liability Companies
6. In respect of the performance by the registrar of his functions in relation to the registration of documents delivered to him in respect of SEs, the fee specified in relation to each matter below is payable on the registration of the documents so delivered relating to that matter—

Matter in relation to which the fee is payable	Amount of fee
(a) for the registration of an SE whose registered office is in the United Kingdom on its formation—	
(i) by merger in accordance with Article 2(1) of the EC Regulation,	£20.00
(ii) by the formation of a holding SE in accordance with Article 2(2) of the EC Regulation,	£20.00
(iii) by the formation of a subsidiary SE in accordance with Article 2(3) of the EC Regulation,	£20.00
(iv) by the transformation of a public company in accordance with Article 2(4) of the EC Regulation,	£20.00
(v) by the formation of a subsidiary SE in accordance with Article 3(2) of the EC Regulation;	£20.00
(b) for the registration of a public company by the conversion of an SE in accordance with Article 66 of the EC Regulation;	£20.00
(c) for the registration of an SE on the transfer of its registered office to the United Kingdom in accordance with Article 8 of the EC Regulation.	£20.00

NOTES

Commencement: 1 October 2009.

SCHEDULE 2
THE PERFORMANCE OF FUNCTIONS RELATING TO THE INSPECTION OR PROVISION OF COPIES OF DOCUMENTS KEPT BY THE REGISTRAR IN RELATION TO EEIGS

Regulation 4

PART 1
INTERPRETATION

[4.584]
1   Means by which the register may be inspected and copies provided

In this Schedule—

    "Companies House Contact Centre" and "CHCC" mean a contact centre maintained by or on behalf of the registrar through which a facility is provided for applying by telephone, fax or e-mail for copies of material on the register;

    "Companies House Information Centre" and "CHIC" mean an office of the registrar where facilities are made available for applicants to inspect the register and to obtain copies of material on the register and "searchroom terminal" means a computer terminal operated by an applicant at a CHIC;

    "WebCHeck" means the service by which information is accessed by the applicant in Hyper Text Markup Language using a website of the registrar with no requirement for the applicant to deliver an access code.

2   Meaning of "same day delivery" and "same day collection"

For the purposes of this Schedule certified copies are provided for "same day delivery" or "same day collection" if—

    (a)   a request for same day delivery or same day collection is received by the registrar before 2.00pm on the day in question; and

    (b)   the appropriate certified copy is issued to the applicant on that day.

NOTES

Commencement: 1 October 2009.

PART 2
FEES PAYABLE

[4.585]
3   Companies House Direct

In respect of the performance of the registrar's function in relation to the inspection of material kept by the registrar and the provision of copies of material kept by the registrar in respect of EEIGs, where an application for inspection or a copy is made by means of CHD, the following fees are payable—

Matter in relation to which the fee is payable	Amount of fee
(a) for subscribing to CHD for each calendar month payable in arrears at the end of that month;	[£4.00]
(b) for the inspection by means of CHD of a statement of particulars of a charge registered in respect of an EEIG;	£1.00
(c) for a copy provided by means of CHD (without prior inspection) of a document in respect of an EEIG;	£1.00
(d) for the inspection and provision of a copy of a document, by means of CHD in respect of an EEIG;	£4.00
(e) for the delivery by post in hard copy form of any document specified in sub-paragraphs (c) and (d) above applied for by means of CHD;	£3.00
(f) for a copy of a document, or extract from a document, in hard copy form, certified under section 1091 of the 2006 Act in relation to EEIGs, applied for by means of CHD—	
(i) where that copy or extract is delivered by post by same day delivery,	[£60.00]
(ii) where that copy or extract is delivered by post other than by same day delivery,	[£20.00]
(iii) where that copy or extract is made available for collection at a CHIC other than for same day collection,	[£20.00]
(iv) where that copy or extract is made available for collection at a CHIC for same day collection.	[£60.00]

4 Extranet

In respect of the performance of the registrar's functions in relation to the inspection of material kept by the registrar and the provision of copies of material kept by the registrar in respect of EEIGs, where an application for inspection or a copy is made by means of Extranet, the following fees are payable—

Matter in relation to which the fee is payable	Amount of fee
(a) for subscribing to Extranet, for each calendar month payable in arrears at the end of that month;	[£4.70]
(b) for the inspection and provision of a copy of a document by means of Extranet in respect of an EEIG;	£4.00
(c) for a copy provided by means of Extranet (without prior inspection) of a document in respect of an EEIG.	£1.00

5 WebCHeck

In respect of the performance of the registrar's functions in relation to the provision of copies of material kept by the registrar in respect of EEIGs, where the application for a copy is made by means of WebCHeck, the following fee is payable—

Matter in relation to which the fee is payable	Amount of fee
(a) for a copy provided by means of WebCHeck (without prior inspection) of a document in respect of an EEIG.	£1.00

6 XML

In respect of the performance of the registrar's functions in relation to the provision of copies of material kept by the registrar in respect of EEIGs, where the application for a copy is made by means of XML, the following fee is payable—

Matter in relation to which the fee is payable	Amount of fee
(a) for subscribing to XML, for each calendar month payable in arrears at the end of that month;	[£4.70]
(b) for a copy provided by means of XML (without prior inspection) of a document in respect of an EEIG.	£1.00

7 Companies House Information Centre

In respect of the performance of the registrar's functions in relation to the inspection of material kept by the registrar and the provision of copies of material kept by the registrar in respect of EEIGs, where the application for inspection or a copy is made at a CHIC, the following fees are payable—

Matter in relation to which the fee is payable	Amount of fee
(a) for the inspection by means of a searchroom terminal of a statement of particulars of a charge registered in respect of an EEIG;	£1.00
(b) for the inspection of a document by means of a searchroom terminal in respect of an EEIG;	£2.00
(c) for a copy, in hard copy form, provided by means of a searchroom terminal (without prior inspection) of a document in respect of an EEIG;	£1.00
(d) for a copy of any document specified in sub-paragraphs (a) and (b) above, applied for at a CHIC and made available at a CHIC;	£3.00
(e) for the inspection, at a CHIC, of an original document delivered to the registrar in hard copy form in respect of an EEIG;	£6.00
(f) for the inspection and for a copy, in hard copy form of a document of the type specified in sub-paragraph (e) above;	£9.00
(g) for a copy in hard copy form of a screen of information in respect of an EEIG displayed on a searchroom terminal and made available for collection at a CHIC;	£0.10
(h) for a copy, in hard copy form, of a document or extract from a document certified under section 1091 of the 2006 Act in relation to an EEIG, applied for at a CHIC and delivered to the applicant by post—	
(i) where the copy or extract consists of up to 10 pages (including the tenth page),	[£20.00]
(ii) for each subsequent page of the copy or extract,	£1.00
(iii) where any copy or extract is delivered by same day delivery;	[£60.00]
(i) for a copy, in hard copy form, of a document or an extract from a document certified under section 1091 of the 2006 Act in relation to an EEIG, applied for at a CHIC and made available for collection at a CHIC—	
(i) where the copy or extract consists of up to 10 pages (including the tenth page),	[£20.00]
(ii) for each subsequent page of the copy or extract,	£1.00
(iii) where the copy or extract is made available for same day collection.	[£60.00]

8 Companies House Contact Centre

In respect of the performance of the registrar's functions in relation to the provision of copies of material kept by the registrar in respect of EEIGs, where the application for a copy is made by means of a CHCC, the following fees are payable—

Matter in relation to which the fee is payable	Amount of fee
(a) for a copy, in hard copy form provided on application to a CHCC, of a statement of particulars of a charge registered in respect of an EEIG delivered by post;	£3.00
(b) for a copy provided on application to a CHCC, of a statement of particulars of a charge registered in respect of an EEIG delivered by e-mail;	£3.00
(c) for a copy, in hard copy form, provided on application to a CHCC of a document in respect of an EEIG delivered by post;	£3.00
(d) for a copy, provided on application to a CHCC of a document in respect of an EEIG delivered by e-mail;	£3.00
(e) for a copy, provided on application to a CHCC of an original document delivered to the registrar and kept by the registrar in hard copy form in respect of an EEIG and delivered by post;	£9.00
(f) for a copy, in hard copy form, provided on application to a CHCC, of a document or extract from a document, certified under section 1091 of the 2006 Act in relation to an EEIG—	

Matter in relation to which the fee is payable	Amount of fee
(i) where that copy or extract is delivered by post other than by same day delivery,	[£20.00]
(ii) where that copy or extract is delivered by post by same day delivery;	[£60.00]
(g) for a copy, in hard copy form, provided on application to a CHCC, of a document or extract from a document of the type specified in sub-paragraph (f) above and made available for collection at a CHIC—	
(i) where that copy or extract is made available for collection other than by same day collection,	[£20.00]
(ii) where that copy or extract is made available for same day collection.	[£60.00]

NOTES

Commencement: 1 October 2009.

Para 3: the fees in the second column in sub-paras (a), (f)(i), (ii), (iii), (iv) were substituted by the Registrar of Companies (Fees) (European Economic Interest Grouping) (Amendment) Regulations 2011, SI 2011/324, reg 2(a), (b), (c), (d), (e) respectively, as from 6 April 2011 (see further the final note below).

Para 4: the fee in the second column in sub-para (a) was substituted by SI 2011/324, reg 2(f), as from 6 April 2011 (see further the final note below).

Para 6: the fee in the second column in sub-para (a) was substituted by SI 2011/324, reg 2(g), as from 6 April 2011 (see further the final note below).

Para 7: the fees in the second column in sub-paras (h)(i), (iii), and (i)(i), (iii) were substituted by SI 2011/324, reg 2(h), (i), (j), (k) respectively, as from 6 April 2011 (see further the final note below).

Para 8: the fees in the second column in sub-paras (f)(i), (ii), and (g)(i), (ii) were substituted by SI 2011/324, reg 2(l), (m), (n), (o) respectively, as from 6 April 2011 (see further the final note below).

Regulation 3 of the Registrar of Companies (Fees) (European Economic Interest Grouping) (Amendment) Regulations 2011, SI 2011/324 provides that the fees prescribed by reg 2 of those Regulations (ie, the amendments noted above) apply: (a) in relation to paras (a), (f) and (g) in respect of a subscription payable on or after 6 April 2011; and (b) in relation to other paragraphs in respect of an application received by the registrar on or after that date.

COMPANIES (AUTHORISED MINIMUM) REGULATIONS 2009

(SI 2009/2425)

NOTES

Made: 4 September 2009.

Authority: Companies Act 2006, ss 763(2)–(4), 766(1)(a), (2), 1292(1), (2).

Commencement: 1 October 2009.

Amendment: as of 1 July 2011 these Regulations had not been amended.

ARRANGEMENT OF REGULATIONS

[4.586]
1 Citation, commencement and interpretation

(1) These Regulations may be cited as the Companies (Authorised Minimum) Regulations 2009 and come into force on 1st October 2009.

(2) In these Regulations—

"the appropriate spot rate of exchange" is to be interpreted in accordance with regulation 4(1);

"the certified spot rate" has the meaning given in regulation 4(3);

"published spot rate" has the meaning given in regulation 4(2);

"reference date" is to be interpreted in accordance with regulation 4(7) and (8);

"relevant day" is to be interpreted in accordance with regulation 4(5) and (6); and "working day" means a day which is not a Saturday or Sunday, Christmas Day, Good Friday or any day that is a bank holiday under the Banking and Financial Dealings Act 1971 in England and Wales.

(3) In these Regulations a reference to any Part or section is, unless otherwise stated, a reference to a Part or section of the Companies Act 2006.

NOTES
Commencement: 1 October 2009.

[4.587]
2 Authorised minimum in euros

For the purposes of the definition of "the authorised minimum" in section 763(1), but subject to regulation 9, the amount in euros that is to be treated as equivalent to the sterling amount is €57,100.

NOTES
Commencement: 1 October 2009.

[4.588]
3 Application of the authorised minimum requirement for certain purposes

(1) This regulation applies for either of the purposes in paragraphs (2) and (3), and is subject to regulation 9.

(2) The first purpose is to determine, for the purposes of section 650, whether a reduction of a public company's share capital confirmed by a court order under section 648 has the effect of bringing the nominal value of the company's allotted share capital below the authorised minimum.

(3) The second purpose is to determine, for the purposes of section 662(2)(b), whether the cancellation of a public company's shares and the diminution of the amount of its share capital under section 662(2)(a) have the effect of bringing the nominal value of the company's allotted share capital below the authorised minimum.

(4) This regulation only applies where the company has allotted share capital denominated in more than one currency, taking account of the effect of the reduction of the company's share capital or (as the case may be) the effect of the cancellation of the company's shares and the diminution of the amount of its allotted share capital.

(5) The nominal value of a public company's allotted share capital is to be treated as being below the authorised minimum if—
    (a) the sterling value is less than £50,000; and
    (b) the euro value is less than €57,100.

(6) The "sterling value" is the sum in sterling of—
    (a) the nominal value of the company's allotted share capital denominated in sterling;
    (b) the nominal value of the company's allotted share capital denominated in euros if it were to be converted into sterling at the appropriate spot rate of exchange; and
    (c) the nominal value of the company's allotted share capital denominated in a currency other than sterling or euros if it were to be converted into sterling at the appropriate spot rate of exchange.

(7) The "euro value" is the sum in euros of—
    (a) the nominal value of the company's allotted share capital denominated in euros;
    (b) the nominal value of the company's allotted share capital denominated in sterling if it were to be converted into euros at the appropriate spot rate of exchange; and
    (c) the nominal value of the company's allotted share capital denominated in a currency other than sterling or euros if it were to be converted into euros at the appropriate spot rate of exchange.

NOTES
Commencement: 1 October 2009.

[4.589]
4 The appropriate spot rate of exchange

(1) The appropriate spot rate of exchange for a currency conversion referred to in regulation 3(6) and (7) is the published spot rate relevant to the currency conversion in question or, where the circumstances in paragraph (4) exist, the certified spot rate relevant to that currency conversion.

(2) The published spot rate is the middle spot exchange rate prevailing on the foreign exchange market at 4pm on the relevant day as published in respect of that day by the Financial Times.

(3) The certified spot rate is the middle spot exchange rate prevailing on the foreign exchange market at 4pm on the relevant day and stated in a certificate obtained by the company from—
    (a) a person, nominated by the company, who under Part 4 of the Financial Services and Markets Act 2000 has permission to accept deposits; or

    (b)   a firm, nominated by the company, which has permission to carry on the activity of accepting deposits in the United Kingdom by virtue of Schedule 3 to that Act.

(4)   The circumstances in this paragraph exist where—

    (a)   the Financial Times has not, on or before the reference date, published an exchange rate referred to in paragraph (2) relevant to the currency conversion in question; or

    (b)   the Financial Times has, on or before the reference date, published what appears to be an exchange rate referred to in paragraph (2) relevant to the currency conversion in question but the company can show that there was a publication error; or

    (c)   there is no evidence of what (if any) was the rate referred to in paragraph (2) relevant to the currency conversion in question as published on or before the reference date by the Financial Times.

(5)   Where the currency conversion is relevant to the calculation of the sterling value or the euro value for the purpose in regulation 3(2), the "relevant day" is the working day which immediately preceded the working day immediately preceding the date of the court order.

(6)   Where the currency conversion is relevant to the calculation of the sterling value or the euro value for the purpose in regulation 3(3), the "relevant day" is—

    (a)   in a case within section 662(1)(a) or (b), the working day immediately preceding the date of the forfeiture or surrender; and

    (b)   in a case within section 662(1)(c), (d) or (e), the working day immediately preceding the date of the acquisition.

(7)   Where the currency calculation is relevant to the calculation of the sterling value or the euro value for the purpose in regulation 3(2), the "reference date" is the date of the court order.

(8)   Where the currency conversion is relevant to the calculation of the sterling value or the euro value for the purpose in regulation 3(3), the "reference date" is—

    (a)   in a case within section 662(1)(a) or (b), the fifth working day following the date of the forfeiture or surrender; and

    (b)   in a case within section 662(1)(c), (d) or (e), the fifth working day following the date of the acquisition.

NOTES

Commencement: 1 October 2009.

[4.590]

5   Registration of a court order confirming a capital reduction: assumptions which may be made by the registrar

(1)   This regulation applies where a public company delivers to the registrar under section 649 a copy of an order of the court confirming a reduction of its share capital and the court has not directed the order to be registered.

(2)   Where the circumstances in paragraph (3), (4) or (5) exist, the registrar may make the assumption in paragraph (6).

(3)   The circumstances in this paragraph are that—

    (a)   taking account of the effect of the reduction of its capital, the company has allotted share capital denominated in more than one currency;

    (b)   either the Financial Times did not publish, on or before the reference date, an exchange rate referred to in regulation 4(2) relevant to converting into sterling a currency in which the company's allotted share capital is denominated or it did not publish, on or before that date, such a rate relevant to converting such a currency into euros; and

    (c)   the company has not delivered to the registrar, in respect of every such currency for which the Financial Times did not publish such an exchange rate on or before the reference date, a copy of a certificate referred to in regulation 4(3).

(4)   The circumstances in this paragraph are that—

    (a)   taking account of the effect of the reduction of its share capital, the company has allotted share capital denominated in more than one currency;

    (b)   the Financial Times published, on or before the reference date, what appears to be an exchange rate referred to in regulation 4(2) relevant to converting into sterling or euros a currency in which the company's allotted share capital is denominated but the company can show that there was a publication error; and

    (c)   the company has not delivered to the registrar, for every currency in respect of which the company can show such a publication error, a copy of a certificate referred to in regulation 4(3).

(5)   The circumstances in this paragraph are that—

    (a)   taking account of the effect of the reduction of its share capital, the company has allotted share capital denominated in more than one currency;

    (b)   in respect of one or more of the exchange rates referred to in regulation 4(2) relevant to converting into sterling or euros the currencies in which the company's allotted share capital is denominated there is no evidence of what (if any) was the rate published on or before the reference date by the Financial Times; and

(c)   the company has not delivered to the registrar, for every such currency in respect of which there is no such evidence, a copy of a certificate referred to in regulation 4(3).

(6)   The registrar may (but is not required to) assume for the purposes of sections 649(1) and 650(1) and (2) that the reduction of the company's share capital has the effect of bringing the nominal value of the company's allotted share capital below the authorised minimum.

NOTES
Commencement: 1 October 2009.

[4.591]
6   Determination of exchange rates by the court in certain proceedings

(1)   This regulation applies to—
    (a)   proceedings against a public company or any officer of a public company for an offence under section 667; and
    (b)   proceedings under section 757 or 758 or Part 30.

(2)   Where the circumstances in paragraph (3) exist, the court may make a determination referred to in paragraph (4) in the proceedings.

(3)   The circumstances are that—
    (a)   in proceedings under section 667 it is alleged that, or in proceedings referred to in paragraph (1)(b) the question arises whether, the effect of a cancellation of the company's shares and diminution of the amount of the company's share capital under section 662(2)(a) was that the nominal value of the company's allotted share capital was brought below the authorised minimum; and
    (b)   as a result of that cancellation and diminution the company had (or continued to have) allotted share capital denominated in more than one currency.

(4)   The court may make such determination as it thinks fit as to the exchange rate to be applied to a currency conversion referred to in regulation 3(6) and (7) where—
    (a)   the Financial Times did not publish, on or before the reference date, an exchange rate referred to in regulation 4(2) relevant to that currency conversion; or
    (b)   the Financial Times published, on or before the reference date, what appears to be an exchange rate referred to in regulation 4(2) relevant to that currency conversion but the company or officer of the company (as the case may be) can show that there was a publication error; or
    (c)   there is no evidence of what (if any) was the exchange rate referred to in regulation 4(2) as published on or before the reference date by the Financial Times relevant to that currency conversion,
and there has not been produced to the court in the proceedings a copy of a certificate referred to in regulation 4(3) in respect of that currency conversion.

(5)   In this regulation, "the court" in relation to proceedings referred to in paragraph (1)(a) means the court of criminal jurisdiction in which the proceedings are brought.

NOTES
Commencement: 1 October 2009.

[4.592]
7   Exclusion of liability in respect of the publication or non-publication of a spot rate

No person shall be liable to any other person as a result of—
    (a)   that or any other person having placed reliance for the purposes of these Regulations upon a rate published by the Financial Times; or
    (b)   any error in a rate published by the Financial Times which is relied upon for the purposes of these Regulations; or
    (c)   any act or omission as a result of which the Financial Times did not publish a rate capable of being relied upon for the purposes of these Regulations.

NOTES
Commencement: 1 October 2009.

8   *(Revokes the Companies (Authorised Minimum) Regulations 2008, SI 2008/729, reg 2.)*

[4.593]
9   Transitional provisions and savings

(1)   The figure of €57,100 in regulation 2 is to be read as €65,600 where that regulation applies for any of the purposes in paragraph (2).

(2)   The purposes are—
    (a)   to determine whether the nominal value of a public company's allotted share capital is less than the authorised minimum for the purposes of an application for a trading certificate under section 761 where the application was received by the registrar before 1st October 2009;

(b) to determine for the purposes of section 91(1)(a) whether the nominal value of a private company's allotted share capital is less than the authorised minimum in a case where the special resolution that the company should be re-registered as a public company was passed before 1st October 2009;

(c) to determine whether, for the purposes of section 139 of the Companies Act 1985 or Article 149 of the Companies (Northern Ireland) Order 1986, the effect of a reduction of share capital is to bring the nominal value of a company's allotted share capital below the authorised minimum;

(d) to determine for the purposes of section 650 whether the effect of a reduction of capital is to bring the nominal value of a company's allotted share capital below the authorised minimum in a case where the special resolution for reducing the company's share capital was passed before 1st October 2009;

(e) to determine for the purposes of section 662(2)(b) whether the effect of cancelling shares and diminishing a company's share capital under section 662(2)(a) is to bring the nominal value of the company's allotted share capital below the authorised minimum in a case where the period for complying with the obligations under section 662(2) began before 1st October 2009.

(3) The figure of €57,100 in regulation 3(5)(b) is to be read as €65,600 where that regulation applies for either of the purposes in paragraph (4).

(4) The purposes are—

(a) to determine for the purposes of section 650 whether the effect of a reduction of capital is to bring the nominal value of a company's allotted share capital below the authorised minimum in a case where the special resolution for reducing the company's share capital was passed before 1st October 2009;

(b) to determine for the purposes of section 662(2)(b) whether the effect of cancelling shares and diminishing a company's share capital under section 662(2)(a) is to bring the nominal value of the company's allotted share capital below the authorised minimum in a case where the period for complying with the obligations under section 662(2) began before 1st October 2009.

NOTES
Commencement: 1 October 2009.

UNREGISTERED COMPANIES REGULATIONS 2009

(SI 2009/2436)

NOTES
Made: 4 September 2009.
Authority: Companies Act 2006, ss 1043, 1210(1)(h), 1292(2).
Commencement: 1 October 2009.
Amendment: as of 1 July 2011 these Regulations had not been amended.

ARRANGEMENT OF REGULATIONS

[4.594]
1 Citation and commencement

(1) These Regulations may be cited as the Unregistered Companies Regulations 2009.

(2) These Regulations come into force on 1st October 2009.

NOTES
Commencement: 1 October 2009.

[4.595]
2   Interpretation

In these Regulations—

   (a)   "unregistered company" means a body corporate incorporated in, and having a principal place of business in, the United Kingdom, other than—

      (i)   a body incorporated by, or registered under, a public general enactment,

      (ii)   a body not formed for the purpose of carrying on a business that has for its object the acquisition of gain by the body or its individual members,

      (iii)   a body for the time being exempted from section 1043 of the Companies Act 2006 by a direction of the Secretary of State under subsection (1)(c) of that section, or

      (iv)   an open-ended investment company;

   (b)   "instrument constituting or regulating the company", in relation to an unregistered company, means any enactment, royal charter, letters patent, deed of settlement, contract of partnership, or other instrument constituting or regulating the company.

NOTES
Commencement: 1 October 2009.

[4.596]
3   Application of provisions of the Companies Acts

The provisions of the Companies Acts specified in Schedule 1 to these Regulations apply to an unregistered company as to a company within the meaning of section 1 of the Companies Act 2006, subject to any limitation, adaptation or modification specified in that Schedule.

NOTES
Commencement: 1 October 2009.

[4.597]
4   References to registered office and registration

For the purposes of the application to an unregistered company of the provisions of the Companies Acts applying to it by virtue of these Regulations—

   (a)   any reference to the company's registered office shall be read as a reference to the company's principal office in the United Kingdom;

   (b)   any reference to the part of the United Kingdom in which the company is registered shall be read as a reference to the part of the United Kingdom in which the company's principal office is situated (and references to the registrar of companies shall be read accordingly);

   (c)   any reference to the company's registered number shall be read as a reference to the reference number allocated to the company by the registrar.

NOTES
Commencement: 1 October 2009.

[4.598]
5   Other general adaptations

(1)   In the application of any provision of the Companies Acts by virtue of these Regulations—

   (a)   any reference to a public company shall be read, in relation to an unregistered company, as referring to a company that has power under its constitution to offer its shares or debentures to the public;

   (b)   any reference to a private company shall be read, in relation to an unregistered company, as referring to a company that does not have power to offer its shares or debentures to the public;

   (c)   any reference to the company's constitution, or to its articles of association, shall be read, in relation to an unregistered company, as referring to any instrument constituting or regulating the company;

   (d)   any reference to the common seal of the company shall be read, in relation to an unregistered company, as referring to the common or authorised seal of the company.

(2)   In the application of any provision of the Companies Acts to an unregistered company by virtue of these Regulations an expression defined, or otherwise having a particular meaning or effect, in relation to a company within the meaning of section 1 of the Companies Act 2006, has effect with any adaptations necessary to ensure a corresponding meaning or effect in relation to an unregistered company.

(3)   Paragraphs (1) and (2) are subject to any specific adaptation or modification provided for in these Regulations.

NOTES
Commencement: 1 October 2009.

[4.599]
6 Application of provisions relating to statutory auditors

For the purposes of section 1210(1)(h) of the Companies Act 2006 (meaning of "statutory auditor")—

   (a)   an unregistered company is a prescribed person, and
   (b)   Part 16 of that Act (audit) as applied to unregistered companies by these Regulations is a prescribed enactment.

(and accordingly a person appointed as auditor of an unregistered company under Part 16 of that Act as so applied is a statutory auditor).

NOTES
   Commencement: 1 October 2009.

[4.600]
7 Saving

Nothing in these Regulations affects the application of any provision to an unregistered company otherwise than by virtue of these Regulations.

NOTES
   Commencement: 1 October 2009.

[4.601]
8 Revocations

The following Regulations are revoked—

   (a)   the Companies (Unregistered Companies) Regulations 1985,
   (b)   the Companies (Unregistered Companies) Regulations (Northern Ireland) 1986, and
   (c)   the Companies Acts (Unregistered Companies) Regulations 2007.

NOTES
   Commencement: 1 October 2009.

[4.602]
9 Transitional provisions and savings

Schedule 2 contains transitional provisions and savings.

NOTES
   Commencement: 1 October 2009.

SCHEDULES

SCHEDULE 1
PROVISIONS OF THE COMPANIES ACTS APPLYING TO
UNREGISTERED COMPANIES

Regulation 3

A company's constitution

[4.603]
1. Sections 26 and 27 of the Companies Act 2006 (filing obligations in connection with company's articles) apply to unregistered companies, modified so that they read as follows—

   "26 Registrar to be sent copy of company's constitution
   (1)   A company must, not later than 15 days after the date of its incorporation, send to the registrar a copy of every instrument constituting or regulating the company.
   (2)   Where a company amends any instrument constituting or regulating the company, it must, not later than 15 days after the amendment takes effect, send to the registrar a copy of the instrument as amended.
   (3)   If a company fails to comply with subsection (1) or (2) an offence is committed by—
      (a)   the company, and
      (b)   every officer of the company who is in default.
   (4)   A person guilty of an offence under this section is liable on summary conviction to a fine not exceeding level 3 on the standard scale and, for continued contravention, a daily default fine not exceeding one-tenth of level 3 on the standard scale.

   27 Registrar's notice to comply in case of failure with respect to company's constitution
   (1)   If it appears to the registrar that a company has failed to comply with—
      (a)   section 26(1) or (2) (registrar to be sent copy of company's constitution), or
      (b)   any enactment requiring the company to send to the registrar—
         (i)   a document making or evidencing an alteration in any instrument constituting or regulating the company, or

(ii)   a copy of any such instrument as amended,

the registrar may give notice to the company requiring it to comply.

(2)   The notice must—

    (a)   state the date on which it is issued, and

    (b)   require the company to comply within 28 days from that date.

(3)   If the company complies with the notice within the specified time, no criminal proceedings may be brought in respect of the failure mentioned in subsection (1).

(4)   If the company does not comply with the notice within the specified time, it is liable to a civil penalty of £200.

(5)   This is in addition to any liability to criminal proceedings in respect of the failure mentioned in subsection (1).

(6)   The penalty may be recovered by the registrar and is to be paid into the Consolidated Fund.".

2. Sections 34 and 35 of the Companies Act 2006 (notice to registrar where company's constitution altered) apply to unregistered companies, modified so that they read as follows—

"34 Notice to registrar where company's constitution altered by enactment

(1)   This section applies where the constitution of a company is altered by an enactment, other than an enactment amending the general law.

(2)   The company must give notice of the alteration to the registrar, specifying the enactment, not later than 15 days after the enactment comes into force.

(3)   In the case of a special enactment the notice must be accompanied by a copy of the enactment.

(4)   If the enactment amends any instrument constituting or regulating the company, the notice must be accompanied by a copy of the instrument in question, as amended.

(5)   A "special enactment" means an enactment that is not a public general enactment, and includes—

    (a)   an Act for confirming a provisional order,

    (b)   any provision of a public general Act in relation to the passing of which any of the standing orders of the House of Lords or the House of Commons relating to Private Business applied, or

    (c)   any enactment to the extent that it is incorporated in or applied for the purposes of a special enactment.

(6)   If a company fails to comply with this section an offence is committed by—

    (a)   the company, and

    (b)   every officer of the company who is in default.

(7)   A person guilty of an offence under this section is liable on summary conviction to a fine not exceeding level 3 on the standard scale and, for continued contravention, a daily default fine not exceeding one-tenth of level 3 on the standard scale.

35 Notice to registrar where company's constitution altered by order

(1)   Where the constitution of a company is altered by an order of a court or other authority, the company must give notice to the registrar of the alteration not later than 15 days after the alteration takes effect.

(2)   The notice must be accompanied by—

    (a)   a copy of the order, and

    (b)   if the order amends any instrument constituting or regulating the company, a copy of the instrument in question, as amended.

(3)   If a company fails to comply with this section an offence is committed by—

    (a)   the company, and

    (b)   every officer of the company who is in default.

(4)   A person guilty of an offence under this section is liable on summary conviction to a fine not exceeding level 3 on the standard scale and, for continued contravention, a daily default fine not exceeding one-tenth of level 3 on the standard scale.

(5)   This section does not apply where provision is made by another enactment for the delivery to the registrar of a copy of the order in question.".

A company's capacity and related matters

3.   The following provisions of the Companies Act 2006 apply to unregistered companies—

    (a)   sections 39 and 40 (a company's capacity and power of directors to bind company);

    (b)   section 41 (constitutional limitations: transactions involving directors or their associates);

    (c)   section 42 (constitutional limitations: companies that are charities);

    (d)   sections 43, 44, 45(1) and 46 (formalities of doing business under the law of England and Wales or Northern Ireland);

    (e)   section 48 (execution of documents under the law of Scotland);

    (f)   section 50 (official seal for share certificates);

    (g)   section 51 (pre-incorporation contracts, deeds and obligations).

Trading disclosures

4. Sections 82 to 85 of the Companies Act 2006 (trading disclosures) apply to unregistered companies, modified so that they read as follows—

"82 Requirement to disclose company name and other particulars

(1) Every company must disclose its corporate name on—
  (a) its business letters, notices and other official publications;
  (b) its bills of exchange, promissory notes, endorsements and order forms;
  (c) cheques purporting to be signed by or on behalf of the company;
  (d) orders for money, goods or services purporting to be signed by or on behalf of the company;
  (e) its bills of parcels, invoices and other demands for payment, receipts and letters of credit;
  (f) its applications for licences to carry on a trade or activity;
  (g) all other forms of its business correspondence and documentation; and
  (h) its websites.

(2) Every company must disclose the further particulars set out in subsection (3) on—
  (a) its business letters;
  (b) its order forms; and
  (c) its websites.

(3) The further particulars required are—
  (a) the part of the United Kingdom in which the company's principal office is situated;
  (b) the reference number allocated to the company by the registrar;
  (c) the address of the company's principal office;
  (d) the manner in which it was incorporated;
  (e) if it is—
    (i) a limited company, or
    (ii) an investment company within the meaning of section 833,
    that fact.

(4) If, in the case of a company having a share capital, there is a reference to the amount of share capital on—
  (a) its business letters,
  (b) its order forms, or
  (c) its websites,
the reference must be to paid up share capital.

(5) In relation to a company, a reference to "its websites" includes a reference to any part of a website relating to that company which that company has caused or authorised to appear.

83 Civil consequences of failure to make required disclosure

(1) This section applies to any legal proceedings brought by a company to enforce a right arising out of a contract made in the course of a business in respect of which the company was, at the time the contract was made, in breach of section 82 (requirement to disclose company name and other particulars).

(2) The proceedings shall be dismissed if the defendant (in Scotland, the defender) to the proceedings shows—
  (a) that he has a claim against the claimant (pursuer) arising out of the contract that he has been unable to pursue by reason of the latter's breach of section 82, or
  (b) that he has suffered some financial loss in connection with the contract by reason of the claimant's (pursuer's) breach of section 82,
unless the court before which the proceedings are brought is satisfied that it is just and equitable to permit the proceedings to continue.

(3) This section does not affect the right of any person to enforce such rights as he may have against another person in any proceedings brought by that person.

84 Criminal consequences of failure to make required disclosure

(1) Where a company fails, without reasonable excuse, to comply with any requirement of section 82, an offence is committed by—
  (a) the company; and
  (b) every officer of the company who is in default.

(2) A person guilty of an offence under this section is liable on summary conviction to—
  (a) a fine not exceeding level 3 on the standard scale; and
  (b) for continued contravention, a daily default fine not exceeding one-tenth of level 3 on the standard scale.

(3) For the purposes of this section a shadow director is to be treated as an officer of the company.

85 Minor variations in form of name to be left out of account

For the purposes of this Chapter, in considering the name of a company no account is to be taken of—
  (a) whether upper or lower case characters (or a combination of the two) are used, or

  (b) whether diacritical marks or punctuation are present or absent,

provided there is no real likelihood of names differing only in those respects being taken to be different names.".

A company's principal office in the United Kingdom

5. Sections 86 and 87 of the Companies Act 2006 (a company's registered office) apply to unregistered companies, modified so that they read as follows—

"86 A company's principal office

(1) Communications and notices may at all times be addressed to a company at its principal office in the United Kingdom.

(2) A company must give notice to the registrar, not later than 15 days after the date of the incorporation of the company, of the address of its principal office in the United Kingdom.

(3) If a company fails to comply with subsection (2) an offence is committed by—

  (a) the company, and

  (b) every officer of the company who is in default.

(4) A person guilty of an offence under subsection (2) is liable on summary conviction to a fine not exceeding level 3 on the standard scale and, for continued contravention, a daily default fine not exceeding one-tenth of level 3 on the standard scale.

87 Change of principal office

(1) Where a company changes its principal office in the United Kingdom, it must send notice of the new address to the registrar not later than 15 days after the change takes effect.

(2) If a company fails to comply with subsection (1) an offence is committed by—

  (a) the company, and

  (b) every officer of the company who is in default.

(3) A person guilty of an offence under subsection (1) is liable on summary conviction to a fine not exceeding level 3 on the standard scale and, for continued contravention, a daily default fine not exceeding one-tenth of level 3 on the standard scale.

(4) Until the end of the period of 14 days beginning with the date on which the new address is registered a person may validly serve any document on the company at the address previously registered.

(5) For the purposes of any duty of a company—

  (a) to keep available for inspection at its principal office in the United Kingdom any register or other document, or

  (b) to mention the address of that office in any document,

a company that changes the address of its principal office in the United Kingdom may make the change as from such date as it may determine, but it is treated as failing to comply with that duty if it does not comply with subsection (1).

(6) Where a company unavoidably ceases to perform at its principal office in the United Kingdom any such duty as is mentioned in subsection (5)(a) but—

  (a) resumes performance of that duty at other premises as soon as practicable, and

  (b) gives notice to the registrar of a change in the address of its principal office in accordance with subsection (1),

it is not to be treated as having failed to comply with that duty.".

Directors and secretaries

6. (1) Sections 162 to 167 of the Companies Act 2006 (register of directors and register of directors' residential addresses) apply to unregistered companies.

(2) Section 162 (register of directors) applies with the following modifications—

 (a) in subsection (3)(b) (places where register may be kept available for inspection), for "specified in regulations under section 1136" substitute "specified in Part 2 of the Companies (Company Records) Regulations 2008 (SI 2008/3006)";

 (b) in subsection (5)(b) (inspection by non-member on payment), for "such fee as may be prescribed" substitute "the fee prescribed by regulation 2(a) of the Companies (Fees for Inspection of Company Records) Regulations 2008 (SI 2008/3007)".

7. (1) Sections 240 to 246 of the Companies Act 2006 (directors' residential addresses: protection from disclosure) apply to unregistered companies.

(2) Section 243 (permitted use or disclosure of protected information by the registrar) applies with the following modifications—

 (a) in subsection (2)(a) for "by regulations made by the Secretary of State" substitute "in the Companies (Disclosure of Address) Regulations 2009 (SI 2009/214)";

 (b) for subsection (3) substitute—

"(3) The provisions of the Companies (Disclosure of Address) Regulations 2009 (SI 2009/214) relating to disclosure of protected information under this section apply.

(3A) Those provisions are—

  (a) Part 2 (disclosure of protected information),

    (b)   Part 4 (matters relating to applications), so far as relating to disclosure under this section, and

    (c)   any other provisions of the Regulations having effect for the purposes of those provisions.";

(c)   omit subsections (4) to (6) and (8).

8. (1)   Sections 275 to 279 of the Companies Act 2006 (register of secretaries) apply to unregistered companies.

(2)   Section 275 applies with the following modifications—

    (a)   in subsection (3)(b) (places where register may be kept available for inspection), for "specified in regulations under section 1136" substitute "specified in Part 2 of the Companies (Company Records) Regulations 2008 (SI 2008/3006)";

    (b)   in subsection (5)(b) (inspection by non-member on payment), for "such fee as may be prescribed" substitute "the fee prescribed by regulation 2(a) of the Companies (Fees for Inspection of Company Records) Regulations 2008 (SI 2008/3007)".

Political donations and expenditure

9. (1)   Sections 362 to 379 of the Companies Act 2006 (control of political donations and expenditure) apply to unregistered companies, with the following modifications.

(2)   In section 369(5) (liability of directors to make good unauthorised donations or expenditure: interest), in paragraph (b) for "such rate as the Secretary of State may prescribe by regulations" substitute, "the rate specified in the Companies (Interest Rate for Unauthorised Political Donations or Expenditure) Regulations 2007 (SI 2007/2242)".

(3)   In section 377 (exemption of certain political expenditure)—

    (a)   in subsection (1) for "an order of the Secretary of State under this section" substitute "articles 3 and 4 of the Companies (Political Expenditure Exemption) Order 2007 (SI 2007/2081)";

    (b)   omit subsection (2);

    (c)   in subsection (3) for "an order under this section" substitute "the articles mentioned in subsection (1)";

    (d)   omit subsection (4).

Accounts

10. (1)   Sections 380 to 416, 418 to 469 and 471 to 474 of the Companies Act 2006 (accounts and reports) apply to unregistered companies, with the following modifications.

(2)   In section 383(6)(a) (small companies: determination of net amounts), for "regulations under section 404" substitute "Part 1 of Schedule 4 to the Small Companies and Groups (Accounts and Directors' Report) Regulations 2008 (SI 2008/409) or Schedule 3 to the Large and Medium-sized Companies and Groups (Accounts and Directors' Reports) Regulations 2008 (SI 2008/410)".

(3)   In section 396 (Companies Act individual accounts)—

    (a)   for subsection (3) (requirements as to form and content of accounts etc) substitute—

"(3)   The accounts must comply with the provisions of—

    (a)   regulation 3 of the Small Companies and Groups (Accounts and Directors' Report) Regulations 2008 (SI 2008/409), or

    (b)   regulations 3 and 4 of the Large and Medium-sized Companies and Groups (Accounts and Directors' Reports) Regulations 2008 (SI 2008/410),

as to the form and content of the balance sheet and profit and loss account, and additional information to be provided by way of notes to the accounts.";

    (b)   in subsection (4) (additional information) after "regulations" insert "specified in subsection (3)".

(4)   In section 404 (Companies Act group accounts)—

    (a)   for subsection (3) (requirements as to form and content of accounts etc) substitute—

"(3)   The accounts must comply with the provisions of—

    (a)   regulation 6 of the Small Companies and Groups (Accounts and Directors' Report) Regulations 2008 (SI 2008/409), or

    (b)   regulation 6 of the Large and Medium-sized Companies and Groups (Accounts and Directors' Reports) Regulations 2008 (SI 2008/410),

as to the form and content of the consolidated balance sheet and consolidated profit and loss account, and additional information to be provided by way of notes to the accounts.";

    (b)   in subsection (4) (additional information) after "regulations" insert "specified in subsection (3)".

(5)   In section 409 (information about related undertakings), for subsections (1) to (3) substitute—

"(1)   The notes to the company's annual accounts must contain the information about related undertakings required by—

    (a)   regulations 4 and 7 of the Small Companies and Groups (Accounts and Directors' Report) Regulations 2008 (SI 2008/409), or

    (b)   regulation 5 of the Large and Medium-sized Companies and Groups (Accounts and Directors' Reports) Regulations 2008 (SI 2008/410).

  (2) That information need not be disclosed with respect to an undertaking that—

    (a)   is established under the law of a country outside the United Kingdom, or

    (b)   carries on business outside the United Kingdom,

  if the following conditions are met.".

(6) In section 412 (information about directors' benefits: remuneration)—

  (a) for subsections (1) to (3) substitute—

  "(1) The information about directors' remuneration required by—

    (a)   the Small Companies and Groups (Accounts and Directors' Report) Regulations 2008 (SI 2008/409), or

    (b)   the Large and Medium-sized Companies and Groups (Accounts and Directors' Reports) Regulations 2008 (SI 2008/410),

  must be given in notes to the company's annual accounts.";

  (b) in subsection (4) for "and regulations made under it" substitute "and the regulations specified in subsection (1)";

  (c) in subsection (5) for "regulations under this section" substitute "and the regulations specified in subsection (1)".

(7) In section 416 (contents of directors' report: general), for subsection (4) substitute—

  "(4) The directors' report must comply with the provisions of—

    (a)   the Small Companies and Groups (Accounts and Directors' Report) Regulations 2008 (SI 2008/409), or

    (b)   the Large and Medium-sized Companies and Groups (Accounts and Directors' Reports) Regulations 2008 (SI 2008/410),

  as to other matters to be included in the report.".

(8) In section 421 (contents of directors' remuneration report), for subsections (1) and (2) substitute—

  "(1) The provisions of the Large and Medium-sized Companies and Groups (Accounts and Directors' Reports) Regulations 2008 (SI 2008/410) apply as to—

    (a)   the information that must be contained in a directors' remuneration report,

    (b)   how information is to be set out in the report, and

    (c)   what is to be the auditable part of the report.".

(9) In section 426 (option to provide summary financial statement)—

  (a) in subsection (1)(a) for "regulations made by the Secretary of State" substitute "the Companies (Summary Financial Statement) Regulations 2008 (SI 2008/374)";

  (b) omit subsections (3) and (6).

(10) In section 427 (form and contents of summary financial statement: unquoted companies)—

  (a) in subsection (1)(b) for "regulations made under it" substitute "the Companies (Summary Financial Statement) Regulations 2008 (SI 2008/374)";

  (b) for subsection (2) substitute—

  "(2) The summary financial statement must be in the form and contain such information as is required in the case of an unquoted company by the Companies (Summary Financial Statement) Regulations 2008 (SI 2008/374).".

(11) In section 428 (form and contents of summary financial statement: quoted companies)—

  (a) in subsection (1)(b) for "regulations made under it" substitute "the Companies (Summary Financial Statement) Regulations 2008 (SI 2008/374)";

  (b) for subsection (2) substitute—

  "(2) The summary financial statement must be in the form and contain such information as is required in the case of a quoted company by the Companies (Summary Financial Statement) Regulations 2008 (SI 2008/374).".

(12) In section 444(3) (filing obligations of companies subject to small companies regime: copies of accounts and reports)—

  (a) in paragraph (a) for "regulations made by the Secretary of State" substitute "regulation 5 of the Small Companies and Groups (Accounts and Directors' Report) Regulations 2008 (SI 2008/409)";

  (b) in paragraph (b) for "the regulations" substitute "that regulation".

(13) In section 445(3) (filing obligations of medium-sized companies: copies of accounts and reports)—

(a) in paragraph (a) for "regulations made by the Secretary of State" substitute "regulation 4 of the Large and Medium-sized Companies and Groups (Accounts and Directors' Reports) Regulations 2008 (SI 2008/410)";

(b) in paragraph (b) for "the regulations" substitute "that regulation".

(14) In section 449(2)(b) (special auditor's report where abbreviated accounts delivered: compliance with regulations), for "regulations under that section" substitute "regulation 5 of the Small Companies and Groups (Accounts and Directors' Report) Regulations 2008 (SI 2008/409) or regulation 4 of the Large and Medium-sized Companies and Groups (Accounts and Directors' Reports) Regulations 2008 (SI 2008/410)".

(15) In section 450(4) (approval and signing of abbreviated accounts: accounts not complying with requirements), for "regulations under the relevant section" substitute "regulation 5 of the Small Companies and Groups (Accounts and Directors' Report) Regulations 2008 (SI 2008/409) or regulation 4 of the Large and Medium-sized Companies and Groups (Accounts and Directors' Reports) Regulations 2008 (SI 2008/410)".

(16) In section 453 (civil penalty for failure to file accounts and reports)—

(a) in subsection (2) (determination of amount), for "regulations made by the Secretary of State" substitute "the relevant provisions of the Companies (Late Filing Penalties) and Limited Liability Partnerships (Filing Periods and Late Filing Penalties) Regulations 2008 (SI 2008/497)";

(b) omit subsection (5).

(17) In section 454 (voluntary revision of accounts), for subsections (3) to (5) substitute—

"(3) The provisions of the Companies (Revision of Defective Accounts) Regulations 2008 (SI 2008/373) apply.".

(18) In section 457 (other persons authorised to apply to the court)—

(a) for subsections (1) to (3) substitute—

"(1) The Companies (Defective Accounts and Directors' Reports) (Authorised Person) and Supervision of Accounts and Reports (Prescribed Body) Order 2008 (SI 2008/623) apply as regards—

(a) the persons authorised by the Secretary of State for the purposes of section 456 (application to court in respect of defective accounts or reports), and

(b) the requirements and other provisions applying to the exercise of functions as an authorised person.";

(b) omit subsections (5) to (7).

(19) In section 464 (accounting standards)—

(a) in subsection (1) for "such body or bodies as may be prescribed by regulations" substitute "the body known as the Accounting Standards Board, as prescribed by the Accounting Standards (Prescribed Body) Regulations 2008 (SI 2008/651)";

(b) omit subsection (3).

Audit

11. (1) Sections 475 to 481 and 484 to 539 of the Companies Act 2006 (audit) apply to unregistered companies, with the following modifications.

(2) Section 494 (disclosure of services provided by auditor or associates and related remuneration) is modified so that it reads as follows—

"494 Disclosure of services provided by auditor or associates and related remuneration
The Companies (Disclosure of Auditor Remuneration and Liability Limitation Agreements) Regulations 2008 (SI 2008/489) apply as regards the disclosure of—

(a) the nature of any services provided for a company by the company's auditor (whether in the capacity as auditor or otherwise) or by the auditor's associates;

(b) the amount of any remuneration received or receivable by the auditor, or the auditor's associates, in respect of any such services.".

(3) In section 504 (meaning of "senior statutory auditor"), in subsection (1)(b)(ii) for "by order of the Secretary of State" substitute "by the Statutory Auditors (Delegation of Functions etc) Order 2008 (SI 2008/496)".

(4) Section 538 (disclosure by company of liability limitation agreement) is modified so that it reads as follows—

"538 Disclosure of agreement by company
A company that has entered into a liability limitation agreement must make the disclosure in connection with the agreement required by the Companies (Disclosure of Auditor Remuneration and Liability Limitation Agreements) Regulations 2008 (SI 2008/489).".

Share certificates

12. (1) The following provisions of the Companies Act 2006 apply to unregistered companies—

(a) section 768 (share certificate to be evidence of title);

(b)   section 778 (issue of certificates etc: allotment or transfer to financial institution).

(2)   In section 778 as it applies to unregistered companies, for "section 769(1) or 776(1) (duty of company as to issue of certificates etc)" substitute "any provision of any instrument constituting or regulating the company".

Annual return

13. (1)   Sections 854 to 859 of the Companies Act 2006 (a company's annual return) apply to unregistered companies.

(2)   Section 855 (contents of annual return: general) applies with the following modifications—

(a)   in subsection (1)(d) (place where company records kept), omit "(in accordance with regulations under section 1136)";

(b)   in subsection (2) (classification of company type), for "prescribed for the purposes of this section" insert "prescribed by regulation 5 of and Schedule 1 to the Companies Act 2006 (Annual Return and Service Addresses) Regulations 2008 (SI 2008/3000)";

(c)   in subsection (3) (classification of business activities), for "any prescribed system of classifying business activities" substitute "the system of classifying business activities prescribed by regulation 6 of and Schedule 2 to the Companies Act 2006 (Annual Return and Service Addresses) Regulations 2008 (SI 2008/3000)".

Takeovers

14. (1)   Sections 966 to 973 of the Companies Act 2006 (impediments to takeovers) apply to unregistered companies.

(2)   Sections 974 to 991 of that Act ("squeeze-out" and "sell-out") apply to unregistered companies, but so far as relating to the offeree company only if the unregistered company has voting shares admitted to trading on a regulated market.

Fraudulent trading

15. Section 993 of the Companies Act 2006 (fraudulent trading) applies to an unregistered company.

Company Investigations

16. Parts 14 and 15 of the Companies Act 1985 (company investigations etc) apply to unregistered companies.

The registrar of companies

17. (1)   The application to unregistered companies by the following paragraphs of certain provisions of Part 35 of the Companies Act 2006 is without prejudice to the application in relation to unregistered companies of the provisions of that Part that are of general application.

(2)   Those provisions are—

(a)   sections 1060(1) and (2) and 1061 to 1063 (the registrar),

(b)   sections 1068 to 1071 (delivery of documents to the registrar),

(c)   sections 1072 to 1076 (requirements for proper delivery),

(d)   sections 1080(1), (4) and (5) and 1092 (keeping and production of records),

(e)   section 1083 (preservation of original documents),

(f)   sections 1108 to 1110 (language requirements: transliteration),

(g)   sections 1111 and 1114 to 1119 (supplementary provisions).

18. Section 1066 of the Companies Act 2006 (registered numbers) applies to unregistered companies, modified so that it reads as follows—

> **"1066 Companies' reference numbers**
>
> (1)   The registrar shall allocate to every company a number, which shall be known as the company's reference number.
>
> (2)   Companies' reference numbers shall be in such form, consisting of one or more sequences of figures or letters, as the registrar may determine.
>
> (3)   The registrar may on adopting a new form of reference number make such changes of existing reference numbers as appear necessary.
>
> (4)   A change of a company's reference number has effect from the date on which the company is notified by the registrar of the change.
>
> (5)   For a period of three years beginning with that date any requirement to disclose the company's reference number imposed by section 82 (trading disclosures) is satisfied by the use of either the old number or the new.".

19. Sections 1077 to 1079 of the Companies Act 2006 (public notice of receipt of certain documents) apply to unregistered companies, modified so that they read as follows—

> **"1077 Public notice of receipt of certain documents**
>
> (1)   The registrar must cause to be published—
>
> (a)   in the Gazette, or
>
> (b)   in accordance with section 1116 (alternative means of giving public notice),

notice of the receipt by the registrar of any document specified in section 1078.

(2) The notice must state the name and reference number of the company, the description of document and the date of receipt.

(3) The registrar is not required to cause notice of the receipt of a document to be published before the date of incorporation of the company to which the document relates.

1078 The section 1077 documents

The following documents are specified for the purposes of section 1077—

Constitutional documents

> 1 Any instrument constituting or regulating the company.
>
> 2 After any alteration of such an instrument, any copy of the instrument as amended.
>
> 3 Any notice of the change of the company's name.

Accounts and returns

> 1 All documents required to be delivered to the registrar under section 441 (annual accounts).
>
> 2 The company's annual return.

Principal office

Notification of any change of the company's principal office in the United Kingdom.

Winding up

> 1 Copy of any winding-up order in respect of the company.
>
> 2 Notice of the appointment of liquidators.
>
> 3 Order for the dissolution of the company on a winding up.
>
> 4 Return by a liquidator of the final meeting of the company on a winding up.

1079 Effect of failure to give public notice

(1) A company is not entitled to rely against other persons on the happening of any event to which this section applies unless—

    (a) the event has been officially notified at the material time, or

    (b) the company shows that the person concerned knew of the event at the material time.

(2) The events to which this section applies are—

    (a) (as regards service of any document on the company) a change of the company's principal office in the United Kingdom,

    (b) the making of a winding-up order in respect of the company, or

    (c) the appointment of a liquidator in a voluntary winding up of the company.

(3) If the material time falls—

    (a) on or before the 15th day after the date of official notification, or

    (b) where the 15th day was not a working day, on or before the next day that was,

the company is not entitled to rely on the happening of the event as against a person who shows that he was unavoidably prevented from knowing of the event at that time.

(4) "Official notification" means—

    (a) in relation to anything stated in a document specified in section 1078, notification of that document in accordance with section 1077;

    (b) in relation to the appointment of a liquidator in a voluntary winding up, notification of that event in accordance with section 109 of the Insolvency Act 1986 (c 45) or Article 95 of the Insolvency (Northern Ireland) Order 1989 (SI 1989/2405 (N.I. 19)).".

20. (1) The following provisions of the Companies Act 2006 apply to unregistered companies—

    (a) section 1080(2) and (4) (meaning of "register" and form in which documents to be recorded and kept);

    (b) sections 1085 and 1086 (inspection of the register and right to take copies on the register);

    (c) sections 1087 and 1088 (material not available for public inspection and application to registrar to make address unavailable for public inspection);

    (d) sections 1089 and 1090 (form and manner of application for inspection or copy);

    (e) section 1091 (certification of copies as accurate).

(2) In section 1087 (material not available for public inspection) as it applies to unregistered companies, in subsection (1)—

    (a) omit paragraph (a);

    (b) in paragraph (b) omit "or any corresponding provision of regulations under section 1046 (overseas companies)";

    (c) in paragraph (ba), omit sub-paragraph (ii);

    (d) omit paragraphs (c) to (h) and (j).

(3) For section 1088 as it applies to unregistered companies substitute—

"1088 Application to registrar to make address unavailable for public inspection

(1) The relevant provisions of the Companies (Disclosure of Address) Regulations 2009 (SI 2009/214) apply with respect to applications to the registrar to make an address on the register unavailable for public inspection.

(2) Those provisions are—
- (a) Part 3 (applications to make address unavailable for public inspection), and
- (b) Part 4 (matters relating to application), so far as relating to such applications, and
- (c) any other provisions of the Regulations having effect for the purposes of those provisions.".

(4) In section 1091 (certification of copies as accurate) as it applies to unregistered companies, for subsection (4) substitute—

"(4) Regulation 2 of the Companies (Registrar, Languages and Trading Disclosures) Regulations 2006 (SI 2006/3429) (certification of electronic copies by registrar) applies where the copy is provided in electronic form.".

Supplementary provisions
21. The provisions of the Companies Acts relating to offences, interpretation and other supplementary matters have effect in relation to unregistered companies so far as necessary for the purposes of the application and enforcement of the provisions applied to unregistered companies by these Regulations.

NOTES
Commencement: 1 October 2009.

SCHEDULE 2
TRANSITIONAL PROVISIONS AND SAVINGS
Regulation 9

Introduction

[4.604]
1. (1) In this Schedule—
- (a) "the 1985 Act" means the Companies Act 1985 and "the 1985 Regulations" means the Companies (Unregistered Companies) Regulations 1985;
- (b) "the 1986 Order" means the Companies (Northern Ireland) Order 1986 and "the 1986 Regulations" means the Companies (Unregistered Companies) Regulations (Northern Ireland) 1986;
- (c) "existing company" means an unregistered company that was incorporated before 1st October 2009.

(2) References in this Schedule to provisions of the 1985 Act or 1986 Order, or to provisions of the Companies Act 2006, are to those provisions as applied to unregistered companies.

A company's constitution
2. (1) Section 26(1) of the Companies Act 2006 (registrar to be sent copy of instruments constituting or regulating company) applies where the company is incorporated on or after 1st October 2009.

(2) Section 18 of the 1985 Act as modified by regulation 6(b)(ii) of the 1985 Regulations or Article 29 of the 1986 Order as modified by regulation 6(b)(ii) of the 1986 Regulations continues to apply where the company was incorporated before that date.

3. (1) Section 26(2) of the Companies Act 2006 (registrar to be sent copy of amended instrument constituting or regulating company) applies where the amendment takes effect on or after 1st October 2009.

(2) Section 18(2) and (3) of the 1985 Act or Article 29(2) and (3) of the 1986 Order continue to apply in relation to amendments taking effect before that date.

4. (1) Section 34 of the Companies Act 2006 (notice to registrar where company's constitution altered by enactment) applies where the enactment in question comes into force on or after 1st October 2009.

(2) Section 18(1) and (3) of the 1985 Act or Article 29(1) and (3) of the 1986 Order continue to apply in relation to alterations made by statutory provisions coming into force before that date.

5. Section 35 of the Companies Act 2006 (notice to registrar where company's constitution altered by order) applies in relation to orders made on or after 1st October 2009.

A company's capacity and related matters
6. (1) Section 39 of the Companies Act 2006 (a company's capacity) applies to acts of a company done on or after 1st October 2009.

(2) Section 35 of the 1985 Act or Article 45 of the 1986 Order continues to apply to acts of a company done before that date.

7. (1) Section 44 of the Companies Act 2006 (execution of documents) applies in relation to the execution of documents on or after 1st October 2009.

(2)   Section 36A of the 1985 Act or Article 46A of the 1986 Order continues to apply in relation to documents executed before that date.

(3)   For the purposes of this paragraph a document signed by one authorised signatory before 1st October 2009 and by another on or after that date is treated as executed on or after 1st October 2009.

A company's principal office in the United Kingdom
8. Section 86(2) of the Companies Act 2006 (registrar to be notified of address of company's principal office in the United Kingdom) applies where the company is incorporated on or after 1st October 2009.

Directors and secretaries
9. On and after 1st October 2009 the register of directors and secretaries kept by a company under section 288(1) of the 1985 Act or Article 296(1) of the 1986 Order shall be treated as two separate registers—
  (a)   a register of directors kept under and for the purposes of section 162 of the Companies Act 2006, and
  (b)   a register of secretaries kept under and for the purposes of section 275 of that Act.

10. (1)   Subject to the following provisions, an existing company need not comply with any provision of the Companies Act 2006 requiring the company's register of directors or secretaries to contain particulars additional to those required by the 1985 Act or the 1986 Order until the earlier of—
  (a)   the date to which the company makes up its first annual return made up to a date on or after 1st October 2009, and
  (b)   the last date to which the company should have made up that return.

(2)   Sub-paragraph (1) does not apply in relation to a director or secretary of whom particulars are first registered on or after 1st October 2009 (whether the director or secretary was appointed before, on or after that date).

(3)   Sub-paragraph (1) ceases to apply in relation to a director or secretary whose registered particulars fall to be altered on or after 1st October 2009 because they have changed (whether the change occurred before, on or after that date).

(4)   This paragraph does not affect the particulars required to be included in the company's annual return.

11. (1)   In the case of an existing company—
  (a)   the relevant existing address of a director or secretary is deemed, on and after 1st October 2009, to be a service address, and
  (b)   any entry in the company's register of directors or secretaries stating that address is treated, on and after that date, as complying with the obligation in section 163(1)(b) or 277(1)(b) of the Companies Act 2006 to state a service address.

(2)   The relevant existing address is—
  (a)   the address that immediately before 1st October 2009 appeared in the company's register of directors and secretaries as having been notified to the company under section 289(1A) or 290(1A) of the 1985 Act (service address notified by individual applying for confidentiality order in respect of usual residential address), or
  (b)   if no such address appeared, the address that immediately before that date appeared in the company's register of directors and secretaries as the director's or secretary's usual residential address.

(3)   Any notification of a change of a relevant existing address occurring before 1st October 2009 that is received by the company on or after that date is treated as being or, as the case may be, including notification of a change of service address.

(4)   The operation of this paragraph does not give rise to any duty to notify the registrar under section 167 or 276 of the Companies Act 2006 (duty to notify registrar of changes in particulars contained in register).

12. (1)   An existing company must remove from its register of directors on 1st October 2009 any entry relating to a shadow director.

(2)   Section 167 of the Companies Act 2006 (duty to notify registrar of changes) applies as if the shadow director had ceased to be a director on that date.

13. The removal by an existing company from its register of directors or secretaries on or after 1st October 2009 of particulars required by the 1985 Act or the 1986 Order but not required by the Companies Act 2006 does not give rise to any duty to notify the registrar under section 167 or 276 of the Companies Act 2006 (duty to notify registrar of changes in particulars contained in register).

14. (1)   The duty of a company to keep a register of directors' residential addresses has effect on and after 1st October 2009.

(2) The entry on that register of information that immediately before that date was contained in the company's register of directors and secretaries does not give rise to any duty to notify the registrar under section 167 of the Companies Act 2006 (duty to notify registrar of changes in particulars contained in register).

15. (1) Sections 167 and 276 of the Companies Act 2006 (duty to notify registrar of changes) apply in relation to—
   (a)   a change among a company's directors or in its secretaries, or
   (b)   a change in the particulars contained in the register,
occurring on or after 1st October 2009.

(2) Sections 288(2), (4) and (6), 289 and 290 of the 1985 Act or Articles 296(2), (4) and (6), 297 and 298 of the 1986 Order (notification to registrar of changes) continue to apply in relation to a change occurring before that date.

16. (1) The registrar may make such entries in the register as appear to be appropriate having regard to paragraphs 10 to 14 and the information appearing on the register immediately before 1st October 2009 or notified to the registrar in accordance with paragraph 15(2).

(2) In particular, the registrar may record as a service address a relevant existing address (within the meaning of paragraph 11).

(3) Any notification of a change of a relevant existing address occurring before 1st October 2009 that is received by the registrar on or after that date is treated as being or, as the case may be, including notification of a change of service address.

17. Where a director's usual residential address appears as a service address—
   (a)   in the company's register of directors by virtue of paragraph 11, or
   (b)   in the register of companies by virtue of paragraph 16,
that address is not protected information for the purposes of Chapter 8 of Part 10 of the Companies Act 2006.

18. (1) Section 242(1) of the Companies Act 2006 (duty of registrar to omit protected information from material available for inspection) does not apply—
   (a)   to material delivered to the registrar before 1st October 2009, or
   (b)   to material delivered to the registrar on or after 1st October 2009 by virtue of paragraph 15(2) (notification of change occurring before that date).

(2) In section 242(2)(b) of the Companies Act 2006 (exclusion of material registered before commencement) the reference to things registered before Chapter 8 of Part 10 of that Act comes into force is treated as including anything registered as a result of a notification in accordance with paragraph 15(2) (notification on or after 1st October 2009 of change occurring before that date).

19. In determining under section 245(1) of the Companies Act 2006 whether to put a director's usual residential address on the public record, the registrar may take into account only—
   (a)   communications sent by the registrar on or after 1st October 2009, and
   (b)   evidence as to the effectiveness of service coming to the registrar's attention on or after that date.

Political donations and expenditure

20. (1) Sections 362 to 379 of the Companies Act 2006 (political donations and expenditure) apply to donations made or expenditure incurred on or after 1st October 2007.

(2) Section 379(2) of that Act applies as to the time when a donation is regarded as made or expenditure as incurred, including where it is made or incurred in pursuance of a contract entered into before that date.

(3) Part 10A of the 1985 Act continues to apply to donations or expenditure in relation to which the relevant time, as defined in section 347A(10) of that Act, is before that date.

(4) The repeal of that Part does not affect paragraph 3(4) of Schedule 7 to the 1985 Act (matters to be dealt with in directors' report: expressions to have same meaning as in Part 10A).

Accounts

21. (1) Sections 380 to 416, 418 to 469 and 471 to 474 of the Companies Act 2006 (accounts and reports) apply to accounts and reports for financial years beginning on or after 1st October 2009.

(2) The corresponding provisions of the 1985 Act or 1986 Order continue to apply to accounts and reports for financial years beginning before that date.

22. Any question whether—
   (a)   for the purposes of section 382, 383, 384(3) or 467(3) of the Companies Act 2006, a company or group qualified as small in a financial year beginning before 1st October 2009, or
   (b)   for the purposes of section 465 or 466 of that Act a company or group qualified as medium-sized in any such financial year,
is to be determined by reference to the corresponding provisions of the 1985 Act or 1986 Order.

Audit

23. (1)   In Chapter 1 of Part 16 of the Companies Act 2006 (requirement for audited accounts)—
   (a)   sections 475 to 481 (general provisions) apply to accounts for financial years beginning on or after 1st October 2009; and
   (b)   section 484 (general power of amendment by regulations) applies accordingly.

(2)   Sections 235(1), 249A(1), (3) and (6) to (7), 249AA and 249B of the 1985 Act or Articles 243(1), 257A(1), (3) and (6) to (7), 257AA and 257B of the 1986 Order continue to apply to accounts for financial years beginning before that date.

24. (1)   Sections 485 to 488 of the Companies Act 2006 (appointment of auditors of private companies) apply in relation to appointments for financial years beginning on or after 1st October 2009.

(2)   Sections 384 to 388A of the 1985 Act or Articles 392 to 396A of the 1986 Order continue to apply in relation to appointments for financial years beginning before that date.

(3)   Where—
   (a)   a private company has elected under section 386 of the 1985 Act or Article 394 of the 1986 Order to dispense with the annual appointment of auditors, and
   (b)   the election is in force immediately before 1st October 2009,
section 487(2)(a) of the Companies Act 2006 (no deemed reappointment of auditors appointed by directors) does not prevent the deemed reappointment under that subsection of auditors first appointed before 1st October 2009.

25. (1)   This paragraph applies where immediately before 1st October 2009 a resolution of a private company under section 390A of the 1985 Act or Article 398A of the 1986 Order (remuneration of auditors) was in force and was expressed (in whatever terms) to continue to have effect so long as a resolution under section 386 of that Act or Article 394 of that Order (election to dispense with annual appointment of auditors) continued in force.

(2)   The repeal of section 386 of the 1985 Act or Article 394 of the 1986 Order does not affect the continued operation of the resolution, which shall continue to have effect until—
   (a)   it is revoked or superseded by a further resolution,
   (b)   the auditors to which it applies cease to hold office, or
   (c)   it otherwise ceases to have effect in accordance with its terms.

26. (1)   In Chapter 2 of Part 16 of the Companies Act 2006 (appointment of auditors)—
   (a)   sections 489 and 490 (appointment of auditors by public companies) apply to appointments for financial years beginning on or after 1st October 2009;
   (b)   section 491 (term of office of auditors of public company) applies to auditors appointed for financial years beginning on or after that date.

(2)   Sections 384, 385, 387 and 388(1), (3) and (4) of the 1985 Act or Articles 392, 393, 395 and 396(1), (3) and (4) of the 1986 Order continue to apply to appointments by public companies for financial years beginning before that date.

27. (1)   The following provisions apply to auditors appointed for financial years beginning on or after 1st October 2009—
   (a)   section 492 (fixing of auditor's remuneration),
   (b)   section 493 (disclosure of terms of audit appointment), and
   (c)   section 494 (disclosure of services provided by auditor or associated and related remuneration).

(2)   Sections 390A and 390B of the 1985 Act or Articles 398A and 398B of the 1986 Order continue to apply to auditors appointed for financial years beginning before that date.

(3)   The repeal of section 390A of the 1985 Act and Article 398A of the 1986 Order (remuneration of auditors) does not affect the operation of any such resolution as is mentioned in paragraph 25 above.

28. (1)   In Chapter 3 of Part 16 of the Companies Act 2006 (functions of auditor)—
   (a)   sections 495 to 498 (auditor's report and duties of auditor) apply to auditors' reports on accounts or reports for financial years beginning on or after 1st October 2009;
   (b)   sections 499 to 501 (rights of auditors) apply to auditors appointed for financial years beginning on or after that date;
   (c)   sections 503 to 509 (signature of auditor's report and offences in connection with auditor's report) apply to auditors' reports on accounts or reports for financial years beginning on or after that date.

(2)   Sections 235 to 237, 389A and 389B of the 1985 Act or Articles 243 to 245, 397A and 397B of the 1986 Order continue to apply as regards financial years beginning before that date.

29. (1)   Section 502 of the Companies Act 2006 (auditor's rights in relation to resolutions and meetings) applies to auditors appointed on or after 1st October 2009.

(2)   Section 390 of the 1985 Act or Article 398 of the 1986 Order continues to apply to auditors appointed before that date.

30. (1) In Chapter 4 of Part 16 of that Act (removal, resignation, etc of auditors), sections 510 to 513 (removal of auditor) apply where notice of the intended resolution is given to the company on or after 1st October 2009.

(2) Sections 391 and 391A of the 1985 Act or Articles 399 and 399A of the 1986 Order continue to apply where notice of the intended resolution is given to the company before that date.

(3) In section 513 (rights of auditor removed from office) as it applies in relation to an auditor appointed before 1st October 2009, the reference to rights under section 502(2) shall be read as a reference to rights under section 390(1) of the 1985 Act or Article 398(1) of the 1986 Order.

31. (1) Sections 514 and 515 of the Companies Act 2006 (failure to re-appoint auditor) apply to appointments for financial years beginning on or after 1st October 2009.

(2) Section 391A of the 1985 Act or Article 399A of the 1986 Order continues to apply to appointments for financial years beginning before that date.

32. (1) Sections 516 to 518 of the Companies Act 2006 (resignation of auditor) apply to resignations occurring on or after 1st October 2009.

(2) Sections 392 and 392A of the 1985 Act or Articles 400 and 400A of the 1986 Order continue to apply to resignations occurring before that date.

(3) In section 518 (rights of resigning auditor) as it applies in relation to an auditor appointed before 1st October 2009, the reference to rights under section 502(2) shall be read as a reference to rights under section 390(1) of the 1985 Act or Article 398(1) of the 1986 Order.

33. (1) Sections 519 to 525 of the Companies Act 2006 (statement by auditor ceasing to hold office) apply where the auditor ceases to hold office on or after 1st October 2009.

(2) Sections 394 and 394A of the 1985 Act or Articles 401A and 401B of the 1986 Order continue to apply where the auditor ceases to hold office before that date.

34. (1) Section 526 of the Companies Act 2006 (effect of casual vacancies) applies where the vacancy occurs on or after 1st October 2009.

(2) Section 388(2) of the 1985 Act or Article 396(2) of the 1986 Order continues to apply where the vacancy occurred before that date.

35. In section 527 of the Companies Act 2006—
- (a) subsection (1)(a) (matters relating to audit of company's accounts) applies to accounts for financial years beginning on or after 1st October 2009, and
- (b) subsection (1)(b) (matters relating to circumstances connected with an auditor of the company) applies to auditors appointed for financial years beginning on or after that date.

36. A resolution passed before 1st October 2009 authorising a liability limitation agreement is effective for the purposes of section 536 of the Companies Act 2006 (authorisation of agreement by members of company) if it complies with the requirements of that section.

Annual return

37. (1) Sections 854 to 859 of the Companies Act 2006 (a company's annual return) apply to annual returns made up to a date on or after 1st October 2009.

(2) Sections 363 to 365 of the 1985 Act or Articles 371 to 373 of the 1986 Order continue to apply to annual returns made up to a date before 1st October 2009.

(3) Any reference in the Companies Act 2006 to a company's last return, or to a return delivered in accordance with Part 24 of that Act, shall be read as including (so far as necessary to ensure the continuity of the law) a return made up to a date before 1st October 2009 or delivered in accordance with the 1985 Act or the 1986 Order.

Fraudulent trading

38. (1) Section 458 of the 1985 Act or Article 451 of the 1986 Order (offences of fraudulent trading) continues to apply to offences completed before 1st October 2009.

(2) Where, in the case of an offence—
- (a) a relevant event occurs before 1st October 2009, and
- (b) another relevant event occurs on or after 1st October 2009,

the offence must be charged under section 993 of the Companies Act 2006 (and not under section 458 of the 1985 Act or Article 451 of the 1986 Order).

(3) If in the case of any such offence a relevant event occurred before 15th January 2007, section 993(3)(a) applies with the substitution of "seven years" for "ten years".

(4) "Relevant event" means an act, omission or other event (including any result of one or more acts or omissions) proof of which is required for conviction of the offence.

Company investigations

39. (1) The extension to Northern Ireland by section 1284 of the Companies Act 2006 of Parts 14 and 15 of the 1985 Act (company investigations) has effect to enable the exercise of the powers conferred by those Parts in relation to unregistered companies having their principal office in Northern Ireland, and otherwise in relation to Northern Ireland, on and after 1st October 2009.

(2) Parts 15 and 16 of the 1986 Order, and any other provision of that Order having effect for the purposes of Part 15, continue to apply (subject to sub-paragraph (3) below)—

(a) in relation to inspectors appointed under Part 15 before 1st October 2009 and matters arising in connection with or in consequence of any such appointment or any report of inspectors so appointed;

(b) in relation to any exercise before 1st October 2009 of any power of the Department of Enterprise, Trade and Investment in Northern Ireland not within paragraph (a), and matters arising in connection with or in consequence of any such exercise.

(3) A direction in force immediately before 1st October 2009 under Article 438(1A) or 449(1A) of the 1986 Order (direction limiting or relaxing restrictions on shares) shall continue in force and have effect on and after that date as if made under the corresponding provision of Part 14 of the 1985 Act, and the provisions of Part 15 of that Act shall apply accordingly.

Saving for provisions as to form or manner in which documents to be delivered

40. (1) Any saving in this Schedule for the effect of a provision of the 1985 Act or 1986 Order requiring use of a prescribed form extends to the form and the power under which it is prescribed.

(2) Any saving in this Schedule for the effect of a provision of the 1985 Act or 1986 Order requiring a document to be delivered to the registrar extends to section 707B of the 1985 Act or Article 656B of the 1986 Order (delivery to the registrar using electronic communications) so far as relating to the provision in question and the delivery of documents under it.

Savings for provisions relating to offences

41. (1) The repeal of any provision of the 1985 Act or 1986 Order creating an offence does not affect the continued operation of that provision in relation to an offence committed before 1st October 2009.

(2) Any saving in this Schedule for the effect of a provision of the 1985 Act or 1986 Order that creates an offence extends to the entry relating to that provision in Schedule 24 to that Act or Schedule 23 to that Order (punishment of offences).

(3) References in this paragraph to provisions of the 1985 Act or 1986 Order include provisions of regulations or orders made under that Act or Order.

NOTES
Commencement: 1 October 2009.

COMPANIES (COMPANIES AUTHORISED TO REGISTER) REGULATIONS 2009

(SI 2009/2437)

NOTES
Made: 4 September 2009.
Authority: European Communities Act 1972, s 2(2); Companies Act 2006, ss 1042, 1292(1).
Commencement: 1 October 2009.
Amendment: as of 1 July 2011 these Regulations had not been amended.

ARRANGEMENT OF REGULATIONS

PART 1
INTRODUCTION

PART 2
REGISTRATION REQUIREMENTS

Introduction

Agreement of members to registration

Requirements for registration

PART 1
INTRODUCTION

[4.605]
1　Citation and commencement

(1)　These Regulations may be cited as the Companies (Companies Authorised to Register) Regulations 2009.

(2)　These Regulations come into force on 1st October 2009.

NOTES
　Commencement: 1 October 2009.

PART 2
REGISTRATION REQUIREMENTS

Introduction

[4.606]
2　Application of this Part

(1)　The provisions of this Part apply in relation to the registration of a company under the Companies Act 2006 in pursuance of section 1040 of that Act (companies not formed under companies legislation but authorised to register).

(2)　In this Part—

　(a)　references to a company are to a company authorised to register under that section (see subsections (1), (4) and (5) of that section); and

　(b)　references to registration are to registration under that section.

NOTES
　Commencement: 1 October 2009.

Agreement of members to registration

[4.607]
3   Agreement of members to registration

(1)   A company must not register without the assent of a majority of such of its members as are present in person or by proxy (in cases where proxies are allowed) at a general meeting summoned for the purpose.

(2)   Where a company not having the liability of its members limited by an enactment or letters patent wishes to register as a limited company, the majority required to assent as required by paragraph (1) is not less than 75% of the members present in person or by proxy at the meeting.

(3)   In computing any majority under this regulation when a poll is demanded, regard is to be had to the number of votes to which each member is entitled according to the company's regulations.

NOTES
Commencement: 1 October 2009.

Requirements for registration

[4.608]
4   Registration documents

(1)   An application for registration of the company must be delivered to the registrar together with the documents required by this regulation and a statement of compliance.

(2)   The application for registration must state—
   (a)   the name with which the company is proposed to be registered,
   (b)   whether the company's registered office is to be situated in England and Wales (or in Wales), in Scotland or in Northern Ireland,
   (c)   whether the liability of the members of the company is to be limited, and if so whether it is to be limited by shares or by guarantee, and
   (d)   whether the company is to be a private or a public company.

(3)   The application must contain—
   (a)   in the case of a joint stock company, a statement of capital and initial shareholdings (see regulation 5);
   (b)   in the case of a company that is to be limited by guarantee, a statement of guarantee (see regulation 6);
   (c)   a statement of the company's proposed officers (see regulation 7).

(4)   The application must contain—
   (a)   a statement of the intended address of the company's registered office, and
   (b)   a copy of any enactment, royal charter, letters patent, deed of settlement, contract of partnership or other instrument constituting or regulating the company.

(5)   The application must be delivered—
   (a)   to the registrar of companies for England and Wales, if the registered office of the company is to be situated in England and Wales (or in Wales);
   (b)   to the registrar of companies for Scotland, if the registered office of the company is to be situated in Scotland;
   (c)   to the registrar of companies for Northern Ireland, if the registered office of the company is to be situated in Northern Ireland.

NOTES
Commencement: 1 October 2009.

[4.609]
5   Statement of capital and initial shareholdings

(1)   The statement of capital and initial shareholdings required to be delivered in the case of a joint stock company must comply with this regulation.

(2)   It must state—
   (a)   the total number of shares of the company that on a date specified in the statement ("the reference date") are held by members of the company,
   (b)   the aggregate nominal value of those shares,
   (c)   for each class of shares—
      (i)   the particulars specified in paragraph (4) below of the rights attached to the shares,
      (ii)   the total number of shares of that class, and
      (iii)   the aggregate nominal value of shares of that class, and
   (d)   the amount to be paid up and the amount (if any) to be unpaid on each share (whether on account of the nominal value of the share or by way of premium).

(3)   The reference date must be not more than 28 days before the date of the application for registration.

(4)   The particulars referred to in paragraph (2)(c)(i) are—

(a)   particulars of any voting rights attached to the shares, including rights that arise only in certain circumstances;

(b)   particulars of any rights attached to the shares, as respects dividends, to participate in a distribution;

(c)   particulars of any rights attached to the shares, as respects capital, to participate in a distribution (including on winding up); and

(d)   whether the shares are to be redeemed or are liable to be redeemed at the option of the company or the shareholder.

(5)   The statement of capital and initial shareholdings must also state—

(a)   the names and service addresses of all persons who on the reference date were members of the company, and

(b)   with respect to each member of the company—

(i)   the number, nominal value (of each share) and class of shares held by that member on that date, and

(ii)   the amount to be paid up and the amount (if any) to be unpaid on each share (whether on account of the nominal value of the share or by way of premium).

(6)   For the purposes of paragraph (5)(a) a person's "name" means his Christian name (or other forename) and surname, except that in the case of—

(a)   a peer, or

(b)   an individual usually known by a title,

the title may be stated instead of his Christian name (or other forename) and surname or in addition to either or both of them.

(7)   Where a member of the company holds shares of more than one class, the information required under paragraph (5)(b)(i) is required for each class.

NOTES

Commencement: 1 October 2009.

[4.610]

6   Statement of guarantee

(1)   Where the company proposes to register as a company limited by guarantee, the members' assent to its being registered (see regulation 3) must be accompanied by a resolution containing a statement of guarantee.

(2)   The statement of guarantee required is a statement that each member undertakes that, if the company is wound up while he is a member, or within one year after he ceases to be a member, he will contribute to the assets of the company such amount as may be required for—

(a)   payment of the debts and liabilities of the company contracted before he ceases to be a member,

(b)   payment of the costs, charges and expenses of winding up, and

(c)   adjustment of the rights of the contributories among themselves,

not exceeding a specified amount.

(3)   The statement of guarantee required to be delivered to the registrar in the case of a company that is to be limited by guarantee is a copy of the resolution containing the statement of guarantee.

NOTES

Commencement: 1 October 2009.

[4.611]

7   Statement of proposed officers

(1)   The statement of the company's proposed officers required to be delivered to the registrar must contain the required particulars of—

(a)   the person who is, or persons who are, to be a director or directors of the company on registration;

(b)   in the case of a company that is to be a private company, any person who is (or any persons who are) to be the secretary (or joint secretaries) of the company on registration;

(c)   in the case of a company that is to be a public company, the person who is (or the persons who are) to be the secretary (or joint secretaries) of the company on registration;

(d)   a consent by each person named as a director, as secretary or as one of joint secretaries, to act in the relevant capacity.

(2)   The required particulars are the particulars that will be required to be stated—

(a)   in the case of a director, in the company's register of directors and register of residential addresses (see sections 162 to 165 of the Companies Act 2006);

(b)   in the case of a secretary, in the company's register of secretaries (see sections 277 to 278 of that Act).

(3)   Regulation 7 of the Companies (Disclosure of Address) Regulations 2009 (disclosure of protected information: application under section 243 on behalf of proposed director) applies as if—

(a) references to a subscriber to the memorandum of association were to any member of the company, and

(b) references to the proposed company were to the company proposing to register.

NOTES
Commencement: 1 October 2009.

[4.612]
8 Statement of compliance

(1) The statement of compliance required to be delivered to the registrar is a statement that the requirements of this Part as to registration have been complied with.

(2) The registrar may accept the statement of compliance as sufficient evidence of compliance.

NOTES
Commencement: 1 October 2009.

Registration as a public company

[4.613]
9 Registration as a public company

(1) A joint stock company may be registered as a public company limited by shares if—
    (a) the following conditions are met, and
    (b) the application for registration is accompanied by the documents specified in paragraph (4) below.

(2) The conditions are—
    (a) that the requirements of section 91 of the Companies Act 2006 are met as regards its share capital;
    (b) the requirements of section 92 of that Act are met as regards its net assets; and
    (c) if section 93 of that Act applies (recent allotment of shares for non-cash consideration), that the requirements of that section are met.

(3) Sections 91 to 93 apply for this purpose as in the case of a private company applying to be re-registered under section 90 of the Companies Act 2006 (re-registration of private company as public), but as if any reference to the special resolution required by section 90 were to the joint stock company's resolution that it be a public company.

(4) The following documents must be delivered to the registrar together with the application for registration (as well as those required by regulation 4)—
    (a) a copy of the resolution that the company be a public company;
    (b) a copy of the balance sheet and other documents referred to in section 92(1); and
    (c) if section 93 applies (recent allotment of shares for non-cash consideration), a copy of the valuation report (if any) under subsection (2)(a) of that section.

(5) The statement of compliance required to be delivered with the application is a statement that the requirements of this Part as to registration as a public company have been complied with.

(6) The registrar may accept the statement of compliance as sufficient evidence that the company is entitled to be registered as a public company.

NOTES
Commencement: 1 October 2009.

Change of name on registration

[4.614]
10 Change of name on registration

(1) Where the name of a company seeking registration is a name by which it is precluded from being registered by any provision of the Companies Acts, either—
    (a) because it is directly prohibited from being registered with that name, or
    (b) because the Secretary of State would not approve the company being registered with that name,
the company may change its name with effect from the date on which it is registered.

(2) A change of name under this regulation requires the like assent of the company's members as is required by regulation 3 for registration.

NOTES
Commencement: 1 October 2009.

Registration

[4.615]
11 Registration

If the registrar is satisfied that the requirements of this Part as to registration are complied with, the registrar shall register the documents delivered to him.

NOTES
Commencement: 1 October 2009.

[4.616]
12   Issue of certificate of incorporation

(1)   On the registration of a company, the registrar shall give a certificate that the company is incorporated.

(2)   The certificate must state—
(a)   the name and registered number of the company,
(b)   the date of its incorporation,
(c)   whether it is a limited or unlimited company, and if it is limited whether it is limited by shares or limited by guarantee,
(d)   whether it is a private or a public company, and
(e)   whether the company's registered office is situated in England and Wales (or in Wales), in Scotland or in Northern Ireland.

(3)   The certificate must be signed by the registrar or authenticated by the registrar's official seal.

(4)   The certificate is conclusive evidence that the requirements of this Part as to registration have been complied with and that the company is duly registered under the Companies Act 2006.

(5)   Section 1064 of that Act (public notice of certificate of incorporation) applies to a certificate of incorporation issued under this regulation.

NOTES
Commencement: 1 October 2009.

PART 3
EFFECT OF REGISTRATION

Introduction

[4.617]
13   Interpretation of this Part

In this Part—
   "registration" means registration under the Companies Act 2006 in pursuance of section 1040 of that Act; and
   "instrument" includes a deed of settlement, a contract of partnership or letters patent.

NOTES
Commencement: 1 October 2009.

Transfer of property, rights and liabilities

[4.618]
14   Transfer of property, rights and liabilities

(1)   All property belonging to or vested in the company at the date of its registration passes to and vests in the company on registration for all the estate and interest of the company in the property.

(2)   Registration does not affect the company's rights or liabilities in respect of any debt or obligation incurred, or contract entered into, by, to, with or on behalf of the company before registration.

NOTES
Commencement: 1 October 2009.

[4.619]
15   Pending legal proceedings

(1)   All actions and other legal proceedings which at the time of the company's registration are pending by or against the company, or the public officer or any member of it, may be continued in the same manner as if the registration had not taken place.

(2)   Execution shall not issue against the effects of any individual member of the company on any judgment, decree or order obtained in such an action or proceeding; but in the event of the company's property and effects being insufficient to satisfy the judgment, decree or order, an order may be obtained for winding up the company.

NOTES
Commencement: 1 October 2009.

The company's constitution

[4.620]
16   Constitutional provisions to have effect as if contained in articles of association
(1)   All provisions contained in any enactment or other instrument constituting or regulating the company are deemed to be conditions and regulations of the company, in the same manner and with the same incidents as if so much of them as would, if the company had been formed and registered under the Companies Act 2006, be contained in registered articles of association.

(2)   The provisions brought in by paragraph (1) include, in the case of a company registered as a company limited by guarantee, those of the resolution declaring the amount of the guarantee.

NOTES
Commencement: 1 October 2009.

[4.621]
17   Power to substitute articles of association
A registered company may by special resolution alter the form of its constitution by substituting articles of association for any instrument constituting or regulating the company, other than an enactment, a royal charter or letters patent.

NOTES
Commencement: 1 October 2009.

Application of the Companies Acts

[4.622]
18   General application of the Companies Acts
(1)   Subject to the following regulations, the provisions of the Companies Acts apply to a registered company, and to its members and contributories, in the same manner as if it had been formed and registered under the Companies Act 2006.

(2)   References in this and the following regulations to the Companies Acts—
  (a)   include the Companies (Cross-Border Mergers) Regulations 2007, and
  (b)   do not include Part 2 of the Companies (Audit, Investigation and Community Enterprise) Act 2004 (community interest companies).

NOTES
Commencement: 1 October 2009.

[4.623]
19   Exclusions
(1)   The model articles of association prescribed by the Secretary of State under section 19 of the Companies Act 2006 do not apply unless adopted by special resolution.

(2)   Provisions relating to the numbering of shares do not apply to a joint stock company whose shares are not numbered.

NOTES
Commencement: 1 October 2009.

[4.624]
20   Restrictions on power to alter company's constitution
(1)   Subject to the provisions of this Part, the company does not have power—
  (a)   to alter any provision contained in an enactment relating to the company,
  (b)   without the consent of the Secretary of State, to alter any provision contained in letters patent relating to the company.

(2)   The company does not have power to alter any provision contained in a royal charter or letters patent with respect to the company's objects.

(3)   Where by virtue of paragraph (1) or (2) a company does not have power to alter a provision, it does not have power to ratify acts of the directors in contravention of the provision.

NOTES
Commencement: 1 October 2009.

[4.625]
21   Provisions as to capital structure
The provisions with respect to—
  (a)   the re-registration of an unlimited company as limited,
  (b)   the powers of an unlimited company on re-registration as a limited company to provide that a portion of its share capital shall not be capable of being called up except in the event of winding up, and

(c)   the power of a limited company to determine that a portion of its share capital shall not be capable of being called up except in that event,

apply notwithstanding any provisions contained in any enactment, royal charter or other instrument constituting or regulating the company.

NOTES
Commencement: 1 October 2009.

[4.626]
22   Saving for other powers to alter company's constitution

(1)   Except as mentioned in paragraph (2), none of the provisions of this Part or of the Companies Acts affects any power of altering the company's constitution or regulations vested in the company by virtue of any enactment or other instrument constituting or regulating it.

(2)   Paragraph (1) does not apply to the power of the court under section 996(2) of the Companies Act 2006 (protection of members against unfair prejudice: power of court to regulate the conduct of the company's affairs).

NOTES
Commencement: 1 October 2009.

[4.627]
23   Status of banking company in Scotland

A banking company in Scotland that is incorporated by virtue of registration under these Regulations is deemed a bank incorporated, constituted or established by or under an Act of Parliament.

NOTES
Commencement: 1 October 2009.

PART 4
TRANSITIONAL PROVISIONS AND SAVINGS

[4.628]
24   Transitional provisions and savings

(1)   Part 2 of these Regulations has effect in accordance with paragraph 93 of Schedule 2 to the Companies Act 2006 (Commencement No 8, Transitional Provisions and Savings) Order 2008 (by virtue of which it applies to applications made on or after 1st October 2009).

(2)   The transitional provisions and savings relating to the coming into force of the provisions of the Companies Acts in relation to companies as defined in section 1 of the Companies Act 2006 (companies formed and registered under that Act) also have effect in relation to those provisions as applied by Part 3 of these Regulations.

(3)   In any such transitional provision or saving as applied by paragraph (2), a reference to a commencement date other than 1st October 2009 shall be read as a reference to 1st October 2009.

NOTES
Commencement: 1 October 2009.

COMPANIES ACT 2006 AND LIMITED LIABILITY PARTNERSHIPS (TRANSITIONAL PROVISIONS AND SAVINGS) (AMENDMENT) REGULATIONS 2009 (NOTE)

(SI 2009/2476)

[4.629]

NOTES
These Regulations were made on 9 September 2009 under the powers conferred by the Companies Act 2006, ss 1292(2), 1296(1), 1300(2), and the Limited Liability Partnerships Act 2000, ss 15, 17.

Regulation 1 provides for citation and commencement. These Regulations come into force on 1 October 2009 (with the exception of the amendment to the Companies Act 2006 (Commencement No 8, Transitional Provisions and Savings) Order 2008, SI 2008/2860, art 3, which comes into force on 30 September 2009).

Regulation 2(1) and (2) amend art 3 of the 2008 Order (at **[2.84]**) so as to stop s 22(2) of CA 2006 coming into force on 1 October 2009.

Regulation 2(1) and (3) replace the transitional provisions and savings relating to ss 1012–1023 of the 2006 Act which come into force on 1 October 2009. Section 1012 provides for the property of a dissolved company to vest in the Crown as if it were bona vacantia. Sections 1013–1022 provide for the disclaimer by the Crown of title to such property and the effects of disclaimer. Sections 1012–1022 re-enact, with modifications, corresponding provisions of the Companies Act 1985 and the Companies (Northern Ireland) Order 1986 (SI 1986/1032). In particular, there are changes to the time periods within which the appropriate Crown representative must disclaim title to such property. Transitional provisions in para 88 of Schedule 2 to the

2008 Order provide for ss 1012–1022 of the 2006 Act to apply in relation to the property of a company dissolved on or after 1 October 2009, and for the provisions replaced by those sections to continue to apply in relation to the property of a company dissolved before that date.

Regulation 2(1) and (3) change the transitional provisions as they relate to the property of a company dissolved before 1 October 2009. The new law on disclaimer will apply in relation to such property if, at that date, the appropriate Crown representative has neither had notice that the property has vested in the Crown, nor received an application to consider disclaimer nor waived the right to disclaim. The old law will continue to apply in cases where the new law does not apply.

Sections 1012–1023 were applied to LLPs by regs 52–55 of the Limited Liability Partnerships (Application of Companies Act 2006) Regulations 2009 (SI 2009/1804). Paragraph 22 of Schedule 1 to those Regulations provides for transitional provisions corresponding to those for company property. Regulation 3 replaces those provisions with transitional provisions corresponding to those substituted, in relation to company property, by reg 2(1) and (3).

Regulation 2(1) and (4) add new savings to the 2008 Order. They relate to s 26(2)(a) of the Companies Act 1985 and s 2(1)(a) of the Business Names Act 1985, which have been repealed with effect from 1 October 2009. The effect is to save prohibitions on companies being registered by, or persons carrying on business under, a name which would be likely to give an impression of a connection with the Welsh Assembly Government. These savings will cease to have effect when equivalent prohibitions are introduced by amendment to the corresponding provisions of the 2006 Act.

COMPANY, LIMITED LIABILITY PARTNERSHIP AND BUSINESS NAMES (SENSITIVE WORDS AND EXPRESSIONS) REGULATIONS 2009

(SI 2009/2615)

NOTES

Made: 25 September 2009.

Authority: Companies Act 2006, ss 55(1), 56(1)(b), 1194(1), 1195(1)(b), 1292(1)

Commencement: 1 October 2009.

These Regulations are reproduced as amended by: the Secretary of State for Education Order 2010, SI 2010/1836.

ARRANGEMENT OF REGULATIONS

SCHEDULES

[4.630]

1 Citation and commencement

These Regulations may be cited as the Company, Limited Liability Partnership and Business Names (Sensitive Words and Expressions) Regulations 2009 and come into force on 1st October 2009.

NOTES

Commencement: 1 October 2009.

[4.631]

2 Interpretation

(1) In these Regulations "the 2006 Act" means the Companies Act 2006.

(2) Any reference in these Regulations to section 55 or 88 of the 2006 Act includes a reference to that section as applied by regulation 8 or 17 of the Limited Liability Partnerships (Application of Companies Act 2006) Regulations 2009.

NOTES
Commencement: 1 October 2009.

[4.632]
3   Specified words and expressions applicable to sections 55 and 1194 of the 2006 Act

(1)   The following words and expressions are specified for the purposes of sections 55(1) and 1194(1) of the 2006 Act—
  (a)   the words and expressions set out in Part 1 of Schedule 1;
  (b)   the plural and possessive forms of those words and expressions, and, where relevant, the feminine form; and
  (c)   in the case of the words and expressions set out in Part 1 of Schedule 1 which are marked with an asterisk, the grammatically mutated forms of those words and expressions.

(2)   For the purposes of section 55(1) of the 2006 Act any word or expression specified in Part 1 of Schedule 1 which contains an accent or other diacritical mark is to be read as though that accent or other diacritical mark were omitted.

NOTES
Commencement: 1 October 2009.

[4.633]
4   Specified words and expressions applicable to section 55 of the 2006 Act

The following words and expressions are specified for the purposes of section 55(1) of the 2006 Act—
  (a)   the words and expressions set out in Part 2 of Schedule 1;
  (b)   the plural and possessive forms of those words and expressions, and, where relevant, the feminine form; and
  (c)   in the case of the words and expressions set out in Part 2 of Schedule 1 which are marked with an asterisk, the grammatically mutated forms of those words and expressions.

NOTES
Commencement: 1 October 2009.

[4.634]
5   Applications where situation of registered office or principal place of business is irrelevant

In connection with an application for the approval of the Secretary of State under section 55 or 1194 of the 2006 Act in relation to a name that includes a word or expression specified in column (1) of Part 1 of Schedule 2 the applicant must seek the view of the Government department or other body set out opposite that word or expression in column (2) of Part 1 of Schedule 2.

NOTES
Commencement: 1 October 2009.

[4.635]
6   Applications where situation of registered office or principal place of business is relevant

In connection with an application for the approval of the Secretary of State under section 55 or 1194 of the 2006 Act in relation to a name that includes a word or expression specified in column (1) of Part 2 of Schedule 2 the applicant must seek the view of a Government department or other body as follows—
  (a)   in the case of—
    (i)   a company or limited liability partnership that has already been registered, whose registered office is situated in England and Wales;
    (ii)   a proposed company or limited liability partnership that has not yet been registered under the 2006 Act, whose registered office is to be situated in England and Wales;
    (iii) a business, whose principal place of business is or is to be situated in England; and
    (iv)   an overseas company (see section 1044 of the 2006 Act),
    the Government department or other body set out in column (2) of Part 2 of Schedule 2 opposite that word or expression;
  (b)   in the case of—
    (i)   a company or limited liability partnership that has already been registered, that is a Welsh company or Welsh LLP (see section 88 of the 2006 Act);
    (ii)   a proposed company or limited liability partnership that has not yet been registered, that is to be a Welsh company or Welsh LLP; and
    (iii) a business, whose principal place of business is or is to be situated in Wales,
    the Government department or other body set out in column (3) of Part 2 of Schedule 2 opposite that word or expression;
  (c)   in the case of—

    (i)   a company or limited liability partnership that has already been registered, whose registered office is situated in Scotland;

    (ii)   a proposed company or limited liability partnership that has not yet been registered, whose registered office is to be situated in Scotland; and

    (iii)   a business, whose principal place of business is or is to be situated in Scotland,

the Government department or other body set out in column (4) of Part 2 of Schedule 2 opposite that word or expression; and

(d)   in the case of—

    (i)   a company or limited liability partnership that has already been registered, whose registered office is situated in Northern Ireland;

    (ii)   a proposed company or limited liability partnership that has not yet been registered, whose registered office is to be situated in Northern Ireland; and

    (iii)   a business, whose principal place of business is or is to be situated in Northern Ireland,

the Government department or other body set out in column (5) of Part 2 of Schedule 2 opposite that word or expression.

NOTES

Commencement: 1 October 2009.

[4.636]
7

The following Regulations are revoked—

(a)   the Company and Business Names Regulations 1981,

(b)   the Company and Business Names (Amendment) Regulations 1982,

(c)   the Company and Business Names (Amendment) Regulations 1992,

(d)   the Company and Business Names (Amendment) Regulations 1995,

(e)   the Company and Business Names (Amendment) Regulations 2001, and

(f)   the Company and Business Names (Amendment) (No 2) Regulations 2007.

NOTES

Commencement: 1 October 2009.

SCHEDULES

SCHEDULE 1
SPECIFIED WORDS AND EXPRESSIONS

Regulations 3 and 4

PART 1
SPECIFIED WORDS AND EXPRESSIONS APPLICABLE TO SECTIONS 55(1) AND 1194(1) OF THE 2006 ACT

[4.637]

Abortion	*Breatainn
Accredit	*Brenhinol
Accreditation	*Brenin
Accredited	*Brenhiniaeth
Accrediting	Britain
Adjudicator	British
Association	*Cenedlaethol
Assurance	Chamber of
Assurer	Charitable
Audit office	Charity
Auditor General	Charter
Authority	Chartered
*Banc	Child maintenance
Bank	Child support
Banking	*Coimisean
Banknote	*Comhairle
Benevolent	*Comisiwn
Board	Commission
*Breatannach	Co-operative

Council
*Cyngor
Data protection
Dental
Dentistry
Disciplinary
Discipline
*Diùc
*Dug
Duke
Ei Fawrhydi
England
English
European
Federation
Friendly Society
Foundation
Fund
Giro
Government
Group
*Gwasanaeth iechyd
*Gwladol
Health centre
Health service
Health visitor
His Majesty
Holding
HPSS
HSC
Human rights
Inspectorate
Institute
Institution
Insurance
Insurer
International
Judicial appointment
King
Licensing
*Llywodraeth
Medical centre
Midwife
Midwifery
*Mòrachd
Mutual
National
NHS
Northern Ireland
Northern Irish
Nurse
Nursing

Oifis sgrùdaidh
*Oilthigh
Ombudsman
*Ombwdsmon
Oversight
*Parlamaid
Parliament
Parliamentarian
Parliamentary
Patent
Patentee
Police
Polytechnic
Post office
Pregnancy termination
*Prifysgol
Prince
*Prionnsa
*Prydain
*Prydeinig
Queen
Reassurance
Reassurer
Register
Registered
Registrar
Registration
Registry
Regulation
Regulator
Reinsurance
Reinsurer
*Riaghaltas
*Rìgh
Rìoghachd Aonaichte
Rìoghail
Rìoghalachd
Royal
Royalty
Rule committee
Scotland
Scottish
Senedd
Sheffield
Siambr
Social service
Society
Special school
Standards
Stock exchange
Swyddfa archwilio
*Teyrnas Gyfunol

*Teyrnas Unedig	United Kingdom
Trade union	University
Tribunal	Wales
Trust	Watchdog
*Tywysog	Welsh
Underwrite	Windsor
Underwriting	

NOTES
Commencement: 1 October 2009.

PART 2
SPECIFIED WORDS AND EXPRESSIONS APPLICABLE TO SECTION 55(1) OF THE 2006 ACT

[4.638]

Alba	*Cymraeg
Albannach	*Cymreig
Na h-Alba	
*Cymru	

NOTES
Commencement: 1 October 2009.

SCHEDULE 2
LIST OF GOVERNMENT DEPARTMENTS AND OTHER BODIES WHOSE VIEWS MUST BE SOUGHT

Regulations 5 and 6

PART 1
APPLICATIONS WHERE SITUATION OF REGISTERED OFFICE OR PRINCIPAL PLACE OF BUSINESS IS IRRELEVANT

[4.639]

Column (1)	Column (2)
Word or expression specified under regulation 3	**Specified Government department or other body whose view must be sought**
Abortion	Department of Health
Accredit	Department for Business, Innovation & Skills
Accreditation	Department for Business, Innovation & Skills
Accredited	Department for Business, Innovation & Skills
Accrediting	Department for Business, Innovation & Skills
Assurance	Financial Services Authority
Assurer	Financial Services Authority
Banc	Financial Services Authority
Bank	Financial Services Authority
Banking	Financial Services Authority
Banknote	The Governor and Company of the Bank of England
Brenhinol	The Welsh Assembly Government
Brenin	The Welsh Assembly Government
Brenhiniaeth	The Welsh Assembly Government
Child maintenance	Child Maintenance and Enforcement Commission
Child support	Child Maintenance and Enforcement Commission
Data protection	Information Commissioner's Office
Dental	General Dental Council
Dentistry	General Dental Council
Diùc	The Scottish Executive
Dug	The Welsh Assembly Government

Column (1)	Column (2)
Word or expression specified under regulation 3	Specified Government department or other body whose view must be sought
Ei Fawrhydi	The Welsh Assembly Government
Friendly Society	Financial Services Authority
Fund	Financial Services Authority
Gwasanaeth iechyd	The Welsh Assembly Government
Health visitor	Nursing & Midwifery Council
HPSS	Department of Health, Social Services and Public Safety
HSC	Department of Health, Social Services and Public Safety
Insurance	Financial Services Authority
Insurer	Financial Services Authority
Judicial appointment	Ministry of Justice
Llywodraeth	The Welsh Assembly Government
Medical centre	Department of Health, Social Services and Public Safety
Midwife	Nursing & Midwifery Council
Midwifery	Nursing & Midwifery Council
Mòrachd	The Scottish Executive
Mutual	Financial Services Authority
NHS	Department of Health
Nurse	Nursing & Midwifery Council
Nursing	Nursing & Midwifery Council
Oifis sgrùdaidh	Audit Scotland
Oilthigh	The Scottish Executive
Parlamaid	The Scottish Parliamentary Corporate Body
Parliament	The Corporate Officer of the House of Lords and
	The Corporate Officer of the House of Commons
Parliamentarian	The Corporate Officer of the House of Lords and
	The Corporate Officer of the House of Commons
Parliamentary	The Corporate Officer of the House of Lords and
	The Corporate Officer of the House of Commons
Patent	The Patent Office
Patentee	The Patent Office
Polytechnic	Department for Business, Innovation & Skills
Pregnancy termination	Department of Health
Prifysgol	The Welsh Assembly Government
Prionnsa	The Scottish Executive
Reassurance	Financial Services Authority
Reassurer	Financial Services Authority
Reinsurance	Financial Services Authority
Reinsurer	Financial Services Authority
Riaghaltas	The Scottish Executive
Rìgh	The Scottish Executive
Rìoghail	The Scottish Executive
Rìoghalachd	The Scottish Executive
Rule committee	Ministry of Justice
Senedd	The National Assembly for Wales
Sheffield	The Company of Cutlers in Hallamshire
Swyddfa archwilio	Auditor General for Wales
Tywysog	The Welsh Assembly Government
Underwrite	Financial Services Authority
Underwriting	Financial Services Authority

NOTES
Commencement: 1 October 2009.

PART 2
APPLICATIONS WHERE SITUATION OF REGISTERED OFFICE OR PRINCIPAL PLACE OF BUSINESS IS RELEVANT

[4.640]

Column (1)	Column (2)	Column (3)	Column (4)	Column (5)
Word or expression specified under regulation 3	Specified Government department or other body whose view must be sought			
	under regulation 6(a)	under regulation 6(b)	under regulation 6(c)	under regulation 6(d)
Audit office	Comptroller & Auditor General	Auditor General for Wales	Audit Scotland	Northern Ireland Audit Office
Charitable Charity	The Charity Commission	The Charity Commission	Office of the Scottish Charity Regulator	The Charity Commission
Duke His Majesty King Prince Queen Royal Royalty Windsor	Ministry of Justice	The Welsh Assembly Government	The Scottish Executive	Ministry of Justice
Health centre Health service	Department of Health	The Welsh Assembly Government	The Scottish Executive	Department of Health, Social Services and Public Safety
Police	The Home Office	The Home Office	The Scottish Executive	Northern Ireland Office
Special school	[Department for Education]	The Welsh Assembly Government	The Scottish Executive	Department of Education
University	Department for Business, Innovation & Skills	The Welsh Assembly Government	The Scottish Executive	Department for Employment and Learning

NOTES
Commencement: 1 October 2009.
Words in square brackets in column 2 of the entry for "Special school" substituted by the Secretary of State for Education Order 2010, SI 2010/1836, art 6, Schedule, Pt 2, para 11, as from 8 August 2010.

COMPANY, LIMITED LIABILITY PARTNERSHIP AND BUSINESS NAMES (PUBLIC AUTHORITIES) REGULATIONS 2009

(SI 2009/2982)

NOTES
Made: 10 November 2009 (at 11.30 am).
Authority: Companies Act 2006, ss 54(1)(c), 56(1)(a), 1193(1)(c), 1195(1)(a), 1292(1).
Commencement: 10 November 2009 (at 11.30 am).
Amendment: as of 1 July 2011 these Regulations had not been amended.

ARRANGEMENT OF REGULATIONS

[4.641]
1   Citation and commencement
These Regulations may be cited as the Company, Limited Liability Partnership and Business Names (Public Authorities) Regulations 2009 and come into force immediately after they are made.

NOTES
Commencement: 10 November 2009 (at 11.30 am).

[4.642]
2   Interpretation
(1)   In these Regulations "the 2006 Act" means the Companies Act 2006.

(2)   Any reference to section 54 of the 2006 Act in these Regulations includes a reference to that section as applied by regulation 8 of the Limited Liability Partnerships (Application of Companies Act 2006) Regulations 2009.

NOTES
Commencement: 10 November 2009 (at 11.30 am).

[4.643]
3   Specified "public authorities"
Each of the persons and bodies set out in column (1) of the Schedule is specified for the purposes of sections 54 and 1193 of the 2006 Act.

NOTES
Commencement: 10 November 2009 (at 11.30 am).

[4.644]
4   Specified Government department or other body whose view must be sought
In connection with an application for the approval of the Secretary of State under section 54 or 1193 of the 2006 Act in relation to a name that would be likely to give the impression of a connection with a public authority set out in column (1) of the Schedule the applicant must seek the view of the Government department or other body set out opposite that public authority in column (2) of the Schedule.

NOTES
Commencement: 10 November 2009 (at 11.30 am).

[4.645]
5   Savings for existing lawful business names
(1)   This Regulation has effect in relation to section 1193 of the 2006 Act.

(2)   These Regulations do not apply to the carrying on of a business by a person who—
   (a)   carried on the business immediately before the date on which these Regulations came into force, and
   (b)   continues to carry it on under the name that immediately before that date was its lawful business name.

(3)   Where—
   (a)   a business is transferred to a person on or after the date on which these Regulations came into force, and
   (b)   that person carries on the business under the name that was its lawful business name immediately before the transfer,
these Regulations do not apply in relation to the carrying on of the business under that name during the period of twelve months beginning with the date of the transfer.

(4)   In this regulation "lawful business name", in relation to a business, means a name under which the business was carried on without contravening the provisions of Chapter 1 of Part 41 of the 2006 Act.

NOTES
Commencement: 10 November 2009 (at 11.30 am).

SCHEDULE
SPECIFIED "PUBLIC AUTHORITIES" AND LIST OF GOVERNMENT DEPARTMENTS AND OTHER BODIES WHOSE VIEWS MUST BE SOUGHT

Regulations 3 and 4

[4.646]

Column (1) Public authority	Column (2) Government department or other body whose view must be sought
Accounts Commission for Scotland	Accounts Commission for Scotland
Audit Commission for Local Authorities and the National Health Service in England	Audit Commission for Local Authorities and the National Health Service in England
Audit Scotland	Audit Scotland
Auditor General for Scotland	Auditor General For Scotland
Auditor General for Wales (known in Welsh as "Archwilydd Cyffredinol Cymru")	Auditor General for Wales (known in Welsh as "Archwilydd Cyffredinol Cymru")
Child Maintenance and Enforcement Commission	Child Maintenance and Enforcement Commission
Comptroller and Auditor General	Comptroller and Auditor General
Comptroller and Auditor General for Northern Ireland	Comptroller and Auditor General for Northern Ireland
Financial Reporting Council	Financial Reporting Council
Financial Services Authority	Financial Services Authority
Health and Safety Executive	Health and Safety Executive
House of Commons	The Corporate Officer of the House of Commons
House of Lords	The Corporate Officer of the House of Lords
Law Commission	Ministry of Justice
National Assembly for Wales (known in Welsh as "Cynulliad Cenedlaethol Cymru")	National Assembly for Wales Commission (known in Welsh as "Comisiwn Cynulliad Cenedlaethol Cymru")
National Assembly for Wales Commission (known in Welsh as "Comisiwn Cynulliad Cenedlaethol Cymru")	National Assembly for Wales Commission (known in Welsh as "Comisiwn Cynulliad Cenedlaethol Cymru")
Northern Ireland Assembly	Northern Ireland Assembly Commission
Northern Ireland Assembly Commission	Northern Ireland Assembly Commission
Northern Ireland Audit Office	Northern Ireland Audit Office
Regional Agency for Public Health and Social Well-being.	Regional Agency for Public Health and Social Well-being.
Regional Health and Social Care Board	Regional Health and Social Care Board
Scottish Law Commission	Scottish Law Commission
The Governor and Company of the Bank of England	The Governor and Company of the Bank of England
The Pensions Advisory Service	Department for Work and Pensions
The Scottish Parliament	The Scottish Parliamentary Corporate Body
The Scottish Parliamentary Corporate Body	The Scottish Parliamentary Corporate Body

NOTES

Commencement: 10 November 2009 (at 11.30 am).

COMPANIES ACT 2006 (AMENDMENT OF SECTION 413) REGULATIONS 2009 (NOTE)

(SI 2009/3022)

[4.647]

NOTES

These Regulations were made on 12 November 2009 under the powers conferred by the Companies Act 2006, s 468(1), (2). They came into force on 12 December 2009. They amend s 413(8) of the 2006 Act (at **[1.413]**) so that banking companies and the holding companies of credit institutions are only required to make aggregate disclosures of the amounts specified in s 413(5)(a) and (c) (correcting an incorrect cross-reference). This is in implementation of the Member State option in Article 40(7) of Council Directive 86/635/EEC on the annual accounts and consolidated accounts of banks and other financial institutions.

COMPANIES ACT 2006 (CONSEQUENTIAL AMENDMENTS AND TRANSITIONAL PROVISIONS) ORDER 2011

(SI 2011/1265)

NOTES

Made: 11 May 2011.
Authority: Companies Act 2006, ss 1292, 1294, 1296.
Commencement: 12 May 2011.
Amendment: as of 1 July 2011 this Order had not been amended.

[4.648]
1   Citation and commencement

(1)   This Order may be cited as the Companies Act 2006 (Consequential Amendments and Transitional Provisions) Order 2011.

(2)   This Order comes into force on the day after the day on which it is made.

NOTES

Commencement: 12 May 2011.

[4.649]
2   Repeal of the Companies Consolidation (Consequential Provisions) Act 1985 (c 9)

The Companies Consolidation (Consequential Provisions) Act 1985 is repealed.

NOTES

Commencement: 12 May 2011.

3, 4   *(Arts 3, 4 contain amendments to the Companies Act 2006 (Commencement No 8, Transitional Provisions and Savings) Order 2008, SI 2008/2860 (at* **[2.82]**) *and the Companies Act 2006 (Consequential Amendments, Transitional Provisions and Savings) Order 2009, SI 2009/1941 (at* **[4.528]**) *consequential on the repeal by art 2 of the Companies Consolidation (Consequential Provisions) Act 1985.)*

[4.650]
5

(1)   Schedule 1 to this Order contains provisions preserving the effect of the provisions of the Companies Consolidation (Consequential Provisions) Act 1985 relating to old public companies.

(2)   The repeal of the other provisions of that Act does not affect the operation of—
    (a)   any provision amending an enactment that remains in force;
    (b)   any transitional provision that remains capable of having effect in relation to the corresponding provision of the Companies Act 2006;
    (c)   any saving that remains capable of having effect in relation to the repeal of an enactment by that Act.

NOTES

Commencement: 12 May 2011.

6–32 *(Arts 6–30 contain various consequential amendments which, in so far as relevant, have been incorporated at the appropriate place; art 31 introduces Sch 3 (transitional provisions and savings in connection with open-ended investment companies in Northern Ireland (outside the scope of this work)); art 32 revokes the Companies (Single Member Private Limited Companies) Regulations 1992, SI 1992/1699 and the Companies (Single Member Private Limited Companies) (Northern Ireland) Regulations 1992.)*

SCHEDULES

SCHEDULE 1
PROVISIONS RELATING TO OLD PUBLIC COMPANIES
Article 5(1)

[4.651]
1 Meaning of "old public company"
For the purposes of this Schedule an "old public company" is a company limited by shares, or a company limited by guarantee and having a share capital, in respect of which the following conditions are met—
  (a)   the company either existed on 22nd December 1980 or was incorporated after that date pursuant to an application made before that date,
  (b)   on that date or, if later, on the day of the company's incorporation, the company was not or (as the case may be) would not have been a private company within the meaning of section 28 of the Companies Act 1948, and
  (c)   the company has not since that date or the day of the company's incorporation (as the case may be) either been re-registered as a public company within the meaning of section 1(3) of the Companies Act 1985 or section 4(2) of the Companies Act 2006 or become a private company within the meaning of section 1(3) of the Companies Act 1985 or section 4(1) of the Companies Act 2006.

2 Application of Companies Acts to old public companies
(1)   References in the Companies Acts to—
  (a)   a public company, or
  (b)   a company other than a private company,
are to be read (unless the context otherwise requires) as including an old public company.
(2)   References in the Companies Acts to a private company are to be read accordingly.
(3)   Sub-paragraphs (1) and (2)—
  (a)   do not apply in relation to—
    (i)   Part 7 of the Companies Act 2006 (re-registration as a means of altering a company's status), and
    (ii)   sections 662 to 669 of that Act (treatment of shares held by or for public company) (see paragraph 7(1) and (2) below), and
  (b)   do not restrict the power to make provision by regulations under section 65 of that Act (inappropriate use of indications of company type or legal form).

3 Old public company re-registering as a public company
(1)   Sections 90 to 96 of the Companies Act 2006 (re-registration as public company limited by shares) apply to an old public company.
(2)   As they so apply—
  (a)   references to a private company shall be read as references to an old public company, and
  (b)   references to a special resolution of the company shall be read as references to a resolution of the directors.
(3)   Chapter 3 of Part 3 of that Act (resolutions affecting a company's constitution) applies to any such resolution.
(4)   References in this Schedule to re-registration as a public company, in relation to an old public company, are to re-registration by virtue of this paragraph.

4 Old public company becoming private: special resolution
(1)   An old public company may pass a special resolution not to be re-registered as a public company.
(2)   Sections 98 and 99 of the Companies Act 2006 (application to court to cancel resolution; notice to registrar of court application or order) apply to such a resolution as they would apply to a special resolution by a public company to be re-registered as private.
(3)   If either—
  (a)   28 days from the passing of the resolution elapse without an application being made under section 98 of the Companies Act 2006 (as applied), or
  (b)   such an application is made and proceedings are concluded on the application without the court making an order for the cancellation of the resolution,

the registrar of companies shall issue the company with a certificate stating that it is a private company.

(4)   The company then becomes a private company by virtue of the issue of the certificate.

(5)   For the purposes of sub-paragraph (3)(b), proceedings on the application are concluded—

(a)   except in a case within the following paragraph, when the period mentioned in section 99(3) of the Companies Act 2006 (as applied) for delivering a copy of the court's order on the application to the registrar has expired, or

(b)   when the company has been notified that the application has been withdrawn.

(6)   A certificate issued to a company under sub-paragraph (3) is conclusive evidence that the requirements of this paragraph have been complied with and that the company is a private company.

5   Old public company becoming private: statutory declaration

(1)   If an old public company delivers to the registrar a statutory declaration by a director or secretary of the company that the company does not at the time of the declaration satisfy the conditions for the company to be re-registered as public, the registrar shall issue the company with a certificate stating that it is a private company.

(2)   The company then becomes a private company by virtue of the issue of the certificate.

(3)   A certificate issued to a company under sub-paragraph (1) is conclusive evidence that the requirements of this paragraph have been complied with and that the company is a private company.

6   Failure by old public company to obtain new classification

(1)   If at any time a company which is an old public company has not delivered to the registrar of companies a declaration under paragraph 5, the company and any officer of it who is in default is guilty of an offence unless at the time the company—

(a)   has applied to be re-registered as a public company, and the application has not been refused or withdrawn, or

(b)   has passed a special resolution not to be re-registered as a public company, and the resolution has not been revoked, and has not been cancelled under section 98 of the Companies Act 2006, as applied by paragraph 4.

(2)   A person guilty of an offence under this paragraph is liable on summary conviction to a fine not exceeding level 3 on the standard scale and, for continued contravention, a daily default fine not exceeding one-tenth of level 3 on the standard scale.

7   Old public company holding, or having charge on, own shares

(1)   In sections 662 to 669 of the Companies Act 2006 (treatment of shares held by or for public company) references to a public company do not include an old public company.

(2)   Section 668 of that Act (application of sections 662 to 667 to private company re-registering as public company) applies to an old public company as to a private company.

(3)   In the case of a company that—

(a)   after 22nd March 1982 remained an old public company, and

(b)   did not before that date apply to be re-registered as a public company,

any charge on its own shares which was in existence on or immediately before that date is a permitted charge and not void under section 670 of the Companies Act 2006.

8   Old public companies: trading under misleading name

(1)   An old public company commits an offence if it carries on a trade, profession or business under a name that includes, as its last part, the words "public limited company" or "cwmni cyfyngedig cyhoeddus".

(2)   Where an offence under this paragraph is committed by a company, an offence is also committed by every officer of the company who is in default.

(3)   A person guilty of an offence under this paragraph is liable on summary conviction to a fine not exceeding level 3 on the standard scale and, for continued contravention, a daily default fine not exceeding one-tenth of level 3 on the standard scale.

9   Old public companies: payment for share capital

Sections 584 to 587 of the Companies Act 2006 (payment for shares: additional rules for public companies) apply to an old public company whose directors have passed and not revoked a resolution to be re-registered as a public company, as those sections apply to a public company.

NOTES

Commencement: 12 May 2011.

SCHEDULES 2 AND 3

(Sch 2 contains consequential amendments to the Open-ended Investment Companies Regulations 2001, SI 2001/1228; Sch 3 contains transitional provisions and savings in connection with open-ended investment companies in Northern Ireland (outside the scope of this work).)

STATUTORY AUDITORS AND THIRD COUNTRY AUDITORS (AMENDMENT) REGULATIONS 2011

(SI 2011/1856)

NOTES

These Regulations were made on 19 July 2011 and published on 27 July 2011 just before this edition of *Butterworths Company Law Handbook* went to press. As the majority of the pages for this edition had already been set at that date, there was not sufficient time to incorporate the amendments made by these Regulations in the Companies Act 2006, the Companies (Audit, Investigations and Community Enterprise) Act 2004, or the Statutory Auditors and Third Country Auditors Regulations 2007 (SI 2007/3494). Accordingly, these Regulations are set out in full text. Note also that, for the same reason, these Regulations are not listed in the complete list of Companies Act 2006 statutory instruments at the start of this Part.

Authority: European Communities Act 1972, s 2(2); Companies Act 2006, ss 1239(1)(b), (2), (5)(d), 1246(1), 1292(1)(c).

Commencement: see reg 1.

PART 1
INTRODUCTION

[4.652]
1   Citation, commencement and application

(1)   These Regulations may be cited as the Statutory Auditors and Third Country Auditors (Amendment) Regulations 2011.

(2)   These Regulations, except for the provisions referred to in paragraphs (3) and (4), come into force on 1st September 2011.

(3)   Regulations 2, 3, 5 and 6 come into force on 1st October 2011.

(4)   Regulation 7(3) comes into force on 31st July 2013.

(5)   A direction given under section 1242(4) of the Companies Act 2006 by virtue of the amendments made by regulation 4 does not apply in respect of the audit of accounts for a period beginning before 2nd July 2010.

(6)   The amendments made by regulations 2, 3, 5 and 6 apply in relation to audits of accounts for periods beginning on or after 1st October 2011.

PART 2
AMENDMENT TO THE COMPANIES (AUDIT, INVESTIGATIONS AND COMMUNITY ENTERPRISE) ACT 2004

[4.653]
2   Grants to bodies concerned with accounting standards etc

In section 16(2)(f) of the Companies (Audit, Investigations and Community Enterprise) Act 2004 (grants to bodies concerned with accounting standards etc) after "23(1)" insert ", 23A(1)".

PART 3
AMENDMENTS TO THE COMPANIES ACT 2006

[4.654]
3   Restrictions on disclosure

In section 1224A(2)(c) of the Companies Act 2006 (restrictions on disclosure), after "(independent monitoring of certain audits)" insert ", paragraph 23A(1) (independent monitoring of third country audits)".

[4.655]
4   Power to disapply duties of registered third country auditors

In section 1242(4) of the Companies Act 2006 (power to disapply duties of registered third country auditors)—

(a)   after "in relation to" insert "(a)"; and

(b)   at the end add—

"(b)   audits of the accounts of a particular UK-traded non-EEA company or class of UK-traded non-EEA companies;

    (c)   audits by a particular registered third country auditor or class of registered third country auditors of the accounts of a particular UK-traded non-EEA company or class of UK-traded non-EEA companies.".

[4.656]
5 Recognised supervisory bodies

(1)   Schedule 10 to the Companies Act 2006 (recognised supervisory bodies) is amended as follows.

(2)   In paragraph 10A(4)(b) after "23" insert ", 23A".

(3)   In paragraph 13 (monitoring of audits)—
    (a)   in sub-paragraph (1)(a)—
        (i)   omit "in the case of members of the body who do not perform any statutory audit functions in respect of major audits,";
        (ii)   after "of statutory audit functions" insert ", other than statutory audit functions in respect of major audits,";
    (b)   omit the "and" at the end of sub-paragraph (1)(b);
    (c)   after sub-paragraph (1)(b) insert—

    "(ba)   in the case of members of the body who perform any third country audit functions, participate in arrangements within paragraph 23A(1); and";

    (d)   in sub-paragraph (1)(c) after "statutory audit functions" insert "or third country audit functions";
    (e)   for sub-paragraph (2) substitute—

    "(2)   Any monitoring of members of the body under the arrangements within paragraph 23(1) or 23A(1) is to be regarded (so far as their performance of statutory audit functions in respect of major audits, or of third country audit functions, is concerned) as monitoring of compliance with the body's rules for the purposes of paragraph 12(1) and (1A).";

    (f)   in sub-paragraph (10) at the end insert—

    ""third country audit function" means any function related to the audit of a UK-traded non-EEA company.".

(4)   After paragraph 23 (arrangements for independent monitoring of major audits) insert—

    "Arrangements for independent monitoring of third country audits

    23A (1)   The arrangements referred to in paragraph 13(1)(ba) are appropriate arrangements—
    (a)   for enabling the performance by members of the body of third country audit functions to be monitored by means of inspections carried out under the arrangements, and
    (b)   for ensuring that the carrying out of such monitoring and inspections is done independently of the body.
    (2)   Those arrangements must provide that the body performing the inspections—
    (a)   may decide that an inspection referred to in sub-paragraph (1) is not required, or that part of an inspection is not required, in relation to a member, and
    (b)   may direct that the arrangements referred to in sub-paragraph (3) apply in relation to the member or apply to such extent as may be specified in the direction.
    (3)   The supervisory body must have adequate arrangements for enabling the performance by its members of third country audit functions to be monitored by means of inspections for cases where a direction is given under sub-paragraph (2)(b).
    (4)   In this paragraph "third country audit function" means any function related to the audit of a UK-traded non-EEA company.".

(5)   In paragraph 24 (arrangements for independent investigation for disciplinary purposes)—
    (a)   in sub-paragraph (1)(a) after "the performance of statutory audit functions" insert "or third country audit functions";
    (b)   in sub-paragraph (2) at the end insert—

    ""third country audit function" means any function related to the audit of a UK-traded non-EEA company.".

(6)   In paragraph 25(1) (arrangements to operate independently of body)—
    (a)   omit the "or" at the end of paragraph (c);
    (b)   after paragraph (c) insert—

    "(ca)   paragraph 23A(1)(b), or".

(7)   In paragraph 26 (funding of arrangements) after "23" insert ", 23A".

(8)   In paragraph 27 (scope of arrangement) after "23" insert ", 23A".

[4.657]
6 Specified persons, descriptions, disclosures etc for the purposes of section 1224A

In Schedule 11A to the Companies Act 2006 (specified persons, descriptions, disclosures etc for the purposes of section 1224A)—

(a) in paragraph 16, after "23" insert "or 23A";

(b) in paragraph 62, after "23(1)" insert "or 23A(1)" and after "bodies" insert "and of UK-traded non-EEA companies".

PART 4
AMENDMENTS TO THE STATUTORY AUDITORS AND THIRD COUNTRY AUDITORS REGULATIONS 2007 (SI 2007/3494)

[4.658]
7 Registration of third country auditors

(1) The Statutory Auditors and Third Country Auditors Regulations 2007 are amended as follows.

(2) In regulation 29 (interpretation)—

(a) at the appropriate places insert the following definitions—

""company" means a UK-traded non-EEA company within the meaning of section 1241 of the Companies Act 2006;"

""equivalent third country" means any of the following countries and territories—
Australia, Canada, China, Croatia, Japan, Singapore, South Africa, South Korea, Switzerland and United States of America;";

(b) for the definition of "the Commission Decision" substitute—

""the Commission Decision" means Commission Decision 2011/30/EU of 19 January 2011 on the equivalence of certain third country public oversight, quality assurance, investigation and penalty systems for auditors and audit entities and a transitional period for audit activities of certain third country auditors and audit entities;";

(c) omit the definition of "exempt third country auditor";

(d) for the definition of "specified third country" substitute—

""specified third country" means any of the Channel Islands, the Isle of Man and the following countries and territories—
Abu Dhabi, Bermuda, Brazil, Cayman Islands, The Dubai International Finance Centre, Egypt, Hong Kong, India, Indonesia, Israel, Malaysia, Mauritius, New Zealand, Russia, Taiwan, Thailand, and Turkey.".

(3) In the definition of "equivalent third country" (inserted by sub-paragraph (2)(a) above) before "Switzerland" insert "and" and at the end omit "and United States of America" (see regulation 1(4)).

(4) In regulation 34 (register of third country auditors)—

(a) at the end of sub-paragraph (2)(e) insert "and";

(b) in sub-paragraph (2)(f) omit "; and";

(c) omit sub-paragraph (2)(g);

(d) for sub-paragraph (3)(h) substitute—

"(h) the name and address of each individual who performs third country audits on behalf of the firm and the registered number allocated to that individual by the third country competent authority with which that individual is registered.";

(e) at the end of sub-paragraph (3)(i) insert "and";

(f) in sub-paragraph (3)(k) omit "; and";

(g) omit sub-paragraph (3)(l).

(5) In regulation 35 (application for registration of third country auditor)—

(a) for sub-paragraph (3)(a) substitute—

"(a) the information required for entry in the register (see regulation 34), other than the registered number;"

(b) for paragraph (3A) substitute—

"(3A) An application for registration must include—
(a) in respect of each UK-traded non-EEA company for which it provides an audit report—
(i) the company's name and any registered number it carries by virtue of its incorporation,
(ii) the third country or territory in which it is incorporated or under the law of which it is formed, and
(iii) the accounting period to which the audit report relates,

(b)   where the company for which it provides an audit report is incorporated or formed in a specified third country or equivalent third country, a statement of the auditing standards and independence requirements applied to the audit,

(c)   a description of the auditor's internal quality control system,

(d)   a statement of whether and (if so) when a quality assurance review has been carried out in respect of the auditor, and

(e)   information required by the designated body about the outcome of a quality assurance review.".

(6)   For regulation 39 (duty to provide updated information) substitute—

"**39** (1)   A registered third country auditor must take all reasonable steps to notify the designated body without undue delay of—

(a)   any change or addition to the information specified in regulation 35(3A)(a);

(b)   any information or event which may lead the designated body to consider that the statement required by regulation 36 (application statement) made by the third country auditor is not correct;

(c)   any information necessary to ensure that the information in the register relating to the third country auditor is correct.

(2)   A registered third country auditor who has provided to the designated body information falling within sub-paragraphs (a) to (d) and the first sentence of sub-paragraph (e) of Article 2.1 of the Commission Decision must take all reasonable steps to notify the designated body without undue delay of any change or addition to that information.".

(7)   For regulation 40(3) (removal of third country auditor from the register) substitute—

"(3)   The designated body may remove a third country auditor from the register if—

(a)   it considers that the auditor—

   (i)   has failed—

      (aa)   to comply with the obligations of the auditor under regulation 39(2) (duty of registered third country auditor to provide updated information), or

      (bb)   to apply the auditing standards and independence requirements set out in the statement provided for in regulation 35(3A)(b), or

   (ii)   is not a fit and proper person to conduct audits of the accounts of UK-traded non-EEA companies, or

(b)   it appears to the designated body that a competent authority which oversees or regulates the auditor considers that the auditor is not—

   (i)   a fit and proper person to conduct audits in the country in which the authority is established, or

   (ii)   eligible to conduct audits of the accounts of bodies corporate incorporated or formed under the law of that country.".

PART 5
FINAL PROVISIONS

[4.659]
8   Exercise of functions of Secretary of State

In article 4(1) of the Statutory Auditors (Delegation of Functions etc) Order 2008 (transfer of Secretary of State functions to Professional Oversight Board) the reference to Part 42 of the Companies Act 2006 includes a reference to that Part as amended by these Regulations.

[4.660]
9   Transitional and saving provisions

The amendments made by regulation 7 to the Statutory Auditors and Third Country Auditors Regulations 2007 do not apply in relation to—

(a)   audits of accounts for periods beginning on or before 1st July 2010; and

(b)   any application for registration delivered to the designated body before 1st September 2011.

PART 5
PRE-2006 COMPANIES PRIMARY LEGISLATION

COMPANIES ACT 1985

(1985 c 6)

NOTES

This Act is reproduced as amended by the following Acts:

1985	Insolvency Act 1985.
1986	FSA 1986; Insolvency Act 1986.
1989	CA 1989.
1990	Law Reform (Miscellaneous Provisions) (Scotland) Act 1990.
1995	Requirements of Writing (Scotland) Act 1995.
1999	Youth Justice and Criminal Evidence Act 1999.
2004	Companies (Audit, Investigations and Community Enterprise) Act 2004; Pensions Act 2004.
2006	Charities Act 2006; Companies Act 2006.
2007	Bankruptcy and Diligence etc (Scotland) Act 2007; Legal Services Act 2007.

This Act is reproduced as amended by the following SIs:

1991	Companies (Disclosure of Interests in Shares) (Orders imposing restrictions on shares) Regulations 1991, SI 1991/1646.
2001	Financial Services and Markets Act 2000 (Consequential Amendments and Repeals) Order 2001, SI 2001/3649.
2003	Companies (Acquisition of Own Shares) (Treasury Shares) Regulations 2003, SI 2003/1116.
2006	Companies (Disclosure of Information) (Designated Authorities) Order 2006, SI 2006/1644.
2007	Companies Act 2006 (Commencement No 3, Consequential Amendments, Transitional Provisions and Savings) Order 2007, SI 2007/2194.
2008	Companies Act 2006 (Consequential Amendments etc) Order 2008, SI 2008/948; Consumer Protection from Unfair Trading Regulations 2008, SI 2008/1277.
2009	Companies Act 2006 (Consequential Amendments, Transitional Provisions and Savings) Order 2009, SI 2009/1941.
2010	Transfer of Tribunal Functions Order 2010, SI 2010/22.
2011	Investment Bank Special Administration Regulations 2011, SI 2011/245.

References to "the European Community", "Community", etc: see the Treaty of Lisbon (Changes in Terminology) Order 2011, SI 2011/1043, which provides that (as from 22 April 2011) "EU" should be substituted for the word "Community" (subject to certain exceptions) in references to "Community treaties", "Community instrument", "Community obligation", "Community law", "Community legislation", etc.

Repeal of this Act by the Companies Act 2006:

In so far as individual provisions of this Act had not already been repealed, the vast majority of this Act was repealed by the Companies Act 2006 (see s 1295 of, and Sch 16 to, the 2006 Act at **[1.1295]**, **[1.1331]** which repeal ss 1–430F, 438, 446, 458–461, 651–746 of, and Schs 1–15B, 20–25 to, this Act). The only provisions not repealed by the 2006 Act are: (a) Part XIV (Investigation of Companies and their Affairs; Requisition of Documents) (including Schs 15C, 15D but not including ss 438, 446 which are repealed); (b) Part XV (Orders Imposing Restrictions on Shares); (c) Part XVIII (Floating Charges and Receivers (Scotland)); and (d) section 747 (citation). For provision relating to the continuity of law, see s 1297 of the 2006 Act at **[1.1297]**.

Note also that Part XVIII (Floating Charges and Receivers (Scotland)) is repealed by the Bankruptcy and Diligence etc (Scotland) Act 2007, s 46(1), as from a day to be appointed. For savings see the introductory note to that Part (preceding **[5.36]**).

Abbreviations used in the notes to this Act are as follows:

— CO No 1: the Companies Act 2006 (Commencement No 1, Transitional Provisions and Savings) Order 2006, SI 2006/3428.

— CO No 2: the Companies Act 2006 (Commencement No 2, Consequential Amendments, Transitional Provisions and Savings) Order 2007, SI 2007/1093.

— CO No 3: the Companies Act 2006 (Commencement No 3, Consequential Amendments, Transitional Provisions and Savings) Order 2007, SI 2007/2194.

— CO No 4: the Companies Act 2006 (Commencement No 4 and Commencement No 3 (Amendment)) Order 2007, SI 2007/2607.

— CO No 5: the Companies Act 2006 (Commencement No 5, Transitional Provisions and Savings) Order 2007, SI 2007/3495.

— CO No 6: the Companies Act 2006 (Commencement No 6, Saving and Commencement Nos 3 and 5 (Amendment)) Order 2008, SI 2008/674.

— CO No 7: the Companies Act 2006 (Commencement No 7, Transitional Provisions and Savings) Order 2008, SI 2008/1886.

— CO No 8: the Companies Act 2006 (Commencement No 8, Transitional Provisions and Savings) Order 2008, SI 2008/2860.

Commencement:

Unless otherwise indicated, this Act came into force on 1 July 1985; see s 746 at **[5.44]**.

Offences under this Act:

See CO No 8, Sch 2, para 116 at **[2.91]** (savings for provisions relating to offences). That paragraph provides that the repeal of any provision of this Act creating an offence does not affect the continued operation of that provision in relation to an offence committed before 1 October 2009. It also provides that such savings extend to Sch 24 to this Act (punishment of offences). Similar provision was made by CO No 5, Sch 4, Pt 1, para 44 at [**2.66**] which provided that the repeal of ss 732–734 of this Act does not affect the operation of those provisions in relation to offences committed before 6 April 2008.

See also the Companies Act 2006, ss 1131 at [**1.1131**] (imprisonment on summary conviction in England and Wales: transitory provision), and CO No 8, art 7 at [**2.88**] (prosecution of offences in transitional cases).

Limited liability partnerships: the provisions of this Act relating to companies were applied with modifications to limited liability partnerships by the Limited Liability Partnerships (Scotland) Regulations 2001, SSI 2001/128 at [**10.802**], and the Limited Liability Partnerships Regulations 2001, SI 2001/1090 at [**10.813**]. Further provisions of this Act were applied to LLPs by the Limited Liability Partnership (No 2) Regulations 2002, SI 2002/913 (revoked as from 1 October 2009).

As the repeals of the provisions of this Act were commenced in stages by the various commencement orders made under the 2006 Act, savings provisions in those orders preserved the operation of the repealed provisions of is Act in so far as they applied to LLPs (see CO No 1, art 8(2) (at [**2.8**]), CO No 2, art 11(1) (at [**2.26**]), CO No 3, art 12(2) (at [**2.42**]), CO No 5, art 12(1) (at [**2.61**]), CO No 6, art 6(1) (at [**2.72**]), and SI 2008/948, art 11 (at [**4.285**])). Those articles provide that nothing in those Orders (which either (i) commence the repeals (or amendments) made to this Act by CA 2006, or (ii) amend this Act) affect the application of any provision of this Act (as applied by the Limited Liability Partnerships Regulations 2001) to LLPs. Art 11(2) of CO No 2 further provides that the repeal of s 723C(1)(a) by CA 2006 (brought into force by art 7(a) of CO No 1) does not apply to the application of the said s 723C(1)(a) to LLPs by the Limited Liability Partnerships (No 2) Regulations 2002. See also CO No 7, art 7(4) (at [**2.81**]) which provides that save as provided by art 2(e) of that Order (the commencement, on 1 October 2008, of s 1286(1)(a), (2)(a) of the 2006 Act in so far as relating to Parts 15, 16 and 42 of that Act) nothing in that Order affects any provision of this Act as applied by 2001 Regulations.

As to the revocation (subject to savings), as from 1 October 2008, of certain Parts of SI 2001/1090 (most notably reg 3 and Sch 1 which applied Part VII of this Act to LLPs) see the Limited Liability Partnerships (Accounts and Audit) (Application of Companies Act 2006) Regulations 2008, SI 2008/1911, reg 58 at [**10.1060**]. See also the Limited Liability Partnerships (Application of Companies Act 2006) Regulations 2009, SI 2009/1804 at [**10.1097**] which applies various provisions of the Companies Act 2006 to LLPs and revokes (as from 1 October 2009) most of Sch 2, Pt I to the 2001 Regulations (application of other provisions of this Act to LLPs) and also revokes SI 2002/913 and the Limited Liability Partnerships (Particulars of Usual Residential Address) (Confidentiality Orders) Regulations 2002, SI 2002/915. Schedule 1 to the 2009 Regulations (at [**10.1181**] et seq) provides for detailed transitional provisions and savings in relation to the application of the 2006 Act to LLPs and the revocation of the 2001 Regulations in so far as they apply provisions of this Act to LLPs.

Currently, Part XIV (Investigation of Companies and their Affairs; Requisition of Documents) (including Schs 15C, 15D) still applies to LLPs by virtue of SI 2001/1090, Sch 2, Pt I. In addition, Part XVIII (Floating Charges and Receivers (Scotland)) still applies to LLPs by virtue of SI 2001/1090, Sch 2, Pt I and SSI 2001/128, Sch 1.

Application of this Act to other companies, etc:
This Act, or particular parts of it, is applied to various other types of companies and bodies, as follows:

European Economic Interest Groupings: as to the application of Parts XIV, XVIII of this Act to European Economic Interest Groupings and their establishments registered, or in the process of being registered, under the European Economic Interest Grouping Regulations 1989, SI 1989/638, see those Regulations at [**10.696**]. Note that the 1989 Regulations were amended by the European Economic Interest Grouping (Amendment) Regulations 2009, SI 2009/2399 which, inter alia, replaced references to provisions of this Act (other than Part XIV) with references to the equivalent provisions of the Companies Act 2006. Regulation 2 of the 2009 Regulations provides that in so far as relating to forms and other documents required to be delivered to the registrar, the amendments made by those Regulations do not have effect in any case where the obligation to deliver the form or other document arose before 1 October 2009 (ie, the date on which the amendments made by SI 2009/2399 took effect).

Unregistered companies: as to the application of Parts XIV, XV of this Act to unregistered companies, see the Unregistered Companies Regulations 2009, SI 2009/2436, Sch 1, para 16 at [**4.603**]. Note that the Companies (Unregistered Companies) Regulations 1985, SI 1985/680 applied certain provisions of this Act to unregistered companies before 1 October 2009. The 1985 Regulations were revoked by the reg 8 of the 2009 Regulations subject to transitional provisions (in Sch 2 to the 2009 Regulations at [**4.604**]) in relation to the application of this Act to unregistered companies before that date.

Societas Europaea: certain provisions of this Act were applied to SEs by the European Public Limited-Liability Company Regulations 2004, SI 2004/2326 at [**10.851**]. Note that the 2004 Regulations were amended by the European Public Limited-Liability Company (Amendment) Regulations 2009, SI 2009/2400 which, inter alia, replaced references to provisions of this Act with references to the equivalent provisions of the Companies Act 2006. Regulation 2 of the 2009 Regulations provides that in so far as relating to forms and other documents required to be delivered to the registrar, the amendments made by those Regulations do not have effect in any case where the obligation to deliver the form or other document arose before 1 October 2009 (ie, the date on which the amendments made by SI 2009/2400 took effect).

Banks: as to the application of certain provisions of this Act to specified banks, see the Banking (Special Provisions) Act 2008 and the Orders made under it. As to the application of this Act to bank insolvency and administration, see the Banking Act 2009 (Parts 2 and 3 Consequential Amendments) Order 2009, SI 2009/317.

ARRANGEMENT OF SECTIONS

PART XIV
INVESTIGATION OF COMPANIES AND THEIR AFFAIRS; REQUISITION OF DOCUMENTS

Appointment and functions of inspectors

SCHEDULES

An Act to consolidate the greater part of the Companies Acts

[11 March 1985]

PART I
FORMATION AND REGISTRATION OF COMPANIES; JURIDICAL STATUS AND MEMBERSHIP

1–42

NOTES
This Part has been repealed as follows:

1 Mode of forming incorporated company	Repealed by CA 2006, as from 1 Oct 2009.
	Savings: CO No 8, Sch 2, para 2(1) (at **[2.91]**) provides that ss 7–16 of the Companies Act 2006 (company formation) apply to applications for registration received by the registrar on or after 1 Oct 2009. Sch 2, para 2(3) further provides that the corresponding provisions of this Act continue to apply to an application for registration if (a) it is received by the registrar, and (b) the requirements as to registration are met in relation to it, before that date. The corresponding provisions of this Act are as follows: ss 1(1), 2(1), (a), (b), (2)–(4), 3(1), 10(1), (2), (3), (4), (6), 12(1)–(3), (3A), 13(1)–(5), (7)(a) (see the table of origins at **[3.52]**).
2 Requirements with respect to memorandum	Repealed by CA 2006, as from 1 Oct 2009. For savings see the note to s 1.
3 Forms of memorandum	Repealed by CA 2006, as from 1 Oct 2009. For savings see the note to s 1.
3A Statement of company's objects: general commercial company	Repealed by CA 2006, as from 1 Oct 2009.
4 Resolution to alter objects	Repealed by CA 2006, as from 1 Oct 2009.
	Savings: CO No 8, Sch 2, para 110 (at **[2.91]**) provides that the repeal of ss 4–6 of this Act does not affect the application of those provisions in relation to a resolution agreed to before 1 Oct 2009.
5 Procedure for objecting to alteration	Repealed by CA 2006, as from 1 Oct 2009. For savings see the savings note to s 4.
6 Provisions supplementing ss 4, 5	Repealed by CA 2006, as from 1 Oct 2009. For savings see the savings note to s 4.
7 Articles prescribing regulations for companies	Repealed by CA 2006, as from 1 Oct 2009.
	Savings: CO No 8, Sch 2, para 3(1) (at **[2.91]**) provides that ss 7, 8 of this Act apply, and ss 18–20 of CA 2006 do not apply, to a company formed and registered under this Act on an application to which para 2(3) of that Schedule applies. Para 2(3) provides that the provisions of this Act corresponding to ss 7–16 of the 2006 Act continue to apply to an application for registration if (a) it is received by the registrar, and (b) the requirements as to registration are met in relation to it, before 1 Oct 2009.
8 Tables A, C, D and E	Repealed by CA 2006, as from 1 Oct 2009. For savings see the note to s 7.
8A Table G	Repealed by CA 2006, as from 1 Oct 2009.
9 Alteration of articles by special resolution	Repealed by CA 2006, as from 1 Oct 2009.
10 Documents to be sent to registrar	Repealed by CA 2006, as from 1 Oct 2009. For savings see the note to s 1.
11 Minimum authorised capital (public companies)	Repealed by CA 2006, as from 1 Oct 2009.
12 Duty of registrar	Repealed by CA 2006, as from 1 Oct 2009. For savings see the note to s 1.
13 Effect of registration	Repealed by CA 2006, as from 1 Oct 2009. For savings see the note to s 1.
14 Effect of memorandum and articles	Repealed by CA 2006, as from 1 Oct 2009:
	Saving for provisions relating to nature of liability of member or contributory: SI 2009/1941, art 11 (at **[4.538]**) provides that the new provisions as to the nature of a member's or contributory's liability (ie, CA 2006, s 33(2) and, in England and Wales, s 80 of the Insolvency Act 1986 as amended by that Order) apply to liabilities arising on or after 1 Oct 2009, and the old provisions (ie, CA 1985, s 14(2) and s 80 of the 1986 Act as it had effect prior to that amendment) continue to apply to liabilities arising before that date. Note also that for the purposes of art 11, a liability is treated as arising when the limitation period starts to run for the purposes of the Limitation Act 1980.

15 Memorandum and articles of company limited by guarantee	Repealed by CA 2006, as from 1 Oct 2009.
16 Effect of alteration on company's members	Repealed by CA 2006, as from 1 Oct 2009.
17 Conditions in memorandum which could have been in articles	Repealed by CA 2006, as from 1 Oct 2009.
18 Amendments of memorandum or articles to be registered	Repealed by CA 2006, as from 1 Oct 2009. Savings: CO No 8, Sch 2, para 6 (at **[2.91]**) provides that sub-ss (2), (3) continue to apply in relation to amendments taking effect before 1 Oct 2009. In addition, sub-ss (1), (3) continue to apply in relation to alterations made by statutory provisions coming into force before that date (see Sch 2, para 12 to that Order).
19 Copies of memorandum and articles to be given to members	Repealed by CA 2006, as from 1 Oct 2009. Savings: CO No 8, Sch 2, para 11 (at **[2.91]**) provides that this section continues to apply where the request was received by the company before 1 Oct 2009.
20 Issued copy of memorandum to embody alterations	Repealed by CA 2006, as from 1 Oct 2009.
21 Registered documentation of Welsh companies.	Repealed by the Welsh Language Act 1993, as from 1 Feb 1994.
22 Definition of "member"	Repealed by CA 2006, as from 1 Oct 2009.
23 Membership of holding company	Repealed by CA 2006, as from 1 Oct 2009.
24 Minimum membership for carrying on business	Repealed by CA 2006, as from 1 Oct 2009. Savings: CO No 8, Sch 2, para 24 (at **[2.91]**) provides that the repeal of this section does not affect any liability for debts of the company contracted before 1 Oct 2009.
25 Name as stated in memorandum	Repealed by CA 2006, as from 1 Oct 2009.
26 Prohibition on registration of certain names	Repealed by CA 2006, as from 1 Oct 2009. Savings: see CO No 8, Sch 2, para 114A (at **[2.91]**) which provides that the repeal of s 26(2)(a) does not affect the operation of that provision in relation to names suggesting a connection with the Welsh Assembly Government.
27 Alternatives of statutory designations	Repealed by CA 2006, as from 1 Oct 2009.
28 Change of name	Repealed by CA 2006, as from 1 Oct 2009. Savings: CO No 8, Sch 2, para 19 (at **[2.91]**) provides that sub-ss (1), (6) and (7) above continue to apply to resolutions of which a copy is received by the registrar before 1 Oct 2009.
29 Regulations about names	Repealed by CA 2006, as from 1 Jan 2007 (in so far as relating to sub-s (4)), and as from 1 Oct 2009 (otherwise). Savings: CO No 8, Sch 2, para 18 (at **[2.91]**) provides that this section continues to apply in relation to applications received by the Secretary of State before 1 Oct 2009.
30 Exemption from requirement of "limited" as part of the name	Repealed by CA 2006, as from 1 Oct 2009.
31 Provisions applying to company exempt under s 30	Repealed by CA 2006, as from 1 Oct 2009. Savings: CO No 8, Sch 2, para 20 (at **[2.91]**) provides that sub-ss (2)–(4), (6) continue to apply where a direction under sub-s (2) was given before 1 October 2009.
32 Power to require company to abandon misleading name	Repealed by CA 2006, as from 1 Oct 2009. Savings: CO No 8, Sch 2, para 21 (at **[2.91]**) provides that this section continues to apply in relation to a direction given before 1 Oct 2009.
33 Prohibition on trading under misleading name	Repealed by CA 2006, as from 1 Oct 2009.
34 Penalty for improper use of "limited" or "cyfyngedig"	Repealed by CA 2006, as from 1 Oct 2009.
34A Penalty for improper use of "community interest company" etc	Repealed by CA 2006, as from 1 Oct 2009.
35 A company's capacity not limited by its memorandum	Repealed by CA 2006, as from 1 Oct 2009. Savings: CO No 8, Sch 2, para 15 (at **[2.91]**) provides that this section continues to apply to acts of a company carried out before 1 Oct 2009.
35A Power of directors to bind the company	Repealed by CA 2006, as from 1 Oct 2009.

35B No duty to enquire as to capacity of company or authority of directors	Repealed by CA 2006, as from 1 Oct 2009.
36 Company contracts: England and Wales	Repealed by CA 2006, as from 1 Oct 2009.
36A Execution of documents: England and Wales	Repealed by CA 2006, s 1295, Sch 16, as from 6 Apr 2008 (in part), and as from 1 Oct 2009 (otherwise). Savings: note that s 36A continues to apply in relation to documents executed before 6 Apr 2008; note also that a document signed by one authorised signatory before 6 Apr 2008 and by another on or after that date is treated as executed on or after 6 Apr 2008 (see CO No 5, Sch 4, Pt 1, para 1 at **[2.66]**).
36AA Execution of deeds: England and Wales	Repealed by CA 2006, as from 1 Oct 2009.
36B Execution of documents by companies	Repealed by CA 2006, as from 1 Oct 2009.
36C Pre-incorporation documents, deeds and obligations	Repealed by CA 2006, as from 1 Oct 2009.
37 Bills of exchange and promissory notes	Repealed by CA 2006, as from 1 Oct 2009.
38 Execution of deeds abroad	Repealed by CA 2006, as from 1 Oct 2009. Savings: CO No 8, Sch 2, para 16 (at **[2.91]**) provides that this section continues to have effect where the power to act as a company's attorney was conferred before 1 Oct 2009 (including in relation to instruments executed by the attorney on behalf of the company on or after that date).
39 Power of company to have official seal for use abroad	Repealed by CA 2006, as from 1 Oct 2009.
40 Official seal for share certificates, etc	Repealed by CA 2006, as from 1 Oct 2009.
41 Authentication of documents	Repealed by CA 2006, as from 6 Apr 2007.
42 Events affecting a company's status	Repealed by CA 2006, as from 1 Jan 2007.

PART II
RE-REGISTRATION AS A MEANS OF ALTERING A COMPANY'S STATUS

43–55

NOTES

This Part has been repealed as follows:

43 Re-registration of private company as public	Repealed by CA 2006, as from 1 Oct 2009. Savings: CO No 8, Sch 2, para 22 (at **[2.91]**) provides that ss 89–108 of CA 2006 (re-registration as a means of altering a company's status) apply to applications for re-registration received by the registrar on or after 1 Oct 2009; and that the corresponding provisions of this Act continue to apply to an application for re-registration if: (a) it is received by the registrar, and (b) the requirements for re-registration are met in relation to it, before that date.
44 Consideration for shares recently allotted to be valued	Repealed by CA 2006, as from 1 Oct 2009. For savings see the note to s 43.
45 Additional requirements relating to share capital	Repealed by CA 2006, as from 1 Oct 2009. For savings see the note to s 43.
46 Meaning of "unqualified report" in s 43(3)	Repealed by CA 2006, as from 1 Oct 2009. For savings see the note to s 43.
47 Certificate of re-registration under s 43	Repealed by CA 2006, as from 1 Oct 2009. For savings see the note to s 43.
48 Modification for unlimited company re-registering	Repealed by CA 2006, as from 1 Oct 2009. For savings see the note to s 43.
49 Re-registration of limited company as unlimited	Repealed by CA 2006, as from 1 Oct 2009. For savings see the note to s 43.
50 Certificate of re-registration under s 49	Repealed by CA 2006, as from 1 Oct 2009. For savings see the note to s 43.
51 Re-registration of unlimited company as limited	Repealed by CA 2006, as from 1 Oct 2009. For savings see the note to s 43.
52 Certificate of re-registration under s 51	Repealed by CA 2006, as from 1 Oct 2009. For savings see the note to s 43.

53 Re-registration of public company as private	Repealed by CA 2006, as from 1 Oct 2009. For savings see the note to s 43.
54 Litigated objection to resolution under s 53	Repealed by CA 2006, as from 1 Oct 2009. For savings see the note to s 43.
55 Certificate of re-registration under s 53	Repealed by CA 2006, as from 1 Oct 2009. For savings see the note to s 43.

PART III
CAPITAL ISSUES

56–79

NOTES

This Part (ie, ss 56–79, Sch 3) (together with the other provisions mentioned in (i) and (ii) below) was repealed (subject to limited savings) in accordance with the notes set out below following the coming into force of the Public Offers of Securities Regulations 1995, SI 1995/1537 (now revoked).

Certain sections in this Part (ie, ss 58, 59, 60, 62 and Sch 3, para 2) were preserved by the Financial Services Act 1986 (Commencement) (No 13) Order 1995, SI 1995/1538 for the sole purpose of interpreting other provisions of this Act (ie, ss 81, 83, 246, 248 and 744).

Subject to the savings mentioned above, this Part was repealed by FSA 1986, s 212(3), Sch 17, Pt I as follows—

(i) to the extent to which they would apply in relation to any investment which is listed or the subject of an application for listing in accordance with FSA 1986, Pt IV—

(a)   *as from 12 January 1987* for the purposes specified in art 5(a) of the Financial Services Act 1986 (Commencement) (No 3) Order 1986, SI 1986/2246, ie for all purposes relating to the admission of securities offered by or on behalf of a Minister of the Crown or a body corporate controlled by a Minister of the Crown or a subsidiary of such a body corporate to the Official List in respect of which an application is made after that date;

(b)   *as from 16 February 1987* for the purposes specified in art 5(b) of SI 1986/2246, ie purposes relating to the admission of securities in respect of which an application is made after that date other than those referred to in art 5(a) of that Order (see (a) above) and otherwise for all purposes;

These repeals also affected ss 81–83, 86, 87, 709(2), (3), and specified words in ss 84, 85, 97, 693

(ii) *as from 29 April 1988* insofar as is necessary to have the effect that they cease to apply to a prospectus offering for subscription, or to any form of application for, units in a body corporate which is an open-ended investment company which is a recognised scheme (Financial Services Act 1986 (Commencement) (No 8) Order 1988, SI 1988/740, art 2, Schedule);

This repeal also affected ss 81–83, 86, 87, and specified words in ss 84, 85, 97, 449, 693, 744.

(iii) subject to NOTES below—

(a)   *as from 31 December 1988* insofar as is necessary to have the effect that, to the extent that they do apply, they cease to apply to a prospectus offering for subscription, or to any application form for, units in an open-ended investment company which *does not* fulfil the conditions described in art 3(a)(i) or (a)(ii) of the Financial Services Act 1986 (Commencement) (No 10) Order 1988, SI 1988/1960. These conditions are—

(1)   it is managed in and authorised under the law of a country or territory in respect of which an order under section 87 of the 1986 Act is in force on 31 December 1988 and which is of a class specified in that Order; or

(2)   it is constituted in a member state in respect of which an order under para 10 of Sch 15 to the 1986 Act is in force on 31 December 1988 and which meets the requirements specified in that Order.

(b)   *as from 1 March 1989* insofar as is necessary to have the effect that, to the extent that they do apply, they cease to apply to a prospectus offering for subscription, or to any application form for, units in an open-ended investment company which *does* fulfil the conditions described in art 3(a)(i) or (a)(ii) of SI 1988/1960 (set out above).

The dates above were appointed by SI 1988/1960, art 4, as amended by SI 1988/2285, art 6. The above repeals also affected s 693.

(iv)—

(a)   *as from 1 May 1989* insofar as is necessary to have the effect that, to the extent that they do apply, they cease to apply to a prospectus offering for subscription, or to any application form for, units in an open-ended investment company falling within art 4(a) of SI 1988/2285, ie an open-ended investment company which fulfils the conditions described in art 2(a) of SI 1988/2285 (which are set out in NOTES to (iii) above), and which is a scheme of a class specified in the Schedule to the Financial Services (Designated Countries and Territories) (Overseas Collective Investment Schemes) (Bermuda) Order 1988, SI 1988/2284;

(b)   *as from 28 February 1989* insofar as is necessary to have the effect that, to the extent that they do apply, they cease to apply to a prospectus offering for subscription, or to any application form for, units in an open-ended investment company falling within art 2(a) of SI 1988/2285 (which is set out in NOTES to (iii) above), but not within art 4(a) (which is set out in (iv)(a) above);

These dates were appointed by SI 1988/2285, art 5.

(v) *as from 19 June 1995* for all remaining purposes except for repeals of ss 58, 59, 60 (so far as necessary for the purposes of ss 81, 83, 246, 248, 744), Sch 3, para 2 (so far as necessary for the purposes of s 83(1)(a)) and s 62 (so far as necessary for the purposes of s 744) (SI 1995/1538, art 2(a)).

(vi) *as from 10 May 1999* so far as relates to repeals of or in (i) ss 82, 83, and the corresponding provisions of the Companies (Northern Ireland) Order 1986, SI 1986/1032, for all remaining purposes except for the purposes of prospectuses to which SI 1995/1537, reg 8 applies; and (ii) ss 86, 87, and the corresponding provisions of SI 1986/1032, for all remaining purposes (SI 1999/727).

NOTES: art 4, cited above, does not have effect in relation to a prospectus offering for subscription, or to any application form for, units in an open-ended investment company which fulfils the conditions described in art 2(a) of the Financial Services Act 1986 (Commencement) (No 11) Order 1988, SI 1988/2285, ie it is an open-ended investment company managed in and authorised under the law of Bermuda, units in which are, on 31 December 1988, included in the Official List of the International Stock Exchange of the United Kingdom and the Republic of Ireland Limited (SI 1988/2285, art 3).

In so far as this Part continued to have effect, it was completely repealed as follows—
(1) by the Financial Services and Markets Act 2000 (Consequential Amendments and Repeals) Order 2001, SI 2001/3649, art 5, as from 1 December 2001 (in the case of ss 59, 60);
(2) by CA 2006, as from 6 April 2008 (in the case of s 58);
(3) by CA 2006, as from 1 October 2009 (in the case of s 62 and Sch 3).

PART IV
ALLOTMENT OF SHARES AND DEBENTURES

80–116

NOTES
This Part has been repealed as follows:

Repeal of certain provisions in this Part for certain purposes: ss 81–83, 86, 87 and specified words in ss 84(1), 85(1) and 97 were repealed by the Financial Services Act 1986, s 212(3), Sch 17, Pt I to the same extent and from the same sates as mentioned in paras (i) and (ii) of the note to Part III *ante*.

80 Authority of company required for certain allotments	Repealed by CA 2006, as from 1 Oct 2009.
	Transitional provisions: see CO No 8, Sch 2, para 45 (at **[2.91]**) which provides that an authorisation in force immediately before 1 Oct 2009 under ss 80, 80A has effect on and after that date as if given under CA 2006, s 551 (power of directors to allot shares etc: authorisation by company).
80A Election by private company as to duration of authority	Repealed by CA 2006, as from 1 Oct 2009. For savings see the note to s 80.
81 Restriction on public offers by private company	Repealed by CA 2006, as from 6 Apr 2008,
	Savings: see CO No 5, Sch 4, Pt 1, para 24 which provides that this section continues to apply to offers made before 6 Apr 2008 (see **[2.66]**). As to the previous repeal of this section by FSA 1986, see the note preceding this table.
82 Application for, and allotment of, shares and debentures	Repealed by CA 2006, as from 1 Oct 2009. As to the previous repeal of this section by FSA 1986, see the note preceding this table.
83 No allotment unless minimum subscription received	Repealed by CA 2006, as from 1 Oct 2009. As to the previous repeal of this section by FSA 1986, see the note preceding this table.
84 Allotment where issue not fully subscribed	Repealed by CA 2006, as from 1 Oct 2009.
	Savings: CO No 8, Sch 2, para 56 (at **[2.91]**) provides that this section and s 85 continue to apply where the offer was made, or a prospectus issued, before 1 Oct 2009.
85 Effect of irregular allotment	Repealed by CA 2006, as from 1 Oct 2009. For savings see the note to s 84.
86 Allotment of shares, etc to be dealt in on stock exchange	Repealed by CA 2006, as from 1 Oct 2009.
87 Operation of s 86 where prospectus offers shares for sale	Repealed by CA 2006, as from 1 Oct 2009.
88 Return as to allotments, etc	Repealed by CA 2006, as from 1 Oct 2009.
	Savings: CO No 8, Sch 2, para 47 (at **[2.91]**) provides that this section continues to apply to shares allotted before 1 Oct 2009.
89 Offers to shareholders to be on pre-emptive basis	Repealed by CA 2006, as from 1 Oct 2009.
	Savings and transitional provisions: for general savings and transitional provisions in connection with the commencement of the equivalent provisions of the 2006 Act (existing shareholders' right of pre-emption (ss 561–577)), see CO No 8, Sch 2, paras 49–55 (at **[2.91]**).
90 Communication of pre-emption offers to shareholders	Repealed by CA 2006, as from 1 Oct 2009. For savings and transitional provisions see the note to s 89.
91 Exclusion of ss 89, 90 by private company	Repealed by CA 2006, as from 1 Oct 2009. For savings and transitional provisions see the note to s 89.
92 Consequences of contravening ss 89, 90	Repealed by CA 2006, as from 1 Oct 2009. For savings and transitional provisions see the note to s 89.
93 Saving for other restrictions as to offers	Repealed by CA 2006, as from 1 Oct 2009. For savings and transitional provisions see the note to s 89.
94 Definitions for ss 89–96	Repealed by CA 2006, as from 1 Oct 2009. For savings and transitional provisions see the note to s 89.
95 Disapplication of pre-emption rights	Repealed by CA 2006, as from 1 Oct 2009. For savings and transitional provisions see the note to s 89.
96 Saving for company's pre-emption procedure operative before 1982	Repealed by CA 2006, as from 1 Oct 2009. For savings and transitional provisions see the note to s 89.
97 Power of company to pay commissions	Repealed by CA 2006, as from 1 Oct 2009. As to the previous repeal of this section by FSA 1986, see the note preceding this table.

98 Apart from s 97, commissions and discounts barred	Repealed by CA 2006, as from 1 Oct 2009.
99 General rules as to payment for shares on allotment	Repealed by CA 2006, as from 1 Oct 2009.
100 Prohibition on allotment of shares at a discount	Repealed by CA 2006, as from 1 Oct 2009.
101 Shares to be allotted as at least one-quarter paid-up	Repealed by CA 2006, as from 1 Oct 2009.
102 Restriction on payment by long-term undertaking	Repealed by CA 2006, as from 1 Oct 2009.
103 Non-cash consideration to be valued before allotment	Repealed by CA 2006, as from 1 Oct 2009.
104 Transfer to public company of non-cash asset in initial period	Repealed by CA 2006, as from 1 Oct 2009.
105 Agreements contravening s 104	Repealed by CA 2006, as from 1 Oct 2009.
106 Shares issued to subscribers of memorandum	Repealed by CA 2006, as from 1 Oct 2009.
107 Meaning of "the appropriate rate"	Repealed by CA 2006, as from 1 Oct 2009.
108 Valuation and report (s 103)	Repealed by CA 2006, as from 1 Oct 2009.
109 Valuation and report (s 104)	Repealed by CA 2006, as from 1 Oct 2009.
110 Entitlement of valuer to full disclosure	Repealed by CA 2006, as from 1 Oct 2009.
111 Matters to be communicated to registrar	Repealed by CA 2006, as from 1 Oct 2009.
111A Right to damages, &c not affected	Repealed by CA 2006, as from 1 Oct 2009.
112 Liability of subsequent holders of shares allotted	Repealed by CA 2006, as from 1 Oct 2009.
113 Relief in respect of certain liabilities under ss 99 ff	Repealed by CA 2006, as from 1 Oct 2009.
114 Penalty for contravention	Repealed by CA 2006, as from 1 Oct 2009.
	Savings: CO No 8, Sch 2, para 57 (at **[2.91]**) provides that this section continues to apply in relation to consideration received in pursuance of an obligation entered into before 1 Oct 2009.
115 Undertakings to do work, etc	Repealed by CA 2006, as from 1 Oct 2009.
116 Application of ss 99 ff to special cases	Repealed by CA 2006, as from 1 Oct 2009.

PART V
SHARE CAPITAL, ITS INCREASE, MAINTENANCE AND REDUCTION

117–197

NOTES

This Part has been repealed as follows:

117 Public company share capital requirements	Repealed by CA 2006, as from 6 Apr 2008.
	Savings: CO No 5, Sch 4, Pt 1, paras 26, 27, 29 (at **[2.66]**) provide (i) that a certificate issued under this section has effect on and after 6 Apr 2008 as issued under CA 2006, s 761, (ii) s 762 of the 2006 Act applies to applications made on or after 6 Apr 2008 and sub-ss (1)–(5), (7A) of this section continue to apply to applications made before that date, and (iii) s 767 of the 2006 Act applies in relation to things done on or after 6 Apr 2008, and sub-ss (6)–(8) of this section continue to apply in relation to things done before that date.
118 The authorised minimum	Repealed by CA 2006, as from 6 Apr 2008.
119 Provision for different amounts to be paid on shares	Repealed by CA 2006, as from 1 Oct 2009.
120 Reserve liability of limited company	Repealed by CA 2006, as from 1 Oct 2009.
	Savings: CO No 8, Sch 2, para 67 (at **[2.91]**) provides that the repeal of this section does not affect the validity of any resolution that is in force immediately before 1 Oct 2009.

121 Alteration of share capital (limited companies)	Repealed by CA 2006, as from 1 Oct 2009. Savings: see CO No 8, Sch 2, para 42 (Saving for provisions as to amount of authorised share capital) at **[2.91]**.
122 Notice to registrar of alteration	Repealed by CA 2006, as from 1 Oct 2009. Savings: see CO No 8, Sch 2, para 41 (at **[2.91]**).
123 Notice to registrar of increased share capital	Repealed by CA 2006, as from 1 Oct 2009.
124 Reserve capital of unlimited company	Repealed by CA 2006, as from 1 Oct 2009. Savings: CO No 8, Sch 2, para 67 (at **[2.91]**) provides that the repeal of this section does not affect the validity of any resolution that is in force immediately before 1 Oct 2009.
125 Variation of class rights	Repealed by CA 2006, as from 1 Oct 2007 (in so far as relating to sub-s (6)), and as from 1 Oct 2009 (otherwise). Savings: sub-s (6) (which applied (with the necessary modifications) ss 369, 370, 376 and 377 and the provisions of the articles relating to general meetings in relation to any meeting of shareholders in connection with the variation of the rights attached to a class of shares) continued to apply to meetings of which notice was given before 1 Oct 2007 (see CO No 3, Sch 3, para 31 at **[2.45]**).
126 Saving for court's powers under other provisions	Repealed by CA 2006, as from 1 Oct 2009.
127 Shareholders' right to object to variation	Repealed by CA 2006, s 1295, Sch 16, as from 1 October 2009.
128 Registration of particulars of special rights	Repealed by CA 2006, as from 1 Oct 2009. Savings: see CO No 8, Sch 2, paras 48, 62, 63 (at **[2.91]**) which respectively provide as follows: (i) sub-ss (1), (2), (5) continue to apply to shares allotted before 1 Oct 2009; (ii) sub-ss (4), (5) continue to apply where the new name or other designation was assigned before that date; (iii) sub-ss (3), (5) continue to apply where the variation was made before that date.
129 Registration of newly created class rights	Repealed by CA 2006, as from 1 Oct 2009. Savings: see CO No 8, Sch 2, paras 64, 65, 66 (at **[2.91]**) which respectively provide as follows: (i) sub-ss (1), (4) continue to apply where a new class of members was created before 1 Oct 2009; (ii) sub-ss (3), (4) continue to apply where the name or other designation, or new name or other designation, was assigned before that date; (iii) sub-ss (2), (4) continue to apply where the variation was made before that date.
130 Application of share premiums	Repealed by CA 2006, as from 1 Oct 2009.
131 Merger relief	Repealed by CA 2006, as from 1 Oct 2009.
132 Relief in respect of group reconstructions	Repealed by CA 2006, as from 1 Oct 2009.
133 Provisions supplementing ss 131, 132	Repealed by CA 2006, as from 1 Oct 2009.
134 Provision for extending or restricting relief from s 130	Repealed by CA 2006, as from 1 Oct 2009.
135 Special resolution for reduction of share capital	Repealed by CA 2006, as from 1 Oct 2009.
136 Application to court for order of confirmation	Repealed by CA 2006, as from 1 Oct 2009. Savings: see CO No 8, Sch 2, paras 68, 69 (Reduction of capital confirmed by the court (ss 645 to 653)) at **[2.91]**.
137 Court order confirming reduction	Repealed by CA 2006, as from 1 Oct 2009. For savings see the note to s 136.
138 Registration of order and minute of reduction	Repealed by CA 2006, as from 1 Oct 2009. For savings see the note to s 136.
139 Public company reducing capital below authorised minimum	Repealed by CA 2006, as from 1 Oct 2009. For savings see the note to s 136.
140 Liability of members on reduced shares	Repealed by CA 2006, as from 1 Oct 2009. For savings see the note to s 136.
141 Penalty for concealing name of creditor, etc	Repealed by CA 2006, as from 1 Oct 2009. For savings see the note to s 136.
142 Duty of directors on serious loss of capital	Repealed by CA 2006, as from 1 Oct 2009.
143 General rule against company acquiring own shares	Repealed by CA 2006, as from 1 Oct 2009.
144 Acquisition of shares by company's nominee	Repealed by CA 2006, as from 1 Oct 2009.
145 Exceptions from s 144	Repealed by CA 2006, as from 1 Oct 2009.

146 Treatment of shares held by or for public company	Repealed by CA 2006, as from 1 Oct 2009.
	Savings: see CO No 8, Sch 2, paras 70, 72 (Cancellation of shares in public company held by or for the company (ss 662 to 668)) at **[2.91]**.
147 Matters arising out of compliance with s 146(2)	Repealed by CA 2006, as from 1 Oct 2009. For savings see the note to s 146.
148 Further provisions supplementing ss 146, 147	Repealed by CA 2006, as from 1 Oct 2009. For savings see the note to s 146.
149 Sanctions for non-compliance	Repealed by CA 2006, as from 1 Oct 2009. For savings see the note to s 146.
150 Charges of public companies on own shares	Repealed by CA 2006, as from 1 Oct 2009.
151 Financial assistance generally prohibited	Repealed by CA 2006, as from 1 Oct 2008 (in relation to the giving of financial assistance (on or after that date) by a private company for the purposes of the acquisition of shares in itself or another private company (see CO No 5, art 5(2) at **[2.54]**) and the savings note below), and as from 1 Oct 2009 (otherwise).
	Savings, etc: see CO No 5, Sch 4, Pt 3, paras 51, 52 (Repeal of prohibition on private companies giving financial assistance for acquisition of shares) at **[2.68]**.
152 Definitions for this Chapter	Repealed by CA 2006, as from 1 Oct 2008 (in relation to the giving of financial assistance (on or after that date) by a private company for the purposes of the acquisition of shares in itself or another private company (see the notes to s 151), and as from 1 Oct 2009 (otherwise).
153 Transactions not prohibited by s 151	Repealed by CA 2006, as from 1 Oct 2008 (in relation to the giving of financial assistance (on or after that date) by a private company for the purposes of the acquisition of shares in itself or another private company (see the notes to s 151), and as from 1 Oct 2009 (otherwise).
154 Special restriction for public companies	Repealed by CA 2006, as from 1 Oct 2009.
155 Relaxation of s 151 for private companies	Repealed by CA 2006, as from 1 Oct 2008 (in relation to the giving of financial assistance (on or after that date) by a private company for the purposes of the acquisition of shares in itself or another private company (see the notes to s 151), and as from 1 Oct 2009 (otherwise).
156 Statutory declaration under s 155	Repealed by CA 2006, as from 1 Oct 2008 (in relation to the giving of financial assistance (on or after that date) by a private company for the purposes of the acquisition of shares in itself or another private company (see the notes to s 151), and as from 1 Oct 2009 (otherwise).
157 Special resolution under s 155	Repealed by CA 2006, as from 1 Oct 2008 (in relation to the giving of financial assistance (on or after that date) by a private company for the purposes of the acquisition of shares in itself or another private company (see the notes to s 151), and as from 1 Oct 2009 (otherwise).
158 Time for giving financial assistance under s 155	Repealed by CA 2006, as from 1 Oct 2008 (in relation to the giving of financial assistance (on or after that date) by a private company for the purposes of the acquisition of shares in itself or another private company (see the notes to s 151), and as from 1 Oct 2009 (otherwise).
159 Power to issue redeemable shares	Repealed by CA 2006, as from 1 Oct 2009.
	Savings: CO No 8, Sch 2, para 73 (at **[2.91]**) provides that CA 2006, s 686(2) (terms allowing for payment on date later than redemption date) applies (a) to shares issued on or after 1 Oct 2009, and (b) to shares issued before that date where the terms of redemption have been amended on or after that date to allow for payment on a date later than the redemption date. Furthermore, so much of sub-s (3) as requires payment on redemption continues to apply in any other case.
159A Terms and manner of redemption	Repealed by CA 2006, as from 1 Oct 2009.
160 Financing etc of redemption	Repealed by CA 2006, as from 1 Oct 2009.
161 Stamp duty on redemption of shares	Repealed by FA 1988, s 148, Sch 14, Pt XI, with effect from 22 Mar 1988.
162 Power of company to purchase own shares	Repealed by CA 2006, as from 1 Oct 2009.
162A Treasury shares	Repealed by CA 2006, as from 1 Oct 2009.
162B Treasury shares: maximum holdings	Repealed by CA 2006, as from 1 Oct 2009.
162C Treasury shares: voting and other rights	Repealed by CA 2006, as from 1 Oct 2009.
162D Treasury shares: disposal and cancellation	Repealed by CA 2006, as from 1 Oct 2009.
	Savings: CO No 8, Sch 2, para 79 (at **[2.91]**) provides that sub-s (1)(a) continues to apply where the contract for the sale of the shares was entered into before 1 Oct 2009.

162E Treasury shares: mandatory cancellation	Repealed by CA 2006, as from 1 Oct 2009.
162F Treasury shares: proceeds of sale	Repealed by CA 2006, as from 1 Oct 2009.
162G Treasury shares: penalty for contravention	Repealed by CA 2006, as from 1 Oct 2009.
163 Definitions of "off-market" and "market" purchase	Repealed by CA 2006, as from 1 Oct 2009.
164 Authority for off-market purchase	Repealed by CA 2006, as from 1 Oct 2009. Savings and transitional provisions: see CO No 8, Sch 2, paras 75–77 (Purchase of own shares (ss 690 to 708)) at **[2.91]**.
165 Authority for contingent purchase contract	Repealed by CA 2006, as from 1 Oct 2009. For savings see the note to s 164.
166 Authority for market purchase	Repealed by CA 2006, as from 1 Oct 2009. Transitional provisions: CO No 8, Sch 2, para 75 (at **[2.91]**) provides that where immediately before 1 Oct 2009 a resolution is in force having been passed under ss 166 or 167(2), the resolution has effect on and after that date as if passed under the corresponding provision of CA 2006 and may be varied, revoked or renewed from time to time accordingly.
167 Assignment or release of company's right to purchase own shares	Repealed by CA 2006, as from 1 Oct 2009. For transitional provisions see the note to s 166.
168 Payments apart from purchase price to be made out of distributable profits	Repealed by CA 2006, as from 1 Oct 2009.
169 Disclosure by company of purchase of own shares	Repealed by CA 2006, as from 1 Oct 2009. For savings see the note to s 164.
169A Disclosure by company of cancellation or disposal of treasury shares	Repealed by CA 2006, as from 1 Oct 2009. Savings: CO No 8, Sch 2, para 80 (at **[2.91]**) provides that this section continues to apply to shares cancelled before 1 Oct 2009.
170 The capital redemption reserve	Repealed by CA 2006, as from 1 Oct 2009.
171 Power of private companies to redeem or purchase own shares out of capital	Repealed by CA 2006, as from 1 Oct 2009. Savings: CO No 8, Sch 2, para 78 (at **[2.91]**) provides that this section and ss 172–178 continue to apply where the statutory declaration required by s 173(3) was made before 1 Oct 2009.
172 Availability of profits for purposes of s 171	Repealed by CA 2006, as from 1 Oct 2009. For savings see the note to s 171.
173 Conditions for payment out of capital	Repealed by CA 2006, as from 1 Oct 2009. For savings see the note to s 171.
174 Procedure for special resolution under s 173	Repealed by CA 2006, as from 1 Oct 2009. For savings see the note to s 171.
175 Publicity for proposed payment out of capital	Repealed by CA 2006, as from 1 Oct 2009. For savings see the note to s 171.
176 Objections by company's members or creditors	Repealed by CA 2006, as from 1 Oct 2009. For savings see the note to s 171.
177 Powers of court on application under s 176	Repealed by CA 2006, as from 1 Oct 2009. For savings see the note to s 171.
178 Effect of company's failure to redeem or purchase	Repealed by CA 2006, as from 1 Oct 2009. For savings see the note to s 171.
179 Power for Secretary of State to modify this Chapter	Repealed by CA 2006, as from 1 Oct 2009.
180 Transitional cases arising under this Chapter; and savings	Repealed by CA 2006, as from 1 Oct 2009.
181 Definitions for Chapter VII	Repealed by CA 2006, as from 1 Oct 2009.
182 Nature, transfer and numbering of shares	Repealed by CA 2006, as from 1 Oct 2009.
183 Transfer and registration	Repealed by CA 2006, as from 6 Apr 2008.
184 Certification of transfers	Repealed by CA 2006, as from 6 Apr 2008.
185 Duty of company as to issue of certificates	Repealed by CA 2006, as from 6 Apr 2008.
186 Certificate to be evidence of title	Repealed by CA 2006, as from 6 Apr 2008.
187 Evidence of grant of probate or confirmation as executor	Repealed by CA 2006, as from 6 Apr 2008.
188 Issue and effect of share warrant to bearer	Repealed by CA 2006, as from 6 Apr 2008.

189 Offences in connection with share warrants (Scotland)	Repealed by CA 2006, as from 6 Apr 2008.
190 Register of debenture holders	Repealed by CA 2006, as from 6 Apr 2008.
191 Right to inspect register	Repealed by CA 2006, as from 6 Apr 2008. Savings: sub-ss (1)–(6) continue to apply to requests made before 6 Apr 2008; see CO No 5, Sch 4, Pt 1, para 22 at **[2.66]**.
192 Liability of trustees of debentures	Repealed by CA 2006, as from 6 Apr 2008.
193 Perpetual debentures	Repealed by CA 2006, as from 6 Apr 2008.
194 Power to re-issue redeemed debentures	Repealed by CA 2006, as from 6 Apr 2008.
195 Contract to subscribe for debentures	Repealed by CA 2006, as from 6 Apr 2008.
196 Payment of debts out of assets subject to floating charge (England and Wales)	Repealed by CA 2006, as from 6 Apr 2008.
197 Debentures to bearer (Scotland)	Repealed by CA 2006, as from 6 Apr 2008.

PART VI
DISCLOSURE OF INTERESTS IN SHARES

198–220

NOTES

This Part has been repealed as follows:

198 Obligation of disclosure: the cases in which it may arise and "the relevant time"	Repealed by the CA 2006, as from 20 Jan 2007. Savings: the repeal of ss 198–210 and 220 does not affect any obligation to which a person became subject under s 198 before 20 Jan 2007; see CO No 1, Sch 5, Pt 2, para 2(1) at **[2.14]**.
199 Interests to be disclosed	Repealed by CA 2006, as from 20 Jan 2007. For savings see the note to s 198.
200 "Percentage level" in relation to notifiable interests	Repealed by CA 2006, as from 20 Jan 2007. For savings see the note to s 198.
201 The notifiable percentage	Repealed by CA 1989, s 212, Sch 24, as from 31 May 1990.
202 Particulars to be contained in notification	Repealed by CA 2006, as from 20 Jan 2007. For savings see the note to s 198.
203 Notification of family and corporate interests	Repealed by CA 2006, as from 20 Jan 2007. For savings see the note to s 198.
204 Agreement to acquire interests in a particular company	Repealed by CA 2006, as from 20 Jan 2007. For savings see the note to s 198.
205 Obligation of disclosure arising under s 204	Repealed by CA 2006, as from 20 Jan 2007. For savings see the note to s 198.
206 Obligation of persons acting together to keep each other informed	Repealed by CA 2006, as from 20 Jan 2007. For savings see the note to s 198.
207 Interests in shares by attribution	Repealed by CA 2006, as from 20 Jan 2007. For savings see the note to s 198.
208 Interests in shares which are to be notified	Repealed by CA 2006, as from 20 Jan 2007. For savings see the note to s 198.
209 Interests to be disregarded	Repealed by CA 2006, as from 20 Jan 2007. For savings see the note to s 198.
210 Other provisions about notification under this Part	Repealed by CA 2006, as from 20 Jan 2007. For savings see the note to s 198.
210A Power to make further provision by regulations	Repealed by CA 2006, as from 20 Jan 2007.
211 Register of interests in shares	Repealed by CA 2006, as from 20 Jan 2007.
212 Company investigations	Repealed by the CA 2006, as from 20 Jan 2007. Savings: the repeal of ss 212–220 does not affect the operation of those sections in relation to a notice issued by a company under s 212 before 20 Jan 2007; see CO No 1, Sch 5, Pt 2, para 2(2) at **[2.14]**.
213 Registration of interests disclosed under s 212	Repealed by CA 2006, as from 20 Jan 2007. For savings see the note to s 212.
214 Company investigation on requisition by members	Repealed by CA 2006, as from 20 Jan 2007. For savings see the note to s 212.
215 Company report to members	Repealed by CA 2006, as from 20 Jan 2007. For savings see the note to s 212.
216 Penalty for failure to provide information	Repealed by CA 2006, as from 20 Jan 2007. For savings see the note to s 212.

217 Removal of entries from register	Repealed by CA 2006, as from 20 Jan 2007. For savings see the note to s 212.
218 Otherwise, entries not to be re-moved	Repealed by CA 2006, as from 20 Jan 2007. For savings see the note to s 212.
219 Inspection of register and reports	Repealed by CA 2006, as from 20 Jan 2007. For savings see the note to s 212.
220 Definitions for Part VI	Repealed by CA 2006, as from 20 Jan 2007. For savings see the notes to ss 198 and 212.

PART VII
ACCOUNTS AND AUDIT

221–262A

NOTES

This Part has been repealed as follows:

221 Duty to keep accounting records	Repealed by CA 2006, as from 6 Apr 2008. Savings: this repeal does not apply in relation to accounts and reports for financial years beginning before 6 Apr 2008; see CO No 5, Sch 4, Pt 1, paras 6–9, 12(1), (2) (at **[2.66]**).
222 Where and for how long records to be kept	Repealed by CA 2006, as from 6 Apr 2008. For savings see the note to s 221.
223 A company's financial year	Repealed by CA 2006, as from 6 Apr 2008. For savings see the note to s 221.
224 Accounting reference periods and accounting reference date	Repealed by CA 2006, as from 6 Apr 2008. For savings see the note to s 221.
225 Alteration of accounting reference date	Repealed by CA 2006, as from 6 Apr 2008. For savings see the note to s 221.
226 Duty to prepare individual accounts	Repealed by CA 2006, as from 6 Apr 2008. For savings see the note to s 221.
226A Companies Act individual accounts	Repealed by CA 2006, as from 6 Apr 2008. For savings see the note to s 221.
226B IAS individual accounts	Repealed by CA 2006, as from 6 Apr 2008. For savings see the note to s 221.
227 Duty to prepare group accounts	Repealed by CA 2006, as from 6 Apr 2008. For savings see the note to s 221.
227A Companies Act group accounts	Repealed by CA 2006, as from 6 Apr 2008. For savings see the note to s 221.
227B IAS group accounts	Repealed by CA 2006, as from 6 Apr 2008. For savings see the note to s 221.
227C Consistency of accounts	Repealed by CA 2006, as from 6 Apr 2008. For savings see the note to s 221.
228 Exemption for parent companies included in accounts of larger group	Repealed by CA 2006, as from 6 Apr 2008. For savings see the note to s 221.
228A Exemption for parent companies included in non-EEA group accounts	Repealed by CA 2006, as from 6 Apr 2008. For savings see the note to s 221.
229 Subsidiary undertakings included in the consolidation	Repealed by CA 2006, as from 6 Apr 2008. For savings see the note to s 221.
230 Treatment of individual profit and loss account where group accounts prepared	Repealed by CA 2006, as from 6 Apr 2008. For savings see the note to s 221.
231 Disclosure required in notes to accounts: related undertakings	Repealed by CA 2006, as from 6 Apr 2008. For savings see the note to s 221.
231A Disclosure required in notes to annual accounts: particulars of staff	Repealed by CA 2006, as from 6 Apr 2008. For savings see the note to s 221.
232 Disclosure required in notes to accounts: emoluments and other benefits of directors and others	Repealed by CA 2006, as from 6 Apr 2008. For savings see the note to s 221.
233 Approval and signing of accounts	Repealed by CA 2006, as from 6 Apr 2008. For savings see the note to s 221.
234 Duty to prepare directors' report	Repealed by CA 2006, as from 6 Apr 2008. For savings see the note to s 221.
234ZZA Directors' report: general requirements	Repealed by CA 2006, as from 6 Apr 2008. For savings see the note to s 221.
234ZZB Directors' report: business review	Repealed by CA 2006, as from 1 Oct 2007. Savings: this repeal does not apply in relation to directors' reports for financial years beginning before 1 Oct 2007; see CO No 3, Sch 3, para 43 at **[2.45]**.
234ZA Statement as to disclosure of information to auditors	Repealed by CA 2006, as from 6 Apr 2008. For savings see the note to s 221.
234A Approval and signing of directors' report	Repealed by CA 2006, as from 6 Apr 2008. For savings see the note to s 221.

234AA Duty to prepare operating and financial review	Repealed by SI 2005/3442, as from 12 Jan 2006.
234AB Approval and signing of operating and financial review	Repealed by SI 2005/3442, as from 12 Jan 2006.
234B Duty to prepare directors' remuneration report	Repealed by CA 2006, as from 6 Apr 2008. For savings see the note to s 221.
234C Approval and signing of directors' remuneration report	Repealed by CA 2006, as from 6 Apr 2008. For savings see the note to s 221.
235 Auditors' report	Repealed by CA 2006, as from 6 Apr 2008. For savings see the note to s 221.
236 Signature of auditors' report	Repealed by CA 2006, as from 6 Apr 2008. For savings see the note to s 221.
237 Duties of auditors	Repealed by CA 2006, as from 6 Apr 2008. For savings see the note to s 221.
238 Persons entitled to receive copies of accounts and reports	Repealed by CA 2006, as from 6 Apr 2008. For savings see the note to s 221.
238A Time allowed for sending out copies of accounts and reports	Repealed by CA 2006, as from 6 Apr 2008. For savings see the note to s 221.
239 Right to demand copies of accounts and reports	Repealed by CA 2006, as from 6 Apr 2008. For savings see the note to s 221.
240 Requirements in connection with publication of accounts	Repealed by CA 2006, as from 6 Apr 2008. For savings see the note to s 221.
241 Accounts and reports to be laid before company in general meeting	Repealed by CA 2006, as from 6 Apr 2008. For savings see the note to s 221.
241A Members' approval of directors' remuneration report	Repealed by CA 2006, as from 6 Apr 2008. For savings see the note to s 221.
242 Accounts and reports to be delivered to the registrar	Repealed by CA 2006, as from 6 Apr 2008. For savings see the note to s 221.
242A Civil penalty for failure to deliver accounts	Repealed by CA 2006, as from 6 Apr 2008. For savings see the note to s 221.
242B Delivery and publication of accounts in ECUs	Repealed by CA 2006, as from 6 Apr 2008. For savings see the note to s 221.
243 Penalty for non-compliance with s 241	Repealed by SI 2004/2947, as from 12 Nov 2004, in relation to companies' financial years which begin on or after 1 Jan 2005.
244 Period allowed for laying and delivering accounts and reports	Repealed by CA 2006, as from 6 Apr 2008. For savings see the note to s 221.
245 Voluntary revision of annual accounts or directors' report	Repealed by CA 2006, as from 6 Apr 2008. For savings see the note to s 221.
245A Secretary of State's notice in respect of annual accounts	Repealed by CA 2006, as from 6 Apr 2008. For savings see the note to s 221.
245B Application to court in respect of defective accounts	Repealed by CA 2006, as from 6 Apr 2008. For savings see the note to s 221.
245C Other persons authorised to apply to court	Repealed by CA 2006, as from 6 Apr 2008. For savings see the note to s 221.
245D Disclosure of information held by Inland Revenue to persons authorised to apply to court	Repealed by CA 2006, as from 6 Apr 2008. For savings see the note to s 221.
245E Restrictions on use and further disclosure of information disclosed under section 245D	Repealed by CA 2006, as from 6 Apr 2008. For savings see the note to s 221.
245F Power of authorised persons to require documents, information and explanations	Repealed by CA 2006, as from 6 Apr 2008. For savings see the note to s 221.
245G Restrictions on further disclosure of information obtained under section 245F	Repealed by CA 2006, as from 6 Apr 2008. For savings see the note to s 221.
246 Special provisions for small companies	Repealed by CA 2006, as from 6 Apr 2008. For savings see the note to s 221.
246A Special provisions for medium-sized companies	Repealed by CA 2006, as from 6 Apr 2008. For savings see the note to s 221.
247 Qualification of company as small or medium-sized	Repealed by CA 2006, as from 6 Apr 2008. For savings see the note to s 221.
247A Cases in which special provisions do not apply	Repealed by CA 2006, as from 6 Apr 2008. For savings see the note to s 221.
247B Special auditors' report	Repealed by CA 2006, as from 6 Apr 2008. For savings see the note to s 221.
248 Exemption for small and medium-sized groups	Repealed by CA 2006, as from 6 Apr 2008. For savings see the note to s 221.

248A Group accounts prepared by small company	Repealed by CA 2006, as from 6 Apr 2008. For savings see the note to s 221.
249 Qualification of group as small or medium-sized	Repealed by CA 2006, as from 6 Apr 2008. For savings see the note to s 221.
249A Exemptions from audit	Repealed by CA 2006, as from 6 Apr 2008. For savings see the note to s 221.
249AA Dormant companies	Repealed by CA 2006, as from 6 Apr 2008. For savings see the note to s 221.
249B Cases where exemptions not available	Repealed by CA 2006, as from 6 Apr 2008. For savings see the note to s 221.
249C The report required for the purposes of section 249A(2)	Repealed by CA 2006, as from 6 Apr 2008. For savings see the note to s 221.
249D The reporting accountant	Repealed by CA 2006, as from 6 Apr 2008. For savings see the note to s 221.
249E Effect of exemptions	Repealed by CA 2006, as from 6 Apr 2008. For savings see the note to s 221.
250 Power of Secretary of State to modify ss 247–250 and Sch 8	Repealed by SI 2000/1430, as from 26 May 2000, in relation to annual accounts and reports in respect of financial years ending two months or more after that date.
251 Provision of summary financial statement to shareholders	Repealed by CA 2006, as from 6 Apr 2008. For savings see the note to s 221.
252 Election to dispense with laying of accounts and reports before general meeting	Repealed by CA 2006, as from 1 Oct 2007. Savings: the repeal of ss 252, 253 have effect in relation to annual accounts and reports for financial years ending on or after 1 Oct 2007; see CO No 3, SI 2007/2194, Sch 3, para 49 at **[2.45]**.
253 Right of shareholder to require laying of accounts	Repealed by CA 2006, as from 1 Oct 2007. For savings see the note to s 252.
254 Exemption from requirement to deliver accounts and reports	Repealed by CA 2006, as from 6 Apr 2008. For savings see the note to s 221.
255 Special provisions for banking and insurance companies	Repealed by CA 2006, as from 6 Apr 2008. For savings see the note to s 221.
255A Special provisions for banking and insurance groups	Repealed by CA 2006, as from 6 Apr 2008. For savings see the note to s 221.
255B Modification of disclosure requirements in relation to banking company or group	Repealed by CA 2006, as from 6 Apr 2008. For savings see the note to s 221.
255C Directors' report where accounts prepared in accordance with special provisions	Repealed by SI 1993/3246, as from 19 Dec 1993,, subject to transitional provisions and exemptions in relation to certain companies.
255D Power to apply provisions to banking partnerships	Repealed by CA 2006, as from 6 Apr 2008. For savings see the note to s 221.
255E Delivery of accounting documents in Welsh only	Repealed by the Welsh Language Act 1993, as from 1 Feb 1994.
256 Accounting standards	Repealed by CA 2006, as from 6 Apr 2008. For savings see the note to s 221.
256A Reporting standards	Repealed by SI 2005/3442, as from 12 Jan 2006.
257 Power of Secretary of State to alter accounting requirements	Repealed by CA 2006, as from 6 Apr 2008. For savings see the note to s 221.
258 Parent and subsidiary undertakings	Repealed by CA 2006, as from 6 Apr 2008. For savings see the note to s 221.
259 Meaning of "undertaking" and related expressions	Repealed by CA 2006, as from 6 Apr 2008. For savings see the note to s 221.
260 Participating interests	Repealed by CA 2006, as from 6 Apr 2008. For savings see the note to s 221.
261 Notes to the accounts	Repealed by CA 2006, as from 6 Apr 2008. For savings see the note to s 221.
262 Minor definitions	Repealed by CA 2006, as from 6 Apr 2008. For savings see the note to s 221.
262A Index of defined expressions	Repealed by CA 2006, as from 6 Apr 2008. For savings see the note to s 221.

PART VIII
DISTRIBUTION OF PROFITS AND ASSETS

263–281

NOTES

This Part has been repealed as follows:

263 Certain distributions prohibited	Repealed by CA2006, as from 6 Apr 2008. Savings: ss 263–281 continue to apply to distributions made before 6 Apr 2008; see CO No 5, Sch 4, Pt 1, para 33 at **[2.66]**.

264 Restriction on distribution of assets	Repealed by CA 2006, as from 6 Apr 2008. For savings see the note to s 263.
265 Other distributions by investment companies	Repealed by CA 2006, as from 6 Apr 2008. For savings see the note to s 263.
266 Meaning of "investment company"	Repealed by CA 2006, as from 6 Apr 2008. For savings see the note to s 263.
267 Extension of ss 265, 266 to other companies	Repealed by CA 2006, as from 6 Apr 2008. For savings see the note to s 263.
268 Realised profits of insurance company with long term business	Repealed by CA 2006, as from 6 Apr 2008. For savings see the note to s 263.
269 Treatment of development costs	Repealed by CA 2006, as from 6 Apr 2008. For savings see the note to s 263.
270 Distribution to be justified by reference to company's accounts	Repealed by CA 2006, as from 6 Apr 2008. For savings see the note to s 263.
271 Requirements for last annual accounts	Repealed by CA 2006, as from 6 Apr 2008. For savings see the note to s 263.
272 Requirements for interim accounts	Repealed by CA 2006, as from 6 Apr 2008. For savings see the note to s 263.
273 Requirements for initial accounts	Repealed by CA 2006, as from 6 Apr 2008. For savings see the note to s 263.
274 Method of applying s 270 to successive distributions	Repealed by CA 2006, as from 6 Apr 2008. For savings see the note to s 263.
275 Treatment of assets in the relevant accounts	Repealed by CA 2006, as from 6 Apr 2008. For savings see the note to s 263.
276 Distributions in kind	Repealed by CA 2006, as from 6 Apr 2008. For savings see the note to s 263.
277 Consequences of unlawful distribution	Repealed by CA 2006, as from 6 Apr 2008. For savings see the note to s 263.
278 Saving for provision in articles operative before Act of 1980	Repealed by CA 2006, as from 6 Apr 2008. For savings see the note to s 263.
279 Distributions by banking or insurance companies	Repealed by CA 2006, as from 6 Apr 2008. For savings see the note to s 263.
280 Definitions for Part VIII	Repealed by CA 2006, as from 6 Apr 2008. For savings see the note to s 263.
281 Saving for other restraints on distribution	Repealed by CA 2006, as from 6 Apr 2008. For savings see the note to s 263.

PART IX
A COMPANY'S MANAGEMENT; DIRECTORS AND SECRETARIES; THEIR QUALIFICATIONS, DUTIES AND RESPONSIBILITIES

282–310

NOTES

This Part has been repealed as follows:

282 Directors	Repealed by CA 2006, as from 1 Oct 2007.
283 Secretary	Repealed by CA 2006, as from 6 Apr 2008.
284 Acts done by person in dual capacity	Repealed by CA 2006, as from 6 Apr 2008.
285 Validity of acts of directors	Repealed by CA 2006, as from 1 Oct 2007. Savings: this repeal does not apply in relation to acts done before 1 Oct 2007; see CO No 3, Sch 3, para 4 at **[2.45]**.
286 Qualifications of company secretaries	Repealed by CA 2006, as from 6 Apr 2008. Savings: this repeal does not apply in relation to company secretaries appointed before 6 Apr 2008; see CO No 5, Sch 4, Pt 1, para 5 at **[2.66]**.
287 Registered office	Repealed by CA 2006, as from 1 Oct 2009.
288 Register of directors and secretaries	Repealed by CA 2006, as from 1 Oct 2009. Savings and transitional provisions: CO No 8, Sch 2, para 25 (at **[2.91]**) provides that on and after 1 Oct 2009 the register of directors and secretaries kept by a company under this section shall be treated as two separate registers: (a) a register of directors kept under and for the purposes of the CA 2006, s 162, and (b) a register of secretaries kept under and for the purposes of s 275 of that Act. See also Sch 2, para 31 to that Order which provides that sub-ss (2), (4) and (6) above continue to apply in relation to a change occurring before 1 Oct 2009.
288A	Repealed by CA 2006, as from 1 Oct 2009.

289 Particulars of directors to be registered under s 288	Repealed by CA 2006, as from 1 Oct 2009.
	Savings: CO No 8, Sch 2, para 31 (at **[2.91]**) provides that this section and s 290 continue to apply in relation to a change occurring before 1 Oct 2009.
290 Particulars of secretaries to be registered under s 288	Repealed by CA 2006, as from 1 Oct 2009. For savings see the note to s 289.
291 Share qualification of directors	Repealed by CA 2006, as from 1 Oct 2009.
292 Appointment of directors to be voted on individually	Repealed by CA 2006, as from 1 Oct 2007.
293 Age limit for directors	Repealed by CA 2006, as from 6 Apr 2007.
	Savings: CO No 1, Sch 5, para 7 (at **[2.15]**) provides that the repeal of sub-s (3) does not affect the validity of acts done by a person acting as director to whom that section applied.
294 Duty of director to disclose his age	Repealed by CA 2006, as from 6 Apr 2007.
295–302	Ss 295–299, 301, 302 repealed with savings by the Company Directors Disqualification Act 1986, as from 29 Dec 1986; s 300 repealed by the Insolvency Act 1985, as from 28 Apr 1986.
303 Resolution to remove director	Repealed by CA 2006, as from 1 Oct 2007.
304 Director's right to protest removal	Repealed by CA 2006, as from 1 Oct 2007.
	Savings: CO No 3, Sch 3, para 5 (at **[2.45]**) provides that sub-s (4) continues to apply where, in the case of an intended resolution to remove a director under s 303, the written representations made by the director concerned are received by the company before 1 Oct 2007.
305 Directors' names on company correspondence, etc	Repealed by CA 2006, as from 1 Oct 2008.
306 Limited company may have directors with unlimited liability	Repealed by CA 2006, as from 1 Oct 2009.
	Savings: SI 2009/1941, art 9 (at **[4.536]**) provides that the repeal of this section (and s 307) does not affect its operation in relation to liabilities arising before 1 Oct 2009 or in connection with the holding of an office to which a person was appointed before that date on the understanding that their liability would be unlimited.
307 Special resolution making liability of directors unlimited	Repealed by CA 2006, as from 1 Oct 2009. For savings see the note to s 306.
308 Assignment of office by directors	Repealed by CA 2006, as from 1 Oct 2009.
309 Directors to have regard to interests of employees	Repealed by CA 2006, as from 1 Oct 2007.
309A Provisions protecting directors from liability	Repealed by CA 2006, as from 1 Oct 2007.
	Savings: ss 309A, 309B and 309C(1)–(3) and (6) continue to apply in relation to any provision to which they applied immediately before 1 Oct 2007; see CO No 3, Sch 3, paras 15–17 (at **[2.45]**).
309B Qualifying third party indemnity provisions	Repealed by CA 2006, as from 1 Oct 2007. For savings see the note to s 309A.
309C Disclosure of qualifying third party indemnity provisions	Repealed by CA 2006, as from 1 Oct 2007. For savings see the note to s 309A.
310 Provisions protecting auditors from liability	Repealed by CA 2006, as from 6 Apr 2008.

PART X
ENFORCEMENT OF FAIR DEALING BY DIRECTORS

311–347

NOTES

This Part has been repealed as follows:

311 Prohibition on tax-free payments to directors	Repealed by CA 2006, as from 6 Apr 2007.
312 Payment to director for loss of office, etc	Repealed by CA 2006, as from 1 Oct 2007.
	Savings: this section and ss 313–316 continue to apply in relation to loss of office or retirement within the meaning of those provisions occurring before 1 Oct 2007; see CO No 3, Sch 3, para 12(3), (4) (at **[2.45]**).
313 Company approval for property transfer	Repealed by CA 2006, as from 1 Oct 2007. For savings see the note to s 311.

314 Director's duty of disclosure on takeover, etc	Repealed by CA 2006, as from 1 Oct 2007. For savings see the note to s 311.
315 Consequences of non-compliance with s 314	Repealed by CA 2006, as from 1 Oct 2007. For savings see the note to s 311.
316 Provisions supplementing ss 312–315	Repealed by CA 2006, as from 1 Oct 2007. For savings see the note to s 311.
317 Directors to disclose interest in contracts	Repealed by CA 2006, as from 1 Oct 2008.
	Savings: this section continues to apply in relation to a duty arising before 1 Oct 2008; see CO No 5, Sch 4, Pt 3, paras 48, 50 (at **[2.68]**).
318 Directors' service contracts to be open to inspection	Repealed by CA 2006, as from 1 Oct 2007.
	Savings: see CO No 3, Sch 3, para 13(4) at **[2.45]** which provides that this section continues to apply to: (a) any default before 1 Oct 2007 in complying with section 318(1) or (5); (b) any request for inspection under s 318(7) made before that date; (c) any duty to give notice under s 318(4) arising before that date.
319 Director's contract of employment for more than 5 years	Repealed by CA 2006, as from 1 Oct 2007.
	Savings: this section continues to apply to agreements made before 1 Oct 2007; see CO No 3, Sch 3, para 6 at **[2.45]**.
320 Substantial property transactions involving directors, etc	Repealed by CA 2006, as from 1 Oct 2007.
	Savings: this section and ss 321, 322 continue to apply in relation to arrangements or transactions entered into before 1 Oct 2007 (see CO No 3, Sch 3, para 7 at **[2.45]**).
321 Exceptions from s 320	Repealed by CA 2006, as from 1 Oct 2007. For savings see the note to s 320.
322 Liabilities arising from contravention of s 320	Repealed by CA 2006, as from 1 Oct 2007. For savings see the note to s 320.
322A Invalidity of certain transactions involving directors, etc	Repealed by CA 2006, as from 1 Oct 2009.
322B Contracts with sole members who are directors	Repealed by CA 2006, as from 1 Oct 2007.
	Savings: this section continues to apply to contracts entered into before 1 Oct 2007 (see CO No 3, Sch 3, para 14 at **[2.45]**).
323 Prohibition on directors dealing in share options	Repealed by CA 2006, as from 6 Apr 2007.
324 Duty of director to disclose shareholdings in own company	Repealed by CA 2006, as from 6 Apr 2007.
325 Register of directors' interests notified under s 324	Repealed by CA 2006, as from 6 Apr 2007.
326 Sanctions for non-compliance	Repealed by CA 2006, as from 6 Apr 2007.
327 Extension of s 323 to spouses, civil partners and children	Repealed by CA 2006, as from 6 Apr 2007.
328 Extension of s 324 to spouses, civil partners and children	Repealed by CA 2006, as from 6 Apr 2007.
329 Duty to notify stock exchange of matters notified under preceding sections	Repealed by CA 2006, as from 6 Apr 2007.
330 General restriction on loans etc to directors and persons connected with them	Repealed by CA 2006, as from 1 Oct 2007.
	Savings: ss 330–342 continue to apply in relation to a contravention occurring before 1 Oct 2007; see CO No 3, Sch 3, paras 8–11 (at **[2.45]**).
331 Definitions for ss 330 ff	Repealed by CA 2006, as from 1 Oct 2007. For savings see the note to s 331.
332 Short-term quasi-loans	Repealed by CA 2006, as from 1 Oct 2007. For savings see the note to s 331.
333 Inter-company loans in same group	Repealed by CA 2006, as from 1 Oct 2007. For savings see the note to s 331.
334 Loans of small amounts	Repealed by CA 2006, as from 1 Oct 2007. For savings see the note to s 331.
335 Minor and business transactions	Repealed by CA 2006, as from 1 Oct 2007. For savings see the note to s 331.
336 Transactions at behest of holding company	Repealed by CA 2006, as from 1 Oct 2007. For savings see the note to s 331.
337 Funding of director's expenditure on duty to company	Repealed by CA 2006, as from 1 Oct 2007. For savings see the note to s 331.
337A Funding of director's expenditure on defending proceedings	Repealed by CA 2006, as from 1 Oct 2007. For savings see the note to s 331.
338 Loan or quasi-loan by money-lending company	Repealed by CA 2006, as from 1 Oct 2007. For savings see the note to s 331.
339 "Relevant amounts" for purposes of ss 334 ff	Repealed by CA 2006, as from 1 Oct 2007. For savings see the note to s 331.

340 "Value" of transactions and arrangements	Repealed by CA 2006, as from 1 Oct 2007. For savings see the note to s 331.
341 Civil remedies for breach of s 330	Repealed by CA 2006, as from 1 Oct 2007. For savings see the note to s 331.
342 Criminal penalties for breach of s 330	Repealed by CA 2006, as from 1 Oct 2007. For savings see the note to s 331.
343 Record of transactions not disclosed in company accounts	Repealed by CA 2006, as from 6 Apr 2007.
344 Exceptions from s 343	Repealed by CA 2006, as from 6 Apr 2007.
345 Power to increase financial limits	Repealed by CA 2006, as from 1 Oct 2007.
346 "Connected persons", etc	Repealed by CA 2006, as from 1 Oct 2007.
	Savings: see CO No 3, Sch 3, para 50 (at [2.45]) which provides that the repeal of this section (and Sch 13) does not affect: (a) s 317(3)(b) (directors to disclose interest in contracts); (b) ss 7E and 7F(3) of the Industrial and Provident Societies Act 1965 (transactions with committee members: whether person "connected with" committee member or "associated with" society); (c) s 96B(2)(a) of FSMA 2000 (disclosure rules: responsibility for compliance: meaning of person connected with person having managerial responsibilities within an issuer).
347 Transactions under foreign law	Repealed by CA 2006, as from 1 Oct 2007.

[PART XA
CONTROL OF POLITICAL DONATIONS

347A–347K

NOTES

This Part has been repealed as follows:

347A Introductory provisions	Repealed by CA 2006, as from 1 Oct 2007.
	Savings: see CO No 3, Sch 3, para 41 (at [2.45]) which provides that this Part continues to apply to donations or expenditure in relation to which the relevant time, as defined in s 347A(10), is before 1 Oct 2007.
347B Exemptions	Repealed by CA 2006, as from 1 Oct 2007. For savings see the note to s 347A.
347C Prohibition on donations and political expenditure by companies	Repealed by CA 2006, as from 1 Oct 2007. For savings see the note to s 347A.
347D Special rules for subsidiaries	Repealed by CA 2006, as from 1 Oct 2007. For savings see the note to s 347A.
347E Special rule for parent company of non-GB subsidiary undertaking	Repealed by CA 2006, as from 1 Oct 2007. For savings see the note to s 347A.
347F Remedies for breach of prohibitions on company donations etc	Repealed by CA 2006, as from 1 Oct 2007. For savings see the note to s 347A.
347G Remedies for unauthorised donation or expenditure by non-GB subsidiary	Repealed by CA 2006, as from 1 Oct 2007. For savings see the note to s 347A.
347H Exemption of directors from liability in respect of unauthorised donation or expenditure	Repealed by CA 2006, as from 1 Oct 2007. For savings see the note to s 347A.
347I Enforcement of directors' liabilities by shareholder action	Repealed by CA 2006, as from 1 Oct 2007. For savings see the note to s 347A.
347J Costs of shareholder action	Repealed by CA 2006, as from 1 Oct 2007. For savings see the note to s 347A.
347K Information for purposes of shareholder action	Repealed by CA 2006, as from 1 Oct 2007. For savings see the note to s 347A.

PART XI
COMPANY ADMINISTRATION AND PROCEDURE

348–394A

NOTES

This Part has been repealed as follows:

348 Company name to appear outside place of business	Repealed by CA 2006, as from 1 Oct 2008.
349 Company's name to appear in its correspondence, etc	Repealed by CA 2006, as from 1 Oct 2008.

350 Company seal	Repealed by CA 2006, as from 1 Oct 2009.
351 Particulars in correspondence etc	Repealed by CA 2006, as from 1 Oct 2008.
352 Obligation to keep and enter up register	Repealed by CA 2006, as from 6 Apr 2008 (in part), and as from 1 Oct 2009 (otherwise).
352A Statement that company has only one member	Repealed by CA 2006, as from 1 Oct 2009.
353 Location of register	Repealed by CA 2006, as from 1 Oct 2009.
354 Index of members	Repealed by CA 2006, as from 1 Oct 2009.
355 Entries in register in relation to share warrants	Repealed by CA 2006, as from 1 Oct 2009.
356 Inspection of register and index	Repealed by CA 2006, as from 1 Oct 2007. Savings: see CO No 3, Sch 3, para 2 at **[2.45]**, which provides that this section and s 357 continue to apply to requests made before 1 Oct 2007 or after that date to a company that is so obliged.
357 Non-compliance with ss 353, 354, 356; agent's default	Repealed by CA 2006, as from 1 Oct 2007. For savings see the note to s 356.
358 Power to close register	Repealed by CA 2006, as from 1 Oct 2009.
359 Power of court to rectify register	Repealed by CA 2006, as from 1 Oct 2009.
360 Trusts not to be entered on register in England and Wales	Repealed by CA 2006, as from 1 Oct 2009.
361 Register to be evidence	Repealed by CA 2006, as from 1 Oct 2009.
362 Overseas branch registers	Repealed by CA 2006, as from 1 Oct 2009.
363 Duty to deliver annual returns	Repealed by CA 2006, as from 1 Oct 2009. Savings: CO No 8, Sch 2, para 81 (at **[2.91]**) provides that ss 363–365 continue to apply to annual returns made up to a date before 1 Oct 2009.
364 Contents of annual return: general	Repealed by CA 2006, as from 1 Oct 2009. For savings see the note to s 363.
364A Contents of annual return: particulars of share capital and shareholders	Repealed by CA 2006, as from 1 Oct 2009. For savings see the note to s 363.
364B Contents of annual return: information about shareholders: non-traded companies	Repealed by CA 2006, as from 1 Oct 2009. For savings see the note to s 363.
364C Contents of annual return: information about shareholders: traded companies	Repealed by CA 2006, as from 1 Oct 2009. For savings see the note to s 363.
364D Contents of annual return: information about shareholders: supplementary	Repealed by CA 2006, as from 1 Oct 2009. For savings see the note to s 363.
365 Supplementary provisions: regulations and interpretation	Repealed by CA 2006, as from 1 Oct 2009. For savings see the note to s 363.
366 Annual general meeting	Repealed by CA 2006, as from 1 Oct 2007. Savings: CO No 3, Sch 3, paras 22–40 (at **[2.45]**) make a variety of savings and transitional provisions in relation to the repeal of Chapter IV (ss 366–383) and the commencement of Part 13 of CA 2006 (Resolutions and Meetings). With regard to this section, see also CO No 3, Sch 3, para 10.
366A Election by private company to dispense with annual general meeting	Repealed by CA 2006, as from 20 Jan 2007 (in part), and as from 1 Oct 2007 (otherwise). For savings see the note to s 366.
367 Secretary of State's power to call meeting in default	Repealed by CA 2006, as from 1 Oct 2007. For savings see the note to s 366.
368 Extraordinary general meeting on members' requisition	Repealed by CA 2006, as from 1 Oct 2007. For savings see the note to s 366. See also CA 2006, s 972 at **[1.972]**.
369 Length of notice for calling meetings	Repealed by CA 2006, as from 20 Jan 2007 (in part), and as from 1 Oct 2007 (otherwise). For savings see the note to s 366. See also CO No 1, Sch 5, Pt 2, paras 4, 5 at **[2.14]**.
370 General provisions as to meetings and votes	Repealed by CA 2006, as from 1 Oct 2007. For savings see the note to s 366.
370A Quorum at meetings of the sole member	Repealed by CA 2006, as from 1 Oct 2007. For savings see the note to s 366.
371 Power of court to order meeting	Repealed by CA 2006, as from 1 Oct 2007. For savings see the note to s 366.
372 Proxies	Repealed by CA 2006, as from 20 Jan 2007 (in part), and as from 1 Oct 2007 (otherwise). For savings see the note to s 366.
373 Right to demand a poll	Repealed by CA 2006, as from 1 Oct 2007. For savings see the note to s 366.

374 Voting on a poll	Repealed by CA 2006, as from 1 Oct 2007. For savings see the note to s 366.
375 Representation of corporations at meetings	Repealed by CA 2006, as from 1 Oct 2007. For savings see the note to s 366.
376 Circulation of members' resolutions	Repealed by CA 2006, as from 1 Oct 2007. For savings see the note to s 366.
377 In certain cases, compliance with s 376 not required	Repealed by CA 2006, as from 1 Oct 2007. For savings see the note to s 366.
378 Extraordinary and special resolutions	Repealed by CA 2006, as from 1 Oct 2007. For savings see the note to s 366.
379 Resolution requiring special notice	Repealed by CA 2006, as from 1 Oct 2007. For savings see the note to s 366.
379A Elective resolution of private company	Repealed by CA 2006, as from 20 Jan 2007 (in part) and 1 Oct 2007 (in part), and as from 1 Oct 2009 (otherwise). For savings see the note to s 366.
380 Registration, etc of resolutions and agreements	Repealed by CA 2006, as from 1 Oct 2007 (in part) and 6 Apr 2008 (in part), and as from 1 Oct 2009 (otherwise). For savings see the note to s 366. Note also that CO No 8, Sch 2, para 14 (at **[2.91]**) provides that sub-ss (2), (6), (7) continue to apply to copies issued before 1 Oct 2009.
381 Resolution passed at adjourned meeting	Repealed by CA 2006, as from 1 Oct 2007. For savings see the note to s 366.
381A Written resolutions of private companies	Repealed by CA 2006, as from 1 Oct 2007. For savings see the note to s 366.
381B Duty to notify auditors of proposed written resolution	Repealed by CA 2006, as from 1 Oct 2007. For savings see the note to s 366.
381C Written resolutions: supplementary provisions	Repealed by CA 2006, as from 1 Oct 2007. For savings see the note to s 366.
382 Minutes of meetings	Repealed by CA 2006, as from 1 Oct 2007. For savings see the note to s 366. Note also CO No 3, Sch 3, para 19 (at **[2.45]**) which provides that this section continues to apply to meetings of directors held before 1 Oct 2007.
382A Recording of written resolutions	Repealed by CA 2006, as from 1 Oct 2007. For savings see the note to s 366.
382B Recording of decisions by the sole member	Repealed by CA 2006, as from 1 Oct 2007. For savings see the note to s 366.
383 Inspection of minute books	Repealed by CA 2006, as from 1 Oct 2007. For savings see the note to s 366.
384 Duty to appoint auditors	Repealed by CA 2006, as from 1 Oct 2007 (in so far as relating to private companies), and as from 6 Apr 2008 (otherwise).
	Savings: see CO No 3, Sch 3, para 44 (at **[2.45]**) which provides that ss 384–388A continue to apply in relation to the appointment of auditors of private companies for financial years beginning before 1 Oct 2007. See also CO No 5, Sch 4, Pt 1, para 10 (at **[2.66]**) which provides that ss 384, 385, 387, 388(1), (3), (4) continue to apply to appointments by public companies for financial years beginning before 6 Apr 2008.
385 Appointment at general meeting at which accounts laid	Repealed by CA 2006, as from 1 Oct 2007 (in so far as relating to private companies), and as from 6 Apr 2008 (otherwise). For savings see the note to s 384.
385A Appointment by private company which is not obliged to lay accounts	Repealed by CA 2006, as from 1 Oct 2007. For savings see the first part of the note to s 384.
386 Election by private company to dispense with annual appointment	Repealed by CA 2006, as from 1 Oct 2007. For savings see the first part of the note to s 384. See also CO No 3, Sch 3, para 45 (at **[2.45]**) which provides that the repeal of this section does not affect the continued operation of the resolution, which shall continue to have effect until (a) it is revoked or superseded by a further resolution, (b) the auditors to which it applies cease to hold office, or (c) it otherwise ceases to have effect in accordance with its terms.
387 Appointment by Secretary of State in default of appointment by company	Repealed by CA 2006, as from 1 Oct 2007 (in so far as relating to private companies), and as from 6 Apr 2008 (otherwise). For savings see the note to s 384.
388 Filling of casual vacancies	Repealed by CA 2006, as from 1 Oct 2007 (in so far as relating to private companies), and as from 6 Apr 2008 (otherwise). For savings see the note to s 384. See also CO No 5, Sch 4, Pt 1, para 17 (at **[2.66]**) which provides that sub-s (2) continues to apply where the vacancy occurred before 6 Apr 2008.
388A Certain companies exempt from obligation to appoint auditors	Repealed by CA 2006, as from 1 Oct 2007 (in so far as relating to private companies), and as from 6 Apr 2008 (otherwise). For savings see the first part of the note to s 384.

389 Qualification for appointment as auditor	Repealed by CA 1989, as from 1 Oct 1991.
389A Rights to information	Repealed by CA 2006, as from 6 Apr 2008.
	Savings: this section and s 389B continue to apply to financial years beginning before 6 Apr 2008 (see CO No 5, Sch 4, Pt 1, para 12(2) (at [2.66])).
389B Offences relating to the provision of information to auditors	Repealed by CA 2006, as from 6 Apr 2008. For savings see the note to s 389A.
390 Right to attend company meetings, &c	Repealed by CA 2006, as from 6 Apr 2008.
	Savings: this section continues to apply to auditors appointed before 6 Apr 2008 (see CO No 5, Sch 4, Pt 1, para 12(4) (at [2.66])).
390A Remuneration of auditors	Repealed by CA 2006, as from 6 Apr 2008.
	Savings: see CO No 5, Sch 4, Pt 1, para 11 (at [2.66]) which provides that this section and s 390B continue to apply to auditors appointed for financial years beginning before 6 Apr 2008, and that the repeal of this section does not affect the operation of any such resolution as is mentioned in Sch 3, para 45 to CO No 3.
390B Disclosure of services provided by auditors or associates and related remuneration	Repealed by CA 2006, as from 6 Apr 2008. For savings see the note to s 390A.
391 Removal of auditors	Repealed by CA 2006, as from 6 Apr 2008.
	Savings: see CO No 5, Sch 4, Pt 1, para 13 (at [2.66]) which provides that ss 391, 391A continue to apply where notice of the intended resolution is given to the company before 6 Apr 2008.
391A Rights of auditors who are removed or not re-appointed	Repealed by CA 2006, as from 6 Apr 2008. For savings see the note to s 391. Note also that this section continues to apply to appointments for financial years beginning before that date; see CO No 5, Sch 4, Pt 1, para 14 (at [2.66]).
392 Resignation of auditors	Repealed by CA 2006, as from 6 Apr 2008.
	Savings: see CO No 5, Sch 4, Pt 1, para 15 (at [2.66]) which provides that ss 392, 392A continue to apply to resignations occurring before 6 Apr 2008.
392A Rights of resigning auditors	Repealed by CA 2006, as from 6 Apr 2008. For savings see the note to s 392.
393 Termination of appointment of auditors not appointed annually	Repealed by CA 2006, as from 1 Oct 2007.
394 Statement by person ceasing to hold office as auditor	Repealed by CA 2006, as from 6 Apr 2008.
	Savings: see CO No 5, Sch 4, Pt 1, para 16 (at [2.66]) which provides that ss 394, 394A continue to apply where the auditor ceases to hold office before 6 Apr 2008.
394A Offences of failing to comply with s 394	Repealed by CA 2006, as from 6 Apr 2008. For savings see the note to s 394.

PART XII
REGISTRATION OF CHARGES

395–424

NOTES
This Part has been repealed as follows:

395 Certain charges void if not registered	Repealed by CA 2006, as from 1 Oct 2009.
	Savings and transitional provisions: in connection with the repeal of this Part, see CO No 8, Sch 2, paras 82–87 (Company charges) at [2.91] and SI 2009/1917, Schedule (Registration of charges; transitional provisions and savings) at [4.527].
396 Charges which have to be registered	Repealed by CA 2006, as from 1 Oct 2009. For savings see the note to s 395.
397 Formalities of registration (debentures)	Repealed by CA 2006, as from 1 Oct 2009. For savings see the note to s 395.
398 Verification of charge on property outside United Kingdom	Repealed by CA 2006, as from 1 Oct 2009. For savings see the note to s 395.
399 Company's duty to register charges it creates	Repealed by CA 2006, as from 1 Oct 2009. For savings see the note to s 395.
400 Charges existing on property acquired	Repealed by CA 2006, as from 1 Oct 2009. For savings see the note to s 395.
401 Register of charges to be kept by registrar of companies	Repealed by CA 2006, as from 1 Oct 2009. For savings see the note to s 395.

402 Endorsement of certificate on debentures	Repealed by CA 2006, as from 1 Oct 2009. For savings see the note to s 395.
403 Entries of satisfaction and release	Repealed by CA 2006, as from 1 Oct 2009. For savings see the note to s 395.
404 Rectification of register of charges	Repealed by CA 2006, as from 1 Oct 2009. For savings see the note to s 395.
405 Registration of enforcement of security	Repealed by CA 2006, as from 1 Oct 2009. For savings see the note to s 395.
406 Companies to keep copies of instruments creating charges	Repealed by CA 2006, as from 1 Oct 2009. For savings see the note to s 395.
407 Company's register of charges	Repealed by CA 2006, as from 1 Oct 2009. For savings see the note to s 395.
408 Right to inspect instruments which create charges, etc	Repealed by CA 2006, as from 1 Oct 2009. For savings see the note to s 395.
409 Charges on property in England and Wales created by overseas company	Repealed by CA 2006, as from 1 Oct 2009. For savings see the note to s 395.
410 Charges void unless registered	Repealed by CA 2006, as from 1 Oct 2009. For savings see the note to s 395.
411 Charges on property outside United Kingdom	Repealed by CA 2006, as from 1 Oct 2009. For savings see the note to s 395.
412 Negotiable instrument to secure book debts	Repealed by CA 2006, as from 1 Oct 2009. For savings see the note to s 395.
413 Charges associated with debentures	Repealed by CA 2006, as from 1 Oct 2009. For savings see the note to s 395.
414 Charge by way of ex facie absolute disposition, etc	Repealed by CA 2006, as from 1 Oct 2009. For savings see the note to s 395.
415 Company's duty to register charges created by it	Repealed by CA 2006, as from 1 Oct 2009. For savings see the note to s 395.
416 Duty to register charges existing on property acquired	Repealed by CA 2006, as from 1 Oct 2009. For savings see the note to s 395.
417 Register of charges to be kept by registrar of companies	Repealed by CA 2006, as from 1 Oct 2009. For savings see the note to s 395.
418 Certificate of registration to be issued	Repealed by CA 2006, as from 1 Oct 2009. For savings see the note to s 395.
419 Entries of satisfaction and relief	Repealed by CA 2006, as from 1 Oct 2009. For savings see the note to s 395.
420 Rectification of register	Repealed by CA 2006, as from 1 Oct 2009. For savings see the note to s 395.
421 Copies of instruments creating charges to be kept by company	Repealed by CA 2006, as from 1 Oct 2009. For savings see the note to s 395.
422 Company's register of charges	Repealed by CA 2006, as from 1 Oct 2009. For savings see the note to s 395.
423 Right to inspect copies of instruments, and company's register	Repealed by CA 2006, as from 1 Oct 2009. For savings see the note to s 395.
424 Extension of Chapter II	Repealed by CA 2006, as from 1 Oct 2009. For savings see the note to s 395.

PART XIII
ARRANGEMENTS AND RECONSTRUCTIONS

425–427A

NOTES

This Part has been repealed as follows:

425 Power of company to compromise with creditors and members	Repealed by CA 2006, as from 6 Apr 2008. Savings and transitional provisions: see CO No 5, Sch 4, Pt 1, para 36 (at **[2.66]**) which provides that (i) s 425(3), (4) continue to apply to orders made before 6 Apr 2008; (ii) s 901 of CA 2006 (obligations of company with respect to articles etc) applies to orders of the court made on or after 6 Apr 2008, including orders made under s 425(2).
426 Information as to compromise to be circulated	Repealed by CA 2006, as from 6 Apr 2008.
427 Provisions for facilitating company reconstruction or amalgamation	Repealed by CA 2006, as from 6 Apr 2008.
427A Application of ss 425–427 to mergers and divisions of public companies	Repealed by CA 2006, as from 6 Apr 2008.

PART XIIIA
TAKEOVER OFFERS

428–430F

NOTES

This Part has been repealed as follows:

428 Takeover offers	Repealed by CA 2006, as from 6 Apr 2007.
	Savings and transitional provisions: for savings regarding the operation of this Part in relation to a takeover offer where the date of the offer (within the meaning of s 428(1)) was before 6 Apr 2007, see CO No 2, Sch 6, para 1 at **[2.30]**. Note also, that this Part was disapplied where a takeover offer (where the date of the offer was on or after 20 May 2006) was made for a company that had securities carrying voting rights admitted to trading on a regulated market; see SI 2006/1183, regs 29, 30. In such circumstances, Sch 2 to those Regulations applied. The 2006 Regulations were revoked, as from 6 Apr 2007, by SI 2007/1093, subject to certain savings in relation to (i) takeover offers (where the date of offer is before 6 Apr 2007) and (ii) offences committed before that date (see Sch 6, paras 2, 3 to the 2007 Order).
429 Right of offeror to buy out minority shareholders	Repealed by CA 2006, as from 6 Apr 2007. For savings see the note to s 428.
430 Effect of notice under s 429	Repealed by CA 2006, as from 6 Apr 2007. For savings see the note to s 428.
430A Right of minority shareholder to be bought out by offeror	Repealed by CA 2006, as from 6 Apr 2007. For savings see the note to s 428.
430B Effect of requirement under s 430A	Repealed by CA 2006, as from 6 Apr 2007. For savings see the note to s 428.
430C Applications to the court	Repealed by CA 2006, as from 6 Apr 2007. For savings see the note to s 428.
430D Joint offers	Repealed by CA 2006, as from 6 Apr 2007. For savings see the note to s 428.
430E Associates	Repealed by CA 2006, as from 6 Apr 2007. For savings see the note to s 428.
430F Convertible securities	Repealed by CA 2006, as from 6 Apr 2007. For savings see the note to s 428.

PART XIV
INVESTIGATION OF COMPANIES AND THEIR AFFAIRS; REQUISITION OF DOCUMENTS

NOTES

Transitional provisions: for transitional provisions in relation to the extension of this Part (and Part XV) to Northern Ireland (by CA 2006, s 1284), see CO No 8, Sch 2, para 114 (at **[2.91]**).

Note also that the Companies (Audit, Investigations and Community Enterprise) Act 2004 (Commencement) and Companies Act 1989 (Commencement No 18) Order 2004, SI 2004/3322, arts 6–13 provided for various transitional provisions relating to company investigations in connection with the amendments made to this Part by the Companies (Audit, Investigations and Community Enterprise) Act 2004. The Act came into force for all purposes on 1 October 2005 and those transitional provisions are now regarded as spent.

Application of this Part to limited liability partnerships, unregistered companies and European Economic Interest Groupings: see the introductory notes to this Act.

Appointment and functions of inspectors

[5.1]
431 Investigation of a company on its own application or that of its members
(1) The Secretary of State may appoint one or more competent inspectors to investigate the affairs of a company and to [report the result of their investigations to him].
(2) The appointment may be made—
  (a) in the case of a company having a share capital, on the application either of not less than 200 members or of members holding not less than one-tenth of the shares issued [(excluding any shares held as treasury shares)],
  (b) in the case of a company not having a share capital, on the application of not less than one-fifth in number of the persons on the company's register of members, and
  (c) in any case, on application of the company.
(3) The application shall be supported by such evidence as the Secretary of State may require for the purpose of showing that the applicant or applicants have good reason for requiring the investigation.
(4) The Secretary of State may, before appointing inspectors, require the applicant or applicants to give security, to an amount not exceeding £5,000, or such other sum as he may by order specify, for payment of the costs of the investigation.

An order under this subsection shall be made by statutory instrument subject to annulment in pursuance of a resolution of either House of Parliament.

NOTES

Sub-s (1): words in square brackets substituted by the Companies Act 2006, s 1035(2), as from 1 October 2007, with effect where an inspector is appointed under a provision of Pt XIV of this Act on or after that date.

Sub-s (2): words in square brackets in para (a) inserted by the Companies (Acquisition of Own Shares) (Treasury Shares) Regulations 2003, SI 2003/1116, reg 4, Schedule, para 28, as from 1 December 2003.

[5.2]

432 Other company investigations

(1) The Secretary of State shall appoint one or more competent inspectors to investigate the affairs of a company and [report the result of their investigations to him], if the court by order declares that its affairs ought to be so investigated.

(2) The Secretary of State may make such an appointment if it appears to him that there are circumstances suggesting—

(a) that the company's affairs are being or have been conducted with intent to defraud its creditors or the creditors of any other person, or otherwise for a fraudulent or unlawful purpose, or in a manner which is unfairly prejudicial to some part of its members, or

(b) that any actual or proposed act or omission of the company (including an act or omission on its behalf) is or would be so prejudicial, or that the company was formed for any fraudulent or unlawful purpose, or

(c) that persons concerned with the company's formation or the management of its affairs have in connection therewith been guilty of fraud, misfeasance or other misconduct towards it or towards its members, or

(d) that the company's members have not been given all the information with respect to its affairs which they might reasonably expect.

[(2A) Inspectors may be appointed under subsection (2) on terms that any report they may make is not for publication; and in such a case, the provisions of section 437(3) (availability and publication of inspectors' reports) do not apply.]

(3) Subsections (1) and (2) are without prejudice to the powers of the Secretary of State under section 431; and the power conferred by subsection (2) is exercisable with respect to a body corporate notwithstanding that it is in course of being voluntarily wound up.

(4) The reference in subsection (2)(a) to a company's members includes any person who is not a member but to whom shares in the company have been transferred or transmitted by operation of law.

NOTES

Sub-s (1): words in square brackets substituted by the Companies Act 2006, s 1035(3), as from 1 October 2007, with effect where an inspector is appointed under a provision of Pt XIV of this Act on or after that date.

Sub-s (2A): inserted by CA 1989, s 55, as from 21 February 1990.

[5.3]

433 Inspectors' powers during investigation

(1) If inspectors appointed under section 431 or 432 to investigate the affairs of a company think it necessary for the purposes of their investigation to investigate also the affairs of another body corporate which is or at any relevant time has been the company's subsidiary or holding company, or a subsidiary of its holding company or a holding company of its subsidiary, they have power to do so; and they shall report on the affairs of the other body corporate so far as they think that the results of their investigation of its affairs are relevant to the investigation of the affairs of the company first mentioned above.

(2) . . .

NOTES

Sub-s (2): repealed by FSA 1986, ss 182, 212(3), Sch 13, para 7, Sch 17, Pt I, as from 27 November 1986.

[5.4]

434 Production of documents and evidence to inspectors

(1) When inspectors are appointed under section 431 or 432, it is the duty of all officers and agents of the company, and of all officers and agents of any other body corporate whose affairs are investigated under section 433(1)—

(a) to produce to the inspectors all [documents] of or relating to the company or, as the case may be, the other body corporate which are in their custody or power,

(b) to attend before the inspectors when required to do so, and

(c) otherwise to give the inspectors all assistance in connection with the investigation which they are reasonably able to give.

[(2) If the inspectors consider that an officer or agent of the company or other body corporate, or any other person, is or may be in possession of information relating to a matter which they believe to be relevant to the investigation, they may require him—

(a) to produce to them any documents in his custody or power relating to that matter,

(b) to attend before them, and

(c)   otherwise to give them all assistance in connection with the investigation which he is reasonably able to give;

and it is that person's duty to comply with the requirement.

(3)   An inspector may for the purposes of the investigation examine any person on oath, and may administer an oath accordingly.]

(4)   In this section a reference to officers or to agents includes past, as well as present, officers or agents (as the case may be); and "agents", in relation to a company or other body corporate, includes its bankers and solicitors and persons employed by it as auditors, whether these persons are or are not officers of the company or other body corporate.

(5)   An answer given by a person to a question put to him in exercise of powers conferred by this section (whether as it has effect in relation to an investigation under any of sections 431 to 433, or as applied by any other section in this Part) may be used in evidence against him.

[(5A)   However, in criminal proceedings in which that person is charged with an offence to which this subsection applies—

(a)   no evidence relating to the answer may be adduced, and

(b)   no question relating to it may be asked,

by or on behalf of the prosecution, unless evidence relating to it is adduced, or a question relating to it is asked, in the proceedings by or on behalf of that person.

(5B)   Subsection (5A) applies to any offence other than—

(a)   an offence under section 2 or 5 of the Perjury Act 1911 (false statements made on oath otherwise than in judicial proceedings or made otherwise than on oath); or

(b)   an offence under section 44(1) or (2) of the Criminal Law (Consolidation) (Scotland) Act 1995 (false statements made on oath or otherwise than on oath)[; or

(c)   an offence under Article 7 or 10 of the Perjury (Northern Ireland) Order 1979 (false statements made on oath otherwise than in judicial proceedings or made otherwise than on oath).]]

[(6)   In this section "document" includes information recorded in any form.

(7)   The power under this section to require production of a document includes power, in the case of a document not in hard copy form, to require the production of a copy of the document—

(a)   in hard copy form, or

(b)   in a form from which a hard copy can be readily obtained.

(8)   An inspector may take copies of or extracts from a document produced in pursuance of this section.]

NOTES

Sub-s (1): word in square brackets substituted by CA 1989, s 56(1), (2), as from 21 February 1990.

Sub-ss (2), (3): substituted by CA 1989, s 56(1), (3), (4), as from 21 February 1990.

Sub-s (5A): inserted, together with sub-s (5B), by the Youth Justice and Criminal Evidence Act 1999, s 59, Sch 3, paras 4, 5, as from 14 April 2000 (in relation to England and Wales), and 1 January 2001 (in relation to Scotland).

Sub-s (5B): inserted as noted above; para (c) (and the word immediately preceding it) inserted by the Companies Act 2006 (Consequential Amendments, Transitional Provisions and Savings) Order 2009, SI 2009/1941, art 2(1), Sch 1, para 57(1), (2), as from 1 October 2009.

Sub-ss (6)–(8): substituted (for the original sub-s (6) as added by CA 1989, s 56(1), (5), as from 21 February 1990) by the Companies Act 2006, s 1038(1), as from 1 October 2007, with effect where an inspector is appointed under a provision of Pt XIV of this Act on or after that date.

Solicitors: the reference to a solicitor in sub-s (4) includes a reference to a recognised body within the meaning of the Administration of Justice Act 1985, s 9; see the Solicitors' Recognised Bodies Order 1991, SI 1991/2684, arts 2–5, Sch 1.

435   (*Repealed by CA 1989, s 212, Sch 24, as from 21 February 1990.*)

[5.5]
436   Obstruction of inspectors treated as contempt of court

[(1)   If any person—

(a)   fails to comply with section 434(1)(a) or (c),

(b)   refuses to comply with a requirement under section 434(1)(b) or (2), or

(c)   refuses to answer any question put to him by the inspectors for the purposes of the investigation,

the inspectors may certify that fact in writing to the court.]

(3)   The court may thereupon enquire into the case; and, after hearing any witnesses who may be produced against or on behalf of the alleged offender and after hearing any statement which may be offered in defence, the court may punish the offender in like manner as if he had been guilty of contempt of the court.

NOTES

Sub-s (1): substituted, for original sub-ss (1), (2), by CA 1989, s 56(6), as from 21 February 1990.

[5.6]
437   Inspectors' reports

(1)   The inspectors may, and if so directed by the Secretary of State shall, make interim reports to the Secretary of State, and on the conclusion of their investigation shall make a final report to him.

. . .

[(1A)   Any persons who have been appointed under section 431 or 432 may at any time and, if the Secretary of State directs them to do so, shall inform him of any matters coming to their knowledge as a result of their investigations.]

[(1B), (1C)   . . .]

(2)   If the inspectors were appointed under section 432 in pursuance of an order of the court, the Secretary of State shall furnish a copy of any report of theirs to the court.

[(2A)   If the company is registered under the Companies Act 2006 in Northern Ireland, the Secretary of State must send a copy of any interim or final report by the inspectors to the Department of Enterprise, Trade and Investment in Northern Ireland.]

(3)   In any case the Secretary of State may, if he thinks fit—

   (a)   forward a copy of any report made by the inspectors to the company's registered office,

   (b)   furnish a copy on request and on payment of the prescribed fee to—

      (i)   any member of the company or other body corporate which is the subject of the report,

      (ii)   any person whose conduct is referred to in the report,

      (iii)   the auditors of that company or body corporate,

      (iv)   the applicants for the investigation,

      (v)   any other person whose financial interests appear to the Secretary of State to be affected by the matters dealt with in the report, whether as a creditor of the company or body corporate, or otherwise, and

   (c)   cause any such report to be printed and published.

NOTES

Sub-s (1): words omitted repealed by the Companies Act 2006, ss 1035(4)(a) 1295, Sch 16, as from 1 October 2007, with effect where an inspector is appointed under a provision of Pt XIV of this Act on or after that date.

Sub-s (1A): inserted by FSA 1986, s 182, Sch 13, para 7, as from 15 November 1986 (for the purposes of anything done or which may be done under, or by virtue of, any provision brought into force by the Financial Services Act 1986 (Commencement No 1) Order 1986, SI 1986/1940), and as from 27 November 1986 (otherwise).

Sub-ss (1B), (1C): inserted by CA 1989, s 57, as from 21 February 1990; repealed by the Companies Act 2006, ss 1035(4)(b) 1295, Sch 16, as from 1 October 2007, with effect where an inspector is appointed under a provision of Pt XIV of this Act on or after that date.

Sub-s (2A): inserted by the Companies Act 2006 (Consequential Amendments, Transitional Provisions and Savings) Order 2009, SI 2009/1941, art 2(1), Sch 1, para 57(1), (3), as from 1 October 2009.

Fees: see [**6.2**].

---

438   *(Repealed by the Companies Act 2006, ss 1176(1), (4), 1295, Sch 16, as from 6 April 2007, except in relation to proceedings brought under this section before that date.)*

[5.7]
439   Expenses of investigating a company's affairs

[(1)   The expenses of an investigation under any of the powers conferred by this Part shall be defrayed in the first instance by the Secretary of State, but he may recover those expenses from the persons liable in accordance with this section.

There shall be treated as expenses of the investigation, in particular, such reasonable sums as the Secretary of State may determine in respect of general staff costs and overheads.]

(2)   A person who is convicted on a prosecution instituted as a result of the investigation,   . . . may in the same proceedings be ordered to pay those expenses to such extent as may be specified in the order.

(3)   . . .

(4)   A body corporate dealt with by [an inspectors' report], where the inspectors were appointed otherwise than of the Secretary of State's own motion, is liable except where it was the applicant for the investigation, and except so far as the Secretary of State otherwise directs.

[(5)   Where inspectors were appointed—

   (a)   under section 431, or

   (b)   on an application under section 442(3),

the applicant or applicants for the investigation is or are liable to such extent (if any) as the Secretary of State may direct.]

(6)   The report of inspectors appointed otherwise than of the Secretary of State's own motion may, if they think fit, and shall if the Secretary of State so directs, include a recommendation as to the directions (if any) which they think appropriate, in the light of their investigation, to be given under subsection (4) or (5) of this section.

(7)   . . .

(8)   Any liability to repay the Secretary of State imposed by [subsection (2)] above is (subject to satisfaction of his right to repayment) a liability also to indemnify all persons against liability under subsections (4) and (5);   . . .

(9)   A person liable under any one of those subsections is entitled to contribution from any other person liable under the same subsection, according to the amount of their respective liabilities under it.

(10)   Expenses to be defrayed by the Secretary of State under this section shall, so far as not recovered under it, be paid out of money provided by Parliament.

NOTES

Sub-ss (1), (5): substituted by CA 1989, s 59(1), (2), (4), as from 21 February 1990.

Sub-s (2): words omitted repealed by the Companies Act 2006, ss 1176(2)(a), (4), 1295, Sch 16, as from 6 April 2007, except in relation to proceedings brought under s 438 before that date.

Sub-ss (3), (7): repealed by the Companies Act 2006, ss 1176(2)(b), (4), 1295, Sch 16, as from 6 April 2007, except in relation to proceedings brought under s 438 before that date.

Sub-s (4): words in square brackets substituted by CA 1989, s 59(1), (3), as from 21 February 1990.

Sub-s (8): words in square brackets substituted, and words omitted repealed, by the Companies Act 2006, ss 1176(2)(c), (4), 1295, Sch 16, as from 6 April 2007, except in relation to proceedings brought under s 438 before that date.

440   *(Repealed by CA 1989, ss 60(1), 212, Sch 24, as from 21 February 1990.)*

[5.8]
441   Inspectors' report to be evidence

(1)   A copy of any report of inspectors appointed under [this Part], certified by the Secretary of State to be a true copy, is admissible in any legal proceedings as evidence of the opinion of the inspectors in relation to any matter contained in the report [and, in proceedings on an application under [section 8 of the Company Directors Disqualification Act 1986] [or Article 11 of the Company Directors Disqualification (Northern Ireland) Order 2002], as evidence of any fact stated therein].

(2)   A document purporting to be such a certificate as is mentioned above shall be received in evidence and be deemed to be such a certificate, unless the contrary is proved.

NOTES

Sub-s (1): words in first pair of square brackets substituted by CA 1989, s 61, as from 21 February 1990; words in second (outer) pair of square brackets added by the Insolvency Act 1985, s 109, Sch 6, para 3, as from 29 December 1986; words in third (inner) pair of square brackets substituted by the Insolvency Act 1986, s 439(1), Sch 13, Pt I, as from 29 December 1986; words in fourth (inner) pair of square brackets inserted by the Companies Act 2006 (Consequential Amendments, Transitional Provisions and Savings) Order 2009, SI 2009/1941, art 2(1), Sch 1, para 57(1), (4), as from 1 October 2009.

Other powers of investigation available to the Secretary of State
[5.9]
442   Power to investigate company ownership

(1)   Where it appears to the Secretary of State that there is good reason to do so, he may appoint one or more competent inspectors to investigate and report on the membership of any company, and otherwise with respect to the company, for the purpose of determining the true persons who are or have been financially interested in the success or failure (real or apparent) of the company or able to control or materially to influence its policy.

(2)   . . .

[(3)   If an application for investigation under this section with respect to particular shares or debentures of a company is made to the Secretary of State by members of the company, and the number of applicants or the amount of shares held by them is not less than that required for an application for the appointment of inspectors under section 431(2)(a) or (b), then, subject to the following provisions, the Secretary of State shall appoint inspectors to conduct the investigation applied for.

(3A)   The Secretary of State shall not appoint inspectors if he is satisfied that the application is vexatious; and where inspectors are appointed their terms of appointment shall exclude any matter in so far as the Secretary of State is satisfied that it is unreasonable for it to be investigated.

(3B)   The Secretary of State may, before appointing inspectors, require the applicant or applicants to give security, to an amount not exceeding £5,000, or such other sum as he may by order specify, for payment of the costs of the investigation.

An order under this subsection shall be made by statutory instrument which shall be subject to annulment in pursuance of a resolution of either House of Parliament.

(3C)   If on an application under subsection (3) it appears to the Secretary of State that the powers conferred by section 444 are sufficient for the purposes of investigating the matters which inspectors would be appointed to investigate, he may instead conduct the investigation under that section.]

(4)   Subject to the terms of their appointment, the inspectors' powers extend to the investigation of any circumstances suggesting the existence of an arrangement or understanding which, though not legally binding, is or was observed or likely to be observed in practice and which is relevant to the purposes of the investigation.

NOTES

Sub-s (2): repealed by the Companies Act 2006, ss 1035(5), 1295, Sch 16, as from 1 October 2007, with effect where an inspector is appointed under a provision of Pt XIV of this Act on or after that date.

Sub-s (3), (3A)–(3C): substituted, for original sub-s (3), by CA 1989, s 62, as from 21 February 1990.

[5.10]
443 Provisions applicable on investigation under s 442
(1) For purposes of an investigation under section 442, sections 433(1), 434, 436 and 437 apply with the necessary modifications of references to the affairs of the company or to those of any other body corporate, subject however to the following subsections.
(2) Those sections apply to—
   (a) all persons who are or have been, or whom the inspector has reasonable cause to believe to be or have been, financially interested in the success or failure or the apparent success or failure of the company or any other body corporate whose membership is investigated with that of the company, or able to control or materially influence its policy (including persons concerned only on behalf of others), and
   (b) any other person whom the inspector has reasonable cause to believe possesses information relevant to the investigation,
as they apply in relation to officers and agents of the company or the other body corporate (as the case may be).
(3) If the Secretary of State is of opinion that there is good reason for not divulging any part of a report made by virtue of section 442 and this section, he may under section 437 disclose the report with the omission of that part; and he may cause to be kept by the registrar of companies a copy of the report with that part omitted or, in the case of any other such report, a copy of the whole report.
(4) . . .

NOTES
   Sub-s (4): repealed by CA 1989, s 212, Sch 24, as from 21 February 1990.

[5.11]
444 Power to obtain information as to those interested in shares, etc
(1) If it appears to the Secretary of State that there is good reason to investigate the ownership of any shares in or debentures of a company and that it is unnecessary to appoint inspectors for the purpose, he may require any person whom he has reasonable cause to believe to have or to be able to obtain any information as to the present and past interests in those shares or debentures and the names and addresses of the persons interested and of any persons who act or have acted on their behalf in relation to the shares or debentures to give any such information to the Secretary of State.
(2) For this purpose a person is deemed to have an interest in shares or debentures if he has any right to acquire or dispose of them or of any interest in them, or to vote in respect of them, or if his consent is necessary for the exercise of any of the rights of other persons interested in them, or if other persons interested in them can be required, or are accustomed, to exercise their rights in accordance with his instructions.
(3) A person who fails to give information required of him under this section, or who in giving such information makes any statement which he knows to be false in a material particular, or recklessly makes any statement which is false in a material particular, [commits an offence].
[(4) A person guilty of an offence under this section is liable—
   (a) on conviction on indictment, to imprisonment for a term not exceeding two years or a fine (or both);
   (b) on summary conviction—
      (i) in England and Wales, to imprisonment for a term not exceeding twelve months or to a fine not exceeding the statutory maximum (or both) and, for continued contravention, a daily default fine not exceeding one- fiftieth of the statutory maximum;
      (ii) in Scotland or Northern Ireland, to imprisonment for a term not exceeding six months, or to a fine not exceeding the statutory maximum (or both) and, for continued contravention, a daily default fine not exceeding one-fiftieth of the statutory maximum.]

NOTES
   Sub-s (3): words in square brackets substituted by the Companies Act 2006, s 1124, Sch 3, para 1(1), as from 1 October 2007 (except in relation to offences committed before that date (see s 1133 of the 2006 Act at **[1.1133]**)).
   Sub-s (4): added by the Companies Act 2006, s 1124, Sch 3, para 1(2), as from 1 October 2007 (except in relation to offences committed before that date (see s 1133 of the 2006 Act at **[1.1133]**)). See also the note below.
   Transitional adaptations: art 6 of the Companies Act 2006 (Commencement No 3, Consequential Amendments, Transitional Provisions and Savings) Order 2007, SI 2007/2194 provides that the provisions brought into force by that Order shall have effect subject to any transitional adaptations specified in Sch 1 to that Order. Schedule 1, para 20 to the Order (at **[2.43]**) provided that in the sub-s (4) added to this section the words "or Northern Ireland" should be omitted from sub-para (b)(ii) (note that this paragraph was revoked by the Companies Act 2006 (Commencement No 8, Transitional Provisions and Savings) Order 2008, SI 2008/2860, art 6, as from 1 October 2009 (subject to any relevant transitional provision or saving in Sch 2 to that Order)).

[5.12]
445 Power to impose restrictions on shares and debentures

(1) If in connection with an investigation under either section 442 or 444 it appears to the Secretary of State that there is difficulty in finding out the relevant facts about any shares (whether issued or to be issued), he may by order direct that the shares shall until further order be subject to the restrictions of Part XV of this Act.

[(1A) If the Secretary of State is satisfied that an order under subsection (1) may unfairly affect the rights of third parties in respect of shares then the Secretary of State, for the purpose of protecting such rights and subject to such terms as he thinks fit, may direct that such acts by such persons or descriptions of persons and for such purposes as may be set out in the order, shall not constitute a breach of the restrictions of Part XV of this Act.]

(2) This section, and Part XV in its application to orders under it, apply in relation to debentures as in relation to shares [save that subsection (1A) shall not so apply].

NOTES

Sub-s (1A): inserted by the Companies (Disclosure of Interests in Shares) (Orders imposing restrictions on shares) Regulations 1991, SI 1991/1646, reg 5(a), as from 18 July 1991.

Sub-s (2): words in square brackets added by SI 1991/1646, reg 5(b), as from 18 July 1991.

446 (*Repealed by the Companies Act 2006, s 1295, Sch 16, as from 1 October 2007.*)

[Powers of Secretary of State to give directions to inspectors

[5.13]
446A General powers to give directions

(1) In exercising his functions an inspector shall comply with any direction given to him by the Secretary of State under this section.

(2) The Secretary of State may give an inspector appointed under section 431, 432(2) or 442(1) a direction—

  (a) as to the subject matter of his investigation (whether by reference to a specified area of a company's operation, a specified transaction, a period of time or otherwise), or

  (b) which requires the inspector to take or not to take a specified step in his investigation.

(3) The Secretary of State may give an inspector appointed under any provision of this Part a direction requiring him to secure that a specified report under section 437—

  (a) includes the inspector's views on a specified matter,

  (b) does not include any reference to a specified matter,

  (c) is made in a specified form or manner, or

  (d) is made by a specified date.

(4) A direction under this section—

  (a) may be given on an inspector's appointment,

  (b) may vary or revoke a direction previously given, and

  (c) may be given at the request of an inspector.

(5) In this section—

  (a) a reference to an inspector's investigation includes any investigation he undertakes, or could undertake, under section 433(1) (power to investigate affairs of holding company or subsidiary);

  (b) "specified" means specified in a direction under this section.]

NOTES

Commencement: 1 October 2007.

Inserted, together with the preceding heading and s 446B, by the Companies Act 2006, s 1035(1), as from 1 October 2007, with effect where an inspector is appointed under a provision of Pt XIV of this Act on or after that date.

[5.14]
[446B Direction to terminate investigation

(1) The Secretary of State may direct an inspector to take no further steps in his investigation.

(2) The Secretary of State may give a direction under this section to an inspector appointed under section 432(1) or 442(3) only on the grounds that it appears to him that—

  (a) matters have come to light in the course of the inspector's investigation which suggest that a criminal offence has been committed, and

  (b) those matters have been referred to the appropriate prosecuting authority.

(3) Where the Secretary of State gives a direction under this section, any direction already given to the inspector under section 437(1) to produce an interim report, and any direction given to him under section 446A(3) in relation to such a report, shall cease to have effect.

(4) Where the Secretary of State gives a direction under this section, the inspector shall not make a final report to the Secretary of State unless—

  (a) the direction was made on the grounds mentioned in subsection (2) and the Secretary of State directs the inspector to make a final report to him, or

  (b) the inspector was appointed under section 432(1) (appointment in pursuance of order of the court).

(5) An inspector shall comply with any direction given to him under this section.

(6) In this section, a reference to an inspector's investigation includes any investigation he undertakes, or could undertake, under section 433(1) (power to investigate affairs of holding company or subsidiary).]

NOTES

Commencement: 1 October 2007.

Inserted as noted to s 446A at **[5.13]**.

[Resignation, removal and replacement of inspectors

[5.15]

446C   Resignation and revocation of appointment

(1)   An inspector may resign by notice in writing to the Secretary of State.

(2)   The Secretary of State may revoke the appointment of an inspector by notice in writing to the inspector.]

NOTES

Commencement: 1 October 2007.

Inserted, together with the preceding heading and s 446D, by the Companies Act 2006, s 1036, as from 1 October 2007, with effect where an inspector is appointed under a provision of Pt XIV of this Act on or after that date.

[5.16]

[446D   Appointment of replacement inspectors

(1)   Where—

    (a)   an inspector resigns,

    (b)   an inspector's appointment is revoked, or

    (c)   an inspector dies,

the Secretary of State may appoint one or more competent inspectors to continue the investigation.

(2)   An appointment under subsection (1) shall be treated for the purposes of this Part (apart from this section) as an appointment under the provision of this Part under which the former inspector was appointed.

(3)   The Secretary of State must exercise his power under subsection (1) so as to secure that at least one inspector continues the investigation.

(4)   Subsection (3) does not apply if—

    (a)   the Secretary of State could give any replacement inspector a direction under section 446B (termination of investigation), and

    (b)   such a direction would (under subsection (4) of that section) result in a final report not being made.

(5)   In this section, references to an investigation include any investigation the former inspector conducted under section 433(1) (power to investigate affairs of holding company or subsidiary).]

NOTES

Commencement: 1 October 2007.

Inserted as noted to s 446C at **[5.15]**.

[Power to obtain information from former inspectors etc

[5.17]

446E   Obtaining information from former inspectors etc

(1)   This section applies to a person who was appointed as an inspector under this Part—

    (a)   who has resigned, or

    (b)   whose appointment has been revoked.

(2)   This section also applies to an inspector to whom the Secretary of State has given a direction under section 446B (termination of investigation).

(3)   The Secretary of State may direct a person to whom this section applies to produce documents obtained or generated by that person during the course of his investigation to—

    (a)   the Secretary of State, or

    (b)   an inspector appointed under this Part.

(4)   The power under subsection (3) to require production of a document includes power, in the case of a document not in hard copy form, to require the production of a copy of the document—

    (a)   in hard copy form, or

    (b)   in a form from which a hard copy can be readily obtained.

(5)   The Secretary of State may take copies of or extracts from a document produced in pursuance of this section.

(6)   The Secretary of State may direct a person to whom this section applies to inform him of any matters that came to that person's knowledge as a result of his investigation.

(7)   A person shall comply with any direction given to him under this section.

(8)   In this section—

    (a)   references to the investigation of a former inspector or inspector include any investigation he conducted under section 433(1) (power to investigate affairs of holding company or subsidiary), and

    (b)   "document" includes information recorded in any form.]

NOTES

Commencement: 1 October 2007.

Inserted, together with the preceding heading, by the Companies Act 2006, s 1037(1), as from 1 October 2007, with effect where an inspector is appointed under a provision of Pt XIV of this Act on or after that date.

Requisition and seizure of books and papers

[5.18]

[447 Power to require documents and information

(1) The Secretary of State may act under subsections (2) and (3) in relation to a company.

(2) The Secretary of State may give directions to the company requiring it—

(a) to produce such documents (or documents of such description) as may be specified in the directions;

(b) to provide such information (or information of such description) as may be so specified.

(3) The Secretary of State may authorise a person (an investigator) to require the company or any other person—

(a) to produce such documents (or documents of such description) as the investigator may specify;

(b) to provide such information (or information of such description) as the investigator may specify[; or

(d) an offence under Article 10 of the Perjury (Northern Ireland) Order 1979 (false statements made otherwise than on oath)].

(4) A person on whom a requirement under subsection (3) is imposed may require the investigator to produce evidence of his authority.

(5) A requirement under subsection (2) or (3) must be complied with at such time and place as may be specified in the directions or by the investigator (as the case may be).

(6) The production of a document in pursuance of this section does not affect any lien which a person has on the document.

(7) The Secretary of State or the investigator (as the case may be) may take copies of or extracts from a document produced in pursuance of this section.

(8) A "document" includes information recorded in any form.

[(9) The power under this section to require production of a document includes power, in the case of a document not in hard copy form, to require the production of a copy of the document—

(a) in hard copy form, or

(b) in a form from which a hard copy can be readily obtained.]]

NOTES

Substituted by the Companies (Audit, Investigations and Community Enterprise) Act 2004, s 21, as from 6 April 2005.

Sub-s (3): para (c) (and the word immediately preceding it) inserted by the Companies Act 2006 (Consequential Amendments, Transitional Provisions and Savings) Order 2009, SI 2009/1941, art 2(1), Sch 1, para 57(1), (5), as from 1 October 2009.

Sub-s (9): substituted by the Companies Act 2006, s 1038(2), as from 1 October 2007.

[5.19]

[447A Information provided: evidence

(1) A statement made by a person in compliance with a requirement under section 447 may be used in evidence against him.

(2) But in criminal proceedings in which the person is charged with a relevant offence—

(a) no evidence relating to the statement may be adduced by or on behalf of the prosecution, and

(b) no question relating to it may be asked by or on behalf of the prosecution,

unless evidence relating to it is adduced or a question relating to it is asked in the proceedings by or on behalf of that person.

(3) A relevant offence is any offence other than the following—

(a) an offence under section 451,

(b) an offence under section 5 of the Perjury Act 1911 (false statement made otherwise than on oath), or

(c) an offence under section 44(2) of the Criminal Law (Consolidation) (Scotland) Act 1995 (false statement made otherwise than on oath)[; or

(d) an offence under Article 10 of the Perjury (Northern Ireland) Order 1979 (false statements made otherwise than on oath)].

NOTES

Inserted by the Companies (Audit, Investigations and Community Enterprise) Act 2004, s 25, Sch 2, Pt 3, paras 16, 17, as from 6 April 2005.

Sub-s (3): para (d) (and the preceding word) added by the Companies Act 2006 (Consequential Amendments, Transitional Provisions and Savings) Order 2009, SI 2009/1941, art 2(1), Sch 1, para 57(1), (5), as from 1 October 2009.

[5.20]
[448 Entry and search of premises
(1)   A justice of the peace may issue a warrant under this section if satisfied on information on oath given by or on behalf of the Secretary of State, or by a person appointed or authorised to exercise powers under this Part, that there are reasonable grounds for believing that there are on any premises documents whose production has been required under this Part and which have not been produced in compliance with the requirement.
(2)   A justice of the peace may also issue a warrant under this section if satisfied on information on oath given by or on behalf of the Secretary of State, or by a person appointed or authorised to exercise powers under this Part—
   (a)   that there are reasonable grounds for believing that an offence has been committed for which the penalty on conviction on indictment is imprisonment for a term of not less than two years and that there are on any premises documents relating to whether the offence has been committed,
   (b)   that the Secretary of State, or the person so appointed or authorised, has power to require the production of the documents under this Part, and
   (c)   that there are reasonable grounds for believing that if production was so required the documents would not be produced but would be removed from the premises, hidden, tampered with or destroyed.
(3)   A warrant under this section shall authorise a constable, together with any other person named in it and any other constables—
   (a)   to enter the premises specified in the information, using such force as is reasonably necessary for the purpose;
   (b)   to search the premises and take possession of any documents appearing to be such documents as are mentioned in subsection (1) or (2), as the case may be, or to take, in relation to any such documents, any other steps which may appear to be necessary for preserving them or preventing interference with them;
   (c)   to take copies of any such documents; and
   (d)   to require any person named in the warrant to provide an explanation of them or to state where they may be found.
(4)   If in the case of a warrant under subsection (2) the justice of the peace is satisfied on information on oath that there are reasonable grounds for believing that there are also on the premises other documents relevant to the investigation, the warrant shall also authorise the actions mentioned in subsection (3) to be taken in relation to such documents.
(5)   A warrant under this section shall continue in force until the end of the period of one month beginning with the day on which it is issued.
(6)   Any documents of which possession is taken under this section may be retained—
   (a)   for a period of three months; or
   (b)   if within that period proceedings to which the documents are relevant are commenced against any person for any criminal offence, until the conclusion of those proceedings.
(7)   Any person who intentionally obstructs the exercise of any rights conferred by a warrant issued under this section or fails without reasonable excuse to comply with any requirement imposed in accordance with subsection (3)(d) is guilty of an offence   . . .
[(7A)   A person guilty of an offence under this section is liable—
   (a)   on conviction on indictment, to a fine;
   (b)   on summary conviction, to a fine not exceeding the statutory maximum.]
(8)   For the purposes of sections 449 and 451A (provision for security of information) documents obtained under this section shall be treated as if they had been obtained under the provision of this Part under which their production was or, as the case may be, could have been required.
(9)   In the application of this section to Scotland for the references to a justice of the peace substitute references to a justice of the peace or a sheriff, and for the references to information on oath substitute references to evidence on oath.
(10)   In this section "document" includes information recorded in any form.]

NOTES
   Substituted by CA 1989, s 64(1), as from 21 February 1990.
   Sub-s (7): words omitted repealed by the Companies Act 2006, ss 1124, 1295, Sch 3, para 2(1), Sch 16, as from 1 October 2007 (except in relation to offences committed before that date (see s 1133 of the 2006 Act at **[1.1133]**)).
   Sub-s (7A): inserted by the Companies Act 2006, s 1124, Sch 3, para 2(2), as from 1 October 2007 (except in relation to offences committed before that date (see s 1133 of the 2006 Act at **[1.1133]**)).
   Take possession of, etc: the power of seizure conferred by sub-s (3) is a power to which Criminal Justice and Police Act 2001, s 50 applies (additional powers of seizure from premises); see s 50 of, and Sch 1, Pt 1, para 35 to, that Act.

[5.21]
[448A   Protection in relation to certain disclosures: information provided to Secretary of State
(1)   A person who makes a relevant disclosure is not liable by reason only of that disclosure in any proceedings relating to a breach of an obligation of confidence.
(2)   A relevant disclosure is a disclosure which satisfies each of the following conditions—

(a) it is made to the Secretary of State otherwise than in compliance with a requirement under this Part;

(b) it is of a kind that the person making the disclosure could be required to make in pursuance of this Part;

(c) the person who makes the disclosure does so in good faith and in the reasonable belief that the disclosure is capable of assisting the Secretary of State for the purposes of the exercise of his functions under this Part;

(d) the information disclosed is not more than is reasonably necessary for the purpose of assisting the Secretary of State for the purposes of the exercise of those functions;

(e) the disclosure is not one falling within subsection (3) or (4).

(3) A disclosure falls within this subsection if the disclosure is prohibited by virtue of any enactment [whenever passed or made].

(4) A disclosure falls within this subsection if—

(a) it is made by a person carrying on the business of banking or by a lawyer, and

(b) it involves the disclosure of information in respect of which he owes an obligation of confidence in that capacity.

[(5) In this section "enactment" has the meaning given by section 1293 of the Companies Act 2006.]]

NOTES

Inserted by the Companies (Audit, Investigations and Community Enterprise) Act 2004, s 22, as from 6 April 2005.

Sub-s (3): words in square brackets inserted by the Companies Act 2006 (Consequential Amendments, Transitional Provisions and Savings) Order 2009, SI 2009/1941, art 2(1), Sch 1, para 57(1), (6)(a), as from 1 October 2009.

Sub-s (5): substituted by SI 2009/1941, art 2(1), Sch 1, para 57(1), (6)(b), as from 1 October 2009.

[5.22]
[449 Provision for security of information obtained

(1) This section applies to information (in whatever form) obtained—

(a) in pursuance of a requirement imposed under section 447;

(b) by means of a relevant disclosure within the meaning of section 448A(2);

(c) by an investigator in consequence of the exercise of his powers under section 453A.

(2) Such information must not be disclosed unless the disclosure—

(a) is made to a person specified in Schedule 15C, or

(b) is of a description specified in Schedule 15D.

(3) The Secretary of State may by order amend Schedules 15C and 15D.

(4) An order under subsection (3) must not—

(a) amend Schedule 15C by specifying a person unless the person exercises functions of a public nature (whether or not he exercises any other function);

(b) amend Schedule 15D by adding or modifying a description of disclosure unless the purpose for which the disclosure is permitted is likely to facilitate the exercise of a function of a public nature.

(5) An order under subsection (3) must be made by statutory instrument subject to annulment in pursuance of a resolution of either House of Parliament.

(6) A person who discloses any information in contravention of this section [is guilty of an offence].

[(6A) A person guilty of an offence under this section is liable—

(a) on conviction on indictment, to imprisonment for a term not exceeding two years or a fine (or both);

(b) on summary conviction—

(i) in England and Wales, to imprisonment for a term not exceeding twelve months or to a fine not exceeding the statutory maximum (or both);

(ii) in Scotland or Northern Ireland, to imprisonment for a term not exceeding six months, or to a fine not exceeding the statutory maximum (or both).]

(7) . . .

(8) Any information which may by virtue of this section be disclosed to a person specified in Schedule 15C may be disclosed to any officer or employee of the person.

(9) This section does not prohibit the disclosure of information if the information is or has been available to the public from any other source.

(10) For the purposes of this section, information obtained by an investigator in consequence of the exercise of his powers under section 453A includes information obtained by a person accompanying the investigator in pursuance of subsection (4) of that section in consequence of that person's accompanying the investigator.

(11) Nothing in this section authorises the making of a disclosure in contravention of the Data Protection Act 1998.]

NOTES

Substituted by the Companies (Audit, Investigations and Community Enterprise) Act 2004, s 25, Sch 2, Pt 3, paras 16, 18, as from 6 April 2005.

Sub-s (6): words in square brackets substituted (for the original paras (a), (b)) by the Companies Act 2006, s 1124, Sch 3, para 3(1), (2), as from 1 October 2007 (except in relation to offences committed before that date (see s 1133 of the 2006 Act at **[1.1133]**)).

Sub-s (6A): inserted by the Companies Act 2006, s 1124, Sch 3, para 3(1), (3), as from 1 October 2007 (except in relation to offences committed before that date (see s 1133 of the 2006 Act at **[1.1133]**)). See also the transitional adaptations note below.

Sub-s (7): repealed by the Companies Act 2006, ss 1124, 1295, Sch 3, para 3(1), (4), Sch 16, as from 1 October 2007 (except in relation to offences committed before that date (see s 1133 of the 2006 Act at **[1.1133]**)).

Transitional adaptations: art 6 of the Companies Act 2006 (Commencement No 3, Consequential Amendments, Transitional Provisions and Savings) Order 2007, SI 2007/2194 provides that the provisions brought into force by that Order shall have effect subject to any transitional adaptations specified in Sch 1 to that Order. Schedule 1, para 20 to the Order (at **[2.43]**) provided that in the sub-s (6A) added to this section the words "or Northern Ireland" should be omitted from sub-para (b)(ii) (note that this paragraph was revoked by the Companies Act 2006 (Commencement No 8, Transitional Provisions and Savings) Order 2008, SI 2008/2860, art 6, as from 1 October 2009 (subject to any relevant transitional provision or saving in Sch 2 to that Order)).

This section has effect in accordance with the Anti-terrorism, Crime and Security Act 2001, s 17. That section, which clarifies and extends a number of information disclosure provisions available to public authorities, permits disclosure to assist any criminal investigation or criminal proceedings being carried out in the UK or abroad or to facilitate determinations of whether or not such investigations or proceedings should begin or end (see Sch 4 to the 2001 Act).

Orders: the Companies (Disclosure of Information) (Designated Authorities) Order 2006, SI 2006/1644. The Order amends Sch 15D *post* by adding a disclosure for the purpose of enabling or assisting the Gambling Commission to exercise its functions under the Gambling Act 2005 to the list of disclosures that are permitted by virtue of this section and Sch 15D of the 1985 Act. It also amends the Table in s 87(4) of the Companies Act 1989 by adding an entry allowing a disclosure to the Gambling Commission for the purpose of its functions under the Gambling Act 2005 to the list of disclosures that are permitted by s 87(1)(b) of the 1989 Act.

[5.23]
450   Punishment for destroying, mutilating etc company documents
(1)   [An officer of a company . . .] . . . who—
   (a)   destroys, mutilates or falsifies, or is privy to the destruction, mutilation or falsification of a document affecting or relating to the [company's] property or affairs, or
   (b)   makes, or is privy to the making of, a false entry in such a document,
is guilty of an offence, unless he proves that he had no intention to conceal the state of affairs of [the company] or to defeat the law.
[(1A)   Subsection (1) applies to an officer of an authorised insurance company which is not a body corporate as it applies to an officer of a company.]
(2)   Such a person as above mentioned who fraudulently either parts with, alters or makes an omission in any such document or is privy to fraudulent parting with, fraudulent altering or fraudulent making of an omission in, any such document, is guilty of an offence.
[(3)   A person guilty of an offence under this section is liable—
   (a)   on conviction on indictment, to imprisonment for a term not exceeding seven years or a fine (or both);
   (b)   on summary conviction—
      (i)   in England and Wales, to imprisonment for a term not exceeding twelve months or to a fine not exceeding the statutory maximum (or both);
      (ii)   in Scotland or Northern Ireland, to imprisonment for a term not exceeding six months, or to a fine not exceeding the statutory maximum (or both).]
[(4)   . . .]
[(5)   In this section "document" includes information recorded in any form.]

NOTES
Sub-s (1): words in square brackets substituted by CA 1989, s 66(1), (2), as from 21 February 1990; words omitted repealed by the Financial Services and Markets Act 2000 (Consequential Amendments and Repeals) Order 2001, SI 2001/3649, art 23(1), (2), as from 1 December 2001.

Sub-s (1A): inserted by SI 2001/3649, art 22(1), (3), as from 1 December 2001.

Sub-s (3): substituted by the Companies Act 2006, s 1124, Sch 3, para 4(1), as from 1 October 2007 (except in relation to offences committed before that date (see s 1133 of the 2006 Act at **[1.1133]**)). See also the transitional adaptations note below.

Sub-s (4): substituted by CA 1989, s 66(1), (3), as from 21 February 1990; repealed by the Companies Act 2006, ss 1124, 1295, Sch 3, para 4(2), Sch 16, as from 1 October 2007 (except in relation to offences committed before that date (see s 1133 of the 2006 Act at **[1.1133]**)).

Sub-s (5): added by CA 1989, s 66(1), (4), as from 21 February 1990.

Transitional adaptations: art 6 of the Companies Act 2006 (Commencement No 3, Consequential Amendments, Transitional Provisions and Savings) Order 2007, SI 2007/2194 provides that the provisions brought into force by that Order shall have effect subject to any transitional adaptations specified in Sch 1 to that Order. Schedule 1, para 20 to the Order (at **[2.43]**) provided that in sub-s (3) the words "or Northern Ireland" should be omitted from sub-para (b)(ii) (note that this paragraph was revoked by the Companies Act 2006 (Commencement No 8, Transitional Provisions and Savings) Order 2008, SI 2008/2860, art 6, as from 1 October 2009 (subject to any relevant transitional provision or saving in Sch 2 to that Order)).

[5.24]
[451   Punishment for furnishing false information
(1)   A person commits an offence if in purported compliance with a requirement under section 447 to provide information—
   (a)   he provides information which he knows to be false in a material particular;
   (b)   he recklessly provides information which is false in a material particular.

[(2)   A person guilty of an offence under this section is liable—
  (a)   on conviction on indictment, to imprisonment for a term not exceeding two years or a fine (or both);
  (b)   on summary conviction—
    (i)   in England and Wales, to imprisonment for a term not exceeding twelve months or to a fine not exceeding the statutory maximum (or both);
    (ii)   in Scotland or Northern Ireland, to imprisonment for a term not exceeding six months, or to a fine not exceeding the statutory maximum (or both).]
(3)   . . .]

NOTES

Substituted by the Companies (Audit, Investigations and Community Enterprise) Act 2004, s 25, Sch 2, Pt 3, paras 16, 19, as from 6 April 2005.

Sub-s (2): substituted by the Companies Act 2006, s 1124, Sch 3, para 5(1), as from 1 October 2007 (except in relation to offences committed before that date (see s 1133 of the 2006 Act at **[1.1133]**)). See also the transitional adaptations note below.

Sub-s (3): repealed by the Companies Act 2006, ss 1124, 1295, Sch 3, para 5(2), Sch 16, as from 1 October 2007 (except in relation to offences committed before that date (see s 1133 of the 2006 Act at **[1.1133]**)).

Transitional adaptations: art 6 of the Companies Act 2006 (Commencement No 3, Consequential Amendments, Transitional Provisions and Savings) Order 2007, SI 2007/2194 provides that the provisions brought into force by that Order shall have effect subject to any transitional adaptations specified in Sch 1 to that Order. Schedule 1, para 20 to the Order (at **[2.43]**) provided that in sub-s (2) the words "or Northern Ireland" should be omitted from sub-para (b)(ii) (note that this paragraph was revoked by the Companies Act 2006 (Commencement No 8, Transitional Provisions and Savings) Order 2008, SI 2008/2860, art 6, as from 1 October 2009 (subject to any relevant transitional provision or saving in Sch 2 to that Order)).

[5.25]
[451A   Disclosure of information by Secretary of State or inspector
[(1)   This section applies to information obtained—
  (a)   under sections 434 to [446E];
  (b)   by an inspector in consequence of the exercise of his powers under section 453A.]
(2)   The Secretary of State may, if he thinks fit—
  (a)   disclose any information to which this section applies to any person to whom, or for any purpose for which, disclosure is permitted under section 449, or
  (b)   authorise or require an inspector appointed under this Part to disclose such information to any such person or for any such purpose.
[(3)   Information to which this section applies may also be disclosed by an inspector appointed under this Part to—
  (a)   another inspector appointed under this Part;
  (b)   a person appointed under—
    (i)   section 167 of the Financial Services and Markets Act 2000 (general investigations),
    (ii)   section 168 of that Act (investigations in particular cases),
    (iii)   section 169(1)(b) of that Act (investigation in support of overseas regulator),
    (iv)   section 284 of that Act (investigations into affairs of certain collective investment schemes), or
    (v)   regulations made as a result of section 262(2)(k) of that Act (investigations into open-ended investment companies),
    to conduct an investigation; or
  (c)   a person authorised to exercise powers under—
    (i)   section 447 of this Act; or
    (ii)   section 84 of the Companies Act 1989 (exercise of powers to assist overseas regulatory authority).]
(4)   Any information which may by virtue of subsection (3) be disclosed to any person may be disclosed to any officer or servant of that person.
(5)   The Secretary of State may, if he thinks fit, disclose any information obtained under section 444 to—
  (a)   the company whose ownership was the subject of the investigation,
  (b)   any member of the company,
  (c)   any person whose conduct was investigated in the course of the investigation,
  (d)   the auditors of the company, or
  (e)   any person whose financial interests appear to the Secretary of State to be affected by matters covered by the investigation.]
[(6)   For the purposes of this section, information obtained by an inspector in consequence of the exercise of his powers under section 453A includes information obtained by a person accompanying the inspector in pursuance of subsection (4) of that section in consequence of that person's accompanying the inspector.
(7)   The reference to an inspector in subsection (2)(b) above includes a reference to a person accompanying an inspector in pursuance of section 453A(4).]

NOTES

Inserted by FSA 1986, s 182, Sch 13, para 10; substituted by CA 1989, s 68, as from 21 February 1990.

Sub-s (1): substituted by the Companies (Audit, Investigations and Community Enterprise) Act 2004, s 25, Sch 2, Pt 3, paras 16, 20(1), (2), as from 6 April 2005; figure "446E" in square brackets substituted by the Companies Act 2006, s 1037(2), as from 1 October 2007, with effect where an inspector is appointed under a provision of Pt XIV of this Act on or after that date.

Sub-s (3): substituted by the Financial Services and Markets Act 2000 (Consequential Amendments and Repeals) Order 2001, SI 2001/3649, art 24, as from 1 December 2001.

Sub-ss (6), (7): added by the Companies (Audit, Investigations and Community Enterprise) Act 2004, s 25, Sch 2, Pt 3, paras 16, 20(1), (3), as from 6 April 2005.

Supplementary

[5.26]
452 Privileged information

[(1) Nothing in sections 431 to [446E] compels the disclosure by any person to the Secretary of State or to an inspector appointed by him of information in respect of which in an action in the High Court a claim to legal professional privilege, or in an action in the Court of Session a claim to confidentiality of communications, could be maintained.]

[(1A) Nothing in sections 434, 443 or 446 requires a person (except as mentioned in subsection (1B) below) to disclose information or produce documents in respect of which he owes an obligation of confidence by virtue of carrying on the business of banking unless—
  (a) the person to whom the obligation of confidence is owed is the company or other body corporate under investigation,
  (b) the person to whom the obligation of confidence is owed consents to the disclosure or production, or
  (c) the making of the requirement is authorised by the Secretary of State.

(1B) Subsection (1A) does not apply where the person owing the obligation of confidence is the company or other body corporate under investigation under section 431, 432 or 433.]

[(2) Nothing in sections 447 to 451—
  (a) compels the production by any person of a document or the disclosure by any person of information in respect of which in an action in the High Court a claim to legal professional privilege, or in an action in the Court of Session a claim to confidentiality of communications, could be maintained;
  (b) authorises the taking of possession of any such document which is in the person's possession.

(3) The Secretary of State must not under section 447 require, or authorise a person to require—
  (a) the production by a person carrying on the business of banking of a document relating to the affairs of a customer of his, or
  (b) the disclosure by him of information relating to those affairs,
unless one of the conditions in subsection (4) is met.

(4) The conditions are—
  (a) the Secretary of State thinks it is necessary to do so for the purpose of investigating the affairs of the person carrying on the business of banking;
  (b) the customer is a person on whom a requirement has been imposed under section 447;
  (c) the customer is a person on whom a requirement to produce information or documents has been imposed by an investigator appointed by the Secretary of State in pursuance of section 171 or 173 of the Financial Services and Markets Act 2000 (powers of persons appointed under section 167 or as a result of section 168(2) to conduct an investigation).

(5) Despite subsections (1) and (2) a person who is a lawyer may be compelled to disclose the name and address of his client.]

NOTES

Sub-s (1): substituted by the Companies (Audit, Investigations and Community Enterprise) Act 2004, s 25, Sch 2, Pt 3, paras 16, 21(a), as from 6 April 2005; figure "446E" in square brackets substituted by the Companies Act 2006, s 1037(3), as from 1 October 2007, with effect where an inspector is appointed under a provision of Pt XIV of this Act on or after that date.

Sub-ss (1A), (1B): inserted by CA 1989, s 69(3), as from 21 February 1990.

Sub-ss (2)–(5): substituted, for original sub-ss (2), (3), by the Companies (Audit, Investigations and Community Enterprise) Act 2004, s 25, Sch 2, Pt 3, paras 16, 21(b), as from 6 April 2005.

[5.27]
453 Investigation of [overseas] companies

[(1) The provisions of this Part apply to bodies corporate incorporated outside [the United Kingdom] which are carrying on business in [the United Kingdom], or have at any time carried on business there, as they apply to companies under this Act; but subject to the following exceptions, adaptations and modifications.

(1A) The following provisions do not apply to such bodies—
  (a) section 431 (investigation on application of company or its members),
  (b) . . .
  (c) sections 442 to 445 (investigation of company ownership and power to obtain information as to those interested in shares, &c), . . .
  (d) . . .

(1B) The other provisions of this Part apply to such bodies subject to such adaptations and modifications as may be specified by regulations made by the Secretary of State.]

(2) Regulations under this section shall be made by statutory instrument subject to annulment in pursuance of a resolution of either House of Parliament.

NOTES

Section heading, sub-s (1): words in square brackets substituted by the Companies Act 2006 (Consequential Amendments, Transitional Provisions and Savings) Order 2009, SI 2009/1941, art 2(1), Sch 1, para 57(1), (7), as from 1 October 2009.

Sub-ss (1), (1B): substituted (together with sub-s (1A)), for original sub-s (1), by CA 1989, s 70, as from 21 February 1990.

Sub-s (1A): substituted as noted above; para (b) repealed by the Companies Act 2006, ss 1176(3), (4), 1295, Sch 16, as from 6 April 2007, except in relation to proceedings brought under s 438 before that date; para (d) (and the word immediately preceding it) repealed by s 1295 of, and Sch 16 to, the 2006 Act, as from 1 October 2007.

[5.28]
[453A   Power to enter and remain on premises
(1) An inspector or investigator may act under subsection (2) in relation to a company if—
   (a) he is authorised to do so by the Secretary of State, and
   (b) he thinks that to do so will materially assist him in the exercise of his functions under this Part in relation to the company.
(2) An inspector or investigator may at all reasonable times—
   (a) require entry to relevant premises, and
   (b) remain there for such period as he thinks necessary for the purpose mentioned in subsection (1)(b).
(3) Relevant premises are premises which the inspector or investigator believes are used (wholly or partly) for the purposes of the company's business.
(4) In exercising his powers under subsection (2), an inspector or investigator may be accompanied by such other persons as he thinks appropriate.
(5) A person who intentionally obstructs a person lawfully acting under subsection (2) or (4) [is guilty of an offence].
[(5A) A person guilty of an offence under this section is liable—
   (a) on conviction on indictment, to a fine;
   (b) on summary conviction, to a fine not exceeding the statutory maximum.]
(6) . . .
(7) An inspector is a person appointed under section 431, 432 or 442.
(8) An investigator is a person authorised for the purposes of section 447.]

NOTES

Inserted, together with s 453B, by the Companies (Audit, Investigations and Community Enterprise) Act 2004, s 23, as from 6 April 2005.

Sub-s (5): words in square brackets substituted (for the original paras (a), (b)) by the Companies Act 2006, s 1124, Sch 3, para 6(1), (2), as from 1 October 2007 (except in relation to offences committed before that date (see s 1133 of the 2006 Act at **[1.1133]**)).

Sub-s (5A): inserted by the Companies Act 2006, s 1124, Sch 3, para 6(1), (3), as from 1 October 2007 (except in relation to offences committed before that date (see s 1133 of the 2006 Act at **[1.1133]**)).

Sub-s (6): repealed by the Companies Act 2006, ss 1124, 1295, Sch 3, para 6(1), (4), Sch 16, as from 1 October 2007 (except in relation to offences committed before that date (see s 1133 of the 2006 Act at **[1.1133]**)).

[5.29]
[453B   Power to enter and remain on premises: procedural
(1) This section applies for the purposes of section 453A.
(2) The requirements of subsection (3) must be complied with at the time an inspector or investigator seeks to enter relevant premises under section 453A(2)(a).
(3) The requirements are—
   (a) the inspector or investigator must produce evidence of his identity and evidence of his appointment or authorisation (as the case may be);
   (b) any person accompanying the inspector or investigator must produce evidence of his identity.
(4) The inspector or investigator must, as soon as practicable after obtaining entry, give to an appropriate recipient a written statement containing such information as to—
   (a) the powers of the investigator or inspector (as the case may be) under section 453A;
   (b) the rights and obligations of the company, occupier and the persons present on the premises,
as may be prescribed by regulations.
(5) If during the time the inspector or investigator is on the premises there is no person present who appears to him to be an appropriate recipient for the purposes of subsection (8), the inspector or investigator must as soon as reasonably practicable send to the company—
   (a) a notice of the fact and time that the visit took place, and
   (b) the statement mentioned in subsection (4).
(6) As soon as reasonably practicable after exercising his powers under section 453A(2), the inspector or investigator must prepare a written record of the visit and—
   (a) if requested to do so by the company he must give it a copy of the record;
   (b) in a case where the company is not the sole occupier of the premises, if requested to do so by an occupier he must give the occupier a copy of the record.

(7)   The written record must contain such information as may be prescribed by regulations.

(8)   If the inspector or investigator thinks that the company is the sole occupier of the premises an appropriate recipient is a person who is present on the premises and who appears to the inspector or investigator to be—

  (a)   an officer of the company, or

  (b)   a person otherwise engaged in the business of the company if the inspector or investigator thinks that no officer of the company is present on the premises.

(9)   If the inspector or investigator thinks that the company is not the occupier or sole occupier of the premises an appropriate recipient is—

  (a)   a person who is an appropriate recipient for the purposes of subsection (8), and (if different)

  (b)   a person who is present on the premises and who appears to the inspector or investigator to be an occupier of the premises or otherwise in charge of them.

(10)   A statutory instrument containing regulations made under this section is subject to annulment in pursuance of a resolution of either House of Parliament.]

NOTES

Inserted as noted to s 453A at **[5.28]**.

Regulations: the Companies Act 1985 (Power to Enter and Remain on Premises: Procedural) Regulations 2005, SI 2005/684 at **[6.110]**.

[5.30]
[453C   Failure to comply with certain requirements

(1)   This section applies if a person fails to comply with a requirement imposed by an inspector, the Secretary of State or an investigator in pursuance of either of the following provisions—

  (a)   section 447;

  (b)   section 453A.

(2)   The inspector, Secretary of State or investigator (as the case may be) may certify the fact in writing to the court.

(3)   If, after hearing—

  (a)   any witnesses who may be produced against or on behalf of the alleged offender;

  (b)   any statement which may be offered in defence,

the court is satisfied that the offender failed without reasonable excuse to comply with the requirement, it may deal with him as if he had been guilty of contempt of the court.]

NOTES

Inserted by the Companies (Audit, Investigations and Community Enterprise) Act 2004, s 24, as from 6 April 2005.

[5.31]
[453D   Offences by bodies corporate

Where an offence under any of sections 448, 449 to 451 and 453A is committed by a body corporate, every officer of the body who is in default also commits the offence.

  For this purpose—

  (a)   any person who purports to act as director, manager or secretary of the body is treated as an officer of the body, and

  (b)   if the body is a company, any shadow director is treated as an officer of the company.]

NOTES

Commencement: 6 April 2008.

Inserted by the Companies Act 2006 (Consequential Amendments etc) Order 2008, SI 2008/948, art 3(1), Sch 1, Pt 2, para 82, as from 6 April 2008.

PART XV
ORDERS IMPOSING RESTRICTIONS ON SHARES
([SECTION 445])

NOTES

Words in square brackets in the Part heading substituted by the Companies Act 2006 (Commencement No 3, Consequential Amendments, Transitional Provisions and Savings) Order 2007, SI 2007/2194, art 10(1), Sch 4, Pt 1, para 11(1), (2), as from 1 October 2007.

Extension of provisions to Northern Ireland: see the note preceding s 431 at **[5.1]**.

Application of this Part to unregistered companies: see the introductory notes to this Act.

[5.32]
454   Consequence of order imposing restrictions

(1)   So long as any shares are directed to be subject to the restrictions of this Part [then, subject to any directions made in relation to an order [pursuant to section 445(1A) or 456(1A)]]—

  (a)   any transfer of those shares or, in the case of unissued shares, any transfer of the right to be issued with them, and any issue of them, is void;

  (b)   no voting rights are exercisable in respect of the shares;

(c) no further shares shall be issued in right of them or in pursuance of any offer made to their holder; and

(d) except in a liquidation, no payment shall be made of any sums due from the company on the shares, whether in respect of capital or otherwise.

(2) Where shares are subject to the restrictions of subsection (1)(a), any agreement to transfer the shares or, in the case of unissued shares, the right to be issued with them is void (except [such agreement or right as may be made or exercised under the terms of directions made by the Secretary of State or the court under [section 445(1A) or 456(1A)] or] an agreement to [transfer] the shares on the making of an order under section 456(3)(b) below).

(3) Where shares are subject to the restrictions of subsection (1)(c) or (d), an agreement to transfer any right to be issued with other shares in right of those shares, or to receive any payment on them (otherwise than in a liquidation) is void (except [such agreement or right as may be made or exercised under the terms of directions made by the Secretary of State or the court under [section 445(1A) or 456(1A)] or] an agreement to transfer any such right on the [transfer] of the shares on the making of an order under section 456(3)(b) below).

NOTES

Sub-s (1): words in first (outer) pair of square brackets inserted by the Companies (Disclosure of Interests in Shares) (Orders imposing restrictions on shares) Regulations 1991, SI 1991/1646, reg 6(a), as from 18 July 1991; words in second (inner) pair of square brackets substituted by the Companies Act 2006 (Commencement No 3, Consequential Amendments, Transitional Provisions and Savings) Order 2007, SI 2007/2194, art 10(1), Sch 4, Pt 1, para 11(1), (3), as from 1 October 2007.

Sub-ss (2), (3): words in first (outer) pair of square brackets inserted by SI 1991/1646, reg 6(b), (c) as from 18 July 1991; words in second (inner) pair of square brackets substituted by SI 2007/2194, art 10(1), Sch 4, Pt 1, para 11(1), (4), (5), as from 1 October 2007; word in final pair of square brackets substituted by CA 1989, s 145, Sch 19, para 10(2), as from 7 January 1991.

[5.33]
455 Punishment for attempted evasion of restrictions
(1) [Subject to the terms of any directions made under [section 445(1A) or 456]] a person [commits an offence if he]—

(a) exercises or purports to exercise any right to dispose of any shares which, to his knowledge, are for the time being subject to the restrictions of this Part or of any right to be issued with any such shares, or

(b) votes in respect of any such shares (whether as holder or proxy), or appoints a proxy to vote in respect of them, or

(c) being the holder of any such shares, fails to notify of their being subject to those restrictions any person whom he does not know to be aware of that fact but does know to be entitled (apart from the restrictions) to vote in respect of those shares whether as holder or as proxy, or

(d) being the holder of any such shares, or being entitled to any right to be issued with other shares in right of them, or to receive any payment on them (otherwise than in a liquidation), enters into any agreement which is void under section 454(2) or (3).

(2) [Subject to the terms of any directions made under [section 445(1A) or 456]] if shares in a company are issued in contravention of the restrictions, [an offence is committed by—

(a) the company, and

(b) every officer of the company who is in default].

[(2A) A person guilty of an offence under this section is liable—

(a) on conviction on indictment, to a fine;

(b) on summary conviction, to a fine not exceeding the statutory maximum.]

(3) . . .

NOTES

Sub-s (1): words in first (outer) pair of square brackets inserted by the Companies (Disclosure of Interests in Shares) (Orders imposing restrictions on shares) Regulations 1991, SI 1991/1646, reg 7, as from 18 July 1991; words in second (inner) pair of square brackets substituted by the Companies Act 2006 (Commencement No 3, Consequential Amendments, Transitional Provisions and Savings) Order 2007, SI 2007/2194, art 10(1), Sch 4, Pt 1, para 11(1), (6), as from 1 October 2007; words in third pair of square brackets substituted by the Companies Act 2006, s 1124, Sch 3, para 7(1), as from 1 October 2007 (except in relation to offences committed before that date (see s 1133 of the 2006 Act at [**1.1133**])).

Sub-s (2): words in first (outer) pair of square brackets inserted by SI 1991/1646, reg 7, as from 18 July 1991; words in second (inner) pair of square brackets substituted by SI 2007/2194, art 10(1), Sch 4, Pt 1, para 11(1), (7), as from 1 October 2007; words in third pair of square brackets substituted by the Companies Act 2006, s 1124, Sch 3, para 7(2), as from 1 October 2007 (except in relation to offences committed before that date (see s 1133 of the 2006 Act at [**1.1133**])).

Sub-s (2A): inserted by the Companies Act 2006, s 1124, Sch 3, para 7(3), as from 1 October 2007 (except in relation to offences committed before that date (see s 1133 of the 2006 Act at [**1.1133**])).

Sub-s (3): repealed by SI 2007/2194, art 10(3), Sch 5, as from 1 October 2007.

[5.34]
456 Relaxation and removal of restrictions
(1) Where shares in a company are by order made subject to the restrictions of this Part, application may be made to the court for an order directing that the shares be no longer so subject.

[(1A) Where the court is satisfied that an order subjecting the shares to the restrictions of this Part unfairly affects the rights of third parties in respect of shares then the court, for the purpose of protecting such rights and subject to such terms as it thinks fit and in addition to any order it may make under subsection (1), may direct on an application made under that subsection that such acts by such persons or descriptions of persons and for such purposes, as may be set out in the order, shall not constitute a breach of the restrictions of Part XV of this Act.

Subsection (3) does not apply to an order made under this subsection.]

(2) If the order applying the restrictions was made by the Secretary of State, or he has refused to make an order disapplying them, the application may be made by any person aggrieved; . . .

(3) Subject as follows, an order of the court or the Secretary of State directing that shares shall cease to be subject to the restrictions may be made only if—

    (a)   the court or (as the case may be) the Secretary of State is satisfied that the relevant facts about the shares have been disclosed to the company and no unfair advantage has accrued to any person as a result of the earlier failure to make that disclosure, or

    (b)   the shares are to be [transferred for valuable consideration] and the court (in any case) or the Secretary of State (if the order was made under section . . . 445) approves the [transfer].

(4) [Without prejudice to the power of the court to give directions under subsection (1A),] where shares in a company are subject to the restrictions, the court may on application order the shares to be sold, subject to the court's approval as to the sale, and may also direct that the shares shall cease to be subject to the restrictions.

An application to the court under this subsection may be made by the Secretary of State . . . , or by the company.

(5) Where an order has been made under subsection (4), the court may on application make such further order relating to the sale or transfer of the shares as it thinks fit.

An application to the court under this subsection may be made—

    (a)   by the Secretary of State . . . , or

    (b)   by the company, or

    (c)   by the person appointed by or in pursuance of the order to effect the sale, or

    (d)   by any person interested in the shares.

(6) An order (whether of the Secretary of State or the court) directing that shares shall cease to be subject to the restrictions of this Part, if it is—

    (a)   expressed to be made with a view to permitting a transfer of the shares, or

    (b)   made under subsection (4) of this section,

may continue the restrictions mentioned in paragraphs (c) and (d) of section 454(1), either in whole or in part, so far as they relate to any right acquired or offer made before the transfer.

(7) Subsection (3) does not apply to an order directing that shares shall cease to be subject to any restrictions which have been continued in force in relation to those shares under subsection (6).

NOTES

Sub-s (1A): inserted by the Companies (Disclosure of Interests in Shares) (Orders imposing restrictions on shares) Regulations 1991, SI 1991/1646, reg 8(a), as from 18 July 1991.

Sub-ss (2), (5): words omitted repealed by the Companies Act 2006 (Commencement No 3, Consequential Amendments, Transitional Provisions and Savings) Order 2007, SI 2007/2194, art 10(1), (3), Sch 4, Pt 1, para 11(1), (8), (11), Sch 5, as from 1 October 2007.

Sub-s (3): words in square brackets in para (b) substituted by CA 1989, s 145, Sch 19, para 10(1), as from 7 January 1991; words omitted repealed by SI 2007/2194, art 10(1), (3), Sch 4, Pt 1, para 11(1), (9), Sch 5, as from 1 October 2007.

Sub-s (4): words in square brackets inserted by SI 1991/1646, reg 8(b), as from 18 July 1991; words omitted repealed by SI 2007/2194, art 10(1), (3), Sch 4, Pt 1, para 11(1), (10), Sch 5, as from 1 October 2007.

Court . . . may direct: by virtue of SI 1991/1646, reg 9, the power of the court to give a direction under sub-s (1A) above is exercisable in respect of any order made under ss 210(5), 216(1) (both repealed) or s 445(1), including such orders as may be in force on 18 July 1991 (commencement of SI 1991/1646).

[5.35]
457 Further provisions on sale by court order of restricted shares

(1) Where shares are sold in pursuance of an order of the court under section 456(4) the proceeds of sale, less the costs of the sale, shall be paid into court for the benefit of the persons who are beneficially interested in the shares; and any such person may apply to the court for the whole or part of those proceeds to be paid to him.

(2) On application under subsection (1) the court shall (subject as provided below) order the payment to the applicant of the whole of the proceeds of sale together with any interest thereon or, if any other person had a beneficial interest in the shares at the time of their sale, such proportion of those proceeds and interest as is equal to the proportion which the value of the applicant's interest in the shares bears to the total value of the shares.

(3) On granting an application for an order under section 456(4) or (5) the court may order that the applicant's costs be paid out of the proceeds of sale; and if that order is made, the applicant is entitled to payment of his costs out of those proceeds before any person interested in the shares in question receives any part of those proceeds.

PART XVI
FRAUDULENT TRADING BY A COMPANY

458   *(S 458 was repealed by CA 2006, s 1295, Sch 16, as from 1 October 2007, except in relation to offences completed before that date (see CO No 3, Sch 3, para 46 (at* **[2.45]***).)*

PART XVII
PROTECTION OF COMPANY'S MEMBERS AGAINST UNFAIR PREJUDICE

459–461   *(Ss 459–461 repealed by CA 2006, s 1295, Sch 16, as from 1 October 2007.)*

PART XVIII
FLOATING CHARGES AND RECEIVERS (SCOTLAND)

NOTES

This Part is repealed by the Bankruptcy and Diligence etc (Scotland) Act 2007, s 46(1), as from a day to be appointed (subject to savings). Note that it was not repealed by the Companies Act 2006. Section 46(2), (3) of the 2007 Act provide that nothing in Part 2 of the 2007 Act (except ss 40, 41 of that Act in so far as they concern the ranking of floating charges subsisting immediately before the coming into force of s 46) affects the validity or operation of floating charges subsisting before the coming into force of s 46 and, therefore, despite the repeal of Chapters I and III of Part XVIII of this Act, those provisions continue to have effect for the purposes of such floating charges. The relevant provisions of the 2007 Act are at **[9.463]** et seq.

Application of this Part to limited liability partnerships and European Economic Interest Groupings: see the introductory notes to this Act.

CHAPTER I
FLOATING CHARGES

[5.36]
462   *Power of incorporated company to create floating charge*
(1)   It is competent under the law of Scotland for an incorporated company (whether a company within the meaning of this Act or not), for the purpose of securing any debt or other obligation (including a cautionary obligation) incurred or to be incurred by, or binding upon, the company or any other person, to create in favour of the creditor in the debt or obligation a charge, in this Part referred to as a floating charge, over all or any part of the property (including uncalled capital) which may from time to time be comprised in its property and undertaking.
(2), (3)   . . .
(4)   References in this Part to the instrument by which a floating charge was created are, in the case of a floating charge created by words in a bond or other written acknowledgment, references to the bond or, as the case may be, the other written acknowledgment.
(5)   Subject to this Act, a floating charge has effect in accordance with this Part [and Part III of the Insolvency Act 1986] in relation to any heritable property in Scotland to which it relates, notwithstanding that the instrument creating it is not recorded in the Register of Sasines or, as appropriate, registered in accordance with the Land Registration (Scotland) Act 1979.

NOTES

Repealed by the Bankruptcy and Diligence etc (Scotland) Act 2007, s 46(1), as from a day to be appointed (for savings see the introductory note to this Part).

Sub-s (2): substituted, for original sub-ss (2), (3), by CA 1989, s 130(7), Sch 17, para 8; repealed by the Law Reform (Miscellaneous Provisions) (Scotland) Act 1990, s 74(1), (2), Sch 8, para 33(6), Sch 9, as from 1 December 1990.

Sub-s (3): substituted as noted above, and repealed again by the Requirements of Writing (Scotland) Act 1995, s 14(2), Sch 5, as from 1 August 1995.

Sub-s (5): words in square brackets inserted by the Insolvency Act 1986, s 439(1), Sch 13, Pt I, as from 29 December 1986.

[5.37]
463   *Effect of floating charge on winding up*
(1)   [Where a company goes into liquidation within the meaning of section 247(2) of the Insolvency Act 1986], a floating charge created by the company attaches to the property then comprised in the company's property and undertaking or, as the case may be, in part of that property and undertaking, but does so subject to the rights of any person who—
     (a)   has effectually executed diligence on the property or any part of it; or
     (b)   holds a fixed security over the property or any part of it ranking in priority to the floating charge; or
     (c)   holds over the property or any part of it another floating charge so ranking.
(2)   The provisions of [Part IV of the Insolvency Act (except section 185)] have effect in relation to a floating charge, subject to subsection (1), as if the charge were a fixed security over the property to which it has attached in respect of the principal of the debt or obligation to which it relates and any interest due or to become due thereon.
[(3)   Nothing in this section derogates from the provisions of sections 53(7) and 54(6) of the Insolvency Act (attachment of floating charge on appointment of receiver), or prejudices the operation of sections 175 and 176 of that Act (payment of preferential debts in winding up).]

(4) . . . interest accrues, in respect of a floating charge which after 16th November 1972 attaches to the property of the company, until payment of the sum due under the charge is made.

NOTES

Repealed by the Bankruptcy and Diligence etc (Scotland) Act 2007, s 46(1), as from a day to be appointed (for savings see the introductory note to this Part).

Sub-s (1): words in square brackets substituted by CA 1989, s 140(1), as from 3 July 1995.

Sub-s (2): words in square brackets substituted by the Insolvency Act 1986, s 439(1), Sch 13, Pt I, as from 29 December 1986.

Sub-s (3): substituted by the Insolvency Act 1986, s 439(1), Sch 13, Pt I, as from 29 December 1986.

Sub-s (4): words omitted repealed by the Insolvency Act 1986, s 438, Sch 12, as from 29 December 1986.

[5.38]
464 Ranking of floating charges
(1)   Subject to subsection (2), the instrument creating a floating charge over all or any part of the company's property under section 462 may contain—
  (a)   provisions prohibiting or restricting the creation of any fixed security or any other floating charge having priority over, or ranking pari passu with, the floating charge; or
  (b)   [with the consent of the holder of any subsisting floating charge or fixed security which would be adversely affected] provisions regulating the order in which the floating charge shall rank with any other subsisting or future floating charges or fixed securities over that property or any part of it.
[(1A)   Where an instrument creating a floating charge contains any such provision as is mentioned in subsection (1)(a), that provision shall be effective to confer priority on the floating charge over any fixed security or floating charge created after the date of the instrument.]
(2)   Where all or any part of the property of a company is subject both to a floating charge and to a fixed security arising by operation of law, the fixed security has priority over the floating charge.
[(3)   The order of ranking of the floating charges with any other subsisting or future floating charges or fixed securities over all or any part of the company's property is determined in accordance with the provisions of subsections (4) and (5) except where it is determined in accordance with any provision such as is mentioned in paragraph (a) or (b) of subsection (1).]
(4)   Subject to the provisions of this section—
  (a)   a fixed security, the right to which has been constituted as a real right before a floating charge has attached to all or any part of the property of the company, has priority of ranking over the floating charge;
  (b)   floating charges rank with one another according to the time of registration in accordance with Chapter II of Part XII;
  (c)   floating charges which have been received by the registrar for registration by the same postal delivery rank with one another equally.
(5)   Where the holder of a floating charge over all or any part of the company's property which has been registered in accordance with Chapter II of Part XII has received intimation in writing of the subsequent registration in accordance with that Chapter of another floating charge over the same property or any part thereof, the preference in ranking of the first-mentioned floating charge is restricted to security for—
  (a)   the holder's present advances;
  (b)   future advances which he may be required to make under the instrument creating the floating charge or under any ancillary document;
  (c)   interest due or to become due on all such advances; . . .
  (d)   any expenses or outlays which may reasonably be incurred by the holder[; and
  (e)   (in the case of a floating charge to secure a contingent liability other than a liability arising under any further advances made from time to time) the maximum sum to which that contingent liability is capable of amounting whether or not it is contractually limited.]
(6)   This section is subject to [Part XII and to] [sections 175 and 176 of the Insolvency Act] (preferential debts in winding up).

NOTES

Repealed by the Bankruptcy and Diligence etc (Scotland) Act 2007, s 46(1), as from a day to be appointed (for savings see the introductory note to this Part).

Sub-s (1): words in square brackets in para (b) inserted by CA 1989, s 140(2), (3), as from 3 July 1995.

Sub-s (1A): inserted by CA 1989, s 140(2), (4), as from 3 July 1995.

Sub-s (3): substituted by CA 1989, s 140(2), (5), as from 3 July 1995.

Sub-s (5): word omitted from para (c) repealed, and para (e) and the word immediately preceding it added, by CA 1989, ss 140(2), (6), 212, Sch 24, as from 3 July 1995.

Sub-s (6): words in first pair of square brackets inserted by CA 1989, s 140(2), (7), as from a day to be appointed; words in second pair of square brackets substituted by the Insolvency Act 1986, s 439(1), Sch 13, Pt I, as from 29 December 1986.

[5.39]
465 Continued effect of certain charges validated by Act of 1972
(1)   Any floating charge which—
  (a)   purported to subsist as a floating charge on 17th November 1972, and

(b)   *if it had been created on or after that date, would have been validly created by virtue of the Companies (Floating Charges and Receivers) (Scotland) Act 1972,*

is deemed to have subsisted as a valid floating charge as from the date of its creation.

(2)   Any provision which—

(a)   *is contained in an instrument creating a floating charge or in any ancillary document executed prior to, and still subsisting at, the commencement of that Act,*

(b)   *relates to the ranking of charges, and*

(c)   *if it had been made after the commencement of that Act, would have been a valid provision,*

is deemed to have been a valid provision as from the date of its making.

NOTES

Repealed by the Bankruptcy and Diligence etc (Scotland) Act 2007, s 46(1), as from a day to be appointed (for savings see the introductory note to this Part).

[5.40]
466   Alteration of floating charges

(1)   The instrument creating a floating charge under section 462 or any ancillary document may be altered by the execution of an instrument of alteration by the company, the holder of the charge and the holder of any other charge (including a fixed security) which would be adversely affected by the alteration.

(2)   [Without prejudice to any enactment or rule of law regarding the execution of documents,] such an instrument of alteration is validly executed if it is executed—

(a)   . . .

(b)   *where trustees for debenture-holders are acting under and in accordance with a trust deed, by those trustees[; or]*

(c)   *where, in the case of a series of secured debentures, no such trustees are acting, by or on behalf of—*

     (i)   *a majority in nominal value of those present or represented by proxy and voting at a meeting of debenture-holders at which the holders of at least one-third in nominal value of the outstanding debentures of the series are present or so represented; or*

     (ii)   *where no such meeting is held, the holders of at least one-half in nominal value of the outstanding debentures of the series; . . .*

(d)   . . .

(3)   Section 464 applies to an instrument of alteration under this section as it applies to an instrument creating a floating charge.

(4)   Subject to the next subsection, section 410(2) and (3) and section 420 apply to an instrument of alteration under this section which—

(a)   *prohibits or restricts the creation of any fixed security or any other floating charge having priority over, or ranking pari passu with, the floating charge; or*

(b)   *varies, or otherwise regulates the order of, the ranking of the floating charge in relation to fixed securities or to other floating charges; or*

(c)   *releases property from the floating charge; or*

(d)   *increases the amount secured by the floating charge.*

(5)   Section 410(2) and (3) and section 420 apply to an instrument of alteration falling under subsection (4) of this section as if references in the said sections to a charge were references to an alteration to a floating charge, and as if in section 410(2) and (3)—

(a)   *references to the creation of a charge were references to the execution of such alteration; and*

(b)   *for the words from the beginning of subsection (2) to the word "applies" there were substituted the words "Every alteration to a floating charge created by a company".*

(6)   Any reference (however expressed) in any enactment, including this Act, to a floating charge is, for the purposes of this section and unless the context otherwise requires, to be construed as including a reference to the floating charge as altered by an instrument of alteration falling under subsection (4) of this section.

NOTES

Repealed by the Bankruptcy and Diligence etc (Scotland) Act 2007, s 46(1), as from a day to be appointed (for savings see the introductory note to this Part).

Sub-s (2): words in square brackets inserted, and words omitted repealed, by CA 1989, ss 130(7), 212, Sch 17, para 9, Sch 24, as from 31 July 1990.

Sub-ss (4), (5): repealed by CA 1989, ss 140(8), 212, Sch 24, as from a day to be appointed.

Sub-s (6): words "falling under subsection (4) of this section" repealed by CA 1989, ss 140(8), 212, Sch 24, as from a day to be appointed.

Particulars of an instrument of alteration to a floating charge: see **[6.10]**.

467–485   *((Chapter II) repealed, with savings, by the Insolvency Act 1986, ss 437, 438, Schs 11, 12, as from 29 December 1986.)*

CHAPTER III
GENERAL

[5.41]
486 Interpretation for Part XVIII generally
(1) In this Part, unless the context otherwise requires, the following expressions have the following meanings respectively assigned to them, that is to say—
"ancillary document" means—
  (a)   a document which relates to the floating charge and which was executed by the
         debtor or creditor in the charge before the registration of the charge in accordance
         with Chapter II of Part XII; or
  (b)   an instrument of alteration such as is mentioned in section 466 in this Part;
"company", . . . means an incorporated company (whether a company within the meaning of
      this Act or not);
"fixed security", in relation to any property of a company, means any security, other than a
      floating charge or a charge having the nature of a floating charge, which on the winding up
      of the company in Scotland would be treated as an effective security over that property, and
      (without prejudice to that generality) includes a security over that property, being a
      heritable security within the meaning of section 9(8) of the Conveyancing and Feudal
      Reform (Scotland) Act 1970;
. . .
"Register of Sasines" means the appropriate division of the General Register of Sasines.

NOTES
    Repealed by the Bankruptcy and Diligence etc (Scotland) Act 2007, s 46(1), as from a day to be appointed (for savings see
the introductory note to this Part).
    Words omitted repealed by the Insolvency Act 1986, s 438, Sch 12, as from 29 December 1986.

[5.42]
487 Extent of Part XVIII
This Part extends to Scotland only.

NOTES
    Repealed by the Bankruptcy and Diligence etc (Scotland) Act 2007, s 46(1), as from a day to be appointed (for savings see
the introductory note to this Part).

PART XIX
RECEIVERS AND MANAGERS (ENGLAND AND WALES)

488–500 *(Repealed, with savings, by the Insolvency Act 1986, ss 437, 438, Schs 11, 12, as from
29 December 1986.)*

PART XX
**WINDING UP OF COMPANIES REGISTERED UNDER THIS ACT OR THE
FORMER COMPANIES ACTS**

501–664

NOTES
    This Part has been repealed as follows:

501–650 (Chapters I–V)	Repealed, with savings, by the Insolvency Act 1986, as from 29 Dec 1986.
651 Power of court to declare dissolution of company void	Repealed by CA 2006, as from 1 Oct 2009. Savings: CO No 8, Sch 2, para 89 (at **[2.91]**) provides that the repeal of this section (and s 653) does not affect an application made before 1 Oct 2009.
652 Registrar may strike defunct company off register	Repealed by CA 2006, as from 1 Oct 2009.
652A Registrar may strike private company off register on application	Repealed by CA 2006, as from 1 Oct 2009.
652B Duties in connection with making application under section 652A	Repealed by CA 2006, as from 1 Oct 2009.
652C Directors' duties following application under section 652A	Repealed by CA 2006, as from 1 Oct 2009.
652D Sections 652B and 652C: supplementary provisions	Repealed by CA 2006, as from 1 Oct 2009.
652E Sections 652B and 652C: enforcement	Repealed by CA 2006, as from 1 Oct 2009.

652F Other offences connected with section 652A	Repealed by CA 2006, as from 1 Oct 2009.
653 Objection to striking off by person aggrieved	Repealed by CA 2006, as from 1 Oct 2009. For savings see the note to s 651.
654 Property of dissolved company to be bona vacantia	Repealed by CA 2006, as from 1 Oct 2009. Savings and transitional provisions: CO No 8, Sch 2, para 88 (at **[2.91]**) provides that (subject to para 88A) CA 2006, ss 1012–1023 (property of dissolved company) apply in relation to the property of a company dissolved on or after 1 Oct 2009, and that the corresponding provisions of this Act continue to apply in relation to the property of a company dissolved before that date.
655 Effect on s 654 of company's revival after dissolution	Repealed by CA 2006, as from 1 Oct 2009.
656 Crown disclaimer of property vesting as bona vacantia	Repealed by CA 2006, as from 1 Oct 2009. For savings see the note to s 654.
657 Effect of Crown disclaimer under s 656	Repealed by CA 2006, as from 1 Oct 2009. For savings see the note to s 654.
658 Liability for rentcharge on company's land after dissolution	Repealed by CA 2006, as from 1 Oct 2009. For savings see the note to s 654.
659–664 (Chapter VII)	Repealed, with savings, by the Insolvency Act 1986, as from 29 Dec 1986. Also repealed by CA 2006, as from 1 Oct 2009.

PART XXI
WINDING UP OF UNREGISTERED COMPANIES

665–674 (*Repealed, with savings, by the Insolvency Act 1986, ss 437, 438, Schs 11, 12, as from 29 December 1986. Also repealed by the Companies Act 2006, s 1295, Sch 16, as from 1 October 2009.*)

PART XXII
BODIES CORPORATE SUBJECT, OR BECOMING SUBJECT, TO THIS ACT
(OTHERWISE THAN BY ORIGINAL FORMATION UNDER PART I)

675–690

NOTES
This Part has been repealed as follows:

675 Companies formed and registered under former Companies Acts	Repealed by CA 2006, as from 1 Oct 2009. Savings: for general savings in relation to existing companies, see CO No 8, Sch 2, para 1 (at **[2.91]**). Note in particular that nothing in CA 2006 affects (a) the registration or re-registration of a company under the former Companies Acts, or the continued existence of a company by virtue of such registration or re-registration, or (b) the application in relation to an existing company of: (i) Table B in the Joint Stock Companies Act 1856, (ii) Table A in any of the former Companies Acts, or (iii) the Companies (Tables A to F) Regulations 1985. Note also that s 1297(3) of the 2006 Act (continuity of the law: etc) applies (a) in relation to a company to which s 675(1) of this Act applied as if the company had been formed and registered under Part I of this Act; (b) in relation to a company to which s 676(1) of this Act applied as if the company had been registered under Chapter II of Part XXII of this Act; (c) in relation to a company to which s 677(1) of this Act applied as if the company had been re-registered under Part II of this Act.
676 Companies registered but not formed under former Companies Acts	Repealed by CA 2006, as from 1 Oct 2009. For savings see the note to s 675.
677 Companies re-registered with altered status under former Companies Acts	Repealed by CA 2006, as from 1 Oct 2009. For savings see the note to s 675.
678 Companies registered under Joint Stock Companies Acts	Repealed by CA 2006, as from 1 Oct 2009. For savings see the note to s 675.
679 Northern Ireland and Irish companies	Repealed by CA 2006, as from 1 Oct 2009. For savings see the note to s 675.

680 Companies capable of being registered under this Chapter	Repealed by CA 2006, as from 1 Oct 2009. Savings: CO No 8, Sch 2, para 93 (at [2.91]) provides that ss 680–690 continue to apply to an application for registration if (a) it is received by the registrar, and (b) the requirements as to registration are met in relation to it, before 1 Oct 2009. Any application for registration under this Act in relation to which the requirements as to registration are not met before that date shall be treated as withdrawn.
681 Procedural requirements for registration	Repealed by CA 2006, as from 1 Oct 2009. For savings see the note to s 680.
682 Change of name on registration	Repealed by CA 2006, as from 1 Oct 2009. For savings see the note to s 680.
683 Definition of "joint stock company"	Repealed by CA 2006, as from 1 Oct 2009. For savings see the note to s 680.
684 Requirements for registration by joint stock companies	Repealed by CA 2006, as from 1 Oct 2009. For savings see the note to s 680.
685 Registration of joint stock company as public company	Repealed by CA 2006, as from 1 Oct 2009. For savings see the note to s 680.
686 Other requirements for registration	Repealed by CA 2006, as from 1 Oct 2009. For savings see the note to s 680.
687 Name of company registering	Repealed by CA 2006, as from 1 Oct 2009. For savings see the note to s 680.
688 Certificate of registration under this Chapter	Repealed by CA 2006, as from 1 Oct 2009. For savings see the note to s 680.
689 Effect of registration	Repealed by CA 2006, as from 1 Oct 2009. For savings see the note to s 680.
690 Power to substitute memorandum and articles for deed of settlement	Repealed by CA 2006, as from 1 Oct 2009. For savings see the note to s 680.

PART XXIII
OVERSEA COMPANIES

690A–703R

NOTES

This Part has been repealed as follows:

690A Branch registration under the Eleventh Company Law Directive (89/666/EEC)	Repealed by CA 2006, as from 1 Oct 2009. Transitional provisions and savings: SI 2009/1801, Sch 8 provides for various transitional provisions and savings in connection with the repeal of Chapter I (Registration, etc) and the commencement of the 2009 Regulations (see [4.482] et seq).
690B Scope of sections 691 and 692	Repealed by CA 2006, as from 1 Oct 2009. For transitional provisions and savings, see the note to s 690A.
691 Documents to be delivered to registrar	Repealed by CA 2006, as from 1 Oct 2009. For transitional provisions and savings, see the note to s 690A.
692 Registration of altered particulars	Repealed by CA 2006, as from 1 Oct 2009. For transitional provisions and savings, see the note to s 690A.
692A Change in registration regime	Repealed by CA 2006, as from 1 Oct 2009. For transitional provisions and savings, see the note to s 690A.
693 Obligation to state name and other particulars	Repealed by CA 2006, as from 1 Oct 2009. For transitional provisions and savings, see the note to s 690A. As to the previous repeal of certain words by FSA 1986, see the notes to Part III ante.
694 Regulation of oversea companies in respect of their names	Repealed by CA 2006, as from 1 Oct 2009. For transitional provisions and savings, see the note to s 690A.
694A Service of documents: companies to which section 690A applies	Repealed by CA 2006, as from 1 Oct 2009. For transitional provisions and savings, see the note to s 690A.
695 Service of documents on oversea company	Repealed by CA 2006, as from 1 Oct 2009. For transitional provisions and savings, see the note to s 690A.
695A Registrar to whom documents to be delivered: companies to which section 690A applies	Repealed by CA 2006, as from 1 Oct 2009. For transitional provisions and savings, see the note to s 690A.
696 Office where documents to be filed	Repealed by CA 2006, as from 1 Oct 2009. For transitional provisions and savings, see the note to s 690A.
697 Penalties for non-compliance	Repealed by CA 2006, as from 1 Oct 2009. For transitional provisions and savings, see the note to s 690A.
698 Definitions	Repealed by CA 2006, as from 1 Oct 2009. For transitional provisions and savings, see the note to s 690A.
699 Channel Islands and Isle of Man companies	Repealed by CA 2006, as from 1 Oct 2009. For transitional provisions and savings, see the note to s 690A.

699A Credit and financial institutions to which the Bank Branches Directive (89/117/EEC) applies	Repealed by CA 2006, as from 1 Oct 2009. Transitional provisions and savings: SI 2009/1801, Sch 8 provides for various transitional provisions and savings in connection with the repeal of Chapter II (Delivery of Accounts and Reports) and the commencement of the 2009 Regulations (see **[4.486]** et seq).
699AA Companies to which the Eleventh Company Law Directive applies	Repealed by CA 2006, as from 1 Oct 2009. For transitional provisions and savings, see the note to s 699A.
699B Scope of sections 700 to 703	Repealed by CA 2006, as from 1 Oct 2009. For transitional provisions and savings, see the note to s 699A.
700 Preparation of accounts and reports by oversea companies	Repealed by CA 2006, as from 1 Oct 2009. For transitional provisions and savings, see the note to s 699A.
701 Oversea company's financial year and accounting reference periods	Repealed by CA 2006, as from 1 Oct 2009. For transitional provisions and savings, see the note to s 699A.
702 Delivery to registrar of accounts and reports of oversea company	Repealed by CA 2006, as from 1 Oct 2009. For transitional provisions and savings, see the note to s 699A.
703 Penalty for non-compliance	Repealed by CA 2006, as from 1 Oct 2009. For transitional provisions and savings, see the note to s 699A.
703A–703N (Chapter III)	Repealed by CA 2006, as from 1 Oct 2009 (without ever coming into force).
703O Scope of Chapter	Repealed by CA 2006, as from 1 Oct 2009.
703P Particulars to be delivered to the registrar: winding up	Repealed by CA 2006, as from 1 Oct 2009. Transitional provisions and savings: see SI 2009/1801, Sch 8, Pt 7, paras 27, 28 at **[4.488]** which provides: (i) sub-s (1) continues to apply in relation to a winding up beginning before 1 Oct 2009; (ii) sub-s (3) continues to apply in relation to an appointment made before that date; (iii) sub-s (5) continues to apply where the event occurred before that date. See also Sch 8, Pt 8 to that Order (at **[4.489]**) for savings as to form or manner in which documents to be delivered.
703Q Particulars to be delivered to the registrar: insolvency proceedings	Repealed by CA 2006, as from 1 Oct 2009. Transitional provisions and savings: see SI 2009/1801, Sch 8, Pt 7, para 29 at **[4.488]** which provides that this section continues to apply where the proceedings began before 1 Oct 2009. See also Sch 8, Pt 8 to that Order (at **[4.489]**) for savings as to form or manner in which documents to be delivered.
703R Penalty for non-compliance	Repealed by CA 2006, as from 1 Oct 2009.

PART XXIV
THE REGISTRAR OF COMPANIES, HIS FUNCTIONS AND OFFICES

704–715A

NOTES

This Part has been repealed as follows:

704 Registration offices	Repealed by CA 2006, as from 1 Oct 2009. Savings, etc: CO No 8, Sch 2, paras 94–109 provide for a variety of savings and transitional provisions in relation to the commencement (also on 1 Oct 2009) of Part 35 of CA 2006 (the Registrar of Companies). See those paragraphs at **[2.91]**.
705 Companies' registered numbers	Repealed by CA 2006, as from 1 Oct 2009. For savings etc, see the note to s 704.
705A Registration of branches of oversea companies	Repealed by CA 2006, as from 1 Oct 2009. For savings etc, see the note to s 704.
706 Delivery to the registrar of documents in legible form	Repealed by CA 2006, as from 1 Oct 2009. For savings etc, see the note to s 704.
707 Delivery to the registrar of documents otherwise than in legible form	Repealed by SI 2000/3373, as from 22 Dec 2000.
707A The keeping of company records by the registrar	Repealed by CA 2006, as from 1 Jan 2007 (in part), and as from 1 Oct 2009 (otherwise). For general transitional provisions, see the note to s 704.

707B Delivery to the registrar using electronic communications	Repealed by CA 2006, as from 1 Oct 2009. For general transitional provisions see the note to s 704. See also CO No 8, Sch 2, para 115 which provides that any saving in that Schedule for the effect of a provision of this Act requiring a document to be delivered to the registrar extends to this section so far as relating to the provision in question and the delivery of documents under it. See also (in relation to overseas companies) the note to s 690A. Note also that various transitional provisions contained in commencement orders made under CA 2006, s 1300 provide that until s 1068 (Registrar's requirements as to form, authentication and manner of delivery) of the 2006 Act comes fully into force (which it did on 1 Oct 2009) this section applies in relation to documents required or authorised to be delivered to the registrar under various provisions of CA 2006 brought into force by those Orders.
708 Fees payable to registrar	Repealed by CA 2006, as from 6 Apr 2007 (in part), and as from 1 Oct 2009 (otherwise). For general transitional provisions see the note to s 704. See, in particular, CO No 8, Sch 2, para 94 which provides that any Regulations made under this section that are in force immediately before 1 Oct 2009 have effect on or after that date as if made under CA 2006, s 1063 (note that SI 2009/1804, Sch 1, Pt 9, para 36 at **[10.1189]** makes similar provisions regarding SIs made under this section that apply to LLPs). Note also that sub-s (5) of this section provided that the registrar may charge a fee for any services provided by him otherwise than in pursuance of an obligation imposed on him by law. CO No 1, Sch 5, Pt 3, para 6(3) (at **[2.15]**) provides that the repeal of that subsection shall not prevent the registrar from continuing to charge fees thereunder of which notice had before the repeal been given to those to whom the services in question have been, are being or are to be provided. See also SI 2009/2101 at **[4.543]**.
709 Inspection, &c of records kept by registrar	Repealed by CA 2006, as from 1 Jan 2007. As to the previous repeal of s 709(2), (3) by FSA 1986, see the notes to Part III ante.
710 Certificate of incorporation	Repealed by CA 2006, as from 1 Oct 2009. For savings etc, see the note to s 704.
710A Provision and authentication by registrar of documents in non-legible form	Repealed by CA 2006, as from 1 Oct 2009. For general transitional provisions see the note to s 704 and see, in particular, CO No 8, Sch 2, para 111 which provides that the repeal of this section does not affect its application on or after 1 Oct 2009 in relation to saved provisions of this Act.
710B Documents relating to Welsh companies	Repealed by CA 2006, as from 1 Jan 2007. For general transitional provisions see the note to s 704. See also CO No 1, Sch 5, para 1 (at **[2.13]**) which provides that regs 4, 5 of the Companies (Welsh Language Forms and Documents) Regulations 1994 continue to have effect notwithstanding the repeal of this section, subject to certain adaptations (note, however, that reg 4 was revoked by SI 2009/1803, as from 1 Oct 2009).
711 Public notice by registrar of receipt and issue of certain documents	Repealed by CA 2006, as from 1 Jan 2007.
711A Exclusion of deemed notice	Repealed by CA 2006, as from 1 Oct 2009 (without ever coming into force).
712 Removal of documents to Public Record Office	Repealed by CA 1989, as from 1 Jul 1991.
713 Enforcement of company's duty to make returns	Repealed by CA 2006, as from 1 Oct 2009. For savings etc, see the note to s 704.
714 Registrar's index of company and corporate names	Repealed by CA 2006, as from 1 Oct 2009. For savings etc, see the note to s 704.
715 Destruction of old records	Repealed by CA 1989, as from 1 Jul 1991.
715A Interpretation	Repealed by CA 2006, as from 1 Oct 2009. For savings etc, see the note to s 704.

PART XXV
MISCELLANEOUS AND SUPPLEMENTARY PROVISIONS

716–734

NOTES

This Part has been repealed as follows. Note that s 726(2) is still in force and that section is reproduced below these notes (at **[5.43]**):

716 Prohibition of partnerships with more than 20 members	Repealed by SI 2002/3203, as from 21 Dec 2002.
717 Limited partnerships: limit on number of members	Repealed by SI 2002/3203, as from 21 Dec 2002.
718 Unregistered companies	Repealed by CA 2006, as from 1 Oct 2009.

719 Power of company to provide for employees on cessation or transfer of business	Repealed by CA 2006, as from 1 Oct 2009. Savings: CO No 8, Sch 2, para 40 (at **[2.91]**) provides that CA 2006, s 247 (power to make provision for employees on cessation or transfer of business) applies to provision made on or after 1 Oct 2009 (subject to para (b) below). This section continues to apply (a) to provision made before that date, and (b) to anything sanctioned in accordance with sub-s (3) before that date.
720 Certain companies to publish periodical statement	Repealed by CA 2006, as from 6 Apr 2007.
721 Production and inspection of books where offence suspected	Repealed by CA 2006, as from 1 Oct 2009.
722 Form of company registers, etc	Repealed by CA 2006, as from 1 Oct 2009.
723 Use of computers for company records	Repealed by CA 2006, as from 1 Oct 2009.
723A Obligations of company as to inspections of register, &c	Repealed by CA 2006, as from 1 Oct 2009.
723B Confidentiality orders	Repealed by CA 2006, as from 1 Oct 2009. Savings: see CO No 8, Sch 2, paras 36–39 (Continuation of protection afforded by confidentiality orders under the 1985 Act) at **[2.91]**. See also, in so far as relating to overseas companies, SI 2009/1801, Sch 8, Pt 4 at **[4.485]**.
723C Effect of confidentiality orders	Repealed by CA 2006, as from 1 Oct 2009. For general savings in relation to the continuation of protection afforded by confidentiality orders, see the note to s 723B.
723D Construction of sections 723B and 723C	Repealed by CA 2006, as from 1 Oct 2009. For general savings in relation to the continuation of protection afforded by confidentiality orders, see the note to s 723B.
723E Sections 723B and 723C: offences	Repealed by CA 2006, as from 1 Oct 2009. For general savings in relation to the continuation of protection afforded by confidentiality orders, see the note to s 723B.
723F Regulations under sections 723B to 723E	Repealed by CA 2006, as from 1 Oct 2009. For general savings in relation to the continuation of protection afforded by confidentiality orders, see the note to s 723B.
724 Cross-border operation of receivership provisions	Repealed, with savings, by the Insolvency Act 1986, as from 29 Dec 1986 (also repealed by CA 2006, as from 1 Oct 2009).
725 Service of documents	Repealed by CA 2006, as from 1 Oct 2009.
726 Costs and expenses in actions by certain limited companies	Still in force for certain purposes see **[5.43]** immediately below this note.
727 Power of court to grant relief in certain cases	Repealed by CA 2006, as from 1 Oct 2008.
728 Enforcement of High Court orders	Repealed by CA 2006, as from 1 Oct 2009.
729 Annual report by Secretary of State	Repealed by CA 2006, as from 6 Apr 2007.
730 Punishment of offences	Repealed by CA 2006, as from 1 Oct 2009.
730A Meaning of "officer in default"	Repealed by CA 2006, as from 1 Oct 2009.
731 Summary proceedings	Repealed by CA 2006, as from 1 Oct 2009.
732 Prosecution by public authorities	Repealed by CA 2006, as from 6 Apr 2008. Savings: this section and ss 733, 734 continue to apply in relation to offences committed before 6 Apr 2008 (see CO No 5, Sch 4, Pt 1, para 44 at **[2.66]** and the introductory notes to this Act).
733 Offences by bodies corporate	Repealed by CA 2006, as from 6 Apr 2008. For savings, see the note to s 732.
734 Criminal proceedings against unincorporated bodies	Repealed by CA 2006, as from 6 Apr 2008. For savings, see the note to s 732.

[5.43]
726   Costs and expenses in actions by certain limited companies
(1)   . . .
(2)   Where in Scotland a limited company is pursuer in an action or other legal proceeding, the court having jurisdiction in the matter may, if it appears by credible testimony that there is reason to believe that the company will be unable to pay the defender's expenses if successful in his defence, order the company to find caution and sist the proceedings until caution is found.

NOTES
Repealed by the Companies Act 2006, s 1295, Sch 16, as from 1 October 2009 (in so far as relating to sub-s (1)), and as from a day to be appointed (otherwise). See further the note below.

The Companies Act 2006 (Commencement No 8, Transitional Provisions and Savings) Order 2008, SI 2008/2860, Sch 1 originally provided that this section would be completely repealed as from 1 October 2009. That Schedule was amended by the Companies Act 2006 (Consequential Amendments, Transitional Provisions and Savings) Order 2009, SI 2009/1941, art 13(1)(a) (as from 1 October 2009). The amendment substitutes a reference to "s 726(1)" for the original reference to "s 726"; the effect being that sub-s (2) above is not repealed as from 1 October 2009.

See also the Companies Act 2006 (Consequential Amendments, Transitional Provisions and Savings) Order 2009, SI 2009/1941, art 13(3) (at **[4.540]**) which provides that sub-s (2) above applies to a LLP registered under the Limited Liability Partnerships Act 2000 as it applies to a limited company.

PART XXVI
INTERPRETATION

735–744A

NOTES

This Part has been repealed as follows:

735 "Company", etc	Repealed by CA 2006, as from 1 Oct 2009.
735A Relationship of this Act to Insolvency Act	Repealed by CA 2006, as from 1 Oct 2009.
735B Relationship of this Act to Part 6 of the Financial Services and Markets Act 2000	Repealed by CA 2006, as from 1 Oct 2009.
736 "Subsidiary", "holding company" and "wholly-owned subsidiary"	Repealed by CA 2006, as from 1 Oct 2009.
736A Provisions supplementing s 736	Repealed by CA 2006, as from 1 Oct 2009.
736B Power to amend ss 736 and 736A	Repealed by CA 2006, as from 1 Oct 2009.
737 "Called-up share capital"	Repealed by CA 2006, as from 1 Oct 2009.
738 "Allotment" and "paid up"	Repealed by CA 2006, as from 1 Oct 2009.
739 "Non-cash asset"	Repealed by CA 2006, as from 1 Oct 2009.
740 "Body corporate" and "corporation"	Repealed by CA 2006, as from 1 Oct 2009.
741 "Director" and "shadow director"	Repealed by CA 2006, as from 1 Oct 2007.
742 Expressions used in connection with accounts	Repealed by CA 2006, as from 1 Oct 2009.
742A Meaning of "offer to the public"	Repealed by CA 2006, as from 6 Apr 2008.
742B Meaning of "banking company"	Repealed by CA 2006, as from 6 Apr 2008.
742C Meaning of "insurance company" and "authorised insurance company"	Repealed by CA 2006, as from 6 Apr 2008.
743 "Employees' share scheme"	Repealed by CA 2006, as from 1 Oct 2009.
743A Meaning of "office copy" in Scotland	Repealed by CA 2006, as from 1 Oct 2009.
744 Expressions used generally in this Act	Repealed by CA 2006, as from 6 Apr 2007 and 6 Apr 2008 (in part), and as from 1 Oct 2009 (otherwise).
744A Index of defined expressions	Repealed by CA 2006, as from 1 Oct 2009.

PART XXVII
FINAL PROVISIONS

745 *(Repealed by the Companies Act 2006, s 1295, Sch 16, as from 1 October 2009.)*

[5.44]
746 Commencement
. . . *this Act comes into force on 1st July 1985.*

NOTES

Repealed by the Companies Act 2006, s 1295, Sch 16, as from a day to be appointed.
Words omitted repealed by CA 1989, s 212, Sch 24, as from 1 April 1990.

[5.45]
747 Citation
This Act may be cited as the Companies Act 1985.

SCHEDULES

SCHEDULES 1–15B

NOTES

These Schedules have been repealed as follows:

Schedule 1—Particulars of Directors etc to be Contained in Statement under Section 10	Repealed by CA 2006, as from 1 Oct 2009. For savings see the note to s 1.
Schedule 2—Interpretation of References to "Beneficial Interest"	
Part I—References in Sections 23, 145, 146 and 148	Repealed by CA 2006, as from 1 Oct 2009. For savings see the note to s 146.
Part II—References in Schedule 5	Repealed by SI 2008/948, as from 6 Apr 2008.
Schedule 3—Mandatory Contents of Prospectus	Repealed, subject to savings in relation to para 2, by FSA 1986, as from the dates, and for the purposes noted in the notes to Part III of this Act ante. In so far as it continued to have effect, it was repealed by CA 2006, as from 1 Oct 2009.
Schedule 4—Form and Content of Company Accounts	
Part I—General rules and formats	Repealed by CA 2006, as from 6 Apr 2008. For savings see the note to s 221.
Part II—Accounting principles and rules	Repealed by CA 2006, as from 6 Apr 2008. For savings see the note to s 221.
Part III—Notes to the accounts	Repealed by CA 2006, as from 6 Apr 2008. For savings see the note to s 221.
Part IV—Special provisions where company is a parent company or subsidiary undertaking	Repealed by CA 2006, as from 6 Apr 2008. For savings see the note to s 221.
Part V—Special provisions where the company is an investment company	Repealed by CA 2006, as from 6 Apr 2008. For savings see the note to s 221.
Part VI	Repealed by CA 1989, as from 1 Apr 1990.
Part VII—Interpretation of Schedule	Repealed by CA 2006, as from 6 Apr 2008. For savings see the note to s 221. Note also that the repeal of Sch 4, Pt VII, paras 88, 89 does not affect the operation of those provisions for the purposes of ss 152(2) or 172(2)(b)(i) of this Act (saving for accounting definitions, see SI 2008/948, art 9(1) at **[4.283]**).
Schedule 4A—Form and Content of Group Accounts	Repealed by CA 2006, as from 6 Apr 2008. For savings see the note to s 221.
Schedule 5—Disclosure of Information: Related Undertakings	Repealed by CA 2006, as from 6 Apr 2008. For savings see the note to s 221.
Schedule 6—Disclosure of Information: Emoluments and Other Benefits of Directors and Others	Repealed by CA 2006, as from 6 Apr 2008. For savings see the note to s 221.
Schedule 7—Matters to be Dealt With in Directors' Report	
Part I—Matters of a general nature	Repealed by CA 2006, as from 6 Apr 2008. For savings see the note to s 221. See also CO No 3, Sch 3, para 41(3) (at **[2.45]**) which provides that the repeal of Part XA of this Act does not affect Sch 7, Pt I, para 3(4) (Political donations and expenditure)
Part II—Disclosure required by company acquiring its own shares, etc	Repealed by CA 2006, as from 6 Apr 2008. For savings see the note to s 221.
Part III—Disclosure concerning employment, etc, of disabled persons	Repealed by CA 2006, as from 6 Apr 2008. For savings see the note to s 221.
Part IV	Repealed, in relation to any financial year ending on or after 2 Feb 1996, by SI 1996/189 (subject to transitional provisions in relation to financial years ending on or before 24 Mar 1996.
Part V—Employee involvement	Repealed by CA 2006, as from 6 Apr 2008. For savings see the note to s 221.
Part VI—Policy and practice on payment of creditors	Repealed by CA 2006, as from 6 Apr 2008. For savings see the note to s 221.
Part VII—Disclosure Required by Certain Publicly-Traded Companies	Repealed by CA 2006, as from 6 Apr 2008. For savings see the note to s 221.
Schedule 7ZA—Operating and Financial Review	Repealed by SI 2005/3442, as from 12 Jan 2006.
Schedule 7A—Directors' remuneration report	Repealed by CA 2006, as from 6 Apr 2008. For savings see the note to s 221.
Schedule 7B—Specified Persons, Descriptions of Disclosures Etc for the Purposes of Section 245G	Repealed by CA 2006, as from 6 Apr 2008. For savings see the note to s 221.

Schedule 8—Form and Content of Accounts Prepared by Small Companies	Repealed by CA 2006, as from 6 Apr 2008. For savings see the note to s 221.
Schedule 8A—Form and Content of Abbreviated Accounts of Small Companies Delivered to Registrar	Repealed by CA 2006, as from 6 Apr 2008. For savings see the note to s 221.
Schedule 9—Special provisions for banking companies and groups	Repealed by CA 2006, as from 6 Apr 2008. For savings see the note to s 221.
Schedule 9A—Form and Content of Accounts of Insurance Companies and Groups	Repealed by CA 2006, as from 6 Apr 2008. For savings see the note to s 221.
Schedule 10—Additional matters to be dealt with in directors' report attached to special category accounts	Repealed by SI 1993/3246, as from 19 Dec 1993, subject to transitional provisions and exemptions in relation to certain companies.
Schedule 10A—Parent and Subsidiary Undertakings: Supplementary Provisions	Repealed by CA 2006, as from 6 Apr 2008. For savings see the note to s 221.
Schedule 11—Modifications of Part VIII Where Company's Accounts Prepared in Accordance with Special Provisions for Banking or Insurance Companies	Repealed by CA 2006, as from 6 Apr 2008. For savings see the note to s 263.
Schedule 12—Supplementary provisions in connection with disqualification orders	Repealed by the Company Directors Disqualification Act 1986, as from 29 Dec 1986, subject to transitional provisions and savings.
Schedule 13—Provisions Supplementing and Interpreting ss 324–328	
Part I—Rules for interpretation of the sections and also section 346(4) and (5)	Repealed by CA 2006, as from 1 Oct 2007. Savings: see CO No 3, Sch 3, para 50 (at **[2.45]**) which provides that the repeal of Sch 13 does not affect (a) s 17(3)(b) of this Act (directors to disclose interest in contracts), (b) the Industrial and Provident Societies Act 1965, ss 7E, 7F(3), (c) FSMA 2000, s 96B(2)(a).
Part II—Periods within which obligations imposed by section 324 must be fulfilled	Repealed by CA 2006, as from 6 Apr 2007.
Part III—Circumstances in which obligation imposed by section 324 is not discharged	Repealed by CA 2006, as from 6 Apr 2007.
Part IV—Provisions with respect to register of directors' interests to be kept under section 325	Repealed by CA 2006, as from 6 Apr 2007.
Schedule 14—Overseas Branch Registers	Repealed by CA 2006, as from 1 Oct 2009.
Schedule 15—Contents of annual return of a company having a share capital.	Repealed by CA 1989, as from 7 Jan 1991.
Schedule 15A—Written Resolutions of Private Companies	Repealed by CA 2006, as from 1 Oct 2007. For savings see the note to s 366.
Schedule 15B—Provisions Subject to which ss 425–427 have Effect in their Application to Mergers and Divisions of Public Companies	Repealed by CA 2006, as from 6 Apr 2008.

[SCHEDULE 15C
SPECIFIED PERSONS

Section 449

[5.46]

1. The Secretary of State.

2. The Department of Enterprise, Trade and Investment for Northern Ireland.

3. The Treasury.

4. The Lord Advocate.

5. The Director of Public Prosecutions.

6. The Director of Public Prosecutions for Northern Ireland.

7. The Financial Services Authority.

8. A constable.

9. A procurator fiscal.

10. The Scottish Ministers.]

NOTES

Inserted, together with Sch 15D, by the Companies (Audit, Investigations and Community Enterprise) Act 2004, s 25, Sch 2, Pt 3, paras 16, 25, as from 6 April 2005 (for transitional provisions see below).

Part 5 Pre-2006 companies legislation

Transitional provisions: note that the Companies (Audit, Investigations and Community Enterprise) Act 2004 (Commencement) and Companies Act 1989 (Commencement No 18) Order 2004, SI 2004/3322, art 10 provides that new s 449 (under which this Schedule takes effect) applies, and old s 449 does not apply, to information to which old s 449(1) applied immediately before 6 April 2005.

[SCHEDULE 15D
DISCLOSURES

Section 449

[5.47]
1. A disclosure for the purpose of enabling or assisting a person authorised under [section 457 of the Companies Act 2006] to exercise his functions.

2. A disclosure for the purpose of enabling or assisting an inspector appointed under Part 14 to exercise his functions.

3. A disclosure for the purpose of enabling or assisting a person authorised under section 447 of this Act or section 84 of the Companies Act 1989 to exercise his functions.

4. A disclosure for the purpose of enabling or assisting a person appointed under section 167 of the Financial Services and Markets Act 2000 (general investigations) to conduct an investigation to exercise his functions.

5. A disclosure for the purpose of enabling or assisting a person appointed under section 168 of the Financial Services and Markets Act 2000 (investigations in particular cases) to conduct an investigation to exercise his functions.

6. A disclosure for the purpose of enabling or assisting a person appointed under section 169(1)(b) of the Financial Services and Markets Act 2000 (investigation in support of overseas regulator) to conduct an investigation to exercise his functions.

7. A disclosure for the purpose of enabling or assisting a person appointed under section 284 of the Financial Services and Markets Act 2000 (investigations into affairs of certain collective investment schemes) to conduct an investigation to exercise his functions.

8. A disclosure for the purpose of enabling or assisting a person appointed under regulations made under sections 262(1) and (2)(k) of the Financial Services and Markets Act 2000 (investigations into open-ended investment companies) to conduct an investigation to exercise his functions.

9. A disclosure for the purpose of enabling or assisting the Secretary of State or the Treasury to exercise any of their functions under any of the following—
[(a) the Companies Acts (as defined in section 2(1) of the Companies Act 2006);]
[(b) Part 5 of the Criminal Justice Act 1993 (insider dealing);]
(c) the Insolvency Act 1986;
(d) the Company Directors Disqualification Act 1986;
[(da) Part 42 of the Companies Act 2006 (statutory auditors);]
[(e) Parts 3 and 7 of the Companies Act 1989 (investigations and powers to obtain information and financial markets and insolvency);]
(f) the Financial Services and Markets Act 2000;
[(g) the Investment Bank Special Administration Regulations 2011].

10. A disclosure for the purpose of enabling or assisting the Scottish Ministers to exercise their functions under the enactments relating to insolvency.

11. A disclosure for the purpose of enabling or assisting the Department of Enterprise, Trade and Investment for Northern Ireland to exercise any powers conferred on it by the enactments relating to companies or insolvency.

12. A disclosure for the purpose of enabling or assisting a person appointed or authorised by the Department of Enterprise, Trade and Investment for Northern Ireland under the enactments relating to companies or insolvency to exercise his functions.

[**13.** A disclosure for the purpose of enabling or assisting the Pensions Regulator to exercise the functions conferred on it by or by virtue of any of the following—
(a) the Pension Schemes Act 1993;
(b) the Pensions Act 1995;
(c) the Welfare Reform and Pensions Act 1999;
(d) the Pensions Act 2004;
(e) any enactment in force in Northern Ireland corresponding to any of those enactments.]

[**13A.** A disclosure for the purpose of enabling or assisting the Board of the Pension Protection Fund to exercise the functions conferred on it by or by virtue of Part 2 of the Pensions Act 2004 or any enactment in force in Northern Ireland corresponding to that Part.]

14. A disclosure for the purpose of enabling or assisting the Bank of England to exercise its functions.

15. A disclosure for the purpose of enabling or assisting the body known as the Panel on Takeovers and Mergers to exercise its functions.

16. A disclosure for the purpose of enabling or assisting organs of the Society of Lloyd's (being organs constituted by or under the Lloyd's Act 1982) to exercise their functions under or by virtue of the Lloyd's Acts 1871 to 1982.

17. A disclosure for the purpose of enabling or assisting the Office of Fair Trading to exercise its functions under any of the following—
  (a) the Fair Trading Act 1973;
  (b) the Consumer Credit Act 1974;
  (c) the Estate Agents Act 1979;
  (d) the Competition Act 1980;
  (e) the Competition Act 1998;
  (f) the Financial Services and Markets Act 2000;
  (g) the Enterprise Act 2002;
  (h)   . . .
  (i) the Unfair Terms in Consumer Contracts Regulations 1999 (SI 1999/2083);
  [(j) the Business Protection from Misleading Marketing Regulations 2008;
  (k) the Consumer Protection from Unfair Trading Regulations 2008].

18. A disclosure for the purpose of enabling or assisting the Competition Commission to exercise its functions under any of the following—
  (a) the Fair Trading Act 1973;
  (b) the Competition Act 1980;
  (c) the Competition Act 1998;
  (d) the Enterprise Act 2002.

19. A disclosure with a view to the institution of, or otherwise for the purposes of, proceedings before the Competition Appeal Tribunal.

20. A disclosure for the purpose of enabling or assisting an enforcer under Part 8 of the Enterprise Act 2002 to exercise its functions under that Part.

21. A disclosure for the purpose of enabling or assisting the [Charity Commission to exercise its] functions.

22. A disclosure for the purpose of enabling or assisting the Attorney General to exercise his functions in connection with charities.

23. A disclosure for the purpose of enabling or assisting the National Lottery Commission to exercise its functions under sections 5 to 10 and 15 of the National Lottery etc Act 1993.

24. A disclosure by the National Lottery Commission to the National Audit Office for the purpose of enabling or assisting the Comptroller and Auditor General to carry out an examination under Part 2 of the National Audit Act 1983 into the economy, effectiveness and efficiency with which the National Lottery Commission has used its resources in discharging its functions under sections 5 to 10 of the National Lottery etc Act 1993.

25. A disclosure for the purpose of enabling or assisting a qualifying body under the Unfair Terms in Consumer Contracts Regulations 1999 (SI 1999/2083) to exercise its functions under those Regulations.

26. A disclosure for the purpose of enabling or assisting an enforcement authority under the Consumer Protection (Distance Selling) Regulations 2000 (SI 2000/2334) to exercise its functions under those Regulations.

27. A disclosure for the purpose of enabling or assisting a local weights and measures authority in England and Wales to exercise its functions under section 230(2) of the Enterprise Act 2002.

28. A disclosure for the purpose of enabling or assisting the Financial Services Authority to exercise its functions under any of the following—
  (a) the legislation relating to friendly societies or to industrial and provident societies;
  (b) the Building Societies Act 1986;
  (c) Part 7 of the Companies Act 1989;
  (d) the Financial Services and Markets Act 2000.

29. A disclosure for the purpose of enabling or assisting the competent authority for the purposes of Part 6 of the Financial Services and Markets Act 2000 to exercise its functions under that Part.

30. A disclosure for the purpose of enabling or assisting a body corporate established in accordance with section 212(1) of the Financial Services and Markets Act 2000 (compensation scheme manager) to exercise its functions.

31. (1) A disclosure for the purpose of enabling or assisting a recognised investment exchange or a recognised clearing house to exercise its functions as such.

(2) Recognised investment exchange and recognised clearing house have the same meaning as in section 285 of the Financial Services and Markets Act 2000.

32. A disclosure for the purpose of enabling or assisting a body designated under section 326(1) of the Financial Services and Markets Act 2000 (designated professional bodies) to exercise its functions in its capacity as a body designated under that section.

33. A disclosure with a view to the institution of, or otherwise for the purposes of, civil proceedings arising under or by virtue of the Financial Services and Markets Act 2000.

34. A disclosure for the purpose of enabling or assisting a body designated by order under [section 1252 of the Companies Act 2006] (delegation of functions of Secretary of State) to exercise its functions under [Part 42 of that Act (statutory auditors)].

35. A disclosure for the purpose of enabling or assisting a recognised supervisory or qualifying body (within the meaning of [Part 42 of the Companies Act 2006]) to exercise its functions as such.

36. A disclosure for the purpose of enabling or assisting an official receiver (including the Accountant in Bankruptcy in Scotland and the Official Assignee in Northern Ireland) to exercise his functions under the enactments relating to insolvency.

37. A disclosure for the purpose of enabling or assisting the Insolvency Practitioners Tribunal to exercise its functions under the Insolvency Act 1986.

38. A disclosure for the purpose of enabling or assisting a body which is for the time being a recognised professional body for the purposes of section 391 of the Insolvency Act 1986 [or Article 350 of the Insolvency (Northern Ireland) Order 1989] (recognised professional bodies) to exercise its functions as such.

39. (1) A disclosure for the purpose of enabling or assisting an overseas regulatory authority to exercise its regulatory functions.

(2) Overseas regulatory authority and regulatory functions have the same meaning as in section 82 of the Companies Act 1989.

40. A disclosure for the purpose of enabling or assisting the Regulator of Community Interest Companies to exercise functions under the Companies (Audit, Investigations and Community Enterprise) Act 2004.

41. A disclosure with a view to the institution of, or otherwise for the purposes of, criminal proceedings.

42. A disclosure with a view to the institution of, or otherwise for the purposes of, proceedings on an application under section 6, 7 or 8 of the Company Directors Disqualification Act 1986 [or Article 9, 10 or 11 of the Company Directors Disqualification (Northern Ireland) Order 2002].

[43. A disclosure with a view to the institution of, or otherwise for the purposes of, proceedings before the Upper Tribunal in respect of—
  (a) a decision of the Financial Services Authority;
  (b) a decision of the Bank of England; or
  (c) a decision of a person relating to the assessment of any compensation or consideration under the Banking (Special Provisions) Act 2008 or the Banking Act 2009.]

44. A disclosure for the purposes of proceedings before the Financial Services Tribunal by virtue of the Financial Services and Markets Act 2000 (Transitional Provisions) (Partly Completed Procedures) Order 2001 (SI 2001/3592).

[44A. A disclosure for the purposes of proceedings before [tribunal in relation to a decision of the Pensions Regulator].]

45. A disclosure for the purpose of enabling or assisting a body appointed under section 14 of the Companies (Audit, Investigations and Community Enterprise) Act 2004 (supervision of periodic accounts and reports of issuers of listed securities) to exercise functions mentioned in subsection (2) of that section.

46. [(1)] A disclosure with a view to the institution of, or otherwise for the purposes of, disciplinary proceedings relating to the performance by a [relevant lawyer], auditor, accountant, valuer or actuary of his professional duties.

[(2) "Relevant lawyer" means—

(a) a person who, for the purposes of the Legal Services Act 2007, is an authorised person in relation to an activity which constitutes a reserved legal activity (within the meaning of that Act),

(b) a solicitor or barrister in Northern Ireland, or

(c) a solicitor or advocate in Scotland.]

47. (1) A disclosure with a view to the institution of, or otherwise for the purposes of, disciplinary proceedings relating to the performance by a public servant of his duties.

(2) Public servant means an officer or employee of the Crown or of any public or other authority for the time being designated for the purposes of this paragraph by the Secretary of State by order.

(3) An order under sub-paragraph (2) must be made by statutory instrument subject to annulment in pursuance of a resolution of either House of Parliament.

48. A disclosure for the purpose of the provision of a summary or collection of information framed in such a way as not to enable the identity of any person to whom the information relates to be ascertained.

49. A disclosure in pursuance of any Community obligation.

[**50.** A disclosure for the purpose of enabling or assisting the Gambling Commission to exercise its functions under the Gambling Act 2005.]]

NOTES

Inserted as noted to Sch 15C at **[5.46]**.

Para 1: words in square brackets substituted by the Companies Act 2006 (Consequential Amendments etc) Order 2008, SI 2008/948, art 3(1), Sch 1, Pt 2, para 92, as from 6 April 2008, in relation to disclosures for the purpose of enabling or assisting a person to exercise functions in relation to accounts for financial years beginning on or after that date (see also see art 6(4) of the 2008 Order (at **[4.280]**) which provides that where by virtue of any transitional provision, a provision of the Companies Act 2006 has effect only (a) on or after a specified date, or (b) in relation to matters occurring or arising on or after a specified date, any amendment substituting or inserting a reference to that provision has effect correspondingly).

Para 9: sub-paras (a), (b), (e) substituted, and sub-para (da) inserted, by the Companies Act 2006 (Consequential Amendments, Transitional Provisions and Savings) Order 2009, SI 2009/1941, art 2(1), Sch 1, para 58(1), (2), as from 1 October 2009; sub-para (g) inserted by the Investment Bank Special Administration Regulations 2011, SI 2011/245, reg 27, Sch 6, Pt 3, para 8, as from 8 February 2011.

Para 13: substituted by the Pensions Act 2004, s 319, Sch 12, para 5(1), (3)(a), as from 6 April 2005.

Para 13A: inserted by the Pensions Act 2004, s 319(1), Sch 12, para 5(1), (3)(b), as from 6 April 2005.

Para 17: sub-para (h) repealed, and sub-paras (j), (k) added, by the Consumer Protection from Unfair Trading Regulations 2008, SI 2008/1277, reg 30(1), (3), Sch 2, Pt 1, para 30, Sch 4, Pt 1, as from 26 May 2008.

Para 21: words in square brackets substituted by the Charities Act 2006, s 75, Sch 8, paras 74, 76, as from 27 February 2007.

Paras 34, 35: words in square brackets substituted by SI 2009/1941, art 2(1), Sch 1, para 58(1), (3), (4), as from 1 October 2009.

Paras 38, 42: words in square brackets inserted by SI 2009/1941, art 2(1), Sch 1, para 58(1), (5), (6), as from 1 October 2009.

Para 43: substituted by the Transfer of Tribunal Functions Order 2010, SI 2010/22, art 5(1), Sch 2, para 5(a), as from 6 April 2010 (for transitional provisions and savings in relation to existing cases and appeals from the Financial Services and Markets Tribunal, see Sch 5 to that Order).

Para 44A: inserted by the Pensions Act 2004, s 102(4), Sch 4, Pt 4, para 19, as from 6 April 2005; words in square brackets substituted by SI 2010/22, art 5(1), Sch 2, para 5(b), as from 6 April 2010 (for transitional provisions and savings in relation to existing cases and appeals from the Pensions Regulator Tribunal, see Sch 5 to that Order).

Para 46: sub-para (1) numbered as such, words in square brackets in that paragraph substituted, and sub-para (2) added, by the Legal Services Act 2007, s 208, Sch 21, para 63, as from 1 January 2010.

Para 50: added by the Companies (Disclosure of Information) (Designated Authorities) Order 2006, SI 2006/1644, art 2, as from 1 October 2006.

Charity Commissioners: as to the abolition of the office of Charity Commissioner for England and Wales, the establishment of the Charity Commission for England and Wales, and the transfer of the functions, rights, liabilities, etc from the Charity Commissioners for England and Wales to the Charity Commission, see the Charities Act 2006, s 6.

SCHEDULES 16–25

NOTES

These Schedules have been repealed as follows:

Schedule 16—Orders in course of winding up pronounced in vacation (Scotland)	Repealed by the Insolvency Act 1986, as from 29 Dec 1986.
Schedule 17—Proceedings of committee of inspection	Repealed by the Insolvency Act 1986, as from 29 Dec 1986.
Schedule 18—Provisions of Part XX not applicable in winding up subject to supervision of the court	Repealed by the Insolvency Act 1986, as from 29 Dec 1986.
Schedule 19—Preference among creditors in company winding up	Repealed by the Insolvency Act 1986, as from 29 Dec 1986.
Schedule 20—Vesting of Disclaimed Property; Protection of Third Parties	
Part I	Repealed by the Insolvency Act 1986, as from 29 Dec 1986.
Part II—Crown Disclaimer Under Section 656 (Scotland Only)	Repealed by CA 2006, as from 1 Oct 2009. For savings see the note to s 654.

Schedule 21—Effect of Registration Under Section 680	Repealed by CA 2006, as from 1 Oct 2009. For savings see the note to s 680.
Schedule 21A—Branch Registration Under the Eleventh Company Law Directive (89/666/EEC)	Repealed by CA 2006, as from 1 Oct 2009. For transitional provisions and savings see the note to s 690A.
Schedule 21B—Change in the Registration Regime: Transitional Provisions	Repealed by CA 2006, as from 1 Oct 2009. For transitional provisions and savings see the note to s 690A.
Schedule 21C—Delivery of Reports and Accounts: Credit and Financial Institutions to which the Bank Branches Directive (89/117/EEC) Applies	Repealed by CA 2006, as from 1 Oct 2009. For transitional provisions and savings see the note to s 699A.
Schedule 21D—Delivery of Reports and Accounts: Companies to which the Eleventh Company Law Directive Applies	Repealed by CA 2006, as from 1 Oct 2009. For transitional provisions and savings see the note to s 699A.
Schedule 22—Provisions of this Act applying to unregistered companies	Repealed by CA 2006, as from 1 Oct 2009.
Schedule 23—Form of statement to be published by certain companies under s 720	Repealed by CA 2006, as from 6 Apr 2007.
Schedule 24—Punishment of Offences Under this Act	Repealed by CA 2006, as from 1 Oct 2007, 6 Apr 2008, and 1 Oct 2008 (certain purposes), and as from 1 Oct 2009 (otherwise). Savings: see CO No 3, Sch 3, para 51 (at **[2.45]**), CO No 5, art 9(1), (2) (at **[2.58]**), CO No 8, art 7 and Sch 2, para 116 (at **[2.88]** and **[2.91]**).
Schedule 25—Companies Act 1981, section 38, as originally enacted.	Repealed by CA 2006, as from 1 Oct 2009.

COMPANY DIRECTORS DISQUALIFICATION ACT 1986

(1986 c 46)

NOTES

This Act is reproduced as amended by: CA 1989; the Friendly Societies Act 1992; the Deregulation and Contracting Out Act 1994; the Youth Justice and Criminal Evidence Act 1999; the Insolvency Act 2000; the Enterprise Act 2002; the Communications Act 2003; the Water Act 2003; the Health and Social Care (Community Health and Standards) Act 2003; the Courts Act 2003; the Railways and Transport Safety Act 2003; the Companies (Audit, Investigations and Community Enterprise) Act 2004; the National Health Service (Consequential Provisions) Act 2006; the Companies Act 2006; the Tribunals, Courts and Enforcement Act 2007; the Banking Act 2009; the Co-operative and Community Benefit Societies and Credit Unions Act 2010; the Open-Ended Investment Companies (Investment Companies with Variable Capital) Regulations 1996, SI 1996/2827; the Open-Ended Investment Companies Regulations 2001, SI 2001/1228; the Financial Services and Markets Act 2000 (Consequential Amendments and Repeals) Order 2001, SI 2001/3649; the Enterprise Act 2002 (Insolvency) Order 2003, SI 2003/2096; the Insolvency Act 2000 (Company Directors Disqualification Undertakings) Order 2004, SI 2004/1941; the Companies Act 2006 (Commencement No 3, Consequential Amendments, Transitional Provisions and Savings) Order 2007, SI 2007/2194; the Companies Act 2006 (Consequential Amendments etc) Order 2008, SI 2008/948; the Building Societies (Insolvency and Special Administration) Order 2009, SI 2009/805; the Companies Act 2006 (Consequential Amendments, Transitional Provisions and Savings) Order 2009, SI 2009/1941.

References to "the European Community", "Community", etc: see the Treaty of Lisbon (Changes in Terminology) Order 2011, SI 2011/1043, which provides that (as from 22 April 2011) "EU" should be substituted for the word "Community" (subject to certain exceptions) in references to "Community treaties", "Community instrument", "Community obligation", "Community law", "Community legislation", etc.

Limited liability partnerships: the Limited Liability Partnerships Regulations 2001, SI 2001/1090, reg 4(2) (at **[10.816]**) provides that the provisions of this Act shall apply to limited liability partnerships, except where the context otherwise requires, with the general modifications specified in that paragraph. See also Sch 2, Pt II to the 2001 Regulations (at **[10.824]**) for specific modifications of Sch 1, Pt II to this Act.

European Economic Interest Groupings: as to the application of certain provisions of this Act to European Economic Interest Groupings, see the European Economic Interest Grouping Regulations 1989, SI 1989/638, reg 20.

Insolvent partnerships: as to the application of certain provisions of this Act to insolvent partnerships, see the Insolvent Partnerships Order 1994, SI 1994/2421, reg 16 (Application of Company Directors Disqualification Act 1986).

Official Receiver: as to the contracting out of certain functions of the Official Receiver conferred by or under this Act, see the Contracting Out (Functions of the Official Receiver) Order 1995, SI 1995/1386 at **[10.755]**.

ARRANGEMENT OF SECTIONS

Preliminary

SCHEDULES

An Act to consolidate certain enactments relating to the disqualification of persons from being directors of companies, and from being otherwise concerned with a company's affairs

[25 July 1986]

Preliminary

[5.48]
1　Disqualification orders: general
(1)　In the circumstances specified below in this Act a court may, and under [sections 6 and 9A] shall, make against a person a disqualification order, that is to say an order that [for a period specified in the order—
　　(a)　he shall not be a director of a company, act as receiver of a company's property or in any way, whether directly or indirectly, be concerned or take part in the promotion, formation or management of a company unless (in each case) he has the leave of the court, and
　　(b)　he shall not act as an insolvency practitioner.]
(2)　In each section of this Act which gives to a court power or, as the case may be, imposes on it the duty to make a disqualification order there is specified the maximum (and, in section 6, the minimum) period of disqualification which may or (as the case may be) must be imposed by means of the order [and, unless the court otherwise orders, the period of disqualification so imposed shall begin at the end of the period of 21 days beginning with the date of the order].
(3)　Where a disqualification order is made against a person who is already subject to such an order [or to a disqualification undertaking], the periods specified in those orders [or, as the case may be, in the order and the undertaking] shall run concurrently.
(4)　A disqualification order may be made on grounds which are or include matters other than criminal convictions, notwithstanding that the person in respect of whom it is to be made may be criminally liable in respect of those matters.

NOTES
　　Sub-s (1): words in first pair of square brackets substituted by the Enterprise Act 2002, s 204(1), (3), as from 20 June 2003; words in second pair of square brackets substituted by the Insolvency Act 2000, s 5(1), as from 2 April 2001.
　　Sub-ss (2), (3): words in square brackets inserted by the Insolvency Act 2000, ss 5(2), 8, Sch 4, Pt I, paras 1, 2, as from 2 April 2001.

[5.49]
[1A　Disqualification undertakings: general
(1)　In the circumstances specified in sections 7 and 8 the Secretary of State may accept a disqualification undertaking, that is to say an undertaking by any person that, for a period specified in the undertaking, the person—
　　(a)　will not be a director of a company, act as receiver of a company's property or in any way, whether directly or indirectly, be concerned or take part in the promotion, formation or management of a company unless (in each case) he has the leave of a court, and
　　(b)　will not act as an insolvency practitioner.
(2)　The maximum period which may be specified in a disqualification undertaking is 15 years; and the minimum period which may be specified in a disqualification undertaking under section 7 is two years.
(3)　Where a disqualification undertaking by a person who is already subject to such an undertaking or to a disqualification order is accepted, the periods specified in those undertakings or (as the case may be) the undertaking and the order shall run concurrently.
(4)　In determining whether to accept a disqualification undertaking by any person, the Secretary of State may take account of matters other than criminal convictions, notwithstanding that the person may be criminally liable in respect of those matters.]

NOTES
　　Inserted by the Insolvency Act 2000, s 6(1), (2), as from 2 April 2001.

Disqualification for general misconduct in connection with companies

[5.50]
2　Disqualification on conviction of indictable offence
(1)　The court may make a disqualification order against a person where he is convicted of an indictable offence (whether on indictment or summarily) in connection with the promotion, formation, management[, liquidation or striking off] of a company [with the receivership of a company's property or with his being an administrative receiver of a company].
(2)　"The court" for this purpose means—
　　(a)　any court having jurisdiction to wind up the company in relation to which the offence was committed, or
　　(b)　the court by or before which the person is convicted of the offence, or
　　(c)　in the case of a summary conviction in England and Wales, any other magistrates' court acting [in the same local justice] area;
and for the purposes of this section the definition of "indictable offence" in Schedule 1 to the Interpretation Act 1978 applies for Scotland as it does for England and Wales.

(3) The maximum period of disqualification under this section is—
(a) where the disqualification order is made by a court of summary jurisdiction, 5 years, and
(b) in any other case, 15 years.

NOTES

Sub-s (1): words in first pair of square brackets substituted by the Deregulation and Contracting Out Act 1994, s 39, Sch 11, para 6, as from 1 July 1995; words in second pair of square brackets substituted by the Insolvency Act 2000, s 8, Sch 4, Pt I, paras 1, 3, as from 2 April 2001.

Sub-s (2): words in square brackets substituted by the Courts Act 2003, s 109(1), Sch 8, para 300, as from 1 April 2005.

[5.51]
3 Disqualification for persistent breaches of companies legislation

(1) The court may make a disqualification order against a person where it appears to it that he has been persistently in default in relation to provisions of the companies legislation requiring any return, account or other document to be filed with, delivered or sent, or notice of any matter to be given, to the registrar of companies.

(2) On an application to the court for an order to be made under this section, the fact that a person has been persistently in default in relation to such provisions as are mentioned above may (without prejudice to its proof in any other manner) be conclusively proved by showing that in the 5 years ending with the date of the application he has been adjudged guilty (whether or not on the same occasion) of three or more defaults in relation to those provisions.

(3) A person is to be treated under subsection (2) as being adjudged guilty of a default in relation to any provision of that legislation if—
(a) he is convicted (whether on indictment or summarily) of an offence consisting in a contravention of or failure to comply with that provision (whether on his own part or on the part of any company), or
(b) a default order is made against him, that is to say an order under any of the following provisions—
(i) [section 452 of the Companies Act 2006] (order requiring delivery of company accounts),
[(ia) [section 456] of that Act (order requiring preparation of revised accounts),]
(ii) [section 1113 of that Act (enforcement of company's filing obligations)],
(iii) section 41 of the Insolvency Act [1986] (enforcement of receiver's or manager's duty to make returns), or
(iv) section 170 of that Act (corresponding provision for liquidator in winding up),
in respect of any such contravention of or failure to comply with that provision (whether on his own part or on the part of any company).

(4) In this section "the court" means any court having jurisdiction to wind up any of the companies in relation to which the offence or other default has been or is alleged to have been committed.

[(4A) In this section "the companies legislation" means the Companies Acts and Parts 1 to 7 of the Insolvency Act 1986 (company insolvency and winding up).]

(5) The maximum period of disqualification under this section is 5 years.

NOTES

Sub-s (3) is amended as follows:

Words in square brackets in paras (b)(i), (ia) substituted by the Companies Act 2006 (Consequential Amendments etc) Order 2008, SI 2008/948, art 3(1), Sch 1, Pt 2, para 106(1), (2)(a), (b), as from 6 April 2008 (for savings see art 6(4) of the 2008 Order (at **[4.280]**)) which provides that where by virtue of any transitional provision, a provision of the Companies Act 2006 has effect only (a) on or after a specified date, or (b) in relation to matters occurring or arising on or after a specified date, any amendment substituting or inserting a reference to that provision has effect correspondingly).

Para (b)(ia) originally inserted by CA 1989, s 23, Sch 10, para 35(2)(b), as from 7 January 1991.

Words in square brackets in para (b)(ii) substituted by the Companies Act 2006 (Consequential Amendments, Transitional Provisions and Savings) Order 2009, SI 2009/1941, art 2(1), Sch 1, para 85(1), (2)(a)(i), as from 1 October 2009.

"1986" in square brackets in para (b)(iii) inserted by SI 2009/1941, art 2(1), Sch 1, para 85(1), (2)(a)(ii), as from 1 October 2009.

Sub-s (4A): inserted by SI 2009/1941, art 2(1), Sch 1, para 85(1), (2)(b), as from 1 October 2009.

[5.52]
4 Disqualification for fraud, etc, in winding up

(1) The court may make a disqualification order against a person if, in the course of the winding up of a company, it appears that he—
(a) has been guilty of an offence for which he is liable (whether he has been convicted or not) under [section 993 of the Companies Act 2006] (fraudulent trading), or
(b) has otherwise been guilty, while an officer or liquidator of the company [receiver of the company's property or administrative receiver of the company], of any fraud in relation to the company or of any breach of his duty as such officer, liquidator, [receiver or administrative receiver].

(2)   In this section "the court" means any court having jurisdiction to wind up any of the companies in relation to which the offence or other default has been or is alleged to have been committed; and "officer" includes a shadow director.

(3)   The maximum period of disqualification under this section is 15 years.

NOTES

Sub-s (1): words in first pair of square brackets substituted by the Companies Act 2006 (Commencement No 3, Consequential Amendments, Transitional Provisions and Savings) Order 2007, SI 2007/2194, art 10(3), Sch 4, Pt 3, para 46, as from 1 October 2007; words in second pair of square brackets substituted by the Insolvency Act 2000, s 8, Sch 4, Pt I, paras 1, 4, as from 2 April 2001.

[5.53]
5   Disqualification on summary conviction
(1)   An offence counting for the purposes of this section is one of which a person is convicted (either on indictment or summarily) in consequence of a contravention of, or failure to comply with, any provision of the companies legislation requiring a return, account or other document to be filed with, delivered or sent, or notice of any matter to be given, to the registrar of companies (whether the contravention or failure is on the person's own part or on the part of any company).
(2)   Where a person is convicted of a summary offence counting for those purposes, the court by which he is convicted (or, in England and Wales, any other magistrates' court acting [in the same local justice] area) may make a disqualification order against him if the circumstances specified in the next subsection are present.
(3)   Those circumstances are that, during the 5 years ending with the date of the conviction, the person has had made against him, or has been convicted of, in total not less than 3 default orders and offences counting for the purposes of this section; and those offences may include that of which he is convicted as mentioned in subsection (2) and any other offence of which he is convicted on the same occasion.
(4)   For the purposes of this section—
    (a)   the definition of "summary offence" in Schedule 1 to the Interpretation Act 1978 applies for Scotland as for England and Wales, and
    (b)   "default order" means the same as in section 3(3)(b).
[(4A)   In this section "the companies legislation" means the Companies Acts and Parts 1 to 7 of the Insolvency Act 1986 (company insolvency and winding up).]
(5)   The maximum period of disqualification under this section is 5 years.

NOTES

Sub-s (2): words in square brackets substituted by the Courts Act 2003, s 109(1), Sch 8, para 300, as from 1 April 2005.
Sub-s (4A): inserted by the Companies Act 2006 (Consequential Amendments, Transitional Provisions and Savings) Order 2009, SI 2009/1941, art 2(1), Sch 1, para 85(1), (3), as from 1 October 2009.

Disqualification for unfitness

[5.54]
6   Duty of court to disqualify unfit directors of insolvent companies
(1)   The court shall make a disqualification order against a person in any case where, on an application under this section, it is satisfied—
    (a)   that he is or has been a director of a company which has at any time become insolvent (whether while he was a director or subsequently), and
    (b)   that his conduct as a director of that company (either taken alone or taken together with his conduct as a director of any other company or companies) makes him unfit to be concerned in the management of a company.
(2)   For the purposes of this section and the next, a company becomes insolvent if—
    (a)   the company goes into liquidation at a time when its assets are insufficient for the payment of its debts and other liabilities and the expenses of the winding up,
    [(b)   the company enters administration,] or
    (c)   an administrative receiver of the company is appointed;
and references to a person's conduct as a director of any company or companies include, where that company or any of those companies has become insolvent, that person's conduct in relation to any matter connected with or arising out of the insolvency of that company.
[(3)   In this section and section 7(2), "the court" means—
    (a)   where the company in question is being or has been wound up by the court, that court,
    (b)   where the company in question is being or has been wound up voluntarily, any court which has or (as the case may be) had jurisdiction to wind it up,
    [(c)   where neither paragraph (a) nor (b) applies but an administrator or administrative receiver has at any time been appointed in respect of the company in question, any court which has jurisdiction to wind it up.]
(3A)   Sections 117 and 120 of the Insolvency Act 1986 (jurisdiction) shall apply for the purposes of subsection (3) as if the references in the definitions of "registered office" to the presentation of the petition for winding up were references—
    (a)   in a case within paragraph (b) of that subsection, to the passing of the resolution for voluntary winding up,

[(b) in a case within paragraph (c) of that subsection, to the appointment of the administrator or (as the case may be) administrative receiver.]

(3B) Nothing in subsection (3) invalidates any proceedings by reason of their being taken in the wrong court; and proceedings—

(a) for or in connection with a disqualification order under this section, or

(b) in connection with a disqualification undertaking accepted under section 7,

may be retained in the court in which the proceedings were commenced, although it may not be the court in which they ought to have been commenced.

(3C) In this section and section 7, "director" includes a shadow director.]

(4) Under this section the minimum period of disqualification is 2 years, and the maximum period is 15 years.

NOTES

Sub-s (2): para (b) substituted by the Enterprise Act 2002, s 248(3), Sch 17, paras 40, 41(a), as from 15 September 2003 (for savings and transitional provisions, see the note to the Insolvency Act 1986, s 8 at [**9.105**]).

Sub-ss (3), (3A)–(3C): substituted, for original sub-s (3), by the Insolvency Act 2000, s 8, Sch 4, Pt I, paras 1, 5, as from 2 April 2001; sub-ss (3)(c), (3A)(b) further substituted by the Enterprise Act 2002, s 248(3), Sch 17, paras 40, 41(b), (c), as from 15 September 2003 (for savings and transitional provisions, see the note to the Insolvency Act 1986, s 8 at [**9.105**]).

[**5.55**]

7 [Disqualification order or undertaking; and reporting provisions]

(1) If it appears to the Secretary of State that it is expedient in the public interest that a disqualification order under section 6 should be made against any person, an application for the making of such an order against that person may be made—

(a) by the Secretary of State, or

(b) if the Secretary of State so directs in the case of a person who is or has been a director of a company which is being [or has been] wound up by the court in England and Wales, by the official receiver.

(2) Except with the leave of the court, an application for the making under that section of a disqualification order against any person shall not be made after the end of the period of 2 years beginning with the day on which the company of which that person is or has been a director became insolvent.

[(2A) If it appears to the Secretary of State that the conditions mentioned in section 6(1) are satisfied as respects any person who has offered to give him a disqualification undertaking, he may accept the undertaking if it appears to him that it is expedient in the public interest that he should do so (instead of applying, or proceeding with an application, for a disqualification order).]

(3) If it appears to the office-holder responsible under this section, that is to say—

(a) in the case of a company which is being wound up by the court in England and Wales, the official receiver,

(b) in the case of a company which is being wound up otherwise, the liquidator,

[(c) in the case of a company which is in administration, the administrator,] or

(d) in the case of a company of which there is an administrative receiver, that receiver,

that the conditions mentioned in section 6(1) are satisfied as respects a person who is or has been a director of that company, the officer-holder shall forthwith report the matter to the Secretary of State.

(4) The Secretary of State or the official receiver may require the liquidator, administrator or administrative receiver of a company, or the former liquidator, administrator or administrative receiver of a company—

(a) to furnish him with such information with respect to any person's conduct as a director of the company, and

(b) to produce and permit inspection of such books, papers and other records relevant to that person's conduct as such a director,

as the Secretary of State or the official receiver may reasonably require for the purpose of determining whether to exercise, or of exercising, any function of his under this section.

NOTES

Section heading: substituted by the Insolvency Act 2000, s 8, Sch 4, Pt I, paras 1, 6(b), as from 2 April 2001.

Sub-s (1): words in square brackets inserted by the Insolvency Act 2000, s 8, Sch 4, Pt I, paras 1, 6(a), as from 2 April 2001.

Sub-s (2A): inserted by the Insolvency Act 2000, s 6(1), (3), as from 2 April 2001.

Sub-s (3): para (c) substituted by the Enterprise Act 2002, s 248(3), Sch 17, paras 40, 42, as from 15 September 2003 (for savings and transitional provisions, see the note to the Insolvency Act 1986, s 8 at [**9.105**]).

[**5.56**]

8 Disqualification after investigation of company

[(1) If it appears to the Secretary of State from investigative material that it is expedient in the public interest that a disqualification order should be made against a person who is, or has been, a director or shadow director of a company, he may apply to the court for such an order.

(1A) "Investigative material" means—

[(a) a report made by inspectors under—

(i) section 437 of the Companies Act 1985, or

       (ii)   section 167, 168, 169 or 284 of the Financial Services and Markets Act 2000; and]

   (b)   information or documents obtained under—

       (i)   section [437, 446E,] 447[, 448[, 451A] or 453A] of the Companies Act 1985;

       (ii)   section 2 of the Criminal Justice Act 1987;

       (iii)   section 28 of the Criminal Law (Consolidation) (Scotland) Act 1995;

       (iv)   section 83 of the Companies Act 1989; or

       (v)   section 165, 171, 172, 173 or 175 of the Financial Services and Markets Act 2000.]

(2)   The court may make a disqualification order against a person where, on an application under this section, it is satisfied that his conduct in relation to the company makes him unfit to be concerned in the management of a company.

[(2A)   Where it appears to the Secretary of State from such report, information or documents that, in the case of a person who has offered to give him a disqualification undertaking—

   (a)   the conduct of the person in relation to a company of which the person is or has been a director or shadow director makes him unfit to be concerned in the management of a company, and

   (b)   it is expedient in the public interest that he should accept the undertaking (instead of applying, or proceeding with an application, for a disqualification order),

he may accept the undertaking.]

(3)   In this section "the court" means the High Court or, in Scotland, the Court of Session.

(4)   The maximum period of disqualification under this section is 15 years.

NOTES

Sub-s (1): substituted, together with sub-s (1A) for original sub-s (1), by the Financial Services and Markets Act 2000 (Consequential Amendments and Repeals) Order 2001, SI 2001/3649, art 39, as from 1 December 2001.

Sub-s (1A): substituted as noted above; para (a) substituted by the Companies Act 2006 (Consequential Amendments, Transitional Provisions and Savings) Order 2009, SI 2009/1941, art 2(1), Sch 1, para 85(1), (4), as from 1 October 2009; figures in first pair and third (inner) pair of square brackets in para (b) inserted by the Companies Act 2006, s 1039, as from 1 October 2007; words in second (outer) pair of square brackets in that paragraph substituted by the Companies (Audit, Investigations and Community Enterprise) Act 2004, s 25, Sch 2, Pt 3, para 28, as from 6 April 2005.

Sub-s (2A): inserted by the Insolvency Act 2000, s 6(1), (4), as from 2 April 2001.

[5.57]

[8A   Variation etc of disqualification undertaking

(1)   The court may, on the application of a person who is subject to a disqualification undertaking—

   (a)   reduce the period for which the undertaking is to be in force, or

   (b)   provide for it to cease to be in force.

(2)   On the hearing of an application under subsection (1), the Secretary of State shall appear and call the attention of the court to any matters which seem to him to be relevant, and may himself give evidence or call witnesses.

[(2A)   Subsection (2) does not apply to an application in the case of an undertaking given under section 9B, and in such a case on the hearing of the application whichever of the OFT or a specified regulator (within the meaning of section 9E) accepted the undertaking—

   (a)   must appear and call the attention of the court to any matters which appear to it or him (as the case may be) to be relevant;

   (b)   may give evidence or call witnesses.]

[(3)   In this section "the court"—

   (a)   in the case of an undertaking given under section 9B means the High Court or (in Scotland) the Court of Session;

   (b)   in any other case has the same meaning as in section 7(2) or 8 (as the case may be).]

NOTES

Inserted by the Insolvency Act 2000, s 6(1), (5), as from 2 April 2001.

Sub-s (2A): inserted by the Enterprise Act 2002, s 204(1), (4), as from 20 June 2003.

Sub-s (3): substituted by the Enterprise Act 2002, s 204(1), (5), as from 20 June 2003.

[5.58]

9   Matters for determining unfitness of directors

(1)   Where it falls to a court to determine whether a person's conduct as a director . . . of any particular company or companies makes him unfit to be concerned in the management of a company, the court shall, as respects his conduct as a director of that company or, as the case may be, each of those companies, have regard in particular—

   (a)   to the matters mentioned in Part I of Schedule 1 to this Act, and

   (b)   where the company has become insolvent, to the matters mentioned in Part II of that Schedule;

and references in that Schedule to the director and the company are to be read accordingly.

[(1A)   In determining whether he may accept a disqualification undertaking from any person the Secretary of State shall, as respects the person's conduct as a director of any company concerned, have regard in particular—

   (a)   to the matters mentioned in Part I of Schedule 1 to this Act, and

(b) where the company has become insolvent, to the matters mentioned in Part II of that Schedule;

and references in that Schedule to the director and the company are to be read accordingly.]

(2) Section 6(2) applies for the purposes of this section and Schedule 1 as it applies for the purposes of sections 6 and 7 [and in this section and that Schedule "director" includes a shadow director].

(3) . . .

(4) The Secretary of State may by order modify any of the provisions of Schedule 1; and such an order may contain such transitional provisions as may appear to the Secretary of State necessary or expedient.

(5) The power to make orders under this section is exercisable by statutory instrument subject to annulment in pursuance of a resolution of either House of Parliament.

NOTES

Sub-s (1): words omitted repealed by the Insolvency Act 2000, ss 8, 15(1), Sch 4, Pt I, paras 1, 7(a), Sch 5, as from 2 April 2001.

Sub-s (1A): inserted by the Insolvency Act 2000, s 6(1), (6), as from 2 April 2001.

Sub-s (2): words in square brackets added by the Insolvency Act 2000, s 8, Sch 4, Pt I, paras 1, 7(b), as from 2 April 2001.

Sub-s (3): repealed by the Companies Act 2006 (Consequential Amendments, Transitional Provisions and Savings) Order 2009, SI 2009/1941, art 2(1), Sch 1, para 85(1), (5), as from 1 October 2009.

[Disqualification for competition infringements

[5.59]

9A Competition disqualification order

(1) The court must make a disqualification order against a person if the following two conditions are satisfied in relation to him.

(2) The first condition is that an undertaking which is a company of which he is a director commits a breach of competition law.

(3) The second condition is that the court considers that his conduct as a director makes him unfit to be concerned in the management of a company.

(4) An undertaking commits a breach of competition law if it engages in conduct which infringes any of the following—

(a) the Chapter 1 prohibition (within the meaning of the Competition Act 1998) (prohibition on agreements, etc preventing, restricting or distorting competition);

(b) the Chapter 2 prohibition (within the meaning of that Act) (prohibition on abuse of a dominant position);

(c) Article 81 of the Treaty establishing the European Community (prohibition on agreements, etc preventing, restricting or distorting competition);

(d) Article 82 of that Treaty (prohibition on abuse of a dominant position).

(5) For the purpose of deciding under subsection (3) whether a person is unfit to be concerned in the management of a company the court—

(a) must have regard to whether subsection (6) applies to him;

(b) may have regard to his conduct as a director of a company in connection with any other breach of competition law;

(c) must not have regard to the matters mentioned in Schedule 1.

(6) This subsection applies to a person if as a director of the company—

(a) his conduct contributed to the breach of competition law mentioned in subsection (2);

(b) his conduct did not contribute to the breach but he had reasonable grounds to suspect that the conduct of the undertaking constituted the breach and he took no steps to prevent it;

(c) he did not know but ought to have known that the conduct of the undertaking constituted the breach.

(7) For the purposes of subsection (6)(a) it is immaterial whether the person knew that the conduct of the undertaking constituted the breach.

(8) For the purposes of subsection (4)(a) or (c) references to the conduct of an undertaking are references to its conduct taken with the conduct of one or more other undertakings.

(9) The maximum period of disqualification under this section is 15 years.

(10) An application under this section for a disqualification order may be made by the OFT or by a specified regulator.

(11) Section 60 of the Competition Act 1998 (c 41) (consistent treatment of questions arising under United Kingdom and Community law) applies in relation to any question arising by virtue of subsection (4)(a) or (b) above as it applies in relation to any question arising under Part 1 of that Act.]

NOTES

Inserted, together with preceding heading and ss 9B–9E, by the Enterprise Act 2002, s 204(1), (2), as from 20 June 2003.

[5.60]

[9B Competition undertakings

(1) This section applies if—

(a)   the OFT or a specified regulator thinks that in relation to any person an undertaking which is a company of which he is a director has committed or is committing a breach of competition law,

(b)   the OFT or the specified regulator thinks that the conduct of the person as a director makes him unfit to be concerned in the management of a company, and

(c)   the person offers to give the OFT or the specified regulator (as the case may be) a disqualification undertaking.

(2)   The OFT or the specified regulator (as the case may be) may accept a disqualification undertaking from the person instead of applying for or proceeding with an application for a disqualification order.

(3)   A disqualification undertaking is an undertaking by a person that for the period specified in the undertaking he will not—

(a)   be a director of a company;

(b)   act as receiver of a company's property;

(c)   in any way, whether directly or indirectly, be concerned or take part in the promotion, formation or management of a company;

(d)   act as an insolvency practitioner.

(4)   But a disqualification undertaking may provide that a prohibition falling within subsection (3)(a) to (c) does not apply if the person obtains the leave of the court.

(5)   The maximum period which may be specified in a disqualification undertaking is 15 years.

(6)   If a disqualification undertaking is accepted from a person who is already subject to a disqualification undertaking under this Act or to a disqualification order the periods specified in those undertakings or the undertaking and the order (as the case may be) run concurrently.

(7)   Subsections (4) to (8) of section 9A apply for the purposes of this section as they apply for the purposes of that section but in the application of subsection (5) of that section the reference to the court must be construed as a reference to the OFT or a specified regulator (as the case may be).]

NOTES

Inserted as noted to s 9A at **[5.59]**.

[5.61]

[9C   Competition investigations

(1)   If the OFT or a specified regulator has reasonable grounds for suspecting that a breach of competition law has occurred it or he (as the case may be) may carry out an investigation for the purpose of deciding whether to make an application under section 9A for a disqualification order.

(2)   For the purposes of such an investigation sections 26 to 30 of the Competition Act 1998 (c 41) apply to the OFT and the specified regulators as they apply to the OFT for the purposes of an investigation under section 25 of that Act.

(3)   Subsection (4) applies if as a result of an investigation under this section the OFT or a specified regulator proposes to apply under section 9A for a disqualification order.

(4)   Before making the application the OFT or regulator (as the case may be) must—

(a)   give notice to the person likely to be affected by the application, and

(b)   give that person an opportunity to make representations.]

NOTES

Inserted as noted to s 9A at **[5.59]**.

[5.62]

[9D   Co-ordination

(1)   The Secretary of State may make regulations for the purpose of co-ordinating the performance of functions under sections 9A to 9C (relevant functions) which are exercisable concurrently by two or more persons.

(2)   Section 54(5) to (7) of the Competition Act 1998 (c 41) applies to regulations made under this section as it applies to regulations made under that section and for that purpose in that section—

(a)   references to Part 1 functions must be read as references to relevant functions;

(b)   references to a regulator must be read as references to a specified regulator;

(c)   a competent person also includes any of the specified regulators.

(3)   The power to make regulations under this section must be exercised by statutory instrument subject to annulment in pursuance of a resolution of either House of Parliament.

(4)   Such a statutory instrument may—

(a)   contain such incidental, supplemental, consequential and transitional provision as the Secretary of State thinks appropriate;

(b)   make different provision for different cases.]

NOTES

Inserted as noted to s 9A at **[5.59]**.

[5.63]
[9E Interpretation
(1)   This section applies for the purposes of sections 9A to 9D.
(2)   Each of the following is a specified regulator for the purposes of a breach of competition law
in relation to a matter in respect of which he or it has a function—
  [(a)   the Office of Communications;]
  (b)   the Gas and Electricity Markets Authority;
  [(c)   the Water Services Regulation Authority;]
  (d)   [the Office of Rail Regulation];
  (e)   the Civil Aviation Authority.
(3)   The court is the High Court or (in Scotland) the Court of Session.
(4)   Conduct includes omission.
(5)   Director includes shadow director.]

NOTES
  Inserted as noted to s 9A at **[5.59]**.
  Sub-s (2): para (a) substituted by the Communications Act 2003, s 406, Sch 17, para 83, as from 29 December 2003; para (c)
substituted by the Water Act 2003, s 101(1), Sch 7, Pt 2, para 25, as from 1 April 2006; words in square brackets in para (d)
substituted by the Railways and Transport Safety Act 2003, s 16, Sch 2, Pt 2. para 19(j), as from 5 July 2004.

Other cases of disqualification

[5.64]
10   Participation in wrongful trading
(1)   Where the court makes a declaration under section 213 or 214 of the Insolvency Act [1986]
that a person is liable to make a contribution to a company's assets, then, whether or not an
application for such an order is made by any person, the court may, if it thinks fit, also make a
disqualification order against the person to whom the declaration relates.
(2)   The maximum period of disqualification under this section is 15 years.

NOTES
  Sub-s (1): date in square brackets inserted by the Companies Act 2006 (Consequential Amendments, Transitional Provisions
and Savings) Order 2009, SI 2009/1941, art 2(1), Sch 1, para 85(1), (6), as from 1 October 2009.

[5.65]
11   Undischarged bankrupts
[(1)   It is an offence for a person to act as director of a company or directly or indirectly to take
part in or be concerned in the promotion, formation or management of a company, without the leave
of the court, at a time when—
  (a)   he is an undischarged bankrupt,
  [(aa) a moratorium period under a debt relief order applies in relation to him,] or
  (b)   a bankruptcy restrictions order [or a debt relief restrictions order] is in force in respect of
        him.]
(2)   "The court" for this purpose is the court by which the person was adjudged bankrupt or, in
Scotland, sequestration of his estates was awarded.
(3)   In England and Wales, the leave of the court shall not be given unless notice of intention to
apply for it has been served on the official receiver; and it is the latter's duty, if he is of opinion that
it is contrary to the public interest that the application should be granted, to attend on the hearing
of the application and oppose it.
[(4)   In this section "company" includes a company incorporated outside Great Britain that has an
established place of business in Great Britain.]

NOTES
  Sub-s (1): substituted, in relation to England and Wales only, by the Enterprise Act 2002, s 257(3), Sch 21, para 5, as from
1 April 2004 (the original sub-s (1) is set out below); para (aa) inserted, and words in square brackets in para (b) inserted, by
the Tribunals, Courts and Enforcement Act 2007, s 108(3), Sch 20, Pt 2, para 16, as from 6 April 2009.
  Sub-s (1) as originally enacted read as follows—

    "(1)   It is an offence for a person who is an undischarged bankrupt to act as director of, or directly or indirectly to take
    part in or be concerned in the promotion, formation or management of, a company, except with the leave of the court.".

  Sub-s (4): added by the Companies Act 2006 (Consequential Amendments, Transitional Provisions and Savings) Order 2009,
SI 2009/1941, art 2(1), Sch 1, para 85(1), (7), as from 1 October 2009.

[5.66]
12   *Failure to pay under county court administration order*
*(1)   The following has effect where a court under section 429 of the Insolvency Act revokes an
administration order under Part VI of the County Courts Act 1984.*
(2)   A person to whom *that section applies by virtue of the order under section 429(2)(b)* shall not,
except with the leave of the court which made the order, act as director or liquidator of, or directly
or indirectly take part or be concerned in the promotion, formation or management of, a company.

NOTES

Section heading: for the words in italics there are substituted the words "Disabilities on revocation of administration order" by the Tribunals, Courts and Enforcement Act 2007, s 106, Sch 16, para 5(1), (2), as from a day to be appointed (except in relation to any case in which an administration order was made, or an application for such an order was made, before the day on which s 106 comes into force).

Sub-s (1): repealed by the Tribunals, Courts and Enforcement Act 2007, ss 106, 146, Sch 16, para 5(1), (3), Sch 23, Pt 5, as from a day to be appointed (subject to the same exception as noted above).

Sub-s (2): for the words in italics there are substituted the words "section 429 of the Insolvency Act applies by virtue of an order under subsection (2) of that section" by the Tribunals, Courts and Enforcement Act 2007, s 106, Sch 16, para 5(1), (4), as from a day to be appointed (subject to the same exception as noted above). Note that the Companies Act 2006 (Consequential Amendments, Transitional Provisions and Savings) Order 2009, SI 2009/1941, art 2(1), Sch 1, para 85(1), (6) provides that "1986" should be inserted after the words "the Insolvency Act" in sub-s (2) of this section (as from 1 October 2009). It is assumed that this amendment should take effect after the substitution noted *ante* comes into force.

[5.67]
[12A　Northern Irish disqualification orders
A person subject to a disqualification order under [the Company Directors Disqualification (Northern Ireland) Order 2002]—

(a)　shall not be a director of a company, act as receiver of a company's property or in any way, whether directly or indirectly, be concerned or take part in the promotion, formation or management of a company unless (in each case) he has the leave of the High Court of Northern Ireland, and

(b)　shall not act as an insolvency practitioner.]

NOTES

Inserted by the Insolvency Act 2000, s 7(1), as from 2 April 2001, except in relation to a person subject to a disqualification order under the Companies (Northern Ireland) Order 1989, Part II made before that date.

Words in square brackets substituted by the Companies Act 2006 (Consequential Amendments, Transitional Provisions and Savings) Order 2009, SI 2009/1941, art 2(1), Sch 1, para 85(1), (8), as from 1 October 2009.

[5.68]
[12B　Northern Irish disqualification undertakings
A person subject to a disqualification undertaking under the Company Directors Disqualification (Northern Ireland) Order 2002—

(a)　shall not be a director of a company, act as receiver of a company's property or in any way, whether directly or indirectly, be concerned or take part in the promotion, formation or management of a company unless (in each case) he has the leave of the High Court of Northern Ireland, and

(b)　shall not act as an insolvency practitioner.]

NOTES

Inserted by the Insolvency Act 2000 (Company Directors Disqualification Undertakings) Order 2004, SI 2004/1941, art 2(1), (2), as from 1 September 2004, in relation to disqualification undertakings under the Company Directors Disqualification (Northern Ireland) Order 2002 accepted on or after that date.

Consequences of contravention

[5.69]
13　Criminal penalties
If a person acts in contravention of a disqualification order or [disqualification undertaking or in contravention] of section 12(2)[, 12A or 12B], or is guilty of an offence under section 11, he is liable—

(a)　on conviction on indictment, to imprisonment for not more than 2 years or a fine, or both; and

(b)　on summary conviction, to imprisonment for not more than 6 months or a fine not exceeding the statutory maximum, or both.

NOTES

Words in first pair of square brackets inserted by the Insolvency Act 2000, s 8, Sch 4, Pt I, paras 1, 8, as from 2 April 2001; words in second pair of square brackets substituted by the Insolvency Act 2000 (Company Directors Disqualification Undertakings) Order 2004, SI 2004/1941, art 2(1), (3), as from 1 September 2004, in relation to disqualification undertakings under the Company Directors Disqualification (Northern Ireland) Order 2002 accepted on or after that date.

[5.70]
14　Offences by body corporate
(1)　Where a body corporate is guilty of an offence of acting in contravention of a disqualification order [or disqualification undertaking or in contravention of section 12A] [or 12B], and it is proved that the offence occurred with the consent or connivance of, or was attributable to any neglect on the part of any director, manager, secretary or other similar officer of the body corporate, or any person who was purporting to act in any such capacity he, as well as the body corporate, is guilty of the offence and liable to be proceeded against and punished accordingly.

(2)   Where the affairs of a body corporate are managed by its members, subsection (1) applies in relation to the acts and defaults of a member in connection with his functions of management as if he were a director of the body corporate.

NOTES

Sub-s (1): words in first pair of square brackets inserted by the Insolvency Act 2000, s 8, Sch 4, Pt I, paras 1, 9, as from 2 April 2001; words in second pair of square brackets inserted by the Insolvency Act 2000 (Company Directors Disqualification Undertakings) Order 2004, SI 2004/1941, art 2(1), (4), as from 1 September 2004, in relation to disqualification undertakings under the Company Directors Disqualification (Northern Ireland) Order 2002 accepted on or after that date.

[5.71]
15   Personal liability for company's debts where person acts while disqualified
(1)   A person is personally responsible for all the relevant debts of a company if at any time—
   (a)   in contravention of a disqualification order or [disqualification undertaking or in contravention] of section 11[, 12A or 12B] of this Act he is involved in the management of the company, or
   [(b)   as a person who is involved in the management of the company, he acts or is willing to act on instructions given without the leave of the court by a person whom he knows at that time—
      (i)   to be the subject of a disqualification order made or disqualification undertaking accepted under this Act or under the Company Directors Disqualification (Northern Ireland) Order 2002, or
      (ii)   to be an undischarged bankrupt.]
(2)   Where a person is personally responsible under this section for the relevant debts of a company, he is jointly and severally liable in respect of those debts with the company and any other person who, whether under this section or otherwise, is so liable.
(3)   For the purposes of this section the relevant debts of a company are—
   (a)   in relation to a person who is personally responsible under paragraph (a) of subsection (1), such debts and other liabilities of the company as are incurred at a time when that person was involved in the management of the company, and
   (b)   in relation to a person who is personally responsible under paragraph (b) of that subsection, such debts and other liabilities of the company as are incurred at a time when that person was acting or was willing to act on instructions given as mentioned in that paragraph.
(4)   For the purposes of this section, a person is involved in the management of a company if he is a director of the company or if he is concerned, whether directly or indirectly, or takes part, in the management of the company.
[(5)   For the purposes of this section a person who, as a person involved in the management of a company, has at any time acted on instructions given without the leave of the court by a person whom he knew at that time—
   (a)   to be the subject of a disqualification order made or disqualification undertaking accepted under this Act or under the Company Directors Disqualification (Northern Ireland) Order 2002, or
   (b)   to be an undischarged bankrupt,
is presumed, unless the contrary is shown, to have been willing at any time thereafter to act on any instructions given by that person.]

NOTES

Sub-s (1): words in first pair of square brackets inserted by the Insolvency Act 2000, s 8, Sch 4, Pt I, paras 1, 10, as from 2 April 2001; words in second pair of square brackets substituted by the Insolvency Act 2000 (Company Directors Disqualification Undertakings) Order 2004, SI 2004/1941, art 2(1), (5)(a), as from 1 September 2004, in relation to disqualification undertakings under the Company Directors Disqualification (Northern Ireland) Order 2002 accepted on or after that date; para (b) substituted by the Companies Act 2006 (Consequential Amendments, Transitional Provisions and Savings) Order 2009, SI 2009/1941, art 2(1), Sch 1, para 85(1), (9)(a), as from 1 October 2009.

Sub-s (5): substituted by SI 2009/1941, art 2(1), Sch 1, para 85(1), (9)(b), as from 1 October 2009.

Supplementary provisions

[5.72]
16   Application for disqualification order
(1)   A person intending to apply for the making of a disqualification order by the court having jurisdiction to wind up a company shall give not less than 10 days' notice of his intention to the person against whom the order is sought; and on the hearing of the application the last-mentioned person may appear and himself give evidence or call witnesses.
(2)   An application to a court with jurisdiction to wind up companies for the making against any person of a disqualification order under any of sections 2 to [4] may be made by the Secretary of State or the official receiver, or by the liquidator or any past or present member or creditor of any company in relation to which that person has committed or is alleged to have committed an offence or other default.
(3)   On the hearing of any application under this Act made by [a person falling within subsection (4)], the applicant shall appear and call the attention of the court to any matters which seem to him to be relevant, and may himself give evidence or call witnesses.

[(4)   The following fall within this subsection—
   (a)   the Secretary of State;
   (b)   the official receiver;
   (c)   the OFT;
   (d)   the liquidator;
   (e)   a specified regulator (within the meaning of section 9E).]

NOTES
  Sub-s (2): figure in square brackets substituted by the Insolvency Act 2000, s 8, Sch 4, Pt I, paras 1, 11, as from 2 April 2001.
  Sub-s (3): words in square brackets substituted by the Enterprise Act 2002, s 204(1), (6), as from 20 June 2003.
  Sub-s (4): added by the Enterprise Act 2002, s 204(1), (7), as from 20 June 2003.

[5.73]
[17   Application for leave under an order or undertaking
(1)   Where a person is subject to a disqualification order made by a court having jurisdiction to wind up companies, any application for leave for the purposes of section 1(1)(a) shall be made to that court.
(2)   Where—
   (a)   a person is subject to a disqualification order made under section 2 by a court other than a court having jurisdiction to wind up companies, or
   (b)   a person is subject to a disqualification order made under section 5,
any application for leave for the purposes of section 1(1)(a) shall be made to any court which, when the order was made, had jurisdiction to wind up the company (or, if there is more than one such company, any of the companies) to which the offence (or any of the offences) in question related.
(3)   Where a person is subject to a disqualification undertaking accepted at any time under section 7 or 8, any application for leave for the purposes of section 1A(1)(a) shall be made to any court to which, if the Secretary of State had applied for a disqualification order under the section in question at that time, his application could have been made.
[(3A)   Where a person is subject to a disqualification undertaking accepted at any time under section 9B any application for leave for the purposes of section 9B(4) must be made to the High Court or (in Scotland) the Court of Session.]
(4)   But where a person is subject to two or more disqualification orders or undertakings (or to one or more disqualification orders and to one or more disqualification undertakings), any application for leave for the purposes of section 1(1)(a) [1A(1)(a) or 9B(4)] shall be made to any court to which any such application relating to the latest order to be made, or undertaking to be accepted, could be made.
(5)   On the hearing of an application for leave for the purposes of section 1(1)(a) or 1A(1)(a), the Secretary of State shall appear and call the attention of the court to any matters which seem to him to be relevant, and may himself give evidence or call witnesses.
[(6)   Subsection (5) does not apply to an application for leave for the purposes of section 1(1)(a) if the application for the disqualification order was made under section 9A.
(7)   In such a case and in the case of an application for leave for the purposes of section 9B(4) on the hearing of the application whichever of the OFT or a specified regulator (within the meaning of section 9E) applied for the order or accepted the undertaking (as the case may be)—
   (a)   must appear and draw the attention of the court to any matters which appear to it or him (as the case may be) to be relevant;
   (b)   may give evidence or call witnesses.]]

NOTES
  Substituted by the Insolvency Act 2000, s 8, Sch 4, Pt I, paras 1, 12, as from 2 April 2001, subject to transitional provisions in relation to cases where a person subject to a disqualification order, made on the application of the Secretary of State, the official receiver or the liquidator, has applied for leave of the court under this section before that date.
  Sub-ss (3A), (6), (7): inserted and added respectively by the Enterprise Act 2002, s 204(1), (8), (10), as from 20 June 2003.
  Sub-s (4): words in square brackets substituted by the Enterprise Act 2002, s 204(1), (9), as from 20 June 2003.

[5.74]
18   [Register of disqualification orders and undertakings]
(1)   The Secretary of State may make regulations requiring officers of courts to furnish him with such particulars as the regulations may specify of cases in which—
   (a)   a disqualification order is made, or
   (b)   any action is taken by a court in consequence of which such an order [or a disqualification undertaking] is varied or ceases to be in force, or
   (c)   leave is granted by a court for a person subject to such an order to do any thing which otherwise the order prohibits him from doing; [or
   (d)   leave is granted by a court for a person subject to such an undertaking to do anything which otherwise the undertaking prohibits him from doing]
and the regulations may specify the time within which, and the form and manner in which, such particulars are to be furnished.

(2) The Secretary of State shall, from the particulars so furnished, continue to maintain the register of orders, and of cases in which leave has been granted as mentioned in subsection (1)(c) . . .

[(2A) The Secretary of State must include in the register such particulars as he considers appropriate of—
  (a) disqualification undertakings accepted by him under section 7 or 8;
  (b) disqualification undertakings accepted by the OFT or a specified regulator under section 9B;
  (c) cases in which leave has been granted as mentioned in subsection (1)(d).]

(3) When an order [or undertaking] of which entry is made in the register ceases to be in force, the Secretary of State shall delete the entry from the register and all particulars relating to it which have been furnished to him under this section or any previous corresponding provision [and, in the case of a disqualification undertaking, any other particulars he has included in the register].

(4) The register shall be open to inspection on payment of such fee as may be specified by the Secretary of State in regulations.

[(4A) Regulations under this section may extend the preceding provisions of this section, to such extent and with such modifications as may be specified in the regulations, to disqualification orders . . . [or disqualification undertakings made under the Company Directors Disqualification (Northern Ireland) Order 2002].]

(5) Regulations under this section shall be made by statutory instrument subject to annulment in pursuance of a resolution of either House of Parliament.

NOTES

Section heading: substituted by the Insolvency Act 2000, s 8, Sch 4, Pt I, paras 1, 13(1), (6), as from 2 April 2001.

Sub-ss (1), (3): words in square brackets inserted by the Insolvency Act 2000, s 8, Sch 4, Pt I, paras 1, 13(1), (2), (4), as from 2 April 2001.

Sub-s (2): words omitted repealed by the Companies Act 2006 (Consequential Amendments, Transitional Provisions and Savings) Order 2009, SI 2009/1941, art 2(1), Sch 1, para 85(1), (10)(a), as from 1 October 2009.

Sub-s (2A): inserted by the Insolvency Act 2000, s 8, Sch 4, Pt I, paras 1, 13(1), (3), as from 2 April 2001; substituted by the Enterprise Act 2002, s 204(1), (11), as from 20 June 2003.

Sub-s (4A): inserted by the Insolvency Act 2000, s 8, Sch 4, Pt I, paras 1, 13(1), (5), as from 2 April 2001; words omitted repealed by SI 2009/1941, art 2(1), Sch 1, para 85(1), (10)(b), as from 1 October 2009; words in square brackets added by the Insolvency Act 2000 (Company Directors Disqualification Undertakings) Order 2004, SI 2004/1941, art 2(1), (6), as from 1 September 2004, in relation to disqualification undertakings under the Company Directors Disqualification (Northern Ireland) Order 2002 accepted on or after that date.

Regulations: the Companies (Disqualification Orders) Regulations 2009, SI 2000/2471 at [**6.161**].

[5.75]
19 Special savings from repealed enactments
Schedule 2 to this Act has effect—
  (a) in connection with certain transitional cases arising under sections 93 and 94 of the Companies Act 1981, so as to limit the power to make a disqualification order, or to restrict the duration of an order, by reference to events occurring or things done before those sections came into force,
  (b) to preserve orders made under section 28 of the Companies Act 1976 (repealed by the Act of 1981), and
  (c) to preclude any applications for a disqualification order under section 6 or 8, where the relevant company went into liquidation before 28th April 1986.

Miscellaneous and general

[5.76]
20 Admissibility in evidence of statements
[(1)] In any proceedings (whether or not under this Act), any statement made in pursuance of a requirement imposed by or under sections 6 to 10, 15 or 19(c) of, or Schedule 1 to, this Act, or by or under rules made for the purposes of this Act under the Insolvency Act [1986], may be used in evidence against any person making or concurring in making the statement.

[(2) However, in criminal proceedings in which any such person is charged with an offence to which this subsection applies—
  (a) no evidence relating to the statement may be adduced, and
  (b) no question relating to it may be asked,
by or on behalf of the prosecution, unless evidence relating to it is adduced, or a question relating to it is asked, in the proceedings by or on behalf of that person.

(3) Subsection (2) applies to any offence other than—
  (a) an offence which is—
    (i) created by rules made for the purposes of this Act under the Insolvency Act [1986], and
    (ii) designated for the purposes of this subsection by such rules or by regulations made by the Secretary of State;
  (b) an offence which is—
    (i) created by regulations made under any such rules, and

        (ii)   designated for the purposes of this subsection by such regulations;
  (c)   an offence under section 5 of the Perjury Act 1911 (false statements made otherwise than on oath); or
  (d)   an offence under section 44(2) of the Criminal Law (Consolidation) (Scotland) Act 1995 (false statements made otherwise than on oath).

(4)   Regulations under subsection (3)(a)(ii) shall be made by statutory instrument and, after being made, shall be laid before each House of Parliament.]

NOTES

Sub-s (1) numbered as such, and sub-ss (2)–(4) added, by the Youth Justice and Criminal Evidence Act 1999, s 59, Sch 3, para 8, as from 14 April 2000 (in relation to England and Wales), and 1 January 2001 (in relation to Scotland).

Date in square brackets in sub-ss (1), (3) inserted by the Companies Act 2006 (Consequential Amendments, Transitional Provisions and Savings) Order 2009, SI 2009/1941, art 2(1), Sch 1, para 85(1), (6), as from 1 October 2009.

[5.77]
[20A   Legal professional privilege

In proceedings against a person for an offence under this Act nothing in this Act is to be taken to require any person to disclose any information that he is entitled to refuse to disclose on grounds of legal professional privilege (in Scotland, confidentiality of communications).]

NOTES

Commencement: 6 April 2008.

Inserted by the Companies Act 2006 (Consequential Amendments etc) Order 2008, SI 2008/948, art 3(1), Sch 1, Pt 2, para 106(1), (3), as from 6 April 2008.

[5.78]
21   Interaction with Insolvency Act [1986]

(1)   References in this Act to the official receiver, in relation to the winding up of a company or the bankruptcy of an individual, are to any person who, by virtue of section 399 of the Insolvency Act [1986], is authorised to act as the official receiver in relation to that winding up or bankruptcy; and, in accordance with section 401(2) of that Act, references in this Act to an official receiver includes a person appointed as his deputy.

(2)   Sections [1A,] 6 to 10, [13, 14,] 15, 19(c) and 20 of, and Schedule 1 to, this Act [and sections 1 and 17 of this Act as they apply for the purposes of those provisions] are deemed included in Parts I to VII of the Insolvency Act [1986] for the purposes of the following sections of that Act—

    section 411 (power to make insolvency rules);
    section 414 (fees orders);
    section 420 (orders extending provisions about insolvent companies to insolvent partnerships);
    section 422 (modification of such provisions in their application to recognised banks); . . .

  . . .

(3)   Section 434 of that Act (Crown application) applies to sections [1A,] 6 to 10, [13, 14,] 15, 19(c) and 20 of, and Schedule 1 to, this Act [and sections 1 and 17 of this Act as they apply for the purposes of those provisions] as it does to the provisions of that Act which are there mentioned.

[(4)   For the purposes of summary proceedings in Scotland, section 431 of that Act applies to summary proceedings for an offence under section 11 or 13 of this Act as it applies to summary proceedings for an offence under Parts I to VII of that Act.]

NOTES

Section heading and sub-s (1): date in square brackets inserted by the Companies Act 2006 (Consequential Amendments, Transitional Provisions and Savings) Order 2009, SI 2009/1941, art 2(1), Sch 1, para 85(1), (6), as from 1 October 2009.

Sub-s (2): date in square brackets inserted by SI 2009/1941, art 2(1), Sch 1, para 85(1), (6), as from 1 October 2009; other words and figures in square brackets inserted by the Insolvency Act 2000, s 8, Sch 4, Pt I, paras 1, 14(1), (2), as from 2 April 2001; words omitted repealed by CA 1989, s 212, Sch 24, as from 1 March 1990.

Sub-s (3): words in square brackets inserted by the Insolvency Act 2000, s 8, Sch 4, Pt I, paras 1, 14(1), (3), as from 2 April 2001.

Sub-s (4): added by CA 1989, s 208, as from 1 March 1990.

As to Rules and Orders having effect under this section, see the notes to the sections listed in sub-s (2) above.

[5.79]
[21A   Bank insolvency

Section 121 of the Banking Act 2009 provides for this Act to apply in relation to bank insolvency as it applies in relation to liquidation.]

NOTES

Commencement: 21 February 2009.

Inserted by the Banking Act 2009, s 121(4), as from 21 February 2009.

[5.80]

[21B   Bank administration

Section 155 of the Banking Act 2009 provides for this Act to apply in relation to bank administration as it applies in relation to liquidation]

NOTES

Commencement: 21 February 2009.

Inserted by the Banking Act 2009, s 155(4), as from 21 February 2009.

[5.81]

[21C   Building society insolvency and special administration

Section 90E of the Building Societies Act 1986 provides for this Act to apply in relation to building society insolvency and building society special administration as it applies in relation to liquidation.]

NOTES

Commencement: 30 March 2009.

Inserted by the Building Societies (Insolvency and Special Administration) Order 2009, SI 2009/805, art 12, as from 30 March 2009.

[5.82]

22   Interpretation

(1)   This section has effect with respect to the meaning of expressions used in this Act, and applies unless the context otherwise requires.

[(2)   "Company" means—

   (a)   a company registered under the Companies Act 2006 in Great Britain, or

   (b)   a company that may be wound up under Part 5 of the Insolvency Act 1986 (unregistered companies).]

(3)   Section 247 in Part VII of the Insolvency Act [1986] (interpretation for the first Group of Parts of that Act) applies as regards references to a company's insolvency and to its going into liquidation; and "administrative receiver" has the meaning given by section 251 of that Act [and references to acting as an insolvency practitioner are to be read in accordance with section 388 of that Act].

(4)   "Director" includes any person occupying the position of director, by whatever name called

(5)   "Shadow director", in relation to a company, means a person in accordance with whose directions or instructions the directors of the company are accustomed to act (but so that a person is not deemed a shadow director by reason only that the directors act on advice given by him in a professional capacity).

[(6)   "Body corporate" and "officer" have the same meaning as in the Companies Acts (see section 1173(1) of the Companies Act 2006).]

[(7)   "The Companies Acts" has the meaning given by section 2(1) of the Companies Act 2006.]

[(8)   Any reference to provisions, or a particular provision, of the Companies Acts or the Insolvency Act 1986 includes the corresponding provisions or provision of corresponding earlier legislation.]

[(9)   Subject to the provisions of this section, expressions that are defined for the purposes of the Companies Acts [(see section 1174 of, and Schedule 8 to, the Companies Act 2006)] have the same meaning in this Act.]

[(10)   Any reference to acting as receiver—

   (a)   includes acting as manager or as both receiver and manager, but

   (b)   does not include acting as administrative receiver;

and "receivership" is to be read accordingly.]

NOTES

Sub-ss (2), (6)–(8): substituted by the Companies Act 2006 (Consequential Amendments, Transitional Provisions and Savings) Order 2009, SI 2009/1941, art 2(1), Sch 1, para 85(1), (11)(a)–(d), as from 1 October 2009.

Sub-s (3): date in square brackets inserted by SI 2009/1941, art 2(1), Sch 1, para 85(1), (6), as from 1 October 2009; other words in square brackets added by the Insolvency Act 2000, s 8, Sch 4, Pt I, paras 1, 15(1), (2), as from 2 April 2001.

Sub-s (4): words omitted repealed by the Insolvency Act 2000, ss 8, 15(1), Sch 4, Pt I, paras 1, 15(1), (3), Sch 5, as from 2 April 2001.

Sub-s (9): substituted by SI 2008/948, art 3(1), Sch 1, Pt 2, para 106(1), (4)(c), as from 6 April 2008; words in square brackets inserted by SI 2009/1941, art 2(1), Sch 1, para 85(1), (11)(e), as from 1 October 2009.

Sub-s (10): added by the Insolvency Act 2000, s 5(3), as from 2 April 2001.

[5.83]

[22A   Application of Act to building societies

(1)   This Act applies to building societies as it applies to companies.

(2)   References in this Act to a company, or to a director or an officer of a company include, respectively, references to a building society within the meaning of the Building Societies Act 1986 or to a director or officer, within the meaning of that Act, of a building society.

(3)　In relation to a building society the definition of "shadow director" in section 22(5) applies with the substitution of "building society" for "company".

(4)　In the application of Schedule 1 to the directors of a building society, references to provisions of [the Companies Act 2006 or the Insolvency Act 1986] include references to the corresponding provisions of the Building Societies Act 1986.]

NOTES

Inserted by CA 1989, s 211(3), as from 31 July 1990.

Sub-s (4): words in square brackets substituted by the Companies Act 2006 (Consequential Amendments, Transitional Provisions and Savings) Order 2009, SI 2009/1941, art 2(1), Sch 1, para 85(1), (12), as from 1 October 2009.

[5.84]

[22B　Application of Act to incorporated friendly societies

(1)　This Act applies to incorporated friendly societies as it applies to companies.

(2)　References in this Act to a company, or to a director or an officer of a company include, respectively, references to an incorporated friendly society within the meaning of the Friendly Societies Act 1992 or to a member of the committee of management or officer, within the meaning of that Act, of an incorporated friendly society.

(3)　In relation to an incorporated friendly society every reference to a shadow director shall be omitted.

(4)　In the application of Schedule 1 to the members of the committee of management of an incorporated friendly society, references to provisions of [the Companies Act 2006 or the Insolvency Act 1986] include references to the corresponding provisions of the Friendly Societies Act 1992.]

NOTES

Inserted by the Friendly Societies Act 1992, s 120(1), Sch 21, Pt I, para 8, as from 1 February 1993.

Sub-s (4): words in square brackets substituted by the Companies Act 2006 (Consequential Amendments, Transitional Provisions and Savings) Order 2009, SI 2009/1941, art 2(1), Sch 1, para 85(1), (12), as from 1 October 2009.

[5.85]

[22C　Application of Act to NHS foundation trusts

(1)　This Act applies to NHS foundation trusts as it applies to companies within the meaning of this Act.

(2)　References in this Act to a company, or to a director or officer of a company, include, respectively, references to an NHS foundation trust or to a director or officer of the trust; but references to shadow directors are omitted.

(3)　In the application of Schedule 1 to the directors of an NHS foundation trust, references to the provisions of [the Companies Act 2006 or the Insolvency Act 1986] include references to the corresponding provisions of [Chapter 5 of Part 2 of the National Health Service Act 2006].]

NOTES

Inserted by the Health and Social Care (Community Health and Standards) Act 2003, s 34, Sch 4, paras 67, 68, as from 1 April 2004.

Sub-s (3): words in first pair of square brackets substituted by the Companies Act 2006 (Consequential Amendments, Transitional Provisions and Savings) Order 2009, SI 2009/1941, art 2(1), Sch 1, para 85(1), (12), as from 1 October 2009; words in second pair of square brackets substituted by the National Health Service (Consequential Provisions) Act 2006, s 2, Sch 1, paras 91, 92, as from 1 March 2007.

[5.86]

[22D　Application of Act to open-ended investment companies

(1)　This Act applies to open-ended investment companies with the following modifications.

(2)　In section 8(1) (disqualification after investigation), the reference to investigative material shall be read as including a report made by inspectors under regulations made by virtue of section 262(2)(k) of the Financial Services and Markets Act 2000.

(3)　In the application of Part 1 of Schedule 1 (matters for determining unfitness of directors: matters applicable in all cases) in relation to a director of an open-ended investment company, a reference to a provision of the Companies Act 2006 is to be taken to be a reference to the corresponding provision of the Open-Ended Investment Companies Regulations 2001 or of rules made under regulation 6 of those Regulations.

(4)　In this section "open-ended investment company" has the meaning given by section 236 of the Financial Services and Markets Act 2000.]

NOTES

Commencement: 1 October 2009.

Inserted by the Companies Act 2006 (Consequential Amendments, Transitional Provisions and Savings) Order 2009, SI 2009/1941, art 2(1), Sch 1, para 85(1), (13), as from 1 October 2009.

[5.87]
[22E   Application of Act to societies registered under the Industrial and Provident Societies Act 1965
(1)   In this section "registered society" means a society registered or deemed to be registered under the Industrial and Provident Societies Act 1965 ("the 1965 Act").
(2)   This Act applies to registered societies as it applies to companies.
(3)   Accordingly, in this Act—
   (a)   references to a company include a registered society, and
   (b)   references to a director or an officer of a company include a member of the committee or an officer of a registered society.
In paragraph (b) "committee" and "officer" have the same meaning as in the 1965 Act: see section 74(1) of that Act.
(4)   As they apply in relation to registered societies, the provisions of this Act have effect with the following modifications—
   (a)   in section 2(1) (disqualification on conviction of indictable offence), the reference to striking off includes cancellation of the registration of a society under the 1965 Act;
   (b)   in section 3 (disqualification for persistent breaches) and section 5 (disqualification on summary conviction), references to the companies legislation shall be read as references to the legislation relating to registered societies;
   (c)   in section 8(1) (disqualification after investigation), the reference to investigative material shall be read as including—
      (i)   any report made under section 47 or 49(1) of the 1965 Act (inspection of books or appointment of inspector), and
      (ii)   any information, books, accounts or other documents obtained under section 48 of the 1965 Act;
   (d)   references to the registrar shall be read as references to the Financial Services Authority;
   (e)   references to a shadow director shall be disregarded.
(5)   In the application of Schedule 1 to the members of the committee of a registered society, references to provisions of the Companies Act 2006 shall be read as including references to the corresponding provisions of the legislation relating to registered societies.
(6)   In this section "the legislation relating to registered societies" means the Industrial and Provident Societies Acts 1965 to 2003, the Credit Unions Act 1979 and the Co-operative and Community Benefit Societies and Credit Unions Act 2010.]

NOTES
   Commencement: to be appointed.
   Inserted by the Co-operative and Community Benefit Societies and Credit Unions Act 2010, s 3, as from a day to be appointed.
   Industrial and Provident Societies Acts 1965 to 2003: see the Co-operative and Community Benefit Societies and Credit Unions Act 2010 which renames these Acts as the Co-operative and Community Benefit Societies and Credit Unions Acts 1965 to 2003. Note that the title of this section will change accordingly.

[5.88]
23   Transitional provisions, savings, repeals
(1)   The transitional provisions and savings in Schedule 3 to this Act have effect, and are without prejudice to anything in the Interpretation Act 1978 with regard to the effect of repeals.
(2)   The enactments specified in the second column of Schedule 4 to this Act are repealed to the extent specified in the third column of that Schedule.

[5.89]
24   Extent
(1)   This Act extends to England and Wales and to Scotland.
(2)   Nothing in this Act extends to Northern Ireland.

[5.90]
25   Commencement
This Act comes into force simultaneously with the Insolvency Act 1986.

[5.91]
26   Citation
This Act may be cited as the Company Directors Disqualification Act 1986.

SCHEDULES

SCHEDULE 1
MATTERS FOR DETERMINING UNFITNESS OF DIRECTORS
Section 9

PART I
MATTERS APPLICABLE IN ALL CASES

[5.92]
1. Any misfeasance or breach of any fiduciary or other duty by the director in relation to the company[, including in particular any breach by the director of a duty under Chapter 2 of Part 10 of the Companies Act 2006 (general duties of directors) owed to the company].

2. Any misapplication or retention by the director of, or any conduct by the director giving rise to an obligation to account for, any money or other property of the company.

3. The extent of the director's responsibility for the company entering into any transaction liable to be set aside under Part XVI of the Insolvency Act [1986] (provisions against debt avoidance).

[**4.** The extent of the director's responsibility for any failure by the company to comply with any of the following provisions of the Companies Act 2006—
- (a)   section 113 (register of members);
- (b)   section 114 (register to be kept available for inspection);
- (c)   section 162 (register of directors);
- (d)   section 165 (register of directors' residential addresses);
- (e)   section 167 (duty to notify registrar of changes: directors);
- (f)   section 275 (register of secretaries);
- (g)   section 276 (duty to notify registrar of changes: secretaries);
- (h)   section 386 (duty to keep accounting records);
- (i)   section 388 (where and for how long accounting records to be kept);
- (j)   section 854 (duty to make annual returns);
- (k)   section 860 (duty to register charges);
- (l)   section 878 (duty to register charges: companies registered in Scotland).]

[**5.** The extent of the director's responsibility for any failure by the directors of the company to comply with the following provisions of the Companies Act 2006—
- (a)   section 394 or 399 (duty to prepare annual accounts);
- (b)   section 414 or 450 (approval and signature of abbreviated accounts); or
- (c)   section 433 (name of signatory to be stated in published copy of accounts).]

[**5A.**   . . .]

NOTES

Paras 1, 3: words in square brackets inserted by the Companies Act 2006 (Consequential Amendments, Transitional Provisions and Savings) Order 2009, SI 2009/1941, art 2(1), Sch 1, para 85(1), (6), (14)(a), as from 1 October 2009.

Para 4: substituted, for paras 4, 4A, by SI 2009/1941, art 2(1), Sch 1, para 85(1), (14)(b), as from 1 October 2009.

Para 5: substituted by SI 2008/948, art 3(1), Sch 1, Pt 2, para 106(1), (8)(b), as from 6 April 2008.

Para 5A: inserted by the Open-Ended Investment Companies (Investment Companies with Variable Capital) Regulations 1996, SI 1996/2827, reg 75, Sch 8, Pt I, para 10, as from 6 January 1997, and repealed by SI 2009/1941, art 2(1), Sch 1, para 85(1), (14)(c), as from 1 October 2009.

PART II
MATTERS APPLICABLE WHERE COMPANY HAS BECOME INSOLVENT

[5.93]
6. The extent of the director's responsibility for the causes of the company becoming insolvent.

7. The extent of the director's responsibility for any failure by the company to supply any goods or services which have been paid for (in whole or in part).

8. The extent of the director's responsibility for the company entering into any transaction or giving any preference, being a transaction or preference—
- (a)   liable to be set aside under section 127 or sections 238 to 240 of the Insolvency Act [1986], or
- (b)   challengeable under section 242 or 243 of that Act or under any rule of law in Scotland.

9. The extent of the director's responsibility for any failure by the directors of the company to comply with section 98 of the Insolvency Act [1986] (duty to call creditors' meeting in creditors' voluntary winding up).

10. Any failure by the director to comply with any obligation imposed on him by or under any of the following provisions of the Insolvency Act [1986]—

(a)   [paragraph 47 of Schedule B1] (company's statement of affairs in administration);
(b)   section 47 (statement of affairs to administrative receiver);
(c)   section 66 (statement of affairs in Scottish receivership);
(d)   section 99 (directors' duty to attend meeting; statement of affairs in creditors' voluntary winding up);
(e)   section 131 (statement of affairs in winding up by the court);
(f)   section 234 (duty of any one with company property to deliver it up);
(g)   section 235 (duty to co-operate with liquidator, etc).

NOTES

Paras 8, 9: date in square brackets inserted by the Companies Act 2006 (Consequential Amendments, Transitional Provisions and Savings) Order 2009, SI 2009/1941, art 2(1), Sch 1, para 85(1), (6), as from 1 October 2009.

Para 10: date in square brackets inserted by SI 2009/1941, art 2(1), Sch 1, para 85(1), (6), as from 1 October 2009; words in square brackets in sub-para (a) substituted by the Enterprise Act 2002 (Insolvency) Order 2003, SI 2003/2096, arts 4, 6, Schedule, Pt 1, para 12, as from 15 September 2003, except in relation to any case where a petition for an administration order was presented before that date.

Limited liability partnerships: see the introductory notes to this Act.

SCHEDULE 2
SAVINGS FROM COMPANIES ACT 1981 SS 93, 94, AND INSOLVENCY ACT 1985 SCHEDULE 9

Section 19

[5.94]

1. Sections 2 and 4(1)(b) do not apply in relation to anything done before 15th June 1982 by a person in his capacity as liquidator of a company or as receiver or manager of a company's property.

2. Subject to paragraph 1—
(a)   section 2 applies in a case where a person is convicted on indictment of an offence which he committed (and, in the case of a continuing offence, has ceased to commit) before 15th June 1982; but in such a case a disqualification order under that section shall not be made for a period in excess of 5 years;
(b)   that section does not apply in a case where a person is convicted summarily—
(i)   in England and Wales, if he had consented so to be tried before that date, or
(ii)   in Scotland, if the summary proceedings commenced before that date.

3. Subject to paragraph 1, section 4 applies in relation to an offence committed or other thing done before 15th June 1982; but a disqualification order made on the grounds of such an offence or other thing done shall not be made for a period in excess of 5 years.

4. The powers of a court under section 5 are not exercisable in a case where a person is convicted of an offence which he committed (and, in the case of a continuing offence, had ceased to commit) before 15th June 1982.

5. For purposes of section 3(1) and section 5, no account is to be taken of any offence which was committed, or any default order which was made, before 1st June 1977.

6. An order made under section 28 of the Companies Act 1976 has effect as if made under section 3 of this Act; and an application made before 15th June 1982 for such an order is to be treated as an application for an order under the section last mentioned.

7. Where—
(a)   an application is made for a disqualification order under section 6 of this Act by virtue of paragraph (a) of subsection (2) of that section, and
(b)   the company in question went into liquidation before 28th April 1986 (the coming into force of the provision replaced by section 6),
the court shall not make an order under that section unless it could have made a disqualification order under section 300 of [the Companies Act 1985] as it had effect immediately before the date specified in sub-paragraph (b) above.

8. An application shall not be made under section 8 of this Act in relation to a report made or information or documents obtained before 28th April 1986.

NOTES

Para 7: words in square brackets substituted by the Companies Act 2006 (Consequential Amendments, Transitional Provisions and Savings) Order 2009, SI 2009/1941, art 2(1), Sch 1, para 85(1), (15), as from 1 October 2009.

SCHEDULE 3
TRANSITIONAL PROVISIONS AND SAVINGS

Section 23(1)

[5.95]

1. In this Schedule, "the former enactments" means so much of [the Companies Act 1985], and so much of [the Insolvency Act 1986], as is repealed and replaced by this Act; and "the appointed day" means the day on which this Act comes into force.

2. So far as anything done or treated as done under or for the purposes of any provision of the former enactments could have been done under or for the purposes of the corresponding provision of this Act, it is not invalidated by the repeal of that provision but has effect as if done under or for the purposes of the corresponding provision; and any order, regulation, rule or other instrument made or having effect under any provision of the former enactments shall, insofar as its effect is preserved by this paragraph, be treated for all purposes as made and having effect under the corresponding provision.

3. Where any period of time specified in a provision of the former enactments is current immediately before the appointed day, this Act has effect as if the corresponding provision had been in force when the period began to run; and (without prejudice to the foregoing) any period of time so specified and current is deemed for the purposes of this Act—
  (a)   to run from the date or event from which it was running immediately before the appointed day, and
  (b)   to expire (subject to any provision of this Act for its extension) whenever it would have expired if this Act had not been passed;
and any rights, priorities, liabilities, reliefs, obligations, requirements, powers, duties or exemptions dependent on the beginning, duration or end of such a period as above mentioned shall be under this Act as they were or would have been under the former enactments.

4. Where in any provision of this Act there is a reference to another such provision, and the first-mentioned provision operates, or is capable of operating, in relation to things done or omitted, or events occurring or not occurring, in the past (including in particular past acts of compliance with any enactment, failures of compliance, contraventions, offences and convictions of offences) the reference to the other provision is to be read as including a reference to the corresponding provision of the former enactments.

5. Offences committed before the appointed day under any provision of the former enactments may, notwithstanding any repeal by this Act, be prosecuted and punished after that day as if this Act had not passed.

6. A reference in any enactment, instrument or document (whether express or implied, and in whatever phraseology) to a provision of the former enactments (including the corresponding provision of any yet earlier enactment) is to be read, where necessary to retain for the enactment, instrument or document the same force and effect as it would have had but for the passing of this Act, as, or as including, a reference to the corresponding provision by which it is replaced in this Act.

NOTES

Para 1: words in square brackets substituted by the Companies Act 2006 (Consequential Amendments, Transitional Provisions and Savings) Order 2009, SI 2009/1941, art 2(1), Sch 1, para 85(1), (16), as from 1 October 2009.

SCHEDULE 4

(Sch 4 repeals CA 1985, ss 295–299, 301, 302, Sch 2 (the entries relating to ss 295(7), 302(1) only), Sch 12, and IA 1985, ss 12–14, 16, 18, 108(2), Sch 2, Sch 6, paras 1, 2, 7, 14, Sch 9, paras 2, 3.)

COMPANIES ACT 1989

(1989 c 40)

NOTES

This Act is reproduced as amended by the following Acts:

1990	Law Reform (Miscellaneous Provisions) (Scotland) Act 1990.
1991	Water Consolidation (Consequential Provisions) Act 1991.
1992	Friendly Societies Act 1992; Trade Union and Labour Relations (Consolidation) Act 1992.
1993	Charities Act 1993; Criminal Justice Act 1993.
1994	Coal Industry Act 1994.
1995	Criminal Procedure (Consequential Provisions) (Scotland) Act 1995; Crown Agents Act 1995; Pensions Act 1995.
1998	Bank of England Act 1998; Competition Act 1998; National Lottery Act 1998; Northern Ireland Act 1998.
1999	Youth Justice and Criminal Evidence Act 1999.
2000	Insolvency Act 2000.
2002	Enterprise Act 2002.
2004	Finance Act 2004; Statute Law (Repeals) Act 2004; Companies (Audit, Investigations and Community Enterprise) Act 2004; Civil Partnership Act 2004; Pensions Act 2004.
2006	Companies Act 2006.
2007	Bankruptcy and Diligence etc (Scotland) Act 2007; Tribunals, Courts and Enforcement Act 2007; Legal Services Act 2007.

This Act is reproduced as amended by the following SIs:

1991	Financial Markets and Insolvency Regulations 1991, SI 1991/880.
1992	Transfer of Functions (Financial Services) Order 1992, SI 1992/1315.
1993	Financial Services (Disclosure of Information) (Designated Authorities) (No 7) Order 1993, SI 1993/1826.
1994	Financial Services (Disclosure of Information) (Designated Authorities) (No 8) Order 1994, SI 1994/340.
1995	Public Offers of Securities Regulations 1995, SI 1995/1537.
1998	Financial Markets and Insolvency Regulations 1998, SI 1998/1748.
1999	Competition Act 1998 (Competition Commission) Transitional, Consequential and Supplemental Provisions Order 1999, SI 1999/506; Scotland Act 1998 (Consequential Modifications) (No 2) Order 1999, SI 1999/1820.
2000	Competition Act 1998 (Transitional, Consequential and Supplemental Provisions) Order 2000, SI 2000/311.
2001	Financial Services and Markets Act 2000 (Dissolution of the Insurance Brokers Registration Council) (Consequential Provisions) Order 2001, SI 2001/1283; Financial Services and Markets Act 2000 (Consequential Amendments and Repeals) Order 2001, SI 2001/3649; Civil Jurisdiction and Judgments Order 2001, SI 2001/3929.
2002	Companies (Disclosure of Information) (Designated Authorities) (No 2) Order 2002, SI 2002/1889.
2003	Companies (Acquisition of Own Shares) (Treasury Shares) Regulations 2003, SI 2003/1116; Enterprise Act 2002 (Consequential and Supplemental Provisions) Order 2003, SI 2003/1398.
2004	Competition Act 1998 and other enactments (Amendment) Regulations 2004, SI 2004/1261.
2005	Regulatory Reform (Trading Stamps) Order 2005, SI 2005/781; Prospectus Regulations 2005, SI 2005/1433; Regulatory Reform (Execution of Deeds and Documents) Order 2005, SI 2005/1906.
2006	Charities and Trustee Investment (Scotland) Act 2005 (Consequential Provisions and Modifications) Order 2006, SI 2006/242; Companies (Disclosure of Information) (Designated Authorities) Order 2006, SI 2006/1644; Financial Services and Markets Act 2000 (Regulated Activities) (Amendment No 3) Order 2006, SI 2006/3384.
2007	Civil Jurisdiction and Judgments Regulations 2007, SI 2007/1655; Companies Act 2006 (Commencement No 3, Consequential Amendments, Transitional Provisions and Savings) Order 2007, SI 2007/2194.
2008	Companies Act 2006 (Consequential Amendments etc) Order 2008, SI 2008/948.
2009	Financial Markets and Insolvency Regulations 2009, SI 2009/853; Companies Act 2006 (Consequential Amendments, Transitional Provisions and Savings) Order 2009, SI 2009/1941.
2010	Transfer of Tribunal Functions Order 2010, SI 2010/22.

References to "the European Community", "Community", etc: see the Treaty of Lisbon (Changes in Terminology) Order 2011, SI 2011/1043, which provides that (as from 22 April 2011) "EU" should be substituted for the word "Community" (subject to certain exceptions) in references to "Community treaties", "Community instrument", "Community obligation", "Community law", "Community legislation", etc.

Commencement: most of this Act came into force between 16 November 1989 (Royal assent) and 3 July 1995, although a limited number of provisions were commenced after 1995, and a few are yet to be brought into force. Extensive transitional provisions and savings were made in connection with the commencement of this Act by the Orders noted to s 215 at **[5.146]**.

Community interest companies: as to the application of this Act (subject to certain modifications) to community interest companies, see the Companies (Audit, Investigations and Community Enterprise) Act 2004. See, in particular, Part 2 of that Act.

Application to bank insolvency and administration: as to the application of this Act to bank insolvency and administration, see the Banking Act 2009 (Parts 2 and 3 Consequential Amendments) Order 2009, SI 2009/317.

Civil Procedure Rules: the Civil Procedure Rules 1998, SI 1998/3132, r 49, states that, as from 26 April 1999, those Rules apply to proceedings under this Act subject to the provisions of the relevant practice direction which applies to those proceedings.

ARRANGEMENT OF SECTIONS

PART III
INVESTIGATIONS AND POWERS TO OBTAIN INFORMATION

Powers exercisable to assist overseas regulatory authorities

PART V
OTHER AMENDMENTS OF COMPANY LAW

A company's capacity and related matters

Miscellaneous

PART VII
FINANCIAL MARKETS AND INSOLVENCY

Introduction

Recognised investment exchanges and clearing houses

Other exchanges and clearing houses

Market charges

An Act to amend the law relating to company accounts; to make new provision with respect to the persons eligible for appointment as company auditors; to amend the Companies Act 1985 and certain other enactments with respect to investigations and powers to obtain information and to confer new powers exercisable to assist overseas regulatory authorities; to make new provision with respect to the registration of company charges and otherwise to amend the law relating to companies; to amend the Fair Trading Act 1973; to enable provision to be made for the payment of fees in connection with the exercise by the Secretary of State, the Director General of Fair Trading and the Monopolies and Mergers Commission of their functions under Part V of that Act; to make provision for safeguarding the operation of certain financial markets; to amend the Financial Services Act 1986; to enable provision to be made for the recording and transfer of title to securities without a written instrument; to amend the Company Directors Disqualification Act 1986, the Company Securities (Insider Dealing) Act 1985, the Policyholders Protection Act 1975 and the law relating to building societies; and for connected purposes

[16 November 1989]

PART I
COMPANY ACCOUNTS

1–23 *(Ss 1–22 amended the Companies Act 1985, Pt VII and were repealed by the Companies Act 2006, s 1295, Sch 16, as from 1 October 2007 (in so far as relating to s 16), and as from 6 April 2008 (otherwise); s 23 introduces Sch 10 to this Act (Consequential amendments on this Part) (as to the repeal of that Schedule, see the Sch 10 note post).)*

PART II
ELIGIBILITY FOR APPOINTMENT AS COMPANY AUDITOR

24–54 *(Part II has been repealed as follows: Ss 24, 35, 36, 39, 51 repealed by the Companies Act 2006, s 1295, Sch 16, as from 6 April 2008. Ss 25–28 repealed by CA 2006, s 1295, Sch 16, as from 6 April 2008, except in relation to auditors appointed for financial years beginning before that date (see the Companies Act 2006 (Commencement No 5, Transitional Provisions and Savings) Order 2007, SI 2007/3495, Sch 4, Pt 1, para 37 at* **[2.66]***). Ss 29, 40–45, 49 repealed by CA 2006, s 1295, Sch 16, as from 6 April 2008, except in relation to auditors, supervisory bodies or qualifying bodies to whom ss 25–28 and 30–39 of this Act apply (see SI 2007/3495, Sch 4, Pt 1, para 41(1), (2)). Ss 30–34, 48 (and Schs 11, 12) repealed by CA 2006, s 1295, Sch 16, as from 6 April 2008, except in relation to the supervision and qualification of auditors appointed for financial years beginning before that date (see SI 2007/3495, Sch 4, Pt 1, para 38; note also that any declaration by the Secretary of State in force under s 33 (approval of overseas qualifications) immediately before 6 April 2008 continues in force on and after that date as if made under s 1221 of CA 2006). Ss 37, 38 repealed by CA 2006, s 1295, Sch 16, as from 6 April 2008, except in relation to the operation of those sections in relation to functions exercised under this Part on or after that date (see SI 2007/3495, Sch 4, Pt 1, para 39). Ss 46, 46A (and Sch 13) repealed by CA 2006, s 1295, Sch 16, as from 6 April 2008, except in relation to the operation of those provisions in relation to functions* *exercised under this Part on or after that date (see SI 2007/3495, Sch 4, Pt 1, para 42(1)). S 47 repealed by the Competition Act 1998 and other enactments (Amendment) Regulations 2004, SI 2004/1261, reg 5, Sch 2, para 2(1), (2), as from 1 May 2004. S 50 repealed by CA 2006, s 1295, Sch 16, as from 6 April 2008 (note that this repeal does not affect any amendments made by Regulations under this section that are in force immediately before that date (see the Companies Act 2006 (Consequential Amendments etc) Order 2008, SI 2008/948, art 10 at [4.284]). Ss 52–54 repealed by CA 2006, s 1295, Sch 16, as from 6 April 2008, except in relation to the operation of those sections for the purposes of interpreting provisions of this Act that continue to apply on or after that date.)*

PART III
INVESTIGATIONS AND POWERS TO OBTAIN INFORMATION

55–81 *(In so far as these sections are still in force they contain amendments to the Companies Act 1985, Pt XIV (Investigation of Companies and their Affairs; Requisition of Documents), other consequential amendments to the 1985 Act, and the Insolvency Act 1986 which have been incorporated at the appropriate place. Note that Pt XIV of the 1985 Act is not repealed by the Companies Act 2006 (see [5.2] et seq). As to the repeal of certain of these sections by the 2006 Act, see Sch 16 to that Act at [1.1331].)*

Powers exercisable to assist overseas regulatory authorities

[5.96]
82 Request for assistance by overseas regulatory authority
(1)   The powers conferred by section 83 are exercisable by the Secretary of State for the purpose of assisting an overseas regulatory authority which has requested his assistance in connection with inquiries being carried out by it or on its behalf.
(2)   An "overseas regulatory authority" means an authority which in a country or territory outside the United Kingdom exercises—
[(a)   any function corresponding to—
    (i)   any function of the Secretary of State under the Companies Act 1985 [or the Companies Act 2006];
    (ii)   any function of the Financial Services Authority under the Financial Services and Markets Act 2000;
    (iii)   any function exercised by the competent authority under Part VI of that Act . . .], or
(b)   any function in connection with the investigation of, or the enforcement of rules (whether or not having the force of law) relating to, conduct of the kind prohibited by [Part V of the Criminal Justice Act 1993 (insider dealing)], or
(c)   any function prescribed for the purposes of this subsection by order of the Secretary of State, being a function which in the opinion of the Secretary of State relates to companies or financial services.
An order under paragraph (c) shall be made by statutory instrument which shall be subject to annulment in pursuance of a resolution of either House of Parliament.
(3)   The Secretary of State shall not exercise the powers conferred by section 83 unless [he and the Financial Services Authority are] satisfied that the assistance requested by the overseas regulatory authority is for the purposes of its regulatory functions.
An authority's "regulatory functions" means any functions falling within subsection (2) and any other functions relating to companies or financial services.
(4)   In deciding whether to exercise those powers the Secretary of State may take into account, in particular—
(a)   whether corresponding assistance would be given in that country or territory to an authority exercising regulatory functions in the United Kingdom;
(b)   whether the inquiries relate to the possible breach of a law, or other requirement, which has no close parallel in the United Kingdom or involves the assertion of a jurisdiction not recognised by the United Kingdom;
(c)   the seriousness of the matter to which the inquiries relate, the importance to the inquiries of the information sought in the United Kingdom and whether the assistance could be obtained by other means;
(d)   whether it is otherwise appropriate in the public interest to give the assistance sought.
(5)   Before deciding whether to exercise those powers in a case where the overseas regulatory authority is a banking supervisor, the Secretary of State shall consult the [Financial Services Authority].
A "banking supervisor" means an overseas regulatory authority with respect to which the [Financial Services Authority] has notified the Secretary of State, for the purposes of this subsection, that it exercises functions corresponding to those of the [Authority] [in relation to authorised persons with permission under the Financial Services and Markets Act 2000 to accept deposits].

[(5A) In subsection (5), "authorised person" has the meaning given in the Financial Services and Markets Act 2000 and the references to deposits and their acceptance must be read with—

(a) section 22 of that Act;

(b) any relevant order under that section; and

(c) Schedule 2 to that Act.]

(6) The Secretary of State may decline to exercise those powers unless the overseas regulatory authority undertakes to make such contribution towards the costs of their exercise as the Secretary of State considers appropriate.

(7) References in this section to financial services include, in particular, investment business, insurance and banking.

NOTES

Sub-s (2): para (a) substituted by the Financial Services and Markets Act 2000 (Consequential Amendments and Repeals) Order 2001, SI 2001/3649, art 76(1), (2), as from 1 December 2001; words in square brackets in sub-para (a)(i) inserted by the Companies Act 2006 (Consequential Amendments etc) Order 2008, SI 2008/948, art 3(1), Sch 1, Pt 2, para 157, as from 6 April 2008; words omitted from sub-para (a)(iii) repealed by the Prospectus Regulations 2005, SI 2005/1433, reg 2(3), Sch 3, para 1, as from 1 July 2005; words in square brackets in para (b) substituted by the Criminal Justice Act 1993, s 79(13), Sch 5, Pt I, para 16, as from 1 March 1994.

Sub-s (3): words in square brackets substituted by SI 2001/3649, art 76(1), (3), as from 1 December 2001.

Sub-s (5): words in first, second and third pairs of square brackets substituted by the Bank of England Act 1998, s 23(1), Sch 5, Pt IV, Ch II, para 66(1), (2)(b), as from 1 June 1998; words in fourth pair of square brackets substituted by SI 2001/3649, art 76(1), (4), as from 1 December 2001.

Sub-s (5A): inserted by SI 2001/3649, art 76(1), (5), as from 1 December 2001.

Transfer of functions: by the Transfer of Functions (Financial Services) Order 1992, SI 1992/1315, art 5, Sch 3, para 3, the function of the Secretary of State under sub-s (3) above is exercisable concurrently by the Secretary of State and the Treasury.

[5.97]
83 Power to require information, documents or other assistance

(1) The following powers may be exercised in accordance with section 82, if the Secretary of State considers there is good reason for their exercise.

(2) The Secretary of State may require any person—

(a) to attend before him at a specified time and place and answer questions or otherwise furnish information with respect to any matter relevant to the inquiries,

(b) to produce at a specified time and place any specified documents which appear to the Secretary of State to relate to any matter relevant to the inquiries, and

(c) otherwise to give him such assistance in connection with the inquiries as he is reasonably able to give.

(3) The Secretary of State may examine a person on oath and may administer an oath accordingly.

(4) Where documents are produced the Secretary of State may take copies or extracts from them.

(5) A person shall not under this section be required to disclose information or produce a document which he would be entitled to refuse to disclose or produce on grounds of legal professional privilege in proceedings in the High Court or on grounds of confidentiality as between client and professional legal adviser in proceedings in the Court of Session, except that a lawyer may be required to furnish the name and address of his client.

(6) A statement by a person in compliance with a requirement imposed under this section may be used in evidence against him.

[(6A) However, in criminal proceedings in which that person is charged with an offence to which this subsection applies—

(a) no evidence relating to the statement may be adduced, and

(b) no question relating to it may be asked,

by or on behalf of the prosecution, unless evidence relating to it is adduced, or a question relating to it is asked, in the proceedings by or on behalf of that person.

(6B) Subsection (6A) applies to any offence other than—

(a) an offence under section 85;

(b) an offence under section 2 or 5 of the Perjury Act 1911 (false statements made on oath otherwise than in judicial proceedings or made otherwise than on oath);

(c) an offence under section 44(1) or (2) of the Criminal Law (Consolidation) (Scotland) Act 1995 (false statements made on oath or otherwise than on oath); or

(d) an offence under Article 7 or 10 of the Perjury (Northern Ireland) Order 1979 (false statements made on oath otherwise than in judicial proceedings or made otherwise than on oath).]

(7) Where a person claims a lien on a document, its production under this section is without prejudice to his lien.

(8) In this section "documents" includes information recorded in any form; and, in relation to information recorded otherwise than in legible form, the power to require its production includes power to require the production of a copy of it in legible form.

NOTES

Sub-ss (6A), (6B): inserted by the Youth Justice and Criminal Evidence Act 1999, s 59, Sch 3, para 21, as from 14 April 2000 (in relation to England and Wales), and as from 1 January 2001 (in relation to Scotland).

[5.98]
84 Exercise of powers by officer, &c
(1)   The Secretary of State may authorise an officer of his or any other competent person to exercise on his behalf all or any of the powers conferred by section 83.
(2)   No such authority shall be granted except for the purpose of investigating—
  (a)   the affairs, or any aspects of the affairs, of a person specified in the authority, or
  (b)   a subject-matter so specified,
being a person who, or subject-matter which, is the subject of the inquiries being carried out by or on behalf of the overseas regulatory authority.
(3)   No person shall be bound to comply with a requirement imposed by a person exercising powers by virtue of an authority granted under this section unless he has, if required, produced evidence of his authority.
(4)   A person shall not by virtue of an authority under this section be required to disclose any information or produce any documents in respect of which he owes an obligation of confidence by virtue of carrying on the business of banking unless—
  (a)   the imposing on him of a requirement with respect to such information or documents has been specifically authorised by the Secretary of State, or
  (b)   the person to whom the obligation of confidence is owed consents to the disclosure or production.
  In this subsection "documents" has the same meaning as in section 83.
(5)   Where the Secretary of State authorises a person other than one of his officers to exercise any powers by virtue of this section, that person shall make a report to the Secretary of State in such manner as he may require on the exercise of those powers and the results of exercising them.

[5.99]
85 Penalty for failure to comply with requirement, &c
(1)   A person who without reasonable excuse fails to comply with a requirement imposed on him under section 83 commits an offence and is liable on summary conviction to imprisonment for a term not exceeding six months or to a fine not exceeding level 5 on the standard scale, or both.
(2)   A person who in purported compliance with any such requirement furnishes information which he knows to be false or misleading in a material particular, or recklessly furnishes information which is false or misleading in a material particular, commits an offence and is liable—
  (a)   on conviction on indictment, to imprisonment for a term not exceeding two years or to a fine, or both;
  (b)   on summary conviction, to imprisonment for a term not exceeding six months or to a fine not exceeding the statutory maximum, or both.

[5.100]
86 Restrictions on disclosure of information
(1)   This section applies to information relating to the business or other affairs of a person which—
  (a)   is supplied by an overseas regulatory authority in connection with a request for assistance, or
  (b)   is obtained by virtue of the powers conferred by section 83, whether or not any requirement to supply it is made under that section.
(2)   Except as permitted by section 87 below, such information shall not be disclosed for any purpose—
  (a)   by the primary recipient, or
  (b)   by any person obtaining the information directly or indirectly from him,
without the consent of the person from whom the primary recipient obtained the information and, if different, the person to whom it relates.
(3)   The "primary recipient" means, as the case may be—
  (a)   the Secretary of State,
  (b)   any person authorised under section 84 to exercise powers on his behalf, and
  (c)   any officer or servant of any such person.
(4)   Information shall not be treated as information to which this section applies if it has been made available to the public by virtue of being disclosed in any circumstances in which, or for any purpose for which, disclosure is not precluded by this section.
(5)   A person who contravenes this section commits an offence and is liable—
  (a)   on conviction on indictment, to imprisonment for a term not exceeding two years or to a fine, or both;
  (b)   on summary conviction, to imprisonment for a term not exceeding three months or to a fine not exceeding the statutory maximum, or both.

[5.101]
87 Exceptions from restrictions on disclosure
(1)   Information to which section 86 applies may be disclosed—
  (a)   to any person with a view to the institution of, or otherwise for the purposes of, relevant proceedings,

(b)   for the purpose of enabling or assisting a relevant authority to discharge any relevant function (including functions in relation to proceedings),

(c)   to the Treasury, if the disclosure is made in the interests of investors or in the public interest,

(d)   if the information is or has been available to the public from other sources,

(e)   in a summary or collection of information framed in such a way as not to enable the identity of any person to whom the information relates to be ascertained, or

(f)   in pursuance of any Community obligation.

(2)   The relevant proceedings referred to in subsection (1)(a) are—

(a)   any criminal proceedings,

[(b)   civil proceedings arising under or by virtue of the Financial Services and Markets Act 2000 and proceedings before the Upper Tribunal in respect of—

    (i)   a decision of the Financial Services Authority;

    (ii)   a decision of the Bank of England; or

    (iii) a decision of a person relating to the assessment of any compensation or consideration under the Banking (Special Provisions) Act 2008 or the Banking Act 2009,]

(c)   disciplinary proceedings relating to—

    (i)   the exercise by a [relevant lawyer], auditor, accountant, valuer or actuary of his professional duties, or

    (ii)   the discharge by a public servant of his duties;

[(d)   proceedings before [a tribunal in relation to a decision of the Pensions Regulator]].

[(2A) In subsection (2)(c)(i) "relevant lawyer" means—

(a)   a person who, for the purposes of the Legal Services Act 2007, is an authorised person in relation to an activity which constitutes a reserved legal activity (within the meaning of that Act),

(b)   a solicitor or barrister in Northern Ireland, or

(c)   a solicitor or advocate in Scotland.]

(3)   In subsection (2)(c)(ii) "public servant" means an officer or servant of the Crown or of any public or other authority for the time being designated for the purposes of that provision by order of the Secretary of State.

(4)   The relevant authorities referred to in subsection (1)(b), and the relevant functions in relation to each such authority, are as follows—

Authority	Functions
[The Secretary of State.	Functions under— (a) the enactments relating to companies or insolvency; (b) Part 2, this Part or Part 7 of this Act; (c) the Financial Services and Markets Act 2000.]
[The Treasury	Functions under— (a) this Part or Part 7 of this Act; (b) the Financial Services and Markets Act 2000.]
[An inspector appointed under Part 14 of the Companies Act 1985.	Functions under that Part.]
[A person authorised to exercise powers under section 447 of the Companies Act 1985 or section 84 of this Act.	Functions under that section.]
[A person appointed under— (a) section 167 of the Financial Services and Markets Act 2000 (general investigations), (b) section 168 of that Act (investigations in particular cases), (c) section 169(1)(b) of that Act (investigation in support of overseas regulator), (d) section 284 of that Act (investigations into affairs of certain collective investment schemes), or (e) regulations made as a result of section 262(2)(k) of that Act (investigations into open-ended investment companies),	Functions in relation to the investigation.]

Part 5   Pre-2006 companies legislation

Authority	Functions
to conduct an investigation.	
An overseas regulatory authority.	Its regulatory functions (within the meaning of section 82 of this Act).
The Department of Economic Development in Northern Ireland or a person appointed or authorised by that Department.	Functions conferred on it or him by the enactments relating to companies or insolvency.
. . .	. . .
. . .	. . .
. . .	. . .
. . .	. . .
. . .	. . .
[. . .]	. . .]
The Bank of England.	[Any of its functions]
[The Financial Services Authority.	Functions under the enactments relating to friendly societies, under the Building Societies Act 1986 and under the Financial Services and Markets Act 2000.]
[A body corporate established in accordance with section 212(1) of that Act.	Functions under the Financial Services Compensation Scheme, established in accordance with section 213 of that Act.]
[A recognised investment exchange or a recognised clearing house (as defined by section 285 of that Act).	Functions in its capacity as an exchange or clearing house recognised under that Act.]
[A body designated under section 326(1) of the Financial Services and Markets Act 2000.	Functions in its capacity as a body designated under that section.]
[A body designated by order under section 1252 of the Companies Act 2006.	Functions under Part 42 of the Companies Act 2006.]
[A recognised supervisory or qualifying body within the meaning of Part 42 of the Companies Act 2006.	Functions as such a body.]
The Official Receiver or, in Northern Ireland, the Official Assignee for company liquidations or for bankruptcy.	Functions under the enactments relating to insolvency.
A recognised professional body (within the meaning of section 391 of the Insolvency Act 1986).	Functions in its capacity as such a body under the Insolvency Act 1986.
. . .	. . .
[The Pensions Regulator	Functions conferred by or by virtue of— (a) the Pension Schemes Act 1993, (b) the Pensions Act 1995, (c) the Welfare Reform and Pensions Act 1999, (d) the Pensions Act 2004, or any enactment in force in Northern Ireland corresponding to an enactment mentioned in paragraphs (a) to (d) above.
The Board of the Pension Protection Fund	Functions conferred by or by virtue of Part 2 of the Pensions Act 2004 or any enactment in force in Northern Ireland corresponding to that Part.]
[The Office of Fair Trading.]	Functions under the [Financial Services and Markets Act 2000].
[A person authorised by the Secretary of State under section 245C of the Companies Act 1985.	Functions relating to the securing of compliance by companies with the accounting requirements of that Act.]

Authority	Functions
[The [Commission] of the National Lottery.	Functions under sections 5 to 10 inclusive and section 15 of the National Lottery etc Act 1993.]
[The Comptroller and Auditor General	Functions under Part 2 of the National Audit Act 1983.]
[The Scottish Ministers	Functions under the enactments relating to insolvency]
[The Accountant in Bankruptcy	Functions he has under the enactments relating to insolvency.]
[The Regulator of Community Interest Companies.	Functions under the Companies (Audit, Investigations and Community Enterprise) Act 2004."
[The Gambling Commission	Functions under the Gambling Act 2005.]
[The Regulator of Community Interest Companies for Northern Ireland.	Functions under the Companies (Audit, Investigations and Community Enterprise) (Northern Ireland) Order 2005.]

[*Note*: Article 3(4) of the Companies (Disclosure of Information) (Designated Authorities) (No 2) Order 2002 restricts the circumstances in which disclosure for the purpose of enabling or assisting the Comptroller and Auditor General to discharge his relevant functions is permitted.]

(5)   The Secretary of State may by order amend the Table in subsection (4) so as to—
  (a)   add any public or other authority to the Table and specify the relevant functions of that authority,
  (b)   remove any authority from the Table, or
  (c)   add functions to, or remove functions from, those which are relevant functions in relation to an authority specified in the Table;
and the order may impose conditions subject to which, or otherwise restrict the circumstances in which, disclosure is permitted.
(6)   An order under this section shall be made by statutory instrument which shall be subject to annulment in pursuance of a resolution of either House of Parliament.

NOTES
  Sub-s (2) is amended as follows:
  Para (b) substituted by the Transfer of Tribunal Functions Order 2010, SI 2010/22, art 5(1), Sch 2, para 9(a), as from 6 April 2010 (for transitional provisions and savings in relation to existing cases and appeals from the Financial Services and Markets Tribunal, see Sch 5 to that Order).
  Words in square brackets in sub-para (c)(i) substituted by the Legal Services Act 2007, s 208, Sch 21, para 82(a), as from 1 January 2010.
  Para (d) added by the Pensions Act 2004, s 102, Sch 4, Pt 4, para 20, as from 6 April 2005.
  Words in square brackets in para (d) substituted by SI 2010/22, art 5(1), Sch 2, para 9(b), as from 6 April 2010 (for transitional provisions and savings in relation to existing cases and appeals from the Pensions Regulator Tribunal, see Sch 5 to that Order).
  Sub-s (2A): inserted by the Legal Services Act 2007, s 208, Sch 21, para 82(b), as from 1 January 2010.
  Sub-s (4) is amended as follows:
  Entry "The Secretary of State" substituted by SI 2001/3649, art 77(1), (3), (5), as from 1 December 2001.
  Entry "The Treasury" inserted by the Transfer of Functions (Financial Services) Order 1992, SI 1992/1315, art 10(1), Sch 4, para 12, as from 7 June 1992; substituted by SI 2001/3649, art 77(1), (3), (6), as from 1 December 2001.
  Entry beginning "An inspector appointed under Part 14" substituted by SI 2001/3649, art 77(1), (3), (7), as from 1 December 2001.
  Entry beginning "A person authorised to exercise powers" and subsequent entry substituted for the original entry beginning with those words by SI 2001/3649, art 77(1), (3), (8), as from 1 December 2001.
  First, second, third, fourth, fifth, seventh, eighth and tenth entries omitted repealed by SI 2001/3649, art 77(1), (3), (4), as from 1 December 2001
  Sixth entry omitted originally inserted by the Friendly Societies Act 1992, s 120, Sch 21, Pt I, para 11, and repealed by SI 2001/3649, 77(1), (3), (4), as from 1 December 2001.
  In entry "The Bank of England" words in square brackets substituted by the Bank of England Act 1998, s 23(1), Sch 5, para 66(1), (3), as from 1 June 1998.
  Entry "The Financial Services Authority" inserted by the Bank of England Act 1998, s 23(1), Sch 5, para 66(1), (3), as from 1 June 1998; substituted by SI 2001/3649, art 77(1), (3), (9), as from 1 December 2001.
  Entry "A body corporate established in accordance with section 212(1) of that Act" inserted by SI 2001/3649, art 77(1), (3), (10), as from 1 December 2001.
  Entry beginning "A recognised investment exchange or a recognised clearing house" inserted by SI 2001/3649, art 77(1), (3), (10), as from 1 December 2001.
  Entry "A body designated under section 326(1) of the Financial Services and Markets Act 2000" inserted by SI 2001/3649, art 77(1), (3), (10), as from 1 December 2001.
  Ninth entry omitted repealed by the Financial Services and Markets Act 2000 (Dissolution of the Insurance Brokers Registration Council) (Consequential Provisions) Order 2001, SI 2001/1283, art 3(4), as from 30 April 2001.

Entries "A body designated by order under section 1252 of the Companies Act 2006" and "A recognised supervisory or qualifying body within the meaning of Part 42 of the Companies Act 2006" substituted (for the original entries "A body designated by order under section 46 of this Act" and "A recognised supervisory or qualifying body within the meaning of Part II of this Act" respectively) by the Companies Act 2006 (Consequential Amendments etc) Order 2008, SI 2008/948, art 3(1), Sch 1, Pt 2, para 158, as from 6 April 2008.

Entries "The Pensions Regulator" and "The Board of the Pension Protection Fund" substituted for the entry "The Occupational Pensions Regulatory Authority" (as inserted by the Pensions Act 1995, s 122, Sch 3, para 19, as from 6 April 1997) by the Pensions Act 2004, s 319, Sch 12, para 6, as from 6 April 2005.

In entry "The Office of Fair Trading" (formerly "The Director General of Fair Trading") words in square brackets in column 1 substituted by the Enterprise Act 2002, s 278(1), Sch 25, para 21(1), (3), as from 1 April 2003; words in square brackets in column 2 substituted by SI 2001/3649, art 77(1), (3), (11), as from 1 December 2001.

Entry beginning "A person authorised by the Secretary of State" inserted by the Financial Services (Disclosure of Information) (Designated Authorities) (No 7) Order 1993, SI 1993/1826, art 3, as from 16 August 1993.

Entry relating to "the National Lottery" inserted by the Financial Services (Disclosure of Information) (Designated Authorities) (No 8) Order 1994, SI 1994/340, art 3, as from 10 March 1994; word in square brackets substituted by the National Lottery Act 1998, s 1(5), Sch 1, para 4, as from 1 April 1999.

Entry "The Comptroller and Auditor General" inserted by the Companies (Disclosure of Information) (Designated Authorities) (No 2) Order 2002, SI 2002/1889, art 3(1), (2), as from 14 August 2002. See further the note relating to the 2002 Order below.

Entry "The Scottish Ministers" added by the Scotland Act 1998 (Consequential Modifications) (No 2) Order 1999, SI 1999/1820, art 4, Sch 2, Pt I, para 96, as from 1 July 1999.

Entry "The Accountant in Bankruptcy" added by the Scotland Act 1998 (Consequential Modifications) (No 2) Order 1999, SI 1999/1820, art 4, Sch 2, Pt I, para 96, as from 1 July 1999.

Entry "The Regulator of Community Interest Companies" added by the Companies (Audit, Investigations and Community Enterprise) Act 2004, s 25, Sch 2, Pt 3, para 29, as from 1 July 2005.

Entry "The Gambling Commission" inserted by the Companies (Disclosure of Information) (Designated Authorities) Order 2006, SI 2006/1644, art 3, as from 1 October 2006.

Entry "The Regulator of Community Interest Companies for Northern Ireland" added by the Companies (Audit, Investigations and Community Enterprise) (Northern Ireland) Order 2005, SI 2005/1967, art 24(1), Sch 2, Pt 2, para 22, as from a day to be appointed.

Table note: added by SI 2002/1889, art 3(1), (3), as from 14 August 2002. See further the note relating to the 2002 Order below.

Note: SI 2002/1889, art 3(4) provides—

"(4)   Disclosure under section 87(1)(b) of the 1989 Act is permitted by virtue of the amendment made by paragraph (2) only where the disclosure is made by the National Lottery Commission to the National Audit Office for the purpose of enabling or assisting the Comptroller and Auditor General to carry out an examination into the economy, efficiency and effectiveness with which the National Lottery Commission has used its resources in discharging its functions under sections 5 to 10 of the National Lottery etc Act 1993."

Sub-s (1) above has effect in accordance with the Anti-terrorism, Crime and Security Act 2001, s 17. That section, which clarifies and extends a number of information disclosure provisions available to public authorities, permits disclosure to assist any criminal investigation or criminal proceedings being carried out in the UK or abroad or to facilitate determinations of whether or not such investigations or proceedings should begin or end (see Sch 4 to the 2001 Act).

Orders: the Financial Services (Disclosure of Information) (Designated Authorities) (No 7) Order 1993, SI 1993/1826; the Financial Services (Disclosure of Information) (Designated Authorities) (No 8) Order 1994, SI 1994/340; the Companies (Disclosure of Information) (Designated Authorities) (No 2) Order 2002, SI 2002/1889; the Companies (Disclosure of Information) (Designated Authorities) Order 2006, SI 2006/1644.

[5.102]
88   Exercise of powers in relation to Northern Ireland

(1)   The following provisions apply where it appears to the Secretary of State that a request for assistance by an overseas regulatory authority may involve the powers conferred by section 83 being exercised in Northern Ireland in relation to matters which are transferred matters within the meaning of the Northern Ireland Constitution Act 1973.

(2)   The Secretary of State shall before deciding whether to accede to the request consult the Department of Economic Development in Northern Ireland, and if he decides to accede to the request and it appears to him—

(a)   that the powers should be exercised in Northern Ireland, and

(b)   that the purposes for which they should be so exercised relate wholly or primarily to transferred matters,

he shall by instrument in writing authorise the Department to exercise in Northern Ireland his powers under section 83.

(3)   The following provisions have effect in relation to the exercise of powers by virtue of such an authority with the substitution for references to the Secretary of State of references to the Department of Economic Development in Northern Ireland—

(a)   section 84 (exercise of powers by officer, &c),

[(b)   section 449 of the Companies Act 1985 and sections 86 and 87 above (restrictions on disclosure of information),] and

(c)   section 89 (authority for institution of criminal proceedings);

and references to the Secretary of State in other enactments which proceed by reference to those provisions shall be construed accordingly as being or including references to the Department.

(4)   The Secretary of State may after consultation with the Department of Economic Development in Northern Ireland revoke an authority given to the Department under this section.

(5)   In that case nothing in the provisions referred to in subsection (3)(b) shall apply so as to prevent the Department from giving the Secretary of State any information obtained by virtue of the authority; and (without prejudice to their application in relation to disclosure by the Department) those provisions shall apply to the disclosure of such information by the Secretary of State as if it had been obtained by him in the first place.

(6)   Nothing in this section affects the exercise by the Secretary of State of any powers in Northern Ireland—

   (a)   in a case where at the time of acceding to the request it did not appear to him that the circumstances were such as to require him to authorise the Department of Economic Development in Northern Ireland to exercise those powers, or

   (b)   after the revocation by him of any such authority;

and no objection shall be taken to anything done by or in relation to the Secretary of State or the Department on the ground that it should have been done by or in relation to the other.

NOTES

Sub-s (3): para (b) substituted by the Financial Services and Markets Act 2000 (Consequential Amendments and Repeals) Order 2001, SI 2001/3649, art 78, as from 1 December 2001.

[5.103]
89   Prosecutions
Proceedings for an offence under section 85 or 86 shall not be instituted—

   (a)   in England and Wales, except by or with the consent of the Secretary of State or the Director of Public Prosecutions;

   (b)   in Northern Ireland, except by or with the consent of the Secretary of State or the Director of Public Prosecutions for Northern Ireland.

[5.104]
90   Offences by bodies corporate, partnerships and unincorporated associations
(1)   Where an offence under section 85 or 86 committed by a body corporate is proved to have been committed with the consent or connivance of, or to be attributable to any neglect on the part of, a director, manager, secretary or other similar officer of the body, or a person purporting to act in any such capacity, he as well as the body corporate is guilty of the offence and liable to be proceeded against and punished accordingly.

(2)   Where the affairs of a body corporate are managed by its members, subsection (1) applies in relation to the acts and defaults of a member in connection with his functions of management as to a director of a body corporate.

(3)   Where an offence under section 85 or 86 committed by a partnership is proved to have been committed with the consent or connivance of, or to be attributable to any neglect on the part of, a partner, he as well as the partnership is guilty of the offence and liable to be proceeded against and punished accordingly.

(4)   Where an offence under section 85 or 86 committed by an unincorporated association (other than a partnership) is proved to have been committed with the consent or connivance of, or to be attributable to any neglect on the part of, any officer of the association or any member of its governing body, he as well as the association is guilty of the offence and liable to be proceeded against and punished accordingly.

[5.105]
91   Jurisdiction and procedure in respect of offences
(1)   Summary proceedings for an offence under section 85 may, without prejudice to any jurisdiction exercisable apart from this section, be taken against a body corporate or unincorporated association at any place at which it has a place of business and against an individual at any place where he is for the time being.

(2)   Proceedings for an offence alleged to have been committed under section 85 or 86 by an unincorporated association shall be brought in the name of the association (and not in that of any of its members), and for the purposes of any such proceedings any rules of court relating to the service of documents apply as in relation to a body corporate.

(3)   Section 33 of the Criminal Justice Act 1925 and Schedule 3 to the Magistrates' Courts Act 1980 (procedure on charge of offence against a corporation) apply in a case in which an unincorporated association is charged in England and Wales with an offence under section 85 or 86 as they apply in the case of a corporation.

(4)   In relation to proceedings on indictment in Scotland for an offence alleged to have been committed under section 85 or 86 by an unincorporated association, section 74 of the Criminal Procedure (Scotland) Act 1975 (proceedings on indictment against bodies corporate) applies as if the association were a body corporate.

(5)   Section 18 of the Criminal Justice Act (Northern Ireland) 1945 and Schedule 4 to the Magistrates' Courts (Northern Ireland) Order 1981 (procedure on charge of offence against a corporation) apply in a case in which an unincorporated association is charged in Northern Ireland with an offence under section 85 or 86 as they apply in the case of a corporation.

(6)   A fine imposed on an unincorporated association on its conviction of such an offence shall be paid out of the funds of the association.

Part 5   Pre-2006 companies legislation

PART IV
REGISTRATION OF COMPANY CHARGES

92–107   *(Repealed by the Companies Act 2006, ss 1180, 1295, Sch 16, as from 1 October 2009 (without ever coming into force).)*

PART V
OTHER AMENDMENTS OF COMPANY LAW

A company's capacity and related matters

108–111   *(Ss 108–110 repealed by the Companies Act 2006, s 1295, Sch 16, as from 1 October 2009. S 111 repealed by the Charities Act 1993, s 98(2), Sch 7, as from 1 August 1993.)*

[5.106]
112   Charitable companies (Scotland)
(1)   In the following provisions (which extend to Scotland only)—
  (a)   "company" means [a company registered under the Companies Act 2006]; and
  (b)   "charity" means a body [entered in the Scottish Charity Register].
(2)   Where a charity is a company or other body corporate having power to alter the instruments establishing or regulating it as a body corporate, no exercise of that power which has the effect of the body ceasing to be a charity shall be valid so as to affect the application of—
  (a)   any property acquired by virtue of any transfer, contract or obligation previously effected otherwise than for full consideration in money or money's worth, or any property representing property so acquired,
  (b)   any property representing income which has accrued before the alteration is made, or
  (c)   the income from any such property as aforesaid.
(3)   [Sections 39 and 40 of the Companies Act 2006 (company's capacity and power of directors to bind company)] do not apply to the acts of a company which is a charity except in favour of a person who—
  (a)   gives full consideration in money or money's worth in relation to the act in question, and
  (b)   does not know that the act is not permitted by the company's [constitution] or, as the case may be, is beyond the powers of the directors,
or who does not know at the time the act is done that the company is a charity.
(4)   However, where such a company purports to transfer or grant an interest in property, the fact that the act was not permitted by the company's [constitution] or, as the case may be, that the directors in connection with the act exceeded any limitation on their powers under the company's constitution, does not affect the title of a person who subsequently acquires the property or any interest in it for full consideration without actual notice of any such circumstances affecting the validity of the company's act.
(5)   In any proceedings arising out of subsection (3) the burden of proving—
  (a)   that a person knew that an act was not permitted by the company's [constitution] or was beyond the powers of the directors, or
  (b)   that a person knew that the company was a charity,
lies on the person making that allegation.
(6)   Where a company is a charity and its name does not include the word "charity" or the word "charitable", the fact that the company is a charity shall be stated in English in legible characters—
  (a)   in all business letters of the company,
  (b)   in all its notices and other official publications,
  (c)   in all bills of exchange, promissory notes, endorsements, cheques and orders for money or goods purporting to be signed by or on behalf of the company,
  (d)   in all conveyances purporting to be executed by the company, and
  (e)   in all its bills of parcels, invoices, receipts and letters of credit.
(7)   In subsection (6)(d) "conveyance" means any document for the creation, transfer, variation or extinction of an interest in land.
[(8)   If a company fails to comply with subsection (6) it commits an offence.
(9)   An officer of a company, or a person acting on its behalf, who—
  (a)   issues or authorises the issue of any business letter of the company, or any notice or other official publication of the company, in which the statement required by subsection (6) does not appear, or
  (b)   issues or authorises the issue of any bill, invoice, receipt or letter of credit in which the statement required by subsection (6) does not appear,
commits an offence.
(10)   An officer of a company, or a person acting on its behalf, who signs or authorises to be signed on behalf of the company any bill of exchange, promissory note, endorsement, cheque or order for money or goods in which the statement required by subsection (6) does not appear—
  (a)   commits an offence, and
  (b)   is personally liable to the holder of the bill of exchange, promissory note, endorsement, cheque or order for money or goods for the amount of it (unless it is duly paid by the company).

(11)   A person guilty of an offence under subsection (8), (9) or (10) is liable on summary conviction to a fine not exceeding level 3 on the standard scale.]

NOTES

Sub-s (1): words in square brackets in para (a) substituted by the Companies Act 2006 (Consequential Amendments, Transitional Provisions and Savings) Order 2009, SI 2009/1941, art 2(1), Sch 1, para 103(1), (2)(a), as from 1 October 2009; words in square brackets in para (b) substituted by the Charities and Trustee Investment (Scotland) Act 2005 (Consequential Provisions and Modifications) Order 2006, SI 2006/242, art 5, Schedule, Pt 1, para 4, as from 1 April 2006.

Sub-s (3)–(5): words in square brackets substituted by SI 2009/1941, art 2(1), Sch 1, para 103(1), (2)(b), (c), as from 1 October 2009.

Sub-ss (8)–(11): substituted, for original sub-s (8), by the Companies Act 2006 (Consequential Amendments etc) Order 2008, SI 2008/948, art 4(1), Sch 3, para 6, as from 1 October 2008.

113–129   *(Ss 113, 114(1), 115(2), (3), 117 repealed by the Companies Act 2006, s 1295, Sch 16, as from 1 October 2007. Ss 114(2),118–122, 123(1)–(4) repealed by CA 2006, s 1295, Sch 16, as from 6 April 2008. Ss 115(1), 117, 123(5), 125(1), 126–129 repealed by CA 2006, s 1295, Sch 16, as from 1 October 2009. S 116 inserted ss 379A, 380(4)(bb) of the Companies Act 1985 Act, and was repealed by CA 2006, s 1295, Sch 16, as from 1 October 2009 (in so far as inserting s 379A) and as from a day to be appointed (in so far as inserting s 380(4)(bb)) (note, however, that s 388 is itself repealed as from 1 October 2009). S 124 repealed by the Trade Union and Labour Relations (Consolidation) Act 1992, s 300(1), Sch 1. S 125(2) substituted CA 1985, s 707 (repealed) and is therefore spent.)*

Miscellaneous

[5.107]
130   Company contracts and execution of documents by companies
(1)–(5)   . . .
(6)   The Secretary of State may make provision by regulations applying sections 36 to 36C of the Companies Act 1985 (company contracts; execution of documents; [execution of deeds;] pre-incorporation contracts, deeds and obligations) to companies incorporated outside Great Britain, subject to such exceptions, adaptations or modifications as may be specified in the regulations.

Regulations under this subsection shall be made by statutory instrument which shall be subject to annulment in pursuance of a resolution of either House of Parliament.
(7)   . . .

NOTES

Repealed by the Companies Act 2006, s 1295, Sch 16, as from 1 October 2009 (in so far as relating to sub-ss (1)–(5), (7)), and as from a day to be appointed (otherwise).

Sub-s (6): words in square brackets inserted by the Regulatory Reform (Execution of Deeds and Documents) Order 2005, SI 2005/1906, art 10(1), Sch 1, para 16, as from 15 September 2005, except in relation to any instrument executed before that date.

131–134   *(Ss 131, 132 repealed by the Companies Act 2006, s 1295, Sch 16, as from 1 October 2009. S 133 was partly repealed by the Companies (Acquisition of Own Shares) (Treasury Shares) Regulations 2003, SI 2003/1116, reg 4, Schedule, para 34, as from 1 December 2003 (and was completely repealed by CA 2006, s 1295, Sch 16, as from 1 October 2009). S 134 repealed by CA 2006, s 1295, Sch 16, as from 20 January 2007.)*

[5.108]
135   Orders imposing restrictions on shares
(1)   The Secretary of State may by regulations made by statutory instrument make such amendments of the provisions of the Companies Act 1985 [and the Companies Act 2006] relating to orders imposing restrictions on shares as appear to him necessary or expedient—
(a)   for enabling orders to be made in a form protecting the rights of third parties;
(b)   with respect to the circumstances in which restrictions may be relaxed or removed;
(c)   with respect to the making of interim orders by a court.
(2)   The provisions referred to in subsection (1) are   . . .   , section 445 and Part XV of the Companies Act 1985 [and section 794 of the Companies Act 2006].
(3)   The regulations may make different provision for different cases and may contain such transitional and other supplementary and incidental provisions as appear to the Secretary of State to be appropriate.
(4)   Regulations under this section shall not be made unless a draft of the regulations has been laid before Parliament and approved by resolution of each House of Parliament.

NOTES

Repealed by the Companies Act 2006, s 1295, Sch 16, as from a day to be appointed.

Sub-s (1): words in square brackets inserted by the Companies Act 2006 (Consequential Amendments etc) Order 2008, SI 2008/948, art 3(1), Sch 1, Pt 2, para 159(1), (2), as from 6 April 2008.

Sub-s (2): words omitted repealed, and words in square brackets inserted, by SI 2008/948, art 3, Sch 1, Pt 2, para 159(1), (3), Sch 2, as from 6 April 2008.

Regulations: the Companies (Disclosure of Interests in Shares) (Orders imposing restrictions on shares) Regulations 1991, SI 1991/1646 (which amends various provisions in Part VI (repealed), and Parts XIV, XV of CA 1985).

136–143 *(Ss 136, 142 repealed by the Companies Act 2006, s 1295, Sch 16, as from 1 October 2009. S 137 repealed by CA 2006, s 1295, Sch 16, as from 6 April 2008. S 138 repealed by CA 2006, s 1295, Sch 16, as from 1 October 2007. S 139(1)–(3) repealed CA 2006, s 1295, Sch 16, as from 1 October 2009. S 139(4) amends the Company Directors Disqualification Act 1986, Sch 1, Pt I, at* **[5.92]***. S 139(5) repealed by the Finance Act 2004, s 326, Sch 42, Part 2 (in relation to payments made on or after 6 April 2007 under contracts relating to construction operations). S 140 amends various provisions in the Companies Act 1985, Pt XVIII (Floating Charges and Receivers (Scotland)) at* **[5.37]** *et seq, and is repealed by the Bankruptcy and Diligence etc (Scotland) Act 2007, s 46(4), as from a day to be appointed (for savings, see the introductory note to Pt XVIII). S 141 repealed by CA 2006, s 1295, Sch 16, as from 1 October 2008 (in part), and as from 1 October 2009 (otherwise). S 143 repealed by CA 2006, s 1295, Sch 16, as from 20 January 2007 (in part), as from 6 April 2007 (in part), as from 1 October 2007 (in part), as from 6 April 2008 (in part), and as from 1 October 2009 (otherwise).)*

[5.109]
144 "Subsidiary", "holding company" and "wholly-owned subsidiary"
(1) . . .
(2) Any reference in any enactment (including any enactment contained in subordinate legislation within the meaning of the Interpretation Act 1978) to a "subsidiary" or "holding company" within the meaning of section 736 of the Companies Act 1985 shall, subject to any express amendment or saving made by or under this Act, be read as referring to a subsidiary or holding company as defined in section 736 as substituted by subsection (1) above.
This applies whether the reference is specific or general, or express or implied.
(3) . . .
(4) Schedule 18 contains amendments and savings consequential on the amendments made by this section; and the Secretary of State may by regulations make such further amendments or savings as appear to him to be necessary or expedient.
(5) Regulations under this section shall be made by statutory instrument which shall be subject to annulment in pursuance of a resolution of either House of Parliament.
(6) So much of section 23(3) of the Interpretation Act 1978 as applies section 17(2)(a) of that Act (presumption as to meaning of references to enactments repealed and re-enacted) to deeds or other instruments or documents does not apply in relation to the repeal and re-enactment by this section of section 736 of the Companies Act 1985.

NOTES
Sub-s (1), (3): repealed by the Companies Act 2006, s 1295, Sch 16, as from 1 October 2009.
Sub-ss (2), (6): repealed by the Companies Act 2006, s 1295, Sch 16, as from a day to be appointed.
Regulations: the Definition of Subsidiary (Consequential Amendments) Regulations 1990, SI 1990/1395 (which amend the Electricity Act 1989, s 77).

145–153 *(S 145 introduces Sch 19 (Minor amendments of CA1985); Pt VII (ie, ss 146–153 (Mergers and related matters)) provides as follows: ss 146–150 amended the Fair Trading Act 1973 and were repealed by the Enterprise Act 2002, s 278(2), Sch 26, as from 20 June 2003 (for all purposes except in relation to the merger of water or sewerage undertakings), and from 29 December 2004 (otherwise) (for transitional provisions see Sch 24 to the 2002 Act, and SI 2003/1397 and SI 2004/3233); s 151 inserts the Fair Trading Act 1973, s 93B; s 152 repealed by the Enterprise Act 2002, s 278(2), Sch 26, as from 29 December 2004; s 153 introduces Sch 20 (Amendments about Mergers and Related Matters).)*

PART VII
FINANCIAL MARKETS AND INSOLVENCY

NOTES
Transfer of functions: by the Transfer of Functions (Financial Services) Order 1992, SI 1992/1315, art 2(1)(c), the functions of the Secretary of State under this Part of this Act are transferred to the Treasury. However, by art 4 of, and Sch 2, para 7 to, that Order, the functions of the Secretary of State under ss 158(4), (5), 160(5), 170 (other than the function under s 170(1) of approving an overseas investment exchange) 171–174, 181, 185, and so much of his functions under s 186 as relate to any function under the aforementioned provisions, are to be exercisable jointly by the Secretary of State and the Treasury. See also the European Communities (Designation) (No 4) Order 2002, SI 2002/2840 in relation to certain open-ended collective investment schemes, and the Financial Markets and Insolvency Regulations 1996, SI 1996/1469.

Introduction

[5.110]
154 Introduction
This Part has effect for the purposes of safeguarding the operation of certain financial markets by provisions with respect to—

(a) the insolvency, winding up or default of a person party to transactions in the market (sections 155 to 172),

(b) the effectiveness or enforcement of certain charges given to secure obligations in connection with such transactions (sections 173 to 176), and

(c) rights and remedies in relation to certain property provided as cover for margin in relation to such transactions [or as default fund contribution,] or subject to such a charge (sections 177 to 181).

NOTES

Words in square brackets in para (c) inserted by the Financial Markets and Insolvency Regulations 2009, SI 2009/853, reg 2(1), (2), as from 15 June 2009.

Recognised investment exchanges and clearing houses

[5.111]
155 Market contracts
(1) This Part applies to the following descriptions of contract connected with a recognised investment exchange or recognised clearing house.

The contracts are referred to in this Part as "market contracts".

[(2) Except as provided in subsection (2A), in relation to a recognised investment exchange this Part applies to—

(a) contracts entered into by a member or designated non-member of the exchange [with a person other than the exchange] which are either
  (i) contracts made on the exchange or an exchange to whose undertaking the exchange has succeeded whether by amalgamation, merger or otherwise; or
  (ii) contracts in the making of which the member or designated non-member was subject to the rules of the exchange or of an exchange to whose undertaking the exchange has succeeded whether by amalgamation, merger or otherwise; . . .

[(b) contracts entered into by the exchange, in its capacity as such, with a member of the exchange or with a recognised clearing house or with another recognised investment exchange for the purpose of enabling the rights and liabilities of that member or clearing house or other investment exchange under a transaction to be settled; and

(c) contracts entered into by the exchange with a member of the exchange or with a recognised clearing house or with another recognised investment exchange for the purpose of providing central counterparty clearing services to that member or clearing house or other investment exchange.]

A "designated non-member" means a person in respect of whom action may be taken under the default rules of the exchange but who is not a member of the exchange.

[(2A) Where the exchange in question is a recognised overseas investment exchange, this Part does not apply to a contract that falls within paragraph (a) of subsection (2) (unless it also falls within subsection (3)).]

[(3) In relation to a recognised clearing house this Part applies to—

(a) contracts entered into by the clearing house, in its capacity as such, with a member of the clearing house or with a recognised investment exchange or with another recognised clearing house for the purpose of enabling the rights and liabilities of that member or investment exchange or other clearing house under a transaction to be settled; and

(b) contracts entered into by the clearing house with a member of the clearing house or with a recognised investment exchange or with another recognised clearing house for the purpose of providing central counterparty clearing services to that member or investment exchange or other clearing house.]

[(3A) In this section "central counterparty clearing services" means—

(a) the services provided by a recognised investment exchange or a recognised clearing house to the parties to a transaction in connection with contracts between each of the parties and the investment exchange or clearing house (in place of, or as an alternative to, a contract directly between the parties),

(b) the services provided by a recognised clearing house to a recognised investment exchange or to another recognised clearing house in connection with contracts between them, or

(c) the services provided by a recognised investment exchange to a recognised clearing house or to another recognised investment exchange in connection with contracts between them.]

(4) The Secretary of State may by regulations make further provision as to the contracts to be treated as "market contracts", for the purposes of this Part, in relation to a recognised investment exchange or recognised clearing house.

(5) The regulations may add to, amend or repeal the provisions of subsections (2) and (3) above.

NOTES

Sub-s (2) is amended as follows:

Substituted, together with sub-s (2A), for original sub-s (2) by the Financial Markets and Insolvency Regulations 1991, SI 1991/880, reg 3, as from 25 April 1991.

Words in first pair of square brackets inserted by the Financial Markets and Insolvency Regulations 1998, SI 1998/1748, reg 3, as from 11 August 1998.

Word omitted from para (a) repealed, and paras (b), (c) substituted (for the original para (b)) by the Financial Markets and Insolvency Regulations 2009, SI 2009/853, reg 2(1), (3)(a), as from 15 June 2009.

Sub-s (2A): substituted as noted above; further substituted by SI 2009/853, reg 2(1), (3)(b), as from 15 June 2009.

Sub-s (3): substituted by SI 1998/1748, reg 4, as from 11 August 1998; further substituted by SI 2009/853, reg 2(1), (3)(c), as from 15 June 2009.

Sub-s (3A): inserted by SI 2009/853, reg 2(1), (3)(d), as from 15 June 2009.

Regulations: the Financial Markets and Insolvency Regulations 1991, SI 1991/880; the Financial Markets and Insolvency Regulations 1998, SI 1998/1748; the Financial Markets and Insolvency Regulations 2009, SI 2009/853.

---

156   (*Repealed by the Financial Services and Markets Act 2000 (Consequential Amendments and Repeals) Order 2001, SI 2001/3649, art 75(e), as from 1 December 2001.*)

[5.112]
157   Change in default rules

(1)   A recognised UK investment exchange or recognised UK clearing house shall give the [Authority] at least 14 days' notice of any proposal to amend, revoke or add to its default rules; and the [Authority] may within 14 days from receipt of the notice direct the exchange or clearing house not to proceed with the proposal, in whole or in part.

(2)   A direction under this section may be varied or revoked.

(3)   Any amendment or revocation of, or addition to, the default rules of an exchange or clearing house in breach of a direction under this section is ineffective.

NOTES

Sub-s (1): words in square brackets substituted by the Financial Services and Markets Act 2000 (Consequential Amendments and Repeals) Order 2001, SI 2001/3649, art 79, as from 1 December 2001.

[5.113]
158   Modifications of the law of insolvency

(1)   The general law of insolvency has effect in relation to market contracts, and action taken under the rules of a recognised investment exchange or recognised clearing house with respect to such contracts, subject to the provisions of sections 159 to 165.

(2)   So far as those provisions relate to insolvency proceedings in respect of a person other than a defaulter, they apply in relation to—

[(a)   proceedings in respect of a recognised investment exchange or a member or designated non-member of a recognised investment exchange,

(aa)   proceedings in respect of a recognised clearing house or a member of a recognised clearing house, and]

(b)   proceedings in respect of a party to a market contract begun after a recognised investment exchange or recognised clearing house has taken action under its default rules in relation to a person party to the contract as principal,

but not in relation to any other insolvency proceedings, notwithstanding that rights or liabilities arising from market contracts fall to be dealt with in the proceedings.

(3)   The reference in subsection (2)(b) to the beginning of insolvency proceedings is to—

(a)   the presentation of a bankruptcy petition or a petition for sequestration of a person's estate, or

[(b)   the application for an administration order or the presentation of a winding-up petition or the passing of a resolution for voluntary winding up,] or

(c)   the appointment of an administrative receiver.

[(3A)   In subsection (3)(b) the reference to an application for an administration order shall be taken to include a reference to—

(a)   in a case where an administrator is appointed under paragraph 14 or 22 of Schedule B1 to the Insolvency Act 1986 (appointment by floating charge holder, company or directors) following filing with the court of a copy of a notice of intention to appoint under that paragraph, the filing of the copy of the notice, and

(b)   in a case where an administrator is appointed under either of those paragraphs without a copy of a notice of intention to appoint having been filed with the court, the appointment of the administrator.]

(4)   The Secretary of State may make further provision by regulations modifying the law of insolvency in relation to the matters mentioned in subsection (1).

(5)   The regulations may add to, amend or repeal the provisions mentioned in subsection (1), and any other provision of this Part as it applies for the purposes of those provisions, or provide that those provisions have effect subject to such additions, exceptions or adaptations as are specified in the regulations.

NOTES

Sub-s (2): paras (a), (aa) substituted, for original para (a), by the Financial Markets and Insolvency Regulations 2009, SI 2009/853, reg 2(1), (4), as from 15 June 2009 (for transitional provisions see the note below).

Sub-s (3): para (b) substituted by the Enterprise Act 2002, s 248(3), Sch 17, paras 43, 44(a), as from 15 September 2003 (for savings and transitional provisions, see the note to the Insolvency Act 1986, s 8 at **[9.105]**).

Sub-s (3A): inserted by the Enterprise Act 2002, s 248(3), Sch 17, paras 43, 44(b), as from 15 September 2003 (for savings and transitional provisions, see the note to the Insolvency Act 1986, s 8 at **[9.105]**).

Transitional provisions: the Financial Markets and Insolvency Regulations 2009, SI 2009/853, reg 1(2), (3) provides as follows—

"(2)   Regulation 2 paragraphs (4), (5), (6), (7), (8), (9), (10) and (12) apply to insolvency proceedings which relate to any of the insolvency events set out in paragraph (3) which take place on or after the date on which these Regulations come into force.

(3)   The insolvency events are—

(a)   an application for an administration order;
(b)   an application for a bank administration order under Part 3 of the Banking Act 2009;
(c)   the filing of a notice of intention to appoint an administrator for an appointment under paragraph 14 or 22 of Schedule B1 to the Insolvency Act 1986;
(d)   where no notice of intention to appoint is filed, the appointment of an administrator under paragraph 14 or 22 of Schedule B1 to the Insolvency Act 1986;
(e)   the presentation of a bankruptcy petition;
(f)   the presentation of a petition for sequestration of a person's estate;
(g)   the presentation of a winding up petition;
(h)   an application for a bank insolvency order under Part 2 of the Banking Act 2009;
(i)   the passing of a resolution for voluntary winding up;
(j)   the appointment of an administrative receiver;
(k)   the making of an order appointing an interim receiver.".

Regulations: the Financial Markets and Insolvency Regulations 1991, SI 1991/880; the Financial Markets and Insolvency Regulations 2009, SI 2009/853.

[5.114]
159   Proceedings of exchange or clearing house take precedence over insolvency procedures
(1)   None of the following shall be regarded as to any extent invalid at law on the ground of inconsistency with the law relating to the distribution of the assets of a person on bankruptcy, winding up or sequestration, or [in the administration of a company or other body or] in the administration of an insolvent estate—

(a)   a market contract,
(b)   the default rules of a recognised investment exchange or recognised clearing house,
(c)   the rules of a recognised investment exchange or recognised clearing house as to the settlement of market contracts not dealt with under its default rules.

(2)   The powers of a relevant office-holder in his capacity as such, and the powers of the court under the Insolvency Act 1986 or the Bankruptcy (Scotland) Act 1985 shall not be exercised in such a way as to prevent or interfere with—

(a)   the settlement in accordance with the rules of a recognised investment exchange or recognised clearing house of a market contract not dealt with under its default rules, or
(b)   any action taken under the default rules of such an exchange or clearing house.

This does not prevent a relevant office-holder from afterwards seeking to recover any amount under section 163(4) or 164(4) or prevent the court from afterwards making any such order or decree as is mentioned in section 165(1) or (2) (but subject to subsections (3) and (4) of that section).

(3)   Nothing in the following provisions of this Part shall be construed as affecting the generality of the above provisions.

(4)   A debt or other liability arising out of a market contract which is the subject of default proceedings may not be proved in a winding up or bankruptcy [or in the administration of a company or other body], or in Scotland claimed in a winding up or sequestration [or in the administration of a company or other body], until the completion of the default proceedings.

A debt or other liability which by virtue of this subsection may not be proved or claimed shall not be taken into account for the purposes of any set-off until the completion of the default proceedings.

[(4A)   However, prior to the completion of default proceedings—

(a)   where it appears to the chairman of the meeting of creditors that a sum will be certified under section 162(1) to be payable, subsection (4) shall not prevent any proof or claim including or consisting of an estimate of that sum which has been lodged or, in Scotland, submitted, from being admitted or, in Scotland, accepted, for the purpose only of determining the entitlement of a creditor to vote at a meeting of creditors; and
(b)   a creditor whose claim or proof has been lodged and admitted or, in Scotland, submitted and accepted, for the purpose of determining the entitlement of a creditor to vote at a meeting of creditors and which has not been subsequently wholly withdrawn, disallowed or rejected, is eligible as a creditor to be a member of a liquidation committee or, in bankruptcy proceedings in England and Wales, [or in the administration of a company or other body] a creditors' committee.]

(5)   For the purposes of [subsections (4) and (4A)] the default proceedings shall be taken to be completed in relation to a person when a report is made under section 162 stating the sum (if any) certified to be due to or from him.

NOTES

Sub-ss (1), (4): words in square brackets inserted by the Financial Markets and Insolvency Regulations 2009, SI 2009/853, reg 2(1), (5)(a), (b), as from 15 June 2009, subject to transitional provisions as noted to s 158 at **[5.113]**.

Sub-s (4A): inserted by the Financial Markets and Insolvency Regulations 1991, SI 1991/880, reg 4(1), (2), as from 25 April 1991; words in square brackets inserted by SI 2009/853, reg 2(1), (5)(c), as from 15 June 2009, subject to transitional provisions as noted to s 158 at **[5.113]**.

Sub-s (5): words in square brackets substituted by SI 1991/880, reg 4(1), (3), as from 25 April 1991.

[5.115]
160 Duty to give assistance for purposes of default proceedings
(1) It is the duty of—
  (a) any person who has or had control of any assets of a defaulter, and
  (b) any person who has or had control of any documents of or relating to a defaulter,
to give a recognised investment exchange or recognised clearing house such assistance as it may reasonably require for the purposes of its default proceedings.

This applies notwithstanding any duty of that person under the enactments relating to insolvency.

(2) A person shall not under this section be required to provide any information or produce any document which he would be entitled to refuse to provide or produce on grounds of legal professional privilege in proceedings in the High Court or on grounds of confidentiality as between client and professional legal adviser in proceedings in the Court of Session.

(3) Where original documents are supplied in pursuance of this section, the exchange or clearing house shall return them forthwith after the completion of the relevant default proceedings, and shall in the meantime allow reasonable access to them to the person by whom they were supplied and to any person who would be entitled to have access to them if they were still in the control of the person by whom they were supplied.

(4) The expenses of a relevant office-holder in giving assistance under this section are recoverable as part of the expenses incurred by him in the discharge of his duties; and he shall not be required under this section to take any action which involves expenses which cannot be so recovered, unless the exchange or clearing house undertakes to meet them.

There shall be treated as expenses of his such reasonable sums as he may determine in respect of time spent in giving the assistance [and for the purpose of determining the priority in which his expenses are payable out of the assets, sums in respect of time spent shall be treated as his remuneration and other sums shall be treated as his disbursements or, in Scotland, outlays].

(5) The Secretary of State may by regulations make further provision as to the duties of persons to give assistance to a recognised investment exchange or recognised clearing house for the purposes of its default proceedings, and the duties of the exchange or clearing house with respect to information supplied to it.

The regulations may add to, amend or repeal the provisions of subsections (1) to (4) above.

(6) In this section "document" includes information recorded in any form.

NOTES
Sub-s (4): words in square brackets inserted by the Financial Markets and Insolvency Regulations 1991, SI 1991/880, reg 5, as from 25 April 1991.

Regulations: the Financial Markets and Insolvency Regulations 1991, SI 1991/880.

[5.116]
161 Supplementary provisions as to default proceedings
(1) If the court is satisfied on an application by a relevant office-holder that a party to a market contract with a defaulter intends to dissipate or apply his assets so as to prevent the officer-holder recovering such sums as may become due upon the completion of the default proceedings, the court may grant such interlocutory relief (in Scotland, such interim order) as it thinks fit.

(2) A liquidator[, administrator] or trustee of a defaulter or, in Scotland, a permanent trustee on the sequestrated estate of the defaulter shall not—
  (a) declare or pay any dividend to the creditors, or
  (b) return any capital to contributories,
unless he has retained what he reasonably considers to be an adequate reserve in respect of any claims arising as a result of the default proceedings of the exchange or clearing house concerned.

(3) The court may on an application by a relevant office-holder make such order as it thinks fit altering or dispensing from compliance with such of the duties of his office as are affected by the fact that default proceedings are pending or could be taken, or have been or could have been taken.

(4) Nothing in [section 126, 128, 130, 185 or 285 of, or paragraph [40, 41,] 42 or 43 ([including those paragraphs as applied by paragraph 44]) of Schedule B1 to, the Insolvency Act 1986] (which restrict the taking of certain legal proceedings and other steps), and nothing in any rule of law in Scotland to the like effect as the said section 285, in the Bankruptcy (Scotland) Act 1985 or in the Debtors (Scotland) Act 1987 as to the effect of sequestration, shall affect any action taken by an exchange or clearing house for the purpose of its default proceedings.

NOTES
Sub-s (2): word in square brackets inserted by the Financial Markets and Insolvency Regulations 2009, SI 2009/853, reg 2(1), (6)(a), as from 15 June 2009, subject to transitional provisions as noted to s 158 at **[5.113]**.

Sub-s (4) is amended as follows:

Words in first (outer) pair of square brackets substituted by the Enterprise Act 2002, s 248(3), Sch 17, paras 43, 45, as from 15 September 2003 (for savings and transitional provisions in relation to a petition for an administration order presented before that date, and in relation to special administration regimes (within the meaning of the Enterprise Act 2002, s 249), see the note to the Insolvency Act 1986, s 8 at **[9.105]**).

Figures "40, 41," in square brackets inserted, and words "including those paragraphs as applied by paragraph 44" in square brackets substituted, by SI 2009/853, reg 2(1), (6)(b), as from 15 June 2009, subject to transitional provisions as noted to s 158 at **[5.113]**.

For an amendment to sub-s (4) as it continues to apply to special administration regimes by virtue of the Enterprise Act 2002, s 249(1), see SI 2009/853, reg 2(1), (6)(c) (as from the same date and subject to the same transitional provisions as noted above).

[5.117]
162 Duty to report on completion of default proceedings
(1) [Subject to subsection (1A),] a recognised investment exchange or recognised clearing house shall, on the completion of proceedings under its default rules, report to the [Authority] on its proceedings stating in respect of each creditor or debtor the sum certified by them to be payable from or to the defaulter or, as the case may be, the fact that no sum is payable.

[(1A) A recognised overseas investment exchange or recognised overseas clearing house shall not be subject to the obligation under subsection (1) unless it has been notified by the [Authority] that a report is required for the purpose of insolvency proceedings in any part of the United Kingdom.]

(2) The exchange or clearing house may make a single report or may make reports from time to time as proceedings are completed with respect to the transactions affecting particular persons.

(3) The exchange or clearing house shall supply a copy of every report under this section to the defaulter and to any relevant office-holder acting in relation to him or his estate.

(4) When a report under this section is received by the [Authority, it] shall publish notice of that fact in such manner as [it] thinks appropriate for bringing [the report] to the attention of creditors and debtors of the defaulter.

(5) An exchange or clearing house shall make available for inspection by a creditor or debtor of the defaulter so much of any report by it under this section as relates to the sum (if any) certified to be due to or from him or to the method by which that sum was determined.

(6) Any such person may require the exchange or clearing house, on payment of such reasonable fee as the exchange or clearing house may determine, to provide him with a copy of any part of a report which he is entitled to inspect.

NOTES
Sub-s (1): words in first pair of square brackets inserted by the Financial Markets and Insolvency Regulations 1991, SI 1991/880, reg 6(1), (2), as from 25 April 1991; word in second pair of square brackets substituted by the Financial Services and Markets Act 2000 (Consequential Amendments and Repeals) Order 2001, SI 2001/3649, art 80(1), (2), as from 1 December 2001.

Sub-s (1A): inserted by SI 1991/880, reg 6(1), (3), as from 25 April 1991; word in square brackets substituted by SI 2001/3649, art 80(1), (3), as from 1 December 2001.

Sub-s (4): words in square brackets substituted by SI 2001/3649, art 80(1), (4), as from 1 December 2001.

[5.118]
163 Net sum payable on completion of default proceedings
(1) The following provisions apply with respect to the net sum certified by a recognised investment exchange or recognised clearing house, upon proceedings under its default rules being duly completed in accordance with this Part, to be payable by or to a defaulter.

(2) If, in England and Wales, a bankruptcy[, winding-up or administration order has been made], or a resolution for voluntary winding up has been passed, the debt—
  (a) is provable in the bankruptcy[, winding up or administration] or, as the case may be, is payable to the relevant officer-holder, and
  (b) shall be taken into account, where appropriate, under section 323 of the Insolvency Act 1986 (mutual dealings and set-off) or the corresponding provision applicable in the case of winding up [or administration],
in the same way as a debt due before the commencement of the bankruptcy, the date on which the body corporate goes into liquidation (within the meaning of section 247 of the Insolvency Act 1986)[, or enters administration] or, in the case of a partnership, the date of the winding-up order [or the date on which the partnership enters administration].

(3) If, in Scotland, an award of sequestration or a winding-up [or administration] order has been made, or a resolution for voluntary winding up has been passed, the debt—
  (a) may be claimed in the sequestration[, winding up or administration] or, as the case may be, is payable to the relevant office-holder, and
  (b) shall be taken into account for the purposes of any rule of law relating to set-off applicable in sequestration[, winding up or administration],
in the same way as a debt due before the date of sequestration (within the meaning of section 73(1) of the Bankruptcy (Scotland) Act 1985) or the commencement of the winding up (within the meaning of section 129 of the Insolvency Act 1986) [or the date on which the body corporate enters administration].

[(3A) In subsections (2) and (3), a reference to the making of an administration order shall be taken to include a reference to the appointment of an administrator under—

(a)   paragraph 14 of Schedule B1 to the Insolvency Act 1986 (appointment by holder of qualifying floating charge); or

(b)   paragraph 22 of that Schedule (appointment by company or directors).]

(4)   However, where (or to the extent that) a sum is taken into account by virtue of subsection (2)(b) or (3)(b) which arises from a contract entered into at a time when the creditor had notice—

(a)   that a bankruptcy petition or, in Scotland, a petition for sequestration was pending, ...

(b)   that a meeting of creditors had been summoned under section 98 of the Insolvency Act 1986 or that a winding-up petition was pending, [or]

[(c)   that an application for an administration order was pending or that any person had given notice of intention to appoint an administrator,]

the value of any profit to him arising from the sum being so taken into account (or being so taken into account to that extent) is recoverable from him by the relevant office-holder unless the court directs otherwise.

(5)   Subsection (4) does not apply in relation to a sum arising from a contract effected under the default rules of a recognised investment exchange or recognised clearing house.

(6)   Any sum recoverable by virtue of subsection (4) ranks for priority, in the event of the insolvency of the person from whom it is due, immediately before preferential or, in Scotland, preferred debts.

NOTES

Sub-s (2): words in first and second pairs of square brackets substituted, and words in other pairs of square brackets inserted, by the Financial Markets and Insolvency Regulations 2009, SI 2009/853, reg 2(1), (7)(a), as from 15 June 2009, subject to transitional provisions as noted to s 158 at **[5.113]**.

Sub-s (3): the words ", winding up or administration" (in both places that they occur) were substituted, and the other words in square brackets were inserted, by SI 2009/853, reg 2(1), (7)(b), as from 15 June 2009, subject to transitional provisions as noted to s 158 at **[5.113]**.

Sub-s (3A): inserted by SI 2009/853, reg 2(1), (7)(c), as from 15 June 2009, subject to transitional provisions as noted to s 158 at **[5.113]**.

Sub-s (4): the word omitted from the end of para (a) was repealed, and the word "or" at the end of para (b) was inserted together with para (c), by SI 2009/853, reg 2(1), (7)(d), as from 15 June 2009, subject to transitional provisions as noted to s 158 at **[5.113]**.

[5.119]

164 Disclaimer of property, rescission of contracts, &c

(1)   Sections 178, 186, 315 and 345 of the Insolvency Act 1986 (power to disclaim onerous property and court's power to order rescission of contracts, &c) do not apply in relation to—

(a)   a market contract, or

(b)   a contract effected by the exchange or clearing house for the purpose of realising property provided as margin in relation to market contracts [or as default fund contribution].

In the application of this subsection in Scotland, the reference to sections 178, 315 and 345 shall be construed as a reference to any rule of law having the like effect as those sections.

(2)   In Scotland, a permanent trustee on the sequestrated estate of a defaulter or a liquidator is bound by any market contract to which that defaulter is a party and by any contract as is mentioned in subsection (1)(b) above notwithstanding section 42 of the Bankruptcy (Scotland) Act 1985 or any rule of law to the like effect applying in liquidations.

(3)   Sections 127 and 284 of the Insolvency Act 1986 (avoidance of property dispositions effected after commencement of winding up or presentation of bankruptcy petition), and section 32(8) of the Bankruptcy (Scotland) Act 1985 (effect of dealing with debtor relating to estate vested in permanent trustee) do not apply to—

(a)   a market contract, or any disposition of property in pursuance of such a contract,

(b)   the provision of margin in relation to market contracts,

[(ba) the provision of default fund contribution to the exchange or clearing house,]

(c)   a contract effected by the exchange or clearing house for the purpose of realising property provided as margin in relation to a market contract [or as default fund contribution], or any disposition of property in pursuance of such a contract, or

(d)   any disposition of property in accordance with the rules of the exchange or clearing house as to the application of property provided as margin [or as default fund contribution].

(4)   However, where—

(a)   a market contract is entered into by a person who has notice that a petition has been presented for the winding up or bankruptcy or sequestration of the estate of the other party to the contract, or

(b)   margin in relation to a market contract [or default fund contribution] is accepted by a person who has notice that such a petition has been presented in relation to the person by whom or on whose behalf the margin [or default fund contribution] is provided,

the value of any profit to him arising from the contract or, as the case may be, the amount or value of the margin [or default fund contribution] is recoverable from him by the relevant office-holder unless the court directs otherwise.

(5) Subsection (4)(a) does not apply where the person entering into the contract is a recognised investment exchange or recognised clearing house acting in accordance with its rules, or where the contract is effected under the default rules of such an exchange or clearing house; but subsection (4)(b) applies in relation to the provision of margin in relation to such a contract [or of default fund contribution].

(6) Any sum recoverable by virtue of subsection (4) ranks for priority, in the event of the insolvency of the person from whom it is due, immediately before preferential or, in Scotland, preferred debts.

NOTES

Sub-ss (1), (3)–(5): words in square brackets inserted by the Financial Markets and Insolvency Regulations 2009, SI 2009/853, reg 2(1), (8), as from 15 June 2009, subject to transitional provisions as noted to s 158 at **[5.113]**.

[5.120]
165 Adjustment of prior transactions
(1) No order shall be made in relation to a transaction to which this section applies under—
- (a)   section 238 or 339 of the Insolvency Act 1986 (transactions at an undervalue),
- (b)   section 239 or 340 of that Act (preferences), or
- (c)   section 423 of that Act (transactions defrauding creditors).

(2) As respects Scotland, no decree shall be granted in relation to any such transaction—
- (a)   under section 34 or 36 of the Bankruptcy (Scotland) Act 1985 or section 242 or 243 of the Insolvency Act 1986 (gratuitous alienations and unfair preferences), or
- (b)   at common law on grounds of gratuitous alienations or fraudulent preferences.

(3) This section applies to—
- (a)   a market contract to which a recognised investment exchange or recognised clearing house is a party or which is entered into under its default rules, and
- (b)   a disposition of property in pursuance of such a market contract.

(4) Where margin is provided in relation to a market contract and (by virtue of subsection (3)(a) or otherwise) no such order or decree as is mentioned in subsection (1) or (2) has been, or could be, made in relation to that contract, this section applies to—
- (a)   the provision of the margin,
- (b)   any contract effected by the exchange or clearing house in question for the purpose of realising the property provided as margin, and
- (c)   any disposition of property in accordance with the rules of the exchange or clearing house [in question] as to the application of property provided as margin.

[(5) This section also applies to—
- (a)   the provision of default fund contribution to a recognised investment exchange or recognised clearing house,
- (b)   any contract effected by a recognised investment exchange or recognised clearing house for the purpose of realising the property provided as default fund contribution, and
- (c)   any disposition of property in accordance with the rules of the recognised investment exchange or recognised clearing house as to the application of property provided as default fund contribution.]

NOTES

Sub-s (4): words in square brackets inserted by the Financial Markets and Insolvency Regulations 2009, SI 2009/853, reg 2(1), (9)(a), as from 15 June 2009, subject to transitional provisions as noted to s 158 at **[5.113]**.

Sub-s (5): added by SI 2009/853, reg 2(1), (9)(b), as from 15 June 2009, subject to transitional provisions as noted to s 158 at **[5.113]**.

[5.121]
166 Powers of Secretary of State to give directions
(1) The powers conferred by this section are exercisable in relation to a recognised UK investment exchange or recognised UK clearing house.

(2) Where in any case an exchange or clearing house has not taken action under its default rules—
- (a)   if it appears to the [Authority] that it could take action, [the Authority] may direct it to do so, and
- (b)   if it appears to the [Authority] that it is proposing to take or may take action, [the Authority] may direct it not to do so.

(3) Before giving such a direction the [Authority] shall consult the exchange or clearing house in question; and [it] shall not give a direction unless [it] is satisfied, in the light of that consultation—
- (a)   in the case of a direction to take action, that failure to take action would involve undue risk to investors or other participants in the market, or
- (b)   in the case of a direction not to take action, that the taking of action would be premature or otherwise undesirable in the interests of investors or other participants in the market.

(4) A direction shall specify the grounds on which it is given.

(5) A direction not to take action may be expressed to have effect until the giving of a further direction (which may be a direction to take action or simply revoking the earlier direction).

(6) No direction shall be given not to take action if, in relation to the person in question—

(a)   a bankruptcy order or an award of sequestration of his estate has been made, or an interim receiver or interim trustee has been appointed, or

(b)   a winding up order has been made, a resolution for voluntary winding up has been passed or an administrator, administrative receiver or provisional liquidator has been appointed;

and any previous direction not to take action shall cease to have effect on the making or passing of any such order, award or appointment.

(7)   Where an exchange or clearing house has taken or been directed to take action under its default rules, the [Authority] may direct it to do or not to do such things (being things which it has power to do under its default rules) as are specified in the direction.

The [Authority] shall not give such a direction unless [it is satisfied that the direction] will not impede or frustrate the proper and efficient conduct of the default proceedings.

(8)   A direction under this section is enforceable, on the application of the [Authority], by injunction or, in Scotland, by an order under section 45 of the Court of Session Act 1988; and where an exchange or clearing house has not complied with a direction, the court may make such order as it thinks fit for restoring the position to what it would have been if the direction had been complied with.

NOTES

Sub-ss (2), (3), (7), (8): words in square brackets substituted by the Financial Services and Markets Act 2000 (Consequential Amendments and Repeals) Order 2001, SI 2001/3649, art 81, as from 1 December 2001.

In consequence of these amendments it is thought that the heading to this section should refer to the powers of the Authority. No amendment was made to the section heading though.

[5.122]
167   Application to determine whether default proceedings to be taken

[(1)   This section applies where a relevant insolvency event has occurred in the case of—

(a)   a recognised investment exchange or a member or designated non-member of a recognised investment exchange, or

(b)   a recognised clearing house or a member of a recognised clearing house.

The investment exchange, member, designated non-member or clearing house in whose case a relevant insolvency event has occurred is referred to below as "the person in default".

(1A)   For the purposes of this section a "relevant insolvency event" occurs where—

(a)   a bankruptcy order is made,

(b)   an award of sequestration is made,

(c)   an order appointing an interim receiver is made,

(d)   an administration or winding up order is made,

(e)   an administrator is appointed under paragraph 14 of Schedule B1 to the Insolvency Act 1986 (appointment by holder of qualifying floating charge) or under paragraph 22 of that Schedule (appointment by company or directors),

(f)   a resolution for voluntary winding up is passed, or

(g)   an order appointing a provisional liquidator is made.

(1B)   Where in relation to a person in default a recognised investment exchange or a recognised clearing house ("the responsible exchange or clearing house")—

(a)   has power under its default rules to take action in consequence of the relevant insolvency event or the matters giving rise to it, but

(b)   has not done so,

a relevant office-holder appointed in connection with or in consequence of the relevant insolvency event may apply to the Authority.]

(2)   The application shall specify [the responsible exchange or clearing house] and the grounds on which it is made.

(3)   On receipt of the application the [Authority] shall notify [the responsible exchange or clearing house], and unless within three business days after the day on which the notice is received [the responsible exchange or clearing house]—

(a)   takes action under its default rules, or

(b)   notifies the [Authority] that it proposes to do so forthwith,

then, subject as follows, the provisions of sections 158 to 165 above do not apply in relation to market contracts to which [the person in default] is a party or to anything done by [the responsible exchange or clearing house] for the purposes of, or in connection with, the settlement of any such contract.

For this purpose a "business day" means any day which is not a Saturday or Sunday, Christmas Day, Good Friday or a bank holiday in any part of the United Kingdom under the Banking and Financial Dealings Act 1971.

(4)   The provisions of sections 158 to 165 are not disapplied if before the end of the period mentioned in subsection (3) the [Authority] gives [the responsible exchange or clearing house] a direction under section 166(2)(a) (direction to take action under default rules).

No such direction may be given after the end of that period.

(5) If [the responsible exchange or clearing house] notifies the [Authority] that it proposes to take action under its default rules forthwith, it shall do so; and that duty is enforceable, on the application of the [Authority], by injunction or, in Scotland, by an order under section 45 of the Court of Session Act 1988.

NOTES

Sub-ss (1), (1A), (1B): substituted (for sub-s (1) and sub-s (1A) (as inserted by the Enterprise Act 2002, s 248(3), Sch 17, paras 43, 46, as from 15 September 200)) by the Financial Markets and Insolvency Regulations 2009, SI 2009/853, reg 2(1), (10)(a), as from 15 June 200, subject to transitional provisions as noted to s 158 at **[5.113]**.

Sub-s (2): words in square brackets substituted by SI 2009/853, reg 2(1), (10)(b), as from 15 June 2009, subject to transitional provisions as noted to s 158 at **[5.113]**.

Sub-s (3): word "Authority" in square brackets (in both places it occurs) substituted by the Financial Services and Markets Act 2000 (Consequential Amendments and Repeals) Order 2001, SI 2001/3649, art 82, as from 1 December 2001. Other words in square brackets substituted by SI 2009/853, reg 2(1), (10)(c), as from 15 June 2009, subject to transitional provisions as noted to s 158 at **[5.113]**.

Sub-ss (4), (5): word "Authority" in square brackets substituted by SI 2001/3649, art 82, as from 1 December 2001. Other words in square brackets substituted by SI 2009/853, reg 2(1), (10)(d), as from 15 June 2009, subject to transitional provisions as noted to s 158 at **[5.113]**.

168 (*Repealed by the Financial Services and Markets Act 2000 (Consequential Amendments and Repeals) Order 2001, SI 2001/3649, art 75(f), as from 1 December 2001.*)

[5.123]
169 Supplementary provisions
(1) . . .
(2) [Sections 296 and 297 of the Financial Services and Markets Act 2000 apply] in relation to a failure by a recognised investment exchange or recognised clearing house to comply with an obligation under this Part as to a failure to comply with an obligation under that Act.
(3) Where the recognition of an investment exchange or clearing house is revoked under the [Financial Services and Markets Act 2000, the appropriate authority] may, before or after the revocation order, give such directions as [it] thinks fit with respect to the continued application of the provisions of this Part, with such exceptions, additions and adaptations as may be specified in the direction, in relation to cases where a relevant event of any description specified in the directions occurred before the revocation order takes effect.
[(3A) "The appropriate authority" means—
   (a) in the case of an overseas investment exchange or clearing house, the Treasury; and
   (b) in the case of a UK investment exchange or clearing house, the Authority.]
(4) . . .
(5) [Regulations under section 414 of the Financial Services and Markets Act 2000 (service of notices) may make provision] in relation to a notice, direction or other document required or authorised by or under this Part to be given to or served on any person other than the [Treasury or the Authority].

NOTES

Sub-s (1): repealed by the Financial Services and Markets Act 2000 (Consequential Amendments and Repeals) Order 2001, SI 2001/3649, art 75(g), as from 1 December 2001.

Sub-ss (2), (3), (5): words in square brackets substituted by SI 2001/3649, art 83(1)–(3), (5), as from 1 December 2001.

Sub-s (3A): inserted by SI 2001/3649, art 83(1), (4), as from 1 December 2001.

Sub-s (4): repealed (without having been brought into force) by SI 2001/3649, art 75(g), as from 1 December 2001.

Other exchanges and clearing houses
[5.124]
170 Certain overseas exchanges and clearing houses
[(1) The Secretary of State and the Treasury may by regulations provide that this Part applies in relation to contracts connected with an overseas investment exchange or overseas clearing house which—
   (a) is not a recognised investment exchange or recognised clearing house, but
   (b) is approved by the Treasury in accordance with such requirements as may be so specified,
as it applies in relation to contracts connected with a recognised investment exchange or recognised clearing house.]
(2) The [Treasury] shall not approve an overseas investment exchange or clearing house unless [they are] satisfied—
   (a) that the rules and practices of the body, together with the law of the country in which the body's head office is situated, provide adequate procedures for dealing with the default of persons party to contracts connected with the body, and
   (b) that it is otherwise appropriate to approve the body.
(3) The reference in subsection (2)(a) to default is to a person being unable to meet his obligations.
(4) The regulations may apply in relation to the approval of a body under this section such of the provisions of the [Financial Services and Markets Act 2000] as the Secretary of State considers appropriate.

(5) The Secretary of State may make regulations which, in relation to a body which is so approved—

   (a) apply such of the provisions of the [Financial Services and Markets Act 2000] as the Secretary of State considers appropriate, and

   (b) provide that the provisions of this Part apply with such exceptions, additions and adaptations as appear to the Secretary of State to be necessary or expedient;

and different provision may be made with respect to different bodies or descriptions of body.

(6) Where the regulations apply any provisions of the [Financial Services and Markets Act 2000], they may provide that those provisions apply with such exceptions, additions and adaptations as appear to the Secretary of State to be necessary or expedient.

NOTES

Commencement: 25 March 1991 (certain purposes); not in force (otherwise); see the final note below.

Sub-s (1): substituted by the Financial Markets and Insolvency Regulations 2009, SI 2009/853, reg 2(1), (11), as from 15 June 2009.

Sub-ss (2), (4)–(6): words in square brackets substituted by SI 2001/3649, art 84(1), (3), (4), as from 1 December 2001.

Note: the Companies Act 1989 (Commencement No 9 and Saving and Transitional Provisions) Order 1991, SI 1991/488 provided that this Part (ie, ss 154–191, Schs 21, 22) comes into force on 25 March 1991 in so far as necessary to enable Regulations to be made under ss 155(4), (5), 158(4), (5), 160(5), 173(4), (5), 174(2)–(4), 185, 186, 187(3), Sch 21, para 2(3). The Companies Act 1989 (Commencement No 10 and Saving Provisions) Order 1991, SI 1991/878 brought most of the remaining provisions of this Part into force on 25 April 1991 but, as of 1 July 2011, this section (and ss 172, 178) had not been commenced for other purposes.

171 (*Repealed by the Financial Services and Markets Act 2000 (Consequential Amendments and Repeals) Order 2001, SI 2001/3649, art 75(h), as from 1 December 2001.*)

[5.125]
172 Settlement arrangements provided by the Bank of England

(1) The Secretary of State may by regulations provide that this Part applies to contracts of any specified description in relation to which settlement arrangements are provided by the Bank of England, as it applies to contracts connected with a recognised investment exchange or recognised clearing house.

(2) Regulations under this section may provide that the provisions of this Part apply with such exceptions, additions and adaptations as appear to the Secretary of State to be necessary or expedient.

(3) Before making any regulations under this section, the Secretary of State [and the Treasury shall consult] the Bank of England.

NOTES

Commencement: 25 March 1991 (certain purposes); not in force (otherwise).

Sub-s (3): words in square brackets substituted by the Transfer of Functions (Financial Services) Order 1992, SI 1992/1315, art 10(1), Sch 4, para 13, as from 7 June 1992.

As to the commencement of this section, see the note to s 170 at **[5.124]**.

Market charges

[5.126]
173 Market charges

(1) In this Part "market charge" means a charge whether fixed or floating, granted—

   (a) in favour of a recognised investment exchange, for the purpose of securing debts or liabilities arising in connection with the settlement of market contracts,

   [(aa) in favour of The Stock Exchange, for the purpose of securing debts or liabilities arising in connection with short term certificates;]

   (b) in favour of a recognised clearing house, for the purpose of securing debts or liabilities arising in connection with their ensuring the performance of market contracts, or

   (c) in favour of a person who agrees to make payments as a result of the transfer [or allotment] of specified securities made through the medium of a computer-based system established by the Bank of England and The Stock Exchange, for the purpose of securing debts or liabilities of the transferee [or allottee] arising in connection therewith.

(2) Where a charge is granted partly for purposes specified in subsection (1)(a), [(aa),] (b) or (c) and partly for other purposes, it is a "market charge" so far as it has effect for the specified purposes.

(3) [In subsection (1)—

"short term certificate" means an instrument issued by The Stock Exchange undertaking to procure the transfer of property of a value and description specified in the instrument to or to the order of the person to whom the instrument is issued or his endorsee or to a person acting on behalf of either of them and also undertaking to make appropriate payments in cash, in the event that the obligation to procure the transfer of property cannot be discharged in whole or in part;]

"specified securities" means securities for the time being specified in the list in Schedule 1 to the Stock Transfer Act 1982, and includes any right to such securities; and

"transfer", in relation to any such securities or right, means a transfer of the beneficial interest.

(4)   The Secretary of State may by regulations make further provision as to the charges granted in favour of any such person as is mentioned in subsection (1)(a), (b) or (c) which are to be treated as "market charges" for the purposes of this Part; and the regulations may add to, amend or repeal the provisions of subsections (1) to (3) above.

(5)   The regulations may provide that a charge shall or shall not be treated as a market charge if or to the extent that it secures obligations of a specified description, is a charge over property of a specified description or contains provisions of a specified description.

(6)   Before making regulations under this section in relation to charges granted in favour of a person within subsection (1)(c), the Secretary of State [and the Treasury shall consult] the Bank of England.

NOTES

Sub-s (1): para (aa), and words in square brackets in para (c), inserted by the Financial Markets and Insolvency Regulations 1991, SI 1991/880, reg 9(a), (b), as from 25 April 1991.

Sub-s (2): words in square brackets inserted by SI 1991/880, reg 9(c), as from 25 April 1991.

Sub-s (3): words in square brackets substituted by SI 1991/880, reg 9(d), as from 25 April 1991.

Sub-s (6): words in square brackets substituted by the Transfer of Functions (Financial Services) Order 1992, SI 1992/1315, art 10(1), Sch 4, para 13, as from 7 June 1992.

Regulations: the Financial Markets and Insolvency Regulations 1991, SI 1991/880; the Financial Markets and Insolvency (CGO Service) Regulations 1999, SI 1999/1209.

[5.127]
174   Modifications of the law of insolvency

(1)   The general law of insolvency has effect in relation to market charges and action taken in enforcing them subject to the provisions of section 175.

(2)   The Secretary of State may by regulations make further provision modifying the law of insolvency in relation to the matters mentioned in subsection (1).

(3)   The regulations may add to, amend or repeal the provisions mentioned in subsection (1), and any other provision of this Part as it applies for the purposes of those provisions, or provide that those provisions have effect with such exceptions, additions or adaptations as are specified in the regulations.

(4)   The regulations may make different provision for cases defined by reference to the nature of the charge, the nature of the property subject to it, the circumstances, nature or extent of the obligations secured by it or any other relevant factor.

(5)   Before making regulations under this section in relation to charges granted in favour of a person within section 173(1)(c), the Secretary of State [and the Treasury shall consult] the Bank of England.

NOTES

Sub-s (5): words in square brackets substituted by the Transfer of Functions (Financial Services) Order 1992, SI 1992/1315, art 10(1), Sch 4, para 13, as from 7 June 1992.

Regulations: the Financial Markets and Insolvency Regulations 1991, SI 1991/880; the Financial Markets and Insolvency (CGO Service) Regulations 1999, SI 1999/1209.

[5.128]
175   Administration orders, &c

[(1)   The following provisions of Schedule B1 to the Insolvency Act 1986 (administration) do not apply in relation to a market charge—

    (a)   paragraph 43(2) and (3) (restriction on enforcement of security or repossession of goods) (including that provision as applied by paragraph 44 (interim moratorium)), and

    (b)   paragraphs 70, 71 and 72 (power of administrator to deal with charged or hire-purchase property).

(1A)   Paragraph 41(2) of that Schedule (receiver to vacate office at request of administrator) does not apply to a receiver appointed under a market charge.]

(2)   However, where a market charge falls to be enforced after [the occurrence of an event to which subsection (2A) applies], and there exists another charge over some or all of the same property ranking in priority to or *pari passu* with the market charge [on the application of any person interested], the court may order that there shall be taken after enforcement of the market charge such steps as the court may direct for the purpose of ensuring that the chargee under the other charge is not prejudiced by the enforcement of the market charge.

[(2A)   This subsection applies to—

    (a)   making an administration application under paragraph 12 of Schedule B1 to the Insolvency Act 1986,

    (b)   appointing an administrator under paragraph 14 or 22 of that Schedule (appointment by floating charge holder, company or directors),

    (c)   filing with the court a copy of notice of intention to appoint an administrator under either of those paragraphs.]

(3)   The following provisions of the Insolvency Act 1986 (which relate to the powers of receivers) do not apply in relation to a market charge—

    (a)   section 43 (power of administrative receiver to dispose of charged property), and

(b)   section 61 (power of receiver in Scotland to dispose of an interest in property).

(4)   Sections 127 and 284 of the Insolvency Act 1986 (avoidance of property dispositions effected after commencement of winding up or presentation of bankruptcy petition), and section 32(8) of the Bankruptcy (Scotland) Act 1985 (effect of dealing with debtor relating to estate vested in permanent trustee), do not apply to a disposition of property as a result of which the property becomes subject to a market charge or any transaction pursuant to which that disposition is made.

(5)   However, if a person (other than the chargee under the market charge) who is party to a disposition mentioned in subsection (4) has notice at the time of the disposition that a petition has been presented for the winding up or bankruptcy or sequestration of the estate of the party making the disposition, the value of any profit to him arising from the disposition is recoverable from him by the relevant office-holder unless the court directs otherwise.

(6)   Any sum recoverable by virtue of subsection (5) ranks for priority, in the event of the insolvency of the person from whom it is due, immediately before preferential or, in Scotland, preferred debts.

(7)   In a case falling within both subsection (4) above (as a disposition of property as a result of which the property becomes subject to a market charge) and section 164(3) (as the provision of margin in relation to a market contract), section 164(4) applies with respect to the recovery of the amount or value of the margin and subsection (5) above does not apply.

NOTES

Sub-ss (1), (1A): substituted, for original sub-s (1), by the Enterprise Act 2002, s 248(3), Sch 17, paras 43, 47(1), (2), as from 15 September 2003 (for savings and transitional provisions, see the note to the Insolvency Act 1986, s 8 at **[9.105]**). Note that the original sub-s (1) (as it continues to apply to special administration regimes by virtue of the Enterprise Act 2002, s 249(1)) is further substituted by the Financial Markets and Insolvency Regulations 2009, SI 2009/853, reg 2(1), (12) (as from 15 June 2009 and subject to the same transitional provisions as noted to s 158 at **[5.113]**).

Sub-s (2): words in first pair of square brackets substituted by the Enterprise Act 2002, s 248(3), Sch 17, paras 43, 47(1), (3), as from 15 September 2003 (for savings and transitional provisions, see the note to the Insolvency Act 1986, s 8 at **[9.105]**); words in second pair of square brackets inserted by the Financial Markets and Insolvency Regulations 1991, SI 1991/880, reg 18, as from 25 April 1991.

Sub-s (2A): inserted by the Enterprise Act 2002, s 248(3), Sch 17, paras 43, 47(1), (4), as from 15 September 2003 (for savings and transitional provisions, see the note to the Insolvency Act 1986, s 8 at **[9.105]**).

[5.129]
176   Power to make provision about certain other charges
(1)   The Secretary of State may by regulations provide that the general law of insolvency has effect in relation to charges of such descriptions as may be specified in the regulations, and action taken in enforcing them, subject to such provisions as may be specified in the regulations.

(2)   The regulations may specify any description of charge granted in favour of—
   (a)   a body approved under section 170 (certain overseas exchanges and clearing houses),
   (b)   a person included in the list maintained by the [. . . Authority] for the purposes of [section 301 of the Financial Services and Markets Act 2000] (certain money market institutions),
   (c)   the Bank of England,
   [(d)   a person who has permission under Part 4 of the Financial Services and Markets Act 2000 to carry on a relevant regulated activity, or
   (e)   an international securities self-regulating organisation approved for the purposes of an order made under section 22 of the Financial Services and Markets Act 2000,]
for the purpose of securing debts or liabilities arising in connection with or as a result of the settlement of contracts or the transfer of assets, rights or interests on a financial market.

(3)   The regulations may specify any description of charge granted for that purpose in favour of any other person in connection with exchange facilities or clearing services provided by a recognised investment exchange or recognised clearing house or by any such body, person, authority or organisation as is mentioned in subsection (2).

(4)   Where a charge is granted partly for the purpose specified in subsection (2) and partly for other purposes, the power conferred by this section is exercisable in relation to the charge so far as it has effect for that purpose.

(5)   The regulations may—
   (a)   make the same or similar provision in relation to the charges to which they apply as is made by or under sections 174 and 175 in relation to market charges, or
   (b)   apply any of those provisions with such exceptions, additions or adaptations as are specified in the regulations.

[(6)   Before making regulations under this section relating to a description of charges defined by reference to their being granted in favour of a person included in the list maintained by the . . . Authority for the purposes of [section 301 of the Financial Services and Markets Act 2000], or in connection with exchange facilities or clearing services provided by a person included in that list, the Secretary of State and the Treasury shall consult the Authority and the Bank of England.

(6A)   Before making regulations under this section relating to a description of charges defined by reference to their being granted in favour of the Bank of England, or in connection with settlement arrangements provided by the Bank, the Secretary of State and the Treasury shall consult the Bank.]

(7)   Regulations under this section may provide that they apply or do not apply to a charge if or to the extent that it secures obligations of a specified description, is a charge over property of a specified description or contains provisions of a specified description.

[(8)   For the purposes of subsection (2)(d), "relevant regulated activity" means—

(a)   dealing in investments as principal or as agent;

(b)   arranging deals in investments;

[(ba) operating a multilateral trading facility;]

(c)   managing investments;

(d)   safeguarding and administering investments;

(e)   sending dematerialised instructions; or

(f)   establishing etc a collective investment scheme.

(9)   Subsection (8) must be read with—

(a)   section 22 of the Financial Services and Markets Act 2000;

(b)   any relevant order under that section; and

(c)   Schedule 2 to that Act.]

NOTES

Sub-s (2): words in first pair of square brackets in para (b) substituted by the Bank of England Act 1998, s 23(1), Sch 5, Pt III, paras 46, 48(1), (2), as from 1 June 1998; words omitted therefrom repealed, and words in second pair of square brackets substituted, by the Financial Services and Markets Act 2000 (Consequential Amendments and Repeals) Order 2001, SI 2001/3649, art 85(1), (2), as from 1 December 2001. Note that the section-heading of the Financial Services and Markets Act 2000, s 301 is "supervision of certain contracts" and not "certain money market institutions" as stated in sub-s (2)(b) above, therefore it is thought that the words "certain money market institutions" should be deleted from the text of this subsection. Paras (d), (e) substituted by SI 2001/3649, art 85(1), (3), as from 1 December 2001.

Sub-s (6): substituted, together with sub-s (6A) for original sub-s (6), by the Bank of England Act 1998, s 23(1), Sch 5, Pt III, paras 46, 48(1), (3), as from 1 June 1998; words omitted repealed, and words in square brackets substituted, by SI 2001/3649, art 85(1), (4), as from 1 December 2001.

Sub-s (6A): substituted as noted above.

Sub-s (8): added, together with sub-s (9), by SI 2001/3649, art 85(1), (5), as from 1 December 2001; para (ba) inserted by the Financial Services and Markets Act 2000 (Regulated Activities) (Amendment No 3) Order 2006, SI 2006/3384, art 32, as from 1 November 2007.

Sub-s (9): added as noted above.

Market property

[5.130]

177   Application of margin [or default fund contribution] not affected by certain other interests

(1)   The following provisions have effect with respect to the application by a recognised investment exchange or recognised clearing house of property (other than land) held by the exchange or clearing house as margin in relation to a market contract [or as default fund contribution].

(2)   So far as necessary to enable the property to be applied in accordance with the rules of the exchange or clearing house, it may be so applied notwithstanding any prior equitable interest or right, or any right or remedy arising from a breach of fiduciary duty, unless the exchange or clearing house had notice of the interest, right or breach of duty at the time the property was provided as margin [or as default fund contribution].

(3)   No right or remedy arising subsequently to the property being provided as margin [or as default fund contribution] may be enforced so as to prevent or interfere with the application of the property by the exchange or clearing house in accordance with its rules.

(4)   Where an exchange or clearing house has power by virtue of the above provisions to apply property notwithstanding an interest, right or remedy, a person to whom the exchange or clearing house disposes of the property in accordance with its rules takes free from that interest, right or remedy.

NOTES

Words in square brackets inserted by the Financial Markets and Insolvency Regulations 2009, SI 2009/853, reg 2(1), (13), as from 15 June 2009.

[5.131]

178   Priority of floating market charge over subsequent charges

(1)   The Secretary of State may by regulations provide that a market charge which is a floating charge has priority over a charge subsequently created or arising, including a fixed charge.

(2)   The regulations may make different provision for cases defined, as regards the market charge or the subsequent charge, by reference to the description of charge, its terms, the circumstances in which it is created or arises, the nature of the charge, the person in favour of whom it is granted or arises or any other relevant factor.

NOTES

Commencement: 25 March 1991 (certain purposes); not in force (otherwise).

As to the commencement of this section, see the note to s 170 at **[5.124]**.

[5.132]
179 Priority of market charge over unpaid vendor's lien
Where property subject to an unpaid vendor's lien becomes subject to a market charge, the charge has priority over the lien unless the chargee had actual notice of the lien at the time the property became subject to the charge.

[5.133]
180 Proceedings against market property by unsecured creditors
(1)   Where property (other than land) is held by a recognised investment exchange or recognised clearing house as margin in relation to market contracts [or as default fund contribution,] or is subject to a market charge, no execution or other legal process for the enforcement of a judgment or order may be commenced or continued, and no distress may be levied, [and no power to use the procedure in Schedule 12 to the Tribunals, Courts and Enforcement Act 2007 (taking control of goods) may be exercised,] against the property by a person not seeking to enforce any interest in or security over the property, except with the consent of—
   (a)   in the case of property provided as cover for margin [or as default fund contribution], the investment exchange or clearing house in question, or
   (b)   in the case of property subject to a market charge, the person in whose favour the charge was granted.
(2)   Where consent is given the proceedings may be commenced or continued notwithstanding any provision of the Insolvency Act 1986 or the Bankruptcy (Scotland) Act 1985.
(3)   Where by virtue of this section a person would not be entitled to enforce a judgment or order against any property, any injunction or other remedy granted with a view to facilitating the enforcement of any such judgment or order shall not extend to that property.
(4)   In the application of this section to Scotland, the reference to execution being commenced or continued includes a reference to diligence being carried out or continued, and the reference to distress being levied shall be omitted.

NOTES
   Sub-s (1): words in first and third pairs of square brackets inserted by the Financial Markets and Insolvency Regulations 2009, SI 2009/853, reg 2(1), (14), as from 15 June 2009; words in second pair of square brackets inserted by the Tribunals, Courts and Enforcement Act 2007, s 62(3), Sch 13, para 91, as from a day to be appointed.

[5.134]
181 Power to apply provisions to other cases
(1)   [A power to which this subsection applies includes the] power to apply sections 177 to 180 to any description of property provided as cover for margin in relation to contracts in relation to which the power is exercised or, as the case may be, property subject to charges in relation to which the power is exercised.
(2)   The regulations may provide that those sections apply with such exceptions, additions and adaptations as may be specified in the regulations.
[(3)   Subsection (1) applies to the powers of the Secretary of State and the Treasury to act jointly under—
   (a)   sections 170, 172 and 176 of this Act; and
   (b)   section 301 of the Financial Services and Markets Act 2000 (supervision of certain contracts).]

NOTES
   Sub-s (1): words in square brackets substituted by the Financial Services and Markets Act 2000 (Consequential Amendments and Repeals) Order 2001, SI 2001/3649, art 86(1), (2), as from 1 December 2001.
   Sub-s (3): added by SI 2001/3649, art 86(1), (3), as from 1 December 2001.

Supplementary provisions

[5.135]
182 Powers of court in relation to certain proceedings begun before commencement
(1)   The powers conferred by this section are exercisable by the court where insolvency proceedings in respect of—
   (a)   a member of a recognised investment exchange or a recognised clearing house, or
   (b)   a person by whom a market charge has been granted,
are begun on or after 22nd December 1988 and before the commencement of this section.
That person is referred to in this section as "the relevant person".
(2)   For the purposes of this section "insolvency proceedings" means proceedings under Part II, IV, V or IX of the Insolvency Act 1986 (administration, winding up and bankruptcy) or under the Bankruptcy (Scotland) Act 1985; and references in this section to the beginning of such proceedings are to—
   (a)   the presentation of a petition on which an administration order, winding-up order, bankruptcy order or award of sequestration is made, or
   (b)   the passing of a resolution for voluntary winding up.
(3)   This section applies in relation to—
   (a)   in England and Wales, the administration of the insolvent estate of a deceased person, and

(b) in Scotland, the administration by a judicial factor appointed under section 11A of the Judicial Factors (Scotland) Act 1889 of the insolvent estate of a deceased person,

as it applies in relation to insolvency proceedings.

In such a case references to the beginning of the proceedings shall be construed as references to the death of the relevant person.

(4) The court may on an application made, within three months after the commencement of this section, by—

(a) a recognised investment exchange or recognised clearing house, or

(b) a person in whose favour a market charge has been granted,

make such order as it thinks fit for achieving, except so far as assets of the relevant person have been distributed before the making of the application, the same result as if the provisions of Schedule 22 had come into force on 22nd December 1988.

(5) The provisions of that Schedule ("the relevant provisions") reproduce the effect of certain provisions of this Part as they appeared in the Bill for this Act as introduced into the House of Lords and published on that date.

(6) The court may in particular—

(a) require the relevant person or a relevant office-holder—

(i) to return property provided as cover for margin or which was subject to a market charge, or to pay to the applicant or any other person the proceeds of realisation of such property, or

(ii) to pay to the applicant or any other person such amount as the court estimates would have been payable to that person if the relevant provisions had come into force on 22nd December 1988 and market contracts had been settled in accordance with the rules of the recognised investment exchange or recognised clearing house, or a proportion of that amount if the property of the relevant person or relevant office-holder is not sufficient to meet the amount in full;

(b) provide that contracts, rules and dispositions shall be treated as not having been void;

(c) modify the functions of a relevant office-holder, or the duties of the applicant or any other person, in relation to the insolvency proceedings, or indemnify any such person in respect of acts or omissions which would have been proper if the relevant provisions had been in force;

(d) provide that conduct which constituted an offence be treated as not having done so;

(e) dismiss proceedings which could not have been brought if the relevant provisions had come into force on 22nd December 1988, and reverse the effect of any order of a court which could not, or would not, have been made if those provisions had come into force on that date.

(7) An order under this section shall not be made against a relevant office-holder if the effect would be that his remuneration, costs and expenses could not be met.

[5.136]
183 Insolvency proceedings in other jurisdictions

(1) The references to insolvency law in section 426 of the Insolvency Act 1986 (co-operation with courts exercising insolvency jurisdiction in other jurisdictions) include, in relation to a part of the United Kingdom, the provisions made by or under this Part and, in relation to a relevant country or territory within the meaning of that section, so much of the law of that country or territory as corresponds to any provisions made by or under this Part.

(2) A court shall not, in pursuance of that section or any other enactment or rule of law, recognise or give effect to—

(a) any order of a court exercising jurisdiction in relation to insolvency law in a country or territory outside the United Kingdom, or

(b) any act of a person appointed in such a country or territory to discharge any functions under insolvency law,

in so far as the making of the order or the doing of the act would be prohibited in the case of a court in the United Kingdom or a relevant office-holder by provisions made by or under this Part.

(3) Subsection (2) does not affect the recognition or enforcement of a judgment required to be recognised or enforced under or by virtue of the Civil Jurisdiction and Judgments Act 1982 [or Council Regulation (EC) No 44/2001 of 22nd December 2000 on jurisdiction and the recognition and enforcement of judgments in civil and commercial matters][, as amended from time to time and as applied by the Agreement made on 19th October 2005 between the European Community and the Kingdom of Denmark on jurisdiction and the recognition and enforcement of judgments in civil and commercial matters (OJ No L299 16.11.2005 at p 62)].

NOTES

Sub-s (3): words in first pair of square brackets added by the Civil Jurisdiction and Judgments Order 2001, SI 2001/3929, art 5, Sch 3, para 21, as from 1 March 2002; words in second pair of square brackets added by the Civil Jurisdiction and Judgments Regulations 2007, SI 2007/1655, reg 5, Schedule, Pt 1, para 15, as from 1 July 2007.

[5.137]
184   Indemnity for certain acts, &c
(1)   Where a relevant office-holder takes any action in relation to property of a defaulter which is liable to be dealt with in accordance with the default rules of a recognised investment exchange or recognised clearing house, and believes and has reasonable grounds for believing that he is entitled to take that action, he is not liable to any person in respect of any loss or damage resulting from his action except in so far as the loss or damage is caused by the office-holder's own negligence.
(2)   Any failure by a recognised investment exchange or recognised clearing house to comply with its own rules in respect of any matter shall not prevent that matter being treated for the purposes of this Part as done in accordance with those rules so long as the failure does not substantially affect the rights of any person entitled to require compliance with the rules.
(3)   No recognised investment exchange or recognised clearing house, nor any officer or servant or member of the governing body of a recognised investment exchange or recognised clearing house, shall be liable in damages for anything done or omitted in the discharge or purported discharge of any functions to which this subsection applies unless the act or omission is shown to have been in bad faith.
(4)   The functions to which subsection (3) applies are the functions of the exchange or clearing house so far as relating to, or to matters arising out of—
(a)   its default rules, or
(b)   any obligations to which it is subject by virtue of this Part.
(5)   No person [to whom the exercise of any function of a recognised investment exchange or recognised clearing house is delegated under its default rules], nor any officer or servant of such a person, shall be liable in damages for anything done or omitted in the discharge or purported discharge of those functions unless the act or omission is shown to have been in bad faith.

NOTES
Sub-s (5): words in square brackets substituted by the Financial Services and Markets Act 2000 (Consequential Amendments and Repeals) Order 2001, SI 2001/3649, art 87, as from 1 December 2001.

[5.138]
185   Power to make further provision by regulations
(1)   The Secretary of State may by regulations make such further provision as appears to him necessary or expedient for the purposes of this Part.
(2)   Provision may, in particular, be made—
(a)   for integrating the provisions of this Part with the general law of insolvency, and
(b)   for adapting the provisions of this Part in their application to overseas investment exchanges and clearing houses.
(3)   Regulations under this section may add to, amend or repeal any of the provisions of this Part or provide that those provisions have effect subject to such additions, exceptions or adaptations as are specified in the regulations.
[(4)   References in this section to the provisions of this Part include any provision made under section 301 of the Financial Services and Markets Act 2000.]

NOTES
Sub-s (4): added by the Financial Services and Markets Act 2000 (Consequential Amendments and Repeals) Order 2001, SI 2001/3649, art 88, as from 1 December 2001.
Regulations: the Financial Markets and Insolvency Regulations 1991, SI 1991/880; the Financial Markets and Insolvency Regulations 1996, SI 1996/1469; the Financial Markets and Insolvency Regulations 1998, SI 1998/1748; the Financial Markets and Insolvency (CGO Service) Regulations 1999, SI 1999/1209; the Financial Markets and Insolvency Regulations 2009, SI 2009/853.

[5.139]
186   Supplementary provisions as to regulations
(1)   Regulations under this Part may make different provision for different cases and may contain such incidental, transitional and other supplementary provisions as appear to the Secretary of State to be necessary or expedient.
(2)   Regulations under this Part shall be made by statutory instrument which shall be subject to annulment in pursuance of a resolution of either House of Parliament.

[5.140]
187   Construction of references to parties to market contracts
(1)   Where a person enters into market contracts in more than one capacity, the provisions of this Part apply (subject as follows) as if the contracts entered into in each different capacity were entered into by different persons.
(2)   References in this Part to a market contract to which a person is a party include (subject as follows, and unless the context otherwise requires) contracts to which he is party as agent.
(3)   The Secretary of State may by regulations—
(a)   modify or exclude the operation of subsections (1) and (2), and
(b)   make provision as to the circumstances in which a person is to be regarded for the purposes of those provisions as acting in different capacities.

NOTES

Regulations: the Financial Markets and Insolvency Regulations 1991, SI 1991/880; the Financial Markets and Insolvency (Amendment) Regulations 1992, SI 1992/716; the Financial Markets and Insolvency Regulations 2009, SI 2009/853.

[5.141]
188   Meaning of "default rules" and related expressions
(1)   In this Part "default rules" means rules of a recognised investment exchange or recognised clearing house which provide for the taking of action in the event of a person [(including another recognised investment exchange or recognised clearing house)] appearing to be unable, or likely to become unable, to meet his obligations in respect of one or more market contracts connected with the exchange or clearing house.
(2)   References in this Part to a "defaulter" are to a person in respect of whom action has been taken by a recognised investment exchange or recognised clearing house under its default rules, whether by declaring him to be a defaulter or otherwise; and references in this Part to "default" shall be construed accordingly.
(3)   In this Part "default proceedings" means proceedings taken by a recognised investment exchange or recognised clearing house under its default rules.
[(3A)   In this Part "default fund contribution" means—
   (a)   contribution by a member or designated non-member of a recognised investment exchange to a fund which—
      (i)   is maintained by that exchange for the purpose of covering losses arising in connection with defaults by any of the members of the exchange, or defaults by any of the members or designated non-members of the exchange, and
      (ii)   may be applied for that purpose under the default rules of the exchange;
   (b)   contribution by a member of a recognised clearing house to a fund which—
      (i)   is maintained by that clearing house for the purpose of covering losses arising in connection with defaults by any of the members of the clearing house, and
      (ii)   may be applied for that purpose under the default rules of the clearing house;
   (c)   contribution by a recognised clearing house to a fund which—
      (i)   is maintained by a recognised investment exchange or another recognised clearing house (A) for the purpose of covering losses arising in connection with defaults by recognised clearing houses or recognised investment exchanges other than A or by any of their members, and
      (ii)   may be applied for that purpose under A's default rules; or
   (d)   contribution by a recognised investment exchange to a fund which—
      (i)   is maintained by a recognised clearing house or another recognised investment exchange (A) for the purpose of covering losses arising in connection with defaults by recognised investment exchanges or recognised clearing houses other than A or by any of their members, and
      (ii)   may be applied for that purpose under A's default rules.]
(4)   If an exchange or clearing house takes action under its default rules in respect of a person, all subsequent proceedings under its rules for the purposes of or in connection with the settlement of market contracts to which the defaulter is a party shall be treated as done under its default rules.

NOTES

Sub-s (1): words in square brackets inserted the Financial Markets and Insolvency Regulations 2009, SI 2009/853, reg 2(1), (15)(a), as from 15 June 2009.

Sub-s (3A): inserted by SI 2009/853, reg 2(1), (15)(b), as from 15 June 2009.

[5.142]
189   Meaning of "relevant office-holder"
(1)   The following are relevant office-holders for the purposes of this Part—
   (a)   the official receiver,
   (b)   any person acting in relation to a company as its liquidator, provisional liquidator, administrator or administrative receiver,
   (c)   any person acting in relation to an individual (or, in Scotland, any debtor within the meaning of the Bankruptcy (Scotland) Act 1985) as his trustee in bankruptcy or interim receiver of his property or as permanent or interim trustee in the sequestration of his estate,
   (d)   any person acting as administrator of an insolvent estate of a deceased person.
(2)   In subsection (1)(b) "company" means any company, society, association, partnership or other body which may be wound up under the Insolvency Act 1986.

[5.143]
190   Minor definitions
(1)   In this Part—
   "administrative receiver" has the meaning given by section 251 of the Insolvency Act 1986;
   ["the Authority" means the Financial Services Authority;]
   "charge" means any form of security, including a mortgage and, in Scotland, a heritable security;

. . .

"interim trustee" and "permanent trustee" have the same meaning as in the Bankruptcy (Scotland) Act 1985;

. . .

"overseas", in relation to an investment exchange or clearing house, means having its head office outside the United Kingdom;

. . .

["recognised clearing house" and "recognised investment exchange" have the same meaning as in the Financial Services and Markets Act 2000;]

"set-off", in relation to Scotland, includes compensation;

["The Stock Exchange" means the London Stock Exchange Limited;]

"UK", in relation to an investment exchange or clearing house, means having its head office in the United Kingdom.

(2) References in this Part to settlement in relation to a market contract are to the discharge of the rights and liabilities of the parties to the contract, whether by performance, compromise or otherwise.

(3) In this Part the expressions "margin" and "cover for margin" have the same meaning.

(4) . . .

(5) For the purposes of this Part a person shall be taken to have notice of a matter if he deliberately failed to make enquiries as to that matter in circumstances in which a reasonable and honest person would have done so.

This does not apply for the purposes of a provision requiring "actual notice".

(6) References in this Part to the law of insolvency include references to every provision made by or under the Insolvency Act 1986 or the Bankruptcy (Scotland) Act 1985; and in relation to a building society references to insolvency law or to any provision of the Insolvency Act 1986 are to that law or provision as modified by the Building Societies Act 1986.

(7) In relation to Scotland, references in this Part—

    (a)   to sequestration include references to the administration by a judicial factor of the insolvent estate of a deceased person, and

    (b)   to an interim or permanent trustee include references to a judicial factor on the insolvent estate of a deceased person,

unless the context otherwise requires.

NOTES

Sub-s (1): definitions "the Authority", "recognised clearing house" and "recognised investment exchange" inserted, definitions "clearing house", "investment", "investment exchange" and "recognised" (omitted) repealed, and definition "The Stock Exchange" substituted, by the Financial Services and Markets Act 2000 (Consequential Amendments and Repeals) Order 2001, SI 2001/3649, art 89(1)–(5), as from 1 December 2001.

Sub-s (4): repealed by SI 2001/3649, art 89(1), (6), as from 1 December 2001.

[5.144]

191   Index of defined expressions

The following Table shows provisions defining or otherwise explaining expressions used in this Part (other than provisions defining or explaining an expression used only in the same section or paragraph)—

administrative receiver	section 190(1)
[the Authority	section 190(1)]
charge	section 190(1)
. . .	. . .
cover for margin	section 190(3)
[default fund contribution	section 188(3A)]
default rules (and related expressions)	section 188
designated non-member	section 155(2)
. . .	. . .
insolvency law (and similar expressions)	section 190(6)
interim trustee	section 190(1) and (7)(b)
. . .	. . .
. . .	. . .
margin	section 190(3)
market charge	section 173
market contract	section 155
notice	section 190(5)
overseas (in relation to an investment exchange or clearing house)	section 190(1)

party (in relation to a market contract)	section 187
permanent trustee	section 190(1) and (7)(b)
. . .	. . .
[recognised clearing house and recognised investment exchange	section 190(1)]
relevant office-holder	section 189
sequestration	section 190(7)(a)
set off (in relation to Scotland)	section 190(1)
settlement and related expressions (in relation to a market contract)	section 190(2)
The Stock Exchange	section 190(1)
trustee, interim or permanent (in relation to Scotland)	section 190(7)(b)
UK (in relation to an investment exchange or clearing house)	section 190(1).

NOTES

Entries relating to "clearing house", "ensuring the performance of a transaction", "investment," "investment exchange" and "recognised" (omitted) repealed, and entries relating to "the Authority" and "recognised clearing house and recognised investment exchange" inserted, by the Financial Services and Markets Act 2000 (Consequential Amendments and Repeals) Order 2001, SI 2001/3649, art 89(7), as from 1 December 2001.

Entry "default fund contribution" inserted by the Financial Markets and Insolvency Regulations 2009, SI 2009/853, reg 2(1), (16), as from 15 June 2009.

192–207   *(Ss 192–206 (Pt VIII: Amendments of FSA 1986): ss 192–197 repealed by the Financial Services and Markets Act 2000 (Consequential Amendments and Repeals) Order 2001, SI 2001/3649, art 75(i), as from 1 December 2001; ss 198, 199 repealed by the Public Offers of Securities Regulations 1995, SI 1995/1537, reg 17, Sch 2, Pt II, para 10, as from 19 June 1995; s 200 repealed in part by SI 2001/3649, art 75(j), as from 1 December 2001 and the reminder of the section is effectively spent (it amended the Civil Jurisdiction and Judgments Act 1982 by inserting a reference to FSA 1986, s 188 into Sch 5 to the 1982 Act – that reference has now been superseded by a reference to FSMA 2000, s 415); ss 201–206 repealed by SI 2001/3649, art 75(k), as from 1 December 2001. S 207 (Pt IX: Transfer of Securities) repealed by the Companies Act 2006, s 1295, Sch 16, as from 6 April 2008. Note that by virtue of the Companies Act 2006, s 1297 (continuity of law) the Uncertificated Securities Regulations 2001, SI 2001/3755 (at [6.42]) and the Uncertificated Securities (Amendment) (Eligible Debt Securities) Regulations 2003, SI 2003/1633 which were made under this section now have effect as if made under ss 783, 784(3), 785 and 788 of the 2006 Act.)*

PART X
MISCELLANEOUS AND GENERAL PROVISIONS

208–212   *(S 208 adds the Company Directors Disqualification Act 1986, s 21(4) at [5.78]; s 209 repealed by the Criminal Justice Act 1993, s 79(14), Sch 6, Pt I, as from 1 March 1994; s 210 spent (amended the Policyholders Protection Act 1975, Sch 3 (repealed)); s 211 amends the Building Societies Act 1986, s 104, Sch 15 and inserts the Company Directors Disqualification Act 1986, s 22A at [5.83]; s 212 introduces Sch 24 (Repeals).)*

General

[5.145]
213   Provisions extending to Northern Ireland
(1)   The provisions of this Act extend to Northern Ireland so far as they amend, or provide for the amendment of, an enactment which so extends.
(2)   So far as any provision of this Act amends . . . the Insolvency Act 1986, its application to companies registered or incorporated in Northern Ireland is subject to . . . section 441(2) of the Insolvency Act 1986 . . .
(3)   In Part III (investigations and powers to obtain information), sections 82 to 91, (powers exercisable to assist overseas regulatory authorities) extend to Northern Ireland.
(4)   Part VI (mergers and related matters) extends to Northern Ireland.
(5)   In Part VII (financial markets and insolvency) the following provisions extend to Northern Ireland—
   (a)   sections 154 and 155 (introductory provisions and definition of "market contract"),
   (b)   . . .
   (c)   sections 157, 160, 162, and 166 to 169 (provisions relating to recognised investment exchanges and clearing houses),
   (d)   sections 170 to 172 (power to extend provisions to other financial markets),
   (e)   section 184 (indemnity for certain acts), and
   (f)   sections 185 to 191 (supplementary provisions).
(6)   . . .
(7)   Part IX (transfer of securities) extends to Northern Ireland.
. . .

(8)   In Part X (miscellaneous and general provisions), this section and sections 214 to 216 (general provisions) extend to Northern Ireland.

(9)   Except as mentioned above, the provisions of this Act do not extend to Northern Ireland.

NOTES

Sub-s (2): words omitted repealed by the Companies Act 2006 (Consequential Amendments, Transitional Provisions and Savings) Order 2009, SI 2009/1941, art 2(1), Sch 1, para 103(1), (3), as from 1 October 2009.

Sub-s (5): para (b) repealed by the Financial Services and Markets Act 2000 (Consequential Amendments and Repeals) Order 2001, SI 2001/3649, art 75(l), as from 1 December 2001.

Sub-s (6): repealed by SI 2001/3649, art 75(l), as from 1 December 2001.

Sub-s (7): words omitted repealed by the Northern Ireland Act 1998, s 100(2), Sch 15, as from 2 December 1999.

214   *(Repealed by the Financial Services and Markets Act 2000 (Consequential Amendments and Repeals) Order 2001, SI 2001/3649, art 75(m), as from 1 December 2001.)*

[5.146]
215   Commencement and transitional provisions

(1)   The following provisions of this Act come into force on Royal Assent—

   (a)   in Part V (amendments of company law), section 141 (application to declare dissolution of company void);

   (b)   in Part VI (mergers)—

       (i)   sections 147 to 150, and

       (ii)   paragraphs 2 to 12, 14 to 16, 18 to 20, 22 to 25 of Schedule 20, and section 153 so far as relating to those paragraphs;

   (c)   in Part VIII (amendments of the Financial Services Act 1986), section 202 (offers of short-dated debentures);

   (d)   in Part X (miscellaneous and general provisions), the repeals made by Schedule 24 in sections 71, 74, 88 and 89 of, and Schedule 9 to, the Fair Trading Act 1973, and section 212 so far as relating to those repeals.

(2)   The other provisions of this Act come into force on such day as the Secretary of State may appoint by order made by statutory instrument; and different days may be appointed for different provisions and different purposes.

(3)   An order bringing into force any provision may contain such transitional provisions and savings as appear to the Secretary of State to be necessary or expedient.

(4)   The Secretary of State may also by order under this section amend any enactment which refers to the commencement of a provision brought into force by the order so as to substitute a reference to the actual date on which it comes into force.

NOTES

Transfer of functions: as to the exercise of functions under this section, see the Transfer of Functions (Financial Services) Order 1992, SI 1992/1315, art 2(2)(c).

Financial Services Act 1986: repealed by the Financial Services and Markets Act 2000 (Consequential Amendments and Repeals) Order 2001, SI 2001/3649, art 3(1)(c), as from 1 December 2001.

Orders: the Companies Act 1989 (Commencement No 1) Order 1990, SI 1990/98; the Companies Act 1989 (Commencement No 2) Order 1990, SI 1990/142 (as amended by SI 1990/355); the Companies Act 1989 (Commencement No 3, Transitional Provisions and Transfer of Functions under the Financial Services Act 1986) Order 1990, SI 1990/354; the Companies Act 1989 (Commencement No 4, Transitional and Saving Provisions) Order 1990, SI 1990/355 (as amended by SI 1990/1707, SI 1990/2569, SI 1993/3246); the Companies Act 1989 (Commencement No 5 and Transitional and Saving Provisions) Order 1990, SI 1990/713; the Companies Act 1989 (Commencement No 6 and Transitional and Savings Provisions) Order 1990, SI 1990/1392 (as amended by SI 1990/1707); the Companies Act 1989 (Commencement No 7, Transitional and Saving Provisions) Order 1990, SI 1990/1707; the Companies Act 1989 (Commencement No 8 and Transitional and Saving Provisions) Order 1990, SI 1990/2569; the Companies Act 1989 (Commencement No 9 and Saving and Transitional Provisions) Order 1991, SI 1991/488; the Companies Act 1989 (Commencement No 10 and Saving Provisions) Order 1991, SI 1991/878; the Companies Act 1989 (Commencement No 11) Order 1991, SI 1991/1452; the Companies Act 1989 (Commencement No 12 and Transitional Provision) Order 1991, SI 1991/1996; the Companies Act 1989 (Commencement No 13) Order 1991, SI 1991/2173; the Companies Act 1989 (Commencement No 14 and Transitional Provision) Order 1991, SI 1991/2945; the Companies Act 1989 (Commencement No 15 and Transitional and Savings Provisions) Order 1995, SI 1995/1352; the Companies Act 1989 (Commencement No 16) Order 1995, SI 1995/1591; the Companies Act 1989 (Commencement No 17) Order 1998, SI 1998/1747; the Companies (Audit, Investigations and Community Enterprise) Act 2004 (Commencement) and Companies Act 1989 (Commencement No 18) Order 2004, SI 2004/3322.

[5.147]
216   Short title

This Act may be cited as the Companies Act 1989.

SCHEDULES

SCHEDULES 1–9

(*Schs 1–9 repealed by the Companies Act 2006, s 1295, Sch 16, as from 6 April 2008. Sch 10 (Amendments consequential on Part I) contains various amendments to CA 1985 and other legislation which, in so far as relevant to this work, and still in force, are incorporated at the appropriate place. Schs 11, 12 repealed by CA 2006, s 1295, Sch 16, as from 6 April 2008 (except in relation to the supervision and qualification of auditors appointed for financial years beginning before that date, see SI 2007/3495, Sch 4, Pt 1, para 38 at [2.66]). Sch 13 repealed by CA 2006, s 1295, Sch 16, as from 6 April 2008 (but this repeal does not affect the operation of this Schedule in relation to functions exercised under Part II of this Act on or after that date, see SI 2007/3495, Sch 4, Pt 1, para 42(1)). Sch 14 repealed by the Competition Act 1998 and other enactments (Amendment) Regulations 2004, SI 2004/1261, reg 5, Sch 2, para 2(1), (2), as from 1 May 2004. Schs 15, 16 repealed by CA 2006, ss 1180, 1295, Sch 16, as from 1 October 2009. Sch 17 repealed by CA 2006, s 1295, Sch 16, as from 6 April 2007 (in part), as from 6 April 2008 (in part), and as from 1 October 2009 (otherwise). Sch 18 (“Subsidiary” and Related Expressions: Consequential Amendments and Savings) was repealed by CA 2006, s 1295, Sch 16, as from 1 October 2007 (in part), and as from 1 October 2009 (in part); in so far as still in force it is now outside the scope of this work. Sch 19 (Minor Amendments of the Companies Act 1985) makes various amendments to CA 1985 which have been incorporated at the appropriate place (note that most of this Schedule is repealed by the Companies Act 2006, s 1295, Sch 16, as from 1 October 2007 (in part), as from 6 April 2008 (in part), and as from 1 October 2009 (otherwise), though a small number of paragraphs remain in force for limited purposes); Sch 20 (Amendments about Mergers and Related Matters) this Schedule has been repealed, or is spent, except in so far as it relates to a minor amendment to the Fair Trading Act 1973, s 132; Schs 21–23 repealed by the Financial Services and Markets Act 2000 (Consequential Amendments and Repeals) Order 2001, SI 2001/3649, art 75(p)–(r), as from 1 December 2001; Sch 24 contains various repeals to the Harbours Act 1964, the Fair Trading Act 1973, CA 1985, IA 1985, IA 1986, the Building Societies Act 1986, the Company Directors Disqualification Act 1986, FSA 1986, the Banking Act 1987, the Criminal Justice (Scotland) Act 1987, ICTA 1988, the Criminal Justice Act 1988, and the Copyright, Designs and Patents Act 1988 and, in so far as relevant to this work, are incorporated at the appropriate place*)

CRIMINAL JUSTICE ACT 1993

(1993 c 36)

NOTES

This Act is reproduced as amended by: the Financial Services and Markets Act 2000 (Consequential Amendments and Repeals) Order 2001, SI 2001/3649; the Financial Services and Markets Act 2000 (Market Abuse) Regulations 2005, SI 2005/381; the Companies Act 2006 (Consequential Amendments, Transitional Provisions and Savings) Order 2009, SI 2009/1941.

Only those provisions of this Act relating to company law are reproduced. Provisions not reproduced are not annotated. The provisions of Part V (including Schs 1, 2) came into force on 1 March 1994 (see the Criminal Justice Act 1993 (Commencement No 5) Order 1994, SI 1994/242 which was made under s 78 of this Act). By virtue of s 79 (Short title, extent etc) Part V applies to the whole of the UK.

ARRANGEMENT OF SECTIONS

PART V
INSIDER DEALING

An Act to make provision about the jurisdiction of courts in England and Wales in relation to certain offences of dishonesty and blackmail; to amend the law about drug trafficking offences and to implement provisions of the Community Council Directive No 91/308/EEC; to amend Part VI of the Criminal Justice Act 1988; to make provision with respect to the financing of terrorism, the proceeds of terrorist-related activities and the investigation of terrorist activities; to amend Part I of the Criminal Justice Act 1991; to implement provisions of the Community Council Directive No 89/592/EEC and to amend and restate the law about insider dealing in securities; to provide for certain offences created by the Banking Coordination (Second Council Directive) Regulations 1992 to be punishable in the same way as offences under sections 39, 40 and 41 of the Banking Act 1987 and to enable regulations implementing Article 15 of the Community Council Directive No 89/646/EEC and Articles 3, 6 and 7 of the Community Council Directive No 92/30/EEC to create offences punishable in that way; to make provision with respect to the penalty for causing death by dangerous driving or causing death by careless driving while under the influence of drink or drugs; to make it an offence to assist in or induce certain conduct which for the purposes of, or in connection with, the provisions of Community law is unlawful in another member State; to provide for the introduction of safeguards in connection with the return of persons under backing of warrants arrangements; to amend the Criminal Procedure (Scotland) Act 1975 and Part I of the Prisoners and Criminal Proceedings (Scotland) Act 1993; and for connected purposes

[27 July 1993]

PART V
INSIDER DEALING

The offence of insider dealing

[5.148]
52 The offence
(1) An individual who has information as an insider is guilty of insider dealing if, in the circumstances mentioned in subsection (3), he deals in securities that are price-affected securities in relation to the information.

(2) An individual who has information as an insider is also guilty of insider dealing if—
- (a) he encourages another person to deal in securities that are (whether or not that other knows it) price-affected securities in relation to the information, knowing or having reasonable cause to believe that the dealing would take place in the circumstances mentioned in subsection (3); or
- (b) he discloses the information, otherwise than in the proper performance of the functions of his employment, office or profession, to another person.

(3) The circumstances referred to above are that the acquisition or disposal in question occurs on a regulated market, or that the person dealing relies on a professional intermediary or is himself acting as a professional intermediary.

(4) This section has effect subject to section 53.

[5.149]
53 Defences
(1) An individual is not guilty of insider dealing by virtue of dealing in securities if he shows—
- (a) that he did not at the time expect the dealing to result in a profit attributable to the fact that the information in question was price-sensitive information in relation to the securities, or
- (b) that at the time he believed on reasonable grounds that the information had been disclosed widely enough to ensure that none of those taking part in the dealing would be prejudiced by not having the information, or
- (c) that he would have done what he did even if he had not had the information.

(2) An individual is not guilty of insider dealing by virtue of encouraging another person to deal in securities if he shows—
- (a) that he did not at the time expect the dealing to result in a profit attributable to the fact that the information in question was price-sensitive information in relation to the securities, or
- (b) that at the time he believed on reasonable grounds that the information had been or would be disclosed widely enough to ensure that none of those taking part in the dealing would be prejudiced by not having the information, or
- (c) that he would have done what he did even if he had not had the information.

(3) An individual is not guilty of insider dealing by virtue of a disclosure of information if he shows—
- (a) that he did not at the time expect any person, because of the disclosure, to deal in securities in the circumstances mentioned in subsection (3) of section 52; or
- (b) that, although he had such an expectation at the time, he did not expect the dealing to result in a profit attributable to the fact that the information was price-sensitive information in relation to the securities.

(4) Schedule 1 (special defences) shall have effect.

(5) The Treasury may by order amend Schedule 1.

(6) In this section references to a profit include references to the avoidance of a loss.

Interpretation

[5.150]
54 Securities to which Part V applies
(1) This Part applies to any security which—
- (a) falls within any paragraph of Schedule 2; and
- (b) satisfies any conditions applying to it under an order made by the Treasury for the purposes of this subsection;

and in the provisions of this Part (other than that Schedule) any reference to a security is a reference to a security to which this Part applies.

(2) The Treasury may by order amend Schedule 2.

NOTES

Orders: the Insider Dealing (Securities and Regulated Markets) Order 1994, SI 1994/187 at **[6.23]**.

[5.151]
55 "Dealing" in securities
(1) For the purposes of this Part, a person deals in securities if—
  (a) he acquires or disposes of the securities (whether as principal or agent); or
  (b) he procures, directly or indirectly, an acquisition or disposal of the securities by any other person.
(2) For the purposes of this Part, "acquire", in relation to a security, includes—
  (a) agreeing to acquire the security; and
  (b) entering into a contract which creates the security.
(3) For the purposes of this Part, "dispose", in relation to a security, includes—
  (a) agreeing to dispose of the security; and
  (b) bringing to an end a contract which created the security.
(4) For the purposes of subsection (1), a person procures an acquisition or disposal of a security if the security is acquired or disposed of by a person who is—
  (a) his agent,
  (b) his nominee, or
  (c) a person who is acting at his direction,
in relation to the acquisition or disposal.
(5) Subsection (4) is not exhaustive as to the circumstances in which one person may be regarded as procuring an acquisition or disposal of securities by another.

[5.152]
56 "Inside information", etc
(1) For the purposes of this section and section 57, "inside information" means information which—
  (a) relates to particular securities or to a particular issuer of securities or to particular issuers of securities and not to securities generally or to issuers of securities generally;
  (b) is specific or precise;
  (c) has not been made public; and
  (d) if it were made public would be likely to have a significant effect on the price of any securities.
(2) For the purposes of this Part, securities are "price-affected securities" in relation to inside information, and inside information is "price-sensitive information" in relation to securities, if and only if the information would, if made public, be likely to have a significant effect on the price of the securities.
(3) For the purposes of this section "price" includes value.

[5.153]
57 "Insiders"
(1) For the purposes of this Part, a person has information as an insider if and only if—
  (a) it is, and he knows that it is, inside information, and
  (b) he has it, and knows that he has it, from an inside source.
(2) For the purposes of subsection (1), a person has information from an inside source if and only if—
  (a) he has it through—
    (i) being a director, employee or shareholder of an issuer of securities; or
    (ii) having access to the information by virtue of his employment, office or profession; or
  (b) the direct or indirect source of his information is a person within paragraph (a).

[5.154]
58 Information "made public"
(1) For the purposes of section 56, "made public", in relation to information, shall be construed in accordance with the following provisions of this section; but those provisions are not exhaustive as to the meaning of that expression.
(2) Information is made public if—
  (a) it is published in accordance with the rules of a regulated market for the purpose of informing investors and their professional advisers;
  (b) it is contained in records which by virtue of any enactment are open to inspection by the public;
  (c) it can be readily acquired by those likely to deal in any securities—
    (i) to which the information relates, or
    (ii) of an issuer to which the information relates; or
  (d) it is derived from information which has been made public.
(3) Information may be treated as made public even though—
  (a) it can be acquired only by persons exercising diligence or expertise;
  (b) it is communicated to a section of the public and not to the public at large;
  (c) it can be acquired only by observation;
  (d) it is communicated only on payment of a fee; or
  (e) it is published only outside the United Kingdom.

[5.155]
59 "Professional intermediary"
(1) For the purposes of this Part, a "professional intermediary" is a person—
   (a) who carries on a business consisting of an activity mentioned in subsection (2) and who holds himself out to the public or any section of the public (including a section of the public constituted by persons such as himself) as willing to engage in any such business; or
   (b) who is employed by a person falling within paragraph (a) to carry out any such activity.
(2) The activities referred to in subsection (1) are—
   (a) acquiring or disposing of securities (whether as principal or agent); or
   (b) acting as an intermediary between persons taking part in any dealing in securities.
(3) A person is not to be treated as carrying on a business consisting of an activity mentioned in subsection (2)—
   (a) if the activity in question is merely incidental to some other activity not falling within subsection (2); or
   (b) merely because he occasionally conducts one of those activities.
(4) For the purposes of section 52, a person dealing in securities relies on a professional intermediary if and only if a person who is acting as a professional intermediary carries out an activity mentioned in subsection (2) in relation to that dealing.

[5.156]
60 Other interpretation provisions
(1) For the purposes of this Part, "regulated market" means any market, however operated, which, by an order made by the Treasury, is identified (whether by name or by reference to criteria prescribed by the order) as a regulated market for the purposes of this Part.
(2) For the purposes of this Part an "issuer", in relation to any securities, means any company, public sector body or individual by which or by whom the securities have been or are to be issued.
(3) For the purposes of this Part—
   (a) "company" means any body (whether or not incorporated and wherever incorporated or constituted) which is not a public sector body; and
   (b) "public sector body" means—
      (i) the government of the United Kingdom, of Northern Ireland or of any country or territory outside the United Kingdom;
      (ii) a local authority in the United Kingdom or elsewhere;
      (iii) any international organisation the members of which include the United Kingdom or another member state;
      (iv) the Bank of England; or
      (v) the central bank of any sovereign State.
(4) For the purposes of this Part, information shall be treated as relating to an issuer of securities which is a company not only where it is about the company but also where it may affect the company's business prospects.

NOTES
Orders: the Insider Dealing (Securities and Regulated Markets) Order 1994, SI 1994/187 at **[6.23]**.

Miscellaneous

[5.157]
61 Penalties and prosecution
(1) An individual guilty of insider dealing shall be liable—
   (a) on summary conviction, to a fine not exceeding the statutory maximum or imprisonment for a term not exceeding six months or to both; or
   (b) on conviction on indictment, to a fine or imprisonment for a term not exceeding seven years or to both.
(2) Proceedings for offences under this Part shall not be instituted in England and Wales except by or with the consent of—
   (a) the Secretary of State; or
   (b) the Director of Public Prosecutions.
(3) In relation to proceedings in Northern Ireland for offences under this Part, subsection (2) shall have effect as if the reference to the Director of Public Prosecutions were a reference to the Director of Public Prosecutions for Northern Ireland.

[5.158]
[61A Summary proceedings: venue and time limit for proceedings
(1) Summary proceedings for an offence of insider dealing may (without prejudice to any jurisdiction exercisable apart from this subsection) be brought against an individual at any place at which the individual is for the time being.
(2) An information relating to an offence of insider dealing that is triable by a magistrates' court in England and Wales may be so tried if it is laid—
   (a) at any time within three years after the commission of the offence, and

(b)   within twelve months after the date on which evidence sufficient in the opinion of the Director of Public Prosecutions or the Secretary of State (as the case may be) to justify the proceedings comes to that person's knowledge.

(3)   Summary proceedings in Scotland for an offence of insider dealing—

   (a)   must not be commenced after the expiration of three years from the commission of the offence;

   (b)   subject to that, may be commenced at any time—

      (i)   within twelve months after the date on which evidence sufficient in the Lord Advocate's opinion to justify the proceedings came to that person's knowledge, or

      (ii)   where such evidence was reported to the Lord Advocate by the Secretary of State, within twelve months after the date on which it came to the knowledge of the latter.

Section 136(3) of the Criminal Procedure (Scotland) Act 1995 (date when proceedings deemed to be commenced) applies for the purposes of this subsection as for the purposes of that section.

(4)   A magistrates' court in Northern Ireland has jurisdiction to hear and determine a complaint charging the commission of a summary offence of insider dealing provided that the complaint is made—

   (a)   within three years from the time when the offence was committed, and

   (b)   within twelve months from the date on which evidence sufficient in the opinion of the Director of Public Prosecutions for Northern Ireland or the Secretary of State (as the case may be) to justify the proceedings comes to that person's knowledge.

(5)   For the purposes of this section a certificate of the Director of Public Prosecutions, the Lord Advocate, the Director of Public Prosecutions for Northern Ireland or the Secretary of State (as the case may be) as to the date on which such evidence as is referred to above came to that person's notice is conclusive evidence.]

NOTES

Commencement: 1 October 2009.

Inserted by the Companies Act 2006 (Consequential Amendments, Transitional Provisions and Savings) Order 2009, SI 2009/1941, art 2(1), Sch 1, para 141, as from 1 October 2009.

[5.159]
62   Territorial scope of offence of insider dealing

(1)   An individual is not guilty of an offence falling within subsection (1) of section 52 unless—

   (a)   he was within the United Kingdom at the time when he is alleged to have done any act constituting or forming part of the alleged dealing;

   (b)   the regulated market on which the dealing is alleged to have occurred is one which, by an order made by the Treasury, is identified (whether by name or by reference to criteria prescribed by the order) as being, for the purposes of this Part, regulated in the United Kingdom; or

   (c)   the professional intermediary was within the United Kingdom at the time when he is alleged to have done anything by means of which the offence is alleged to have been committed.

(2)   An individual is not guilty of an offence falling within subsection (2) of section 52 unless—

   (a)   he was within the United Kingdom at the time when he is alleged to have disclosed the information or encouraged the dealing; or

   (b)   the alleged recipient of the information or encouragement was within the United Kingdom at the time when he is alleged to have received the information or encouragement.

NOTES

Orders: the Insider Dealing (Securities and Regulated Markets) Order 1994, SI 1994/187 at **[6.23]**.

[5.160]
63   Limits on section 52

(1)   Section 52 does not apply to anything done by an individual acting on behalf of a public sector body in pursuit of monetary policies or policies with respect to exchange rates or the management of public debt or foreign exchange reserves.

(2)   No contract shall be void or unenforceable by reason only of section 52.

[5.161]
64   Orders

(1)   Any power under this Part to make an order shall be exercisable by statutory instrument.

(2)   No order shall be made under this Part unless a draft of it has been laid before and approved by a resolution of each House of Parliament.

(3)   An order under this Part—

   (a)   may make different provision for different cases; and

   (b)   may contain such incidental, supplemental and transitional provisions as the Treasury consider expedient.

SCHEDULES

SCHEDULE 1
SPECIAL DEFENCES

Section 53(4)

Market makers

[5.162]

1. (1) An individual is not guilty of insider dealing by virtue of dealing in securities or encouraging another person to deal if he shows that he acted in good faith in the course of—

    (a)   his business as a market maker, or

    (b)   his employment in the business of a market maker.

(2) A market maker is a person who—

    (a)   holds himself out at all normal times in compliance with the rules of a regulated market or an approved organisation as willing to acquire or dispose of securities; and

    (b)   is recognised as doing so under those rules.

(3) In this paragraph "approved organisation" means an international securities self-regulating organisation approved [by the Treasury under any relevant order under section 22 of the Financial Services and Markets Act 2000].

Market information

2. (1) An individual is not guilty of insider dealing by virtue of dealing in securities or encouraging another person to deal if he shows that—

    (a)   the information which he had as an insider was market information; and

    (b)   it was reasonable for an individual in his position to have acted as he did despite having that information as an insider at the time.

(2) In determining whether it is reasonable for an individual to do any act despite having market information at the time, there shall, in particular, be taken into account—

    (a)   the content of the information;

    (b)   the circumstances in which he first had the information and in what capacity; and

    (c)   the capacity in which he now acts.

3. An individual is not guilty of insider dealing by virtue of dealing in securities or encouraging another person to deal if he shows—

    (a)   that he acted—

        (i)   in connection with an acquisition or disposal which was under consideration or the subject of negotiation, or in the course of a series of such acquisitions or disposals; and

        (ii)   with a view to facilitating the accomplishment of the acquisition or disposal or the series of acquisitions or disposals; and

    (b)   that the information which he had as an insider was market information arising directly out of his involvement in the acquisition or disposal or series of acquisitions or disposals.

4. For the purposes of paragraphs 2 and 3 market information is information consisting of one or more of the following facts—

    (a)   that securities of a particular kind have been or are to be acquired or disposed of, or that their acquisition or disposal is under consideration or the subject of negotiation;

    (b)   that securities of a particular kind have not been or are not to be acquired or disposed of;

    (c)   the number of securities acquired or disposed of or to be acquired or disposed of or whose acquisition or disposal is under consideration or the subject of negotiation;

    (d)   the price (or range of prices) at which securities have been or are to be acquired or disposed of or the price (or range of prices) at which the securities whose acquisition or disposal is under consideration or the subject of negotiation may be acquired or disposed of;

    (e)   the identity of the persons involved or likely to be involved in any capacity in an acquisition or disposal.

Price stabilisation

5. (1) An individual is not guilty of insider dealing by virtue of dealing in securities or encouraging another person to deal if he shows that he acted in conformity with the price stabilisation rules [or with the relevant provisions of Commission Regulation (EC) No 2273/2003 of 22 December 2003 implementing Directive 2003/6/EC of the European Parliament and of the Council as regards exemptions for buy-back programmes and stabilisation of financial instruments].

[(2) "Price stabilisation rules" means rules made under section 144(1) of the Financial Services and Markets Act 2000.]

NOTES

Para 1: words in square brackets in sub-para (3) substituted by the Financial Services and Markets Act 2000 (Consequential Amendments and Repeals) Order 2001, SI 2001/3649, art 341(1), (2), as from 1 December 2001.

Para 5: words in square brackets in sub-para (1) added by the Financial Services and Markets Act 2000 (Market Abuse) Regulations 2005, SI 2005/381, reg 3, as from 17 March 2005; sub-para (2) substituted by SI 2001/3649, art 341(1), (3), as from 1 December 2001.

SCHEDULE 2
SECURITIES

Section 54

Shares

[5.163]

1. Shares and stock in the share capital of a company ("shares").

Debt securities

2. Any instrument creating or acknowledging indebtedness which is issued by a company or public sector body, including, in particular, debentures, debenture stock, loan stock, bonds and certificates of deposit ("debt securities").

Warrants

3. Any right (whether conferred by warrant or otherwise) to subscribe for shares or debt securities ("warrants").

Depositary receipts

4. (1) The rights under any depositary receipt.

(2) For the purposes of sub-paragraph (1) a "depositary receipt" means a certificate or other record (whether or not in the form of a document)—

 (a) which is issued by or on behalf of a person who holds any relevant securities of a particular issuer; and

 (b) which acknowledges that another person is entitled to rights in relation to the relevant securities or relevant securities of the same kind.

(3) In sub-paragraph (2) "relevant securities" means shares, debt securities and warrants.

Options

5. Any option to acquire or dispose of any security falling within any other paragraph of this Schedule.

Futures

6. (1) Rights under a contract for the acquisition or disposal of relevant securities under which delivery is to be made at a future date and at a price agreed when the contract is made.

(2) In sub-paragraph (1)—

 (a) the references to a future date and to a price agreed when the contract is made include references to a date and a price determined in accordance with terms of the contract; and

 (b) "relevant securities" means any security falling within any other paragraph of this Schedule.

Contracts for differences

7. (1) Rights under a contract which does not provide for the delivery of securities but whose purpose or pretended purpose is to secure a profit or avoid a loss by reference to fluctuations in—

 (a) a share index or other similar factor connected with relevant securities;

 (b) the price of particular relevant securities; or

 (c) the interest rate offered on money placed on deposit.

(2) In sub-paragraph (1) "relevant securities" means any security falling within any other paragraph of this Schedule.

NOTES

Modification: the reference in para 2 to securities, instruments or investments creating or acknowledging indebtedness (or creating or acknowledging a present or future indebtedness) includes a reference to uncertificated units of eligible debt securities; see the Uncertificated Securities (Amendment) (Eligible Debt Securities) Regulations 2003, SI 2003/1633, reg 15, Sch 2, para 8.

COMPANIES (AUDIT, INVESTIGATIONS AND COMMUNITY ENTERPRISE) ACT 2004

(2004 c 27)

NOTES

This Act is reproduced as amended by: the Charities Act 2006; the Companies Act 2006; the Corporation Tax Act 2010; the Prospectus Regulations 2005, SI 2005/1433; the Companies (Audit, Investigations and Community Enterprise) (Northern Ireland) Order 2005, SI 2005/1967; the Charities and Trustee Investment (Scotland) Act 2005 (Consequential Provisions and Modifications) Order 2006, SI 2006/242; the Companies Act 2006 (Commencement No 2, Consequential Amendments, Transitional Provisions and Savings) Order 2007, SI 2007/1093; the Companies Act 2006 (Commencement No 3, Consequential Amendments, Transitional Provisions and Savings) Order 2007, SI 2007/2194; the Companies Act 2006 (Consequential Amendments etc) Order 2008, SI 2008/948; the Companies Act 2006 (Consequential Amendments, Transitional Provisions and Savings) Order 2009, SI 2009/1941; the Community Interest Company (Amendment) Regulations 2009, SI 2009/1942; the Charities (Pre-consolidation Amendments) Order 2011, SI 2011/1396.

References to "the European Community", "Community", etc: see the Treaty of Lisbon (Changes in Terminology) Order 2011, SI 2011/1043, which provides that (as from 22 April 2011) "EU" should be substituted for the word "Community" (subject to certain exceptions) in references to "Community treaties", "Community instrument", "Community obligation", "Community law", "Community legislation", etc.

Commencement: see s 65 at **[5.223]** and the Orders noted thereto.

Offences under this Act: see further the Companies Act 2006, ss 1131 at **[1.1131]**.

ARRANGEMENT OF SECTIONS

PART 1
AUDITORS, ACCOUNTS, DIRECTORS' LIABILITIES AND INVESTIGATIONS

CHAPTER 2
ACCOUNTS AND REPORTS

CHAPTER 5
SUPPLEMENTARY

PART 2
COMMUNITY INTEREST COMPANIES

An Act to amend the law relating to company auditors and accounts, to the provision that may be made in respect of certain liabilities incurred by a company's officers, and to company investigations; to make provision for community interest companies; and for connected purposes
[28 October 2004]

PART 1
AUDITORS, ACCOUNTS, DIRECTORS' LIABILITIES AND INVESTIGATIONS

1–7   *(Ss 1–7 (Chap 1) repealed by the Companies Act 2006, s 1295, Sch 16, as from 6 April 2008.)*

CHAPTER 2
ACCOUNTS AND REPORTS

8–13   *(Ss 8–13 repealed by the Companies Act 2006, s 1295, Sch 16, as from 6 April 2008.)*

Supervision of accounts and reports

[5.164]
14   Supervision of periodic accounts and reports of issuers of listed securities
(1)   The Secretary of State may make an order appointing a body ("the prescribed body") to exercise the functions mentioned in subsection (2).
(2)   The functions are—
   (a)   keeping under review periodic accounts and reports that are produced by issuers of [transferable] securities and are required to comply with any accounting requirements imposed by [Part 6] rules; and
   (b)   if the prescribed body thinks fit, informing the Financial Services Authority of any conclusions reached by the body in relation to any such accounts or report.
(3)   A body may be appointed under this section if it is a body corporate or an unincorporated association which appears to the Secretary of State—
   (a)   to have an interest in, and to have satisfactory procedures directed to, monitoring compliance by issuers of [transferable] securities with accounting requirements imposed by [Part 6] rules in relation to periodic accounts and reports produced by such issuers; and
   (b)   otherwise to be a fit and proper body to be appointed.
(4)   But where the order is to contain any requirements or other provisions specified under subsection (8), the Secretary of State may not appoint a body unless, in addition, it appears to him that the body would, if appointed, exercise its functions as a prescribed body in accordance with any such requirements or provisions.
(5)   A body may be appointed either generally or in respect of any of the following, namely—
   (a)   any particular class or classes of issuers,
   (b)   any particular class or classes of periodic accounts or reports,
and different bodies may be appointed in respect of different classes within either or both of paragraphs (a) and (b).
(6)   In relation to the appointment of a body in respect of any such class or classes, subsections (2) and (3) are to be read as referring to issuers, or (as the case may be) to periodic accounts or reports, of the class or classes concerned.
(7)   Where—
   (a)   a body is so appointed, but
   (b)   the Financial Services Authority requests the body to exercise its functions under subsection (2) in relation to any particular issuer of [transferable] securities in relation to whom those functions would not otherwise be exercisable,
the body is to exercise those functions in relation to that issuer as well.
(8)   An order under this section may contain such requirements or other provisions relating to the exercise of functions by the prescribed body as appear to the Secretary of State to be appropriate.
(9)   If the prescribed body is an unincorporated association, any relevant proceedings may be brought by or against that body in the name of any body corporate whose constitution provides for the establishment of the body.
   For this purpose "relevant proceedings" means proceedings brought in or in connection with the exercise of any function by the body as a prescribed body.
(10)   Where an appointment is revoked, the revoking order may make such provision as the Secretary of State thinks fit with respect to pending proceedings.
(11)   The power to make an order under this section is exercisable by statutory instrument subject to annulment in pursuance of a resolution of either House of Parliament.
(12)   In this section [and sections 15A to 15E below]—
   [["Part 6 Rules" has] have the meaning given by section 103(1) of the Financial Services and Markets Act 2000 (c 8) (interpretation of Part 6);
   ["issuer" has the meaning given by section 102A(6) of that Act;]]
   "periodic" accounts and reports means accounts and reports which are required by [Part 6] rules to be produced periodically;
   ["transferable securities" has the meaning given by section 102A(3) of that Act].

NOTES

   Sub-ss (2), (3), (7): words in square brackets substituted by the Companies Act 2006, s 1272, Sch 15, Pt 2, paras 13, 14(1)–(4), as from 8 November 2006.

   Sub-s (12): words in first pair of square brackets substituted by the Companies Act 2006 (Consequential Amendments etc) Order 2008, SI 2008/948, art 3(1), Sch 1, Pt 2, para 232(1), as from 6 April 2008; words in second (outer) pair of square brackets substituted by the Prospectus Regulations 2005, SI 2005/1433, reg 2(3), Sch 3, para 5, as from 1 July 2005; other words in square brackets substituted, and definition "transferable securities" inserted, by the Companies Act 2006, s 1272, Sch 15, Pt 2, paras 13, 14(1), (5), as from 8 November 2006.

Orders: the Companies (Defective Accounts and Directors' Reports) (Authorised Person) and Supervision of Accounts and Reports (Prescribed Body) Order 2008, SI 2008/623 at **[4.258]**. See further art 3 (Appointment in relation to issuers) and art 4 (Appointment in relation to accounts) of the 2008 Order (at **[4.260]**, **[4.261]**) which appoint the Financial Reporting Review Panel established under the articles of association of The Financial Reporting Council Limited for the purposes of sub-s (2) above.

[5.165]
[15　Application of sections 15A to 15E
(1)　The provisions of sections 15A to 15E have effect in relation to bodies appointed under section 14 (supervision of accounts and reports of issuers of transferable securities).
(2)　In those sections—
   (a)　"prescribed body" means a body appointed under that section; and
   (b)　references to the functions of a prescribed body are to its functions under that section.]

NOTES
Commencement: 6 April 2008.
This section together with ss 15A–15E were substituted (for the original s 15) by the Companies Act 2006 (Consequential Amendments etc) Order 2008, SI 2008/948, art 3(1), Sch 1, Pt 2, para 232(2), as from 6 April 2008.
Note: the Companies Act 2006 (Consequential Amendments etc) Order 2008, SI 2008/948, art 3, Sch 2 also repeals s 15 (as from 6 April 2008) in relation to Northern Ireland only.

[5.166]
[15A　Disclosure of information by tax authorities
(1)　The Commissioners for Her Majesty's Revenue and Customs may disclose information to a prescribed body for the purposes of its functions.
(2)　This section applies despite any statutory or other restriction on the disclosure of information. Provided that, in the case of personal data within the meaning of the Data Protection Act 1998, information is not to be disclosed in contravention of that Act.
(3)　Information disclosed to a prescribed body under this section—
   (a)　may only be used for the purposes of its functions, and
   (b)　must not be further disclosed except to the person to whom the information relates.
(4)　A person who contravenes subsection (3) commits an offence unless—
   (a)　the person did not know, and had no reason to suspect, that the information had been disclosed under this section, or
   (b)　the person took all reasonable steps and exercised all due diligence to avoid the commission of the offence.
(5)　A person guilty of an offence under subsection (4) is liable—
   (a)　on conviction on indictment, to imprisonment for a term not exceeding two years or a fine (or both);
   (b)　on summary conviction—
      (i)　in England and Wales or Scotland, to imprisonment for a term not exceeding twelve months or to a fine not exceeding the statutory maximum (or both);
      (ii)　in Northern Ireland, to imprisonment for a term not exceeding three months, or to a fine not exceeding the statutory maximum (or both).
(6)　In subsection (5)(b)(i) as it applies in relation to England and Wales in the case of an offence committed before section 154(1) of the Criminal Justice Act 2003 comes into force, for "twelve months" substitute "six months".
(7)　Sections 400, 401 and 403 of the Financial Services and Markets Act 2000 (supplementary provisions relating to offences) apply in relation to an offence under this section.]

NOTES
Commencement: 6 April 2008.
Substituted as noted to s 15 at **[5.165]**.

[5.167]
[15B　Power of prescribed body to require documents, information and explanations
(1)　This section applies where it appears to a prescribed body that there is, or may be, a question whether the periodic accounts and reports produced by an issuer of transferable securities comply with any accounting requirements imposed by Part 6 rules.
(2)　The prescribed body may require any of the persons mentioned in subsection (3) to produce any document, or to provide any information or explanations, that the body may reasonably require for the purpose of its functions.
(3)　Those persons are—
   (a)　the issuer;
   (b)　any officer, employee, or auditor of the issuer;
   (c)　any persons who fell within paragraph (b) at a time to which the document or information required by the prescribed body relates.

(4)   If a person fails to comply with such a requirement, the prescribed body may apply to the court.

(5)   If it appears to the court that the person has failed to comply with a requirement under subsection (2), it may order the person to take such steps as it directs for securing that the documents are produced or the information or explanations are provided.

(6)   A statement made by a person in response to a requirement under subsection (2) or an order under subsection (5) may not be used in evidence against him in any criminal proceedings.

(7)   Nothing in this section compels any person to disclose documents or information in respect of which a claim to legal professional privilege (in Scotland, to confidentiality of communications) could be maintained in legal proceedings.

(8)   In this section—

"the court" means the High Court or the Court of Session; and

"document" includes information recorded in any form.]

NOTES

Commencement: 6 April 2008.

Substituted as noted to s 15 at **[5.165]**.

[5.168]
[15C   Restrictions on disclosure of information obtained under compulsory powers

(1)   This section applies to information (in whatever form) obtained in pursuance of a requirement or order under section 15B (power of prescribed body to require documents etc) that relates to the private affairs of an individual or to any particular business.

(2)   No such information may, during the lifetime of that individual or so long as that business continues to be carried on, be disclosed without the consent of that individual or the person for the time being carrying on that business.

(3)   This does not apply—

(a)   to disclosure permitted by section 15D (permitted disclosure of information obtained under compulsory powers), or

(b)   to the disclosure of information that is or has been available to the public from another source.

(4)   A person who discloses information in contravention of this section commits an offence, unless—

(a)   the person did not know, and had no reason to suspect, that the information had been disclosed under section 15B, or

(b)   the person took all reasonable steps and exercised all due diligence to avoid the commission of the offence.

(5)   A person guilty of an offence under this section is liable—

(a)   on conviction on indictment, to imprisonment for a term not exceeding two years or a fine (or both);

(b)   on summary conviction—

(i)   in England and Wales or Scotland, to imprisonment for a term not exceeding twelve months or to a fine not exceeding the statutory maximum (or both);

(ii)   in Northern Ireland, to imprisonment for a term not exceeding six months, or to a fine not exceeding the statutory maximum (or both).

(6)   In subsection (5)(b)(i) as it applies in relation to England and Wales in the case of an offence committed before section 154(1) of the Criminal Justice Act 2003 comes into force, for "twelve months" substitute "six months".]

NOTES

Commencement: 6 April 2008.

Substituted as noted to s 15 at **[5.165]**.

[5.169]
[15D   Permitted disclosure of information obtained under compulsory powers

(1)   The prohibition in section 15C of the disclosure of information obtained in pursuance of a requirement or order under section 15B (power of prescribed body to require documents etc) that relates to the private affairs of an individual or to any particular business has effect subject to the following exceptions.

(2)   It does not apply to the disclosure of information for the purpose of facilitating the carrying out by the prescribed body of its functions.

(3)   It does not apply to disclosure to—

(a)   the Secretary of State,

(b)   the Department of Enterprise, Trade and Investment for Northern Ireland,

(c)   the Treasury,

(d)   the Bank of England,

(e)   the Financial Services Authority, or

(f)   the Commissioners for Her Majesty's Revenue and Customs.

(4)   It does not apply to disclosure—

(a)   for the purpose of assisting a body designated by an order under section 1252 of the Companies Act 2006 (delegation of functions of the Secretary of State) to exercise its functions under Part 42 of that Act (statutory auditors);

(b)   with a view to the institution of, or otherwise for the purposes of, disciplinary proceedings relating to the performance by an accountant or auditor of his professional duties;

(c)   for the purpose of enabling or assisting the Secretary of State or the Treasury to exercise any of their functions under any of the following—

     (i)   the Companies Acts (as defined in section 2 of the Companies Act 2006),

     (ii)   Part 5 of the Criminal Justice Act 1993 (insider dealing),

     (iii)   the Insolvency Act 1986 or the Insolvency (Northern Ireland) Order 1989,

     (iv)   the Company Directors Disqualification Act 1986 or the Company Directors Disqualification (Northern Ireland) Order 2002,

     (v)   the Financial Services and Markets Act 2000;

(d)   for the purpose of enabling or assisting the Department of Enterprise, Trade and Investment for Northern Ireland to exercise any powers conferred on it by the enactments relating to companies, directors' disqualification or insolvency;

(e)   for the purpose of enabling or assisting the Bank of England to exercise its functions;

(f)   for the purpose of enabling or assisting the Commissioners for Her Majesty's Revenue and Customs to exercise their functions;

(g)   for the purpose of enabling or assisting the Financial Services Authority to exercise its functions under any of the following—

     (i)   the legislation relating to friendly societies or to industrial and provident societies,

     (ii)   the Building Societies Act 1986,

     (iii)   Part 7 of the Companies Act 1989,

     (iv)   the Financial Services and Markets Act 2000; or

(h)   in pursuance of any Community obligation.

(5)   It does not apply to disclosure to a body exercising functions of a public nature under legislation in any country or territory outside the United Kingdom that appear to the prescribed body to be similar to its functions for the purpose of enabling or assisting that body to exercise those functions.

(6)   In determining whether to disclose information to a body in accordance with subsection (5), the prescribed body must have regard to the following considerations—

(a)   whether the use which the other body is likely to make of the information is sufficiently important to justify making the disclosure;

(b)   whether the other body has adequate arrangements to prevent the information from being used or further disclosed other than—

     (i)   for the purposes of carrying out the functions mentioned in that subsection, or

     (ii)   for other purposes substantially similar to those for which information disclosed to the prescribed body could be used or further disclosed.

(7)   Nothing in this section authorises the making of a disclosure in contravention of the Data Protection Act 1998.]

NOTES
Commencement: 6 April 2008.
Substituted as noted to s 15 at **[5.165]**.

[5.170]
[15E   Power to amend categories of permitted disclosure
(1)   The Secretary of State may by order amend section 15D(3), (4) and (5).

(2)   An order under this section must not—

(a)   amend subsection (3) of that section (UK public authorities) by specifying a person unless the person exercises functions of a public nature (whether or not he exercises any other function);

(b)   amend subsection (4) of that section (purposes for which disclosure permitted) by adding or modifying a description of disclosure unless the purpose for which the disclosure is permitted is likely to facilitate the exercise of a function of a public nature;

(c)   amend subsection (5) of that section (overseas regulatory authorities) so as to have the effect of permitting disclosures to be made to a body other than one that exercises functions of a public nature in a country or territory outside the United Kingdom.

(3)   The power to make an order under this section is exercisable by statutory instrument subject to annulment in pursuance of a resolution of either House of Parliament.]

NOTES
Commencement: 6 April 2008.
Substituted as noted to s 15 at **[5.165]**.

Bodies concerned with accounting standards etc

[5.171]
16   Grants to bodies concerned with accounting standards etc
(1)   The Secretary of State may make grants to any body carrying on activities concerned with any of the matters set out in subsection (2).
(2)   The matters are—
  (a)   issuing accounting standards;
  (b)   issuing standards in respect of matters to be contained in reports required to be produced by auditors or company directors;
  (c)   investigating departures from standards within paragraph (a) or (b) or from the accounting requirements of [the Companies Act 2006] or any requirements of directly applicable Community legislation relating to company accounts;
  (d)   taking steps to secure compliance with such standards or requirements;
  (e)   keeping under review periodic accounts and reports that are produced by issuers of listed securities and are required to comply with any accounting requirements imposed by listing rules;
  (f)   establishing, maintaining or carrying out arrangements within [paragraph 21, 22, 23(1) or 24(1) of Schedule 10 to the Companies Act 2006];
  (g)   exercising functions of the Secretary of State under [Part 42 of that Act];
  (h)   carrying out investigations into public interest cases arising in connection with the performance of accountancy functions by members of professional accountancy bodies;
  (i)   holding disciplinary hearings relating to members of such bodies following the conclusion of such investigations;
  (j)   deciding whether (and, if so, what) disciplinary action should be taken against members of such bodies to whom such hearings related;
  (k)   supervising the exercise by such bodies of regulatory functions in relation to their members;
  [(ka) exercising functions of the Independent Supervisor appointed under Chapter 3 of Part 42 of the Companies Act 2006;]
  [(kb) establishing, maintaining or carrying out arrangements within paragraph 1 or 2 of Schedule 12 to the Companies Act 2006;]
  [(l)   issuing standards to be applied in actuarial work;
  (m)   issuing standards in respect of matters to be contained in reports or other communications required to be produced or made by actuaries or in accordance with standards within paragraph (l);
  (n)   investigating departures from standards within paragraph (l) or (m);
  (o)   taking steps to secure compliance with standards within paragraph (l) or (m);
  (p)   carrying out investigations into public interest cases arising in connection with the performance of actuarial functions by members of professional actuarial bodies;
  (q)   holding disciplinary hearings relating to members of professional actuarial bodies following the conclusion of investigations within paragraph (p);
  (r)   deciding whether (and, if so, what) disciplinary action should be taken against members of professional actuarial bodies to whom hearings within paragraph (q) related;
  (s)   supervising the exercise by professional actuarial bodies of regulatory functions in relation to their members;
  (t)   overseeing or directing any of the matters mentioned above.]
(3)   A grant may be made to a body within subsection (1) in respect of any of its activities.
(4)   For the purposes of this section—
  (a)   a body is to be regarded as carrying on any subsidiary activities of the body; and
  (b)   a body's "subsidiary activities" are activities carried on by any of its subsidiaries or by any body established under its constitution or under the constitution of such a subsidiary.
(5)   In this section—
  "accountancy functions" means functions performed as an accountant, whether in the capacity of auditor or otherwise;
  "company" means a company [as defined in section 1(1) of the Companies Act 2006];
  ["listed securities" and "listing rules" have the meaning given by section 103(1) of the Financial Services and Markets Act 2000 (c 8) (interpretation of Part 6);
  "issuer", in relation to listed securities, has the meaning given by section 102A(6)(b) of the Financial Services and Markets Act 2000 (meaning of "securities" etc,);]
  "professional accountancy body" means—
      (a)   a supervisory body which is recognised for the purposes of [Part 42 of the Companies Act 2006], or
      (b)   a qualifying body, as defined by [section 1220] of that Act, which enforces rules as to the performance of accountancy functions by its members,
      and references to the members of professional accountancy bodies include persons who, although not members of such bodies, are subject to their rules in performing accountancy functions;
  ["professional actuarial body" means—

    (a)   the Institute of Actuaries, or

    (b)   the Faculty of Actuaries in Scotland,

and the "members" of a professional actuarial body include persons who, although not members of the body, are subject to its rules in performing actuarial functions;]

"public interest cases" means matters which raise or appear to raise important issues affecting the public interest;

"regulatory functions", in relation to professional accountancy bodies, means any of the following functions—

    (a)   investigatory or disciplinary functions exercised by such bodies in relation to the performance by their members of accountancy functions,

    (b)   the setting by such bodies of standards in relation to the performance by their members of accountancy functions, and

    (c)   the determining by such bodies of requirements in relation to the education and training of their members;

["regulatory functions", in relation to professional actuarial bodies, means any of the following—

    (a)   investigatory or disciplinary functions exercised by such bodies in relation to the performance by their members of actuarial functions,

    (b)   the setting by such bodies of standards in relation to the performance by their members of actuarial functions, and

    (c)   the determining by such bodies of requirements in relation to the education and training of their members;]

"subsidiary" has the meaning given by [section 1159 of the Companies Act 2006];

[(6)   In their application to Scotland, subsection (2)(a) to (t) are to be read as referring only to matters provision relating to which would be outside the legislative competence of the Scottish Parliament.]

(7)   . . .

NOTES

Sub-s (2) is amended as follows:

Words in square brackets in para (c) substituted by the Companies Act 2006 (Consequential Amendments etc) Order 2008, SI 2008/948, art 3(1), Sch 1, Pt 2, para 233, as from 6 April 2008.

Words in square brackets in paras (f), (g) substituted by the Companies Act 2006, s 1264, Sch 14, paras 1(1), (2), as from 6 April 2008.

Paras (ka), (kb) inserted by the Companies Act 2006, s 1238, 1247, as from 6 April 2008.

Paras (l)–(t) substituted, for original para (l), by the Companies Act 2006, s 1274(1), (2), as from 8 November 2006.

Sub-s (5) is amended as follows:

Words in square brackets in definitions "company" and "subsidiary" substituted by the Companies Act 2006 (Consequential Amendments, Transitional Provisions and Savings) Order 2009, SI 2009/1941, art 2(1), Sch 1, para 222(1)–(3), as from 1 October 2009.

Definitions "listed securities", "listing rules" and "issuer" substituted for the original definitions "issuer", "listing rules" and "security" by the Prospectus Regulations 2005, SI 2005/1433, reg 2(3), Sch 3, para 6, as from 1 July 2005.

Words in square brackets in the definition "professional accountancy body" substituted by the Companies Act 2006, s 1264, Sch 14, paras 1(1), (2), as from 6 April 2008.

Definitions "professional actuarial body" and "regulatory functions" (in relation to professional actuarial bodies) inserted by the Companies Act 2006, s 1274(1), (3), as from 8 November 2006.

Definition "the 1986 Order" (omitted) inserted by the Companies Act 2006, s 1276(1), (4)(c), as from 8 November 2006, and repealed by SI 2009/1941, art 2(1), Sch 1, para 222(1), (4), as from 1 October 2009.

Sub-s (6): substituted by the Companies Act 2006, s 1276(1), (2), as from 8 November 2006.

Sub-s (7): repeals the Companies Act 1985, s 256(3).

[5.172]

17   Levy to pay expenses of bodies concerned with accounting standards etc

(1)   For the purpose of meeting any part of the expenses of a grant-aided body, the Secretary of State may by regulations provide for a levy to be payable to that body ("the specified recipient") by bodies or persons which are specified, or are of a description specified, in the regulations.

(2)   For the purposes of this section—

    (a)   "grant-aided body" means a body to whom the Secretary of State has paid, or is proposing to pay, grant under section 16; and

    (b)   any expenses of any body carrying on subsidiary activities of the grant-aided body (within the meaning of that section) are to be regarded as expenses of the grant-aided body.

(3)   The power to specify (or to specify descriptions of) bodies or persons must be exercised in such a way that the levy is only payable by—

    (a)   bodies corporate to which[, or persons within subsection (3A) to whom,] the Secretary of State considers that any of the activities of the specified recipient, or any of its subsidiary activities, are relevant to a significant extent, or

    (b)   bodies or persons who the Secretary of State considers have a major interest in any of those activities being carried on.

[(3A)   The following persons are within this subsection—

(a) the administrators of a public service pension scheme (within the meaning of section 1 of the Pension Schemes Act 1993);

(b) the trustees or managers of an occupational or personal pension scheme (within the meaning of that section).]

(4) Regulations under this section may in particular—

(a) specify the rate of the levy and the period in respect of which it is payable at that rate;

(b) make provision as to the times when, and the manner in which, payments are to be made in respect of the levy;

[(c) make different provision for different cases].

(5) In determining the rate of the levy payable in respect of a particular period, the Secretary of State—

(a) must take into account the amount of any grant which is to be or has been made to the specified recipient in respect of that period under section 16;

(b) may take into account estimated as well as actual expenses of that body in respect of that period.

(6) Any amount of levy payable by any body or person is a debt due from the body or person to the specified recipient, and is recoverable accordingly.

(7) The specified recipient must—

(a) keep proper accounts in respect of amounts of levy received, and

(b) prepare in relation to each levy period a statement of account relating to such amounts in such form and manner as is specified in the regulations.

(8) Those accounts must be audited, and the statement certified, by persons appointed by the Secretary of State.

(9) The power to make regulations under this section is exercisable by statutory instrument.

(10) Regulations to which this subsection applies may not be made unless a draft of the regulations has been laid before, and approved by a resolution of, each House of Parliament.

(11) Subsection (10) applies to—

(a) the first regulations under this section, and

(b) any other regulations under this section that would result in any change in the bodies or persons by whom the levy is payable.

(12) Otherwise, any statutory instrument containing regulations under this section is subject to annulment in pursuance of a resolution of either House of Parliament.

[(13) If a draft of any regulations to which subsection (10) applies would, apart from this subsection, be treated for the purposes of the standing orders of either House of Parliament as a hybrid instrument, it is to proceed in that House as if it were not such an instrument.]

NOTES

Sub-ss (3), (4): words in square brackets inserted by the Companies Act 2006, s 1275(1), (2), (4), (6), as from 1 October 2009, subject to transitional provisions as noted below.

Sub-ss (3A), (13): inserted and added respectively by the Companies Act 2006, s 1275(1), (3), (5), (6), as from 1 October 2009, subject to transitional provisions as noted below.

Transitional provisions: the Companies Act 2006, s 1275(6) provides that the amendments made to this section by s 1275(1)–(5) of the 2006 Act have effect in relation to any exercise of the power to make Regulations under this section after s 1275 comes into force, regardless of when the expenses to be met by the levy in respect of which the Regulations are made were incurred. Section 1275 came into force on 1 October 2009.

[5.173]
18 Exemption from liability

(1) Where a grant has been paid by the Secretary of State to a body under section 16, this section prevents any liability in damages arising in respect of certain acts or omissions occurring during the period of 12 months beginning with the date on which the grant was paid.

(2) In this section—

"the exemption period" means the period of 12 months mentioned in subsection (1);

"a relevant body" means the body mentioned in that subsection or a body carrying on any subsidiary activities of that body (within the meaning of section 16);

"section 16(2) activities" means activities concerned with any of the matters set out in section 16(2).

(3) Neither a relevant body, nor any person who is (or is acting as) a member, officer or member of staff of a relevant body, is to be liable in damages for anything done, or omitted to be done, during the exemption period for the purposes of or in connection with—

(a) the carrying on of any section 16(2) activities of the body, or

(b) the purported carrying on of any such activities.

(4) Subsection (3) does not apply—

(a) if the act or omission is shown to have been in bad faith; or

(b) so as to prevent an award of damages in respect of the act or omission on the grounds that it was unlawful as a result of section 6(1) of the Human Rights Act 1998 (c 42) (acts of public authorities incompatible with Convention rights).

19–24 (*(Chaps 3, 4): s 19 repealed by the Companies Act 2006, s 1295, Sch 16, as from 1 October 2007 (in part), and as from 6 April 2008 (otherwise); s 20 repealed by CA 2006, s 1295, Sch 16, as* *from 1 October 2007; s 21 substitutes CA 1985, s 447 at* **[5.18]***; s 22 inserts CA 1985, s 448A at* **[5.21]***; s 23 inserts CA 1985, ss 453A, 453B at* **[5.28]**, **[5.29]***; s 24 inserts CA 1985, s 453C at* **[5.30]**.)

CHAPTER 5

SUPPLEMENTARY

[5.174]

25   Minor and consequential amendments

(1)   Schedule 2 (minor and consequential amendments relating to Part 1) has effect.

(2)   That Schedule has effect subject to the modifications set out in subsection (3)—

   (a)   in relation to England and Wales, in the case of an offence committed before section 154(1) of the Criminal Justice Act 2003 (c 44) comes into force, and

   (b)   in relation to Scotland.

(3)   The modifications are—

   (a)   the amendment in paragraph 10(2) has effect as if for "12 months" there were substituted "6 months";

   (b)   the amendment in paragraph 10(3) has effect as if for "12 months", in both places where it occurs, there were substituted "3 months";

   (c)   the amendment in paragraph 10(4) has effect as if for "12 months" there were substituted "6 months";

   (d)   the amendment in paragraph 26(2) has effect as if for "12 months" there were substituted "6 months"; and

   (e)   the amendment in paragraph 26(3) has effect as if for "12 months" there were substituted "6 months".

PART 2

COMMUNITY INTEREST COMPANIES

Introductory

[5.175]

26   Community interest companies

(1)   There is to be a new type of company to be known as the community interest company.

(2)   In accordance with this Part—

   (a)   a company limited by shares or a company limited by guarantee and not having a share capital may be formed as or become a community interest company, and

   (b)   a company limited by guarantee and having a share capital may become a community interest company.

(3)   A community interest company established for charitable purposes is to be treated as not being so established and accordingly—

   (a)   is not [an English charity or a Northern Ireland charity], and

   (b)   must not be [entered in the Scottish Charity Register].

NOTES

Sub-s (3): words in square brackets in para (a) substituted by the Companies Act 2006 (Commencement No 2, Consequential Amendments, Transitional Provisions and Savings) Order 2007, SI 2007/1093, art 6(2), Sch 4, Pt 1, para 1, as from 6 April 2007; words in square brackets in para (b) substituted by the Charities and Trustee Investment (Scotland) Act 2005 (Consequential Provisions and Modifications) Order 2006, SI 2006/242, art 5, Schedule, Pt 1, para 8(1), (2), as from 1 April 2006.

[5.176]

27   Regulator

(1)   There is to be an officer known as the Regulator of Community Interest Companies (referred to in this Part as "the Regulator").

(2)   The Secretary of State must appoint a person to be the Regulator.

(3)   The Regulator has such functions relating to community interest companies as are conferred or imposed by or by virtue of this Act or any other enactment.

(4)   The Regulator must adopt an approach to the discharge of those functions which is based on good regulatory practice, that is an approach adopted having regard to—

   (a)   the likely impact on those who may be affected by the discharge of those functions,

   (b)   the outcome of consultations with, and with organisations representing, community interest companies and others with relevant experience, and

   (c)   the desirability of using the Regulator's resources in the most efficient and economic way.

(5)   The Regulator may issue guidance, or otherwise provide assistance, about any matter relating to community interest companies.

(6)   The Secretary of State may require the Regulator to issue guidance or otherwise provide assistance about any matter relating to community interest companies which is specified by the Secretary of State.

(7)   Any guidance issued under this section must be such that it is readily accessible to, and capable of being easily understood by, those at whom it is aimed; and any other assistance provided under this section must be provided in the manner which the Regulator considers is most likely to be helpful to those to whom it is provided.

(8)   Schedule 3 (further provisions about the Regulator) has effect.

[5.177]
28   Appeal Officer
(1)   There is to be an officer known as the Appeal Officer for Community Interest Companies (referred to in this Part as "the Appeal Officer").

(2)   The Secretary of State must appoint a person to be the Appeal Officer.

(3)   The Appeal Officer has the function of determining appeals against decisions and orders of the Regulator which under or by virtue of this Act or any other enactment lie to the Appeal Officer.

(4)   An appeal to the Appeal Officer against a decision or order of the Regulator may be brought on the ground that the Regulator made a material error of law or fact.

(5)   On such an appeal the Appeal Officer must—
  (a)   dismiss the appeal,
  (b)   allow the appeal, or
  (c)   remit the case to the Regulator.

(6)   Where a case is remitted the Regulator must reconsider it in accordance with any rulings of law and findings of fact made by the Appeal Officer.

(7)   Schedule 4 (further provisions about the Appeal Officer) has effect.

[5.178]
29   Official Property Holder
(1)   There is to be an officer known as the Official Property Holder for Community Interest Companies (referred to in this Part as "the Official Property Holder").

(2)   The Regulator must appoint a member of the Regulator's staff to be the Official Property Holder.

(3)   The Official Property Holder has such functions relating to property of community interest companies as are conferred or imposed by or by virtue of this Act or any other enactment.

(4)   Schedule 5 (further provisions about the Official Property Holder) has effect.

Requirements

[5.179]
30   Cap on distributions and interest
(1)   Community interest companies must not distribute assets to their members unless regulations make provision authorising them to do so.

(2)   If regulations authorise community interest companies to distribute assets to their members, the regulations may impose limits on the extent to which they may do so.

(3)   Regulations may impose limits on the payment of interest on debentures issued by, or debts of, community interest companies.

(4)   Regulations under this section may make provision for limits to be set by the Regulator.

(5)   The Regulator—
  (a)   may set a limit by reference to a rate determined by any other person (as it has effect from time to time), and
  (b)   may set different limits for different descriptions of community interest companies.

(6)   The Regulator must (in accordance with section 27)—
  (a)   undertake appropriate consultation before setting a limit, and
  (b)   in setting a limit, have regard to its likely impact on community interest companies.

(7)   Regulations under this section may include power for the Secretary of State to require the Regulator to review a limit or limits.

(8)   Where the Regulator sets a limit he must publish notice of it in the Gazette.

NOTES
  Regulations: the Community Interest Company Regulations 2005, SI 2005/1788 at **[6.113]**; the Community Interest Company (Amendment) Regulations 2009, SI 2009/1942.

[5.180]
31   Distribution of assets on winding up
(1)   Regulations may make provision for and in connection with the distribution, on the winding up of a community interest company, of any assets of the company which remain after satisfaction of the company's liabilities.

(2)   The regulations may, in particular, amend or modify the operation of any enactment or instrument.

NOTES
  Regulations: the Community Interest Company Regulations 2005, SI 2005/1788 at **[6.113]**; the Community Interest Company (Amendment) Regulations 2009, SI 2009/1942.

[5.181]
32   [Articles of association]
(1)   The [articles] of a community interest company must state that the company is to be a community interest company.

(2)   . . .

(3)   The [articles] of a community interest company of any description—

    (a)   must at all times include such provisions as regulations require to be included in the [articles] of every community interest company or a community interest company of that description, and

    (b)   must not include such provisions as regulations require not to be so included.

(4)   The provisions required by regulations under subsection (3)(a) to be included in the [articles] of a community interest company may (in particular) include—

    (a)   provisions about the transfer and distribution of the company's assets (including their distribution on a winding up),

    (b)   provisions about the payment of interest on debentures issued by the company or debts of the company,

    (c)   provisions about membership of the company,

    (d)   provisions about the voting rights of members of the company,

    (e)   provisions about the appointment and removal of directors of the company, and

    (f)   provisions about voting at meetings of directors of the company.

(5)   The [articles] of a community interest company are of no effect to the extent that they—

    (a)   are inconsistent with provisions required to be included in the [articles] of the company by regulations under subsection (3)(a), or

    (b)   include provisions required not to be included by regulations under subsection (3)(b).

(6)   Regulations may make provision for and in connection with restricting the ability of a community interest company [to amend its articles so as to add, remove or alter a statement of the company's objects].

NOTES

All words in square brackets wee substituted, and sub-s (2) was repealed, by the Companies Act 2006 (Consequential Amendments, Transitional Provisions and Savings) Order 2009, SI 2009/1941, art 2(1), Sch 1, para 223, as from 1 October 2009.

Regulations: the Community Interest Company Regulations 2005, SI 2005/1788 at **[6.113]**; the Community Interest Company (Amendment) Regulations 2009, SI 2009/1942.

[5.182]
33   Names
(1)   The name of a community interest company which is not a public company must end with—

    (a)   "community interest company", or

    (b)   "cic".

(2)   [In the case of a Welsh company, its name may instead] end with—

    (a)   "cwmni buddiant cymunedol", or

    (b)   "cbc",

. . .

(3)   The name of a community interest company which is a public company must end with—

    (a)   "community interest public limited company", or

    (b)   "community interest plc".

(4)   [In the case of a Welsh company, its name may instead] end with—

    (a)   "cwmni buddiant cymunedol cyhoeddus cyfyngedig", or

    (b)   "cwmni buddiant cymunedol ccc",

. . .

(5)   . . .

(6)   Schedule 6 (further provisions about names) has effect.

NOTES

Words in square brackets in sub-ss (2), (4) substituted, and words omitted from those subsections and the whole of sub-s (5) repealed, by the Companies Act 2006 (Consequential Amendments, Transitional Provisions and Savings) Order 2009, SI 2009/1941, art 2(1), Sch 1, para 224, as from 1 October 2009.

[5.183]
34   Community interest company reports
(1)   The directors of a community interest company must prepare in respect of each financial year a report about the company's activities during the financial year (a "community interest company report").

(2)   [Regulations must make provision] requiring the directors of a community interest company to deliver to the registrar of companies a copy of the community interest company report.

(3)   Regulations—

    (a)   must make provision requiring community interest company reports to include information about the remuneration of directors,

(b)   may make provision as to the form of, and other information to be included in, community interest company reports, and

(c)   may apply provisions of [. . . . the Companies Act 2006] relating to directors' reports to community interest company reports (with any appropriate modifications).

(4)   The registrar of companies must forward to the Regulator a copy of each community interest company report delivered to the registrar by virtue of this section.

NOTES

Sub-s (2): words in square brackets substituted by the Companies Act 2006 (Consequential Amendments etc) Order 2008, SI 2008/948, art 3(1), Sch 1, Pt 2, para 234(1), (2)(a), as from 6 April 2008.

Sub-s (3): words in square brackets substituted by the Companies Act 2006 (Commencement No 3, Consequential Amendments, Transitional Provisions and Savings) Order 2007, SI 2007/2194, art 10(1), Sch 4, Pt 3, para 104, as from 1 October 2007; words omitted therefrom repealed by SI 2008/948, art 3, Sch 1, Pt 2, para 234(1), (2)(b), Sch 2, as from 6 April 2008.

Regulations: the Community Interest Company Regulations 2005, SI 2005/1788 at **[6.113]**.

[5.184]
35   Community interest test and excluded companies
(1)   This section has effect for the purposes of this Part.
(2)   A company satisfies the community interest test if a reasonable person might consider that its activities are being carried on for the benefit of the community.
(3)   An object stated in the [articles] of a company is a community interest object of the company if a reasonable person might consider that the carrying on of activities by the company in furtherance of the object is for the benefit of the community.
(4)   Regulations may provide that activities of a description prescribed by the regulations are to be treated as being, or as not being, activities which a reasonable person might consider are activities carried on for the benefit of the community.
(5)   "Community" includes a section of the community (whether in [the United Kingdom] or anywhere else); and regulations may make provision about what does, does not or may constitute a section of the community.
(6)   A company is an excluded company if it is a company of a description prescribed by regulations.

NOTES

Sub-s (3): word in square brackets substituted by the Companies Act 2006 (Consequential Amendments, Transitional Provisions and Savings) Order 2009, SI 2009/1941, art 2(1), Sch 1, para 225, as from 1 October 2009.

Sub-s (5): words in square brackets substituted by the Companies Act 2006 (Commencement No 2, Consequential Amendments, Transitional Provisions and Savings) Order 2007, SI 2007/1093, art 6(2), Sch 4, Pt 1, para 5, as from 6 April 2007.

Regulations: the Community Interest Company Regulations 2005, SI 2005/1788 at **[6.113]**; the Community Interest Company (Amendment) Regulations 2009, SI 2009/1942.

Becoming a community interest company

[5.185]
[36   Formation of company as a community interest company
(1)   If a company is to be formed as a community interest company, the documents delivered to the registrar of companies under section 9 of the Companies Act 2006 (registration documents) must be accompanied by the prescribed formation documents.
(2)   The "prescribed formation documents" means such declarations or statements as are required by regulations to accompany the application, in such form as may be approved in accordance with the regulations.
(3)   On receiving the documents delivered under that section and the prescribed formation documents, the registrar must (instead of registering the documents)—
(a)   forward a copy of each of the documents to the Regulator, and
(b)   retain the documents pending the Regulator's decision.]

NOTES

Commencement: 1 October 2009.

Substituted (together with ss 36A, 36B for the original s 36) by the Companies Act 2006 (Consequential Amendments, Transitional Provisions and Savings) Order 2009, SI 2009/1941, art 2(1), Sch 1, para 226,as from 1 October 2009.

Regulations: the Community Interest Company Regulations 2005, SI 2005/1788 at **[6.113]**.

[5.186]
[36A   Formation as community interest company: decision on eligibility
(1)   The Regulator must decide whether the company is eligible to be formed as a community interest company.
(2)   A company is eligible to be formed as a community interest company if—
(a)   its articles comply with the requirements imposed by and by virtue of section 32,
(b)   its proposed name complies with section 33, and
(c)   the Regulator, having regard to the application and accompanying documents and any other relevant considerations, considers that the company—

Part 5   Pre-2006 companies legislation

      (i)   will satisfy the community interest test, and

      (ii)   is not an excluded company.

(3)   The Regulator must give notice of the decision to the registrar of companies (but the registrar is not required to record it).]

NOTES

Commencement: 1 October 2009.

Substituted as noted to s 36 at **[5.185]**.

[5.187]

[36B   Formation as community interest company: implementation of decision on eligibility

(1)   If the Regulator decides that the company is eligible to be formed as a community interest company, the registrar of companies must—

   (a)   proceed in accordance with sections 14 and 15 of the Companies Act 2006 (registration and issue of certificate of incorporation), and

   (b)   if the company is entered on the register, retain and record the prescribed formation documents.

(2)   The certificate of incorporation must state that the company is a community interest company and is conclusive evidence that the company is a community interest company.

(3)   If the Regulator decides that the company is not eligible to be formed as a community interest company, any subscriber to the memorandum of association may appeal to the Appeal Officer against the decision.]

NOTES

Commencement: 1 October 2009.

Substituted as noted to s 36 at **[5.185]**.

[5.188]

[37   Company becoming a community interest company

(1)   If a company is to become a community interest company—

   (a)   the company must by special resolution—

      (i)   state that it is to be a community interest company,

      (ii)   make such alterations of its articles as it considers necessary to comply with requirements imposed by and by virtue of section 32 or otherwise appropriate in connection with becoming a community interest company, and

      (iii) change its name to comply with section 33;

   (b)   the conditions specified below must be met; and

   (c)   an application must be delivered to the registrar of companies in accordance with section 37C together with the other documents required by that section.

(2)   The conditions referred to in subsection (1)(b) are that—

   (a)   where no application under section 37A for cancellation of the special resolutions has been made—

      (i)   having regard to the number of members who consented to or voted in favour of the resolutions, no such application may be made, or

      (ii)   the period within which such an application could be made has expired, or

   (b)   where such an application has been made—

      (i)   the application has been withdrawn, or

      (ii)   an order has been made confirming the resolutions and a copy of that order has been delivered to the registrar.

(3)   Section 30 of the Companies Act 2006 (copies of resolutions to be forwarded to the registrar) applies to the special resolutions as follows—

   (a)   that section is complied with by forwarding copies of the resolutions together with the application in accordance with section 37C,

   (b)   copies of the resolutions must not be so forwarded before the relevant date, and

   (c)   subsection (1) of that section has effect in relation to the resolutions as if it referred to 15 days after the relevant date.

(4)   The relevant date is—

   (a)   if an application is made under section 37A for cancellation of the special resolutions—

      (i)   the date on which the court determines the application (or if there is more than one application, the date on which the last to be determined by the court is determined), or

      (ii)   such later date as the court may order;

   (b)   if there is no such application—

      (i)   if having regard to the number of members who consented to or voted in favour of the resolutions, no such application may be made, the date on which the resolutions were passed or made (or, if the resolutions were passed or made on different days, the date on which the last of them was passed or made);

      (ii)   in any other case, the end of the period for making such an application.]

NOTES

Commencement: 1 October 2009.

Substituted (together with ss 37A–37C for the original s 37) by the Companies Act 2006 (Consequential Amendments, Transitional Provisions and Savings) Order 2009, SI 2009/1941, art 2(1), Sch 1, para 226,as from 1 October 2009.

[5.189]
[37A   Becoming a community interest company: application to court to cancel resolutions
(1)   Where special resolutions have been passed with a view to the company becoming a community interest company, an application to the court for the cancellation of the resolutions may be made—
  (a)   by the holders of not less in the aggregate than 15% in nominal value of the company's issued share capital or any class of the company's issued share capital (disregarding any shares held by the company as treasury shares);
  (b)   if the company is not limited by shares, by not less than 15% of its members; or
  (c)   by the holders of not less than 15% of the company's debentures entitling the holders to object to an alteration of its objects;
but not by a person who has consented to or voted in favour of the resolutions.
(2)   The application—
  (a)   must be made within 28 days after the date on which the resolutions are passed or made (or, if the resolutions are passed or made on different days, the date on which the last of them is passed or made), and
  (b)   may be made on behalf of the persons entitled to make it by such one or more of their number as they may appoint for the purpose.
(3)   On the hearing of the application the court shall make an order either cancelling or confirming the resolutions.
(4)   The court may—
  (a)   make that order on such terms and conditions as it thinks fit,
  (b)   if it thinks fit adjourn the proceedings in order that an arrangement may be made to the satisfaction of the court for the purchase of the interests of dissentient members, and
  (c)   give such directions, and make such orders, as it thinks expedient for facilitating or carrying into effect any such arrangement.
(5)   The court's order may, if the court thinks fit—
  (a)   provide for the purchase by the company of the shares of any of its members and for the reduction accordingly of the company's capital; and
  (b)   make such alteration in the company's articles as may be required in consequence of that provision.
(6)   The court's order may, if the court thinks fit, require the company not to make any, or any specified, amendments to its articles without the leave of the court.]

NOTES

Commencement: 1 October 2009.

Substituted as noted to s 37 at **[5.188]**.

[5.190]
[37B   Becoming a community interest company: notice to registrar of court application or order
(1)   On making an application under section 37A (application to court to cancel resolutions) the applicants, or the person making the application on their behalf, must immediately give notice to the registrar of companies.
  This is without prejudice to any provision of rules of court as to service of notice of the application.
(2)   On being served with notice of any such application, the company must immediately give notice to the registrar.
(3)   Within 15 days of the making of the court's order on the application, or such longer period as the court may at any time direct, the company must deliver to the registrar a copy of the order.
(4)   If a company fails to comply with subsection (2) or (3) an offence is committed by—
  (a)   the company, and
  (b)   every officer of the company who is in default.
(5)   A person guilty of an offence under this section is liable on summary conviction to a fine not exceeding level 3 on the standard scale and, for continued contravention, a daily default fine not exceeding one-tenth of level 3 on the standard scale.]

NOTES

Commencement: 1 October 2009.

Substituted as noted to s 37 at **[5.188]**.

Part 5 Pre-2006 companies legislation

[5.191]
[37C Becoming a community interest company: application and accompanying documents
(1) An application to become a community interest company must be accompanied by—
 (a) a copy of the special resolutions,
 (b) a copy of the company's articles as proposed to be amended, and
 (c) the prescribed conversion documents.
(2) The "prescribed conversion documents" means such declarations or statements as are required by regulations to accompany the application, in such form as may be approved in accordance with the regulations.
(3) On receiving an application to become a community interest company together with the other documents required to accompany it, the registrar of companies must (instead of recording the documents and entering a new name on the register)—
 (a) forward a copy of each of the documents to the Regulator, and
 (b) retain the documents pending the Regulator's decision.]

NOTES
Commencement: 1 October 2009.
Substituted as noted to s 37 at **[5.188]**.

[5.192]
[38 Becoming a community interest company: decision by Regulator
(1) The Regulator must decide whether the company is eligible to become a community interest company.
(2) A company is eligible to become a community interest company if—
 (a) its articles as proposed to be amended comply with the requirements imposed by and by virtue of section 32,
 (b) its proposed name complies with section 33, and
 (c) the Regulator, having regard to the application and accompanying documents and any other relevant considerations, considers that the company—
  (i) will satisfy the community interest test, and
  (ii) is not an excluded company.
(3) The Regulator must give notice of the decision to the registrar of companies (but the registrar is not required to record it).]

NOTES
Commencement: 1 October 2009.
Substituted (together with s 38A for the original s 38) by the Companies Act 2006 (Consequential Amendments, Transitional Provisions and Savings) Order 2009, SI 2009/1941, art 2(1), Sch 1, para 227(2), as from 1 October 2009.

[5.193]
[38A Becoming a community interest company: implementation of decision on eligibility
(1) If the Regulator gives notice of a decision that the company is eligible to become a community interest company, the registrar of companies must—
 (a) proceed in accordance with section 80 of the Companies Act 2006 (change of name: registration and issue of new certificate of incorporation), and
 (b) if the registrar enters the new name of the company on the register, retain and record the documents mentioned in section 37C(3).
(2) The new certificate of incorporation must state—
 (a) that it is issued on the company's conversion to a community interest company,
 (b) the date on which it is issued, and
 (c) that the company is a community interest company.
(3) On the issue of the certificate—
 (a) the company by virtue of the issue of the certificate becomes a community interest company, and
 (b) the changes in the company's name and articles take effect.
(4) The certificate is conclusive evidence that the company is a community interest company.
(5) If the Regulator decides that the company is not eligible to become a community interest company, the company may appeal to the Appeal Officer against the decision.]

NOTES
Commencement: 1 October 2009.
Substituted as noted to s 38 at **[5.192]**.

[5.194]
39 [Becoming a community interest company: English charities]
(1) A [company that is an English charity] may not [become a community interest company] without the prior written consent of the [Charity Commission].
(2) If a [company that is an English charity] contravenes subsection (1), the [Charity Commission] may apply to the High Court for an order quashing any altered certificate of incorporation issued under [section 38A].

(3) If a [company that is an English charity] becomes a community interest company, that does not affect the application of—

(a) any property acquired under any disposition or agreement previously made otherwise than for full consideration in money or money's worth, or any property representing property so acquired,

(b) any property representing income which has previously accrued, or

(c) the income from any such property.

(4) . . .

NOTES

Section heading substituted, words in second pair of square brackets in sub-s (1) substituted, and final words in square brackets in sub-s (2) substituted, by the Companies Act 2006 (Consequential Amendments, Transitional Provisions and Savings) Order 2009, SI 2009/1941, art 2(1), Sch 1, para 228, as from 1 October 2009.

Words "Charity Commission" in square brackets in sub-ss (1), (2) substituted by the Charities Act 2006, s 75, Sch 8, paras 200, 201, as from 27 February 2007.

All other words in square bracket substituted, and sub-s (4) repealed, by the Companies Act 2006 (Commencement No 2, Consequential Amendments, Transitional Provisions and Savings) Order 2007, SI 2007/1093, art 6(2), Sch 4, Pt 1, para 9, as from 6 April 2007.

[5.195]

40 [Becoming a community interest company: Scottish charities]

(1), (2) . . .

(3) Regulations may repeal subsections (1) and (2); and subsections (4) to (7) have effect on and after the day on which regulations under this subsection come into force.

(4) A [company that is a Scottish charity] may not [become a community interest company] without the prior written consent—

(a) if the company's registered office is situated in Scotland, of the Scottish Charity Regulator, or

(b) if the company's registered office is situated in England and Wales (or Wales), of both the Scottish Charity Regulator and the [Charity Commission].

(5) If a [company that is a Scottish charity] contravenes subsection (4)(a), the Scottish Charity Regulator may apply to the Court of Session for an order quashing any altered certificate of incorporation issued under [section 38A].

(6) If a [company that is a Scottish charity] contravenes subsection (4)(b), the Scottish Charity Regulator or the [Charity Commission] may apply to the High Court for such an order.

(7) If a [company that is a Scottish charity] becomes a community interest company, [it shall continue to be under a duty to apply—

(a) any property previously acquired, or any property representing property previously acquired,

(b) any property representing income which has previously accrued, and

(c) the income from any such property,

in accordance with its purposes as set out in its entry in the Scottish Charity Register immediately before it became a community interest company.]

(8), (9) . . .

NOTES

Section heading: substituted by the Companies Act 2006 (Consequential Amendments, Transitional Provisions and Savings) Order 2009, SI 2009/1941, art 2(1), Sch 1, para 229(1), (2), as from 1 October 2009.

Sub-ss (1), (2): repealed by the Community Interest Company (Amendment) Regulations 2009, SI 2009/1942, reg 2, as from 1 October 2009.

Sub-s (4): words in first pair of square brackets substituted by the Companies Act 2006 (Commencement No 2, Consequential Amendments, Transitional Provisions and Savings) Order 2007, SI 2007/1093, art 6(2), Sch 4, Pt 1, para 10(a), as from 6 April 2007; words in second pair of square brackets substituted by SI 2009/1941, art 2(1), Sch 1, para 229(1), (3), as from 1 October 2009; words in final pair of square brackets substituted by the Charities Act 2006, s 75, Sch 8, paras 200, 202, as from 27 February 2007.

Sub-s (5): words in first pair of square brackets substituted by SI 2007/1093, art 6(2), Sch 4, Pt 1, para 10(a), (b), as from 6 April 2007; words in second pair of square brackets substituted by SI 2009/1941, art 2(1), Sch 1, para 229(1), (4), as from 1 October 2009.

Sub-s (6): words in first pair of square brackets substituted by SI 2007/1093, art 6(2), Sch 4, Pt 1, para 10(a), as from 6 April 2007; words in second pair of square brackets substituted by the Charities Act 2006, s 75, Sch 8, paras 200, 202, as from 27 February 2007.

Sub-s (7): words in first pair of square brackets substituted by SI 2007/1093, art 6(2), Sch 4, Pt 1, para 10(a), as from 6 April 2007; words in second pair of square brackets substituted by the Charities and Trustee Investment (Scotland) Act 2005 (Consequential Provisions and Modifications) Order 2006, SI 2006/242, art 5, Schedule, Pt 1, para 8(1), (3)(a), as from 1 April 2006.

Sub-s (8): repealed by SI 2007/1093, art 6(2), Sch 4, Pt 1, para 10(c), as from 6 April 2007.

Sub-s (9): repealed by SI 2006/242, art 5, Schedule, Pt 1, para 8(1), (3)(c), as from 1 April 2006.

Commissioners of Inland Revenue: a reference to the Commissioners of Inland Revenue is now to be taken as a reference to the Commissioners for Her Majesty's Revenue and Customs; see the Commissioners for Revenue and Customs Act 2005, s 50(1), (7).

Regulations: the Community Interest Company Regulations 2005, SI 2005/1788 at **[6.113]**; the Community Interest Company (Amendment) Regulations 2009, SI 2009/1942.

[5.196]
[40A   [Becoming a community interest company: Northern Ireland charities]
(1)   A company that is a Northern Ireland charity may not become a community interest company.
(2)   If a company that is a Northern Ireland charity purports [to become a community interest company], the Commissioners of Her Majesty's Revenue and Customs may apply to the High Court for an order quashing any altered certificate of incorporation under [section 38A].]

NOTES
Commencement: 6 April 2007.
Inserted by the Companies Act 2006 (Commencement No 2, Consequential Amendments, Transitional Provisions and Savings) Order 2007, SI 2007/1093, art 6(2), Sch 4, Pt 1, para 11, as from 6 April 2007.
Section heading, sub-s (2): words in square brackets substituted by the Companies Act 2006 (Consequential Amendments, Transitional Provisions and Savings) Order 2009, SI 2009/1941, art 2(1), Sch 1, para 230, as from 1 October 2009.

Supervision by Regulator

[5.197]
41   Conditions for exercise of supervisory powers
(1)   In deciding whether and how to exercise the powers conferred by sections 42 to 51 the Regulator must adopt an approach which is based on the principle that those powers should be exercised only to the extent necessary to maintain confidence in community interest companies.
(2)   No power conferred on the Regulator by—
   (a)   section 45 (appointment of director),
   (b)   section 46 (removal of director),
   (c)   section 47 (appointment of manager), or
   (d)   section 48 (property),
is exercisable in relation to a community interest company unless the company default condition is satisfied in relation to the power and the company.
(3)   The company default condition is satisfied in relation to a power and a company if it appears to the Regulator necessary to exercise the power in relation to the company because—
   (a)   there has been misconduct or mismanagement in the administration of the company,
   (b)   there is a need to protect the company's property or to secure the proper application of that property,
   (c)   the company is not satisfying the community interest test, or
   (d)   if the company has community interest objects, the company is not carrying on any activities in pursuit of those objects.
(4)   The power conferred on the Regulator by section 49 (transfer of shares etc) is not exercisable in relation to a community interest company unless it appears to the Regulator that the company is an excluded company.

[5.198]
42   Investigation
(1)   The Regulator may—
   (a)   investigate the affairs of a community interest company, or
   (b)   appoint any person (other than a member of the Regulator's staff) to investigate the affairs of a community interest company on behalf of the Regulator.
(2)   Subsection (1)(b) is in addition to paragraph 5 of Schedule 3 (powers of Regulator exercisable by authorised members of staff) and does not affect the application of that paragraph to the Regulator's power under subsection (1)(a).
(3)   Schedule 7 (further provision about investigations under this section) has effect.

[5.199]
43   Audit
(1)   The Regulator may by order require a community interest company to allow the annual accounts of the company to be audited by a qualified auditor appointed by the Regulator.
(2)   A person is a qualified auditor if he is eligible for appointment [as a statutory auditor under Part 42 of the Companies Act 2006].
(3)   [Sections 499 to 501 of the Companies Act 2006] (auditor's rights to information) apply in relation to an auditor appointed under this section . . .
(4)   On completion of the audit the auditor must make a report to the Regulator on such matters and in such form as the Regulator specifies.
(5)   The expenses of the audit, including the remuneration of the auditor, are to be paid by the Regulator.
(6)   An audit under this section is in addition to, and does not affect, any audit required by or by virtue of any other enactment.

NOTES
Sub-s (2): words in square brackets substituted by the Companies Act 2006 (Consequential Amendments etc) Order 2008, SI 2008/948, art 3(1), Sch 1, Pt 1, para 31, as from 6 April 2008 (for savings see art 6(4) of the 2008 Order (at **[4.280]**)) which provides that where by virtue of any transitional provision, a provision of the Companies Act 2006 has effect only (a) on or after a specified date, or (b) in relation to matters occurring or arising on or after a specified date, any amendment substituting or inserting a reference to that provision has effect correspondingly)

Sub-s (3): words in square brackets substituted by SI 2008/948, art 3(1), Sch 1, Pt 2, para 234(1), (3), as from 6 April 2008 (for savings see the note for sub-s (1) above); words omitted repealed by the Companies Act 2006 (Commencement No 3, Consequential Amendments, Transitional Provisions and Savings) Order 2007, SI 2007/2194, art 10(1), (3), Sch 4, Pt 3, para 106, Sch 5, as from 1 October 2007.

[5.200]
44 Civil proceedings
(1)   The Regulator may bring civil proceedings in the name and on behalf of a community interest company.
(2)   Before instituting proceedings under this section the Regulator must give written notice to the company stating—
  (a)   the cause of action,
  (b)   the remedy sought, and
  (c)   a summary of the facts on which the proceedings are to be based.
(3)   Any director of the company may apply to the court for an order—
  (a)   that proposed proceedings are not to be instituted under this section, or
  (b)   that proceedings instituted under this section are to be discontinued.
(4)   On an application under subsection (3) the court may make such order as it thinks fit.
(5)   In particular the court may (as an alternative to ordering that proposed proceedings are not to be instituted under this section or that proceedings instituted under this section are to be discontinued) order—
  (a)   that the proposed proceedings may be instituted under this section, or the proceedings instituted under this section may be continued, on such terms and conditions as the court thinks fit,
  (b)   that any proceedings instituted by the company are to be discontinued, or
  (c)   that any proceedings instituted by the company may be continued on such terms and conditions as the court thinks fit.
(6)   The Regulator must indemnify the company against any costs (or expenses) incurred by it in connection with proceedings brought under this section.
(7)   Any costs (or expenses)—
  (a)   awarded to the company in connection with proceedings brought under this section, or
  (b)   incurred by the company in connection with the proceedings and which it is agreed should be paid by a defendant (or defender),
are to be paid to the Regulator.

[5.201]
45 Appointment of director
(1)   The Regulator may by order appoint a director of a community interest company.
(2)   The person appointed may be anyone whom the Regulator thinks appropriate, other than a member of the Regulator's staff.
(3)   A person may be appointed as a director of a company under this section—
  (a)   whether or not the person is a member of the company, and
  (b)   irrespective of any provision made by the [articles] of the company or a resolution of the company   . . .
(4)   An order appointing a person to be a director of a company under this section must specify the terms on which the director is to hold office; and those terms have effect as if contained in a contract between the director and the company.
(5)   The terms specified must include the period for which the director is to hold office, and may include terms as to the remuneration of the director by the company.
(6)   A director appointed under this section has all the powers of the directors appointed by the company (including powers exercisable only by a particular director or class of directors).
(7)   A director appointed under this section may not be removed by the company, but may be removed by the Regulator at any time.
(8)   Where—
  (a)   a person is appointed to be a director of the company under this section, or
  (b)   a person so appointed ceases to be a director of the company,
the obligation which would otherwise be imposed on the company under [section 167(1)(a) of the Companies Act 2006] (requirement that company notify change among directors to registrar) is instead an obligation of the Regulator.
(9)   But if subsection (10) applies, [section 167(1)(a)] applies as if the period within which the Regulator must send a notification to the registrar of companies is 14 days from the date on which the Regulator receives notification under that subsection.
(10)   Where a person appointed to be a director of the company under this section ceases to be a director of the company (otherwise than by removal under subsection (7)), the company must give notification of that fact to the Regulator in a form approved by the Regulator before the end of the period of 14 days beginning with the date on which the person ceases to be a director.
[(11)   If default is made in complying with subsection (10) an offence is committed by—
  (a)   the company, and
  (b)   every officer of the company who is in default.

For this purpose a shadow director is treated as an officer of the company.

(12)   A person guilty of an offence under subsection (11) is liable on summary conviction to a fine not exceeding level 5 on the standard scale and, for continued contravention, a daily default fine not exceeding one-tenth of level 5 on the standard scale.]

(13)   The company may appeal to the Appeal Officer against an order under this section.

NOTES

Sub-s (3): word in square brackets substituted by the Companies Act 2006 (Consequential Amendments, Transitional Provisions and Savings) Order 2009, SI 2009/1941, art 2(1), Sch 1, para 231(1), (2), as from 1 October 2009; words omitted repealed by the Companies Act 2006 (Consequential Amendments etc) Order 2008, SI 2008/948, art 3, Sch 1, Pt 2, para 234(1), (4), Sch 2, as from 6 April 2008.

Sub-s (8), (9): words in square brackets substituted by SI 2009/1941, art 2(1), Sch 1, para 231(1), (3), (4), as from 1 October 2009.

Sub-s (11), (12): substituted by SI 2009/1941, art 2(1), Sch 1, para 231(1), (5), as from 1 October 2009.

[5.202]
46   Removal of director
(1)   The Regulator may by order remove a director of a community interest company.
(2)   If a person has been removed under subsection (1)—
   (a)   the company may not subsequently appoint him a director of the company, and
   (b)   any assignment to the person of the office of director of the company is of no effect (even if approved by special resolution of the company).
(3)   The Regulator may by order suspend a director of the company pending a decision whether to remove him.
(4)   The maximum period for which a director may be suspended under subsection (3) is one year.
(5)   If the Regulator suspends a director under subsection (3) the Regulator may give directions in relation to the performance of the director's functions.
(6)   The Regulator may discharge an order made under subsection (1).
(7)   The discharge of an order made under subsection (1) does not reinstate the person removed by the order as a director of the company, but on the discharge of the order subsection (2) ceases to apply to the person.
(8)   The Regulator must from time to time review any order made under subsection (3) and, if it is appropriate to do so, discharge the order.
(9)   Before making an order under subsection (1) or (3) in relation to a director, the Regulator must give at least 14 days' notice to—
   (a)   the director, and
   (b)   the company.
(10)   Where an order is made in relation to a director under subsection (1) or (3) the director may appeal against the order—
   (a)   in England and Wales [or Northern Ireland], to the High Court, or
   (b)   in Scotland, to the Court of Session.
(11)   The Regulator must, before the end of the period of 14 days beginning with the date on which—
   (a)   an order under subsection (1) is made or discharged,
   (b)   an order under subsection (3) is made or discharged or expires, or
   (c)   an order under subsection (1) or (3) is quashed on appeal,
give notification of that event to the registrar of companies in a form approved by the registrar of companies.
(12)   Where subsection (11) imposes an obligation to notify the registrar of companies of an event, [section 167(1)(a) of the Companies Act 2006] (requirement that company notify change among directors to registrar) does not apply in respect of the event.

NOTES

Sub-s (10): words in square brackets inserted by the Companies Act 2006 (Commencement No 2, Consequential Amendments, Transitional Provisions and Savings) Order 2007, SI 2007/1093, art 6(2), Sch 4, Pt 1, para 14(a), as from 6 April 2007.

Sub-s (12): words in square brackets substituted by the Companies Act 2006 (Consequential Amendments, Transitional Provisions and Savings) Order 2009, SI 2009/1941, art 2(1), Sch 1, para 232, as from 1 October 2009.

[5.203]
47   Appointment of manager
(1)   The Regulator may by order appoint a manager in respect of the property and affairs of a community interest company.
(2)   The person appointed may be anyone whom the Regulator thinks appropriate, other than a member of the Regulator's staff.
(3)   An order under subsection (1) may make provision as to the functions to be exercised by, and the powers of, the manager.
(4)   The order may in particular provide—
   (a)   for the manager to have such of the functions of the company's directors as are specified in the order, and

(b)   for the company's directors to be prevented from exercising any of those functions.

(5)   In carrying out his functions the manager acts as the company's agent; and a person dealing with the manager in good faith and for value need not inquire whether the manager is acting within his powers.

(6)   The appointment of the manager does not affect—

(a)   any right of any person to appoint a receiver or manager of the company's property (including any right under section 51 of the Insolvency Act 1986 (c 45) [(power to appoint receiver under law of Scotland)]), or

(b)   the rights of a receiver or manager appointed by a person other than the Regulator.

(7)   The manager's functions are to be discharged by him under the supervision of the Regulator; and the Regulator must from time to time review the order by which the manager is appointed and, if it is appropriate to do so, discharge it in whole or in part.

(8)   In particular, the Regulator must discharge the order on the appointment of a person to act as administrative receiver, administrator, provisional liquidator or liquidator of the company.

(9)   The Regulator may apply to the court for directions in relation to any matter arising in connection with the manager's functions or powers.

(10)   On an application under subsection (9) the court may give such directions or make such orders as it thinks fit.

(11)   The costs of any application under subsection (9) are to be paid by the company.

(12)   Regulations may authorise the Regulator—

(a)   to require a manager to make reports,

(b)   to require a manager to give security (or, in Scotland, to find caution) for the due exercise of the manager's functions, and

(c)   to remove a manager in circumstances prescribed by the regulations.

(13)   Regulations may—

(a)   provide for a manager's remuneration to be payable from the property of the company, and

(b)   authorise the Regulator to determine the amount of a manager's remuneration and to disallow any amount of remuneration in circumstances prescribed by the regulations.

(14)   The company may appeal to the Appeal Officer against an order under this section.

NOTES

Sub-s (6): words in square brackets inserted by the Companies Act 2006 (Commencement No 2, Consequential Amendments, Transitional Provisions and Savings) Order 2007, SI 2007/1093, art 6(2), Sch 4, Pt 1, para 15, as from 6 April 2007.

Regulations: the Community Interest Company Regulations 2005, SI 2005/1788 at **[6.113]**.

[5.204]
48   Property

(1)   The Regulator may by order—

(a)   vest in the Official Property Holder any property held by or in trust for a community interest company, or

(b)   require persons in whom such property is vested to transfer it to the Official Property Holder.

(2)   The Regulator—

(a)   may order a person who holds property on behalf of a community interest company, or on behalf of a trustee of a community interest company, not to part with the property without the Regulator's consent, and

(b)   may order any debtor of a community interest company not to make any payment in respect of the debtor's liability to the company without the Regulator's consent.

(3)   The Regulator may by order restrict—

(a)   the transactions which may be entered into by a community interest company, or

(b)   the nature or amount of the payments that a community interest company may make,

and the order may in particular provide that transactions may not be entered into or payments made without the Regulator's consent.

(4)   The vesting or transfer of property under subsection (1) does not constitute a breach of a covenant or condition against alienation, and no right listed in subsection (5) operates or becomes exercisable as a result of the vesting or transfer.

(5)   The rights are—

(a)   a right of reverter (or, in Scotland, the right of the fiar on the termination of a liferent),

(b)   a right of pre-emption,

(c)   a right of forfeiture,

(d)   a right of re-entry,

(e)   a right of irritancy,

(f)   an option, and

(g)   any right similar to those listed in paragraphs (a) to (f).

(6)   The Regulator must from time to time review any order under this section and, if it is appropriate to do so, discharge the order in whole or in part.

(7)   On discharging an order under subsection (1) the Regulator may make any order as to the vesting or transfer of the property, and give any directions, which he considers appropriate.

(8)   If a person fails to comply with an order under subsection (1)(b), the Regulator may certify that fact in writing to the court.

(9)   If, after hearing—

    (a)   any witnesses who may be produced against or on behalf of the alleged offender, and

    (b)   any statement which may be offered in defence,

the court is satisfied that the offender failed without reasonable excuse to comply with the order, it may deal with him as if he had been guilty of contempt of the court.

(10)   A person who contravenes an order under subsection (2) or (3) commits an offence, but a prosecution may be instituted[—

    (a)   in England and Wales, only with the consent of the Regulator or the Director of Public Prosecutions;

    (b)   in Northern Ireland, only with the consent of the Regulator or the Director of Public Prosecutions for Northern Ireland].

(11)   A person guilty of an offence under subsection (10) is liable on summary conviction to a fine not exceeding level 5 on the standard scale.

(12)   Subsections (8) to (10) do not prevent the bringing of civil proceedings in respect of a contravention of an order under subsection (1)(b), (2) or (3).

(13)   The company and any person to whom the order is directed may appeal to the Appeal Officer against an order under subsection (1) or (2).

(14)   The company may appeal to the Appeal Officer against an order under subsection (3).

NOTES

    Sub-s (10): words in square brackets substituted by the Companies Act 2006 (Commencement No 2, Consequential Amendments, Transitional Provisions and Savings) Order 2007, SI 2007/1093, art 6(2), Sch 4, Pt 1, para 16, as from 6 April 2007.

[5.205]
49   Transfer of shares etc

(1)   If a community interest company has a share capital, the Regulator may by order transfer specified shares in the company to specified persons.

(2)   If a community interest company is a company limited by guarantee, the Regulator may by order—

    (a)   extinguish the interests in the company of specified members of the company (otherwise than as shareholders), and

    (b)   appoint a new member in place of each member whose interest has been extinguished.

(3)   An order under subsection (1) may not transfer any shares in respect of which—

    (a)   a dividend may be paid, or

    (b)   a distribution of the company's assets may be made if the company is wound up.

(4)   An order under this section in relation to a company—

    (a)   may only transfer shares to, and appoint as new members, persons who have consented to the transfer or appointment, and

    (b)   may be made irrespective of any provision made by the [articles] of the company or a resolution of the company in general meeting.

(5)   The company and any person from whom shares are transferred by the order may appeal to the Appeal Officer against an order under subsection (1).

(6)   The company and any person whose interest is extinguished by the order may appeal to the Appeal Officer against an order under subsection (2).

(7)   "Specified", in relation to an order, means specified in the order.

NOTES

    Sub-s (4): word in square brackets substituted by the Companies Act 2006 (Consequential Amendments, Transitional Provisions and Savings) Order 2009, SI 2009/1941, art 2(1), Sch 1, para 233, as from 1 October 2009.

[5.206]
50   Petition for winding up

(1)   The Regulator may present a petition for a community interest company to be wound up if the court is of the opinion that it is just and equitable that the company should be wound up.

(2)   Subsection (1) does not apply if the company is already being wound up by the court.

(3)   (*Amends the Insolvency Act 1986, s 124 at* **[9.213]**.)

[5.207]
51   Dissolution and striking off

[(1)   If a community interest company has been—

    (a)   dissolved, or

    (b)   struck off the register under section 1000 or 1001 of the Companies Act 2006,

the Regulator may apply to the court under section 1029 of that Act for an order restoring the company's name to the register.]

(3) If an application under [section 1003 of the Companies Act 2006 (striking off on application by company)] is made on behalf of a community interest company, [section 1006 of the Companies Act 2006] (persons to be notified of application) is to be treated as also requiring a copy of the application to be given to the Regulator.

NOTES

Sub-s (1): substituted (for original sub-ss (1), (2)) by the Companies Act 2006 (Consequential Amendments, Transitional Provisions and Savings) Order 2009, SI 2009/1941, art 2(1), Sch 1, para 234(1), (2), as from as from 1 October 2009.

Sub-s (3): words in square brackets substituted by SI 2009/1941, art 2(1), Sch 1, para 234(1), (3), as from as from 1 October 2009.

Change of status

[5.208]
52 Re-registration
(1) A community interest company is excluded from re-registering under [section 102 of the Companies Act 2006] (re-registration of limited company as unlimited).
(2) If a community interest company which is not a public company re-registers as a public company under [section 90 of the Companies Act 2006], or a community interest company which is a public company re-registers as a private company under [section 97 of the Companies Act 2006], the certificate of incorporation issued under [section 96(2) or 101(2) of the Companies Act 2006] is to contain a statement that the company is a community interest company.
(3) The fact that the certificate of incorporation contains such a statement is conclusive evidence that the company is a community interest company.

NOTES

Sub-ss (1), (2): words in square brackets substituted by the Companies Act 2006 (Consequential Amendments, Transitional Provisions and Savings) Order 2009, SI 2009/1941, art 2(1), Sch 1, para 235, as from 1 October 2009.

[5.209]
53 Ceasing to be a community interest company
A community interest company may not cease to be a community interest company except by dissolution or as provided—
   (a)   by [sections 54 to 55A] (becoming a charity . . .), or
   (b)   if regulations are made under section 56 (becoming an industrial and provident society), by the regulations.

NOTES

Words in square brackets in para (a) substituted by the Companies Act 2006 (Consequential Amendments, Transitional Provisions and Savings) Order 2009, SI 2009/1941, art 2(1), Sch 1, para 236, as from 1 October 2009; words omitted from para (a) repealed by the Companies Act 2006 (Consequential Amendments etc) Order 2008, SI 2008/948, art 3, Sch 1, Pt 2, para 234(1), (4), Sch 2, as from 6 April 2008.

[5.210]
[54 Ceasing to be a community interest company and becoming a charity
(1) If a company is to cease to be a community interest company and become a charity—
   (a)   the company must by special resolution—
      (i)   state that it is to cease to be a community interest company,
      (ii)   make such alterations of its articles as it considers appropriate, and
      (iii)   change its name so that it does not comply with section 33;
   (b)   the conditions specified below must be met; and
   (c)   an application must be delivered to the registrar of companies in accordance with section 54C together with the other documents required by that section.
(2) The conditions referred to in subsection (1)(b) are that—
   (a)   where no application under section 54A for cancellation of the special resolutions has been made—
      (i)   having regard to the number of members who consented to or voted in favour of the resolutions, no such application may be made, or
      (ii)   the period within which such an application could be made has expired, or
   (b)   where such an application has been made—
      (i)   the application has been withdrawn, or
      (ii)   an order has been made confirming the resolutions and a copy of that order has been delivered to the registrar.
(3) Section 30 of the Companies Act 2006 (copies of resolutions to be forwarded to the registrar) applies to the special resolutions as follows—
   (a)   that section is complied with by forwarding copies of the resolutions together with the application in accordance with section 54C,
   (b)   copies of the resolutions must not be so forwarded before the relevant date, and
   (c)   subsection (1) of that section has effect in relation to the resolutions as if it referred to 15 days after the relevant date.
(4) The relevant date is—

(a)   if an application is made under section 54A for cancellation of the resolutions—
     (i)   the date on which the court determines the application (or if there is more than one application, the date on which the last to be determined by the court is determined), or
     (ii)   such later date as the court may order;
(b)   if there is no such application—
     (i)   if having regard to the number of members who consented to or voted in favour of the resolutions, no such application may be made, the date on which the resolutions were passed or made (or, if the resolutions were passed or made on different days, the date on which the last of them was passed or made);
     (ii)   in any other case, the end of the period for making such an application.]

NOTES
Commencement: 1 October 2009.
Substituted (together with ss 54A–54C for the original s 54) by the Companies Act 2006 (Consequential Amendments, Transitional Provisions and Savings) Order 2009, SI 2009/1941, art 2(1), Sch 1, para 237(1), as from 1 October 2009.

[5.211]
[54A   Ceasing to be a community interest company and becoming a charity: application to court to cancel resolutions
(1)   Where special resolutions have been passed with a view to a company ceasing to be a community interest company and becoming a charity, an application to the court for the cancellation of the resolutions may be made—
   (a)   by the holders of not less in the aggregate than 15% in nominal value of the company's issued share capital or any class of the company's issued share capital (disregarding any shares held by the company as treasury shares);
   (b)   if the company is not limited by shares, by not less than 15% of its members; or
   (c)   by the holders of not less than 15% of the company's debentures entitling the holders to object to an alteration of its objects;
but not by a person who has consented to or voted in favour of the resolutions.
(2)   The application—
   (a)   must be made within 28 days after the date on which the resolutions were passed or made (or, if the resolutions were passed or made on different days, the date on which the last of them was passed or made), and
   (b)   may be made on behalf of the persons entitled to make it by such one or more of their number as they may appoint for the purpose.
(3)   On the hearing of the application the court shall make an order either cancelling or confirming the resolutions.
(4)   The court may—
   (a)   make that order on such terms and conditions as it thinks fit,
   (b)   if it thinks fit adjourn the proceedings in order that an arrangement may be made to the satisfaction of the court for the purchase of the interests of dissentient members, and
   (c)   give such directions, and make such orders, as it thinks expedient for facilitating or carrying into effect any such arrangement.
(5)   The court's order may, if the court thinks fit—
   (a)   provide for the purchase by the company of the shares of any of its members and for the reduction accordingly of the company's capital; and
   (b)   make such alteration in the company's articles as may be required in consequence of that provision.
(6)   The court's order may, if the court thinks fit, require the company not to make any, or any specified, amendments to its articles without the leave of the court.]

NOTES
Commencement: 1 October 2009.
Substituted as noted to s 54 at **[5.210]**.

[5.212]
[54B   Ceasing to be a community interest company and becoming a charity: notice to registrar of court application or order
(1)   On making an application under section 54A (application to court to cancel resolutions) the applicants, or the person making the application on their behalf, must immediately give notice to the registrar of companies.
This is without prejudice to any provision of rules of court as to service of notice of the application.
(2)   On being served with notice of any such application, the company must immediately give notice to the registrar.
(3)   Within 15 days of the making of the court's order on the application, or such longer period as the court may at any time direct, the company must deliver to the registrar a copy of the order.
(4)   If a company fails to comply with subsection (2) or (3) an offence is committed by—

(a)   the company, and

(b)   every officer of the company who is in default.

(5)   A person guilty of an offence under this section is liable on summary conviction to a fine not exceeding level 3 on the standard scale and, for continued contravention, a daily default fine not exceeding one-tenth of level 3 on the standard scale.]

NOTES

Commencement: 1 October 2009.

Substituted as noted to s 54 at **[5.210]**.

[5.213]
[54C   Ceasing to be a community interest company and becoming a charity: application and accompanying documents

(1)   An application to cease to be a community interest company and become a charity must be accompanied by—

(a)   a copy of the special resolutions,

(b)   a copy of the company's articles as proposed to be amended, and

(c)   the statement required by subsection (2).

(2)   The statement required is—

(a)   where the company is to become an English charity, a statement by the Charity Commission that, in its opinion, if the proposed changes take effect the company will be an English charity and will not be an exempt charity;

(b)   where the company is to become a Scottish charity, a statement by the Scottish Charity Regulator that if the proposed changes take effect the company will be entered in the Scottish Charity Register;

(c)   where the company is to become a Northern Ireland charity, a statement by the Commissioners of Her Majesty's Revenue and Customs that the company has claimed exemption under [a relevant provision of Part 11 of the Corporation Tax Act 2010].

(3)   In subsection (2)(a) "exempt charity" has the same meaning as in the Charities Act 1993 (see section 96 of that Act).

[(3A)   For the purposes of subsection (2)(c) all the provisions of Part 11 of the Corporation Tax Act 2010 under which exemption may be claimed are relevant provisions except—

(a)   section 480 (exemption for profits of small-scale trades), and

(b)   section 481 (exemption from charges under provisions to which section 1173 applies).]

(4)   On receiving an application to cease to be a community interest company and become a charity, together with the other documents required to accompany it, the registrar of companies must (instead of recording the documents and entering a new name on the register)—

(a)   forward a copy of each of the documents to the Regulator, and

(b)   retain the documents pending the Regulator's decision.]

NOTES

Commencement: 1 October 2009.

Substituted as noted to s 54 at **[5.210]**.

Sub-s (2): words in square brackets in para (c) substituted by the Corporation Tax Act 2010, s 1177, Sch 1, Pt 2, para 439(1), (2) (note that the 2010 Act comes into force on 1 April 2010 and has effect, for corporation tax purposes for accounting periods ending on or after that day, and for income tax and capital gains tax purposes for the tax year 2010–11 and subsequent tax years; see s 1184(1) of the 2010 Act (and for transitional provisions and savings, see Sch 2 to that Act)).

Sub-s (3A): inserted by the Corporation Tax Act 2010, s 1177, Sch 1, Pt 2, para 439(1), (3) (see the note above with regard to the commencement of this amendment).

[5.214]
[55   Ceasing to be a community interest company and becoming a charity: decision by Regulator

(1)   The Regulator must decide whether the company is eligible to cease being a community interest company.

(2)   A company is eligible to cease being a community interest company if it has complied with sections 54 and 54C and none of the following applies—

(a)   the Regulator has under section 43 appointed an auditor to audit the company's annual accounts and the audit has not been completed,

(b)   civil proceedings instituted by the Regulator in the name of the company under section 44 have not been determined or discontinued,

(c)   a director of the company holds office by virtue of an order under section 45,

(d)   a director of the company is suspended under section 46(3),

(e)   there is a manager in respect of the property and affairs of the company appointed under section 47,

(f)   the Official Property Holder holds property as trustee for the company,

(g)   an order under section 48(2) or (3) is in force in relation to the company,

(h)   a petition has been presented for the company to be wound up.

(3)   The Regulator must give notice of the decision to the registrar of companies (but the registrar is not required to record it).]

Part 5 Pre-2006 companies legislation

NOTES

Commencement: 1 October 2009.

Substituted (together with ss 55A for the original s 55) by the Companies Act 2006 (Consequential Amendments, Transitional Provisions and Savings) Order 2009, SI 2009/1941, art 2(1), Sch 1, para 237(2), as from 1 October 2009.

[5.215]
[55A Ceasing to be a community interest company and becoming a charity: consequences of Regulator's decision
(1) If the Regulator gives notice of a decision that the company is eligible to cease being a community interest company, the registrar of companies must—
  (a) proceed in accordance with section 80 of the Companies Act 2006 (change of name: registration and issue of new certificate of incorporation), and
  (b) if the registrar enters the new name of the company on the register, retain and record the documents mentioned in section 54C(4).
(2) The new certificate of incorporation must state—
  (a) that it is issued on the company's ceasing to be a community interest company, and
  (b) the date on which it is issued.
(3) On the issue of the certificate—
  (a) the changes in the company's name and articles take effect, and
  (b) the company ceases to be a community interest company.
(4) If the Regulator decides that the company is not eligible to cease being a community interest company, the company may appeal to the Appeal Officer against the decision.]

NOTES

Commencement: 1 October 2009.

Substituted as noted to s 55 at **[5.214]**.

[5.216]
56 Becoming an industrial and provident society
(1) Unless regulations make provision to the contrary, a community interest company may not convert itself into a registered society under section 53 of the Industrial and Provident Societies Act 1965 (c 12) [or section 62 of the Industrial and Provident Societies Act (Northern Ireland) 1969].
(2) If regulations make provision allowing the conversion of community interest companies under that section they may include provision modifying that section in its application by virtue of the regulations.

NOTES

Sub-s (1): words in square brackets inserted by the Companies Act 2006 (Commencement No 2, Consequential Amendments, Transitional Provisions and Savings) Order 2007, SI 2007/1093, art 6(2), Sch 4, Pt 1, para 21, as from 6 April 2007.

Industrial and Provident Societies Act 1965: see the Co-operative and Community Benefit Societies and Credit Unions Act 2010 which renames this Act as the Co-operative and Community Benefit Societies and Credit Unions Act 1965.

Regulations: the Community Interest Company (Amendment) Regulations 2009, SI 2009/1942.

Supplementary

[5.217]
57 Fees
(1) Regulations may require the payment of such fees in connection with the Regulator's functions as may be specified in the regulations.
(2) The regulations may provide for fees to be paid to the registrar of companies (rather than to the Regulator).
(3) The Regulator may charge a fee for any service which is provided otherwise than in pursuance of an obligation imposed by law, other than the provision of guidance which the Regulator considers to be of general interest.
(4) Fees paid by virtue of this section are to be paid into the Consolidated Fund.

NOTES

Regulations: the Community Interest Company Regulations 2005, SI 2005/1788 at **[6.113]**; the Community Interest Company (Amendment) Regulations 2009, SI 2009/1942.

58 *(Repealed by the Companies Act 2006 (Consequential Amendments, Transitional Provisions and Savings) Order 2009, SI 2009/1941, art 2(1), Sch 1, para 238, as from 1 October 2009.)*

[5.218]
59 Information
(1) Regulations may require the registrar of companies—
  (a) to notify the Regulator of matters specified in the regulations, and
  (b) to provide the Regulator with copies of documents specified in the regulations.

(2), (3) *(Insert the Bankruptcy (Scotland) Act 1985, s 71A, and amend the Data Protection Act 1998, s 31.)*

(4) A public authority may disclose to the Regulator, for any purpose connected with the exercise of the Regulator's functions, information received by the authority in connection with its functions.

(5) The Regulator may disclose to a public authority any information received by the Regulator in connection with the functions of the Regulator—

(a) for a purpose connected with the exercise of those functions, or

(b) for a purpose connected with the exercise by the authority of its functions.

(6) In deciding whether to disclose information to a public authority in a country or territory outside the United Kingdom the Regulator must have regard to the considerations listed in section 243(6) of the Enterprise Act 2002 (c 40) (overseas disclosures), but as if the reference to information of a kind to which section 237 of that Act applies were to information of the kind the Regulator is considering disclosing.

(7) The powers to disclose information in subsections (4) and (5) are subject to—

(a) any restriction on disclosure imposed by or by virtue of an enactment, and

(b) any express restriction on disclosure subject to which information was supplied.

(8) Information may be disclosed under subsection (4) or (5) subject to a restriction on its further disclosure.

(9) A person who discloses information in contravention of a restriction imposed under subsection (8) is guilty of an offence, but a prosecution may be instituted[—

(a) in England and Wales, only with the consent of the Regulator or the Director of Public Prosecutions;

(b) in Northern Ireland, only with the consent of the Regulator or the Director of Public Prosecutions for Northern Ireland].

(10) A person guilty of an offence under subsection (9) is liable on summary conviction to a fine not exceeding level 3 on the standard scale.

(11) "Public authority" means a person or body having functions of a public nature.

NOTES

Sub-s (9): words in square brackets substituted by the Companies Act 2006 (Commencement No 2, Consequential Amendments, Transitional Provisions and Savings) Order 2007, SI 2007/1093, art 6(2), Sch 4, Pt 1, para 23, as from 6 April 2007.

Regulations: the Community Interest Company Regulations 2005, SI 2005/1788 at **[6.113]**; the Community Interest Company (Amendment) Regulations 2009, SI 2009/1942.

[5.219]
60 Offences
(1) If an offence under [section 48 or 59 or paragraph 5 of Schedule 7] committed by a body corporate is proved—

(a) to have been committed with the consent or connivance of an officer, or

(b) to be attributable to any neglect on the part of an officer,

the officer as well as the body corporate is guilty of the offence and liable to be proceeded against and punished accordingly.

(2) "Officer" means a director, manager, secretary or other similar officer of the body corporate, or a person purporting to act in any such capacity.

(3) "Director"—

(a) includes a shadow director, and

(b) if the affairs of a body corporate are managed by its members, means a member of the body.

NOTES

Sub-s (1): words in square brackets substituted by the Companies Act 2006 (Consequential Amendments, Transitional Provisions and Savings) Order 2009, SI 2009/1941, art 2(1), Sch 1, para 239, as from 1 October 2009.

[5.220]
61 Orders made by Regulator
(1) An order made by the Regulator under this Part must be given to the community interest company in relation to which it is made and—

(a) if the order is under section 46(1) or (3), to the director removed or suspended,

(b) if the order is under section 48(1)(b) or (2), to the person to whom the order is directed,

(c) if the order is under section 49(1), to the persons from and to whom shares are transferred,

(d) if the order is under section 49(2), to the person whose interest is extinguished and any person appointed in his place.

(2) Orders made by the Regulator under or by virtue of this Part may contain any incidental or supplementary provisions the Regulator considers expedient.

(3) When discharging an order made under or by virtue of this Part, the Regulator may make savings and transitional provisions.

(4) A document certified by the Regulator to be a true copy of an order made by the Regulator is evidence of the order without further proof; and a document purporting to be so certified shall, unless the contrary is proved, be taken to be so certified.

(5) Where the Regulator makes an order or decision against which an appeal lies under or by virtue of this Part, the Regulator must give reasons for the order or decision to the persons entitled to appeal against it.

[5.221]
62 Regulations
(1) Any power to make regulations under this Part is exercisable by the Secretary of State by statutory instrument.

(2) Regulations under this Part may make different provision for different cases.

(3) Regulations under this Part may confer or impose functions on the Regulator or any other person specified in the regulations (and, unless made under paragraph 4 of Schedule 4, may provide for appeals to the Appeal Officer from a person on whom functions are conferred by the regulations).

(4) No regulations to which this subsection applies are to be made unless a draft of the statutory instrument containing the regulations (whether or not together with other provisions) has been laid before, and approved by a resolution of, each House of Parliament.

(5) Subsection (4) applies to regulations under—
  (a) section 30,
  (b) section 31,
  (c) section 32,
  (d) section 34,
  (e) section 35,
  (f) section 36,
  (g) [section 37C],
  (h) section 47, and
  (i) section 56.

(6) A statutory instrument containing regulations under this Part is (unless a draft of it has been approved by each House of Parliament under subsection (4)) subject to annulment in pursuance of a resolution of either House of Parliament.

NOTES
Sub-s (5): words in square brackets substituted by the Companies Act 2006 (Consequential Amendments, Transitional Provisions and Savings) Order 2009, SI 2009/1941, art 2(1), Sch 1, para 240, as from 1 October 2009.

[5.222]
63 Interpretation
(1) In this Part—

. . . .
. . .

  "administrative receiver" has the meaning given[—
      (a) in England and Wales or Scotland, by section 251 of the Insolvency Act 1986, and
      (b) in Northern Ireland, by Article 5 of the Insolvency (Northern Ireland) Order 1989;]
  "the Appeal Officer" has the meaning given by section 28(1),
  ["charity" means an English charity, a Scottish charity or a Northern Ireland charity, as defined below;]
  "community interest object" is to be construed in accordance with section 35(3),
  "the community interest test" is to be construed in accordance with section 35(2),
  "enactment" includes an Act of the Scottish Parliament,
  ["English charity" means a charity *within the meaning of the Charities Act 1993 (see section 96 of that Act)*;]
  "excluded company" is to be construed in accordance with section 35(6),
. . .
  ["Northern Ireland charity" means a charity within the meaning of the Charities Act (Northern Ireland) 1964 (see section 35 of that Act);]
  "the Official Property Holder" has the meaning given by section 29(1),
  "the Regulator" has the meaning given by section 27(1), and
  ["Scottish charity" means a body entered in the Scottish Charity Register].
[(2), (3) . . .]

NOTES
Sub-s (1) is amended as follows:
Definitions omitted repealed by the Companies Act 2006 (Consequential Amendments, Transitional Provisions and Savings) Order 2009, SI 2009/1941, art 2(1), Sch 1, para 241(1), as from 1 October 2009.
Words in square brackets in definition "administrative receiver" substituted, definition "charity" substituted, and definitions "the 1985 Act" (omitted), "the 1986 Order" (omitted), "English charity", "the Gazette" (omitted), and "Northern Ireland charity" inserted, by the Companies Act 2006 (Commencement No 2, Consequential Amendments, Transitional Provisions and Savings) Order 2007, SI 2007/1093, art 6(2), Sch 4, Pt 1, para 24(1)–(4), as from 6 April 2007.
For the words in italics in the definition "English charity" there are substituted the words "as defined by section 1(1) of the Charities Act 2006" by the Charities (Pre-consolidation Amendments) Order 2011, SI 2011/1396, art 2, Schedule, Pt 4, para 47, as from a day to be appointed.

Definition "Scottish charity" substituted by the Charities and Trustee Investment (Scotland) Act 2005 (Consequential Provisions and Modifications) Order 2006, SI 2006/242, art 5, Schedule, Pt 1, para 8(1), (5), as from 1 April 2006.

Sub-ss (2), (3): substituted, for original sub-s (2), by SI 2007/1093, art 6(2), Sch 4, Pt 1, para 24(1), (5), as from 6 April 2007, and repealed by SI 2009/1941, art 2(1), Sch 1, para 241(2), as from 1 October 2009.

PART 3
SUPPLEMENTARY

64 (*Introduces Schedule 8 to this Act (repeals and revocations).*)

[5.223]
65 Commencement etc
(1) This Act (apart from this section and sections 66 and 67) does not come into force until such day as the Secretary of State may by order made by statutory instrument appoint; and different days may be appointed for different provisions or otherwise for different purposes.
(2) The Secretary of State may by order made by statutory instrument make any transitional provisions or savings which appear appropriate in connection with the commencement of any provision of this Act.

NOTES

Orders: the Companies (Audit, Investigations and Community Enterprise) Act 2004 (Commencement) and Companies Act 1989 (Commencement No 18) Order 2004, SI 2004/3322.

[5.224]
66 Extent
(1) Any amendment made by this Act has the same extent as the provision to which it relates.
(2) Sections 14, 15(1)(b), (3) and (7) and [16 to 18] [and Part 2] extend to Northern Ireland.
(3) Subject to that, this Act (apart from section 65, this section and section 67) does not extend to Northern Ireland.

NOTES

Sub-s (2): words in first pair of square brackets substituted by the Companies Act 2006, s 1276(5), as from 8 November 2006; words in second pair of square brackets inserted by the Companies Act 2006 (Commencement No 2, Consequential Amendments, Transitional Provisions and Savings) Order 2007, SI 2007/1093, art 6(2), Sch 4, Pt 1, para 25, as from 6 April 2007.

As to the application of this Act to Northern Ireland, see also the Companies Act 2006, s 1284(1) at **[1.1284]**.

[5.225]
67 Short title
This Act may be cited as the Companies (Audit, Investigations and Community Enterprise) Act 2004.

SCHEDULES

SCHEDULES 1, 2

(*Sch 1 repealed by the Companies Act 2006, s 1295, Sch 16, as from 6 April 2008; Sch 2 Pt 1 (Amendments Relating to Auditors) and Sch 2, Pt 2 (Amendments Relating to Accounts and Reports) make various amendments to CA 1985, CA 1989, the Companies (Northern Ireland) Order 1986, SI 1986/1032, and the Companies (Northern Ireland) Order 1990, SI 1990/593, and are repealed by CA 2006, s 1295, Sch 16, as from 1 October 2007 (in part), as from 6 April 2008 (in part), and as from a day to be appointed (otherwise); Sch 2, Pt 3 (Amendments Relating to Investigations) amends Part XIV of CA 1985 (Investigation of Companies and their Affairs; Requisition of Documents at* **[5.1]** *et seq), contains other consequential amendments to the 1985 Act, and consequential amendments to the Insolvency Act 1986, the Company Directors Disqualification Act 1986, the Criminal Justice and Police Act 2001, and the Anti-terrorism, Crime and Security Act 2001, and is partly repealed by CA 2006, as from 1 October 2007, 6 April 2008, and as from a day to be appointed.*)

SCHEDULE 3
REGULATOR OF COMMUNITY INTEREST COMPANIES
Section 27

Regulator's terms of appointment

[5.226]
1. (1) The period for which a person is appointed as Regulator must not exceed five years.

(2) A person who has held office as Regulator may be re-appointed, once only, for a further period not exceeding five years.

(3) The Regulator may at any time resign the office by giving notice in writing to the Secretary of State.

(4)   The Secretary of State may at any time remove the Regulator on the ground of incapacity or misbehaviour.

(5)   Subject to that, the Regulator holds and vacates office on the terms determined by the Secretary of State.

Remuneration and pensions

2. (1)   The Secretary of State may pay remuneration and travelling and other allowances to the Regulator.

(2)   The Secretary of State may—
- (a)   pay a pension, allowance or gratuity to or in respect of a person who is or has been the Regulator, or
- (b)   make contributions or payments towards provision for a pension, allowance or gratuity for or in respect of such a person.

Staff

3. (1)   The Regulator may, after consulting the Minister for the Civil Service as to numbers and terms and conditions of service, appoint such staff as the Regulator may determine.

(2)   The members of staff must include a deputy to the Regulator who is to act as Regulator—
- (a)   during any vacancy in that office, or
- (b)   if the Regulator is absent, subject to suspension or unable to act.

(3)   Where a participant in a scheme under section 1 of the Superannuation Act 1972 (c 11) is appointed as the Regulator, the Minister for the Civil Service may determine that the person's term of office as the Regulator is to be treated for the purposes of the scheme as service in the employment by reference to which he was a participant (whether or not any benefits are payable by virtue of paragraph 2(2)).

4.   The [chairman of the Charity Commission] may make available to the Regulator, to assist in the exercise of the Regulator's functions, [any other member of the Commission appointed under paragraph 1(2) of Schedule 1A to the Charities Act 1993 or any member of staff of the Commission appointed under paragraph 5(1) of that Schedule].

Delegation of functions

5.   Anything which the Regulator is authorised or required to do may be done by a member of the Regulator's staff if authorised by the Regulator (generally or specifically) for that purpose.

Finance

6.   The Secretary of State may make payments to the Regulator.

Reports and other information

7. (1)   The Regulator must, in respect of each financial year, prepare a report on the exercise of the Regulator's functions during the financial year.

(2)   The Regulator must prepare accounts in respect of a financial year if the Secretary of State so directs.

(3)   The Regulator must send a copy of the accounts to the Comptroller and Auditor General.

(4)   The Comptroller and Auditor General must examine, certify and report on the accounts and send a copy of the report to the Regulator.

(5)   The Regulator must include the accounts and the Comptroller and Auditor General's report on them in the report prepared by the Regulator in respect of the financial year to which the accounts relate.

(6)   The Regulator must prepare that report as soon as possible after the end of the financial year to which it relates.

(7)   The Regulator must send to the Secretary of State a copy of—
- (a)   each report prepared by the Regulator under sub-paragraph (1), and
- (b)   each report prepared by the Official Property Holder under paragraph 6 of Schedule 5.

(8)   The Secretary of State must lay before each House of Parliament a copy of each of those reports.

(9)   The Regulator must supply the Secretary of State with such other reports and information relating to the exercise of the Regulator's functions as the Secretary of State may require.

(10)   "Financial year" means—
- (a)   the period beginning with the date on which a person is first appointed as the Regulator and ending with the next 31st March, and
- (b)   each successive period of 12 months beginning with 1st April.

Amendments

8, 9.   . . .

NOTES

Para 4: words in square brackets substituted by the Charities Act 2006, s 75, Sch 8, paras 200, 204, as from 27 February 2007.
Para 8: amended the Parliamentary Commissioner Act 1967, Sch 2 (and is superseded by the Parliamentary Commissioner Order 2005, SI 2005/249, art 2, Sch 1).
Para 9: amends the House of Commons Disqualification Act 1975, Sch 1, Pt III.

SCHEDULE 4
APPEAL OFFICER FOR COMMUNITY INTEREST COMPANIES
Section 28

Appeal Officer's terms of appointment

[5.227]
1. (1)   The Appeal Officer holds office for the period determined by the Secretary of State on appointment (or re-appointment).

(2)   But—
  (a)   the Appeal Officer may at any time resign the office by giving notice in writing to the Secretary of State, and
  (b)   the Secretary of State may at any time remove the Appeal Officer on the ground of incapacity or misbehaviour.

(3)   Subject to that, the Appeal Officer holds and vacates office on the terms determined by the Secretary of State.

Remuneration and pensions

2. (1)   The Secretary of State may pay remuneration and travelling and other allowances to the Appeal Officer.

(2)   The Secretary of State may—
  (a)   pay a pension, allowance or gratuity to or in respect of a person who is or has been the Appeal Officer, or
  (b)   make contributions or payments towards provision for a pension, allowance or gratuity for or in respect of such a person.

Finance

3. The Secretary of State may make payments to the Appeal Officer.

Procedure

4. (1)   Regulations may make provision about the practice and procedure to be followed by the Appeal Officer.

(2)   Regulations under this paragraph may in particular impose time limits for bringing appeals.

Amendments

5, 6.   . . .

NOTES

Paras 5, 6: amend the Parliamentary Commissioner Act 1967, Sch 2, and the House of Commons Disqualification Act 1975, Sch 1, Pt III.
Regulations: the Community Interest Company Regulations 2005, SI 2005/1788 at **[6.113]**.

SCHEDULE 5
OFFICIAL PROPERTY HOLDER FOR COMMUNITY INTEREST COMPANIES
Section 29

Status

[5.228]
1. (1)   The Official Property Holder is a corporation sole.

(2)   A document purporting to be—
  (a)   duly executed under the seal of the Official Property Holder, or
  (b)   signed on behalf of the Official Property Holder,
shall be received in evidence and shall, unless the contrary is proved, be taken to be so executed or signed.

Relationship with Regulator

2. The Regulator must make available to the Official Property Holder such members of the Regulator's staff as the Official Property Holder may require in order to exercise the functions of the office.

Effect of vacancy

3. The Regulator must appoint a member of the Regulator's staff who is to act as Official Property Holder—

    (a)   during any vacancy in the office, or

    (b)   if the Official Property Holder is absent, subject to suspension or unable to act.

Property

4. (1)   The Official Property Holder holds property vested in or transferred to him as a trustee.

(2)   The Official Property Holder may release or deal with the property—

    (a)   to give effect to any interest in or right over the property of any person (other than the community interest company by which, or in trust for which, the property was held before it was vested or transferred), or

    (b)   at the request of a person appointed to act as administrative receiver, administrator, provisional liquidator or liquidator of the company.

(3)   Subject to sub-paragraph (2), the Official Property Holder may not release or deal with the property except in accordance with directions given by the Regulator.

Finance

5. (1)   The Official Property Holder may recover his expenses in respect of property held by him from the property or from the community interest company by which, or in trust for which, the property was held before it was vested in or transferred to the Official Property Holder.

(2)   Any expenses of the Official Property Holder not recovered under sub-paragraph (1) are to be met by the Regulator.

Reports

6. (1)   As soon as possible after the end of each financial year, the Official Property Holder must prepare a report on the exercise of the Official Property Holder's functions during the financial year.

(2)   The Official Property Holder must send a copy of the report to the Regulator.

(3)   "Financial year" means—

    (a)   the period beginning with the date on which a person is first appointed as the Official Property Holder and ending with the next 31st March, and

    (b)   each successive period of 12 months beginning with 1st April.

SCHEDULE 6

(Sch 6 repealed by a combination of the Companies Act 2006, s 1295, Sch 16 and the Companies Act 2006 (Consequential Amendments, Transitional Provisions and Savings) Order 2009, SI 2009/1941, art 2(2), Sch 2, as from 1 October 2008 (in part), and as from 1 October 2009 (otherwise).)

SCHEDULE 7
COMMUNITY INTEREST COMPANIES: INVESTIGATIONS

Section 42

Power to require documents and information

[5.229]

1. (1)   The investigator of a community interest company may require the company or any other person—

    (a)   to produce such documents (or documents of such description) as the investigator may specify;

    (b)   to provide such information (or information of such description) as the investigator may specify.

(2)   A person on whom a requirement is imposed under sub-paragraph (1) may require the investigator to produce evidence of his authority.

(3)   A requirement under sub-paragraph (1) must be complied with at such time and place as may be specified by the investigator.

(4)   The production of a document in pursuance of this paragraph does not affect any lien which a person has on the document.

(5)   The investigator may take copies of or extracts from a document produced in pursuance of this paragraph.

(6)   In relation to information recorded otherwise than in legible form, the power to require production of it includes power to require the production of a copy of it in legible form or in a form from which it can readily be produced in visible and legible form.

(7)   In this Schedule—

- (a) "the investigator of a community interest company" means a person investigating the company's affairs under section 42, and
- (b) "document" includes information recorded in any form.

Privileged information

2. (1) Nothing in paragraph 1 requires a person to produce a document or provide information in respect of which a claim could be maintained—

- (a) in an action in the High Court, to legal professional privilege, or
- (b) in an action in the Court of Session, to confidentiality of communications,

but a person who is a lawyer may be required to provide the name and address of his client.

(2) Nothing in paragraph 1 requires a person carrying on the business of banking to produce a document, or provide information, relating to the affairs of a customer unless a requirement to produce the document, or provide the information, has been imposed on the customer under that paragraph.

Use of information as evidence

3. (1) A statement made by a person in compliance with a requirement imposed under paragraph 1 may be used in evidence against the person.

(2) But in criminal proceedings—

- (a) no evidence relating to the statement may be adduced by or on behalf of the prosecution, and
- (b) no question relating to it may be asked by or on behalf of the prosecution,

unless evidence relating to it is adduced or a question relating to it is asked in the proceedings by or on behalf of that person.

(3) However, sub-paragraph (2) does not apply to proceedings in which a person is charged with—

- [(a) an offence under paragraph 5 below (false information), or
- (b) an offence under section 5 of the Perjury Act 1911, section 44(2) of the Criminal Law (Consolidation) (Scotland) Act 1995 or Article 10 of the Perjury (Northern Ireland) Order 1979 (false statement made otherwise than on oath).]

Failure to comply with requirement

4. (1) This paragraph applies if a person fails to comply with a requirement imposed under paragraph 1.

(2) The investigator may certify that fact in writing to the court.

(3) If, after hearing—

- (a) any witnesses who may be produced against or on behalf of the alleged offender, and
- (b) any statement which may be offered in defence,

the court is satisfied that the offender failed without reasonable excuse to comply with the requirement, it may deal with him as if he had been guilty of contempt of the court.

False information

5. (1) A person commits an offence if in purported compliance with a requirement under paragraph 1 to provide information, the person—

- (a) provides information which the person knows to be false in a material particular, or
- (b) recklessly provides information which is false in a material particular,

. . .

[(1A) A prosecution for an offence under sub-paragraph (1) may be instituted—

- (a) in England and Wales, only with the consent of the Director of Public Prosecutions;
- (b) in Northern Ireland, only with the consent of the Director of Public Prosecutions for Northern Ireland.]

(2) A person guilty of an offence under sub-paragraph (1) is liable—

- (a) on conviction on indictment to imprisonment for a term not exceeding two years or a fine or to both,
- (b) on summary conviction in England and Wales, to imprisonment for a term not exceeding twelve months or a fine of an amount not exceeding the statutory maximum or to both, and
- (c) on summary conviction in Scotland [or Northern Ireland], to imprisonment for a term not exceeding six months or a fine of an amount not exceeding the statutory maximum or to both.

(3) In relation to an offence committed before section 154(1) of the Criminal Justice Act 2003 (c 44) comes into force, sub-paragraph (2)(b) has effect as if for "twelve" there were substituted "six".

NOTES

Para 3: words in square brackets in sub-para (3) substituted by the Companies Act 2006 (Commencement No 2, Consequential Amendments, Transitional Provisions and Savings) Order 2007, SI 2007/1093, art 6(2), Sch 4, Pt 1, para 26(1), (2), as from 6 April 2007.

Para 5: words omitted from sub-para (1) repealed, sub-para (1A) inserted, and words in square brackets in sub-para (2) inserted, by SI 2007/1093, art 6(2), Sch 4, Pt 1, para 26(1), (3), as from 6 April 2007.

SCHEDULE 8

(*Sch 8 contains repeals of or in CA 1985, ss 27, 245C, 256, 310, 390A, 734, Schs 4A, 24, IA 1986, Sch 13, and CA 1989, s 48, 63, 65, 67, 69, 120. Other repeals in this Schedule are outside the scope of this work.*)

PART 6
STATUTORY INSTRUMENTS MADE UNDER PRE-2006 COMPANIES LEGISLATION

INTRODUCTORY NOTE

The statutory instruments contained in this Part were made under the pre-2006 companies legislation; ie, the Companies Act 1985, the Company Directors Disqualification Act 1986, the Companies Act 1989, the Companies (Audit, Investigations and Community Enterprise) Act 2004, and Part V of the Criminal Justice Act 1993.

COMPANIES (INSPECTORS' REPORTS) (FEES) REGULATIONS 1981

(SI 1981/1686)

NOTES

Made: 24 November 1981.
Authority: Originally made under CA 1948, ss 168(2), 455(1) (repealed); now have effect under CA 1985, s 437(3)(b).
Commencement: 22 December 1981.
As of 1 July 2011, these Regulations had not been amended.

[6.1]
1.

These Regulations may be cited as the Companies (Inspectors' Reports) (Fees) Regulations 1981 and shall come into operation on 22nd December 1981.

[6.2]
2.

The fee prescribed for the furnishing of a copy of a report under section 168(2) of the Companies Act 1948 or for furnishing a copy of a report or part of a report under that section as it applies for the purposes of section 172 of that Act shall be 10 pence for each page copied.

NOTES

CA 1948, ss 168(2), 172 (repealed): see now CA 1985, ss 437(3)(b), 443, respectively.

COMPANIES (TABLES A TO F) REGULATIONS 1985

(SI 1985/805)

NOTES

Made: 22 May 1985.
Authority: Companies Act 1985, ss 3, 8 (repealed by the Companies Act 2006, s 1295, Sch 16, as from 1 October 2009 (for savings see the note below)).
Commencement: 1 July 1985.
Savings: the Companies Act 2006 (Commencement No 8, Transitional Provisions and Savings) Order 2008, SI 2008/2860, Sch 2, para 1(1) (at **[2.91]**) provides as follows—

"(1)   Nothing in the Companies Act 2006 affects—
(a)   the registration or re-registration of a company under the former Companies Acts, or the continued existence of a company by virtue of such registration or re-registration, or
(b)   the application in relation to an existing company of—
(i)   Table B in the Joint Stock Companies Act 1856,
(ii)   Table A in any of the former Companies Acts, or
(iii)   the Companies (Tables A to F) Regulations 1985 or the Companies (Tables A to F) Regulations (Northern Ireland) 1986.".

Note also that Sch 2, para 2(1) provides that ss 7–16 of the Companies Act 2006 (company formation) apply to applications for registration received by the registrar on or after 1 October 2009. Sch 2, para 2(3) further provides that the corresponding provisions of the 1985 Act continue to apply to an application for registration if (a) it is received by the registrar, and (b) the requirements as to registration are met in relation to it, before that date. The corresponding provisions of this Act include s 3(1) (see the table of origins at **[3.52]**).
Note that Table A is at **[A2]**.
These Regulations are reproduced as amended by: the Companies (Tables A to F) (Amendment) Regulations 2007, SI 2007/2541; the Companies (Tables A to F) (Amendment) Regulations 2008, SI 2008/739.

[6.3]
1

These Regulations may be cited as the Companies (Tables A to F) Regulations 1985 and shall come into operation on 1st July 1985.

Part 6   Pre-2006 companies SIs

[6.4]
2

The regulations in Table A and the forms in Tables B, C, D, E and F in the Schedule to these Regulations shall be the regulations and forms of memorandum and articles of association for the purposes of sections 3 and 8 of the Companies Act 1985.

3 *(Revokes the Companies (Alteration of Table A etc) Regulations 1984, SI 1984/717.)*

SCHEDULE

(Table A reproduced at **[A2]**.*)*

TABLE B

A PRIVATE COMPANY LIMITED BY SHARES

Memorandum of Association

[6.5]

1. The company's name is "The South Wales Motor Transport Company cyfyngedig".

2. The company's registered office is to be situated in Wales.

3. The company's objects are the carriage of passengers and goods in motor vehicles between such places as the company may from time to time determine and the doing of all such other things as are incidental or conducive to the attainment of that object.

4. The liability of the members is limited.

5. The company's share capital is £50,000 divided into 50,000 shares of £1 each.

We, the subscribers to this memorandum of association, wish to be formed into a company pursuant to this memorandum; and we agree to take the number of shares shown opposite our respective names.

Names and Addresses of Subscribers	Number of shares taken by each Subscriber
1. Thomas Jones, 138 Mountfield Street, Tredegar.	1
2. Mary Evans, 19 Merthyr Road, Aberystwyth.	1
Total shares taken	2
Dated. . . . . 19.	
Witness to the above signatures,	
Anne Brown, "Woodlands", Fieldside Road, Bryn Mawr.	

TABLE C

A COMPANY LIMITED BY GUARANTEE AND NOT HAVING A SHARE CAPITAL

Memorandum of Association

[6.6]
[A1. References in these Articles to Table A are to that Table so far as it relates to private companies limited by shares.]

1. The company's name is "The Dundee School Association Limited".

2. The company's registered office is to be situated in Scotland.

3. The company's objects are the carrying on of a school for boys and girls in Dundee and the doing of all such other things as are incidental or conducive to the attainment of that object.

4. The liability of the members is limited.

5. Every member of the company undertakes to contribute such amount as may be required (not exceeding £100) to the company's assets if it should be wound up while he is a member or within one year after he ceases to be a member, for payment of the company's debts and liabilities contracted before he ceases to be a member, and of the costs, charges and expenses of winding up, and for the adjustment of the rights of the contributories among themselves.

We, the subscribers to this memorandum of association, wish to be formed into a company pursuant to this memorandum.

Names and Addresses of Subscribers.

1. Kenneth Brodie, 14 Bute Street, Dundee.

2. Ian Davis, 2 Burns Avenue, Dundee.

Dated . . . . 19. . . . .

Witness to the above signatures.

Anne Brown, 149 Princes Street, Edinburgh.

Articles of Association

Preliminary

1. Regulations 2 to 35 inclusive, 54, 55, 57, 59, 102 to 108 inclusive, 110, 114, 116 and 117 of Table A, shall not apply to the company but the articles hereinafter contained and, subject to the modifications hereinafter expressed, the remaining regulations of Table A shall constitute the articles of association of the company.

Interpretation

2. In regulation 1 of Table A, the definition of "the holder" shall be omitted.

Members

3. The subscribers to the memorandum of association of the company and such other persons as are admitted to membership in accordance with the articles shall be members of the company. No person shall be admitted a member of the company unless he is approved by the directors. Every person who wishes to become a member shall deliver to the company an application for membership in such form as the directors require executed by him.

4. A member may at any time withdraw from the company by giving at least seven clear days' notice to the company. Membership shall not be transferable and shall cease on death.

Notice of General Meetings

5. In regulation 38 of Table A—
- (a) in paragraph (b) the words "of the total voting rights at the meeting of all the members" shall be substituted for "in nominal value of the shares giving that right" and
- (b) the words "The notice shall be given to all the members and to the directors and auditors" shall be substituted for the last sentence.

Proceedings at General Meetings

6. The words "and at any separate meeting of the holders of any class of shares in the company" shall be omitted from regulation 44 of Table A.

7. Paragraph (d) of regulation 46 of Table A shall be omitted.

Votes of Members

8. On a show of hands every member present in person [or by proxy] shall have one vote. On a poll every member present in person or by proxy shall have one vote.

Directors' Expenses

9. The words "of any class of shares or" shall be omitted from regulation 83 of Table A.

Proceedings of Directors

10. In paragraph (c) of regulation 94 of Table A the word "debentures" shall be substituted for the words "shares, debentures or other securities" in both places where they occur.

Minutes

11. The words "of the holders of any class of shares in the company" shall be omitted from regulation 100 of Table A.

Notices

12. The second sentence of regulation 112 of Table A shall be omitted.

13. The words "or of the holders of any class of shares in the company" shall be omitted from regulation 113 of Table A.

NOTES

Para A1 of the Memorandum of Association inserted by the Companies (Tables A to F) (Amendment) Regulations 2007, SI 2007/2541, reg 23, with effect from 1 October 2007.

Words in square brackets in Article 8 of the Articles of Association inserted by the Companies (Tables A to F) (Amendment) Regulations 2008, SI 2008/739, reg 2, with effect from 6 April 2008.

TABLE D

PART I
A PUBLIC COMPANY LIMITED BY GUARANTEE AND HAVING A SHARE CAPITAL

Memorandum of Association

1. The company's name is "Gwestai Glyndwr, cwmni cyfyngedig cyhoeddus".

2. The company is to be a public company.

3. The company's registered office is to be situated in Wales.

4. The company's objects are facilitating travelling in Wales by providing hotels and conveyances by sea and by land for the accommodation of travellers and the doing of all such other things as are incidental or conducive to the attainment of those objects.

5. The liability of the members is limited.

6. Every member of the company undertakes to contribute such amount as may be required (not exceeding £100) to the company's assets if it should be wound up while he is a member or within one year after he ceases to be a member, for payment of the company's debts and liabilities contracted before he ceases to be a member, and of the costs, charges and expenses of winding up, and for the adjustment of the rights of the contributories among themselves.

7. The company's share capital is £50,000 divided into 50,000 shares of £1 each.

We, the subscribers to this memorandum of association, wish to be formed into a company pursuant to this memorandum; and we agree to take the number of shares shown opposite our respective names.

Names and Addresses of Subscribers	Number of shares taken by each Subscriber
1. Thomas Jones, 138 Mountfield Street, Tredegar.	1
2. Mary Evans, 19 Merthyr Road, Aberystwyth.	1
Total shares taken	2
Dated. . . . . 19.	

Witness to the above signatures,

Anne Brown, "Woodlands", Fieldside Road, Bryn Mawr.

PART II
A PRIVATE COMPANY LIMITED BY GUARANTEE AND HAVING A SHARE CAPITAL

Memorandum of Association

1. The company's name is "The Highland Hotel Company Limited".

2. The company's registered office is to be situated in Scotland.

3. The company's objects are facilitating travelling in the Highlands of Scotland by providing hotels and conveyances by sea and by land for the accommodation of travellers and the doing of all such other things as are incidental or conducive to the attainment of those objects.

4. The liability of the members is limited.

5. Every member of the company undertakes to contribute such amount as may be required (not exceeding £100) to the company's assets if it should be wound up while he is a member or within one year after he ceases to be a member, for payment of the company's debts and liabilities contracted before he ceases to be a member, and of the costs, charges and expenses of winding up, and for the adjustment of the rights of the contributories among themselves.

6. The company's share capital is £50,000 divided into 50,000 shares of £1 each.

We, the subscribers to this memorandum of association, wish to be formed into a company pursuant to this memorandum; and we agree to take the number of shares shown opposite our respective names.

Names and Addresses of Subscribers	Number of shares taken by each Subscriber
Kenneth Brodie, 14 Bute Street, Dundee.	1
Ian Davis, 2 Burns Avenue, Dundee.	1
Total shares taken	2

Names and Addresses of Subscribers	Number of shares taken by each Subscriber

Dated. . . . . 19. . . . .

Witness to the above signatures,

Anne Brown, 149 Princes Street, Edinburgh.

Part 6   Pre-2006 companies SIs

PART III

A COMPANY (PUBLIC OR PRIVATE) LIMITED BY GUARANTEE AND HAVING A SHARE CAPITAL

Articles of Association

[6.7]

The regulations of Table A shall constitute the articles of association of the company.

TABLE E

AN UNLIMITED COMPANY HAVING A SHARE CAPITAL

Memorandum of Association

[6.8]

1. The company's name is "The Woodford Engineering Company".

2. The company's registered office is to be situated in England and Wales.

3. The company's objects are the working of certain patented inventions relating to the application of microchip technology to the improvement of food processing, and the doing of all such other things as are incidental or conducive to the attainment of that object.

We, the subscribers to this memorandum of association, wish to be formed into a company pursuant to this memorandum; and we agree to take the number of shares shown opposite our respective names.

Names and Addresses of Subscribers	Number of shares taken by each Subscriber
1. Brian Smith, 24 Nibley Road, Wotton-under-Edge, Gloucester-shire.	3
2. William Green, 278 High Street, Chipping Sodbury, Avon.	5
Total shares taken	8

Dated. . . . . 19. . . . .

Witness to the above signatures,

Anne Brown, 108 Park Way, Bristol 8.

Articles of Association

1. Regulations 3, 32, 34 and 35 of Table A shall not apply to the company, but the articles hereinafter contained and, subject to the modification hereinafter expressed, the remaining regulations of Table A shall constitute the articles of association of the company.

2. . . . .

3. The share capital of the company is £20,000 divided into 20,000 shares of £1 each.

4. The company may by special resolution—

    (a)   increase the share capital by such sum to be divided into shares of such amount as the resolution may prescribe;

    (b)   consolidate and divide all or any of its share capital into shares of a larger amount than its existing shares;

    (c)   subdivide its shares, or any of them, into shares of a smaller amount than its existing shares;

    (d)   cancel any shares which at the date of the passing of the resolution have not been taken or agreed to be taken by any person;

    (e)   reduce its share capital and any share premium account in any way.

NOTES

Article 2 of the Articles of Association revoked by the Companies (Tables A to F) (Amendment) Regulations 2008, SI 2008/739, reg 3, with effect from 6 April 2008.

TABLE F

A PUBLIC COMPANY LIMITED BY SHARES

Memorandum of Association

[6.9]

1. The company's name is "Western Electronics Public Limited Company".

2. The company is to be a public company.

3. The company's registered office is to be situated in England and Wales.

4. The company's objects are the manufacture and development of such descriptions of electronic equipment, instruments and appliances as the company may from time to time determine, and the doing of all such other things as are incidental or conducive to the attainment of that object.

5. The liability of the members is limited.

6. The company's share capital is £5,000,000 divided into 5,000,000 shares of £1 each.

We, the subscribers of this memorandum of association, wish to be formed into a company pursuant to this memorandum; and we agree to take the number of shares shown opposite our respective names.

Names and Addresses of Subscribers	Number of shares taken by each Subscriber
1. James White, 12 Broadmead, Birmingham.	1
2. Patrick Smith, 145A Huntley House, London Wall, London EC2.	1
Total shares taken	2

Dated. . . . . 19. . . . .

Witness to the above signatures,

Anne Brown, 13 Hute Street, London WC2.

COMPANIES (FORMS) REGULATIONS 1985 (AND GENERAL NOTE REGARDING FORMS)

(SI 1985/854)

[6.10]

NOTES

These Regulations were made on 4 June 1985 and came into force on 1 July 1985. They were made under the provisions listed below (see Sch 1 to these Regulations):

Authority: originally made under CA 1985, ss 6(1)(b)(i), 10(2), 12(3), 21(5), 30(5), 43(3), 49(4), (8)(a), 51(4), 53(1)(b), 54(4), 65(3)(b), 72(2)(c), 77(5)(a), 88(2)(a), (3), 97(3)(a), 117(2), (3), 122(1), 123(2), 128(1), (3), (4), 129(1), (2), (3), 139(4), 147(3), 155(6), 156(1), 157(3), 169(1), 173(5), 176(3)(a), 190(5), 224(2), 225(1), (2), 241(3)(b), 242(3), 266(1), (3), 272(5), 273(7), 287(2), 288(2), 318(4), 325(5), 353(2), 362(3), 363(2), 364(1), 386(2), 395(1), 397(1), 398(1), (4), 400(2), 401(1), 403(1), 405(3), 409(1), 410(2), 413(2), 416(1), 417(1), 419(1), (5), 424(1), 428(2), 429(2), (3), 466(4), (5), 469(1), 470(3), 481(1)(b), (2), 482(1), 485(1), 486, 495(2)(a), (b), 496(1)(e), 497(2), 498(3), 600(1), 680(1), 681(6), 684(1)(a), (b), (2), 685(4), (4)(e), 686(1)(a), (2), 690(2), 691(1)(a), (b), 692(1), (2), 694(4)(a), (b), 698, 700(2), 701(2), (6), 744, Sch 13, para 27, Sch 14, para 1(1) (all of which (with the exception of s 466) were repealed by CA 2006); the Companies Consolidation (Consequential Provisions) Act 1985, ss 2(1)(b), (4)(b), 4(1), (4) (repealed by SI 2011/1265, as from 12 May 2011).

General note regarding forms: numerous provisions of the Companies Act 1985 provided for forms to be prescribed by Regulations for the purposes of those provisions; such forms have been prescribed by the Companies (Forms) Regulations 1985, SI 1985/854 and various subsequent instruments (ie, SI 1987/752, SI 1988/1359, SI 1990/572, SI 1990/1766, SI 1991/879, SI 1991/1259, SI 1992/3006, SI 1995/736, SI 1995/1479, SI 1996/594, SI 1998/1702, SI 1999/2356, SI 1999/2678, SI 2002/691, SI 2003/2982, and SI 2005/2747). The provisions of the 1985 Act under which these Regulations were made were in some cases substituted or repealed by subsequent legislation and are now (mostly) repealed by the Companies Act 2006, s 1295, Sch 16 (see further the notes above). Various transitional provisions are contained in commencement orders made under the Companies Act 2006 having effect until s 1068 of the 2006 Act came into force (this section came fully into force on 1 October 2009). See, in particular:

— the Companies Act 2006 (Commencement No 3, Consequential Amendments, Transitional Provisions and Savings) Order 2007, SI 2007/2194, Sch 3 at **[2.45]**,

— the Companies Act 2006 (Commencement No 5, Transitional Provisions and Savings) Order 2007, SI 2007/3495, art 9, Sch 4, Pt 1 at **[2.58]**, **[2.66]**,

— the Companies Act 2006 (Commencement No 8, Transitional Provisions and Savings) Order 2008, SI 2008/2860, Sch 2, para 115 (at **[2.91]**) which provides (i) that any saving in that Schedule for the effect of a provision of the 1985 Act requiring use of a prescribed form extends to the form and the power under which it is prescribed; and (ii) any saving in that Schedule for the effect of a provision of the 1985 Act requiring a document to be delivered to the registrar extends to s 707B of the 1985 Act (delivery to the registrar using electronic communications) so far as relating to the provision in question and the delivery of documents under it. Similar provisions are contained in relation to overseas companies in the Overseas Companies Regulations 2009, SI 2009/1801, Sch 8, Pt 8, para 31 at **[4.489]**.

Of the forms prescribed by the Regulations noted above, Form 466 Scot (prescribed by SI 1985/854) continues to be used for the purposes of a provision of the 1985 Act, the repeal of which has not yet been brought into force (s 466, which applies to Scotland only and is repealed by the Bankruptcy and Diligence etc (Scotland) Act 2007, s 46(1), as from a day to be appointed).

Form 980(1) (Notice to non-assenting shareholders), Form 980(dec) (Statutory Declaration relating to a notice to non-assenting shareholders) and Form 984 (Notice to non-assenting shareholders) continue to be used for the purposes of the 2006 Act. Forms 980(1), 980dec, 984 were formerly Forms 429(4), 429dec and 430(A) respectively. They were originally prescribed by SI 1987/752 and were renumbered (and amended) by SI 2007/1093 following the repeal of Part XIIIA of the 1985 Act (Takeovers) and its replacement by Part 28 (ss 942–992) of the 2006 Act.

The following forms are also listed on the Companies House website as Companies Act 2006 forms implemented prior to 1 October 2009: Form 128(1) (statement of rights attached to allotted shares), Form 128(3) (statement of particulars of variation of rights attached to shares), Form 128(4) (notice of assignment of name or new name to any class of shares), Form 129(1) (statement by a company without share capital of rights attached to newly created class of members), Form 129(2) (statement by a company without share capital of particulars of a variation of members' class rights), Form 129(3) (notice by a company without share capital of assignment of a name or other designation to a class of members) (all originally prescribed by SI 1985/854). They now take effect for the purposes of ss 556(3), 637(1), 636(1), 638(1), 640(1) and 639(1) of the 2006 Act respectively.

It should be noted that forms which are no longer required have not been specifically revoked. Forms which are still relevant, including those referred to above, may be found on the Companies House website.

The 2006 Act does not provide for forms to be prescribed by Regulations but in s 1068 provides that the registrar may impose requirements as to the form, authentication and manner of delivery of documents required or authorised to be delivered to the registrar under any enactment. By s 1117 of the 2006 Act, where any provision of Part 35 of the Act (ss 1059A–1120) enables the registrar to make provision, or impose requirements, as to any matter, the registrar may make such provision or impose such requirements by means of rules under that section; such rules are not statutory instruments. The appropriate 2006 Act forms may be found on the Companies House website.

Additional forms in Welsh, made in accordance with the requirements of the Welsh Language Act 1993 were prescribed for the purposes of the Companies Act 1985 by the Companies (Welsh Language Forms and Documents) Regulations 1994, SI 1994/117 and by subsequent statutory instruments. The 1994 Regulations were made under the Companies Act 1985, ss 287(3), 288(2), 363(2), 710B(3), (8), 744, as extended by the Welsh Language Act 1993, s 26(3). These provisions of the 1985 Act have all been repealed by the Companies Act 2006, s 1295, Sch 16. Note also that by virtue of SI 2006/3428, art 8(1), Sch 5, Pt 1, para 1, notwithstanding the repeal of s 710B of the 1985 Act by s 1295 of, and Sch 16 to, the 2006 Act, reg 5 of SI 1994/117, which deals with translation of documents into English, continues to have effect as if the requirements imposed by it were imposed by the registrar under the Companies Act 2006, s 1111, by means of rules under s 1117 thereof.

Note also that the Companies (Registers and Other Records) Regulations 1985, SI 1985/724 specified various requirements with respect to registers kept otherwise than in a legible form. It also prescribed the following forms: Form 325a (Notice of place for inspection of register of directors' interests in shares etc which is kept in non-legible form, or of any change in that place); Form 353a (Notice of place for inspection of register of members which is kept in non-legible form, or of any change in that place); Form 362a (Notice of place for inspection of overseas branch register which is kept in non-legible form, or of any change in that place); and Form 190a (Notice of place for inspection of register of holders of debentures which is kept in non-legible form, or of any change in that place). These Regulations are now effectively spent and lapsed on the repeal of s 723(4) of the 1985 Act.

FINANCIAL MARKETS AND INSOLVENCY REGULATIONS 1991

(SI 1991/880)

NOTES

Made: 27 March 1991.

Authority: Companies Act 1989, ss 155(4), (5), 158(4), (5), 160(5), 173(4), (5), 174(2)–(4), 185, 186, 187(3).

Commencement: 25 April 1991.

These Regulations are reproduced as amended by: the Financial Markets and Insolvency (Amendment) Regulations 1992, SI 1992/716; the Financial Markets and Insolvency (CGO Service) Regulations 1999, SI 1999/1209; the Financial Services and Markets Act 2000 (Consequential Amendments and Repeals) Order 2001, SI 2001/3649; the Enterprise Act 2002 (Insolvency) Order 2003, SI 2003/2096; the Financial Markets and Insolvency Regulations 2009, SI 2009/853.

Application to bank insolvency and administration: as to the application of these Regulations to bank insolvency and administration, see the Banking Act 2009 (Parts 2 and 3 Consequential Amendments) Order 2009, SI 2009/317.

ARRANGEMENT OF REGULATIONS

PART I
GENERAL

PART V
MARKET CHARGES

PART I
GENERAL

[6.11]
1   Citation and commencement
These Regulations may be cited as the Financial Markets and Insolvency Regulations 1991 and shall come into force on 25th April 1991.

[6.12]
2   Interpretation: general
(1)   In these Regulations "the Act" means the Companies Act 1989.

[(1A)   In these Regulations "the Recognition Requirements Regulations" means the Financial Services and Markets Act 2000 (Recognition Requirements for Investment Exchanges and Clearing Houses) Regulations 2001.]

(2)   A reference in any of these Regulations to a numbered regulation shall be construed as a reference to the regulation bearing that number in these Regulations.

(3)   A reference in any of these Regulations to a numbered paragraph shall, unless the reference is to a paragraph of a specified regulation, be construed as a reference to the paragraph bearing that number in the regulation in which the reference is made.

NOTES
Para (1A): inserted by the Financial Markets and Insolvency Regulations 2009, SI 2009/853, reg 3(1), (2), as from 15 June 2009.

3–6   ((*Pts II–IV*) *amend CA 1989, ss 155, 159, 160, 162 at* **[5.111]**, **[5.114]**, **[5.115]**, **[5.117]**.)

PART V
MARKET CHARGES

[6.13]
7   Interpretation of Part V
In this Part of these Regulations, unless the context otherwise requires—
   "the Bank" means the Bank of England;
   "business day" has the same meaning as in section 167(3) of the Act;
   . . .
   "CGO" means the Central Gilts Office of the Bank;
   "CGO Service" means the computer-based system established by the Bank and The Stock Exchange to facilitate the transfer of specified securities;
   "CGO Service charge" means a charge of the kind described in section 173(1)(c) of the Act;
   "CGO Service member" means a person who is entitled by contract with [CRESTCo Limited (which is now responsible for operating the CGO Service)] to use the CGO Service;
   ["default fund contribution" has the same meaning as in section 188(3A) of the Act;]
   "former CGO Service member" means a person whose entitlement   . . .   to use the CGO Service has been terminated or suspended;
   "market charge" means a charge which is a market charge for the purposes of Part VII of the Act;
   "settlement bank" means a person who has agreed under a contract with [CRESTCo Limited (which is now responsible for operating the CGO Service)] to make payments of the kind mentioned in section 173(1)(c) of the Act;
   "specified securities" has the meaning given in section 173(3) of the Act;
   "Talisman" means The Stock Exchange settlement system known as Talisman;

"Talisman charge" means a charge granted in favour of The Stock Exchange over property credited to an account within Talisman maintained in the name of the chargor in respect of certain property beneficially owned by the chargor; and

"transfer" when used in relation to specified securities has the meaning given in section 173(3) of the Act.

NOTES

Definition "CGO" (omitted) revoked, words in square brackets in definitions "CGO Service member" and "settlement bank" substituted, and words omitted from definition "former CGO Service member" revoked, by the Financial Markets and Insolvency (CGO Service) Regulations 1999, SI 1999/1209, reg 3(1), as from 24 May 1999.

Definition "default fund contribution" inserted by the Financial Markets and Insolvency Regulations 2009, SI 2009/853, reg 3(1), (3), as from 15 June 2009.

[6.14]
8   Charges on land or any interest in land not to be treated as market charges

(1)   No charge, whether fixed or floating, shall be treated as a market charge to the extent that it is a charge on land or any interest in land.

(2)   For the purposes of paragraph (1), a charge on a debenture forming part of an issue or series shall not be treated as a charge on land or any interest in land by reason of the fact that the debenture is secured by a charge on land or any interest in land.

9   (*Amends CA 1989, s 173 at* **[5.126]**.)

[6.15]
10   Extent to which charge granted in favour of recognised investment exchange to be treated as market charge

(1)   A charge granted in favour of a recognised investment exchange other than The Stock Exchange shall be treated as a market charge only to the extent that—
  (a)   it is a charge over property provided as margin in respect of market contracts entered into by the exchange for the purposes of or in connection with the provision of clearing services [or over property provided as a default fund contribution to the exchange];
  (b)   in the case of a recognised UK investment exchange, it secures the obligation to pay to the exchange [any sum due to the exchange from a member or designated non-member of the exchange or from a recognised clearing house or from another recognised investment exchange in respect of unsettled market contracts to which the member, designated non-member, clearing house or investment exchange is a party under the rules referred to in paragraph 12 of the Schedule to the Recognition Requirements Regulations]; and
  (c)   in the case of a recognised overseas investment exchange, it secures the obligation to reimburse the cost (other than fees and other incidental expenses) incurred by the exchange in settling unsettled market contracts in respect of which the charged property is provided as margin.

(2)   A charge granted in favour of The Stock Exchange shall be treated as a market charge only to the extent that—
  (a)   it is a charge of the kind described in paragraph (1); or
  (b)   it is a Talisman charge and secures an obligation of either or both of the kinds mentioned in paragraph (3).

(3)   The obligations mentioned in this paragraph are—
  (a)   the obligation of the chargor to reimburse The Stock Exchange for payments (including stamp duty and taxes but excluding Stock Exchange fees and incidental expenses arising from the operation by The Stock Exchange of settlement arrangements) made by The Stock Exchange in settling, through Talisman, market contracts entered into by the chargor; and
  (b)   the obligation of the chargor to reimburse The Stock Exchange the amount of any payment it has made pursuant to a short term certificate.

(4)   In paragraph (3), "short term certificate" means an instrument issued by The Stock Exchange undertaking to procure the transfer of property of a value and description specified in the instrument to or to the order of the person to whom the instrument is issued or his endorsee or to a person acting on behalf of either of them and also undertaking to make appropriate payments in cash, in the event that the obligation to procure the transfer of property cannot be discharged in whole or in part.

NOTES

Para (1): words in square brackets in para (a) inserted, and words in square brackets in para (b) substituted, by the Financial Markets and Insolvency Regulations 2009, SI 2009/853, reg 3(1), (4), as from 15 June 2009.

[6.16]
11   Extent to which charge granted in favour of recognised clearing house to be treated as market charge

A charge granted in favour of a recognised clearing house shall be treated as a market charge only to the extent that—

(a)   it is a charge over property provided as margin in respect of market contracts entered into by the clearing house [or over property provided as a default fund contribution to the clearing house];

(b)   in the case of a recognised UK clearing house, it secures the obligation to pay to the clearing house [any sum due to the clearing house from a member of the clearing house or from a recognised investment exchange or from another recognised clearing house in respect of unsettled market contracts to which the member, clearing house or investment exchange is a party under the rules referred to in paragraph 25 of the Schedule to the Recognition Requirements Regulations]; and

(c)   in the case of a recognised overseas clearing house, it secures the obligation to reimburse the cost (other than fees or other incidental expenses) incurred by the clearing house in settling unsettled market contracts in respect of which the charged property is provided as margin.

NOTES

Para (1): words in square brackets in para (a) inserted, and words in square brackets in para (b) substituted, by the Financial Markets and Insolvency Regulations 2009, SI 2009/853, reg 3(1), (5), as from 15 June 2009.

[6.17]
12   Circumstances in which CGO Service charge to be treated as market charge

A CGO Service charge shall be treated as a market charge only if—

(a)   it is granted to a settlement bank by a person for the purpose of securing debts or liabilities of the kind mentioned in section 173(1)(c) of the Act incurred by that person through his use of the CGO Service as a CGO Service member; and

(b)   it contains provisions which refer expressly to the [CGO Service].

NOTES

Words in square brackets substituted by the Financial Markets and Insolvency (CGO Service) Regulations 1999, SI 1999/1209, reg 3(2), as from 24 May 1999.

[6.18]
13   Extent to which CGO Service charge to be treated as market charge

A CGO Service charge shall be treated as a market charge only to the extent that—

(a)   it is a charge over any one or more of the following—

  (i)   specified securities held within the CGO Service to the account of a CGO Service member or a former CGO Service member;

  (ii)   specified securities which were held as mentioned in sub-paragraph (i) above immediately prior to their being removed from the CGO Service consequent upon the person in question becoming a former CGO Service member;

  (iii)   sums receivable by a CGO Service member or former CGO Service member representing interest accrued on specified securities held within the CGO Service to his account or which were so held immediately prior to their being removed from the CGO Service consequent upon his becoming a former CGO Service member;

  (iv)   sums receivable by a CGO Service member or former CGO Service member in respect of the redemption or conversion of specified securities which were held within the CGO Service to his account at the time that the relevant securities were redeemed or converted or which were so held immediately prior to their being removed from the CGO Service consequent upon his becoming a former CGO Service member; and

  (v)   sums receivable by a CGO Service member or former CGO Service member in respect of the transfer by him of specified securities through the medium of the CGO Service; and

(b)   it secures the obligation of a CGO Service member or former CGO Service member to reimburse a settlement bank for the amount due from him to the settlement bank as a result of the settlement bank having discharged or become obliged to discharge payment obligations in respect of transfers or allotments of specified securities made to him through the medium of the CGO Service.

[6.19]
14   [Limitation on disapplication of moratorium on certain legal processes under Schedule B1 to the Insolvency Act 1986 (administration) in relation to CGO Service charges]

(1)   In this regulation "qualifying period" means the period beginning with the fifth business day before the day on which [an application] for the making of an administration order in relation to the relevant CGO Service member or former CGO Service member is presented and ending with the second business day after the day on which an administration order is made in relation to the relevant CGO Service member or former CGO Service member pursuant to the petition.

[(1A)   A reference in paragraph (1) to an application for an administration order shall be treated as including a reference to—

(a)   appointing an administrator under paragraph 14 or 22 of Schedule B1 to the Insolvency Act 1986, or

(b)   filing with the court a notice of intention to appoint an administrator under either of those paragraphs,

and a reference to "an administration order" shall include the appointment of an administrator under paragraph 14 or 22 of Schedule B1 to the Insolvency Act 1986.]

(2)   [The disapplication of paragraph 43(2) of Schedule B1 to the Insolvency Act 1986 (including that provisions as applied by paragraph 44 of that Schedule)] by section 175(1)(a) of the Act shall be limited in respect of a CGO Service charge so that it has effect only to the extent necessary to enable there to be realised, whether through the sale of specified securities or otherwise, a sum equal to whichever is less of the following—

(a)   the total amount of payment obligations discharged by the settlement bank in respect of transfers and allotments of specified securities made during the qualifying period to the relevant CGO Service member or former CGO Service member through the medium of the CGO Service less the total amount of payment obligations discharged to the settlement bank in respect of transfers of specified securities made during the qualifying period by the relevant CGO Service member or former CGO Service member through the medium of the CGO Service; and

(b)   the amount (if any) described in regulation 13(b) due to the settlement bank from the relevant CGO Service member or former CGO Service member.

NOTES

Regulation heading: substituted by the Enterprise Act 2002 (Insolvency) Order 2003, SI 2003/2096, arts 5, 6, Schedule, Pt 2, paras 47, 48(a), as from 15 September 2003, except in relation to any case where a petition for an administration order was presented before that date.

Paras (1), (2): words in square brackets substituted by SI 2003/2096, arts 5, 6, Schedule, Pt 2, paras 47, 48(b), (d), as from 15 September 2003, except in relation to any case where a petition for an administration order was presented before that date. Note, it is assumed that the words "the petition" at the end of para (1) should have been similarly substituted, but the Queen's Printer's copy of SI 2003/2096 made no such provision.

Para (1A): inserted by SI 2003/2096, arts 5, 6, Schedule, Pt 2, paras 47, 48(c), as from 15 September 2003, except in relation to any case where a petition for an administration order was presented before that date.

[6.20]
15   Ability of administrator or receiver to recover assets in case of property subject to CGO Service charge or Talisman charge

(1)   [The disapplication—

(a)   by section 175(1)(b) of the Act, of paragraphs 70, 71 and 72 of Schedule B1 to the Insolvency Act 1986, and

(b)   by section 175(3) of the Act, of sections 43 and 61 of the 1986 Act,

shall cease to have effect] in respect of a charge which is either a CGO Service charge or a Talisman charge after the end of the second business day after the day on which an administration order is made or, as the case may be, an administrative receiver or a receiver is appointed, in relation to the grantor of the charge, in relation to property subject to it which—

(a)   in the case of a CGO Service charge, is not, on the basis of a valuation in accordance with paragraph (2), required for the realisation of whichever is the less of the sum referred to in regulation 14(2)(a) and the amount referred to in regulation 14(2)(b) due to the settlement bank at the close of business on the second business day referred to above; and

(b)   in the case of a Talisman charge is not, on the basis of a valuation in accordance with paragraph (2), required to enable The Stock Exchange to reimburse itself for any payment it has made of the kind referred to in regulation 10(3).

[(1A)   A reference in paragraph (1) to "an administration order" shall include the appointment of an administrator under paragraph 14 or 22 of Schedule B1 to the Insolvency Act 1986.]

(2)   For the purposes of paragraph (1) the value of property shall, except in a case falling within paragraph (3), be such as may be agreed between whichever is relevant of the administrator, administrative receiver or receiver on the one hand and the settlement bank or The Stock Exchange on the other.

(3)   For the purposes of paragraph (1), the value of any investment for which a price for the second business day referred to above is quoted in the Daily Official List of The Stock Exchange shall—

(a)   in a case in which two prices are so quoted, be an amount equal to the average of those two prices, adjusted where appropriate to take account of any accrued interest; and

(b)   in a case in which one price is so quoted, be an amount equal to that price, adjusted where appropriate to take account of any accrued interest.

NOTES

Para (1): words in square brackets substituted by the Enterprise Act 2002 (Insolvency) Order 2003, SI 2003/2096, arts 5, 6, Schedule, Pt 2, paras 47, 49(a), as from 15 September 2003, except in relation to any case where a petition for an administration order was presented before that date.

Para (1A): inserted by SI 2003/2096, arts 5, 6, Schedule, Pt 2, paras 47, 49(b), as from 15 September 2003, except in relation to any case where a petition for an administration order was presented before that date.

PART VI
CONSTRUCTION OF REFERENCES TO PARTIES TO MARKET CONTRACTS

[6.21]
16   Circumstances in which member or designated non-member dealing as principal to be treated as acting in different capacities

(1)   In this regulation "relevant transaction" means—
[(a)   a market contract, effected as principal by a member or designated non-member of a recognised investment exchange or a member of a recognised clearing house, in relation to which money received by the member or designated non-member is—
(i)   clients' money for the purposes of rules relating to clients' money, or
(ii)   would be clients' money for the purposes of those rules were it not money which, in accordance with those rules, may be regarded as immediately due and payable to the member or designated non-member for its own account; and]
(b)   a market contract which would be regarded as a relevant transaction by virtue of sub-paragraph (a) above were it not for the fact that no money is received by the member or designated non-member in relation to the contract

[(1A)   In addition "relevant transaction" means a market contract entered into by a recognised clearing house effected as principal in relation to which money is received by the recognised clearing house from a recognised investment exchange or from another recognised clearing house.

(1B)   In addition "relevant transaction" means a market contract entered into by a recognised investment exchange effected as principal in relation to which money is received by the recognised investment exchange from a recognised clearing house or from another recognised investment exchange.

(1C)   Where paragraph (1A) or (1B) apply paragraph (1) applies to the recognised clearing house or recognised investment exchange as it does to a member of the clearing house or investment exchange, and as if the clearing house or investment exchange were subject to the rules referred to in paragraph (1)(a)(i).

(1D)   In paragraph (1), "rules relating to clients' money" are rules made by the Financial Services Authority, in particular, under section 138 or 139 of the Financial Services and Markets Act 2000.]

[(2)   For the purposes of section 187(1) of the Act (construction of references to parties to market contracts)—
(a)   a recognised investment exchange or a member or designated non-member of a recognised investment exchange, or
(b)   a recognised clearing house or a member of a recognised clearing house,
shall be treated as effecting relevant transactions in a different capacity from other market contracts it has effected as principal,]

[(3), (4)   . . .]

NOTES
   Para (1): sub-para (a) substituted by the Financial Markets and Insolvency Regulations 2009, SI 2009/853, reg 3(1), (6)(a), as from 15 June 2009.
   Paras (1A)–(1D): inserted by SI 2009/853, reg 3(1), (6)(b), as from 15 June 2009.
   Para (2): substituted by SI 2009/853, reg 3(1), (6)(c), as from 15 June 2009.
   Paras (3), (4): added by SI 2001/3649, art 415(1), (3), as from 1 December 2001, and revoked by SI 2009/853, reg 3(1), (6)(d), as from 15 June 2009.

17   *((Pt VII) Amends CA 1989, Sch 21.)*

PART VIII
LEGAL PROCEEDINGS

18   *(Amends CA 1989, s 175 at* **[5.128]**.)

[6.22]
19   Court having jurisdiction in respect of proceedings under Part VII of Act

(1)   For the purposes of sections 161, 163, 164, 175(5) and 182 of the Act (various legal proceedings under Part VII of Act) "the court" shall be the court which has last heard an application in the proceedings under the Insolvency Act 1986 or the Bankruptcy (Scotland) Act 1985 in which the relevant office-holder is acting or, as the case may be, any court having jurisdiction to hear applications in those proceedings.

(2)   For the purposes of subsection (2) [and (2A)] of section 175 of the Act (administration orders etc), "the court" shall be the court which has made the administration order or, as the case may be, to which the [application] for an administration order has been presented [or the notice of intention to appoint has been filed].

(3)   The rules regulating the practice and procedure of the court in relation to applications to the court in England and Wales under sections 161, 163, 164, 175 and 182 of the Act shall be the rules applying in relation to applications to that court under the Insolvency Act 1986.

NOTES

Para (2): words in first and third pairs of square brackets inserted, and word in second pair of square brackets substituted, by the Enterprise Act 2002 (Insolvency) Order 2003, SI 2003/2096, arts 5, 6, Schedule, Pt 2, paras 47, 50, as from 15 September 2003, except in relation to any case where a petition for an administration order was presented before that date.

INSIDER DEALING (SECURITIES AND REGULATED MARKETS) ORDER 1994

(SI 1994/187)

NOTES

Made: 1 February 1994.

Authority: Criminal Justice Act 1993, ss 54(1), 60(1), 62(1), 64(3).

Commencement: 1 March 1994.

This Order is reproduced as amended by: the Insider Dealing (Securities and Regulated Markets) (Amendment) Order 1996, SI 1996/1561; the Insider Dealing (Securities and Regulated Markets) (Amendment) Order 2000, SI 2000/1923; the Insider Dealing (Securities and Regulated Markets) (Amendment) Order 2002, SI 2002/1874.

References to "the European Community", "Community", etc: see the Treaty of Lisbon (Changes in Terminology) Order 2011, SI 2011/1043, which provides that (as from 22 April 2011) "EU" should be substituted for the word "Community" (subject to certain exceptions) in references to "Community treaties", "Community instrument", "Community obligation", "Community law", "Community legislation", etc.

ARRANGEMENT OF ARTICLES

[6.23]
1 Title, commencement and interpretation

This Order may be cited as the Insider Dealing (Securities and Regulated Markets) Order 1994 and shall come into force on the twenty eighth day after the day on which it is made.

[6.24]
2

In this Order a "State within the European Economic Area" means a State which is a member of the European Communities and the Republics of Austria, Finland and Iceland, the Kingdoms of Norway and Sweden and the Principality of Liechtenstein.

[6.25]
3 Securities

Articles 4 to 8 set out conditions for the purposes of section 54(1) of the Criminal Justice Act 1993 (securities to which Part V of the Act of 1993 applies).

[6.26]
4

The following condition applies in relation to any security which falls within any paragraph of Schedule 2 to the Act of 1993, that is, that it is officially listed in a State within the European Economic Area or that it is admitted to dealing on, or has its price quoted on or under the rules of, a regulated market.

[6.27]
5

The following alternative condition applies in relation to a warrant, that is, that the right under it is a right to subscribe for any share or debt security of the same class as a share or debt security which satisfies the condition in article 4.

[6.28]
6

The following alternative condition applies in relation to a depositary receipt, that is, that the rights under it are in respect of any share or debt security which satisfies the condition in article 4.

Part 6   Pre-2006 companies SIs

[6.29]

7

The following alternative conditions apply in relation to an option or a future, that is, that the option or rights under the future are in respect of—

(a)   any share or debt security which satisfies the condition in article 4, or

(b)   any depositary receipt which satisfies the condition in article 4 or article 6.

[6.30]

8

The following alternative condition applies in relation to a contract for differences, that is, that the purpose or pretended purpose of the contract is to secure a profit or avoid a loss by reference to fluctuations in—

(a)   the price of any shares or debt securities which satisfy the condition in article 4, or

(b)   an index of the price of such shares or debt securities.

[6.31]

9   Regulated markets

The following markets are regulated markets for the purposes of Part V of the Act of 1993—

[(a)]   any market which is established under the rules of an investment exchange specified in the Schedule to this Order

(b)   the market known as OFEX . . .]

NOTES

Para (a) designated as such, and para (b) added, by the Insider Dealing (Securities and Regulated Markets) (Amendment) Order 2000, SI 2000/1923, art 2(1), (2), as from 20 July 2000; words omitted from para (b) revoked by the Insider Dealing (Securities and Regulated Markets) (Amendment) Order 2002, SI 2002/1874, art 2(1), (2), as from 19 July 2002.

[6.32]

10   United Kingdom regulated markets

The regulated markets which are regulated in the United Kingdom for the purposes of Part V of the Act of 1993 are any market which is established under the rules of—

[(a)   the London Stock Exchange Limited;]

(b)   LIFFE Administration & Management; . . .

(c)   OMLX, the London Securities and Derivatives Exchange Limited [. . .

(d)   [virt-x Exchange Limited].]

[(e)   [the exchange known as COREDEALMTS]; together with the market known as OFEX . . .]

NOTES

Para (a) substituted, word omitted from para (b) revoked, and para (d) and the word immediately preceding it added, by the Insider Dealing (Securities and Regulated Markets) (Amendment) Order 1996, SI 1996/1561, art 3, as from 1 July 1996; word omitted from para (c) revoked, and para (e) added, by the Insider Dealing (Securities and Regulated Markets) (Amendment) Order 2000, SI 2000/1923, art 2(1), (3), as from 20 July 2000; words in square brackets in paras (d), (e) substituted, and words omitted from para (e) revoked, by the Insider Dealing (Securities and Regulated Markets) (Amendment) Order 2002, SI 2002/1874, art 2(1), (3) as from 19 July 2002.

SCHEDULE
REGULATED MARKETS

Article 9

[6.33]

Any market which is established under the rules of one of the following investment exchanges:

Amsterdam Stock Exchange	[The exchange known as COREDEALMTS]
Antwerp Stock Exchange	Dusseldorf Stock Exchange
Athens Stock Exchange	[The exchange known as EASDAQ]
Barcelona Stock Exchange	Florence Stock Exchange
Bavarian Stock Exchange	Frankfurt Stock Exchange
Berlin Stock Exchange	Genoa Stock Exchange
Bilbao Stock Exchange	. . .
Bologna Stock Exchange	Hamburg Stock Exchange
. . .	Hanover Stock Exchange
Bremen Stock Exchange	Helsinki Stock Exchange
Brussels Stock Exchange	[Iceland Stock Exchange]
Copenhagen Stock Exchange	[The Irish Stock Exchange Limited]

. . .

. . .

Lisbon Stock Exchange

LIFFE Administration & Management

[The London Stock Exchange Limited]

Luxembourg Stock Exchange

Lyon Stock Exchange

Madrid Stock Exchange

. . .

Milan Stock Exchange

. . .

. . .

Naples Stock Exchange

The exchange known as NASDAQ

[The exchange known as the Nouveau Marché]

OMLX, the London Securities and Derivatives Exchange Limited

Oporto Stock Exchange

Oslo Stock Exchange

Palermo Stock Exchange

Paris Stock Exchange

Rome Stock Exchange

. . .

Stockholm Stock Exchange

Stuttgart Stock Exchange

[The exchange known as SWX Swiss Exchange]

[. . .]

Trieste Stock Exchange

Turin Stock Exchange

Valencia Stock Exchange

Venice Stock Exchange

Vienna Stock Exchange

[virt-x Exchange Limited]

Part 6   Pre-2006 companies SIs

NOTES

First to seventh entries omitted revoked, entries "Iceland Stock Exchange" and "The Irish Stock Exchange Limited" substituted, and entries "The London Stock Exchange Limited" and "The exchange known as the Nouveau Marché inserted, by the Insider Dealing (Securities and Regulated Markets) (Amendment) Order 1996, SI 1996/1561, art 4, as from 1 July 1996; entry "The exchange known as COREDEALMTS" originally inserted by the Insider Dealing (Securities and Regulated Markets) (Amendment) Order 2000, SI 2000/1923, art 2(1), (4)(a), as from 20 July 2000, and substituted by the Insider Dealing (Securities and Regulated Markets) (Amendment) Order 2002, SI 2002/1874, art 2(1), (4)(a) as from 19 July 2002; entry "The exchange known as EASDAQ" inserted, and eighth entry omitted revoked, by SI 2000/1923, art 2(1), (4)(b), (c), as from 20 July 2000; entries "The exchange known as SWX Swiss Exchange" and "virt-x Exchange Limited" inserted by SI 2002/1874, art 2(1), (4)(b), (d) as from 19 July 2002; final entry omitted originally inserted by SI 1996/1561, art 4, as from 1 July 1996, and revoked by SI 2002/1874, art 2(1), (4)(c) as from 19 July 2002.

Note that on 3 March 2008 virt-x Exchange Limited changed its name to SWX Europe Limited and, in mid-2009, SWX Europe Limited merged and became part of SIX Swiss Exchange in Zurich. This Order does not appear to have been amended to reflect this.

FINANCIAL MARKETS AND INSOLVENCY REGULATIONS 1996

(SI 1996/1469)

NOTES

Made: 5 June 1996.

Authority: Companies Act 1989, ss 185, 186.

Commencement: 15 July 1996.

These Regulations are reproduced as amended by: the Uncertificated Securities Regulations 2001, SI 2001/3755; the Enterprise Act 2002 (Insolvency) Order 2003, SI 2003/2096; the Enterprise Act 2002 (Insolvency) Order 2004, SI 2004/2312.

Application to bank insolvency and administration: as to the application of this SI to bank insolvency and administration, see the Banking Act 2009 (Parts 2 and 3 Consequential Amendments) Order 2009, SI 2009/317.

ARRANGEMENT OF REGULATIONS

PART I
GENERAL

PART II
SYSTEM-CHARGES

PART I
GENERAL

[6.34]
1   Citation and commencement

These Regulations may be cited as the Financial Markets and Insolvency Regulations 1996 and shall come into force on 15th July 1996.

[6.35]
2   Interpretation

(1)   In these Regulations—

"the Act" means the Companies Act 1989;

"business day" means any day which is not a Saturday or Sunday, Christmas Day, Good Friday or a bank holiday in any part of the United Kingdom under the Banking and Financial Dealings Act 1971;

"issue", in relation to an uncertificated unit of a security, means to confer on a person title to a new unit;

"register of securities"—

    (a)   in relation to shares, means a register of members; and

    (b)   in relation to units of a security other than shares, means [a register, whether maintained by virtue of the Uncertificated Securities Regulations 2001 or otherwise], of persons holding the units;

. . .

"relevant nominee" means a system-member who is a subsidiary undertaking of the Operator designated by him as such in accordance with such rules and practices as are mentioned in [paragraph 25(f) of Schedule 1 to the Uncertificated Securities Regulations 2001];

"settlement bank" means a person who has contracted with an Operator to make payments in connection with transfers, by means of a relevant system, of title to uncertificated units of a security and of interests of system-beneficiaries in relation to such units;

"system-beneficiary" means a person on whose behalf a system-member or former system-member holds or held uncertificated units of a security;

"system-charge" means a charge of a kind to which regulation 3(2) applies;

"system-member" means a person who is permitted by an Operator to transfer by means of a relevant system title to uncertificated units of a security held by him; and "former system-member" means a person whose participation in the relevant system is terminated or suspended;

"transfer", in relation to title to uncertificated units of a security, means [the registration of a transfer of title to those units in the relevant Operator register of securities;] and in relation to an interest of a system-beneficiary in relation to uncertificated units of a security, means the transfer of the interest to another system-beneficiary by means of a relevant system; and

other expressions used in these Regulations which are also used in [the Uncertificated Securities Regulations 2001] have the same meanings as in those Regulations.

(2)   For the purposes of these Regulations, a person holds a unit of a security if—

    (a)   in the case of an uncertificated unit, he is entered on a register of securities in relation to the unit in accordance with [regulation 20, 21 or 22 of the Uncertificated Securities Regulations 2001]; and

    (b)   in the case of a certificated unit, he has title to the unit.

(3)   A reference in any of these Regulations to a numbered regulation shall be construed as a reference to the regulation bearing that number in these Regulations.

(4)   A reference in any of these Regulations to a numbered paragraph shall, unless the reference is to a paragraph of a specified regulation, be construed as a reference to the paragraph bearing that number in the regulation in which the reference is made.

NOTES

    Para (1): words in square brackets substituted, and definition "the 1995 Regulations" (omitted) revoked, by the Uncertificated Securities Regulations 2001, SI 2001/3755, reg 51, Sch 7, Pt 2, para 20(a), as from 26 November 2001.

    Para (2): words in square brackets substituted by SI 2001/3755, reg 51, Sch 7, Pt 2, para 20(b), as from 26 November 2001.

PART II
SYSTEM-CHARGES

[6.36]
3   Application of Part VII of the Act in relation to system-charges

(1)   Subject to the provisions of these Regulations, Part VII of the Act shall apply in relation to—

    (a)   a charge to which paragraph (2) applies ("a system-charge") and any action taken to enforce such a charge; and

    (b)   any property subject to a system-charge,

in the same way as it applies in relation to a market charge, any action taken to enforce a market charge and any property subject to a market charge.

(2)   This paragraph applies in relation to a charge granted in favour of a settlement bank for the purpose of securing debts or liabilities arising in connection with any of the following—

- (a)   a transfer of uncertificated units of a security to a system-member by means of a relevant system whether the system-member is acting for himself or on behalf of a system-beneficiary;
- (b)   a transfer, by one system-beneficiary to another and by means of a relevant system, of his interests in relation to uncertificated units of a security held by a relevant nominee where the relevant nominee will continue to hold the units;
- (c)   an agreement to make a transfer of the kind specified in paragraph (a);
- (d)   an agreement to make a transfer of the kind specified in paragraph (b); and
- (e)   an issue of uncertificated units of a security to a system-member by means of a relevant system whether the system-member is acting for himself or on behalf of a system-beneficiary.

(3)   In its application, by virtue of these Regulations, in relation to a system-charge, section 173(2) of the Act shall have effect as if the references to "purposes specified" and "specified purposes" were references to any one or more of the purposes specified in paragraph (2).

[6.37]

4   Circumstances in which Part VII applies in relation to system-charge

(1)   Part VII of the Act shall apply in relation to a system-charge granted by a system-member and in relation to property subject to such a charge only if—

- (a)   it is granted to a settlement bank by a system-member for the purpose of securing debts or liabilities arising in connection with any of the transactions specified in regulation 3(2), being debts or liabilities incurred by that system-member or by a system-beneficiary on whose behalf he holds uncertificated units of a security; and
- (b)   it contains provisions which refer expressly to the relevant system in relation to which the grantor is a system-member.

(2)   Part VII of the Act shall apply in relation to a system-charge granted by a system-beneficiary and in relation to property subject to such a charge only if—

- (a)   it is granted to a settlement bank by a system-beneficiary for the purpose of securing debts or liabilities arising in connection with any of the transactions specified in regulation 3(2), incurred by that system-beneficiary or by a system-member who holds uncertificated units of a security on his behalf; and
- (b)   it contains provisions which refer expressly to the relevant system in relation to which the system-member who holds the uncertificated units of a security in relation to which the system-beneficiary has the interest is a system-member.

[6.38]

5   Extent to which Part VII applies to a system-charge

Part VII of the Act shall apply in relation to a system-charge only to the extent that—

- (a)   it is a charge over any one or more of the following—
  - (i)   uncertificated units of a security held by a system-member or a former system-member;
  - (ii)   interests of a kind specified in [regulation 31(2)(b) or 31(4)(b) of the Uncertificated Securities Regulations 2001] in uncertificated units of a security in favour of a system member or a former system-member;
  - (iii)   interests of a system-beneficiary in relation to uncertificated units of a security;
  - (iv)   units of a security which are no longer in uncertificated form because the person holding the units has become a former system-member;
  - (v)   sums or other benefits receivable by a system-member or former system-member by reason of his holding uncertificated units of a security, or units which are no longer in uncertificated form because the person holding the units has become a former system-member;
  - (vi)   sums or other benefits receivable by a system-beneficiary by reason of his having an interest in relation to uncertificated units of a security or in relation to units which are no longer in uncertificated form because the person holding the units has become a former system-member;
  - (vii)   sums or other benefits receivable by a system-member or former system-member by way of repayment, bonus, preference, redemption, conversion or accruing or offered in respect of uncertificated units of a security, or units which are no longer in uncertificated form because the person holding the units has become a former system-member;
  - (viii)   sums or other benefits receivable by a system-beneficiary by way of repayment, bonus, preference, redemption, conversion or accruing or offered in respect of uncertificated units of a security in relation to which he has an interest or in respect

of units in relation to which the system-beneficiary has an interest and which are no longer in uncertificated form because the person holding the units has become a former system-member;

(ix)   sums or other benefits receivable by a system-member or former system-member in respect of the transfer of uncertificated units of a security by or to him by means of a relevant system;

(x)   sums or other benefits receivable by a system-member or former system-member in respect of an agreement to transfer uncertificated units of a security by or to him by means of a relevant system;

(xi)   sums or other benefits receivable by a system-beneficiary in respect of the transfer of the interest of a system-beneficiary in relation to uncertificated units of a security by or to him by means of a relevant system or in respect of the transfer of uncertificated units of a security by or to a system-member acting on his behalf by means of a relevant system;

(xii) sums or other benefits receivable by a system-beneficiary in respect of an agreement to transfer the interest of a system-beneficiary in relation to uncertificated units of a security by or to him by means of a relevant system, or in respect of an agreement to transfer uncertificated units of a security by or to a system-member acting on his behalf by means of a relevant system; and

(b)   it secures—

(i)   the obligation of a system-member or former system-member to reimburse a settlement bank, being an obligation which arises in connection with any of the transactions specified in regulation 3(2) and whether the obligation was incurred by the system-member when acting for himself or when acting on behalf of a system-beneficiary; or

(ii)   the obligation of a system-beneficiary to reimburse a settlement bank, being an obligation which arises in connection with any of the transactions specified in regulation 3(2) and whether the obligation was incurred by the system-beneficiary when acting for himself or by reason of a system-member acting on his behalf.

NOTES

Words in square brackets in sub-para (a)(ii) substituted by the Uncertificated Securities Regulations 2001, SI 2001/3755, reg 51, Sch 7, Pt 2, para 20(c), as from 26 November 2001.

[6.39]

6   [Limitation on disapplication of moratorium on certain legal processes under Schedule B1 to the Insolvency Act 1986 (administration) in relation to system-charges]

(1)   This regulation applies where an administration order is made in relation to a system-member or former system-member.

[(1A)   A reference in paragraph (1) to "an administration order" shall include the appointment of an administrator under paragraph 14 or 22 of Schedule B1 to the Insolvency Act 1986].

(2)   [The disapplication of paragraph 43(2) of Schedule B1 to the Insolvency Act 1986 (including that provision as applied by paragraph 44 of that Schedule)] by section 175(1)(a) of the Act shall have effect, in relation to a system-charge granted by a system-member or former system-member, only to the extent necessary to enable there to be realised, whether through the sale of uncertificated units of a security or otherwise, the lesser of the two sums specified in paragraphs (3) and (4).

(3)   The first sum of the two sums referred to in paragraph (2) is the net sum of—

(a)   all payment obligations discharged by the settlement bank in connection with—

(i)   transfers of uncertificated units of a security by means of a relevant system made during the qualifying period to or by the relevant system-member or former system-member, whether acting for himself or on behalf of a system-beneficiary;

(ii)   agreements made during the qualifying period to transfer uncertificated units of a security by means of a relevant system to or from the relevant system-member or former system-member, whether acting for himself or on behalf of a system-beneficiary; and

(iii) issues of uncertificated units of a security by means of a relevant system made during the qualifying period to the relevant system-member or former system-member, whether acting for himself or on behalf of a system-beneficiary; less

(b)   all payment obligations discharged to the settlement bank in connection with transactions of any kind described in paragraph (3)(a)(i) and (ii).

(4)   The second of the two sums referred to in paragraph (2) is the sum (if any) due to the settlement bank from the relevant system-member or former system-member by reason of an obligation of the kind described in regulation 5(b)(i).

(5)   In this regulation and regulation 7, "qualifying period" means the period—

(a)   beginning with the fifth business day before the day on which [an application] for the making of the administration order was presented; and

(b)   ending with the second business day after the day on which the administration order is made.

[(5A)　A reference in paragraph (5) to an application for an administration order shall be treated as including a reference to—

(a)　appointing an administrator under [paragraph 14] or 22 of Schedule B1 to the Insolvency Act 1986, or

(b)　filing with the court a notice of intention to appoint an administrator under either of those paragraphs,

and a reference to "an administration order" shall include the appointment of an administrator under paragraph 14 or 22 of Schedule B1 to the Insolvency Act 1986.]

NOTES

Regulation heading: substituted by the Enterprise Act 2002 (Insolvency) Order 2003, SI 2003/2096, arts 5, 6, Schedule, Pt 2, paras 61, 62(a), as from 15 September 2003, except in relation to any case where a petition for an administration order was presented before that date.

Para (1A): inserted by SI 2003/2096, arts 5, 6, Schedule, Pt 2, paras 61, 62(b), as from 15 September 2003, except in relation to any case where a petition for an administration order was presented before that date.

Paras (2), (5): words in square brackets substituted by SI 2003/2096, arts 5, 6, Schedule, Pt 2, paras 61, 62(c), (d), as from 15 September 2003, except in relation to any case where a petition for an administration order was presented before that date.

Para (5A): added by SI 2003/2096, arts 5, 6, Schedule, Pt 2, paras 61, 62(e), as from 15 September 2003, except in relation to any case where a petition for an administration order was presented before that date; words in square brackets substituted by the Enterprise Act 2002 (Insolvency) Order 2004, SI 2004/2312, art 3, as from 15 October 2004.

[6.40]

7　[Limitation on disapplication of moratorium on certain legal processes under Schedule B1 to the Insolvency Act 1986 (administration) in relation to system-charges granted by a system-beneficiary]

(1)　This regulation applies where an administration order is made in relation to a system-beneficiary.

[(1A)　A reference in paragraph (1) to "an administration order" shall include the appointment of an administrator under paragraph 14 or 22 of Schedule B1 to the Insolvency Act 1986].

(2)　[The disapplication of paragraph 43(2) of Schedule B1 to the Insolvency Act 1986 (including that provision as applied by paragraph 44 of that Schedule)] by section 175(1)(a) of the Act shall have effect, in relation to a system-charge granted by a system-beneficiary, only to the extent necessary to enable there to be realised, whether through the sale of interests of a system-beneficiary in relation to uncertificated units of a security or otherwise, the lesser of the two sums specified in paragraphs (3) and (4).

(3)　The first of the two sums referred to in paragraph (2) is the net sum of—

(a)　all payment obligations discharged by the settlement bank in connection with—

(i)　transfers, to or by the relevant system-beneficiary by means of a relevant system made during the qualifying period, of interests of the system-beneficiary in relation to uncertificated units of a security held by a relevant nominee, where the relevant nominee has continued to hold the units;

(ii)　agreements made during the qualifying period to transfer, to or from the relevant system-beneficiary by means of a relevant system, interests of the system-beneficiary in relation to uncertificated units of a security held by a relevant nominee, where the relevant nominee will continue to hold the units;

(iii)　transfers, during the qualifying period and by means of a relevant system, of uncertificated units of a security, being transfers made to or by a system-member acting on behalf of the relevant system-beneficiary;

(iv)　agreements made during the qualifying period to transfer uncertificated units of a security by means of a relevant system to or from a system-member acting on behalf of the relevant system-beneficiary; and

(v)　issues of uncertificated units of a security made during the qualifying period and by means of a relevant system, being issues to a system-member acting on behalf of the relevant system-beneficiary; less

(b)　all payment obligations discharged to the settlement bank in connection with transactions of any kind described in paragraph (3)(a)(i) to (iv).

(4)　The second of the two sums referred to in paragraph (2) is the sum (if any) due to the settlement bank from the relevant system-beneficiary by reason of an obligation of the kind described in regulation 5(b)(ii).

NOTES

Regulation heading: substituted by the Enterprise Act 2002 (Insolvency) Order 2003, SI 2003/2096, arts 5, 6, Schedule, Pt 2, paras 61, 63(a), as from 15 September 2003, except in relation to any case where a petition for an administration order was presented before that date.

Para (1A): inserted by SI 2003/2096, arts 5, 6, Schedule, Pt 2, paras 61, 63(b), as from 15 September 2003, except in relation to any case where a petition for an administration order was presented before that date.

Para (2): words in square brackets substituted by SI 2003/2096, arts 5, 6, Schedule, Pt 2, paras 61, 63(c), as from 15 September 2003, except in relation to any case where a petition for an administration order was presented before that date.

[6.41]

8   Ability of administrator or receiver to recover assets in case of property subject to system-charge

(1)   This regulation applies where an administration order is made or an administrator or an administrative receiver or a receiver is appointed, in relation to a system-member, former system-member or system-beneficiary.

[(1A)   A reference in paragraph (1) to "an administration order" shall include the appointment of an administrator under paragraph 14 or 22 of Schedule B1 to the Insolvency Act 1986.]

(2)   [The disapplication—

 (a)   by section 175(1)(b) of the Act, of paragraphs 70, 71 and 72 of Schedule B1 to the Insolvency Act 1986, and

 (b)   by section 175(3) of the Act, of sections 43 and 61 of the 1986 Act,

shall cease to have effect] after the end of the relevant day in respect of any property which is subject to a system-charge granted by the system-member, former system-member or system-beneficiary if on the basis of a valuation in accordance with paragraph (3), the charge is not required for the realisation of the sum specified in paragraph (4) or (5).

(3)   For the purposes of paragraph (2), the value of property shall, except in a case falling within paragraph (6), be such as may be agreed between the administrator, administrative receiver or receiver on the one hand and the settlement bank on the other.

(4)   Where the system-charge has been granted by a system-member or former system-member, the sum referred to in paragraph (2) is whichever is the lesser of—

 (a)   the sum referred to in regulation 6(3);

 (b)   the sum referred to in regulation 6(4) due to the settlement bank at the close of business on the relevant day.

(5)   Where the system-charge has been granted by a system-beneficiary, the sum referred to in paragraph (2) is whichever is the lesser of—

 (a)   the sum referred to in regulation 7(3);

 (b)   the sum referred to in regulation 7(4) due to the settlement bank at the close of business on the relevant day.

(6)   For the purposes of paragraph (2), the value of any property for which a price for the relevant day is quoted in the Daily Official List of The London Stock Exchange Limited shall—

 (a)   in a case in which two prices are so quoted, be an amount equal to the average of those two prices, adjusted where appropriate to take account of any accrued dividend or interest; and

 (b)   in a case in which one price is so quoted, be an amount equal to that price, adjusted where appropriate to take account of any accrued dividend or interest.

(7)   In this regulation "the relevant day" means the second business day after the day on which the [company enters administration], or the administrative receiver or receiver is appointed.

NOTES

Para (1A): inserted by the Enterprise Act 2002 (Insolvency) Order 2003, SI 2003/2096, arts 5, 6, Schedule, Pt 2, paras 61, 64(a), as from 15 September 2003, except in relation to any case where a petition for an administration order was presented before that date.

Paras (2), (7): words in square brackets substituted by SI 2003/2096, arts 5, 6, Schedule, Pt 2, paras 61, 64(b), (c), as from 15 September 2003, except in relation to any case where a petition for an administration order was presented before that date.

9   ((*Pt III*) *spent; amended CA 1989, s 156 (repealed).*)

UNCERTIFICATED SECURITIES REGULATIONS 2001

(SI 2001/3755)

NOTES

Made: 23 November 2001.

Authority: Companies Act 1989, s 207. Note that s 207 is repealed by the Companies Act 2006, s 1295, Sch 16, as from 6 April 2008. By virtue of s 1297 of that Act at **[1.1297]** (continuity of law) these Regulations have effect as if made under ss 784(3), 785 and 788 of the 2006 Act.

Commencement: 26 November 2001.

These Regulations are reproduced as amended by: the Enterprise Act 2002 (Consequential and Supplemental Provisions) Order 2003, SI 2003/1398; the Uncertificated Securities (Amendment) (Eligible Debt Securities) Regulations 2003, SI 2003/1633; the Enterprise Act 2002 and Media Mergers (Consequential Amendments) Order 2003, SI 2003/3180; the Government Stock (Consequential and Transitional Provision) (No 2) Order 2004, SI 2004/1662; the Local Authorities (Capital Finance) (Further Consequential and Saving Provisions) Order 2004, SI 2004/2044; the Capital Requirements Regulations 2006, SI 2006/3221; the Uncertificated Securities (Amendment) Regulations 2007, SI 2007/124; the Companies Act 2006 (Commencement No 2, Consequential Amendments, Transitional Provisions and Savings) Order 2007, SI 2007/1093; the Companies Act 2006 (Commencement No 3, Consequential Amendments, Transitional Provisions and Savings) Order 2007, SI 2007/2194; the Companies Act 2006 (Consequential Amendments) (Uncertificated Securities) Order 2009, SI 2009/1889; the Capital Requirements (Amendment) Regulations 2010, SI 2010/2628.

References to "the European Community", "Community", etc: see the Treaty of Lisbon (Changes in Terminology) Order 2011, SI 2011/1043, which provides that (as from 22 April 2011) "EU" should be substituted for the word "Community" (subject to certain exceptions) in references to "Community treaties", "Community instrument", "Community obligation", "Community law", "Community legislation", etc.

Limited liability partnerships: this Order applies, with modifications, to limited liability partnerships; see the Limited Liability Partnerships Regulations 2001, SI 2001/1090, reg 10, Sch 6, Pt III (at **[10.830]**), and the Interpretation Act 1978, ss 17(2)(a), 23(1), (2).

Part 6   Pre-2006 companies SIs

ARRANGEMENT OF REGULATIONS

PART 1
CITATION, COMMENCEMENT AND INTERPRETATION

PART 2
THE OPERATOR

Approval and compliance

Supervision

Miscellaneous

PART 3
PARTICIPATING SECURITIES

Participation by issuers

Keeping of registers and records

Conversions and new issues

PART 4
DEMATERIALISED INSTRUCTIONS ETC

PART 5

MISCELLANEOUS AND SUPPLEMENTAL

Miscellaneous

Defaults and contraventions

Amendments and revocations

SCHEDULES

PART 1

CITATION, COMMENCEMENT, AND INTERPRETATION

[6.42]

1   Citation and commencement

These Regulations may be cited as the Uncertificated Securities Regulations 2001 and shall come into force on 26th November 2001.

[6.43]

2   Purposes and basic definition

(1)   These Regulations enable title to units of a security to be evidenced otherwise than by a certificate and transferred otherwise than by a written instrument, and make provision for certain supplementary and incidental matters; and in these Regulations "relevant system" means a computer-based system, and procedures, which enable title to units of a security to be evidenced and transferred without a written instrument, and which facilitate supplementary and incidental matters.

(2)   Where a title to a unit of a security is evidenced otherwise than by a certificate by virtue of these Regulations, the transfer of title to such a unit of a security shall be subject to these Regulations.

[6.44]

3   Interpretation

(1)   In these Regulations—

["the 1877 Act" means the Treasury Bills Act 1877;
   "the 1950 Act" means the Exchequer and Financial Provisions Act (Northern Ireland) 1950;]

. . .

"the 1986 Act" means the Financial Services Act 1986;
[. . .]
"the 2000 Act" means the Financial Services and Markets Act 2000;
["the 2006 Act" means the Companies Act 2006;];

. . .

["the 1968 Regulations" means the Treasury Bills Regulations 1968;]
"the 1974 Regulations" means the Local Authority (Stocks and Bonds) Regulations 1974;

. . .

[. . .]
"the 1995 Regulations" means the Uncertificated Securities Regulations 1995;

["the 2003 Regulations" means the Uncertificated Securities (Amendment) (Eligible Debt Securities) Regulations 2003;]

["the 2004 Regulations" means the Government Stock Regulations 2004;]

"the Authority" means the Financial Services Authority referred to in section 1 of the 2000 Act;

"certificate" means any certificate, instrument or other document of, or evidencing, title to units of a security;

"company" means a company within the meaning of [section 1(1) of the 2006 Act];

"dematerialised instruction" means an instruction sent or received by means of a relevant system;
[. . .]

"designated agency" has the meaning given by regulation 11(1);

["eligible debt security" means—

    (a)   a security that satisfies the following conditions—

        (i)   the security is constituted by an order, promise, engagement or acknowledgement to pay on demand, or at a determinable future time, a sum in money to, or to the order of, the holder of one or more units of the security; and

        (ii) the current terms of issue of the security provide that its units may only be held in uncertificated form and title to them may only be transferred by means of a relevant system;

    (b)   an eligible Northern Ireland Treasury Bill; or

    (c)   an eligible Treasury bill;

"eligible Northern Ireland Treasury Bill" means a security—

    (a)   constituted by a Northern Ireland Treasury Bill issued in accordance with the 1950 Act as modified by Part 2 of Schedule 1 to the 2003 Regulations; and

    (b)   whose current terms of issue provide that its units may only be held in uncertificated form and title to them may only be transferred by means of a relevant system;

"eligible Treasury bill" means a security—

    (a)   constituted by a Treasury bill issued in accordance with the 1877 Act and the 1968 Regulations as modified by Part 1 of Schedule 1 to the 2003 Regulations; and

    (b)   whose current terms of issue provide that its units may only be held in uncertificated form and title to them may only be transferred by means of a relevant system;]

"enactment" includes an enactment comprised in any subordinate legislation within the meaning of the Interpretation Act 1978, and an enactment comprised in, or in an instrument made under, an Act of the Scottish Parliament;

["general local authority security" means a local authority security that is not an eligible debt security;

"general public sector security" means a public sector security that is not an eligible debt security;

"general UK Government security" means a UK Government security that is not an eligible debt security;]

"generate", in relation to an Operator-instruction, means to initiate the procedures by which the Operator-instruction comes to be sent;

"guidance", in relation to an Operator, means guidance issued by him which is intended to have continuing effect and is issued in writing or other legible form, which if it were a rule, would come within the definition of a rule;

"instruction" includes any instruction, election, acceptance or any other message of any kind;

"interest in a security" means any legal or equitable interest or right in relation to a security, including—

    (a)   an absolute or contingent right to acquire a security created, allotted or issued or to be created, allotted or issued; and

    (b)   the interests or rights of a person for whom a security is held on trust or by a custodian or depositary;

"issue", in relation to a new unit of a security, means to confer title to a new unit on a person;

"issuer-instruction" means a properly authenticated dematerialised instruction attributable to a participating issuer;

"issuer register of members" has the meaning given by regulation 20(1)(a);

"issuer register of securities"—

    (a)   in relation to shares, means an issuer register of members; and

    [(b)   in relation to units of securities other than—

        (i)   shares,

        (ii) securities in respect of which regulation 22(3) applies, or

        (iii) wholly dematerialised securities,

means a register of persons holding the units, maintained by or on behalf of the issuer or, in the case of general public sector securities, by or on behalf of the person specified in regulation 21(3);]

["local authority"—

    (a)   in relation to a security referred to in paragraph (a)(i) of the definition of "local authority security", has the same meaning as in the 1974 Regulations;

[(b)   in relation to a security referred to in paragraph (b) of the definition of "local authority security", has the same meaning as in section 23 of the Local Government Act 2003 ("local authority");]

["local authority security" means a security which is either—

(a)   a security other than an eligible debt security which, when held in certificated form is—

    (i)   transferable in accordance with regulation 7(1) of the 1974 Regulations and title to which must be registered in accordance with regulation 5 of those Regulations; or

    (ii)   . . .

(b)   an eligible debt security issued by a local authority;]

"officer", in relation to an Operator or a participating issuer, includes—

(a)   where the Operator or the participating issuer is a company, such persons as are mentioned in [section 1173(1) of the 2006 Act];

(b)   where the Operator or the participating issuer is a partnership, a partner; or in the event that no partner is situated in the United Kingdom, a person in the United Kingdom who is acting on behalf of a partner; and

(c)   where the Operator or the participating issuer is neither a company nor a partnership, any member of its governing body; or in the event that no member of its governing body is situated in the United Kingdom, a person in the United Kingdom who is acting on behalf of any member of its governing body;

"Operator" means a person approved by the Treasury under these Regulations as Operator of a relevant system (and in Schedule 1 includes a person who has applied to the Treasury under regulation 4 for their approval of him as an Operator);

"Operator-instruction" means a properly authenticated dematerialised instruction attributable to an Operator;

"Operator register of corporate securities" has the meaning given by regulation 22(2)(a)(i);

["Operator register of eligible debt securities" has the meaning given by regulation 22(3A)(a);

"Operator register of general public sector securities" has the meaning given by regulation 21(1)(a);]

"Operator register of members" has the meaning given by regulation 20(1)(b);

. . .

"Operator register of securities"—

(a)   in relation to shares, means an Operator register of members;

(b)   in relation to units of a security other than shares, means an Operator register of corporate securities, an Operator register of [general public sector securities, an Operator register of eligible debt securities or, as the case may be, a register maintained by an Operator in accordance with regulation 22(3)(a)];

"Operator's conversion rules" means the rules made and practices instituted by the Operator in order to comply with paragraph 18 of Schedule 1;

"Operator-system" means those facilities and procedures which are part of the relevant system, which are maintained and operated by or for an Operator, by which he generates Operator-instructions and receives dematerialised instructions from system-participants and by which persons change the form in which units of a participating security are held;

"participating issuer" means (subject to paragraph (3)) a person who has issued a security which is a participating security;

"participating security" means a security title to units of which is permitted by an Operator to be transferred by means of a relevant system;

"public sector securities" means UK Government securities and local authority securities;

["record of uncertificated general public sector securities" has the meaning given by regulation 21(2)(a);]

"record of securities" means any of a record of uncertificated corporate securities, a record of uncertificated shares and a record of uncertificated [general public sector securities];

"record of uncertificated corporate securities" has the meaning given by regulation 22(2)(b)(ii);

"record of uncertificated shares" has the meaning given by regulation 20(6)(a);

"register of members" means either or both of an issuer register of members and an Operator register of members;

"register of securities" means either or both of an issuer register of securities and an Operator register of securities;

"relevant system" has the meaning given by regulation 2(1); and "relevant system" includes an Operator-system;

"rules", in relation to an Operator, means rules made or conditions imposed by him with respect to the provision of the relevant system;

"securities" means shares, stock, debentures, debenture stock, loan stock, bonds, units of a collective investment scheme within the meaning of section 235 of the 2000 Act, rights under a depositary receipt within the meaning of paragraph 4 of Schedule 2 to the Criminal Justice Act 1993, and other securities of any description, and interests in a security;

"settlement", [except in paragraph 28 of Schedule 1,] in relation to a transfer of uncertificated units of a security between two system-members by means of a relevant system, means the delivery of those units to the transferee and, where appropriate, the creation of any associated obligation to make payments, in accordance with the rules and practices of the Operator; and "settle" shall be construed accordingly;

"settlement bank", in relation to a relevant system, means a person who has contracted to make payments in connection with transfers of title to uncertificated units of a security by means of that system;

"share" means share (or stock) in the share capital of a company;

"system-member", in relation to a relevant system, means a person who is permitted by an Operator to transfer by means of that system title to uncertificated units of a security held by him, and shall include, where relevant, two or more persons who are jointly so permitted;

"system-member instruction" means a properly authenticated dematerialised instruction attributable to a system-member;

"system-participant", in relation to a relevant system, means a person who is permitted by an Operator to send and receive properly authenticated dematerialised instructions; and "sponsoring system-participant" means a system-participant who is permitted by an Operator to send properly authenticated dematerialised instructions attributable to another person and to receive properly authenticated dematerialised instructions on another person's behalf;

"system-user", in relation to a relevant system, means a person who as regards that system is a participating issuer, a system-member, system-participant or settlement bank;

"UK Government security" means a security issued by Her Majesty's Government in the United Kingdom or by a Northern Ireland department;

"uncertificated", in relation to a unit of a security, means (subject to Regulation 42(11)(a)) that title to the unit is recorded on the relevant Operator register of securities, and may, by virtue of these Regulations, be transferred by means of a relevant system; and "certificated", in relation to a unit of a security, means that the unit is not an uncertificated unit;

"unit", in relation to a security, means the smallest possible transferable unit of the security (for example a single share);

"wholly dematerialised security" means—

(a)   a strip, in relation to any stock or bond, within the meaning of section 47(1B) of the Finance Act 1942; or

(b)   a participating security whose terms of issue (or, in the case of shares, where its terms of issue or the articles of association of the company in question) provide that its units may only be held in uncertificated form and title to them may only be transferred by means of a relevant system;

and other expressions have the meanings given to them by the [Companies Acts (as defined by section 2 of the 2006 Act)].

(2)   For the purposes of these Regulations—

(a)   a dematerialised instruction is properly authenticated if it complies with the specifications referred to in paragraph 5(3) of Schedule 1; or if it was given, and not withdrawn, before these Regulations came into force and was properly authenticated within the meaning of regulation 3(2)(a) of the 1995 Regulations;

(b)   a dematerialised instruction is attributable to a person if it is expressed to have been sent by that person, or if it is expressed to have been sent on behalf of that person, in accordance with the rules and specifications referred to in paragraph 5(4) of Schedule 1; and a dematerialised instruction may be attributable to more than one person.

(3)   In respect of a participating security which is a [general] public sector security, references in these Regulations to the participating issuer shall, other than in Regulation 41, be taken to be references—

(a)   in the case of a local authority security—

(i)   to the relevant local authority; or

(ii)   if the local authority has appointed another person to act as registrar for the purpose of the 1974 Regulations in respect of that security, to the person so appointed [. . .

(iii)   . . .]; and

(b)   in the case of any other [general] public sector security, to [the Registrar of Government Stock].

[(4)   In respect of a security which is an eligible debt security, references in these regulations to the issuer or the participating issuer of that security (or units of that security) shall be taken to be references to—

(a)   a person ("P") who undertakes as principal to perform the payment obligation constituted by the security in accordance with its current terms of issue; and

(b)   any other person who undertakes as principal to perform that obligation in accordance with those terms in the event that P fails to do so.

(5)   For the purposes of paragraph (4)(b), a person who undertakes to perform an obligation under a contract of guarantee or other contract of suretyship is not to be regarded as undertaking to perform it as principal.

(6)   For the purposes of paragraph (a) of the definition of "eligible debt security" in paragraph (1), a sum of money—

(a)   is to be regarded as payable at a determinable future time if it is payable—

    (i)   at a future time fixed by or in accordance with the current terms of issue of the security; or

    (ii)   at the expiry of a fixed period after the occurrence of a specified event which is certain to happen, though the time of happening may be uncertain; and

(b)   is not to be regarded as payable at a determinable future time if it is payable on a contingency.]

NOTES

Para (1) is amended as follows:

Definitions "the 1877 Act", "the 1950 Act", "the 1968 Regulations", "the 2003 Regulations", "eligible debt security", "eligible Northern Ireland Treasury Bill", "eligible Treasury bill", "general local authority security", "general public sector security", "general UK Government security", "local authority", "Operator register of eligible debt securities" and "Operator register of general public sector securities" inserted, words omitted from definition "the 1974 Regulations", and the definition "Operator register of public sector securities" (omitted) revoked, words in square brackets in definitions "issuer register of securities", "Operator register of securities" and "record of securities" substituted, and definition "record of uncertificated general public sector securities" substituted (for original definition "record of uncertificated public sector securities"), by the Uncertificated Securities (Amendment) (Eligible Debt Securities) Regulations 2003, SI 2003/1633, reg 3, as from 24 June 2003.

Definitions "the 1985 Act" and "the 1986 Order" (omitted) revoked, definition "the 2006 Act" inserted, and words in square brackets in the definitions "company" and "officer" and the final words in square brackets substituted, by the Companies Act 2006 (Consequential Amendments) (Uncertificated Securities) Order 2009, SI 2009/1889, art 2(1), (2), as from 1 October 2009.

Definitions "the 1989 Act", "the 1990 Regulations" and "dematerialised loan instrument" (omitted) inserted by SI 2003/1633, reg 3, as from 24 June 2003, and revoked by the Local Authorities (Capital Finance) (Further Consequential and Saving Provisions) Order 2004, SI 2004/2044, art 6(1)(a), as from 1 October 2004.

Definition "the 1965 Regulations" (omitted) revoked, and definition "the 2004 Regulations" inserted, by the Government Stock (Consequential and Transitional Provision) (No 2) Order 2004, SI 2004/1662, art 2, Schedule, Pt 3, para 29(1), (2)(a), as from 1 July 2004.

In definition "local authority" para (b) substituted by SI 2004/2044, art 6(1)(b), as from 1 October 2004.

Definition "local authority security" substituted by SI 2003/1633, reg 3, as from 24 June 2003; para (a)(ii) revoked by SI 2004/2044, art 6(1)(c), as from 1 October 2004.

Words in square brackets in definition "settlement" inserted by the Uncertificated Securities (Amendment) Regulations 2007, SI 2007/124, reg 2, as from 1 November 2007.

Para (3): the word "general" in square brackets in both places it occurs inserted by SI 2003/1633, reg 4(1)(a), as from 24 June 2003; para (a)(iii) and the word immediately preceding it originally inserted by SI 2003/1633, reg 4(1)(b), as from 24 June 2003, and revoked by SI 2004/2044, art 6(1)(d), as from 1 October 2004; words in final pair of square brackets substituted by SI 2004/1662, art 2, Schedule, Pt 3, para 29(1), (2)(b), as from 1 July 2004.

Paras (4)–(6): added by SI 2003/1633, reg 4(2), as from 24 June 2003.

Note: in the original Queen's Printer's copy of these Regulations there were two definitions of "record of securities" in para (1) above. It is believed that the second one (ie, the one that followed the definition "register of members") should be the definition "*register* of securities". The above text has been changed accordingly, but no correction slip has been issued to confirm this.

Financial Services Act 1986: repealed by the Financial Services and Markets Act 2000 (Consequential Amendments and Repeals) Order 2001, SI 2001/3649, art 3(1)(c), as from 1 December 2001.

Uncertificated Securities Regulations 1995, SI 1995/3272: revoked by these Regulations.

PART 2
THE OPERATOR

Approval and compliance

[6.45]
4   Applications for approval

(1)   Any person may apply to the Treasury for their approval of him as Operator of a relevant system.

(2)   The application shall be made in such manner as the Treasury may direct and shall be accompanied by—

(a)   a copy of the rules and any guidance to be issued by the applicant; and

(b)   such other information as the Treasury may reasonably require for the purpose of determining the application.

(3)   At any time after receiving an application and before determining it, the Treasury may require the applicant to provide such further information as they reasonably consider necessary to enable them to determine the application.

(4)   Information which the Treasury require under this regulation shall, if they so require, be provided in such form, or verified in such manner, as they may direct.

(5)   Different directions may be given, or requirements imposed, by the Treasury with respect to different applications.

[6.46]
5 Grant and refusal of approval

(1)   If, on an application made under regulation 4, it appears to the Treasury that the requirements of Schedule 1 (which imposes requirements which must appear to the Treasury to be satisfied with respect to an Operator, his rules and practices and the relevant system) are satisfied with respect to the application, they may—

    (a)   subject to the payment of any fee charged by virtue of regulation 6(1); and

    (b)   subject to the provisions of Schedule 2,

approve the applicant as Operator of a relevant system.

(2)   In considering an application, the Treasury may have regard to any information which they consider is relevant to the application.

(3)   An approval under this regulation shall be by instrument in writing and shall state the date on which it is to take effect.

(4)   Schedule 3 shall have effect in relation to a decision to refuse an application made under regulation 4 as if references to an Operator were to the applicant.

(5)   Provided that it had not been withdrawn before these Regulations came into force, an approval granted to a person under regulation 5 of the 1995 Regulations shall be treated as having been granted under this regulation.

[6.47]
6 Fees charged by the Treasury

(1)   The Treasury may charge a fee to a person seeking approval as Operator of a relevant system.

(2)   The Treasury may charge an Operator a periodical fee.

(3)   Any fee chargeable by the Treasury under this regulation shall not exceed an amount which reasonably represents the amount of costs incurred—

    (a)   in the case of a fee charged to a person seeking approval, in determining whether to grant approval; and

    (b)   in the case of a periodical fee, in satisfying themselves that the Operator, his rules and practices and the relevant system continue to meet the requirements of Schedule 1 and that the Operator is complying with any obligations imposed on him by or under these Regulations.

(4)   For the purposes of paragraph (3), the costs incurred by the Treasury shall be determined on the basis that they include such proportion of the following matters as are properly attributable to the performance of the relevant function—

    (a)   expenditure on staff, equipment, premises, facilities, research and development;

    (b)   the allocation, over a period of years, whether before or after the coming into force of these Regulations, of any initial expenditure incurred wholly and exclusively to perform the function or to prepare for its performance;

    (c)   any notional interest incurred on any capital expended on or in connection with the performance of the function or in preparing for its performance and, in a case in which any function is exercisable by the designated agency, any actual interest payable on any sums borrowed which have been so expended; and

    (d)   any other matter which, in accordance with generally accepted accounting principles, may properly be taken account of in ascertaining the costs properly attributable to the performance of the function.

(5)   For the purposes of paragraph (4)(c)—

    (a)   "notional interest" means any interest which that person might reasonably have been expected to have been liable to pay had the sums expended been borrowed at arm's length; and

    (b)   "actual interest" means the actual interest paid on sums borrowed in a transaction at arm's length and, where a sum has been borrowed otherwise than in such a transaction, means whichever is the lesser of the interest actually paid and the interest that might reasonably have been expected to be paid had the transaction been at arm's length.

(6)   Any fee received by the Treasury under this regulation shall be paid into the Consolidated Fund.

(7)   Any fee received by the designated agency under this regulation may be retained by it.

Supervision

[6.48]
7 Withdrawal of approval

(1)   The Treasury may withdraw an Operator's approval at the request, or with the consent, of the Operator.

(2)   If it appears to the Treasury that—

    (a)   any requirement of Schedule 1 is not satisfied in relation to an Operator; or

    (b)   an Operator is failing or has failed to comply with any obligation imposed on him by or under these Regulations, they may withdraw approval from that Operator by written instrument even though the Operator does not wish his approval to be withdrawn.

(3)   Schedule 3 shall have effect as regards the procedure to be followed before withdrawing an Operator's approval under paragraph (2).

(4)   An instrument withdrawing an Operator's approval shall state the date on which it is to take effect.

(5)   In the case of an instrument withdrawing an Operator's approval under paragraph (2), the date stated shall not be earlier than the end of the period of three months beginning with the day on which the instrument is executed.

(6)   An instrument withdrawing an Operator's approval may contain such transitional provisions as the Treasury think necessary or expedient.

[6.49]
8   Compliance orders and directions
(1)   This regulation applies if it appears to the Treasury that—
  (a)   any requirement of Schedule 1 is not satisfied, or is likely not to be satisfied, in relation to an Operator; or
  (b)   an Operator has failed to comply with any obligation imposed on him by or under these Regulations.

(2)   The Treasury may—
  (a)   make an application to the court; or
  (b)   subject to paragraph (4), direct the Operator to take specified steps for the purpose of securing—
    (i)   that the relevant requirement of Schedule 1 is satisfied in relation to the Operator; or
    (ii)   the Operator's compliance with any obligation of the kind in question.

(3)   If on any application by the Treasury under paragraph (2)(a) the court is satisfied that the relevant requirement of Schedule 1 is not satisfied or is likely not to be satisfied, or, as the case may be, that the Operator has failed to comply with the obligation in question, it may order the Operator to take such steps as the court directs for securing that the requirement is satisfied or that the obligation is complied with.

(4)   Schedule 3 shall have effect as regards the procedure to be followed before giving a direction under paragraph (2)(b).

(5)   A direction under paragraph (2)(b) is enforceable, on the application of the Treasury, by an injunction or, in Scotland, by an order for specific performance under section 45 of the Court of Session Act 1988.

(6)   The jurisdiction conferred by paragraph (3) shall be exercisable by the High Court and the Court of Session.

(7)   The fact that a rule made or condition imposed by an Operator has been altered in response to a direction given by the Treasury under paragraph (2)(b) or an order of the court under paragraph (3) does not prevent it from being subsequently altered or revoked by the Operator.

[6.50]
9   Injunctions and restitution orders
(1)   If on the application of the Treasury the court is satisfied—
  (a)   that there is a reasonable likelihood that any person will contravene a relevant rule; or
  (b)   that any person has contravened a relevant rule, and that there is a reasonable likelihood that the contravention will continue or be repeated,
the court may make an order restraining (or in Scotland an interdict prohibiting) the contravention.

(2)   If on the application of the Treasury the court is satisfied—
  (a)   that any person has contravened a relevant rule; and
  (b)   that there are steps which could be taken for remedying the contravention,
the court may make an order requiring that person and any other person who appears to the court to have been knowingly concerned in the contravention to take such steps as the court may direct to remedy it.

(3)   No application shall be made by the Treasury under paragraph (1) or (2) in respect of a relevant rule unless it appears to them that the Operator of the relevant system is unable or unwilling to take appropriate steps to restrain the contravention or to require the person concerned to take such steps as are mentioned in paragraph (2)(b).

(4)   If on the application of the Treasury the court is satisfied that any person may have—
  (a)   contravened a relevant rule; or
  (b)   been knowingly concerned in the contravention of a relevant rule,
the court may make an order restraining (or in Scotland an interdict prohibiting) him from disposing of, or otherwise dealing with, any assets of his which it is satisfied he is reasonably likely to dispose of or otherwise deal with.

(5)   The court may, on the application of the Treasury, make an order under paragraph (6) if it is satisfied that a person has contravened a relevant rule, or been knowingly concerned in the contravention of such a rule, and—

   (a)   that profits have accrued to him as a result of the contravention; or
   (b)   that one or more persons have suffered loss or been otherwise adversely affected as a result of the contravention.

(6)   The court may order the person concerned to pay to the Treasury such sum as appears to the court to be just having regard—

   (a)   in a case within subparagraph (a) of paragraph (5), to the profits appearing to the court to have accrued;
   (b)   in a case within subparagraph (b) of that paragraph, to the extent of the loss or other adverse effect; or
   (c)   in a case within both of those subparagraphs, to the profits appearing to the court to have accrued and to the extent of the loss or other adverse effect.

(7)   Subsections (3) to (5) and (8) of section 382 of the 2000 Act shall apply in relation to an application of the Treasury under paragraph (5) as they have effect in relation to an application of the Authority under subsection (1) of that section; and in those subsections as they so apply—

   (a)   the references to subsections (1) and (2) shall be taken to be references to paragraphs (5) and (6) respectively;
   (b)   the references to paragraphs (a) and (b) of subsection (1) shall be taken to be references to subparagraphs (a) and (b) respectively of paragraph (5).

(8)   The jurisdiction conferred by this Regulation shall be exercisable by the High Court and the Court of Session.

(9)   Nothing in this regulation affects the right of any person other than the Treasury to bring proceedings in respect of matters to which this regulation applies.

(10)   In this regulation, "relevant rule" means any provision of the rules of an Operator to which the person in question is subject and which regulate the carrying on by that person of business of any of the following kinds—

   (a)   dealing in investments as principal;
   (b)   dealing in investments as agent;
   (c)   arranging deals in investments;
   (d)   managing investments;
   (e)   safeguarding and administering investments;
   (f)   sending dematerialised instructions;
   (g)   establishing etc a collective investment scheme;
   (h)   advising on investments; or
   (i)   agreeing to carry on any of the activities mentioned in paragraphs (a) to (h).

(11)   In paragraph (2), references to remedying a contravention include references to mitigating its effect.

(12)   Paragraph (10) shall be read with—

   (a)   section 22 of the 2000 Act;
   (b)   any relevant order under that section; and
   (c)   Schedule 2 to that Act.

[6.51]
10   Provision of information by Operators

(1)   The Treasury may, in writing, require an Operator to give them such information as they may specify.

(2)   The Treasury may also, in writing, require an Operator to give them, at such times or in respect of such periods as they may specify, such information relating to that Operator as they may specify.

(3)   Any information required to be given under this regulation shall be only such as the Treasury may reasonably require for the exercise of their functions under these Regulations.

(4)   The Treasury may require information to be given by a specified time, in a specified form and to be verified in a specified manner.

(5)   If an Operator—

   (a)   alters or revokes any of his rules or guidance; or
   (b)   makes new rules or issues new guidance,

he shall give written notice to the Treasury without delay.

[6.52]
11   Delegation of Treasury functions

(1)   Subject to paragraphs (2) and (5), the Treasury may by instrument in writing delegate all or any of the functions conferred by this Part of these Regulations to the Authority; and references in these Regulations to the "designated agency" are references to the Authority so far as such functions are so delegated.

Part 6   Pre-2006 companies SIs

(2)   The functions conferred on the Treasury by regulation 12 may not be delegated.

(3)   The designated agency shall send to the Treasury a copy of any guidance issued by virtue of these Regulations and any requirements imposed by it on an Operator by virtue of regulation 10, and give them written notice of any amendment or revocation of, or addition to, any such guidance or requirements.

(4)   The designated agency shall—

  (a)   send to the Treasury a copy of any guidance issued by it which is intended to have continuing effect and is issued in writing or other legible form; and

  (b)   give them written notice of any amendment or revocation of, or addition to, guidance issued by it,

but notice need not be given of the revocation of guidance other than is mentioned in subparagraph (a) or of any amendment or addition which does not result in or consist of such guidance as is there mentioned.

(5)   The Treasury shall not delegate any function to the Authority unless they are satisfied that—

  (a)   any guidance issued by it in the exercise of its functions under these Regulations;

  (b)   any requirements imposed by it on an Operator by virtue of regulation 10;

  (c)   any guidance proposed to be issued by it in the exercise of its functions under these Regulations; and

  (d)   any requirements it proposes to impose on an Operator by virtue of regulation 10,

do not have, and are not intended or likely to have, to any significant extent the effect of restricting, distorting or preventing competition, or if they have or are intended or likely to have that effect to any significant extent, that the effect is not greater than is necessary for the protection of investors.

(6)   The powers conferred by paragraph (7) shall be exercisable by the Treasury if at any time it appears to them that—

  (a)   any guidance issued by the designated agency in the exercise of its functions under these Regulations;

  (b)   any requirements imposed by the designated agency on an Operator by virtue of regulation 10; or

  (c)   any practices of the designated agency followed in the exercise of its functions under these Regulations,

have, or are intended or likely to have, to any significant extent the effect of restricting, distorting or preventing competition and that the effect is greater than is necessary for the protection of investors.

(7)   The powers exercisable under this paragraph are—

  (a)   to resume all or any of the functions delegated to the designated agency by the written instrument referred to in paragraph (1); or

  (b)   to direct the designated agency to take specified steps for the purpose of securing that the guidance, requirements or practices in question do not have the effect mentioned in paragraph (6).

(8)   The Treasury may by written instrument—

  (a)   at the request or with the consent of the designated agency; or

  (b)   if at any time it appears to them that the designated agency is unable or unwilling to discharge all or any of the functions delegated to it,

resume all or any of the functions delegated to the designated agency under paragraph (1).

(9)   Neither the designated agency nor any person who is, or is acting as, a member, officer or member of staff of the designated agency shall be liable in damages for anything done or omitted in the discharge or purported discharge of functions delegated under paragraph (1) unless the act or omission is shown to have been in bad faith.

(10)   In this regulation—

  (a)   any reference to guidance issued to an Operator by the designated agency is a reference to any guidance issued or any recommendation made by the designated agency in writing, or other legible form, which is intended to have continuing effect, and is issued or made to an Operator; and

  (b)   references to the practices of the designated agency are references to the practices of the designated agency in its capacity as such.

(11)   If under paragraph (1) the Treasury delegate to the designated agency the Treasury's function of making applications to the court under regulation 9(5), the reference to the Treasury in regulation 9(6) shall, unless the Treasury otherwise provide in the instrument by which that function is delegated, be taken as a reference to the designated agency.

[6.53]
12   International obligations

(1)   If it appears to the Treasury that any action proposed to be taken by an Operator or the designated agency would be incompatible with Community obligations or any other international obligations of the United Kingdom they may direct the Operator or the designated agency, as the case may be, not to take that action.

(2)   If it appears to the Treasury that any action which an Operator or the designated agency has power to take is required for the purpose of implementing any such obligations, they may direct the Operator or the designated agency, as the case may be, to take that action.

(3)   A direction under this regulation—

    (a)   may include such supplemental or incidental requirements as the Treasury consider necessary or expedient; and

    (b)   is enforceable, on an application made by the Treasury, by injunction or, in Scotland, by an order for specific performance under section 45 of the Court of Session Act 1988.

[6.54]
13   Prevention of restrictive practices

Schedule 2 (prevention of restrictive practices) shall have effect.

PART 3
PARTICIPATING SECURITIES

Participation by issuers

[6.55]
14   Participation in respect of shares

Where—

    (a)   an Operator permits title to shares of a class in relation to which regulation 15 applies, or in relation to which a directors' resolution passed in accordance with regulation 16 is effective, to be transferred by means of a relevant system; and

    (b)   the company in question permits the holding of shares of that class in uncertificated form and the transfer of title to any such shares by means of a relevant system,

title to shares of that class which are recorded on an Operator register of members may be transferred by means of that relevant system.

[6.56]
15

This regulation applies to a class of shares if the company's articles of association are in all respects consistent with—

    (a)   the holding of shares of that class in uncertificated form;

    (b)   the transfer of title to shares of that class by means of a relevant system; and

    (c)   these Regulations.

[6.57]
16

(1)   This regulation applies to a class of shares if a company's articles of association in any respect are inconsistent with—

    (a)   the holding of shares of that class in uncertificated form;

    (b)   the transfer of title to shares of that class by means of a relevant system; or

    (c)   any provision of these Regulations.

(2)   A company may resolve, subject to paragraph (6)(a), by resolution of its directors (in this Part referred to as a "director's resolution") that title to shares of a class issued or to be issued by it may be transferred by means of a relevant system.

(3)   Upon a directors' resolution becoming effective in accordance with its terms, and for as long as it is in force, the articles of association in relation to the class of shares which were the subject of the directors' resolution shall not apply to any uncertificated shares of that class to the extent that they are inconsistent with—

    (a)   the holding of shares of that class in uncertificated form;

    (b)   the transfer of title to shares of that class by means of a relevant system; or

    (c)   any provision of these Regulations.

(4)   Unless a company has given notice to every member of the company in accordance with its articles of association of its intention to pass a directors' resolution before the passing of such a resolution, it shall give such notice within 60 days of the passing of the resolution.

(5)   Notice given by the company before the coming into force of these Regulations of its intention to pass a directors' resolution which, if it had been given after the coming into force of these Regulations would have satisfied the requirements of paragraph (4), shall be taken to satisfy the requirements of that paragraph.

(6)   In respect of a class of shares, the members of a company may by ordinary resolution—

    (a)   if a directors' resolution has not been passed, resolve that the directors of the company shall not pass a directors' resolution;

    (b)   if a directors' resolution has been passed but not yet come into effect in accordance with its terms, resolve that it shall not come into effect;

(c)   if a directors' resolution has been passed and is effective in accordance with its terms but the class of shares has not yet been permitted by the Operator to be a participating security, resolve that the directors' resolution shall cease to have effect; or

(d)   if a directors' resolution has been passed and is effective in accordance with its terms and the class of shares has been permitted by the Operator to be a participating security, resolve that the directors shall take the necessary steps to ensure that title to shares of the class that was the subject of the directors' resolution shall cease to be transferable by means of a relevant system and that the directors' resolution shall cease to have effect,

and the directors shall be bound by the terms of any such ordinary resolution.

[(7)   In the event of default in complying with paragraph (4), an offence is committed by every officer of the issuer who is in default.

(7A)   A person guilty of such an offence is liable—

(a)   on conviction on indictment, to a fine;

(b)   on summary conviction, to a fine not exceeding the statutory maximum.]

(8)   A company shall not permit the holding of shares in such a class as is referred to in paragraph (1) in uncertificated form, or the transfer of title to shares in such a class by means of a relevant system, unless in relation to that class of shares a directors' resolution is effective.

[(8A)   Chapter 3 of Part 3 of [the 2006 Act] (resolutions affecting a company's constitution) applies to—

(a)   a directors' resolution passed by virtue of paragraph (2), or

(b)   a resolution of a company passed by virtue of paragraph (6) preventing or reversing such a resolution.]

(9)   This regulation shall not be taken to exclude the right of the members of a company to amend the articles of association of the company, in accordance with the articles, to allow the holding of any class of its shares in uncertificated form and the transfer of title to shares in such a class by means of a relevant system.

NOTES

Paras (7), (7A): substituted, for original para (7), by the Companies Act 2006 (Commencement No 3, Consequential Amendments, Transitional Provisions and Savings) Order 2007, SI 2007/2194, art 10(1), Sch 4, Pt 3, para 97(1), (2), as from 1 October 2007.

Para (8A): inserted by SI 2007/2194, art 10(1), Sch 4, Pt 3, para 97(1), (3), as from 1 October 2007; words in square brackets substituted by the Companies Act 2006 (Consequential Amendments) (Uncertificated Securities) Order 2009, SI 2009/1889, art 2(1), (3), as from 1 October 2009.

[6.58]

17

(1)   A class of shares in relation to which, immediately before the coming into force of these Regulations—

(a)   regulation 15 of the 1995 Regulations applied; or

(b)   a directors' resolution passed in accordance with regulation 16 of the 1995 Regulations was effective,

shall be taken to be a class of shares in relation to which regulation 15 of these Regulations applies or, as the case may be, a directors' resolution passed in accordance with regulation 16 is effective.

(2)   On the coming into force of these Regulations a company's articles of association in relation to any such class of shares, and the terms of issue of any such class of shares, shall cease to apply to the extent that they are inconsistent with any provision of these Regulations.

[6.59]

18   Interpretation of regulations 15, 16 and 17

For the purposes of regulations 15, 16 and 17 any shares with respect to which share warrants to bearer are issued under [section 779 of the 2006 Act] shall be regarded as forming a separate class of shares.

NOTES

Words in square brackets substituted by the Companies Act 2006 (Consequential Amendments) (Uncertificated Securities) Order 2009, SI 2009/1889, art 2(1), (4), as from 1 October 2009.

[6.60]

19   Participation in respect of securities other than shares

(1)   Subject to paragraph (2), where—

(a)   an Operator permits title to a security other than a share to be transferred by means of a relevant system; and

(b)   the issuer permits the holding of units of that security in uncertificated form and the transfer of title to units of that security by means of a relevant system,

title to units of that security which are recorded on an Operator register of securities may be transferred by means of that relevant system.

(2) In relation to any security other than a share, if the law under which it is constituted is not the law of England and Wales, Northern Ireland or Scotland, or if the current terms of its issue are in any respect inconsistent with—

    (a) the holding of title to units of that security in uncertificated form;

    (b) the transfer of title to units of that security by means of a relevant system; or

    (c) subject to paragraph (3), these Regulations,

[an issuer of that security] shall not permit the holding of units of that security in uncertificated form, or the transfer of title to units of that security by means of a relevant system.

(3) On the coming into force of these Regulations the current terms of issue of a relevant participating security shall cease to apply to the extent that they are inconsistent with any provision of these Regulations.

(4) For the purposes of this regulation—

    (a) a relevant participating security is a participating security (other than a share) the terms of issue of which, immediately before the coming into force of these Regulations, were in all respects consistent with the 1995 Regulations; and

    (b) the terms of issue of a security shall be taken to include the terms prescribed by the issuer on which units of the security are held and title to them is transferred.

NOTES

Para (2): words in square brackets substituted by the Uncertificated Securities (Amendment) (Eligible Debt Securities) Regulations 2003, SI 2003/1633, regs 2, 5, as from 24 June 2004.

Keeping of registers and records

[6.61]

20 Entries on registers and records in respect of shares

(1) In respect of every company which is a participating issuer, there shall be—

    (a) a register maintained by the participating issuer, and such a register is referred to in these Regulations as an "issuer register of members"; and

    (b) a register maintained by the Operator, and such a register is referred to in these Regulations as an "Operator register of members".

(2) A participating issuer which is a company shall keep and enter up the issuer register of members in accordance with paragraph 2 of Schedule 4.

(3) In respect of every company which is a participating issuer, the Operator shall keep and enter up the Operator register of members in accordance with paragraph 4 of Schedule 4.

(4) References in any enactment or instrument to a company's register of members shall, unless the context otherwise requires, be construed in relation to a company which is a participating issuer as referring to the company's issuer register of members and Operator register of members.

(5) Paragraph (4) does not apply in relation to a company's issuer register of members to the extent that any of the particulars entered in that register in accordance with paragraph 2(1) of Schedule 4 are inconsistent with the company's Operator register of members.

(6) A participating issuer which is a company shall—

    (a) maintain a record of the entries made in its Operator register of members; and such a record is referred to in these Regulations as a "record of uncertificated shares"; and

    (b) keep and enter up that record in accordance with paragraph 5 of Schedule 4.

(7) Such sanctions as apply to a company and its officers in the event of a default in complying with [section 113 of the 2006 Act] shall apply to—

    (a) a company which is a participating issuer and its officers in the event of a default in complying with paragraph (1)(a) or (6)(a), or

    (b) an Operator and his officers in the event of a default in complying with paragraph (1)(b).

NOTES

Para (7): words in square brackets substituted by the Companies Act 2006 (Consequential Amendments) (Uncertificated Securities) Order 2009, SI 2009/1889, art 2(1), (5), as from 1 October 2009.

[6.62]

21 Entries on registers and records in respect of [general] public sector securities

(1) In respect of every participating security which is a [general] public sector security the Operator shall—

    (a) maintain a register, and such a register is referred to in these Regulations as an "Operator register of [general] public sector securities"; and

    (b) keep and enter up the Operator register of [general] public sector securities in accordance with paragraph 12 of Schedule 4.

(2) The person specified in paragraph (3) shall—

    (a) maintain a record of the entries made in an Operator register of [general] public sector securities; and such a record is referred to in these Regulations as a "record of uncertificated [general] public sector securities"; and

    (b) keep and enter up that record in accordance with paragraph 13 of Schedule 4.

(3)   The person referred to in paragraph (2) is [the Registrar of Government Stock], except where the security to which an Operator register of [general] public sector securities relates is a [general] local authority security, in which case it is—

(a)   the relevant local authority; or

(b)   if the local authority has appointed another person to act as registrar for the purpose of the 1974 Regulations in respect of that security, the person so appointed [. . .

(c)   . . .].

(4)   Such sanctions as apply to a company and its officers in the event of a default in complying with [section 113 of the 2006 Act] shall apply to an Operator and his officers in the event of a default in complying with paragraph (1)(a).

(5)   Such sanctions as apply to the registrar, within the meaning of the 1974 Regulations, in the event of a default in complying with regulation 5 of those Regulations shall apply to a participating issuer and his officers in the event of a default in complying with paragraph (2)(a) in respect of a local authority security [falling within paragraph (a)(i) of the definition of "local authority security" in regulation 3(1)].

[(6)   . . .]

NOTES

Regulation heading, paras (1), (2), (5): words in square brackets inserted by the Uncertificated Securities (Amendment) (Eligible Debt Securities) Regulations 2003, SI 2003/1633, regs 6(1), (2), 8(2), as from 24 June 2003.

Para (3): words in first pair of square brackets substituted by the Government Stock (Consequential and Transitional Provision) (No 2) Order 2004, SI 2004/1662, art 2, Schedule, Pt 3, para 29(1), (3), as from 1 July 2004; the word "general" in square brackets in both places it occurs inserted by SI 2003/1633, regs 6(2), 8(1)(a), (2), as from 24 June 2003; para (c) and the word immediately preceding it originally inserted by SI 2003/1633, art 8(1)(b), as from 24 June 2003, and revoked by the Local Authorities (Capital Finance) (Further Consequential and Saving Provisions) Order 2004, SI 2004/2044, art 6(2)(a), as from 1 October 2004.

Para (4): words in square brackets substituted by the Companies Act 2006 (Consequential Amendments) (Uncertificated Securities) Order 2009, SI 2009/1889, art 2(1), (6), as from 1 October 2009.

Para (6): added by SI 2003/1633, reg 8(3), as from 24 June 2003, and revoked by SI 2004/2044, art 6(2)(b), as from 1 October 2004.

[6.63]

22   Entries on registers and records in respect of other securities

(1)   Paragraph (2) applies where a participating issuer is required by or under an enactment or instrument to maintain in the United Kingdom a register of persons holding securities (other than shares[, general public sector securities or eligible debt securities]) issued by him.

(2)   Where this paragraph applies, then in so far as the register in question relates to any class of security which is a participating security—

(a)   the Operator shall—

(i)   maintain a register, and such a register is referred to in these Regulations as an "Operator register of corporate securities"; and

(ii)   keep and enter up the Operator register of corporate securities in accordance with paragraph 14 of Schedule 4;

(b)   the participating issuer—

(i)   shall not maintain the register to the extent that it relates to securities held in uncertificated form;

(ii)   shall maintain a record of the entries made in any Operator register of corporate securities, and such a record is referred to in these Regulations as a "record of uncertificated corporate securities"; and

(iii)   shall keep and enter up that record in accordance with paragraph 15 of Schedule 4.

(3)   Where a participating issuer is not required by or under an enactment or instrument to maintain in the United Kingdom in respect of a participating security [(other than an eligible debt security)] issued by him a register of persons holding units of that participating security, the Operator shall—

(a)   maintain a register in respect of that participating security; and

(b)   record in that register—

(i)   the names and addresses of the persons holding units of that security in uncertificated form, and

(ii)   how many units of that security each such person holds in that form.

[(3A)   In respect of every participating security which is an eligible debt security, the Operator shall—

(a)   maintain a register, and such a register is referred to in these Regulations as an "Operator register of eligible debt securities"; and

(b)   record in that register—

(i)   the names and addresses of the persons holding units of that security; and

(ii)   how many units of that security each such person holds.]

(4)   Such sanctions as apply to a company and its officers in the event of a default in complying with [section 113 of the 2006 Act] shall apply to an Operator and his officers in the event of a default in complying with paragraph [(2)(a)(i), (3) or (3A)].

(5)   Such sanctions as apply in the event of a default in complying with the requirement to maintain a register imposed by the relevant enactment or instrument referred to in paragraph (1) shall apply to a participating issuer and his officers in the event of a default in complying with paragraph (2)(b)(ii).

NOTES

Para (1): words in square brackets substituted by the Uncertificated Securities (Amendment) (Eligible Debt Securities) Regulations 2003, SI 2003/1633, reg 6(3), as from 24 June 2003.

Para (3): words in square brackets inserted by SI 2003/1633, reg 9(1), as from 24 June 2003.

Para (3A): inserted by SI 2003/1633, reg 9(2), as from 24 June 2003.

Para (4): words in first pair of square brackets substituted by the Companies Act 2006 (Consequential Amendments) (Uncertificated Securities) Order 2009, SI 2009/1889, art 2(1), (6), as from 1 October 2009; words in second pair of square brackets substituted by SI 2003/1633, reg 9(3), as from 24 June 2003.

[6.64]
23   General provisions concerning keeping registers and records

(1)   The obligations of an Operator to maintain and to keep and enter up any register of securities, imposed by these Regulations—

    (a)   shall not give rise to any form of duty or liability on the Operator, except such as is expressly provided for in these Regulations or as arises from fraud or other wilful default, or negligence, on the part of the Operator;

    (b)   shall not give rise to any form of duty or liability on a participating issuer, other than where the Operator acts on the instructions of that participating issuer, in the absence of fraud or other wilful default, or negligence, on the part of that participating issuer; and

    (c)   shall not give rise to any form of duty or liability enforceable by civil proceedings for breach of statutory duty.

(2)   Without prejudice to paragraph (1) or to any lesser period of limitation and to any rule as to the prescription of rights, liability incurred by a participating issuer or by an Operator arising—

    (a)   from the making or deletion of an entry in a register of securities or record of securities pursuant to these Regulations; or

    (b)   from a failure to make or delete any such entry,

shall not be enforceable more than [10 years] after the date on which the entry was made or deleted or, in the case of a failure, the failure first occurred.

(3)   No notice of any trust, expressed, implied or constructive, shall be entered on an Operator register of securities, or a part of such a register, or be receivable by an Operator.

(4)   Schedule 4 (which provides for the keeping of registers and records of participating securities, and which excludes, or applies with appropriate modifications, certain provisions of [the 2006 Act]) shall have effect.

[(5)   Section 120 of the 2006 Act shall not apply with respect to a company which is a participating issuer.]

NOTES

Paras (2), (4): words in square brackets substituted by the Companies Act 2006 (Consequential Amendments) (Uncertificated Securities) Order 2009, SI 2009/1889, art 2(1), (8), as from 1 October 2009.

Para (5): added by SI 2009/1889, art 2(1), (9), as from 1 October 2009.

[6.65]
24   Effect of entries on registers

(1)   Subject to regulation 29 and to paragraphs (2) and (3) below, a register of members is prima facie evidence, and in Scotland sufficient evidence unless the contrary is shown, of any matters which are by these Regulations directed or authorised to be inserted in it.

(2)   Paragraph (1) does not apply to a company's issuer register of members to the extent that any of the particulars entered in that register in accordance with paragraph 2(1) of Schedule 4 are inconsistent with the company's Operator register of members.

(3)   The entry of a person's name and address in a company's issuer register of members shall not be treated as showing that person to be a member of the company unless—

    (a)   the issuer register of members also shows him as holding shares in the company in certificated form;

    (b)   the Operator register of members shows him as holding shares in the company in uncertificated form; or

    (c)   he is deemed to be a member of the company by regulation 32(6)(b).

(4)   [Section 127 of the 2006 Act] shall not apply with respect to a company which is a participating issuer.

Part 6   Pre-2006 companies SIs

(5)   Subject to regulation 29, an Operator register of [general] public sector securities is prima facie evidence, and in Scotland sufficient evidence unless the contrary is shown, of any matters which are by these Regulations directed or authorised to be inserted in it.

(6)   Subject to regulation 29, an entry on an Operator register of corporate securities which records a person as holding units of a security in uncertificated form shall be evidence of such title to the units as would be evidenced if the entry on that register—

   (a)   were an entry on the part maintained by the participating issuer of such register as is mentioned in regulation 22(1); and

   (b)   where appropriate, related to units of that security held in certificated form.

(7)   Subject to regulation 29, an entry on a register maintained by virtue of regulation 22(3)(a) shall (where the units are capable of being held in certificated form) be prima facie evidence, and in Scotland sufficient evidence unless the contrary is shown, that the person to whom the entry relates has such title to the units of the security which he is recorded as holding in uncertificated form as he would have if he held the units in certificated form.

[(8)   Subject to regulation 29, an entry on an Operator register of eligible debt securities shall be prima facie evidence, and in Scotland sufficient evidence unless the contrary is shown, of any matters which are by these Regulations directed or authorised to be inserted in it.]

NOTES

Para (4): words in square brackets substituted by the Companies Act 2006 (Consequential Amendments) (Uncertificated Securities) Order 2009, SI 2009/1889, art 2(1), (10), as from 1 October 2009.

Para (5): word in square brackets inserted by the Uncertificated Securities (Amendment) (Eligible Debt Securities) Regulations 2003, SI 2003/1633, reg 6(4), as from 24 June 2003.

Para (8): added by SI 2003/1633, reg 10, as from 24 June 2003.

[6.66]
25 Rectification of registers of securities

(1)   Unless the circumstances described in paragraph (2) apply, a participating issuer shall not rectify an issuer register of securities if such rectification would also require the rectification of an Operator register of securities.

(2)   The circumstances referred to in paragraph (1) are that the rectification of an issuer register of securities is effected—

   (a)   with the consent of the Operator; or

   (b)   by order of a court in the United Kingdom.

(3)   A participating issuer who rectifies an issuer register of securities in order to give effect to an order of a court in the United Kingdom shall immediately give the Operator written notification of the change to the entry, if any rectification of the Operator register of securities may also be required (unless the change to the issuer register is made in response to an Operator-instruction).

(4)   An Operator who rectifies an Operator register of securities shall immediately—

   (a)   generate an Operator-instruction to inform the relevant participating issuer of the change to the entry (unless the change is made in response to an issuer-instruction); and

   (b)   generate an Operator-instruction to inform the system-members concerned of the change to the entry.

[6.67]
26 Closing registers

Notwithstanding . . . any other enactment, a participating issuer shall not close a register of securities relating to a participating security without the consent of the Operator.

NOTES

Words omitted revoked by the Companies Act 2006 (Consequential Amendments) (Uncertificated Securities) Order 2009, SI 2009/1889, art 2(1), (11), as from 1 October 2009.

[6.68]
27 Registration by an Operator of transfers of securities

(1)   Except where relevant units of a security are transferred by means of a relevant system to a person who is to hold them thereafter in certificated form (and subject to paragraphs (2) and (4))—

   (a)   upon settlement of a transfer of uncertificated units of a security in accordance with his rules;

   (b)   following receipt of an issuer-instruction notifying him that the circumstances specified in regulation 33(2)(b) have arisen in respect of a transfer of units of a participating security; or

   (c)   following receipt of an issuer-instruction given under Regulation 42(8)(b),

an Operator shall register on the relevant Operator register of securities the transfer of title to those units of that security.

(2)   An Operator shall refuse to register a transfer of title to units of a participating security in accordance with a system-member instruction or an issuer-instruction (as the case may be) if he has actual notice that the transfer is—

(a)   prohibited by order of a court in the United Kingdom;
(b)   prohibited or avoided by or under an enactment;
(c)   a transfer to a deceased person; or
(d)   where the participating issuer is constituted under the law of Scotland, prohibited by or under an arrestment.

(3)   Notwithstanding that an Operator has received, in respect of a transfer of title to units of a participating security, actual notice of the kind referred to in paragraph (2), the Operator may register that transfer of title on the relevant Operator register of securities if at the time that he received the actual notice it was not practicable for him to halt the process of registration.

(4)   Without prejudice to his rules, an Operator may refuse to register a transfer of title to units of a participating security in accordance with a system-member instruction or an issuer-instruction (as the case may be) if the instruction requires a transfer of units—

(a)   to an entity which is not a natural or legal person;
(b)   to a minor (which, in relation to a participating issuer constituted under the law of Scotland, shall mean a person under 16 years of age);
(c)   to be held jointly in the names of more persons than is permitted under the terms of the issue of the security; or
(d)   where, in relation to the system-member instruction or the issuer-instruction (as the case may be), the Operator has actual notice of any of the matters specified in regulation 35(5)(a)(i) to (iii).

(5)   An Operator shall not register a transfer of title to uncertificated units of a security on an Operator register of securities otherwise than in accordance with paragraph (1) unless he is required to do so by order of a court in the United Kingdom or by or under an enactment.

(6)   Paragraph (5) shall not be taken to prevent an Operator from entering on an Operator register of securities a person who is a system-member to whom title to uncertificated units of a security has been transmitted by operation of law.

(7)   [Subject to paragraph (7A), immediately upon]—

(a)   the registration by an Operator of the transfer of title to units of a participating security in accordance with—
    (i)   paragraph (1);
    (ii)   an order of a court in the United Kingdom; or
    (iii)   a requirement arising by or under an enactment; or
(b)   the making or deletion by an Operator of an entry on an Operator register of securities—
    (i)   following the transmission of title to uncertificated units of a security by operation of law; or
    (ii)   upon the transfer of uncertificated units of a security to a person who is to hold them thereafter in certificated form,

the Operator shall generate an Operator-instruction to inform the relevant participating issuer of the registration, or of the making or deletion of the entry (as the case may be); and where appropriate the participating issuer shall register the transfer or transmission of title to those units on an issuer register of securities in accordance with regulation 28.

[(7A)   Paragraph (7) does not apply in relation to units of an eligible debt security.]

[(8)   If an Operator refuses to register a transfer of securities in any of the circumstances specified in paragraphs (2) and (4), the Operator shall, within 2 months of the date on which the relevant system-member instruction or issuer-instruction (as the case may be) was received by the Operator, send an Operator-instruction, or written notification, informing the relevant system-member or participating issuer (as the case may be) of the refusal.]

(9)   Such sanctions as apply to a company and its officers in the event of a default in complying with [subsections (1) and (2) of section 771 of the 2006 Act] shall apply to an Operator and his officers in the event of a default in complying with that subsection as applied by paragraph (8).

NOTES

Para (7): words in square brackets substituted by the Uncertificated Securities (Amendment) (Eligible Debt Securities) Regulations 2003, SI 2003/1633, reg 11(a), as from 24 June 2003.

Para (7A): added by SI 2003/1633, reg 11(b), as from 24 June 2003.

Para (8): substituted by the Companies Act 2006 (Consequential Amendments) (Uncertificated Securities) Order 2009, SI 2009/1889, art 2(1), (12)(a), as from 1 October 2009.

Para (9): words in square brackets substituted by SI 2009/1889, art 2(1), (12)(b), as from 1 October 2009.

[6.69]
28   Registration by a participating issuer of transfers of securities upon conversion into certificated form

(1)   Paragraphs (2) to (5) apply where relevant units of a security are transferred by means of a relevant system to a person who is to hold them thereafter in certificated form.

(2)   Subject to paragraphs (3) and (4), a participating issuer shall (where appropriate) register a transfer of title to relevant units of a security on an issuer register of securities in accordance with an Operator-instruction.

(3)   A participating issuer shall refuse to register a transfer of title to relevant units of a security in accordance with an Operator-instruction if he has actual notice that the transfer is—
- (a)   prohibited by order of a court in the United Kingdom;
- (b)   prohibited or avoided by or under an enactment;
- (c)   a transfer to a deceased person; or
- (d)   where the participating issuer is constituted under the law of Scotland, prohibited by or under an arrestment.

(4)   A participating issuer may refuse to register a transfer of title to relevant units of a security in accordance with an Operator-instruction if the instruction requires a transfer of units—
- (a)   to an entity which is not a natural or legal person;
- (b)   to a minor (which, in relation to a participating issuer constituted under the law of Scotland, shall mean a person under 16 years of age);
- (c)   to be held jointly in the names of more persons than is permitted under the terms of the issue of the security; or
- (d)   where, in relation to the Operator-instruction, the participating issuer has actual notice from the Operator of any of the matters specified in regulation 35(5)(a)(i) to (iii).

(5)   A participating issuer shall notify the Operator by issuer-instruction whether he has registered a transfer in response to an Operator-instruction to do so.

(6)   A participating issuer shall not register a transfer of title to relevant units of a security on an issuer register of securities unless he is required to do so—
- (a)   by an Operator-instruction;
- (b)   by an order of a court in the United Kingdom; or
- (c)   by or under an enactment.

(7)   A unit of a security is a relevant unit for the purposes of this regulation if, immediately before the transfer in question, it was held by the transferor in uncertificated form.

[(8)   If a participating issuer refuses to register under paragraph (2) a transfer of securities in any of the circumstances specified in paragraphs (3) and (4), the participating issuer shall, within 2 months of the date on which the Operator-instruction was received by the participating issuer, send to the transferee notice of the refusal.]

(9)   Such sanctions as apply to a company and its officers in the event of a default in complying with [subsections (1) and (2) of section 771 of the 2006 Act] shall apply to a participating issuer and his officers in the event of a default in complying with that subsection as applied by paragraph (8).

NOTES

Para (8): substituted by the Companies Act 2006 (Consequential Amendments) (Uncertificated Securities) Order 2009, SI 2009/1889, art 2(1), (13)(a), as from 1 October 2009.

Para (9): words in square brackets substituted by SI 2009/1889, art 2(1), (13)(b), as from 1 October 2009.

[6.70]
29   Registration to be in accordance with regulations 27 and 28

Any purported registration of a transfer of title to an uncertificated unit of a security other than in accordance with regulation 27 or 28 shall be of no effect.

[6.71]
30   Registration of linked transfers

(1)   Paragraph (2) applies where an Operator receives two or more system-member instructions requesting him to register two or more transfers of title to uncertificated units of a security, and it appears to the Operator—
- (a)   either—
  - (i)   that there are fewer units of the security registered on an Operator register of securities in the name of a person identified in any of the system-member instructions as a transferor than the number of units to be transferred from him under those system-member instructions; or
  - (ii)   that it has not been established in accordance with paragraph 21(1)(c) of Schedule 1, in relation to any of the transfers taken without regard to the other transfers, that a settlement bank has agreed to make a payment; and
- (b)   that registration of all of the transfers would result in each of the persons identified in the system-member instructions as a transferor having title to a number of uncertificated units of a security equal to or greater than nil; and
- (c)   that the combined effect of all the transfers taken together would result in paragraph 21(1)(c) of Schedule 1 being satisfied.

(2)   Where this paragraph applies, the Operator may either—
- (a)   register the combined effect of all the transfers taken together; or
- (b)   register all the transfers simultaneously,

unless one or more of those transfers may not be registered by virtue of the fact that the Operator has actual notice of any of the circumstances specified in regulation 27(2), or is to be refused registration by virtue of regulation 27(4).

(3) Notwithstanding that an Operator has received, in respect of two or more such system-member instructions as are referred to in paragraph (1), actual notice of the kind referred to in paragraph (2), the Operator may register all the transfers in question or their combined effect if at the time that he received the actual notice it was not practicable for him to halt the process of registration.

[6.72]
31   Position of a transferee prior to entry on an issuer register of securities

(1) Paragraph (2) applies when an Operator deletes an entry on an Operator register of securities in consequence of which—

   (a) the Operator must generate an Operator-instruction in accordance with regulation 27(7); and

   (b) by virtue of that instruction a participating issuer must register, on an issuer register of securities, a transfer of title to units of a participating security constituted under the law of England and Wales or Northern Ireland.

(2) Where this paragraph applies—

   (a) subject to—

      (i) subparagraph (b); and

      (ii) any enactment or rule of law,

      the transferor shall, notwithstanding the deletion of the entry in the Operator register of securities, retain title to the requisite number of units of the relevant participating security until the transferee is entered on the relevant issuer register of securities as the holder thereof; and

   (b) the transferee shall acquire an equitable interest in the requisite number of units of that security.

(3) Paragraph (4) applies when an Operator deletes an entry on an Operator register of securities in consequence of which—

   (a) the Operator must generate an Operator-instruction in accordance with regulation 27(7); and

   (b) by virtue of that instruction a participating issuer must register, on an issuer register of securities, a transfer of title to units of a participating security constituted under the law of Scotland.

(4) Where this paragraph applies—

   (a) subject to—

      (i) subparagraph (b); and

      (ii) any enactment or rule of law,

      the transferor shall, notwithstanding the deletion of the entry in the Operator register of securities, retain title to the requisite number of units of the relevant participating security until the transferee is entered on the relevant issuer register of securities as the holder thereof; and

   (b) the transferor shall hold the requisite number of units of that security on trust for the benefit of the transferee.

(5) The requisite number for the purposes of this regulation is the number of units which are to be specified in the Operator-instruction which the Operator must generate in accordance with regulation 27(7).

(6) This regulation has effect notwithstanding that the units to which the deletion of the entry in the Operator register of securities relates, or in which an interest arises by virtue of paragraph (2)(b) or (4)(b), or any of them, may be unascertained.

(7) In Scotland—

   (a) this regulation has effect notwithstanding that the requirements relating to the creation of a trust under any enactment or rule of law have not been complied with; and

   (b) as from the time the trust referred to in paragraph (4)(b) arises, any holder, or any holder thereafter, of a floating charge over any part of the property of the transferor shall be deemed to have received notice of the trust's existence and of the property to which it relates.

(8) Subject to paragraphs (6) and (7), this regulation shall not be construed as conferring a proprietary interest (whether of the kind referred to in paragraph (2)(b) or (4)(b), or of any other kind) in units of a security if the conferring of such an interest at the time specified in these Regulations would otherwise be void by or under any enactment or rule of law.

(9) In this regulation—

   (a) "the transferee" means the person to be identified in the Operator-instruction as the transferee; and

   (b) "the transferor" means the person to be identified in the Operator-instruction as the transferor.

Conversions and New Issues

[6.73]
32   Conversion of securities into certificated form

(1)   Except as provided in regulation 42, a unit of a participating security shall not be converted from uncertificated form into certificated form unless an Operator generates an Operator-instruction to notify the relevant participating issuer that a conversion event has occurred; and in this regulation such an Operator-instruction is referred to as a "rematerialisation notice".

(2)   A conversion event occurs—
- (a)   where such a conversion is permitted by the Operator's conversion rules; or
- (b)   following receipt by an Operator of a system-member instruction requiring the conversion into certificated form of uncertificated units of a participating security registered in the name of the system-member; or
- (c)   following receipt by an Operator of written notification from a participating issuer which is a company requiring the conversion into certificated form of uncertificated units of a participating security, issued by that participating issuer and registered in the name of a system-member, and which contains a statement that the conversion is required to enable the participating issuer to deal with the units in question in accordance with provisions in that participating issuer's memorandum or articles or in the terms of issue of the units in question.

(3)   An Operator—
- (a)   may generate a rematerialisation notice following a conversion event occurring in the circumstances specified in paragraph (2)(a);
- (b)   shall generate a rematerialisation notice following a conversion event occurring in the circumstances specified in paragraph (2)(b) unless the participation in the relevant system, by the system-member in whose name the uncertificated units in question are registered, has been suspended pursuant to the Operator's rules; and
- (c)   shall generate a rematerialisation notice following a conversion event occurring in the circumstances specified in paragraph (2)(c).

(4)   On the generation of a rematerialisation notice, the Operator shall delete any entry in an Operator register of securities which shows the relevant system-member as the holder of the unit or units specified in the rematerialisation notice.

(5)   On receipt of a rematerialisation notice, the participating issuer to whom the rematerialisation notice is addressed shall, where relevant, enter the name of the system-member on an issuer register of securities as the holder of the unit or units specified in the rematerialisation notice.

(6)   During any period between the deletion of any entry in an Operator register of securities required to be made by paragraph (4) and the making of the entry in an issuer register of securities required to be made by paragraph (5)—
- (a)   the relevant system-member shall retain title to the units of the security specified in the rematerialisation notice notwithstanding the deletion of any entry in the Operator register of securities; and
- (b)   where those units are shares, the relevant system-member shall be deemed to continue to be a member of the company.

(7)   Following—
- (a)   the making of an entry in an issuer register of securities in accordance with paragraph (5); or
- (b)   registration of a transfer of title to units of a security in accordance with regulation 28,

the relevant participating issuer shall, where the terms of issue of the security in question provide for a certificate to be issued, issue a certificate in respect of the units of the security to the relevant person.

(8)   [Subsection (1) of section 776 of the 2006 Act] shall apply in relation to the issue of a certificate by a participating issuer pursuant to paragraph (7) as it applies in relation to the completion and having ready for delivery by a company of share certificates, debentures or certificates of debenture stock; and in that subsection as it so applies the reference to the date on which a transfer is lodged with the company shall be a reference to the date on which the participating issuer receives the relevant rematerialisation notice in accordance with this regulation, or the relevant Operator-instruction in accordance with regulation 27(7).

(9)   Such sanctions as apply to a company and its officers in the event of a default in complying with [subsections (1) and (2) of section 771 of the 2006 Act] shall apply—
- (a)   to an Operator and his officers in the event of a default in complying with paragraph (4); and
- (b)   to a participating issuer and his officers in the event of a default in complying with paragraph (5).

(10)   Such sanctions as apply to a company and its officers in the event of a default in complying with [subsection (1) of section 776 of the 2006 Act] shall apply to a participating issuer and his officers in the event of a default in complying with paragraph (7) in accordance with the requirements laid down in paragraph (8).

NOTES

Paras (8)–(10): words in square brackets substituted by the Companies Act 2006 (Consequential Amendments) (Uncertificated Securities) Order 2009, SI 2009/1889, art 2(1), (14), as from 1 October 2009.

[6.74]

33 Conversion of securities into uncertificated form

(1) A unit of a participating security shall not be converted from certificated form into uncertificated form unless the participating issuer notifies the Operator by means of an issuer-instruction that any of the circumstances specified in paragraph (2) have arisen; and in this regulation such an issuer-instruction is referred to as a "dematerialisation notice".

(2) The circumstances referred to in paragraph (1) are—

   (a) where the unit of the participating security is held by a system-member, that the participating issuer has received—

      (i) a request in writing from the system-member in the form required by the Operator's conversion rules that the unit be converted from certificated form to uncertificated form; and

      (ii) subject to paragraph (4), the certificate relating to that unit; or

   (b) where the unit of the participating security is to be registered on an Operator register of securities in the name of a system-member following a transfer of the unit to him, that the participating issuer—

      (i) subject to paragraph (3), has received (by means of the Operator-system unless the Operator's conversion rules permit otherwise) a proper instrument of transfer in favour of the system-member relating to the unit to be transferred;

      (ii) subject to paragraph (4), has received (by means of the Operator-system unless the Operator's conversion rules permit otherwise) the certificate relating to that unit; and

      (iii) may accept by virtue of the Operator's conversion rules that the system-member to whom the unit is to be transferred wishes to hold it in uncertificated form.

(3) The requirement in paragraph (2)(b)(i) that the participating issuer shall have received an instrument of transfer relating to the unit of the participating security shall not apply in a case where for a transfer of a unit of that security no instrument of transfer is required.

(4) The requirements in paragraphs (2)(a)(ii) and (2)(b)(ii) that the participating issuer shall have received a certificate relating to the unit of the participating security shall not apply in a case where the system-member or transferor (as the case may be) does not have a certificate in respect of the unit to be converted into uncertificated form because no certificate has yet been issued to him or is due to be issued to him in accordance with the terms of issue of the relevant participating security.

(5) Subject to paragraphs (3) and (4), a participating issuer shall not give a dematerialisation notice except in the circumstances specified in paragraph (2).

(6) Upon giving a dematerialisation notice, a participating issuer shall delete any entry in any issuer register of securities which evidences title to the unit or units of the participating security in question.

(7) Following receipt of a dematerialisation notice, an Operator shall enter the name of the relevant system-member on an Operator register of securities as the holder of the relevant unit or units of the participating security in question, provided that this obligation shall be subject to regulation 27 if the notice was given in the circumstances specified in paragraph (2)(b).

(8) When a dematerialisation notice is given, the relevant system-member, or the transferor of the unit or units of the security in question, as the case may be, shall (without prejudice to any equitable interest which the transferee may have acquired in the unit or units in question)—

   (a) retain title to the units of the security specified in the dematerialisation notice notwithstanding the deletion of any entry in any issuer register of securities required to be made by paragraph (6); and

   (b) where those units are shares, be deemed to continue to be a member of the company.

(9) Where a dematerialisation notice is given in the circumstances specified in paragraph (2)(b), such title shall be retained, and (where appropriate) such membership shall be deemed to continue, until the time at which the Operator enters the name of the relevant system-member on an Operator register of securities in accordance with paragraph (7).

(10) Within 2 months of receiving a dematerialisation notice, an Operator shall generate an Operator-instruction informing the participating issuer whether an entry has been made in an Operator register of securities in response to the dematerialisation notice.

(11) Such sanctions as apply to a company and its officers in the event of a default in complying with [subsections (1) and (2) of section 771 of the 2006 Act] shall apply—

   (a) to a participating issuer and his officers in the event of a default in complying with paragraph (6); and

   (b) to an Operator and his officers in the event of a default in complying with paragraph (7) or (10).

Part 6   Pre-2006 companies SIs

NOTES

Para (11): words in square brackets substituted by the Companies Act 2006 (Consequential Amendments) (Uncertificated Securities) Order 2009, SI 2009/1889, art 2(1), (15), as from 1 October 2009.

[6.75]
34 New issues in uncertificated form

(1) For the purposes of an issue of units of a participating security, a participating issuer may require the Operator to enter the name of a person in an Operator register of securities as the holder of new units of that security in uncertificated form if, and only if, that person is a system-member; and provided that compliance with any such requirement shall be subject to the rules of the Operator.

(2) For the purposes of calculating the number of new units to which a system-member is entitled a participating issuer may treat a system-member's holdings of certificated and uncertificated units of a security as if they were separate holdings.

(3) A requirement made by a participating issuer under paragraph (1) may be made by means of an issuer-instruction and shall specify the names of the persons to be entered in the Operator register of securities as the holders of new uncertificated units of the security, and the number of such units to be issued to each of those persons.

(4) An Operator who receives a requirement made by a participating issuer under paragraph (1) shall notify the participating issuer, by Operator-instruction or in writing, if he has not entered the name of any one or more of the persons in question in the Operator register of securities as the holder of new units of the security.

PART 4
DEMATERIALISED INSTRUCTIONS ETC

[6.76]
35 Properly authenticated dematerialised instructions, etc

(1) This regulation has effect for the purpose of determining the rights and obligations of persons to whom properly authenticated dematerialised instructions are attributable and of persons to whom properly authenticated dematerialised instructions are addressed, when such instructions relate to an uncertificated unit of a security, or relate to a right, benefit or privilege attaching to or arising from such a unit, or relate to the details of a holder of such a unit.

(2) Where a properly authenticated dematerialised instruction is expressed to have been sent on behalf of a person by a sponsoring system-participant or the Operator—
   (a) the person on whose behalf the instruction is expressed to have been sent shall not be able to deny to the addressee—
      (i) that the properly authenticated dematerialised instruction was sent with his authority; or
      (ii) that the information contained in the properly authenticated dematerialised instruction is correct; and
   (b) the sponsoring system-participant or the Operator (as the case may be) shall not be able to deny to the addressee—
      (i) that he has authority to send the properly authenticated dematerialised instruction; or
      (ii) that he has sent the properly authenticated dematerialised instruction.

(3) Where a properly authenticated dematerialised instruction is expressed to have been sent by a person, and the properly authenticated dematerialised instruction is not expressed to have been sent on behalf of another person, the person shall not be able to deny to the addressee—
   (a) that the information contained in the properly authenticated dematerialised instruction is correct; or
   (b) that he has sent the properly authenticated dematerialised instruction.

(4) An addressee who receives (whether directly, or by means of the facilities of a sponsoring system-participant acting on his behalf) a properly authenticated dematerialised instruction may, subject to paragraph (5), accept that at the time at which the properly authenticated dematerialised instruction was sent or at any time thereafter—
   (a) the information contained in the instruction was correct;
   (b) the system-participant or the Operator (as the case may be) identified in the instruction as having sent the instruction sent the instruction; and
   (c) the instruction, where relevant, was sent with the authority of the person on whose behalf it is expressed to have been sent.

(5) Subject to paragraph (6), an addressee may not accept any of the matters specified in paragraph (4) if at the time he received the properly authenticated dematerialised instruction or at any time thereafter—
   (a) he was a person other than a participating issuer or a sponsoring system-participant receiving properly authenticated dematerialised instructions on behalf of a participating issuer, and he had actual notice—

        (i)   that any information contained in it was incorrect;

        (ii)   that the system-participant or the Operator (as the case may be) expressed to have sent the instruction did not send the instruction; or

        (iii)   where relevant, that the person on whose behalf it was expressed to have been sent had not given to the Operator or the sponsoring system-participant (as the case may be), identified in the properly authenticated dematerialised instruction as having sent it, his authority to send the properly authenticated dematerialised instruction on his behalf; or

    (b)   he was a participating issuer, or a sponsoring system-participant receiving properly authenticated dematerialised instructions on behalf of a participating issuer, and—

        (i)   he had actual notice from the Operator of any of the matters specified in subparagraph (a)(i) to (iii); or

        (ii)   if the instruction was an Operator-instruction requiring the registration of a transfer of title, he had actual notice of any of the circumstances specified in regulation 28(3); or

    (c)   he was an Operator and the instruction related to a transfer of units of a security which was in excess of any limit imposed by virtue of paragraph 15 of Schedule 1; or

    (d)   he was an Operator and he had actual notice of any of the circumstances specified in regulation 27(2) in a case where the instruction was—

        (i)   a system-member instruction requesting him to settle a transfer in accordance with his rules; or

        (ii)   an issuer-instruction given in the circumstances specified in regulation 33(2)(b) requesting him to register a transfer of title.

(6) Notwithstanding that an addressee has received, in respect of a properly authenticated dematerialised instruction, actual notice of the kind referred to in paragraph (5), the addressee may accept the matters specified in paragraph (4) if at the time that he received the actual notice it was not practicable for him to halt the processing of the instruction.

(7) Subject to paragraph (8), this regulation has effect without prejudice to the liability of any person for causing or permitting a dematerialised instruction—

    (a)   to be sent without authority; or

    (b)   to contain information which is incorrect; or

    (c)   to be expressed to have been sent by a person who did not send it.

(8) Subject to paragraph (9), a person who is permitted by this regulation to accept any matter shall not be liable in damages or otherwise to any person by reason of his having relied on the matter that he was permitted to accept.

(9) The provisions of paragraph (8) do not affect—

    (a)   any liability of the Operator to pay compensation under regulation 36; or

    (b)   any liability of a participating issuer under regulation 46 arising by reason of a default in complying with, or contravention of, regulation 28(6).

(10) For the purposes of this regulation—

    (a)   a properly authenticated dematerialised instruction is expressed to have been sent by a person or on behalf of a person if it is attributable to that person; and

    (b)   an addressee is the person to whom a properly authenticated dematerialised instruction indicates it is addressed in accordance with the rules and specifications referred to in paragraph 5(5) of Schedule 1.

(11) Nothing in this regulation shall be taken, in respect of any authority, to modify or derogate from the protections to a donee or third person given by or under any enactment or to prohibit a donee or third person so protected from accepting any of the matters specified in paragraph (4).

(12) Paragraphs (2) to (4), (5)(a), (6) to (9) and (11) of this regulation shall apply in relation to a written notification given under regulation 25(3) or 32(2)(c) as if—

    (a)   each reference to a properly authenticated dematerialised instruction were to such a notification which has been authenticated by the Operator in accordance with rules made and practices instituted by the Operator in order to comply with paragraph 25(g) of Schedule 1;

    (b)   each reference to information contained in the properly authenticated dematerialised instruction being correct (or incorrect) included, in the case of written notification given under subparagraph (c) of regulation 32(2), a reference to any statement of the sort referred to in that subparagraph being true (or untrue, as the case may be);

    (c)   each reference to an addressee were a reference to the Operator; and

    (d)   the reference in paragraph (6) to the processing of the instruction were to acting on the written notification.

[6.77]

36 Liability for forged dematerialised instructions, induced amendments to Operator registers of securities, and induced Operator-instructions

(1) For the purpose of this regulation—

    (a)   a dematerialised instruction is a forged dematerialised instruction if—

    (i)   it was not sent from the computers of a system-participant or the computers comprising an Operator-system; or

    (ii)   it was not sent from the computers of the system-participant or the computers comprising an Operator-system (as the case may be) from which it is expressed to have been sent;

  (b)   an act is a causative act if, not being a dematerialised instruction and not being an act which causes a dematerialised instruction to be sent from the computer of a system-participant, it unlawfully causes the Operator—

    (i)   to make, delete or amend an entry on an Operator register of securities; or

    (ii)   to send an Operator-instruction to a participating issuer;

  (c)   an entry on, deletion from, or amendment to an Operator register of securities is an induced amendment if it is an entry on, deletion from, or amendment to an Operator register of securities which results from a causative act or a forged dematerialised instruction; and

  (d)   an Operator-instruction is an induced Operator-instruction if it is an Operator-instruction to a participating issuer which results from a causative act or a forged dematerialised instruction.

(2)   If, as a result of a forged dematerialised instruction (not being one which results in an induced amendment to an Operator register of securities or an induced Operator-instruction), an induced amendment to an Operator register of securities, or an induced Operator-instruction, any one or more of the following events occurs—

  (a)   the name of any person remains on, is entered on, or is removed or omitted from, a register of securities;

  (b)   the number of units of a security in relation to which the name of any person is entered on a register of securities is increased, reduced, or remains unaltered;

  (c)   the description of any units of a security in relation to which the name of any person is entered on a register of securities is changed or remains unaltered,

and that person suffers loss as a result, he may apply to the court for an order that the Operator compensate him for his loss.

(3)   It is immaterial for the purposes of subparagraphs (a) to (c) of paragraph (2) whether the event is permanent or temporary.

(4)   The court shall not make an order under paragraph (2)—

  (a)   if the Operator identifies a person as being responsible (whether alone or with others) for the forged dematerialised instruction (not being one which results in an induced amendment to an Operator register of securities or an induced Operator-instruction) or the causative act or forged dematerialised instruction resulting in the induced amendment to the Operator register of securities or the induced Operator-instruction (as the case may be) notwithstanding that it is impossible (for whatever reason) for the applicant to obtain satisfactory compensation from that person; or

  (b)   if the Operator shows that a participating issuer would be liable under regulation 46 to compensate the applicant for the loss in respect of which the application is made, by reason of the participating issuer's default in complying with, or contravention of, regulation 28(6).

(5)   Subject to paragraphs (6) and (7), the court may award to an applicant compensation for—

  (a)   each forged dematerialised instruction (not being one which results in an induced amendment to an Operator register of securities or an induced Operator-instruction);

  (b)   each induced amendment to an Operator register of securities; and

  (c)   each induced Operator-instruction,

resulting in an event mentioned in subparagraph (a), (b) or (c) of paragraph (2).

(6)   The court shall not under paragraph (5) award to an applicant—

  (a)   more than £50,000 for each such forged dematerialised instruction, induced amendment to an Operator register of securities, or induced Operator-instruction;

  (b)   compensation for both an induced amendment to an Operator register of securities and an induced Operator-instruction if that induced amendment and that induced Operator-instruction resulted from the same causative act or the same forged dematerialised instruction.

(7)   In respect of liability arising under this regulation the court shall—

  (a)   in awarding compensation only order the Operator to pay such amount of compensation as it appears to it to be just and equitable in all the circumstances having regard to the loss sustained by the applicant as a result of the forged dematerialised instruction, induced amendment to the Operator register of securities, or induced Operator-instruction;

  (b)   in ascertaining the loss, apply the same rules concerning the duty of a person to mitigate his loss as apply to damages recoverable under the common law of England and Wales, Northern Ireland, or Scotland, (as the case may be); and

  (c)   where it finds that the loss was to any extent caused or contributed to by any act or omission of the applicant, reduce the amount of the award by such proportion as it thinks just and equitable having regard to that finding.

(8)   An application to the court for an order under paragraph (2) shall not prejudice any right of the Operator to recover from a third party any sum that he may be ordered to pay.

(9)   An event mentioned in subparagraph (a), (b) or (c) of paragraph (2) shall not give rise to any liability on the Operator other than such as is expressly provided for in this regulation, except such as may arise from fraud or other wilful default, or negligence, on the part of the Operator.

(10)   Subject to paragraph (9), this regulation does not affect—
(a)   any right which any person may have other than under this regulation (not being a right against the Operator); or
(b)   any liability which any person other than the Operator may incur other than under this regulation.

(11)   Where an application is made under paragraph (2), and the Operator receives from the applicant a request for information or documents relating to—
(a)   a forged dematerialised instruction;
(b)   an induced amendment to an Operator register of securities; or
(c)   an induced Operator-instruction,
in respect of which the application is made, the Operator shall, in so far as he is able, and in so far as the request is reasonable, within one month give the applicant the information and documents.

(12)   The applicant shall, in so far as he is able, within one month give the Operator such information or documents as the Operator reasonably requests in connection with an application under paragraph (2) with respect to—
(a)   steps taken by the applicant to prevent the giving of any forged dematerialised instruction (whether of the kind referred to in paragraph (2) or of any other kind); and
(b)   steps taken by the applicant to mitigate the loss suffered by him,
provided that the applicant need not give information or documents pursuant to this paragraph until the Operator has complied with any request made by virtue of paragraph (11).

(13)   Neither the Operator nor the applicant shall be required to disclose any information by virtue of, respectively, paragraph (11) or (12) which would be privileged in the course of civil proceedings, or, in Scotland, which they would be entitled to refuse to disclose—
(a)   on grounds of confidentiality as between client and professional legal adviser in proceedings in the Court of Session; or
(b)   on grounds of confidentiality of communications made in connection with, or in contemplation of, such proceedings and for the purposes of those proceedings.

(14)   The jurisdiction conferred by this regulation shall be exercisable, in the case of a participating security constituted under the law of England and Wales, or Northern Ireland, by the High Court; and in the case of a participating security constituted under the law of Scotland by the Court of Session.

PART 5
MISCELLANEOUS AND SUPPLEMENTAL

Miscellaneous

[6.78]
37   Construction of references to transfers etc

References in any enactment or rule of law to a proper instrument of transfer or to a transfer with respect to securities, or any expression having like meaning, shall be taken to include a reference to an Operator-instruction to a participating issuer to register a transfer of title on the relevant issuer register of securities in accordance with the Operator-instruction.

[6.79]
38   Certain formalities and requirements not to apply

(1)   Any requirements in an enactment or rule of law which apply in respect of the transfer of securities otherwise than by means of a relevant system shall not prevent—
(a)   an Operator from registering a transfer of title to uncertificated units of a security upon settlement of a transfer of such units in accordance with his rules; or
(b)   an Operator-instruction from requiring a participating issuer to register a transfer of title to uncertificated units of a security.

(2)   Subject to regulation 32(7), notwithstanding any enactment, instrument or rule of law, a participating issuer shall not issue a certificate in relation to any uncertificated units of a participating security.

(3)   A document issued by or on behalf of a participating issuer purportedly evidencing title to an uncertificated unit of a participating security shall not be evidence of title to the unit of the security; and in particular—
(a)   [section 768 of the 2006 Act] shall not apply to any document issued with respect to uncertificated shares; and
(b)   [regulation 9(3) of the 2004 Regulations] and regulation 6(3) of the 1974 Regulations shall not apply to any document issued with respect to uncertificated units of a public sector security.

(4)   Any requirement in or under any enactment to endorse any statement or information on a certificate evidencing title to a unit of a security—

    (a)   shall not prohibit the conversion into, or issue of, units of the security in uncertificated form; and

    (b)   in relation to uncertificated units of the security, shall be taken to be a requirement for the relevant participating issuer to provide the holder of the units with the statement or information on request by him.

(5)   Sections 53(1)(c) and 136 of the Law of Property Act 1925 (which impose requirements for certain dispositions and assignments to be in writing) shall not apply (if they would otherwise do so) to—

    (a)   any transfer of title to uncertificated units of a security by means of a relevant system; and

    (b)   any disposition or assignment of an interest in uncertificated units of a security title to which is held by a relevant nominee.

(6)   In paragraph (5) "relevant nominee" means a subsidiary undertaking of an Operator designated by him as a relevant nominee in accordance with such rules and practices as are mentioned in paragraph 25(f) of Schedule 1.

(7)   [Section 772 of the 2006 Act] shall not apply in relation to the transfer of uncertificated units of a security by means of a relevant system.

NOTES

   Para (3): words in first pair of square brackets substituted by the Companies Act 2006 (Consequential Amendments) (Uncertificated Securities) Order 2009, SI 2009/1889, art 2(1), (16)(a), as from 1 October 2009; words in second pair of square brackets substituted by the Government Stock (Consequential and Transitional Provision) (No 2) Order 2004, SI 2004/1662, art 2, Schedule, Pt 3, para 29(1), (4), as from 1 July 2004.

   Para (7): words in square brackets substituted by SI 2009/1889, art 2(1), (16)(b), as from 1 October 2009.

[6.80]
39   Fees charged by Operators

(1)   Subject to paragraph (2), nothing in these Regulations prevents an Operator from charging a fee for carrying out any function under Part 3 of these Regulations.

(2)   An Operator may not charge a fee to a participating issuer for maintaining or keeping and entering up an Operator register of securities.

[6.81]
40   Trusts, trustees and personal representatives etc

(1)   Unless expressly prohibited from transferring units of a security by means of any computer-based system, a trustee or personal representative shall not be chargeable with a breach of trust or, as the case may be, with default in administering the estate by reason only of the fact that—

    (a)   for the purpose of acquiring units of a security which he has the power to acquire in connection with the trust or estate, he has paid for the units under arrangements which provide for them to be transferred to him from a system-member but not to be so transferred until after the payment of the price;

    (b)   for the purpose of disposing of units of a security which he has power to dispose of in connection with the trust or estate, he has transferred the units to a system-member under arrangements which provide that the price is not to be paid to him until after the transfer is made; or

    (c)   for the purpose of holding units of a security belonging to the trust or estate in uncertificated form and for transferring title to them by means of a relevant system, he has become a system-member.

(2)   Notwithstanding [sections 750 and 751 of the 2006 Act], a trustee of a trust deed for securing an issue of debentures shall not be chargeable with a breach of trust by reason only of the fact that he has assented to an amendment of the trust deed only for the purposes of—

    (a)   allowing the holding of debentures in uncertificated form;

    (b)   allowing the exercise of rights attaching to the debentures by means of a relevant system; or

    (c)   allowing the transfer of title to the debentures by means of a relevant system, provided that he has given or caused to be given notice of the amendment in accordance with the trust deed not less than 30 days prior to its becoming effective to all persons registered as holding the debentures on a date not more than 21 days before the dispatch of the notice.

(3)   Without prejudice to regulation 23(3) or [section 126 of the 2006 Act], the Operator shall not be bound by or compelled to recognise any express, implied or constructive trust or other interest in respect of uncertificated units of a security, even if he has actual or constructive notice of the said trust or interest.

(4)   Paragraph (3) shall not prevent, in the case of a participating issuer constituted under the law of Scotland, an Operator giving notice of a trust to the participating issuer on behalf of a system-member.

NOTES

Paras (2), (3): words in square brackets substituted by the Companies Act 2006 (Consequential Amendments) (Uncertificated Securities) Order 2009, SI 2009/1889, art 2(1), (17), as from 1 October 2009.

[6.82]
41 Notices of meetings etc

(1) For the purposes of determining which persons are entitled to attend or vote at a meeting, and how many votes such persons may cast, the participating issuer may specify in the notice of the meeting a time, not more than 48 hours before the time fixed for the meeting, by which a person must be entered on the relevant register of securities in order to have the right to attend or vote at the meeting.

(2) Changes to entries on the relevant register of securities after the time specified by virtue of paragraph (1) shall be disregarded in determining the rights of any person to attend or vote at the meeting, notwithstanding any provisions in any enactment, articles of association or other instrument to the contrary.

(3) For the purposes of—
   (a) serving notices of meetings, whether under [section 310(1) of the 2006 Act], any other enactment, a provision in the articles of association or any other instrument; or
   (b) sending copies of the documents required to be sent to any person by [section 423(1) of the 2006 Act],
a participating issuer may determine that persons entitled to receive such notices, or copies of such documents (as the case may be), are those persons entered on the relevant register of securities at the close of business on a day determined by him.

(4) The day determined by a participating issuer under paragraph (3) may not be more than 21 days before the day that the notices of the meeting, or the copies of the documents as the case may be, are sent.

(5) This regulation is without prejudice to the protection afforded—
   (a) by paragraph 5(3) of Schedule 4, to a participating issuer which is a company; and
   (b) by paragraph 13(4) or 15(3) of Schedule 4, to a participating issuer.

[(6) In calculating the period mentioned in paragraph (1) above no account shall be taken of any part of a day that is not a working day.]

NOTES

Para (3): words in square brackets substituted by the Companies Act 2006 (Consequential Amendments) (Uncertificated Securities) Order 2009, SI 2009/1889, art 2(1), (18)(a), (b), as from 1 October 2009.
Para (6): added by SI 2009/1889, art 2(1), (18)(c), as from 1 October 2009.

[6.83]
42 Notices to minority shareholders

(1) Paragraphs (2) to (4) shall apply in relation to any uncertificated units of a security (other than a wholly dematerialised security) to which a notice given under [section 979 of the [2006 Act]] relates, in place of the provisions of [section 981(7)] of that Act.

(2) Immediately on receipt of a copy sent under [section 981(6)(a) of the [2006 Act]] of a notice given under [section 979] relating to uncertificated units of a participating security (whether or not it also relates to certificated units of the security), a company which is a participating issuer shall—
   (a) by issuer-instruction—
      (i) inform the Operator that the copy notice has been received, and
      (ii) identify the holding of uncertificated units of the participating security to which the notice relates; and
   (b) enter the name of the relevant system-member on an issuer register of securities as the holder of those uncertificated units.

(3) On receipt of an issuer-instruction under paragraph (2)(a), the Operator shall delete any entry in an Operator register of securities which shows the relevant system-member as the holder of the uncertificated units of the participating security to which the notice relates.

(4) On registration on an issuer register of securities (in accordance with paragraph (2)(b)) of the relevant system-member as the holder of the uncertificated units of the participating security to which the notice relates, the participating issuer—
   (a) shall be under the same obligation to enter the offeror on that register as the holder of those units, in place of the relevant system-member, as it would be if it had received an Operator-instruction under regulation 28(2) requiring it to register a transfer of title to those units in that manner; and regulation 28(9) shall have effect accordingly; and
   (b) where the terms of issue of the security in question provide for a certificate to be issued, shall issue to the offeror a certificate in respect of those units.

(5) [Subsection (1) of section 776 of the 2006 Act] shall apply in relation to the issue of a certificate by a participating issuer pursuant to paragraph (4)(b) as it applies in relation to the completion and having ready for delivery by a company of share certificates, debentures or

certificates of debenture stock; and in that subsection as it so applies the reference to the date on which a transfer is lodged with the company shall be a reference to the date on which the participating issuer receives the copy notice sent under [section 981(6)(a) of the [2006 Act]].

(6)   Such sanctions as apply to a company and its officers in the event of a default in complying with [subsection (1) of section 776 of the 2006 Act] shall apply to a participating issuer and his officers in the event of a default in complying with paragraph (4)(b) in accordance with the requirements laid down in paragraph (5).

(7)   Paragraphs (8) to (11) shall apply in relation to any units of a wholly dematerialised security to which a notice given under [section 979 of the [2006 Act]] relates, in place of the provisions of [section 981(7)] of that Act.

(8)   Immediately on receipt of a copy sent under [section 981(6)(a) of the [2006 Act]] of a notice given under [section 979] relating to units of a wholly dematerialised security, a company which is a participating issuer shall—

(a)   by issuer-instruction—
    (i)   inform the Operator that the copy notice has been received; and
    (ii)   identify the holding of units of the wholly dematerialised security to which the notice relates; and

(b)   by a further issuer-instruction, inform the Operator of the name of the transferee.

(9)   On receipt of an issuer-instruction under paragraph (8)(a), the Operator shall delete any entry in an Operator register of securities which shows the relevant system-member as the holder of the units to which the notice relates.

(10)   On receipt of an issuer-instruction under paragraph (8)(b), the Operator shall enter the transferee on the relevant Operator register of securities as the holder of the units to which the notice relates, in place of the relevant system-member.

(11)   Where an Operator deletes an entry in an Operator register of securities pursuant to paragraph (9)—

(a)   the units of the wholly dematerialised security to which the notice relates shall notwithstanding that deletion, continue to be regarded as uncertificated units for the purposes of these Regulations until the Operator enters the transferee on the relevant Operator register of securities as the holder of those units;

(b)   subject to—
    (i)   subparagraph (c) or (d), as the case may be; and
    (ii)   any enactment or rule of law,
    the relevant system-member shall, notwithstanding that deletion, retain title to the units of the wholly dematerialised security to which the notice relates until the transferee is entered on the relevant Operator register of securities pursuant to paragraph (10);

(c)   in the case of a security constituted under the law of England and Wales or Northern Ireland, the transferee shall acquire an equitable interest in the units of the wholly dematerialised security to which the notice relates;

(d)   in the case of a security constituted under the law of Scotland, the relevant system-member shall hold the units of the wholly dematerialised security to which the notice relates on trust for the benefit of the transferee.

(12)   Such sanctions as apply to a company and its officers in the event of a default in complying with [subsections (1) and (2) of section 771 of the 2006 Act] shall apply—

(a)   to a participating issuer and his officers in the event of a default in complying with paragraph (2)(b) or (8); and

(b)   to an Operator and his officers in the event of a default in complying with paragraph (3), (9) or (10).

(13)   For the purposes of this regulation—

(a)   "offeror" has the meaning [in section 991(1) of the [2006 Act];]

(b)   "relevant system-member" means the system-member identified in the copy notice sent under [section 981(6)(a) of the [2006 Act]] as the holder of the uncertificated units, or as the case may be the units of the wholly dematerialised security, to which the notice relates; and

(c)   "transferee" means the offeror or, if the offeror is not a system-member, the system-member in whose name the units of the wholly dematerialised security to which the notice given under [section 979 of the [2006 Act]] relates are to be registered on the Operator register of securities.

(14)   The reference in [section 987(8) of the [2006 Act] to section 981(7)] shall be taken to include a reference to the provisions of paragraphs (4), (8) and (9).

NOTES

Paras (1), (2), (7), (8), (13), (14): words "2006 Act" in square brackets substituted by the Companies Act 2006 (Consequential Amendments) (Uncertificated Securities) Order 2009, SI 2009/1889, art 2(1), (19)(a), as from 1 October 2009; other words in square brackets substituted by the Companies Act 2006 (Commencement No 2, Consequential Amendments, Transitional Provisions and Savings) Order 2007, SI 2007/1093, art 6(1), Sch 3, para 9, as from 6 April 2007.

Para (5): words in first pair of square brackets and third (inner) pair of square brackets substituted by SI 2009/1889, art 2(1), (19)(a), (b), as from 1 October 2009; words in second(outer) pair of square brackets substituted by the Companies Act 2006 (Commencement No 2, Consequential Amendments, Transitional Provisions and Savings) Order 2007, SI 2007/1093, art 6(1), Sch 3, para 9, as from 6 April 2007.

Paras (6), (12): words in square brackets substituted by SI 2009/1889, art 2(1), (19)(c), (d), as from 1 October 2009.

[6.84]
43 Irrevocable powers of attorney

(1) This regulation applies where the terms of an offer for all or any uncertificated units of a participating security provide that a person accepting the offer creates an irrevocable power of attorney in favour of the offeror, or a person nominated by the offeror, in the terms set out in the offer.

(2) An acceptance communicated by properly authenticated dematerialised instruction in respect of uncertificated units of a security shall constitute a grant of an irrevocable power of attorney by the system-member accepting the offer in favour of the offeror, or person nominated by the offeror, in the terms set out in the offer.

(3) Where the contract constituted by such offer and acceptance as are referred to in paragraphs (1) and (2) respectively is governed by the law of England and Wales, section 4 of the Powers of Attorney Act 1971 shall apply to a power of attorney constituted in accordance with this regulation.

(4) A declaration in writing by the offeror stating the terms of a power of attorney and that it has been granted by virtue of this regulation and stating the name and address of the grantor shall be prima facie evidence, and in Scotland sufficient evidence unless the contrary is shown, of the grant; and any requirement in any enactment, rule of law, or instrument to produce a copy of the power of attorney, or such a copy certified in a particular manner, shall be satisfied by the production of the declaration or a copy of the declaration certified in that manner.

(5) In the application of this regulation to an offer, acceptance or contract governed by the law of Scotland, any reference to an irrevocable power of attorney shall mean and include reference to an irrevocable mandate, however expressed.

[6.85]
44 Actual notice

For the purpose of determining under these Regulations whether a person has actual notice of a fact, matter or thing that person shall not under any circumstances be taken to be concerned to establish whether or not it exists or has occurred.

[6.86]
45 Participating securities issued in uncertificated form

Nothing in these Regulations shall require—
   (a)   a participating issuer or its officers to maintain a register which records how many units of a wholly dematerialised security are held in certificated form; or
   (b)   an Operator or participating issuer, or their officers, to take any action to change a unit of a wholly dematerialised security from uncertificated form to certificated form or vice versa.

Defaults and Contraventions

[6.87]
46 Breaches of statutory duty

(1) A default in complying with, or a contravention of, regulation 16(8), 19(2), 25(1), 26, 28(5) or (6), 32(5), 33(5), or 42(2) or (8) shall be actionable at the suit of a person who suffers loss as a result of the default or contravention, or who is otherwise adversely affected by it, subject to the defences and other incidents applying to actions for breach of statutory duty.

(2) Paragraph (1) shall not affect the liability which any person may incur, nor affect any right which any person may have, apart from paragraph (1).

[6.88]
47 Liability of officers for contraventions

(1) In regulation 16(7), 20(7), 21(5), 22(5), 28(9), 32(9) or (10), 33(11) or 42(6) or (12) an officer of a participating issuer shall be in default in complying with, or in contravention of, the provision mentioned in that regulation if, and only if, he knowingly and wilfully authorised or permitted the default or contravention.

(2) In regulation 20(7), 21(4), 22(4), 27(9), 32(9), 33(11) or 42(12) an officer of an Operator shall be in default in complying with, or in contravention of, the provision mentioned in that regulation if, and only if, he knowingly and wilfully authorised or permitted the default or contravention.

[6.89]
48 Exemption from liability

Regulations 21(5), 28(9), 32(9) and (10), and 33(11) shall not apply to any of the following or its officers—

(a)   the Crown;
(b)   any person acting on behalf of the Crown;
[(c)   the Bank of England;
(d)   the Registrar of Government Stock;
(e)   any previous Registrar of Government Stock; or
(f)   in respect of a security which immediately before it became a participating security was transferable by exempt transfer within the meaning of the Stock Transfer Act 1982, a participating issuer].

NOTES

Paras (c)–(f) substituted, for original paras (c), (d), by the Government Stock (Consequential and Transitional Provision) (No 2) Order 2004, SI 2004/1662, art 2, Schedule, Pt 3, para 29(1), (5), as from 1 July 2004.

49   *(Reg 49 (Application to Northern Ireland) outside the scope of this work.)*

Transitory Provisions, Amendments and Revocations

[6.90]
50   Transitory provisions
Schedule 6 (transitory provisions) shall have effect.

[6.91]
51   Minor and consequential amendments
Schedule 7 (minor and consequential amendments) shall have effect.

52   *(Revokes the Government Stock Regulations 1965, SI 1965/1420, regs 4(3), (4), 4A, 4B, 6(5), 17(7), 18(5), 19(2), 20(2), Sch 1, the Local Authority (Stocks and Bonds) Regulations 1974, SI 1974/519, reg 6(6), 6A, 7(1)(b), (4), (5), 8(2), (3), 9(4), 10(3), 16(4), 21(3), Sch 2, the Uncertificated Securities Regulations 1995, SI 1995/3272, the Open-Ended Investment Companies Regulations 2001, SI 2001/1228, reg 47(1), Sch 3, paras 2(2), 5(1)(c), 6(3)(d), Sch 4, para 3, Sch 7, para 12.)*

SCHEDULES

SCHEDULE 1
REQUIREMENTS FOR APPROVAL OF A PERSON AS OPERATOR
Regulation 5(1)

Arrangements and resources

[6.92]
1. An Operator must have adequate arrangements and resources for the effective monitoring and enforcement of compliance with his rules or, as respects monitoring, arrangements providing for that function to be performed on his behalf (and without affecting his responsibility) by another body or person who is able and willing to perform it.

Financial resources

2. An Operator must have financial resources sufficient for the proper performance of his functions as an Operator.

Promotion and maintenance of standards

3. An Operator must be able and willing to promote and maintain high standards of integrity and fair dealing in the operation of the relevant system and to cooperate, by the sharing of information or otherwise, with the Treasury and any other authority, body or person having responsibility for the supervision or regulation of investment business or other financial services.

Operation of the relevant system

4. (1)   Except in the circumstances referred to in subparagraph (2), where an Operator causes or permits a part of the relevant system which is not the Operator-system to be operated by another person (other than as his agent) the Operator—
(a)   shall monitor compliance by the person and that part with the requirements of this Schedule; and
(b)   shall have arrangements to ensure that the person provides him with such information and such assistance as he may require in order to meet his obligations under these Regulations.

(2)   Where a part of the relevant system which is not the Operator-system comprises procedures which enable dematerialised instructions to be authenticated in accordance with paragraph 5(3)(b), the Operator shall have arrangements to ensure that he is provided with such information and such assistance as he may require in order to keep under review his agreement to the specifications by which those dematerialised instructions may be authenticated.

System security

5. (1) A relevant system must be so constructed and operate in such a way that it satisfies the requirements of subparagraphs (2) to (6).

(2) The relevant system must minimise the possibility of unauthorised access to, or modification of, any program or data held in any computer forming part of the Operator-system.

(3) Each dematerialised instruction must be authenticated—
- (a) in accordance with the specifications of the Operator, and those specifications shall provide that each dematerialised instruction—
  - (i) is identifiable as being from the computers of the Operator or of a particular system-participant; and
  - (ii) is designed to minimise fraud and forgery; or
- (b) if it is sent to the Operator by, or by the Operator to, a depositary, a clearing house or an exchange, in accordance with specifications of that depositary, clearing house or exchange to which the Operator has agreed and which provide that each dematerialised instruction—
  - (i) is identifiable as being from the computers of the Operator or of the depositary, clearing house or exchange which sent it; and
  - (ii) is designed to minimise fraud and forgery.

(4) Each dematerialised instruction must, in accordance with any relevant rules of the Operator and with the specifications of the Operator or the specifications referred to in subparagraph (3)(b) (as the case may be), express by whom it has been sent and, where relevant, on whose behalf it has been sent.

(5) Each dematerialised instruction must, in accordance with any relevant rules of the Operator and with the specifications of the Operator or the specifications referred to in subparagraph (3)(b) (as the case may be), indicate—
- (a) where it is sent to a system-participant or the Operator, that it is addressed to that system-participant or the Operator;
- (b) where it is sent to a person who is using the facilities of a sponsoring system-participant to receive dematerialised instructions, that it is addressed to that person and the sponsoring system-participant; and
- (c) where it is sent to the Operator in order for him to send an Operator-instruction to a system-participant, that it is addressed to the Operator, to the system-participant and, if the system-participant is acting as a sponsoring system-participant, to the relevant person on whose behalf the sponsoring system-participant receives dematerialised instructions; and

(6) The relevant system must minimise the possibility for a system-participant to send a dematerialised instruction on behalf of a person from whom he has no authority.

(7) For the purposes of this paragraph—
"clearing house" means a body or association—
- (a) which is a recognised clearing house within section 285(1)(b) of the 2000 Act;
- (b) which is authorised under that Act to provide clearing services in the United Kingdom; or
- (c) which provides services outside the United Kingdom which are similar in nature to those provided by any such body or association, and which is regulated or supervised in the provision of those services by a regulatory body or agency of government;

"depositary" means a body or association carrying on business outside the United Kingdom with whom an Operator has made arrangements—
- (a) to enable system-members to hold (whether directly or indirectly) and transfer title to securities (other than participating securities) by means of facilities provided by that body or association; or
- (b) to enable that body or association to permit persons to whom it provides services in the course of its business to hold (whether directly or indirectly) and transfer title to participating securities by means of the Operator's relevant system; and

"exchange" means a body or association—
- (a) which is a recognised investment exchange within section 285(1)(a) of the 2000 Act;
- (b) which is authorised under that Act to provide a facility for the matching and execution of transactions in securities in the United Kingdom; or
- (c) which provides services outside the United Kingdom which are similar in nature to those provided by any such body or association, and which is regulated or supervised in the provision of those services by a regulatory body or agency of government.

System capabilities

6. A relevant system must ensure that the Operator-system can send and respond to properly authenticated dematerialised instructions in sufficient volume and speed.

7. Before an Operator registers a transfer of title to uncertificated units of a security, a relevant system must be able to establish—

(a)   that the transferor has title to such number of units of the security as is in aggregate at least equal to the number to be transferred; or

(b)   that the transfer is one of two or more transfers which may be registered in accordance with regulation 30(2).

8. Before an Operator-instruction to a participating issuer to register a transfer of title to uncertificated units of a security is generated, a relevant system must be able to establish that the transferor has title to such number of units of the security as is in aggregate at least equal to the number to be transferred.

9. A relevant system must enable an Operator to comply with his obligations to keep all necessary Operator registers of securities in accordance with these Regulations.

10. A relevant system must maintain adequate records of all dematerialised instructions.

11. A relevant system must—
(a)   enable each system-member to obtain a copy of any records relating to him as are maintained by the relevant system in order to comply with paragraph 7(a), 8 or 10; and
(b)   be able to make correcting entries in such records as are maintained in order to comply with paragraph 7(a) or 8 which are inaccurate.

12. A relevant system must be able to permit each participating issuer to inspect the entries from time to time appearing in an Operator register of securities [(other than an Operator register of eligible debt securities)] relating to any participating security issued by him.

13. A relevant system must be able to establish, where there is a transfer of uncertificated units of a security to a system-member for value, that a settlement bank has agreed to make payment in respect of the transfer, whether alone or taken together with another transfer for value.

14. A relevant system must ensure that the Operator-system is able to generate Operator-instructions—
(a)   requiring participating issuers to amend the appropriate issuer registers of securities kept by them;
(b)   informing participating issuers in a way which enables them to amend the appropriate records of securities kept by them; and
(c)   informing settlement banks of their payment obligations.

15. A relevant system must—
(a)   enable a system-member—
    (i)   to grant authority to a sponsoring system-participant to send properly authenticated dematerialised instructions on his behalf; and
    (ii)   to limit such authority by reference to the net value of the units of the securities to be transferred in any one day; and
(b)   prevent the transfer of units in excess of that limit.

16. For the purposes of paragraph 15(a)(ii), once authority is granted pursuant to a system charge (within the meaning of regulation 3 of the Financial Markets and Insolvency Regulations 1996) a limit of such authority shall not be imposed or changed without the consent of the donee of that authority.

17. Nothing in paragraph 15 or 16 shall be taken, in respect of an authority, to modify or derogate from the protections given by or under any enactment to a donee of the authority or a third person.

18. A relevant system must enable system-members—
(a)   to change the form in which they hold units of a participating security; and
(b)   where appropriate, to require participating issuers to issue certificates relating to units of a participating security held or to be held by them.

19. Paragraph 18 shall not apply to any wholly dematerialised security.

Operating procedures

20. A relevant system must comprise procedures which provide that it responds only to properly authenticated dematerialised instructions which are attributable to a system-user or an Operator.

21. (1)   Subject to subparagraphs (2) to (5), a relevant system must comprise procedures which provide that an Operator only registers a transfer of title to uncertificated units of a security or generates an Operator-instruction requiring a participating issuer to register such a transfer, and only generates an Operator-instruction informing a settlement bank of its payment obligations in respect of such a transfer, if—
(a)   it has—
    (i)   received a system-member instruction which is attributable to the transferor; or
    (ii)   been required to do so by a court in the United Kingdom or by or under an enactment;

(b)   it has—
  (i)   established that the transferor has title to such number of units as is in aggregate at least equal to the number to be transferred; or
  (ii)   established that the transfer is one of two or more transfers which may be registered in accordance with regulation 30(2);
(c)   in the case of a transfer to a system-member for value, it has established that a settlement bank has agreed to make payment in respect of the transfer, whether alone or taken together with another transfer for value; and
(d)   the transfer is not in excess of any limit which by virtue of paragraph 15(a)(ii) the transferor has set on an authority given by him to a sponsoring system-participant.

(2)   Subparagraph (1)(a) shall not prevent the registration by an Operator of a transfer of title to uncertificated units of a security, or the generation of an Operator-instruction, in accordance with procedures agreed between the Operator and the transferor to enable the transfer by means of a relevant system of uncertificated units of a security provided that such transfer is for the purpose of, or relates to, facilitating the provision of financial credit or financial liquidity to the transferor by a settlement bank, the Bank of England, the European Central Bank, any other central bank, or any other body having functions as a monetary authority.

(3)   A relevant system must comprise procedures which provide that—
  (a)   the Operator may amend an Operator register of securities; and
  (b)   an Operator-instruction requiring a participating issuer to register a transfer of uncertificated units of a security, or informing a settlement bank of its payment obligations in respect of such a transfer, may be generated,
if necessary to correct an error and if in accordance with the rules made and practices instituted by the Operator in order to comply with this Schedule.

(4)   A relevant system must comprise procedures which provide that—
  (a)   the Operator may amend an Operator register of securities; and
  (b)   an Operator-instruction requiring a participating issuer to register a transfer of units of a wholly dematerialised security, or informing a settlement bank of its payment obligations in respect of such a transfer, may be generated,
if necessary to effect a transfer of such units, on the termination of participation in the relevant system by the system-member by whom those units are held and if in accordance with the rules made and practices instituted by the Operator in order to comply with this Schedule, to a person nominated under the Operator's rules.

(5)   Subparagraph (1)(a) shall not prevent the registration by an Operator of a transfer of title to uncertificated units of a security, or the generation of an Operator-instruction, in order to give effect to the procedures referred to in subparagraph (3) or (4).

22. (1)   Subject to subparagraph (2), a relevant system must comprise procedures which provide that an Operator-instruction to a participating issuer relating to a right, privilege or benefit attaching to or arising from an uncertificated unit of a security, is generated only if it has—
  (a)   received a properly authenticated dematerialised instruction attributable to the system-member having the right, privilege or benefit requiring the Operator to generate an Operator-instruction to the participating issuer; or
  (b)   been required to do so by a court in the United Kingdom or by or under an enactment.

(2)   A relevant system must comprise procedures which provide that an Operator-instruction to a participating issuer relating to a right, privilege or benefit attaching to or arising from an uncertificated unit of a security, may be generated if necessary to correct an error and if in accordance with the rules made and practices instituted by an Operator in order to comply with this Schedule.

23. A relevant system must comprise procedures which ensure that, where participating issuers keep records of securities, those records are regularly reconciled with the relevant Operator registers of securities.

24. A relevant system must comprise procedures which—
  (a)   enable system-users to notify the Operator of an error in or relating to a dematerialised instruction; and
  (b)   ensure that, where the Operator becomes aware of an error in or relating to a dematerialised instruction, he takes appropriate corrective action.

Rules and Practices

25. An Operator's rules and practices—
  (a)   must bind system-members and participating issuers—
  (i)   so as to ensure the efficient processing of transfers of title to uncertificated units of a security in response to Operator-instructions; and
  (ii)   as to the action to be taken where transfer of title in response to a system-member instruction or an Operator-instruction cannot be effected;

(b)   must make provision as to the manner in which a system-member or the relevant participating issuer may change the form in which that system-member holds units of a participating security (other than a wholly dematerialised security);

(c)   must make provision for a participating issuer to cease to participate in respect of a participating security so as—

    (i)   to minimise so far as practicable any disruption to system-members in respect of their ability to transfer the relevant security; and

    (ii)   to provide the participating issuer with any relevant information held by the Operator relating to the uncertificated units of the relevant security held by system-members;

(d)   must make provision for the orderly termination of participation by system-members and system-participants whose participation is disruptive to other system-members or system-participants or to participating issuers;

(e)   must make provision—

    (i)   as to which of the Operator's records are to constitute an Operator register of securities in relation to a participating security, or a participating security of a particular kind; and

    (ii)   as to the times at which, and the manner in which, a participating issuer may inspect an Operator register of securities [(other than an Operator register of eligible debt securities)] in accordance with paragraph 12;

(f)   if they make provision for the designation of a subsidiary undertaking as a relevant nominee, must require that the relevant nominee maintain adequate records of—

    (i)   the names of the persons who have an interest in the securities it holds; and

    (ii)   the nature and extent of their interests; and

(g)   must make provision for the authentication by the Operator of any written notification given under regulation 25(3) or 32(2)(c).

26. An Operator's rules and practices must require—

(a)   that each system-participant is able to send and receive properly authenticated dematerialised instructions;

(b)   that each system-member has arrangements—

    (i)   for properly authenticated dematerialised instructions attributable to him to be sent;

    (ii)   for properly authenticated dematerialised instructions to be received by or for him; and

    (iii)   with a settlement bank for payments to be made, where appropriate, for units of a security transferred by means of the relevant system; and

(c)   that each participating issuer is able to respond with sufficient speed to Operator-instructions.

27. An Operator must have rules which require system-users and former system-users to provide him with such information in their possession as he may require in order to meet his obligations under these Regulations.

[Access to central counterparty, clearing and settlement facilities

28. (1) The Operator must make transparent and non-discriminatory rules, based on objective criteria, governing access to his settlement facilities.

(2)   The rules under sub-paragraph (1) must enable an investment firm or a credit institution authorised by the competent authority of another EEA State (including a branch established in the United Kingdom of such a firm or institution) to have access to those facilities on the same terms as a UK firm for the purposes of finalising or arranging the finalisation of transactions in financial instruments.

(3)   The Operator may refuse access to those facilities on legitimate commercial grounds.

(4)   In this paragraph—

"banking consolidation directive" means Directive 2006/48/EC of the European Parliament and of the Council of 14th June 2006 relating to the taking up and pursuit of the business of credit institutions [as last amended by Directive 2009/111 of the European Parliament and of the Council];

"branch" in relation to an investment firm has the meaning given in Article 4.1.26 of the markets in financial instruments directive and in relation to a credit institution has the meaning given in Article 4.3 of the banking consolidation directive;

"competent authority", in relation to an investment firm or credit institution, means the competent authority in relation to that firm or institution for the purposes of the markets in financial instruments directive;

"credit institution" means—

(a)   a credit institution authorised under the banking consolidation directive, or

(b)   an institution which would satisfy the requirements for authorisation as a credit institution under that directive if it had its registered office (or if it does not have a registered office, its head office) in an EEA State;

"EEA State" has the meaning given by paragraph 8 of Schedule 3 to the 2000 Act;

"financial instrument" has the meaning given by Article 4.1.17 of the markets in financial instruments directive;

"investment firm" has the meaning given by section 424A of the 2000 Act;

"markets in financial instruments directive" means Directive 2004/39/EC of the European Parliament and of the Council of 21st April 2004 on markets in financial instruments;

"regulated activity" has the meaning given by section 22 of the 2000 Act;

"settlement" has the same meaning as in the markets in financial instruments directive;

"UK firm" means an investment firm or credit institution which has a permission given by the Authority under Part 4 of the 2000 Act (or having effect as if so given) to carry on one or more regulated activities.]

NOTES

Paras 12, 25: words in square brackets inserted by the Uncertificated Securities (Amendment) (Eligible Debt Securities) Regulations 2003, SI 2003/1633, reg 12, as from 24 June 2003.

Para 28: added by the Uncertificated Securities (Amendment) Regulations 2007, SI 2007/124, reg 3, as from 1 November 2007; words in square brackets in the definition "banking consolidation directive" in sub-para (4) inserted by the Capital Requirements (Amendment) Regulations 2010, SI 2010/2628, regs 2, 14, Sch 2, para 4(a), as from 31 December 2010.

SCHEDULE 2
PREVENTION OF RESTRICTIVE PRACTICES

Regulation 13

Examination of rules and practices

[6.93]

1. (1) The Treasury shall not approve a person as Operator of a relevant system unless they are satisfied that the rules and any guidance of which copies are furnished with the application for approval—

(a) do not have, and are not intended or likely to have, to any significant extent the effect of restricting, distorting or preventing competition; or

(b) if they have or are intended to have that effect to any significant extent, that the effect is not greater than is necessary for the protection of investors, or for compliance with [Directive 2006/48/EC of the European Parliament and of the Council of 14 June 2006 relating to the taking up and pursuit of the business of credit institutions] [as last amended by Directive 2009/111/EC of the European Parliament and of the Council].

(2) Subject to subparagraph (5), the powers conferred by subparagraph (3) shall be exercisable by the Treasury if at any time it appears to them that—

(a) any rules made or guidance issued by an Operator;

(b) any practices of an Operator in his capacity as such; or

(c) any practices of a system-user,

have, or are intended or likely to have, to a significant extent the effect of restricting, distorting or preventing competition and that the effect is greater than is necessary for the protection of investors or for compliance with [Directive 2006/48/EC] of the European Parliament and of the Council.

(3) the powers exercisable under this paragraph are—

(a) to withdraw approval from the Operator;

(b) to direct the Operator to take specified steps for the purpose of securing that the rules, guidance or practices in question do not have the effect mentioned in subparagraph (2); or

(c) to make alterations in the rules of the Operator for that purpose.

(4) The practices referred to in subparagraph (2)(c) are practices in relation to business in respect of which system-users are subject to the rules of the Operator and which are required or contemplated by his rules or guidance or otherwise attributable to his conduct in his capacity as Operator.

(5) The provisions of Schedule 3 shall apply as regards the procedure to be followed before—

(a) refusing to approve a person as Operator of a relevant system pursuant to subparagraph (1); or

(b) exercising any of the powers conferred by subparagraph (3).

Modification of paragraph 1 where delegation order is made

2. (1) This paragraph applies instead of paragraph 1 where the function of approving a person as Operator has been delegated to the designated agency by virtue of regulation 11.

(2) The designated agency—

(a) shall send to the Treasury a copy of the rules and any guidance copies of which accompany the application for approval together with any other information supplied with or in connection with the application; and

(b) shall not grant the approval without the leave of the Treasury,

and the Treasury shall not give leave in any case in which they would (apart from the delegation of functions to the designated agency) have been precluded by paragraph 1(1) from granting approval.

(3) The designated agency shall send to the Treasury a copy of any notice received by it from an Operator under regulation 10(5).

(4)   If at any time it appears to the Treasury that there are circumstances such that (apart from the delegation of functions to the designated agency) they would have been able to exercise any of the powers conferred by paragraph 1(3) they may, notwithstanding the delegation of functions to the designated agency but subject to paragraph 1(5)—

(a)   themselves exercise the power conferred by paragraph 1(3)(a); or

(b)   direct the designated agency to exercise the power conferred by paragraph 1(3)(b) or (c) in such manner as they may specify.

(5)   The provisions of Schedule 3 shall apply as regards the procedure to be followed before the Treasury exercise their power to refuse leave under subparagraph (2), or their power to give a direction under subparagraph (4), in respect of an Operator.

Reports by the [Office of Fair Trading]

3. (1)   The Treasury shall before deciding—

(a)   whether to refuse to approve a person as Operator of a relevant system pursuant to paragraph 1(1); or

(b)   whether to refuse for the granting of an approval pursuant to paragraph 2(2),

send to the [Office of Fair Trading (in this Schedule referred to as "the OFT")] a copy of the rules and of any guidance which the Treasury are required to consider in making that decision together with such other information as the Treasury consider will assist in discharging [its] functions under subparagraph (2).

(2)   The [OFT] shall report to the Treasury whether, in [its] opinion, the rules and guidance copies of which are sent to [it] under subparagraph (1) have, or are intended or likely to have, to any significant extent the effect of restricting, distorting or preventing competition and, if so, what that effect is likely to be; and in making any decision as is mentioned in subparagraph (1) the Treasury shall have regard to the [OFT's] report.

(3)   The Treasury shall send to the [OFT] copies of any notice received by them under regulation 10(5) or paragraph 2(3) together with such other information as the Treasury consider will assist the [OFT] in discharging [its] functions under subparagraphs (4) and (5).

(4)   The [OFT] shall keep under review—

(a)   the rules, guidance and practices mentioned in paragraph 1(2); and

(b)   the matters specified in the notices of which copies are sent to [it] under subparagraph (3),

and if at any time [it] is of the opinion that any such rules or guidance taken together with any such matters, have, or are intended or likely to have, to any significant extent the effect mentioned in subparagraph (2), [it] shall report [its] opinion to the Treasury stating what in [its] opinion that effect is or is likely to be.

(5)   The [OFT] may report to the Treasury [its] opinion that any such matter as is mentioned in subparagraph (4)(b) does not in [its] opinion have, and is not intended or likely to have, to any significant extent the effect mentioned in subparagraph (2).

(6)   The [OFT] may from time to time consider whether any such practices as are mentioned in paragraph 1(2) have, or are intended or likely to have, to any significant extent the effect mentioned in subparagraph (2) and, if so, what that effect is or is likely to be; and if [it] is of that opinion [it] shall make a report to the Treasury stating [its] opinion and what the effect is or is likely to be.

(7)   The Treasury shall not exercise their powers under paragraph 1(3) or 2(4) except after receiving a report from the [OFT] under subparagraph (4) or (6).

(8)   The [OFT] may, if [it] thinks fit, publish any report made by [it] under this paragraph but shall exclude from a published report, so far as practicable, any matter which relates to the affairs of a particular person (other than the person seeking approval as an Operator) the publication of which would or might in [its] opinion seriously and prejudicially affect the interests of that person.

Investigations by the [Office of Fair Trading]

4. (1)   For the purpose of investigating any matter with a view to [its] consideration under paragraph 3 the [OFT] may by a notice in writing—

(a)   require any person to produce, at any time and place specified in the notice, to the [OFT] or to any person appointed by [it] for the purpose, any documents which are specified or described in the notice and which are documents in his custody or under his control and relating to any matter relevant to the investigation; or

(b)   require any person carrying on business to furnish to the [OFT] such information as may be specified or described in the notice, and specify the time within which, and the manner and form in which, any such information is to be furnished.

(2)   A person shall not under this paragraph be required to produce any document or disclose any information which he would be entitled to refuse to produce or disclose on grounds of legal professional privilege in proceedings in the High Court or on grounds of confidentiality as between client and professional legal adviser proceedings in the Court of Session.

(3)   . . .

[Enforcement

4A. (1)   The court may, on an application by the OFT, enquire into whether any person ("the defaulter") has refused or otherwise failed, without reasonable excuse, to comply with a notice under paragraph 4(1).

(2)   An application under sub-paragraph (1) shall include details of the possible failure which the OFT considers has occurred.

(3)   In enquiring into a case under sub-paragraph (1), the court shall hear any witness who may be produced against or on behalf of the defaulter and any statement which may be offered in defence.

(4)   Sub-paragraphs (5) and (6) apply where the court is satisfied, after hearing any witnesses and statements as mentioned in sub-paragraph (3), that the defaulter has refused or otherwise failed, without reasonable excuse, to comply with a notice under paragraph 4(1).

(5)   The court may punish the defaulter as it would have been able to punish him had he been guilty of contempt of court.

(6)   Where the defaulter is a body corporate or is a partnership constituted under the law of Scotland, the court may punish any director, officer or (as the case may be) partner of the defaulter as it would have been able to punish that director, officer or partner had he been guilty of contempt of court.

(7)   In this paragraph "the court"—
   (a)   in relation to England and Wales or Northern Ireland, means the High Court, and
   (b)   in relation to Scotland, means the Court of Session.

4B. (1)   A person commits an offence if he intentionally alters, suppresses or destroys a document which he has been required to produce by a notice under paragraph 4(1).

(2)   A person who commits an offence under sub-paragraph (1) shall be liable—
   (a)   on summary conviction, to a fine not exceeding the statutory maximum;
   (b)   on conviction on indictment, to imprisonment for a term not exceeding two years or to a fine or to both.]

. . .

5.

Exemptions from the Competition Act 1998

6. (1)   The Chapter I prohibition does not apply to—
   (a)   an agreement for the constitution of an Operator; or
   (b)   an agreement for the constitution of a person who has applied for approval as an Operator in accordance with these Regulations and whose application has not yet been determined,
to the extent to which the agreement relates to rules made or guidance issued by the Operator.

(2)   The Chapter I prohibition does not apply to a decision made by an Operator to the extent to which the decision relates to any of the rules made or guidance issued by that Operator or to the Operator's specified practices.

(3)   The Chapter I prohibition does not apply to the specified practices of—
   (a)   an Operator; or
   (b)   a person who is subject to the rules of an Operator.

(4)   The Chapter I prohibition does not apply to any agreement the parties to which consist of or include—
   (a)   an Operator; or
   (b)   a person who is subject to the rules of an Operator,
to the extent to which the agreement consists of provisions the inclusion of which is required or contemplated by these Regulations or by any rules made or guidance issued by the Operator or by the Operator's specified practices.

(5)   In this paragraph—
   "the Chapter I prohibition" means the prohibition imposed by section 2(1) of the Competition Act 1998; and
   "specified practices" means—
      (a)   any practices of an Operator in its capacity as such; or
      (b)   any practices of persons who are members of, or otherwise subject to rules made by, an Operator and which are practices—
         (i)   in relation to business in respect of which the persons in question are subject to the rules of the Operator where those practices are required or contemplated by the rules of the Operator or by guidance issued by the Operator; or
         (ii)   otherwise attributable to the conduct of the Operator as such;
and expressions used in this paragraph which are also used in Part I of the Competition Act 1998 are to be interpreted in same way as for the purposes of that Part of that Act.

Supplementary provisions

7. (1)   Any direction given under this Schedule shall, on the application of the person by whom it was given, be enforceable by injunction or, in Scotland, by an order for specific performance under section 45 of the Court of Session Act 1988.

(2)   The fact that any rules made by an Operator have been altered by or pursuant to a direction given by the Treasury under this Schedule shall not preclude their subsequent alteration or revocation by the Operator.

(3)   In determining under this Schedule whether any guidance has, or is likely to have, any particular effect the Treasury and the [OFT] may assume that the persons to whom it is addressed will act in conformity with it.

NOTES

Para 1: words in first pair of square brackets substituted by the Capital Requirements Regulations 2006, SI 2006/3221, reg 29(4), Sch 6, para 12, as from 1 January 2007; words in second pair of square brackets inserted, and words in third pair of square brackets substituted, by the Capital Requirements (Amendment) Regulations 2010, SI 2010/2628, regs 2, 14, Sch 2, para 4(b), as from 31 December 2010.

Para 3: all words in square brackets (with the exception of the penultimate word in square brackets in sub-para (8)) substituted by the Enterprise Act 2002 (Consequential and Supplemental Provisions) Order 2003, SI 2003/1398, art 2, Schedule, para 43(1), (2)(a), as from 20 June 2003; penultimate word in square brackets in sub-para (8) substituted by the Enterprise Act 2002 and Media Mergers (Consequential Amendments) Order 2003, SI 2003/3180, art 2, Schedule, para 9, as from 29 December 2003.

Para 4: words in square brackets substituted, and sub-para (3) revoked, by SI 2003/1398, art 2, Schedule, para 43(1), (2)(b), as from 20 June 2003.

Paras 4A, 4B: inserted by SI 2003/1398, art 2, Schedule, para 43(1), (2)(c), as from 20 June 2003.

Para 5: revoked by SI 2003/1398, art 2, Schedule, para 43(1), (2)(d), as from 20 June 2003.

Para 7: reference to "OFT" in square brackets substituted by virtue of the Enterprise Act 2002, s 2(1), as from 1 April 2003.

SCHEDULE 3
PROCEDURE FOR REFUSAL OR WITHDRAWAL OF APPROVAL AS AN OPERATOR, OR FOR GIVING DIRECTIONS, ETC

Regulations 5(4), 7(3) and 8(4)

[6.94]

1. Before—
(a)   refusing an application for approval as an Operator made under regulation 4 (whether or not pursuant to paragraph 1(1) of Schedule 2);
(b)   withdrawing an Operator's approval under regulation 7(2);
(c)   giving a direction under regulation 8;
(d)   exercising any power conferred by paragraph 1(3) of Schedule 2;
(e)   exercising the power to refuse leave under paragraph 2(2) of Schedule 2; or
(f)   giving a direction under paragraph 2(4) of Schedule 2, the Treasury shall—
    (i)   give written notice of their intention to do so to the Operator;
    (ii)   take such steps as they consider reasonably practicable to bring the notice to the attention of system-users; and
    (iii) publish the notice in such manner as they think appropriate for bringing it to the attention of other persons who are, in their opinion, likely to be affected.

2. A notice under paragraph 1 shall—
(a)   state why the Treasury intend to refuse the application, withdraw the approval, give the direction, or exercise the power in question; and
(b)   draw attention to the right to make representations conferred by paragraph 3.

3. Before the end of the period for making representations—
(a)   the Operator,
(b)   any system-user, and
(c)   any other person who is likely to be affected by the proposed withdrawal or direction, may make representations to the Treasury.

4. The period for making representations is—
(a)   two months beginning—
    (i)   with the date on which the notice under paragraph 1 is served on the Operator; or
    (ii)   if later, with the date on which that notice is published; or
(b)   such longer period as the Treasury may allow in the particular case.

5. In deciding whether to refuse the application, withdraw the approval, give the direction, or exercise the power in question, the Treasury shall have regard to any representations made in accordance with paragraph 3.

6. When the Treasury have decided whether to refuse the application, withdraw the approval, give the direction, or exercise the power in question they shall, if they have decided to refuse the application, withdraw the Operator's approval under regulation 7(2), give a direction under regulation 8 or exercise a power conferred by paragraph 1(3) of Schedule 2—

(a)   give the Operator written notice of their decision; and

(b)   take such steps as they consider reasonably practicable for bringing their decision to the attention of system-users and of any other persons who are, in the Treasury's opinion, likely to be affected.

7. If the Treasury consider it essential to do so, they may withdraw an Operator's approval under regulation 7(2) or give a direction under regulation 8—

(a)   without following the procedure set out in this Schedule; or

(b)   if the Treasury have begun to follow that procedure, regardless of whether the period for making representations has expired.

8. If the Treasury have, in relation to a particular matter, followed the procedure set out in paragraphs 1 to 5, they need not follow it again if, in relation to that matter, they decide to take action other than that specified in their notice under paragraph 1.

SCHEDULE 4
KEEPING OF REGISTERS AND RECORDS OF PARTICIPATING SECURITIES
Regulation 23(4)

Interpretation

[6.95]
1. In this Schedule—

"uncertificated shares" means shares title to which may be transferred by means of a relevant system; and

"certificated shares" means shares which are not uncertificated shares; and "uncertificated stock" means stock title to which may be transferred by means of a relevant system; and "certificated stock" means stock which is not uncertificated stock.

Registers of members

2. (1) Every participating issuer which is a company shall enter in its issuer register of members—

(a)   the names and addresses of the members;

(b)   the date on which each person was registered as a member; and

(c)   the date at which any person ceased to be a member.

(2)   With the names and addresses of the members there shall be entered a statement—

(a)   of the certificated shares held by each member, distinguishing each share by its number (so long as the share has a number) and, where the company has more than one class of issued shares, by its class; and

(b)   of the amount paid or agreed to be considered as paid on the certificated shares of each member.

(3)   Where the company has converted any of its shares into stock and given notice of the conversion to the registrar of companies, the issuer register of members shall show the amount and class of the certificated stock held by each member, instead of the amount of shares and the particulars relating to shares specified in subparagraph (2).

(4)   Subject to subparagraph (5), [section 113 of the 2006 Act] shall not apply to a company which is a participating issuer, other than as respects any overseas branch register.

(5)   [Section 113(7) and (8) of the 2006 Act]shall apply to a participating issuer which is a company which makes default in complying with this paragraph and every officer of it who is in default as if such a default were a default in complying with [section 113] of the Act.

(6)   An entry relating to a former member of the company may be removed from the issuer register of members after the expiration of [10 years] beginning with the day on which he ceased to be a member.

(7)   For the purposes of this paragraph references to an issuer register of members shall not be taken to include an overseas branch register.

3. [Section 123 of the 2006 Act] shall apply to a participating issuer which is a private company limited by shares as if references therein to the company's register of members were references to its issuer register of members.

4. (1)   In relation to every participating issuer which is a company, an Operator of a relevant system shall, in respect of any class of shares which is a participating security for the purposes of that system, enter on an Operator register of members—

(a)   the names and addresses of the members who hold uncertificated shares in the company;

(b)   with those names and addresses a statement of the uncertificated shares held by each member and, where the company has more than one class of issued uncertificated shares, distinguishing each share by its class; and

(c)   where the company has converted any of its shares into stock and given notice of the conversion to the registrar of companies, the Operator register of members shall show the amount and class of uncertificated stock held by each member, instead of the amount of shares and the particulars relating to shares specified in subparagraph (b).

(2)   An entry relating to a member of a company who has ceased to hold any uncertificated shares in the company may be removed from the Operator register of members after the expiration of [10 years] beginning with the day on which he ceased to hold any such shares.

(3)   For the purposes of this paragraph references to an Operator register of members shall not be taken to include an overseas branch register.

(4)   Members of a company who hold shares in uncertificated form may not be entered as holders of those shares on an overseas branch register.

Records of uncertificated shares

5. (1)   Every participating issuer which is a company shall enter in its record of uncertificated shares—
  (a)   the same particulars, so far as practicable, as are required by paragraph 4(1) to be entered in the Operator register of members; and
  (b)   a statement of the amount paid or agreed to be considered as paid on the uncertificated shares of each member.

(2)   A company to which this paragraph applies shall, unless it is impracticable to do so by virtue of circumstances beyond its control, ensure that the record of uncertificated shares is regularly reconciled with the Operator register of members.

(3)   Provided that it has complied with subparagraph (2), a company shall not be liable in respect of any act or thing done or omitted to be done by or on behalf of the company in reliance upon the assumption that the particulars entered in any record of uncertificated shares which the company is required to keep by these Regulations accord with the particulars entered in its Operator register of members.

(4)   [Section 113(7) and (8) of the 2006 Act] shall apply to a participating issuer which is a company which makes default in complying with this paragraph and every officer of it who is in default as if such a default were a default in complying with [section 113] of that Act.

Location of issuer register of members and records of uncertificated shares, and ancillary matters

6. (1)   Subject to subparagraph (2), a company's issuer register of members and its record of uncertificated shares shall be [kept available for inspection] at its registered office, [or at a place specified in regulations made under section 1136 of the 2006 Act].
  (a), (b) . . .
but the issuer register of members must not be [kept available for inspection], in the case of a company registered in England and Wales, at any place elsewhere than in England and Wales or, in the case of a company registered in Scotland, at any place elsewhere than in Scotland.

(2)   A company's issuer register of members and its record of uncertificated shares shall at all times be [kept available for inspection] at the same place.

(3)   Subject as follows, every participating issuer which is a company shall send notice . . . to the registrar of companies of the place where its issuer register of members and its record of uncertificated shares are [kept available for inspection], and of any change in that place, provided that any notice sent by such a company in accordance with [section 114(2) of the 2006 Act], and which has effect on the coming into force of these Regulations, shall be treated as being a notice sent in compliance with this subparagraph.

(4)   The notice need not be sent if the issuer register of members and the record of uncertificated shares have at all times since they came into existence been [kept available for inspection] at the company's registered office.

(5)   Subject to subparagraph (6), [section 114 of the 2006 Act] shall not apply to a company which is a participating issuer.

(6)   [Section 114 (6) of the 2006 Act] shall apply to a participating issuer which is a company which makes default in complying with subparagraph (2) at any time, or makes default for 14 days in complying with subparagraph (3), and every officer of it who is in default as if such a default were a default in complying with [section 114(2)] of that Act.

7. (1)   Every participating issuer which is a company having more than 50 members shall, unless the particulars required by paragraph 2(1) to be entered in the issuer register of members are kept in such a form as to constitute in themselves an index, keep an index of the names of the members of the company and shall, within 14 days after the date on which any alteration is made in the issuer register of members or the Operator register of members, make any necessary alteration in the index.

(2) The index shall in respect of each member contain a sufficient indication to enable the account of that member in the issuer register of members and, in the case of a member who holds uncertificated shares in the company, in the record of uncertificated shares, to be readily found.

(3) The index shall be at all times [kept available for inspection] at the same place as the issuer register of members and the record of uncertificated shares.

(4) Subject to subparagraph (5), [section 115 of the 2006 Act] shall not apply to a company which is a participating issuer.

(5) [Section 115(5) and (6) of the 2006 Act] shall apply to a participating issuer which is a company which makes default in complying with this paragraph and every officer of it who is in default as if such a default were a default in complying with [section 115] of that Act.

8. [Section 122 of the 2006 Act] shall apply to a company which is a participating issuer as if references in that section to the company's register of members were references instead to its issuer register of members.

9. [Sections 115 to 118 of the 2006 Act] shall apply to a company which is a participating issuer as if—

(a) references in those provisions to the company's register of members were references to its issuer register of members and its record of uncertificated shares; and

(b) references in [section 116] to the company's [index of members' names] were references to the index required to be kept by paragraph 7,

and references to [the 2006 Act in the Companies (Fees for Inspection and Copying of Company Records) Regulations 2007 and the Companies (Fees for Inspection and Copying of Company Records) Regulations 2008] shall be construed accordingly.

10. Where under [paragraph 6(1)], a company's issuer register of members and record of uncertificated shares is [kept available for inspection] at the office of some person other than the company, and by reason of any default of his the company fails to comply with—

paragraph 6(2) (record of uncertificated shares to be [kept available for inspection] with issuer register of members);

paragraph 6(3) (notice to registrar);

paragraph 7(3) (index to be [kept available for inspection] with issuer register of members and record of uncertificated shares); or

[section 116 of the 2006 Act (rights to inspect and require copies)],

or with any requirement of the [the 2006 Act] as to the production of the register of members or any part thereof, that other person is liable to the same penalties as if he were an officer of the company who was in default, and the power of the court under [section 118(3) of the 2006 Act] extends to the making of orders against that other and his officers and servants.

11. Where, under [section 125 of the 2006 Act], the court orders rectification of the register of members of a company which is a participating issuer, it shall not order the payment of any damages under subsection (2) of that section to the extent that such rectification relates to the company's Operator register of members and does not arise from an act or omission of the Operator on the instructions of that company or from fraud or other wilful default, or negligence, on the part of that company.

Registers of [general] public sector securities

12. (1) Where an Operator of a relevant system is required to maintain an Operator register of [general] public sector securities that register shall comprise the following particulars which the Operator shall enter on it, namely—

(a) the names and address of the persons holding units of the relevant participating security in uncertificated form; and

(b) how many units of that security each such person holds in that form.

[(2) The following provisions of the 2004 Regulations shall not apply in respect of units of general UK Government securities held in uncertificated form—

regulations 7 to 9;

regulations 12 to 14;

regulations 16 to 24;

regulation 28; and

regulations 30 to 31.]

(3) The following provisions of the 1974 Regulations shall not apply in respect of units of [general] local authority securities held in uncertificated form—

regulations 5 and 6;

regulations 8 to 14;

regulation 16; and

regulation 21.

Records of uncertificated [general] public sector securities

13. (1)   The participating issuer shall enter in a record of uncertificated [general] public sector securities the same particulars, so far as is practicable, as are required by paragraph 12(1) to be entered in the relevant Operator register of [general] public sector securities.

(2)   In respect of every participating security which is a [general] UK Government security, the record of uncertificated [general] public sector securities shall be kept [by the Registrar of Government Stock].

(3)   The participating issuer shall, unless it is impracticable to do so by virtue of circumstances beyond his control, ensure that the record of uncertificated [general] public sector securities is regularly reconciled with the Operator register of [general] public sector securities.

(4)   Provided that he has complied with subparagraph (3), a participating issuer shall not be liable in respect of any act or thing done or omitted to be done by him or on his behalf in reliance upon the assumption that the particulars entered in any record of uncertificated [general] public sector securities which he is required to keep by these Regulations accord with particulars entered in the Operator register of [general] public sector securities to which the record relates.

(5)   The provisions of the Bankers' Books Evidence Act 1879 shall apply for the purpose of proving any entry in the record of uncertificated [general] public sector securities as if the participating issuer were a bank and a banker within the meaning of that Act, and as if such entry in the record, or, where the information recorded therein is not in readable form and is later transcribed into readable form, the transcribed version of such entry, were an entry in a banker's book.

Registers of corporate securities

14. (1)   Where an Operator of a relevant system is required to maintain an Operator register of corporate securities, that register shall comprise the following particulars which the Operator shall enter on it, namely—

(a)   the names and addresses of the persons holding units of the relevant participating security in uncertificated form; and

(b)   how many units of that security each such person holds in that form.

(2)   [Sections 743 to 748 of the 2006 Act] shall not apply to any part of an Operator register of corporate securities.

Records of uncertificated corporate securities

15. (1)   A participating issuer shall enter in a record of uncertificated corporate securities the same particulars, so far as practicable, as are required by paragraph 14(1) to be entered in the relevant Operator register of corporate securities.

(2)   A participating issuer to which this paragraph applies shall, unless it is impracticable to do so by virtue of circumstances beyond its control, ensure that the record of uncertificated corporate securities is regularly reconciled with the Operator register of corporate securities.

(3)   Provided that it has complied with subparagraph (2), a participating issuer shall not be liable in respect of any act or thing done or omitted to be done by it or on its behalf in reliance upon the assumption that the particulars entered in any record of uncertificated corporate securities which the participating issuer is required to keep by these Regulations accord with particulars entered in any Operator register of corporate securities relating to it.

(4)   In the case of a participating issuer which is a company, the record of uncertificated corporate securities shall be kept at the same place as the part of any register of debenture holders maintained by the company would be required to be kept.

(5)   [Sections 744(1) to (4) and 746 of the 2006 Act] shall apply in relation to a record of uncertificated corporate securities maintained by a participating issuer which is a company, so far as that record relates to debentures, [as they apply] or would apply to any register of debenture holders maintained by the company; and references to [the 2006 Act in the Companies (Fees for Inspection and Copying of Company Records) Regulations 2007 and the Companies (Fees for Inspection and Copying of Company Records) Regulations 2008] shall be construed accordingly.

(6)   Any provision of an enactment or instrument which requires a register of persons holding securities (other than shares or public sector securities) to be open to inspection shall also apply to the record of uncertificated corporate securities relating to any units of those securities which are participating securities.

Miscellaneous

16. (1)   . . .

(2)   [Every register which an Operator is required to maintain by virtue of these Regulations] [(other than an Operator register of eligible debt securities)] which relates to securities issued by a company shall be deemed to be kept—

(a)   in the case of a company registered in England and Wales, in England and Wales; or

(b)   in the case of a company registered in Scotland, in Scotland.

17. (1) An entry in a register of securities or in a record of securities relating to a person who no longer holds the securities which are the subject of the entry may be removed from the register or the record (as the case may be) after the expiration of 20 years beginning with the day on which the person ceased to hold any of those securities.

(2) Subparagraph (1) does not apply in respect of an entry in a register of members.

18. [Sections 1134, 1135 and 1138 of the 2006 Act] shall apply—
- (a) to any register, record or index required to be kept by any person in accordance with these Regulations as they apply to any register, record or index required to be kept by the Companies Acts to be kept by a company; and
- (b) to an Operator and its officers as they apply to a company and its officers.

19. (1) Such sanctions as apply to a company and its officers in the event of a default in complying with [section 113 of the 2006 Act] shall apply to an Operator and his officers in the event of a default in complying with paragraph 4, 12 or 14.

(2) Such sanctions as apply to the registrar, within the meaning of the 1974 Regulations, in the event of a default in complying with regulation 5 of those Regulations shall apply to a participating issuer and his officers in the event of a default in complying with paragraph 13 in respect of a local authority security [falling within paragraph (a)(i) of the definition of "local authority security" in regulation 3(1)].

[(2A) . . .]

(3) Such sanctions as apply in the event of a default in complying with the requirement to maintain a register imposed by the relevant enactment or instrument referred to in Regulation 22(1) shall apply to—
- (a) a participating issuer other than a company; and
- (b) a participating issuer which is a company, in relation to so much of the record of uncertificated corporate securities as does not relate to debentures,

and his officers in the event of a default in complying with paragraph 15.

(4) Subparagraphs (2) and (3) shall not apply to any of the following or its officers—
- (a) the Crown;
- (b) any person acting on behalf of the Crown;
- [(c) the Bank of England;
- (d) the Registrar of Government Stock;
- (e) any previous Registrar of Government Stock; or
- (f) in respect of a security which immediately before it became a participating security was transferable by exempt transfer within the meaning of the Stock Transfer Act 1982, a participating issuer].

20. An officer of a participating issuer shall be in default in complying with, or in contravention of paragraph 2, 5, 6, 7, 13 or 15, or [section 1138 of the 2006 Act] as applied by paragraph 18, if, and only if, he knowingly and wilfully authorised or permitted the default or contravention.

21. An officer of an Operator shall be in default in complying with, or in contravention of, the provisions referred to in paragraph 19(1) of this Schedule, or of [section 1138 of the 2006 Act] as applied by paragraph 18, if, and only if, he knowingly and wilfully authorised or permitted the default or contravention.

NOTES

Paras 2–5, 8–11, 14, 15, 18, 20, 21: words in square brackets substituted by the Companies Act 2006 (Consequential Amendments) (Uncertificated Securities) Order 2009, SI 2009/1889, art 2(1), (21)(a)–(f), (o)–(v), (y), (aa), (bb), as from 1 October 2009.

Para 6: words in square brackets substituted, and words omitted revoked, by SI 2009/1889, art 2(1), (21)(g)–(k), as from 1 October 2009.

Para 7: words in square brackets substituted by SI 2009/1889, art 2(1), (21)(l)–(n), as from 1 October 2009. Note that sub-para (n) actually provided "in paragraph 7(5), for "Section 354(4)" substitute "Section 115(5) and (6)". It is believed that references to the '1985 Act' and '2006 Act' were inadvertently omitted from this sub-paragraph.

Para 12: word "general" in square brackets in every place it occurs substituted by the Uncertificated Securities (Amendment) (Eligible Debt Securities) Regulations 2003, SI 2003/1633, regs 6(5)(a), (b), 7, 8(4)(a), as from 24 June 2003; sub-para (2) substituted by the Government Stock (Consequential and Transitional Provision) (No 2) Order 2004, SI 2004/1662, art 2, Schedule, Pt 3, para 29(1), (6)(a), as from 1 July 2004.

Para 13: word "general" in square brackets in every place it occurs substituted by SI 2003/1633, regs 6(5)(c), (d), 7, as from 24 June 2003; final words in square brackets in sub-para (2) substituted by SI 2004/1662, art 2, Schedule, Pt 3, para 29(1), (6)(b), as from 1 July 2004.

Para 16: sub-para (1) revoked, and words in first pair of square brackets in sub-para (2) substituted, by SI 2009/1889, art 2(1), (21)(w), (x), as from 1 October 2009; words in second pair of square brackets in sub-para (2) inserted by SI 2003/1633, reg 13, as from 24 June 2003.

Para 19: words in square brackets in sub-para (1) substituted by SI 2009/1889, art 2(1), (21)(z), as from 1 October 2009; words in square brackets in sub-para (2) and the whole of sub-para (2A) inserted by SI 2003/1633, reg 8(4)(b), (c), as from 24 June 2003; sub-para (2A) revoked by the Local Authorities (Capital Finance) (Further Consequential and Saving Provisions) Order 2004, SI 2004/2044, art 6(3), as from 1 October 2004; sub-para (4)(c)–(f) substituted, for original sub-para (4)(c), (d), by SI 2004/1662, art 2, Schedule, Pt 3, para 29(1), (6)(c), as from 1 July 2004.

SCHEDULES 5–7

(Sch 5 revoked by the Companies Act 2006 (Consequential Amendments) (Uncertificated Securities) Order 2009, SI 2009/1889, art 2(1), (22), as from 1 October 2009; Sch 6 contains transitory modifications of these Regulations which had effect until the date upon which the Financial Services and Markets Act 2000, s 19 came into force (this was 1 December 2001 and this Schedule is now regarded as spent); Sch 7 (minor and consequential amendments to statutes and secondary legislation); in so far as these are relevant to this work, they have been incorporated at the appropriate place.)

COMPANIES (FEES) REGULATIONS 2004 (NOTE)

(SI 2004/2621)

[6.96]

NOTES

These Regulations were made under the Companies Act 1985, s 708(1) (repealed) and came into in force on 1 February 2005. They were amended by the Secretaries of State for Children, Schools and Families, for Innovation, Universities and Skills and for Business, Enterprise and Regulatory Reform Order 2007, SI 2007/3224 (which is spent in so far as it amended these Regulations). These Regulations, which revoked and replaced the Companies (Fees) Regulations 1991, SI 1991/1206 (and the amending SI 1992/2876, SI 1994/2217, SI 1995/1423, SI 1996/1444, SI 1998/3088, SI 2000/3325, SI 2002/317, and SI 2002/2894) provided for a revised scale of fees payable to the registrar of companies for the purposes of the Companies Act 1985. Section 708 of the 1985 Act was repealed by the Companies Act 2006, s 1295, Sch 16, subject to savings in the Companies Act 2006 (Commencement No 1, Transitional Provisions and Savings) Order 2006, SI 2006/3428, art 8(1), Sch 5, Pt 3, para 6 (at **[2.8]** and **[2.15]**). By virtue of s 1297 of the 2006 Act and the Companies Act 2006 (Commencement No 8, Transitional Provisions and Savings) Order 2008, SI 2008/2860, art 5, Sch 2, para 94 (at **[2.86]** and **[2.91]**), any Regulations under the Companies Act 1985, s 708 which were in force immediately before 1 October 2009 have effect on or after that date as if made under s 1063 of the 2006 Act. These Regulations were revoked by SI 2009/2101 (except in so far as relating to Fees Nos 5 (5(a) and 5(b)), 6, and 9 in Sch 4). For transitional provisions see regs 6–8 of, and Schs 4, 5 to the 2009 Regulations. Fees Nos 5, 6, and 9 are set out below.

Matter in relation to which fee is payable	Amount of fee
5. Delivery by a company of all relevant documents during a relevant period, payable on delivery by the company of its annual return under section 363 at the end of that period—	
(a) where the annual return is delivered using electronic communications	£15.00
(b) where the annual return is delivered not using electronic communications	£30.00
6. Delivery by an oversea company of all relevant documents during a relevant period, payable on delivery of accounts by the company at the end of that period	£30.00
9. Registration of a charge under Part XII	£13.00

COMPANIES (AUDIT, INVESTIGATIONS AND COMMUNITY ENTERPRISE) ACT 2004 (COMMENCEMENT) AND COMPANIES ACT 1989 (COMMENCEMENT NO 18) ORDER 2004

(SI 2004/3322)

NOTES

Made: 9 December 2004.
Authority: CA 1989, s 215(2); Companies (Audit, Investigations and Community Enterprise) Act 2004, s 65.
Amendment: as of 1 July 2011 this Order had not been amended.

ARRANGEMENT OF ARTICLES

[6.97]
1 Citation and interpretation

(1)   This Order may be cited as the Companies (Audit, Investigations and Community Enterprise) Act 2004 (Commencement) and Companies Act 1989 (Commencement No 18) Order 2004.

(2)   In this Order—
   "the 1985 Act" means the Companies Act 1985; and
   "the 2004 Act" means the Companies (Audit, Investigations and Community Enterprise) Act 2004.

(3)   References in articles 3 to 11 to sections are references to those sections of the 1985 Act; and the references in article 3 to Schedule 4A and in article 7 to Schedule 24 are references to those Schedules to that Act.

(4)   References in this Order to old sections of the 1985 Act are references to the sections in question as they had effect before their amendment by the 2004 Act; and references to new sections of that Act are references to the sections in question as inserted by the 2004 Act.

[6.98]
2 Commencement

(1)   Section 46 of and Schedule 13 to the Companies Act 1989 and the provisions of the 2004 Act set out in Schedule 1 hereto shall come into force on 1st January 2005.

(2)   The provisions of the 2004 Act set out in Schedule 2 hereto shall, subject to articles 4 to 13 below, come into force on 6th April 2005.

(3)   The provisions of the 2004 Act set out in Schedule 3 hereto shall come into force on 1st July 2005.

(4)   The provisions of the 2004 Act set out in Schedule 4 hereto shall, subject to article 3 below, come into force on 1st October 2005.

[6.99]
3 Transitional provision for section 7 of the 2004 Act

New section 390B, and the repeal of old section 390A(3) and of words in paragraph 1(1) of Schedule 4A relating thereto, shall have no effect in relation to the accounts of a company for a financial year beginning before 1st October 2005.

[6.100]
4 Transitional provision for section 9 of the 2004 Act

New sections 234(2A) and 234ZA shall not apply in relation to any report of the directors of a company prepared under section 234 concerning a financial year beginning before 1st April 2005 or ending before 6th April 2005.

[6.101]
5 Transitional provision for section 19 of the 2004 Act

New section 309A shall have no effect in relation to provisions made before 29th October 2004 which are not void under old section 310.

[6.102]
6 Authorisations under old section 447 of the 1985 Act effective immediately before 6th April 2005

An authorisation under old section 447(3) which was effective immediately before 6th April 2005 shall have effect on and after 6th April 2005 as though it were an authorisation under new section 447(3).

[6.103]
7 Outstanding requirements under old section 447 of the 1985 Act

(1)   An outstanding requirement imposed under old section 447 shall be treated, on and after 6th April 2005, as a requirement imposed under new section 447, whether or not the requirement could have been imposed under new section 447.

(2)   But old section 447(6) and (7) shall apply, and section 453C shall not apply, in relation to a failure to comply with such an outstanding requirement.

(3)   The following shall continue to have effect for the purposes of paragraph (2):

(a)   the references to section 447 in sections 732, 733 and 734; and

(b)   the entry in Schedule 24 relating to old section 447(6).

(4)   Where a person provides information on or after 6th April 2005 in purported compliance with an outstanding requirement and in doing so commits an offence under section 451, the court, on summary conviction of that person for that offence, may not impose a term of imprisonment greater than six months.

(5)   For the purposes of this article, an outstanding requirement is a requirement imposed under old section 447, either in directions given by the Secretary of State or by a person authorised by the Secretary of State, which—

(a)   was imposed before 6th April 2005;

(b)   was required to be complied with on or after that date; and

(c)   had not been complied with before that date.

[6.104]
8   Power to take copies of or extracts from documents produced under old section 447 of the 1985 Act before 6th April 2005

The powers in new section 447(7) are exercisable on and after 6th April 2005 in relation to any document produced before that date in pursuance of old section 447.

[6.105]
9   Use in evidence of statements made in compliance with requirements under section 447 of the 1985 Act

(1)   Subsections (8) to (8B) of old section 447 continue to have effect on and after 6th April 2005 in relation to any statement made before that date as if the reference in subsection (8B)(a) to section 451 were a reference to old or new section 451.

(2)   In its application to any statement made on or after 6th April 2005 by a person in compliance with an outstanding requirement imposed under old section 447 or a requirement imposed under new section 447, section 447A has effect as if the relevant offences in section 447A(3) included the offences under old sections 451 and 447(6).

[6.106]
10   Security of information obtained under old section 447 of the 1985 Act

New section 449 applies, and old section 449 does not apply, to information to which old section 449(1) applied immediately before 6th April 2005.

[6.107]
11   Power to enter and remain on premises: persons authorised under old section 447 of the 1985 Act

For the purposes of sections 453A and 453B, and for the purposes of section 453C as it relates to section 453A, an investigator includes a person authorised for the purposes of old section 447 whose authorisation was effective immediately before 6th April 2005.

[6.108]
12   Use of information obtained under the 1985 Act for the purposes of proceedings under section 8 of the Company Directors Disqualification Act 1986

The references to sections 447 and 448 of the 1985 Act in section 8(1A)(b)(i) of the Company Directors Disqualification Act 1986 are references to either the old or the new sections.

[6.109]
13   Use of information obtained under Part 14 of the 1985 Act for the purposes of proceedings under section 124A of the Insolvency Act 1986

The reference to information obtained under Part 14 of the 1985 Act in section 124A(1)(a) of the Insolvency Act 1986, insofar as it is a reference to information obtained under section 447 or 448 of the 1985 Act, is a reference to information obtained either the old or the new section.

SCHEDULES 1–4

(Sch 1 brings the following provisions of the 2004 Act into force on 1 January 2005: ss 3–5, 10, 13, 14, 16–18, 25 (in respect of the provisions of Sch 2 mentioned below), 27, 64 (in respect of the provisions of Sch 8 mentioned below), Sch 2, paras 1, 3, 4, Sch 3, and Sch 8 (in respect of the entries relating to the 1985 Act, ss 245C(6), 256(3), CA 1989, s 48(3), the Companies (Northern Ireland) Order 1990, the Competition Act 1998, the Competition Act 1998 (Competition Commission) Transitional, Consequential and Supplemental Provisions Order 1999, and the Enterprise Act 2002); Sch 2 brings the following provisions of the 2004 Act into force on 6 April 2005: ss 1,

2, 6, 8, 9, 11, 12, 15, 19–24, 25 (in respect of the provisions of Sch 2 mentioned below), 64 (in respect of the provisions of Sch 8 mentioned below), Sch 1, Sch 2, paras 2, 5–24, 25 (except in respect of paras 40 and 45 of new Sch 15D to the 1985 Act), 26–28, 30, 31, and Sch 8 (in respect of the entries relating to the 1985 Act, ss 310, 734(1), Sch 24, IA 1986, IA 1986, CA 1989, ss 63, 65, 67, 69, 120, the Friendly Societies Act 1992, the Pensions Act 1995, the Bank of England Act 1998, and the Youth Justice and Criminal Evidence Act 1999); Sch 3 brings the following provisions of the 2004 Act into force on 1 July 2005: ss 25 (so far as not already in force), 26, 28–63, 64 (in respect of the provisions of Sch 8 mentioned below), Sch 2 (so far as not already in force), Schs 4–7, and Sch 8 (in respect of the entry relating to the 1985 Act, s 27(4)); Sch 4 brings the following provisions of the 2004 Act into force on 1 October 2005: ss 7, 64 (so far as not already in force), Sch 8 (so far as not already in force).)

COMPANIES ACT 1985 (POWER TO ENTER AND REMAIN ON PREMISES: PROCEDURAL) REGULATIONS 2005

(SI 2005/684)

NOTES
Made: 9 March 2005.
Authority: Companies Act 1985, s 453B(4), (7).
Commencement: 6 April 2005.
Amendment: as of 1 July 2011, these Regulations had not been amended.
Limited liability partnerships: these Regulations apply, with modifications, to limited liability partnerships; see the Limited Liability Partnerships Regulations 2001, SI 2001/1090, reg 10, Sch 6, Pt I (at **[10.828]**).

[6.110]
1   Citation, commencement and interpretation
(1)   These Regulations may be cited as the Companies Act 1985 (Power to Enter and Remain on Premises: Procedural) Regulations 2005 and shall come into force on 6 April 2005.

(2)   In these Regulations "the 1985 Act" means the Companies Act 1985.

(3)   References in regulations 2 and 3 to sections are references to those sections of the 1985 Act.

[6.111]
2   Prescribed contents of the written statement given under section 453B(4) or sent under section 453B(5)
The written statement which section 453B(4) requires the inspector or investigator to give to an appropriate recipient (or which section 453B(5), where it applies, requires him to send to the company) must contain the following information—
(a)   a statement that the inspector or investigator has been appointed or (as the case may be) authorised by the Secretary of State to carry out an investigation and a reference to the enactment under which that appointment or authorisation was made;
(b)   a statement that the inspector or investigator has been authorised by the Secretary of State under section 453A to exercise the powers in that section;
(c)   a description of the conditions which are required by section 453A(1) to be satisfied before an inspector or investigator can act under section 453A(2);
(d)   a description of the powers in sub-section 453A(2);
(e)   a statement that the inspector or investigator must, at the time he seeks to enter premises under section 453A, produce evidence of his identity and evidence of his appointment or authorisation (as the case may be);
(f)   a statement that any person accompanying the inspector or investigator when the inspector or investigator seeks to enter the premises must, at that time, produce evidence of his identity;
(g)   a statement that entry to premises under section 453A may be refused to an inspector, investigator or other person who fails to produce the evidence referred to (in the case of an inspector or investigator) in paragraph (e) or (in the case of any other person) in paragraph (f);
(h)   a statement that the company, occupier and the persons present on the premises may be required by the inspector or investigator, while he is on the premises, to comply with any powers the inspector or investigator may have by virtue of his appointment or authorisation (as the case may be) to require documents or information;
(i)   a statement that the inspector or investigator is not permitted to use any force in exercising his powers under section 453A and is not permitted during the course of his visit to search the premises or to seize any document or other thing on the premises;
(j)   a description of the effect of section 453C as it relates to a requirement imposed by an inspector or investigator under section 453A;
(k)   a statement that it is an offence under section 453A(5) intentionally to obstruct an inspector, investigator or other person lawfully acting under section 453A;

(l)   a description of the inspector's or investigator's obligations under section 453B(6) and (7) to prepare a written record of the visit and to give a copy of the record, when requested, to the company and any other occupier of the premises; and

(m)   information about how any person entitled under section 453B(6) to receive a copy of that record can request it.

[6.112]

3 Prescribed contents of the written record prepared under section 453B(6)

The written record which section 453B(6) requires an inspector or investigator to prepare must contain the following information—

(a)   the name by which the company in relation to which the powers under section 453A were exercised was registered at the time of the authorisation under section 453A(1)(a);

(b)   the company's registered number at that time;

(c)   the postal address of the premises visited;

(d)   the name of the inspector or investigator who visited the premises and the name of any person accompanying him;

(e)   the date and time when the inspector or investigator entered the premises and the duration of his visit;

(f)   the name (if known by the inspector or investigator) of the person to whom the inspector or investigator and any person accompanying him produced evidence of their identity under section 453B(3);

(g)   the name (if known by the inspector or investigator) of the person to whom the inspector or investigator produced evidence of his appointment or authorisation (as the case may be) as required by section 453B(3);

(h)   if the inspector or investigator does not know the name of the person to whom he produced evidence of his identity and appointment or authorisation as required by section 453B(3), an account of how he produced that evidence under that section;

(i)   if the inspector or investigator does not know the name of the person to whom any person accompanying the inspector or investigator produced evidence of his identity under section 453B(3), an account of how that evidence was produced under that section;

(j)   the name (if known by the inspector or investigator) of the person who admitted the inspector or investigator to the premises or, if the inspector or investigator does not know that person's name, an account of how he was admitted to the premises;

(k)   the name (if known by the inspector or investigator) of every appropriate recipient to whom the inspector or investigator, while on the premises, gave a written statement of powers, rights and obligations as required by section 453B(4);

(l)   if the inspector or investigator does not know the name of a person referred to in paragraph (k), an account of how the written statement was given to that person;

(m)   the name (if known by the inspector or investigator) of any person physically present on the premises (to the inspector's or investigator's knowledge) at any time during the inspector's or investigator's visit (other than another inspector or investigator, a person accompanying the inspector or investigator or a person referred to in paragraph (k)) and with whom the inspector or investigator communicated in relation to the inspector's or investigator's presence on the premises;

(n)   a record of any apparent failure by any person during the course of the inspector's or investigator's visit to the premises to comply with any requirement imposed by the inspector or investigator under Part 14 of the 1985 Act; and

(o)   a record of any conduct by any person during the course of the inspector's or investigator's visit to the premises which the inspector or investigator believes amounted to the intentional obstruction of him, or anyone accompanying him, in the lawful exercise of the power to enter and remain on the premises under section 453A.

COMMUNITY INTEREST COMPANY REGULATIONS 2005

(SI 2005/1788)

NOTES

Made: 30 June 2005.

Authority: Companies (Audit, Investigations and Community Enterprise) Act 2004, ss 30(1)–(4), (7), 31, 32(3), (4), (6), 34(3), 35(4)–(6), 36(2), 37(7), 47(12), (13), 57(1), (2), 58, 59(1), 62(2), (3), Sch 4, para 4.

Commencement: 1 July 2005.

These Regulations are reproduced as amended by: the Charities and Trustee Investment (Scotland) Act 2005 (Consequential Provisions and Modifications) Order 2006, SI 2006/242; the Companies Act 2006 (Commencement No 2, Consequential Amendments, Transitional Provisions and Savings) Order 2007, SI 2007/1093; the Companies Act 2006 (Consequential Amendments etc) Order 2008, SI 2008/948; the Community Interest Company (Amendment) Regulations 2009, SI 2009/1942; the Housing and Regeneration Act 2008 (Consequential Provisions) (No 2) Order 2010, SI 2010/671.

References to "the European Community", "Community", etc: see the Treaty of Lisbon (Changes in Terminology) Order 2011, SI 2011/1043, which provides that (as from 22 April 2011) "EU" should be substituted for the word "Community" (subject to certain exceptions) in references to "Community treaties", "Community instrument", "Community obligation", "Community law", "Community legislation", etc.

ARRANGEMENT OF REGULATIONS

PART 1
CITATION, COMMENCEMENT AND INTERPRETATION

[6.113]
1   Citation and commencement
These Regulations may be cited as the Community Interest Company Regulations 2005 and shall come into force on 1 July 2005.

[6.114]
2   Interpretation
In these Regulations—
   ["the 1965 Act" means the Industrial and Provident Societies Act 1965;]
   ["the 1969 Northern Ireland Act" means the Industrial and Provident Societies Act (Northern Ireland) 1969;]

   [. . .]
   "the 2004 Act" means the Companies (Audit, Investigations and Community Enterprise) Act 2004;
   ["the 2006 Act" means the Companies Act 2006;]
   "aggregate dividend cap" means a cap set under regulation 22 for the purposes of determining maximum aggregate dividends;
   "appellant" means, in respect of an appeal to the Appeal Officer, the person bringing the appeal;
   "applicable share dividend cap" has the meaning given in regulation 18(2) and (3);
   "applicable interest cap" has the meaning given in regulation 21(3);
   "asset-locked body" means—
      (a)   a community interest company, [a charity or a permitted industrial and provident society]; or
      (b)   a body established outside [the United Kingdom] that is equivalent to [either of those];
   ["the Authority" means the Financial Services Authority;]
   "community interest statement" means a statement in a form approved by the Regulator which—
      (a)   contains a declaration that the company will carry on its activities for the benefit of the community or a section of the community; and
      (b)   indicates how it is proposed that the company's activities will benefit the community (or a section of the community);
   "distributable profits" means, in relation to a company, its accumulated, realised profits, so far as not previously utilised by distribution or capitalisation, less its accumulated, realised losses, so far as not previously written off in a reduction or reorganisation of capital duly made . . .
   "election" means any election to public office held in [the United Kingdom] or elsewhere;
   "employee" means a person who has entered into or works under (or, where the employment has ceased, worked under)—

(a)   a contract of service or apprenticeship; or

(b)   a contract for services under which it is agreed that a specified individual is to perform services,

whether express or implied, and (if it is express) whether oral or in writing;

"employer" means the person by whom an employee is (or, where the employment has ceased, was) employed;

"exempt dividend" has the meaning given in regulation 17(3);

["governmental authority" includes—

(a)   any national, regional or local government in the United Kingdom or elsewhere;

(b)   the European Community;

(c)   any inter-governmental organisation; and

(d)   any organisation which is able to make rules or adopt decisions which are legally binding on any governmental authority falling within sub-paragraph (a), (b) or (c);

or any of their organs, institutions or agencies;]

"interest cap" means a cap set under regulation 22 for the purpose of determining the maximum rate of interest payable under regulation 21;

"manager" means a person appointed by order under section 47(1) of the 2004 Act;

"maximum aggregate dividend" has the meaning given to it in regulation 19;

"maximum dividend per share" has the meaning given to it in regulation 18(1);

"paid up value" means, in respect of any share in a company, the sum of—

(a)   so much of the share's nominal value as has been paid up; and

(b)   any premium on that share paid to the company;

["permitted industrial and provident society" means an industrial and provident society which has a restriction on the use of its assets in accordance with regulation 4 of the Community Benefit Societies (Restriction on Use of Assets) Regulations 2006 or regulation 4 of the Community Benefit Societies (Restriction on Use of Assets) Regulations (Northern Ireland) 2006;]

"performance-related rate" means any rate which is linked to the company's profits or turnover or to any item in the balance sheet of the company;

"political party" includes any person standing, or proposing to stand, as a candidate at any election, and any person holding public office following his election to that office;

"political campaigning organisation" means any person carrying on, or proposing to carry on activities—

(a)   to promote, or oppose, changes in any law applicable in [the United Kingdom] or elsewhere, or any policy of a governmental or public authority (unless such activities are incidental to other activities carried on by that person); or

(b)   which could reasonably be regarded as intended to affect public support for a political party, or to influence voters in relation to any election or referendum (unless such activities are incidental to other activities carried on by that person);

["public authority" includes—

(a)   a court or tribunal; and

(b)   any person certain of whose functions are functions of a public nature,

whether in the United Kingdom or elsewhere;]

"referendum" includes any national or regional referendum or other poll held in pursuance of any provision made by or under the law of any state on one or more questions or propositions specified in or in accordance with any such provision;

"relevant company" means a community interest company which is a company limited by shares or a company limited by guarantee with a share capital;

"share dividend cap" means a cap set under regulation 22 for the purpose of determining maximum dividends per share;

"subsidiary" has the meaning [given to it by section 1159 of the 2006 Act]; and

"unused dividend capacity" has the meaning given to it in regulation 20(2).

NOTES

Definitions "the 1965 Act", "the 1969 Northern Ireland Act", "the Authority", and "permitted industrial and provident society" inserted by the Community Interest Company (Amendment) Regulations 2009, SI 2009/1942, reg 3(1), (2), as from 1 October 2009.

Definition "the 1985 Act" (omitted) revoked by SI 2009/1942, reg 3(1), (3), as from 1 October 2009.

Definition "the 1986 Order" (omitted) originally inserted by the Companies Act 2006 (Commencement No 2, Consequential Amendments, Transitional Provisions and Savings) Order 2007, SI 2007/1093, art 6(2), Sch 4, Pt 2, para 27(a), as from 6 April 2007, and revoked by SI 2009/1942, reg 3(1), (3), as from 1 October 2009.

Definition "the 2006 Act" inserted by the Companies Act 2006 (Consequential Amendments etc) Order 2008, SI 2008/948, art 3(1), Sch 1, Pt 2, para 242(1), (2), as from 6 April 2008.

Words in first pair of square brackets in definition "asset-locked body" substituted by SI 2009/1942, reg 3(1), (4), as from 1 October 2009; other words in square brackets substituted by SI 2007/1093, art 6(2), Sch 4, Pt 2, para 27(b), as from 6 April 2007.

Words omitted from the definition "distributable profits" revoked by SI 2008/948, art 3(1), Sch 1, Pt 2, para 242(1), (2), as from 6 April 2008.

Words in square brackets in definition "election" substituted by SI 2007/1093, art 6(2), Sch 4, Pt 2, para 27(d), as from 6 April 2007.

Definitions "governmental authority" and "public authority" substituted by SI 2009/1942, reg 3(1), (5), (6), as from 1 October 2009.

Words in square brackets in definition "political campaigning organisation" substituted by SI 2007/1093, art 6(2), Sch 4, Pt 2, para 27(f), as from 6 April 2007.

Words in square brackets in definition "subsidiary" substituted by SI 2009/1942, reg 3(1), (7), as from 1 October 2009.

Industrial and Provident Societies Act 1965: see the Co-operative and Community Benefit Societies and Credit Unions Act 2010 which renames this Act as the Co-operative and Community Benefit Societies and Credit Unions Act 1965.

PART 2
THE COMMUNITY INTEREST TEST AND EXCLUDED COMPANIES

[6.115]
3   Political activities not to be treated as being carried on for the benefit of the community

(1)   For the purposes of the community interest test the following activities are to be treated as not being activities which a reasonable person might consider are activities carried on for the benefit of the community:

   (a)   the promotion of, or the opposition to, changes in—
      (i)   any law applicable in [the United Kingdom] or elsewhere; or
      (ii)   the policy adopted by any governmental or public authority in relation to any matter;
   (b)   the promotion of, or the opposition (including the promotion of changes) to, the policy which any governmental or public authority proposes to adopt in relation to any matter; and
   (c)   activities which can reasonably be regarded as intended or likely to—
      (i)   provide or affect support (whether financial or otherwise) for a political party or political campaigning organisation; or
      (ii)   influence voters in relation to any election or referendum.

(2)   But activities of the descriptions prescribed in paragraph (1) are to be treated as being activities which a reasonable person might consider are activities carried on for the benefit of the community if—

   (a)   they can reasonably be regarded as incidental to other activities, which a reasonable person might consider are being carried on for the benefit the community; and
   (b)   those other activities cannot reasonably be regarded as incidental to activities of any of the descriptions prescribed in paragraph (1).

NOTES

Para (1): words in square brackets substituted by the Companies Act 2006 (Commencement No 2, Consequential Amendments, Transitional Provisions and Savings) Order 2007, SI 2007/1093, art 6(2), Sch 4, Pt 2, para 28, as from 6 April 2007.

[6.116]
4   Other activities not to be treated as being carried on for the benefit of the community

For the purposes of the community interest test, an activity is to be treated as not being an activity which a reasonable person might consider is an activity carried on for the benefit of the community if, or to the extent that, a reasonable person might consider that that activity benefits only the members of a particular body or the employees of a particular employer.

NOTES

Para (1): words in square brackets substituted by the Companies Act 2006 (Commencement No 2, Consequential Amendments, Transitional Provisions and Savings) Order 2007, SI 2007/1093, art 6(2), Sch 4, Pt 2, para 28, as from 6 April 2007.

[6.117]
[5   Section of the community

For the purposes of the community interest test, any group of individuals may constitute a section of the community if—

   (a)   they share a common characteristic which distinguishes them from other members of the community; and
   (b)   a reasonable person might consider that they constitute a section of the community.]

NOTES

Commencement: 1 October 2009.

Substituted by the Community Interest Company (Amendment) Regulations 2009, SI 2009/1942, reg 4, as from 1 October 2009.

[6.118]
6   Excluded companies

For the purposes of section 35(6) of the 2004 Act, the following are excluded companies:

   (a)   a company which is (or when formed would be) a political party;
   (b)   a company which is (or when formed would be) a political campaigning organisation; or

(c) a company which is (or when formed would be) a subsidiary of a political party or of a political campaigning organisation.

[PART 2A
CONVERSION TO AN INDUSTRIAL AND PROVIDENT SOCIETY

[6.119]
6A Becoming an industrial and provident society

Pursuant to section 56 of the 2004 Act, a community interest company may convert itself into a permitted industrial and provident society and section 53 of the 1965 Act and section 62 of the 1969 Northern Ireland Act apply to community interest companies, modified so that they read as follows—

(a) section 53 of the 1965 Act—

"53 Conversion of company into registered society
(1) A company registered under the Companies Acts which is a community interest company may, by special resolution, determine to convert itself into a registered society which has a restriction on use of assets in accordance with the provisions of the Community Benefit Societies (Restriction on Use of Assets) Regulations 2006; and for this purpose, in any case where the nominal value of the company's shares held by any member other than a registered society exceeds the maximum for the time being permitted by section 6(1) of this Act in the case of a member of a registered society the resolution may provide for the conversion of the shares representing that excess into a transferable loan stock bearing such rate of interest as may be fixed, and repayable on such conditions only as are determined by the resolution.
(2) Any such resolution as aforesaid shall be accompanied by a copy of the rules of the society therein referred to and shall appoint three persons, being members of the company, who, together with a director, shall sign the rules and who may either—
    (a) be authorised to accept any alterations made by the Authority therein without further consulting the company; or
    (b) be required to lay any such alterations before the company in general meeting for acceptance as the resolution may direct.
(2A) The following documents shall be sent to the registrar of companies—
    (a) a copy of the resolution;
    (b) a copy of the rules of the society therein referred to; and
    (c) a statement by the Authority that, in its opinion, if those rules take effect, the company will become a registered society which has a restriction on use of assets in accordance with the provisions of the Community Benefit Societies (Restriction on Use of Assets) Regulations 2006,
and, on receiving them, the registrar of companies must forward each of the documents to the Regulator.
(2B) The Regulator must decide whether the company is eligible to cease being a community interest company.
(2C) The company is eligible to cease being a community interest company if none of the following applies—
    (a) the Regulator has under section 43 of the 2004 Act appointed an auditor to audit the company's annual accounts and the audit has not been completed,
    (b) civil proceedings instituted by the Regulator in the name of the company under section 44 of the 2004 Act have not been determined or discontinued,
    (c) a director of the company holds office by virtue of an order under section 45 of the 2004 Act,
    (d) a director of the company is suspended under section 46(3) of the 2004 Act,
    (e) there is a manager in respect of the property and affairs of the company appointed under section 47 of the 2004 Act,
    (f) the Official Property Holder holds property as trustee for the company,
    (g) an order under section 48(2) or (3) of the 2004 Act is in force in relation to the company,
    (h) a petition has been presented for the company to be wound up.
(2D) The Regulator must give notice of the decision to the company.
(2E) The Authority shall register the community interest company as a registered society under this Act if the following conditions are met—
    (a) a copy of the resolution aforesaid and a copy of the rules aforesaid is delivered to the Authority;
    (b) a copy of the decision of the Regulator that the company is eligible to cease being a community interest company is delivered to the Authority;
    (c) the company has a restriction on use of assets in accordance with the provisions of the Community Benefit Societies (Restriction on Use of Assets) Regulations 2006.
(3) The Authority upon the registration of the society under this Act, shall give to it, in addition to an acknowledgement of registration under section 2(3) of this Act, a certificate similarly sealed or signed that the rules of the society referred to in the resolution have been

registered.

(4)   A copy of any such resolution as aforesaid together with a copy of the notice of the decision issued by the Regulator and the certificate issued as aforesaid by the Authority shall be sent to the registrar of companies and, upon his registering that resolution and certificate (but not the notice of the decision issued by the Regulator), the conversion shall take effect.

(5)   The name under which any community interest company is registered under this section as a registered society shall not include any of the following words, expressions or abbreviations—

    (a)   "company",

    (b)   "community interest company" or (with or without full stops) the abbreviation "cic",

    (c)   "cwmni buddiant cymunedol" or (with or without full stops) the abbreviation "cbc",

    (d)   "community interest public limited company" or (with or without full stops) the abbreviation "community interest plc", or

    (e)   "cwmni buddiant cymunedol cyhoeddus cyfyngedig" or (with or without full stops) the abbreviation "cwmni buddiant cymunedol ccc".

(6)   Subject to the next following subsection, upon the conversion of a community interest company into a registered society under this section, the registration of the company under the Companies Acts shall become void and shall be cancelled by the registrar of companies.

(7)   The registration of a community interest company as a registered society shall not affect any right or claim for the time being subsisting against the company or any penalty for the time being incurred by the company; and—

    (a)   for the purpose of enforcing any such right, penalty or claim the company may be sued and proceeded against in the same manner as if it had not been registered as a society;

    (b)   any such right or claim and the liability to any such penalty shall have priority as against the property of the registered society over all other rights or claims against or liabilities of the society.

(8)   In this section—

"the 2004 Act" means the Companies (Audit, Investigations and Community Enterprise) Act 2004;

"the Official Property Holder" has the meaning given in section 29 of the 2004 Act; and

"the Regulator" has the meaning given in section 27 of the 2004 Act.",

(b)   . . .

NOTES

Commencement: 1 October 2009.

Inserted, together with the preceding Part heading, by the Community Interest Company (Amendment) Regulations 2009, SI 2009/1942, reg 5, as from 1 October 2009.

Para (b) sets out s 62 of the Industrial and Provident Societies Act (Northern Ireland) 1969 as it applies to community interest companies, and is outside the scope of this work.

Industrial and Provident Societies Act 1965: see the Co-operative and Community Benefit Societies and Credit Unions Act 2010 which renames this Act as the Co-operative and Community Benefit Societies and Credit Unions Act 1965.

PART 3
REQUIREMENTS CONCERNING THE [ARTICLES OF ASSOCIATION]

NOTES

Words in square brackets in the Part heading substituted by the Community Interest Company (Amendment) Regulations 2009, SI 2009/1942, reg 6(1), as from 1 October 2009.

Saving for provisions relating to community interest companies: the Companies Act 2006 (Commencement No 2, Consequential Amendments, Transitional Provisions and Savings) Order 2007, SI 2007/1093, Sch 6, para 4 (at **[2.30]**) provides as follows (note that the 2007 Order came into force on 6 April 2007)—

"**4   Saving for provisions relating to community interest companies**

A community interest company in relation to which regulations 7 to 9 of the 2005 Regulations (matters to be included in memorandum and articles) were complied with immediately before the coming into force of this Order need not alter its memorandum or articles to take account of any amendment made by this Order.".

[6.120]
[7   Company without share capital

A community interest company which is a company limited by guarantee without a share capital must include in its articles the provisions prescribed by Schedule 1, but if the company is a community interest company immediately prior to 1st October 2009 it may continue to comply with Schedule 1, as Schedule 1 read immediately prior to that date.]

NOTES

Commencement: 1 October 2009.

Substituted by the Community Interest Company (Amendment) Regulations 2009, SI 2009/1942, reg 7, as from 1 October 2009.

[6.121]
[8   Company with share capital
A community interest company which is a company limited by shares or a company limited by guarantee with a share capital must include in its articles either—
   (a)   the provisions prescribed by Schedule 2; or
   (b)   the provisions prescribed by Schedule 3,
but if the company is a community interest company immediately prior to 1st October 2009 it may continue to comply with Schedule 2 or Schedule 3 (as the case may be), as Schedule 2 or Schedule 3 read immediately prior to that date.]

NOTES
Commencement: 1 October 2009.
Substituted by the Community Interest Company (Amendment) Regulations 2009, SI 2009/1942, reg 8, as from 1 October 2009.

[6.122]
9   Alternative provisions
(1)   For paragraph 1(4)(a) of the provisions prescribed by Schedule 1, 2 or 3 a community interest company may substitute—

        ""charitable body" means [a charity or an equivalent body established outside the United Kingdom;]"

(2)   If a community interest company makes the substitution permitted by paragraph (1), it must also for every reference to "asset-locked body" in paragraph 1(2) of the provisions prescribed by Schedule 1, 2 or 3 substitute a reference to "charitable body".

NOTES
Para (1): words in square brackets substituted by the Companies Act 2006 (Commencement No 2, Consequential Amendments, Transitional Provisions and Savings) Order 2007, SI 2007/1093, art 6(2), Sch 4, Pt 2, para 29, as from 6 April 2007.

[6.123]
10   Declaration of dividends
A relevant company must not include in its . . .   articles any provision which purports to permit a dividend to be declared otherwise than by an ordinary or special resolution of its members.

NOTES
Words omitted revoked by the Community Interest Company (Amendment) Regulations 2009, SI 2009/1942, reg 6(2), as from 1 October 2009.

PART 4
PRESCRIBED DOCUMENTS

[6.124]
11   Prescribed formation documents
(1)   For the purposes of section 36 of the 2004 Act, the prescribed formation documents are—
   (a)   a community interest statement signed by each person who is to be a first director of the company; and
   (b)   a declaration that the company, when formed, will not be an excluded company.
(2)   The declaration referred to in paragraph (1)(b) must be in a form approved by the Regulator and must be made by each person who is to be a first director of the company.

[6.125]
12   Prescribed conversion documents
(1)   For the purposes of section 37 of the 2004 Act, the prescribed conversion documents are—
   (a)   a community interest statement signed by each person who is a director of the company;
   (b)   a declaration that the company is not an excluded company; and
  [(c)   either—
      (i)   a declaration that the company is not a charity, . . .
      (ii)   in the case of a company that is an English charity, a declaration that [the Charity Commission] have given the company the written consent required by section 39 of the 2004 Act] [, or]
    [(iii)   in the case of a company that is a Scottish charity, a declaration that the Scottish Charity Regulator, and, where applicable, the Charity Commission, has given the company the written consent required by section 40 of the 2004 Act]].
(2)   The declarations referred to in sub-paragraphs (b) and (c) of paragraph (1) must be in a form approved by the Regulator and must be made by each person who is a director of the company.

NOTES
Para (1): sub-para (c) substituted by the Companies Act 2006 (Commencement No 2, Consequential Amendments, Transitional Provisions and Savings) Order 2007, SI 2007/1093, art 6(2), Sch 4, Pt 2, para 30, as from 6 April 2007; all other amendments to this sub-paragraph were made by the Community Interest Company (Amendment) Regulations 2009, SI 2009/1942, reg 9, as from 1 October 2009.

PART 5
ALTERATION OF OBJECTS

[6.126]
13   Requirement for Regulator's approval

An alteration of the [articles] of a community interest company with respect to the statement of the company's objects does not have effect except in so far as it is approved by the Regulator.

NOTES
Word in square brackets substituted by the Community Interest Company (Amendment) Regulations 2009, SI 2009/1942, reg 10, as from 1 October 2009.

[6.127]
14   Documents to be delivered to registrar of companies

(1)   If [notice under section 31(2)(a) of the 2006 Act (notice of amendment of articles so as to add, remove or alter a statement of the company's objects) is given to the registrar of companies], the company must also deliver—
  (a)   a community interest statement; and
  (b)   a statement, in a form approved by the Regulator, of the steps that have been taken to bring the proposed alteration to the notice of persons affected by the company's activities.

(2)   The community interest statement and the statement under paragraph (1)(b) must be signed by each person who is a director of the company.

NOTES
Para (1): words in square brackets substituted by the Community Interest Company (Amendment) Regulations 2009, SI 2009/1942, reg 11, as from 1 October 2009.

[6.128]
15   Decisions etc

(1)   On receiving [notice under section 31(2)(a) of the 2006 Act], the community interest statement delivered under regulation 14(1)(a) and the statement delivered under regulation 14(1)(b), the registrar of companies must—
  (a)   forward a copy of each of the documents to the Regulator; and
  (b)   retain the documents pending the Regulator's decision.

(2)   The Regulator must decide whether to approve the proposed alteration of the [articles] of the community interest company with respect to the statement of the company's objects.

(3)   The Regulator may approve the proposed alteration if he considers that—
  (a)   the statement of the company's objects as altered by the special resolution will comply with the requirements imposed by and by virtue of section 32 of the 2004 Act;
  (b)   the company will satisfy the community interest test; and
  (c)   the company has taken reasonable steps to bring the proposed alteration to the notice of persons affected by its activities.

(4)   In considering whether the company will satisfy the community interest test, the Regulator shall have regard to—
  (a)   the statement of the company's objects as altered by the special resolution;
  (b)   the community interest statement; and
  (c)   any other relevant considerations.

(5)   The Regulator must give notice of the decision to the registrar (but the registrar is not required to record it).

(6)   The registrar shall not—
  [(a)   register the notice under section 31(2)(a) of the 2006 Act;
  (b)   register any copy of the amended articles delivered pursuant to section 26(1) of that Act;]
  (c)   cause notice of that alteration to be published pursuant to [section 1077 of the Companies Act 2006] (public notice by registrar of receipt of documents),
unless and until the Regulator has given notice of a decision to approve the proposed alteration.

(7)   If the Regulator gives notice of a decision to approve the proposed alteration, the registrar shall also—
  (a)   record the community interest statement; and
  (b)   record the statement delivered under regulation 14(1)(b).

(8)   If the Regulator decides not to approve the proposed alteration of the memorandum of the community interest company with respect to the statement of the company's objects, the company may appeal to the Appeal Officer against the decision.

NOTES

Paras (1), (2): words in square brackets substituted by the Community Interest Company (Amendment) Regulations 2009, SI 2009/1942, reg 12(a), (b), as from 1 October 2009.

Para (6): sub-paras (a), (b) substituted by SI 2009/1942, reg 12(c), as from 1 October 2009; words in square brackets in sub-para (c) substituted by SI 2007/1093, art 6(2), Sch 4, Pt 2, para 32(d), as from 6 April 2007.

[6.129]
16   Exemptions

Regulations 13 to 15 do not apply where a community interest company is to cease being a community interest company by becoming a charity or . . . and the special resolution to alter the [articles] of the company with respect to the statement of its objects is forwarded to the registrar of companies in accordance with section 54 of the 2004 Act.

NOTES

Words omitted revoked by the Companies Act 2006 (Commencement No 2, Consequential Amendments, Transitional Provisions and Savings) Order 2007, SI 2007/1093, art 6(2), Sch 4, Pt 2, para 33, as from 6 April 2007; word in square brackets substituted by the Community Interest Company (Amendment) Regulations 2009, SI 2009/1942, reg 13, as from 1 October 2009.

PART 6
RESTRICTIONS ON DISTRIBUTIONS AND INTEREST

[6.130]
17   Declaration of dividends

(1)   A relevant company may declare a dividend to its members only—
    (a)   to the extent that its . . . articles permit it to do so;
    (b)   if an ordinary or special resolution of the company's members has approved the declaration of the dividend; and
    (c)   if the declaration of the dividend does not cause—
        (i)   the total amount of dividend declared on any of the company's shares for the financial year for which it is declared to exceed the maximum dividend per share for that financial year; or
        (ii)   the total amount of all the dividends declared on shares in the relevant company for the financial year for which it is declared to exceed the maximum aggregate dividend for that financial year.

(2)   Paragraph (1)(c) does not apply to a dividend if, or to the extent that, it is an exempt dividend.

(3)   A dividend declared on a share in a relevant company is an exempt dividend if one of the conditions specified in paragraph (4) and one of the conditions specified in paragraph (5) is satisfied in respect of it.

(4)   The conditions specified in this paragraph are—
    (a)   that the dividend is declared on a share which is held by an asset-locked body (but this condition is not satisfied in respect of a share which the directors recommending the dividend are aware is being held on trust for a person who is not an asset-locked body);
    (b)   that the dividend is declared on a share which is held on behalf of an asset-locked body (or is believed by the directors recommending the dividend to be so held).

(5)   The conditions specified in this paragraph are—
    (a)   that the Regulator has consented to the declaration of the dividend;
    (b)   that the asset-locked body by or on behalf of which the share on which the dividend is declared is held (or on behalf of which the directors declaring the dividend believe that it is held) is named in the memorandum or articles of the company as a possible recipient of the assets of the company.

(6)   If a relevant company has made the substitutions prescribed in regulation 9(2), references to "asset-locked body" in this article shall have effect as if there were substituted for them references to "charitable body", with the meaning prescribed in regulation 9(1).

NOTES

Para (1): words omitted revoked by the Community Interest Company (Amendment) Regulations 2009, SI 2009/1942, reg 14, as from 1 October 2009.

[6.131]
18   Maximum dividend per share

(1)   The maximum dividend per share for a financial year is the dividend which a relevant company declares on a share when the total amount of dividend declared on that share for that year (when expressed as a percentage of the paid up value of the share) equals that share's applicable share dividend cap.

(2)   The applicable share dividend cap of a share in a relevant company is the share dividend cap which had effect in relation to that share at the time that the share was issued or the company became a community interest company, whichever is the later.

(3)   Where the expression of the applicable dividend cap includes reference to a rate or figure determined by any person other than the company, the Regulator or the Secretary of State [(in Northern Ireland, the Department of Enterprise, Trade and Investment for Northern Ireland)], the maximum dividend per share for any financial year shall be calculated by reference to that rate or figure as it had effect at the beginning of the first day of that financial year.

NOTES
Para (3): words in square brackets inserted by the Companies Act 2006 (Commencement No 2, Consequential Amendments, Transitional Provisions and Savings) Order 2007, SI 2007/1093, art 6(2), Sch 4, Pt 2, para 34, as from 6 April 2007.

[6.132]
19   Maximum aggregate dividend

The maximum aggregate dividend for a financial year of a relevant company is declared when the total amount of all dividends declared on its shares for that year, less the amount of any exempt dividends, equals (when expressed as a percentage of the relevant company's distributable profits) the aggregate dividend cap which had effect in relation to that company on the first day of the financial year in respect of which the dividends are declared.

[6.133]
20   Carrying forward of unused dividend capacity from previous financial years

(1)   Notwithstanding regulation 17(1)(c)(i), but subject to regulation 17(1)(c)(ii), the total amount of dividends declared on a share in a relevant company for a financial year may, subject to the company's articles, include the whole or any part of the share's unused dividend capacity.

(2)   For the purposes of this regulation, a share's unused dividend capacity is A minus B where—
   A is the aggregate of any sums by which, for any of the four financial years immediately preceding the financial year for which a dividend is to be declared under this regulation, the total amount of dividend declared and paid on the share for that financial year was less than the maximum dividend per share for that financial year; and
   B is any part of A which has already been distributed by way of a dividend declared and paid for a previous financial year.

[6.134]
21   The interest cap

(1)   This regulation applies to debentures issued by, and debts of, a community interest company in respect of which—
   (a)   a performance-related rate of interest is payable; and
   (b)   the agreement to pay interest at a performance-related rate was entered into by the company on or after the date on which it became a community interest company.

(2)   In connection with debentures and debts of the kind specified in paragraph (1), a community interest company shall not be liable to pay, and shall not pay, interest at a higher rate than the applicable interest cap.

(3)   The applicable interest cap is the interest cap which had effect at the time that the agreement to pay interest at a performance-related rate was made.

(4)   Where the expression of the interest cap includes reference to a rate or figure determined by any person other than the company, the Regulator or the Secretary of State [(in Northern Ireland, the Department of Enterprise, Trade and Investment for Northern Ireland)], the interest payable on any debt or debenture to which the interest cap applies shall be calculated by reference to that rate or figure as it had effect at the beginning of the first day of the financial year in which the interest became due.

(5)   Nothing in paragraph (2) shall be taken as releasing a community interest company from liability to pay, or as preventing a community interest company from paying—
   (a)   interest which accrued before the company became a community interest company; or
   (b)   arrears of interest which if it had been paid at the time it became due would not have breached paragraph (2).

NOTES
Para (4): words in square brackets inserted by the Companies Act 2006 (Commencement No 2, Consequential Amendments, Transitional Provisions and Savings) Order 2007, SI 2007/1093, art 6(2), Sch 4, Pt 2, para 35, as from 6 April 2007.

[6.135]
22 Initial level and subsequent variation of dividend caps and interest cap

(1) Subject to paragraph (3)—

    (a) the share dividend cap shall be that percentage of the paid up value of a share in a relevant company which is 5 percentage points higher than the Bank of England's base lending rate;

    (b) the aggregate dividend cap shall be 35 per cent of a relevant company's distributable profits; and

    (c) the interest cap shall be that percentage of the average amount of a community interest company's debt, or the sum outstanding under a debenture issued by it, during the 12 month period immediately preceding the date on which the interest on that debt or debenture becomes due (determined in accordance with Schedule 4) which is 4 percentage points higher than the Bank of England's base lending rate.

(2) For the purposes of paragraph (1), the Bank of England's base lending rate is the base lending rate most recently set by the Monetary Policy Committee of the Bank of England in connection with its responsibilities under Part II of the Bank of England Act 1998.

(3) The Regulator may from time to time, with the approval of the Secretary of State, set a new share dividend cap, aggregate dividend cap, or interest cap.

(4) A new cap set under paragraph (3)—

    (a) shall not take effect from a date less than three months after it is published; and

    (b) subject to paragraphs (5) to (7), may result in a change to both the level of any cap and the way in which it is expressed.

(5) The share dividend cap must be expressed as a percentage of the paid up value of the shares to which it applies.

(6) The aggregate dividend cap must be expressed as a percentage of distributable profits.

(7) The interest cap must be expressed as a percentage of the average amount of a debt, or the sum outstanding under a debenture, during the 12 month period immediately preceding the date on which the interest on that debt or debenture becomes due (determined in accordance with Schedule 4).

(8) The Secretary of State may from time to time require the Regulator to review any cap set under this regulation.

[6.136]
23 Distribution of assets on a winding up

(1) This regulation applies where—

    (a) a community interest company is wound up under the Insolvency Act 1986 [or the Insolvency (Northern Ireland) Order 1989]; and

    (b) some property of the company (the "residual assets") remains after satisfaction of the company's liabilities.

(2) Subject to paragraph (3), the residual assets shall be distributed to those members of the community interest company (if any) who are entitled to share in any distribution of assets on the winding up of the company according to their rights and interests in the company.

(3) No member shall receive under paragraph (2) an amount which exceeds the paid up value of the shares which he holds in the company.

(4) If any residual assets remain after any distribution to members under paragraph (2) (the "remaining residual assets"), they shall be distributed in accordance with paragraphs (5) and (6).

(5) If the . . . articles of the company specify an asset-locked body to which any remaining residual assets of the company should be distributed, then, unless either of the conditions specified in sub-paragraphs (b) and (c) of paragraph (6) is satisfied, the remaining residual assets shall be distributed to that asset-locked body in such proportions or amounts as the Regulator shall direct.

(6) If—

    (a) the . . . articles of the company do not specify an asset-locked body to which any remaining residual assets of the company should be distributed;

    (b) the Regulator is aware that the asset-locked body to which the . . . articles of the company specify that the remaining residual assets of the company should be distributed is itself in the process of being wound up; or

    (c) the Regulator—

       (i) has received representations from a member or director of the company stating, with reasons, that the asset-locked body to which the . . . articles of the company specify that the remaining residual assets of the company should be distributed is not an appropriate recipient of the company's remaining residual assets; and

       (ii) has agreed with those representations,

    then the remaining residual assets shall be distributed to such asset-locked bodies, and in such proportions or amounts, as the Regulator shall direct.

(7) In considering any direction to be made under this regulation, the Regulator must—

(a)   consult the directors and members of the company, to the extent that he considers it practicable and appropriate to do so; and

(b)   have regard to the desirability of distributing assets in accordance with any relevant provisions of the company's . . . articles.

(8)   The Regulator must give notice of any direction under this regulation to the company and the liquidator.

(9)   This regulation has effect notwithstanding anything in the Insolvency Act 1986 [or the Insolvency (Northern Ireland) Order 1989].

(10)   This regulation has effect subject to the provisions of the Housing Act 1996[, Part 2 of the Housing and Regeneration Act 2008] and the Housing (Scotland) Act 2001.

(11)   Any member or director of the company may appeal to the Appeal Officer against a direction of the Regulator made under this regulation.

NOTES

Paras (1), (9): words in square brackets inserted by the Companies Act 2006 (Commencement No 2, Consequential Amendments, Transitional Provisions and Savings) Order 2007, SI 2007/1093, art 6(2), Sch 4, Pt 2, para 36, as from 6 April 2007.

Paras (5)–(7): words omitted revoked by the Community Interest Company (Amendment) Regulations 2009, SI 2009/1942, reg 15, as from 1 October 2009.

Para (10): words in square brackets inserted by the Housing and Regeneration Act 2008 (Consequential Provisions) (No 2) Order 2010, SI 2010/671, art 4, Sch 1, para 42, as from 1 April 2010.

[6.137]
24   Redemption and purchase of shares

A relevant company may not distribute assets to its members by way of the redemption or purchase of the company's own shares, unless the amount to be paid by the company in respect of any such share does not exceed the paid up value of the share.

[6.138]
25   Reduction of share capital

A relevant company may not distribute assets to its members by way of a reduction of the company's share capital unless—

(a)   the reduction is made by extinguishing or reducing the liability of any of the members on any of the company's shares in respect of share capital not paid up; or

(b)   the amount to be paid by the company to members in paying off paid up share capital does not exceed the paid up value of their respective shares.

PART 7
COMMUNITY INTEREST COMPANY REPORT

[6.139]
26   General

(1)   Every community interest company report shall contain—

(a)   a fair and accurate description of the manner in which the company's activities during the financial year have benefited the community;

(b)   a description of the steps, if any, which the company has taken during the financial year to consult persons affected by the company's activities, and the outcome of any such consultation; and

[(c)   the information specified in—

(i)   Schedule 3 to the Small Companies and Groups (Accounts and Directors' Report) Regulations 2008, or

(ii)   Schedule 5 to the Large and Medium-Sized Companies and Groups (Accounts and Reports) Regulations 2008 save that the information specified in Part 2 of that Schedule shall be given only in the case of a company which is not a quoted company.]

(2)   If, during a financial year, a community interest company has transferred any of its assets other than for full consideration—

(a)   to any asset-locked body (other than by way of an exempt dividend); or

(b)   for the benefit of the community other than by way of transfer to an asset-locked body,

its community interest report for that financial year shall specify the amount, or contain a fair estimate of the value, of such transfer.

[(3)   If—

(a)   a community interest company has provided the information required by paragraph (1)(c) in its copy of the annual accounts for the year delivered to the registrar of companies under section 441 of the 2006 Act; and

(b)   its community interest company report contains a statement that details of the remuneration of the directors of the company during the financial year may be found in the notes to the annual accounts of the company, the community interest report need not contain the information required by paragraph (1)(c).

(4)   Paragraphs (1)(c) and (3) have effect for financial years ending on or after 1st October 2009.]

NOTES

Para (1): sub-para (c) added by the Community Interest Company (Amendment) Regulations 2009, SI 2009/1942, reg 16(1), (2), as from 1 October 2009. Note that there was an original sub-para (c), which was revoked by the Companies Act 2006 (Consequential Amendments etc) Order 2008, SI 2008/948, art 3, Sch 1, Pt 2, para 242(1), (3), Sch 2, as from 6 April 2008.

Paras (3), (4): added by SI 2009/1942, reg 16(1), (3), as from 1 October 2009. Note that there was an original para (3), which was revoked by SI 2008/948, art 3, Sch 1, Pt 2, para 242(1), (3), Sch 2, as from 6 April 2008.

[6.140]
27   Information about dividends

(1)   This regulation applies to the community interest company report of any community interest company—
   (a)   which has declared, or whose directors propose to declare, a dividend for the financial year to which the report relates; or
   (b)   which has declared a dividend for any of the four financial years immediately preceding that financial year.

(2)   The report must state—
   (a)   the amount of any dividend declared, or proposed to be declared, by the company on each of its shares for the financial year to which the report relates; and
   (b)   for each of the four financial years immediately preceding the financial year to which the report relates (in so far as the company was formed and trading during that period)—
      (i)   the amount of any dividend declared and paid on each of the company's shares; and
      (ii)   the maximum dividend per share in respect of each of the company's shares.

(3)   The report must also explain how the declaration or proposed declaration of any dividend declared, or proposed to be declared, by the company in respect of the financial year to which the report relates complies, or will comply, with regulations 17 to 20.

(4)   The explanation provided under paragraph (3) must include details of—
   (a)   in the case of an exempt dividend, why it is an exempt dividend;
   (b)   in the case of any other dividend—
      (i)   the applicable share dividend cap and the maximum dividend per share for each share on which the dividend has been, or is to be, declared;
      (ii)   the amount of any unused dividend capacity distributed or to be distributed as part of the dividend declared, or proposed to be declared; and
      (iii)   the maximum aggregate dividend,
      and how each of these has been determined.

[6.141]
28   Information about debts or debentures on which a performance-related rate is payable

(1)   Where a community interest company has at any time during the financial year a debt outstanding, or a debenture in issue, to which regulation 21 applies, its community interest company report must state—
   (a)   the rate of interest payable on that debt or debenture as calculated over a 12 month period ending with the most recent date on which interest became payable in respect of that debt or debenture during the financial year; and
   (b)   the applicable interest cap applying to that debt or debenture,
and how each of these has been determined.

(2)   Where the company has at any time during the financial year a debt outstanding, or a debenture in issue, to which regulation 21 does not apply, but on which a performance-related rate is payable, its community interest company report must state—
   (a)   the rate of interest payable on that debt or debenture as calculated over a 12 month period ending with the most recent date on which interest became payable in respect of that debt or debenture during the financial year; and
   (b)   why regulation 21 does not apply to that debt or debenture.

[6.142]
[29   Application of provisions relating to directors' report
The following provisions of the 2006 Act apply to the community interest company report as they apply to the directors' report—
   section 419 (approval and signing);
   sections 423 to 425, 430 to 433 and 436 (publication);
   sections 437 and 438 (public companies: laying before general meeting);
   sections 441 to 448 and 451 to 453 (filing obligations);
   section 454 (voluntary revision).]

Part 6   Pre-2006 companies SIs

NOTES

Commencement: 6 April 2008.

Substituted by the Companies Act 2006 (Consequential Amendments etc) Order 2008, SI 2008/948, art 3(1), Sch 1, Pt 2, para 242(1), (4), as from 6 April 2008 (for savings see art 6(4) of the 2008 Order (at **[4.280]**) which provides that where by virtue of any transitional provision, a provision of the Companies Act 2006 has effect only (a) on or after a specified date, or (b) in relation to matters occurring or arising on or after a specified date, any amendment substituting or inserting a reference to that provision has effect correspondingly).

PART 8
MANAGERS

[6.143]
30   Remuneration

(1)   The Regulator is authorised to determine the amount of a manager's remuneration.

(2)   The remuneration of a manager shall be payable out of the income of the community interest company in respect of which the manager was appointed.

(3)   The Regulator is authorised to disallow any amount of remuneration of a manager if—
   (a)   the time specified in the notice referred to in regulation 32(2) has expired; and
   (b)   the Regulator—
      (i)   has considered such representations, if any, as are duly made in response to such a notice; and
      (ii)   is satisfied that the manager has failed in such manner as is set out in sub-paragraph (a)(i) or (ii) of regulation 32(1) and specified in such a notice.

[6.144]
31   Security

The Regulator is authorised to require the manager to give security to him for the due discharge of the manager's functions within such time and in such form as the Regulator may specify.

[6.145]
32   Failure and removal

(1)   Where—
   (a)   it appears to the Regulator that a manager has failed—
      (i)   to give security within such time or in such form as the Regulator has specified; or
      (ii)   satisfactorily to discharge any function imposed on the manager by or by virtue of the order by which the manager was appointed or by regulation 33; and
   (b)   the Regulator wishes to consider exercising his powers under regulation 30(3) or paragraph (3) of this regulation,
the Regulator shall give the manager, whether in person or by post, a written notice complying with paragraph (2).

(2)   A notice given to a manager under paragraph (1) shall inform the manager of—
   (a)   any failure under paragraph (1)(a) in respect of which the notice is issued;
   (b)   the Regulator's power under regulation 30(3) to authorise the disallowance of any amount of remuneration if satisfied as to any such failure;
   (c)   the Regulator's power under paragraph (3) to remove the manager if satisfied as to any such failure; and
   (d)   the manager's right to make representations to the Regulator in respect of any such alleged failure within such reasonable time as is specified in the notice.

(3)   The Regulator may remove a manager (whether or not he also exercises the power conferred by regulation 30(3)) if—
   (a)   the time specified in the notice referred to in paragraph (2) has expired; and
   (b)   the Regulator—
      (i)   has considered such representations, if any, as are duly made in response to such a notice; and
      (ii)   is satisfied that the manager has failed in such manner as is set out in paragraph (1)(a)(i) or (ii) and specified in such notice.

[6.146]
33   Reports

The manager must make such reports to the Regulator as the Regulator may from time to time require on such matters and in such form as the Regulator specifies.

PART 9
THE REGISTRAR OF COMPANIES

[6.147]
34 Modifications and amendments

[(1) The registrar of companies shall not cause to be published in the Gazette notice pursuant to section 1077 of the Companies Act 2006 of the receipt of documents under section 37C(3) or 54C(4) of the 2004 Act unless the registrar records those documents pursuant to section 38A(1)(b) or 55A(1)(b) of the 2004 Act.]

(2)–(4) . . .

NOTES

Para (1): substituted by the Community Interest Company (Amendment) Regulations 2009, SI 2009/1942, reg 17(a), as from 1 October 2009.
Para (2): amended CA 1985, ss 715A (repealed).
Para (3): revoked by SI 2007/1093, art 6(2), Sch 4, Pt 2, para 39(b), as from 6 April 2007.
Para (4): revoked by SI 2009/1942, reg 17(b), as from 1 October 2009.

[6.148]
35 Documents

(1) The registrar of companies shall, on receiving any notice under section 109(1) of the Insolvency Act 1986 [or Article 95 of the Insolvency (Northern Ireland) Order 1989] (notice by liquidator of his appointment) in relation to a community interest company, provide a copy of that notice to the Regulator.

(2) The registrar of companies shall, on receiving any copy of a winding-up order forwarded under section 130(1) of the Insolvency Act 1986 [or Article 110 of the Insolvency (Northern Ireland) Order 1989] (consequences of a winding-up order) in relation to a community interest company, provide the Regulator with a copy of that winding-up order.

NOTES

Words in square brackets inserted by the Companies Act 2006 (Commencement No 2, Consequential Amendments, Transitional Provisions and Savings) Order 2007, SI 2007/1093, art 6(2), Sch 4, Pt 2, para 40, as from 6 April 2007.

PART 10
FEES

[6.149]
36 Fees payable by a community interest company

The fees set out in the second column of Schedule 5—
(a) shall be the fees payable in connection with the Regulator's functions in relation to the matters set out in the first column of that Schedule;
(b) shall be payable as stated in the third column of that Schedule; and
(c) shall be paid to the registrar of companies.

PART 11
THE APPEAL OFFICER

[6.150]
37 Time limits

(1) Unless paragraph (2) applies, an appeal to the Appeal Officer must be made by sending a notice of appeal to the Regulator so that it is received within two months of the date upon which the appellant was given reasons for the disputed order or decision in accordance with section 61(5) of the 2004 Act.

(2) When an appeal is brought against a direction of the Regulator made under regulation 23, it must be made by sending a notice of appeal to the Regulator so that it is received within three weeks of the date upon which notice of the disputed direction was given to the community interest company in accordance with regulation 23(8).

(3) On receiving the notice of appeal, the Regulator must—
(a) send an acknowledgement of its receipt to the appellant together with a copy of any statement made under paragraph (4); and
(b) forward the notice of appeal to the Appeal Officer endorsed with the date of receipt.

(4) Where paragraph (2) applies, the Regulator must forward with the notice of appeal a statement—
(a) of the date upon which notice of the disputed direction or decision was given to the community interest company in accordance with regulation 23(8); or
(b) that no such notice was given.

[6.151]
38   Notice of appeal

(1)   The notice of appeal must state—
   (a)   the name and address of the appellant; and
   (b)   an address for service in [the United Kingdom].

(2)   Unless regulation 37(2) applies, the notice of appeal must—
   (a)   specify as precisely as the appellant is able the date or dates on which the appellant was given reasons by the Regulator for the disputed order or decision; or
   (b)   include a statement that no such reasons were given.

(3)   The notice of appeal must contain—
   (a)   a statement of the grounds for the appeal;
   (b)   details of the disputed order, decision or direction;
   (c)   a succinct presentation of the arguments supporting each of the grounds of appeal; and
   (d)   a schedule listing all the documents annexed to the notice of appeal.

(4)   There shall be annexed to the notice of appeal—
   (a)   in the case of a disputed order or decision, a copy of any reasons given by the Regulator under section 61(5) of the 2004 Act; and
   (b)   as far as practicable a copy of every document on which the appellant relies.

(5)   The notice of appeal must be signed and dated by the appellant, or on his behalf by his duly authorised officer or his legal representative.

NOTES
  Para (1): words in square brackets substituted by the Companies Act 2006 (Commencement No 2, Consequential Amendments, Transitional Provisions and Savings) Order 2007, SI 2007/1093, art 6(2), Sch 4, Pt 2, para 41, as from 6 April 2007.

[6.152]
39   Appeal procedure etc

(1)   The Regulator may make a written response to the notice of appeal.

(2)   Any such written response must be sent to the Appeal Officer so that it is received by him within two weeks of the date on which the Regulator received the notice of appeal or such further time as the Appeal Officer may allow.

(3)   The Appeal Officer must send a copy of the written response to the appellant.

(4)   The Appeal Officer may give the appellant and the Regulator the opportunity to make further written or oral representations.

(5)   The Appeal Officer may specify the time and manner in which such further representations are to be made.

(6)   The Appeal Officer may—
   (a)   make enquiries of any person;
   (b)   receive representations from any person;
   (c)   hold any meeting or hearing; and
   (d)   subject to these Regulations, follow such practice and procedure,
as he thinks fit, having regard to the just, expeditious and economical conduct of the appeal.

(7)   The Appeal Officer may specify the time and place at which any meeting or hearing is to be held.

[6.153]
40   Determination of appeal

In determining an appeal, the Appeal Officer shall have regard to all matters that appear to him to be relevant.

[6.154]
41   Dismissal of appeal

(1)   The Appeal Officer may dismiss an appeal at any stage if he considers that—
   (a)   the notice of appeal discloses no valid ground of appeal;
   (b)   the notice of appeal fails to comply with the requirements of regulation 38; or
   (c)   the appellant is not entitled to bring the appeal.

(2)   The Appeal Officer must dismiss an appeal if he considers that the appeal was not brought within the time limits imposed by regulation 37 unless he is satisfied that the circumstances are exceptional.

(3)   The Appeal Officer may dismiss an appeal at any stage at the request of the appellant.

[6.155]
42   Reasons

(1)   The Appeal Officer must give reasons for a decision to—
   (a)   dismiss an appeal;

(b)   allow an appeal; or

(c)   remit a case to the Regulator.

(2)   The reasons must be given to the Regulator and to the person bringing the appeal.

(3)   The Appeal Officer must make such arrangements for the publication of the decisions listed in paragraph (1) and his reasons for them as he considers appropriate.

SCHEDULES

SCHEDULE 1

PROVISIONS PRESCRIBED FOR THE . . . ARTICLES OF A COMMUNITY INTEREST COMPANY LIMITED BY GUARANTEE WITHOUT A SHARE CAPITAL

Regulation 7

[6.156]

1. (1)   The company shall not transfer any of its assets other than for full consideration.

(2)   Provided the conditions in sub-paragraph (3) are satisfied, sub-paragraph (1) shall not apply to—

(a)   the transfer of assets to any specified asset-locked body, or (with the consent of the Regulator) to any other asset-locked body; and

(b)   the transfer of assets made for the benefit of the community other than by way of a transfer of assets to an asset-locked body.

(3)   The conditions are that the transfer of assets must comply with any restrictions on the transfer of assets for less than full consideration which may be set out elsewhere in the memorandum or articles of the company.

(4)   In this paragraph—

(a)   "asset-locked body" means—

(i)   a community interest company, [a charity, or a permitted industrial and provident society]; or

(ii)   a body established outside the United Kingdom that is equivalent to [either of those];

(b)   "community" is to be construed in accordance with section 35(5) of the Companies (Audit, Investigations and Community Enterprise) Act 2004;

[(ba) "permitted industrial and provident society" means an industrial and provident society which has a restriction on the use of its assets in accordance with regulation 4 of the Community Benefit Societies (Restriction on Use of Assets) Regulations 2006 or regulation 4 of the Community Benefit Societies (Restriction on Use of Assets) Regulations (Northern Ireland) 2006;]

(c)   . . .

(d)   "the Regulator" means the Regulator of Community Interest Companies;

[(e)   . . .]

(f)   "specified" means specified in the memorandum or articles of association of the company for the purposes of this paragraph; and

(g)   "transfer" includes every description of disposition, payment, release or distribution, and the creation or extinction of an estate or interest in, or a right over, any property.

2. (1)   The subscribers to the memorandum are the first members of the company.

(2)   Such other persons as are admitted to membership in accordance with the articles shall be members of the company.

(3)   No person shall be admitted a member of the company unless he is approved by the directors.

(4)   Every person who wishes to become a member shall deliver to the company an application for membership in such form (and containing such information) as the directors require and executed by him.

(5)   Membership is not transferable to anyone else.

(6)   Membership is terminated if:

(a)   the member dies or ceases to exist; or

(b)   otherwise in accordance with the articles.

3. (1)   A person who is not a member of the company shall not have any right to vote at a general meeting of the company; but this is without prejudice to any right to vote on a resolution affecting the rights attached to a class of the company's debentures.

(2)–(5)   . . .

4. (1)   Questions arising at a meeting of directors shall be decided by a majority of votes . . .

(2)   . . .

(3)   Except as provided by sub-paragraphs (1) and (2) in all proceedings of directors each director must not have more than one vote.

Part 6   Pre-2006 companies SIs

NOTES

Schedule heading: words omitted revoked by the Community Interest Company (Amendment) Regulations 2009, SI 2009/1942, reg 18, as from 1 October 2009.

Para 1 is amended as follows:

Words in square brackets in sub-para (4)(a)(i) substituted, and sub-para (ba) inserted, by SI 2009/1942, regs 19, 20, as from 1 October 2009.

Words in square brackets in sub-para (4)(a)(ii) substituted, and sub-paras (4)(c), (e) revoked, by the Companies Act 2006 (Commencement No 2, Consequential Amendments, Transitional Provisions and Savings) Order 2007, SI 2007/1093, art 6(2), Sch 4, Pt 2, para 42(a)–(c), as from 6 April 2007 (sub-para (4)(e) was previously substituted by the Charities and Trustee Investment (Scotland) Act 2005 (Consequential Provisions and Modifications) Order 2006, SI 2006/242, art 5, Schedule, Pt 2, para 12, as from 1 April 2006).

Para 3: sub-paras (2)–(5) revoked by SI 2009/1942, reg 21, as from 1 October 2009.

Para 4: words omitted from sub-para (1), and the whole of sub-para (2), revoked by SI 2009/1942, reg 22, as from 1 October 2009.

SCHEDULE 2
PROVISIONS PRESCRIBED FOR THE . . . ARTICLES OF A COMMUNITY INTEREST COMPANY LIMITED BY SHARES, OR LIMITED BY GUARANTEE WITH A SHARE CAPITAL

Regulation 8(a)

[6.157]

1. (1)   The company shall not transfer any of its assets other than for full consideration.

(2)   Provided the conditions in sub-paragraph (3) are satisfied, sub-paragraph (1) shall not apply to—

(a)   the transfer of assets to any specified asset-locked body, or (with the consent of the Regulator) to any other asset-locked body; and

(b)   the transfer of assets made for the benefit of the community other than by way of a transfer of assets to an asset-locked body.

(3)   The conditions are that the transfer of assets must comply with any restrictions on the transfer of assets for less than full consideration which may be set out elsewhere in the memorandum or articles of the company.

(4)   In this paragraph—

(a)   "asset-locked body" means—

(i)   a community interest company, [a charity, or a permitted industrial and provident society]; or

(ii)   a body established outside [the United Kingdom] that is equivalent to [either of those];

(b)   "community" is to be construed in accordance with section 35(5) of the Companies (Audit, Investigations and Community Enterprise) Act 2004;

[(ba)   "permitted industrial and provident society" means an industrial and provident society which has a restriction on the use of its assets in accordance with regulation 4 of the Community Benefit Societies (Restriction on Use of Assets) Regulations 2006 or regulation 4 of the Community Benefit Societies (Restriction on Use of Assets) Regulations (Northern Ireland) 2006;]

(c)   . . .

(d)   "the Regulator" means the Regulator of Community Interest Companies;

[(e)   . . .]

(f)   "specified" means specified in the memorandum or articles of association of the company for the purposes of this paragraph; and

(g)   "transfer" includes every description of disposition, payment, release or distribution, and the creation or extinction of an estate or interest in, or a right over, any property.

2. (1)   The directors may refuse to register the transfer of a share to a person of whom they do not approve.

(2)   They may also refuse to register the transfer unless it is lodged at the registered office of the company or at such other place as the directors may appoint and is accompanied by such evidence as the directors may reasonably require to show the right of the transferor to make the transfer, and by such other information as they may reasonably require.

(3)   If the directors refuse to register such a transfer, they shall within two months after the date on which the transfer was lodged with the company send to the transferee notice of the refusal.

(4)   The provisions of this paragraph apply in addition to any restrictions on the transfer of a share which may be set out elsewhere in the memorandum or articles of the company.

3. (1)   A person who is not a member of the company shall not have any right to vote at a general meeting of the company; but this is without prejudice to any right to vote on a resolution affecting the rights attached to a class of the company's debentures.

(2)–(5)   . . .

4. (1)   Questions arising at a meeting of directors shall be decided by a majority of votes . . .

(2)   . . .

(3)   Except as provided by sub-paragraphs (1) and (2) in all proceedings of directors each director must not have more than one vote.

NOTES

Schedule heading: words omitted revoked by the Community Interest Company (Amendment) Regulations 2009, SI 2009/1942, reg 18, as from 1 October 2009.

Para 1: words in square brackets in sub-para (4)(a)(i) substituted, and sub-para (ba) inserted, by SI 2009/1942, regs 19, 20, as from 1 October 2009; words in square brackets in sub-para (4)(a)(ii) substituted, and sub-paras (4)(c), (e) revoked, by the Companies Act 2006 (Commencement No 2, Consequential Amendments, Transitional Provisions and Savings) Order 2007, SI 2007/1093, art 6(2), Sch 4, Pt 2, para 43(a)–(c), as from 6 April 2007 (sub-para (4)(e) was previously substituted by the Charities and Trustee Investment (Scotland) Act 2005 (Consequential Provisions and Modifications) Order 2006, SI 2006/242, art 5, Schedule, Pt 2, para 12, as from 1 April 2006).

Para 3: sub-paras (2)–(5) revoked by SI 2009/1942, reg 21, as from 1 October 2009.

Para 4: words omitted from sub-para (1), and the whole of sub-para (2), revoked by SI 2009/1942, reg 22, as from 1 October 2009.

SCHEDULE 3

ALTERNATIVE PROVISIONS PRESCRIBED FOR THE . . . ARTICLES OF A COMMUNITY INTEREST COMPANY LIMITED BY SHARES, OR LIMITED BY GUARANTEE WITH A SHARE CAPITAL

Regulation 8(b)

[6.158]

1. (1)   The company shall not transfer any of its assets other than for full consideration.

(2)   Provided the conditions in sub-paragraph (3) are satisfied, sub-paragraph (1) shall not apply to—

   (a)   the transfer of assets to any specified asset-locked body, or (with the consent of the Regulator) to any other asset-locked body;

   (b)   the transfer of assets made for the benefit of the community other than by way of a transfer of assets to an asset-locked body;

   (c)   the payment of dividends in respect of shares in the company;

   (d)   the distribution of assets on a winding up;

   (e)   payments on the redemption or purchase of the company's own shares;

   (f)   payments on the reduction of share capital; and

   (g)   the extinguishing or reduction of the liability of members in respect of share capital not paid up on the reduction of share capital.

(3)   The conditions are that the transfer of assets—

   (a)   must comply with any restrictions on the transfer of assets for less than full consideration which may be set out elsewhere in the memorandum or articles of the company; and

   (b)   must not exceed any limits imposed by, or by virtue of, Part 2 of the Companies (Audit, Investigations and Community Enterprise) Act 2004.

(4)   In this paragraph—

   (a)   "asset-locked body" means—

      (i)   a community interest company, [a charity, or a permitted industrial and provident society]; or

      (ii)   a body established outside [the United Kingdom] that is equivalent to [either of those];

   (b)   "community" is to be construed in accordance with section 35(5) of the Companies (Audit, Investigations and Community Enterprise) Act 2004;

   [(ba)   "permitted industrial and provident society" means an industrial and provident society which has a restriction on the use of its assets in accordance with regulation 4 of the Community Benefit Societies (Restriction on Use of Assets) Regulations 2006 or regulation 4 of the Community Benefit Societies (Restriction on Use of Assets) Regulations (Northern Ireland) 2006;]

   (c)   . . .

   (d)   "the Regulator" means the Regulator of Community Interest Companies;

   [(e)   . . .]

   (f)   "specified" means specified in the memorandum or articles of association of the company for the purposes of this paragraph; and

   (g)   "transfer" includes every description of disposition, payment, release or distribution, and the creation or extinction of an estate or interest in, or a right over, any property.

2. (1)   The directors may refuse to register the transfer of a share to a person of whom they do not approve.

(2)   They may also refuse to register the transfer unless it is lodged at the registered office of the company or at such other place as the directors may appoint and is accompanied by such evidence as the directors may reasonably require to show the right of the transferor to make the transfer, and by such other information as they may reasonably require.

(3)   If the directors refuse to register such a transfer, they shall within two months after the date on which the transfer was lodged with the company send to the transferee notice of the refusal.

(4)   The provisions of this paragraph apply in addition to any restrictions on the transfer of a share which may be set out elsewhere in the memorandum or articles of the company.

3. (1)   A person who is not a member of the company shall not have any right to vote at a general meeting of the company; but this is without prejudice to any right to vote on a resolution affecting the rights attached to a class of the company's debentures.

(2)–(5)   . . .

4. (1)   Questions arising at a meeting of directors shall be decided by a majority of votes   . . .

(2)   . . .

(3)   Except as provided by sub-paragraphs (1) and (2) in all proceedings of directors each director must not have more than one vote.

NOTES

Schedule heading: words omitted revoked by the Community Interest Company (Amendment) Regulations 2009, SI 2009/1942, reg 18, as from 1 October 2009.

Para 1: words in square brackets in sub-para (4)(a)(i) substituted, and sub-para (ba) inserted, by SI 2009/1942, regs 19, 20, as from 1 October 2009; words in square brackets in sub-para (4)(a)(ii) substituted, and sub-paras (4)(c), (e) revoked, by the Companies Act 2006 (Commencement No 2, Consequential Amendments, Transitional Provisions and Savings) Order 2007, SI 2007/1093, art 6(2), Sch 4, Pt 2, para 44(a)–(c), as from 6 April 2007 (sub-para (4)(e) was previously substituted by the Charities and Trustee Investment (Scotland) Act 2005 (Consequential Provisions and Modifications) Order 2006, SI 2006/242, art 5, Schedule, Pt 2, para 12, as from 1 April 2006).

Para 3: sub-paras (2)–(5) revoked by SI 2009/1942, reg 21, as from 1 October 2009.

Para 4: words omitted from sub-para (1), and the whole of sub-para (2), revoked by SI 2009/1942, reg 22, as from 1 October 2009.

SCHEDULE 4
CALCULATION OF THE AVERAGE DEBT OR SUM OUTSTANDING UNDER A DEBENTURE DURING A 12 MONTH PERIOD
Regulation 22(7)

[6.159]
1. (1)   The average amount of a debt or sum outstanding under a debenture during any 12 month period is the amount which satisfies the calculation set out in sub-paragraph (2).

(2)   The calculation referred to in sub-paragraph (1) is A divided by B where:
A is the aggregate of the amount of the debt or the sum outstanding under the debenture as at the end of each day during the 12 month period; and
B is the number of days during that 12 month period.

(3)   For the purposes of A in sub-paragraph (2) there shall be excluded any sums which represent interest which has accrued on that debt or debenture within that 12 month period.

(4)   For the purposes of A in sub-paragraph (2) where the debt or debenture did not exist at the end of any day during the 12 month period, the amount of the debt or the sum outstanding under the debenture as at the end of that day shall be treated as being zero for the purposes of the calculation in A.

2.   Where the amount of the debt or the sum outstanding under the debenture is not known as at the end of any particular date, the directors of the community interest company may, for the purposes of the calculation referred to in paragraph 1, substitute for the debt or the sum outstanding under the debenture such amount or sum as they estimate to be the amount of the debt or the sum outstanding under the debenture as at the end of that particular date.

SCHEDULE 5
FEES PAYABLE TO THE REGISTRAR OF COMPANIES
Regulation 36
[6.160]

[Matter in relation to which fee is payable	Amount of fee	When payable
Decision under section 36A(1) of the 2004 Act as to whether a company is eligible to be formed as a community interest company	£15.00	On delivery to the registrar under section 9 of the 2006 Act, section 36 of the 2004 Act and regulation 11 of the documents constituting an application to form a community interest company

[Matter in relation to which fee is payable	Amount of fee	When payable
Decision under section 38(1) of the 2004 Act as to whether a company is eligible to become a community interest company	£15.00	On delivery to the registrar under section 30 of the 2006 Act, section 37 of the 2004 Act and regulation 12 of the documents constituting an application to the registrar to become a community interest company
Consideration of a community interest company report forwarded by the registrar under section 34(4) of the 2004 Act	£15.00	On delivery of the report to the registrar]

NOTES

Commencement:

Substituted by the Community Interest Company (Amendment) Regulations 2009, SI 2009/1942, reg 23, as from 1 October 2009.

COMPANIES (DISQUALIFICATION ORDERS) REGULATIONS 2009

(SI 2009/2471)

NOTES

Made: 8 September 2009.

Authority: Company Directors Disqualification Act 1986, s 18.

Commencement: 1 October 2009 (see reg 1 at **[6.161]**).

Amendment: as of 1 July 2011 these Regulations had not been amended.

ARRANGEMENT OF REGULATIONS

[6.161]
1   Citation and commencement

These Regulations may be cited as the Companies (Disqualification Orders) Regulations 2009 and come into force on 1st October 2009.

NOTES

Commencement: 1 October 2009.

[6.162]
2   Definitions

(1)   In these Regulations—

"the Act" means the Company Directors Disqualification Act 1986;

"disqualification order" means an order of the court under any of sections 2 to 6, 8, 9A and 10 of the Act;

"disqualification undertaking" means an undertaking accepted by the Secretary of State under section 7, 8 or 9B of the Act;

"grant of leave" means a grant by the court of leave under section 17 of the Act to any person in relation to a disqualification order or a disqualification undertaking.

(2)   For the purposes of regulations 5 and 9, "leave granted"—

(a)   in relation to a disqualification order granted under Part 2 of the Companies (Northern Ireland) Order 1989 means leave granted by a court for a person subject to such an order to do anything which otherwise the order prohibits that person from doing; and

(b)   in relation to a disqualification undertaking accepted under the Company Directors Disqualification (Northern Ireland) Order 2002 means leave granted by a court for a person subject to such an undertaking to do anything which otherwise the undertaking prohibits that person from doing.

Part 6   Pre-2006 companies SIs

NOTES
Commencement: 1 October 2009.

[6.163]
3   Revocations

The following instruments are revoked—
- (a)   the Companies (Disqualification Orders) Regulations 2001;
- (b)   the Companies (Disqualification Orders) (Amendment No 2) Regulations 2002; and
- (c)   the Companies (Disqualification Orders) (Amendment) Regulations 2004.

NOTES
Commencement: 1 October 2009.

[6.164]
4   Transitional provisions

Other than regulation 9, these Regulations apply—
- (a)   in relation to a disqualification order made after the coming into force of these Regulations; and
- (b)   in relation to—
  - (i)   a grant of leave made after the coming into force of these Regulations; or
  - (ii)   any action taken by a court after the coming into force of these Regulations in consequence of which a disqualification order or a disqualification undertaking is varied or ceases to be in force,

whether the disqualification order or disqualification undertaking to which the grant of leave or the action relates was made by the court or accepted by the Secretary of State before or after the coming into force of these Regulations.

NOTES
Commencement: 1 October 2009.

[6.165]
5

Regulation 9 applies to—
- (a)   particulars of disqualification orders made and leave granted under Part 2 of the Companies (Northern Ireland) Order 1989 received by the Secretary of State on or after 1st October 2009 other than particulars of disqualification orders made and leave granted under that Order which relate to disqualification orders made by the courts of Northern Ireland before 2nd April 2001; and
- (b)   particulars of undertakings accepted under the Company Directors Disqualification (Northern Ireland) Order 2002 on or after 1st October 2009, and to leave granted under that Order in relation to such undertakings.

NOTES
Commencement: 1 October 2009.

[6.166]
6   Particulars to be furnished by officers of the court

(1)   The following officers of the court must furnish to the Secretary of State the particulars specified in regulation 7(a) to (c) in the form and manner there specified—
- (a)   where a disqualification order is made by the Crown Court, the Court Manager;
- (b)   where a disqualification order or grant of leave is made by the High Court, the Court Manager;
- (c)   where a disqualification order or grant of leave is made by a County Court, the Court Manager;
- (d)   where a disqualification order is made by a Magistrates' Court, the designated officer for a Magistrates' Court;
- (e)   where a disqualification order is made by the High Court of Justiciary, the Deputy Principal Clerk of Justiciary;
- (f)   where a disqualification order or grant of leave is made by a Sheriff Court, the Sheriff Clerk;
- (g)   where a disqualification order or grant of leave is made by the Court of Session, the Deputy Principal Clerk of Session;
- (h)   where a disqualification order or grant of leave is made by the Court of Appeal, the Court Manager; and
- (i)   where a disqualification order or grant of leave is made by the Supreme Court, the Registrar of the Supreme Court.

(2)   Where—

(a)   a disqualification order has been made by any of the courts mentioned in paragraph (1), or
(b)   a disqualification undertaking has been accepted by the Secretary of State,

and subsequently any action is taken by a court in consequence of which that order or that undertaking is varied or ceases to be in force, the officer specified in paragraph (1) of the court which takes such action must furnish to the Secretary of State the particulars specified in regulation 7(d) in the form and manner there specified.

NOTES

Commencement: 1 October 2009.

[6.167]
7

The form in which the particulars are to be furnished is—

(a)   that set out in Schedule 1 to these Regulations with such variations as circumstances require when the person against whom the disqualification order is made is an individual, and the particulars contained therein are the particulars specified for that purpose;

(b)   that set out in Schedule 2 to these Regulations with such variations as circumstances require when the person against whom the disqualification order is made is a body corporate, and the particulars contained therein are the particulars specified for that purpose;

(c)   that set out in Schedule 3 to these Regulations with such variations as circumstances require when a grant of leave is made by the court in relation to a disqualification order or a disqualification undertaking, and the particulars contained therein are the particulars specified for that purpose;

(d)   that set out in Schedule 4 to these Regulations with such variations as circumstances require when any action is taken by a court in consequence of which a disqualification order or a disqualification undertaking is varied or ceases to be in force, and the particulars contained therein are the particulars specified for that purpose.

NOTES

Commencement: 1 October 2009.

[6.168]
8

The time within which the officer specified in regulation 6(1) is to furnish the Secretary of State with the said particulars is the period of 14 days beginning with the day on which the disqualification order or grant of leave is made or on which action is taken by a court in consequence of which the disqualification order or disqualification undertaking is varied or ceases to be in force.

NOTES

Commencement: 1 October 2009.

[6.169]
9   Extension of certain of the provisions of section 18 of the Act to orders made, undertakings accepted and leave granted in Northern Ireland

(1)   Section 18(2) of the Act is extended to the particulars furnished to the Secretary of State of disqualification orders made and leave granted under Part 2 of the Companies (Northern Ireland) Order 1989.

(2)   Section 18(2A) of the Act is extended to the particulars of disqualification undertakings accepted under and leave granted in relation to disqualification undertakings under the Company Directors Disqualification (Northern Ireland) Order 2002.

(3)   Section 18(3) of the Act is extended to all entries in the register and particulars relating to them furnished to the Secretary of State in respect of orders made under Part 2 of the Companies (Northern Ireland) Order 1989 or disqualification undertakings accepted under the Company Directors Disqualification (Northern Ireland) Order 2002.

NOTES

Commencement: 1 October 2009.

SCHEDULES

SCHEDULES 1–4

NOTES

Regulation 7 of these Regulations (at **[6.167]**) specifies the form and manner in which certain particulars must be furnished to the Secretary of State. Schs 1 to 4 contain the forms to be used when furnishing such particulars. Those forms are not reproduced here, but their names and numbers are listed below:

Companies (Disqualification Orders) Regulations 2001	
Form No	*Description*
DQO1	Disqualification order against an individual
DQO2	Disqualification order against a corporate body or firm
DQO3	Grant of leave in relation to a disqualification order or disqualification undertaking
DQO4	Variation or cessation of a disqualification order or disqualification undertaking

PART 7
THE FINANCIAL SERVICES AND MARKETS ACT 2000

PART 7
THE FINANCIAL SERVICES AND MARKETS ACT 2000

FINANCIAL SERVICES AND MARKETS ACT 2000

(2000 c 8)

NOTES

Only those provisions of this Act of most relevance to company law are reproduced in this edition. Certain provisions, which were printed in earlier editions of the *Company Law Handbook*, have been omitted from this edition in order to create space for other, more relevant, legislation. The provisions not reproduced are as follows—

- Part IX—Hearings and Appeals (ss 132–137 and Sch 13);
- Part X—Rules and Guidance (ss 138–164 and Sch 14);
- Part XI—Information Gathering and Investigations (ss 165–177 and Sch 15);
- Part XIII—Incoming Firms: Intervention by Authority (ss 193–204 and Sch 16);
- Part XIV—Disciplinary Measures (ss 205–211);
- Part XV—The Financial Services Compensation Scheme (ss 212–224A);
- Part 15A—Power to Require FSCS Manager to Act in Relation to Other Schemes (ss 224B–224F);
- Part XVI—The Ombudsman Scheme (ss 225–234A and Sch 17);
- Part 18A—Suspension and Removal of Financial Instruments from Trading (ss 313A–313D);
- Part XIX—Lloyd's (ss 314–324);
- Part XXI—Mutual Societies (ss 334–339 and Sch 18);
- Part XXIII—Public Record, Disclosure of Information and Co-operation (ss 347–354);
- Part XXIV—Insolvency (ss 355–379);
- Part XXVI—Notices (ss 387–396);
- Part XXVIII—Miscellaneous (ss 404–416);
- Part XXX—Supplemental (ss 426–433 and Schs 20–22);
- Sch 1A—Further Provision about the Consumer Financial Education Body.

The Act is reproduced in full in *Butterworths Securities & Financial Services Law Handbook*.

Commencement: The main provisions of this Act came into force on 1 December 2001, ie, the date on which s 19 (the general prohibition) came into force (see s 432 and Orders made under that section).

Extent: this Act extends to the whole of the United Kingdom with the exception of Chapter IV of Part XVII which does not extend to Northern Ireland; see s 430 (not printed).

Limited liability partnerships: ss 215(3), (4), (6), 356, 359(1)–(4), 361–365, 367, 370, and 371 of this Act apply to limited liability partnerships (except where the context otherwise requires and subject to certain modifications); see the Limited Liability Partnerships Regulations 2001, SI 2001/1090, reg 6 at **[10.818]**.

Application of Act to certain overseas investment exchanges and clearing houses: see the Companies Act 1989, s 170 at **[5.124]**.

Application of Act to payment service providers, etc: see the Payment Services Regulations 2009, SI 2009/209. In particular, see Sch 5, Pt 1 to those Regulations ("Application and Modification of the 2000 Act"). See also the Cross-Border Payments in Euro Regulations 2010, SI 2010/89. The 2010 Regulations apply (with modifications) this Act in respect of the FSA's functions under the 2010 Regulations.

Banking (Special Provisions) Act 2008 and Banking Act 2009: various Orders made under the 2008 and 2009 Acts apply and modify certain provisions of this Act in relation to the banks and building societies that are the subject of the Orders.

Exemption from requirement for contract for sale etc of land to be in writing: a contract regulated under this Act, other than a regulated mortgage contract, a regulated home reversion plan, a regulated home purchase plan or a regulated sale and rent back agreement, is exempt from the Law of Property (Miscellaneous Provisions) Act 1989, s 2 (contracts for sale etc of land to be made by writing); see s 2(5) of that Act.

Credit rating agencies: the Credit Rating Agencies Regulations 2010, SI 2010/906 designates the FSA as the competent authority in the UK for the purposes of Regulation 1060/2009/EC of the European Parliament and of the Council on credit rating agencies. For consequential modifications of this Act with regard to the FSA's functions relating to credit rating agencies, see those Regulations.

Regulated claims management services: with effect from 23 April 2007 (the day on which the Compensation Act 2006, s 4(1) came into force), a person who provides "regulated claims management services" (i) must be authorised under the 2006 Act to do so, or (ii) be exempted, or (iii) have the benefit of a waiver of the obligation to be authorised, or (iv) be an individual acting otherwise than in the course of business. The Compensation (Regulated Claims Management Services) Order 2006, SI 2006/3319 sets out the kinds of services to be regulated when provided in connection with certain kinds of claim, and this includes claims relating to financial products and services (see art 4(3)(f) of the 2006 Order). The Compensation (Exemptions) Order 2007, SI 2007/209, art 5 exempts a person who is carrying out a regulated claims management service if in providing that service he is carrying on a regulated activity or would be doing so except that he is exempt from the general prohibition under FSMA, or he has the benefit of an exclusion under the Financial Services and Markets Act 2000 (Regulated Activities) Order 2001.

References to solicitors, etc: a registered European lawyer may provide professional activities by way of legal advice and assistance or legal aid under this Act and references to a solicitor, counsel or legal representative shall be interpreted accordingly: see the European Communities (Lawyer's Practice) Regulations 2000, SI 2000/1119, reg 14, Sch 3, Pt 1 (as amended by the European Communities (Lawyer's Practice) (Amendment) Regulations 2004, SI 2004/1628).

Offences under this Act: generally, see Pt XXVII at **[7.352]** et seq. As to offences committed by bodies corporate etc, see s 400 at **[7.355]**; as to proceedings for offences, see s 401 at **[7.356]**; and as to jurisdiction and procedure in respect of offences, see s 403 at **[7.358]**. See also s 28(9) at **[7.29]**, as to the illegality or invalidity of agreements.

The Provisions of this Act included in this work are reproduced as amended by the following Acts:

2001	Criminal Justice and Police Act 2001.
2002	Enterprise Act 2002; Proceeds of Crime Act 2002.
2004	Civil Partnership Act 2004.
2005	Inquiries Act 2005; Regulation of Financial Services (Land Transactions) Act 2005.
2006	Consumer Credit Act 2006; Companies Act 2006; Investment Exchanges and Clearing Houses Act 2006.
2007	Consumers, Estate Agents and Redress Act 2007.

2008	Dormant Bank and Building Society Accounts Act 2008.
2009	Banking Act 2009.
2010	Financial Services Act 2010.

The Provisions of this Act included in this work are reproduced as amended by the following SIs:

2000	Banking Consolidation Directive (Consequential Amendments) Regulations 2000, SI 2000/2952.
2001	Financial Services and Markets Act 2000 (Regulated Activities) Order 2001, SI 2001/544; Financial Services (EEA Passport Rights) Regulations 2001, SI 2001/1376; Financial Services and Markets Act 2000 (Variation of Threshold Conditions) Order 2001, SI 2001/2507.
2002	Financial Services and Markets Act 2000 (Regulated Activities) (Amendment) Order 2002, SI 2002/682; Electronic Commerce Directive (Financial Services and Markets) Regulations 2002, SI 2002/1775; Financial Services and Markets Act 2000 (Variation of Threshold Conditions) Order 2002, SI 2002/2707.
2003	Insurance Mediation Directive (Miscellaneous Amendments) Regulations 2003, SI 2003/1473; Financial Services and Markets Act 2000 (Regulated Activities) (Amendment) (No 2) Order 2003, SI 2003/1476; Collective Investment Schemes (Miscellaneous Amendments) Regulations 2003, SI 2003/2066.
2004	Life Assurance Consolidation Directive (Consequential Amendments) Regulations 2004, SI 2004/3379.
2005	Financial Services and Markets Act 2000 (Market Abuse) Regulations 2005, SI 2005/381; Prospectus Regulations 2005, SI 2005/1433.
2006	Charities and Trustee Investment (Scotland) Act 2005 (Consequential Provisions and Modifications) Order 2006, SI 2006/242; Taxation of Pension Schemes (Consequential Amendments) Order 2006, SI 2006/745; Financial Services and Markets Act 2000 (Regulated Activities) (Amendment) (No 2) Order 2006, SI 2006/2383; Financial Services and Markets Act 2000 (Markets in Financial Instruments) (Modification of Powers) Regulations 2006, SI 2006/2975; the Capital Requirements Regulations 2006, SI 2006/3221.
2007	Financial Services (EEA State) Regulations 2007, SI 2007/108; Financial Services and Markets Act 2000 (Markets in Financial Instruments) Regulations 2007, SI 2007/126; Regulatory Reform (Financial Services and Markets Act 2000) Order 2007, SI 2007/1973; Financial Services and Markets Act 2000 (Motor Insurance) Regulations 2007, SI 2007/2403; Reinsurance Directive Regulations 2007, SI 2007/3253.
2008	Companies Act 2006 (Consequential Amendments etc) Order 2008, SI 2008/948; Financial Services and Markets Act 2000 (Market Abuse) Regulations 2008, SI 2008/1439; Financial Services and Markets Act 2000 (Amendments to Part 7) Regulations 2008, SI 2008/1468; Definition of Financial Instrument Order 2008, SI 2008/3053.
2009	Financial Services and Markets Act 2000 (Controllers) Regulations 2009, SI 2009/534; Financial Services and Markets Act 2000 (Regulated Activities) (Amendment) Order 2009, SI 2009/1342; Companies Act 2006 (Consequential Amendments, Transitional Provisions and Savings) Order 2009, SI 2009/1941; Financial Services and Markets Act 2000 (Amendment) Regulations 2009, SI 2009/2461; Financial Services and Markets Act 2000 (Market Abuse) Regulations 2009, SI 2009/3128.
2010	Transfer of Tribunal Functions Order 2010, SI 2010/22; Financial Services and Markets Act 2000 (Liability of Issuers) Regulations 2010, SI 2010/1192; Capital Requirements (Amendment) Regulations 2010, SI 2010/2628.
2011	Electronic Money Regulations 2011, SI 2011/99; Companies Act 2006 (Consequential Amendments and Transitional Provisions) Order 2011, SI 2011/1265; Undertakings for Collective Investment in Transferable Securities Regulations 2011, SI 2011/1613; Prospectus Regulations 2011, SI 2011/1668.

References to the "European Community", "Community", etc: see the Treaty of Lisbon (Changes in Terminology) Order 2011, SI 2011/1043, which provides (with effect from 22 April 2011): (1) that for references to the "European Communities" or to the "European Community" (including references to "the Communities", "the Community", "the EC" or "the EEC") substitute references to the European Union; and (2) that "EU" should be substituted for the word "Community" (subject to certain exceptions) in references to "Community treaties", "Community customs duty", "Community institution", "Community instrument", "Community obligation", "enforceable Community right", "Community law", "Community legislation", and "Community provision". Also, where such a term is preceded by the word "a", for "a" substitute "an".

ARRANGEMENT OF SECTIONS

PART I
THE REGULATOR

PART IV
PERMISSION TO CARRY ON REGULATED ACTIVITIES

PART V
PERFORMANCE OF REGULATED ACTIVITIES

PART VI
OFFICIAL LISTING

Part 7   FSMA 2000

PART XVII
COLLECTIVE INVESTMENT SCHEMES

CHAPTER I
INTERPRETATION

CHAPTER II
RESTRICTIONS ON PROMOTION

CHAPTER III
AUTHORISED UNIT TRUST SCHEMES

Part 7   FSMA 2000

CHAPTER 1A
CONTROL OVER RECOGNISED INVESTMENT EXCHANGE

Notices of acquisitions of control over recognised investment exchanges

Acquiring and increasing control

Assessment procedure

Enforcement procedures

Offences

Interpretation

CHAPTER II
COMPETITION SCRUTINY

Role of Office of Fair Trading

Role of Competition Commission

An Act to make provision about the regulation of financial services and markets; to provide for the transfer of certain statutory functions relating to building societies, friendly societies, industrial and provident societies and certain other mutual societies; and for connected purposes

[14 June 2000]

PART I
THE REGULATOR

[7.1]
1   The Financial Services Authority
(1)   The body corporate known as the Financial Services Authority ("the Authority") is to have the functions conferred on it by or under this Act.
(2)   The Authority must comply with the requirements as to its constitution set out in Schedule 1.
(3)   Schedule 1 also makes provision about the status of the Authority and the exercise of certain of its functions.
[(4)   Section 249 of the Banking Act 2009 provides for references to functions of the Authority (whether generally or under this Act) to include references to functions conferred on the Authority by that Act (subject to any order under that section).]

NOTES

Sub-s (4): added by the Banking Act 2009, s 249, as from 21 February 2009.

Note: the FSA is the same corporate entity as the former Securities and Investments Board and later assumed functions under the Banking Act 1985 and exercised other functions on behalf of the Treasury under other financial services legislation.

The self regulating bodies (the Securities and Futures Authority, the Investment Management Regulatory Organisation and the Personal Investment Authority) established under the Financial Services Act 1986 were constituted as companies limited by guarantee and were wound up on the designated dates specified under the Financial Services and Markets Act 2000 (Transitional Provisions) (Designated Date for The Securities and Futures Authority) Order 2001, SI 2001/2255, and the Financial Services and Markets (Transitional Provisions) (Designated Date for Certain Self-Regulating Organisations) Order 2000, SI 2000/1734.

The Authority's general duties

[7.2]
2   The Authority's general duties
(1)   In discharging its general functions the Authority must, so far as is reasonably possible, act in a way—
    (a)   which is compatible with the regulatory objectives; and
    (b)   which the Authority considers most appropriate for the purpose of meeting those objectives.
(2)   The regulatory objectives are—
    (a)   market confidence;
    [(ab) financial stability;]
    (b)   . . .
    (c)   the protection of consumers; and
    (d)   the reduction of financial crime.
(3)   In discharging its general functions the Authority must have regard to—
    (a)   the need to use its resources in the most efficient and economic way;
    (b)   the responsibilities of those who manage the affairs of authorised persons;
    (c)   the principle that a burden or restriction which is imposed on a person, or on the carrying on of an activity, should be proportionate to the benefits, considered in general terms, which are expected to result from the imposition of that burden or restriction;
    (d)   the desirability of facilitating innovation in connection with regulated activities;
    (e)   the international character of financial services and markets and the desirability of maintaining the competitive position of the United Kingdom;
    (f)   the need to minimise the adverse effects on competition that may arise from anything done in the discharge of those functions;
    (g)   the desirability of facilitating competition between those who are subject to any form of regulation by the Authority;
    [(h)   the desirability of enhancing the understanding and knowledge of members of the public of financial matters (including the UK financial system)].
(4)   The Authority's general functions are—
    (a)   its function of making rules under this Act (considered as a whole);
    (b)   its function of preparing and issuing codes under this Act (considered as a whole);
    (c)   its functions in relation to the giving of general guidance (considered as a whole); and
    (d)   its function of determining the general policy and principles by reference to which it performs particular functions.
(5)   "General guidance" has the meaning given in section 158(5).

Part 7   FSMA 2000

NOTES

Sub-s (2): para (ab) inserted by the Financial Services Act 2010, s 1(1), (2), as from 8 April 2010; para (b) repealed by the Financial Services Act 2010, s 2(1), (2)(a), as from 12 October 2010.

Sub-s (3): para (h) added by the Financial Services Act 2010, s 2(1), (2)(b), as from 12 October 2010.

The regulatory objectives

[7.3]

3 Market confidence

(1)   The market confidence objective is: maintaining confidence in [the UK financial system].

(2)   [In this Act "the UK financial system"] means the financial system operating in the United Kingdom and includes—

    (a)   financial markets and exchanges;

    (b)   regulated activities; and

    (c)   other activities connected with financial markets and exchanges.

NOTES

Words in square brackets substituted by the Financial Services Act 2010, s 24(1), (2), Sch 2, Pt 1, paras 1, 2, as from 8 April 2010.

[7.4]

[3A Financial stability

(1)   The financial stability objective is: contributing to the protection and enhancement of the stability of the UK financial system.

(2)   In considering that objective the Authority must have regard to—

    (a)   the economic and fiscal consequences for the United Kingdom of instability of the UK financial system;

    (b)   the effects (if any) on the growth of the economy of the United Kingdom of anything done for the purpose of meeting that objective; and

    (c)   the impact (if any) on the stability of the UK financial system of events or circumstances outside the United Kingdom (as well as in the United Kingdom).

(3)   The Authority must, consulting the Treasury, determine and review its strategy in relation to the financial stability objective.]

NOTES

Commencement: 8 April 2010.

Inserted by the Financial Services Act 2010, s 1(1), (3), as from 8 April 2010.

4   (*Repealed by the Financial Services Act 2010, s 2(1), (3), as from 12 October 2010.*)

[7.5]

5 The protection of consumers

(1)   The protection of consumers objective is: securing the appropriate degree of protection for consumers.

(2)   In considering what degree of protection may be appropriate, the Authority must have regard to—

    (a)   the differing degrees of risk involved in different kinds of investment or other transaction;

    (b)   the differing degrees of experience and expertise that different consumers may have in relation to different kinds of regulated activity;

    [(ba) any information which the consumer financial education body has provided to the Authority in the exercise of the consumer financial education function;]

    (c)   the needs that consumers may have for advice and accurate information; and

    (d)   the general principle that consumers should take responsibility for their decisions.

[(3)   Sections 425A and 425B (meaning of "consumers") apply for the purposes of this section.]

NOTES

Sub-s (2): para (ba) inserted by the Financial Services Act 2010, s 2(1), (4), as from 12 October 2010.

Sub-s (3): substituted by the Financial Services Act 2010, s 24(1), (2), Sch 2, Pt 1, paras 1, 4, as from 8 April 2010.

[7.6]

6 The reduction of financial crime

(1)   The reduction of financial crime objective is: reducing the extent to which it is possible for a business carried on—

    (a)   by a regulated person, or

    (b)   in contravention of the general prohibition,

to be used for a purpose connected with financial crime.

(2)   In considering that objective the Authority must, in particular, have regard to the desirability of—

    (a)   regulated persons being aware of the risk of their businesses being used in connection with the commission of financial crime;

   (b)   regulated persons taking appropriate measures (in relation to their administration and employment practices, the conduct of transactions by them and otherwise) to prevent financial crime, facilitate its detection and monitor its incidence;

   (c)   regulated persons devoting adequate resources to the matters mentioned in paragraph (b).

(3)   "Financial crime" includes any offence involving—

   (a)   fraud or dishonesty;

   (b)   misconduct in, or misuse of information relating to, a financial market; or

   (c)   handling the proceeds of crime.

(4)   "Offence" includes an act or omission which would be an offence if it had taken place in the United Kingdom.

(5)   "Regulated person" means an authorised person, a recognised investment exchange or a recognised clearing house.

NOTES

Note: a "regulated person" for these purposes includes an authorised person, a recognised investment exchange and a recognised clearing house, but the position of exempt persons under s 38 (exemption orders) or s 39 (appointed representatives) is not clear.

[Enhancing public understanding of financial matters etc

[7.7]

6A Enhancing public understanding of financial matters etc

(1)   The Authority must establish a body corporate ("the consumer financial education body") whose function ("the consumer financial education function") is to enhance—

   (a)   the understanding and knowledge of members of the public of financial matters (including the UK financial system); and

   (b)   the ability of members of the public to manage their own financial affairs.

(2)   The consumer financial education function includes, in particular—

   (a)   promoting awareness of the benefits of financial planning;

   (b)   promoting awareness of the financial advantages and disadvantages in relation to the supply of particular kinds of goods or services;

   (c)   promoting awareness of the benefits and risks associated with different kinds of financial dealing (which includes informing the Authority and other bodies of those benefits and risks);

   (d)   the publication of educational materials or the carrying out of other educational activities; and

   (e)   the provision of information and advice to members of the public.

(3)   Schedule 1A makes further provision about the consumer financial education body.]

NOTES

Commencement: 8 April 2010.

Inserted, together with the preceding heading, by the Financial Services Act 2010, s 2(1), (5), as from 8 April 2010.

Corporate governance

[7.8]

7 Duty of Authority to follow principles of good governance

In managing its affairs, the Authority must have regard to such generally accepted principles of good corporate governance as it is reasonable to regard as applicable to it.

Arrangements for consulting practitioners and consumers

[7.9]

8 The Authority's general duty to consult

The Authority must make and maintain effective arrangements for consulting practitioners and consumers on the extent to which its general policies and practices are consistent with its general duties under section 2.

[7.10]

9 The Practitioner Panel

(1)   Arrangements under section 8 must include the establishment and maintenance of a panel of persons (to be known as "the Practitioner Panel") to represent the interests of practitioners.

(2)   The Authority must appoint one of the members of the Practitioner Panel to be its chairman.

(3)   The Treasury's approval is required for the appointment or dismissal of the chairman.

(4)   The Authority must have regard to any representations made to it by the Practitioner Panel.

(5)   The Authority must appoint to the Practitioner Panel such—

   (a)   individuals who are authorised persons,

   (b)   persons representing authorised persons,

   (c)   persons representing recognised investment exchanges, and

   (d)   persons representing recognised clearing houses,

as it considers appropriate.

Note: Information regarding the Practitioner Panel can be obtained through its website at http://www.fs-pp.org.uk.

[7.11]
10 The Consumer Panel
(1) Arrangements under section 8 must include the establishment and maintenance of a panel of persons (to be known as "the Consumer Panel") to represent the interests of consumers.
(2) The Authority must appoint one of the members of the Consumer Panel to be its chairman.
(3) The Treasury's approval is required for the appointment or dismissal of the chairman.
(4) The Authority must have regard to any representations made to it by the Consumer Panel.
(5) The Authority must appoint to the Consumer Panel such consumers, or persons representing the interests of consumers, as it considers appropriate.
[(5A) The Secretary of State may direct the Authority to appoint as a member of the Consumer Panel a person specified by the Secretary of State who—
    (a) is a non-executive member of the National Consumer Council, and
    (b) is nominated for the purposes of this subsection by the National Consumer Council after consultation with the Authority.
(5B) Only one person may, at any time, be a member of the Consumer Panel appointed in accordance with a direction under subsection (5A); but that does not prevent the Authority appointing as a member of the Consumer Panel any person who is also a member of the National Consumer Council.
(5C) A person appointed in accordance with a direction under subsection (5A) ceases to be a member of the Panel on ceasing to be a non-executive member of the National Consumer Council.]
(6) The Authority must secure that the membership of the Consumer Panel is such as to give a fair degree of representation to those who are using, or are or may be contemplating using, services otherwise than in connection with businesses carried on by them.
[(7) Sections 425A and 425B (meaning of "consumers") apply for the purposes of this section, but the references to consumers in this section do not include consumers who are authorised persons.]

Sub-ss (5A)–(5C): inserted by the Consumers, Estate Agents and Redress Act 2007, s 39, as from 21 December 2007.
Sub-s (7): substituted by the Financial Services Act 2010, s 24(1), (2), Sch 2, Pt 1, paras 1, 5, as from 8 April 2010.
Note: Information regarding the Consumer Panel can be obtained through its website at http://www.fs-cp.org.uk.

[7.12]
11 Duty to consider representations by the Panels
(1) This section applies to a representation made, in accordance with arrangements made under section 8, by the Practitioner Panel or by the Consumer Panel.
(2) The Authority must consider the representation.
(3) If the Authority disagrees with a view expressed, or proposal made, in the representation, it must give the Panel a statement in writing of its reasons for disagreeing.

Reviews

[7.13]
12 Reviews
(1) The Treasury may appoint an independent person to conduct a review of the economy, efficiency and effectiveness with which the Authority has used its resources in discharging its functions.
(2) A review may be limited by the Treasury to such functions of the Authority (however described) as the Treasury may specify in appointing the person to conduct it.
(3) A review is not to be concerned with the merits of the Authority's general policy or principles in pursuing regulatory objectives or in exercising functions under Part VI.
(4) On completion of a review, the person conducting it must make a written report to the Treasury—
    (a) setting out the result of the review; and
    (b) making such recommendations (if any) as he considers appropriate.
(5) A copy of the report must be—
    (a) laid before each House of Parliament; and
    (b) published in such manner as the Treasury consider appropriate.
(6) Any expenses reasonably incurred in the conduct of a review are to be met by the Treasury out of money provided by Parliament.
(7) "Independent" means appearing to the Treasury to be independent of the Authority.

[7.14]
13 Right to obtain documents and information
(1) A person conducting a review under section 12—
    (a) has a right of access at any reasonable time to all such documents as he may reasonably require for purposes of the review; and

(b)   may require any person holding or accountable for any such document to provide such information and explanation as are reasonably necessary for that purpose.

(2)   Subsection (1) applies only to documents in the custody or under the control of the Authority.

(3)   An obligation imposed on a person as a result of the exercise of powers conferred by subsection (1) is enforceable by injunction or, in Scotland, by an order for specific performance under section 45 of the Court of Session Act 1988.

Inquiries

[7.15]
14   Cases in which the Treasury may arrange independent inquiries

(1)   This section applies in two cases.

(2)   The first is where it appears to the Treasury that—

    (a)   events have occurred in relation to—

        (i)   a collective investment scheme, or

        (ii)   a person who is, or was at the time of the events, carrying on a regulated activity (whether or not as an authorised person),

    which posed or could have posed a grave risk to [the UK financial system] or caused or risked causing significant damage to the interests of consumers; and

    (b)   those events might not have occurred, or the risk or damage might have been reduced, but for a serious failure in—

        (i)   the system established by this Act[, or by any previous statutory provision,] for the regulation of such schemes or of such persons and their activities; or

        (ii)   the operation of that system.

(3)   The second is where it appears to the Treasury that—

    (a)   events have occurred in relation to listed securities or an issuer of listed securities which caused or could have caused significant damage to holders of listed securities; and

    (b)   those events might not have occurred but for a serious failure [in—

        (i)   the regulatory system established by Part 6 or by any previous statutory provision concerned with the official listing of securities; or

        (ii)   the operation of that system].

(4)   If the Treasury consider that it is in the public interest that there should be an independent inquiry into the events and the circumstances surrounding them, they may arrange for an inquiry to be held under section 15.

[(5)   Sections 425A and 425B (meaning of "consumers") apply for the purposes of this section.]

[(5A)   "Event" does not include any event occurring before 1st December 2001 (but no such limitation applies to the reference in subsection (4) to surrounding circumstances).]

(6)   . . .

(7)   "Listed securities" means anything which has been admitted to the official list under Part VI.

NOTES

Sub-s (2): words in square brackets in para (a) substituted by the Financial Services Act 2010, s 24(1), (2), Sch 2, Pt 1, paras 1, 6(1), (2), as from 8 April 2010; words in square brackets in para (b) inserted by the Inquiries Act 2005, s 46(1), (2), as from 7 June 2005.

Sub-s (3): words in square brackets substituted by the Inquiries Act 2005, s 46(1), (3), as from 7 June 2005.

Sub-s (5): substituted by the Financial Services Act 2010, s 24(1), (2), Sch 2, Pt 1, paras 1, 6(1), (3), as from 8 April 2010.

Sub-s (5A): inserted by the Inquiries Act 2005, s 46(1), (4), as from 7 June 2005.

Sub-s (6): repealed by the Financial Services Act 2010, s 24(1), Sch 2, Pt 1, paras 1, 6(1), (4), as from 8 April 2010.

[7.16]
15   Power to appoint person to hold an inquiry

(1)   If the Treasury decide to arrange for an inquiry to be held under this section, they may appoint such person as they consider appropriate to hold the inquiry.

(2)   The Treasury may, by a direction to the appointed person, control—

    (a)   the scope of the inquiry;

    (b)   the period during which the inquiry is to be held;

    (c)   the conduct of the inquiry; and

    (d)   the making of reports.

(3)   A direction may, in particular—

    (a)   confine the inquiry to particular matters;

    (b)   extend the inquiry to additional matters;

    (c)   require the appointed person to discontinue the inquiry or to take only such steps as are specified in the direction;

    (d)   require the appointed person to make such interim reports as are so specified.

[7.17]
16   Powers of appointed person and procedure

(1)   The person appointed to hold an inquiry under section 15 may—

    (a)   obtain such information from such persons and in such manner as he thinks fit;

    (b)   make such inquiries as he thinks fit; and

    (c)   determine the procedure to be followed in connection with the inquiry.

(2) The appointed person may require any person who, in his opinion, is able to provide any information, or produce any document, which is relevant to the inquiry to provide any such information or produce any such document.

(3) For the purposes of an inquiry, the appointed person has the same powers as the court in respect of the attendance and examination of witnesses (including the examination of witnesses abroad) and in respect of the production of documents.

(4) "Court" means—

    (a) the High Court; or

    (b) in Scotland, the Court of Session.

[7.18]

17 Conclusion of inquiry

(1) On completion of an inquiry under section 15, the person holding the inquiry must make a written report to the Treasury—

    (a) setting out the result of the inquiry; and

    (b) making such recommendations (if any) as he considers appropriate.

(2) The Treasury may publish the whole, or any part, of the report and may do so in such manner as they consider appropriate.

(3) Subsection (4) applies if the Treasury propose to publish a report but consider that it contains material—

    (a) which relates to the affairs of a particular person whose interests would, in the opinion of the Treasury, be seriously prejudiced by publication of the material; or

    (b) the disclosure of which would be incompatible with an international obligation of the United Kingdom.

(4) The Treasury must ensure that the material is removed before publication.

(5) The Treasury must lay before each House of Parliament a copy of any report or part of a report published under subsection (2).

(6) Any expenses reasonably incurred in holding an inquiry are to be met by the Treasury out of money provided by Parliament.

[7.19]

18 Obstruction and contempt

(1) If a person ("A")—

    (a) fails to comply with a requirement imposed on him by a person holding an inquiry under section 15, or

    (b) otherwise obstructs such an inquiry,

the person holding the inquiry may certify the matter to the High Court (or, in Scotland, the Court of Session).

(2) The court may enquire into the matter.

(3) If, after hearing—

    (a) any witnesses who may be produced against or on behalf of A, and

    (b) any statement made by or on behalf of A,

the court is satisfied that A would have been in contempt of court if the inquiry had been proceedings before the court, it may deal with him as if he were in contempt.

PART II
REGULATED AND PROHIBITED ACTIVITIES

The general prohibition

[7.20]

19 The general prohibition

(1) No person may carry on a regulated activity in the United Kingdom, or purport to do so, unless he is—

    (a) an authorised person; or

    (b) an exempt person.

(2) The prohibition is referred to in this Act as the general prohibition.

Requirement for permission

[7.21]

20 Authorised persons acting without permission

(1) If an authorised person carries on a regulated activity in the United Kingdom, or purports to do so, otherwise than in accordance with permission—

    (a) given to him by the Authority under Part IV, or

    (b) resulting from any other provision of this Act,

he is to be taken to have contravened a requirement imposed on him by the Authority under this Act.

(2) The contravention does not—

    (a) make a person guilty of an offence;

    (b) make any transaction void or unenforceable; or

    (c) (subject to subsection (3)) give rise to any right of action for breach of statutory duty.

(3) In prescribed cases the contravention is actionable at the suit of a person who suffers loss as a result of the contravention, subject to the defences and other incidents applying to actions for breach of statutory duty.

NOTES

Application in relation to interim permissions and interim approvals: see the notes preceding s 40 at **[7.42]**.
Regulations: the Financial Services and Markets Act 2000 (Rights of Action) Regulations 2001, SI 2001/2256.

Financial promotion

[7.22]
21 Restrictions on financial promotion
(1) A person ("A") must not, in the course of business, communicate an invitation or inducement to engage in investment activity.
(2) But subsection (1) does not apply if—
  (a) A is an authorised person; or
  (b) the content of the communication is approved for the purposes of this section by an authorised person.
(3) In the case of a communication originating outside the United Kingdom, subsection (1) applies only if the communication is capable of having an effect in the United Kingdom.
(4) The Treasury may by order specify circumstances in which a person is to be regarded for the purposes of subsection (1) as—
  (a) acting in the course of business;
  (b) not acting in the course of business.
(5) The Treasury may by order specify circumstances (which may include compliance with financial promotion rules) in which subsection (1) does not apply.
(6) An order under subsection (5) may, in particular, provide that subsection (1) does not apply in relation to communications—
  (a) of a specified description;
  (b) originating in a specified country or territory outside the United Kingdom;
  (c) originating in a country or territory which falls within a specified description of country or territory outside the United Kingdom; or
  (d) originating outside the United Kingdom.
(7) The Treasury may by order repeal subsection (3).
(8) "Engaging in investment activity" means—
  (a) entering or offering to enter into an agreement the making or performance of which by either party constitutes a controlled activity; or
  (b) exercising any rights conferred by a controlled investment to acquire, dispose of, underwrite or convert a controlled investment.
(9) An activity is a controlled activity if—
  (a) it is an activity of a specified kind or one which falls within a specified class of activity; and
  (b) it relates to an investment of a specified kind, or to one which falls within a specified class of investment.
(10) An investment is a controlled investment if it is an investment of a specified kind or one which falls within a specified class of investment.
(11) Schedule 2 (except paragraph 26) applies for the purposes of subsections (9) and (10) with references to section 22 being read as references to each of those subsections.
(12) Nothing in Schedule 2, as applied by subsection (11), limits the powers conferred by subsection (9) or (10).
(13) "Communicate" includes causing a communication to be made.
(14) "Investment" includes any asset, right or interest.
(15) "Specified" means specified in an order made by the Treasury.

NOTES

Application in relation to interim permissions and interim approvals: see the notes preceding s 40 at **[7.42]**.
Orders: the Financial Services and Markets Act 2000 (Miscellaneous Provisions) Order 2001, SI 2001/3650; the Financial Services and Markets Act 2000 (Financial Promotion) Order 2005, SI 2005/1529 at **[8.250]**.
Note that the following amending Orders have also been made under this section: the Financial Services and Markets Act 2000 (Financial Promotion and Miscellaneous Amendments) Order 2002, SI 2002/1310; the Financial Services and Markets Act 2000 (Commencement of Mortgage Regulation) (Amendment) Order 2002, SI 2002/1777; the Financial Services and Markets Act 2000 (Promotion of Collective Investment Schemes etc) (Exemptions) (Amendment) Order 2003, SI 2003/2067; the Financial Services and Markets Act 2000 (Financial Promotion and Promotion of Collective Investment Schemes) (Miscellaneous Amendments) Order 2005, SI 2005/270; the Financial Services and Markets Act 2000 (Financial Promotion) (Amendment) Order 2005, SI 2005/3392; the Financial Services and Markets Act 2000 (Financial Promotion) (Amendment) Order 2007, SI 2007/1083; the Financial Services and Markets Act 2000 (Financial Promotion) (Amendment No 2) Order 2007, SI 2007/2615; the Financial Services and Markets Act 2000 (Financial Promotion) (Amendment) Order 2010, SI 2010/905.

Regulated activities

[7.23]

22 The classes of activity and categories of investment

(1) An activity is a regulated activity for the purposes of this Act if it is an activity of a specified kind which is carried on by way of business and—

    (a) relates to an investment of a specified kind; or

    (b) in the case of an activity of a kind which is also specified for the purposes of this paragraph, is carried on in relation to property of any kind.

(2) Schedule 2 makes provision supplementing this section.

(3) Nothing in Schedule 2 limits the powers conferred by subsection (1).

(4) "Investment" includes any asset, right or interest.

(5) "Specified" means specified in an order made by the Treasury.

NOTES

See further, the Gambling Act 2005, s 10(2) which provides that an order under this section which has the effect that a class of bet becomes or ceases to be a regulated activity may, in particular, include transitional provision relating to the application of the 2005 Act to that class of bet.

Orders: the Financial Services and Markets Act 2000 (Regulated Activities) Order 2001, SI 2001/544 at **[8.1]**.

Note that the following amending Orders have also been made under this section: the Financial Services and Markets Act 2000 (Regulated Activities) (Amendment) Order 2001, SI 2001/3544; the Financial Services and Markets Act 2000 (Regulated Activities) (Amendment) Order 2002, SI 2002/682; the Financial Services and Markets Act 2000 (Financial Promotion and Miscellaneous Amendments) Order 2002, SI 2002/1310; the Financial Services and Markets Act 2000 (Regulated Activities) (Amendment) (No 2) Order 2002, SI 2002/1776; the Financial Services and Markets Act 2000 (Commencement of Mortgage Regulation) (Amendment) Order 2002, SI 2002/1777; the Financial Services and Markets Act 2000 (Regulated Activities) (Amendment) (No 1) Order 2003, SI 2003/1475; the Financial Services and Markets Act 2000 (Regulated Activities) (Amendment) (No 2) Order 2003, SI 2003/1476; the Financial Services and Markets Act 2000 (Regulated Activities) (Amendment) (No 3) Order 2003, SI 2003/2822; the Financial Services and Markets Act 2000 (Regulated Activities) (Amendment) Order 2004, SI 2004/1610; the Financial Services and Markets Act 2000 (Regulated Activities) (Amendment) (No 2) Order 2004, SI 2004/2737; the Financial Services and Markets Act 2000 (Regulated Activities) (Amendment) Order 2005, SI 2005/593; the Financial Services and Markets Act 2000 (Regulated Activities) (Amendment) (No 2) Order 2005, SI 2005/1518; the Financial Services and Markets Act 2000 (Regulated Activities) (Amendment) Order 2006, SI 2006/1969; the Financial Services and Markets Act 2000 (Regulated Activities) (Amendment) (No 2) Order 2006, SI 2006/2383; the Financial Services and Markets Act 2000 (Regulated Activities) (Amendment No 3) Order 2006, SI 2006/3384; the Financial Services and Markets Act 2000 (Regulated Activities) (Amendment) Order 2007, SI 2007/1339; the Financial Services and Markets Act 2000 (Reinsurance Directive) Order 2007, SI 2007/3254; the Financial Services and Markets Act 2000 (Regulated Activities) (Amendment) (No 2) Order 2007, SI 2007/3510; the Financial Services and Markets Act 2000 (Regulated Activities) (Amendment) Order 2009, SI 2009/1342; the Financial Services and Markets Act 2000 (Regulated Activities) (Amendment) (No 2) Order 2009, SI 2009/1389; the Financial Services and Markets Act 2000 (Regulated Activities) (Amendment) Order 2010, SI 2010/86; the Financial Services and Markets Act 2000 (Regulated Activities) (Amendment) Order 2011, SI 2011/133.

Offences

[7.24]

23 Contravention of the general prohibition

(1) A person who contravenes the general prohibition is guilty of an offence and liable—

    (a) on summary conviction, to imprisonment for a term not exceeding six months or a fine not exceeding the statutory maximum, or both;

    (b) on conviction on indictment, to imprisonment for a term not exceeding two years or a fine, or both.

(2) In this Act "an authorisation offence" means an offence under this section.

(3) In proceedings for an authorisation offence it is a defence for the accused to show that he took all reasonable precautions and exercised all due diligence to avoid committing the offence.

[7.25]

24 False claims to be authorised or exempt

(1) A person who is neither an authorised person nor, in relation to the regulated activity in question, an exempt person is guilty of an offence if he—

    (a) describes himself (in whatever terms) as an authorised person;

    (b) describes himself (in whatever terms) as an exempt person in relation to the regulated activity; or

    (c) behaves, or otherwise holds himself out, in a manner which indicates (or which is reasonably likely to be understood as indicating) that he is—

        (i) an authorised person; or

        (ii) an exempt person in relation to the regulated activity.

(2) In proceedings for an offence under this section it is a defence for the accused to show that he took all reasonable precautions and exercised all due diligence to avoid committing the offence.

(3) A person guilty of an offence under this section is liable on summary conviction to imprisonment for a term not exceeding six months or a fine not exceeding level 5 on the standard scale, or both.

(4)   But where the conduct constituting the offence involved or included the public display of any material, the maximum fine for the offence is level 5 on the standard scale multiplied by the number of days for which the display continued.

[7.26]
25 Contravention of section 21

(1)   A person who contravenes section 21(1) is guilty of an offence and liable—
   (a)   on summary conviction, to imprisonment for a term not exceeding six months or a fine not exceeding the statutory maximum, or both;
   (b)   on conviction on indictment, to imprisonment for a term not exceeding two years or a fine, or both.

(2)   In proceedings for an offence under this section it is a defence for the accused to show—
   (a)   that he believed on reasonable grounds that the content of the communication was prepared, or approved for the purposes of section 21, by an authorised person; or
   (b)   that he took all reasonable precautions and exercised all due diligence to avoid committing the offence.

NOTES

Application in relation to interim permissions and interim approvals: see the notes preceding s 40 at **[7.42]**.

Enforceability of agreements

[7.27]
26 Agreements made by unauthorised persons

(1)   An agreement made by a person in the course of carrying on a regulated activity in contravention of the general prohibition is unenforceable against the other party.

(2)   The other party is entitled to recover—
   (a)   any money or other property paid or transferred by him under the agreement; and
   (b)   compensation for any loss sustained by him as a result of having parted with it.

(3)   "Agreement" means an agreement—
   (a)   made after this section comes into force; and
   (b)   the making or performance of which constitutes, or is part of, the regulated activity in question.

(4)   This section does not apply if the regulated activity is accepting deposits.

NOTES

Application to certain agreements: sub-ss (1), (2) above (and, subject to certain modifications, s 28 below) apply to certain agreements entered into in contravention of the Financial Services Act 1986, s 3 (repealed by the Financial Services and Markets Act 2000 (Consequential Amendments and Repeals) Order 2001, SI 2001/3649, art 3(1)(c)), or the Insurance Companies Act 1982, s 2 (repealed by art 3(1)(b) of that Order) as they apply to an agreement in contravention of the general prohibition; see the Financial Services and Markets Act 2000 (Transitional Provisions and Savings) (Civil Remedies, Discipline, Criminal Offences etc) (No 2) Order 2001, SI 2001/3083, art 5(1), (3), (4).

[7.28]
27 Agreements made through unauthorised persons

(1)   An agreement made by an authorised person ("the provider")—
   (a)   in the course of carrying on a regulated activity (not in contravention of the general prohibition), but
   (b)   in consequence of something said or done by another person ("the third party") in the course of a regulated activity carried on by the third party in contravention of the general prohibition,
is unenforceable against the other party.

(2)   The other party is entitled to recover—
   (a)   any money or other property paid or transferred by him under the agreement; and
   (b)   compensation for any loss sustained by him as a result of having parted with it.

(3)   "Agreement" means an agreement—
   (a)   made after this section comes into force; and
   (b)   the making or performance of which constitutes, or is part of, the regulated activity in question carried on by the provider.

(4)   This section does not apply if the regulated activity is accepting deposits.

NOTES

Application to certain agreements: sub-ss (1), (2) above (and, subject to certain modifications, s 28 below) apply to certain agreements entered into in contravention of the Financial Services Act 1986, s 3 (repealed by the Financial Services and Markets Act 2000 (Consequential Amendments and Repeals) Order 2001, SI 2001/3649, art 3(1)(c)) as they apply to an agreement in contravention of the general prohibition; see the Financial Services and Markets Act 2000 (Transitional Provisions and Savings) (Civil Remedies, Discipline, Criminal Offences etc) (No 2) Order 2001, SI 2001/3083, art 5(2), (3), (5).

[7.29]
28 Agreements made unenforceable by section 26 or 27

(1)   This section applies to an agreement which is unenforceable because of section 26 or 27.

(2)   The amount of compensation recoverable as a result of that section is—

(a) the amount agreed by the parties; or

(b) on the application of either party, the amount determined by the court.

(3) If the court is satisfied that it is just and equitable in the circumstances of the case, it may allow—

(a) the agreement to be enforced; or

(b) money and property paid or transferred under the agreement to be retained.

(4) In considering whether to allow the agreement to be enforced or (as the case may be) the money or property paid or transferred under the agreement to be retained the court must—

(a) if the case arises as a result of section 26, have regard to the issue mentioned in subsection (5); or

(b) if the case arises as a result of section 27, have regard to the issue mentioned in subsection (6).

(5) The issue is whether the person carrying on the regulated activity concerned reasonably believed that he was not contravening the general prohibition by making the agreement.

(6) The issue is whether the provider knew that the third party was (in carrying on the regulated activity) contravening the general prohibition.

(7) If the person against whom the agreement is unenforceable—

(a) elects not to perform the agreement, or

(b) as a result of this section, recovers money paid or other property transferred by him under the agreement,

he must repay any money and return any other property received by him under the agreement.

(8) If property transferred under the agreement has passed to a third party, a reference in section 26 or 27 or this section to that property is to be read as a reference to its value at the time of its transfer under the agreement.

(9) The commission of an authorisation offence does not make the agreement concerned illegal or invalid to any greater extent than is provided by section 26 or 27.

NOTES

Application to certain agreements: see the notes to ss 26 and 27 at **[7.27]** and **[7.28]**.

[7.30]

29 Accepting deposits in breach of general prohibition

(1) This section applies to an agreement between a person ("the depositor") and another person ("the deposit-taker") made in the course of the carrying on by the deposit-taker of accepting deposits in contravention of the general prohibition.

(2) If the depositor is not entitled under the agreement to recover without delay any money deposited by him, he may apply to the court for an order directing the deposit-taker to return the money to him.

(3) The court need not make such an order if it is satisfied that it would not be just and equitable for the money deposited to be returned, having regard to the issue mentioned in subsection (4).

(4) The issue is whether the deposit-taker reasonably believed that he was not contravening the general prohibition by making the agreement.

(5) "Agreement" means an agreement—

(a) made after this section comes into force; and

(b) the making or performance of which constitutes, or is part of, accepting deposits.

[7.31]

30 Enforceability of agreements resulting from unlawful communications

(1) In this section—

"unlawful communication" means a communication in relation to which there has been a contravention of section 21(1);

"controlled agreement" means an agreement the making or performance of which by either party constitutes a controlled activity for the purposes of that section; and

"controlled investment" has the same meaning as in section 21.

(2) If in consequence of an unlawful communication a person enters as a customer into a controlled agreement, it is unenforceable against him and he is entitled to recover—

(a) any money or other property paid or transferred by him under the agreement; and

(b) compensation for any loss sustained by him as a result of having parted with it.

(3) If in consequence of an unlawful communication a person exercises any rights conferred by a controlled investment, no obligation to which he is subject as a result of exercising them is enforceable against him and he is entitled to recover—

(a) any money or other property paid or transferred by him under the obligation; and

(b) compensation for any loss sustained by him as a result of having parted with it.

(4) But the court may allow—

(a) the agreement or obligation to be enforced, or

(b) money or property paid or transferred under the agreement or obligation to be retained,

if it is satisfied that it is just and equitable in the circumstances of the case.

(5) In considering whether to allow the agreement or obligation to be enforced or (as the case may be) the money or property paid or transferred under the agreement to be retained the court must have regard to the issues mentioned in subsections (6) and (7).

(6) If the applicant made the unlawful communication, the issue is whether he reasonably believed that he was not making such a communication.

(7) If the applicant did not make the unlawful communication, the issue is whether he knew that the agreement was entered into in consequence of such a communication.

(8) "Applicant" means the person seeking to enforce the agreement or obligation or retain the money or property paid or transferred.

(9) Any reference to making a communication includes causing a communication to be made.

(10) The amount of compensation recoverable as a result of subsection (2) or (3) is—

    (a)   the amount agreed between the parties; or

    (b)   on the application of either party, the amount determined by the court.

(11) If a person elects not to perform an agreement or an obligation which (by virtue of subsection (2) or (3)) is unenforceable against him, he must repay any money and return any other property received by him under the agreement.

(12) If (by virtue of subsection (2) or (3)) a person recovers money paid or property transferred by him under an agreement or obligation, he must repay any money and return any other property received by him as a result of exercising the rights in question.

(13) If any property required to be returned under this section has passed to a third party, references to that property are to be read as references to its value at the time of its receipt by the person required to return it.

PART III
AUTHORISATION AND EXEMPTION

NOTES

    Transitional provisions: see the Financial Services and Markets Act 2000 (Transitional Provisions) (Authorised Persons etc) Order 2001, SI 2001/2636. That Order sets out the transitional arrangements for ensuring that people who have been authorised to carry on particular business under the various regulatory regimes replaced by this Act are treated as authorised persons with the appropriate permission for the purposes of this Act. The regulatory regimes covered by the Order are the Financial Services Act 1986, the Banking Act 1987, the Insurance Companies Act 1982, the Friendly Societies Act 1992, the Building Societies Act 1986, the Banking Coordination (Second Council Directive) Regulations 1992 (SI 1992/3218) and the Investment Services Regulations 1995 (SI 1995/3275).

Authorisation

[7.32]
31 Authorised persons

(1) The following persons are authorised for the purposes of this Act—

    (a)   a person who has a Part IV permission to carry on one or more regulated activities;

    (b)   an EEA firm qualifying for authorisation under Schedule 3;

    (c)   a Treaty firm qualifying for authorisation under Schedule 4;

    (d)   a person who is otherwise authorised by a provision of, or made under, this Act.

(2) In this Act "authorised person" means a person who is authorised for the purposes of this Act.

NOTES

    Application in relation to interim permissions and interim approvals: see the notes preceding s 40 at **[7.42]**.

[7.33]
32 Partnerships and unincorporated associations

(1) If a firm is authorised—

    (a)   it is authorised to carry on the regulated activities concerned in the name of the firm; and

    (b)   its authorisation is not affected by any change in its membership.

(2) If an authorised firm is dissolved, its authorisation continues to have effect in relation to any [individual or] firm which succeeds to the business of the dissolved firm.

[(3) For the purposes of this section, an individual or firm is to be regarded as succeeding to the business of a dissolved firm only if succession is to the whole or substantially the whole of the business of the former firm.]

(4) "Firm" means—

    (a)   a partnership; or

    (b)   an unincorporated association of persons.

(5) "Partnership" does not include a partnership which is constituted under the law of any place outside the United Kingdom and is a body corporate.

NOTES

    Para (2): words in square brackets inserted by the Regulatory Reform (Financial Services and Markets Act 2000) Order 2007, SI 2007/1973, arts 2, 3(a), as from 12 July 2007.

    Para (3): substituted by SI 2007/1973, arts 2, 3(b), as from 12 July 2007.

Part 7 FSMA 2000

Ending of authorisation

[7.34]
33 Withdrawal of authorisation by the Authority
(1) This section applies if—
  (a) an authorised person's Part IV permission is cancelled; and
  (b) as a result, there is no regulated activity for which he has permission.
(2) The Authority must give a direction withdrawing that person's status as an authorised person.

[7.35]
34 EEA firms
(1) An EEA firm ceases to qualify for authorisation under Part II of Schedule 3 if it ceases to be an EEA firm as a result of—
  (a) having its EEA authorisation withdrawn; or
  (b) ceasing to have an EEA right in circumstances in which EEA authorisation is not required.
(2) At the request of an EEA firm, the Authority may give a direction cancelling its authorisation under Part II of Schedule 3.
(3) If an EEA firm has a Part IV permission, it does not cease to be an authorised person merely because it ceases to qualify for authorisation under Part II of Schedule 3.

[7.36]
35 Treaty firms
(1) A Treaty firm ceases to qualify for authorisation under Schedule 4 if its home State authorisation is withdrawn.
(2) At the request of a Treaty firm, the Authority may give a direction cancelling its Schedule 4 authorisation.
(3) If a Treaty firm has a Part IV permission, it does not cease to be an authorised person merely because it ceases to qualify for authorisation under Schedule 4.

[7.37]
36 Persons authorised as a result of paragraph 1(1) of Schedule 5
(1) At the request of a person authorised as a result of paragraph 1(1) of Schedule 5, the Authority may give a direction cancelling his authorisation as such a person.
(2) If a person authorised as a result of paragraph 1(1) of Schedule 5 has a Part IV permission, he does not cease to be an authorised person merely because he ceases to be a person so authorised.

NOTES
  Note: under Sch 5, para 1(1) the operator, trustee or depositary of a collective investment scheme recognised by virtue of s 264 is deemed to be an authorised person (Sch 5, para 1(1), (2)) so far as it is a regulated activity, any activity appropriate to the capacity in which he acts in relation to the scheme, of the kind described in para 8 of Sch 2, or any activity in connection with, or for the purposes of, the scheme or in the case of an authorised OEIC which is an authorised person by virtue of Sch 5, para 1(3) so far as it is a regulated activity, the operation of the scheme or any activity in connection with, or for the purposes of, the operation of the scheme.

Exercise of EEA rights by UK firms

[7.38]
37 Exercise of EEA rights by UK firms
Part III of Schedule 3 makes provision in relation to the exercise outside the United Kingdom of EEA rights by UK firms.

Exemption

[7.39]
38 Exemption orders
(1) The Treasury may by order ("an exemption order") provide for—
  (a) specified persons, or
  (b) persons falling within a specified class,
to be exempt from the general prohibition.
(2) But a person cannot be an exempt person as a result of an exemption order if he has a Part IV permission.
(3) An exemption order may provide for an exemption to have effect—
  (a) in respect of all regulated activities;
  (b) in respect of one or more specified regulated activities;
  (c) only in specified circumstances;
  (d) only in relation to specified functions;
  (e) subject to conditions.
(4) "Specified" means specified by the exemption order.

NOTES
  Application in relation to interim permissions and interim approvals: see the notes preceding s 40 at **[7.42]**.
  Orders: the Financial Services and Markets Act 2000 (Exemption) Order 2001, SI 2001/1201 at **[8.220]**.
  Note that the following amending Orders have also been made under this section: the Financial Services and Markets Act 2000 (Exemption) (Amendment) Order 2001, SI 2001/3623; the Financial Services and Markets Act 2000 (Financial

Promotion and Miscellaneous Amendments) Order 2002, SI 2002/1310; the Financial Services and Markets Act 2000 (Exemption) (Amendment) Order 2003, SI 2003/47; the Financial Services and Markets Act 2000 (Exemption) (Amendment) (No 2) Order 2003, SI 2003/1675; the Financial Services and Markets Act 2000 (Exemption) (Amendment) Order 2005, SI 2005/592; the Financial Services and Markets Act 2000 (Exemption) (Amendment) Order 2007, SI 2007/125; the Financial Services and Markets Act 2000 (Exemption) (Amendment No 2) Order 2007, SI 2007/1821; the Financial Services and Markets Act 2000 (Exemption) (Amendment) Order 2008, SI 2008/682; the Financial Services and Markets Act 2000 (Exemption) (Amendment) Order 2009, SI 2009/118; the Financial Services and Markets Act 2000 (Exemption) (Amendment) (No 2) Order 2009, SI 2009/264.

[7.40]
39 Exemption of appointed representatives

(1) If a person (other than an authorised person)—
  (a) is a party to a contract with an authorised person ("his principal") which—
    (i) permits or requires him to carry on business of a prescribed description, and
    (ii) complies with such requirements as may be prescribed, and
  (b) is someone for whose activities in carrying on the whole or part of that business his principal has accepted responsibility in writing,
he is exempt from the general prohibition in relation to any regulated activity comprised in the carrying on of that business for which his principal has accepted responsibility.

[(1A) But a person is not exempt as a result of subsection (1)—
  (a) if his principal is an investment firm or a credit institution, and
  (b) so far as the business for which his principal has accepted responsibility is investment services business,
unless he is entered on the applicable register.

(1B) The "applicable register" is—
  (a) in the case of a person established in an EEA State (other than the United Kingdom) which permits investment firms authorised by the competent authority of that State to appoint tied agents, the register of tied agents maintained in that State pursuant to Article 23 of the markets in financial instruments directive;
  (b) in the case of a person established in an EEA State which does not permit investment firms authorised as mentioned in paragraph (a) to appoint tied agents—
    (i) if his principal has his relevant office in the United Kingdom, the record maintained by the Authority by virtue of section 347(1)(ha), and
    (ii) if his principal is established in an EEA State (other than the United Kingdom) which permits investment firms authorised by the competent authority of the State to appoint tied agents, the register of tied agents maintained by that State pursuant to Article 23 of the markets in financial instruments directive; and
  (c) in any other case, the record maintained by the Authority by virtue of section 347(1)(ha).]

(2) A person who is exempt as a result of subsection (1) is referred to in this Act as an appointed representative.

(3) The principal of an appointed representative is responsible, to the same extent as if he had expressly permitted it, for anything done or omitted by the representative in carrying on the business for which he has accepted responsibility.

(4) In determining whether an authorised person has complied with a provision contained in or made under this Act, [or with a provision contained in any directly applicable Community regulation made under the markets in financial instruments directive,] anything which a relevant person has done or omitted as respects business for which the authorised person has accepted responsibility is to be treated as having been done or omitted by the authorised person.

(5) "Relevant person" means a person who at the material time is or was an appointed representative by virtue of being a party to a contract with the authorised person.

(6) Nothing in subsection (4) is to cause the knowledge or intentions of an appointed representative to be attributed to his principal for the purpose of determining whether the principal has committed an offence, unless in all the circumstances it is reasonable for them to be attributed to him.

[(7) A person carries on "investment services business" if—
  (a) the business includes providing services or carrying on activities of the kind mentioned in Article 4.1.25 of the markets in financial instruments directive, and
  (b) as a result of providing such services or carrying on such activities he is a tied agent or would be if he were established in an EEA State.

(8) In this section—
"competent authority" has the meaning given in Article 4.1.22 of the markets in financial instruments directive;
"credit institution" means—
  (a) a credit institution authorised under the banking consolidation directive, or
  (b) an institution which would satisfy the requirements for authorisation as a credit institution under that directive if it had its relevant office in an EEA State;
"relevant office" means—
  (a) in relation to a body corporate, its registered office or, if it has no registered office, its head office, and

Part 7 FSMA 2000

(b)   in relation to a person other than a body corporate, the person's head office.]

NOTES

Sub-s (1A), (1B), (7), (8): inserted and added respectively by the Financial Services and Markets Act 2000 (Markets in Financial Instruments) Regulations 2007, SI 2007/126, reg 3(5), Sch 5, paras 1, 2(a), (c), as from 1 April 2007 (certain purposes), and as from 1 November 2007 (otherwise).

Sub-s (4): words in square brackets inserted by SI 2007/126, reg 3(5), Sch 5, paras 1, 2(b), as from 1 April 2007 (certain purposes), and as from 1 November 2007 (otherwise).

Transitional provisions: see the Financial Services and Markets Act 2000 (Markets in Financial Instruments) Regulations 2007, SI 2007/126, reg 9 (Transitional provision: appointed representatives and tied agents).

Application in relation to interim permissions and interim approvals: see the notes preceding s 40 at **[7.42]**.

Regulations: the Financial Services and Markets Act 2000 (Appointed Representatives) Regulations 2001, SI 2001/1217.

Note that the following amending Regulations have also been made under this section: the Financial Services and Markets Act 2000 (Appointed Representatives) (Amendment) Regulations 2001, SI 2001/2508; the Financial Services and Markets Act 2000 (Appointed Representatives) (Amendment) Regulations 2004, SI 2004/453; the Financial Services and Markets Act 2000 (Appointed Representatives) (Amendment) Regulations 2006, SI 2006/3414; the Financial Services and Markets Act 2000 (Markets in Financial Instruments) (Amendment) Regulations 2007, SI 2007/763.

[7.41]
[39A   Certain tied agents operating outside United Kingdom
(1)   This section applies to an authorised person whose relevant office is in the United Kingdom if—
(a)   he is a party to a contract with a person (other than an authorised person) who is established—
    (i)   in the United Kingdom, or
    (ii)   in an EEA State which does not permit investment firms authorised by the competent authority of the State to appoint tied agents; and
(b)   the contract is a relevant contract.
(2)   A contract is a "relevant contract" if it satisfies conditions A to C
(3)   Condition A is that the contract permits or requires the person mentioned in subsection (1)(a) (the "agent") to carry on investment services business.
(4)   Condition B is that either—
(a)   it is a condition of the contract that such business may only be carried on by the agent in an EEA State other than the United Kingdom; or
(b)   in a case not falling within paragraph (a), the Authority is satisfied that no such business is, or is likely to be, carried on by the agent in the United Kingdom.
(5)   Condition C is that the business is of a description that, if carried on in the United Kingdom, would be prescribed for the purposes of section 39(1)(a)(i).
(6)   An authorised person to whom this section applies who—
(a)   enters into or continues to perform a relevant contract with an agent which does not comply with the applicable requirements,
(b)   enters into or continues to perform a relevant contract without accepting or having accepted responsibility in writing for the agent's activities in carrying on investment services business,
(c)   enters into a relevant contract with an agent who is not entered on the record maintained by the Authority by virtue of section 347(1)(ha), or
(d)   continues to perform a relevant contract with an agent when he knows or ought to know that the agent is not entered on that record,
is to be taken for the purposes of this Act to have contravened a requirement imposed on him by or under this Act.
(7)   The "applicable requirements" are the requirements prescribed for the purposes of subsection (1)(a)(ii) of section 39 which have effect in the case of a person to whom subsection (1A) of that section applies.
(8)   A person carries on "investment services business" if—
(a)   his business includes providing services or carrying on activities of the kind mentioned in Article 4.1.25 of the markets in financial instruments directive, and
(b)   as a result of providing such services or carrying on such activities he is a tied agent.
(9)   In this section—
"competent authority" has the meaning given in Article 4.1.22 of the markets in financial instruments directive;
"relevant office" means—
    (a)   in relation to a body corporate, its registered office or, if it has no registered office, its head office, and
    (b)   in relation to a person other than a body corporate, the person's head office.]

NOTES

Commencement: 1 April 2007 (certain purposes); 1 November 2007 (otherwise).

Inserted by the Financial Services and Markets Act 2000 (Markets in Financial Instruments) Regulations 2007, SI 2007/126, reg 3(5), Sch 5, paras 1, 3, as from 1 April 2007 (certain purposes), and as from 1 November 2007 (otherwise).

Transitional provisions: see the Financial Services and Markets Act 2000 (Markets in Financial Instruments) Regulations 2007, SI 2007/126, reg 9 (Transitional provision: appointed representatives and tied agents).

PART IV
PERMISSION TO CARRY ON REGULATED ACTIVITIES

NOTES

Transitional provisions: the Financial Services and Markets Act 2000 (Transitional Provisions) (Authorised Persons etc) Order 2001, SI 2001/2636, Pt II, Chapter I provides that persons who are authorised or exempted from the need for authorisation under provisions of the previous regulatory regimes are treated, as from 1 December 2001, as having permission under Pt IV of this Act to carry on the activities they were lawfully able to carry on immediately before that date by reason of that authorisation or exemption. Pt II of SI 2001/2636 applies to: (a) persons authorised or exempted under the Financial Services Act 1986 (repealed by the Financial Services and Markets Act 2000 (Consequential Amendments and Repeals) Order 2001, SI 2001/3649, art 3(1)(c)); (b) persons authorised under the Banking Act 1987 (repealed by SI 2001/3649, art 3(1)(d)); (c) insurance companies; (d) friendly societies; and (e) building societies.

Pt III of SI 2001/2636 provides that restrictions and prohibitions imposed under provisions of the previous regulatory regimes on authorised persons are to have effect after 1 December 2001 as if they were requirements imposed under s 43 (in relation to persons with a permission under Pt IV of this Act). Pt III of SI 2001/2636 applies to: (a) prohibitions and requirements under the Financial Services Act 1986 (repealed as noted above); (b) restrictions and directions under the Banking Act 1987 (repealed as noted above); (c) directions and requirements under the Insurance Companies Act 1982 (repealed by SI 2001/3649, art 3(1)(b)); (d) conditions and directions under the Friendly Societies Act 1992; (e) conditions and directions under the Building Societies Act 1986; and (f) prohibitions and restrictions under the Banking Coordination (Second Council Directive) Regulations 1992, SI 1992/3218 (revoked by SI 2001/3649, art 3(2)(a)) and the Investment Services Regulations 1995, SI 1995/3275 (revoked by SI 2001/3649, art 3(2)(c)).

See also, the Financial Services and Markets Act 2000 (Permission and Applications) (Credit Unions etc) Order 2002, SI 2002/704 (transitional provisions relating to the expiry, on 2 July 2002, of the transitional exemption of credit unions from the general prohibition imposed by s 19 of this Act (see the Financial Services and Markets Act 2000 (Exemption) Order 2001, SI 2001/1201).

See also, the Financial Services and Markets Act 2000 (Consequential and Transitional Provisions) (Miscellaneous) (No 2) Order 2001, SI 2001/2659 (transitional provisions in consequence of the Financial Services and Markets Act 2000 (Commencement No 5) Order (SI 2001/2632). That Order brings into force the provisions of the Act relating to (among other things) the making of applications under the Act for permission or authorisation coming into force on 1 December 2001).

Interim permissions and interim approvals: see the Financial Services and Markets Act 2000 (Interim Permissions) Order 2001, SI 2001/3374. This Order conferred an interim permission on certain applicants who applied to the FSA for permission under this Part and whose application was pending on the date when the main provisions of the Act come into force (1 December 2001). The scope of the Order is limited by arts 3–5 to those applicants who were lawfully carrying on the activity which was regulated for the first time under this Act. In order to ensure that their business was not disrupted by the fact that the activity became a regulated activity while their application for permission was pending, an applicant who applied for permission before 31 October 2001 and who opted to benefit from the provisions of this Order had an interim permission to enable him to continue to carry on that activity until his application was determined. The Order does not apply to those who were carrying on an activity which was regulated under previous legislation since they benefited from a Part IV permission conferred by the Financial Services and Markets Act 2000 (Transitional Provisions) (Authorised Persons etc) Order 2001, SI 2001/2636 (see above). See also art 8 of SI 2001/3374 (interim permission lapses at the time when it is superseded by the grant of the application or when the application is withdrawn or refused), and art 9 (which conferred interim approval on people who were working for a person who benefited from interim permission if those people would have needed approval under this Part). Article 12 conferred a power on the Authority to modify the rules and guidance it makes under this Act as it applies to persons with interim permission. Article 13 and the Schedule to the Order provided for the application of provisions in this Part and Part V (and various other provisions of this Act and the Regulated Activities Order) to persons who have interim permission under this Order.

As to interim permissions, interim approvals and the application of this Part and Part V (and various other provisions of this Act) to various activities that have become regulated activities following the amendment of the Regulated Activities Order, see the table below:

Order	Regulated Activity
Financial Services and Markets Act 2000 (Transitional Provisions) (Mortgages) Order 2004, SI 2004/2615	Certain mortgage mediation activities
Financial Services and Markets Act 2000 (Regulated Activities) (Amendment) (No 2) Order 2004, SI 2004/2737	Advice on stakeholder products
Financial Services and Markets Act 2000 (Transitional Provisions) (General Insurance Intermediaries) Order 2004, SI 2004/3351	Certain general insurance mediation activities
Financial Services and Markets Act 2000 (Regulated Activities) (Amendment) Order 2006, SI 2006/1969	Establishing, operating or winding up a personal pension scheme, or activities which relate to the specified investment of rights under a personal pension scheme
Financial Services and Markets Act 2000 (Regulated Activities) (Amendment) (No 2) Order 2006, SI 2006/2383	Administering, arranging or advising on regulated home reversion plans or regulated home purchase plans
Financial Services and Markets Act 2000 (Regulated Activities) (Amendment) (No 2) Order 2007, SI 2007/3510	Provision of travel insurance in certain circumstances

Order	Regulated Activity
Financial Services and Markets Act 2000 (Regulated Activities) (Amendment) Order 2009, SI 2009/1342	Entering into, administering, arranging and advising on regulated sale and rent back agreements

Investment firms, etc: see the Financial Services and Markets Act 2000 (Markets in Financial Instruments) Regulations 2007, SI 2007/126, reg 4 (General restriction on giving Part IV permission) which requires the FSA to be satisfied that the authorisation requirements of MiFID (as to which see Chapter I of Title II of MiFID and Commission Regulation 1287/2006) are met before giving permission under this Part to an investment firm (as defined in s 424A) or varying the permission of such a firm. See also reg 4A (Applications to be an exempt investment firm), reg 4B (Limitation on exempt investment firms), reg 4C (Requirements to be applied to exempt investment firms) and reg 9 (Transitional provision: appointed representatives and tied agents), reg 9A (Transitional provision: exempt investment firms), reg 9B (Transitional provision: operators of alternative trading systems), reg 9C (Transitional provision for investment firms and credit institutions in relation to options, futures and contracts for differences), reg 9D (Transitional provision for management companies in relation to options, futures and contracts for differences), and reg 9E (Transitional provision in relation to client classification).

Application for permission

[7.42]
40   Application for permission
(1)   An application for permission to carry on one or more regulated activities may be made to the Authority by—
   (a)   an individual;
   (b)   a body corporate;
   (c)   a partnership; or
   (d)   an unincorporated association.
(2)   An authorised person may not apply for permission under this section if he has a permission—
   (a)   given to him by the Authority under this Part, or
   (b)   having effect as if so given,
which is in force.
(3)   An EEA firm may not apply for permission under this section to carry on a regulated activity which it is, or would be, entitled to carry on in exercise of an EEA right, whether through a United Kingdom branch or by providing services in the United Kingdom.
(4)   A permission given by the Authority under this Part or having effect as if so given is referred to in this Act as "a Part IV permission".

NOTES
   Interim permissions: see the notes preceding this section.

[7.43]
41   The threshold conditions
(1)   "The threshold conditions", in relation to a regulated activity, means the conditions set out in Schedule 6.
(2)   In giving or varying permission, or imposing or varying any requirement, under this Part the Authority must ensure that the person concerned will satisfy, and continue to satisfy, the threshold conditions in relation to all of the regulated activities for which he has or will have permission.
(3)   But the duty imposed by subsection (2) does not prevent the Authority, having due regard to that duty, from taking such steps as it considers are necessary, in relation to a particular authorised person, in order to secure its regulatory objective of the protection of consumers.

Permission

[7.44]
42   Giving permission
(1)   "The applicant" means an applicant for permission under section 40.
(2)   The Authority may give permission for the applicant to carry on the regulated activity or activities to which his application relates or such of them as may be specified in the permission.
(3)   If the applicant—
   (a)   in relation to a particular regulated activity, is exempt from the general prohibition as a result of section 39(1) or an order made under section 38(1), but
   (b)   has applied for permission in relation to another regulated activity,
the application is to be treated as relating to all the regulated activities which, if permission is given, he will carry on.
(4)   If the applicant—
   (a)   in relation to a particular regulated activity, is exempt from the general prohibition as a result of section 285(2) or (3), but
   (b)   has applied for permission in relation to another regulated activity,
the application is to be treated as relating only to that other regulated activity.
(5)   If the applicant—
   (a)   is a person to whom, in relation to a particular regulated activity, the general prohibition does not apply as a result of Part XIX, but
   (b)   has applied for permission in relation to another regulated activity,

the application is to be treated as relating only to that other regulated activity.

(6)   If it gives permission, the Authority must specify the permitted regulated activity or activities, described in such manner as the Authority considers appropriate.

(7)   The Authority may—

    (a)   incorporate in the description of a regulated activity such limitations (for example as to circumstances in which the activity may, or may not, be carried on) as it considers appropriate;

    (b)   specify a narrower or wider description of regulated activity than that to which the application relates;

    (c)   give permission for the carrying on of a regulated activity which is not included among those to which the application relates.

NOTES

Application in relation to interim permissions and interim approvals: see the notes preceding s 40 at **[7.42]**.

[7.45]
43   Imposition of requirements

(1)   A Part IV permission may include such requirements as the Authority considers appropriate.

(2)   A requirement may, in particular, be imposed—

    (a)   so as to require the person concerned to take specified action; or

    (b)   so as to require him to refrain from taking specified action.

(3)   A requirement may extend to activities which are not regulated activities.

(4)   A requirement may be imposed by reference to the person's relationship with—

    (a)   his group; or

    (b)   other members of his group.

(5)   A requirement expires at the end of such period as the Authority may specify in the permission.

(6)   But subsection (5) does not affect the Authority's powers under section 44 or 45.

NOTES

Application in relation to interim permissions and interim approvals: see the notes preceding s 40 at **[7.42]**.

Variation and cancellation of Part IV permission

[7.46]
44   Variation etc at request of authorised person

(1)   The Authority may, on the application of an authorised person with a Part IV permission, vary the permission by—

    (a)   adding a regulated activity to those for which it gives permission;

    (b)   removing a regulated activity from those for which it gives permission;

    (c)   varying the description of a regulated activity for which it gives permission;

    (d)   cancelling a requirement imposed under section 43; or

    (e)   varying such a requirement.

(2)   The Authority may, on the application of an authorised person with a Part IV permission, cancel the permission.

(3)   The Authority may refuse an application under this section if it appears [to it that it is desirable to refuse the application in order to meet any of its regulatory objectives].

(4)   If, as a result of a variation of a Part IV permission under this section, there are no longer any regulated activities for which the authorised person concerned has permission, the Authority must, once it is satisfied that it is no longer necessary to keep the permission in force, cancel it.

(5)   The Authority's power to vary a Part IV permission under this section extends to including any provision in the permission as varied that could be included if a fresh permission were being given in response to an application under section 40.

NOTES

Sub-s (3): words in square brackets substituted by the Financial Services Act 2010, s 3(1), (2), as from 8 June 2010.

Application in relation to interim permissions and interim approvals: see the notes preceding s 40 at **[7.42]**.

[7.47]
45   Variation etc on the Authority's own initiative

(1)   The Authority may exercise its power under this section in relation to an authorised person if it appears to it that—

    (a)   he is failing, or is likely to fail, to satisfy the threshold conditions;

    (b)   he has failed, during a period of at least 12 months, to carry on a regulated activity for which he has a Part IV permission; or

    [(c)   it is desirable to exercise the power in order to meet any of its regulatory objectives].

[(1A)   For the purposes of subsection (1)(c) it does not matter whether there is a relationship between the authorised person and the persons whose interests will be protected by the exercise of the power under this section.]

(2)   The Authority's power under this section is the power to vary a Part IV permission in any of the ways mentioned in section 44(1) or to cancel it.

[(2A)   Without prejudice to the generality of subsections (1) and (2), the Authority may, in relation to an authorised person who is an investment firm, exercise its power under this section to cancel the Part IV permission of the firm if it appears to it that—

  (a)   the firm has failed, during a period of at least six months, to carry on a regulated activity which is an investment service or activity for which it has a Part IV permission;

  (b)   the firm obtained the Part IV permission by making a false statement or by other irregular means;

  (c)   the firm no longer satisfies the requirements for authorisation pursuant to Chapter I of Title II of the markets in financial instruments directive, or pursuant to or contained in any Community legislation made under that Chapter, in relation to a regulated activity which is an investment service or activity for which it has a Part IV permission; or

  (d)   the firm has seriously and systematically infringed the operating conditions pursuant to Chapter II of Title II of the markets in financial instruments directive, or pursuant to or contained in any Community legislation made under that Chapter, in relation to a regulated activity which is an investment service or activity for which it has a Part IV permission.

(2B)   For the purposes of subsection (2A) a regulated activity is an investment service or activity if it falls within the definition of "investment services and activities" in section 417(1).]

(3)   If, as a result of a variation of a Part IV permission under this section, there are no longer any regulated activities for which the authorised person concerned has permission, the Authority must, once it is satisfied that it is no longer necessary to keep the permission in force, cancel it.

(4)   The Authority's power to vary a Part IV permission under this section extends to including any provision in the permission as varied that could be included if a fresh permission were being given in response to an application under section 40.

(5)   The Authority's power under this section is referred to in this Part as its own-initiative power.

NOTES

Sub-s (1): para (c) substituted by the Financial Services Act 2010, s 3(1), (3)(a), as from 8 June 2010.

Sub-s (1A): inserted by the Financial Services Act 2010, s 3(1), (3)(b), as from 8 June 2010.

Sub-ss (2A), (2B): inserted by the Financial Services and Markets Act 2000 (Markets in Financial Instruments) Regulations 2007, SI 2007/126, reg 3(5), Sch 5, paras 1, 4, as from 1 April 2007 (certain purposes), and as from 1 November 2007 (otherwise).

Application in relation to interim permissions and interim approvals: see the notes preceding s 40 at **[7.42]**.

[7.48]

46   Variation of permission on acquisition of control

(1)   This section applies if it appears to the Authority that—

  (a)   a person has acquired control over a UK authorised person who has a Part IV permission; but

  (b)   there are no grounds for exercising its own-initiative power.

(2)   If it appears to the Authority that the likely effect of the acquisition of control on the authorised person, or on any of its activities, is uncertain the Authority may vary the authorised person's permission by—

  (a)   imposing a requirement of a kind that could be imposed under section 43 on giving permission; or

  (b)   varying a requirement included in the authorised person's permission under that section.

(3)   Any reference to a person having acquired control is to be read in accordance with Part XII.

[7.49]

47   Exercise of power in support of overseas regulator

(1)   The Authority's own-initiative power may be exercised in respect of an authorised person at the request of, or for the purpose of assisting, a regulator who is—

  (a)   outside the United Kingdom; and

  (b)   of a prescribed kind.

(2)   Subsection (1) applies whether or not the Authority has powers which are exercisable in relation to the authorised person by virtue of any provision of Part XIII.

(3)   If a request to the Authority for the exercise of its own-initiative power has been made by a regulator who is—

  (a)   outside the United Kingdom,

  (b)   of a prescribed kind, and

  (c)   acting in pursuance of provisions of a prescribed kind,

the Authority must, in deciding whether or not to exercise that power in response to the request, consider whether it is necessary to do so in order to comply with a Community obligation.

(4)   In deciding in any case in which the Authority does not consider that the exercise of its own-initiative power is necessary in order to comply with a Community obligation, it may take into account in particular—

  (a)   whether in the country or territory of the regulator concerned, corresponding assistance would be given to a United Kingdom regulatory authority;

(b)　whether the case concerns the breach of a law, or other requirement, which has no close parallel in the United Kingdom or involves the assertion of a jurisdiction not recognised by the United Kingdom;

(c)　the seriousness of the case and its importance to persons in the United Kingdom;

(d)　whether it is otherwise appropriate in the public interest to give the assistance sought.

(5)　The Authority may decide not to exercise its own-initiative power, in response to a request, unless the regulator concerned undertakes to make such contribution towards the cost of its exercise as the Authority considers appropriate.

(6)　Subsection (5) does not apply if the Authority decides that it is necessary for it to exercise its own-initiative power in order to comply with a Community obligation.

(7)　In subsections (4) and (5) "request" means a request of a kind mentioned in subsection (1).

NOTES

Regulations: the Financial Services and Markets Act 2000 (Own-initiative Power) (Overseas Regulators) Regulations 2001, SI 2001/2639.

[7.50]
48　Prohibitions and restrictions
(1)　This section applies if the Authority—

(a)　on giving a person a Part IV permission, imposes an assets requirement on him; or

(b)　varies an authorised person's Part IV permission so as to alter an assets requirement imposed on him or impose such a requirement on him.

(2)　A person on whom an assets requirement is imposed is referred to in this section as "A".

(3)　"Assets requirement" means a requirement under section 43—

(a)　prohibiting the disposal of, or other dealing with, any of A's assets (whether in the United Kingdom or elsewhere) or restricting such disposals or dealings; or

(b)　that all or any of A's assets, or all or any assets belonging to consumers but held by A or to his order, must be transferred to and held by a trustee approved by the Authority.

(4)　If the Authority—

(a)　imposes a requirement of the kind mentioned in subsection (3)(a), and

(b)　gives notice of the requirement to any institution with whom A keeps an account,

the notice has the effects mentioned in subsection (5).

(5)　Those effects are that—

(a)　the institution does not act in breach of any contract with A if, having been instructed by A (or on his behalf) to transfer any sum or otherwise make any payment out of A's account, it refuses to do so in the reasonably held belief that complying with the instruction would be incompatible with the requirement; and

(b)　if the institution complies with such an instruction, it is liable to pay to the Authority an amount equal to the amount transferred from, or otherwise paid out of, A's account in contravention of the requirement.

(6)　If the Authority imposes a requirement of the kind mentioned in subsection (3)(b), no assets held by a person as trustee in accordance with the requirement may, while the requirement is in force, be released or dealt with except with the consent of the Authority.

(7)　If, while a requirement of the kind mentioned in subsection (3)(b) is in force, A creates a charge over any assets of his held in accordance with the requirement, the charge is (to the extent that it confers security over the assets) void against the liquidator and any of A's creditors.

(8)　Assets held by a person as trustee ("T") are to be taken to be held by T in accordance with a requirement mentioned in subsection (3)(b) only if—

(a)　A has given T written notice that those assets are to be held by T in accordance with the requirement; or

(b)　they are assets into which assets to which paragraph (a) applies have been transposed by T on the instructions of A.

(9)　A person who contravenes subsection (6) is guilty of an offence and liable on summary conviction to a fine not exceeding level 5 on the standard scale.

(10)　"Charge" includes a mortgage (or in Scotland a security over property).

(11)　Subsections (6) and (8) do not affect any equitable interest or remedy in favour of a person who is a beneficiary of a trust as a result of a requirement of the kind mentioned in subsection (3)(b).

Connected persons

[7.51]
49　Persons connected with an applicant
(1)　In considering—

(a)　an application for a Part IV permission, or

(b)　whether to vary or cancel a Part IV permission,

the Authority may have regard to any person appearing to it to be, or likely to be, in a relationship with the applicant or person given permission which is relevant.

(2)　Before—

(a) giving permission in response to an application made by a person who is connected with an EEA firm [(other than an EEA firm falling within paragraph 5(e) of Schedule 3 (insurance and reinsurance intermediaries))], or

[(b) varying any permission given by the Authority to such a person, where the effect of the variation is to grant permission for the purposes of a single market directive other than the one for the purposes of which the existing permission was granted,]

the Authority must consult the firm's home state regulator.

[(2A) But subsection (2) does not apply to the extent that the permission relates to—

(a) an insurance mediation activity (within the meaning given by paragraph 2(5) of Schedule 6); or

(b) a regulated activity involving a regulated mortgage contract[, a regulated home reversion plan[, a regulated home purchase plan or a regulated sale and rent back agreement]].]

(3) A person ("A") is connected with an EEA firm if—

(a) A is a subsidiary undertaking of the firm; or

(b) A is a subsidiary undertaking of a parent undertaking of the firm.

[(4) In subsection (2A)(b) "regulated mortgage contract", "regulated home reversion plan", "regulated home purchase plan" and "regulated sale and rent back agreement" shall be construed in accordance with—

(a) section 22;

(b) any relevant order under that section; and

(c) Schedule 2.]

NOTES

Sub-s (2): words in square brackets in para (a) inserted by the Financial Services and Markets Act 2000 (Regulated Activities) (Amendment) (No 2) Order 2003, SI 2003/1476, art 20(1), (2), as from 31 October 2004 (in so far as relating to contracts of long-term care insurance), and as from 14 January 2005 (otherwise) (for transitional provisions in relation to applications for Part IV permissions and applications for approval, etc, see arts 22–27 of that Order); para (b) substituted by the Regulatory Reform (Financial Services and Markets Act 2000) Order 2007, SI 2007/1973, arts 2, 4, as from 12 July 2007.

Sub-s (2A): inserted by the Financial Services and Markets Act 2000 (Regulated Activities) Order 2001, SI 2001/544, art 97, as from 15 July 2004 (see further the note below); words in first (outer) pair of square brackets inserted by the Financial Services and Markets Act 2000 (Regulated Activities) (Amendment) (No 2) Order 2006, SI 2006/2383, art 28, as from 6 November 2006 (for the purposes of enabling applications to be made for (i) a Pt IV permission, or a variation of a Pt IV permission, in relation to activities of the kind specified by arts 25B, 25C, 53B, 53C, 63B or 63F or, so far as relevant to any such activity, art 64 of the Regulated Activities Order; or (ii) the Authority's approval under s 59 of this Act in relation to any of those activities), and as from 6 April 2007 (otherwise) (for transitional provisions in relation to interim permissions and interim approvals, etc, see arts 36–40 of, and the Schedule to, the 2006 Order); words in second (inner) pair of square brackets substituted by the Financial Services and Markets Act 2000 (Regulated Activities) (Amendment) Order 2009, SI 2009/1342, art 25(a), as from 1 July 2009 (other than for the purposes of enabling applications to be made for a Part IV permission, or a variation of a Part IV permission, in relation to activities of the kind specified by arts 25E, 53D or 63J or, so far as relevant to any such activity, art 64 of this Order), and as from 30 June 2010 (for those purposes) (for transitional provisions in relation to applications for Part IV permissions, etc, see arts 1, 32–34 of that Order).

Para (4): added by SI 2009/1342, art 25(b), as from the same dates and for the same purposes, etc, as mentioned in the note relating to this Order above.

Note: sub-s (2A) was originally inserted by the Financial Services and Markets Act 2000 (Regulated Activities) (Amendment) (No 2) Order 2003, SI 2003/1476, art 20(1), (3), as from 31 October 2004 (in so far as relating to contracts of long-term care insurance), and as from 14 January 2005 (otherwise). Article 20(3) of SI 2003/1476 was subsequently revoked by the Financial Services and Markets Act 2000 (Regulated Activities) (Amendment) Order 2004, SI 2004/1610, art 2, as from 15 July 2004. Article 3 of SI 2004/1610 also amended the Financial Services and Markets Act 2000 (Regulated Activities) Order 2001, SI 2001/544 by adding a new art 97 which, in turn, inserted the new sub-s (2A) as noted above.

Additional permissions

[7.52]

50 Authority's duty to consider other permissions etc

(1) "Additional Part IV permission" means a Part IV permission which is in force in relation to an EEA firm, a Treaty firm or a person authorised as a result of paragraph 1(1) of Schedule 5.

(2) If the Authority is considering whether, and if so how, to exercise its own-initiative power under this Part in relation to an additional Part IV permission, it must take into account—

(a) the home State authorisation of the authorised person concerned;

(b) any relevant directive; and

(c) relevant provisions of the Treaty.

Procedure

[7.53]

51 Applications under this Part

(1) An application for a Part IV permission must—

(a) contain a statement of the regulated activity or regulated activities which the applicant proposes to carry on and for which he wishes to have permission; and

(b) give the address of a place in the United Kingdom for service on the applicant of any notice or other document which is required or authorised to be served on him under this Act.

(2) An application for the variation of a Part IV permission must contain a statement—

(a) of the desired variation; and

(b)   of the regulated activity or regulated activities which the applicant proposes to carry on if his permission is varied.

(3)   Any application under this Part must—
  (a)   be made in such manner as the Authority may direct; and
  (b)   contain, or be accompanied by, such other information as the Authority may reasonably require.

(4)   At any time after receiving an application and before determining it, the Authority may require the applicant to provide it with such further information as it reasonably considers necessary to enable it to determine the application.

(5)   Different directions may be given, and different requirements imposed, in relation to different applications or categories of application.

(6)   The Authority may require an applicant to provide information which he is required to provide under this section in such form, or to verify it in such a way, as the Authority may direct.

[7.54]
52   Determination of applications

(1)   An application under this Part must be determined by the Authority before the end of the period of six months beginning with the date on which it received the completed application.

(2)   The Authority may determine an incomplete application if it considers it appropriate to do so; and it must in any event determine such an application within twelve months beginning with the date on which it received the application.

(3)   The applicant may withdraw his application, by giving the Authority written notice, at any time before the Authority determines it.

(4)   If the Authority grants an application for, or for variation of, a Part IV permission, it must give the applicant written notice.

(5)   The notice must state the date from which the permission, or the variation, has effect.

(6)   If the Authority proposes—
  (a)   to give a Part IV permission but to exercise its power under section 42(7)(a) or (b) or 43(1), or
  (b)   to vary a Part IV permission on the application of an authorised person but to exercise its power under any of those provisions (as a result of section 44(5)),
it must give the applicant a warning notice.

(7)   If the Authority proposes to refuse an application made under this Part, it must (unless subsection (8) applies) give the applicant a warning notice.

(8)   This subsection applies if it appears to the Authority that—
  (a)   the applicant is an EEA firm; and
  (b)   the application is made with a view to carrying on a regulated activity in a manner in which the applicant is, or would be, entitled to carry on that activity in the exercise of an EEA right whether through a United Kingdom branch or by providing services in the United Kingdom.

(9)   If the Authority decides—
  (a)   to give a Part IV permission but to exercise its power under section 42(7)(a) or (b) or 43(1),
  (b)   to vary a Part IV permission on the application of an authorised person but to exercise its power under any of those provisions (as a result of section 44(5)), or
  (c)   to refuse an application under this Part,
it must give the applicant a decision notice.

NOTES

  Application in relation to interim permissions and interim approvals: see the notes preceding s 40 at **[7.42]**.

[7.55]
53   Exercise of own-initiative power: procedure

(1)   This section applies to an exercise of the Authority's own-initiative power to vary an authorised person's Part IV permission.

(2)   A variation takes effect—
  (a)   immediately, if the notice given under subsection (4) states that that is the case;
  (b)   on such date as may be specified in the notice; or
  (c)   if no date is specified in the notice, when the matter to which the notice relates is no longer open to review.

(3)   A variation may be expressed to take effect immediately (or on a specified date) only if the Authority, having regard to the ground on which it is exercising its own-initiative power, reasonably considers that it is necessary for the variation to take effect immediately (or on that date).

(4)   If the Authority proposes to vary the Part IV permission, or varies it with immediate effect, it must give the authorised person written notice.

(5)   The notice must—
  (a)   give details of the variation;
  (b)   state the Authority's reasons for the variation and for its determination as to when the variation takes effect;

(c) inform the authorised person that he may make representations to the Authority within such period as may be specified in the notice (whether or not he has referred the matter to the Tribunal);

(d) inform him of when the variation takes effect; and

(e) inform him of his right to refer the matter to the Tribunal.

(6) The Authority may extend the period allowed under the notice for making representations.

(7) If, having considered any representations made by the authorised person, the Authority decides—

(a) to vary the permission in the way proposed, or

(b) if the permission has been varied, not to rescind the variation,

it must give him written notice.

(8) If, having considered any representations made by the authorised person, the Authority decides—

(a) not to vary the permission in the way proposed,

(b) to vary the permission in a different way, or

(c) to rescind a variation which has effect,

it must give him written notice.

(9) A notice given under subsection (7) must inform the authorised person of his right to refer the matter to the Tribunal.

(10) A notice under subsection (8)(b) must comply with subsection (5).

(11) If a notice informs a person of his right to refer a matter to the Tribunal, it must give an indication of the procedure on such a reference.

(12) For the purposes of subsection (2)(c), whether a matter is open to review is to be determined in accordance with section 391(8).

NOTES

Application in relation to interim permissions and interim approvals: see the notes preceding s 40 at **[7.42]**.

[7.56]

54 Cancellation of Part IV permission: procedure

(1) If the Authority proposes to cancel an authorised person's Part IV permission otherwise than at his request, it must give him a warning notice.

(2) If the Authority decides to cancel an authorised person's Part IV permission otherwise than at his request, it must give him a decision notice.

NOTES

Application in relation to interim permissions and interim approvals: see the notes preceding s 40 at **[7.42]**.

References to the Tribunal

[7.57]

55 Right to refer matters to the Tribunal

(1) An applicant who is aggrieved by the determination of an application made under this Part may refer the matter to the Tribunal.

(2) An authorised person who is aggrieved by the exercise of the Authority's own-initiative power may refer the matter to the Tribunal.

NOTES

Application in relation to interim permissions and interim approvals: see the notes preceding s 40 at **[7.42]**.

PART V
PERFORMANCE OF REGULATED ACTIVITIES

NOTES

Transitional provisions: the Financial Services and Markets Act 2000 (Transitional Provisions) (Authorised Persons etc) Order 2001, SI 2001/2636, Pt VI makes transitional provisions for people working for authorised persons who will be covered by the regime for approved persons in Pt V of the Act after commencement. Where someone is working for an authorised person before commencement in a post for which they would need to be approved under Pt V after commencement, that person is treated has having been approved for the purpose of working in that post. This deemed approval applies unless the person was working before commencement in contravention of certain provisions of the regulatory rules or of rules made by a self-regulating organisation. The Part also carries forward approvals given under the Insurance Companies Act 1982 and the Banking Act 1987 where the person approved did not take up the appointment before commencement.

See also the notes relating to interim permissions and interim approvals preceding s 40 at **[7.42]**.

Prohibition orders

[7.58]

56 Prohibition orders

(1) Subsection (2) applies if it appears to the Authority that an individual is not a fit and proper person to perform functions in relation to a regulated activity carried on by an authorised person.

(2) The Authority may make an order ("a prohibition order") prohibiting the individual from performing a specified function, any function falling within a specified description or any function.

(3)　A prohibition order may relate to—

(a)　a specified regulated activity, any regulated activity falling within a specified description or all regulated activities;

(b)　authorised persons generally or any person within a specified class of authorised person.

(4)　An individual who performs or agrees to perform a function in breach of a prohibition order is guilty of an offence and liable on summary conviction to a fine not exceeding level 5 on the standard scale.

(5)　In proceedings for an offence under subsection (4) it is a defence for the accused to show that he took all reasonable precautions and exercised all due diligence to avoid committing the offence.

(6)　An authorised person must take reasonable care to ensure that no function of his, in relation to the carrying on of a regulated activity, is performed by a person who is prohibited from performing that function by a prohibition order.

(7)　The Authority may, on the application of the individual named in a prohibition order, vary or revoke it.

(8)　This section applies to the performance of functions in relation to a regulated activity carried on by—

(a)　a person who is an exempt person in relation to that activity, and

(b)　a person to whom, as a result of Part XX, the general prohibition does not apply in relation to that activity,

as it applies to the performance of functions in relation to a regulated activity carried on by an authorised person.

(9)　"Specified" means specified in the prohibition order.

NOTES

Transitional provisions: the Financial Services and Markets Act 2000 (Transitional Provisions) (Authorised Persons etc) Order 2001, SI 2001/2636, art 79 provides that where, on 1 December 2001, a person is the subject of a disqualification direction made under the Financial Services Act 1986, s 59, the direction has effect after that date as a prohibition order made under this section. The 1986 Act was repealed by the Financial Services and Markets Act 2000 (Consequential Amendments and Repeals) Order 2001, SI 2001/3649, art 3(1)(c).

[7.59]

57　Prohibition orders: procedure and right to refer to Tribunal

(1)　If the Authority proposes to make a prohibition order it must give the individual concerned a warning notice.

(2)　The warning notice must set out the terms of the prohibition.

(3)　If the Authority decides to make a prohibition order it must give the individual concerned a decision notice.

(4)　The decision notice must—

(a)　name the individual to whom the prohibition order applies;

(b)　set out the terms of the order; and

(c)　be given to the individual named in the order.

(5)　A person against whom a decision to make a prohibition order is made may refer the matter to the Tribunal.

[7.60]

58　Applications relating to prohibitions: procedure and right to refer to Tribunal

(1)　This section applies to an application for the variation or revocation of a prohibition order.

(2)　If the Authority decides to grant the application, it must give the applicant written notice of its decision.

(3)　If the Authority proposes to refuse the application, it must give the applicant a warning notice.

(4)　If the Authority decides to refuse the application, it must give the applicant a decision notice.

(5)　If the Authority gives the applicant a decision notice, he may refer the matter to the Tribunal.

Approval

[7.61]

59　Approval for particular arrangements

(1)　An authorised person ("A") must take reasonable care to ensure that no person performs a controlled function under an arrangement entered into by A in relation to the carrying on by A of a regulated activity, unless the Authority approves the performance by that person of the controlled function to which the arrangement relates.

(2)　An authorised person ("A") must take reasonable care to ensure that no person performs a controlled function under an arrangement entered into by a contractor of A in relation to the carrying on by A of a regulated activity, unless the Authority approves the performance by that person of the controlled function to which the arrangement relates.

(3)　"Controlled function" means a function of a description specified in rules.

(4)　The Authority may specify a description of function under subsection (3) only if, in relation to the carrying on of a regulated activity by an authorised person, it is satisfied that the first, second or third condition is met.

(5) The first condition is that the function is likely to enable the person responsible for its performance to exercise a significant influence on the conduct of the authorised person's affairs, so far as relating to the regulated activity.

(6) The second condition is that the function will involve the person performing it in dealing with customers of the authorised person in a manner substantially connected with the carrying on of the regulated activity.

(7) The third condition is that the function will involve the person performing it in dealing with property of customers of the authorised person in a manner substantially connected with the carrying on of the regulated activity.

(8) Neither subsection (1) nor subsection (2) applies to an arrangement which allows a person to perform a function if the question of whether he is a fit and proper person to perform the function is reserved under any of the single market directives to an authority in a country or territory outside the United Kingdom.

(9) In determining whether the first condition is met, the Authority may take into account the likely consequences of a failure to discharge that function properly.

(10) "Arrangement"—

  (a) means any kind of arrangement for the performance of a function of A which is entered into by A or any contractor of his with another person; and

  (b) includes, in particular, that other person's appointment to an office, his becoming a partner or his employment (whether under a contract of service or otherwise).

(11) "Customer", in relation to an authorised person, means a person who is using, or who is or may be contemplating using, any of the services provided by the authorised person.

NOTES

Transitional provisions: the Financial Services and Markets Act 2000 (Transitional Provisions) (Authorised Persons etc) Order 2001, SI 2001/2636, Pt VI applies where a person is performing a function for another person at 1 December 2001, and provides for the continued performance of that function after that date to be taken to be approved by the Authority for the purposes of this section.

Note: "person" includes both individuals (natural persons) and bodies corporate or unincorporate; see the Interpretation Act 1978, Sch 1.

Application in relation to interim permissions and interim approvals: see the notes preceding s 40 at **[7.42]**.

[7.62]

60 Applications for approval

(1) An application for the Authority's approval under section 59 may be made by the authorised person concerned.

(2) The application must—

  (a) be made in such manner as the Authority may direct; and

  (b) contain, or be accompanied by, such information as the Authority may reasonably require.

(3) At any time after receiving the application and before determining it, the Authority may require the applicant to provide it with such further information as it reasonably considers necessary to enable it to determine the application.

(4) The Authority may require an applicant to present information which he is required to give under this section in such form, or to verify it in such a way, as the Authority may direct.

(5) Different directions may be given, and different requirements imposed, in relation to different applications or categories of application.

(6) "The authorised person concerned" includes a person who has applied for permission under Part IV and will be the authorised person concerned if permission is given.

NOTES

The authorised person concerned: as to the meaning of this, see also the Financial Services and Markets Act 2000 (EEA Passport Rights) Regulations 2001, SI 2001/2511, reg 10 which (as amended) provides as follows—

"In section 60 of the Act (applications for approval for persons to perform controlled functions), "the authorised person concerned" includes—

  (a) an EEA firm with respect to which the Authority has received a consent notice or regulator's notice under paragraph 13 of Schedule 3 or a regulator's notice under paragraph 14 of that Schedule, and which will be the authorised person concerned if it qualifies for authorisation under that Schedule; and

  (b) an EEA firm which falls within paragraph 5(da) of Schedule 3 which establishes a branch in the United Kingdom.".

See also the notes relating to interim permissions and interim approvals preceding s 40 at **[7.42]**.

[7.63]

61 Determination of applications

(1) The Authority may grant an application made under section 60 only if it is satisfied that the person in respect of whom the application is made ("the candidate") is a fit and proper person to perform the function to which the application relates.

(2) In deciding that question, the Authority may have regard (among other things) to whether the candidate, or any person who may perform a function on his behalf—

  (a) has obtained a qualification,

  (b) has undergone, or is undergoing, training, or

(c)   possesses a level of competence,
required by general rules in relation to persons performing functions of the kind to which the application relates.
(3)   The Authority must, before the end of the period of three months beginning with the date on which it receives an application made under section 60 ("the period for consideration"), determine whether—
(a)   to grant the application; or
(b)   to give a warning notice under section 62(2).
(4)   If the Authority imposes a requirement under section 60(3), the period for consideration stops running on the day on which the requirement is imposed but starts running again—
(a)   on the day on which the required information is received by the Authority; or
(b)   if the information is not provided on a single day, on the last of the days on which it is received by the Authority.
(5)   A person who makes an application under section 60 may withdraw his application by giving written notice to the Authority at any time before the Authority determines it, but only with the consent of—
(a)   the candidate; and
(b)   the person by whom the candidate is to be retained to perform the function concerned, if not the applicant.

NOTES
Application in relation to interim permissions and interim approvals: see the notes preceding s 40 at **[7.42]**.

[7.64]
62   Applications for approval: procedure and right to refer to Tribunal
(1)   If the Authority decides to grant an application made under section 60 ("an application"), it must give written notice of its decision to each of the interested parties.
(2)   If the Authority proposes to refuse an application, it must give a warning notice to each of the interested parties.
(3)   If the Authority decides to refuse an application, it must give a decision notice to each of the interested parties.
(4)   If the Authority decides to refuse an application, each of the interested parties may refer the matter to the Tribunal.
(5)   "The interested parties", in relation to an application, are—
(a)   the applicant;
(b)   the person in respect of whom the application is made ("A"); and
(c)   the person by whom A's services are to be retained, if not the applicant.

NOTES
Application in relation to interim permissions and interim approvals: see the notes preceding s 40 at **[7.42]**.

[7.65]
63   Withdrawal of approval
(1)   The Authority may withdraw an approval given under section 59 if it considers that the person in respect of whom it was given is not a fit and proper person to perform the function to which the approval relates.
(2)   When considering whether to withdraw its approval, the Authority may take into account any matter which it could take into account if it were considering an application made under section 60 in respect of the performance of the function to which the approval relates.
(3)   If the Authority proposes to withdraw its approval, it must give each of the interested parties a warning notice.
(4)   If the Authority decides to withdraw its approval, it must give each of the interested parties a decision notice.
(5)   If the Authority decides to withdraw its approval, each of the interested parties may refer the matter to the Tribunal.
(6)   "The interested parties", in relation to an approval, are—
(a)   the person on whose application it was given ("A");
(b)   the person in respect of whom it was given ("B"); and
(c)   the person by whom B's services are retained, if not A.

NOTES
Application in relation to interim permissions and interim approvals: see the notes preceding s 40 at **[7.42]**.

[Performance of controlled functions without approval
[7.66]
63A   Power to impose penalties
(1)   If the Authority is satisfied that—
(a)   a person ("P") has at any time performed a controlled function without approval, and

(b)   at that time P knew, or could reasonably be expected to have known, that P was performing a controlled function without approval,

it may impose a penalty on P of such amount as it considers appropriate.

(2)   For the purposes of this section P performs a controlled function without approval at any time if at that time—

(a)   P performs a controlled function under an arrangement entered into by an authorised person ("A"), or by a contractor of A, in relation to the carrying on by A of a regulated activity; and

(b)   the performance by P of the function was not approved under section 59.

(3)   The Authority may not impose a penalty under this section after the end of the limitation period unless, before the end of that period, it has given a warning notice to the person concerned under section 63B(1).

(4)   "The limitation period" means the period of three years beginning with the first day on which the Authority knew that the person concerned had performed a controlled function without approval.

(5)   For this purpose the Authority is to be treated as knowing that a person has performed a controlled function without approval if it has information from which that can reasonably be inferred.

(6)   Any expression which is used both in this section and section 59 has the same meaning in this section as in that section.]

NOTES

Commencement: 8 June 2010.

Inserted, together with the preceding heading and ss 63B–63D, by the Financial Services Act 2010, s 11, as from 8 June 2010.

[7.67]
[63B   Procedure and right to refer to Tribunal
(1)   If the Authority proposes to impose a penalty on a person under section 63A, it must give the person a warning notice.

(2)   A warning notice must state the amount of the penalty.

(3)   If the Authority decides to impose a penalty on a person under section 63A, it must give the person a decision notice.

(4)   A decision notice must state the amount of the penalty.

(5)   If the Authority decides to impose a penalty on a person under section 63A, the person may refer the matter to the Tribunal.]

NOTES

Commencement: 8 June 2010.

Inserted as noted to s 63A at **[7.66]**.

[7.68]
[63C   Statement of policy
(1)   The Authority must prepare and issue a statement of its policy with respect to—

(a)   the imposition of penalties under section 63A; and

(b)   the amount of penalties under that section.

(2)   The Authority's policy in determining whether a penalty should be imposed, and what the amount of a penalty should be, must include having regard to—

(a)   the conduct of the person on whom the penalty is to be imposed;

(b)   the extent to which the person could reasonably be expected to have known that a controlled function was performed without approval;

(c)   the length of the period during which the person performed a controlled function without approval; and

(d)   whether the person on whom the penalty is to be imposed is an individual.

(3)   The Authority's policy in determining whether a penalty should be imposed on a person must also include having regard to the appropriateness of taking action against the person instead of, or in addition to, taking action against an authorised person.

(4)   A statement issued under this section must include an indication of the circumstances in which the Authority would expect to be satisfied that a person could reasonably be expected to have known that the person was performing a controlled function without approval.

(5)   The Authority may at any time alter or replace a statement issued under this section.

(6)   If a statement issued under this section is altered or replaced, the Authority must issue the altered or replaced statement.

(7)   The Authority must, without delay, give the Treasury a copy of any statement which it publishes under this section.

(8)   A statement issued under this section must be published by the Authority in the way appearing to the Authority to be best calculated to bring it to the attention of the public.

(9)   The Authority may charge a reasonable fee for providing a person with a copy of the statement.

(10) In exercising, or deciding whether to exercise, its power under section 63A in the case of any particular person, the Authority must have regard to any statement of policy published under this section and in force at a time when the person concerned performed a controlled function without approval.]

NOTES
Commencement: 8 June 2010.
Inserted as noted to s 63A at **[7.66]**.

[7.69]
[63D Statement of policy: procedure
(1) Before issuing a statement under section 63C, the Authority must publish a draft of the proposed statement in the way appearing to the Authority to be best calculated to bring it to the attention of the public.
(2) The draft must be accompanied by notice that representations about the proposal may be made to the Authority within a specified time.
(3) Before issuing the proposed statement, the Authority must have regard to any representations made to it in accordance with subsection (2).
(4) If the Authority issues the proposed statement it must publish an account, in general terms, of—
   (a) the representations made to it in accordance with subsection (2); and
   (b) its response to them.
(5) If the statement differs from the draft published under subsection (1) in a way which is, in the opinion of the Authority, significant, the Authority must (in addition to complying with subsection (4)) publish details of the difference.
(6) The Authority may charge a reasonable fee for providing a person with a copy of a draft published under subsection (1).
(7) This section also applies to a proposal to alter or replace a statement.]

NOTES
Commencement: 8 June 2010.
Inserted as noted to s 63A at **[7.66]**.

Conduct [of approved persons]

NOTES
Words in square brackets in the above heading added by the Financial Services Act 2010, s 24(1), (2), Sch 2, Pt 1, paras 1, 7, as from 8 June 2010.

[7.70]
64 Conduct: statements and codes
(1) The Authority may issue statements of principle with respect to the conduct expected of approved persons.
(2) If the Authority issues a statement of principle under subsection (1), it must also issue a code of practice for the purpose of helping to determine whether or not a person's conduct complies with the statement of principle.
(3) A code issued under subsection (2) may specify—
   (a) descriptions of conduct which, in the opinion of the Authority, comply with a statement of principle;
   (b) descriptions of conduct which, in the opinion of the Authority, do not comply with a statement of principle;
   (c) factors which, in the opinion of the Authority, are to be taken into account in determining whether or not a person's conduct complies with a statement of principle.
(4) The Authority may at any time alter or replace a statement or code issued under this section.
(5) If a statement or code is altered or replaced, the altered or replacement statement or code must be issued by the Authority.
(6) A statement or code issued under this section must be published by the Authority in the way appearing to the Authority to be best calculated to bring it to the attention of the public.
(7) A code published under this section and in force at the time when any particular conduct takes place may be relied on so far as it tends to establish whether or not that conduct complies with a statement of principle.
(8) Failure to comply with a statement of principle under this section does not of itself give rise to any right of action by persons affected or affect the validity of any transaction.
(9) A person is not to be taken to have failed to comply with a statement of principle if he shows that, at the time of the alleged failure, it or its associated code of practice had not been published.
(10) The Authority must, without delay, give the Treasury a copy of any statement or code which it publishes under this section.
(11) The power under this section to issue statements of principle and codes of practice—
   (a) includes power to make different provision in relation to persons, cases or circumstances of different descriptions; and

(b)   is to be treated for the purposes of section 2(4)(a) as part of the Authority's rule-making functions.

(12)   The Authority may charge a reasonable fee for providing a person with a copy of a statement or code published under this section.

(13)   "Approved person" means a person in relation to whom the Authority has given its approval under section 59.

[7.71]
65   Statements and codes: procedure

(1)   Before issuing a statement or code under section 64, the Authority must publish a draft of it in the way appearing to the Authority to be best calculated to bring it to the attention of the public.

(2)   The draft must be accompanied by—
  (a)   a cost benefit analysis; and
  (b)   notice that representations about the proposal may be made to the Authority within a specified time.

(3)   Before issuing the proposed statement or code, the Authority must have regard to any representations made to it in accordance with subsection (2)(b).

(4)   If the Authority issues the proposed statement or code it must publish an account, in general terms, of—
  (a)   the representations made to it in accordance with subsection (2)(b); and
  (b)   its response to them.

(5)   If the statement or code differs from the draft published under subsection (1) in a way which is, in the opinion of the Authority, significant—
  (a)   the Authority must (in addition to complying with subsection (4)) publish details of the difference; and
  (b)   those details must be accompanied by a cost benefit analysis.

(6)   Neither subsection (2)(a) nor subsection (5)(b) applies if the Authority considers—
  (a)   that, making the appropriate comparison, there will be no increase in costs; or
  (b)   that, making that comparison, there will be an increase in costs but the increase will be of minimal significance.

(7)   Subsections (1) to (6) do not apply if the Authority considers that the delay involved in complying with them would prejudice the interests of consumers.

(8)   A statement or code must state that it is issued under section 64.

(9)   The Authority may charge a reasonable fee for providing a copy of a draft published under subsection (1).

(10)   This section also applies to a proposal to alter or replace a statement or code.

(11)   "Cost benefit analysis" means an estimate of the costs together with an analysis of the benefits that will arise—
  (a)   if the proposed statement or code is issued; or
  (b)   if subsection (5)(b) applies, from the statement or code that has been issued.

(12)   "The appropriate comparison" means—
  (a)   in relation to subsection (2)(a), a comparison between the overall position if the statement or code is issued and the overall position if it is not issued;
  (b)   in relation to subsection (5)(b), a comparison between the overall position after the issuing of the statement or code and the overall position before it was issued.

NOTES

Application in relation to interim permissions and interim approvals: see the notes preceding s 40 at **[7.42]**.

[7.72]
66   Disciplinary powers

(1)   The Authority may take action against a person under this section if—
  (a)   it appears to the Authority that he is guilty of misconduct; and
  (b)   the Authority is satisfied that it is appropriate in all the circumstances to take action against him.

(2)   A person is guilty of misconduct if, while an approved person—
  (a)   he has failed to comply with a statement of principle issued under section 64; or
  (b)   he has been knowingly concerned in a contravention by the relevant authorised person of a requirement imposed on that authorised person by or under this Act [or by any directly applicable Community regulation [or decision] made under the markets in financial instruments directive] [or the UCITS directive].

(3)   If the Authority is entitled to take action under this section against a person, [it may do one or more of the following—]
  (a)   impose a penalty on him of such amount as it considers appropriate;
  [(aa)   suspend, for such period as it considers appropriate, any approval of the performance by him of any function to which the approval relates;
  (ab)   impose, for such period as it considers appropriate, such limitations or other restrictions in relation to the performance by him of any function to which any approval relates as it considers appropriate;] or

(b)   publish a statement of his misconduct.

[(3A)   The period for which a suspension or restriction is to have effect may not exceed two years.

(3B)   A suspension or restriction may have effect in relation to part of a function.

(3C)   A restriction may, in particular, be imposed so as to require any person to take, or refrain from taking, specified action.

(3D)   The Authority may—
(a)   withdraw a suspension or restriction; or
(b)   vary a suspension or restriction so as to reduce the period for which it has effect or otherwise to limit its effect.]

(4)   The Authority may not take action under this section after the end of the period of [three years] beginning with the first day on which the Authority knew of the misconduct, unless proceedings in respect of it against the person concerned were begun before the end of that period.

(5)   For the purposes of subsection (4)—
(a)   the Authority is to be treated as knowing of misconduct if it has information from which the misconduct can reasonably be inferred; and
(b)   proceedings against a person in respect of misconduct are to be treated as begun when a warning notice is given to him under section 67(1).

[(5A)   Approval" means an approval given under section 59.]

(6)   "Approved person" has the same meaning as in section 64.

(7)   "Relevant authorised person", in relation to an approved person, means the person on whose application approval   .   .   .   was given.

[(8)   In relation to any time while a suspension is in force under subsection (3)(aa) in relation to part of a function, any reference in section 59 or 63A to the performance of a function includes the performance of part of a function.

(9)   If at any time a restriction imposed under subsection (3)(ab) is contravened, the approval in relation to the person concerned is to be treated for the purposes of sections 59 and 63A as if it had been withdrawn at that time.]

NOTES

Sub-s (2): words in first (outer) pair of square brackets inserted by the Financial Services and Markets Act 2000 (Markets in Financial Instruments) Regulations 2007, SI 2007/126, reg 3(5), Sch 5, paras 1, 5, as from 1 April 2007 (certain purposes), and as from 1 November 2007 (otherwise); words in second (inner) pair of square brackets and words in third pair of square brackets inserted by the Undertakings for Collective Investment in Transferable Securities Regulations 2011, SI 2011/1613, reg 2(1), (2), as from 1 July 2011.

Sub-s (3): words in first pair of square brackets substituted, and paras (aa), (ab) inserted, by the Financial Services Act 2010, s 12(1), (2), as from 8 June 2010.

Sub-ss (3A)–(3D): inserted by the Financial Services Act 2010, s 12(1), (3), as from 8 June 2010.

Sub-s (4): words in square brackets substituted by the Financial Services Act 2010, s 12(1), (4), as from 8 June 2010.

Sub-s (5A): inserted by the Financial Services Act 2010, s 24(1), (2), Sch 2, Pt 1, paras 1, 8(1), (2), as from 8 June 2010.

Sub-s (7): words omitted repealed by the Financial Services Act 2010, s 24(1), (2), Sch 2, Pt 1, paras 1, 8(1), (3), as from 8 June 2010.

Sub-ss (8), (9): added by the Financial Services Act 2010, s 24(1), (2), Sch 2, Pt 1, paras 1, 8(1), (4), as from 8 June 2010.

As to the power of the Financial Services Authority to take action under this section in relation to persons who were formerly registered individuals (or registered persons) under the rules of a self-regulating organisation, in the case of a failure to comply with, or an act of misconduct or a contravention under, those rules, see the Financial Services and Markets Act 2000 (Transitional Provisions and Savings) (Civil Remedies, Discipline, Criminal Offences etc) (No 2) Order 2001, SI 2001/3083, art 9.

[7.73]
67   Disciplinary measures: procedure and right to refer to Tribunal

(1)   If the Authority proposes to take action against a person under section 66, it must give him a warning notice[; and if it proposes to take action under subsection (3)(aa) or (ab) of that section, it must also give each of the other interested parties a warning notice].

(2)   A warning notice about a proposal to impose a penalty must state the amount of the penalty.

[(2A)   A warning notice about a proposal—
(a)   to suspend an approval, or
(b)   to impose a restriction in relation to the performance of a function,
must state the period for which the suspension or restriction is to have effect.]

(3)   A warning notice about a proposal to publish a statement must set out the terms of the statement.

(4)   If the Authority decides to take action against a person under section 66, it must give him a decision notice[; and if it decides to take action under subsection (3)(aa) or (ab) of that section, it must also give each of the other interested parties a decision notice].

(5)   A decision notice about the imposition of a penalty must state the amount of the penalty.

[(5A)   A decision notice about—
(a)   the suspension of an approval, or
(b)   the imposition of a restriction in relation to the performance of a function,
must state the period for which the suspension or restriction is to have effect.]

(6)   A decision notice about the publication of a statement must set out the terms of the statement.

(7)   If the Authority decides to take action against a person under section 66, he may refer the matter to the Tribunal[; and if the Authority decides to take action under section 66(3)(aa) or (ab), each of the other interested parties may also refer the matter to the Tribunal].

[(8)   Approval" means an approval given under section 59.

(9)   "Other interested parties", in relation to an approved person ("A"), are—

   (a)   the person on whose application the approval was given ("B"); and

   (b)   the person by whom A's services are retained, if not B.

The reference in this subsection to an approved person has the same meaning as in section 64.]

NOTES

Sub-ss (1), (4), (7): words in square brackets added by the Financial Services Act 2010, s 24(1), (2), Sch 2, Pt 1, paras 1, 9(1), (2), (4), (6), as from 8 June 2010.

Sub-s (2A), (5A), (8), (9): inserted and added respectively by the Financial Services Act 2010, s 24(1), (2), Sch 2, Pt 1, paras 1, 9(1), (3), (5), (7), as from 8 June 2010.

[7.74]
68   Publication
After a statement under section 66 is published, the Authority must send a copy of it to the person concerned and to any person to whom a copy of the decision notice was given.

[7.75]
69   Statement of policy
(1)   The Authority must prepare and issue a statement of its policy with respect to—

   [(a)   the imposition of penalties, suspensions or restrictions under section 66;

   (b)   the amount of penalties under that section; and

   (c)   the period for which suspensions or restrictions under that section are to have effect.]

(2)   The Authority's policy in determining what the amount of a penalty should be[, or what the period for which a suspension or restriction is to have effect should be,] must include having regard to—

   (a)   the seriousness of the misconduct in question in relation to the nature of the principle or requirement concerned;

   (b)   the extent to which that misconduct was deliberate or reckless; and

   (c)   whether [the person against whom action is to be taken] is an individual.

(3)   The Authority may at any time alter or replace a statement issued under this section.

(4)   If a statement issued under this section is altered or replaced, the Authority must issue the altered or replacement statement.

(5)   The Authority must, without delay, give the Treasury a copy of any statement which it publishes under this section.

(6)   A statement issued under this section must be published by the Authority in the way appearing to the Authority to be best calculated to bring it to the attention of the public.

(7)   The Authority may charge a reasonable fee for providing a person with a copy of the statement.

(8)   In exercising, or deciding whether to exercise, its power under section 66 in the case of any particular misconduct, the Authority must have regard to any statement of policy published under this section and in force at the time when the misconduct in question occurred.

NOTES

Sub-s (1): paras (a)–(c) substituted for original paras (a), (b), by the Financial Services Act 2010, s 24(1), (2), Sch 2, Pt 1, paras 1, 10(1), (2), as from 8 June 2010.

Sub-s (2): words in first pair of square brackets inserted, and words in second pair of square brackets substituted, by the Financial Services Act 2010, s 24(1), (2), Sch 2, Pt 1, paras 1, 10(1), (3), as from 8 June 2010.

[7.76]
70   Statements of policy: procedure
(1)   Before issuing a statement under section 69, the Authority must publish a draft of the proposed statement in the way appearing to the Authority to be best calculated to bring it to the attention of the public.

(2)   The draft must be accompanied by notice that representations about the proposal may be made to the Authority within a specified time.

(3)   Before issuing the proposed statement, the Authority must have regard to any representations made to it in accordance with subsection (2).

(4)   If the Authority issues the proposed statement it must publish an account, in general terms, of—

   (a)   the representations made to it in accordance with subsection (2); and

   (b)   its response to them.

(5)   If the statement differs from the draft published under subsection (1) in a way which is, in the opinion of the Authority, significant, the Authority must (in addition to complying with subsection (4)) publish details of the difference.

(6)   The Authority may charge a reasonable fee for providing a person with a copy of a draft published under subsection (1).

(7)   This section also applies to a proposal to alter or replace a statement.

Breach of statutory duty

[7.77]
71   Actions for damages
(1)   A contravention of section 56(6) or 59(1) or (2) is actionable at the suit of a private person who suffers loss as a result of the contravention, subject to the defences and other incidents applying to actions for breach of statutory duty.

(2)   In prescribed cases, a contravention of that kind which would be actionable at the suit of a private person is actionable at the suit of a person who is not a private person, subject to the defences and other incidents applying to actions for breach of statutory duty.

(3)   "Private person" has such meaning as may be prescribed.

NOTES

Regulations: the Financial Services and Markets Act 2000 (Rights of Action) Regulations 2001, SI 2001/2256.

PART VI
OFFICIAL LISTING

NOTES

Transitional provisions: see the Financial Services and Markets Act 2000 (Official Listing of Securities) (Transitional Provisions) Order 2001, SI 2001/2957 which makes transitional provisions in relation to the listing of securities under this Act instead of the Financial Services Act 1986 (repealed).

The competent authority

[7.78]
72   The competent authority
(1)   On the coming into force of this section, the functions conferred on the competent authority by this Part are to be exercised by the Authority.

(2)   Schedule 7 modifies this Act in its application to the Authority when it acts as the competent authority.

(3)   But provision is made by Schedule 8 allowing some or all of those functions to be transferred by the Treasury so as to be exercisable by another person.

[7.79]
73   General duty of the competent authority
(1)   In discharging its general functions the competent authority must have regard to—
  (a)   the need to use its resources in the most efficient and economic way;
  (b)   the principle that a burden or restriction which is imposed on a person should be proportionate to the benefits, considered in general terms, which are expected to arise from the imposition of that burden or restriction;
  [(c)   the desirability of facilitating innovation in respect of listed securities and in respect of financial instruments which have otherwise been admitted to trading on a regulated market or for which a request for admission to trading on such a market has been made;]
  (d)   the international character of capital markets and the desirability of maintaining the competitive position of the United Kingdom;
  (e)   the need to minimise the adverse effects on competition of anything done in the discharge of those functions;
  [(f)   the desirability of facilitating competition in relation to listed securities and in relation to financial instruments which have otherwise been admitted to trading on a regulated market or for which a request for admission to trading on such a market has been made.]

[(1A)   To the extent that those general functions are functions under or relating to transparency rules, subsection (1)(c) and (f) have effect as if the references to a regulated market were references to a market.]

(2)   The competent authority's general functions are—
  (a)   its function of making rules under this Part (considered as a whole);
  (b)   its functions in relation to the giving of general guidance in relation to this Part (considered as a whole);
  (c)   its function of determining the general policy and principles by reference to which it performs particular functions under this Part.

NOTES

Sub-s (1): paras (c), (f) substituted by the Financial Services and Markets Act 2000 (Market Abuse) Regulations 2005, SI 2005/381, reg 4, Sch 1, para 1, as from 1 July 2005.

Sub-s (1A): inserted by the Companies Act 2006, s 1272, Sch 15, Pt 1, paras 1, 2, as from 8 November 2006.

[7.80]
[73A   Part 6 Rules
(1)   The competent authority may make rules ("Part 6 rules") for the purposes of this Part.

(2) Provisions of Part 6 rules expressed to relate to the official list are referred to in this Part as "listing rules".

(3) Provisions of Part 6 rules expressed to relate to disclosure of information in respect of financial instruments which have been admitted to trading on a regulated market or for which a request for admission to trading on such a market has been made, are referred to in this Part as "disclosure rules".

[(4) Provisions of Part 6 rules expressed to relate to transferable securities are referred to in this Part as "prospectus rules".

(5) In relation to prospectus rules, the purposes of this Part include the purposes of the prospectus directive.]

[(6) Transparency rules and corporate governance rules are not listing rules, disclosure rules or prospectus rules, but are Part 6 rules.]]

NOTES

Inserted by the Financial Services and Markets Act 2000 (Market Abuse) Regulations 2005, SI 2005/381, reg 4, Sch 1, para 2, as from 17 March 2005.

Sub-ss (4), (5): added by the Prospectus Regulations 2005, SI 2005/1433, reg 2(1), Sch 1, para 1, as from 1 July 2005.

Sub-s (6): added by the Companies Act 2006, s 1272, Sch 15, Pt 1, paras 1, 3, as from 8 November 2006.

The official list

[7.81]
74 The official list

(1) The competent authority must maintain the official list.

(2) The competent authority may admit to the official list such securities and other things as it considers appropriate.

(3) But—
  (a) nothing may be admitted to the official list except in accordance with this Part; and
  (b) the Treasury may by order provide that anything which falls within a description or category specified in the order may not be admitted to the official list.

(4) . . .

(5) In the following provisions of this Part—

  . . .

  "listing" means being included in the official list in accordance with this Part.

NOTES

Sub-s (4): repealed by the Financial Services and Markets Act 2000 (Market Abuse) Regulations 2005, SI 2005/381, reg 4, Sch 1, para 3, as from 17 March 2005.

Sub-s (5): definition "security" (omitted) repealed by the Prospectus Regulations 2005, SI 2005/1433, reg 2(1), Sch 1, para 2, as from 1 July 2005.

Note: the Financial Services and Markets Act 2000 (Official Listing of Securities) Regulations 2001, SI 2001/2956 at **[8.237]** prescribes certain bodies whose securities may not be considered for listing under this Part.

Listing

[7.82]
75 Applications for listing

(1) Admission to the official list may be granted only on an application made to the competent authority in such manner as may be required by listing rules.

(2) No application for listing may be entertained by the competent authority unless it is made by, or with the consent of, the issuer of the securities concerned.

(3) No application for listing may be entertained by the competent authority in respect of securities which are to be issued by a body of a prescribed kind.

(4) The competent authority may not grant an application for listing unless it is satisfied that—
  (a) the requirements of listing rules (so far as they apply to the application), and
  (b) any other requirements imposed by the authority in relation to the application,
are complied with.

(5) An application for listing may be refused if, for a reason relating to the issuer, the competent authority considers that granting it would be detrimental to the interests of investors.

(6) An application for listing securities which are already officially listed in another EEA State may be refused if the issuer has failed to comply with any obligations to which he is subject as a result of that listing.

NOTES

Regulations: the Financial Services and Markets Act 2000 (Official Listing of Securities) Regulations 2001, SI 2001/2956 at **[8.237]**.

Note that the following amending Regulations have also been made under this section: the Financial Services and Markets Act 2000 (Official Listing of Securities) (Amendment) Regulations 2001, SI 2001/3439.

[7.83]

76 Decision on application

(1) The competent authority must notify the applicant of its decision on an application for listing—

 (a) before the end of the period of six months beginning with the date on which the application is received; or

 (b) if within that period the authority has required the applicant to provide further information in connection with the application, before the end of the period of six months beginning with the date on which that information is provided.

(2) If the competent authority fails to comply with subsection (1), it is to be taken to have decided to refuse the application.

(3) If the competent authority decides to grant an application for listing, it must give the applicant written notice.

(4) If the competent authority proposes to refuse an application for listing, it must give the applicant a warning notice.

(5) If the competent authority decides to refuse an application for listing, it must give the applicant a decision notice.

(6) If the competent authority decides to refuse an application for listing, the applicant may refer the matter to the Tribunal.

(7) If securities are admitted to the official list, their admission may not be called in question on the ground that any requirement or condition for their admission has not been complied with.

[7.84]

77 Discontinuance and suspension of listing

(1) The competent authority may, in accordance with listing rules, discontinue the listing of any securities if satisfied that there are special circumstances which preclude normal regular dealings in them.

(2) The competent authority may, in accordance with listing rules, suspend the listing of any securities.

[(2A) The competent authority may discontinue under subsection (1) or suspend under subsection (2) the listing of any securities on its own initiative or on the application of the issuer of those securities.]

(3) If securities are suspended under subsection (2) they are to be treated, for the purposes of sections 96 and 99, as still being listed.

(4) This section applies to securities whenever they were admitted to the official list.

(5) If the competent authority discontinues or suspends the listing of any securities, [on its own initiative,] the issuer may refer the matter to the Tribunal.

NOTES

Sub-s (2A): inserted by the Regulatory Reform (Financial Services and Markets Act 2000) Order 2007, SI 2007/1973, arts 2, 5(a), as from 12 July 2007.

Sub-s (5): words in square brackets inserted by SI 2007/1973, arts 2, 5(b), as from 12 July 2007.

[7.85]

78 Discontinuance or suspension: procedure

(1) A discontinuance or suspension [by the competent authority on its own initiative] takes effect—

 (a) immediately, if the notice under subsection (2) states that that is the case;

 (b) in any other case, on such date as may be specified in that notice.

(2) If [on its own initiative] the competent authority—

 (a) proposes to discontinue or suspend the listing of securities, or

 (b) discontinues or suspends the listing of securities with immediate effect,

it must give the issuer of the securities written notice.

(3) The notice must—

 (a) give details of the discontinuance or suspension;

 (b) state the competent authority's reasons for the discontinuance or suspension and for choosing the date on which it took effect or takes effect;

 (c) inform the issuer of the securities that he may make representations to the competent authority within such period as may be specified in the notice (whether or not he has referred the matter to the Tribunal);

 (d) inform him of the date on which the discontinuance or suspension took effect or will take effect; and

 (e) inform him of his right to refer the matter to the Tribunal.

(4) The competent authority may extend the period within which representations may be made to it.

(5) If, having considered any representations made by the issuer of the securities, the competent authority decides—

 (a) to discontinue or suspend the listing of the securities, or

 (b) if the discontinuance or suspension has taken effect, not to cancel it, the competent authority must give the issuer of the securities written notice.

(6) A notice given under subsection (5) must inform the issuer of the securities of his right to refer the matter to the Tribunal.

(7) If a notice informs a person of his right to refer a matter to the Tribunal, it must give an indication of the procedure on such a reference.

(8) If the competent authority decides—

   (a)   not to discontinue or suspend the listing of the securities, or

   (b)   if the discontinuance or suspension has taken effect, to cancel it,

the competent authority must give the issuer of the securities written notice.

(9) The effect of cancelling a discontinuance is that the securities concerned are to be readmitted, without more, to the official list.

(10) If the competent authority has suspended the listing of securities [on its own initiative] and proposes to refuse an application by the issuer of the securities for the cancellation of the suspension, it must give him a warning notice.

(11) The competent authority must, having considered any representations made in response to the warning notice—

   (a)   if it decides to refuse the application, give the issuer of the securities a decision notice;

   (b)   if it grants the application, give him written notice of its decision.

(12) If the competent authority decides to refuse an application for the cancellation of the suspension of listed securities, the applicant may refer the matter to the Tribunal.

(13) "Discontinuance" means a discontinuance of listing under section 77(1).

(14) "Suspension" means a suspension of listing under section 77(2).

NOTES

Sub-ss (1), (2), (10): words in square brackets inserted by the Regulatory Reform (Financial Services and Markets Act 2000) Order 2007, SI 2007/1973, arts 2, 6, as from 12 July 2007.

[7.86]
[78A   Discontinuance or suspension at the request of the issuer: procedure

(1) A discontinuance or suspension by the competent authority on the application of the issuer of the securities takes effect—

   (a)   immediately, if the notice under subsection (2) states that this is the case;

   (b)   in any other case, on such date as may be specified in that notice.

(2) If the competent authority discontinues or suspends the listing of securities on the application of the issuer of the securities it must give him written notice.

(3) The notice must—

   (a)   give details of the discontinuance or suspension;

   (b)   inform the issuer of the securities of the date on which the discontinuance or suspension took effect or will take effect; and

   (c)   inform the issuer of his right to apply for the cancellation of the suspension.

(4) If the competent authority proposes to refuse an application by the issuer of the securities for the discontinuance or suspension of the listing of the securities, it must give him a warning notice.

(5) The competent authority must, having considered any representations made in response to the warning notice, if it decides to refuse the application, give the issuer of the securities a decision notice.

(6) If the competent authority decides to refuse an application by the issuer of the securities for the discontinuance or suspension of the listing of the securities, the issuer may refer the matter to the Tribunal.

(7) If the competent authority has suspended the listing of securities on the application of the issuer of the securities and proposes to refuse an application by the issuer for the cancellation of the suspension, it must give him a warning notice.

(8) The competent authority must, having considered any representations made in response to the warning notice—

   (a)   if it decides to refuse the application for the cancellation of the suspension, give the issuer of the securities a decision notice;

   (b)   if it grants the application, give him written notice of its decision.

(9) If the competent authority decides to refuse an application for the cancellation of the suspension of listed securities, the applicant may refer the matter to the Tribunal.

(10) "Discontinuance" means a discontinuance of listing under section 77(1).

(11) "Suspension" means a suspension of listing under section 77(2).]

NOTES

Commencement: 12 July 2007.

Inserted by the Regulatory Reform (Financial Services and Markets Act 2000) Order 2007, SI 2007/1973, arts 2, 7, as from 12 July 2007.

Listing particulars

[7.87]
79 Listing particulars and other documents

(1) Listing rules may provide that securities . . . of a kind specified in the rules may not be admitted to the official list unless—

    (a) listing particulars have been submitted to, and approved by, the competent authority and published; or

    (b) in such cases as may be specified by listing rules, such document (other than listing particulars or a prospectus of a kind required by listing rules) as may be so specified has been published.

(2) "Listing particulars" means a document in such form and containing such information as may be specified in listing rules.

(3) For the purposes of this Part, the persons responsible for listing particulars are to be determined in accordance with regulations made by the Treasury.

[(3A) Listing rules made under subsection (1) may not specify securities of a kind for which an approved prospectus is required as a result of section 85.]

(4) Nothing in this section affects the competent authority's general power to make listing rules.

NOTES

    Sub-s (1): words omitted repealed by the Prospectus Regulations 2005, SI 2005/1433, reg 2(1), Sch 1, para 3(1), (2), as from 1 July 2005.

    Sub-s (3A): inserted by SI 2005/1433, reg 2(1), Sch 1, para 3(1), (3), as from 1 July 2005.

    Regulations: the Financial Services and Markets Act 2000 (Official Listing of Securities) Regulations 2001, SI 2001/2956 at **[8.237]**.

[7.88]
80 General duty of disclosure in listing particulars

(1) Listing particulars submitted to the competent authority under section 79 must contain all such information as investors and their professional advisers would reasonably require, and reasonably expect to find there, for the purpose of making an informed assessment of—

    (a) the assets and liabilities, financial position, profits and losses, and prospects of the issuer of the securities; and

    (b) the rights attaching to the securities.

(2) That information is required in addition to any information required by—

    (a) listing rules, or

    (b) the competent authority,

as a condition of the admission of the securities to the official list.

(3) Subsection (1) applies only to information—

    (a) within the knowledge of any person responsible for the listing particulars; or

    (b) which it would be reasonable for him to obtain by making enquiries.

(4) In determining what information subsection (1) requires to be included in listing particulars, regard must be had (in particular) to—

    (a) the nature of the securities and their issuer;

    (b) the nature of the persons likely to consider acquiring them;

    (c) the fact that certain matters may reasonably be expected to be within the knowledge of professional advisers of a kind which persons likely to acquire the securities may reasonably be expected to consult; and

    (d) any information available to investors or their professional advisers as a result of requirements imposed on the issuer of the securities by a recognised investment exchange, by listing rules or by or under any other enactment.

[7.89]
81 Supplementary listing particulars

(1) If at any time after the preparation of listing particulars which have been submitted to the competent authority under section 79 and before the commencement of dealings in the securities concerned following their admission to the official list—

    (a) there is a significant change affecting any matter contained in those particulars the inclusion of which was required by—

        (i) section 80,

        (ii) listing rules, or

        (iii) the competent authority, or

    (b) a significant new matter arises, the inclusion of information in respect of which would have been so required if it had arisen when the particulars were prepared,

the issuer must, in accordance with listing rules, submit supplementary listing particulars of the change or new matter to the competent authority, for its approval and, if they are approved, publish them.

(2) "Significant" means significant for the purpose of making an informed assessment of the kind mentioned in section 80(1).

(3)   If the issuer of the securities is not aware of the change or new matter in question, he is not under a duty to comply with subsection (1) unless he is notified of the change or new matter by a person responsible for the listing particulars.

(4)   But it is the duty of any person responsible for those particulars who is aware of such a change or new matter to give notice of it to the issuer.

(5)   Subsection (1) applies also as respects matters contained in any supplementary listing particulars previously published under this section in respect of the securities in question.

[7.90]
82   Exemptions from disclosure

(1)   The competent authority may authorise the omission from listing particulars of any information, the inclusion of which would otherwise be required by section 80 or 81, on the ground—

   (a)   that its disclosure would be contrary to the public interest;

   (b)   that its disclosure would be seriously detrimental to the issuer; or

   (c)   in the case of securities of a kind specified in listing rules, that its disclosure is unnecessary for persons of the kind who may be expected normally to buy or deal in securities of that kind.

(2)   But—

   (a)   no authority may be granted under subsection (1)(b) in respect of essential information; and

   (b)   no authority granted under subsection (1)(b) extends to any such information.

(3)   The Secretary of State or the Treasury may issue a certificate to the effect that the disclosure of any information (including information that would otherwise have to be included in listing particulars for which they are themselves responsible) would be contrary to the public interest.

(4)   The competent authority is entitled to act on any such certificate in exercising its powers under subsection (1)(a).

(5)   This section does not affect any powers of the competent authority under listing rules made as a result of section 101(2).

(6)   "Essential information" means information which a person considering acquiring securities of the kind in question would be likely to need in order not to be misled about any facts which it is essential for him to know in order to make an informed assessment.

(7)   "Listing particulars" includes supplementary listing particulars.

83   *(Repealed by the Prospectus Regulations 2005, SI 2005/1433, reg 2(1), Sch 1, para 4, as from 1 July 2005.)*

[Transferable securities: public offers and admission to trading

[7.91]
84   Matters which may be dealt with by prospectus rules

(1)   Prospectus rules may make provision as to—

   (a)   the required form and content of a prospectus (including a summary);

   (b)   the cases in which a summary need not be included in a prospectus;

   (c)   the languages which may be used in a prospectus (including a summary);

   (d)   the determination of the persons responsible for a prospectus;

   (e)   the manner in which applications to the competent authority for the approval of a prospectus are to be made.

(2)   Prospectus rules may also make provision as to—

   (a)   the period of validity of a prospectus;

   (b)   the disclosure of the maximum price or of the criteria or conditions according to which the final offer price is to be determined, if that information is not contained in a prospectus;

   (c)   the disclosure of the amount of the transferable securities which are to be offered to the public or of the criteria or conditions according to which that amount is to be determined, if that information is not contained in a prospectus;

   (d)   the required form and content of other summary documents (including the languages which may be used in such a document);

   (e)   the ways in which a prospectus that has been approved by the competent authority may be made available to the public;

   (f)   the disclosure, publication or other communication of such information as the competent authority may reasonably stipulate;

   (g)   the principles to be observed in relation to advertisements in connection with an offer of transferable securities to the public or admission of transferable securities to trading on a regulated market and the enforcement of those principles;

   (h)   the suspension of trading in transferable securities where continued trading would be detrimental to the interests of investors;

   (i)   elections under section 87 or under Article 2.1(m)(iii) of the prospectus directive as applied for the purposes of this Part by section 102C

(3)   Prospectus rules may also make provision as to—

   (a)   access to the register of investors maintained under section 87R; and

(b)   the supply of information from that register.

(4)   Prospectus rules may make provision for the purpose of dealing with matters arising out of or related to any provision of the prospectus directive.

(5)   In relation to cases where the home State in relation to an issuer of transferable securities is an EEA State other than the United Kingdom, prospectus rules may make provision for the recognition of elections made in relation to such securities under the law of that State in accordance with Article 1.3 or 2.1(m)(iii) of the prospectus directive.

(6)   In relation to a document relating to transferable securities issued by an issuer incorporated in a non-EEA State and drawn up in accordance with the law of that State, prospectus rules may make provision as to the approval of that document as a prospectus.

(7)   Nothing in this section affects the competent authority's general power to make prospectus rules.]

NOTES

Sections 84–87, 87A–87R substituted (together with the preceding heading) for original ss 84–87, by the Prospectus Regulations 2005, SI 2005/1433, reg 2(1), Sch 1, para 5, as from 1 July 2005.

[7.92]
[85   Prohibition of dealing etc in transferable securities without approved prospectus

(1)   It is unlawful for transferable securities to which this subsection applies to be offered to the public in the United Kingdom unless an approved prospectus has been made available to the public before the offer is made.

(2)   It is unlawful to request the admission of transferable securities to which this subsection applies to trading on a regulated market situated or operating in the United Kingdom unless an approved prospectus has been made available to the public before the request is made.

(3)   A person who contravenes subsection (1) or (2) is guilty of an offence and liable—

   (a)   on summary conviction, to imprisonment for a term not exceeding 3 months or a fine not exceeding the statutory maximum or both;

   (b)   on conviction on indictment, to imprisonment for a term not exceeding 2 years or a fine or both.

(4)   A contravention of subsection (1) or (2) is actionable, at the suit of a person who suffers loss as a result of the contravention, subject to the defences and other incidents applying to actions for breach of statutory duty.

(5)   Subsection (1) applies to all transferable securities other than—

   (a)   those listed in Schedule 11A;

   (b)   such other transferable securities as may be specified in prospectus rules.

(6)   Subsection (2) applies to all transferable securities other than—

   (a)   those listed in Part 1 of Schedule 11A;

   (b)   such other transferable securities as may be specified in prospectus rules.

(7)   "Approved prospectus" means, in relation to transferable securities to which this section applies, a prospectus approved by the competent authority of the home State in relation to the issuer of the securities.]

NOTES

Substituted as noted to s 84 at **[7.91]**.

[7.93]
[86   Exempt offers to the public

(1)   A person does not contravene section 85(1) if—

   (a)   the offer is made to or directed at qualified investors only;

   (b)   the offer is made to or directed at fewer than [150 persons], other than qualified investors, per EEA State;

   (c)   the minimum consideration which may be paid by any person for transferable securities acquired by him pursuant to the offer is at least 50,000 euros (or an equivalent amount);

   (d)   the transferable securities being offered are denominated in amounts of at least 50,000 euros (or equivalent amounts); or

   (e)   the total consideration for the transferable securities being offered cannot exceed 100,000 euros (or an equivalent amount).

(2)   Where—

   (a)   a person who is not a qualified investor ("the client") has engaged a qualified investor falling within Article 2.1(e)(i) of the prospectus directive to act as his agent, and

   (b)   the terms on which the qualified investor is engaged enable him to make decisions concerning the acceptance of offers of transferable securities on the client's behalf without reference to the client,

an offer made to or directed at the qualified investor is not to be regarded for the purposes of subsection (1) as also having been made to or directed at the client.

(3)   For the purposes of subsection (1)(b), the making of an offer of transferable securities to—

   (a)   trustees of a trust,

   (b)   members of a partnership in their capacity as such, or

    (c)   two or more persons jointly,
is to be treated as the making of an offer to a single person.

(4)   In determining whether subsection (1)(e) is satisfied in relation to an offer ("offer A"), offer A is to be taken together with any other offer of transferable securities of the same class made by the same person which—

    (a)   was open at any time within the period of 12 months ending with the date on which offer A is first made; and

    (b)   had previously satisfied subsection (1)(e).

(5)   For the purposes of this section, an amount (in relation to an amount denominated in euros) is an "equivalent amount" if it is an amount of equal value denominated wholly or partly in another currency or unit of account.

(6)   The equivalent is to be calculated at the latest practicable date before (but in any event not more than 3 working days before) the date on which the offer is first made.

(7)   "Qualified investor" means—

    (a)   an entity falling within Article 2.1(e)(i), (ii) or (iii) of the prospectus directive;

    (b)   an investor registered on the register maintained by the competent authority under section 87R;

    (c)   an investor authorised by an EEA State other than the United Kingdom to be considered as a qualified investor for the purposes of the prospectus directive.]

NOTES

Substituted as noted to s 84 at **[7.91]**.

Sub-s (1): words in square brackets substituted by the Prospectus Regulations 2011, SI 2011/1668, reg 2(2), as from 31 July 2011.

[7.94]
[87   Election to have prospectus

(1)   A person who proposes—

    (a)   to issue transferable securities to which this section applies,

    (b)   to offer to the public transferable securities to which this section applies, or

    (c)   to request the admission to a regulated market of transferable securities to which this section applies,

may elect, in accordance with prospectus rules, to have a prospectus in relation to the securities.

(2)   If a person makes such an election, the provisions of this Part and of prospectus rules apply in relation to those transferable securities as if, in relation to an offer of the securities to the public or the admission of the securities to trading on a regulated market, they were transferable securities for which an approved prospectus would be required as a result of section 85.

(3)   Listing rules made under section 79 do not apply to securities which are the subject of an election.

(4)   The transferable securities to which this section applies are those which fall within any of the following paragraphs of Schedule 11A—

    (a)   paragraph 2,

    (b)   paragraph 4,

    (c)   paragraph 8, or

    (d)   paragraph 9,

where the United Kingdom is the home State in relation to the issuer of the securities.]

NOTES

Substituted as noted to s 84 at **[7.91]**.

[Approval of prospectus]

[7.95]
87A   Criteria for approval of prospectus by competent authority

(1)   The competent authority may not approve a prospectus unless it is satisfied that—

    (a)   the United Kingdom is the home State in relation to the issuer of the transferable securities to which it relates,

    (b)   the prospectus contains the necessary information, and

    (c)   all of the other requirements imposed by or in accordance with this Part or the prospectus directive have been complied with (so far as those requirements apply to a prospectus for the transferable securities in question).

(2)   The necessary information is the information necessary to enable investors to make an informed assessment of—

    (a)   the assets and liabilities, financial position, profits and losses, and prospects of the issuer of the transferable securities and of any guarantor; and

    (b)   the rights attaching to the transferable securities.

(3)   The necessary information must be presented in a form which is comprehensible and easy to analyse.

(4)   The necessary information must be prepared having regard to the particular nature of the transferable securities and their issuer.

(5)   The prospectus must include a summary (unless the transferable securities in question are ones in relation to which prospectus rules provide that a summary is not required).

(6)   The summary must, briefly and in non-technical language, convey the essential characteristics of, and risks associated with, the issuer, any guarantor and the transferable securities to which the prospectus relates.

(7)   Where the prospectus for which approval is sought does not include the final offer price or the amount of transferable securities to be offered to the public, the applicant must inform the competent authority in writing of that information as soon as that element is finalised.

(8)   "Prospectus" (except in subsection (5)) includes a supplementary prospectus.]

NOTES

Substituted as noted to s 84 at **[7.91]**.

[7.96]
[87B   Exemptions from disclosure

(1)   The competent authority may authorise the omission from a prospectus of any information, the inclusion of which would otherwise be required, on the ground—

   (a)   that its disclosure would be contrary to the public interest;

   (b)   that its disclosure would be seriously detrimental to the issuer, provided that the omission would be unlikely to mislead the public with regard to any facts or circumstances which are essential for an informed assessment of the kind mentioned in section 87A(2); or

   (c)   that the information is only of minor importance for a specific offer to the public or admission to trading on a regulated market and unlikely to influence an informed assessment of the kind mentioned in section 87A(2).

(2)   The Secretary of State or the Treasury may issue a certificate to the effect that the disclosure of any information would be contrary to the public interest.

(3)   The competent authority is entitled to act on any such certificate in exercising its powers under subsection (1)(a).

(4)   This section does not affect any powers of the competent authority under prospectus rules.

(5)   "Prospectus" includes a supplementary prospectus.]

NOTES

Substituted as noted to s 84 at **[7.91]**.

[7.97]
[87C   Consideration of application for approval

(1)   The competent authority must notify the applicant of its decision on an application for approval of a prospectus before the end of the period for consideration.

(2)   The period for consideration—

   (a)   begins with the first working day after the date on which the application is received; but

   (b)   if the competent authority gives a notice under subsection (4), is to be treated as beginning with the first working day after the date on which the notice is complied with.

(3)   The period for consideration is—

   (a)   except in the case of a new issuer, 10 working days; or

   (b)   in that case, 20 working days.

(4)   The competent authority may by notice in writing require a person who has applied for approval of a prospectus to provide—

   (a)   specified documents or documents of a specified description, or

   (b)   specified information or information of a specified description.

(5)   No notice under subsection (4) may be given after the end of the period, beginning with the first working day after the date on which the application is received, of—

   (a)   except in the case of a new issuer, 10 working days; or

   (b)   in that case, 20 working days.

(6)   Subsection (4) applies only to information and documents reasonably required in connection with the exercise by the competent authority of its functions in relation to the application.

(7)   The competent authority may require any information provided under this section to be provided in such form as it may reasonably require.

(8)   The competent authority may require—

   (a)   any information provided, whether in a document or otherwise, to be verified in such manner, or

   (b)   any document produced to be authenticated in such manner,

as it may reasonably require.

(9)   The competent authority must notify the applicant of its decision on an application for approval of a supplementary prospectus before the end of the period of 7 working days beginning with the date on which the application is received; and subsections (4) and (6) to (8) apply to such an application as they apply to an application for approval of a prospectus.

(10)   The competent authority's failure to comply with subsection (1) or (9) does not constitute approval of the application in question.

(11)   "New issuer" means an issuer of transferable securities which—

(a)   does not have transferable securities admitted to trading on any regulated market; and

(b)   has not previously offered transferable securities to the public.]

NOTES
Substituted as noted to s 84 at **[7.91]**.

[7.98]
[87D   Procedure for decision on application for approval
(1)   If the competent authority approves a prospectus, it must give the applicant written notice.
(2)   If the competent authority proposes to refuse to approve a prospectus, it must give the applicant written notice.
(3)   The notice must state the competent authority's reasons for the proposed refusal.
(4)   If the competent authority decides to refuse to approve a prospectus, it must give the applicant written notice.
(5)   The notice must—
     (a)   give the competent authority's reasons for refusing the application; and
     (b)   inform the applicant of his right to refer the matter to the Tribunal.
(6)   If the competent authority refuses to approve a prospectus, the applicant may refer the matter to the Tribunal.
(7)   In this section "prospectus" includes a supplementary prospectus.]

NOTES
Substituted as noted to s 84 at **[7.91]**.

[Transfer of application for approval of a prospectus

[7.99]
87E   Transfer by competent authority of application for approval
(1)   The competent authority may transfer an application for the approval of a prospectus or a supplementary prospectus to the competent authority of another EEA State ("the transferee authority").
(2)   Before doing so, the competent authority must obtain the agreement of the transferee authority.
(3)   The competent authority must inform the applicant of the transfer within 3 working days beginning with the first working day after the date of the transfer.
(4)   On making a transfer under subsection (1), the competent authority ceases to have functions under this Part in relation to the application transferred.]

NOTES
Substituted as noted to s 84 at **[7.91]**.

[7.100]
[87F   Transfer to competent authority of application for approval
(1)   Where the competent authority agrees to the transfer to it of an application for the approval of a prospectus made to the competent authority of another EEA State—
     (a)   the United Kingdom is to be treated for the purposes of this Part as the home State in relation to the issuer of the transferable securities to which the prospectus relates, and
     (b)   this Part applies to the application as if it had been made to the competent authority but with the modification in subsection (2).
(2)   Section 87C applies as if the date of the transfer were the date on which the application was received by the competent authority.]

NOTES
Substituted as noted to s 84 at **[7.91]**.

[Supplementary prospectus

[7.101]
87G   Supplementary prospectus
(1)   Subsection (2) applies if, during the relevant period, there arises or is noted a significant new factor, material mistake or inaccuracy relating to the information included in a prospectus approved by the competent authority.
(2)   The person on whose application the prospectus was approved must, in accordance with prospectus rules, submit a supplementary prospectus containing details of the new factor, mistake or inaccuracy to the competent authority for its approval.
(3)   The relevant period begins when the prospectus is approved and ends—
     (a)   with the closure of the offer of the transferable securities to which the prospectus relates; or
     (b)   when trading in those securities on a regulated market begins.
(4)   "Significant" means significant for the purposes of making an informed assessment of the kind mentioned in section 87A(2).

(5) Any person responsible for the prospectus who is aware of any new factor, mistake or inaccuracy which may require the submission of a supplementary prospectus in accordance with subsection (2) must give notice of it to—

   (a) the issuer of the transferable securities to which the prospectus relates, and

   (b) the person on whose application the prospectus was approved.

(6) A supplementary prospectus must provide sufficient information to correct any mistake or inaccuracy which gave rise to the need for it.

Subsection (1) applies also to information contained in any supplementary prospectus approved under this section.]

NOTES

Substi... to s 84 at **[7.91]**.

[7.102]
87H   *[Passporting*

Prospectus approved...

(1) A prospectus approved...
Kingdom is not an appr... another EEA State
provided the competent author... competent authority of an EEA State other than the United
... tus for the purposes of section 85 unless that authority has

   (a) a certificate of approval;

   (b) a copy of the prospectus as appr...

   (c) if requested by the competent authority;

(2) A document is not a certificate of approval unless... lation of the summary of the prospectus.

   (a) has been drawn up in accordance with the prospectus... ates that the prospectus—

   (b) has been approved, in accordance with that directive, by the... irective; and the certificate. ... competent authority providing

(3) A document is not a certificate of approval... unless it states whether (and, if so, why) the
competent authority providing... authorised, in ac... rdance with the prospectus directive, the
omission from the prospectus of information which... uld otherwise have been required to be
included.

(4) "Prospectus" includes a supplementary prospectus.]

NOTES

Substituted as noted to s 84 at **[7.91]**.

[7.103]
[87I   Provision of information to host Member State

(1) The competent authority must, if requested to do so, supply the competent authority of a specified EEA State with—

   (a) a certificate of approval;

   (b) a copy of the specified prospectus (as approved by the competent authority); and

   (c) a translation of the summary of the specified prospectus (if the request states that one has been requested by the other competent authority).

(2) Only the following may make a request under this section—

   (a) the issuer of the transferable securities to which the specified prospectus relates;

   (b) a person who wishes to offer the transferable securities to which the specified prospectus relates to the public in an EEA State other than (or as well as) the United Kingdom;

   (c) a person requesting the admission of the transferable securities to which the specified prospectus relates to a regulated market situated or operating in an EEA State other than (or as well as) the United Kingdom.

(3) A certificate of approval must state that the prospectus—

   (a) has been drawn up in accordance with this Part and the prospectus directive; and

   (b) has been approved, in accordance with those provisions, by the competent authority.

(4) A certificate of approval must state whether (and, if so, why) the competent authority authorised, in accordance with section 87B, the omission from the prospectus of information which would otherwise have been required to be included.

(5) The competent authority must comply with a request under this section—

   (a) if the prospectus has been approved before the request is made, within 3 working days beginning with the date of the request; or

   (b) if the request is submitted with an application for the approval of the prospectus, on the first working day after the date on which it approves the prospectus.

(6) "Prospectus" includes a supplementary prospectus.

(7) "Specified" means specified in a request made for the purposes of this section.]

NOTES

Substituted as noted to s 84 at **[7.91]**.

[Transferable securities: powers of competent authority

[7.104]

87J Requirements imposed as condition of approval

(1) As a condition of approving a prospectus, the competent authority may by notice in writing—

   (a) require the inclusion in the prospectus of such supplementary information necessary for investor protection as the competent authority may specify;

   (b) require a person controlling, or controlled by, the applicant to provide specified information or documents;

   (c) require an auditor or manager of the applicant to provide specified information or documents;

   (d) require a financial intermediary commissioned to assist either in carrying out the offer to the public of the transferable securities to which the prospectus relates, or in requesting their admission to trading on a regulated market, to provide specified information or documents.

(2) "Specified" means specified in the notice.

(3) "Prospectus" includes a supplementary prospectus.]

NOTES

Substituted as noted to s 84 at **[7.91]**.

[7.105]

[87K Power to suspend or prohibit offer to public

(1) This section applies where a person ("the offeror") has made an offer of transferable securities to the public in the United Kingdom ("the offer").

(2) If the competent authority has reasonable grounds for suspecting that an applicable provision has been infringed, it may—

   (a) require the offeror to suspend the offer for a period not exceeding 10 working days;

   (b) require a person not to advertise the offer, or to take such steps as the authority may specify to suspend any existing advertisement of the offer, for a period not exceeding 10 working days.

(3) If the competent authority has reasonable grounds for suspecting that it is likely that an applicable provision will be infringed, it may require the offeror to withdraw the offer.

(4) If the competent authority finds that an applicable provision has been infringed, it may require the offeror to withdraw the offer.

(5) "An applicable provision" means—

   (a) a provision of this Part,

   (b) a provision contained in prospectus rules,

   (c) any other provision made in accordance with the prospectus directive,

applicable in relation to the offer.]

NOTES

Substituted as noted to s 84 at **[7.91]**.

[7.106]

[87L Power to suspend or prohibit admission to trading on a regulated market

(1) This section applies where a person has requested the admission of transferable securities to trading on a regulated market situated or operating in the United Kingdom.

(2) If the competent authority has reasonable grounds for suspecting that an applicable provision has been infringed and the securities have not yet been admitted to trading on the regulated market in question, it may—

   (a) require the person requesting admission to suspend the request for a period not exceeding 10 working days;

   (b) require a person not to advertise the securities to which it relates, or to take such steps as the authority may specify to suspend any existing advertisement in connection with those securities, for a period not exceeding 10 working days.

(3) If the competent authority has reasonable grounds for suspecting that an applicable provision has been infringed and the securities have been admitted to trading on the regulated market in question, it may—

   (a) require the market operator to suspend trading in the securities for a period not exceeding 10 working days;

   (b) require a person not to advertise the securities, or to take such steps as the authority may specify to suspend any existing advertisement in connection with those securities, for a period not exceeding 10 working days.

(4) If the competent authority finds that an applicable provision has been infringed, it may require the market operator to prohibit trading in the securities on the regulated market in question.

(5) "An applicable provision" means—

   (a) a provision of this Part,

   (b) a provision contained in prospectus rules,

   (c) any other provision made in accordance with the prospectus directive, applicable in relation to the admission of the transferable securities to trading on the regulated market in question.]

NOTES
Substituted as noted to s 84 at **[7.91]**.

[7.107]
[87M   Public censure of issuer
(1)   If the competent authority finds that—
  (a)   an issuer of transferable securities,
  (b)   a person offering transferable securities to the public, or
  (c)   a person requesting the admission of transferable securities to trading on a regulated market,
is failing or has failed to comply with his obligations under an applicable provision, it may publish a statement to that effect.
(2)   If the competent authority proposes to publish a statement, it must give the person a warning notice setting out the terms of the proposed statement.
(3)   If, after considering any representations made in response to the warning notice, the competent authority decides to make the proposed statement, it must give the person a decision notice setting out the terms of the statement.
(4)   "An applicable provision" means—
  (a)   a provision of this Part,
  (b)   a provision contained in prospectus rules,
  (c)   any other provision made in accordance with the prospectus directive,
applicable to a prospectus in relation to the transferable securities in question.
(5)   "Prospectus" includes a supplementary prospectus.]

NOTES
Substituted as noted to s 84 at **[7.91]**.

[7.108]
[87N   Right to refer matters to the Tribunal
(1)   A person to whom a decision notice is given under section 87M may refer the matter to the Tribunal.
(2)   A person to whom a notice is given under section 87O may refer the matter to the Tribunal.]

NOTES
Substituted as noted to s 84 at **[7.91]**.

[7.109]
[87O   Procedure under sections 87K and 87L
(1)   A requirement under section 87K or 87L takes effect—
  (a)   immediately, if the notice under subsection (2) states that that is the case;
  (b)   in any other case, on such date as may be specified in that notice.
(2)   If the competent authority—
  (a)   proposes to exercise the powers in section 87K or 87L in relation to a person, or
  (b)   exercises any of those powers in relation to a person with immediate effect,
it must give that person written notice.
(3)   The notice must—
  (a)   give details of the competent authority's action or proposed action;
  (b)   state the competent authority's reasons for taking the action in question and choosing the date on which it took effect or takes effect;
  (c)   inform the recipient that he may make representations to the competent authority within such period as may be specified by the notice (whether or not he has referred the matter to the Tribunal);
  (d)   inform him of the date on which the action took effect or takes effect; and
  (e)   inform him of his right to refer the matter to the Tribunal.
(4)   The competent authority may extend the period within which representations may be made to it.
(5)   If, having considered any representations made to it, the competent authority decides to maintain, vary or revoke its earlier decision, it must give written notice to that effect to the person mentioned in subsection (2).
(6)   A notice given under subsection (5) must inform that person, where relevant, of his right to refer the matter to the Tribunal.
(7)   If a notice informs a person of his right to refer a matter to the Tribunal, it must give an indication of the procedure on such a reference.
(8)   If a notice under this section relates to the exercise of the power conferred by section 87L(3), the notice must also be given to the person at whose request the transferable securities were admitted to trading on the regulated market.]

NOTES

Substituted as noted to s 84 at **[7.91]**.

[7.110]

[87P Exercise of powers at request of competent authority of another EEA State

(1) This section applies if—

    (a) the competent authority of an EEA State other than the United Kingdom has approved a prospectus,

    (b) the transferable securities to which the prospectus relates have been offered to the public in the United Kingdom or their admission to trading on a regulated market has been requested, and

    (c) that competent authority makes a request that the competent authority assist it in the performance of its functions under the law of that State in connection with the prospectus directive.

(2) For the purpose of complying with the request mentioned in subsection (1)(c), the powers conferred by sections 87K and 87L may be exercised as if the prospectus were one which had been approved by the competent authority.

(3) Section 87N does not apply to an exercise of those powers as a result of this section.

(4) Section 87O does apply to such an exercise of those powers but with the omission of subsections (3)(e), (6) and (7).]

NOTES

Substituted as noted to s 84 at **[7.91]**.

[Rights of investors

[7.111]

87Q Right of investor to withdraw

(1) Where a person agrees to buy or subscribe for transferable securities in circumstances where the final offer price or the amount of transferable securities to be offered to the public is not included in the prospectus, he may withdraw his acceptance before the end of the withdrawal period.

(2) The withdrawal period—

    (a) begins with the investor's acceptance; and

    (b) ends at the end of the second working day after the date on which the competent authority is informed of the information in accordance with section 87A(7).

(3) Subsection (1) does not apply if the prospectus contains—

    (a) in the case of the amount of transferable securities to be offered to the public, the criteria or conditions (or both) according to which that element will be determined, or

    (b) in the case of price, the criteria or conditions (or both) according to which that element will be determined or the maximum price.

(4) Where a supplementary prospectus has been published and, prior to the publication, a person agreed to buy or subscribe for transferable securities to which it relates, he may withdraw his acceptance before the end of the period of 2 working days beginning with the first working day after the date on which the supplementary prospectus was published.]

NOTES

Substituted as noted to s 84 at **[7.91]**.

[Registered investors

[7.112]

87R Register of investors

(1) The competent authority must establish and maintain, in accordance with this section and prospectus rules, a register of investors for the purposes of section 86.

(2) An individual may not be entered in the register unless—

    (a) he is resident in the United Kingdom; and

    (b) he meets at least two of the criteria mentioned in Article 2.2 of the prospectus directive.

(3) A company may not be entered in the register unless—

    (a) it falls within the meaning of "small and medium-sized enterprises" in Article 2.1 of the prospectus directive; and

    (b) its registered office is in the United Kingdom.

(4) A person who does not fall within subsection (2) or (3) may not be entered in the register.]

NOTES

Substituted as noted to s 84 at **[7.91]**.

Sponsors

(c) require a person to make arrangements with sponsor for the performance of services in relation to him as may be specified in the rules.
(d) specify the approved by the competent authority for the purposes of the rules.
(4) If the competent authority to maintain a list of sponsors;
(a) to refuse a person's a performed by a sponsor;
(b) to cancel a person's approval in relation to the provision of services or specified
it must give him a warning notice. son is qualified for being approved as a sponsor.
(5) If, after considering any representations is a sponsor, or
competent authority decides— wise than at his best],
(a) to grant the application for approval, or conse to the warning notice, the
(b) not to cancel the approval,
it must give the person concerned, and any person to whom a copy of the warning notice was given, written notice of its decision.
(6) If, after considering any representations made in response to the warning notice, the competent authority decides—
(a) to refuse to grant the application for approval, or
(b) to cancel the approval,
it must give the person concerned a decision notice.
(7) A person to whom a decision notice is given under this section may refer the matter to the Tribunal.

NOTES

Sub-s (4): words in square brackets inserted by the Regulatory Reform (Financial Services and Markets Act 2000) Order 2007, SI 2007/1973, arts 2, 9, as from 12 July 2007.

[7.114]
89 Public censure of sponsor
(1) Listing rules may make provision for the competent authority if it considers that a sponsor has contravened a requirement imposed on him by rules made as a result of section 88(3)(c), to publish a statement to that effect.
(2) If the competent authority proposes to publish a statement it must give the sponsor a warning notice setting out the terms of the proposed statement.
(3) If, after considering any representations made in response to the warning notice, the competent authority decides to make the proposed statement, it must give the sponsor a decision notice setting out the terms of the statement.
(4) A sponsor to whom a decision notice is given under this section may refer the matter to the Tribunal.

[Transparency obligations

[7.115]
89A Transparency rules
(1) The competent authority may make rules for the purposes of the transparency obligations directive.
(2) The rules may include provision for dealing with any matters arising out of or related to any provision of the transparency obligations directive.
(3) The competent authority may also make rules—
(a) for the purpose of ensuring that voteholder information in respect of voting shares traded on a UK market other than a regulated market is made public or notified to the competent authority;
(b) providing for persons who hold comparable instruments (see section 89F(1)(c)) in respect of voting shares to be treated, in the circumstances specified in the rules, as holding some or all of the voting rights in respect of those shares.
(4) Rules under this section may, in particular, make provision—
(a) specifying how the proportion of—
(i) the total voting rights in respect of shares in an issuer, or
(ii) the total voting rights in respect of a particular class of shares in an issuer,
held by a person is to be determined;

(b) specifying the circumstances in which, for the purposes of voting shar and the period within
rights held by a person ("P") in respect of voting shar and the period within
or treated by virtue of subsection (3)(b) as held,
(c) shares in the issuer re to be regarded as held by
(d) specifying the nature of the information which imposed by rules under this
about the form of any notification;
(e) requiring any notation to be given withi
(f) specifying the manner in which any information transparency rules".
which it must made public;
(g) specifying circumstances in which any of the power to make rules under this
(5) Rules under the section does apply.
(6) Nothing in ses 89B to 89G af
section.]

NOTES

Commencement: 8 ember 2006.

Inserted, to and ss 89B–89G, by the Companies Act 2006, s 1266(1), as from 8 November 2006. See further the preceding
Section 1266(te below.

2006 A ovides as follows—

"(2) The effe of the purposes section 155 of the Financial Services and Markets Act 2000 (c 8) (consultation on proposed ru f the Financial Services Authority before this section comes into force with a view to making transpa is done defined in the provisions to be inserted in that Act by subsection (1) above) is not affected by the fact that the prov were not then in force.".

[7.116]
[89B Provision of voteholder information

(1) Transparency rules may make provision for voteholder information in respect of voting shares to be notified, in circumstances specified in the rules—
(a) to the issuer, or
(b) to the public,
or to both.
(2) Transparency rules make provision for voteholder information notified to the issuer to be notified at the same time e competent authority.
(3) In this Part "voteholder information" in respect of voting shares means information relating to the proportion of voting rights held by a person in respect of the shares.
(4) Transparency rules may require notification of voteholder information relating to a person—
(a) initially, not later than ch date as may be specified in the rules for the purposes of the first in dent of Article 30.2 of the transparency obligations directive, and
(b) subsequently, in accordance with the following provisions.
(5) Transparency rules under subsection (4)(b) may require notification of voteholder information relating to a person only where there is a notifiable change in the proportion of—
(a) the total voting rights in respect of shares in the issuer, or
(b) the total voting rights in respect of a particular class of share in the issuer,
held by the person.
(6) For this purpose there is a "notifiable change" in the proportion of voting rights held by a person when the proportion changes—
(a) from being a proportion less than a designated proportion to a proportion equal to or greater than that designated proportion,
(b) from being a proportion equal to a designated proportion to a proportion greater or less than that designated proportion, or
(c) from being a proportion greater than a designated proportion to a proportion equal to or less than that designated proportion.
(7) In subsection (6) "designated" means designated by the rules.]

NOTES

Commencement: 8 November 2006.

Inserted as noted to s 89A at [7.115].

[7.117]
[89C Provision of information by issuers of transferable securities

(1) Transparency rules may make provision requiring the issuer of transferable securities, in circumstances specified in the rules—
(a) to make public information to which this section applies, or
(b) to notify to the competent authority information to which this section applies,
or to do both.
(2) In the case of every issuer, this section applies to—
(a) information required by Article 4 of the transparency obligations directive;

(b)　information relating to the rights attached to the transferable securities, including information about the terms and conditions of those securities which could indirectly affect those rights; and

(c)　information about new loan issues and about any guarantee or security in connection with any such issue.

(3)　In the case of an issuer of debt securities, this section also applies to information required by Article 5 of the transparency obligations directive.

(4)　In the case of an issuer of shares, this section also applies to—

　(a)　information required by Article 5 of the transparency obligations directive;

　(b)　information required by Article 6 of that directive;

　(c)　voteholder information—

　　(i)　notified to the issuer, or

　　(ii)　relating to the proportion of voting rights held by the issuer in respect of shares in the issuer;

　(d)　information relating to the issuer's capital; and

　(e)　information relating to the total number of voting rights in respect of shares or shares of a particular class.]

NOTES

Commencement: 8 November 2006.
Inserted as noted to s 89A at **[7.115]**.

[7.118]
[89D　Notification of voting rights held by issuer

(1)　Transparency rules may require notification of voteholder information relating to the proportion of voting rights held by an issuer in respect of voting shares in the issuer—

　(a)　initially, not later than such date as may be specified in the rules for the purposes of the second indent of Article 30.2 of the transparency obligations directive, and

　(b)　subsequently, in accordance with the following provisions.

(2)　Transparency rules under subsection (1)(b) may require notification of voteholder information relating to the proportion of voting rights held by an issuer in respect of voting shares in the issuer only where there is a notifiable change in the proportion of—

　(a)　the total voting rights in respect of shares in the issuer, or

　(b)　the total voting rights in respect of a particular class of share in the issuer,

held by the issuer.

(3)　For this purpose there is a "notifiable change" in the proportion of voting rights held by a person when the proportion changes—

　(a)　from being a proportion less than a designated proportion to a proportion equal to or greater than that designated proportion,

　(b)　from being a proportion equal to a designated proportion to a proportion greater or less than that designated proportion, or

　(c)　from being a proportion greater than a designated proportion to a proportion equal to or less than that designated proportion.

(4)　In subsection (3) "designated" means designated by the rules.]

NOTES

Commencement: 8 November 2006.
Inserted as noted to s 89A at **[7.115]**.

[7.119]
[89E　Notification of proposed amendment of issuer's constitution

Transparency rules may make provision requiring an issuer of transferable securities that are admitted to trading on a regulated market to notify a proposed amendment to its constitution—

　(a)　to the competent authority, and

　(b)　to the market on which the issuer's securities are admitted,

at times and in circumstances specified in the rules.]

NOTES

Commencement: 8 November 2006.
Inserted as noted to s 89A at **[7.115]**.

[7.120]
[89F　Transparency rules: interpretation etc

(1)　For the purposes of sections 89A to 89G—

　(a)　the voting rights in respect of any voting shares are the voting rights attached to those shares,

　(b)　a person is to be regarded as holding the voting rights in respect of the shares—

　　(i)　if, by virtue of those shares, he is a shareholder within the meaning of Article 2.1(e) of the transparency obligations directive;

(ii)　if, and to the extent that, he is entitled to acquire, dispose of or exercise those voting rights in one or more of the cases mentioned in Article 10(a) to (h) of the transparency obligations directive;

(iii)　if he holds, directly or indirectly, a financial instrument which results in an entitlement to acquire the shares and is an Article 13 instrument, and

(c)　a person holds a "comparable instrument" in respect of voting shares if he holds, directly or indirectly, a financial instrument in relation to the shares which has similar economic effects to an Article 13 instrument (whether or not the financial instrument results in an entitlement to acquire the shares).

(2)　Transparency rules under section 89A(3)(b) may make different provision for different descriptions of comparable instrument.

(3)　For the purposes of sections 89A to 89G two or more persons may, at the same time, each be regarded as holding the same voting rights.

(4)　In those sections—

"Article 13 instrument" means a financial instrument of a type determined by the European Commission under Article 13.2 of the transparency obligations directive;

["financial instrument" has the meaning given in Article 4.1(17) of Directive 2004/39/EC on markets in financial instruments;]

"UK market" means a market that is situated or operating in the United Kingdom;

"voting shares" means shares of an issuer to which voting rights are attached.]

NOTES

Commencement: 8 November 2006.

Inserted as noted to s 89A at **[7.115]**.

Sub-s (4): definition "financial instrument" inserted by the Definition of Financial Instrument Order 2008, SI 2008/3053, art 2, as from 31 January 2009.

[7.121]

[89G　Transparency rules: other supplementary provisions

(1)　Transparency rules may impose the same obligations on a person who has applied for the admission of transferable securities to trading on a regulated market without the issuer's consent as they impose on an issuer of transferable securities.

(2)　Transparency rules that require a person to make information public may include provision authorising the competent authority to make the information public in the event that the person fails to do so.

(3)　The competent authority may make public any information notified to the authority in accordance with transparency rules.

(4)　Transparency rules may make provision by reference to any provision of any rules made by the Panel on Takeovers and Mergers under Part 28 of the Companies Act 2006.

(5)　Sections 89A to 89F and this section are without prejudice to any other power conferred by this Part to make Part 6 rules.]

NOTES

Commencement: 8 November 2006.

Inserted as noted to s 89A at **[7.115]**.

[Power of competent authority to call for information

[7.122]

89H　Competent authority's power to call for information

(1)　The competent authority may by notice in writing given to a person to whom this section applies require him—

(a)　to provide specified information or information of a specified description, or

(b)　to produce specified documents or documents of a specified description.

(2)　This section applies to—

(a)　an issuer in respect of whom transparency rules have effect;

(b)　a voteholder;

(c)　an auditor of—

(i)　an issuer to whom this section applies, or

(ii)　a voteholder;

(d)　a person who controls a voteholder;

(e)　a person controlled by a voteholder;

(f)　a director or other similar officer of an issuer to whom this section applies;

(g)　a director or other similar officer of a voteholder or, where the affairs of a voteholder are managed by its members, a member of the voteholder.

(3)　This section applies only to information and documents reasonably required in connection with the exercise by the competent authority of functions conferred on it by or under sections 89A to 89G (transparency rules).

(4)　Information or documents required under this section must be provided or produced—

(a)　before the end of such reasonable period as may be specified, and

(b) at such place as may be specified.

(5) If a person claims a lien on a document, its production under this section does not affect the lien.]

NOTES

Commencement: 8 November 2006.

Inserted, together with the preceding heading and ss 89I, 89J, by the Companies Act 2006, s 1267, as from 8 November 2006.

[7.123]
[89I Requirements in connection with call for information

(1) The competent authority may require any information provided under section 89H to be provided in such form as it may reasonably require.

(2) The competent authority may require—

(a) any information provided, whether in a document or otherwise, to be verified in such manner as it may reasonably require;

(b) any document produced to be authenticated in such manner as it may reasonably require.

(3) If a document is produced in response to a requirement imposed under section 89H, the competent authority may—

(a) take copies of or extracts from the document; or

(b) require the person producing the document, or any relevant person, to provide an explanation of the document.

(4) In subsection (3)(b) "relevant person", in relation to a person who is required to produce a document, means a person who—

(a) has been or is a director or controller of that person;

(b) has been or is an auditor of that person;

(c) has been or is an actuary, accountant or lawyer appointed or instructed by that person; or

(d) has been or is an employee of that person.

(5) If a person who is required under section 89H to produce a document fails to do so, the competent authority may require him to state, to the best of his knowledge and belief, where the document is.]

NOTES

Commencement: 8 November 2006.

Inserted as noted to s 89H at **[7.122]**.

[7.124]
[89J Power to call for information: supplementary provisions

(1) The competent authority may require an issuer to make public any information provided to the authority under section 89H.

(2) If the issuer fails to comply with a requirement under subsection (1), the competent authority may, after seeking representations from the issuer, make the information public.

(3) In sections 89H and 89I (power of competent authority to call for information)—

"control" and "controlled" have the meaning given by subsection (4) below;

"specified" means specified in the notice;

"voteholder" means a person who—

(a) holds voting rights in respect of any voting shares for the purposes of sections 89A to 89G (transparency rules), or

(b) is treated as holding such rights by virtue of rules under section 89A(3)(b).

(4) For the purposes of those sections a person ("A") controls another person ("B") if—

(a) A holds a majority of the voting rights in B,

(b) A is a member of B and has the right to appoint or remove a majority of the members of the board of directors (or, if there is no such board, the equivalent management body) of B,

(c) A is a member of B and controls alone, pursuant to an agreement with other shareholders or members, a majority of the voting rights in B, or

(d) A has the right to exercise, or actually exercises, dominant influence or control over B.

(5) For the purposes of subsection (4)(b)—

(a) any rights of a person controlled by A, and

(b) any rights of a person acting on behalf of A or a person controlled by A,

are treated as held by A.]

NOTES

Commencement: 8 November 2006.

Inserted as noted to s 89H at **[7.122]**.

[Powers exercisable in case of infringement of transparency obligation

[7.125]
89K Public censure of issuer

(1) If the competent authority finds that an issuer of securities admitted to trading on a regulated market is failing or has failed to comply with an applicable transparency obligation, it may publish a statement to that effect.

(2)   If the competent authority proposes to publish a statement, it must give the issuer a warning notice setting out the terms of the proposed statement.

(3)   If, after considering any representations made in response to the warning notice, the competent authority decides to make the proposed statement, it must give the issuer a decision notice setting out the terms of the statement.

(4)   A notice under this section must inform the issuer of his right to refer the matter to the Tribunal (see section 89N) and give an indication of the procedure on such a reference.

(5)   In this section "transparency obligation" means an obligation under—

    (a)   a provision of transparency rules, or

    (b)   any other provision made in accordance with the transparency obligations directive.

(6)   In relation to an issuer whose home State is a member State other than the United Kingdom, any reference to an applicable transparency obligation must be read subject to section 100A(2).]

NOTES

Commencement: 8 November 2006.

Inserted, together with the preceding heading and ss 89L–89N, by the Companies Act 2006, s 1268, as from 8 November 2006.

[7.126]

[89L   Power to suspend or prohibit trading of securities

(1)   This section applies to securities admitted to trading on a regulated market.

(2)   If the competent authority has reasonable grounds for suspecting that an applicable transparency obligation has been infringed by an issuer, it may—

    (a)   suspend trading in the securities for a period not exceeding 10 days,

    (b)   prohibit trading in the securities, or

    (c)   make a request to the operator of the market on which the issuer's securities are traded—

        (i)   to suspend trading in the securities for a period not exceeding 10 days, or

        (ii)   to prohibit trading in the securities.

(3)   If the competent authority has reasonable grounds for suspecting that a provision required by the transparency obligations directive has been infringed by a voteholder of an issuer, it may—

    (a)   prohibit trading in the securities, or

    (b)   make a request to the operator of the market on which the issuer's securities are traded to prohibit trading in the securities.

(4)   If the competent authority finds that an applicable transparency obligation has been infringed, it may require the market operator to prohibit trading in the securities.

(5)   In this section "transparency obligation" means an obligation under—

    (a)   a provision contained in transparency rules, or

    (b)   any other provision made in accordance with the transparency obligations directive.

(6)   In relation to an issuer whose home State is a member State other than the United Kingdom, any reference to an applicable transparency obligation must be read subject to section 100A(2).]

NOTES

Commencement: 8 November 2006.

Inserted as noted to s 89K at **[7.125]**.

[7.127]

[89M   Procedure under section 89L

(1)   A requirement under section 89L takes effect—

    (a)   immediately, if the notice under subsection (2) states that that is the case;

    (b)   in any other case, on such date as may be specified in the notice.

(2)   If the competent authority—

    (a)   proposes to exercise the powers in section 89L in relation to a person, or

    (b)   exercises any of those powers in relation to a person with immediate effect,

it must give that person written notice.

(3)   The notice must—

    (a)   give details of the competent authority's action or proposed action;

    (b)   state the competent authority's reasons for taking the action in question and choosing the date on which it took effect or takes effect;

    (c)   inform the recipient that he may make representations to the competent authority within such period as may be specified by the notice (whether or not he had referred the matter to the Tribunal);

    (d)   inform him of the date on which the action took effect or takes effect;

    (e)   inform him of his right to refer the matter to the Tribunal (see section 89N) and give an indication of the procedure on such a reference.

(4)   The competent authority may extend the period within which representations may be made to it.

(5)   If, having considered any representations made to it, the competent authority decides to maintain, vary or revoke its earlier decision, it must give written notice to that effect to the person mentioned in subsection (2).]

NOTES
Commencement: 8 November 2006.
Inserted as noted to s 89K at **[7.125]**.

[7.128]
[89N   Right to refer matters to the Tribunal
A person—
   (a)   to whom a decision notice is given under section 89K (public censure), or
   (b)   to whom a notice is given under section 89M (procedure in connection with suspension or prohibition of trading),
may refer the matter to the Tribunal.]

NOTES
Commencement: 8 November 2006.
Inserted as noted to s 89K at **[7.125]**.

[Corporate governance

[7.129]
89O   Corporate governance rules
(1)   The competent authority may make rules ("corporate governance rules")—
   (a)   for the purpose of implementing, enabling the implementation of or dealing with matters arising out of or related to, any Community obligation relating to the corporate governance of issuers who have requested or approved admission of their securities to trading on a regulated market;
   (b)   about corporate governance in relation to such issuers for the purpose of implementing, or dealing with matters arising out of or related to, any Community obligation.
(2)   "Corporate governance", in relation to an issuer, includes—
   (a)   the nature, constitution or functions of the organs of the issuer;
   (b)   the manner in which organs of the issuer conduct themselves;
   (c)   the requirements imposed on organs of the issuer;
   (d)   the relationship between the different organs of the issuer;
   (e)   the relationship between the organs of the issuer and the members of the issuer or holders of the issuer's securities.
(3)   The burdens and restrictions imposed by rules under this section on foreign-traded issuers must not be greater than the burdens and restrictions imposed on UK-traded issuers by—
   (a)   rules under this section, and
   (b)   listing rules.
(4)   For this purpose—
   "foreign-traded issuer" means an issuer who has requested or approved admission of the issuer's securities to trading on a regulated market situated or operating outside the United Kingdom;
   "UK-traded issuer" means an issuer who has requested or approved admission of the issuer's securities to trading on a regulated market situated or operating in the United Kingdom.
(5)   This section is without prejudice to any other power conferred by this Part to make Part 6 rules.]

NOTES
Commencement: 8 November 2006.
Inserted, together with the preceding heading, by the Companies Act 2006, s 1269, as from 8 November 2006.

[Compensation for false or misleading statements etc]

[7.130]
90   [Compensation for statements in listing particulars or prospectus]
(1)   Any person responsible for listing particulars is liable to pay compensation to a person who has—
   (a)   acquired securities to which the particulars apply; and
   (b)   suffered loss in respect of them as a result of—
      (i)   any untrue or misleading statement in the particulars; or
      (ii)   the omission from the particulars of any matter required to be included by section 80 or 81.
(2)   Subsection (1) is subject to exemptions provided by Schedule 10.
(3)   If listing particulars are required to include information about the absence of a particular matter, the omission from the particulars of that information is to be treated as a statement in the listing particulars that there is no such matter.
(4)   Any person who fails to comply with section 81 is liable to pay compensation to any person who has—
   (a)   acquired securities of the kind in question; and

(b)   suffered loss in respect of them as a result of the failure.

(5)   Subsection (4) is subject to exemptions provided by Schedule 10.

(6)   This section does not affect any liability which may be incurred apart from this section.

(7)   References in this section to the acquisition by a person of securities include references to his contracting to acquire them or any interest in them.

(8)   No person shall, by reason of being a promoter of a company or otherwise, incur any liability for failing to disclose information which he would not be required to disclose in listing particulars in respect of a company's securities—

(a)   if he were responsible for those particulars; or

(b)   if he is responsible for them, which he is entitled to omit by virtue of section 82.

(9)   The reference in subsection (8) to a person incurring liability includes a reference to any other person being entitled as against that person to be granted any civil remedy or to rescind or repudiate an agreement.

(10)   "Listing particulars", in subsection (1) and Schedule 10, includes supplementary listing particulars.

[(11)   This section applies in relation to a prospectus as it applies to listing particulars, with the following modifications—

(a)   references in this section or in Schedule 10 to listing particulars, supplementary listing particulars or sections 80, 81 or 82 are to be read, respectively, as references to a prospectus, supplementary prospectus and sections 87A, 87G and 87B;

(b)   references in Schedule 10 to admission to the official list are to be read as references to admission to trading on a regulated market;

(c)   in relation to a prospectus, "securities" means "transferable securities".

(12)   A person is not to be subject to civil liability solely on the basis of a summary in a prospectus unless the summary is misleading, inaccurate or inconsistent when read with the rest of the prospectus; and, in this subsection, a summary includes any translation of it.]

NOTES

The section heading and the heading preceding this section were substituted by the Companies Act 2006, s 1272, Sch 15, Pt 1, paras 1, 4, 5, as from 8 November 2006.

Sub-ss (11), (12): added by SI 2005/1433, reg 2(1), Sch 1, para 6(1), (2), as from 1 July 2005.

[7.131]
[90ZA   Liability for key investor information

(1)   A person is not to be subject to civil liability solely on the basis of the key investor information produced in relation to a collective investment scheme or a sub-fund of such a scheme in accordance with rules or other provisions implementing Chapter IX of the UCITS directive, or of any translation of that information, unless the key investor information is misleading, inaccurate or inconsistent with the relevant parts of the prospectus published for that collective investment scheme or sub-fund in accordance with rules made by the Authority under section 248 of this Act.

(2)   In this section, a reference to a sub-fund of a collective investment scheme is a reference to a part of the property of the collective investment scheme which forms a separate pool where—

(a)   the collective investment scheme provides arrangements for separate pooling of the contributions of the participants and the profits and income out of which payments are made to them; and

(b)   the participants are entitled to exchange rights in one pool for rights in another.]

NOTES

Commencement: 1 July 2011.

Inserted by the Undertakings for Collective Investment in Transferable Securities Regulations 2011, SI 2011/1613, reg 2(1), (3), as from 1 July 2011.

[7.132]
[90A   Liability of issuers in connection with published information

Schedule 10A makes provision about the liability of issuers of securities to pay compensation to persons who have suffered loss as a result of—

(a)   a misleading statement or dishonest omission in certain published information relating to the securities, or

(b)   a dishonest delay in publishing such information.]

NOTES

Commencement: 1 October 2010.

This section was originally inserted, together with s 90B, by the Companies Act 2006, s 1270, as from 8 November 2006. It was subsequently substituted by the Financial Services and Markets Act 2000 (Liability of Issuers) Regulations 2010, SI 2010/1192, reg 2(1), (2), as from 1 October 2010. Note that reg 3 of the 2010 Regulations provides that this substitution has effect in relation to information first published on or after 1 October 2010 and that the original section (as inserted by CA 2006) continues to apply to information first published before that date. That section read as follows—

"90A   Compensation for statements in certain publications

(1)   The publications to which this section applies are—

  (a)   any reports and statements published in response to a requirement imposed by a provision implementing Article 4, 5 or 6 of the transparency obligations directive, and

  (b)   any preliminary statement made in advance of a report or statement to be published in response to a requirement imposed by a provision implementing Article 4 of that directive, to the extent that it contains information that it is intended—

     (i)   will appear in the report or statement, and

     (ii)   will be presented in the report or statement in substantially the same form as that in which it is presented in the preliminary statement.

  (2)   The securities to which this section applies are—

  (a)   securities that are traded on a regulated market situated or operating in the United Kingdom, and

  (b)   securities that—

     (i)   are traded on a regulated market situated or operating outside the United Kingdom, and

     (ii)   are issued by an issuer for which the United Kingdom is the home Member State within the meaning of Article 2.1(i) of the transparency obligations directive.

  (3)   The issuer of securities to which this section applies is liable to pay compensation to a person who has—

  (a)   acquired such securities issued by it, and

  (b)   suffered loss in respect of them as a result of—

     (i)   any untrue or misleading statement in a publication to which this section applies, or

     (ii)   the omission from any such publication of any matter required to be included in it.

  (4)   The issuer is so liable only if a person discharging managerial responsibilities within the issuer in relation to the publication—

  (a)   knew the statement to be untrue or misleading or was reckless as to whether it was untrue or misleading, or

  (b)   knew the omission to be dishonest concealment of a material fact.

  (5)   A loss is not regarded as suffered as a result of the statement or omission in the publication unless the person suffering it acquired the relevant securities—

  (a)   in reliance on the information in the publication, and

  (b)   at a time when, and in circumstances in which, it was reasonable for him to rely on that information.

  (6)   Except as mentioned in subsection (8)—

  (a)   the issuer is not subject to any other liability than that provided for by this section in respect of loss suffered as a result of reliance by any person on—

     (i)   an untrue or misleading statement in a publication to which this section applies, or

     (ii)   the omission from any such publication of any matter required to be included in it, and

  (b)   a person other than the issuer is not subject to any liability, other than to the issuer, in respect of any such loss.

  (7)   Any reference in subsection (6) to a person being subject to a liability includes a reference to another person being entitled as against him to be granted any civil remedy or to rescind or repudiate an agreement.

  (8)   This section does not affect—

  (a)   the powers conferred by section 382 and 384 (powers of the court to make a restitution order and of the Authority to require restitution);

  (b)   liability for a civil penalty;

  (c)   liability for a criminal offence.

  (9)   For the purposes of this section—

  (a)   the following are persons "discharging managerial responsibilities" in relation to a publication—

     (i)   any director of the issuer (or person occupying the position of director, by whatever name called),

     (ii)   in the case of an issuer whose affairs are managed by its members, any member of the issuer,

     (iii)   in the case of an issuer that has no persons within sub-paragraph (i) or (ii), any senior executive of the issuer having responsibilities in relation to the publication;

  (b)   references to the acquisition by a person of securities include his contracting to acquire them or any interest in them.".

[7.133]
[90B   Power to make further provision about liability for published information

(1)   The Treasury may by regulations make provision about the liability of issuers of securities traded on a regulated market, and other persons, in respect of information published to holders of securities, to the market or to the public generally.

(2)   Regulations under this section may amend any primary or subordinate legislation, including any provision of, or made under, this Act.]

NOTES

Commencement: 8 November 2006.

Inserted as noted to s 90A at **[7.132]**.

Regulations: the Financial Services and Markets Act 2000 (Liability of Issuers) Regulations 2010, SI 2010/1192 (which substitute s 90A of this Act as noted *ante* and insert Sch 10A to this Act).

Penalties

[7.134]
91   [Penalties for breach of Part 6 rules]

[[(1)   If the competent authority considers that—

  (a)   an issuer of listed securities, or

  (b)   an applicant for listing,

has contravened any provision of listing rules, it may impose on him a penalty of such amount as it considers appropriate.

(1ZA)   If the competent authority considers that—

  (a)   an issuer who has requested or approved the admission of a financial instrument to trading on a regulated market,

   (b)   a person discharging managerial responsibilities within such an issuer, or

   (c)   a person connected with such a person discharging managerial responsibilities,

has contravened any provision of disclosure rules, it may impose on him a penalty of such amount as it considers appropriate.]]

[(1A)   If the competent authority considers that—

   (a)   an issuer of transferable securities,

   (b)   a person offering transferable securities to the public or requesting their admission to trading on a regulated market,

   (c)   an applicant for the approval of a prospectus in relation to transferable securities,

   (d)   a person on whom a requirement has been imposed under section 87K or 87L, or

   (e)   any other person to whom a provision of the prospectus directive applies,

has contravened a provision of this Part or of prospectus rules, or a provision otherwise made in accordance with the prospectus directive or a requirement imposed on him under such a provision, it may impose on him a penalty of such amount as it considers appropriate.]

[(1B)   If the competent authority considers—

   (a)   that a person has contravened—

      (i)   a provision of transparency rules or a provision otherwise made in accordance with the transparency obligations directive, or

      (ii)   a provision of corporate governance rules, or

   (b)   that a person on whom a requirement has been imposed under section 89L (power to suspend or prohibit trading of securities in case of infringement of applicable transparency obligation), has contravened that requirement,

it may impose on the person a penalty of such amount as it considers appropriate.]

(2)   If, in the case of a contravention [by a person] referred to in subsection [[(1), (1ZA)(a), (1A) or (1B)] ("P")], the competent authority considers that [another person] who was at the material time a director of [P] was knowingly concerned in the contravention, it may impose upon him a penalty of such amount as it considers appropriate.]

(3)   If the competent authority is entitled to impose a penalty on a person under this section in respect of a particular matter it may, instead of imposing a penalty on him in respect of that matter, publish a statement censuring him.

(4)   Nothing in this section prevents the competent authority from taking any other steps which it has power to take under this Part.

(5)   A penalty under this section is payable to the competent authority.

(6)   The competent authority may not take action against a person under this section after the end of the period of two years beginning with the first day on which it knew of the contravention unless proceedings against that person, in respect of the contravention, were begun before the end of that period.

(7)   For the purposes of subsection (6)—

   (a)   the competent authority is to be treated as knowing of a contravention if it has information from which the contravention can reasonably be inferred; and

   (b)   proceedings against a person in respect of a contravention are to be treated as begun when a warning notice is given to him under section 92.

NOTES

Section heading: substituted by the Prospectus Regulations 2005, SI 2005/1433, reg 2(1), Sch 1, para 7(1), (4), as from 1 July 2005.

Sub-s (1): originally substituted (by a new sub-s (1) and (2)) by the Financial Services and Markets Act 2000 (Market Abuse) Regulations 2005, SI 2005/381, reg 4, Sch 1, para 4, as from 1 July 2005; further substituted (by a new sub-s (1) and (1ZA)) by the Companies Act 2006, s 1272, Sch 15, Pt 1, paras 1, 6(1), (2), as from 8 November 2006.

Sub-s (1ZA): substituted as noted above.

Sub-s (1A): inserted by SI 2005/1433, reg 2(1), Sch 1, para 7(1), (2), as from 1 July 2005.

Sub-s (1B): inserted by the Companies Act 2006, s 1272, Sch 15, Pt 1, paras 1, 6(1), (3), as from 8 November 2006.

Sub-s (2): substituted as noted above; words "(1), (1ZA)(a), (1A) or (1B)" in square brackets substituted by the Companies Act 2006, s 1272, Sch 15, Pt 1, paras 1, 6(1), (4), as from 8 November 2006; other words in square brackets substituted by SI 2005/1433, reg 2(1), Sch 1, para 6(1), (3), as from 1 July 2005.

[7.135]
92 Procedure

(1)   If the competent authority proposes to take action against a person under section 91, it must give him a warning notice.

(2)   A warning notice about a proposal to impose a penalty must state the amount of the proposed penalty.

(3)   A warning notice about a proposal to publish a statement must set out the terms of the proposed statement.

(4)   If the competent authority decides to take action against a person under section 91, it must give him a decision notice.

(5)   A decision notice about the imposition of a penalty must state the amount of the penalty.

(6)   A decision notice about the publication of a statement must set out the terms of the statement.

(7)   If the competent authority decides to take action against a person under section 91, he may refer the matter to the Tribunal.

[7.136]
93   Statement of policy
(1)   The competent authority must prepare and issue a statement ("its policy statement") of its policy with respect to—
- (a)   the imposition of penalties under section 91; and
- (b)   the amount of penalties under that section.

(2)   The competent authority's policy in determining what the amount of a penalty should be must include having regard to—
- (a)   the seriousness of the contravention in question in relation to the nature of the requirement contravened;
- (b)   the extent to which that contravention was deliberate or reckless; and
- (c)   whether the person on whom the penalty is to be imposed is an individual.

(3)   The competent authority may at any time alter or replace its policy statement.
(4)   If its policy statement is altered or replaced, the competent authority must issue the altered or replacement statement.
(5)   In exercising, or deciding whether to exercise, its power under section 91 in the case of any particular contravention, the competent authority must have regard to any policy statement published under this section and in force at the time when the contravention in question occurred.
(6)   The competent authority must publish a statement issued under this section in the way appearing to the competent authority to be best calculated to bring it to the attention of the public.
(7)   The competent authority may charge a reasonable fee for providing a person with a copy of the statement.
(8)   The competent authority must, without delay, give the Treasury a copy of any policy statement which it publishes under this section.

[7.137]
94   Statements of policy: procedure
(1)   Before issuing a statement under section 93, the competent authority must publish a draft of the proposed statement in the way appearing to the competent authority to be best calculated to bring it to the attention of the public.
(2)   The draft must be accompanied by notice that representations about the proposal may be made to the competent authority within a specified time.
(3)   Before issuing the proposed statement, the competent authority must have regard to any representations made to it in accordance with subsection (2).
(4)   If the competent authority issues the proposed statement it must publish an account, in general terms, of—
- (a)   the representations made to it in accordance with subsection (2); and
- (b)   its response to them.

(5)   If the statement differs from the draft published under subsection (1) in a way which is, in the opinion of the competent authority, significant, the competent authority must (in addition to complying with subsection (4)) publish details of the difference.
(6)   The competent authority may charge a reasonable fee for providing a person with a copy of a draft published under subsection (1).
(7)   This section also applies to a proposal to alter or replace a statement.

Competition

[7.138]
95   Competition scrutiny
(1)   The Treasury may by order provide for—
- (a)   regulating provisions, and
- (b)   the practices of the competent authority in exercising its functions under this Part ("practices"),

to be kept under review.
(2)   Provision made as a result of subsection (1) must require the person responsible for keeping regulating provisions and practices under review to consider—
- (a)   whether any regulating provision or practice has a significantly adverse effect on competition; or
- (b)   whether two or more regulating provisions or practices taken together have, or a particular combination of regulating provisions and practices has, such an effect.

(3)   An order under this section may include provision corresponding to that made by any provision of Chapter III of Part X.
(4)   Subsection (3) is not to be read as in any way restricting the power conferred by subsection (1).
(5)   Subsections (6) to (8) apply for the purposes of provision made by or under this section.
(6)   Regulating provisions or practices have a significantly adverse effect on competition if—
- (a)   they have, or are intended or likely to have, that effect; or
- (b)   the effect that they have, or are intended or likely to have, is to require or encourage behaviour which has, or is intended or likely to have, a significantly adverse effect on competition.

(7)   If regulating provisions or practices have, or are intended or likely to have, the effect of requiring or encouraging exploitation of the strength of a market position they are to be taken to have, or be intended or be likely to have, an adverse effect on competition.

(8)   In determining whether any of the regulating provisions or practices have, or are intended or likely to have, a particular effect, it may be assumed that the persons to whom the provisions concerned are addressed will act in accordance with them.

(9)   "Regulating provisions" means—

  (a)   [Part 6 rules],

  (b)   general guidance given by the competent authority in connection with its functions under this Part.

NOTES

Sub-s (9): words in square brackets substituted by the Financial Services and Markets Act 2000 (Market Abuse) Regulations 2005, SI 2005/381, reg 4, Sch 1, para 5, as from 1 July 2005.

Miscellaneous

[7.139]
96   Obligations of issuers of listed securities
(1)   Listing rules may—

  (a)   specify requirements to be complied with by issuers of listed securities; and

  (b)   make provision with respect to the action that may be taken by the competent authority in the event of non-compliance.

(2)   If the rules require an issuer to publish information, they may include provision authorising the competent authority to publish it in the event of his failure to do so.

(3)   This section applies whenever the listed securities were admitted to the official list.

[7.140]
[96A   Disclosure of information requirements
(1)   Disclosure rules must include provision specifying the disclosure of information requirements to be complied with by—

  (a)   issuers who have requested or approved admission of their financial instruments to trading on a regulated market in the United Kingdom;

  (b)   persons acting on behalf of or for the account of such issuers;

  (c)   persons discharging managerial responsibilities within an issuer—

    (i)   who is registered in the United Kingdom and who has requested or approved admission of its shares to trading on a regulated market; or

    (ii)   who is not registered in the United Kingdom or any other EEA State but who has requested or approved admission of its shares to trading on a regulated market and who is required to file annual information in relation to the shares in the United Kingdom in accordance with Article 10 of the prospectus directive;

  (d)   persons connected to such persons discharging managerial responsibilities.

(2)   The rules must in particular—

  (a)   require an issuer to publish specified inside information;

  (b)   require an issuer to publish any significant change concerning information it has already published in accordance with paragraph (a);

  (c)   allow an issuer to delay the publication of inside information in specified circumstances;

  (d)   require an issuer (or a person acting on his behalf or for his account) who discloses inside information to a third party to publish that information without delay in specified circumstances;

  (e)   require an issuer (or person acting on his behalf or for his account) to draw up a list of those persons working for him who have access to inside information relating directly or indirectly to that issuer; and

  (f)   require persons discharging managerial responsibilities within an issuer falling within subsection (1)(c)(i) or (ii), and persons connected to such persons discharging managerial responsibilities, to disclose transactions conducted on their own account in shares of the issuer, or derivatives or any other financial instrument relating to those shares.

(3)   Disclosure rules may make provision with respect to the action that may be taken by the competent authority in respect of non-compliance.]

NOTES

Inserted, together with ss 96B, 96C, by the Financial Services and Markets Act 2000 (Market Abuse) Regulations 2005, SI 2005/381, reg 4, Sch 1, para 6, as from 17 March 2005.

[7.141]
[96B   [Disclosure rules: persons responsible for compliance]
(1)   [For the purposes of the provisions of this Part relating to disclosure rules], a "person discharging managerial responsibilities within an issuer" means—

  (a)   a director of an issuer falling within section 96A(1)(c)(i) or (ii); or

  (b)   a senior executive of such an issuer who—

   (i)　　has regular access to inside information relating, directly or indirectly, to the issuer, and

   (ii)　　has power to make managerial decisions affecting the future development and business prospects of the issuer.

[(2)　Schedule 11B (connected persons) has effect for the purposes of the provisions of this Part relating to disclosure rules.]]

NOTES

Inserted as noted to s 96A at **[7.140]**.

Section heading: substituted by the Companies Act 2006, s 1272, Sch 15, Pt 1, paras 1, 7(a), as from 8 November 2006.

Sub-s (1): words in square brackets substituted by the Companies Act 2006, s 1272, Sch 15, Pt 1, paras 1, 7(b), as from 8 November 2006.

Sub-s (2): substituted by the Financial Services and Markets Act 2000 (Amendment) Regulations 2009, SI 2009/2461, reg 2(1), as from 1 October 2009.

[7.142]
[96C　Suspension of trading
(1)　The competent authority may, in accordance with disclosure rules, suspend trading in a financial instrument.
(2)　If the competent authority does so, the issuer of that financial instrument may refer the matter to the Tribunal.
(3)　The provisions relating to suspension of listing of securities in section 78 apply to the suspension of trading in a financial instrument and the references to listing and securities are to be read as references to trading and financial instruments respectively for the purposes of this section.]

NOTES

Inserted as noted to s 96A at **[7.140]**.

[7.143]
97　Appointment by competent authority of persons to carry out investigations
(1)　Subsection (2) applies if it appears to the competent authority that there are circumstances suggesting that—
   [(a)　there may have been a contravention of—
      (i)　a provision of this Part or of Part 6 rules, or
      (ii)　a provision otherwise made in accordance with the prospectus directive or the transparency obligations directive;
   (b)　a person who was at the material time a director of a person mentioned in section 91(1), (1ZA)(a), (1A) or (1B) has been knowingly concerned in a contravention by that person of—
      (i)　a provision of this Part or of Part 6 rules, or
      (ii)　a provision otherwise made in accordance with the prospectus directive or the transparency obligations directive;]
   (c)　. . .
   (d)　there may have been a contravention of section 83, 85[, 87G] or 98.
(2)　The competent authority may appoint one or more competent persons to conduct an investigation on its behalf.
(3)　Part XI applies to an investigation under subsection (2) as if—
   (a)　the investigator were appointed under section 167(1);
   (b)　references to the investigating authority in relation to him were to the competent authority;
   (c)　references to the offences mentioned in section 168 were to those mentioned in subsection (1)(d);
   (d)　references to an authorised person were references to the person under investigation.

NOTES

Sub-s (1): paras (a), (b) substituted by the Companies Act 2006, s 1272, Sch 15, Pt 1, paras 1, 8, as from 8 November 2006; para (c) repealed by the Financial Services and Markets Act 2000 (Market Abuse) Regulations 2005, SI 2005/381, reg 4, Sch 1, para 7, as from 1 July 2005; figure in square brackets in para (d) inserted by the Prospectus Regulations 2005, SI 2005/1433, reg 2(1), Sch 1, para 8, as from 1 July 2005.

98　*(Repealed by the Prospectus Regulations 2005, SI 2005/1433, reg 2(1), Sch 1, para 9, as from 1 July 2005.)*

[7.144]
99　Fees
(1)　Listing rules may require the payment of fees to the competent authority in respect of—
   (a)　applications for listing;
   (b)　the continued inclusion of securities in the official list;
   (c)　applications under section 88 for approval as a sponsor; and
   (d)　continued inclusion of sponsors in the list of sponsors.
[(1A)　Disclosure rules may require the payment of fees to the competent authority in respect of the continued admission of financial instruments to trading on a regulated market.]

[(1B) Prospectus rules may require the payment of fees to the competent authority in respect of—
  (a) applications for approval of a prospectus or a supplementary prospectus;
  (b) applications for inclusion in the register of investors;
  (c) the continued inclusion of investors in that register;
  (d) access to that register.]
[(1C) Transparency rules may require the payment of fees to the competent authority in respect of the continued admission of financial instruments to trading on a regulated market.]
(2) In exercising its powers under subsection (1), the competent authority may set such fees as it considers will (taking account of the income it expects as the competent authority) enable it—
  (a) to meet expenses incurred in carrying out its functions under this Part or for any incidental purpose;
  (b) to maintain adequate reserves; and
  (c) in the case of the Authority, to repay the principal of, and pay any interest on, any money which it has borrowed and which has been used for the purpose of meeting expenses incurred in relation to—
      (i) its assumption of functions from the London Stock Exchange Limited in relation to the official list; and
      (ii) its assumption of functions under this Part.
(3) In fixing the amount of any fee which is to be payable to the competent authority, no account is to be taken of any sums which it receives, or expects to receive, by way of penalties imposed by it under this Part.
(4) Subsection (2)(c) applies whether expenses were incurred before or after the coming into force of this Part.
(5) Any fee which is owed to the competent authority under any provision made by or under this Part may be recovered as a debt due to it.

NOTES
  Sub-s (1A): inserted by the Financial Services and Markets Act 2000 (Market Abuse) Regulations 2005, SI 2005/381, reg 4, Sch 1, para 8, as from 1 July 2005.
  Sub-s (1B): inserted by the Prospectus Regulations 2005, SI 2005/1433, reg 2(1), Sch 1, para 10, as from 1 July 2005.
  Sub-s (1C): inserted by the Companies Act 2006, s 1272, Sch 15, Pt 1, paras 1, 9, as from 8 November 2006.

[7.145]
100 Penalties
(1) In determining its policy with respect to the amount of penalties to be imposed by it under this Part, the competent authority must take no account of the expenses which it incurs, or expects to incur, in discharging its functions under this Part.
(2) The competent authority must prepare and operate a scheme for ensuring that the amounts paid to it by way of penalties imposed under this Part are applied for the benefit of issuers of securities admitted to the official list[, and issuers who have requested or approved the admission of financial instruments to trading on a regulated market].
(3) The scheme may, in particular, make different provision with respect to different classes of issuer.
(4) Up to date details of the scheme must be set out in a document ("the scheme details").
(5) The scheme details must be published by the competent authority in the way appearing to it to be best calculated to bring them to the attention of the public.
(6) Before making the scheme, the competent authority must publish a draft of the proposed scheme in the way appearing to it to be best calculated to bring it to the attention of the public.
(7) The draft must be accompanied by notice that representations about the proposals may be made to the competent authority within a specified time.
(8) Before making the scheme, the competent authority must have regard to any representations made to it under subsection (7).
(9) If the competent authority makes the proposed scheme, it must publish an account, in general terms, of—
  (a) the representations made to it in accordance with subsection (7); and
  (b) its response to them.
(10) If the scheme differs from the draft published under subsection (6) in a way which is, in the opinion of the competent authority, significant the competent authority must (in addition to complying with subsection (9)) publish details of the difference.
(11) The competent authority must, without delay, give the Treasury a copy of any scheme details published by it.
(12) The competent authority may charge a reasonable fee for providing a person with a copy of—
  (a) a draft published under subsection (6);
  (b) scheme details.
(13) Subsections (6) to (10) and (12) apply also to a proposal to alter or replace the scheme.

NOTES

Sub-s (2): words in square brackets added by the Financial Services and Markets Act 2000 (Market Abuse) Regulations 2005, SI 2005/381, reg 4, Sch 1, para 9, as from 1 July 2005.

[7.146]
[100A Exercise of powers where UK is host member state
(1) This section applies to the exercise by the competent authority of any power under this Part exercisable in case of infringement of—
  (a) a provision of prospectus rules or any other provision made in accordance with the prospectus directive, or
  (b) a provision of transparency rules or any other provision made in accordance with the transparency obligations directive,
in relation to an issuer whose home State is a member State other than the United Kingdom.
(2) The competent authority may act in such a case only in respect of the infringement of a provision required by the relevant directive.

Any reference to an applicable provision or applicable transparency obligation shall be read accordingly.
(3) If the authority finds that there has been such an infringement, it must give a notice to that effect to the competent authority of the person's home State requesting it—
  (a) to take all appropriate measures for the purpose of ensuring that the person remedies the situation that has given rise to the notice, and
  (b) to inform the authority of the measures it proposes to take or has taken or the reasons for not taking such measures.
(4) The authority may not act further unless satisfied—
  (a) that the competent authority of the person's home State has failed or refused to take measures for the purpose mentioned in subsection (3)(a), or
  (b) that the measures taken by that authority have proved inadequate for that purpose.

This does not affect exercise of the powers under section 87K(2), 87L(2) or (3) or 89L(2) or (3) (powers to protect market).
(5) If the authority is so satisfied, it must, after informing the competent authority of the person's home State, take all appropriate measures to protect investors.
(6) In such a case the authority must inform the Commission of the measures at the earliest opportunity.]

NOTES

Commencement: 8 November 2006.
Inserted by the Companies Act 2006, s 1271, as from 8 November 2006.

[7.147]
101 [Part 6 rules]: general provisions
(1) [Part 6 rules] may make different provision for different cases.
(2) [Part 6 rules] may authorise the competent authority to dispense with or modify the application of the rules in particular cases and by reference to any circumstances.
(3) [Part 6 rules] must be made by an instrument in writing.
(4) Immediately after an instrument containing [Part 6 rules] is made, it must be printed and made available to the public with or without payment.
(5) A person is not to be taken to have contravened [any Part 6 rule] if he shows that at the time of the alleged contravention the instrument containing the rule had not been made available as required by subsection (4).
(6) The production of a printed copy of an instrument purporting to be made by the competent authority on which is endorsed a certificate signed by an officer of the authority authorised by it for that purpose and stating—
  (a) that the instrument was made by the authority,
  (b) that the copy is a true copy of the instrument, and
  (c) that on a specified date the instrument was made available to the public as required by subsection (4),
is evidence (or in Scotland sufficient evidence) of the facts stated in the certificate.
(7) A certificate purporting to be signed as mentioned in subsection (6) is to be treated as having been properly signed unless the contrary is shown.
(8) A person who wishes in any legal proceedings to rely on a rule-making instrument may require the Authority to endorse a copy of the instrument with a certificate of the kind mentioned in subsection (6).

NOTES

Section heading: words in square brackets substituted by virtue of the Financial Services and Markets Act 2000 (Market Abuse) Regulations 2005, SI 2005/381, reg 4, Sch 1, para 10, as from 1 July 2005. Note that SI 2005/381 makes no provision for the section name to be amended, but in consequence of the amendments noted below, it is believed that it should be.
Sub-ss (1)–(5): words in square brackets substituted by SI 2005/381, reg 4, Sch 1, para 10, as from 1 July 2005.

[7.148]
102   Exemption from liability in damages
(1)   Neither the competent authority nor any person who is, or is acting as, a member, officer or member of staff of the competent authority is to be liable in damages for anything done or omitted in the discharge, or purported discharge, of the authority's functions.
(2)   Subsection (1) does not apply—
  (a)   if the act or omission is shown to have been in bad faith; or
  (b)   so as to prevent an award of damages made in respect of an act or omission on the ground that the act or omission was unlawful as a result of section 6(1) of the Human Rights Act 1998.

[Interpretative provisions

[7.149]
102A   Meaning of "securities" etc
(1)   This section applies for the purposes of this Part.
(2)   "Securities" means (except in section 74(2) and the expression "transferable securities") anything which has been, or may be, admitted to the official list.
(3)   "Transferable securities" means anything which is a transferable security for the purposes of [Directive 2004/39/EC of the European Parliament and of the Council on markets in financial instruments], other than money-market instruments for the purposes of that directive which have a maturity of less than 12 months.
[(3A)   "Debt securities" has the meaning given in Article 2.1(b) of the transparency obligations directive.]
(4)   "Financial instrument" has [(except in section 89F)] the meaning given in Article 1.3 of Directive 2003/6/EC of the European Parliament and of the Council of 28 January 2003 on insider dealing and market manipulation [(as modified by Article 69 of Directive 2004/39/EC on markets in financial instruments)].
(5)   "Non-equity transferable securities" means all transferable securities that are not equity securities; and for this purpose "equity securities" has the meaning given in Article 2.1(b) of the prospectus directive.
(6)   "Issuer"—
  (a)   in relation to an offer of transferable securities to the public or admission of transferable securities to trading on a regulated market for which an approved prospectus is required as a result of section 85, means a legal person who issues or proposes to issue the transferable securities in question,
  [(aa)   in relation to transparency rules, means a legal person whose securities are admitted to trading on a regulated market or whose voting shares are admitted to trading on a UK market other than a regulated market, and in the case of depository receipts representing securities, the issuer is the issuer of the securities represented,]
  (b)   in relation to anything else which is or may be admitted to the official list, has such meaning as may be prescribed by the Treasury, and
  (c)   in any other case, means a person who issues financial instruments.]

NOTES

Sections 102A–102C, 103 substituted (together with the preceding heading) for original s 103, by the Prospectus Regulations 2005, SI 2005/1433, reg 2(1), Sch 1, para 11, as from 1 July 2005.

Sub-s (3): words in square brackets substituted by the Companies Act 2006, s 1272, Sch 15, Pt 1, paras 1, 10(1), (3), as from 8 November 2006.

Sub-s (3A): inserted by the Companies Act 2006, s 1272, Sch 15, Pt 1, paras 1, 10(1), (2), as from 8 November 2006.

Sub-s (4): words in square brackets inserted by the Definition of Financial Instrument Order 2008, SI 2008/3053, art 3, as from 31 January 2009.

Sub-s (6): para (aa) inserted by the Companies Act 2006, s 1272, Sch 15, Pt 1, paras 1, 10(1), (4), as from 8 November 2006.

[7.150]
[102B   Meaning of "offer of transferable securities to the public" etc
(1)   For the purposes of this Part there is an offer of transferable securities to the public if there is a communication to any person which presents sufficient information on—
  (a)   the transferable securities to be offered, and
  (b)   the terms on which they are offered,
to enable an investor to decide to buy or subscribe for the securities in question.
(2)   For the purposes of this Part, to the extent that an offer of transferable securities is made to a person in the United Kingdom it is an offer of transferable securities to the public in the United Kingdom.
(3)   The communication may be made—
  (a)   in any form;
  (b)   by any means.
(4)   Subsection (1) includes the placing of securities through a financial intermediary.
(5)   Subsection (1) does not include a communication in connection with trading on—
  (a)   a regulated market;
  (b)   a multilateral trading facility; or

(c)   a market prescribed by an order under section 130A(3).

(6) "Multilateral trading facility" means a multilateral system, operated by an investment firm . . . or a market operator, which brings together multiple third-party buying and selling interests in financial instruments in accordance with non-discretionary rules so as to result in a contract.]

NOTES

Substituted as noted to s 102A at **[7.149]**.

Sub-s (6): words omitted repealed by the Financial Services and Markets Act 2000 (Markets in Financial Instruments) Regulations 2007, SI 2007/126, reg 3(5), Sch 5, paras 1, 6, as from 1 April 2007 (certain purposes), and as from 1 November 2007 (otherwise).

[7.151]
[102C   Meaning of "home State" in relation to transferable securities
In this Part, in relation to an issuer of transferable securities, the "home-State" is the EEA State which is the "home Member State" for the purposes of the prospectus directive (which is to be determined in accordance with Article 2.1(m) of that directive).]

NOTES

Substituted as noted to s 102A at **[7.149]**.

[7.152]
[103   Interpretation of this Part
(1)   In this Part, save where the context otherwise requires—
   "disclosure rules" has the meaning given in section 73A;
   "inside information" has the meaning given in section 118C;
   "listed securities" means anything which has been admitted to the official list;
   "listing" has the meaning given in section 74(5);
   "listing particulars" has the meaning given in section 79(2);
   "listing rules" has the meaning given in section 73A;
   "market operator" means a person who manages or operates the business of a regulated market;
   "offer of transferable securities to the public" has the meaning given in section 102B;
   "the official list" means the list maintained by the competent authority as that list has effect for
        the time being;
   "Part 6 rules" has the meaning given in section 73A;
   "the prospectus directive" means Directive 2003/71/EC of the European Parliament and of
        the Council of 4 November 2003 on the prospectus to be published when securities are
        offered to the public or admitted to trading;
   "prospectus rules" has the meaning given in section 73A;
   "regulated market" has the meaning given in [Article 4.1(14) of Directive 2004/39/EC of the
        European Parliament and of the Council on markets in financial instruments];
   "supplementary prospectus" has the meaning given in section 87G;
   ["the transparency obligations directive" means Directive 2004/ 109/EC of the European
        Parliament and of the Council relating to the harmonisation of transparency requirements
        in relation to information about issuers whose securities are admitted to trading on a
        regulated market;]
   ["transparency rules" has the meaning given by section 89A(5);
   "voteholder information" has the meaning given by section 89B(3);]
   "working day" means any day other that a Saturday, a Sunday, Christmas Day, Good Friday or
        a day which is a bank holiday under the Banking and Financial Dealings Act 1971 (c 80)
        in any part of the United Kingdom.
(2)   In relation to any function conferred on the competent authority by this Part, any reference in this Part to the competent authority is to be read as a reference to the person by whom that function is for the time being exercisable.
(3)   If, as a result of an order under Schedule 8, different functions conferred on the competent authority by this Part are exercisable by different persons, the powers conferred by section 91 are exercisable by such person as may be determined in accordance with the provisions of the order.]

NOTES

Substituted as noted to s 102A at **[7.149]**.

Sub-s (1): words in square brackets in the definition "regulated market" substituted by the Companies Act 2006, s 1272, Sch 15, Pt 1, paras 1, 11(1), (2), as from 1 October 2008; definitions "the transparency obligations directive", "transparency rules", and "voteholder information" inserted by the Companies Act 2006, ss 1265, 1272, Sch 15, Pt 1, paras 1, 11(1), (3), as from 8 November 2006.

Part 7   FSMA 2000

PART VII
CONTROL OF BUSINESS TRANSFERS

[7.153]
104 Control of business transfers

No insurance business transfer scheme or banking business transfer scheme is to have effect unless an order has been made in relation to it under section 111(1).

NOTES

Commencement: 1 December 2001 (for the purpose of insurance business transfer schemes); to be appointed (otherwise).

[7.154]
105 Insurance business transfer schemes

(1)   A scheme is an insurance business transfer scheme if it—
   (a)   satisfies one of the conditions set out in subsection (2);
   (b)   results in the business transferred being carried on from an establishment of the transferee in an EEA State; and
   (c)   is not an excluded scheme.
(2)   The conditions are that—
   (a)   the whole or part of the business carried on in one or more member States by a UK authorised person who has permission to effect or carry out contracts of insurance ("the authorised person concerned") is to be transferred to another body ("the transferee");
   (b)   the whole or part of the business, so far as it consists of reinsurance, carried on in the United Kingdom through an establishment there by an EEA firm [falling within paragraph 5(d) of Schedule 3 and qualifying for authorisation under that Schedule] ("the authorised person concerned") is to be transferred to another body ("the transferee");
   (c)   the whole or part of the business carried on in the United Kingdom by an authorised person who is neither a UK authorised person nor an EEA firm but who has permission to effect or carry out contracts of insurance ("the authorised person concerned") is to be transferred to another body ("the transferee").
(3)   A scheme is an excluded scheme for the purposes of this section if it falls within any of the following cases:
CASE 1
Where the authorised person concerned is a friendly society.
CASE 2
Where—
   (a)   the authorised person concerned is a UK authorised person;
   [(aa) the authorised person concerned is not a reinsurance undertaking (within the meaning of Article 2.1(c) of the reinsurance directive);]
   (b)   the business to be transferred under the scheme is business which consists of the effecting or carrying out of contracts of reinsurance in one or more EEA States other than the United Kingdom; and
   (c)   the scheme has been approved by a court in an EEA State other than the United Kingdom or by the host state regulator.
CASE 3
Where—
   (a)   the authorised person concerned is a UK authorised person;
   (b)   the business to be transferred under the scheme is carried on in one or more countries or territories (none of which is an EEA State) and does not include policies of insurance . . . against risks arising in an EEA State; and
   (c)   the scheme has been approved by a court in a country or territory other than an EEA State or by the authority responsible for the supervision of that business in a country or territory in which it is carried on.
CASE 4
Where[—
   (a)   the business to be transferred under the scheme is the whole of the business of the authorised person concerned;]
   (b)   all the policyholders are controllers of the firm or of firms within the same group as the firm which is the transferee, and
   [(c)] all of the policyholders who will be affected by the transfer have consented to it.
[CASE 5
Where—
   (a)   the business of the authorised person concerned consists solely of the effecting or carrying out of contracts of reinsurance;
   (b)   the business to be transferred is the whole or part of that business;
   (c)   the scheme does not fall within Case 4;
   (d)   all of the policyholders who will be affected by the transfer have consented to it; and
   (e)   a certificate has been obtained under paragraph 2 of Schedule 12 in relation to the proposed transfer.]

(4)   The parties to a scheme which falls within Case 2, [3, 4 or 5] may apply to the court for an order sanctioning the scheme as if it were an insurance business transfer scheme.

[(5)   If the scheme involves a compromise or arrangement falling within Part 27 of the Companies Act 2006 (mergers and divisions of public companies), the provisions of that Part (and Part 26 of that Act) apply accordingly but this does not affect the operation of this Part in relation to the scheme.]

(8)   "UK authorised person" means a body which is an authorised person and which—
   (a)   is incorporated in the United Kingdom; or
   (b)   is an unincorporated association formed under the law of any part of the United Kingdom.
(9)   "Establishment" means, in relation to a person, his head office or a branch of his.

NOTES

Sub-ss (2), (4): words in square brackets substituted by the Reinsurance Directive Regulations 2007, SI 2007/3253, reg 2(1), Sch 1, paras 1, 2(1)(a), (f), as from 10 December 2007.

Sub-s (3): words in square brackets substituted or inserted, and words omitted repealed, by SI 2007/3253, reg 2(1), Sch 1, paras 1, 2(1)(b)–(e), as from 10 December 2007.

Sub-s (5): substituted, for original sub-ss (5)–(7), by the Companies Act 2006 (Consequential Amendments etc) Order 2008, SI 2008/948, art 3(1), Sch 1, Pt 2, para 211(1), as from 6 April 2008.

Transitional provisions: see the Financial Services and Markets Act 2000 (Transitional Provisions and Savings) (Business Transfers) Order 2001, SI 2001/3639. That Order makes savings and transitional provision for applications under the Insurance Companies Act 1982, Sch 2C (repealed) for approval of a transfer of the whole or part of the long term business carried on by an insurance company or approval of the transfer of rights and obligations under contracts of general insurance (including transfers of business to or from members of Lloyd's). In relation to any application that has been made but not determined before 1 December 2001, the relevant provisions of Sch 2C are saved, subject to the general modifications in art 2 of the Order and the specific modifications in arts 3 and 5.

[7.155]
106   Banking business transfer schemes
(1)   A scheme is a banking business transfer scheme if it—
   (a)   satisfies one of the conditions set out in subsection (2);
   (b)   is one under which the whole or part of the business to be transferred includes the accepting of deposits; and
   (c)   is not an excluded scheme.
(2)   The conditions are that—
   (a)   the whole or part of the business carried on by a UK authorised person who has permission to accept deposits ("the authorised person concerned") is to be transferred to another body ("the transferee");
   (b)   the whole or part of the business carried on in the United Kingdom by an authorised person who is not a UK authorised person but who has permission to accept deposits ("the authorised person concerned") is to be transferred to another body which will carry it on in the United Kingdom ("the transferee").
(3)   A scheme is an excluded scheme for the purposes of this section if—
   (a)   the authorised person concerned is a building society or a credit union; or
   [(b)   the scheme is a compromise or arrangement to which Part 27 of the Companies Act 2006 (mergers and divisions of public companies) applies.]
(4)   For the purposes of subsection (2)(a) it is immaterial whether or not the business to be transferred is carried on in the United Kingdom.
(5)   "UK authorised person" has the same meaning as in section 105.
(6)   "Building society" has the meaning given in the Building Societies Act 1986.
(7)   "Credit union" means a credit union within the meaning of—
   (a)   the Credit Unions Act 1979;
   (b)   the Credit Unions (Northern Ireland) Order 1985.

NOTES

Sub-s (3): para (b) substituted by the Companies Act 2006 (Consequential Amendments etc) Order 2008, SI 2008/948, art 3(1), Sch 1, Pt 2, para 211(2), as from 6 April 2008.

[7.156]
[106A   Reclaim fund business transfer scheme
(1)   A scheme is a reclaim fund business transfer scheme if, under the scheme, the whole or part of the business carried on by a reclaim fund is to be transferred to one or more other reclaim funds.
(2)   "Reclaim fund" has the meaning given by section 5(1) of the Dormant Bank and Building Society Accounts Act 2008.]

NOTES

Commencement: 12 March 2009.

Inserted by the Dormant Bank and Building Society Accounts Act 2008, s 15, Sch 2, para 2, as from 12 March 2009.

[7.157]
107   Application for order sanctioning transfer scheme
(1)   An application may be made to the court for an order sanctioning an insurance business transfer scheme[, a banking business transfer scheme or a reclaim fund business transfer scheme].
(2)   An application may be made by—
  (a)   the authorised person concerned;
  (b)   the transferee; or
  (c)   both.
(3)   The application must be made—
  (a)   if the authorised person concerned and the transferee are registered or have their head offices in the same jurisdiction, to the court in that jurisdiction;
  (b)   if the authorised person concerned and the transferee are registered or have their head offices in different jurisdictions, to the court in either jurisdiction;
  (c)   if the transferee is not registered in the United Kingdom and does not have his head office there, to the court which has jurisdiction in relation to the authorised person concerned.
(4)   "Court" means—
  (a)   the High Court; or
  (b)   in Scotland, the Court of Session.

NOTES
Sub-s (1): words in square brackets substituted by the Dormant Bank and Building Society Accounts Act 2008, s 15, Sch 2, para 3, as from 12 March 2009.

[7.158]
108   Requirements on applicants
(1)   The Treasury may by regulations impose requirements on applicants under section 107.
(2)   The court may not determine an application under that section if the applicant has failed to comply with a prescribed requirement.
(3)   The regulations may, in particular, include provision—
  (a)   as to the persons to whom, and periods within which, notice of an application must be given;
  (b)   enabling the court to waive a requirement of the regulations in prescribed circumstances.

NOTES
Regulations: the Financial Services and Markets Act 2000 (Control of Business Transfers) (Requirements on Applicants) Regulations 2001, SI 2001/3625.
Note that the following amending Regulations have also been made under this section: the Financial Services and Markets Act 2000 (Reinsurance Directive) Regulations 2007, SI 2007/3255; the Financial Services and Markets Act 2000 (Control of Business Transfers) (Requirements on Applicants) (Amendment) Regulations 2008, SI 2008/1467; the Financial Services and Markets Act 2000 (Control of Business Transfers) (Requirements on Applicants) (Amendment) Regulations 2009, SI 2009/1390.

[7.159]
109   Scheme reports
(1)   An application under section 107 in respect of an insurance business transfer scheme must be accompanied by a report on the terms of the scheme ("a scheme report").
(2)   A scheme report may be made only by a person—
  (a)   appearing to the Authority to have the skills necessary to enable him to make a proper report; and
  (b)   nominated or approved for the purpose by the Authority.
(3)   A scheme report must be made in a form approved by the Authority.

[7.160]
110   Right to participate in proceedings
On an application under section 107, the following are also entitled to be heard—
  (a)   the Authority, and
  (b)   any person (including an employee of the authorised person concerned or of the transferee) who alleges that he would be adversely affected by the carrying out of the scheme.

[7.161]
111   Sanction of the court for business transfer schemes
(1)   This section sets out the conditions which must be satisfied before the court may make an order under this section sanctioning an insurance business transfer scheme[, a banking business transfer scheme or a reclaim fund business transfer scheme].
(2)   The court must be satisfied that—
  (a)   [in the case of an insurance business transfer scheme or a banking business transfer scheme,] the appropriate certificates have been obtained (as to which see Parts I and II of Schedule 12);
  [(aa) in the case of a reclaim fund business transfer scheme, the appropriate certificate has been obtained (as to which see Part 2A of that Schedule);]

   (b)   the transferee has the authorisation required (if any) to enable the business, or part, which is to be transferred to be carried on in the place to which it is to be transferred (or will have it before the scheme takes effect).

(3)   The court must consider that, in all the circumstances of the case, it is appropriate to sanction the scheme.

NOTES

  Sub-s (1): words in square brackets substituted by the Dormant Bank and Building Society Accounts Act 2008, s 15, Sch 2, para 4(1), (2), as from 12 March 2009.

  Sub-s (2): words in square brackets in para (a), and the whole of para (aa), inserted by the Dormant Bank and Building Society Accounts Act 2008, s 15, Sch 2, para 4(1), (3), as from 12 March 2009.

[7.162]
112   Effect of order sanctioning business transfer scheme

(1)   If the court makes an order under section 111(1), it may by that or any subsequent order make such provision (if any) as it thinks fit—

   (a)   for the transfer to the transferee of the whole or any part of the undertaking concerned and of any property or liabilities of the authorised person concerned;

   (b)   for the allotment or appropriation by the transferee of any shares, debentures, policies or other similar interests in the transferee which under the scheme are to be allotted or appropriated to or for any other person;

   (c)   for the continuation by (or against) the transferee of any pending legal proceedings by (or against) the authorised person concerned;

   (d)   with respect to such incidental, consequential and supplementary matters as are, in its opinion, necessary to secure that the scheme is fully and effectively carried out.

(2)   An order under subsection (1)(a) may—

   (a)   transfer property or liabilities whether or not the authorised person concerned otherwise has the capacity to effect the transfer in question;

   (b)   make provision in relation to property which was held by the authorised person concerned as trustee;

   (c)   make provision as to future or contingent rights or liabilities of the authorised person concerned, including provision as to the construction of instruments (including wills) under which such rights or liabilities may arise;

   (d)   make provision as to the consequences of the transfer in relation to any [occupational pension scheme (within the meaning of section 150(5) of the Finance Act 2004)] operated by or on behalf of the authorised person concerned.

[(2A)   Subsection (2)(a) is to be taken to include power to make provision in an order—

   (a)   for the transfer of property or liabilities which would not otherwise be capable of being transferred or assigned;

   (b)   for a transfer of property or liabilities to take effect as if there were—

      (i)   no such requirement to obtain a person's consent or concurrence, and

      (ii)   no such contravention, liability or interference with any interest or right,

      as there would otherwise be (in the case of a transfer apart from this section) by reason of any provision falling within subsection (2B).

(2B)   A provision falls within this subsection to the extent that it has effect (whether under an enactment or agreement or otherwise) in relation to the terms on which the authorised person concerned is entitled to the property or subject to the liabilities in question.

(2C)   Nothing in subsection (2A) or (2B) is to be read as limiting the scope of subsection (1).]

(3)   If an order under subsection (1) makes provision for the transfer of property or liabilities—

   (a)   the property is transferred to and vests in, and

   (b)   the liabilities are transferred to and become liabilities of,

the transferee as a result of the order.

(4)   But if any property or liability included in the order is governed by the law of any country or territory outside the United Kingdom, the order may require the authorised person concerned, if the transferee so requires, to take all necessary steps for securing that the transfer to the transferee of the property or liability is fully effective under the law of that country or territory.

(5)   Property transferred as the result of an order under subsection (1) may, if the court so directs, vest in the transferee free from any charge which is (as a result of the scheme) to cease to have effect.

(6)   An order under subsection (1) which makes provision for the transfer of property is to be treated as an instrument of transfer for the purposes of [section 770(1) of the Companies Act 2006] and any other enactment requiring the delivery of an instrument of transfer for the registration of property.

(7)   . . .

(8)   If the court makes an order under section 111(1) in relation to an insurance business transfer scheme, it may by that or any subsequent order make such provision (if any) as it thinks fit—

   (a)   for dealing with the interests of any person who, within such time and in such manner as the court may direct, objects to the scheme;

   (b)   for the dissolution, without winding up, of the authorised person concerned;

    (c)   for the reduction, on such terms and subject to such conditions (if any) as it thinks fit, of the benefits payable under—

        (i)   any description of policy, or

        (ii)   policies generally,

    entered into by the authorised person concerned and transferred as a result of the scheme.

(9)   If, in the case of an insurance business transfer scheme, the authorised person concerned is not an EEA firm, it is immaterial for the purposes of subsection (1)(a), (c) or (d) or subsection (2), [(2A),] (3) or (4) that the law applicable to any of the contracts of insurance included in the transfer is the law of an EEA State other than the United Kingdom.

(10)   The transferee must, if an insurance or banking business transfer scheme is sanctioned by the court, deposit two office copies of the order made under subsection (1) with the Authority within 10 days of the making of the order.

(11)   But the Authority may extend that period.

(12)   "Property" includes property, rights and powers of any description.

(13)   "Liabilities" includes duties.

(14)   "Shares" and "debentures" have the same meaning as in [the Companies Acts (see sections 540 and 738 of the Companies Act 2006).]

(15)   "Charge" includes a mortgage (or, in Scotland, a security over property).

NOTES

Sub-s (2): words in square brackets substituted by the Taxation of Pension Schemes (Consequential Amendments) Order 2006, SI 2006/745, art 17, as from 6 April 2006.

Sub-ss (2A)–(2C): inserted by the Financial Services and Markets Act 2000 (Amendments to Part 7) Regulations 2008, SI 2008/1468, reg 2(1), as from 30 June 2008.

Sub-ss (6), (14): words in square brackets substituted by the Companies Act 2006 (Consequential Amendments etc) Order 2008, SI 2008/948, art 3(1), Sch 1, Pt 2, para 211(3)(a), (c), as from 6 April 2008.

Sub-s (7): repealed by SI 2008/948, art 3, Sch 1, Pt 2, para 211(3)(b), Sch 2, as from 6 April 2008.

Sub-s (9): figure in square brackets inserted by SI 2008/1468, reg 2(2), as from 30 June 2008.

[7.163]
[112A   Rights to terminate etc

(1)   Subsection (2) applies where (apart from that subsection) a person would be entitled, in consequence of anything done or likely to be done by or under this Part in connection with an insurance business transfer scheme or a banking business transfer scheme—

    (a)   to terminate, modify, acquire or claim an interest or right; or

    (b)   to treat an interest or right as terminated or modified.

(2)   The entitlement—

    (a)   is not enforceable in relation to that interest or right until after an order has been made under section 112(1) in relation to the scheme; and

    (b)   is then enforceable in relation to that interest or right only insofar as the order contains provision to that effect.

(3)   Nothing in subsection (1) or (2) is to be read as limiting the scope of section 112(1).]

NOTES

Commencement: 30 June 2008.

Inserted by the Financial Services and Markets Act 2000 (Amendments to Part 7) Regulations 2008, SI 2008/1468, reg 2(3), as from 30 June 2008.

[7.164]
113   Appointment of actuary in relation to reduction of benefits

(1)   This section applies if an order has been made under section 111(1).

(2)   The court making the order may, on the application of the Authority, appoint an independent actuary—

    (a)   to investigate the business transferred under the scheme; and

    (b)   to report to the Authority on any reduction in the benefits payable under policies entered into by the authorised person concerned that, in the opinion of the actuary, ought to be made.

[7.165]
114   Rights of certain policyholders

(1)   This section applies in relation to an insurance business transfer scheme if—

    (a)   the authorised person concerned is an authorised person other than an EEA firm qualifying for authorisation under Schedule 3;

    (b)   the court has made an order under section 111 in relation to the scheme; and

    (c)   an EEA State other than the United Kingdom is, as regards any policy included in the transfer which evidences a contract of insurance [(other than a contract of reinsurance)], the State of the commitment or the EEA State in which the risk is situated ("the EEA State concerned").

(2) The court must direct that notice of the making of the order, or the execution of any instrument, giving effect to the transfer must be published by the transferee in the EEA State concerned.

(3) A notice under subsection (2) must specify such period as the court may direct as the period during which the policyholder may exercise any right which he has to cancel the policy.

(4) The order or instrument mentioned in subsection (2) does not bind the policyholder if—
  (a) the notice required under that subsection is not published; or
  (b) the policyholder cancels the policy during the period specified in the notice given under that subsection.

(5) The law of the EEA State concerned governs—
  (a) whether the policyholder has a right to cancel the policy; and
  (b) the conditions, if any, subject to which any such right may be exercised.

(6) Paragraph 6 of Schedule 12 applies for the purposes of this section as it applies for the purposes of that Schedule.

NOTES

Sub-s (1): words in square brackets in para (c) inserted by the Reinsurance Directive Regulations 2007, SI 2007/3253, reg 2(1), Sch 1, paras 1, 2(1), (2), as from 10 December 2007.

[7.166]
[114A   Notice of transfer of reinsurance contracts
(1) This section applies in relation to an insurance business transfer scheme if—
  (a) the authorised person concerned is an authorised person other than an EEA firm qualifying for authorisation under Schedule 3;
  (b) the court has made an order under section 111 in relation to the scheme; and
  (c) an EEA State other than the United Kingdom is, as regards any policy included in the transfer which evidences a contract of reinsurance, the State in which the establishment of the policyholder to which the policy relates is situated at the date when the contract was entered into ("the EEA State concerned").

(2) The court may direct that notice of the making of the order, or the execution of any instrument, giving effect to the transfer must be published by the transferee in the EEA State concerned.]

NOTES

Commencement: 10 December 2007.

Inserted by the Reinsurance Directive Regulations 2007, SI 2007/3253, reg 2(1), Sch 1, paras 1, 2(1), (3), as from 10 December 2007.

Business transfers outside the United Kingdom

[7.167]
115   Certificates for purposes of insurance business transfers overseas
Part III of Schedule 12 makes provision about certificates which the Authority may issue in relation to insurance business transfers taking place outside the United Kingdom.

[7.168]
116   Effect of insurance business transfers authorised in other EEA States
(1) This section applies if, as a result of an authorised transfer, an EEA firm falling within paragraph 5(d) [or (da)] of Schedule 3 transfers to another body all its rights and obligations under any UK policies.

[(2) This section also applies if, as a result of an authorised transfer, any of the following transfers to another body all its rights and obligations under any UK policies—
  (a) an undertaking authorised in an EEA State other than the United Kingdom under Article 51 of the life assurance consolidation directive;
  (b) an undertaking authorised in an EEA State other than the United Kingdom under Article 23 of the first non-life insurance directive;
  (c) an undertaking, whose head office is not within the EEA, authorised under the law of an EEA State other than the United Kingdom to carry out reinsurance activities in its territory (as mentioned in Article 49 of the reinsurance directive).]

(3) If appropriate notice of the execution of an instrument giving effect to the transfer is published, the instrument has the effect in law—
  (a) of transferring to the transferee all the transferor's rights and obligations under the UK policies to which the instrument applies, and
  (b) if the instrument so provides, of securing the continuation by or against the transferee of any legal proceedings by or against the transferor which relate to those rights and obligations.

(4) No agreement or consent is required before subsection (3) has the effects mentioned.

(5) "Authorised transfer" means—
  (a) in subsection (1), a transfer authorised in the home State of the EEA firm in accordance with—
    [(i) Article 14 of the life assurance consolidation directive; . . .]

     (ii)   Article 12 of the third non-life directive; [or]
     [(iii) Article 18 of the reinsurance directive; and]
  (b)   in subsection (2), a transfer authorised in an EEA State other than the United Kingdom in accordance with—
     [(i)   Article 53 of the life assurance consolidation directive; . . .]
     (ii)   Article 28a of the first non-life directive; [or
     (iii)   the provisions in the law of that EEA State which provide for the authorisation of transfers of all or part of a portfolio of contracts of an undertaking authorised to carry out reinsurance activities in its territory (as mentioned in Article 49 of the reinsurance directive)].
[(6) "UK policy" means—
  (a)   in the case of an authorised transfer within the meaning of paragraph (a)(i) or (ii) or (b)(i) or (ii) of subsection (5), a policy evidencing a contract of insurance (other than a contract of reinsurance) to which the applicable law is the law of a part of the United Kingdom;
  (b)   in the case of an authorised transfer within the meaning of paragraph (a)(iii) or (b)(iii) of that subsection, a policy evidencing a contract of reinsurance to which the applicable law is the law of a part of the United Kingdom.]
(7) "Appropriate notice" means—
  (a)   if the UK policy evidences a contract of insurance in relation to which an EEA State other than the United Kingdom is the State of the commitment, notice given in accordance with the law of that State;
  (b)   if the UK policy evidences a contract of insurance where the risk is situated in an EEA State other than the United Kingdom, notice given in accordance with the law of that EEA State;
  (c)   in any other case, notice given in accordance with the applicable law.
(8) Paragraph 6 of Schedule 12 applies for the purposes of this section as it applies for the purposes of that Schedule.

NOTES

Sub-s (1): words in square brackets inserted by the Reinsurance Directive Regulations 2007, SI 2007/3253, reg 2(1), Sch 1, paras 1, 2(4)(a), as from 10 December 2007.

Sub-ss (2), (6): substituted by SI 2007/3253, reg 2(1), Sch 1, paras 1, 2(4)(b), (d), as from 10 December 2007.

Sub-s (5): sub-paras (a)(i), (b)(i) substituted by the Life Assurance Consolidation Directive (Consequential Amendments) Regulations 2004, SI 2004/3379, reg 6(1), (2)(b), (c), as from 11 January 2005; words omitted from sub-paras (a)(i), (b)(i) repealed, word in square brackets in sub-paras (a)(ii) substituted, and sub-paras (a)(iii) and (b)(iii) (and the word preceding sub-para (b)(iii)) inserted, by SI 2007/3253, reg 2(1), Sch 1, paras 1, 2(4)(c), as from 10 December 2007.

Modifications

[7.169]
117 Power to modify this Part
The Treasury may by regulations—
  (a)   provide for prescribed provisions of this Part to have effect in relation to prescribed cases with such modifications as may be prescribed;
  (b)   make such amendments to any provision of this Part as they consider appropriate for the more effective operation of that or any other provision of this Part.

NOTES

Regulations: the Financial Services and Markets Act 2000 (Motor Insurance) Regulations 2007, SI 2007/2403 (these Regulations amend this Act and the Financial Services and Markets Act 2000 (Law Applicable to Contracts of Insurance) Regulations 2001, SI 2001/2635 to change the meaning of "EEA State in which a risk is situated" in certain circumstances in the context of vehicle insurance); the Financial Services and Markets Act 2000 (Amendments to Part 7) Regulations 2008, SI 2008/1468.

PART VIII
PENALTIES FOR MARKET ABUSE

Market abuse

[7.170]
[118 Market abuse
(1) For the purposes of this Act, market abuse is behaviour (whether by one person alone or by two or more persons jointly or in concert) which—
  (a)   occurs in relation to—
     (i)   qualifying investments admitted to trading on a prescribed market,
     (ii)   qualifying investments in respect of which a request for admission to trading on such a market has been made, or
     (iii)   in the case of subsection (2) or (3) behaviour, investments which are related investments in relation to such qualifying investments, and
  (b)   falls within any one or more of the types of behaviour set out in subsections (2) to (8).

(2)   The first type of behaviour is where an insider deals, or attempts to deal, in a qualifying investment or related investment on the basis of inside information relating to the investment in question.

(3)   The second is where an insider discloses inside information to another person otherwise than in the proper course of the exercise of his employment, profession or duties.

(4)   The third is where the behaviour (not falling within subsection (2) or (3))—

    (a)   is based on information which is not generally available to those using the market but which, if available to a regular user of the market, would be, or would be likely to be, regarded by him as relevant when deciding the terms on which transactions in qualifying investments should be effected, and

    (b)   is likely to be regarded by a regular user of the market as a failure on the part of the person concerned to observe the standard of behaviour reasonably expected of a person in his position in relation to the market.

(5)   The fourth is where the behaviour consists of effecting transactions or orders to trade (otherwise than for legitimate reasons and in conformity with accepted market practices on the relevant market) which—

    (a)   give, or are likely to give, a false or misleading impression as to the supply of, or demand for, or as to the price of, one or more qualifying investments, or

    (b)   secure the price of one or more such investments at an abnormal or artificial level.

(6)   The fifth is where the behaviour consists of effecting transactions or orders to trade which employ fictitious devices or any other form of deception or contrivance.

(7)   The sixth is where the behaviour consists of the dissemination of information by any means which gives, or is likely to give, a false or misleading impression as to a qualifying investment by a person who knew or could reasonably be expected to have known that the information was false or misleading.

(8)   The seventh is where the behaviour (not falling within subsection (5), (6) or (7))—

    (a)   is likely to give a regular user of the market a false or misleading impression as to the supply of, demand for or price or value of, qualifying investments, or

    (b)   would be, or would be likely to be, regarded by a regular user of the market as behaviour that would distort, or would be likely to distort, the market in such an investment,

and the behaviour is likely to be regarded by a regular user of the market as a failure on the part of the person concerned to observe the standard of behaviour reasonably expected of a person in his position in relation to the market.

(9)   Subsections (4) and (8) and the definition of "regular user" in section 130A(3) cease to have effect on [31 December 2011] and subsection (1)(b) is then to be read as no longer referring to those subsections.]

NOTES

   Substituted, together with ss 118B–118C for original s 118, by the Financial Services and Markets Act 2000 (Market Abuse) Regulations 2005, SI 2005/381, reg 5, Sch 2, para 1, as from 1 July 2005.

   Sub-ss (4), (8): repealed as from 31 December 2011 by subsection (9) of this section.

   Sub-s (9): words in square brackets substituted by the Financial Services and Markets Act 2000 (Market Abuse) Regulations 2009, SI 2009/3128, reg 2(1), (2), as from 31 December 2009.

   Orders: the Financial Services and Markets Act 2000 (Prescribed Markets and Qualifying Investments) Order 2001, SI 2001/996 at **[8.167]**. Note, the 2001 Order was originally made under s 118(3) but, following the substitution of this section as noted above, now has effect as if made under s 130A(1) at **[7.186]**.

[7.171]

[118A   Supplementary provision about certain behaviour

(1)   Behaviour is to be taken into account for the purposes of this Part only if it occurs—

    (a)   in the United Kingdom, or

    (b)   in relation to—

        (i)   qualifying investments which are admitted to trading on a prescribed market situated in, or operating in, the United Kingdom,

        (ii)   qualifying investments for which a request for admission to trading on such a prescribed market has been made, or

        (iii)   in the case of section 118(2) and (3), investments which are related investments in relation to such qualifying investments.

(2)   For the purposes of subsection (1), as it applies in relation to section 118(4) and (8), a prescribed market accessible electronically in the United Kingdom is to be treated as operating in the United Kingdom.

(3)   For the purposes of section 118(4) and (8), the behaviour that is to be regarded as occurring in relation to qualifying investments includes behaviour which—

    (a)   occurs in relation to anything that is the subject matter, or whose price or value is expressed by reference to the price or value of the qualifying investments, or

    (b)   occurs in relation to investments (whether or not they are qualifying investments) whose subject matter is the qualifying investments.

Part 7   FSMA 2000

(4)   For the purposes of section 118(7), the dissemination of information by a person acting in the capacity of a journalist is to be assessed taking into account the codes governing his profession unless he derives, directly or indirectly, any advantage or profits from the dissemination of the information.

(5)   Behaviour does not amount to market abuse for the purposes of this Act if—

- (a)   it conforms with a rule which includes a provision to the effect that behaviour conforming with the rule does not amount to market abuse,
- (b)   it conforms with the relevant provisions of Commission Regulation (EC) No 2273/2003 of 22 December 2003 implementing Directive 2003/6/EC of the European Parliament and of the Council as regards exemptions for buy-back programmes and stabilisation of financial instruments, or
- (c)   it is done by a person acting on behalf of a public authority in pursuit of monetary policies or policies with respect to exchange rates or the management of public debt or foreign exchange reserves.

(6)   Subsections (2) and (3) cease to have effect on [31 December 2011].]

NOTES

Substituted as noted to s 118 at **[7.170]**.

Sub-ss (2), (4): repealed as from 31 December 2011 by subsection (6) of this section.

Sub-s (6): words in square brackets substituted by the Financial Services and Markets Act 2000 (Market Abuse) Regulations 2009, SI 2009/3128, reg 2(1), (3), as from 31 December 2009.

[7.172]
[118B   Insiders

For the purposes of this Part an insider is any person who has inside information—

- (a)   as a result of his membership of an administrative, management or supervisory body of an issuer of qualifying investments,
- (b)   as a result of his holding in the capital of an issuer of qualifying investments,
- (c)   as a result of having access to the information through the exercise of his employment, profession or duties,
- (d)   as a result of his criminal activities, or
- (e)   which he has obtained by other means and which he knows, or could reasonably be expected to know, is inside information.]

NOTES

Substituted as noted to s 118 at **[7.170]**.

[7.173]
[118C   Inside information

(1)   This section defines "inside information" for the purposes of this Part.

(2)   In relation to qualifying investments, or related investments, which are not commodity derivatives, inside information is information of a precise nature which—

- (a)   is not generally available,
- (b)   relates, directly or indirectly, to one or more issuers of the qualifying investments or to one or more of the qualifying investments, and
- (c)   would, if generally available, be likely to have a significant effect on the price of the qualifying investments or on the price of related investments.

(3)   In relation to qualifying investments or related investments which are commodity derivatives, inside information is information of a precise nature which—

- (a)   is not generally available,
- (b)   relates, directly or indirectly, to one or more such derivatives, and
- (c)   users of markets on which the derivatives are traded would expect to receive in accordance with any accepted market practices on those markets.

(4)   In relation to a person charged with the execution of orders concerning any qualifying investments or related investments, inside information includes information conveyed by a client and related to the client's pending orders which—

- (a)   is of a precise nature,
- (b)   is not generally available,
- (c)   relates, directly or indirectly, to one or more issuers of qualifying investments or to one or more qualifying investments, and
- (d)   would, if generally available, be likely to have a significant effect on the price of those qualifying investments or the price of related investments.

(5)   Information is precise if it—

- (a)   indicates circumstances that exist or may reasonably be expected to come into existence or an event that has occurred or may reasonably be expected to occur, and
- (b)   is specific enough to enable a conclusion to be drawn as to the possible effect of those circumstances or that event on the price of qualifying investments or related investments.

(6) Information would be likely to have a significant effect on price if and only if it is information of a kind which a reasonable investor would be likely to use as part of the basis of his investment decisions.

(7) For the purposes of subsection (3)(c), users of markets on which investments in commodity derivatives are traded are to be treated as expecting to receive information relating directly or indirectly to one or more such derivatives in accordance with any accepted market practices, which is—

 (a) routinely made available to the users of those markets, or

 (b) required to be disclosed in accordance with any statutory provision, market rules, or contracts or customs on the relevant underlying commodity market or commodity derivatives market.

(8) Information which can be obtained by research or analysis conducted by, or on behalf of, users of a market is to be regarded, for the purposes of this Part, as being generally available to them.]

NOTES

Substituted as noted to s 118 at **[7.170]**.

The code

[7.174]

119 The code

(1) The Authority must prepare and issue a code containing such provisions as the Authority considers will give appropriate guidance to those determining whether or not behaviour amounts to market abuse.

(2) The code may among other things specify—

 (a) descriptions of behaviour that, in the opinion of the Authority, amount to market abuse;

 (b) descriptions of behaviour that, in the opinion of the Authority, do not amount to market abuse;

 (c) factors that, in the opinion of the Authority, are to be taken into account in determining whether or not behaviour amounts to market abuse;

 [(d) descriptions of behaviour that are accepted market practices in relation to one or more specified markets;

 (e) descriptions of behaviour that are not accepted market practices in relation to one or more specified markets].

[(2A) In determining, for the purposes of subsections (2)(d) and (2)(e) or otherwise, what are and what are not accepted market practices, the Authority must have regard to the factors and procedures laid down in Articles 2 and 3 respectively of Commission Directive 2004/72/EC of 29 April 2004 implementing Directive 2003/6/EC of the European Parliament and of the Council.]

(3) The code may make different provision in relation to persons, cases or circumstances of different descriptions.

(4) The Authority may at any time alter or replace the code.

(5) If the code is altered or replaced, the altered or replacement code must be issued by the Authority.

(6) A code issued under this section must be published by the Authority in the way appearing to the Authority to be best calculated to bring it to the attention of the public.

(7) The Authority must, without delay, give the Treasury a copy of any code published under this section.

(8) The Authority may charge a reasonable fee for providing a person with a copy of the code.

NOTES

Sub-s (2): paras (d), (e) added by the Financial Services and Markets Act 2000 (Market Abuse) Regulations 2005, SI 2005/381, reg 5, Sch 2, para 2(1), (2), as from 1 July 2005.

Sub-s (2A): inserted by SI 2005/381, reg 5, Sch 2, para 2(1), (3), as from 1 July 2005.

[7.175]

120 Provisions included in the Authority's code by reference to the City Code

(1) The Authority may include in a code issued by it under section 119 ("the Authority's code") provision to the effect that in its opinion behaviour conforming with the City Code—

 (a) does not amount to market abuse;

 (b) does not amount to market abuse in specified circumstances; or

 (c) does not amount to market abuse if engaged in by a specified description of person.

(2) But the Treasury's approval is required before any such provision may be included in the Authority's code.

(3) If the Authority's code includes provision of a kind authorised by subsection (1), the Authority must keep itself informed of the way in which the Panel on Takeovers and Mergers interprets and administers the relevant provisions of the City Code.

(4) "City Code" means the City Code on Takeovers and Mergers issued by the Panel as it has effect at the time when the behaviour occurs.

(5) "Specified" means specified in the Authority's code.

Part 7 FSMA 2000

[7.176]
121 Codes: procedure

(1) Before issuing a code under section 119, the Authority must publish a draft of the proposed code in the way appearing to the Authority to be best calculated to bring it to the attention of the public.

(2) The draft must be accompanied by—

    (a) a cost benefit analysis; and

    (b) notice that representations about the proposal may be made to the Authority within a specified time.

(3) Before issuing the proposed code, the Authority must have regard to any representations made to it in accordance with subsection (2)(b).

(4) If the Authority issues the proposed code it must publish an account, in general terms, of—

    (a) the representations made to it in accordance with subsection (2)(b); and

    (b) its response to them.

(5) If the code differs from the draft published under subsection (1) in a way which is, in the opinion of the Authority, significant—

    (a) the Authority must (in addition to complying with subsection (4)) publish details of the difference; and

    (b) those details must be accompanied by a cost benefit analysis.

(6) Subsections (1) to (5) do not apply if the Authority considers that there is an urgent need to publish the code.

(7) Neither subsection (2)(a) nor subsection (5)(b) applies if the Authority considers—

    (a) that, making the appropriate comparison, there will be no increase in costs; or

    (b) that, making that comparison, there will be an increase in costs but the increase will be of minimal significance.

(8) The Authority may charge a reasonable fee for providing a person with a copy of a draft published under subsection (1).

(9) This section also applies to a proposal to alter or replace a code.

(10) "Cost benefit analysis" means an estimate of the costs together with an analysis of the benefits that will arise—

    (a) if the proposed code is issued; or

    (b) if subsection (5)(b) applies, from the code that has been issued.

(11) "The appropriate comparison" means—

    (a) in relation to subsection (2)(a), a comparison between the overall position if the code is issued and the overall position if it is not issued;

    (b) in relation to subsection (5)(b), a comparison between the overall position after the issuing of the code and the overall position before it was issued.

[7.177]
122 Effect of the code

(1) If a person behaves in a way which is described (in the code in force under section 119 at the time of the behaviour) as behaviour that, in the Authority's opinion, does not amount to market abuse that behaviour of his is to be taken, for the purposes of this Act, as not amounting to market abuse.

(2) Otherwise, the code in force under section 119 at the time when particular behaviour occurs may be relied on so far as it indicates whether or not that behaviour should be taken to amount to market abuse.

Power to impose penalties

[7.178]
123 Power to impose penalties in cases of market abuse

(1) If the Authority is satisfied that a person ("A")—

    (a) is or has engaged in market abuse, or

    (b) by taking or refraining from taking any action has required or encouraged another person or persons to engage in behaviour which, if engaged in by A, would amount to market abuse,

it may impose on him a penalty of such amount as it considers appropriate.

(2) But the Authority may not impose a penalty on a person if, having considered any representations made to it in response to a warning notice, there are reasonable grounds for it to be satisfied that—

    (a) he believed, on reasonable grounds, that his behaviour did not fall within paragraph (a) or (b) of subsection (1), or

    (b) he took all reasonable precautions and exercised all due diligence to avoid behaving in a way which fell within paragraph (a) or (b) of that subsection.

(3) If the Authority is entitled to impose a penalty on a person under this section it may, instead of imposing a penalty on him, publish a statement to the effect that he has engaged in market abuse.

Statement of policy

[7.179]
124   Statement of policy
(1)   The Authority must prepare and issue a statement of its policy with respect to—
  (a)   the imposition of penalties under section 123; and
  (b)   the amount of penalties under that section.
(2)   The Authority's policy in determining what the amount of a penalty should be must include having regard to—
  (a)   whether the behaviour in respect of which the penalty is to be imposed had an adverse effect on the market in question and, if it did, how serious that effect was;
  (b)   the extent to which that behaviour was deliberate or reckless; and
  (c)   whether the person on whom the penalty is to be imposed is an individual.
(3)   A statement issued under this section must include an indication of the circumstances in which the Authority is to be expected to regard a person as—
  (a)   having a reasonable belief that his behaviour did not amount to market abuse; or
  (b)   having taken reasonable precautions and exercised due diligence to avoid engaging in market abuse.
(4)   The Authority may at any time alter or replace a statement issued under this section.
(5)   If a statement issued under this section is altered or replaced, the Authority must issue the altered or replacement statement.
(6)   In exercising, or deciding whether to exercise, its power under section 123 in the case of any particular behaviour, the Authority must have regard to any statement published under this section and in force at the time when the behaviour concerned occurred.
(7)   A statement issued under this section must be published by the Authority in the way appearing to the Authority to be best calculated to bring it to the attention of the public.
(8)   The Authority may charge a reasonable fee for providing a person with a copy of a statement published under this section.
(9)   The Authority must, without delay, give the Treasury a copy of any statement which it publishes under this section.

[7.180]
125   Statement of policy: procedure
(1)   Before issuing a statement of policy under section 124, the Authority must publish a draft of the proposed statement in the way appearing to the Authority to be best calculated to bring it to the attention of the public.
(2)   The draft must be accompanied by notice that representations about the proposal may be made to the Authority within a specified time.
(3)   Before issuing the proposed statement, the Authority must have regard to any representations made to it in accordance with subsection (2).
(4)   If the Authority issues the proposed statement it must publish an account, in general terms, of—
  (a)   the representations made to it in accordance with subsection (2); and
  (b)   its response to them.
(5)   If the statement differs from the draft published under subsection (1) in a way which is, in the opinion of the Authority, significant, the Authority must (in addition to complying with subsection (4)) publish details of the difference.
(6)   The Authority may charge a reasonable fee for providing a person with a copy of a draft published under subsection (1).
(7)   This section also applies to a proposal to alter or replace a statement.

Procedure

[7.181]
126   Warning notices
(1)   If the Authority proposes to take action against a person under section 123, it must give him a warning notice.
(2)   A warning notice about a proposal to impose a penalty must state the amount of the proposed penalty.
(3)   A warning notice about a proposal to publish a statement must set out the terms of the proposed statement.

[7.182]
127   Decision notices and right to refer to Tribunal
(1)   If the Authority decides to take action against a person under section 123, it must give him a decision notice.
(2)   A decision notice about the imposition of a penalty must state the amount of the penalty.
(3)   A decision notice about the publication of a statement must set out the terms of the statement.
(4)   If the Authority decides to take action against a person under section 123, that person may refer the matter to the Tribunal.

Miscellaneous

[7.183]
128 Suspension of investigations
(1) If the Authority considers it desirable or expedient because of the exercise or possible exercise of a power relating to market abuse, it may direct a recognised investment exchange or recognised clearing house—
  (a) to terminate, suspend or limit the scope of any inquiry which the exchange or clearing house is conducting under its rules; or
  (b) not to conduct an inquiry which the exchange or clearing house proposes to conduct under its rules.
(2) A direction under this section—
  (a) must be given to the exchange or clearing house concerned by notice in writing; and
  (b) is enforceable, on the application of the Authority, by injunction or, in Scotland, by an order under section 45 of the Court of Session Act 1988.
(3) The Authority's powers relating to market abuse are its powers—
  (a) to impose penalties under section 123; or
  (b) to appoint a person to conduct an investigation under section 168 in a case falling within subsection (2)(d) of that section.

[7.184]
129 Power of court to impose penalty in cases of market abuse
(1) The Authority may on an application to the court under section 381 or 383 request the court to consider whether the circumstances are such that a penalty should be imposed on the person to whom the application relates.
(2) The court may, if it considers it appropriate, make an order requiring the person concerned to pay to the Authority a penalty of such amount as it considers appropriate.

[7.185]
130 Guidance
(1) The Treasury may from time to time issue written guidance for the purpose of helping relevant authorities to determine the action to be taken in cases where behaviour occurs which is behaviour—
  (a) with respect to which the power in section 123 appears to be exercisable; and
  (b) which appears to involve the commission of an offence under section 397 of this Act or Part V of the Criminal Justice Act 1993 (insider dealing).
(2) The Treasury must obtain the consent of the Attorney General and the Secretary of State before issuing any guidance under this section.
(3) In this section "relevant authorities"—
  (a) in relation to England and Wales, means the Secretary of State, the Authority, the Director of the Serious Fraud Office and the Director of Public Prosecutions;
  (b) in relation to Northern Ireland, means the Secretary of State, the Authority, the Director of the Serious Fraud Office and the Director of Public Prosecutions for Northern Ireland.
(4) Subsections (1) to (3) do not apply to Scotland.
(5) In relation to Scotland, the Lord Advocate may from time to time, after consultation with the Treasury, issue written guidance for the purpose of helping the Authority to determine the action to be taken in cases where behaviour mentioned in subsection (1) occurs.

NOTES
Attorney General: any function of the Attorney General may be exercised by the Solicitor General; see the Law Officers Act 1997, s 1.

[7.186]
[130A Interpretation and supplementary provision
(1) The Treasury may by order specify (whether by name or description)—
  (a) the markets which are prescribed markets for the purposes of specified provisions of this Part, and
  (b) the investments that are qualifying investments in relation to the prescribed markets.
(2) An order may prescribe different investments or descriptions of investment in relation to different markets or descriptions of market.
(3) In this Part—
  "accepted market practices" means practices that are reasonably expected in the financial market or markets in question and are accepted by the Authority or, in the case of a market situated in another EEA State, the competent authority of that EEA State within the meaning of Directive 2003/6/EC of the European Parliament and of the Council of 28 January 2003 on insider dealing and market manipulation (market abuse),
  "behaviour" includes action or inaction,
  "dealing", in relation to an investment, means acquiring or disposing of the investment whether as principal or agent or directly or indirectly, and includes agreeing to acquire or dispose of the investment, and entering into and bringing to an end a contract creating it,

"investment" is to be read with section 22 and Schedule 2,
*"regular user", in relation to a particular market, means a reasonable person who regularly
    deals on that market in investments of the kind in question,*
"related investment", in relation to a qualifying investment, means an investment whose price or
    value depends on the price or value of the qualifying investment.
(4)   Any reference in this Act to a person engaged in market abuse is to a person engaged in
market abuse either alone or with one or more other persons.]

NOTES

Inserted by the Financial Services and Markets Act 2000 (Market Abuse) Regulations 2005, SI 2005/381, reg 5, Sch 2, para 3, as from 1 July 2005.

Definition "regular user" repealed by s 118(9) of this Act (at **[7.170]**), as from 31 December 2011.

Orders: the Financial Services and Markets Act 2000 (Prescribed Markets and Qualifying Investments) Order 2001, SI 2001/996 at **[8.167]**. Note that the 2001 Order was originally made under s 118(3) of this Act but, following the substitution of that section as noted thereto, now has effect as if made under sub-s (1) above.

[7.187]
131   Effect on transactions
The imposition of a penalty under this Part does not make any transaction void or unenforceable.

[7.188]
[131A   Protected Disclosures
(1)   A disclosure which satisfies the following three conditions is not to be taken to breach any
restriction on the disclosure of information (however imposed).
(2)   The first condition is that the information or other matter—
   (a)   causes the person making the disclosure (the discloser) to know or suspect, or
   (b)   gives him reasonable grounds for knowing or suspecting, that another person has engaged
         in market abuse.
(3)   The second condition is that the information or other matter disclosed came to the discloser in
the course of his trade, profession, business or employment.
(4)   The third condition is that the disclosure is made to the Authority or to a nominated officer as
soon as is practicable after the information or other matter comes to the discloser.
(5)   A disclosure to a nominated officer is a disclosure which is made to a person nominated by the
discloser's employer to receive disclosures under this section, and is made in the course of the
discloser's employment and in accordance with the procedure established by the employer for the
purpose.
(6)   For the purposes of this section, references to a person's employer include any body,
association or organisation (including a voluntary organisation) in connection with whose activities
the person exercises a function (whether or not for gain or reward) and references to employment
must be construed accordingly.]

NOTES

Inserted by the Financial Services and Markets Act 2000 (Market Abuse) Regulations 2005, SI 2005/381, reg 5, Sch 2, para 4, as from 1 July 2005.

[PART 8A
SHORT SELLING

Short selling rules

[7.189]
131B   Short selling rules
(1)   The Authority may make rules prohibiting in specified cases persons from engaging in short
selling in relation to relevant financial instruments (or relevant financial instruments of a specified
description).
(2)   The Authority may make rules requiring—
   (a)   a person who has engaged in short selling in relation to relevant financial instruments (or
         relevant financial instruments of a specified description), or
   (b)   an authorised person of a specified description who has acted on behalf of such a person,
to disclose in specified cases specified information, or information of a specified description, about
the short selling.
(3)   Rules under subsection (2) may specify the time by which, and the way in which, the
disclosure must be made (and may in particular provide for the information to be disclosed to the
Authority or published in a specified way).
(4)   Rules under subsection (2) may apply in relation to short selling engaged in before the
rules are made where the resulting short position is still open when the rules are made.
(5)   The reference to a short position being open is to be read in accordance with provision made
by the rules.
(6)   Rules under this section may apply to short selling wholly outside the United Kingdom by
persons outside the United Kingdom, but only in so far as the rules relate to UK financial
instruments.

(7) The description of relevant financial instruments that may be specified by the rules includes relevant financial instruments issued by a specified person.

(8) Rules under this section are referred to in this Part as "short selling rules".

(9) The Authority must, when making short selling rules, have regard to any international agreement as to measures to be taken in respect of short selling.]

NOTES

Commencement: 8 June 2010.

Part 8A (ss 131B–131K) inserted by the Financial Services Act 2010, s 8, as from 8 June 2010.

[7.190]
[131C   Short selling rules: definitions etc

(1)   This section supplements section 131B.

(2)   The cases in which a person ("S") engages in short selling in relation to a financial instrument (a "shorted instrument") include any case where—

(a)   S enters into a transaction which creates, or relates to, another financial instrument; and

(b)   the effect (or one of the effects) of the transaction is to confer a financial advantage on S in the event of a decrease in the price or value of the shorted instrument.

(3)   "Financial instrument" has the meaning given by Article 4.1(17) of the markets in financial instruments directive.

(4)   "Relevant financial instrument" means a financial instrument that—

(a)   is admitted to trading on a regulated market or on any other prescribed market in an EEA State; or

(b)   has such other connection with a market in an EEA State as may be specified.

(5)   "Specified" means specified by short selling rules.

(6)   "UK financial instrument" means a financial instrument that is admitted to trading on a market in the United Kingdom.

(7)   In the case of a financial instrument that is admitted to trading on—

(a)   a market in the United Kingdom or another EEA State, and

(b)   one or more markets in a country or territory, or countries or territories, anywhere else in the world,

short selling rules may apply in relation to trading on both or all markets.

(8)   In any case where—

(a)   a financial instrument ("instrument A") is admitted to trading on a market in the United Kingdom or another EEA State,

(b)   another financial instrument ("instrument B") is admitted to trading on one or more markets in a country or territory, or countries or territories, anywhere else in the world, and

(c)   the price or value of instrument A depends on the price or value of instrument B (or vice versa),

short selling rules may apply in relation to trading on both or all markets.

(9)   In subsection (4)(a) "regulated market" has the meaning given by Article 4.1(14) of the markets in financial instruments directive.

(10)   References in this section to a market in a country or territory are to a market situated or operating in the country or territory.]

NOTES

Commencement: 8 June 2010.

Inserted as noted to s 131B at **[7.189]**.

[7.191]
[131D   Short selling rules: procedure in urgent cases

(1)   The Authority may make short selling rules (and may subsequently amend those rules) without complying with section 155 (consultation in relation to proposed rules) if it considers that it is necessary to do so, in order to—

(a)   maintain confidence in the UK financial system; or

(b)   protect the stability of the UK financial system.

(2)   Any rules made by virtue of subsection (1) ("emergency rules") cease to have effect at the end of the period of three months beginning with the day on which the rules are made ("the relevant day"); but this is subject as follows.

(3)   The Authority may direct that emergency rules are to cease to have effect at the end of a period (not exceeding six months beginning with the relevant day) specified in the direction.

(4)   A direction under subsection (3) may be made only if, immediately before the end of the period mentioned in subsection (2), the Authority considers that it is necessary to do so, in order to—

(a)   maintain confidence in the UK financial system; or

(b)   protect the stability of the UK financial system.

(5)   Such a direction must be published by the Authority in the way appearing to the Authority to be best calculated to bring it to the attention of the public.

(6)   Nothing in subsection (2) or (3) prevents the Authority from revoking emergency rules before the end of the periods referred to there.]

NOTES
Commencement: 8 June 2010.
Inserted as noted to s 131B at **[7.189]**.

[Power to require information

[7.192]
131E   Power to require information
(1)   The Authority may, by notice in writing, require a person ("P")—
   (a)   to provide specified information or information of a specified description; or
   (b)   to produce specified documents or documents of a specified description.
(2)   This section applies only to information and documents that the Authority reasonably requires for the purpose of determining whether P, or a person connected with P, has contravened any provision of short selling rules.
(3)   Information or documents required under this section must be provided or produced—
   (a)   before the end of such reasonable period as may be specified; and
   (b)   at such place as may be specified.
(4)   The Authority may require any information provided under this section to be provided in such form as it may reasonably require.
(5)   The Authority may require—
   (a)   any information provided, whether in a document or otherwise, to be verified in such manner as it may reasonably require; or
   (b)   any document produced to be authenticated in such manner as it may reasonably require.
(6)   In this section "specified" means specified in the notice.
(7)   For the purposes of this section a person is connected with another person ("P") if the person is or has at any relevant time been—
   (a)   a member of P's group;
   (b)   a controller of P;
   (c)   any other member of a partnership of which P is a member; or
   (d)   in relation to P, a person mentioned in Part 1 of Schedule 15 (reading references in that Part to the authorised person as references to P).]

NOTES
Commencement: 8 June 2010.
Inserted as noted to s 131B at **[7.189]**.

[7.193]
[131F   Power to require information: supplementary
(1)   If the Authority has power under section 131E to require a person to produce a document but it appears that the document is in the possession of a third person, that power may be exercised in relation to the third person.
(2)   If a document is produced in response to a requirement imposed under section 131E, the Authority may—
   (a)   take copies of or extracts from the document; or
   (b)   require the person producing the document, or any relevant person, to provide an explanation of the document.
(3)   In subsection (2)(b) "relevant person", in relation to a person who is required to produce a document, means a person who—
   (a)   has been or is or is proposed to be a director or controller of that person;
   (b)   has been or is an auditor of that person;
   (c)   has been or is an actuary, accountant or lawyer appointed or instructed by that person; or
   (d)   has been or is an employee of that person.
(4)   If a person who is required under section 131E to produce a document fails to do so, the Authority may require the person to state, to the best of the person's knowledge and belief, where the document is.
(5)   A lawyer may be required under section 131E to provide the name and address of the lawyer's client.
(6)   A person ("P") may not be required under section 131E to disclose information or produce a document in respect of which P owes an obligation of confidence by virtue of carrying on the business of banking unless—
   (a)   P is the person under investigation or a member of that person's group;
   (b)   the person to whom the obligation of confidence is owed is the person under investigation or a member of that person's group; or
   (c)   the person to whom the obligation of confidence is owed consents to the disclosure or production.
(7)   If a person claims a lien on a document, its production under section 131E does not affect the lien.]

NOTES
Commencement: 8 June 2010.
Inserted as noted to s 131B at **[7.189]**.

[Breach of short selling rules etc

[7.194]
131G   Power to impose penalty or issue censure
(1)   This section applies if the Authority is satisfied that a person has contravened—
   (a)   any provision of short selling rules; or
   (b)   any requirement imposed on the person under section 131E or 131F.
(2)   The Authority may impose a penalty of such amount as it considers appropriate on—
   (a)   the person who contravened the provision or requirement; or
   (b)   any person who was knowingly concerned in the contravention.
(3)   It may, instead of imposing a penalty on a person, publish a statement censuring the person.
(4)   The Authority may not take action against a person under this section after the end of the limitation period unless, before the end of that period, it has given a warning notice to the person under section 131H.
(5)   "The limitation period" means the period of three years beginning with the first day on which the Authority knew of the contravention.
(6)   For this purpose the Authority is to be treated as knowing of a contravention if it has information from which the contravention can reasonably be inferred.]

NOTES
Commencement: 8 June 2010.
Inserted as noted to s 131B at **[7.189]**.

[7.195]
[131H   Procedure and right to refer to Tribunal
(1)   If the Authority proposes to take action against a person under section 131G, it must give the person a warning notice.
(2)   A warning notice about a proposal to impose a penalty must state the amount of the penalty.
(3)   A warning notice about a proposal to publish a statement must set out the terms of the statement.
(4)   If the Authority decides to take action against a person under section 131G, it must give the person a decision notice.
(5)   A decision notice about the imposition of a penalty must state the amount of the penalty.
(6)   A decision notice about the publication of a statement must set out the terms of the statement.
(7)   If the Authority decides to take action against a person under section 131G, the person may refer the matter to the Tribunal.]

NOTES
Commencement: 8 June 2010.
Inserted as noted to s 131B at **[7.189]**.

[7.196]
[131I   Duty on publication of statement
After a statement under section 131G(3) is published, the Authority must send a copy of the statement to—
   (a)   the person in respect of whom it is made; and
   (b)   any person to whom a copy of the decision notice was given under section 393(4).]

NOTES
Commencement: 8 June 2010.
Inserted as noted to s 131B at **[7.189]**.

[7.197]
[131J   Imposition of penalties under section 131G: statement of policy
(1)   The Authority must prepare and issue a statement of its policy with respect to—
   (a)   the imposition of penalties under section 131G; and
   (b)   the amount of penalties under that section.
(2)   The Authority's policy in determining what the amount of a penalty should be must include having regard to—
   (a)   the seriousness of the contravention;
   (b)   the extent to which the contravention was deliberate or reckless; and
   (c)   whether the person on whom the penalty is to be imposed is an individual.
(3)   The Authority may at any time alter or replace a statement issued under this section.
(4)   If a statement issued under this section is altered or replaced, the Authority must issue the altered or replaced statement.

(5) The Authority must, without delay, give the Treasury a copy of any statement which it publishes under this section.

(6) A statement issued under this section must be published by the Authority in the way appearing to the Authority to be best calculated to bring it to the attention of the public.

(7) The Authority may charge a reasonable fee for providing a person with a copy of the statement.

(8) In exercising, or deciding whether to exercise, a power under section 131G in the case of any particular contravention, the Authority must have regard to any statement of policy published under this section and in force at a time when the contravention occurred.]

NOTES
Commencement: 8 June 2010.
Inserted as noted to s 131B at **[7.189]**.

[7.198]
[131K   Statement of policy: procedure
(1) Before issuing a statement under section 131J, the Authority must publish a draft of the proposed statement in the way appearing to the Authority to be best calculated to bring it to the attention of the public.

(2) The draft must be accompanied by notice that representations about the proposal may be made to the Authority within a specified time.

(3) Before issuing the proposed statement, the Authority must have regard to any representations made to it in accordance with subsection (2).

(4) If the Authority issues the proposed statement it must publish an account, in general terms, of—
    (a) the representations made to it in accordance with subsection (2); and
    (b) its response to them.

(5) If the statement differs from the draft published under subsection (1) in a way which is, in the opinion of the Authority, significant, the Authority must (in addition to complying with subsection (4)) publish details of the difference.

(6) The Authority may charge a reasonable fee for providing a person with a copy of a draft published under subsection (1).

(7) This section also applies to a proposal to alter or replace a statement.]

NOTES
Commencement: 8 June 2010.
Inserted as noted to s 131B at **[7.189]**.

132–177 *(Part IX—Hearings and Appeals (ss 132–137 and Sch 13), Part X—Rules and Guidance (ss 138–164 and Sch 14), and Part XI—Information Gathering and Investigations (ss 165–177 and Sch 15) omitted for reasons of space; see further, the introductory notes to this Act.)*

PART XII
CONTROL OVER AUTHORISED PERSONS

NOTES
Transitional provisions: see the Financial Services and Markets Act 2000 (Transitional Provisions) (Controllers) Order 2001, SI 2001/2637 which makes transitional provisions for people who are subject to a regime requiring them to notify a significant shareholding in an authorised person and who will fall within this Part. The Order deals both with the status after commencement of people who have been approved as shareholder controllers under existing regimes and with partly completed procedures. It also provides that the FSA can exercise its powers under this Act in respect of a person who has failed to comply with obligations under the pre-existing regimes, in circumstances where that person would have been subject to an equivalent obligation under this Part after commencement.
See also s 192 at **[7.220]** with regard to the Treasury's power to change the definition of "control".

[Notices of acquisitions of control over UK authorised persons

[7.199]
178   Obligation to notify the Authority: acquisitions of control
(1) A person who decides to acquire or increase control over a UK authorised person must give the Authority notice in writing before making the acquisition.

(2) For the purposes of calculations relating to this section, the holding of shares or voting power by a person ("A1") includes any shares or voting power held by another ("A2") if A1 and A2 are acting in concert.

(3) In this Part, a notice given under this section is a "section 178 notice" and a person giving notice is a "section 178 notice-giver".]

NOTES
Commencement: 21 March 2009.
Sections 178–191G were substituted (for the original ss 178–191) by the Financial Services and Markets Act 2000 (Controllers) Regulations 2009, SI 2009/534, reg 3, Sch 1, as from 21 March 2009, subject to transitional provisions in reg 8 of

those Regulations which provide that Part XII of this Act, as it stood immediately before that date, applies in respect of any notification submitted to the FSA under those provisions before that date.

[7.200]
[179   Requirements for section 178 notices
(1)   A section 178 notice must be in such form, include such information and be accompanied by such documents as the Authority may reasonably require.
(2)   The Authority must publish a list of its requirements as to the form, information and accompanying documents for a section 178 notice.
(3)   The Authority may impose different requirements for different cases and may vary or waive requirements in particular cases.]

NOTES
Commencement: 21 March 2009.
Substituted, subject to transitional provisions, as noted to s 178 at **[7.199]**.

[7.201]
[180   Acknowledgment of receipt
(1)   The Authority must acknowledge receipt of a completed section 178 notice in writing before the end of the second working day following receipt.
(2)   If the Authority receives an incomplete section 178 notice it must inform the section 178 notice-giver as soon as reasonably practicable.]

NOTES
Commencement: 21 March 2009.
Substituted, subject to transitional provisions, as noted to s 178 at **[7.199]**.

[Acquiring control and other changes of holding
[7.202]
181   Acquiring control
(1)   For the purposes of this Part, a person ("A") acquires control over a UK authorised person ("B") if any of the cases in subsection (2) begin to apply.
(2)   The cases are where A holds—
    (a)   10% or more of the shares in B or in a parent undertaking of B ("P");
    (b)   10% or more of the voting power in B or P; or
    (c)   shares or voting power in B or P as a result of which A is able to exercise significant influence over the management of B.]

NOTES
Commencement: 21 March 2009.
Substituted, subject to transitional provisions, as noted to s 178 at **[7.199]**.

[7.203]
[182   Increasing control
(1)   For the purposes of this Part, a person ("A") increases control over a UK authorised person ("B") whenever—
    (a)   the percentage of shares which A holds in B or in a parent undertaking of B ("P") increases by any of the steps mentioned in subsection (2);
    (b)   the percentage of voting power A holds in B or P increases by any of the steps mentioned in subsection (2); or
    (c)   A becomes a parent undertaking of B.
(2)   The steps are—
    (a)   from less than 20% to 20% or more;
    (b)   from less than 30% to 30% or more;
    (c)   from less than 50% to 50% or more.]

NOTES
Commencement: 21 March 2009.
Substituted, subject to transitional provisions, as noted to s 178 at **[7.199]**.

[7.204]
[183   Reducing or ceasing to have control
(1)   For the purposes of this Part, a person ("A") reduces control over a UK authorised person ("B") whenever—
    (a)   the percentage of shares which A holds in B or in a parent undertaking of B ("P") decreases by any of the steps mentioned in subsection (2);
    (b)   the percentage of voting power which A holds in B or P decreases by any of the steps mentioned in subsection (2); or
    (c)   A ceases to be a parent undertaking of B.
(2)   The steps are—

(a)   from 50% or more to less than 50%;
(b)   from 30% or more to less than 30%;
(c)   from 20% or more to less than 20%.

(3)   For the purposes of this Part, a person ("A") ceases to have control over a UK authorised person ("B") if A ceases to be in the position of holding—

(a)   10% or more of the shares in B or in a parent undertaking of B ("P");
(b)   10% or more of the voting power in B or P; or
(c)   shares or voting power in B or P as a result of which A is able to exercise significant influence over the management of B.]

NOTES

Commencement: 21 March 2009.

Substituted, subject to transitional provisions, as noted to s 178 at **[7.199]**.

[7.205]
[184   Disregarded holdings
(1)   For the purposes of sections 181 to 183, shares and voting power that a person holds in a UK authorised person ("B") or in a parent undertaking of B ("P") are disregarded in the following circumstances.

(2)   Shares held only for the purposes of clearing and settling within a short settlement cycle are disregarded.

(3)   Shares held by a custodian or its nominee in a custodian capacity are disregarded, provided that the custodian or nominee is only able to exercise voting power represented by the shares in accordance with instructions given in writing.

(4)   Shares representing no more than 5% of the total voting power in B or P held by an investment firm are disregarded, provided that it—

(a)   holds the shares in the capacity of a market maker (as defined in article 4.1(8) of the markets in financial instruments directive);
(b)   is authorised by its home state regulator under the markets in financial instruments directive; and
(c)   neither intervenes in the management of B or P nor exerts any influence on B or P to buy the shares or back the share price.

(5)   Shares held by a credit institution or investment firm in its trading book are disregarded, provided that—

(a)   the shares represent no more than 5% of the total voting power in B or P; and
(b)   the credit institution or investment firm ensures that the voting power is not used to intervene in the management of B or P.

(6)   Shares held by a credit institution or an investment firm are disregarded, provided that—

(a)   the shares are held as a result of performing the investment services and activities of—
    (i)   underwriting a share issue; or
    (ii)   placing shares on a firm commitment basis in accordance with Annex I, section A.6 of the markets in financial instruments directive; and
(b)   the credit institution or investment firm—
    (i)   does not exercise voting power represented by the shares or otherwise intervene in the management of the issuer; and
    (ii)   retains the holding for a period of less than one year.

(7)   Where a management company (as defined in [Article 2.1(b)] of the UCITS directive) and its parent undertaking both hold shares or voting power, each may disregard holdings of the other, provided that each exercises its voting power independently of the other.

(8)   But subsection (7) does not apply if the management company—

(a)   manages holdings for its parent undertaking or an undertaking in respect of which the parent undertaking is a controller;
(b)   has no discretion as to the exercise of the voting power attached to such holdings; and
(c)   may only exercise the voting power in relation to such holdings under direct or indirect instruction from—
    (i)   the parent undertaking; or
    (ii)   an undertaking in respect of which of the parent undertaking is a controller.

(9)   Where an investment firm and its parent undertaking both hold shares or voting power, the parent undertaking may disregard holdings managed by the investment firm on a client by client basis and the investment firm may disregard holdings of the parent undertaking, provided that the investment firm—

(a)   has permission to provide portfolio management;
(b)   exercises its voting power independently from the parent undertaking; and
(c)   may only exercise the voting power under instructions given in writing, or has appropriate mechanisms in place for ensuring that individual portfolio management services are conducted independently of any other services.]

NOTES
Commencement: 21 March 2009.
Substituted, subject to transitional provisions, as noted to s 178 at **[7.199]**.
Sub-s (7): words in square brackets substituted by the Undertakings for Collective Investment in Transferable Securities
Regulations 2011, SI 2011/1613, reg 2(1), (6), as from 1 July 2011.

[Assessment procedure

[7.206]
185   Assessment: general
(1)   Where the Authority receives a section 178 notice, it must—
   (a)   determine whether to approve the acquisition to which it relates unconditionally; or
   (b)   propose to—
      (i)   approve the acquisition subject to conditions (see section 187); or
      (ii)   object to the acquisition.
(2)   The Authority must—
   (a)   consider the suitability of the section 178 notice-giver and the financial soundness of the
      acquisition in order to ensure the sound and prudent management of the UK authorised
      person;
   (b)   have regard to the likely influence that the section 178 notice-giver will have on the UK
      authorised person; and
   (c)   disregard the economic needs of the market.
(3)   The Authority may only object to an acquisition—
   (a)   if there are reasonable grounds for doing so on the basis of the matters set out in
      section 186; or
   (b)   if the information provided by the section 178 notice-giver is incomplete.]

NOTES
Commencement: 21 March 2009.
Substituted, subject to transitional provisions, as noted to s 178 at **[7.199]**.

[7.207]
[186   Assessment criteria
The matters specified in section 185(3)(a) are—
   (a)   the reputation of the section 178 notice-giver;
   (b)   the reputation and experience of any person who will direct the business of the UK
      authorised person as a result of the proposed acquisition;
   (c)   the financial soundness of the section 178 notice-giver, in particular in relation to the type
      of business that the UK authorised person pursues or envisages pursuing;
   (d)   whether the UK authorised person will be able to comply with its prudential requirements
      (including the threshold conditions in relation to all of the regulated activities for which it
      has or will have permission);
   (e)   if the UK authorised person is to become part of a group as a result of the acquisition,
      whether that group has a structure which makes it possible to—
      (i)   exercise effective supervision;
      (ii)   exchange information among regulators; and
      (iii)   determine the allocation of responsibility among regulators; and
   (f)   whether there are reasonable grounds to suspect that in connection with the proposed
      acquisition—
      (i)   money laundering or terrorist financing (within the meaning of Article 1 of Directive
         2005/60/EC of the European Parliament and of the Council of 26th October 2005 on
         the prevention of the use of the financial system for the purpose of money laundering
         and terrorist financing) is being or has been committed or attempted; or
      (ii)   the risk of such activity could increase.]

NOTES
Commencement: 21 March 2009.
Substituted, subject to transitional provisions, as noted to s 178 at **[7.199]**.

[7.208]
[187   Approval with conditions
(1)   The Authority may impose conditions on its approval of an acquisition.
(2)   The Authority may only impose conditions where, if it did not impose those conditions, it
would propose to object to the acquisition.
(3)   The Authority may not impose conditions requiring a particular level of holding to be
acquired.
(4)   The Authority may vary or cancel the conditions.]

NOTES
Commencement: 21 March 2009.

Substituted, subject to transitional provisions, as noted to s 178 at **[7.199]**.

[7.209]
[188 Assessment: consultation with EC competent authorities
(1) The Authority must consult any appropriate home state regulator before making a determination under section 185 and, in doing so, must comply with such requirements as to consultation as may be prescribed.
(2) Where the Authority makes a determination under section 185, it must indicate any views or reservations received from any home state regulator it consults in accordance with subsection (1).
(3) The Authority must cooperate with any equivalent consultation by a host state regulator in relation to a UK authorised person.
(4) In order to comply with an obligation under subsection (1) or (3), the Authority must provide the regulator with—
   (a) any relevant information that it requests; and
   (b) any information that the Authority considers that it needs.]

NOTES
Commencement: 21 March 2009.
Substituted, subject to transitional provisions, as noted to s 178 at **[7.199]**.
Regulations: the Financial Services and Markets Act 2000 (Consultation with Competent Authorities) Regulations 2001, SI 2001/2509; the Financial Conglomerates and Other Financial Groups Regulations 2004, SI 2004/1862. Note that these Regulations were originally made under ss 183 and 188 of this Act (prior to the substitution of those sections as noted above). These Regulations now have effect under this section and s 191A *post*. Note also that the following amending Regulations were also made under the original ss 183, 188, ie, the Collective Investment Schemes (Miscellaneous Amendments) Regulations 2003, SI 2003/2066; the Financial Services and Markets Act 2000 (Reinsurance Directive) Regulations 2007, SI 2007/3255.

[7.210]
[189 Assessment: Procedure
(1) The Authority must act under section 185 within a period of 60 working days beginning with the day on which the Authority acknowledges receipt of the section 178 notice ("the assessment period").
(2) The assessment period may be interrupted, no more than once, in accordance with section 190.
(3) The Authority must inform the section 178 notice-giver in writing of—
   (a) the duration of the assessment period;
   (b) its expiry date; and
   (c) any change to the expiry date by virtue of section 190.
(4) The Authority must, within two working days of acting under section 185 (and in any event no later than the expiry date of the assessment period)—
   (a) notify the section 178 notice-giver that it has determined to approve the acquisition unconditionally; or
   (b) give a warning notice stating that it proposes to—
      (i) approve the acquisition subject to conditions; or
      (ii) object to the acquisition.
(5) Where the Authority gives a warning notice stating that it proposes to approve the acquisition subject to conditions—
   (a) it must, in the warning notice, specify those conditions; and
   (b) the conditions take effect as interim conditions.
(6) The Authority is treated as having approved the acquisition if, at the expiry of the assessment period, it has neither—
   (a) given notice under subsection (4); nor
   (b) informed the section 178 notice-giver that the section 178 notice is incomplete.
(7) If the Authority decides to approve an acquisition subject to conditions or to object to an acquisition it must give the section 178 notice-giver a decision notice.
(8) Following receipt of a decision notice under this section, the section 178 notice-giver may refer the Authority's decision to the Tribunal.]

NOTES
Commencement: 21 March 2009.
Substituted, subject to transitional provisions, as noted to s 178 at **[7.199]**.

[7.211]
[190 Requests for further information
(1) The Authority may, no later than the 50th working day of the assessment period, in writing ask the section 178 notice-giver to provide any further information necessary to complete its assessment.
(2) On the first occasion that the Authority asks for further information, the assessment period is interrupted from the date of the request until the date the Authority receives the requested information ("the interruption period").
(3) But the interruption period may not exceed 20 working days, unless subsection (4) applies.

(4)   The interruption period may not exceed 30 working days if the notice-giver—
  (a)   is situated or regulated outside the European Community; or
  (b)   is not subject to supervision under—
    (i)   the UCITS directive;
    (ii)   the insurance directives;
    (iii)   the markets in financial instruments directive;
    (iv)   the reinsurance directive; or
    (v)   the banking consolidation directive.
(5)   The Authority may make further requests for information (but a further request does not result in a further interruption of the assessment period).
(6)   The Authority must acknowledge in writing receipt of further information before the end of the second working day following receipt.]

NOTES
  Commencement: 21 March 2009.
  Substituted, subject to transitional provisions, as noted to s 178 at **[7.199]**.

[7.212]
[191   Duration of approval
(1)   Approval of an acquisition (whether granted unconditionally or subject to conditions) is effective for such period as the Authority may specify in writing.
(2)   Where the Authority has specified a period under subsection (1), it may extend the period.
(3)   Where the Authority has not specified a period, the approval is effective for one year beginning with the date—
  (a)   of the notice given under section 189(4)(a) or (b)(i);
  (b)   on which the Authority is treated as having given approval under section 189(6); or
  (c)   of a decision on a reference to the Tribunal which results in the person receiving approval.]

NOTES
  Commencement: 21 March 2009.
  Substituted, subject to transitional provisions, as noted to s 178 at **[7.199]**.

[Enforcement procedures

[7.213]
191A   Objection by the Authority
(1)   The Authority may object to a person's control over a UK authorised person in any of the circumstances specified in subsection (2).
(2)   The circumstances are that the Authority reasonably believes that—
  (a)   the person acquired or increased control without giving notice under section 178(1) in circumstances where notice was required;
  (b)   the person is in breach of a condition imposed under section 187; or
  (c)   there are grounds for objecting to control on the basis of the matters in section 186.
(3)   The Authority—
  (a)   must take into account whether influence exercised by the person is likely to operate to the detriment of the sound and prudent management of the UK authorised person; and
  (b)   may take into account whether the person has co-operated with any information requests made or requirements imposed by the Authority.
(4)   If the Authority proposes to object to a person's control over a UK authorised person, it must give that person a warning notice.
(5)   The Authority must consult any appropriate home state regulator before giving a warning notice under this section and, in doing so, must comply with such requirements as to consultation as may be prescribed.
(6)   If the Authority decides to object to a person's control over a UK authorised person, it must give that person a decision notice.
(7)   A person to whom the Authority gives a decision notice under this section may refer the matter to the Tribunal.]

NOTES
  Commencement: 21 March 2009.
  Substituted, subject to transitional provisions, as noted to s 178 at **[7.199]**.
  Regulations: see the note to s 188 at **[7.209]**.

[7.214]
[191B   Restriction notices
(1)   The Authority may give notice in writing (a "restriction notice") to a person in the following circumstances.
(2)   The circumstances are that—
  (a)   the person has control over a UK authorised person by virtue of holding shares or voting power; and

(b)   in relation to the shares or voting power, the Authority has given the person a warning notice or a decision notice under section 189 or 191A or a final notice which confirms a decision notice given under section 189 or 191A.

(3)   In a restriction notice, the Authority may direct that shares or voting power to which the notice relates are, until further notice, subject to one or more of the following restrictions—

(a)   except by court order, an agreement to transfer or a transfer of any such shares or voting power or, in the case of unissued shares, any agreement to transfer or transfer of the right to be issued with them, is void;

(b)   no voting power is to be exercisable;

(c)   no further shares are to be issued in pursuance of any right of the holder of any such shares or voting power or in pursuance of any offer made to their holder;

(d)   except in a liquidation, no payment is to be made of any sums due from the body corporate on any such shares, whether in respect of capital or otherwise.

(4)   A restriction notice takes effect—

(a)   immediately; or

(b)   on such date as may be specified in the notice.

(5)   A restriction notice does not extinguish rights which would be enjoyable but for the notice.

(6)   A copy of the restriction notice must be served on—

(a)   the UK authorised person in question; and

(b)   in the case of shares or voting power held in a parent undertaking of a UK authorised person, the parent undertaking.

(7)   A person to whom the Authority gives a restriction notice may refer the matter to the Tribunal.]

NOTES

Commencement: 21 March 2009.

Substituted, subject to transitional provisions, as noted to s 178 at **[7.199]**.

[7.215]

[191C   Orders for sale of shares

(1)   The court may, on the application of the Authority, order the sale of shares or the disposition of voting power in the following circumstances.

(2)   The circumstances are that—

(a)   a person has control over a UK authorised person by virtue of holding the shares or voting power; and

(b)   the acquisition or continued holding of the shares or voting power by that person is in contravention of a final notice which confirms a decision notice given under section 189 or section 191A.

(3)   Where the court orders the sale of shares or disposition of voting power it may—

(a)   if a restriction notice has been given in relation to the shares or voting power, order that the restrictions cease to apply; and

(b)   make any further order.

(4)   Where the court makes an order under this section, it must take into account the level of holding that the person would have been entitled to acquire, or to continue to hold, without contravening the final notice.

(5)   If shares are sold or voting power disposed of in pursuance of an order under this section, any proceeds, less the costs of the sale or disposition, must be paid into court for the benefit of the persons beneficially interested in them; and any such person may apply to the court for payment of a whole or part of the proceeds.

(6)   The jurisdiction conferred by this section may be exercised by the High Court and the Court of Session.]

NOTES

Commencement: 21 March 2009.

Substituted, subject to transitional provisions, as noted to s 178 at **[7.199]**.

[Notice of reductions of control of UK authorised persons

[7.216]

191D   Obligation to notify the Authority: dispositions of control

(1)   A person who decides to reduce or cease to have control over a UK authorised person must give the Authority notice in writing before making the disposition.

(2)   For the purposes of calculations relating to this section, the holding of shares or voting power by a person ("A1") includes any shares or voting power held by another ("A2") if A1 and A2 are acting in concert.]

NOTES

Commencement: 21 March 2009.

Substituted, subject to transitional provisions, as noted to s 178 at **[7.199]**.

[7.217]
[191E Requirements for notices under section 191D
(1) A notice under section 191D must be in such form, include such information and be accompanied by such documents as the Authority may reasonably require.
(2) The Authority must publish a list of its requirements as to the form, information and accompanying documents for a notice under section 191D.
(3) The Authority may impose different requirements for different cases and may vary or waive requirements in particular cases.]

NOTES
Commencement: 21 March 2009.
Substituted, subject to transitional provisions, as noted to s 178 at **[7.199]**.

[Offences

[7.218]
191F Offences under this Part
(1) A person who fails to comply with an obligation to notify the Authority under section 178(1) or 191D(1) is guilty of an offence.
(2) A person who gives notice to the Authority under section 178(1) and makes the acquisition to which the notice relates before the expiry date of the assessment period is guilty of an offence unless the Authority has approved the acquisition or given a warning notice under section 189(4)(b)(i).
(3) A person who contravenes an interim condition in a warning notice given under section 189(4)(b)(i) or a condition in a decision notice given under section 189(7) or a final notice which confirms a decision notice under that section is guilty of an offence.
(4) A person who makes an acquisition in contravention of a warning notice given under section 189(4)(b)(ii) or a decision notice given under section 189(7) or a final notice which confirms a decision notice under that section is guilty of an offence.
(5) A person who makes an acquisition after the Authority's approval for the acquisition has ceased to be effective by virtue of section 191 is guilty of an offence.
(6) A person who provides information to the Authority which is false in a material particular is guilty of an offence.
(7) A person who breaches a direction contained in a restriction notice given under section 191B is guilty of an offence.
(8) A person guilty of an offence under subsection (1) to (3) or (5) to (7) is liable—
   (a) on summary conviction to a fine not exceeding the statutory maximum; or
   (b) on conviction on indictment, to a fine.
(9) A person guilty of an offence under subsection (4) is liable—
   (a) on summary conviction, to a fine not exceeding the statutory maximum; or
   (b) on conviction on indictment, to imprisonment for a term not exceeding two years or a fine, or both.]

NOTES
Commencement: 21 March 2009.
Substituted, subject to transitional provisions, as noted to s 178 at **[7.199]**.

[Interpretation

[7.219]
191G Interpretation
(1) In this Part—
   "acquisition" means the acquisition of control or of an increase in control over a UK authorised person;
   "credit institution" means—
      (a) a credit institution authorised under the banking consolidation directive; or
      (b) an institution which would satisfy the requirements for authorisation as a credit institution under that directive if it had its registered office (or if it does not have a registered office, its head office) in an EEA State;
   "shares" has the same meaning as in section 422;
   "UK authorised person" means an authorised person who—
      (a) is a body incorporated in, or an unincorporated association formed under the law of, any part of the United Kingdom; and
      (b) is not a person authorised as a result of paragraph 1 of Schedule 5; and
   "voting power" has the same meaning as in section 422.
(2) For the purposes of this Part, a "working day" is a day other than—
   (a) a Saturday or a Sunday; or
   (b) a day which is a bank holiday in England and Wales under the Banking and Financial Dealings Act 1971.]

NOTES
Commencement: 21 March 2009.

Substituted, subject to transitional provisions, as noted to s 178 at **[7.199]**.

Miscellaneous

[7.220]
192   Power to change definitions of control etc
The Treasury may by order—
(a)   provide for exemptions from the obligations to notify imposed by sections 178 and [191D];
(b)   amend section [181] by varying, or removing, any of the cases in which a person is treated as [acquiring] control over a UK authorised person or by adding a case;
(c)   amend section [182] by varying, or removing, any of the cases in which a person is treated as increasing control over a UK authorised person or by adding a case;
(d)   amend section [183] by varying, or removing, any of the cases in which a person is treated as [reducing or ceasing to have] control over a UK authorised person or by adding a case;
(e)   amend section 422 by varying, or removing, any of the cases in which a person is treated as being a controller of a person or by adding a case.

NOTES
Words and figures in square brackets substituted by the Financial Services and Markets Act 2000 (Controllers) Regulations 2009, SI 2009/534, reg 4, as from 21 March 2009.
Orders: the Financial Services and Markets Act 2000 (Controllers) (Exemption) Order 2009, SI 2009/774.
Note that the following amending Orders have also been made under this section: the Financial Services and Markets Act 2000 (Regulated Activities) (Amendment) (No 2) Order 2003, SI 2003/1476.

193–234   *(Part XIII—Incoming Firms: Intervention by Authority (ss 193–204 and Sch 16), Part XIV—Disciplinary Measures (ss 205–211), Part XV—The Financial Services Compensation Scheme (ss 212–224A), Part 15A—Power to Require FSCS Manager to Act in Relation to Other Schemes (ss 224B–224F) and Part XVI—The Ombudsman Scheme (ss 225–234A and Sch 17) omitted for reasons of space; see further, the introductory notes to this Act.)*

PART XVII
COLLECTIVE INVESTMENT SCHEMES

NOTES
Transitional provisions: the Financial Services and Markets Act 2000 (Transitional Provisions) (Authorised Persons etc) Order 2001, SI 2001/2636, Pt V provides that collective investment schemes that were authorised or recognised under the Financial Services Act 1986, Pt I, Chapter VIII immediately before 1 December 2001 are to be treated as from that date as if authorised and recognised under Pt XVII of this Act. Directions imposed on schemes under the 1986 Act have effect, as from 1 December 2001, as directions imposed under Pt XVII of this Act. The 1986 Act was repealed by the Financial Services and Markets Act 2000 (Consequential Amendments and Repeals) Order 2001, SI 2001/3649, art 3(1)(c).

CHAPTER I
INTERPRETATION

[7.221]
235   Collective investment schemes
(1)   In this Part "collective investment scheme" means any arrangements with respect to property of any description, including money, the purpose or effect of which is to enable persons taking part in the arrangements (whether by becoming owners of the property or any part of it or otherwise) to participate in or receive profits or income arising from the acquisition, holding, management or disposal of the property or sums paid out of such profits or income.
(2)   The arrangements must be such that the persons who are to participate ("participants") do not have day-to-day control over the management of the property, whether or not they have the right to be consulted or to give directions.
(3)   The arrangements must also have either or both of the following characteristics—
(a)   the contributions of the participants and the profits or income out of which payments are to be made to them are pooled;
(b)   the property is managed as a whole by or on behalf of the operator of the scheme.
(4)   If arrangements provide for such pooling as is mentioned in subsection (3)(a) in relation to separate parts of the property, the arrangements are not to be regarded as constituting a single collective investment scheme unless the participants are entitled to exchange rights in one part for rights in another.
(5)   The Treasury may by order provide that arrangements do not amount to a collective investment scheme—
(a)   in specified circumstances; or
(b)   if the arrangements fall within a specified category of arrangement.

NOTES
Orders: the Financial Services and Markets Act 2000 (Collective Investment Schemes) Order 2001, SI 2001/1062 at **[8.208]**; the Financial Services and Markets Act 2000 (Miscellaneous Provisions) Order 2001, SI 2001/3650.
Note that the following amending Orders have also been made under this section: the Financial Services and Markets Act 2000 (Collective Investment Schemes) (Amendment) Order 2005, SI 2005/57; the Financial Services and Markets Act 2000

(Collective Investment Schemes) (Amendment) Order 2007, SI 2007/800; the Financial Services and Markets Act 2000 (Collective Investment Schemes) (Amendment) Order 2008, SI 2008/1641; the Financial Services and Markets Act 2000 (Collective Investment Schemes) (Amendment) (No 2) Order 2008, SI 2008/1813.

[7.222]
236 Open-ended investment companies

(1) In this Part "an open-ended investment company" means a collective investment scheme which satisfies both the property condition and the investment condition.

(2) The property condition is that the property belongs beneficially to, and is managed by or on behalf of, a body corporate ("BC") having as its purpose the investment of its funds with the aim of—
  (a) spreading investment risk; and
  (b) giving its members the benefit of the results of the management of those funds by or on behalf of that body.

(3) The investment condition is that, in relation to BC, a reasonable investor would, if he were to participate in the scheme—
  (a) expect that he would be able to realize, within a period appearing to him to be reasonable, his investment in the scheme (represented, at any given time, by the value of shares in, or securities of, BC held by him as a participant in the scheme); and
  (b) be satisfied that his investment would be realized on a basis calculated wholly or mainly by reference to the value of property in respect of which the scheme makes arrangements.

(4) In determining whether the investment condition is satisfied, no account is to be taken of any actual or potential redemption or repurchase of shares or securities under—
  [(a) Chapters 3 to 7 of Part 18 of the Companies Act 2006;]
  (c) corresponding provisions in force in another EEA State; or
  (d) provisions in force in a country or territory other than an EEA state which the Treasury have, by order, designated as corresponding provisions.

(5) The Treasury may by order amend the definition of "an open-ended investment company" for the purposes of this Part.

NOTES

Sub-s (4): para (a) substituted (for the original paras (a), (b)) by the Companies Act 2006 (Consequential Amendments, Transitional Provisions and Savings) Order 2009, SI 2009/1941, art 2(1), Sch 1, para 181(1), (3), as from 1 October 2009.

[7.223]
237 Other definitions

(1) In this Part "unit trust scheme" means a collective investment scheme under which the property is held on trust for the participants.

(2) In this Part—
  "trustee", in relation to a unit trust scheme, means the person holding the property in question on trust for the participants;
  "depositary", in relation to—
    (a) a collective investment scheme which is constituted by a body incorporated by virtue of regulations under section 262, or
    (b) any other collective investment scheme which is not a unit trust scheme,
    means any person to whom the property subject to the scheme is entrusted for safekeeping;
  ["management company" has the meaning given in Article 2.1(b) of the UCITS directive;]
  ["the operator"—
    (a) in relation to a unit trust scheme with a separate trustee, means the manager;
    (b) in relation to an open-ended investment company, means that company; and
    (c) in relation to an EEA UCITS which is not an open-ended investment company or unit trust scheme, means the management company for that UCITS;]
  "units" means the rights or interests (however described) of the participants in a collective investment scheme;
  ["working day" has the meaning given in section 191G(2)].

(3) In this Part—
  "an authorised unit trust scheme" means a unit trust scheme which is authorised for the purposes of this Act by an authorisation order in force under section 243;
  "an authorised open-ended investment company" means a body incorporated by virtue of regulations under section 262 in respect of which an authorisation order is in force under any provision made in such regulations by virtue of subsection (2)(l) of that section;
  ["EEA UCITS" means a UCITS which is authorised pursuant to Article 5 of the UCITS directive in an EEA State other than the United Kingdom;
  "feeder UCITS" means a UCITS, or a sub-fund of a UCITS, which has been approved by the Authority or (where relevant) by its home state regulator to invest 85% or more of the total property which is subject to the collective investment scheme constituted by the UCITS in units of another UCITS or UCITS sub-fund (the "master UCITS");]
  "a recognised scheme" means a scheme recognised under section 264, 270 or 272.
  ["UCITS" has the meaning given in Article 1.2 of the UCITS directive;

"UK UCITS" means a UCITS which is an authorised unit trust scheme or an authorised open-ended investment company.]

[(4)   In this Part, references to a sub-fund of a UCITS are references to a part of the property of the UCITS which forms a separate pool where—

(a)   the UCITS provides arrangements for separate pooling of the contributions of the participants and the profits and income out of which payments are made to them; and

(b)   the participants are entitled to exchange rights in one pool for rights in another.]

NOTES

The definition "the operator" in sub-s (1) was substituted, all other definitions in square brackets in sub-ss (1) and (3) were inserted, and sub-s (4) was added, by the Undertakings for Collective Investment in Transferable Securities Regulations 2011, SI 2011/1613, reg 2(1), (14), as from 1 July 2011.

CHAPTER II
RESTRICTIONS ON PROMOTION

NOTES

Application of this Chapter in relation to interim permissions and interim approvals: see the notes preceding s 40 at **[7.42]**.

[7.224]
238   Restrictions on promotion

(1)   An authorised person must not communicate an invitation or inducement to participate in a collective investment scheme.

(2)   But that is subject to the following provisions of this section and to section 239.

(3)   Subsection (1) applies in the case of a communication originating outside the United Kingdom only if the communication is capable of having an effect in the United Kingdom.

(4)   Subsection (1) does not apply in relation to—

(a)   an authorised unit trust scheme;

(b)   a scheme constituted by an authorised open-ended investment company; or

(c)   a recognised scheme.

(5)   Subsection (1) does not apply to anything done in accordance with rules made by the Authority for the purpose of exempting from that subsection the promotion otherwise than to the general public of schemes of specified descriptions.

(6)   The Treasury may by order specify circumstances in which subsection (1) does not apply.

(7)   An order under subsection (6) may, in particular, provide that subsection (1) does not apply in relation to communications—

(a)   of a specified description;

(b)   originating in a specified country or territory outside the United Kingdom;

(c)   originating in a country or territory which falls within a specified description of country or territory outside the United Kingdom; or

(d)   originating outside the United Kingdom.

(8)   The Treasury may by order repeal subsection (3).

(9)   "Communicate" includes causing a communication to be made.

(10)   "Promotion otherwise than to the general public" includes promotion in a way designed to reduce, so far as possible, the risk of participation by persons for whom participation would be unsuitable.

(11)   "Participate", in relation to a collective investment scheme, means become a participant (within the meaning given by section 235(2)) in the scheme.

NOTES

Orders: the Financial Services and Markets Act 2000 (Promotion of Collective Investment Schemes) (Exemptions) Order 2001, SI 2001/1060 at **[8.172]**.

Note that the following amending Orders have also been made under this section: the Financial Services and Markets Act 2000 (Financial Promotion and Miscellaneous Amendments) Order 2002, SI 2002/1310; the Financial Services and Markets Act 2000 (Promotion of Collective Investment Schemes etc) (Exemptions) (Amendment) Order 2003, SI 2003/2067; the Financial Services and Markets Act 2000 (Financial Promotion and Promotion of Collective Investment Schemes) (Miscellaneous Amendments) Order 2005, SI 2005/270; the Financial Services and Markets Act 2000 (Promotion of Collective Investment Schemes) (Exemptions) (Amendment) Order 2005, SI 2005/1532.

[7.225]
239   Single property schemes

(1)   The Treasury may by regulations make provision for exempting single property schemes from section 238(1).

(2)   For the purposes of subsection (1) a single property scheme is a scheme which has the characteristics mentioned in subsection (3) and satisfies such other requirements as are prescribed by the regulations conferring the exemption.

(3)   The characteristics are—

(a)   that the property subject to the scheme (apart from cash or other assets held for management purposes) consists of—

(i)   a single building (or a single building with ancillary buildings) managed by or on behalf of the operator of the scheme, or

(ii)   a group of adjacent or contiguous buildings managed by him or on his behalf as a single enterprise,

with or without ancillary land and with or without furniture, fittings or other contents of the building or buildings in question; and

(b)   that the units of the participants in the scheme are either dealt in on a recognised investment exchange or offered on terms such that any agreement for their acquisition is conditional on their admission to dealings on such an exchange.

(4)   If regulations are made under subsection (1), the Authority may make rules imposing duties or liabilities on the operator and (if any) the trustee or depositary of a scheme exempted by the regulations.

(5)   The rules may include, to such extent as the Authority thinks appropriate, provision for purposes corresponding to those for which provision can be made under section 248 in relation to authorised unit trust schemes.

[7.226]
240   Restriction on approval of promotion
(1)   An authorised person may not approve for the purposes of section 21 the content of a communication relating to a collective investment scheme if he would be prohibited by section 238(1) from effecting the communication himself or from causing it to be communicated.

(2)   For the purposes of determining in any case whether there has been a contravention of section 21(1), an approval given in contravention of subsection (1) is to be regarded as not having been given.

[7.227]
241   Actions for damages
If an authorised person contravenes a requirement imposed on him by section 238 or 240, section 150 applies to the contravention as it applies to a contravention mentioned in that section.

CHAPTER III
AUTHORISED UNIT TRUST SCHEMES
Applications for authorisation

[7.228]
242   Applications for authorisation of unit trust schemes
(1)   Any application for an order declaring a unit trust scheme to be an authorised unit trust scheme must be made to the Authority by the manager and trustee, or proposed manager and trustee, of the scheme.

(2)   The manager and trustee (or proposed manager and trustee) must be different persons.

(3)   The application—
(a)   must be made in such manner as the Authority may direct; and
(b)   must contain or be accompanied by such information as the Authority may reasonably require for the purpose of determining the application.

(4)   At any time after receiving an application and before determining it, the Authority may require the applicants to provide it with such further information as it reasonably considers necessary to enable it to determine the application.

(5)   Different directions may be given, and different requirements imposed, in relation to different applications.

(6)   The Authority may require applicants to present information which they are required to give under this section in such form, or to verify it in such a way, as the Authority may direct.

[7.229]
243   Authorisation orders
(1)   If, on an application under section 242 in respect of a unit trust scheme, the Authority—
(a)   is satisfied that the scheme complies with the requirements set out in this section,
(b)   is satisfied that the scheme complies with the requirements of the trust scheme rules, and
(c)   has been provided with a copy of the trust deed and a certificate signed by a solicitor to the effect that it complies with such of the requirements of this section or those rules as relate to its contents,

the Authority may make an order declaring the scheme to be an authorised unit trust scheme.

(2)   If the Authority makes an order under subsection (1), it must give written notice of the order to the applicant.

(3)   In this Chapter "authorisation order" means an order under subsection (1).

(4)   The manager and the trustee must be persons who are independent of each other.

[(5)   The manager and the trustee must each be a body corporate incorporated in the United Kingdom or another EEA State, and the affairs of each must be administered in the country in which it is incorporated.

(5A)   The trustee must have a place of business in the United Kingdom, and the manager must have a place of business in the United Kingdom or in another EEA State.]

(6)   If the manager is incorporated in another EEA State, the scheme must not be one which satisfies the requirements prescribed for the purposes of section 264.

(7)   The manager and the trustee must each be an authorised person and the manager must have permission to act as manager and the trustee must have permission to act as trustee.

[(7A)   The manager must be a fit and proper person to manage the unit trust scheme to which the application relates.]

(8)   The name of the scheme must not be undesirable or misleading.

(9)   The purposes of the scheme must be reasonably capable of being successfully carried into effect.

(10)   The participants must be entitled to have their units redeemed in accordance with the scheme at a price—
   (a)   related to the net value of the property to which the units relate; and
   (b)   determined in accordance with the scheme.

(11)   But a scheme is to be treated as complying with subsection (10) if it requires the manager to ensure that a participant is able to sell his units on an investment exchange at a price not significantly different from that mentioned in that subsection.

NOTES
   Sub-ss (5), (5A) were substituted (for the original sub-s (5)), and sub-s (7A) was inserted, by the Undertakings for Collective Investment in Transferable Securities Regulations 2011, SI 2011/1613, reg 2(1), (15), as from 1 July 2011.

[7.230]
244   Determination of applications
(1)   [Subject to subsection (1A),] an application under section 242 must be determined by the Authority before the end of the period of six months beginning with the date on which it receives the completed application.

[(1A)   An application under section 242 for authorisation of a unit trust scheme which is a UCITS must be determined by the Authority before the end of two months beginning with the date on which it receives the application.]

(2)   The Authority may determine an incomplete application if it considers it appropriate to do so; and it must in any event determine such an application within twelve months beginning with the date on which it first receives the application.

(3)   The applicant may withdraw his application, by giving the Authority written notice, at any time before the Authority determines it.

NOTES
   Words in square brackets in sub-s (1) inserted, and sub-s (1A) inserted, by the Undertakings for Collective Investment in Transferable Securities Regulations 2011, SI 2011/1613, reg 2(1), (16), as from 1 July 2011.

Applications refused

[7.231]
245   Procedure when refusing an application
(1)   If the Authority proposes to refuse an application made under section 242 it must give each of the applicants a warning notice.

(2)   If the Authority decides to refuse the application—
   (a)   it must give each of the applicants a decision notice; and
   (b)   either applicant may refer the matter to the Tribunal.

Certificates

[7.232]
246   Certificates
(1)   If the manager or trustee of a unit trust scheme which complies with the conditions necessary for it to enjoy the rights conferred by any relevant Community instrument so requests, the Authority may issue a certificate to the effect that the scheme complies with those conditions.

(2)   Such a certificate may be issued on the making of an authorisation order in respect of the scheme or at any subsequent time.

Rules

[7.233]
247   Trust scheme rules
(1)   The Authority may make rules ("trust scheme rules") as to—
   (a)   the constitution, management and operation of authorised unit trust schemes;
   (b)   the powers, duties, rights and liabilities of the manager and trustee of any such scheme;
   (c)   the rights and duties of the participants in any such scheme; and
   (d)   the winding up of any such scheme.

(2)   Trust scheme rules may, in particular, make provision—
   (a)   as to the issue and redemption of the units under the scheme;
   (b)   as to the expenses of the scheme and the means of meeting them;

    (c)   for the appointment, removal, powers and duties of an auditor for the scheme;

    (d)   for restricting or regulating the investment and borrowing powers exercisable in relation to the scheme;

    (e)   requiring the keeping of records with respect to the transactions and financial position of the scheme and for the inspection of those records;

    (f)   requiring the preparation of periodical reports with respect to the scheme and the provision of those reports to the participants and to the Authority; and

    (g)   with respect to the amendment of the scheme.

(3)   Trust scheme rules may make provision as to the contents of the trust deed, including provision requiring any of the matters mentioned in subsection (2) to be dealt with in the deed.

(4)   But trust scheme rules are binding on the manager, trustee and participants independently of the contents of the trust deed and, in the case of the participants, have effect as if contained in it.

(5)   If—

    (a)   a modification is made of the statutory provisions in force in [the United Kingdom] relating to companies,

    (b)   the modification relates to the rights and duties of persons who hold the beneficial title to any shares in a company without also holding the legal title, and

    (c)   it appears to the Treasury that, for the purpose of assimilating the law relating to authorised unit trust schemes to the law relating to companies as so modified, it is expedient to modify the rule-making powers conferred on the Authority by this section,

the Treasury may by order make such modifications of those powers as they consider appropriate.

NOTES

Sub-s (5): words in square brackets substituted by the Companies Act 2006 (Consequential Amendments and Transitional Provisions) Order 2011, SI 2011/1265, art 12(1), (2), as from 12 May 2011.

[7.234]
248 Scheme particulars rules

(1)   The Authority may make rules ("scheme particulars rules") requiring the manager of an authorised unit trust scheme—

    (a)   to submit scheme particulars to the Authority; and

    (b)   to publish scheme particulars or make them available to the public on request.

(2)   "Scheme particulars" means particulars in such form, containing such information about the scheme and complying with such requirements, as are specified in scheme particulars rules.

(3)   Scheme particulars rules may require the manager of an authorised unit trust scheme to submit, and to publish or make available, revised or further scheme particulars if there is a significant change affecting any matter—

    (a)   which is contained in scheme particulars previously published or made available; and

    (b)   whose inclusion in those particulars was required by the rules.

(4)   Scheme particulars rules may require the manager of an authorised unit trust scheme to submit, and to publish or make available, revised or further scheme particulars if—

    (a)   a significant new matter arises; and

    (b)   the inclusion of information in respect of that matter would have been required in previous particulars if it had arisen when those particulars were prepared.

(5)   Scheme particulars rules may provide for the payment, by the person or persons who in accordance with the rules are treated as responsible for any scheme particulars, of compensation to any qualifying person who has suffered loss as a result of—

    (a)   any untrue or misleading statement in the particulars; or

    (b)   the omission from them of any matter required by the rules to be included.

(6)   "Qualifying person" means a person who—

    (a)   has become or agreed to become a participant in the scheme; or

    (b)   although not being a participant, has a beneficial interest in units in the scheme.

(7)   Scheme particulars rules do not affect any liability which any person may incur apart from the rules.

[7.235]
249 Disqualification of auditor for breach of trust scheme rules

(1)   If it appears to the Authority that an auditor has failed to comply with a duty imposed on him by trust scheme rules, it may disqualify him from being the auditor for any authorised unit trust scheme or authorised open-ended investment company.

(2)   Subsections (2) to (5) of section 345 have effect in relation to disqualification under subsection (1) as they have effect in relation to disqualification under subsection (1) of that section.

[7.236]
250 Modification or waiver of rules

(1)   In this section "rules" means—

    (a)   trust scheme rules; or

    (b)   scheme particulars rules.

(2)   The Authority may, on the application or with the consent of any person to whom any rules apply, direct that all or any of the rules—
    (a)   are not to apply to him as respects a particular scheme; or
    (b)   are to apply to him, as respects a particular scheme, with such modifications as may be specified in the direction.
(3)   The Authority may, on the application or with the consent of the manager and trustee of a particular scheme acting jointly, direct that all or any of the rules—
    (a)   are not to apply to the scheme; or
    (b)   are to apply to the scheme with such modifications as may be specified in the direction.
(4)   Subsections (3) to (9) and (11) of section 148 have effect in relation to a direction under subsection (2) as they have effect in relation to a direction under section 148(2) but with the following modifications—
    (a)   . . .
    (b)   any reference to the [person] is to be read as a reference to the person mentioned in subsection (2); and
    (c)   subsection (7)(b) is to be read, in relation to a participant of the scheme, as if the word "commercial" were omitted.
(5)   Subsections (3) to (9) and (11) of section 148 have effect in relation to a direction under subsection (3) as they have effect in relation to a direction under section 148(2) but with the following modifications—
    (a)   subsection (4)(a) is to be read as if the words "by the . . . person" were omitted;
    (b)   subsections (7)(b) and (11) are to be read as if references to the . . . person were references to each of the manager and the trustee of the scheme;
    (c)   subsection (7)(b) is to be read, in relation to a participant of the scheme, as if the word "commercial" were omitted;
    (d)   subsection (8) is to be read as if the reference to the . . . person concerned were a reference to the scheme concerned and to its manager and trustee; and
    (e)   subsection (9) is to be read as if the reference to the . . . person were a reference to the manager and trustee of the scheme acting jointly.

NOTES
    Sub-s (4): para (a) repealed, and word in square brackets in para (b) substituted, by the Regulatory Reform (Financial Services and Markets Act 2000) Order 2007, SI 2007/1973, arts 2, 11(a), (b), as from 12 July 2007.
    Sub-s (5): words omitted repealed by SI 2007/1973, arts 2, 11(c), as from 12 July 2007.

Alterations

[7.237]
251   Alteration of schemes and changes of manager or trustee
[(A1)   This section applies where the manager of an authorised unit trust scheme proposes—
    (a)   to make an alteration to the scheme, other than an alteration—
        (i)   to which section 252A applies; or
        (ii)   to which Part 4 of the Undertakings for Collective Investment in Transferable Securities Regulations 2011 (mergers) applies; or
    (b)   to replace its trustee.
(1)   The manager must give written notice of the proposal to the Authority.]
(2)   Any notice given in respect of a proposal to alter the scheme involving a change in the trust deed must be accompanied by a certificate signed by a solicitor to the effect that the change will not affect the compliance of the deed with the trust scheme rules.
(3)   The trustee of an authorised unit trust scheme must give written notice to the Authority of any proposal to replace the manager of the scheme.
(4)   Effect is not to be given to any proposal of which notice has been given under subsection (1) or (3) unless—
    (a)   the Authority, by written notice, has given its approval to the proposal; or
    (b)   one month, beginning with the date on which the notice was given, has expired without the manager or trustee having received from the Authority a warning notice under section 252 in respect of the proposal.
(5)   The Authority must not approve a proposal to replace the manager or the trustee of an authorised unit trust scheme unless it is satisfied that, if the proposed replacement is made, the scheme will continue to comply with the requirements of section 243(4) to (7).

NOTES
    Sub-ss (A1), (1): substituted (for the original sub-s (1)) by the Undertakings for Collective Investment in Transferable Securities Regulations 2011, SI 2011/1613, reg 2(1), (17), as from 1 July 2011.

[7.238]
252   Procedure when refusing approval [of a proposal under section 251]
(1)   If the Authority proposes to refuse approval of a proposal [under section 251] to replace the trustee or manager of an authorised unit trust scheme, it must give a warning notice to the person by whom notice of the proposal was given under section 251(1) or (3).

(2) If the Authority proposes to refuse approval of a proposal [under section 251] to alter an authorised unit trust scheme it must give separate warning notices to the manager and the trustee of the scheme.

(3) To be valid the warning notice must be received by that person before the end of one month beginning with the date on which notice of the proposal was given.

(4) If, having given a warning notice to a person, the Authority decides to refuse approval—
  (a) it must give him a decision notice; and
  (b) he may refer the matter to the Tribunal.

NOTES

The words in square brackets in the section heading were substituted, and the words in square brackets in sub-ss (1), (2) were added, by the Undertakings for Collective Investment in Transferable Securities Regulations 2011, SI 2011/1613, reg 2(1), (18), as from 1 July 2011.

[7.239]
[252A Proposal to convert to a non-feeder UCITS
(1) This section applies where the manager of an authorised unit trust scheme which is a feeder UCITS proposes to make an alteration to the scheme which—
  (a) involves a change in the trust deed, and
  (b) will enable the scheme to convert into a UCITS which is not a feeder UCITS.
(2) The manager must give written notice of the proposal to the Authority.
(3) Any notice given in respect of such a proposal must be accompanied by—
  (a) a certificate signed by a solicitor to the effect that the change will not affect the compliance of the deed with the trust scheme rules; and
  (b) the specified information.
(4) The Authority must, within 15 working days after the date on which it received the notice under subsection (2), give—
  (a) written notice to the manager of the scheme that the Authority approves the proposed amendments to the trust deed, or
  (b) separate warning notices to the manager and trustee of the scheme that the Authority proposes to refuse approval of the proposed amendments.
(5) Effect is not to be given to any proposal of which notice has been given under subsection (2) unless the Authority, by written notice, has given its approval to the proposal.
(6) If, having given a warning notice to a person, the Authority decides to refuse approval—
  (a) it must give that person a decision notice; and
  (b) that person may refer the matter to the Tribunal.
(7) Subsection (8) applies where—
  (a) the notice given under subsection (2) relates to a proposal to amend the trust deed of a feeder UCITS to enable it to convert into a UCITS which is not a feeder UCITS following the winding-up of its master UCITS; and
  (b) the proceeds of the winding-up are to be paid to the feeder UCITS before the date on which the feeder UCITS proposes to start investing in accordance with the new investment objectives and policy provided for in its amended trust deed and scheme rules.
(8) Where this subsection applies, the Authority may only approve the proposal subject to the conditions set out in section 283A(5) and (6).
(9) In this section, "specified" means—
  (a) specified in rules made by the Authority to implement the UCITS directive, or
  (b) specified in any directly applicable Community regulation or decision made under the UCITS directive.]

NOTES

Commencement: 1 July 2011.

Inserted by the Undertakings for Collective Investment in Transferable Securities Regulations 2011, SI 2011/1613, reg 2(1), (19), as from 1 July 2011.

Exclusion clauses

[7.240]
253 Avoidance of exclusion clauses
Any provision of the trust deed of an authorised unit trust scheme is void in so far as it would have the effect of exempting the manager or trustee from liability for any failure to exercise due care and diligence in the discharge of his functions in respect of the scheme.

Ending of authorisation

[7.241]
254 Revocation of authorisation order otherwise than by consent
(1) An authorisation order may be revoked by an order made by the Authority if it appears to the Authority that—
  (a) one or more of the requirements for the making of the order are no longer satisfied;
  (b) the manager or trustee of the scheme concerned has contravened a requirement imposed on him by or under this Act;

   (c)   the manager or trustee of the scheme has, in purported compliance with any such requirement, knowingly or recklessly given the Authority information which is false or misleading in a material particular;

   (d)   no regulated activity is being carried on in relation to the scheme and the period of that inactivity began at least twelve months earlier; or

   (e)   none of paragraphs (a) to (d) applies, but it is desirable to revoke the authorisation order in order to protect the interests of participants or potential participants in the scheme.

(2)   For the purposes of subsection (1)(e), the Authority may take into account any matter relating to—

   (a)   the scheme;

   (b)   the manager or trustee;

   (c)   any person employed by or associated with the manager or trustee in connection with the scheme;

   (d)   any director of the manager or trustee;

   (e)   any person exercising influence over the manager or trustee;

   (f)   any body corporate in the same group as the manager or trustee;

   (g)   any director of any such body corporate;

   (h)   any person exercising influence over any such body corporate.

[7.242]
255 Procedure

(1)   If the Authority proposes to make an order under section 254 revoking an authorisation order ("a revoking order"), it must give separate warning notices to the manager and the trustee of the scheme.

(2)   If the Authority decides to make a revoking order, it must without delay give each of them a decision notice and either of them may refer the matter to the Tribunal.

[7.243]
256 Requests for revocation of authorisation order

(1)   An authorisation order may be revoked by an order made by the Authority at the request of the manager or trustee of the scheme concerned.

(2)   If the Authority makes an order under subsection (1), it must give written notice of the order to the manager and trustee of the scheme concerned.

(3)   The Authority may refuse a request to make an order under this section if it considers that—

   (a)   the public interest requires that any matter concerning the scheme should be investigated before a decision is taken as to whether the authorisation order should be revoked; or

   (b)   revocation would not be in the interests of the participants or would be incompatible with a Community obligation.

(4)   If the Authority proposes to refuse a request under this section, it must give separate warning notices to the manager and the trustee of the scheme.

(5)   If the Authority decides to refuse the request, it must without delay give each of them a decision notice and either of them may refer the matter to the Tribunal.

Powers of intervention

[7.244]
257 Directions

(1)   The Authority may give a direction under this section if it appears to the Authority that—

   (a)   one or more of the requirements for the making of an authorisation order are no longer satisfied;

  [(b)   the manager or trustee of an authorised unit trust scheme has contravened, or is likely to contravene, a requirement imposed—

     (i)   by or under this Act; or

     (ii)   by any directly applicable Community regulation or decision made under the UCITS directive;]

   (c)   the manager or trustee of such a scheme has, in purported compliance with any such requirement, knowingly or recklessly given the Authority information which is false or misleading in a material particular; or

   (d)   none of paragraphs (a) to (c) applies, but it is desirable to give a direction in order to protect the interests of participants or potential participants in such a scheme.

(2)   A direction under this section may—

   (a)   require the manager of the scheme to cease the issue or redemption, or both the issue and redemption, of units under the scheme;

   (b)   require the manager and trustee of the scheme to wind it up.

(3)   If the authorisation order is revoked, the revocation does not affect any direction under this section which is then in force.

(4)   A direction may be given under this section in relation to a scheme in the case of which the authorisation order has been revoked if a direction under this section was already in force at the time of revocation.

(5) If a person contravenes a direction under this section, section 150 applies to the contravention as it applies to a contravention mentioned in that section.

(6) The Authority may, either on its own initiative or on the application of the manager or trustee of the scheme concerned, revoke or vary a direction given under this section if it appears to the Authority—

(a) in the case of revocation, that it is no longer necessary for the direction to take effect or continue in force;

(b) in the case of variation, that the direction should take effect or continue in force in a different form.

NOTES

Sub-s (1): para (b) substituted by the Undertakings for Collective Investment in Transferable Securities Regulations 2011, SI 2011/1613, reg 2(1), (20), as from 1 July 2011.

[7.245]
258 Applications to the court

(1) If the Authority could give a direction under section 257, it may also apply to the court for an order—

(a) removing the manager or the trustee, or both the manager and the trustee, of the scheme; and

(b) replacing the person or persons removed with a suitable person or persons nominated by the Authority.

(2) The Authority may nominate a person for the purposes of subsection (1)(b) only if it is satisfied that, if the order was made, the requirements of section 243(4) to (7) would be complied with.

(3) If it appears to the Authority that there is no person it can nominate for the purposes of subsection (1)(b), it may apply to the court for an order—

(a) removing the manager or the trustee, or both the manager and the trustee, of the scheme; and

(b) appointing an authorised person to wind up the scheme.

(4) On an application under this section the court may make such order as it thinks fit.

(5) The court may, on the application of the Authority, rescind any such order as is mentioned in subsection (3) and substitute such an order as is mentioned in subsection (1).

(6) The Authority must give written notice of the making of an application under this section to the manager and trustee of the scheme concerned.

(7) The jurisdiction conferred by this section may be exercised by—

(a) the High Court;

(b) in Scotland, the Court of Session.

[7.246]
[258A Winding up or merger of master UCITS

(1) Subsection (2) applies if a master UCITS which has one or more feeder UCITS which are authorised unit trust schemes is wound up, whether as a result of a direction given by the Authority under section 257, an order of the court under section 258, rules made by the Authority or otherwise.

(2) The Authority must direct the manager and trustee of any authorised unit trust scheme which is a feeder UCITS of the master UCITS to wind up the feeder UCITS unless—

(a) the Authority approves under section 283A the investment by the feeder UCITS of at least 85% of the total property which is subject to the collective investment scheme constituted by the feeder UCITS in units of another UCITS or master UCITS; or

(b) the Authority approves under section 252A an amendment of the trust deed of the feeder UCITS which would enable it to convert into a UCITS which is not a feeder UCITS.

(3) Subsection (4) applies if a master UCITS which has one or more feeder UCITS which are authorised unit trust schemes—

(a) merges with another UCITS, or

(b) is divided into two or more UCITS.

(4) The Authority must direct the manager and trustee of any authorised unit trust scheme which is a feeder UCITS of the master UCITS to wind up the scheme unless—

(a) the Authority approves under section 283A the investment by the scheme of at least 85% of the total property which is subject to the collective investment scheme constituted by the feeder UCITS in the units of—

(i) the master UCITS which results from the merger;

(ii) one of the UCITS resulting from the division; or

(iii) another UCITS or master UCITS;

(b) the Authority approves under section 252A an amendment of the trust deed of the scheme which would enable it to convert into a UCITS which is not a feeder UCITS.]

NOTES
Commencement: 1 July 2011.

Inserted by the Undertakings for Collective Investment in Transferable Securities Regulations 2011, SI 2011/1613, reg 2(1), (21), as from 1 July 2011.

[7.247]
259 Procedure on giving directions under section 257 [or 258A] and varying them on Authority's own initiative
(1) A direction [under section 257 or 258A] takes effect—
  (a) immediately, if the notice given under subsection (3) states that that is the case;
  (b) on such date as may be specified in the notice; or
  (c) if no date is specified in the notice, when the matter to which it relates is no longer open to review.
(2) A direction may be expressed to take effect immediately (or on a specified date) only if the Authority, having regard to the ground on which it is exercising its power under section 257, considers that it is necessary for the direction to take effect immediately (or on that date).
(3) If the Authority proposes to give a direction under section 257, or gives such a direction with immediate effect, it must give separate written notice to the manager and the trustee of the scheme concerned.
(4) The notice must—
  (a) give details of the direction;
  (b) inform the person to whom it is given of when the direction takes effect;
  (c) state the Authority's reasons for giving the direction and for its determination as to when the direction takes effect;
  (d) inform the person to whom it is given that he may make representations to the Authority within such period as may be specified in it (whether or not he has referred the matter to the Tribunal); and
  (e) inform him of his right to refer the matter to the Tribunal.
(5) If the direction imposes a requirement under section 257(2)(a), the notice must state that the requirement has effect until—
  (a) a specified date; or
  (b) a further direction.
(6) If the direction [is given under section 257(2)(b) or section 258A(2) or (4)], the scheme must be wound up—
  (a) by a date specified in the notice; or
  (b) if no date is specified, as soon as practicable.
(7) The Authority may extend the period allowed under the notice for making representations.
(8) If, having considered any representations made by a person to whom the notice was given, the Authority decides—
  (a) to give the direction in the way proposed, or
  (b) if it has been given, not to revoke the direction,
it must give separate written notice to the manager and the trustee of the scheme concerned.
(9) If, having considered any representations made by a person to whom the notice was given, the Authority decides—
  (a) not to give the direction in the way proposed,
  (b) to give the direction in a way other than that proposed, or
  (c) to revoke a direction which has effect,
it must give separate written notice to the manager and the trustee of the scheme concerned.
(10) A notice given under subsection (8) must inform the person to whom it is given of his right to refer the matter to the Tribunal.
(11) A notice under subsection (9)(b) must comply with subsection (4).
(12) If a notice informs a person of his right to refer a matter to the Tribunal, it must give an indication of the procedure on such a reference.
(13) This section applies to the variation of a direction on the Authority's own initiative as it applies to the giving of a direction.
(14) For the purposes of subsection (1)(c), whether a matter is open to review is to be determined in accordance with section 391(8).

NOTES
  The words in square brackets in the section heading and in sub-s (1) were inserted, and the words in square brackets in sub-s (6) were substituted, by the Undertakings for Collective Investment in Transferable Securities Regulations 2011, SI 2011/1613, reg 2(1), (22), as from 1 July 2011.

[7.248]
260 Procedure: refusal to revoke or vary direction
(1) If on an application under section 257(6) for a direction to be revoked or varied the Authority proposes—
  (a) to vary the direction otherwise than in accordance with the application, or
  (b) to refuse to revoke or vary the direction,
it must give the applicant a warning notice.
(2) If the Authority decides to refuse to revoke or vary the direction—

(a) it must give the applicant a decision notice; and

(b) the applicant may refer the matter to the Tribunal.

[7.249]

261 Procedure: revocation of direction and grant of request for variation

(1) If the Authority decides on its own initiative to revoke a direction under section 257 it must give separate written notices of its decision to the manager and trustee of the scheme.

(2) If on an application under section 257(6) for a direction to be revoked or varied the Authority decides to revoke the direction or vary it in accordance with the application, it must give the applicant written notice of its decision.

(3) A notice under this section must specify the date on which the decision takes effect.

(4) The Authority may publish such information about the revocation or variation, in such way, as it considers appropriate.

[7.250]

[261A Information for home state regulator

(1) Subsection (2) applies if, in accordance with rules made by the Authority to implement Article 66 of the UCITS directive, the Authority is informed by the manager of an authorised unit trust scheme which is a master UCITS that a feeder UCITS which invests in units of the scheme is an EEA UCITS.

(2) The Authority must immediately inform the home state regulator of the feeder UCITS of the investment made by that UCITS in the master UCITS.]

NOTES

Commencement: 1 July 2011.

Inserted, together with s 261B, by the Undertakings for Collective Investment in Transferable Securities Regulations 2011, SI 2011/1613, reg 2(1), (23), as from 1 July 2011.

[7.251]

[261B Information for feeder UCITS

(1) The Authority must immediately inform the operator of any authorised unit trust scheme which is a feeder UCITS of an authorised unit trust scheme or an authorised open-ended investment company (the master UCITS) of—

(a) any failure of which the Authority becomes aware by the master UCITS to comply with a provision made in implementation of Chapter VIII of the UCITS directive;

(b) any warning notice or decision notice given to the master UCITS in relation to a contravention of any provision made in implementation of Chapter VIII of the UCITS directive by or under any enactment or in rules of the Authority;

(c) any information reported to the Authority pursuant to rules of the Authority made to implement Article 106(1) of the UCITS directive which relates to the master UCITS, or to one or more of its directors, or its management company, trustee, depositary or auditor.

(2) The Authority must immediately inform the operator of any authorised unit trust scheme which is a feeder UCITS of an EEA UCITS of any information received from the home state regulator of the EEA UCITS in relation to—

(a) any failure by the EEA UCITS to comply with any requirement in Chapter VIII of the UCITS directive;

(b) any decision or measure imposed on the EEA UCITS under provisions implementing Chapter VIII of the UCITS directive;

(c) any information reported to the home state regulator pursuant to Article 106(1) of the UCITS directive relating to the EEA UCITS, its operator, depositary or auditor.

(3) Where the Authority has the information described in subsection (1)(a), (b) or (c) in relation to an authorised unit trust scheme which is a master UCITS for one or more feeder UCITS which are EEA UCITS, the Authority must immediately give that information to the home state regulator of each feeder UCITS established outside the United Kingdom.]

NOTES

Commencement: 1 July 2011.

Inserted as noted to s 261A at **[7.250]**.

CHAPTER IV
OPEN-ENDED INVESTMENT COMPANIES

[7.252]

262 Open-ended investment companies

(1) The Treasury may by regulations make provision for—

(a) facilitating the carrying on of collective investment by means of open-ended investment companies;

(b) regulating such companies.

(2) The regulations may, in particular, make provision—

(a) for the incorporation and registration in [the United Kingdom] of bodies corporate;

(b)   for a body incorporated by virtue of the regulations to take such form as may be determined in accordance with the regulations;

(c)   as to the purposes for which such a body may exist, the investments which it may issue and otherwise as to its constitution;

(d)   as to the management and operation of such a body and the management of its property;

(e)   as to the powers, duties, rights and liabilities of such a body and of other persons, including—

     (i)   the directors or sole director of such a body;

     (ii)   its depositary (if any);

     (iii)   its shareholders, and persons who hold the beneficial title to shares in it without holding the legal title;

     (iv)   its auditor; and

     (v)   any persons who act or purport to act on its behalf;

(f)   as to the merger of one or more such bodies and the division of such a body;

(g)   for the appointment and removal of an auditor for such a body;

(h)   as to the winding up and dissolution of such a body;

(i)   for such a body, or any director or depositary of such a body, to be required to comply with directions given by the Authority;

(j)   enabling the Authority to apply to a court for an order removing and replacing any director or depositary of such a body;

(k)   for the carrying out of investigations by persons appointed by the Authority or the Secretary of State;

(l)   corresponding to any provision made in relation to unit trust schemes by Chapter III of this Part.

(3)   Regulations under this section may—

(a)   impose criminal liability;

(b)   confer functions on the Authority;

(c)   in the case of provision made by virtue of subsection (2)(l), authorise the making of rules by the Authority;

(d)   confer jurisdiction on any court or on the Tribunal;

(e)   provide for fees to be charged by the Authority in connection with the carrying out of any of its functions under the regulations (including fees payable on a periodical basis);

(f)   modify, exclude or apply (with or without modifications) any primary or subordinate legislation (including any provision of, or made under, this Act);

(g)   make consequential amendments, repeals and revocations of any such legislation;

(h)   modify or exclude any rule of law.

(4)   The provision that may be made by virtue of subsection (3)(f) includes provision extending or adapting any power to make subordinate legislation.

(5)   Regulations under this section may, in particular—

(a)   revoke the Open-Ended Investment Companies (Investment Companies with Variable Capital) Regulations 1996; and

(b)   provide for things done under or in accordance with those regulations to be treated as if they had been done under or in accordance with regulations under this section.

NOTES

Sub-s (2): words in square brackets in para (a) substituted by the Companies Act 2006 (Consequential Amendments and Transitional Provisions) Order 2011, SI 2011/1265, art 12(1), (3), as from 12 May 2011.

Open-Ended Investment Companies (Investment Companies with Variable Capital) Regulations 1996 (SI 1996/2827): revoked, subject to transitional provisions and savings, by the Open-Ended Investment Companies Regulations 2001, SI 2001/1228, reg 85.

Regulations: the Open-Ended Investment Companies Regulations 2001, SI 2001/1228.

Note that the following amending Regulations have also been made under this section: the Open-Ended Investment Companies (Amendment) Regulations 2005, SI 2005/923; the Open-Ended Investment Companies (Amendment) Regulations 2009, SI 2009/553.

---

263   (*Spent; this section amended the Companies Act 1985, s 716 (s 716 was repealed by the Regulatory Reform (Removal of 20 Member Limit in Partnerships etc) Order 2002, SI 2002/3203, art 2, as from 21 December 2002). This section is also repealed by the Companies Act 2006, s 1295, Sch 16.*)

CHAPTER V
RECOGNISED OVERSEAS SCHEMES

Schemes constituted in other EEA States

[7.253]
264   Schemes constituted in other EEA States
(1)   A collective investment scheme constituted in another EEA State is a recognised scheme if—

(a)   it satisfies such requirements as are prescribed for the purposes of this section; . . .

[(b)   the home state regulator of the operator of the scheme has transmitted to the Authority notice of the operator's intention to invite persons in the United Kingdom to participate in the scheme; and

(c)   the notice from the home state regulator—

   (i)   complies with the requirements of any directly applicable Community regulation or decision made under the UCITS directive, and

   (ii)   is accompanied by such other information as may be prescribed].

(2)–(4)   . . .

(5)   For the purposes of this section a collective investment scheme is constituted in another EEA State if—

(a)   it is constituted under the law of that State by a contract or under a trust and is managed by a body corporate incorporated under that law; or

(b)   it takes the form of an open-ended investment company incorporated under that law.

(6)   The operator of a recognised scheme may give written notice to the Authority that he desires the scheme to be no longer recognised by virtue of this section.

(7)   On the giving of notice under subsection (6), the scheme ceases to be a recognised scheme.

NOTES

The word omitted from sub-s (1)(a) was repealed, sub-s (1)(b), (c) were substituted (for the original sub-s (1)(b)), and sub-ss (2)–(4) were repealed, by the Undertakings for Collective Investment in Transferable Securities Regulations 2011, SI 2011/1613, reg 2(1), (24), as from 1 July 2011.

Regulations: the Financial Services and Markets Act 2000 (Collective Investment Schemes Constituted in Other EEA States) Regulations 2001, SI 2001/2383 at **[8.232]**.

Note that the following amending Regulations have also been made under this section: the Collective Investment Schemes (Miscellaneous Amendments) Regulations 2003, SI 2003/2066.

265   *(Repealed by the Undertakings for Collective Investment in Transferable Securities Regulations 2011, SI 2011/1613, reg 2(1), (25), as from 1 July 2011.)*

[7.254]
266   Disapplication of rules

(1)   Apart from—

(a)   financial promotion rules, and

(b)   rules under section 283(1),

rules made by the Authority under this Act do not apply to the operator, trustee or depositary of a scheme in relation to the carrying on by him of regulated activities for which he has permission in that capacity.

[(1A)   But subsection (1) does not affect the application of rules to an operator of a scheme if the operator is an EEA firm falling within paragraph 5(f) of Schedule 3 who qualifies for authorisation under that Schedule.]

(2)   "Scheme" means a scheme which is a recognised scheme by virtue of section 264.

NOTES

Sub-s (1A): inserted by the Collective Investment Schemes (Miscellaneous Amendments) Regulations 2003, SI 2003/2066, reg 9, as from 13 February 2004.

[7.255]
267   Power of Authority to suspend promotion of scheme

(1)   Subsection (2) applies if it appears to the Authority that the operator of a scheme has communicated an invitation or inducement in relation to the scheme in a manner contrary to financial promotion rules.

(2)   The Authority may direct that—

(a)   the exemption from subsection (1) of section 238 provided by subsection (4)(c) of that section is not to apply in relation to the scheme; and

(b)   subsection (5) of that section does not apply with respect to things done in relation to the scheme.

(3)   A direction under subsection (2) has effect—

(a)   for a specified period;

(b)   until the occurrence of a specified event; or

(c)   until specified conditions are complied with.

(4)   The Authority may, either on its own initiative or on the application of the operator of the scheme concerned, vary a direction given under subsection (2) if it appears to the Authority that the direction should take effect or continue in force in a different form.

(5)   The Authority may, either on its own initiative or on the application of the operator of the recognised scheme concerned, revoke a direction given under subsection (2) if it appears to the Authority—

(a)   that the conditions specified in the direction have been complied with; or

(b)   that it is no longer necessary for the direction to take effect or continue in force.

(6)   If an event is specified, the direction ceases to have effect (unless revoked earlier) on the occurrence of that event.

(7)   For the purposes of this section and sections 268 and 269—
  (a)   the scheme's home State is the EEA State in which the scheme is constituted (within the meaning given by section 264);
  (b)   the competent authorities in the scheme's home State are the authorities in that State who are responsible for the authorisation of collective investment schemes.
(8)   "Scheme" means a scheme which is a recognised scheme by virtue of section 264.
(9)   "Specified", in relation to a direction, means specified in it.

[7.256]
268   Procedure on giving directions under section 267 and varying them on Authority's own initiative
(1)   A direction under section 267 takes effect—
  (a)   immediately, if the notice given under subsection (3)(a) states that that is the case;
  (b)   on such date as may be specified in the notice; or
  (c)   if no date is specified in the notice, when the matter to which it relates is no longer open to review.
(2)   A direction may be expressed to take effect immediately (or on a specified date) only if the Authority, having regard to its reasons for exercising its power under section 267, considers that it is necessary for the direction to take effect immediately (or on that date).
(3)   If the Authority proposes to give a direction under section 267, or gives such a direction with immediate effect, it must—
  (a)   give the operator of the scheme concerned written notice; and
  (b)   inform the competent authorities in the scheme's home State of its proposal or (as the case may be) of the direction.
(4)   The notice must—
  (a)   give details of the direction;
  (b)   inform the operator of when the direction takes effect;
  (c)   state the Authority's reasons for giving the direction and for its determination as to when the direction takes effect;
  (d)   inform the operator that he may make representations to the Authority within such period as may be specified in it (whether or not he has referred the matter to the Tribunal); and
  (e)   inform him of his right to refer the matter to the Tribunal.
(5)   The Authority may extend the period allowed under the notice for making representations.
(6)   Subsection (7) applies if, having considered any representations made by the operator, the Authority decides—
  (a)   to give the direction in the way proposed, or
  (b)   if it has been given, not to revoke the direction.
(7)   The Authority must—
  (a)   give the operator of the scheme concerned written notice; and
  (b)   inform the competent authorities in the scheme's home State of the direction.
(8)   Subsection (9) applies if, having considered any representations made by a person to whom the notice was given, the Authority decides—
  (a)   not to give the direction in the way proposed,
  (b)   to give the direction in a way other than that proposed, or
  (c)   to revoke a direction which has effect.
(9)   The Authority must—
  (a)   give the operator of the scheme concerned written notice; and
  (b)   inform the competent authorities in the scheme's home State of its decision.
(10)   A notice given under subsection (7)(a) must inform the operator of his right to refer the matter to the Tribunal.
(11)   A notice under subsection (9)(a) given as a result of subsection (8)(b) must comply with subsection (4).
(12)   If a notice informs a person of his right to refer a matter to the Tribunal, it must give an indication of the procedure on such a reference.
(13)   This section applies to the variation of a direction on the Authority's own initiative as it applies to the giving of a direction.
(14)   For the purposes of subsection (1)(c), whether a matter is open to review is to be determined in accordance with section 391(8).

[7.257]
269   Procedure on application for variation or revocation of direction
(1)   If, on an application under subsection (4) or (5) of section 267, the Authority proposes—
  (a)   to vary a direction otherwise than in accordance with the application, or
  (b)   to refuse the application,
it must give the operator of the scheme concerned a warning notice.
(2)   If, on such an application, the Authority decides—
  (a)   to vary a direction otherwise than in accordance with the application, or
  (b)   to refuse the application,
it must give the operator of the scheme concerned a decision notice.

(3) If the application is refused, the operator of the scheme may refer the matter to the Tribunal.

(4) If, on such an application, the Authority decides to grant the application it must give the operator of the scheme concerned written notice.

(5) If the Authority decides on its own initiative to revoke a direction given under section 267 it must give the operator of the scheme concerned written notice.

(6) The Authority must inform the competent authorities in the scheme's home State of any notice given under this section.

Schemes authorised in designated countries or territories

[7.258]
270 Schemes authorised in designated countries or territories

(1) A collective investment scheme which is not a recognised scheme by virtue of section 264 but is managed in, and authorised under the law of, a country or territory outside the United Kingdom is a recognised scheme if—

(a) that country or territory is designated for the purposes of this section by an order made by the Treasury;

(b) the scheme is of a class specified by the order;

(c) the operator of the scheme has given written notice to the Authority that he wishes it to be recognised; and

(d) either—

    (i) the Authority, by written notice, has given its approval to the scheme's being recognised; or

    (ii) two months, beginning with the date on which notice was given under paragraph (c), have expired without the operator receiving a warning notice from the Authority under section 271.

(2) The Treasury may not make an order designating any country or territory for the purposes of this section unless satisfied—

(a) that the law and practice under which relevant collective investment schemes are authorised and supervised in that country or territory affords to investors in the United Kingdom protection at least equivalent to that provided for them by or under this Part in the case of comparable authorised schemes; and

(b) that adequate arrangements exist, or will exist, for co-operation between the authorities of the country or territory responsible for the authorisation and supervision of relevant collective investment schemes and the Authority.

(3) "Relevant collective investment schemes" means collective investment schemes of the class or classes to be specified by the order.

(4) "Comparable authorised schemes" means whichever of the following the Treasury consider to be the most appropriate, having regard to the class or classes of scheme to be specified by the order—

(a) authorised unit trust schemes;

(b) authorised open-ended investment companies;

(c) both such unit trust schemes and such companies.

(5) If the Treasury are considering whether to make an order designating a country or territory for the purposes of this section—

(a) the Treasury must ask the Authority for a report—

    (i) on the law and practice of that country or territory in relation to the authorisation and supervision of relevant collective investment schemes,

    (ii) on any existing or proposed arrangements for co-operation between it and the authorities responsible in that country or territory for the authorisation and supervision of relevant collective investment schemes,

    having regard to the Treasury's need to be satisfied as mentioned in subsection (2);

(b) the Authority must provide the Treasury with such a report; and

(c) the Treasury must have regard to it in deciding whether to make the order.

(6) The notice to be given by the operator under subsection (1)(c)—

(a) must contain the address of a place in the United Kingdom for the service on the operator of notices or other documents required or authorised to be served on him under this Act; and

(b) must contain or be accompanied by such information and documents as may be specified by the Authority.

NOTES

Orders: the Financial Services and Markets Act 2000 (Collective Investment Schemes) (Designated Countries and Territories) Order 2003, SI 2003/1181 at **[8.246]**. See also, the Financial Services (Designated Countries and Territories) (Overseas Collective Investment Schemes) (Bermuda) Order 1988, SI 1988/2284 (made under FSA 1986, s 87) which continues in force and has effect as if made under sub-s (1)(a) above by virtue of the Financial Services and Markets Act 2000 (Transitional Provisions) (Authorised Persons etc) Order 2001, SI 2001/2636, art 67(1).

[7.259]
271   Procedure
(1)   If the Authority proposes to refuse approval of a scheme's being a recognised scheme by virtue of section 270, it must give the operator of the scheme a warning notice.
(2)   To be valid the warning notice must be received by the operator before the end of two months beginning with the date on which notice was given under section 270(1)(c).
(3)   If, having given a warning notice, the Authority decides to refuse approval—
    (a)   it must give the operator of the scheme a decision notice; and
    (b)   the operator may refer the matter to the Tribunal.

Individually recognised overseas schemes

[7.260]
272   Individually recognised overseas schemes
(1)   The Authority may, on the application of the operator of a collective investment scheme which—
    (a)   is managed in a country or territory outside the United Kingdom,
    (b)   does not satisfy the requirements prescribed for the purposes of section 264,
    (c)   is not managed in a country or territory designated for the purposes of section 270 or, if it is so managed, is of a class not specified by the designation order, and
    (d)   appears to the Authority to satisfy the requirements set out in the following provisions of this section,
make an order declaring the scheme to be a recognised scheme.
(2)   Adequate protection must be afforded to participants in the scheme.
(3)   The arrangements for the scheme's constitution and management must be adequate.
(4)   The powers and duties of the operator and, if the scheme has a trustee or depositary, of the trustee or depositary must be adequate.
(5)   In deciding whether the matters mentioned in subsection (3) or (4) are adequate, the Authority must have regard to—
    (a)   any rule of law, and
    (b)   any matters which are, or could be, the subject of rules,
applicable in relation to comparable authorised schemes.
(6)   "Comparable authorised schemes" means whichever of the following the Authority considers the most appropriate, having regard to the nature of scheme in respect of which the application is made—
    (a)   authorised unit trust schemes;
    (b)   authorised open-ended investment companies;
    (c)   both such unit trust schemes and such companies.
(7)   The scheme must take the form of an open-ended investment company or (if it does not take that form) the operator must be a body corporate.
(8)   The operator of the scheme must—
    (a)   if an authorised person, have permission to act as operator;
    (b)   if not an authorised person, be a fit and proper person to act as operator.
(9)   The trustee or depositary (if any) of the scheme must—
    (a)   if an authorised person, have permission to act as trustee or depositary;
    (b)   if not an authorised person, be a fit and proper person to act as trustee or depositary.
(10)   The operator and the trustee or depositary (if any) of the scheme must be able and willing to co-operate with the Authority by the sharing of information and in other ways.
(11)   The name of the scheme must not be undesirable or misleading.
(12)   The purposes of the scheme must be reasonably capable of being successfully carried into effect.
(13)   The participants must be entitled to have their units redeemed in accordance with the scheme at a price related to the net value of the property to which the units relate and determined in accordance with the scheme.
(14)   But a scheme is to be treated as complying with subsection (13) if it requires the operator to ensure that a participant is able to sell his units on an investment exchange at a price not significantly different from that mentioned in that subsection.
(15)   Subsection (13) is not to be read as imposing a requirement that the participants must be entitled to have their units redeemed (or sold as mentioned in subsection (14)) immediately following a demand to that effect.

NOTES
Application in relation to interim permissions and interim approvals: see the notes preceding s 40 at **[7.42]**.

[7.261]
273   Matters that may be taken into account
For the purposes of subsections (8)(b) and (9)(b) of section 272, the Authority may take into account any matter relating to—
    (a)   any person who is or will be employed by or associated with the operator, trustee or depositary in connection with the scheme;

(b)   any director of the operator, trustee or depositary;

(c)   any person exercising influence over the operator, trustee or depositary;

(d)   any body corporate in the same group as the operator, trustee or depositary;

(e)   any director of any such body corporate;

(f)   any person exercising influence over any such body corporate.

[7.262]
274   Applications for recognition of individual schemes

(1)   An application under section 272 for an order declaring a scheme to be a recognised scheme must be made to the Authority by the operator of the scheme.

(2)   The application—

(a)   must be made in such manner as the Authority may direct;

(b)   must contain the address of a place in the United Kingdom for the service on the operator of notices or other documents required or authorised to be served on him under this Act;

(c)   must contain or be accompanied by such information as the Authority may reasonably require for the purpose of determining the application.

(3)   At any time after receiving an application and before determining it, the Authority may require the applicant to provide it with such further information as it reasonably considers necessary to enable it to determine the application.

(4)   Different directions may be given, and different requirements imposed, in relation to different applications.

(5)   The Authority may require an applicant to present information which he is required to give under this section in such form, or to verify it in such a way, as the Authority may direct.

[7.263]
275   Determination of applications

(1)   An application under section 272 must be determined by the Authority before the end of the period of six months beginning with the date on which it receives the completed application.

(2)   The Authority may determine an incomplete application if it considers it appropriate to do so; and it must in any event determine such an application within twelve months beginning with the date on which it first receives the application.

(3)   If the Authority makes an order under section 272(1), it must give written notice of the order to the applicant.

[7.264]
276   Procedure when refusing an application

(1)   If the Authority proposes to refuse an application made under section 272 it must give the applicant a warning notice.

(2)   If the Authority decides to refuse the application—

(a)   it must give the applicant a decision notice; and

(b)   the applicant may refer the matter to the Tribunal.

[7.265]
277   Alteration of schemes and changes of operator, trustee or depositary

(1)   The operator of a scheme recognised by virtue of section 272 must give written notice to the Authority of any proposed alteration to the scheme.

(2)   Effect is not to be given to any such proposal unless—

(a)   the Authority, by written notice, has given its approval to the proposal; or

(b)   one month, beginning with the date on which notice was given under subsection (1), has expired without the Authority having given written notice to the operator that it has decided to refuse approval.

(3)   At least one month before any replacement of the operator, trustee or depositary of such a scheme, notice of the proposed replacement must be given to the Authority—

(a)   by the operator, trustee or depositary (as the case may be); or

(b)   by the person who is to replace him.

Schemes recognised under sections 270 and 272

[7.266]
278   Rules as to scheme particulars

The Authority may make rules imposing duties or liabilities on the operator of a scheme recognised under section 270 or 272 for purposes corresponding to those for which rules may be made under section 248 in relation to authorised unit trust schemes.

[7.267]
279   Revocation of recognition

The Authority may direct that a scheme is to cease to be recognised by virtue of section 270 or revoke an order under section 272 if it appears to the Authority—

(a)   that the operator, trustee or depositary of the scheme has contravened a requirement imposed on him by or under this Act;

(b)   that the operator, trustee or depositary of the scheme has, in purported compliance with any such requirement, knowingly or recklessly given the Authority information which is false or misleading in a material particular;

(c)   in the case of an order under section 272, that one or more of the requirements for the making of the order are no longer satisfied; or

(d)   that none of paragraphs (a) to (c) applies, but it is undesirable in the interests of the participants or potential participants that the scheme should continue to be recognised.

[7.268]
280   Procedure
(1)   If the Authority proposes to give a direction under section 279 or to make an order under that section revoking a recognition order, it must give a warning notice to the operator and (if any) the trustee or depositary of the scheme.

(2)   If the Authority decides to give a direction or make an order under that section—

(a)   it must without delay give a decision notice to the operator and (if any) the trustee or depositary of the scheme; and

(b)   the operator or the trustee or depositary may refer the matter to the Tribunal.

[7.269]
281   Directions
(1)   In this section a "relevant recognised scheme" means a scheme recognised under section 270 or 272.

(2)   If it appears to the Authority that—

(a)   the operator, trustee or depositary of a relevant recognised scheme has contravened, or is likely to contravene, a requirement imposed on him by or under this Act,

(b)   the operator, trustee or depositary of such a scheme has, in purported compliance with any such requirement, knowingly or recklessly given the Authority information which is false or misleading in a material particular,

(c)   one or more of the requirements for the recognition of a scheme under section 272 are no longer satisfied, or

(d)   none of paragraphs (a) to (c) applies, but the exercise of the power conferred by this section is desirable in order to protect the interests of participants or potential participants in a relevant recognised scheme who are in the United Kingdom,

it may direct that the scheme is not to be a recognised scheme for a specified period or until the occurrence of a specified event or until specified conditions are complied with.

[7.270]
282   Procedure on giving directions under section 281 and varying them otherwise than as requested
(1)   A direction takes effect—

(a)   immediately, if the notice given under subsection (3) states that that is the case;

(b)   on such date as may be specified in the notice; or

(c)   if no date is specified in the notice, when the matter to which it relates is no longer open to review.

(2)   A direction may be expressed to take effect immediately (or on a specified date) only if the Authority, having regard to the ground on which it is exercising its power under section 281, considers that it is necessary for the direction to take effect immediately (or on that date).

(3)   If the Authority proposes to give a direction under section 281, or gives such a direction with immediate effect, it must give separate written notice to the operator and (if any) the trustee or depositary of the scheme concerned.

(4)   The notice must—

(a)   give details of the direction;

(b)   inform the person to whom it is given of when the direction takes effect;

(c)   state the Authority's reasons for giving the direction and for its determination as to when the direction takes effect;

(d)   inform the person to whom it is given that he may make representations to the Authority within such period as may be specified in it (whether or not he has referred the matter to the Tribunal); and

(e)   inform him of his right to refer the matter to the Tribunal.

(5)   The Authority may extend the period allowed under the notice for making representations.

(6)   If, having considered any representations made by a person to whom the notice was given, the Authority decides—

(a)   to give the direction in the way proposed, or

(b)   if it has been given, not to revoke the direction,

it must give separate written notice to the operator and (if any) the trustee or depositary of the scheme concerned.

(7)   If, having considered any representations made by a person to whom the notice was given, the Authority decides—

(a)   not to give the direction in the way proposed,

(b)   to give the direction in a way other than that proposed, or

(c)   to revoke a direction which has effect,

it must give separate written notice to the operator and (if any) the trustee or depositary of the scheme concerned.

(8)   A notice given under subsection (6) must inform the person to whom it is given of his right to refer the matter to the Tribunal.

(9)   A notice under subsection (7)(b) must comply with subsection (4).

(10)   If a notice informs a person of his right to refer a matter to the Tribunal, it must give an indication of the procedure on such a reference.

(11)   This section applies to the variation of a direction on the Authority's own initiative as it applies to the giving of a direction.

(12)   For the purposes of subsection (1)(c), whether a matter is open to review is to be determined in accordance with section 391(8).

Facilities and information in UK

[7.271]

283   Facilities and information in UK

(1)   The Authority may make rules requiring operators of recognised schemes to maintain in the United Kingdom, or in such part or parts of it as may be specified, such facilities as the Authority thinks desirable in the interests of participants and as are specified in rules.

(2)   The Authority may by notice in writing require the operator of any recognised scheme to include such explanatory information as is specified in the notice in any communication of his which—

(a)   is a communication of an invitation or inducement of a kind mentioned in section 21(1); and

(b)   names the scheme.

(3)   In the case of a communication originating outside the United Kingdom, subsection (2) only applies if the communication is capable of having an effect in the United Kingdom.

[CHAPTER 5A
MASTER-FEEDER STRUCTURES

[7.272]

283A   Master-feeder structures

(1)   The operator of a UK UCITS may not invest a higher proportion of the property which is subject to the collective investment scheme constituted by that UCITS in units of another UCITS than is permitted by rules made by the Authority implementing Article 55 of the UCITS directive unless the investment is approved by the Authority in accordance with this section.

(2)   An application for approval under subsection (1) of an investment must be made by the operator of the UK UCITS in such manner, and accompanied by such information, as is required by rules made by the Authority.

(3)   The Authority must grant an application made under subsection (2) if it is satisfied—

(a)   that the UCITS, its operator, trustee or depositary and auditor and the UCITS in which it proposes to invest, and its operator, have complied with—

(i)   the requirements laid down in Chapter VIII of the UCITS directive, and

(ii)   any other requirements imposed by the Authority in relation to the application;

(b)   in a case where the application is made by the operator of a feeder UCITS in respect of the investment of the proceeds of the winding-up of its master UCITS, that the proceeds of the winding up are to be paid to the feeder UCITS before the date on which the investment is to be made.

(4)   In a case within subsection (3)(b), approval must be subject to the conditions in subsections (5) and (6).

(5)   The first condition is that the feeder UCITS is to receive the proceeds of the winding-up—

(a)   in cash; or

(b)   wholly or partly in assets other than cash in a case where the feeder UCITS so elects and each of the following so permits—

(i)   the decision of the master UCITS that it should be wound up;

(ii)   the trust deed or instrument of incorporation of the feeder UCITS; and

(iii)   either the agreement between the feeder UCITS and its master UCITS, or the internal conduct of business rules operated by the feeder UCITS and the master UCITS in accordance with rules made by the Authority.

(6)   The second condition is that cash received by the feeder UCITS in accordance with paragraph (5)(a) may not be reinvested before the date on which the feeder UCITS proposes to invest in the new UCITS, except for the purpose of efficient cash management.

(7)   The Authority must, within 15 working days of the date on which the Authority had received all the information required in relation to the application, give written notice to the operator—

(a)   that the Authority approves its application, or

(b)   that the Authority objects to the application.

(8)   Following receipt of notice that the Authority objects to the application, the operator may refer the Authority's decision to the Tribunal.]

NOTES

Commencement: 1 July 2011.

Chapter 5A (ss 283A, 283B) was inserted by the Undertakings for Collective Investment in Transferable Securities Regulations 2011, SI 2011/1613, reg 2(1), (26), as from 1 July 2011.

[7.273]
[283B   Reports on derivative instruments
(1)   An authorised person who is the management company in relation to a UCITS must report to the Authority at specified intervals of not more than 12 months about any investment in derivative instruments during the specified period to which the report relates.
(2)   The report must be in the specified form and contain the specified information.
(3)   The Authority must review the regularity and completeness of the information provided by each management company under subsection (1).
(4)   In this section, "specified" means specified—
     (a)   in rules made by the Authority to implement the UCITS directive, or
     (b)   in any directly applicable Community regulation or decision made under the UCITS directive.]

NOTES

Commencement: 1 July 2011.
Inserted as noted to s 283A at **[7.272]**.

CHAPTER VI
INVESTIGATIONS

[7.274]
284   Power to investigate
(1)   An investigating authority may appoint one or more competent persons to investigate on its behalf—
     (a)   the affairs of, or of the manager or trustee of, any authorised unit trust scheme,
     (b)   the affairs of, or of the operator, trustee or depositary of, any recognised scheme so far as relating to activities carried on in the United Kingdom, or
     (c)   the affairs of, or of the operator, trustee or depositary of, any other collective investment scheme except a body incorporated by virtue of regulations under section 262,
if it appears to the investigating authority that it is in the interests of the participants or potential participants to do so or that the matter is of public concern.
(2)   A person appointed under subsection (1) to investigate the affairs of, or of the manager, trustee, operator or depositary of, any scheme (scheme "A"), may also, if he thinks it necessary for the purposes of that investigation, investigate—
     (a)   the affairs of, or of the manager, trustee, operator or depositary of, any other such scheme as is mentioned in subsection (1) whose manager, trustee, operator or depositary is the same person as the manager, trustee, operator or depositary of scheme A;
     (b)   the affairs of such other schemes and persons (including bodies incorporated by virtue of regulations under section 262 and the directors and depositaries of such bodies) as may be prescribed.
(3)   If the person appointed to conduct an investigation under this section ("B") considers that a person ("C") is or may be able to give information which is relevant to the investigation, B may require C—
     (a)   to produce to B any documents in C's possession or under his control which appear to B to be relevant to the investigation,
     (b)   to attend before B, and
     (c)   otherwise to give B all assistance in connection with the investigation which C is reasonably able to give,
and it is C's duty to comply with that requirement.
(4)   Subsections (5) to (9) of section 170 apply if an investigating authority appoints a person under this section to conduct an investigation on its behalf as they apply in the case mentioned in subsection (1) of that section.
(5)   Section 174 applies to a statement made by a person in compliance with a requirement imposed under this section as it applies to a statement mentioned in that section.
(6)   Subsections (2) to (4) and (6) of section 175 and section 177 have effect as if this section were contained in Part XI.
(7)   Subsections (1) to (9) of section 176 apply in relation to a person appointed under subsection (1) as if—
     (a)   references to an investigator were references to a person so appointed;
     (b)   references to an information requirement were references to a requirement imposed under section 175 or under subsection (3) by a person so appointed;

   (c)   the premises mentioned in subsection (3)(a) were the premises of a person whose affairs are the subject of an investigation under this section or of an appointed representative of such a person.

(8)   No person may be required under this section to disclose information or produce a document in respect of which he owes an obligation of confidence by virtue of carrying on the business of banking unless subsection (9) or (10) applies.

(9)   This subsection applies if—
   (a)   the person to whom the obligation of confidence is owed consents to the disclosure or production; or
   (b)   the imposing on the person concerned of a requirement with respect to information or a document of a kind mentioned in subsection (8) has been specifically authorised by the investigating authority.

(10)   This subsection applies if the person owing the obligation of confidence or the person to whom it is owed is—
   (a)   the manager, trustee, operator or depositary of any collective investment scheme which is under investigation;
   (b)   the director of a body incorporated by virtue of regulations under section 262 which is under investigation;
   (c)   any other person whose own affairs are under investigation.

(11)   "Investigating authority" means the Authority or the Secretary of State.

NOTES

The business of banking: this phrase is not defined in this Act and it is not clear whether it applies to all those who have permission or authorisation to accept deposits.

PART XVIII
RECOGNISED INVESTMENT EXCHANGES AND CLEARING HOUSES

CHAPTER I
EXEMPTION

General

[7.275]
285   Exemption for recognised investment exchanges and clearing houses
(1)   In this Act—
   (a)   "recognised investment exchange" means an investment exchange in relation to which a recognition order is in force; and
   (b)   "recognised clearing house" means a clearing house in relation to which a recognition order is in force.

(2)   A recognised investment exchange is exempt from the general prohibition as respects any regulated activity—
   (a)   which is carried on as a part of the exchange's business as an investment exchange; or
   (b)   which is carried on for the purposes of, or in connection with, the provision of clearing services by the exchange.

(3)   A recognised clearing house is exempt from the general prohibition as respects any regulated activity which is carried on for the purposes of, or in connection with, the provision of clearing services by the clearing house.

[7.276]
286   Qualification for recognition
(1)   The Treasury may make regulations setting out the requirements—
   (a)   which must be satisfied by an investment exchange or clearing house if it is to qualify as a body in respect of which the Authority may make a recognition order under this Part; and
   (b)   which, if a recognition order is made, it must continue to satisfy if it is to remain a recognised body.

(2)   But if regulations contain provision as to the default rules of an investment exchange or clearing house, or as to proceedings taken under such rules by such a body, they require the approval of the Secretary of State.

(3)   "Default rules" means rules of an investment exchange or clearing house which provide for the taking of action in the event of a person's appearing to be unable, or likely to become unable, to meet his obligations in respect of one or more market contracts connected with the exchange or clearing house.

(4)   "Market contract" means—
   (a)   a contract to which Part VII of the Companies Act 1989 applies as a result of section 155 of that Act or a contract to which Part V of the Companies (No 2) (Northern Ireland) Order 1990 applies as a result of Article 80 of that Order; and
   (b)   such other kind of contract as may be prescribed.

[(4A)   If regulations under subsection (1) require an investment exchange to make information available to the public in accordance with—

(a)   Article 29.1 of the markets in financial instruments directive and the Commission Regulation, or

(b)   Article 44.1 of that directive and that Regulation,

the regulations may authorise the Authority to waive the requirement in the circumstances specified in the relevant provisions.

(4B)   The "relevant provisions" for the purposes of subsection (4A) are—

(a)   in a case falling within paragraph (a) of that subsection, Article 29.2 of the markets in financial instruments directive and the Commission Regulation, and

(b)   in a case falling within paragraph (b) of that subsection, Article 44.2 of that directive and that Regulation.

(4C)   If regulations under subsection (1) require an investment exchange to make information available to the public in accordance with—

(a)   Article 30.1 of the markets in financial instruments directive and the Commission Regulation, or

(b)   Article 45.1 of that directive and that Regulation,

the regulations may authorise the Authority to defer the requirement in the circumstances specified, and subject to the requirements contained, in the relevant provisions.

(4D)   The "relevant provisions" for the purposes of subsection (4C) are—

(a)   in a case falling within paragraph (a) of that subsection, Article 30.2 of the markets in financial instruments directive and the Commission Regulation, and

(b)   in a case falling within paragraph (b) of that subsection, Article 45.2 of that directive and that Regulation.

(4E)   "The Commission Regulation" means Commission Regulation 1287/2006 of 10 August 2006.]

(5)   Requirements resulting from this section are referred to in this Part as "recognition requirements".

[(6)   In the case of an investment exchange, requirements resulting from this section are in addition to requirements which must be satisfied by the exchange as a result of section 290(1A) before the Authority may make a recognition order declaring the exchange to be a recognised investment exchange.]

NOTES

Sub-ss (4A)–(4E): inserted by the Financial Services and Markets Act 2000 (Markets in Financial Instruments) (Modification of Powers) Regulations 2006, SI 2006/2975, regs 2, 8, as from 6 December 2006.

Sub-s (6): added by the Financial Services and Markets Act 2000 (Markets in Financial Instruments) Regulations 2007, SI 2007/126, reg 3(2), Sch 2, paras 1, 2, as from 1 April 2007 (certain purposes), and as from 1 November 2007 (otherwise).

Regulations: the Financial Services and Markets Act 2000 (Recognition Requirements for Investment Exchanges and Clearing Houses) Regulations 2001, SI 2001/995.

Note that the following amending Regulations have also been made under this section: the Financial Services and Markets Act 2000 (Recognition Requirements for Investment Exchanges and Clearing Houses) (Amendment) Regulations 2006, SI 2006/3386; the Financial Markets and Insolvency Regulations 2009, SI 2009/853.

Applications for recognition

[7.277]

287   Application by an investment exchange

(1)   Any body corporate or unincorporated association may apply to the Authority for an order declaring it to be a recognised investment exchange for the purposes of this Act.

(2)   The application must be made in such manner as the Authority may direct and must be accompanied by—

(a)   a copy of the applicant's rules;

(b)   a copy of any guidance issued by the applicant;

(c)   the required particulars; and

(d)   such other information as the Authority may reasonably require for the purpose of determining the application.

(3)   The required particulars are—

(a)   particulars of any arrangements which the applicant has made, or proposes to make, for the provision of clearing services in respect of transactions effected on the exchange;

(b)   if the applicant proposes to provide clearing services in respect of transactions other than those effected on the exchange, particulars of the criteria which the applicant will apply when determining to whom it will provide those services[;

(c)   a programme of operations which includes the types of business the applicant proposes to undertake and the applicant's proposed organisational structure;

(d)   such particulars of the persons who effectively direct the business and operations of the exchange as the Authority may reasonably require;

(e)   such particulars of the ownership of the exchange, and in particular of the identity and scale of interests of the persons who are in a position to exercise significant influence over the management of the exchange, whether directly or indirectly, as the Authority may reasonably require].

[(4)   Subsection (3)(c) to (e) does not apply to an application by an overseas applicant.]

NOTES

Sub-s (3): paras (c)–(e) added by the Financial Services and Markets Act 2000 (Markets in Financial Instruments) Regulations 2007, SI 2007/126, reg 3(2), Sch 2, paras 1, 3(a), as from 1 April 2007 (certain purposes), and as from 1 November 2007 (otherwise).

Sub-s (4): added by SI 2007/126, reg 3(2), Sch 2, paras 1, 3(b), as from 1 April 2007 (certain purposes), and as from 1 November 2007 (otherwise).

[7.278]
288 Application by a clearing house
(1) Any body corporate or unincorporated association may apply to the Authority for an order declaring it to be a recognised clearing house for the purposes of this Act.
(2) The application must be made in such manner as the Authority may direct and must be accompanied by—
  (a) a copy of the applicant's rules;
  (b) a copy of any guidance issued by the applicant;
  (c) the required particulars; and
  (d) such other information as the Authority may reasonably require for the purpose of determining the application.
(3) The required particulars are—
  (a) if the applicant makes, or proposes to make, clearing arrangements with a recognised investment exchange, particulars of those arrangements;
  (b) if the applicant proposes to provide clearing services for persons other than recognised investment exchanges, particulars of the criteria which it will apply when determining to whom it will provide those services.

[7.279]
289 Applications: supplementary
(1) At any time after receiving an application and before determining it, the Authority may require the applicant to provide such further information as it reasonably considers necessary to enable it to determine the application.
(2) Information which the Authority requires in connection with an application must be provided in such form, or verified in such manner, as the Authority may direct.
(3) Different directions may be given, or requirements imposed, by the Authority with respect to different applications.

[7.280]
290 Recognition orders
(1) If it appears to the Authority that the applicant satisfies the recognition requirements applicable in its case, the Authority may make a recognition order declaring the applicant to be—
  (a) a recognised investment exchange, if the application is made under section 287;
  (b) a recognised clearing house, if it is made under section 288.
[(1A) In the case of an application for an order declaring the applicant to be a recognised investment exchange, the reference in subsection (1) to the recognition requirements applicable in its case includes a reference to requirements contained in any directly applicable Community regulation made under the markets in financial instruments directive.
(1B) In the case mentioned in subsection (1A), the application must be determined by the Authority before the end of the period of six months beginning with the date on which it receives the completed application.
(1C) Subsection (1B) does not apply in the case of an application by an overseas applicant.]
(2) The Treasury's approval of the making of a recognition order is required under section 307.
(3) In considering an application, the Authority may have regard to any information which it considers is relevant to the application.
(4) A recognition order must specify a date on which it is to take effect.
(5) Section 298 has effect in relation to a decision to refuse to make a recognition order—
  (a) as it has effect in relation to a decision to revoke such an order; and
  (b) as if references to a recognised body were references to the applicant.
(6) Subsection (5) does not apply in a case in which the Treasury have failed to give their approval under section 307.

NOTES

Sub-ss (1A)–(1C): inserted by the Financial Services and Markets Act 2000 (Markets in Financial Instruments) Regulations 2007, SI 2007/126, reg 3(2), Sch 2, paras 1, 4, as from 1 April 2007 (certain purposes), and as from 1 November 2007 (otherwise).

[7.281]
[290A Refusal of recognition on ground of excessive regulatory provision
(1) The Authority must not make a recognition order if it appears to the Authority that an existing or proposed regulatory provision of the applicant in connection with—
  (a) the applicant's business as an investment exchange, or

(b)   the provision by the applicant of clearing services,

imposes or will impose an excessive requirement on the persons affected (directly or indirectly) by it.

(2)   The reference in section 290(1) (making of recognition order) to satisfying the applicable recognition requirements shall be read accordingly.

(3)   Expressions used in subsection (1) above that are defined for the purposes of section 300A (power of Authority to disallow excessive regulatory provision) have the same meaning as in that section.

(4)   The provisions of section 300A(3) and (4) (determination whether regulatory provision excessive) apply for the purposes of this section as for the purposes of section 300A.

(5)   Section 298 has effect in relation to a decision under this section to refuse a recognition order—

(a)   as it has effect in relation to a decision to revoke such an order, and

(b)   as if references to a recognised body were references to the applicant.

(6)   This section does not apply to an application for recognition as an overseas investment exchange or overseas clearing house.]

NOTES

Commencement: 20 December 2006.

Inserted by the Investment Exchanges and Clearing Houses Act 2006, s 4, as from 20 December 2006.

[7.282]

291   Liability in relation to recognised body's regulatory functions

(1)   A recognised body and its officers and staff are not to be liable in damages for anything done or omitted in the discharge of the recognised body's regulatory functions unless it is shown that the act or omission was in bad faith.

(2)   But subsection (1) does not prevent an award of damages made in respect of an act or omission on the ground that the act or omission was unlawful as a result of section 6(1) of the Human Rights Act 1998.

(3)   "Regulatory functions" means the functions of the recognised body so far as relating to, or to matters arising out of, the obligations to which the body is subject under or by virtue of this Act.

[7.283]

292   Overseas investment exchanges and overseas clearing houses

(1)   An application under section 287 or 288 by an overseas applicant must contain the address of a place in the United Kingdom for the service on the applicant of notices or other documents required or authorised to be served on it under this Act.

(2)   If it appears to the Authority that an overseas applicant satisfies the requirements of subsection (3) it may make a recognition order declaring the applicant to be—

(a)   a recognised investment exchange;

(b)   a recognised clearing house.

(3)   The requirements are that—

(a)   investors are afforded protection equivalent to that which they would be afforded if the body concerned were required to comply with recognition requirements[, other than any such requirements which are expressed in regulations under section 286 not to apply for the purposes of this paragraph];

(b)   there are adequate procedures for dealing with a person who is unable, or likely to become unable, to meet his obligations in respect of one or more market contracts connected with the investment exchange or clearing house;

(c)   the applicant is able and willing to co-operate with the Authority by the sharing of information and in other ways;

(d)   adequate arrangements exist for co-operation between the Authority and those responsible for the supervision of the applicant in the country or territory in which the applicant's head office is situated.

(4)   In considering whether it is satisfied as to the requirements mentioned in subsection (3)(a) and (b), the Authority is to have regard to—

(a)   the relevant law and practice of the country or territory in which the applicant's head office is situated;

(b)   the rules and practices of the applicant.

(5)   In relation to an overseas applicant and a body or association declared to be a recognised investment exchange or recognised clearing house by a recognition order made by virtue of subsection (2)—

(a)   the reference in section 313(2) to recognition requirements is to be read as a reference to matters corresponding to the matters in respect of which provision is made in the recognition requirements;

(b)   sections 296(1) and 297(2) have effect as if the requirements mentioned in section 296(1)(a) and section 297(2)(a) were those of subsection (3)(a), (b), and (c) of this section;

(c)   section 297(2) has effect as if the grounds on which a recognition order may be revoked under that provision included the ground that in the opinion of the Authority arrangements of the kind mentioned in subsection (3)(d) no longer exist.

NOTES

Sub-s (3): words in square brackets in para (a) inserted by the Financial Services and Markets Act 2000 (Markets in Financial Instruments) (Modification of Powers) Regulations 2006, SI 2006/2975, regs 2, 9, as from 6 December 2006.

[Publication of information by recognised investment exchange

[7.284]
292A   Publication of information by recognised investment exchange
(1)   A recognised investment exchange must as soon as practicable after a recognition order is made in respect of it publish such particulars of the ownership of the exchange as the Authority may reasonably require.
(2)   The particulars published under subsection (1) must include particulars of the identity and scale of interests of the persons who are in a position to exercise significant influence over the management of the exchange, whether directly or indirectly.
(3)   If an ownership transfer takes place in relation to a recognised investment exchange, the exchange must as soon as practicable after becoming aware of the transfer publish such particulars relating to the transfer as the Authority may reasonably require.
(4)   "Ownership transfer", in relation to an exchange, means a transfer of ownership which gives rise to a change in the persons who are in a position to exercise significant influence over the management of the exchange, whether directly or indirectly.
(5)   A recognised investment exchange must publish such particulars of any decision it makes to suspend or remove a financial instrument from trading on a regulated market operated by it as the Authority may reasonably require.
(6)   The Authority may determine the manner of publication under subsections (1), (3) and (5) and the timing of publication under subsection (5).
(7)   This section does not apply to an overseas investment exchange.]

NOTES

Commencement: 1 April 2007 (certain purposes); 1 November 2007 (otherwise).

Inserted, together with the preceding heading, by the Financial Services and Markets Act 2000 (Markets in Financial Instruments) Regulations 2007, SI 2007/126, reg 3(2), Sch 2, paras 1, 5, as from 1 April 2007 (certain purposes), and as from 1 November 2007 (otherwise).

Supervision

[7.285]
293   Notification requirements
(1)   The Authority may make rules requiring a recognised body to give it—
    (a)   notice of such events relating to the body as may be specified; and
    (b)   such information in respect of those events as may be specified.
(2)   The rules may also require a recognised body to give the Authority, at such times or in respect of such periods as may be specified, such information relating to the body as may be specified.
(3)   An obligation imposed by the rules extends only to a notice or information which the Authority may reasonably require for the exercise of its functions under this Act.
(4)   The rules may require information to be given in a specified form and to be verified in a specified manner.
(5)   If a recognised body—
    (a)   alters or revokes any of its rules or guidance, or
    (b)   makes new rules or issues new guidance,
it must give written notice to the Authority without delay.
(6)   If a recognised investment exchange makes a change—
    (a)   in the arrangements it makes for the provision of clearing services in respect of transactions effected on the exchange, or
    (b)   in the criteria which it applies when determining to whom it will provide clearing services,
it must give written notice to the Authority without delay.
(7)   If a recognised clearing house makes a change—
    (a)   in the recognised investment exchanges for whom it provides clearing services, or
    (b)   in the criteria which it applies when determining to whom (other than recognised investment exchanges) it will provide clearing services,
it must give written notice to the Authority without delay.
(8)   Subsections (5) to (7) do not apply to an overseas investment exchange or an overseas clearing house.
(9)   "Specified" means specified in the Authority's rules.

[7.286]
[293A Information: compliance of recognised investment exchanges with directly applicable Community regulations
The Authority may require a recognised investment exchange to give the Authority such information as it reasonably requires in order to satisfy itself that the exchange is complying with any directly applicable Community regulation made under the markets in financial instruments directive.]

NOTES
Commencement: 1 April 2007 (certain purposes); 1 November 2007 (otherwise).
Inserted by the Financial Services and Markets Act 2000 (Markets in Financial Instruments) Regulations 2007, SI 2007/126, reg 3(2), Sch 2, paras 1, 6, as from 1 April 2007 (certain purposes), and as from 1 November 2007 (otherwise).

[7.287]
294   Modification or waiver of rules
(1)   The Authority may, on the application or with the consent of a recognised body, direct that rules made under section 293 or 295—
   (a)   are not to apply to the body; or
   (b)   are to apply to the body with such modifications as may be specified in the direction.
(2)   An application must be made in such manner as the Authority may direct.
(3)   Subsections (4) to (6) apply to a direction given under subsection (1).
(4)   The Authority may not give a direction unless it is satisfied that—
   (a)   compliance by the recognised body with the rules, or with the rules as unmodified, would be unduly burdensome or would not achieve the purpose for which the rules were made; and
   (b)   the direction would not result in undue risk to persons whose interests the rules are intended to protect.
(5)   A direction may be given subject to conditions.
(6)   The Authority may—
   (a)   revoke a direction; or
   (b)   vary it on the application, or with the consent, of the recognised body to which it relates.

[7.288]
295   Notification: overseas investment exchanges and overseas clearing houses
(1)   At least once a year, every overseas investment exchange and overseas clearing house must provide the Authority with a report.
(2)   The report must contain a statement as to whether any events have occurred which are likely—
   (a)   to affect the Authority's assessment of whether it is satisfied as to the requirements set out in section 292(3); or
   (b)   to have any effect on competition.
(3)   The report must also contain such information as may be specified in rules made by the Authority.
(4)   The investment exchange or clearing house must provide the Treasury and the [OFT] with a copy of the report.

NOTES
Sub-s (4): word in square brackets substituted by the Enterprise Act 2002, s 278(1), Sch 25, para 40(1), (9), as from 1 April 2003.

[7.289]
296   Authority's power to give directions
(1)   This section applies if it appears to the Authority that a recognised body—
   (a)   has failed, or is likely to fail, to satisfy the recognition requirements; or
   (b)   has failed to comply with any other obligation imposed on it by or under this Act.
[(1A)   This section also applies in the case of a recognised body which is a recognised investment exchange if it appears to the Authority that the body has failed, or is likely to fail, to comply with any obligation imposed on it by any directly applicable Community regulation made under the markets in financial instruments directive.]
(2)   The Authority may direct the body to take specified steps for the purpose of securing the body's compliance with—
   (a)   the recognition requirements; or
   (b)   any obligation of the kind in question.
[(2A)   In the case of a recognised investment exchange other than an overseas investment exchange, those steps may include—
   (a)   the granting to the Authority of access to the premises of the exchange for the purpose of inspecting—
     (i)   those premises; or
     (ii)   any documents on the premises which appear to the Authority to be relevant for the purpose mentioned in subsection (2);

Part 7   FSMA   2000

(b) the suspension of the carrying on of any regulated activity by the exchange for the period specified in the direction.]

(3) A direction under this section is enforceable, on the application of the Authority, by an injunction or, in Scotland, by an order for specific performance under section 45 of the Court of Session Act 1988.

(4) The fact that a rule made by a recognised body has been altered in response to a direction given by the Authority does not prevent it from being subsequently altered or revoked by the recognised body.

NOTES

Sub-ss (1A), (2A): inserted by the Financial Services and Markets Act 2000 (Markets in Financial Instruments) Regulations 2007, SI 2007/126, reg 3(2), Sch 2, paras 1, 7, as from 1 April 2007 (certain purposes), and as from 1 November 2007 (otherwise).

Application: this section and s 297 apply in relation to a failure by a recognised investment exchange or recognised clearing house to comply with an obligation under the CA 1989, Pt VII, as to a failure to comply with an obligation under this Act; see s 169(2) of the 1989 Act at **[5.123]**.

[7.290]
297 Revoking recognition

(1) A recognition order may be revoked by an order made by the Authority at the request, or with the consent, of the recognised body concerned.

(2) If it appears to the Authority that a recognised body—
  (a) is failing, or has failed, to satisfy the recognition requirements, or
  (b) is failing, or has failed, to comply with any other obligation imposed on it by or under this Act,
it may make an order revoking the recognition order for that body even though the body does not wish the order to be made.

[(2A) If it appears to the Authority that a recognised body which is a recognised investment exchange—
  (a) has not carried on the business of an investment exchange during the period of twelve months beginning with the day on which the recognition order took effect in relation to it,
  (b) has not carried on the business of an investment exchange at any time during the period of six months ending with the relevant day, or
  (c) has failed, or is likely to fail, to comply with any obligation imposed on it by a directly applicable Community regulation made under the markets in financial instruments directive,
it may make an order revoking the recognition order for that body even though the body does not wish the order to be made.

(2B) The "relevant day", for the purposes of paragraph (b) of subsection (2A), is the day on which the power to make an order under that subsection is exercised.

(2C) Subsection (2A) does not apply to an overseas investment exchange.]

(3) An order under this section ("a revocation order") must specify the date on which it is to take effect.

(4) In the case of a revocation order made under subsection (2) [or (2A)], the specified date must not be earlier than the end of the period of three months beginning with the day on which the order is made.

(5) A revocation order may contain such transitional provisions as the Authority thinks necessary or expedient.

NOTES

Sub-ss (2A)–(2C): inserted by the Financial Services and Markets Act 2000 (Markets in Financial Instruments) Regulations 2007, SI 2007/126, reg 3(2), Sch 2, paras 1, 8(a), as from 1 April 2007 (certain purposes), and as from 1 November 2007 (otherwise).

Sub-s (4): words in square brackets inserted by SI 2007/126, reg 3(2), Sch 2, paras 1, 8(b), as from 1 April 2007 (certain purposes), and as from 1 November 2007 (otherwise).

Application: see the note to s 296 at **[7.289]**.

[7.291]
298 Directions and revocation: procedure

(1) Before giving a direction under section 296, or making a revocation order under section 297(2) [or (2A)], the Authority must—
  (a) give written notice of its intention to do so to the recognised body concerned;
  (b) take such steps as it considers reasonably practicable to bring the notice to the attention of members (if any) of that body; and
  (c) publish the notice in such manner as it thinks appropriate for bringing it to the attention of other persons who are, in its opinion, likely to be affected.

(2) A notice under subsection (1) must—
  (a) state why the Authority intends to give the direction or make the order; and
  (b) draw attention to the right to make representations conferred by subsection (3).

(3) Before the end of the period for making representations—

  (a)　　the recognised body,
  (b)　　any member of that body, and
  (c)　　any other person who is likely to be affected by the proposed direction or revocation order,
may make representations to the Authority.
(4)　The period for making representations is—
  (a)　　two months beginning—
    (i)　　with the date on which the notice is served on the recognised body; or
    (ii)　　if later, with the date on which the notice is published; or
  (b)　　such longer period as the Authority may allow in the particular case.
(5)　In deciding whether to—
  (a)　　give a direction, or
  (b)　　make a revocation order,
the Authority must have regard to any representations made in accordance with subsection (3).
(6)　When the Authority has decided whether to give a direction under section 296 or to make the
proposed revocation order, it must—
  (a)　　give the recognised body written notice of its decision; and
  (b)　　if it has decided to give a direction or make an order, take such steps as it considers
        reasonably practicable for bringing its decision to the attention of members of the body or
        of other persons who are, in the Authority's opinion, likely to be affected.
(7)　If the Authority considers it essential to do so, it may give a direction under section 296—
  (a)　　without following the procedure set out in this section; or
  (b)　　if the Authority has begun to follow that procedure, regardless of whether the period for
        making representations has expired.
(8)　If the Authority has, in relation to a particular matter, followed the procedure set out in
subsections (1) to (5), it need not follow it again if, in relation to that matter, it decides to take
action other than that specified in its notice under subsection (1).

NOTES

Sub-s (1): words in square brackets inserted by the Financial Services and Markets Act 2000 (Markets in Financial
Instruments) Regulations 2007, SI 2007/126, reg 3(2), Sch 2, paras 1, 9, as from 1 April 2007 (certain purposes), and as from
1 November 2007 (otherwise).

[7.292]
299　Complaints about recognised bodies
(1)　The Authority must make arrangements for the investigation of any relevant complaint about
a recognised body.
(2)　"Relevant complaint" means a complaint which the Authority considers is relevant to the
question of whether the body concerned should remain a recognised body.

[7.293]
300　Extension of functions of Tribunal
(1)　If the Treasury are satisfied that the condition mentioned in subsection (2) is satisfied, they
may by order confer functions on the Tribunal with respect to disciplinary proceedings—
  (a)　　of one or more investment exchanges in relation to which a recognition order under
        section 290 is in force or of such investment exchanges generally, or
  (b)　　of one or more clearing houses in relation to which a recognition order under that section is
        in force or of such clearing houses generally.
(2)　The condition is that it is desirable to exercise the power conferred under subsection (1) with
a view to ensuring that—
  (a)　　decisions taken in disciplinary proceedings with respect to which functions are to be
        conferred on the Tribunal are consistent with—
    (i)　　decisions of the Tribunal in cases arising under Part VIII; and
    (ii)　　decisions taken in other disciplinary proceedings with respect to which the Tribunal
          has functions as a result of an order under this section; or
  (b)　　the disciplinary proceedings are in accordance with the Convention rights.
(3)　An order under this section may modify or exclude any provision made by or under this Act
with respect to proceedings before the Tribunal.
(4)　"Disciplinary proceedings" means proceedings under the rules of an investment exchange or
clearing house in relation to market abuse by persons subject to the rules.
(5)　"The Convention rights" has the meaning given in section 1 of the Human Rights Act 1998.

[Power to disallow excessive regulatory provision
[7.294]
300A　Power of Authority to disallow excessive regulatory provision
(1)　This section applies where a recognised body proposes to make any regulatory provision in
connection with its business as an investment exchange or the provision by it of clearing services.
(2)　If it appears to the Authority—
  (a)　　that the proposed provision will impose a requirement on persons affected (directly or
        indirectly) by it, and
  (b)　　that the requirement is excessive,

the Authority may direct that the proposed provision must not be made.

(3) A requirement is excessive if—

  (a) it is not required under Community law or any enactment or rule of law in the United Kingdom, and

  (b) either—

    (i) it is not justified as pursuing a reasonable regulatory objective, or

    (ii) it is disproportionate to the end to be achieved.

(4) In considering whether a requirement is excessive the Authority must have regard to all the relevant circumstances, including—

  (a) the effect of existing legal and other requirements,

  (b) the global character of financial services and markets and the international mobility of activity,

  (c) the desirability of facilitating innovation, and

  (d) the impact of the proposed provision on market confidence.

(5) In this section "requirement" includes any obligation or burden.

(6) Any provision made in contravention of a direction under this section is of no effect.]

NOTES

Commencement: 20 December 2006.

Inserted, together with the preceding heading, by the Investment Exchanges and Clearing Houses Act 2006, s 1, as from 20 December 2006. Note that by virtue of s 5(3) of the 2006 Act, this section (a) does not apply to regulatory provision made before that day, and (b) applies to regulatory provision proposed on or after that day, whenever originally proposed.

[7.295]
[300B Duty to notify proposal to make regulatory provision

(1) A recognised body that proposes to make any regulatory provision must give written notice of the proposal to the Authority without delay.

(2) The Authority may by rules under section 293 (notification requirements)—

  (a) specify descriptions of regulatory provision in relation to which, or circumstances in which, the duty in subsection (1) above does not apply, or

  (b) provide that the duty applies only to specified descriptions of regulatory provision or in specified circumstances.

(3) The Authority may also by rules under that section—

  (a) make provision as to the form and contents of the notice required, and

  (b) require the body to provide such information relating to the proposal as may be specified in the rules or as the Authority may reasonably require.]

NOTES

Commencement: 20 December 2006.

Inserted, together with ss 300C–300E, by the Investment Exchanges and Clearing Houses Act 2006, s 2, as from 20 December 2006. Note that by virtue of s 5(3) of the 2006 Act, this section (and ss 300C–300E) (a) does not apply to regulatory provision made before that day, and (b) applies to regulatory provision proposed on or after that day, whenever originally proposed.

[7.296]
[300C Restriction on making provision before Authority decides whether to act

(1) Where notice of a proposal to make regulatory provision is required to be given to the Authority under section 300B, the provision must not be made—

  (a) before that notice is given, or

  (b) subject to the following provisions of this section, before the end of the initial period.

(2) The initial period is—

  (a) the period of 30 days beginning with the day on which the Authority receives notice of the proposal, or

  (b) if any consultation period announced by the body in relation to the proposal ends after that 30-day period, the end of the consultation period.

(3) If before the end of the initial period the Authority notifies the body that it is calling in the proposal, the provisions of section 300D (consideration by Authority whether to disallow proposed provision) apply as to when the provision may be made.

(4) If—

  (a) before the end of the initial period the Authority notifies the body that it is not calling in the proposal, or

  (b) the initial period ends without the Authority having notified the body that it is calling in the proposal,

the body may then make the proposed provision.

(5) Any provision made in contravention of this section is of no effect.]

NOTES

Commencement: 20 December 2006.

Inserted as noted to s 300B at **[7.295]**.

[7.297]
[300D   Consideration by Authority whether to disallow proposed provision
(1)   This section applies where the Authority notifies a recognised body that it is calling in a proposal to make regulatory provision.
(2)   The Authority must publish a notice—
  (a)   giving details of the proposed provision,
  (b)   stating that it has called in the proposal in order to consider whether to disallow it, and
  (c)   specifying a period during which representations with respect to that question may be made to it.
(3)   The Authority may extend the period for making representations.
(4)   The Authority must notify the body of its decision whether to disallow the provision not later than 30 days after the end of the period for making representations, and must publish the decision and the reasons for it.
(5)   The body must not make the provision unless and until—
  (a)   the Authority notifies it of its decision not to disallow it, or
  (b)   the 30-day period specified in subsection (4) ends without the Authority having notified any decision.
(6)   If the Authority notifies the body of its decision to disallow the provision and that decision is questioned in legal proceedings—
  (a)   the body must not make the provision until those proceedings, and any proceedings on appeal, are finally determined,
  (b)   if the Authority's decision is quashed and the matter is remitted to it for reconsideration, the court may give directions as to the period within which the Authority is to complete its reconsideration, and
  (c)   the body must not make the provision until—
    (i)   the Authority notifies it of its decision on reconsideration not to disallow the provision, or
    (ii)   the period specified by the court ends without the Authority having notified any decision.
(7)   Any provision made in contravention of subsection (5) or (6) is of no effect.]

NOTES
Commencement: 20 December 2006.
Inserted as noted to s 300B at **[7.295]**.

[7.298]
[300E   Power to disallow excessive regulatory provision: supplementary
(1)   In sections 300A to 300D—
  (a)   "regulatory provision" means any rule, guidance, arrangements, policy or practice, and
  (b)   references to making provision shall be read accordingly as including, as the case may require, issuing guidance, entering into arrangements or adopting a policy or practice.
(2)   For the purposes of those sections a variation of a proposal is treated as a new proposal.
(3)   Those sections do not apply to an overseas investment exchange or overseas clearing house.]

NOTES
Commencement: 20 December 2006.
Inserted as noted to s 300B at **[7.295]**.

Other matters
[7.299]
301   Supervision of certain contracts
(1)   The Secretary of State and the Treasury, acting jointly, may by regulations provide for—
  (a)   Part VII of the Companies Act 1989 (financial markets and insolvency), and
  (b)   Part V of the Companies (No 2) (Northern Ireland) Order 1990,
to apply to relevant contracts as it applies to contracts connected with a recognised body.
(2)   "Relevant contracts" means contracts of a prescribed description in relation to which settlement arrangements are provided by a person for the time being included in a list ("the list") maintained by the Authority for the purposes of this section.
(3)   Regulations may be made under this section only if the Secretary of State and the Treasury are satisfied, having regard to the extent to which the relevant contracts concerned are contracts of a kind dealt in by persons supervised by the Authority, that it is appropriate for the arrangements mentioned in subsection (2) to be supervised by the Authority.
(4)   The approval of the Treasury is required for—
  (a)   the conditions set by the Authority for admission to the list; and
  (b)   the arrangements for admission to, and removal from, the list.
(5)   If the Treasury withdraw an approval given by them under subsection (4), all regulations made under this section and then in force are to be treated as suspended.
(6)   But if—
  (a)   the Authority changes the conditions or arrangements (or both), and

(b)   the Treasury give a fresh approval under subsection (4),

the suspension of the regulations ends on such date as the Treasury may, in giving the fresh approval, specify.

(7)   The Authority must—

(a)   publish the list as for the time being in force; and

(b)   provide a certified copy of it to any person who wishes to refer to it in legal proceedings.

(8)   A certified copy of the list is evidence (or in Scotland sufficient evidence) of the contents of the list.

(9)   A copy of the list which purports to be certified by or on behalf of the Authority is to be taken to have been duly certified unless the contrary is shown.

(10)   Regulations under this section may, in relation to a person included in the list—

(a)   apply (with such exceptions, additions and modifications as appear to the Secretary of State and the Treasury to be necessary or expedient) such provisions of, or made under, this Act as they consider appropriate;

(b)   provide for the provisions of Part VII of the Companies Act 1989 and Part V of the Companies (No 2)(Northern Ireland) Order 1990 to apply (with such exceptions, additions or modifications as appear to the Secretary of State and the Treasury to be necessary or expedient).

[CHAPTER 1A
CONTROL OVER RECOGNISED INVESTMENT EXCHANGE

Notices of acquisitions of control over recognised investment exchanges

[7.300]
301A   Obligation to notify the Authority: acquisitions of control
(1)   A person who decides to acquire or increase control over a recognised investment exchange must give the Authority notice in writing before making the acquisition.

(2)   A person who acquires or increases control over a recognised investment exchange in circumstances where notice is not required under subsection (1) must give the Authority notice in writing before the end of 14 days beginning with—

(a)   the day the person acquired or increased the control; or

(b)   if later, the day on which the person first became aware that the control had been acquired or increased.

(3)   For the purposes of calculations relating to this section, the holding of shares or voting power by a person ("A1") includes any shares or voting power held by another ("A2") if A1 and A2 are acting in concert.

(4)   A notice given under this section is a "section 301A notice" and a person giving notice is a "section 301A notice-giver".]

NOTES
Commencement: 21 March 2009.

The original Chapter 1A (ie, ss 301A–301G) was inserted by the Financial Services and Markets Act 2000 (Markets in Financial Instruments) Regulations 2007, SI 2007/126, reg 3(2), Sch 2, paras 1, 10, as from 1 April 2007 (certain purposes), and as from 1 November 2007 (otherwise). It was subsequently substituted (by new ss 301A–301M) by the Financial Services and Markets Act 2000 (Controllers) Regulations 2009, SI 2009/534, reg 5, Sch 2, as from 21 March 2009, subject to transitional provisions in reg 8 of those Regulations which provide that this Chapter, as it stood immediately before that date, applies in respect of any notification submitted to the FSA under those provisions before that date.

[7.301]
[301B   Requirements for section 301A notices
(1)   A section 301A notice must be in such form, include such information and be accompanied by such documents as the Authority may reasonably require.

(2)   The Authority must publish a list of its requirements as to the form, information and accompanying documents for a section 301A notice.

(3)   The Authority may impose different requirements for different cases and may vary or waive requirements in particular cases.]

NOTES
Commencement: 21 March 2009.
Inserted and substituted, subject to transitional provisions, as noted to s 301A at **[7.300]**.

[7.302]
[301C   Acknowledgment of receipt
(1)   The Authority must acknowledge receipt of a section 301A notice in writing before the end of the second working day following receipt.

(2)   If the Authority receives an incomplete section 301A notice it must inform the section 301A notice-giver as soon as reasonably practicable.]

NOTES
Commencement: 21 March 2009.

Inserted and substituted, subject to transitional provisions, as noted to s 301A at **[7.300]**.

[Acquiring and increasing control

[7.303]
301D   Acquiring and increasing control
(1)   For the purposes of this Chapter, a person ("A") acquires control over a recognised investment exchange ("B") if any of the cases in subsection (2) begin to apply.
(2)   The cases are where A holds—
  (a)   20% or more of the shares in B or in a parent undertaking of B ("P");
  (b)   20% or more of the voting power in B or P; or
  (c)   shares or voting power in B or P as a result of which A is able to exercise significant influence over the management of B.
(3)   For the purposes of this Chapter, a person ("A") increases control over a recognised investment exchange ("B") whenever—
  (a)   the percentage of shares which A holds in B or in a parent undertaking of B ("P") increases from less than 50% to 50% or more;
  (b)   the percentage of voting power A holds in B or P increases from less than 50% to 50% or more; or
  (c)   A becomes a parent undertaking of B.]

NOTES
  Commencement: 21 March 2009.
  Inserted and substituted, subject to transitional provisions, as noted to s 301A at **[7.300]**.

[7.304]
[301E   Disregarded holdings
(1)   For the purpose of section 301D, shares and voting power that a person holds in a recognised investment exchange ("B") or in a parent undertaking of B ("P") are disregarded in the following circumstances.
(2)   Shares held only for the purposes of clearing and settling within a short settlement cycle are disregarded.
(3)   Shares held by a custodian or its nominee in a custodian capacity are disregarded, provided that the custodian or nominee is only able to exercise voting power represented by the shares in accordance with instructions given in writing.
(4)   Shares representing no more than 5% of the total voting power in B or P held by an investment firm are disregarded, provided that it—
  (a)   holds the shares in the capacity of a market maker (as defined in article 4.1(8) of the markets in financial instruments directive);
  (b)   is authorised by its home state regulator under the markets in financial instruments directive; and
  (c)   neither intervenes in the management of B or P nor exerts any influence on B or P to buy the shares or back the share price.
(5)   Shares held by a credit institution or investment firm in its trading book are disregarded, provided that—
  (a)   the shares represent no more than 5% of the total voting power in B or P; and
  (b)   the credit institution or investment firm ensures that the voting power is not exercised nor otherwise used to intervene in the management of B or P.
(6)   Shares held by a credit institution or an investment firm are disregarded, provided that—
  (a)   the shares are held as a result of performing the investment services and activities of—
    (i)   underwriting a share issue; or
    (ii)   placing shares on a firm commitment basis in accordance with Annex I, section A.6 of the markets in financial instruments directive; and
  (b)   the credit institution or investment firm—
    (i)   does not exercise voting power represented by the shares or otherwise intervene in the management of the issuer; and
    (ii)   retains the holding for a period of less than one year.
(7)   Where a management company (as defined in [Article 2.1(b)] of the UCITS directive) and its parent undertaking both hold shares or voting power, each may disregard holdings of the other, provided that each exercises its voting power independently of the other.
(8)   But subsection (7) does not apply if the management company—
  (a)   manages holdings for its parent undertaking or an undertaking in respect of which the parent undertaking is a controller;
  (b)   has no discretion as to the exercise of the voting power attached to such holdings; and
  (c)   may only exercise the voting power in relation to such holdings under direct or indirect instruction from—
    (i)   the parent undertaking; or
    (ii)   an undertaking in respect of which of the parent undertaking is a controller.

Part 7   FSMA   2000

(9)　Where an investment firm and its parent undertaking both hold shares or voting power, the parent undertaking may disregard holdings managed by the investment firm on a client by client basis and the investment firm may disregard holdings of the parent undertaking, provided that the investment firm—
  (a)　has permission to provide portfolio management;
  (b)　exercises its voting power independently from the parent undertaking; and
  (c)　may only exercise the voting power under instructions given in writing, or has appropriate mechanisms in place for ensuring that individual portfolio management services are conducted independently of any other services.]

NOTES
Commencement: 21 March 2009.
Inserted and substituted, subject to transitional provisions, as noted to s 301A at [**7.300**].
Sub-s (7): words in square brackets substituted by the Undertakings for Collective Investment in Transferable Securities Regulations 2011, SI 2011/1613, reg 2(1), (27), as from 1 July 2011.

[Assessment procedure

[7.305]
301F　Assessment: general
(1)　Where the Authority receives a section 301A notice, it must—
  (a)　determine whether to approve the acquisition to which it relates; or
  (b)　propose to object to the acquisition.
(2)　In making its determination the Authority must—
  (a)　consider the suitability of the section 301A notice-giver and the financial soundness of the acquisition in order to ensure the sound and prudent management of the recognised investment exchange in question; and
  (b)　have regard to the likely influence that the section 301A notice-giver will have on the recognised investment exchange.
(3)　The Authority may only object to an acquisition if it is not satisfied that the approval requirement is met.
(4)　The approval requirement is that the acquisition in question by the notice-giver does not pose a threat to the sound and prudent management of any financial market operated by the recognised investment exchange.]

NOTES
Commencement: 21 March 2009.
Inserted and substituted, subject to transitional provisions, as noted to s 301A at [**7.300**].

[7.306]
[301G　Assessment: Procedure
(1)　The Authority must act under section 301F within a period three months from the date the Authority receives the completed section 301A notice ("the assessment period").
(2)　The Authority must inform the section 301A notice-giver in writing of—
  (a)　the duration of the assessment period; and
  (b)　its expiry date.
(3)　The Authority must, within two working days of acting under section 301F (and in any event no later than the expiry date of the assessment period)—
  (a)　notify the section 301A notice-giver that it has determined to approve the acquisition; or
  (b)　in the case of a proposed objection to an acquisition, give a warning notice.
(4)　The Authority is treated as having approved the acquisition if, at the expiry of the assessment period, it has neither—
  (a)　given notice under subsection (3); nor
  (b)　informed the section 301A notice-giver that the notice is incomplete.
(5)　If the Authority decides to object to an acquisition it must give the section 301A notice-giver a decision notice.
(6)　Following receipt of a decision notice under this section, the section 301A notice-giver may refer the Authority's decision to the Tribunal.]

NOTES
Commencement: 21 March 2009.
Inserted and substituted, subject to transitional provisions, as noted to s 301A at [**7.300**].

[7.307]
[301H　Duration of approval
(1)　Approval of an acquisition is effective for such period as the Authority may specify in writing.
(2)　Where the Authority has specified a period under subsection (1), it may extend the period.
(3)　Where the Authority has not specified a period, the approval is effective for one year beginning with the date—
  (a)　of the notice given under section 301G(3)(a);
  (b)　on which the Authority is treated as having given approval under section 301G(5); or

(c)   of a decision on a reference to the Tribunal which results in the person receiving approval.]

NOTES
Commencement: 21 March 2009.
Substituted, subject to transitional provisions, as noted to s 301A at **[7.300]**.

[Enforcement procedures

[7.308]
301I   Objections by the Authority
(1)   The Authority may object to a person's control over a recognised investment exchange in any of the circumstances specified in subsection (2).
(2)   The circumstances are that the Authority reasonably believes that—
    (a)   the person acquired or increased control without giving notice under section 301A in circumstances where notice was required; and
    (b)   there are grounds for objecting to control on the basis of the approval requirement in section 301F(4).
(3)   If the Authority proposes to object to a person's control over a recognised investment exchange, it must give that person a warning notice.
(4)   If the Authority decides to object to a person's control over a UK authorised person, it must give that person a decision notice.
(5)   A person to whom the Authority gives a decision notice under this section may refer the matter to the Tribunal.]

NOTES
Commencement: 21 March 2009.
Substituted, subject to transitional provisions, as noted to s 301A at **[7.300]**.

[7.309]
[301J   Restriction notices
(1)   The Authority may give notice in writing (a "restriction notice") to a person in the following circumstances.
(2)   The circumstances are that—
    (a)   the person has control over a recognised investment exchange by virtue of holding shares or voting power; and
    (b)   in relation to the shares or voting power, the Authority has given the person a warning notice or a decision notice under section 301G or 301I or a final notice which confirms a decision notice given under section 301G or 301I.
(3)   In a restriction notice, the Authority may direct that shares or voting power to which the notice relates are, until further notice, subject to one or more of the following restrictions—
    (a)   except by court order, an agreement to transfer or a transfer of any such shares or voting power or, in the case of unissued shares, any agreement to transfer or transfer of the right to be issued with them, is void;
    (b)   no voting power is to be exercisable;
    (c)   no further shares are to be issued in pursuance of any right of the holder of any such shares or voting power or in pursuance of any offer made to their holder;
    (d)   except in a liquidation, no payment is to be made of any sums due from the body corporate on any such shares, whether in respect of capital or otherwise.
(4)   A restriction notice takes effect—
    (a)   immediately; or
    (b)   on such date as may be specified in the notice.
(5)   A restriction notice does not extinguish rights which would be enjoyable but for the notice.
(6)   A copy of the restriction notice must be served on—
    (a)   the recognised investment exchange in question; and
    (b)   in the case of shares or voting power held in a parent undertaking of a recognised investment exchange, the parent undertaking.
(7)   A person to whom the Authority gives a restriction notice may refer the matter to the Tribunal.]

NOTES
Commencement: 21 March 2009.
Substituted, subject to transitional provisions, as noted to s 301A at **[7.300]**.

[7.310]
[301K   Orders for sale of shares
(1)   The court may, on the application of the Authority, order the sale of shares or the disposition of voting power in the following circumstances.
(2)   The circumstances are that—
    (a)   a person has control over a recognised investment exchange by virtue of holding the shares or voting power; and

Part 7   FSMA 2000

(b)   the acquisition or continued holding of the shares or voting power by that person is in contravention of a final notice which confirms a decision notice given under section 301G or section 301I.

(3)   Where the court orders the sale of shares or disposition of voting power it may—

(a)   if a restriction notice has been given in relation to the shares or voting power, order that the restrictions cease to apply; and

(b)   make any further order.

(4)   Where the court makes an order under this section, it must take into account the level of holding that the person would have been entitled to acquire, or to continue to hold, without contravening the final notice.

(5)   If shares are sold or voting power disposed of in pursuance of an order under this section, any proceeds, less the costs of the sale or disposition, must be paid into court for the benefit of the persons beneficially interested in them; and any such person may apply to the court for payment of a whole or part of the proceeds.

(6)   The jurisdiction conferred by this section may be exercised by the High Court and the Court of Session.]

NOTES

Commencement: 21 March 2009.

Substituted, subject to transitional provisions, as noted to s 301A at **[7.300]**.

[Offences

[7.311]

301L   Offences under this Chapter

(1)   A person who fails to comply with an obligation to notify the Authority under section 301A(1) or (2) is guilty of an offence.

(2)   A person who gives notice to the Authority under section 301A(1) and makes the acquisition to which the notice relates before the expiry date of the assessment period is guilty of an offence unless the Authority has approved the acquisition.

(3)   A person who makes an acquisition in contravention of a warning notice or a decision notice given under section 301G or a final notice which confirms a decision notice under that section is guilty of an offence.

(4)   A person who makes an acquisition after the Authority's approval for the acquisition has ceased to be effective by virtue of section 301H is guilty of an offence.

(5)   A person who provides information to the Authority which is false in a material particular is guilty of an offence.

(6)   A person who breaches a direction contained in a restriction notice given under section 301J is guilty of an offence.

(7)   A person guilty of an offence under subsection (1), (2) or (4) to (6) is liable—

(a)   on summary conviction to a fine not exceeding the statutory maximum; or

(b)   on conviction on indictment, to a fine.

(8)   A person guilty of an offence under subsection (3) is liable—

(a)   on summary conviction, to a fine not exceeding the statutory maximum; or

(b)   on conviction on indictment, to imprisonment for a term not exceeding two years or a fine, or both.

(9)   It is a defence for a person charged with an offence under subsection (1) in relation to section 301A(2) to show that the person had, at the time of the alleged offence, no knowledge of the act or circumstances by virtue of which the duty to notify the Authority arose.]

NOTES

Commencement: 21 March 2009.

Substituted, subject to transitional provisions, as noted to s 301A at **[7.300]**.

[Interpretation

[7.312]

301M   Interpretation

(1)   In this Chapter—

"acquisition" means the acquisition of control or of an increase in control over a recognised investment exchange;

"credit institution" means—

(a)   a credit institution authorised under the banking consolidation directive; or

(b)   an institution which would satisfy the requirements for authorisation as a credit institution under that directive if it had its registered office (or if it does not have a registered office, its head office) in an EEA State; and

"shares" and "voting power" have the same meaning as in section 422.

(2)   For the purposes of this Chapter, a "working day" is a day other than—

(a)   a Saturday or a Sunday; or

(b)   a day which is a bank holiday in England and Wales under the Banking and Financial Dealings Act 1971.]

NOTES

Commencement: 21 March 2009.

Substituted, subject to transitional provisions, as noted to s 301A at **[7.300]**.

CHAPTER II
COMPETITION SCRUTINY

[7.313]
302 Interpretation

(1) In this Chapter and Chapter III—

"practices" means—

    (a)   in relation to a recognised investment exchange, the practices of the exchange in its capacity as such; and

    (b)   in relation to a recognised clearing house, the practices of the clearing house in respect of its clearing arrangements;

"regulatory provisions" means—

    (a)   the rules of an investment exchange or a clearing house;

    (b)   any guidance issued by an investment exchange or clearing house;

    (c)   in the case of an investment exchange, the arrangements and criteria mentioned in section [287(3)(a) and (b)];

    (d)   in the case of a clearing house, the arrangements and criteria mentioned in section 288(3).

(2) For the purposes of this Chapter, regulatory provisions or practices have a significantly adverse effect on competition if—

    (a)   they have, or are intended or likely to have, that effect; or

    (b)   the effect that they have, or are intended or likely to have, is to require or encourage behaviour which has, or is intended or likely to have, a significantly adverse effect on competition.

(3) If regulatory provisions or practices have, or are intended or likely to have, the effect of requiring or encouraging exploitation of the strength of a market position they are to be taken, for the purposes of this Chapter, to have an adverse effect on competition.

(4) In determining under this Chapter whether any regulatory provisions have, or are intended or likely to have, a particular effect, it may be assumed that persons to whom the provisions concerned are addressed will act in accordance with them.

NOTES

Sub-s (1): words in square brackets substituted by the Financial Services and Markets Act 2000 (Markets in Financial Instruments) Regulations 2007, SI 2007/126, reg 3(2), Sch 2, paras 1, 11, as from 1 April 2007 (certain purposes), and as from 1 November 2007 (otherwise).

Role of [Office of Fair Trading]

[7.314]
303 Initial report by [OFT]

(1) The Authority must send to the Treasury and to the [OFT] a copy of any regulatory provisions with which it is provided on an application for recognition under section 287 or 288.

(2) The Authority must send to the [OFT] such information in its possession as a result of the application for recognition as it considers will assist [the OFT] in discharging [its] functions in connection with the application.

(3) The [OFT] must issue a report as to whether—

    (a)   a regulatory provision of which a copy has been sent to [it] under subsection (1) has a significantly adverse effect on competition; or

    (b)   a combination of regulatory provisions so copied to [it] have such an effect.

(4) If the [OFT's] conclusion is that one or more provisions have a significantly adverse effect on competition, [it] must state [its] reasons for that conclusion.

(5) When the [OFT] issues a report under subsection (3), [the OFT] must send a copy of it to the Authority, the Competition Commission and the Treasury.

[(6) In the case of an application for recognition under section 287, the OFT must issue its report under subsection (3) before the end of the period of 12 weeks beginning with the date on which it receives the copy sent to it under subsection (1).

(7) Subsection (6) does not apply if the application is made by an overseas investment exchange.]

NOTES

Sub-ss (6), (7): added by the Financial Services and Markets Act 2000 (Markets in Financial Instruments) Regulations 2007, SI 2007/126, reg 3(2), Sch 2, paras 1, 12, as from 1 April 2007 (certain purposes), and as from 1 November 2007 (otherwise).

All other words in square brackets (including the words in the heading preceding this section) substituted by the Enterprise Act 2002, s 278(1), Sch 25, para 40(1), (10), as from 1 April 2003.

Part 7   **FSMA 2000**

[7.315]
304 Further reports by [OFT]
(1) The [OFT] must keep under review the regulatory provisions and practices of recognised bodies.
(2) If at any time the [OFT] considers that—
(a) a regulatory provision or practice has a significantly adverse effect on competition, or
(b) regulatory provisions or practices, or a combination of regulating provisions and practices have such an effect,
[the OFT] must make a report.
(3) If at any time the [OFT] considers that—
(a) a regulatory provision or practice does not have a significantly adverse effect on competition, or
(b) regulatory provisions or practices, or a combination of regulatory provisions and practices do not have any such effect,
[the OFT] may make a report to that effect.
(4) A report under subsection (2) must contain details of the adverse effect on competition.
(5) If the [OFT] makes a report under subsection (2), [the OFT] must—
(a) send a copy of it to the Treasury, to the Competition Commission and to the Authority; and
(b) publish it in the way appearing to [the OFT] to be best calculated to bring it to the attention of the public.
(6) If the [OFT] makes a report under subsection (3)—
(a) [the OFT] must send a copy of it to the Treasury, to the Competition Commission and to the Authority; and
(b) [the OFT] may publish it.
(7) Before publishing a report under this section, the [OFT] must, so far as practicable, exclude any matter which relates to the private affairs of a particular individual the publication of which, in the opinion of the [OFT], would or might seriously and prejudicially affect his interests.
(8) Before publishing such a report, the [OFT] must exclude any matter which relates to the affairs of a particular body the publication of which, in the opinion of the [OFT], would or might seriously and prejudicially affect its interests.
(9) Subsections (7) and (8) do not apply to the copy of a report which the [OFT] is required to send to the Treasury, the Competition Commission and the Authority under subsection (5)(a) or (6)(a).
(10) For the purposes of the law of defamation, absolute privilege attaches to any report of the [OFT] under this section.

NOTES
Words in square brackets substituted by the Enterprise Act 2002, s 278(1), Sch 25, para 40(1), (11), as from 1 April 2003.

[7.316]
305 Investigations by [OFT]
(1) For the purpose of investigating any matter with a view to its consideration under section 303 or 304, the [OFT] may exercise the powers conferred on [it] by this section.
(2) The [OFT] may by notice in writing require any person to produce to [it] or to a person appointed by [it] for the purpose, at a time and place specified in the notice, any document which—
(a) is specified or described in the notice; and
(b) is a document in that person's custody or under his control.
(3) The [OFT] may by notice in writing—
(a) require any person carrying on any business to provide [it] with such information as may be specified or described in the notice; and
(b) specify the time within which, and the manner and form in which, any such information is to be provided.
(4) A requirement may be imposed under subsection (2) or (3)(a) only in respect of documents or information which relate to any matter relevant to the investigation.
(5) If a person ("the defaulter") refuses, or otherwise fails, to comply with a notice under this section, the [OFT] may certify that fact in writing to the court and the court may enquire into the case.
(6) If, after hearing any witness who may be produced against or on behalf of the defaulter and any statement which may be offered in defence, the court is satisfied that the defaulter did not have a reasonable excuse for refusing or otherwise failing to comply with the notice, the court may deal with the defaulter as if he were in contempt.
(7) In this section, "the court" means—
(a) the High Court; or
(b) in Scotland, the Court of Session.

NOTES
Words in square brackets substituted by the Enterprise Act 2002, s 278(1), Sch 25, para 40(1), (12), as from 1 April 2003.

Role of Competition Commission

[7.317]
306 Consideration by Competition Commission
(1)   If subsection (2) or (3) applies, the Commission must investigate the matter which is the subject of the [OFT's] report.
(2)   This subsection applies if the [OFT] sends to the Competition Commission a report—
   (a)   issued by [the OFT] under section 303(3) which concludes that one or more regulatory provisions have a significantly adverse effect on competition, or
   (b)   made by [the OFT] under section 304(2).
(3)   This subsection applies if the [OFT] asks the Commission to consider a report—
   (a)   issued by [the OFT] under section 303(3) which concludes that one or more regulatory provisions do not have a significantly adverse effect on competition, or
   (b)   made by [the OFT] under section 304(3).
(4)   The Commission must then make its own report on the matter unless it considers that, as a result of a change of circumstances, no useful purpose would be served by a report.
(5)   If the Commission decides in accordance with subsection (4) not to make a report, it must make a statement setting out the change of circumstances which resulted in that decision.
(6)   A report made under this section must state the Commission's conclusion as to whether—
   (a)   the regulatory provision or practice which is the subject of the report has a significantly adverse effect on competition, or
   (b)   the regulatory provisions or practices or combination of regulatory provisions and practices which are the subject of the report have such an effect.
(7)   A report under this section stating the Commission's conclusion that there is a significantly adverse effect on competition must also—
   (a)   state whether the Commission considers that that effect is justified; and
   (b)   if it states that the Commission considers that it is not justified, state its conclusion as to what action, if any, the Treasury ought to direct the Authority to take.
(8)   Subsection (9) applies whenever the Commission is considering, for the purposes of this section, whether a particular adverse effect on competition is justified.
(9)   The Commission must ensure, so far as that is reasonably possible, that the conclusion it reaches is compatible with the obligations imposed on the recognised body concerned by or under this Act.
(10)   A report under this section must contain such an account of the Commission's reasons for its conclusions as is expedient, in the opinion of the Commission, for facilitating proper understanding of them.
(11)   The provisions of Schedule 14 (except paragraph 2(b)) apply for the purposes of this section as they apply for the purposes of section 162.
(12)   If the Commission makes a report under this section it must send a copy to the Treasury, the Authority and the [OFT].
[(13)   Subsection (14) applies if—
   (a)   the case relates to an application for recognition under section 287, other than an application by an overseas applicant; and
   (b)   subsection (2)(a) or (3)(a) of this section applies.
(14)   The Commission must—
   (a)   make a report under this section, or a statement under subsection (5), before the end of the period of 12 weeks beginning with the date on which it receives a copy of the OFT's report under section 303(3); and
   (b)   if it makes a statement under subsection (5), send a copy to the Authority and the Treasury.]

NOTES
Sub-ss (13), (14): added by the Financial Services and Markets Act 2000 (Markets in Financial Instruments) Regulations 2007, SI 2007/126, reg 3(2), Sch 2, paras 1, 13, as from 1 April 2007 (certain purposes), and as from 1 November 2007 (otherwise).
   All other words in square brackets substituted by the Enterprise Act 2002, s 278(1), Sch 25, para 40(1), (13), as from 1 April 2003.

Role of the Treasury

[7.318]
307 Recognition orders: role of the Treasury
(1)   Subsection (2) applies if, on an application for a recognition order—
   (a)   the [OFT] makes a report under section 303 but does not ask the Competition Commission to consider it under section 306;
   (b)   the Competition Commission concludes—
      (i)   that the applicant's regulatory provisions do not have a significantly adverse effect on competition; or
      (ii)   that if those provisions do have that effect, the effect is justified.
(2)   The Treasury may refuse to approve the making of the recognition order only if they consider that the exceptional circumstances of the case make it inappropriate for them to give their approval.

(3) Subsection (4) applies if, on an application for a recognition order, the Competition Commission concludes—

  (a) that the applicant's regulatory provisions have a significantly adverse effect on competition; and

  (b) that that effect is not justified.

(4) The Treasury must refuse to approve the making of the recognition order unless they consider that the exceptional circumstances of the case make it inappropriate for them to refuse their approval.

[(5) Subsection (6) applies in the case of an application for recognition under section 287, other than an application by an overseas applicant.

(6) The Treasury must decide whether to approve the application before the end of the period of 10 days beginning with—

  (a) in a case falling within subsection (2)(a) or (3)(a) of section 306, the date on which they receive a copy of the report under that section or, if no such report was made, of the statement under subsection (5) of that section;

  (b) in any other case, the date on which they receive a copy of the report from the OFT under section 303.]

NOTES

Sub-s (1): word in square brackets substituted by the Enterprise Act 2002, s 278(1), Sch 25, para 40(1), (14)(a), as from 1 April 2003.

Sub-ss (5), (6): added by the Financial Services and Markets Act 2000 (Markets in Financial Instruments) Regulations 2007, SI 2007/126, reg 3(2), Sch 2, paras 1, 14, as from 1 April 2007 (certain purposes), and as from 1 November 2007 (otherwise).

[7.319]
308 Directions by the Treasury

(1) This section applies if the Competition Commission makes a report under section 306(4) (other than a report on an application for a recognition order) which states the Commission's conclusion that there is a significantly adverse effect on competition.

(2) If the Commission's conclusion, as stated in the report, is that the adverse effect on competition is not justified, the Treasury must give a remedial direction to the Authority.

(3) But subsection (2) does not apply if the Treasury consider—

  (a) that, as a result of action taken by the Authority or the recognised body concerned in response to the Commission's report, it is unnecessary for them to give a direction; or

  (b) that the exceptional circumstances of the case make it inappropriate or unnecessary for them to do so.

(4) In considering the action to be specified in a remedial direction, the Treasury must have regard to any conclusion of the Commission included in the report because of section 306(7)(b).

(5) Subsection (6) applies if—

  (a) the Commission's conclusion, as stated in its report, is that the adverse effect on competition is justified; but

  (b) the Treasury consider that the exceptional circumstances of the case require them to act.

(6) The Treasury may give a direction to the Authority requiring it to take such action—

  (a) as they consider to be necessary in the light of the exceptional circumstances of the case; and

  (b) as may be specified in the direction.

(7) If the action specified in a remedial direction is the giving by the Authority of a direction—

  (a) the direction to be given must be compatible with the recognition requirements applicable to the recognised body in relation to which it is given; and

  (b) subsections (3) and (4) of section 296 apply to it as if it were a direction given under that section.

(8) "Remedial direction" means a direction requiring the Authority—

  (a) to revoke the recognition order for the body concerned; or

  (b) to give such directions to the body concerned as may be specified in it.

[7.320]
309 Statements by the Treasury

(1) If, in reliance on subsection (3)(a) or (b) of section 308, the Treasury decline to act under subsection (2) of that section, they must make a statement to that effect, giving their reasons.

(2) If the Treasury give a direction under section 308 they must make a statement giving—

  (a) details of the direction; and

  (b) if the direction is given under subsection (6) of that section, their reasons for giving it.

(3) The Treasury must—

  (a) publish any statement made under this section in the way appearing to them best calculated to bring it to the attention of the public; and

  (b) lay a copy of it before Parliament.

[7.321]
310 Procedure on exercise of certain powers by the Treasury

(1) Subsection (2) applies if the Treasury are considering—

(a)   whether to refuse their approval under section 307;

(b)   whether section 308(2) applies; or

(c)   whether to give a direction under section 308(6).

(2)   The Treasury must—

    (a)   take such steps as they consider appropriate to allow the exchange or clearing house concerned, and any other person appearing to the Treasury to be affected, an opportunity to make representations—

        (i)   about any report made by the [OFT] under section 303 or 304 or by the Competition Commission under section 306;

        (ii)   as to whether, and if so how, the Treasury should exercise their powers under section 307 or 308; and

    (b)   have regard to any such representations.

NOTES

Sub-s (2): word in square brackets substituted by the Enterprise Act 2002, s 278(1), Sch 25, para 40(1), (14)(b), as from 1 April 2003.

CHAPTER III
EXCLUSION FROM THE COMPETITION ACT 1998

[7.322]
311 The Chapter I prohibition

(1)   The Chapter I prohibition does not apply to an agreement for the constitution of a recognised body to the extent to which the agreement relates to the regulatory provisions of that body.

(2)   If the conditions set out in subsection (3) are satisfied, the Chapter I prohibition does not apply to an agreement for the constitution of—

    (a)   an investment exchange which is not a recognised investment exchange, or

    (b)   a clearing house which is not a recognised clearing house,

to the extent to which the agreement relates to the regulatory provisions of that body.

(3)   The conditions are that—

    (a)   the body has applied for a recognition order in accordance with the provisions of this Act; and

    (b)   the application has not been determined.

(4)   The Chapter I prohibition does not apply to a recognised body's regulatory provisions.

(5)   The Chapter I prohibition does not apply to a decision made by a recognised body to the extent to which the decision relates to any of that body's regulatory provisions or practices.

(6)   The Chapter I prohibition does not apply to practices of a recognised body.

(7)   The Chapter I prohibition does not apply to an agreement the parties to which consist of or include—

    (a)   a recognised body, or

    (b)   a person who is subject to the rules of a recognised body,

to the extent to which the agreement consists of provisions the inclusion of which is required or encouraged by any of the body's regulatory provisions or practices.

(8)   If a recognised body's recognition order is revoked, this section is to have effect as if that body had continued to be recognised until the end of the period of six months beginning with the day on which the revocation took effect.

(9)   "The Chapter I prohibition" means the prohibition imposed by section 2(1) of the Competition Act 1998.

(10)   Expressions used in this section which are also used in Part I of the Competition Act 1998 are to be interpreted in the same way as for the purposes of that Part of that Act.

[7.323]
312 The Chapter II prohibition

(1)   The Chapter II prohibition does not apply to—

    (a)   practices of a recognised body;

    (b)   the adoption or enforcement of such a body's regulatory provisions;

    (c)   any conduct which is engaged in by such a body or by a person who is subject to the rules of such a body to the extent to which it is encouraged or required by the regulatory provisions of the body.

(2)   The Chapter II prohibition means the prohibition imposed by section 18(1) of the Competition Act 1998.

[CHAPTER 3A
PASSPORT RIGHTS

EEA market operators in United Kingdom

[7.324]
312A   Exercise of passport rights by EEA market operator
(1)   An EEA market operator may, in pursuance of the right under the applicable provision, make arrangements in the United Kingdom to facilitate access to, or use of, a specified regulated market or specified multilateral trading facility operated by it if—
   (a)   the operator has given its home state regulator notice of its intention to make such arrangements; and
   (b)   the home state regulator has given the Authority notice of the operator's intention.
(2)   In making arrangements under subsection (1), the operator is exempt from the general prohibition as respects any regulated activity which is carried on as a part of its business of operating the market or facility in question, or in connection with, or for the purposes of, that business.
(3)   "Specified" means specified in the notice referred to in subsection (1)(a).
(4)   This section does not apply to an overseas investment exchange.]

NOTES
Commencement: 1 April 2007 (certain purposes); 1 November 2007 (otherwise).
Chapter 3A (ss 312A–312D) was inserted by the Financial Services and Markets Act 2000 (Markets in Financial Instruments) Regulations 2007, SI 2007/126, reg 3(2), Sch 2, paras 1, 15, as from 1 April 2007 (certain purposes), and as from 1 November 2007 (otherwise).
Transitional provisions: the Financial Services and Markets Act 2000 (Markets in Financial Instruments) Regulations 2007, SI 2007/126, reg 5 (Transitional and saving provisions: market operators) provides that sub-s (2) above applies to arrangements made on or before 31 October 2007, in the UK, by an EEA market operator to facilitate access to, or use of, a regulated market or multilateral trading facility operated by it as it applies to arrangements under sub-s (1) above.

[7.325]
[312B   Removal of passport rights from EEA market operator
(1)   The Authority may prohibit an EEA market operator from making or, as the case may be, continuing arrangements in the United Kingdom, in pursuance of the applicable provision, to facilitate access to, or use of, a regulated market or multilateral trading facility operated by the operator if—
   (a)   the Authority has clear and demonstrable grounds for believing that the operator has contravened a relevant requirement, and
   (b)   the Authority has first complied with subsections (3) to (9).
(2)   A requirement is relevant if it is imposed—
   (a)   by the operator's home state regulator in the implementation of the markets in financial instruments directive or any Community legislation made under that directive;
   (b)   by provision implementing that directive, or any Community legislation made under it, in the operator's home state; or
   (c)   by any directly applicable Community regulation made under that directive.
(3)   The Authority must notify the operator and its home state regulator of its finding under subsection (1)(a).
(4)   The notice to the home state regulator under subsection (3) must—
   (a)   request that the home state regulator take all appropriate measures for the purpose of ensuring that the operator puts an end to the contravention; and
   (b)   state that the Authority proposes to exercise the power under subsection (1) if the operator continues the contravention.
(5)   The Authority may not exercise the power under subsection (1) unless satisfied—
   (a)   either—
      (i)   that the home state regulator has failed or refused to take measures for the purpose mentioned in subsection (4)(a); or
      (ii)   that the measures taken by the home state regulator have proved inadequate for that purpose; and
   (b)   that the operator is acting in a manner which is clearly prejudicial to the interests of investors in the United Kingdom or the orderly functioning of the financial markets.
(6)   If the Authority is satisfied as mentioned in subsection (5), it must give written notice to—
   (a)   the operator, and
   (b)   the home state regulator,
of its intention to exercise the power under subsection (1).
(7)   A notice under subsection (6) must—
   (a)   state why the Authority intends to exercise its power under subsection (1), and
   (b)   in the case of the notice to the operator, inform the operator that it may make representations to the Authority before the end of the representation period.
(8)   The representation period is—
   (a)   the period of two months beginning with the date on which the notice is given to the operator; or

(b) such longer period as the Authority may allow in a particular case.

(9) If, having considered any representations made by the operator, the Authority decides to exercise the power under subsection (1), it must—

    (a) notify the operator in writing that it will be prohibited from making or, as the case may be, continuing the arrangements mentioned in that subsection from the date specified in the notice; and

    (b) notify the home state regulator of the action to be taken in relation to the operator.

(10) If the Authority exercises the power under subsection (1) it must at the earliest opportunity notify the Commission of the action taken in relation to the operator.

(11) The exemption conferred on an operator by section 312A(2) ceases to apply if the Authority exercises the power under subsection (1) in relation to the operator.

(12) The right to make the arrangements mentioned in subsection (1) may be reinstated in relation to the operator (together with the exemption mentioned in subsection (11)) if the Authority is satisfied that the contravention which led to the Authority exercising the power under subsection (1) has been remedied.]

NOTES

Commencement: 1 April 2007 (certain purposes); 1 November 2007 (otherwise).
Inserted as noted to s 312A at **[7.324]**.

[Recognised investment exchanges operating in EEA States
(other than the United Kingdom)

[7.326]
312C　Exercise of passport rights by recognised investment exchange
(1) Subject to subsection (4), a recognised investment exchange may, in pursuance of the right under the applicable provision, make arrangements in an EEA State (other than the United Kingdom) to facilitate access to, or use of, a regulated market or multilateral trading facility operated by the exchange ("the relevant arrangements").

(2) The exchange must give the Authority written notice of its intention to make the relevant arrangements which—

    (a) describes the arrangements, and

    (b) identifies the EEA State in which it intends to make them.

(3) The Authority must, within one month of receiving a notice under subsection (2), send a copy of it to the host state regulator.

(4) The exchange may not make the relevant arrangements until the Authority has complied with subsection (3).

(5) Subsection (6) applies if the Authority receives a request for information—

    (a) under the second sub-paragraph of Article 31.6 of the markets in financial instruments directive (in the case of relevant arrangements relating to a multilateral trading facility), or

    (b) under the third sub-paragraph of Article 42.6 of that directive (in the case of relevant arrangements relating to a regulated market),

from the host state regulator.

(6) The Authority must, as soon as reasonably practicable, comply with the request.

(7) "Host state regulator" means the competent authority (within the meaning of Article 4.1.22 of the markets in financial instruments directive) of the EEA State in which the exchange intends to make, or has made, the relevant arrangements.

(8) This section does not apply to an overseas investment exchange.]

NOTES

Commencement: 1 April 2007 (certain purposes); 1 November 2007 (otherwise).
Inserted as noted to s 312A at **[7.324]**.
Transitional provisions: the Financial Services and Markets Act 2000 (Markets in Financial Instruments) Regulations 2007, SI 2007/126, reg 5 (Transitional and saving provisions: market operators) provides that sub-ss (2), (4) above do not apply in relation to arrangements made by a recognised investment exchange on or before 31 October 2007 in the territory of another EEA State to facilitate access to, or use of, a regulated market or multilateral trading facility operated by it by persons established in that State.

[Interpretation

[7.327]
312D　Interpretation of Chapter 3A
In this Chapter—

    "the applicable provision" means—

        (a) in the case of arrangements relating to a multilateral trading facility, Article 31.5 of the markets in financial instruments directive; and

        (b) in the case of arrangements relating to a regulated market, the first sub-paragraph of Article 42.6 of that directive;

    "EEA market operator" means a person who is a market operator (within the meaning of Article 4.1.13 of the markets in financial instruments directive) whose home state is an EEA State other than the United Kingdom;

"home state", in relation to an EEA market operator, means the EEA State in which it has its registered office, or if it has no registered office, its head office;

"home state regulator" means the competent authority (within the meaning of Article 4.1.22 of the markets in financial instruments directive) of the EEA State which is the home state in relation to the EEA market operator concerned.]

NOTES

Commencement: 1 April 2007 (certain purposes); 1 November 2007 (otherwise).
Inserted as noted to s 312A at **[7.324]**.

CHAPTER IV

Interpretation

[7.328]
313 Interpretation of Part XVIII

(1)   In this Part—

"application" means an application for a recognition order made under section 287 or 288;

"applicant" means a body corporate or unincorporated association which has applied for a recognition order;

["multilateral trading facility" has the meaning given in Article 4.1.15 of the markets in financial instruments directive;]

["OFT" means the Office of Fair Trading;]

"overseas applicant" means a body corporate or association which has neither its head office nor its registered office in the United Kingdom and which has applied for a recognition order;

"overseas investment exchange" means a body corporate or association which has neither its head office nor its registered office in the United Kingdom and in relation to which a recognition order is in force;

"overseas clearing house" means a body corporate or association which has neither its head office nor its registered office in the United Kingdom and in relation to which a recognition order is in force;

"recognised body" means a recognised investment exchange or a recognised clearing house;

"recognised clearing house" has the meaning given in section 285;

"recognised investment exchange" has the meaning given in section 285;

"recognition order" means an order made under section 290 or 292;

"recognition requirements" has the meaning given by section 286;

["regulated market" has the meaning given in Article 4.1.14 of the markets in financial instruments directive;]

"remedial direction" has the meaning given in section 308(8);

"revocation order" has the meaning given in section 297.

(2)   References in this Part to rules of an investment exchange (or a clearing house) are to rules made, or conditions imposed, by the investment exchange (or the clearing house) with respect to—

(a)   recognition requirements;

(b)   admission of persons to, or their exclusion from the use of, its facilities; or

(c)   matters relating to its constitution.

(3)   References in this Part to guidance issued by an investment exchange are references to guidance issued, or any recommendation made, in writing or other legible form and intended to have continuing effect, by the investment exchange to—

(a)   all or any class of its members or users, or

(b)   persons seeking to become members of the investment exchange or to use its facilities,

with respect to any of the matters mentioned in subsection (2)(a) to (c).

(4)   References in this Part to guidance issued by a clearing house are to guidance issued, or any recommendation made, in writing or other legible form and intended to have continuing effect, by the clearing house to—

(a)   all or any class of its members, or

(b)   persons using or seeking to use its services,

with respect to the provision by it or its members of clearing services.

NOTES

Sub-s (1): definition "OFT" substituted by the Enterprise Act 2002, s 278(1), Sch 25, para 40(1), (15), as from 1 April 2003; definitions "multilateral trading facility" and "regulated market" inserted by the Financial Services and Markets Act 2000 (Markets in Financial Instruments) Regulations 2007, SI 2007/126, reg 3(2), Sch 2, paras 1, 16, as from 1 April 2007 (certain purposes), and as from 1 November 2007 (otherwise).

313A–324 (*Part 18A—Suspension and Removal of Financial Instruments from Trading (ss 313A–313D) and Part XIX—Lloyd's (ss 314–32) omitted for reasons of space; see further, the introductory notes to this Act.*)

PART XX
PROVISION OF FINANCIAL SERVICES BY MEMBERS OF THE PROFESSIONS

[7.329]
325 Authority's general duty

(1) The Authority must keep itself informed about—

    (a)   the way in which designated professional bodies supervise and regulate the carrying on of exempt regulated activities by members of the professions in relation to which they are established;

    (b)   the way in which such members are carrying on exempt regulated activities.

(2) In this Part—

    "exempt regulated activities" means regulated activities which may, as a result of this Part, be carried on by members of a profession which is supervised and regulated by a designated professional body without breaching the general prohibition; and

    "members", in relation to a profession, means persons who are entitled to practise the profession in question and, in practising it, are subject to the rules of the body designated in relation to that profession, whether or not they are members of that body.

(3) The Authority must keep under review the desirability of exercising any of its powers under this Part.

(4) Each designated professional body must co-operate with the Authority, by the sharing of information and in other ways, in order to enable the Authority to perform its functions under this Part.

[7.330]
326 Designation of professional bodies

(1) The Treasury may by order designate bodies for the purposes of this Part.

(2) A body designated under subsection (1) is referred to in this Part as a designated professional body.

(3) The Treasury may designate a body under subsection (1) only if they are satisfied that—

    (a)   the basic condition, and

    (b)   one or more of the additional conditions,

are met in relation to it.

(4) The basic condition is that the body has rules applicable to the carrying on by members of the profession in relation to which it is established of regulated activities which, if the body were to be designated, would be exempt regulated activities.

(5) The additional conditions are that—

    (a)   the body has power under any enactment to regulate the practice of the profession;

    (b)   being a member of the profession is a requirement under any enactment for the exercise of particular functions or the holding of a particular office;

    (c)   the body has been recognised for the purpose of any enactment other than this Act and the recognition has not been withdrawn;

    (d)   the body is established in an EEA State other than the United Kingdom and in that State—

        (i)   the body has power corresponding to that mentioned in paragraph (a);

        (ii)   there is a requirement in relation to the body corresponding to that mentioned in paragraph (b); or

        (iii)   the body is recognised in a manner corresponding to that mentioned in paragraph (c).

(6) "Enactment" includes an Act of the Scottish Parliament, Northern Ireland legislation and subordinate legislation (whether made under an Act, an Act of the Scottish Parliament or Northern Ireland legislation).

(7) "Recognised" means recognised by—

    (a)   a Minister of the Crown;

    (b)   the Scottish Ministers;

    (c)   a Northern Ireland Minister;

    (d)   a Northern Ireland department or its head.

NOTES

Orders: the Financial Services and Markets Act 2000 (Designated Professional Bodies) Order 2001, SI 2001/1226 at **[8.230]**.

[7.331]
327 Exemption from the general prohibition

(1) The general prohibition does not apply to the carrying on of a regulated activity by a person ("P") if—

    (a)   the conditions set out in subsections (2) to (7) are satisfied; and

    (b)   there is not in force—

        (i)   a direction under section 328, or

        (ii)   an order under section 329,

        which prevents this subsection from applying to the carrying on of that activity by him.

(2) P must be—

    (a)   a member of a profession; or

Part 7   FSMA 2000

(b)   controlled or managed by one or more such members.

(3)   P must not receive from a person other than his client any pecuniary reward or other advantage, for which he does not account to his client, arising out of his carrying on of any of the activities.

(4)   The manner of the provision by P of any service in the course of carrying on the activities must be incidental to the provision by him of professional services.

(5)   P must not carry on, or hold himself out as carrying on, a regulated activity other than—
   (a)   one which rules made as a result of section 332(3) allow him to carry on; or
   (b)   one in relation to which he is an exempt person.

(6)   The activities must not be of a description, or relate to an investment of a description, specified in an order made by the Treasury for the purposes of this subsection.

(7)   The activities must be the only regulated activities carried on by P (other than regulated activities in relation to which he is an exempt person).

(8)   "Professional services" means services—
   (a)   which do not constitute carrying on a regulated activity, and
   (b)   the provision of which is supervised and regulated by a designated professional body.

NOTES

Orders: the Financial Services and Markets Act 2000 (Professions) (Non-Exempt Activities) Order 2001, SI 2001/1227; the Financial Services and Markets Act 2000 (Miscellaneous Provisions) Order 2001, SI 2001/3650; the Financial Services and Markets Act 2000 (Commencement of Mortgage Regulation) (Amendment) Order 2002, SI 2002/1777.

[7.332]
328   Directions in relation to the general prohibition

(1)   The Authority may direct that section 327(1) is not to apply to the extent specified in the direction.

(2)   A direction under subsection (1)—
   (a)   must be in writing;
   (b)   may be given in relation to different classes of person or different descriptions of regulated activity.

(3)   A direction under subsection (1) must be published in the way appearing to the Authority to be best calculated to bring it to the attention of the public.

(4)   The Authority may charge a reasonable fee for providing a person with a copy of the direction.

(5)   The Authority must, without delay, give the Treasury a copy of any direction which it gives under this section.

[(6)   The Authority may exercise the power conferred by subsection (1) only if it is satisfied either—
   (a)   that it is desirable to do so in order to protect the interests of clients; or
   (b)   that it is necessary to do so in order to comply with a Community obligation imposed by the insurance mediation directive.]

(7)   In considering whether it is [satisfied of the matter specified in subsection (6)(a)], the Authority must have regard amongst other things to the effectiveness of any arrangements made by any designated professional body—
   (a)   for securing compliance with rules made under section 332(1);
   (b)   for dealing with complaints against its members in relation to the carrying on by them of exempt regulated activities;
   (c)   in order to offer redress to clients who suffer, or claim to have suffered, loss as a result of misconduct by its members in their carrying on of exempt regulated activities;
   (d)   for co-operating with the Authority under section 325(4).

(8)   In this Part "clients" means—
   (a)   persons who use, have used or are or may be contemplating using, any of the services provided by a member of a profession in the course of carrying on exempt regulated activities;
   (b)   persons who have rights or interests which are derived from, or otherwise attributable to, the use of any such services by other persons; or
   (c)   persons who have rights or interests which may be adversely affected by the use of any such services by persons acting on their behalf or in a fiduciary capacity in relation to them.

(9)   If a member of a profession is carrying on an exempt regulated activity in his capacity as a trustee, the persons who are, have been or may be beneficiaries of the trust are to be treated as persons who use, have used or are or may be contemplating using services provided by that person in his carrying on of that activity.

NOTES

Sub-s (6): substituted by the Insurance Mediation Directive (Miscellaneous Amendments) Regulations 2003, SI 2003/1473, reg 9(a), as from 14 January 2005.

Sub-s (7): words in square brackets substituted by SI 2003/1473, reg 9(b), as from 14 January 2005.

[7.333]
329 Orders in relation to the general prohibition
(1) Subsection (2) applies if it appears to the Authority that a person to whom, as a result of section 327(1), the general prohibition does not apply is not a fit and proper person to carry on regulated activities in accordance with that section.
(2) The Authority may make an order disapplying section 327(1) in relation to that person to the extent specified in the order.
(3) The Authority may, on the application of the person named in an order under subsection (1), vary or revoke it.
(4) "Specified" means specified in the order.
(5) If a partnership is named in an order under this section, the order is not affected by any change in its membership.
(6) If a partnership named in an order under this section is dissolved, the order continues to have effect in relation to any partnership which succeeds to the business of the dissolved partnership.
(7) For the purposes of subsection (6), a partnership is to be regarded as succeeding to the business of another partnership only if—
    (a)   the members of the resulting partnership are substantially the same as those of the former partnership; and
    (b)   succession is to the whole or substantially the whole of the business of the former partnership.

[7.334]
330 Consultation
(1) Before giving a direction under section 328(1), the Authority must publish a draft of the proposed direction.
(2) The draft must be accompanied by—
    (a)   a cost benefit analysis; and
    (b)   notice that representations about the proposed direction may be made to the Authority within a specified time.
(3) Before giving the proposed direction, the Authority must have regard to any representations made to it in accordance with subsection (2)(b).
(4) If the Authority gives the proposed direction it must publish an account, in general terms, of—
    (a)   the representations made to it in accordance with subsection (2)(b); and
    (b)   its response to them.
(5) If the direction differs from the draft published under subsection (1) in a way which is, in the opinion of the Authority, significant—
    (a)   the Authority must (in addition to complying with subsection (4)) publish details of the difference; and
    (b)   those details must be accompanied by a cost benefit analysis.
(6) Subsections (1) to (5) do not apply if the Authority considers that the delay involved in complying with them would prejudice the interests of consumers.
(7) Neither subsection (2)(a) nor subsection (5)(b) applies if the Authority considers—
    (a)   that, making the appropriate comparison, there will be no increase in costs; or
    (b)   that, making that comparison, there will be an increase in costs but the increase will be of minimal significance.
(8) The Authority may charge a reasonable fee for providing a person with a copy of a draft published under subsection (1).
(9) When the Authority is required to publish a document under this section it must do so in the way appearing to it to be best calculated to bring it to the attention of the public.
(10) "Cost benefit analysis" means an estimate of the costs together with an analysis of the benefits that will arise—
    (a)   if the proposed direction is given; or
    (b)   if subsection (5)(b) applies, from the direction that has been given.
(11) "The appropriate comparison" means—
    (a)   in relation to subsection (2)(a), a comparison between the overall position if the direction is given and the overall position if it is not given;
    (b)   in relation to subsection (5)(b), a comparison between the overall position after the giving of the direction and the overall position before it was given.

[7.335]
331 Procedure on making or varying orders under section 329
(1) If the Authority proposes to make an order under section 329, it must give the person concerned a warning notice.
(2) The warning notice must set out the terms of the proposed order.
(3) If the Authority decides to make an order under section 329, it must give the person concerned a decision notice.
(4) The decision notice must—
    (a)   name the person to whom the order applies;
    (b)   set out the terms of the order; and

Part 7   FSMA 2000

    (c)   be given to the person named in the order.

(5)   Subsections (6) to (8) apply to an application for the variation or revocation of an order under section 329.

(6)   If the Authority decides to grant the application, it must give the applicant written notice of its decision.

(7)   If the Authority proposes to refuse the application, it must give the applicant a warning notice.

(8)   If the Authority decides to refuse the application, it must give the applicant a decision notice.

(9)   A person—

    (a)   against whom the Authority have decided to make an order under section 329, or

    (b)   whose application for the variation or revocation of such an order the Authority had decided to refuse,

may refer the matter to the Tribunal.

(10)   The Authority may not make an order under section 329 unless—

    (a)   the period within which the decision to make to the order may be referred to the Tribunal has expired and no such reference has been made; or

    (b)   if such a reference has been made, the reference has been determined.

[7.336]

332   Rules in relation to persons to whom the general prohibition does not apply

(1)   The Authority may make rules applicable to persons to whom, as a result of section 327(1), the general prohibition does not apply.

(2)   The power conferred by subsection (1) is to be exercised for the purpose of ensuring that clients are aware that such persons are not authorised persons.

(3)   A designated professional body must make rules—

    (a)   applicable to members of the profession in relation to which it is established who are not authorised persons; and

    (b)   governing the carrying on by those members of regulated activities (other than regulated activities in relation to which they are exempt persons).

(4)   Rules made in compliance with subsection (3) must be designed to secure that, in providing a particular professional service to a particular client, the member carries on only regulated activities which arise out of, or are complementary to, the provision by him of that service to that client.

(5)   Rules made by a designated professional body under subsection (3) require the approval of the Authority.

[7.337]

333   False claims to be a person to whom the general prohibition does not apply

(1)   A person who—

    (a)   describes himself (in whatever terms) as a person to whom the general prohibition does not apply, in relation to a particular regulated activity, as a result of this Part, or

    (b)   behaves, or otherwise holds himself out, in a manner which indicates (or which is reasonably likely to be understood as indicating) that he is such a person,

is guilty of an offence if he is not such a person.

(2)   In proceedings for an offence under this section it is a defence for the accused to show that he took all reasonable precautions and exercised all due diligence to avoid committing the offence.

(3)   A person guilty of an offence under this section is liable on summary conviction to imprisonment for a term not exceeding six months or a fine not exceeding level 5 on the standard scale, or both.

(4)   But where the conduct constituting the offence involved or included the public display of any material, the maximum fine for the offence is level 5 on the standard scale multiplied by the number of days for which the display continued.

334–339   *(Part XXI—Mutual Societies (ss 334–339 and Sch 18) omitted for reasons of space; see further, the introductory notes to this Act.)*

PART XXII
AUDITORS AND ACTUARIES

Appointment

[7.338]

340   Appointment

(1)   Rules may require an authorised person, or an authorised person falling within a specified class—

    (a)   to appoint an auditor, or

    (b)   to appoint an actuary,

if he is not already under an obligation to do so imposed by another enactment.

(2)   Rules may require an authorised person, or an authorised person falling within a specified class—

    (a)   to produce periodic financial reports; and

    (b)   to have them reported on by an auditor or an actuary.

(3)   Rules may impose such other duties on auditors of, or actuaries acting for, authorised persons as may be specified.

(4)   Rules under subsection (1) may make provision—

(a)   specifying the manner in which and time within which an auditor or actuary is to be appointed;

(b)   requiring the Authority to be notified of an appointment;

(c)   enabling the Authority to make an appointment if no appointment has been made or notified;

(d)   as to remuneration;

(e)   as to the term of office, removal and resignation of an auditor or actuary.

(5)   An auditor or actuary appointed as a result of rules under subsection (1), or on whom duties are imposed by rules under subsection (3)—

(a)   must act in accordance with such provision as may be made by rules; and

(b)   is to have such powers in connection with the discharge of his functions as may be provided by rules.

(6)   In subsections (1) to (3) "auditor" or "actuary" means an auditor, or actuary, who satisfies such requirements as to qualifications, experience and other matters (if any) as may be specified.

(7)   "Specified" means specified in rules.

Information

[7.339]

341   Access to books etc

(1)   An appointed auditor of, or an appointed actuary acting for, an authorised person—

(a)   has a right of access at all times to the authorised person's books, accounts and vouchers; and

(b)   is entitled to require from the authorised person's officers such information and explanations as he reasonably considers necessary for the performance of his duties as auditor or actuary.

(2)   "Appointed" means appointed under or as a result of this Act.

[7.340]

342   Information given by auditor or actuary to the Authority

(1)   This section applies to a person who is, or has been, an auditor of an authorised person appointed under or as a result of a statutory provision.

(2)   This section also applies to a person who is, or has been, an actuary acting for an authorised person and appointed under or as a result of a statutory provision.

(3)   An auditor or actuary does not contravene any duty to which he is subject merely because he gives to the Authority—

(a)   information on a matter of which he has, or had, become aware in his capacity as auditor of, or actuary acting for, the authorised person, or

(b)   his opinion on such a matter,

if he is acting in good faith and he reasonably believes that the information or opinion is relevant to any functions of the Authority.

(4)   Subsection (3) applies whether or not the auditor or actuary is responding to a request from the Authority.

(5)   The Treasury may make regulations prescribing circumstances in which an auditor or actuary must communicate matters to the Authority as mentioned in subsection (3).

(6)   It is the duty of an auditor or actuary to whom any such regulations apply to communicate a matter to the Authority in the circumstances prescribed by the regulations.

(7)   The matters to be communicated to the Authority in accordance with the regulations may include matters relating to persons other than the authorised person concerned.

NOTES

Regulations: the Financial Services and Markets Act 2000 (Communications by Auditors) Regulations 2001, SI 2001/2587; the Financial Services and Markets Act 2000 (Communications by Actuaries) Regulations 2003, SI 2003/1294.

[7.341]

343   Information given by auditor or actuary to the Authority: persons with close links

(1)   This section applies to a person who—

(a)   is, or has been, an auditor of an authorised person appointed under or as a result of a statutory provision; and

(b)   is, or has been, an auditor of a person ("CL") who has close links with the authorised person.

(2)   This section also applies to a person who—

(a)   is, or has been, an actuary acting for an authorised person and appointed under or as a result of a statutory provision; and

(b)   is, or has been, an actuary acting for a person ("CL") who has close links with the authorised person.

(3) An auditor or actuary does not contravene any duty to which he is subject merely because he gives to the Authority—

(a) information on a matter concerning the authorised person of which he has, or had, become aware in his capacity as auditor of, or actuary acting for, CL, or

(b) his opinion on such a matter,

if he is acting in good faith and he reasonably believes that the information or opinion is relevant to any functions of the Authority.

(4) Subsection (3) applies whether or not the auditor or actuary is responding to a request from the Authority.

(5) The Treasury may make regulations prescribing circumstances in which an auditor or actuary must communicate matters to the Authority as mentioned in subsection (3).

(6) It is the duty of an auditor or actuary to whom any such regulations apply to communicate a matter to the Authority in the circumstances prescribed by the regulations.

(7) The matters to be communicated to the Authority in accordance with the regulations may include matters relating to persons other than the authorised person concerned.

(8) CL has close links with the authorised person concerned ("A") if CL is—

(a) a parent undertaking of A;

(b) a subsidiary undertaking of A;

(c) a parent undertaking of a subsidiary undertaking of A; or

(d) a subsidiary undertaking of a parent undertaking of A.

(9) "Subsidiary undertaking" includes all the instances mentioned in Article 1(1) and (2) of the Seventh Company Law Directive in which an entity may be a subsidiary of an undertaking.

NOTES

Regulations: the Financial Services and Markets Act 2000 (Communications by Auditors) Regulations 2001, SI 2001/2587; the Financial Services and Markets Act 2000 (Communications by Actuaries) Regulations 2003, SI 2003/1294.

[7.342]
344 Duty of auditor or actuary resigning etc to give notice

(1) This section applies to an auditor or actuary to whom section 342 applies.

(2) He must without delay notify the Authority if he—

(a) is removed from office by an authorised person;

(b) resigns before the expiry of his term of office with such a person; or

(c) is not re-appointed by such a person.

(3) If he ceases to be an auditor of, or actuary acting for, such a person, he must without delay notify the Authority—

(a) of any matter connected with his so ceasing which he thinks ought to be drawn to the Authority's attention; or

(b) that there is no such matter.

Disqualification

[7.343]
345 Disqualification

(1) If it appears to the Authority that an auditor or actuary to whom section 342 applies has failed to comply with a duty imposed on him under this Act, it may disqualify him from being the auditor of, or (as the case may be) from acting as an actuary for, any authorised person or any particular class of authorised person.

(2) If the Authority proposes to disqualify a person under this section it must give him a warning notice.

(3) If it decides to disqualify him it must give him a decision notice.

(4) The Authority may remove any disqualification imposed under this section if satisfied that the disqualified person will in future comply with the duty in question.

(5) A person who has been disqualified under this section may refer the matter to the Tribunal.

NOTES

Transitional provisions: the Financial Services and Markets Act 2000 (Transitional Provisions) (Authorised Persons etc) Order 2001, SI 2001/2636, art 78, provides for the disqualification under this section of an auditor who, at 1 December 2001, has been disqualified pursuant to the Financial Services Act 1986, s 111(3) (repealed by the Financial Services and Markets Act 2000 (Consequential Amendments and Repeals) Order 2001, SI 2001/3649, art 3(1)(c), or the Insurance Companies Act 1982, s 21A(5) (repealed by art 3(1)(b) of that Order).

Offence

[7.344]
346 Provision of false or misleading information to auditor or actuary

(1) An authorised person who knowingly or recklessly gives an appointed auditor or actuary information which is false or misleading in a material particular is guilty of an offence and liable—

(a) on summary conviction, to imprisonment for a term not exceeding six months or a fine not exceeding the statutory maximum, or both;

(b) on conviction on indictment, to imprisonment for a term not exceeding two years or a fine, or both.

(2) Subsection (1) applies equally to an officer, controller or manager of an authorised person.

(3) "Appointed" means appointed under or as a result of this Act.

347–379 *(Part XXIII—Public Record, Disclosure of Information and Co-operation (ss 347–354) and Part XXIV—Insolvency (ss 355–379) omitted for reasons of space; see further, the introductory notes to this Act.)*

PART XXV
INJUNCTIONS AND RESTITUTION

Injunctions

[7.345]
380 Injunctions

(1) If, on the application of the Authority or the Secretary of State, the court is satisfied—
(a) that there is a reasonable likelihood that any person will contravene a relevant requirement, or
(b) that any person has contravened a relevant requirement and that there is a reasonable likelihood that the contravention will continue or be repeated,

the court may make an order restraining (or in Scotland an interdict prohibiting) the contravention.

(2) If on the application of the Authority or the Secretary of State the court is satisfied—
(a) that any person has contravened a relevant requirement, and
(b) that there are steps which could be taken for remedying the contravention,

the court may make an order requiring that person, and any other person who appears to have been knowingly concerned in the contravention, to take such steps as the court may direct to remedy it.

(3) If, on the application of the Authority or the Secretary of State, the court is satisfied that any person may have—
(a) contravened a relevant requirement, or
(b) been knowingly concerned in the contravention of such a requirement,

it may make an order restraining (or in Scotland an interdict prohibiting) him from disposing of, or otherwise dealing with, any assets of his which it is satisfied he is reasonably likely to dispose of or otherwise deal with.

(4) The jurisdiction conferred by this section is exercisable by the High Court and the Court of Session.

(5) In subsection (2), references to remedying a contravention include references to mitigating its effect.

(6) "Relevant requirement"—
(a) in relation to an application by the Authority, means a requirement—
(i) which is imposed by or under this Act [or by any directly applicable Community regulation [or decision] made under the markets in financial instruments directive] [or the UCITS directive]; or
(ii) which is imposed by or under any other Act and whose contravention constitutes an offence which the Authority has power to prosecute under this Act;
(b) in relation to an application by the Secretary of State, means a requirement which is imposed by or under this Act and whose contravention constitutes an offence which the Secretary of State has power to prosecute under this Act.

(7) In the application of subsection (6) to Scotland—
(a) in paragraph (a)(ii) for "which the Authority has power to prosecute under this Act" substitute "mentioned in paragraph (a) or (b) of section 402(1)"; and
(b) in paragraph (b) omit "which the Secretary of State has power to prosecute under this Act".

NOTES

Sub-s (6): words in first (outer) pair of square brackets inserted by the Financial Services and Markets Act 2000 (Markets in Financial Instruments) Regulations 2007, SI 2007/126, reg 3(5), Sch 5, paras 1, 13, as from 1 April 2007 (certain purposes), and as from 1 November 2007 (otherwise); words in second (inner) pair of square brackets and words in third pair of square brackets inserted by the Undertakings for Collective Investment in Transferable Securities Regulations 2011, SI 2011/1613, reg 2(1), (29), as from 1 July 2011.

Transitional provisions: any requirement, condition or prohibition imposed before 1 December 2001 by or under certain specified provisions is to be treated as a relevant requirement for the purposes of sub-s (2) above, and any restriction or requirement imposed by or under certain other provisions is to be treated as a relevant requirement for the purposes of sub-s (3)(a) above; see, in general, the Financial Services and Markets Act 2000 (Transitional Provisions and Savings) (Civil Remedies, Discipline, Criminal Offences etc) (No 2) Order 2001, SI 2001/3083, arts 2, 4. The specified provisions for the purposes of sub-ss (2), (3)(a) are listed in arts 2(3), 4(3) of the 2001 Order.

Note: for the purposes of this section a requirement imposed by the FSA under the Electronic Commerce Directive (Financial Services and Markets) Regulations 2002, SI 2002/1775 upon an incoming provider is to be treated as imposed on him by or under this Act; see reg 12(2) of those Regulations.

[7.346]
381 Injunctions in cases of market abuse

(1) If, on the application of the Authority, the court is satisfied—
(a) that there is a reasonable likelihood that any person will engage in market abuse, or

(b)   that any person is or has engaged in market abuse and that there is a reasonable likelihood that the market abuse will continue or be repeated,

the court may make an order restraining (or in Scotland an interdict prohibiting) the market abuse.

(2)   If on the application of the Authority the court is satisfied—

(a)   that any person is or has engaged in market abuse, and

(b)   that there are steps which could be taken for remedying the market abuse,

the court may make an order requiring him to take such steps as the court may direct to remedy it.

(3)   Subsection (4) applies if, on the application of the Authority, the court is satisfied that any person—

(a)   may be engaged in market abuse; or

(b)   may have been engaged in market abuse.

(4)   The court make an order restraining (or in Scotland an interdict prohibiting) the person concerned from disposing of, or otherwise dealing with, any assets of his which it is satisfied that he is reasonably likely to dispose of, or otherwise deal with.

(5)   The jurisdiction conferred by this section is exercisable by the High Court and the Court of Session.

(6)   In subsection (2), references to remedying any market abuse include references to mitigating its effect.

Restitution orders

[7.347]

382   Restitution orders

(1)   The court may, on the application of the Authority or the Secretary of State, make an order under subsection (2) if it is satisfied that a person has contravened a relevant requirement, or been knowingly concerned in the contravention of such a requirement, and—

(a)   that profits have accrued to him as a result of the contravention; or

(b)   that one or more persons have suffered loss or been otherwise adversely affected as a result of the contravention.

(2)   The court may order the person concerned to pay to the Authority such sum as appears to the court to be just having regard—

(a)   in a case within paragraph (a) of subsection (1), to the profits appearing to the court to have accrued;

(b)   in a case within paragraph (b) of that subsection, to the extent of the loss or other adverse effect;

(c)   in a case within both of those paragraphs, to the profits appearing to the court to have accrued and to the extent of the loss or other adverse effect.

(3)   Any amount paid to the Authority in pursuance of an order under subsection (2) must be paid by it to such qualifying person or distributed by it among such qualifying persons as the court may direct.

(4)   On an application under subsection (1) the court may require the person concerned to supply it with such accounts or other information as it may require for any one or more of the following purposes—

(a)   establishing whether any and, if so, what profits have accrued to him as mentioned in paragraph (a) of that subsection;

(b)   establishing whether any person or persons have suffered any loss or adverse effect as mentioned in paragraph (b) of that subsection and, if so, the extent of that loss or adverse effect; and

(c)   determining how any amounts are to be paid or distributed under subsection (3).

(5)   The court may require any accounts or other information supplied under subsection (4) to be verified in such manner as it may direct.

(6)   The jurisdiction conferred by this section is exercisable by the High Court and the Court of Session.

(7)   Nothing in this section affects the right of any person other than the Authority or the Secretary of State to bring proceedings in respect of the matters to which this section applies.

(8)   "Qualifying person" means a person appearing to the court to be someone—

(a)   to whom the profits mentioned in subsection (1)(a) are attributable; or

(b)   who has suffered the loss or adverse effect mentioned in subsection (1)(b).

(9)   "Relevant requirement"—

(a)   in relation to an application by the Authority, means a requirement—

(i)   which is imposed by or under this Act [or by any directly applicable Community regulation [or decision] made under the markets in financial instruments directive] [or the UCITS directive]; or

(ii)   which is imposed by or under any other Act and whose contravention constitutes an offence which the Authority has power to prosecute under this Act;

(b)   in relation to an application by the Secretary of State, means a requirement which is imposed by or under this Act and whose contravention constitutes an offence which the Secretary of State has power to prosecute under this Act.

(10) In the application of subsection (9) to Scotland—

   (a)   in paragraph (a)(ii) for "which the Authority has power to prosecute under this Act" substitute "mentioned in paragraph (a) or (b) of section 402(1); and

   (b)   in paragraph (b) omit "which the Secretary of State has power to prosecute under this Act".

NOTES

Sub-s (9): words in first (outer) pair of square brackets inserted by the Financial Services and Markets Act 2000 (Markets in Financial Instruments) Regulations 2007, SI 2007/126, reg 3(5), Sch 5, paras 1, 14, as from 1 April 2007 (certain purposes), and as from 1 November 2007 (otherwise); words in second (inner) pair of square brackets and words in third pair of square brackets inserted by the Undertakings for Collective Investment in Transferable Securities Regulations 2011, SI 2011/1613, reg 2(1), (29), as from 1 July 2011.

Transitional provisions: any requirement, condition or prohibition imposed before 1 December 2001 by or under certain specified provisions is to be treated as a relevant requirement for the purposes of this section; see the Financial Services and Markets Act 2000 (Transitional Provisions and Savings) (Civil Remedies, Discipline, Criminal Offences etc) (No 2) Order 2001, SI 2001/3083, art 2. The specified provisions are listed in art 2(3) of the 2001 Order.

Note: for the purposes of this section a requirement imposed by the FSA under the Electronic Commerce Directive (Financial Services and Markets) Regulations 2002, SI 2002/1775 upon an incoming provider is to be treated as imposed on him by or under this Act; see reg 12(2) of those Regulations.

[7.348]
383   Restitution orders in cases of market abuse

(1)   The court may, on the application of the Authority, make an order under subsection (4) if it is satisfied that a person ("the person concerned")—

   (a)   has engaged in market abuse, or

   (b)   by taking or refraining from taking any action has required or encouraged another person or persons to engage in behaviour which, if engaged in by the person concerned, would amount to market abuse,

and the condition mentioned in subsection (2) is fulfilled.

(2)   The condition is—

   (a)   that profits have accrued to the person concerned as a result; or

   (b)   that one or more persons have suffered loss or been otherwise adversely affected as a result.

(3)   But the court may not make an order under subsection (4) if it is satisfied that—

   (a)   the person concerned believed, on reasonable grounds, that his behaviour did not fall within paragraph (a) or (b) of subsection (1); or

   (b)   he took all reasonable precautions and exercised all due diligence to avoid behaving in a way which fell within paragraph (a) or (b) of subsection (1).

(4)   The court may order the person concerned to pay to the Authority such sum as appears to the court to be just having regard—

   (a)   in a case within paragraph (a) of subsection (2), to the profits appearing to the court to have accrued;

   (b)   in a case within paragraph (b) of that subsection, to the extent of the loss or other adverse effect;

   (c)   in a case within both of those paragraphs, to the profits appearing to the court to have accrued and to the extent of the loss or other adverse effect.

(5)   Any amount paid to the Authority in pursuance of an order under subsection (4) must be paid by it to such qualifying person or distributed by it among such qualifying persons as the court may direct.

(6)   On an application under subsection (1) the court may require the person concerned to supply it with such accounts or other information as it may require for any one or more of the following purposes—

   (a)   establishing whether any and, if so, what profits have accrued to him as mentioned in subsection (2)(a);

   (b)   establishing whether any person or persons have suffered any loss or adverse effect as mentioned in subsection (2)(b) and, if so, the extent of that loss or adverse effect; and

   (c)   determining how any amounts are to be paid or distributed under subsection (5).

(7)   The court may require any accounts or other information supplied under subsection (6) to be verified in such manner as it may direct.

(8)   The jurisdiction conferred by this section is exercisable by the High Court and the Court of Session.

(9)   Nothing in this section affects the right of any person other than the Authority to bring proceedings in respect of the matters to which this section applies.

(10)   "Qualifying person" means a person appearing to the court to be someone—

   (a)   to whom the profits mentioned in paragraph (a) of subsection (2) are attributable; or

   (b)   who has suffered the loss or adverse effect mentioned in paragraph (b) of that subsection.

Restitution required by Authority

[7.349]
384   Power of Authority to require restitution
(1)   The Authority may exercise the power in subsection (5) if it is satisfied that an authorised person ("the person concerned") has contravened a relevant requirement, or been knowingly concerned in the contravention of such a requirement, and—
  (a)   that profits have accrued to him as a result of the contravention; or
  (b)   that one or more persons have suffered loss or been otherwise adversely affected as a result of the contravention.
(2)   The Authority may exercise the power in subsection (5) if it is satisfied that a person ("the person concerned")—
  (a)   has engaged in market abuse, or
  (b)   by taking or refraining from taking any action has required or encouraged another person or persons to engage in behaviour which, if engaged in by the person concerned, would amount to market abuse,
and the condition mentioned in subsection (3) is fulfilled.
(3)   The condition is—
  (a)   that profits have accrued to the person concerned as a result of the market abuse; or
  (b)   that one or more persons have suffered loss or been otherwise adversely affected as a result of the market abuse.
(4)   But the Authority may not exercise that power as a result of subsection (2) if, having considered any representations made to it in response to a warning notice, there are reasonable grounds for it to be satisfied that—
  (a)   the person concerned believed, on reasonable grounds, that his behaviour did not fall within paragraph (a) or (b) of that subsection; or
  (b)   he took all reasonable precautions and exercised all due diligence to avoid behaving in a way which fell within paragraph (a) or (b) of that subsection.
(5)   The power referred to in subsections (1) and (2) is a power to require the person concerned, in accordance with such arrangements as the Authority considers appropriate, to pay to the appropriate person or distribute among the appropriate persons such amount as appears to the Authority to be just having regard—
  (a)   in a case within paragraph (a) of subsection (1) or (3), to the profits appearing to the Authority to have accrued;
  (b)   in a case within paragraph (b) of subsection (1) or (3), to the extent of the loss or other adverse effect;
  (c)   in a case within paragraphs (a) and (b) of subsection (1) or (3), to the profits appearing to the Authority to have accrued and to the extent of the loss or other adverse effect.
(6)   "Appropriate person" means a person appearing to the Authority to be someone—
  (a)   to whom the profits mentioned in paragraph (a) of subsection (1) or (3) are attributable; or
  (b)   who has suffered the loss or adverse effect mentioned in paragraph (b) of subsection (1) or (3).
(7)   "Relevant requirement" means—
  (a)   a requirement imposed by or under this Act [or by any directly applicable Community regulation [or decision] made under the markets in financial instruments directive] [or the UCITS directive]; and
  (b)   a requirement which is imposed by or under any other Act and whose contravention constitutes an offence in relation to which this Act confers power to prosecute on the Authority.
(8)   In the application of subsection (7) to Scotland, in paragraph (b) for "in relation to which this Act confers power to prosecute on the Authority" substitute "mentioned in paragraph (a) or (b) of section 402(1)".

NOTES

Sub-s (7): words in first (outer) pair of square brackets inserted by the Financial Services and Markets Act 2000 (Markets in Financial Instruments) Regulations 2007, SI 2007/126, reg 3(5), Sch 5, paras 1, 15, as from 1 April 2007 (certain purposes), and as from 1 November 2007 (otherwise); words in second (inner) pair of square brackets and words in third pair of square brackets inserted by the Undertakings for Collective Investment in Transferable Securities Regulations 2011, SI 2011/1613, reg 2(1), (29), as from 1 July 2011.

Transitional provisions: as to the power of the Authority under sub-s (5) in relation to certain conduct before 1 December 2001, see the Financial Services and Markets Act 2000 (Transitional Provisions and Savings) (Civil Remedies, Discipline, Criminal Offences etc) (No 2) Order 2001, SI 2001/3083, art 3.

Note: for the purposes of this section a requirement imposed by the FSA under the Electronic Commerce Directive (Financial Services and Markets) Regulations 2002, SI 2002/1775 upon an authorised incoming provider is to be treated as imposed on him by or under this Act; see reg 12(1) of those Regulations.

[7.350]
385   Warning notices
(1)   If the Authority proposes to exercise the power under section 384(5) in relation to a person, it must give him a warning notice.

(2)   A warning notice under this section must specify the amount which the Authority proposes to require the person concerned to pay or distribute as mentioned in section 384(5).

[7.351]
386   Decision notices
(1)   If the Authority decides to exercise the power under section 384(5), it must give a decision notice to the person in relation to whom the power is exercised.
(2)   The decision notice must—
(a)   state the amount that he is to pay or distribute as mentioned in section 384(5);
(b)   identify the person or persons to whom that amount is to be paid or among whom that amount is to be distributed; and
(c)   state the arrangements in accordance with which the payment or distribution is to be made.
(3)   If the Authority decides to exercise the power under section 384(5), the person in relation to whom it is exercised may refer the matter to the Tribunal.

387–396   *(Part XXVI—Notices (ss 387–396) omitted for reasons of space; see further, the introductory notes to this Act.)*

PART XXVII
OFFENCES

Miscellaneous offences

[7.352]
397   Misleading statements and practices
(1)   This subsection applies to a person who—
(a)   makes a statement, promise or forecast which he knows to be misleading, false or deceptive in a material particular;
(b)   dishonestly conceals any material facts whether in connection with a statement, promise or forecast made by him or otherwise; or
(c)   recklessly makes (dishonestly or otherwise) a statement, promise or forecast which is misleading, false or deceptive in a material particular.
(2)   A person to whom subsection (1) applies is guilty of an offence if he makes the statement, promise or forecast or conceals the facts for the purpose of inducing, or is reckless as to whether it may induce, another person (whether or not the person to whom the statement, promise or forecast is made)—
(a)   to enter or offer to enter into, or to refrain from entering or offering to enter into, a relevant agreement; or
(b)   to exercise, or refrain from exercising, any rights conferred by a relevant investment.
(3)   Any person who does any act or engages in any course of conduct which creates a false or misleading impression as to the market in or the price or value of any relevant investments is guilty of an offence if he does so for the purpose of creating that impression and of thereby inducing another person to acquire, dispose of, subscribe for or underwrite those investments or to refrain from doing so or to exercise, or refrain from exercising, any rights conferred by those investments.
(4)   In proceedings for an offence under subsection (2) brought against a person to whom subsection (1) applies as a result of paragraph (a) of that subsection, it is a defence for him to show that the statement, promise or forecast was made in conformity with[—
(a)   price stabilising rules;
(b)   control of information rules; or
(c)   the relevant provisions of Commission Regulation (EC) No 2273/2003 of 22 December 2003 implementing Directive 2003/6/EC of the European Parliament and of the Council as regards exemptions for buy-back programmes and stabilisation of financial instruments].
(5)   In proceedings brought against any person for an offence under subsection (3) it is a defence for him to show—
(a)   that he reasonably believed that his act or conduct would not create an impression that was false or misleading as to the matters mentioned in that subsection;
(b)   that he acted or engaged in the conduct—
(i)   for the purpose of stabilising the price of investments; and
(ii)   in conformity with price stabilising rules;   . . .
(c)   that he acted or engaged in the conduct in conformity with control of information rules[; or
(d)   that he acted or engaged in the conduct in conformity with the relevant provisions of Commission Regulation (EC) No 2273/2003 of 22 December 2003 implementing Directive 2003/6/EC of the European Parliament and of the Council as regards exemptions for buy-back programmes and stabilisation of financial instruments].
(6)   Subsections (1) and (2) do not apply unless—
(a)   the statement, promise or forecast is made in or from, or the facts are concealed in or from, the United Kingdom or arrangements are made in or from the United Kingdom for the statement, promise or forecast to be made or the facts to be concealed;
(b)   the person on whom the inducement is intended to or may have effect is in the United Kingdom; or

(c) the agreement is or would be entered into or the rights are or would be exercised in the United Kingdom.

(7) Subsection (3) does not apply unless—

  (a) the act is done, or the course of conduct is engaged in, in the United Kingdom; or
  (b) the false or misleading impression is created there.

(8) A person guilty of an offence under this section is liable—

  (a) on summary conviction, to imprisonment for a term not exceeding six months or a fine not exceeding the statutory maximum, or both;
  (b) on conviction on indictment, to imprisonment for a term not exceeding seven years or a fine, or both.

(9) "Relevant agreement" means an agreement—

  (a) the entering into or performance of which by either party constitutes an activity of a specified kind or one which falls within a specified class of activity; and
  (b) which relates to a relevant investment.

(10) "Relevant investment" means an investment of a specified kind or one which falls within a prescribed class of investment.

(11) Schedule 2 (except paragraphs 25 and 26) applies for the purposes of subsections (9) and (10) with references to section 22 being read as references to each of those subsections.

(12) Nothing in Schedule 2, as applied by subsection (11), limits the power conferred by subsection (9) or (10).

(13) "Investment" includes any asset, right or interest.

(14) "Specified" means specified in an order made by the Treasury.

NOTES

Sub-s (4): words in square brackets substituted by the Financial Services and Markets Act 2000 (Market Abuse) Regulations 2005, SI 2005/381, reg 8(1), (2), as from 17 March 2005.

Sub-s (5): word omitted from para (b) repealed, and para (d) and the word immediately preceding it added, by SI 2005/381, reg 8(1), (3), as from 17 March 2005.

Orders: Financial Services and Markets Act 2000 (Misleading Statements and Practices) Order 2001, SI 2001/3645.

Note that the following amending Orders have also been made under this section: the Financial Services and Markets Act 2000 (Commencement of Mortgage Regulation) (Amendment) Order 2002, SI 2002/1777; the Financial Services and Markets Act 2000 (Misleading Statements and Practices) (Amendment) Order 2003, SI 2003/1474.

[7.353]
398 Misleading the Authority: residual cases

(1) A person who, in purported compliance with any requirement imposed by or under this Act, knowingly or recklessly gives the Authority information which is false or misleading in a material particular is guilty of an offence.

(2) Subsection (1) applies only to a requirement in relation to which no other provision of this Act creates an offence in connection with the giving of information.

(3) A person guilty of an offence under this section is liable—

  (a) on summary conviction, to a fine not exceeding the statutory maximum;
  (b) on conviction on indictment, to a fine.

NOTES

Note: for the purposes of this section a requirement imposed by the FSA under the Electronic Commerce Directive (Financial Services and Markets) Regulations 2002, SI 2002/1775 upon an incoming provider is to be treated as imposed on him by or under this Act; see reg 12(2) of those Regulations.

[7.354]
399 Misleading [the OFT]

Section 44 of the Competition Act 1998 (offences connected with the provision of false or misleading information) applies in relation to any function of [the Office of Fair Trading] under this Act as if it were a function under Part I of that Act.

NOTES

Words in square brackets substituted by the Enterprise Act 2002, s 278(1), Sch 25, para 40(1), (16), as from 1 April 2003.

Bodies corporate and partnerships

[7.355]
400 Offences by bodies corporate etc

(1) If an offence under this Act committed by a body corporate is shown—

  (a) to have been committed with the consent or connivance of an officer, or
  (b) to be attributable to any neglect on his part,

the officer as well as the body corporate is guilty of the offence and liable to be proceeded against and punished accordingly.

(2) If the affairs of a body corporate are managed by its members, subsection (1) applies in relation to the acts and defaults of a member in connection with his functions of management as if he were a director of the body.

(3) If an offence under this Act committed by a partnership is shown—

(a)   to have been committed with the consent or connivance of a partner, or

(b)   to be attributable to any neglect on his part,

the partner as well as the partnership is guilty of the offence and liable to be proceeded against and punished accordingly.

(4)   In subsection (3) "partner" includes a person purporting to act as a partner.

(5)   "Officer", in relation to a body corporate, means—

(a)   a director, member of the committee of management, chief executive, manager, secretary or other similar officer of the body, or a person purporting to act in any such capacity; and

(b)   an individual who is a controller of the body.

(6)   If an offence under this Act committed by an unincorporated association (other than a partnership) is shown—

(a)   to have been committed with the consent or connivance of an officer of the association or a member of its governing body, or

(b)   to be attributable to any neglect on the part of such an officer or member,

that officer or member as well as the association is guilty of the offence and liable to be proceeded against and punished accordingly.

(7)   Regulations may provide for the application of any provision of this section, with such modifications as the Treasury consider appropriate, to a body corporate or unincorporated association formed or recognised under the law of a territory outside the United Kingdom.

Institution of proceedings

[7.356]

401   Proceedings for offences

(1)   In this section "offence" means an offence under this Act or subordinate legislation made under this Act.

(2)   Proceedings for an offence may be instituted in England and Wales only—

(a)   by the Authority or the Secretary of State; or

(b)   by or with the consent of the Director of Public Prosecutions.

(3)   Proceedings for an offence may be instituted in Northern Ireland only—

(a)   by the Authority or the Secretary of State; or

(b)   by or with the consent of the Director of Public Prosecutions for Northern Ireland.

(4)   Except in Scotland, proceedings for an offence under section 203 may also be instituted by [the Office of Fair Trading].

(5)   In exercising its power to institute proceedings for an offence, the Authority must comply with any conditions or restrictions imposed in writing by the Treasury.

(6)   Conditions or restrictions may be imposed under subsection (5) in relation to—

(a)   proceedings generally; or

(b)   such proceedings, or categories of proceedings, as the Treasury may direct.

NOTES

Sub-s (4): words in square brackets substituted by the Enterprise Act 2002, s 278(1), Sch 25, para 40(1), (17), as from 1 April 2003.

Transitional provisions: this section and s 403 have effect as if offences committed before 1 December 2001 under certain provisions (the Insurance Companies Act 1982, the Financial Services Act 1986, the Banking Act 1987, and certain related provisions) were an offence under this Act; see the Financial Services and Markets Act 2000 (Transitional Provisions and Savings) (Civil Remedies, Discipline, Criminal Offences etc) (No 2) Order 2001, SI 2001/3083, art 13. The 1982, 1986 and 1987 Acts were repealed by the Financial Services and Markets Act 2000 (Consequential Amendments and Repeals) Order 2001, SI 2001/3649, art 3(1)(b)–(d).

[7.357]

402   Power of the Authority to institute proceedings for certain other offences

(1)   Except in Scotland, the Authority may institute proceedings for an offence under—

(a)   Part V of the Criminal Justice Act 1993 (insider dealing); . . .

(b)   prescribed regulations relating to money laundering; [or

(c)   Schedule 7 to the Counter-Terrorism Act 2008 (terrorist financing or money laundering)].

(2)   In exercising its power to institute proceedings for any such offence, the Authority must comply with any conditions or restrictions imposed in writing by the Treasury.

(3)   Conditions or restrictions may be imposed under subsection (2) in relation to—

(a)   proceedings generally; or

(b)   such proceedings, or categories of proceedings, as the Treasury may direct.

NOTES

Sub-s (1): word omitted repealed, and para (c) (and the word immediately preceding it) inserted, by the Counter-Terrorism Act 2008, s 62, Sch 7, Pt 7, para 33(4), as from 27 November 2008.

Note: the Money Laundering Regulations 2007, SI 2007/2157 have been prescribed for the purposes of sub-s (1)(b) above by reg 1(2) of those Regulations.

Regulations: the Money Laundering Regulations 2007, SI 2007/2157.

[7.358]

403 Jurisdiction and procedure in respect of offences

(1) A fine imposed on an unincorporated association on its conviction of an offence is to be paid out of the funds of the association.

(2) Proceedings for an offence alleged to have been committed by an unincorporated association must be brought in the name of the association (and not in that of any of its members).

(3) Rules of court relating to the service of documents are to have effect as if the association were a body corporate.

(4) In proceedings for an offence brought against an unincorporated association—

    (a) section 33 of the Criminal Justice Act 1925 and Schedule 3 to the Magistrates' Courts Act 1980 (procedure) apply as they do in relation to a body corporate;

    (b) section 70 of the Criminal Procedure (Scotland) Act 1995 (procedure) applies as if the association were a body corporate;

    (c) section 18 of the Criminal Justice (Northern Ireland) Act 1945 and Schedule 4 to the Magistrates' Courts (Northern Ireland) Order 1981 (procedure) apply as they do in relation to a body corporate.

(5) Summary proceedings for an offence may be taken—

    (a) against a body corporate or unincorporated association at any place at which it has a place of business;

    (b) against an individual at any place where he is for the time being.

(6) Subsection (5) does not affect any jurisdiction exercisable apart from this section.

(7) "Offence" means an offence under this Act.

NOTES

Transitional provisions: see the note to s 401 at **[7.356]**.

404–416 (Part XXVIII—Miscellaneous (ss 404–416) omitted for reasons of space; see further, the introductory notes to this Act.)

PART XXIX
INTERPRETATION

[7.359]

417 Definitions

(1) In this Act—

    "appointed representative" has the meaning given in section 39(2);

    "auditors and actuaries rules" means rules made under section 340;

    "authorisation offence" has the meaning given in section 23(2);

    "authorised open-ended investment company" has the meaning given in section 237(3);

    "authorised person" has the meaning given in section 31(2);

    "the Authority" means the Financial Services Authority;

    "body corporate" includes a body corporate constituted under the law of a country or territory outside the United Kingdom;

    "chief executive"—

        (a) in relation to a body corporate whose principal place of business is within the United Kingdom, means an employee of that body who, alone or jointly with one or more others, is responsible under the immediate authority of the directors, for the conduct of the whole of the business of that body; and

        (b) in relation to a body corporate whose principal place of business is outside the United Kingdom, means the person who, alone or jointly with one or more others, is responsible for the conduct of its business within the United Kingdom;

    ["claim", in relation to the Financial Services Compensation Scheme under Part XV, is to be construed in accordance with section 214(1B);]

    "collective investment scheme" has the meaning given in section 235;

    "the Commission" means the European Commission (except in provisions relating to the Competition Commission);

    "the compensation scheme" has the meaning given in section 213(2);

    "control of information rules" has the meaning given in section 147(1);

    "director", in relation to a body corporate, includes—

        (a) a person occupying in relation to it the position of a director (by whatever name called); and

        (b) a person in accordance with whose directions or instructions (not being advice given in a professional capacity) the directors of that body are accustomed to act;

    "documents" includes information recorded in any form and, in relation to information recorded otherwise than in legible form, references to its production include references to producing a copy of the information in legible form[, or in a form from which it can readily be produced in visible and legible form];

["electronic commerce directive" means Directive 2000/31/EC of the European Parliament and
the Council of 8 June 2000 on certain legal aspects of information society services, in
particular electronic commerce, in the Internal Market (Directive on electronic
commerce);]

"exempt person", in relation to a regulated activity, means a person who is exempt from the
general prohibition in relation to that activity as a result of an exemption order made under
section 38(1) or as a result of section 39(1) or 285(2) or (3);

"financial promotion rules" means rules made under section 145;

"friendly society" means an incorporated or registered friendly society;

"general prohibition" has the meaning given in section 19(2);

"general rules" has the meaning given in section 138(2);

"incorporated friendly society" means a society incorporated under the Friendly Societies
Act 1992;

"industrial and provident society" means a society registered or deemed to be registered under
the Industrial and Provident Societies Act 1965 or the Industrial and Provident Societies
Act (Northern Ireland) 1969;

["information society service" means an information society service within the meaning of
Article 2(a) of the electronic commerce directive;]

["investment services and activities" has the meaning given in Article 4.1.2 of the markets in
financial instruments directive, read with—
    (a)   Chapter VI of Commission Regulation 1287/2006 of 10 August 2006, and
    (b)   Article 52 of Commission Directive 2006/73/EC of 10 August 2006;]

"market abuse" has the meaning given in section 118;

"Minister of the Crown" has the same meaning as in the Ministers of the Crown Act 1975;

"money laundering rules" means rules made under section 146;

"notice of control" [(except in Chapter 1A of Part 18)] has the meaning given in section 178(5);

"the ombudsman scheme" has the meaning given in section 225(3);

"open-ended investment company" has the meaning given in section 236;

"Part IV permission" has the meaning given in section 40(4);

"partnership" includes a partnership constituted under the law of a country or territory outside
the United Kingdom;

"prescribed" (where not otherwise defined) means prescribed in regulations made by the
Treasury;

"price stabilising rules" means rules made under section 144;

"private company" has [the same meaning as in the Companies Acts (see section 4 of
the Companies Act 2006)];

"prohibition order" has the meaning given in section 56(2);

"recognised clearing house" and "recognised investment exchange" have the meaning given in
section 285;

"registered friendly society" means a society which is—
    (a)   a friendly society within the meaning of section 7(1)(a) of the Friendly Societies
            Act 1974; and
    (b)   registered within the meaning of that Act;

"regulated activity" has the meaning given in section 22;

"regulating provisions" has the meaning given in section 159(1);

"regulatory objectives" means the objectives mentioned in section 2;

"regulatory provisions" has the meaning given in section 302;

"rule" means a rule made by the Authority under this Act;

"rule-making instrument" has the meaning given in section 153;

"the scheme manager" has the meaning given in section 212(1);

"the scheme operator" has the meaning given in section 225(2);

"scheme particulars rules" has the meaning given in section 248(1);

"Seventh Company Law Directive" means the European Council Seventh Company Law
Directive of 13 June 1983 on consolidated accounts (No 83/349/EEC);

["Takeovers Directive" means Directive 2004/25/EC of the European Parliament and of
the Council;]

"threshold conditions", in relation to a regulated activity, has the meaning given in section 41;

"the Treaty" means the treaty establishing the European Community;

["the Tribunal" means the Upper Tribunal;]

"trust scheme rules" has the meaning given in section 247(1);

"UK authorised person" has the meaning given in section 178(4);

["the UK financial system" has the meaning given in section 3;] and

"unit trust scheme" has the meaning given in section 237.

(2)   In the application of this Act to Scotland, references to a matter being actionable at the suit of
a person are to be read as references to the matter being actionable at the instance of that person.

(3)   For the purposes of any provision of this Act [(other than a provision of Part 6)] authorising
or requiring a person to do anything within a specified number of days no account is to be taken of
any day which is a public holiday in any part of the United Kingdom.

[(4)   For the purposes of this Act—

   (a)   an information society service is provided from an EEA State if it is provided from an establishment in that State;

   (b)   an establishment, in connection with an information society service, is the place at which the provider of the service (being a national of an EEA State or a company or firm as mentioned in Article 48 of the Treaty) effectively pursues an economic activity for an indefinite period;

   (c)   the presence or use in a particular place of equipment or other technical means of providing an information society service does not, of itself, constitute that place as an establishment of the kind mentioned in paragraph (b);

   (d)   where it cannot be determined from which of a number of establishments a given information society service is provided, that service is to be regarded as provided from the establishment where the provider has the centre of his activities relating to the service.]

NOTES

Sub-s (1) is amended as follows:

Definition "claim" inserted by the Banking Act 2009, s 174(2), as from 21 February 2009.

Words in square brackets in definition "documents" inserted by the Criminal Justice and Police Act 2001, s 70, Sch 2, Pt 2, para 16(1), (2)(f), as from 1 April 2003.

Definitions "electronic commerce directive" and "information society service" inserted by the Electronic Commerce Directive (Financial Services and Markets) Regulations 2002, SI 2002/1775, reg 13(1), (2)(a), (b), as from 21 August 2002.

Definition "investment services and activities" inserted, and words in square brackets in definition "notice of control" inserted, by the Financial Services and Markets Act 2000 (Markets in Financial Instruments) Regulations 2007, SI 2007/126, reg 3(5), Sch 5, paras 1, 19, as from 1 April 2007 (certain purposes), and as from 1 November 2007 (otherwise).

Words in square brackets in the definition "private company" substituted by the Companies Act 2006 (Consequential Amendments, Transitional Provisions and Savings) Order 2009, SI 2009/1941, art 2(1), Sch 1, para 181(1), (4), as from 1 October 2009.

Definition "Takeovers Directive" inserted by the Companies Act 2006, s 964(1), (6), as from 6 April 2007.

Definition "the Tribunal" inserted by the Transfer of Tribunal Functions Order 2010, SI 2010/22, art 5(1), Sch 2, paras 43, 48, as from 6 April 2010 (for transitional provisions and savings in relation to existing cases and appeals from the tribunals whose functions were transferred by the 2010 Order, see Sch 5 to that Order).

Definition "the UK financial system" inserted by the Financial Services Act 2010, s 24(1), (2), Sch 2, Pt 1, paras 1, 31, as from 8 April 2010.

Sub-s (3): words in square brackets inserted by the Prospectus Regulations 2005, SI 2005/1433, reg 2(1), Sch 1, para 15, as from 1 July 2005.

Sub-s (4): added by SI 2002/1775, reg 13(1), (2)(c), as from 21 August 2002.

Industrial and Provident Societies Act 1965: see the Co-operative and Community Benefit Societies and Credit Unions Act 2010 which renames this Act as the Co-operative and Community Benefit Societies and Credit Unions Act 1965.

[7.360]

418 Carrying on regulated activities in the United Kingdom

(1) In the [five] cases described in this section, a person who—

   (a)   is carrying on a regulated activity, but

   (b)   would not otherwise be regarded as carrying it on in the United Kingdom,

is, for the purposes of this Act, to be regarded as carrying it on in the United Kingdom.

(2) The first case is where—

   (a)   his registered office (or if he does not have a registered office his head office) is in the United Kingdom;

   (b)   he is entitled to exercise rights under a single market directive as a UK firm; and

   (c)   he is carrying on in another EEA State a regulated activity to which that directive applies.

(3) The second case is where—

   (a)   his registered office (or if he does not have a registered office his head office) is in the United Kingdom;

   (b)   he is the manager of a scheme which is entitled to enjoy the rights conferred by an instrument which is a relevant Community instrument for the purposes of section 264; and

   (c)   persons in another EEA State are invited to become participants in the scheme.

(4) The third case is where—

   (a)   his registered office (or if he does not have a registered office his head office) is in the United Kingdom;

   (b)   the day-to-day management of the carrying on of the regulated activity is the responsibility of—

      (i)   his registered office (or head office); or

      (ii)   another establishment maintained by him in the United Kingdom.

(5) The fourth case is where—

   (a)   his head office is not in the United Kingdom; but

   (b)   the activity is carried on from an establishment maintained by him in the United Kingdom.

[(5A) The fifth case is any other case where the activity—

   (a)   consists of the provision of an information society service to a person or persons in one or more EEA States; and

   (b)   is carried on from an establishment in the United Kingdom.]

(6) For the purposes of subsections (2) to [(5A)] it is irrelevant where the person with whom the activity is carried on is situated.

Part 7   FSMA   2000

NOTES

Sub-ss (1), (6): word in square brackets substituted by the Electronic Commerce Directive (Financial Services and Markets) Regulations 2002, SI 2002/1775, reg 13(1), (3)(a), (c), as from 21 August 2002.

Sub-s (5A): inserted by SI 2002/1775, reg 13(1), (3)(b), as from 21 August 2002.

[7.361]
419   Carrying on regulated activities by way of business

(1)   The Treasury may by order make provision—
  (a)   as to the circumstances in which a person who would otherwise not be regarded as carrying on a regulated activity by way of business is to be regarded as doing so;
  (b)   as to the circumstances in which a person who would otherwise be regarded as carrying on a regulated activity by way of business is to be regarded as not doing so.

(2)   An order under subsection (1) may be made so as to apply—
  (a)   generally in relation to all regulated activities;
  (b)   in relation to a specified category of regulated activity; or
  (c)   in relation to a particular regulated activity.

(3)   An order under subsection (1) may be made so as to apply—
  (a)   for the purposes of all provisions;
  (b)   for a specified group of provisions; or
  (c)   for a specified provision.

(4)   "Provision" means a provision of, or made under, this Act.

(5)   Nothing in this section is to be read as affecting the provisions of section 428(3).

NOTES

Orders: the Financial Services and Markets Act 2000 (Carrying on Regulated Activities by Way of Business) Order 2001, SI 2001/1177 at **[8.212]**.

Note that the following amending Orders have also been made under this section: the Financial Services and Markets Act 2000 (Carrying on Regulated Activities by Way of Business) (Amendment) Order 2005, SI 2005/922.

[7.362]
420   Parent and subsidiary undertaking

(1)   In this Act, except in relation to an incorporated friendly society, "parent undertaking" and "subsidiary undertaking" have the same meaning as in [the Companies Acts (see section 1162 of, and Schedule 7 to, the Companies Act 2006)].

(2)   But—
  (a)   "parent undertaking" also includes an individual who would be a parent undertaking for the purposes of those provisions if he were taken to be an undertaking (and "subsidiary undertaking" is to be read accordingly);
  (b)   "subsidiary undertaking" also includes, in relation to a body incorporated in or formed under the law of an EEA State other than the United Kingdom, an undertaking which is a subsidiary undertaking within the meaning of any rule of law in force in that State for purposes connected with implementation of the Seventh Company Law Directive (and "parent undertaking" is to be read accordingly).

(3)   In this Act "subsidiary undertaking", in relation to an incorporated friendly society, means a body corporate of which the society has control within the meaning of section 13(9)(a) or (aa) of the Friendly Societies Act 1992 (and "parent undertaking" is to be read accordingly).

NOTES

Sub-s (1): words in square brackets substituted by the Companies Act 2006 (Consequential Amendments etc) Order 2008, SI 2008/948, art 3(1), Sch 1, Pt 2, para 212(1), as from 6 April 2008.

[7.363]
421   Group

(1)   In this Act "group", in relation to a person ("A"), means A and any person who is—
  (a)   a parent undertaking of A;
  (b)   a subsidiary undertaking of A;
  (c)   a subsidiary undertaking of a parent undertaking of A;
  (d)   a parent undertaking of a subsidiary undertaking of A;
  (e)   an undertaking in which A or an undertaking mentioned in paragraph (a), (b), (c) or (d) has a participating interest;
  (f)   if A or an undertaking mentioned in paragraph (a) or (d) is a building society, an associated undertaking of the society; or
  (g)   if A or an undertaking mentioned in paragraph (a) or (d) is an incorporated friendly society, a body corporate of which the society has joint control (within the meaning of section 13(9)(c) or (cc) of the Friendly Societies Act 1992).

(2)   "Participating interest" [has the meaning given in section 421A]; but also includes an interest held by an individual which would be a participating interest for the purposes of those provisions if he were taken to be an undertaking.

(3) "Associated undertaking" has the meaning given in section 119(1) of the Building Societies Act 1986.

NOTES

Sub-s (2): words in square brackets substituted by the Companies Act 2006 (Consequential Amendments etc) Order 2008, SI 2008/948, art 3(1), Sch 1, Pt 2, para 212(2), as from 6 April 2008.

[7.364]
[421A Meaning of "participating interest"
(1) In section 421 a "participating interest" means an interest held by an undertaking in the shares of another undertaking which it holds on a long-term basis for the purpose of securing a contribution to its activities by the exercise of control or influence arising from or related to that interest.
(2) A holding of 20% or more of the shares of an undertaking is presumed to be a participating interest unless the contrary is shown.
(3) The reference in subsection (1) to an interest in shares includes—
  (a) an interest which is convertible into an interest in shares, and
  (b) an option to acquire shares or any such interest;
And an interest or option falls within paragraph (a) or (b) notwithstanding that the shares to which it relates are, until the conversion or the exercise of the option, unissued.
(4) For the purposes of this section an interest held on behalf of an undertaking shall be treated as held by it.
(5) In this section "undertaking" has the same meaning as in the Companies Acts (see section 1161(1) of the Companies Act 2006).]

NOTES

Commencement: 6 April 2008.

Inserted by the Companies Act 2006 (Consequential Amendments etc) Order 2008, SI 2008/948, art 3(1), Sch 1, Pt 2, para 212(3), as from 6 April 2008.

[7.365]
[422 Controller
(1) In this Act "controller", in relation to an undertaking ("B"), means a person ("A") who falls within any of the cases in subsection (2).
(2) The cases are where A holds—
  (a) 10% or more of the shares in B or in a parent undertaking of B ("P");
  (b) 10% or more of the voting power in B or P; or
  (c) shares or voting power in B or P as a result of which A is able to exercise significant influence over the management of B.
(3) For the purposes of calculations relating to this section, the holding of shares or voting power by a person ("A1") includes any shares or voting power held by another ("A2") if A1 and A2 are acting in concert.
(4) In this section "shares"—
  (a) in relation to an undertaking with a share capital, means allotted shares;
  (b) in relation to an undertaking with capital but no share capital, means rights to share in the capital of the undertaking;
  (c) in relation to an undertaking without capital, means interests—
    (i)   conferring any right to share in the profits, or liability to contribute to the losses, of the undertaking; or
    (ii) giving rise to an obligation to contribute to the debts or expenses of the undertaking in the event of a winding up.
(5) In this section "voting power"—
  (a) includes, in relation to a person ("H")—
    (i)   voting power held by a third party with whom H has concluded an agreement, which obliges H and the third party to adopt, by concerted exercise of the voting power they hold, a lasting common policy towards the management of the undertaking in question;
    (ii)   voting power held by a third party under an agreement concluded with H providing for the temporary transfer for consideration of the voting power in question;
    (iii) voting power attaching to shares which are lodged as collateral with H, provided that H controls the voting power and declares an intention to exercise it;
    (iv)   voting power attaching to shares in which H has a life interest;
    (v)   voting power which is held, or may be exercised within the meaning of subparagraphs (i) to (iv), by a subsidiary undertaking of H;
    (vi)   voting power attaching to shares deposited with H which H has discretion to exercise in the absence of specific instructions from the shareholders;
    (vii) voting power held in the name of a third party on behalf of H;

(viii) voting power which H may exercise as a proxy where H has discretion about the exercise of the voting power in the absence of specific instructions from the shareholders; and

(b) in relation to an undertaking which does not have general meetings at which matters are decided by the exercise of voting rights, means the right under the constitution of the undertaking to direct the overall policy of the undertaking or alter the terms of its constitution.]

NOTES

Commencement: 21 March 2009.

The original s 422 was substituted by new ss 422, 422A by the Financial Services and Markets Act 2000 (Controllers) Regulations 2009, SI 2009/534, reg 7, Sch 3, as from 21 March 2009, subject to transitional provisions in reg 8 of those Regulations which provide that this section, as it stood immediately before that date, applies in respect of any notification submitted to the FSA before that date.

[7.366]
[422A   Disregarded holdings
(1)   For the purposes of section 422, shares and voting power that a person holds in an undertaking ("B") or in a parent undertaking of B ("P") are disregarded in the following circumstances.
(2)   Shares held only for the purposes of clearing and settling within a short settlement cycle are disregarded.
(3)   Shares held by a custodian or its nominee in a custodian capacity are disregarded, provided that the custodian or nominee is only able to exercise voting power attached to the shares in accordance with instructions given in writing.
(4)   Shares representing no more than 5% of the total voting power in B or P held by an investment firm are disregarded, provided that it—
(a)   holds the shares in the capacity of a market maker (as defined in article 4.1(8) of the markets in financial instruments directive);
(b)   is authorised by its home state regulator under the markets in financial instruments directive; and
(c)   neither intervenes in the management of B or P nor exerts any influence on B or P to buy the shares or back the share price.
(5)   Shares held by a credit institution or investment firm in its trading book are disregarded, provided that—
(a)   the shares represent no more than 5% of the total voting power in B or P; and
(b)   the credit institution or investment firm ensures that the voting power is not used to intervene in the management of B or P.
(6)   Shares held by a credit institution or an investment firm are disregarded, provided that—
(a)   the shares are held as a result of performing the investment services and activities of—
(i)   underwriting shares; or
(ii)   placing shares on a firm commitment basis in accordance with Annex I, section A.6 of the markets in financial instruments directive; and
(b)   the credit institution or investment firm—
(i)   does not exercise voting power represented by the shares or otherwise intervene in the management of the issuer; and
(ii)   retains the holding for a period of less than one year.
(7)   Where a management company (as defined in [Article 1a.2] of the UCITS directive) and its parent undertaking both hold shares or voting power, each may disregard holdings of the other, provided that each exercises its voting power independently of the other.
(8)   But subsection (7) does not apply if the management company—
(a)   manages holdings for its parent undertaking or an undertaking in respect of which the parent undertaking is a controller;
(b)   has no discretion to exercise the voting power attached to such holdings; and
(c)   may only exercise the voting power in relation to such holdings under direct or indirect instruction from—
(i)   its parent undertaking; or
(ii)   an undertaking in respect of which of the parent undertaking is a controller.
(9)   Where an investment firm and its parent undertaking both hold shares or voting power, the parent undertaking may disregard holdings managed by the investment firm on a client by client basis and the investment firm may disregard holdings of the parent undertaking, provided that the investment firm—
(a)   has permission to provide portfolio management;
(b)   exercises its voting power independently from the parent undertaking; and
(c)   may only exercise the voting power under instructions given in writing, or has appropriate mechanisms in place for ensuring that individual portfolio management services are conducted independently of any other services.
(10)   In this section "credit institution" means—
(a)   a credit institution authorised under the banking consolidation directive; or

(b) an institution which would satisfy the requirements for authorisation as a credit institution under that directive if it had its registered office (or if it does not have a registered office, its head office) in an EEA State.]

NOTES

Commencement: 21 March 2009.

Substituted, subject to transitional provisions, as noted to s 422 at **[7.365]**.

Sub-s (7): words in square brackets substituted by the Undertakings for Collective Investment in Transferable Securities Regulations 2011, SI 2011/1613, reg 2(1), (31), as from 1 July 2011.

[7.367]
423 Manager
(1) In this Act, except in relation to a unit trust scheme or a registered friendly society, "manager" means an employee who—
  (a) under the immediate authority of his employer is responsible, either alone or jointly with one or more other persons, for the conduct of his employer's business; or
  (b) under the immediate authority of his employer or of a person who is a manager by virtue of paragraph (a) exercises managerial functions or is responsible for maintaining accounts or other records of his employer.
(2) If the employer is not an individual, references in subsection (1) to the authority of the employer are references to the authority—
  (a) in the case of a body corporate, of the directors;
  (b) in the case of a partnership, of the partners; and
  (c) in the case of an unincorporated association, of its officers or the members of its governing body.
(3) "Manager", in relation to a body corporate, means a person (other than an employee of the body) who is appointed by the body to manage any part of its business and includes an employee of the body corporate (other than the chief executive) who, under the immediate authority of a director or chief executive of the body corporate, exercises managerial functions or is responsible for maintaining accounts or other records of the body corporate.

[7.368]
424 Insurance
(1) In this Act, references to—
  (a) contracts of insurance,
  (b) reinsurance,
  (c) contracts of long-term insurance,
  (d) contracts of general insurance,
are to be read with section 22 and Schedule 2.
(2) In this Act "policy" and "policyholder", in relation to a contract of insurance, have such meaning as the Treasury may by order specify.
(3) The law applicable to a contract of insurance, the effecting of which constitutes the carrying on of a regulated activity, is to be determined, if it is of a prescribed description, in accordance with regulations made by the Treasury.

NOTES

Regulations/Orders: the Financial Services and Markets Act 2000 (Meaning of "Policy" and "Policyholder") Order 2001, SI 2001/2361; the Financial Services and Markets Act 2000 (Law Applicable to Contracts of Insurance) Regulations 2001, SI 2001/2635; the Financial Services and Markets Act 2000 (Law Applicable to Contracts of Insurance) Regulations 2009, SI 2009/3075.

Note that the following amending Regulations have also been made under this section: the Financial Services and Markets Act 2000 (Law Applicable to Contracts of Insurance) (Amendment) Regulations 2001, SI 2001/3542; the Financial Services and Markets Act 2000 (Motor Insurance) Regulations 2007, SI 2007/2403.

[7.369]
[424A Investment firm
(1) In this Act, "investment firm" has the meaning given in Article 4.1.1 of the markets in financial instruments directive.
(2) Subsection (1) is subject to subsections (3) to (5).
[(3) References in this Act to an "investment firm" include references to a person who would be an investment firm (within the meaning of Article 4.1.1 of the markets in financial instruments directive) if—
  (a) in the case of a body corporate, his registered office or, if he has no registered office, his head office, and
  (b) in the case of a person other than a body corporate, his head office,
were in an EEA State.]
(4) But subsection (3) does not apply if the person in question is one to whom the markets in financial instruments directive would not apply by virtue of Article 2 of that directive.
(5) References in this Act to an "investment firm" do not include references to—

  (a)   a person to whom the markets in financial instruments directive does not apply by virtue of Article 2 of the directive; or

  (b)   a person whose home Member State (within the meaning of Article 4.1.20 of the markets in financial instruments directive) is an EEA State and to whom, by reason of the fact that the State has given effect to Article 3 of that directive, that directive does not apply by virtue of that Article.]

NOTES

Commencement: 6 December 2006.

Inserted by the Financial Services and Markets Act 2000 (Markets in Financial Instruments) (Modification of Powers) Regulations 2006, SI 2006/2975, regs 2, 10, as from 6 December 2006.

Sub-s (3): substituted by the Financial Services and Markets Act 2000 (Markets in Financial Instruments) Regulations 2007, SI 2007/126, reg 3(5), Sch 5, paras 1, 21, as from 1 April 2007 (certain purposes), and as from 1 November 2007 (otherwise).

[7.370]

425   Expressions relating to authorisation elsewhere in the single market

(1)   In this Act—

  [(a)   "banking consolidation directive", ["life assurance consolidation directive",] "EEA authorisation", "EEA firm", "EEA right", "EEA State", . . . , "first non-life insurance directive", "insurance directives", ["reinsurance directive",] "insurance mediation directive", . . . ["markets in financial instruments directive",] "single market directives"[, " tied agent"] and "UCITS directive" have the meaning given in Schedule 3; and]

  (b)   "home state regulator", in relation to an EEA firm, has the meaning given in Schedule 3.

(2)   In this Act—

  (a)   "home state authorisation" has the meaning given in Schedule 4;

  (b)   "Treaty firm" has the meaning given in Schedule 4; and

  (c)   "home state regulator", in relation to a Treaty firm, has the meaning given in Schedule 4.

NOTES

Sub-s (1) is amended as follows:

Para (a) substituted by the Collective Investment Schemes (Miscellaneous Amendments) Regulations 2003, SI 2003/2066, reg 2(1), as from 13 February 2004.

Words in first pair of square brackets in para (a) inserted, and first words omitted from that paragraph repealed, by the Life Assurance Consolidation Directive (Consequential Amendments) Regulations 2004, SI 2004/3379, reg 6(1), (5), as from 11 January 2005.

Words in second pair of square brackets in para (a) inserted by the Reinsurance Directive Regulations 2007, SI 2007/3253, reg 2(1), Sch 1, paras 1, 5, as from 10 December 2007.

Words in third pair of square brackets in para (a) inserted by the Financial Services and Markets Act 2000 (Markets in Financial Instruments) (Modification of Powers) Regulations 2006, SI 2006/2975, regs 2, 11, as from 6 December 2006.

Second words omitted from para (a) repealed, and words in final pair of square brackets in that paragraph inserted, by the Financial Services and Markets Act 2000 (Markets in Financial Instruments) Regulations 2007, SI 2007/126, reg 3(5), Sch 5, paras 1, 22, as from 1 April 2007 (certain purposes), and as from 1 November 2007 (otherwise).

[7.371]

[425A   Consumers: regulated activities etc carried on by authorised persons

(1)   This section has effect for the purposes of the provisions of this Act which apply this section.

(2)   "Consumers" means persons who—

  (a)   use, have used or may use any of the services within subsection (3); or

  (b)   have relevant rights or interests in relation to any of those services.

(3)   The services within this subsection are services provided by—

  (a)   authorised persons in carrying on regulated activities;

  (b)   authorised persons who are investment firms, or credit institutions, in providing relevant ancillary services; or

  (c)   persons acting as appointed representatives.

(4)   A person ("P") has a "relevant right or interest" in relation to any services within subsection (3) if P has a right or interest—

  (a)   which is derived from, or is otherwise attributable to, the use of the services by others; or

  (b)   which may be adversely affected by the use of the services by persons acting on P's behalf or in a fiduciary capacity in relation to P.

(5)   If a person is providing a service within subsection (3) as a trustee, the persons who are, have been or may be beneficiaries of the trust are to be treated as persons who use, have used or may use the service.

(6)   A person who deals with another person ("A") in the course of A providing a service within subsection (3) is to be treated as using the service.

(7)   In this section—

"credit institution" means—

    (a)   a credit institution authorised under the banking consolidation directive; or

    (b)   an institution which would satisfy the requirements for authorisation as a credit institution under that directive if it had its registered office (or if does not have one, its head office) in an EEA State;

"relevant ancillary service" means any service of a kind mentioned in Section B of Annex I to the markets in financial instruments directive the provision of which does not involve the carrying on of a regulated activity.]

NOTES
Commencement: 8 April 2010.
Inserted, together with s 425B, by the Financial Services Act 2010, s 24(1), (2), Sch 2, Pt 1, paras 1, 32, as from 8 April 2010.

[7.372]
[425B Consumers: regulated activities carried on by others
(1) This section has effect for the purposes of the provisions of this Act which apply this section.
(2) "Consumers" means persons who, in relation to regulated activities carried on otherwise than by authorised persons, would be consumers as defined by section 425A if the activities were carried on by authorised persons.]

NOTES
Commencement: 8 April 2010.
Inserted as noted to s 425A at **[7.371]**.

426–433 *(Part XXX—Supplemental (ss 426–433 and Schs 20–22) omitted for reasons of space; see further, the introductory notes to this Act.)*

SCHEDULES

SCHEDULE 1
THE FINANCIAL SERVICES AUTHORITY

Section 1

NOTES
Note: the functions of the FSA under the Transfer of Funds (Information on the Payer) Regulations 2007, SI 2007/3298 shall be treated for the purposes of Parts 1, 2 and 4 of this Schedule as functions conferred on the Authority under this Act; see reg 4(4) of the 2007 Regulations.
The functions of the FSA under the Counter-Terrorism Act 2008, Sch 7 shall be treated for the purposes of Parts 1, 2 and 4 of this Schedule as functions conferred on the Authority under that Act; see Sch 7, Pt 8, para 41.
The functions of the FSA under Regulation 1060/2009/EC of the European Parliament and of the Council on credit rating agencies are to be treated for the purposes of Part 1, and para 13 (in Part II) and para 19 (in Part IV) of this Schedule as functions conferred on the Authority under this Act; see the Credit Rating Agencies Regulations 2010, SI 2010/906, reg 7.

PART I
GENERAL

Interpretation

[7.373]
1. (1) In this Schedule—

. . .

"non-executive committee" means the committee maintained under paragraph 3;
"functions", in relation to the Authority, means functions conferred on the Authority by or under any provision of this Act.

(2) For the purposes of this Schedule, the following are the Authority's legislative functions—
(a) making rules;
(b) issuing codes under section 64 or 119;
(c) issuing statements under section 64, 69, 124 or 210;
(d) giving directions under section 316, 318 or 328;
(e) issuing general guidance (as defined by section 158(5)) [or guidance under section 158A].

Constitution

2. (1) The constitution of the Authority must continue to provide for the Authority to have—
(a) a chairman; and
(b) a governing body.

(2) The governing body must include the chairman.

(3) The chairman and other members of the governing body must be appointed, and be liable to removal from office, by the Treasury.

(4) The validity of any act of the Authority is not affected—
(a) by a vacancy in the office of chairman; or
(b) by a defect in the appointment of a person as a member of the governing body or as chairman.

Non-executive members of the governing body

3. (1) The Authority must secure—

(a)   that the majority of the members of its governing body are non-executive members; and

(b)   that a committee of its governing body, consisting solely of the non-executive members, is set up and maintained for the purposes of discharging the functions conferred on the committee by this Schedule.

(2)   The members of the non-executive committee are to be appointed by the Authority.

(3)   The non-executive committee is to have a chairman appointed by the Treasury from among its members.

Functions of the non-executive committee

4. (1)   In this paragraph "the committee" means the non-executive committee.

(2)   The non-executive functions are functions of the Authority but must be discharged by the committee.

(3)   The non-executive functions are—

(a)   keeping under review the question whether the Authority is, in discharging its functions in accordance with decisions of its governing body, using its resources in the most efficient and economic way;

(b)   keeping under review the question whether the Authority's internal financial controls secure the proper conduct of its financial affairs; and

(c)   determining the remuneration of—

(i)   the chairman of the Authority's governing body; and

(ii)   the executive members of that body.

(4)   The function mentioned in sub-paragraph (3)(b) and those mentioned in sub-paragraph (3)(c) may be discharged on behalf of the committee by a sub-committee.

(5)   Any sub-committee of the committee—

(a)   must have as its chairman the chairman of the committee; but

(b)   may include persons other than members of the committee.

(6)   The committee must prepare a report on the discharge of its functions for inclusion in the Authority's annual report to the Treasury under paragraph 10.

(7)   The committee's report must relate to the same period as that covered by the Authority's report.

Arrangements for discharging functions

5. (1)   The Authority may make arrangements for any of its functions to be discharged by a committee, sub-committee, officer or member of staff of the Authority.

[(2)   But—

(a)   in exercising the legislative functions mentioned in paragraph 1(2)(a) to (d) [or in determining or reviewing its strategy in relation to the financial stability objective], the Authority must act through its governing body; and

(b)   the legislative function mentioned in paragraph 1(2)(e) may not be discharged by an officer or member of staff of the Authority.]

(3)   Sub-paragraph (1) does not apply to the non-executive functions.

Monitoring and enforcement

6. (1)   The Authority must maintain arrangements designed to enable it to determine whether persons on whom requirements are imposed by or under this Act[, or by any directly applicable [Community regulation or decision] made under the markets in financial instruments directive,] are complying with them.

(2)   Those arrangements may provide for functions to be performed on behalf of the Authority by any body or person who, in its opinion, is competent to perform them.

(3)   The Authority must also maintain arrangements for enforcing the provisions of, or made under, this Act [or of any directly applicable [Community regulation or decision] made under the markets in financial instruments directive].

(4)   Sub-paragraph (2) does not affect the Authority's duty under sub-paragraph (1).

Arrangements for the investigation of complaints

7. (1)   The Authority must—

(a)   make arrangements ("the complaints scheme") for the investigation of complaints arising in connection with the exercise of, or failure to exercise, any of its functions (other than its legislative functions); and

(b)   appoint an independent person ("the investigator") to be responsible for the conduct of investigations in accordance with the complaints scheme.

(2)   The complaints scheme must be designed so that, as far as reasonably practicable, complaints are investigated quickly.

(3)   The Treasury's approval is required for the appointment or dismissal of the investigator.

Part 7   FSMA 2000

(4)   The terms and conditions on which the investigator is appointed must be such as, in the opinion of the Authority, are reasonably designed to secure—

(a)   that he will be free at all times to act independently of the Authority; and

(b)   that complaints will be investigated under the complaints scheme without favouring the Authority.

(5)   Before making the complaints scheme, the Authority must publish a draft of the proposed scheme in the way appearing to the Authority best calculated to bring it to the attention of the public.

(6)   The draft must be accompanied by notice that representations about it may be made to the Authority within a specified time.

(7)   Before making the proposed complaints scheme, the Authority must have regard to any representations made to it in accordance with sub-paragraph (6).

(8)   If the Authority makes the proposed complaints scheme, it must publish an account, in general terms, of—

(a)   the representations made to it in accordance with sub-paragraph (6); and

(b)   its response to them.

(9)   If the complaints scheme differs from the draft published under sub-paragraph (5) in a way which is, in the opinion of the Authority, significant the Authority must (in addition to complying with sub-paragraph (8)) publish details of the difference.

(10)   The Authority must publish up-to-date details of the complaints scheme including, in particular, details of—

(a)   the provision made under paragraph 8(5); and

(b)   the powers which the investigator has to investigate a complaint.

(11)   Those details must be published in the way appearing to the Authority to be best calculated to bring them to the attention of the public.

(12)   The Authority must, without delay, give the Treasury a copy of any details published by it under this paragraph.

(13)   The Authority may charge a reasonable fee for providing a person with a copy of—

(a)   a draft published under sub-paragraph (5);

(b)   details published under sub-paragraph (10).

(14)   Sub-paragraphs (5) to (9) and (13)(a) also apply to a proposal to alter or replace the complaints scheme.

Investigation of complaints

8. (1)   The Authority is not obliged to investigate a complaint in accordance with the complaints scheme which it reasonably considers would be more appropriately dealt with in another way (for example by referring the matter to the Tribunal or by the institution of other legal proceedings).

(2)   The complaints scheme must provide—

(a)   for reference to the investigator of any complaint which the Authority is investigating; and

(b)   for him—

(i)   to have the means to conduct a full investigation of the complaint;

(ii)   to report on the result of his investigation to the Authority and the complainant; and

(iii)   to be able to publish his report (or any part of it) if he considers that it (or the part) ought to be brought to the attention of the public.

(3)   If the Authority has decided not to investigate a complaint, it must notify the investigator.

(4)   If the investigator considers that a complaint of which he has been notified under sub-paragraph (3) ought to be investigated, he may proceed as if the complaint had been referred to him under the complaints scheme.

(5)   The complaints scheme must confer on the investigator the power to recommend, if he thinks it appropriate, that the Authority—

(a)   makes a compensatory payment to the complainant,

(b)   remedies the matter complained of,

or takes both of those steps.

(6)   The complaints scheme must require the Authority, in a case where the investigator—

(a)   has reported that a complaint is well-founded, or

(b)   has criticised the Authority in his report,

to inform the investigator and the complainant of the steps which it proposes to take in response to the report.

(7)   The investigator may require the Authority to publish the whole or a specified part of the response.

(8)   The investigator may appoint a person to conduct the investigation on his behalf but subject to his direction.

(9)   Neither an officer nor an employee of the Authority may be appointed under sub-paragraph (8).

(10)   Sub-paragraph (2) is not to be taken as preventing the Authority from making arrangements for the initial investigation of a complaint to be conducted by the Authority.

Records

9. The Authority must maintain satisfactory arrangements for—
- (a)   recording decisions made in the exercise of its functions; and
- (b)   the safe-keeping of those records which it considers ought to be preserved.

Annual report

10. (1)   At least once a year the Authority must make a report to the Treasury on—
- (a)   the discharge of its functions;
- (b)   the extent to which, in its opinion, the regulatory objectives have been met;
- (c)   its consideration of the matters mentioned in section 2(3); and
- (d)   such other matters as the Treasury may from time to time direct.

(2)   The report must be accompanied by—
- (a)   the report prepared by the non-executive committee under paragraph 4(6); and
- (b)   such other reports or information, prepared by such persons, as the Treasury may from time to time direct.

(3)   The Treasury must lay before Parliament a copy of each report received by them under this paragraph.

(4)   The Treasury may—
- (a)   require the Authority to comply with any provisions of [the Companies Act 2006] about accounts and their audit which would not otherwise apply to it; or
- (b)   direct that any such provision of that Act is to apply to the Authority with such modifications as are specified in the direction.

(5)   Compliance with any requirement imposed under sub-paragraph (4)(a) or (b) is enforceable by injunction or, in Scotland, an order under section 45(b) of the Court of Session Act 1988.

(6)   Proceedings under sub-paragraph (5) may be brought only by the Treasury.

Annual public meeting

11. (1)   Not later than three months after making a report under paragraph 10, the Authority must hold a public meeting ("the annual meeting") for the purposes of enabling that report to be considered.

(2)   The Authority must organise the annual meeting so as to allow—
- (a)   a general discussion of the contents of the report which is being considered; and
- (b)   a reasonable opportunity for those attending the meeting to put questions to the Authority about the way in which it discharged, or failed to discharge, its functions during the period to which the report relates.

(3)   But otherwise the annual meeting is to be organised and conducted in such a way as the Authority considers appropriate.

(4)   The Authority must give reasonable notice of its annual meeting.

(5)   That notice must—
- (a)   give details of the time and place at which the meeting is to be held;
- (b)   set out the proposed agenda for the meeting;
- (c)   indicate the proposed duration of the meeting;
- (d)   give details of the Authority's arrangements for enabling persons to attend; and
- (e)   be published by the Authority in the way appearing to it to be most suitable for bringing the notice to the attention of the public.

(6)   If the Authority proposes to alter any of the arrangements which have been included in the notice given under sub-paragraph (4) it must—
- (a)   give reasonable notice of the alteration; and
- (b)   publish that notice in the way appearing to the Authority to be best calculated to bring it to the attention of the public.

Report of annual meeting

12. Not later than one month after its annual meeting, the Authority must publish a report of the proceedings of the meeting.

Part 7   **FSMA   2000**

NOTES

Para 1: definition "the 1985 Act" (omitted) repealed by the Companies Act 2006 (Consequential Amendments, Transitional Provisions and Savings) Order 2009, SI 2009/1941, art 2(1), Sch 1, para 181(1), (5)(a), as from 1 October 2009; words in square brackets in sub-para (2)(e) inserted by the Financial Services and Markets Act 2000 (Markets in Financial Instruments) (Modification of Powers) Regulations 2006, SI 2006/2975, regs 2, 12, as from 6 December 2006.

Para 5: sub-para (2) substituted by the Regulatory Reform (Financial Services and Markets Act 2000) Order 2007, SI 2007/1973, arts 2, 14, as from 12 July 2007; words in square brackets in sub-para (2)(a) inserted by the Financial Services Act 2010, s 24(1), (2), Sch 2, Pt 1, paras 1, 34(1), (2), as from 8 April 2010.

Para 6: words in first (outer) pair of square brackets in sub-paras (1), (3) inserted by the Financial Services and Markets Act 2000 (Markets in Financial Instruments) Regulations 2007, SI 2007/126, reg 3(5), Sch 5, paras 1, 23, as from 1 April 2007 (certain purposes), and as from 1 November 2007 (otherwise); words in second (inner) pair of square brackets in those sub-paragraphs substituted by the Undertakings for Collective Investment in Transferable Securities Regulations 2011, SI 2011/1613, reg 2(1), (32), as from 1 July 2011.

Para 10: words in square brackets substituted by the Companies Act 2006 (Consequential Amendments etc) Order 2008, SI 2008/948, art 3(1), Sch 1, Pt 2, para 213, as from 6 April 2008 (for savings see art 6(4) of the 2008 Order (at **[4.280]**) which provides that where by virtue of any transitional provision, a provision of the Companies Act 2006 has effect only (a) on or after a specified date, or (b) in relation to matters occurring or arising on or after a specified date, any amendment substituting or inserting a reference to that provision has effect correspondingly).

Transitional provisions: see the Financial Services and Markets Act 2000 (Transitional Provisions and Savings) (Rules) Order 2001, SI 2001/1534, art 4(7), the Financial Services and Markets Act 2000 (Transitional Provisions) (Reviews of Pensions Business) Order 2001, SI 2001/2512, and the Financial Services and Markets Act 2000 (Interim Permissions) Order 2001, SI 2001/3374, art 12(3). Note also that the reference to the Authority's functions includes its functions as a designated agency under the Financial Services Act 1986 (repealed by the Financial Services and Markets Act 2000 (Consequential Amendments and Repeals) Order 2001, SI 2001/3649, art 3(1)(c)) and the reference to the Authority's legislative functions includes its functions of issuing statements of principle, rules, regulations and codes of practice under that Act; see the Financial Services and Markets Act 2000 (Consequential and Transitional Provisions) (Miscellaneous) Order 2001, SI 2001/1821, art 2(1)(b), (c).

Note: for the purposes of para 6 a requirement imposed by the FSA under the Electronic Commerce Directive (Financial Services and Markets) Regulations 2002, SI 2002/1775 upon an incoming provider is to be treated as imposed on him by or under this Act; see reg 12(2) of those Regulations.

Note: FSA 1986, s 190 was repealed by the Data Protection Act 1998, s 74(2), Sch 16, Pt I, as from 1 March 2000. Section 31(1) of the 1998 Act provides that personal data processed for the purposes of discharging functions to which that subsection applies are exempt from the subject information provisions in any case to the extent to which the application of those provisions to the data would be likely to prejudice the proper discharge of those functions.

PART II
STATUS

[7.374]
13. In relation to any of its functions—
    (a)   the Authority is not to be regarded as acting on behalf of the Crown; and
    (b)   its members, officers and staff are not to be regarded as Crown servants.

Exemption from requirement of "limited" in Authority's name

14. The Authority is to continue to be exempt from the requirements of [the Companies Act 2006] relating to the use of "limited" as part of its name.

15. If the Secretary of State is satisfied that any action taken by the Authority makes it inappropriate for the exemption given by paragraph 14 to continue he may, after consulting the Treasury, give a direction removing it.

NOTES

Para 14: words in square brackets substituted by the Companies Act 2006 (Consequential Amendments, Transitional Provisions and Savings) Order 2009, SI 2009/1941, art 2(1), Sch 1, para 181(1), (5)(b), as from 1 October 2009.

Transitional provisions: see the note to Pt I of this Schedule at **[7.373]**.

PART III
PENALTIES AND FEES

Penalties

[7.375]
16. (1)   In determining its policy with respect to the amounts of penalties to be imposed by it under this Act, the Authority must take no account of the expenses which it incurs, or expects to incur, in discharging its functions.

(2)   The Authority must prepare and operate a scheme for ensuring that the amounts paid to the Authority by way of penalties imposed under this Act are applied for the benefit of authorised persons.

(3)   The scheme may, in particular, make different provision with respect to different classes of authorised person.

(4)   Up to date details of the scheme must be set out in a document ("the scheme details").

(5)   The scheme details must be published by the Authority in the way appearing to it to be best calculated to bring them to the attention of the public.

(6)   Before making the scheme, the Authority must publish a draft of the proposed scheme in the way appearing to the Authority to be best calculated to bring it to the attention of the public.

(7)   The draft must be accompanied by notice that representations about the proposals may be made to the Authority within a specified time.

(8)   Before making the scheme, the Authority must have regard to any representations made to it in accordance with sub-paragraph (7).

(9)   If the Authority makes the proposed scheme, it must publish an account, in general terms, of—

   (a)   the representations made to it in accordance with sub-paragraph (7); and

   (b)   its response to them.

(10)   If the scheme differs from the draft published under sub-paragraph (6) in a way which is, in the opinion of the Authority, significant the Authority must (in addition to complying with sub-paragraph (9)) publish details of the difference.

(11)   The Authority must, without delay, give the Treasury a copy of any scheme details published by it.

(12)   The Authority may charge a reasonable fee for providing a person with a copy of—

   (a)   a draft published under sub-paragraph (6);

   (b)   scheme details.

(13)   Sub-paragraphs (6) to (10) and (12)(a) also apply to a proposal to alter or replace the complaints scheme.

Fees

17. (1)   The Authority may make rules providing for the payment to it of such fees, in connection with the discharge of any of its functions under or as a result of this Act, as it considers will (taking account of its expected income from fees and charges provided for by any other provision of this Act) enable it—

   (a)   to meet expenses incurred in carrying out its functions or for any incidental purpose;

   (b)   to repay the principal of, and pay any interest on, any money which it has borrowed and which has been used for the purpose of meeting expenses incurred in relation to its assumption of functions under this Act or the Bank of England Act 1998; and

   (c)   to maintain adequate reserves.

(2)   In fixing the amount of any fee which is to be payable to the Authority, no account is to be taken of any sums which the Authority receives, or expects to receive, by way of penalties imposed by it under this Act.

(3)   Sub-paragraph (1)(b) applies whether expenses were incurred before or after the coming into force of this Act or the Bank of England Act 1998.

(4)   Any fee which is owed to the Authority under any provision made by or under this Act may be recovered as a debt due to the Authority.

Services for which fees may not be charged

18. The power conferred by paragraph 17 may not be used to require—

   (a)   a fee to be paid in respect of the discharge of any of the Authority's functions under paragraphs 13, 14, 19 or 20 of Schedule 3; or

   (b)   a fee to be paid by any person whose application for approval under section 59 has been granted.

NOTES

   Transitional provisions: see the note to Pt I of this Schedule at **[7.373]**.

PART IV
MISCELLANEOUS

Exemption from liability in damages

[7.376]

19. (1)   Neither the Authority nor any person who is, or is acting as, a member, officer or member of staff of the Authority is to be liable in damages for anything done or omitted in the discharge, or purported discharge, of the Authority's functions.

(2)   Neither the investigator appointed under paragraph 7 nor a person appointed to conduct an investigation on his behalf under paragraph 8(8) is to be liable in damages for anything done or omitted in the discharge, or purported discharge, of his functions in relation to the investigation of a complaint.

(3)   Neither sub-paragraph (1) nor sub-paragraph (2) applies—

   (a)   if the act or omission is shown to have been in bad faith; or

   (b)   so as to prevent an award of damages made in respect of an act or omission on the ground that the act or omission was unlawful as a result of section 6(1) of the Human Rights Act 1998.

[19A. For the purposes of this Act anything done by an accredited financial investigator within the meaning of the Proceeds of Crime Act 2002 who is—

   (a)   a member of the staff of the Authority, or

   (b)   a person appointed by the Authority under section 97, 167 or 168 to conduct an investigation,

must be treated as done in the exercise or discharge of a function of the Authority.]

[Amounts required by rules to be paid to the Authority

19B. Any amount (other than a fee) which is required by rules to be paid to the Authority may be recovered as a debt due to the Authority.]

20, 21. . . .

NOTES

Para 19A: inserted by the Proceeds of Crime Act 2002, s 456, Sch 11, para 38, as from 24 February 2003.

Para 19B: inserted by the Financial Services Act 2010, s 24(1), (2), Sch 2, Pt 1, paras 1, 34(1), (3), as from 8 April 2010.

Paras 20, 21: amend the House of Commons Disqualification Act 1975, Sch 1, Pt III, and the Northern Ireland Assembly Disqualification Act 1975, Sch 1, Pt III.

Transitional provisions: see the note to Pt I of this Schedule at **[7.373]**.

SCHEDULE 1A

(Sch 1A—Further Provision about the Consumer Financial Education Body (as inserted by the Financial Services Act 2010) omitted for reasons of space; see further, the introductory notes to this Act.)

SCHEDULE 2
REGULATED ACTIVITIES

Section 22(2)

NOTES

The regulated activities for the purposes of s 22 of this Act are set out in the Financial Services and Markets Act 2000 (Regulated Activities) Order 2001, SI 2001/544 at **[8.1]**.

PART I
[REGULATED ACTIVITIES: GENERAL]

General

[7.377]

1. The matters with respect to which provision may be made under section 22(1) in respect of activities include, in particular, those described in general terms in this Part of this Schedule.

Dealing in investments

2. (1) Buying, selling, subscribing for or underwriting investments or offering or agreeing to do so, either as a principal or as an agent.

(2) In the case of an investment which is a contract of insurance, that includes carrying out the contract.

Arranging deals in investments

3. Making, or offering or agreeing to make—
   (a) arrangements with a view to another person buying, selling, subscribing for or underwriting a particular investment;
   (b) arrangements with a view to a person who participates in the arrangements buying, selling, subscribing for or underwriting investments.

Deposit taking

4. Accepting deposits.

Safekeeping and administration of assets

5. (1) Safeguarding and administering assets belonging to another which consist of or include investments or offering or agreeing to do so.

(2) Arranging for the safeguarding and administration of assets belonging to another, or offering or agreeing to do so.

Managing investments

6. Managing, or offering or agreeing to manage, assets belonging to another person where—
   (a) the assets consist of or include investments; or
   (b) the arrangements for their management are such that the assets may consist of or include investments at the discretion of the person managing or offering or agreeing to manage them.

Investment advice

7. Giving or offering or agreeing to give advice to persons on—
   (a) buying, selling, subscribing for or underwriting an investment; or

(b)   exercising any right conferred by an investment to acquire, dispose of, underwrite or convert an investment.

Establishing collective investment schemes

8. Establishing, operating or winding up a collective investment scheme, including acting as—
- (a)   trustee of a unit trust scheme;
- (b)   depositary of a collective investment scheme other than a unit trust scheme; or
- (c)   sole director of a body incorporated by virtue of regulations under section 262.

Using computer-based systems for giving investment instructions

9. (1)   Sending on behalf of another person instructions relating to an investment by means of a computer-based system which enables investments to be transferred without a written instrument.

(2)   Offering or agreeing to send such instructions by such means on behalf of another person.

(3)   Causing such instructions to be sent by such means on behalf of another person.

(4)   Offering or agreeing to cause such instructions to be sent by such means on behalf of another person.

NOTES

Part heading: words in square brackets substituted by the Dormant Bank and Building Society Accounts Act 2008, s 15, Sch 2, para 1(1), (2), as from 12 March 2009.

[PART 1A
REGULATED ACTIVITIES: RECLAIM FUNDS

Activities of reclaim funds
[7.378]
9A. (1)   The matters with respect to which provision may be made under section 22(1) in respect of activities include, in particular, any of the activities of a reclaim fund.

(2)   "Reclaim fund" has the meaning given by section 5(1) of the Dormant Bank and Building Society Accounts Act 2008.]

NOTES

Commencement: 12 March 2009.

Pt 1A inserted by the Dormant Bank and Building Society Accounts Act 2008, s 15, Sch 2, para 1(1), (3), as from 12 March 2009.

PART II
INVESTMENTS

General

[7.379]
10. The matters with respect to which provision may be made under section 22(1) in respect of investments include, in particular, those described in general terms in this Part of this Schedule.

Securities

11. (1)   Shares or stock in the share capital of a company.

(2)   "Company" includes—
- (a)   any body corporate (wherever incorporated), and
- (b)   any unincorporated body constituted under the law of a country or territory outside the United Kingdom,

other than an open-ended investment company.

Instruments creating or acknowledging indebtedness

12. Any of the following—
- (a)   debentures;
- (b)   debenture stock;
- (c)   loan stock;
- (d)   bonds;
- (e)   certificates of deposit;
- (f)   any other instruments creating or acknowledging a present or future indebtedness.

Government and public securities

13. (1)   Loan stock, bonds and other instruments—
- (a)   creating or acknowledging indebtedness; and
- (b)   issued by or on behalf of a government, local authority or public authority.

(2)   "Government, local authority or public authority" means—

    (a)   the government of the United Kingdom, of Northern Ireland, or of any country or territory outside the United Kingdom;

    (b)   a local authority in the United Kingdom or elsewhere;

    (c)   any international organisation the members of which include the United Kingdom or another member State.

Instruments giving entitlement to investments

14. (1)   Warrants or other instruments entitling the holder to subscribe for any investment.

(2)   It is immaterial whether the investment is in existence or identifiable.

Certificates representing securities

15. Certificates or other instruments which confer contractual or property rights—

    (a)   in respect of any investment held by someone other than the person on whom the rights are conferred by the certificate or other instrument; and

    (b)   the transfer of which may be effected without requiring the consent of that person.

Units in collective investment schemes

16. (1)   Shares in or securities of an open-ended investment company.

(2)   Any right to participate in a collective investment scheme.

Options

17. Options to acquire or dispose of property.

Futures

18. Rights under a contract for the sale of a commodity or property of any other description under which delivery is to be made at a future date.

Contracts for differences

19. Rights under—

    (a)   a contract for differences; or

    (b)   any other contract the purpose or pretended purpose of which is to secure a profit or avoid a loss by reference to fluctuations in—

        (i)   the value or price of property of any description; or

        (ii)   an index or other factor designated for that purpose in the contract.

Contracts of insurance

20. Rights under a contract of insurance, including rights under contracts falling within head C of Schedule 2 to the Friendly Societies Act 1992.

Participation in Lloyd's syndicates

21. (1)   The underwriting capacity of a Lloyd's syndicate.

(2)   A person's membership (or prospective membership) of a Lloyd's syndicate.

Deposits

22. Rights under any contract under which a sum of money (whether or not denominated in a currency) is paid on terms under which it will be repaid, with or without interest or a premium, and either on demand or at a time or in circumstances agreed by or on behalf of the person making the payment and the person receiving it.

Loans secured on land

23. (1)   Rights under any contract under which—

    (a)   one person provides another with credit; and

    (b)   the obligation of the borrower to repay is secured on land.

(2)   "Credit" includes any cash loan or other financial accommodation.

(3)   "Cash" includes money in any form.

[Other finance arrangements involving land

23A. (1)   Rights under any arrangement for the provision of finance under which the person providing the finance either—

    (a)   acquires a major interest in land from the person to whom the finance is provided, or

    (b)   disposes of a major interest in land to that person,

as part of the arrangement.

(2)   References in sub-paragraph (1) to a "major interest" in land are to—

    (a)   in relation to land in England or Wales—

        (i)   an estate in fee simple absolute, or

      (ii)   a term of years absolute,
      whether subsisting at law or in equity;
  (b)   in relation to land in Scotland—
      (i)   the interest of an owner of land, or
      (ii)   the tenant's right over or interest in a property subject to a lease;
  (c)   in relation to land in Northern Ireland—
      (i)   any freehold estate, or
      (ii)   any leasehold estate,
      whether subsisting at law or in equity.

(3)   It is immaterial for the purposes of sub-paragraph (1) whether either party acquires or (as the case may be) disposes of the interest in land—
  (a)   directly, or
  (b)   indirectly.]

Rights in investments

24.   Any right or interest in anything which is an investment as a result of any other provision made under section 22(1).

NOTES

Para 23A: inserted by the Regulation of Financial Services (Land Transactions) Act 2005, s 1, as from 19 February 2006.

Modifications to para 12(e): (i) a reference to a certificate of deposit includes a reference to uncertificated units of an eligible debt security where the issue of those units corresponds, in accordance with the current terms of issue of the security, to the issue of a certificate of deposit which is a certificate of deposit for the purposes of that enactment; (ii) a reference to an amount stated in a certificate of deposit includes a reference to a principal amount stated in, or determined in accordance with, the current terms of issue of an eligible debt security of the kind referred to in (i) above; see the Uncertificated Securities (Amendment) (Eligible Debt Securities) Regulations 2003, SI 2003/1633, reg 15, Sch 2, para 6.

Modifications to para 12(f): the reference to securities, instruments or investments creating or acknowledging indebtedness (or creating or acknowledging a present or future indebtedness) includes a reference to uncertificated units of eligible debt securities; see SI 2003/1633, reg 15, Sch 2, para 8.

PART III
SUPPLEMENTAL PROVISIONS

The order-making power

[7.380]

25.   (1)   An order under section 22(1) may—
  (a)   provide for exemptions;
  (b)   confer powers on the Treasury or the Authority;
  (c)   authorise the making of regulations or other instruments by the Treasury for purposes of, or connected with, any relevant provision;
  (d)   authorise the making of rules or other instruments by the Authority for purposes of, or connected with, any relevant provision;
  (e)   make provision in respect of any information or document which, in the opinion of the Treasury or the Authority, is relevant for purposes of, or connected with, any relevant provision;
  (f)   make such consequential, transitional or supplemental provision as the Treasury consider appropriate for purposes of, or connected with, any relevant provision.

(2)   Provision made as a result of sub-paragraph (1)(f) may amend any primary or subordinate legislation, including any provision of, or made under, this Act.

(3)   "Relevant provision" means any provision—
  (a)   of section 22 or this Schedule; or
  (b)   made under that section or this Schedule.

Parliamentary control

26.   (1)   This paragraph applies to the first order made under section 22(1).

(2)   This paragraph also applies to any subsequent order made under section 22(1) which contains a statement by the Treasury that, in their opinion, the effect (or one of the effects) of the proposed order would be that an activity which is not a regulated activity would become a regulated activity.

(3)   An order to which this paragraph applies—
  (a)   must be laid before Parliament after being made; and
  (b)   ceases to have effect at the end of the relevant period unless before the end of that period the order is approved by a resolution of each House of Parliament (but without that affecting anything done under the order or the power to make a new order).

(4)   "Relevant period" means a period of twenty-eight days beginning with the day on which the order is made.

(5)   In calculating the relevant period no account is to be taken of any time during which Parliament is dissolved or prorogued or during which both Houses are adjourned for more than four days.

Part 7   FSMA 2000

Interpretation

27. (1)   In this Schedule—

"buying" includes acquiring for valuable consideration;

"offering" includes inviting to treat;

"property" includes currency of the United Kingdom or any other country or territory; and

"selling" includes disposing for valuable consideration.

(2)   In sub-paragraph (1) "disposing" includes—

(a)   in the case of an investment consisting of rights under a contract—

    (i)   surrendering, assigning or converting those rights; or

    (ii)   assuming the corresponding liabilities under the contract;

(b)   in the case of an investment consisting of rights under other arrangements, assuming the corresponding liabilities under the contract or arrangements;

(c)   in the case of any other investment, issuing or creating the investment or granting the rights or interests of which it consists.

(3)   In this Schedule references to an instrument include references to any record (whether or not in the form of a document).

NOTES

Order under section 22: see that section at **[7.23]**.

SCHEDULE 3
EEA PASSPORT RIGHTS

Sections 31(1)(b) and 37

NOTES

Transitional provisions: the Financial Services and Markets Act 2000 (Transitional Provisions) (Authorised Persons etc) Order 2001, SI 2001/2636, Pt II, Chapter II, provides that EEA firms with "passports" before 1 December 2001 under the Insurance Companies Act 1982, the Banking Coordination (Second Council Directive) Regulations 1992, SI 1992/3218, or the Investment Services Regulations 1995, SI 1995/3275, are to be treated after that date as having complied with the procedures in this Schedule. In relation to UK firms with "passports" before 1 December 2001, see art 77 of the 2001 Order. The 1982 Act was repealed, and SI 1992/3218 and SI 1995/3275 were revoked, by the Financial Services and Markets Act 2000 (Consequential Amendments and Repeals) Order 2001, SI 2001/3649, art 3(1)(b), (2)(a), (c).

PART I
DEFINED TERMS

The single market directives

[7.381]

1. "The single market directives" means—

[(a)   the banking consolidation directive;]

(c)   the insurance directives;   . . .

[(ca) the reinsurance directive;]

(d)   the [markets in financial instruments directive][;   . . .

(e)   the insurance mediation directive][; and

(f)   the UCITS directive.]

The banking [consolidation directive]

[2. The banking consolidation directive" means Directive 2006/48/EC of the European Parliament and of the Council of 14 June 2006 relating to the taking up and pursuit of the business of credit institutions [as last amended by Directive 2009/111/EC of the European Parliament and of the Council].]

The insurance directives

3. (1)   "The insurance directives" means the first, second and third non-life insurance directives and the [life assurance consolidation directive].

(2)   "First non-life insurance directive" means the Council Directive of 24 July 1973 on the co-ordination of laws, regulations and administrative provisions relating to the taking up and pursuit of the business of direct insurance other than life assurance (No 73/239/EEC).

(3)   "Second non-life insurance directive" means the Council Directive of 22 June 1988 on the co-ordination of laws, etc, and laying down provisions to facilitate the effective exercise of freedom to provide services and amending Directive 73/239/EEC (No 88/357/EEC).

(4)   "Third non-life insurance directive" means the Council Directive of 18 June 1992 on the co-ordination of laws, etc, and amending Directives 73/239/EEC and 88/357/EEC (No 92/49/EEC).

[(8)   "Life assurance consolidation directive" means Directive 2002/83/EC of the European Parliament and of the Council of 5th November 2002 concerning life assurance.]

[The reinsurance directive

3A. "The reinsurance directive" means Directive 2005/68/EC of the European Parliament and of the Council of 16 November 2005 on reinsurance and amending Council Directives 73/239/EEC, 92/49/EEC as well as Directives 98/78/EC and 2002/83/EC.]

4. . . .

[The insurance mediation directive

4A. "The insurance mediation directive" means the European Parliament and Council Directive of 9th December 2002 on insurance mediation (No 2002/92/EC).]

[The UCITS directive

4B. "The UCITS directive" means the Directive of the European Parliament and of the Council of 13 July 2009 on the coordination of laws, regulations and administrative provisions relating to undertakings for collective investment in transferable securities (No 2009/65/EC).]

[The markets in financial instruments directive

4C. "The markets in financial instruments directive" means Directive 2004/39/EC of the European Parliament and of the Council of 21 April 2004 on markets in financial instruments.]

EEA firm

5. "EEA firm" means any of the following if it does not have its [relevant office] in the United Kingdom—
   (a)   an investment firm (as defined in [Article 4.1.1 of the markets in financial instruments directive]) which is authorised (within the meaning of [Article 5]) by its home state regulator;
   [(b)   a credit institution (as defined in Article 4.1 of the banking consolidation directive) which is authorised (within the meaning of Article 4.2) by its home state regulator,
   (c)   a financial institution (as defined in Article 4.5 of the banking consolidation directive) which is a subsidiary of the kind mentioned in Article 24 and which fulfils the conditions in that Article;]
   (d)   an undertaking pursuing the activity of direct insurance (within the meaning of [Article 2 of the life assurance consolidation directive or Article 1 of the first non-life insurance directive]) which has received authorisation under [Article 4 of the life assurance consolidation directive or Article 6 of the first non-life insurance directive] from its home state regulator[; . . .
   [(da) an undertaking pursuing the activity of reinsurance (within the meaning of Article 2.1(a) of the reinsurance directive) which has received authorisation under (or is deemed to be authorised in accordance with) Article 3 of the reinsurance directive from its home state regulator;]
   (e)   an insurance intermediary (as defined in Article 2.5 of the insurance mediation directive), or a reinsurance intermediary (as defined in Article 2.6) which is registered with its home state regulator under Article 3][; or
   [(f)   a management company (as defined in paragraph 11B) which is authorised (within the meaning of Article 6 of the UCITS directive) by its home state regulator.]]

[5A.   In paragraph 5, "relevant office" means—
   (a)   in relation to a firm falling within sub-paragraph (e) of that paragraph which has a registered office, its registered office;
   (b)   in relation to any other firm, its head office.]

EEA authorisation

[6. "EEA authorisation" means—
   (a)   in relation to an EEA firm falling within paragraph 5(e), registration with its home state regulator under Article 3 of the insurance mediation directive;
   (b)   in relation to any other EEA firm, authorisation granted to an EEA firm by its home state regulator for the purpose of the relevant single market directive.]

EEA right

7. "EEA right" means the entitlement of a person to establish a branch, or provide services, in an EEA State other than that in which he has his [relevant office]—
   (a)   in accordance with the Treaty as applied in the EEA; and
   (b)   subject to the conditions of the relevant single market directive.

[7A.   In paragraph 7, "relevant office" means—

(a) in relation to a person who has a registered office and whose entitlement is subject to the conditions of the insurance mediation directive, his registered office;

(b) in relation to any other person, his head office.]

EEA State

[8. "EEA State" has the meaning given by Schedule 1 to the Interpretation Act 1978.]

Home state regulator

9. "Home state regulator" means the competent authority (within the meaning of the relevant single market directive) of an EEA State (other than the United Kingdom) in relation to the EEA firm concerned.

UK firm

10. "UK firm" means a person whose [relevant office] is in the UK and who has an EEA right to carry on activity in an EEA State other than the United Kingdom.

[**10A.** In paragraph 10, "relevant office" means—

(a) in relation to a firm whose EEA right derives from the insurance mediation directive and which has a registered office, its registered office;

(b) in relation to any other firm, its head office.]

[UK investment firm

10B. "UK investment firm" means a UK firm—

(a) which is an investment firm, and

(b) whose EEA right derives from the markets in financial instruments directive.]

11. "Host state regulator" means the competent authority (within the meaning of the relevant single market directive) of an EEA State (other than the United Kingdom) in relation to a UK firm's exercise of EEA rights there.

[Tied agent

11A. "Tied agent" has the meaning given in Article 4.1.25 of the markets in financial instruments directive.]

[Management company

11B. "Management company" has the meaning given in Article 2.1(b) of the UCITS directive.

UCITS

11C "UCITS" has the meaning given in Article 1.2 of the UCITS directive.]

NOTES

Para 1 is amended as follows:

Sub-para (a) substituted, for original sub-paras (a), (b), by the Banking Consolidation Directive (Consequential Amendments) Regulations 2000, SI 2000/2952, reg 8(1), (5)(a), as from 22 November 2000.

Word omitted from sub-para (c) repealed, and sub-para (e) and the word immediately preceding it inserted, by the Insurance Mediation Directive (Miscellaneous Amendments) Regulations 2003, SI 2003/1473, reg 2(2)(a), as from 14 January 2005.

Sub-para (ca) inserted by the Reinsurance Directive Regulations 2007, SI 2007/3253, reg 2(1), Sch 1, paras 1, 6(a), as from 10 December 2007.

Words in square brackets in sub-para (d) substituted by the Financial Services and Markets Act 2000 (Markets in Financial Instruments) Regulations 2007, SI 2007/126, reg 3(4), Sch 4, paras 1, 2, as from 1 April 2007 (certain purposes), and as from 1 November 2007 (otherwise).

Word omitted from sub-para (d) repealed, and sub-para (f) and the word immediately preceding it inserted, by the Collective Investment Schemes (Miscellaneous Amendments) Regulations 2003, SI 2003/2066, reg 2(2)(a), as from 13 February 2004.

Para 2: substituted by the Capital Requirements Regulations 2006, SI 2006/3221, reg 29(1), Sch 3, para 2(1), (2), as from 1 January 2007; words in square brackets in the heading preceding para 2 substituted by virtue of SI 2000/2952, reg 8(1), (5)(b), as from 22 November 2000; words in square brackets added by the Capital Requirements (Amendment) Regulations 2010, SI 2010/2628, regs 2, 13, Sch 1, para 2, as from 31 December 2010.

Para 3: words in square brackets in sub-para (1) substituted, and sub-para (8) substituted for the original sub-paras (5)–(7), by the Life Assurance Consolidation Directive (Consequential Amendments) Regulations 2004, SI 2004/3379, reg 6(1), (6)(a), as from 11 January 2005.

Para 3A: inserted by SI 2007/3253, reg 2(1), Sch 1, paras 1, 6(b), as from 10 December 2007.

Para 4: repealed by SI 2007/126, reg 3(4), Sch 4, paras 1, 3, as from 1 April 2007 (certain purposes), and as from 1 November 2007 (otherwise).

Paras 4A, 5A, 7A, 10A: inserted by SI 2003/1473, reg 2(2)(b), (d), (g), (i), as from 14 January 2005.

Para 4B: inserted by SI 2003/2066, reg 2(2)(b), as from 13 February 2004, and substituted by the Undertakings for Collective Investment in Transferable Securities Regulations 2011, SI 2011/1613, reg 2(1), (33)(a), as from 1 July 2011.

Para 4C: inserted by the Financial Services and Markets Act 2000 (Markets in Financial Instruments) (Modification of Powers) Regulations 2006, SI 2006/2975, regs 2, 13, as from 6 December 2006.

Para 5 is amended as follows:

Words in first pair of square brackets substituted, and sub-para (e) and the word immediately preceding it inserted, by SI 2003/1473, reg 2(2)(c), as from 14 January 2005.

Words in square brackets in sub-para (a) substituted by SI 2007/126, reg 3(4), Sch 4, paras 1, 4, as from 1 April 2007 (certain purposes), and as from 1 November 2007 (otherwise).

Sub-paras (b), (c) substituted by SI 2006/3221, reg 29(1), Sch 3, para 2(1), (3), as from 1 January 2007.

Words in square brackets in sub-para (d) substituted by SI 2004/3379, reg 6(1), (6)(b), as from 11 January 2005.

Word omitted from sub-para (d) repealed, and sub-para (f) and the word immediately preceding it inserted, by SI 2003/2066, reg 2(2)(c), as from 13 February 2004.

Sub-para (da) inserted by SI 2007/3253, reg 2(1), Sch 1, paras 1, 6(c), as from 10 December 2007.

Sub-para (f) substituted by SI 2011/1613, reg 2(1), (33)(b), as from 1 July 2011.

Para 6: substituted by SI 2003/1473, reg 2(2)(e), as from 14 January 2005.

Paras 7, 10: words in square brackets substituted by SI 2003/1473, reg 2(2)(f), (h), as from 14 January 2005.

Para 8: substituted by the Financial Services (EEA State) Regulations 2007, SI 2007/108, reg 2, as from 13 February 2007.

Paras 10B, 11A: inserted by SI 2007/126, reg 3(4), Sch 4, paras 1, 5, 6, as from 1 April 2007 (certain purposes), and as from 1 November 2007 (otherwise).

Paras 11B, 11C: inserted by SI 2011/1613, reg 2(1), (33)(c), as from 1 July 2011.

EEA firm: (para 5): Regulations made under the Income Tax (Trading and Other Income) Act 2005, s 694, may provide that an EEA firm of the kind mentioned in para 5(a)–(c) of this Schedule that qualifies for authorisation under para 12 *post* may only be an individual investment plan manager if certain requirements specified in those Regulations are met; see ss 697, 698 of the 2005 Act.

"The banking consolidation directive", ie, Directive 2000/12/EC: repealed and replaced by European Parliament and Council Directive 2006/48/EC relating to the taking up and pursuit of the business of credit institutions (recast).

"The investment services directive", ie, Directive 93/22/EEC: repealed by European Parliament and Council Directive 2004/39/EC on markets in financial instruments amending Council Directives 85/611/EEC and 93/6/EEC and Directive 2000/12/EC of the European Parliament and of the Council and repealing Council Directive 93/22/EEC (the MiFID Directive).

PART II
EXERCISE OF PASSPORT RIGHTS BY EEA FIRMS

Firms qualifying for authorisation

[7.382]

12. (1)   Once an EEA firm which is seeking to establish a branch in the United Kingdom in exercise of an EEA right satisfies the establishment conditions, it qualifies for authorisation.

(2)   Once an EEA firm which is seeking to provide services in the United Kingdom in exercise of an EEA right satisfies the service conditions, it qualifies for authorisation.

[(3)   If an EEA firm falling within paragraph 5(a) is seeking to use a tied agent established in the United Kingdom in connection with the exercise of an EEA right deriving from the markets in financial instruments directive, this Part of this Schedule applies as if the firm were seeking to establish a branch in the United Kingdom.

(4)   But if—
   (a)   an EEA firm already qualifies for authorisation by virtue of sub-paragraph (1); and
   (b)   the EEA right which it is exercising derives from the markets in financial instruments directive,
sub-paragraph (3) does not require the firm to satisfy the establishment conditions in respect of its use of the tied agent in question.]

[(5)   An EEA firm which falls within paragraph 5(da) which establishes a branch in the United Kingdom, or provides services in the United Kingdom, in exercise of an EEA right qualifies for authorisation.

(6)   Sub-paragraphs (1) and (2) do not apply to an EEA firm falling within paragraph 5(da).]

Establishment

13. (1)   [If the firm falls within paragraph 5(a), (b), [(c), (d) or (f)],] The establishment conditions are that—
   (a)   the Authority has received notice ("a consent notice") from the firm's home state regulator that it has given the firm consent to establish a branch in the United Kingdom;
   (b)   the consent notice—
      (i)   is given in accordance with the relevant single market directive;
      (ii)   identifies the activities to which consent relates; and
      (iii)   includes such other information as may be prescribed;   . . .
   [(ba) in the case of a firm falling within paragraph 5(a), the Authority has given the firm notice for the purposes of this paragraph or two months have elapsed beginning with the date when the home state regulator gave the consent notice; and"]
   (c)   [in the case of a firm falling within paragraph 5(b), (c), (d) or (f),] the firm has been informed of the applicable provisions or two months have elapsed beginning with the date when the Authority received the consent notice.

[(1A)   If the firm falls within paragraph 5(e), the establishment conditions are that—
   (a)   the firm has given its home state regulator notice of its intention to establish a branch in the United Kingdom;
   (b)   the Authority has received notice ("a regulator's notice") from the firm's home state regulator that the firm intends to establish a branch in the United Kingdom;

(c)   the firm's home state regulator has informed the firm that the regulator's notice has been sent to the Authority; and

(d)   one month has elapsed beginning with the date on which the firm's home state regulator informed the firm that the regulator's notice has been sent to the Authority.]

(2)   If the Authority has received a consent notice, it must—

(a)   prepare for the firm's supervision;

(b)   [except if the firm falls within paragraph 5(a),] notify the firm of the applicable provisions (if any); and

(c)   if the firm falls within paragraph 5(d), notify its home state regulator of the applicable provisions (if any).

(3)   A notice under sub-paragraph (2)(b) or (c) must be given before the end of the period of two months beginning with the day on which the Authority received the consent notice.

(4)   For the purposes of this paragraph—

"applicable provisions" means the host state rules with which the firm is required to comply when carrying on a permitted activity through a branch in the United Kingdom;

"host state rules" means rules—

(a)   made in accordance with the relevant single market directive; and

(b)   which are the responsibility of the United Kingdom (both as to implementation and as to supervision of compliance) in accordance with that directive; and

"permitted activity" means an activity identified in the consent notice [or regulator's notice, as the case may be].

Services

14. (1)   The service conditions are that—

(a)   the firm has given its home state regulator notice of its intention to provide services in the United Kingdom ("a notice of intention");

(b)   if the firm falls within [paragraph 5(a), [(d), (e) or (f)]], the Authority has received notice ("a regulator's notice") from the firm's home state regulator containing such information as may be prescribed;

[(ba) if the firm falls within paragraph 5(b) and is seeking to provide services in exercise of the right under Article 31.5 of the markets in financial instruments directive, the Authority has received notice ("a regulator's notice") from the firm's home state regulator stating that the firm intends to exercise that right in the United Kingdom;]

(c)   if the firm falls within [paragraph 5(d) or (e)], its home state regulator has informed it that the regulator's notice has been sent to the Authority[; and

(d)   if the firm falls within paragraph 5(e), one month has elapsed beginning with the date on which the firm's home state regulator informed the firm that the regulator's notice has been sent to the Authority].

(2)   If the Authority has received a regulator's notice or, where none is required by sub-paragraph (1), has been informed of the firm's intention to provide services in the United Kingdom, it must[, unless the firm falls within paragraph 5(e),]—

(a)   prepare for the firm's supervision; and

(b)   notify the firm of the applicable provisions (if any).

[(2A) Sub-paragraph (2)(b) does not apply in the case of a firm falling within paragraph 5(a).]

(3)   A notice under sub-paragraph (2)(b) must be given before the end of the period of two months beginning on the day on which the Authority received the regulator's notice, or was informed of the firm's intention.

(4)   For the purposes of this paragraph—

"applicable provisions" means the host state rules with which the firm is required to comply when carrying on a permitted activity by providing services in the United Kingdom;

"host state rules" means rules—

(a)   made in accordance with the relevant single market directive; and

(b)   which are the responsibility of the United Kingdom (both as to implementation and as to supervision of compliance) in accordance with that directive; and

"permitted activity" means an activity identified in—

(a)   the regulator's notice; or

(b)   where none is required by sub-paragraph (1), the notice of intention.

Grant of permission

15. (1)   On qualifying for authorisation as a result of [paragraph 12(1), (2) or (3)], a firm has, in respect of each permitted activity which is a regulated activity, permission to carry it on through its United Kingdom branch (if it satisfies the establishment conditions) or by providing services in the United Kingdom (if it satisfies the service conditions).

[(1A) Sub-paragraph (1) is to be read subject to paragraph 15A(3).]

(2)   The permission is to be treated as being on terms equivalent to those appearing from the consent notice, regulator's notice or notice of intention.

(3)   Sections [21 and 39(1)] of the Consumer Credit Act 1974 (business requiring a licence under that Act) do not apply in relation to the carrying on of a permitted activity which is Consumer Credit Act business by a firm which qualifies for authorisation as a result of paragraph 12, unless [the Office of Fair Trading] has exercised the power conferred on [it] by section 203 in relation to the firm.

(4)   "Consumer Credit Act business" has the same meaning as in section 203.

[(5)   A firm which qualifies for authorisation as a result of paragraph 12(5) has, in respect of each permitted activity which is a regulated activity, permission to carry it on through its United Kingdom branch or by providing services in the United Kingdom.

(6)   The permission is to be treated as being on terms equivalent to those appearing in the authorisation granted to the firm under Article 3 of the reinsurance directive by its home state regulator ("its home authorisation").

(7)   For the purposes of sub-paragraph (5), "permitted activity" means an activity which the firm is permitted to carry on under its home authorisation.]

[Application for approval to manage UCITS

15A.   (1)   An EEA firm falling within paragraph 5(f) which wishes to manage a UK UCITS must apply to the Authority in the specified form for approval to manage that UCITS.

(2)   Where the EEA firm satisfies the conditions in paragraph 13 (establishment conditions) or paragraph 14 (service conditions), the Authority may only refuse the application if it determines that one of the grounds set out in sub-paragraph (3) applies.

(3)   The grounds referred to in sub-paragraph (2) are—
   (a)   that the EEA firm does not comply with the UCITS home state rules;
   (b)   that the firm is not authorised by its home state regulator to manage the type of collective investment scheme for which authorisation is requested; or
   (c)   that the firm has not provided the documentation required under Article 20(1) of the UCITS directive.

(4)   The Authority must give a notice to the EEA firm, the firm's home state regulator and the Commission of the Authority's determination under sub-paragraph (2).

(5)   Before giving a notice under sub-paragraph (4), the Authority must consult the home state regulator of the firm.

(6)   A notice given by the Authority under sub-paragraph (4) must—
   (a)   give the Authority's reasons for considering that one of the grounds set out in sub-paragraph (3) is satisfied; and
   (b)   specify a reasonable period (which may not be less than 28 days) within which any person to whom it is given may make representations to the Authority.

(7)   In this paragraph—
   "specified" means specified—
      (a)   in rules made by the Authority to implement the UCITS directive, or
      (b)   in any directly applicable Community regulation or decision made under the UCITS directive;
   "UCITS home state rules" means requirements which are imposed by or under this Act so far as relating to matters falling within Article 19(3) and (4) of the UCITS directive.

Representations and references to the Tribunal

15B.   (1)   Within a reasonable time after the end of the period for making representations, the Authority must decide, in the light of any representations made to it during that period by a person to whom notice has been given under paragraph 15A(4), whether to withdraw the notice.

(2)   If the Authority decides not to withdraw its notice, it must—
   (a)   give a decision notice to each person to whom the notice under paragraph 15A(4) was given, and
   (b)   inform the firm's home state regulator and the Commission that authorisation has been refused, and of the grounds for the refusal.

(3)   The management company to whom the decision notice is given may refer the matter to the Tribunal.

Information to home state regulator

15C.   (1)   Where an EEA firm falling within paragraph 5(f) has applied to manage a UCITS established in the United Kingdom, the Authority must without delay inform the home state regulator of that firm of any problem of which they are aware that may materially affect the ability of the firm—
   (a)   to perform its duties properly, or
   (b)   to comply with the home state rules.

(2)   In sub-paragraph (1), "home state rules" means rules—
   (a)   made by the EEA State concerned in accordance with the UCITS directive; and

(b)   which are the responsibility of that EEA State (both as to implementation and as to supervision of compliance) in accordance with that directive.]

Effect of carrying on regulated activity when not qualified for authorisation

16. (1)   This paragraph applies to an EEA firm which is not qualified for authorisation under paragraph 12.

(2)   Section 26 does not apply to an agreement entered into by the firm.

(3)   Section 27 does not apply to an agreement in relation to which the firm is a third party for the purposes of that section.

(4)   Section 29 does not apply to an agreement in relation to which the firm is the deposit-taker.

Continuing regulation of EEA firms

17. Regulations may—
    (a)   modify any provision of this Act which is an applicable provision (within the meaning of paragraph 13 or 14) in its application to an EEA firm qualifying for authorisation;
    (b)   make provision as to any change (or proposed change) of a prescribed kind relating to an EEA firm or to an activity that it carries on in the United Kingdom and as to the procedure to be followed in relation to such cases;
    (c)   provide that the Authority may treat an EEA firm's notification that it is to cease to carry on regulated activity in the United Kingdom as a request for cancellation of its qualification for authorisation under this Schedule.

Giving up right to authorisation

18. Regulations may provide that in prescribed circumstances an EEA firm falling within paragraph 5(c) may, on following the prescribed procedure—
    (a)   have its qualification for authorisation under this Schedule cancelled; and
    (b)   seek to become an authorised person by applying for a Part IV permission.

NOTES

Para 12: sub-paras (3), (4) added by the Financial Services and Markets Act 2000 (Markets in Financial Instruments) Regulations 2007, SI 2007/126, reg 3(4), Sch 4, paras 1, 7, as from 1 April 2007 (certain purposes), and as from 1 November 2007 (otherwise); sub-paras (5), (6) added by the Reinsurance Directive Regulations 2007, SI 2007/3253, reg 2(1), Sch 1, paras 1, 6(d), as from 10 December 2007.

Para 13 is amended as follows:

Words in first (outer) pair of square brackets in sub-para (1), words in square brackets in sub-para (4), and the whole of sub-para (1A), inserted by the Insurance Mediation Directive (Miscellaneous Amendments) Regulations 2003, SI 2003/1473, reg 3, as from 14 January 2005.

Words in second (inner) pair of square brackets in sub-para (1) substituted by the Collective Investment Schemes (Miscellaneous Amendments) Regulations 2003, SI 2003/2066, reg 3(1)(a), as from 13 February 2004.

Word omitted from sub-para (1)(b)(iii) repealed, and sub-para (1)(ba) and the words in square brackets in sub-paras (1)(c), (2)(a) inserted, by SI 2007/126, reg 3(4), Sch 4, paras 1, 8, as from 1 April 2007 (certain purposes), and as from 1 November 2007 (otherwise) (for transitional provisions, see the note below).

Para 14: words in first (outer) pair of square brackets in sub-para (1)(b) substituted, and word omitted from that paragraph repealed, by SI 2003/1473, reg 4(1), (2)(a), (b), as from 14 January 2005; words in second (inner) pair of square brackets in sub-para (1)(b) substituted by SI 2003/2066, reg 3(1)(b), as from 13 February 2004; sub-paras (1)(ba), (2A) inserted by SI 2007/126, reg 3(4), Sch 4, paras 1, 9, as from 1 April 2007 (certain purposes), and as from 1 November 2007 (otherwise); words in square brackets in sub-para (1)(c) substituted, sub-para (1)(d) and the word immediately preceding it inserted, and words in square brackets in sub-para (2) inserted, by SI 2003/1473, reg 4(1), (2)(c), (d), (3), as from 14 January 2005.

Para 15: words in square brackets in sub-para (1) substituted, and sub-paras (5)–(7) added, by SI 2007/3253, reg 2(1), Sch 1, paras 1, 6(e), as from 10 December 2007; sub-para (1A) inserted by SI 2003/2066, reg 3(1)(c), as from 13 February 2004; words in first pair of square brackets in sub-para (3) substituted by the Consumer Credit Act 2006, s 33(9), as from 6 April 2008; other words in square brackets in sub-para (3) substituted by the Enterprise Act 2002, s 278(1), Sch 25, para 40(1), (19)(a), as from 1 April 2003.

Paras 15A–15C: substituted (for para 15A as inserted by SI 2003/2066, reg 3(1)(d), as from 13 February 2004) by the Undertakings for Collective Investment in Transferable Securities Regulations 2011, SI 2011/1613, reg 2(1), (33)(d), as from 1 July 2011.

Transitional provisions: the Financial Services and Markets Act 2000 (Markets in Financial Instruments) Regulations 2007, SI 2007/126, reg 6 (Transitional and saving provisions: EEA firms) provides that where the Authority has received a consent notice of the sort referred to in para 13(1)(a) from the home state regulator of an EEA investment firm on or before 31 October 2007, para 13 applies as if it had not been amended by Sch 4, para 8 to the 2007 Regulations.

Regulations: the Financial Services and Markets Act 2000 (EEA Passport Rights) Regulations 2001, SI 2001/2511.

Note that the following amending Regulations have also been made under this Part: the Electronic Money (Miscellaneous Amendments) Regulations 2002, SI 2002/765; the Insurance Mediation Directive (Miscellaneous Amendments) Regulations 2003, SI 2003/1473; the Collective Investment Schemes (Miscellaneous Amendments) Regulations 2003, SI 2003/2066; the Financial Services and Markets Act 2000 (EEA Passport Rights) (Amendment) Regulations 2006, SI 2006/3385.

PART III
EXERCISE OF PASSPORT RIGHTS BY UK FIRMS
Establishment

[7.383]

19. (1) [Subject to [sub-paragraphs (5ZA) and (5A)],] A UK firm may not exercise an EEA right to establish a branch unless three conditions are satisfied.

(2) The first is that the firm has given the Authority, in the specified way, notice of its intention to establish a branch ("a notice of intention") which—
- (a) identifies the activities which it seeks to carry on through the branch; and
- (b) includes such other information as may be specified.

(3) [Subject to sub-paragraph (5B), the] activities identified in a notice of intention may include activities which are not regulated activities.

[(4) The second is that—
- (a) the Authority has given notice in specified terms ("a consent notice") to the host state regulator; and
- (b) where the firm is a management company which wishes to pursue the activity of collective portfolio management referred to in Annex II to the UCITS directive, the Authority has provided to the host state regulator—
  - (i) confirmation that the firm has been authorised as a management company pursuant to the provisions of the UCITS directive;
  - (ii) a description of the scope of the management company's authorisation; and
  - (iii) details of any restriction on the types of UCITS that the management company is authorised to manage.]

[(5) The third is—
- (a) if the EEA right in question derives from the insurance mediation directive, that one month has elapsed beginning with the date on which the firm received notice, in accordance with sub-paragraph (11), that the Authority has given a consent notice;
- (b) in any other case, that either—
  - (i) the host state regulator has notified the firm (or, where the EEA right in question derives from any of the insurance directives, the Authority) of the applicable provisions; or
  - (ii) two months have elapsed beginning with the date on which the Authority gave the consent notice.]

[(5ZA) This paragraph does not apply to a UK firm having an EEA right which is subject to the conditions of the reinsurance directive.]

[(5A) If—
- (a) the EEA right in question derives from the insurance mediation directive, and
- (b) the EEA State in which the firm intends to establish a branch has not notified the Commission, in accordance with Article 6(2) of that directive, of its wish to be informed of the intention of any UK firm to establish a branch in its territory,

the second and third conditions do not apply (and so the firm may establish the branch to which its notice of intention relates as soon as the first condition is satisfied).]

[(5B) If the firm is a UK investment firm, a notice of intention may not include ancillary services unless such services are to be provided in connection with the carrying on of one or more investment services and activities.

(5C) In sub-paragraph (5B) "ancillary services" has the meaning given in Article 4.1.3 of the markets in financial instruments directive.]

(6) If the firm's EEA right derives from [the banking consolidation directive, [. . . or, in the case of a credit institution authorised under the banking consolidation directive, the markets in financial instruments directive]] and the first condition is satisfied, the Authority must give a consent notice to the host state regulator unless it has reason to doubt the adequacy of the firm's resources or its administrative structure.

[(6A) If the firm's EEA right derives from the UCITS directive and the first condition is satisfied, the Authority must give a consent notice and information about the compensation scheme to the host state regulator unless it has reason to doubt the adequacy of the firm's resources or its administrative structure, and must do so within two months beginning with the date on which it received the firm's notice of intention.]

(7) If the firm's EEA right derives from any of the insurance directives and the first condition is satisfied, the Authority must give a consent notice unless it has reason—
- (a) to doubt the adequacy of the firm's resources or its administrative structure, or
- (b) to question the reputation, qualifications or experience of the directors or managers of the firm or the person proposed as the branch's authorised agent for the purposes of those directives,

in relation to the business to be conducted through the proposed branch.

[(7A) If—

    (a)   the firm's EEA right derives from the insurance mediation directive,

    (b)   the first condition is satisfied, and

    (c)   the second condition applies,

the Authority must give a consent notice, and must do so within one month beginning with the date on which it received the firm's notice of intention.]

[(7B) If the firm is a UK investment firm and the first condition is satisfied, the Authority must give a consent notice to the host state regulator within three months beginning with the date on which it received the firm's notice of intention unless the Authority has reason to doubt the adequacy of the firm's resources or its administrative structure.]

(8) If the Authority proposes to refuse to give a consent notice it must give the firm concerned a warning notice.

(9) If the firm's EEA right derives from any of the insurance directives and the host state regulator has notified it of the applicable provisions, the Authority must inform the firm of those provisions.

(10) Rules may specify the procedure to be followed by the Authority in exercising its functions under this paragraph.

(11) If the Authority gives a consent notice it must give written notice that it has done so to the firm concerned.

(12) If the Authority decides to refuse to give a consent notice—

    (a)   it must, [within the relevant period], give the person who gave that notice a decision notice to that effect; and

    (b)   that person may refer the matter to the Tribunal.

[(12ZA) If the firm's EEA right derives from the UCITS directive, the Authority must inform the Commission if it decides to refuse to give a consent notice, giving the reasons for that refusal.]

[(12A) In sub-paragraph (12), "the relevant period" means—

    (a)   if the firm's EEA right derives from the UCITS directive, two months beginning with the date on which the Authority received the notice of intention;

    (b)   in any other case, three months beginning with that date.]

(13) In this paragraph, "applicable provisions" means the host state rules with which the firm will be required to comply when conducting business through the proposed branch in the EEA State concerned.

(14) In sub-paragraph (13), "host state rules" means rules—

    (a)   made in accordance with the relevant single market directive; and

    (b)   which are the responsibility of the EEA State concerned (both as to implementation and as to supervision of compliance) in accordance with that directive.

(15) "Specified" means specified in rules.

Services

20. (1) [Subject to sub-paragraph (4D),] a UK firm may not exercise an EEA right to provide services unless the firm has given the Authority, in the specified way, notice of its intention to provide services ("a notice of intention") which—

    (a)   identifies the activities which it seeks to carry out by way of provision of services; and

    (b)   includes such other information as may be specified.

(2) [Subject to sub-paragraph (2A), the] activities identified in a notice of intention may include activities which are not regulated activities.

[(2A) If the firm is a UK investment firm, a notice of intention may not include ancillary services unless such services are to be provided in connection with the carrying on of one or more investment services and activities.

(2B) In sub-paragraph (2A) "ancillary services" has the meaning given in Article 4.1.3 of the markets in financial instruments directive.]

(3) If the firm's EEA right derives from [the banking consolidation directive, the [markets in financial instruments directive] or the UCITS directive], the Authority must, within one month of receiving a notice of intention, send a copy of it to the host state regulator [with such other information as may be specified].

[(3ZA) If the firm's EEA right derives from the UCITS directive, the Authority must provide information about the compensation scheme with the information provided to the host state regulator under sub-paragraph (3).]

[(3A) If the firm's EEA right derives from any of the insurance directives, the Authority must, within one month of receiving the notice of intention—

    (a)   give notice in specified terms ("a consent notice") to the host state regulator; or

    (b)   give written notice to the firm of—

        (i)   its refusal to give a consent notice; and

        (ii)   its reasons for that refusal.]

[(3B)   If the firm's EEA right derives from the insurance mediation directive and the EEA State in which the firm intends to provide services has notified the Commission, in accordance with Article 6(2) of that directive, of its wish to be informed of the intention of any UK firm to provide services in its territory—

(a)   the Authority must, within one month of receiving the notice of intention, send a copy of it to the host state regulator;

(b)   the Authority, when it sends the copy in accordance with sub-paragraph (a), must give written notice to the firm concerned that it has done so; and

(c)   the firm concerned must not provide the services to which its notice of intention relates until one month, beginning with the date on which it receives the notice under sub-paragraph (b), has elapsed.]

[(3C)   If the firm is a management company which wishes to pursue the activity of collective portfolio management referred to in Annex II to the UCITS directive, the Authority must send with the documentation provided to the host state regulator under sub-paragraph (3)—

(a)   confirmation that the firm has been authorised as a management company pursuant to the provisions of the UCITS directive;

(b)   a description of the scope of the management company's authorisation; and

(c)   details of any restriction on the types of UCITS that the management company is authorised to manage.]

(4)   When the Authority sends the copy under sub-paragraph (3) [or gives a consent notice], it must give written notice to the firm concerned.

[(4A)   If the firm is given notice under sub-paragraph (3A)(b), it may refer the matter to the Tribunal.

(4B)   If the firm's EEA right derives from any of the insurance directives [or from the markets in financial instruments directive] [or the UCITS directive], it must not provide the services to which its notice of intention relates until it has received written notice under sub-paragraph (4).

[(4BA)   If the firm's EEA right derives from the markets in financial instruments directive, the Authority must comply as soon as reasonably practicable with a request for information under the second sub-paragraph of Article 31.6 of that directive from the host state regulator.]

(4C)   Rules may specify the procedure to be followed by the Authority under this paragraph.]

[(4D)   This paragraph does not apply to a UK firm having an EEA right which is subject to the conditions of the reinsurance directive.]

(5)   . . .

(6)   "Specified" means specified in rules.

[Information for host state regulator]

20ZA. (1)   The Authority must keep a record of the confirmation and other information provided to the host state regulator under paragraph 19(4) or paragraph 20(3C) in relation to a UK firm which is a management company.

(2)   The Authority must inform the host state regulator whenever there is a change in the confirmation or other information referred to in sub-paragraph (1).]

[Tied agents]

20A. (1)   If a UK investment firm is seeking to use a tied agent established in an EEA State (other than the United Kingdom) in connection with the exercise of an EEA right deriving from the markets in financial instruments directive, this Part of this Schedule applies as if the firm were seeking to establish a branch in that State.

(2)   But if—

(a)   a UK investment firm has already established a branch in an EEA State other than the United Kingdom in accordance with paragraph 19; and

(b)   the EEA right which it is exercising derives from the markets in financial instruments directive,

paragraph 19 does not apply in respect of its use of the tied agent in question.]

[Notice of intention to market]

20B. (1)   The operator of a UCITS established in the United Kingdom may not exercise an EEA right to market the units of that UCITS in the territory of another EEA State unless the operator has given the Authority, in the specified way, notice of its intention to market the units ("notice of intention") which contains, and is accompanied by, such information as may be specified in rules, or in regulations made by the European Commission under the UCITS directive.

(2)   The Authority must ensure that the information referred to in sub-paragraph (1) may be transmitted to it electronically.

(3)   The Authority must verify whether the information submitted with the notice of intention is complete and, within 10 days of the date on which the Authority received the complete information required, send to the host state regulator—

(a)　a copy of the notice of intention;

(b)　the accompanying information; and

(c)　confirmation that the operator and the UCITS fulfil the conditions imposed by the UCITS directive.

(4)　The Authority must ensure that the host state regulator has electronic access to the information and documents referred to in sub-paragraph (3).

(5)　The Authority must notify the operator immediately that the information referred to in sub-paragraph (3) has been sent to the competent authorities of the host state regulator.

(6)　The operator may market the units of the UCITS in the territory of the host state regulator from the moment it receives the notification referred to in sub-paragraph (5).

(7)　In this paragraph—

　　"operator" has the same meaning as in section 237 of this Act;

　　"specified" means specified in rules.]

Offence relating to exercise of passport rights

21.　(1)　If a UK firm which is not an authorised person contravenes the prohibition imposed by—

(a)　sub-paragraph (1) of paragraph 19, or

(b)　[sub-paragraph (1), (3B)(c) or (4B)] of paragraph 20,

it is guilty of an offence.

(2)　A firm guilty of an offence under sub-paragraph (1) is liable—

(a)　on summary conviction, to a fine not exceeding the statutory maximum; or

(b)　on conviction on indictment, to a fine.

(3)　In proceedings for an offence under sub-paragraph (1), it is a defence for the firm to show that it took all reasonable precautions and exercised all due diligence to avoid committing the offence.

Continuing regulation of UK firms

22.　(1)　Regulations may make such provision as the Treasury consider appropriate in relation to a UK firm's exercise of EEA rights, and may in particular provide for the application (with or without modification) of any provision of, or made under, this Act in relation to an activity of a UK firm.

(2)　Regulations may—

(a)　make provision as to any change (or proposed change) of a prescribed kind relating to a UK firm or to an activity that it carries on and as to the procedure to be followed in relation to such cases;

(b)　make provision with respect to the consequences of the firm's failure to comply with a provision of the regulations.

(3)　Where a provision of the kind mentioned in sub-paragraph (2) requires the Authority's consent to a change (or proposed change)—

(a)　consent may be refused only on prescribed grounds; and

(b)　if the Authority decides to refuse consent, the firm concerned may refer the matter to the Tribunal.

23.　(1)　[Sub-paragraphs (2) and (2A) apply] if a UK firm—

(a)　has a Part IV permission; and

(b)　is exercising an EEA right to carry on any Consumer Credit Act business in an EEA State other than the United Kingdom.

(2)　The Authority may exercise its power under section 45 in respect of the firm if [the Office of Fair Trading] has informed the Authority that—

(a)　the firm,

(b)　any of the firm's employees, agents or associates (whether past or present), or

(c)　if the firm is a body corporate, a controller of the firm or an associate of such a controller,

has done any of the things specified in paragraphs [(a) to (e) of section 25(2A)] of the Consumer Credit Act 1974.

[(2A)　The Authority may also exercise its power under section 45 in respect of the firm if the Office of Fair Trading has informed the Authority that it has concerns about any of the following—

(a)　the firm's skills, knowledge and experience in relation to Consumer Credit Act businesses;

(b)　such skills, knowledge and experience of other persons who are participating in any Consumer Credit Act business being carried on by the firm;

(c)　practices and procedures that the firm is implementing in connection with any such business.]

(3)　"Associate", "Consumer Credit Act business" and "controller" have the same meaning as in section 203.

24.　(1)　Sub-paragraph (2) applies if a UK firm—

(a)　is not required to have a Part IV permission in relation to the business which it is carrying on; and

(b)   is exercising the right conferred by [[Article 24] of the banking consolidation directive] to carry on that business in an EEA State other than the United Kingdom.

(2)   If requested to do so by the host state regulator in the EEA State in which the UK firm's business is being carried on, the Authority may impose any requirement in relation to the firm which it could impose if—

(a)   the firm had a Part IV permission in relation to the business which it is carrying on; and

(b)   the Authority was entitled to exercise its power under that Part to vary that permission.

[Information to be included in the public record

25. The Authority must include in the record that it maintains under section 347 in relation to any UK firm whose EEA right derives from the insurance mediation directive information as to each EEA State in which the UK firm, in accordance with such a right—

(a)   has established a branch; or

(b)   is providing services.]

[UK management companies: delegation of functions

26. Where a UK firm which is a management company and is providing services in the exercise of an EEA right to an EEA UCITS informs the Authority that it has delegated one or more of its functions to a third party, the Authority must transmit that information to the home state regulator of the EEA UCITS without delay.

UK management companies: withdrawal of authorisation

27. Where a UK firm which is a management company has exercised an EEA right deriving from the UCITS directive to establish a branch or to provide services in another EEA State, the Authority must consult the home state regulator of any UCITS managed by that management company before taking a decision to withdraw the authorisation of the management company under section 33.

Management companies: request for information

28. (1)   Where a UK firm has applied to manage a UCITS which is established in another EEA State, the home state regulator of the UCITS may—

(a)   request further information from the Authority regarding the documents referred to in Article 20.1 of the UCITS directive, and

(b)   ask the Authority whether the type of UCITS for which the UK firm has applied to provide its services falls within the scope of the authorisation of the UK firm.

(2)   The Authority must respond to a request under sub-paragraph (1)(a) or (b) within 10 working days of the date on which the request was received.]

NOTES

Para 19 is amended as follows:

Words in first (outer) pair of square brackets in sub-para (1), and the whole of sub-paras (5A), (7A) inserted, and sub-para (5) substituted, by the Insurance Mediation Directive (Miscellaneous Amendments) Regulations 2003, SI 2003/1473, reg 5, as from 14 January 2005.

Words in second (inner) pair of square brackets in sub-para (1) substituted, and sub-para (5ZA) inserted, by the Reinsurance Directive Regulations 2007, SI 2007/3253, reg 2(1), Sch 1, paras 1, 6(f), (g), as from 10 December 2007.

Words in square brackets in sub-para (3), and words in second (inner) pair of square brackets in sub-para (6) substituted, and sub-paras (5B), (5C), (7B) inserted, by SI 2007/126, reg 3(4), Sch 4, paras 1, 10, as from 1 April 2007 (certain purposes), and as from 1 November 2007 (otherwise) (for transitional provisions, see the note below).

Sub-para (4) substituted, words omitted from sub-para (6) repealed, and sub-paras (6A), (12ZA) inserted, by the Undertakings for Collective Investment in Transferable Securities Regulations 2011, SI 2011/1613, reg 2(1), (33)(e)–(h), as from 1 July 2011.

Words in first (outer) pair of square brackets in sub-para (6) and words in square brackets in sub-para (12) substituted, and sub-para (12A) inserted, by the Collective Investment Schemes (Miscellaneous Amendments) Regulations 2003, SI 2003/2066, reg 4(1)(a), as from 13 February 2004.

Para 20 is amended as follows:

Words in square brackets in sub-para (1), and sub-para (4D), inserted by SI 2007/3253, reg 2(1), Sch 1, paras 1, 6(h), (i), as from 10 December 2007.

Words in square brackets in sub-para (2), and words in second (inner) pair of square brackets in sub-para (3), substituted, sub-pars (2A), (2B), (4BA) inserted, and words in first pair of square brackets in sub-para (4B) inserted, by SI 2007/126, reg 3(4), Sch 4, paras 1, 11, as from 1 April 2007 (certain purposes), and as from 1 November 2007 (otherwise) (for transitional provisions, see the note below).

Words in first (outer) pair of square brackets in sub-para (3) substituted, and words in third pair of square brackets in that paragraph added, by SI 2003/2066, reg 4(1)(b), as from 13 February 2004.

Sub-paras (3A), (4A)–(4C) inserted, words in square brackets in sub-para (4) inserted, and sub-para (5) repealed, by the Financial Services (EEA Passport Rights) Regulations 2001, SI 2001/1376, reg 2(1)–(5), as from 30 April 2001; sub-para (3B) inserted by SI 2003/1473, reg 6(1), as from 14 January 2005.

Sub-paras (3ZA), (3C) inserted, and words in second pair of square brackets in sub-para (4B) inserted, by SI 2011/1613, reg 2(1), (33)(i)–(k), as from 1 July 2011.

Paras 20ZA, 20B, 26–28: inserted by SI 2011/1613, reg 2(1), (33)(l)–(n), as from 1 July 2011.

Para 20A: inserted and added respectively by SI 2007/126, reg 3(4), Sch 4, paras 1, 12, as from 1 April 2007 (certain purposes), and as from 1 November 2007 (otherwise).

Para 21: words in square brackets substituted by SI 2003/1473, reg 6(2), as from 14 January 2005.

Para 23: words in square brackets sub-para (1) and words in second pair of square brackets in sub-para (2) substituted, and sub-para (2A) inserted, by the Consumer Credit Act 2006, s 33(10)–(12), as from 6 April 2008; words in first pair of square brackets in sub-para (2) substituted by the Enterprise Act 2002, s 278(1), Sch 25, para 40(1), (19)(b), as from 1 April 2003.

Para 24: words in first (outer) pair of square brackets substituted by the Banking Consolidation Directive (Consequential Amendments) Regulations 2000, SI 2000/2952, reg 8(1), (5)(f), as from 22 November 2000; words in second (inner) pair of square brackets substituted by the Capital Requirements Regulations 2006, SI 2006/3221, reg 29(1), Sch 3, para 2(1), (4), as from 1 January 2007.

Para 25: inserted, together with preceding heading, by SI 2003/1473, reg 7, as from 14 January 2005.

Transitional provisions: the Financial Services and Markets Act 2000 (Markets in Financial Instruments) Regulations 2007, SI 2007/126 provide for various transitional provisions in connection with the amendments made by those Regulations to this Schedule. For transitional provisions in connection with paras 19, 20 above, see reg 7 (Transitional provisions: UK investment firms exercising passport rights under the investment services directive), and reg 8 (Additional saving provision: UK investment firms) of the 2007 Regulations.

Regulations: the Financial Services and Markets Act 2000 (EEA Passport Rights) Regulations 2001, SI 2001/2511.

Note that the following amending Regulations have also been made under this Part: the Collective Investment Schemes (Miscellaneous Amendments) Regulations 2003, SI 2003/2066; the Financial Services and Markets Act 2000 (EEA Passport Rights) (Amendment) Regulations 2006, SI 2006/3385; the Financial Services and Markets Act 2000 (Markets in Financial Instruments) (Amendment) Regulations 2007, SI 2007/763.

SCHEDULE 4
TREATY RIGHTS

Section 31(1)(c)

NOTES

Transitional provisions: the Financial Services and Markets Act 2000 (Transitional Provisions) (Authorised Persons etc) Order 2001, SI 2001/2636, Pt II, Chapter III, provides that treaty firms authorised before 1 December 2001 under the Financial Services Act 1986, s 31 and certain treaty firms which were authorised insurance companies before that date are to be treated after 1 December 2001 as having complied with the procedures of this Schedule. The 1986 Act was repealed by the Financial Services and Markets Act 2000 (Consequential Amendments and Repeals) Order 2001, SI 2001/3649, art 3(1)(c).

Definitions

[7.384]

1. [(1)]   In this Schedule—

. . .

"Treaty firm" means a person—
- (a)   whose head office is situated in an EEA State (its "home state") other than the United Kingdom; and
- (b)   which is recognised under the law of that State as its national; and

"home state regulator", in relation to a Treaty firm, means the competent authority of the firm's home state for the purpose of its home state authorisation (as to which see paragraph 3(1)(a)).

[(2)   Section 425A (meaning of "consumers") applies for the purposes of this Schedule.]

Firms qualifying for authorisation

2. Once a Treaty firm which is seeking to carry on a regulated activity satisfies the conditions set out in paragraph 3(1), it qualifies for authorisation.

Exercise of Treaty rights

3. (1)   The conditions are that—
- (a)   the firm has received authorisation ("home state authorisation") under the law of its home state to carry on the regulated activity in question ("the permitted activity");
- (b)   the relevant provisions of the law of the firm's home state—
  - (i)   afford equivalent protection; or
  - (ii)   satisfy the conditions laid down by a Community instrument for the co-ordination or approximation of laws, regulations or administrative provisions of member States relating to the carrying on of that activity; and
- (c)   the firm has no EEA right to carry on that activity in the manner in which it is seeking to carry it on.

(2)   A firm is not to be regarded as having home state authorisation unless its home state regulator has so informed the Authority in writing.

(3)   Provisions afford equivalent protection if, in relation to the firm's carrying on of the permitted activity, they afford consumers protection which is at least equivalent to that afforded by or under this Act in relation to that activity.

(4)   A certificate issued by the Treasury that the provisions of the law of a particular EEA State afford equivalent protection in relation to the activities specified in the certificate is conclusive evidence of that fact.

Permission

4. (1)   On qualifying for authorisation under this Schedule, a Treaty firm has permission to carry on each permitted activity through its United Kingdom branch or by providing services in the United Kingdom.

(2)   The permission is to be treated as being on terms equivalent to those to which the firm's home state authorisation is subject.

(3)   If, on qualifying for authorisation under this Schedule, a firm has a Part IV permission which includes permission to carry on a permitted activity, the Authority must give a direction cancelling the permission so far as it relates to that activity.

(4)   The Authority need not give a direction under sub-paragraph (3) if it considers that there are good reasons for not doing so.

Notice to Authority

5. (1)   Sub-paragraph (2) applies to a Treaty firm which—
   (a)   qualifies for authorisation under this Schedule, but
   (b)   is not carrying on in the United Kingdom the regulated activity, or any of the regulated activities, which it has permission to carry on there.

(2)   At least seven days before it begins to carry on such a regulated activity, the firm must give the Authority written notice of its intention to do so.

(3)   If a Treaty firm to which sub-paragraph (2) applies has given notice under that sub-paragraph, it need not give such a notice if it again becomes a firm to which that sub-paragraph applies.

(4)   Subsections (1), (3) and (6) of section 51 apply to a notice under sub-paragraph (2) as they apply to an application for a Part IV permission.

Offences

6. (1)   A person who contravenes paragraph 5(2) is guilty of an offence.

(2)   In proceedings against a person for an offence under sub-paragraph (1) it is a defence for him to show that he took all reasonable precautions and exercised all due diligence to avoid committing the offence.

(3)   A person is guilty of an offence if in, or in connection with, a notice given by him under paragraph 5(2) he—
   (a)   provides information which he knows to be false or misleading in a material particular; or
   (b)   recklessly provides information which is false or misleading in a material particular.

(4)   A person guilty of an offence under this paragraph is liable—
   (a)   on summary conviction, to a fine not exceeding the statutory maximum;
   (b)   on conviction on indictment, to a fine.

NOTES

Para 1: sub-para (1) numbered as such, definition "consumers" (omitted) repealed, and sub-para (2) added, by the Financial Services Act 2010, s 24(1), (2), Sch 2, Pt 1, paras 1, 35, as from 8 April 2010.

Qualifies for authorisation (para 2): regulations made under the Income Tax (Trading and Other Income) Act 2005, s 694, may provide that a firm which is an authorised person as a result of qualifying for authorisation under para 2 of this Schedule may only be a plan manager if certain requirements specified in those regulations are met; see ss 697, 698 of the 2005 Act.

SCHEDULE 5
PERSONS CONCERNED IN COLLECTIVE INVESTMENT SCHEMES

Section 36

Authorisation

[7.385]
1. (1)   A person who for the time being is an operator, trustee or depositary of a recognised collective investment scheme is an authorised person.

(2)   "Recognised" means recognised by virtue of section 264.

(3)   An authorised open-ended investment company is an authorised person.

[(4)   A body—
   (a)   incorporated by virtue of regulations made under section 1 of the Open-Ended Investment Companies Act (Northern Ireland) 2002 in respect of which an authorisation order is in force, and
   (b)   to which the UCITS directive applies,
is an authorised person.

(5)   "Authorisation order" means an order made under (or having effect as made under) any provision of those regulations which is made by virtue of section 1(2)(1) of that Act (provision corresponding to Chapter 3 of Part 17 of the Act).]

Permission

2. (1) A person authorised as a result of paragraph 1(1) has permission to carry on, so far as it is a regulated activity—

    (a)   any activity, appropriate to the capacity in which he acts in relation to the scheme, of the kind described in paragraph 8 of Schedule 2;

    (b)   any activity in connection with, or for the purposes of, the scheme.

(2) A person authorised as a result of paragraph 1(3) [or (4)] has permission to carry on, so far as it is a regulated activity—

    (a)   the operation of the scheme;

    (b)   any activity in connection with, or for the purposes of, the operation of the scheme.

NOTES

Para 1: sub-paras (4), (5) added by the Collective Investment Schemes (Miscellaneous Amendments) Regulations 2003, SI 2003/2066, reg 10(a), as from 13 February 2004.

Para 2: words in square brackets inserted by SI 2003/2066, reg 10(b), as from 13 February 2004.

SCHEDULE 6
THRESHOLD CONDITIONS
Section 41

PART I
PART IV PERMISSION
Legal status

[7.386]
1. (1) If the regulated activity concerned is the effecting or carrying out of contracts of insurance the authorised person must be a body corporate [(other than a limited liability partnership)], a registered friendly society or a member of Lloyd's.

(2) If the person concerned appears to the Authority to be seeking to carry on, or to be carrying on, a regulated activity constituting accepting deposits [or issuing electronic money], it must be—

    (a)   a body corporate; or

    (b)   a partnership.

Location of offices

2. (1) [Subject to [sub-paragraphs (2A) and (3)],] If the person concerned is a body corporate constituted under the law of any part of the United Kingdom—

    (a)   its head office, and

    (b)   if it has a registered office, that office,

must be in the United Kingdom.

(2) If the person concerned has its head office in the United Kingdom but is not a body corporate, it must carry on business in the United Kingdom.

[(2A) If—

    (a)   the regulated activity concerned is any of the investment services and activities, and

    (b)   the person concerned is a body corporate with no registered office,

sub-paragraph (2B) applies in place of sub-paragraph (1).

(2B) If the person concerned has its head office in the United Kingdom, it must carry on business in the United Kingdom.]

[(3) If the regulated activity concerned is an insurance mediation activity, sub-paragraph (1) does not apply.

(4) If the regulated activity concerned is an insurance mediation activity, the person concerned—

    (a)   if he is a body corporate constituted under the law of any part of the United Kingdom, must have its registered office, or if it has no registered office, its head office, in the United Kingdom;

    (b)   if he is a natural person, is to be treated for the purposes of sub-paragraph (2), as having his head office in the United Kingdom if his residence is situated there.

(5) "Insurance mediation activity" means any of the following activities—

    (a)   dealing in rights under a contract of insurance as agent;

    (b)   arranging deals in rights under a contract of insurance;

    (c)   assisting in the administration and performance of a contract of insurance;

    (d)   advising on buying or selling rights under a contract of insurance;

    (e)   agreeing to do any of the activities specified in sub-paragraph (a) to (d).

(6) Paragraph (5) must be read with—

    (a)   section 22;

    (b)   any relevant order under that section; and

    (c)   Schedule 2.]

[Appointment of claims representatives

2A. (1)   If it appears to the Authority that—

(a)   the regulated activity that the person concerned is carrying on, or is seeking to carry on, is the effecting or carrying out of contracts of insurance, and

(b)   contracts of insurance against damage arising out of or in connection with the use of motor vehicles on land (other than carrier's liability) are being, or will be, effected or carried out by the person concerned,

that person must have a claims representative in each EEA State other than the United Kingdom.

(2)   For the purposes of sub-paragraph (1)(b), contracts of reinsurance are to be disregarded.

(3)   A claims representative is a person with responsibility for handling and settling claims arising from accidents of the kind mentioned in Article 1(2) of the fourth motor insurance directive.

(4)   In this paragraph "fourth motor insurance directive" means Directive 2000/26/EC of the European Parliament and of the Council of 16th May 2000 on the approximation of the laws of the Member States relating to insurance against civil liability in respect of the use of motor vehicles and amending Council Directives 73/239/EEC and 88/357/EEC.]

Close links

3. (1)   If the person concerned ("A") has close links with another person ("CL") the Authority must be satisfied—

(a)   that those links are not likely to prevent the Authority's effective supervision of A; and

(b)   if it appears to the Authority that CL is subject to the laws, regulations or administrative provisions of a territory which is not an EEA State ("the foreign provisions"), that neither the foreign provisions, nor any deficiency in their enforcement, would prevent the Authority's effective supervision of A.

(2)   A has close links with CL if—

(a)   CL is a parent undertaking of A;

(b)   CL is a subsidiary undertaking of A;

(c)   CL is a parent undertaking of a subsidiary undertaking of A;

(d)   CL is a subsidiary undertaking of a parent undertaking of A;

(e)   CL owns or controls 20% or more of the voting rights or capital of A; or

(f)   A owns or controls 20% or more of the voting rights or capital of CL.

(3)   "Subsidiary undertaking" includes all the instances mentioned in Article 1(1) and (2) of the Seventh Company Law Directive in which an entity may be a subsidiary of an undertaking.

Adequate resources

4. (1)   The resources of the person concerned must, in the opinion of the Authority, be adequate in relation to the regulated activities that he seeks to carry on, or carries on.

(2)   In reaching that opinion, the Authority may—

(a)   take into account the person's membership of a group and any effect which that membership may have; and

(b)   have regard to—

(i)   the provision he makes and, if he is a member of a group, which other members of the group make in respect of liabilities (including contingent and future liabilities); and

(ii)   the means by which he manages and, if he is a member of a group, which other members of the group manage the incidence of risk in connection with his business.

Suitability

5. The person concerned must satisfy the Authority that he is a fit and proper person having regard to all the circumstances, including—

(a)   his connection with any person;

(b)   the nature of any regulated activity that he carries on or seeks to carry on; and

(c)   the need to ensure that his affairs are conducted soundly and prudently.

NOTES

Para 1: words in first pair of square brackets inserted by the Financial Services and Markets Act 2000 (Variation of Threshold Conditions) Order 2001, SI 2001/2507, art 2, as from 3 September 2001; words in second pair of square brackets inserted by the Financial Services and Markets Act 2000 (Regulated Activities) (Amendment) Order 2002, SI 2002/682, art 8, as from 27 April 2002.

Para 2: words in first (outer) pair of square brackets in sub-para (1), and the whole of sub-paras (3)–(6), inserted by the Financial Services and Markets Act 2000 (Regulated Activities) (Amendment) (No 2) Order 2003, SI 2003/1476, art 19, as from 31 October 2004 (in so far as relating to contracts of long-term care insurance), and as from 14 January 2005 (otherwise) (for transitional provisions in relation to applications for Part IV permissions and applications for approval, etc, see arts 22–27 of that Order); words in second (inner) pair of square brackets in sub-para (1) substituted, and sub-paras (2A), (2B) inserted, by the Financial Services and Markets Act 2000 (Markets in Financial Instruments) Regulations 2007, SI 2007/126, reg 3(5), Sch 5, paras 1, 24, as from 1 April 2007 (certain purposes), and as from 1 November 2007 (otherwise).

Para 2A: inserted by the Financial Services and Markets Act 2000 (Variation of Threshold Conditions) Order 2002, SI 2002/2707, art 2, as from 19 January 2003.

Swiss general insurance companies: the conditions in paras 4, 5 have been removed in relation to a Swiss general insurance company; see the Financial Services and Markets Act 2000 (Variation of Threshold Conditions) Order 2001, SI 2001/2507, art 3(3) (as substituted by the Financial Services and Markets Act 2000 (Variation of Threshold Conditions) (Amendment) Order 2005, SI 2005/680). See also art 4 of that Order for additional conditions imposed on such companies.

PART II
AUTHORISATION
Authorisation under Schedule 3

[7.387]
6. In relation to an EEA firm qualifying for authorisation under Schedule 3, the conditions set out in paragraphs 1 and 3 to 5 apply, so far as relevant, to—
 (a) an application for permission under Part IV;
 (b) exercise of the Authority's own-initiative power under section 45 in relation to a Part IV permission.

Authorisation under Schedule 4

7. In relation to a person who qualifies for authorisation under Schedule 4, the conditions set out in paragraphs 1 and 3 to 5 apply, so far as relevant, to—
 (a) an application for an additional permission;
 (b) the exercise of the Authority's own-initiative power under section 45 in relation to additional permission.

PART III
ADDITIONAL CONDITIONS

[7.388]
8. (1) If this paragraph applies to the person concerned, he must, for the purposes of such provisions of this Act as may be specified, satisfy specified additional conditions.

(2) This paragraph applies to a person who—
 (a) has his head office outside the EEA; and
 (b) appears to the Authority to be seeking to carry on a regulated activity relating to insurance business.

(3) "Specified" means specified in, or in accordance with, an order made by the Treasury.

9. The Treasury may by order—
 (a) vary or remove any of the conditions set out in Parts I and II;
 (b) add to those conditions.

NOTES
 Orders: the Financial Services and Markets Act 2000 (Variation of Threshold Conditions) Order 2001, SI 2001/2507.
 Note that the following amending Orders have also been made under this Part: the Financial Services and Markets Act 2000 (Variation of Threshold Conditions) Order 2002, SI 2002/2707; the Financial Services and Markets Act 2000 (Variation of Threshold Conditions) (Amendment) Order 2005, SI 2005/680.

SCHEDULE 7
THE AUTHORITY AS COMPETENT AUTHORITY FOR PART VI
Section 72(2)

General

[7.389]
1. This Act applies in relation to the Authority when it is exercising functions under Part VI as the competent authority subject to the following modifications.

The Authority's general functions

2. In section 2—
 (a) subsection (4)(a) does not apply to [Part 6 rules];
 (b) subsection (4)(c) does not apply to general guidance given in relation to Part VI; and
 (c) subsection (4)(d) does not apply to functions under Part VI.

Duty to consult

3. Section 8 does not apply.

Rules

4. (1) Sections 149, 153, 154 and 156 do not apply.
(2) Section 155 has effect as if—
 (a) the reference in subsection (2)(c) to the general duties of the Authority under section 2 were a reference to its duty under section 73; and
 (b) section 99 were included in the provisions referred to in subsection (9).

Statements of policy

5. (1) Paragraph 5 of Schedule 1 has effect as if the requirement to act through the Authority's governing body applied also to the exercise of its functions of publishing statements under section 93.

(2) Paragraph 1 of Schedule 1 has effect as if section 93 were included in the provisions referred to in sub-paragraph (2)(d).

Penalties

6. Paragraph 16 of Schedule 1 does not apply in relation to penalties under Part VI (for which separate provision is made by section 100).

Fees

7. Paragraph 17 of Schedule 1 does not apply in relation to fees payable under Part VI (for which separate provision is made by section 99).

Exemption from liability in damages

8. Schedule 1 has effect as if—
   (a)   sub-paragraph (1) of paragraph 19 were omitted (similar provision being made in relation to the competent authority by section 102); and
   (b)   for the words from the beginning to "(a)" in sub-paragraph (3) of that paragraph, there were substituted "Sub-paragraph (2) does not apply".

NOTES

Para 2: words in square brackets in sub-para (a) substituted by the Financial Services and Markets Act 2000 (Market Abuse) Regulations 2005, SI 2005/381, reg 4, Sch 1, para 12, as from 1 July 2005.

SCHEDULE 8
TRANSFER OF FUNCTIONS UNDER PART VI

Section 72(3)

The power to transfer

[7.390]
1. (1)   The Treasury may by order provide for any function conferred on the competent authority which is exercisable for the time being by a particular person to be transferred so as to be exercisable by another person.

(2)   An order may be made under this paragraph only if—
   (a)   the person from whom the relevant functions are to be transferred has agreed in writing that the order should be made;
   (b)   the Treasury are satisfied that the manner in which, or efficiency with which, the functions are discharged would be significantly improved if they were transferred to the transferee; or
   (c)   the Treasury are satisfied that it is otherwise in the public interest that the order should be made.

Supplemental

2. (1)   An order under this Schedule does not affect anything previously done by any person ("the previous authority") in the exercise of functions which are transferred by the order to another person ("the new authority").

(2)   Such an order may, in particular, include provision—
   (a)   modifying or excluding any provision of Part VI, IX or XXVI in its application to any such functions;
   (b)   for reviews similar to that made, in relation to the Authority, by section 12;
   (c)   imposing on the new authority requirements similar to those imposed, in relation to the Authority, by sections 152, 155 and 354;
   (d)   as to the giving of guidance by the new authority;
   (e)   for the delegation by the new authority of the exercise of functions under Part VI and as to the consequences of delegation;
   (f)   for the transfer of any property, rights or liabilities relating to any such functions from the previous authority to the new authority;
   (g)   for the carrying on and completion by the new authority of anything in the process of being done by the previous authority when the order takes effect;
   (h)   for the substitution of the new authority for the previous authority in any instrument, contract or legal proceedings;
   (i)   for the transfer of persons employed by the previous authority to the new authority and as to the terms on which they are to transfer;

(j) making such amendments to any primary or subordinate legislation (including any provision of, or made under, this Act) as the Treasury consider appropriate in consequence of the transfer of functions effected by the order.

(3) Nothing in this paragraph is to be taken as restricting the powers conferred by section 428.

3. If the Treasury have made an order under paragraph 1 ("the transfer order") they may, by a separate order made under this paragraph, make any provision of a kind that could have been included in the transfer order.

<h2 style="text-align:center">SCHEDULE 9</h2>

(Sch 9 repealed by the Prospectus Regulations 2005, SI 2005/1433, reg 2(1), Sch 1, para 16, as from 1 July 2005.)

<h2 style="text-align:center">SCHEDULE 10
COMPENSATION: EXEMPTIONS</h2>

Section 90(2) and (5)

Statements believed to be true

[7.391]
1. (1) In this paragraph "statement" means—
  (a) any untrue or misleading statement in listing particulars; or
  (b) the omission from listing particulars of any matter required to be included by section 80 or 81.

(2) A person does not incur any liability under section 90(1) for loss caused by a statement if he satisfies the court that, at the time when the listing particulars were submitted to the competent authority, he reasonably believed (having made such enquiries, if any, as were reasonable) that—
  (a) the statement was true and not misleading, or
  (b) the matter whose omission caused the loss was properly omitted,
and that one or more of the conditions set out in sub-paragraph (3) are satisfied.

(3) The conditions are that—
  (a) he continued in his belief until the time when the securities in question were acquired;
  (b) they were acquired before it was reasonably practicable to bring a correction to the attention of persons likely to acquire them;
  (c) before the securities were acquired, he had taken all such steps as it was reasonable for him to have taken to secure that a correction was brought to the attention of those persons;
  (d) he continued in his belief until after the commencement of dealings in the securities following their admission to the official list and they were acquired after such a lapse of time that he ought in the circumstances to be reasonably excused.

Statements by experts

2. (1) In this paragraph "statement" means a statement included in listing particulars which—
  (a) purports to be made by, or on the authority of, another person as an expert; and
  (b) is stated to be included in the listing particulars with that other person's consent.

(2) A person does not incur any liability under section 90(1) for loss in respect of any securities caused by a statement if he satisfies the court that, at the time when the listing particulars were submitted to the competent authority, he reasonably believed that the other person—
  (a) was competent to make or authorise the statement, and
  (b) had consented to its inclusion in the form and context in which it was included,
and that one or more of the conditions set out in sub-paragraph (3) are satisfied.

(3) The conditions are that—
  (a) he continued in his belief until the time when the securities were acquired;
  (b) they were acquired before it was reasonably practicable to bring the fact that the expert was not competent, or had not consented, to the attention of persons likely to acquire the securities in question;
  (c) before the securities were acquired he had taken all such steps as it was reasonable for him to have taken to secure that that fact was brought to the attention of those persons;
  (d) he continued in his belief until after the commencement of dealings in the securities following their admission to the official list and they were acquired after such a lapse of time that he ought in the circumstances to be reasonably excused.

Corrections of statements

3. (1) In this paragraph "statement" has the same meaning as in paragraph 1.

(2) A person does not incur liability under section 90(1) for loss caused by a statement if he satisfies the court—
  (a) that before the securities in question were acquired, a correction had been published in a manner calculated to bring it to the attention of persons likely to acquire the securities; or

(b)   that he took all such steps as it was reasonable for him to take to secure such publication and reasonably believed that it had taken place before the securities were acquired.

(3)   Nothing in this paragraph is to be taken as affecting paragraph 1.

Corrections of statements by experts

4. (1)   In this paragraph "statement" has the same meaning as in paragraph 2.

(2)   A person does not incur liability under section 90(1) for loss caused by a statement if he satisfies the court—

(a)   that before the securities in question were acquired, the fact that the expert was not competent or had not consented had been published in a manner calculated to bring it to the attention of persons likely to acquire the securities; or

(b)   that he took all such steps as it was reasonable for him to take to secure such publication and reasonably believed that it had taken place before the securities were acquired.

(3)   Nothing in this paragraph is to be taken as affecting paragraph 2.

Official statements

5. A person does not incur any liability under section 90(1) for loss resulting from—

(a)   a statement made by an official person which is included in the listing particulars, or

(b)   a statement contained in a public official document which is included in the listing particulars,

if he satisfies the court that the statement is accurately and fairly reproduced.

False or misleading information known about

6. A person does not incur any liability under section 90(1) or (4) if he satisfies the court that the person suffering the loss acquired the securities in question with knowledge—

(a)   that the statement was false or misleading,

(b)   of the omitted matter, or

(c)   of the change or new matter,

as the case may be.

Belief that supplementary listing particulars not called for

7. A person does not incur any liability under section 90(4) if he satisfies the court that he reasonably believed that the change or new matter in question was not such as to call for supplementary listing particulars.

Meaning of "expert"

8. "Expert" includes any engineer, valuer, accountant or other person whose profession, qualifications or experience give authority to a statement made by him.

[SCHEDULE 10A
LIABILITY OF ISSUERS IN CONNECTION WITH PUBLISHED INFORMATION
Section 90A

PART 1
SCOPE OF THIS SCHEDULE

Securities to which this Schedule applies

[7.392]

1. (1)   This Schedule applies to securities that are, with the consent of the issuer, admitted to trading on a securities market, where—

(a)   the market is situated or operating in the United Kingdom, or

(b)   the United Kingdom is the issuer's home State.

(2)   For the purposes of this Schedule—

(a)   an issuer of securities is not taken to have consented to the securities being admitted to trading on a securities market by reason only of having consented to their admission to trading on another market as a result of which they are admitted to trading on the first-mentioned market;

(b)   an issuer who has accepted responsibility (to any extent) for any document prepared for the purposes of the admission of the securities to trading on a securities market (such as a prospectus or listing particulars) is taken to have consented to their admission to trading on that market.

(3)   For the purposes of this Schedule the United Kingdom is the home State of an issuer—

(a)   in the case of securities in relation to which the transparency obligations directive applies, if the United Kingdom is the home Member State for the purposes of that directive (see Article 2.1 of the directive);

(b)   in any other case, if the issuer has its registered office (or, if it does not have a registered office, its head office) in the United Kingdom.

Published information to which this Schedule applies

2. (1)   This Schedule applies to information published by the issuer of securities to which this Schedule applies—

   (a)   by recognised means, or

   (b)   by other means where the availability of the information has been announced by the issuer by recognised means.

(2)   It is immaterial whether the information is required to be published (by recognised means or otherwise).

(3)   The following are "recognised means"—

   (a)   a recognised information service;

   (b)   other means required or authorised to be used to communicate information to the market in question, or to the public, when a recognised information service is unavailable.

(4)   A "recognised information service" means—

   (a)   in relation to a securities market situated or operating in the EEA, a service used for the dissemination of information in accordance with Article 21 of the transparency obligations directive;

   (b)   in relation to a securities market situated or operating outside the EEA, a service used for the dissemination of information corresponding to that required to be disclosed under that directive; or

   (c)   in relation to any securities market, any other service used by issuers of securities for the dissemination of information required to be disclosed by the rules of the market.]

NOTES

Commencement: 1 October 2010.

Inserted by the Financial Services and Markets Act 2000 (Liability of Issuers) Regulations 2010, SI 2010/1192, reg 2(1), (3), Schedule, as from 1 October 2010 (for transitional provisions see the note below).

Transitional provisions: the Financial Services and Markets Act 2000 (Liability of Issuers) Regulations 2010, SI 2010/1192, reg 3 provides as follows—

"3   Transitional provision

(1)   The amendments made to the Financial Services and Markets Act 2000 by these Regulations have effect in relation to information first published on or after 1st October 2010.

(2)   Section 90A of that Act, in the form inserted by the Companies Act 2006, continues to apply to information first published before that date.".

Note that para 2 above is actually numbered as para 4 in the Queen's Printer's Copy of these Regulations. It is assumed that this is an error and it has been changed accordingly.

[PART 2
LIABILITY IN CONNECTION WITH PUBLISHED INFORMATION

Liability of issuer for misleading statement or dishonest omission

[7.393]

3. (1)   An issuer of securities to which this Schedule applies is liable to pay compensation to a person who—

   (a)   acquires, continues to hold or disposes of the securities in reliance on published information to which this Schedule applies, and

   (b)   suffers loss in respect of the securities as a result of—

      (i)   any untrue or misleading statement in that published information, or

      (ii)   the omission from that published information of any matter required to be included in it.

(2)   The issuer is liable in respect of an untrue or misleading statement only if a person discharging managerial responsibilities within the issuer knew the statement to be untrue or misleading or was reckless as to whether it was untrue or misleading.

(3)   The issuer is liable in respect of the omission of any matter required to be included in published information only if a person discharging managerial responsibilities within the issuer knew the omission to be a dishonest concealment of a material fact.

(4)   A loss is not regarded as suffered as a result of the statement or omission unless the person suffering it acquired, continued to hold or disposed of the relevant securities—

   (a)   in reliance on the information in question, and

   (b)   at a time when, and in circumstances in which, it was reasonable for him to rely on it.

4. An issuer of securities to which this Schedule applies is not liable under paragraph 3 to pay compensation to a person for loss suffered as a result of an untrue or misleading statement in, or omission from, published information to which this Schedule applies if—

   (a)   the published information is contained in listing particulars or a prospectus (or supplementary listing particulars or a supplementary prospectus), and

   (b)   the issuer is liable under section 90 (compensation for statements in listing particulars or prospectus) to pay compensation to the person in respect of the statement or omission.

Liability of issuer for dishonest delay in publishing information

5. (1)   An issuer of securities to which this Schedule applies is liable to pay compensation to a person who—
  (a)   acquires, continues to hold or disposes of the securities, and
  (b)   suffers loss in respect of the securities as a result of delay by the issuer in publishing information to which this Schedule applies.

(2)   The issuer is liable only if a person discharging managerial responsibilities within the issuer acted dishonestly in delaying the publication of the information.

Meaning of dishonesty

6.   For the purposes of paragraphs 3(3) and 5(2) a person's conduct is regarded as dishonest if (and only if)—
  (a)   it is regarded as dishonest by persons who regularly trade on the securities market in question, and
  (b)   the person was aware (or must be taken to have been aware) that it was so regarded.

Exclusion of certain other liabilities

7. (1)   The issuer is not subject—
  (a)   to any liability other than that provided for by paragraph 3 in respect of loss suffered as a result of reliance by any person on—
    (i)   an untrue or misleading statement in published information to which this Schedule applies, or
    (ii)   the omission from any such published information of any matter required to be included in it;
  (b)   to any liability other than that provided for by paragraph 5 in respect of loss suffered as a result of delay in the publication of information to which this Schedule applies.

(2)   A person other than the issuer is not subject to any liability, other than to the issuer, in respect of any such loss.

(3)   This paragraph does not affect—
  (a)   civil liability—
    (i)   under section 90 (compensation for statements in listing particulars or prospectus),
    (ii)   under rules made by virtue of section 954 of the Companies Act 2006 (compensation),
    (iii)   for breach of contract,
    (iv)   under the Misrepresentation Act 1967, or
    (v)   arising from a person's having assumed responsibility, to a particular person for a particular purpose, for the accuracy or completeness of the information concerned;
  (b)   liability to a civil penalty; or
  (c)   criminal liability.

(4)   This paragraph does not affect the powers conferred by sections 382 and 384 (powers of the court to make a restitution order and of the Authority to require restitution).

(5)   References in this paragraph to liability, in relation to a person, include a reference to another person being entitled as against that person to be granted any civil remedy or to rescind or repudiate an agreement.]

NOTES

Commencement: 1 October 2010.

Inserted, subject to transitional provisions, as noted to Part 1 of this Schedule at **[7.392]**.

[PART 3
SUPPLEMENTARY PROVISIONS

Interpretation

[7.394]
8. (1)   In this Schedule—
  (a)   "securities" means transferable securities within the meaning of Article 4.1.18 of the markets in financial instruments directive, other than money-market instruments as defined in Article 4.1.19 of that directive that have a maturity of less than 12 months (and includes instruments outside the EEA);
  (b)   "securities market" means—
    (i)   a regulated market as defined in Article 4.1.14 of the markets in financial instruments directive,
    (ii)   a multilateral trading facility as defined in Article 4.1.15 of the markets in financial instruments directive, or
    (iii)   a market or facility of a corresponding description outside the EEA.

(2)   References in this Schedule to the issuer of securities are—

(a)   in relation to a depositary receipt, derivative instrument or other financial instrument representing securities where the issuer of the securities represented has consented to the admission of the instrument to trading as mentioned in paragraph 1(1), to the issuer of the securities represented;

(b)   in any other case, to the person who issued the securities.

(3)   References in this Schedule to the acquisition or disposal of securities include—

(a)   acquisition or disposal of any interest in securities, or

(b)   contracting to acquire or dispose of securities or of any interest in securities,

except where what is acquired or disposed of (or contracted to be acquired or disposed of) is a depositary receipt, derivative instrument or other financial instrument representing securities.

(4)   References to continuing to hold securities have a corresponding meaning.

(5)   For the purposes of this Schedule the following are persons "discharging managerial responsibilities" within an issuer—

(a)   any director of the issuer (or person occupying the position of director, by whatever name called);

(b)   in the case of an issuer whose affairs are managed by its members, any member of the issuer;

(c)   in the case of an issuer that has no persons within paragraph (a) or (b), any senior executive of the issuer having responsibilities in relation to the information in question or its publication.

(6)   The following definitions (which apply generally for the purposes of Part 6 of this Act) do not apply for the purposes of this Schedule:

(a)   section 102A(1), (2) and (6) (meaning of "securities" and "issuer");

(b)   section 102C (meaning of "home State" in relation to transferable securities).]

NOTES

Commencement: 1 October 2010.

Inserted, subject to transitional provisions, as noted to Part 1 of this Schedule at **[7.392]**.

[SCHEDULE 11

(Sch 11 repealed by the Prospectus Regulations 2005, SI 2005/1433, reg 2(1), Sch 1, para 16, as from 1 July 2005.)

[SCHEDULE 11A
TRANSFERABLE SECURITIES

Section 85(5)(a)

PART 1

[7.395]

1. Units (within the meaning in section 237(2)) in an open-ended collective investment scheme.

2. Non-equity transferable securities issued by

(a)   the government of an EEA State;

(b)   a local or regional authority of an EEA State;

(c)   a public international body of which an EEA State is a member;

(d)   the European Central Bank;

(e)   the central bank of an EEA State.

3. Shares in the share capital of the central bank of an EEA State.

4. Transferable securities unconditionally and irrevocably guaranteed by the government, or a local or regional authority, of an EEA State.

5. (1)   Non-equity transferable securities, issued in a continuous or repeated manner by a credit institution, which satisfy the conditions in sub-paragraph (2).

(2)   The conditions are that the transferable securities—

(a)   are not subordinated, convertible or exchangeable;

(b)   do not give a right to subscribe to or acquire other types of securities and are not linked to a derivative instrument;

(c)   materialise reception of repayable deposits; and

(d)   are covered by a deposit guarantee under directive 94/19/EC of the European Parliament and of the Council on deposit-guarantee schemes.

6. Non-fungible shares of capital—

(a)   the main purpose of which is to provide the holder with a right to occupy any immoveable property, and

(b)   which cannot be sold without that right being given up.]

NOTES
Inserted by the Prospectus Regulations 2005, SI 2005/1433, reg 2(2), Sch 2, as from 1 July 2005.

[PART 2

[7.396]
7. (1)   Transferable securities issued by a body specified in sub-paragraph (2) if, and only if, the proceeds of the offer of the transferable securities to the public will be used solely for the purposes of the issuer's objectives.

(2)   The bodies are
  (a)   a charity within the meaning of—
    (i)   section 96(1) of the Charities Act 1993 (c 10), or
    (ii)   section 35 of the Charities Act (Northern Ireland) 1964 (c 33 (NI));
  [(b)   a body entered in the Scottish Charity Register;]
  (c)   a housing association within the meaning of—
    (i)   section 5(1) of the Housing Act 1985 (c 68),
    (ii)   section 1 of the Housing Associations Act 1985 (c 69), or
    (iii) Article 3 of the Housing (Northern Ireland) Order 1992 (SI 1992/1725 (NI 15));
  (d)   an industrial and provident society registered in accordance with—
    (i)   section 1(2)(b) of the Industrial and Provident Societies Act 1965 (c 12), or
    (ii)   section 1(2)(b) of the Industrial and Provident Societies Act (Northern Ireland) 1969 (c 24 (NI));
  (e)   a non-profit making association or body recognised by an EEA State with objectives similar to those of a body falling within any of sub-paragraphs (a) to (d).

8. (1)   Non-equity transferable securities, issued in a continuous or repeated manner by a credit institution, which satisfy the conditions in sub-paragraph (2).

(2)   The conditions are—
  (a)   that the total consideration of the offer is less than 50,000,000 euros (or an equivalent amount); and
  (b)   those mentioned in paragraph 5(2)(a) and (b).

(3)   In determining whether sub-paragraph (2)(a) is satisfied in relation to an offer ("offer A"), offer A is to be taken together with any other offer of transferable securities of the same class made by the same person which—
  (a)   was open at any time within the period of 12 months ending with the date on which offer A is first made; and
  (b)   had previously satisfied sub-paragraph (2)(a).

(4)   For the purposes of this paragraph, an amount (in relation to an amount denominated in euros) is an "equivalent amount" if it is an amount of equal value denominated wholly or partly in another currency or unit of account.

(5)   The equivalent is to be calculated at the latest practicable date before (but in any event not more than 3 working days before) the date on which the offer is first made.

(6)   "Credit institution" means a credit institution as defined in [Article [4(1)]] of the banking consolidation directive.

9. (1)   Transferable securities included in an offer where [the total consideration of the offer in the European Union is less than 5,000,000 euros (or an equivalent amount)].

(2)   Sub-paragraphs (3) to (5) of paragraph 8 apply for the purposes of this paragraph but with the references in sub-paragraph (3) to "sub-paragraph (2)(a)" being read as references to "paragraph 9(1)".]

NOTES
Inserted by the Prospectus Regulations 2005, SI 2005/1433, reg 2(2), Sch 2, as from 1 July 2005.
Para 7: sub-para (2)(b) substituted by the Charities and Trustee Investment (Scotland) Act 2005 (Consequential Provisions and Modifications) Order 2006, SI 2006/242, art 5, Schedule, Pt 1, para 7, as from 1 April 2006.
Para 8: words in first (outer) pair of square brackets in sub-para (6) substituted by the Capital Requirements Regulations 2006, SI 2006/3221, reg 29(1), Sch 3, para 3, as from 1 January 2007; number in second (inner) pair of square brackets substituted by the Electronic Money Regulations 2011, SI 2011/99, reg 79, Sch 4, Pt 1, para 2(7), as from 9 February 2011.
Para 9: words in square brackets substituted by the Prospectus Regulations 2011, SI 2011/1668, reg 2(3), as from 31 July 2011.
Industrial and Provident Societies Act 1965: see the Co-operative and Community Benefit Societies and Credit Unions Act 2010 which renames this Act as the Co-operative and Community Benefit Societies and Credit Unions Act 1965.

[SCHEDULE 11B
CONNECTED PERSONS

Section 96B(2)

PART 1
MEANING OF "CONNECTED PERSON"

Introduction

[7.397]
1. (1)   In this Schedule "manager" means a person discharging managerial responsibilities within an issuer.

(2)   This Schedule defines what is meant by references in the provisions of this Part relating to disclosure rules to a person being "connected" with a manager (or a manager being "connected" with a person).

Meaning of "connected person"

2. (1)   The following persons (and only those persons) are connected with a manager—
   (a)   members of the manager's family (see paragraph 3);
   (b)   a body corporate with which the manager is associated (as defined in paragraph 4);
   (c)   a person acting in his capacity as trustee of a trust—
      (i)   the beneficiaries of which include the manager or a person who by virtue of paragraph (a) or (b) is connected with him, or
      (ii)   the terms of which confer a power on the trustees that may be exercised for the benefit of the manager or any such person,
   other than a trust for the purposes of an employees' share scheme or a pension scheme;
   (d)   a person acting in his capacity as partner—
      (i)   of the manager, or
      (ii)   of a person who, by virtue of paragraph (a), (b) or (c), is connected with that manager;
   (e)   a firm that is a legal person under the law by which it is governed and in which—
      (i)   the manager is a partner,
      (ii)   a partner is a person who, by virtue of paragraph (a), (b) or (c) is connected with the manager, or
      (iii)   a partner is a firm in which the manager is a partner or in which there is a partner who, by virtue of paragraph (a), (b) or (c), is connected with the director.

(2)   References to a person connected with a manager do not include a person who is also a manager of the issuer in question.

Family members

3. (1)   This paragraph defines what is meant by references to members of a manager's family.

(2)   The members of a manager's family are—
   (a)   the manager's spouse or civil partner;
   (b)   any relative of the manager who, on the date of the transaction in question, has shared the same household as the manager for at least 12 months;
   (c)   the manager's children or step-children under the age of 18.

Associated bodies corporate

4. (1)   This paragraph defines what is meant by a manager being "associated" with a body corporate.

(2)   A manager is associated with a body corporate if, but only if—
   (a)   the manager, or a person connected with the manager, is a director or senior executive who has the power to make management decisions affecting the future development and business prospects of the body corporate; or
   (b)   the manager and the persons connected with the manager together—
      (i)   are interested in shares comprised in the equity share capital of that body corporate of a nominal value equal to at least 20% of that share capital, or
      (ii)   are entitled to exercise or control the exercise of more than 20% of the voting power at any general meeting of that body.

(3)   The rules set out in Part 2 of this Schedule (references to interest in shares or debentures) apply for the purposes of this paragraph.

(4)   References in this paragraph to voting power the exercise of which is controlled by a manager include voting power whose exercise is controlled by a body corporate controlled by the manager.

(5)   Shares in a company held as treasury shares, and any voting rights attached to such shares, are disregarded for the purposes of this paragraph.

Control of a body corporate

5. (1)   This paragraph defines what is meant by a manager "controlling" a body corporate.

(2)   A manager is taken to control a body corporate if, but only if—
- (a)   the manager or a person connected with the manager—
    - (i)   is interested in any part of the equity share capital of that body, or
    - (ii)   is entitled to exercise or control the exercise of any part of the voting power at any general meeting of that body, and
- (b)   the manager, the persons connected with the manager and the other managers of the issuer in question, together—
    - (i)   are interested in more than 50% of that share capital, or
    - (ii)   are entitled to exercise or control the exercise of more than 50% of that voting power.

(3)   The rules set out in Part 2 of this Schedule (references to interest in shares or debentures) apply for the purposes of this paragraph.

(4)   References in this paragraph to voting power the exercise of which is controlled by a manager include voting power whose exercise is controlled by a body corporate controlled by the manager.

(5)   Shares in a company held as treasury shares, and any voting rights attached to such shares, are disregarded for the purposes of this paragraph.

Supplementary provisions

6. For the purposes of paragraphs 4 and 5 (associated bodies corporate and control of a body corporate)—
- (a)   a body corporate with which a manager is associated is not treated as connected with that manager unless it is also connected with that manager by virtue of sub-paragraph (1)(c) or (d) of that paragraph (connection as trustee or partner); and
- (b)   a trustee of a trust the beneficiaries of which include (or may include) a body corporate with which a manager is associated is not treated as connected with a manager by reason only of that fact.]

NOTES

Commencement: 1 October 2009.

Inserted by the Financial Services and Markets Act 2000 (Amendment) Regulations 2009, SI 2009/2461, reg 2(2), Schedule, as from 1 October 2009.

[PART 2
CONNECTED PERSONS: REFERENCES TO AN INTEREST IN SHARES
OR DEBENTURES

Introduction

[7.398]
7. (1)   The provisions of this Part of this Schedule have effect for the interpretation of references in paragraphs 4 and 5 (associated bodies corporate and control of a body corporate) to an interest in shares or debentures.

(2)   The provisions are expressed in relation to shares but apply to debentures as they apply to shares.

General provisions

8. (1)   A reference to an interest in shares includes any interest of any kind whatsoever in shares.

(2)   Any restraints or restrictions to which the exercise of any right attached to the interest is or may be subject shall be disregarded.

(3)   It is immaterial that the shares in which a person has an interest are not identifiable.

(4)   Persons having a joint interest in shares are deemed each of them to have that interest.

Rights to acquire shares

9. (1)   A person who enters into a contract to acquire shares is taken to have an interest in the shares.

(2)   A person who—
- (a)   has a right to call for delivery of shares to the person or to the person's order, or
- (b)   has a right to acquire an interest in shares or is under an obligation to take an interest in shares,

is taken to have an interest in the shares, whether the right or obligation is conditional or absolute.

(3)   Rights or obligations to subscribe for shares are not to be taken for the purposes of sub-paragraph (2) to be rights to acquire or obligations to take an interest in shares.

(4)   A person ("A") ceases to have an interest in shares by virtue of this paragraph—
- (a)   on the shares being delivered to another person at A's order—
    - (i)   in fulfilment of a contract for their acquisition by A, or

    (ii)   in satisfaction of a right of A's to call for their delivery;

(b)   on a failure to deliver the shares in accordance with the terms of such a contract or on which such a right falls to be satisfied;

(c)   on the lapse of A's right to call for the delivery of shares.

Right to exercise or control exercise of rights

10. (1)   A person who, not being the registered holder, is entitled—

(a)   to exercise any right conferred by the holding of the shares, or

(b)   to control the exercise of any such right.

is taken to have an interest in the shares.

(2)   For this purpose a person is taken to be entitled to exercise or control the exercise of a right conferred by the holding of shares who—

(a)   has a right (whether subject to conditions or not) the exercise of which would make the person so entitled, or

(b)   is under an obligation (whether or not so subject) the fulfilment of which would make the person so entitled.

(3)   A person who—

(a)   has been appointed a proxy to exercise any of the rights attached to the shares, or

(b)   has been appointed by a body corporate to act as its representative at any meeting of a company or of any class of its members,

is not, by reason only of that fact, to be taken by virtue of this paragraph to be interested in the shares.

Bodies corporate

11. (1)   A person is taken to be interested in shares if a body corporate is interested in them and—

(a)   the body corporate or its directors are accustomed to act in accordance with the person's directions or instructions, or

(b)   the person is entitled to exercise or control the exercise of more than one-half of the voting power at general meetings of the body corporate.

(2)   For the purposes of sub-paragraph (1)(b) where—

(a)   a person is entitled to exercise or control the exercise of more than one-half of the voting power at general meetings of a body corporate, and

(b)   that body corporate is entitled to exercise or control the exercise of any of the voting power at general meetings of another body corporate,

the voting power mentioned in paragraph (b) above is taken to be exercisable by that person.

Trusts

12. (1)   Where an interest in shares is comprised in property held on trust, every beneficiary of the trust is taken to have an interest in shares, subject as follows.

(2)   So long as a person is entitled to receive, during the lifetime of that person or another, income from trust property comprising shares, an interest in the shares in reversion or remainder or (as regards Scotland) in fee shall be disregarded.

(3)   A person is treated as not interested in shares if and so long as the person holds them—

(a)   under the law in force in any part of the United Kingdom, as a bare trustee or as a custodian trustee, or

(b)   under the law in force in Scotland, as a simple trustee.

(4)   There shall be disregarded any interest of a person subsisting by virtue of—

(a)   an authorised unit trust scheme (within the meaning of section 237 (other definitions));

(b)   a scheme made under section 22 or 22A of the Charities Act 1960 (c 58), section 25 of the Charities Act (Northern Ireland) 1964 (c 33 (NI)) or section 24 or 25 of the Charities Act 1993 (c 10), section 11 of the Trustee Investments Act 1961 (c 62) or section 42 of the Administration of Justice Act 1982 (c 53); or

(c)   the scheme set out in the Schedule to the Church Funds Investment Measure 1958 (1958 No 1).

(5)   There shall be disregarded any interest—

(a)   of the Church of Scotland General Trustees or of the Church of Scotland Trust in shares held by them;

(b)   of any other person in shares held by those Trustees or that Trust otherwise than as simple trustees.

"The Church of Scotland General Trustees" are the body incorporated by the order confirmed by the Church of Scotland (General Trustees) Order Confirmation Act 1921 (1921 c xxv), and "the Church of Scotland Trust" is the body incorporated by the order confirmed by the Church of Scotland Trust Order Confirmation Act 1932 (1932 c xxi).]

NOTES

Commencement: 1 October 2009.

Inserted by the Financial Services and Markets Act 2000 (Amendment) Regulations 2009, SI 2009/2461, reg 2(2), Schedule, as from 1 October 2009.

Note: this Part as originally enacted contained paragraphs 6 to 11. This error was corrected by a correction slip issued in October 2010.

SCHEDULE 12
TRANSFER SCHEMES: CERTIFICATES
Sections 111(2) and 115

PART I
INSURANCE BUSINESS TRANSFER SCHEMES

[7.399]

1. (1)   For the purposes of section 111(2) the appropriate certificates, in relation to an insurance business transfer scheme, are—

(a)   a certificate under paragraph 2;

(b)   if sub-paragraph (2) applies, a certificate under paragraph 3;

(c)   if sub-paragraph (3) applies, a certificate under paragraph 4;

(d)   if sub-paragraph (4) applies, a certificate under paragraph 5;

[(e)   if sub-paragraph (5) applies, the certificates under paragraph 5A].

(2)   This sub-paragraph applies if—

(a)   the authorised person concerned is a UK authorised person which has received authorisation under [Article 4 of the life assurance consolidation directive or Article 6] of the first non-life insurance directive from the Authority; and

(b)   the establishment from which the business is to be transferred under the proposed insurance business transfer scheme is in an EEA State other than the United Kingdom.

(3)   This sub-paragraph applies if—

(a)   the authorised person concerned has received authorisation under [Article 4 [or Article 51] of the life assurance consolidation directive] from the Authority;

(b)   the proposed transfer relates to business which consists of the effecting or carrying out of contracts of long-term insurance; and

(c)   as regards any policy which is included in the proposed transfer and which evidences a contract of insurance (other than reinsurance), an EEA State other than the United Kingdom is the State of the commitment.

(4)   This sub-paragraph applies if—

(a)   the authorised person concerned has received authorisation under Article 6 [or Article 23] of the first non-life insurance directive from the Authority;

(b)   the business to which the proposed insurance business transfer scheme relates is business which consists of the effecting or carrying out of contracts of general insurance; and

(c)   as regards any policy which is included in the proposed transfer and which evidences a contract of insurance (other than reinsurance), the risk is situated in an EEA State other than the United Kingdom.

[(5)   This sub-paragraph applies if—

(a)   the authorised person concerned has received authorisation under Article 23 of the first non-life insurance directive or Article 51 of the life assurance consolidation directive from the Authority; and

(b)   the proposed transfer is to a branch or agency, in an EEA State other than the United Kingdom, authorised under the same Article.]

Certificates as to margin of solvency

2. (1)   A certificate under this paragraph is to be given—

(a)   by the relevant authority; or

(b)   in a case in which there is no relevant authority, by the Authority.

(2)   A certificate given under sub-paragraph (1)(a) is one certifying that, taking the proposed transfer into account—

(a)   the transferee possesses, or will possess before the scheme takes effect, the necessary margin of solvency; or

(b)   there is no necessary margin of solvency applicable to the transferee.

(3)   A certificate under sub-paragraph (1)(b) is one certifying that the Authority has received from the authority which it considers to be the authority responsible for supervising persons who effect or carry out contracts of insurance in the place to which the business is to be transferred that, taking the proposed transfer into account—

(a)   the transferee possesses or will possess before the scheme takes effect the margin of solvency required under the law applicable in that place; or

(b)   there is no such margin of solvency applicable to the transferee.

Part 7 · FSMA 2000

(4) "Necessary margin of solvency" means the margin of solvency required in relation to the transferee, taking the proposed transfer into account, under the law which it is the responsibility of the relevant authority to apply.

(5) "Margin of solvency" means the excess of the value of the assets of the transferee over the amount of its liabilities.

(6) "Relevant authority" means—
    (a)   if the transferee is an EEA firm falling within paragraph 5(d) [or (da)] of Schedule 3, its home state regulator;
   [(aa) if the transferee is a non-EEA branch, the competent authorities of the EEA State in which the transferee is situated or, where appropriate, the competent authorities of an EEA State which supervises the state of solvency of the entire business of the transferee's agencies and branches within the EEA in accordance with Article 26 of the first non-life insurance directive or Article 56 of the life assurance consolidation directive;]
    (b)   if the transferee is a Swiss general insurer, the authority responsible in Switzerland for supervising persons who effect or carry out contracts of insurance;
    (c)   if the transferee is an authorised person not falling within [paragraph (a), (aa)] or (b), the Authority.

(7) In sub-paragraph (6), any reference to a transferee of a particular description includes a reference to a transferee who will be of that description if the proposed scheme takes effect.

[(7A) "Competent authorities" has the same meaning as in the insurance directives.]

(8) "Swiss general insurer" means a body—
    (a)   whose head office is in Switzerland;
    (b)   which has permission to carry on regulated activities consisting of the effecting and carrying out of contracts of general insurance; and
    (c)   whose permission is not restricted to the effecting or carrying out of contracts of reinsurance.

[(9) "Non-EEA branch" means a branch or agency which has received authorisation under Article 23 of the first non-life insurance directive or Article 51 of the life assurance consolidation directive.]

Certificates as to consent

3. A certificate under this paragraph is one given by the Authority and certifying that the host State regulator has been notified of the proposed scheme and that—
    (a)   that regulator has responded to the notification; or
    (b)   that it has not responded but the period of three months beginning with the notification has elapsed.

Certificates as to long-term business

4. A certificate under this paragraph is one given by the Authority and certifying that the authority responsible for supervising persons who effect or carry out contracts of insurance in the State of the commitment has been notified of the proposed scheme and that—
    (a)   that authority has consented to the proposed scheme; or
    (b)   the period of three months beginning with the notification has elapsed and that authority has not refused its consent.

Certificates as to general business

5. A certificate under this paragraph is one given by the Authority and certifying that the authority responsible for supervising persons who effect or carry out contracts of insurance in the EEA State in which the risk is situated has been notified of the proposed scheme and that—
    (a)   that authority has consented to the proposed scheme; or
    (b)   the period of three months beginning with the notification has elapsed and that authority has not refused its consent.

[Certificates as to legality and as to consent

5A. (1) The certificates under this paragraph are to be given—
    (a)   in the case of the certificate under sub-paragraph (2), by the Authority;
    (b)   in the case of the certificate under sub-paragraph (3), by the relevant authority.

(2) A certificate given under this sub-paragraph is one certifying that the relevant authority has been notified of the proposed scheme and that—
    (a)   the relevant authority has consented to the proposed scheme; or
    (b)   the period of three months beginning with the notification has elapsed and that relevant authority has not refused its consent.

(3) A certificate given under this sub-paragraph is one certifying that the law of the EEA State in which the transferee is set up permits such a transfer.

(4) "Relevant authority" means the competent authorities (within the meaning of the insurance directives) of the EEA State in which the transferee is set up.]

Interpretation of Part I

6. (1)   "State of the commitment", in relation to a commitment entered into at any date, means—

(a)   if the policyholder is an individual, the State in which he had his habitual residence at that date;

(b)   if the policyholder is not an individual, the State in which the establishment of the policyholder to which the commitment relates was situated at that date.

(2)   "Commitment" means a commitment represented by contracts of insurance of a prescribed class.

(3)   References to the EEA State in which a risk is situated are—

(a)   if the insurance relates to a building or to a building and its contents (so far as the contents are covered by the same policy), to the EEA State in which the building is situated;

(b)   if the insurance relates to a vehicle of any type, to the EEA State of registration;

(c)   in the case of policies of a duration of four months or less covering travel or holiday risks (whatever the class concerned), to the EEA State in which the policyholder took out the policy;

(d)   in a case not covered by paragraphs (a) to (c)—

(i)   if the policyholder is an individual, to the EEA State in which he has his habitual residence at the date when the contract is entered into; and

(ii)   otherwise, to the EEA State in which the establishment of the policyholder to which the policy relates is situated at that date.

[(4)   If the insurance relates to a vehicle dispatched from one EEA State to another, in respect of the period of 30 days beginning with the day on which the purchaser accepts delivery a reference to the EEA State in which a risk is situated is a reference to the State of destination (and not, as provided by sub-paragraph (3)(b), to the State of registration).]

NOTES

Para 1: sub-para (1)(e), words in second (inner) pair of square brackets in sub-para (3)(a), words in square brackets in sub-para (4)(a), and sub-para (5) inserted by the Reinsurance Directive Regulations 2007, SI 2007/3253, reg 2(1), Sch 1, paras 1, 2(5)(a)–(d), as from 10 December 2007; words in square brackets in sub-para (2)(a) and words in first (outer) pair of square brackets in sub-para (3)(a) substituted by the Life Assurance Consolidation Directive (Consequential Amendments) Regulations 2004, SI 2004/3379, reg 6(1), (7)(a), as from 11 January 2005.

Para 2: words in square brackets in sub-para (6)(a), sub-para (6)(aa), and sub-paras (7A), (9) inserted, and words in square brackets in sub-para (6)(c) substituted, by SI 2007/3253, reg 2(1), Sch 1, paras 1, 2(5)(e), as from 10 December 2007.

Para 5A: inserted by SI 2007/3253, reg 2(1), Sch 1, paras 1, 2(5)(f), as from 10 December 2007.

Para 6: sub-para (4) added by the Financial Services and Markets Act 2000 (Motor Insurance) Regulations 2007, SI 2007/2403, reg 2, as from 5 September 2007.

Regulations: the Financial Services and Markets Act 2000 (Control of Business Transfers) (Requirements on Applicants) Regulations 2001, SI 2001/3625.

PART II
BANKING BUSINESS TRANSFER SCHEMES

[7.400]

7. (1)   For the purposes of section 111(2) the appropriate certificates, in relation to a banking business transfer scheme, are—

(a)   a certificate under paragraph 8; and

(b)   if sub-paragraph (2) applies, a certificate under paragraph 9.

(2)   This sub-paragraph applies if the authorised person concerned or the transferee is an EEA firm falling within paragraph 5(b) of Schedule 3.

Certificates as to financial resources

8. (1)   A certificate under this paragraph is one given by the relevant authority and certifying that, taking the proposed transfer into account, the transferee possesses, or will possess before the scheme takes effect, adequate financial resources.

(2)   "Relevant authority" means—

(a)   if the transferee is a person with a Part IV permission or with permission under Schedule 4, the Authority;

(b)   if the transferee is an EEA firm falling within paragraph 5(b) of Schedule 3, its home state regulator;

(c)   if the transferee does not fall within paragraph (a) or (b), the authority responsible for the supervision of the transferee's business in the place in which the transferee has its head office.

(3)   In sub-paragraph (2), any reference to a transferee of a particular description of person includes a reference to a transferee who will be of that description if the proposed banking business transfer scheme takes effect.

Certificates as to consent of home state regulator

9. A certificate under this paragraph is one given by the Authority and certifying that the home State regulator of the authorised person concerned or of the transferee has been notified of the proposed scheme and that—

(a) the home State regulator has responded to the notification; or

(b) the period of three months beginning with the notification has elapsed.

[PART 2A
RECLAIM FUND BUSINESS TRANSFER SCHEMES

Certificate as to financial resources

[7.401]

9A. For the purposes of section 111(2) the appropriate certificate, in relation to a reclaim fund business transfer scheme, is a certificate given by the Authority certifying that, taking the proposed transfer into account, the transferee possesses, or will possess before the scheme takes effect, adequate financial resources.]

NOTES

Commencement: 12 March 2009.

Inserted by the Dormant Bank and Building Society Accounts Act 2008, s 15, Sch 2, para 5, as from 12 March 2009.

PART III
INSURANCE BUSINESS TRANSFERS EFFECTED OUTSIDE THE UNITED KINGDOM

[7.402]

10. (1) This paragraph applies to a proposal to execute under provisions corresponding to Part VII in a country or territory other than the United Kingdom an instrument transferring all the rights and obligations of the transferor under general or long-term insurance policies, or under such descriptions of such policies as may be specified in the instrument, to the transferee if any of the conditions in sub-paragraphs (2), (3) or (4) is met in relation to it.

(2) The transferor is an EEA firm falling within paragraph 5(d) [or (da)] of Schedule 3 and the transferee is an authorised person whose margin of solvency is supervised by the Authority.

(3) The transferor is a company authorised in an EEA State other than the United Kingdom under [Article 51 of the life assurance consolidation directive], or Article 23 of the first non-life insurance directive and the transferee is a UK authorised person which has received authorisation under [Article 4 of the life assurance consolidation directive or Article 6 of the first non-life insurance directive].

(4) The transferor is a Swiss general insurer and the transferee is a UK authorised person which has received authorisation under [Article 4 of the life assurance consolidation directive or Article 6 of the first non-life insurance directive].

(5) In relation to a proposed transfer to which this paragraph applies, the Authority may, if it is satisfied that the transferee possesses the necessary margin of solvency, issue a certificate to that effect.

(6) "Necessary margin of solvency" means the margin of solvency which the transferee, taking the proposed transfer into account, is required by the Authority to maintain.

(7) "Swiss general insurer" has the same meaning as in paragraph 2.

(8) "General policy" means a policy evidencing a contract which, if it had been effected by the transferee, would have constituted the carrying on of a regulated activity consisting of the effecting of contracts of general insurance.

(9) "Long-term policy" means a policy evidencing a contract which, if it had been effected by the transferee, would have constituted the carrying on of a regulated activity consisting of the effecting of contracts of long-term insurance.

NOTES

Para 10: words in square brackets in sub-para (2) inserted by the Reinsurance Directive Regulations 2007, SI 2007/3253, reg 2(1), Sch 1, paras 1, 2(5)(g), as from 10 December 2007; other words in square brackets substituted by the Life Assurance Consolidation Directive (Consequential Amendments) Regulations 2004, SI 2004/3379, reg 6(1), (7)(b), (c), as from 11 January 2005.

SCHEDULES 13–22

(Schs 13–18, 20–22 omitted for reasons of space (see further, the introductory notes to this Act); Sch 19 repealed by the Enterprise Act 2002, ss 247(k), 278(2), Sch 26, as from 23 June 2003.)

PART 8
FINANCIAL SERVICES AND MARKETS ACT 2000: STATUTORY INSTRUMENTS

FINANCIAL SERVICES AND MARKETS ACT 2000 (REGULATED ACTIVITIES) ORDER 2001

(SI 2001/544)

NOTES

Made: 26 February 2001.

Authority: Financial Services and Markets Act 2000, ss 22(1), (5), 426, 428(3), Sch 2, para 25.

Commencement: 1 December 2001 (being the date on which the Financial Services and Markets Act 2000, s 19 came into force) and subject as follows; 1 January 2002 (arts 59, 60, 87); 31 October 2004 (arts 61–63, 88, 90, 91).

This Order is reproduced as amended by the following SIs:

2001	Financial Services and Markets Act 2000 (Regulated Activities) (Amendment) Order 2001, SI 2001/3544.
2002	Financial Services and Markets Act 2000 (Regulated Activities) (Amendment) Order 2002, SI 2002/682; Financial Services and Markets Act 2000 (Financial Promotion and Miscellaneous Amendments) Order 2002, SI 2002/1310; Financial Services and Markets Act 2000 (Regulated Activities) (Amendment) (No 2) Order 2002, SI 2002/1776; Financial Services and Markets Act 2000 (Commencement of Mortgage Regulation) (Amendment) Order 2002, SI 2002/1777.
2003	Financial Services and Markets Act 2000 (Regulated Activities) (Amendment) (No 1) Order 2003, SI 2003/1475; Financial Services and Markets Act 2000 (Regulated Activities) (Amendment) (No 2) Order 2003, SI 2003/1476; Financial Services and Markets Act 2000 (Regulated Activities) (Amendment) (No 3) Order 2003, SI 2003/2822.
2004	Financial Services and Markets Act 2000 (Regulated Activities) (Amendment) Order 2004, SI 2004/1610; Financial Services and Markets Act 2000 (Regulated Activities) (Amendment) (No 2) Order 2004, SI 2004/2737; Life Assurance Consolidation Directive (Consequential Amendments) Regulations 2004, SI 2004/3379.
2005	Financial Services and Markets Act 2000 (Regulated Activities) (Amendment) Order 2005, SI 2005/593; Financial Services and Markets Act 2000 (Regulated Activities) (Amendment) (No 2) Order 2005, SI 2005/1518; Civil Partnership Act 2004 (Amendments to Subordinate Legislation) Order 2005, SI 2005/2114.
2006	Financial Services and Markets Act 2000 (Regulated Activities) (Amendment) Order 2006, SI 2006/1969; Financial Services and Markets Act 2000 (Regulated Activities) (Amendment) (No 2) Order 2006, SI 2006/2383; Capital Requirements Regulations 2006, SI 2006/3221; Financial Services and Markets Act 2000 (Regulated Activities) (Amendment No 3) Order 2006, SI 2006/3384.
2007	Companies Act 2006 (Commencement No 2, Consequential Amendments, Transitional Provisions and Savings) Order 2007, SI 2007/1093; Financial Services and Markets Act 2000 (Regulated Activities) (Amendment) Order 2007, SI 2007/1339; Money Laundering Regulations 2007, SI 2007/2157; Financial Services and Markets Act 2000 (Reinsurance Directive) Order 2007, SI 2007/3254; Financial Services and Markets Act 2000 (Regulated Activities) (Amendment) (No 2) Order 2007, SI 2007/3510.
2008	Companies Act 2006 (Consequential Amendments etc) Order 2008, SI 2008/948.
2009	Payment Services Regulations 2009, SI 2009/209; Solicitors' Recognised Bodies (Amendment) Order 2009, SI 2009/500; Financial Services and Markets Act 2000 (Regulated Activities) (Amendment) Order 2009, SI 2009/1342; Financial Services and Markets Act 2000 (Regulated Activities) (Amendment) (No 2) Order 2009, SI 2009/1389.
2010	Financial Services and Markets Act 2000 (Regulated Activities) (Amendment) Order 2010, SI 2010/86; Timeshare, Holiday Products, Resale and Exchange Contracts Regulations 2010, SI 2010/2960.
2011	Electronic Money Regulations 2011, SI 2011/99; Financial Services and Markets Act 2000 (Regulated Activities) (Amendment) Order 2011, SI 2011/133; Companies Act 2006 (Consequential Amendments and Transitional Provisions) Order 2011, SI 2011/1265; Undertakings for Collective Investment in Transferable Securities Regulations 2011, SI 2011/1613.

References to the "European Community", "Community", etc: see the Treaty of Lisbon (Changes in Terminology) Order 2011, SI 2011/1043, which provides (with effect from 22 April 2011): (1) that for references to the "European Communities" or to the "European Community" (including references to "the Communities", "the Community", "the EC" or "the EEC") substitute references to the European Union; and (2) that "EU" should be substituted for the word "Community" (subject to certain exceptions) in references to "Community treaties", "Community customs duty", "Community institution", "Community instrument", "Community obligation", "enforceable Community right", "Community law", "Community legislation", and "Community provision". Also, where such a term is preceded by the word "a", for "a" substitute "an".

Transitional provisions (interim permissions and interim approvals): for transitional provisions relating to interim permissions and interim approvals and the application of Parts IV, V of FSMA 2000 (and various other provisions of that Act) to various activities that have become regulated activities following the amendment of this Order, see the table below:

Order	Regulated Activity
Financial Services and Markets Act 2000 (Transitional Provisions) (Mortgages) Order 2004, SI 2004/2615	Certain mortgage mediation activities
Financial Services and Markets Act 2000 (Regulated Activities) (Amendment) (No 2) Order 2004, SI 2004/2737	Advice on stakeholder products
Financial Services and Markets Act 2000 (Transitional Provisions) (General Insurance Intermediaries) Order 2004, SI 2004/3351	Certain general insurance mediation activities

Order	Regulated Activity
Financial Services and Markets Act 2000 (Regulated Activities) (Amendment) Order 2006, SI 2006/1969	Establishing, operating or winding up a personal pension scheme, or activities which relate to the specified investment of rights under a personal pension scheme
Financial Services and Markets Act 2000 (Regulated Activities) (Amendment) (No 2) Order 2006, SI 2006/2383	Administering, arranging or advising on regulated home reversion plans or regulated home purchase plans
Financial Services and Markets Act 2000 (Regulated Activities) (Amendment) (No 2) Order 2007, SI 2007/3510	Provision of travel insurance in certain circumstances
Financial Services and Markets Act 2000 (Regulated Activities) (Amendment) Order 2009, SI 2009/1342	Entering into, administering, arranging and advising on regulated sale and rent back agreements

ARRANGEMENT OF ARTICLES

PART I
GENERAL

PART II
SPECIFIED ACTIVITIES

CHAPTER I
GENERAL

CHAPTER II
ACCEPTING DEPOSITS

The activity

Exclusions

CHAPTER IIA
ELECTRONIC MONEY

The activity

Exclusions

Supplemental

CHAPTER III
INSURANCE

The activities

Exclusions

CHAPTER IV
DEALING IN INVESTMENTS AS PRINCIPAL

The activity

Exclusions

CHAPTER V
DEALING IN INVESTMENTS AS AGENT

The activity

Exclusions

CHAPTER VI
ARRANGING DEALS IN INVESTMENTS

The activities

Exclusions

CHAPTER VII
MANAGING INVESTMENTS

The activity

Exclusions

PART I
GENERAL

[8.1]
1 Citation

This Order may be cited as the Financial Services and Markets Act 2000 (Regulated Activities) Order 2001.

[8.2]
2 Commencement

(1)   Except as provided by paragraph (2), this Order comes into force on the day on which section 19 of the Act comes into force.

(2)   This Order comes into force—
   (a)   for the purposes of articles 59, 60 and 87 (funeral plan contracts) on 1st January 2002; and
   (b)   for the purposes of articles 61 to 63, 88, 90 and 91 (regulated mortgage contracts) [on such a day as the Treasury may specify].

[(3)   Any day specified under paragraph 2(b) must be caused to be notified in the London, Edinburgh and Belfast Gazettes published not later than one week before that day.]

NOTES

  Para (2): words in square brackets in sub-para (b) substituted by the Financial Services and Markets Act 2000 (Commencement of Mortgage Regulation) (Amendment) Order 2002, SI 2002/1777, art 2(1), (2), as from 30 August 2002.

  Para (3): added by SI 2002/1777, art 2(1), (3), as from 30 August 2002.

  FSMA 2000, s 19 came into force on 1 December 2001 (see the Financial Services and Markets Act 2000 (Commencement No 7) Order 2001, SI 2001/3538).

  On such a day as the Treasury may specify: 31 October 2004 (see the London Gazette, 14 July 2003).

[8.3]
3 Interpretation

(1)   In this Order—
   "the Act" means the Financial Services and Markets Act 2000;
   ["agreement provider" has the meaning given by article 63J(3);
   "agreement seller" has the meaning given by article 63J(3);]
   "annuities on human life" does not include superannuation allowances and annuities payable out of any fund applicable solely to the relief and maintenance of persons engaged, or who have been engaged, in any particular profession, trade or employment, or of the dependants of such persons;
   "buying" includes acquiring for valuable consideration;
   "close relative" in relation to a person means—
      (a)   his spouse [or civil partner];
      (b)   his children and step children, his parents and step-parents, his brothers and sisters and his step-brothers and step-sisters; and
      (c)   the spouse [or civil partner] of any person within sub-paragraph (b);
   ["the Commission Regulation" means Commission Regulation 1287/2006 of 10 August 2006;]
   "contract of general insurance" means any contract falling within Part I of Schedule 1;
   "contract of insurance" means any contract of insurance which is a contract of long-term insurance or a contract of general insurance, and includes—
      (a)   fidelity bonds, performance bonds, administration bonds, bail bonds, customs bonds or similar contracts of guarantee, where these are—
         (i)   effected or carried out by a person not carrying on a banking business;
         (ii)   not effected merely incidentally to some other business carried on by the person effecting them; and
         (iii)   effected in return for the payment of one or more premiums;
      (b)   tontines;
      (c)   capital redemption contracts or pension fund management contracts, where these are effected or carried out by a person who—
         (i)   does not carry on a banking business; and
         (ii)   otherwise carries on a regulated activity of the kind specified by article 10(1) or (2);
      (d)   contracts to pay annuities on human life;
      (e)   contracts of a kind referred to in article 1(2)(e) of the first life insurance directive (collective insurance etc); and
      (f)   contracts of a kind referred to in article 1(3) of the first life insurance directive (social insurance);

but does not include a funeral plan contract (or a contract which would be a funeral plan contract but for the exclusion in article 60);

"contract of long-term insurance" means any contract falling within Part II of Schedule 1;

"contractually based investment" means—

    (a)   rights under a qualifying contract of insurance;

    (b)   any investment of the kind specified by any of articles 83, 84, 85 and 87; or

    (c)   any investment of the kind specified by article 89 so far as relevant to an investment falling within (a) or (b);

["credit institution" means—

    (a)   a credit institution authorised under the banking consolidation directive [(as last amended by Directive 2009/111/EC)] other than an institution to which Article 2.1 of the markets in financial instruments directive (the text of which is set out in Schedule 3) applies, or

    (b)   an institution which would satisfy the requirements for authorisation as a credit institution under that directive (other than an institution to which Article 2.1 of the markets in financial instruments directive would apply) if it had its registered office (or if it does not have a registered office, its head office) in an EEA State;]

"deposit" has the meaning given by article 5;

["electronic money" has the meaning given by regulation 2(1) of the Electronic Money Regulations 2011;]

["financial instrument" means any instrument listed in Section C of Annex I to the markets in financial instruments directive (the text of which is set out in Part 1 of Schedule 2) read with Chapter VI of the Commission Regulation (the text of which is set out in Part 2 of Schedule 2);]

"funeral plan contract" has the meaning given by article 59;

["home Member State", in relation to an investment firm, has the meaning given by Article 4.1.20 of the markets in financial instruments directive, and in relation to a credit institution, has the meaning given by Article 4.7 of the banking consolidation directive;]

["home purchase provider" has the meaning given by article 63F(3);

"home purchaser" has the meaning given by article 63F(3);]

"instrument" includes any record whether or not in the form of a document;

["investment firm" means a person whose regular occupation or business is the provision or performance of investment services and activities on a professional basis but does not include—

    (a)   a person to whom the markets in financial instruments directive does not apply by virtue of Article 2 of that directive (the text of which is set out in Schedule 3);

    (b)   a person whose home Member State is an EEA State other than the United Kingdom and to whom, by reason of the fact that the State has given effect to Article 3 of that directive, that directive does not apply by virtue of that Article;

    (c)   a person who does not have a home Member State and to whom (if he had his registered office in an EEA State, or, being a person other than a body corporate or a body corporate not having a registered office, if he had his head office in an EEA State) the markets in financial instruments directive would not apply by virtue of Article 2 of that directive;]

["investment services and activities" means—

    (a)   any service provided to third parties listed in Section A of Annex I to the markets in financial instruments directive (the text of which is set out in Part 3 of Schedule 2) read with Article 52 of Commission Directive 2006/73/EC of 10 August 2006 (the text of which is set out in Part 4 of Schedule 2), or

    (b)   any activity listed in Section A of Annex I to that directive,

    relating to any financial instrument;]

"joint enterprise" means an enterprise into which two or more persons ("the participators") enter for commercial purposes related to a business or businesses (other than the business of engaging in a regulated activity) carried on by them; and, where a participator is a member of a group, each other member of the group is also to be regarded as a participator in the enterprise;

"local authority" means—

    (a)   in England and Wales, a local authority within the meaning of the Local Government Act 1972, the Greater London Authority, the Common Council of the City of London or the Council of the Isles of Scilly;

    (b)   in Scotland, a local authority within the meaning of the Local Government (Scotland) Act 1973;

    (c)   in Northern Ireland, a district council within the meaning of the Local Government Act (Northern Ireland) 1972;

["management company" has the meaning given by Article 2.1(b) of the UCITS directive;]

"managing agent" means a person who is permitted by the Council of Lloyd's in the conduct of his business as an underwriting agent to perform for a member of Lloyd's one or more of the following functions—

(a)   underwriting contracts of insurance at Lloyd's;

(b)   reinsuring such contracts in whole or in part;

(c)   paying claims on such contracts;

["market operator" means a market operator within the meaning of Article 4.1.13 of the markets in financial instruments directive, or a person who would be a market operator if he had his registered office, or if he does not have a registered office his head office, in an EEA State, but does not include—

(a)   a person to whom the markets in financial instruments directive does not apply by virtue of Article 2 of that directive (the text of which is set out in Schedule 3);

(b)   a person who does not have a home Member State to whom (if he had his registered office, or if he does not have a registered office his head office, in an EEA State) the markets in financial instruments directive would not apply by virtue of Article 2 of that directive;]

["multilateral trading facility" means—

(a)   a multilateral trading facility (within the meaning of Article 4.1.15 of the markets in financial instruments directive) operated by an investment firm, a credit institution or a market operator, or

(b)   a facility which—

(i)   is operated by an investment firm, a credit institution or market operator which does not have a home Member State, and

(ii)   if its operator had a home Member State, would be a multilateral trading facility within the meaning of Article 4.1.15 of the markets in financial instruments directive;]

["occupational pension scheme" has the meaning given by section 1 of the Pension Schemes Act 1993 but with paragraph (b) of the definition omitted;]

"overseas person" means a person who—

(a)   carries on activities of the kind specified by any of articles 14, 21, 25, [25A,] [25B, 25C,] [25D,] [25E,] 37[, 39A], 40, 45, 51, 52[, 53, 53A[, 53B, 53C, [53D,] 61, 63B[, 63F and 63J]]] or, so far as relevant to any of those articles, article 64 (or activities of a kind which would be so specified but for the exclusion in article 72); but

(b)   does not carry on any such activities, or offer to do so, from a permanent place of business maintained by him in the United Kingdom;

"pension fund management contract" means a contract to manage the investments of pension funds (other than funds solely for the benefit of the officers or employees of the person effecting or carrying out the contract and their dependants or, in the case of a company, partly for the benefit of officers and employees and their dependants of its subsidiary or holding company or a subsidiary of its holding company); and for the purposes of this definition, "subsidiary" and "holding company" are to be construed in accordance with [section 1159 of the Companies Act 2006];

["personal pension scheme" means a scheme or arrangement which is not an occupational pension scheme or a stakeholder pension scheme and which is comprised in one or more instruments or agreements, having or capable of having effect so as to provide benefits to or in respect of people—

(a)   on retirement,

(b)   on having reached a particular age, or

(c)   on termination of service in an employment;]

["plan provider" has the meaning given by paragraph (3) of article 63B, read with paragraphs (7) and (8) of that article;]

"property" includes currency of the United Kingdom or any other country or territory;

"qualifying contract of insurance" means a contract of long-term insurance which is not—

(a)   a reinsurance contract; nor

(b)   a contract in respect of which the following conditions are met—

(i)   the benefits under the contract are payable only on death or in respect of incapacity due to injury, sickness or infirmity;

(ii)   . . .

(iii)   the contract has no surrender value, or the consideration consists of a single premium and the surrender value does not exceed that premium; and

(iv)   the contract makes no provision for its conversion or extension in a manner which would result in it ceasing to comply with any of the above conditions;

["regulated home purchase plan" has the meaning given by article 63F(3);

"regulated home reversion plan" has the meaning given by article 63B(3);]

"regulated mortgage contract" has the meaning given by article 61(3);

["regulated sale and rent back agreement" has the meaning given by article 63J(3);]

["relevant investment" means—

(a)   rights under a qualifying contract of insurance;

(b)   rights under any other contract of insurance;

(c)   any investment of the kind specified by any of articles 83, 84, 85 and 87; or

      (d)   any investment of the kind specified by article 89 so far as relevant to an investment falling within (a) or (c);]

["reversion seller" has the meaning given by article 63B(3);]

"security" means (except where the context otherwise requires) any investment of the kind specified by any of articles 76 to 82 or, so far as relevant to any such investment, article 89;

"selling", in relation to any investment, includes disposing of the investment for valuable consideration, and for these purposes "disposing" includes—

      (a)   in the case of an investment consisting of rights under a contract—

          (i)   surrendering, assigning or converting those rights; or

          (ii)   assuming the corresponding liabilities under the contract;

      (b)   in the case of an investment consisting of rights under other arrangements, assuming the corresponding liabilities under the arrangements; and

      (c)   in the case of any other investment, issuing or creating the investment or granting the rights or interests of which it consists;

"stakeholder pension scheme" has the meaning given by section 1 of the Welfare Reform and Pensions Act 1999 [in relation to Great Britain and has the meaning given by article 3 of the Welfare Reform and Pensions (Northern Ireland) Order 1999 in relation to Northern Ireland];

"syndicate" means one or more persons, to whom a particular syndicate number has been assigned by or under the authority of the Council of Lloyd's, carrying out or effecting contracts of insurance written at Lloyd's;

"voting shares", in relation to a body corporate, means shares carrying voting rights attributable to share capital which are exercisable in all circumstances at any general meeting of that body corporate.

(2)   For the purposes of this Order, a transaction is entered into through a person if he enters into it as agent or arranges, in a manner constituting the carrying on of an activity of the kind specified by article 25(1)[, 25A(1), 25B(1)[, 25C(1) or 25E(1)]], for it to be entered into by another person as agent or principal.

(3)   For the purposes of this Order, a contract of insurance is to be treated as falling within Part II of Schedule 1, notwithstanding the fact that it contains related and subsidiary provisions such that it might also be regarded as falling within Part I of that Schedule, if its principal object is that of a contract falling within Part II and it is effected or carried out by an authorised person who has permission to effect or carry out contracts falling within paragraph I of Part II of Schedule 1.

NOTES

Para (1) is amended as follows:

Definitions "agreement provider", "agreement seller", and "regulated sale and rent back agreement" inserted by the Financial Services and Markets Act 2000 (Regulated Activities) (Amendment) Order 2009, SI 2009/1342, arts 2, 3(1)(a), (b), as from 1 July 2009 (other than for the purposes of enabling applications to be made for a Part IV permission, or a variation of a Part IV permission, in relation to activities of the kind specified by arts 25E, 53D or 63J or, so far as relevant to any such activity, art 64 of this Order), and as from 30 June 2010 (for those purposes) (for transitional provisions in relation to applications for Part IV permissions, etc, see arts 1, 32–34 of that Order).

Words in square brackets in definition "close relative" inserted by the Civil Partnership Act 2004 (Amendments to Subordinate Legislation) Order 2005, SI 2005/2114, art 2(16), Sch 16, Pt 1, para 1(1), (2), as from 5 December 2005.

Definitions "the Commission Regulation", "credit institution", "financial instrument", "home Member State", "investment firm", "investment services and activities", "management company", "market operator", and "multilateral trading facility" inserted by the Financial Services and Markets Act 2000 (Regulated Activities) (Amendment No 3) Order 2006, SI 2006/3384, arts 2, 3(b), as from 1 April 2007 (for the purposes of enabling applications to be made for (i) a Part IV permission, (ii) a variation of a Part IV permission, and (iii) the Authority's approval under s 59 of the 2000 Act, in relation to an activity of the kind specified by art 25D of this Order, or in relation to an investment of the kind specified by arts 83, 84 or 85 of this Order), and as from 1 November 2007 (otherwise).

Words in square brackets in the definition "credit institution" inserted by the Electronic Money Regulations 2011, SI 2011/99, reg 79, Sch 4, Pt 2, para 12(a)(i), as from 30 April 2011.

Definition "electronic money" inserted by the Financial Services and Markets Act 2000 (Regulated Activities) (Amendment) Order 2002, SI 2002/682, art 2, as from 27 April 2002; substituted by SI 2011/99, reg 79, Sch 4, Pt 2, para 12(a)(ii), as from 30 April 2011.

Definitions "home purchase provider", "home purchaser", "plan provider", "regulated home purchase plan", "regulated home reversion plan", and "reversion seller" inserted by the Financial Services and Markets Act 2000 (Regulated Activities) (Amendment) (No 2) Order 2006, SI 2006/2383, arts 2, 3(1)(a), (c)–(e), as from 6 November 2006 (for the purposes of enabling applications to be made for (i) a Pt IV permission, or a variation of a Pt IV permission, in relation to activities of the kind specified by arts 25B, 25C, 53B, 53C, 63B or 63F or, so far as relevant to any such activity, art 64 of this Order; or (ii) the Authority's approval under FSMA 2000, s 59 in relation to any of those activities), and as from 6 April 2007 (otherwise) (for transitional provisions in relation to interim permissions and interim approvals, etc, see arts 36–40 of, and the Schedule to, the 2006 Order).

Definition "management company" substituted by the Undertakings for Collective Investment in Transferable Securities Regulations 2011, SI 2011/1613, reg 16, Schedule, para 1(1), (2), as from 1 July 2011.

Definition "occupational pension scheme" substituted by the Financial Services and Markets Act 2000 (Regulated Activities) (Amendment) Order 2006, SI 2006/1969, art 2(1), (2)(a), as from 1 October 2006 (for the purposes of enabling applications to be made for Part IV permission or for a variation of Part IV permission in relation to the regulated activity specified by art 52(b) of this Order (as amended by SI 2006/1969) or in relation to an investment specified by art 82(2) of this Order (as so amended)), and as from 6 April 2007 (otherwise) (for transitional provisions in relation to interim permissions and interim approvals, etc, see arts 3–7 of, and the Schedule to, the 2006 Order).

Definition "overseas person" is amended as follows:

Figure "25A," in square brackets inserted by the Financial Services and Markets Act 2000 (Regulated Activities) (Amendment) (No 1) Order 2003, SI 2003/1475, art 3(a), as from 31 October 2004 (for transitional provisions in relation to applications for Part IV permissions and applications for approvals, etc, see arts 26–29 of the 2003 Order).

Figures "25B, 25C," in square brackets inserted by SI 2006/2383, arts 2, 3(1)(b)(i), as from the same dates and for the same purposes, etc, as mentioned in the note relating to this Order above.

Figure "25D," in square brackets inserted by SI 2006/3384, arts 2, 3(a), as from the same dates and for the same purposes, etc, as mentioned in the note relating to this Order above.

Figure "25E," in square brackets inserted by SI 2009/1342, arts 2, 3(1)(c)(i), as from the same dates and for the same purposes, etc, as mentioned in the note relating to this Order above.

Figure ", 39A" in square brackets inserted by SI 2003/1476, arts 2, 3(1)(a), as from 31 October 2004 (in so far as relating to contracts of long-term care insurance), and as from 14 January 2005 (otherwise) (for transitional provisions in relation to applications for Part IV permissions and applications for approvals, etc, see arts 22–27 of the 2003 Order).

Words in square brackets beginning with the figures ", 53, 53A" substituted by SI 2003/1475, art 3(b), as from 31 October 2004 (for transitional provisions in relation to applications for Part IV permissions and applications for approvals, etc, see arts 26–29 of the 2003 Order).

Words in square brackets beginning with the figures ", 53B, 53C" substituted by SI 2006/2383, arts 2, 3(1)(b)(ii), as from the same dates and for the same purposes as mentioned in the note relating to this Order above.

Figure "53D," in square brackets inserted by SI 2009/1342, arts 2, 3(1)(c)(ii), as from the same dates and for the same purposes, etc, as mentioned in the note relating to this Order above.

Words "63F and 63J" substituted by SI 2009/1342, arts 2, 3(1)(c)(iii), as from the same dates and for the same purposes, etc, as mentioned in the note relating to this Order above.

Words in square brackets in definition "pension fund management contract" substituted by the Companies Act 2006 (Consequential Amendments and Transitional Provisions) Order 2011, SI 2011/1265, art 13(1), (2), as from 12 May 2011.

Definition "personal pension scheme" inserted by SI 2006/1969, art 2(1), (2)(a), as from the same dates and for the same purposes, etc, as mentioned in the note relating to this Order above.

In definition "qualifying contract of insurance" sub-para (b)(ii) revoked by the Financial Services and Markets Act 2000 (Regulated Activities) (Amendment) Order 2007, SI 2007/1339, arts 2, 3, as from 6 June 2007.

Definition "relevant investment", inserted by SI 2003/1476, art 3(1)(b), as from 31 October 2004 (in so far as relating to contracts of long-term care insurance), and as from 14 January 2005 (otherwise) (for transitional provisions in relation to applications for Part IV permissions and applications for approvals, etc, see arts 22–27 of the 2003 Order).

Words in square brackets in definition "stakeholder pension scheme" added by SI 2005/593, art 2(1), (2)(b), as from 6 April 2005.

Para (2): words in first (outer) pair of square brackets inserted by SI 2006/2383, arts 2, 3(2), as from the same dates and for the same purposes, etc, as mentioned in the note relating to this Order above; words in second (inner) pair of square brackets substituted by SI 2009/1342, arts 2, 3(2), as from the same dates and for the same purposes, etc, as mentioned in the note relating to this Order above.

Close relative: as to the meaning of "step-children", and related expressions, see the Civil Partnership Act 2004, s 246 (as applied to this Order by the Civil Partnership Act 2004 (Relationships Arising Through Civil Partnership) Order 2005, SI 2005/3137, art 3, Schedule).

PART II
SPECIFIED ACTIVITIES

CHAPTER I
GENERAL

[8.4]
4 Specified activities: general

(1)   The following provisions of this Part specify kinds of activity for the purposes of section 22 of the Act (and accordingly any activity of one of those kinds, which is carried on by way of business, and relates to an investment of a kind specified by any provision of Part III and applicable to that activity, is a regulated activity for the purposes of the Act).

(2)   The kinds of activity specified by articles [51, 52 and 63N] are also specified for the purposes of section 22(1)(b) of the Act (and accordingly any activity of one of those kinds, when carried on by way of business, is a regulated activity when carried on in relation to property of any kind).

(3)   Subject to paragraph (4), each provision specifying a kind of activity is subject to the exclusions applicable to that provision (and accordingly any reference in this Order to an activity of the kind specified by a particular provision is to be read subject to any such exclusions).

[(4)   Where an investment firm or credit institution—
   (a)   provides or performs investment services and activities on a professional basis, and
   (b)   in doing so would be treated as carrying on an activity of a kind specified by a provision of this Part but for an exclusion in any of articles 15, 16, 19, 22, 23, 29, 38, 67, 68, 69, 70 and 72E,
that exclusion is to be disregarded and, accordingly, the investment firm or credit institution is to be treated as carrying on an activity of the kind specified by the provision in question.]

[(4A)   Where a person, other than a person specified by Article 1.2 of the insurance mediation directive (the text of which is set out in Part 1 of Schedule 4)—
   (a)   for remuneration, takes up or pursues insurance mediation or reinsurance mediation in relation to a risk or commitment located in an EEA State, and
   (b)   in doing so would be treated as carrying on an activity of a kind specified by a provision of this Part but for an exclusion in any of articles 30, 66 and 67,

that exclusion is to be disregarded (and accordingly that person is to be treated as carrying on an activity of the kind specified by the provision in question).]

(5) In this article—

. . .

["insurance mediation" has the meaning given by Article 2.3 of the insurance mediation directive, the text of which is set out in Part II of Schedule 4;]

. . .

["reinsurance mediation" has the meaning given by Article 2.4 of the insurance mediation directive, the text of which is set out in Part III of Schedule 4.]

NOTES

Para (2): words in square brackets substituted by the Financial Services and Markets Act 2000 (Regulated Activities) (Amendment) (No 2) Order 2009, SI 2009/1389, arts 2, 3, as from 13 July 2009.

Para (4): substituted by the Financial Services and Markets Act 2000 (Regulated Activities) (Amendment No 3) Order 2006, SI 2006/3384, arts 2, 4(a), as from 1 April 2007 (for the purposes of enabling applications to be made for (i) a Part IV permission, (ii) a variation of a Part IV permission, and (iii) the Authority's approval under s 59 of the 2000 Act, in relation to an activity of the kind specified by art 25D of this Order, or in relation to an investment of the kind specified by arts 83, 84 or 85 of this Order), and as from 1 November 2007 (otherwise).

Para (4A): inserted by the Financial Services and Markets Act 2000 (Regulated Activities) (Amendment) (No 2) Order 2003, SI 2003/1476, art 3(2)(a), as from 31 October 2004 (in so far as relating to contracts of long-term care insurance), and as from 14 January 2005 (otherwise) (for transitional provisions in relation to applications for Part IV permissions and applications for approvals, etc, see arts 22–27 of the 2003 Order).

Para (5): definitions "insurance mediation" and "reinsurance mediation" inserted by SI 2003/1476, art 3(2)(b), as from 31 October 2004, as from the same dates and for the same purposes, etc, as mentioned in the note relating to this Order above; definitions "core investment service" and "investment firm" revoked by SI 2006/3384, arts 2, 4(a), as from the same dates and for the same purposes, etc, as mentioned in the note relating to this Order above.

CHAPTER II
ACCEPTING DEPOSITS

The activity

[8.5]
5 Accepting deposits

(1) Accepting deposits is a specified kind of activity if—
  (a) money received by way of deposit is lent to others; or
  (b) any other activity of the person accepting the deposit is financed wholly, or to a material extent, out of the capital of or interest on money received by way of deposit.

(2) In paragraph (1), "deposit" means a sum of money, other than one excluded by any of [articles 6 to 9A], paid on terms—
  (a) under which it will be repaid, with or without interest or premium, and either on demand or at a time or in circumstances agreed by or on behalf of the person making the payment and the person receiving it; and
  (b) which are not referable to the provision of property (other than currency) or services or the giving of security.

(3) For the purposes of paragraph (2), money is paid on terms which are referable to the provision of property or services or the giving of security if, and only if—
  (a) it is paid by way of advance or part payment under a contract for the sale, hire or other provision of property or services, and is repayable only in the event that the property or services is or are not in fact sold, hired or otherwise provided;
  (b) it is paid by way of security for the performance of a contract or by way of security in respect of loss which may result from the non-performance of a contract; or
  (c) without prejudice to sub-paragraph (b), it is paid by way of security for the delivery up or return of any property, whether in a particular state of repair or otherwise.

NOTES

Para (2): words in square brackets substituted by the Financial Services and Markets Act 2000 (Regulated Activities) (Amendment) Order 2002, SI 2002/682, art 3(1), as from 27 April 2002, subject to transitional provisions in relation to persons issuing electronic money immediately before that date contained in art 9.

Exclusions

[8.6]
6 Sums paid by certain persons

(1) A sum is not a deposit for the purposes of article 5 if it is—
  (a) paid by any of the following persons—
    (i) the Bank of England, the central bank of an EEA State other than the United Kingdom, or the European Central Bank;
    (ii) an authorised person who has permission to accept deposits, or to effect or carry out contracts of insurance;
    (iii) an EEA firm falling within paragraph 5(b), (c) or (d) of Schedule 3 to the Act (other than one falling within paragraph (ii) above);

(iv)   the National Savings Bank;

(v)   a municipal bank, that is to say a company which was, immediately before the coming into force of this article, exempt from the prohibition in section 3 of the Banking Act 1987 by virtue of section 4(1) of, and paragraph 4 of Schedule 2 to, that Act;

(vi)   Keesler Federal Credit Union;

(vii) a body of persons certified as a school bank by the National Savings Bank or by an authorised person who has permission to accept deposits;

(viii) a local authority;

(ix)   any body which by virtue of any enactment has power to issue a precept to a local authority in England and Wales or a requisition to a local authority in Scotland, or to the expenses of which, by virtue of any enactment, a local authority in the United Kingdom is or can be required to contribute (and in this paragraph, "enactment" includes an enactment comprised in, or in an instrument made under, an Act of the Scottish Parliament);

(x)   the European Community, the European Atomic Energy Community or the European Coal and Steel Community;

(xi)   the European Investment Bank;

(xii) the International Bank for Reconstruction and Development;

(xiii) the International Finance Corporation;

(xiv) the International Monetary Fund;

(xv)   the African Development Bank;

(xvi) the Asian Development Bank;

(xvii) the Caribbean Development Bank;

(xviii) the Inter-American Development Bank;

(xix) the European Bank for Reconstruction and Development;

[(xx) the Council of Europe Development Bank;]

(b)   paid by a person other than one mentioned in sub-paragraph (a) in the course of carrying on a business consisting wholly or to a significant extent of lending money;

(c)   paid by one company to another at a time when both are members of the same group or when the same individual is a majority shareholder controller of both of them; or

(d)   paid by a person who, at the time when it is paid, is a close relative of the person receiving it or who is, or is a close relative of, a director or manager of that person or who is, or is a close relative of, a controller of that person.

(2)   For the purposes of paragraph (1)(c), an individual is a majority shareholder controller of a company if he is a controller of the company by virtue of paragraph (a), (c), (e) or (g) of section 422(2) of the Act, and if in his case the greatest percentage of those referred to in those paragraphs is 50 or more.

(3)   In the application of sub-paragraph (d) of paragraph (1) to a sum paid by a partnership, that sub-paragraph is to have effect as if, for the reference to the person paying the sum, there were substituted a reference to each of the partners.

NOTES

Para (1): sub-para (a)(xx) substituted by the Financial Services and Markets Act 2000 (Financial Promotion and Miscellaneous Amendments) Order 2002, SI 2002/1310, art 4(1), as from 5 June 2002.

[8.7]
7   Sums received by solicitors etc

(1)   A sum is not a deposit for the purposes of article 5 if it is received by a practising solicitor acting in the course of his profession.

(2)   In paragraph (1), "practising solicitor" means—

(a)   a solicitor who is qualified to act as such under section 1 of the Solicitors Act 1974, article 4 of the Solicitors (Northern Ireland) Order 1976 or section 4 of the Solicitors (Scotland) Act 1980;

(b)   a recognised body;

(c)   a registered foreign lawyer in the course of providing professional services as a member of a multi-national partnership;

(d)   a registered European lawyer; or

(e)   a partner of a registered European lawyer who is providing professional services in accordance with—

(i)   rules made under section 31 of the Solicitors Act 1974;

(ii)   regulations made under article 26 of the Solicitors (Northern Ireland) Order 1976; or

(iii) rules made under section 34 of the Solicitors (Scotland) Act 1980.

(3)   In this article—

(a)   "a recognised body" means a body   . . .   recognised by—

(i)   the Council of the Law Society under section 9 of the Administration of Justice Act 1985;

      (ii)   the Incorporated Law Society of Northern Ireland under article 26A of the Solicitors (Northern Ireland) Order 1976; or

      (iii)   the Council of the Law Society of Scotland under section 34 of the Solicitors (Scotland) Act 1980;

  (b)   "registered foreign lawyer" has the meaning given by section 89 of the Courts and Legal Services Act 1990 or, in Scotland, section 65 of the Solicitors (Scotland) Act 1980;

  (c)   "multi-national partnership" has the meaning given by section 89 of the Courts and Legal Services Act 1990 but, in Scotland, is a reference to a "multi-national practice" within the meaning of section 60A of the Solicitors (Scotland) Act 1980; and

  (d)   "registered European lawyer" has the meaning given by regulation 2(1) of the European Communities (Lawyer's Practice) Regulations 2000 or regulation 2(1) of the European Communities (Lawyer's Practice) (Scotland) Regulation 2000.

NOTES

Para (3): word omitted from the definition "a recognised body" revoked by the Solicitors' Recognised Bodies (Amendment) Order 2009, SI 2009/500, art 3, as from 31 March 2009.

[8.8]
8 Sums received by persons authorised to deal etc

A sum is not a deposit for the purposes of article 5 if it is received by a person who is—

  (a)   an authorised person with permission to carry on an activity of the kind specified by any of articles 14, 21, 25, 37, 51 and 52, or

  (b)   an exempt person in relation to any such activity,

in the course of, or for the purpose of, [carrying on any such activity (or any activity which would be such an activity but for any exclusion made by this Part)] with or on behalf of the person by or on behalf of whom the sum is paid.

NOTES

Words in square brackets substituted by the Financial Services and Markets Act 2000 (Regulated Activities) (Amendment) Order 2001, SI 2001/3544, arts 2, 3, as from 1 December 2001.

[8.9]
9 Sums received in consideration for the issue of debt securities

(1)   Subject to paragraph (2), a sum is not a deposit for the purposes of article 5 if it is received by a person as consideration for the issue by him of any investment of the kind specified by article 77 or 78.

(2)   The exclusion in paragraph (1) does not apply to the receipt by a person of a sum as consideration for the issue by him of commercial paper unless—

  (a)   the commercial paper is issued to persons—

      (i)   whose ordinary activities involve them in acquiring, holding, managing or disposing of investments (as principal or agent) for the purposes of their businesses; or

      (ii)   who it is reasonable to expect will acquire, hold, manage or dispose of investments (as principal or agent) for the purposes of their businesses; and

  (b)   the redemption value of the commercial paper is not less than £100,000 (or an amount of equivalent value denominated wholly or partly in a currency other than sterling), and no part of the commercial paper may be transferred unless the redemption value of that part is not less than £100,000 (or such an equivalent amount).

[(3)   In paragraph (2), "commercial paper" means an investment of the kind specified by article 77 or 78 having a maturity of less than one year from the date of issue.]

NOTES

Para (3): substituted by the Financial Services and Markets Act 2000 (Regulated Activities) (Amendment) Order 2002, SI 2002/682, art 12, as from 27 April 2002.

[8.10]
[9A Sums received in exchange for electronic money

A sum is not a deposit for the purposes of article 5 if it is immediately exchanged for electronic money.]

NOTES

Inserted by the Financial Services and Markets Act 2000 (Regulated Activities) (Amendment) Order 2002, SI 2002/682, art 3(2), as from 27 April 2002, subject to transitional provisions in relation to persons issuing electronic money immediately before that date contained in art 9.

[8.11]
[9AA Information society services

Article 5 is subject to the exclusion in article 72A (information society services).]

NOTES

Inserted by the Financial Services and Markets Act 2000 (Regulated Activities) (Amendment) (No 2) Order 2002, SI 2002/1776, art 3(1), (2), as from 21 August 2002.

[8.12]
[9AB   Funds received for payment services

(1)   A sum is not a deposit for the purposes of article 5 if it is received by an authorised payment institution, an EEA authorised payment institution[, a small payment institution, an electronic money institution or an EEA authorised electronic money institution] from a payment service user with a view to the provision of payment services.

(2)   For the purposes of paragraph (1), "authorised payment institution", "EEA authorised payment institution", "small payment institution", "payment services" and "payment service user" have the meanings given in the Payment Services Regulations 2009 [and "electronic money institution" and "EEA authorised electronic money institution" have the meanings given in the Electronic Money Regulations 2011].]

NOTES

Commencement: 1 November 2009.

Inserted by the Payment Services Regulations 2009, SI 2009/209, reg 126, Sch 6, Pt 2, para 4(a), as from 1 November 2009 (for the full commencement details of the 2009 Regulations, see reg 1 of those Regulations).

Para (1): words in square brackets substituted by the Electronic Money Regulations 2011, SI 2011/99, reg 79, Sch 4, Pt 2, para 12(b)(i), as from 30 April 2011.

Para (2): words in square brackets inserted by SI 2011/99, reg 79, Sch 4, Pt 2, para 12(b)(ii), as from 30 April 2011.

[CHAPTER IIA
ELECTRONIC MONEY

The activity

[8.13]
9B   Issuing electronic money

Issuing electronic money [by—
     (a)   a credit institution, a credit union or a municipal bank; or
     (b)   a person who is deemed to have been granted authorisation under regulation 74 of the Electronic Money Regulations 2011 or who falls within regulation 76(1) of those Regulations,]
is a specified kind of activity.]

NOTES

Inserted, together with arts 9C–9K and the preceding heading, by the Financial Services and Markets Act 2000 (Regulated Activities) (Amendment) Order 2002, SI 2002/682, art 4, as from 27 April 2002, subject to transitional provisions in relation to persons issuing electronic money immediately before that date contained in art 9.

Words in square brackets inserted by the Electronic Money Regulations 2011, SI 2011/99, reg 79, Sch 4, Pt 2, para 12(c), as from 30 April 2011.

[8.14]
[9BA

Articles 9C to 9I and 9K apply only in the case of a person falling within regulation 76(1) of the Electronic Money Regulations 2011.

NOTES

Commencement: 30 April 2011.

Inserted by the Electronic Money Regulations 2011, SI 2011/99, reg 79, Sch 4, Pt 2, para 12(c), as from 30 April 2011.

[Exclusions

[8.15]
9C   Persons certified as small issuers etc

(1)   There is excluded from article 9B the issuing of electronic money by a person to whom the Authority has given a certificate under this article (provided the certificate has not been revoked).

(2)   An application for a certificate may be made by—
     (a)   a body corporate, or
     (b)   a partnership,
(other than a credit institution as defined in [Article 4(1)(a)] of the banking consolidation directive) which has its head office in the United Kingdom.

(3)   The authority must, on the application of such a person ("A"), give A a certificate if it appears to the Authority that paragraph (4), (5) or (6) applies.

(4)   This paragraph applies if—

(a)　A does not issue electronic money except on terms that the electronic device on which the monetary value is stored is subject to a maximum storage amount of not more than 150 euro; and

(b)　A's total liabilities with respect to the issuing of electronic money do not (or will not) usually exceed 5 million euro and do not (or will not) ever exceed 6 million euro.

(5)　This paragraph applies if—
(a)　the condition in paragraph (4)(a) is met;
(b)　A's total liabilities with respect to the issuing of electronic money do not (or will not) exceed 10 million euro; and
(c)　electronic money issued by A is accepted as a means of payment only by—
(i)　subsidiaries of A which perform operational or other ancillary functions related to electronic money issued or distributed by A; or
(ii)　other members of the same group as A (other than subsidiaries of A).

(6)　This paragraph applies if—
(a)　the conditions in paragraphs (4)(a) and (5)(b) are met; and
(b)　electronic money issued by A is accepted as a means of payment, in the course of business, by not more than one hundred persons where—
(i)　those persons accept such electronic money only at locations within the same premises or limited local area; or
(ii)　those persons have a close financial or business relationship with A, such as a common marketing or distribution scheme.

(7)　For the purposes of paragraph (6)(b)(i), locations are to be treated as situated within the same premises or limited local area if they are situated within—
(a)　a shopping centre, airport, railway station, bus station, or campus of a university, polytechnic, college, school or similar educational establishment; or
(b)　an area which does not exceed four square kilometres;
but sub-paragraphs (a) and (b) are illustrative only and are not to be treated as limiting the scope of paragraph (6)(b)(i).

(8)　For the purposes of paragraph (6)(b)(ii), persons are not to be treated as having a close financial or business relationship with A merely because they participate in arrangements for the acceptance of electronic money issued by A.

(9)　In this article, references to amounts in euro include references to equivalent amounts in sterling.

(10)　A person to whom a certificate has been given under this article (and whose certificate has not been revoked) is referred to in this Chapter as a "certified person".]

NOTES

Inserted as noted to art 9B at **[8.13]**.

Para (2): words in square brackets substituted the Capital Requirements Regulations 2006, SI 2006/3221, reg 29(4), Sch 6, para 6(1), (2), as from 1 January 2007.

[8.16]
[9D　Applications for certificates
The following provisions of the Act apply to applications to the Authority for certificates under 9C (and the determination of such applications) as they apply to applications for Part IV permissions (and the determination of such applications)—
(a)　section 51(1)(b) and (3) to (6);
(b)　section 52, except subsections (6), (8) and (9)(a) and (b); and
(c)　section 55(1).]

NOTES

Inserted as noted to art 9B at **[8.13]**.

[8.17]
[9E　Revocation of certificate on Authority's own initiative
(1)　The Authority may revoke a certificate given to a person ("A") under article 9C if—
(a)　it appears to it that A does not meet the relevant conditions, or has failed to meet the relevant conditions at any time since the certificate was given; or
(b)　the person to whom the certificate was given has contravened any rule or requirement to which he is subject as a result of article 9G.

(2)　For the purposes of paragraph (1), A meets the relevant conditions at any time if, at that time, paragraph (4), (5) or (6) of article 9C applies.

(3)　Sections 54 and 55(2) of the Act apply to the revocation of a certificate under paragraph (1) as they apply to the cancellation of a Part IV permission on the Authority's own initiative, as if references in those sections to an authorised person were references to a certified person.]

NOTES
Inserted as noted to art 9B at **[8.13]**.

[8.18]
[9F   Revocation of certificate on request

(1)   A certified person ("B") may apply to the Authority for his certificate to be revoked, and the Authority must then revoke the certificate and give B written notice that it has done so.

(2)   An application under paragraph (1) must be made in such manner as the Authority may direct.

(3)   If—
    (a)   B has made an application under Part IV of the Act for permission to carry on a regulated activity of the kind specified by article 9B (or for variation of an existing permission so as to add a regulated activity of that kind), and
    (b)   on making an application for revocation of his certificate under paragraph (1), he requests that the revocation be conditional on the granting of his application under Part IV of the Act,

the revocation of B's certificate is to be conditional on the granting of his application under Part IV of the Act.]

NOTES
Inserted as noted to art 9B at **[8.13]**.

[8.19]
[9G   Obtaining information from certified persons etc

(1)   The Authority may make rules requiring certified persons to provide information to the Authority about their activities so far as relating to the issuing of electronic money, including the amount of their liabilities with respect to the issuing of electronic money.

(2)   Section 148 of the Act (modification or waiver of rules) applies in relation to rules made under paragraph (1) as if references in that section to an authorised person were references to a certified person.

(3)   Section 150 of the Act (actions for damages) applies in relation to a rule made under paragraph (1) as if the reference in subsection (1) of that section to an authorised person were a reference to a certified person.

(4)   The Authority may, by notice in writing given to a certified person, require him—
    (a)   to provide specified information or information of a specified description; or
    (b)   to produce specified documents or documents of a specified description.

(5)   Paragraph (4) applies only to information or documents reasonably required for the purposes of determining whether the certified person meets, or has met, the relevant conditions.

(6)   Subsections (2), (5) and (6) of section 165 of the Act (Authority's power to require information) apply to a requirement imposed under paragraph (4) as they apply to a requirement imposed under that section.

(7)   Section 166 of the Act (reports by skilled persons) has effect as if—
    (a)   the reference in subsection (1) of that section to section 165 included a reference to paragraph (4) above; and
    (b)   the reference in section 166(2)(a) of the Act to an authorised person included a reference to a certified person.

(8)   Subsection (4) of section 168 of the Act (appointment of persons to carry out investigations in particular cases) has effect as if it provided for subsection (5) of that section to apply if it appears to the Authority that there are circumstances suggesting that a certified person may not meet, or may not have met, the relevant conditions.

(9)   Sections 175 (information and documents: supplemental provisions), 176 (entry of premises under warrant) and 177 (offences) of the Act apply to a requirement imposed under paragraph (4) as they apply to a requirement imposed under section 165 of the Act (the reference in section 176(3)(a) to an authorised person being read as a reference to a certified person).

(10)   In this article—
    (a)   "specified", in paragraph (4), means specified in the notice mentioned in that paragraph;
    (b)   a certified person ("A") meets the relevant conditions at any time if, at that time, paragraph (4), (5) or (6) of article 9C applies.]

NOTES
Inserted as noted to art 9B at **[8.13]**.

[Supplemental

[8.20]
9H Rules prohibiting the issue of electronic money at a discount

(1)   The Authority may make rules applying to authorised persons with permission to carry on an activity of the kind specified by article 9B, prohibiting the issue of electronic money having a monetary value greater than the funds received.

(2)   Section 148 of the Act (modification or waiver of rules) applies in relation to rules made under paragraph (1).]

NOTES
Inserted as noted to art 9B at **[8.13]**.

[8.21]
[9I False claims to be a certified person

A person who is not a certified person is to be treated as guilty of an offence under section 24 of the Act (false claims to be authorised or exempt) if he—
   (a)   describes himself (in whatever terms) as a certified person;
   (b)   behaves, or otherwise holds himself out, in a manner which indicates (or which is reasonably likely to be understood as indicating) that he is a certified person.]

NOTES
Inserted as noted to art 9B at **[8.13]**.

[8.22]
[9J Exclusion of electronic money from the compensation scheme

The compensation scheme established under Part XV of the Act is not to provide for the compensation of persons in respect of claims made in connection with any activity of the kind specified by article 9B.]

NOTES
Inserted as noted to art 9B at **[8.13]**.

[8.23]
[9K Record of certified persons

The record maintained by the Authority under section 347 of the Act (public record of authorised persons etc) must include every certified person.]

NOTES
Inserted as noted to art 9B at **[8.13]**.

9L *(Inserted by the Payment Services Regulations 2009, SI 2009/209, reg 126, Sch 6, Pt 2, para 4(b), as from 1 November 2009, and revoked by the Electronic Money Regulations 2011, SI 2011/99, reg 79, Sch 4, Pt 2, para 12(e), as from 30 April 2011.)*

CHAPTER III
INSURANCE

The activities

[8.24]
10 Effecting and carrying out contracts of insurance

(1)   Effecting a contract of insurance as principal is a specified kind of activity.

(2)   Carrying out a contract of insurance as principal is a specified kind of activity.

Exclusions

[8.25]
11 Community co-insurers

(1)   There is excluded from article 10(1) or (2) the effecting or carrying out of a contract of insurance by an EEA firm falling within paragraph 5(d) of Schedule 3 to the Act—
   (a)   other than through a branch in the United Kingdom; and
   (b)   pursuant to a Community co-insurance operation in which the firm is participating otherwise than as the leading insurer.

(2)   In paragraph (1), "Community co-insurance operation" and "leading insurer" have the same meaning as in the Council Directive of 30 May 1978 on the co-ordination of laws, regulations and administrative provisions relating to Community co-insurance (No 78/473/EEC).

[8.26]

12   Breakdown insurance

(1)   There is excluded from article 10(1) or (2) the effecting or carrying out, by a person who does not otherwise carry on an activity of the kind specified by that article, of a contract of insurance which—

    (a)   is a contract under which the benefits provided by that person ("the provider") are exclusively or primarily benefits in kind in the event of accident to or breakdown of a vehicle; and

    (b)   contains the terms mentioned in paragraph (2).

(2)   Those terms are that—

    (a)   the assistance takes either or both of the forms mentioned in paragraph (3)(a) and (b);

    (b)   the assistance is not available outside the United Kingdom and the Republic of Ireland except where it is provided without the payment of additional premium by a person in the country concerned with whom the provider has entered into a reciprocal agreement; and

    (c)   assistance provided in the case of an accident or breakdown occurring in the United Kingdom or the Republic of Ireland is, in most circumstances, provided by the provider's servants.

(3)   The forms of assistance are—

    (a)   repairs to the relevant vehicle at the place where the accident or breakdown has occurred; this assistance may also include the delivery of parts, fuel, oil, water or keys to the relevant vehicle;

    (b)   removal of the relevant vehicle to the nearest or most appropriate place at which repairs may be carried out, or to—

        (i)   the home, point of departure or original destination within the United Kingdom of the driver and passengers, provided the accident or breakdown occurred within the United Kingdom;

        (ii)   the home, point of departure or original destination within the Republic of Ireland of the driver and passengers, provided the accident or breakdown occurred within the Republic of Ireland or within Northern Ireland;

        (iii)   the home, point of departure or original destination within Northern Ireland of the driver and passengers, provided the accident or breakdown occurred within the Republic of Ireland;

    and this form of assistance may include the conveyance of the driver or passengers of the relevant vehicle, with the vehicle, or (where the vehicle is to be conveyed only to the nearest or most appropriate place at which repairs may be carried out) separately, to the nearest location from which they may continue their journey by other means.

(4)   A contract does not fail to meet the condition in paragraph (1)(a) solely because the provider may reimburse the person entitled to the assistance for all or part of any sums paid by him in respect of assistance either because he failed to identify himself as a person entitled to the assistance or because he was unable to get in touch with the provider in order to claim the assistance.

(5)   In this article—

    "the assistance" means the benefits to be provided under a contract of the kind mentioned in paragraph (1);

    "breakdown" means an event—

    (a)   which causes the driver of the relevant vehicle to be unable to start a journey in the vehicle or involuntarily to bring the vehicle to a halt on a journey because of some malfunction of the vehicle or failure of it to function, and

    (b)   after which the journey cannot reasonably be commenced or continued in the relevant vehicle;

    "the relevant vehicle" means the vehicle (including a trailer or caravan) in respect of which the assistance is required.

[8.27]

[12A   Information society services

Article 10 is subject to the exclusion in article 72A (information society services), as qualified by paragraph (2) of that article.]

NOTES

Inserted by the Financial Services and Markets Act 2000 (Regulated Activities) (Amendment) (No 2) Order 2002, SI 2002/1776 art 3(1), (3), as from 21 August 2002.

Supplemental

[8.28]

13 Application of sections 327 and 332 of the Act to insurance market activities

(1) In sections 327(5) and (7) and 332(3)(b) of the Act (exemption from the general prohibition for members of the professions, and rules in relation to such persons), the references to "a regulated activity" and "regulated activities" do not include—

    (a) any activity of the kind specified by article 10(1) or (2), where—
        (i) P is a member of the Society; and
        (ii) by virtue of section 316 of the Act (application of the Act to Lloyd's underwriting), the general prohibition does not apply to the carrying on by P of that activity; or
    (b) any activity of the kind specified by article 10(2), where—
        (i) P is a former underwriting member; and
        (ii) the contract of insurance in question is one underwritten by P at Lloyd's.

(2) In paragraph (1)—

"member of the Society" has the same meaning as in Lloyd's Act 1982; and

"former underwriting member" has the meaning given by section 324(1) of the Act.

CHAPTER IV
DEALING IN INVESTMENTS AS PRINCIPAL

The activity

[8.29]

14 Dealing in investments as principal

[(1)] Buying, selling, subscribing for or underwriting securities or contractually based investments (other than investments of the kind specified by article 87, or article 89 so far as relevant to that article) as principal is a specified kind of activity.

[(2) Paragraph (1) does not apply to a kind of activity to which article 25D applies.]

NOTES

Para (1) numbered as such, and para (2) added, by the Financial Services and Markets Act 2000 (Regulated Activities) (Amendment No 3) Order 2006, SI 2006/3384, arts 2, 5, as from 1 April 2007 (for the purposes of enabling applications to be made for (i) a Part IV permission, (ii) a variation of a Part IV permission, and (iii) the Authority's approval under s 59 of the 2000 Act, in relation to an activity of the kind specified by art 25D of this Order, or in relation to an investment of the kind specified by arts 83, 84 or 85 of this Order), and as from 1 November 2007 (otherwise).

Exclusions

[8.30]

15 Absence of holding out etc

(1) Subject to paragraph (3), a person ("A") does not carry on an activity of the kind specified by article 14 by entering into a transaction which relates to a security or is the assignment (or, in Scotland, the assignation) of a qualifying contract of insurance (or an investment of the kind specified by article 89, so far as relevant to such a contract), unless—

    (a) A holds himself out as willing, as principal, to buy, sell or subscribe for investments of the kind to which the transaction relates at prices determined by him generally and continuously rather than in respect of each particular transaction;
    (b) A holds himself out as engaging in the business of buying investments of the kind to which the transaction relates, with a view to selling them;
    (c) A holds himself out as engaging in the business of underwriting investments of the kind to which the transaction relates; or
    (d) A regularly solicits members of the public with the purpose of inducing them, as principals or agents, to enter into transactions constituting activities of the kind specified by article 14, and the transaction is entered into as a result of his having solicited members of the public in that manner.

(2) In paragraph (1)(d), "members of the public" means any persons other than—

    (a) authorised persons or persons who are exempt persons in relation to activities of the kind specified by article 14;
    (b) members of the same group as A;
    (c) persons who are or who propose to become participators with A in a joint enterprise;
    (d) any person who is solicited by A with a view to the acquisition by A of 20 per cent or more of the voting shares in a body corporate;
    (e) if A (either alone or with members of the same group as himself) holds more than 20 per cent of the voting shares in a body corporate, any person who is solicited by A with a view to—
        (i) the acquisition by A of further shares in the body corporate; or
        (ii) the disposal by A of shares in the body corporate to the person solicited or to a member of the same group as the person solicited;
    (f) any person who—

         (i)   is solicited by A with a view to the disposal by A of shares in a body corporate to the person solicited or to a member of the same group as that person; and

         (ii)   either alone or with members of the same group holds 20 per cent or more of the voting shares in the body corporate;

    (g)   any person whose head office is outside the United Kingdom, who is solicited by an approach made or directed to him at a place outside the United Kingdom and whose ordinary business involves him in carrying on activities of the kind specified by any of articles 14, 21, 25, 37, 40, 45, 51, 52 and 53 or (so far as relevant to any of those articles) article 64, or would do so apart from any exclusion from any of those articles made by this Order.

(3)   This article does not apply where A enters into the transaction as bare trustee or, in Scotland, as nominee for another person and is acting on that other person's instructions (but the exclusion in article 66(1) applies if the conditions set out there are met).

[(4)   This article is subject to article 4(4).]

NOTES

Para (4): added by the Financial Services and Markets Act 2000 (Regulated Activities) (Amendment No 3) Order 2006, SI 2006/3384, arts 2, 6, as from 1 April 2007 (for the purposes of enabling applications to be made for (i) a Part IV permission, (ii) a variation of a Part IV permission, and (iii) the Authority's approval under s 59 of the 2000 Act, in relation to an activity of the kind specified by art 25D of this Order, or in relation to an investment of the kind specified by arts 83, 84 or 85 of this Order), and as from 1 November 2007 (otherwise).

[8.31]

16 Dealing in contractually based investments

[(1)]   A person who is not an authorised person does not carry on an activity of the kind specified by article 14 by entering into a transaction relating to a contractually based investment—

    (a)   with or through an authorised person, or an exempt person acting in the course of a business comprising a regulated activity in relation to which he is exempt; or

    (b)   through an office outside the United Kingdom maintained by a party to the transaction, and with or through a person whose head office is situated outside the United Kingdom and whose ordinary business involves him in carrying on activities of the kind specified by any of articles 14, 21, 25, 37, 40, 45, 51, 52 and 53 or, so far as relevant to any of those articles, article 64 (or would do so apart from any exclusion from any of those articles made by this Order).

[(2)   This article is subject to article 4(4).]

NOTES

Para (1) numbered as such, and para (2) added, by the Financial Services and Markets Act 2000 (Regulated Activities) (Amendment No 3) Order 2006, SI 2006/3384, arts 2, 7, as from 1 April 2007 (for the purposes of enabling applications to be made for (i) a Part IV permission, (ii) a variation of a Part IV permission, and (iii) the Authority's approval under s 59 of the 2000 Act, in relation to an activity of the kind specified by art 25D of this Order, or in relation to an investment of the kind specified by arts 83, 84 or 85 of this Order), and as from 1 November 2007 (otherwise).

[8.32]

17 Acceptance of instruments creating or acknowledging indebtedness

(1)   A person does not carry on an activity of the kind specified by article 14 by accepting an instrument creating or acknowledging indebtedness in respect of any loan, credit, guarantee or other similar financial accommodation or assurance which he has made, granted or provided.

(2)   The reference in paragraph (1) to a person accepting an instrument includes a reference to a person becoming a party to an instrument otherwise than as a debtor or a surety.

NOTES

Modification: references in para (1) to securities, instruments or investments creating or acknowledging indebtedness (or creating or acknowledging a present or future indebtedness) includes a reference to uncertificated units of eligible debt securities; see the Uncertificated Securities (Amendment) (Eligible Debt Securities) Regulations 2003, SI 2003/1633, reg 15, Sch 2, para 8.

Modification: references in para (2) to a person becoming party to an instrument includes a reference to a person assuming rights and obligations in respect of uncertificated units of an eligible debt security in accordance with its current terms of issue; see the Uncertificated Securities (Amendment) (Eligible Debt Securities) Regulations 2003, SI 2003/1633, reg 15, Sch 2, para 9.

[8.33]

18 Issue by a company of its own shares etc

(1)   There is excluded from article 14 the issue by a company of its own shares or share warrants, and the issue by any person of his own debentures or debenture warrants.

(2)   In this article—

    (a)   "company" means any body corporate other than an open-ended investment company;

    (b)   "shares" and "debentures" include any investment of the kind specified by article 76[, 77 or 77A];

(c) "share warrants" and "debenture warrants" mean any investment of the kind specified by article 79 which relates to shares in the company concerned or, as the case may be, debentures issued by [the person concerned].

NOTES

Para (2): words in square brackets in sub-para (b) substituted by the Financial Services and Markets Act 2000 (Regulated Activities) (Amendment) Order 2010, SI 2010/86, art 4, Schedule, para 5(a), as from 24 February 2010; words in square brackets in sub-para (c) substituted by the Financial Services and Markets Act 2000 (Regulated Activities) (Amendment) Order 2001, SI 2001/3544, arts 2, 4, as from 1 December 2001.

[8.34]
[18A   Dealing by a company in its own shares

(1)   A company does not carry on an activity of the kind specified by article 14 by purchasing its own shares where [section 724 of the Companies Act 2006] (Treasury shares) applies to the shares purchased.

(2)   A company does not carry on an activity of the kind specified by article 14 by dealing in its own shares held as treasury shares, in accordance with [section 727 (Treasury shares: disposal) or 729 (Treasury shares: cancellation) of that Act].

(3)   In this article "shares held as treasury shares" has the same meaning as in that Act.]

NOTES

Inserted by the Financial Services and Markets Act 2000 (Regulated Activities) (Amendment) (No 3) Order 2003, SI 2003/2822, arts 2, 3, as from 1 December 2003.

Paras (1), (2): words in square brackets substituted by the Companies Act 2006 (Consequential Amendments and Transitional Provisions) Order 2011, SI 2011/1265, art 13(1), (3), as from 12 May 2011.

[8.35]
19   Risk management

(1)   A person ("B") does not carry on an activity of the kind specified by article 14 by entering as principal into a transaction with another person ("C") if—
   (a)   the transaction relates to investments of the kind specified by any of articles 83 to 85 (or article 89 so far as relevant to any of those articles);
   (b)   neither B nor C is an individual;
   (c)   the sole or main purpose for which B enters into the transaction (either by itself or in combination with other such transactions) is that of limiting the extent to which a relevant business will be affected by any identifiable risk arising otherwise than as a result of the carrying on of a regulated activity; and
   (d)   the relevant business consists mainly of activities other than—
      (i)   regulated activities; or
      (ii)   activities which would be regulated activities but for any exclusion made by this Part.

(2)   In paragraph (1), "relevant business" means a business carried on by—
   (a)   B;
   (b)   a member of the same group as B; or
   (c)   where B and another person are, or propose to become, participators in a joint enterprise, that other person.

[(3)   This article is subject to article 4(4).]

NOTES

Para (3): added by the Financial Services and Markets Act 2000 (Regulated Activities) (Amendment No 3) Order 2006, SI 2006/3384, arts 2, 8, as from 1 April 2007 (for the purposes of enabling applications to be made for (i) a Part IV permission, (ii) a variation of a Part IV permission, and (iii) the Authority's approval under s 59 of the 2000 Act, in relation to an activity of the kind specified by art 25D of this Order, or in relation to an investment of the kind specified by arts 83, 84 or 85 of this Order), and as from 1 November 2007 (otherwise).

[8.36]
20   Other exclusions

Article 14 is also subject to the exclusions in articles 66 (trustees etc), 68 (sale of goods and supply of services), 69 (groups and joint enterprises), 70 (sale of body corporate), 71 (employee share schemes)[, 72 (overseas persons) and 72A (information society services)].

NOTES

Words in square brackets substituted by the Financial Services and Markets Act 2000 (Regulated Activities) (Amendment) (No 2) Order 2002, SI 2002/1776, art 3(1), (4), as from 21 August 2002.

CHAPTER V
DEALING IN INVESTMENTS AS AGENT

The activity

[8.37]
21　Dealing in investments as agent

[(1)]　Buying, selling, subscribing for or underwriting securities or [relevant investments] (other than investments of the kind specified by article 87, or article 89 so far as relevant to that article) as agent is a specified kind of activity.

[(2)　Paragraph (1) does not apply to a kind of activity to which article 25D applies.]

NOTES

Para (1) numbered as such, and para (2) added, by the Financial Services and Markets Act 2000 (Regulated Activities) (Amendment No 3) Order 2006, SI 2006/3384, arts 2, 9, as from 1 April 2007 (for the purposes of enabling applications to be made for (i) a Part IV permission, (ii) a variation of a Part IV permission, and (iii) the Authority's approval under s 59 of the 2000 Act, in relation to an activity of the kind specified by art 25D of this Order, or in relation to an investment of the kind specified by arts 83, 84 or 85 of this Order), and as from 1 November 2007 (otherwise).

Words in square brackets in para (1) substituted by the Financial Services and Markets Act 2000 (Regulated Activities) (Amendment) (No 2) Order 2003, SI 2003/1476, art 4(1), as from 31 October 2004 (in so far as relating to contracts of long-term care insurance), and as from 14 January 2005 (otherwise) (for transitional provisions in relation to applications for Part IV permissions and applications for approvals, etc, see arts 22–27 of the 2003 Order).

Exclusions

[8.38]
22　Deals with or through authorised persons

(1)　A person who is not an authorised person does not carry on an activity of the kind specified by article 21 by entering into a transaction as agent for another person ("the client") with or through an authorised person if—

    (a)　the transaction is entered into on advice given to the client by an authorised person; or

    (b)　it is clear, in all the circumstances, that the client, in his capacity as an investor, is not seeking and has not sought advice from the agent as to the merits of the client's entering into the transaction (or, if the client has sought such advice, the agent has declined to give it but has recommended that the client seek such advice from an authorised person).

[(2)　But the exclusion in paragraph (1) does not apply if—

    (a)　the transaction relates to a contract of insurance; or

    (b)　the agent receives from any person other than the client any pecuniary reward or other advantage, for which he does not account to the client, arising out of his entering into the transaction.]

[(3)　This article is subject to article 4(4).]

NOTES

Para (2): substituted by the Financial Services and Markets Act 2000 (Regulated Activities) (Amendment) (No 2) Order 2003, SI 2003/1476, art 4(2), as from 31 October 2004 (in so far as relating to contracts of long-term care insurance), and as from 14 January 2005 (otherwise) (for transitional provisions in relation to applications for Part IV permissions and applications for approvals, etc, see arts 22–27 of the 2003 Order).

Para (3): added by the Financial Services and Markets Act 2000 (Regulated Activities) (Amendment No 3) Order 2006, SI 2006/3384, arts 2, 10, as from 1 April 2007 (for the purposes of enabling applications to be made for (i) a Part IV permission, (ii) a variation of a Part IV permission, and (iii) the Authority's approval under s 59 of the 2000 Act, in relation to an activity of the kind specified by art 25D of this Order, or in relation to an investment of the kind specified by arts 83, 84 or 85 of this Order), and as from 1 November 2007 (otherwise).

[8.39]
23　Risk management

(1)　A person ("B") does not carry on an activity of the kind specified by article 21 by entering as agent for a relevant person into a transaction with another person ("C") if—

    (a)　the transaction relates to investments of the kind specified by any of articles 83 to 85 (or article 89 so far as relevant to any of those articles);

    (b)　neither B nor C is an individual;

    (c)　the sole or main purpose for which B enters into the transaction (either by itself or in combination with other such transactions) is that of limiting the extent to which a relevant business will be affected by any identifiable risk arising otherwise than as a result of the carrying on of a regulated activity; and

    (d)　the relevant business consists mainly of activities other than—

        (i)　regulated activities; or

        (ii)　activities which would be regulated activities but for any exclusion made by this Part.

(2)　In paragraph (1), "relevant person" means—

    (a)　a member of the same group as B; or

(b) where B and another person are, or propose to become, participators in a joint enterprise, that other person;

and "relevant business" means a business carried on by a relevant person.

[(3) This article is subject to article 4(4).]

NOTES

Para (3): added by the Financial Services and Markets Act 2000 (Regulated Activities) (Amendment No 3) Order 2006, SI 2006/3384, arts 2, 11, as from 1 April 2007 (for the purposes of enabling applications to be made for (i) a Part IV permission, (ii) a variation of a Part IV permission, and (iii) the Authority's approval under s 59 of the 2000 Act, in relation to an activity of the kind specified by art 25D of this Order, or in relation to an investment of the kind specified by arts 83, 84 or 85 of this Order), and as from 1 November 2007 (otherwise).

[8.40]
24 Other exclusions

Article 21 is also subject to the exclusions in articles 67 (profession or non-investment business), 68 (sale of goods and supply of services), 69 (groups and joint enterprises), 70 (sale of body corporate), 71 (employee share schemes)[, 72 (overseas persons)[, 72A (information society services), 72B (activities carried on by a provider of relevant goods or services) and 72D (large risks contracts where risk situated outside the EEA)]].

NOTES

Words in first (outer) pair of square brackets substituted by the Financial Services and Markets Act 2000 (Regulated Activities) (Amendment) (No 2) Order 2002, SI 2002/1776, art 3(1), (5), as from 21 August 2002; words in second (inner) pair of square brackets substituted by the Financial Services and Markets Act 2000 (Regulated Activities) (Amendment) (No 2) Order 2003, SI 2003/1476, art 4(3), as from 31 October 2004 (in so far as relating to contracts of long-term care insurance), and as from 14 January 2005 (otherwise) (for transitional provisions in relation to applications for Part IV permissions and applications for approvals, etc, see arts 22–27 of the 2003 Order).

CHAPTER VI
ARRANGING DEALS IN INVESTMENTS
The activities

[8.41]
25 Arranging deals in investments

(1) Making arrangements for another person (whether as principal or agent) to buy, sell, subscribe for or underwrite a particular investment which is—
(a) a security,
(b) a [relevant investment], or
(c) an investment of the kind specified by article 86, or article 89 so far as relevant to that article,
is a specified kind of activity.

(2) Making arrangements with a view to a person who participates in the arrangements buying, selling, subscribing for or underwriting investments falling within paragraph (1)(a), (b) or (c) (whether as principal or agent) is also a specified kind of activity.

[(3) Paragraphs (1) and (2) do not apply to a kind of activity to which article 25D applies.]

NOTES

Para (1): words in square brackets substituted by the Financial Services and Markets Act 2000 (Regulated Activities) (Amendment) (No 2) Order 2003, SI 2003/1476, art 5(1), as from 31 October 2004 (in so far as relating to contracts of long-term care insurance), and as from 14 January 2005 (otherwise) (for transitional provisions in relation to applications for Part IV permissions and applications for approvals, etc, see arts 22–27 of the 2003 Order).

Para (3): added by the Financial Services and Markets Act 2000 (Regulated Activities) (Amendment No 3) Order 2006, SI 2006/3384, arts 2, 12, as from 1 April 2007 (for the purposes of enabling applications to be made for (i) a Part IV permission, (ii) a variation of a Part IV permission, and (iii) the Authority's approval under s 59 of the 2000 Act, in relation to an activity of the kind specified by art 25D of this Order, or in relation to an investment of the kind specified by arts 83, 84 or 85 of this Order), and as from 1 November 2007 (otherwise).

[8.42]
[25A Arranging regulated mortgage contracts

(1) Making arrangements—
(a) for another person to enter into a regulated mortgage contract as borrower; or
(b) for another person to vary the terms of a regulated mortgage contract entered into by him as borrower after the coming into force of article 61, in such a way as to vary his obligations under that contract,
is a specified kind of activity.

(2) Making arrangements with a view to a person who participates in the arrangements entering into a regulated mortgage contract as borrower is also a specified kind of activity.

(3) In this article "borrower" has the meaning given by article 61(3)(a)(i).]

NOTES

Inserted by the Financial Services and Markets Act 2000 (Regulated Activities) (Amendment) (No 1) Order 2003, SI 2003/1475, art 4, as from 31 October 2004 (for transitional provisions in relation to applications for Part IV permissions and applications for approvals, etc, see arts 26–29 of the 2003 Order).

[8.43]
[25B Arranging regulated home reversion plans

(1) Making arrangements—
  (a)   for another person to enter into a regulated home reversion plan as reversion seller or as plan provider; or
  (b)   for another person to vary the terms of a regulated home reversion plan, entered into on or after 6th April 2007 by him as reversion seller or as plan provider, in such a way as to vary his obligations under that plan,
is a specified kind of activity.

(2) Making arrangements with a view to a person who participates in the arrangements entering into a regulated home reversion plan as reversion seller or as plan provider is also a specified kind of activity.]

NOTES

Commencement: 6 November 2006 (certain purposes); 6 April 2007 (otherwise) (for more information see the note below).
Inserted, together with art 25C, by the Financial Services and Markets Act 2000 (Regulated Activities) (Amendment) (No 2) Order 2006, SI 2006/2383, arts 2, 4, as from 6 November 2006 (for the purposes of enabling applications to be made for (i) a Pt IV permission, or a variation of a Pt IV permission, in relation to activities of the kind specified by arts 25B, 25C, 53B, 53C, 63B or 63F or, so far as relevant to any such activity, art 64 of this Order; or (ii) the Authority's approval under FSMA 2000, s 59 in relation to any of those activities), and as from 6 April 2007 (otherwise) (for transitional provisions in relation to interim permissions and interim approvals, etc, see arts 36–40 of, and the Schedule to, the 2006 Order).

[8.44]
[25C Arranging regulated home purchase plans

(1) Making arrangements—
  (a)   for another person to enter into a regulated home purchase plan as home purchaser; or
  (b)   for another person to vary the terms of a regulated home purchase plan, entered into on or after 6th April 2007 by him as home purchaser, in such a way as to vary his obligations under that plan,
is a specified kind of activity.

(2) Making arrangements with a view to a person who participates in the arrangements entering into a regulated home purchase plan as home purchaser is also a specified kind of activity.]

NOTES

Commencement: 6 November 2006 (certain purposes); 6 April 2007 (otherwise) (for more information see the note to art 25B at **[8.43]**).
Inserted as noted to art 25B at **[8.43]**.

[8.45]
[25D Operating a multilateral trading facility

(1) The operation of a multilateral trading facility on which MiFID instruments are traded is a specified kind of activity.

(2) In paragraph (1), "MiFID instrument" means any investment—
  (a)   of the kind specified by article 76, 77, [77A,] 78, 79, 80, 81, 83, 84 or 85; or
  (b)   of the kind specified by article 89 so far as relevant to an investment falling within sub-paragraph (a),
that is a financial instrument.]

NOTES

Commencement: 1 April 2007 (certain purposes); 1 November 2007 (otherwise) (for more information see below).
Inserted by the Financial Services and Markets Act 2000 (Regulated Activities) (Amendment No 3) Order 2006, SI 2006/3384, arts 2, 13, as from 1 April 2007 (for the purposes of enabling applications to be made for (i) a Part IV permission, (ii) a variation of a Part IV permission, and (iii) the Authority's approval under s 59 of the 2000 Act, in relation to an activity of the kind specified by art 25D of this Order, or in relation to an investment of the kind specified by arts 83, 84 or 85 of this Order), and as from 1 November 2007 (otherwise).
Para (2): figure in square brackets inserted by the Financial Services and Markets Act 2000 (Regulated Activities) (Amendment) Order 2010, SI 2010/86, art 4, Schedule, para 5(b), as from 24 February 2010.

[8.46]
[25E Arranging regulated sale and rent back agreements

(1) Making arrangements—
  (a)   for another person to enter into a regulated sale and rent back agreement as an agreement seller or as an agreement provider; or

Part 8   FSMA 2000: SIs

(b)　for another person ("A") to vary the terms of a regulated sale and rent back agreement, entered into on or after 1st July 2009 by A as agreement seller or agreement provider, in such a way as to vary A's obligations under that agreement,

is a specified kind of activity.

(2)　Making arrangements with a view to a person who participates in the arrangements entering into a regulated sale and rent back agreement as agreement seller or agreement provider is also a specified kind of activity.]

NOTES

Commencement: 1 July 2009 (certain purposes); 30 June 2010 (otherwise) (see below).

Inserted by the Financial Services and Markets Act 2000 (Regulated Activities) (Amendment) Order 2009, SI 2009/1342, arts 2, 4, as from 1 July 2009 (other than for the purposes of enabling applications to be made for a Part IV permission, or a variation of a Part IV permission, in relation to activities of the kind specified by arts 25E, 53D or 63J or, so far as relevant to any such activity, art 64 of this Order), and as from 30 June 2010 (for those purposes) (for transitional provisions in relation to applications for Part IV permissions, etc, see arts 1, 32–34 of that Order).

Exclusions

[8.47]
26　Arrangements not causing a deal

There are excluded from [articles 25(1), 25A(1), 25B(1)[, 25C(1) and 25E(1)]] arrangements which do not or would not bring about the transaction to which the arrangements relate.

NOTES

Words in first (outer) pair of square brackets substituted by the Financial Services and Markets Act 2000 (Regulated Activities) (Amendment) (No 2) Order 2006, SI 2006/2383, arts 2, 5, as from 6 November 2006 (for the purposes of enabling applications to be made for (i) a Pt IV permission, or a variation of a Pt IV permission, in relation to activities of the kind specified by arts 25B, 25C, 53B, 53C, 63B or 63F or, so far as relevant to any such activity, art 64 of this Order; or (ii) the Authority's approval under FSMA 2000, s 59 in relation to any of those activities), and as from 6 April 2007 (otherwise) (for transitional provisions in relation to interim permissions and interim approvals, etc, see arts 36–40 of, and the Schedule to, the 2006 Order).

Words in second (inner) pair of square brackets substituted by the Financial Services and Markets Act 2000 (Regulated Activities) (Amendment) Order 2009, SI 2009/1342, arts 2, 5, as from 1 July 2009 (other than for the purposes of enabling applications to be made for a Part IV permission, or a variation of a Part IV permission, in relation to activities of the kind specified by arts 25E, 53D or 63J or, so far as relevant to any such activity, art 64 of this Order), and as from 30 June 2010 (for those purposes) (for transitional provisions in relation to applications for Part IV permissions, etc, see arts 1, 32–34 of that Order).

[8.48]
27　Enabling parties to communicate

A person does not carry on an activity of the kind specified by [article 25(2), 25A(2), 25B(2)[, 25C(2) or 25E(2)]] merely by providing means by which one party to a transaction (or potential transaction) is able to communicate with other such parties.

NOTES

Words in first (outer) pair of square brackets substituted by the Financial Services and Markets Act 2000 (Regulated Activities) (Amendment) (No 2) Order 2006, SI 2006/2383, arts 2, 6, as from 6 November 2006 (for the purposes of enabling applications to be made for (i) a Pt IV permission, or a variation of a Pt IV permission, in relation to activities of the kind specified by arts 25B, 25C, 53B, 53C, 63B or 63F or, so far as relevant to any such activity, art 64 of this Order; or (ii) the Authority's approval under FSMA 2000, s 59 in relation to any of those activities), and as from 6 April 2007 (otherwise) (for transitional provisions in relation to interim permissions and interim approvals, etc, see arts 36–40 of, and the Schedule to, the 2006 Order).

Words in second (inner) pair of square brackets substituted by the Financial Services and Markets Act 2000 (Regulated Activities) (Amendment) Order 2009, SI 2009/1342, arts 2, 6, as from 1 July 2009 (other than for the purposes of enabling applications to be made for a Part IV permission, or a variation of a Part IV permission, in relation to activities of the kind specified by arts 25E, 53D or 63J or, so far as relevant to any such activity, art 64 of this Order), and as from 30 June 2010 (for those purposes) (for transitional provisions in relation to applications for Part IV permissions, etc, see arts 1, 32–34 of that Order).

[8.49]
28　Arranging transactions to which the arranger is a party

(1)　There are excluded from article 25(1) any arrangements for a transaction into which the person making the arrangements enters or is to enter as principal or as agent for some other person.

(2)　There are excluded from article 25(2) any arrangements which a person makes with a view to transactions into which he enters or is to enter as principal or as agent for some other person.

[(3)　But the exclusions in paragraphs (1) and (2) do not apply to arrangements made for or with a view to a transaction which relates to a contract of insurance, unless the person making the arrangements either—

(a)　is the only policyholder; or
(b)　as a result of the transaction, would become the only policyholder.]

NOTES

Para (3): added by the Financial Services and Markets Act 2000 (Regulated Activities) (Amendment) (No 2) Order 2003, SI 2003/1476, art 5(2), as from 31 October 2004 (in so far as relating to contracts of long-term care insurance), and as from 14 January 2005 (otherwise) (for transitional provisions in relation to applications for Part IV permissions and applications for approvals, etc, see arts 22–27 of the 2003 Order).

[8.50]
[28A Arranging contracts[, plans or agreements] to which the arranger is a party]

[(1)   There are excluded from [articles 25A(1), 25B(1)[, 25C(1) and 25E(1)]] any arrangements—
   (a)   for a [contract][, plan or agreement] into which the person making the arrangements enters or is to enter; or
   (b)   for a variation of a [contract][, plan or agreement] to which that person is (or is to become) a party.

(2)   There are excluded from [articles 25A(2), 25B(2)][, 25C(2) and 25E(2)]] any arrangements which a person makes with a view to contracts[, plans or agreements] into which he enters or is to enter.]

NOTES

Inserted by the Financial Services and Markets Act 2000 (Regulated Activities) (Amendment) (No 1) Order 2003, SI 2003/1475, art 7, as from 31 October 2004 (for transitional provisions in relation to applications for Part IV permissions and applications for approvals, etc, see arts 26–29 of the 2003 Order).

Article heading: words in square brackets inserted by the Financial Services and Markets Act 2000 (Regulated Activities) (Amendment) (No 2) Order 2006, SI 2006/2383, arts 2, 7(1), as from 6 November 2006 (for the purposes of enabling applications to be made for (i) a Pt IV permission, or a variation of a Pt IV permission, in relation to activities of the kind specified by arts 25B, 25C, 53B, 53C, 63B or 63F or, so far as relevant to any such activity, art 64 of this Order; or (ii) the Authority's approval under FSMA 2000, s 59 in relation to any of those activities), and as from 6 April 2007 (otherwise) (for transitional provisions in relation to interim permissions and interim approvals, etc, see arts 36–40 of, and the Schedule to, the 2006 Order). Those words were substituted by the Financial Services and Markets Act 2000 (Regulated Activities) (Amendment) Order 2009, SI 2009/1342, arts 2, 7(1), as from 1 July 2009 (other than for the purposes of enabling applications to be made for a Part IV permission, or a variation of a Part IV permission, in relation to activities of the kind specified by arts 25E, 53D or 63J or, so far as relevant to any such activity, art 64 of this Order), and as from 30 June 2010 (for those purposes) (for transitional provisions in relation to applications for Part IV permissions, etc, see arts 1, 32–34 of that Order).

Para (1): words in first (outer), third and fifth pairs of square brackets substituted by SI 2006/2383, arts 2, 7(1)(a), as from 6 November 2006 (certain purposes), and as from 6 April 2007 (otherwise) (for purposes, transitional provisions, and effect, see the note "Article heading" above); other words in square brackets substituted by SI 2009/1342, arts 2, 7(2)(a), as from the same dates and for the same purposes, etc, as mentioned in the note relating to this Order above.

Para (2): words in first pair of square brackets substituted by SI 2006/2383, arts 2, 7(1)(b)(i), as from 6 November 2006 (certain purposes), and as from 6 April 2007 (otherwise) (for purposes, transitional provisions, and effect, see the note "Article heading" above); words in second and third pairs of square brackets substituted by SI 2009/1342, arts 2, 7(2)(b), as from the same dates and for the same purposes, etc, as mentioned in the note relating to this Order above.

[8.51]
29 Arranging deals with or through authorised persons

(1)   There are excluded from [articles 25(1) and (2), 25A(1) and (2), 25B(1) and (2)[, 25C(1) and (2) and 25E(1) and (2)]] arrangements made by a person ("A") who is not an authorised person for or with a view to a transaction which is or is to be entered into by a person ("the client") with or though an authorised person if—
   (a)   the transaction is or is to be entered into on advice to the client by an authorised person; or
   (b)   it is clear, in all the circumstances, that the client, in his capacity as an [investor, borrower, reversion seller, plan provider, home purchaser, agreement provider or (as the case may be) agreement seller], is not seeking and has not sought advice from A as to the merits of the client's entering into the transaction (or, if the client has sought such advice, A has declined to give it but has recommended that the client seek such advice from an authorised person).

[(2)   But the exclusion in paragraph (1) does not apply if—
   (a)   the transaction relates, or would relate, to a contract of insurance; or
   (b)   A receives from any person other than the client any pecuniary reward or other advantage, for which he does not account to the client, arising out of his making the arrangements.]

[(3)   This article is subject to article 4(4).]

NOTES

Para (1): words in first (outer) pair of square brackets substituted by the Financial Services and Markets Act 2000 (Regulated Activities) (Amendment) (No 2) Order 2006, SI 2006/2383, arts 2, 8, as from 6 November 2006 (for the purposes of enabling applications to be made for (i) a Pt IV permission, or a variation of a Pt IV permission, in relation to activities of the kind specified by arts 25B, 25C, 53B, 53C, 63B or 63F or, so far as relevant to any such activity, art 64 of this Order; or (ii) the Authority's approval under FSMA 2000, s 59 in relation to any of those activities), and as from 6 April 2007 (otherwise) (for transitional provisions in relation to interim permissions and interim approvals, etc, see arts 36–40 of, and the Schedule to, the 2006 Order); words in second (inner) and third pairs of square brackets substituted by the Financial Services and Markets Act 2000 (Regulated Activities) (Amendment) Order 2009, SI 2009/1342, arts 2, 8, as from 1 July 2009 (other than for the purposes of enabling applications to be made for a Part IV permission, or a variation of a Part IV permission, in relation to activities of the kind specified by arts 25E, 53D or 63J or, so far as relevant to any such activity, art 64 of this Order), and as from 30 June 2010 (for those purposes) (for transitional provisions in relation to applications for Part IV permissions, etc, see arts 1, 32–34 of that Order).

Para (2): substituted by the Financial Services and Markets Act 2000 (Regulated Activities) (Amendment) (No 2) Order 2003, SI 2003/1476, art 5(3), as from 31 October 2004 (in so far as relating to contracts of long-term care insurance), and as from 14 January 2005 (otherwise) (for transitional provisions in relation to applications for Part IV permissions and applications for approvals, etc, see arts 22–27 of the 2003 Order).

Para (3): added by the Financial Services and Markets Act 2000 (Regulated Activities) (Amendment No 3) Order 2006, SI 2006/3384, arts 2, 14, as from 1 April 2007 (for the purposes of enabling applications to be made for (i) a Part IV permission, (ii) a variation of a Part IV permission, and (iii) the Authority's approval under s 59 of the 2000 Act, in relation to an activity of the kind specified by art 25D of this Order, or in relation to an investment of the kind specified by arts 83, 84 or 85 of this Order), and as from 1 November 2007 (otherwise).

[8.52]
[29A   Arrangements made in the course of administration by authorised person

[(1)]   A person who is not an authorised person ("A") does not carry on an activity of the kind specified by article 25A(1)(b) as a result of—

(a)   anything done by an authorised person ("B") in relation to a regulated mortgage contract which B is administering pursuant to an arrangement of the kind mentioned in article 62(a); or

(b)   anything A does in connection with the administration of a regulated mortgage contract in circumstances falling within article 62(b).

[(2)   A person who is not an authorised person ("A") does not carry on an activity of the kind specified by article 25B(1)(b) as a result of—

(a)   anything done by an authorised person ("B") in relation to a regulated home reversion plan which B is administering pursuant to an arrangement of the kind mentioned in article 63C(a); or

(b)   anything A does in connection with the administration of a regulated home reversion plan in circumstances falling within article 63C(b).

(3)   A person who is not an authorised person ("A") does not carry on an activity of the kind specified by article 25C(1)(b) as a result of—

(a)   anything done by an authorised person ("B") in relation to a regulated home purchase plan which B is administering pursuant to an arrangement of the kind mentioned in article 63G(a); or

(b)   anything A does in connection with the administration of a regulated home purchase plan in circumstances falling within article 63G(b).]]

[(4)   A person who is not an authorised person ("A") does not carry on an activity of the kind specified by article 25E(1)(b) as a result of—

(a)   anything done by an authorised person ("B") in relation to a regulated sale and rent back agreement which B is administering pursuant to an arrangement of the kind mentioned in article 63K(a); or

(b)   anything A does in connection with the administration of a regulated sale and rent back agreement in circumstances falling within article 63K(b).]

NOTES
Inserted by the Financial Services and Markets Act 2000 (Regulated Activities) (Amendment) (No 1) Order 2003, SI 2003/1475, art 9, as from 31 October 2004 (for transitional provisions in relation to applications for Part IV permissions and applications for approvals, etc, see arts 26–29 of the 2003 Order).

Para (1) numbered as such, and paras (2), (3) added, by the Financial Services and Markets Act 2000 (Regulated Activities) (Amendment) (No 2) Order 2006, SI 2006/2383, arts 2, 9, as from 6 November 2006 (for the purposes of enabling applications to be made for (i) a Pt IV permission, or a variation of a Pt IV permission, in relation to activities of the kind specified by arts 25B, 25C, 53B, 53C, 63B or 63F or, so far as relevant to any such activity, art 64 of this Order; or (ii) the Authority's approval under FSMA 2000, s 59 in relation to any of those activities), and as from 6 April 2007 (otherwise) (for transitional provisions in relation to interim permissions and interim approvals, etc, see arts 36–40 of, and the Schedule to, the 2006 Order).

Para (4): added by the Financial Services and Markets Act 2000 (Regulated Activities) (Amendment) Order 2009, SI 2009/1342, arts 2, 9, as from 1 July 2009 (other than for the purposes of enabling applications to be made for a Part IV permission, or a variation of a Part IV permission, in relation to activities of the kind specified by arts 25E, 53D or 63J or, so far as relevant to any such activity, art 64 of this Order), and as from 30 June 2010 (for those purposes) (for transitional provisions in relation to applications for Part IV permissions, etc, see arts 1, 32–34 of that Order).

[8.53]
30   Arranging transactions in connection with lending on the security of insurance policies

(1)   There are excluded from article 25(1) and (2) arrangements made by a money-lender under which either—

[(a)   a relevant authorised person or a person acting on his behalf will introduce to the money-lender persons with whom the relevant authorised person has entered, or proposes to enter, into a relevant transaction, or will advise such persons to approach the money-lender, with a view to the money-lender lending money on the security of any contract effected pursuant to a relevant transaction;]

(b)　a relevant authorised person gives an assurance to the money-lender as to the amount which, on the security of any contract effected pursuant to a relevant transaction, will or may be received by the money-lender should the money-lender lend money to a person introduced to him pursuant to the arrangements.

(2)　In paragraph (1)—

"money-lender" means a person who is—

    (a)　a money-lending company within the meaning of [section 209 of the Companies Act 2006];

    (b)　a body corporate incorporated under the law of, or of any part of, the United Kingdom relating to building societies; or

    (c)　a person whose ordinary business includes the making of loans or the giving of guarantees in connection with loans;

"relevant authorised person" means an authorised person who has permission to effect [contracts of insurance] or to sell investments of the kind specified by article 89, so far as relevant to such contracts;

"relevant transaction" means the effecting of a [contract of insurance] or the sale of an investment of the kind specified by article 89, so far as relevant to such contracts.

[(3)　This article is subject to article 4(4A).]

NOTES

Para (1): sub-para (a) substituted by the Financial Services and Markets Act 2000 (Regulated Activities) (Amendment) Order 2001, SI 2001/3544, arts 2, 5, as from 1 December 2001.

Para (2): words in square brackets in definition "money-lender" substituted by the Companies Act 2006 (Consequential Amendments and Transitional Provisions) Order 2011, SI 2011/1265, art 13(1), (4), as from 12 May 2011; words in square brackets in definitions "relevant authorised person" and "relevant transaction" substituted by the Financial Services and Markets Act 2000 (Regulated Activities) (Amendment) (No 2) Order 2003, SI 2003/1476, art 5(4), as from 31 October 2004 (in so far as relating to contracts of long-term care insurance), and as from 14 January 2005 (otherwise) (for transitional provisions in relation to applications for Part IV permissions and applications for approvals, etc, see arts 22–27 of the 2003 Order).

Para (3): added by the Financial Services and Markets Act 2000 (Regulated Activities) (Amendment No 3) Order 2006, SI 2006/3384, arts 2, 15, as from 1 April 2007 (for the purposes of enabling applications to be made for (i) a Part IV permission, (ii) a variation of a Part IV permission, and (iii) the Authority's approval under s 59 of the 2000 Act, in relation to an activity of the kind specified by art 25D of this Order, or in relation to an investment of the kind specified by arts 83, 84 or 85 of this Order), and as from 1 November 2007 (otherwise).

[8.54]

31　Arranging the acceptance of debentures in connection with loans

(1)　There are excluded from article 25(1) and (2) arrangements under which a person accepts or is to accept, whether as principal or agent, an instrument creating or acknowledging indebtedness in respect of any loan, credit, guarantee or other similar financial accommodation or assurance which is, or is to be, made, granted or provided by that person or his principal.

(2)　The reference in paragraph (1) to a person accepting an instrument includes a reference to a person becoming a party to an instrument otherwise than as a debtor or a surety.

NOTES

Modification: references in para (1) to securities, instruments or investments creating or acknowledging indebtedness (or creating or acknowledging a present or future indebtedness) includes a reference to uncertificated units of eligible debt securities; see the Uncertificated Securities (Amendment) (Eligible Debt Securities) Regulations 2003, SI 2003/1633, reg 15, Sch 2, para 8.

Modification: references in para (2) to a person becoming party to an instrument includes a reference to a person assuming rights and obligations in respect of uncertificated units of an eligible debt security in accordance with its current terms of issue; see the Uncertificated Securities (Amendment) (Eligible Debt Securities) Regulations 2003, SI 2003/1633, reg 15, Sch 2, para 9.

[8.55]

32　Provision of finance

There are excluded from article 25(2) arrangements having as their sole purpose the provision of finance to enable a person to buy, sell, subscribe for or underwrite investments.

[8.56]

33　Introducing

There are excluded from [articles 25(2), 25A(2), 25B(2)[, 25C(2) and 25E(2)]] arrangements where—

    (a)　they are arrangements under which persons ("clients") will be introduced to another person;

    (b)　the person to whom introductions are to be made is—

        (i)　an authorised person;

        (ii)　an exempt person acting in the course of a business comprising a regulated activity in relation to which he is exempt; or

        (iii)　a person who is not unlawfully carrying on regulated activities in the United Kingdom and whose ordinary business involves him in engaging in an activity of the kind specified by any of articles 14, 21, 25, [25A,] [25B, 25C,] [25E,] 37[, 39A], 40,

45, 51, [52, 53[, 53A, 53B][, 53C and 53D]] (or, so far as relevant to any of those articles, article 64), or would do so apart from any exclusion from any of those articles made by this Order; . . .

(c)   the introduction is made with a view to the provision of independent advice or the independent exercise of discretion in relation to investments generally or in relation to any class of investments to which the arrangements relate[; and

(d)   the arrangements are made with a view to a person entering into a transaction which does not relate to a contract of insurance].

NOTES

Words in first (outer) pair of square brackets substituted by the Financial Services and Markets Act 2000 (Regulated Activities) (Amendment) (No 2) Order 2006, SI 2006/2383, arts 2, 10(a), as from 6 November 2006 (for the purposes of enabling applications to be made for (i) a Pt IV permission, or a variation of a Pt IV permission, in relation to activities of the kind specified by arts 25B, 25C, 53B, 53C, 63B or 63F or, so far as relevant to any such activity, art 64 of this Order; or (ii) the Authority's approval under FSMA 2000, s 59 in relation to any of those activities), and as from 6 April 2007 (otherwise) (for transitional provisions in relation to interim permissions and interim approvals, etc, see arts 36–40 of, and the Schedule to, the 2006 Order).

Words in second (inner) pair of square brackets substituted by the Financial Services and Markets Act 2000 (Regulated Activities) (Amendment) Order 2009, SI 2009/1342, arts 2, 10(a), as from 1 July 2009 (other than for the purposes of enabling applications to be made for a Part IV permission, or a variation of a Part IV permission, in relation to activities of the kind specified by arts 25E, 53D or 63J or, so far as relevant to any such activity, art 64 of this Order), and as from 30 June 2010 (for those purposes) (for transitional provisions in relation to applications for Part IV permissions, etc, see arts 1, 32–34 of that Order).

Figure in first pair of square brackets in para (b)(iii) inserted, and words in the fifth (outer) pair of square brackets in that paragraph substituted, by the Financial Services and Markets Act 2000 (Regulated Activities) (Amendment) (No 1) Order 2003, SI 2003/1475, art 10, as from 31 October 2004 (for transitional provisions in relation to applications for Part IV permissions and applications for approvals, etc, see arts 26–29 of the 2003 Order).

Figures in second pair of square brackets in para (b)(iii) inserted, and words in sixth (inner) pair of square brackets substituted, by SI 2006/2383, arts 2, 10(b), as from 6 November 2006 (certain purposes), and as from 6 April 2007 (otherwise) (for purposes, transitional provisions, and effect, see the note above).

Figure in third pair of square brackets in para (b)(iii) inserted, and words in final pair of square brackets in para (b)(iii) substituted, by SI 2009/1342, arts 2, 10(b), as from the same dates and for the same purposes, etc, as mentioned in the note relating to this Order above.

Figure in fourth pair of square brackets in para (b)(iii) inserted, word omitted from that paragraph revoked, and para (d) and the word immediately preceding it added, by the Financial Services and Markets Act 2000 (Regulated Activities) (Amendment) (No 2) Order 2003, SI 2003/1476, art 5(5), as from 31 October 2004 (in so far as relating to contracts of long-term care insurance), and as from 14 January 2005 (otherwise) (for transitional provisions in relation to applications for Part IV permissions and applications for approvals, etc, see arts 22–27 of the 2003 Order).

[8.57]
[33A   Introducing to authorised persons etc

(1)   There are excluded from article 25A(2) arrangements where—

(a)   they are arrangements under which a client is introduced to a person ("N") who is—

(i)   an authorised person who has permission to carry on a regulated activity of the kind specified by any of articles 25A, 53A, and 61(1),

(ii)   an appointed representative who may carry on a regulated activity of the kind specified by either of articles 25A and 53A without contravening the general prohibition, or

(iii)   an overseas person who carries on activities specified by any of articles 25A, 53A and 61(1); and

(b)   the conditions mentioned in paragraph (2) are satisfied.

[(1A)   There are excluded from article 25B(2) arrangements where—

(a)   they are arrangements under which a client is introduced to a person ("N") who is—

(i)   an authorised person who has permission to carry on a regulated activity of the kind specified by any of articles 25B, 53B and 63B(1),

(ii)   an appointed representative who may carry on a regulated activity of the kind specified by either of articles 25B and 53B without contravening the general prohibition, or

(iii)   an overseas person who carries on activities specified by any of articles 25B, 53B and 63B(1); and

(b)   the conditions mentioned in paragraph (2) are satisfied.

(1B)   There are excluded from article 25C(2) arrangements where—

(a)   they are arrangements under which a client is introduced to a person ("N") who is—

(i)   an authorised person who has permission to carry on a regulated activity of the kind specified by any of articles 25C, 53C and 63F(1),

(ii)   an appointed representative who may carry on a regulated activity of the kind specified by either of articles 25C and 53C without contravening the general prohibition, or

(iii)   an overseas person who carries on activities specified by any of articles 25C, 53C and 63F(1); and

(b)   the conditions mentioned in paragraph (2) are satisfied.]

[(1C)   There are excluded from article 25E(2) arrangements where—
    (a)   they are arrangements under which a client is introduced to a person ("N") who is—
        (i)   an authorised person who has permission to carry on a regulated activity of the kind specified by any of articles 25E, 53D and 63J(1),
        (ii)   an appointed representative who may carry on a regulated activity of the kind specified by either of articles 25E or 53D without contravening the general prohibition, or
        (iii) an overseas person who carries on activities specified by any of articles 25E, 53D and 63J(1); and
    (b)   the conditions mentioned in paragraph (2) are satisfied.]

(2)   Those conditions are—
    (a)   that the person making the introduction ("P") does not receive any money, other than money payable to P on his own account, paid by the client for or in connection with any transaction which the client enters into with or through N as a result of the introduction; and
    (b)   that before making the introduction P discloses to the client such of the information mentioned in paragraph (3) as applies to P.

(3)   That information is—
    (a)   that P is a member of the same group as N;
    (b)   details of any payment which P will receive from N, by way of fee or commission, for introducing the client to N;
    (c)   an indication of any other reward or advantage received or to be received by P that arises out of his introducing clients to N.

[(4)   In this article, "client" means—
    (a)   for the purposes of paragraph (1), a borrower within the meaning given by article 61(3)(a)(i), or a person who is or may be contemplating entering into a regulated mortgage contract as such a borrower;
    (b)   for the purposes of paragraph (1A), a reversion seller, a plan provider or a person who is or may be contemplating entering into a regulated home reversion plan as a reversion seller or as a plan provider;
    (c)   for the purposes of paragraph (1B), a home purchaser or a person who is or may be contemplating entering into a regulated home purchase plan as a home purchaser[;
    (d)   for the purposes of paragraph (1C), an agreement provider, an agreement seller or a person who is or may be contemplating entering into a regulated sale and rent back agreement as an agreement provider or agreement seller.]]

NOTES

Inserted by the Financial Services and Markets Act 2000 (Regulated Activities) (Amendment) (No 1) Order 2003, SI 2003/1475, art 11, as from 31 October 2004 (for transitional provisions in relation to applications for Part IV permissions and applications for approvals, etc, see arts 26–29 of the 2003 Order).

Paras (1A), (1B) inserted by the Financial Services and Markets Act 2000 (Regulated Activities) (Amendment) (No 2) Order 2006, SI 2006/2383, arts 2, 11(a), as from 6 November 2006 (for the purposes of enabling applications to be made for (i) a Pt IV permission, or a variation of a Pt IV permission, in relation to activities of the kind specified by arts 25B, 25C, 53B, 53C, 63B or 63F or, so far as relevant to any such activity, art 64 of this Order; or (ii) the Authority's approval under FSMA 2000, s 59 in relation to any of those activities), and as from 6 April 2007 (otherwise) (for transitional provisions in relation to interim permissions and interim approvals, etc, see arts 36–40 of, and the Schedule to, the 2006 Order).

Para (1C): inserted by the Financial Services and Markets Act 2000 (Regulated Activities) (Amendment) Order 2009, SI 2009/1342, arts 2, 11(a), as from 1 July 2009 (other than for the purposes of enabling applications to be made for a Part IV permission, or a variation of a Part IV permission, in relation to activities of the kind specified by arts 25E, 53D or 63J or, so far as relevant to any such activity, art 64 of this Order), and as from 30 June 2010 (for those purposes) (for transitional provisions in relation to applications for Part IV permissions, etc, see arts 1, 32–34 of that Order).

Para (4): substituted by SI 2006/2383, arts 2, 11(b), as from 6 November 2006 (certain purposes), and as from 6 April 2007 (otherwise) (for purposes, transitional provisions, and effect, see the note above); sub-para (d) inserted by SI 2009/1342, arts 2, 11(b), as from the same dates and for the same purposes, etc, as mentioned in the note relating to this Order above.

[8.58]
34   Arrangements for the issue of shares etc
(1)   There are excluded from article 25(1) and (2)—
    (a)   arrangements made by a company for the purposes of issuing its own shares or share warrants; and
    (b)   arrangements made by any person for the purposes of issuing his own debentures or debenture warrants;
and for the purposes of article 25(1) and (2), a company is not, by reason of issuing its own shares or share warrants, and a person is not, by reason of issuing his own debentures or debenture warrants, to be treated as selling them.
(2)   In paragraph (1), "company", "shares", "debentures", "share warrants" and "debenture warrants" have the meanings given by article 18(2).

[8.59]

35 International securities self-regulating organisations

(1) There are excluded from article 25(1) and (2) any arrangements made for the purposes of carrying out the functions of a body or association which is approved under this article as an international securities self-regulating organisation, whether the arrangements are made by the organisation itself or by a person acting on its behalf.

(2) The Treasury may approve as an international securities self-regulating organisation any body corporate or unincorporated association with respect to which the conditions mentioned in paragraph (3) appear to them to be met if, having regard to such matters affecting international trade, overseas earnings and the balance of payments or otherwise as they consider relevant, it appears to them that to do so would be desirable and not result in any undue risk to investors.

(3) The conditions are that—

(a) the body or association does not have its head office in the United Kingdom;

(b) the body or association is not eligible for recognition under section 287 or 288 of the Act (applications by investment exchanges and clearing houses) on the ground that (whether or not it has applied, and whether or not it would be eligible on other grounds) it is unable to satisfy the requirements of one or both of paragraphs (a) and (b) of section 292(3) of the Act (requirements for overseas investment exchanges and overseas clearing houses);

(c) the body or association is able and willing to co-operate with the Authority by the sharing of information and in other ways;

(d) adequate arrangements exist for co-operation between the Authority and those responsible for the supervision of the body or association in the country or territory in which its head office is situated;

(e) the body or association has a membership composed of persons falling within any of the following categories, that is to say, authorised persons, exempt persons, and persons whose head offices are outside the United Kingdom and whose ordinary business involves them in engaging in activities which are activities of a kind specified by this Order (or would be apart from any exclusion made by this Part); and

(f) the body or association facilitates and regulates the activity of its members in the conduct of international securities business.

(4) In paragraph (3)(f), "international securities business" means the business of buying, selling, subscribing for or underwriting investments (or agreeing to do so), either as principal or agent, where—

(a) the investments are securities or [relevant investments] and are of a kind which, by their nature, and the manner in which the business is conducted, may be expected normally to be bought or dealt in by persons sufficiently expert to understand the risks involved; and

(b) either the transaction is international or each of the parties may be expected to be indifferent to the location of the other;

and, for the purposes of this definition, it is irrelevant that the investments may ultimately be bought otherwise than in the course of such business by persons not so expert.

(5) Any approval under this article is to be given by notice in writing; and the Treasury may by a further notice in writing withdraw any such approval if for any reason it appears to them that it is not appropriate to it to continue in force.

NOTES

Para (4): words in square brackets in sub-para (a) substituted by the Financial Services and Markets Act 2000 (Regulated Activities) (Amendment) (No 2) Order 2003, SI 2003/1476, art 5(6), as from 31 October 2004 (in so far as relating to contracts of long-term care insurance), and as from 14 January 2005 (otherwise) (for transitional provisions in relation to applications for Part IV permissions and applications for approvals, etc, see arts 22–27 of the 2003 Order).

[8.60]

36 Other exclusions

[(1)] Article 25 is also subject to the exclusions in articles 66 (trustees etc), 67 (profession or non-investment business), 68 (sale of goods and supply of services), 69 (groups and joint enterprises), 70 (sale of body corporate), 71 (employee share schemes)[, 72 (overseas persons)[, 72A (information society services), 72B (activities carried on by a provider of relevant goods or services), 72C (provision of information about contracts of insurance on an incidental basis) and 72D (large risks contracts where risk situated outside the EEA)]].

[(2) [Articles 25A, 25B[, 25C and 25E] are] also subject to the exclusions in articles 66 (trustees etc), 67 (profession or non-investment business), 72 (overseas persons) and 72A (information society services).]

[(3) Article 25D is also subject to the exclusion in article 72 (overseas persons).]

NOTES

Para (1): numbered as such by the Financial Services and Markets Act 2000 (Regulated Activities) (Amendment) (No 1) Order 2003, SI 2003/1475, art 12(a), as from 31 October 2004 (for transitional provisions in relation to applications for Part IV permissions and applications for approvals, etc, see arts 26–29 of the 2003 Order); words in first (outer) pair of square brackets substituted by the Financial Services and Markets Act 2000 (Regulated Activities) (Amendment) (No 2) Order 2002,

SI 2002/1776, art 3(1), (6), as from 21 August 2002; words in second (inner) pair of square brackets substituted by the Financial Services and Markets Act 2000 (Regulated Activities) (Amendment) (No 2) Order 2003, SI 2003/1476, art 5(7), as from 31 October 2004 (in so far as relating to contracts of long-term care insurance), and as from 14 January 2005 (otherwise) (for transitional provisions in relation to applications for Part IV permissions and applications for approvals, etc, see arts 22–27 of the 2003 Order).

Para (2): added by SI 2003/1475, art 12(b), as from 31 October 2004 (for transitional provisions in relation to applications for Part IV permissions and applications for approvals, etc, see arts 26–29 of the 2003 Order); words in first (outer) pair of square brackets substituted by the Financial Services and Markets Act 2000 (Regulated Activities) (Amendment) (No 2) Order 2006, SI 2006/2383, arts 2, 12, as from 6 November 2006 (for the purposes of enabling applications to be made for (i) a Pt IV permission, or a variation of a Pt IV permission, in relation to activities of the kind specified by arts 25B, 25C, 53B, 53C, 63B or 63F or, so far as relevant to any such activity, art 64 of this Order; or (ii) the Authority's approval under FSMA 2000, s 59 in relation to any of those activities), and as from 6 April 2007 (otherwise) (for transitional provisions in relation to interim permissions and interim approvals, etc, see arts 36–40 of, and the Schedule to, the 2006 Order); words in second (inner) pair of square brackets substituted by the Financial Services and Markets Act 2000 (Regulated Activities) (Amendment) Order 2009, SI 2009/1342, arts 2, 12, as from 1 July 2009 (other than for the purposes of enabling applications to be made for a Part IV permission, or a variation of a Part IV permission, in relation to activities of the kind specified by arts 25E, 53D or 63J or, so far as relevant to any such activity, art 64 of this Order), and as from 30 June 2010 (for those purposes) (for transitional provisions in relation to applications for Part IV permissions, etc, see arts 1, 32–34 of that Order).

Para (3): added by the Financial Services and Markets Act 2000 (Regulated Activities) (Amendment No 3) Order 2006, SI 2006/3384, arts 2, 16, as from 1 April 2007 (for the purposes of enabling applications to be made for (i) a Part IV permission, (ii) a variation of a Part IV permission, and (iii) the Authority's approval under s 59 of the 2000 Act, in relation to an activity of the kind specified by art 25D of this Order, or in relation to an investment of the kind specified by arts 83, 84 or 85 of this Order), and as from 1 November 2007 (otherwise).

CHAPTER VII
MANAGING INVESTMENTS

The activity

[8.61]
37 Managing investments

Managing assets belonging to another person, in circumstances involving the exercise of discretion, is a specified kind of activity if—

(a)   the assets consist of or include any investment which is a security or a contractually based investment; or

(b)   the arrangements for their management are such that the assets may consist of or include such investments, and either the assets have at any time since 29th April 1988 done so, or the arrangements have at any time (whether before or after that date) been held out as arrangements under which the assets would do so.

Exclusions

[8.62]
38 Attorneys

[(1)]   A person does not carry on an activity of the kind specified by article 37 if—

(a)   he is a person appointed to manage the assets in question under a power of attorney; and

(b)   all routine or day-to-day decisions, so far as relating to investments of a kind mentioned in article 37(a), are taken on behalf of that person by—

(i)   an authorised person with permission to carry on activities of the kind specified by article 37;   . . .

(ii)   a person who is an exempt person in relation to activities of that kind[; or

(iii)   an overseas person.]

[(2)   This article is subject to article 4(4).]

NOTES

Para (1) numbered as such, and para (2) added, by the Financial Services and Markets Act 2000 (Regulated Activities) (Amendment No 3) Order 2006, SI 2006/3384, arts 2, 17, as from 1 April 2007 (for the purposes of enabling applications to be made for (i) a Part IV permission, (ii) a variation of a Part IV permission, and (iii) the Authority's approval under s 59 of the 2000 Act, in relation to an activity of the kind specified by art 25D of this Order, or in relation to an investment of the kind specified by arts 83, 84 or 85 of this Order), and as from 1 November 2007 (otherwise). Note that the Queen's Printer's copy of SI 2006/3384 does not actually specify that the words "This article is subject to article 4(4)" should be numbered as paragraph (2) even though it does provide that the original text should be numbered as paragraph (1). It is assumed that this is an error.

Word omitted from para (1)(b)(i) revoked, and para (1)(b)(iii) and the word immediately preceding it added, by the Financial Services and Markets Act 2000 (Regulated Activities) (Amendment) Order 2001, SI 2001/3544, arts 2, 6, as from 1 December 2001.

[8.63]
39 Other exclusions

Article 37 is also subject to the exclusions in articles 66 (trustees etc), 68 (sale of goods and supply of services)[, 69 (groups and joint enterprises)[, 72A (information society services) and 72C (provision of information about contracts of insurance on an incidental basis)]].

NOTES

Words in first (outer) pair of square brackets substituted by the Financial Services and Markets Act 2000 (Regulated Activities) (Amendment) (No 2) Order 2002, SI 2002/1776, art 3(1), (7), as from 21 August 2002; words in second (inner) pair of square brackets substituted by the Financial Services and Markets Act 2000 (Regulated Activities) (Amendment) (No 2) Order 2003, SI 2003/1476, art 6, as from 31 October 2004 (in so far as relating to contracts of long-term care insurance), and as from 14 January 2005 (otherwise) (for transitional provisions in relation to applications for Part IV permissions and applications for approvals, etc, see arts 22–27 of the 2003 Order).

[CHAPTER VIIA
ASSISTING IN THE ADMINISTRATION AND PERFORMANCE OF A
CONTRACT OF INSURANCE

The Activity

[8.64]
39A   Assisting in the administration and performance of a contract of insurance

Assisting in the administration and performance of a contract of insurance is a specified kind of activity.]

NOTES

Chapter VIIA (arts 39A–39C and the preceding headings) inserted by the Financial Services and Markets Act 2000 (Regulated Activities) (Amendment) (No 2) Order 2003, SI 2003/1476, art 7, as from 31 October 2004 (in so far as relating to contracts of long-term care insurance), and as from 14 January 2005 (otherwise) (for transitional provisions in relation to applications for Part IV permissions and applications for approvals, etc, see arts 22–27 of the 2003 Order).

[Exclusions

[8.65]
39B   Claims management on behalf of an insurer etc

(1)   A person does not carry on an activity of the kind specified by article 39A if he acts in the course of carrying on the activity of—
  (a)   expert appraisal;
  (b)   loss adjusting on behalf of a relevant insurer; or
  (c)   managing claims on behalf of a relevant insurer,
and that activity is carried on in the course of carrying on any profession or business.

(2)   In this article—
  (a)   "relevant insurer" means—
    (i)   a person who has Part IV permission to carry on an activity of the kind specified by article 10;
    (ii)   a person to whom the general prohibition does not apply by virtue of section 316(1)(a) of the Act (members of the Society of Lloyd's);
    (iii)   an EEA firm falling within paragraph 5(d) of Schedule 3 to the Act (insurance undertaking); or
    (iv)   a relevant reinsurer;
  (b)   "relevant reinsurer" means a person whose main business consists of accepting risks ceded by—
    (i)   a person falling within sub-paragraph (i), (ii) or (iii) of the definition of "relevant insurer"; . . .
    [(ii)   an EEA firm falling within paragraph 5(da) of Schedule 3 to the Act (reinsurance undertaking); or
    (iii)   a person established outside the United Kingdom and not falling within paragraph (ii) who carries on an activity of the kind specified by article 10 by way of business].]

NOTES

Inserted as noted to art 39A at **[8.64]**.
Para (2): word omitted from sub-para (b)(i) revoked, and sub-paras (b)(ii), (iii) substituted (for the original sub-para (b)(ii)) by the Financial Services and Markets Act 2000 (Reinsurance Directive) Order 2007, SI 2007/3254, reg 2, as from 10 December 2007.

[8.66]
[39C   Other exclusions

Article 39A is also subject to the exclusions in articles 66 (trustees etc), 67 (profession or non-investment business), 72A (information society services), 72B (activities carried on by a provider of relevant goods or services), 72C (provision of information about contracts of insurance on an incidental basis) and 72D (large risks contracts where risk situated outside the EEA).]

NOTES

Inserted as noted to art 39A at **[8.64]**.

CHAPTER VIII
SAFEGUARDING AND ADMINISTERING INVESTMENTS

The activity

[8.67]
40　Safeguarding and administering investments

(1)　The activity consisting of both—

(a)　the safeguarding of assets belonging to another, and

(b)　the administration of those assets,

or arranging for one or more other persons to carry on that activity, is a specified kind of activity if the condition in sub-paragraph (a) or (b) of paragraph (2) is met.

(2)　The condition is that—

(a)　the assets consist of or include any investment which is a security or a contractually based investment; or

(b)　the arrangements for their safeguarding and administration are such that the assets may consist of or include such investments, and either the assets have at any time since 1st June 1997 done so, or the arrangements have at any time (whether before or after that date) been held out as ones under which such investments would be safeguarded and administered.

(3)　For the purposes of this article—

(a)　it is immaterial that title to the assets safeguarded and administered is held in uncertificated form;

(b)　it is immaterial that the assets safeguarded and administered may be transferred to another person, subject to a commitment by the person safeguarding and administering them, or arranging for their safeguarding and administration, that they will be replaced by equivalent assets at some future date or when so requested by the person to whom they belong.

Exclusions

[8.68]
41　Acceptance of responsibility by third party

(1)　There are excluded from article 40 any activities which a person carries on pursuant to arrangements which—

(a)　are ones under which a qualifying custodian undertakes to the person to whom the assets belong a responsibility in respect of the assets which is no less onerous than the qualifying custodian would have if the qualifying custodian were safeguarding and administering the assets; and

(b)　are operated by the qualifying custodian in the course of carrying on in the United Kingdom an activity of the kind specified by article 40.

(2)　In paragraph (1), "qualifying custodian" means a person who is—

(a)　an authorised person who has permission to carry on an activity of the kind specified by article 40, or

(b)　an exempt person acting in the course of a business comprising a regulated activity in relation to which he is exempt.

[8.69]
42　Introduction to qualifying custodians

(1)　There are excluded from article 40 any arrangements pursuant to which introductions are made by a person ("P") to a qualifying custodian with a view to the qualifying custodian providing in the United Kingdom a service comprising an activity of the kind specified by article 40, where the qualifying person (or other person who is to safeguard and administer the assets in question) is not connected with P.

(2)　For the purposes of paragraph (1)—

(a)　"qualifying custodian" has the meaning given by article 41(2); and

(b)　a person is connected with P if either he is a member of the same group as P, or P is remunerated by him.

[8.70]
43　Activities not constituting administration

The following activities do not constitute the administration of assets for the purposes of article 40—

(a)　providing information as to the number of units or the value of any assets safeguarded;

(b)　converting currency;

(c)　receiving documents relating to an investment solely for the purpose of onward transmission to, from or at the direction of the person to whom the investment belongs.

[8.71]
44 Other exclusions

Article 40 is also subject to the exclusions in articles 66 (trustees etc), 67 (profession or non-investment business), 68 (sale of goods and supply of services), 69 (groups and joint enterprises)[, 71 (employee share schemes)[, 72A (information society services) and 72C (provision of information about contracts of insurance on an incidental basis)]].

NOTES

Words in first (outer) pair of square brackets substituted by the Financial Services and Markets Act 2000 (Regulated Activities) (Amendment) (No 2) Order 2002, SI 2002/1776, art 3(1), (8), as from 21 August 2002; words in second (inner) pair of square brackets substituted by the Financial Services and Markets Act 2000 (Regulated Activities) (Amendment) (No 2) Order 2003, SI 2003/1476, art 8, as from 31 October 2004 (in so far as relating to contracts of long-term care insurance), and as from 14 January 2005 (otherwise) (for transitional provisions in relation to applications for Part IV permissions and applications for approvals, etc, see arts 22–27 of the 2003 Order).

CHAPTER IX
SENDING DEMATERIALISED INSTRUCTIONS
The activities

[8.72]
45 Sending dematerialised instructions

(1) Sending, on behalf of another person, dematerialised instructions relating to a security [or a contractually based investment] is a specified kind of activity, where those instructions are sent by means of a relevant system in respect of which an Operator is approved under the [2001] Regulations.

(2) Causing dematerialised instructions relating to a security [or a contractually based investment] to be sent [on behalf of another person] by means of such a system is also a specified kind of activity where the person causing them to be sent is a system-participant.

(3) In this Chapter—
   [(a) "the 2001 Regulations" means the Uncertificated Securities Regulations 2001;]
   (b) "dematerialised instruction", "Operator", "settlement bank" and "system-participant" have the meaning given by regulation 3 of the [2001] Regulations.

NOTES

Para (1): words in first pair of square brackets inserted, and date in second pair of square brackets substituted, by the Financial Services and Markets Act 2000 (Regulated Activities) (Amendment) Order 2002, SI 2002/682, art 13(1), as from 27 April 2002.

Para (2): words in first pair of square brackets inserted by SI 2002/682, art 13(2), as from 27 April 2002; words in second pair of square brackets inserted by the Financial Services and Markets Act 2000 (Regulated Activities) (Amendment) Order 2001, SI 2001/3544, arts 2, 7, as from 1 December 2001.

Para (3): words in square brackets substituted by SI 2002/682, art 13(3), as from 27 April 2002.

Exclusions

[8.73]
46 Instructions on behalf of participating issuers

There is excluded from article 45 the act of sending, or causing to be sent, a dematerialised instruction where the person on whose behalf the instruction is sent or caused to be sent is a participating issuer within the meaning of the [2001] Regulations.

NOTES

Date in square brackets substituted by the Financial Services and Markets Act 2000 (Regulated Activities) (Amendment) Order 2002, SI 2002/682, art 13(4), as from 27 April 2002.

[8.74]
47 Instructions on behalf of settlement banks

There is excluded from article 45 the act of sending, or causing to be sent, a dematerialised instruction where the person on whose behalf the instruction is sent or caused to be sent is a settlement bank in its capacity as such.

[8.75]
48 Instructions in connection with takeover offers

(1) There is excluded from article 45 of the act of sending, or causing to be sent, a dematerialised instruction where the person on whose behalf the instruction is sent or caused to be sent is an offeror making a takeover offer.

(2) In this article—
   (a) "offeror" means, in the case of a takeover offer made by two or more persons jointly, the joint offers or any of them;
   (b) "takeover offer" means—

(i)   an offer to acquire shares (which in this sub-paragraph has the same meaning as in [section 974 of the Companies Act 2006]) in a body corporate incorporated in the United Kingdom which is a takeover offer within the meaning of [Chapter 3 of Part 28] of that Act (or would be such an offer if that Part of that Act applied in relation to any body corporate);

(ii)   an offer to acquire all or substantially all the shares, or all the shares of a particular class, in a body corporate incorporated outside the United Kingdom; or

(iii)   an offer made to all the holders of shares, or shares of a particular class, in a body corporate to acquire a specified proportion of those shares;

but in determining whether an offer falls within paragraph (ii) there are to be disregarded any shares which the offeror or any associate of his (within the meaning of [section 988 of the Companies Act 2006]) holds or has contracted to acquire; and in determining whether an offer falls within paragraph (iii) the offeror, any such associate and any person whose shares the offeror or any such associate has contracted to acquire is not to be regarded as a holder of shares.

NOTES

Para (2): words in square brackets in sub-para (b) substituted the Companies Act 2006 (Commencement No 2, Consequential Amendments, Transitional Provisions and Savings) Order 2007, SI 2007/1093, art 6(1), Sch 3, para 8, as from 6 April 2007, subject to transitional provisions in relation to a takeover offer where the date of the offer is before that date.

[8.76]

49   Instructions in the course of providing a network

There is excluded from article 45 the act of sending, or causing to be sent, a dematerialised instruction as a necessary part of providing a network, the purpose of which is to carry dematerialised instructions which are at all time properly authenticated (within the meaning of the [2001] Regulations).

NOTES

Date in square brackets substituted by the Financial Services and Markets Act 2000 (Regulated Activities) (Amendment) Order 2002, SI 2002/682, art 13(4), as from 27 April 2002.

[8.77]

50   Other exclusions

Article 45 is also subject to the exclusions in articles 66 (trustees etc)[, 69 (groups and joint enterprises) and 72A (information society services)].

NOTES

Words in square brackets substituted by the Financial Services and Markets Act 2000 (Regulated Activities) (Amendment) (No 2) Order 2002, SI 2002/1776, art 3(1), (9), as from 21 August 2002.

CHAPTER X
COLLECTIVE INVESTMENT SCHEMES

The activities

[8.78]

51   Establishing etc a collective investment scheme

(1)   The following are specified kinds of activity—

(a)   establishing, operating or winding up a collective investment scheme;

(b)   acting as trustee of an authorised unit trust scheme;

(c)   acting as the depositary or sole director of an open-ended investment company.

(2)   In this article, "trustee", "authorised unit trust scheme" and "depositary" have the meaning given by section 237 of the Act.

[Exclusion

[8.79]

51A   Information society services

Article 51 is subject to the exclusion in article 72A (information society services).]

NOTES

Inserted, together with the preceding heading, by the Financial Services and Markets Act 2000 (Regulated Activities) (Amendment) (No 2) Order 2002, SI 2002/1776, art 3(1), (10), as from 21 August 2002.

CHAPTER XI
. . . PENSION SCHEMES

The activities

[8.80]
[52   Establishing etc a pension scheme
The following are specified kinds of activity—
- (a)   establishing, operating or winding up a stakeholder pension scheme;
- (b)   establishing, operating or winding up a personal pension scheme.]

NOTES
Commencement: 1 October 2006 (certain purposes); 6 April 2007 (otherwise) (see below).

The word omitted from the Chapter heading preceding this article was revoked, and this article was substituted, by the Financial Services and Markets Act 2000 (Regulated Activities) (Amendment) Order 2006, SI 2006/1969, art 2(1), (3), (4), as from 1 October 2006 (for the purposes of enabling applications to be made for Part IV permission or for a variation of Part IV permission in relation to the regulated activity specified by art 52(b) of this Order (as so substituted)), and as from 6 April 2007 (otherwise) (for transitional provisions in relation to interim permissions and interim approvals, etc, see arts 3–7 of, and the Schedule to, the 2006 Order).

[Exclusion

[8.81]
52A   Information society services
Article 52 is subject to the exclusion in article 72A (information society services).]

NOTES
Inserted by the Financial Services and Markets Act 2000 (Regulated Activities) (Amendment) (No 2) Order 2002, SI 2002/1776, art 3(1), (11), as from 21 August 2002.

[CHAPTER XIA
PROVIDING BASIC ADVICE ON STAKEHOLDER PRODUCTS

The Activity

[8.82]
52B   Providing basic advice on stakeholder products
(1)   Providing basic advice to a retail consumer on a stakeholder product is a specified kind of activity.

(2)   For the purposes of paragraph (1), a person ("P") provides basic advice when—
- (a)   he asks a retail consumer questions to enable him to assess whether a stakeholder product is appropriate for that consumer; and
- (b)   relying on the information provided by the retail consumer P assesses that a stakeholder product is appropriate for the retail consumer and—
  - (i)   describes that product to that consumer;
  - (ii)   gives a recommendation of that product to that consumer; and
- (c)   the retail consumer has indicated to P that he has understood the description and the recommendation in sub-paragraph (b).

(3)   In this article—
"retail consumer" means any person who is advised by P on the merits of opening or buying a stakeholder product in the course of a business carried on by P and who does not receive the advice in the course of a business carried on by him;
"stakeholder product" means—
- (a)   an account which qualifies as a stakeholder child trust fund within the meaning given by the Child Trust Funds Regulations 2004;
- [(b)   rights under a stakeholder pension scheme;]
- (c)   an investment of a kind specified in regulations made by the Treasury.]

NOTES
Inserted, together with the preceding headings, by the Financial Services and Markets Act 2000 (Regulated Activities) (Amendment) (No 2) Order 2004, SI 2004/2737, arts, 2, 3, as from 6 April 2005. For transitional provisions, see the note below.

Para (3): in definition "stakeholder product", para (b) substituted by the Financial Services and Markets Act 2000 (Regulated Activities) (Amendment) Order 2005, SI 2005/593, art 2(3), as from 6 April 2005.

Transitional provisions: SI 2004/2737, art 4, provides that Part IV of FSMA 2000 applies in the case of persons who have permission on 6 April 2005 to carry out the activity specified in art 53 of this Order and who wish to carry out the activity specified in art 52B as follows: if "P" is such a person then (a) the procedures established under ss 44, 45 of the 2000 Act in respect of application for permission shall not apply in respect of permission to carry out the art 52B activity, and (b) P shall be deemed to have such a permission if he has notified the Authority in writing of his wish to undertake the activity and the Authority has acknowledged receipt of P's notification in writing from the date of the acknowledgement.

Regulations: the Financial Services and Markets Act 2000 (Stakeholder Products) Regulations 2004, SI 2004/2738.

CHAPTER XII
ADVISING ON INVESTMENTS

The activity

[8.83]

53 Advising on investments

Advising a person is a specified kind of activity if the advice is—

(a) given to the person in his capacity as an investor or potential investor, or in his capacity as agent for an investor or a potential investor; and

(b) advice on the merits of his doing any of the following (whether as principal or agent)—

   (i) buying, selling, subscribing for or underwriting a particular investment which is a security or a [relevant investment], or

   (ii) exercising any right conferred by such an investment to buy, sell, subscribe for or underwrite such an investment.

NOTES

Words in square brackets substituted by the Financial Services and Markets Act 2000 (Regulated Activities) (Amendment) (No 2) Order 2003, SI 2003/1476, art 9(1), as from 31 October 2004 (in so far as relating to contracts of long-term care insurance), and as from 14 January 2005 (otherwise) (for transitional provisions in relation to applications for Part IV permissions and applications for approvals, etc, see arts 22–27 of the 2003 Order).

Transitional provisions: see the note to art 52B at **[8.82]**.

[8.84]

[53A Advising on regulated mortgage contracts

(1) Advising a person is a specified kind of activity if the advice—

(a) is given to the person in his capacity as a borrower or potential borrower; and

(b) is advice on the merits of his doing any of the following—

   (i) entering into a particular regulated mortgage contract, or

   (ii) varying the terms of a regulated mortgage contract entered into by him after the coming into force of article 61 in such a way as to vary his obligations under that contract.

(2) In this article, "borrower" has the meaning given by article 61(3)(a)(i).]

NOTES

Inserted by the Financial Services and Markets Act 2000 (Regulated Activities) (Amendment) (No 1) Order 2003, SI 2003/1475, art 13, as from 31 October 2004 (for transitional provisions in relation to applications for Part IV permissions and applications for approvals, etc, see arts 26–29 of the 2003 Order).

[8.85]

[53B Advising on regulated home reversion plans

Advising a person is a specified kind of activity if the advice—

(a) is given to the person in his capacity as—

   (i) a reversion seller or potential reversion seller, or

   (ii) a plan provider or potential plan provider; and

(b) is advice on the merits of his doing either of the following—

   (i) entering into a particular regulated home reversion plan, or

   (ii) varying the terms of a regulated home reversion plan, entered into on or after 6th April 2007 by him, in such a way as to vary his obligations under that plan.]

NOTES

Commencement: 6 November 2006 (certain purposes); 6 April 2007 (otherwise) (for more information see the note below).

Inserted, together with art 53C, by the Financial Services and Markets Act 2000 (Regulated Activities) (Amendment) (No 2) Order 2006, SI 2006/2383, arts 2, 13, as from 6 November 2006 (for the purposes of enabling applications to be made for (i) a Pt IV permission, or a variation of a Pt IV permission, in relation to activities of the kind specified by arts 25B, 25C, 53B, 53C, 63B or 63F or, so far as relevant to any such activity, art 64 of this Order; or (ii) the Authority's approval under FSMA 2000, s 59 in relation to any of those activities), and as from 6 April 2007 (otherwise) (for transitional provisions in relation to interim permissions and interim approvals, etc, see arts 36–40 of, and the Schedule to, the 2006 Order).

[8.86]

[53C Advising on regulated home purchase plans

Advising a person is a specified kind of activity if the advice—

(a) is given to the person in his capacity as a home purchaser or potential home purchaser; and

(b) is advice on the merits of his doing either of the following—

   (i) entering into a particular regulated home purchase plan, or

   (ii) varying the terms of a regulated home purchase plan, entered into on or after 6th April 2007 by him, in such a way as to vary his obligations under that plan.]

NOTES

Commencement: 6 November 2006 (certain purposes); 6 April 2007 (otherwise) (for more information see the note to art 53B at **[8.85]**).

Inserted as noted to art 53B at **[8.85]**.

[8.87]
[53D Advising on regulated sale and rent back agreements

Advising a person is a specified kind of activity if the advice—
- (a) is given to the person ("A") in A's capacity as—
  - (i)   an agreement seller or potential agreement seller, or
  - (ii) an agreement provider or potential agreement provider; and
- (b) is advice on the merits of A doing either of the following—
  - (i)   entering into a particular regulated sale and rent back agreement; or
  - (ii) varying the terms of a regulated sale and rent back agreement entered into on or after 1st July 2009 by A as agreement seller or agreement provider, in such a way so as to vary A's obligations under that agreement.]

NOTES

Commencement: 1 July 2009 (certain purposes); 30 June 2010 (otherwise) (see below).

Inserted by the Financial Services and Markets Act 2000 (Regulated Activities) (Amendment) Order 2009, SI 2009/1342, arts 2, 13, as from 1 July 2009 (other than for the purposes of enabling applications to be made for a Part IV permission, or a variation of a Part IV permission, in relation to activities of the kind specified by arts 25E, 53D or 63J or, so far as relevant to any such activity, art 64 of this Order), and as from 30 June 2010 (for those purposes) (for transitional provisions in relation to applications for Part IV permissions, etc, see arts 1, 32–34 of that Order)

Exclusions

[8.88]
54 Advice given in newspapers etc

(1)   There is excluded from [articles 53, 53A, 53B[, 53C and 53D]] the giving of advice in writing or other legible form if the advice is contained in a newspaper, journal, magazine, or other periodical publication, or is given by way of a service comprising regularly updated news or information, if the principal purpose of the publication or service, taken as a whole and including any advertisements or other promotional material contained in it, is neither—
- (a) that of giving advice of a kind mentioned in article 53[, 53A, 53B[, 53C or 53D,] as the case may be]; nor
- [(b) that of leading or enabling persons—
  - (i)   to buy, sell, subscribe for or underwrite securities or [relevant investments], or (as the case may be),
  - (ii)   to enter as borrower into regulated mortgage contracts, or vary the terms of regulated mortgage contracts entered into by them as borrower;
  - [(iii) to enter as reversion seller or plan provider into regulated home reversion plans, or vary the terms of regulated home reversion plans entered into by them as reversion seller or plan provider,
  - (iv)   to enter as home purchaser into regulated home purchase plans, or vary the terms of regulated home purchase plans entered into by them as home purchaser][;
  - (v)   to enter as agreement seller or agreement provider into regulated sale and rent back agreements, or vary the terms of regulated sale and rent back agreements entered into by them as agreement seller or agreement provider]].

(2)   There is also excluded from [articles 53, 53A, 53B[, 53C and 53D]] the giving of advice in any service consisting of the broadcast or transmission of television or radio programmes, if the principal purpose of the service, taken as a whole and including any advertisements or other promotional material contained in it, is neither of those mentioned in paragraph (1)(a) and (b).

(3)   The Authority may, on the application of the proprietor of any such publication or service as is mentioned in paragraph (1) or (2), certify that it is of the nature described in that paragraph, and may revoke any such certificate if it considers that it is no longer justified.

(4)   A certificate given under paragraph (3) and not revoked is conclusive evidence of the matters certified.

NOTES

Para (1) is amended as follows:

Words in first and third (both outer) pairs of square brackets substituted by the Financial Services and Markets Act 2000 (Regulated Activities) (Amendment) (No 2) Order 2006, SI 2006/2383, arts 2, 14(a)(i), (ii), as from 6 November 2006 (for the purposes of enabling applications to be made for (i) a Pt IV permission, or a variation of a Pt IV permission, in relation to activities of the kind specified by arts 25B, 25C, 53B, 53C, 63B or 63F or, so far as relevant to any such activity, art 64 of this Order; or (ii) the Authority's approval under FSMA 2000, s 59 in relation to any of those activities), and as from 6 April 2007 (otherwise) (for transitional provisions in relation to interim permissions and interim approvals, etc, see arts 36–40 of, and the Schedule to, the 2006 Order).

Words in second and fourth (both inner) pairs of square brackets substituted, and sub-para (b)(v) added by the Financial Services and Markets Act 2000 (Regulated Activities) (Amendment) Order 2009, SI 2009/1342, arts 2, 14(a)–(c), as from 1 July 2009 (other than for the purposes of enabling applications to be made for a Part IV permission, or a variation of a Part IV permission, in relation to activities of the kind specified by arts 25E, 53D or 63J or, so far as relevant to any such activity, art 64 of this Order), and as from 30 June 2010 (for those purposes) (for transitional provisions in relation to applications for Part IV permissions, etc, see arts 1, 32–34 of that Order).

Sub-para (b) substituted by the Financial Services and Markets Act 2000 (Regulated Activities) (Amendment) (No 1) Order 2003, SI 2003/1475, art 14, as from 31 October 2004 (for transitional provisions in relation to applications for Part IV permissions and applications for approvals, etc, see arts 26–29 of the 2003 Order).

Words in square brackets in sub-para (b)(i) substituted by the Financial Services and Markets Act 2000 (Regulated Activities) (Amendment) (No 2) Order 2003, SI 2003/1476, art 9(2), as from 31 October 2004 (in so far as relating to contracts of long-term care insurance), and as from 14 January 2005 (otherwise) (for transitional provisions in relation to applications for Part IV permissions and applications for approvals, etc, see arts 22–27 of the 2003 Order).

Sub-paras (b)(iii), (iv) inserted by SI 2006/2383, arts 2, 14(a)(iii), as from 6 November 2006 (certain purposes), and as from 6 April 2007 (otherwise) (for purposes, transitional provisions, and effect, see the note above).

Para (2): words in first (outer) pair of square brackets substituted by SI 2006/2383, arts 2, 14(b), as from 6 November 2006 (certain purposes), and as from 6 April 2007 (otherwise) (for purposes, transitional provisions, and effect, see the note above); words in second (inner) pair of square brackets substituted by SI 2009/1342, arts 2, 14(d), as from the same dates and for the same purposes, etc, as mentioned in the note relating to this Order above.

[8.89]

[54A   Advice given in the course of administration by authorised person

[(1)   A person who is not an authorised person ("A") does not carry on an activity of the kind specified by article 53A by reason of—

    (a)   anything done by an authorised person ("B") in relation to a regulated mortgage contract which B is administering pursuant to arrangements of the kind mentioned in article 62(a); or

    (b)   anything A does in connection with the administration of a regulated mortgage contract in circumstances falling within article 62(b).

[(2)   A person who is not an authorised person ("A") does not carry on an activity of the kind specified by article 53B by reason of—

    (a)   anything done by an authorised person ("B") in relation to a regulated home reversion plan which B is administering pursuant to arrangements of the kind mentioned in article 63C(a); or

    (b)   anything A does in connection with the administration of a regulated home reversion plan in circumstances falling within article 63C(b).

(3)   A person who is not an authorised person ("A") does not carry on an activity of the kind specified by article 53C by reason of—

    (a)   anything done by an authorised person ("B") in relation to a regulated home purchase plan which B is administering pursuant to arrangements of the kind mentioned in article 63G(a); or

    (b)   anything A does in connection with the administration of a regulated home purchase plan in circumstances falling within article 63G(b).]]

[(4)   A person who is not an authorised person ("A") does not carry on an activity of the kind specified by article 53D by reason of

    (a)   anything done by an authorised person ("B") in relation to a regulated sale and rent back agreement which B is administering pursuant to arrangements of the kind mentioned in article 63K(a); or

    (b)   anything A does in connection with the administration of a regulated sale and rent back agreement in circumstances falling within article 63K(b).]

NOTES

Inserted by the Financial Services and Markets Act 2000 (Regulated Activities) (Amendment) (No 1) Order 2003, SI 2003/1475, art 15, as from 31 October 2004 (for transitional provisions in relation to applications for Part IV permissions and applications for approvals, etc, see arts 26–29 of the 2003 Order).

Para (1) numbered as such, and paras (2), (3) added, by the Financial Services and Markets Act 2000 (Regulated Activities) (Amendment) (No 2) Order 2006, SI 2006/2383, arts 2, 15, as from 6 November 2006 (for the purposes of enabling applications to be made for (i) a Pt IV permission, or a variation of a Pt IV permission, in relation to activities of the kind specified by arts 25B, 25C, 53B, 53C, 63B or 63F or, so far as relevant to any such activity, art 64 of this Order; or (ii) the Authority's approval under FSMA 2000, s 59 in relation to any of those activities), and as from 6 April 2007 (otherwise) (for transitional provisions in relation to interim permissions and interim approvals, etc, see arts 36–40 of, and the Schedule to, the 2006 Order).

Para (4): added by the Financial Services and Markets Act 2000 (Regulated Activities) (Amendment) Order 2009, SI 2009/1342, arts 2, 15, as from 1 July 2009 (other than for the purposes of enabling applications to be made for a Part IV permission, or a variation of a Part IV permission, in relation to activities of the kind specified by arts 25E, 53D or 63J or, so far as relevant to any such activity, art 64 of this Order), and as from 30 June 2010 (for those purposes) (for transitional provisions in relation to applications for Part IV permissions, etc, see arts 1, 32–34 of that Order).

[8.90]
55   Other exclusions

[(1)   Article 53 is also subject to the exclusions in articles 66 (trustees etc), 67, (profession or non-investment business), 68 (sale of goods and supply of services), 69 (groups and joint enterprises), 70 (sale of body corporate)[, 72 (overseas persons)[, 72A (information society services), 72B (activities carried on by a provider of relevant goods or services) and 72D (large risks contracts where risk situated outside the EEA)]]

[(2)   [Articles 53A, 53B[, 53C and 53D] are] also subject to the exclusions in articles 66 (trustees etc), 67 (profession or non-investment business) and 72A (information society services).]

NOTES

Para (1): numbered as such by the Financial Services and Markets Act 2000 (Regulated Activities) (Amendment) (No 1) Order 2003, SI 2003/1475, art 16(a), as from 31 October 2004 (for transitional provisions in relation to applications for Part IV permissions and applications for approvals, etc, see arts 26–29 of the 2003 Order); words in first (outer) pair of square brackets substituted by the Financial Services and Markets Act 2000 (Regulated Activities) (Amendment) (No 2) Order 2002, SI 2002/1776, art 3(1), (12), as from 21 August 2002; words in second (inner) pair of square brackets substituted by the Financial Services and Markets Act 2000 (Regulated Activities) (Amendment) (No 2) Order 2003, SI 2003/1476, art 9(3), as from 31 October 2004 (in so far as relating to contracts of long-term care insurance), and as from 14 January 2005 (otherwise) (for transitional provisions in relation to applications for Part IV permissions and applications for approvals, etc, see arts 22–27 of the 2003 Order).

Para (2): added by SI 2003/1475, art 16(b), as from 31 October 2004 (for transitional provisions in relation to applications for Part IV permissions and applications for approvals, etc, see arts 26–29 of the 2003 Order); words in first (outer) pair of square brackets substituted by the Financial Services and Markets Act 2000 (Regulated Activities) (Amendment) (No 2) Order 2006, SI 2006/2383, arts 2, 16, as from 6 November 2006 (for the purposes of enabling applications to be made for (i) a Pt IV permission, or a variation of a Pt IV permission, in relation to activities of the kind specified by arts 25B, 25C, 53B, 53C, 63B or 63F or, so far as relevant to any such activity, art 64 of this Order; or (ii) the Authority's approval under FSMA 2000, s 59 in relation to any of those activities), and as from 6 April 2007 (otherwise) (for transitional provisions in relation to interim permissions and interim approvals, etc, see arts 36–40 of, and the Schedule to, the 2006 Order); words in second (inner) pair of square brackets substituted by the Financial Services and Markets Act 2000 (Regulated Activities) (Amendment) Order 2009, SI 2009/1342, arts 2, 16, as from 1 July 2009 (other than for the purposes of enabling applications to be made for a Part IV permission, or a variation of a Part IV permission, in relation to activities of the kind specified by arts 25E, 53D or 63J or, so far as relevant to any such activity, art 64 of this Order), and as from 30 June 2010 (for those purposes) (for transitional provisions in relation to applications for Part IV permissions, etc, see arts 1, 32–34 of that Order).

CHAPTER XIII
LLOYD'S

The activities

[8.91]
56   Advice on syndicate participation at Lloyd's

Advising a person to become, or continue or cease to be, a member of a particular Lloyd's syndicate is a specified kind of activity.

[8.92]
57   Managing the underwriting capacity of a Lloyd's syndicate

Managing the underwriting capacity of a Lloyd's syndicate as a managing agent at Lloyd's is a specified kind of activity.

[8.93]
58   Arranging deals in contracts of insurance written at Lloyd's

The arranging, by the society incorporated by Lloyd's Act 1871 by the name of Lloyd's, of deals in contracts of insurance written at Lloyd's, is a specified kind of activity.

[Exclusion

[8.94]
58A   Information society services

Articles 56 to 58 are subject to the exclusion in article 72A (information society services).]

NOTES

Inserted, together with the preceding heading, by the Financial Services and Markets Act 2000 (Regulated Activities) (Amendment) (No 2) Order 2002, SI 2002/1776, art 3(1), (13), as from 21 August 2002.

CHAPTER XIV
FUNERAL PLAN CONTRACTS

The activity

[8.95]
59   Funeral plan contracts

(1)   Entering as provider into a funeral plan contract is a specified kind of activity.

(2)   A "funeral plan contract" is a contract (other than one excluded by article 60) under which—

   (a)   a person ("the customer") makes one or more payments to another person ("the provider"); and

   (b)   the provider undertakes to provide, or secure that another person provides, a funeral in the United Kingdom for the customer (or some other person who is living at the date when the contract is entered into) on his death;

unless, at the time of entering into the contract, the customer and the provider intend or expect the funeral to occur within one month.

[Exclusions]

[8.96]
60   Plans covered by insurance or trust arrangements

(1)   There is excluded from article 59 any contract under which—

   (a)   the provider undertakes to secure that sums paid by the customer under the contract will be applied towards a contract of whole life insurance on the life of the customer (or other person for whom the funeral is to be provided), effected and carried out by an authorised person who has permission to effect and carry out such contracts of insurance, for the purpose of providing the funeral; or

   (b)   the provider undertakes to secure that sums paid by the customer under the contract will be held on trust for the purpose of providing the funeral, and that the following requirements are or will be met with respect to the trust—

     (i)   the trust must be established by a written instrument;

     (ii)   more than half of the trustees must be unconnected with the provider;

     (iii)   the trustees must appoint, or have appointed, an independent fund manager who is an authorised person who has permission to carry on an activity of the kind specified by article 37, and who is a person who is unconnected with the provider, to manage the assets of the trust;

     (iv)   annual accounts must be prepared, and audited by a person who is eligible for appointment as a [statutory auditor under Part 42 of the Companies Act 2006], with respect to the assets and liabilities of the trust; and

     (v)   the assets and liabilities of the trust must, at least once every three years, be determined, calculated and verified by an actuary who is a Fellow of the Institute of Actuaries or of the Faculty of Actuaries.

(2)   For the purposes of paragraph (1)(b)(ii) and (iii), a person is unconnected with the provider if he is a person other than—

   (a)   the provider;

   (b)   a member of the same group as the provider;

   (c)   a director, other officer or employee of the provider, or of any member of the same group as the provider;

   (d)   a partner of the provider;

   (e)   a close relative of a person falling within sub-paragraph (a), (c) or (d); or

   (f)   an agent of any person falling within sub-paragraphs (a) to (e).

NOTES

The heading preceding this article was substituted by the Financial Services and Markets Act 2000 (Regulated Activities) (Amendment) (No 2) Order 2002, art 3(1), (14), as from 21 August 2002.

Para (1): words in square brackets substituted by the Companies Act 2006 (Consequential Amendments etc) Order 2008, SI 2008/948, art 3(1), Sch 1, Pt 1, para 1(tt), as from 6 April 2008 (for savings see art 6(4) of the 2008 Order (at **[4.280]**) which provides that where by virtue of any transitional provision, a provision of the Companies Act 2006 has effect only (a) on or after a specified date, or (b) in relation to matters occurring or arising on or after a specified date, any amendment substituting or inserting a reference to that provision has effect correspondingly).

[8.97]
[60A   Information society services

Article 59 is subject to the exclusion in article 72A (information society services).]

NOTES

Inserted by the Financial Services and Markets Act 2000 (Regulated Activities) (Amendment) (No 2) Order 2002, SI 2002/1776, art 3(1), (15), as from 21 August 2002.

CHAPTER XV
REGULATED MORTGAGE CONTRACTS

The activities

[8.98]
61   Regulated mortgage contracts

(1)   Entering into a regulated mortgage contract as lender is a specified kind of activity.

(2)   Administering a regulated mortgage contract is also a specified kind of activity, where the contract was entered into [by way of business] after the coming into force of this article.

(3)   In this Chapter—

   [(a)   a contract is a "regulated mortgage contract" if, at the time it is entered into, the following conditions are met—

     (i)   the contract is one under which a person ("the lender") provides credit to an individual or to trustees ("the borrower");

     (ii)   the contract provides for the obligation of the borrower to repay to be secured by a first legal mortgage on land (other than timeshare accommodation) in the United Kingdom;

      (iii)   at least 40% of that land is used, or is intended to be used, as or in connection with a dwelling by the borrower or (in the case of credit provided to trustees) by an individual who is a beneficiary of the trust, or by a related person;

    [but such a contract is not a regulated mortgage contract if it is a regulated home purchase plan;]]

  (b)   "administering" a regulated mortgage contract means either or both of—

      (i)   notifying the borrower of changes in interest rates or payments due under the contract, or of other matters of which the contract requires him to be notified; and

      (ii)   taking any necessary steps for the purposes of collecting or recovering payments due under the contract from the borrower;

    but a person is not to be treated as administering a regulated mortgage contract merely because he has, or exercises, a right to take action for the purposes of enforcing the contract (or to require that such action is or is not taken);

  (c)   "credit" includes a cash loan, and any other form of financial accommodation.

(4) For the purposes of [paragraph 3(a)]—

  (a)   a "first legal mortgage" means a legal mortgage ranking in priority ahead of all other mortgages (if any) affecting the land in question, where "mortgage" includes charge and (in Scotland) a heritable security;

  (b)   the area of any land which comprises a building or other structure containing two or more storeys is to be taken to be the aggregate of the floor areas of each of those storeys;

  (c)   "related person", in relation to the borrower or (in the case of credit provided to trustees) a beneficiary of the trust, means—

      (i)   that person's spouse [or civil partner];

      (ii)   a person (whether or not of the opposite sex) whose relationship with that person has the characteristics of the relationship between husband and wife; or

      (iii) that person's parent, brother, sister, child, grandparent or grandchild; and

  [(d) "timeshare accommodation" means overnight accommodation which is the subject of a timeshare contract within the meaning of the Timeshare, Holiday Products, Resale and Exchange Contracts Regulations 2010].

NOTES

Para (2): words in square brackets inserted by the Financial Services and Markets Act 2000 (Regulated Activities) (Amendment) Order 2001, SI 2001/3544, arts 2, 8(a), as from 1 September 2002.

Para (3): sub-para (a) substituted by SI 2001/3544, arts 2, 8(b), as from 1 September 2002; words in square brackets inserted by the Financial Services and Markets Act 2000 (Regulated Activities) (Amendment) (No 2) Order 2006, SI 2006/2383, arts 2, 17, as from 6 November 2006 (for the purposes of enabling applications to be made for (i) a Pt IV permission, or a variation of a Pt IV permission, in relation to activities of the kind specified by arts 25B, 25C, 53B, 53C, 63B or 63F or, so far as relevant to any such activity, art 64 of this Order; or (ii) the Authority's approval under FSMA 2000, s 59 in relation to any of those activities), and as from 6 April 2007 (otherwise) (for transitional provisions in relation to interim permissions and interim approvals, etc, see arts 36–40 of, and the Schedule to, the 2006 Order).

Para (4): words in first pair of square brackets substituted by SI 2001/3544, arts 2, 8(c), as from 1 September 2002; words in second pair of square brackets inserted by the Civil Partnership Act 2004 (Amendments to Subordinate Legislation) Order 2005, SI 2005/2114, art 2(16), Sch 16, Pt 1, para 1(1), (3), as from 5 December 2005; sub-para (d) substituted by the Timeshare, Holiday Products, Resale and Exchange Contracts Regulations 2010, SI 2010/2960, reg 36(3), Sch 6, para 7(1), (2), as from 23 February 2011.

Exclusions

[8.99]

62 Arranging administration by authorised person

A person who is not an authorised person does not carry on an activity of the kind specified by article 61(2) in relation to a regulated mortgage contract where he—

  (a)   arranges for another person, being an authorised person with permission to carry on an activity of that kind, to administer the contract; or

  (b)   administers the contract himself during a period of not more than one month beginning with the day on which any such arrangement comes to an end.

[8.100]

63 Administration pursuant to agreement with authorised person

A person who is not an authorised person does not carry on an activity of the kind specified by article 61(2) in relation to a regulated mortgage contract where he administers the contract pursuant to an agreement with an authorised person who has permission to carry on an activity of that kind.

[8.101]

[63A Other exclusions

Article 61 is also subject to the exclusions in articles 66 (trustees etc), 72 (overseas persons) and 72A (information society services).]

NOTES

Inserted by the Financial Services and Markets Act 2000 (Regulated Activities) (Amendment) (No 2) Order 2002, SI 2002/1776, art 3(1), (16), as from 21 August 2002; substituted by the Financial Services and Markets Act 2000 (Regulated

Activities) (Amendment) (No 1) Order 2003, SI 2003/1475, art 17, as from 31 October 2004 (for transitional provisions in relation to applications for Part IV permissions and applications for approvals, etc, see arts 26–29 of the 2003 Order).

[CHAPTER 15A
REGULATED HOME REVERSION PLANS

The activities

[8.102]

63B   Entering into and administering regulated home reversion plans

(1)   Entering into a regulated home reversion plan as plan provider is a specified kind of activity.

(2)   Administering a regulated home reversion plan is also a specified kind of activity where the plan was entered into on or after 6th April 2007.

(3)   In this Chapter—

(a)   a "regulated home reversion plan" is an arrangement comprised in one or more instruments or agreements, in relation to which the following conditions are met at the time it is entered into—

    (i)   the arrangement is one under which a person (the "plan provider") buys all or part of a qualifying interest in land (other than timeshare accommodation) in the United Kingdom from an individual or trustees (the "reversion seller");

    (ii)   the reversion seller (if he is an individual) or an individual who is a beneficiary of the trust (if the reversion seller is a trustee), or a related person, is entitled under the arrangement to occupy at least 40% of the land in question as or in connection with a dwelling, and intends to do so; and

    (iii)   the arrangement specifies one or more qualifying termination events, on the occurrence of which that entitlement will end;

(b)   "administering" a regulated home reversion plan means any of—

    (i)   notifying the reversion seller of changes in payments due under the plan, or of other matters of which the plan requires him to be notified;

    (ii)   taking any necessary steps for the purposes of making payments to the reversion seller under the plan; and

    (iii)   taking any necessary steps for the purposes of collecting or recovering payments due under the plan from the reversion seller,

but a person is not to be treated as administering a regulated home reversion plan merely because he has, or exercises, a right to take action for the purposes of enforcing the plan (or to require that such action is or is not taken).

(4)   For the purposes of paragraph (3)—

(a)   the reference to a "qualifying interest" in land—

    (i)   in relation to land in England or Wales, is to an estate in fee simple absolute or a term of years absolute, whether subsisting at law or in equity;

    (ii)   in relation to land in Scotland, is to the interest of an owner in land or the tenant's right over or interest in a property subject to a lease;

    (iii)   in relation to land in Northern Ireland, is to any freehold estate or any leasehold estate, whether subsisting at law or in equity;

(b)   "timeshare accommodation" has the meaning given by section 1 of the Timeshare Act 1992;

(c)   "related person" in relation to the reversion seller or, where the reversion seller is a trustee, a beneficiary of the trust, means—

    (i)   that person's spouse or civil partner;

    (ii)   a person (whether or not of the opposite sex) whose relationship with that person has the characteristics of the relationship between husband and wife; or

    (iii)   that person's parent, brother, sister, child, grandparent or grandchild; and

(d)   "qualifying termination event", in relation to a person's entitlement to occupy land, means—

    (i)   the person becomes a resident of a care home;

    (ii)   the person dies;

    (iii)   the end of a specified period of at least twenty years beginning with the day on which the reversion seller entered into the arrangement.

(5)   For the purposes of paragraph (3)(a)(ii), the area of any land which comprises a building or other structure containing two or more storeys is to be taken to be the aggregate of the floor areas of each of those storeys.

(6)   For the purposes of the definition of "qualifying termination event" in paragraph (4), "care home"—

(a)   in relation to England and Wales, has the meaning given by section 3 of the Care Standards Act 2000;

(b)   in relation to Scotland, means accommodation provided by a "care home" within the meaning of section 2(3)of the Regulation of Care (Scotland) Act 2001;

(c)   in relation to Northern Ireland, means—

    (i)   a residential care home within the meaning of article 10 of the Health and Personal
           Social Services (Quality, Improvement and Regulation) (Northern Ireland)
           Order 2003; or
    (ii)   a nursing home within the meaning of article 11 of that Order.
(7) In this Order—
    (a)   references to entering into a regulated home reversion plan as plan provider include
           acquiring any obligations or rights (including his interest in land) of the plan provider,
           under such a plan; but
    (b)   in relation to a person who acquires any such obligations or rights, an activity is a specified
           kind of activity for the purposes of articles 25B(1)(b) and 53B(b)(ii) and paragraph (2) only
           if the plan was entered into by the plan provider (rather than the obligations or rights
           acquired) on or after 6th April 2007.
(8) Accordingly, references in this Order to a plan provider, other than in paragraph (7), include
a person who acquires any such obligations or rights.]

NOTES

Commencement: 6 November 2006 (certain purposes); 6 April 2007 (otherwise) (for more information see the note below).
Chapters 15A, 15B (arts 63B–63I and the preceding headings) inserted by the Financial Services and Markets Act 2000
(Regulated Activities) (Amendment) (No 2) Order 2006, SI 2006/2383, arts 2, 18, as from 6 November 2006 (for the purposes
of enabling applications to be made for (i) a Pt IV permission, or a variation of a Pt IV permission, in relation to activities of
the kind specified by arts 25B, 25C, 53B, 53C, 63B or 63F or, so far as relevant to any such activity, art 64 of this Order; or
(ii) the Authority's approval under FSMA 2000, s 59 in relation to any of those activities), and as from 6 April 2007 (otherwise)
(for transitional provisions in relation to interim permissions and interim approvals, etc, see arts 36–40 of, and the Schedule to,
the 2006 Order).

[Exclusions

[8.103]
63C   Arranging administration by authorised person
A person who is not an authorised person does not carry on an activity of the kind specified by
article 63B(2) in relation to a regulated home reversion plan where he—
    (a)   arranges for another person, being an authorised person with permission to carry on an
           activity of that kind, to administer the plan; or
    (b)   administers the plan himself during a period of not more than one month beginning with
           the day on which any such arrangement comes to an end.]

NOTES

Commencement: 6 November 2006 (certain purposes); 6 April 2007 (otherwise) (for more information see the note to art 63B
at **[8.102]**).
Inserted as noted to art 63B at **[8.102]**.

[8.104]
[63D   Administration pursuant to agreement with authorised person
A person who is not an authorised person does not carry on an activity of the kind specified by
article 63B(2) in relation to a regulated home reversion plan where he administers the plan pursuant
to an agreement with an authorised person who has permission to carry on an activity of that kind.]

NOTES

Commencement: 6 November 2006 (certain purposes); 6 April 2007 (otherwise) (for more information see the note to art 63B
at **[8.102]**).
Inserted as noted to art 63B at **[8.102]**.

[8.105]
[63E   Other exclusions
Article 63B is also subject to the exclusions in articles 66 (trustees etc), 72 (overseas persons)
and 72A (information society services).]

NOTES

Commencement: 6 November 2006 (certain purposes); 6 April 2007 (otherwise) (for more information see the note to art 63B
at **[8.102]**).
Inserted as noted to art 63B at **[8.102]**.

[CHAPTER 15B
REGULATED HOME PURCHASE PLANS

The activities

[8.106]
63F   Entering into and administering regulated home purchase plans
(1) Entering into a regulated home purchase plan as home purchase provider is a specified kind of
activity.

(2)   Administering a regulated home purchase plan is also a specified kind of activity where the plan was entered into by way of business on or after 6th April 2007.

(3)   In this Chapter—

(a)   a "regulated home purchase plan" is an arrangement comprised in one or more instruments or agreements, in relation to which the following conditions are met at the time it is entered into—

(i)   the arrangement is one under which a person (the "home purchase provider") buys a qualifying interest or an undivided share of a qualifying interest in land (other than timeshare accommodation) in the United Kingdom;

(ii)   where an undivided share of a qualifying interest in land is bought, the interest is held on trust for the home purchase provider and the individual or trustees mentioned in paragraph (iii) as beneficial tenants in common;

(iii)   the arrangement provides for the obligation of an individual or trustees (the "home purchaser") to buy the interest bought by the home purchase provider over the course of or at the end of a specified period; and

(iv)   the home purchaser (if he is an individual) or an individual who is a beneficiary of the trust (if the home purchaser is a trustee), or a related person, is entitled under the arrangement to occupy at least 40% of the land in question as or in connection with a dwelling during that period, and intends to do so;

(b)   "administering" a regulated home purchase plan means either or both of—

(i)   notifying the home purchaser of changes in payments due under the plan, or of other matters of which the plan requires him to be notified; and

(ii)   taking any necessary steps for the purposes of collecting or recovering payments due under the plan from the home purchaser;

but a person is not to be treated as administering a regulated home purchase plan merely because he has, or exercises, a right to take action for the purposes of enforcing the plan or to require that such action is or is not taken.

(4)   Article 63B(4)(a) to (c) applies for the purposes of paragraph (3)(a) with references to the "reversion seller" being read as references to the "home purchaser".

(5)   Article 63B(5) applies for the purposes of paragraph (3)(a)(iv) with the reference to "paragraph (3)(a)(ii)" being read as a reference to "paragraph (3)(a)(iv)".]

NOTES

Commencement: 6 November 2006 (certain purposes); 6 April 2007 (otherwise) (for more information see the note to art 63B at **[8.102]**).

Inserted as noted to art 63B at **[8.102]**.

[Exclusions

[8.107]
63G   Arranging administration by authorised person
A person who is not an authorised person does not carry on an activity of the kind specified by article 63F(2) in relation to a regulated home purchase plan where he—

(a)   arranges for another person, being an authorised person with permission to carry on an activity of that kind, to administer the plan; or

(b)   administers the plan himself during a period of not more than one month beginning with the day on which any such arrangement comes to an end.]

NOTES

Commencement: 6 November 2006 (certain purposes); 6 April 2007 (otherwise) (for more information see the note to art 63B at **[8.102]**).

Inserted as noted to art 63B at **[8.102]**.

[8.108]
[63H   Administration pursuant to agreement with authorised person
A person who is not an authorised person does not carry on an activity of the kind specified by article 63F(2) in relation to a regulated home purchase plan where he administers the plan pursuant to an agreement with an authorised person who has permission to carry on an activity of that kind.]

NOTES

Commencement: 6 November 2006 (certain purposes); 6 April 2007 (otherwise) (for more information see the note to art 63B at **[8.102]**).

Inserted as noted to art 63B at **[8.102]**.

[8.109]
[63I   Other exclusions
Article 63F is also subject to the exclusions in articles 66 (trustees etc), 72 (overseas persons) and 72A (information society services).]

NOTES

Commencement: 6 November 2006 (certain purposes); 6 April 2007 (otherwise) (for more information see the note to art 63B at **[8.102]**).

Inserted as noted to art 63B at **[8.102]**.

[CHAPTER 15C]
REGULATED SALE AND RENT BACK AGREEMENTS THE ACTIVITIES

The activities

[8.110]
63J   Entering into and administering regulated sale and rent back agreements

(1)   Entering into a regulated sale and rent back agreement as an agreement provider is a specified kind of activity.

(2)   Administering a regulated sale and rent back agreement is also a specified kind of activity when the agreement was entered into on or after 1st July 2009.

(3)   In this Chapter—
   (a)   a "regulated sale and rent back agreement" is an arrangement comprised in one or more instruments or agreements, in relation to which the following conditions are met at the time it is entered into—
      (i)   the arrangement is one under which a person (the "agreement provider") buys all or part of the qualifying interest in land (other than timeshare accommodation) in the United Kingdom from an individual or trustees (the "agreement seller"); and
      (ii)   the agreement seller (if the agreement seller is an individual) or an individual who is the beneficiary of the trust (if the agreement seller is a trustee), or a related person, is entitled under the arrangement to occupy at least 40% of the land in question as or in connection with a dwelling, and intends to do so;
   but such an arrangement is not a regulated sale and rent back agreement if it is a regulated home reversion plan;
   (b)   "administering" a regulated sale and rent back agreement means any of—
      (i)   notifying the agreement seller of changes in payments due under the agreement, or of other matters of which the agreement requires the agreement seller to be notified;
      (ii)   taking any necessary steps for the purpose of making payments to the agreement seller under the agreement; and
      (iii)   taking any necessary steps for the purposes of collecting or recovering payments due under the agreement from the agreement seller,
   but a person is not to be treated as administering a regulated sale and rent back agreement because that person has, or exercises, a right to take action for the purposes of enforcing the agreement (or to require that such action is or is not taken).

(4)   For the purposes of paragraph (3)—
   (a)   the reference to a "qualifying interest" in land—
      (i)   in relation to land in England and Wales, is to an estate in fee simple absolute or a term of years absolute, whether subsisting at law or in equity;
      (ii)   in relation to land in Scotland, is to the interest of an owner in land or the tenant's right over or interest in a property subject to a lease;
      (iii)   in relation to land in Northern Ireland, is to any freehold estate or any leasehold estate, whether subsisting at law or in equity;
   [(b)   "timeshare accommodation" means overnight accommodation which is the subject of a timeshare contract within the meaning of the Timeshare, Holiday Products, Resale and Exchange Contracts Regulations 2010; and]
   (c)   "related person" in relation to the agreement seller or, where the agreement seller is a trustee, a beneficiary of the trust, means—
      (i)   that person's spouse or civil partner;
      (ii)   a person (whether or not of the opposite sex) whose relationship with that person has the characteristic of the relationship between husband and wife;
      (iii)   that person's parent, brother, sister, child, grandparent or grandchild.

(5)   For the purposes of paragraph (3)(a)(ii), the area of any land which compromises a building or other structure containing two or more storeys is to be taken to be the aggregate of the floor areas of each of those storeys.

(6)   In this Order—
   (a)   references to entering into a regulated sale and rent back agreement as agreement provider include acquiring any obligations or rights of the agreement provider, including the agreement provider's interest in land or interests under one or more of the instruments or agreements referred to in paragraph (3)(a); but

    (b)   in relation to a person who acquires any such obligations or rights, an activity is a specified kind of activity for the purposes of articles 25E(1)(b) and 53D(b)(ii) and paragraph (2) only if the agreement was entered into by the agreement provider (rather than the obligations or rights acquired) on or after 1st July 2009.

(7)   Accordingly, references in this Order to an agreement provider, other than in paragraph (6), include a person who acquires any such obligations or rights.]

NOTES

Commencement: 1 July 2009 (certain purposes); 30 June 2010 (otherwise) (see below).

Chapter 15C (arts 63J–63M and the preceding headings) inserted by the Financial Services and Markets Act 2000 (Regulated Activities) (Amendment) Order 2009, SI 2009/1342, arts 2, 17, as from 1 July 2009 (other than for the purposes of enabling applications to be made for a Part IV permission, or a variation of a Part IV permission, in relation to activities of the kind specified by arts 25E, 53D or 63J or, so far as relevant to any such activity, art 64 of this Order), and as from 30 June 2010 (for those purposes) (for transitional provisions in relation to applications for Part IV permissions, etc, see arts 1, 32–34 of that Order)

Para (4): sub-para (b) substituted by the Timeshare, Holiday Products, Resale and Exchange Contracts Regulations 2010, SI 2010/2960, reg 36(3), Sch 6, para 7(1), (3), as from 23 February 2011.

[Exclusions

[8.111]
63K   Arranging administration by authorised person

A person who is not an authorised person does not carry on an activity of the kind specified by article 63J(2) in relation to a regulated sale and rent back agreement where that person—

    (a)   arranges for another person, being an authorised person with permission to carry on an activity of that kind, to administer the agreement; or

    (b)   administers the agreement during a period of not more than one month beginning with the day on which any such arrangement comes to an end.]

NOTES

Commencement: 1 July 2009 (certain purposes); 30 June 2010 (otherwise) (see art 63J at **[8.110]**).
Inserted as noted to art 63J at **[8.110]**.

[8.112]
[63L   Administration pursuant to agreement with authorised person

A person who is not an authorised person does not carry on an activity of the kind specified by article 63J(2) in relation to a regulated sale and rent back agreement where that person administers the agreement pursuant to an agreement with an authorised person who has permission to carry on activity of that kind.]

NOTES

Commencement: 1 July 2009 (certain purposes); 30 June 2010 (otherwise) (see art 63J at **[8.110]**).
Inserted as noted to art 63J at **[8.110]**.

[8.113]
[63M   Other exclusions

Article 63J is also subject to the exclusions in article 66 (trustees etc), 72 (overseas persons) and 72A (information society services).]

NOTES

Commencement: 1 July 2009 (certain purposes); 30 June 2010 (otherwise) (see art 63J at **[8.110]**).
Inserted as noted to art 63J at **[8.110]**.

[CHAPTER 15D
ACTIVITIES OF RECLAIM FUNDS
The activities

[8.114]
63N   Dormant account funds

(1)   The following are specified kinds of activity—

    (a)   the meeting of repayment claims by a reclaim fund;

    (b)   the management of dormant account funds (including the investment of such funds) by a reclaim fund.

(2)   In this article—

"account", "balance", "dormant" and "reclaim fund" have the same meaning as in Part 1 of the Dormant Bank and Building Society Accounts Act 2008 (transfer of balances in dormant accounts) (see section 6 of that Act);

"dormant account funds" and "repayment claims" have the same meaning as in section 5 of that Act;

"management of dormant account funds" means the acceptance of a transfer from a bank or building society of the balance of a dormant account, or a proportion of such a balance, and the management of those funds in such a way as to enable the reclaim fund to meet whatever repayment claims it is prudent to anticipate.]

NOTES

Commencement: 13 July 2009.

Inserted, together with the preceding headings, by the Financial Services and Markets Act 2000 (Regulated Activities) (Amendment) (No 2) Order 2009, SI 2009/1389, arts 2, 4, as from 13 July 2009.

CHAPTER XVI
AGREEING TO CARRY ON ACTIVITIES

The activity

[8.115]
64 Agreeing to carry on specified kinds of activity

Agreeing to carry on an activity of the kind specified by any other provision of this Part (other than article 5, [9B,] 10, [25D,] [51, 52 and 63N]) is a specified kind of activity.

NOTES

First figure in square brackets inserted by the Financial Services and Markets Act 2000 (Regulated Activities) (Amendment) Order 2002, SI 2002/682, art 5, as from 27 April 2002, subject to transitional provisions in relation to persons issuing electronic money immediately before that date contained in art 9.

Second figure in square brackets inserted by the Financial Services and Markets Act 2000 (Regulated Activities) (Amendment No 3) Order 2006, SI 2006/3384, arts 2, 18, as from 1 April 2007 (for the purposes of enabling applications to be made for (i) a Part IV permission, (ii) a variation of a Part IV permission, and (iii) the Authority's approval under s 59 of the 2000 Act, in relation to an activity of the kind specified by art 25D of this Order, or in relation to an investment of the kind specified by arts 83, 84 or 85 of this Order), and as from 1 November 2007 (otherwise).

Words in third pair of square brackets substituted by the Financial Services and Markets Act 2000 (Regulated Activities) (Amendment) (No 2) Order 2009, SI 2009/1389, arts 2, 5, as from 13 July 2009.

[Exclusions

[8.116]
65 Overseas persons etc

Article 64 is subject to the exclusions in articles 72 (overseas persons) and 72A (information society services).]

NOTES

Substituted, together with the preceding heading, by the Financial Services and Markets Act 2000 (Regulated Activities) (Amendment) (No 2) Order 2002, SI 2002/1776, art 3(1), (17), as from 21 August 2002.

CHAPTER XVII
EXCLUSIONS APPLYING TO SEVERAL SPECIFIED KINDS OF ACTIVITY

[8.117]
66 Trustees, nominees and personal representatives

(1) A person ("X") does not carry on an activity of the kind specified by article 14 where he enters into a transaction as bare trustee or, in Scotland, as nominee for another person ("Y") and—
   (a) X is acting on Y's instructions; and
   (b) X does not hold himself out as providing a service of buying and selling securities or contractually based investments.

(2) Subject to paragraph (7), there are excluded from [articles 25(1) and (2)[, 25A(1) and (2), 25B(1) and (2)][, 25C(1) and (2) and 25E (1) and (2)]] arrangements made by a person acting as trustee or personal representative for or with a view to a transaction which is or is to be entered into—
   (a) by that person and a fellow trustee or personal representative (acting in their capacity as such); or
   (b) by a beneficiary under the trust, will or intestacy.

(3) Subject to paragraph (7), there is excluded from article 37 any activity carried on by a person acting as trustee or personal representative, unless—
   (a) he holds himself out as providing a service comprising an activity of the kind specified by article 37; or
   (b) the assets in question are held for the purposes of an occupational pension scheme, and, by virtue of article 4 of the Financial Services and Markets Act 2000 (Carrying on Regulated Activities by Way of Business) Order 2001, he is to be treated as carrying on that activity by way of business.

[(3A) Subject to paragraph (7), there is excluded from article 39A any activity carried on by a person acting as trustee or personal representative, unless he holds himself out as providing a service comprising an activity of the kind specified by article 39A.]

(4) Subject to paragraph (7), there is excluded from article 40 any activity carried on by a person acting as trustee or personal representative, unless he holds himself out as providing a service comprising an activity of the kind specified by article 40.

[(4A) There is excluded from article 40 any activity carried on by a person acting as trustee which consists of arranging for one or more other persons to safeguard and administer trust assets where—
  (a) that other person is a qualifying custodian; or
  (b) that safeguarding and administration is also arranged by a qualifying custodian.
  In this paragraph, "qualifying custodian" has the meaning given by article 41(2).]

(5) A person does not, by sending or causing to be sent a dematerialised instruction (within the meaning of article 45), carry on an activity of the kind specified by that article if the instruction relates to an investment which that person holds as trustee or personal representative.

(6) Subject to paragraph (7), there is excluded from [articles 53[, 53A, 53B][, 53C and 53D]] the giving of advice by a person acting as trustee or personal representative where he gives the advice to—
  (a) a fellow trustee or personal representative for the purposes of the trust or the estate; or
  (b) a beneficiary under the trust, will or intestacy concerning his interest in the trust fund or estate.

[(6A) Subject to paragraph (7), a person acting as trustee or personal representative does not carry on an activity of the kind specified by article 61(1) or (2) where the borrower under the regulated mortgage contract in question is a beneficiary under the trust, will or intestacy.]

[(6B) Subject to paragraph (7), a person acting as trustee or personal representative does not carry on an activity of the kind specified by article 63B(1) or (2) where the reversion seller under the regulated home reversion plan in question is a beneficiary under the trust, will or intestacy.

(6C) Subject to paragraph (7), a person acting as trustee or personal representative does not carry on an activity of the kind specified by article 63F(1) or (2) where the home purchaser under the regulated home purchase plan in question is a beneficiary under the trust, will or intestacy.]

[(6D) Subject to paragraph (7), a person acting as a trustee or personal representative does not carry on an activity of the kind specified by article 63J(1) or (2) where the agreement seller under the regulated sale and rent back agreement is a beneficiary under the trust, will or intestacy.]

(7) Paragraphs (2), (3)[, (3A)], [(4), (6)[, (6A), (6B)][, (6C) and (6D)]] do not apply if the person carrying on the activity is remunerated for what he does in addition to any remuneration he receives as trustee or personal representative, and for these purposes a person is not to be regarded as receiving additional remuneration merely because his remuneration is calculated by reference to time spent.

[(8) This article is subject to article 4(4A).]

NOTES

Para (2): words in first (outer) pair of square brackets substituted by the Financial Services and Markets Act 2000 (Regulated Activities) (Amendment) (No 1) Order 2003, SI 2003/1475, art 18(a), as from 31 October 2004 (for transitional provisions in relation to applications for Part IV permissions and applications for approvals, etc, see arts 26–29 of the 2003 Order); words in second (inner) pair of square brackets substituted by the Financial Services and Markets Act 2000 (Regulated Activities) (Amendment) (No 2) Order 2006, SI 2006/2383, arts 2, 19(a), as from 6 November 2006 (for the purposes of enabling applications to be made for (i) a Pt IV permission, or a variation of a Pt IV permission, in relation to activities of the kind specified by arts 25B, 25C, 53B, 53C, 63B or 63F or, so far as relevant to any such activity, art 64 of this Order; or (ii) the Authority's approval under FSMA 2000, s 59 in relation to any of those activities), and as from 6 April 2007 (otherwise) (for transitional provisions in relation to interim permissions and interim approvals, etc, see arts 36–40 of, and the Schedule to, the 2006 Order); words in third (inner) pair of square brackets substituted by the Financial Services and Markets Act 2000 (Regulated Activities) (Amendment) Order 2009, SI 2009/1342, arts 2, 18(a), as from 1 July 2009 (other than for the purposes of enabling applications to be made for a Part IV permission, or a variation of a Part IV permission, in relation to activities of the kind specified by arts 25E, 53D or 63J or, so far as relevant to any such activity, art 64 of this Order), and as from 30 June 2010 (for those purposes) (for transitional provisions in relation to applications for Part IV permissions, etc, see arts 1, 32–34 of that Order).

Para (3A): inserted by the Financial Services and Markets Act 2000 (Regulated Activities) (Amendment) (No 2) Order 2003, SI 2003/1476, art 10(1)(a), as from 31 October 2004 (in so far as relating to contracts of long-term care insurance), and as from 14 January 2005 (otherwise) (for transitional provisions in relation to applications for Part IV permissions and applications for approvals, etc, see arts 22–27 of the 2003 Order).

Para (4A): inserted by the Financial Services and Markets Act 2000 (Regulated Activities) (Amendment) Order 2005, SI 2005/593, art 2(4), as from 6 April 2005.

Para (6): words in first (outer) pair of square brackets substituted by SI 2003/1475, art 18(b), as from 31 October 2004 (for transitional provisions in relation to applications for Part IV permissions and applications for approvals, etc, see arts 26–29 of the 2003 Order); words in second (inner) pair of square brackets substituted by SI 2006/2383, arts 2, 19(b), as from 6 November 2006 (certain purposes), and as from 6 April 2007 (otherwise) (for purposes, transitional provisions, and effect, see the para (2) note above); words in second (inner) pair of square brackets substituted by SI 2009/1342, arts 2, 18(b), as from the same dates and for the same purposes, etc, as mentioned in the note relating to this Order above.

Para (6A): inserted by SI 2003/1475, art 18(c), as from 31 October 2004 (for transitional provisions in relation to applications for Part IV permissions and applications for approvals, etc, see arts 26–29 of the 2003 Order).

Paras (6B), (6C): inserted by SI 2006/2383, arts 2, 19(c), as from 6 November 2006 (certain purposes), and as from 6 April 2007 (otherwise) (for purposes, transitional provisions, and effect, see the para (2) note above).

Para (6D): inserted by SI 2009/1342, arts 2, 18(c), as from the same dates and for the same purposes, etc, as mentioned in the note relating to this Order above.

Para (7): figure in first pair of square brackets inserted by SI 2003/1476, art 10(1)(b), as from 31 October 2004 (in so far as relating to contracts of long-term care insurance), and as from 14 January 2005 (otherwise) (for transitional provisions in relation to applications for Part IV permissions and applications for approvals, etc, see arts 22–27 of the 2003 Order); words in second (outer) pair of square brackets substituted by SI 2003/1475, art 18(d), as from 31 October 2004 (for transitional provisions in relation to applications for Part IV permissions and applications for approvals, etc, see arts 26–29 of the 2003 Order); words in third (inner) pair of square brackets substituted by SI 2006/2383, arts 2, 19(d), as from 6 November 2006 (certain purposes), and as from 6 April 2007 (otherwise) (for purposes, transitional provisions, and effect, see the para (2) note above); words in fourth (inner) pair of square brackets substituted by SI 2009/1342, arts 2, 18(d), as from the same dates and for the same purposes, etc, as mentioned in the note relating to this Order above.

Para (8): added by the Financial Services and Markets Act 2000 (Regulated Activities) (Amendment No 3) Order 2006, SI 2006/3384, arts 2, 19, as from 1 April 2007 (for the purposes of enabling applications to be made for (i) a Part IV permission, (ii) a variation of a Part IV permission, and (iii) the Authority's approval under s 59 of the 2000 Act, in relation to an activity of the kind specified by art 25D of this Order, or in relation to an investment of the kind specified by arts 83, 84 or 85 of this Order), and as from 1 November 2007 (otherwise).

[8.118]
67 Activities carried on in the course of a profession or non-investment business

(1)   There is excluded from articles 21, 25(1) and (2)[, 25A], [25B, 25C,] [25E,] [39A, 40] [53[, 53A, 53B]][, 53C and 53D] any activity which—

(a)   is carried on in the course of carrying on any profession or business which does not otherwise consist of [the carrying on of regulated activities in the United Kingdom]; and

(b)   may reasonably be regarded as a necessary part of other services provided in the course of that profession or business.

(2)   But the exclusion in paragraph (1) does not apply if the activity in question is remunerated separately from the other services.

[(3)   This article is subject to article 4(4) and (4A).]

NOTES
Para (1) is amended as follows:

Figure in first pair of square brackets inserted, and words in fifth (outer) pair of square brackets substituted, by the Financial Services and Markets Act 2000 (Regulated Activities) (Amendment) (No 1) Order 2003, SI 2003/1475, art 19, as from 31 October 2004 (for transitional provisions in relation to applications for Part IV permissions and applications for approvals, etc, see arts 26–29 of the 2003 Order).

Figures in second pair of square brackets inserted and words in sixth (inner) pair of square brackets substituted by the Financial Services and Markets Act 2000 (Regulated Activities) (Amendment) (No 2) Order 2006, SI 2006/2383, arts 2, 20, as from 6 November 2006 (for the purposes of enabling applications to be made for (i) a Pt IV permission, or a variation of a Pt IV permission, in relation to activities of the kind specified by arts 25B, 25C, 53B, 53C, 63B or 63F or, so far as relevant to any such activity, art 64 of this Order; or (ii) the Authority's approval under FSMA 2000, s 59 in relation to any of those activities), and as from 6 April 2007 (otherwise) (for transitional provisions in relation to interim permissions and interim approvals, etc, see arts 36–40 of, and the Schedule to, the 2006 Order).

Figure in third pair of square brackets inserted, and words in seventh pair of square brackets substituted by the Financial Services and Markets Act 2000 (Regulated Activities) (Amendment) Order 2009, SI 2009/1342, arts 2, 19, as from 1 July 2009 (other than for the purposes of enabling applications to be made for a Part IV permission, or a variation of a Part IV permission, in relation to activities of the kind specified by arts 25E, 53D or 63J or, so far as relevant to any such activity, art 64 of this Order), and as from 30 June 2010 (for those purposes) (for transitional provisions in relation to applications for Part IV permissions, etc, see arts 1, 32–34 of that Order).

Figures in fourth pair of square brackets substituted by the Financial Services and Markets Act 2000 (Regulated Activities) (Amendment) (No 2) Order 2003, SI 2003/1476, art 10(2), as from 31 October 2004 (in so far as relating to contracts of long-term care insurance), and as from 14 January 2005 (otherwise) (for transitional provisions in relation to applications for Part IV permissions and applications for approvals, etc, see arts 22–27 of the 2003 Order).

Words in square brackets in sub-para (a) substituted by the Financial Services and Markets Act 2000 (Regulated Activities) (Amendment) Order 2001, SI 2001/3544, arts 2, 9, as from 1 December 2001.

Para (3): added by the Financial Services and Markets Act 2000 (Regulated Activities) (Amendment No 3) Order 2006, SI 2006/3384, arts 2, 20, as from 1 April 2007 (for the purposes of enabling applications to be made for (i) a Part IV permission, (ii) a variation of a Part IV permission, and (iii) the Authority's approval under s 59 of the 2000 Act, in relation to an activity of the kind specified by art 25D of this Order, or in relation to an investment of the kind specified by arts 83, 84 or 85 of this Order), and as from 1 November 2007 (otherwise).

[8.119]
68 Activities carried on in connection with the sale of goods or supply of services

(1)   Subject to paragraphs (9), (10) and (11), this article concerns certain activities carried on for the purposes of or in connection with the sale of goods or supply of services by a supplier to a customer, where—

"supplier" means a person whose main business is to sell goods or supply services and not to carry on any activities of the kind specified by any of articles 14, 21, 25, 37[, 39A], 40, 45, 51, 52 and 53 and, where the supplier is a member of a group, also means any other member of that group; and

"customer" means a person, other than an individual, to whom a supplier sells goods or supplies services, or agrees to do so, and, where the customer is a member of a group, also means any other member of that group;

and in this article "related sale or supply" means a sale of goods or supply of services to the customer otherwise than by the supplier, but for or in connection with the same purpose as the sale or supply mentioned above.

(2)   There is excluded from article 14 any transaction entered into by a supplier with a customer, if the transaction is entered into for the purposes of or in connection with the sale of goods or supply of services, or a related sale or supply.

(3)   There is excluded from article 21 any transaction entered into [by a supplier as agent for a customer], if the transaction is entered into for the purposes of or in connection with the sale of goods or supply of services, or a related sale or supply, and provided that—

   (a)   where the investment to which the transaction relates is a security, the supplier does not hold himself out (other than to the customer) as engaging in the business of buying securities of the kind to which the transaction relates with a view to selling them, and does not regularly solicit members of the public for the purpose of inducing them (as principals or agents) to buy, sell, subscribe for or underwrite securities;

   (b)   where the investment to which the transaction relates is a contractually based investment, the supplier enters into the transaction—

      (i)   with or through an authorised person, or an exempt person acting in the course of a business comprising a regulated activity in relation to which he is exempt; or

      (ii)   through an office outside the United Kingdom maintained by a party to the transaction, and with or through a person whose head office is situated outside the United Kingdom and whose ordinary business involves him in carrying on activities of the kind specified by any of articles 14, 21, 25, 37, 40, 45, 51, 52 and 53 or, so far as relevant to any of those articles, article 64, or would do so apart from any exclusion from any of those articles made by this Order.

(4)   In paragraph (3)(a), "members of the public" has the meaning given by article 15(2), references to "A" being read as references to the supplier.

(5)   There are excluded from article 25(1) and (2) arrangements made by a supplier for, or with a view to, a transaction which is or is to be entered into by a customer for the purposes of or in connection with the sale of goods or supply of services, or a related sale or supply.

(6)   There is excluded from article 37 any activity carried on by a supplier where the assets in question—

   (a)   are those of a customer; and

   (b)   are managed for the purposes of or in connection with the sale of goods or supply of services, or a related sale or supply.

(7)   There is excluded from article 40 any activity carried on by a supplier where the assets in question are or are to be safeguarded and administered for the purposes of or in connection with the sale of goods or supply of services, or a related sale or supply.

(8)   There is excluded from article 53 the giving of advice by a supplier to a customer for the purposes of or in connection with the sale of goods or supply of services, or a related sale or supply, or to a person with whom the customer proposes to enter into a transaction for the purposes of or in connection with such a sale or supply or related sale or supply.

(9)   Paragraphs (2), (3) and (5) do not apply in the case of a transaction for the sale or purchase of a [contract of insurance], an investment of the kind specified by article 81, or an investment of the kind specified by article 89 so far as relevant to such a contract or such an investment.

(10)   Paragraph (6) does not apply where the assets managed consist of qualifying contracts of insurance, investments of the kind specified by article 81, or investments of the kind specified by article 89 so far as relevant to such contracts or such investments.

(11)   Paragraph (8) does not apply in the case of advice in relation to an investment which is a [contract of insurance], is of the kind specified by article 81, or is of the kind specified by article 89 so far as relevant to such a contract or such an investment.

[(12)   This article is subject to article 4(4).]

NOTES

Para (1): figure in square brackets in definition "supplier" inserted by the Financial Services and Markets Act 2000 (Regulated Activities) (Amendment) (No 2) Order 2003, SI 2003/1476, art 10(3)(a), as from 31 October 2004 (in so far as relating to contracts of long-term care insurance), and as from 14 January 2005 (otherwise) (for transitional provisions in relation to applications for Part IV permissions and applications for approvals, etc, see arts 22–27 of the 2003 Order).

Para (3): words in square brackets substituted by the Financial Services and Markets Act 2000 (Regulated Activities) (Amendment) Order 2001, SI 2001/3544, arts 2, 10, as from 1 December 2001.

Paras (9), (11): words in square brackets substituted by SI 2003/1476, art 10(3)(b), (c), as from the same dates and for the same purposes, etc, as mentioned in the note relating to this Order above.

Para (12): added by the Financial Services and Markets Act 2000 (Regulated Activities) (Amendment No 3) Order 2006, SI 2006/3384, arts 2, 21, as from 1 April 2007 (for the purposes of enabling applications to be made for (i) a Part IV permission, (ii) a variation of a Part IV permission, and (iii) the Authority's approval under s 59 of the 2000 Act, in relation to an activity of the kind specified by art 25D of this Order, or in relation to an investment of the kind specified by arts 83, 84 or 85 of this Order), and as from 1 November 2007 (otherwise).

[8.120]

69 Groups and joint enterprises

(1)   There is excluded from article 14 any transaction into which a person enters as principal with another person if that other person is also acting as principal and—

   (a)   they are members of the same group; or

   (b)   they are, or propose to become, participators in a joint enterprise and the transaction is entered into for the purposes of or in connection with that enterprise.

(2)   There is excluded from article 21 any transaction into which a person enters as agent for another person if that other person is acting as principal, and the condition in paragraph (1)(a) or (b) is met, provided that—

   (a)   where the investment to which the transaction relates is a security, the agent does not hold himself out (other than to members of the same group or persons who are or propose to become participators with him in a joint enterprise) as engaging in the business of buying securities of the kind to which the transaction relates with a view to selling them, and does not regularly solicit members of the public for the purpose of inducing them (as principals or agents) to buy, sell, subscribe for or underwrite securities;

   (b)   where the investment to which the transaction relates is a contractually based investment, the agent enters into the transaction—

      (i)   with or through an authorised person, or an exempt person acting in the course of a business comprising a regulated activity in relation to which he is exempt; or

      (ii)   through an office outside the United Kingdom maintained by a party to the transaction, and with or through a person whose head office is situated outside the United Kingdom and whose ordinary business involves him in carrying on activities of the kind specified by any of articles 14, 21, 25, 37, 40, 45, 51, 52 and 53 or, so far as relevant to any of those articles, article 64, or would do so apart from any exclusion from any of those articles made by this Order.

(3)   In paragraph (2)(a), "members of the public" has the meaning given by article 15(2), references to "A" being read as references to the agent.

(4)   There are excluded from article 25(1) and (2) arrangements made by a person if—

   (a)   he is a member of a group and the arrangements in question are for, or with a view to, a transaction which is or is to be entered into, as principal, by another member of the same group; or

   (b)   he is or proposes to become a participator in a joint enterprise, and the arrangements in question are for, or with a view to, a transaction which is or is to be entered into, as principal, by another person who is or proposes to become a participator in that enterprise, for the purposes of or in connection with that enterprise.

(5)   There is excluded from article 37 any activity carried on by a person if—

   (a)   he is a member of a group and the assets in question belong to another member of the same group; or

   (b)   he is or proposes to become a participator in a joint enterprise with the person to whom the assets belong, and the assets are managed for the purposes of or in connection with that enterprise.

(6)   There is excluded from article 40 any activity carried on by a person if—

   (a)   he is a member of a group and the assets in question belong to another member of the same group; or

   (b)   he is or proposes to become a participator in a joint enterprise, and the assets in question—

      (i)   belong to another person who is or proposes to become a participator in that joint enterprise; and

      (ii)   are or are to be safeguarded and administered for the purposes of or in connection with that enterprise.

(7)   A person who is a member of a group does not carry on an activity of the kind specified by article 45 where he sends a dematerialised instruction, or causes one to be sent, on behalf of another member of the same group, if the investment to which the instruction relates is one in respect of which a member of the same group is registered as holder in the appropriate register of securities, or will be so registered as a result of the instruction.

(8)   In paragraph (7), "dematerialised instruction" and "register of securities" have the meaning given by regulation 3 of the Uncertificated Securities Regulations [2001].

(9)   There is excluded from article 53 the giving of advice by a person if—

   (a)   he is a member of a group and gives the advice in question to another member of the same group; or

   (b)   he is, or proposes to become, a participator in a joint enterprise and the advice in question is given to another person who is, or proposes to become, a participator in that enterprise for the purposes of or in connection with that enterprise.

[(10)   Paragraph (2) does not apply to a transaction for the sale or purchase of a contract of insurance.

(11)   Paragraph (4) does not apply to arrangements for, or with a view to, a transaction for the sale or purchase of a contract of insurance.

(12)   Paragraph (9) does not apply where the advice relates to a transaction for the sale or purchase of a contract of insurance.]

[(13)   This article is subject to article 4(4).]

NOTES

Para (8): date in square brackets substituted by the Financial Services and Markets Act 2000 (Regulated Activities) (Amendment) Order 2002, SI 2002/682, art 13(4), as from 27 April 2002.

Paras (10)–(12): added by the Financial Services and Markets Act 2000 (Regulated Activities) (Amendment) (No 2) Order 2003, SI 2003/1476, art 10(4), as from 31 October 2004 (in so far as relating to contracts of long-term care insurance), and as from 14 January 2005 (otherwise) (for transitional provisions in relation to applications for Part IV permissions and applications for approvals, etc, see arts 22–27 of the 2003 Order).

Para (13): added by the Financial Services and Markets Act 2000 (Regulated Activities) (Amendment No 3) Order 2006, SI 2006/3384, arts 2, 22, as from 1 April 2007 (for the purposes of enabling applications to be made for (i) a Part IV permission, (ii) a variation of a Part IV permission, and (iii) the Authority's approval under s 59 of the 2000 Act, in relation to an activity of the kind specified by art 25D of this Order, or in relation to an investment of the kind specified by arts 83, 84 or 85 of this Order), and as from 1 November 2007 (otherwise).

[8.121]
70   Activities carried on in connection with the sale of a body corporate

(1)   A person does not carry on an activity of the kind specified by article 14 by entering as principal into a transaction if—

(a)   the transaction is one to acquire or dispose of shares in a body corporate other than an open-ended investment company, or is entered into for the purposes of such an acquisition or disposal; and

(b)   either—

(i)   the conditions set out in paragraph (2) are met; or

(ii)   those conditions are not met, but the object of the transaction may nevertheless reasonably be regarded as being the acquisition of day to day control of the affairs of the body corporate.

(2)   The conditions mentioned in paragraph (1)(b) are that—

(a)   the shares consist of or include 50 per cent or more of the voting shares in the body corporate; or

(b)   the shares, together with any already held by the person acquiring them, consist of or include at least that percentage of such shares; and

(c)   in either case, the acquisition or disposal is between parties each of whom is a body corporate, a partnership, a single individual or a group of connected individuals.

(3)   In paragraph (2)(c), "a group of connected individuals" means—

(a)   in relation to a party disposing of shares in a body corporate, a single group of persons each of whom is—

(i)   a director or manager of the body corporate;

(ii)   a close relative of any such director or manager;

(iii)   a person acting as trustee for any person falling within paragraph (i) or (ii); and

(b)   in relation to a party acquiring shares in a body corporate, a single group of persons each of whom is—

(i)   a person who is or is to be a director or manager of the body corporate;

(ii)   a close relative of any such person; or

(iii)   a person acting as trustee for any person falling within paragraph (i) or (ii).

(4)   A person does not carry on an activity of the kind specified by article 21 by entering as agent into a transaction of the kind described in paragraph (1).

(5)   There are excluded from article 25(1) and (2) arrangements made for, or with a view to, a transaction of the kind described in paragraph (1).

(6)   There is excluded from article 53 the giving of advice in connection with a transaction (or proposed transaction) of the kind described in paragraph (1).

[(7)   Paragraphs (4), (5) and (6) do not apply in the case of a transaction for the sale or purchase of a contract of insurance.]

[(8)   This article is subject to article 4(4).]

NOTES

Para (7): added by the Financial Services and Markets Act 2000 (Regulated Activities) (Amendment) (No 2) Order 2003, SI 2003/1476, art 10(5), as from 31 October 2004 (in so far as relating to contracts of long-term care insurance), and as from 14 January 2005 (otherwise) (for transitional provisions in relation to applications for Part IV permissions and applications for approvals, etc, see arts 22–27 of the 2003 Order).

Para (8): added by the Financial Services and Markets Act 2000 (Regulated Activities) (Amendment No 3) Order 2006, SI 2006/3384, arts 2, 23, as from 1 April 2007 (for the purposes of enabling applications to be made for (i) a Part IV permission, (ii) a variation of a Part IV permission, and (iii) the Authority's approval under s 59 of the 2000 Act, in relation to an activity of the kind specified by art 25D of this Order, or in relation to an investment of the kind specified by arts 83, 84 or 85 of this Order), and as from 1 November 2007 (otherwise).

[8.122]
71 Activities carried on in connection with employee share schemes

(1)   A person ("C"), a member of the same group as C or a relevant trustee does not carry on an activity of the kind specified by article 14 by entering as principal into a transaction the purpose of which is to enable or facilitate—

(a)   transactions in shares in, or debentures issued by, C between, or for the benefit of, any of the persons mentioned in paragraph (2); or

(b)   the holding of such shares or debentures by, or for the benefit of, such persons.

(2)   The persons referred to in paragraph (1) are—

(a)   the bona fide employees or former employees of C or of another member of the same group as C;

(b)   the wives, husbands, widows, widowers, [civil partners, surviving civil partners,] or children or step-children under the age of eighteen of such employees or former employees.

(3)   C, a member of the same group as C or a relevant trustee does not carry on an activity of the kind specified by article 21 by entering as agent into a transaction of the kind described in paragraph (1).

(4)   There are excluded from article 25(1) or (2) arrangements made by C, a member of the same group as C or a relevant trustee if the arrangements in question are for, or with a view to, a transaction of the kind described in paragraph (1).

(5)   There is excluded from article 40 any activity if the assets in question are, or are to be, safeguarded and administered by C, a member of the same group as C or a relevant trustee for the purpose of enabling or facilitating transactions of the kind described in paragraph (1).

(6)   In this article—

(a)   "shares" and "debentures" include—

(i)   any investment of the kind specified by article 76[, 77 or 77A];

(ii)   any investment of the kind specified by article 79 or 80 so far as relevant to articles 76[, 77 and 77A]; and

(iii) any investment of the kind specified by article 89 so far as relevant to investments of the kind mentioned in paragraph (i) or (ii);

(b)   "relevant trustee" means a person who, in pursuance of the arrangements made for the purpose mentioned in paragraph (1), holds, as trustee, shares in or debentures issued by C.

NOTES

Para (2): words in square brackets in sub-para (b) inserted by the Civil Partnership Act 2004 (Amendments to Subordinate Legislation) Order 2005, SI 2005/2114, art 2(16), Sch 16, Pt 1, para 1(1), (4), as from 5 December 2005.

Para (6): words in square brackets substituted by the Financial Services and Markets Act 2000 (Regulated Activities) (Amendment) Order 2010, SI 2010/86, art 4, Schedule, para 5(c), (d), as from 24 February 2010.

Step-children, etc: as to the meaning of this, and related expressions, see the Civil Partnership Act 2004, s 246 (as applied to this Order by the Civil Partnership Act 2004 (Relationships Arising Through Civil Partnership) Order 2005, SI 2005/3137, art 3, Schedule).

[8.123]
72 Overseas persons

(1)   An overseas person does not carry on an activity of the kind specified by article 14 [or 25D] by—

(a)   entering into a transaction as principal with or though an authorised person, or an exempt person acting in the course of a business comprising a regulated activity in relation to which he is exempt; or

(b)   entering into a transaction as principal with a person in the United Kingdom, if the transaction is the result of a legitimate approach.

(2)   An overseas person does not carry on an activity of the kind specified by article 21 [or 25D] by—

(a)   entering into a transaction as agent for any person with or through an authorised person or an exempt person acting in the course of a business comprising a regulated activity in relation to which he is exempt; or

(b)   entering into a transaction with another party ("X") as agent for any person ("Y"), other than with or through an authorised person or such an exempt person, unless—

(i)   either X or Y is in the United Kingdom; and

(ii)   the transaction is the result of an approach (other than a legitimate approach) made by or on behalf of, or to, whichever of X or Y is in the United Kingdom.

(3)   There are excluded from article 25(1) [or 25D] arrangements made by an overseas person with an authorised person, or an exempt person acting in the course of a business comprising a regulated activity in relation to which he is exempt.

(4)   There are excluded from article 25(2) [or 25D] arrangements made by an overseas person with a view to transactions which are, as respects transactions in the United Kingdom, confined to—

(a)   transactions entered into by authorised persons as principal or agent; and

(b)   transactions entered into by exempt persons, as principal or agent, in the course of business comprising regulated activities in relation to which they are exempt.

(5)   There is excluded from article 53 the giving of advice by an overseas person as a result of a legitimate approach.

[(5A)   An overseas person does not carry on an activity of the kind specified by article 25A(1)(a), 25B(1)(a)[, 25C(1)(a) or 25E(1)(a)] if each person who may be contemplating entering into the relevant type of agreement in the relevant capacity is non-resident.

(5B)   There are excluded from articles 25A(1)(b), 25B(1)(b)[, 25C(1)(b) and 25E(1)(b)] arrangements made by an overseas person to vary the terms of a qualifying agreement.

(5C)   There are excluded from articles 25A(2), 25B(2)[, 25C(2) and 25E(2)], arrangements made by an overseas person which are made solely with a view to non-resident persons who participate in those arrangements entering, in the relevant capacity, into the relevant type of agreement.

(5D)   An overseas person does not carry on an activity of the kind specified in article 61(1), 63B(1)[, 63F(1) or 63J(1)] by entering into a qualifying agreement.

(5E)   An overseas person does not carry on an activity of the kind specified in article 61(2), 63B(2)[, 63F(2) or 63J(2)] where he administers a qualifying agreement.

(5F)   In paragraphs (5A) to (5E)—
    (a)   "non-resident" means not normally resident in the United Kingdom;
    (b)   "qualifying agreement" means—
        (i)   in relation to articles 25A and 61, a regulated mortgage contract where the borrower (or each borrower) is non-resident when he enters into it;
        (ii)   in relation to articles 25B and 63B, a regulated home reversion plan where the reversion seller (or each reversion seller) is non-resident when he enters into it;
        (iii)   in relation to articles 25C and 63F, a regulated home purchase plan where the home purchaser (or each home purchaser) is non-resident when he enters into it;
        [(iv)   in relation to articles 25E and 63J, a regulated sale and rent back agreement where the agreement seller (or each agreement seller) is non-resident when the agreement seller enters into it;]
    (c)   "the relevant capacity" means—
        (i)   in the case of a regulated mortgage contract, as borrower;
        (ii)   in the case of a regulated home reversion plan, as reversion seller or plan provider;
        (iii)   in the case of a regulated home purchase plan, as home purchaser;
        [(iv)   in the case of a regulated sale and rent back agreement, as agreement seller or agreement provider;]
    (d)   "the relevant type of agreement" means—
        (i)   in relation to article 25A, a regulated mortgage contract;
        (ii)   in relation to article 25B, a regulated home reversion plan;
        (iii)   in relation to article 25C, a regulated home purchase plan[;
        (iv)   in relation to article 25E, a regulated sale and rent back agreement]].

(6)   There is excluded from article 64 any agreement made by an overseas person to carry on an activity of the kind specified by article 25(1) or (2), 37[, 39A], 40 or 45 if the agreement is the result of a legitimate approach.

(7)   In this article, "legitimate approach" means—
    (a)   an approach made to the overseas person which has not been solicited by him in any way, or has been solicited by him in a way which does not contravene section 21 of the Act; or
    (b)   an approach made by or on behalf of the overseas person in a way which does not contravene that section.

[(8)   Paragraphs (1) to (5) do not apply where the overseas person is an investment firm or credit institution—
    (a)   who is providing or performing investment services and activities on a professional basis; and
    (b)   whose home Member State is the United Kingdom.]

NOTES

Paras (1)–(4): figures in square brackets inserted by the Financial Services and Markets Act 2000 (Regulated Activities) (Amendment No 3) Order 2006, SI 2006/3384, arts 2, 24(a)–(d), as from 1 April 2007 (for the purposes of enabling applications to be made for (i) a Part IV permission, (ii) a variation of a Part IV permission, and (iii) the Authority's approval under s 59 of the 2000 Act, in relation to an activity of the kind specified by art 25D of this Order, or in relation to an investment of the kind specified by arts 83, 84 or 85 of this Order), and as from 1 November 2007 (otherwise).

Paras (5A)–(5F): inserted by the Financial Services and Markets Act 2000 (Regulated Activities) (Amendment) (No 1) Order 2003, SI 2003/1475, art 20, as from 31 October 2004 (for transitional provisions in relation to applications for Part IV permissions and applications for approvals, etc, see arts 26–29 of the 2003 Order); and substituted by the Financial Services and Markets Act 2000 (Regulated Activities) (Amendment) (No 2) Order 2006, SI 2006/2383, arts 2, 21, as from 6 November 2006 (for the purposes of enabling applications to be made for (i) a Pt IV permission, or a variation of a Pt IV permission, in relation to activities of the kind specified by arts 25B, 25C, 53B, 53C, 63B or 63F or, so far as relevant to any such activity, art 64 of this Order; or (ii) the Authority's approval under FSMA 2000, s 59 in relation to any of those activities), and as from 6 April 2007 (otherwise) (for transitional provisions in relation to interim permissions and interim approvals, etc, see arts 36–40 of, and the Schedule to, the 2006 Order). These paragraphs have subsequently been amended as follows—

Words in square brackets in paras (5A)–(5E) substituted by the Financial Services and Markets Act 2000 (Regulated Activities) (Amendment) Order 2009, SI 2009/1342, arts 2, 20(a)–(e), as from 1 July 2009 (other than for the purposes of enabling applications to be made for a Part IV permission, or a variation of a Part IV permission, in relation to activities of the kind specified by arts 25E, 53D or 63J or, so far as relevant to any such activity, art 64 of this Order), and as from 30 June 2010 (for those purposes) (for transitional provisions in relation to applications for Part IV permissions, etc, see arts 1, 32–34 of that Order).

In para (5F), sub-paras (b)(iv), (c)(iv), and (d)(iv) inserted by SI 2009/1342, arts 2, 20(f)–(h), as from the same dates and for the same purposes, etc, as mentioned in the note relating to this Order above.

Para (6): figure in square brackets inserted by the Financial Services and Markets Act 2000 (Regulated Activities) (Amendment) (No 2) Order 2003, SI 2003/1476, art 10(6), as from 31 October 2004 (in so far as relating to contracts of long-term care insurance), and as from 14 January 2005 (otherwise) (for transitional provisions in relation to applications for Part IV permissions and applications for approvals, etc, see arts 22–27 of the 2003 Order).

Para (8): added by SI 2006/3384, arts 2, 24(e), as from 1 April 2007 (for the purposes of enabling applications to be made for (i) a Part IV permission, (ii) a variation of a Part IV permission, and (iii) the Authority's approval under s 59 of the 2000 Act, in relation to an activity of the kind specified by art 25D of this Order, or in relation to an investment of the kind specified by arts 83, 84 or 85 of this Order), and as from 1 November 2007 (otherwise).

[8.124]
[72A   Information society services

(1)   There is excluded from this Part any activity consisting of the provision of an information society service from an EEA State other than the United Kingdom.

(2)   The exclusion in paragraph (1) does not apply to the activity of effecting or carrying out a contract of insurance as principal, where—

    (a)   the activity is carried on by an undertaking which has received official authorisation in accordance with [Article 4 of the life assurance consolidation directive] or the first non-life insurance directive, and

    (b)   the insurance falls within the scope of any of the insurance directives.]

NOTES

Inserted by the Financial Services and Markets Act 2000 (Regulated Activities) (Amendment) (No 2) Order 2002, SI 2002/1776, art 2, as from 21 August 2002.

Para (2): words in square brackets substituted by the Life Assurance Consolidation Directive (Consequential Amendments) Regulations 2004, SI 2004/3379, reg 17, as from 11 January 2005.

[8.125]
[72B   Activities carried on by a provider of relevant goods or services

(1)   In this article—

"connected contract of insurance" means a contract of insurance which—

    (a)   is not a contract of long-term insurance;

    (b)   has a total duration (or would have a total duration were any right to renew conferred by the contract exercised) of five years or less;

    (c)   has an annual premium (or, where the premium is paid otherwise than by way of annual premium, the equivalent of an annual premium) of 500 euro or less, or the equivalent amount in sterling or other currency;

    (d)   covers the risk of—

        (i)   breakdown, loss of, or damage to, non-motor goods supplied by the provider; or

        [(ii)   damage to, or loss of, baggage and other risks linked to the travel booked with the provider ("travel risks") in circumstances where—

            (aa)   the travel booked with the provider relates to attendance at an event organised or managed by that provider and the party seeking insurance is not an individual (acting in his private capacity) or a small business; or

            (bb)   the travel booked with the provider is only the hire of an aircraft, vehicle or vessel which does not provide sleeping accommodation;]

    (e)   does not cover any liability risks (except, in the case of a contract which covers travel risks, where that cover is ancillary to the main cover provided by the contract);

    (f)   is complementary to the non-motor goods being supplied or service being provided by the provider; and

    (g)   is of such a nature that the only information that a person requires in order to carry on an activity of the kind specified by article 21, 25, 39A or 53 in relation to it is the cover provided by the contract;

"non-motor goods" means goods which are not mechanically propelled road vehicles;

"provider" means a person who supplies non-motor goods or provides services related to travel in the course of carrying on a profession or business which does not otherwise consist of the carrying on of regulated activities.

[For these purposes, the transfer of possession of an aircraft, vehicle or vessel under an agreement for hire which is not—

    (a)   a hire-purchase agreement within the meaning of section 189(1) of the Consumer Credit Act 1974, or

    (b)   any other agreement which contemplates that the property in those goods will also pass at some time in the future,

is the provision of a service related to travel, not a supply of goods.]

["small business" means—

    (a)   subject to paragraph (b) a sole trader, body corporate, partnership or an unincorporated association which had a turnover in the last financial year of less than £1,000,000;

    (b)   where the business concerned is a member of a group within the meaning of [section 474(1) of the Companies Act 2006], reference to its turnover means the combined turnover of the group;

"turnover" means the amounts derived from the provision of goods and services falling within the business's ordinary activities, after deduction of trade discounts, value added tax and any other taxes based on the amounts so derived].

(2) There is excluded from article 21 any transaction for the sale or purchase of a connected contract of insurance into which a provider enters as agent.

(3) There are excluded from article 25(1) and (2) any arrangements made by a provider for, or with a view to, a transaction for the sale or purchase of a connected contract of insurance.

(4) There is excluded from article 39A any activity carried on by a provider where the contract of insurance in question is a connected contract of insurance.

(5) There is excluded from article 53 the giving of advice by a provider in relation to a transaction for the sale or purchase of a connected contract of insurance.

(6) For the purposes of this article, a contract of insurance which covers travel risks is not to be treated as a contract of long-term insurance, notwithstanding the fact that it contains related and subsidiary provisions such that it might be regarded as a contract of long-term insurance, if the cover to which those provisions relate is ancillary to the main cover provided by the contract.]

NOTES

Inserted, together with arts 72C, 72D, by the Financial Services and Markets Act 2000 (Regulated Activities) (Amendment) (No 2) Order 2003, SI 2003/1476, art 11, as from 31 October 2004 (in so far as relating to contracts of long-term care insurance), and as from 14 January 2005 (otherwise) (for transitional provisions in relation to applications for Part IV permissions and applications for approvals, etc, see arts 22–27 of the 2003 Order).

Para (1) is amended as follows:

In definition "connected contract of insurance" sub-para (d)(ii) substituted by the Financial Services and Markets Act 2000 (Regulated Activities) (Amendment) (No 2) Order 2007, SI 2007/3510, art 2(1), (2), as from 30 June 2008 (for the purposes of enabling applications to be made, pursuant to this amendment, for (i) a Pt IV permission, or a variation of a Pt IV permission, in relation to activities of the kind specified by arts 21, 25(1), 25(2), 39A, 53 or, so far as relevant to any such activity, art 64 of this Order, or (ii) the Authority's approval under s 59 of FSMA 2000 in relation to any of those activities), and as from 1 January 2009 (otherwise) (for transitional provisions in relation to interim permissions and interim approvals, etc, see arts 3–9 of that Order).

Words in square brackets in definition "provider" inserted, and definitions "small business" and "turnover" added, by SI 2007/3510, art 2(1), (3), as from the same dates and for the same purposes as noted above (for transitional provisions in relation to interim permissions and interim approvals, etc, see arts 3–9 of that Order).

Words in square brackets in definition "small business" substituted by the Companies Act 2006 (Consequential Amendments and Transitional Provisions) Order 2011, SI 2011/1265, art 13(1), (5), as from 12 May 2011.

[8.126]
[72C   Provision of information on an incidental basis

(1) There is excluded from articles 25(1) and (2) the making of arrangements for, or with a view to, a transaction for the sale or purchase of a contract of insurance or an investment of the kind specified by article 89, so far as relevant to such a contract, where that activity meets the conditions specified in paragraph (4).

(2) There is excluded from articles 37 and 40 any activity—

    (a)   where the assets in question are rights under a contract of insurance or an investment of the kind specified by article 89, so far as relevant to such a contract; and

    (b)   which meets the conditions specified in paragraph (4).

(3) There is excluded from article 39A any activity which meets the conditions specified in paragraph (4).

(4) The conditions specified in this paragraph are that the activity—

    (a)   consists of the provision of information to the policyholder or potential policyholder;

    (b)   is carried on by a person in the course of carrying on a profession or business which does not otherwise consist of the carrying on of regulated activities; and

    (c)   may reasonably be regarded as being incidental to that profession or business.]

NOTES

Inserted as noted to art 72B at **[8.125]**.

[8.127]
[72D   Large risks contracts where risk situated outside the EEA

(1)   There is excluded from articles 21, 25(1) and (2), 39A and 53 any activity which is carried on in relation to a large risks contract of insurance, to the extent that the risk or commitment covered by the contract is not situated in an EEA State.

(2)   In this article, a "large risks contract of insurance" is a contract of insurance the principal object of which is to cover—

(a)   risks falling within paragraph 4 (railway rolling stock), 5 (aircraft), 6 (ships), 7 (goods in transit), 11 (aircraft liability) or 12 (liability of ships) of Part 1 of Schedule 1;

(b)   risks falling within paragraph 14 (credit) or 15 (suretyship) of that Part provided that the risks relate to a business carried on by the policyholder; or

(c)   risks falling within paragraph 3 (land vehicles), 8 (fire and natural forces), 9 (damage to property), 10 (motor vehicle liability), 13 (general liability) or 16 (miscellaneous financial loss) of that Part provided that the risks relate to a business carried on by the policyholder and that the condition specified in paragraph (3) is met in relation to that business.

(3)   The condition specified in this paragraph is that at least two of the three following criteria were met in the most recent financial year for which information is available—

(a)   the balance sheet total of the business [(within the meaning of section 382(5) or 465(5) of the Companies Act 2006)] exceeded 6.2 million euro,

(b)   the net turnover [(within the meaning given to "turnover" by section 474(1) of the Companies Act 2006)] exceeded 12.8 million euro,

(c)   the number of employees [(within the meaning given by sections 382(6) and 465(6) of the Companies Act 2006)] exceeded 250,

and for a financial year which is a company's financial year but not in fact a year, the net turnover of the policyholder shall be proportionately adjusted.

(4)   For the purposes of paragraph (3), where the policyholder is a member of a group for which consolidated accounts (within the meaning of the Seventh Company Law Directive) are drawn up, the question whether the condition specified by that paragraph is met is to be determined by reference to those accounts.]

NOTES

Inserted as noted to art 72B at **[8.125]**.

Para (3): words in square brackets substituted by the Companies Act 2006 (Consequential Amendments and Transitional Provisions) Order 2011, SI 2011/1265, art 13(1), (6), as from 12 May 2011.

[8.128]
[72E   Business Angel-led Enterprise Capital Funds

(1)   A body corporate of a type specified in paragraph (7) does not carry on the activity of the kind specified by article 21 by entering as agent into a transaction on behalf of the participants of a Business Angel-led Enterprise Capital Fund.

(2)   There are excluded from article 25(1) and (2) arrangements, made by a body corporate of a type specified in paragraph (7), for or with a view to a transaction which is or is to be entered into by or on behalf of the participants in a Business Angel-led Enterprise Capital Fund.

(3)   There is excluded from article 37 any activity, carried on by a body corporate of a type specified in paragraph (7), which consists in the managing of assets belonging to the participants in a Business Angel-led Enterprise Capital Fund.

(4)   There is excluded from article 40 any activity, carried on by a body corporate of a type specified in paragraph (7), in respect of assets belonging to the participants in a Business Angel-led Enterprise Capital Fund.

(5)   A body corporate of a type specified in paragraph (7) does not carry on the activity of the kind specified in article 51(1)(a) where it carries on the activity of establishing, operating or winding up a Business Angel-led Enterprise Capital Fund.

(6)   A body corporate of a type specified in paragraph (7) does not carry on the activity of the kind specified in article 53 where it is advising the participants in a Business Angel-led Enterprise Capital Fund on investments to be made by or on behalf of the participants of that Business Angel-led Enterprise Capital Fund.

(7)   The type of body corporate specified is a limited company—

(i)   which operates a Business Angel-led Enterprise Capital Fund; and

(ii)   the members of which are participants in the Business Angel-led Enterprise Capital Fund operated by that limited company and between them have invested at least 50 per cent of the total investment in that Business Angel-led Enterprise Capital Fund excluding any investment made by the Secretary of State.

(8)   For the purposes of paragraph (7), "a limited company" means a body corporate with limited liability which is a company or firm formed in accordance with the law of an EEA State and having its registered office, central administration or principal place of business within the territory of an EEA State.

(9)   Nothing in this article has the effect of excluding a body corporate from the application of the Money Laundering Regulations [2007], in so far as those Regulations would have applied to it but for this article.

(10)   Nothing in this article has the effect of excluding a body corporate from the application of section 397 of the Act (misleading statements and practices), in so far as that section would have applied to it but for this article.]

[(11)   This article is subject to article 4(4).]

NOTES

Inserted, together with art 72F, by the Financial Services and Markets Act 2000 (Regulated Activities) (Amendment) (No 2) Order 2005, SI 2005/1518, art 2(1), (3), as from 1 October 2005.

Para (9): date in square brackets substituted by the Money Laundering Regulations 2007, SI 2007/2157, reg 51, Sch 6, Pt 2, para 10, as from 15 December 2007.

Para (11): added by the Financial Services and Markets Act 2000 (Regulated Activities) (Amendment No 3) Order 2006, SI 2006/3384, arts 2, 25, as from 1 April 2007 (for the purposes of enabling applications to be made for (i) a Part IV permission, (ii) a variation of a Part IV permission, and (iii) the Authority's approval under s 59 of the 2000 Act, in relation to an activity of the kind specified by art 25D of this Order, or in relation to an investment of the kind specified by arts 83, 84 or 85 of this Order), and as from 1 November 2007 (otherwise).

[8.129]
[72F   Interpretation

(1)   For the purposes of this article and of article 72E—

"Business Angel-led Enterprise Capital Fund" means a collective investment scheme which—

   (a)   is established for the purpose of enabling participants to participate in or receive profits or income arising from the acquisition, holding, management or disposal of investments falling within one or more of—

      (i)   article 76, being shares in an unlisted company;

      (ii)   article 77, being instruments creating or acknowledging indebtedness in respect of an unlisted company; and

      [(iia)   article 77A, being rights under an alternative finance investment bond issued by an unlisted company;]

      (iii)   article 79, being warrants or other instruments entitling the holder to subscribe for shares in an unlisted company;

   (b)   has only the following as its participants—

      (i)   the Secretary of State;

      (ii)   a body corporate of a type specified in article 72E(7); and

      (iii)   one or more persons each of whom at the time they became a participant was—

         (aa)   a sophisticated investor;

         (bb)   a high net worth individual;

         (cc)   a high net worth company;

         (dd)   a high net worth unincorporated association;

         (ee)   a trustee of a high value trust; or

         (ff)   a self-certified sophisticated investor;

   (c)   is prevented, by the arrangements by which it is established, from—

      (i)   acquiring investments, other than those falling within paragraphs (i) to (iii) of sub-paragraph (a); and

      (ii)   acquiring investments falling within paragraphs (i) to (iii) of sub-paragraph (a) in an unlisted company, where the aggregated cost of those investments exceeds £2 million, unless that acquisition is necessary to prevent or reduce the dilution of an existing share-holding in that unlisted company;

"high net worth company" means a body corporate which—

   (a)   falls within article 49(2)(a) of the Financial Services and Markets Act 2000 (Financial Promotion) Order 2001 (high net worth companies, unincorporated associations etc); and

   (b)   has executed a document [(in a manner which binds the company)] in the following terms:

"This company is a high net worth company and falls within article 49(2)(a) of the Financial Services and Markets Act 2000 (Financial Promotion) Order 2001. We understand that any Business Angel-led Enterprise Capital Fund (within the meaning of article 72F of the Financial Services and Markets Act 2000 (Regulated Activities) Order 2001), in which this company participates, or any person who operates that Business Angel-led Enterprise Capital Fund, in which this company participates, will not be authorised under the Financial Services and Markets Act 2000 (and so will not have to satisfy the threshold conditions set out in Part I of Schedule 6 to that Act and will not be subject to Financial Services Authority rules such as those on holding client money). We understand that this means that redress through the Financial Services Authority, the Financial Ombudsman Scheme or the Financial Services Compensation Scheme will not be available. We also understand the risks associated in investing in a Business Angel-led Enterprise Capital Fund and are aware that it is open to us to seek advice from someone who is authorised under the Financial Services and Markets Act 2000 and who specialises in advising on this kind of investment."

"high net worth individual" means an individual who—

(a)   is a "certified high net worth individual" within the meaning of article 48(2) of the Financial Services and Markets Act 2000 (Financial Promotion) Order 2001 (certified high net worth individuals); and

(b)   has signed a statement in the following terms:

"I declare that I am a certified high net worth individual within the meaning of article 48(2) of the Financial Services and Markets Act 2000 (Financial Promotion) Order 2001 and that I understand that any Business Angel-led Enterprise Capital Fund (within the meaning of article 72F of the Financial Services and Markets Act 2000 (Regulated Activities) Order 2001), in which I participate, or any person who operates that Business Angel-led Enterprise Capital Fund, in which I participate, will not be authorised under the Financial Services and Markets Act 2000 (and so will not have to satisfy the threshold conditions set out in Part I of Schedule 6 to that Act and will not be subject to Financial Services Authority rules such as those on holding client money). I understand that this means that redress through the Financial Services Authority, the Financial Ombudsman Scheme or the Financial Services Compensation Scheme will not be available. I also understand the risks associated in investing in a Business Angel-led Enterprise Capital Fund and am aware that it is open to me to seek advice from someone who is authorised under the Financial Services and Markets Act 2000 and who specialises in advising on this kind of investment.";

"high net worth unincorporated association" means an unincorporated association—

(a)   which falls within article 49(2)(b) of the Financial Services and Markets Act 2000 (Financial Promotion) Order 2001; and

(b)   on behalf of which an officer of that association or a member of its governing body has signed a statement in the following terms:

"This unincorporated association is a high net worth unincorporated association and falls within article 49(2)(b) of the Financial Services and Markets Act 2000 (Financial Promotion) Order 2001. I understand that any Business Angel-led Enterprise Capital Fund (within the meaning of article 72F of the Financial Services and Markets Act 2000 (Regulated Activities) Order 2001), in which this association participates, or any person who operates that Business Angel-led Enterprise Capital Fund, in which this association participates, will not be authorised under the Financial Services and Markets Act 2000 (and so will not have to satisfy the threshold conditions set out in Part I of Schedule 6 to that Act and will not be subject to Financial Services Authority rules such as those on holding client money). I understand that this means that redress through the Financial Services Authority, the Financial Ombudsman Scheme or the Financial Services Compensation Scheme will not be available. I also understand the risks associated in investing in a Business Angel-led Enterprise Capital Fund and am aware that it is open to the association to seek advice from someone who is authorised under the Financial Services and Markets Act 2000 and who specialises in advising on this kind of investment.";

"high value trust" means a trust—

(a)   where the aggregate value of the cash and investments which form a part of the trust's assets (before deducting the amount of its liabilities) is £10 million or more;

(b)   on behalf of which a trustee has signed a statement in the following terms:

"This trust is a high value trust. I understand that any Business Angel-led Enterprise Capital Fund (within the meaning of article 72F of the Financial Services and Markets Act 2000 (Regulated Activities) Order 2001), in which this trust participates, or any person who operates that Business Angel-led Enterprise Capital Fund, in which this trust participates, will not be authorised under the Financial Services and Markets Act 2000 (and so will not have to satisfy the threshold conditions set out in Part I of Schedule 6 to that Act and will not be subject to Financial Services Authority rules such as those on holding client money). I understand that this means that redress through the Financial Services Authority, the Financial Ombudsman Scheme or the Financial Services Compensation Scheme will not be available. I also understand the risks associated in investing in a Business Angel-led Enterprise Capital Fund and am aware that it is open to the trust to seek advice from someone who is authorised under the Financial Services and Markets Act 2000 and who specialises in advising on this kind of investment.";

"self-certified sophisticated investor" means an individual who—

(a)   is a "self-certified sophisticated investor" within the meaning of article 50A of the Financial Services and Markets Act 2000 (Financial Promotion) Order 2001;

(b)   has signed a statement in the following terms:

"I declare that I am a self-certified sophisticated investor within the meaning of article 50A of the Financial Services and Markets Act 2000 (Financial Promotion) Order 2001 and that I understand that any Business Angel-led Enterprise Capital Fund (within the meaning of article 72F of the Financial Services and Markets Act 2000 (Regulated Activities) Order 2001), in which I participate, or any person who operates that Business Angel-led Enterprise Capital Fund, in which I participate, will not be authorised under the Financial Services and Markets Act 2000 (and so will not have to satisfy the threshold conditions set out in Part I of Schedule 6 to that Act and will not be subject to Financial Services Authority rules such as those on holding client money). I understand that this means that redress through the Financial Services Authority, the Financial Ombudsman Scheme or the Financial Services Compensation Scheme will not be available. I also understand the risks associated in investing in a Business Angel-led Enterprise Capital Fund and am aware that it is open to me to seek advice from someone who is authorised under the Financial Services and Markets Act 2000 and who specialises in advising on this kind of investment.";

"sophisticated investor" means an individual who—

(a)   is a "certified sophisticated investor" within the meaning of article 50(1) of the Financial Services and Markets Act 2000 (Financial Promotion) Order 2001; and

(b)   has signed a statement in the following terms:

"I declare that I am a certified sophisticated investor within the meaning of article 50(1) of the Financial Services and Markets Act 2000 (Financial Promotion) Order 2001 and that I understand that any Business Angel-led Enterprise Capital Fund (within the meaning of article 72F of the Financial Services and Markets Act 2000 (Regulated Activities) Order 2001), in which I participate, or any person who operates that Business Angel-led Enterprise Capital Fund, in which I participate, will not be authorised under the Financial Services and Markets Act 2000 (and so will not have to satisfy the threshold conditions set out in Part I of Schedule 6 to that Act and will not be subject to Financial Services Authority rules such as those on holding client money). I understand that this means that redress through the Financial Services Authority, the Financial Ombudsman Scheme or the Financial Services Compensation Scheme will not be available. I also understand the risks associated in investing in a Business Angel-led Enterprise Capital Fund and am aware that it is open to me to seek advice from someone who is authorised under the Financial Services and Markets Act 2000 and who specialises in advising on this kind of investment.";

"unlisted company" has the meaning given by article 3 of the Financial Services and Markets Act 2000 (Financial Promotion) Order 2001.

(2)   References in this Article and in Article 72E to a participant in a Business Angel-led Enterprise Capital Fund, doing things on behalf of such a participant and property belonging to such a participant are, respectively, references to that participant in that capacity, to doing things on behalf of that participant in that capacity or to the property of that participant held in that capacity.]

NOTES

Inserted as noted to art 72E at **[8.128]**.

Para (1): sub-para (iia) of the definition "Business Angel-led Enterprise Capital Fund" inserted by the Financial Services and Markets Act 2000 (Regulated Activities) (Amendment) Order 2010, SI 2010/86, art 4, Schedule, para 5(e), as from 24 February 2010; words in square brackets in definition "high net worth company" substituted by the Financial Services and Markets Act 2000 (Regulated Activities) (Amendment) (No 2) Order 2006, SI 2006/2383, arts 2, 22, as from 6 November 2006 (for the purposes of enabling applications to be made for (i) a Pt IV permission, or a variation of a Pt IV permission, in relation to activities of the kind specified by arts 25B, 25C, 53B, 53C, 63B or 63F or, so far as relevant to any such activity, art 64 of this Order; or (ii) the Authority's approval under FSMA 2000, s 59 in relation to any of those activities), and as from 6 April 2007 (otherwise) (for transitional provisions in relation to interim permissions and interim approvals, etc, see arts 36–40 of, and the Schedule to, the 2006 Order).

PART III
SPECIFIED INVESTMENTS

[8.130]
73   Investments: general

The following kinds of investment are specified for the purposes of section 22 of the Act.

[8.131]
74   Deposits

A deposit.

[8.132]
[74A   Electronic money

Electronic money.]

NOTES

Inserted by the Financial Services and Markets Act 2000 (Regulated Activities) (Amendment) Order 2002, SI 2002/682, art 6, as from 27 April 2002, subject to transitional provisions in relation to persons issuing electronic money immediately before that date contained in art 9.

[8.133]

75 Contracts of insurance

Rights under a contract of insurance.

[8.134]

76 Shares etc

(1) Shares or stock in the share capital of—

  (a) any body corporate (wherever incorporated), and

  (b) any unincorporated body constituted under the law of a country or territory outside the United Kingdom.

(2) Paragraph (1) includes—

  (a) any shares of a class defined as deferred shares for the purposes of section 119 of the Building Societies Act 1986; and

  (b) any transferable shares in a body incorporated under the law of, or any part of, the United Kingdom relating to industrial and provident societies or credit unions, or in a body constituted under the law of another EEA State for purposes equivalent to those of such a body.

(3) But subject to paragraph (2) there are excluded from paragraph (1) shares or stock in the share capital of—

  (a) an open-ended investment company;

  (b) a building society incorporated under the law of, or any part of, the United Kingdom;

  (c) a body incorporated under the law of, or any part of, the United Kingdom relating to industrial and provident societies or credit unions;

  (d) any body constituted under the law of an EEA State for purposes equivalent to those of a body falling within sub-paragraph (b) or (c).

[8.135]

77 Instruments creating or acknowledging indebtedness

(1) Subject to paragraph (2), such of the following as do not fall within [article . . . 78]—

  (a) debentures;

  (b) debenture stock;

  (c) loan stock;

  (d) bonds;

  (e) certificates of deposit;

  (f) any other instrument creating or acknowledging indebtedness.

(2) If and to the extent that they would otherwise fall within paragraph (1), there are excluded from that paragraph—

  (a) an instrument acknowledging or creating indebtedness for, or for money borrowed to defray, the consideration payable under a contract for the supply of goods or services;

  (b) a cheque or other bill of exchange, a banker's draft or a letter of credit (but not a bill of exchange accepted by a banker);

  (c) a banknote, a statement showing a balance on a current, deposit or savings account, a lease or other disposition of property, or a heritable security; and

  (d) a contract of insurance;

  [(e) . . .]

(3) An instrument excluded from paragraph (1) of article 78 by paragraph (2)(b) of that article is not thereby to be taken to fall within paragraph (1) of this article.

NOTES

Para (1): words in square brackets substituted by the Financial Services and Markets Act 2000 (Regulated Activities) (Amendment) Order 2010, SI 2010/86, art 2(1), (2)(a), as from 24 February 2010; words omitted revoked by the Financial Services and Markets Act 2000 (Regulated Activities) (Amendment) Order 2011, SI 2011/133, art 2(1), (2)(a), as from 16 February 2011 (note also art 4 of the 2011 Order which provides that the instruments to which the amendments made by that Order apply from its commencement include existing instruments which fall within (a) arts 77 or 77A of this Order; or (b) paras 15 or 15A of Sch 1 to the Financial Services and Markets Act 2000 (Financial Promotion) Order 2005 (in each case as amended by that Order)).

Para (2): sub para (e) added by SI 2010/86, art 2(1), (2)(b), as from 24 February 2010, and revoked by SI 2011/133, art 2(1), (2)(b), as from 16 February 2011 (subject to the same transitional provisions in art 4 as noted above).

Modification: references in para (1) to securities, instruments or investments creating or acknowledging indebtedness (or creating or acknowledging a present or future indebtedness) includes a reference to uncertificated units of eligible debt securities; see the Uncertificated Securities (Amendment) (Eligible Debt Securities) Regulations 2003, SI 2003/1633, reg 15, Sch 2, para 8.

[8.136]

[77A   Alternative finance investment bonds

(1)   Rights under an alternative finance investment bond, to the extent that they do not fall within article [77 or] 78.

(2)   For the purposes of this article, arrangements constitute an alternative finance investment bond if—

  (a)   the arrangements provide for a person ("the bond-holder") to pay a sum of money ("the capital") to another ("the bond-issuer");

  (b)   the arrangements identify assets, or a class of assets, which the bond-issuer will acquire for the purpose of generating income or gains directly or indirectly ("the bond assets");

  (c)   the arrangements specify a period at the end of which they cease to have effect ("the bond term");

  (d)   the bond-issuer undertakes under the arrangements—

    (i)   to make a repayment in respect of the capital ("the redemption payment") to the bond-holder during or at the end of the bond term (whether or not in instalments); and

    (ii)   to pay to the bond-holder other payments on one or more occasions during or at the end of the bond term ("the additional payments");

  (e)   the amount of the additional payments does not exceed an amount which would, at the time at which the bond is issued, be a reasonable commercial return on a loan of the capital; and

  (f)   the arrangements are a security admitted to—

    (i)   an official list (in accordance with the provisions of Directive 2001/34/EC of the European Parliament and of the Council on the admission of securities to official stock exchange listing and on information to be published on those securities); or

    (ii)   trading on a regulated market (within the meaning of Article 4.1(14) of Directive 2004/39/EC of the European Parliament and of the Council on markets in financial instruments) or on a recognised investment exchange (within the meaning of section 285 of the Act).

(3)   For the purposes of paragraph (2)—

  (a)   the bond-issuer may acquire the bond assets before or after the arrangements take effect;

  (b)   the bond assets may be property of any kind, including rights in relation to property owned by someone other than the bond-issuer;

  (c)   the identification of the bond assets mentioned in paragraph (2)(b) and the undertakings mentioned in paragraph (2)(d) may (but need not) be described as, or accompanied by a document described as, a declaration of trust;

  (d)   the reference to a period in paragraph (2)(c) includes any period specified to end upon the redemption of the bond by the bond-issuer;

  (e)   the bond-holder may (but need not) be entitled under the arrangements to terminate them, or participate in terminating them, before the end of the bond term;

  (f)   the amount of the additional payments may be—

    (i)   fixed at the beginning of the bond term;

    (ii)   determined wholly or partly by reference to the value of or income generated by the bond assets; or

    (iii) determined in some other way;

  (g)   if the amount of the additional payments is not fixed at the beginning of the bond term, the reference in paragraph (2)(e) to the amount of the additional payments is a reference to the maximum amount of the additional payments;

  (h)   the amount of the redemption payment may (but need not) be subject to reduction in the event of a fall in the value of the bond assets or in the rate of income generated by them; and

  (i)   entitlement to the redemption payment may (but need not) be capable of being satisfied (whether or not at the option of the bond-issuer or the bond-holder) by the issue or transfer of shares or other securities.

(4)   An instrument excluded from paragraph (1) of article 78 by paragraph (2)(b) of that article is not thereby taken to fall within paragraph (1) of this article.]

NOTES

  Commencement: 24 February 2010.

  Inserted by the Financial Services and Markets Act 2000 (Regulated Activities) (Amendment) Order 2010, SI 2010/86, art 2(1), (3), as from 24 February 2010.

  Para (1): words in square brackets inserted by the Financial Services and Markets Act 2000 (Regulated Activities) (Amendment) Order 2011, SI 2011/133, art 2(3), as from 16 February 2011 (note also art 4 of the 2011 Order which provides that the instruments to which the amendments made by that Order apply from its commencement include existing instruments which fall within (a) arts 77 or 77A of this Order; or (b) paras 15 or 15A of Sch 1 to the Financial Services and Markets Act 2000 (Financial Promotion) Order 2005 (in each case as amended by that Order)).

  The reference in this article to an alternative finance investment bond includes a reference to uncertificated units of eligible debt securities; see the Uncertificated Securities (Amendment) (Eligible Debt Securities) Regulations 2003, SI 2003/1633, Schedule, para 8(3) (as inserted by SI 2010/86).

[8.137]
78   Government and public securities

(1)   Subject to paragraph (2), loan stock, bonds and other instruments creating or acknowledging indebtedness, issued by or on behalf of any of the following—

   (a)   the government of the United Kingdom;

   (b)   the Scottish Administration;

   (c)   the Executive Committee of the Northern Ireland Assembly;

   (d)   the National Assembly for Wales;

   (e)   the government of any country or territory outside the United Kingdom;

   (f)   a local authority in the United Kingdom or elsewhere; or

   (g)   a body the members of which comprise—

      (i)   states including the United Kingdom or another EEA State; or

      (ii)   bodies whose members comprise states including the United Kingdom or another EEA State.

(2)   [Subject to paragraph (3),] there are excluded from paragraph (1)—

   (a)   so far as applicable, the instruments mentioned in article 77(2)(a) to (d);

   (b)   any instrument creating or acknowledging indebtedness in respect of—

      (i)   money received by the Director of Savings as deposits or otherwise in connection with the business of the National Savings Bank;

      (ii)   money raised under the National Loans Act 1968 under the auspices of the Director of Savings or treated as so raised by virtue of section 11(3) of the National Debt Act 1972.

[(3)   Paragraph (2)(a) does not exclude an instrument which meets the requirements set out in sub-paragraphs (a) to (e) of article 77A(2).]

NOTES

   Para (2): words in square brackets inserted by the Financial Services and Markets Act 2000 (Regulated Activities) (Amendment) Order 2010, SI 2010/86, art 2(1), (4), as from 24 February 2010.

   Para (3): added by SI 2010/86, art 2(1), (5), as from 24 February 2010.

   Modification: references in this article to securities, instruments or investments creating or acknowledging indebtedness (or creating or acknowledging a present or future indebtedness) includes a reference to uncertificated units of eligible debt securities; see the Uncertificated Securities (Amendment) (Eligible Debt Securities) Regulations 2003, SI 2003/1633, reg 15, Sch 2, para 8.

[8.138]
79   Instruments giving entitlements to investments

(1)   Warrants and other instruments entitling the holder to subscribe for any investment of the kind specified by article 76, 77[, 77A] or 78.

(2)   It is immaterial whether the investment to which the entitlement relates is in existence or identifiable.

(3)   An investment of the kind specified by this article is not to be regarded as falling within article 83, 84 or 85.

NOTES

   Para (1): figure in square brackets inserted by the Financial Services and Markets Act 2000 (Regulated Activities) (Amendment) Order 2010, SI 2010/86, art 4, Schedule, para 5(f), as from 24 February 2010.

[8.139]
80   Certificates representing certain securities

(1)   Subject to paragraph (2), certificates or other instruments which confer contractual or property rights (other than rights consisting of an investment of the kind specified by article 83)—

   (a)   in respect of any investment of the kind specified by any of articles 76 to 79, being an investment held by a person other than the person on whom the rights are conferred by the certificate or instrument; and

   (b)   the transfer of which may be effected without the consent of that person.

(2)   There is excluded from paragraph (1) any certificate or other instrument which confers rights in respect of two or more investments issued by different persons, or in respect of two or more different investments of the kind specified by article 78 and issued by the same person.

[8.140]
81   Units in a collective investment scheme

Units in a collective investment scheme (within the meaning of Part XVII of the Act).

[8.141]
[82   Rights under a pension scheme

(1)   Rights under a stakeholder pension scheme.

(2)   Rights under a personal pension scheme.]

NOTES

Commencement: 1 October 2006 (certain purposes); 6 April 2007 (otherwise) (see below).

Substituted by the Financial Services and Markets Act 2000 (Regulated Activities) (Amendment) Order 2006, SI 2006/1969, art 2(1), (5), as from 1 October 2006 (for the purposes of enabling applications to be made for Part IV permission or for a variation of Part IV permission in relation to an investment specified by art 82(2) of this Order (as so substituted)), and as from 6 April 2007 (otherwise) (for transitional provisions in relation to interim permissions and interim approvals, etc, see arts 3–7 of, and the Schedule to, the 2006 Order).

[8.142]
83 Options

[(1)]   Options to acquire or dispose of—
     (a)   a security or contractually based investment (other than one of a kind specified by this article);
     (b)   currency of the United Kingdom or any other country or territory;
     (c)   palladium, platinum, gold or silver; . . .
     (d)   an option to acquire or dispose of an investment of the kind specified by this article by virtue of paragraph (a), (b) or (c);
     [(e)   subject to paragraph (4), an option to acquire or dispose of an option to which paragraph 5, 6, 7 or 10 of Section C of Annex I to the markets in financial instruments directive (the text of which is set out in Part I of Schedule 2) applies].

[(2)   Subject to paragraph (4), options—
     (a)   to which paragraph (1) does not apply;
     (b)   which relate to commodities;
     (c)   which may be settled physically; and
     (d)   either—
         (i)   to which paragraph 5 or 6 of Section C of Annex I to the markets in financial instruments directive, the text of which is set out in Part 1 of Schedule 2, applies, or
         (ii)   which in accordance with Article 38 of the Commission Regulation (the text of which is set out in Part 2 of Schedule 2) are to be considered as having the characteristics of other derivative financial instruments and not being for commercial purposes, and to which paragraph 7 of Section C of Annex I to the markets in financial instruments directive applies.

(3)   Subject to paragraph (4), options—
     (a)   to which paragraph (1) does not apply;
     (b)   which may be settled physically; and
     (c)   to which paragraph 10 of Section C of Annex I to the markets in financial instruments directive (read with the Commission Regulation) applies.

(4)   Paragraphs (1)(e), (2) and (3) only apply to options in relation to which—
     (a)   an investment firm or credit institution is providing or performing investment services and activities on a professional basis,
     (b)   a management company is providing, in accordance with [Article 6(3)] of the UCITS directive, the investment service specified in paragraph 4 or 5 of Section A, or the ancillary service specified in paragraph 1 of Section B, of Annex I to the markets in financial instruments directive, or
     (c)   a market operator is providing the investment service specified in paragraph 8 of Section A of Annex I to the markets in financial instruments directive.

(5)   Expressions used in paragraphs (1)(e), (2) and (3) and in the markets in financial instruments directive have the same meaning as in that directive.]

NOTES

Para (1): numbered as such, word omitted from sub-para (c) revoked, and sub-para (e) inserted, by the Financial Services and Markets Act 2000 (Regulated Activities) (Amendment No 3) Order 2006, SI 2006/3384, arts 2, 26(a), (b), as from 1 April 2007 (for the purposes of enabling applications to be made for (i) a Part IV permission, (ii) a variation of a Part IV permission, and (iii) the Authority's approval under s 59 of the 2000 Act, in relation to an activity of the kind specified by art 25D of this Order, or in relation to an investment of the kind specified by arts 83, 84 or 85 of this Order), and as from 1 November 2007 (otherwise).

Paras (2)–(5): added by SI 2006/3384, arts 2, 26(c), as from the same dates and for the same purposes as noted above.

Words in square brackets in para (4)(b) substituted by the Undertakings for Collective Investment in Transferable Securities Regulations 2011, SI 2011/1613, reg 16, Schedule, para 1(1), (3), as from 1 July 2011.

[8.143]
84 Futures

(1)   Subject to paragraph (2), rights under a contract for the sale of a commodity or property of any other description under which delivery is to be made at a future date and at a price agreed on when the contract is made.

[(1A)   Subject to paragraph (1D), futures—
     (a)   to which paragraph (1) does not apply;
     (b)   which relate to commodities;

    (c)   which may be settled physically; and

    (d)   to which paragraph 5 or 6 of Section C of Annex I to the markets in financial instruments directive applies.

(1B)   Subject to paragraph (1D), futures and forwards—

    (a)   to which paragraph (1) does not apply;

    (b)   which relate to commodities;

    (c)   which may be settled physically;

    (d)   which in accordance with Article 38 of the Commission Regulation (the text of which is set out in Part 2 of Schedule 2) are to be considered as having the characteristics of other derivative financial instruments and not being for commercial purposes; and

    (e)   to which paragraph 7 of Section C of Annex I to the markets in financial instruments directive applies.

(1C)   Subject to paragraph (1D), futures—

    (a)   to which paragraph (1) does not apply;

    (b)   which may be settled physically; and

    (c)   to which paragraph 10 of Section C of Annex I to the markets in financial instruments directive (read with the Commission Regulation) applies.

(1D)   Paragraph (1A), (1B) and (1C) only apply to futures or forwards in relation to which—

    (a)   an investment firm or credit institution is providing or performing investment services and activities on a professional basis,

    (b)   a management company is providing, in accordance with [Article 6(3)] of the UCITS directive, the investment service specified in paragraph 4 or 5 of Section A, or the ancillary service specified in paragraph 1 of Section B, of Annex I to the markets in financial instruments directive, or

    (c)   a market operator is providing the investment service specified in paragraph 8 of Section A of Annex I to the markets in financial instruments directive.

(1E)   Expressions used in paragraphs (1A) to (1C) and in the markets in financial instruments directive have the same meaning as in that directive.]

(2)   There are excluded from paragraph (1) rights under any contract which is made for commercial and not investment purposes.

(3)   A contract is to be regarded as made for investment purposes if it is made or traded on a recognised investment exchange, or is made otherwise than on a recognised investment exchange but is expressed to be as traded on such an exchange or on the same terms as those on which an equivalent contract would be made on such an exchange.

(4)   A contract not falling within paragraph (3) is to be regarded as made for commercial purposes if under the terms of the contract delivery is to be made within seven days, unless it can be shown that there existed an understanding that (notwithstanding the express terms of the contract) delivery would not be made within seven days.

(5)   The following are indications that a contract not falling within paragraph (3) or (4) is made for commercial purposes and the absence of them is an indication that it is made for investment purposes—

    (a)   one or more of the parties is a producer of the commodity or other property, or uses it in his business;

    (b)   the seller delivers or intends to deliver the property or the purchaser takes or intends to take delivery of it.

(6)   It is an indication that a contract is made for commercial purposes that the prices, the lot, the delivery date or other terms are determined by the parties for the purposes of the particular contract and not by reference (or not solely by reference) to regularly published prices, to standard lots or delivery dates or to standard terms.

(7)   The following are indications that a contract is made for investment purposes—

    (a)   it is expressed to be as traded on an investment exchange;

    (b)   performance of the contract is ensured by an investment exchange or a clearing house;

    (c)   there are arrangements for the payment or provision of margin.

(8)   For the purposes of paragraph (1), a price is to be taken to be agreed on when a contract is made—

    (a)   notwithstanding that it is left to be determined by reference to the price at which a contract is to be entered into on a market or exchange or could be entered into at a time and place specified in the contract; or

    (b)   in a case where the contract is expressed to be by reference to a standard lot and quality, notwithstanding that provision is made for a variation in the price to take account of any variation in quantity or quality on delivery.

NOTES

    Paras (1A)–(1E): inserted by the Financial Services and Markets Act 2000 (Regulated Activities) (Amendment No 3) Order 2006, SI 2006/3384, arts 2, 27, as from 1 April 2007 (for the purposes of enabling applications to be made for (i) a Part IV permission, (ii) a variation of a Part IV permission, and (iii) the Authority's approval under s 59 of the 2000 Act, in relation to an activity of the kind specified by art 25D of this Order, or in relation to an investment of the kind specified by arts 83, 84 or 85 of this Order), and as from 1 November 2007 (otherwise).

Words in square brackets in para (1D)(b) substituted by the Undertakings for Collective Investment in Transferable Securities Regulations 2011, SI 2011/1613, reg 16, Schedule, para 1(1), (4), as from 1 July 2011.

[8.144]
85   Contracts for differences etc
(1)   Subject to paragraph (2), rights under—
   (a)   a contract for differences; or
   (b)   any other contract the purpose or pretended purpose of which is to secure a profit or avoid a loss by reference to fluctuations in—
      (i)   the value or price of property of any description; or
      (ii)   an index or other factor designated for that purpose in the contract.
(2)   There are excluded from paragraph (1)—
   (a)   rights under a contract if the parties intend that the profit is to be secured or the loss is to be avoided by one or more of the parties taking delivery of any property to which the contract relates;
   (b)   rights under a contract under which money is received by way of deposit on terms that any interest or other return to be paid on the sum deposited will be calculated by reference to fluctuations in an index or other factor;
   (c)   rights under any contract under which—
      (i)   money is received by the Director of Savings as deposits or otherwise in connection with the business of the National Savings Bank; or
      (ii)   money is raised under the National Loans Act 1968 under the auspices of the Director of Savings or treated as so raised by virtue of section 11(3) of the National Debt Act 1972;
   (d)   rights under a qualifying contract of insurance.
[(3)   Subject to paragraph (4), derivative instruments for the transfer of credit risk—
   (a)   to which neither article 83 nor paragraph (1) applies; and
   (b)   to which paragraph 8 of Section C of Annex I to the markets in financial instruments directive applies.
(4)   Paragraph (3) only applies to derivatives in relation to which—
   (a)   an investment firm or credit institution is providing or performing investment services and activities on a professional basis,
   (b)   a management company is providing, in accordance with [Article 6(3)] of the UCITS directive, the investment service specified in paragraph 4 or 5 of Section A, or the ancillary service specified in paragraph 1 of Section B, of Annex I to the markets in financial instruments directive, or
   (c)   a market operator is providing the investment service specified in paragraph 8 of Section A of Annex I to the markets in financial instruments directive.
(5)   "Derivative instruments for the transfer of credit risk" has the same meaning as in the markets in financial instruments directive.]

NOTES

Paras (3)–(5): added by the Financial Services and Markets Act 2000 (Regulated Activities) (Amendment No 3) Order 2006, SI 2006/3384, arts 2, 28, as from 1 April 2007 (for the purposes of enabling applications to be made for (i) a Part IV permission, (ii) a variation of a Part IV permission, and (iii) the Authority's approval under s 59 of the 2000 Act, in relation to an activity of the kind specified by art 25D of this Order, or in relation to an investment of the kind specified by arts 83, 84 or 85 of this Order), and as from 1 November 2007 (otherwise).

Words in square brackets in para (4)(b) substituted by the Undertakings for Collective Investment in Transferable Securities Regulations 2011, SI 2011/1613, reg 16, Schedule, para 1(1), (5), as from 1 July 2011.

[8.145]
86   Lloyd's syndicate capacity and syndicate membership
(1)   The underwriting capacity of a Lloyd's syndicate.
(2)   A person's membership (or prospective membership) of a Lloyd's syndicate.

[8.146]
87   Funeral plan contracts
Rights under a funeral plan contract.

[8.147]
88   Regulated mortgage contracts
Rights under a regulated mortgage contract.

[8.148]
[88A Regulated home reversion plans

Rights under a regulated home reversion plan.]

NOTES

Commencement: 6 November 2006 (certain purposes); 6 April 2007 (otherwise) (for more information see the note below).

Inserted, together with art 88B, by the Financial Services and Markets Act 2000 (Regulated Activities) (Amendment) (No 2) Order 2006, SI 2006/2383, arts 2, 23, as from 6 November 2006 (for the purposes of enabling applications to be made for (i) a Pt IV permission, or a variation of a Pt IV permission, in relation to activities of the kind specified by arts 25B, 25C, 53B, 53C, 63B or 63F or, so far as relevant to any such activity, art 64 of this Order; or (ii) the Authority's approval under FSMA 2000, s 59 in relation to any of those activities), and as from 6 April 2007 (otherwise) (for transitional provisions in relation to interim permissions and interim approvals, etc, see arts 36–40 of, and the Schedule to, the 2006 Order).

[8.149]
[88B Regulated home purchase plans

Rights under a regulated home purchase plan.]

NOTES

Commencement: 6 November 2006 (certain purposes); 6 April 2007 (otherwise) (for more information see the note to art 88A at **[8.148]**).

Inserted as noted to art 88A at **[8.148]**.

[8.150]
[88C Regulated sale and rent back agreements

Rights under a regulated sale and rent back agreement.]

NOTES

Commencement: 1 July 2009 (certain purposes); 30 June 2010 (otherwise) (see below).

Inserted by the Financial Services and Markets Act 2000 (Regulated Activities) (Amendment) Order 2009, SI 2009/1342, arts 2, 21, as from 1 July 2009 (other than for the purposes of enabling applications to be made for a Part IV permission, or a variation of a Part IV permission, in relation to activities of the kind specified by arts 25E, 53D or 63J or, so far as relevant to any such activity, art 64 of this Order), and as from 30 June 2010 (for those purposes) (for transitional provisions in relation to applications for Part IV permissions, etc, see arts 1, 32–34 of that Order).

[8.151]
89 Rights to or interests in investments

(1)   Subject to paragraphs (2) to (4), any right to or interest in anything which is specified by any other provision of this Part (other than [article 88,] [88A, 88B or 88C]).

(2)   Paragraph (1) does not include interests under the trusts of an occupational pension scheme.

(3)   Paragraph (1) does not include—
   (a)   rights to or interests in a contract of insurance of the kind referred to in paragraph (1)(a) of article 60; or.
   (b)   interests under a trust of the kind referred to in paragraph (1)(b) of that article.

(4)   Paragraph (1) does not include anything which is specified by any other provision of this Part.

NOTES

Para (1): words in first pair of square brackets substituted by the Financial Services and Markets Act 2000 (Regulated Activities) (Amendment) (No 2) Order 2006, SI 2006/2383, arts 2, 24, as from 6 November 2006 (for the purposes of enabling applications to be made for (i) a Pt IV permission, or a variation of a Pt IV permission, in relation to activities of the kind specified by arts 25B, 25C, 53B, 53C, 63B or 63F or, so far as relevant to any such activity, art 64 of this Order; or (ii) the Authority's approval under FSMA 2000, s 59 in relation to any of those activities), and as from 6 April 2007 (otherwise) (for transitional provisions in relation to interim permissions and interim approvals, etc, see arts 36–40 of, and the Schedule to, the 2006 Order); words in second pair of square brackets substituted by the Financial Services and Markets Act 2000 (Regulated Activities) (Amendment) Order 2009, SI 2009/1342, arts 2, 22, as from 1 July 2009 (other than for the purposes of enabling applications to be made for a Part IV permission, or a variation of a Part IV permission, in relation to activities of the kind specified by arts 25E, 53D or 63J or, so far as relevant to any such activity, art 64 of this Order), and as from 30 June 2010 (for those purposes) (for transitional provisions in relation to applications for Part IV permissions, etc, see arts 1, 32–34 of that Order).

90, 91 *((Pt IV) reg 90 amends the Consumer Credit Act 1974, ss 16, 43, 52, 53, 137, 151; reg 91 amended the Consumer Credit (Advertisements) Regulations 1989, SI 1989/1125 (revoked) and amends the Consumer Credit (Content of Quotations) and Consumer Credit (Advertisements) (Amendment) Regulations 1999, SI 1999/2725.)*

[PART V
UNAUTHORISED PERSONS CARRYING ON INSURANCE MEDIATION ACTIVITIES

[8.152]
92 Interpretation

In this Part—

"designated professional body" means a body which is for the time being designated by the Treasury under section 326 of the Act (designation of professional bodies);

"insurance mediation activity" means any regulated activity of the kind specified by article 21, 25(1) or (2), 39A or 53, or, so far as relevant to any of those articles, article 64, which is carried on in relation to a contract of insurance;

"the record" means the record maintained by the Authority under section 347 of the Act (public record of authorised persons etc);

"recorded insurance intermediary" has the meaning given by article 93(4);

"a relevant member", in relation to a designated professional body, means a member (within the meaning of section 325(2) of the Act) of the profession in relation to which that designated professional body is established, or a person who is controlled or managed by one or more such members.]

NOTES

Added, together with the preceding heading and arts 93–96, by the Financial Services and Markets Act 2000 (Regulated Activities) (Amendment) (No 2) Order 2003, SI 2003/1476, art 13, as from 31 October 2004 (in so far as relating to contracts of long-term care insurance), and as from 14 January 2005 (otherwise) (for transitional provisions in relation to applications for Part IV permissions and applications for approvals, etc, see arts 22–27 of the 2003 Order).

[8.153]
[93   Duty to maintain a record of persons carrying on insurance mediation activities

(1)   Subject to articles 95 and 96, the Authority must include in the record every person who—
  (a)   as a result of information obtained by virtue of its rules or by virtue of a direction given, or requirement imposed, under section 51(3) of the Act (procedure for applications under Part IV), appears to the Authority to fall within paragraph (2); or
  (b)   as a result of information obtained by virtue of article 94, appears to the Authority to fall within paragraph (3).

(2)   A person falls within this paragraph if he is, or has entered into a contract by virtue of which he will be, an appointed representative who carries on any insurance mediation activity.

(3)   A person falls within this paragraph if—
  (a)   he is a relevant member of a designated professional body who carries on, or is proposing to carry on, any insurance mediation activity; and
  (b)   the general prohibition does not (or will not) apply to the carrying on of those activities by virtue of section 327 of the Act (exemption from the general prohibition).

(4)   In this Part, "recorded insurance intermediary" means a person who is included in the record by virtue of paragraph (1).

(5)   The record must include—
  (a)   in the case of any recorded insurance intermediary, its address; and
  (b)   in the case of a recorded insurance intermediary which is not an individual, the name of the individuals who are responsible for the management of the business carried on by the intermediary, so far as it relates to insurance mediation activities.]

NOTES
Added as noted to art 92 at **[8.152]**.

[8.154]
[94   Members of designated professional bodies

(1)   A designated professional body must, by notice in writing, inform the Authority of—
  (a)   the name,
  (b)   the address, and
  (c)   in the case of a relevant member which is not an individual, the name of the individuals who are responsible for the management of the business carried on by the member, so far as it relates to insurance mediation activities,
of any relevant member who falls within paragraph (2).

(2)   A relevant member of a designated professional body falls within this paragraph if, in accordance with the rules of that body, he carries on, or proposes to carry on any insurance mediation activity but does not have, and does not propose to apply for, Part IV permission on the basis that the general prohibition does not (or will not) apply to the carrying on of that activity by virtue of section 327 of the Act.

(3)   A designated professional body must also, by notice in writing, inform the Authority of any change in relation to the matters specified in sub-paragraphs (a) to (c) of paragraph (1).

(4)   A designated professional body must inform the Authority when a relevant member to whom paragraph (2) applies ceases, for whatever reason, to carry on insurance mediation activities.

(5)   The Authority may give directions to a designated professional body as to the manner in which the information referred to in paragraphs (1), (3) and (4) must be provided.]

NOTES
Added as noted to art 92 at **[8.152]**.

[8.155]
[95 Exclusion from record where not fit and proper to carry on insurance mediation activities

(1) If it appears to the Authority that a person who falls within article 93(2) (appointed representatives) ("AR") is not a fit and proper person to carry on insurance mediation activities, it may decide not to include him in the record or, if that person is already included in the record, to remove him from the record.

(2) Where the Authority proposes to make a determination under paragraph (1), it must give AR a warning notice.

(3) If the Authority makes a determination under paragraph (1), it must give AR a decision notice.

(4) If the Authority gives AR a decision notice under paragraph (3), AR may refer the matter to the Tribunal.

(5) The Authority may, on the application of AR, revoke a determination under paragraph (1).

(6) If the Authority decides to grant the application, it must give AR written notice of its decision.

(7) If the Authority proposes to refuse the application, it must give AR a warning notice.

(8) If the Authority decides to refuse the application, it must give AR a decision notice.

(9) If the Authority gives AR a decision notice under paragraph (8), AR may refer the matter to the Tribunal.

(10) Sections 393 and 394 of the Act (third party rights and access to Authority material) apply to a warning notice given in accordance with paragraph (2) or (7) and to a decision notice given in accordance with paragraph (3) or (8).]

NOTES
Added as noted to art 92 at **[8.152]**.

[8.156]
[96 Exclusion from the record where Authority has exercised its powers under Part XX of the Act

(1) If a person who appears to the Authority to fall within article 93(3) (member of a designated professional body) falls within paragraph (2) or (3), the Authority must not include him in the record or, if that person is already included in the record, must remove him from the record.

(2) A person falls within this paragraph if, by virtue of a direction given by the Authority under section 328(1) of the Act (directions in relation to the general prohibition), section 327(1) of the Act does not apply in relation to the carrying on by him of any insurance mediation activity.

(3) A person falls within this paragraph if the Authority has made an order under section 329(2) of the Act (orders in relation to the general prohibition) disapplying section 327(1) of the Act in relation to the carrying on by him of any insurance mediation activity.]

NOTES
Added as noted to art 92 at **[8.152]**.

97 (*Art 97 (Pt VI) added by the Financial Services and Markets Act 2000 (Regulated Activities) (Amendment) Order 2004, SI 2004/1610, art 3, as from 15 July 2004, and inserts the Financial Services and Markets Act 2000, s 49(2A) at **[7.51]**.)

SCHEDULES
SCHEDULE 1
CONTRACTS OF INSURANCE
Article 3(1)

PART I
CONTRACTS OF GENERAL INSURANCE

[8.157]
1 Accident
Contracts of insurance providing fixed pecuniary benefits or benefits in the nature of indemnity (or a combination of both) against risks of the person insured or, in the case of a contract made by virtue of section 140, 140A or 140B of the Local Government Act 1972 (or, in Scotland, section 86(1) of the Local Government (Scotland) Act 1973), a person for whose benefit the contract is made—
(a) sustaining injury as the result of an accident or of an accident of a specified class; or

(b)   dying as a result of an accident or of an accident of a specified class; or

(c)   becoming incapacitated in consequence of disease or of disease of a specified class,

including contracts relating to industrial injury and occupational disease but excluding contracts falling within paragraph 2 of Part I of, or paragraph IV of Part II of, this Schedule.

2   Sickness

Contracts of insurance providing fixed pecuniary benefits or benefits in the nature of indemnity (or a combination of both) against risks of loss to the persons insured attributable to sickness or infirmity but excluding contracts falling within paragraph IV of Part II of this Schedule.

3   Land vehicles

Contracts of insurance against loss of or damage to vehicles used on land, including motor vehicles but excluding railway rolling stock.

4   Railway rolling stock

Contract of insurance against loss of or damage to railway rolling stock.

5   Aircraft

Contracts of insurance upon aircraft or upon the machinery, tackle, furniture or equipment of aircraft.

6   Ships

Contracts of insurance upon vessels used on the sea or on inland water, or upon the machinery, tackle, furniture or equipment of such vessels.

7   Goods in transit

Contracts of insurance against loss of or damage to merchandise, baggage and all other goods in transit, irrespective of the form of transport.

8   Fire and natural forces

Contracts of insurance against loss of or damage to property (other than property to which paragraphs 3 to 7 relate) due to fire, explosion, storm, natural forces other than storm, nuclear energy or land subsidence.

9   Damage to property

Contracts of insurance against loss of or damage to property (other than property to which paragraphs 3 to 7 relate) due to hail or frost or any other event (such as theft) other than those mentioned in paragraph 8.

10   Motor vehicle liability

Contracts of insurance against damage arising out of or in connection with the use of motor vehicles on land, including third-party risks and carrier's liability.

11   Aircraft liability

Contracts of insurance against damage arising out of or in connection with the use of aircraft, including third-party risks and carrier's liability.

12   Liability of ships

Contracts of insurance against damage arising out of or in connection with the use of vessels on the sea or on inland water, including third party risks and carrier's liability.

13   General liability

Contracts of insurance against risks of the persons insured incurring liabilities to third parties, the risks in question not being risks to which paragraph 10, 11 or 12 relates.

14   Credit

Contracts of insurance against risks of loss to the persons insured arising from the insolvency of debtors of theirs or from the failure (otherwise than through insolvency) of debtors of theirs to pay their debts when due.

15   Suretyship

(1)   Contracts of insurance against the risks of loss to the persons insured arising from their having to perform contracts of guarantee entered into by them.

(2)   Fidelity bonds, performance bonds, administration bonds, bail bonds or customs bonds or similar contracts of guarantee, where these are—

(a)   effected or carried out by a person not carrying on a banking business;

(b)   not effected merely incidentally to some other business carried on by the person effecting them; and

(c)   effected in return for the payment of one or more premiums.

16 Miscellaneous financial loss

Contracts of insurance against any of the following risks, namely—

    (a)   risks of loss to the persons insured attributable to interruptions of the carrying on of business carried on by them or to reduction of the scope of business so carried on;

    (b)   risks of loss to the persons insured attributable to their incurring unforeseen expense (other than loss such as is covered by contracts falling within paragraph 18);

    (c)   risks which do not fall within sub-paragraph (a) or (b) and which are not of a kind such that contracts of insurance against them fall within any other provision of this Schedule.

17 Legal expenses

Contracts of insurance against risks of loss to the persons insured attributable to their incurring legal expenses (including costs of litigation).

18 Assistance

Contracts of insurance providing either or both of the following benefits, namely—

    (a)   assistance (whether in cash or in kind) for persons who get into difficulties while travelling, while away from home or while away from their permanent residence; or

    (b)   assistance (whether in cash or in kind) for persons who get into difficulties otherwise than as mentioned in sub-paragraph (a).

PART II
CONTRACTS OF LONG-TERM INSURANCE

[8.158]

I Life and annuity

Contracts of insurance on human life or contracts to pay annuities on human life, but excluding (in each case) contracts within paragraph III.

II Marriage and birth

Contract of insurance to provide a sum on marriage [or the formation of a civil partnership] or on the birth of a child, being contracts expressed to be in effect for a period of more than one year.

III Linked long term

Contracts of insurance on human life or contracts to pay annuities on human life where the benefits are wholly or partly to be determined by references to the value of, or the income from, property of any description (whether or not specified in the contracts) or by reference to fluctuations in, or in an index of, the value of property of any description (whether or not so specified).

IV Permanent health

Contracts of insurance providing specified benefits against risks of persons becoming incapacitated in consequence of sustaining injury as a result of an accident or of an accident of a specified class or of sickness or infirmity, being contracts that—

    (a)   are expressed to be in effect for a period of not less than five years, or until the normal retirement age for the persons concerned, or without limit of time; and

    (b)   either are not expressed to be terminable by the insurer, or are expressed to be so terminable only in special circumstances mentioned in the contract.

V Tontines

Tontines.

VI Capital redemption contracts

Capital redemption contracts, where effected or carried out by a person who does not carry on a banking business, and otherwise carries on a regulated activity of the kind specified by article 10(1) or (2).

VII Pension fund management

    (a)   Pension fund management contracts, and

    (b)   pension fund management contracts which are combined with contracts of insurance covering either conservation of capital or payment of a minimum interest, where effected or carried out by a person who does not carry on a banking business, and otherwise carries on a regulated activity of the kind specified by article 10(1) or (2).

VIII Collective insurance etc

Contracts of a kind referred to in article 1(2)(e) of the first life insurance directive.

IX Social insurance

Contracts of a kind referred to in article 1(3) of the first life insurance directive.

NOTES

II Marriage and birth: words in square brackets inserted by the Civil Partnership Act 2004 (Amendments to Subordinate Legislation) Order 2005, SI 2005/2114, art 2(16), Sch 16, Pt 1, para 1(1), (5), as from 5 December 2005. Note it is unclear whether these words should also be inserted after the word "Marriage" in the heading to this paragraph.

[SCHEDULE 2
SECTIONS A AND C OF ANNEX I TO THE MARKETS IN FINANCIAL INSTRUMENTS DIRECTIVE AND RELATED COMMUNITY SUBORDINATE LEGISLATION

Article 3(1)

PART 1
SECTION C OF ANNEX I TO THE MARKETS IN FINANCIAL INSTRUMENTS DIRECTIVE

Financial Instruments

[8.159]

1. Transferable securities;

2. Money-market instruments;

3. Units in collective investment undertakings;

4. Options, futures, swaps, forward rate agreements and any other derivative contracts relating to securities, currencies, interest rates or yields, or other derivatives instruments, financial indices or financial measures which may be settled physically or in cash;

5. Options, futures, swaps, forward rate agreements and any other derivative contracts relating to commodities that must be settled in cash or may be settled in cash at the option of one of the parties (otherwise than by reason of a default or other termination event);

6. Options, futures, swaps, and any other derivative contracts relating to commodities that can be physically settled provided that they are traded on a regulated market and/or an MTF;

7. Options, futures, swaps, forwards and any other derivative contracts relating to commodities, that can be physically settled not otherwise mentioned in C6 and not being for commercial purposes, which have the characteristics of other derivative financial instruments, having regard to whether, inter alia, they are cleared and settled through recognised clearing houses or are subject to regular margin calls;

8. Derivative instruments for the transfer of credit risk;

9. Financial contracts for differences;

10. Options, futures, swaps, forward rate agreements and any other derivative contracts relating to climatic variables, freight rates, emission allowances or inflation rates or other official economic statistics that must be settled in cash or may be settled in cash at the option of one of the parties (otherwise than by reason of a default or other termination event), as well as any other derivative contracts relating to assets, rights, obligations, indices and measures not otherwise mentioned in this Section, which have the characteristics of other derivative financial instruments, having regard to whether, inter alia, they are traded on a regulated market or an MTF, are cleared and settled through recognised clearing houses or are subject to regular margin calls.]

NOTES

Commencement: 1 April 2007 (certain purposes); 1 November 2007 (otherwise); see the note below.

Substituted by the Financial Services and Markets Act 2000 (Regulated Activities) (Amendment No 3) Order 2006, SI 2006/3384, arts 2, 29, as from 1 April 2007 (for the purposes of enabling applications to be made for (i) a Part IV permission, (ii) a variation of a Part IV permission, and (iii) the Authority's approval under s 59 of the 2000 Act, in relation to an activity of the kind specified by art 25D of this Order, or in relation to an investment of the kind specified by arts 83, 84 or 85 of this Order), and as from 1 November 2007 (otherwise).

[PART 2
CHAPTER VI OF THE COMMISSION REGULATION

DERIVATIVE FINANCIAL INSTRUMENTS
ARTICLE 38

Characteristics of other derivative financial instruments

[8.160]

1. For the purposes of Section C(7) of Annex I to Directive 2004/39/EC, a contract which is not a spot contract within the meaning of paragraph 2 of this Article and which is not covered by paragraph 4 shall be considered as having the characteristics of other derivative financial instruments and not being for commercial purposes if it satisfies the following conditions:

  (a) it meets one of the following sets of criteria:

    (i) it is traded on a third country trading facility that performs a similar function to a regulated market or an MTF;

    (ii) it is expressly stated to be traded on, or is subject to the rules of, a regulated market, an MTF or such a third country trading facility;

    (iii) it is expressly stated to be equivalent to a contract traded on a regulated market, MTF or such a third country trading facility;

  (b) it is cleared by a clearing house or other entity carrying out the same functions as a central counterparty, or there are arrangements for the payment or provision of margin in relation to the contract;

  (c) it is standardised so that, in particular, the price, the lot, the delivery date or other terms are determined principally by reference to regularly published prices, standard lots or standard delivery dates.

2. A spot contract for the purposes of paragraph 1 means a contract for the sale of a commodity, asset or right, under the terms of which delivery is scheduled to be made within the longer of the following periods:

  (a) two trading days;

  (b) the period generally accepted in the market for that commodity, asset or right as the standard delivery period.

However, a contract is not a spot contract if, irrespective of its explicit terms, there is an understanding between the parties to the contract that delivery of the underlying is to be postponed and not to be performed within the period mentioned in the first subparagraph.

3. For the purposes of Section C(10) of Annex I to Directive 2004/39/EC, a derivative contract relating to an underlying referred to in that Section or in Article 39 shall be considered to have the characteristics of other derivative financial instruments if one of the following conditions is satisfied:

  (a) that contract is settled in cash or may be settled in cash at the option of one or more of the parties, otherwise than by reason of a default or other termination event;

  (b) that contract is traded on a regulated market or an MTF;

  (c) the conditions laid down in paragraph 1 are satisfied in relation to that contract.

4. A contract shall be considered to be for commercial purposes for the purposes of Section C(7) of Annex I to Directive 2004/39/EC, and as not having the characteristics of other derivative financial instruments for the purposes of Sections C(7) and (10) of that Annex, if it is entered into with or by an operator or administrator of an energy transmission grid, energy balancing mechanism or pipeline network, and it is necessary to keep in balance the supplies and uses of energy at a given time.

ARTICLE 39
DERIVATIVES WITHIN SECTION C(10) OF ANNEX I TO DIRECTIVE 2004/39/EC

In addition to derivative contracts of a kind referred to in Section C(10) of Annex I to Directive 2004/39/EC, a derivative contract relating to any of the following shall fall within that Section if it meets the criteria set out in that Section and in Article 38(3):

  (a) telecommunications bandwidth;

  (b) commodity storage capacity;

  (c) transmission or transportation capacity relating to commodities, whether cable, pipeline or other means;

  (d) an allowance, credit, permit, right or similar asset which is directly linked to the supply, distribution or consumption of energy derived from renewable resources;

  (e) a geological, environmental or other physical variable;

  (f) any other asset or right of a fungible nature, other than a right to receive a service, that is capable of being transferred;

  (g) an index or measure related to the price or value of, or volume of transactions in any asset, right, service or obligation.]

NOTES

Commencement: 1 April 2007 (certain purposes); 1 November 2007 (otherwise); see the note at **[8.159]**.
Substituted as noted to Part 1 at **[8.159]**.

[PART 3
SECTION A OF ANNEX I TO THE MARKETS IN FINANCIAL
INSTRUMENTS DIRECTIVE

INVESTMENT SERVICES AND ACTIVITIES

[8.161]

1. Reception and transmission of orders in relation to one or more financial instruments.

2. Execution of orders on behalf of clients.

3. Dealing on own account.

4. Portfolio management.

5. Investment advice.

6. Underwriting of financial instruments and/or placing of financial instruments on a firm commitment basis.

7. Placing of financial instruments without a firm commitment basis.

8. Operation of Multilateral Trading Facilities.]

NOTES

Commencement: 1 April 2007 (certain purposes); 1 November 2007 (otherwise); see the note at **[8.159]**.
Substituted as noted to Part 1 at **[8.159]**.

[PART 4
ARTICLE 52 OF COMMISSION DIRECTIVE 2006/73/EC

ARTICLE 52
INVESTMENT ADVICE

[8.162]

For the purposes of the definition of "investment advice" in Article 4(1)(4) of Directive 2004/39/EC, a personal recommendation is a recommendation that is made to a person in his capacity as an investor or potential investor, or in his capacity as an agent for an investor or potential investor.

That recommendation must be presented as suitable for that person, or must be based on a consideration of the circumstances of that person, and must constitute a recommendation to take one of the following sets of steps:

(a) to buy, sell, subscribe for, exchange, redeem, hold or underwrite a particular financial instrument;

(b) to exercise or not to exercise any right conferred by a particular financial instrument to buy, sell, subscribe for, exchange, or redeem a financial instrument.

A recommendation is not a personal recommendation if it is issued exclusively through distribution channels or to the public.]

NOTES

Commencement: 1 April 2007 (certain purposes); 1 November 2007 (otherwise); see the note at **[8.159]**.
Substituted as noted to Part 1 at **[8.159]**.

[SCHEDULE 3
ARTICLE 2 OF THE MARKETS IN FINANCIAL INSTRUMENTS DIRECTIVE

Article 2
Exemptions

[8.163]

1. This Directive shall not apply to:

(a) insurance undertakings as defined in Article 1 of Directive 73/239/EEC or assurance undertakings as defined in Article 1 of Directive 2002/83/EC or undertakings carrying on the reinsurance and retrocession activities referred to in Directive 64/225/EEC;

(b) persons which provide investment services exclusively for their parent undertakings, for their subsidiaries or for other subsidiaries of their parent undertakings;

(c)   persons providing an investment service where that service is provided in an incidental manner in the course of a professional activity and that activity is regulated by legal or regulatory provisions or a code of ethics governing the profession which do not exclude the provision of that service;

(d)   persons who do not provide any investment services or activities other than dealing on own account unless they are market makers or deal on own account outside a regulated market or an MTF on an organised, frequent and systematic basis by providing a system accessible to third parties in order to engage in dealings with them;

(e)   persons which provide investment services consisting exclusively in the administration of employee-participation schemes;

(f)   persons which provide investment services which only involve both administration of employee-participation schemes and the provision of investment services exclusively for their parent undertakings, for their subsidiaries or for other subsidiaries of their parent undertakings;

(g)   the members of the European System of Central Banks and other national bodies performing similar functions and other public bodies charged with or intervening in the management of the public debt;

(h)   collective investment undertakings and pension funds whether coordinated at Community level or not and the depositaries and managers of such undertakings;

(i)   persons dealing on own account in financial instruments, or providing investment services in commodity derivatives or derivative contracts included in Annex I, Section C10 to the clients of their main business, provided this is an ancillary activity to their main business, when considered on a group basis, and that main business is not the provision of investment services within the meaning of this Directive or banking services under Directive 2000/12/EC;

(j)   persons providing investment advice in the course of providing another professional activity not covered by this Directive provided that the provision of such advice is not specifically remunerated;

(k)   persons whose main business consists of dealing on own account in commodities and/or commodity derivatives. This exception shall not apply where the persons that deal on own account in commodities and/or commodity derivatives are part of a group the main business of which is the provision of other investment services within the meaning of this Directive or banking services under Directive 2000/12/EC;

(l)   firms which provide investment services and/or perform investment activities consisting exclusively in dealing on own account on markets in financial futures or options or other derivatives and on cash markets for the sole purpose of hedging positions on derivatives markets or which deal for the accounts of other members of those markets or make prices for them and which are guaranteed by clearing members of the same markets, where responsibility for ensuring the performance of contracts entered into by such firms is assumed by clearing members of the same markets;

(m)   associations set up by Danish and Finnish pensions funds with the sole aim of managing the assets of pension funds that are members of those associations;

(n)   'agenti di cambio' whose activities and functions are governed by Article 201 of Italian Legislative Decree No 58 of 24 February 1998.

2. The rights conferred by this Directive shall not extend to the provision of services as counterparty in transactions carried out by public bodies dealing with public debt or by members of the European System of Central Banks performing their tasks as provided for by the Treaty and the Statute of the European System of Central Banks and of the European Central Bank or performing equivalent functions under national provisions.

3. In order to take account of developments on financial markets, and to ensure the uniform application of this Directive, the Commission, acting in accordance with the procedure referred to in Article 64(2), may, in respect of exemptions (c), (i) and (k) define the criteria for determining when an activity is to be considered as ancillary to the main business on a group level as well as for determining when an activity is provided in an incidental manner.]

NOTES

Commencement: 1 April 2007 (certain purposes); 1 November 2007 (otherwise); see the note below.

Substituted by the Financial Services and Markets Act 2000 (Regulated Activities) (Amendment No 3) Order 2006, SI 2006/3384, arts 2, 30, as from 1 April 2007 (for the purposes of enabling applications to be made for (i) a Part IV permission, (ii) a variation of a Part IV permission, and (iii) the Authority's approval under s 59 of the 2000 Act, in relation to an activity of the kind specified by art 25D of this Order, or in relation to an investment of the kind specified by arts 83, 84 or 85 of this Order), and as from 1 November 2007 (otherwise).

[SCHEDULE 4
RELEVANT TEXT OF THE INSURANCE MEDIATION DIRECTIVE
Article 4

PART I
ARTICLE 1.2

[8.164]

"This Directive shall not apply to persons providing mediation services for insurance contracts if all the following conditions are met:

(a)   the insurance contract only requires knowledge of the insurance cover that is provided;
(b)   the insurance contract is not a life assurance contract;
(c)   the insurance contract does not cover any liability risks;
(d)   the principal professional activity of the person is other than insurance mediation;
(e)   the insurance is complementary to the product or service supplied by any provider, where such insurance covers:
    (i)   the risk of breakdown, loss of or damage to goods supplied by that provider; or
    (ii)   damage to or loss of baggage and other risks linked to the travel booked with that provider, even if the insurance covers life assurance or liability risks, provided that the cover is ancillary to the main cover for the risks linked to that travel;
(f)   the amount of the annual premium does not exceed EUR 500 and the total duration of the insurance contract, including any renewals, does not exceed five years."]

NOTES

Inserted by the Financial Services and Markets Act 2000 (Regulated Activities) (Amendment) (No 2) Order 2003, SI 2003/1476, art 12, as from 31 October 2004 (in so far as relating to contracts of long-term care insurance), and as from 14 January 2005 (otherwise) (for transitional provisions in relation to applications for Part IV permissions and applications for approvals, etc, see arts 22–27 of the 2003 Order).

[PART II
ARTICLE 2.3

[8.165]

""Insurance mediation" means the activities of introducing, proposing or carrying out other work preparatory to the conclusion of contracts of insurance, or of concluding such contracts, or of assisting in the administration and performance of such contracts, in particular in the event of a claim.

These activities when undertaken by an insurance undertaking or an employee of an insurance undertaking who is acting under the responsibility of the insurance undertaking shall not be considered as insurance mediation.

The provision of information on an incidental basis in the context of another professional activity provided that the purpose of that activity is not to assist the customer in concluding or performing an insurance contract, the management of claims of an insurance undertaking on a professional basis, and loss adjusting and expert appraisal of claims shall also not be considered as insurance mediation."]

NOTES

Inserted as noted to Sch 4, Pt I at **[8.164]**.

[PART III
ARTICLE 2.4

[8.166]

""Reinsurance mediation" means the activities of introducing, proposing or carrying out other work preparatory to the conclusion of contracts of reinsurance, or of concluding such contracts, or of assisting in the administration and performance of such contracts, in particular in the event of a claim.

These activities when undertaken by a reinsurance undertaking or an employee of a reinsurance undertaking who is acting under the responsibility of the reinsurance undertaking are not considered as reinsurance mediation.

The provision of information on an incidental basis in the context of another professional activity provided that the purpose of that activity is not to assist the customer in concluding or performing a reinsurance contract, the management of claims of a reinsurance undertaking on a professional basis, and loss adjusting and expert appraisal of claims shall also not be considered as reinsurance mediation."]

NOTES

Inserted as noted to Sch 4, Pt I at **[8.164]**.

FINANCIAL SERVICES AND MARKETS ACT 2000 (PRESCRIBED MARKETS AND QUALIFYING INVESTMENTS) ORDER 2001

(SI 2001/996)

NOTES

Made: 15 March 2001.

Authority: Financial Services and Markets Act 2000, s 118(3).

Commencement: 1 December 2001.

This Order is reproduced as amended by: the Financial Services and Markets Act 2000 (Prescribed Markets and Qualifying Investments) (Amendment) Order 2001, SI 2001/3681; the Financial Services and Markets Act 2000 (Market Abuse) Regulations 2005, SI 2005/381; the Financial Services and Markets Act 2000 (Markets in Financial Instruments) Regulations 2007, SI 2007/126; the Definition of Financial Instrument Order 2008 SI 2008/3053.

[8.167]
1 Citation

This Order may be cited as the Financial Services and Markets Act 2000 (Prescribed Markets and Qualifying Investments) Order 2001.

[8.168]
2 Commencement

This Order comes into force on the day on which section 123 of the Act (power to impose penalties in cases of market abuse) comes into force.

NOTES

FSMA 2000, s 123 came into force on 1 December 2001 (see the Financial Services and Markets Act 2000 (Commencement No 7) Order 2001, SI 2001/3538).

[8.169]
3 Interpretation

In this Order—

"the Act" means the Financial Services and Markets Act 2000; and

["regulated market" has the meaning given in [Article 4.1.14 of the markets in financial instruments directive];]

"UK recognised investment exchange" means a body corporate or unincorporated association in respect of which there is in effect a recognition order made under section 290(1)(a) of the Act (recognition orders in respect of investment exchanges other than overseas investment exchanges).

NOTES

Definition "regulated market" inserted by the Financial Services and Markets Act 2000 (Market Abuse) Regulations 2005, SI 2005/381, reg 10(1), as from 1 July 2005; words in square brackets in that definition substituted by the Financial Services and Markets Act 2000 (Markets in Financial Instruments) Regulations 2007, SI 2007/126, reg 3(6), Sch 6, Pt 2, para 15, as from 1 November 2007.

[8.170]
[4 Prescribed Markets

(1) There are prescribed, as markets to which subsections (2), (3), (5), (6) and (7) of section 118 apply—

    (a) all markets which are established under the rules of a UK recognised investment exchange,

    (b) the market known as OFEX,

    (c) all other markets which are regulated markets.

(2) There are prescribed, as markets to which subsections (4) and (8) of section 118 apply—

    (a) all markets which are established under the rules of a UK recognised investment exchange;

    (b) the market known as OFEX.]

NOTES

Articles 4, 5 substituted for original arts 4, 4A, 5, by the Financial Services and Markets Act 2000 (Market Abuse) Regulations 2005, SI 2005/381, reg 10(2), as from 1 July 2005. Art 4A was previously inserted by the Financial Services and Markets Act 2000 (Prescribed Markets and Qualifying Investments) (Amendment) Order 2001, SI 2001/3681, art 2, as from 5 December 2001.

4A (*See the note to art 4 at* **[8.170]**.)

[8.171]
[5 Qualifying Investments

There are prescribed, as qualifying investments in relation to the markets prescribed by article 4, all financial instruments within the meaning given in Article 1(3) of Directive 2003/6/EC of the European Parliament and the Council of 28 January 2003 on insider dealing and market manipulation (market abuse) [as modified by Article 69 of Directive 2004/39/EC on markets in financial instruments].]

NOTES
Substituted as noted to art 4 at **[8.170]**.
Words in square brackets added by the Definition of Financial Instrument Order 2008 SI 2008/3053, art 4, as from 31 January 2009.

FINANCIAL SERVICES AND MARKETS ACT 2000 (PROMOTION OF COLLECTIVE INVESTMENT SCHEMES) (EXEMPTIONS) ORDER 2001

(SI 2001/1060)

NOTES
Made: 19 March 2001.
Authority: Financial Services and Markets Act 2000, s 238(6), (7).
Commencement: 1 December 2001.
This Order is reproduced as amended by: the Financial Services and Markets Act 2000 (Financial Promotion) (Amendment) Order 2001, SI 2001/2633; the Financial Services and Markets Act 2000 (Financial Promotion and Miscellaneous Amendments) Order 2002, SI 2002/1310; the Financial Services and Markets Act 2000 (Financial Promotion) (Amendment) (Electronic Commerce Directive) Order 2002, SI 2002/2157; the Financial Services and Markets Act 2000 (Promotion of Collective Investment Schemes etc) (Exemptions) (Amendment) Order 2003, SI 2003/2067; the Financial Services and Markets Act 2000 (Financial Promotion and Promotion of Collective Investment Schemes) (Miscellaneous Amendments) Order 2005, SI 2005/270; the Financial Services and Markets Act 2000 (Promotion of Collective Investment Schemes) (Exemptions) (Amendment) Order 2005, SI 2005/1532; the Civil Partnership Act 2004 (Amendments to Subordinate Legislation) Order 2005, SI 2005/2114; the Companies Act 2006 (Consequential Amendments and Transitional Provisions) Order 2011, SI 2011/1265; the Undertakings for Collective Investment in Transferable Securities Regulations 2011, SI 2011/1613.

ARRANGEMENT OF ARTICLES

PART I
GENERAL AND INTERPRETATION

PART I
GENERAL AND INTERPRETATION

[8.172]
1   Citation and commencement

(1)   This Order may be cited as the Financial Services and Markets Act 2000 (Promotion of Collective Investment Schemes) (Exemptions) Order 2001.

(2)   This Order comes into force on the day on which section 19 of the Act comes into force.

[8.173]
2   Interpretation: general

(1)   In this Order—
"the Act" means the Financial Services and Markets Act 2000;
"authorised unit trust scheme" has the meaning given by section 237 of the Act;
"close relative", in relation to a person means—
    (a)   his spouse [or civil partner];
    (b)   his children and step-children, his parents and step-parents, his brothers and sisters and his step-brothers and step-sisters; and
    (c)   the spouse [or civil partner] of any person within sub-paragraph (b);
"overseas scheme" means an unregulated scheme which is operated and managed in a country or territory outside the United Kingdom;
"publication" means—
    (a)   a newspaper, journal, magazine or other periodical publication;
    (b)   a web site [or similar system for the electronic display of information];
    (c)   any programme forming part of a service consisting of the broadcast or transmission of television or radio programmes; and
    (d)   any teletext service, that is to say a service consisting of television transmissions consisting of a succession of visual displays (with or without accompanying sound) capable of being selected and held for separate viewing or other use;
"qualifying contract of insurance" has the meaning given in the Regulated Activities Order;
"the Regulated Activities Order" means the Financial Services and Markets Act 2000 (Regulated Activities) Order 2001;
"relevant scheme activities" means—
    (i)   the activity specified by article 51 of the Regulated Activities Order; or
    (ii)   any activity specified by article 14, 21, 25, 37 or 53 of that Order when carried on in relation to units;
"solicited real time communication" has the meaning given by article 5;
"units" has the meaning given by section 237(2) of the Act;
"unregulated scheme" means a collective investment scheme which is not an authorised unit trust scheme nor a scheme constituted by an authorised open-ended investment company nor a recognised scheme for the purposes of Part XVII of the Act;
"unsolicited real time communication" has the meaning given by article 5.

(2)   In this Order, any reference to the "scheme promotion restriction" means the restriction imposed by section 238(1) of the Act.

NOTES

Para (1): words in square brackets in definition "close relative" inserted by the Civil Partnership Act 2004 (Amendments to Subordinate Legislation) Order 2005, SI 2005/2114, art 2(16), Sch 16, Pt 1, para 2, as from 5 December 2005; words in square brackets in definition "publication" inserted by the Financial Services and Markets Act 2000 (Financial Promotion and Miscellaneous Amendments) Order 2002, SI 2002/1310, art 3(1), (2), as from 5 June 2002.

Step-children, etc: as to the meaning of this and related expressions, see the Civil Partnership Act 2004, s 246 (as applied to this Order by the Civil Partnership Act 2004 (Relationships Arising Through Civil Partnership) Order 2005, SI 2005/3137, art 3, Schedule).

[8.174]

3 Interpretation: communications

In this Order—

  (a)   any reference to a communication is a reference to the communication, by an authorised person in the course of business, of an invitation or inducement to participate in an unregulated scheme;

  (b)   any reference to a communication being made to another person is a reference to a communication being addressed, whether verbally or in legible form, to a particular person or persons (for example where it is contained in a telephone call or letter);

  (c)   any reference to a communication being directed at persons is a reference to a communication being addressed to persons generally (for example where it is contained in a television broadcast or web site);

  (d)   "communicate" includes causing a communication to be made;

  (e)   a "recipient" of a communication is a person to whom the communication is made or, in the case of a non-real time communication which is directed at persons generally, any person who reads or hears the communication;

  [(f)   "electronic commerce communication" means a communication, the making of which constitutes the provision of an information society service;

  (g)   "incoming electronic commerce communication" means an electronic commerce communication made from an establishment in an EEA State other than the United Kingdom;

  (h)   "outgoing electronic commerce communication" means an electronic commerce communication made from an establishment in the United Kingdom to a person in an EEA State other than the United Kingdom].

NOTES

Paras (f)–(h) added by the Financial Services and Markets Act 2000 (Financial Promotion) (Amendment) (Electronic Commerce Directive) Order 2002, SI 2002/2157, arts 7, 8(1), as from 21 August 2002.

[8.175]

4 Interpretation: real time communications

(1)   In this Order, references to a real time communication are references to any communication made in the course of a personal visit, telephone conversation or other interactive dialogue.

(2)   A non-real time communication is a communication not falling within paragraph (1).

(3)   For the purposes of this Order, non-real time communications include communications made by letter or e-mail or contained in a publication.

(4)   For the purposes of this Order, the factors in paragraph (5) are to be treated as indications that a communication is a non-real time communication.

(5)   The factors are that—

  (a)   the communication is made to or directed at more than one recipient in identical terms (save for details of the recipient's identity);

  (b)   the communication is made or directed by way of a system which in the normal course constitutes or creates a record of the communication which is available to the recipient to refer to at a later time;

  (c)   the communication is made or directed by way of a system which in the normal course does not enable or require the recipient to respond immediately to it.

[8.176]

5 Interpretation: solicited and unsolicited real time communications

(1)   A real time communication is solicited where it is made in the course of a personal visit, telephone call or other interactive dialogue if that call, visit or dialogue—

  (a)   was initiated by the recipient of the communication; or

  (b)   takes place in response to an express request from the recipient of the communication.

(2)   A real time communication is unsolicited where it is made otherwise than as described in paragraph (1).

(3)   For the purposes of paragraph (1)—

  (a)   a person is not to be treated as expressly requesting a call, visit or dialogue—

     (i)   because he omits to indicate that he does not wish to receive any or any further visits or calls or to engage in any or any further dialogue;

     (ii)   because he agrees to standard terms that state that such visits, calls or dialogue will take place, unless he has signified clearly that, in addition to agreeing to the terms, he is willing for them to take place;

  (b)   a communication is solicited only if it is clear from all the circumstances when the call, visit or dialogue is initiated or requested that during the course of the visit, call or dialogue communications will be made concerning the kind of activities or investments to which the communications in fact made relate;

(c) it is immaterial whether the express request is made before or after this Order comes into force.

(4) Where a real time communication is solicited by a recipient ("R"), it is treated as having also been solicited by any other person to whom it is made at the same time as it is made to R if that other recipient is—

(a) a close relative of R; or

(b) expected to participate in the unregulated scheme jointly with R.

[8.177]
[5A Interpretation: outgoing electronic commerce communications

(1) For the purposes of the application of those articles to outgoing electronic commerce communications—

(a) any reference in article 21(4)(d) or 23(1)(a) or (3)(d) to an authorised person includes a reference to a person who is entitled, under the law of an EEA State other than the United Kingdom, to carry on regulated activities in that State;

(b) any reference in article 21 or 22 to an amount in pounds sterling includes a reference to an equivalent amount in another currency.

(2) For the purposes of the application of article 22 to outgoing electronic commerce communications, any reference in [section 547 or 831(2) and (3) of the Companies Act 2006] to a company includes a reference to a company registered under the law of an EEA State other than the United Kingdom.]

NOTES

Inserted by the Financial Services and Markets Act 2000 (Financial Promotion) (Amendment) (Electronic Commerce Directive) Order 2002, SI 2002/2157, arts 7, 8(2), as from 21 August 2002.

Para (2): words in square brackets substituted by the Companies Act 2006 (Consequential Amendments and Transitional Provisions) Order 2011, SI 2011/1265, art 14(1), (2), as from 12 May 2011.

[8.178]
6 Degree of prominence to be given to required indications

Where a communication must, if it is to fall within any provision of this Order, be accompanied by an indication of any matter, the indication must be presented to the recipient—

(a) in a way that can be easily understood; and

(b) in such manner as, depending on the means by which the communication is made or directed, is best calculated to bring the matter in question to the attention of the recipient and to allow him to consider it.

[8.179]
7 Combination of different exemptions

Nothing in this Order is to be construed as preventing a person from relying on more than one exemption in respect of the same communication.

PART II
TERRITORIAL SCOPE

[8.180]
8 Communications to overseas recipients

(1) Subject to [paragraphs (2) and (7)], the scheme promotion restriction does not apply to any communication—

(a) which is made (whether from inside or outside the United Kingdom) to a person who receives the communication outside the United Kingdom; or

(b) which is directed (whether from inside or outside the United Kingdom) only at persons outside the United Kingdom.

(2) Paragraph (1) does not apply to an unsolicited real time communication unless—

(a) it is made from a place outside the United Kingdom; and

(b) it relates to an overseas scheme.

(3) For the purposes of paragraph (1)(b)—

(a) if the conditions set out in paragraph (4)(a), (b), (c) and (d) are met, a communication directed from a place inside the United Kingdom is to be regarded as directed only at persons outside the United Kingdom;

(b) if the conditions set out in paragraph (4)(c) and (d) are met, a communication directed from a place outside the United Kingdom is to be regarded as directed only at persons outside the United Kingdom;

(c) in any other case where one or more of the conditions in paragraph (4)(a) to (e) are met, that fact shall be taken into account in determining whether the communication is to be regarded as directed only at persons outside the United Kingdom (but a communication may still be regarded as directed only at persons outside the United Kingdom even if none of the conditions in paragraph (4) is met).

(4)   The conditions are that—

(a)   the communication is accompanied by an indication that it is directed only at persons outside the United Kingdom;

(b)   the communication is accompanied by an indication that it must not be acted upon by persons in the United Kingdom;

(c)   the communication is not referred to in, or directly accessible from, any other communication which is made to a person or directed at persons in the United Kingdom by or on behalf of the same person;

(d)   there are in place proper systems and procedures to prevent recipients in the United Kingdom (other than those to whom the communication might otherwise lawfully have been made or directed) acquiring from the person directing the communication, a close relative of his or a company in the same group, units in the scheme to which the communication relates;

(e)   the communication is included in—

(i)   a web site, newspaper, journal, magazine or periodical publication which is principally accessed in or intended for a market outside the United Kingdom;

(ii)   a radio or television broadcast or teletext service transmitted principally for reception outside the United Kingdom.

(5)   For the purposes of paragraph (1)(b), a communication may be treated as directed only at persons outside the United Kingdom even if—

(a)   it is also directed, for the purposes of article 14(1)(b), at investment professionals falling within article 14(5) (but disregarding paragraph (6) of that article for this purpose);

(b)   it is also directed, for the purposes of article 22(1)(b), at high net worth persons to whom article 22 applies (but disregarding paragraph (2)(e) of that article for this purpose).

(6)   Where a communication falls within paragraph (5)—

(a)   the condition in paragraph (4)(a) is to be construed as requiring an indication that the communication is directed only at persons outside the United Kingdom or persons having professional experience in matters relating to investments or high net worth persons (as the case may be);

(b)   the condition in paragraph (4)(b) is to be construed as requiring an indication that the communication must not be acted upon by persons in the United Kingdom or by persons who do not have professional experience in matters relating to investments or who are not high net worth persons (as the case may be).

[(7)   Paragraph (1) does not apply to an outgoing electronic commerce communication.]

NOTES

Para (1): words in square brackets substituted by the Financial Services and Markets Act 2000 (Financial Promotion) (Amendment) (Electronic Commerce Directive) Order 2002, SI 2002/2157, arts 7, 9(a), as from 21 August 2002.

Para (7): added by SI 2002/2157, arts 7, 9(b), as from 21 August 2002.

[8.181]
9   Solicited real time communications from overseas

The scheme promotion restriction does not apply to any solicited real time communication which is made from outside the United Kingdom and which relates to units in an overseas scheme.

[8.182]
10   Communications from overseas to previously overseas customers

(1)   The scheme promotion restriction does not apply to a non-real time or unsolicited real time communication which—

(a)   is made from outside the United Kingdom by an authorised person to a previously overseas customer of his; and

(b)   relates to units in an overseas scheme.

(2)   In this article—

"previously overseas customer" means a person with whom the authorised person has done business within the period of twelve months ending with the day on which the communication was made ("the earlier business") and where—

(a)   at the time that the earlier business was done, the customer was neither resident in the United Kingdom nor had a place of business there; or

(b)   at the time the earlier business was done, the authorised person had on a former occasion done business with the customer, being business of the same description as the business to which the communication relates, and on that former occasion the customer was neither resident in the United Kingdom nor had a place of business there.

(3)   For the purposes of this article, an authorised person has done business with a customer if, in the course of his overseas business, he has—

(a)   effected a transaction, or arranged for a transaction to be effected, with the customer in respect of units in an overseas scheme; or

(b) given, outside the United Kingdom, any advice on the merits of the customer buying or selling units in an overseas scheme.

[8.183]
[10A Incoming electronic commerce communications

(1) The scheme promotion restriction does not apply to an incoming electronic commerce communication.

(2) Paragraph (1) does not apply to—
  (a) a communication which constitutes an advertisement by the operator of a UCITS Directive scheme of units in that scheme; or
  (b) an unsolicited communication made by electronic mail.

(3) In this article, "UCITS Directive scheme" means an undertaking for collective investment in transferable securities which is subject to [the UCITS directive], and has been authorised in accordance with [Article 5] of that Directive.

(4) For the purposes of this article, a communication by electronic mail is to be regarded as unsolicited, unless it is made in response to an express request from the recipient of the communication.]

NOTES

Inserted by the Financial Services and Markets Act 2000 (Financial Promotion) (Amendment) (Electronic Commerce Directive) Order 2002, SI 2002/2157, arts 7, 10, as from 21 August 2002.

Para (3): words in first pair of square brackets substituted by the Financial Services and Markets Act 2000 (Promotion of Collective Investment Schemes etc) (Exemptions) (Amendment) Order 2003, SI 2003/2067, art 2(1), (2), as from 13 February 2004; words in second pair of square brackets substituted by the Undertakings for Collective Investment in Transferable Securities Regulations 2011, SI 2011/1613, reg 16, Schedule, para 2(1), (2), as from 1 July 2011.

PART III
OTHER EXEMPTIONS

[8.184]
11 Follow up non-real time communications and solicited real time communications

(1) Where an authorised person makes or directs a communication ("the first communication") which is exempt from the scheme promotion restriction because, in compliance with the requirements of another provision of this Order, it is accompanied by certain indications or contains certain information, then the scheme promotion restriction does not apply to any subsequent communication which complies with the requirements of paragraph (2).

(2) The requirements of this paragraph are that the subsequent communication—
  (a) is a non-real time communication or a solicited real time communication;
  (b) is made by the same person who made the first communication;
  (c) is made to a recipient of the first communication;
  (d) relates to the same unregulated scheme as the first communication; and
  (e) is made within 12 months of the recipient receiving the first communication.

(3) A communication made or directed before this Order comes into force is to be treated as a first communication falling within paragraph (1) if it would have fallen within that paragraph had it been made or directed after this Order comes into force.

[8.185]
12 Introductions

(1) If the requirements of paragraph (2) are met, the scheme promotion restriction does not apply to any real time communication which is made with a view to or for the purposes of introducing the recipient to—
  (a) an authorised person who carries on one or more relevant scheme activities in relation to units in unregulated schemes; or
  (b) a person who is exempt, as a result of an exemption order made under section 38(1) of the Act, in relation to one or more relevant scheme activities.

(2) The requirements of this paragraph are that—
  (a) the maker of the communication ("A") is not a close relative of, nor a member of the same group as, the person to whom the introduction is, or is to be, made;
  (b) A does not carry on business in relevant scheme activities in relation to units in unregulated schemes;
  (c) A does not receive from any person other than the recipient any pecuniary reward or other advantage arising out of his making the introduction; and
  (d) it is clear in all the circumstances that the recipient, in his capacity as an investor, is not seeking and has not sought advice from A as to the merits of participating in an unregulated scheme (or, if the client has sought such advice, A has declined to give it, but has recommended that the recipient seek such advice from an authorised person specialising in that kind of investment).

[8.186]

13 Generic promotions

The scheme promotion restriction does not apply to any communication which—

    (a)   does not relate to units of a particular unregulated scheme identified (directly or indirectly) in the communication; and

    (b)   does not identify (directly or indirectly) any person who operates a collective investment scheme or sells units.

[8.187]

14 Investment professionals

(1)   The scheme promotion restriction does not apply to any communication which—

    (a)   is made only to recipients whom the person making the communication believes on reasonable grounds to be investment professionals; or

    (b)   may reasonably be regarded as directed only at such recipients.

(2)   For the purposes of paragraph (1)(b), if all the conditions set out in paragraph (4)(a) to (c) are met in relation to the communication, it is to be regarded as directed only at investment professionals.

(3)   In any other case in which one or more of the conditions set out in paragraph (4)(a) to (c) are met, that fact shall be taken into account in determining whether the communication is directed only at investment professionals (but a communication may still be regarded as so directed even if none of the conditions in paragraph (4) is met).

(4)   The conditions are that—

    (a)   the communication is accompanied by an indication that it is directed at persons having professional experience of participating in unregulated schemes and that the units to which the communication relates are available only to such persons;

    (b)   the communication is accompanied by an indication that persons who do not have professional experience in participating in unregulated schemes should not rely on it;

    (c)   there are in place proper systems and procedures to prevent recipients other than investment professionals from acquiring from the person directing the communication, a close relative of his or a company in the same group, units in the scheme to which the communication relates.

(5)   "Investment professionals" means—

    (a)   an authorised person;

    (b)   a person who is exempt, as a result of an exemption order made under section 38(1) of the Act, in relation to one or more relevant scheme activities;

    (c)   any other person—

        (i)   whose ordinary activities involve him in participating in unregulated schemes for the purposes of a business carried on by him; or

        (ii)   who it is reasonable to expect will so participate for the purposes of a business carried on by him;

    (d)   a government, local authority (whether in the United Kingdom or elsewhere) or an international organisation;

    (e)   a person ("A") who is a director, officer or employee of a person ("B") falling within any of sub-paragraphs (a) to (d), when the communication is made to A in that capacity and where A's responsibilities when acting in that capacity involve him in B's participation in unregulated schemes.

(6)   For the purposes of paragraph (1), a communication is to be treated as made only to or directed only at investment professionals even if it also made to or directed at other persons to whom it may lawfully be communicated.

(7)   In this article—

"government" means the government of the United Kingdom, the Scottish Administration, the Executive Committee of the Northern Ireland Assembly, the National Assembly for Wales and any government of any country or territory outside the United Kingdom;

"international organisation" means any body the members of which comprise—

    (a)   states including the United Kingdom or another EEA State; or

    (b)   bodies whose members comprise states including the United Kingdom or another EEA State.

[8.188]

15 One off non-real time communications and solicited real time communications

(1)   The scheme promotion restriction does not apply to a one off communication which is either a non-real time communication or a solicited real time communication.

(2)   If both the conditions set out in paragraph (3) are met in relation to a communication it is to be regarded as a one off communication. In any other case in which either of those conditions is met, that fact is to be taken into account in determining whether the communication is a one off communication (but a communication may still be regarded as a one off communication even if neither of the conditions in paragraph (3) is met).

(3)   The conditions are that—

    (a)   the communication is made only to one recipient or only to one group of recipients in the expectation that they would engage in any investment activity jointly;

    (b)   the communication is not part of an organised marketing campaign.

[8.189]
[15A   One off unsolicited real time communications

(1)   The scheme promotion restriction does not apply to an unsolicited real time communication if the conditions in paragraph (2) are met.

(2)   The conditions in this paragraph are that—

    (a)   the communication is a one off communication;

    (b)   the communicator believes on reasonable grounds that the recipient understands the risks associated with engaging in the investment activity to which the communication relates;

    (c)   at the time the communication is made, the communicator believes on reasonable grounds that the recipient would expect to be contacted by him in relation to the investment activity to which the communication relates.

(3)   Paragraphs (2) and (3) of article 15 apply in determining whether a communication is a one off communication for the purposes of this article as they apply for the purposes of article 15.]

NOTES

Inserted by the Financial Services and Markets Act 2000 (Financial Promotion) (Amendment) Order 2001, SI 2001/2633, art 3, as from 1 December 2001.

[8.190]
16   Communications required or authorised by enactments

The scheme promotion restriction does not apply to any communication which is required or authorised to be communicated by or under any enactment other than the Act.

[8.191]
17   Persons in the business of placing promotional material

The scheme promotion restriction does not apply to any communication which is made to a person whose business it is to place, or arrange for the placing of, promotional material provided that it is communicated so that he can place or arrange for placing it.

[8.192]
18   Existing participants in an unregulated scheme

The scheme promotion restriction does not apply to any communication which is—

    (a)   a non-real time communication or a solicited real time communication;

    (b)   communicated by the operator of an unregulated scheme; and

    (c)   communicated to persons whom the person making the communication believes on reasonable grounds to be persons who are entitled to units in that scheme.

[8.193]
19   Group companies

The scheme promotion restriction does not apply to any communication made by one body corporate in a group to another body corporate in the same group.

[8.194]
20   Persons in the business of disseminating information

(1)   The scheme promotion restriction does not apply to any communication which is made only to recipients whom the person making the communication believes on reasonable grounds to be persons to whom paragraph (2) applies.

(2)   This paragraph applies to—

    (a)   a person who receives the communication in the course of a business which involves the dissemination through a publication of information concerning investments;

    (b)   a person whilst acting in the capacity of director, officer or employee of a person falling within sub-paragraph (a) being a person whose responsibilities when acting in that capacity involve him in the business referred to in that sub-paragraph;

    (c)   any person to whom the communication may otherwise lawfully be made.

[8.195]
[21   Certified high net worth individuals

(1)   If the requirements of paragraphs (4) and (7) are met, the scheme promotion restriction does not apply to any communication which—

    (a)   is a non-real time communication or a solicited real time communication;

    (b)   is made to an individual whom the person making the communication believes on reasonable grounds to be a certified high net worth individual;

    (c)   relates only to units falling within paragraph (8); and

    (d)   does not invite or induce the recipient to enter into an agreement under the terms of which he can incur a liability or obligation to pay or contribute more than he commits by way of investment.

(2)   "Certified high net worth individual" means an individual who has signed, within the period of twelve months ending with the day on which the communication is made, a statement complying with Part I of the Schedule.

(3)   The validity of a statement signed for the purposes of paragraph (2) is not affected by a defect in the form or wording of the statement, provided that the defect does not alter the statement's meaning and that the words shown in bold type in Part I of the Schedule are so shown in the statement.

(4)   The requirements of this paragraph are that either the communication is accompanied by the giving of a warning in accordance with paragraphs (5) and (6) or, where because of the nature of the communication this is not reasonably practicable,—

    (a)   a warning in accordance with paragraph (5) is given to the recipient orally at the beginning of the communication together with an indication that he will receive the warning in legible form and that, before receipt of that warning, he should consider carefully any decision to participate in a collective investment scheme to which the communication relates; and

    (b)   a warning in accordance with paragraphs (5) and (6) (d) to (h) is sent to the recipient of the communication within two business days of the day on which the communication is made.

(5)   The warning must be in the following terms—

    "Reliance on this promotion for the purpose of buying the units to which the promotion relates may expose an individual to a significant risk of losing all of the property or other assets invested.".

But, where a warning is sent pursuant to paragraph (4)(b), for the words "this promotion" in both places where they occur there must be substituted wording which clearly identifies the promotion which is the subject of the warning.

(6)   The warning must—

    (a)   be given at the beginning of the communication;

    (b)   precede any other written or pictorial matter;

    (c)   be in a font size consistent with the text forming the remainder of the communication;

    (d)   be indelible;

    (e)   be legible;

    (f)   be printed in black, bold type;

    (g)   be surrounded by a black border which does not interfere with the text of the warning; and

    (h)   not be hidden, obscured or interrupted by any other written or pictorial matter.

(7)   The requirements of this paragraph are that the communication is accompanied by an indication—

    (a)   that it is exempt from the restriction on the promotion of unregulated schemes (in section 238 of the Act) on the grounds that the communication is made to a certified high net worth individual;

    (b)   of the requirements that must be met for an individual to qualify as a certified high net worth individual;

    (c)   that any individual who is in any doubt about the units to which the communication relates should consult an authorised person specialising in advising in participation in unregulated schemes.

(8)   A unit falls within this paragraph if it is in an unregulated scheme which invests wholly or predominantly in the shares in or debentures of one or more unlisted companies.

(9)   "Business day" means any day except a Saturday, a Sunday, Christmas Day, Good Friday or a day which is a bank holiday under the Banking and Financial Dealings Act 1971 in any part of the United Kingdom.

(10)   "Unlisted company" has the meaning given in the Financial Services and Markets Act 2000 (Financial Promotion) Order 2001.]

NOTES

Substituted by the Financial Services and Markets Act 2000 (Financial Promotion and Promotion of Collective Investment Schemes) (Miscellaneous Amendments) Order 2005, SI 2005/270, art 3, Sch 2, para 1, as from 3 March 2005, subject to transitional provisions in art 5 of that Order in relation to an individual who is a certified high net worth individual within the meaning of art 21 of the CIS Exemptions Order immediately before that date.

[8.196]

22 High net worth companies, unincorporated associations etc

(1)   The scheme promotion restriction does not apply to any communication which—

    (a)   is made only to recipients whom the person making the communication believes on reasonable grounds to be persons to whom paragraph (2) applies; or

    (b)   may reasonably be regarded as directed only at persons to whom paragraph (2) applies.

(2)   This paragraph applies to—

[(a) any body corporate which has, or which is a member of the same group as an undertaking which has, a called-up share capital or net assets of not less than—
  (i) if the body corporate has more than 20 members or is a subsidiary undertaking of an undertaking which has more than 20 members, £500,000;
  (ii) otherwise, £5 million;]
(b) any unincorporated association or partnership which has net assets of not less than £5 million;
(c) the trustee of a high value trust;
(d) any person ("A") whilst acting in the capacity of director, officer or employee of a person ("B") falling within any of sub-paragraphs (a) to (c), where A's responsibilities, when acting in that capacity, involve him in B's participation in unregulated schemes;
(e) any person to whom the communication might otherwise lawfully be made.

(3) For the purposes of paragraph (1)(b)—
(a) if all the conditions set out in paragraph (4)(a) to (c) are met in relation to the communication, it is to be regarded as directed at persons to whom paragraph (2) applies;
(b) in any other case in which one or more of those conditions are met, that fact is to be taken into account in determining whether the communication is directed at persons to whom paragraph (2) applies (but a communication may still be regarded as so directed even if none of the conditions in paragraph (4) is met).

(4) The conditions are that—
(a) the communication includes an indication of the description of persons to whom it is directed and an indication of the fact that the units to which it relates are available only to such persons;
(b) the communication includes an indication that persons of any other description should not rely upon it;
(c) there are in place proper systems and procedures to prevent recipients other than persons to whom paragraph (2) applies from acquiring from the person directing the communication, a close relative of his or a company in the same group, units in the scheme to which the communication relates.

(5) In this article—
"called-up share capital" has the meaning given in [section 547 of the Companies Act 2006];
"high value trust" means a trust where the aggregate value of the cash and investments which form part of the trust's assets (before deducing the amount of its liabilities)—
(a) is £10 million or more; or
(b) has been £10 million or more at any time during the year immediately preceding the date on which communication in question was first made or directed;
"net assets" has the meaning given in [section 831 of the Companies Act 2006].

NOTES

Para (2): sub-para (a) substituted by the Financial Services and Markets Act 2000 (Financial Promotion and Miscellaneous Amendments) Order 2002, SI 2002/1310, art 3(1), (3), as from 5 June 2002.

Para (5): words in square brackets in definitions "called-up share capital" and "net assets" substituted by the Companies Act 2006 (Consequential Amendments and Transitional Provisions) Order 2011, SI 2011/1265, art 14(1), 3), as from 12 May 2011.

[8.197]
23 Sophisticated investors
(1) "Certified sophisticated investor" means a person—
(a) who has a current certificate in writing or other legible form signed by an authorised person to the effect that he is sufficiently knowledgeable to understand the risks associated with participating in unregulated schemes; and
(b) who has signed, within the period of twelve months ending with the day on which the communication is made, a statement in the following terms—

"I make this statement so that I can receive promotions which are exempt from the restriction on promotion of unregulated schemes in the Financial Services and Markets Act 2000. The exemption relates to certified sophisticated investors and I declare that I qualify as such. I accept that the schemes to which the promotions will relate are not authorised or recognised for the purposes of that Act. I am aware that it is open to me to seek advice from an authorised person who specialises in advising on this kind of investment".

[(1A) The validity of a statement signed in accordance with paragraph (1)(b) is not affected by a defect in the wording of the statement, provided that the defect does not alter the statement's meaning.]
(2) If the requirements of paragraph (3) are met, the scheme promotion restriction does not apply to any communication which—
(a) is made to a certified sophisticated investor; and

(b)   does not invite or induce the recipient to participate in an unregulated scheme operated by the person who has signed the certificate referred to in paragraph (1)(a) or to acquire units from that person.

(3)   The requirements of this paragraph are that the communication is accompanied by an indication—

    (a)   that it is exempt from the scheme promotion restriction (in section 238 of the Financial Services and Markets Act 2000) on the communication of invitations or inducements to participate in unregulated schemes on the ground that it is made to a certified sophisticated investor;

    (b)   of the requirements that must be met for a person to qualify as a certified sophisticated investor;

    (c)   that buying the units to which the communication relates may expose the individual to a significant risk of losing all of the property invested;

    (d)   that any individual who is in any doubt about the investment to which the invitation or inducement relates should consult an authorised person specialising in advising on investments of the kind in question.

(4)   For the purposes of paragraph (1)(a), a certificate is current if it is signed and dated not more than three years before the date on which the communication is made.

NOTES

Para (1A): inserted by the Financial Services and Markets Act 2000 (Financial Promotion and Promotion of Collective Investment Schemes) (Miscellaneous Amendments) Order 2005, SI 2005/270, art 3, Sch 2, para 2, as from 3 March 2005.

[8.198]
[23A   Self-certified sophisticated investors

(1)   "Self-certified sophisticated investor" means an individual who has signed, within the period of twelve months ending with the day on which the communication is made, a statement complying with Part II of the Schedule.

(2)   The validity of a statement signed for the purposes of paragraph (1) is not affected by a defect in the form or wording of the statement, provided that the defect does not alter the statement's meaning and that the words shown in bold type in Part II of the Schedule are so shown in the statement.

(3)   If the requirements of paragraphs (4) and (7) are met, the scheme promotion restriction does not apply to any communication which—

    (a)   is made to an individual whom the person making the communication believes on reasonable grounds to be a self-certified sophisticated investor;

    (b)   relates only to units falling within paragraph (8); and

    (c)   does not invite or induce the recipient to enter into an agreement under the terms of which he can incur a liability or obligation to pay or contribute more than he commits by way of investment.

(4)   The requirements of this paragraph are—

    (a)   . . .

    (b)   . . . that either the communication is accompanied by the giving of a warning in accordance with paragraphs (5) and (6) or, where because of the nature of the communication this is not reasonably practicable,—

       (i)   a warning in accordance with paragraph (5) is given to the recipient orally at the beginning of the communication together with an indication that he will receive the warning in legible form and that, before receipt of that warning, he should consider carefully any decision to participate in a collective investment scheme to which the communication relates; and

       (ii)   a warning in accordance with paragraphs (5) and (6) (d) to (h) is sent to the recipient of the communication within two business days of the day on which the communication is made.

(5)   The warning must be in the following terms—

"Reliance on this promotion for the purpose of buying [the] units to which the promotion relates may expose an individual to a significant risk of losing all of the property or other assets invested.".

But, where a warning is sent pursuant to paragraph (4)(b), for the words "this promotion" in both places where they occur there must be substituted wording which clearly identifies the promotion which is the subject of the warning.

(6)   The warning must—

    (a)   be given at the beginning of the communication;

    (b)   precede any other written or pictorial matter;

    (c)   be in a font size consistent with the text forming the remainder of the communication;

    (d)   be indelible;

    (e)   be legible;

   (f)   be printed in black, bold type;

   (g)   be surrounded by a black border which does not interfere with the text of the warning; and

   (h)   not be hidden, obscured or interrupted by any other written or pictorial matter.

(7) The requirements of this paragraph are that the communication is accompanied by an indication—

   (a)   that it is exempt from the scheme promotion restriction (in section 238 of the Act) on the communication of invitations or inducements to participate in unregulated schemes on the ground that it is made to a self-certified sophisticated investor;

   (b)   of the requirements that must be met for an individual to qualify as a self-certified sophisticated investor;

   (c)   that any individual who is in any doubt about the investment to which the invitation or inducement relates should consult an authorised person specialising in advising on investments of the kind in question.

(8) A unit falls within this paragraph if it is in an unregulated scheme which invests wholly or predominantly in the shares in or debentures of one or more an unlisted companies.

(9) "Business day" means any day except a Saturday, a Sunday, Christmas Day, Good Friday or a day which is a bank holiday under the Banking and Financial Dealings Act 1971 in any part of the United Kingdom.

(10) "Unlisted company" has the meaning given in the Financial Services and Markets Act 2000 (Financial Promotion) Order 2001.]

NOTES

Inserted by the Financial Services and Markets Act 2000 (Financial Promotion and Promotion of Collective Investment Schemes) (Miscellaneous Amendments) Order 2005, SI 2005/270, art 3, Sch 2, para 3, as from 3 March 2005.

Para (4): words omitted revoked by the Financial Services and Markets Act 2000 (Promotion of Collective Investment Schemes) (Exemptions) (Amendment) Order 2005, SI 2005/1532, art 2(1), (2)(a), (b), as from 1 July 2005.

Para (5): word in square brackets substituted by SI 2005/1532, art 2(1), (2)(c), as from 1 July 2005.

[8.199]

24 Associations of high net worth or sophisticated investors

The scheme promotion restriction does not apply to any non-real time communication or solicited real time communication which—

   (a)   is made to an association[, or to a member of an association,] the membership of which the person making the communication believes on reasonable grounds comprises wholly or predominantly persons who are—

      (i)   certified high net worth individuals within the meaning of article 21;

      (ii) high net worth persons falling within article 22(2)(a) to (d);

      (iii) certified sophisticated investors within the meaning of article 23 [or 23A]; and

   (b)   does not invite or induce the recipient to enter into an agreement under the terms of which he can incur a liability or obligation to pay or contribute more than he commits by way of investment.

NOTES

Words in square brackets inserted by the Financial Services and Markets Act 2000 (Promotion of Collective Investment Schemes) (Exemptions) (Amendment) Order 2005, SI 2005/1532, art 2(1), (3), as from 1 July 2005.

[8.200]

25 Settlors, trustees and personal representatives

The scheme promotion restriction does not apply to any communication which is made—

   (a)   by an authorised person when acting as a settlor or grantor of a trust, a trustee or a personal representative;

   (b)   to a trustee of the trust, a fellow trustee or a fellow personal representative (as the case may be),

if the communication is made for the purposes of the trust or estate.

[8.201]

26 Beneficiaries of trust, will or intestacy

The scheme promotion restriction does not apply to any communication which is made—

   (a)   by an authorised person when acting as a settlor of a trust, trustee or personal representative to a beneficiary under the trust, will or intestacy; or

   (b)   by an authorised person who is a beneficiary under a trust, will or intestacy to another beneficiary under the same trust, will or intestacy,

if the communication relates to the management or distribution of that trust fund or estate.

[8.202]

27 Remedy following report by Parliamentary Commissioner for Administration

The scheme promotion restriction does not apply to any communication made or directed by a person for the purpose of enabling any injustice, stated by the Parliamentary Commissioner for

Administration in a report under section 10 of the Parliamentary Commissioner Act 1967 to have occurred, to be remedied with respect to the recipient.

[8.203]
28   Persons placing promotional material in particular publications
The scheme promotion restriction does not apply to any communication received by a person who receives the publication in which the communication is contained because he has himself placed an advertisement in that publication.

[8.204]
[29   Open-ended investment companies authorised in Northern Ireland
(1)   The scheme promotion restriction does not apply in relation to a scheme constituted by an authorised Northern Ireland open-ended investment company.
(2)   In this article—
   (a)   "authorised Northern Ireland open-ended investment company" means a body incorporated by virtue of regulations made under section 1 of the Open-Ended Investment Companies Act (Northern Ireland) 2002 in respect of which an authorisation order is in force; and
   (b)   "authorisation order" means an order made under (or having effect as made under) any provision of those regulations which is made by virtue of section 1(2)(1) of that Act (provision corresponding to Chapter 3 of Part 17 of the Act).]

NOTES
   Added by the Financial Services and Markets Act 2000 (Promotion of Collective Investment Schemes etc) (Exemptions) (Amendment) Order 2003, SI 2003/2067, art 2(1), (3), as from 5 September 2003.

[8.205]
[30   EEA management companies
The scheme promotion restriction does not apply to any communication which is made by an EEA firm which—
   (a)   falls within paragraph 5(f) of Schedule 3 to the Act (management companies of UCITS), and
   (b)   qualifies for authorisation by virtue of paragraph 12 of that Schedule,
unless the Authority has given (and not withdrawn) a notice to that firm under paragraph 15A(2) of that Schedule [(notice indicating the existence of grounds for refusal of an application for authorisation)].]

NOTES
   Added by the Financial Services and Markets Act 2000 (Promotion of Collective Investment Schemes etc) (Exemptions) (Amendment) Order 2003, SI 2003/2067, art 2(1), (4), as from 13 February 2004.
   Words in square brackets substituted by the Undertakings for Collective Investment in Transferable Securities Regulations 2011, SI 2011/1613, reg 16, Schedule, para 2(1), (3), as from 1 July 2011.

[SCHEDULE
STATEMENTS FOR CERTIFIED HIGH NET WORTH INDIVIDUALS AND
SELF-CERTIFIED SOPHISTICATED INVESTORS
Articles 21 and 23A

PART I
STATEMENT FOR CERTIFIED HIGH NET WORTH INDIVIDUALS

[8.206]
1. The statement to be signed for the purposes of article 21(2) (definition of high net worth individual) must be in the following form and contain the following content—

"STATEMENT FOR CERTIFIED HIGH NET WORTH INDIVIDUAL
   I declare that I am a certified high net worth individual for the purposes of the Financial Services and Markets Act 2000 (Promotion of Collective Investment Schemes) (Exemptions) Order 2001.
   I understand that this means—
   (a)   I can receive promotions, made by a person who is authorised by the Financial Services Authority, which relate to units in unregulated collective investment schemes that invest wholly or predominantly in unlisted companies;
   (b)   the schemes to which the promotions will relate are not authorised or recognised for the purposes of the Financial Services and Markets Act 2000.
   I am a certified high net worth individual because **at least one of the following applies**—
   (a)   I had, during the financial year immediately preceding the date below, an annual income to the value of £100,000 or more;

(b)   I held, throughout the financial year immediately preceding the date below, net assets to the value of £250,000 or more. Net assets for these purposes do not include—

   (i)   the property which is my primary residence or any loan secured on that residence;

   (ii) any rights of mine under a qualifying contract of insurance within the meaning of the Financial Services and Markets Act 2000 (Regulated Activities) Order 2001; or

   (iii) any benefits (in the form of pensions or otherwise) which are payable on the termination of my service or on my death or retirement and to which I am (or my dependants are), or may be, entitled.

I accept that I can lose my property and other assets from making investment decisions based on financial promotions.

I am aware that it is open to me to seek advice from someone who specialises in advising on unregulated collective investment schemes.

Signature . . . .

Date . . . ."]

NOTES

Added by the Financial Services and Markets Act 2000 (Financial Promotion and Promotion of Collective Investment Schemes) (Miscellaneous Amendments) Order 2005, SI 2005/270, art 3, Sch 2, para 4, as from 3 March 2005.

[PART II
STATEMENT FOR SELF-CERTIFIED SOPHISTICATED INVESTORS

[8.207]

2. The statement to be signed for the purposes of article 23A(1) (definition of self-certified sophisticated investor) must be in the following form and contain the following content—

"STATEMENT FOR SELF-CERTIFIED SOPHISTICATED INVESTOR

I declare that I am a self-certified sophisticated investor for the purposes of the Financial Services and Markets Act 2000 (Promotion of Collective Investment Schemes) (Exemptions) Order 2001.

I understand that this means—

(a)   I can receive promotions, made by a person who is authorised by the Financial Services Authority, which relate to units in unregulated collective investment schemes that invest wholly or predominantly in unlisted companies;

(b)   the schemes to which the promotions will relate are not authorised or recognised for the purposes of the Financial Services and Markets Act 2000.

I am a self-certified sophisticated investor because **at least one of the following applies**—

(a)   I am a member of a network or syndicate of business angels and have been so for at least the last six months prior to the date below;

(b)   I have made more than one investment in an unlisted company in the two years prior to the date below;

(c)   I am working, or have worked in the two years prior to the date below, in a professional capacity in the private equity sector, or in the provision of finance for small and medium enterprises;

(d)   I am currently, or have been in the two years prior to the date below, a director of a company with an annual turnover of at least £1 million.

I accept that I can lose my property and other assets from making investment decisions based on financial promotions.

I am aware that it is open to me to seek advice from someone who specialises in advising on unregulated collective investment schemes.

Signature . . . .

Date . . . ."]

NOTES

Added as noted to Pt I at **[7.228]**.

FINANCIAL SERVICES AND MARKETS ACT 2000 (COLLECTIVE INVESTMENT SCHEMES) ORDER 2001

(SI 2001/1062)

NOTES

Made: 19 March 2001.

Authority: Financial Services and Markets Act 2000, s 235(5).

Commencement: 1 December 2001.

This Order is reproduced as amended by: the Financial Services and Markets Act 2000 (Miscellaneous Provisions) Order 2001, SI 2001/3650; the Financial Services and Markets Act 2000 (Collective Investment Schemes) (Amendment) Order 2005, SI 2005/57; the Civil Partnership Act 2004 (Amendments to Subordinate Legislation) Order 2005, SI 2005/2114; the Financial Services and Markets Act 2000 (Regulated Activities) (Amendment) Order 2006, SI 2006/1969; the Financial Services and Markets Act 2000 (Regulated Activities) (Amendment No 3) Order 2006, SI 2006/3384; the Financial Services and Markets Act 2000 (Collective Investment Schemes) (Amendment) Order 2007, SI 2007/800; the Financial Services and Markets Act 2000 (Collective Investment Schemes) (Amendment) Order 2008, SI 2008/1641; the Financial Services and Markets Act 2000 (Regulated Activities) (Amendment) Order 2010, SI 2010/86; the Timeshare, Holiday Products, Resale and Exchange Contracts Regulations 2010, SI 2010/2960.

[8.208]
1   Citation and commencement
This Order may be cited as the Financial Services and Markets Act 2000 (Collective Investment Schemes) Order 2001 and comes into force on the day on which section 19 of the Act comes into force.

[8.209]
2   Interpretation
In this Order—
   "the Act" means the Financial Services and Markets Act 2000;
   "the 1988 Act" means the Income and Corporation Taxes Act 1988;
   "authorised unit trust scheme" has the meaning given by section 237(3) of the Act;
   "contract of insurance" and "contract of long term insurance" have the meaning given by
      article 3(1) of the Regulated Activities Order;
   "feeder fund" means an authorised unit trust scheme the sole object of which is investment in
      units of a single authorised unit trust scheme or shares in a single open-ended investment
      company;
   "franchise arrangements" means arrangements under which a person earns profits or income by
      exploiting a right conferred by the arrangements to use a trade mark or design or other
      intellectual property or the good-will attached to it;
   "funeral plan contract" has the meaning given by article 59 of the Regulated Activities Order;
   "individual pension account" has the meaning given by regulation 4 of the Personal Pension
      Schemes   (Restriction   on   Discretion   to   Approve)   (Permitted   Investments)
      Regulations 2001;
   ["long-term holiday product contract" has the meaning given by regulation 8 of the Timeshare,
      Holiday Products, Resale and Exchange Contracts Regulations 2010;]
      . . .
   ["occupational pension scheme" has the meaning given by section 1 of the Pension Schemes
      Act 1993 but with paragraph (b) of the definition omitted;]
   "the operator" has the meaning given by section 237(2) of the Act;
   ["personal pension scheme" means a scheme or arrangement which is not an occupational
      pension scheme and which is comprised in one or more instruments or agreements, having
      or capable of having effect so as to provide benefits to or in respect of people—
      (a)   on retirement,
      (b)   on having reached a particular age, or
      (c)   on termination of service in an employment;]
   "personal pension unit trust" means a personal pension scheme which is an authorised unit trust
      scheme of a kind mentioned in Part I of Schedule 1 to the Personal Pension Schemes
      (Appropriate Schemes) Regulations 1997;
   "recognised scheme" has the meaning given by section 237(3) of the Act;
   "the Regulated Activities Order" means the Financial Services and Markets Act 2000 (Regulated
      Activities) Order 2001;
   ["timeshare contract" has the meaning given by regulation 7 of the Timeshare, Holiday Products,
      Resale and Exchange Contracts Regulations 2010].

NOTES
Definition "long-term holiday product contract" inserted, and definition "timeshare rights" substituted by the Timeshare, Holiday Products, Resale and Exchange Contracts Regulations 2010, SI 2010/2960, reg 36(3), Sch 6, para 8(1), (2), as from 23 February 2011.
Original (joint) definition "occupational pension scheme" and "personal pension scheme" (omitted) revoked, and new (separate) definitions "occupational pension scheme" and "personal pension scheme" inserted, by the Financial Services and Markets Act 2000 (Regulated Activities) (Amendment) Order 2006, SI 2006/1969, art 8, as from 6 April 2007.

[8.210]
3   Arrangements not amounting to a collective investment scheme
Arrangements of the kind specified by the Schedule to this Order do not amount to a collective investment scheme.

SCHEDULE
ARRANGEMENTS NOT AMOUNTING TO A COLLECTIVE INVESTMENT SCHEME
Article 3

[8.211]
1 Individual investment management arrangements

Arrangements do not amount to a collective investment scheme if—
- (a) the property to which the arrangements relate (other than cash awaiting investment) consists of investments of one or more of the following kinds:
  - (i) an investment of the kind specified by any of articles 76 to 80 of the Regulated Activities Order;
  - (ii) an investment of the kind specified by article 81 of that Order (units in a collective investment scheme) so far as relating to authorised unit trust schemes, recognised schemes or shares in an open-ended investment company; or
  - (iii) a contract of long term insurance;
- (b) each participant is entitled to a part of that property and to withdraw that part at any time; and
- (c) the arrangements do not have the characteristics mentioned in section 235(3)(a) of the Act and have those mentioned in section 235(3)(b) only because the parts of the property to which different participants are entitled are not bought and sold separately except where a person becomes or ceases to be a participant.

2 Enterprise initiative schemes

(1) Arrangements do not amount to a collective investment scheme if—
- (a) the property to which the arrangements relate (other than cash awaiting investment) consists of shares;
- (b) the arrangements constitute a complying fund;
- (c) each participant is entitled to a part of the property to which the arrangements relate and—
  - (i) to the extent that the property to which he is entitled comprises relevant shares of a class which are admitted to official listing in an EEA State or to dealings on a recognised investment exchange, he is entitled to withdraw it at any time after the end of the period of five years beginning with the date on which the shares in question were issued;
  - (ii) to the extent that the property to which he is entitled comprises other relevant shares, he is entitled to withdraw it at any time after the end of the period of seven years beginning with the date on which the shares in question were issued;
  - (iii) to the extent that the property to which he is entitled comprises shares other than relevant shares, he is entitled to withdraw it at any time after the end of the period of six months beginning with the date on which the shares in question ceased to be relevant shares; and
  - (iv) to the extent that the property comprises cash which the operator has agreed (conditionally or unconditionally) to apply in subscribing for shares, he is entitled to withdraw it at any time; and
- (d) the arrangements would meet the conditions described in paragraph 1(c) were it not for the fact that the operator is entitled to exercise all or any of the rights conferred by shares included in the property to which the arrangements relate.

(2) In sub-paragraph (1)—
- (a) "shares" means investments of the kind specified by article 76 of the Regulated Activities Order (shares etc) and shares are to be regarded as relevant shares if and so long as they are shares in respect of which neither—
  - (i) a claim for relief made in accordance with section 306 of the 1988 Act has been disallowed; nor
  - (ii) an assessment has been made pursuant to section 307 of the 1988 Act withdrawing or refusing relief by reason of the body corporate in which the shares are held having ceased to be a body corporate which is a qualifying company for the purposes of that Act;
- (b) "complying fund" means arrangements which provide that—
  - (i) the operator will, so far as is practicable, make investments each of which, subject to each participant's individual circumstances, qualify for relief by virtue of Chapter III of Part VII of the 1988 Act; and
  - (ii) the minimum contribution to the arrangements which each participant must make is not less than £2000.

3 Pure deposit based schemes

Arrangements do not amount to a collective investment scheme if the whole amount of each participant's contribution is a deposit which is accepted by an authorised person with permission to carry on an activity of the kind specified by article 5 of the Regulated Activities Order (accepting deposits) or a person who is an exempt person in relation to such an activity.

4 Schemes not operated by way of business

Arrangements do not amount to a collective investment scheme if they are operated otherwise than by way of business.

5 Debt issues

(1)   Arrangements do not amount to a collective investment scheme if they are arrangements under which the rights or interests of participants are, except as provided in sub-paragraph (2), represented by investments of one, and only one, of the following descriptions:

(a)   investments of the kind specified by article 77 [or 77A] of the Regulated Activities Order [(debt instruments)] which are—

   (i)   issued by a single body corporate other than an open-ended investment company; or

   (ii)   issued by a single issuer who is not a body corporate and which are guaranteed by the government of the United Kingdom, the Scottish Administration, the Executive Committee of the Northern Ireland Assembly, the National Assembly for Wales or the government of any country or territory outside the United Kingdom;

   and which are not convertible into or exchangeable for investments of any other description;

(b)   investments falling within sub-paragraph (a)(i) or (ii) ("the former investments") which are convertible into or exchangeable for investments of the kind specified by article 76 of the Regulated Activities Order ("the latter investments") provided that the latter investments are issued by the same person who issued the former investments or are issued by a single other issuer;

(c)   investments of the kind specified by article 78 of the Regulated Activities Order (government and public securities) which are issued by a single issuer; or

(d)   investments of the kind specified by article 79 of the Regulated Activities Order (instruments giving entitlement to investments) which are issued otherwise than by an open-ended investment company and which confer rights in respect of investments, issued by the same issuer, of the kind specified by article 76 of that Order or within any of paragraphs (a) to (c).

(2)   Arrangements which would otherwise not amount to a collective investment scheme by virtue of the provisions of sub-paragraph (1) are not to be regarded as amounting to such a scheme by reason only that one or more of the participants ("the counterparty") is a person—

(a)   whose ordinary business involves him in carrying on activities of the kind specified by any of articles 14 (dealing in investments as principal), 21 (dealing in investments as agent), 25 (arranging deals in investments), [25D (operating a multilateral trading facility),] 37 (managing investments), 40 (safeguarding and administering investments), 45 (sending dematerialised instructions), 51 (establishing etc a collective investment scheme), 52 (establishing etc a stakeholder pension scheme) and 53 (advising on investments) or, so far as relevant to any of those articles, article 64 of the Regulated Activities Order (agreeing to carry on specified kinds of activities), or would do so apart from any exclusion from any of those articles made by that Order; and

(b)   whose rights or interests in the arrangements are or include rights or interests under a swap arrangement.

(3)   In sub-paragraph (2), "swap arrangement" means an arrangement the purpose of which is to facilitate the making of payments to participants whether in a particular amount or currency or at a particular time or rate of interest or all or any combination of those things, being an arrangement under which the counterparty—

(a)   is entitled to receive amounts, whether representing principal or interest, payable in respect of any property subject to the arrangements or sums determined by reference to such amounts; and

(b)   makes payments, whether or not of the same amount or in the same currency as the amounts or sums referred to in paragraph (a), which are calculated in accordance with an agreed formula by reference to those amounts or sums.

6 Common accounts

Arrangements do not amount to a collective investment scheme if—

(a)   they are arrangements under which the rights or interests of participants are rights to or interests in money held in a common account; and

(b)   that money is held in the account on the understanding that an amount representing the contribution of each participant is to be applied—

   (i)   in making payments to him;

   (ii)   in satisfaction of sums owed by him; or

   (iii) in the acquisition of property for him or the provision of services to him.

[7 Certain funds relating to leasehold property

Arrangements do not amount to a collective investment scheme if the rights or interests of the participants are rights or interests—

(a) in a fund which is a trust fund within the meaning of section 42(1) of the Landlord and Tenant Act 1987 or which would be such a trust fund if the landlord were not an exempt landlord within the meaning of section 58(1) of that Act; or

(b) in money held in a designated account by the scheme administrator under a tenancy deposit scheme within the meaning of section 212(2) of the Housing Act 2004.]

8 Certain employee share schemes

(1) Arrangements do not amount to a collective investment scheme if they are operated by a person ("A"), a member of the same group as A or a relevant trustee for the purpose of enabling or facilitating—

(a) transactions in shares in, or debentures issued by, A between, or for the benefit of, any of the persons mentioned in sub-paragraph (2); or

(b) the holding of such shares or debentures by, or for the benefit of, any such persons.

(2) The persons referred to in sub-paragraph (1) are—

(a) the bona fide employees or former employees of A or of another member of the same group; or

(b) the wives, husbands, widows, widowers, [civil partners, surviving civil partners,] or children or step-children under the age of eighteen of such employees or former employees.

(3) For the purposes of this paragraph—

(a) "shares" and "debentures" have the meaning given by article 71(6)(a) of the Regulated Activities Order:

(b) "relevant trustee" means a person who, in pursuance of the arrangements, holds shares in or debentures issued by A.

[9 Schemes entered into for commercial purposes wholly or mainly related to existing business

(1) Arrangements first entered into before 15th July 2008 do not amount to a collective investment scheme if—

(a) by virtue of paragraph 9 of the Schedule to the Financial Services and Markets Act 2000 (Collective Investment Schemes) Order 2001 as it had effect immediately before 15th July 2008 they did not then do so provided that all participants are permitted participants; or

(b) in the case of arrangements which amounted to a collective investment scheme immediately before 15th July 2008—

(i) all participants are permitted participants; and

(ii) at any time each person which is at that time a participant [agrees in writing in respect of the remaining life of the arrangements] that the arrangements do not amount to a collective investment scheme.

(2) Arrangements first entered into on or after 15th July 2008 do not amount to a collective investment scheme if all participants are permitted participants.

(3) The exclusion in sub-paragraph (2) shall not apply to arrangements falling within that sub-paragraph if [at any time each person which is at that time a permitted participant agrees in writing in respect of the life of the arrangements that the arrangements amount to a collective investment scheme].

(4) If at any time a person which is not a permitted participant participates in arrangements then for as long as that person is a participant but not a permitted participant the exclusion in sub-paragraph (1) or, as the case may be, sub-paragraph (2) shall not apply to the arrangements.

(5) For the purposes of this paragraph—

"permitted participant" means a participant which—

(a) at the time of entering into the arrangements carries on a business which is not a specified business (the "first business") but which may be in addition to any specified business carried on by that participant at that time and—

(i) does not carry on that first business solely by virtue of being—

(a) a participant in the arrangements; or

(b) a member, partner or trust beneficiary of a body corporate, unincorporated association, partnership or trust which is itself a participant in the arrangements; and

(ii) enters into the arrangements for commercial purposes wholly or mainly related to the first business; or

(b) is a body corporate, unincorporated association[,] partnership, or trustee of a trust (unless that trustee is an individual) which—

(i) does not carry on a specified business; and

(ii) only has as its members, partners or trust beneficiaries persons which themselves qualify, or would qualify if they participated in the arrangements, as participants of the kind mentioned in paragraph (a) of this paragraph; and "specified business" means the business of engaging in any regulated activity of the kind specified by any of articles 14, 21, 25, 25D, 37, 40, 45, 51 to 53 or, so far as relevant to any of those articles, article 64 of the Regulated Activities Order.

(6) For the purposes of this paragraph, neither the entry into arrangements by any person as a further participant nor the exit from arrangements by any participant shall in itself constitute the creation of new arrangements.

[(7) An agreement made in respect of any arrangements in accordance with the provisions of sub-paragraph (1)(b)(ii) or sub-paragraph (3) is not affected by—

    (a)   the entry into such arrangements by any person as a further participant;

    (b)   the exit from such arrangements of any participant;

    (c)   any later agreement in writing or otherwise under which, contrary to the earlier agreement, such arrangements do or, as the case may be, do not amount to a collective investment scheme.]]

10   Group schemes

Arrangements do not amount to a collective investment scheme if each of the participants is a body corporate in the same group as the operator.

11   Franchise arrangements

Franchise arrangements do not amount to a collective investment scheme.

12   Trading schemes

Arrangements do not amount to a collective investment scheme if—

    (a)   the purpose of the arrangements is that participants should receive, by way of reward, payments or other benefits in respect of the introduction by any person of other persons who become participants;

    (b)   the arrangements are such that the payments or other benefits referred to in paragraph (a) are to be wholly or mainly funded out of the contributions of other participants; and

    (c)   the only reason why the arrangements have either or both of the characteristics mentioned in section 235(3) of the Act is because, pending their being used to fund those payments or other benefits, contributions of participants are managed as a whole by or on behalf of the operator of the scheme.

[13   Timeshare and long-term holiday product schemes

Arrangements do not amount to a collective investment scheme if the rights or interests of the participants are rights under a timeshare contract or a long-term holiday product contract.]

14   Other schemes relating to use or enjoyment of property

Arrangements do not amount to a collective investment scheme if—

    (a)   the predominant purpose of the arrangements is to enable the participants to share in the use or enjoyment of property or to make its use or enjoyment available gratuitously to others; and

    (b)   the property to which the arrangements relate does not consist of the currency of any country or territory and does not consist of or include any investment of the kind specified by Part III of the Regulated Activities Order or which would be of such a kind apart from any exclusion made by that Part of the Order.

15   Schemes involving the issue of certificates representing investments

Arrangements do not amount to a collective investment scheme if the rights or interests of the participants are investments of the kind specified by article 80 of the Regulated Activities Order (certificates representing certain securities).

16   Clearing services

Arrangements do not amount to a collective investment scheme if their purpose is the provision of clearing services and they are operated by an authorised person, a recognised clearing house or a recognised investment exchange.

17   Contracts of insurance

A contract of insurance does not amount to a collective investment scheme.

[18   Funeral plan contracts

Arrangements do not amount to a collective investment scheme if they consist of, or are made pursuant to—

    (a)   a funeral plan contract; or

    (b)   a contract which would be a funeral plan contract but for—

       (i)   the proviso to article 59(2) of the Regulated Activities Order, or

       (ii)   the exclusion in article 60 of that Order.]

19   Individual pension accounts

An individual pension account does not amount to a collective investment scheme.

20   Occupational and personal pension schemes

(1)   An occupational pension scheme does not amount to a collective investment scheme.

(2)   A personal pension scheme does not amount to a collective investment scheme.

(3)   Sub-paragraph (2) does not extend to a personal pension unit trust which is constituted as a feeder fund or comprises feeder funds.

[21   Bodies corporate etc

(1)   Subject to sub-paragraph (2), no body incorporated under the law of, or any part of, the United Kingdom relating to building societies or industrial and provident societies or registered under any such law relating to friendly societies, and no other body corporate other than an open-ended investment company, amounts to a collective investment scheme.

(2)   Sub-paragraph (1) does not apply to any body incorporated as a limited liability partnership.]

NOTES

Para 5: words in first pair of square brackets in sub-para (1)(a) inserted, and words in second pair of square brackets in that sub-para substituted, by the Financial Services and Markets Act 2000 (Regulated Activities) (Amendment) Order 2010, SI 2010/86, art 3, as from 24 February 2010; words in square brackets in sub-para (2)(a) inserted by the Financial Services and Markets Act 2000 (Regulated Activities) (Amendment No 3) Order 2006, SI 2006/3384, art 36(1), (2), as from 1 November 2007.

Para 7: substituted by the Financial Services and Markets Act 2000 (Collective Investment Schemes) (Amendment) Order 2007, SI 2007/800, art 2, as from 6 April 2007.

Para 8: words in square brackets in sub-para (2)(b) inserted by the Civil Partnership Act 2004 (Amendments to Subordinate Legislation) Order 2005, SI 2005/2114, art 2(16), Sch 16, Pt 1, para 3, as from 5 December 2005.

Para 9: substituted by the Financial Services and Markets Act 2000 (Collective Investment Schemes) (Amendment) Order 2008, SI 2008/1641, art 2, as from 15 July 2008 (as amended by the Financial Services and Markets Act 2000 (Collective Investment Schemes) (Amendment) (No 2) Order 2008, SI 2008/1813, art 2, as from 14 July 2008).

Para 13: substituted by the Timeshare, Holiday Products, Resale and Exchange Contracts Regulations 2010, SI 2010/2960, reg 36(3), Sch 6, para 8(3), as from 23 February 2011.

Paras 18, 21: substituted by SI 2001/3650, art 2(1), (3), (4), as from 1 December 2001.

Step-children, etc: as to the meaning of this and related expressions, see the Civil Partnership Act 2004, s 246 (as applied to this Order by the Civil Partnership Act 2004 (Relationships Arising Through Civil Partnership) Order 2005, SI 2005/3137, art 3, Schedule).

FINANCIAL SERVICES AND MARKETS ACT 2000 (CARRYING ON REGULATED ACTIVITIES BY WAY OF BUSINESS) ORDER 2001

(SI 2001/1177)

NOTES

Made: 26 March 2001.

Authority: Financial Services and Markets Act 2000, ss 419, 428(3).

Commencement: 1 December 2001.

This Order is reproduced as amended by: the Financial Services and Markets Act 2000 (Regulated Activities) (Amendment) (No 1) Order 2003, SI 2003/1475; the Financial Services and Markets Act 2000 (Regulated Activities) (Amendment) (No 2) Order 2003, SI 2003/1476; the Financial Services and Markets Act 2000 (Carrying on Regulated Activities by Way of Business) (Amendment) Order 2005, SI 2005/922; the Financial Services and Markets Act 2000 (Regulated Activities) (Amendment) Order 2006, SI 2006/1969; the Financial Services and Markets Act 2000 (Regulated Activities) (Amendment) (No 2) Order 2006, SI 2006/2383; the Financial Services and Markets Act 2000 (Regulated Activities) (Amendment No 3) Order 2006, SI 2006/3384; the Financial Services and Markets Act 2000 (Regulated Activities) (Amendment) Order 2009, SI 2009/1342; the Financial Services and Markets Act 2000 (Regulated Activities) (Amendment) Order 2010, SI 2010/86.

ARRANGEMENT OF ARTICLES

[8.212]
1 Citation, commencement and interpretation

(1) This Order may be cited as the Financial Services and Markets Act 2000 (Carrying on Regulated Activities by Way of Business) Order 2001, and comes into force on the day on which section 19 of the Financial Services and Markets Act 2000 comes into force.

(2) In this Order—
- (a) the "Regulated Activities Order" means the Financial Services and Markets Act 2000 (Regulated Activities) Order 2001;
- (b) ["contract of insurance",] "contractually based investment", "deposit", "overseas person" and "security" have the same meaning as in that Order;
- (c) "shares" and "debentures" mean any investment of the kind specified by article 76[, 77 or 77A] of that Order;
- (d) "units in a collective investment scheme" means any investment of the kind specified by article 81 of that Order;
- (e) "warrants" means any investment of the kind specified by article 79 of that Order.

NOTES

Para (2): words in square brackets in sub-para (b) inserted by the Financial Services and Markets Act 2000 (Regulated Activities) (Amendment) (No 2) Order 2003, SI 2003/1476, art 18(1), (2), as from 31 October 2004 (in so far as relating to contracts of long-term care insurance), and as from 14 January 2005 (otherwise); words in square brackets in para (c) substituted by the Financial Services and Markets Act 2000 (Regulated Activities) (Amendment) Order 2010, SI 2010/86, art 4, Schedule, para 6, as from 24 February 2010.

FSMA 2000, s 19 came into force on 1 December 2001 (see the Financial Services and Markets Act 2000 (Commencement No 7) Order 2001, SI 2001/3538).

[8.213]
2 Deposit taking business

(1) A person who carries on an activity of the kind specified by article 5 of the Regulated Activities Order (accepting deposits) is not to be regarded as doing so by way of business if—
- (a) he does not hold himself out as accepting deposits on a day to day basis; and
- (b) any deposits which he accepts are accepted only on particular occasions, whether or not involving the issue of any securities.

(2) In determining for the purposes of paragraph (1)(b) whether deposits are accepted only on particular occasions, regard is to be had to the frequency of those occasions and to any characteristics distinguishing them from each other.

[8.214]
3 Investment business

(1) A person is not to be regarded as carrying on by way of business an activity to which [paragraph (2) applies], unless he carries on the business of engaging in one or more such activities.

(2) [This paragraph] applies to an activity of the kind specified by any of the following provisions of the Regulated Activities Order, namely—
- (a) article 14 (dealing in investments as principal);
- (b) article 21 (dealing in investments as agent);
- (c) article 25 (arranging deals in investments), except in so far as that activity relates to an investment of the kind specified by article 86 of that Order (Lloyd's syndicate capacity and syndicate membership), or article 89 of that Order (rights and interests) so far as relevant to that article;
- [(ca) article 25D (operating a multilateral trading facility);]
- (d) article 37 (managing investments);
- (e) article 40 (safeguarding and administering investments);
- (f) article 45 (sending dematerialised instructions);
- (g) article 51 (establishing etc a collective investment scheme);
- (h) article 52 (establishing etc a . . . pension scheme);
- (i) article 53 (advising on investments); and
- [(j) article 64 (agreeing) so far as relevant to any of the articles mentioned in sub-paragraphs (a) to (i),

but does not apply to any insurance mediation activity].

(3) [Paragraph (1)] is without prejudice to article 4 of this Order.

[(4) A person is not to be regarded as carrying on by way of business any insurance mediation activity unless he takes up or pursues that activity for remuneration.

(5) In this article, "insurance mediation activity" means any activity of the kind specified by article 21, 25(1) or (2), 39A or 53 of the Regulated Activities Order, or, so far as relevant to any of those articles, article 64 of that Order, which is carried on in relation to a contract of insurance.]

NOTES

Paras (1), (3): words in square brackets substituted by the Financial Services and Markets Act 2000 (Regulated Activities) (Amendment) (No 2) Order 2003, SI 2003/1476, art 18(1), (3)(a), (c), as from 31 October 2004 (in so far as relating to contracts of long-term care insurance), and as from 14 January 2005 (otherwise).

Para (2): words in first pair of square brackets and sub-para (j) (and the following words) substituted by SI 2003/1476, art 18(1), (3)(b), as from 31 October 2004 (in so far as relating to contracts of long-term care insurance), and as from 14 January 2005 (otherwise); sub-para (ca) inserted by the Financial Services and Markets Act 2000 (Regulated Activities) (Amendment No 3) Order 2006, SI 2006/3384, art 37, as from 1 November 2007; word omitted from sub-para (h) revoked by the Financial Services and Markets Act 2000 (Regulated Activities) (Amendment) Order 2006, SI 2006/1969, art 9(1), (2), as from 6 April 2007.

Paras (4), (5): added by SI 2003/1476, art 18(1), (3)(d), as from 31 October 2004 (in so far as relating to contracts of long-term care insurance), and as from 14 January 2005 (otherwise).

[8.215]

[3A   Arranging and advising on regulated mortgage contracts

A person is not to be regarded as carrying on by way of business an activity of the kind specified by—

(a)   article 25A of the Regulated Activities Order (arranging regulated mortgage contracts);

(b)   article 53A of that Order (advising on regulated mortgage contracts); or

(c)   article 64 of that Order (agreeing), so far as relevant to any of the articles mentioned in sub-paragraphs (a) and (b),

unless he carries on the business of engaging in that activity.]

NOTES

Inserted by the Financial Services and Markets Act 2000 (Regulated Activities) (Amendment) (No 1) Order 2003, SI 2003/1475, art 25, as from 31 October 2004.

[8.216]

[3B   Arranging and advising on regulated home reversion plans

A person is not to be regarded as carrying on by way of business an activity specified by—

(a)   article 25B of the Regulated Activities Order (arranging regulated home reversion plans);

(b)   article 53B of that Order (advising on regulated home reversion plans); or

(c)   article 64 of that Order (agreeing), so far as relevant to either of the articles mentioned in sub-paragraphs (a) and (b),

unless he carries on the business of engaging in that activity.]

NOTES

Commencement: 6 April 2007.

Inserted, together with art 3C, by the Financial Services and Markets Act 2000 (Regulated Activities) (Amendment) (No 2) Order 2006, SI 2006/2383, art 29, as from 6 April 2007.

[8.217]

[3C   Arranging and advising on regulated home purchase plans

A person is not to be regarded as carrying on by way of business an activity specified by—

(a)   article 25C of the Regulated Activities Order (arranging regulated home purchase plans);

(b)   article 53C of that Order (advising on regulated home purchase plans); or

(c)   article 64 of that Order (agreeing), so far as relevant to either of the articles mentioned in sub-paragraphs (a) and (b),

unless he carries on the business of engaging in that activity.]

NOTES

Commencement: 6 April 2007.

Inserted as noted to art 3B at **[8.216]**.

[8.218]

[3D   Arranging and advising on regulated sale and rent back agreements

A person is not to be regarded as carrying on by way of business an activity specified by—

(a)   article 25E of the Regulated Activities Order (arranging regulated sale and rent back agreements);

(b)   article 53D of that Order (advising on regulated sale and rent back agreements); or

(c)   article 64 of that Order (agreeing), so far as relevant to either of the articles mentioned in sub-paragraphs (a) and (b),

unless that person carries on the business of engaging in that activity.]

NOTES

Commencement: 1 July 2009 (certain purposes); 30 June 2010 (otherwise) (see below).

Inserted by the Financial Services and Markets Act 2000 (Regulated Activities) (Amendment) Order 2009, SI 2009/1342, art 27, as from 1 July 2009 (certain purposes), and as from 30 June 2010 (otherwise).

[8.219]

4   Managing investments: occupational pension schemes

(1)   A person who carries on an activity of the kind specified by article 37 of the Regulated Activities Order (managing investments), where the assets in question are held for the purposes of an occupational pension scheme, is to be regarded as carrying on that activity by way of business, except where—

   (a)   he is a person to whom paragraph (2) applies; or

   (b)   all . . . day to day decisions in the carrying on of that activity (other than decisions falling within paragraph (6)), so far as relating to relevant assets, are taken on his behalf by—

      (i)   an authorised person who has permission to carry on activities of the kind specified by article 37 of the Regulated Activities Order;

      (ii)   a person who is an exempt person in relation to activities of that kind; or

      (iii)   an overseas person.

(2)   This paragraph applies to—

   (a)   any trustee of a relevant scheme who is a beneficiary or potential beneficiary under the scheme; and

   (b)   any other trustee of a relevant scheme who takes no . . . day to day decisions relating to the management of any relevant assets.

(3)   In this article—

   ["occupational pension scheme" has the meaning given by section 1 of the Pension Schemes Act 1993 but with paragraph (b) of the definition omitted;]

   "relevant assets" means assets of the scheme in question which are securities or contractually based investments;

   "relevant scheme" means any occupational pension scheme of a kind falling within paragraph (4) or (5).

(4)   A scheme falls within this paragraph if—

   (a)   it is constituted under an irrevocable trust:

   (b)   it has no more than twelve relevant members;

   (c)   all relevant members, other than any relevant member who is unfit to act, or is incapable of acting, as trustee of the scheme, are trustees of it; and

   (d)   all . . . day to day decisions relating to the management of the assets of the scheme which are relevant assets are required to be taken by all, or a majority of, relevant members who are trustees of the scheme or by a person of a kind falling within paragraph (1)(b)(i) or (ii) acting alone or jointly with all, or a majority of, such relevant members;

and for these purposes a person is a relevant member of a scheme if he is an employee or former employee by or in respect of whom contributions to the scheme are being or have been made and to or in respect of whom benefits are or may become payable under the scheme.

(5)   A scheme falls within this paragraph if—

   (a)   it has no more than fifty members;

   (b)   the contributions made by or in respect of each member of the scheme are used in the acquisition of a contract of insurance on the life of that member or in the acquisition of a contract to pay an annuity on that life;

   (c)   the only decision of a kind described in paragraph (1)(b) which may be taken in relation to the scheme is the selection of such contracts; and

   (d)   each member is given the opportunity to select the contract which the contributions made by or in respect of him will be used to acquire.

(6)   A decision falls within this paragraph if—

   [(a)   it is a decision by the trustees of an occupational pension scheme to buy, sell or subscribe for—

      (i)   units in a collective investment scheme;

      (ii)   shares or debentures (or warrants relating to such shares or debentures) issued by a body corporate having as its purpose the investment of its funds with the aim of spreading investment risk and giving its members the benefit of the results of the management of those funds by or on behalf of that body; or

      (iii)   rights under (or rights to or interests in) any contract of insurance;]

     . . .

   [(b)   the decision is taken after advice has been obtained and considered from a person who falls within any of the cases in paragraph (7);]

   (c), (d) . . .

[(7)   The cases are where the person is—

   (a)   an authorised person who has permission to carry on activities of the kind specified by article 53 of the Regulated Activities Order in relation to the decision in question;

   (b)   an exempt person in relation to such activities;

   (c)   exempt from the general prohibition by virtue of section 327 of the Financial Services and Markets Act 2000; or

   (d)   an overseas person.]

Part 8   FSMA 2000: SIs

NOTES

Paras (1), (2), (4): words omitted revoked by the Financial Services and Markets Act 2000 (Carrying on Regulated Activities by Way of Business) (Amendment) Order 2005, SI 2005/922, art 2(1), (2), as from 6 April 2005.

Para (3): definition "occupational pension scheme" substituted by the Financial Services and Markets Act 2000 (Regulated Activities) (Amendment) Order 2006, SI 2006/1969, art 9(1), (3), as from 6 April 2007.

Para (6): sub-paras (a), (b) substituted, omitted words following sub-para (a) revoked, and sub-paras (c), (d) revoked, by SI 2005/922, art 2(1), (4)–(7), as from 6 April 2005.

Para (7): substituted by SI 2005/922, art 2(1), (8), as from 6 April 2005.

FINANCIAL SERVICES AND MARKETS ACT 2000 (EXEMPTION) ORDER 2001

(SI 2001/1201)

NOTES

Made: 26 March 2001.

Authority: Financial Services and Markets Act 2000, ss 38, 428(3).

Commencement: 1 December 2001.

This Order is reproduced as amended by: the Tourist Boards (Scotland) Act 2006; the Financial Services and Markets Act 2000 (Exemption) (Amendment) Order 2001, SI 2001/3623; the Financial Services and Markets Act 2000 (Financial Promotion and Miscellaneous Amendments) Order 2002, SI 2002/1310; the Financial Services and Markets Act 2000 (Exemption) (Amendment) Order 2003, SI 2003/47; the Financial Services and Markets Act 2000 (Exemption) (Amendment) (No 2) Order 2003, SI 2003/1675; the Financial Services and Markets Act 2000 (Exemption) (Amendment) Order 2005, SI 2005/592; the Civil Partnership Act 2004 (Amendments to Subordinate Legislation) Order 2005, SI 2005/2114; the Wales Tourist Board (Transfer of Functions to the National Assembly for Wales and Abolition) Order 2005, SI 2005/3225; the Charities and Trustee Investment (Scotland) Act 2005 (Consequential Provisions and Modifications) Order 2006, SI 2006/242; the Financial Services and Markets Act 2000 (Regulated Activities) (Amendment) Order 2006, SI 2006/1969; the Financial Services and Markets Act 2000 (Regulated Activities) (Amendment) (No 2) Order 2006, SI 2006/2383; the Financial Services and Markets Act 2000 (Exemption) (Amendment) Order 2007, SI 2007/125; the Tourist Boards (Scotland) Act 2006 (Consequential Modifications) Order 2007, SI 2007/1103; the Financial Services and Markets Act 2000 (Exemption) (Amendment No 2) Order 2007, SI 2007/1821; the Financial Services and Markets Act 2000 (Exemption) (Amendment) Order 2008, SI 2008/682; the Housing and Regeneration Act 2008 (Consequential Provisions) (No 2) Order 2008, SI 2008/2831; the Financial Services and Markets Act 2000 (Exemption) (Amendment) Order 2009, SI 2009/118; the Financial Services and Markets Act 2000 (Exemption) (Amendment) Order 2009, SI 2009/264; the Financial Services and Markets Act 2000 (Regulated Activities) (Amendment) Order 2009, SI 2009/1342; the Financial Services and Markets Act 2000 (Regulated Activities) (Amendment) Order 2010, SI 2010/86; the Housing and Regeneration Act 2008 (Consequential Provisions) (No 2) Order 2010, SI 2010/671; the Financial Services and Markets Act 2000 (Exemption) (Amendment) Order 2011, SI 2011/1626.

References to the "European Community", "Community", etc: see the Treaty of Lisbon (Changes in Terminology) Order 2011, SI 2011/1043, which provides (with effect from 22 April 2011): (1) that for references to the "European Communities" or to the "European Community" (including references to "the Communities", "the Community", "the EC" or "the EEC") substitute references to the European Union; and (2) that "EU" should be substituted for the word "Community" (subject to certain exceptions) in references to "Community treaties", "Community customs duty", "Community institution", "Community instrument", "Community obligation", "enforceable Community right", "Community law", "Community legislation", and "Community provision". Also, where such a term is preceded by the word "a", for "a" substitute "an".

ARRANGEMENT OF ARTICLES

[8.220]

1   Citation and commencement

This Order may be cited as the Financial Services and Markets Act 2000 (Exemption) Order 2001 and comes into force on the day on which section 19 of the Act comes into force.

NOTES

FSMA 2000, s 19 came into force on 1 December 2001 (see the Financial Services and Markets Act 2000 (Commencement No 7) Order 2001, SI 2001/3538).

[8.221]
2   Interpretation

In this Order—

"the Act" means the Financial Services and Markets Act 2000;

"charity"—
    (a)   in relation to Scotland, means a [body entered in the Scottish Charity Register]; and
    (b)   otherwise, has the meaning given by section 96(1) of the Charities Act 1993 or by section 35 of the Charities Act (Northern Ireland) 1964;

["credit institution" has the meaning given by the Regulated Activities Order;]

"deposit" has the meaning given by the Regulated Activities Order;

"industrial and provident society" has the meaning given by section 417(1) of the Act but does not include a credit union within the meaning of the Credit Unions Act 1979 or the Credit Unions (Northern Ireland) Order 1985;

["investment firm" has the meaning given by the Regulated Activities Order;]

"local authority" means—
    (a)   in England and Wales, a local authority within the meaning of the Local Government Act 1972, the Greater London Authority, the Common Council of the City of London or the Council of the Isles of Scilly;
    (b)   in Scotland, a local authority within the meaning of the Local Government (Scotland) Act 1973; and
    (c)   in Northern Ireland, a district council within the meaning of the Local Government Act (Northern Ireland) 1972;

["non-qualifying contract of insurance" means a contract of insurance (within the meaning of the Regulated Activities Order) which is not a qualifying contract of insurance (within the meaning of that Order);]

"the Regulated Activities Order" means the Financial Services and Markets Act 2000 (Regulated Activities) Order 2001.

NOTES

Words in square brackets in definition "charity" substituted by the Charities and Trustee Investment (Scotland) Act 2005 (Consequential Provisions and Modifications) Order 2006, SI 2006/242, art 5, Schedule, Pt 2, para 11, as from 1 April 2006; definitions "credit institution" and "investment firm" inserted by the Financial Services and Markets Act 2000 (Exemption) (Amendment) Order 2007, SI 2007/125, art 3, as from 1 November 2007; definition "non-qualifying contract of insurance" inserted by the Financial Services and Markets Act 2000 (Exemption) (Amendment) (No 2) Order 2003, SI 2003/1675, art 2(1), (2), as from 14 January 2005.

[8.222]
3   Persons exempt in respect of any regulated activity other than insurance business

Each of the persons listed in Part I of the Schedule is exempt from the general prohibition in respect of any regulated activity other than an activity of the kind specified by article 10 of the Regulated Activities Order (effecting and carrying out contracts of insurance).

[8.223]
4   Persons exempt in respect of accepting deposits

Subject to the limitations, if any, expressed in relation to him, each of the persons listed in Part II of the Schedule is exempt from the general prohibition in respect of any regulated activity of the kind specified by article 5 of the Regulated Activities Order (accepting deposits).

[8.224]
5   Persons exempt in respect of particular regulated activities

(1)   Subject to the limitation, if any, expressed in relation to him, each of the persons listed in Part III of the Schedule is exempt from the general prohibition in respect of any regulated activity of the kind specified by any of the following provisions of the Regulated Activities Order, or article 64 of that Order (agreeing to carry on specified kinds of activity) so far as relevant to any such activity—
    (a)   article 14 (dealing in investments as principal);
    (b)   article 21 (dealing in investments as agent);
    (c)   article 25 (arranging deals in investments);
    [(ca) article 25D (operating a multilateral trading facility);]
    (d)   article 37 (managing investments);
    [(da) article 39A (assisting in the administration and performance of a contract of insurance);]
    (e)   article 40 (safeguarding and administering investments);
    (f)   article 45 (sending dematerialised instructions);
    (g)   article 51 (establishing etc a collective investment scheme);

(h)   article 52 (establishing etc a . . . pension scheme);

(i)   article 53 (advising on investments).

(2)   Subject to the limitation, if any, expressed in relation to him, each of the persons listed in Part IV of the Schedule is exempt from the general prohibition in respect of any regulated activity of the kind referred to in relation to him, or an activity of the kind specified by article 64 of the Regulated Activities Order so far as relevant to any such activity.

NOTES

Para (1): sub-para (ca) inserted by the Financial Services and Markets Act 2000 (Exemption) (Amendment) Order 2007, SI 2007/125, art 4, as from 1 November 2007; sub-para (da) inserted by the Financial Services and Markets Act 2000 (Exemption) (Amendment) (No 2) Order 2003, SI 2003/1675, art 2(1), (3), as from 14 January 2005; word omitted from sub-para (h) revoked by the Financial Services and Markets Act 2000 (Regulated Activities) (Amendment) Order 2006, SI 2006/1969, art 10, as from 6 April 2007.

[8.225]

6   Transitional exemption for credit unions

A credit union, within the meaning of the Credit Unions Act 1979 . . . , is exempt from the general prohibition in respect of any regulated activity of the kind specified by article 5 of the Regulated Activities Order, but only until 1st July 2002.

NOTES

Words omitted revoked by the Financial Services and Markets Act 2000 (Exemption) (Amendment) Order 2001, SI 2001/3623, arts 2, 3, as from 1 December 2001.

SCHEDULE

Articles 3 to 5

PART I

PERSONS EXEMPT IN RESPECT OF ANY REGULATED ACTIVITY OTHER THAN INSURANCE BUSINESS

[8.226]

1. The Bank of England.

2. The central bank of an EEA State other than the United Kingdom.

3. The European Central Bank.

4. The European Community.

5. The European Atomic Energy Community.

6. The European Coal and Steel Community.

7. The European Investment Bank.

8. The International Bank for Reconstruction and Development.

9. The International Finance Corporation.

10. The International Monetary Fund.

11. The African Development Bank.

12. The Asian Development Bank.

13. The Caribbean Development Bank.

14. The Inter-American Development Bank.

15. The European Bank for Reconstruction and Development.

[15A. Bank for International Settlements.]

[15B. Bank of England Asset Purchase Facility Fund Limited.]

NOTES

Para 15A: added by the Financial Services and Markets Act 2000 (Exemption) (Amendment) Order 2003, SI 2003/47, art 2, as from 1 March 2003.

Para 15B: added by the Financial Services and Markets Act 2000 (Exemption) (Amendment) Order 2009, SI 2009/118, art 2, as from 2 February 2009.

PART II
PERSONS EXEMPT IN RESPECT OF ACCEPTING DEPOSITS

[8.227]

16. A municipal bank, that is to say a company which was, immediately before the coming into force of this Order, exempted from the prohibition in section 3 of the Banking Act 1987 by virtue of section 4(1) of, and paragraph 4 of Schedule 2 to, that Act.

17. (1) Keesler Federal Credit Union, in so far as it accepts deposits from members, or dependants of members, of a visiting force of the United States of America, or from members, or dependants of members, of a civilian component of such a force.

(2) In sub-paragraph (1), "member", "dependent" and "visiting force" have the meanings given by section 12 of the Visiting Forces Act 1952 and "member of a civilian component" has the meaning given by section 10 of that Act.

18. A body of persons certified as a school bank by the National Savings Bank or by an authorised person who has permission to accept deposits.

19. A local authority.

20. (1) Any body which by virtue of any enactment has power to issue a precept to a local authority in England or Wales or a requisition to a local authority in Scotland, or to the expenses of which, by virtue of any enactment, a local authority in the United Kingdom is or can be required to contribute.

(2) In sub-paragraph (1), "enactment" includes an enactment comprised in, or in an instrument made under, an Act of the Scottish Parliament.

[21. The Council of Europe Development Bank.**]**

22. A charity, in so far as it accepts deposits—
(a)   from another charity; or
(b)   in respect of which no interest or premium is payable.

23. The National Children's Charities Fund in so far as—
(a)   it accepts deposits in respect of which no interest or premium is payable; and
(b)   the total value of the deposits made by any one person does not exceed £10,000.

24. An industrial and provident society, in so far as it accepts deposits in the form of withdrawable share capital.

[24A. A credit union, within the meaning of the Credit Unions (Northern Ireland) Order 1985.**]**

25. (1) The Student Loans Company Limited, in so far as it accepts deposits from the Secretary of State or the Scottish Ministers in connection with, or for the purposes of, enabling eligible students to receive loans.

(2) In sub-paragraph (1), "eligible student" means—
(a)   any person who is an eligible student pursuant to regulations made under Part II of the Teaching and Higher Education Act 1998;
(b)   any person to whom, or in respect of whom, loans may be paid under section 73(f) of the Education (Scotland) Act 1980;
(c)   any person who is an eligible student pursuant to regulations made under article 3 of the Education (Student Support) (Northern Ireland) Order 1998; or
(d)   any person who is in receipt of or who is eligible to receive a loan of the kind mentioned in article 3(1) of the Teaching and Higher Education Act 1998 (Commencement No 2 and Transitional Provisions) Order 1998 or article 3(1) of the Education (Student Support) (Northern Ireland) Order 1998 (Commencement and Transitional Provisions) Order (Northern Ireland) 1998.

NOTES

Para 21: substituted by the Financial Services and Markets Act 2000 (Financial Promotion and Miscellaneous Amendments) Order 2002, SI 2002/1310, art 4(2), as from 5 June 2002.

Para 24A: inserted by the Financial Services and Markets Act 2000 (Exemption) (Amendment) Order 2001, SI 2001/3623, arts 2, 4, as from 1 December 2001.

PART III
PERSONS EXEMPT IN RESPECT OF ANY REGULATED ACTIVITY MENTIONED IN ARTICLE 5(1)

[8.228]

26. The National Debt Commissioners.

[27. Partnerships UK.**]**

28. The International Development Association.

29. The English Tourist Board.

30. ....

[31. VisitScotland.]

32. The Northern Ireland Tourist Board.

33. Scottish Enterprise.

[33A. Invest Northern Ireland.]

34. The Multilateral Investment Guarantee Agency.

[34A. The Board of the Pension Protection Fund.]

[34B. Capital for Enterprise Limited, in so far as in carrying on any regulated activity it provides services only to the Crown.]

35. A person acting as an official receiver within the meaning of section 399 of the Insolvency Act 1986 or article 2 of the Insolvency (Northern Ireland) Order 1989.

36. ....

37. [(1) An Operator, in so far as he carries on—
   (a) any regulated activity for the purposes of the performance of his functions as an Operator under the Uncertificated Securities Regulations 1995; or
   (b) any other regulated activity for the purposes of operating a computer-based system and procedures which—
       (i) enable title to investments to be evidenced and transferred without a written instrument; or
       (ii) facilitate matters supplementary or incidental to those specified in sub-paragraph (i),
other than a regulated activity in respect of which a recognised clearing house is exempt from the general prohibition by virtue of section 285(3) of the Act.]
(2) In sub-paragraph (1), "Operator" means a person approved as such by the Treasury under the Uncertificated Securities Regulations 1995.

38. A person acting as a judicial factor.

39. A person acting as an insolvency practitioner within the meaning of section 388 of the Insolvency Act 1986 [or article 3 of the Insolvency (Northern Ireland) Order 1989].

NOTES

Para 27: substituted by the Financial Services and Markets Act 2000 (Exemption) (Amendment) (No 2) Order 2003, SI 2003/1675, art 2(1), (4)(a), as from 13 July 2003.

Para 30: revoked by the Wales Tourist Board (Transfer of Functions to the National Assembly for Wales and Abolition) Order 2005, SI 2005/3225, art 6(2), Sch 2, Pt 2, para 4, as from 1 April 2006.

Para 31: substituted by the Tourist Boards (Scotland) Act 2006, s 4, Sch 2, Pt 2, para 10, as from 1 April 2007 (in relation to Scotland), and by the Tourist Boards (Scotland) Act 2006 (Consequential Modifications) Order 2007, SI 2007/1103, art 2, Schedule, Pt 2, para 6, as from 29 March 2007 (in relation to England and Wales).

Para 33A: inserted by the Financial Services and Markets Act 2000 (Exemption) (Amendment No 2) Order 2007, SI 2007/1821, art 2(1), (2), as from 20 July 2007.

Para 34A: inserted by the Financial Services and Markets Act 2000 (Exemption) (Amendment) Order 2005, SI 2005/592, art 2(1), as from 6 April 2005.

Para 34B: inserted by the Financial Services and Markets Act 2000 (Exemption) (Amendment) Order 2008, SI 2008/682, art 2, as from 1 April 2008.

Para 36: revoked by the Financial Services and Markets Act 2000 (Exemption) (Amendment) Order 2007, SI 2007/125, art 5, as from 1 November 2007.

Para 37: sub-para (1) substituted by the Financial Services and Markets Act 2000 (Exemption) (Amendment) Order 2001, SI 2001/3623, arts 2, 5, as from 1 December 2001.

Para 39: words in square brackets added by SI 2001/3623, arts 2, 6, as from 1 December 2001.

Uncertificated Securities Regulations 1995 (SI 1995/3272): revoked and replaced by the Uncertificated Securities Regulations 2001, SI 2001/3755.

PART IV
PERSONS EXEMPT IN RESPECT OF PARTICULAR REGULATED ACTIVITIES

Enterprise schemes

[8.229]
40. (1) Any body corporate which has as its principal object (or one of its principal objects)—
   (a) the promotion or encouragement of industrial or commercial activity or enterprise in the United Kingdom or in any particular area of it; or
   (b) the dissemination of information concerning persons engaged in such activity or enterprise or requiring capital to become so engaged;

is exempt from the general prohibition in respect of any regulated activity of the kind specified by article 25 of the Regulated Activities Order (arranging deals in investments) so long as it does not carry on that activity for, or with the prospect of, direct or indirect pecuniary gain.

(2)   For the purposes of this paragraph, such sums as may reasonably be regarded as necessary to meet the costs of carrying on the activity mentioned in sub-paragraph (1) do not constitute a pecuniary gain.

[(3)   This paragraph does not apply where an investment firm or credit institution—

    (a)   provides or performs investment services and activities on a professional basis, and

    (b)   in doing so, but for the operation of [sub-paragraph (1)], it would be treated as carrying on an activity of a kind specified by Part 2 of the Regulated Activities Order [in breach of the general prohibition].]

Employee share schemes in electricity industry shares

41. (1)   Each of the persons to whom this paragraph applies is exempt from the general prohibition in respect of any regulated activity of the kind specified by article 14, 21 or 25 of the Regulated Activities Order (dealing in investments as principal or agent or arranging deals in investments) which he carries on for the purpose of—

    (a)   enabling or facilitating transactions in electricity industry shares or debentures between or for the benefit of any qualifying person; or

    (b)   the holding of electricity industry shares or debentures by or for the benefit of any qualifying person.

(2)   This paragraph applies to—

    (a)   The National Grid Holding plc;

    (b)   Electricity Association Limited;

    (c)   any body corporate in the same group as the person mentioned in sub-paragraph (a) or (b);

    (d)   any company listed in Schedule 1 to the Electricity Act 1989 (Nominated Companies) (England and Wales) Order 1990; and

    (e)   a person holding shares in or debentures of a body corporate as trustee in pursuance of arrangements made for either of the purposes mentioned in sub-paragraph (1) by the Secretary of State, by any of the bodies mentioned in sub-paragraphs (a) to (c) or by an electricity successor company or by some or all of them.

(3)   In this paragraph—

    (a)   "electricity industry shares or debentures" means—

        (i)   any investment of the kind specified by article 76[, 77 or 77A] of the Regulated Activities Order (shares or instruments creating or acknowledging indebtedness [or alternative finance investment bond]) in or of an electricity successor company;

        (ii)   any investment of the kind specified by article 79 or 80 of that Order (instruments giving entitlement to investments and certificates representing certain securities), so far as relevant to the investments mentioned in sub-paragraph (i); and

        (iii)   any investment of the kind specified by article 89 of that Order (rights to or interests in investments) so far as relevant to the investments mentioned in sub-paragraphs (i) and (ii);

    (b)   "qualifying person" means—

        (i)   the bona fide employees or former employees of The National Grid Holding plc, Electricity Association Limited or any other body corporate in the same group as either of them; and

        (ii)   the wives, husbands, widows, widowers[, civil partners, surviving civil partners,] or children (including, in Northern Ireland, adopted children) or step-children under the age of eighteen of such employees or former employees;

    (c)   references to an electricity successor company include any body corporate that is in the same group and "electricity successor company" means a body corporate which is a successor company for the purposes of Part II of the Electricity Act 1989;

    (d)   "former employees" of a person ("the employer") include any person who has never been employed by the employer so long as he occupied a position in relation to some other person of such a kind that it may reasonably be assumed that he would have been a former employee of the employer had the reorganisation of the electricity industry under Part II of the Electricity Act 1989 been affected before he ceased to occupy the relevant position.

Gas industry

42. (1)   Transco plc is exempt from the general prohibition in respect of any regulated activity of the kind specified by article 14, 21[, 25 or 25D] of the Regulated Activities Order (dealing in investments as principal or agent[, arranging deals in investments or operating a multilateral trading facility]) which it carries on—

    (a)   in its capacity as a gas transporter under the Transco Licence; and

    (b)   for the purposes of enabling or facilitating gas shippers to buy or sell an investment of the kind specified by article 84 or 85 of the Regulated Activities Order (futures or contracts for differences etc).

(2)   ENMO Ltd is exempt from the general prohibition in respect of any regulated activity of the kind specified by article 14, 21[, 25 or 25D] of the Regulated Activities Order (dealing in investments as principal or agent[, arranging deals in investments or operating a multilateral trading facility]) which it carries on—

- (a)   in its capacity as the operator of the balancing market; and
- (b)   for the purpose of enabling or facilitating Transco plc and relevant gas shippers, for the purpose of participating in the balancing market, to buy or sell investments of the kind specified by article 84 or 85 of that Order (futures or contracts for differences etc).

(3)   Transco plc and relevant gas shippers are exempt from the general prohibition in respect of any regulated activity of the kind specified by article 14 or 21 of the Regulated Activities Order (dealing in investments as principal or agent) in so far as that activity relates to an investment of the kind specified by article 84 or 85 of that Order (futures or contracts for differences etc) and is carried on for the purpose of participating in the balancing market.

(4)   In this paragraph—

- (a)   "the balancing market" means the market to regulate the delivery and off-take of gas in Transco plc's pipeline system for the purpose of balancing the volume of gas in that system;
- (b)   "gas shipper" has the same meaning as in Part I of the Gas Act 1986;
- (c)   "relevant gas shippers" means gas shippers who have entered into a subscription agreement with ENMO Ltd for the purpose of participating in the balancing market;
- (d)   "Transco Licence" means the licence treated as granted to Transco plc as a gas transporter under section 7 of the Gas Act 1986;
- (e)   the reference to enabling or facilitating includes acting pursuant to rules governing the operation of the balancing market which apply in the event of one of the participants appearing to be unable, or likely to become unable, to meet his obligations in respect of one or more contracts entered into through the balancing market.

Trade unions and employers' associations

43.   (1)   A trade union or employers' association is exempt from the general prohibition in respect of any regulated activity of the kind specified by article 10 of the Regulated Activities Order (effecting and carrying out contracts of insurance) which it carries on in order to provide provident benefits or strike benefits for its members.

(2)   In sub-paragraph (1), "trade union" and "employers' association" have the meanings given by section 1 and section 122(1) of the Trade Union and Labour Relations (Consolidation) Act 1992 or, in Northern Ireland, the meanings given by article 3(1) and article 4(1) of the Industrial Relations (Northern Ireland) Order 1992.

Charities

44.   (1)   A charity is exempt from the general prohibition in respect of any regulated activity of the kind specified by article 51 of the Regulated Activities Order (establishing etc a collective investment scheme) which it carries on in relation to a fund established under—

- (a)   section 22A of the Charities Act 1960;
- (b)   section 25 of the Charities Act 1993; or
- (c)   section 25 of the Charities Act (Northern Ireland) 1964.

(2)   A charity is exempt from the general prohibition in respect of any regulated activity of the kind specified by article 51 of the Regulated Activities Order (establishing etc a collective investment scheme) which it carries on in relation to a pooling scheme fund established under—

- (a)   section 22 of the Charities Act 1960; or
- (b)   section 24 of the Charities Act 1993.

(3)   In sub-paragraph (2), "pooling scheme fund" means a fund established by a common investment scheme the trusts of which provide that property is not to be transferred to the fund except by or on behalf of a charity, the charity trustees (within the meaning of section 97(1) of the Charities Act 1993) of which are the trustees appointed to manage the fund.

Schemes established under the Trustee Investments Act 1961

45.   A person acting in his capacity as manager or operator of a fund established under section 11 of the Trustee Investments Act 1961 is exempt from the general prohibition in respect of any regulated activity of the kind specified by article 51 of the Regulated Activities Order (establishing etc a collective investment scheme) which he carries on in relation to that fund.

Former members of Lloyd's

46.   Any person who ceased to be an underwriting member (within the meaning of Lloyd's Act 1982) of Lloyd's before 24th December 1996 is exempt from the general prohibition in respect of any regulated activity of the kind specified by article 10(2) of the Regulated Activities Order (carrying out contracts of insurance) which relates to contracts of insurance that he has underwritten at Lloyd's.

Local authorities

[47. A local authority is exempt from the general prohibition in respect of any regulated activity of the kind specified by—
   (a)   article 21, 25(1) or (2), 39A or 53 of the Regulated Activities Order (dealing in investments as agent, arranging deals in investments, assisting in the administration and performance of a contract of insurance or advising on investments) which relates to a non-qualifying contract of insurance; . . .
   (b)   article 25A, 53A or 61 of that Order (arranging, advising on, entering into or administering a regulated mortgage contract)[;
   (c)   article 25B, 53B or 63B of that Order (arranging, advising on, entering into or administering a regulated home reversion plan); . . .
   (d)   article 25C, 53C or 63F of that Order (arranging, advising on, entering into or administering a regulated home purchase plan)][;
   [(e)   article 25E, 53D or 63J of that Order (arranging, advising on, entering into or administering a regulated sale and rent back agreement)].]

Social housing

[48. (1)   A relevant housing body is exempt from the general prohibition in respect of any regulated activity of the kind specified by—
   (a)   article 21, 25(1) or (2), 39A or 53 of the Regulated Activities Order (dealing in investments as agent, arranging deals in investments, assisting in the administration and performance of a contract of insurance or advising on investments) which relates to a non-qualifying contract of insurance; . . .
   (b)   article 25A, 53A or 61 of that Order (arranging, advising on, entering into or administering a regulated mortgage contract)[;
   (c)   article 25B, 53B or 63B of that Order (arranging, advising on, entering into or administering a regulated home reversion plan); . . .
   (d)   article 25C, 53C or 63F of that Order (arranging, advising on, entering into or administering a regulated home purchase plan)[;
   [(e)   article 25E, 53D or 63J of that Order (arranging, advising on, entering into or administering a regulated sale and rent back agreement)]].

(2)   In this paragraph, "relevant housing body" means any of the following—
   (a)   a registered social landlord within the meaning of Part I of the Housing Act 1996;
   [(aa) a non-profit registered provider of social housing;]
   (b)   a registered social landlord within the meaning of the Housing (Scotland) Act 2001;
   (c)   [The Regulator of Social Housing];
   [(ca) the Homes and Communities Agency;]
   (d)   Scottish Homes;
   (e)   the body established under article 9 of the Housing (Northern Ireland) Order 1981 known as the Northern Ireland Housing Executive;
   [(f)   Communities Scotland];
   [(g)   a housing association within the meaning of Part 2 of the Housing (Northern Ireland) Order 1992].]

[Electricity industry

49. (1)   NGC is exempt from the general prohibition in respect of any regulated activity of the kind specified by article 14, 21, 25[, 25D] or 53 of the Regulated Activities Order (dealing in investments as principal or agent, arranging deals in investments or advising on investments) which it carries on in the course of—
   (a)   its participation in the Balancing and Settlement Arrangements as operator of the electricity transmission system in [Great Britain] under the Transmission Licence; or
   (b)   the acquisition by it of Balancing Services in accordance with the Electricity Act 1989 and the Transmission Licence.

(2)   ELEXON Clear Limited is exempt from the general prohibition in respect of any regulated activity of the kind specified by article 14, 21[, 25 or 25D] of that Order which it carries on in the course of its participation in the Balancing and Settlement Arrangements as clearer for the purposes of (among other things) receiving from and paying to BSC Parties trading and reconciliation charges arising under the Balancing and Settlement Arrangements.

(3)   Each BSC Party is exempt from the general prohibition in respect of any regulated activity of the kind specified by article 14, 21, 25[, 25D] or 53 of that Order which it carries on in the course of—
   (a)   its participation in the Balancing and Settlement Arrangements; or
   (b)   the provision by it (or, in the case of an activity of the kind specified by article 21 of that Order, its principal) of Balancing Services to NGC.

(4)   ELEXON Limited is exempt from the general prohibition in respect of any regulated activity of the kind specified by article 25[, 25D] of that Order which it carries on in the course of its participation in the Balancing and Settlement Arrangements as administrator.

(5) Each BSC Agent and each Volume Notification Agent is exempt from the general prohibition in respect of any regulated activity of the kind specified by article 25[, 25D] of that Order which it carries on in that capacity.

(6) . . .

(7) In this paragraph—

"Ancillary Services" means services which generators and suppliers of electricity and those making transfers of electricity across an Interconnector are required (as a condition of their connection to the transmission system in [Great Britain]), or have agreed, to make available to NGC for the purpose of securing the stability of the electricity transmission or any distribution system in [Great Britain] or any system linked to it by an Interconnector;

"Balancing and Settlement Arrangements" means—
    (a)   the Balancing Mechanism; and
    (b)   arrangements—
        (i)   for the determination and allocation to BSC Parties of the quantities of electricity that have been delivered to and taken off the electricity transmission system and any distribution system in [Great Britain]; and
        (ii)   which set, and provide for the determination and financial settlement of, BSC Parties' obligations arising by reference to the quantities referred to in sub-paragraph (i), including the difference between such quantities (after taking account of accepted bids and offers in the Balancing Mechanism) and the quantities of electricity contracted for sale and purchase between BSC Parties;

"Balancing Mechanism" means the arrangements pursuant to which BSC Parties may make, and NGC may accept, offers or bids to increase or decrease the quantities of electricity to be delivered to or taken off the electricity transmission system or any distribution system in [Great Britain] at any time or during any period so as to assist NGC in operating and balancing the electricity transmission system, and arrangements for the settlement of financial obligations arising from the acceptance of such offers and bids;

"Balancing Services" means—
    (a)   offers and bids made in the Balancing Mechanism;
    (b)   Ancillary Services; and
    (c)   other services available to NGC which assist it in operating the electricity transmission system in accordance with the Electricity Act 1989 and the Transmission Licence;

"BSC Agents" means the persons for the time being engaged by or on behalf of ELEXON Limited for the purpose of providing services to all BSC Parties, NGC, ELEXON Limited and ELEXON Clear Limited in connection with the operation of the Balancing and Settlement Arrangements;

["BSC Framework Agreement" means the agreement of that title in the form approved by the Secretary of State for the purpose of conditions of the Transmission Licence and which is dated 14 August 2000; and "conditions" for the purposes of this definition means conditions determined by the Secretary of State under powers granted by section 137(1) of the Energy Act 2004. and incorporated into existing electricity transmission licences by a scheme made by the Secretary of State pursuant to section 138 of, and Schedule 17 to, that Act;]

"BSC Parties" means those persons (other than NGC, ELEXON Limited and ELEXON Clear Limited) who have signed or acceded to (in accordance with the terms of the BSC Framework Agreement), and not withdrawn from, the BSC Framework Agreement;

"Interconnector" means the electric lines and electrical plant [and meters] used [solely] for the transfer of electricity to or from the electricity transmission system . . . in [Great Britain] into or out of [Great Britain];

"NGC" means . . . National Grid Company plc;

. . . .
"the Transmission Licence" means the licence to [participate in the transmission of] electricity in [Great Britain] granted[, or treated as granted,] to NGC under section 6(1)(b) of the Electricity Act 1989; and

"Volume Notification Agents" means the persons for the time being appointed and authorised under and in accordance with the Balancing and Settlement Arrangements on behalf of BSC Parties to notify to the BSC Agent designated for that purpose pursuant to the Balancing and Settlement Arrangements quantities of electricity contracted for the sale and purchase between those BSC Parties to be taken into account for the purposes of the Balancing and Settlement Arrangements.]

[Freight Forwarders and Storage Firms

50. (1) A freight forwarder or storage firm is exempt from the general prohibition in respect of any regulated activity of the kind specified by article 21, 25, 39A or 53 of the Regulated Activities Order (dealing in investments as agent, arranging deals in investments, assisting in the administration and performance of a contract of insurance or advising on investments) in the circumstances referred to in paragraph 2.

(2)   The circumstances are—

    (a)   where a freight forwarder ("F")—

        (i)   holds a policy of insurance which insures F in respect of loss of or damage to goods which F transports or of which F arranges the transportation, and

        (ii) makes available to a customer rights under that policy to enable the customer to claim directly against the insurer in respect of loss or damage to those goods; or

    (b)   where a storage firm ("S")—

        (i)   holds a policy of insurance which insures S in respect of loss of or damage to goods which S stores or for which S arranges storage, and

        (ii) makes available to a customer rights under that policy to enable the customer to claim directly against the insurer in respect of loss or damage to those goods.

(3)   In this paragraph—

    (a)   "freight forwarder" means a person whose principal business is arranging or carrying out the transportation of goods;

    (b)   "storage firm" means a person whose principal business is storing goods or arranging storage for goods;

    (c)   "customer" means a person . . . who uses the service of a freight forwarder or storage firm.

Policyholder Advocates

51. (1)   A person acting as a policyholder advocate is exempt from the general prohibition in respect of any regulated activity of the kind specified by article 25 or 53 of the Regulated Activities Order (arranging deals in investments or advising on investments) in so far as he carries on these activities in connection with, or for the purposes of, his role as policyholder advocate.

(2)   In sub-paragraph (1), "policyholder advocate" means a person who is—

    (a)   appointed by an insurer ("I") to represent the interests of policyholders in negotiations with I about I's proposals to redefine the rights and interests in any surplus assets arising in I's with-profits fund; and

    (b)   approved or nominated by the Authority to carry out that role.

(3)   In sub-paragraph (2), "with-profits fund" means a long-term insurance fund in which policyholders are eligible to participate in surplus assets of the fund.]

NOTES

Para 40: sub-para (3) added by the Financial Services and Markets Act 2000 (Exemption) (Amendment) Order 2007, SI 2007/125, art 6(a), as from 1 November 2007; words in first pair of square brackets substituted, and words in second pair of square brackets added, by the Financial Services and Markets Act 2000 (Exemption) (Amendment No 2) Order 2007, SI 2007/1821, art 2(1), (3), as from 1 November 2007.

Para 41: words in first pair of square brackets in sub-para (3)(a) substituted, and words in second pair of square brackets in that sub-para inserted, by the Financial Services and Markets Act 2000 (Regulated Activities) (Amendment) Order 2010, SI 2010/86, art 4, Schedule, para 7, as from 24 February 2010; words in square brackets in sub-para (3)(b)(ii) inserted by the Civil Partnership Act 2004 (Amendments to Subordinate Legislation) Order 2005, SI 2005/2114, art 2(16), Sch 16, Pt 1, para 4, as from 5 December 2005.

Para 42: words in square brackets substituted by SI 2007/125, art 6(b), as from 1 November 2007.

Para 47: substituted by the Financial Services and Markets Act 2000 (Exemption) (Amendment) (No 2) Order 2003, SI 2003/1675, art 2(1), (4)(b), as from 31 October 2004 (in so far as providing for an exemption in relation to any mortgage activity), and as from 14 January 2005 (otherwise); word omitted from sub-para (a) revoked, and sub-paras (c), (d) inserted, by the Financial Services and Markets Act 2000 (Regulated Activities) (Amendment) (No 2) Order 2006, SI 2006/2383, art 30(a), as from 6 April 2007; word "or" omitted from sub-para (c) revoked, and sub-para (e) inserted, by the Financial Services and Markets Act 2000 (Regulated Activities) (Amendment) Order 2009, SI 2009/1342, art 28(a), as from 1 July 2009 (certain purposes), and as from 30 June 2010 (otherwise).

Para 48: substituted by SI 2003/1675, art 2(1), (4)(c), as from 31 October 2004 (in so far as providing for an exemption in relation to any mortgage activity), and as from 14 January 2005 (otherwise); word omitted from sub-para (1)(a) revoked, and sub-paras (1)(c), (d) inserted, by SI 2006/2383, art 30(b), as from 6 April 2007; word omitted from sub-para (1)(c) revoked, and sub-para (1)(e) inserted, by the Financial Services and Markets Act 2000 (Regulated Activities) (Amendment) Order 2009, SI 2009/1342, art 28(b), as from 1 July 2009 (certain purposes), and as from 30 June 2010 (otherwise); sub-para (2)(aa) inserted by the Housing and Regeneration Act 2008 (Consequential Provisions) (No 2) Order 2010, SI 2010/671, art 4, Sch 1, para 27, as from 1 April 2010; words in square brackets in sub-para (2)(c) substituted, and sub-para (2)(ca) inserted, by the Housing and Regeneration Act 2008 (Consequential Provisions) (No 2) Order 2008, SI 2008/2831, arts 3, 4, Sch 1, para 11, Sch 2, para 4, as from 1 December 2008; sub-para (2)(f) added by the Financial Services and Markets Act 2000 (Exemption) (Amendment) Order 2005, SI 2005/592, art 2(2), as from 6 April 2005; sub-para (2)(g) added by the Financial Services and Markets Act 2000 (Exemption) (Amendment) Order 2011, SI 2011/1626, art 2, as from 26 July 2011.

Para 49: added by the Financial Services and Markets Act 2000 (Exemption) (Amendment) Order 2001, SI 2001/3623, arts 2, 8, as from 1 December 2001, and subsequently amended as follows:

Words ", operating a multilateral trading facility" in square brackets in sub-para (1), and the figure ", 25D" in square brackets in sub-paras (1), (3)–(5), inserted by SI 2007/125, art 6(c)(i), (iii)–(v), as from 1 November 2007.

Words in square brackets in sub-para (2) substituted by SI 2007/125, art 6(c)(ii), as from 1 November 2007.

Other words in square brackets substituted or inserted, and words omitted revoked, by the Financial Services and Markets Act 2000 (Exemption) (Amendment) Order 2005, SI 2005/592, art 3, as from 1 April 2005.

Para 50: added, together with para 51, by SI 2007/1821, art 2(1), (4), as from 20 July 2007; words omitted from the definition "customer" revoked by the Financial Services and Markets Act 2000 (Exemption) (Amendment) Order 2009, SI 2009/264, art 2, as from 6 April 2009.

Para 51: added as noted above.

Transfer of functions: by the Housing (Scotland) Act 2001, s 84, the functions of Scottish Homes are transferred to the Scottish Ministers.

Step-children, etc: as to the meaning of this, and related expressions, see the Civil Partnership Act 2004, s 246 (as applied to this Order by the Civil Partnership Act 2004 (Relationships Arising Through Civil Partnership) Order 2005, SI 2005/3137, art 3, Schedule).

FINANCIAL SERVICES AND MARKETS ACT 2000 (DESIGNATED PROFESSIONAL BODIES) ORDER 2001

(SI 2001/1226)

NOTES
Made: 27 March 2001.
Authority: Financial Services and Markets Act 2000, s 326.
Commencement: 28 March 2001.
This Order is reproduced as amended by: the Financial Services and Markets Act 2000 (Designated Professional Bodies) (Amendment) Order 2004, SI 2004/3352; the Financial Services and Markets Act 2000 (Designated Professional Bodies) (Amendment) Order 2006, SI 2006/58.

[8.230]
1 Citation, commencement and interpretation
(1) This Order may be cited as the Financial Services and Markets Act 2000 (Designated Professional Bodies) Order 2001.
(2) This Order comes into force on the day after the day on which it is made.
(3) In this Order, "the Act" means the Financial Services and Markets Act 2000.

[8.231]
2 Designated professional bodies
The following bodies are designated under section 326(1) of the Act for the purposes of Part XX of the Act—
 (a) the Law Society;
 (b) the Law Society of Scotland;
 (c) the Law Society of Northern Ireland;
 (d) the Institute of Chartered Accountants in England and Wales;
 (e) the Institute of Chartered Accountants of Scotland;
 (f) the Institute of Chartered Accountants in Ireland;
 (g) the Association of Chartered Certified Accountants;
 (h) the Institute of Actuaries;
 [(i) the Council for Licensed Conveyancers][;
 (j) the Royal Institution of Chartered Surveyors].

NOTES
Para (i) added by the Financial Services and Markets Act 2000 (Designated Professional Bodies) (Amendment) Order 2004, SI 2004/3352, art 2, as from 14 January 2005; para (j) added by the Financial Services and Markets Act 2000 (Designated Professional Bodies) (Amendment) Order 2006, SI 2006/58, art 2, as from 10 February 2006.

FINANCIAL SERVICES AND MARKETS ACT 2000 (COLLECTIVE INVESTMENT SCHEMES CONSTITUTED IN OTHER EEA STATES) REGULATIONS 2001

(SI 2001/2383)

NOTES
Made: 4 July 2001.
Authority: Financial Services and Markets Act 2000, ss 264, 417(1).
Commencement: 1 December 2001.
These Regulations are reproduced as amended by: the Collective Investment Schemes (Miscellaneous Amendments) Regulations 2003, SI 2003/2066; the Undertakings for Collective Investment in Transferable Securities Regulations 2011, SI 2011/1613.

[8.232]
1

These Regulations may be cited as the Financial Services and Markets Act 2000 (Collective Investment Schemes Constituted in Other EEA States) Regulations 2001 and come into force on the day on which section 19 of the Act comes into force.

[8.233]

2

In these Regulations—

"the Act" means the Financial Services and Markets Act 2000;

. . .

["the UCITS 1985 directive" means the Council Directive of 20 December 1985 on the coordination of laws, regulations and administrative provisions relating to undertakings for collective investment in transferable securities (No 85/61/EEC)].

NOTES

Definition "the UCITS Directive" (omitted) revoked by the Collective Investment Schemes (Miscellaneous Amendments) Regulations 2003, SI 2003/2066, reg 11(a), as from 13 February 2004.

Definition "the UCITS 1985 directive" added by the Undertakings for Collective Investment in Transferable Securities Regulations 2011, SI 2011/1613, reg 6(1), (2), as from 1 July 2011.

[8.234]

3

The requirements prescribed for the purposes of section 264 of the Act are that a collective investment scheme is one which, in accordance with [the UCITS directive], is an undertaking for collective investment in transferable securities subject to [that directive] ("the undertaking").

NOTES

Words in square brackets substituted by the Collective Investment Schemes (Miscellaneous Amendments) Regulations 2003, SI 2003/2066, reg 11(b), as from 13 February 2004.

[8.235]

4

The notice to be given to the Authority under section 264(1) of the Act must contain or be accompanied by—

    (a)   the undertaking's fund rules or instrument of incorporation;

    [(b)   its prospectus and, subject to regulation 5, the key investor information referred to in Article 78 of the UCITS directive;]

    (c)   where appropriate, its latest annual report and any subsequent half-yearly report.

NOTES

Para (b): substituted by the Undertakings for Collective Investment in Transferable Securities Regulations 2011, SI 2011/1613, reg 6(1), (3), as from 1 July 2011.

[8.236]

[5

The notice to be given to the Authority under section 264(1) may be submitted with the simplified prospectus (within the meaning of Section VI of the UCITS 1985 directive) until 30 June 2012.]

NOTES

Commencement: 1 July 2011.

Inserted by the Undertakings for Collective Investment in Transferable Securities Regulations 2011, SI 2011/1613, reg 6(1), (4), as from 1 July 2011.

FINANCIAL SERVICES AND MARKETS ACT 2000 (OFFICIAL LISTING OF SECURITIES) REGULATIONS 2001

(SI 2001/2956)

NOTES

Made: 22 August 2001.

Authority: Financial Services and Markets Act 2000, ss 75(3), 79(3), 103(1), 417(1), 428(3), Sch 10, para 9, Sch 11, paras 16(3), (4), 20(2).

Commencement: 1 December 2001.

These Regulations are reproduced as amended by: the Financial Services and Markets Act 2000 (Official Listing of Securities) (Amendment) Regulations 2001, SI 2001/3439; the Prospectus Regulations 2005, SI 2005/1433; the Companies Act 2006 (Consequential Amendments and Transitional Provisions) Order 2011, SI 2011/1265.

ARRANGEMENT OF REGULATIONS

PART 1
GENERAL

PART 1
GENERAL

[8.237]
1   Citation and commencement

These Regulations may be cited as the Financial Services and Markets Act 2000 (Official Listing of Securities) Regulations 2001 and come into force on the day on which section 74(1) comes into force.

NOTES

FSMA 2000, s 74(1) came into force on 1 December 2001 (see the Financial Services and Markets Act 2000 (Commencement No 7) Order 2001, SI 2001/3538).

[8.238]
2   Interpretation

(1)   In these Regulations—

"the Act" means the Financial Services and Markets Act 2000;

"competent authority" is to be construed in accordance with section 72;

"the Financial Promotion Order" means the Financial Services and Markets Act 2000 (Financial Promotion) Order 2001;

"issuer" has the same meaning as is given, for the purposes of section 103(1), in regulation 4 below;

"non-listing prospectus" has the meaning given in section 87(2); and

"the Regulated Activities Order" means the Financial Services and Markets Act 2000 (Regulated Activities) Order 2001.

(2)   Any reference in these Regulations to a section or Schedule is, unless otherwise stated or unless the context otherwise requires, a reference to that section of or Schedule to the Act.

PART 2
MISCELLANEOUS MATTERS PRESCRIBED FOR THE PURPOSES OF PART VI OF THE ACT

[8.239]
3   Bodies whose securities may not be listed

For the purposes of section 75(3) (which provides that no application for listing may be entertained in respect of securities issued by a body of a prescribed kind) there are prescribed the following kinds of body—

(a)   [where the securities are securities within the meaning of the Regulated Activities Order,] a private company within the meaning of [section 4(1) of the Companies Act 2006];

(b)   an old public company within the meaning of section 1 of the Companies Consolidation (Consequential Provisions) Act 1985 or article 3 of the Companies Consolidation (Consequential Provisions) (Northern Ireland) Order 1986.

NOTES

Words in first pair of square brackets in para (a) inserted by the Financial Services and Markets Act 2000 (Official Listing of Securities) (Amendment) Regulations 2001, SI 2001/3439, reg 2, as from 1 December 2001; words in second pair of square brackets substituted by the Companies Act 2006 (Consequential Amendments and Transitional Provisions) Order 2011, SI 2011/1265, art 19(1), (2), as from 12 May 2011.

Old public companies: as to the meaning of this, see now the Companies Act 2006 (Consequential Amendments and Transitional Provisions) Order 2011, SI 2011/1265, Sch 1 at **[4.651]**. Note that the Companies Consolidation (Consequential Provisions) Act 1985 was repealed by the 2011 Order, as from 12 May 2011.

[8.240]

4 Meaning of "issuer"

(1) For the purposes of section 103(1), "issuer" has the meaning given in this regulation.

(2) In relation to certificates or other instruments falling within article 80 of the Regulated Activities Order (certificates representing certain securities), "issuer" means—

   (a)   . . .

   (b)   for all other purposes, the person who issued or is to issue the securities to which the certificates or instruments relate.

(3) In relation to any other securities, "issuer" means the person by whom the securities have been or are to be issued.

NOTES

Para (2): sub-para (a) revoked by the Prospectus Regulations 2005, SI 2005/1433, reg 2(3), Sch 3, para 3, as from 1 July 2005.

[8.241]

5 Meaning of "approved exchange"

For the purposes of paragraph 9 of Schedule 10, "approved exchange" means a recognised investment exchange approved by the Treasury for the purposes of the Public Offers of Securities Regulations 1995 (either generally or in relation to dealings in securities).

PART 3
PERSONS RESPONSIBLE FOR LISTING PARTICULARS, PROSPECTUSES AND NON-LISTING PROSPECTUSES

[8.242]

6 Responsibility for listing particulars

(1) Subject to the following provisions of this Part, for the purposes of Part VI of the Act the persons responsible for listing particulars (including supplementary listing particulars) are—

   (a)   the issuer of the securities to which the particulars relate;

   (b)   where the issuer is a body corporate, each person who is a director of that body at the time when the particulars are submitted to the competent authority;

   (c)   where the issuer is a body corporate, each person who has authorised himself to be named, and is named, in the particulars as a director or as having agreed to become a director of that body either immediately or at a future time;

   (d)   each person who accepts, and is stated in the particulars as accepting, responsibility for the particulars;

   (e)   each person not falling within any of the foregoing sub-paragraphs who has authorised the contents of the particulars.

(2) A person is not to be treated as responsible for any particulars by virtue of paragraph (1)(b) above if they are published without his knowledge or consent and on becoming aware of their publication he forthwith gives reasonable public notice that they were published without his knowledge or consent.

(3) When accepting responsibility for particulars under paragraph (1)(d) above or authorising their contents under paragraph (1)(e) above, a person may state that he does so only in relation to certain specified parts of the particulars, or only in certain specified respects, and in such a case he is responsible under paragraph (1)(d) or (e) above—

   (a)   only to the extent specified; and

   (b)   only if the material in question is included in (or substantially in) the form and context to which he has agreed.

(4) Nothing in this regulation is to be construed as making a person responsible for any particulars by reason of giving advice as to their contents in a professional capacity.

(5) Where by virtue of this regulation the issuer of any shares pays or is liable to pay compensation under section 90 for loss suffered in respect of shares for which a person has subscribed no account is to be taken of that liability or payment in determining any question as to the amount paid on subscription for those shares or as to the amount paid up or deemed to be paid up on them.

[8.243]

7 Securities issued in connection with takeovers and mergers

(1) This regulation applies where—

   (a)   listing particulars relate to securities which are to be issued in connection with—

      (i)   an offer by the issuer (or by a wholly-owned subsidiary of the issuer) for securities issued by another person ("A");

      (ii)   an agreement for the acquisition by the issuer (or by a wholly-owned subsidiary of the issuer) of securities issued by another person ("A"); or

      (iii)   any arrangement whereby the whole of the undertaking of another person ("A") is to become the undertaking of the issuer (or of a wholly-owned subsidiary of the issuer, or of a body corporate which will become such a subsidiary by virtue of the arrangement); and

    (b)   each of the specified persons is responsible by virtue of regulation 6(1)(d) above for any part ("the relevant part") of the particulars relating to A or to the securities or undertaking to which the offer, agreement or arrangement relates.

(2)   In paragraph (1)(b) above the "specified persons" are—

    (a)   A; and

    (b)   where A is a body corporate—

        (i)   each person who is a director of A at the time when the particulars are submitted to the competent authority; and

        (ii)   each other person who has authorised himself to be named, and is named, in the particulars as a director of A.

(3)   Where this regulation applies, no person is to be treated as responsible for the relevant part of the particulars under regulation 6(1)(a), (b) or (c) above but without prejudice to his being responsible under regulation 6(1)(d).

(4)   In this regulation—

    (a)   "listing particulars" includes supplementary listing particulars; and

    (b)   "wholly-owned subsidiary" is to be construed in accordance with [section 1159 of the Companies Act 2006] (and, in relation to an issuer which is not a body corporate, means a body corporate which would be a wholly-owned subsidiary of the issuer within the meaning of that section if the issuer were a body corporate).

NOTES

Para (4): words in square brackets substituted by the Companies Act 2006 (Consequential Amendments and Transitional Provisions) Order 2011, SI 2011/1265, art 19(1), (3), as from 12 May 2011.

[8.244]
8 Successor companies under legislation relating to electricity

(1)   Where—

    (a)   the same document contains listing particulars relating to the securities of—

        (i)   two or more successor companies within the meaning of Part II of the Electricity Act 1989, or

        (ii)   two or more successor companies within the meaning of Part III of the Electricity (Northern Ireland) Order 1992; and

    (b)   the responsibility of any person for any information included in the document ("the relevant information") is stated in the document to be confined to its inclusion as part of the particulars relating to the securities of any one of those companies,

that person is not to be treated as responsible, by virtue of regulation 6 above, for the relevant information in so far as it is stated in the document to form part of the particulars relating to the securities of any other of those companies.

(2)   "Listing particulars" includes supplementary listing particulars.

[8.245]
9 Specialist securities

(1)   This regulation applies where listing particulars relate to securities of a kind specified by listing rules for the purposes of section 82(1)(c), other than securities which are to be issued in the circumstances mentioned in regulation 7(1)(a) above.

(2)   No person is to be treated as responsible for the particulars under regulation 6(1)(a), (b) or (c) above but without prejudice to his being responsible under regulation 6(1)(d).

(3)   "Listing particulars" includes supplementary listing particulars.

10–12   *(Revoked by the Prospectus Regulations 2005, SI 2005/1433, reg 2(3), Sch 3, para 3, as from 1 July 2005.)*

FINANCIAL SERVICES AND MARKETS ACT 2000 (COLLECTIVE INVESTMENT SCHEMES) (DESIGNATED COUNTRIES AND TERRITORIES) ORDER 2003

(SI 2003/1181)

NOTES

Made: 29 April 2003.
Authority: Financial Services and Markets Act 2000, ss 270, 426, 428(3).
Commencement: 21 May 2003.
Amendment: as of 1 July 2011, this Order had not been amended.

[8.246]

1   Citation and commencement

This Order may be cited as the Financial Services and Markets Act 2000 (Collective Investment Schemes) (Designated Countries and Territories) Order 2003 and comes into force on 21st May 2003.

[8.247]

2   Designation of territories

Guernsey, Jersey and the Isle of Man are designated for the purposes of section 270 of the Act (collective investment schemes authorised in designated countries or territories).

[8.248]

3   Specification of classes of collective investment schemes

(1)   The following classes of collective investment scheme are specified for the purposes of subsection (1)(b) of section 270 of the Act—

- (a)   where the scheme is managed in, and authorised under the law of, Guernsey, any authorised scheme (within the meaning of the Collective Investment Schemes (Class A) Rules 2002, as amended by the Collective Investment Schemes (Class A) Rules 2002 (Amendment) Rules 2003) which is not—
  - (i)   a feeder-fund; or
  - (ii)   a protected cell scheme;
- (b)   where the scheme is managed in, and authorised under the law of, Jersey, any scheme which is a recognised fund within the meaning of the Collective Investment Funds (Recognised Funds) (Rules) (Jersey) Order 2003 and which is not a feeder-fund; and
- (c)   where the scheme is managed in, and authorised under the law of, the Isle of Man, any scheme which is an authorised scheme within the meaning of the Financial Supervision Act 1988 (an Act of Tynwald) (as last amended by the Corporate Service Providers Act 2000) and which is not a feeder-fund.

(2)   For the purposes of this article—

- (a)   "feeder-fund" means a collective investment scheme which has as its purpose the investment of its funds in securities (within the meaning of article 3 of the Financial Services and Markets Act 2000 (Regulated Activities) Order 2001) issued by one other collective investment scheme; and
- (b)   "protected cell scheme" means a collective investment scheme which, under the law of Guernsey, has been incorporated as, or converted into, a protected cell company under the Protected Cell Companies Ordinance 1997 (as last amended by the Protected Cell Companies (Amendment) Ordinance 1998).

[8.249]

4   Revocation of transitional provisions

Article 67(1) of the Financial Services and Markets Act 2000 (Transitional Provisions) (Authorised Persons etc) Order 2001, in so far as it relates to any order under section 87(1) of the Financial Services Act 1986 which designated Guernsey, Jersey or the Isle of Man for the purposes of that section, is revoked.

FINANCIAL SERVICES AND MARKETS ACT 2000 (FINANCIAL PROMOTION) ORDER 2005

(SI 2005/1529)

NOTES

Made: 8 June 2005.

Authority: Financial Services and Markets Act 2000, ss 21(5), (6), (9), (10), 428(3), Sch 2, para 25.

Commencement: 1 July 2005.

Note: this Order revokes and re-enacts, with certain amendments, the Financial Services and Markets Act 2000 (Financial Promotion) Order 2001, SI 2001/1335 (as amended).

This Order is reproduced as amended by: the Financial Services and Markets Act 2000 (Financial Promotion) (Amendment) Order 2005, SI 2005/3392; the Financial Services and Markets Act 2000 (Regulated Activities) (Amendment) Order 2006, SI 2006/1969; the Financial Services and Markets Act 2000 (Regulated Activities) (Amendment) (No 2) Order 2006, SI 2006/2383; the Financial Services and Markets Act 2000 (Regulated Activities) (Amendment No 3) Order 2006, SI 2006/3384; the Financial Services and Markets Act 2000 (Financial Promotion) (Amendment) Order 2007, SI 2007/1083; the Companies Act 2006 (Commencement No 2, Consequential Amendments, Transitional Provisions and Savings) Order 2007, SI 2007/1093; the Financial Services and Markets Act 2000 (Financial Promotion) (Amendment No 2) Order 2007, SI 2007/2615; the Financial Services and Markets Act 2000 (Regulated Activities) (Amendment) Order 2009, SI 2009/1342; the Financial Services and Markets Act 2000 (Regulated Activities) (Amendment) Order 2010, SI 2010/86; the Financial Services and Markets Act 2000 (Financial Promotion) (Amendment) Order 2010, SI 2010/905; the Financial Services and Markets Act 2000 (Regulated Activities) (Amendment) Order 2011, SI 2011/133; the Companies Act 2006 (Consequential Amendments and Transitional Provisions) Order 2011, SI 2011/1265; the Undertakings for Collective Investment in Transferable Securities Regulations 2011, SI 2011/1613.

ARRANGEMENT OF ARTICLES

PART I
CITATION, COMMENCEMENT AND INTERPRETATION

PART II
CONTROLLED ACTIVITIES AND CONTROLLED INVESTMENTS

PART III
EXEMPTIONS: INTERPRETATION AND APPLICATION

PART IV
EXEMPT COMMUNICATIONS: ALL CONTROLLED ACTIVITIES

PART V
EXEMPT COMMUNICATIONS: DEPOSITS AND INSURANCE

PART VI
EXEMPT COMMUNICATIONS: CERTAIN CONTROLLED ACTIVITIES

SCHEDULES

PART I
CITATION, COMMENCEMENT AND INTERPRETATION

[8.250]
1 Citation and commencement

This Order may be cited as the Financial Services and Markets Act 2000 (Financial Promotion) Order 2005 and comes into force on 1st July 2005.

[8.251]
2 Interpretation: general

(1) In this Order, except where the context otherwise requires—

. . .

. . .

["the 2006 Act" means the Companies Act 2006;]

"the Act" means the Financial Services and Markets Act 2000;

"close relative" in relation to a person means—

    (a)   his spouse [or civil partner];

    (b)   his children and step-children, his parents and step-parents, his brothers and sisters and his step-brothers and step-sisters; and

    (c)   the spouse [or civil partner] of any person within sub-paragraph (b);

"controlled activity" has the meaning given by article 4 and Schedule 1;

"controlled investment" has the meaning given by article 4 and Schedule 1;

"deposit" means a sum of money which is a deposit for the purposes of article 5 of the Regulated Activities Order;

["direct financial benefit" includes any commission, discount, remuneration or reduction in premium;]

"equity share capital" has the meaning given in [the 2006 Act (see section 548)];

"financial promotion restriction" has the meaning given by article 5;

"government" means the government of the United Kingdom, the Scottish Administration, the Executive Committee of the Northern Ireland Assembly, the National Assembly for Wales and any government of any country or territory outside the United Kingdom;

"instrument" includes any record whether or not in the form of a document;

"international organisation" means any body the members of which comprise—

    (a)   states including the United Kingdom or another EEA State; or

    (b)   bodies whose members comprise states including the United Kingdom or another EEA State;

"overseas communicator" has the meaning given by article 30;

"previously overseas customer" has the meaning given by article 31;

"publication" means—

    (a)   a newspaper, journal, magazine or other periodical publication;

    (b)   a web site or similar system for the electronic display of information;

    (c)   any programme forming part of a service consisting of the broadcast or transmission of television or radio programmes;

    (d)   any teletext service, that—is to say a service consisting of television transmissions consisting of a succession of visual displays (with or without accompanying sound) capable of being selected and held for separate viewing or other use;

"qualifying contract of insurance" has the meaning given in the Regulated Activities Order;

"qualifying credit" has the meaning given by paragraph 10 of Schedule 1;

"the Regulated Activities Order" means the Financial Services and Markets Act 2000 (Regulated Activities) Order 2001;

"relevant insurance activity" has the meaning given by article 21;

"relevant investment activities" has the meaning given by article 30;

"solicited real time communication" has the meaning given by article 8;

"units", in a collective investment scheme, has the meaning given by Part XVII of the Act;

"unsolicited real time communication" has the meaning given by article 8.

(2) References to a person engaging in investment activity are to be construed in accordance with subsection (8) of section 21 of the Act; and for these purposes, "controlled activity" and "controlled investment" in that subsection have the meaning given in this Order.

NOTES

Para (1): definitions "the 1985 Act" and "the 1986 Order" (omitted) revoked, definition the 2006 Act" inserted, and words in square brackets in definition "equity share capital" substituted, by the Companies Act 2006 (Consequential Amendments and Transitional Provisions) Order 2011, SI 2011/1265, art 26(1), (2), as from 12 May 2011; words in square brackets in definition "close relative" inserted by the Financial Services and Markets Act 2000 (Financial Promotion) (Amendment) Order 2005, SI 2005/3392, art 2(1), (2), as from 21 December 2005; definition "direct financial benefit" inserted by the Financial Services and Markets Act 2000 (Financial Promotion) (Amendment) Order 2010, SI 2010/905, arts 2, 3, as from 13 April 2010.

"Close relative": as to the meaning of "step-children", and related expressions, see the Civil Partnership Act 2004, s 246 (as applied to this Order by the Civil Partnership Act 2004 (Relationships Arising Through Civil Partnership) Order 2005, SI 2005/3137, art 3, Schedule).

[8.252]

3   Interpretation: unlisted companies

(1)   In this Order, an "unlisted company" means a body corporate the shares in which are not—

(a)   listed or quoted on an investment exchange whether in the United Kingdom or elsewhere;

(b)   shares in respect of which information is, with the agreement or approval of any officer of the company, published for the purpose of facilitating deals in the shares indicating prices at which persons have dealt or are willing to deal in them other than persons who, at the time the information is published, are existing members of a relevant class; or

(c)   subject to a marketing arrangement which accords to the company the facilities referred to in [section 693(3)(b) of the 2006 Act].

(2)   For the purpose of paragraph (1)(b), a person is to be regarded as a member of a relevant class if he was, at the relevant time—

(a)   an existing member or debenture holder of the company;

(b)   an existing employee of the company;

(c)   a close relative of such a member or employee; or

(d)   a trustee (acting in his capacity as such) of a trust, the principal beneficiary of which is a person within any of sub-paragraphs (a), (b) and (c).

(3)   In this Order references to shares in and debentures of an unlisted company are references to—

(a)   in the case of a body corporate which is a company within the meaning of [the 2006 Act (see section 1)], shares and debentures within the meaning of that Act [(see sections 540(1) and (4) and 738)];

(b)   . . .

(c)   in the case of any other body corporate, investments falling within paragraph 14[, 15 or 15A] of Schedule 1 to this Order.

NOTES

Para (1): words in square brackets substituted by the Companies Act 2006 (Consequential Amendments and Transitional Provisions) Order 2011, SI 2011/1265, art 26(1), (3)(a), as from 12 May 2011.

Para (3): words in first pair of square brackets in sub-para (a) substituted, words in second pair of square brackets in that paragraph inserted, and sub-para (b) revoked, by SI 2011/1265, art 26(1), (3)(b), as from 12 May 2011; words in square brackets in sub-para (c) substituted by the Financial Services and Markets Act 2000 (Regulated Activities) (Amendment) Order 2010, SI 2010/86, art 4, Schedule, para 9(a)(i), as from 24 February 2010.

PART II
CONTROLLED ACTIVITIES AND CONTROLLED INVESTMENTS

[8.253]

4   Definition of controlled activities and controlled investments

(1)   For the purposes of section 21(9) of the Act, a controlled activity is an activity which falls within any of paragraphs 1 to 11 of Schedule 1.

(2)   For the purposes of section 21(10) of the Act, a controlled investment is an investment which falls within any of paragraphs 12 to 27 of Schedule 1.

PART III
EXEMPTIONS: INTERPRETATION AND APPLICATION

[8.254]

5   Interpretation: financial promotion restriction

In this Order, any reference to the financial promotion restriction is a reference to the restriction in section 21(1) of the Act.

[8.255]

6   Interpretation: communications

In this Order—

(a)   any reference to a communication is a reference to the communication, in the course of business, of an invitation or inducement to engage in investment activity;

(b)   any reference to a communication being made to another person is a reference to a communication being addressed, whether orally or in legible form, to a particular person or persons (for example where it is contained in a telephone call or letter);

(c)   any reference to a communication being directed at persons is a reference to a communication being addressed to persons generally (for example where it is contained in a television broadcast or web site);

(d)   "communicate" includes causing a communication to be made or directed;

(e)   a "recipient" of a communication is the person to whom the communication is made or, in the case of a non-real time communication which is directed at persons generally, any person who reads or hears the communication;

(f) "electronic commerce communication" means a communication, the making of which constitutes the provision of an information society service;

(g) "incoming electronic commerce communication" means an electronic commerce communication made from an establishment in an EEA State other than the United Kingdom;

(h) "outgoing electronic commerce communication" means an electronic commerce communication made from an establishment in the United Kingdom to a person in an EEA State other than the United Kingdom.

[8.256]

7 Interpretation: real time communications

(1) In this Order, references to a real time communication are references to any communication made in the course of a personal visit, telephone conversation or other interactive dialogue.

(2) A non-real time communication is a communication not falling within paragraph (1).

(3) For the purposes of this Order, non-real time communications include communications made by letter or e-mail or contained in a publication.

(4) For the purposes of this Order, the factors in paragraph (5) are to be treated as indications that a communication is a non-real time communication.

(5) The factors are that—

(a) the communication is made to or directed at more than one recipient in identical terms (save for details of the recipient's identity);

(b) the communication is made or directed by way of a system which in the normal course constitutes or creates a record of the communication which is available to the recipient to refer to at a later time;

(c) the communication is made or directed by way of a system which in the normal course does not enable or require the recipient to respond immediately to it.

[8.257]

8 Interpretation: solicited and unsolicited real time communications

(1) A real time communication is solicited where it is made in the course of a personal visit, telephone call or other interactive dialogue if that call, visit or dialogue—

(a) was initiated by the recipient of the communication; or

(b) takes place in response to an express request from the recipient of the communication.

(2) A real time communication is unsolicited where it is made otherwise than as described in paragraph (1).

(3) For the purposes of paragraph (1)—

(a) a person is not to be treated as expressly requesting a call, visit or dialogue—

(i) because he omits to indicate that he does not wish to receive any or any further visits or calls or to engage in any or any further dialogue;

(ii) because he agrees to standard terms that state that such visits, calls or dialogue will take place, unless he has signified clearly that, in addition to agreeing to the terms, he is willing for them to take place;

(b) a communication is solicited only if it is clear from all the circumstances when the call, visit or dialogue is initiated or requested that during the course of the visit, call or dialogue communications will be made concerning the kind of controlled activities or investments to which the communications in fact made relate;

(c) it is immaterial whether the express request was made before or after this article comes into force.

(4) Where a real time communication is solicited by a recipient ("R"), it is treated as having also been solicited by any other person to whom it is made at the same time as it is made to R if that other recipient is—

(a) a close relative of R; or

(b) expected to engage in any investment activity jointly with R.

[8.258]

8A Interpretation: outgoing electronic commerce communications

(1) For the purposes of the application of those articles to outgoing electronic commerce communications—

(a) any reference in article 48(7)(c), 50(1)(a) or (3)(e) or 52(3)(c) to an authorised person includes a reference to a person who is entitled, under the law of an EEA State other than the United Kingdom, to carry on regulated activities in that State;

(b) any reference in article 68(1) or 71 to rules or legislation includes a reference to provisions corresponding to those rules or legislation in the law of an EEA State other than the United Kingdom;

(c) any reference in article 49 to an amount in pounds sterling includes a reference to an equivalent amount in another currency.

(2) For the purposes of the application of article 49 to outgoing electronic commerce communications, any reference in [section 831(2) and (3) of the 2006 Act] to a body corporate or company includes a reference to a body corporate or company registered under the law of an EEA State other than the United Kingdom.

(3) For the purposes of the application of article 3 in respect of outgoing electronic commerce communications—

    (a)   any reference in [section 693(3)(b) of the 2006 Act] to a company includes a reference to a company registered under the law of an EEA State other than the United Kingdom;

    (b)   any reference in that section to an investment exchange includes a reference to an investment exchange which is recognised as an investment exchange under the law of an EEA State other than the United Kingdom.

NOTES

Paras (2), (3): words in square brackets substituted by the Companies Act 2006 (Consequential Amendments and Transitional Provisions) Order 2011, SI 2011/1265, art 26(1), (4), as from 12 May 2011.

[8.259]
9 Degree of prominence to be given to required indications

Where a communication must, if it is to fall within any provision of this Order, be accompanied by an indication of any matter, the indication must be presented to the recipient—

    (a)   in a way that can be easily understood; and

    (b)   in such manner as, depending on the means by which the communication is made or directed, is best calculated to bring the matter in question to the attention of the recipient and to allow him to consider it.

[8.260]
10 Application to qualifying contracts of insurance

(1) Nothing in this Order exempts from the application of the financial promotion restriction a communication which invites or induces a person to enter into a qualifying contract of insurance with a person who is not—

    (a)   an authorised person;

    (b)   an exempt person who is exempt in relation to effecting or carrying out contracts of insurance of the class to which the communication relates;

    (c)   a company which has its head office in an EEA State other than the United Kingdom and which is entitled under the law of that State to carry on there insurance business of the class to which the communication relates;

    (d)   a company which has a branch or agency in an EEA State other than the United Kingdom and is entitled under the law of that State to carry on there insurance business of the class to which the communication relates;

    (e)   a company authorised to carry on insurance business of the class to which the communication relates in any country or territory which is listed in Schedule 2.

(2) In this article, references to a class of insurance are references to the class of insurance contract described in Schedule 1 to the Regulated Activities Order into which the effecting or carrying out of the contract to which the communication relates would fall.

[8.261]
11 Combination of different exemptions

(1) In respect of a communication relating to—

    (a)   a controlled activity falling within paragraph 2 of Schedule 1 carried on in relation to a qualifying contract of insurance; or

    (b)   a controlled activity falling within any of paragraphs 3 to 11 of Schedule 1,

a person may rely on the application of one or more of the exemptions in Parts IV and VI.

(2) In respect of a communication relating to—

    (a)   an activity falling within paragraph 1 of Schedule 1; or

    (b)   a relevant insurance activity,

a person may rely on one or more of the exemptions in Parts IV and V; and, where a communication relates to any such activity and also to an activity mentioned in paragraph (1)(a) or (b), a person may rely on one or more of the exemptions in Parts IV and V in respect of the former activity and on one or more of the exemptions in Parts V and VI in respect of the latter activity.

PART IV
EXEMPT COMMUNICATIONS: ALL CONTROLLED ACTIVITIES

[8.262]
12 Communications to overseas recipients

(1) Subject to paragraphs (2) and (7), the financial promotion restriction does not apply to any communication—

(a) which is made (whether from inside or outside the United Kingdom) to a person who receives the communication outside the United Kingdom; or

(b) which is directed (whether from inside or outside the United Kingdom) only at persons outside the United Kingdom.

(2) Paragraph (1) does not apply to an unsolicited real time communication unless—

(a) it is made from a place outside the United Kingdom; and

(b) it is made for the purposes of a business which is carried on outside the United Kingdom and which is not carried on in the United Kingdom.

(3) For the purposes of paragraph (1)(b)—

(a) if the conditions set out in paragraph (4)(a), (b), (c) and (d) are met, a communication directed from a place inside the United Kingdom is to be regarded as directed only at persons outside the United Kingdom;

(b) if the conditions set out in paragraph (4)(c) and (d) are met, a communication directed from a place outside the United Kingdom is to be regarded as directed only at persons outside the United Kingdom;

(c) in any other case where one or more of the conditions in paragraph (4)(a) to (e) are met, that fact is to be taken into account in determining whether or not a communication is to be regarded as directed only at persons outside the United Kingdom (but a communication may still be regarded as directed only at persons outside the United Kingdom even if none of the conditions in paragraph (4) is met).

(4) The conditions are that—

(a) the communication is accompanied by an indication that it is directed only at persons outside the United Kingdom;

(b) the communication is accompanied by an indication that it must not be acted upon by persons in the United Kingdom;

(c) the communication is not referred to in, or directly accessible from, any other communication made to a person or directed at persons in the United Kingdom by the person directing the communication;

(d) there are in place proper systems and procedures to prevent recipients in the United Kingdom (other than those to whom the communication might otherwise lawfully have been made by the person directing it or a member of the same group) engaging in the investment activity to which the communication relates with the person directing the communication, a close relative of his or a member of the same group;

(e) the communication is included in—

(i) a web site, newspaper, journal, magazine or periodical publication which is principally accessed in or intended for a market outside the United Kingdom;

(ii) a radio or television broadcast or teletext service transmitted principally for reception outside the United Kingdom.

(5) For the purpose of paragraph (1)(b), a communication may be treated as directed only at persons outside the United Kingdom even if—

(a) it is also directed, for the purposes of article 19(1)(b), at investment professionals falling within article 19(5) (but disregarding paragraph (6) of that article for this purpose);

(b) it is also directed, for the purposes of article 49(1)(b), at high net worth persons to whom article 49 applies (but disregarding paragraph (2)(e) of that article for this purpose) and it relates to a controlled activity to which article 49 applies;

(c) it is a communication to which article 31 applies.

(6) Where a communication falls within paragraph (5)(a) or (b)—

(a) the condition in paragraph (4)(a) is to be construed as requiring an indication that the communication is directed only at persons outside the United Kingdom or persons having professional experience in matters relating to investments or high net worth persons (as the case may be);

(b) the condition in paragraph (4)(b) is to be construed as requiring an indication that the communication must not be acted upon by persons in the United Kingdom except by persons who have professional experience in matters relating to investments or who are not high net worth persons (as the case may be);

(c) the condition in paragraph (4)(c) will not apply where the other communication referred to in that paragraph is made to a person or directed at a person in the United Kingdom to whom paragraph (5) applies.

(7) Paragraph (1) does not apply to an outgoing electronic commerce communication.

[8.263]
13 Communications from customers and potential customers

(1) The financial promotion restriction does not apply to any communication made by or on behalf of a person ("customer") to one other person ("supplier")—

(a) in order to obtain information about a controlled investment available from or a controlled service provided by the supplier; or

   (b)   in order that the customer can acquire a controlled investment from that supplier or be supplied with a controlled service by that supplier.

(2)   For the purposes of paragraph (1), a controlled service is a service the provision of which constitutes engaging in a controlled activity by the supplier.

[8.264]
14 Follow up non-real time communications and solicited real time communications

(1)   Where a person makes or directs a communication ("the first communication") which is exempt from the financial promotion restriction because, in compliance with the requirements of another provision of this Order, it is accompanied by certain indications or contains certain information, then the financial promotion restriction does not apply to any subsequent communication which complies with the requirements of paragraph (2).

(2)   The requirements of this paragraph are that the subsequent communication—
   (a)   is a non-real time communication or a solicited real time communication;
   (b)   is made by, or on behalf of, the same person who made the first communication;
   (c)   is made to a recipient of the first communication;
   (d)   relates to the same controlled activity and the same controlled investment as the first communication; and
   (e)   is made within 12 months of the recipient receiving the first communication.

(3)   The provisions of this article only apply in the case of a person who makes or directs a communication on behalf of another where the first communication is made by that other person.

(4)   Where a person makes or directs a communication on behalf of another person in reliance on the exemption contained in this article the person on whose behalf the communication was made or directed remains responsible for the content of that communication.

(5)   A communication made or directed before this article comes into force is to be treated as a first communication falling within paragraph (1) if it would have fallen within that paragraph had it been made or directed after this article comes into force.

[8.265]
15 Introductions

(1)   If the requirements of paragraph (2) are met, the financial promotion restriction does not apply to any communication which is made with a view to or for the purposes of introducing the recipient to—
   (a)   an authorised person who carries on the controlled activity to which the communication relates; or
   (b)   an exempt person where the communication relates to a controlled activity which is also a regulated activity in relation to which he is an exempt person.

(2)   The requirements of this paragraph are that—
   (a)   the maker of the communication ("A") is not a close relative of, nor a member of the same group as, the person to whom the introduction is, or is to be, made;
   (b)   A does not receive from any person other than the recipient any pecuniary reward or other advantage arising out of his making the introduction; and
   (c)   it is clear in all the circumstances that the recipient, in his capacity as an investor, is not seeking and has not sought advice from A as to the merits of the recipient engaging in investment activity (or, if the client has sought such advice, A has declined to give it, but has recommended that the recipient seek such advice from an authorised person).

[8.266]
16 Exempt persons

(1)   The financial promotion restriction does not apply to any communication which—
   (a)   is a non-real time communication or a solicited real time communication;
   (b)   is made or directed by an exempt person; and
   (c)   is for the purposes of that exempt person's business of carrying on a controlled activity which is also a regulated activity in relation to which he is an exempt person.

(2)   The financial promotion restriction does not apply to any unsolicited real time communication made by a person ("AR") who is an appointed representative (within the meaning of section 39(2) of the Act) where—
   (a)   the communication is made by AR in carrying on the business—
      (i)   for which his principal ("P") has accepted responsibility for the purposes of section 39 of the Act; and
      (ii)   in relation to which AR is exempt from the general prohibition by virtue of that section; and
   (b)   the communication is one which, if it were made by P, would comply with any rules made by the Authority under section 145 of the Act (financial promotion rules) which are relevant to a communication of that kind.

[8.267]
17 Generic promotions

The financial promotion restriction does not apply to any communication which—
- (a) does not identify (directly or indirectly) a person who provides the controlled investment to which the communication relates; and
- (b) does not identify (directly or indirectly) any person as a person who carries on a controlled activity in relation to that investment.

[8.268]
17A Communications caused to be made or directed by unauthorised persons

(1) If a condition in paragraph (2) is met, the financial promotion restriction does not apply to a communication caused to be made or directed by an unauthorised person which is made or directed by an authorised person.

(2) The conditions in this paragraph are that—
- (a) the authorised person prepared the content of the communication; or
- (b) it is a real-time communication.

[8.269]
18 Mere conduits

(1) Subject to paragraph (4), the financial promotion restriction does not apply to any communication which is made or directed by a person who acts as a mere conduit for it.

(2) A person acts as a mere conduit for a communication if—
- (a) he communicates it in the course of an activity carried on by him, the principal purpose of which is transmitting or receiving material provided to him by others;
- (b) the content of the communication is wholly devised by another person; and
- (c) the nature of the service provided by him in relation to the communication is such that he does not select, modify or otherwise exercise control over its content prior to its transmission or receipt.

(3) For the purposes of paragraph (2)(c) a person does not select, modify or otherwise exercise control over the content of a communication merely by removing or having the power to remove material—
- (a) which is, or is alleged to be, illegal, defamatory or in breach of copyright;
- (b) in response to a request to a body which is empowered by or under any enactment to make such a request; or
- (c) when otherwise required to do so by law.

(4) Nothing in paragraph (1) prevents the application of the financial promotion restriction in so far as it relates to the person who has caused the communication to be made or directed.

(5) This article does not apply to an electronic commerce communication.

[8.270]
18A Electronic commerce communications: mere conduits, caching and hosting

The financial promotion restriction does not apply to an electronic commerce communication in circumstances where—
- (a) the making of the communication constitutes the provision of an information society service of a kind falling within paragraph 1 of Article 12, 13 or 14 of the electronic commerce directive ("mere conduit", "caching" and "hosting"); and
- (b) the conditions mentioned in the paragraph in question, to the extent that they are applicable at the time of, or prior to, the making of the communication, are or have been met at that time.

[8.271]
19 Investment professionals

(1) The financial promotion restriction does not apply to any communication which—
- (a) is made only to recipients whom the person making the communication believes on reasonable grounds to be investment professionals; or
- (b) may reasonably be regarded as directed only at such recipients.

(2) For the purposes of paragraph (1)(b), if all the conditions set out in paragraph (4)(a) to (c) are met in relation to the communication, it is to be regarded as directed only at investment professionals.

(3) In any other case in which one or more of the conditions set out in paragraph (4)(a) to (c) are met, that fact is to be taken into account in determining whether the communication is directed only at investment professionals (but a communication may still be regarded as so directed even if none of the conditions in paragraph (4) is met).

(4) The conditions are that—

  (a)   the communication is accompanied by an indication that it is directed at persons having professional experience in matters relating to investments and that any investment or investment activity to which it relates is available only to such persons or will be engaged in only with such persons;

  (b)   the communication is accompanied by an indication that persons who do not have professional experience in matters relating to investments should not rely on it;

  (c)   there are in place proper systems and procedures to prevent recipients other than investment professionals engaging in the investment activity to which the communication relates with the person directing the communication, a close relative of his or a member of the same group.

(5)   "Investment professionals" means—

  (a)   an authorised person;

  (b)   an exempt person where the communication relates to a controlled activity which is a regulated activity in relation to which the person is exempt;

  (c)   any other person—

    (i)   whose ordinary activities involve him in carrying on the controlled activity to which the communication relates for the purpose of a business carried on by him; or

    (ii)   who it is reasonable to expect will carry on such activity for the purposes of a business carried on by him;

  (d)   a government, local authority (whether in the United Kingdom or elsewhere) or an international organisation;

  (e)   a person ("A") who is a director, officer or employee of a person ("B") falling within any of sub-paragraphs (a) to (d) where the communication is made to A in that capacity and where A's responsibilities when acting in that capacity involve him in the carrying on by B of controlled activities.

(6)   For the purposes of paragraph (1), a communication may be treated as made only to or directed only at investment professionals even if it is also made to or directed at other persons to whom it may lawfully be communicated.

[8.272]
20   Communications by journalists

(1)   Subject to paragraph (2), the financial promotion restriction does not apply to any non-real time communication if—

  (a)   the content of the communication is devised by a person acting in the capacity of a journalist;

  (b)   the communication is contained in a qualifying publication; and

  (c)   in the case of a communication requiring disclosure, one of the conditions in paragraph (2) is met.

(2)   The conditions in this paragraph are that—

  (a)   the communication is accompanied by an indication explaining the nature of the author's financial interest or that of a member of his family (as the case may be);

  (b)   the authors are subject to proper systems and procedures which prevent the publication of communications requiring disclosure without the explanation referred to in sub-paragraph (a); or

  (c)   the qualifying publication in which the communication appears falls within the remit of—

    (i)   the Code of Practice issued by the Press Complaints Commission;

    (ii)   the OFCOM Broadcasting Code; or

    (iii)   the Producers' Guidelines issued by the British Broadcasting Corporation.

(3)   For the purposes of this article, a communication requires disclosure if—

  (a)   an author of the communication or a member of his family is likely to obtain a financial benefit or avoid a financial loss if people act in accordance with the invitation or inducement contained in the communication;

  (b)   the communication relates to a controlled investment of a kind falling within paragraph (4); and

  (c)   the communication identifies directly a person who issues or provides the controlled investment to which the communication relates.

(4)   A controlled investment falls within this paragraph if it is—

  (a)   an investment falling within paragraph 14 of Schedule 1 (shares or stock in share capital);

  (b)   an investment falling within paragraph 21 of that Schedule (options) to acquire or dispose of an investment falling within sub-paragraph (a);

  (c)   an investment falling within paragraph 22 of that Schedule (futures) being rights under a contract for the sale of an investment falling within sub-paragraph (a); or

  (d)   an investment falling within paragraph 23 of that Schedule (contracts for differences etc) being rights under a contract relating to, or to fluctuations in, the value or price of an investment falling within sub-paragraph (a).

(5)   For the purposes of this article—

   (a)   the authors of the communication are the person who devises the content of the communication and the person who is responsible for deciding to include the communication in the qualifying publication;

   (b)   a "qualifying publication" is a publication or service of the kind mentioned in paragraph (1) or (2) of article 54 of the Regulated Activities Order and which is of the nature described in that article, and for the purposes of this article, a certificate given under paragraph (3) of article 54 of that Order and not revoked is conclusive evidence of the matters certified;

   (c)   the members of a person's family are his spouse [or civil partner] and any children of his under the age of 18 years.

NOTES

Para (5): words in square brackets in sub-para (c) inserted by the Financial Services and Markets Act 2000 (Financial Promotion) (Amendment) Order 2005, SI 2005/3392, art 2(1), (3), as from 21 December 2005.

[8.273]
20A Promotion broadcast by company director etc

(1) The financial promotion restriction does not apply to a communication which is communicated as part of a qualifying service by a person ("D") who is a director or employee of an undertaking ("U") where—

   (a)   the communication invites or induces the recipient to acquire—

      (i)   a controlled investment of the kind falling within article 20(4) which is issued by U (or by an undertaking in the same group as U); or

      (ii)   a controlled investment issued or provided by an authorised person in the same group as U;

   (b)   the communication—

      (i)   comprises words which are spoken by D and not broadcast, transmitted or displayed in writing; or

      (ii)   is displayed in writing only because it forms part of an interactive dialogue to which D is a party and in the course of which D is expected to respond immediately to questions put by a recipient of the communication;

   (c)   the communication is not part of an organised marketing campaign; and

   (d)   the communication is accompanied by an indication that D is a director or employee (as the case may be) of U.

(2) For the purposes of this article, a "qualifying service" is a service—

   (a)   which is broadcast or transmitted in the form of television or radio programmes; or

   (b)   displayed on a web site (or similar system for the electronic display of information) comprising regularly updated news and information,

provided that the principal purpose of the service, taken as a whole and including any advertisements and other promotional material contained in it, is neither of the purposes described in article 54(1)(a) or (b) of the Regulated Activities Order.

(3) For the purposes of paragraph (2), a certificate given under article 54(3) of the Regulated Activities Order and not revoked is conclusive evidence of the matters certified.

[8.274]
20B Incoming electronic commerce communications

(1) The financial promotion restriction does not apply to an incoming electronic commerce communication.

(2) Paragraph (1) does not apply to—

   (a)   a communication which constitutes an advertisement by the operator of a UCITS directive scheme of units in that scheme;

   (b)   a communication consisting of an invitation or inducement to enter into a contract of insurance, where—

      (i)   the communication is made by an undertaking which has received official authorisation in accordance with Article 4 of the life assurance consolidation directive or the first non-life insurance directive, and

      (ii)   the insurance falls within the scope of any of the insurance directives; or

   (c)   an unsolicited communication made by electronic mail.

[(3) In this article, "UCITS directive scheme" means an undertaking for collective investment in transferable securities which is subject to Directive 2009/65/EC of the European Parliament and of the Council of 13th July 2009 on the co-ordination of laws, regulations and administrative provisions relating to undertakings for collective investment in transferable securities and has been authorised in accordance with Article 5 of that Directive.]

(4) For the purposes of this article, a communication by electronic mail is to be regarded as unsolicited, unless it is made in response to an express request from the recipient of the communication.

NOTES

Para (3): substituted by the Undertakings for Collective Investment in Transferable Securities Regulations 2011, SI 2011/1613, reg 16, Schedule, para 7(1), (2), as from 1 July 2011.

PART V
EXEMPT COMMUNICATIONS: DEPOSITS AND INSURANCE

[8.275]
21 Interpretation: relevant insurance activity

In this Part, a "relevant insurance activity" means a controlled activity falling within paragraph 2 of Schedule 1 carried on in relation to an investment falling within paragraph 13 of that Schedule where that investment is not a qualifying contract of insurance.

[8.276]
22 Deposits: non-real time communications

(1)   If the requirements of paragraph (2) are met, the financial promotion restriction does not apply to any non-real time communication which relates to a controlled activity falling within paragraph 1 of Schedule 1.

(2)   The requirements of this paragraph are that the communication is accompanied by an indication—

  (a)   of the full name of the person with whom the investment which is the subject of the communication is to be made ("deposit-taker");

  (b)   of the country or territory in which a deposit-taker that is a body corporate is incorporated (described as such);

  (c)   if different, of the country or territory in which the deposit-taker's principal place of business is situated (described as such);

  (d)   whether or not the deposit-taker is regulated in respect of his deposit-taking business;

  (e)   if the deposit-taker is so regulated, of the name of the regulator in the deposit-taker's principal place of business, or if there is more than one such regulator, the prudential regulator;

  (f)   whether any transaction to which the communication relates would, if entered into by the recipient and the deposit-taker, fall within the jurisdiction of any dispute resolution scheme or deposit guarantee scheme and if so, identifying each such scheme;

  (g)   the necessary capital information.

(3)   In this article—

"full name", in relation to a person, means the name under which that person carries on business and, if different, that person's corporate name;

"liabilities" includes provisions where such provisions have not been deducted from the value of the assets;

"necessary capital information" means—

  (a)   in relation to a deposit-taker which is a body corporate, either the amount of its paid up capital and reserves, described as such, or a statement that the amount of its paid up capital and reserves exceeds a particular amount (stating it);

  (b)   in relation to a deposit-taker which is not a body corporate, either the amount of the total assets less liabilities (described as such) or a statement that the amount of its total assets exceeds a particular amount (stating it) and that its total liabilities do not exceed a particular amount (stating it).

[8.277]
23 Deposits: real time communications

The financial promotion restriction does not apply to any real time communication (whether solicited or unsolicited) which relates to an activity falling within paragraph 1 of Schedule 1.

[8.278]
24 Relevant insurance activity: non-real time communications

(1)   If the requirements of paragraph (2) are met, the financial promotion restriction does not apply to any non-real time communication which relates to a relevant insurance activity.

(2)   The requirements of this paragraph are that the communication is accompanied by an indication—

  (a)   of the full name of the person with whom the investment which is the subject of the communication is to be made ("the insurer");

  (b)   of the country or territory in which the insurer is incorporated (described as such);

  (c)   if different, of the country or territory in which the insurer's principal place of business is situated (described as such);

  (d)   whether or not the insurer is regulated in respect of its insurance business;

(e) if the insurer is so regulated, of the name of the regulator of the insurer in its principal place of business or, if there is more than one such regulator, the name of the prudential regulator;

(f) whether any transaction to which the communication relates would, if entered into by the recipient and the insurer, fall within the jurisdiction of any dispute resolution scheme or compensation scheme and if so, identifying each such scheme.

(3) In this article "full name", in relation to a person, means the name under which that person carries on business and, if different, that person's corporate name.

[8.279]
25 Relevant insurance activity: non-real time communications: reinsurance and large risks

(1) The financial promotion restriction does not apply to any non-real time communication which relates to a relevant insurance activity and concerns only—

(a) a contract of reinsurance; or

(b) a contract that covers large risks.

(2) "Large risks" means—

(a) risks falling within paragraph 4 (railway rolling stock), 5 (aircraft), 6 (ships), 7 (goods in transit), 11 (aircraft liability) or 12 (liability of ships) of Schedule 1 to the Regulated Activities Order;

(b) risks falling within paragraph 14 (credit) or 15 (suretyship) of that Schedule provided that the risks relate to a business carried on by the recipient;

(c) risks falling within paragraph 3 (land vehicles), 8 (fire and natural forces), 9 (damage to property), 10 (motor vehicle liability), 13 (general liability) or 16 (miscellaneous financial loss) of that Schedule provided that the risks relate to a business carried on by the recipient and that the condition specified in paragraph (3) is met in relation to that business.

(3) The condition specified in this paragraph is that at least two of the three following criteria were exceeded in the most recent financial year for which information is available prior to the making of the communication—

[(a) the aggregate of the amounts shown as assets in the balance sheet of the business was 6.2 million euros;]

(b) the net turnover (within the meaning given to "turnover" by [section 474(1) of the 2006 Act] was 12.8 million euros;

(c) the number of employees (within the meaning given by [section 465(6) of the 2006 Act] was 250;

and for a financial year which is a company's financial year but not in fact a year, the net turnover of the recipient shall be proportionately adjusted.

(4) For the purposes of paragraph (3), where the recipient is a member of a group for which consolidated accounts (within the meaning of the Seventh Company Law Directive) are drawn up, the question whether the condition met in that paragraph is met is to be determined by reference to those accounts.

NOTES

Para (3): words in square brackets substituted by the Companies Act 2006 (Consequential Amendments and Transitional Provisions) Order 2011, SI 2011/1265, art 26(1), (5), as from 12 May 2011.

[8.280]
26 Relevant insurance activity: real time communication

The financial promotion restriction does not apply to any real time communication (whether solicited or unsolicited) which relates to a relevant insurance activity.

PART VI
EXEMPT COMMUNICATIONS: CERTAIN CONTROLLED ACTIVITIES

[8.281]
27 Application of exemptions in this Part

Except where otherwise stated, the exemptions in this Part apply to communications which relate to—

(a) a controlled activity falling within paragraph 2 of Schedule 1 carried on in relation to a qualifying contract of insurance;

(b) controlled activities falling within any of paragraphs 3 to 11 of Schedule 1.

[8.282]
28 One off non-real time communications and solicited real time communications

(1) The financial promotion restriction does not apply to a one off communication which is either a non-real time communication or a solicited real time communication.

(2) If all the conditions set out in paragraph (3) are met in relation to a communication it is to be regarded as a one off communication. In any other case in which one or more of those conditions are met, that fact is to be taken into account in determining whether the communication is a one off communication (but a communication may still be regarded as a one off communication even if none of the conditions in paragraph (3) is met).

(3) The conditions are that—

    (a) the communication is made only to one recipient or only to one group of recipients in the expectation that they would engage in any investment activity jointly;

    (b) the identity of the product or service to which the communication relates has been determined having regard to the particular circumstances of the recipient;

    (c) the communication is not part of an organised marketing campaign.

[8.283]
28A One off unsolicited real time communications

(1) The financial promotion restriction does not apply to an unsolicited real time communication if the conditions in paragraph (2) are met.

(2) The conditions in this paragraph are that—

    (a) the communication is a one off communication;

    (b) the communicator believes on reasonable grounds that the recipient understands the risks associated with engaging in the investment activity to which the communication relates;

    (c) at the time that the communication is made, the communicator believes on reasonable grounds that the recipient would expect to be contacted by him in relation to the investment activity to which the communication relates.

(3) Paragraphs (2) and (3) of article 28 apply in determining whether a communication is a one off communication for the purposes of this article as they apply for the purposes of article 28.

[8.284]
28B Real time communications: introductions . . .

(1) If the requirements of paragraph (2) are met, the financial promotion restriction does not apply to any real time communication which—

    (a) relates to a controlled activity falling within [paragraph 10, 10A, 10B, 10C, 10D, 10E, 10F, [10G, 10H, 10I, 10J or 10K]] of Schedule 1; and

    (b) is made for the purpose of, or with a view to, introducing the recipient to a person ("N") who is—

       (i) an authorised person who carries on the controlled activity to which the communication relates,

       (ii) an appointed representative, where the controlled activity to which the communication relates is also a regulated activity in respect of which he is exempt from the general prohibition, or

       (iii) an overseas person who carries on the controlled activity to which the communication relates.

(2) The requirements of this paragraph are that the maker of the communication ("M")—

    (a) does not receive any money, other than money payable to M on his own account, paid by the recipient for or in connection with any transaction which the recipient enters into with or through N as a result of the introduction; and

    (b) before making the introduction, discloses to the recipient such of the information mentioned in paragraph (3) as applies to M.

(3) That information is—

    (a) that M is a member of the same group as N;

    (b) details of any payment which M will receive from N, by way of fee or commission, for introducing the recipient to N;

    (c) an indication of any other reward or advantage received or to be received by M that arises out of his making introductions to N.

(4) In this article, "overseas person" means a person who carries on controlled activities which fall within paragraph 10, 10A or 10B of Schedule 1, but who does not carry on any such activity, or offer to do so, from a permanent place of business maintained by him in the United Kingdom.

NOTES

Article heading: words omitted revoked by the Financial Services and Markets Act 2000 (Regulated Activities) (Amendment) (No 2) Order 2006, SI 2006/2383, art 35(1), (2), as from 6 April 2007.

Para (1): words in first (outer) pair of square brackets substituted by SI 2006/2383, art 35(1), (3), as from 6 April 2007; words in second (inner) pair of square brackets substituted by the Financial Services and Markets Act 2000 (Regulated Activities) (Amendment) Order 2009, SI 2009/1342, art 30(1), (2), as from 1 July 2009 (certain purposes), and as from 30 June 2010 (otherwise).

[8.285]
29 Communications required or authorised by enactments

(1) Subject to paragraph (2), the financial promotion restriction does not apply to any communication which is required or authorised by or under any enactment other than the Act.

(2) This article does not apply to a communication which relates to a controlled activity falling within paragraph 10, 10A or 10B of Schedule 1 or within paragraph 11 in so far as it relates to that activity.

[8.286]
30 Overseas communicators: solicited real time communications

(1) The financial promotion restriction does not apply to any solicited real time communication which is made by an overseas communicator from outside the United Kingdom in the course of or for the purposes of his carrying on the business of engaging in relevant investment activities outside the United Kingdom.

(2) In this article—
"overseas communicator" means a person who carries on relevant investment activities outside the United Kingdom but who does not carry on any such activity from a permanent place of business maintained by him in the United Kingdom;
"relevant investment activities" means controlled activities which fall within paragraphs 3 to 7 or 10 to 10B of Schedule 1 or, so far as relevant to any of those paragraphs, paragraph 11 of that Schedule.

[8.287]
31 Overseas communicators: non-real time communications to previously overseas customers

(1) The financial promotion restriction does not apply to any non-real time communication which is communicated by an overseas communicator from outside the United Kingdom to a previously overseas customer of his.

(2) In this article a "previously overseas customer" means a person with whom the overseas communicator has done business within the period of twelve months ending with the day on which the communication was received ("the earlier business") and where—
 (a) at the time that the earlier business was done, the customer was neither resident in the United Kingdom nor had a place of business there; or
 (b) at the time the earlier business was done, the overseas communicator had on a former occasion done business with the customer, being business of the same description as the business to which the communication relates, and on that former occasion the customer was neither resident in the United Kingdom nor had a place of business there.

(3) For the purposes of this article, an overseas communicator has done business with a customer if, in the course of carrying on his relevant investment activities outside the United Kingdom, he has—
 (a) effected a transaction, or arranged for a transaction to be effected, with the customer;
 (b) provided, outside the United Kingdom; a service to the customer as described in paragraph 6 of Schedule 1 (whether or not that paragraph was in force at the time the business was done); or
 (c) given, outside the United Kingdom, any advice to the customer as described in paragraph 7 of that Schedule (whether or not that paragraph was in force at the time the business was done).

[8.288]
32 Overseas communicators: unsolicited real time communications to previously overseas customers

(1) If the requirements of paragraphs (2) and (3) are met, the financial promotion restriction does not apply to an unsolicited real time communication which is made by an overseas communicator from outside the United Kingdom to a previously overseas customer of his.

(2) The requirements of this paragraph are that the terms on which previous transactions and services had been effected or provided by the overseas communicator to the previously overseas customer were such that the customer would reasonably expect, at the time that the unsolicited real time communication is made, to be contacted by the overseas communicator in relation to the investment activity to which the communication relates.

(3) The requirements of this paragraph are that the previously overseas customer has been informed by the overseas communicator on an earlier occasion—
 (a) that the protections conferred by or under the Act will not apply to any unsolicited real time communication which is made by the overseas communicator and which relates to that investment activity;
 (b) that the protections conferred by or under the Act may not apply to any investment activity that may be engaged in as a result of the communication; and

(c)   whether any transaction between them resulting from the communication would fall within the jurisdiction of any dispute resolution scheme or compensation scheme or, if there is no such scheme, of that fact.

[8.289]
33 Overseas communicators: unsolicited real time communications to knowledgeable customers

(1)   If the requirements of paragraphs (2), (3) and (4) are met, the financial promotion restriction does not apply to an unsolicited real time communication which is made by an overseas communicator from outside the United Kingdom in the course of his carrying on relevant investment activities outside the United Kingdom.

(2)   The requirements of this paragraph are that the overseas communicator believes on reasonable grounds that the recipient is sufficiently knowledgeable to understand the risks associated with engaging in the investment activity to which the communication relates.

(3)   The requirements of this paragraph are that, in relation to any particular investment activity, the recipient has been informed by the overseas communicator on an earlier occasion—
- (a)   that the protections conferred by or under the Act will not apply to any unsolicited real time communication which is made by him and which relates to that activity;
- (b)   that the protections conferred by or under the Act may not apply to any investment activity that may be engaged in as a result of the communication; and
- (c)   whether any transaction between them resulting from the communication would fall within the jurisdiction of any dispute resolution scheme or compensation scheme or, if there is no such scheme, of that fact.

(4)   The requirements of this paragraph are that the recipient, after being given a proper opportunity to consider the information given to him in accordance with paragraph (3), has clearly signified that he understands the warnings referred to in paragraph (3)(a) and (b) and that he accepts that he will not benefit from the protections referred to.

[8.290]
34   Governments, central banks etc

The financial promotion restriction does not apply to any communication which—
- (a)   is a non-real time communication or a solicited real time communication;
- (b)   is communicated by and relates only to controlled investments issued, or to be issued, by—
  - (i)   any government;
  - (ii)   any local authority (in the United Kingdom or elsewhere);
  - (iii)   any international organisation;
  - (iv)   the Bank of England;
  - (v)   the European Central Bank;
  - (vi)   the central bank of any country or territory outside the United Kingdom.

[8.291]
35   Industrial and provident societies

The financial promotion restriction does not apply to any communication which—
- (a)   is a non-real time communication or a solicited real time communication;
- (b)   is communicated by an industrial and provident society; and
- (c)   relates only to an investment falling within paragraph 15 [or 15A] of Schedule 1 issued, or to be issued, by the society in question.

NOTES

Words in square brackets in para (c) inserted by the Financial Services and Markets Act 2000 (Regulated Activities) (Amendment) Order 2010, SI 2010/86, art 4, Schedule, para 9(b), as from 24 February 2010.

[8.292]
36   Nationals of EEA States other than United Kingdom

The financial promotion restriction does not apply to any communication which—
- (a)   is a non-real time communication or a solicited real time communication;
- (b)   is communicated by a national of an EEA State other than the United Kingdom in the course of any controlled activity lawfully carried on by him in that State; and
- (c)   conforms with any rules made by the Authority under section 145 of the Act (financial promotion rules) which are relevant to a communication of that kind.

[8.293]
37   Financial markets

(1)   The financial promotion restriction does not apply to any communication—
- (a)   which is a non-real time communication or a solicited real time communication;
- (b)   which is communicated by a relevant market; and
- (c)   to which paragraph (2) or (3) applies.

(2)   This paragraph applies to a communication if—

(a) it relates only to facilities provided by the market; and

(b) it does not identify (directly or indirectly)—

    (i) any particular investment issued, or to be issued, by or available from an identified person as one that may be traded or dealt in on the market; or

    (ii) any particular person as a person through whom transactions on the market may be effected.

(3) This paragraph applies to a communication if—

(a) it relates only to a particular investment falling within paragraph 21, 22 or 23 of Schedule 1; and

(b) it identifies the investment as one that may be traded or dealt in on the market.

(4) "Relevant market" means a market which—

(a) meets the criteria specified in Part I of Schedule 3; or

(b) is specified in, or is established under the rules of an exchange specified in, Part II, III or IV of that Schedule.

[8.294]
38 Persons in the business of placing promotional material

The financial promotion restriction does not apply to any communication which is made to a person whose business it is to place, or arrange for the placing of, promotional material provided that it is communicated so that he can place or arrange for placing it.

[8.295]
39 Joint enterprises

(1) The financial promotion restriction does not apply to any communication which is made or directed by a participator in a joint enterprise to or at another participator in the same joint enterprise in connection with, or for the purposes of, that enterprise.

(2) "Joint enterprise" means an enterprise into which two or more persons ("the participators") enter for commercial purposes related to a business or businesses (other than the business of engaging in a controlled activity) carried on by them; and, where a participator is a member of a group, each other member of the group is also to be regarded as a participator in the enterprise.

(3) "Participator" includes potential participator.

[8.296]
40 Participants in certain recognised collective investment schemes

The financial promotion restriction does not apply to any non-real time communication or solicited real time communication which is made—

(a) by a person who is the operator of a scheme recognised under section 270 or 272 of the Act; and

(b) to persons in the United Kingdom who are participants in any such recognised scheme operated by the person making the communication,

and which relates only to such recognised schemes as are operated by that person or to units in such schemes.

[8.297]
41 Bearer instruments: promotions required or permitted by market rules

(1) The financial promotion restriction does not apply to any communication which—

(a) is a non-real time communication or a solicited real time communication;

(b) is communicated by a body corporate ("A") that is not an open-ended investment company;

(c) is made to or may reasonably be regarded as directed at persons entitled to bearer instruments issued by A, a parent undertaking of A or a subsidiary undertaking of A; and

(d) is required or permitted by the rules of a relevant market to be communicated to holders of instruments of a class which consists of or includes the bearer instruments in question.

(2) "Bearer instrument" means any of the following investments title to which is capable of being transferred by delivery—

(a) any investment falling within paragraph 14[, 15 or 15A] of Schedule 1;

(b) any investment falling within paragraph 17 or 18 of that Schedule which confers rights in respect of an investment falling within paragraph 14[, 15 or 15A].

(3) For the purposes of this article, a bearer instrument falling within paragraph 17 or 18 of Schedule 1 is treated as issued by the person ("P") who issued the investment in respect of which the bearer instrument confers rights if it is issued by—

(a) an undertaking in the same group as P; or

(b) a person acting on behalf of, or pursuant to arrangements made with, P.

(4) "Relevant market", in relation to instruments of any particular class, means any market on which instruments of that class can be traded or dealt in and which—

(a) meets the criteria specified in Part I of Schedule 3; or

(b)   is specified in, or established under the rules of an exchange specified in, Part II or III of that Schedule.

NOTES

Para (2): words in square brackets in sub-paras (a), (b) substituted by the Financial Services and Markets Act 2000 (Regulated Activities) (Amendment) Order 2010, SI 2010/86, art 4, Schedule, para 9(a)(ii), as from 24 February 2010.

[8.298]

42   Bearer instruments: promotions to existing holders

(1)   The financial promotion restriction does not apply to any communication which—

(a)   is a non-real time communication or a solicited real time communication;

(b)   is communicated by a body corporate ("A") that is not an open-ended investment company;

(c)   is made to or may reasonably be regarded as directed at persons entitled to bearer instruments issued by A, a parent undertaking of A or a subsidiary undertaking of A;

(d)   relates only to instruments of a class which consists of or includes either the bearer instruments to which the communication relates or instruments in respect of which those bearer instruments confer rights; and

(e)   is capable of being accepted or acted on only by persons who are entitled to instruments (whether or not bearer instruments) issued by A, a parent undertaking of A or a subsidiary undertaking of A.

(2)   "Bearer instruments" has the meaning given by article 41.

(3)   For the purposes of this article, an instrument falling within paragraph 17 or 18 of Schedule 1 is treated as issued by the person ("P") who issued the investment in respect of which the bearer instrument confers rights if it is issued by—

(a)   an undertaking in the same group as P; or

(b)   a person acting on behalf of, or pursuant to arrangements made with, P.

[8.299]

43   Members and creditors of certain bodies corporate

(1)   The financial promotion restriction does not apply to any non-real time communication or solicited real time communication which is communicated—

(a)   by, or on behalf of, a body corporate ("A") that is not an open-ended investment company; and

(b)   to persons whom the person making or directing the communication believes on reasonable grounds to be persons to whom paragraph (2) applies,

and which relates only to a relevant investment which is issued or to be issued by A, or by an undertaking ("U") in the same group as A that is not an open-ended investment company.

(2)   This paragraph applies to—

(a)   a creditor or member of A or of U;

(b)   a person who is entitled to a relevant investment which is issued, or to be issued, by A or by U;

(c)   a person who is entitled, whether conditionally or unconditionally, to become a member of A or of U but who has not yet done so;

(d)   a person who is entitled, whether conditionally or unconditionally, to have transferred to him title to a relevant investment which is issued by A or by U but has not yet acquired title to the investment.

(3)   "Relevant investment" means—

(a)   an investment falling within paragraph 14[, 15 or 15A] of Schedule 1;

(b)   an investment falling within paragraph 17 or 18 of that Schedule so far as relating to any investments within sub-paragraph (a).

(4)   For the purposes of this article, an investment falling within paragraph 17 or 18 of Schedule 1 is treated as issued by the person ("P") who issued the investment in respect of which the instrument confers rights if it is issued by—

(a)   an undertaking in the same group as P; or

(b)   a person acting on behalf of, or pursuant to arrangements made with, P.

NOTES

Para (3): words in square brackets in sub-para (a) substituted by the Financial Services and Markets Act 2000 (Regulated Activities) (Amendment) Order 2010, SI 2010/86, art 4, Schedule, para 9(a)(iii), as from 24 February 2010.

[8.300]

44   Members and creditors of open-ended investment companies

(1)   The financial promotion restriction does not apply to any communication which—

(a)   is a non-real time communication or a solicited real time communication;

(b)   is communicated by, or on behalf of, a body corporate ("A") that is an open-ended investment company;

(c) is communicated to persons whom the person making or directing the communication believes on reasonable grounds to be persons to whom paragraph (2) applies; and

(d) relates only to an investment falling within paragraph 15, [15A,] 17 or 19 of Schedule 1 which is issued, or to be issued, by A.

(2) This paragraph applies to—

 (a) a creditor or member of A;

 (b) a person who is entitled to an investment falling within paragraph 15, [15A,] 17 or 19 of Schedule 1 which is issued, or to be issued, by A;

 (c) a person who is entitled, whether conditionally or unconditionally, to become a member of A but who has not yet done so;

 (d) a person who is entitled, whether conditionally or unconditionally, to have transferred to him title to an investment falling within paragraph 15, [15A,] 17 or 19 of Schedule 1 which is issued by A but has not yet acquired title to the investment.

(3) For the purposes of this article, an investment falling within paragraph 17 of Schedule 1 is treated as issued by the person ("P") who issued the investment in respect of which the instrument confers rights if it is issued by—

 (a) an undertaking in the same group as P; or

 (b) a person acting on behalf of, or pursuant to arrangements made with, P.

NOTES

Paras (1), (2): figures in square brackets inserted by the Financial Services and Markets Act 2000 (Regulated Activities) (Amendment) Order 2010, SI 2010/86, art 4, Schedule, para 9(c), as from 24 February 2010.

[8.301]
45 Group companies

The financial promotion restriction does not apply to any communication made by one body corporate in a group to another body corporate in the same group.

[8.302]
46 Qualifying credit to bodies corporate

The financial promotion restriction does not apply to any communication which relates to a controlled activity falling within paragraph 10, 10A or 10B of Schedule 1 (or within paragraph 11 so far as it relates to that activity) if the communication is—

 (a) made to or directed at bodies corporate only; or

 (b) accompanied by an indication that the qualifying credit to which it relates is only available to bodies corporate.

[8.303]
47 Persons in the business of disseminating information

(1) The financial promotion restriction does not apply to any communication which is made only to recipients whom the person making the communication believes on reasonable grounds to be persons to whom paragraph (2) applies.

(2) This paragraph applies to—

 (a) a person who receives the communication in the course of a business which involves the dissemination through a publication of information concerning controlled activities;

 (b) a person whilst acting in the capacity of director, officer or employee of a person falling within sub-paragraph (a) being a person whose responsibilities when acting in that capacity involve him in the business referred to in that sub-paragraph;

 (c) any person to whom the communication may otherwise lawfully be made.

[8.304]
48 Certified high net worth individuals

(1) If the requirements of paragraphs (4) and (7) are met, the financial promotion restriction does not apply to any communication which—

 (a) is a non-real time communication or a solicited real time communication;

 (b) is made to an individual whom the person making the communication believes on reasonable grounds to be a certified high net worth individual, and

 (c) relates only to one or more investments falling within paragraph (8).

(2) "Certified high net worth individual" means an individual who has signed, within the period of twelve months ending with the day on which the communication is made, a statement complying with Part I of Schedule 5.

(3) The validity of a statement signed for the purposes of paragraph (2) is not affected by a defect in the form or wording of the statement, provided that the defect does not alter the statement's meaning and that the words shown in bold type in Part I of Schedule 5 are so shown in the statement.

(4) The requirements of this paragraph are that either the communication is accompanied by the giving of a warning in accordance with paragraphs (5) and (6) or where, because of the nature of the communication, this is not reasonably practicable,—

(a) a warning in accordance with paragraph (5) is given to the recipient orally at the beginning of the communication together with an indication that he will receive the warning in legible form and that, before receipt of that warning, he should consider carefully any decision to engage in investment activity to which the communication relates; and

(b) a warning in accordance with paragraphs (5) and (6) (d) to (h) is sent to the recipient of the communication within two business days of the day on which the communication is made.

(5) The warning must be in the following terms—

"The content of this promotion has not been approved by an authorised person within the meaning of the Financial Services and Markets Act 2000. Reliance on this promotion for the purpose of engaging in any investment activity may expose an individual to a significant risk of losing all of the property or other assets invested.".

But where a warning is sent pursuant to paragraph (4)(b), for the words "this promotion" in both places where they occur there must be substituted wording which clearly identifies the promotion which is the subject of the warning.

(6) The warning must—
  (a) be given at the beginning of the communication;
  (b) precede any other written or pictorial matter;
  (c) be in a font size consistent with the text forming the remainder of the communication;
  (d) be indelible;
  (e) be legible;
  (f) be printed in black, bold type;
  (g) be surrounded by a black border which does not interfere with the text of the warning; and
  (h) not be hidden, obscured or interrupted by any other written or pictorial matter.

(7) The requirements of this paragraph are that the communication is accompanied by an indication—
  (a) that it is exempt from the general restriction (in section 21 of the Act) on the communication of invitations or inducements to engage in investment activity on the ground that it is made to a certified high net worth individual;
  (b) of the requirements that must be met for an individual to qualify as a certified high net worth individual; and
  (c) that any individual who is in any doubt about the investment to which the communication relates should consult an authorised person specialising in advising on investments of the kind in question.

(8) An investment falls within this paragraph if—
  (a) it is an investment falling within paragraph 14 of Schedule 1 being stock or shares in an unlisted company;
  (b) it is an investment falling within paragraph 15 of Schedule 1 being an investment acknowledging the indebtedness of an unlisted company;
  [(ba) it is an investment falling within paragraph 15A of Schedule 1 being an investment constituting an alternative finance investment bond issued by an unlisted company;]
  (c) it is an investment falling within paragraph 17 or 18 of Schedule 1 conferring entitlement or rights with respect to investments falling within sub-paragraph (a) or (b);
  (d) it comprises units in a collective investment scheme being a scheme which invests wholly or predominantly in investments falling within sub-paragraph (a) or (b);
  (e) it is an investment falling within paragraph 21 of Schedule 1 being an option to acquire or dispose of an investment falling within sub-paragraph (a), (b) or (c);
  (f) it is an investment falling within paragraph 22 of Schedule 1 being rights under a contract for the sale of an investment falling within sub-paragraph (a), (b) or (c);
  (g) it is an investment falling within paragraph 23 of Schedule 1 being a contract relating to, or to fluctuations in value or price of, an investment falling within sub-paragraph (a), (b) or (c),

provided in each case that it is an investment under the terms of which the investor cannot incur a liability or obligation to pay or contribute more than he commits by way of investment.

(9) "Business day" means any day except a Saturday, a Sunday, Christmas Day, Good Friday or a day which is a bank holiday under the Banking and Financial Dealings Act 1971 in any part of the United Kingdom.

NOTES

Para (8): sub-para (ba) inserted by the Financial Services and Markets Act 2000 (Regulated Activities) (Amendment) Order 2010, SI 2010/86, art 4, Schedule, para 9(d), as from 24 February 2010.

[8.305]
49 High net worth companies, unincorporated associations etc

(1) The financial promotion restriction does not apply to any communication which—
  (a) is made only to recipients whom the person making the communication believes on reasonable grounds to be persons to whom paragraph (2) applies; or
  (b) may reasonably be regarded as directed only at persons to whom paragraph (2) applies.

(2)   This paragraph applies to—

  (a)   any body corporate which has, or which is a member of the same group as an undertaking which has, a called-up share capital or net assets of not less than—

    (i)   if the body corporate has more than 20 members or is a subsidiary undertaking of an undertaking which has more than 20 members, £500,000;

    (ii)   otherwise, £5 million;

  (b)   any unincorporated association or partnership which has net assets of not less than £5 million;

  (c)   the trustee of a high value trust;

  (d)   any person ("A") whilst acting in the capacity of director, officer or employee of a person ("B") falling within any of sub-paragraphs (a) to (c) where A's responsibilities, when acting in that capacity, involve him in B's engaging in investment activity;

  (e)   any person to whom the communication may otherwise lawfully be made.

(3)   For the purposes of paragraph (1)(b)—

  (a)   if all the conditions set out in paragraph (4)(a) to (c) are met, the communication is to be regarded as directed at persons to whom paragraph (2) applies;

  (b)   in any other case in which one or more of those conditions are met, that fact is to be taken into account in determining whether the communication is directed at persons to whom paragraph (2) applies (but a communication may still be regarded as so directed even if none of the conditions in paragraph (4) is met).

(4)   The conditions are that—

  (a)   the communication includes an indication of the description of persons to whom it is directed and an indication of the fact that the controlled investment or controlled activity to which it relates is available only to such persons;

  (b)   the communication includes an indication that persons of any other description should not act upon it;

  (c)   there are in place proper systems and procedures to prevent recipients other than persons to whom paragraph (2) applies engaging in the investment activity to which the communication relates with the person directing the communication, a close relative of his or a member of the same group.

(5)   "Called-up share capital" has the meaning given in [the 2006 Act (see section 547)].

(6)   "High value trust" means a trust where the aggregate value of the cash and investments which form part of the trust's assets (before deducting the amount of its liabilities)—

  (a)   is £10 million or more; or

  (b)   has been £10 million or more at anytime during the year immediately preceding the date on which the communication in question was first made or directed.

(7)   "Net assets" has the meaning given by [section 831 of the 2006 Act].

NOTES

Paras (5), (7): words in square brackets substituted by the Companies Act 2006 (Consequential Amendments and Transitional Provisions) Order 2011, SI 2011/1265, art 26(1), (6), as from 12 May 2011.

[8.306]
50   Sophisticated investors

(1)   "Certified sophisticated investor", in relation to any description of investment, means a person—

  (a)   who has a current certificate in writing or other legible form signed by an authorised person to the effect that he is sufficiently knowledgeable to understand the risks associated with that description of investment; and

  (b)   who has signed, within the period of twelve months ending with the day on which the communication is made, a statement in the following terms:

"I make this statement so that I am able to receive promotions which are exempt from the restrictions on financial promotion in the Financial Services and Markets Act 2000. The exemption relates to certified sophisticated investors and I declare that I qualify as such in relation to investments of the following kind [list them]. I accept that the contents of promotions and other material that I receive may not have been approved by an authorised person and that their content may not therefore be subject to controls which would apply if the promotion were made or approved by an authorised person. I am aware that it is open to me to seek advice from someone who specialises in advising on this kind of investment.".

(1A)   The validity of a statement signed in accordance with paragraph (1)(b) is not affected by a defect in the wording of the statement, provided that the defect does not alter the statement's meaning.

(2)   If the requirements of paragraph (3) are met, the financial promotion restriction does not apply to any communication which—

  (a)   is made to a certified sophisticated investor;

(b)   does not invite or induce the recipient to engage in investment activity with the person who has signed the certificate referred to in paragraph (1)(a); and

(c)   relates only to a description of investment in respect of which that investor is certified.

(3)   The requirements of this paragraph are that the communication is accompanied by an indication—

(a)   that it is exempt from the general restriction (in section 21 of the Act) on the communication of invitations or inducements to engage in investment activity on the ground that it is made to a certified sophisticated investor;

(b)   of the requirements that must be met for a person to qualify as a certified sophisticated investor;

(c)   that the content of the communication has not been approved by an authorised person and that such approval is, unless this exemption or any other exemption applies, required by section 21 of the Act;

(d)   that reliance on the communication for the purpose of engaging in any investment activity may expose the individual to a significant risk of losing all of the property invested or of incurring additional liability;

(e)   that any person who is in any doubt about the investment to which the communication relates should consult an authorised person specialising in advising on investments of the kind in question.

(4)   For the purposes of paragraph (1)(a), a certificate is current if it is signed and dated not more than three years before the date on which the communication is made.

[8.307]
50A   Self-certified sophisticated investors

(1)   "Self-certified sophisticated investor" means an individual who has signed within the period of twelve months ending with the day on which the communication is made, a statement complying with Part II of Schedule 5.

(2)   The validity of a statement signed for the purposes of paragraph (1) is not affected by a defect in the form or wording of the statement, provided that the defect does not alter the statement's meaning and that the words shown in bold type in Part II of Schedule 5 are so shown in the statement.

(3)   If the requirements of paragraphs (4) and (7) are met, the financial promotion restriction does not apply to any communication which—

(a)   is made to an individual whom the person making the communication believes on reasonable grounds to be a self-certified sophisticated investor; and

(b)   relates only to one or more investments falling within paragraph (8).

(4)   The requirements of this paragraph are that either the communication is accompanied by the giving of a warning in accordance with paragraphs (5) and (6) or where, because of the nature of the communication this is not reasonably practicable—

(a)   a warning in accordance with paragraph (5) is given to the recipient orally at the beginning of the communication together with an indication that he will receive the warning in legible form and that, before receipt of that warning, he should consider carefully any decision to engage in investment activity to which the communication relates; and

(b)   a warning in accordance with paragraphs (5) and (6) (d) to (h) is sent to the recipient of the communication within two business days of the day on which the communication is made.

(5)   The warning must be in the following terms—

"The content of this promotion has not been approved by an authorised person within the meaning of the Financial Services and Markets Act 2000. Reliance on this promotion for the purpose of engaging in any investment activity may expose an individual to a significant risk of losing all of the property or other assets invested.".

But where a warning is sent pursuant to paragraph (4)(b), for the words "this promotion" in both places where they occur there must be substituted wording which clearly identifies the promotion which is the subject of the warning.

(6)   The warning must—

(a)   be given at the beginning of the communication;

(b)   precede any other written or pictorial matter;

(c)   be in a font size consistent with the text forming the remainder of the communication;

(d)   be indelible;

(e)   be legible;

(f)   be printed in black, bold type;

(g)   be surrounded by a black border which does not interfere with the text of the warning; and

(h)   not be hidden, obscured or interrupted by any other written or pictorial matter.

(7)   The requirements of this paragraph are that the communication is accompanied by an indication—

   (a) that it is exempt from the general restriction (in section 21 of the Act) on the communication of invitations or inducements to engage in investment activity on the ground that it is made to a self-certified sophisticated investor;

   (b) of the requirements that must be met for an individual to qualify as a self-certified sophisticated investor;

   (c) that any individual who is in any doubt about the investment to which the communication relates should consult an authorised person specialising in advising on investments of the kind in question.

(8) An investment falls within this paragraph if—

   (a) it is an investment falling within paragraph 14 of Schedule 1 being stock or shares in an unlisted company;

   (b) it is an investment falling within paragraph 15 of Schedule I being an investment acknowledging the indebtedness of an unlisted company;

  [(ba) it is an investment falling within paragraph 15A of Schedule 1 being an investment constituting an alternative finance investment bond issued by an unlisted company;]

   (c) it is an investment falling within paragraph 17 or 18 of Schedule 1 conferring entitlement or rights with respect to investments falling within sub-paragraph (a) or (b);

   (d) it comprises units in a collective investment scheme being a scheme which invests wholly or predominantly in investments falling within sub-paragraph (a) or (b);

   (e) it is an investment falling within paragraph 21 of Schedule 1 being an option to acquire or dispose of an investment falling within sub-paragraph (a), (b) or (c);

   (f) it is an investment falling within paragraph 22 of Schedule 1 being rights under a contract for the sale of an investment falling within sub-paragraph (a), (b) or (c);

   (g) it is an investment falling within paragraph 23 of Schedule 1 being a contract relating to, or to fluctuations in value or price of, an investment falling within sub-paragraph (a), (b) or (c),

provided in each case that it is an investment under the terms of which the investor cannot incur a liability or obligation to pay or contribute more than he commits by way of investment.

(9) "Business day" means any day except a Saturday, a Sunday, Christmas Day, Good Friday or a day which is a bank holiday under the Banking and Financial Dealings Act 1971 in any part of the United Kingdom.

NOTES

Para (8): sub-para (ba) inserted by the Financial Services and Markets Act 2000 (Regulated Activities) (Amendment) Order 2010, SI 2010/86, art 4, Schedule, para 9(e), as from 24 February 2010.

[8.308]
51 Associations of high net worth or sophisticated investors

The financial promotion restriction does not apply to any non-real time communication or solicited real time communication which—

   (a) is made to an association, or to a member of an association, the membership of which the person making the communication believes on reasonable grounds comprises wholly or predominantly persons who are—

      (i) certified or self-certified high net worth individuals within the meaning of article 48;

     (ii) high net worth persons falling within article 49(2)(a) to (d);

    (iii) certified or self-certified sophisticated investors within the meaning of article 50 or 50A; and

   (b) relates only to an investment under the terms of which a person cannot incur a liability or obligation to pay or contribute more than he commits by way of investment.

[8.309]
52 Common interest group of a company

(1) "Common interest group", in relation to a company, means an identified group of persons who at the time the communication is made might reasonably be regarded as having an existing and common interest with each other and that company in—

   (a) the affairs of the company; and

   (b) what is done with the proceeds arising from any investment to which the communication relates.

(2) If the requirements of paragraphs (3) and either (4) or (5) are met, the financial promotion restriction does not apply to any communication which—

   (a) is a non-real time communication or a solicited real time communication;

   (b) is made only to persons who are members of a common interest group of a company, or may reasonably be regarded as directed only at such persons; and

   (c) relates to investments falling within paragraph 14[, 15 or 15A] of Schedule 1 which are issued, or to be issued, by that company.

(3) The requirements of this paragraph are that the communication is accompanied by an indication—

(a)   that the directors of the company (or its promoters named in the communication) have taken all reasonable care to ensure that every statement of fact or opinion included in the communication is true and not misleading given the form and context in which it appears;

(b)   that the directors of the company (or its promoters named in the communication) have not limited their liability with respect to the communication; and

(c)   that any person who is in any doubt about the investment to which the communication relates should consult an authorised person specialising in advising on investments of the kind in question.

(4)   The requirements of this paragraph are that the communication is accompanied by an indication—

(a)   that the directors of the company (or its promoters named in the communication) have taken all reasonable care to ensure that any person belonging to the common interest group (and his professional advisers) can have access, at all reasonable times, to all the information that he or they would reasonably require, and reasonably expect to find, for the purpose of making an informed assessment of the assets and liabilities, financial position, profits and losses and prospects of the company and of the rights attaching to the investments in question; and

(b)   describing the means by which such information can be accessed.

(5)   The requirements of this paragraph are that the communication is accompanied by an indication that any person considering subscribing for the investments in question should regard any subscription as made primarily to assist the furtherance of the company's objectives (other than any purely financial objectives) and only secondarily, if at all, as an investment.

(6)   For the purposes of paragraph (2)(b)—

(a)   if all the conditions set out in paragraph (7) are met, the communication is to be regarded as directed at persons who are members of the common interest group;

(b)   in any other case in which one or more of those conditions are met, that fact shall be taken into account in determining whether the communication is directed at persons who are members of the common interest group (but a communication may still be regarded as directed only at such persons even if none of the conditions in paragraph (7) is met).

(7)   The conditions are that—

(a)   the communication is accompanied by an indication that it is directed at persons who are members of the common interest group and that any investment or activity to which it relates is available only to such persons;

(b)   the communication is accompanied by an indication that it must not be acted upon by persons who are not members of the common interest group;

(c)   there are in place proper systems and procedures to prevent recipients other than members of the common interest group engaging in the investment activity to which the communication relates with the person directing the communication, a close relative of his or a member of the same group.

(8)   Persons are not to be regarded as having an interest of the kind described in paragraph (1) if the only reason why they would be so regarded is that—

(a)   they will have such an interest if they become members or creditors of the company;

(b)   they all carry on a particular trade or profession; or

(c)   they are persons with whom the company has an existing business relationship, whether by being its clients, customers, contractors, suppliers or otherwise.

NOTES

Para (2): words in square brackets in sub-para (c) substituted by the Financial Services and Markets Act 2000 (Regulated Activities) (Amendment) Order 2010, SI 2010/86, art 4, Schedule, para 9(a)(iv), as from 24 February 2010.

[8.310]
53   Settlors, trustees and personal representatives

The financial promotion restriction does not apply to any communication which is made between—

(a)   a person when acting as a settlor or grantor of a trust, a trustee or a personal representative; and

(b)   a trustee of the trust, a fellow trustee or a fellow personal representative (as the case may be),

if the communication is made for the purposes of the trust or estate.

[8.311]
54   Beneficiaries of trust, will or intestacy

The financial promotion restriction does not apply to any communication which is made—

(a)   between a person when acting as a settlor or grantor of a trust, trustee or personal representative and a beneficiary under the trust, will or intestacy; or

(b)   between a beneficiary under a trust, will or intestacy and another beneficiary under the same trust, will or intestacy,

if the communication relates to the management or distribution of that trust fund or estate.

[8.312]
55 Communications by members of professions

(1) The financial promotion restriction does not apply to a real time communication (whether solicited or unsolicited) which—

(a) is made by a person ("P") who carries on a regulated activity to which the general prohibition does not apply by virtue of section 327 of the Act; and

(b) is made to a recipient who has, prior to the communication being made, engaged P to provide professional services,

where the controlled activity to which the communication relates is an excluded activity which would be undertaken by P for the purposes of, and incidental to, the provision by him of professional services to or at the request of the recipient.

(2) "Professional services" has the meaning given in section 327 of the Act.

(3) An "excluded activity" is an activity to which the general prohibition would apply but for the application of—

(a) section 327 of the Act; or

(b) article 67 of the Regulated Activities Order.

[8.313]
55A Non-real time communication by members of professions

(1) The financial promotion restriction does not apply to a non-real time communication which is—

(a) made by a person ("P") who carries on Part XX activities; and

(b) limited to what is required or permitted by paragraphs (2) and (3).

(2) The communication must be in the following terms—

"This [firm/company] is not authorised under the Financial Services and Markets Act 2000 but we are able in certain circumstances to offer a limited range of investment services to clients because we are members of [relevant designated professional body]. We can provide these investment services if they are an incidental part of the professional services we have been engaged to provide."

(3) The communication may in addition set out the Part XX activities which P is able to offer to his clients, provided it is clear that these are the investment services to which the statement in paragraph (2) relates.

(4) The validity of a communication made in accordance with paragraph (2) is not affected by a defect in the wording of it provided that the defect does not alter the communication's meaning.

(5) "Part XX activities" means the regulated activities to which the general prohibition does not apply when they are carried on by P by virtue of section 327 of the Act.

[8.314]
56 Remedy following report by Parliamentary Commissioner for Administration

The financial promotion restriction does not apply to any communication made or directed by a person for the purpose of enabling any injustice, stated by the Parliamentary Commissioner for Administration in a report under section 10 of the Parliamentary Commissioner Act 1967 to have occurred, to be remedied with respect to the recipient.

[8.315]
57 Persons placing promotional material in particular publications

The financial promotion restriction does not apply to any communication received by a person who receives the publication in which the communication is contained because he has himself placed an advertisement in that publication.

[8.316]
58 Acquisition of interest in premises run by management companies

(1) "Management company" means a company established for the purpose of—

(a) managing the common parts or fabric of premises used for residential or business purposes; or

(b) supplying services to such premises.

(2) The financial promotion restriction does not apply to any non-real time communication or solicited real time communication if it relates to an investment falling within paragraph 14 of Schedule 1 which—

(a) is issued, or to be issued, by a management company; and

(b) is to be acquired by any person in connection with the acquisition of an interest in the premises in question.

[8.317]

59   Annual accounts and directors' report

(1)   If the requirements in paragraphs (2) to (5) are met, the financial promotion restriction does not apply to any communication by a body corporate (other than an open-ended investment company) which—

    (a)   consists of, or is accompanied by, the whole or any part of the annual accounts of a body corporate (other than an open-ended investment company); or

    (b)   is accompanied by any report which is prepared and approved by the directors of such a body corporate under—

        [(i)   sections 415 and 419 of the 2006 Act; or]

        (ii)   . . .

        (iii)   the law of an EEA State other than the United Kingdom which corresponds to the provisions mentioned in paragraph (i) . . .

(2)   The requirements of this paragraph are that the communication—

    (a)   does not contain any invitation to persons to underwrite, subscribe for, or otherwise acquire or dispose of, a controlled investment; and

    (b)   does not advise persons to engage in any of the activities within sub-paragraph (a).

(3)   The requirements of this paragraph are that the communication does not contain any invitation to persons to—

    (a)   effect any transaction with the body corporate (or with any named person) in the course of that body's (or person's) carrying on of any activity falling within any of paragraphs 3 to 11 of Schedule 1; or

    (b)   make use of any services provided by that body corporate (or by any named person) in the course of carrying on such activity.

(4)   The requirements of this paragraph are that the communication does not contain any inducement relating to an investment other than one issued, or to be issued, by the body corporate (or another body corporate in the same group) which falls within—

    (a)   paragraph 14[, 15 or 15A] of Schedule 1; or

    (b)   paragraph 17 or 18 of that Schedule, so far as relating to any investments within sub-paragraph (a).

(5)   The requirements of this paragraph are that the communication does not contain any reference to—

    (a)   the price at which investments issued by the body corporate have in the past been bought or sold; or

    (b)   the yield on such investments,

unless it is also accompanied by an indication that past performance cannot be relied on as a guide to future performance.

(6)   For the purposes of paragraph (5)(b), a reference, in relation to an investment, to earnings, dividend or nominal rate of interest payable shall not be taken to be a reference to the yield on the investment.

(7)   "Annual accounts" means—

    (a)   accounts produced by virtue of [Part 15 of the 2006 Act] (or of that Part as applied by virtue of any other enactment);

    (b)   . . .

    (c)   a summary financial statement prepared under [section 426 of the 2006 Act];

    [(d)   accounts produced in accordance with Chapter 3 of Part 5 of the Overseas Companies Regulations 2009 and filed with the registrar under section 441 of the 2006 Act as applied and modified by regulation 40 of those Regulations;]

    (e)   accounts which are produced or published by virtue of the law of an EEA State other than the United Kingdom and which correspond to accounts within any of sub-paragraphs (a) to (d).

NOTES

All amendments to paras (1), (7) were made by the Companies Act 2006 (Consequential Amendments and Transitional Provisions) Order 2011, SI 2011/1265, art 26(1), (7), (8), as from 12 May 2011.

Words in square brackets in para (4)(c) substituted by the Financial Services and Markets Act 2000 (Regulated Activities) (Amendment) Order 2010, SI 2010/86, art 4, Schedule, para 9(a)(v), as from 24 February 2010.

[8.318]

60   Participation in employee share schemes

(1)   The financial promotion restriction does not apply to any communication by a person ("C"), a member of the same group as C or a relevant trustee where the communication is for the purposes of an employee share scheme and relates to any of the following investments issued, or to be issued, by C—

    (a)   investments falling within paragraph 14[, 15 or 15A] of Schedule 1;

    (b)   investments falling within paragraph 17 or 18 so far as relating to any investments within sub-paragraph (a); or

Part 8   **FSMA 2000: SIs**

(c) investments falling within paragraph 21 or 27 so far as relating to any investments within sub-paragraph (a) or (b).

(2) "Employee share scheme", in relation to any investments issued by C, means arrangements made or to be made by C or by a person in the same group as C to enable or facilitate—

    (a) transactions in the investments specified in paragraphs (1)(a) or (b) between or for the benefit of—

        (i) the bona fide employees or former employees of C or of another member of the same group as C;

        (ii) the wives, husbands, widows, widowers[, civil partners, surviving civil partners] or children or step-children under the age of eighteen of such employees or former employees; or

    (b) the holding of those investments by, or for the benefit of, such persons.

(3) "Relevant trustee" means a person who, in pursuance of an actual or proposed employee share scheme, holds as trustee or will hold as trustee investments issued by C.

NOTES

Para (1): words in square brackets in sub-para (a) substituted by the Financial Services and Markets Act 2000 (Regulated Activities) (Amendment) Order 2010, SI 2010/86, art 4, Schedule, para 9(a)(vi), as from 24 February 2010.

Para (2): words in square brackets in sub-para (a)(ii) inserted by the Financial Services and Markets Act 2000 (Financial Promotion) (Amendment) Order 2005, SI 2005/3392, art 2(1), (4), as from 21 December 2005.

Step-children, etc: as to the meaning of this, and related expressions, see the Civil Partnership Act 2004, s 246 (as applied to this Order by the Civil Partnership Act 2004 (Relationships Arising Through Civil Partnership) Order 2005, SI 2005/3137, art 3, Schedule).

[8.319]
61 Sale of goods and supply of services

(1) In this article—

"supplier" means a person whose main business is to sell goods or supply services and not to carry on controlled activities falling within any of paragraphs 3 to 7 of Schedule 1 and, where the supplier is a member of a group, also means any other member of that group;

"customer" means a person, other than an individual, to whom a supplier sells goods or supplies services, or agrees to do so, and, where the customer is a member of a group, also means any other member of that group;

"a related sale or supply" means a sale of goods or supply of services to the customer otherwise than by the supplier, but for or in connection with the same purpose as the sale or supply mentioned above.

(2) The financial promotion restriction does not apply to any non-real time communication or any solicited real time communication made by a supplier to a customer of his for the purposes of, or in connection with, the sale of goods or supply of services or a related sale or supply.

(3) But the exemption in paragraph (2) does not apply if the communication relates to—

    (a) a qualifying contract of insurance or units in a collective investment scheme; or

    (b) investments falling within paragraph 27 of Schedule 1 so far as relating to investments within paragraph (a).

[8.320]
62 Sale of body corporate

(1) The financial promotion restriction does not apply to any communication by, or on behalf of, a body corporate, a partnership, a single individual or a group of connected individuals which relates to a transaction falling within paragraph (2).

(2) A transaction falls within this paragraph if—

    (a) it is one to acquire or dispose of shares in a body corporate other than an open-ended investment company, or is entered into for the purposes of such an acquisition or disposal; and

    (b) either—

        (i) the conditions set out in paragraph (3) are met; or

        (ii) those conditions are not met, but the object of the transaction may nevertheless reasonably be regarded as being the acquisition of day to day control of the affairs of the body corporate.

(3) The conditions mentioned in paragraph (2)(b) are that—

    (a) the shares consist of or include 50 per cent or more of the voting shares in the body corporate; or

    (b) the shares, together with any already held by the person acquiring them, consist of or include at least that percentage of such shares; and

    (c) in either case, the acquisition or disposal is, or is to be, between parties each of whom is a body corporate, a partnership, a single individual or a group of connected individuals.

(4) "A group of connected individuals" means—

    (a) in relation to a party disposing of shares in a body corporate, a single group of persons each of whom is—

(i)   a director or manager of the body corporate;
(ii) a close relative of any such director or manager; or
(iii) a person acting as trustee for, or nominee of, any person falling within paragraph (i) or (ii); and
(b)   in relation to a party acquiring shares in a body corporate, a single group of persons each of whom is—
(i)   a person who is or is to be a director or manager of the body corporate;
(ii) a close relative of any such person; or
(iii) a person acting as trustee for or nominee of any person falling within paragraph (i) or (ii).

(5)   "Voting shares" in relation to a body corporate, means shares carrying voting rights attributable to share capital which are exercisable in all circumstances at any general meeting of that body corporate.

[8.321]
63   Takeovers of relevant unlisted companies: interpretation

(1)   In this article and in articles 64, 65 and 66, a "relevant unlisted company", in relation to a takeover offer, means a company which is an unlisted company at the time that the offer is made and which has been an unlisted company throughout the period of ten years immediately preceding the date of the offer.

(2)   In this article and in articles 64, 65 and 66, references to a takeover offer for a relevant unlisted company are references to an offer which meets the requirements of Part I of Schedule 4 and which is an offer—
(a)   for all the shares in, or all the shares comprised in the equity or non-equity share capital of, a relevant unlisted company (other than any shares already held by or on behalf of the person making the offer); or
(b)   for all the debentures of such a company (other than debentures already held by or on behalf of the person making the offer).

(3)   Shares in or debentures of an unlisted company are to be regarded as being held by or on behalf of the person making the offer if the person who holds them, or on whose behalf they are held, has agreed that an offer should not be made in respect of them.

[8.322]
64   Takeovers of relevant unlisted companies

(1)   If the requirements of paragraphs (2) and (3) are met, the financial promotion restriction does not apply to any communication which is communicated in connection with a takeover offer for a relevant unlisted company.

(2)   The requirements of this paragraph are that the communication is accompanied by the material listed in Part II of Schedule 4.

(3)   The requirements of this paragraph are that the material listed in Part III of Schedule 4 is available at a place in the United Kingdom at all times during normal office hours for inspection free of charge.

[8.323]
65   Takeovers of relevant unlisted companies: warrants etc

The financial promotion restriction does not apply to any communication which—
(a)   is communicated at the same time as, or after, a takeover offer for a relevant unlisted company is made; and
(b)   relates to investments falling within paragraph 17 or 18 of Schedule 1 so far as relating to the shares in or debentures of the unlisted company which are the subject of the offer.

[8.324]
66   Takeovers of relevant unlisted companies: application forms

The financial promotion restriction does not apply to any communication made in connection with a takeover offer for a relevant unlisted company which is a form of application for—
(a)   shares in or debentures of the unlisted company; or
(b)   investments falling within paragraphs 17 or 18 of Schedule 1 so far as relating to the shares in or debentures of the company which are the subject of the offer.

[8.325]
67   Promotions required or permitted by market rules

(1)   The financial promotion restriction does not apply to any communication which—
(a)   is a non-real time communication or a solicited real time communication;
(b)   relates to an investment which falls within any of paragraphs 14 to 18 of Schedule 1 and which is permitted to be traded or dealt in on a relevant market; and
(c)   is required or permitted to be communicated by—
(i)   the rules of the relevant market;
(ii) a body which regulates the market; or

    (iii) a body which regulates offers or issues of investments to be traded on such a market.

(2) "Relevant market" means a market which—
- (a) meets the criteria specified in Part I of Schedule 3; or
- (b) is specified in, or established under the rules of an exchange specified in, Part II or III of that Schedule.

[8.326]
68 Promotions in connection with admission to certain EEA markets

(1) The financial promotion restriction does not apply to any communication—
- (a) which is a non-real time communication or a solicited real time communication;
- (b) which a relevant EEA market requires to be communicated before an investment can be admitted to trading on that market;
- (c) which, if it were included in a prospectus issued in accordance with prospectus rules made under Part VI of the Act, would be required to be communicated by those rules; and
- (d) which is not accompanied by any information other than information which is required or permitted to be published by the rules of that market.

(2) In this article "relevant EEA market" means any market on which investments can be traded or dealt in and which—
- (a) meets the criteria specified in Part I of Schedule 3; or
- (b) is specified in, or established under the rules of an exchange specified in, Part II of that Schedule.

[8.327]
69 Promotions of securities already admitted to certain markets

(1) In this article—
"relevant investment" means any investment falling within—
- (a) paragraph 14[, 15 or 15A] of Schedule 1; or
- (b) paragraph 17 or 18 of that Schedule so far as relating to any investment mentioned in sub-paragraph (a);

"relevant market" means any market on which investments can be traded and which—
- (a) meets the criteria specified in Part I of Schedule 3; or
- (b) is specified in, or established under, the rules of an exchange specified in, Part II or III of that Schedule.

(2) If the requirements of paragraph (3) are met, the financial promotion restriction does not apply to any communication which—
- (a) is a non-real time communication or a solicited real time communication;
- (b) is communicated by a body corporate ("A"), other than an open-ended investment company; and
- (c) relates only to relevant investments issued, or to be issued, by A or by another body corporate in the same group,

if relevant investments issued by A or by any such body corporate are permitted to be traded on a relevant market.

(3) The requirements of this paragraph are that the communication—
- (a) is not, and is not accompanied by, an invitation to engage in investment activity;
- (b) is not, and is not accompanied by, an inducement relating to an investment other than one issued, or to be issued, by A (or another body corporate in the same group);
- (c) is not, and is not accompanied by, an inducement relating to a relevant investment which refers to—
  - (i) the price at which relevant investments have been bought or sold in the past, or
  - (ii) the yield on such investments,
  unless the inducement also contains an indication that past performance cannot be relied on as a guide to future performance.

(4) For the purposes of this article, an investment falling within paragraph 17 or 18 of Schedule 1 is treated as issued by the person ("P") who issued the investment in respect of which the investment confers rights if it is issued by—
- (a) an undertaking in the same group as P; or
- (b) a person acting on behalf of, or pursuant to, arrangements made with P.

(5) For the purposes of paragraph (3)(a), "engaging in investment activity" has the meaning given in section 21(8) of the Act; and for the purposes of paragraph (3)(c)(ii), a reference, in relation to an investment, to earnings, dividend or nominal rate of interest payable shall not be taken to be a reference to the yield on the investment.

NOTES
  Para (1): words in square brackets in sub-para (a) substituted by the Financial Services and Markets Act 2000 (Regulated Activities) (Amendment) Order 2010, SI 2010/86, art 4, Schedule, para 9(a), as from 24 February 2010.

[8.328]

70   Promotions included in listing particulars etc

(1)   The financial promotion restriction does not apply to any non-real time communication which is included in—

    (a)   listing particulars;

    (b)   supplementary listing particulars;

    [(c)   a prospectus or supplementary prospectus approved—

        (i)   by the competent authority in accordance with Part 6 of the Act; or

        (ii)   by the competent authority of an EEA State other than the United Kingdom, provided the requirements of section 87H of the Act have been met,

        or part of such a prospectus or supplementary prospectus; or]

    (d)   any other document required or permitted to be published by listing rules or prospectus rules under Part VI of the Act (except an advertisement within the meaning of the prospectus directive).

[(1A)   The financial promotion restriction does not apply to any non-real time communication—

    (a)   comprising the final terms of an offer or the final offer price or amount of securities which will be offered to the public; and

    (b)   complying with Articles 5(4), 8(1) and 14(2) of the prospectus directive.]

(2)   In this article "listing particulars", "listing rules", "the prospectus directive" and "prospectus rules" have the meaning given by Part VI of the Act.

NOTES

Para (1): sub-para (c) substituted by the Financial Services and Markets Act 2000 (Financial Promotion) (Amendment No 2) Order 2007, SI 2007/2615, art 2(1), (2), as from 1 October 2007.

Para (1A): inserted by SI 2007/2615, art 2(1), (3), as from 1 October 2007.

[8.329]

71   Material relating to prospectus for public offer of unlisted securities

(1)   The financial promotion restriction does not apply to any non-real time communication relating to a prospectus or supplementary prospectus where the only reason for considering it to be an invitation or inducement is that it does one or more of the following—

    (a)   it states the name and address of the person by whom the transferable securities to which the prospectus or supplementary prospectus relates are to be offered;

    (b)   it gives other details for contacting that person;

    (c)   it states the nature and the nominal value of the transferable securities to which the prospectus or supplementary prospectus relates, the number offered and the price at which they are offered;

    (d)   it states that a prospectus or supplementary prospectus is or will be available (and, if it is not yet available, when it is expected to be);

    (e)   it gives instructions for obtaining a copy of the prospectus or supplementary prospectus.

(2)   In this article—

    (a)   "transferable securities" has the same meaning as in section 102A(3) of the Act;

    (b)   references to a prospectus or supplementary prospectus are references to a prospectus or supplementary prospectus which is published in accordance with prospectus rules made under Part VI of the Act.

[8.330]

72   Pension products offered by employers

(1)   If the requirements of paragraph (2) are met, the financial promotion restriction does not apply to any communication which is made by an employer to an employee in relation to a group personal pension scheme or a stakeholder pension scheme.

(2)   The requirements of this paragraph are that—

    (a)   the employer will make a contribution to the group personal pension scheme or stakeholder pension scheme to which the communication relates in the event of the employee becoming a member of the scheme and the communication contains a statement informing the employee of this;

    [(b)   the employer has not received, and will not receive, any direct financial benefit as a result of making the communication;]

    (c)   the employer notifies the employee in writing prior to the employee becoming a member of the scheme of the amount of the contribution that the employer will make to the scheme in respect of that employee [or the basis on which the contribution will be calculated]; and

    (d)   in the case of a non-real time communication, the communication contains, or is accompanied by, a statement informing the employee of his right to seek advice from an authorised person or an appointed representative.

(3)   . . .

(4)   In this article—

"group personal pension scheme" means arrangements administered on a group basis under a personal pension scheme and which are available to employees of the same employer or of employers within a group;

["personal pension scheme" means a scheme or arrangement which is not an occupational pension scheme or a stakeholder pension scheme and which is comprised in one or more instruments or agreements, having or capable of having effect so as to provide benefits to or in respect of people—

    (a)   on retirement,

    (b)   on having reached a particular age, or

    (c)   on termination of service in an employment.]

"stakeholder pension scheme" has the meaning given by section 1 of the Welfare Reform and Pensions Act 1999.

NOTES

Para (2): sub-para (b) substituted, and words in square brackets in sub-para (c) inserted, by the Financial Services and Markets Act 2000 (Financial Promotion) (Amendment) Order 2010, SI 2010/905, arts 2, 4(a), as from 13 April 2010.

Para (3): revoked by SI 2010/905, arts 2, 4(b), as from 13 April 2010.

Para (4): definition "personal pension scheme" substituted by the Financial Services and Markets Act 2000 (Regulated Activities) (Amendment) Order 2006, SI 2006/1969, art 12(1), (2), as from 6 April 2007.

[8.331]

[72A Pension product offers communicated to employees by third parties

(1) If the requirements of paragraph (2) are met, the financial promotion restriction does not apply to any communication which is made to an employee by or on behalf of a person ("A") in relation to a group personal pension scheme or a stakeholder pension scheme.

(2) The requirements of this paragraph are that—

    (a)   the employer and A have entered into a written contract specifying the terms on which the communication may be made;

    (b)   in the case of a communication made by a person ("B") on behalf of A, A and B have also entered into a written contract specifying the terms on which the communication may be made;

    (c)   the employer has not received, and will not receive, any direct financial benefit as a result of the communication being made;

    (d)   the employer will make a contribution to the scheme in the event of the employee becoming a member of the scheme and the communication contains a statement informing the employee of this;

    (e)   in the case of a non-real time communication, the communication contains, or is accompanied by, a statement informing the employee of their right to seek advice from an authorised person or an appointed representative; and

    (f)   the employer or A notifies the employee in writing prior to the employee becoming a member of the scheme of—

        (i)   the amount of the contribution that the employer will make to the scheme in respect of that employee, or the basis on which the contribution will be calculated; and

        (ii)   any remuneration A or B has received, or will receive, as a consequence of the employee becoming a member of the scheme, or the basis on which any such remuneration will be calculated.

(3) In this article "group personal pension scheme" and "stakeholder pension scheme" have the meaning given by article 72(4).]

NOTES

Commencement: 13 April 2010.

Inserted, together with arts 72B–72E, by the Financial Services and Markets Act 2000 (Financial Promotion) (Amendment) Order 2010, SI 2010/905, arts 2, 5, as from 13 April 2010.

[8.332]

[72B Insurance product offers communicated to employees by employers

(1) If the requirements of paragraph (2) are met, the financial promotion restriction does not apply to any communication which is made by an employer to an employee in relation to work-related insurance.

(2) The requirements of this paragraph are that—

    (a)   where the provider of the insurance is not the employer, the employer has not received, and will not receive, any direct financial benefit as a result of making the communication; and

    (b)   in the case of a non-real time communication, the communication contains, or is accompanied by, a statement informing the employee of their right to seek advice from an authorised person or an appointed representative.

(3) In this article "work-related insurance" includes—

    (a)   life assurance;

    (b)   long term disability insurance (also known as permanent health insurance); and

(c)   accidental death, injury, critical illness, medical, dental, income protection or travel insurance.]

NOTES
Commencement: 13 April 2010.
Inserted as noted to art 72A at **[8.331]**.

[8.333]
[72C   Insurance product offers communicated to employees by third parties

(1)   If the requirements of paragraph (2) are met, the financial promotion restriction does not apply to any communication which is made to an employee by or on behalf of a person ("A") in relation to work-related insurance.

(2)   The requirements of this paragraph are that—
(a)   the employer and A have entered into a written contract specifying the terms on which the communication may be made;
(b)   in the case of a communication made by a person ("B") on behalf of A, A and B have also entered into a written contract specifying the terms on which the communication may be made;
(c)   the employer has not received, and will not receive, any direct financial benefit as a result of the communication being made;
(d)   in the case of a non-real time communication, the communication contains, or is accompanied by, a statement informing the employee of their right to seek advice from an authorised person or an appointed representative; and
(e)   the employer or A notifies the employee in writing prior to the employee entering into a contract for the work-related insurance of any remuneration A or B has received, or will receive, as a consequence of the employee entering into the contract, or the basis on which any such remuneration will be calculated.

(3)   In this article "work-related insurance" has the meaning given by article 72B(3).]

NOTES
Commencement: 13 April 2010.
Inserted as noted to art 72A at **[8.331]**.

[8.334]
[72D   Staff mortgage offers communicated to employees by employers

(1)   If the requirements of paragraph (2) are met, the financial promotion restriction does not apply to any communication which is made by an employer to an employee in relation to a staff mortgage.

(2)   The requirements of this paragraph are that—
(a)   where the provider of the staff mortgage is an undertaking in the same group as the employer, the employer has not received, and will not receive, any direct financial benefit as a result of making the communication; and
(b)   in the case of a non-real time communication, the communication contains or is accompanied by a statement informing the employee of their right to seek advice from an authorised person or an appointed representative.

(3)   In this article, "staff mortgage" means a regulated mortgage contract between the employer, or an undertaking in the same group as the employer, as lender and the employee (alone or with another person) as borrower to defray money applied for any of the following purposes—
(a)   acquiring any residential land which was intended, at the time of the acquisition, for occupation by the employee as their home;
(b)   carrying out repairs or improvements to any residential land which was intended, at the time of taking out the loan, for occupation by the employee as their home; or
(c)   payments in respect of a loan (whether of interest or capital).

(4)   In this article, "borrower", "lender" and "regulated mortgage contract" have the meaning given by article 61(3)(a) (regulated mortgage contracts) of the Financial Services and Markets Act 2000 (Regulated Activities) Order 2001.]

NOTES
Commencement: 13 April 2010.
Inserted as noted to art 72A at **[8.331]**.

[8.335]
[72E   Staff mortgage offers communicated to employees by third parties

(1)   If the requirements of paragraph (2) are met, the financial promotion restriction does not apply to any communication which is made to an employee by or on behalf of a person ("A") in relation to a staff mortgage.

(2)   The requirements of this paragraph are that—

(a) the employer and A have entered into a written contract specifying the terms on which the communication may be made;

(b) in the case of a communication made by a person ("B") on behalf of A, A and B have also entered into a written contract specifying the terms on which the communication may be made;

(c) where the provider of the staff mortgage is an undertaking in the same group as the employer, the employer has not received, and will not receive, any direct financial benefit as a result of the communication being made;

(d) in the case of a non-real time communication, the communication contains, or is accompanied by, a statement informing the employee of their right to seek advice from an authorised person or an appointed representative; and

(e) the employer or A notifies the employee in writing prior to the employee entering into the staff mortgage of any remuneration A or B has received, or will receive, as a consequence of the employee entering into the staff mortgage, or the basis on which any such remuneration will be calculated.

(3) In this article "staff mortgage" has the same meaning as in article 72D(3).]

NOTES
Commencement: 13 April 2010.
Inserted as noted to art 72A at **[8.331]**.

[8.336]
73 Advice centres
(1) If the requirements of paragraph (2) are met, the financial promotion restriction does not apply to any communication which is made by a person in the course of carrying out his duties as an adviser for, or employee of, an advice centre.

(2) The requirements of this paragraph are that the communication relates to—
(a) qualifying credit;
(b) rights under, or rights to or interests in rights under, qualifying contracts of insurance; . . .
(c) a child trust fund[;
(d) a regulated home reversion plan; . . .
(e) a regulated home purchase plan][; or
(f) a regulated sale and rent back agreement].

(3) In this article—
"adequate professional indemnity insurance", in relation to an advice centre, means insurance providing cover that is adequate having regard to—
(a) the claims record of the centre;
(b) the financial resources of the centre; and
(c) the right of clients of the centre to be compensated for loss arising from the negligent provision of financial advice;
"advice centre" means a body which—
(a) gives advice which is free and in respect of which the centre does not receive any fee, commission or other reward;
(b) provides debt advice as its principal financial services activity; and
(c) in the case of a body which is not part of a local authority, holds adequate professional indemnity insurance or a guarantee providing comparable cover;
"child trust fund" has the meaning given by section 1(2) of the Child Trust Funds Act 2004;
"local authority" has the meaning given in article 2 of the Financial Services and Markets Act 2000 (Exemption) Order 2001.

NOTES
Para (2): word omitted from sub-para (b) revoked, and sub-paras (d), (e) inserted, by the Financial Services and Markets Act 2000 (Regulated Activities) (Amendment) (No 2) Order 2006, SI 2006/2383, art 35(1), (4), as from 6 April 2007; word "or" omitted from sub-para (d) revoked, and sub-para (f) (and the word preceding it) inserted, by the Financial Services and Markets Act 2000 (Regulated Activities) (Amendment) Order 2009, SI 2009/1342, art 30(1), (3), as from 1 July 2009 (certain purposes), and as from 30 June 2010 (otherwise).

[8.337]
74 Revocation
The Orders specified in the first column of Schedule 6 are revoked to the extent specified in the third column of that Schedule.

SCHEDULES
SCHEDULE 1

Article 4

PART I
CONTROLLED ACTIVITIES

Accepting deposits

[8.338]
1. Accepting deposits is a controlled activity if—
(a) money received by way of deposit is lent to others; or
(b) any other activity of the person accepting the deposit is financed wholly, or to a material extent, out of the capital of or interest on money received by way of deposit,
and the person accepting the deposit holds himself out as accepting deposits on a day to day basis.

Effecting or carrying out contracts of insurance

2. (1) Effecting a contract of insurance as principal is a controlled activity.

(2) Carrying out a contract of insurance as principal is a controlled activity.

(3) There is excluded from sub-paragraph (1) or (2) the effecting or carrying out of a contract of insurance of the kind described in article 12 of the Regulated Activities Order by a person who does not otherwise carry on an activity falling within those sub-paragraphs.

Dealing in securities and contractually based investments

3. (1) Buying, selling, subscribing for or underwriting securities or contractually based investments (other than investments of the kind specified by paragraph 25, or paragraph 27 so far as relevant to that paragraph) as principal or agent is a controlled activity.

(2) A person does not carry on the activity in sub-paragraph (1) by accepting an instrument creating or acknowledging indebtedness in respect of any loan, credit, guarantee or other similar financial accommodation or assurance which he has made, granted or provided.

(3) The reference in sub-paragraph (2) to a person accepting an instrument includes a reference to a person becoming a party to an instrument otherwise than as a debtor or a surety.

Arranging deals in investments

4. (1) Making arrangements for another person (whether as principal or agent) to buy, sell, subscribe for or underwrite a particular investment which is—
(a) a security;
(b) a contractually based investment; or
(c) an investment of the kind specified by paragraph 24, or paragraph 27 so far as relevant to that paragraph,
is a controlled activity.

(2) Making arrangements with a view to a person who participates in the arrangements buying, selling, subscribing for or underwriting investments falling within sub-paragraph (1)(a), (b) or (c) (whether as principal or agent) is a controlled activity.

(3) A person does not carry on an activity falling within paragraph (2) merely by providing means by which one party to a transaction (or potential transaction) is able to communicate with other such parties.

Operating a multilateral trading facility

[4A. Operating a multilateral trading facility on which MiFID instruments are traded is a controlled activity.]

Managing investments

5. Managing assets belonging to another person, in circumstances involving the exercise of discretion, is a controlled activity if—
(a) the assets consist of or include any investment which is a security or a contractually based investment; or
(b) the arrangements for their management are such that the assets may consist of or include such investments, and either the assets have at any time since 29th April 1988 done so, or the arrangements have at any time (whether before or after that date) been held out as arrangements under which the assets would do so.

Safeguarding and administering investments

6. (1) The activity consisting of both—
(a) the safeguarding of assets belonging to another; and
(b) the administration of those assets,
or arranging for one or more other persons to carry on that activity, is a controlled activity if either the condition in paragraph (a) or (b) of sub-paragraph (2) is met.

(2) The condition is that—
  (a) the assets consist of or include any investment which is a security or a contractually based investment; or
  (b) the arrangements for their safeguarding and administration are such that the assets may consist of or include investments of the kind mentioned in sub-paragraph (a) and either the assets have at any time since 1st June 1997 done so, or the arrangements have at any time (whether before or after that date) been held out as ones under which such investments would be safeguarded and administered.

(3) For the purposes of this article—
  (a) it is immaterial that title to the assets safeguarded and administered is held in uncertificated form;
  (b) it is immaterial that the assets safeguarded and administered may be transferred to another person, subject to a commitment by the person safeguarding and administering them, or arranging for their safeguarding and administration, that they will be replaced by equivalent assets at some future date or when so requested by the person to whom they belong.

(4) For the purposes of this article, the following activities do not constitute the administration of assets—
  (a) providing information as to the number of units or the value of any assets safeguarded;
  (b) converting currency;
  (c) receiving documents relating to an investment solely for the purpose of onward transmission to, from or at the direction of the person to whom the investment belongs.

Advising on investments
7. Advising a person is a controlled activity if the advice is—
  (a) given to the person in his capacity as an investor or potential investor, or in his capacity as agent for an investor or a potential investor; and
  (b) advice on the merits of his doing any of the following (whether as principal or agent)—
    (i) buying, selling, subscribing for or underwriting a particular investment which is a security or a contractually based investment; or
    (ii) exercising any right conferred by such an investment to buy, sell, subscribe for or underwrite such an investment.

Advising on syndicate participation at Lloyd's
8. Advising a person to become, or continue or cease to be, a member of a particular Lloyd's syndicate is a controlled activity.

Providing funeral plan contracts
9. (1) Entering as provider into a qualifying funeral plan contract is a controlled activity.

(2) A "qualifying funeral plan contract" is a contract under which—
  (a) a person ("the customer") makes one or more payments to another person ("the provider");
  (b) the provider undertakes to provide, or to secure that another person provides, a funeral in the United Kingdom for the customer (or some other person who is living at the date when the contract is entered into) on his death; and
  (c) the provider is a person who carries on the regulated activity specified in article 59 of the Regulated Activities Order.

Providing qualifying credit
10. (1) Providing qualifying credit is a controlled activity.

(2) "Qualifying credit" is a credit provided pursuant to an agreement under which—
  (a) the lender is a person who carries on the regulated activity specified in article 61 of the Regulated Activities Order; and
  (b) the obligation of the borrower to repay is secured (in whole or in part) on land.

(3) "Credit" includes a cash loan and any other form of financial accommodation.

Arranging qualifying credit etc
10A. Making arrangements—
  (a) for another person to enter as borrower into an agreement for the provision of qualifying credit; or
  (b) for a borrower under a regulated mortgage contract, within the meaning of article 61(3) of the Regulated Activities Order, entered into after the coming into force of that article, to vary the terms of that contract in such a way as to vary his obligations under that contract, is a controlled activity.

Advising on qualifying credit etc
10B. (1) Advising a person is a controlled activity if the advice is—
  (a) given to the person in his capacity as a borrower or potential borrower; and
  (b) advice on the merits of his doing any of the following—
    (i) entering into an agreement for the provision of qualifying credit, or

(ii)   varying the terms of a regulated mortgage contract entered into by him after the coming into force of article 61 of the Regulated Activities Order in such a way as to vary his obligations under that contract.

(2)   In this paragraph, "borrower" and "regulated mortgage contract" have the meaning given by article 61(3) of the Regulated Activities Order.

Providing a regulated home reversion plan
[10C. Entering into a regulated home reversion plan as plan provider is a controlled activity.

Arranging a regulated home reversion plan
10D.   Making arrangements—
(a)   for another person to enter as reversion seller or plan provider into a regulated home reversion plan; or
(b)   for a reversion seller or a plan provider under a regulated home reversion plan, entered into on or after 6th April 2007 by him, to vary the terms of that plan in such a way as to vary his obligations under that plan,
is a controlled activity.

Advising on a regulated home reversion plan
10E.   Advising a person is a controlled activity if the advice is—
(a)   given to the person in his capacity as reversion seller, potential reversion seller, plan provider or potential plan provider; and
(b)   advice on the merits of his doing either of the following—
(i)   entering into a regulated home reversion plan, or
(ii)   varying the terms of a regulated home reversion plan, entered into on or after 6th April 2007 by him, in such a way as to vary his obligations under that plan.

Providing a regulated home purchase plan
10F. Entering into a regulated home purchase plan as home purchase provider is a controlled activity.

Arranging a regulated home purchase plan
10G.   Making arrangements—
(a)   for another person to enter as home purchaser into a regulated home purchase plan; or
(b)   for a home purchaser under a regulated home purchase plan, entered into on or after 6th April 2007 by him, to vary the terms of that plan in such a way as to vary his obligations under that plan,
is a controlled activity.

Advising on a regulated home purchase plan
10H.   Advising a person is a controlled activity if the advice is—
(a)   given to the person in his capacity as home purchaser or potential home purchaser; and
(b)   advice on the merits of his doing either of the following—
(i)   entering into a regulated home purchase plan, or
(ii)   varying the terms of a regulated home purchase plan, entered into on or after 6th April 2007 by him, in such a way as to vary his obligations under that plan.]

[Providing a regulated sale and rent back agreement
10I. Entering into a regulated sale and rent back agreement as agreement provider is a controlled activity.

Arranging a regulated sale and rent back agreement
10J. Making arrangements—
(a)   for another person to enter as agreement seller or agreement provider into a regulated sale and rent back agreement; or
(b)   for an agreement seller or an agreement provider under a regulated sale and rent back agreement, entered into on or after 1st July 2009, to vary the terms of that plan in such a way as to vary the obligations of the agreement seller or the agreement provider under that plan,
is a controlled activity.

Advising on a regulated sale and rent back agreement
10K.   Advising a person ("A") is a controlled activity if the advice is—
(a)   given to A in A's capacity as agreement seller, potential agreement seller, agreement provider or potential agreement provider; and
(b)   advice on the merits of A doing either of the following—
(i)   entering into a regulated sale and rent back agreement, or
(ii)   varying the terms of a regulated sale and rent back agreement, entered into on or after 1st July 2009 by A, in such a way as to vary A's obligations under that agreement.]

Agreeing to carry on specified kinds of activity

11. Agreeing to carry on any controlled activity falling within any of paragraphs 3 to 10B [(other than paragraph 4A)] above is a controlled activity.

NOTES

Para 4A: inserted by the Financial Services and Markets Act 2000 (Regulated Activities) (Amendment No 3) Order 2006, SI 2006/3384, art 40(1), (2)(a), as from 1 November 2007.

Paras 10C–10H: inserted by the Financial Services and Markets Act 2000 (Regulated Activities) (Amendment) (No 2) Order 2006, SI 2006/2383, art 35(1), (5), as from 6 April 2007.

Paras 10I–10K: inserted by the Financial Services and Markets Act 2000 (Regulated Activities) (Amendment) Order 2009, SI 2009/1342, art 30(1), (4), as from 1 July 2009 (certain purposes), and as from 30 June 2010 (otherwise).

Para 11: words in square brackets inserted by SI 2006/3384, art 40(1), (2)(b), as from 1 November 2007.

PART II
CONTROLLED INVESTMENTS

[8.339]
12. A deposit.

13. Rights under a contract of insurance.

14. (1) Shares or stock in the share capital of—
(a) any body corporate (wherever incorporated);
(b) any unincorporated body constituted under the law of a country or territory outside the United Kingdom.

(2) Sub-paragraph (1) includes—
(a) any shares of a class defined as deferred shares for the purposes of section 119 of the Building Societies Act 1986;
(b) any transferable shares in a body incorporated under the law of, or any part of, the United Kingdom relating to industrial and provident societies or credit unions or in a body constituted under the law of another EEA State for purposes equivalent to those of such a body.

(3) But subject to sub-paragraph (2) there are excluded from sub-paragraph (1) shares or stock in the share capital of—
(a) an open-ended investment company;
(b) a building society incorporated under the law of, or any part of, the United Kingdom;
(c) any body incorporated under the law of, or any part of, the United Kingdom relating to industrial and provident societies or credit unions;
(d) any body constituted under the law of an EEA State for purposes equivalent to those of a body falling within paragraph (b) or (c).

Instruments creating or acknowledging indebtedness

15. (1) Subject to sub-paragraph (2), such of the following as do not fall within [paragraph . . . 16]—
(a) debentures;
(b) debenture stock;
(c) loan stock;
(d) bonds;
(e) certificates of deposit;
(f) any other instrument creating or acknowledging a present or future indebtedness.

(2) If and to the extent that they would otherwise fall within sub-paragraph (1), there are excluded from that sub-paragraph—
(a) any instrument acknowledging or creating indebtedness for, or for money borrowed to defray, the consideration payable under a contract for the supply of goods or services;
(b) a cheque or other bill of exchange, a banker's draft or a letter of credit (but not a bill of exchange accepted by a banker);
(c) a banknote, a statement showing a balance on a current, deposit or saving account, a lease or other disposition of property, a heritable security; and
(d) a contract of insurance;
[(e) . . .].

(3) An instrument excluded from sub-paragraph (1) of paragraph 16 by paragraph 16(2)(b) is not thereby to be taken to fall within sub-paragraph (1) of this paragraph.

[Alternative finance investment bonds
15A. (1) Rights under an alternative finance investment bond, to the extent that they do not fall within paragraph [15 or] 16.

(2) For the purposes of this paragraph, arrangements constitute an alternative finance investment bond if—
(a) the arrangements provide for a person ("the bond-holder") to pay a sum of money ("the capital") to another ("the bond-issuer");

(b)   the arrangements identify assets, or a class of assets, which the bond-issuer will acquire for the purpose of generating income or gains directly or indirectly ("the bond assets");

(c)   the arrangements specify a period at the end of which they cease to have effect ("the bond term");

(d)   the bond-issuer undertakes under the arrangements—

    (i)   to make a repayment in respect of the capital ("the redemption payment") to the bond-holder during or at the end of the bond term (whether or not in instalments); and

    (ii)   to pay to the bond-holder other payments on one or more occasions during or at the end of the bond term ("the additional payments");

(e)   the amount of the additional payments does not exceed an amount which would, at the time at which the bond is issued, be a reasonable commercial return on a loan of the capital; and

(f)   the arrangements are a security admitted to—

    (i)   an official list (in accordance with the provisions of Directive 2001/34/EC of the European Parliament and of the Council on the admission of securities to official stock exchange listing and on information to be published on those securities); or

    (ii)   trading on a regulated market (within the meaning of Article 4.1(14) of Directive 2004/39/EC of the European Parliament and of the Council on markets in financial instruments) or on a recognised investment exchange (within the meaning of section 285 of the Act).

(3)   For the purposes of sub-paragraph (2)—

(a)   the bond-issuer may acquire the bond assets before or after the arrangements take effect;

(b)   the bond assets may be property of any kind, including rights in relation to property owned by someone other than the bond-issuer;

(c)   the identification of the bond assets mentioned in sub-paragraph (2)(b) and the undertakings mentioned in sub-paragraph (2)(d) may (but need not) be described as, or accompanied by a document described as, a declaration of trust;

(d)   the reference to a period in sub-paragraph (2)(c) includes any period specified to end upon the redemption of the bond by the bond-issuer;

(e)   the bond-holder may (but need not) be entitled under the arrangements to terminate them, or participate in terminating them, before the end of the bond term;

(f)   the amount of the additional payments may be—

    (i)   fixed at the beginning of the bond term;

    (ii)   determined wholly or partly by reference to the value of or income generated by the bond assets; or

    (iii)   determined in some other way;

(g)   if the amount of the additional payments is not fixed at the beginning of the bond term, the reference in sub-paragraph (2)(e) to the amount of the additional payments is a reference to the maximum amount of the additional payments;

(h)   the amount of the redemption payment may (but need not) be subject to reduction in the event of a fall in the value of the bond assets or in the rate of income generated by them; and

(i)   entitlement to the redemption payment may (but need not) be capable of being satisfied (whether or not at the option of the bond-issuer or the bond-holder) by the issue or transfer of shares or other securities.

(4)   An instrument excluded from sub-paragraph (1) of paragraph 16 by sub-paragraph (2)(b) of that paragraph is not thereby taken to fall within sub-paragraph (1) of this paragraph.]

Government and public securities
16. (1)   Subject to sub-paragraph (2), loan stock, bonds and other instruments—

(a)   creating or acknowledging indebtedness; and

(b)   issued by or on behalf of a government, local authority (whether in the United Kingdom or elsewhere) or international organisation.

(2)   [Subject to sub-paragraph (3),] there are excluded from sub-paragraph (1)—

(a)   so far as applicable, the instruments mentioned in paragraph 15(2)(a) to (d);

(b)   any instrument creating or acknowledging indebtedness in respect of—

    (i)   money received by the Director of Savings as deposits or otherwise in connection with the business of the National Savings Bank;

    (ii)   money raised under the National Loans Act 1968 under the auspices of the Director of Savings or treated as so raised by virtue of section 11(3) of the National Debt Act 1972.

[(3)   Sub-paragraph (2)(a) does not exclude an instrument which meets the requirements set out in paragraphs (a) to (e) of paragraph 15A(2).]

Instruments giving entitlements to investments
17. (1)   Warrants and other instruments entitling the holder to subscribe for any investment falling within paragraph 14, 15 or 16.

(2)   It is immaterial whether the investment to which the entitlement relates is in existence or identifiable.

(3)   An investment falling within this paragraph shall not be regarded as falling within paragraph 21, 22 or 23.

Certificates representing certain securities

18. (1)   Subject to sub-paragraph (2), certificates or other instruments which confer contractual or property rights (other than rights consisting of an investment of the kind specified by paragraph 21)—

    (a)   in respect of any investment of the kind specified by any of paragraphs 14 to 17 being an investment held by a person other than the person on whom the rights are conferred by the certificate or instrument; and

    (b)   the transfer of which may be effected without the consent of that person.

(2)   There is excluded from sub-paragraph (1) any instrument which confers rights in respect of two or more investments issued by different persons, or in respect of two or more different investments of the kind specified by paragraph 16 and issued by the same person.

Units in a collective investment scheme

19.   Units in a collective investment scheme.

Rights under a pension scheme

[20. (1)   Rights under a stakeholder pension scheme.

(2)   Rights under a personal pension scheme.

(3)   "Stakeholder pension scheme" and "personal pension scheme" have the meanings given by article 72(4).]

Options

21.   [(1)]   Options to acquire or dispose of—

    (a)   a security or contractually based investment (other than one of a kind specified in this paragraph);

    (b)   currency of the United Kingdom or of any other country or territory;

    (c)   palladium, platinum, gold or silver; . . .

    (d)   an option to acquire or dispose of an investment falling within this paragraph by virtue of sub-paragraph (a), (b) or (c)[;

    (e)   subject to sub-paragraph (4), an option to acquire or dispose of an option to which paragraph 5, 6, 7 or 10 of Section C of Annex I to the markets in financial instruments directive applies].

[(2)   Subject to sub-paragraph (4), options—

    (a)   to which sub-paragraph (1) does not apply;

    (b)   which relate to commodities;

    (c)   which may be settled physically; and

    (d)   either—

        (i)   to which paragraph 5 or 6 of Section C of Annex I to the markets in financial instruments directive applies, or

        (ii)   which in accordance with Article 38 of the Commission Regulation are to be considered as having the characteristics of other derivative financial instruments and not being for commercial purposes, and to which paragraph 7 of Section C of Annex I to the markets in financial instruments directive applies.

(3)   Subject to sub-paragraph (4), options—

    (a)   to which sub-paragraph (1) does not apply;

    (b)   which may be settled physically; and

    (c)   to which paragraph 10 of Section C of Annex I to the markets in financial instruments directive (read with the Commission Regulation) applies.

(4)   Sub-paragraphs (1)(e), (2) and (3) only apply to options in relation to which—

    (a)   an investment firm or credit institution is providing or performing investment services and activities on a professional basis,

    (b)   a management company is providing, in accordance with [Article 6(3)] of the UCITS directive, the investment service specified in paragraph 4 or 5 of Section A, or the ancillary service specified in paragraph 1 of Section B, of Annex I to the markets in financial instruments directive, or

    (c)   a market operator is providing the investment service specified in paragraph 8 of Section A of Annex I to the markets in financial instruments directive.

(5)   Expressions used in sub-paragraphs (1)(e), (2) and (3) and in the markets in financial instruments directive have the same meaning as in that directive.]

Futures

22. (1) Subject to sub-paragraph (2), rights under a contract for the sale of a commodity or property of any other description under which delivery is to be made at a future date and at a price agreed on when the contract is made.

[(1A) Subject to sub-paragraph (1D), futures—
  (a) to which sub-paragraph (1) does not apply;
  (b) which relate to commodities;
  (c) which may be settled physically; and
  (d) to which paragraph 5 or 6 of Section C of Annex I to the markets in financial instruments directive applies.

(1B) Subject to sub-paragraph (1D), futures and forwards—
  (a) to which sub-paragraph (1) does not apply;
  (b) which relate to commodities;
  (c) which may be settled physically;
  (d) which in accordance with Article 38 of the Commission Regulation are to be considered as having the characteristics of other derivative financial instruments and not being for commercial purposes; and
  (e) to which paragraph 7 of Section C of Annex I to the markets in financial instruments directive applies.

(1C) Subject to sub-paragraph (1D), futures—
  (a) to which sub-paragraph (1) does not apply;
  (b) which may be settled physically; and
  (c) to which paragraph 10 of Section C of Annex I to the markets in financial instruments directive (read with the Commission Regulation) applies.

(1D) Sub-paragraphs (1A), (1B) and (1C) only apply to futures or forwards in relation to which—
  (a) an investment firm or credit institution is providing or performing investment services and activities on a professional basis,
  (b) a management company is providing, in accordance with Article 5(3) of the UCITS directive, the investment service specified in paragraph 4 or 5 of Section A, or the ancillary service specified in paragraph 1 of Section B, of Annex I to the markets in financial instruments directive, or
  (c) a market operator is providing the investment service specified in paragraph 8 of Section A of Annex I to the markets in financial instruments directive.

(1E) Expressions used in sub-paragraphs (1A) to (1C) and in the markets in financial instruments directive have the same meaning as in that directive.]

(2) There are excluded from sub-paragraph (1) rights under any contract which is made for commercial and not investment purposes.

(3) For the purposes of sub-paragraph (2), in considering whether a contract is to be regarded as made for investment purposes or for commercial purposes, the indicators set out in article 84 of the Regulated Activities Order shall be applied in the same way as they are applied for the purposes of that article.

Contracts for differences etc

23. (1) Subject to sub-paragraph (2), rights under—
  (a) a contract for differences; or
  (b) any other contract the purpose or pretended purpose of which is to secure a profit or avoid a loss by reference to fluctuations in—
    (i) the value or price of property of any description;
    (ii) an index or other factor designated for that purpose in the contract.

(2) There are excluded from sub-paragraph (1)—
  (a) rights under a contract if the parties intend that the profit is to be secured or the loss is to be avoided by one or more of the parties taking delivery of any property to which the contract relates;
  (b) rights under a contract under which money is received by way of deposit on terms that any interest or other return to be paid on the sum deposited will be calculated by reference to fluctuations in an index or other factor;
  (c) rights under any contract under which—
    (i) money is received by the Director of Savings as deposits or otherwise in connection with the business of the National Savings Bank; or
    (ii) money is raised under the National Loans Act 1968 under the auspices of the Director of Savings or treated as so raised by virtue of section 11(3) of the National Debt Act 1972;
  (d) rights under a qualifying contract of insurance.

[(3) Subject to sub-paragraph (4), derivative instruments for the transfer of credit risk—
  (a) to which neither paragraph 21 nor sub-paragraph (1) applies; and
  (b) to which paragraph 8 of Section C of Annex I to the markets in financial instruments directive applies.

(4) Sub-paragraph (3) only applies to derivatives in relation to which—

(a) an investment firm or credit institution is providing or performing investment services and activities on a professional basis,

(b) a management company is providing, in accordance with Article 5(3) of the UCITS directive, the investment service specified in paragraph 4 or 5 of Section A, or the ancillary service specified in paragraph 1 of Section B, of Annex I to the markets in financial instruments directive, or

(c) a market operator is providing the investment service specified in paragraph 8 of Section A of Annex I to the markets in financial instruments directive.

(5) "Derivative instruments for the transfer of credit risk" has the same meaning as in the markets in financial instruments directive.]

Lloyd's syndicate capacity and syndicate membership
24. (1) The underwriting capacity of a Lloyd's syndicate.

(2) A person's membership (or prospective membership) of a Lloyd's syndicate.

Funeral plan contracts
25. Rights under a qualifying funeral plan contract.

Agreements for qualifying credit
26. Rights under an agreement for qualifying credit.

Regulated home reversion plans
[26A. Rights under a regulated home reversion plan.

Regulated home purchase plans
26B. Rights under a regulated home purchase plan.]

[Regulated sale and rent back agreement
26C. Rights under a regulated sale and rent back agreement.]

Rights to or interests in investments
27. (1) Subject to sub-paragraphs (2) and (3), any right to or interest in anything which is specified by any other provision of this Part of this Schedule (other than [paragraph 26, [26A, 26B or 26C]]).

(2) Sub-paragraph (1) does not apply to interests under the trusts of an occupational pension scheme.

(2A) Sub-paragraph (1) does not apply to any right or interest acquired as a result of entering into a funeral plan contract (and for this purpose a "funeral plan contract" is a contract of a kind described in paragraph 9(2)(a) and (b)).

(3) Sub-paragraph (1) does not apply to anything which falls within any other provision of this Part of this Schedule.

Interpretation
28. In this Schedule—

["agreement provider" has the meaning given in paragraph (3) of article 63J of the Regulated Activities Order, read with paragraphs (6) and (7) of that article;

"agreement seller" has the meaning given in article 63J(3) of the Regulated Activities Order;]

"buying" includes acquiring for valuable consideration;

["Commission Regulation" means Commission Regulation 1287/2006 of 10 August 2006;]

"contract of insurance" has the meaning given in the Regulated Activities Order;

"contractually based investment" means—

(a) rights under a qualifying contract of insurance;

(b) any investment of the kind specified by any of paragraphs 21, 22, 23 and 25;

(c) any investment of the kind specified by paragraph 27 so far as relevant to an investment falling within (a) or (b);

["credit institution" has the meaning given in the Regulated Activities Order;]

["home purchase provider" and "home purchaser" have the meanings given in article 63F(3) of the Regulated Activities Order;]

["investment firm" has the meaning given in the Regulated Activities Order;]

["investment services and activities" has the meaning given in the Regulated Activities Order;]

["management company" has the meaning given in the Regulated Activities Order;]

["market operator" has the meaning given in the Regulated Activities Order;]

["MiFID instrument" has the meaning given in article 25D(2) of the Regulated Activities Order;]

["multilateral trading facility" has the meaning given in the Regulated Activities Order;]

["occupational pension scheme" has the meaning given by section 1 of the Pension Schemes Act 1993 but with paragraph (b) of the definition omitted;]

["plan provider" has the meaning given by paragraph (3) of article 63B of the Regulated Activities Order, read with paragraphs (7) and (8) of that article;]

"property" includes currency of the United Kingdom or any other country or territory;

"qualifying funeral plan contract" has the meaning given by paragraph 9;

["regulated home purchase plan" has the meaning given in article 63F(3) of the Regulated Activities Order;

"regulated home reversion plan" and "reversion seller" have the meanings given in article 63B(3) of the Regulated Activities Order;]

["regulated sale and rent back agreement" has the meaning given in article 63J(3) of the Regulated Activities Order;]

"security" means a controlled investment falling within any of paragraphs 14 to 20 or, so far as relevant to any such investment, paragraph 27;

"selling", in relation to any investment, includes disposing of the investment for valuable consideration, and for these purposes "disposing" includes—

(a)   in the case of an investment consisting of rights under a contract—

     (i)   surrendering, assigning or converting those rights; or

     (ii)   assuming the corresponding liabilities under the contract;

(b)   in the case of an investment consisting of rights under other arrangements, assuming the corresponding liabilities under the arrangements; and

(c)   in the case of any other investment, issuing or creating the investment or granting the rights or interests of which it consists;

"syndicate" has the meaning given in the Regulated Activities Order.

NOTES

Para 15: words in square brackets in sub-para (1) substituted, and sub-para (2)(e) added, by the Financial Services and Markets Act 2000 (Regulated Activities) (Amendment) Order 2010, SI 2010/86, art 4, Schedule, para 9(f)(i), (ii), as from 24 February 2010; words omitted from sub-para (1) revoked, and sub-para (2)(e) revoked, by the Financial Services and Markets Act 2000 (Regulated Activities) (Amendment) Order 2011, SI 2011/133, art 3(1), (2)(a), (b), as from 16 February 2011 (note also art 4 of the 2011 Order which provides that the instruments to which the amendments made by that Order apply from its commencement include existing instruments which fall within (a) paras 15 or 15A of this Schedule; or (b) arts 77 or 77A of the RAO (in each case as amended by that Order)).

Para 15A: inserted by SI 2010/86, art 4, Schedule, para 9(f)(iii), as from 24 February 2010; words in square brackets in sub-para (1) inserted by SI 2011/133, art 3(1), (2)(c), as from 16 February 2011 (subject to the same transitional provisions in art 4 as noted above).

Para 16: words in square brackets in sub-para (2) inserted, and sub-para (3) added, by SI 2010/86, art 4, Schedule, para 9(f)(iv), (v), as from 24 February 2010.

Para 20: substituted by the Financial Services and Markets Act 2000 (Regulated Activities) (Amendment) Order 2006, SI 2006/1969, art 12(1), (3), as from 6 April 2007.

Para 21: sub-para (1) numbered as such, word omitted from sub-para (1)(c) revoked, and sub-paras (1)(e), (2)–(5) inserted, by the Financial Services and Markets Act 2000 (Regulated Activities) (Amendment No 3) Order 2006, SI 2006/3384, art 40(1), (3), as from 1 November 2007; words in square brackets in sub-para (4)(b) substituted by the Undertakings for Collective Investment in Transferable Securities Regulations 2011, SI 2011/1613, reg 16, Schedule, para 7(1), (3), as from 1 July 2011.

Para 22: sub-paras (1A)–(1E) inserted by SI 2006/3384, art 40(1), (4), as from 1 November 2007.

Para 23: sub-paras (3)–(5) added by SI 2006/3384, art 40(1), (5), as from 1 November 2007.

Paras 26A, 26B: inserted by the Financial Services and Markets Act 2000 (Regulated Activities) (Amendment) (No 2) Order 2006, SI 2006/2383, art 35(1), (6)(a), as from 6 April 2007.

Para 26C: inserted by the Financial Services and Markets Act 2000 (Regulated Activities) (Amendment) Order 2009, SI 2009/1342, art 30(1), (5)(a), as from 1 July 2009 (certain purposes), and as from 30 June 2010 (otherwise).

Para 27: words in first (outer) pair of square brackets substituted by SI 2006/2383, art 35(1), (6)(b), as from 6 April 2007; words in second (inner) pair of square brackets substituted by SI 2009/1342, art 30(1), (5)(b), as from the same dates and for the same purposes, etc, as mentioned in the note relating to this Order above.

Para 28 is amended as follows:

Definitions "agreement provider", "agreement seller", and "regulated sale and rent back agreement" inserted by SI 2009/1342, art 30(1), (5)(c), as from the same dates and for the same purposes, etc, as mentioned in the note relating to this Order above.

Definitions "Commission Regulation", "credit institution", "investment firm", "investment services and activities", "management company", "market operator", "MiFID instrument", and "multilateral trading facility" inserted by SI 2006/3384, art 40(1), (6), as from 1 November 2007.

Definitions "home purchase provider", "home purchaser", "plan provider", "regulated home purchase plan", "regulated home reversion plan", and "reversion seller" inserted by SI 2006/2383, art 35(1), (6)(c), as from 6 April 2007.

Definition "occupational pension scheme" substituted by SI 2006/1969, art 12(1), (4), as from 6 April 2007.

SCHEDULE 2
COUNTRIES AND TERRITORIES

Article 10

[8.340]

1. The Bailiwick of Guernsey.

2. The Isle of Man.

3. The Commonwealth of Pennsylvania.

4. The State of Iowa.

5. The Bailiwick of Jersey.

SCHEDULE 3
MARKETS AND EXCHANGES

Articles 37, 41, 67, 68 and 69

PART I
CRITERIA FOR RELEVANT EEA MARKETS

[8.341]

The criteria are—
  (a) the head office of the market must be situated in an EEA State; and
  (b) the market must be subject to requirements in the EEA State in which its head office is
       situated as to—
       (i)   the manner in which it operates;
       (ii) the means by which access may be had to the facilities it provides;
       (iii) the conditions to be satisfied before an investment may be traded or dealt in by
             means of its facilities;
       (iv) the reporting and publication of transactions effected by means of its facilities.

[PART II
CERTAIN INVESTMENT EXCHANGES OPERATING RELEVANT EEA MARKETS

[8.342]

Aktietorget I Norden (Sweden).

Amsterdam Options Exchange (Netherlands).

Athens Stock Exchange (Greece).

Athens Derivative Exchange (Greece).

Barcelona Stock Exchange (Spain).

Bavarian Stock Exchange (Germany).

Belgian Secondary Market for Treasury Certificates (Belgium).

Berlin-Bremen Stock Exchange (Germany).

Bilbao Stock Exchange (Spain).

Böag Borsen AG (Germany).

Bratislava Stock Exchange (Slovakia).

Bucharest Stock Exchange (Romania).

Budapest Stock Exchange (Hungary).

Bulgaria Stock Exchange (Bulgaria).

Copenhagen Stock Exchange (Denmark).

Cyprus Stock Exchange (Cyprus).

Danish Authorised Market Place (Denmark).

Dusseldorf Stock Market (Germany).

EDX (UK).

Eurex Deutschland (Germany).

Euronext Amsterdam (Netherlands).

Euronext Brussels (Belgium).

Euronext Lisbon (Portugal).

Euronext Paris (France).

Frankfurt Stock Exchange (Germany).

Helsinki Stock Exchange and Securities and Derivatives Exchange (Finland).

Irish Stock Exchange (Ireland).

Italian and Foreign Government Bonds Market (Italy).

Italian Stock Exchange (Italy).

Ljubliana Stock Exchange (Slovenia).

London International Financial Futures and Options Exchange (UK).

London Stock Exchange (UK).

Luxembourg Stock Exchange (Luxembourg).

Madrid Stock Exchange (Spain)

Malta Stock Exchange (Malta).

Market for Public Debt (Spain).

MEFF Renta Variable Futures Options Exchange (Spain).

MEFF Renta Fija Equity Futures Exchange (Spain).

MTS Italy (Italy).

MTS Poland (Poland).

MTS Portugal (Portugal).

National Stock Exchange of Lithuania (Lithuania).

Nordic Growth Market (Sweden).

PLUS (UK).

Prague Stock Exchange (Czech Republic).

Riga Stock Exchange (Latvia).

ShareMark (UK).

Stockholm Stock Exchange (Sweden).

Stuttgart Stock Exchange (Germany).

Tallinn Stock Exchange (Estonia).

Valencia Stock Exchange (Spain).

Vienna Stock Exchange (Austria).

Virt-x (UK).

Warsaw Stock Exchange (Poland).]

NOTES

Commencement: 20 April 2007.

Substituted by the Financial Services and Markets Act 2000 (Financial Promotion) (Amendment) Order 2007, SI 2007/1083, art 2, as from 20 April 2007.

PART III
CERTAIN NON-EEA INVESTMENT EXCHANGES OPERATING RELEVANT MARKETS

[8.343]

America Stock Exchange.

Australian Stock Exchange.

Basler Effektenbourse.

Boston Stock Exchange.

Bourse de Geneve.

Buenos Aires Stock Exchange.

Canadian Venture Exchange.

Chicago Board Options Exchange.

Chicago Stock Exchange.

Effektenborsenverein Zurich.

Fukuoka Stock Exchange.

Hiroshima Stock Exchange.

Iceland Stock Exchange.

Johannesburg Stock Exchange.

Korean Stock Exchange.

Kuala Lumpur Stock Exchange.

Kyoto Stock Exchange.

Midwest Stock Exchange.

Montreal Stock Exchange.

Nagoya Stock Exchange.

NASDAQ.

National Stock Exchange.

New York Stock Exchange.

New Zealand Stock Exchange Limited.

Niigita Stock Exchange.

Osaka Stock Exchange.

Oslo Stock Exchange.

Pacific Stock Exchange.

Philadelphia Stock Exchange.

Sapporo Stock Exchange.

Singapore Stock Exchange.

Stock Exchange of Hong Kong Limited.

Stock Exchange of Thailand.

Tokyo Stock Exchange.

Toronto Stock Exchange.

PART IV
OTHER RELEVANT MARKETS

[8.344]

American Commodity Exchange.

Australian Financial Futures Market.

Chicago Board of Trade.

Chicago Mercantile Exchange.

Chicago Rice and Cotton Exchange.

Commodity Exchange Inc.

Eurex US.

Eurex Zurich.

International Securities Market Association.

International Petroleum Exchange.

Kansas City Board of Trade.

London Metal Exchange.

Minneapolis Grain Exchange.

New York Board of Trade.

New York Futures Exchange.

New York Mercantile Exchange.

New Zealand Futures Exchange.

Pacific Commodity Exchange.

Philadelphia Board of Trade.

Singapore International Monetary Exchange.

Sydney Futures Exchange.

Toronto Futures Exchange.

SCHEDULE 4
TAKEOVERS OF RELEVANT UNLISTED COMPANIES
Articles 63 and 64

PART I
REQUIREMENTS RELATING TO THE OFFER

[8.345]
1. The terms of the offer must be recommended by all the directors of the company other than any director who is—
    (a)   the person by whom, or on whose behalf, an offer is made ("offeror"); or
    (b)   a director of the offeror.

2. (1) This paragraph applies to an offer for debentures or for non-equity share capital.

(2) Where, at the date of the offer, shares carrying 50 per cent or less of the voting rights attributable to the equity share capital are held by or on behalf of the offeror, the offer must include or be accompanied by an offer made by the offeror for the rest of the shares comprised in the equity share capital.

3. (1) This paragraph applies to an offer for shares comprised in the equity share capital.

(2) Where, at the date of the offer, shares which carry 50 per cent or less of the categories of voting rights described in sub-paragraph (3) are held by or on behalf of the offeror, it must be a condition of the offer that sufficient shares will be acquired or agreed to be acquired by the offeror pursuant to or during the offer so as to result in shares carrying more than 50 per cent of one or both categories of relevant voting rights being held by him or on his behalf.

(3) The categories of voting rights mentioned in sub-paragraph (2) are—
    (a)   voting rights exercisable in general meetings of the company;
    (b)   voting rights attributable to the equity share capital.

4. (1) Subject to sub-paragraph (2), the offer must be open for acceptance by every recipient for the period of at least 21 days beginning with the day after the day on which the invitation or inducement in question was first communicated to recipients of the offer.

(2) Sub-paragraph (1) does not apply if the offer is totally withdrawn and all persons are released from any obligation incurred under it.

5. The acquisition of the shares or debentures to which the offer relates must not be conditional upon the recipients approving, or consenting, to any payment or other benefit being made or given to any director or former director of the company in connection with, or as compensation or consideration for—
    (a)   his ceasing to be a director;
    (b)   his ceasing to hold any office held in conjunction with any directorship; or
    (c)   in the case of a former director, his ceasing to hold any office which he held in conjunction with his former directorship and which he continued to hold after ceasing to be a director.

6. The consideration for the shares or debentures must be—
    (a)   cash; or
    (b)   in the case of an offeror which is a body corporate other than an open-ended investment company, either cash or shares in, or debentures of, the body corporate or any combination of such cash, shares or debentures.

PART II
ACCOMPANYING MATERIAL

[8.346]
7. An indication of the identity of the offeror and, if the offer is being made on behalf of another person, the identity of that person.

8. An indication of the fact that the terms of the offer are recommended by all directors of the company other than (if that is the case) any director who is the offeror or a director of the offeror.

9. An indication to the effect that any person who is in any doubt about the invitation or inducement should consult a person authorised under the Act.

10. An indication that, except insofar as the offer may be totally withdrawn and all persons released from any obligation incurred under it, the offer is open for acceptance by every recipient for the period of at least 21 days beginning with the day after the day on which the invitation or inducement in question was first communicated to recipients of the offer.

11. An indication of the date on which the invitation or inducement was first communicated to the recipients of the offer.

12. An indication that the acquisition of the shares or debentures to which the offer relates is not conditional upon the recipients approving, or consenting, to any payment or other benefit being made or given to any director or former director of the company in connection with, or as compensation or consideration for—
    (a)   his ceasing to be a director;
    (b)   his ceasing to hold any office held in conjunction with any directorship; or
    (c)   in the case of a former director, his ceasing to hold any office which he held in conjunction with his former directorship and which he continued to hold after ceasing to be a director.

13. An indication of the place where additional material listed in Part III may be inspected.

14. The audited accounts of the company in respect of the latest accounting reference period for which the period for laying and delivering accounts under [the 2006 Act] has passed or, if accounts in respect of a later accounting reference period have been delivered under the relevant legislation, as shown in those accounts and not the earlier accounts.

15. Advice to the directors of the company on the financial implications of the offer which is given by a competent person who is independent of and who has no substantial financial interest in the company or the offeror, being advice which gives the opinion of that person in relation to the offer.

16. An indication by the directors of the company, acting as a board, of the following matters—
    (a)   whether or not there has been any material change in the financial position or prospects of the company since the end of the latest accounting reference period in respect of which audited accounts have been delivered to the relevant registrar of companies under the relevant legislation;
    (b)   if there has been any such change, the particulars of it;
    (c)   any interests, in percentage terms, which any of them have in the shares in or debentures of the company . . .
    (d)   any interests, in percentage terms, which any of them have in the shares in or debentures of any offeror which is a body corporate . . .

17. An indication of any material interest which any director has in any contract entered into by the offeror and in any contract entered into by any member of any group of which the offeror is a member.

18. An indication as to whether or not each director intends to accept the offer in respect of his own beneficial holdings in the company.

19. In the case of an offeror which is a body corporate and the shares in or debentures of which are to be the consideration or any part of the consideration for the offer, an indication by the directors of the offeror that the information concerning the offeror and those shares or debentures contained in the document is correct.

20. If the offeror is making the offer on behalf of another person—
    (a)   an indication by the offeror as to whether or not he has taken any steps to ascertain whether that person will be in a position to implement the offer;
    (b)   if he has taken any such steps, an indication by him as to what those steps are; and
    (c)   the offeror's opinion as to whether that person will be in a position to implement the offer.

21. An indication that each of the following—
    (a)   each of the directors of the company;
    (b)   the offeror; and
    (c)   if the offeror is a body corporate, each of the directors of the offeror;
is responsible for the information required by Part I and this Part of this Schedule insofar as it relates to themselves or their respective bodies corporate and that, to the best of their knowledge and belief (having taken all reasonable care to ensure that such is the case) the information is in accordance with the facts and that no material fact has been omitted.

22. The particulars of—
    (a)   all shares in or debentures of the company; and
    (b)   all investments falling within paragraph 17, 19 or 21 of Schedule 1 so far as relating to shares in or debentures of the company;

which are held by or on behalf of the offeror or each offeror, if there is more than one, or if none are so held an appropriate negative statement.

23. An indication as to whether or not the offer is conditional upon acceptance in respect of a minimum number of shares or debentures being received and, if the offer is so conditional, what the minimum number is.

24. Where the offer is conditional upon acceptances, an indication of the date which is the latest date on which it can become unconditional.

25. If the offer is, or has become, unconditional an indication of the fact that it will remain open until further notice and that at least 14 days' notice will be given before it is closed.

26. An indication as to whether or not, if circumstances arise in which an offeror is able compulsorily to acquire shares of any dissenting minority under [Chapter 3 of Part 28 of the Companies Act 2006 (c 46)], that offeror intends to so acquire those shares.

27. If shares or debentures are to be acquired for cash, an indication of the period within which the payment will be made.

28. (1) Subject to sub-paragraph (2), if the consideration or any part of the consideration for the shares or debentures to be acquired is shares in or debentures of an offeror—
  (a) an indication of the nature and particulars of the offeror's business, its financial and trading prospects and its place of incorporation;
  (b) the following information, in respect of any offeror which is a body corporate and in respect of the company, for the period of five years immediately preceding the date on which the invitation or inducement in question was first communicated to recipients of the offer—
    (i) turnover,
    (ii) profit on ordinary activities before and after tax,
    (iii) extraordinary items,
    (iv) profits and loss, and
    (v) the rate per cent of any dividends paid, adjusted as appropriate to take account of relevant changes over the period and the total amount absorbed thereby.
(2) In the case of a body corporate—
  (a) which was incorporated during the period of five years immediately preceding the date on which the invitation or inducement in question was first communicated to recipients of the offer; or
  (b) which has, at any time during that period, been exempt from the provisions of [Part 15 of the 2006 Act] relating to the audit of accounts by virtue of [section 477 or 480] of that Act . . .
the information described in sub-paragraph (1) with respect to that body corporate need be included only in relation to the period since its incorporation or since it last ceased to be exempt from those provisions of [Part 15 of the 2006 Act].

29. Particulars of the first dividend in which any such shares or debentures will participate and of the rights attaching to them (including in the case of debentures, rights as to interest) and of any restrictions on their transfer.

30. An indication of the effect of the acceptance on the capital and income position of the holder of the shares in or debentures of the company.

31. Particulars of all material contracts (not being contracts which were entered into in the ordinary course of business) which were entered into by each of the company and the offeror during the period of two years immediately preceding the date on which the invitation or inducement in question was first communicated to recipients of the offer.

32. Particulars of the terms on which shares in or debentures of the company acquired in pursuance of the offer will be transferred and any restrictions on their transfer.

33. An indication as to whether or not it is proposed, in connection with the offer, that any payment or other benefit be made or given to any director or former director of the company in connection with, or as compensation or consideration for—
  (a) his ceasing to be a director;
  (b) his ceasing to hold any office held in conjunction with any directorship; or
  (c) in the case of a former director, his ceasing to hold any office which he held in conjunction with his former directorship and which he continued to hold after ceasing to be a director;
and, if such payments or benefits are proposed, details of each one.

34. An indication as to whether or not there exists any agreement or arrangement between—

    (a)   the offeror or any person with whom the offeror has an agreement of the kind described in [section 824 of the 2006 Act]; and

    (b)   any director or shareholder of the company or any person who has been such a director or shareholder;

at any time during the period of twelve months immediately preceding the date on which the invitation or inducement in question was first communicated to recipients of the offer, being an agreement or arrangement which is connected with or dependent on the offer and, if there is any such agreement or arrangement, particulars of it.

35. An indication whether or not the offeror has reason to believe that there has been any material change in the financial position or prospects of the company since the end of the accounting reference period to which the accounts referred to in paragraph 14 relate, and if the offeror has reason to believe that there has been such a change, the particulars of it.

36. An indication as to whether or not there is any agreement or arrangement whereby any shares or debentures acquired by the offeror in pursuance of the offer will or may be transferred to any other person, together with the names of the parties to any such agreement or arrangement and particulars of all shares and debentures in the company held by such persons.

37. Particulars of any dealings—

    (a)   in the shares in or debentures of the company; and

    (b)   if the offeror is a body corporate, in the shares in or debentures of the offeror;

which took place during the period of twelve months immediately preceding the date on which the invitation or inducement in question was first communicated to recipients of the offer and which were entered into by every person who was a director of either the company or the offeror during that period; and, if there have been no such dealings, an indication to that effect.

38. In a case in which the offeror is a body corporate which is required to deliver accounts under [the 2006 Act], particulars of the assets and liabilities as shown in its audited accounts in respect of the latest accounting reference period for which the period for laying and delivering accounts under the relevant legislation has passed or, if accounts in respect of a later accounting reference period have been delivered under the relevant legislation, as shown in those accounts and not the earlier accounts.

39. Where valuations of assets are given in connection with the offer, the basis on which the valuation was made and the names and addresses of the persons who valued them and particulars of any relevant qualifications.

40. If any profit forecast is given in connection with the offer, an indication of the assumptions on which the forecast is based.

NOTES

    The amendments to paras 14, 16, 28, 34 and 38 were made by the Companies Act 2006 (Consequential Amendments and Transitional Provisions) Order 2011, SI 2011/1265, art 26(1), (9), as from 12 May 2011.

    The words in square brackets in para 26 were substituted by the Companies Act 2006 (Commencement No 2, Consequential Amendments, Transitional Provisions and Savings) Order 2007, SI 2007/1093, art 6(1), Sch 3, para 10, as from 6 April 2007.

PART III
ADDITIONAL MATERIAL AVAILABLE FOR INSPECTION

[8.347]
41. The memorandum and articles of association of the company.

42. If the offeror is a body corporate, the memorandum and articles of association of the offeror or, if there is no such memorandum and articles, any instrument constituting or defining the constitution of the offeror and, in either case, if the relevant document is not written in English, a certified translation in English.

43. In the case of a company that does not fall within paragraph 45—

    (a)   the audited accounts of the company in respect of the last two accounting reference periods for which the laying and delivering of accounts under [the 2006 Act] has passed; and

    (b)   if accounts have been delivered to the relevant registrar of companies, in respect of a later accounting reference period, a copy of those accounts.

44. In the case of an offeror which is required to deliver accounts to the registrar of companies and which does not fall within paragraph 45—

    (a)   the audited accounts of the offeror in respect of the last two accounting reference periods for which the laying and delivering of accounts under [the 2006 Act] has passed; and

    (b)   if accounts have been delivered to the relevant registrar of companies in respect of a later accounting reference period, a copy of those accounts.

45. In the case of a company or an offeror—

(a)   which was incorporated during the period of three years immediately preceding the date on which the invitation or inducement in question was first communicated to recipients of the offer; or

(b)   which has, at any time during that period, been exempt from the provisions of [Part 15 of the 2006 Act] relating to the audit of accounts by virtue of [section 477 or 480] of that Act . . .

the information described in whichever is relevant of paragraph 43 or 44 with respect to that body corporate need be included only in relation to the period since its incorporation or since it last ceased to be exempt from those provisions of [Part 15 of the 2006 Act].

46. All existing contracts of service entered into for a period of more than one year between the company and any of its directors and, if the offeror is a body corporate, between the offeror and any of its directors.

47. Any report, letter, valuation or other document any part of which is exhibited or referred to in the information required to be made available by Part II and this Part of this Schedule.

48. If the offer document contains any statement purporting to have been made by an expert, that expert's written consent to the inclusion of that statement.

49. All material contracts (if any) of the company and of the offeror (not, in either case, being contracts which were entered into in the ordinary course of business) which were entered into during the period of two years immediately preceding the date on which the invitation or inducement in question was first communicated to recipients of the offer.

NOTES

The amendments to paras 43, 44, 45 were made by the Companies Act 2006 (Consequential Amendments and Transitional Provisions) Order 2011, SI 2011/1265, art 26(1), (10), as from 12 May 2011.

SCHEDULE 5
STATEMENTS FOR CERTIFIED HIGH NET WORTH INDIVIDUALS
AND SELF-CERTIFIED SOPHISTICATED INVESTORS
Articles 48 and 50A

PART I
STATEMENT FOR CERTIFIED HIGH NET WORTH INDIVIDUALS

[8.348]
1. The statement to be signed for the purposes of article 48(2) (definition of high net worth individual) must be in the following form and contain the following content—

"STATEMENT FOR CERTIFIED HIGH NET WORTH INDIVIDUAL
    I declare that I am a certified high net worth individual for the purposes of the Financial Services and Markets Act 2000 (Financial Promotion) Order 2005.
    I understand that this means:
    (a)   I can receive financial promotions that may not have been approved by a person authorised by the Financial Services Authority;
    (b)   the content of such financial promotions may not conform to rules issued by the Financial Services Authority;
    (c)   by signing this statement I may lose significant rights;
    (d)   I may have no right to complain to either of the following—
           (i)   the Financial Services Authority; or
           (ii)   the Financial Ombudsman Scheme;
    (e)   I may have no right to seek compensation from the Financial Services Compensation Scheme.
    I am a certified high net worth individual because **at least one of the following applies**—
    (a)   I had, during the financial year immediately preceding the date below, an annual income to the value of £100,000 or more;
    (b)   I held, throughout the financial year immediately preceding the date below, net assets to the value of £250,000 or more. Net assets for these purposes do not include—
           (i)   the property which is my primary residence or any loan secured on that residence;
           (ii)   any rights of mine under a qualifying contract of insurance within the meaning of the Financial Services and Markets Act 2000 (Regulated Activities) Order 2001; or
           (iii) any benefits (in the form of pensions or otherwise) which are payable on the termination of my service or on my death or retirement and to which I am (or my dependants are), or may be, entitled.
    I accept that I can lose my property and other assets from making investment decisions

based on financial promotions.
I am aware that it is open to me to seek advice from someone who specialises in advising on investments.
Signature. . . . .
Date . . . . ,,

PART II
STATEMENT FOR SELF-CERTIFIED SOPHISTICATED INVESTORS

[8.349]
2. The statement to be signed for the purposes of article 50A(1) (definition of self-certified sophisticated investor) must be in the following form and contain the following content—

"STATEMENT FOR SELF-CERTIFIED SOPHISTICATED INVESTOR
I declare that I am a self-certified sophisticated investor for the purposes of the Financial Services and Markets Act (Financial Promotion) Order 2005.
I understand that this means:

(a)   I can receive financial promotions that may not have been approved by a person authorised by the Financial Services Authority;

(b)   the content of such financial promotions may not conform to rules issued by the Financial Services Authority;

(c)   by signing this statement I may lose significant rights;

(d)   I may have no right to complain to either of the following—
(i)   the Financial Services Authority; or
(ii)   the Financial Ombudsman Scheme;

(e)   I may have no right to seek compensation from the Financial Services Compensation Scheme.

I am a self-certified sophisticated investor because **at least one of the following applies—**

(a)   I am a member of a network or syndicate of business angels and have been so for at least the last six months prior to the date below;

(b)   I have made more than one investment in an unlisted company in the two years prior to the date below;

(c)   I am working, or have worked in the two years prior to the date below, in a professional capacity in the private equity sector, or in the provision of finance for small and medium enterprises;

(d)   I am currently, or have been in the two years prior to the date below, a director of a company with an annual turnover of at least £1 million.

I accept that I can lose my property and other assets from making investment decisions based on financial promotions.
I am aware that it is open to me to seek advice from someone who specialises in advising on investments.
Signature. . . . .
Date . . . .

SCHEDULE 6
REVOCATION

Article 74
[8.350]

Order	Reference	Extent of revocation
The Financial Services and Markets Act 2000 (Financial Promotion) Order 2001	SI 2001/1335	The whole Order
The Financial Services and Markets Act 2000 (Financial Promotion) (Amendment) Order 2001	SI 2001/2633	The whole Order
The Financial Services and Markets Act 2000 (Miscellaneous Provisions) Order 2001	SI 2001/3650	Article 4 and 5
The Financial Services and Markets Act 2000 (Financial Promotion) (Amendment No 2) Order 2001	SI 2001/3800	The whole Order
The Financial Services and Markets Act 2000 (Financial Promotion and Miscellaneous Amendments) Order 2002	SI 2002/1310	Article 2
The Financial Services and Markets Act 2000 (Commencement of Mortgage Regulation) (Amendment) Order 2002	SI 2002/1777	Article 4
The Financial Services and Markets Act 2000 (Financial Promotion) (Amendment) (Electronic Communications Directive) Order 2002	SI 2002/2157	The whole Order

Order	Reference	Extent of revocation
The Financial Services and Markets Act 2000 (Financial Promotion) (Amendment) Order 2003	SI 2003/1676	The whole Order
The Financial Services and Markets Act 2000 (Financial Promotion and Promotion of Collective Investment Schemes) (Miscellaneous Amendments) Order 2005	SI 2005/270	Article 2 and Schedule 1

Order	Reference	Extent of revocation
The Financial Services and Markets Act 2000 (Financial Promotion) (Amendment) Order 2005	SI 2005/1676	The whole Order
The Financial Services and Markets Act 2000 (Financial Promotion and Promotion of Collective Investment Schemes) (Miscellaneous Amendments) Order 2005	SI 2005/270	Article 2 and Schedule 1

PART 9
MISCELLANEOUS OTHER PRIMARY LEGISLATION

PARTNERSHIP ACT 1890

(1890 c 39)

Part 9   Misc primary legislation

NOTES

This Act is reproduced as amended by: the Statute Law Revision Act 1908; the Mental Health Act 1959; the Decimal Currency Act 1969; the Courts Act 1971; the Trusts of Land and Appointment of Trustees Act 1996; the Statute Law (Repeals) Act 1998; the Civil Partnership Act 2004; the Companies Act 2006 (Consequential Amendments, Transitional Provisions and Savings) Order 2009, SI 2009/1941.

ARRANGEMENT OF SECTIONS

An Act to declare and amend the Law of Partnership

[14 August 1890]

Nature of Partnership

[9.1]
1 Definition of Partnership
(1)   Partnership is the relation which subsists between persons carrying on a business in common with a view of profit.
(2)   But the relation between members of any company or association which is—
[(a)   registered under the Companies Act 2006, or]
   (b)   Formed or incorporated by or in pursuance of any other Act of Parliament or letters patent, or Royal Charter   . . .
   (c)   . . .
is not a partnership within the meaning of this Act.

NOTES
Sub-s (2): para (a) substituted by the Companies Act 2006 (Consequential Amendments, Transitional Provisions and Savings) Order 2009, SI 2009/1941, art 2(1), Sch 1, para 2, as from 1 October 2009; para (c) and the word immediately preceding it repealed by the Statute Law (Repeals) Act 1998, as from 19 November 1998.
Companies Act 1862: repealed by the Companies (Consolidation) Act 1908, s 286, Sch 6, Pt I.

[9.2]
2 Rules for determining existence of partnership
In determining whether a partnership does or does not exist, regard shall be had to the following rules—
   (1)   Joint tenancy, tenancy in common, joint property, common property, or part ownership does not of itself create a partnership as to anything so held or owned, whether the tenants or owners do or do not share any profits made by the use thereof.
   (2)   The sharing of gross returns does not of itself create a partnership, whether the persons sharing such returns have or have not a joint or common right or interest in any property from which or from the use of which the returns are derived.
   (3)   The receipt by a person of a share of the profits of a business is *prima facie* evidence that he is a partner in the business, but receipt of such a share, or of a payment contingent on or varying with the profits of a business, does not of itself make him a partner in the business; and in particular—
      (a)   The receipt by a person of a debt or other liquidated amount by instalments or otherwise out of the accruing profits of a business does not of itself make him a partner in the business or liable as such:
      (b)   A contract for the remuneration of a servant or agent of a person engaged in a business by a share of the profits of the business does not of itself make the servant or agent a partner in the business or liable as such:
      (c)   A person being the widow[, widower, surviving civil partner] or child of a deceased partner, and receiving by way of annuity a portion of the profits made in the business in which the deceased person was a partner, is not by reason only of such receipt a partner in the business or liable as such:
      (d)   The advance of money by way of loan to a person engaged or about to engage in any business on a contract with that person that the lender shall receive a rate of interest varying with the profits, or shall receive a share of the profits arising from carrying on the business, does not of itself make the lender a partner with the person or persons carrying on the business or liable as such. Provided that the contract is in writing, and signed by or on behalf of all the parties thereto:
      (e)   A person receiving by way of annuity or otherwise a portion of the profits of a business in consideration of the sale by him of the goodwill of the business is not by reason only of such receipt a partner in the business or liable as such.

NOTES
Words in square brackets inserted by the Civil Partnership Act 2004, s 261(1), Sch 27, para 2, as from 5 December 2005.

[9.3]
3 Postponement of rights of person lending or selling in consideration of share of profits in case of insolvency
In the event of any person to whom money has been advanced by way of loan upon such a contract as is mentioned in the last foregoing section, or of any buyer of a goodwill in consideration of a share of the profits of the business, being adjudged a bankrupt, entering into an arrangement to pay his creditors less than [100p] in the pound, or dying in insolvent circumstances, the lender of the

loan shall not be entitled to recover anything in respect of his loan, and the seller of the goodwill shall not be entitled to recover anything in respect of the share of profits contracted for, until the claims of the other creditors of the borrower or buyer for valuable consideration in money or money's worth have been satisfied.

NOTES

Sum in square brackets substituted by virtue of the Decimal Currency Act 1969, s 10(1), as from 16 May 1969.

[9.4]
4 Meaning of firm
(1) Persons who have entered into partnership with one another are for the purposes of this Act called collectively a firm, and the name under which their business is carried on is called the firm-name.
(2) In Scotland a firm is a legal person distinct from the partners of whom it is composed, but an individual partner may be charged on a decree or diligence directed against the firm, and on payment of the debts is entitled to relief pro rata from the firm and its other members.

Relations of Partners to persons dealing with them

[9.5]
5 Power of partner to bind the firm
Every partner is an agent of the firm and his other partners for the purpose of the business of the partnership; and the acts of every partner who does any act for carrying on in the usual way business of the kind carried on by the firm of which he is a member bind the firm and his partners, unless the partner so acting has in fact no authority to act for the firm in the particular matter, and the person with whom he is dealing either knows that he has no authority, or does not know or believe him to be a partner.

[9.6]
6 Partners bound by acts on behalf of firm
An act or instrument relating to the business of the firm done or executed in the firm-name, or in any other manner showing an intention to bind the firm, by any person thereto authorised, whether a partner or not, is binding on the firm and all the partners.

Provided that this section shall not affect any general rule of law relating to the execution of deeds or negotiable instruments.

[9.7]
7 Partner using credit of firm for private purposes
Where one partner pledges the credit of the firm for a purpose apparently not connected with the firm's ordinary course of business, the firm is not bound, unless he is in fact specially authorised by the other partners; but this section does not affect any personal liability incurred by an individual partner.

[9.8]
8 Effect of notice that firm will not be bound by acts of partner
If it has been agreed between the partners that any restriction shall be placed on the power of any one or more of them to bind the firm, no act done in contravention of the agreement is binding on the firm with respect to persons having notice of the agreement.

[9.9]
9 Liability of partners
Every partner in a firm is liable jointly with the other partners, and in Scotland severally also, for all debts and obligations of the firm incurred while he is a partner; and after his death his estate is also severally liable in a due course of administration for such debts and obligations, so far as they remain unsatisfied, but subject in England or Ireland to the prior payment of his separate debts.

[9.10]
10 Liability of the firm for wrongs
Where, by any wrongful act or omission of any partner acting in the ordinary course of the business of the firm, or with the authority of his co-partners, loss or injury is caused to any person not being a partner in the firm, or any penalty is incurred, the firm is liable therefor to the same extent as the partner so acting or omitting to act.

[9.11]
11 Misapplication of money or property received for or in custody of the firm
In the following cases; namely—
(a) Where one partner acting within the scope of his apparent authority receives the money or property of a third person and misapplies it; and
(b) Where a firm in the course of its business receives money or property of a third person, and the money or property so received is misapplied by one or more of the partners while it is in the custody of the firm;

the firm is liable to make good the loss.

[9.12]
12 Liability for wrongs joint and several
Every partner is liable jointly with his co-partners and also severally for everything for which the firm while he is a partner therein becomes liable under either of the two last preceding sections.

[9.13]
13 Improper employment of trust-property for partnership purposes
If a partner, being a trustee, improperly employs trust-property in the business or on the account of the partnership, no other partner is liable for the trust property to the persons beneficially interested therein:
Provided as follows—
(1) This section shall not affect any liability incurred by any partner by reason of his having notice of a breach of trust; and
(2) Nothing in this section shall prevent trust money from being followed and recovered from the firm if still in its possession or under its control.

[9.14]
14 Persons liable by "holding out"
(1) Every one who by words spoken or written or by conduct represents himself, or who knowingly suffers himself to be represented, as a partner in a particular firm, is liable as a partner to any one who has on the faith of any such representation given credit to the firm, whether the representation has or has not been made or communicated to the person so giving credit by or with the knowledge of the apparent partner making the representation or suffering it to be made.
(2) Provided that where after a partner's death the partnership business is continued in the old firm's name, the continued use of that name or of the deceased partner's name as part thereof shall not of itself make his executors or administrators estate or effects liable for any partnership debts contracted after his death.

[9.15]
15 Admissions and representation of partners
An admission or representation made by any partner concerning the partnership affairs, and in the ordinary course of its business, is evidence against the firm.

[9.16]
16 Notice to acting partner to be notice to the firm
Notice to any partner who habitually acts in the partnership business of any matter relating to partnership affairs operates as notice to the firm, except in the case of a fraud on the firm committed by or with the consent of that partner.

[9.17]
17 Liabilities of incoming and outgoing partners
(1) A person who is admitted as a partner into an existing firm does not thereby become liable to the creditors of the firm for anything done before he became a partner.
(2) A partner who retires from a firm does not thereby cease to be liable for partnership debts or obligations incurred before his retirement.
(3) A retiring partner may be discharged from any existing liabilities, by an agreement to that effect between himself and the members of the firm as newly constituted and the creditors, and this agreement may be either expressed or inferred as a fact from the course of dealing between the creditors and the firm as newly constituted.

[9.18]
18 Revocation of continuing guaranty by change in firm
A continuing guaranty or cautionary obligation given either to a firm or to a third person in respect of the transactions of a firm is, in the absence of agreement to the contrary, revoked as to future transactions by any change in the constitution of the firm to which, or of the firm in respect of the transactions of which, the guaranty or obligation was given.

Relations of Partners to one another

[9.19]
19 Variation by consent of terms of partnership
The mutual rights and duties of partners, whether ascertained by agreement or defined by this Act, may be varied by the consent of all the partners, and such consent may be either express or inferred from a course of dealing.

[9.20]
20 Partnership property
(1)   All property and rights and interests in property originally brought into the partnership stock or acquired, whether by purchase or otherwise, on account of the firm, or for the purposes and in the course of the partnership business, are called in this Act partnership property, and must be held and applied by the partners exclusively for the purposes of the partnership and in accordance with the partnership agreement.
(2)   Provided that the legal estate or interest in any land, or in Scotland the title to and interest in any heritable estate, which belongs to the partnership shall devolve according to the nature and tenure thereof, and the general rules of law thereto applicable, but in trust, so far as necessary, for the persons beneficially interested in the land under this section.
(3)   Where co-owners of an estate or interest in any land, or in Scotland of any heritable estate, not being itself partnership property, are partners as to profits made by the use of that land or estate, and purchase other land or estate out of the profits to be used in like manner, the land or estate so purchased belongs to them, in the absence of an agreement to the contrary, not as partners, but as co-owners for the same respective estates and interests as are held by them in the land or estate first mentioned at the date of the purchase.

[9.21]
21 Property bought with partnership money
Unless the contrary intention appears, property bought with money belonging to the firm is deemed to have been bought on account of the firm.

22   *(Repealed by the Trusts of Land and Appointment of Trustees Act 1996, s 25(2), (5), Sch 4, except in relation to any circumstances involving the personal representatives of a partner who died before 1 July 1997.)*

[9.22]
23 Procedure against partnership property for a partner's separate judgement debt
(1)   . . .   A writ of execution shall not issue against any partnership property except on a judgment against the firm.
(2)   The High Court, or a judge thereof,   . . . , or a county court, may, on the application by summons of any judgment creditor of a partner, make an order charging that partner's interest in the partnership property and profits with payment of the amount of the judgment debt and interest thereon, and may by the same or a subsequent order appoint a receiver of that partner's share of profits (whether already declared or accruing), and of any other money which may be coming to him in respect of the partnership, and direct all accounts and inquiries, and give all other orders and directions which might have been directed or given if the charge had been made in favour of the judgment creditor by the partner, or which the circumstances of the case may require.
(3)   The other partner or partners shall be at liberty at any time to redeem the interest charged, or in case of a sale being directed, to purchase the same.
(4)   . . .
(5)   This section shall not apply to Scotland.

NOTES
Sub-s (1): words omitted repealed by the Statute Law Revision Act 1908, as from 21 December 1908.
Sub-s (2): words omitted repealed by the Courts Act 1971, s 56(4), Sch 11, Pt II, as from 1 January 1972.
Sub-s (4): repealed by the Statute Law (Repeals) Act 1998, as from 19 November 1998.

[9.23]
24 Rules as to interests and duties of partners subject to special agreement
The interests of partners in the partnership property and their rights and duties in relation to the partnership shall be determined, subject to any agreement express or implied between the partners, by the following rules—
  (1)   All the partners are entitled to share equally in the capital and profits of the business, and must contribute equally towards the losses whether of capital or otherwise sustained by the firm.
  (2)   The firm must indemnify every partner in respect of payments made and personal liabilities incurred by him—
      (a)   In the ordinary and proper conduct of the business of the firm; or,
      (b)   In or about anything necessarily done for the preservation of the business or property of the firm.
  (3)   A partner making, for the purpose of the partnership, any actual payment or advance beyond the amount of capital which he has agreed to subscribe, is entitled to interest at the rate of five per cent per annum from the date of the payment or advance.
  (4)   A partner is not entitled, before the ascertainment of profits, to interest on the capital subscribed by him.
  (5)   Every partner may take part in the management of the partnership business.
  (6)   No partner shall be entitled to remuneration for acting in the partnership business.
  (7)   No person may be introduced as a partner without the consent of all existing partners.

(8)   Any difference arising as to ordinary matters connected with the partnership business may be decided by a majority of the partners, but no change may be made in the nature of the partnership business without the consent of all existing partners.

(9)   The partnership books are to be kept at the place of business of the partnership (or the principal place, if there is more than one), and every partner may, when he thinks fit, have access to and inspect and copy any of them.

[9.24]
25   Expulsion of partner
No majority of the partners can expel any partner unless a power to do so has been conferred by express agreement between the partners.

[9.25]
26   Retirement from partnership at will
(1)   Where no fixed term has been agreed upon for the duration of the partnership, any partner may determine the partnership at any time on giving notice of his intention so to do to all the other partners.

(2)   Where the partnership has originally been constituted by deed, a notice in writing, signed by the partner giving it, shall be sufficient for this purpose.

[9.26]
27   Where partnership for term is continued over, continuance on old terms presumed
(1)   Where a partnership entered into for a fixed term is continued after the term has expired, and without any express new agreement, the rights and duties of the partners remain the same as they were at the expiration of the term, so far as is consistent with the incidents of a partnership at will.

(2)   A continuance of the business by the partners or such of them as habitually acted therein during the term, without any settlement or liquidation of the partnership affairs, is presumed to be a continuance of the partnership.

[9.27]
28   Duty of partners to render accounts, etc
Partners are bound to render true accounts and full information of all things affecting the partnership to any partner or his legal representatives.

[9.28]
29   Accountability of partners for private profits
(1)   Every partner must account to the firm for any benefit derived by him without the consent of the other partners from any transaction concerning the partnership, or from any use by him of the partnership property name or business connexion.

(2)   This section applies also to transactions undertaken after a partnership has been dissolved by the death of a partner, and before the affairs thereof have been completely wound up, either by any surviving partner or by the representatives of the deceased partner.

[9.29]
30   Duty of partner not to compete with firm
If a partner, without the consent of the other partners, carries on any business of the same nature as and competing with that of the firm, he must account for and pay over to the firm all profits made by him in that business.

[9.30]
31   Rights of assignee of share in partnership
(1)   An assignment by any partner of his share in the partnership, either absolute or by way of mortgage or redeemable charge, does not, as against the other partners, entitle the assignee, during the continuance of the partnership, to interfere in the management or administration of the partnership business or affairs, or to require any accounts of the partnership transactions, or to inspect the partnership books, but entitles the assignee only to receive the share of profits to which the assigning partner would otherwise be entitled, and the assignee must accept the account of profits agreed to by the partners.

(2)   In case of a dissolution of the partnership, whether as respects all the partners or as respects the assigning partner, the assignee is entitled to receive the share of the partnership assets to which the assigning partner is entitled as between himself and the other partners, and, for the purpose of ascertaining that share, to an account as from the date of the dissolution.

Dissolution of Partnership, and its consequences

[9.31]
32   Dissolution by expiration or notice
Subject to any agreement between the partners, a partnership is dissolved—
(a)   If entered into for a fixed term, by the expiration of that term:
(b)   If entered into for a single adventure or undertaking, by the termination of that adventure or undertaking:

(c)   If entered into for an undefined time, by any partner giving notice to the other or others of his intention to dissolve the partnership.

In the last-mentioned case the partnership is dissolved as from the date mentioned in the notice as the date of dissolution, or, if no date is so mentioned, as from the date of the communication of the notice.

[9.32]
33 Dissolution by bankruptcy, death or charge
(1)   Subject to any agreement between the partners, every partnership is dissolved as regards all the partners by the death or bankruptcy of any partner.
(2)   A partnership may, at the option of the other partners, be dissolved if any partner suffers his share of the partnership property to be charged under this Act for his separate debt.

[9.33]
34 Dissolution by illegality of partnership
A partnership is in every case dissolved by the happening of any event which makes it unlawful for the business of the firm to be carried on or for the members of the firm to carry it on in partnership.

[9.34]
35 Dissolution by the Court
On application by a partner the Court may decree a dissolution of the partnership in any of the following cases—
(a)   . . .
(b)   When a partner, other than the partner suing, becomes in any other way permanently incapable of performing his part of the partnership contract;
(c)   When a partner, other than the partner suing, has been guilty of such conduct as, in the opinion of the Court, regard being had to the nature of the business, is calculated to prejudicially affect the carrying on of the business;
(d)   When a partner, other than the partner suing, wilfully or persistently commits a breach of the partnership agreement, or otherwise so conducts himself in matters relating to the partnership business that it is not reasonably practicable for the other partner or partners to carry on the business in partnership with him;
(e)   When the business of the partnership can only be carried on at a loss;
(f)   Whenever in any case circumstances have arisen which, in the opinion of the Court, render it just and equitable that the partnership be dissolved.

NOTES
Para (a) repealed by the Mental Health Act 1959, s 149(2), Sch 8, as from 1 November 1960.

[9.35]
36 Rights of persons dealing with firm against apparent members of firm
(1)   Where a person deals with a firm after a change in its constitution he is entitled to treat all apparent members of the old firm as still being members of the firm until he has notice of the change.
(2)   An advertisement in the London Gazette as to a firm whose principal place of business is in England or Wales, in the Edinburgh Gazette as to a firm whose principal place of business is in Scotland, and in the Dublin Gazette as to a firm whose principal place of business is in Ireland, shall be notice as to persons who had not dealings with the firm before the date of the dissolution or change so advertised.
(3)   The estate of a partner who dies, or who becomes bankrupt, or of a partner who, not having been known to the person dealing with the firm to be a partner, retires from the firm, is not liable for partnership debts contracted after the date of the death, bankruptcy, or retirement respectively.

NOTES
Dublin Gazette: this should now be construed as a reference to the Belfast Gazette: see the General Adaptation of Enactments (Northern Ireland) Order 1921, SR & O 1921/1804.

[9.36]
37 Right of partners to notify dissolution
On the dissolution of a partnership or retirement of a partner any partner may publicly notify the same, and may require the other partner or partners to concur for that purpose in all necessary or proper acts, if any, which cannot be done without his or their concurrence.

[9.37]
38 Continuing authority of partners for purposes of winding up
After the dissolution of a partnership the authority of each partner to bind the firm, and the other rights and obligations of the partners, continue notwithstanding the dissolution so far as may be necessary to wind up the affairs of the partnership, and to complete transactions begun but unfinished at the time of the dissolution, but not otherwise.

Provided that the firm is in no case bound by the acts of a partner who has become bankrupt; but this proviso does not affect the liability of any person who has after the bankruptcy represented himself or knowingly suffered himself to be represented as a partner of the bankrupt.

[9.38]
39   Rights of partners as to application of partnership property
On the dissolution of a partnership every partner is entitled, as against the other partners in the firm, and all persons claiming through them in respect of their interests as partners, to have the property of the partnership applied in payment of the debts and liabilities of the firm, and to have the surplus assets after such payment applied in payment of what may be due to the partners respectively after deducting what may be due from them as partners to the firm; and for that purpose any partner or his representatives may on the termination of the partnership apply to the Court to wind up the business and affairs of the firm.

[9.39]
40   Apportionment of premium where partnership prematurely dissolved
Where one partner has paid a premium to another on entering into a partnership for a fixed term, and the partnership is dissolved before the expiration of that term otherwise than by the death of a partner, the Court may order the repayment of the premium, or of such part thereof as it thinks just, having regard to the terms of the partnership contract and to the length of time during which the partnership has continued; unless—
    (a)   the dissolution is, in the judgment of the Court, wholly or chiefly due to the misconduct of the partner who paid the premium; or
    (b)   the partnership has been dissolved by an agreement containing no provision for a return of any part of the premium.

[9.40]
41   Rights where partnership dissolved for fraud or misrepresentation
Where a partnership contract is rescinded on the ground of the fraud or misrepresentation of one of the parties thereto, the party entitled to rescind is, without prejudice to any other right, entitled—
    (a)   to a lien on, or right of retention of, the surplus of the partnership assets, after satisfying the partnership liabilities, for any sum of money paid by him for the purchase of a share in the partnership and for any capital contributed by him, and is
    (b)   to stand in the place of the creditors of the firm for any payments made by him in respect of the partnership liabilities, and
    (c)   to be indemnified by the person guilty of the fraud or making the representation against all the debts and liabilities of the firm.

[9.41]
42   Right of outgoing partner in certain cases to share profits made after dissolution
(1)   Where any member of a firm has died or otherwise ceased to be a partner, and the surviving or continuing partners carry on the business of the firm with its capital or assets without any final settlement of accounts as between the firm and the outgoing partner or his estate, then, in the absence of any agreement to the contrary, the outgoing partner or his estate is entitled at the option of himself or his representatives to such share of the profits made since the dissolution as the Court may find to be attributable to the use of his share of the partnership assets, or to interest at the rate of five per cent per annum on the amount of his share of the partnership assets.
(2)   Provided that where by the partnership contract an option is given to surviving or continuing partners to purchase the interest of a deceased or outgoing partner, and that option is duly exercised, the estate of the deceased partner, or the outgoing partner or his estate, as the case may be, is not entitled to any further or other share of profits; but if any partner assuming to act in exercise of the option does not in all material respects comply with the terms thereof, he is liable to account under the foregoing provisions of this section.

[9.42]
43   Retiring or deceased partner's share to be a debt
Subject to any agreement between the partners, the amount due from surviving or continuing partners to an outgoing partner or the representatives of a deceased partner in respect of the outgoing or deceased partner's share is a debt accruing at the date of the dissolution or death.

[9.43]
44   Rule for distribution of assets on final settlement of accounts
In settling accounts between the partners after a dissolution of partnership, the following rules shall, subject to any agreement, be observed—
    (a)   Losses, including losses and deficiencies of capital, shall be paid first out of profits, next out of capital, and lastly, if necessary, by the partners individually in the proportion in which they were entitled to share profits;
    (b)   The assets of the firm including the sums, if any, contributed by the partners to make up losses or deficiencies of capital, shall be applied in the following manner and order—
        1.   In paying the debts and liabilities of the firm to persons who are not partners therein:

2. In paying to each partner rateably what is due from the firm to him for advances as distinguished from capital:

3. In paying to each partner rateably what is due from the firm to him in respect of capital:

4. The ultimate residue, if any, shall be divided among the partners in the proportion in which profits are divisible.

Supplemental

[9.44]
45   Definitions of "court" and "business"
In this Act, unless the contrary intention appears,—

The expression "court" includes every court and judge having jurisdiction in the case;

The expression "business" includes every trade, occupation, or profession.

[9.45]
46   Saving for rules of equity and common law
The rules of equity and of common law applicable to partnership shall continue in force except so far as they are inconsistent with the express provisions of this Act.

[9.46]
47   Provision as to bankruptcy in Scotland
(1)   In the application of this Act to Scotland the bankruptcy of a firm or of an individual shall mean sequestration under the Bankruptcy (Scotland) Acts, and also in the case of an individual the issue against him of a decree of cessio bonorum.

(2)   Nothing in this Act shall alter the rules of the law of Scotland relating to the bankruptcy of a firm or of the individual partners thereof.

48, 49   *(Repealed by the Statute Law Revision Act 1908.)*

[9.47]
50   Short title
This Act may be cited as the Partnership Act 1890.

SCHEDULE

(Schedule repealed by the Statute Law Revision Act 1908.)

FORGED TRANSFERS ACT 1891

(54 & 55 Vict c 43)

NOTES
This Act is reproduced as amended by: the Forged Transfers Act 1892; the Decimal Currency Act 1969; the Stock Transfer Act 1982; the Local Government Finance Act 1992; the Police and Magistrates' Courts Act 1994; the Statute Law (Repeals) Act 1998; the Fire and Rescue Services Act 2004; the Statute Law (Repeals) Act 2004; the Local Government Finance (Miscellaneous Amendments and Repeal) Order 1990, SI 1990/1285; the Local Government (Translation Amendments) (Scotland) Order 1996, SI 1996/974.

An Act for preserving Purchasers of Stock from Losses by Forged Transfers

[5 August 1891]

[9.48]
1   Power to make compensation for losses from forged transfer
(1)   Where a company or local authority issue or have issued shares, stock, or securities transferable by an instrument in writing [or by an exempt transfer within the meaning of the Stock Transfer Act 1982] or by an entry, in any books or register kept by or on behalf of the company or local authority, they shall have power to make compensation by a cash payment out of their funds for any loss arising from a transfer of any such shares, stock, or securities, in pursuance of a [forged instrument] or of a transfer under a forged power of attorney, [. . . and whether the person receiving such compensation, or any person through whom he claims, has or has not paid any fee or otherwise contributed to any fund out of which the compensation is paid].

[(1A)   In subsection (1) above "instrument" has the same meaning as in Part I of the Forgery and Counterfeiting Act 1981.]

(2)   Any company or local authority may, if they think fit, provide, either by fees not exceeding the rate of [5p] on every one hundred pounds transferred [with a minimum charge equal to that for twenty-five pounds] to be paid by the transferee upon the entry of the transfer in the books of the company or local authority, or by insurance, reservation of capital, accumulation of income, or in any other manner which they may resolve upon, a fund to meet claims for such compensation.

(3)   For the purpose of providing such compensation any company may borrow on the security of their property, and any local authority may borrow with the like consent and on the like security and subject to the like conditions as to repayment by means of instalments or the provision of a sinking fund and otherwise as in the case of the securities in respect of which compensation is to be provided, but any money so borrowed by a local authority shall be repaid within a term not longer than five years. Any expenses incurred by a local authority in making compensation, or in the repayment of, or the payment of interest on, or otherwise in connexion with, any loan raised as aforesaid, shall, except so far as they may be met by such fees as aforesaid, be paid out of the [revenue] on which the security in respect of which compensation is to be made is charged.

(4)   Any such company or local authority may impose such reasonable restrictions on the transfer of their shares, stock, or securities, or with respect to powers of attorney for the transfer thereof, as they may consider requisite for guarding against losses arising from forgery.

(5)   Where a company or local authority compensate a person under this Act for any loss arising from forgery, the company or local authority shall, without prejudice to any other rights or remedies, have the same rights and remedies against the person liable for the loss as the person compensated would have had.

NOTES

Sub-s (1): words in first pair of square brackets inserted, and words in second and fourth (inner) pairs of square brackets substituted, by the Stock Transfer Act 1982, s 3, Sch 2, para 1, as from 23 July 1985; words in third (outer) pair of square brackets added by the Forged Transfers Act 1892, s 2, as from 27 June 1892; words omitted repealed by the Statute Law (Repeals) Act 2004, as from 22 July 2004.

Sub-s (1A): inserted by the Stock Transfer Act 1982, s 3, Sch 2, para 1, as from 23 July 1985.

Sub-s (2): reference to "5p" substituted by virtue of the Decimal Currency Act 1969, s 10(1), as from 16 May 1969; words in square brackets added by the Forged Transfers Act 1892, s 3, as from 27 June 1892.

Sub-s (3): words in square brackets substituted by the Local Government Finance (Miscellaneous Amendments and Repeal) Order 1990, SI 1990/1285, art 2, Schedule, Pt I, para 1, as from 19 July 1990.

[9.49]
2   Definitions
For the purposes of this Act—
   The expression "company" shall mean any company incorporated by or in pursuance of any Act of Parliament, or by royal charter.
   [The expression "local authority" shall mean—
      [(a)   a billing authority or a precepting authority, as defined in section 69 of the Local Government Finance Act 1992;
      [(aa)   a council constituted under section 2 of the Local Government etc (Scotland) Act 1994;]
      [(ab)   a fire and rescue authority in Wales constituted by a scheme under section 2 of the Fire and Rescue Services Act 2004 or a scheme to which section 4 of that Act applies;]]
      (b)   a levying body within the meaning of section 74 of [the Local Government Finance Act 1988]; and
      (c)   a body as regards which section 75 of that Act applies.]

NOTES

Definition "local authority" substituted by the Local Government Finance Act (Miscellaneous Amendments and Repeal) Order 1990, SI 1990/1285, art 2, Schedule, Pt I, para 2, as from 19 July 1990.

Paras (a), (aa), (ab) of definition "local authority" further substituted, for original para (a), by the Local Government Finance Act 1992, s 117(1), Sch 13, para 1, as from 1 April 1993.

Para (aa) of definition "local authority" further substituted by the Local Government (Translation Amendments) (Scotland) Order 1996, SI 1996/974, art 2(1), Sch 1, Pt I, para 1, as from 1 April 1996.

Para (ab) of definition "local authority" further substituted by the Fire and Rescue Services Act 2004, s 53, Sch 1, para 2(1), (2), as from 1 October 2004 (in relation to England and Scotland), and as from 10 November 2004 (in relation to Wales).

Words in square brackets in para (c) of definition "local authority" substituted by the Fire and Rescue Services Act 2004, s 53, Sch 1, para 2(1), (3), as from 1 October 2004 (in relation to England and Scotland), and as from 10 November 2004 (in relation to Wales).

[9.50]
3   Application to industrial societies, etc
This Act shall apply to any industrial provident, friendly benefit, building . . . society incorporated by or in pursuance of any Act of Parliament as if the society were a company.

NOTES

Words omitted repealed by the Statute Law (Repeals) Act 2004, as from 22 July 2004.

[9.51]
4   Application to harbour and conservancy authorities
(1)   This Act shall apply to any harbour authority or conservancy authority as if the authority were a company.

(2)   For the purposes of this Act the expression "harbour authority" includes all persons, being proprietors of, or entrusted with the duty or invested with the power of constructing, improving, managing, regulating, maintaining, or lighting any harbour otherwise than for profit, and not being a joint stock company.

(3)   For the purposes of this Act the expression "conservancy authority" includes all persons entrusted with the duty or invested with the power of conserving, maintaining, or improving the navigation of any tidal water otherwise than for profit, and not being a joint stock company.

5   *(Repealed by the Statute Law (Repeals) Act 1998, as from 19 November 1998.)*

[9.52]
6   Short title
This Act may be cited as the Forged Transfers Act 1891.

FORGED TRANSFERS ACT 1892

(55 & 56 Vict c 36)

NOTES
This Act is reproduced as amended by: the Statute Law (Repeals) Act 2004.

An Act to remove doubts as to the meaning of the Forged Transfers Act 1891

[27 June 1892]

[9.53]
1   Short title
This Act may be cited as the Forged Transfers Act 1892 and this Act and the Forged Transfers Act 1891 may be cited together as the Forged Transfers Acts 1891 and 1892.

2, 3   *(S 2 amends the Forged Transfers Act 1891, s 1, and is repealed in part by the Statute Law (Repeals) Act 2004, as from 22 July 2004; s 3 also amends s 1 of the 1891 Act.)*

[9.54]
4   Provision where one company takes over shares, etc, of another company
Where the shares, stock, or securities of a company or local authority have by amalgamation or otherwise become the shares, stock, or securities of another company or local authority, the last-mentioned company and authority shall have the same power under the Forged Transfers Act 1891 and this Act, as the original company or authority would have had if it had continued.

LIMITED PARTNERSHIPS ACT 1907

(1907 c 24)

NOTES
This Act is reproduced as amended by: the Companies (Consolidation) Act 1908; the Perjury Act 1911; the Statute Law Revision Act 1927; the Perjury Act (Northern Ireland) 1946; the Decimal Currency Act 1969; the Finance Act 1973; the Banking Act 1979; the Companies Act 2006; the Finance (Miscellaneous Provisions) (Northern Ireland) Order 1973, SI 1973/1323; the Regulatory Reform (Removal of 20 Member Limit in Partnerships etc) Order 2002, SI 2002/3203; the Legislative Reform (Limited Partnerships) Order 2009, SI 2009/1940; the Companies Act 2006 (Consequential Amendments, Transitional Provisions and Savings) Order 2009, SI 2009/1941.

As to the repeal of this Act as it formerly had effect in relation to Northern Ireland (as from 1 October 2009), see the Companies Act 2006, s 1286(2) at **[1.1286]**.

ARRANGEMENT OF SECTIONS

An Act to establish Limited Partnership

[28 August 1907]

[9.55]
1 Short title
This Act may be cited for all purposes as the Limited Partnerships Act 1907.

2 *(Repealed by the Statute Law Revision Act 1927.)*

[9.56]
3 Interpretation of terms
In the construction of this Act the following words and expressions shall have the meanings respectively assigned to them in this section, unless there be something in the subject or context repugnant to such construction—

"Firm," "firm name," and "business" have the same meanings as in the Partnership Act 1890;

"General partner" shall mean any partner who is not a limited partner as defined by this Act.

[9.57]
4 Definition and constitution of limited partnership
(1)   . . . Limited partnerships may be formed in the manner and subject to the conditions by this Act provided.

(2) A limited partnership . . . must consist of one or more persons called general partners, who shall be liable for all debts and obligations of the firm, and one or more persons to be called limited partners, who shall at the time of entering into such partnership contribute thereto a sum or sums as capital or property valued at a stated amount, and who shall not be liable for the debts or obligations of the firm beyond the amount so contributed.

(3) A limited partner shall not during the continuance of the partnership, either directly or indirectly, draw out or receive back any part of his contribution, and if he does so draw out or receive back any such part shall be liable for the debts and obligations of the firm up to the amount so drawn out or received back.

(4) A body corporate may be a limited partner.

NOTES

Sub-s (1): words omitted repealed by the Statute Law Revision Act 1927, as from 22 December 1927.

Sub-s (2): words omitted repealed by a combination of the Banking Act 1979, ss 46(b), 51(2), Sch 7, as from 19 February 1982, the Regulatory Reform (Removal of 20 Member Limit in Partnerships etc) Order 2002, SI 2002/3203, art 3, as from 21 December 2002, and the Partnerships etc (Removal of Twenty Member Limit) (Northern Ireland) Order 2003, SI 2003/2904, arts 3(1), 4, Schedule, as from 13 January 2004.

Note: the Regulatory Reform (Removal of 20 Member Limit in Partnerships etc) Order 2002, SI 2002/3203 reforms the law relating to the maximum limit of 20 on the numbers of persons who can be members of partnerships (including limited partnerships), and of certain companies or associations. It does so by repealing CA 1985, ss 716, 717 and amending sub-s (2) above, thereby removing the maximum limits on the number of members in a partnership or limited partnership, company or association.

[9.58]
5 Registration of limited partnership required
Every limited partnership must be registered as such in accordance with the provisions of this Act, . . .

NOTES

Words omitted repealed by the Legislative Reform (Limited Partnerships) Order 2009, SI 2009/1940, arts 2, 8, as from 1 October 2009, in relation to limited partnerships for which registration applications are received on or after that day.

[9.59]
6 Modifications of general law in case of limited partnerships
(1) A limited partner shall not take part in the management of the partnership business, and shall not have power to bind the firm—

Provided that a limited partner may by himself or his agent at any time inspect the books of the firm and examine into the state and prospects of the partnership business, and may advise with the partners thereon.

If a limited partner takes part in the management of the partnership business he shall be liable for all debts and obligations of the firm incurred while he so takes part in the management as though he were a general partner.

(2) A limited partnership shall not be dissolved by the death or bankruptcy of a limited partner, and the lunacy of a limited partner shall not be a ground for dissolution of the partnership by the court unless the lunatic's share cannot be otherwise ascertained and realised.

(3) In the event of the dissolution of a limited partnership its affairs shall be wound up by the general partners unless the court otherwise orders.

(4) . . .

(5) Subject to any agreement expressed or implied between the partners—
  (a) Any difference arising as to ordinary matters connected with the partnership business may be decided by a majority of the general partners;
  (b) A limited partner may, with the consent of the general partners, assign his share in the partnership, and upon such an assignment the assignee shall become a limited partner with all the rights of the assignor;
  (c) The other partners shall not be entitled to dissolve the partnership by reason of any limited partner suffering his share to be charged for his separate debt;
  (d) A person may be introduced as a partner without the consent of the existing limited partners;
  (e) A limited partner shall not be entitled to dissolve the partnership by notice.

NOTES
Sub-s (4): repealed by the Companies (Consolidation) Act 1908, s 286, Sch 6, Pt I, as from 21 December 1908.

[9.60]
7 Law as to private partnerships to apply where not excluded by this Act
Subject to the provisions of this Act, the Partnership Act 1890 and the rules of equity and of common law applicable to partnerships, except so far as they are inconsistent with the express provisions of the last-mentioned Act, shall apply to limited partnerships.

[9.61]
[8 Duty to register
The registrar shall register a limited partnership if an application is made to the registrar in accordance with section 8A.]

NOTES
Commencement: 1 October 2009.
Substituted by the Legislative Reform (Limited Partnerships) Order 2009, SI 2009/1940, arts 2, 4, as from 1 October 2009, in relation to limited partnerships for which registration applications are received on or after that day.

[9.62]
[8A Application for registration
(1) An application for registration must—
  (a) specify the firm name, complying with section 8B, under which the limited partnership is to be registered,
  (b) contain the details listed in subsection (2),
  (c) be signed or otherwise authenticated by or on behalf of each partner, and
  (d) be made to the registrar for the part of the United Kingdom in which the principal place of business of the limited partnership is to be situated.
(2) The required details are—
  (a) the general nature of the partnership business,
  (b) the name of each general partner,
  (c) the name of each limited partner,
  (d) the amount of the capital contribution of each limited partner (and whether the contribution is paid in cash or in another specified form),
  (e) the address of the proposed principal place of business of the limited partnership, and
  (f) the term (if any) for which the limited partnership is to be entered into (beginning with the date of registration).]

NOTES
Commencement: 1 October 2009.
Inserted by the Legislative Reform (Limited Partnerships) Order 2009, SI 2009/1940, arts 2, 5, as from 1 October 2009, in relation to limited partnerships for which registration applications are received on or after that day.

[9.63]
[8B Name of limited partnership
(1) This section sets out conditions which must be satisfied by the firm name of a limited partnership as specified in the application for registration.
(2) The name must end with—
  (a) the words "limited partnership" (upper or lower case, or any combination), or
  (b) the abbreviation "LP" (upper or lower case, or any combination, with or without punctuation).

(3)   But if the principal place of business of a limited partnership is to be in Wales, its firm name may end with—
    (a)   the words "partneriaeth cyfyngedig" (upper or lower case, or any combination), or
    (b)   the abbreviation "PC" (upper or lower case, or any combination, with or without punctuation).]

NOTES
Commencement: 1 October 2009.
Inserted by the Legislative Reform (Limited Partnerships) Order 2009, SI 2009/1940, arts 2, 6, as from 1 October 2009, in relation to limited partnerships for which registration applications are received on or after that day.

[9.64]
[8C   Certificate of registration
(1)   On registering a limited partnership the registrar shall issue a certificate of registration.
(2)   The certificate must be—
    (a)   signed by the registrar, or
    (b)   authenticated with the registrar's seal.
(3)   The certificate must state—
    (a)   the firm name of the limited partnership given in the application for registration,
    (b)   the limited partnership's registration number,
    (c)   the date of registration, and
    (d)   that the limited partnership is registered as a limited partnership under this Act.
(4)   The certificate is conclusive evidence that a limited partnership came into existence on the date of registration.]

NOTES
Commencement: 1 October 2009.
Inserted by the Legislative Reform (Limited Partnerships) Order 2009, SI 2009/1940, arts 2, 7, as from 1 October 2009, in relation to limited partnerships for which registration applications are received on or after that day.

[9.65]
9   Registration of changes in partnerships
(1)   If during the continuance of a limited partnership any change is made or occurs in—
    (a)   the firm name,
    (b)   the general nature of the business,
    (c)   the principal place of business,
    (d)   the partners or the name of any partner,
    (e)   the term or character of the partnership,
    (f)   the sum contributed by any limited partner,
    (g)   the liability of any partner by reason of his becoming a limited instead of a general partner or a general instead of a limited partner,
a statement, signed by the firm, specifying the nature of the change shall within seven days be sent by post or delivered to the registrar   . . .
(2)   If default is made in compliance with the requirements of this section each of the general partners shall, on conviction under the Summary Jurisdiction Acts, be liable to a fine not exceeding one pound for each day during which the default continues.

NOTES
Sub-s (1): words omitted repealed by the Companies Act 2006 (Consequential Amendments, Transitional Provisions and Savings) Order 2009, SI 2009/1941, art 2(1), Sch 1, para 3(1), (2), as from 1 October 2009.

[9.66]
10   Advertisement in Gazette of statement of general partner becoming a limited partner and of assignment of share of limited partner
(1)   Notice of any arrangement or transaction under which any person will cease to be a general partner in any firm, and will become a limited partner in that firm, or under which the share of a limited partner in a firm will be assigned to any person, shall be forthwith advertised in the Gazette, and until notice of the arrangement or transaction is so advertised the arrangement or transaction shall, for the purposes of this Act, be deemed to be of no effect.
(2)   For the purposes of this section, the expression "the Gazette" means—
In the case of a limited partnership registered in England, the London Gazette.
In the case of a limited partnership registered in Scotland, the Edinburgh Gazette.
In the case of a limited partnership registered in [Northern Ireland], the [Belfast] Gazette.

NOTES
Sub-s (2): words in square brackets substituted by the Companies Act 2006 (Consequential Amendments, Transitional Provisions and Savings) Order 2009, SI 2009/1941, art 2(1), Sch 1, para 3(1), (3), as from 1 October 2009.

11, 12   *(S 11 repealed by the Finance Act 1973, s 59(7), Sch 22, Pt V and the Finance (Miscellaneous Provisions) (Northern Ireland) Order 1973, SI 1973/1323, art 10(1), Sch 4, as from*

1 August 1973; s 12 repealed by the Perjury Act 1911, s 17, Schedule and the Perjury Act (Northern Ireland) 1946, s 16(3), Schedule, as from 1 January 1912.)

[9.67]
13   Registrar to file statement and issue certificate of registration
On receiving any statement made in pursuance of this Act the registrar shall cause the same to be filed, and he shall send by post to the firm from whom such statement shall have been received a certificate of the registration thereof.

[9.68]
14   Register and index to be kept
. . .   the registrar shall keep   . . .   a register and an index of all the limited partnerships registered as aforesaid, and of all the statements registered in relation to such partnerships.

NOTES
Words omitted repealed by the Companies Act 2006 (Consequential Amendments, Transitional Provisions and Savings) Order 2009, SI 2009/1941, art 2(1), Sch 1, para 3(1), (4), as from 1 October 2009.

[9.69]
[15   The registrar
(1)   The registrar of companies is the registrar of limited partnerships.
(2)   In this Act—
(a)   references to the registrar in relation to the registration of a limited partnership are to the registrar to whom the application for registration is to be made (see section 8A(1)(d)[(1)]);
(b)   references to registration in a particular part of the United Kingdom are to registration by the registrar for that part of the United Kingdom;
(c)   references to the registrar in relation to any other matter relating to a limited partnership are to the registrar for the part of the United Kingdom in which the partnership is registered.]

NOTES
Commencement: 1 October 2009.
Substituted by the Companies Act 2006 (Consequential Amendments, Transitional Provisions and Savings) Order 2009, SI 2009/1941, art 2(1), Sch 1, para 3(1), (5), as from 1 October 2009.

[9.70]
16   Inspection of statements registered
(1)   Any person may inspect the statements filed by the registrar . . .   . . . and any person may require a certificate of the registration of any limited partnership, or a copy of or extract from any registered statement, to be certified by the registrar   . . .
(2)   A certificate of registration or a copy of or extract from any statement registered under this Act, if duly certified to be a true copy under the hand of the registrar   . . .   (whom it shall not be necessary to prove to be the registrar   . . .   ) shall, in all legal proceedings, civil or criminal, and in all cases whatsoever be received in evidence.

NOTES
Sub-s (1): first words omitted repealed by the Companies Act 2006 (Consequential Amendments, Transitional Provisions and Savings) Order 2009, SI 2009/1941, art 2(1), Sch 1, para 3(1), (6)(a), as from 1 October 2009; other words omitted repealed by the Companies Act 2006, ss 1063(7)(a), 1295, Sch 16, as from 6 April 2007 (for transitional provisions see the note below).
Sub-s (2): words omitted repealed by SI 2009/1941, art 2(1), Sch 1, para 3(1), (6)(b), as from 1 October 2009.
Transitional provisions: the Companies Act 2006 (Commencement No 1, Transitional Provisions and Savings) Order 2006, SI 2006/3428, Sch 5, para 6(2) provided as follows (as to the revocation of this provision, see the notes below)—

(2)   Notwithstanding the coming into force of the repeals in section 16 of the Limited Partnerships Act 1907 and the repeal of section 17(a) of that Act, the fees appointed under the said section 16 and having effect immediately before 6th April 2007 shall continue to be payable, and the rules in force under the said section 17(a) immediately before 6th April 2007 shall continue to have effect.

Note that Sch 5, para 6(2) to the 2006 Order was revoked by the Registrar of Companies (Fees) (Limited Partnerships and Newspaper Proprietors) Regulations 2009, SI 2009/2392, regs 6, 7, as from 1 October 2009, subject to transitional provisions in relation to cases where any application is made to the registrar on or before 30 September 2009 in respect of the inspection of, or the provision of copies of, material kept by the registrar. The fees specified in the 2009 Regulations replace the fees set under this section and the Limited Partnerships Rules 1907, SR & O 1907/1020 (made under s 17 *post*). See **[4.566]**.
Note also that SI 2006/3428, art 4(4) provided that the commencement of CA 2006, s 1063 did not extend to Northern Ireland. That section was commenced for all purposes on 1 October 2009.

[9.71]
17   Power to Board of Trade to make rules
The Board of Trade may make rules   . . .   concerning any of the following matters:—
(a)   . . .
(b)   The duties or additional duties to be performed by the registrar for the purposes of this Act;
(c)   The performance by assistant registrars and other officers of acts by this Act required to be done by the registrar;

(d)   The forms to be used for the purposes of this Act;

(e)   Generally, the conduct and regulation of registration under this Act and any matters incidental thereto.

NOTES

Words omitted repealed by the Companies Act 2006, ss 1063(7)(b), 1295, Sch 16, as from 6 April 2007 (for transitional provisions see the note to s 16 at **[9.70]**).

See further, the Legislative Reform (Limited Partnerships) Order 2009, SI 2009/1940, art 9, which provides that nothing in that Order (which amends s 5 of this Act, substitutes s 8, and inserts ss 8A–8C (as noted *ante*)) permits anything to be done under this section that could not otherwise have been done.

Rules: the Limited Partnerships Rules 1907, SR & O 1907/1020; the Limited Partnerships (Forms) Rules 2009, SI 2009/2160 at **[10.1192]** (which revoke, as from 1 October 2009, the 1907 Rules (with the exception of r 3)).

STOCK TRANSFER ACT 1963

(1963 c 18)

NOTES

This Act is reproduced as amended by: FA 1964; the Post Office Act 1969; the Northern Ireland Constitution Act 1973; the Stock Exchange (Completion of Bargains) Act 1976; the Companies Consolidation (Consequential Provisions) Act 1985; the Building Societies Act 1986; FSA 1986; the Local Government Finance Act 1992; the Police and Magistrates' Courts Act 1994; the Requirements of Writing (Scotland) Act 1995; FA 1999; the Fire and Rescue Services Act 2004; the Stock Transfer (Amendment of Forms) Order 1974, SI 1974/1214; the Local Government Finance (Repeals, Savings and Consequential Amendments) Order 1990, SI 1990/776; the Stock Transfer (Addition and Substitution of Forms) Order 1996, SI 1996/1571; the Open Ended Investment Companies (Investment Companies with Variable Capital) Regulations 1996, SI 1996/2827; the Open-Ended Investment Companies Regulations 2001, SI 2001, SI 2001/1228; the Financial Services and Markets Act 2000 (Consequential Amendments and Repeals) Order 2001, SI 2001/3649; the Companies Act 2006 (Consequential Amendments etc) Order 2008, SI 2008/948; the Companies Act 2006 (Consequential Amendments, Transitional Provisions and Savings) Order 2009, SI 2009/1941.

ARRANGEMENT OF SECTIONS

An Act to amend the law with respect to the transfer of securities

[10 July 1963]

[9.72]
1   Simplified transfer of securities

(1)   Registered securities to which this section applies may be transferred by means of an instrument under hand in the form set out in Schedule 1 to this Act (in this Act referred to as a stock transfer), executed by the transferor only and specifying (in addition to the particulars of the consideration, of the description and number or amount of the securities, and of the person by whom the transfer is made) the full name and address of the transferee.

(2)   The execution of a stock transfer need not be attested; and where such a transfer has been executed for the purpose of a stock exchange transaction, the particulars of the consideration and of the transferee may either be inserted in that transfer or, as the case may require, supplied by means of separate instruments in the form set out in Schedule 2 to this Act (in this Act referred to as brokers transfers), identifying the stock transfer and specifying the securities to which each such instrument relates and the consideration paid for those securities.

(3)   Nothing in this section shall be construed as affecting the validity of any instrument which would be effective to transfer securities apart from this section; and any instrument purporting to be made in any form which was common or usual before the commencement of this Act, or in any other form authorised or required for that purpose apart from this section, shall be sufficient, whether or not it is completed in accordance with the form, if it complies with the requirements as to execution and contents which apply to a stock transfer.

(4)   This section applies to fully paid up registered securities of any description, being—

(a)   securities issued by any company [as defined in section 1(1) of the Companies Act 2006] except a company limited by guarantee or an unlimited company;

(b)   securities issued by any body (other than a company [as so defined]) incorporated in Great Britain by or under any enactment or by Royal Charter except a building society within the meaning of the Building Societies Act [1986] or a society registered under the Industrial and Provident Societies Act 1893;

(c)   securities issued by the Government of the United Kingdom, except stock or bonds in [the National Savings Stock Register]   . . . , and except national savings certificates;

(d)   securities issued by any local authority;

[(e)   units of an authorised unit trust scheme or a recognised scheme within the meaning of [Part 17 of the Financial Services and Markets Act 2000]];

[(f)   shares issued by an open-ended investment company within the meaning of the Open-Ended Investment Companies Regulations 2001.]

NOTES

Sub-s (4) is amended as follows:

Words in square brackets in para (a), and words in first pair of square brackets in para (b), substituted by the Companies Act 2006 (Consequential Amendments, Transitional Provisions and Savings) Order 2009, SI 2009/1941, art 2(1), Sch 1, para 10, as from 1 October 2009.

Words in second pair of square brackets in para (b) substituted by the Building Societies Act 1986, s 120(1), Sch 18, Pt I, para 5, as from 1 January 1987.

Words in square brackets in para (c) substituted by the Post Office Act 1969, s 108(1)(f), as from 25 July 1969, and words omitted from that paragraph repealed by FA 1964, ss 24, 26(7), Sch 8, para 10, Sch 9, as from 16 July 1964.

Para (e) substituted by FSA 1986, s 212(2), Sch 16, para 4(a), as from 29 April 1988, and words in square brackets in that paragraph substituted by the Financial Services and Markets Act 2000 (Consequential Amendments and Repeals) Order 2001, SI 2001/3649, art 270, as from 1 December 2001.

Para (f) added by the Open-Ended Investment Companies (Investment Companies with Variable Capital) Regulations 1996, SI 1996/2827, reg 75, Sch 8, Pt I, para 2, as from 6 January 1997, and substituted by the Open-Ended Investment Companies Regulations 2001, SI 2001, SI 2001/1228, reg 84, Sch 7, Pt I, para 2, as from 1 December 2001.

Modifications: the Stock Transfer (Substitution of Forms) Order 1990, SI 1990/18, art 3 provides as follows—

"Section 1(3) of the Act shall apply in relation to the form for which the form set out in the Schedule to this Order is substituted as it applies to any form which was common or usual before the commencement of the Act with the modification that for the words "which was common or usual before the commencement of this Act" there shall be substituted the words "for which the form set out in the Schedule to the Stock Transfer (Substitution of Forms) Order 1990 is substituted".".

The Stock Transfer (Addition and Substitution of Forms) Order 1996, SI 1996/1571, art 3(2), (3) further provides as follows—

"(2)   Subsection (3) of section 1 of the Stock Transfer Act 1963 shall apply in relation to the form for which the form set out in Schedule 2 to this Order is substituted as it applies to any form for which the form set out in the Schedule to the Stock Transfer (Substitution of Forms) Order 1990 was substituted but with the modification mentioned in paragraph (3) below.
(3)   The modification referred to in paragraph (2) above is the substitution for the words "for which the form set out in the Schedule to the Stock Transfer (Substitution of Forms) Order 1990 is substituted" of the words "for which the form set out in Schedule 2 to the Stock Transfer (Addition and Substitution of Forms) Order 1996 is substituted".".

[9.73]
2   Supplementary provisions as to simplified transfer

(1)   Section 1 of this Act shall have effect in relation to the transfer of any securities to which that section applies notwithstanding anything to the contrary in any enactment or instrument relating to the transfer of those securities; but nothing in that section affects—

(a)   any right to refuse to register a person as the holder of any securities on any ground other than the form in which those securities purport to be transferred to him: or

(b)   any enactment or rule of law regulating the execution of documents by companies or other bodies corporate, or any articles of association or other instrument regulating the execution of documents by any particular company or body corporate.

(2)   Subject to the provisions of this section, any enactment or instrument relating to the transfer of securities to which section 1 of this Act applies shall, with any necessary modifications, apply in relation to an instrument of transfer authorised by that section as it applies in relation to an instrument of transfer to which it applies apart from this subsection; and without prejudice to the generality of the foregoing provision, [the references to an instrument of transfer in section 775 of the Companies Act 2006 (certification of instrument of transfer)] shall be construed as including a reference to a brokers transfer.

(3)   In relation to the transfer of securities by means of a stock transfer and a brokers transfer—

(a)   any reference in any enactment or instrument (including in particular [section 770(1)(a) of the Companies Act 2006 (registration of transfer)]   . . .) to the delivery or lodging of an instrument (or proper instrument) of transfer shall be construed as a reference to the delivery or lodging of the stock transfer and the brokers transfer;

(b)   any such reference to the date on which an instrument of transfer is delivered or lodged shall be construed as a reference to the date by which the later of those transfers to be delivered or lodged has been delivered or lodged; and

(c)   subject to the foregoing provisions of this subsection, the brokers transfer (and not the stock transfer) shall be deemed to be the conveyance or transfer for the purposes of the enactments relating to stamp duty.

(4)   . . .

NOTES

Sub-s (2): words in square brackets substituted by the Companies Act 2006 (Consequential Amendments etc) Order 2008, SI 2008/948, art 3(1), Sch 1, Pt 2, para 37(a), as from 6 April 2008.

Sub-s (3): words in square brackets substituted by SI 2008/948, art 3(1), Sch 1, Pt 2, para 37(b), as from 6 April 2008; words omitted from para (a) repealed by FA 1999, s 139, Sch 20, Pt V(5), with effect in relation to instruments executed from 6 February 2000. Note that these words and para (c) were to be repealed by FA 1990, s 132, Sch 19, Pt VI, with effect from an appointed day in accordance with FA 1990, ss 107–111. The Treasury order specifying the appointed day for the purposes of FA 1990, ss 107–110 was to coincide with the start of paperless trading under the Stock Exchange's planned TAURUS system (IR press release, 20.3.1990). However, on 11.3.1993 the London Stock Exchange News Release 6/93 announced that TAURUS had been abandoned.

Sub-s (4): repealed by the Requirements of Writing (Scotland) Act 1995, s 14(2), Sch 5, as from 1 August 1995.

[9.74]
3   Additional provisions as to transfer forms
(1)   References in this Act to the forms set out in Schedule 1 and Schedule 2 include references to forms substantially corresponding to those forms respectively.

(2)   The Treasury may by order amend the said Schedules either by altering the forms set out therein or by substituting different forms for those forms or by the addition of forms for use as alternatives to those forms; and references in this Act to the forms set out in those Schedules (including references in this section) shall be construed accordingly.

(3)   Any order under subsection (2) of this section which substitutes a different form for a form set out in Schedule 1 to this Act may direct that subsection (3) of section 1 of this Act shall apply, with any necessary modifications, in relation to the form for which that form is substituted as it applies to any form which was common or usual before the commencement of this Act.

(4)   Any order of the Treasury under this section shall be made by statutory instrument, and may be varied or revoked by a subsequent order; and any statutory instrument made by virtue of this section shall be subject to annulment in pursuance of a resolution of either House of Parliament.

[(5)   An order under subsection (2) of this section may—
   (a)   provide for forms on which some of the particulars mentioned in subsection (1) of section 1 of this Act are not required to be specified;
   (b)   provide for that section to have effect, in relation to such forms as are mentioned in the preceding paragraph or other forms specified in the order, subject to such amendments as are so specified (which may include an amendment of the reference in subsection (1) of that section to an instrument under hand);
   (c)   provide for all or any of the provisions of the order to have effect in such cases only as are specified in the order.]

NOTES

Sub-s (5): added by the Stock Exchange (Completion of Bargains) Act 1976, s 6, as from 12 February 1979.

Orders: the Stock Transfer (Amendment of Forms) Order 1974, SI 1974/1214; the Stock Transfer (Addition of Forms) Order 1979, SI 1979/277; the Stock Transfer (Substitution of Forms) Order 1990, SI 1990/18; the Stock Transfer (Addition and Substitution of Forms) Order 1996, SI 1996/1571.

[9.75]
4   Interpretation
(1)   In this Act the following expressions have the meanings hereby respectively assigned to them, that is to say—
   "local authority" means, in relation to England and Wales—
      [[(a)   a billing authority or a precepting authority as defined in section 69 of the Local Government Finance Act 1992;
      [(aa)   a fire and rescue authority in Wales constituted by a scheme under section 2 of the Fire and Rescue Services Act 2004 or a scheme to which section 4 of that Act applies;]]
      (b)   a levying body within the meaning of section 74 of [the Local Government Finance Act 1988]; and
      (c)   a body as regards which section 75 of that Act applies,]
      and, in relation to Scotland, a county council, a town council and any statutory authority, commissioners or trustees to whom section 270 of the Local Government (Scotland) Act 1947 applies;
   "registered securities" means transferable securities the holders of which are entered in a register (whether maintained in Great Britain or not);
   "securities" means shares, stock, debentures, debenture stock, loan stock, bonds, units of a [collective investment scheme within the meaning of the [Financial Services and Markets Act 2000]], and other securities of any description;
   "stock exchange transaction" means a sale and purchase of securities in which each of the parties is a member of a stock exchange acting in the ordinary course of his business as such or is acting through the agency of such a member;

"stock exchange" means the Stock Exchange, London, and any other stock exchange (whether in Great Britain or not) which is declared by order of the Treasury to be a recognised stock exchange for the purposes of this Act.

(2)   Any order of the Treasury under this section shall be made by statutory instrument and may be varied or revoked by a subsequent order.

NOTES

Definition "local authority" in sub-s (1) amended as follows—

Paras (a)–(c) substituted by the Local Government Finance (Repeals, Savings and Consequential Amendments) Order 1990, SI 1990/776, art 8, Sch 3, para 8, as from 1 April 1990.

Paras (a), (aa) further substituted, for para (a), by the Local Government Finance Act 1992, s 117(1), Sch 13, para 12, as from 2 November 1992.

Para (aa) further substituted by the Fire and Rescue Services Act 2004, s 53, Sch 1, para 18(1), (2), as from 1 October 2004 (in relation to England and Scotland), and as from 10 November 2004 (in relation to Wales).

Words in square brackets in para (b) substituted by the Fire and Rescue Services Act 2004, s 53, Sch 1, para 18(1), (3), as from 1 October 2004 (in relation to England and Scotland), and as from 10 November 2004 (in relation to Wales).

In definition "securities" in sub-s (1) words in first (outer) pair of square brackets substituted by FSA 1986, s 212(2), Sch 16, para 4(b), as from 29 April 1988, words in second (inner) pair of square brackets substituted by the Financial Services and Markets Act 2000 (Consequential Amendments and Repeals) Order 2001, SI 2001/3649, art 271, as from 1 December 2001.

Orders: the Stock Transfer (Recognised Stock Exchanges) Order 1973, SI 1973/536.

5   *((Application to Northern Ireland) outside the scope of this work.)*

[9.76]
6   Short title and commencement
(1)   This Act may be cited as the Stock Transfer Act 1963.
(2)   Subsection (3) of section 5 of this Act shall come into force on the passing of this Act, and the remaining provisions of this Act shall come into force on such date as the Treasury may by order made by statutory instrument direct.

NOTES

Orders: the Stock Transfer Act 1963 (Commencement) Order 1963, SI 1963/1592 (bringing provisions of this Act, other than s 5(3), into force on 26 October 1963).

SCHEDULE I

[9.77]

STOCK TRANSFER FORM	Certificate lodged with the Registrar
Consideration Money £...............................	(For completion by the Registrar/ Stock Exchange)

Name of Undertaking.	
Description of Security.	

Number or amount of Shares, Stock or other security and, in figures column only, number and denomination of units, if any.	Words	Figures
		(units of)

Name(s) of registered holder(s) should be given in full: the address should be given where there is only one holder. If the transfer is not made by the registered holder(s) insert also the name(s) and capacity (eg, Executor(s)), of the person(s) making the transfer.	in the name(s) of

Delete words in italics except for stock exchange transactions.	I/We hereby transfer the above security out of the name(s) aforesaid to the person(s) named below *or to the several persons named in Parts 2 of Brokers Transfer Forms relating to the above security.* Signature(s) of transferor(s) 1..................................... 3..................................... 2..................................... 4.....................................	Stamp of Selling Broker(s) or, for transactions which are not stock exchange transactions, of Agent(s), if any, acting for the Transferor(s).

A body corporate should execute this transfer under its common seal or otherwise in accordance with applicable statutory requirements.	Date

Full name(s), full postal address(es) (including County or, if applicable, Postal District number) of the person(s) to whom the security is transferred. Please state title, if any, or whether Mr, Mrs or Miss. Please complete in type or in Block Capitals.	

I/We request that such entries be made in the register as are necessary to give effect to this transfer.

Stamp of Buying Broker(s) (if any).	Stamp or name and address of person lodging this form (if other than the Buying Broker(s)).

Reference to the Registrar in this form means the registrar or registration agent of the undertaking, <u>not</u> the Registrar of Companies at Companies House.

(Endorsement for use only in stock exchange transactions)
The security represented by the transfer overleaf has been sold as follows:—

.................................*Shares/Stock*   ....*Shares/Stock*

.................................*Shares/Stock*   ....*Shares/Stock*

.................................*Shares/Stock*   ....*Shares/Stock*

.................................*Shares/Stock*   ....*Shares/Stock*

.................................*Shares/Stock*   ....*Shares/Stock*

.................................*Shares/Stock*   ....*Shares/Stock*

Balance (if any) due to Selling Broker(s)

Amount of Certificate(s)

Brokers Transfer Forms for above amounts certified

Stamp of certifying Stock Exchange   *Stamp of Selling Broker(s)*

NOTES

Substituted by the Stock Transfer (Addition and Substitution of Forms) Order 1996, SI 1996/1571, art 3(1), Sch 2, as from 15 July 1996, subject to art 3(2), (3) of the 1996 Order. For the effect of art 3 see s 1(3) of this Act at **[9.72]**.

[9.78]

TRANSFER	Counter Location Stamp	Barcode or reference

Above this line for Registrar's use

RN

Above this line for completion by the depositing system-user only.

	Consideration Money	Certificate(s) lodged with Registrar (To be completed by Registrar)

Name of Undertaking.

Description of Security.

Please complete form in type or in block capitals.

Amount of shares or other security in words	Figures

Name(s) of registered holder(s) should be given in full: the address should be given where there is only one holder.

If the transfer is not made by the registered holder(s) insert also the name(s) and capacity (eg executor(s)) of the person(s) making the transfer.

In the name(s) of	Designation (if any)

Balance certificate(s) required

Please Sign Here

I/We hereby transfer the above security out of the name(s) aforesaid into the name(s) of the system-member set out below and request that the necessary entries be made in the undertaking's own register of members.

Signature(s) of transferor(s)

1.

2.

3.

4.

A body corporate should execute this transfer under its common seal or otherwise in accordance with applicable statutory requirements.

Stamp of depositing system-user

Date

Full name(s) of the person(s) to whom the security is transferred.

Such person(s) must be a system-member.

	Participant ID
	Member Account ID

Reference to the Registrar in this form means the registrar or registration agent of the undertaking, not the Registrar of the Companies at Company House.

...... is delivering this transfer at the direction and on behalf of the depositing system-user whose stamp appears herein and does not in any manner or to any extent warrant or represent the validity, genuineness or correctness of the transfer instructions contained herein or the genuineness of the signature(s) of the transferor(s). The depositing system-user by delivering this transfer to ...... authorises ...... to deliver this transfer for registration and agrees to be deemed for all the purposes to be the person(s) actually so delivering this transfer for registration.

NOTES

Added by the Stock Transfer (Addition and Substitution of Forms) Order 1996, SI 1996/1571, art 2(1), Sch 1, as from 15 July 1996, for use where units of a registered security to which s 1 of this Act applies are transferred to a system-member to be held by him as uncertificated units of that security. By art 2(2) of the 1996 Order, an instrument in that form is not required to specify the address of the transferee.

The Talisman Sold Transfer Forms which were inserted and substituted by SI 1979/277 and SI 1990/18 are not reproduced. The Talisman Bought Transfer Form which was inserted by SI 1979/277 is not reproduced. See the tenth edition for these Forms.

SCHEDULE II

[9.79]

BROKERS TRANSFER FORM	Certificate lodged with the Registrar
Consideration Money £...............	*(For completion by the Registrar/ Stock Exchange)*

Part 1		
[Name of Undertaking.]		
[Description of Security.]		
Number or amount of Shares, Stock or other security and, in figures column only, number and denomination of units, if any.	Words	Figures
		(units of)
Name(s) of registered holder(s) should be given in full: the address should be given where there is only one holder. If the transfer is not made by the registered holder(s) insert also the name(s) and capacity (eg, Executor(s)), of the person(s) making the transfer.	in the name(s) of	

I/We confirm that the Stock Transfer Form relating to the security set out above has been lodged with the Registrar, and that the said security has been sold by me/us by a stock exchange transaction within the meaning of the Stock Transfer Act 1963.

Date and Stamp of Selling Broker(s)

Part 2
Full name(s), full postal address(es) (including County or, if applicable, Postal District number) of the person(s) to whom the security is transferred. Please state title, if any, or whether Mr, Mrs or Miss. Please complete in typewriting or in Block Capitals.

I/We confirm that the security set out in Part 1 above has been purchased by a stock exchange transaction within the meaning of the Stock Transfer Act 1963, and I/we request that such entries be made in the register as are necessary to give effect to this transfer.

Stamp of Buying Broker(s).	Stamp of Lodging Agent (if other than the Buying Broker(s))

NOTES

Words in square brackets substituted by the Stock Transfer (Amendment of Forms) Order 1974, SI 1974/1214, art 3(2), as from 3 August 1974.

THEFT ACT 1968

(1968 c 60)

NOTES
   This Act is reproduced as amended by: the Northern Ireland Constitution Act 1973; the Theft Act 1978; the Criminal Justice Act 1991; the Theft (Amendment) Act 1996; the Fraud Act 2006; the Financial Services and Markets Act 2000 (Consequential Amendments and Repeals) Order 2001, SI 2001/3649.

ARRANGEMENT OF SECTIONS

An Act to revise the law of England and Wales as to theft and similar or associated offences, and in connection therewith to make provision as to criminal proceedings by one party to a marriage against the other, and to make certain amendments extending beyond England and Wales in the Post Office Act 1953 and other enactments; and for other purposes connected therewith

[26 July 1968]

NOTES
   Only those provisions of this Act relating to company law are reproduced. Provisions not reproduced are not annotated.

Definition of "Theft"

[9.80]
1   Basic definition of theft
(1)   A person is guilty of theft if he dishonestly appropriates property belonging to another with the intention of permanently depriving the other of it; and "thief" and "steal" shall be construed accordingly.
(2)   It is immaterial whether the appropriation is made with a view to gain, or is made for the thief's own benefit.
(3)   The five following sections of this Act shall have effect as regards the interpretation and operation of this section (and, except as otherwise provided by this Act, shall apply only for purposes of this section).

[9.81]
2   "Dishonestly"
(1)   A person's appropriation of property belonging to another is not to be regarded as dishonest—
   (a)   if he appropriates the property in the belief that he has in law the right to deprive the other of it, on behalf of himself or of a third person; or
   (b)   if he appropriates the property in the belief that he would have the other's consent if the other knew of the appropriation and the circumstances of it; or
   (c)   (except where the property came to him as trustee or personal representative) if he appropriates the property in the belief that the person to whom the property belongs cannot be discovered by taking reasonable steps.
(2)   A person's appropriation of property belonging to another may be dishonest notwithstanding that he is willing to pay for the property.

[9.82]
3   "Appropriates"
(1)   Any assumption by a person of the rights of an owner amounts to an appropriation, and this includes, where he has come by the property (innocently or not) without stealing it, any later assumption of a right to it by keeping or dealing with it as owner.

(2)   Where property or a right or interest in property is or purports to be transferred for value to a person acting in good faith, no later assumption by him of rights which he believed himself to be acquiring shall, by reason of any defect in the transferor's title, amount to theft of the property.

[9.83]
4   "Property"
(1)   "Property" includes money and all other property, real or personal, including things in action and other intangible property.

(2)   A person cannot steal land, or things forming part of land and severed from it by him or by his directions, except in the following cases, that is to say—

- (a)   when he is a trustee or personal representative, or is authorised by power of attorney, or as liquidator of a company, or otherwise, to sell or dispose of land belonging to another, and he appropriates the land or anything forming part of it by dealing with it in breach of the confidence reposed in him; or
- (b)   when he is not in possession of the land and appropriates anything forming part of the land by severing it or causing it to be severed, or after it has been severed; or
- (c)   when, being in possession of the land under a tenancy, he appropriates the whole or part of any fixture or structure let to be used with the land.

For purposes of this subsection "land" does not include incorporeal hereditaments; "tenancy" means a tenancy for years or any less period and includes an agreement for such a tenancy, but a person who after the end of a tenancy remains in possession as statutory tenant or otherwise is to be treated as having possession under the tenancy, and "let" shall be construed accordingly.

(3)   A person who picks mushrooms growing wild on any land, or who picks flowers, fruit or foliage from a plant growing wild on any land, does not (although not in possession of the land) steal what he picks, unless he does it for reward or for sale or other commercial purpose.

For purposes of this subsection "mushroom" includes any fungus, and "plant" includes any shrub or tree.

(4)   Wild creatures, tamed or untamed, shall be regarded as property; but a person cannot steal a wild creature not tamed nor ordinarily kept in captivity, or the carcase of any such creature, unless either it has been reduced into possession by or on behalf of another person and possession of it has not since been lost or abandoned, or another person is in course of reducing it into possession.

[9.84]
5   "Belonging to another"
(1)   Property shall be regarded as belonging to any person having possession or control of it, or having in it any proprietary right or interest (not being an equitable interest arising only from an agreement to transfer or grant an interest).

(2)   Where property is subject to a trust, the persons to whom it belongs shall be regarded as including any person having a right to enforce the trust, and an intention to defeat the trust shall be regarded accordingly as an intention to deprive of the property any person having that right.

(3)   Where a person receives property from or on account of another, and is under an obligation to the other to retain and deal with that property or its proceeds in a particular way, the property or proceeds shall be regarded (as against him) as belonging to the other.

(4)   Where a person gets property by another's mistake, and is under an obligation to make restoration (in whole or in part) of the property or its proceeds or of the value thereof, then to the extent of that obligation the property or proceeds shall be regarded (as against him) as belonging to the person entitled to restoration, and an intention not to make restoration shall be regarded accordingly as an intention to deprive that person of the property or proceeds.

(5)   Property of a corporation sole shall be regarded as belonging to the corporation notwithstanding a vacancy in the corporation.

[9.85]
6   "With the intention of permanently depriving the other of it"
(1)   A person appropriating property belonging to another without meaning the other permanently to lose the thing itself is nevertheless to be regarded as having the intention of permanently depriving the other of it if his intention is to treat the thing as his own to dispose of regardless of the other's rights; and a borrowing or lending of it may amount to so treating it if, but only if, the borrowing or lending is for a period and in circumstances making it equivalent to an outright taking or disposal.

(2)   Without prejudice to the generality of subsection (1) above, where a person, having possession or control (lawfully or not) of property belonging to another, parts with the property under a condition as to its return which he may not be able to perform, this (if done for purposes of his own and without the other's authority) amounts to treating the property as his own to dispose of regardless of the other's rights.

Theft, Robbery, Burglary, etc

[9.86]
7   Theft

A person guilty of theft shall on conviction on indictment be liable to imprisonment for a term not exceeding [seven years].

NOTES

Words in square brackets substituted by the Criminal Justice Act 1991, s 26(1), as from 1 October 1992.

Fraud and blackmail

15, 15A, 15B, 16   *(Repealed by the Fraud Act 2006, s 14(1), (3), Sch 1, paras 1(a), 3, Sch 3, as from 15 January 2007 (subject to savings and transitional provisions in relation to any liability, investigation, legal proceeding or penalty for, or in respect of, any offence partly committed before that date; see Sch 2, para 3 to the 2006 Act).)*

[9.87]
17   False accounting

(1)   Where a person dishonestly, with a view to gain for himself or another or with intent to cause loss to another,—

  (a)   destroys, defaces, conceals or falsifies any account or any record or document made or required for any accounting purpose; or

  (b)   in furnishing information for any purpose produces or makes use of any account, or any such record or document as aforesaid, which to his knowledge is or may be misleading, false or deceptive in a material particular;

he shall, on conviction on indictment, be liable to imprisonment for a term not exceeding seven years.

(2)   For purposes of this section a person who makes or concurs in making in an account or other document an entry which is or may be misleading, false or deceptive in a material particular, or who omits or concurs in omitting a material particular from an account or other document, is to be treated as falsifying the account or document.

NOTES

Serious crime prevention orders: a court may make a serious crime prevention order under the Serious Crime Act 2007, ss 1, 19 if it is satisfied that a person has been involved in serious crime, and it has reasonable grounds to believe that the order would protect the public by preventing, restricting or disrupting involvement by the person in serious crime. By virtue of s 2 of, and Sch 1 to, the 2007 Act, the offence under this section is a serious crime.

[9.88]
18   Liability of company officers for certain offences by company

(1)   Where an offence committed by a body corporate under section . . . 17 of this Act is proved to have been committed with the consent or connivance of any director, manager, secretary or other similar officer of the body corporate, or any person who was purporting to act in any such capacity, he as well as the body corporate shall be guilty of that offence, and shall be liable to be proceeded against and punished accordingly.

(2)   Where the affairs of a body corporate are managed by its members, this section shall apply in relation to the acts and defaults of a member in connection with his functions of management as if he were a director of the body corporate.

NOTES

Sub-s (1): words omitted repealed by the Fraud Act 2006, s 14(1), (3), Sch 1, para 4, Sch 3, as from 15 January 2007.

[9.89]
19   False statements by company directors, etc

(1)   Where an officer of a body corporate or unincorporated association (or person purporting to act as such), with intent to deceive members or creditors of the body corporate or association about its affairs, publishes or concurs in publishing a written statement or account which to his knowledge is or may be misleading, false or deceptive in a material particular, he shall on conviction on indictment be liable to imprisonment for a term not exceeding seven years.

(2)   For purposes of this section a person who has entered into a security for the benefit of a body corporate or association is to be treated as a creditor of it.

(3)   Where the affairs of a body corporate or association are managed by its members, this section shall apply to any statement which a member publishes or concurs in publishing in connection with his functions of management as if he were an officer of the body corporate or association.

[9.90]

20   Suppression, etc of documents

(1)   A person who dishonestly, with a view to gain for himself or another or with intent to cause loss to another, destroys, defaces or conceals any valuable security, any will or other testamentary document or any original document of or belonging to, or filed or deposited in, any court of justice or any government department shall on conviction on indictment be liable to imprisonment for a term not exceeding seven years.

(2)   . . .

(3)   For purposes of this section   . . .   "valuable security" means any document creating, transferring, surrendering or releasing any right to, in or over property, or authorising the payment of money or delivery of any property, or evidencing the creation, transfer, surrender or release of any such right, or the payment of money or delivery of any property, or the satisfaction of any obligation.

NOTES

Sub-s (2): repealed by the Fraud Act 2006, s 14(1), (3), Sch 1, para 1(a)(iv), Sch 3, as from 15 January 2007 (subject to savings and transitional provisions in relation to any liability, investigation, legal proceeding or penalty for, or in respect of, any offence partly committed before the commencement of this repeal, see Sch 2, para 3 to the 2006 Act).

Sub-s (3): words omitted repealed by the Fraud Act 2006, s 14(1), (3), Sch 1, para 5, Sch 3, as from 15 January 2007.

Supplementary

[9.91]

35   Commencement and transitional provisions

(1)   This Act shall come into force on the 1st January 1969 and, save as otherwise provided by this Act, shall have effect only in relation to offences wholly or partly committed on or after that date.

(2), (3)   (*Outside the scope of this work.*)

[9.92]

36   Short title, and general provisions as to Scotland and Northern Ireland

(1)   This Act may be cited as the Theft Act 1968.

(2)   . . .

(3)   This Act does not extend to Scotland or,   . . .   to Northern Ireland, except as regards any amendment or repeal which in accordance with section 33 above is to extend to Scotland or Northern Ireland.

NOTES

Sub-s (2): repealed by the Northern Ireland Constitution Act 1973, s 41(1), Sch 6, Pt I, as from 18 July 1973.

Sub-s (3): words omitted repealed by the Northern Ireland Constitution Act 1973, s 41(1), Sch 6, Pt I, as from 18 July 1973.

INSOLVENCY ACT 1986

(1986 c 45)

NOTES

Commencement: this Act came into force on 29 December 1986 by virtue of s 443 and the Insolvency Act 1985 (Commencement No 5) Order 1986, SI 1986/1924.

Rules: see the Insolvency Rules 1986, SI 1986/1925 at **[10.1]**.

Application of this Act: this Act is applied, with certain modifications, to various types of business and financial sectors, etc, as follows:

Limited liability partnerships: as to the application of this Act to LLPs, see the notes below:

(1) The Limited Liability Partnerships Regulations 2001, SI 2001/1090, reg 5(1) applies Parts I, II, III, IV, VI and VII of the First Group of Parts, and the whole of the Third Group of Parts, to limited liability partnerships (see reg 5(1) at **[10.817]**). For general modifications of this Act in its application to LLPs see reg 5(2) of those Regulations, and for specific modifications see Sch 3 (at **[10.825]**). See also reg 5(3) of, and Sch 4 to, those Regulations (which provide that certain provisions of the First and Third Groups of Parts which are applied to LLPs by reg 5(1) do not apply to Scotland).

(2) As to the application of this Act in relation to LLPs in Scotland, see also the Limited Liability Partnerships (Scotland) Regulations 2001, SSI 2001/128. Regulation 4(1) of those Regulations (at **[10.805]**) applies the provisions of this Act specified in Sch 2 to those Regulations (at **[10.809]**) to Scotland, subject to the general modifications provided for by reg 4(2), and the specific modifications provided for by Sch 3 (at **[10.810]**).

(3) In so far as s 201 applies to LLPs by virtue of the Limited Liability Partnerships Regulations 2001, SI 2001/1090, the substitution of the words "a copy" for the original words "an office copy" in sub-s (4) has no effect; see the Companies (Registrar, Languages and Trading Disclosures) Regulations 2006, SI 2006/3429, reg 3(3) at **[4.4]**.

Banks: as to the application of certain provisions of this Act to particular banks, see the Banking (Special Provisions) Act 2008 and the Orders made under it. As to the application of this Act to banks generally, see the Banking Act 2009 and see, in particular Part 2 of that Act (bank insolvency) and Part 3 (bank administration) and the Orders and Regulations made under those Parts.

Former authorised institutions: see the Banks (Former Authorised Institutions) (Insolvency) Order 2006, SI 2006/3107 as to the application of Part II of, and Sch B1 to, this Act, to any company within the meaning of s 735(1) of the Companies Act 1985 that (a) has a liability in respect of a deposit which it accepted in accordance with the Banking Act 1979 or Banking Act 1987, but (b) does not have permission under Part IV of the Financial Services and Markets Act 2000 to accept deposits.

EEA credit institutions: as to the application of this Act to EEA credit institutions or any branch of an EEA credit institution, see the Credit Institutions (Reorganisation and Winding up) Regulations 2004, SI 2004/1045.

Insurers: as to the application of this Act to insurers, see the Insurers (Reorganisation and Winding Up) Regulations 2004, SI 2004/353, and the Financial Services and Markets Act 2000 (Administration Orders Relating to Insurers) Order 2010, SI 2010/3023.

European Economic Interest Groupings: as to the application of this Act to European Economic Interest Groupings, see the European Economic Interest Grouping Regulations 1989, SI 1989/638, reg 19.

Open-ended investment companies: as to the application of this Act to open-ended investment companies, see the Open-Ended Investment Companies Regulations 2001, SI 2001/1228, reg 31.

Companies incorporated outside Great Britain: the Enterprise Act 2002, s 254 provides that the Secretary of State may by order provide for a provision of this Act to apply (with or without modification) in relation to a company incorporated outside Great Britain. As of 1 July 2011 no Orders had been made under that section.

Non-companies: the Enterprise Act 2002, s 255 provides that the Treasury may with the concurrence of the Secretary of State by order provide for a company arrangement or administration provision to apply (ie, Pts I, II) in relation to (a) a society registered under the Industrial and Provident Societies Act 1965 (see the Co-operative and Community Benefit Societies and Credit Unions Act 2010 which renames this Act as the Co-operative and Community Benefit Societies and Credit Unions Act 1965); (b) a society registered under the Friendly Societies Act 1974, s 7(1)(b), (c), (d), (e) or (f); (c) a friendly society within the meaning of the Friendly Societies Act 1992; (d) an unregistered friendly society. As of 1 July 2011 no Orders had been made under that section.

Special administration regimes: see the notes to s 8 of this Act at **[9.105]**; and, with regard to companies which hold a licence under the Electricity Act 1989, s 6(1)(b) or (c) (transmission and distribution licences for electricity) or the Gas Act 1986, s 7 (licensing of gas transporters), see the Energy Act 2004, ss 154–171, Schs 20, 21.

European Grouping of Territorial Cooperation: see the European Grouping of Territorial Cooperation Regulations 2007, SI 2007/1949.

Banks authorised to issue banknotes in Scotland and Northern Ireland (other than the Bank of England): see the Scottish and Northern Ireland Banknote Regulations 2009, SI 2009/3056.

Other bodies etc: see (i) the Friendly Societies Act 1992, ss 23, 52, Sch 10 (application to incorporated and registered friendly societies) (see also the note 'Non companies' above); (ii) the Industrial and Provident Societies Act 1965, ss 55–58 (application to industrial and provident societies) (see also the note 'Non companies' above); (iii) the Agricultural Marketing Act 1958, s 3(3), Sch 2, para 4 (application to agricultural marketing boards); (iv) the European Public Limited-Liability Company Regulations 2004, SI 2004/2326 at **[10.851]** (application to Societas Europaea); (v) CA 1989, s 182 at **[5.135]** (application to certain proceedings begun before the commencement of that section in respect of insolvency proceedings regarding members of recognised investment exchanges and clearing houses and persons to whom market charges have been granted); (vi) the Solicitors' Incorporated Practices Order 1991, SI 1991/2684, arts 2–5, Sch 1 (application to a "recognised body" within the meaning of the Administration of Justice Act 1985, s 9); (vi) the National Health Service Act 2006, ss 52–55 (application to NHS foundation trusts); (vii) the Postal Services Act 2011 (Postal administration orders).

See also the powers to apply this Act in s 420 at **[9.382]** (insolvent partnerships) and s 422 at **[9.383]** (formerly authorised banks).

Other Modifications, etc:

Cross-Border insolvency proceedings: British insolvency law (as defined in Article 2 of the UNCITRAL Model Law as set out in Schedule 1 to the Cross-Border Insolvency Regulations 2006, SI 2006/1030) and Part III of this Act shall apply with such modifications as the context requires for the purpose of giving effect to the provisions of the 2006 Regulations; see reg 2 of the 2006 Regulations.

Scotland: by virtue of the Scotland Act 1998, s 125, Sch 8, para 23 (as amended): (i) anything directed to be done, or which may be done, to or by the registrar of companies in Scotland by virtue of ss 53(1), 54(3), 61(6), 62(5) (so far as relating to the giving of notice), 67(1), 69(2), 84(3), 94(3), 106(3) and (5), 112(3), 130(1), 147(3), 170(2) and 172(8), or by the FSA by virtue of any of those provisions as applied (with or without modification) in relation to friendly societies, industrial and provident societies or building societies, shall, or (as the case may be) may, also be done to or by the Accountant in Bankruptcy, and (ii) anything directed to be done to or by the registrar of companies in Scotland by virtue of ss 89(3), 109(1), 171(5) and (6), 173(2)(a) and 192(1), or by the FSA by virtue of any of those provisions as applied (with or without modification) in relation to friendly societies, industrial and provident societies or building societies, shall instead be done to or by the Accountant in Bankruptcy.

Miscellaneous:

Registrar of companies: as to the contracting out of certain functions of the registrar of companies in relation to Scotland conferred by or under this Act, see the Contracting Out (Functions in relation to the Registration of Companies) Order 1995, SI 1995/1013, art 4, Sch 2 at **[10.750]**, **[10.753]**.

Official Receiver: as to the contracting out of functions of the Official Receiver conferred by or under this Act, see the Contracting Out (Functions of the Official Receiver) Order 1995, SI 1995/1386 at **[10.755]**.

Proceeds of crime: if an order for the winding up of a company is made or it passes a resolution for its voluntary winding up, the functions of the liquidator (or any provisional liquidator) are not exercisable in relation to property deemed to be the proceeds of crime; see the Proceeds of Crime Act 2002, Pt 9 (ss 417–434).

See the Serious Crime Act 2007, ss 27, 29 in relation to the power of the Director of Public Prosecutions, the Director of Revenue and Customs Prosecutions and the Director of the Serious Fraud Office to present a petition to the court for the winding up of a company, partnership (etc) where the company, partnership (etc) has been convicted of an offence under s 25 of that Act (offence of failing to comply with serious crime prevention order) and the Director concerned considers that it would be in the public interest for the company, partnership (etc) to be wound up.

Only those provisions of this Act relating to company law are reproduced. Provisions not reproduced are not annotated.

This Act is reproduced as amended by the following Acts:

1988	Court of Session Act 1988; Criminal Justice Act 1988; ICTA 1988.
1989	CA 1989; Water Act 1989.
1990	Broadcasting Act 1990; Courts and Legal Services Act 1990; Law Reform (Miscellaneous Provisions) (Scotland) Act 1990.
1991	FA 1991; Water Consolidation (Consequential Provisions) Act 1991.
1992	F (No 2) A 1992; Social Security (Consequential Provisions) Act 1992; Transport and Works Act 1992; Tribunals and Inquiries Act 1992.

1993	Bankruptcy (Scotland) Act 1993; FA 1993; Pension Schemes Act 1993; Railways Act 1993; Statute Law (Repeals) Act 1993.
1994	FA 1994; Insolvency Act 1994; Insolvency (No 2) Act 1994; Value Added Tax Act 1994.
1995	Criminal Procedure (Consequential Provisions) (Scotland) Act 1995; FA 1995; Gas Act 1995; Requirements of Writing (Scotland) Act 1995.
1996	Employment Rights Act 1996; FA 1996.
1997	FA 1997.
1998	Bank of England Act 1998; Government of Wales Act 1998; Northern Ireland Act 1998; Scotland Act 1998.
1999	Access to Justice Act 1999; Youth Justice and Criminal Evidence Act 1999.
2000	Abolition of Feudal Tenure etc (Scotland) Act 2000; Adults with Incapacity (Scotland) Act 2000; FA 2000; Insolvency Act 2000; Utilities Act 2000.
2001	FA 2001.
2002	Commonhold and Leasehold Reform Act 2002; Enterprise Act 2002; Income Tax (Earnings and Pensions) Act 2003.
2003	Communications Act 2003; Courts Act 2003.
2004	Companies (Audit, Investigations and Community Enterprise) Act 2004; Civil Partnership Act 2004.
2005	Constitutional Reform Act 2005; Mental Capacity Act 2005.
2006	Government of Wales Act 2006; Companies Act 2006.
2007	Bankruptcy and Diligence etc (Scotland) Act 2007; Tribunals, Courts and Enforcement Act 2007.
2009	Banking Act 2009.

This Act is reproduced as amended by the following SIs:

1986	Insolvency Proceedings (Monetary Limits) Order 1986, SI 1986/1996.
1987	Insolvency (ECSC Levy Debts) Regulations 1987, SI 1987/2093.
1989	Companies (Northern Ireland) Order 1989, SI 1989/2404; Insolvency (Northern Ireland) Order 1989, SI 1989/2405.
1992	Companies (Single Member Private Limited Companies) Regulations 1992, SI 1992/1699.
1994	Insolvent Partnerships Order 1994, SI 1994/2421.
1999	Scotland Act 1998 (Consequential Modifications) (No 2) Order 1999, SI 1999/1820.
2001	Limited Liability Partnerships (Scotland) Regulations 2001, SSI 2001/128; Limited Liability Partnerships Regulations 2001, SI 2001/1090; Financial Services and Markets Act 2000 (Consequential Amendments and Repeals) Order 2001, SI 2001/3649.
2002	Insolvency Act 1986 (Amendment) Regulations 2002, SI 2002/1037; Insolvency Act 1986 (Amendment) (No 2) Regulations 2002, SI 2002/1240; Financial Services and Markets Act 2000 (Consequential Amendments) Order 2002, SI 2002/1555; Insolvency Act 1986 (Amendment) (No 3) Regulations 2002, SI 2002/1990; Insolvent Partnerships (Amendment) (No 2) Order 2002, SI 2002/2708; Company Directors Disqualification (Northern Ireland) Order 2002, SI 2002/3150.
2003	Insolvency Act 1986 (Amendment) (Administrative Receivership and Capital Market Arrangements) Order 2003, SI 2003/1468; Insolvency Act 1986 (Amendment) (Administrative Receivership and Urban Regeneration etc) Order 2003, SI 2003/1832; Enterprise Act 2002 (Insolvency) Order 2003, SI 2003/2096.
2004	Water Industry (Scotland) Act 2002 (Consequential Modifications) Order 2004, SI 2004/1822; Insolvency Act 2000 (Company Directors Disqualification Undertakings) Order 2004, SI 2004/1941; Enterprise Act 2002 (Insolvency) Order 2004, SI 2004/2312; European Public Limited-Liability Company Regulations 2004, SI 2004/2326.
2005	Insolvency Act 1986 (Amendment) Regulations 2005, SI 2005/879; Mental Health (Care and Treatment) (Scotland) Act 2003 (Consequential Provisions) Order 2005, SI 2005/2078; Mental Health (Care and Treatment) (Scotland) Act 2003 (Modification of Enactments) Order 2005, SSI 2005/486; Railway (Licensing of Railway Undertakings) Regulations 2005, SI 2005/3050; Civil Partnership Act 2004 (Overseas Relationships and Consequential, etc Amendments) Order 2005, SI 2005/3129.
2006	European Cooperative Society Regulations 2006, SI 2006/2078; Companies (Registrar, Languages and Trading Disclosures) Regulations 2006, SI 2006/3429.
2007	Companies Act 2006 (Commencement No 3, Consequential Amendments, Transitional Provisions and Savings) Order 2007, SI 2007/2194; Companies (Cross-Border Mergers) Regulations 2007, SI 2007/2974.
2008	Companies Act 2006 (Consequential Amendments etc) Order 2008, SI 2008/948; the Companies (Trading Disclosures) (Insolvency) Regulations 2008, SI 2008/1897.
2009	Building Societies (Insolvency and Special Administration) Order 2009, SI 2009/805; Legislative Reform (Insolvency) (Advertising Requirements) Order 2009, SI 2009/864; Companies Act 2006 (Consequential Amendments, Transitional Provisions and Savings) Order 2009, SI 2009/1941; Provision of Services (Insolvency Practitioners) Regulations 2009, SI 2009/3081.
2010	Legislative Reform (Insolvency) (Miscellaneous Provisions) Order 2010, SI 2010/18; Financial Services and Markets Act 2000 (Regulated Activities) (Amendment) Order 2010, SI 2010/86; Housing and Regeneration Act 2008 (Consequential Provisions) Order 2010, SI 2010/866.
2011	Insolvency Act 1986 Amendment (Appointment of Receivers) (Scot) Regulations 2011, SSI 2011/140; Companies Act 2006 (Consequential Amendments and Transitional Provisions) Order 2011, SI 2011/1265.

CHAPTER III
RECEIVERS' POWERS IN GREAT BRITAIN AS A WHOLE

CHAPTER IV
PROHIBITION OF APPOINTMENT OF ADMINISTRATIVE RECEIVER

PART IV
WINDING UP OF COMPANIES REGISTERED UNDER THE COMPANIES ACTS

CHAPTER I
PRELIMINARY

Introductory

Contributories

CHAPTER II
VOLUNTARY WINDING UP (INTRODUCTORY AND GENERAL)

Resolutions for, and commencement of, voluntary winding up

Consequences of resolution to wind up

CHAPTER VII
LIQUIDATORS

An Act to consolidate the enactments relating to company insolvency and winding up (including the winding up of companies that are not insolvent, and of unregistered companies); enactments relating to the insolvency and bankruptcy of individuals; and other enactments bearing on those two subject matters, including the functions and qualification of insolvency practitioners, the public administration of insolvency, the penalisation and redress of malpractice and wrongdoing, and the avoidance of certain transactions at an undervalue

[25 July 1986]

THE FIRST GROUP OF PARTS
COMPANY INSOLVENCY; COMPANIES WINDING UP

PART I
COMPANY VOLUNTARY ARRANGEMENTS

The proposal

[9.93]
1   Those who may propose an arrangement
(1)   The directors of a company [(other than one which is in administration or being wound up)] may make a proposal under this Part to the company and to its creditors for a composition in satisfaction of its debts or a scheme of arrangement of its affairs (from here on referred to, in either case, as a "voluntary arrangement").

(2)   A proposal under this Part is one which provides for some person ("the nominee") to act in relation to the voluntary arrangement either as trustee or otherwise for the purpose of supervising its implementation; and the nominee must be a person who is qualified to act as an insolvency practitioner [or authorised to act as nominee, in relation to the voluntary arrangement].

(3)   Such a proposal may also be made—
   [(a)   where the company is in administration, by the administrator,] and
   (b)   where the company is being wound up, by the liquidator.
[(4)   In this Part "company" means—
   [(a)   a company registered under the Companies Act 2006 in England and Wales or Scotland;]
   (b)   a company incorporated in an EEA State other than the United Kingdom; or
   (c)   a company not incorporated in an EEA State but having its centre of main interests in a member State other than Denmark.
(5)   In subsection (4), in relation to a company, "centre of main interests" has the same meaning as in the EC Regulation and, in the absence of proof to the contrary, is presumed to be the place of its registered office (within the meaning of that Regulation).
(6)   If a company incorporated outside the United Kingdom has a principal place of business in Northern Ireland, no proposal under this Part shall be made in relation to it unless it also has a principal place of business in England and Wales or Scotland (or both in England and Wales or Scotland).]

NOTES
Sub-s (1): words in square brackets substituted by the Enterprise Act 2002, s 248(3), Sch 17, paras 9, 10(a), as from 15 September 2003 (for savings and transitional provisions, see the note to s 8 at **[9.105]**).

Sub-s (2): words in square brackets substituted by the Insolvency Act 2000, s 2, Sch 2, Pt I, paras 1, 2, as from 1 January 2003 (for transitional provisions see the note below).

Sub-s (3): para (a) substituted by the Enterprise Act 2002, s 248(3), Sch 17, paras 9, 10(b), as from 15 September 2003 (for savings and transitional provisions, see the note to s 8 at **[9.105]**).

Sub-ss (4)–(6): substituted (for the original sub-s (4) as added by the Insolvency Act 1986 (Amendment) (No 2) Regulations 2002, SI 2002/1240, regs 3, 4, as from 31 May 2002) by the Insolvency Act 1986 (Amendment) Regulations 2005, SI 2005/879, reg 2(1), (2), as from 13 April 2005, except in relation to any voluntary arrangement under this Part that took effect before that date. Sub-s (4)(a) subsequently substituted by the Companies Act 2006 (Consequential Amendments, Transitional Provisions and Savings) Order 2009, SI 2009/1941, art 2(1), Sch 1, para 71(1), (2), as from 1 October 2009 (for transitional provisions see the note to s 7A at **[9.103]**).

Transitional provisions: the Insolvency Act 2000 (Commencement No 3 and Transitional Provisions) Order 2002, SI 2002/2711, art 3 provides for the following transitional provisions (note that by virtue of arts 1, 2, the "appointed day" means 1 January 2003):

   "(1)   In a case where—
      (a)   a proposal is made by the directors of a company and before the appointed day the intended nominee has endorsed a copy of the written notice of the proposal under Rule 1.4(3) of the Insolvency Rules, or, in Scotland, under Rule 1.4(3) of the Insolvency (Scotland) Rules;
      (b)   a proposal is made by the liquidator or the administrator (acting as nominee) and before the appointed day the liquidator or administrator (as the case may be) has sent out a notice summoning the meetings under section 3 of the Act as required by Rule 1.11 of the Insolvency Rules, or, in Scotland, by Rule 1.11 of the Insolvency (Scotland) Rules; or
      (c)   a proposal is made by the liquidator or the administrator of a company (not acting as the nominee) and before the appointed day the intended nominee has endorsed a copy of the written notice of the proposal under Rule 1.12(2) of the Insolvency Rules, or, in Scotland, Rule 1.12(2) of the Insolvency (Scotland) Rules,
   the amendments made to the Act by Part I of Schedule 2 and the repeal made by section 15(1) and Schedule 5 in respect of section 5(2) and (3) of the Act shall not apply and the provisions of the Act as they have effect immediately before the appointed day shall continue to have effect.
   (2)   The provisions of paragraph (1) shall—
      (a)   apply in relation to building societies as they apply in relation to companies; and
      (b)   in their application to building societies, have effect with the substitution for "company" of "building society".
   (3)   In this article "proposal" has the same meaning as it has in section 1(2) of the Act.".

[9.94]

[1A Moratorium

(1) Where the directors of an eligible company intend to make a proposal for a voluntary arrangement, they may take steps to obtain a moratorium for the company.

(2) The provisions of Schedule A1 to this Act have effect with respect to—

(a) companies eligible for a moratorium under this section,

(b) the procedure for obtaining such a moratorium,

(c) the effects of such a moratorium, and

(d) the procedure applicable (in place of sections 2 to 6 and 7) in relation to the approval and implementation of a voluntary arrangement where such a moratorium is or has been in force.]

NOTES

Inserted by the Insolvency Act 2000, s 1, Sch 1, paras 1, 2, as from 1 January 2003.

[9.95]

2   Procedure where nominee is not the liquidator or administrator

(1) This section applies where the nominee under section 1 is not the liquidator or administrator of the company [and the directors do not propose to take steps to obtain a moratorium under section 1A for the company].

(2) The nominee shall, within 28 days (or such longer period as the court may allow) after he is given notice of the proposal for a voluntary arrangement, submit a report to the court stating—

(a) [whether, in his opinion, the proposed voluntary arrangement has a reasonable prospect of being approved and implemented,

(aa)] whether, in his opinion, meetings of the company and of its creditors should be summoned to consider the proposal, and

(b) if in his opinion such meetings should be summoned, the date on which, and time and place at which, he proposes the meetings should be held.

(3) For the purposes of enabling the nominee to prepare his report, the person intending to make the proposal shall submit to the nominee—

(a) a document setting out the terms of the proposed voluntary arrangement, and

(b) a statement of the company's affairs containing—

    (i) such particulars of its creditors and of its debts and other liabilities and of its assets as may be prescribed, and

    (ii) such other information as may be prescribed.

[(4) The court may—

(a) on an application made by the person intending to make the proposal, in a case where the nominee has failed to submit the report required by this section or has died, or

(b) on an application made by that person or the nominee, in a case where it is impracticable or inappropriate for the nominee to continue to act as such,

direct that the nominee be replaced as such by another person qualified to act as an insolvency practitioner, or authorised to act as nominee, in relation to the voluntary arrangement.]

NOTES

Sub-s (1): words in square brackets added by the Insolvency Act 2000, s 1, Sch 1, paras 1, 3, as from 1 January 2003.

Sub-s (2): words in square brackets inserted by the Insolvency Act 2000, s 2, Sch 2, Pt I, paras 1, 3(a), as from 1 January 2003 (for transitional provisions see the note to s 1 at **[9.93]**).

Sub-s (4): substituted by the Insolvency Act 2000, s 2, Sch 2, Pt I, paras 1, 3(b), as from 1 January 2003 (for transitional provisions see the note to s 1 at **[9.93]**).

[9.96]

3   Summoning of meetings

(1) Where the nominee under section 1 is not the liquidator or administrator, and it has been reported to the court that such meetings as are mentioned in section 2(2) should be summoned, the person making the report shall (unless the court otherwise directs) summon those meetings for the time, date and place proposed in the report.

(2) Where the nominee is the liquidator or administrator, he shall summon meetings of the company and of its creditors to consider the proposal for such a time, date and place as he thinks fit.

(3) The persons to be summoned to a creditors' meeting under this section are every creditor of the company of whose claim and address the person summoning the meeting is aware.

Consideration and implementation of proposal

[9.97]

4   Decisions of meetings

(1) The meetings summoned under section 3 shall decide whether to approve the proposed voluntary arrangement (with or without modifications).

(2) The modifications may include one conferring the functions proposed to be conferred on the nominee on another person qualified to act as an insolvency practitioner [or authorised to act as nominee, in relation to the voluntary arrangement].

But they shall not include any modification by virtue of which the proposal ceases to be a proposal such as is mentioned in section 1.

(3)   A meeting so summoned shall not approve any proposal or modification which affects the right of a secured creditor of the company to enforce his security, except with the concurrence of the creditor concerned.

(4)   Subject as follows, a meeting so summoned shall not approve any proposal or modification under which—

    (a)   any preferential debt of the company is to be paid otherwise than in priority to such of its debts as are not preferential debts, or

    (b)   a preferential creditor of the company is to be paid an amount in respect of a preferential debt that bears to that debt a smaller proportion than is borne to another preferential debt by the amount that is to be paid in respect of that other debt.

However, the meeting may approve such a proposal or modification with the concurrence of the preferential creditor concerned.

(5)   Subject as above, each of the meetings shall be conducted in accordance with the rules.

(6)   After the conclusion of either meeting in accordance with the rules, the chairman of the meeting shall report the result of the meeting to the court, and, immediately after reporting to the court, shall give notice of the result of the meeting to such persons as may be prescribed.

(7)   References in this section to preferential debts and preferential creditors are to be read in accordance with section 386 in Part XII of this Act.

NOTES

    Sub-s (2): words in square brackets substituted by the Insolvency Act 2000, s 2, Sch 2, Pt I, paras 1, 4, as from 1 January 2003 (for transitional provisions see the note to s 1 at **[9.93]**).

[9.98]
[4A   Approval of arrangement

(1)   This section applies to a decision, under section 4, with respect to the approval of a proposed voluntary arrangement.

(2)   The decision has effect if, in accordance with the rules—

    (a)   it has been taken by both meetings summoned under section 3, or

    (b)   (subject to any order made under subsection (4)) it has been taken by the creditors' meeting summoned under that section.

(3)   If the decision taken by the creditors' meeting differs from that taken by the company meeting, a member of the company may apply to the court.

(4)   An application under subsection (3) shall not be made after the end of the period of 28 days beginning with—

    (a)   the day on which the decision was taken by the creditors' meeting, or

    (b)   where the decision of the company meeting was taken on a later day, that day.

(5)   Where a member of a regulated company, within the meaning given by paragraph 44 of Schedule A1, applies to the court under subsection (3), the Financial Services Authority is entitled to be heard on the application.

(6)   On an application under subsection (3), the court may—

    (a)   order the decision of the company meeting to have effect instead of the decision of the creditors' meeting, or

    (b)   make such other order as it thinks fit.]

NOTES

    Inserted by the Insolvency Act 2000, s 2, Sch 2, Pt I, paras 1, 5, as from 1 January 2003 (for transitional provisions see the note to s 1 at **[9.93]**).

[9.99]
5   Effect of approval

[(1)   This section applies where a decision approving a voluntary arrangement has effect under section 4A.]

(2)   The . . . voluntary arrangement—

    (a)   takes effect as if made by the company at the creditors' meeting, and

    [(b)   binds every person who in accordance with the rules—

        (i)   was entitled to vote at that meeting (whether or not he was present or represented at it), or

        (ii)   would have been so entitled if he had had notice of it,

    as if he were a party to the voluntary arrangement.]

[(2A)   If—

    (a)   when the arrangement ceases to have effect any amount payable under the arrangement to a person bound by virtue of subsection (2)(b)(ii) has not been paid, and

    (b)   the arrangement did not come to an end prematurely,

the company shall at that time become liable to pay to that person the amount payable under the arrangement.]

(3)   Subject as follows, if the company is being wound up or [is in administration], the court may do one or both of the following, namely—

  (a)   by order stay or sist all proceedings in the winding up or [provide for the appointment of the administrator to cease to have effect];

  (b)   give such directions with respect to the conduct of the winding up or the administration as it thinks appropriate for facilitating the implementation of the . . . voluntary arrangement.

(4)   The court shall not make an order under subsection (3)(a)—

  (a)   at any time before the end of the period of 28 days beginning with the first day on which each of the reports required by section 4(6) has been made to the court, or

  (b)   at any time when an application under the next section or an appeal in respect of such an application is pending, or at any time in the period within which such an appeal may be brought.

NOTES

Sub-s (1): substituted by the Insolvency Act 2000, s 2, Sch 2, Pt I, paras 1, 6(a), as from 1 January 2003 (for transitional provisions see the note to s 1 at **[9.93]**).

Sub-s (2): word omitted repealed, and para (b) substituted (together with sub-s (2A) for original para (b)), by the Insolvency Act 2000, ss 2, 15(1), Sch 2, Pt I, paras 1, 6(b), (c), Sch 5, as from 1 January 2003 (for transitional provisions see the note to s 1 at **[9.93]**).

Sub-s (2A): substituted as noted above.

Sub-s (3): words in square brackets substituted by the Enterprise Act 2002, s 248(3), Sch 17, paras 9, 11, as from 15 September 2003 (for savings and transitional provisions, see the note to s 8 at **[9.105]**); word omitted repealed by the Insolvency Act 2000, ss 2, 15(1), Sch 2, Pt I, paras 1, 6(b), Sch 5, as from 1 January 2003 (for transitional provisions see the note to s 1 at **[9.93]**).

[9.100]
6   Challenge of decisions

(1)   Subject to this section, an application to the court may be made, by any of the persons specified below, on one or both of the following grounds, namely—

  (a)   that a voluntary arrangement [which has effect under section 4A] unfairly prejudices the interests of a creditor, member or contributory of the company;

  (b)   that there has been some material irregularity at or in relation to either of the meetings.

(2)   The persons who may apply under this section are—

  (a)   a person entitled, in accordance with the rules, to vote at either of the meetings;

  [(aa) a person who would have been entitled, in accordance with the rules, to vote at the creditors' meeting if he had had notice of it]

  (b)   the nominee or any person who has replaced him under section 2(4) or 4(2); and

  (c)   if the company is being wound up or [is in administration], the liquidator or administrator.

(3)   An application under this section shall not be made

  [(a)] after the end of the period of 28 days beginning with the first day on which each of the reports required by section 4(6) has been made to the court [or

  (b)   in the case of a person who was not given notice of the creditors' meeting, after the end of the period of 28 days beginning with the day on which he became aware that the meeting had taken place,

but (subject to that) an application made by a person within subsection (2)(aa) on the ground that the voluntary arrangement prejudices his interests may be made after the arrangement has ceased to have effect, unless it came to an end prematurely.]

(4)   Where on such an application the court is satisfied as to either of the grounds mentioned in subsection (1), it may do one or both of the following, namely—

  (a)   revoke or suspend [any decision approving the voluntary arrangement which has effect under section 4A] or, in a case falling within subsection (1)(b), any [decision taken by the meeting in question which has effect under that section];

  (b)   give a direction to any person for the summoning of further meetings to consider any revised proposal the person who made the original proposal may make or, in a case falling within subsection (1)(b), a further company or (as the case may be) creditors' meeting to reconsider the original proposal.

(5)   Where at any time after giving a direction under subsection (4)(b) for the summoning of meetings to consider a revised proposal the court is satisfied that the person who made the original proposal does not intend to submit a revised proposal, the court shall revoke the direction and revoke or suspend any [decision approving the voluntary arrangement which has effect under section 4A].

(6)   In a case where the court, on an application under this section with respect to any meeting—

  (a)   gives a direction under subsection (4)(b), or

  (b)   revokes or suspends an approval under subsection (4)(a) or (5),

the court may give such supplemental directions as it thinks fit and, in particular, directions with respect to things done [under the voluntary arrangement since it took effect].

(7)   Except in pursuance of the preceding provisions of this section, [a decision taken] at a meeting summoned under section 3 is not invalidated by any irregularity at or in relation to the meeting.

NOTES

Sub-ss (1), (4)–(7): words in square brackets substituted by the Insolvency Act 2000, s 2, Sch 2, Pt I, paras 1, 7(1), (2), (5)–(8), as from 1 January 2003 (for transitional provisions see the note to s 1 at **[9.93]**).

Sub-s (2): para (aa) inserted by the Insolvency Act 2000, s 2, Sch 2, Pt I, paras 1, 7(1), (3), as from 1 January 2003 (for transitional provisions see the note to s 1 at **[9.93]**); words in square brackets in para (c) substituted by the Enterprise Act 2002, s 248(3), Sch 17, paras 9, 12, as from 15 September 2003 (for savings and transitional provisions, see the note to s 8 at **[9.105]**).

Sub-s (3): words in square brackets inserted by the Insolvency Act 2000, s 2, Sch 2, Pt I, paras 1, 7(1), (4), as from 1 January 2003 (for transitional provisions see the note to s 1 at **[9.93]**).

[9.101]
[6A   False representations, etc
(1)   If, for the purpose of obtaining the approval of the members or creditors of a company to a proposal for a voluntary arrangement, a person who is an officer of the company—
   (a)   makes any false representation, or
   (b)   fraudulently does, or omits to do, anything,
he commits an offence.
(2)   Subsection (1) applies even if the proposal is not approved.
(3)   For purposes of this section "officer" includes a shadow director.
(4)   A person guilty of an offence under this section is liable to imprisonment or a fine, or both.]

NOTES

Inserted by the Insolvency Act 2000, s 2, Sch 2, Pt I, paras 1, 8, as from 1 January 2003 (for transitional provisions see the note to s 1 at **[9.93]**).

[9.102]
7   Implementation of proposal
(1)   This section applies where a voluntary arrangement [has effect under section 4A].
(2)   The person who is for the time being carrying out in relation to the voluntary arrangement the functions conferred—
   [(a)   on the nominee by virtue of the approval given at one or both of the meetings summoned under section 3]
   (b)   by virtue of section 2(4) or 4(2) on a person other than the nominee,
shall be known as the supervisor of the voluntary arrangement.
(3)   If any of the company's creditors or any other person is dissatisfied by any act, omission or decision of the supervisor, he may apply to the court; and on the application the court may—
   (a)   confirm, reverse or modify any act or decision of the supervisor,
   (b)   give him directions, or
   (c)   make such other order as it thinks fit.
(4)   The supervisor—
   (a)   may apply to the court for directions in relation to any particular matter arising under the voluntary arrangement, and
   (b)   is included among the persons who may apply to the court for the winding up of the company or for an administration order to be made in relation to it.
(5)   The court may, whenever—
   (a)   it is expedient to appoint a person to carry out the functions of the supervisor, and
   (b)   it is inexpedient, difficult or impracticable for an appointment to be made without the assistance of the court,
make an order appointing a person who is qualified to act as an insolvency practitioner [or authorised to act as supervisor, in relation to the voluntary arrangement] either in substitution for the existing supervisor or to fill a vacancy.
(6)   The power conferred by subsection (5) is exercisable so as to increase the number of persons exercising the functions of supervisor or, where there is more than one person exercising those functions, so as to replace one or more of those persons.

NOTES

Sub-ss (1), (5): words in square brackets substituted by the Insolvency Act 2000, s 2, Sch 2, Pt I, paras 1, 9(a), (c), as from 1 January 2003 (for transitional provisions see the note to s 1 at **[9.93]**).

Sub-s (2): para (a) substituted by the Insolvency Act 2000, s 2, Sch 2, Pt I, paras 1, 9(b), as from 1 January 2003 (for transitional provisions see the note to s 1 at **[9.93]**).

[9.103]
[7A   Prosecution of delinquent officers of company
(1)   This section applies where a moratorium under section 1A has been obtained for a company or the approval of a voluntary arrangement in relation to a company has taken effect under section 4A or paragraph 36 of Schedule A1.
(2)   If it appears to the nominee or supervisor that any past or present officer of the company has been guilty of any offence in connection with the moratorium or, as the case may be, voluntary arrangement for which he is criminally liable, the nominee or supervisor shall forthwith—

    (a)   report the matter to the appropriate authority, and

    (b)   provide the appropriate authority with such information and give the authority such access to and facilities for inspecting and taking copies of documents (being information or documents in the possession or under the control of the nominee or supervisor and relating to the matter in question) as the authority requires.

    In this subsection, "the appropriate authority" means—

      (i)   in the case of a company registered in England and Wales, the Secretary of State, and

      (ii)   in the case of a company registered in Scotland, the Lord Advocate.

(3)   Where a report is made to the Secretary of State under subsection (2), he may, for the purpose of investigating the matter reported to him and such other matters relating to the affairs of the company as appear to him to require investigation, exercise any of the powers which are exercisable by inspectors appointed under section 431 or 432 of [the Companies Act 1985] to investigate a company's affairs.

(4)   For the purpose of such an investigation any obligation imposed on a person by any provision of [the Companies Acts] to produce documents or give information to, or otherwise to assist, inspectors so appointed is to be regarded as an obligation similarly to assist the Secretary of State in his investigation.

(5)   An answer given by a person to a question put to him in exercise of the powers conferred by subsection (3) may be used in evidence against him.

(6)   However, in criminal proceedings in which that person is charged with an offence to which this subsection applies—

    (a)   no evidence relating to the answer may be adduced, and

    (b)   no question relating to it may be asked,

by or on behalf of the prosecution, unless evidence relating to it is adduced, or a question relating to it is asked, in the proceedings by or on behalf of that person.

(7)   Subsection (6) applies to any offence other than—

    (a)   an offence under section 2 or 5 of the Perjury Act 1911 (false statements made on oath otherwise than in judicial proceedings or made otherwise than on oath), or

    (b)   an offence under section 44(1) or (2) of the Criminal Law (Consolidation) (Scotland) Act 1995 (false statements made on oath or otherwise than on oath).

(8)   Where a prosecuting authority institutes criminal proceedings following any report under subsection (2), the nominee or supervisor, and every officer and agent of the company past and present (other than the defendant or defender), shall give the authority all assistance in connection with the prosecution which he is reasonably able to give.

    For this purpose—

    "agent" includes any banker or solicitor of the company and any person employed by the company as auditor, whether that person is or is not an officer of the company,

    "prosecuting authority" means the Director of Public Prosecutions, the Lord Advocate or the Secretary of State.

(9)   The court may, on the application of the prosecuting authority, direct any person referred to in subsection (8) to comply with that subsection if he has failed to do so.]

NOTES

Inserted, together with s 7B, by the Insolvency Act 2000, s 2, Sch 2, Pt I, paras 1, 10, as from 1 January 2003 (for transitional provisions see the note to s 1 at **[9.93]**).

Sub-ss (3), (4): words in square brackets substituted by the Companies Act 2006 (Consequential Amendments, Transitional Provisions and Savings) Order 2009, SI 2009/1941, art 2(1), Sch 1, para 71(1), (3), as from 1 October 2009 (for transitional provisions see the note below).

Transitional provisions: the Companies Act 2006 (Consequential Amendments, Transitional Provisions and Savings) Order 2009, SI 2009/1941, art 8 (at **[4.535]**) provides as follows—

"8   Amendments of insolvency legislation

(1)   The amendments by this Order of the Insolvency Act 1986 ("the 1986 Act") and the Insolvency (Northern Ireland) Order 1989 ("the 1989 Order") apply as follows.

(2)   They apply where, in a company voluntary arrangement, a moratorium comes into force in relation to a company on or after 1st October 2009.

(3)   They apply where a company enters administration on or after 1st October 2009, except where—

    (a)   it enters administration by virtue of an administration order under paragraph 10 of Schedule B1 to the 1986 Act (or paragraph 11 of Schedule B1 to the 1989 Order) on an application made before 1st October 2009,

    (b)   the administration is immediately preceded by a voluntary liquidation in respect of which the resolution to wind up was passed before 1st October 2009, or

    (c)   the administration is immediately preceded by a liquidation on the making of a winding-up order on a petition which was presented before 1st October 2009.

(4)   They apply where, in a receivership, a receiver or manager is appointed in respect of a company on or after 1st October 2009.

(5)   They apply where a company goes into liquidation upon the passing on or after 1st October 2009 of a resolution to wind up.

(6)   They apply where a company goes into voluntary liquidation under paragraph 83 of Schedule B1 to the 1986 Act (or paragraph 84 of Schedule B1 to the 1989 Order), except where the preceding administration—

    (a)   commenced before 1st October 2009, or

    (b)   is an administration which commenced by virtue of an administration order under paragraph 10 of Schedule B1 to the 1986 Act (or paragraph 11 of Schedule B1 to the 1989 Order) on an application which was made before

1st October 2009.

(7)   They apply where a company goes into liquidation on the making of a winding-up order on a petition presented on or after 1st October 2009, except where the liquidation is immediately preceded by—

(a)   an administration under paragraph 10 of Schedule B1 to the 1986 Act (or paragraph 11 of Schedule B1 to the 1989 Order) where the administration order was made on an application made before 1st October 2009,

(b)   an administration in respect of which the appointment of an administrator under paragraph 14 or 22 of Schedule B1 to the 1986 Act (or paragraph 15 or 23 of Schedule B1 to the 1989 Order) took effect before 1st October 2009, or

(c)   a voluntary liquidation in respect of which the resolution to wind up was passed before 1st October 2009.".

[9.104]
[7B   Arrangements coming to an end prematurely
For the purposes of this Part, a voluntary arrangement the approval of which has taken effect under section 4A or paragraph 36 of Schedule A1 comes to an end prematurely if, when it ceases to have effect, it has not been fully implemented in respect of all persons bound by the arrangement by virtue of section 5(2)(b)(i) or, as the case may be, paragraph 37(2)(b)(i) of Schedule A1.]

NOTES
Inserted as noted to s 7A at **[9.103]**.

[PART II
ADMINISTRATION

[9.105]
8   Administration
Schedule B1 to this Act (which makes provision about the administration of companies) shall have effect.]

NOTES
This section was substituted for the original Pt II of this Act (ss 8–27) by the Enterprise Act 2002, s 248(1), as from 15 September 2003, subject to the following savings and transitional provisions.

Savings in relation to special administration regimes:
The Enterprise Act 2002, s 249(1), (2) (Special administration regimes) provides as follows (note that para (aa) was inserted by the Water Act 2003, s 101(1), Sch 8, para 55(1), (3), as from 1 December 2005, and that that paragraph (and para (a)) are repealed by the Flood and Water Management Act 2010, s 34, Sch 5, para 6(3), as from a day to be appointed)—

"(1)   Section 248 shall have no effect in relation to—

(a)   a company holding an appointment under Chapter I of Part II of the Water Industry Act 1991 (c 56) (water and sewerage undertakers),

[(aa)   a qualifying licensed water supplier within the meaning of subsection (6) of section 23 of the Water Industry Act 1991 (meaning and effect of special administration order),]

(b)   a protected railway company within the meaning of section 59 of the Railways Act 1993 (c 43) (railway administration order) (including that section as it has effect by virtue of section 19 of the Channel Tunnel Rail Link Act 1996 (c 61) (administration)),

(c)   a licence company within the meaning of section 26 of the Transport Act 2000 (c 38) (air traffic services),

(d)   a public-private partnership company within the meaning of section 210 of the Greater London Authority Act 1999 (c 29) (public-private partnership agreement), or

(e)   a building society within the meaning of section 119 of the Building Societies Act 1986 (c 53) (interpretation).

(2)   A reference in an Act listed in subsection (1) to a provision of Part II of the Insolvency Act 1986 (or to a provision which has effect in relation to a provision of that Part of that Act) shall, in so far as it relates to a company or society listed in subsection (1), continue to have effect as if it referred to Part II as it had effect immediately before the coming into force of section 248.".

See the Companies Act 2006 (Consequential Amendments etc) Order 2008, SI 2008/948, art 3(1), Sch 1, Pt 2, para 101, which (as from 6 April 2008) amends this section, and the original s 27, as they stood without the amendment made by the Enterprise Act 2002 (ie, as they apply by virtue of s 249(1) of the 2002 Act, and art 3(2) or (3) of the Enterprise Act 2002 (Commencement No 4 and Transitional Provisions and Savings) Order 2003 (as to which, see below)).

See the Companies Act 2006 (Consequential Amendments, Transitional Provisions and Savings) Order 2009, SI 2009/1941, art 2(1), Sch 1, para 73, which (as from 1 October 2009) amends the original ss 14, 15, 18, 21, 24, 27, as they stood without the amendment made by the Enterprise Act 2002 (ie, as they apply by virtue of s 249(1) of the 2002 Act, and art 3(2) or (3) of the Enterprise Act 2002 (Commencement No 4 and Transitional Provisions and Savings) Order 2003 (as to which, see below)).

See the Companies Act 2006 (Consequential Amendments and Transitional Provisions) Order 2011, SI 2011/1265, art 6(1) which (as from 12 May 2011) amends the original s 24, as it stood without the amendment made by the Enterprise Act 2002 (ie, as they apply by virtue of s 249(1) of the 2002 Act, and art 3(2) or (3) of the Enterprise Act 2002 (Commencement No 4 and Transitional Provisions and Savings) Order 2003 (as to which, see below)).

See also the Insolvency (Amendment) Rules 2010, SI 2010/686, Sch 5 (Special Administration Regimes and Old Administrations).

As to special administration regimes, see also the Energy Act 2004, Pt 3, Chapter 3 (in particular, s 159 of, and Sch 20 to, that Act).

Transitional provisions:
The Enterprise Act 2002 (Commencement No 4 and Transitional Provisions and Savings) Order 2003, SI 2003/2093, art 3, provides as follows (note that by virtue of art 2(1) "the first commencement date" means 15 September 2003)—

"3   Administration—transitional provisions
(1)   In this article "the former administration provisions" means the law relating to administration under Part II of the Insolvency Act 1986 and section 62(2)(a) of the Criminal Justice Act 1988 without the amendments and repeals made by the

provisions of the Enterprise Act 2002 mentioned in paragraph (2).

(2)   In a case where a petition for an administration order has been presented before the first commencement date—

    (a)   section 248 and Schedules 16 and 17; and

    (b)   section 278(2) and Schedule 26 as respects the repeals relating to sections 212, 230(1), 231, 232, 240(1) and 245(3) of the Insolvency Act 1986, the entries in Schedule 10 to the Insolvency Act 1986 in respect of sections 12(2), 15(8), 18(5), 21(3), 22(6), 23(3), 24(7) and 27(6) of that Act and section 62(2)(a) of the Criminal Justice Act 1988,

shall have no effect.

(3)   The former administration provisions shall continue to apply insofar as is necessary to give effect to—

    (a)   the Insolvent Partnerships Order 1994;

    (b)   regulation 5 of the Limited Liability Partnerships Regulations 2001; and

    (c)   the Financial Services and Markets Act 2000 (Administration Orders relating to Insurers) Order 2002.".

The Enterprise Act 2002, Sch 17, para 1 provides that in any instrument made before s 248(1)–(3) of the 2002 Act comes into force: (a) a reference to the making of an administration order shall be treated as including a reference to the appointment of an administrator under Sch B1, para 14 or 22 to this Act (as inserted by s 248(2) of the 2002 Act), and (b) a reference to making an application for an administration order by petition shall be treated as including a reference to making an administration application under that Schedule, appointing an administrator under para 14 or 22 of that Schedule or giving notice under para 15 or 26 of that Schedule.

PART III
RECEIVERSHIP

CHAPTER I
RECEIVERS AND MANAGERS (ENGLAND AND WALES)

Preliminary and general provisions

[9.106]
[28   Extent of this Chapter
(1)   In this Chapter "company" means a company registered under the Companies Act 2006 in England and Wales or Scotland.
(2)   This Chapter does not apply to receivers appointed under Chapter 2 of this Part (Scotland).]

NOTES
Commencement: 1 October 2009.
Substituted by the Companies Act 2006 (Consequential Amendments, Transitional Provisions and Savings) Order 2009, SI 2009/1941, art 2(1), Sch 1, para 74(1), (2), as from 1 October 2009 (for transitional provisions see the note to s 7A at **[9.103]**).

[9.107]
29   Definitions
(1)   It is hereby declared that, except where the context otherwise requires—

    (a)   any reference in . . . this Act to a receiver or manager of the property of a company, or to a receiver of it, includes a receiver or manager, or (as the case may be) a receiver of part only of that property and a receiver only of the income arising from the property or from part of it; and

    (b)   any reference in . . . this Act to the appointment of a receiver or manager under powers contained in an instrument includes an appointment made under powers which, by virtue of an enactment, are implied in and have effect as if contained in an instrument.

(2)   In this Chapter "administrative receiver" means—

    (a)   a receiver or manager of the whole (or substantially the whole) of a company's property appointed by or on behalf of the holders of any debentures of the company secured by a charge which, as created, was a floating charge, or by such a charge and one or more other securities; or

    (b)   a person who would be such a receiver or manager but for the appointment of some other person as the receiver of part of the company's property.

NOTES
Sub-s (1): words omitted repealed by the Companies Act 2006 (Consequential Amendments, Transitional Provisions and Savings) Order 2009, SI 2009/1941, art 2(1), Sch 1, para 74(1), (3), as from 1 October 2009 (for transitional provisions see the note to s 7A at **[9.103]**).

[9.108]
30   Disqualification of body corporate from acting as receiver
A body corporate is not qualified for appointment as receiver of the property of a company, and any body corporate which acts as such a receiver is liable to a fine.

[9.109]
[31   Disqualification of bankrupt [or person in respect of whom a debt relief order is made]
(1)   A person commits an offence if he acts as receiver or manager of the property of a company on behalf of debenture holders while—

    (a)   he is an undischarged bankrupt,

[(aa) a moratorium period under a debt relief order applies in relation to him,] or

(b) a bankruptcy restrictions order [or a debt relief restrictions order] is in force in respect of him.

(2) A person guilty of an offence under subsection (1) shall be liable to imprisonment, a fine or both.

(3) This section does not apply to a receiver or manager acting under an appointment made by the court.]

NOTES

Substituted by the Enterprise Act 2002, s 257(3), Sch 21, para 1, as from 1 April 2004.

Section heading: words in square brackets inserted by the Tribunals, Courts and Enforcement Act 2007, s 108(3), Sch 20, Pt 1, paras 1, 2(2), as from 6 April 2009.

Sub-s (1): para (aa) inserted, and words in square brackets in para (b) inserted, by the Tribunals, Courts and Enforcement Act 2007, s 108(3), Sch 20, Pt 1, paras 1, 2(1), as from 6 April 2009.

[9.110]
32   Power for court to appoint official receiver

Where application is made to the court to appoint a receiver on behalf of the debenture holders or other creditors of a company which is being wound up by the court, the official receiver may be appointed.

Receivers and managers appointed out of court

[9.111]
33   Time from which appointment is effective

(1) The appointment of a person as a receiver or manager of a company's property under powers contained in an instrument—

(a) is of no effect unless it is accepted by that person before the end of the business day next following that on which the instrument of appointment is received by him or on his behalf, and

(b) subject to this, is deemed to be made at the time at which the instrument of appointment is so received.

(2) This section applies to the appointment of two or more persons as joint receivers or managers of a company's property under powers contained in an instrument, subject to such modifications as may be prescribed by the rules.

[9.112]
34   Liability for invalid appointment

Where the appointment of a person as the receiver or manager of a company's property under powers contained in an instrument is discovered to be invalid (whether by virtue of the invalidity of the instrument or otherwise), the court may order the person by whom or on whose behalf the appointment was made to indemnify the person appointed against any liability which arises solely by reason of the invalidity of the appointment.

[9.113]
35   Application to court for directions

(1) A receiver or manager of the property of a company appointed under powers contained in an instrument, or the persons by whom or on whose behalf a receiver or manager has been so appointed, may apply to the court for directions in relation to any particular matter arising in connection with the performance of the functions of the receiver or manager.

(2) On such an application, the court may give such directions, or may make such order declaring the rights of persons before the court or otherwise, as it thinks just.

[9.114]
36   Court's power to fix remuneration

(1) The court may, on an application made by the liquidator of a company, by order fix the amount to be paid by way of remuneration to a person who, under powers contained in an instrument, has been appointed receiver or manager of the company's property.

(2) The court's power under subsection (1), where no previous order has been made with respect thereto under the subsection—

(a) extends to fixing the remuneration for any period before the making of the order or the application for it,

(b) is exercisable notwithstanding that the receiver or manager has died or ceased to act before the making of the order or the application, and

(c) where the receiver or manager has been paid or has retained for his remuneration for any period before the making of the order any amount in excess of that so fixed for that period, extends to requiring him or his personal representatives to account for the excess or such part of it as may be specified in the order.

But the power conferred by paragraph (c) shall not be exercised as respects any period before the making of the application for the order under this section, unless in the court's opinion there are special circumstances making it proper for the power to be exercised.

(3)   The court may from time to time on an application made either by the liquidator or by the receiver or manager, vary or amend an order made under subsection (1).

[9.115]
37   Liability for contracts, etc
(1)   A receiver or manager appointed under powers conferred in an instrument (other than an administrative receiver) is, to the same extent as if he had been appointed by order of the court—
  (a)   personally liable on any contract entered into by him in the performance of his functions (except in so far as the contract otherwise provides) and on any contract of employment adopted by him in the performance of those functions, and
  (b)   entitled in respect of that liability to indemnity out of the assets.
(2)   For the purposes of subsection (1)(a), the receiver or manager is not to be taken to have adopted a contract of employment by reason of anything done or omitted to be done within 14 days after his appointment.
(3)   Subsection (1) does not limit any right to indemnity which the receiver or manager would have apart from it, nor limit his liability on contracts entered into without authority, nor confer any right to indemnity in respect of that liability.
(4)   Where at any time the receiver or manager so appointed vacates office—
  (a)   his remuneration and any expenses properly incurred by him, and
  (b)   any indemnity to which he is entitled out of the assets of the company,
shall be charged on and paid out of any property of the company which is in his custody or under his control at that time in priority to any charge or other security held by the person by or on whose behalf he was appointed.

[9.116]
38   Receivership accounts to be delivered to registrar
(1)   Except in the case of an administrative receiver, every receiver or manager of a company's property who has been appointed under powers contained in an instrument shall deliver to the registrar of companies for registration the requisite accounts of his receipts and payments.
(2)   The accounts shall be delivered within one month (or such longer period as the registrar may allow) after the expiration of 12 months from the date of his appointment and of every subsequent period of 6 months, and also within one month after he ceases to act as receiver or manager.
(3)   The requisite accounts shall be an abstract in the prescribed form showing—
  (a)   receipts and payments during the relevant period of 12 or 6 months, or
  (b)   where the receiver or manager ceases to act, receipts and payments during the period from the end of the period of 12 or 6 months to which the last preceding abstract related (or, if no preceding abstract has been delivered under this section, from the date of his appointment) up to the date of his so ceasing, and the aggregate amount of receipts and payments during all preceding periods since his appointment.
(4)   In this section "prescribed" means prescribed by regulations made by statutory instrument by the Secretary of State.
(5)   A receiver or manager who makes default in complying with this section is liable to a fine and, for continued contravention, to a daily default fine.

Provisions applicable to every receivership

[9.117]
39   Notification that receiver or manager appointed
[(1)   Where a receiver or manager of the property of a company has been appointed—
  (a)   every invoice, order for goods or services, business letter or order form (whether in hard copy, electronic or any other form) issued by or on behalf of the company or the receiver or manager or the liquidator of the company; and
  (b)   all the company's websites,
must contain a statement that a receiver or manager has been appointed.]
(2)   If default is made in complying with this section, the company and any of the following persons, who knowingly and wilfully authorises or permits the default, namely, any officer of the company, any liquidator of the company and any receiver or manager, is liable to a fine.

NOTES
Sub-s (1): substituted by the Companies (Trading Disclosures) (Insolvency) Regulations 2008, SI 2008/1897, reg 2(1), as from 1 October 2008.

[9.118]
40   Payment of debts out of assets subject to floating charge
(1)   The following applies, in the case of a company, where a receiver is appointed on behalf of the holders of any debentures of the company secured by a charge which, as created, was a floating charge.
(2)   If the company is not at the time in course of being wound up, its preferential debts (within the meaning given to that expression by section 386 in Part XII) shall be paid out of the assets coming to the hands of the receiver in priority to any claims for principal or interest in respect of the debentures.

(3)   Payments made under this section shall be recouped, as far as may be, out of the assets of the company available for payment of general creditors.

[9.119]
41   Enforcement of duty to make returns
(1)   If a receiver or manager of a company's property—
  (a)   having made default in filing, delivering or making any return, account or other document, or in giving any notice, which a receiver or manager is by law required to file, deliver, make or give, fails to make good the default within 14 days after the service on him of a notice requiring him to do so, or
  (b)   having been appointed under powers contained in an instrument, has, after being required at any time by the liquidator of the company to do so, failed to render proper accounts of his receipts and payments and to vouch them and pay over to the liquidator the amount properly payable to him,
the court may, on an application made for the purpose, make an order directing the receiver or manager (as the case may be) to make good the default within such time as may be specified in the order.
(2)   In the case of the default mentioned in subsection (1)(a), application to the court may be made by any member or creditor of the company or by the registrar of companies; and in the case of the default mentioned in subsection (1)(b), the application shall be made by the liquidator.
  In either case the court's order may provide that all costs of and incidental to the application shall be borne by the receiver or manager, as the case may be.
(3)   Nothing in this section prejudices the operation of any enactment imposing penalties on receivers in respect of any such default as is mentioned in subsection (1).

Administrative receivers: general
[9.120]
42   General powers
(1)   The powers conferred on the administrative receiver of a company by the debentures by virtue of which he was appointed are deemed to include (except in so far as they are inconsistent with any of the provisions of those debentures) the powers specified in Schedule 1 to this Act.
(2)   In the application of Schedule 1 to the administrative receiver of a company—
  (a)   the words "he" and "him" refer to the administrative receiver, and
  (b)   references to the property of the company are to the property of which he is or, but for the appointment of some other person as the receiver of part of the company's property, would be the receiver or manager.
(3)   A person dealing with the administrative receiver in good faith and for value is not concerned to inquire whether the receiver is acting within his powers.

[9.121]
43   Power to dispose of charged property, etc
(1)   Where, on an application by the administrative receiver, the court is satisfied that the disposal (with or without other assets) of any relevant property which is subject to a security would be likely to promote a more advantageous realisation of the company's assets than would otherwise be effected, the court may by order authorise the administrative receiver to dispose of the property as if it were not subject to the security.
(2)   Subsection (1) does not apply in the case of any security held by the person by or on whose behalf the administrative receiver was appointed, or of any security to which a security so held has priority.
(3)   It shall be a condition of an order under this section that—
  (a)   the net proceeds of the disposal, and
  (b)   where those proceeds are less than such amount as may be determined by the court to be the net amount which would be realised on a sale of the property in the open market by a willing vendor, such sums as may be required to make good the deficiency,
shall be applied towards discharging the sums secured by the security.
(4)   Where a condition imposed in pursuance of subsection (3) relates to two or more securities, that condition shall require the net proceeds of the disposal and, where paragraph (b) of that subsection applies, the sums mentioned in that paragraph to be applied towards discharging the sums secured by those securities in the order of their priorities.
(5)   [A copy] of an order under this section shall, within 14 days of the making of the order, be sent by the administrative receiver to the registrar of companies.
(6)   If the administrative receiver without reasonable excuse fails to comply with subsection (5), he is liable to a fine and, for continued contravention, to a daily default fine.
(7)   In this section "relevant property", in relation to the administrative receiver, means the property of which he is or, but for the appointment of some other person as the receiver of part of the company's property, would be the receiver or manager.

NOTES
Sub-s (5): words in square brackets substituted by the Companies Act 2006 (Consequential Amendments, Transitional Provisions and Savings) Order 2009, SI 2009/1941, art 2(1), Sch 1, para 74(1), (4), as from 1 October 2009 (for transitional

provisions see the note to s 7A at **[9.103]**).

[9.122]
44   Agency and liability for contracts
(1)   The administrative receiver of a company—
  (a)   is deemed to be the company's agent, unless and until the company goes into liquidation;
  (b)   is personally liable on any contract entered into by him in the carrying out of his functions (except in so far as the contract otherwise provides) and[, to the extent of any qualifying liability,] on any contract of employment adopted by him in the carrying out of those functions; and
  (c)   is entitled in respect of that liability to an indemnity out of the assets of the company.
(2)   For the purposes of subsection (1)(b) the administrative receiver is not to be taken to have adopted a contract of employment by reason of anything done or omitted to be done within 14 days after his appointment.
[(2A)   For the purposes of subsection (1)(b), a liability under a contract of employment is a qualifying liability if—
  (a)   it is a liability to pay a sum by way of wages or salary or contribution to an occupational pension scheme,
  (b)   it is incurred while the administrative receiver is in office, and
  (c)   it is in respect of services rendered wholly or partly after the adoption of the contract.
(2B)   Where a sum payable in respect of a liability which is a qualifying liability for the purposes of subsection (1)(b) is payable in respect of services rendered partly before and partly after the adoption of the contract, liability under subsection (1)(b) shall only extend to so much of the sum as is payable in respect of services rendered after the adoption of the contract.
(2C)   For the purposes of subsections (2A) and (2B)—
  (a)   wages or salary payable in respect of a period of holiday or absence from work through sickness or other good cause are deemed to be wages or (as the case may be) salary in respect of services rendered in that period, and
  (b)   a sum payable in lieu of holiday is deemed to be wages or (as the case may be) salary in respect of services rendered in the period by reference to which the holiday entitlement arose.
(2D)   In subsection (2C)(a), the reference to wages or salary payable in respect of a period of holiday includes any sums which, if they had been paid, would have been treated for the purposes of the enactments relating to social security as earnings in respect of that period.]
(3)   This section does not limit any right to indemnity which the administrative receiver would have apart from it, nor limit his liability on contracts entered into or adopted without authority, nor confer any right to indemnity in respect of that liability.

NOTES
  Sub-s (1): words in square brackets in para (b) inserted by the Insolvency Act 1994, s 2(1), (2), (4), in relation to contracts of employment adopted on or after 15 March 1994.
  Sub-ss (2A)–(2D): inserted by the Insolvency Act 1994, s 2(1), (3), (4), in relation to contracts of employment adopted on or after 15 March 1994.

[9.123]
45   Vacation of office
(1)   An administrative receiver of a company may at any time be removed from office by order of the court (but not otherwise) and may resign his office by giving notice of his resignation in the prescribed manner to such persons as may be prescribed.
(2)   An administrative receiver shall vacate office if he ceases to be qualified to act as an insolvency practitioner in relation to the company.
(3)   Where at any time an administrative receiver vacates office—
  (a)   his remuneration and any expenses properly incurred by him, and
  (b)   any indemnity to which he is entitled out of the assets of the company,
shall be charged on and paid out of any property of the company which is in his custody or under his control at that time in priority to any security held by the person by or on whose behalf he was appointed.
(4)   Where an administrative receiver vacates office otherwise than by death, he shall, within 14 days after his vacation of office, send a notice to that effect to the registrar of companies.
(5)   If an administrative receiver without reasonable excuse fails to comply with subsection (4), he is liable to a fine *and, for continued contravention, to a daily default fine.*

NOTES
  Sub-s (5): the words in italics are repealed by CA 1989, ss 107, 212, Sch 16, para 3, Sch 24, as from a day to be appointed. Note that s 107 of, and Sch 16 to, the 1989 Act (in Part IV of that Act) made amendments consequential on the other provisions of Part IV (Registration of company charges) and that the whole of that Part was repealed by CA 2006, as from 1 October 2009, without coming into force. It is believed that this amendment will not be brought into force.

Administrative receivers: ascertainment and investigation of company's affairs

[9.124]
46 Information to be given by administrative receiver

(1) Where an administrative receiver is appointed, he shall—

- (a) forthwith send to the company and publish in the prescribed manner a notice of his appointment, and
- (b) within 28 days after his appointment, unless the court otherwise directs, send such a notice to all the creditors of the company (so far as he is aware of their addresses).

(2) This section and the next do not apply in relation to the appointment of an administrative receiver to act—

- (a) with an existing administrative receiver, or
- (b) in place of an administrative receiver dying or ceasing to act,

except that, where they apply to an administrative receiver who dies or ceases to act before they have been fully complied with, the references in this section and the next to the administrative receiver include (subject to the next subsection) his successor and any continuing administrative receiver.

(3) If the company is being wound up, this section and the next apply notwithstanding that the administrative receiver and the liquidator are the same person, but with any necessary modifications arising from that fact.

(4) If the administrative receiver without reasonable excuse fails to comply with this section, he is liable to a fine and, for continued contravention, to a daily default fine.

[9.125]
47 Statement of affairs to be submitted

(1) Where an administrative receiver is appointed, he shall forthwith require some or all of the persons mentioned below to make out and submit to him a statement in the prescribed form as to the affairs of the company.

(2) A statement submitted under this section shall be verified by [a statement of truth] by the persons required to submit it and shall show—

- (a) particulars of the company's assets, debts and liabilities;
- (b) the names and addresses of its creditors;
- (c) the securities held by them respectively;
- (d) the dates when the securities were respectively given; and
- (e) such further or other information as may be prescribed.

(3) The persons referred to in subsection (1) are—

- (a) those who are or have been officers of the company;
- (b) those who have taken part in the company's formation at any time within one year before the date of the appointment of the administrative receiver;
- (c) those who are in the company's employment, or have been in its employment within that year, and are in the administrative receiver's opinion capable of giving the information required;
- (d) those who are or have been within that year officers of or in the employment of a company which is, or within that year was, an officer of the company.

In this subsection "employment" includes employment under a contract for services.

(4) Where any persons are required under this section to submit a statement of affairs to the administrative receiver, they shall do so (subject to the next subsection) before the end of the period of 21 days beginning with the day after that on which the prescribed notice of the requirement is given to them by the administrative receiver.

(5) The administrative receiver, if he thinks fit, may—

- (a) at any time release a person from an obligation imposed on him under subsection (1) or (2), or
- (b) either when giving notice under subsection (4) or subsequently, extend the period so mentioned;

and where the administrative receiver has refused to exercise a power conferred by this subsection, the court, if it thinks fit, may exercise it.

(6) If a person without reasonable excuse fails to comply with any obligation imposed under this section, he is liable to a fine and, for continued contravention, to a daily default fine.

NOTES

Sub-s (2): words in square brackets substituted by the Legislative Reform (Insolvency) (Miscellaneous Provisions) Order 2010, SI 2010/18, arts 2, 5(1), as from 6 April 2010.

[9.126]
48 Report by administrative receiver

(1) Where an administrative receiver is appointed, he shall, within 3 months (or such longer period as the court may allow) after his appointment, send to the registrar of companies, to any trustees for secured creditors of the company and (so far as he is aware of their addresses) to all such creditors a report as to the following matters, namely—

- (a) the events leading up to his appointment, so far as he is aware of them;

(b) the disposal or proposed disposal by him of any property of the company and the carrying on or proposed carrying on by him of any business of the company;

(c) the amounts of principal and interest payable to the debenture holders by whom or on whose behalf he was appointed and the amounts payable to preferential creditors; and

(d) the amount (if any) likely to be available for the payment of other creditors.

(2) The administrative receiver shall also, within 3 months (or such longer period as the court may allow) after his appointment, either—

(a) send a copy of the report (so far as he is aware of their addresses) to all unsecured creditors of the company; or

(b) publish in the prescribed manner a notice stating an address to which unsecured creditors of the company should write for copies of the report to be sent to them free of charge,

and (in either case), unless the court otherwise directs, lay a copy of the report before a meeting of the company's unsecured creditors summoned for the purpose on not less than 14 days' notice.

(3) The court shall not give a direction under subsection (2) unless—

(a) the report states the intention of the administrative receiver to apply for the direction, and

(b) a copy of the report is sent to the persons mentioned in paragraph (a) of that subsection, or a notice is published as mentioned in paragraph (b) of that subsection, not less than 14 days before the hearing of the application.

(4) Where the company has gone or goes into liquidation, the administrative receiver—

(a) shall, within 7 days after his compliance with subsection (1) or, if later, the nomination or appointment of the liquidator, send a copy of the report to the liquidator, and

(b) where he does so within the time limited for compliance with subsection (2), is not required to comply with that subsection.

(5) A report under this section shall include a summary of the statement of affairs made out and submitted to the administrative receiver under section 47 and of his comments (if any) upon it.

(6) Nothing in this section is to be taken as requiring any such report to include any information the disclosure of which would seriously prejudice the carrying out by the administrative receiver of his functions.

(7) Section 46(2) applies for the purposes of this section also.

(8) If the administrative receiver without reasonable excuse fails to comply with this section, he is liable to a fine and, for continued contravention, to a daily default fine.

[9.127]
49 Committee of creditors

(1) Where a meeting of creditors is summoned under section 48, the meeting may, if it thinks fit, establish a committee ("the creditors' committee") to exercise the functions conferred on it by or under this Act.

(2) If such a committee is established, the committee may, on giving not less than 7 days' notice, require the administrative receiver to attend before it at any reasonable time and furnish it with such information relating to the carrying out by him of his functions as it may reasonably require.

CHAPTER II

RECEIVERS (SCOTLAND)

[9.128]
50 Extent of this Chapter

This Chapter extends to Scotland only.

[9.129]
51 Power to appoint receiver

(1) It is competent under the law of Scotland for the holder of a floating charge over all or any part of the property (including uncalled capital), which may from time to time be comprised in the property and undertaking of an incorporated company (whether [a company registered under the Companies Act 2006] or not)—

[(a) which the Court of Session has jurisdiction to wind up; or

(b) where paragraph (a) does not apply, in respect of which a court of a member state other than the United Kingdom has under the EU Regulation jurisdiction to open insolvency proceedings,

to appoint a receiver of such part of the property of the company as is subject to the charge].

(2) It is competent under the law of Scotland for the court, on the application of the holder of such a floating charge, to appoint a receiver of such part of the property of the company as is subject to the charge.

[(2ZA) But, in relation to a company mentioned in subsection (1)(b), a receiver may be appointed under subsection (1) or (2) only in respect of property situated in Scotland.]

[(2A) Subsections (1) and (2) are subject to section 72A.]

(3) The following are disqualified from being appointed as receiver—

(a) a body corporate;

(b) an undischarged bankrupt; and

[(ba) a person subject to a bankruptcy restrictions order;]

(c)   a firm according to the law of Scotland.

(4)   A body corporate or a firm according to the law of Scotland which acts as a receiver is liable to a fine.

(5)   An undischarged bankrupt [or a person subject to a bankruptcy restrictions order] who so acts is liable to imprisonment or a fine, or both.

(6)   In this section, "receiver" includes joint receivers[; and

"bankruptcy restrictions order" means—

(a)   a bankruptcy restrictions order made under section 56A of the Bankruptcy (Scotland) Act 1985 (c 66);

(b)   a bankruptcy restrictions undertaking entered into under section 56G of that Act;

(c)   a bankruptcy restrictions order made under paragraph 1 of Schedule 4A to this Act; or

(d)   a bankruptcy restrictions undertaking entered into under paragraph 7 of that Schedule

["the EU Regulation" is the Regulation of the Council of the European Union published as Council Regulation (EC) No 1346/2000 on insolvency proceedings;

"court" is to be construed in accordance with Article 2(d) of the EU Regulation;

"insolvency proceedings" is to be construed in accordance with Article 2(a) of the EU Regulation]].

NOTES

Sub-s (1): words in first pair of square brackets substituted by the Companies Act 2006 (Consequential Amendments, Transitional Provisions and Savings) Order 2009, SI 2009/1941, art 2(1), Sch 1, para 74(1), (5), as from 1 October 2009 (for transitional provisions see the note to s 7A at **[9.103]**); words in second pair of square brackets substituted by the Insolvency Act 1986 Amendment (Appointment of Receivers) (Scotland) Regulations 2011, SSI 2011/140, reg 2(a), as from 17 March 2011.

Sub-s (2ZA): inserted by SSI 2011/140, reg 2(b), as from 17 March 2011.

Sub-s (2A): inserted by the Enterprise Act 2002, s 248(3), Sch 17, paras 9, 13, as from 15 September 2003 (for savings and transitional provisions, see the note to s 8 at **[9.105]**).

Sub-ss (3), (5): words in square brackets inserted by the Bankruptcy and Diligence etc (Scotland) Act 2007, s 3(1)–(3), as from 1 April 2008.

Sub-s (6): words in first (outer) pair of square brackets inserted by the Bankruptcy and Diligence etc (Scotland) Act 2007, s 3(1), (4), as from 1 April 2008; definitions "the EU Regulation", "court", and "insolvency proceedings" inserted by SSI 2011/140, reg 2(c), as from 17 March 2011.

[9.130]
52   Circumstances justifying appointment
(1)   A receiver may be appointed under section 51(1) by the holder of the floating charge on the occurrence of any event which, by the provisions of the instrument creating the charge, entitles the holder of the charge to make that appointment and, in so far as not otherwise provided for by the instrument, on the occurrence of any of the following events, namely—

(a)   the expiry of a period of 21 days after the making of a demand for payment of the whole or any part of the principal sum secured by the charge, without payment having been made;

(b)   the expiry of a period of 2 months during the whole of which interest due and payable under the charge has been in arrears;

(c)   the making of an order or the passing of a resolution to wind up the company;

(d)   the appointment of a receiver by virtue of any other floating charge created by the company.

(2)   A receiver may be appointed by the court under section 51(2) on the occurrence of any event which, by the provisions of the instrument creating the floating charge, entitles the holder of the charge to make that appointment and, in so far as not otherwise provided for by the instrument on the occurrence of any of the following events, namely—

(a)   where the court, on the application of the holder of the charge, pronounces itself satisfied that the position of the holder of the charge is likely to be prejudiced if no such appointment is made;

(b)   any of the events referred to in paragraphs (a) to (c) of subsection (1).

[9.131]
53   Mode of appointment by holder of charge
(1)   The appointment of a receiver by the holder of the floating charge under section 51(1) shall be by means of [an instrument subscribed in accordance with the Requirements of Writing (Scotland) Act 1995] ("the instrument of appointment"), a copy (certified in the prescribed manner to be a correct copy) whereof shall be delivered by or on behalf of the person making the appointment to the registrar of companies for registration within 7 days of its execution and shall be accompanied by a notice in the prescribed form.

(2)   If any person without reasonable excuse makes default in complying with the requirements of subsection (1), he is liable to a fine *and, for continued contravention, to a daily default fine*.

(3)   . . .

[(4) If the receiver is to be appointed by the holders of a series of secured debentures, the instrument of appointment may be executed on behalf of the holders of the floating charge by any person authorised by resolution of the debenture-holders to execute the instrument.]

(5) On receipt of the certified copy of the instrument of appointment in accordance with subsection (1), the registrar shall, on payment of the prescribed fee, enter the particulars of the appointment in the register of charges.

(6) The appointment of a person as a receiver by an instrument of appointment in accordance with subsection (1)—

    (a)   is of no effect unless it is accepted by that person before the end of the business day next following that on which the instrument of appointment is received by him or on his behalf, and

    (b)   subject to paragraph (a), is deemed to be made on the day on and at the time at which the instrument of appointment is so received, as evidence by a written docquet by that person or on his behalf;

and this subsection applies to the appointment of joint receivers subject to such modifications as may be prescribed.

(7) On the appointment of a receiver under this section, the floating charge by virtue of which he was appointed attaches to the property then subject to the charge; and such attachment has effect as if the charge was a fixed security over the property to which it has attached.

NOTES

Sub-s (1): words in square brackets substituted by the Requirements of Writing (Scotland) Act 1995, s 14(1), Sch 4, para 58(a), as from 1 August 1995.

Sub-s (2): words in italics repealed by CA 1989, ss 107, 212, Sch 16, para 3, Sch 24, as from a day to be appointed (see further the note to s 45 at **[9.123]**).

Sub-s (3): repealed by the Law Reform (Miscellaneous Provisions) (Scotland) Act 1990, s 74, Sch 8, Pt II, para 35, Sch 9, as from 1 December 1990.

Sub-s (4): substituted by the Requirements of Writing (Scotland) Act 1995, s 14(1), Sch 4, para 58(b), as from 1 August 1995.

Modification (by virtue of the Scotland Act 1998): see the Note at the beginning of this Act.

Regulations: the Receivers (Scotland) Regulations 1986, SI 1986/1917.

[9.132]
54 Appointment by court

(1) Application for the appointment of a receiver by the court under section 51(2) shall be by petition to the court, which shall be served on the company.

(2) On such an application, the court shall, if it thinks fit, issue an interlocutor making the appointment of the receiver.

(3) A copy (certified by the clerk of the court to be a correct copy) of the court's interlocutor making the appointment shall be delivered by or on behalf of the petitioner to the registrar of companies for registration, accompanied by a notice in the prescribed form within 7 days of the date of the interlocutor or such longer period as the court may allow.

If any person without reasonable excuse makes default in complying with the requirements of this subsection, he is liable to a fine *and, for continued contravention, to a daily default fine.*

(4) On receipt of the certified copy interlocutor in accordance with subsection (3), the registrar shall, on payment of the prescribed fee, enter the particulars of the appointment in the register of charges.

(5) The receiver is to be regarded as having been appointed on the date of his being appointed by the court.

(6) On the appointment of a receiver under this section, the floating charge by virtue of which he was appointed attaches to the property then subject to the charge; and such attachment has effect as if the charge were a fixed security over the property to which it has attached.

(7) In making rules of court for the purposes of this section, the Court of Session shall have regard to the need for special provision for cases which appear to the court to require to be dealt with as a matter of urgency.

NOTES

Sub-s (3): words in italics repealed by CA 1989, ss 107, 212, Sch 16, para 3, Sch 24, as from a day to be appointed (see further the note to s 45 at **[9.123]**).

Modification (by virtue of the Scotland Act 1998): see the Note at the beginning of this Act.

Regulations: the Receivers (Scotland) Regulations 1986, SI 1986/1917.

[9.133]
55 Powers of receiver

(1) Subject to the next subsection, a receiver has in relation to such part of the property of the company as is attached by the floating charge by virtue of which he was appointed, the powers, if any, given to him by the instrument creating that charge.

(2) In addition, the receiver has under this Chapter the powers as respects that property (in so far as these are not inconsistent with any provision contained in that instrument) which are specified in Schedule 2 to this Act.

(3) Subsections (1) and (2) apply—

(a)   subject to the rights of any person who has effectually executed diligence on all or any part of the property of the company prior to the appointment of the receiver, and

(b)   subject to the rights of any person who holds over all or any part of the property of the company a fixed security or floating charge having priority over, or ranking pari passu with, the floating charge by virtue of which the receiver was appointed.

(4)   A person dealing with a receiver in good faith and for value is not concerned to enquire whether the receiver is acting within his powers.

[9.134]
56   Precedence among receivers

(1)   Where there are two or more floating charges subsisting over all or any part of the property of the company, a receiver may be appointed under this Chapter by virtue of each such charge; but a receiver appointed by, or on the application of, the holder of a floating charge having priority of ranking over any other floating charge by virtue of which a receiver has been appointed has the powers given to a receiver by section 55 and Schedule 2 to the exclusion of any other receiver.

(2)   Where two or more floating charges rank with one another equally, and two or more receivers have been appointed by virtue of such charges, the receivers so appointed are deemed to have been appointed as joint receivers.

(3)   Receivers appointed, or deemed to have been appointed, as joint receivers shall act jointly unless the instrument of appointment or respective instruments of appointment otherwise provide.

(4)   Subject to subsection (5) below, the powers of a receiver appointed by, or on the application of, the holder of a floating charge are suspended by, and as from the date of, the appointment of a receiver by, or on the application of, the holder of a floating charge having priority of ranking over that charge to such extent as may be necessary to enable the receiver second mentioned to exercise his powers under section 55 and Schedule 2; and any powers so suspended take effect again when the floating charge having priority of ranking ceases to attach to the property then subject to the charge, whether such cessation is by virtue of section 62(6) or otherwise.

(5)   The suspension of the powers of a receiver under subsection (4) does not have the effect of requiring him to release any part of the property (including any letters or documents) of the company from his control until he receives from the receiver superseding him a valid indemnity (subject to the limit of the value of such part of the property of the company as is subject to the charge by virtue of which he was appointed) in respect of any expenses, charges and liabilities he may have incurred in the performance of his functions as receiver.

(6)   The suspension of the powers of a receiver under subsection (4) does not cause the floating charge by virtue of which he was appointed to cease to attach to the property to which it attached by virtue of section 53(7) or 54(6).

(7)   Nothing in this section prevents the same receiver being appointed by virtue of two or more floating charges.

[9.135]
57   Agency and liability of receiver for contracts

(1)   A receiver is deemed to be the agent of the company in relation to such property of the company as is attached by the floating charge by virtue of which he was appointed.

[(1A)   Without prejudice to subsection (1), a receiver is deemed to be the agent of the company in relation to any contract of employment adopted by him in the carrying out of his functions.]

(2)   A receiver (including a receiver whose powers are subsequently suspended under section 56) is personally liable on any contract entered into by him in the performance of his functions, except in so far as the contract otherwise provides, and[, to the extent of any qualifying liability,] on any contract of employment adopted by him in the carrying out of those functions.

[(2A)   For the purposes of subsection (2), a liability under a contract of employment is a qualifying liability if—

(a)   it is a liability to pay a sum by way of wages or salary or contribution to an occupational pension scheme,

(b)   it is incurred while the receiver is in office, and

(c)   it is in respect of services rendered wholly or partly after the adoption of the contract.

(2B)   Where a sum payable in respect of a liability which is a qualifying liability for the purposes of subsection (2) is payable in respect of services rendered partly before and partly after the adoption of the contract, liability under that subsection shall only extend to so much of the sum as is payable in respect of services rendered after the adoption of the contract.

(2C)   For the purposes of subsections (2A) and (2B)—

(a)   wages or salary payable in respect of a period of holiday or absence from work through sickness or other good cause are deemed to be wages or (as the case may be) salary in respect of services rendered in that period, and

(b)   a sum payable in lieu of holiday is deemed to be wages or (as the case may be) salary in respect of services rendered in the period by reference to which the holiday entitlement arose.

(2D)   In subsection (2C)(a), the reference to wages or salary payable in respect of a period of holiday includes any sums which, if they had been paid, would have been treated for the purposes of the enactments relating to social security as earnings in respect of that period.]

(3)   A receiver who is personally liable by virtue of subsection (2) is entitled to be indemnified out of the property in respect of which he was appointed.

(4)   Any contract entered into by or on behalf of the company prior to the appointment of a receiver continues in force (subject to its terms) notwithstanding that appointment, but the receiver does not by virtue only of his appointment incur any personal liability on any such contract.

(5)   For the purposes of subsection (2), a receiver is not to be taken to have adopted a contract of employment by reason of anything done or omitted to be done within 14 days after his appointment.

(6)   This section does not limit any right to indemnity which the receiver would have apart from it, nor limit his liability on contracts entered into or adopted without authority, nor confer any right to indemnity in respect of that liability.

(7)   Any contract entered into by a receiver in the performance of his functions continues in force (subject to its terms) although the powers of the receiver are subsequently suspended under section 56.

NOTES

Sub-ss (1A), (2A)–(2D): inserted by the Insolvency Act 1994, s 3(1), (2), (4), (5), in relation to contracts of employment adopted on or after 15 March 1994.

Sub-s (2): words in square brackets inserted by the Insolvency Act 1994, s 3(1), (3), (5), in relation to contracts of employment adopted on or after 15 March 1994.

[9.136]
58 Remuneration of receiver

(1)   The remuneration to be paid to a receiver is to be determined by agreement between the receiver and the holder of the floating charge by virtue of which he was appointed.

(2)   Where the remuneration to be paid to the receiver has not been determined under subsection (1), or where it has been so determined but is disputed by any of the persons mentioned in paragraphs (a) to (d) below, it may be fixed instead by the Auditor of the Court of Session on application made to him by—

   (a)   the receiver;

   (b)   the holder of any floating charge or fixed security over all or any part of the property of the company;

   (c)   the company; or

   (d)   the liquidator of the company.

(3)   Where the receiver has been paid or has retained for his remuneration for any period before the remuneration has been fixed by the Auditor of the Court of Session under subsection (2) any amount in excess of the remuneration so fixed for that period, the receiver or his personal representatives shall account for the excess.

[9.137]
59 Priority of debts

(1)   Where a receiver is appointed and the company is not at the time of the appointment in course of being wound up, the debts which fall under subsection (2) of this section shall be paid out of any assets coming to the hands of the receiver in priority to any claim for principal or interest by the holder of the floating charge by virtue of which the receiver was appointed.

(2)   Debts falling under this subsection are preferential debts (within the meaning given by section 386 in Part XII) which, by the end of a period of 6 months after advertisement by the receiver for claims in the Edinburgh Gazette and in a newspaper circulating in the district where the company carries on business either—

   (i)   have been intimated to him, or

   (ii)   have become known to him.

(3)   Any payments made under this section shall be recouped as far as may be out of the assets of the company available for payment of ordinary creditors.

[9.138]
60 Distribution of moneys

(1)   Subject to the next section, and to the rights of any of the following categories of persons (which rights shall, except to the extent otherwise provided in any instrument, have the following order of priority), namely—

   (a)   the holder of any fixed security which is over property subject to the floating charge and which ranks prior to, or pari passu with, the floating charge;

   (b)   all persons who have effectually executed diligence on any part of the property of the company which is subject to the charge by virtue of which the receiver was appointed;

   (c)   creditors in respect of all liabilities, charges and expenses incurred by or on behalf of the receiver;

   (d)   the receiver in respect of his liabilities, expenses and remuneration, and any indemnity to which he is entitled out of the property of the company; and

   (e)   the preferential creditors entitled to payment under section 59,

the receiver shall pay moneys received by him to the holder of the floating charge by virtue of which the receiver was appointed in or towards satisfaction of the debt secured by the floating charge.

(2)   Any balance of moneys remaining after the provisions of subsection (1) and section 61 below have been satisfied shall be paid in accordance with their respective rights and interests to the following persons, as the case may require—

  (a)   any other receiver;

  (b)   the holder of a fixed security which is over property subject to the floating charge;

  (c)   the company or its liquidator, as the case may be.

(3)   Where any question arises as to the person entitled to a payment under this section, or where a receipt or a discharge of a security cannot be obtained in respect of any such payment, the receiver shall consign the amount of such payment in any joint stock bank of issue in Scotland in name of the Accountant of Court for behoof of the person or persons entitled thereto.

[9.139]
61   Disposal of interest in property

(1)   Where the receiver sells or disposes, or is desirous of selling or disposing, of any property or interest in property of the company which is subject to the floating charge by virtue of which the receiver was appointed and which is—

  (a)   subject to any security or interest of, or burden or encumbrance in favour of, a creditor the ranking of which is prior to, or pari passu with, or postponed to the floating charge, or

  (b)   property or an interest in property affected or attached by effectual diligence executed by any person,

and the receiver is unable to obtain the consent of such creditor or, as the case may be, such person to such a sale or disposal, the receiver may apply to the court for authority to sell or dispose of the property or interest in property free of such security, interest, burden, encumbrance or diligence.

[(1A)   For the purposes of subsection (1) above, an inhibition which takes effect after the creation of the floating charge by virtue of which the receiver was appointed is not an effectual diligence.]

[(1B)   For the purposes of subsection (1) above, an arrestment is an effectual diligence only where it is executed before the floating charge, by virtue of which the receiver was appointed, attaches to the property comprised in the company's property and undertaking.]

(2)   Subject to the next subsection, on such an application the court may, if it thinks fit, authorise the sale or disposal of the property or interest in question free of such security, interest, burden, encumbrance or diligence, and such authorisation may be on such terms or conditions as the court thinks fit.

(3)   In the case of an application where a fixed security over the property or interest in question which ranks prior to the floating charge has not been met or provided for in full, the court shall not authorise the sale or disposal of the property or interest in question unless it is satisfied that the sale or disposal would be likely to provide a more advantageous realisation of the company's assets than would otherwise be effected.

(4)   It shall be a condition of an authorisation to which subsection (3) applies that—

  (a)   the net proceeds of the disposal, and

  (b)   where those proceeds are less than such amount as may be determined by the court to be the net amount which would be realised on a sale of the property or interest in the open market by a willing seller, such sums as may be required to make good the deficiency,

shall be applied towards discharging the sums secured by the fixed security.

(5)   Where a condition imposed in pursuance of subsection (4) relates to two or more such fixed securities, that condition shall require the net proceeds of the disposal and, where paragraph (b) of that subsection applies, the sums mentioned in that paragraph to be applied towards discharging the sums secured by those fixed securities in the order of their priorities.

(6)   A copy of an authorisation under subsection (2) . . . shall, within 14 days of the granting of the authorisation, be sent by the receiver to the registrar of companies.

(7)   If the receiver without reasonable excuse fails to comply with subsection (6), he is liable to a fine and, for continued contravention, to a daily default fine.

(8)   Where any sale or disposal is effected in accordance with the authorisation of the court under subsection (2), the receiver shall grant to the purchaser or disponee an appropriate document of transfer or conveyance of the property or interest in question, and that document has the effect, or, where recording, intimation or registration of that document is a legal requirement for completion of title to the property or interest, then that recording, intimation or registration (as the case may be) has the effect, of—

  (a)   disencumbering the property or interest of the security, interest, burden or encumbrance affecting it, and

  (b)   freeing the property or interest from the diligence executed upon it.

(9)   Nothing in this section prejudices the right of any creditor of the company to rank for his debt in the winding up of the company.

NOTES

Sub-s (1A): inserted by the Bankruptcy and Diligence etc (Scotland) Act 2007, s 155(1), (2), as from 22 April 2009.

Sub-s (1B): inserted by the Bankruptcy and Diligence etc (Scotland) Act 2007, s 226, Sch 5, para 14(1), (2), as from a day to be appointed (note that Sch 5, para 14 actually provides that this subsection should be inserted after sub-s (1)).

Sub-s (6): words omitted repealed by the Companies Act 2006 (Consequential Amendments, Transitional Provisions and Savings) Order 2009, SI 2009/1941, art 2(1), Sch 1, para 74(1), (6), as from 1 October 2009 (for transitional provisions see the note to s 7A at **[9.103]**).

Modification (by virtue of the Scotland Act 1998): see the Note at the beginning of this Act.

[9.140]
62 Cessation of appointment of receiver
(1)   A receiver may be removed from office by the court under subsection (3) below and may resign his office by giving notice of his resignation in the prescribed manner to such persons as may be prescribed.
(2)   A receiver shall vacate office if he ceases to be qualified to act as an insolvency practitioner in relation to the company.
(3)   Subject to the next subsection, a receiver may, on application to the court by the holder of the floating charge by virtue of which he was appointed, be removed by the court on cause shown.
(4)   Where at any time a receiver vacates office—
   (a)   his remuneration and any expenses properly incurred by him, and
   (b)   any indemnity to which he is entitled out of the property of the company,
shall be paid out of the property of the company which is subject to the floating charge and shall have priority as provided for in section 60(1).
(5)   When a receiver ceases to act as such otherwise than by death he shall, and, when a receiver is removed by the court, the holder of the floating charge by virtue of which he was appointed shall, within 14 days of the cessation or removal (as the case may be) give the registrar of companies notice to that effect, and the registrar shall enter the notice in the register of charges.
   If the receiver or the holder of the floating charge (as the case may require) makes default in complying with the requirements of this subsection, he is liable to a fine *and, for continued contravention, to a daily default fine.*
(6)   If by the expiry of a period of one month following upon the removal of the receiver or his ceasing to act as such no other receiver has been appointed, the floating charge by virtue of which the receiver was appointed—
   (a)   thereupon ceases to attach to the property then subject to the charge, and
   (b)   again subsists as a floating charge;
and for the purposes of calculating the period of one month under this subsection no account shall be taken of any period during which [the company is in administration,] under Part II of this Act . . .

NOTES
   Sub-s (5): words in italics repealed by CA 1989, ss 107, 212, Sch 16, para 3, Sch 24, as from a day to be appointed (see further the note to s 45 at **[9.123]**).
   Sub-s (6): words in square brackets substituted, and words omitted repealed, by the Enterprise Act 2002 (Insolvency) Order 2003, SI 2003/2096, arts 4, 6, Schedule, Pt 1, paras 8, 9, as from 15 September 2003, except in relation to any case where a petition for an administration order was presented before that date.
   Modification (by virtue of the Scotland Act 1998): see the Note at the beginning of this Act.
   Regulations: the Receivers (Scotland) Regulations 1986, SI 1986/1917.

[9.141]
63 Powers of court
(1)   The court on the application of—
   (a)   the holder of a floating charge by virtue of which a receiver was appointed, or
   (b)   a receiver appointed under section 51,
may give directions to the receiver in respect of any matter arising in connection with the performance by him of his functions.
(2)   Where the appointment of a person as a receiver by the holder of a floating charge is discovered to be invalid (whether by virtue of the invalidity of the instrument or otherwise), the court may order the holder of the floating charge to indemnify the person appointed against any liability which arises solely by reason of the invalidity of the appointment.

[9.142]
64 Notification that receiver appointed
[(1)   Where a receiver has been appointed—
   (a)   every invoice, order for goods or services, business letter or order form (whether in hard copy, electronic or any other form) issued by or on behalf of the company or the receiver or the liquidator of the company; and
   (b)   all the company's websites,
must contain a statement that a receiver has been appointed.]
(2)   If default is made in complying with the requirements of this section, the company and any of the following persons who knowingly and wilfully authorises or permits the default, namely any officer of the company, any liquidator of the company and any receiver, is liable to a fine.

NOTES
   Sub-s (1): substituted by the Companies (Trading Disclosures) (Insolvency) Regulations 2008, SI 2008/1897, reg 2(2), as from 1 October 2008.

[9.143]
65   Information to be given by receiver
(1)   Where a receiver is appointed, he shall—
   (a)   forthwith send to the company and publish notice of his appointment, and
   (b)   within 28 days after his appointment, unless the court otherwise directs, send such notice
         to all the creditors of the company (so far as he is aware of their addresses).
(2)   This section and the next do not apply in relation to the appointment of a receiver to act—
   (a)   with an existing receiver, or
   (b)   in place of a receiver who has died or ceased to act,
except that, where they apply to a receiver who dies or ceases to act before they have been fully
complied with, the references in this section and the next to the receiver include (subject to
subsection (3) of this section) his successor and any continuing receiver.
(3)   If the company is being wound up, this section and the next apply notwithstanding that the
receiver and the liquidator are the same person, but with any necessary modifications arising from
that fact.
(4)   If a person without reasonable excuse fails to comply with this section, he is liable to a fine
and, for continued contravention, to a daily default fine.

NOTES
   Regulations: the Receivers (Scotland) Regulations 1986, SI 1986/1917.

[9.144]
66   Company's statement of affairs
(1)   Where a receiver of a company is appointed, the receiver shall forthwith require some or all
of the persons mentioned in subsection (3) below to make out and submit to him a statement in the
prescribed form as to the affairs of the company.
(2)   A statement submitted under this section shall be verified by affidavit by the persons required
to submit it and shall show—
   (a)   particulars of the company's assets, debts and liabilities;
   (b)   the names and addresses of its creditors;
   (c)   the securities held by them respectively;
   (d)   the dates when the securities were respectively given; and
   (e)   such further or other information as may be prescribed.
(3)   The persons referred to in subsection (1) are—
   (a)   those who are or have been officers of the company;
   (b)   those who have taken part in the company's formation at any time within one year before
         the date of the appointment of the receiver;
   (c)   those who are in the company's employment or have been in its employment within that
         year, and are in the receiver's opinion capable of giving the information required;
   (d)   those who are or have been within that year officers of or in the employment of a company
         which is, or within that year was, an officer of the company.
   In this subsection "employment" includes employment under a contract for services.
(4)   Where any persons are required under this section to submit a statement of affairs to the
receiver they shall do so (subject to the next subsection) before the end of the period of 21 days
beginning with the day after that on which the prescribed notice of the requirement is given to them
by the receiver.
(5)   The receiver, if he thinks fit, may—
   (a)   at any time release a person from an obligation imposed on him under subsection (1) or (2),
         or
   (b)   either when giving the notice mentioned in subsection (4) or subsequently extend the
         period so mentioned,
and where the receiver has refused to exercise a power conferred by this subsection, the court, if it
thinks fit, may exercise it.
(6)   If a person without reasonable excuse fails to comply with any obligation imposed under this
section, he is liable to a fine and, for continued contravention to a daily default fine.

NOTES
   Regulations: the Receivers (Scotland) Regulations 1986, SI 1986/1917.

[9.145]
67   Report by receiver
(1)   Where a receiver is appointed under section 51, he shall within 3 months (or such longer
period as the court may allow) after his appointment, send to the registrar of companies, to the
holder of the floating charge by virtue of which he was appointed and to any trustees for secured
creditors of the company and (so far as he is aware of their addresses) to all such creditors a report
as to the following matters, namely—
   (a)   the events leading up to his appointment, so far as he is aware of them;
   (b)   the disposal or proposed disposal by him of any property of the company and the carrying
         on or proposed carrying on by him of any business of the company;

   (c)   the amounts of principal and interest payable to the holder of the floating charge by virtue of which he was appointed and the amounts payable to preferential creditors; and

   (d)   the amount (if any) likely to be available for the payment of other creditors.

(2)   The receiver shall also, within 3 months (or such longer period as the court may allow) after his appointment, either—

   (a)   send a copy of the report (so far as he is aware of their addresses) to all unsecured creditors of the company, or

   (b)   publish in the prescribed manner a notice stating an address to which unsecured creditors of the company should write for copies of the report to be sent to them free of charge,

and (in either case), unless the court otherwise directs, lay a copy of the report before a meeting of the company's unsecured creditors summoned for the purpose on not less than 14 days' notice.

(3)   The court shall not give a direction under subsection (2) unless—

   (a)   the report states the intention of the receiver to apply for the direction, and

   (b)   a copy of the report is sent to the persons mentioned in paragraph (a) of that subsection, or a notice is published as mentioned in paragraph (b) of that subsection, not less than 14 days before the hearing of the application.

(4)   Where the company has gone or goes into liquidation, the receiver—

   (a)   shall, within 7 days after his compliance with subsection (1) or, if later, the nomination or appointment of the liquidator, send a copy of the report to the liquidator, and

   (b)   where he does so within the time limited for compliance with subsection (2), is not required to comply with that subsection.

(5)   A report under this section shall include a summary of the statement of affairs made out and submitted under section 66 and of his comments (if any) on it.

(6)   Nothing in this section shall be taken as requiring any such report to include any information the disclosure of which would seriously prejudice the carrying out by the receiver of his functions.

(7)   Section 65(2) applies for the purposes of this section also.

(8)   If a person without reasonable excuse fails to comply with this section, he is liable to a fine and, for continued contravention, to a daily default fine.

(9)   In this section "secured creditor", in relation to a company, means a creditor of the company who holds in respect of his debt a security over property of the company, and "unsecured creditor" shall be construed accordingly.

NOTES

   Modification (by virtue of the Scotland Act 1998): see the Note at the beginning of this Act.

   Regulations: the Receivers (Scotland) Regulations 1986, SI 1986/1917.

[9.146]
68　Committee of creditors

(1)   Where a meeting of creditors is summoned under section 67, the meeting may, if it thinks fit, establish a committee ("the creditors' committee") to exercise the functions conferred on it by or under this Act.

(2)   If such a committee is established, the committee may on giving not less than 7 days' notice require the receiver to attend before it at any reasonable time and furnish it with such information relating to the carrying out by him of his functions as it may reasonably require.

[9.147]
69　Enforcement of receiver's duty to make returns, etc

(1)   If any receiver—

   (a)   having made default in filing, delivering or making any return, account or other document, or in giving any notice, which a receiver is by law required to file, deliver, make or give, fails to make good the default within 14 days after the service on him of a notice requiring him to do so; or

   (b)   has, after being required at any time by the liquidator of the company so to do, failed to render proper accounts of his receipts and payments and to vouch the same and to pay over to the liquidator the amount properly payable to him,

the court may, on an application made for the purpose, make an order directing the receiver to make good the default within such time as may be specified in the order.

(2)   In the case of any such default as is mentioned in subsection (1)(a), an application for the purposes of this section may be made by any member or creditor of the company or by the registrar of companies; and, in the case of any such default as is mentioned in subsection (1)(b), the application shall be made by the liquidator; and, in either case, the order may provide that all expenses of and incidental to the application shall be borne by the receiver.

(3)   Nothing in this section prejudices the operation of any enactments imposing penalties on receivers in respect of any such default as is mentioned in subsection (1).

NOTES

   Modification (by virtue of the Scotland Act 1998): see the Note at the beginning of this Act.

[9.148]
70   Interpretation for Chapter II
(1)   In this Chapter, unless the contrary intention appears, the following expressions have the following meanings respectively assigned to them—

"company" means an incorporated company (whether or not [a company registered under the Companies Act 2006]) which the Court of Session has jurisdiction to wind up;

"fixed security", in relation to any property of a company, means any security, other than a floating charge or a charge having the nature of a floating charge, which on the winding up of the company in Scotland would be treated as an effective security over that property, and (without prejudice to that generality) includes a security over that property, being a heritable security within the meaning of the Conveyancing and Feudal Reform (Scotland) Act 1970;

"instrument of appointment" has the meaning given by section 53(1);

"prescribed" means prescribed by regulations made under this Chapter by the Secretary of State;

"receiver" means a receiver of such part of the property of the company as is subject to the floating charge by virtue of which he has been appointed under section 51;

"register of charges" means the register kept by the registrar of companies for the purposes of [Chapter 2 of Part 25 of the Companies Act 2006];

"secured debenture" means a bond, debenture, debenture stock or other security which, either itself or by reference to any other instrument, creates a floating charge over all or any part of the property of the company, but does not include a security which creates no charge other than a fixed security; and

"series of secured debentures" means two or more secured debentures created as a series by the company in such a manner that the holders thereof are entitled pari passu to the benefit of the floating charge.

(2)   Where a floating charge, secured debenture or series of secured debentures has been created by the company, then, except where the context otherwise requires, any reference in this Chapter to the holder of the floating charge shall—

(a)   where the floating charge, secured debenture or series of secured debentures provides for a receiver to be appointed by any person or body, be construed as a reference to that person or body;

(b)   where, in the case of a series of secured debentures, no such provision has been made therein but—

(i)   there are trustees acting for the debenture-holders under and in accordance with a trust deed, be construed as a reference to those trustees, and

(ii)   where no such trustees are acting, be construed as a reference to—

(aa)   a majority in nominal value of those present or represented by proxy and voting at a meeting of debenture-holders at which the holders of at least one-third in nominal value of the outstanding debentures of the series are present or so represented, or

(bb)   where no such meeting is held, the holders of at least one-half in nominal value of the outstanding debentures of the series.

(3)   Any reference in this Chapter to a floating charge, secured debenture, series of secured debentures or instrument creating a charge includes, except where the context otherwise requires, a reference to that floating charge, debenture, series of debentures or instrument as varied by any instrument.

(4)   References in this Chapter to the instrument by which a floating charge was created are, in the case of a floating charge created by words in a bond or other written acknowledgement, references to the bond or, as the case may be, the other written acknowledgement.

NOTES

Sub-s (1): words in square brackets in the definitions "company" and "register of charges" substituted by the Companies Act 2006 (Consequential Amendments, Transitional Provisions and Savings) Order 2009, SI 2009/1941, art 2(1), Sch 1, para 74(1), (7), as from 1 October 2009 (for transitional provisions see the note to s 7A at **[9.103]**).

[9.149]
71   Prescription of forms, etc; regulations
(1)   The notice referred to in section 62(5), and the notice referred to in section 65(1)(a) shall be in such form as may be prescribed.

(2)   Any power conferred by this Chapter on the Secretary of State to make regulations is exercisable by statutory instrument; and a statutory instrument made in the exercise of the power so conferred to prescribe a fee is subject to annulment in pursuance of a resolution of either House of Parliament.

CHAPTER III
RECEIVERS' POWERS IN GREAT BRITAIN AS A WHOLE

[9.150]
72   Cross-border operation of receivership provisions
(1)   A receiver appointed under the law of either part of Great Britain in respect of the whole or any part of any property or undertaking of a company and in consequence of the company having created a charge which, as created, was a floating charge may exercise his powers in the other part of Great Britain so far as their exercise is not inconsistent with the law applicable there.
(2)   In subsection (1) "receiver" includes a manager and a person who is appointed both receiver and manager.

[CHAPTER IV
PROHIBITION OF APPOINTMENT OF ADMINISTRATIVE RECEIVER

[9.151]
72A   Floating charge holder not to appoint administrative receiver
(1)   The holder of a qualifying floating charge in respect of a company's property may not appoint an administrative receiver of the company.
(2)   In Scotland, the holder of a qualifying floating charge in respect of a company's property may not appoint or apply to the court for the appointment of a receiver who on appointment would be an administrative receiver of property of the company.
(3)   In subsections (1) and (2)—
   "holder of a qualifying floating charge in respect of a company's property" has the same meaning as in paragraph 14 of Schedule B1 to this Act, and
   "administrative receiver" has the meaning given by section 251.
(4)   This section applies—
   (a)   to a floating charge created on or after a date appointed by the Secretary of State by order made by statutory instrument, and
   (b)   in spite of any provision of an agreement or instrument which purports to empower a person to appoint an administrative receiver (by whatever name).
(5)   An order under subsection (4)(a) may—
   (a)   make provision which applies generally or only for a specified purpose;
   (b)   make different provision for different purposes;
   (c)   make transitional provision.
(6)   This section is subject to the exceptions specified in [sections 72B to 72GA].]

NOTES
   Inserted, together with the preceding heading and ss 72B–72D, 72E–72G, 72H, by the Enterprise Act 2002, s 250(1), as from 15 September 2003.
   Sub-s (6): words in square brackets substituted by the Insolvency Act 1986 (Amendment) (Administrative Receivership and Urban Regeneration etc) Order 2003, SI 2003/1832, art 2(a), as from 15 September 2003 (ie, immediately after the coming into force of ss 72A–72G of, and Sch 2A to, this Act).
   Orders: the Insolvency Act 1986, Section 72A (Appointed Date) Order 2003, SI 2003/2095, appointing 15 September 2003 for the purposes of sub-s (4)(a) above.

[9.152]
[72B   First exception: capital market
(1)   Section 72A does not prevent the appointment of an administrative receiver in pursuance of an agreement which is or forms part of a capital market arrangement if—
   (a)   a party incurs or, when the agreement was entered into was expected to incur, a debt of at least £50 million under the arrangement, and
   (b)   the arrangement involves the issue of a capital market investment.
(2)   In subsection (1)—
   "capital market arrangement" means an arrangement of a kind described in paragraph 1 of Schedule 2A, and
   "capital market investment" means an investment of a kind described in paragraph 2 or 3 of that Schedule.]

NOTES
   Inserted as noted to s 72A at **[9.151]**.

[9.153]
[72C   Second exception: public-private partnership
(1)   Section 72A does not prevent the appointment of an administrative receiver of a project company of a project which—
   (a)   is a public-private partnership project, and
   (b)   includes step-in rights.
(2)   In this section "public-private partnership project" means a project—

(a) the resources for which are provided partly by one or more public bodies and partly by one or more private persons, or

(b) which is designed wholly or mainly for the purpose of assisting a public body to discharge a function.

(3) In this section—

"step-in rights" has the meaning given by paragraph 6 of Schedule 2A, and

"project company" has the meaning given by paragraph 7 of that Schedule.]

NOTES

Inserted as noted to s 72A at **[9.151]**.

[9.154]

[72D Third exception: utilities

(1) Section 72A does not prevent the appointment of an administrative receiver of a project company of a project which—

(a) is a utility project, and

(b) includes step-in rights.

(2) In this section—

(a) "utility project" means a project designed wholly or mainly for the purpose of a regulated business,

(b) "regulated business" means a business of a kind listed in paragraph 10 of Schedule 2A,

(c) "step-in rights" has the meaning given by paragraph 6 of that Schedule, and

(d) "project company" has the meaning given by paragraph 7 of that Schedule.]

NOTES

Inserted as noted to s 72A at **[9.151]**.

[9.155]

[72DA Exception in respect of urban regeneration projects

(1) Section 72A does not prevent the appointment of an administrative receiver of a project company of a project which—

(a) is designed wholly or mainly to develop land which at the commencement of the project is wholly or partly in a designated disadvantaged area outside Northern Ireland, and

(b) includes step-in rights.

(2) In subsection (1) "develop" means to carry out—

(a) building operations,

(b) any operation for the removal of substances or waste from land and the levelling of the surface of the land, or

(c) engineering operations in connection with the activities mentioned in paragraph (a) or (b).

(3) In this section—

"building" includes any structure or erection, and any part of a building as so defined, but does not include plant and machinery comprised in a building,

"building operations" includes—

(a) demolition of buildings,

(b) filling in of trenches,

(c) rebuilding,

(d) structural alterations of, or additions to, buildings and

(e) other operations normally undertaken by a person carrying on business as a builder,

"designated disadvantaged area" means an area designated as a disadvantaged area under section 92 of the Finance Act 2001,

"engineering operations" includes the formation and laying out of means of access to highways,

"project company" has the meaning given by paragraph 7 of Schedule 2A,

"step-in rights" has the meaning given by paragraph 6 of that Schedule,

"substance" means any natural or artificial substance whether in solid or liquid form or in the form of a gas or vapour, and

"waste" includes any waste materials, spoil, refuse or other matter deposited on land.]

NOTES

Inserted by the Insolvency Act 1986 (Amendment) (Administrative Receivership and Urban Regeneration etc) Order 2003, SI 2003/1832, art 2(b), as from 15 September 2003 (ie, immediately after the coming into force of ss 72A–72G of, and Sch 2A to, this Act).

[9.156]

[72E Fourth exception: project finance

(1) Section 72A does not prevent the appointment of an administrative receiver of a project company of a project which—

(a) is a financed project, and

(b) includes step-in rights.

(2) In this section—

(a)   a project is "financed" if under an agreement relating to the project a project company incurs, or when the agreement is entered into is expected to incur, a debt of at least £50 million for the purposes of carrying out the project,

(b)   "project company" has the meaning given by paragraph 7 of Schedule 2A, and

(c)   "step-in rights" has the meaning given by paragraph 6 of that Schedule.]

NOTES

Inserted as noted to s 72A at **[9.151]**.

[9.157]
[72F   Fifth exception: financial market
Section 72A does not prevent the appointment of an administrative receiver of a company by virtue of—

(a)   a market charge within the meaning of section 173 of the Companies Act 1989 (c 40),

(b)   a system-charge within the meaning of the Financial Markets and Insolvency Regulations 1996 (SI 1996/1469),

(c)   a collateral security charge within the meaning of the Financial Markets and Insolvency (Settlement Finality) Regulations 1999 (SI 1999/2979).]

NOTES

Inserted as noted to s 72A at **[9.151]**.

[9.158]
[72G   Sixth exception: [social landlords]
Section 72A does not prevent the appointment of an administrative receiver of a company which is[—

(a)   a private registered provider of social housing, or

(b)]   registered as a social landlord under Part I of the Housing Act 1996 (c 52) or under Part 3 of the Housing (Scotland) Act 2001 (asp 10).]

NOTES

Inserted as noted to s 72A at **[9.151]**.

Words in square brackets in the section heading substituted, and other words in square brackets inserted, by the Housing and Regeneration Act 2008 (Consequential Provisions) Order 2010, SI 2010/866, art 5, Sch 2, para 61, as from 1 April 2010.

[9.159]
[72GA   Exception in relation to protected railway companies etc
Section 72A does not prevent the appointment of an administrative receiver of—

(a)   a company holding an appointment under Chapter I of Part II of the Water Industry Act 1991,

(b)   a protected railway company within the meaning of section 59 of the Railways Act 1993 (including that section as it has effect by virtue of section 19 of the Channel Tunnel Rail Link Act 1996, or

(c)   a licence company within the meaning of section 26 of the Transport Act 2000.]

NOTES

Inserted by the Insolvency Act 1986 (Amendment) (Administrative Receivership and Urban Regeneration etc) Order 2003, SI 2003/1832, art 2(c), as from 15 September 2003 (ie, immediately after the coming into force of ss 72A–72G of, and Sch 2A to, this Act).

[9.160]
[72H   Sections 72A to 72G: supplementary
(1)   Schedule 2A (which supplements sections 72B to 72G) shall have effect.

(2)   The Secretary of State may by order—

(a)   insert into this Act provision creating an additional exception to section 72A(1) or (2);

(b)   provide for a provision of this Act which creates an exception to section 72A(1) or (2) to cease to have effect;

(c)   amend section 72A in consequence of provision made under paragraph (a) or (b);

(d)   amend any of sections 72B to 72G;

(e)   amend Schedule 2A.

(3)   An order under subsection (2) must be made by statutory instrument.

(4)   An order under subsection (2) may make—

(a)   provision which applies generally or only for a specified purpose;

(b)   different provision for different purposes;

(c)   consequential or supplementary provision;

(d)   transitional provision.

(5)   An order under subsection (2)—

(a)   in the case of an order under subsection (2)(e), shall be subject to annulment in pursuance of a resolution of either House of Parliament,

(b)   in the case of an order under subsection (2)(d) varying the sum specified in section 72B(1)(a) or 72E(2)(a) (whether or not the order also makes consequential or transitional provision), shall be subject to annulment in pursuance of a resolution of either House of Parliament, and

(c)   in the case of any other order under subsection (2)(a) to (d), may not be made unless a draft has been laid before and approved by resolution of each House of Parliament.]

NOTES

Inserted as noted to s 72A at **[9.151]**.

Orders: the Insolvency Act 1986 (Amendment) (Administrative Receivership and Capital Market Arrangements) Order 2003, SI 2003/1468; the Insolvency Act 1986 (Amendment) (Administrative Receivership and Urban Regeneration etc) Order 2003, SI 2003/1832.

PART IV
WINDING UP OF COMPANIES REGISTERED UNDER THE COMPANIES ACTS

CHAPTER I
PRELIMINARY

[Introductory

[9.161]
73   Scheme of this Part
(1)   This Part applies to the winding up of a company registered under the Companies Act 2006 in England and Wales or Scotland.
(2)   The winding up may be either—
(a)   voluntary (see Chapters 2 to 5), or
(b)   by the court (see Chapter 6).
(3)   This Chapter and Chapters 7 to 10 relate to winding up generally, except where otherwise stated.]

NOTES

Substituted (together with the heading preceding this section) by the Companies Act 2006 (Consequential Amendments, Transitional Provisions and Savings) Order 2009, SI 2009/1941, art 2(1), Sch 1, para 75(1), (2), as from 1 October 2009 (for transitional provisions see the note to s 7A at **[9.103]**).

Contributories

[9.162]
74   Liability as contributories of present and past members
(1)   When a company is wound up, every present and past member is liable to contribute to its assets to any amount sufficient for payment of its debts and liabilities, and the expenses of the winding up, and for the adjustment of the rights of the contributories among themselves.
(2)   This is subject as follows—
(a)   a past member is not liable to contribute if he has ceased to be a member for one year or more before the commencement of the winding up;
(b)   a past member is not liable to contribute in respect of any debt or liability of the company contracted after he ceased to be a member;
(c)   a past member is not liable to contribute, unless it appears to the court that the existing members are unable to satisfy the contributions required to be made by them   . . . ;
(d)   in the case of a company limited by shares, no contribution is required from any member exceeding the amount (if any) unpaid on the shares in respect of which he is liable as a present or past member;
(e)   nothing in [the Companies Acts] or this Act invalidates any provision contained in a policy of insurance or other contract whereby the liability of individual members on the policy or contract is restricted, or whereby the funds of the company are alone made liable in respect of the policy or contract;
(f)   a sum due to any member of the company (in his character of a member) by way of dividends, profits or otherwise is not deemed to be a debt of the company, payable to that member in a case of competition between himself and any other creditor not a member of the company, but any such sum may be taken into account for the purpose of the final adjustment of the rights of the contributories among themselves.
(3)   In the case of a company limited by guarantee, no contribution is required from any member exceeding the amount undertaken to be contributed by him to the company's assets in the event of its being wound up; but if it is a company with a share capital, every member of it is liable (in addition to the amount so undertaken to be contributed to the assets), to contribute to the extent of any sums unpaid on shares held by him.

NOTES

Sub-s (2): words omitted from para (c) repealed, and words in square brackets in para (e) substituted, by the Companies Act 2006 (Consequential Amendments, Transitional Provisions and Savings) Order 2009, SI 2009/1941, art 2(1), Sch 1, para 75(1), (3), as from 1 October 2009 (for transitional provisions see the note to s 7A at **[9.103]**).

75 *(Repealed by the Companies Act 2006 (Consequential Amendments, Transitional Provisions and Savings) Order 2009, SI 2009/1941, art 2(1), Sch 1, para 75(1), (4), as from 1 October 2009 (for transitional provisions see the note to s 7A at* **[9.103]***). Note also that the Companies Act 2006 (Consequential Amendments, Transitional Provisions and Savings) Order 2009, SI 2009/1941, art 9 (at* **[4.536]***) provides that the repeal of this section does not affect its operation in relation to liabilities arising before 1 October 2009 or in connection with the holding of an office to which a person was appointed before that date on the understanding that their liability would be unlimited..)*

[9.163]
76 Liability of past directors and shareholders

(1) This section applies where a company is being wound up and—
   (a) it has under [Chapter 5 of Part 18 of the Companies Act 2006 (acquisition by limited company of its own shares: redemption or purchase by private company out of capital)] made a payment out of capital in respect of the redemption or purchase of any of its own shares (the payment being referred to below as "the relevant payment"), and
   (b) the aggregate amount of the company's assets and the amounts paid by way of contribution to its assets (apart from this section) is not sufficient for payment of its debts and liabilities, and the expenses of the winding up.

(2) If the winding up commenced within one year of the date on which the relevant payment was made, then—
   (a) the person from whom the shares were redeemed or purchased, and
   (b) the directors who signed the [statement] made in accordance with [section 714(1) to (3) of the Companies Act 2006] for purposes of the redemption or purchase (except a director who shows that he had reasonable grounds for forming the opinion set out in the [statement]),
are, so as to enable that insufficiency to be met, liable to contribute to the following extent to the company's assets.

(3) A person from whom any of the shares were redeemed or purchased is liable to contribute an amount not exceeding so much of the relevant payment as was made by the company in respect of his shares; and the directors are jointly and severally liable with that person to contribute that amount.

(4) A person who has contributed any amount to the assets in pursuance of this section may apply to the court for an order directing any other person jointly and severally liable in respect of that amount to pay him such amount as the court thinks just and equitable.

(5) [Section 74 does not apply] in relation to liability accruing by virtue of this section.

(6) . . .

NOTES
   Sub-ss (1), (5): words in square brackets substituted by the Companies Act 2006 (Consequential Amendments, Transitional Provisions and Savings) Order 2009, SI 2009/1941, art 2(1), Sch 1, para 75(1), (5)(a), (c), as from 1 October 2009 (for transitional provisions see the note to s 7A at **[9.103]**).
   Sub-s (2): words in second pair of square brackets substituted by SI 2009/1941, art 2(1), Sch 1, para 75(1), (5)(b), as from 1 October 2009 (for transitional provisions see the note to s 7A at **[9.103]**). Other words in square brackets substituted by the Companies Act 2006 (Consequential Amendments and Transitional Provisions) Order 2011, SI 2011/1265, art 6(3), as from 12 May 2011.
   Sub-s (6): repealed by SI 2009/1941, art 2(1), Sch 1, para 75(1), (5)(d), as from 1 October 2009 (for transitional provisions see the note to s 7A at **[9.103]**).

[9.164]
77 Limited company formerly unlimited

(1) This section applies in the case of a company being wound up which was at some former time registered as unlimited but has [re-registered as a limited company].

(2) Notwithstanding section 74(2)(a) above, a past member of the company who was a member of it at the time of re-registration, if the winding up commences within the period of 3 years beginning with the day on which the company was re-registered, is liable to contribute to the assets of the company in respect of debts and liabilities contracted before that time.

(3) If no persons who were members of the company at that time are existing members of it, a person who at that time was a present or past member is liable to contribute as above notwithstanding that the existing members have satisfied the contributions required to be made by them . . .

   This applies subject to section 74(2)(a) above and to subsection (2) of this section, but notwithstanding section 74(2)(c).

(4) Notwithstanding section 74(2)(d) and (3), there is no limit on the amount which a person who, at that time, was a past or present member of the company is liable to contribute as above.

NOTES
   Sub-s (1): words in square brackets substituted by the Companies Act 2006 (Consequential Amendments, Transitional Provisions and Savings) Order 2009, SI 2009/1941, art 2(1), Sch 1, para 75(1), (6)(a), as from 1 October 2009 (for transitional provisions see the note to s 7A at **[9.103]**).

Sub-s (3): words omitted repealed by SI 2009/1941, art 2(1), Sch 1, para 75(1), (6)(b), as from 1 October 2009 (for transitional provisions see the note to s 7A at **[9.103]**).

[9.165]
78 Unlimited company formerly limited
(1)   This section applies in the case of a company being wound up which was at some former time registered as limited but has been re-registered as unlimited . . .
(2)   A person who, at the time when the application for the company to be re-registered was lodged, was a past member of the company and did not after that again become a member of it is not liable to contribute to the assets of the company more than he would have been liable to contribute had the company not been re-registered.

NOTES
Sub-s (1): words omitted repealed by the Companies Act 2006 (Consequential Amendments, Transitional Provisions and Savings) Order 2009, SI 2009/1941, art 2(1), Sch 1, para 75(1), (7), as from 1 October 2009 (for transitional provisions see the note to s 7A at **[9.103]**).

[9.166]
79 Meaning of "contributory"
(1)   In this Act . . . the expression "contributory" means every person liable to contribute to the assets of a company in the event of its being wound up, and for the purposes of all proceedings for determining, and all proceedings prior to the final determination of, the persons who are to be deemed contributories, includes any person alleged to be a contributory.
(2)   The reference in subsection (1) to persons liable to contribute to the assets does not include a person so liable by virtue of a declaration by the court under section 213 (imputed responsibility for company's fraudulent trading) or section 214 (wrongful trading) in Chapter X of this Part.
(3)   A reference in a company's articles to a contributory does not (unless the context requires) include a person who is a contributory only by virtue of section 76.

NOTES
Sub-ss (1), (3): words omitted repealed by the Companies Act 2006 (Consequential Amendments, Transitional Provisions and Savings) Order 2009, SI 2009/1941, art 2(1), Sch 1, para 75(1), (8), as from 1 October 2009 (for transitional provisions see the note to s 7A at **[9.103]**).

[9.167]
80 Nature of contributory's liability
The liability of a contributory creates a debt (in England and Wales in the nature of [an ordinary contract debt]) accruing due from him at the time when his liability commenced, but payable at the times when calls are made for enforcing the liability.

NOTES
Words in square brackets substituted by the Companies Act 2006 (Consequential Amendments, Transitional Provisions and Savings) Order 2009, SI 2009/1941, art 2(1), Sch 1, para 75(1), (9), as from 1 October 2009 (for savings and transitional provisions see the note to s 7A at **[9.103]** and the note below).
Saving for provisions relating to nature of liability of member or contributory: the Companies Act 2006 (Consequential Amendments, Transitional Provisions and Savings) Order 2009, SI 2009/1941, art 11 (at **[4.538]**) provides that the new provisions as to the nature of a member's or contributory's liability (ie, the Companies Act 2006, s 33(2) and, in England and Wales, s 80 of the Insolvency Act 1986 as amended by that Order) apply to liabilities arising on or after 1 October 2009, and the old provisions (ie, CA 1985, s 14(2) and s 80 of the 1986 Act as it had effect prior to that amendment) continue to apply to liabilities arising before that date. Note also that for the purposes of art 11, a liability is treated as arising when the limitation period starts to run for the purposes of the Limitation Act 1980.

[9.168]
81 Contributories in case of death of a member
(1)   If a contributory dies either before or after he has been placed on the list of contributories, his personal representatives, and the heirs and legatees of heritage of his heritable estate in Scotland, are liable in a due course of administration to contribute to the assets of the company in discharge of his liability and are contributories accordingly.
(2)   Where the personal representatives are placed on the list of contributories, the heirs or legatees of heritage need not be added, but they may be added as and when the court thinks fit.
(3)   If in England and Wales the personal representatives make default in paying any money ordered to be paid by them, proceedings may be taken for administering the estate of the deceased contributory and for compelling payment out of it of the money due.

[9.169]
82 Effect of contributory's bankruptcy
(1)   The following applies if a contributory becomes bankrupt, either before or after he has been placed on the list of contributories.
(2)   His trustee in bankruptcy represents him for all purposes of the winding up, and is a contributory accordingly.

(3)   The trustee may be called on to admit to proof against the bankrupt's estate, or otherwise allow to be paid out of the bankrupt's assets in due course of law, any money due from the bankrupt in respect of his liability to contribute to the company's assets.

(4)   There may be proved against the bankrupt's estate the estimated value of his liability to future calls as well as calls already made.

[9.170]

83   [Companies registered but not formed under the Companies Act 2006]

(1)   The following applies in the event of a company being wound up which [is registered but not formed under the Companies Act 2006].

(2)   Every person is a contributory, in respect of the company's debts and liabilities contracted before registration, who is liable—

(a)   to pay, or contribute to the payment of, any debt or liability so contracted, or

(b)   to pay, or contribute to the payment of, any sum for the adjustment of the rights of the members among themselves in respect of any such debt or liability, or

(c)   to pay, or contribute to the amount of, the expenses of winding up the company, so far as relates to the debts or liabilities above-mentioned.

(3)   Every contributory is liable to contribute to the assets of the company, in the course of the winding up, all sums due from him in respect of any such liability.

(4)   In the event of the death, bankruptcy or insolvency of any contributory, provisions of this Act, with respect to the personal representatives, to the heirs and legatees of heritage of the heritable estate in Scotland of deceased contributories and to the trustees of bankrupt or insolvent contributories respectively, apply.

NOTES

Words in square brackets substituted by the Companies Act 2006 (Consequential Amendments, Transitional Provisions and Savings) Order 2009, SI 2009/1941, art 2(1), Sch 1, para 75(1), (10), as from 1 October 2009 (for transitional provisions see the note to s 7A at **[9.103]**).

CHAPTER II

VOLUNTARY WINDING UP (INTRODUCTORY AND GENERAL)

Resolutions for, and commencement of, voluntary winding up

[9.171]

84   Circumstances in which company may be wound up voluntarily

(1)   A company may be wound up voluntarily—

(a)   when the period (if any) fixed for the duration of the company by the articles expires, or the event (if any) occurs, on the occurrence of which the articles provide that the company is to be dissolved, and the company in general meeting has passed a resolution requiring it to be wound up voluntarily;

(b)   if the company resolves by special resolution that it be wound up voluntarily;

(c)   . . .

(2)   In this Act the expression "a resolution for voluntary winding up" means a resolution passed under [either of the paragraphs] of subsection (1).

[(2A)   Before a company passes a resolution for voluntary winding up it must give written notice of the resolution to the holder of any qualifying floating charge to which section 72A applies.

(2B)   Where notice is given under subsection (2A) a resolution for voluntary winding up may be passed only—

(a)   after the end of the period of five business days beginning with the day on which the notice was given, or

(b)   if the person to whom the notice was given has consented in writing to the passing of the resolution.]

[(3)   Chapter 3 of Part 3 of the Companies Act 2006 (resolutions affecting a company's constitution) applies to a resolution under paragraph (a) of subsection (1) as well as a special resolution under paragraph (b).]

[(4)   This section has effect subject to section 43 of the Commonhold and Leasehold Reform Act 2002.]

NOTES

Sub-s (1): para (c) repealed by the Companies Act 2006 (Commencement No 3, Consequential Amendments, Transitional Provisions and Savings) Order 2007, SI 2007/2194, art 10(1), Sch 4, Pt 3, para 39(1), (2), Sch 5, as from 1 October 2007 (for transitional provisions see the note below).

Sub-s (2): words in square brackets substituted by SI 2007/2194, art 10(1), Sch 4, Pt 3, para 39(1), (3), as from 1 October 2007 (for transitional provisions see the note below).

Sub-ss (2A), (2B): inserted by the Enterprise Act 2002 (Insolvency) Order 2003, SI 2003/2096, arts 4, 6, Schedule, Pt 1, paras 8, 10, as from 15 September 2003, except in relation to any case where a petition for an administration order was presented before that date.

Sub-s (3): substituted by SI 2007/2194, art 10(1), Sch 4, Pt 3, para 39(1), (4), as from 1 October 2007 (for transitional provisions see the note below).

Sub-s (4): added by the Commonhold and Leasehold Reform Act 2002, s 68, Sch 5, para 6, as from 27 September 2004, in relation to England and Wales only.

Transitional provisions: with regard to the amendments made by SI 2007/2194, Sch 4, Pt 3, para 39(1)–(4) above, note that Sch 4, Pt 3, para 39(5) provides that they apply in relation to (a) written resolutions for which the circulation date (see s 290 of CA 2006) is on or after 1 October 2007, and (b) to resolutions passed at a meeting of which notice is given on or after that date
Modification in relation to Scotland: see the Note at the beginning of this Act.

[9.172]
85 Notice of resolution to wind up
(1) When a company has passed a resolution for voluntary winding up, it shall, within 14 days after the passing of the resolution, give notice of the resolution by advertisement in the Gazette.
(2) If default is made in complying with this section, the company and every officer of it who is in default is liable to a fine and, for continued contravention, to a daily default fine.
For purposes of this subsection the liquidator is deemed an officer of the company.

[9.173]
86 Commencement of winding up
A voluntary winding up is deemed to commence at the time of the passing of the resolution for voluntary winding up.

Consequences of resolution to wind up

[9.174]
87 Effect on business and status of company
(1) In case of a voluntary winding up, the company shall from the commencement of the winding up cease to carry on its business, except so far as may be required for its beneficial winding up.
(2) However, the corporate state and corporate powers of the company, notwithstanding anything to the contrary in its articles, continue until the company is dissolved.

[9.175]
88 Avoidance of share transfers, etc after winding-up resolution
Any transfer of shares, not being a transfer made to or with the sanction of the liquidator, and any alteration in the status of the company's members, made after the commencement of a voluntary winding up, is void.

Declaration of solvency

[9.176]
89 Statutory declaration of solvency
(1) Where it is proposed to wind up a company voluntarily, the directors (or, in the case of a company having more than two directors, the majority of them) may at a directors' meeting make a statutory declaration to the effect that they have made a full inquiry into the company's affairs and that, having done so, they have formed the opinion that the company will be able to pay its debts in full, together with interest at the official rate (as defined in section 251), within such period, not exceeding 12 months from the commencement of the winding up, as may be specified in the declaration.
(2) Such a declaration by the directors has no effect for purposes of this Act unless—
    (a)   it is made within the 5 weeks immediately preceding the date of the passing of the resolution for winding up, or on that date but before the passing of the resolution, and
    (b)   it embodies a statement of the company's assets and liabilities as at the latest practicable date before the making of the declaration.
(3) The declaration shall be delivered to the registrar of companies before the expiration of 15 days immediately following the date on which the resolution for winding up is passed.
(4) A director making a declaration under this section without having reasonable grounds for the opinion that the company will be able to pay its debts in full, together with interest at the official rate, within the period specified is liable to imprisonment or a fine, or both.
(5) If the company is wound up in pursuance of a resolution passed within 5 weeks after the making of the declaration, and its debts (together with interest at the official rate) are not paid or provided for in full within the period specified, it is to be presumed (unless the contrary is shown) that the director did not have reasonable grounds for his opinion.
(6) If a declaration required by subsection (3) to be delivered to the registrar is not so delivered within the time prescribed by that subsection, the company and every officer in default is liable to a fine and, for continued contravention, to a daily default fine.

NOTES
Modification in relation to Scotland: see the Note at the beginning of this Act.

[9.177]
90 Distinction between "members'" and "creditors'" voluntary winding up
A winding up in the case of which a directors' statutory declaration under section 89 has been made is a "members' voluntary winding up"; and a winding up in the case of which such a declaration has not been made is a "creditors' voluntary winding up".

CHAPTER III
MEMBERS' VOLUNTARY WINDING UP

[9.178]
91 Appointment of liquidator
(1) In a members' voluntary winding up, the company in general meeting shall appoint one or more liquidators for the purpose of winding up the company's affairs and distributing its assets.
(2) On the appointment of a liquidator all the powers of the directors cease, except so far as the company in general meeting or the liquidator sanctions their continuance.

[9.179]
92 Power to fill vacancy in office of liquidator
(1) If a vacancy occurs by death, resignation or otherwise in the office of liquidator appointed by the company, the company in general meeting may, subject to any arrangement with its creditors, fill the vacancy.
(2) For that purpose a general meeting may be convened by any contributory or, if there were more liquidators than one, by the continuing liquidators.
(3) The meeting shall be held in manner provided by this Act or by the articles, or in such manner as may, on application by any contributory or by the continuing liquidators, be determined by the court.

NOTES

Meeting held in manner provided by this Act: it is thought that the reference in sub-s (3) above to "this Act" should originally have been a reference to CA 1985.

[9.180]
[92A Progress report to company at year's end (England and Wales)
(1) Subject to sections 96 and 102, in the event of the winding up of a company registered in England and Wales continuing for more than one year, the liquidator must—
    (a) for each prescribed period produce a progress report relating to the prescribed matters; and
    (b) within such period commencing with the end of the period referred to in paragraph (a) as may be prescribed send a copy of the progress report to—
        (i) the members of the company; and
        (ii) such other persons as may be prescribed.
(2) A liquidator who fails to comply with this section is liable to a fine.]

NOTES

Commencement: 6 April 2010.
Inserted by the Legislative Reform (Insolvency) (Miscellaneous Provisions) Order 2010, SI 2010/18, arts 2, 6(1), as from 6 April 2010 (for transitional provisions see art 12(1) of the 2010 Order which provides that this section does not apply in respect of a company in voluntary winding up where the resolution to wind up was passed before 6 April 2010).

[9.181]
93 General company meeting at each year's end [(Scotland)]
(1) Subject to sections 96 and 102, in the event of the winding up [of a company registered in Scotland] continuing for more than one year, the liquidator shall summon a general meeting of the company at the end of the first year from the commencement of the winding up, and of each succeeding year, or at the first convenient date within 3 months from the end of the year or such longer period as the Secretary of State may allow.
(2) The liquidator shall lay before the meeting an account of his acts and dealings, and of the conduct of the winding up, during the preceding year.
(3) If the liquidator fails to comply with this section, he is liable to a fine.

NOTES

Section heading, sub-s (1): words in square brackets inserted by the Legislative Reform (Insolvency) (Miscellaneous Provisions) Order 2010, SI 2010/18, arts 2, 6(2), as from 6 April 2010 (for transitional provisions see art 12(2) of the 2010 Order which provides that these amendments do not apply in respect of a company in voluntary winding up where the resolution to wind up was passed before 6 April 2010).

[9.182]
94 Final meeting prior to dissolution
(1) As soon as the company's affairs are fully wound up, the liquidator shall make up an account of the winding up, showing how it has been conducted and the company's property has been disposed of, and thereupon shall call a general meeting of the company for the purpose of laying before it the account, and giving an explanation of it.
(2) The meeting shall be called by advertisement in the Gazette, specifying its time, place and object and published at least one month before the meeting.
(3) Within one week after the meeting, the liquidator shall send to the registrar of companies a copy of the account, and shall make a return to him of the holding of the meeting and of its date.
(4) If the copy is not sent or the return is not made in accordance with subsection (3), the liquidator is liable to a fine and, for continued contravention, to a daily default fine.

(5)   If a quorum is not present at the meeting, the liquidator shall, in lieu of the return mentioned above, make a return that the meeting was duly summoned and that no quorum was present; and upon such a return being made, the provisions of subsection (3) as to the making of the return are deemed complied with.

(6)   If the liquidator fails to call a general meeting of the company as required by subsection (1), he is liable to a fine.

NOTES

Modification in relation to Scotland: see the Note at the beginning of this Act.

[9.183]
95   Effect of company's insolvency

(1)   This section applies where the liquidator is of the opinion that the company will be unable to pay its debts in full (together with interest at the official rate) within the period stated in the directors' declaration under section 89.

(2)   [In the case of the winding up of a company registered in Scotland, the liquidator] shall—

    (a)   summon a meeting of creditors for a day not later than the 28th day after the day on which he formed that opinion;

    (b)   send notices of the creditors' meeting to the creditors by post not less than 7 days before the day on which that meeting is to be held;

    (c)   cause notice of the creditors' meeting to be advertised once in the Gazette and once at least in 2 newspapers circulating in the relevant locality (that is to say the locality in which the company's principal place of business in Great Britain was situated during the relevant period); and

    (d)   during the period before the day on which the creditors' meeting is to be held, furnish creditors free of charge with such information concerning the affairs of the company as they may reasonably require;

and the notice of the creditors' meeting shall state the duty imposed by paragraph (d) above.

[(2A)   In the case of the winding up of a company registered in England and Wales, the liquidator—

    (a)   shall summon a meeting of creditors for a day not later than the 28th day after the day on which he formed that opinion;

    (b)   shall send notices of the creditors' meeting to the creditors   . . .   not less than 7 days before the day on which that meeting is to be held;

    (c)   shall cause notice of the creditors' meeting to be advertised once in the Gazette;

    (d)   may cause notice of the meeting to be advertised in such other manner as he thinks fit; and

    (e)   shall during the period before the day on which the creditors' meeting is to be held, furnish creditors free of charge with such information concerning the affairs of the company as they may reasonably require;

and the notice of the creditors' meeting shall state the duty imposed by paragraph (e) above.]

(3)   The liquidator shall also—

    (a)   make out a statement in the prescribed form as to the affairs of the company;

    (b)   lay that statement before the creditors' meeting; and

    (c)   attend and preside at that meeting.

(4)   The statement as to the affairs of the company   . . .   shall show—

    (a)   particulars of the company's assets, debts and liabilities;

    (b)   the names and addresses of the company's creditors;

    (c)   the securities held by them respectively;

    (d)   the dates when the securities were respectively given; and

    (e)   such further or other information as may be prescribed.

[(4A)   The statement as to the affairs of the company shall be verified by the liquidator—

    (a)   in the case of a winding up of a company registered in England and Wales, by a statement of truth; and

    (b)   in the case of a winding up of a company registered in Scotland, by affidavit.]

(5)   Where the company's principal place of business in Great Britain was situated in different localities at different times during the relevant period, the duty imposed by subsection (2)(c) applies separately in relation to each of those localities.

(6)   Where the company had no place of business in Great Britain during the relevant period, references in subsections (2)(c) and (5) to the company's principal place of business in Great Britain are replaced by references to its registered office.

(7)   In this section "the relevant period" means the period of 6 months immediately preceding the day on which were sent the notices summoning the company meeting at which it was resolved that the company be wound up voluntarily.

(8)   If the liquidator without reasonable excuse fails to comply with this section, he is liable to a fine.

NOTES

Sub-s (2): words in square brackets substituted by the Legislative Reform (Insolvency) (Advertising Requirements) Order 2009, SI 2009/864, arts 2, 3(1)(a), 4, as from 6 April 2009, except in respect of a company in voluntary winding up where the resolution to wind up was passed before that date.

Sub-s (2A): inserted by SI 2009/864, arts 2, 3(1)(b), 4, as from 6 April 2009, except in respect of a company in voluntary winding up where the resolution to wind up was passed before that date; words omitted repealed by the Legislative Reform (Insolvency) (Miscellaneous Provisions) Order 2010, SI 2010/18, arts 2, 7, as from 6 April 2010 (for transitional provisions see art 12(3) of the 2010 Order which provides that this amendment does not apply in respect of a company in voluntary winding up where the resolution to wind up was passed before 6 April 2010).

Sub-s (4): words omitted repealed by SI 2010/18, arts 2, 5(2)(a), as from 6 April 2010.

Sub-s (4A): inserted by SI 2010/18, arts 2, 5(2)(b), as from 6 April 2010.

[9.184]
96 Conversion to creditors' voluntary winding up
As from the day on which the creditors' meeting is held under section 95, this Act has effect as if—
 (a) the directors' declaration under section 89 had not been made; and
 (b) the creditors' meeting and the company meeting at which it was resolved that the company be wound up voluntarily were the meetings mentioned in section 98 in the next Chapter;
and accordingly the winding up becomes a creditors' voluntary winding up.

CHAPTER IV
CREDITORS' VOLUNTARY WINDING UP

[9.185]
97 Application of this Chapter
(1) Subject as follows, this Chapter applies in relation to a creditors' voluntary winding up.
(2) Sections 98 and 99 do not apply where, under section 96 in Chapter III, a members' voluntary winding up has become a creditors' voluntary winding up.

[9.186]
98 Meeting of creditors
(1) [In the case of the winding up of a company registered in Scotland, the company] shall—
 (a) cause a meeting of its creditors to be summoned for a day not later than the 14th day after the day on which there is to be held the company meeting at which the resolution for voluntary winding up is to be proposed;
 (b) cause the notices of the creditors' meeting to be sent by post to the creditors not less than 7 days before the day on which that meeting is to be held; and
 (c) cause notice of the creditors' meeting to be advertised once in the Gazette and once at least in two newspapers circulating in the relevant locality (that is to say the locality in which the company's principal place of business in Great Britain was situated during the relevant period).
[(1A) In the case of the winding up of a company registered in England and Wales, the company—
 (a) shall cause a meeting of its creditors to be summoned for a day not later than the 14th day after the day on which there is to be held the company meeting at which the resolution for voluntary winding up is to be proposed;
 (b) shall cause the notices of the creditors' meeting to be sent . . . to the creditors not less than 7 days before the day on which that meeting is to be held;
 (c) shall cause notice of the creditors' meeting to be advertised once in the Gazette; and
 (d) may cause notice of the meeting to be advertised in such other manner as the directors think fit.]
(2) The notice of the creditors' meeting shall state either—
 (a) the name and address of a person qualified to act as an insolvency practitioner in relation to the company who, during the period before the day on which that meeting is to be held, will furnish creditors free of charge with such information concerning the company's affairs as they may reasonably require; or
 (b) a place in the relevant locality where, on the two business days falling next before the day on which that meeting is to be held, a list of the names and addresses of the company's creditors will be available for inspection free of charge.
(3) Where the company's principal place of business in Great Britain was situated in different localities at different times during the relevant period, the duties imposed by subsections (1)(c) and (2)(b) above apply separately in relation to each of those localities.
(4) Where the company had no place of business in Great Britain during the relevant period, references in subsections (1)(c) and (3) to the company's principal place of business in Great Britain are replaced by references to its registered office.
(5) In this section "the relevant period" means the period of 6 months immediately preceding the day on which were sent the notices summoning the company meeting at which it was resolved that the company be wound up voluntarily.
(6) If the company without reasonable excuse fails to comply with subsection (1)[, (1A)] or (2), it is guilty of an offence and liable to a fine.

NOTES

Sub-s (1): words in square brackets substituted by the Legislative Reform (Insolvency) (Advertising Requirements) Order 2009, SI 2009/864, arts 2, 3(2)(a), 4, as from 6 April 2009, except in respect of a company in voluntary winding up where the resolution to wind up was passed before that date.

Sub-s (1A): inserted by SI 2009/864, arts 2, 3(2)(b), 4, as from 6 April 2009, except in respect of a company in voluntary winding up where the resolution to wind up was passed before that date; words omitted repealed by the Legislative Reform (Insolvency) (Miscellaneous Provisions) Order 2010, SI 2010/18, arts 2, 7, as from 6 April 2010 (for transitional provisions see art 12(3) of the 2010 Order which provides that this amendment does not apply in respect of a company in voluntary winding up where the resolution to wind up was passed before 6 April 2010).

Sub-s (6): figure in square brackets inserted by SI 2009/864, arts 2, 3(2)(c), 4, as from 6 April 2009, except in respect of a company in voluntary winding up where the resolution to wind up was passed before that date.

[9.187]
99   Directors to lay statement of affairs before creditors
(1)   The directors of the company shall—
   (a)   make out a statement in the prescribed form as to the affairs of the company;
   (b)   cause that statement to be laid before the creditors' meeting under section 98; and
   (c)   appoint one of their number to preside at that meeting;
and it is the duty of the director so appointed to attend the meeting and preside over it.
(2)   The statement as to the affairs of the company   . . .   shall show—
   (a)   particulars of the company's assets, debts and liabilities;
   (b)   the names and addresses of the company's creditors;
   (c)   the securities held by them respectively;
   (d)   the dates when the securities were respectively given; and
   (e)   such further or other information as may be prescribed.
[(2A)   The statement as to the affairs of the company shall be verified by some or all of the directors—
   (a)   in the case of a winding up of a company registered in England and Wales, by a statement of truth; and
   (b)   in the case of a winding up of a company registered in Scotland, by affidavit.]
(3)   If—
   (a)   the directors without reasonable excuse fail to comply with subsection (1)[, (2) or (2A)]; or
   (b)   any director without reasonable excuse fails to comply with subsection (1), so far as requiring him to attend and preside at the creditors' meeting,
the directors are or (as the case may be) the director is guilty of an offence and liable to a fine.

NOTES

Sub-s (2): words omitted repealed by the Legislative Reform (Insolvency) (Miscellaneous Provisions) Order 2010, SI 2010/18, arts 2, 5(3)(a), as from 6 April 2010.

Sub-s (2A): inserted by SI 2010/18, arts 2, 5(3)(b), as from 6 April 2010.

Sub-s (3): words in square brackets in para (a) substituted by SI 2010/18, arts 2, 5(3)(c), as from 6 April 2010.

[9.188]
100   Appointment of liquidator
(1)   The creditors and the company at their respective meetings mentioned in section 98 may nominate a person to be liquidator for the purpose of winding up the company's affairs and distributing its assets.
(2)   The liquidator shall be the person nominated by the creditors or, where no person has been so nominated, the person (if any) nominated by the company.
(3)   In the case of different persons being nominated, any director, member or creditor of the company may, within 7 days after the date on which the nomination was made by the creditors, apply to the court for an order either—
   (a)   directing that the person nominated as liquidator by the company shall be liquidator instead of or jointly with the person nominated by the creditors, or
   (b)   appointing some other person to be liquidator instead of the person nominated by the creditors.
[(4)   The court shall grant an application under subsection (3) made by the holder of a qualifying floating charge in respect of the company's property (within the meaning of paragraph 14 of Schedule B1) unless the court thinks it right to refuse the application because of the particular circumstances of the case.]

NOTES

Sub-s (4): added by the Enterprise Act 2002, s 248(3), Sch 17, paras 9, 14, as from a day to be appointed (for savings and transitional provisions, see the note to s 8 at **[9.105]**).

[9.189]
101   Appointment of liquidation committee

(1) The creditors at the meeting to be held under section 98 or at any subsequent meeting may, if they think fit, appoint a committee ("the liquidation committee") of not more than 5 persons to exercise the functions conferred on it by or under this Act.

(2) If such a committee is appointed, the company may, either at the meeting at which the resolution for voluntary winding up is passed or at any time subsequently in general meeting, appoint such number of persons as they think fit to act as members of the committee, not exceeding 5.

(3) However, the creditors may, if they think fit, resolve that all or any of the persons so appointed by the company ought not to be members of the liquidation committee; and if the creditors so resolve—

  (a) the persons mentioned in the resolution are not then, unless the court otherwise directs, qualified to act as members of the committee; and

  (b) on any application to the court under this provision the court may, if it thinks fit, appoint other persons to act as such members in place of the persons mentioned in the resolution.

(4) In Scotland, the liquidation committee has, in addition to the powers and duties conferred and imposed on it by this Act, such of the powers and duties of commissioners on a bankrupt estate as may be conferred and imposed on liquidation committees by the rules.

[9.190]
102   Creditors' meeting where winding up converted under s 96

Where, in the case of a winding up which was, under section 96 in Chapter III, converted to a creditors' voluntary winding up, a creditors' meeting is held in accordance with section 95, any appointment made or committee established by that meeting is deemed to have been made or established by a meeting held in accordance with section 98 in this Chapter.

[9.191]
103   Cesser of directors' powers

On the appointment of a liquidator, all the powers of the directors cease, except so far as the liquidation committee (or, if there is no such committee, the creditors) sanction their continuance.

[9.192]
104   Vacancy in office of liquidator

If a vacancy occurs, by death, resignation or otherwise, in the office of a liquidator (other than a liquidator appointed by, or by the direction of, the court), the creditors may fill the vacancy.

[9.193]
[104A   Progress report to company and creditors at year's end (England and Wales)

(1) If the winding up of a company registered in England and Wales continues for more than one year, the liquidator must—

  (a) for each prescribed period produce a progress report relating to the prescribed matters; and

  (b) within such period commencing with the end of the period referred to in paragraph (a) as may be prescribed send a copy of the progress report to—

    (i) the members and creditors of the company; and

    (ii) such other persons as may be prescribed.

(2) A liquidator who fails to comply with this section is liable to a fine.]

NOTES

Commencement: 6 April 2010.

Inserted by the Legislative Reform (Insolvency) (Miscellaneous Provisions) Order 2010, SI 2010/18, arts 2, 6(3), as from 6 April 2010 (for transitional provisions see art 12(1) of the 2010 Order which provides that this section does not apply in respect of a company in voluntary winding up where the resolution to wind up was passed before 6 April 2010).

[9.194]
105   Meetings of company and creditors at each year's end [(Scotland)]

(1) If the winding up [of a company registered in Scotland] continues for more than one year, the liquidator shall summon a general meeting of the company and a meeting of the creditors at the end of the first year from the commencement of the winding up, and of each succeeding year, or at the first convenient date within 3 months from the end of the year or such longer period as the Secretary of State may allow.

(2) The liquidator shall lay before each of the meetings an account of his acts and dealings and of the conduct of the winding up during the preceding year.

(3) If the liquidator fails to comply with this section, he is liable to a fine.

(4) Where under section 96 a members' voluntary winding up has become a creditors' voluntary winding up, and the creditors' meeting under section 95 is held 3 months or less before the end of the first year from the commencement of the winding up, the liquidator is not required by this section to summon a meeting of creditors at the end of that year.

NOTES

Section heading, sub-s (1): words in square brackets inserted by the Legislative Reform (Insolvency) (Miscellaneous Provisions) Order 2010, SI 2010/18, arts 2, 6(4), as from 6 April 2010 (for transitional provisions see art 12(2) of the 2010 Order which provides that these amendments do not apply in respect of a company in voluntary winding up where the resolution to wind up was passed before 6 April 2010).

[9.195]
106 Final meeting prior to dissolution
(1)   As soon as the company's affairs are fully wound up, the liquidator shall make up an account of the winding up, showing how it has been conducted and the company's property has been disposed of, and thereupon shall call a general meeting of the company and a meeting of the creditors for the purpose of laying the account before the meetings and giving an explanation of it.
(2)   Each such meeting shall be called by advertisement in the Gazette specifying the time, place and object of the meeting, and published at least one month before it.
(3)   Within one week after the date of the meetings (or, if they are not held on the same date, after the date on the later one) the liquidator shall send to the registrar of companies a copy of the account, and shall make a return to him of the holding of the meetings and of their dates.
(4)   If the copy is not sent or the return is not made in accordance with subsection (3), the liquidator is liable to a fine and, for continued contravention, to a daily default fine.
(5)   However, if a quorum is not present at either such meeting, the liquidator shall, in lieu of the return required by subsection (3), make a return that the meeting was duly summoned and that no quorum was present; and upon such return being made the provisions of that subsection as to the making of the return are, in respect of that meeting, deemed complied with.
(6)   If the liquidator fails to call a general meeting of the company or a meeting of the creditors as required by this section, he is liable to a fine.

NOTES

Modification in relation to Scotland: see the Note at the beginning of this Act.

CHAPTER V
PROVISIONS APPLYING TO BOTH KINDS OF VOLUNTARY WINDING UP

[9.196]
107 Distribution of company's property
Subject to the provisions of this Act as to preferential payments, the company's property in a voluntary winding up shall on the winding up be applied in satisfaction of the company's liabilities pari passu and, subject to that application, shall (unless the articles otherwise provide) be distributed among the members according to their rights and interests in the company.

[9.197]
108 Appointment or removal of liquidator by the court
(1)   If from any cause whatever there is no liquidator acting, the court may appoint a liquidator.
(2)   The court may, on cause shown, remove a liquidator and appoint another.

[9.198]
109 Notice by liquidator of his appointment
(1)   The liquidator shall, within 14 days after his appointment, publish in the Gazette and deliver to the registrar of companies for registration a notice of his appointment in the form prescribed by statutory instrument made by the Secretary of State.
(2)   If the liquidator fails to comply with this section, he is liable to a fine and, for continued contravention, to a daily default fine.

NOTES

Modification in relation to Scotland: see the Note at the beginning of this Act.
Deliver to the registrar of companies: the Accountant in Bankruptcy in Scotland must forward copies of notices of the appointment of a liquidator of a community interest company to the Regulator of Community Interest Companies (since in Scotland such notices are received by the Accountant in Bankruptcy and not the registrar of companies); see the Bankruptcy (Scotland) Act 1985, s 71A (as inserted by the Companies (Audit, Investigations and Community Enterprise) Act 2004, s 59(2)

[9.199]
110 Acceptance of shares, etc, as consideration for sale of company property
(1)   This section applies, in the case of a company proposed to be, or being, wound up voluntarily, where the whole or part of the company's business or property is proposed to be transferred or sold
   [(a)   to another company ("the transferee company"), whether or not the latter is a [company registered under the Companies Act 2006][, or
   (b)   to a limited liability partnership (the "transferee limited liability partnership")].
(2)   With the requisite sanction, the liquidator of the company being, or proposed to be, wound up ("the transferor company") may receive, in compensation or part compensation for the transfer or [sale—

(a)　in the case of the transferee company, shares, policies or other like interests in the company for distribution among the members of the transferor company, or

(b)　in the case of the transferee limited liability partnership, membership in the limited liability partnership for distribution among the members of the transferor company.]

(3)　The sanction requisite under subsection (2) is—

(a)　in the case of a members' voluntary winding up, that of a special resolution of the company, conferring either a general authority on the liquidator or an authority in respect of any particular arrangement, and

(b)　in the case of a creditors' voluntary winding up, that of either the court or the liquidation committee.

(4)　Alternatively to subsection (2), the liquidator may (with that sanction) enter into any other arrangement whereby the members of the transferor [company may—

(a)　in the case of the transferee company, in lieu of receiving cash, shares, policies or other like interests (or in addition thereto) participate in the profits of, or receive any other benefit from, the company, or

(b)　in the case of the transferee limited liability partnership, in lieu of receiving cash, or membership (or in addition thereto) participate in some other way in the profits of, or receive any other benefit from, the limited liability partnership.]

(5)　A sale or arrangement in pursuance of this section is binding on members of the transferor company.

(6)　A special resolution is not invalid for purposes of this section by reason that it is passed before or concurrently with a resolution for voluntary winding up or for appointing liquidators; but, if an order is made within a year for winding up the company by the court, the special resolution is not valid unless sanctioned by the court.

NOTES

Sub-s (1): para (a) designated as such, and para (b) (and the preceding word) added by the Limited Liability Partnerships Regulations 2001, SI 2001/1090, reg 9, Sch 5, para 15(1), (2), as from 6 April 2001 (in relation to England and Wales) and by the Limited Liability Partnerships (Scotland) Regulations 2001, SSI 2001/128, reg 5, Sch 4, para 1(1), (2), as from 6 April 2001 (in relation to Scotland); words in square brackets in para (a) substituted by the Companies Act 2006 (Consequential Amendments, Transitional Provisions and Savings) Order 2009, SI 2009/1941, art 2(1), Sch 1, para 75(1), (11), as from 1 October 2009 (for transitional provisions see the note to s 7A at **[9.103]**).

Sub-ss (2), (4): words in square brackets substituted, in relation to England and Wales, by SI 2001/1090, reg 9, Sch 5, para 15(1), (3), (4), as from 6 April 2001, and in relation to Scotland, by SSI 2001/128, reg 5, Sch 4, para 1(1), (3), (4), as from 6 April 2001.

[9.200]
111　Dissent from arrangement under s 110

(1)　This section applies in the case of a voluntary winding up where, for the purposes of section 110(2) or (4), there has been passed a special resolution of the transferor company providing the sanction requisite for the liquidator under that section.

(2)　If a member of the transferor company who did not vote in favour of the special resolution expresses his dissent from it in writing, addressed to the liquidator and left at the company's registered office within 7 days after the passing of the resolution, he may require the liquidator either to abstain from carrying the resolution into effect or to purchase his interest at a price to be determined by agreement or by arbitration under this section.

(3)　If the liquidator elects to purchase the member's interest, the purchase money must be paid before the company is dissolved and be raised by the liquidator in such manner as may be determined by special resolution.

(4)　For purposes of an arbitration under this section, the provisions of the Companies Clauses Consolidation Act 1845 or, in the case of a winding up in Scotland, the Companies Clauses Consolidation (Scotland) Act 1845 with respect to the settlement of disputes by arbitration are incorporated with this Act, and—

(a)　in the construction of those provisions this Act is deemed the special Act and "the company" means the transferor company, and

(b)　any appointment by the incorporated provisions directed to be made under the hand of the secretary or any two of the directors may be made in writing by the liquidator (or, if there is more than one liquidator, then any two or more of them).

[9.201]
112　Reference of questions to court

(1)　The liquidator or any contributory or creditor may apply to the court to determine any question arising in the winding up of a company, or to exercise, as respects the enforcing of calls or any other matter, all or any of the powers which the court might exercise if the company were being wound up by the court.

(2)　The court, if satisfied that the determination of the question or the required exercise of power will be just and beneficial, may accede wholly or partially to the application on such terms and conditions as it thinks fit, or may make such other order on the application as it thinks just.

(3)   A copy of an order made by virtue of this section staying the proceedings in the winding up shall forthwith be forwarded by the company, or otherwise as may be prescribed, to the registrar of companies, who shall enter it in his records relating to the company.

NOTES

Modification in relation to Scotland: see the Note at the beginning of this Act.

[9.202]
113   Court's power to control proceedings (Scotland)
If the court, on the application of the liquidator in the winding up of a company registered in Scotland, so directs, no action or proceeding shall be proceeded with or commenced against the company except by leave of the court and subject to such terms as the court may impose.

[9.203]
114   No liquidator appointed or nominated by company
(1)   This section applies where, in the case of a voluntary winding up, no liquidator has been appointed or nominated by the company.
(2)   The powers of the directors shall not be exercised, except with the sanction of the court or (in the case of a creditors' voluntary winding up) so far as may be necessary to secure compliance with sections 98 (creditors' meeting) and 99 (statement of affairs), during the period before the appointment or nomination of a liquidator of the company.
(3)   Subsection (2) does not apply in relation to the powers of the directors—
   (a)   to dispose of perishable goods and other goods the value of which is likely to diminish if they are not immediately disposed of, and
   (b)   to do all such other things as may be necessary for the protection of the company's assets.
(4)   If the directors of the company without reasonable excuse fail to comply with this section, they are liable to a fine.

[9.204]
115   Expenses of voluntary winding up
All expenses properly incurred in the winding up, including the remuneration of the liquidator, are payable out of the company's assets in priority to all other claims.

[9.205]
116   Saving for certain rights
The voluntary winding up of a company does not bar the right of any creditor or contributory to have it wound up by the court; but in the case of an application by a contributory the court must be satisfied that the rights of the contributories will be prejudiced by a voluntary winding up.

CHAPTER VI
WINDING UP BY THE COURT

Jurisdiction (England and Wales)

[9.206]
117   High Court and county court jurisdiction
(1)   The High Court has jurisdiction to wind up any company registered in England and Wales.
(2)   Where the amount of a company's share capital paid up or credited as paid up does not exceed £120,000, then (subject to this section) the county court of the district in which the company's registered office is situated has concurrent jurisdiction with the High Court to wind up the company.
(3)   The money sum for the time being specified in subsection (2) is subject to increase or reduction by order under section 416 in Part XV.
(4)   The Lord Chancellor [may, with the concurrence of the Lord Chief Justice, by order] in a statutory instrument exclude a county court from having winding-up jurisdiction, and for the purposes of that jurisdiction may attach its district, or any part thereof, to any other county court, and may by statutory instrument revoke or vary any such order.
   In exercising the powers of this section, the Lord Chancellor shall provide that a county court is not to have winding-up jurisdiction unless it has for the time being jurisdiction for the purposes of Parts VIII to XI of this Act (individual insolvency).
(5)   Every court in England and Wales having winding-up jurisdiction has for the purposes of that jurisdiction all the powers of the High Court; and every prescribed officer of the court shall perform any duties which an officer of the High Court may discharge by order of a judge of that court or otherwise in relation to winding up.
(6)   For the purposes of this section, a company's "registered office" is the place which has longest been its registered office during the 6 months immediately preceding the presentation of the petition for winding up.
[(7)   This section is subject to Article 3 of the EC Regulation (jurisdiction under EC Regulation).]
[(8)   The Lord Chief Justice may nominate a judicial office holder (as defined in section 109(4) of the Constitutional Reform Act 2005) to exercise his functions under this section.]

NOTES

Sub-s (4): words in square brackets substituted by the Constitutional Reform Act 2005, s 15, Sch 4, Pt 1, paras 185, 186(1), (2), as from 3 April 2006.

Sub-s (7): added by the Insolvency Act 1986 (Amendment) (No 2) Regulations 2002, SI 2002/1240, regs 3, 6, as from 31 May 2002.

Sub-s (8): added by the Constitutional Reform Act 2005, s 15, Sch 4, Pt 1, paras 185, 186(1), (3), as from 3 April 2006.

Orders: the Civil Courts Order 1983, SI 1983/713.

[9.207]
118 Proceedings taken in wrong court
(1) Nothing in section 117 invalidates a proceeding by reason of its being taken in the wrong court.

(2) The winding up of a company by the court in England and Wales, or any proceedings in the winding up, may be retained in the court in which the proceedings were commenced, although it may not be the court in which they ought to have been commenced.

[9.208]
119 Proceedings in county court; case stated for High Court
(1) If any question arises in any winding-up proceedings in a county court which all the parties to the proceedings, or which one of them and the judge of the court, desire to have determined in the first instance in the High Court, the judge shall state the facts in the form of a special case for the opinion of the High Court.

(2) Thereupon the special case and the proceedings (or such of them as may be required) shall be transmitted to the High Court for the purposes of the determination.

Jurisdiction (Scotland)

[9.209]
120 Court of Session and sheriff court jurisdiction
(1) The Court of Session has jurisdiction to wind up any company registered in Scotland.

(2) When the Court of Session is in vacation, the jurisdiction conferred on that court by this section may (subject to the provisions of this Part) be exercised by the judge acting as vacation judge . . .

(3) Where the amount of a company's share capital paid up or credited as paid up does not exceed £120,000, the sheriff court of the sheriffdom in which the company's registered office is situated has concurrent jurisdiction with the Court of Session to wind up the company; but—

   (a)   the Court of Session may, if it thinks expedient having regard to the amount of the company's assets to do so—

       (i)   remit to a sheriff court any petition presented to the Court of Session for winding up such a company, or

      (ii)   require such a petition presented to a sheriff court to be remitted to the Court of Session; and

   (b)   the Court of Session may require any such petition as above-mentioned presented to one sheriff court to be remitted to another sheriff court; and

   (c)   in a winding up in the sheriff court the sheriff may submit a stated case for the opinion of the Court of Session on any question of law arising in that winding up.

(4) For purposes of this section, the expression "registered office" means the place which has longest been the company's registered office during the 6 months immediately preceding the presentation of the petition for winding up.

(5) The money sum for the time being specified in subsection (3) is subject to increase or reduction by order under section 416 in Part XV.

[(6) This section is subject to Article 3 of the EC Regulation (jurisdiction under EC Regulation).]

NOTES

Sub-s (2): words omitted repealed by the Court of Session Act 1988, s 52(2), Sch 2, Pt III, as from 29 September 1988.

Sub-s (6): added by the Insolvency Act 1986 (Amendment) (No 2) Regulations 2002, SI 2002/1240, regs 3, 7, as from 31 May 2002.

[9.210]
121 Power to remit winding up to Lord Ordinary
(1) The Court of Session may, by Act of Sederunt, make provision for the taking of proceedings in a winding up before one of the Lords Ordinary; and, where provision is so made, the Lord Ordinary has, for the purposes of the winding up, all the powers and jurisdiction of the court.

(2) However, the Lord Ordinary may report to the Inner House any matter which may arise in the course of a winding up.

Grounds and effect of winding-up petition

[9.211]
122 Circumstances in which company may be wound up by the court
(1) A company may be wound up by the court if—

(a)   the company has by special resolution resolved that the company be wound up by the court,

(b)   being a public company which was registered as such on its original incorporation, the company has not been issued with [a trading certificate under section 761 of the Companies Act 2006 (requirement as to minimum share capital)] and more than a year has expired since it was so registered,

(c)   it is an old public company, within the meaning of [Schedule 3 to the Companies Act 2006 (Consequential Amendments, Transitional Provisions and Savings) Order 2009],

(d)   the company does not commence its business within a year from its incorporation or suspends its business for a whole year,

(e)   . . .

(f)   the company is unable to pay its debts,

[(fa) at the time at which a moratorium for the company under section 1A comes to an end, no voluntary arrangement approved under Part I has effect in relation to the company]

(g)   the court is of the opinion that it is just and equitable that the company should be wound up.

(2)   In Scotland, a company which the Court of Session has jurisdiction to wind up may be wound up by the Court if there is subsisting a floating charge over property comprised in the company's property and undertaking, and the court is satisfied that the security of the creditor entitled to the benefit of the floating charge is in jeopardy.

For this purpose a creditor's security is deemed to be in jeopardy if the Court is satisfied that events have occurred or are about to occur which render it unreasonable in the creditor's interests that the company should retain power to dispose of the property which is subject to the floating charge.

NOTES

Sub-s (1): words in square brackets in para (b) substituted by the Companies Act 2006 (Consequential Amendments etc) Order 2008, SI 2008/948, art 3(1), Sch 1, Pt 2, para 102, as from 6 April 2008; words in square brackets in para (c) substituted by the Companies Act 2006 (Consequential Amendments, Transitional Provisions and Savings) Order 2009, SI 2009/1941, art 2(1), Sch 1, para 75(1), (12), as from 1 October 2009 (for transitional provisions see the note to s 7A at **[9.103]**); para (e) repealed by the Companies Act 2006 (Consequential Amendments and Transitional Provisions) Order 2011, SI 2011/1265, art 6(4), as from 12 May 2011; para (fa) inserted by the Insolvency Act 2000, s 1, Sch 1, paras 1, 6, as from 1 January 2003.

Old public companies: as to the meaning of this, see also the Companies Act 2006 (Consequential Amendments and Transitional Provisions) Order 2011, SI 2011/1265, Sch 1 at **[4.651]**.

[9.212]
123   Definition of inability to pay debts

(1)   A company is deemed unable to pay its debts—

(a)   if a creditor (by assignment or otherwise) to whom the company is indebted in a sum exceeding £750 then due has served on the company, by leaving it at the company's registered office, a written demand (in the prescribed form) requiring the company to pay the sum so due and the company has for 3 weeks thereafter neglected to pay the sum or to secure or compound for it to the reasonable satisfaction of the creditor, or

(b)   if, in England and Wales, execution or other process issued on a judgment, decree or order of any court in favour of a creditor of the company is returned unsatisfied in whole or in part, or

(c)   if, in Scotland, the induciae of a charge for payment on an extract decree, or an extract registered bond, or an extract registered protest, have expired without payment being made, or

(d)   if, in Northern Ireland, a certificate of unenforceability has been granted in respect of a judgment against the company, or

(e)   if it is proved to the satisfaction of the court that the company is unable to pay its debts as they fall due.

(2)   A company is also deemed unable to pay its debts if it is proved to the satisfaction of the court that the value of the company's assets is less than the amount of its liabilities, taking into account its contingent and prospective liabilities.

(3)   The money sum for the time being specified in subsection (1)(a) is subject to increase or reduction by order under section 416 in Part XV.

[9.213]
124   Application for winding up

(1)   Subject to the provisions of this section, an application to the court for the winding up of a company shall be by petition presented either by the company, or the directors, or by any creditor or creditors (including any contingent or prospective creditor or creditors), contributory or contributories[, or by a liquidator (within the meaning of Article 2(b) of the EC Regulation) appointed in proceedings by virtue of Article 3(1) of the EC Regulation or a temporary

administrator (within the meaning of Article 38 of the EC Regulation)] [or by [the designated officer for a magistrates' court] in the exercise of the power conferred by section 87A of the Magistrates' Courts Act 1980 (enforcement of fines imposed on companies)], or by all or any of those parties, together or separately.

(2)   Except as mentioned below, a contributory is not entitled to present a winding-up petition unless either—

(a)   the number of members is reduced below 2, or

(b)   the shares in respect of which he is a contributory, or some of them, either were originally allotted to him, or have been held by him, and registered in his name, for at least 6 months during the 18 months before the commencement of the winding up, or have devolved on him through the death of a former holder.

(3)   A person who is liable under section 76 to contribute to a company's assets in the event of its being wound up may petition on either of the grounds set out in section 122(1)(f) and (g), and subsection (2) above does not then apply; but unless the person is a contributory otherwise than under section 76, he may not in his character as contributory petition on any other ground.
. . .

[(3A)   A winding-up petition on the ground set out in section 122(1)(fa) may only be presented by one or more creditors.]

(4)   A winding-up petition may be presented by the Secretary of State—

(a)   if the ground of the petition is that in section 122(1)(b) or (c), or

[(b)   in a case falling within section 124A [or 124B] below.]

[(4AA)   A winding up petition may be presented by the Financial Services Authority in a case falling within section 124C(1) or (2).]

[(4A)   A winding-up petition may be presented by the Regulator of Community Interest Companies in a case falling within section 50 of the Companies (Audit, Investigations and Community Enterprise) Act 2004.]

(5)   Where a company is being wound up voluntarily in England and Wales, a winding-up petition may be presented by the official receiver attached to the court as well as by any other person authorised in that behalf under the other provisions of this section; but the court shall not make a winding-up order on the petition unless it is satisfied that the voluntary winding up cannot be continued with due regard to the interests of the creditors or contributories.

NOTES

Sub-s (1): words in first pair of square brackets inserted by the Insolvency Act 1986 (Amendment) (No 2) Regulations 2002, SI 2002/1240, regs 3, 8, as from 31 May 2002; words in second (outer) pair of square brackets inserted by the Criminal Justice Act 1988, s 62(2)(b), as from 5 January 1989; words in third (inner) pair of square brackets substituted by the Courts Act 2003, s 109(1), Sch 8, para 294, as from 1 April 2005.

Sub-s (3): words omitted repealed by the Companies Act 2006 (Consequential Amendments, Transitional Provisions and Savings) Order 2009, SI 2009/1941, art 2(1), Sch 1, para 75(1), (13), as from 1 October 2009 (for transitional provisions see the note to s 7A at **[9.103]**).

Sub-s (3A): inserted by the Insolvency Act 2000, s 1, Sch 1, paras 1, 7, as from 1 January 2003.

Sub-s (4): para (b) substituted by CA 1989, s 60(2), as from 21 February 1990; words in square brackets in para (b) inserted by the European Public Limited-Liability Company Regulations 2004, SI 2004/2326, reg 73(4)(a), as from 8 October 2004.

Sub-s (4AA): inserted by the European Cooperative Society Regulations 2006, SI 2006/22078, reg 33(2), as from 18 August 2006.

Sub-s (4A): inserted by the Companies (Audit, Investigations and Community Enterprise) Act 2004, s 50(3), as from 1 July 2005.

[9.214]
[124A   Petition for winding up on grounds of public interest
(1)   Where it appears to the Secretary of State from—

(a)   any report made or information obtained under Part XIV [(except section 448A)] of the Companies Act 1985 (company investigations, &c),

[(b)   any report made by inspectors under—

(i)   section 167, 168, 169 or 284 of the Financial Services and Markets Act 2000, or

(ii)   where the company is an open-ended investment company (within the meaning of that Act), regulations made as a result of section 262(2)(k) of that Act;

(bb)   any information or documents obtained under section 165, 171, 172, 173 or 175 of that Act,]

(c)   any information obtained under section 2 of the Criminal Justice Act 1987 or section 52 of the Criminal Justice (Scotland) Act 1987 (fraud investigations), or

(d)   any information obtained under section 83 of the Companies Act 1989 (powers exercisable for purpose of assisting overseas regulatory authorities),

that it is expedient in the public interest that a company should be wound up, he may present a petition for it to be wound up if the court thinks it just and equitable for it to be so.

(2)   This section does not apply if the company is already being wound up by the court.]

NOTES

Inserted by CA 1989, s 60(3), as from 21 February 1990.

Sub-s (1): words in square brackets in para (a) inserted by the Companies (Audit, Investigations and Community Enterprise) Act 2004, s 25, Sch 2, Pt 3, para 27, as from 6 April 2005; paras (b), (bb) substituted, for original para (b), by the Financial Services and Markets Act 2000 (Consequential Amendments and Repeals) Order 2001, SI 2001/3649, art 305, as from 1 December 2001.

Information obtained under Part XIV: in so far as this means information obtained under ss 447 or 448 of the 1985 Act, it is a reference to information obtained under those sections whether before or after their amendment by the Companies (Audit, Investigations and Community Enterprise) Act 2004; see SI 2004/3322, art 13.

[9.215]
[124B   Petition for winding up of SE
(1)   Where—
- (a)   an SE whose registered office is in Great Britain is not in compliance with Article 7 of Council Regulation (EC) No 2157/2001 on the Statute for a European company (the "EC Regulation") (location of head office and registered office), and
- (b)   it appears to the Secretary of State that the SE should be wound up, he may present a petition for it to be wound up if the court thinks it is just and equitable for it to be so.

(2)   This section does not apply if the SE is already being wound up by the court.

(3)   In this section "SE" has the same meaning as in the EC Regulation.]

NOTES

Inserted by the European Public Limited-Liability Company Regulations 2004, SI 2004/2326, reg 73(3), as from 8 October 2004.

[9.216]
[124C   Petition for winding up of SCE
(1)   Where, in the case of an SCE whose registered office is in Great Britain—
- (a)   there has been such a breach as is mentioned in Article 73(1) of Council Regulation (EC) No 1435/2003 on the Statute for a European Cooperative Society (SCE) (the "European Cooperative Society Regulation") (winding up by the court or other competent authority), and
- (b)   it appears to the Financial Services Authority that the SCE should be wound up,

the Authority may present a petition for the SCE to be wound up if the court thinks it is just and equitable for it to be so.

(2)   Where, in the case of an SCE whose registered office is in Great Britain—
- (a)   the SCE is not in compliance with Article 6 of the European Cooperative Society Regulation (location of head office and registered office, and
- (b)   it appears to the Financial Service Authority that the SCE should be wound up,

the Authority may present a petition for the SCE to be wound up if the court thinks it is just and equitable for it to be so.

(3)   This section does not apply if the SCE is already being wound up by the court.

(4)   In this section "SCE" has the same meaning as in the European Cooperative Society Regulation.]

NOTES

Commencement: 18 August 2006.

Inserted by the European Cooperative Society Regulations 2006, SI 2006/22078, reg 33(1), as from 18 August 2006.

[9.217]
125   Powers of court on hearing of petition
(1)   On hearing a winding-up petition the court may dismiss it, or adjourn the hearing conditionally or unconditionally, or make an interim order, or any other order that it thinks fit; but the court shall not refuse to make a winding-up order on the ground only that the company's assets have been mortgaged to an amount equal to or in excess of those assets, or that the company has no assets.

(2)   If the petition is presented by members of the company as contributories on the ground that it is just and equitable that the company should be wound up, the court, if it is of opinion—
- (a)   that the petitioners are entitled to relief either by winding up the company or by some other means, and
- (b)   that in the absence of any other remedy it would be just and equitable that the company should be wound up,

shall make a winding-up order; but this does not apply if the court is also of the opinion both that some other remedy is available to the petitioners and that they are acting unreasonably in seeking to have the company wound up instead of pursuing that other remedy.

[9.218]
126   Power to stay or restrain proceedings against company
(1)   At any time after the presentation of a winding-up petition, and before a winding-up order has been made, the company, or any creditor or contributory, may—

(a)   where any action or proceeding against the company is pending in the High Court or Court of Appeal in England and Wales or Northern Ireland, apply to the court in which the action or proceeding is pending for a stay of proceedings therein, and

(b)   where any other action or proceeding is pending against the company, apply to the court having jurisdiction to wind up the company to restrain further proceedings in the action or proceeding;

and the court to which application is so made may (as the case may be) stay, sist or restrain the proceedings accordingly on such terms as it thinks fit.

(2)   In the case of [a company registered but not formed under the Companies Act 2006], where the application to stay, sist or restrain is by a creditor, this section extends to actions and proceedings against any contributory of the company.

NOTES

Sub-s (2): words in square brackets substituted by the Companies Act 2006 (Consequential Amendments, Transitional Provisions and Savings) Order 2009, SI 2009/1941, art 2(1), Sch 1, para 75(1), (14), as from 1 October 2009 (for transitional provisions see the note to s 7A at **[9.103]**).

[9.219]
127   Avoidance of property dispositions, etc
[(1)]   In a winding up by the court, any disposition of the company's property, and any transfer of shares, or alteration in the status of the company's members, made after the commencement of the winding up is, unless the court otherwise orders, void.

[(2)   This section has no effect in respect of anything done by an administrator of a company while a winding-up petition is suspended under paragraph 40 of Schedule B1.]

NOTES

Sub-s (1) numbered as such, and sub-s (2) added, by the Enterprise Act 2002, s 248(3), Sch 17, paras 9, 15, as from 15 September 2003 (for savings and transitional provisions, see the note to s 8 at **[9.105]**).

[9.220]
128   Avoidance of attachments, etc
(1)   Where a company registered in England and Wales is being wound up by the court, any attachment, sequestration, distress or execution put in force against the estate or effects of the company after the commencement of the winding up is void.

(2)   This section, so far as relates to any estate or effects of the company situated in England and Wales, applies in the case of a company registered in Scotland as it applies in the case of a company registered in England and Wales.

Commencement of winding up

[9.221]
129   Commencement of winding up by the court
(1)   If, before the presentation of a petition for the winding up of a company by the court, a resolution has been passed by the company for voluntary winding up, the winding up of the company is deemed to have commenced at the time of the passing of the resolution; and unless the court, on proof of fraud or mistake, directs otherwise, all proceedings taken in the voluntary winding up are deemed to have been validly taken.

[(1A)   Where the court makes a winding-up order by virtue of paragraph 13(1)(e) of Schedule B1, the winding up is deemed to commence on the making of the order.]

(2)   In any other case, the winding up of a company by the court is deemed to commence at the time of the presentation of the petition for winding up.

NOTES

Sub-s (1A): inserted by the Enterprise Act 2002, s 248(3), Sch 17, paras 9, 16, as from 15 September 2003 (for savings and transitional provisions, see the note to s 8 at **[9.105]**).

[9.222]
130   Consequences of winding-up order
(1)   On the making of a winding-up order, a copy of the order must forthwith be forwarded by the company (or otherwise as may be prescribed) to the registrar of companies, who shall enter it in his records relating to the company.

(2)   When a winding-up order has been made or a provisional liquidator has been appointed, no action or proceeding shall be proceeded with or commenced against the company or its property, except by leave of the court and subject to such terms as the court may impose.

(3)   When an order has been made for winding up a company [registered but not formed under the Companies Act 2006], no action or proceeding shall be commenced or proceeded with against the company or its property or any contributory of the company, in respect of any debt of the company, except by leave of the court, and subject to such terms as the court may impose.

(4)   An order for winding up a company operates in favour of all the creditors and of all contributories of the company as if made on the joint petition of a creditor and of a contributory.

NOTES

  Sub-s (3): words in square brackets substituted by the Companies Act 2006 (Consequential Amendments, Transitional Provisions and Savings) Order 2009, SI 2009/1941, art 2(1), Sch 1, para 75(1), (15), as from 1 October 2009 (for transitional provisions see the note to s 7A at **[9.103]**).

  Modification in relation to Scotland: see the Note at the beginning of this Act.

Investigation procedures

[9.223]

131   Company's statement of affairs

(1)   Where the court has made a winding-up order or appointed a provisional liquidator, the official receiver may require some or all of the persons mentioned in subsection (3) below to make out and submit to him a statement in the prescribed form as to the affairs of the company.

(2)   The statement . . . . shall show—

  (a)   particulars of the company's assets and liabilities;

  (b)   the names and addresses of the company's creditors;

  (c)   the securities held by them respectively;

  (d)   the dates when the securities were respectively given; and

  (e)   such further or other information as may be prescribed or as the official receiver may require.

[(2A)   The statement shall be verified by the persons required to submit it—

  (a)   in the case of an appointment of a provisional liquidator or a winding up by the court in England and Wales, by a statement of truth; and

  (b)   in the case of an appointment of a provisional liquidator or a winding by the court in Scotland, by affidavit.]

(3)   The persons referred to in subsection (1) are—

  (a)   those who are or have been officers of the company;

  (b)   those who have taken part in the formation of the company at any time within one year before the relevant date;

  (c)   those who are in the company's employment, or have been in its employment within that year, and are in the official receiver's opinion capable of giving the information required;

  (d)   those who are or have been within that year officers of, or in the employment of, a company which is, or within that year was, an officer of the company.

(4)   Where any persons are required under this section to submit a statement of affairs to the official receiver, they shall do so (subject to the next subsection) before the end of the period of 21 days beginning with the day after that on which the prescribed notice of the requirement is given to them by the official receiver.

(5)   The official receiver, if he thinks fit, may—

  (a)   at any time release a person from an obligation imposed on him under subsection (1) or (2) above; or

  (b)   either when giving the notice mentioned in subsection (4) or subsequently, extend the period so mentioned;

and where the official receiver has refused to exercise a power conferred by this subsection, the court, if it thinks fit, may exercise it.

(6)   In this section—

  "employment" includes employment under a contract for services; and

  "the relevant date" means—

    (a)   in a case where a provisional liquidator is appointed, the date of his appointment; and

    (b)   in a case where no such appointment is made, the date of the winding-up order.

(7)   If a person without reasonable excuse fails to comply with any obligation imposed under this section, he is liable to a fine and, for continued contravention, to a daily default fine.

(8)   In the application of this section to Scotland references to the official receiver are to the liquidator or, in a case where a provisional liquidator is appointed, the provisional liquidator.

NOTES

  Sub-s (2): words omitted repealed by the Legislative Reform (Insolvency) (Miscellaneous Provisions) Order 2010, SI 2010/18, arts 2, 5(4)(a), as from 6 April 2010.

  Sub-s (2A): inserted by SI 2010/18, arts 2, 5(4)(b), as from 6 April 2010.

[9.224]

132   Investigation by official receiver

(1)   Where a winding-up order is made by the court in England and Wales, it is the duty of the official receiver to investigate—

  (a)   if the company has failed, the causes of the failure; and

  (b)   generally, the promotion, formation, business, dealings and affairs of the company,

and to make such report (if any) to the court as he thinks fit.

(2)   The report is, in any proceedings, prima facie evidence of the facts stated in it.

[9.225]
133 Public examination of officers
(1) Where a company is being wound up by the court, the official receiver or, in Scotland, the liquidator may at any time before the dissolution of the company apply to the court for the public examination of any person who—
- (a) is or has been an officer of the company; or
- (b) has acted as liquidator or administrator of the company or as receiver or manager or, in Scotland, receiver of its property; or
- (c) not being a person falling within paragraph (a) or (b), is or has been concerned, or has taken part, in the promotion, formation or management of the company.

(2) Unless the court otherwise orders, the official receiver or, in Scotland, the liquidator shall make an application under subsection (1) if he is requested in accordance with the rules to do so by—
- (a) one-half, in value, of the company's creditors; or
- (b) three-quarters, in value, of the company's contributories.

(3) On an application under subsection (1), the court shall direct that a public examination of the person to whom the application relates shall be held on a day appointed by the court; and that person shall attend on that day and be publicly examined as to the promotion, formation or management of the company or as to the conduct of its business and affairs, or his conduct or dealings in relation to the company.

(4) The following may take part in the public examination of a person under this section and may question that person concerning the matters mentioned in subsection (3), namely—
- (a) the official receiver;
- (b) the liquidator of the company;
- (c) any person who has been appointed as special manager of the company's property or business;
- (d) any creditor of the company who has tendered a proof or, in Scotland, submitted a claim in the winding up;
- (e) any contributory of the company.

[9.226]
134 Enforcement of s 133
(1) If a person without reasonable excuse fails at any time to attend his public examination under section 133, he is guilty of a contempt of court and liable to be punished accordingly.

(2) In a case where a person without reasonable excuse fails at any time to attend his examination under section 133 or there are reasonable grounds for believing that a person has absconded, or is about to abscond, with a view to avoiding or delaying his examination under that section, the court may cause a warrant to be issued to a constable or prescribed officer of the court—
- (a) for the arrest of that person; and
- (b) for the seizure of any books, papers, records, money or goods in that person's possession.

(3) In such a case the court may authorise the person arrested under the warrant to be kept in custody, and anything seized under such a warrant to be held, in accordance with the rules, until such time as the court may order.

Appointment of liquidator

[9.227]
135 Appointment and powers of provisional liquidator
(1) Subject to the provisions of this section, the court may, at any time after the presentation of a winding-up petition, appoint a liquidator provisionally.

(2) In England and Wales, the appointment of a provisional liquidator may be made at any time before the making of a winding-up order; and either the official receiver or any other fit person may be appointed.

(3) In Scotland, such an appointment may be made at any time before the first appointment of liquidators.

(4) The provisional liquidator shall carry out such functions as the court may confer on him.

(5) When a liquidator is provisionally appointed by the court, his powers may be limited by the order appointing him.

[9.228]
136 Functions of official receiver in relation to office of liquidator
(1) The following provisions of this section have effect, subject to section 140 below, on a winding-up order being made by the court in England and Wales.

(2) The official receiver, by virtue of his office, becomes the liquidator of the company and continues in office until another person becomes liquidator under the provisions of this Part.

(3) The official receiver is, by virtue of his office, the liquidator during any vacancy.

(4) At any time when he is the liquidator of the company, the official receiver may summon separate meetings of the company's creditors and contributories for the purpose of choosing a person to be liquidator of the company in place of the official receiver.

(5) It is the duty of the official receiver—

(a)   as soon as practicable in the period of 12 weeks beginning with the day on which the winding-up order was made, to decide whether to exercise his power under subsection (4) to summon meetings, and

(b)   if in pursuance of paragraph (a) he decides not to exercise that power, to give notice of his decision, before the end of that period, to the court and to the company's creditors and contributories, and

(c)   (whether or not he has decided to exercise that power) to exercise his power to summon meetings under subsection (4) if he is at any time requested, in accordance with the rules, to do so by one-quarter, in value, of the company's creditors;

and accordingly, where the duty imposed by paragraph (c) arises before the official receiver has performed a duty imposed by paragraph (a) or (b), he is not required to perform the latter duty.

(6)   A notice given under subsection (5)(b) to the company's creditors shall contain an explanation of the creditors' power under subsection (5)(c) to require the official receiver to summon meetings of the company's creditors and contributories.

[9.229]
137   Appointment by Secretary of State
(1)   In a winding up by the court in England and Wales the official receiver may, at any time when he is the liquidator of the company, apply to the Secretary of State for the appointment of a person as liquidator in his place.

(2)   If meetings are held in pursuance of a decision under section 136(5)(a), but no person is chosen to be liquidator as a result of those meetings, it is the duty of the official receiver to decide whether to refer the need for an appointment to the Secretary of State.

(3)   On an application under subsection (1), or a reference made in pursuance of a decision under subsection (2), the Secretary of State shall either make an appointment or decline to make one.

(4)   Where a liquidator has been appointed by the Secretary of State under subsection (3), the liquidator shall give notice of his appointment to the company's creditors or, if the court so allows, shall advertise his appointment in accordance with the directions of the court.

(5)   In that notice or advertisement the liquidator shall—

(a)   state whether he proposes to summon a general meeting of the company's creditors under section 141 below for the purpose of determining (together with any meeting of contributories) whether a liquidation committee should be established under that section, and

(b)   if he does not propose to summon such a meeting, set out the power of the company's creditors under that section to require him to summon one.

[9.230]
138   Appointment of liquidator in Scotland
(1)   Where a winding-up order is made by the court in Scotland, a liquidator shall be appointed by the court at the time when the order is made.

(2)   The liquidator so appointed (here referred to as "the interim liquidator") continues in office until another person becomes liquidator in his place under this section or the next.

(3)   The interim liquidator shall (subject to the next subsection) as soon as practicable in the period of 28 days beginning with the day on which the winding-up order was made or such longer period as the court may allow, summon separate meetings of the company's creditors and contributories for the purpose of choosing a person (who may be the person who is the interim liquidator) to be liquidator of the company in place of the interim liquidator.

(4)   If it appears to the interim liquidator, in any case where a company is being wound up on grounds including its inability to pay its debts, that it would be inappropriate to summon under subsection (3) a meeting of the company's contributories, he may summon only a meeting of the company's creditors for the purpose mentioned in that subsection.

(5)   If one or more meetings are held in pursuance of this section but no person is appointed or nominated by the meeting or meetings, the interim liquidator shall make a report to the court which shall appoint either the interim liquidator or some other person to be liquidator of the company.

(6)   A person who becomes liquidator of the company in place of the interim liquidator shall, unless he is appointed by the court, forthwith notify the court of that fact.

[9.231]
139   Choice of liquidator at meetings of creditors and contributories
(1)   This section applies where a company is being wound up by the court and separate meetings of the company's creditors and contributories are summoned for the purpose of choosing a person to be liquidator of the company.

(2)   The creditors and the contributories at their respective meetings may nominate a person to be liquidator.

(3)   The liquidator shall be the person nominated by the creditors or, where no person has been so nominated, the person (if any) nominated by the contributories.

(4)   In the case of different persons being nominated, any contributory or creditor may, within 7 days after the date on which the nomination was made by the creditors, apply to the court for an order either—

(a) appointing the person nominated as liquidator by the contributories to be a liquidator instead of, or jointly with, the person nominated by the creditors; or

(b) appointing some other person to be liquidator instead of the person nominated by the creditors.

[9.232]
140 Appointment by the court following administration or voluntary arrangement

[(1) Where a winding-up order is made immediately upon the appointment of an administrator ceasing to have effect, the court may appoint as liquidator of the company the person whose appointment as administrator has ceased to have effect.]

(2) Where a winding-up order is made at a time when there is a supervisor of a voluntary arrangement approved in relation to the company under Part I, the court may appoint as liquidator of the company the person who is the supervisor at the time when the winding-up order is made.

(3) Where the court makes an appointment under this section, the official receiver does not become the liquidator as otherwise provided by section 136(2), and he has no duty under section 136(5)(a) or (b) in respect of the summoning of creditors' or contributories' meetings.

NOTES

Sub-s (1): substituted by the Enterprise Act 2002, s 248(3), Sch 17, paras 9, 17, as from 15 September 2003 (for savings and transitional provisions, see the note to s 8 at **[9.105]**).

Liquidation committees

[9.233]
141 Liquidation committee (England and Wales)

(1) Where a winding-up order has been made by the court in England and Wales and separate meetings of creditors and contributories have been summoned for the purpose of choosing a person to be liquidator, those meetings may establish a committee ("the liquidation committee") to exercise the functions conferred on it by or under this Act.

(2) The liquidator (not being the official receiver) may at any time, if he thinks fit, summon separate general meetings of the company's creditors and contributories for the purpose of determining whether such a committee should be established and, if it is so determined, of establishing it.

The liquidator (not being the official receiver) shall summon such a meeting if he is requested, in accordance with the rules, to do so by one-tenth, in value, of the company's creditors.

(3) Where meetings are summoned under this section, or for the purpose of choosing a person to be liquidator, and either the meeting of creditors or the meeting of contributories decides that a liquidation committee should be established, but the other meeting does not so decide or decides that a committee should not be established, the committee shall be established in accordance with the rules, unless the court otherwise orders.

(4) The liquidation committee is not to be able or required to carry out its functions at any time when the official receiver is liquidator; but at any such time its functions are vested in the Secretary of State except to the extent that the rules otherwise provide.

(5) Where there is for the time being no liquidation committee, and the liquidator is a person other than the official receiver, the functions of such a committee are vested in the Secretary of State except to the extent that the rules otherwise provide.

[9.234]
142 Liquidation committee (Scotland)

(1) Where a winding-up order has been made by the court in Scotland and separate meetings of creditors and contributories have been summoned for the purpose of choosing a person to be liquidator or, under section 138(4), only a meeting of creditors has been summoned for that purpose, those meetings or (as the case may be) that meeting may establish a committee ("the liquidation committee") to exercise the functions conferred on it by or under this Act.

(2) The liquidator may at any time, if he thinks fit, summon separate general meetings of the company's creditors and contributories for the purpose of determining whether such a committee should be established and, if it is so determined, of establishing it.

(3) The liquidator, if appointed by the court otherwise than under section 139(4)(a), is required to summon meetings under subsection (2) if he is requested, in accordance with the rules, to do so by one-tenth, in value, of the company's creditors.

(4) Where meetings are summoned under this section, or for the purpose of choosing a person to be liquidator, and either the meeting of creditors or the meeting of contributories decides that a liquidation committee should be established, but the other meeting does not so decide or decides that a committee should not be established, the committee shall be established in accordance with the rules, unless the court otherwise orders.

(5) Where in the case of any winding up there is for the time being no liquidation committee, the functions of such a committee are vested in the court except to the extent that the rules otherwise provide.

(6) In addition to the powers and duties conferred and imposed on it by this Act, a liquidation committee has such of the powers and duties of commissioners in a sequestration as may be conferred and imposed on such committees by the rules.

The liquidator's functions

[9.235]
143 General functions in winding up by the court
(1) The functions of the liquidator of a company which is being wound up by the court are to secure that the assets of the company are got in, realised and distributed to the company's creditors and, if there is a surplus, to the persons entitled to it.
(2) It is the duty of the liquidator of a company which is being wound up by the court in England and Wales, if he is not the official receiver—
   (a) to furnish the official receiver with such information,
   (b) to produce to the official receiver, and permit inspection by the official receiver of, such books, papers and other records, and
   (c) to give the official receiver such other assistance,
as the official receiver may reasonably require for the purposes of carrying out his functions in relation to the winding up.

[9.236]
144 Custody of company's property
(1) When a winding-up order has been made, or where a provisional liquidator has been appointed, the liquidator or the provisional liquidator (as the case may be) shall take into his custody or under his control all the property and things in action to which the company is or appears to be entitled.
(2) In a winding up by the court in Scotland, if and so long as there is no liquidator, all the property of the company is deemed to be in the custody of the court.

[9.237]
145 Vesting of company property in liquidator
(1) When a company is being wound up by the court, the court may on the application of the liquidator by order direct that all or any part of the property of whatsoever description belonging to the company or held by trustees on its behalf shall vest in the liquidator by his official name; and thereupon the property to which the order relates vests accordingly.
(2) The liquidator may, after giving such indemnity (if any) as the court may direct, bring or defend in his official name any action or other legal proceeding which relates to that property or which it is necessary to bring or defend for the purpose of effectually winding up the company and recovering its property.

[9.238]
146 Duty to summon final meeting
(1) Subject to the next subsection, if it appears to the liquidator of a company which is being wound by the court that the winding up of the company is for practical purposes complete and the liquidator is not the official receiver, the liquidator shall summon a final general meeting of the company's creditors which—
   (a) shall receive the liquidator's report of the winding up, and
   (b) shall determine whether the liquidator should have his release under section 174 in Chapter VII of this Part.
(2) The liquidator may, if he thinks fit, give the notice summoning the final general meeting at the same time as giving notice of any final distribution of the company's property but, if summoned for an earlier date, that meeting shall be adjourned (and, if necessary, further adjourned) until a date on which the liquidator is able to report to the meeting that the winding up of the company is for practical purposes complete.
(3) In the carrying out of his functions in the winding up it is the duty of the liquidator to retain sufficient sums from the company's property to cover the expenses of summoning and holding the meeting required by this section.

General powers of court

[9.239]
147 Power to stay or sist winding up
(1) The court may at any time after an order for winding up, on the application either of the liquidator or the official receiver or any creditor or contributory, and on proof to the satisfaction of the court that all proceedings in the winding up ought to be stayed or sisted, make an order staying or sisting the proceedings, either altogether or for a limited time, on such terms and conditions as the court thinks fit.
(2) The court may, before making an order, require the official receiver to furnish to it a report with respect to any facts or matters which are in his opinion relevant to the application.
(3) A copy of every order made under this section shall forthwith be forwarded by the company, or otherwise as may be prescribed, to the registrar of companies, who shall enter it in his records relating to the company.

NOTES

Modification in relation to Scotland: see the Note at the beginning of this Act.

[9.240]
148   Settlement of list of contributories and application of assets
(1)   As soon as may be after making a winding-up order, the court shall settle a list of contributories, with power to rectify the register of members in all cases where rectification is required . . . , and shall cause the company's assets to be collected, and applied in discharge of its liabilities.
(2)   If it appears to the court that it will not be necessary to make calls on or adjust the rights of contributories, the court may dispense with the settlement of a list of contributories.
(3)   In settling the list, the court shall distinguish between persons who are contributories in their own right and persons who are contributories as being representatives of or liable for the debts of others.

NOTES

Sub-s (1): words omitted repealed by the Companies Act 2006 (Consequential Amendments, Transitional Provisions and Savings) Order 2009, SI 2009/1941, art 2(1), Sch 1, para 75(1), (16), as from 1 October 2009 (for transitional provisions see the note to s 7A at **[9.103]**).

[9.241]
149   Debts due from contributory to company
(1)   The court may, at any time after making a winding-up order, make an order on any contributory for the time being on the list of contributories to pay, in manner directed by the order, any money due from him (or from the estate of the person who he represents) to the company, exclusive of any money payable by him or the estate by virtue of any call . . .
(2)   The court in making such an order may—
   (a)   in the case of an unlimited company, allow to the contributory by way of set-off any money due to him or the estate which he represents from the company on any independent dealing or contract with the company, but not any money due to him as a member of the company in respect of any dividend or profit, and
   (b)   in the case of a limited company, make to any director or manager whose liability is unlimited or to his estate the like allowance.
(3)   In the case of any company, whether limited or unlimited, when all the creditors are paid in full (together with interest at the official rate), any money due on any account whatever to a contributory from the company may be allowed to him by way of set-off against any subsequent call.

NOTES

Sub-s (1): words omitted repealed by the Companies Act 2006 (Consequential Amendments, Transitional Provisions and Savings) Order 2009, SI 2009/1941, art 2(1), Sch 1, para 75(1), (16), as from 1 October 2009 (for transitional provisions see the note to s 7A at **[9.103]**).

[9.242]
150   Power to make calls
(1)   The court may, at any time after making a winding-up order, and either before or after it has ascertained the sufficiency of the company's assets, make calls on all or any of the contributories for the time being settled on the list of the contributories to the extent of their liability, for payment of any money which the court considers necessary to satisfy the company's debts and liabilities, and the expenses of winding up, and for the adjustment of the rights of the contributories among themselves, and make an order for payment of any calls so made.
(2)   In making a call the court may take into consideration the probability that some of the contributories may partly or wholly fail to pay it.

[9.243]
151   Payment into bank of money due to company
(1)   The court may order any contributory, purchaser or other person from whom money is due to the company to pay the amount due into the Bank of England (or any branch of it) to the account of the liquidator instead of to the liquidator, and such an order may be enforced in the same manner as if it had directed payment to the liquidator.
(2)   All money and securities paid or delivered into the Bank of England (or branch) in the event of a winding up by the court are subject in all respects to the orders of the court.

[9.244]
152   Order on contributory to be conclusive evidence
(1)   An order made by the court on a contributory is conclusive evidence that the money (if any) thereby appearing to be due or ordered to be paid is due, but subject to any right of appeal.
(2)   All other pertinent matters stated in the order are to be taken as truly stated as against all persons and in all proceedings except proceedings in Scotland against the heritable estate of a deceased contributory; and in that case the order is only prima facie evidence for the purpose of charging his heritable estate, unless his heirs or legatees of heritage were on the list of contributories at the time of the order being made.

[9.245]
153   Power to exclude creditors not proving in time
The court may fix a time or times within which creditors are to prove their debts or claims or to be excluded from the benefit of any distribution made before those debts are proved.

[9.246]
154   Adjustment of rights of contributories
The court shall adjust the rights of the contributories among themselves and distribute any surplus among the persons entitled to it.

[9.247]
155   Inspection of books by creditors, etc
(1)   The court may, at any time after making a winding-up order, make such order for inspection of the company's books and papers by creditors and contributories as the court thinks just; and any books and papers in the company's possession may be inspected by creditors and contributories accordingly, but not further or otherwise.
(2)   Nothing in this section excludes or restricts any statutory rights of a government department or person acting under the authority of a government department.
[(3)   For the purposes of subsection (2) above, references to a government department shall be construed as including references to any part of the Scottish Administration.]

NOTES
Sub-s (3): added by the Scotland Act 1998 (Consequential Modifications) (No 2) Order 1999, SI 1999/1820, art 4, Sch 2, Pt I, para 85, as from 1 July 1999.

[9.248]
156   Payment of expenses of winding up
The court may, in the event of the assets being insufficient to satisfy the liabilities, make an order as to the payment out of the assets of the expenses incurred in the winding up in such order of priority as the court thinks just.

[9.249]
157   Attendance at company meetings (Scotland)
In the winding up by the court of a company registered in Scotland, the court has power to require the attendance of any officer of the company at any meeting of creditors or of contributories, or of a liquidation committee, for the purpose of giving information as to the trade, dealings, affairs or property of the company.

[9.250]
158   Power to arrest absconding contributory
The court, at any time either before or after making a winding-up order, on proof of probable cause for believing that a contributory is about to quit the United Kingdom or otherwise to abscond or to remove or conceal any of his property for the purpose of evading payment of calls, may cause the contributory to be arrested and his books and papers and moveable personal property to be seized and him and them to be kept safely until such time as the court may order.

[9.251]
159   Powers of court to be cumulative
Powers conferred [on the court by this Act] are in addition to, and not in restriction of, any existing powers of instituting proceedings against a contributory or debtor of the company, or the estate of any contributory or debtor, for the recovery of any call or other sums.

NOTES
Words in square brackets substituted by the Companies Act 2006 (Consequential Amendments, Transitional Provisions and Savings) Order 2009, SI 2009/1941, art 2(1), Sch 1, para 75(1), (17), as from 1 October 2009 (for transitional provisions see the note to s 7A at **[9.103]**).

[9.252]
160   Delegation of powers to liquidator (England and Wales)
(1)   Provision may be made by rules for enabling or requiring all or any of the powers and duties conferred and imposed on the court in England and Wales . . . in respect of the following matters—
   (a)   the holding and conducting of meetings to ascertain the wishes of creditors and contributories,
   (b)   the settling of lists of contributories and the rectifying of the register of members where required, and the collection and application of the assets,
   (c)   the payment, delivery, conveyance, surrender or transfer of money, property, books or papers to the liquidator,
   (d)   the making of calls,
   (e)   the fixing of a time within which debts and claims must be proved,

to be exercised or performed by the liquidator as an officer of the court, and subject to the court's control.

(2) But the liquidator shall not, without the special leave of the court, rectify the register of members, and shall not make any call without either that special leave or the sanction of the liquidation committee.

NOTES

Sub-s (1): words omitted repealed by the Companies Act 2006 (Consequential Amendments, Transitional Provisions and Savings) Order 2009, SI 2009/1941, art 2(1), Sch 1, para 75(1), (18), as from 1 October 2009 (for transitional provisions see the note to s 7A at **[9.103]**).

Enforcement of, and appeal from, orders

[9.253]
161 Orders for calls on contributories (Scotland)

(1) In Scotland, where an order, interlocutor or decree has been made for winding up a company by the court, it is competent to the court, on production by the liquidators of a list certified by them of the names of the contributories liable in payment of any calls, and of the amount due by each contributory, and of the date when that amount became due, to pronounce forthwith a decree against those contributories for payment of the sums so certified to be due, with interest from that date until payment (at 5 per cent. per annum) in the same way and to the same effect as if they had severally consented to registration for execution, on a charge of 6 days, of a legal obligation to pay those calls and interest.

(2) The decree may be extracted immediately, and no suspension of it is competent, except on caution or consignation, unless with special leave of the court.

[9.254]
162 Appeals from orders in Scotland

(1) Subject to the provisions of this section and to rules of court, an appeal from any order or decision made or given in the winding up of a company by the court in Scotland under this Act lies in the same manner and subject to the same conditions as an appeal from an order or decision of the court in cases within its ordinary jurisdiction.

(2) In regard to orders or judgments pronounced by the judge acting as vacation judge . . . —
  (a) none of the orders specified in Part I of Schedule 3 to this Act are subject to review, reduction, suspension or stay of execution, and
  (b) every other order or judgment (except as mentioned below) may be submitted to review by the Inner House by reclaiming motion enrolled within 14 days from the date of the order or judgment.

(3) However, an order being one of those specified in Part II of that Schedule shall, from the date of the order and notwithstanding that it has been submitted to review as above, be carried out and receive effect until the Inner House have disposed of the matter.

(4) In regard to orders or judgments pronounced in Scotland by a Lord Ordinary before whom proceedings in a winding up are being taken, any such order or judgment may be submitted to review by the Inner House by reclaiming motion enrolled within 14 days from its date; but should it not be so submitted to review during session, the provisions of this section in regard to orders or judgments pronounced by the judge acting as vacation judge apply.

(5) Nothing in this section affects provisions of [the Companies Acts] or this Act in reference to decrees in Scotland for payment of calls in the winding up of companies, whether voluntary or by the court.

NOTES

Sub-s (2): words omitted repealed by the Court of Session Act 1988, s 52(2), Sch 2, Pt III, as from 29 September 1988.

Sub-s (5): words in square brackets substituted by the Companies Act 2006 (Consequential Amendments, Transitional Provisions and Savings) Order 2009, SI 2009/1941, art 2(1), Sch 1, para 75(1), (19), as from 1 October 2009 (for transitional provisions see the note to s 7A at **[9.103]**).

CHAPTER VII
LIQUIDATORS

Preliminary

[9.255]
163 Style and title of liquidators

The liquidator of a company shall be described—
  (a) where a person other than the official receiver is liquidator, by the style of "the liquidator" of the particular company, or
  (b) where the official receiver is liquidator, by the style of "the official receiver and liquidator" of the particular company;
and in neither case shall he be described by an individual name.

[9.256]
164   Corrupt inducement affecting appointment
A person who gives, or agrees or offers to give, to any member or creditor of a company any valuable consideration with a view to securing his own appointment or nomination, or to securing or preventing the appointment or nomination of some person other than himself, as the company's liquidator is liable to a fine.

Liquidator's powers and duties

[9.257]
165   Voluntary winding up
(1)   This section has effect where a company is being wound up voluntarily, but subject to section 166 below in the case of a creditors' voluntary winding up.
(2)   The liquidator may—
  (a)   in the case of a members' voluntary winding up, with the sanction of an [special resolution] of the company, and
  (b)   in the case of a creditors' voluntary winding up, with the sanction of the court or the liquidation committee (or, if there is no such committee, a meeting of the company's creditors),
exercise any of the powers specified in Part I of Schedule 4 to this Act (payment of debts, compromise of claims, etc).
(3)   The liquidator may, without sanction, exercise either of the powers specified in Part II of that Schedule (institution and defence of proceedings; carrying on the business of the company) and any of the general powers specified in Part III of that Schedule.
(4)   The liquidator may—
  (a)   exercise the court's power of settling a list of contributories (which list is prima facie evidence of the liability of the persons named in it to be contributories),
  (b)   exercise the court's power of making calls,
  (c)   summon general meetings of the company for the purpose of obtaining its sanction by [special resolution] or for any other purpose he may think fit.
(5)   The liquidator shall pay the company's debts and adjust the rights of the contributories among themselves.
(6)   Where the liquidator in exercise of the powers conferred on him by this Act disposes of any property of the company to a person who is connected with the company (within the meaning of section 249 in Part VII), he shall, if there is for the time being a liquidation committee, give notice to the committee of that exercise of his powers.

NOTES
  Sub-ss (2), (4): words in square brackets substituted by the Companies Act 2006 (Commencement No 3, Consequential Amendments, Transitional Provisions and Savings) Order 2007, SI 2007/2194, art 10(1), Sch 4, Pt 3, para 41(1), as from 1 October 2007, in relation to (a) written resolutions for which the circulation date (see s 290 of CA 2006) is on or after that date, and (b) to resolutions passed at a meeting of which notice is given on or after that date.

[9.258]
166   Creditors' voluntary winding up
(1)   This section applies where, in the case of a creditors' voluntary winding up, a liquidator has been nominated by the company.
[(1A)   The exercise by the liquidator of the power specified in paragraph 6 of Schedule 4 to this Act (power to sell any of the company's property) shall not be challengeable on the ground of any prior inhibition.]
(2)   The powers conferred on the liquidator by section 165 shall not be exercised, except with the sanction of the court, during the period before the holding of the creditors' meeting under section 98 in Chapter IV.
(3)   Subsection (2) does not apply in relation to the power of the liquidator—
  (a)   to take into his custody or under his control all the property to which the company is or appears to be entitled;
  (b)   to dispose of perishable goods and other goods the value of which is likely to diminish if they are not immediately disposed of; and
  (c)   to do all such other things as may be necessary for the protection of the company's assets.
(4)   The liquidator shall attend the creditors' meeting held under section 98 and shall report to the meeting on any exercise by him of his powers (whether or not under this section or under section 112 or 165).
(5)   If default is made—
  (a)   by the company in complying with subsection (1)[, (1A)] or (2) of section 98, or
  (b)   by the directors in complying with subsection (1)[, (2) or (2A)] of section 99,
the liquidator shall, within 7 days of the relevant day, apply to the court for directions as to the manner in which that default is to be remedied.
(6)   "The relevant day" means the day on which the liquidator was nominated by the company or the day on which he first became aware of the default, whichever is the later.

(7)   If the liquidator without reasonable excuse fails to comply with this section, he is liable to a fine.

NOTES

Sub-s (1A): inserted by the Bankruptcy and Diligence etc (Scotland) Act 2007, s 155(1), (3), as from 22 April 2009.

Sub-s (5): figure in square brackets in para (a) inserted by the Legislative Reform (Insolvency) (Advertising Requirements) Order 2009, SI 2009/864, arts 2, 3(3), 4, as from 6 April 2009, except in respect of a company in voluntary winding up where the resolution to wind up was passed before that date; words in square brackets in para (b) substituted by the Legislative Reform (Insolvency) (Miscellaneous Provisions) Order 2010, SI 2010/18, arts 2, 5(5), as from 6 April 2010.

[9.259]
167   Winding up by the court
(1)   Where a company is being wound up by the court, the liquidator may—
- (a)   with the sanction of the court or the liquidation committee, exercise any of the powers specified in Parts I and II of Schedule 4 to this Act (payment of debts; compromise of claims, etc; institution and defence of proceedings; carrying on of the business of the company), and
- (b)   with or without that sanction, exercise any of the general powers specified in Part III of that Schedule.

(2)   Where the liquidator (not being the official receiver), in exercise of the powers conferred on him by this Act—
- (a)   disposes of any property of the company to a person who is connected with the company (within the meaning of section 249 in Part VII), or
- (b)   employs a solicitor to assist him in the carrying out of his functions,

he shall, if there is for the time being a liquidation committee, give notice to the committee of that exercise of his powers.

(3)   The exercise by the liquidator in a winding up by the court of the powers conferred by this section is subject to the control of the court, and any creditor or contributory may apply to the court with respect to any exercise or proposed exercise of any of those powers.

[9.260]
168   Supplementary powers (England and Wales)
(1)   This section applies in the case of a company which is being wound up by the court in England and Wales.

(2)   The liquidator may summon general meetings of the creditors or contributories for the purpose of ascertaining their wishes; and it is his duty to summon meetings at such times as the creditors or contributories by resolution (either at the meeting appointing the liquidator or otherwise) may direct, or whenever requested in writing to do so by one-tenth in value of the creditors or contributories (as the case may be).

(3)   The liquidator may apply to the court (in the prescribed manner) for directions in relation to any particular matter arising in the winding up.

(4)   Subject to the provisions of this Act, the liquidator shall use his own discretion in the management of the assets and their distribution among the creditors.

(5)   If any person is aggrieved by an act or decision of the liquidator, that person may apply to the court; and the court may confirm, reverse or modify the act or decision complained of, and make such order in the case as it thinks just.

[(5A)   Where at any time after a winding-up petition has been presented to the court against any person (including an insolvent partnership or other body which may be wound up under Part V of the Act as an unregistered company), whether by virtue of the provisions of the Insolvent Partnerships Order 1994 or not, the attention of the court is drawn to the fact that the person in question is a member of an insolvent partnership, the court may make an order as to the future conduct of the insolvency proceedings and any such order may apply any provisions of that Order with any necessary modifications.

(5B)   Any order or directions under subsection (5A) may be made or given on the application of the official receiver, any responsible insolvency practitioner, the trustee of the partnership or any other interested person and may include provisions as to the administration of the joint estate of the partnership, and in particular how it and the separate estate of any member are to be administered.

[(5C)   Where the court makes an order for the winding up of an insolvent partnership under—
- (a)   section 72(1)(a) of the Financial Services Act 1986;
- (b)   section 92(1)(a) of the Banking Act 1987; or
- (c)   section 367(3)(a) of the Financial Services and Markets Act 2000,

the court may make an order as to the future conduct of the winding up proceedings, and any such order may apply any provisions of the Insolvent Partnerships Order 1994 with any necessary modifications.]]

NOTES

Sub-ss (5A), (5B): added, together with sub-s (5C), by the Insolvent Partnerships Order 1994, SI 1994/2421, art 14(1), as from 1 December 1994.

Sub-s (5C): added as noted above. It was repealed by the Financial Services and Markets Act 2000 (Consequential Amendments and Repeals) Order 2001, SI 2001/3649, art 306, as from 1 December 2001, but was subsequently substituted by the Financial Services and Markets Act 2000 (Consequential Amendments) Order 2002, SI 2002/1555, art 15, as from 3 July 2002, which further provided that the repeal by SI 2001/3649 was to be treated as if it had not been made.

[9.261]
169   Supplementary powers (Scotland)
(1)   In the case of a winding up in Scotland, the court may provide by order that the liquidator may, where there is no liquidation committee, exercise any of the following powers, namely—
    (a)   to bring or defend any action or other legal proceeding in the name and on behalf of the company, or
    (b)   to carry on the business of the company so far as may be necessary for its beneficial winding up,
without the sanction or intervention of the court.
(2)   In a winding up by the court in Scotland, the liquidator has (subject to the rules) the same powers as a trustee on a bankrupt estate.

[9.262]
170   Enforcement of liquidator's duty to make returns, etc
(1)   If a liquidator who has made any default—
    (a)   in filing, delivering or making any return, account or other document, or
    (b)   in giving any notice which he is by law required to file, deliver, make or give,
fails to make good the default within 14 days after the service on him of a notice requiring him to do so, the court has the following powers.
(2)   On an application made by any creditor or contributory of the company, or by the registrar of companies, the court may make an order directing the liquidator to make good the default within such time as may be specified in the order.
(3)   The court's order may provide that all costs of and incidental to the application shall be borne by the liquidator.
(4)   Nothing in this section prejudices the operation of any enactment imposing penalties on a liquidator in respect of any such default as is mentioned above.

NOTES
Modification in relation to Scotland: see the Note at the beginning of this Act.

Removal; vacation of office

[9.263]
171   Removal, etc (voluntary winding up)
(1)   This section applies with respect to the removal from office and vacation of office of the liquidator of a company which is being wound up voluntarily.
(2)   Subject to the next subsection, the liquidator may be removed from office only by an order of the court or—
    (a)   in the case of a members' voluntary winding up, by a general meeting of the company summoned specially for that purpose, or
    (b)   in the case of a creditors' voluntary winding up, by a general meeting of the company's creditors summoned specially for that purpose in accordance with the rules.
(3)   Where the liquidator was appointed by the court under section 108 in Chapter V, a meeting such as is mentioned in subsection (2) above shall be summoned for the purpose of replacing him only if he thinks fit or the court so directs or the meeting is requested, in accordance with the rules—
    (a)   in the case of a members' voluntary winding up, by members representing not less than one-half of the total voting rights of all the members having at the date of the request a right to vote at the meeting, or
    (b)   in the case of a creditors' voluntary winding up, by not less than one-half, in value, of the company's creditors.
(4)   A liquidator shall vacate office if he ceases to be a person who is qualified to act as an insolvency practitioner in relation to the company.
(5)   A liquidator may, in the prescribed circumstances, resign his office by giving notice of his resignation to the registrar of companies.
(6)   Where—
    (a)   in the case of a members' voluntary winding up, a final meeting of the company has been held under section 94 in Chapter III, or
    (b)   in the case of a creditors' voluntary winding up, final meetings of the company and of the creditors have been held under section 106 in Chapter IV,
the liquidator whose report was considered at the meeting or meetings shall vacate office as soon as he has complied with subsection (3) of that section and has given notice to the registrar of companies that the meeting or meetings have been held and of the decisions (if any) of the meeting or meetings.

NOTES
Modification in relation to Scotland: see the Note at the beginning of this Act.

[9.264]
172   Removal, etc (winding up by the court)

(1)   This section applies with respect to the removal from office and vacation of office of the liquidator of a company which is being wound up by the court, or of a provisional liquidator.

(2)   Subject as follows, the liquidator may be removed from office only by an order of the court or by a general meeting of the company's creditors summoned specially for that purpose in accordance with the rules; and a provisional liquidator may be removed from office only by an order of the court.

(3)   Where—

   (a)   the official receiver is liquidator otherwise than in succession under section 136(3) to a person who held office as a result of a nomination by a meeting of the company's creditors or contributories, or

   (b)   the liquidator was appointed by the court otherwise than under section 139(4)(a) or 140(1), or was appointed by the Secretary of State,

a general meeting of the company's creditors shall be summoned for the purpose of replacing him only if he thinks fit, or the court so directs, or the meeting is requested, in accordance with the rules, by not less than one-quarter, in value, of the creditors.

(4)   If appointed by the Secretary of State, the liquidator may be removed from office by a direction of the Secretary of State.

(5)   A liquidator or provisional liquidator, not being the official receiver, shall vacate office if he ceases to be a person who is qualified to act as an insolvency practitioner in relation to the company.

(6)   A liquidator may, in the prescribed circumstances, resign his office by giving notice of his resignation to the court.

(7)   Where an order is made under section 204 (early dissolution in Scotland) for the dissolution of the company, the liquidator shall vacate office when the dissolution of the company takes effect in accordance with that section.

(8)   Where a final meeting has been held under section 146 (liquidator's report on completion of winding up), the liquidator whose report was considered at the meeting shall vacate office as soon as he has given notice to the court and the registrar of companies that the meeting has been held and of the decisions (if any) of the meeting.

NOTES

Modification in relation to Scotland: see the Note at the beginning of this Act.

Release of liquidator

[9.265]
173   Release (voluntary winding up)

(1)   This section applies with respect to the release of the liquidator of a company which is being wound up voluntarily.

(2)   A person who has ceased to be a liquidator shall have his release with effect from the following time, that is to say—

   (a)   in the case of a person who has been removed from office by a general meeting of the company or by a general meeting of the company's creditors that has not resolved against his release or who has died, the time at which notice is given to the registrar of companies in accordance with the rules that that person has ceased to hold office;

   (b)   in the case of a person who has been removed from office by a general meeting of the company's creditors that has resolved against his release, or by the court, or who has vacated office under section 171(4) above, such time as the Secretary of State may, on the application of that person, determine;

   (c)   in the case of a person who has resigned, such time as may be prescribed;

   (d)   in the case of a person who has vacated office under subsection (6)(a) of section 171, the time at which he vacated office;

   (e)   in the case of a person who has vacated office under subsection (6)(b) of that section—

      (i)   if the final meeting of the creditors referred to in that subsection has resolved against that person's release, such time as the Secretary of State may, on an application by that person, determine, and

      (ii)   if that meeting has not resolved against that person's release, the time at which he vacated office.

(3)   In the application of subsection (2) to the winding up of a company registered in Scotland, the references to a determination by the Secretary of State as to the time from which a person who has ceased to be liquidator shall have his release are to be read as references to such a determination by the Accountant of Court.

(4)   Where a liquidator has his release under subsection (2), he is, with effect from the time specified in that subsection, discharged from all liability both in respect of acts or omissions of his in the winding up and otherwise in relation to his conduct as liquidator.

But nothing in this section prevents the exercise, in relation to a person who has had his release under subsection (2), of the court's powers under section 212 of this Act (summary remedy against delinquent directors, liquidators, etc).

NOTES

Modification in relation to Scotland: see the Note at the beginning of this Act.

[9.266]
174 Release (winding up by the court)

(1) This section applies with respect to the release of the liquidator of a company which is being wound up by the court, or of a provisional liquidator.

(2) Where the official receiver has ceased to be liquidator and a person becomes liquidator in his stead, the official receiver has his release with effect from the following time, that is to say—

    (a) in a case where that person was nominated by a general meeting of creditors or contributories, or was appointed by the Secretary of State, the time at which the official receiver gives notice to the court that he has been replaced;

    (b) in a case where that person is appointed by the court, such time as the court may determine.

(3) If the official receiver while he is a liquidator gives notice to the Secretary of State that the winding up is for practical purposes complete, he has his release with effect from such time as the Secretary of State may determine.

(4) A person other than the official receiver who has ceased to be a liquidator has his release with effect from the following time, that is to say—

    (a) in the case of a person who has been removed from office by a general meeting of creditors that has not resolved against his release or who has died, the time at which notice is given to the court in accordance with the rules that that person has ceased to hold office;

    (b) in the case of a person who has been removed from office by a general meeting of creditors that has resolved against his release, or by the court or the Secretary of State, or who has vacated office under section 172(5) or (7), such time as the Secretary of State may, on an application by that person, determine;

    (c) in the case of a person who has resigned, such time as may be prescribed;

    (d) in the case of a person who has vacated office under section 172(8)—

        (i) if the final meeting referred to in that subsection has resolved against that person's release, such time as the Secretary of State may, on an application by that person, determine, and

        (ii) if that meeting has not so resolved, the time at which that person vacated office.

(5) A person who has ceased to hold office as a provisional liquidator has his release with effect from such time as the court may, on an application by him, determine.

(6) Where the official receiver or a liquidator or provisional liquidator has his release under this section, he is, with effect from the time specified in the preceding provisions of this section, discharged from all liability both in respect of acts or omissions of his in the winding up and otherwise in relation to his conduct as liquidator or provisional liquidator.

But nothing in this section prevents the exercise, in relation to a person who has had his release under this section, of the court's powers under section 212 (summary remedy against delinquent directors, liquidators, etc).

(7) In the application of this section to a case where the order for winding up has been made by the court in Scotland, the references to a determination by the Secretary of State as to the time from which a person who has ceased to be liquidator has his release are to such a determination by the Accountant of Court.

CHAPTER VIII
PROVISIONS OF GENERAL APPLICATION IN WINDING UP

Preferential debts

[9.267]
175 Preferential debts (general provision)

(1) In a winding up the company's preferential debts (within the meaning given by section 386 in Part XII) shall be paid in priority to all other debts.

(2) Preferential debts—

    (a) rank equally among themselves after the expenses of the winding up and shall be paid in full, unless the assets are insufficient to meet them, in which case they abate in equal proportions; and

    (b) so far as the assets of the company available for payment of general creditors are insufficient to meet them, have priority over the claims of holders of debentures secured by, or holders of, any floating charge created by the company, and shall be paid accordingly out of any property comprised in or subject to that charge.

[9.268]
176 Preferential charge on goods distrained

(1) This section applies where a company is being wound up by the court in England and Wales, and is without prejudice to section 128 (avoidance of attachments, etc).

(2)   Where any person (whether or not a landlord or person entitled to rent) has distrained upon the goods or effects of the company in the period of 3 months ending with the date of the winding-up order, those goods or effects, or the proceeds of their sale, shall be charged for the benefit of the company with the preferential debts of the company to the extent that the company's property is for the time being insufficient for meeting them.

(3)   Where by virtue of a charge under subsection (2) any person surrenders any goods or effects to a company or makes a payment to a company, that person ranks, in respect of the amount of the proceeds of sale of those goods or effects by the liquidator or (as the case may be) the amount of the payment, as a preferential creditor of the company, except as against so much of the company's property as is available for the payment of preferential creditors by virtue of the surrender or payment.

[Property subject to floating charge

NOTES

    See further, as to the effect of floating charges on winding up, the Bankruptcy and Diligence etc (Scotland) Act 2007, s 45.

[9.269]

[176ZA   Payment of expenses of winding up (England and Wales)

(1)   The expenses of winding up in England and Wales, so far as the assets of the company available for payment of general creditors are insufficient to meet them, have priority over any claims to property comprised in or subject to any floating charge created by the company and shall be paid out of any such property accordingly.

(2)   In subsection (1)—

    (a)   the reference to assets of the company available for payment of general creditors does not include any amount made available under section 176A(2)(a);

    (b)   the reference to claims to property comprised in or subject to a floating charge is to the claims of—

       (i)   the holders of debentures secured by, or holders of, the floating charge, and

       (ii)   any preferential creditors entitled to be paid out of that property in priority to them.

(3)   Provision may be made by rules restricting the application of subsection (1), in such circumstances as may be prescribed, to expenses authorised or approved—

    (a)   by the holders of debentures secured by, or holders of, the floating charge and by any preferential creditors entitled to be paid in priority to them, or

    (b)   by the court.

(4)   References in this section to the expenses of the winding up are to all expenses properly incurred in the winding up, including the remuneration of the liquidator.]

NOTES

    Commencement: 6 April 2008.

    Inserted by the Companies Act 2006, s 1282(1), as from 6 April 2008, subject to transitional provisions as noted below.

    Transitional provisions: Sch 4, Pt 1, para 43(1) to the Companies Act 2006 (Commencement No 5, Transitional Provisions and Savings) Order 2007, SI 2007/3495 (at **[2.66]**) (as substituted by the Companies Act 2006 (Commencement No 6, Saving and Commencement Nos 3 and 5 (Amendment)) Order 2008, SI 2008/674, art 5, Sch 3, para 6(1), (5), as from 6 April 2008) provides as follows—

    "**Expenses of winding up (s 1282)**

    [43.—(1)   The amendment made to the Insolvency Act 1986 by section 1282(1) of the Companies Act 2006 (expenses of winding up) applies—

      (a)   to a creditors' voluntary winding up—

        (i)   for which the resolution is passed, or

        (ii)   where commenced as a members' voluntary winding up, for which the conversion to a creditors' voluntary winding up under section 96 of the Insolvency Act 1986 takes effect, or

        (iii)   in respect of which a notice is registered under paragraph 83 of Schedule B1 to the Insolvency Act 1986, on or after 6th April 2008;

      (b)   to a members' voluntary winding up for which the resolution is passed on or after 6th April 2008;

      (c)   to the winding up of a company by the court where the winding-up order is made on or after 6th April 2008, except where the order is made following a resolution for voluntary winding up passed by the company before 6th April 2008.]".

    See also the Insolvency (Amendment) Rules 2008, SI 2008/737 which amend the Insolvency Rules 1986, SI 1986/1925. The 2008 Rules amend r 4.218 of the Insolvency Rules 1986 so as to provide expressly for the expenses of a liquidation to be payable out of the proceeds of any legal proceedings which the liquidator has power to bring in his own name or bring or defend in the name of the company and also for the recovery of expenses and costs relating not only to the conduct, but also to the preparation, of any such legal proceedings. The provision is extended so to apply also to proceeds arising out of any awards made under arbitration or dispute resolution procedures or of any compromise or settlement of any legal action or dispute reached prior to a judgment or award being made. Correspondingly also included as costs or expenses of liquidation are those properly incurred in the preparation or conduct of arbitration or dispute resolution procedures and negotiations leading to a settlement or compromise of any legal action or dispute. The 2008 Rules also insert new rr 4.218A–4.218E into the 1986 Rules. These new provisions are derived from the power to make exceptions to the amendment made by CA 2006, s 1282(1) to this Act. The insertion of this section by s 1282(1) of the 2006 Act followed the judgment of the House of Lords in *Buchler and another (as joint liquidators of Leyland Daf Ltd) v Talbot and another (as joint administrative receivers of Leyland Daf Ltd) and Stichting Ofasec and others* [2004] UKHL 9 where the court held, on an interpretation of s 175 of this Act, that it could not be relied upon to support the deduction of expenses of a liquidation from property comprised in, or subject to, a floating charge created by the company. Where the assets of a company available for the payment of general creditors are insufficient to make payments in respect of preferential debts after the expenses of the winding up have been met, s 175 of this Act makes provision for payment of those preferential debts to be made out of property comprised in, or subject to, a floating charge created by the company and for those debts to have priority over the claims of holders of debentures secured by, or holders of, that floating charge. In the same judgment the court confirmed that liquidation expenses could be paid out of, and had priority as against preferential debts in relation to such assets as were available for the payment of general creditors. The new s 176ZA provides for expenses of a winding up in England and Wales, so far as the assets of the company available for the payment of general creditors are insufficient to meet them, to have priority over any claims to property comprised in, or subject to, a floating charge created by the company and to be paid out of such property. This is made expressly subject to any rules restricting the application of this section in such circumstances as may be prescribed, to expenses authorised or approved by the holders of debentures secured by, or holders of, the floating charge or by any preferential creditors entitled to be paid in priority to them or by the court. New rr 4.218A–4.218E restrict this section in its application to litigation expenses, which may not be paid out of property comprised in, or subject to, a floating charge without the approval or authorisation of the holder of a debenture secured by, or holder, of the floating charge or any preferential creditor or the court, as the case may be. The new rules set out the scope of the exception and the procedure for obtaining approval or authorisation of litigation expenses for the purpose of deducting them as liquidation expenses from property subject to a floating charge.

[9.270]
[176A Share of assets for unsecured creditors
(1)   This section applies where a floating charge relates to property of a company—
   (a)   which has gone into liquidation,
   (b)   which is in administration,
   (c)   of which there is a provisional liquidator, or
   (d)   of which there is a receiver.
(2)   The liquidator, administrator or receiver—
   (a)   shall make a prescribed part of the company's net property available for the satisfaction of unsecured debts, and
   (b)   shall not distribute that part to the proprietor of a floating charge except in so far as it exceeds the amount required for the satisfaction of unsecured debts.
(3)   Subsection (2) shall not apply to a company if—
   (a)   the company's net property is less than the prescribed minimum, and
   (b)   the liquidator, administrator or receiver thinks that the cost of making a distribution to unsecured creditors would be disproportionate to the benefits.
(4)   Subsection (2) shall also not apply to a company if or in so far as it is disapplied by—
   (a)   a voluntary arrangement in respect of the company, or
   (b)   a compromise or arrangement agreed under [Part 26 of the Companies Act 2006 (arrangements and reconstructions)].
(5)   Subsection (2) shall also not apply to a company if—
   (a)   the liquidator, administrator or receiver applies to the court for an order under this subsection on the ground that the cost of making a distribution to unsecured creditors would be disproportionate to the benefits, and
   (b)   the court orders that subsection (2) shall not apply.
(6)   In subsections (2) and (3) a company's net property is the amount of its property which would, but for this section, be available for satisfaction of claims of holders of debentures secured by, or holders of, any floating charge created by the company.
(7)   An order under subsection (2) prescribing part of a company's net property may, in particular, provide for its calculation—
   (a)   as a percentage of the company's net property, or
   (b)   as an aggregate of different percentages of different parts of the company's net property.
(8)   An order under this section—
   (a)   must be made by statutory instrument, and
   (b)   shall be subject to annulment pursuant to a resolution of either House of Parliament.
(9)   In this section—
   "floating charge" means a charge which is a floating charge on its creation and which is created after the first order under subsection (2)(a) comes into force, and
   "prescribed" means prescribed by order by the Secretary of State.
(10)   An order under this section may include transitional or incidental provision.]

NOTES
   Inserted, together with the heading preceding s 176ZA, by the Enterprise Act 2002, s 252, as from 15 September 2003.
   Sub-s (4): words in square brackets in para (b) substituted by the Companies Act 2006 (Consequential Amendments etc) Order 2008, SI 2008/948, art 3(1), Sch 1, Pt 2, para 103, as from 6 April 2008.
   Orders: the Insolvency Act 1986 (Prescribed Part) Order 2003, SI 2003/2097 at **[10.831]**.

Special managers

[9.271]
177 Power to appoint special manager
(1)   Where a company has gone into liquidation or a provisional liquidator has been appointed, the court may, on an application under this section, appoint any person to be the special manager of the business or property of the company.

(2) The application may be made by the liquidator or provisional liquidator in any case where it appears to him that the nature of the business or property of the company, or the interests of the company's creditors or contributories or members generally, require the appointment of another person to manage the company's business or property.

(3) The special manager has such powers as may be entrusted to him by the court.

(4) The court's power to entrust powers to the special manager includes power to direct that any provision of this Act that has effect in relation to the provisional liquidator or liquidator of a company shall have the like effect in relation to the special manager for the purposes of the carrying out by him of any of the functions of the provisional liquidator or liquidator.

(5) The special manager shall—

    (a) give such security or, in Scotland, caution as may be prescribed;

    (b) prepare and keep such accounts as may be prescribed; and

    (c) produce those accounts in accordance with the rules to the Secretary of State or to such other persons as may be prescribed.

Disclaimer (England and Wales only)

[9.272]

178 Power to disclaim onerous property

(1) This and the next two sections apply to a company that is being wound up in England and Wales.

(2) Subject as follows, the liquidator may, by the giving of the prescribed notice, disclaim any onerous property and may do so notwithstanding that he has taken possession of it, endeavoured to sell it, or otherwise exercised rights of ownership in relation to it.

(3) The following is onerous property for the purposes of this section—

    (a) any unprofitable contract, and

    (b) any other property of the company which is unsaleable or not readily saleable or is such that it may give rise to a liability to pay money or perform any other onerous act.

(4) A disclaimer under this section—

    (a) operates so as to determine, as from the date of the disclaimer, the rights, interests and liabilities of the company in or in respect of the property disclaimed; but

    (b) does not, except so far as is necessary for the purpose of releasing the company from any liability, affect the rights or liabilities of any other person.

(5) A notice of disclaimer shall not be given under this section in respect of any property if—

    (a) a person interested in the property has applied in writing to the liquidator or one of his predecessors as liquidator requiring the liquidator or that predecessor to decide whether he will disclaim or not, and

    (b) the period of 28 days beginning with the day on which that application was made, or such longer period as the court may allow, has expired without a notice of disclaimer having been given under this section in respect of that property.

(6) Any person sustaining loss or damage in consequence of the operation of a disclaimer under this section is deemed a creditor of the company to the extent of the loss or damage and accordingly may prove for the loss or damage in the winding up.

[9.273]

179 Disclaimer of leaseholds

(1) The disclaimer under section 178 of any property of a leasehold nature does not take effect unless a copy of the disclaimer has been served (so far as the liquidator is aware of their addresses) on every person claiming under the company as underlessee or mortgagee and either—

    (a) no application under section 181 below is made with respect to that property before the end of the period of 14 days beginning with the day on which the last notice served under this subsection was served; or

    (b) where such an application has been made, the court directs that the disclaimer shall take effect.

(2) Where the court gives a direction under subsection (1)(b) it may also, instead of or in addition to any order it makes under section 181, make such orders with respect to fixtures, tenant's improvements and other matters arising out of the lease as it thinks fit.

[9.274]

180 Land subject to rentcharge

(1) The following applies where, in consequence of the disclaimer under section 178 of any land subject to a rentcharge, that land vests by operation of law in the Crown or any other person (referred to in the next subsection as "the proprietor").

(2) The proprietor and the successors in title of the proprietor are not subject to any personal liability in respect of any sums becoming due under the rentcharge except sums becoming due after the proprietor, or some person claiming under or through the proprietor, has taken possession or control of the land or has entered into occupation of it.

[9.275]
181   Powers of court (general)
(1)   This section and the next apply where the liquidator has disclaimed property under section 178.
(2)   An application under this section may be made to the court by—
  (a)   any person who claims an interest in the disclaimed property, or
  (b)   any person who is under any liability in respect of the disclaimed property, not being a liability discharged by the disclaimer.
(3)   Subject as follows, the court may on the application make an order, on such terms as it thinks fit, for the vesting of the disclaimed property in, or for its delivery to—
  (a)   a person entitled to it or a trustee for such a person, or
  (b)   a person subject to such a liability as is mentioned in subsection (2)(b) or a trustee for such a person.
(4)   The court shall not make an order under subsection (3)(b) except where it appears to the court that it would be just to do so for the purpose of compensating the person subject to the liability in respect of the disclaimer.
(5)   The effect of any order under this section shall be taken into account in assessing for the purpose of section 178(6) the extent of any loss or damage sustained by any person in consequence of the disclaimer.
(6)   An order under this section vesting property in any person need not be completed by conveyance, assignment or transfer.

[9.276]
182   Powers of court (leaseholds)
(1)   The court shall not make an order under section 181 vesting property of a leasehold nature in any person claiming under the company as underlessee or mortgagee except on terms making that person—
  (a)   subject to the same liabilities and obligations as the company was subject to under the lease at the commencement of the winding up, or
  (b)   if the court thinks fit, subject to the same liabilities and obligations as that person would be subject to if the lease had been assigned to him at the commencement of the winding up.
(2)   For the purposes of an order under section 181 relating to only part of any property comprised in a lease, the requirements of subsection (1) apply as if the lease comprised only the property to which the order relates.
(3)   Where subsection (1) applies and no person claiming under the company as underlessee or mortgagee is willing to accept an order under section 181 on the terms required by virtue of that subsection, the court may, by order under that section, vest the company's estate or interest in the property in any person who is liable (whether personally or in a representative capacity, and whether alone or jointly with the company) to perform the lessee's covenants in the lease.
  The court may vest that estate and interest in such a person freed and discharged from all estates, incumbrances and interests created by the company.
(4)   Where subsection (1) applies and a person claiming under the company as underlessee or mortgagee declines to accept an order under section 181, that person is excluded from all interest in the property.

Execution, attachment and the Scottish equivalents

[9.277]
183   Effect of execution or attachment (England and Wales)
(1)   Where a creditor has issued execution against the goods or land of a company or has attached any debt due to it, and the company is subsequently wound up, he is not entitled to retain the benefit of the execution or attachment against the liquidator unless he has completed the execution or attachment before the commencement of the winding up.
(2)   However—
  (a)   if a creditor has had notice of a meeting having been called at which a resolution for voluntary winding up is to be proposed, the date on which he had notice is substituted, for the purpose of subsection (1), for the date of commencement of the winding up;
  (b)   a person who purchases in good faith under a sale by the [enforcement officer or other officer charged with the execution of the writ] any goods of a company on which execution has been levied in all cases acquires a good title to them against the liquidator; and
  (c)   the rights conferred by subsection (1) on the liquidator may be set aside by the court in favour of the creditor to such extent and subject to such terms as the court thinks fit.
(3)   For purposes of this Act—
  (a)   an execution against goods is completed by seizure and sale, or by the making of a charging order under section 1 of the Charging Orders Act 1979;
  (b)   an attachment of a debt is completed by receipt of the debt; and
  (c)   an execution against land is completed by seizure, by the appointment of a receiver, or by the making of a charging order under section 1 of the Act above-mentioned.
(4)   In this section, "goods" includes all chattels personal; and ["enforcement officer" means an individual who is authorised to act as an enforcement officer under the Courts Act 2003].

(5)   This section does not apply in the case of a winding up in Scotland.

NOTES

   Sub-ss (2), (4): words in square brackets substituted by the Courts Act 2003, s 109(1), Sch 8, para 295, as from 15 March 2004.

[9.278]
184   Duties of [officers charged with execution of writs and other processes] (England and Wales)
(1)   The following applies where a company's goods are taken in execution and, before their sale or the completion of the execution (by the receipt or recovery of the full amount of the levy), notice is served on the [enforcement officer, or other officer, charged with execution of the writ or other process,] that a provisional liquidator has been appointed or that a winding-up order has been made, or that a resolution for voluntary winding up has been passed.
(2)   The [enforcement officer or other officer] shall, on being so required, deliver the goods and any money seized or received in part satisfaction of the execution to the liquidator; but the costs of execution are a first charge on the goods or money so delivered, and the liquidator may sell the goods, or a sufficient part of them, for the purpose of satisfying the charge.
(3)   If under an execution in respect of a judgment for a sum exceeding [£500] a company's goods are sold or money is paid in order to avoid sale, the [enforcement officer or other officer] shall deduct the costs of the execution from the proceeds of sale or the money paid and retain the balance for 14 days.
(4)   If within that time notice is served on the [enforcement officer or other officer] of a petition for the winding up of the company having been presented, or of a meeting having been called at which there is to be proposed a resolution for voluntary winding up, and an order is made or a resolution passed (as the case may be), the [enforcement officer or other officer] shall pay the balance to the liquidator, who is entitled to retain it as against the execution creditor.
(5)   The rights conferred by this section on the liquidator may be set aside by the court in favour of the creditor to such extent and subject to such terms as the court thinks fit.
(6)   In this section, "goods" includes all chattels personal; and ["enforcement officer" means an individual who is authorised to act as an enforcement officer under the Courts Act 2003].
(7)   The money sum for the time being specified in subsection (3) is subject to increase or reduction by order under section 416 in Part XV.
(8)   This section does not apply in the case of a winding up in Scotland.

NOTES

   Section heading, sub-ss (1), (2), (4), (6): words in square brackets substituted by the Courts Act 2003, s 109(1), Sch 8, para 296, as from 15 March 2004.
   Sub-s (3): sum in first pair of square brackets increased from £250 by the Insolvency Proceedings (Monetary Limits) Order 1986, SI 1986/1996, art 2, Schedule, Pt I (but this amendment is not to affect any case where the goods are sold or payment to avoid sale is made before 29 December 1986); words in second pair of square brackets substituted by the Courts Act 2003, s 109(1), Sch 8, para 296(1), (3), as from 15 March 2004.

[9.279]
185   Effect of diligence (Scotland)
(1)   In the winding up of a company registered in Scotland, the following provisions of the Bankruptcy (Scotland) Act 1985—
   (a)   subsections (1) to (6)[, (8A) to (8F) and (10)] of section 37 (effect of sequestration on diligence); and
   (b)   subsections (3), (4), (7) and (8) of section 39 (realisation of estate),
apply, so far as consistent with this Act, in like manner as they apply in the sequestration of a debtor's estate, with the substitutions specified below and with any other necessary modifications.
(2)   The substitutions to be made in those sections of the Act of 1985 are as follows—
   (a)   for references to the debtor, substitute references to the company;
   (b)   for references to the sequestration, substitute references to the winding up;
   (c)   for references to the date of sequestration, substitute references to the commencement of the winding up of the company; and
   (d)   for references to the . . . trustee, substitute references to the liquidator.
(3)   In this section, "the commencement of the winding up of the company" means, where it is being wound up by the court, the day on which the winding-up order is made.
(4)   This section, so far as relating to any estate or effects of the company situated in Scotland, applies in the case of a company registered in England and Wales as in the case of one registered in Scotland.

NOTES

   Sub-s (1): words in square brackets inserted by the Bankruptcy and Diligence etc (Scotland) Act 2007, s 226, Sch 5, para 14(1), (3), as from a day to be appointed.
   Sub-s (2): word omitted from para (d) repealed by the Bankruptcy and Diligence etc (Scotland) Act 2007, s 226, Sch 6, Pt 1, as from 1 April 2008.

Miscellaneous matters

[9.280]
186   Rescission of contracts by the court
(1)   The court may, on the application of a person who is, as against the liquidator, entitled to the benefit or subject to the burden of a contract made with the company, make an order rescinding the contract on such terms as to payment by or to either party of damages for the non-performance of the contract, or otherwise as the court thinks just.
(2)   Any damages payable under the order to such a person may be proved by him as a debt in the winding up.

[9.281]
187   Power to make over assets to employees
(1)   On the winding up of a company (whether by the court or voluntarily), the liquidator may, subject to the following provisions of this section, make any payment which the company has, before the commencement of the winding up, decided to make under [section 247 of the Companies Act 2006] (power to provide for employees or former employees on cessation or transfer of business).
[(2)   The liquidator may, after the winding up has commenced, make any such provision as is mentioned in section 247(1) if—
   (a)   the company's liabilities have been fully satisfied and provision has been made for the expenses of the winding up,
   (b)   the exercise of the power has been sanctioned by a resolution of the company, and
   (c)   any requirements of the company's [articles] as to the exercise of the power conferred by section 247(1) are complied with.]
(3)   Any payment which may be made by a company under this section (that is, a payment after the commencement of its winding up) may be made out of the company's assets which are available to the members on the winding up.
(4)   On a winding up by the court, the exercise by the liquidator of his powers under this section is subject to the court's control, and any creditor or contributory may apply to the court with respect to any exercise or proposed exercise of the power.
(5)   Subsections (1) and (2) above have effect notwithstanding anything in any rule of law or in section 107 of this Act (property of company after satisfaction of liabilities to be distributed among members).

NOTES
   Sub-s (1): words in square brackets substituted by the Companies Act 2006 (Commencement No 3, Consequential Amendments, Transitional Provisions and Savings) Order 2007, SI 2007/2194, art 10(1), Sch 4, Pt 3, para 42(1), (2), as from 1 October 2007.
   Sub-s (2): substituted by SI 2007/2194, art 10(1), Sch 4, Pt 3, para 42(1), (3), as from 1 October 2007; word in square brackets substituted by the Companies Act 2006 (Consequential Amendments, Transitional Provisions and Savings) Order 2009, SI 2009/1941, art 2(1), Sch 1, para 75(1), (20), as from 1 October 2009 (for transitional provisions see the note to s 7A at **[9.103]**).

[9.282]
188   Notification that company is in liquidation
[(1)   When a company is being wound up, whether by the court or voluntarily—
   (a)   every invoice, order for goods [or services], business letter or order form (whether in hard copy, electronic or any other form) issued by or on behalf of the company, or a liquidator of the company or a receiver or manager of the company's property, . . . and
   (b)   all the company's websites,
must contain a statement that the company is being wound up.]
(2)   If default is made in complying with this section, the company and any of the following persons who knowingly and wilfully authorises or permits the default, namely, any officer of the company, any liquidator of the company and any receiver or manager, is liable to a fine.

NOTES
   Sub-s (1): substituted by the Companies (Registrar, Languages and Trading Disclosures) Regulations 2006, SI 2006/3429, reg 7(1), as from 1 January 2007; words in square brackets inserted, and words omitted repealed, by the Companies (Trading Disclosures) (Insolvency) Regulations 2008, SI 2008/1897, reg 5(1), as from 1 October 2008.

[9.283]
189   Interest on debts
(1)   In a winding up interest is payable in accordance with this section on any debt proved in the winding up, including so much of any such debt as represents interest on the remainder.
(2)   Any surplus remaining after the payment of the debts proved in a winding up shall, before being applied for any other purpose, be applied in paying interest on those debts in respect of the periods during which they have been outstanding since the company went into liquidation.
(3)   All interest under this section ranks equally, whether or not the debts on which it is payable rank equally.

(4)   The rate of interest payable under this section in respect of any debt ("the official rate" for the purposes of any provision of this Act in which that expression is used) is whichever is the greater of—

    (a)   the rate specified in section 17 of the Judgments Act 1838 on the day on which the company went into liquidation, and

    (b)   the rate applicable to that debt apart from the winding up.

(5)   In the application of this section to Scotland—

    (a)   references to a debt proved in a winding up have effect as references to a claim accepted in a winding up, and

    (b)   the reference to section 17 of the Judgments Act 1838 has effect as a reference to the rules.

[9.284]
190   Documents exempt from stamp duty

(1)   In the case of a winding up by the court, or of a creditors' voluntary winding up, the following has effect as regards exemption from duties chargeable under the enactments relating to stamp duties.

(2)   If the company is registered in England and Wales, the following documents are exempt from stamp duty—

    (a)   every assurance relating solely to freehold or leasehold property, or to any estate, right or interest in, any real or personal property, which forms part of the company's assets and which, after the execution of the assurance, either at law or in equity, is or remains part of those assets, and

    (b)   every writ, order, certificate, or other instrument or writing relating solely to the property of any company which is being wound up as mentioned in subsection (1), or to any proceeding under such a winding up.

"Assurance" here includes deed, conveyance, assignment and surrender.

(3)   If the company is registered in Scotland, the following documents are exempt from stamp duty—

    (a)   every conveyance relating solely to property which forms part of the company's assets and which, after the execution of the conveyance, is or remains the company's property for the benefit of its creditors,

    (b)   any article of roup or sale, submission and every other instrument and writing whatsoever relating solely to the company's property, and

    (c)   every deed or writing forming part of the proceedings in the winding up.

"Conveyance" here includes assignation, instrument, discharge, writing and deed.

[9.285]
191   Company's books to be evidence

Where a company is being wound up, all books and papers of the company and of the liquidators are, as between the contributories of the company, prima facie evidence of the truth of all matters purporting to be recorded in them.

[9.286]
192   Information as to pending liquidations

(1)   If the winding up of a company is not concluded within one year after its commencement, the liquidator shall, at such intervals as may be prescribed, until the winding up is concluded, send to the registrar of companies a statement in the prescribed form and containing the prescribed particulars with respect to the proceedings in, and position of, the liquidation.

(2)   If a liquidator fails to comply with this section, he is liable to a fine and, for continued contravention, to a daily default fine.

NOTES

Modification in relation to Scotland: see the Note at the beginning of this Act.

[9.287]
193   Unclaimed dividends (Scotland)

(1)   The following applies where a company registered in Scotland has been wound up, and is about to be dissolved.

(2)   The liquidator shall lodge in an appropriate bank or institution as defined in section 73(1) of the Bankruptcy (Scotland) Act 1985 (not being a bank or institution in or of which the liquidator is acting partner, manager, agent or cashier) in the name of the Accountant of Court the whole unclaimed dividends and unapplied or undistributable balances, and the deposit receipts shall be transmitted to the Accountant of Court.

(3)   The provisions of section 58 of the Bankruptcy (Scotland) Act 1985 (so far as consistent with this Act and [the Companies Acts]) apply with any necessary modifications to sums lodged in a bank or institution under this section as they apply to sums deposited under section 57 of the Act first mentioned.

NOTES

Sub-s (3): words in square brackets substituted by the Companies Act 2006 (Consequential Amendments, Transitional Provisions and Savings) Order 2009, SI 2009/1941, art 2(1), Sch 1, para 75(1), (21), as from 1 October 2009 (for transitional provisions see the note to s 7A at **[9.103]**).

[9.288]
194 Resolutions passed at adjourned meetings
Where a resolution is passed at an adjourned meeting of a company's creditors or contributories, the resolution is treated for all purposes as having been passed on the date on which it was in fact passed, and not as having been passed on any earlier date.

[9.289]
195 Meetings to ascertain wishes of creditors or contributories
(1)   The court may—
  (a)   as to all matters relating to the winding up of a company, have regard to the wishes of the creditors or contributories (as proved to it by any sufficient evidence), and
  (b)   if it thinks fit, for the purpose of ascertaining those wishes, direct meetings of the creditors or contributories to be called, held and conducted in such manner as the court directs, and appoint a person to act as chairman of any such meeting and report the result of it to the court.
(2)   In the case of creditors, regard shall be had to the value of each creditor's debt.
(3)   In the case of contributories, regard shall be had to the number of votes conferred on each contributory . . .

NOTES

Sub-s (3): words omitted repealed by the Companies Act 2006 (Consequential Amendments, Transitional Provisions and Savings) Order 2009, SI 2009/1941, art 2(1), Sch 1, para 75(1), (22), as from 1 October 2009 (for transitional provisions see the note to s 7A at **[9.103]**).

[9.290]
196 Judicial notice of court documents
In all proceedings under this Part, all courts, judges and persons judicially acting, and all officers, judicial or ministerial, of any court, or employed in enforcing the process of any court shall take judicial notice—
  (a)   of the signature of any officer of the High Court or of a county court in England and Wales, or of the Court of Session or a sheriff court in Scotland, or of the High Court in Northern Ireland, and also
  (b)   of the official seal or stamp of the several offices of the High Court in England and Wales or Northern Ireland, or of the Court of Session, appended to or impressed on any document made, issued or signed under the provisions of this Act or [the Companies Acts], or any official copy of such a document.

NOTES

Words in square brackets substituted by the Companies Act 2006 (Consequential Amendments, Transitional Provisions and Savings) Order 2009, SI 2009/1941, art 2(1), Sch 1, para 75(1), (23), as from 1 October 2009 (for transitional provisions see the note to s 7A at **[9.103]**).

[9.291]
197 Commission for receiving evidence
(1)   When a company is wound up in England and Wales or in Scotland, the court may refer the whole or any part of the examination of witnesses—
  (a)   to a specified county court in England and Wales, or
  (b)   to the sheriff principal for a specified sheriffdom in Scotland, or
  (c)   to the High Court in Northern Ireland or a specified Northern Ireland County Court,
("specified" meaning specified in the order of the winding-up court).
(2)   Any person exercising jurisdiction as a judge of the court to which the reference is made (or, in Scotland, the sheriff principal to whom it is made) shall then, by virtue of this section, be a commissioner for the purpose of taking the evidence of those witnesses.
(3)   The judge or sheriff principal has in the matter referred the same power of summoning and examining witnesses, of requiring the production and delivery of documents, of punishing defaults by witnesses, and of allowing costs and expenses to witnesses, as the court which made the winding-up order.
These powers are in addition to any which the judge or sheriff principal might lawfully exercise apart from this section.
(4)   The examination so taken shall be returned or reported to that court which made the order in such manner as the court requests.
(5)   This section extends to Northern Ireland.

[9.292]
198   Court order for examination of persons in Scotland

(1)   The court may direct the examination in Scotland of any person for the time being in Scotland (whether a contributory of the company or not), in regard to the trade, dealings, affairs or property of any company in course of being wound up, or of any person being a contributory of the company, so far as the company may be interested by reason of his being a contributory.

(2)   The order or commission to take the examination shall be directed to the sheriff principal of the sheriffdom in which the person to be examined is residing or happens to be for the time; and the sheriff principal shall summon the person to appear before him at a time and place to be specified in the summons for examination on oath as a witness or as a haver, and to produce any books or papers called for which are in his possession or power.

(3)   The sheriff principal may take the examination either orally or on written interrogatories, and shall report the same in writing in the usual form to the court, and shall transmit with the report the books and papers produced, if the originals are required and specified by the order or commission, or otherwise copies or extracts authenticated by the sheriff.

(4)   If a person so summoned fails to appear at the time and place specified, or refuses to be examined or to make the production required, the sheriff principal shall proceed against him as a witness or haver duly cited; and failing to appear or refusing to give evidence or make production may be proceeded against by the law of Scotland.

(5)   The sheriff principal is entitled to such fees, and the witness is entitled to such allowances, as sheriffs principal when acting as commissioners under appointment from the Court of Session and as witnesses and havers are entitled to in the like cases according to the law and practice of Scotland.

(6)   If any objection is stated to the sheriff principal by the witness, either on the ground of his incompetency as a witness, or as to the production required, or on any other ground, the sheriff principal may, if he thinks fit, report the objection to the court, and suspend the examination of the witness until it has been disposed of by the court.

[9.293]
199   Costs of application for leave to proceed (Scottish companies)
Where a petition or application for leave to proceed with an action or proceeding against a company which is being wound up in Scotland is unopposed and is granted by the court, the costs of the petition or application shall, unless the court otherwise directs, be added to the amount of the petitioner's or applicant's claim against the company.

[9.294]
200   Affidavits etc in United Kingdom and overseas

(1)   An affidavit required to be sworn under or for the purposes of this Part may be sworn in the United Kingdom, or elsewhere in Her Majesty's dominions, before any court, judge or person lawfully authorised to take and receive affidavits, or before any of Her Majesty's consuls or vice-consuls in any place outside Her dominions.

(2)   All courts, judges, justices, commissioners and persons acting judicially shall take judicial notice of the seal or stamp or signature (as the case may be) of any such court, judge, person, consul or vice-consul attached, appended or subscribed to any such affidavit, or to any other document to be used for the purposes of this Part.

CHAPTER IX
DISSOLUTION OF COMPANIES AFTER WINDING UP

[9.295]
201   Dissolution (voluntary winding up)

(1)   This section applies, in the case of a company wound up voluntarily, where the liquidator has sent to the registrar of companies his final account and return under section 94 (members' voluntary) or section 106 (creditors' voluntary).

(2)   The registrar on receiving the account and return shall forthwith register them; and on the expiration of 3 months from the registration of the return the company is deemed to be dissolved.

(3)   However, the court may, on the application of the liquidator or any other person who appears to the court to be interested, make an order deferring the date at which the dissolution of the company is to take effect for such time as the court thinks fit.

(4)   It is the duty of the person on whose application an order of the court under this section is made within 7 days after the making of the order to deliver to the registrar [a copy] of the order for registration; and if that person fails to do so he is liable to a fine and, for continued contravention, to a daily default fine.

NOTES

Sub-s (4): words in square brackets substituted by the Companies (Registrar, Languages and Trading Disclosures) Regulations 2006, SI 2006/3429, reg 3(1)(d), as from 1 January 2007.

[9.296]
202   Early dissolution (England and Wales)
(1)   This section applies where an order for the winding up of a company has been made by the court in England and Wales.
(2)   The official receiver, if—
  (a)   he is the liquidator of the company, and
  (b)   it appears to him—
      (i)   that the realisable assets of the company are insufficient to cover the expenses of the winding up, and
      (ii)   that the affairs of the company do not require any further investigation,
may at any time apply to the registrar of companies for the early dissolution of the company.
(3)   Before making that application, the official receiver shall give not less than 28 days' notice of his intention to do so to the company's creditors and contributories and, if there is an administrative receiver of the company, to that receiver.
(4)   With the giving of that notice the official receiver ceases (subject to any directions under the next section) to be required to perform any duties imposed on him in relation to the company, its creditors or contributories by virtue of any provision of this Act, apart from a duty to make an application under subsection (2) of this section.
(5)   On the receipt of the official receiver's application under subsection (2) the registrar shall forthwith register it and, at the end of the period of 3 months beginning with the day of the registration of the application, the company shall be dissolved.
  However, the Secretary of State may, on the application of the official receiver or any other person who appears to the Secretary of State to be interested, give directions under section 203 at any time before the end of that period.

[9.297]
203   Consequence of notice under s 202
(1)   Where a notice has been given under section 202(3), the official receiver or any creditor or contributory of the company, or the administrative receiver of the company (if there is one) may apply to the Secretary of State for directions under this section.
(2)   The grounds on which that application may be made are—
  (a)   that the realisable assets of the company are sufficient to cover the expenses of the winding up;
  (b)   that the affairs of the company do require further investigation; or
  (c)   that for any other reason the early dissolution of the company is inappropriate.
(3)   Directions under this section—
  (a)   are directions making such provision as the Secretary of State thinks fit for enabling the winding up of the company to proceed as if no notice had been given under section 202(3), and
  (b)   may, in the case of an application under section 202(5), include a direction deferring the date at which the dissolution of the company is to take effect for such period as the Secretary of State thinks fit.
(4)   An appeal to the court lies from any decision of the Secretary of State on an application for directions under this section.
(5)   It is the duty of the person on whose application any directions are given under this section, or in whose favour an appeal with respect to an application for such directions is determined, within 7 days after the giving of the directions or the determination of the appeal, to deliver to the registrar of companies for registration such a copy of the directions or determination as is prescribed.
(6)   If a person without reasonable excuse fails to deliver a copy as required by subsection (5), he is liable to a fine and, for continued contravention, to a daily default fine.

[9.298]
204   Early dissolution (Scotland)
(1)   This section applies where a winding-up order has been made by the court in Scotland.
(2)   If after a meeting or meetings under section 138 (appointment of liquidator in Scotland) it appears to the liquidator that the realisable assets of the company are insufficient to cover the expenses of the winding up, he may apply to the court for an order that the company be dissolved.
(3)   Where the liquidator makes that application, if the court is satisfied that the realisable assets of the company are insufficient to cover the expenses of the winding up and it appears to the court appropriate to do so, the court shall make an order that the company be dissolved in accordance with this section.
(4)   A copy of the order shall within 14 days from its date be forwarded by the liquidator to the registrar of companies, who shall forthwith register it; and, at the end of the period of 3 months beginning with the day of the registration of the order, the company shall be dissolved.
(5)   The court may, on an application by any person who appears to the court to have an interest, order that the date at which the dissolution of the company is to take effect shall be deferred for such period as the court thinks fit.

(6)   It is the duty of the person on whose application an order is made under subsection (5), within 7 days after the making of the order, to deliver to the registrar of companies such a copy of the order as is prescribed.

(7)   If the liquidator without reasonable excuse fails to comply with the requirements of subsection (4), he is liable to a fine and, for continued contravention, to a daily default fine.

(8)   If a person without reasonable excuse fails to deliver a copy as required by subsection (6), he is liable to a fine and, for continued contravention, to a daily default fine.

[9.299]
205   Dissolution otherwise than under ss 202–204

(1)   This section applies where the registrar of companies receives—
  (a)   a notice served for the purposes of section 172(8) (final meeting of creditors and vacation of office by liquidator), or
  (b)   a notice from the official receiver that the winding up of a company by the court is complete.

(2)   The registrar shall, on receipt of the notice, forthwith register it; and, subject as follows, at the end of the period of 3 months beginning with the day of the registration of the notice, the company shall be dissolved.

(3)   The Secretary of State may, on the application of the official receiver or any other person who appears to the Secretary of State to be interested, give a direction deferring the date at which the dissolution of the company is to take effect for such period as the Secretary of State thinks fit.

(4)   An appeal to the court lies from any decision of the Secretary of State on an application for a direction under subsection (3).

(5)   Subsection (3) does not apply in a case where the winding-up order was made by the court in Scotland, but in such a case the court may, on an application by any person appearing to the court to have an interest, order that the date at which the dissolution of the company is to take effect shall be deferred for such period as the court thinks fit.

(6)   It is the duty of the person—
  (a)   on whose application a direction is given under subsection (3);
  (b)   in whose favour an appeal with respect to an application for such a direction is determined; or
  (c)   on whose application an order is made under subsection (5),
within 7 days after the giving of the direction, the determination of the appeal or the making of the order, to deliver to the registrar for registration such a copy of the direction, determination or order as is prescribed.

(7)   If a person without reasonable excuse fails to deliver a copy as required by subsection (6), he is liable to a fine and, for continued contravention, to a daily default fine.

CHAPTER X
MALPRACTICE BEFORE AND DURING LIQUIDATION; PENALISATION OF COMPANIES
AND COMPANY OFFICERS; INVESTIGATIONS AND PROSECUTIONS

Offences of fraud, deception, etc

[9.300]
206   Fraud, etc in anticipation of winding up

(1)   When a company is ordered to be wound up by the court, or passes a resolution for voluntary winding up, any person, being a past or present officer of the company, is deemed to have committed an offence if, within the 12 months immediately preceding the commencement of the winding up, he has—
  (a)   concealed any part of the company's property to the value of [£500] or more, or concealed any debt due to or from the company, or
  (b)   fraudulently removed any part of the company's property to the value of [£500] or more, or
  (c)   concealed, destroyed, mutilated or falsified any book or paper affecting or relating to the company's property or affairs, or
  (d)   made any false entry in any book or paper affecting or relating to the company's property or affairs, or
  (e)   fraudulently parted with, altered or made any omission in any document affecting or relating to the company's property or affairs, or
  (f)   pawned, pledged or disposed of any property of the company which has been obtained on credit and has not been paid for (unless the pawning, pledging or disposal was in the ordinary way of the company's business).

(2)   Such a person is deemed to have committed an offence if within the period above mentioned he has been privy to the doing by others of any of the things mentioned in paragraphs (c), (d) and (e) of subsection (1); and he commits an offence if, at any time after the commencement of the winding up, he does any of the things mentioned in paragraphs (a) to (f) of that subsection, or is privy to the doing by others of any of the things mentioned in paragraphs (c) to (e) of it.

(3)   For purposes of this section, "officer" includes a shadow director.

(4)   It is a defence—

(a)   for a person charged under paragraph (a) or (f) of subsection (1) (or under subsection (2) in respect of the things mentioned in either of those two paragraphs) to prove that he had no intent to defraud, and

(b)   for a person charged under paragraph (c) or (d) of subsection (1) (or under subsection (2) in respect of the things mentioned in either of those two paragraphs) to prove that he had no intent to conceal the state of affairs of the company or to defeat the law.

(5)   Where a person pawns, pledges or disposes of any property in circumstances which amount to an offence under subsection (1)(f), every person who takes in pawn or pledge, or otherwise receives, the property knowing it to be pawned, pledged or disposed of in such circumstances, is guilty of an offence.

(6)   A person guilty of an offence under this section is liable to imprisonment or a fine, or both.

(7)   The money sums specified in paragraphs (a) and (b) of subsection (1) are subject to increase or reduction by order under section 416 in Part XV.

NOTES

Sub-s (1): sums in square brackets in sub-paras (a), (b) increased from £120 by the Insolvency Proceedings (Monetary Limits) Order 1986, SI 1986/1996, art 2(1), Schedule, Pt I.

[9.301]
207   Transactions in fraud of creditors
(1)   When a company is ordered to be wound up by the court or passes a resolution for voluntary winding up, a person is deemed to have committed an offence if he, being at the time an officer of the company—

(a)   has made or caused to be made any gift or transfer of, or charge on, or has caused or connived at the levying of any execution against, the company's property, or

(b)   has concealed or removed any part of the company's property since, or within 2 months before, the date of any unsatisfied judgment or order for the payment of money obtained against the company.

(2)   A person is not guilty of an offence under this section—

(a)   by reason of conduct constituting an offence under subsection (1)(a) which occurred more than 5 years before the commencement of the winding up, or

(b)   if he proves that, at the time of the conduct constituting the offence, he had no intent to defraud the company's creditors.

(3)   A person guilty of an offence under this section is liable to imprisonment or a fine, or both.

[9.302]
208   Misconduct in course of winding up
(1)   When a company is being wound up, whether by the court or voluntarily, any person, being a past or present officer of the company, commits an offence if he—

(a)   does not to the best of his knowledge and belief fully and truly discover to the liquidator all the company's property, and how and to whom and for what consideration and when the company disposed of any part of that property (except such part as has been disposed of in the ordinary way of the company's business), or

(b)   does not deliver up to the liquidator (or as he directs) all such part of the company's property as is in his custody or under his control, and which he is required by law to deliver up, or

(c)   does not deliver up to the liquidator (or as he directs) all books and papers in his custody or under his control belonging to the company and which he is required by law to deliver up, or

(d)   knowing or believing that a false debt has been proved by any person in the winding up, fails to inform the liquidator as soon as practicable, or

(e)   after the commencement of the winding up, prevents the production of any book or paper affecting or relating to the company's property or affairs.

(2)   Such a person commits an offence if after the commencement of the winding up he attempts to account for any part of the company's property by fictitious losses or expenses; and he is deemed to have committed that offence if he has so attempted at any meeting of the company's creditors within the 12 months immediately preceding the commencement of the winding up.

(3)   For purposes of this section, "officer" includes a shadow director.

(4)   It is a defence—

(a)   for a person charged under paragraph (a), (b) or (c) of subsection (1) to prove that he had no intent to defraud, and

(b)   for a person charged under paragraph (e) of that subsection to prove that he had no intent to conceal the state of affairs of the company or to defeat the law.

(5)   A person guilty of an offence under this section is liable to imprisonment or a fine, or both.

[9.303]
209 Falsification of company's books
(1)   When a company is being wound up, an officer or contributory of the company commits an offence if he destroys, mutilates, alters or falsifies any books, papers or securities, or makes or is privy to the making of any false or fraudulent entry in any register, book of account or document belonging to the company with intent to defraud or deceive any person.
(2)   A person guilty of an offence under this section is liable to imprisonment or a fine, or both.

[9.304]
210 Material omissions from statement relating to company's affairs
(1)   When a company is being wound up, whether by the court or voluntarily, any person, being a past or present officer of the company, commits an offence if he makes any material omission in any statement relating to the company's affairs.
(2)   When a company has been ordered to be wound up by the court, or has passed a resolution for voluntary winding up, any such person is deemed to have committed that offence if, prior to the winding up, he has made any material omission in any such statement.
(3)   For purposes of this section, "officer" includes a shadow director.
(4)   It is a defence for a person charged under this section to prove that he had no intent to defraud.
(5)   A person guilty of an offence under this section is liable to imprisonment or a fine, or both.

[9.305]
211 False representations to creditors
(1)   When a company is being wound up, whether by the court or voluntarily, any person, being a past or present officer of the company—
   (a)   commits an offence if he makes any false representation or commits any other fraud for the purpose of obtaining the consent of the company's creditors or any of them to an agreement with reference to the company's affairs or to the winding up, and
   (b)   is deemed to have committed that offence if, prior to the winding up, he has made any false representation, or committed any other fraud, for that purpose.
(2)   For purposes of this section, "officer" includes a shadow director.
(3)   A person guilty of an offence under this section is liable to imprisonment or a fine, or both.

Penalisation of directors and officers
[9.306]
212 Summary remedy against delinquent directors, liquidators, etc
(1)   This section applies if in the course of the winding up of a company it appears that a person who—
   (a)   is or has been an officer of the company,
   (b)   has acted as liquidator   . . .   or administrative receiver of the company, or
   (c)   not being a person falling within paragraph (a) or (b), is or has been concerned, or has taken part, in the promotion, formation or management of the company,
has misapplied or retained, or become accountable for, any money or other property of the company, or been guilty of any misfeasance or breach of any fiduciary or other duty in relation to the company.
(2)   The reference in subsection (1) to any misfeasance or breach of any fiduciary or other duty in relation to the company includes, in the case of a person who has acted as liquidator   . . .   of the company, any misfeasance or breach of any fiduciary or other duty in connection with the carrying out of his functions as liquidator   . . .   of the company.
(3)   The court may, on the application of the official receiver or the liquidator, or of any creditor or contributory, examine into the conduct of the person falling within subsection (1) and compel him—
   (a)   to repay, restore or account for the money or property or any part of it, with interest at such rate as the court thinks just, or
   (b)   to contribute such sum to the company's assets by way of compensation in respect of the misfeasance or breach of fiduciary or other duty as the court thinks just.
(4)   The power to make an application under subsection (3) in relation to a person who has acted as liquidator   . . .   of the company is not exercisable, except with the leave of the court, after [he] has had his release.
(5)   The power of a contributory to make an application under subsection (3) is not exercisable except with the leave of the court, but is exercisable notwithstanding that he will not benefit from any order the court may make on the application.

NOTES
Sub-ss (1), (2): words omitted repealed by the Enterprise Act 2002, ss 248(3), 278(2), Sch 17, paras 9, 18(a), (b), Sch 26, as from 15 September 2003 (for savings and transitional provisions, see the note to s 8 at **[9.105]**).
Sub-s (4): words omitted repealed, and word in square brackets substituted, by the Enterprise Act 2002, ss 248(3), 278(2), Sch 17, paras 9, 18(c), Sch 26, as from 15 September 2003 (for savings and transitional provisions, see the note to s 8 at **[9.105]**).

[9.307]

213   Fraudulent trading

(1)   If in the course of the winding up of a company it appears that any business of the company has been carried on with intent to defraud creditors of the company or creditors of any other person, or for any fraudulent purpose, the following has effect.

(2)   The court, on the application of the liquidator may declare that any persons who were knowingly parties to the carrying on of the business in the manner above-mentioned are to be liable to make such contributions (if any) to the company's assets as the court thinks proper.

[9.308]

214   Wrongful trading

(1)   Subject to subsection (3) below, if in the course of the winding up of a company it appears that subsection (2) of this section applies in relation to a person who is or has been a director of the company, the court, on the application of the liquidator, may declare that that person is to be liable to make such contribution (if any) to the company's assets as the court thinks proper.

(2)   This subsection applies in relation to a person if—

   (a)   the company has gone into insolvent liquidation,

   (b)   at some time before the commencement of the winding up of the company, that person knew or ought to have concluded that there was no reasonable prospect that the company would avoid going into insolvent liquidation, and

   (c)   that person was a director of the company at that time;

but the court shall not make a declaration under this section in any case where the time mentioned in paragraph (b) above was before 28th April 1986.

(3)   The court shall not make a declaration under this section with respect to any person if it is satisfied that after the condition specified in subsection (2)(b) was first satisfied in relation to him that person took every step with a view to minimising the potential loss to the company's creditors as (assuming him to have known that there was no reasonable prospect that the company would avoid going into insolvent liquidation) he ought to have taken.

(4)   For the purposes of subsections (2) and (3), the facts which a director of a company ought to know or ascertain, the conclusions which he ought to reach and the steps which he ought to take are those which would be known or ascertained, or reached or taken, by a reasonably diligent person having both—

   (a)   the general knowledge, skill and experience that may reasonably be expected of a person carrying out the same functions as are carried out by that director in relation to the company, and

   (b)   the general knowledge, skill and experience that that director has.

(5)   The reference in subsection (4) to the functions carried out in relation to a company by a director of the company includes any functions which he does not carry out but which have been entrusted to him.

(6)   For the purposes of this section a company goes into insolvent liquidation if it goes into liquidation at a time when its assets are insufficient for the payment of its debts and other liabilities and the expenses of the winding up.

(7)   In this section "director" includes a shadow director.

(8)   This section is without prejudice to section 213.

[9.309]

215   Proceedings under ss 213, 214

(1)   On the hearing of an application under section 213 or 214, the liquidator may himself give evidence or call witnesses.

(2)   Where under either section the court makes a declaration, it may give such further directions as it thinks proper for giving effect to the declaration; and in particular, the court may—

   (a)   provide for the liability of any person under the declaration to be a charge on any debt or obligation due from the company to him, or on any mortgage or charge or any interest in a mortgage or charge on assets of the company held by or vested in him, or any person on his behalf, or any person claiming as assignee from or through the person liable or any person acting on his behalf, and

   (b)   from time to time make such further order as may be necessary for enforcing any charge imposed under this subsection.

(3)   For the purposes of subsection (2), "assignee"—

   (a)   includes a person to whom or in whose favour, by the directions of the person made liable, the debt, obligation, mortgage or charge was created, issued or transferred or the interest created, but

   (b)   does not include an assignee for valuable consideration (not including consideration by way of marriage [or the formation of a civil partnership]) given in good faith and without notice of any of the matters on the ground of which the declaration is made.

(4)   Where the court makes a declaration under either section in relation to a person who is a creditor of the company, it may direct that the whole or any part of any debt owed by the company to that person and any interest thereon shall rank in priority after all other debts owed by the company and after any interest on those debts.

(5)   Sections 213 and 214 have effect notwithstanding that the person concerned may be criminally liable in respect of matters on the ground of which the declaration under the section is to be made.

NOTES

Sub-s (3): words in square brackets inserted by the Civil Partnership Act 2004, s 261(1), Sch 27, para 112, as from 5 December 2005.

[9.310]
216   Restriction on re-use of company names
(1)   This section applies to a person where a company ("the liquidating company") has gone into insolvent liquidation on or after the appointed day and he was a director or shadow director of the company at any time in the period of 12 months ending with the day before it went into liquidation.
(2)   For the purposes of this section, a name is a prohibited name in relation to such a person if—
  (a)   it is a name by which the liquidating company was known at any time in that period of 12 months, or
  (b)   it is a name which is so similar to a name falling within paragraph (a) as to suggest an association with that company.
(3)   Except with leave of the court or in such circumstances as may be prescribed, a person to whom this section applies shall not at any time in the period of 5 years beginning with the day on which the liquidating company went into liquidation—
  (a)   be a director of any other company that is known by a prohibited name, or
  (b)   in any way, whether directly or indirectly, be concerned or take part in the promotion, formation or management of any such company, or
  (c)   in any way, whether directly or indirectly, be concerned or take part in the carrying on of a business carried on (otherwise than by a company) under a prohibited name.
(4)   If a person acts in contravention of this section, he is liable to imprisonment or a fine, or both.
(5)   In subsection (3) "the court" means any court having jurisdiction to wind up companies; and on an application for leave under that subsection, the Secretary of State or the official receiver may appear and call the attention of the court to any matters which seem to him to be relevant.
(6)   References in this section, in relation to any time, to a name by which a company is known are to the name of the company at that time or to any name under which the company carries on business at that time.
(7)   For the purposes of this section a company goes into insolvent liquidation if it goes into liquidation at a time when its assets are insufficient for the payment of its debts and other liabilities and the expenses of the winding up.
(8)   In this section "company" includes a company which may be wound up under Part V of this Act.

[9.311]
217   Personal liability for debts, following contravention of s 216
(1)   A person is personally responsible for all the relevant debts of a company if at any time—
  (a)   in contravention of section 216, he is involved in the management of the company, or
  (b)   as a person who is involved in the management of the company, he acts or is willing to act on instructions given (without the leave of the court) by a person whom he knows at that time to be in contravention in relation to the company of section 216.
(2)   Where a person is personally responsible under this section for the relevant debts of a company, he is jointly and severally liable in respect of those debts with the company and any other person who, whether under this section or otherwise, is so liable.
(3)   For the purposes of this section the relevant debts of a company are—
  (a)   in relation to a person who is personally responsible under paragraph (a) of subsection (1), such debts and other liabilities of the company as are incurred at a time when that person was involved in the management of the company, and
  (b)   in relation to a person who is personally responsible under paragraph (b) of that subsection, such debts and other liabilities of the company as are incurred at a time when that person was acting or was willing to act on instructions given as mentioned in that paragraph.
(4)   For the purposes of this section, a person is involved in the management of a company if he is a director of the company or if he is concerned, whether directly or indirectly, or takes part, in the management of the company.
(5)   For the purposes of this section a person who, as a person involved in the management of a company, has at any time acted on instructions given (without the leave of the court) by a person whom he knew at that time to be in contravention in relation to the company of section 216 is presumed, unless the contrary is shown, to have been willing at any time thereafter to act on any instructions given by that person.
(6)   In this section "company" includes a company which may be wound up under Part V.

Investigation and prosecution of malpractice

[9.312]

218   Prosecution of delinquent officers and members of company

(1)   If it appears to the court in the course of a winding up by the court that any past or present officer, or any member, of the company has been guilty of any offence in relation to the company for which he is criminally liable, the court may (either on the application of a person interested in the winding up or of its own motion) direct the liquidator to refer the matter—

[(a)   in the case of a winding up in England and Wales, to the Secretary of State, and

(b)   in the case of a winding up in Scotland, to the Lord Advocate.]

(2)   . . .

(3)   If in the case of a winding up by the court in England and Wales it appears to the liquidator, not being the official receiver, that any past or present officer of the company, or any member of it, has been guilty of an offence in relation to the company for which he is criminally liable, the liquidator shall report the matter to the official receiver.

(4)   If it appears to the liquidator in the course of a voluntary winding up that any past or present officer of the company, or any member of it, has been guilty of an offence in relation to the company for which he is criminally liable, he shall [forthwith report the matter—

(a)   in the case of a winding up in England and Wales, to the Secretary of State, and

(b)   in the case of a winding up in Scotland, to the Lord Advocate,

and shall furnish to the Secretary of State or (as the case may be) the Lord Advocate] such information and give to him such access to and facilities for inspecting and taking copies of documents (being information or documents in the possession or under the control of the liquidator and relating to the matter in question) as [the Secretary of State or (as the case may be) the Lord Advocate] requires.

[(5)   Where a report is made to the Secretary of State under subsection (4) he may, for the purpose of investigating the matter reported to him and such other matters relating to the affairs of the company as appear to him to require investigation, exercise any of the powers which are exercisable by inspectors appointed under section 431 or 432 of [the Companies Act 1985] to investigate a company's affairs.]

(6)   If it appears to the court in the course of a voluntary winding up that—

(a)   any past or present officer of the company, or any member of it, has been guilty as above-mentioned, and

(b)   no report with respect to the matter has been made by the liquidator . . . under subsection (4),

the court may (on the application of any person interested in the winding up or of its own motion) direct the liquidator to make such a report.

On a report being made accordingly, this section has effect as though the report had been made in pursuance of subsection (4).

NOTES

Sub-ss (1), (4): words in square brackets substituted by the Insolvency Act 2000, s 10(1), (2), (4), as from 2 April 2001.

Sub-s (2): repealed by the Insolvency Act 2000, ss 10(1), (3), 15(1), Sch 5, as from 2 April 2001.

Sub-s (5): substituted by the Insolvency Act 2000, s 10(1), (5), as from 2 April 2001; words in square brackets substituted by the Companies Act 2006 (Consequential Amendments, Transitional Provisions and Savings) Order 2009, SI 2009/1941, art 2(1), Sch 1, para 75(1), (24), as from 1 October 2009 (for transitional provisions see the note to s 7A at **[9.103]**).

Sub-s (6): words omitted repealed by the Insolvency Act 2000, ss 10(1), (6), 15(1), Sch 5, as from 2 April 2001.

[9.313]

219   Obligations arising under s 218

(1)   For the purpose of an investigation by the Secretary of State [in consequence of a report made to him under section 218(4)], any obligation imposed on a person by any provision of [the Companies Act 1985] to produce documents or give information to, or otherwise to assist, inspectors appointed as mentioned in [section 218(5)] is to be regarded as an obligation similarly to assist the Secretary of State in his investigation.

(2)   An answer given by a person to a question put to him in exercise of the powers conferred by section 218(5) may be used in evidence against him.

[(2A)   However, in criminal proceedings in which that person is charged with an offence to which this subsection applies—

(a)   no evidence relating to the answer may be adduced, and

(b)   no question relating to it may be asked,

by or on behalf of the prosecution, unless evidence relating to it is adduced, or a question relating to it is asked, in the proceedings by or on behalf of that person.

(2B)   Subsection (2A) applies to any offence other than—

(a)   an offence under section 2 or 5 of the Perjury Act 1911 (false statements made on oath otherwise than in judicial proceedings or made otherwise than on oath), or

(b)   an offence under section 44(1) or (2) of the Criminal Law (Consolidation) (Scotland) Act 1995 (false statements made on oath or otherwise than on oath).]

(3) Where criminal proceedings are instituted by [the Director of Public Prosecutions, the Lord Advocate] or the Secretary of State following any report or reference under section 218, it is the duty of the liquidator and every officer and agent of the company past and present (other than the defendant or defender) to give to [the Director of Public Prosecutions, the Lord Advocate] or the Secretary of State (as the case may be) all assistance in connection with the prosecution which he is reasonably able to give.

For this purpose "agent" includes any banker or solicitor of the company and any person employed by the company as auditor, whether that person is or is not an officer of the company.

(4) If a person fails or neglects to give assistance in the manner required by subsection (3), the court may, on the application of the [Director of Public Prosecutions, the Lord Advocate] or the Secretary of State (as the case may be) direct the person to comply with that subsection; and if the application is made with respect to a liquidator, the court may (unless it appears that the failure or neglect to comply was due to the liquidator not having in his hands sufficient assets of the company to enable him to do so) direct that the costs shall be borne by the liquidator personally.

NOTES

Sub-s (1): words in first and third pairs of square brackets substituted by the Insolvency Act 2000, s 10(1), (7), as from 2 April 2001; words in second pair of square brackets substituted by the Companies Act 2006 (Consequential Amendments, Transitional Provisions and Savings) Order 2009, SI 2009/1941, art 2(1), Sch 1, para 75(1), (24), as from 1 October 2009 (for transitional provisions see the note to s 7A at **[9.103]**).

Sub-ss (3), (4): words in square brackets substituted by the Insolvency Act 2000, s 10(1), (7), as from 2 April 2001.

Sub-ss (2A), (2B): inserted by the Insolvency Act 2000, s 11, as from 2 April 2001.

PART V
WINDING UP OF UNREGISTERED COMPANIES

[9.314]
[220 Meaning of "unregistered company"
For the purposes of this Part "unregistered company" includes any association and any company, with the exception of a company registered under the Companies Act 2006 in any part of the United Kingdom.]

NOTES

Commencement: 1 October 2009.

Substituted by the Companies Act 2006 (Consequential Amendments, Transitional Provisions and Savings) Order 2009, SI 2009/1941, art 2(1), Sch 1, para 76(1), (2), as from 1 October 2009 (for transitional provisions see the note to s 7A at **[9.103]**).

[9.315]
221 Winding up of unregistered companies
(1) Subject to the provisions of this Part, any unregistered company may be wound up under this Act; and all the provisions of this Act . . . winding up apply to an unregistered company with the exceptions and additions mentioned in the following subsections.

(2) If an unregistered company has a principal place of business situated in Northern Ireland, it shall not be wound up under this Part unless it has a principal place of business situated in England and Wales or Scotland, or in both England and Wales and Scotland.

(3) For the purpose of determining a court's winding-up jurisdiction, an unregistered company is deemed—

(a) to be registered in England and Wales or Scotland, according as its principal place of business is situated in England and Wales or Scotland, or

(b) if it has a principal place of business situated in both countries, to be registered in both countries;

and the principal place of business situated in that part of Great Britain in which proceedings are being instituted is, for all purposes of the winding up, deemed to be the registered office of the company.

(4) No unregistered company shall be wound up under this Act voluntarily[, except in accordance with the EC Regulation].

(5) The circumstances in which an unregistered company may be wound up are as follows—

(a) if the company is dissolved, or has ceased to carry on business, or is carrying on business only for the purpose of winding up its affairs;

(b) if the company is unable to pay its debts;

(c) if the court is of opinion that it is just and equitable that the company should be wound up.

(6) A petition for winding up a trustee savings bank may be presented by the Trustee Savings Banks Central Board or by a commissioner appointed under section 35 of the Trustee Savings Banks Act 1981 as well as by any person authorised under Part IV of this Act to present a petition for the winding up of a company.

On such day as the Treasury appoints by order under section 4(3) of the Trustee Savings Banks Act 1985, this subsection ceases to have effect and is hereby repealed.

(7)   In Scotland, an unregistered company which the Court of Session has jurisdiction to wind up may be wound up by the court if there is subsisting a floating charge over property comprised in the company's property and undertaking, and the court is satisfied that the security of the creditor entitled to the benefit of the floating charge is in jeopardy.

For this purpose a creditor's security is deemed to be in jeopardy if the court is satisfied that events have occurred or are about to occur which render it unreasonable in the creditor's interests that the company should retain power to dispose of the property which is subject to the floating charge.

NOTES

Sub-s (1): words omitted repealed by the Companies Act 2006 (Consequential Amendments, Transitional Provisions and Savings) Order 2009, SI 2009/1941, art 2(1), Sch 1, para 76(1), (3), as from 1 October 2009 (for transitional provisions see the note to s 7A at **[9.103]**).

Sub-s (4): words in square brackets added by the Insolvency Act 1986 (Amendment) (No 2) Regulations 2002, SI 2002/1240, regs 3, 9, as from 31 May 2002.

Sub-s (6): CA 1985, s 666(6), from which sub-s (6) above was principally derived, was repealed by the Trustee Savings Banks Act 1985, ss 4(3), 7(3), Sch 4, as from 21 July 1986 by virtue of the Trustee Savings Banks Act 1985 (Appointed Day) (No 4) Order 1986, SI 1986/1223 (made under s 4(3) of that Act). It is thought, therefore, that, as construed in accordance with s 437, Sch 11, para 27, sub-s (6) above has ceased to have effect and is thus repealed.

[9.316]
222   Inability to pay debts; unpaid creditor for £750 or more
(1)   An unregistered company is deemed (for the purposes of section 221) unable to pay its debts if there is a creditor, by assignment or otherwise, to whom the company is indebted in a sum exceeding £750 then due and—
   (a)   the creditor has served on the company, by leaving at its principal place of business, or by delivering to the secretary or some director, manager or principal officer of the company, or by otherwise serving in such manner as the court may approve or direct, a written demand in the prescribed form requiring the company to pay the sum due, and
   (b)   the company has for 3 weeks after the service of the demand neglected to pay the sum or to secure or compound for it to the creditor's satisfaction.
(2)   The money sum for the time being specified in subsection (1) is subject to increase or reduction by regulations under section 417 in Part XV; but no increase in the sum so specified affects any case in which the winding-up petition was presented before the coming into force of the increase.

[9.317]
223   Inability to pay debts: debt remaining unsatisfied after action brought
An unregistered company is deemed (for the purposes of section 221) unable to pay its debts if an action or other proceeding has been instituted against any member for any debt or demand due, or claimed to be due, from the company, or from him in his character of member, and—
   (a)   notice in writing of the institution of the action or proceeding has been served on the company by leaving it at the company's principal place of business (or by delivering it to the secretary, or some director, manager or principal officer of the company, or by otherwise serving it in such manner as the court may approve or direct), and
   (b)   the company has not within 3 weeks after service of the notice paid, secured or compounded for the debt or demand, or procured the action or proceeding to be stayed or sisted, or indemnified the defendant or defender to his reasonable satisfaction against the action or proceeding, and against all costs, damages and expenses to be incurred by him because of it.

[9.318]
224   Inability to pay debts: other cases
(1)   An unregistered company is deemed (for purposes of section 221) unable to pay its debts—
   (a)   if in England and Wales execution or other process issued on a judgment, decree or order obtained in any court in favour of a creditor against the company, or any member of it as such, or any person authorised to be sued as nominal defendant on behalf of the company, is returned unsatisfied;
   (b)   if in Scotland the induciae of a charge for payment on an extract decree, or an extract registered bond, or an extract registered protest, have expired without payment being made;
   (c)   if in Northern Ireland a certificate of unenforceability has been granted in respect of any judgment, decree or order obtained as mentioned in paragraph (a);
   (d)   it is otherwise proved to the satisfaction of the court that the company is unable to pay its debts as they fall due.
(2)   An unregistered company is also deemed unable to pay its debts if it is proved to the satisfaction of the court that the value of the company's assets is less than the amount of its liabilities, taking into account its contingent and prospective liabilities.

[9.319]
225 [Company incorporated outside Great Britain] may be wound up though dissolved
[(1)] Where a company incorporated outside Great Britain which has been carrying on business in Great Britain ceases to carry on business in Great Britain, it may be wound up as an unregistered company under this Act, notwithstanding that it has been dissolved or otherwise ceased to exist as a company under or by virtue of the laws of the country under which it was incorporated.
[(2) This section is subject to the EC Regulation.]

NOTES
Section heading: words in square brackets substituted by the Companies Act 2006 (Consequential Amendments, Transitional Provisions and Savings) Order 2009, SI 2009/1941, art 2(1), Sch 1, para 76(1), (4), as from 1 October 2009 (for transitional provisions see the note to s 7A at **[9.103]**).
Sub-s (1) numbered as such, and sub-s (2) added, by the Insolvency Act 1986 (Amendment) (No 2) Regulations 2002, SI 2002/1240, regs 3, 10, as from 31 May 2002.

[9.320]
226 Contributories in winding up of unregistered company
(1) In the event of an unregistered company being wound up, every person is deemed a contributory who is liable to pay or contribute to the payment of any debt or liability of the company, or to pay or contribute to the payment of any sum for the adjustment of the rights of members among themselves, or to pay or contribute to the payment of the expenses of winding up the company.
(2) Every contributory is liable to contribute to the company's assets all sums due from him in respect of any such liability as is mentioned above.
(3) In the case of an unregistered company engaged in or formed for working mines within the stannaries, a past member is not liable to contribute to the assets if he has ceased to be a member for 2 years or more either before the mine ceased to be worked or before the date of the winding-up order.
(4) . . .

NOTES
Sub-s (4): repealed by the Companies Act 2006 (Consequential Amendments, Transitional Provisions and Savings) Order 2009, SI 2009/1941, art 2(1), Sch 1, para 76(1), (5), as from 1 October 2009 (for transitional provisions see the note to s 7A at **[9.103]**).

[9.321]
227 Power of court to stay, sist or restrain proceedings
The provisions of this Part with respect to staying, sisting or restraining actions and proceedings against a company at any time after the presentation of a petition for winding up and before the making of a winding-up order extend, in the case of an unregistered company, where the application to stay, sist or restrain is presented by a creditor, to actions and proceedings against any contributory of the company.

[9.322]
228 Actions stayed on winding-up order
Where an order has been made for winding up an unregistered company, no action or proceeding shall be proceeded with or commenced against any contributory of the company in respect of any debt of the company, except by leave of the court, and subject to such terms as the court may impose.

[9.323]
229 Provisions of this Part to be cumulative
(1) The provisions of this Part with respect to unregistered companies are in addition to and not in restriction of any provisions in Part IV with respect to winding up companies by the court; and the court or liquidator may exercise any powers or do any act in the case of unregistered companies which might be exercised or done by it or him in winding up [companies registered under the Companies Act 2006 in England and Wales or Scotland].
(2) . . .

NOTES
Sub-s (1): words in square brackets substituted by the Companies Act 2006 (Consequential Amendments, Transitional Provisions and Savings) Order 2009, SI 2009/1941, art 2(1), Sch 1, para 76(1), (6)(a), as from 1 October 2009 (for transitional provisions see the note to s 7A at **[9.103]**).
Sub-s (2): repealed by SI 2009/1941, art 2(1), Sch 1, para 76(1), (6)(b), as from 1 October 2009 (for transitional provisions see the note to s 7A at **[9.103]**).

PART VI
MISCELLANEOUS PROVISIONS APPLYING TO COMPANIES WHICH ARE INSOLVENT OR IN LIQUIDATION

Office-holders

[9.324]
230   Holders of office to be qualified insolvency practitioners
(1)   . . .
(2)   Where an administrative receiver of a company is appointed, he must be a person who is so qualified.
(3)   Where a company goes into liquidation, the liquidator must be a person who is so qualified.
(4)   Where a provisional liquidator is appointed, he must be a person who is so qualified.
(5)   Subsections (3) and (4) are without prejudice to any enactment under which the official receiver is to be, or may be, liquidator or provisional liquidator.

NOTES
Sub-s (1): repealed by the Enterprise Act 2002, ss 248(3), 287(2), Sch 17, paras 9, 19, Sch 26, as from 15 September 2003 (for savings and transitional provisions, see the note to s 8 at **[9.105]**).

[9.325]
231   Appointment to office of two or more persons
(1)   This section applies if an appointment or nomination of any person to the office of   . . .
administrative receiver, liquidator or provisional liquidator—
   (a)   relates to more than one person, or
   (b)   has the effect that the office is to be held by more than one person.
(2)   The appointment or nomination shall declare whether any act required or authorised under any enactment to be done by the   . . .   administrative receiver, liquidator or provisional liquidator is to be done by all or any one or more of the persons for the time being holding the office in question.

NOTES
Sub-ss (1), (2): words omitted repealed by the Enterprise Act 2002, ss 248(3), 287(2), Sch 17, paras 9, 20, Sch 26, as from 15 September 2003 (for savings and transitional provisions, see the note to s 8 at **[9.105]**).

[9.326]
232   Validity of office-holder's acts
The acts of an individual as   . . .   administrative receiver, liquidator or provisional liquidator of a company are valid notwithstanding any defect in his appointment, nomination or qualifications.

NOTES
Word omitted repealed by the Enterprise Act 2002, ss 248(3), 287(2), Sch 17, paras 9, 21, Sch 26, as from 15 September 2003 (for savings and transitional provisions, see the note to s 8 at **[9.105]**).

Management by administrators, liquidators, etc

[9.327]
233   Supplies of gas, water, electricity, etc
(1)   This section applies in the case of a company where—
  [(a)   the company enters administration,]
   (b)   an administrative receiver is appointed, or
  [(ba) a moratorium under section 1A is in force, or]
   (c)   a voluntary arrangement [approved under Part I], has taken effect, or
   (d)   the company goes into liquidation, or
   (e)   a provisional liquidator is appointed;
and "the office-holder" means the administrator, the administrative receiver, [the nominee,] the supervisor of the voluntary arrangement, the liquidator or the provisional liquidator, as the case may be.
(2)   If a request is made by or with the concurrence of the office-holder for the giving, after the effective date, of any of the supplies mentioned in the next subsection, the supplier—
   (a)   may make it a condition of the giving of the supply that the office-holder personally guarantees the payment of any charges in respect of the supply, but
   (b)   shall not make it a condition of the giving of the supply, or do anything which has the effect of making it a condition of the giving of the supply, that any outstanding charges in respect of a supply given to the company before the effective date are paid.
(3)   The supplies referred to in subsection (2) are—
  [(a)   a supply of gas by a gas supplier within the meaning of Part I of the Gas Act 1986;]
  [(b)   a supply of electricity by an electricity supplier within the meaning of Part I of the Electricity Act 1989;]
   (c)   a supply of water by [a water undertaker] or, in Scotland, [Scottish Water],
  [(d)   a supply of communications services by a provider of a public electronic communications service.]

(4)   "The effective date" for the purposes of this section is whichever is applicable of the following dates—
   [(a)   the date on which the company entered administration,]
   (b)   the date on which the administrative receiver was appointed (or, if he was appointed in succession to another administrative receiver, the date on which the first of his predecessors was appointed),
   [(ba) the date on which the moratorium came into force]
   (c)   the date on which the voluntary arrangement [took effect],
   (d)   the date on which the company went into liquidation,
   (e)   the date on which the provisional liquidator was appointed.
(5)   The following applies to expressions used in subsection (3)—
   (a)–(c)   . . .
   [(d)   "communications services" do not include electronic communications services to the extent that they are used to broadcast or otherwise transmit programme services (within the meaning of the Communications Act 2003).]

NOTES
   Sub-s (1): para (a) substituted by the Enterprise Act 2002, s 248(3), Sch 17, paras 9, 22(a), as from 15 September 2003 (for savings and transitional provisions, see the note to s 8 at **[9.105]**); para (ba) and final words in square brackets inserted, and second words in square brackets substituted, by the Insolvency Act 2000, s 1, Sch 1, paras 1, 8(1), (2), as from 1 January 2003.
   Sub-s (3): para (a) substituted by the Gas Act 1995, s 16(1), Sch 4, para 14(1), as from 1 March 1996; para (b) substituted by the Utilities Act 2000, s 108, Sch 6, para 47(1), (2)(a), as from 1 October 2001; words in first pair of square brackets in para (c) substituted by the Water Act 1989, s 190(1), Sch 25, para 78(1), as from 1 September 1989; words in second pair of square brackets in para (c) substituted by the Water Industry (Scotland) Act 2002 (Consequential Modifications) Order 2004, SI 2004/1822, art 2, Schedule, Pt 1, para 14(a), as from 14 July 2004; para (d) substituted by the Communications Act 2003, s 406, Sch 17, para 82(1), (2)(a), as from 25 July 2003 (certain purposes), and as from 29 December 2003 (otherwise).
   Sub-s (4): para (a) substituted by the Enterprise Act 2002, s 248(3), Sch 17, paras 9, 22(b), as from 15 September 2003 (for savings and transitional provisions, see the note to s 8 at **[9.105]**); para (ba) inserted, and words in square brackets in para (c) substituted, by the Insolvency Act 2000, s 1, Sch 1, paras 1, 8(1), (3), as from 1 January 2003.
   Sub-s (5): para (a) repealed by the Gas Act 1995, ss 16(1), 17(5), Sch 4, para 14(2), Sch 6, as from 1 March 1996; para (b) repealed by the Utilities Act 2000, s 108, Sch 6, para 47(1), (2)(b), Sch 8, as from 1 October 2001; para (c) repealed by SI 2004/1822, art 2, Schedule, Pt 1, para 14(b), as from 14 July 2004; para (d) substituted by the Communications Act 2003, s 406, Sch 17, para 82(1), (2)(b), as from 25 July 2003 (certain purposes), and as from 29 December 2003 (otherwise).

[9.328]
234   Getting in the company's property
(1)   This section applies in the case of a company where—
   [(a)   the company enters administration,] or
   (b)   an administrative receiver is appointed, or
   (c)   the company goes into liquidation, or
   (d)   a provisional liquidator is appointed;
and "the office-holder" means the administrator, the administrative receiver, the liquidator or the provisional liquidator, as the case may be.
(2)   Where any person has in his possession or control any property, books, papers or records to which the company appears to be entitled, the court may require that person forthwith (or within such period as the court may direct) to pay, deliver convey, surrender or transfer the property, books, papers or records to the office-holder.
(3)   Where the office-holder—
   (a)   seizes or disposes of any property which is not property of the company, and
   (b)   at the time of seizure or disposal believes, and has reasonable grounds for believing, that he is entitled (whether in pursuance of an order of the court or otherwise) to seize or dispose of that property,
the next subsection has effect.
(4)   In that case the office-holder—
   (a)   is not liable to any person in respect of any loss or damage resulting from the seizure or disposal except in so far as that loss or damage is caused by the office-holder's own negligence, and
   (b)   has a lien on the property, or the proceeds of its sale, for such expenses as were incurred in connection with the seizure or disposal.

NOTES
   Sub-s (1): para (a) substituted by the Enterprise Act 2002, s 248(3), Sch 17, paras 9, 23, as from 15 September 2003 (for savings and transitional provisions, see the note to s 8 at **[9.105]**).

[9.329]
235   Duty to co-operate with office-holder
(1)   This section applies as does section 234; and it also applies, in the case of a company in respect of which a winding-up order has been made by the court in England and Wales, as if references to the office-holder included the official receiver, whether or not he is the liquidator.
(2)   Each of the persons mentioned in the next subsection shall—

(a)   give to the office-holder such information concerning the company and its promotion, formation, business, dealings, affairs or property as the office-holder may at any time after the effective date reasonably require, and

(b)   attend on the office-holder at such times as the latter may reasonably require.

(3)   The persons referred to above are—

(a)   those who are or have at any time been officers of the company,

(b)   those who have taken part in the formation of the company at any time within one year before the effective date,

(c)   those who are in the employment of the company, or have been in its employment (including employment under a contract for services) within that year, and are in the office-holder's opinion capable of giving information which he requires,

(d)   those who are, or have within that year been, officers of, or in the employment (including employment under a contract for services) of, another company which is, or within that year was, an officer of the company in question, and

(e)   in the case of a company being wound up by the court, any person who has acted as administrator, administrative receiver or liquidator of the company.

(4)   For the purposes of subsections (2) and (3), "the effective date" is whichever is applicable of the following dates—

[(a)   the date on which the company entered administration,]

(b)   the date on which the administrative receiver was appointed or, if he was appointed in succession to another administrative receiver, the date on which the first of his predecessors was appointed,

(c)   the date on which the provisional liquidator was appointed, and

(d)   the date on which the company went into liquidation.

(5)   If a person without reasonable excuse fails to comply with any obligation imposed by this section, he is liable to a fine and, for continued contravention, to a daily default fine.

NOTES

Sub-s (4): para (a) substituted by the Enterprise Act 2002, s 248(3), Sch 17, paras 9, 24, as from 15 September 2003 (for savings and transitional provisions, see the note to s 8 at **[9.105]**).

[9.330]
236   Inquiry into company's dealings, etc

(1)   This section applies as does section 234; and it also applies in the case of a company in respect of which a winding-up order has been made by the court in England and Wales as if references to the office-holder included the official receiver, whether or not he is the liquidator.

(2)   The court may, on the application of the office-holder, summon to appear before it—

(a)   any officer of the company,

(b)   any person known or suspected to have in his possession any property of the company or supposed to be indebted to the company, or

(c)   any person whom the court thinks capable of giving information concerning the promotion, formation, business, dealings, affairs or property of the company.

(3)   The court may require any such person as is mentioned in subsection (2)(a) to (c) to submit [to the court] an account of his dealings with the company or to produce any books, papers or other records in his possession or under his control relating to the company or the matters mentioned in paragraph (c) of the subsection.

[(3A)   An account submitted to the court under subsection (3) must be contained in—

(a)   a witness statement verified by a statement of truth (in England and Wales), and

(b)   an affidavit (in Scotland).]

(4)   The following applies in a case where—

(a)   a person without reasonable excuse fails to appear before the court when he is summoned to do so under this section, or

(b)   there are reasonable grounds for believing that a person has absconded, or is about to abscond, with a view to avoiding his appearance before the court under this section.

(5)   The court may, for the purpose of bringing that person and anything in his possession before the court, cause a warrant to be issued to a constable or prescribed officer of the court—

(a)   for the arrest of that person, and

(b)   for the seizure of any books, papers, records, money or goods in that person's possession.

(6)   The court may authorise a person arrested under such a warrant to be kept in custody, and anything seized under such a warrant to be held, in accordance with the rules, until that person is brought before the court under the warrant or until such other time as the court may order.

NOTES

Sub-s (3): words in square brackets substituted by the Legislative Reform (Insolvency) (Miscellaneous Provisions) Order 2010, SI 2010/18, arts 2, 5(6)(a), as from 6 April 2010.

Sub-s (3A): inserted by SI 2010/18, arts 2, 5(6)(b), as from 6 April 2010.

[9.331]
237   Court's enforcement powers under s 236

(1)   If it appears to the court, on consideration of any evidence obtained under section 236 or this section, that any person has in his possession any property of the company, the court may, on the application of the office-holder, order that person to deliver the whole or any part of the property to the officer-holder at such time, in such manner and on such terms as the court thinks fit.

(2)   If it appears to the court, on consideration of any evidence so obtained, that any person is indebted to the company, the court may, on the application of the office-holder, order that person to pay to the office-holder, at such time and in such manner as the court may direct, the whole or any part of the amount due, whether in full discharge of the debt or otherwise, as the court thinks fit.

(3)   The court may, if it thinks fit, order that any person who if within the jurisdiction of the court would be liable to be summoned to appear before it under section 236 or this section shall be examined in any part of the United Kingdom where he may for the time being be, or in a place outside the United Kingdom.

(4)   Any person who appears or is brought before the court under section 236 or this section may be examined on oath, either orally or (except in Scotland) by interrogatories, concerning the company or the matters mentioned in section 236(2)(c).

Adjustment of prior transactions (administration and liquidation)

[9.332]
238   Transactions at an undervalue (England and Wales)

(1)   This section applies in the case of a company where—
  [(a)   the company enters administration,] or
  (b)   the company goes into liquidation;
and "the office-holder" means the administrator or the liquidator, as the case may be.

(2)   Where the company has at a relevant time (defined in section 240) entered into a transaction with any person at an undervalue, the office-holder may apply to the court for an order under this section.

(3)   Subject as follows, the court shall, on such an application, make such order as it thinks fit for restoring the position to what it would have been if the company had not entered into that transaction.

(4)   For the purposes of this section and section 241, a company enters into a transaction with a person at an undervalue if—
  (a)   the company makes a gift to that person or otherwise enters into a transaction with that person on terms that provide for the company to receive no consideration, or
  (b)   the company enters into a transaction with that person for a consideration the value of which, in money or money's worth, is significantly less than the value, in money or money's worth, of the consideration provided by the company.

(5)   The court shall not make an order under this section in respect of a transaction at an undervalue if it is satisfied—
  (a)   that the company which entered into the transaction did so in good faith and for the purpose of carrying on its business, and
  (b)   that at the time it did so there were reasonable grounds for believing that the transaction would benefit the company.

NOTES

Sub-s (1): para (a) substituted by the Enterprise Act 2002, s 248(3), Sch 17, paras 9, 25, as from 15 September 2003 (for savings and transitional provisions, see the note to s 8 at **[9.105]**).

[9.333]
239   Preferences (England and Wales)

(1)   This section applies as does section 238.

(2)   Where the company has at a relevant time (defined in the next section) given a preference to any person, the office-holder may apply to the court for an order under this section.

(3)   Subject as follows, the court shall, on such an application, make such order as it thinks fit for restoring the position to what it would have been if the company had not given that preference.

(4)   For the purposes of this section and section 241, a company gives a preference to a person if—
  (a)   that person is one of the company's creditors or a surety or guarantor for any of the company's debts or other liabilities, and
  (b)   the company does anything or suffers anything to be done which (in either case) has the effect of putting that person into a position which, in the event of the company going into insolvent liquidation, will be better than the position he would have been in if that thing had not been done.

(5)   The court shall not make an order under this section in respect of a preference given to any person unless the company which gave the preference was influenced in deciding to give it by a desire to produce in relation to that person the effect mentioned in subsection (4)(b).

(6)   A company which has given a preference to a person connected with the company (otherwise than by reason only of being its employee) at the time the preference was given is presumed, unless the contrary is shown, to have been influenced in deciding to give it by such a desire as is mentioned in subsection (5).

(7)   The fact that something has been done in pursuance of the order of a court does not, without more, prevent the doing or suffering of that thing from constituting the giving of a preference.

[9.334]
240   "Relevant time" under ss 238, 239
(1)   Subject to the next subsection, the time at which a company enters into a transaction at an undervalue or gives a preference is a relevant time if the transaction is entered into, or the preference given—

   (a)   in the case of a transaction at an undervalue or of a preference which is given to a person who is connected with the company (otherwise than by reason only of being its employee), at a time in the period of 2 years ending with the onset of insolvency (which expression is defined below),

   (b)   in the case of a preference which is not such a transaction and is not so given, at a time in the period of 6 months ending with the onset of insolvency,

   [(c)   in either case, at a time between the making of an administration application in respect of the company and the making of an administration order on that application, and

   (d)   in either case, at a time between the filing with the court of a copy of notice of intention to appoint an administrator under paragraph 14 or 22 of Schedule B1 and the making of an appointment under that paragraph.]

(2)   Where a company enters into a transaction at an undervalue or gives a preference at a time mentioned in subsection (1)(a) or (b), that time is not a relevant time for the purposes of section 238 or 239 unless the company—

   (a)   is at that time unable to pay its debts within the meaning of section 123 in Chapter VI of Part IV, or

   (b)   becomes unable to pay its debts within the meaning of that section in consequence of the transaction or preference;

but the requirements of this subsection are presumed to be satisfied, unless the contrary is shown, in relation to any transaction at an undervalue which is entered into by a company with a person who is connected with the company.

(3)   For the purposes of subsection (1), the onset of insolvency is—

   [(a)   in a case where section 238 or 239 applies by reason of an administrator of a company being appointed by administration order, the date on which the administration application is made,

   (b)   in a case where section 238 or 239 applies by reason of an administrator of a company being appointed under paragraph 14 or 22 of Schedule B1 following filing with the court of a copy of a notice of intention to appoint under that paragraph, the date on which the copy of the notice is filed,

   (c)   in a case where section 238 or 239 applies by reason of an administrator of a company being appointed otherwise than as mentioned in paragraph (a) or (b), the date on which the appointment takes effect,

   (d)   in a case where section 238 or 239 applies by reason of a company going into liquidation either following conversion of administration into winding up by virtue of Article 37 of the EC Regulation or at the time when the appointment of an administrator ceases to have effect, the date on which the company entered administration (or, if relevant, the date on which the application for the administration order was made or a copy of the notice of intention to appoint was filed), and

   (e)   in a case where section 238 or 239 applies by reason of a company going into liquidation at any other time, the date of the commencement of the winding up.]

NOTES
   Sub-s (1): word omitted from para (b) repealed, and paras (c), (d) substituted for the original para (c), by the Enterprise Act 2002, ss 248(3), 278(2), Sch 17, paras 9, 26(1)–(3), Sch 26, as from 15 September 2003 (for savings and transitional provisions, see the note to s 8 at **[9.105]**).
   Sub-s (3): paras (a)–(e) substituted, for paras (a), (aa), (b), by the Enterprise Act 2002, s 248(3), Sch 17, paras 9, 26(1), (4), as from 15 September 2003 (for savings and transitional provisions, see the note to s 8 at **[9.105]**); the original para (aa) was inserted by the Insolvency Act 1986 (Amendment) (No 2) Regulations 2002, SI 2002/1240, regs 3, 11, as from 31 May 2002.

[9.335]
241   Orders under ss 238, 239
(1)   Without prejudice to the generality of sections 238(3) and 239(3), an order under either of those sections with respect to a transaction or preference entered into or given by a company may (subject to the next subsection)—

   (a)   require any property transferred as part of the transaction, or in connection with the giving of the preference, to be vested in the company,

   (b)   require any property to be so vested if it represents in any person's hands the application either of the proceeds of sale of property so transferred or of money so transferred,

- (c)　release or discharge (in whole or in part) any security given by the company,
- (d)　require any person to pay, in respect of benefits received by him from the company, such sums to the office-holder as the court may direct,
- (e)　provide for any surety or guarantor whose obligations to any person were released or discharged (in whole or in part) under the transaction, or by the giving of the preference, to be under such new or revived obligations to that person as the court thinks appropriate,
- (f)　provide for security to be provided for the discharge of any obligation imposed by or arising under the order, for such an obligation to be charged on any property and for the security or charge to have the same priority as a security or charge released or discharged (in whole or in part) under the transaction or by the giving of the preference, and
- (g)　provide for the extent to which any person whose property is vested by the order in the company, or on whom obligations are imposed by the order, is to be able to prove in the winding up of the company for debts or other liabilities which arose from, or were released or discharged (in whole or in part) under or by, the transaction or the giving of the preference.

(2)　An order under section 238 or 239 may affect the property of, or impose any obligation on, any person whether or not he is the person with whom the company in question entered into the transaction or (as the case may be) the person to whom the preference was given; but such an order—

- (a)　shall not prejudice any interest in property which was acquired from a person other than the company and was acquired [in good faith and for value], or prejudice any interest deriving from such an interest, and
- (b)　shall not require a person who received a benefit from the transaction or preference [in good faith and for value] to pay a sum to the office-holder, except where that person was a party to the transaction or the payment is to be in respect of a preference given to that person at a time when he was a creditor of the company.

[(2A)　Where a person has acquired an interest in property from a person other than the company in question, or has received a benefit from the transaction or preference, and at the time of that acquisition or receipt—

- (a)　he had notice of the relevant surrounding circumstances and of the relevant proceedings, or
- (b)　he was connected with, or was an associate of, either the company in question or the person with whom that company entered into the transaction or to whom that company gave the preference,

then, unless the contrary is shown, it shall be presumed for the purposes of paragraph (a) or (as the case may be) paragraph (b) of subsection (2) that the interest was acquired or the benefit was received otherwise than in good faith.]

[(3)　For the purposes of subsection (2A)(a), the relevant surrounding circumstances are (as the case may require)—

- (a)　the fact that the company in question entered into the transaction at an undervalue; or
- (b)　the circumstances which amounted to the giving of the preference by the company in question;

and subsections (3A) to (3C) have effect to determine whether, for those purposes, a person has notice of the relevant proceedings.

[(3A)　Where section 238 or 239 applies by reason of a company's entering administration, a person has notice of the relevant proceedings if he has notice that—

- (a)　an administration application has been made,
- (b)　an administration order has been made,
- (c)　a copy of a notice of intention to appoint an administrator under paragraph 14 or 22 of Schedule B1 has been filed, or
- (d)　notice of the appointment of an administrator has been filed under paragraph 18 or 29 of that Schedule.]

[(3B)　Where section 238 or 239 applies by reason of a company's going into liquidation at the time when the appointment of an administrator of the company ceases to have effect, a person has notice of the relevant proceedings if he has notice that—

- (a)　an administration application has been made,
- (b)　an administration order has been made,
- (c)　a copy of a notice of intention to appoint an administrator under paragraph 14 or 22 of Schedule B1 has been filed,
- (d)　notice of the appointment of an administrator has been filed under paragraph 18 or 29 of that Schedule, or
- (e)　the company has gone into liquidation.]

(3C)　In a case where section 238 or 239 applies by reason of the company in question going into liquidation at any other time, a person has notice of the relevant proceedings if he has notice—

- (a)　where the company goes into liquidation on the making of a winding-up order, of the fact that the petition on which the winding-up order is made has been presented or of the fact that the company has gone into liquidation;
- (b)　in any other case, of the fact that the company has gone into liquidation.]

(4)   The provisions of sections 238 to 241 apply without prejudice to the availability of any other remedy, even in relation to a transaction or preference which the company had no power to enter into or give.

NOTES

Sub-s (2): words in square brackets in paras (a), (b) substituted by the Insolvency (No 2) Act 1994, s 1(1), in relation to interests acquired and benefits received after 26 July 1994.

Sub-s (2A): inserted by the Insolvency (No 2) Act 1994, s 1(2), in relation to interests acquired and benefits received after 26 July 1994.

Sub-ss (3), (3C): substituted together with sub-ss (3A), (3B), for sub-s (3) as originally enacted, by the Insolvency (No 2) Act 1994, s 1(3), in relation to interests acquired and benefits received after 26 July 1994.

Sub-ss (3A), (3B): substituted as noted above; further substituted by the Enterprise Act 2002, s 248(3), Sch 17, paras 9, 27, as from 15 September 2003 (for savings and transitional provisions, see the note to s 8 at **[9.105]**).

[9.336]
242   Gratuitous alienations (Scotland)
(1)   Where this subsection applies and—
  (a)   the winding up of a company has commenced, an alienation by the company is challengeable by—
     (i)   any creditor who is a creditor by virtue of a debt incurred on or before the date of such commencement, or
     (ii)   the liquidator;
  (b)   [a company enters administration], an alienation by the company is challengeable by the administrator.
(2)   Subsection (1) applies where—
  (a)   by the alienation, whether before or after 1st April 1986 (the coming into force of section 75 of the Bankruptcy (Scotland) Act 1985), any part of the company's property is transferred or any claim or right of the company is discharged or renounced, and
  (b)   the alienation takes place on a relevant day.
(3)   For the purposes of subsection (2)(b), the day on which an alienation takes place is the day on which it becomes completely effectual; and in that subsection "relevant day" means, if the alienation has the effect of favouring—
  (a)   a person who is an associate (within the meaning of the Bankruptcy (Scotland) Act 1985) of the company, a day not earlier than 5 years before the date on which—
     (i)   the winding up of the company commences, or
     (ii)   as the case may be, [the company enters administration]; or
  (b)   any other person, a day not earlier than 2 years before that date.
(4)   On a challenge being brought under subsection (1), the court shall grant decree of reduction or for such restoration of property to the company's assets or other redress as may be appropriate; but the court shall not grant such a decree if the person seeking to uphold the alienation establishes—
  (a)   that immediately, or at any other time, after the alienation the company's assets were greater than its liabilities, or
  (b)   that the alienation was made for adequate consideration, or
  (c)   that the alienation—
     (i)   was a birthday, Christmas or other conventional gift, or
     (ii)   was a gift made, for a charitable purpose, to a person who is not an associate of the company,
     which, having regard to all the circumstances, it was reasonable for the company to make:
  Provided that this subsection is without prejudice to any right or interest acquired in good faith and for value from or through the transferee in the alienation.
(5)   In subsection (4) above, "charitable purpose" means any charitable, benevolent or philanthropic purpose, whether or not it is charitable within the meaning of any rule of law.
(6)   For the purposes of the foregoing provisions of this section, an alienation in implementation of a prior obligation is deemed to be one for which there was no consideration or no adequate consideration to the extent that the prior obligation was undertaken for no consideration or no adequate consideration.
(7)   A liquidator and an administrator have the same right as a creditor has under any rule of law to challenge an alienation of a company made for no consideration or no adequate consideration.
(8)   This section applies to Scotland only.

NOTES

Sub-ss (1), (3): words in square brackets substituted by the Enterprise Act 2002, s 248(3), Sch 17, paras 9, 28, as from 15 September 2003 (for savings and transitional provisions, see the note to s 8 at **[9.105]**).

[9.337]

243   Unfair preferences (Scotland)

(1)   Subject to subsection (2) below, subsection (4) below applies to a transaction entered into by a company, whether before or after 1st April 1986, which has the effect of creating a preference in favour of a creditor to the prejudice of the general body of creditors, being a preference created not earlier than 6 months before the commencement of the winding up of the company or [the company enters administration].

(2)   Subsection (4) below does not apply to any of the following transactions—

- (a)   a transaction in the ordinary course of trade or business;
- (b)   a payment in cash for a debt which when it was paid had become payable, unless the transaction was collusive with the purpose of prejudicing the general body of creditors;
- (c)   a transaction whereby the parties to it undertake reciprocal obligations (whether the performance by the parties of their respective obligations occurs at the same time or at different times) unless the transaction was collusive as aforesaid;
- (d)   the granting of a mandate by a company authorising an arrestee to pay over the arrested funds or part thereof to the arrester where—
  - (i)   there has been a decree for payment or a warrant for summary diligence, and
  - (ii)   the decree or warrant has been preceded by an arrestment on the dependence of the action or followed by an arrestment in execution.

(3)   For the purposes of subsection (1) above, the day on which a preference was created is the day on which the preference became completely effectual.

(4)   A transaction to which this subsection applies is challengeable by—

- (a)   in the case of a winding up—
  - (i)   any creditor who is a creditor by virtue of a debt incurred on or before the date of commencement of the winding up, or
  - (ii)   the liquidator; and
- (b)   [where the company has entered administration], the administrator.

(5)   On a challenge being brought under subsection (4) above, the court, if satisfied that the transaction challenged is a transaction to which this section applies, shall grant decree of reduction or for such restoration of property to the company's assets or other redress as may be appropriate:

Provided that this subsection is without prejudice to any right or interest acquired in good faith and for value from or through the creditor in whose favour the preference was created.

(6)   A liquidator and an administrator have the same right as a creditor has under any rule of law to challenge a preference created by a debtor.

(7)   This section applies to Scotland only.

NOTES

Sub-ss (1), (4): words in square brackets substituted by the Enterprise Act 2002, s 248(3), Sch 17, paras 9, 29, as from 15 September 2003 (for savings and transitional provisions, see the note to s 8 at **[9.105]**).

[9.338]

244   Extortionate credit transactions

(1)   This section applies as does section 238, and where the company is, or has been, a party to a transaction for, or involving, the provision of credit to the company.

(2)   The court may, on the application of the office-holder, make an order with respect to the transaction if the transaction is or was extortionate and was entered into in the period of 3 years ending with [the day on which the company entered administration or went into liquidation].

(3)   For the purposes of this section a transaction is extortionate if, having regard to the risk accepted by the person providing the credit—

- (a)   the terms of it are or were such as to require grossly exorbitant payments to be made (whether unconditionally or in certain contingencies) in respect of the provision of the credit, or
- (b)   it otherwise grossly contravened ordinary principles of fair dealing;

and it shall be presumed, unless the contrary is proved, that a transaction with respect to which an application is made under this section is or, as the case may be, was extortionate.

(4)   An order under this section with respect to any transaction may contain such one or more of the following as the court thinks fit, that is to say—

- (a)   provision setting aside the whole or part of any obligation created by the transaction,
- (b)   provision otherwise varying the terms of the transaction or varying the terms on which any security for the purposes of the transaction is held,
- (c)   provision requiring any person who is or was a party to the transaction to pay to the office-holder any sums paid to that person, by virtue of the transaction, by the company,
- (d)   provision requiring any person to surrender to the office-holder any property held by him as security for the purposes of the transaction,
- (e)   provision directing accounts to be taken between any persons.

(5)   The powers conferred by this section are exercisable in relation to any transaction concurrently with any powers exercisable in relation to that transaction as a transaction at an undervalue or under section 242 (gratuitous alienations in Scotland).

NOTES

Sub-s (2): words in square brackets substituted by the Enterprise Act 2002, s 248(3), Sch 17, paras 9, 30, as from 15 September 2003 (for savings and transitional provisions, see the note to s 8 at [**9.105**]).

[9.339]

245   Avoidance of certain floating charges

(1)   This section applies as does section 238, but applies to Scotland as well as to England and Wales.

(2)   Subject as follows, a floating charge on the company's undertaking or property created at a relevant time is invalid except to the extent of the aggregate of—

    (a)   the value of so much of the consideration for the creation of the charge as consists of money paid, or goods or services supplied, to the company at the same time as, or after, the creation of the charge,

    (b)   the value of so much of that consideration as consists of the discharge or reduction, at the same time as, or after, the creation of the charge, of any debt of the company, and

    (c)   the amount of such interest (if any) as is payable on the amount falling within paragraph (a) or (b) in pursuance of any agreement under which the money was so paid, the goods or services were so supplied or the debt was so discharged or reduced.

(3)   Subject to the next subsection, the time at which a floating charge is created by a company is a relevant time for the purposes of this section if the charge is created—

    (a)   in the case of a charge which is created in favour of a person who is connected with the company, at a time in the period of 2 years ending with the onset of insolvency,

    (b)   in the case of a charge which is created in favour of any other person, at a time in the period of 12 months ending with the onset of insolvency,   . . .

    [(c)   in either case, at a time between the making of an administration application in respect of the company and the making of an administration order on that application, or

    (d)   in either case, at a time between the filing with the court of a copy of notice of intention to appoint an administrator under paragraph 14 or 22 of Schedule B1 and the making of an appointment under that paragraph.]

(4)   Where a company creates a floating charge at a time mentioned in subsection (3)(b) and the person in favour of whom the charge is created is not connected with the company, that time is not a relevant time for the purposes of this section unless the company—

    (a)   is at that time unable to pay its debts within the meaning of section 123 in Chapter VI of Part IV, or

    (b)   becomes unable to pay its debts within the meaning of that section in consequence of the transaction under which the charge is created.

(5)   For the purposes of subsection (3), the onset of insolvency is—

    [(a)   in a case where this section applies by reason of an administrator of a company being appointed by administration order, the date on which the administration application is made,

    (b)   in a case where this section applies by reason of an administrator of a company being appointed under paragraph 14 or 22 of Schedule B1 following filing with the court of a copy of notice of intention to appoint under that paragraph, the date on which the copy of the notice is filed,

    (c)   in a case where this section applies by reason of an administrator of a company being appointed otherwise than as mentioned in paragraph (a) or (b), the date on which the appointment takes effect, and

    (d)   in a case where this section applies by reason of a company going into liquidation, the date of the commencement of the winding up.]

(6)   For the purposes of subsection (2)(a) the value of any goods or services supplied by way of consideration for a floating charge is the amount in money which at the time they were supplied could reasonably have been expected to be obtained for supplying the goods or services in the ordinary course of business and on the same terms (apart from the consideration) as those on which they were supplied to the company.

NOTES

Sub-s (3): word omitted from para (b) repealed, and paras (c), (d) substituted for the original para (c), by the Enterprise Act 2002, ss 248(3), 278(2), Sch 17, paras 9, 31(1)–(3), Sch 26, as from 15 September 2003 (for savings and transitional provisions, see the note to s 8 at [**9.105**]).

Sub-s (5): paras (a)–(d) substituted, for original paras (a), (b), by the Enterprise Act 2002, s 248(3), Sch 17, paras 9, 31(1), (4), as from 15 September 2003 (for savings and transitional provisions, see the note to s 8 at [**9.105**]).

[9.340]

246   Unenforceability of liens on books, etc

(1)   This section applies in the case of a company where—

    [(a)   the company enters administration,] or

    (b)   the company goes into liquidation, or

    (c)   a provisional liquidator is appointed;

and "the office-holder" means the administrator, the liquidator or the provisional liquidator, as the case may be.

(2)   Subject as follows, a lien or other right to retain possession of any of the books, papers or other records of the company is unenforceable to the extent that its enforcement would deny possession of any books, papers or other records to the office-holder.

(3)   This does not apply to a lien on documents which give a title to property and are held as such.

NOTES

Sub-s (1): para (a) substituted by the Enterprise Act 2002, s 248(3), Sch 17, paras 9, 32, as from 15 September 2003 (for savings and transitional provisions, see the note to s 8 at **[9.105]**).

[Remote attendance at meetings

[9.341]

246A   Remote attendance at meetings

(1)   Subject to subsection (2), this section applies to—

     (a)   any meeting of the creditors of a company summoned under this Act or the rules, or

     (b)   any meeting of the members or contributories of a company summoned by the office-holder under this Act or the rules, other than a meeting of the members of a company in a members' voluntary winding up.

(2)   This section does not apply where—

     (a)   a company is being wound up in Scotland, or

     (b)   a receiver is appointed under section 51 in Chapter 2 of Part 3.

(3)   Where the person summoning a meeting ("the convener") considers it appropriate, the meeting may be conducted and held in such a way that persons who are not present together at the same place may attend it.

(4)   Where a meeting is conducted and held in the manner referred to in subsection (3), a person attends the meeting if that person is able to exercise any rights which that person may have to speak and vote at the meeting.

(5)   For the purposes of this section—

     (a)   a person is able to exercise the right to speak at a meeting when that person is in a position to communicate to all those attending the meeting, during the meeting, any information or opinions which that person has on the business of the meeting; and

     (b)   a person is able to exercise the right to vote at a meeting when—

         (i)   that person is able to vote, during the meeting, on resolutions put to the vote at the meeting, and

         (ii)   that person's vote can be taken into account in determining whether or not such resolutions are passed at the same time as the votes of all the other persons attending the meeting.

(6)   The convener of a meeting which is to be conducted and held in the manner referred to in subsection (3) shall make whatever arrangements the convener considers appropriate to—

     (a)   enable those attending the meeting to exercise their rights to speak or vote, and

     (b)   ensure the identification of those attending the meeting and the security of any electronic means used to enable attendance.

(7)   Where in the reasonable opinion of the convener—

     (a)   a meeting will be attended by persons who will not be present together at the same place, and

     (b)   it is unnecessary or inexpedient to specify a place for the meeting,

any requirement under this Act or the rules to specify a place for the meeting may be satisfied by specifying the arrangements the convener proposes to enable persons to exercise their rights to speak or vote.

(8)   In making the arrangements referred to in subsection (6) and in forming the opinion referred to in subsection (7)(b), the convener must have regard to the legitimate interests of the creditors, members or contributories and others attending the meeting in the efficient despatch of the business of the meeting.

(9)   If—

     (a)   the notice of a meeting does not specify a place for the meeting,

     (b)   the convener is requested in accordance with the rules to specify a place for the meeting, and

     (c)   that request is made—

         (i)   in the case of a meeting of creditors or contributories, by not less than ten percent in value of the creditors or contributories, or

         (ii)   in the case of a meeting of members, by members representing not less than ten percent of the total voting rights of all the members having at the date of the request a right to vote at the meeting,

it shall be the duty of the convener to specify a place for the meeting.

(10)   In this section, "the office-holder", in relation to a company, means—

     (a)   its liquidator, provisional liquidator, administrator, or administrative receiver, or

     (b)   where a voluntary arrangement in relation to the company is proposed or has taken effect under Part 1, the nominee or the supervisor of the voluntary arrangement.]

NOTES

Commencement: 6 April 2010.

Inserted, together with the preceding heading and s 246B, by the Legislative Reform (Insolvency) (Miscellaneous Provisions) Order 2010, SI 2010/18, arts 2, 3(1), as from 6 April 2010.

[Use of websites

[9.342]

246B   Use of websites

(1)   Subject to subsection (2), where any provision of this Act or the rules requires the office-holder to give, deliver, furnish or send a notice or other document or information to any person, that requirement is satisfied by making the notice, document or information available on a website—

    (a)   in accordance with the rules, and

    (b)   in such circumstances as may be prescribed.

(2)   This section does not apply where—

    (a)   a company is being wound up in Scotland, or

    (b)   a receiver is appointed under section 51 in Chapter 2 of Part 3.

(3)   In this section, "the office-holder" means—

    (a)   the liquidator, provisional liquidator, administrator, or administrative receiver of a company, or

    (b)   where a voluntary arrangement in relation to a company is proposed or has taken effect under Part 1, the nominee or the supervisor of the voluntary arrangement.]

NOTES

Commencement: 6 April 2010.

Inserted as noted to s 246A at **[9.341]**.

PART VII
INTERPRETATION FOR FIRST GROUP OF PARTS

[9.343]

247   "Insolvency" and "go into liquidation"

(1)   In this Group of Parts, except in so far as the context otherwise requires, "insolvency", in relation to a company, includes the approval of a voluntary arrangement under Part I, [or the appointment of an administrator or administrative receiver].

(2)   For the purposes of any provision in this Group of Parts, a company goes into liquidation if it passes a resolution for voluntary winding up or an order for its winding up is made by the court at a time when it has not already gone into liquidation by passing such a resolution.

[(3)   The reference to a resolution for voluntary winding up in subsection (2) includes a reference to a resolution which is deemed to occur by virtue of—

    (a)   paragraph 83(6)(b) of Schedule B1, or

    (b)   an order made following conversion of administration or a voluntary arrangement into winding up by virtue of Article 37 of the EC Regulation.]

NOTES

Sub-s (1): words in square brackets substituted by the Enterprise Act 2002, s 248(3), Sch 17, paras 9, 33(1), (2), as from 15 September 2003 (for savings and transitional provisions, see the note to s 8 at **[9.105]**).

Sub-s (3): added by the Insolvency Act 1986 (Amendment) (No 2) Regulations 2002, SI 2002/1240, regs 3, 12, as from 31 May 2002; substituted by the Enterprise Act 2002, s 248(3), Sch 17, paras 9, 33(1), (3), as from 15 September 2003 (for savings and transitional provisions, see the note to s 8 at **[9.105]**).

[9.344]

248   "Secured creditor", etc

In this Group of Parts, except in so far as the context otherwise requires—

    (a)   "secured creditor", in relation to a company, means a creditor of the company who holds in respect of his debt a security over property of the company, and "unsecured creditor" is to be read accordingly; and

    (b)   "security" means—

        (i)   in relation to England and Wales, any mortgage, charge, lien or other security, and

        (ii)   in relation to Scotland, any security (whether heritable or moveable), any floating charge and any right of lien or preference and any right of retention (other than a right of compensation or set off).

[9.345]

249   "Connected" with a company

For the purposes of any provision in this Group of Parts, a person is connected with a company if—

    (a)   he is a director or shadow director of the company or an associate of such a director or shadow director, or

    (b)   he is an associate of the company;

and "associate" has the meaning given by section 435 in Part XVIII of this Act.

[9.346]
250   "Member" of a company
For the purposes of any provision in this Group of Parts, a person who is not a member of a company but to whom shares in the company have been transferred, or transmitted by operation of law, is to be regarded as a member of the company, and references to a member or members are to be read accordingly.

[9.347]
251   Expressions used generally
In this Group of Parts, except in so far as the context otherwise requires—

"administrative receiver" means—

     (a)   an administrative receiver as defined by section 29(2) in Chapter I of Part III, or

     (b)   a receiver appointed under section 51 in Chapter II of that Part in a case where the whole (or substantially the whole) of the company's property is attached by the floating charge;

["agent" does not include a person's counsel acting as such;]

["books and papers" and "books or papers" includes accounts, deeds, writing and documents;]

"business day" means any day other than a Saturday, a Sunday, Christmas Day, Good Friday or a day which is a bank holiday in any part of Great Britain;

"chattel leasing agreement" means an agreement for the bailment or, in Scotland, the hiring of goods which is capable of subsisting for more than 3 months;

"contributory" has the meaning given by section 79;

["the court", in relation to a company, means a court having jurisdiction to wind up the company;]

"director" includes any person occupying the position of director, by whatever name called;

["document" includes summons, notice, order and other legal process, and registers;]

"floating charge" means a charge which, as created, was a floating charge and includes a floating charge within section 462 of the Companies Act (Scottish floating charges);

["the Gazette" means—

     (a)   as respects companies registered in England and Wales, the London Gazette;

     (b)   as respects companies registered in Scotland, the Edinburgh Gazette;]

. . .

["officer", in relation to a body corporate, includes a director, manager or secretary;]

"the official rate", in relation to interest, means the rate payable under section 189(4);

"prescribed" means prescribed by the rules;

"receiver", in the expression "receiver or manager", does not include a receiver appointed under section 51 in Chapter II of Part III;

"retention of title agreement" means an agreement for the sale of goods to a company, being an agreement—

     (a)   which does not constitute a charge on the goods, but

     (b)   under which, if the seller is not paid and the company is wound up, the seller will have priority over all other creditors of the company as respects the goods or any property representing the goods;

"the rules" means rules under section 411 in Part XV; and

"shadow director", in relation to a company, means a person in accordance with whose directions or instructions the directors of the company are accustomed to act (but so that a person is not deemed a shadow director by reason only that the directors act on advice given by him in a professional capacity);

[. . .]

NOTES

   All definitions in square brackets inserted, and the definition "office copy" (omitted) repealed, by the Companies Act 2006 (Consequential Amendments, Transitional Provisions and Savings) Order 2009, SI 2009/1941, art 2(1), Sch 1, para 77(1)–(3), as from 1 October 2009 (for transitional provisions see the note to s 7A at **[9.103]**).

   Final words in square brackets substituted by the Companies Act 2006 (Commencement No 3, Consequential Amendments, Transitional Provisions and Savings) Order 2007, SI 2007/2194, art 10(1), Sch 4, Pt 3, para 43, as from 1 October 2007, and repealed by SI 2009/1941, art 2(1), Sch 1, para 77(1), (4), as from 1 October 2009 (for transitional provisions see the note to s 7A at **[9.103]**).

THE THIRD GROUP OF PARTS
MISCELLANEOUS MATTERS BEARING ON BOTH COMPANY
AND INDIVIDUAL INSOLVENCY;
GENERAL INTERPRETATION; FINAL PROVISIONS

PART XII
PREFERENTIAL DEBTS IN COMPANY AND INDIVIDUAL INSOLVENCY

[9.348]
386   Categories of preferential debts
(1)   A reference in this Act to the preferential debts of a company or an individual is to the debts listed in Schedule 6 to this Act [(contributions to occupational pension schemes; remuneration, &c. of employees; levies on coal and steel production)]; and references to preferential creditors are to be read accordingly.
(2)   In that Schedule "the debtor" means the company or the individual concerned.
(3)   Schedule 6 is to be read with [Schedule 4 to the Pension Schemes Act 1993] (occupational pension scheme contributions).

NOTES
   Sub-s (1): words in square brackets substituted by the Enterprise Act 2002, s 251(3), as from 15 September 2003 (for savings and transitional provisions, see the note to Sch 6 at **[9.421]**).
   Sub-s (3): words in square brackets substituted by the Pension Schemes Act 1993, s 190, Sch 8, para 8, as from 7 February 1994.

[9.349]
387   "The relevant date"
(1)   This section explains references in Schedule 6 to the relevant date (being the date which determines the existence and amount of a preferential debt).
(2)   For the purposes of section 4 in Part I (meetings to consider company voluntary arrangement), the relevant date in relation to a company which is not being wound up is—
   [(a)   if the company is in administration, the date on which it entered administration, and
   (b)   if the company is not in administration, the date on which the voluntary arrangement takes effect.]
[(2A)   For the purposes of paragraph 31 of Schedule A1 (meetings to consider company voluntary arrangement where a moratorium under section 1A is in force), the relevant date in relation to a company is the date of filing.]
(3)   In relation to a company which is being wound up, the following applies—
   (a)   if the winding up is by the court, and the winding-up order was made immediately upon the discharge of an administration order, the relevant date is [the date on which the company entered administration];
   [(aa)   if the winding up is by the court and the winding-up order was made following conversion of administration into winding up by virtue of Article 37 of the EC Regulation, the relevant date is [the date on which the company entered administration];
   (ab)   if the company is deemed to have passed a resolution for voluntary winding up by virtue of an order following conversion of administration into winding up under Article 37 of the EC Regulation, the relevant date is [the date on which the company entered administration];]
   (b)   if the case does not fall within paragraph (a)[, (aa) or (ab)] and the company—
      (i)   is being wound up by the court, and
      (ii)   had not commenced to be wound up voluntarily before the date of the making of the winding-up order,
      the relevant date is the date of the appointment (or first appointment) of a provisional liquidator or, if no such appointment has been made, the date of the winding-up order;
   [(ba)   if the case does not fall within paragraph (a), (aa), (ab) or (b) and the company is being wound up following administration pursuant to paragraph 83 of Schedule B1, the relevant date is the date on which the company entered administration;]
   (c)   if the case does not fall within [paragraph (a), (aa), (ab), (b) or (ba)], the relevant date is the date of the passing of the resolution for the winding up of the company.
[(3A)   In relation to a company which is in administration (and to which no other provision of this section applies) the relevant date is the date on which the company enters administration.]
(4)   In relation to a company in receivership (where section 40 or, as the case may be, section 59 applies), the relevant date is—
   (a)   in England and Wales, the date of the appointment of the receiver by debenture-holders, and
   (b)   in Scotland, the date of the appointment of the receiver under section 53(6) or (as the case may be) 54(5).
(5)   For the purposes of section 258 in Part VIII (individual voluntary arrangements), the relevant date is, in relation to a debtor who is not an undischarged bankrupt

[(a)　where an interim order has been made under section 252 with respect to his proposal, the date of that order, and

(b)　in any other case, the date on which the voluntary arrangement takes effect.]

(6)　In relation to a bankrupt, the following applies—

(a)　where at the time the bankruptcy order was made there was an interim receiver appointed under section 286, the relevant date is the date on which the interim receiver was first appointed after the presentation of the bankruptcy petition;

(b)　otherwise, the relevant date is the date of the making of the bankruptcy order.

NOTES

Sub-s (2): paras (a), (b) substituted by the Enterprise Act 2002, s 248(3), Sch 17, paras 9, 34(1), (2), as from 15 September 2003 (for savings and transitional provisions, see the note to s 8 at **[9.105]**).

Sub-s (2A): inserted by the Insolvency Act 2000, s 1, Sch 1, paras 1, 9, as from 1 January 2003.

Sub-s (3): paras (aa), (ab) and words in square brackets in para (b) inserted by the Insolvency Act 1986 (Amendment) (No 2) Regulations 2002, SI 2002/1240, regs 3, 16, as from 31 May 2002; words in square brackets in paras (a), (aa), (ab) (c) substituted, and para (ba) inserted, by the Enterprise Act 2002, s 248(3), Sch 17, paras 9, 34(1), (3), as from 15 September 2003 (for savings and transitional provisions, see the note to s 8 at **[9.105]**).

Sub-s (3A): inserted by the Enterprise Act 2002, s 248(3), Sch 17, paras 9, 34(1), (4), as from 15 September 2003 (for savings and transitional provisions, see the note to s 8 at **[9.105]**).

Sub-s (5): words in square brackets substituted by the Insolvency Act 2000, s 3, Sch 3, paras 1, 15, as from 1 January 2003, subject to savings in relation to cases where a proposal is made by a debtor and, before that date, the intended nominee has endorsed a copy of the written notice of the proposal under r 5.4(3) of the Insolvency Rules (see SI 2002/2711, art 4).

PART XIII
INSOLVENCY PRACTITIONERS AND THEIR QUALIFICATION

Restrictions on unqualified persons acting as liquidator, trustee in bankruptcy, etc

[9.350]
388　Meaning of "act as insolvency practitioner"

(1)　A person acts as an insolvency practitioner in relation to a company by acting—

(a)　as its liquidator, provisional liquidator, administrator or administrative receiver, or

[(b)　where a voluntary arrangement in relation to the company is proposed or approved under Part I, as nominee or supervisor].

(2)　A person acts as an insolvency practitioner in relation to an individual by acting—

(a)　as his trustee in bankruptcy or interim receiver of his property or as permanent or interim trustee in the sequestration of his estate; or

(b)　as trustee under a deed which is a deed of arrangement made for the benefit of his creditors or, in Scotland, a trust deed for his creditors; or

[(c)　where a voluntary arrangement in relation to the individual is proposed or approved under Part VIII, as nominee or supervisor]

(d)　in the case of a deceased individual to the administration of whose estate this section applies by virtue of an order under section 421 (application of provisions of this Act to insolvent estates of deceased persons), as administrator of that estate.

[(2A)　A person acts as an insolvency practitioner in relation to an insolvent partnership by acting—

(a)　as its liquidator, provisional liquidator or administrator, or

(b)　as trustee of the partnership under article 11 of the Insolvent Partnerships Order 1994, or

[(c)　where a voluntary arrangement in relation to the insolvent partnership is proposed or approved under Part I of the Act, as nominee or supervisor].]

[(2B)　In relation to a voluntary arrangement proposed under Part I or VIII, a person acts as nominee if he performs any of the functions conferred on nominees under the Part in question.]

(3)　References in this section to an individual include, except in so far as the context otherwise requires, references . . . . to any debtor within the meaning of the Bankruptcy (Scotland) Act 1985.

(4)　In this section—

"administrative receiver" has the meaning given by section 251 in Part VII;

["company" means—

(a)　a company registered under the Companies Act 2006 in England and Wales or Scotland, or

(b)　a company that may be wound up under Part 5 of this Act (unregistered companies);]

"interim trustee" and "permanent trustee" mean the same as in the Bankruptcy (Scotland) Act 1985.

[(5)　Nothing in this section applies to anything done by—

(a)　the official receiver; or

(b)　the Accountant in Bankruptcy (within the meaning of the Bankruptcy (Scotland) Act 1985).]

[(6)　Nothing in this section applies to anything done (whether in the United Kingdom or elsewhere) in relation to insolvency proceedings under the EC Regulation in a member State other than the United Kingdom.]

NOTES

Sub-s (1): para (b) substituted by the Insolvency Act 2000, s 4(1), (2)(a), as from 1 January 2003 (for transitional provisions see the note below).

Sub-s (2): para (c) substituted by the Insolvency Act 2000, s 4(1), (2)(b), as from 1 January 2003 (for transitional provisions see the note below).

Sub-s (2A): inserted by the Insolvent Partnerships Order 1994, SI 1994/2421, art 15(1), as from 1 December 1994; para (c) substituted by the Insolvent Partnerships (Amendment) (No 2) Order 2002, SI 2002/2708, art 3, as from 1 January 2003. Note: SI 2002/2708 (which also amends the Insolvent Partnerships Order 1994, SI 1994/2421) provides (in art 11) that "the amendments to the 1994 Order set out in articles 3, 4, 5, 6, 8, 9 and 10 of, and Schedules 1 and 2 to, this Order" do not apply where, in relation to a voluntary arrangement under the Insolvency Act 1986, Pt I, as the case may be, a proposal is made by (a) the members of a partnership and before 1 January 2003 the intended nominee has endorsed a copy of the written notice of the proposal under r 1.4(3) (of the Insolvency Rules 1986, SI 1986/1925), (b) the liquidator or the administrator (acting as nominee) and before 1 January 2003 the liquidator or administrator (as the case may be) has sent out a notice summoning the meetings under s 3 of the 1986 Act as required by r 1.11, or (c) the liquidator or the administrator of a partnership (not acting as the nominee) and before 1 January 2003 the intended nominee has endorsed a copy of the written notice of the proposal under rule 1.12(2). It should be noted that art 3 of the 2002 Order amends this section and not the Insolvent Partnerships Order 1994.

Sub-s (2B): inserted by the Insolvency Act 2000, s 4(1), (2)(c), as from 1 January 2003 (for transitional provisions see the note below).

Sub-s (3): words omitted repealed by SI 1994/2421, art 15(2), as from 1 December 1994.

Sub-s (4): definition "company" substituted by the Companies Act 2006 (Consequential Amendments, Transitional Provisions and Savings) Order 2009, SI 2009/1941, art 2(1), Sch 1, para 78(1), (2), as from 1 October 2009 (for transitional provisions see the note to s 7A at **[9.103]**).

Sub-s (5): substituted by the Bankruptcy (Scotland) Act 1993, s 11(1), as from 1 April 1993.

Sub-s (6): added by the Insolvency Act 1986 (Amendment) (No 2) Regulations 2002, SI 2002/1240, regs 3, 17, as from 31 May 2002.

Transitional provisions: the Insolvency Act 2000 (Commencement No 3 and Transitional Provisions) Order 2002, SI 2002/2711, art 5 provides for the following transitional provisions (note that by virtue of arts 1 and 2, the "appointed day" means 1 January 2003):

> "(1)   The amendments made by section 4(1) and 4(2) to section 388 of the Act shall not apply in any case where—
>
> (a)   a person acts as a nominee (within the meaning of section 1(2) of the Act) and that case falls within paragraph (1) of article 3; or
>
> (b)   a person acts as a nominee (within the meaning of section 253(2) of the Act) and that case falls within paragraph (1) of article 4,
>
> and in such cases section 388 of the Act as it has effect immediately before the appointed day shall continue to have effect.".

[9.351]
389   Acting without qualification an offence

(1)   A person who acts as an insolvency practitioner in relation to a company or an individual at a time when he is not qualified to do so is liable to imprisonment or a fine, or to both.

[(1A)   This section is subject to section 389A.]

(2)   This section does not apply to the official receiver [or the Accountant in Bankruptcy (within the meaning of the Bankruptcy (Scotland) Act 1985)].

NOTES

Sub-s (1A): inserted by the Insolvency Act 2000, s 4(1), (3), as from 1 January 2003.

Sub-s (2): words in square brackets added by the Bankruptcy (Scotland) Act 1993, s 11(2), as from 1 April 1993.

[9.352]
[389A   Authorisation of nominees and supervisors

(1)   Section 389 does not apply to a person acting, in relation to a voluntary arrangement proposed or approved under Part I or Part VIII, as nominee or supervisor if he is authorised so to act.

(2)   For the purposes of subsection (1) and those Parts, an individual to whom subsection (3) does not apply is authorised to act as nominee or supervisor in relation to such an arrangement if—

(a)   he is a member of a body recognised for the purpose by the Secretary of State [or of a body recognised for the purpose of Article 348A(2)(a) of the Insolvency (Northern Ireland) Order 1989 by the Department of Enterprise, Trade and Investment for Northern Ireland], and

(b)   there is in force security (in Scotland, caution) for the proper performance of his functions and that security or caution meets the prescribed requirements with respect to his so acting in relation to the arrangement.

(3)   This subsection applies to a person if—

(a)   he has been adjudged bankrupt or sequestration of his estate has been awarded and (in either case) he has not been discharged,

[(b)   he is subject to a disqualification order made or a disqualification undertaking accepted under the Company Directors Disqualification Act 1986 or the Company Directors Disqualification (Northern Ireland) Order 2002,]

(c)   he is a patient within the meaning of . . . [section 329(1) of the Mental Health (Care and Treatment) (Scotland) Act 2003][, or

(d)   he lacks capacity (within the meaning of the Mental Capacity Act 2005) to act as nominee or supervisor].

(4)   The Secretary of State may by order declare a body which appears to him to fall within subsection (5) to be a recognised body for the purposes of subsection (2)(a).

(5)   A body may be recognised if it maintains and enforces rules for securing that its members—
   (a)   are fit and proper persons to act as nominees or supervisors, and
   (b)   meet acceptable requirements as to education and practical training and experience.

(6)   For the purposes of this section, a person is a member of a body only if he is subject to its rules when acting as nominee or supervisor (whether or not he is in fact a member of the body).

(7)   An order made under subsection (4) in relation to a body may be revoked by a further order if it appears to the Secretary of State that the body no longer falls within subsection (5).

(8)   An order of the Secretary of State under this section has effect from such date as is specified in the order; and any such order revoking a previous order may make provision for members of the body in question to continue to be treated as members of a recognised body for a specified period after the revocation takes effect.]

NOTES

Inserted by the Insolvency Act 2000, s 4(1), (4), as from 1 January 2003.

Sub-s (2): words in square brackets in para (a) inserted by the Provision of Services (Insolvency Practitioners) Regulations 2009, SI 2009/3081, reg 2(1), (2), as from 28 December 2009 (except in relation to an application for authorisation to act as an insolvency practitioner under s 393 of this Act made or granted before that date).

Sub-s (3) is amended as follows:

Para (b) substituted by the Companies Act 2006 (Consequential Amendments, Transitional Provisions and Savings) Order 2009, SI 2009/1941, art 2(1), Sch 1, para 78(1), (3), as from 1 October 2009 (for transitional provisions see the note to s 7A at **[9.103]**).

Words omitted repealed, and para (d) and the word immediately preceding it inserted, by the Mental Capacity Act 2005, s 67(1), (2), Sch 6, para 31(1), (2), Sch 7, as from 1 October 2007.

Words in square brackets in para (c) substituted, in relation to Scotland, by the Mental Health (Care and Treatment) (Scotland) Act 2003 (Modification of Enactments) Order 2005, SSI 2005/486, art 2, Sch 1, para 18(1), (2), as from 27 September 2005, and, in relation to England and Wales, by the Mental Health (Care and Treatment) (Scotland) Act 2003 (Consequential Provisions) Order 2005, SI 2005/2078, art 15, Sch 1, para 3(1), (2), as from 5 October 2005.

Regulations: the Provision of Services (Insolvency Practitioners) Regulations 2009, SI 2009/3081.

[9.353]
[389B   Official receiver as nominee or supervisor

(1)   The official receiver is authorised to act as nominee or supervisor in relation to a voluntary arrangement approved under Part VIII provided that the debtor is an undischarged bankrupt when the arrangement is proposed.

(2)   The Secretary of State may by order repeal the proviso in subsection (1).

(3)   An order under subsection (2)—
   (a)   must be made by statutory instrument, and
   (b)   shall be subject to annulment in pursuance of a resolution of either House of Parliament.]

NOTES

Inserted, in relation to England and Wales only, by the Enterprise Act 2002, s 264(1), Sch 22, para 3, as from 1 April 2004.

The requisite qualification, and the means of obtaining it
[9.354]
390   Persons not qualified to act as insolvency practitioners

(1)   A person who is not an individual is not qualified to act as an insolvency practitioner.

(2)   A person is not qualified to act as an insolvency practitioner at any time unless at that time—
   (a)   he is authorised so to act by virtue of membership of a professional body recognised under section 391 below, being permitted so to act by or under the rules of that body, or
   (b)   he holds an authorisation granted by a competent authority under section 393[; or
   (c)   he holds an authorisation granted by the Department of Enterprise, Trade and Investment for Northern Ireland under Article 352 of the Insolvency (Northern Ireland) Order 1989].

(3)   A person is not qualified to act as an insolvency practitioner in relation to another person at any time unless—
   (a)   there is in force at that time security or, in Scotland, caution for the proper performance of his functions, and
   (b)   that security or caution meets the prescribed requirements with respect to his so acting in relation to that other person.

(4)   A person is not qualified to act as an insolvency practitioner at any time if at that time—
   (a)   he has been adjudged bankrupt or sequestration of his estate has been awarded and (in either case) he has not been discharged,
   [(aa)   a moratorium period under a debt relief order applies in relation of him,]
   [(b)   he is subject to a disqualification order made or a disqualification undertaking accepted under the Company Directors Disqualification Act 1986 or the Company Directors Disqualification (Northern Ireland) Order 2002,]
   (c)   he is a patient within the meaning of   . . .   [section 329(1) of the Mental Health (Care and Treatment) (Scotland) Act 2003] [or has had a guardian appointed to him under the Adults with Incapacity (Scotland) Act 2000 (asp 4)][, or

    (d) he lacks capacity (within the meaning of the Mental Capacity Act 2005) to act as an insolvency practitioner].

[(5) A person is not qualified to act as an insolvency practitioner while a bankruptcy restrictions order [or a debt relief restrictions order] is in force in respect of him.]

NOTES

Sub-s (2): para (c) and the word immediately preceding it inserted by the Provision of Services (Insolvency Practitioners) Regulations 2009, SI 2009/3081, reg 2(1), (3), as from 28 December 2009 (except in relation to an application for authorisation to act as an insolvency practitioner under s 393 of this Act made or granted before that date).

Sub-s (4) is amended as follows:

Para (aa) inserted by the Tribunals, Courts and Enforcement Act 2007, s 108(3), Sch 20, Pt 1, paras 1, 5(1), (2), as from 6 April 2009.

Para (b) substituted by the Companies Act 2006 (Consequential Amendments, Transitional Provisions and Savings) Order 2009, SI 2009/1941, art 2(1), Sch 1, para 78(1), (4), as from 1 October 2009 (for transitional provisions see the note to s 7A at **[9.103]**).

Para (d) and the word immediately preceding it inserted, by the Mental Capacity Act 2005, s 67(1), (2), Sch 6, para 31(1), (3), Sch 7, as from 1 October 2007.

Words in first pair of square brackets in para (c) substituted, in relation to Scotland, by the Mental Health (Care and Treatment) (Scotland) Act 2003 (Modification of Enactments) Order 2005, SSI 2005/486, art 2, Sch 1, para 18(1), (3), as from 27 September 2005, and, in relation to England and Wales, by the Mental Health (Care and Treatment) (Scotland) Act 2003 (Consequential Provisions) Order 2005, SI 2005/2078, art 15, Sch 1, para 3(1), (3), as from 5 October 2005.

Words in second pair of square brackets in para (c) added by the Adults with Incapacity (Scotland) Act 2000, s 88(2), Sch 5, para 18, as from 1 April 2002.

Sub-s (5): added, in relation to England and Wales only, by the Enterprise Act 2002, s 257(3), Sch 21, para 4, as from 1 April 2004; words in square brackets inserted by the Tribunals, Courts and Enforcement Act 2007, s 108(3), Sch 20, Pt 1, paras 1, 5(1), (3), as from 6 April 2009.

Regulations: the Insolvency Practitioners Regulations 2005, SI 2005/524; the Provision of Services (Insolvency Practitioners) Regulations 2009, SI 2009/3081.

[9.355]
391 Recognised professional bodies

(1) The Secretary of State may by order declare a body which appears to him to fall within subsection (2) below to be a recognised professional body for the purposes of this section.

(2) A body may be recognised if it regulates the practice of a profession and maintains and enforces rules for securing that such of its members as are permitted by or under the rules to act as insolvency practitioners—

    (a) are fit and proper persons so to act, and

    (b) meet acceptable requirements as to education and practical training and experience.

(3) References to members of a recognised professional body are to persons who, whether members of that body or not, are subject to its rules in the practice of the profession in question.

The reference in section 390(2) above to membership of a professional body recognised under this section is to be read accordingly.

(4) An order made under subsection (1) in relation to a professional body may be revoked by a further order if it appears to the Secretary of State that the body no longer falls within subsection (2).

(5) An order of the Secretary of State under this section has effect from such date as is specified in the order; and any such order revoking a previous order may make provision whereby members of the body in question continue to be treated as authorised to act as insolvency practitioners for a specified period after the revocation takes effect.

NOTES

Orders: the Insolvency Practitioners (Recognised Professional Bodies) Order 1986, SI 1986/1764 recognising the following bodies for the purposes of this section: the Chartered Association of Certified Accountants; the Insolvency Practitioners Association; the Institute of Chartered Accountants in England and Wales; the Institute of Chartered Accountants in Ireland; the Institute of Chartered Accountants of Scotland; the Law Society; the Law Society of Scotland.

[9.356]
392 Authorisation by competent authority

(1) Application may be made to a competent authority for authorisation to act as an insolvency practitioner.

(2) The competent authorities for this purpose are—

    (a) in relation to a case of any description specified in directions given by the Secretary of State, the body or person so specified in relation to cases of that description, and

    (b) in relation to a case not falling within paragraph (a), the Secretary of State.

(3) The application—

    (a) shall be made in such manner as the competent authority may direct,

    (b) shall contain or be accompanied by such information as that authority may reasonably require for the purpose of determining the application, and

    (c) shall be accompanied by the prescribed fee;

and the authority may direct that notice of the making of the application shall be published in such manner as may be specified in the direction.

(4)   At any time after receiving the application and before determining it the authority may require the applicant to furnish additional information.

(5)   Directions and requirements given or imposed under subsection (3) or (4) may differ as between different applications.

(6)   Any information to be furnished to the competent authority under this section shall, if it so requires, be in such form or verified in such manner as it may specify.

(7)   An application may be withdrawn before it is granted or refused.

(8)   Any sums received under this section by a competent authority other than the Secretary of State may be retained by the authority; and any sums so received by the Secretary of State shall be paid into the Consolidated Fund.

[(9)   Subsection (3)(c) shall not have effect in respect of an application made to the Secretary of State (but this subsection is without prejudice to section 415A).]

NOTES

Sub-s (9): added by the Enterprise Act 2002, s 270(3), as from 1 April 2004.

Regulations: the Insolvency Practitioners Regulations 2005, SI 2005/524; the Provision of Services (Insolvency Practitioners) Regulations 2009, SI 2009/3081.

[9.357]
393   Grant, refusal and withdrawal of authorisation

(1)   The competent authority may, on an application duly made in accordance with section 392 and after being furnished with all such information as it may require under that section, grant or refuse the application.

(2)   The authority shall grant the application if it appears to it from the information furnished by the applicant and having regard to such other information, if any, as it may have—

   (a)   that the applicant is a fit and proper person to act as an insolvency practitioner, and
   (b)   that the applicant meets the prescribed requirements with respect to education and practical training and experience.

[(3)   An authorisation granted under this section, if not previously withdrawn, continues in force for one year.

(3A)   But where an authorisation is granted under this section the competent authority must, before its expiry (and without a further application made in accordance with section 392) grant a further authorisation under this section taking effect immediately after the expiry of the previous authorisation, unless it appears to the authority that the subject of the authorisation no longer complies with subsection (2)(a) and (b).]

(4)   An authorisation [granted under this section] may be withdrawn by the competent authority if it appears to it—

   (a)   that the holder of the authorisation is no longer a fit and proper person to act as an insolvency practitioner, or
   (b)   without prejudice to paragraph (a), that the holder—
      (i)   has failed to comply with any provision of this Part or of any regulations made under this Part or Part XV, or
      (ii)   in purported compliance with any such provision, has furnished the competent authority with false, inaccurate or misleading information.

(5)   An authorisation granted under this section may be withdrawn by the competent authority at the request or with the consent of the holder of the authorisation.

[(6)   Where an authorisation granted under this section is withdrawn—

   (a)   subsection (3A) does not require a further authorisation to be granted, or
   (b)   if a further authorisation has already been granted at the time of the withdrawal, the further authorisation is also withdrawn.]

NOTES

Sub-ss (3), (3A): substituted for original sub-s (3) by the Provision of Services (Insolvency Practitioners) Regulations 2009, SI 2009/3081, reg 2(1), (4)(a), as from 28 December 2009 (except in relation to an application for authorisation to act as an insolvency practitioner under this section made or granted before that date).

Sub-s (4): words in square brackets substituted by SI 2009/3081, reg 2(1), (4)(b), as from 28 December 2009 (except in relation to an application for authorisation to act as an insolvency practitioner under this section made or granted before that date).

Sub-s (6): added by SI 2009/3081, reg 2(1), (4)(c), as from 28 December 2009 (except in relation to an application for authorisation to act as an insolvency practitioner under this section made or granted before that date).

Regulations: the Insolvency Practitioners Regulations 2005, SI 2005/524; the Provision of Services (Insolvency Practitioners) Regulations 2009, SI 2009/3081.

[9.358]
394   Notices

(1)   Where a competent authority grants an authorisation under section 393, it shall give written notice of that fact to the applicant, specifying the date on which the authorisation takes effect.

(2)   Where the authority proposes to refuse an application, or to withdraw an authorisation under section 393(4), it shall give the applicant or holder of the authorisation written notice of its intention to do so, setting out particulars of the grounds on which it proposes to act.

(3)   In the case of a proposed withdrawal the notice shall state the date on which it is proposed that the withdrawal should take effect.

(4)   A notice under subsection (2) shall give particulars of the rights exercisable under the next two sections by a person on whom the notice is served.

[9.359]
395   Right to make representations
(1)   A person on whom a notice is served under section 394(2) may within 14 days after the date of service make written representations to the competent authority.

(2)   The competent authority shall have regard to any representations so made in determining whether to refuse the application or withdraw the authorisation, as the case may be.

[9.360]
396   Reference to Tribunal
(1)   The Insolvency Practitioners Tribunal ("the Tribunal") continues in being; and the provisions of Schedule 7 apply to it.

(2)   Where a person is served with a notice under section 394(2), he may—
   (a)   at any time within 28 days after the date of service of the notice, or
   (b)   at any time after the making by him of representations under section 395 and before the end of the period of 28 days after the date of the service on him of a notice by the competent authority that the authority does not propose to alter its decision in consequence of the representations,
give written notice to the authority requiring the case to be referred to the Tribunal.

(3)   Where a requirement is made under subsection (2), then, unless the competent authority—
   (a)   has decided or decides to grant the application or, as the case may be, not to withdraw the authorisation, and
   (b)   within 7 days after the date of the making of the requirement, gives written notice of that decision to the person by whom the requirement was made,
it shall refer the case to the Tribunal.

NOTES
   Rules: the Insolvency Practitioners Tribunal (Conduct of Investigations) Rules 1986, SI 1986/952.

[9.361]
397   Action of Tribunal on reference
(1)   On a reference under section 396 the Tribunal shall—
   (a)   investigate the case, and
   (b)   make a report to the competent authority stating what would in their opinion be the appropriate decision in the matter and the reasons for that opinion,
and it is the duty of the competent authority to decide the matter accordingly.

(2)   The Tribunal shall send a copy of the report to the applicant or, as the case may be, the holder of the authorisation; and the competent authority shall serve him with a written notice of the decision made by it in accordance with the report.

(3)   The competent authority may, if he thinks fit, publish the report of the Tribunal.

[9.362]
398   Refusal or withdrawal without reference to Tribunal
Where in the case of any proposed refusal or withdrawal of an authorisation either—
   (a)   the period mentioned in section 396(2)(a) has expired without the making of any requirement under that subsection or of any representations under section 395, or
   (b)   the competent authority has given a notice such as is mentioned in section 396(2)(b) and the period so mentioned has expired without the making of any such requirement,
the competent authority may give written notice of the refusal or withdrawal to the person concerned in accordance with the proposal in the notice given under section 394(2).

PART XIV
PUBLIC ADMINISTRATION (ENGLAND AND WALES)
Official Receivers

[9.363]
399   Appointment, etc of official receivers
(1)   For the purposes of this Act the official receiver, in relation to any bankruptcy[, winding up[, individual voluntary arrangement, debt relief order or application for such an order]], is any person who by virtue of the following provisions of this section or section 401 below is authorised to act as the official receiver in relation to that bankruptcy[, winding up[, individual voluntary arrangement, debt relief order or application for such an order]].

(2)   The Secretary of State may (subject to the approval of the Treasury as to numbers) appoint persons to the office of official receiver, and a person appointed to that office (whether under this section or section 70 of the Bankruptcy Act 1914)—

(a)   shall be paid out of money provided by Parliament such salary as the Secretary of State may with the concurrence of the Treasury direct,

(b)   shall hold office on such other terms and conditions as the Secretary of State may with the concurrence of the Treasury direct, and

(c)   may be removed from office by a direction of the Secretary of State.

(3)   Where a person holds the office of official receiver, the Secretary of State shall from time to time attach him either to the High Court or to a county court having jurisdiction for the purposes of the second Group of Parts of this Act.

(4)   Subject to any directions under subsection (6) below, an official receiver attached to a particular court is the person authorised to act as the official receiver in relation to every bankruptcy[, winding up[, individual voluntary arrangement, debt relief order or application for such an order]] falling within the jurisdiction of that court.

(5)   The Secretary of State shall ensure that there is, at all times, at least one official receiver attached to the High Court and at least one attached to each county court having jurisdiction for the purposes of the second Group of Parts; but he may attach the same official receiver to two or more different courts.

(6)   The Secretary of State may give directions with respect to the disposal of the business of official receivers, and such directions may, in particular—

(a)   authorise an official receiver attached to one court to act as the official receiver in relation to any case or description of cases falling within the jurisdiction of another court;

(b)   provide, where there is more than one official receiver authorised to act as the official receiver in relation to cases falling within the jurisdiction of any court, for the distribution of their business between or among themselves.

(7)   A person who at the coming into force of section 222 of the Insolvency Act 1985 (replaced by this section) is an official receiver attached to a court shall continue in office after the coming into force of that section as an official receiver attached to that court under this section.

NOTES

Sub-s (1): words in first and third (outer) pairs of square brackets substituted by the Enterprise Act 2002, s 269, Sch 23, paras 1, 14, as from 1 April 2004; words in second and fourth (inner) pairs of square brackets substituted by the Tribunals, Courts and Enforcement Act 2007, s 108(3), Sch 20, Pt 1, paras 1, 7, as from 6 April 2009.

Sub-s (4): words in first (outer) pair of square brackets substituted by the Enterprise Act 2002, s 269, Sch 23, paras 1, 14, as from 1 April 2004; words in second (inner) pair of square brackets substituted by the Tribunals, Courts and Enforcement Act 2007, s 108(3), Sch 20, Pt 1, paras 1, 7, as from 6 April 2009.

[9.364]
400   Functions and status of official receivers

(1)   In addition to any functions conferred on him by this Act, a person holding the office of official receiver shall carry out such other functions as may from time to time be conferred on him by the Secretary of State.

(2)   In the exercise of the functions of his office a person holding the office of official receiver shall act under the general directions of the Secretary of State and shall also be an officer of the court in relation to which he exercises those functions.

(3)   Any property vested in his official capacity in a person holding the office of official receiver shall, on his dying, ceasing to hold office or being otherwise succeeded in relation to the bankruptcy or winding up in question by another official receiver, vest in his successor without any conveyance, assignment or transfer.

[9.365]
401   Deputy official receivers and staff

(1)   The Secretary of State may, if he thinks it expedient to do so in order to facilitate the disposal of the business of the official receiver attached to any court, appoint an officer of his department to act as deputy to that official receiver.

(2)   Subject to any directions given by the Secretary of State under section 399 or 400, a person appointed to act as deputy to an official receiver has, on such conditions and for such period as may be specified in the terms of his appointment, the same status and functions as the official receiver to whom he is appointed deputy.

Accordingly, references in this Act (except section 399(1) to (5)) to an official receiver include a person appointed to act as his deputy.

(3)   An appointment made under subsection (1) may be terminated at any time by the Secretary of State.

(4)   The Secretary of State may, subject to the approval of the Treasury as to numbers and remuneration and as to the other terms and conditions of the appointments, appoint officers of his department to assist official receivers in the carrying out of their functions.

The Official Petitioner

[9.366]
402 Official Petitioner
(1) There continues to be an officer known as the Official Petitioner for the purpose of discharging, in relation to cases in which a criminal bankruptcy order is made, the functions assigned to him by or under this Act; and the Director of Public Prosecutions continues, by virtue of his office, to be the Official Petitioner.
(2) The functions of the Official Petitioner include the following—
 (a) to consider whether, in a case in which a criminal bankruptcy order is made, it is in the public interest that he should himself present a petition under section 264(1)(d) of this Act;
 (b) to present such a petition in any case where he determines that it is in the public interest for him to do so;
 (c) to make payments, in such cases as he may determine, towards expenses incurred by other persons in connection with proceedings in pursuance of such a petition; and
 (d) to exercise, so far as he considers it in the public interest to do so, any of the powers conferred on him by or under this Act.
(3) Any functions of the Official Petitioner may be discharged on his behalf by any person acting with his authority.
(4) Neither the Official Petitioner nor any person acting with his authority is liable to any action or proceeding in respect of anything done or omitted to be done in the discharge, or purported discharge, of the functions of the Official Petitioner.
(5) In this section "criminal bankruptcy order" means an order under section 39(1) of the Powers of Criminal Courts Act 1973.

NOTES
Repealed by the Criminal Justice Act 1988, s 170(2), Sch 16, as from a day to be appointed.

Insolvency Service finance, accounting and investment

[9.367]
403 Insolvency Services Account
(1) All money received by the Secretary of State in respect of proceedings under this Act as it applies to England and Wales shall be paid into the Insolvency Services Account kept by the Secretary of State with the Bank of England; and all payments out of money standing to the credit of the Secretary of State in that account shall be made by the Bank of England in such manner as he may direct.
(2) Whenever the cash balance standing to the credit of the Insolvency Services Account is in excess of the amount which in the opinion of the Secretary of State is required for the time being to answer demands in respect of bankrupts' estates or companies' estates, the Secretary of State shall—
 (a) notify the excess to the National Debt Commissioners, and
 (b) pay into the Insolvency Services Investment Account ("the Investment Account") kept by the Commissioners with the Bank of England the whole or any part of the excess as the Commissioners may require for investment in accordance with the following provisions of this Part.
(3) Whenever any part of the money so invested is, in the opinion of the Secretary of State, required to answer any demand in respect of bankrupt's estates or companies' estates, he shall notify to the National Debt Commissioners the amount so required and the Commissioners—
 (a) shall thereupon repay to the Secretary of State such sum as may be required to the credit of the Insolvency Services Account, and
 (b) for that purpose may direct the sale of such part of the securities in which the money has been invested as may be necessary.

[9.368]
404 Investment Account
Any money standing to the credit of the Investment Account (including any money received by the National Debt Commissioners by way of interest on or proceeds of any investment under this section) may be invested by the Commissioners, in accordance with such directions as may be given by the Treasury, in any manner for the time being specified in Part II of Schedule 1 to the Trustee Investments Act 1961.

405 *(Repealed by the Enterprise Act 2002, ss 272(1), 278(2), Sch 26, as from 1 April 2004.)*

[9.369]
406 [Interest on money received by liquidators or trustees in bankruptcy and invested]
Where under rules made by virtue of paragraph 16 of Schedule 8 to this Act (investment of money received by company liquidators) [or paragraph 21 of Schedule 9 to this Act (investment of money received by trustee in bankruptcy) a company or a bankrupt's estate] has become entitled to any

sum by way of interest, the Secretary of State shall certify that sum and the amount of tax payable on it to the National Debt Commissioners; and the Commissioners shall pay, out of the Investment Account—

(a)   into the Insolvency Services Account, the sum so certified less the amount of tax so certified, and

(b)   to the Commissioners of Inland Revenue, the amount of tax so certified.

NOTES

Words in square brackets substituted by the Insolvency Act 2000, s 13(2), as from 2 April 2001.

Commissioners of Inland Revenue: a reference to the Commissioners of Inland Revenue is now to be taken as a reference to the Commissioners for Her Majesty's Revenue and Customs; see the Commissioners for Revenue and Customs Act 2005, s 50(1), (7).

[9.370]
407   Unclaimed dividends and undistributed balances
(1)   The Secretary of State shall from time to time pay into the Consolidated Fund out of the Insolvency Services Account so much of the sums standing to the credit of that Account as represents—

(a)   dividends which were declared before such date as the Treasury may from time to time determine and have not been claimed, and

(b)   balances ascertained before that date which are too small to be divided among the persons entitled to them.

(2)   For the purposes of this section the sums standing to the credit of the Insolvency Services Account are deemed to include any sums paid out of that Account and represented by any sums or securities standing to the credit of the Investment Account.

(3)   The Secretary of State may require the National Debt Commissioners to pay out of the Investment Account into the Insolvency Services Account the whole or part of any sum which he is required to pay out of that account under subsection (1); and the Commissioners may direct the sale of such securities standing to the credit of the Investment Account as may be necessary for that purpose.

[9.371]
[408   Adjustment of balances
(1)   The Treasury may direct the payment out of the Consolidated Fund of sums into—

(a)   the Insolvency Services Account;

(b)   the Investment Account.

(2)   The Treasury shall certify to the House of Commons the reason for any payment under subsection (1).

(3)   The Secretary of State may pay sums out of the Insolvency Services Account into the Consolidated Fund.

(4)   The National Debt Commissioners may pay sums out of the Investment Account into the Consolidated Fund.]

NOTES

Substituted by the Enterprise Act 2002, s 272(2), as from 1 April 2004.

[9.372]
409   Annual financial statement and audit
(1)   The National Debt Commissioners shall for each year ending on 31st March prepare a statement of the sums credited and debited to the Investment Account in such form and manner as the Treasury may direct and shall transmit it to the Comptroller and Auditor General before the end of November next following the year.

(2)   The Secretary of State shall for each year ending 31st March prepare a statement of the sums received or paid by him under section 403 above in such form and manner as the Treasury may direct and shall transmit each statement to the Comptroller and Auditor General before the end of November next following the year.

(3)   Every such statement shall include such additional information as the Treasury may direct.

(4)   The Comptroller and Auditor General shall examine, certify and report on every such statement and shall lay copies of it, and of his report, before Parliament.

Supplementary

[9.373]
410   Extent of this Part
This Part of this Act extends to England and Wales only.

PART XV
SUBORDINATE LEGISLATION

General insolvency rules

[9.374]
411   Company insolvency rules
(1)   Rules may be made—
   (a)   in relation to England and Wales, by the Lord Chancellor with the concurrence of the Secretary of State [and, in the case of rules that affect court procedure, with the concurrence of the Lord Chief Justice], or
   (b)   in relation to Scotland, by the Secretary of State,
for the purpose of giving effect to Parts I to VII of this Act [or the EC Regulation].
[(1A)   Rules may also be made for the purpose of giving effect to Part 2 of the Banking Act 2009 (bank insolvency orders); and rules for that purpose shall be made—
   (a)   in relation to England and Wales, by the Lord Chancellor with the concurrence of—
      (i)   the Treasury, and
      (ii)   in the case of rules that affect court procedure, the Lord Chief Justice, or
   (b)   in relation to Scotland, by the Treasury.]
[(1B)   Rules may also be made for the purpose of giving effect to Part 3 of the Banking Act 2009 (bank administration); and rules for that purpose shall be made—
   (a)   in relation to England and Wales, by the Lord Chancellor with the concurrence of—
      (i)   the Treasury, and
      (ii)   in the case of rules that affect court procedure, the Lord Chief Justice, or
   (b)   in relation to Scotland, by the Treasury.]
(2)   Without prejudice to the generality of subsection (1), [(1A)] [or (1B)] or to any provision of those Parts by virtue of which rules under this section may be made with respect to any matter, rules under this section may contain—
   (a)   any such provision as is specified in Schedule 8 to this Act or corresponds to provision contained immediately before the coming into force of section 106 of the Insolvency Act 1985 in rules made, or having effect as if made, under section 663(1) or (2) of [the Companies Act 1985] (old winding-up rules), and
   (b)   such incidental, supplemental and transitional provisions as may appear to the Lord Chancellor or, as the case may be, the Secretary of State [or the Treasury] necessary or expedient.
[(2A)   For the purposes of subsection (2), a reference in Schedule 8 to this Act to doing anything under or for the purposes of a provision of this Act includes a reference to doing anything under or for the purposes of the EC Regulation (in so far as the provision of this Act relates to a matter to which the EC Regulation applies).
(2B)   Rules under this section for the purpose of giving effect to the EC Regulation may not create an offence of a kind referred to in paragraph 1(1)(d) of Schedule 2 to the European Communities Act 1972.]
[(2C)   For the purposes of subsection (2), a reference in Schedule 8 to this Act to doing anything under or for the purposes of a provision of this Act includes a reference to doing anything under or for the purposes of Part 2 of the Banking Act 2009.]
[(2D)   For the purposes of subsection (2), a reference in Schedule 8 to this Act to doing anything under or for the purposes of a provision of this Act includes a reference to doing anything under or for the purposes of Part 3 of the Banking Act 2009.]
(3)   In Schedule 8 to this Act "liquidator" includes a provisional liquidator [or bank liquidator] [or administrator]; and references above in this section to Parts I to VII of this Act [or Part 2 [or 3] of the Banking Act 2009] are to be read as including [the Companies Acts] so far as relating to, and to matters connected with or arising out of, the insolvency or winding up of companies.
[(3A)   In this section references to Part 2 or 3 of the Banking Act 2009 include references to those Parts as applied to building societies (see section 90C of the Building Societies Act 1986).]
(4)   Rules under this section shall be made by statutory instrument subject to annulment in pursuance of a resolution of either House of Parliament.
(5)   Regulations made by the Secretary of State [or the Treasury] under a power conferred by rules under this section shall be made by statutory instrument and, after being made, shall be laid before each House of Parliament.
(6)   Nothing in this section prejudices any power to make rules of court.
[(7)   The Lord Chief Justice may nominate a judicial office holder (as defined in section 109(4) of the Constitutional Reform Act 2005) to exercise his functions under this section.]

NOTES
   Sub-s (1): words in square brackets in para (a) inserted by the Constitutional Reform Act 2005, s 15, Sch 4, Pt 1, paras 185, 188(1), (2), as from 3 April 2006; words in second pair of square brackets inserted by the Insolvency Act 1986 (Amendment) Regulations 2002, SI 2002/1037, regs 2, 3(1), as from 3 May 2002.
   Sub-ss (1A), (1B), (2C), (2D): inserted by the Banking Act 2009, ss 125(1), (2), (4), 160(1), (2), (4), as from 17 February 2009 (in so far as conferring or relating to any power to make subordinate legislation), and as from 21 February 2009 (otherwise).

Sub-s (2): words in square brackets in the introductory wording and in para (b) inserted by the Banking Act 2009, ss 125(1), (3), (6), 160(1), (3), as from 17 February 2009 (in so far as conferring or relating to any power to make subordinate legislation), and as from 21 February 2009 (otherwise); words in square brackets in para (a) substituted by the Companies Act 2006 (Consequential Amendments, Transitional Provisions and Savings) Order 2009, SI 2009/1941, art 2(1), Sch 1, para 79, as from 1 October 2009 (for transitional provisions see the note to s 7A at **[9.103]**).

Sub-ss (2A), (2B): inserted by SI 2002/1037, regs 2, 3(2), as from 3 May 2002.

Sub-s (3): words in the final pair of square brackets substituted by the Companies Act 2006 (Commencement No 3, Consequential Amendments, Transitional Provisions and Savings) Order 2007, SI 2007/2194, art 10(1), Sch 4, Pt 3, para 44, as from 1 October 2007; all other words in square brackets inserted by the Banking Act 2009, ss 125(1), (5). 160(1), (5), as from 21 February 2009.

Sub-s (3A): inserted by the Building Societies (Insolvency and Special Administration) Order 2009, SI 2009/805, art 13, as from 30 March 2009.

Sub-s (5): words in square brackets inserted by the Banking Act 2009, ss 125(1), (3), (6), 160(1), (3), as from 17 February 2009 (in so far as conferring or relating to any power to make subordinate legislation), and as from 21 February 2009 (otherwise).

Sub-s (7): added by the Constitutional Reform Act 2005, s 15, Sch 4, Pt 1, paras 185, 188(1), (3), as from 3 April 2006.

Rules: the Insolvency (Scotland) Rules 1986, SI 1986/1915; the Insolvency Rules 1986, SI 1986/1925 at **[10.1]**; the Insolvent Companies (Disqualification of Unfit Directors) Proceedings Rules 1987, SI 1987/2023 at **[10.676]**; the Insolvent Companies (Reports on Conduct of Directors) Rules 1996, SI 1996/1909 at **[10.759]**; the Insolvent Companies (Reports on Conduct of Directors) (Scotland) Rules 1996, SI 1996/1910 at **[10.767]**; the Railway Administration Order Rules 2001, SI 2001/3352; the Insurers (Winding Up) Rules 2001, SI 2001/3635; the Insurers (Winding Up) (Scotland) Rules 2001, SI 2001/4040; the Energy Administration Rules 2005, SI 2005/2483; the Energy Administration (Scotland) Rules 2006, SI 2006/772; the PPP Administration Order Rules 2007, SI 2007/3141; the Bank Administration (Scotland) Rules 2009, SI 2009/350; the Bank Insolvency (Scotland) Rules 2009, SI 2009/351; the Bank Insolvency (England and Wales) Rules 2009, SI 2009/356; the Bank Administration (England and Wales) Rules 2009, SI 2009/357; the Building Society Special Administration (Scotland) Rules 2009, SI 2009/806; the Companies (Unfair Prejudice Applications) Proceedings Rules 2009, SI 2009/2469 at **[10.1233]**; the Water Industry (Special Administration) Rules 2009, SI 2009/2477; the Building Society Special Administration (England and Wales) Rules 2010, SI 2010/2580; the Building Society Insolvency (England and Wales) Rules 2010, SI 2010/2581; the Building Society Insolvency (Scotland) Rules 2010, SI 2010/2584; the Investment Bank Special Administration (England and Wales) Rules 2011, SI 2011/1301.

Regulations: the Insolvency Regulations 1994, SI 1994/2507 at **[10.720]**.

[9.375]
413 Insolvency Rules Committee
(1) The committee established under section 10 of the Insolvency Act 1976 (advisory committee on bankruptcy and winding-up rules) continues to exist for the purpose of being consulted under this section.

(2) The Lord Chancellor shall consult the committee before making any rules under section 411 or 412 [other than rules which contain a statement that the only provision made by the rules is provision applying rules made under section 411, with or without modifications, for the purposes of provision made by [any of sections 23 to 26 of the Water Industry Act 1991 or Schedule 3 to that Act]] [or by any of sections 59 to 65 of, or Schedule 6 or 7 to, the Railways Act 1993].

(3) Subject to the next subsection, the committee shall consist of—
 (a) a judge of the High Court attached to the Chancery Division;
 (b) a circuit judge;
 (c) a registrar in bankruptcy of the High Court;
 (d) the registrar of a county court;
 (e) a practising barrister;
 (f) a practising solicitor; and
 (g) a practising accountant;
and the appointment of any person as a member of the committee shall be made [in accordance with subsection (3A) or (3B)].

[(3A) The Lord Chief Justice must appoint the persons referred to in paragraphs (a) to (d) of subsection (3), after consulting the Lord Chancellor.

(3B) The Lord Chancellor must appoint the persons referred to in paragraphs (e) to (g) of subsection (3), after consulting the Lord Chief Justice.]

(4) The Lord Chancellor may appoint as additional members of the committee any persons appearing to him to have qualifications or experience that would be of value to the committee in considering any matter with which it is concerned.

[(5) The Lord Chief Justice may nominate a judicial office holder (as defined in section 109(4) of the Constitutional Reform Act 2005) to exercise his functions under this section.]

NOTES

Sub-s (2): words in first (outer) pair of square brackets substituted by the Water Act 1989, s 190(1), Sch 25, para 78(2), as from 1 September 1989; words in second (inner) pair of square brackets substituted by the Water Consolidation (Consequential Provisions) Act 1991, s 2(1), Sch 1, para 46, as from 1 December 1991; words in third pair of square brackets added by the Railways Act 1993, s 152, Sch 12, para 25, as from 1 April 1994.

Sub-s (3): words in square brackets substituted by the Constitutional Reform Act 2005, s 15, Sch 4, Pt 1, paras 185, 190(1), (2), as from 3 April 2006.

Sub-ss (3A), (3B), (5): inserted and added respectively by the Constitutional Reform Act 2005, s 15, Sch 4, Pt 1, paras 185, 190(1), (3), (4), as from 3 April 2006.

[9.376]
414   Fees orders (company insolvency proceedings)
(1)   There shall be paid in respect of—
  (a)   proceedings under any of Parts I to VII of this Act, and
  (b)   the performance by the official receiver or the Secretary of State of functions under those Parts,
such fees as the competent authority may with the sanction of the Treasury by order direct.
(2)   That authority is—
  (a)   in relation to England and Wales, the Lord Chancellor, and
  (b)   in relation to Scotland, the Secretary of State.
(3)   The Treasury may by order direct by whom and in what manner the fees are to be collected and accounted for.
(4)   The Lord Chancellor may, with the sanction of the Treasury, by order provide for sums to be deposited, by such persons, in such manner and in such circumstances as may be specified in the order, by way of security for fees payable by virtue of this section.
(5)   An order under this section may contain such incidental, supplemental and transitional provisions as may appear to the Lord Chancellor, the Secretary of State or (as the case may be) the Treasury necessary or expedient.
(6)   An order under this section shall be made by statutory instrument and, after being made, shall be laid before each House of Parliament.
(7)   Fees payable by virtue of this section shall be paid into the Consolidated Fund.
(8)   References in subsection (1) to Parts I to VII of this Act are to be read as including [the Companies Acts] so far as relating to, and to matters connected with or arising out of, the insolvency or winding up of companies.
[(8A)   This section applies in relation to Part 2 of the Banking Act 2009 (bank insolvency) as in relation to Parts I to VII of this Act.]
[(8B)   This section applies in relation to Part 3 of the Banking Act 2009 (bank administration) as in relation to Parts I to VII of this Act.]
[(8C)   In subsections (8A) and (8B) the reference to Parts 2 and 3 of the Banking Act 2009 include references to those Parts as applied to building societies (see section 90C of the Building Societies Act 1986).]
(9)   Nothing in this section prejudices any power to make rules of court; and the application of this section to Scotland is without prejudice to section 2 of the Courts of Law Fees (Scotland) Act 1985.

NOTES
  Sub-s (8): words in square brackets substituted by the Companies Act 2006 (Commencement No 3, Consequential Amendments, Transitional Provisions and Savings) Order 2007, SI 2007/2194, art 10(1), Sch 4, Pt 3, para 44, as from 1 October 2007.
  Sub-ss (8A), (8B): inserted by the Banking Act 2009, ss 126, 161, as from 17 February 2009 (in so far as conferring or relating to any power to make subordinate legislation), and as from 21 February 2009 (otherwise).
  Sub-s (8C): inserted by the Building Societies (Insolvency and Special Administration) Order 2009, SI 2009/805, art 14, as from 30 March 2009.
  Orders: the Insolvency Proceedings (Fees) Order 2004, SI 2004/593 at **[10.841]**; the Civil Proceedings Fees Order 2008, SI 2008/1053.

[9.377]
[415A   Fees orders (general)
[(A1)   The Secretary of State—
  (a)   may by order require a person or body to pay a fee in connection with the grant or maintenance of a designation of that person or body as a competent authority under section 251U, and
  (b)   may refuse to grant, or may withdraw, any such designation where a fee is not paid.]
(1)   The Secretary of State—
  (a)   may by order require a body to pay a fee in connection with the grant or maintenance of recognition of the body under section 391, and
  (b)   may refuse recognition, or revoke an order of recognition under section 391(1) by a further order, where a fee is not paid.
(2)   The Secretary of State—
  (a)   may by order require a person to pay a fee in connection with the grant or maintenance of authorisation of the person under section 393, and
  (b)   may disregard an application or withdraw an authorisation where a fee is not paid.
(3)   The Secretary of State may by order require the payment of fees in respect of—
  (a)   the operation of the Insolvency Services Account;
  (b)   payments into and out of that Account.
(4)   The following provisions of section 414 apply to fees under this section as they apply to fees under that section—
  (a)   subsection (3) (manner of payment),
  (b)   subsection (5) (additional provision),

(c)   subsection (6) (statutory instrument),
(d)   subsection (7) (payment into Consolidated Fund), and
(e)   subsection (9) (saving for rules of court).]

NOTES

   Inserted by the Enterprise Act 2002, s 270(1), as from 18 December 2003, subject to s 270(2) of that Act which provides that an Order made under this section may relate to the maintenance of recognition or authorisation granted before that date.
   Sub-s (A1): inserted by the Tribunals, Courts and Enforcement Act 2007, s 108(3), Sch 20, Pt 1, paras 1, 10, as from 24 February 2009 (for the purpose of making orders), and as from 6 April 2009 (otherwise).
   Orders: the Insolvency Practitioners and Insolvency Services Account (Fees) Order 2003, SI 2003/3363 at **[10.834]**.
   Regulations: the Provision of Services (Insolvency Practitioners) Regulations 2009, SI 2009/3081.

Specification, increase and reduction of money sums relevant in the operation of this Act

[9.378]
416   Monetary limits (companies winding up)
(1)   The Secretary of State may by order in a statutory instrument increase or reduce any of the money sums for the time being specified in the following provisions in the first Group of Parts—
   section 117(2) (amount of company's share capital determining whether county court has jurisdiction to wind it up);
   section 120(3) (the equivalent as respects sheriff court jurisdiction in Scotland);
   section 123(1)(a) (minimum debt for service of demand on company by unpaid creditor);
   section 184(3) (minimum value of judgment, affecting sheriff's duties on levying execution);
   section 206(1)(a) and (b) (minimum value of company property concealed or fraudulently removed, affecting criminal liability of company's officer).
(2)   An order under this section may contain such transitional provisions as may appear to the Secretary of State necessary or expedient.
(3)   No order under this section increasing or reducing any of the money sums for the time being specified in section 117(2), 120(3) or 123(1)(a) shall be made unless a draft of the order has been laid before and approved by a resolution of each House of Parliament.
(4)   A statutory instrument containing an order under this section, other than an order to which subsection (3) applies, is subject to annulment in pursuance of a resolution of either House of Parliament.

NOTES

   Orders: the Insolvency Proceedings (Monetary Limits) Order 1986, SI 1986/1996 (increasing the sums specified in ss 184(3), 206(1)(a), (b)).

[9.379]
417   Money sum in s 222
The Secretary of State may by regulations in a statutory instrument increase or reduce the money sum for the time being specified in section 222(1) (minimum debt for service of demand on unregistered company by unpaid creditor); but such regulations shall not be made unless a draft of the statutory instrument containing them has been approved by resolution of each House of Parliament.

[9.380]
[417A   Money sums (company moratorium)
(1)   The Secretary of State may by order increase or reduce any of the money sums for the time being specified in the following provisions of Schedule A1 to this Act—
   paragraph 17(1) (maximum amount of credit which company may obtain without disclosure of moratorium);
   paragraph 41(4) (minimum value of company property concealed or fraudulently removed, affecting criminal liability of company's officer).
(2)   An order under this section may contain such transitional provisions as may appear to the Secretary of State necessary or expedient.
(3)   An order under this section shall be made by statutory instrument subject to annulment in pursuance of a resolution of either House of Parliament.]

NOTES

   Inserted by the Insolvency Act 2000, s 1, Sch 1, paras 1, 10, as from 1 January 2003.

Insolvency practice

[9.381]
419   Regulations for purposes of Part XIII
(1)   The Secretary of State may make regulations for the purpose of giving effect to Part XIII of this Act; and "prescribed" in that Part means prescribed by regulations made by the Secretary of State.
(2)   Without prejudice to the generality of subsection (1) or to any provision of that Part by virtue of which regulations may be made with respect to any matter, regulations under this section may contain—

    (a)   provision as to the matters to be taken into account in determining whether a person is a fit and proper person to act as an insolvency practitioner;

    (b)   provision prohibiting a person from so acting in prescribed cases, being cases in which a conflict of interest will or may arise;

    (c)   provision imposing requirements with respect to—

        (i)   the preparation and keeping by a person who acts as an insolvency practitioner of prescribed books, accounts and other records, and

        (ii)   the production of those books, accounts and records to prescribed persons;

    (d)   provision conferring power on prescribed persons—

        (i)   to require any person who acts or has acted as an insolvency practitioner to answer any inquiry in relation to a case in which he is so acting or has so acted, and

        (ii)   to apply to a court to examine such a person or any other person on oath concerning such a case;

    (e)   provision making non-compliance with any of the regulations a criminal offence; and

    (f)   such incidental, supplemental and transitional provisions as may appear to the Secretary of State necessary or expedient.

(3)   Any power conferred by Part XIII or this Part to make regulations, rules or orders is exercisable by statutory instrument subject to annulment by resolution of either House of Parliament.

(4)   Any rule or regulation under Part XIII or this Part may make different provision with respect to different cases or descriptions of cases, including different provision for different areas.

NOTES

    Regulations: the Insolvency Practitioners (Recognised Professional Bodies) Order 1986, SI 1986/1764; the Insolvency Practitioners Regulations 2005, SI 2005/524; the Provision of Services (Insolvency Practitioners) Regulations 2009, SI 2009/3081.

Other order making powers

[9.382]
420   Insolvent partnerships
(1)   The Lord Chancellor may, by order made with the concurrence of the Secretary of State [and the Lord Chief Justice], provide that such provisions of this Act as may be specified in the order shall apply in relation to insolvent partnerships with such modifications as may be so specified.

[(1A)   An order under this section may make provision in relation to the EC Regulation.

(1B)   But provision made by virtue of this section in relation to the EC Regulation may not create an offence of a kind referred to in paragraph 1(1)(d) of Schedule 2 to the European Communities Act 1972.]

(2)   An order under this section may make different provision for different cases and may contain such incidental, supplemental and transitional provisions as may appear to the Lord Chancellor [and the Lord Chief Justice] necessary or expedient.

(3)   An order under this section shall be made by statutory instrument subject to annulment in pursuance of a resolution of either House of Parliament.

[(4)   The Lord Chief Justice may nominate a judicial office holder (as defined in section 109(4) of the Constitutional Reform Act 2005) to exercise his functions under this section.]

NOTES

    Sub-ss (1), (2): words in square brackets inserted by the Constitutional Reform Act 2005, s 15(1), Sch 4, Pt 1, paras 185, 191(1)–(3), as from 3 April 2006.

    Sub-ss (1A), (1B): inserted by the Insolvency Act 1986 (Amendment) Regulations 2002, SI 2002/1037, regs 2, 3(5), as from 3 May 2002.

    Sub-s (4): added by the Constitutional Reform Act 2005, s 15(1), Sch 4, Pt 1, paras 185, 191(1), (4), as from 3 April 2006.

    Orders: the Insolvent Partnerships Order 1994, SI 1994/2421.

[9.383]
422   [Formerly authorised banks]
[(1)   The Secretary of State may by order made with the concurrence of the Treasury and after consultation with the Financial Services Authority provide that specified provisions in the first Group of Parts shall apply with specified modifications in relation to any person who—

    (a)   has a liability in respect of a deposit which he accepted in accordance with the Banking Act 1979 (c 37) or 1987 (c 22), but

    (b)   does not have permission under Part IV of the Financial Services and Markets Act 2000 (c 8) (regulated activities) to accept deposits.

(1A)   Subsection (1)(b) shall be construed in accordance with—

    (a)   section 22 of the Financial Services and Markets Act 2000 (classes of regulated activity and categories of investment),

    (b)   any relevant order under that section, and

    (c)   Schedule 2 to that Act (regulated activities).]

[(1A)   . . .]

Part 9   Misc primary legislation

(2)   An order under this section may make different provision for different cases and may contain such incidental, supplemental and transitional provisions as may appear to the Secretary of State necessary or expedient.

(3)   An order under this section shall be made by statutory instrument subject to annulment in pursuance of a resolution of either House of Parliament.

NOTES

Section heading: substituted by the Financial Services and Markets Act 2000 (Consequential Amendments) Order 2002, SI 2002/1555, art 16(1), (2), as from 3 July 2002.

Sub-ss (1), (1A): substituted, for original sub-s (1), by the Enterprise Act 2002, s 248(3), Sch 17, paras 9, 35, as from 15 September 2003 (for savings and transitional provisions, see the note to s 8 at **[9.105]**).

Second sub-s (1A): inserted by SI 2002/1555, art 16(1), (4), as from 3 July 2002; repealed by the Enterprise Act 2002 (Insolvency) Order 2003, SI 2003/2096, arts 4, 6, Schedule, Pt 1, paras 8, 11, as from 15 September 2003, except in relation to any case where a petition for an administration order was presented before that date.

Banking Act 1987: repealed by SI 2001/3649, art 3(1)(d), as from 1 December 2001.

Orders: the Banks (Former Authorised Institutions) (Insolvency) Order 2006, SI 2006/3107.

PART XVI
PROVISIONS AGAINST DEBT AVOIDANCE
(ENGLAND AND WALES ONLY)

[9.384]
423   Transactions defrauding creditors

(1)   This section relates to transactions entered into at an undervalue; and a person enters into such a transaction with another person if—

(a)   he makes a gift to the other person or he otherwise enters into a transaction with the other on terms that provide for him to receive no consideration;

(b)   he enters into a transaction with the other in consideration of marriage [or the formation of a civil partnership]; or

(c)   he enters into a transaction with the other for a consideration the value of which, in money or money's worth, is significantly less than the value, in money or money's worth, of the consideration provided by himself.

(2)   Where a person has entered into such a transaction, the court may, if satisfied under the next subsection, make such order as it thinks fit for—

(a)   restoring the position to what it would have been if the transaction had not been entered into, and

(b)   protecting the interests of persons who are victims of the transaction.

(3)   In the case of a person entering into such a transaction, an order shall only be made if the court is satisfied that it was entered into by him for the purpose—

(a)   of putting assets beyond the reach of a person who is making, or may at some time make, a claim against him, or

(b)   of otherwise prejudicing the interests of such a person in relation to the claim which he is making or may make.

(4)   In this section "the court" means the High Court or—

(a)   if the person entering into the transaction is an individual, any other court which would have jurisdiction in relation to a bankruptcy petition relating to him;

(b)   if that person is a body capable of being wound up under Part IV or V of this Act, any other court having jurisdiction to wind it up.

(5)   In relation to a transaction at an undervalue, references here and below to a victim of the transaction are to a person who is, or is capable of being, prejudiced by it; and in the following two sections the person entering into the transaction is referred to as "the debtor".

NOTES

Sub-s (1): words in square brackets inserted by the Civil Partnership Act 2004, s 261(1), Sch 27, para 121, as from 5 December 2005.

[9.385]
424   Those who may apply for an order under s 423

(1)   An application for an order under section 423 shall not be made in relation to a transaction except—

(a)   in a case where the debtor has been adjudged bankrupt or is a body corporate which is being wound up or [is in administration], by the official receiver, by the trustee of the bankrupt's estate or the liquidator or administrator of the body corporate or (with the leave of the court) by a victim of the transaction;

(b)   in a case where a victim of the transaction is bound by a voluntary arrangement approved under Part I or Part VIII of this Act, by the supervisor of the voluntary arrangement or by any person who (whether or not so bound) is such a victim; or

(c)   in any other case, by a victim of the transaction.

(2)   An application made under any of the paragraphs of subsection (1) is to be treated as made on behalf of every victim of the transaction.

NOTES

Sub-s (1): words in square brackets substituted by the Enterprise Act 2002, s 248(3), Sch 17, paras 9, 36, as from 15 September 2003 (for savings and transitional provisions, see the note to s 8 at **[9.105]**).

[9.386]
425   Provision which may be made by order under s 423

(1)   Without prejudice to the generality of section 423, an order made under that section with respect to a transaction may (subject as follows)—

 (a)   require any property transferred as part of the transaction to be vested in any person, either absolutely or for the benefit of all the persons on whose behalf the application for the order is treated as made;

 (b)   require any property to be so vested if it represents, in any person's hands, the application either of the proceeds of sale of property so transferred or of money so transferred;

 (c)   release or discharge (in whole or in part) any security given by the debtor;

 (d)   require any person to pay to any other person in respect of benefits received from the debtor such sums as the court may direct;

 (e)   provide for any surety or guarantor whose obligations to any person were released or discharged (in whole or in part) under the transaction to be under such new or revived obligations as the court thinks appropriate;

 (f)   provide for security to be provided for the discharge of any obligation imposed by or arising under the order, for such an obligation to be charged on any property and for such security or charge to have the same priority as a security or charge released or discharged (in whole or in part) under the transaction.

(2)   An order under section 423 may affect the property of, or impose any obligation on, any person whether or not he is the person with whom the debtor entered into the transaction; but such an order—

 (a)   shall not prejudice any interest in property which was acquired from a person other than the debtor and was acquired in good faith, for value and without notice of the relevant circumstances, or prejudice any interest deriving from such an interest, and

 (b)   shall not require a person who received a benefit from the transaction in good faith, for value and without notice of the relevant circumstances to pay any sum unless he was a party to the transaction.

(3)   For the purposes of this section the relevant circumstances in relation to a transaction are the circumstances by virtue of which an order under section 423 may be made in respect of the transaction.

(4)   In this section "security" means any mortgage, charge, lien or other security.

PART XVII
MISCELLANEOUS AND GENERAL

[9.387]
426   Co-operation between courts exercising jurisdiction in relation to insolvency

(1)   An order made by a court in any part of the United Kingdom in the exercise of jurisdiction in relation to insolvency law shall be enforced in any other part of the United Kingdom as if it were made by a court exercising the corresponding jurisdiction in that other part.

(2)   However, without prejudice to the following provisions of this section, nothing in subsection (1) requires a court in any part of the United Kingdom to enforce, in relation to property situated in that part, any order made by a court in any other part of the United Kingdom.

(3)   The Secretary of State, with the concurrence in relation to property situated in England and Wales of the Lord Chancellor, may by order make provision for securing that a trustee or assignee under the insolvency law of any part of the United Kingdom has, with such modifications as may be specified in the order, the same rights in relation to any property situated in another part of the United Kingdom as he would have in the corresponding circumstances if he were a trustee or assignee under the insolvency law of that other part.

(4)   The courts having jurisdiction in relation to insolvency law in any part of the United Kingdom shall assist the courts having the corresponding jurisdiction in any other part of the United Kingdom or any relevant country or territory.

(5)   For the purposes of subsection (4) a request made to a court in any part of the United Kingdom by a court in any other part of the United Kingdom or in a relevant country or territory is authority for the court to which the request is made to apply, in relation to any matters specified in the request, the insolvency law which is applicable by either court in relation to comparable matters falling within its jurisdiction.

In exercising its discretion under this subsection, a court shall have regard in particular to the rules of private international law.

Part 9 Misc primary legislation

(6) Where a person who is a trustee or assignee under the insolvency law of any part of the United Kingdom claims property situated in any other part of the United Kingdom (whether by virtue of an order under subsection (3) or otherwise), the submission of that claim to the court exercising jurisdiction in relation to insolvency law in that other part shall be treated in the same manner as a request made by a court for the purpose of subsection (4).

(7) Section 38 of the Criminal Law Act 1977 (execution of warrant of arrest throughout the United Kingdom) applies to a warrant which, in exercise of any jurisdiction in relation to insolvency law, is issued in any part of the United Kingdom for the arrest of a person as it applies to a warrant issued in that part of the United Kingdom for the arrest of a person charged with an offence.

(8) Without prejudice to any power to make rules of court, any power to make provision by subordinate legislation for the purpose of giving effect in relation to companies or individuals to the insolvency law of any part of the United Kingdom includes power to make provisions for the purpose of giving effect in that part to any provision made by or under the preceding provisions of this section.

(9) An order under subsection (3) shall be made by statutory instrument subject to annulment in pursuance of a resolution of either House of Parliament.

(10) In this section, "insolvency law" means—

(a) in relation to England and Wales, provision [extending to England and Wales and] made by or under this Act or sections [1A,] 6 to 10, [12 to 15], 19(c) and 20 (with Schedule 1) of the Company Directors Disqualification Act 1986 [and sections 1 to 17 of that Act as they apply for the purposes of those provisions of that Act];

(b) in relation to Scotland, provision extending to Scotland and made by or under this Act, sections [1A,] 6 to 10, [12 to 15], 19(c) and 20 (with Schedule 1) of the Company Directors Disqualification Act 1986 [and sections 1 to 17 of that Act as they apply for the purposes of those provisions of that Act], Part XVIII of the Companies Act or the Bankruptcy (Scotland) Act 1985;

(c) in relation to Northern Ireland, provision made by or under [the Insolvency (Northern Ireland) Order 1989] [or the Company Directors Disqualification (Northern Ireland) Order 2002];

(d) in relation to any relevant country or territory, so much of the law of that country or territory as corresponds to provisions falling within any of the foregoing paragraphs;

and references in this subsection to any enactment include, in relation to any time before the coming into force of that enactment the corresponding enactment in force at that time.

(11) In this section "relevant country or territory" means—

(a) any of the Channel Islands or the Isle of Man, or

(b) any country or territory designated for the purposes of this section by the Secretary of State by order made by statutory instrument.

[(12) In the application of this section to Northern Ireland—

(a) for any reference to the Secretary of State there is substituted a reference to the Department of Economic Development in Northern Ireland;

(b) in subsection (3) for the words "another part of the United Kingdom" and the words "that other part" there are substituted the words "Northern Ireland";

(c) for subsection (9) there is substituted the following subsection—

"(9) An order made under subsection (3) by the Department of Economic Development in Northern Ireland shall be a statutory rule for the purposes of the Statutory Rules (Northern Ireland) Order 1979 and shall be subject to negative resolution within the meaning of section 41(6) of the Interpretation Act (Northern Ireland) 1954.".]

[(13) Section 129 of the Banking Act 2009 provides for provisions of that Act about bank insolvency to be "insolvency law" for the purposes of this section.]

[(14) Section 165 of the Banking Act 2009 provides for provisions of that Act about bank administration to be "insolvency law" for the purposes of this section.]

NOTES

Sub-s (10): words in square brackets in paras (a), (b) inserted or substituted by the Insolvency Act 2000, s 8, Sch 4, Pt II, para 16(1), (3), as from 2 April 2001; words in first pair of square brackets in para (c) substituted by the Insolvency (Northern Ireland) Order 1989, SI 1989/2405, art 381(2), Sch 9, Pt II, para 41(a); words in second pair of square brackets in para (c) added by the Companies (Northern Ireland) Order 1989, SI 1989/2404, arts 25(2), 36, Sch 4, Pt I, para 1, and substituted by the Company Directors Disqualification (Northern Ireland) Order 2002, SI 2002/3150, art 26(2), Sch 3, para 2.

Sub-s (12): added by SI 1989/2405, art 381(2), Sch 9, Pt II, para 41(b), but not yet in operation so far as amends sub-s (11)(b) to give the Department of Economic Development in Northern Ireland power to make an order designating relevant countries for the purposes of this section as it applies to Northern Ireland.

Sub-ss (13), (14): added by the Banking Act 2009, ss 129, 165, as from 21 February 2009.

Criminal Law Act 1977, s 38: repealed by the Criminal Justice and Public Order Act 1994, s 168(3), Sch 11.

Orders: the Co-operation of Insolvency Courts (Designation of Relevant Countries and Territories) Order 1986, SI 1986/2123 designating the following countries and territories for the purposes of this section: Anguilla; Australia; the Bahamas; Bermuda; Botswana; Canada; Cayman Islands; Falkland Islands; Gibraltar; Hong Kong; Republic of Ireland; Montserrat; New Zealand; St Helena; Turks and Caicos Islands; Tuvalu; Virgin Islands; the Co-operation of Insolvency Courts (Designation of Relevant Countries) Order 1996, SI 1996/253 designating Malaysia and the Republic of South Africa as relevant countries for the purposes of this section; the Co-operation of Insolvency Courts (Designation of Relevant Country) Order 1998, SI 1998/2766 designating Brunei Darussalam as a relevant country for the purposes of this section.

[9.388]
430   Provision introducing Schedule of punishments
(1)   Schedule 10 to this Act has effect with respect to the way in which offences under this Act are punishable on conviction.
(2)   In relation to an offence under a provision of this Act specified in the first column of the Schedule (the general nature of the offence being described in the second column), the third column shows whether the offence is punishable on conviction on indictment, or on summary conviction, or either in the one way or the other.
(3)   The fourth column of the Schedule shows, in relation to an offence, the maximum punishment by way of fine or imprisonment under this Act which may be imposed on a person convicted of the offence in the way specified in relation to it in the third column (that is to say, on indictment or summarily), a reference to a period of years or months being to a term of imprisonment of that duration.
(4)   The fifth column shows (in relation to an offence for which there is an entry in that column) that a person convicted of the offence after continued contravention is liable to a daily default fine; that is to say, he is liable on a second or subsequent conviction of the offence to the fine specified in that column for each day on which the contravention is continued (instead of the penalty specified for the offence in the fourth column of the Schedule).
(5)   For the purpose of any enactment in this Act whereby an officer of a company who is in default is liable to a fine or penalty, the expression "officer who is in default" means any officer of the company who knowingly and wilfully authorises or permits the default, refusal or contravention mentioned in the enactment.

[9.389]
431   Summary proceedings
(1)   Summary proceedings for any offence under any of Parts I to VII of this Act may (without prejudice to any jurisdiction exercisable apart from this subsection) be taken against a body corporate at any place at which the body has a place of business, and against any other person at any place at which he is for the time being.
(2)   Notwithstanding anything in section 127(1) of the Magistrates' Courts Act 1980, an information relating to such an offence which is triable by a magistrates' court in England and Wales may be so tried if it is laid at any time within 3 years after the commission of the offence and within 12 months after the date on which evidence sufficient in the opinion of the Director of Public Prosecutions or the Secretary of State (as the case may be) to justify the proceedings comes to his knowledge.
(3)   Summary proceedings in Scotland for such an offence shall not be commenced after the expiration of 3 years from the commission of the offence.
   Subject to this (and notwithstanding anything in [section 136 of the Criminal Procedure (Scotland) Act 1995]), such proceedings may (in Scotland) be commenced at any time within 12 months after the date on which evidence sufficient in the Lord Advocate's opinion to justify the proceedings came to his knowledge or, where such evidence was reported to him by the Secretary of State, within 12 months after the date on which it came to the knowledge of the latter; and subsection (3) of that section applies for the purpose of this subsection as it applies for the purpose of that section.
(4)   For purposes of this section, a certificate of the Director of Public Prosecutions, the Lord Advocate or the Secretary of State (as the case may be) as to the date on which such evidence as is referred to above came to his knowledge is conclusive evidence.

NOTES
   Sub-s (3): words in square brackets substituted by the Criminal Procedure (Consequential Provisions) (Scotland) Act 1995, s 5, Sch 4, para 61, as from 1 April 1996.

[9.390]
432   Offences by bodies corporate
(1)   This section applies to offences under this Act other than those excepted by subsection (4).
(2)   Where a body corporate is guilty of an offence to which this section applies and the offence is proved to have been committed with the consent or connivance of, or to be attributable to any neglect on the part of, any director, manager, secretary or other similar officer of the body corporate or any person who was purporting to act in any such capacity he, as well as the body corporate, is guilty of the offence and liable to be proceeded against and punished accordingly.
(3)   Where the affairs of a body corporate are managed by its members, subsection (2) applies in relation to the acts and defaults of a member in connection with his functions of management as if he were a director of the body corporate.
(4)   The offences excepted from this section are those under sections 30, 39, 51, 53, 54, 62, 64, 66, 85, 89, 164, 188, 201, 206, 207, 208, 209, 210 and 211 [and those under paragraphs 16(2), 17(3)(a), 18(3)(a), 19(3)(a), 22(1) and 23(1)(a) of Schedule A1].

NOTES

Sub-s (4): words in square brackets added by the Insolvency Act 2000, s 1, Sch 1, paras 1, 11, as from 1 January 2003.

[9.391]

433 Admissibility in evidence of statements of affairs, etc

[(1)] In any proceedings (whether or not under this Act)—

(a) a statement of affairs prepared for the purposes of any provision of this Act which is derived from the Insolvency Act 1985,

[(aa) a statement made in pursuance of a requirement imposed by or under Part 2 of the Banking Act 2009 (bank insolvency),]

[(ab) a statement made in pursuance of a requirement imposed by or under Part 3 of that Act (bank administration),] and

(b) any other statement made in pursuance of a requirement imposed by or under any such provision or by or under rules made under this Act,

may be used in evidence against any person making or concurring in making the statement.

[(2) However, in criminal proceedings in which any such person is charged with an offence to which this subsection applies—

(a) no evidence relating to the statement may be adduced, and

(b) no question relating to it may be asked,

by or on behalf of the prosecution, unless evidence relating to it is adduced, or a question relating to it is asked, in the proceedings by or on behalf of that person.

(3) Subsection (2) applies to any offence other than—

(a) an offence under section 22(6), 47(6), 48(8), 66(6), 67(8), 95(8), 98(6), 99(3)(a), 131(7), 192(2), 208(1)(a) or (d) or (2), 210, 235(5), 353(1), 354(1)(b) or (3) or 356(1) or (2)(a) or (b) or paragraph 4(3)(a) of Schedule 7;

(b) an offence which is—

(i) created by rules made under this Act, and

(ii) designated for the purposes of this subsection by such rules or by regulations made by the Secretary of State;

(c) an offence which is—

(i) created by regulations made under any such rules, and

(ii) designated for the purposes of this subsection by such regulations;

(d) an offence under section 1, 2 or 5 of the Perjury Act 1911 (false statements made on oath or made otherwise than on oath); or

(e) an offence under section 44(1) or (2) of the Criminal Law (Consolidation) (Scotland) Act 1995 (false statements made on oath or otherwise than on oath).

(4) Regulations under subsection (3)(b)(ii) shall be made by statutory instrument and, after being made, shall be laid before each House of Parliament.]

NOTES

Sub-s (1): numbered as such by the Youth Justice and Criminal Evidence Act 1999, s 59, Sch 3, para 7, as from 14 April 2000 (in relation to England and Wales), and 1 January 2001 (in relation to Scotland); paras (aa), (ab) inserted by the Banking Act 2009, ss 128, 162, as from 21 February 2009.

Sub-ss (2)–(4): added by the Youth Justice and Criminal Evidence Act 1999, s 59, Sch 3, para 7, as from 14 April 2000 (in relation to England and Wales), and 1 January 2001 (in relation to Scotland).

[9.392]

434 Crown application

For the avoidance of doubt it is hereby declared that provisions of this Act which derive from the Insolvency Act 1985 bind the Crown so far as affecting or relating to the following matters, namely—

(a) remedies against, or against the property of, companies or individuals;

(b) priorities of debts;

(c) transactions at an undervalue or preferences;

(d) voluntary arrangements approved under Part I or Part VIII, and

(e) discharge from bankruptcy.

[PART 17A
SUPPLEMENTARY PROVISIONS

[9.393]

434A Introductory

The provisions of this Part have effect for the purposes of—

(a) the First Group of Parts, and

(b) sections 411, 413, 414, 416 and 417 in Part 15.]

NOTES

Commencement: 6 April 2008.

Inserted, together with the preceding heading and ss 434B, 434C, by the Companies Act 2006 (Consequential Amendments etc) Order 2008, SI 2008/948, art 3(1), Sch 1, Pt 2, para 105, as from 6 April 2008.

[9.394]
[434B   Representation of corporations at meetings
(1)   If a corporation is a creditor or debenture-holder, it may by resolution of its directors or other governing body authorise a person or persons to act as its representative or representatives—
  (a)   at any meeting of the creditors of a company held in pursuance of this Act or of rules made under it, or
  (b)   at any meeting of a company held in pursuance of the provisions contained in a debenture or trust deed.
(2)   Where the corporation authorises only one person, that person is entitled to exercise the same powers on behalf of the corporation as the corporation could exercise if it were an individual creditor or debenture-holder.
(3)   Where the corporation authorises more than one person, any one of them is entitled to exercise the same powers on behalf of the corporation as the corporation could exercise if it were an individual creditor or debenture-holder.
(4)   Where the corporation authorises more than one person and more than one of them purport to exercise a power under subsection (3)—
  (a)   if they purport to exercise the power in the same way, the power is treated as exercised in that way;
  (b)   if they do not purport to exercise the power in the same way, the power is treated as not exercised.]

NOTES
Commencement: 6 April 2008.
Inserted as noted to s 434A at **[9.393]**.

[9.395]
[434C   Legal professional privilege
In proceedings against a person for an offence under this Act nothing in this Act is to be taken to require any person to disclose any information that he is entitled to refuse to disclose on grounds of legal professional privilege (in Scotland, confidentiality of communications).]

NOTES
Commencement: 6 April 2008.
Inserted as noted to s 434A at **[9.393]**.

[9.396]
434D   Enforcement of company's filing obligations
(1)   This section applies where a company has made default in complying with any obligation under this Act—
  (a)   to deliver a document to the registrar, or
  (b)   to give notice to the registrar of any matter.
(2)   The registrar, or any member or creditor of the company, may give notice to the company requiring it to comply with the obligation.
(3)   If the company fails to make good the default within 14 days after service of the notice, the registrar, or any member or creditor of the company, may apply to the court for an order directing the company, and any specified officer of it, to make good the default within a specified time.
(4)   The court's order may provide that all costs (in Scotland, expenses) of or incidental to the application are to be borne by the company or by any officers of it responsible for the default.
(5)   This section does not affect the operation of any enactment imposing penalties on a company or its officers in respect of any such default.]

NOTES
Commencement: 1 October 2009.
Inserted, together with s 434E, by the Companies Act 2006 (Consequential Amendments, Transitional Provisions and Savings) Order 2009, SI 2009/1941, art 2(1), Sch 1, para 81, as from 1 October 2009 (for transitional provisions see the note to s 7A at **[9.103]**).

[9.397]
[434E   Application of filing obligations to overseas companies
The provisions of this Act requiring documents to be forwarded or delivered to, or filed with, the registrar of companies apply in relation to an overseas company that is required to register particulars under section 1046 of the Companies Act 2006 as they apply in relation to a company registered under that Act in England and Wales or Scotland.]

NOTES
Commencement: 1 October 2009.
Inserted, subject to transitional provisions, as noted to s 434D at **[9.396]**.

PART XVIII
INTERPRETATION

[9.398]

435 Meaning of "associate"

(1) For the purposes of this Act any question whether a person is an associate of another person is to be determined in accordance with the following provisions of this section (any provision that a person is an associate of another person being taken to mean that they are associates of each other).

[(2) A person is an associate of an individual if that person is—
  (a) the individual's husband or wife or civil partner,
  (b) a relative of—
    (i) the individual, or
    (ii) the individual's husband or wife or civil partner, or
  (c) the husband or wife or civil partner of a relative of—
    (i) the individual, or
    (ii) the individual's husband or wife or civil partner.]

(3) A person is an associate of any person with whom he is in partnership, and of the husband or wife [or civil partner] or a relative of any individual with whom he is in partnership; and a Scottish firm is an associate of any person who is a member of the firm.

(4) A person is an associate of any person whom he employs or by whom he is employed.

(5) A person in his capacity as trustee of a trust other than—
  (a) a trust arising under any of the second Group of Parts or the Bankruptcy (Scotland) Act 1985, or
  (b) a pension scheme or an employees' share scheme . . . ,
is an associate of another person if the beneficiaries of the trust include, or the terms of the trust confer a power that may be exercised for the benefit of, that other person or an associate of that other person.

(6) A company is an associate of another company—
  (a) if the same person has control of both, or a person has control of one and persons who are his associates, or he and persons who are his associates, have control of the other, or
  (b) if a group of two or more persons has control of each company, and the groups either consist of the same persons or could be regarded as consisting of the same persons by treating (in one or more cases) a member of either group as replaced by a person of whom he is an associate.

(7) A company is an associate of another person if that person has control of it or if that person and persons who are his associates together have control of it.

(8) For the purposes of this section a person is a relative of an individual if he is that individual's brother, sister, uncle, aunt, nephew, niece, lineal ancestor or lineal descendant, treating—
  (a) any relationship of the half blood as a relationship of the whole blood and the stepchild or adopted child of any person as his child, and
  (b) an illegitimate child as the legitimate child of his mother and reputed father;
and references in this section to a husband or wife include a former husband or wife and a reputed husband or wife [and references to a civil partner include a former civil partner] [and a reputed civil partner].

(9) For the purposes of this section any director or other officer of a company is to be treated as employed by that company.

(10) For the purposes of this section a person is to be taken as having control of a company if—
  (a) the directors of the company or of another company which has control of it (or any of them) are accustomed to act in accordance with his directions or instructions, or
  (b) he is entitled to exercise, or control the exercise of, one third or more of the voting power at any general meeting of the company or of another company which has control of it;
and where two or more persons together satisfy either of the above conditions, they are to be taken as having control of the company.

(11) In this section "company" includes any body corporate (whether incorporated in Great Britain or elsewhere); and references to directors and other officers of a company and to voting power at any general meeting of a company have effect with any necessary modifications.

NOTES

Sub-s (2): substituted by the Civil Partnership Act 2004, s 261(1), Sch 27, para 122(1), (2), as from 5 December 2005.

Sub-s (3): words in square brackets inserted by the Civil Partnership Act 2004, s 261(1), Sch 27, para 122(1), (3), as from 5 December 2005.

Sub-s (5): words omitted repealed by the Companies Act 2006 (Consequential Amendments, Transitional Provisions and Savings) Order 2009, SI 2009/1941, art 2(1), Sch 1, para 82(1), (2), as from 1 October 2009 (for transitional provisions see the note to s 7A at **[9.103]**).

Sub-s (8): words in first pair of square brackets inserted by the Civil Partnership Act 2004, s 261(1), Sch 27, para 122(1), (4), as from 5 December 2005; words in second pair of square brackets inserted by the Civil Partnership Act 2004 (Overseas Relationships and Consequential, etc Amendments) Order 2005, SI 2005/3129, art 4(4), Sch 4, para 8, as from 5 December 2005.

Stepchild: this includes relationships arising through civil partnerships; see the Civil Partnership Act 2004, ss 246, 247, Sch 21.

[9.399]
436 Expressions used generally

[(1)] In this Act, except in so far as the context otherwise requires (and subject to Parts VII and XI)—

"the appointed day" means the day on which this Act comes into force under section 443;

"associate" has the meaning given by section 435;

["body corporate" includes a body incorporated outside Great Britain, but does not include—
   (a) a corporation sole, or
   (b) a partnership that, whether or not a legal person, is not regarded as a body corporate under the law by which it is governed;]

"business" includes a trade or profession;

. . .

["the Companies Acts" means the Companies Acts (as defined in section 2 of the Companies Act 2006) as they have effect in Great Britain;]

"conditional sale agreement" and "hire-purchase agreement" have the same meanings as in the Consumer Credit Act 1974;

["distress" includes use of the procedure in Schedule 12 to the Tribunals, Courts and Enforcement Act 2007, and references to levying distress, seizing goods and related expressions shall be construed accordingly;]

["the EC Regulation" means Council Regulation (EC) No 1346/2000;]

["EEA State" means a state that is a Contracting Party to the Agreement on the European Economic Area signed at Oporto on 2nd May 1992 as adjusted by the Protocol signed at Brussels on 17th March 1993;]

["employees' share scheme" means a scheme for encouraging or facilitating the holding of shares in or debentures of a company by or for the benefit of—
   (a) the bona fide employees or former employees of—
      (i) the company,
      (ii) any subsidiary of the company, or
      (iii) the company's holding company or any subsidiary of the company's holding company, or
   (b) the spouses, civil partners, surviving spouses, surviving civil partners, or minor children or step-children of such employees or former employees.]

"modifications" includes additions, alterations and omissions and cognate expressions shall be construed accordingly;

"property" includes money, goods, things in action, land and every description of property wherever situated and also obligations and every description of interest, whether present or future or vested or contingent, arising out of, or incidental to, property;

"records" includes computer records and other non-documentary records;

"subordinate legislation" has the same meaning as in the Interpretation Act 1978; and

"transaction" includes a gift, agreement or arrangement, and references to entering into a transaction shall be construed accordingly.

[(2) The following expressions have the same meaning in this Act as in the Companies Acts—

"articles", in relation to a company (see section 18 of the Companies Act 2006);

"debenture" (see section 738 of that Act);

"holding company" (see sections 1159 and 1160 of, and Schedule 6 to, that Act);

"the Joint Stock Companies Acts" (see section 1171 of that Act);

"overseas company" (see section 1044 of that Act);

"paid up" (see section 583 of that Act);

"private company" and "public company" (see section 4 of that Act);

"registrar of companies" (see section 1060 of that Act);

"share" (see section 540 of that Act);

"subsidiary" (see sections 1159 and 1160 of, and Schedule 6 to, that Act).]

NOTES

Sub-s (1) numbered as such, definitions "body corporate" and "employees' share scheme" inserted, definition "the Companies Act" (omitted) repealed, and sub-s (2) added, by the Companies Act 2006 (Consequential Amendments, Transitional Provisions and Savings) Order 2009, SI 2009/1941, art 2(1), Sch 1, para 82(1), (3), as from 1 October 2009 (for transitional provisions see the note to s 7A at **[9.103]**).

Definition "distress" inserted by the Tribunals, Courts and Enforcement Act 2007, s 62(3), Sch 13, para 85, as from a day to be appointed.

Definition "the EC Regulation" inserted by the Insolvency Act 1986 (Amendment) Regulations 2002, SI 2002/1037, regs 2, 4, as from 3 May 2002.

Definition "EEA State" inserted by the Insolvency Act 1986 (Amendment) Regulations 2005, SI 2005/879, reg 2(1), (3), as from 13 April 2005, except in relation to any voluntary arrangement under Part I, or the appointment of an administrator under Part II, that took effect before that date.

[9.400]
[436A Proceedings under EC Regulation: modified definition of property
In the application of this Act to proceedings by virtue of Article 3 of the EC Regulation, a reference to property is a reference to property which may be dealt with in the proceedings.]

NOTES
Inserted by the Insolvency Act 1986 (Amendment) (No 2) Regulations 2002, SI 2002/1240, regs 3, 18, as from 31 May 2002.

[9.401]
[436B References to things in writing
(1) A reference in this Act to a thing in writing includes that thing in electronic form.
(2) Subsection (1) does not apply to the following provisions—
  (a) section 53 (mode of appointment by holder of charge),
  (b) section 67(2) (report by receiver),
  (c) section 70(4) (reference to instrument creating a charge),
  (d) section 111(2) (dissent from arrangement under s 110),
  (e) in the case of a winding up of a company registered in Scotland, section 111(4),
  (f) section 123(1) (definition of inability to pay debts),
  (g) section 198(3) (duties of sheriff principal as regards examination),
  (h) section 222(1) (inability to pay debts: unpaid creditor for £750 or more), and
  (i) section 223 (inability to pay debts: debt remaining unsatisfied after action brought).]

NOTES
Commencement: 6 April 2010.
Inserted by the Legislative Reform (Insolvency) (Miscellaneous Provisions) Order 2010, SI 2010/18, arts 2, 4(1), as from 6 April 2010.

PART XIX
FINAL PROVISIONS

[9.402]
440 Extent (Scotland)
(1) Subject to the next subsection, provisions of this Act contained in the first Group of Parts extend to Scotland except where otherwise stated.
(2) The following provisions of this Act do not extend to Scotland—
  (a) In the first Group of Parts—
    section 43;
    sections 238 to 241; and
    section 246;
  (b) the second Group of Parts;
  (c) in the third Group of Parts—
    sections 399 to 402,
    sections 412, 413, 415, [415A(3),] 418, 420 and 421,
    sections 423 to 425, and
    section 429(1) and (2); and
  (d) in the Schedules—
    Parts II and III of Schedule 11; and
    Schedules 12 and 14 so far as they repeal or amend enactments which extend to England
    and Wales only.

NOTES
Sub-s (2): figure in square brackets inserted by the Enterprise Act 2002, s 270(4), as from 18 December 2003; for the words in italics there are substituted the words "section 429(1) to (2A)" by the Tribunals, Courts and Enforcement Act 2007, s 106, Sch 16, para 4, as from a day to be appointed (except in relation to any case in which an administration order was made, or an application for such an order was made, before the day on which s 106 comes into force).

[9.403]
442 Extent (other territories)
Her Majesty may, by Order in Council, direct that such of the provisions of this Act as are specified in the Order, being provisions formerly contained in the Insolvency Act 1985, shall extend to any of the Channel Islands or any colony with such modifications as may be so specified.

NOTES
Orders: the Insolvency Act 1986 (Guernsey) Order 1989, SI 1989/2409.

[9.404]
443 Commencement
This Act comes into force on the day appointed under section 236(2) of the Insolvency Act 1985 for the coming into force of Part III of that Act (individual insolvency and bankruptcy), immediately after that Part of that Act comes into force for England and Wales.

NOTES
See the note "Commencement" at the beginning of this Act.

[9.405]
444 Citation
This Act may be cited as the Insolvency Act 1986.

SCHEDULES

[SCHEDULE A1]
MORATORIUM WHERE DIRECTORS PROPOSE VOLUNTARY ARRANGEMENT

Section 1A

PART I
INTRODUCTORY

Interpretation

[9.406]
1. In this Schedule—
"the beginning of the moratorium" has the meaning given by paragraph 8(1),
"the date of filing" means the date on which the documents for the time being referred to in
paragraph 7(1) are filed or lodged with the court,
"hire-purchase agreement" includes a conditional sale agreement, a chattel leasing agreement
and a retention of title agreement,
"market contract" and "market charge" have the meanings given by Part VII of the Companies
Act 1989,
. . .
"moratorium" means a moratorium under section 1A,
"the nominee" includes any person for the time being carrying out the functions of a nominee
under this Schedule,
"the settlement finality regulations" means the Financial Markets and Insolvency (Settlement
Finality) Regulations 1999,
"system-charge" has the meaning given by the Financial Markets and Insolvency
Regulations 1996.

Eligible companies

2. (1) A company is eligible for a moratorium if it meets the requirements of paragraph 3,
unless—
    (a)   it is excluded from being eligible by virtue of paragraph 4, or
    (b)   it falls within sub-paragraph (2).
(2) A company falls within this sub-paragraph if—
    [(a) it effects or carries out contracts of insurance, but is not exempt from the general
          prohibition, within the meaning of section 19 of the Financial Services and Markets
          Act 2000, in relation to that activity,
    (b) it has permission under Part IV of that Act to accept deposits,
    (bb) it has a liability in respect of a deposit which it accepted in accordance with the Banking
          Act 1979 (c 37) or 1987 (c 22),]
    (c) it is a party to a market contract . . . or any of its property is subject to a market charge
          . . . or a system-charge, or
    (d) it is a participant (within the meaning of the settlement finality regulations) or any of its
          property is subject to a collateral security charge (within the meaning of those regulations).
[(3) Paragraphs (a), (b) and (bb) of sub-paragraph (2) must be read with—
    (a) section 22 of the Financial Services and Markets Act 2000;
    (b) any relevant order under that section; and
    (c) Schedule 2 to that Act.]

3. (1) A company meets the requirements of this paragraph if the qualifying conditions are met—
    (a) in the year ending with the date of filing, or
    (b) in the financial year of the company which ended last before that date.
(2) For the purposes of sub-paragraph (1)—
    (a) the qualifying conditions are met by a company in a period if, in that period, it satisfies two
          or more of the requirements for being a small company specified for the time being in
          [section 382(3) of the Companies Act 2006], and
    (b) a company's financial year is to be determined in accordance with that Act.
(3) [Section 382(4), (5) and (6)] of that Act apply for the purposes of this paragraph as they apply
for the purposes of that section.

[(4)   A company does not meet the requirements of this paragraph if it is a [parent company] of a group of companies which does not qualify as a small group or a medium-sized group [in relation to] the financial year of the company which ended last before the date of filing.

[(5)   For the purposes of sub-paragraph (4)—
  (a)   "group" has the same meaning as in Part 15 of the Companies Act 2006 (see section 474(1) of that Act); and
  (b)   a group qualifies as small in relation to a financial year if it so qualifies under section 383(2) to (7) of that Act, and qualifies as medium-sized in relation to a financial year if it so qualifies under section 466(2) to (7) of that Act.]]

[(6)   Expressions used in this paragraph that are defined expressions in Part 15 of the Companies Act 2006 (accounts and reports) have the same meaning in this paragraph as in that Part.]

4. (1)   A company is excluded from being eligible for a moratorium if, on the date of filing—
  [(a)   the company is in administration,]
  (b)   the company is being wound up,
  (c)   there is an administrative receiver of the company,
  (d)   a voluntary arrangement has effect in relation to the company,
  (e)   there is a provisional liquidator of the company,
  (f)   a moratorium has been in force for the company at any time during the period of 12 months ending with the date of filing and—
    (i)   no voluntary arrangement had effect at the time at which the moratorium came to an end, or
    (ii)   a voluntary arrangement which had effect at any time in that period has come to an end prematurely,
  [(fa)   an administrator appointed under paragraph 22 of Schedule B1 has held office in the period of 12 months ending with the date of filing,] or
  (g)   a voluntary arrangement in relation to the company which had effect in pursuance of a proposal under section 1(3) has come to an end prematurely and, during the period of 12 months ending with the date of filing, an order under section 5(3)(a) has been made.

(2)   Sub-paragraph (1)(b) does not apply to a company which, by reason of a winding-up order made after the date of filing, is treated as being wound up on that date.

[Capital market arrangement

4A.   A company is also excluded from being eligible for a moratorium if, on the date of filing, it is a party to an agreement which is or forms part of a capital market arrangement under which—
  (i)   a party has incurred, or when the agreement was entered into was expected to incur, a debt of at least £10 million under the arrangement, and
  (ii)   the arrangement involves the issue of a capital market investment.

Public private partnership

4B.   A company is also excluded from being eligible for a moratorium if, on the date of filing, it is a project company of a project which—
  (i)   is a public-private partnership project, and
  (ii)   includes step-in rights.

Liability under an arrangement

4C. (1)   A company is also excluded from being eligible for a moratorium if, on the date of filing, it has incurred a liability under an agreement of £10 million or more.

(2)   Where the liability in sub-paragraph (1) is a contingent liability under or by virtue of a guarantee or an indemnity or security provided on behalf of another person, the amount of that liability is the full amount of the liability in relation to which the guarantee, indemnity or security is provided.

(3)   In this paragraph—
  (a)   the reference to "liability" includes a present or future liability whether, in either case, it is certain or contingent,
  (b)   the reference to "liability" includes a reference to a liability to be paid wholly or partly in foreign currency (in which case the sterling equivalent shall be calculated as at the time when the liability is incurred).

Interpretation of capital market arrangement

4D. (1)   For the purposes of paragraph 4A an arrangement is a capital market arrangement if—
  (a)   it involves a grant of security to a person holding it as trustee for a person who holds a capital market investment issued by a party to the arrangement, or
  (b)   at least one party guarantees the performance of obligations of another party, or
  (c)   at least one party provides security in respect of the performance of obligations of another party, or

(d)   the arrangement involves an investment of a kind described in articles 83 to 85 of the Financial Services and Markets Act 2000 (Regulated Activities) Order 2001 (SI 2001/544) (options, futures and contracts for differences).

(2)   For the purposes of sub-paragraph (1)—

(a)   a reference to holding as trustee includes a reference to holding as nominee or agent,

(b)   a reference to holding for a person who holds a capital market investment includes a reference to holding for a number of persons at least one of whom holds a capital market investment, and

(c)   a person holds a capital market investment if he has a legal or beneficial interest in it.

(3)   In paragraph 4A, 4C, 4J and this paragraph—

"agreement" includes an agreement or undertaking effected by—

   (a)   contract,

   (b)   deed, or

   (c)   any other instrument intended to have effect in accordance with the law of England and Wales, Scotland or another jurisdiction, and

"party" to an arrangement includes a party to an agreement which—

   (a)   forms part of the arrangement,

   (b)   provides for the raising of finance as part of the arrangement, or

   (c)   is necessary for the purposes of implementing the arrangement.

Capital market investment

4E.   (1)   For the purposes of paragraphs 4A and 4D, an investment is a capital market investment if—

(a)   it is within article 77 [or 77A] of the Financial Services and Markets Act 2000 (Regulated Activities) Order 2001 (SI 2001/544) (debt instruments) and

(b)   it is rated, listed or traded or designed to be rated, listed or traded.

(2)   In sub-paragraph (1)—

"listed" means admitted to the official list within the meaning given by section 103(1) of the Financial Services and Markets Act 2000 (c 8) (interpretation),

"rated" means rated for the purposes of investment by an internationally recognised rating agency,

"traded" means admitted to trading on a market established under the rules of a recognised investment exchange or on a foreign market.

(3)   In sub-paragraph (2)—

"foreign market" has the same meaning as "relevant market" in article 67(2) of the Financial Services and Markets Act 2000 (Financial Promotion) Order 2001 (SI 2001/1335) (foreign markets),

"recognised investment exchange" has the meaning given by section 285 of the Financial Services and Markets Act 2000 (recognised investment exchange).

4F.   (1)   For the purposes of paragraphs 4A and 4D an investment is also a capital market investment if it consists of a bond or commercial paper issued to one or more of the following—

(a)   an investment professional within the meaning of article 19(5) of the Financial Services and Markets Act 2000 (Financial Promotion) Order 2001,

(b)   a person who is, when the agreement mentioned in paragraph 4A is entered into, a certified high net worth individual in relation to a communication within the meaning of article 48(2) of that order,

(c)   a person to whom article 49(2) of that order applies (high net worth company, &c.),

(d)   a person who is, when the agreement mentioned in paragraph 4A is entered into, a certified sophisticated investor in relation to a communication within the meaning of article 50(1) of that order, and

(e)   a person in a State other than the United Kingdom who under the law of that State is not prohibited from investing in bonds or commercial paper.

(2)   For the purposes of sub-paragraph (1)—

(a)   in applying article 19(5) of the Financial Services and Markets Act 2000 (Financial Promotion) Order 2001 for the purposes of sub-paragraph (1)(a)—

   (i)   in article 19(5)(b), ignore the words after "exempt person",

   (ii)   in article 19(5)(c)(i), for the words from "the controlled activity" to the end substitute "a controlled activity", and

   (iii)   in article 19(5)(e) ignore the words from "where the communication" to the end, and

(b)   in applying article 49(2) of that order for the purposes of sub-paragraph (1)(c), ignore article 49(2)(e).

(3)   In sub-paragraph (1)—

"bond" shall be construed in accordance with article 77 of the Financial Services and Markets Act 2000 (Regulated Activities) Order 2001 (SI 2001/544)[, and includes any instrument falling within article 77A of that Order], and

"commercial paper" has the meaning given by article 9(3) of that order.

Debt

4G. The debt of at least £10 million referred to in paragraph 4A—

    (a)   may be incurred at any time during the life of the capital market arrangement, and

    (b)   may be expressed wholly or partly in a foreign currency (in which case the sterling equivalent shall be calculated as at the time when the arrangement is entered into).

Interpretation of project company

4H. (1) For the purposes of paragraph 4B a company is a "project company" of a project if—

    (a)   it holds property for the purpose of the project,

    (b)   it has sole or principal responsibility under an agreement for carrying out all or part of the project,

    (c)   it is one of a number of companies which together carry out the project,

    (d)   it has the purpose of supplying finance to enable the project to be carried out, or

    (e)   it is the holding company of a company within any of paragraphs (a) to (d).

(2) But a company is not a "project company" of a project if—

    (a)   it performs a function within sub-paragraph (1)(a) to (d) or is within sub-paragraph (1)(e), but

    (b)   it also performs a function which is not—

        (i)   within sub-paragraph (1)(a) to (d),

        (ii)   related to a function within sub-paragraph (1)(a) to (d), or

        (iii)   related to the project.

(3) For the purposes of this paragraph a company carries out all or part of a project whether or not it acts wholly or partly through agents.

Public-private partnership project

4I. (1) In paragraph 4B "public-private partnership project" means a project—

    (a)   the resources for which are provided partly by one or more public bodies and partly by one or more private persons, or

    (b)   which is designed wholly or mainly for the purpose of assisting a public body to discharge a function.

(2) In sub-paragraph (1) "resources" includes—

    (a)   funds (including payment for the provision of services or facilities),

    (b)   assets,

    (c)   professional skill,

    (d)   the grant of a concession or franchise, and

    (e)   any other commercial resource.

(3) In sub-paragraph (1) "public body" means—

    (a)   a body which exercises public functions,

    (b)   a body specified for the purposes of this paragraph by the Secretary of State, and

    (c)   a body within a class specified for the purposes of this paragraph by the Secretary of State.

(4) A specification under sub-paragraph (3) may be—

    (a)   general, or

    (b)   for the purpose of the application of paragraph 4B to a specified case.

Step-in rights

4J. (1) For the purposes of paragraph 4B a project has "step-in rights" if a person who provides finance in connection with the project has a conditional entitlement under an agreement to—

    (i)   assume sole or principal responsibility under an agreement for carrying out all or part of the project, or

    (ii)   make arrangements for carrying out all or part of the project.

(2) In sub-paragraph (1) a reference to the provision of finance includes a reference to the provision of an indemnity.

"Person"

4K. For the purposes of paragraphs 4A to 4J, a reference to a person includes a reference to a partnership or another unincorporated group of persons.]

5. The Secretary of State may by regulations modify the qualifications for eligibility of a company for a moratorium.]

NOTES

Inserted by the Insolvency Act 2000, s 1, Sch 1, paras 1, 4.

Para 1: definitions omitted repealed by virtue of the Financial Services and Markets Act 2000 (Consequential Amendments) Order 2002, SI 2002/1555, art 28(1), (2), as from 3 July 2002.

Para 2: sub-paras (2)(a)–(bb) substituted for original sub-paras (2)(a), (b), words omitted from sub-para (2)(c) repealed, and sub-para (3) added, by virtue of SI 2002/1555, arts 28(1), (3), 29, as from 3 July 2002.

Para 3 is amended as follows:

Words in square brackets in sub-paras (2), (3) substituted by the Companies Act 2006 (Consequential Amendments etc) Order 2008, SI 2008/948, art 3(1), Sch 1, Pt 2, para 99(1)–(3), as from 6 April 2008; for transitional provisions and savings see the note below.

Sub-paras (4), (5) originally added by the Insolvency Act 1986 (Amendment) (No 3) Regulations 2002, SI 2002/1990, reg 3(1), (2), as from 1 January 2003 (being the day on which the Insolvency Act 2000, s 1 comes into force for the purpose of giving effect to para 4 of this Schedule; see reg 2 of the 2002 Regulations).

Words in square brackets in sub-para (4) substituted, and the whole of sub-para (5) substituted, by SI 2008/948, art 3(1), Sch 1, Pt 2, para 99(1), (4), (5), as from 6 April 2008; for transitional provisions and savings see the note below.

Sub-para (6) added by the Companies Act 2006 (Consequential Amendments, Transitional Provisions and Savings) Order 2009, SI 2009/1941, art 2(1), Sch 1, para 71(1), (4)(a), as from 1 October 2009 (for transitional provisions see the note to s 7A at **[9.103]**).

Para 4: sub-para (1)(a) substituted, and sub-para (1)(fa) inserted, by the Enterprise Act 2002, s 248(3), Sch 17, paras 9, 37(1), (2), as from 15 September 2003 (for savings and transitional provisions, see the note to s 8 at **[9.105]**).

Paras 4A–4K: inserted by SI 2002/1990, reg 3(1), (3), as from 1 January 2003 (being the day on which the Insolvency Act 2000, s 1 comes into force for the purpose of giving effect to para 4 of this Schedule; see reg 2 of the 2002 Regulations); words in square brackets in paras 4E, 4F inserted by the Financial Services and Markets Act 2000 (Regulated Activities) (Amendment) Order 2010, SI 2010/86, art 4, Schedule, para 1, as from 24 February 2010.

Transitional provisions and savings: the Companies Act 2006 (Consequential Amendments etc) Order 2008, SI 2008/948, Sch 1, Pt 2, para 99(6) provides that the amendments made by para 99 as noted above apply only in relation to periods, or parts of periods, falling on or after 6 April 2008. See also art 6(4) of the 2008 Order (at **[4.280]**) which provides that where by virtue of any transitional provision, a provision of the Companies Act 2006 has effect only (a) on or after a specified date, or (b) in relation to matters occurring or arising on or after a specified date, any amendment substituting or inserting a reference to that provision has effect correspondingly).

Modification: a reference to commercial paper in this Schedule includes a reference to uncertificated units of an eligible debt security where the issue of the units corresponds, in accordance with the current terms of issue of the security, to the issue of commercial paper within the meaning of the Financial Services and Markets Act 2000 (Regulated Activities) Order 2001, SI 2001/544, art 9(3); see the Uncertificated Securities (Amendment) (Eligible Debt Securities) Regulations 2003, SI 2003/1633, reg 15, Sch 2, para 7.

Banking Act 1987, Insurance Companies Act 1982: repealed by the Financial Services and Markets Act 2000 (Consequential Amendments and Repeals) Order 2001, SI 2001/3649, art 3(1)(b), (d), as from 1 December 2001.

Financial Services and Markets Act 2000 (Financial Promotion) Order 2001, SI 2001/1335: revoked and replaced by the Financial Services and Markets Act 2000 (Financial Promotion) Order 2005, SI 2005/1529.

Regulations: the Insolvency Act 1986 (Amendment) (No 3) Regulations 2002, SI 2002/1990.

[PART II
OBTAINING A MORATORIUM
Nominee's statement

[9.407]
6. (1) Where the directors of a company wish to obtain a moratorium, they shall submit to the nominee—
   (a) a document setting out the terms of the proposed voluntary arrangement,
   (b) a statement of the company's affairs containing—
      (i)   such particulars of its creditors and of its debts and other liabilities and of its assets as may be prescribed, and
      (ii) such other information as may be prescribed, and
   (c) any other information necessary to enable the nominee to comply with sub-paragraph (2) which he requests from them.

(2) The nominee shall submit to the directors a statement in the prescribed form indicating whether or not, in his opinion—
   (a) the proposed voluntary arrangement has a reasonable prospect of being approved and implemented,
   (b) the company is likely to have sufficient funds available to it during the proposed moratorium to enable it to carry on its business, and
   (c) meetings of the company and its creditors should be summoned to consider the proposed voluntary arrangement.

(3) In forming his opinion on the matters mentioned in sub-paragraph (2), the nominee is entitled to rely on the information submitted to him under sub-paragraph (1) unless he has reason to doubt its accuracy.

(4) The reference in sub-paragraph (2)(b) to the company's business is to that business as the company proposes to carry it on during the moratorium.

Documents to be submitted to court

7. (1) To obtain a moratorium the directors of a company must file (in Scotland, lodge) with the court—
   (a) a document setting out the terms of the proposed voluntary arrangement,
   (b) a statement of the company's affairs containing—
      (i)   such particulars of its creditors and of its debts and other liabilities and of its assets as may be prescribed, and
      (ii) such other information as may be prescribed,
   (c) a statement that the company is eligible for a moratorium,

(d) a statement from the nominee that he has given his consent to act, and

(e) a statement from the nominee that, in his opinion—

    (i) the proposed voluntary arrangement has a reasonable prospect of being approved and implemented,

    (ii) the company is likely to have sufficient funds available to it during the proposed moratorium to enable it to carry on its business, and

    (iii) meetings of the company and its creditors should be summoned to consider the proposed voluntary arrangement.

(2) Each of the statements mentioned in sub-paragraph (1)(b) to (e), except so far as it contains the particulars referred to in paragraph (b)(i), must be in the prescribed form.

(3) The reference in sub-paragraph (1)(e)(ii) to the company's business is to that business as the company proposes to carry it on during the moratorium.

(4) The Secretary of State may by regulations modify the requirements of this paragraph as to the documents required to be filed (in Scotland, lodged) with the court in order to obtain a moratorium.

Duration of moratorium

8. (1) A moratorium comes into force when the documents for the time being referred to in paragraph 7(1) are filed or lodged with the court and references in this Schedule to "the beginning of the moratorium" shall be construed accordingly.

(2) A moratorium ends at the end of the day on which the meetings summoned under paragraph 29(1) are first held (or, if the meetings are held on different days, the later of those days), unless it is extended under paragraph 32.

(3) If either of those meetings has not first met before the end of the period of 28 days beginning with the day on which the moratorium comes into force, the moratorium ends at the end of the day on which those meetings were to be held (or, if those meetings were summoned to be held on different days, the later of those days), unless it is extended under paragraph 32.

(4) If the nominee fails to summon either meeting within the period required by paragraph 29(1), the moratorium ends at the end of the last day of that period.

(5) If the moratorium is extended (or further extended) under paragraph 32, it ends at the end of the day to which it is extended (or further extended).

(6) Sub-paragraphs (2) to (5) do not apply if the moratorium comes to an end before the time concerned by virtue of—

(a) paragraph 25(4) (effect of withdrawal by nominee of consent to act),

(b) an order under paragraph 26(3), 27(3) or 40 (challenge of actions of nominee or directors), or

(c) a decision of one or both of the meetings summoned under paragraph 29.

(7) If the moratorium has not previously come to an end in accordance with sub-paragraphs (2) to (6), it ends at the end of the day on which a decision under paragraph 31 to approve a voluntary arrangement takes effect under paragraph 36.

(8) The Secretary of State may by order increase or reduce the period for the time being specified in sub-paragraph (3).

Notification of beginning of moratorium

9. (1) When a moratorium comes into force, the directors shall notify the nominee of that fact forthwith.

(2) If the directors without reasonable excuse fail to comply with sub-paragraph (1), each of them is liable to imprisonment or a fine, or both.

10. (1) When a moratorium comes into force, the nominee shall, in accordance with the rules—

(a) advertise that fact forthwith, and

(b) notify the registrar of companies, the company and any petitioning creditor of the company of whose claim he is aware of that fact.

(2) In sub-paragraph (1)(b), "petitioning creditor" means a creditor by whom a winding-up petition has been presented before the beginning of the moratorium, as long as the petition has not been dismissed or withdrawn.

(3) If the nominee without reasonable excuse fails to comply with sub-paragraph (1)(a) or (b), he is liable to a fine.

Notification of end of moratorium

11. (1) When a moratorium comes to an end, the nominee shall, in accordance with the rules—

(a) advertise that fact forthwith, and

(b) notify the court, the registrar of companies, the company and any creditor of the company of whose claim he is aware of that fact.

(2) If the nominee without reasonable excuse fails to comply with sub-paragraph (1)(a) or (b), he is liable to a fine.]

NOTES
Inserted as noted to Pt I of this Schedule at **[9.406]**.

**[PART III
EFFECTS OF MORATORIUM**

Effect on creditors, etc

[9.408]

12. (1)   During the period for which a moratorium is in force for a company—

(a)   no petition may be presented for the winding up of the company,

(b)   no meeting of the company may be called or requisitioned except with the consent of the nominee or the leave of the court and subject (where the court gives leave) to such terms as the court may impose,

(c)   no resolution may be passed or order made for the winding up of the company,

[(d)   no administration application may be made in respect of the company,

(da)   no administrator of the company may be appointed under paragraph 14 or 22 of Schedule B1,]

(e)   no administrative receiver of the company may be appointed,

(f)   no landlord or other person to whom rent is payable may exercise any right of forfeiture by peaceable re-entry in relation to premises let to the company in respect of a failure by the company to comply with any term or condition of its tenancy of such premises, except with the leave of the court and subject to such terms as the court may impose,

(g)   no other steps may be taken to enforce any security over the company's property, or to repossess goods in the company's possession under any hire-purchase agreement, except with the leave of the court and subject to such terms as the court may impose, and

(h)   no other proceedings and no execution or other legal process may be commenced or continued, and no distress may be levied, against the company or its property except with the leave of the court and subject to such terms as the court may impose.

(2)   Where a petition, other than an excepted petition, for the winding up of the company has been presented before the beginning of the moratorium, section 127 shall not apply in relation to any disposition of property, transfer of shares or alteration in status made during the moratorium or at a time mentioned in paragraph 37(5)(a).

(3)   In the application of sub-paragraph (1)(h) to Scotland, the reference to execution being commenced or continued includes a reference to diligence being carried out or continued, and the reference to distress being levied is omitted.

(4)   Paragraph (a) of sub-paragraph (1) does not apply to an excepted petition and, where such a petition has been presented before the beginning of the moratorium or is presented during the moratorium, paragraphs (b) and (c) of that sub-paragraph do not apply in relation to proceedings on the petition.

(5)   For the purposes of this paragraph, "excepted petition" means a petition under—

(a)   section 124A [or 124B] of this Act,

(b)   section 72 of the Financial Services Act 1986 on the ground mentioned in subsection (1)(b) of that section, or

(c)   section 92 of the Banking Act 1987 on the ground mentioned in subsection (1)(b) of that section,

[(d)   section 367 of the Financial Services and Markets Act 2000 on the ground mentioned in subsection (3)(b) of that section.]

13. (1)   This paragraph applies where there is an uncrystallised floating charge on the property of a company for which a moratorium is in force.

(2)   If the conditions for the holder of the charge to give a notice having the effect mentioned in sub-paragraph (4) are met at any time, the notice may not be given at that time but may instead be given as soon as practicable after the moratorium has come to an end.

(3)   If any other event occurs at any time which (apart from this sub-paragraph) would have the effect mentioned in sub-paragraph (4), then—

(a)   the event shall not have the effect in question at that time, but

(b)   if notice of the event is given to the company by the holder of the charge as soon as is practicable after the moratorium has come to an end, the event is to be treated as if it had occurred when the notice was given.

(4)   The effect referred to in sub-paragraphs (2) and (3) is—

(a)   causing the crystallisation of the floating charge, or

(b)   causing the imposition, by virtue of provision in the instrument creating the charge, of any restriction on the disposal of any property of the company.

(5)   Application may not be made for leave under paragraph 12(1)(g) or (h) with a view to obtaining—

(a)   the crystallisation of the floating charge, or

(b)   the imposition, by virtue of provision in the instrument creating the charge, of any restriction on the disposal of any property of the company.

14.   Security granted by a company at a time when a moratorium is in force in relation to the company may only be enforced if, at that time, there were reasonable grounds for believing that it would benefit the company.

Effect on company

15.   (1)   Paragraphs 16 to 23 apply in relation to a company for which a moratorium is in force.

(2)   The fact that a company enters into a transaction in contravention of any of paragraphs 16 to 22 does not—
(a)   make the transaction void, or
(b)   make it to any extent unenforceable against the company.

Company invoices, etc

16.   [(1)   Every invoice, order for goods or services, business letter or order form (whether in hard copy, electronic or any other form) issued by or on behalf of the company, and all the company's websites, must also contain the nominee's name and a statement that the moratorium is in force for the company.]

(2)   If default is made in complying with sub-paragraph (1), the company and (subject to sub-paragraph (3)) any officer of the company is liable to a fine.

(3)   An officer of the company is only liable under sub-paragraph (2) if, without reasonable excuse, he authorises or permits the default.

Obtaining credit during moratorium

17.   (1)   The company may not obtain credit to the extent of £250 or more from a person who has not been informed that a moratorium is in force in relation to the company.

(2)   The reference to the company obtaining credit includes the following cases—
(a)   where goods are bailed (in Scotland, hired) to the company under a hire-purchase agreement, or agreed to be sold to the company under a conditional sale agreement, and
(b)   where the company is paid in advance (whether in money or otherwise) for the supply of goods or services.

(3)   Where the company obtains credit in contravention of sub-paragraph (1)—
(a)   the company is liable to a fine, and
(b)   if any officer of the company knowingly and wilfully authorised or permitted the contravention, he is liable to imprisonment or a fine, or both.

(4)   The money sum specified in sub-paragraph (1) is subject to increase or reduction by order under section 417A in Part XV.

Disposals and payments

18.   (1)   Subject to sub-paragraph (2), the company may only dispose of any of its property if—
(a)   there are reasonable grounds for believing that the disposal will benefit the company, and
(b)   the disposal is approved by the committee established under paragraph 35(1) or, where there is no such committee, by the nominee.

(2)   Sub-paragraph (1) does not apply to a disposal made in the ordinary way of the company's business.

(3)   If the company makes a disposal in contravention of sub-paragraph (1) otherwise than in pursuance of an order of the court—
(a)   the company is liable to a fine, and
(b)   if any officer of the company authorised or permitted the contravention, without reasonable excuse, he is liable to imprisonment or a fine, or both.

19.   (1)   Subject to sub-paragraph (2), the company may only make any payment in respect of any debt or other liability of the company in existence before the beginning of the moratorium if—
(a)   there are reasonable grounds for believing that the payment will benefit the company, and
(b)   the payment is approved by the committee established under paragraph 35(1) or, where there is no such committee, by the nominee.

(2)   Sub-paragraph (1) does not apply to a payment required by paragraph 20(6).

(3)   If the company makes a payment in contravention of sub-paragraph (1) otherwise than in pursuance of an order of the court—
(a)   the company is liable to a fine, and
(b)   if any officer of the company authorised or permitted the contravention, without reasonable excuse, he is liable to imprisonment or a fine, or both.

Disposal of charged property, etc

20.   (1)   This paragraph applies where—

(a)   any property of the company is subject to a security, or

(b)   any goods are in the possession of the company under a hire-purchase agreement.

(2)   If the holder of the security consents, or the court gives leave, the company may dispose of the property as if it were not subject to the security.

(3)   If the owner of the goods consents, or the court gives leave, the company may dispose of the goods as if all rights of the owner under the hire-purchase agreement were vested in the company.

(4)   Where property subject to a security which, as created, was a floating charge is disposed of under sub-paragraph (2), the holder of the security has the same priority in respect of any property of the company directly or indirectly representing the property disposed of as he would have had in respect of the property subject to the security.

(5)   Sub-paragraph (6) applies to the disposal under sub-paragraph (2) or (as the case may be) sub-paragraph (3) of—

(a)   any property subject to a security other than a security which, as created, was a floating charge, or

(b)   any goods in the possession of the company under a hire-purchase agreement.

(6)   It shall be a condition of any consent or leave under sub-paragraph (2) or (as the case may be) sub-paragraph (3) that—

(a)   the net proceeds of the disposal, and

(b)   where those proceeds are less than such amount as may be agreed, or determined by the court, to be the net amount which would be realised on a sale of the property or goods in the open market by a willing vendor, such sums as may be required to make good the deficiency,

shall be applied towards discharging the sums secured by the security or payable under the hire-purchase agreement.

(7)   Where a condition imposed in pursuance of sub-paragraph (6) relates to two or more securities, that condition requires—

(a)   the net proceeds of the disposal, and

(b)   where paragraph (b) of sub-paragraph (6) applies, the sums mentioned in that paragraph,

to be applied towards discharging the sums secured by those securities in the order of their priorities.

(8)   Where the court gives leave for a disposal under sub-paragraph (2) or (3), the directors shall, within 14 days after leave is given, send [a copy] of the order giving leave to the registrar of companies.

(9)   If the directors without reasonable excuse fail to comply with sub-paragraph (8), they are liable to a fine.

21.   (1)   Where property is disposed of under paragraph 20 in its application to Scotland, the company shall grant to the disponee an appropriate document of transfer or conveyance of the property, and

(a)   that document, or

(b)   where any recording, intimation or registration of the document is a legal requirement for completion of title to the property, that recording, intimation or registration,

has the effect of disencumbering the property of, or (as the case may be) freeing the property from, the security.

(2)   Where goods in the possession of the company under a hire-purchase agreement are disposed of under paragraph 20 in its application to Scotland, the disposal has the effect of extinguishing, as against the disponee, all rights of the owner of the goods under the agreement.

22.   (1)   If the company—

(a)   without any consent or leave under paragraph 20, disposes of any of its property which is subject to a security otherwise than in accordance with the terms of the security,

(b)   without any consent or leave under paragraph 20, disposes of any goods in the possession of the company under a hire-purchase agreement otherwise than in accordance with the terms of the agreement, or

(c)   fails to comply with any requirement imposed by paragraph 20 or 21,

it is liable to a fine.

(2)   If any officer of the company, without reasonable excuse, authorises or permits any such disposal or failure to comply, he is liable to imprisonment or a fine, or both.

Market contracts, etc

23.   (1)   If the company enters into any transaction to which this paragraph applies—

(a)   the company is liable to a fine, and

(b)   if any officer of the company, without reasonable excuse, authorised or permitted the company to enter into the transaction, he is liable to imprisonment or a fine, or both.

(2)   A company enters into a transaction to which this paragraph applies if it—

(a)   enters into a market contract,   . . .

(b)   gives a transfer order,

(c)   grants a market charge   . . . .   or a system-charge, or

(d)   provides any collateral security.

(3)   The fact that a company enters into a transaction in contravention of this paragraph does not—

(a)   make the transaction void, or

(b)   make it to any extent unenforceable by or against the company.

(4)   Where during the moratorium a company enters into a transaction to which this paragraph applies, nothing done by or in pursuance of the transaction is to be treated as done in contravention of paragraphs 12(1)(g), 14 or 16 to 22.

(5)   Paragraph 20 does not apply in relation to any property which is subject to a market charge, . . . a system-charge or a collateral security charge.

(6)   In this paragraph, "transfer order", "collateral security" and "collateral security charge" have the same meanings as in the settlement finality regulations.]

NOTES

Inserted as noted to Pt I of this Schedule at **[9.406]**.

Para 12: sub-paras (1)(d), (da) substituted, for original sub-para (1)(d), by the Enterprise Act 2002, s 248(3), Sch 17, paras 9, 37(1), (3), as from 15 September 2003 (for savings and transitional provisions, see the note to s 8 at **[9.105]**); words in square brackets in sub-para (5)(a) inserted by the European Public Limited-Liability Company Regulations 2004, SI 2004/2326, reg 73(4)(b), as from 8 October 2004; sub-para (5)(d) inserted by virtue of the Financial Services and Markets Act 2000 (Consequential Amendments) Order 2002, SI 2002/1555, art 30, as from 3 July 2002.

Para 16: sub-para (1) substituted by the Companies (Trading Disclosures) (Insolvency) Regulations 2008, SI 2008/1897, reg 3(1), as from 1 October 2008.

Para 20: words in square brackets in sub-para (8) substituted by the Companies Act 2006 (Consequential Amendments, Transitional Provisions and Savings) Order 2009, SI 2009/1941, art 2(1), Sch 1, para 71(1), (4)(b), as from 1 October 2009 (for transitional provisions see the note to s 7A at **[9.103]**).

Para 23: words omitted from sub-paras (2), (5) repealed by virtue of SI 2002/1555, art 28(1), (4), as from 3 July 2002.

Banking Act 1987, Financial Services Act 1986: repealed by the Financial Services and Markets Act 2000 (Consequential Amendments and Repeals) Order 2001, SI 2001/3649, art 3(1)(c), (d), as from 1 December 2001.

[PART IV
NOMINEES
Monitoring of company's activities

[9.409]

24. (1)   During a moratorium, the nominee shall monitor the company's affairs for the purpose of forming an opinion as to whether—

(a)   the proposed voluntary arrangement or, if he has received notice of proposed modifications under paragraph 31(7), the proposed arrangement with those modifications has a reasonable prospect of being approved and implemented, and

(b)   the company is likely to have sufficient funds available to it during the remainder of the moratorium to enable it to continue to carry on its business.

(2)   The directors shall submit to the nominee any information necessary to enable him to comply with sub-paragraph (1) which he requests from them.

(3)   In forming his opinion on the matters mentioned in sub-paragraph (1), the nominee is entitled to rely on the information submitted to him under sub-paragraph (2) unless he has reason to doubt its accuracy.

(4)   The reference in sub-paragraph (1)(b) to the company's business is to that business as the company proposes to carry it on during the remainder of the moratorium.

Withdrawal of consent to act

25. (1)   The nominee may only withdraw his consent to act in the circumstances mentioned in this paragraph.

(2)   The nominee must withdraw his consent to act if, at any time during a moratorium—

(a)   he forms the opinion that—

(i)   the proposed voluntary arrangement or, if he has received notice of proposed modifications under paragraph 31(7), the proposed arrangement with those modifications no longer has a reasonable prospect of being approved or implemented, or

(ii)   the company will not have sufficient funds available to it during the remainder of the moratorium to enable it to continue to carry on its business,

(b)   he becomes aware that, on the date of filing, the company was not eligible for a moratorium, or

(c)   the directors fail to comply with their duty under paragraph 24(2).

(3)   The reference in sub-paragraph (2)(a)(ii) to the company's business is to that business as the company proposes to carry it on during the remainder of the moratorium.

(4)   If the nominee withdraws his consent to act, the moratorium comes to an end.

(5)   If the nominee withdraws his consent to act he must, in accordance with the rules, notify the court, the registrar of companies, the company and any creditor of the company of whose claim he is aware of his withdrawal and the reason for it.

(6)   If the nominee without reasonable excuse fails to comply with sub-paragraph (5), he is liable to a fine.

Challenge of nominee's actions, etc

26. (1)   If any creditor, director or member of the company, or any other person affected by a moratorium, is dissatisfied by any act, omission or decision of the nominee during the moratorium, he may apply to the court.

(2)   An application under sub-paragraph (1) may be made during the moratorium or after it has ended.

(3)   On an application under sub-paragraph (1) the court may—
  (a)   confirm, reverse or modify any act or decision of the nominee,
  (b)   give him directions, or
  (c)   make such other order as it thinks fit.

(4)   An order under sub-paragraph (3) may (among other things) bring the moratorium to an end and make such consequential provision as the court thinks fit.

27. (1)   Where there are reasonable grounds for believing that—
  (a)   as a result of any act, omission or decision of the nominee during the moratorium, the company has suffered loss, but
  (b)   the company does not intend to pursue any claim it may have against the nominee,
any creditor of the company may apply to the court.

(2)   An application under sub-paragraph (1) may be made during the moratorium or after it has ended.

(3)   On an application under sub-paragraph (1) the court may—
  (a)   order the company to pursue any claim against the nominee,
  (b)   authorise any creditor to pursue such a claim in the name of the company, or
  (c)   make such other order with respect to such a claim as it thinks fit,
unless the court is satisfied that the act, omission or decision of the nominee was in all the circumstances reasonable.

(4)   An order under sub-paragraph (3) may (among other things)—
  (a)   impose conditions on any authority given to pursue a claim,
  (b)   direct the company to assist in the pursuit of a claim,
  (c)   make directions with respect to the distribution of anything received as a result of the pursuit of a claim,
  (d)   bring the moratorium to an end and make such consequential provision as the court thinks fit.

(5)   On an application under sub-paragraph (1) the court shall have regard to the interests of the members and creditors of the company generally.

Replacement of nominee by court

28. (1)   The court may—
  (a)   on an application made by the directors in a case where the nominee has failed to comply with any duty imposed on him under this Schedule or has died, or
  (b)   on an application made by the directors or the nominee in a case where it is impracticable or inappropriate for the nominee to continue to act as such,
direct that the nominee be replaced as such by another person qualified to act as an insolvency practitioner, or authorised to act as nominee, in relation to the voluntary arrangement.

(2)   A person may only be appointed as a replacement nominee under this paragraph if he submits to the court a statement indicating his consent to act.]

NOTES

Inserted as noted to Pt I of this Schedule at **[9.406]**.

[PART V
CONSIDERATION AND IMPLEMENTATION OF VOLUNTARY ARRANGEMENT

Summoning of meetings

[9.410]
29. (1)   Where a moratorium is in force, the nominee shall summon meetings of the company and its creditors for such a time, date (within the period for the time being specified in paragraph 8(3)) and place as he thinks fit.

(2)   The persons to be summoned to a creditors' meeting under this paragraph are every creditor of the company of whose claim the nominee is aware.

Conduct of meetings

30. (1) Subject to the provisions of paragraphs 31 to 35, the meetings summoned under paragraph 29 shall be conducted in accordance with the rules.

(2) A meeting so summoned may resolve that it be adjourned (or further adjourned).

(3) After the conclusion of either meeting in accordance with the rules, the chairman of the meeting shall report the result of the meeting to the court, and, immediately after reporting to the court, shall give notice of the result of the meeting to such persons as may be prescribed.

Approval of voluntary arrangement

31. (1) The meetings summoned under paragraph 29 shall decide whether to approve the proposed voluntary arrangement (with or without modifications).

(2) The modifications may include one conferring the functions proposed to be conferred on the nominee on another person qualified to act as an insolvency practitioner, or authorised to act as nominee, in relation to the voluntary arrangement.

(3) The modifications shall not include one by virtue of which the proposal ceases to be a proposal such as is mentioned in section 1.

(4) A meeting summoned under paragraph 29 shall not approve any proposal or modification which affects the right of a secured creditor of the company to enforce his security, except with the concurrence of the creditor concerned.

(5) Subject to sub-paragraph (6), a meeting so summoned shall not approve any proposal or modification under which—

    (a) any preferential debt of the company is to be paid otherwise than in priority to such of its debts as are not preferential debts, or

    (b) a preferential creditor of the company is to be paid an amount in respect of a preferential debt that bears to that debt a smaller proportion than is borne to another preferential debt by the amount that is to be paid in respect of that other debt.

(6) The meeting may approve such a proposal or modification with the concurrence of the preferential creditor concerned.

(7) The directors of the company may, before the beginning of the period of seven days which ends with the meetings (or either of them) summoned under paragraph 29 being held, give notice to the nominee of any modifications of the proposal for which the directors intend to seek the approval of those meetings.

(8) References in this paragraph to preferential debts and preferential creditors are to be read in accordance with section 386 in Part XII of this Act.

Extension of moratorium

32. (1) Subject to sub-paragraph (2), a meeting summoned under paragraph 29 which resolves that it be adjourned (or further adjourned) may resolve that the moratorium be extended (or further extended), with or without conditions.

(2) The moratorium may not be extended (or further extended) to a day later than the end of the period of two months which begins—

    (a) where both meetings summoned under paragraph 29 are first held on the same day, with that day,

    (b) in any other case, with the day on which the later of those meetings is first held.

(3) At any meeting where it is proposed to extend (or further extend) the moratorium, before a decision is taken with respect to that proposal, the nominee shall inform the meeting—

    (a) of what he has done in order to comply with his duty under paragraph 24 and the cost of his actions for the company, and

    (b) of what he intends to do to continue to comply with that duty if the moratorium is extended (or further extended) and the expected cost of his actions for the company.

(4) Where, in accordance with sub-paragraph (3)(b), the nominee informs a meeting of the expected cost of his intended actions, the meeting shall resolve whether or not to approve that expected cost.

(5) If a decision not to approve the expected cost of the nominee's intended actions has effect under paragraph 36, the moratorium comes to an end.

(6) A meeting may resolve that a moratorium which has been extended (or further extended) be brought to an end before the end of the period of the extension (or further extension).

(7) The Secretary of State may by order increase or reduce the period for the time being specified in sub-paragraph (2).

33. (1) The conditions which may be imposed when a moratorium is extended (or further extended) include a requirement that the nominee be replaced as such by another person qualified to act as an insolvency practitioner, or authorised to act as nominee, in relation to the voluntary arrangement.

(2)   A person may only be appointed as a replacement nominee by virtue of sub-paragraph (1) if he submits to the court a statement indicating his consent to act.

(3)   At any meeting where it is proposed to appoint a replacement nominee as a condition of extending (or further extending) the moratorium—

- (a)   the duty imposed by paragraph 32(3)(b) on the nominee shall instead be imposed on the person proposed as the replacement nominee, and
- (b)   paragraphs 32(4) and (5) and 36(1)(e) apply as if the references to the nominee were to that person.

34. (1)   If a decision to extend, or further extend, the moratorium takes effect under paragraph 36, the nominee shall, in accordance with the rules, notify the registrar of companies and the court.

(2)   If the moratorium is extended, or further extended, by virtue of an order under paragraph 36(5), the nominee shall, in accordance with the rules, send [a copy] of the order to the registrar of companies.

(3)   If the nominee without reasonable excuse fails to comply with this paragraph, he is liable to a fine.

Moratorium committee

35. (1)   A meeting summoned under paragraph 29 which resolves that the moratorium be extended (or further extended) may, with the consent of the nominee, resolve that a committee be established to exercise the functions conferred on it by the meeting.

(2)   The meeting may not so resolve unless it has approved an estimate of the expenses to be incurred by the committee in the exercise of the proposed functions.

(3)   Any expenses, not exceeding the amount of the estimate, incurred by the committee in the exercise of its functions shall be reimbursed by the nominee.

(4)   The committee shall cease to exist when the moratorium comes to an end.

Effectiveness of decisions

36. (1)   Sub-paragraph (2) applies to references to one of the following decisions having effect, that is, a decision, under paragraph 31, 32 or 35, with respect to—

- (a)   the approval of a proposed voluntary arrangement,
- (b)   the extension (or further extension) of a moratorium,
- (c)   the bringing of a moratorium to an end,
- (d)   the establishment of a committee, or
- (e)   the approval of the expected cost of a nominee's intended actions.

(2)   The decision has effect if, in accordance with the rules—

- (a)   it has been taken by both meetings summoned under paragraph 29, or
- (b)   (subject to any order made under sub-paragraph (5)) it has been taken by the creditors' meeting summoned under that paragraph.

(3)   If a decision taken by the creditors' meeting under any of paragraphs 31, 32 or 35 with respect to any of the matters mentioned in sub-paragraph (1) differs from one so taken by the company meeting with respect to that matter, a member of the company may apply to the court.

(4)   An application under sub-paragraph (3) shall not be made after the end of the period of 28 days beginning with—

- (a)   the day on which the decision was taken by the creditors' meeting, or
- (b)   where the decision of the company meeting was taken on a later day, that day.

(5)   On an application under sub-paragraph (3), the court may—

- (a)   order the decision of the company meeting to have effect instead of the decision of the creditors' meeting, or
- (b)   make such other order as it thinks fit.

Effect of approval of voluntary arrangement

37. (1)   This paragraph applies where a decision approving a voluntary arrangement has effect under paragraph 36.

(2)   The approved voluntary arrangement—

- (a)   takes effect as if made by the company at the creditors' meeting, and
- (b)   binds every person who in accordance with the rules—
  - (i)   was entitled to vote at that meeting (whether or not he was present or represented at it), or
  - (ii)   would have been so entitled if he had had notice of it,
  - as if he were a party to the voluntary arrangement.

(3)   If—

- (a)   when the arrangement ceases to have effect any amount payable under the arrangement to a person bound by virtue of sub-paragraph (2)(b)(ii) has not been paid, and
- (b)   the arrangement did not come to an end prematurely,

the company shall at that time become liable to pay to that person the amount payable under the arrangement.

(4) Where a petition for the winding up of the company, other than an excepted petition within the meaning of paragraph 12, was presented before the beginning of the moratorium, the court shall dismiss the petition.

(5) The court shall not dismiss a petition under sub-paragraph (4)—

    (a)   at any time before the end of the period of 28 days beginning with the first day on which each of the reports of the meetings required by paragraph 30(3) has been made to the court, or

    (b)   at any time when an application under paragraph 38 or an appeal in respect of such an application is pending, or at any time in the period within which such an appeal may be brought.

Challenge of decisions

38. (1) Subject to the following provisions of this paragraph, any of the persons mentioned in sub-paragraph (2) may apply to the court on one or both of the following grounds—

    (a)   that a voluntary arrangement approved at one or both of the meetings summoned under paragraph 29 and which has taken effect unfairly prejudices the interests of a creditor, member or contributory of the company,

    (b)   that there has been some material irregularity at or in relation to either of those meetings.

(2) The persons who may apply under this paragraph are—

    (a)   a person entitled, in accordance with the rules, to vote at either of the meetings,

    (b)   a person who would have been entitled, in accordance with the rules, to vote at the creditors' meeting if he had had notice of it, and

    (c)   the nominee.

(3) An application under this paragraph shall not be made—

    (a)   after the end of the period of 28 days beginning with the first day on which each of the reports required by paragraph 30(3) has been made to the court, or

    (b)   in the case of a person who was not given notice of the creditors' meeting, after the end of the period of 28 days beginning with the day on which he became aware that the meeting had taken place,

but (subject to that) an application made by a person within sub-paragraph (2)(b) on the ground that the arrangement prejudices his interests may be made after the arrangement has ceased to have effect, unless it came to an end prematurely.

(4) Where on an application under this paragraph the court is satisfied as to either of the grounds mentioned in sub-paragraph (1), it may do any of the following—

    (a)   revoke or suspend—

        (i)   any decision approving the voluntary arrangement which has effect under paragraph 36, or

        (ii)   in a case falling within sub-paragraph (1)(b), any decision taken by the meeting in question which has effect under that paragraph,

    (b)   give a direction to any person—

        (i)   for the summoning of further meetings to consider any revised proposal for a voluntary arrangement which the directors may make, or

        (ii)   in a case falling within sub-paragraph (1)(b), for the summoning of a further company or (as the case may be) creditors' meeting to reconsider the original proposal.

(5) Where at any time after giving a direction under sub-paragraph (4)(b)(i) the court is satisfied that the directors do not intend to submit a revised proposal, the court shall revoke the direction and revoke or suspend any decision approving the voluntary arrangement which has effect under paragraph 36.

(6) Where the court gives a direction under sub-paragraph (4)(b), it may also give a direction continuing or, as the case may require, renewing, for such period as may be specified in the direction, the effect of the moratorium.

(7) Sub-paragraph (8) applies in a case where the court, on an application under this paragraph—

    (a)   gives a direction under sub-paragraph (4)(b), or

    (b)   revokes or suspends a decision under sub-paragraph (4)(a) or (5).

(8) In such a case, the court may give such supplemental directions as it thinks fit and, in particular, directions with respect to—

    (a)   things done under the voluntary arrangement since it took effect, and

    (b)   such things done since that time as could not have been done if a moratorium had been in force in relation to the company when they were done.

(9) Except in pursuance of the preceding provisions of this paragraph, a decision taken at a meeting summoned under paragraph 29 is not invalidated by any irregularity at or in relation to the meeting.

Implementation of voluntary arrangement

39. (1)   This paragraph applies where a voluntary arrangement approved by one or both of the meetings summoned under paragraph 29 has taken effect.

(2)   The person who is for the time being carrying out in relation to the voluntary arrangement the functions conferred—

(a)   by virtue of the approval of the arrangement, on the nominee, or

(b)   by virtue of paragraph 31(2), on a person other than the nominee,

shall be known as the supervisor of the voluntary arrangement.

(3)   If any of the company's creditors or any other person is dissatisfied by any act, omission or decision of the supervisor, he may apply to the court.

(4)   On an application under sub-paragraph (3) the court may—

(a)   confirm, reverse or modify any act or decision of the supervisor,

(b)   give him directions, or

(c)   make such other order as it thinks fit.

(5)   The supervisor—

(a)   may apply to the court for directions in relation to any particular matter arising under the voluntary arrangement, and

(b)   is included among the persons who may apply to the court for the winding up of the company or for an administration order to be made in relation to it.

(6)   The court may, whenever—

(a)   it is expedient to appoint a person to carry out the functions of the supervisor, and

(b)   it is inexpedient, difficult or impracticable for an appointment to be made without the assistance of the court,

make an order appointing a person who is qualified to act as an insolvency practitioner, or authorised to act as supervisor, in relation to the voluntary arrangement, either in substitution for the existing supervisor or to fill a vacancy.

(7)   The power conferred by sub-paragraph (6) is exercisable so as to increase the number of persons exercising the functions of supervisor or, where there is more than one person exercising those functions, so as to replace one or more of those persons.

NOTES

Inserted as noted to Pt I of this Schedule at **[9.406]**.

Para 34: words in square brackets in sub-para (2) substituted by the Companies Act 2006 (Consequential Amendments, Transitional Provisions and Savings) Order 2009, SI 2009/1941, art 2(1), Sch 1, para 71(1), (4)(b), as from 1 October 2009 (for transitional provisions see the note to s 7A at **[9.103]**).

[PART VI
MISCELLANEOUS

Challenge of directors' actions

[9.411]

40. (1)   This paragraph applies in relation to acts or omissions of the directors of a company during a moratorium.

(2)   A creditor or member of the company may apply to the court for an order under this paragraph on the ground—

(a)   that the company's affairs, business and property are being or have been managed by the directors in a manner which is unfairly prejudicial to the interests of its creditors or members generally, or of some part of its creditors or members (including at least the petitioner), or

(b)   that any actual or proposed act or omission of the directors is or would be so prejudicial.

(3)   An application for an order under this paragraph may be made during or after the moratorium.

(4)   On an application for an order under this paragraph the court may—

(a)   make such order as it thinks fit for giving relief in respect of the matters complained of,

(b)   adjourn the hearing conditionally or unconditionally, or

(c)   make an interim order or any other order that it thinks fit.

(5)   An order under this paragraph may in particular—

(a)   regulate the management by the directors of the company's affairs, business and property during the remainder of the moratorium,

(b)   require the directors to refrain from doing or continuing an act complained of by the petitioner, or to do an act which the petitioner has complained they have omitted to do,

(c)   require the summoning of a meeting of creditors or members for the purpose of considering such matters as the court may direct,

(d)   bring the moratorium to an end and make such consequential provision as the court thinks fit.

(6)   In making an order under this paragraph the court shall have regard to the need to safeguard the interests of persons who have dealt with the company in good faith and for value.

[(7)   Sub-paragraph (8) applies where—
  [(a)   the appointment of an administrator has effect in relation to the company and that appointment was in pursuance of—
      (i)   an administration application made, or
      (ii)   a notice of intention to appoint filed,
      before the moratorium came into force, or]
  (b)   the company is being wound up in pursuance of a petition presented before the moratorium came into force.

(8)   No application for an order under this paragraph may be made by a creditor or member of the company; but such an application may be made instead by the administrator or (as the case may be) the liquidator.]

Offences

41.   (1)   This paragraph applies where a moratorium has been obtained for a company.

(2)   If, within the period of 12 months ending with the day on which the moratorium came into force, a person who was at the time an officer of the company—
  (a)   did any of the things mentioned in paragraphs (a) to (f) of sub-paragraph (4), or
  (b)   was privy to the doing by others of any of the things mentioned in paragraphs (c), (d) and (e) of that sub-paragraph,
he is to be treated as having committed an offence at that time.

(3)   If, at any time during the moratorium, a person who is an officer of the company—
  (a)   does any of the things mentioned in paragraphs (a) to (f) of sub-paragraph (4), or
  (b)   is privy to the doing by others of any of the things mentioned in paragraphs (c), (d) and (e) of that sub-paragraph,
he commits an offence.

(4)   Those things are—
  (a)   concealing any part of the company's property to the value of £500 or more, or concealing any debt due to or from the company, or
  (b)   fraudulently removing any part of the company's property to the value of £500 or more, or
  (c)   concealing, destroying, mutilating or falsifying any book or paper affecting or relating to the company's property or affairs, or
  (d)   making any false entry in any book or paper affecting or relating to the company's property or affairs, or
  (e)   fraudulently parting with, altering or making any omission in any document affecting or relating to the company's property or affairs, or
  (f)   pawning, pledging or disposing of any property of the company which has been obtained on credit and has not been paid for (unless the pawning, pledging or disposal was in the ordinary way of the company's business).

(5)   For the purposes of this paragraph, "officer" includes a shadow director.

(6)   It is a defence—
  (a)   for a person charged under sub-paragraph (2) or (3) in respect of the things mentioned in paragraph (a) or (f) of sub-paragraph (4) to prove that he had no intent to defraud, and
  (b)   for a person charged under sub-paragraph (2) or (3) in respect of the things mentioned in paragraph (c) or (d) of sub-paragraph (4) to prove that he had no intent to conceal the state of affairs of the company or to defeat the law.

(7)   Where a person pawns, pledges or disposes of any property of a company in circumstances which amount to an offence under sub-paragraph (2) or (3), every person who takes in pawn or pledge, or otherwise receives, the property knowing it to be pawned, pledged or disposed of in circumstances which—
  (a)   would, if a moratorium were obtained for the company within the period of 12 months beginning with the day on which the pawning, pledging or disposal took place, amount to an offence under sub-paragraph (2), or
  (b)   amount to an offence under sub-paragraph (3),
commits an offence.

(8)   A person guilty of an offence under this paragraph is liable to imprisonment or a fine, or both.

(9)   The money sums specified in paragraphs (a) and (b) of sub-paragraph (4) are subject to increase or reduction by order under section 417A in Part XV.

42.   (1)   If, for the purpose of obtaining a moratorium, or an extension of a moratorium, for a company, a person who is an officer of the company—
  (a)   makes any false representation, or
  (b)   fraudulently does, or omits to do, anything,
he commits an offence.

(2)   Sub-paragraph (1) applies even if no moratorium or extension is obtained.

(3)   For the purposes of this paragraph, "officer" includes a shadow director.

(4)   A person guilty of an offence under this paragraph is liable to imprisonment or a fine, or both.

Void provisions in floating charge documents

43. (1) A provision in an instrument creating a floating charge is void if it provides for—

(a) obtaining a moratorium, or

(b) anything done with a view to obtaining a moratorium (including any preliminary decision or investigation),

to be an event causing the floating charge to crystallise or causing restrictions which would not otherwise apply to be imposed on the disposal of property by the company or a ground for the appointment of a receiver.

(2) In sub-paragraph (1), "receiver" includes a manager and a person who is appointed both receiver and manager.

Functions of the Financial Services Authority

44. (1) This Schedule has effect in relation to a moratorium for a regulated company with the modifications in sub-paragraphs (2) to (16) below.

(2) Any notice or other document required by virtue of this Schedule to be sent to a creditor of a regulated company must also be sent to the Authority.

(3) The Authority is entitled to be heard on any application to the court for leave under paragraph 20(2) or 20(3) (disposal of charged property, etc).

(4) Where paragraph 26(1) (challenge of nominee's actions, etc) applies, the persons who may apply to the court include the Authority.

(5) If a person other than the Authority applies to the court under that paragraph, the Authority is entitled to be heard on the application.

(6) Where paragraph 27(1) (challenge of nominee's actions, etc) applies, the persons who may apply to the court include the Authority.

(7) If a person other than the Authority applies to the court under that paragraph, the Authority is entitled to be heard on the application.

(8) The persons to be summoned to a creditors' meeting under paragraph 29 include the Authority.

(9) A person appointed for the purpose by the Authority is entitled to attend and participate in (but not to vote at)—

(a) any creditors' meeting summoned under that paragraph,

(b) any meeting of a committee established under paragraph 35 (moratorium committee).

(10) The Authority is entitled to be heard on any application under paragraph 36(3) (effectiveness of decisions).

(11) Where paragraph 38(1) (challenge of decisions) applies, the persons who may apply to the court include the Authority.

(12) If a person other than the Authority applies to the court under that paragraph, the Authority is entitled to be heard on the application.

(13) Where paragraph 39(3) (implementation of voluntary arrangement) applies, the persons who may apply to the court include the Authority.

(14) If a person other than the Authority applies to the court under that paragraph, the Authority is entitled to be heard on the application.

(15) Where paragraph 40(2) (challenge of directors' actions) applies, the persons who may apply to the court include the Authority.

(16) If a person other than the Authority applies to the court under that paragraph, the Authority is entitled to be heard on the application.

(17) This paragraph does not prejudice any right the Authority has (apart from this paragraph) as a creditor of a regulated company.

(18) In this paragraph—

"the Authority" means the Financial Services Authority, and

"regulated company" means a company which—

(a) is, or has been, an authorised person within the meaning given by section 31 of the Financial Services and Markets Act 2000,

(b) is, or has been, an appointed representative within the meaning given by section 39 of that Act, or

(c) is carrying on, or has carried on, a regulated activity, within the meaning given by section 22 of that Act, in contravention of the general prohibition within the meaning given by section 19 of that Act.

Subordinate legislation

45. (1) Regulations or an order made by the Secretary of State under this Schedule may make different provision for different cases.

(2) Regulations so made may make such consequential, incidental, supplemental and transitional provision as may appear to the Secretary of State necessary or expedient.

(3)   Any power of the Secretary of State to make regulations under this Schedule may be exercised by amending or repealing any enactment contained in this Act (including one contained in this Schedule) or contained in the Company Directors Disqualification Act 1986.

(4)   Regulations (except regulations under paragraph 5) or an order made by the Secretary of State under this Schedule shall be made by statutory instrument subject to annulment in pursuance of a resolution of either House of Parliament.

(5)   Regulations under paragraph 5 of this Schedule are to be made by statutory instrument and shall only be made if a draft containing the regulations has been laid before and approved by resolution of each House of Parliament.]

NOTES

Inserted as noted to Pt I of this Schedule at **[9.406]**.

Para 40: sub-paras (7), (8) substituted, for original sub-para (7), by the Enterprise Act 2002, s 248(3), Sch 17, paras 9, 37(1), (4), as from 15 September 2003 (for savings and transitional provisions, see the note to s 8 at **[9.105]**); sub-para (7)(a) further substituted by the Enterprise Act 2002 (Insolvency) Order 2004, SI 2004/2312, art 2, as from 15 October 2004.

Regulations under paragraph 5: see Part I of this Schedule *ante*.

[SCHEDULE B1
ADMINISTRATION

Section 8

[9.412]

Arrangement of Schedule

NATURE OF ADMINISTRATION

Administration

1.   (1)   For the purposes of this Act "administrator" of a company means a person appointed under this Schedule to manage the company's affairs, business and property.

(2)   For the purposes of this Act—

(a)   a company is "in administration" while the appointment of an administrator of the company has effect,

(b)   a company "enters administration" when the appointment of an administrator takes effect,

(c)   a company ceases to be in administration when the appointment of an administrator of the company ceases to have effect in accordance with this Schedule, and

(d)   a company does not cease to be in administration merely because an administrator vacates office (by reason of resignation, death or otherwise) or is removed from office.

2.   A person may be appointed as administrator of a company—

(a)   by administration order of the court under paragraph 10,

(b)   by the holder of a floating charge under paragraph 14, or

(c)   by the company or its directors under paragraph 22.

Purpose of administration

3.   (1)   The administrator of a company must perform his functions with the objective of—

(a)   rescuing the company as a going concern, or

(b)   achieving a better result for the company's creditors as a whole than would be likely if the company were wound up (without first being in administration), or

(c)   realising property in order to make a distribution to one or more secured or preferential creditors.

(2)   Subject to sub-paragraph (4), the administrator of a company must perform his functions in the interests of the company's creditors as a whole.

(3)   The administrator must perform his functions with the objective specified in sub-paragraph (1)(a) unless he thinks either—

(a)   that it is not reasonably practicable to achieve that objective, or

(b)   that the objective specified in sub-paragraph (1)(b) would achieve a better result for the company's creditors as a whole.

(4)   The administrator may perform his functions with the objective specified in sub-paragraph (1)(c) only if—

(a)   he thinks that it is not reasonably practicable to achieve either of the objectives specified in sub-paragraph (1)(a) and (b), and

(b)   he does not unnecessarily harm the interests of the creditors of the company as a whole.

4. The administrator of a company must perform his functions as quickly and efficiently as is reasonably practicable.

Status of administrator

5. An administrator is an officer of the court (whether or not he is appointed by the court).

General restrictions

6. A person may be appointed as administrator of a company only if he is qualified to act as an insolvency practitioner in relation to the company.

7. A person may not be appointed as administrator of a company which is in administration (subject to the provisions of paragraphs 90 to 97 and 100 to 103 about replacement and additional administrators).

8. (1)   A person may not be appointed as administrator of a company which is in liquidation by virtue of—

(a)   a resolution for voluntary winding up, or

(b)   a winding-up order.

(2)   Sub-paragraph (1)(a) is subject to paragraph 38.

(3)   Sub-paragraph (1)(b) is subject to paragraphs 37 and 38.

9. (1)   A person may not be appointed as administrator of a company which—

(a)   has a liability in respect of a deposit which it accepted in accordance with the Banking Act 1979 (c 37) or 1987 (c 22), but

(b)   is not an authorised deposit taker.

(2)   A person may not be appointed as administrator of a company which effects or carries out contracts of insurance.

(3)   But sub-paragraph (2) does not apply to a company which—

(a)   is exempt from the general prohibition in relation to effecting or carrying out contracts of insurance, or

(b)   is an authorised deposit taker effecting or carrying out contracts of insurance in the course of a banking business.

(4)   In this paragraph—

"authorised deposit taker" means a person with permission under Part IV of the Financial Services and Markets Act 2000 (c 8) to accept deposits, and

"the general prohibition" has the meaning given by section 19 of that Act.

(5)   This paragraph shall be construed in accordance with—

(a)   section 22 of the Financial Services and Markets Act 2000 (classes of regulated activity and categories of investment),

(b)   any relevant order under that section, and

(c)   Schedule 2 to that Act (regulated activities).

APPOINTMENT OF ADMINISTRATOR BY COURT

Administration order

10. An administration order is an order appointing a person as the administrator of a company.

Conditions for making order

11. The court may make an administration order in relation to a company only if satisfied—

(a)   that the company is or is likely to become unable to pay its debts, and

(b)   that the administration order is reasonably likely to achieve the purpose of administration.

Administration application

12. (1)   An application to the court for an administration order in respect of a company (an "administration application") may be made only by—

(a)   the company,

(b)   the directors of the company,

(c)   one or more creditors of the company,

(d)   the [designated officer] for a magistrates' court in the exercise of the power conferred by section 87A of the Magistrates' Courts Act 1980 (c 43) (fine imposed on company), or

(e)   a combination of persons listed in paragraphs (a) to (d).

(2)   As soon as is reasonably practicable after the making of an administration application the applicant shall notify—

(a)   any person who has appointed an administrative receiver of the company,

(b)   any person who is or may be entitled to appoint an administrative receiver of the company,

(c)   any person who is or may be entitled to appoint an administrator of the company under paragraph 14, and

(d)   such other persons as may be prescribed.

(3)   An administration application may not be withdrawn without the permission of the court.

(4)   In sub-paragraph (1) "creditor" includes a contingent creditor and a prospective creditor.

[(5)   Sub-paragraph (1) is without prejudice to section 7(4)(b).]

Powers of court

13. (1)   On hearing an administration application the court may—

(a)   make the administration order sought;

(b)   dismiss the application;

(c)   adjourn the hearing conditionally or unconditionally;

(d)   make an interim order;

(e)   treat the application as a winding-up petition and make any order which the court could make under section 125;

(f)   make any other order which the court thinks appropriate.

(2)   An appointment of an administrator by administration order takes effect—

(a)   at a time appointed by the order, or

(b)   where no time is appointed by the order, when the order is made.

(3)   An interim order under sub-paragraph (1)(d) may, in particular—

(a)   restrict the exercise of a power of the directors or the company;

(b)   make provision conferring a discretion on the court or on a person qualified to act as an insolvency practitioner in relation to the company.

(4)   This paragraph is subject to paragraph 39.

APPOINTMENT OF ADMINISTRATOR BY HOLDER OF FLOATING CHARGE

Power to appoint

14. (1)   The holder of a qualifying floating charge in respect of a company's property may appoint an administrator of the company.

(2)   For the purposes of sub-paragraph (1) a floating charge qualifies if created by an instrument which—

(a)   states that this paragraph applies to the floating charge,

(b)   purports to empower the holder of the floating charge to appoint an administrator of the company,

(c)   purports to empower the holder of the floating charge to make an appointment which would be the appointment of an administrative receiver within the meaning given by section 29(2), or

(d)   purports to empower the holder of a floating charge in Scotland to appoint a receiver who on appointment would be an administrative receiver.

(3)   For the purposes of sub-paragraph (1) a person is the holder of a qualifying floating charge in respect of a company's property if he holds one or more debentures of the company secured—

(a)   by a qualifying floating charge which relates to the whole or substantially the whole of the company's property,

(b)   by a number of qualifying floating charges which together relate to the whole or substantially the whole of the company's property, or

(c)   by charges and other forms of security which together relate to the whole or substantially the whole of the company's property and at least one of which is a qualifying floating charge.

Restrictions on power to appoint

15. (1)   A person may not appoint an administrator under paragraph 14 unless—

(a)   he has given at least two business days' written notice to the holder of any prior floating charge which satisfies paragraph 14(2), or

(b)   the holder of any prior floating charge which satisfies paragraph 14(2) has consented in writing to the making of the appointment.

(2)   One floating charge is prior to another for the purposes of this paragraph if—

(a)   it was created first, or

(b)   it is to be treated as having priority in accordance with an agreement to which the holder of each floating charge was party.

(3)   Sub-paragraph (2) shall have effect in relation to Scotland as if the following were substituted for paragraph (a)—

"(a)   it has priority of ranking in accordance with section 464(4)(b) of the Companies Act 1985 (c 6),

16. An administrator may not be appointed under paragraph 14 while a floating charge on which the appointment relies is not enforceable.

17. An administrator of a company may not be appointed under paragraph 14 if—
(a)   a provisional liquidator of the company has been appointed under section 135, or
(b)   an administrative receiver of the company is in office.

Notice of appointment

18. (1)   A person who appoints an administrator of a company under paragraph 14 shall file with the court—
(a)   a notice of appointment, and
(b)   such other documents as may be prescribed.

(2)   The notice of appointment must include a statutory declaration by or on behalf of the person who makes the appointment—
(a)   that the person is the holder of a qualifying floating charge in respect of the company's property,
(b)   that each floating charge relied on in making the appointment is (or was) enforceable on the date of the appointment, and
(c)   that the appointment is in accordance with this Schedule.

(3)   The notice of appointment must identify the administrator and must be accompanied by a statement by the administrator—
(a)   that he consents to the appointment,
(b)   that in his opinion the purpose of administration is reasonably likely to be achieved, and
(c)   giving such other information and opinions as may be prescribed.

(4)   For the purpose of a statement under sub-paragraph (3) an administrator may rely on information supplied by directors of the company (unless he has reason to doubt its accuracy).

(5)   The notice of appointment and any document accompanying it must be in the prescribed form.

(6)   A statutory declaration under sub-paragraph (2) must be made during the prescribed period.

(7)   A person commits an offence if in a statutory declaration under sub-paragraph (2) he makes a statement—
(a)   which is false, and
(b)   which he does not reasonably believe to be true.

Commencement of appointment

19. The appointment of an administrator under paragraph 14 takes effect when the requirements of paragraph 18 are satisfied.

20. A person who appoints an administrator under paragraph 14—
(a)   shall notify the administrator and such other persons as may be prescribed as soon as is reasonably practicable after the requirements of paragraph 18 are satisfied, and
(b)   commits an offence if he fails without reasonable excuse to comply with paragraph (a).

Invalid appointment: indemnity

21. (1)   This paragraph applies where—
(a)   a person purports to appoint an administrator under paragraph 14, and
(b)   the appointment is discovered to be invalid.

(2)   The court may order the person who purported to make the appointment to indemnify the person appointed against liability which arises solely by reason of the appointment's invalidity.

APPOINTMENT OF ADMINISTRATOR BY COMPANY OR DIRECTORS

Power to appoint

22. (1)   A company may appoint an administrator.
(2)   The directors of a company may appoint an administrator.

Restrictions on power to appoint

23. (1)   This paragraph applies where an administrator of a company is appointed—
(a)   under paragraph 22, or
(b)   on an administration application made by the company or its directors.

(2)   An administrator of the company may not be appointed under paragraph 22 during the period of 12 months beginning with the date on which the appointment referred to in sub-paragraph (1) ceases to have effect.

24. (1)   If a moratorium for a company under Schedule A1 ends on a date when no voluntary arrangement is in force in respect of the company, this paragraph applies for the period of 12 months beginning with that date.

(2)   This paragraph also applies for the period of 12 months beginning with the date on which a voluntary arrangement in respect of a company ends if—
- (a)   the arrangement was made during a moratorium for the company under Schedule A1, and
- (b)   the arrangement ends prematurely (within the meaning of section 7B).

(3)   While this paragraph applies, an administrator of the company may not be appointed under paragraph 22.

25.   An administrator of a company may not be appointed under paragraph 22 if—
- (a)   a petition for the winding up of the company has been presented and is not yet disposed of,
- (b)   an administration application has been made and is not yet disposed of, or
- (c)   an administrative receiver of the company is in office.

Notice of intention to appoint

26. (1)   A person who proposes to make an appointment under paragraph 22 shall give at least five business days' written notice to—
- (a)   any person who is or may be entitled to appoint an administrative receiver of the company, and
- (b)   any person who is or may be entitled to appoint an administrator of the company under paragraph 14.

(2)   A person who proposes to make an appointment under paragraph 22 shall also give such notice as may be prescribed to such other persons as may be prescribed.

(3)   A notice under this paragraph must—
- (a)   identify the proposed administrator, and
- (b)   be in the prescribed form.

27. (1)   A person who gives notice of intention to appoint under paragraph 26 shall file with the court as soon as is reasonably practicable a copy of—
- (a)   the notice, and
- (b)   any document accompanying it.

(2)   The copy filed under sub-paragraph (1) must be accompanied by a statutory declaration made by or on behalf of the person who proposes to make the appointment—
- (a)   that the company is or is likely to become unable to pay its debts,
- (b)   that the company is not in liquidation, and
- (c)   that, so far as the person making the statement is able to ascertain, the appointment is not prevented by paragraphs 23 to 25, and
- (d)   to such additional effect, and giving such information, as may be prescribed.

(3)   A statutory declaration under sub-paragraph (2) must—
- (a)   be in the prescribed form, and
- (b)   be made during the prescribed period.

(4)   A person commits an offence if in a statutory declaration under sub-paragraph (2) he makes a statement—
- (a)   which is false, and
- (b)   which he does not reasonably believe to be true.

28. (1)   An appointment may not be made under paragraph 22 unless the person who makes the appointment has complied with any requirement of paragraphs 26 and 27 and—
- (a)   the period of notice specified in paragraph 26(1) has expired, or
- (b)   each person to whom notice has been given under paragraph 26(1) has consented in writing to the making of the appointment.

(2)   An appointment may not be made under paragraph 22 after the period of ten business days beginning with the date on which the notice of intention to appoint is filed under paragraph 27(1).

Notice of appointment

29. (1)   A person who appoints an administrator of a company under paragraph 22 shall file with the court—
- (a)   a notice of appointment, and
- (b)   such other documents as may be prescribed.

(2)   The notice of appointment must include a statutory declaration by or on behalf of the person who makes the appointment—
- (a)   that the person is entitled to make an appointment under paragraph 22,
- (b)   that the appointment is in accordance with this Schedule, and

(c)   that, so far as the person making the statement is able to ascertain, the statements made and information given in the statutory declaration filed with the notice of intention to appoint remain accurate.

(3)   The notice of appointment must identify the administrator and must be accompanied by a statement by the administrator—

(a)   that he consents to the appointment,

(b)   that in his opinion the purpose of administration is reasonably likely to be achieved, and

(c)   giving such other information and opinions as may be prescribed.

(4)   For the purpose of a statement under sub-paragraph (3) an administrator may rely on information supplied by directors of the company (unless he has reason to doubt its accuracy).

(5)   The notice of appointment and any document accompanying it must be in the prescribed form.

(6)   A statutory declaration under sub-paragraph (2) must be made during the prescribed period.

(7)   A person commits an offence if in a statutory declaration under sub-paragraph (2) he makes a statement—

(a)   which is false, and

(b)   which he does not reasonably believe to be true.

30.   In a case in which no person is entitled to notice of intention to appoint under paragraph 26(1) (and paragraph 28 therefore does not apply)—

(a)   the statutory declaration accompanying the notice of appointment must include the statements and information required under paragraph 27(2), and

(b)   paragraph 29(2)(c) shall not apply.

Commencement of appointment

31.   The appointment of an administrator under paragraph 22 takes effect when the requirements of paragraph 29 are satisfied.

32.   A person who appoints an administrator under paragraph 22—

(a)   shall notify the administrator and such other persons as may be prescribed as soon as is reasonably practicable after the requirements of paragraph 29 are satisfied, and

(b)   commits an offence if he fails without reasonable excuse to comply with paragraph (a).

33.   If before the requirements of paragraph 29 are satisfied the company enters administration by virtue of an administration order or an appointment under paragraph 14—

(a)   the appointment under paragraph 22 shall not take effect, and

(b)   paragraph 32 shall not apply.

Invalid appointment: indemnity

34.   (1)   This paragraph applies where—

(a)   a person purports to appoint an administrator under paragraph 22, and

(b)   the appointment is discovered to be invalid.

(2)   The court may order the person who purported to make the appointment to indemnify the person appointed against liability which arises solely by reason of the appointment's invalidity.

ADMINISTRATION APPLICATION—SPECIAL CASES

Application by holder of floating charge

35.   (1)   This paragraph applies where an administration application in respect of a company—

(a)   is made by the holder of a qualifying floating charge in respect of the company's property, and

(b)   includes a statement that the application is made in reliance on this paragraph.

(2)   The court may make an administration order—

(a)   whether or not satisfied that the company is or is likely to become unable to pay its debts, but

(b)   only if satisfied that the applicant could appoint an administrator under paragraph 14.

Intervention by holder of floating charge

36.   (1)   This paragraph applies where—

(a)   an administration application in respect of a company is made by a person who is not the holder of a qualifying floating charge in respect of the company's property, and

(b)   the holder of a qualifying floating charge in respect of the company's property applies to the court to have a specified person appointed as administrator (and not the person specified by the administration applicant).

(2)   The court shall grant an application under sub-paragraph (1)(b) unless the court thinks it right to refuse the application because of the particular circumstances of the case.

Application where company in liquidation

37. (1)   This paragraph applies where the holder of a qualifying floating charge in respect of a company's property could appoint an administrator under paragraph 14 but for paragraph 8(1)(b).

(2)   The holder of the qualifying floating charge may make an administration application.

(3)   If the court makes an administration order on hearing an application made by virtue of sub-paragraph (2)—
- (a)   the court shall discharge the winding-up order,
- (b)   the court shall make provision for such matters as may be prescribed,
- (c)   the court may make other consequential provision,
- (d)   the court shall specify which of the powers under this Schedule are to be exercisable by the administrator, and
- (e)   this Schedule shall have effect with such modifications as the court may specify.

38. (1)   The liquidator of a company may make an administration application.

(2)   If the court makes an administration order on hearing an application made by virtue of sub-paragraph (1)—
- (a)   the court shall discharge any winding-up order in respect of the company,
- (b)   the court shall make provision for such matters as may be prescribed,
- (c)   the court may make other consequential provision,
- (d)   the court shall specify which of the powers under this Schedule are to be exercisable by the administrator, and
- (e)   this Schedule shall have effect with such modifications as the court may specify.

Effect of administrative receivership

39. (1)   Where there is an administrative receiver of a company the court must dismiss an administration application in respect of the company unless—
- (a)   the person by or on behalf of whom the receiver was appointed consents to the making of the administration order,
- (b)   the court thinks that the security by virtue of which the receiver was appointed would be liable to be released or discharged under sections 238 to 240 (transaction at undervalue and preference) if an administration order were made,
- (c)   the court thinks that the security by virtue of which the receiver was appointed would be avoided under section 245 (avoidance of floating charge) if an administration order were made, or
- (d)   the court thinks that the security by virtue of which the receiver was appointed would be challengeable under section 242 (gratuitous alienations) or 243 (unfair preferences) or under any rule of law in Scotland.

(2)   Sub-paragraph (1) applies whether the administrative receiver is appointed before or after the making of the administration application.

EFFECT OF ADMINISTRATION

Dismissal of pending winding-up petition

40. (1)   A petition for the winding up of a company—
- (a)   shall be dismissed on the making of an administration order in respect of the company, and
- (b)   shall be suspended while the company is in administration following an appointment under paragraph 14.

(2)   Sub-paragraph (1)(b) does not apply to a petition presented under—
- (a)   section 124A (public interest),
- [(aa)   section 124B (SEs),] or
- (b)   section 367 of the Financial Services and Markets Act 2000 (c 8) (petition by Financial Services Authority).

(3)   Where an administrator becomes aware that a petition was presented under a provision referred to in sub-paragraph (2) before his appointment, he shall apply to the court for directions under paragraph 63.

Dismissal of administrative or other receiver

41. (1)   When an administration order takes effect in respect of a company any administrative receiver of the company shall vacate office.

(2)   Where a company is in administration, any receiver of part of the company's property shall vacate office if the administrator requires him to.

(3)   Where an administrative receiver or receiver vacates office under sub-paragraph (1) or (2)—
- (a)   his remuneration shall be charged on and paid out of any property of the company which was in his custody or under his control immediately before he vacated office, and
- (b)   he need not take any further steps under section 40 or 59.

(4)   In the application of sub-paragraph (3)(a)—

(a)   "remuneration" includes expenses properly incurred and any indemnity to which the administrative receiver or receiver is entitled out of the assets of the company,

(b)   the charge imposed takes priority over security held by the person by whom or on whose behalf the administrative receiver or receiver was appointed, and

(c)   the provision for payment is subject to paragraph 43.

Moratorium on insolvency proceedings

42. (1)   This paragraph applies to a company in administration.

(2)   No resolution may be passed for the winding up of the company.

(3)   No order may be made for the winding up of the company.

(4)   Sub-paragraph (3) does not apply to an order made on a petition presented under—
(a)   section 124A (public interest),
[(aa) section 124B (SEs),] or
(b)   section 367 of the Financial Services and Markets Act 2000 (c 8) (petition by Financial Services Authority).

(5)   If a petition presented under a provision referred to in sub-paragraph (4) comes to the attention of the administrator, he shall apply to the court for directions under paragraph 63.

Moratorium on other legal process

43. (1)   This paragraph applies to a company in administration.

(2)   No step may be taken to enforce security over the company's property except—
(a)   with the consent of the administrator, or
(b)   with the permission of the court.

(3)   No step may be taken to repossess goods in the company's possession under a hire-purchase agreement except—
(a)   with the consent of the administrator, or
(b)   with the permission of the court.

(4)   A landlord may not exercise a right of forfeiture by peaceable re-entry in relation to premises let to the company except—
(a)   with the consent of the administrator, or
(b)   with the permission of the court.

(5)   In Scotland, a landlord may not exercise a right of irritancy in relation to premises let to the company except—
(a)   with the consent of the administrator, or
(b)   with the permission of the court.

(6)   No legal process (including legal proceedings, execution, distress and diligence) may be instituted or continued against the company or property of the company except—
(a)   with the consent of the administrator, or
(b)   with the permission of the court.

[(6A)   An administrative receiver of the company may not be appointed.]

(7)   Where the court gives permission for a transaction under this paragraph it may impose a condition on or a requirement in connection with the transaction.

(8)   In this paragraph "landlord" includes a person to whom rent is payable.

Interim moratorium

44. (1)   This paragraph applies where an administration application in respect of a company has been made and—
(a)   the application has not yet been granted or dismissed, or
(b)   the application has been granted but the administration order has not yet taken effect.

(2)   This paragraph also applies from the time when a copy of notice of intention to appoint an administrator under paragraph 14 is filed with the court until—
(a)   the appointment of the administrator takes effect, or
(b)   the period of five business days beginning with the date of filing expires without an administrator having been appointed.

(3)   Sub-paragraph (2) has effect in relation to a notice of intention to appoint only if it is in the prescribed form.

(4)   This paragraph also applies from the time when a copy of notice of intention to appoint an administrator is filed with the court under paragraph 27(1) until—
(a)   the appointment of the administrator takes effect, or
(b)   the period specified in paragraph 28(2) expires without an administrator having been appointed.

(5)   The provisions of paragraphs 42 and 43 shall apply (ignoring any reference to the consent of the administrator).

(6)   If there is an administrative receiver of the company when the administration application is made, the provisions of paragraphs 42 and 43 shall not begin to apply by virtue of this paragraph until the person by or on behalf of whom the receiver was appointed consents to the making of the administration order.

(7)   This paragraph does not prevent or require the permission of the court for—
  (a)   the presentation of a petition for the winding up of the company under a provision mentioned in paragraph 42(4),
  (b)   the appointment of an administrator under paragraph 14,
  (c)   the appointment of an administrative receiver of the company, or
  (d)   the carrying out by an administrative receiver (whenever appointed) of his functions.

Publicity

[**45.** (1)   While a company is in administration, every business document issued by or on behalf of the company or the administrator, and all the company's websites, must state—
  (a)   the name of the administrator, and
  (b)   that the affairs, business and property of the company are being managed by the administrator.

(2)   Any of the following persons commits an offence if without reasonable excuse the person authorises or permits a contravention of sub-paragraph (1)—
  (a)   the administrator,
  (b)   an officer of the company, and
  (c)   the company.

(3)   In sub-paragraph (1) "business document" means—
  (a)   an invoice,
  (b)   an order for goods or services,
  (c)   a business letter, and
  (d)   an order form,
whether in hard copy, electronic or any other form.]

PROCESS OF ADMINISTRATION

Announcement of administrator's appointment

46. (1)   This paragraph applies where a person becomes the administrator of a company.

(2)   As soon as is reasonably practicable the administrator shall—
  (a)   send a notice of his appointment to the company, and
  (b)   publish a notice of his appointment in the prescribed manner.

(3)   As soon as is reasonably practicable the administrator shall—
  (a)   obtain a list of the company's creditors, and
  (b)   send a notice of his appointment to each creditor of whose claim and address he is aware.

(4)   The administrator shall send a notice of his appointment to the registrar of companies before the end of the period of 7 days beginning with the date specified in sub-paragraph (6).

(5)   The administrator shall send a notice of his appointment to such persons as may be prescribed before the end of the prescribed period beginning with the date specified in sub-paragraph (6).

(6)   The date for the purpose of sub-paragraphs (4) and (5) is—
  (a)   in the case of an administrator appointed by administration order, the date of the order,
  (b)   in the case of an administrator appointed under paragraph 14, the date on which he receives notice under paragraph 20, and
  (c)   in the case of an administrator appointed under paragraph 22, the date on which he receives notice under paragraph 32.

(7)   The court may direct that sub-paragraph (3)(b) or (5)—
  (a)   shall not apply, or
  (b)   shall apply with the substitution of a different period.

(8)   A notice under this paragraph must—
  (a)   contain the prescribed information, and
  (b)   be in the prescribed form.

(9)   An administrator commits an offence if he fails without reasonable excuse to comply with a requirement of this paragraph.

Statement of company's affairs

47. (1)   As soon as is reasonably practicable after appointment the administrator of a company shall by notice in the prescribed form require one or more relevant persons to provide the administrator with a statement of the affairs of the company.

(2)   The statement must—
  (a)   be verified by a statement of truth in accordance with Civil Procedure Rules,
  (b)   be in the prescribed form,
  (c)   give particulars of the company's property, debts and liabilities,

(d)   give the names and addresses of the company's creditors,

(e)   specify the security held by each creditor,

(f)   give the date on which each security was granted, and

(g)   contain such other information as may be prescribed.

(3)   In sub-paragraph (1) "relevant person" means—

(a)   a person who is or has been an officer of the company,

(b)   a person who took part in the formation of the company during the period of one year ending with the date on which the company enters administration,

(c)   a person employed by the company during that period, and

(d)   a person who is or has been during that period an officer or employee of a company which is or has been during that year an officer of the company.

(4)   For the purpose of sub-paragraph (3) a reference to employment is a reference to employment through a contract of employment or a contract for services.

(5)   In Scotland, a statement of affairs under sub-paragraph (1) must be a statutory declaration made in accordance with the Statutory Declarations Act 1835 (c 62) (and sub-paragraph (2)(a) shall not apply).

48.   (1)   A person required to submit a statement of affairs must do so before the end of the period of 11 days beginning with the day on which he receives notice of the requirement.

(2)   The administrator may—

(a)   revoke a requirement under paragraph 47(1), or

(b)   extend the period specified in sub-paragraph (1) (whether before or after expiry).

(3)   If the administrator refuses a request to act under sub-paragraph (2)—

(a)   the person whose request is refused may apply to the court, and

(b)   the court may take action of a kind specified in sub-paragraph (2).

(4)   A person commits an offence if he fails without reasonable excuse to comply with a requirement under paragraph 47(1).

Administrator's proposals

49.   (1)   The administrator of a company shall make a statement setting out proposals for achieving the purpose of administration.

(2)   A statement under sub-paragraph (1) must, in particular—

(a)   deal with such matters as may be prescribed, and

(b)   where applicable, explain why the administrator thinks that the objective mentioned in paragraph 3(1)(a) or (b) cannot be achieved.

(3)   Proposals under this paragraph may include—

(a)   a proposal for a voluntary arrangement under Part I of this Act (although this paragraph is without prejudice to section 4(3));

(b)   a proposal for a compromise or arrangement to be sanctioned under [Part 26 of the Companies Act 2006 (arrangements and reconstructions)].

(4)   The administrator shall send a copy of the statement of his proposals—

(a)   to the registrar of companies,

(b)   to every creditor of the company of whose claim and address he is aware, and

(c)   to every member of the company of whose address he is aware.

(5)   The administrator shall comply with sub-paragraph (4)—

(a)   as soon as is reasonably practicable after the company enters administration, and

(b)   in any event, before the end of the period of eight weeks beginning with the day on which the company enters administration.

(6)   The administrator shall be taken to comply with sub-paragraph (4)(c) if he publishes in the prescribed manner a notice undertaking to provide a copy of the statement of proposals free of charge to any member of the company who applies in writing to a specified address.

(7)   An administrator commits an offence if he fails without reasonable excuse to comply with sub-paragraph (5).

(8)   A period specified in this paragraph may be varied in accordance with paragraph 107.

Creditors' meeting

50.   (1)   In this Schedule "creditors' meeting" means a meeting of creditors of a company summoned by the administrator—

(a)   in the prescribed manner, and

(b)   giving the prescribed period of notice to every creditor of the company of whose claim and address he is aware.

(2)   A period prescribed under sub-paragraph (1)(b) may be varied in accordance with paragraph 107.

(3)   A creditors' meeting shall be conducted in accordance with the rules.

Requirement for initial creditors' meeting

51. (1) Each copy of an administrator's statement of proposals sent to a creditor under paragraph 49(4)(b) must be accompanied by an invitation to a creditors' meeting (an "initial creditors' meeting").

(2) The date set for an initial creditors' meeting must be—

    (a) as soon as is reasonably practicable after the company enters administration, and

    (b) in any event, within the period of ten weeks beginning with the date on which the company enters administration.

(3) An administrator shall present a copy of his statement of proposals to an initial creditors' meeting.

(4) A period specified in this paragraph may be varied in accordance with paragraph 107.

(5) An administrator commits an offence if he fails without reasonable excuse to comply with a requirement of this paragraph.

52. (1) Paragraph 51(1) shall not apply where the statement of proposals states that the administrator thinks—

    (a) that the company has sufficient property to enable each creditor of the company to be paid in full,

    (b) that the company has insufficient property to enable a distribution to be made to unsecured creditors other than by virtue of section 176A(2)(a), or

    (c) that neither of the objectives specified in paragraph 3(1)(a) and (b) can be achieved.

(2) But the administrator shall summon an initial creditors' meeting if it is requested—

    (a) by creditors of the company whose debts amount to at least 10% of the total debts of the company,

    (b) in the prescribed manner, and

    (c) in the prescribed period.

(3) A meeting requested under sub-paragraph (2) must be summoned for a date in the prescribed period.

(4) The period prescribed under sub-paragraph (3) may be varied in accordance with paragraph 107.

Business and result of initial creditors' meeting

53. (1) An initial creditors' meeting to which an administrator's proposals are presented shall consider them and may—

    (a) approve them without modification, or

    (b) approve them with modification to which the administrator consents.

(2) After the conclusion of an initial creditors' meeting the administrator shall as soon as is reasonably practicable report any decision taken to—

    (a) the court,

    (b) the registrar of companies, and

    (c) such other persons as may be prescribed.

(3) An administrator commits an offence if he fails without reasonable excuse to comply with sub-paragraph (2).

Revision of administrator's proposals

54. (1) This paragraph applies where—

    (a) an administrator's proposals have been approved (with or without modification) at an initial creditors' meeting,

    (b) the administrator proposes a revision to the proposals, and

    (c) the administrator thinks that the proposed revision is substantial.

(2) The administrator shall—

    (a) summon a creditors' meeting,

    (b) send a statement in the prescribed form of the proposed revision with the notice of the meeting sent to each creditor,

    (c) send a copy of the statement, within the prescribed period, to each member of the company of whose address he is aware, and

    (d) present a copy of the statement to the meeting.

(3) The administrator shall be taken to have complied with sub-paragraph (2)(c) if he publishes a notice undertaking to provide a copy of the statement free of charge to any member of the company who applies in writing to a specified address.

(4) A notice under sub-paragraph (3) must be published—

    (a) in the prescribed manner, and

    (b) within the prescribed period.

(5) A creditors' meeting to which a proposed revision is presented shall consider it and may—

    (a) approve it without modification, or

    (b)   approve it with modification to which the administrator consents.

(6) After the conclusion of a creditors' meeting the administrator shall as soon as is reasonably practicable report any decision taken to—

    (a)   the court,

    (b)   the registrar of companies, and

    (c)   such other persons as may be prescribed.

(7) An administrator commits an offence if he fails without reasonable excuse to comply with sub-paragraph (6).

Failure to obtain approval of administrator's proposals

55. (1) This paragraph applies where an administrator reports to the court that—

    (a)   an initial creditors' meeting has failed to approve the administrator's proposals presented to it, or

    (b)   a creditors' meeting has failed to approve a revision of the administrator's proposals presented to it.

(2) The court may—

    (a)   provide that the appointment of an administrator shall cease to have effect from a specified time;

    (b)   adjourn the hearing conditionally or unconditionally;

    (c)   make an interim order;

    (d)   make an order on a petition for winding up suspended by virtue of paragraph 40(1)(b);

    (e)   make any other order (including an order making consequential provision) that the court thinks appropriate.

Further creditors' meetings

56. (1) The administrator of a company shall summon a creditors' meeting if—

    (a)   it is requested in the prescribed manner by creditors of the company whose debts amount to at least 10% of the total debts of the company, or

    (b)   he is directed by the court to summon a creditors' meeting.

(2) An administrator commits an offence if he fails without reasonable excuse to summon a creditors' meeting as required by this paragraph.

Creditors' committee

57. (1) A creditors' meeting may establish a creditors' committee.

(2) A creditors' committee shall carry out functions conferred on it by or under this Act.

(3) A creditors' committee may require the administrator—

    (a)   to attend on the committee at any reasonable time of which he is given at least seven days' notice, and

    (b)   to provide the committee with information about the exercise of his functions.

Correspondence instead of creditors' meeting

58. (1) Anything which is required or permitted by or under this Schedule to be done at a creditors' meeting may be done by correspondence between the administrator and creditors—

    (a)   in accordance with the rules, and

    (b)   subject to any prescribed condition.

(2) A reference in this Schedule to anything done at a creditors' meeting includes a reference to anything done in the course of correspondence in reliance on sub-paragraph (1).

(3) A requirement to hold a creditors' meeting is satisfied by conducting correspondence in accordance with this paragraph.

FUNCTIONS OF ADMINISTRATOR

General powers

59. (1) The administrator of a company may do anything necessary or expedient for the management of the affairs, business and property of the company.

(2) A provision of this Schedule which expressly permits the administrator to do a specified thing is without prejudice to the generality of sub-paragraph (1).

(3) A person who deals with the administrator of a company in good faith and for value need not inquire whether the administrator is acting within his powers.

60. The administrator of a company has the powers specified in Schedule 1 to this Act.

61. The administrator of a company—

    (a)   may remove a director of the company, and

    (b)   may appoint a director of the company (whether or not to fill a vacancy).

62. The administrator of a company may call a meeting of members or creditors of the company.

63. The administrator of a company may apply to the court for directions in connection with his functions.

64. (1) A company in administration or an officer of a company in administration may not exercise a management power without the consent of the administrator.

(2) For the purpose of sub-paragraph (1)—
- (a) "management power" means a power which could be exercised so as to interfere with the exercise of the administrator's powers,
- (b) it is immaterial whether the power is conferred by an enactment or an instrument, and
- (c) consent may be general or specific.

Distribution

65. (1) The administrator of a company may make a distribution to a creditor of the company.

(2) Section 175 shall apply in relation to a distribution under this paragraph as it applies in relation to a winding up.

(3) A payment may not be made by way of distribution under this paragraph to a creditor of the company who is neither secured nor preferential unless the court gives permission.

66. The administrator of a company may make a payment otherwise than in accordance with paragraph 65 or paragraph 13 of Schedule 1 if he thinks it likely to assist achievement of the purpose of administration.

General duties

67. The administrator of a company shall on his appointment take custody or control of all the property to which he thinks the company is entitled.

68. (1) Subject to sub-paragraph (2), the administrator of a company shall manage its affairs, business and property in accordance with—
- (a) any proposals approved under paragraph 53,
- (b) any revision of those proposals which is made by him and which he does not consider substantial, and
- (c) any revision of those proposals approved under paragraph 54.

(2) If the court gives directions to the administrator of a company in connection with any aspect of his management of the company's affairs, business or property, the administrator shall comply with the directions.

(3) The court may give directions under sub-paragraph (2) only if—
- (a) no proposals have been approved under paragraph 53,
- (b) the directions are consistent with any proposals or revision approved under paragraph 53 or 54,
- (c) the court thinks the directions are required in order to reflect a change in circumstances since the approval of proposals or a revision under paragraph 53 or 54, or
- (d) the court thinks the directions are desirable because of a misunderstanding about proposals or a revision approved under paragraph 53 or 54.

Administrator as agent of company

69. In exercising his functions under this Schedule the administrator of a company acts as its agent.

Charged property: floating charge

70. (1) The administrator of a company may dispose of or take action relating to property which is subject to a floating charge as if it were not subject to the charge.

(2) Where property is disposed of in reliance on sub-paragraph (1) the holder of the floating charge shall have the same priority in respect of acquired property as he had in respect of the property disposed of.

(3) In sub-paragraph (2) "acquired property" means property of the company which directly or indirectly represents the property disposed of.

Charged property: non-floating charge

71. (1) The court may by order enable the administrator of a company to dispose of property which is subject to a security (other than a floating charge) as if it were not subject to the security.

(2) An order under sub-paragraph (1) may be made only—
- (a) on the application of the administrator, and
- (b) where the court thinks that disposal of the property would be likely to promote the purpose of administration in respect of the company.

(3) An order under this paragraph is subject to the condition that there be applied towards discharging the sums secured by the security—
- (a) the net proceeds of disposal of the property, and

   (b)   any additional money required to be added to the net proceeds so as to produce the amount determined by the court as the net amount which would be realised on a sale of the property at market value.

(4)   If an order under this paragraph relates to more than one security, application of money under sub-paragraph (3) shall be in the order of the priorities of the securities.

(5)   An administrator who makes a successful application for an order under this paragraph shall send a copy of the order to the registrar of companies before the end of the period of 14 days starting with the date of the order.

(6)   An administrator commits an offence if he fails to comply with sub-paragraph (5) without reasonable excuse.

Hire-purchase property

72. (1)   The court may by order enable the administrator of a company to dispose of goods which are in the possession of the company under a hire-purchase agreement as if all the rights of the owner under the agreement were vested in the company.

(2)   An order under sub-paragraph (1) may be made only—
   (a)   on the application of the administrator, and
   (b)   where the court thinks that disposal of the goods would be likely to promote the purpose of administration in respect of the company.

(3)   An order under this paragraph is subject to the condition that there be applied towards discharging the sums payable under the hire-purchase agreement—
   (a)   the net proceeds of disposal of the goods, and
   (b)   any additional money required to be added to the net proceeds so as to produce the amount determined by the court as the net amount which would be realised on a sale of the goods at market value.

(4)   An administrator who makes a successful application for an order under this paragraph shall send a copy of the order to the registrar of companies before the end of the period of 14 days starting with the date of the order.

(5)   An administrator commits an offence if he fails without reasonable excuse to comply with sub-paragraph (4).

Protection for secured or preferential creditor

73. (1)   An administrator's statement of proposals under paragraph 49 may not include any action which—
   (a)   affects the right of a secured creditor of the company to enforce his security,
   (b)   would result in a preferential debt of the company being paid otherwise than in priority to its non-preferential debts, or
   (c)   would result in one preferential creditor of the company being paid a smaller proportion of his debt than another.

(2)   Sub-paragraph (1) does not apply to—
   (a)   action to which the relevant creditor consents,
   (b)   a proposal for a voluntary arrangement under Part I of this Act (although this sub-paragraph is without prejudice to section 4(3)), . . .
   (c)   a proposal for a compromise or arrangement to be sanctioned under [Part 26 of the Companies Act 2006 (arrangements and reconstructions)]; [or
   (d)   a proposal for a cross-border merger within the meaning of regulation 2 of the Companies (Cross-Border Mergers) Regulations 2007].

(3)   The reference to a statement of proposals in sub-paragraph (1) includes a reference to a statement as revised or modified.

Challenge to administrator's conduct of company

74. (1)   A creditor or member of a company in administration may apply to the court claiming that—
   (a)   the administrator is acting or has acted so as unfairly to harm the interests of the applicant (whether alone or in common with some or all other members or creditors), or
   (b)   the administrator proposes to act in a way which would unfairly harm the interests of the applicant (whether alone or in common with some or all other members or creditors).

(2)   A creditor or member of a company in administration may apply to the court claiming that the administrator is not performing his functions as quickly or as efficiently as is reasonably practicable.

(3)   The court may—
   (a)   grant relief;
   (b)   dismiss the application;
   (c)   adjourn the hearing conditionally or unconditionally;
   (d)   make an interim order;
   (e)   make any other order it thinks appropriate.

(4)   In particular, an order under this paragraph may—
  (a)   regulate the administrator's exercise of his functions;
  (b)   require the administrator to do or not do a specified thing;
  (c)   require a creditors' meeting to be held for a specified purpose;
  (d)   provide for the appointment of an administrator to cease to have effect;
  (e)   make consequential provision.

(5)   An order may be made on a claim under sub-paragraph (1) whether or not the action complained of—
  (a)   is within the administrator's powers under this Schedule;
  (b)   was taken in reliance on an order under paragraph 71 or 72.

(6)   An order may not be made under this paragraph if it would impede or prevent the implementation of—
  (a)   a voluntary arrangement approved under Part I,
  (b)   a compromise or arrangement sanctioned under [Part 26 of the Companies Act 2006 (arrangements and reconstructions)],   . . .
  [(ba) a cross-border merger within the meaning of regulation 2 of the Companies (Cross-Border Mergers) Regulations 2007, or].
  (c)   proposals or a revision approved under paragraph 53 or 54 more than 28 days before the day on which the application for the order under this paragraph is made.

Misfeasance

75.   (1)   The court may examine the conduct of a person who—
  (a)   is or purports to be the administrator of a company, or
  (b)   has been or has purported to be the administrator of a company.

(2)   An examination under this paragraph may be held only on the application of—
  (a)   the official receiver,
  (b)   the administrator of the company,
  (c)   the liquidator of the company,
  (d)   a creditor of the company, or
  (e)   a contributory of the company.

(3)   An application under sub-paragraph (2) must allege that the administrator—
  (a)   has misapplied or retained money or other property of the company,
  (b)   has become accountable for money or other property of the company,
  (c)   has breached a fiduciary or other duty in relation to the company, or
  (d)   has been guilty of misfeasance.

(4)   On an examination under this paragraph into a person's conduct the court may order him—
  (a)   to repay, restore or account for money or property;
  (b)   to pay interest;
  (c)   to contribute a sum to the company's property by way of compensation for breach of duty or misfeasance.

(5)   In sub-paragraph (3) "administrator" includes a person who purports or has purported to be a company's administrator.

(6)   An application under sub-paragraph (2) may be made in respect of an administrator who has been discharged under paragraph 98 only with the permission of the court.

ENDING ADMINISTRATION
Automatic end of administration

76.   (1)   The appointment of an administrator shall cease to have effect at the end of the period of one year beginning with the date on which it takes effect.

(2)   But—
  (a)   on the application of an administrator the court may by order extend his term of office for a specified period, and
  (b)   an administrator's term of office may be extended for a specified period not exceeding six months by consent.

77.   (1)   An order of the court under paragraph 76—
  (a)   may be made in respect of an administrator whose term of office has already been extended by order or by consent, but
  (b)   may not be made after the expiry of the administrator's term of office.

(2)   Where an order is made under paragraph 76 the administrator shall as soon as is reasonably practicable notify the registrar of companies.

(3)   An administrator who fails without reasonable excuse to comply with sub-paragraph (2) commits an offence.

78.   (1)   In paragraph 76(2)(b) "consent" means consent of—
  (a)   each secured creditor of the company, and

(b)   if the company has unsecured debts, creditors whose debts amount to more than 50% of the company's unsecured debts, disregarding debts of any creditor who does not respond to an invitation to give or withhold consent.

(2)   But where the administrator has made a statement under paragraph 52(1)(b) "consent" means—

(a)   consent of each secured creditor of the company, or

(b)   if the administrator thinks that a distribution may be made to preferential creditors, consent of—

(i)   each secured creditor of the company, and

(ii)   preferential creditors whose debts amount to more than 50% of the preferential debts of the company, disregarding debts of any creditor who does not respond to an invitation to give or withhold consent.

(3)   Consent for the purposes of paragraph 76(2)(b) may be—

(a)   written, or

(b)   signified at a creditors' meeting.

(4)   An administrator's term of office—

(a)   may be extended by consent only once,

(b)   may not be extended by consent after extension by order of the court, and

(c)   may not be extended by consent after expiry.

(5)   Where an administrator's term of office is extended by consent he shall as soon as is reasonably practicable—

(a)   file notice of the extension with the court, and

(b)   notify the registrar of companies.

(6)   An administrator who fails without reasonable excuse to comply with sub-paragraph (5) commits an offence.

Court ending administration on application of administrator

79. (1)   On the application of the administrator of a company the court may provide for the appointment of an administrator of the company to cease to have effect from a specified time.

(2)   The administrator of a company shall make an application under this paragraph if—

(a)   he thinks the purpose of administration cannot be achieved in relation to the company,

(b)   he thinks the company should not have entered administration, or

(c)   a creditors' meeting requires him to make an application under this paragraph.

(3)   The administrator of a company shall make an application under this paragraph if—

(a)   the administration is pursuant to an administration order, and

(b)   the administrator thinks that the purpose of administration has been sufficiently achieved in relation to the company.

(4)   On an application under this paragraph the court may—

(a)   adjourn the hearing conditionally or unconditionally;

(b)   dismiss the application;

(c)   make an interim order;

(d)   make any order it thinks appropriate (whether in addition to, in consequence of or instead of the order applied for).

Termination of administration where objective achieved

80. (1)   This paragraph applies where an administrator of a company is appointed under paragraph 14 or 22.

(2)   If the administrator thinks that the purpose of administration has been sufficiently achieved in relation to the company he may file a notice in the prescribed form—

(a)   with the court, and

(b)   with the registrar of companies.

(3)   The administrator's appointment shall cease to have effect when the requirements of sub-paragraph (2) are satisfied.

(4)   Where the administrator files a notice he shall within the prescribed period send a copy to every creditor of the company of whose claim and address he is aware.

(5)   The rules may provide that the administrator is taken to have complied with sub-paragraph (4) if before the end of the prescribed period he publishes in the prescribed manner a notice undertaking to provide a copy of the notice under sub-paragraph (2) to any creditor of the company who applies in writing to a specified address.

(6)   An administrator who fails without reasonable excuse to comply with sub-paragraph (4) commits an offence.

Court ending administration on application of creditor

81. (1)   On the application of a creditor of a company the court may provide for the appointment of an administrator of the company to cease to have effect at a specified time.

(2) An application under this paragraph must allege an improper motive—
- (a) in the case of an administrator appointed by administration order, on the part of the applicant for the order, or
- (b) in any other case, on the part of the person who appointed the administrator.

(3) On an application under this paragraph the court may—
- (a) adjourn the hearing conditionally or unconditionally;
- (b) dismiss the application;
- (c) make an interim order;
- (d) make any order it thinks appropriate (whether in addition to, in consequence of or instead of the order applied for).

Public interest winding-up

82. (1) This paragraph applies where a winding-up order is made for the winding up of a company in administration on a petition presented under—
- (a) section 124A (public interest),
- [(aa) section 124B (SEs),] or
- (b) section 367 of the Financial Services and Markets Act 2000 (c 8) (petition by Financial Services Authority).

(2) This paragraph also applies where a provisional liquidator of a company in administration is appointed following the presentation of a petition under any of the provisions listed in sub-paragraph (1).

(3) The court shall order—
- (a) that the appointment of the administrator shall cease to have effect, or
- (b) that the appointment of the administrator shall continue to have effect.

(4) If the court makes an order under sub-paragraph (3)(b) it may also—
- (a) specify which of the powers under this Schedule are to be exercisable by the administrator, and
- (b) order that this Schedule shall have effect in relation to the administrator with specified modifications.

Moving from administration to creditors' voluntary liquidation

83. (1) This paragraph applies in England and Wales where the administrator of a company thinks—
- (a) that the total amount which each secured creditor of the company is likely to receive has been paid to him or set aside for him, and
- (b) that a distribution will be made to unsecured creditors of the company (if there are any).

(2) This paragraph applies in Scotland where the administrator of a company thinks—
- (a) that each secured creditor of the company will receive payment in respect of his debt, and
- (b) that a distribution will be made to unsecured creditors (if there are any).

(3) The administrator may send to the registrar of companies a notice that this paragraph applies.

(4) On receipt of a notice under sub-paragraph (3) the registrar shall register it.

(5) If an administrator sends a notice under sub-paragraph (3) he shall as soon as is reasonably practicable—
- (a) file a copy of the notice with the court, and
- (b) send a copy of the notice to each creditor of whose claim and address he is aware.

(6) On the registration of a notice under sub-paragraph (3)—
- (a) the appointment of an administrator in respect of the company shall cease to have effect, and
- (b) the company shall be wound up as if a resolution for voluntary winding up under section 84 were passed on the day on which the notice is registered.

(7) The liquidator for the purposes of the winding up shall be—
- (a) a person nominated by the creditors of the company in the prescribed manner and within the prescribed period, or
- (b) if no person is nominated under paragraph (a), the administrator.

(8) In the application of Part IV to a winding up by virtue of this paragraph—
- (a) section 85 shall not apply,
- (b) section 86 shall apply as if the reference to the time of the passing of the resolution for voluntary winding up were a reference to the beginning of the date of registration of the notice under sub-paragraph (3),
- (c) section 89 does not apply,
- (d) sections 98, 99 and 100 shall not apply,
- (e) section 129 shall apply as if the reference to the time of the passing of the resolution for voluntary winding up were a reference to the beginning of the date of registration of the notice under sub-paragraph (3), and

(f)   any creditors' committee which is in existence immediately before the company ceases to be in administration shall continue in existence after that time as if appointed as a liquidation committee under section 101.

Moving from administration to dissolution

84. (1)   If the administrator of a company thinks that the company has no property which might permit a distribution to its creditors, he shall send a notice to that effect to the registrar of companies.

(2)   The court may on the application of the administrator of a company disapply sub-paragraph (1) in respect of the company.

(3)   On receipt of a notice under sub-paragraph (1) the registrar shall register it.

(4)   On the registration of a notice in respect of a company under sub-paragraph (1) the appointment of an administrator of the company shall cease to have effect.

(5)   If an administrator sends a notice under sub-paragraph (1) he shall as soon as is reasonably practicable—
   (a)   file a copy of the notice with the court, and
   (b)   send a copy of the notice to each creditor of whose claim and address he is aware.

(6)   At the end of the period of three months beginning with the date of registration of a notice in respect of a company under sub-paragraph (1) the company is deemed to be dissolved.

(7)   On an application in respect of a company by the administrator or another interested person the court may—
   (a)   extend the period specified in sub-paragraph (6),
   (b)   suspend that period, or
   (c)   disapply sub-paragraph (6).

(8)   Where an order is made under sub-paragraph (7) in respect of a company the administrator shall as soon as is reasonably practicable notify the registrar of companies.

(9)   An administrator commits an offence if he fails without reasonable excuse to comply with sub-paragraph (5).

Discharge of administration order where administration ends

85. (1)   This paragraph applies where—
   (a)   the court makes an order under this Schedule providing for the appointment of an administrator of a company to cease to have effect, and
   (b)   the administrator was appointed by administration order.

(2)   The court shall discharge the administration order.

Notice to Companies Registrar where administration ends

86. (1)   This paragraph applies where the court makes an order under this Schedule providing for the appointment of an administrator to cease to have effect.

(2)   The administrator shall send a copy of the order to the registrar of companies within the period of 14 days beginning with the date of the order.

(3)   An administrator who fails without reasonable excuse to comply with sub-paragraph (2) commits an offence.

REPLACING ADMINISTRATOR

Resignation of administrator

87. (1)   An administrator may resign only in prescribed circumstances.

(2)   Where an administrator may resign he may do so only—
   (a)   in the case of an administrator appointed by administration order, by notice in writing to the court,
   (b)   in the case of an administrator appointed under paragraph 14, by notice in writing to the [holder of the floating charge by virtue of which the appointment was made],
   (c)   in the case of an administrator appointed under paragraph 22(1), by notice in writing to the company, or
   (d)   in the case of an administrator appointed under paragraph 22(2), by notice in writing to the directors of the company.

Removal of administrator from office

88.   The court may by order remove an administrator from office.

Administrator ceasing to be qualified

89. (1)   The administrator of a company shall vacate office if he ceases to be qualified to act as an insolvency practitioner in relation to the company.

(2) Where an administrator vacates office by virtue of sub-paragraph (1) he shall give notice in writing—
- (a) in the case of an administrator appointed by administration order, to the court,
- (b) in the case of an administrator appointed under paragraph 14, to the [holder of the floating charge by virtue of which the appointment was made],
- (c) in the case of an administrator appointed under paragraph 22(1), to the company, or
- (d) in the case of an administrator appointed under paragraph 22(2), to the directors of the company.

(3) An administrator who fails without reasonable excuse to comply with sub-paragraph (2) commits an offence.

Supplying vacancy in office of administrator

90. Paragraphs 91 to 95 apply where an administrator—
- (a) dies,
- (b) resigns,
- (c) is removed from office under paragraph 88, or
- (d) vacates office under paragraph 89.

91. (1) Where the administrator was appointed by administration order, the court may replace the administrator on an application under this sub-paragraph made by—
- (a) a creditors' committee of the company,
- (b) the company,
- (c) the directors of the company,
- (d) one or more creditors of the company, or
- (e) where more than one person was appointed to act jointly or concurrently as the administrator, any of those persons who remains in office.

(2) But an application may be made in reliance on sub-paragraph (1)(b) to (d) only where—
- (a) there is no creditors' committee of the company,
- (b) the court is satisfied that the creditors' committee or a remaining administrator is not taking reasonable steps to make a replacement, or
- (c) the court is satisfied that for another reason it is right for the application to be made.

92. Where the administrator was appointed under paragraph 14 the holder of the floating charge by virtue of which the appointment was made may replace the administrator.

93. (1) Where the administrator was appointed under paragraph 22(1) by the company it may replace the administrator.

(2) A replacement under this paragraph may be made only—
- (a) with the consent of each person who is the holder of a qualifying floating charge in respect of the company's property, or
- (b) where consent is withheld, with the permission of the court.

94. (1) Where the administrator was appointed under paragraph 22(2) the directors of the company may replace the administrator.

(2) A replacement under this paragraph may be made only—
- (a) with the consent of each person who is the holder of a qualifying floating charge in respect of the company's property, or
- (b) where consent is withheld, with the permission of the court.

95. The court may replace an administrator on the application of a person listed in paragraph 91(1) if the court—
- (a) is satisfied that a person who is entitled to replace the administrator under any of paragraphs 92 to 94 is not taking reasonable steps to make a replacement, or
- (b) that for another reason it is right for the court to make the replacement.

Substitution of administrator: competing floating charge-holder

96. (1) This paragraph applies where an administrator of a company is appointed under paragraph 14 by the holder of a qualifying floating charge in respect of the company's property.

(2) The holder of a prior qualifying floating charge in respect of the company's property may apply to the court for the administrator to be replaced by an administrator nominated by the holder of the prior floating charge.

(3) One floating charge is prior to another for the purposes of this paragraph if—
- (a) it was created first, or
- (b) it is to be treated as having priority in accordance with an agreement to which the holder of each floating charge was party.

(4) Sub-paragraph (3) shall have effect in relation to Scotland as if the following were substituted for paragraph (a)—

"(a)   it has priority of ranking in accordance with section 464(4)(b) of the Companies Act 1985 (c 6),

Substitution of administrator appointed by company or directors: creditors' meeting

97. (1)   This paragraph applies where—
  (a)   an administrator of a company is appointed by a company or directors under paragraph 22, and
  (b)   there is no holder of a qualifying floating charge in respect of the company's property.
(2)   A creditors' meeting may replace the administrator.
(3)   A creditors' meeting may act under sub-paragraph (2) only if the new administrator's written consent to act is presented to the meeting before the replacement is made.

Vacation of office: discharge from liability

98. (1)   Where a person ceases to be the administrator of a company (whether because he vacates office by reason of resignation, death or otherwise, because he is removed from office or because his appointment ceases to have effect) he is discharged from liability in respect of any action of his as administrator.
(2)   The discharge provided by sub-paragraph (1) takes effect—
  (a)   in the case of an administrator who dies, on the filing with the court of notice of his death,
  (b)   in the case of an administrator appointed under paragraph 14 or 22, at a time appointed by resolution of the creditors' committee or, if there is no committee, by resolution of the creditors, or
  (c)   in any case, at a time specified by the court.
(3)   For the purpose of the application of sub-paragraph (2)(b) in a case where the administrator has made a statement under paragraph 52(1)(b), a resolution shall be taken as passed if (and only if) passed with the approval of—
  (a)   each secured creditor of the company, or
  (b)   if the administrator has made a distribution to preferential creditors or thinks that a distribution may be made to preferential creditors—
    (i)   each secured creditor of the company, and
    (ii)   preferential creditors whose debts amount to more than 50% of the preferential debts of the company, disregarding debts of any creditor who does not respond to an invitation to give or withhold approval.
(4)   Discharge—
  (a)   applies to liability accrued before the discharge takes effect, and
  (b)   does not prevent the exercise of the court's powers under paragraph 75.

Vacation of office: charges and liabilities

99. (1)   This paragraph applies where a person ceases to be the administrator of a company (whether because he vacates office by reason of resignation, death or otherwise, because he is removed from office or because his appointment ceases to have effect).
(2)   In this paragraph—
  "the former administrator" means the person referred to in sub-paragraph (1), and
  "cessation" means the time when he ceases to be the company's administrator.
(3)   The former administrator's remuneration and expenses shall be—
  (a)   charged on and payable out of property of which he had custody or control immediately before cessation, and
  (b)   payable in priority to any security to which paragraph 70 applies.
(4)   A sum payable in respect of a debt or liability arising out of a contract entered into by the former administrator or a predecessor before cessation shall be—
  (a)   charged on and payable out of property of which the former administrator had custody or control immediately before cessation, and
  (b)   payable in priority to any charge arising under sub-paragraph (3).
(5)   Sub-paragraph (4) shall apply to a liability arising under a contract of employment which was adopted by the former administrator or a predecessor before cessation; and for that purpose—
  (a)   action taken within the period of 14 days after an administrator's appointment shall not be taken to amount or contribute to the adoption of a contract,
  (b)   no account shall be taken of a liability which arises, or in so far as it arises, by reference to anything which is done or which occurs before the adoption of the contract of employment, and
  (c)   no account shall be taken of a liability to make a payment other than wages or salary.
(6)   In sub-paragraph (5)(c) "wages or salary" includes—
  (a)   a sum payable in respect of a period of holiday (for which purpose the sum shall be treated as relating to the period by reference to which the entitlement to holiday accrued),
  (b)   a sum payable in respect of a period of absence through illness or other good cause,
  (c)   a sum payable in lieu of holiday,

(d)   in respect of a period, a sum which would be treated as earnings for that period for the purposes of an enactment about social security, and

(e)   a contribution to an occupational pension scheme.

GENERAL

Joint and concurrent administrators

100. (1)   In this Schedule—

(a)   a reference to the appointment of an administrator of a company includes a reference to the appointment of a number of persons to act jointly or concurrently as the administrator of a company, and

(b)   a reference to the appointment of a person as administrator of a company includes a reference to the appointment of a person as one of a number of persons to act jointly or concurrently as the administrator of a company.

(2)   The appointment of a number of persons to act as administrator of a company must specify—

(a)   which functions (if any) are to be exercised by the persons appointed acting jointly, and

(b)   which functions (if any) are to be exercised by any or all of the persons appointed.

101. (1)   This paragraph applies where two or more persons are appointed to act jointly as the administrator of a company.

(2)   A reference to the administrator of the company is a reference to those persons acting jointly.

(3)   But a reference to the administrator of a company in paragraphs 87 to 99 of this Schedule is a reference to any or all of the persons appointed to act jointly.

(4)   Where an offence of omission is committed by the administrator, each of the persons appointed to act jointly—

(a)   commits the offence, and

(b)   may be proceeded against and punished individually.

(5)   The reference in paragraph 45(1)(a) to the name of the administrator is a reference to the name of each of the persons appointed to act jointly.

(6)   Where persons are appointed to act jointly in respect of only some of the functions of the administrator of a company, this paragraph applies only in relation to those functions.

102. (1)   This paragraph applies where two or more persons are appointed to act concurrently as the administrator of a company.

(2)   A reference to the administrator of a company in this Schedule is a reference to any of the persons appointed (or any combination of them).

103. (1)   Where a company is in administration, a person may be appointed to act as administrator jointly or concurrently with the person or persons acting as the administrator of the company.

(2)   Where a company entered administration by administration order, an appointment under sub-paragraph (1) must be made by the court on the application of—

(a)   a person or group listed in paragraph 12(1)(a) to (e), or

(b)   the person or persons acting as the administrator of the company.

(3)   Where a company entered administration by virtue of an appointment under paragraph 14, an appointment under sub-paragraph (1) must be made by—

(a)   the holder of the floating charge by virtue of which the appointment was made, or

(b)   the court on the application of the person or persons acting as the administrator of the company.

(4)   Where a company entered administration by virtue of an appointment under paragraph 22(1), an appointment under sub-paragraph (1) above must be made either by the court on the application of the person or persons acting as the administrator of the company or—

(a)   by the company, and

(b)   with the consent of each person who is the holder of a qualifying floating charge in respect of the company's property or, where consent is withheld, with the permission of the court.

(5)   Where a company entered administration by virtue of an appointment under paragraph 22(2), an appointment under sub-paragraph (1) must be made either by the court on the application of the person or persons acting as the administrator of the company or—

(a)   by the directors of the company, and

(b)   with the consent of each person who is the holder of a qualifying floating charge in respect of the company's property or, where consent is withheld, with the permission of the court.

(6)   An appointment under sub-paragraph (1) may be made only with the consent of the person or persons acting as the administrator of the company.

Presumption of validity

104. An act of the administrator of a company is valid in spite of a defect in his appointment or qualification.

Majority decision of directors

105. A reference in this Schedule to something done by the directors of a company includes a reference to the same thing done by a majority of the directors of a company.

Penalties

106. (1)   A person who is guilty of an offence under this Schedule is liable to a fine (in accordance with section 430 and Schedule 10).

(2)   A person who is guilty of an offence under any of the following paragraphs of this Schedule is liable to a daily default fine (in accordance with section 430 and Schedule 10)—
   (a)   paragraph 20,
   (b)   paragraph 32,
   (c)   paragraph 46,
   (d)   paragraph 48,
   (e)   paragraph 49,
   (f)   paragraph 51,
   (g)   paragraph 53,
   (h)   paragraph 54,
   (i)   paragraph 56,
   (j)   paragraph 71,
   (k)   paragraph 72,
   (l)   paragraph 77,
   (m)   paragraph 78,
   (n)   paragraph 80,
   (o)   paragraph 84,
   (p)   paragraph 86, and
   (q)   paragraph 89.

Extension of time limit

107. (1)   Where a provision of this Schedule provides that a period may be varied in accordance with this paragraph, the period may be varied in respect of a company—
   (a)   by the court, and
   (b)   on the application of the administrator.

(2)   A time period may be extended in respect of a company under this paragraph—
   (a)   more than once, and
   (b)   after expiry.

108. (1)   A period specified in paragraph 49(5), 50(1)(b) or 51(2) may be varied in respect of a company by the administrator with consent.

(2)   In sub-paragraph (1) "consent" means consent of—
   (a)   each secured creditor of the company, and
   (b)   if the company has unsecured debts, creditors whose debts amount to more than 50% of the company's unsecured debts, disregarding debts of any creditor who does not respond to an invitation to give or withhold consent.

(3)   But where the administrator has made a statement under paragraph 52(1)(b) "consent" means—
   (a)   consent of each secured creditor of the company, or
   (b)   if the administrator thinks that a distribution may be made to preferential creditors, consent of—
      (i)   each secured creditor of the company, and
      (ii)   preferential creditors whose debts amount to more than 50% of the total preferential debts of the company, disregarding debts of any creditor who does not respond to an invitation to give or withhold consent.

(4)   Consent for the purposes of sub-paragraph (1) may be—
   (a)   written, or
   (b)   signified at a creditors' meeting.

(5)   The power to extend under sub-paragraph (1)—
   (a)   may be exercised in respect of a period only once,
   (b)   may not be used to extend a period by more than 28 days,
   (c)   may not be used to extend a period which has been extended by the court, and
   (d)   may not be used to extend a period after expiry.

109. Where a period is extended under paragraph 107 or 108, a reference to the period shall be taken as a reference to the period as extended.

Amendment of provision about time

110. (1)   The Secretary of State may by order amend a provision of this Schedule which—
   (a)   requires anything to be done within a specified period of time,

(b)   prevents anything from being done after a specified time, or
(c)   requires a specified minimum period of notice to be given.

(2)   An order under this paragraph—
(a)   must be made by statutory instrument, and
(b)   shall be subject to annulment in pursuance of a resolution of either House of Parliament.

Interpretation

111. (1)   In this Schedule—
"administrative receiver" has the meaning given by section 251,
"administrator" has the meaning given by paragraph 1 and, where the context requires, includes
     a reference to a former administrator,

. . .
"correspondence" includes correspondence by telephonic or other electronic means,
"creditors' meeting" has the meaning given by paragraph 50,
"enters administration" has the meaning given by paragraph 1,
"floating charge" means a charge which is a floating charge on its creation,
"in administration" has the meaning given by paragraph 1,
"hire-purchase agreement" includes a conditional sale agreement, a chattel leasing agreement
     and a retention of title agreement,
"holder of a qualifying floating charge" in respect of a company's property has the meaning
     given by paragraph 14,
"market value" means the amount which would be realised on a sale of property in the open
     market by a willing vendor,
"the purpose of administration" means an objective specified in paragraph 3, and
"unable to pay its debts" has the meaning given by section 123.

[(1A)   In this Schedule, "company" means—
[(a)   a company registered under the Companies Act 2006 in England and Wales or Scotland,]
(b)   a company incorporated in an EEA State other than the United Kingdom, or
(c)   a company not incorporated in an EEA State but having its centre of main interests in a
     member State other than Denmark.

(1B)   In sub-paragraph (1A), in relation to a company, "centre of main interests" has the same
meaning as in the EC Regulation and, in the absence of proof to the contrary, is presumed to be the
place of its registered office (within the meaning of that Regulation).]

(2)   . . .

(3)   In this Schedule a reference to action includes a reference to inaction.

[Non-UK companies

111A.   A company incorporated outside the United Kingdom that has a principal place of business
in Northern Ireland may not enter administration under this Schedule unless it also has a principal
place of business in England and Wales or Scotland (or both in England and Wales and in
Scotland).]

Scotland

112. In the application of this Schedule to Scotland—
(a)   a reference to filing with the court is a reference to lodging in court, and
(b)   a reference to a charge is a reference to a right in security.

113. Where property in Scotland is disposed of under paragraph 70 or 71, the administrator shall
grant to the disponee an appropriate document of transfer or conveyance of the property, and—
(a)   that document, or
(b)   recording, intimation or registration of that document (where recording, intimation or
     registration of the document is a legal requirement for completion of title to the property),
has the effect of disencumbering the property of or, as the case may be, freeing the property from,
the security.

114. In Scotland, where goods in the possession of a company under a hire-purchase agreement are
disposed of under paragraph 72, the disposal has the effect of extinguishing as against the disponee
all rights of the owner of the goods under the agreement.

115. (1)   In Scotland, the administrator of a company may make, in or towards the satisfaction of
the debt secured by the floating charge, a payment to the holder of a floating charge which has
attached to the property subject to the charge.

(2)   In Scotland, where the administrator thinks that the company has insufficient property to
enable a distribution to be made to unsecured creditors other than by virtue of section 176A(2)(a),
he may file a notice to that effect with the registrar of companies.

(3)   On delivery of the notice to the registrar of companies, any floating charge granted by the company shall, unless it has already so attached, attach to the property which is subject to the charge and that attachment shall have effect as if each floating charge is a fixed security over the property to which it has attached.

116. In Scotland, the administrator in making any payment in accordance with paragraph 115 shall make such payment subject to the rights of any of the following categories of persons (which rights shall, except to the extent provided in any instrument, have the following order of priority)—

(a)   the holder of any fixed security which is over property subject to the floating charge and which ranks prior to, or pari passu with, the floating charge,

(b)   creditors in respect of all liabilities and expenses incurred by or on behalf of the administrator,

(c)   the administrator in respect of his liabilities, expenses and remuneration and any indemnity to which he is entitled out of the property of the company,

(d)   the preferential creditors entitled to payment in accordance with paragraph 65,

(e)   the holder of the floating charge in accordance with the priority of that charge in relation to any other floating charge which has attached, and

(f)   the holder of a fixed security, other than one referred to in paragraph (a), which is over property subject to the floating charge.]

NOTES

Inserted by the Enterprise Act 2002, s 248(2), Sch 16, as from 15 September 2003 (for savings and transitional provisions, see the note to s 8 at **[9.105]**).

Para 12: words in square brackets in sub-para (1)(d) substituted by the Courts Act 2003, s 109(1), Sch 8, para 299, as from 1 April 2005; sub-para (5) added by the Enterprise Act 2002 (Insolvency) Order 2003, SI 2003/2096, arts 2(1), (2), 6, as from 15 September 2003, except in relation to any case where a petition for an administration order was presented before that date.

Para 40: sub-para (2)(aa) inserted by the European Public Limited-Liability Company Regulations 2004, SI 2004/2326, reg 73(4)(c), as from 8 October 2004.

Para 42: sub-para (4)(aa) inserted by SI 2004/2326, reg 73(4)(c), as from 8 October 2004.

Para 43: sub-para (6A) inserted by SI 2003/2096, art 2(1), (3) as from 15 September 2003, except in relation to any case where a petition for an administration order was presented before that date.

Para 45: substituted by the Companies (Trading Disclosures) (Insolvency) Regulations 2008, SI 2008/1897, reg 4(1), as from 1 October 2008.

Para 49: words in square brackets in sub-para (3) substituted by the Companies Act 2006 (Consequential Amendments etc) Order 2008, SI 2008/948, art 3(1), Sch 1, Pt 2, para 100(a), as from 6 April 2008.

Para 73: word omitted from sub-para (2)(b) repealed, and sub-para (2)(d) (and the word immediately preceding it) added, by the Companies (Cross-Border Mergers) Regulations 2007, SI 2007/2974, reg 65(1)–(3), as from 15 December 2007; words in square brackets in sub-para (2)(c) substituted by SI 2008/948, art 3(1), Sch 1, Pt 2, para 100(a), as from 6 April 2008.

Para 74: word omitted from sub-para (6)(b) repealed, and sub-para (6)(ba) added, by SI 2007/2974, reg 65(1), (4), (5), as from 15 December 2007; words in square brackets in sub-para (6)(b) substituted by SI 2008/948, art 3(1), Sch 1, Pt 2, para 100(b), as from 6 April 2008.

Para 82: sub-para (1)(aa) inserted by SI 2004/2326, reg 73(4)(c), as from 8 October 2004.

Paras 87, 89: words in square brackets in sub-para (2)(b) substituted by SI 2003/2096, arts 2(1), (4), (5), 6, as from 15 September 2003, except in relation to any case where a petition for an administration order was presented before that date.

Para 111 is amended as follows:

Definition omitted from sub-para (1) repealed, and sub-paras (1A), (1B) inserted, by the Insolvency Act 1986 (Amendment) Regulations 2005, SI 2005/879, reg 2(1), (4)(a), (b), as from 13 April 2005, except in relation to the appointment of an administrator under Part II that took effect before that date.

Sub-para (1A)(a) substituted by the Companies Act 2006 (Consequential Amendments, Transitional Provisions and Savings) Order 2009, SI 2009/1941, art 2(1), Sch 1, para 72, as from 1 October 2009 (for transitional provisions see the note to s 7A at **[9.103]**).

Sub-para (2) repealed by the Legislative Reform (Insolvency) (Miscellaneous Provisions) Order 2010, SI 2010/18, arts 2, 4(2), as from 6 April 2010. Note that this paragraph is effectively replaced by a new s 436B of this Act that was also added by the 2010 Order as from 6 April 2010. That section provides that a reference in this Act to a thing in writing includes that thing in electronic form (except in certain specified sections).

Para 111A: inserted by SI 2005/879, reg 2(1), (4)(c), as from 13 April 2005, except in relation to the appointment of an administrator under Part II that took effect before that date.

SCHEDULE 1
POWERS OF ADMINISTRATOR OR ADMINISTRATIVE RECEIVER

Sections 14, 42

[9.413]

1. Power to take possession of, collect and get in the property of the company and, for that purpose, to take such proceedings as may seem to him expedient.

2. Power to sell or otherwise dispose of the property of the company by public auction or private contract or, in Scotland, to sell, . . . hire out or otherwise dispose of the property of the company by public roup or private bargain.

3. Power to raise or borrow money and grant security therefor over the property of the company.

4. Power to appoint a solicitor or accountant or other professionally qualified person to assist him in the performance of his functions.

5. Power to bring or defend any action or other legal proceedings in the name and on behalf of the company.

6. Power to refer to arbitration any question affecting the company.

7. Power to effect and maintain insurances in respect of the business and property of the company.

8. Power to use the company's seal.

9. Power to do all acts and to execute in the name and on behalf of the company any deed, receipt or other document.

10. Power to draw, accept, make and endorse any bill of exchange or promissory note in the name and on behalf of the company.

11. Power to appoint any agent to do any business which he is unable to do himself or which can more conveniently be done by an agent and power to employ and dismiss employees.

12. Power to do all such things (including the carrying out of works) as may be necessary for the realisation of the property of the company.

13. Power to make any payment which is necessary or incidental to the performance of his functions.

14. Power to carry on the business of the company.

15. Power to establish subsidiaries of the company.

16. Power to transfer to subsidiaries of the company the whole or any part of the business and property of the company.

17. Power to grant or accept a surrender of a lease or tenancy of any of the property of the company, and to take a lease or tenancy of any property required or convenient for the business of the company.

18. Power to make any arrangement or compromise on behalf of the company.

19. Power to call up any uncalled capital of the company.

20. Power to rank and claim in the bankruptcy, insolvency, sequestration or liquidation of any person indebted to the company and to receive dividends, and to accede to trust deeds for the creditors of any such person.

21. Power to present or defend a petition for the winding up of the company.

22. Power to change the situation of the company's registered office.

23. Power to do all other things incidental to the exercise of the foregoing powers.

NOTES

Para 2: word omitted repealed by the Abolition of Feudal Tenure etc (Scotland) Act 2000, s 76(2), Sch 13, Pt I, as from 28 November 2004.

SCHEDULE 2
POWERS OF A SCOTTISH RECEIVER (ADDITIONAL TO THOSE CONFERRED ON HIM BY THE INSTRUMENT OF CHARGE)

Section 55

[9.414]

1. Power to take possession of, collect and get in the property from the company or a liquidator thereof or any other person, and for that purpose, to take such proceedings as may seem to him expedient.

2. Power to sell, . . . hire out or otherwise dispose of the property by public roup or private bargain and with or without advertisement.

3. Power to raise or borrow money and grant security therefor over the property.

4. Power to appoint a solicitor or accountant or other professionally qualified person to assist him in the performance of his functions.

5. Power to bring or defend any action or other legal proceedings in the name and on behalf of the company.

6. Power to refer to arbitration all questions affecting the company.

7. Power to effect and maintain insurances in respect of the business and property of the company.

8. Power to use the company's seal.

9. Power to do all acts and to execute in the name and on behalf of the company any deed, receipt or other document.

10. Power to draw, accept, make and endorse any bill of exchange or promissory note in the name and on behalf of the company.

11. Power to appoint any agent to do any business which he is unable to do himself or which can more conveniently be done by an agent, and power to employ and dismiss employees.

12. Power to do all such things (including the carrying out of works), as may be necessary for the realisation of the property.

13. Power to make any payment which is necessary or incidental to the performance of his functions.

14. Power to carry on the business of the company or any part of it.

15. Power to grant or accept a surrender of a lease or tenancy of any of the property, and to take a lease or tenancy of any property required or convenient for the business of the company.

16. Power to make any arrangement or compromise on behalf of the company.

17. Power to call up any uncalled capital of the company.

18. Power to establish subsidiaries of the company.

19. Power to transfer to subsidiaries of the company the business of the company or any part of it and any of the property.

20. Power to rank and claim in the bankruptcy, insolvency, sequestration or liquidation of any person or company indebted to the company and to receive dividends, and to accede to trust deeds for creditors of any such person.

21. Power to present or defend a petition for the winding up of the company.

22. Power to change the situation of the company's registered office.

23. Power to do all other things incidental to the exercise of the powers mentioned in section 55(1) of this Act or above in this Schedule.

NOTES

Para 2: word omitted repealed by the Abolition of Feudal Tenure etc (Scotland) Act 2000, s 76(2), Sch 13, Pt I, as from 28 November 2004.

[SCHEDULE 2A
EXCEPTIONS TO PROHIBITION ON APPOINTMENT OF ADMINISTRATIVE
RECEIVER: SUPPLEMENTARY PROVISIONS

Section 72H

Capital market arrangement

[9.415]

1. (1)   For the purposes of section 72B an arrangement is a capital market arrangement if—
  (a)   it involves a grant of security to a person holding it as trustee for a person who holds a capital market investment issued by a party to the arrangement, or
  [(aa)   it involves a grant of security to—
    (i)   a party to the arrangement who issues a capital market investment, or
    (ii)   a person who holds the security as trustee for a party to the arrangement in connection with the issue of a capital market investment, or
  (ab)   it involves a grant of security to a person who holds the security as trustee for a party to the arrangement who agrees to provide finance to another party, or]
  (b)   at least one party guarantees the performance of obligations of another party, or
  (c)   at least one party provides security in respect of the performance of obligations of another party, or
  (d)   the arrangement involves an investment of a kind described in articles 83 to 85 of the Financial Services and Markets Act 2000 (Regulated Activities) Order 2001 (SI 2001/544) (options, futures and contracts for differences).
  (2)   For the purposes of sub-paragraph (1)—
  (a)   a reference to holding as trustee includes a reference to holding as nominee or agent,
  (b)   a reference to holding for a person who holds a capital market investment includes a reference to holding for a number of persons at least one of whom holds a capital market investment, and
  (c)   a person holds a capital market investment if he has a legal or beneficial interest in it[; and

(d)   the reference to the provision of finance includes the provision of an indemnity].

(3)   In section 72B(1) and this paragraph "party" to an arrangement includes a party to an agreement which—

(a)   forms part of the arrangement,

(b)   provides for the raising of finance as part of the arrangement, or

(c)   is necessary for the purposes of implementing the arrangement.

Capital market investment

2. (1)   For the purposes of section 72B an investment is a capital market investment if it—

(a)   is within article 77 [or 77A] of the Financial Services and Markets Act 2000 (Regulated Activities) Order 2001 (SI 2001/544) (debt instruments), and

(b)   is rated, listed or traded or designed to be rated, listed or traded.

(2)   In sub-paragraph (1)—

"rated" means rated for the purposes of investment by an internationally recognised rating agency,

"listed" means admitted to the official list within the meaning given by section 103(1) of the Financial Services and Markets Act 2000 (c 8) (interpretation), and

"traded" means admitted to trading on a market established under the rules of a recognised investment exchange or on a foreign market.

(3)   In sub-paragraph (2)—

"recognised investment exchange" has the meaning given by section 285 of the Financial Services and Markets Act 2000 (recognised investment exchange), and

"foreign market" has the same meaning as "relevant market" in article 67(2) of the Financial Services and Markets Act 2000 (Financial Promotion) Order 2001 (SI 2001/1335) (foreign markets).

3. (1)   An investment is also a capital market investment for the purposes of section 72B if it consists of a bond or commercial paper issued to one or more of the following—

(a)   an investment professional within the meaning of article 19(5) of the Financial Services and Markets Act 2000 (Financial Promotion) Order 2001,

(b)   a person who is, when the agreement mentioned in section 72B(1) is entered into, a certified high net worth individual in relation to a communication within the meaning of article 48(2) of that order,

(c)   a person to whom article 49(2) of that order applies (high net worth company, &c),

(d)   a person who is, when the agreement mentioned in section 72B(1) is entered into, a certified sophisticated investor in relation to a communication within the meaning of article 50(1) of that order, and

(e)   a person in a State other than the United Kingdom who under the law of that State is not prohibited from investing in bonds or commercial paper.

(2)   In sub-paragraph (1)—

"bond" shall be construed in accordance with article 77 of the Financial Services and Markets Act 2000 (Regulated Activities) Order 2001 (SI 2001/544)[, and includes any instrument falling within article 77A of that Order], and

"commercial paper" has the meaning given by article 9(3) of that order.

(3)   For the purposes of sub-paragraph (1)—

(a)   in applying article 19(5) of the Financial Promotion Order for the purposes of sub-paragraph (1)(a)—

(i)   in article 19(5)(b), ignore the words after "exempt person",

(ii)   in article 19(5)(c)(i), for the words from "the controlled activity" to the end substitute "a controlled activity", and

(iii)   in article 19(5)(e) ignore the words from "where the communication" to the end, and

(b)   in applying article 49(2) of that order for the purposes of sub-paragraph (1)(c), ignore article 49(2)(e).

"Agreement"

4. For the purposes of sections 72B and 72E and this Schedule "agreement" includes an agreement or undertaking effected by—

(a)   contract,

(b)   deed, or

(c)   any other instrument intended to have effect in accordance with the law of England and Wales, Scotland or another jurisdiction.

Debt

5. The debt of at least £50 million referred to in section 72B(1)(a) or 72E(2)(a)—

(a)   may be incurred at any time during the life of the capital market arrangement or financed project, and

(b)   may be expressed wholly or partly in foreign currency (in which case the sterling equivalent shall be calculated as at the time when the arrangement is entered into or the project begins).

Step-in rights

6. (1)   For the purposes of sections 72C to 72E a project has "step-in rights" if a person who provides finance in connection with the project has a conditional entitlement under an agreement to—

(a)   assume sole or principal responsibility under an agreement for carrying out all or part of the project, or

(b)   make arrangements for carrying out all or part of the project.

(2)   In sub-paragraph (1) a reference to the provision of finance includes a reference to the provision of an indemnity.

Project company

7. (1)   For the purposes of sections 72C to 72E a company is a "project company" of a project if—

(a)   it holds property for the purpose of the project,

(b)   it has sole or principal responsibility under an agreement for carrying out all or part of the project,

(c)   it is one of a number of companies which together carry out the project,

(d)   it has the purpose of supplying finance to enable the project to be carried out, or

(e)   it is the holding company of a company within any of paragraphs (a) to (d).

(2)   But a company is not a "project company" of a project if—

(a)   it performs a function within sub-paragraph (1)(a) to (d) or is within sub-paragraph (1)(e), but

(b)   it also performs a function which is not—

(i)   within sub-paragraph (1)(a) to (d),

(ii)   related to a function within sub-paragraph (1)(a) to (d), or

(iii)   related to the project.

(3)   For the purposes of this paragraph a company carries out all or part of a project whether or not it acts wholly or partly through agents.

"Resources"

8. In section 72C "resources" includes—

(a)   funds (including payment for the provision of services or facilities),

(b)   assets,

(c)   professional skill,

(d)   the grant of a concession or franchise, and

(e)   any other commercial resource.

"Public body"

9. (1)   In section 72C "public body" means—

(a)   a body which exercises public functions,

(b)   a body specified for the purposes of this paragraph by the Secretary of State, and

(c)   a body within a class specified for the purposes of this paragraph by the Secretary of State.

(2)   A specification under sub-paragraph (1) may be—

(a)   general, or

(b)   for the purpose of the application of section 72C to a specified case.

Regulated business

10. (1)   For the purposes of section 72D a business is regulated if it is carried on—

(a)   . . .

(b)   in reliance on a licence under section 7 or 7A of the Gas Act 1986 (c 44) (transport and supply of gas),

(c)   in reliance on a licence granted by virtue of section 41C of that Act (power to prescribe additional licensable activity),

(d)   in reliance on a licence under section 6 of the Electricity Act 1989 (c 29) (supply of electricity),

(e)   by a water undertaker,

(f)   by a sewerage undertaker,

(g)   by a universal service provider within the meaning given by section 4(3) and (4) of the Postal Services Act 2000 (c 26),

(h)   by the Post Office company within the meaning given by section 62 of that Act (transfer of property),

(i)   by a relevant subsidiary of the Post Office Company within the meaning given by section 63 of that Act (government holding),

(j)   in reliance on a licence under section 8 of the Railways Act 1993 (c 43) (railway services),

(k)   in reliance on a licence exemption under section 7 of that Act (subject to sub-paragraph (2) below),

(l)   by the operator of a system of transport which is deemed to be a railway for a purpose of Part I of that Act by virtue of section 81(2) of that Act (tramways, &c),   . . .

(m)   by the operator of a vehicle carried on flanged wheels along a system within paragraph (l); [or

(n)   in reliance on a European licence granted pursuant to a provision contained in any instrument made for the purpose of implementing Council Directive 1995/18/EC dated 19th June 1995 on the licensing of railway undertakings, as amended by Directive 2001/13/EC dated 26th February 2001 and Directive 2004/49/EC dated 29th April 2004, both of the European Parliament and of the Council, or pursuant to any action taken by an EEA State for that purpose].

(2)   Sub-paragraph (1)(k) does not apply to the operator of a railway asset on a railway unless on some part of the railway there is a permitted line speed exceeding 40 kilometres per hour.

[(2A)   For the purposes of section 72D a business is also regulated to the extent that it consists in the provision of a public electronic communications network or a public electronic communications service.]

[(2B)   In sub-paragraph (1)(n), an "EEA State" means a member State, Norway, Iceland or Liechtenstein.]

"Person"

11.   A reference to a person in this Schedule includes a reference to a partnership or another unincorporated group of persons.]

NOTES

Inserted by the Enterprise Act 2002, s 250(2), Sch 18, as from 15 September 2003.

Para 1: sub-paras (1)(aa), (ab), (2)(d) (and the word immediately preceding it) inserted by the Insolvency Act 1986 (Amendment) (Administrative Receivership and Capital Market Arrangements) Order 2003, SI 2003/1468, arts 2, 3, as from 15 September 2003 (ie, immediately after the coming into force of this Schedule and ss 72A–72G of this Act).

Paras 2, 3: words in square brackets inserted by the Financial Services and Markets Act 2000 (Regulated Activities) (Amendment) Order 2010, SI 2010/86, art 4, Schedule, para 2, as from 24 February 2010.

Para 10: sub-para (1)(a) repealed, and sub-para (2A) inserted, by the Communications Act 2003, s 406, Sch 17, para 82(1), (4), Sch 19, as from 25 July 2003 (certain purposes), and as from 29 December 2003 (otherwise); word omitted from sub-para (1)(l) repealed, and sub-para (1)(n) (and the word immediately preceding it) and sub-para (2B) inserted, by the Railway (Licensing of Railway Undertakings) Regulations 2005, SI 2005/3050, as from 28 November 2005.

Modification: a reference to commercial paper in this Schedule includes a reference to uncertificated units of an eligible debt security where the issue of the units corresponds, in accordance with the current terms of issue of the security, to the issue of commercial paper within the meaning of the Financial Services and Markets Act 2000 (Regulated Activities) Order 2001, SI 2001/544, art 9(3); see the Uncertificated Securities (Amendment) (Eligible Debt Securities) Regulations 2003, SI 2003/1633, reg 15, Sch 2, para 7.

Financial Services and Markets Act 2000 (Financial Promotion) Order 2001, SI 2001/1335: revoked and replaced by the Financial Services and Markets Act 2000 (Financial Promotion) Order 2005, SI 2005/1529.

SCHEDULE 3
ORDERS IN COURSE OF WINDING UP PRONOUNCED IN VACATION (SCOTLAND)
Section 162

PART I
ORDERS WHICH ARE TO BE FINAL

[9.416]

Orders under section 153, as to the time for proving debts and claims.

Orders under section 195 as to meetings for ascertaining wishes of creditors or contributories.

Orders under section 198, as to the examination of witnesses in regard to the property or affairs of a company.

PART II
ORDERS WHICH ARE TO TAKE EFFECT UNTIL MATTER DISPOSED OF BY INNER HOUSE

[9.417]

Orders under section 126(1), 130(2) or (3), 147, 227 or 228, restraining or permitting the commencement or the continuance of legal proceedings.

Orders under section 135(5), limiting the powers of provisional liquidators.

Orders under section 108, appointing a liquidator to fill a vacancy.

Orders under section 167 or 169, sanctioning the exercise of any powers by a liquidator, other than the powers specified in paragraphs 1, 2 and 3 of Schedule 4 to this Act.

Orders under section 158, as to the arrest and detention of an absconding contributory and his property.

SCHEDULE 4
POWERS OF LIQUIDATOR IN A WINDING UP

Sections 165, 167

PART I
POWERS EXERCISABLE WITH SANCTION

[9.418]
1. Power to pay any class of creditors in full.

2. Power to make any compromise or arrangement with creditors or persons claiming to be creditors, or having or alleging themselves to have any claim (present or future, certain or contingent, ascertained or sounding only in damages) against the company, or whereby the company may be rendered liable.

3. [In the case of a winding up in Scotland,] power to compromise, on such terms as may be agreed—
  (a)   all calls and liabilities to calls, all debts and liabilities capable of resulting in debts, and all claims (present or future, certain or contingent, ascertained or sounding only in damages) subsisting or supposed to subsist between the company and a contributory or alleged contributory or other debtor or person apprehending liability to the company, and
  (b)   all questions in any way relating to or affecting the assets or the winding up of the company,
and take any security for the discharge of any such call, debt, liability or claim and give a complete discharge in respect of it.

[3A.   Power to bring legal proceedings under section 213, 214, 238, 239, 242, 243 or 423.]

NOTES
  Para 3: words in square brackets inserted by the Legislative Reform (Insolvency) (Miscellaneous Provisions) Order 2010, SI 2010/18, arts 2, 10(1), as from 6 April 2010 (for transitional provisions see the note below).
  Para 3A: added by the Enterprise Act 2002, s 253, as from 15 September 2003, except in relation to any proceedings of a kind mentioned in para 3A which were commenced prior to that date.
  Transitional provisions: the Legislative Reform (Insolvency) (Miscellaneous Provisions) Order 2010, SI 2010/18, art 12(5) provides as follows—

  "(5)   The amendments made to Schedules 4 and 5 to the 1986 Act by articles 10 and 11 respectively do not apply in respect of any proceedings under the 1986 Act where—
    (a)   in the case of a company in voluntary winding up, the resolution to wind up was passed before 6th April 2010;
    (b)   in the case of a company in voluntary winding up pursuant to paragraph 83 of Schedule B1 to the 1986 Act, the preceding administration commenced before 6th April 2010;
    (c)   in the case of a company in winding up following an order for the conversion of administration or a voluntary arrangement into winding up by virtue of article 37 of Council Regulation (EC) No 1346/2000 on insolvency proceedings, the order for conversion was made before 6th April 2010;
    (d)   in the case of a company being wound up by the court, the winding-up order was made before 6th April 2010;
    (e)   in the case of a bankruptcy, the debtor was adjudged bankrupt before 6th April 2010; and
    (f)   in the case of a bankruptcy following an order for the conversion of a voluntary arrangement into a bankruptcy by virtue of article 37 of Council Regulation (EC) No 1346/2000, the order for conversion was made before 6th April 2010.".

PART II
POWERS EXERCISABLE WITHOUT SANCTION IN VOLUNTARY WINDING UP,
WITH SANCTION IN WINDING UP BY THE COURT

[9.419]
4. Power to bring or defend any action or other legal proceeding in the name and on behalf of the company.

5. Power to carry on the business of the company so far as may be necessary for its beneficial winding up.

PART III
POWERS EXERCISABLE WITHOUT SANCTION IN ANY WINDING UP

[9.420]
6. Power to sell any of the company's property by public auction or private contract with power to transfer the whole of it to any person or to sell the same in parcels.

[6A.   In the case of a winding up in England and Wales, power to compromise, on such terms as may be agreed—

(a) all calls and liabilities to calls, all debts and liabilities capable of resulting in debts, and all claims (present or future, certain or contingent, ascertained or sounding only in damages) subsisting or supposed to subsist between the company and a contributory or alleged contributory or other debtor or person apprehending liability to the company, and

(b) subject to paragraph 2 in Part 1 of this Schedule, all questions in any way relating to or affecting the assets or the winding up of the company,

and take any security for the discharge of any such call, debt, liability or claim and give a complete discharge in respect of it.]

7. Power to do all acts and execute, in the name and on behalf of the company, all deeds, receipts and other documents and for that purpose to use, when necessary, the company's seal.

8. Power to prove, rank and claim in the bankruptcy, insolvency or sequestration of any contributory for any balance against his estate, and to receive dividends in the bankruptcy, insolvency or sequestration in respect of that balance, as a separate debt due from the bankrupt or insolvent, and rateably with the other separate creditors.

9. Power to draw, accept, make and indorse any bill of exchange or promissory note in the name and on behalf of the company, with the same effect with respect to the company's liability as if the bill or note had been drawn, accepted, made or indorsed by or on behalf of the company in the course of its business.

10. Power to raise on the security of the assets of the company any money requisite.

11. Power to take out in his official name letters of administration to any deceased contributory, and to do in his official name any other act necessary for obtaining payment of any money due from a contributory or his estate which cannot conveniently be done in the name of the company.

In all such cases the money due is deemed, for the purpose of enabling the liquidator to take out the letters of administration or recover the money, to be due to the liquidator himself.

12. Power to appoint an agent to do any business which the liquidator is unable to do himself.

13. Power to do all such other things as may be necessary for winding up the company's affairs and distributing its assets.

NOTES

Para 6A: inserted by the Legislative Reform (Insolvency) (Miscellaneous Provisions) Order 2010, SI 2010/18, arts 2, 10(2), as from 6 April 2010 (for transitional provisions see the note to Part I of this Schedule at **[9.418]**).

SCHEDULE 6
THE CATEGORIES OF PREFERENTIAL DEBTS

Section 386

[9.421]
1–7. . . .

Category 4: Contributions to occupational pension schemes, etc

8. Any sum which is owed by the debtor and is a sum to which [Schedule 4 to the Pension Schemes Act 1993] applies (contributions to occupational pension schemes and state scheme premiums).

Category 5: Remuneration, etc, of employees

9. So much of any amount which—
(a) is owed by the debtor to a person who is or has been an employee of the debtor, and
(b) is payable by way of remuneration in respect of the whole or any part of the period of 4 months next before the relevant date,
as does not exceed so much as may be prescribed by order made by the Secretary of State.

10. An amount owed by way of accrued holiday remuneration, in respect of any period of employment before the relevant date, to a person whose employment by the debtor has been terminated, whether before, on or after that date.

11. So much of any sum owed in respect of money advanced for the purpose as has been applied for the payment of a debt which, if it had not been paid, would have been a debt falling within paragraph 9 or 10.

12. So much of any amount which—
(a) is ordered (whether before or after the relevant date) to be paid by the debtor under the Reserve Forces (Safeguard of Employment) Act 1985, and
(b) is so ordered in respect of a default made by the debtor before that date in the discharge of his obligations under that Act,
as does not exceed such amount as may be prescribed by order made by the Secretary of State.

Interpretation for Category 5

13. (1)   For the purposes of paragraphs 9 to 12, a sum is payable by the debtor to a person by way of remuneration in respect of any period if—

(a)   it is paid as wages or salary (whether payable for time or for piece work or earned wholly or partly by way of commission) in respect of services rendered to the debtor in that period, or

(b)   it is an amount falling within the following sub-paragraph and is payable by the debtor in respect of that period.

[(2)   An amount falls within this sub-paragraph if it is—

(a)   a guarantee payment under Part III of the Employment Rights Act 1996 (employee without work to do);

(b)   any payment for time off under section 53 (time off to look for work or arrange training) or section 56 (time off for ante-natal care) of that Act or under section 169 of the Trade Union and Labour Relations (Consolidation) Act 1992 (time off for carrying out trade union duties etc);

(c)   remuneration on suspension on medical grounds, or on maternity grounds, under Part VII of the Employment Rights Act 1996; or

(d)   remuneration under a protective award under section 189 of the Trade Union and Labour Relations (Consolidation) Act 1992 (redundancy dismissal with compensation).]

14. (1)   This paragraph relates to a case in which a person's employment has been terminated by or in consequence of his employer going into liquidation or being adjudged bankrupt or (his employer being a company not in liquidation) by or in consequence of—

(a)   a receiver being appointed as mentioned in section 40 of this Act (debenture-holders secured by floating charge), or

(b)   the appointment of a receiver under section 53(6) or 54(5) of this Act (Scottish company with property subject to floating charge), or

(c)   the taking of possession by debenture-holders (so secured), as mentioned in [section 754 of the Companies Act 2006].

(2)   For the purposes of paragraphs 9 to 12, holiday remuneration is deemed to have accrued to that person in respect of any period of employment if, by virtue of his contract of employment or of any enactment that remuneration would have accrued in respect of that period if his employment had continued until he became entitled to be allowed the holiday.

(3)   The reference in sub-paragraph (2) to any enactment includes an order or direction made under an enactment.

15. Without prejudice to paragraphs 13 and 14—

(a)   any remuneration payable by the debtor to a person in respect of a period of holiday or of absence from work through sickness or other good cause is deemed to be wages or (as the case may be) salary in respect of services rendered to the debtor in that period, and

(b)   references here and in those paragraphs to remuneration in respect of a period of holiday include any sums which, if they had been paid, would have been treated for the purposes of the enactments relating to social security as earnings in respect of that period.

[Category 6: Levies on coal and steel production

15A.   Any sums due at the relevant date from the debtor in respect of:

(a)   the levies on the production of coal and steel referred to in Articles 49 and 50 of the ECSC Treaty, or

(b)   any surcharge for delay provided for in Article 50(3) of that Treaty and Article 6 of Decision 3/52 of the High Authority of the Coal and Steel Community.]

Orders

16. An order under paragraph 9 or 12—

(a)   may contain such transitional provisions as may appear to the Secretary of State necessary or expedient;

(b)   shall be made by statutory instrument subject to annulment in pursuance of a resolution of either House of Parliament.

NOTES

Paras 1–7: repealed by the Enterprise Act 2002, ss 251(1), 278(2), Sch 26, as from 15 September 2003. Note that art 4 of the Enterprise Act 2002 (Commencement No 4 and Transitional Provisions and Savings) Order 2003, SI 2003/2093 (as amended) contains detailed transitional provisions in relation to the abolition of preferential status for Crown debts. Broadly speaking, preferential status will continue to apply in those cases which were started before 15 September 2003.

Para 8: words in square brackets substituted by the Pension Schemes Act 1993, s 190, Sch 8, para 18, as from 7 February 1994.

Para 13: sub-para (2) substituted by the Employment Rights Act 1996, s 240, Sch 1, para 29, as from 22 August 1996.

Para 14: words in square brackets in sub-para (1)(c) substituted the Companies Act 2006 (Consequential Amendments etc) Order 2008, SI 2008/948, art 3(1), Sch 1, Pt 2, para 104, as from 6 April 2008.

Para 15A: inserted by the Insolvency (ECSC Levy Debts) Regulations 1987, SI 1987/2093, reg 2(1), (3), as from 1 January 1988.

Orders: the Insolvency Proceedings (Monetary Limits) Order 1986, SI 1986/1996 prescribing £800 for the purposes of paras 9, 12 above.

SCHEDULE 7
INSOLVENCY PRACTITIONERS TRIBUNAL
Section 396

Panels of members

[9.422]
1. (1)   The Secretary of State shall draw up and from time to time revise—
    (a)   a panel of persons who—
        [[(i)   satisfy the judicial-appointment eligibility condition on a 5-year basis;]
        (ii)   are advocates or solicitors in Scotland of at least [5] years' standing],
        and are nominated for the purpose by the Lord Chancellor or the Lord President of the Court of Session, and
    (b)   a panel of persons who are experienced in insolvency matters;
and the members of the Tribunal shall be selected from those panels in accordance with this Schedule.

(2)   The power to revise the panels includes power to terminate a person's membership of either of them, and is accordingly to that extent subject to [section 7 of the Tribunals and Inquiries Act 1992] (which makes it necessary to obtain the concurrence of the Lord Chancellor and the Lord President of the Court of Session to dismissals in certain cases).

Remuneration of members

2. The Secretary of State may out of money provided by Parliament pay to members of the Tribunal such remuneration as he may with the approval of the Treasury determine; and such expenses of the Tribunal as the Secretary of State and the Treasury may approve shall be defrayed by the Secretary of State out of money so provided.

Sittings of Tribunal

3. (1)   For the purposes of carrying out their functions in relation to any cases referred to them, the Tribunal may sit either as a single tribunal or in two or more divisions.

(2)   The functions of the Tribunal in relation to any case referred to them shall be exercised by three members consisting of—
    (a)   a chairman selected by the Secretary of State from the panel drawn up under paragraph 1(1)(a) above, and
    (b)   two other members selected by the Secretary of State from the panel drawn up under paragraph 1(1)(b).

Procedure of Tribunal

4. (1)   Any investigation by the Tribunal shall be so conducted as to afford a reasonable opportunity for representations to be made to the Tribunal by or on behalf of the person whose case is the subject of the investigation.

(2)   For the purposes of any such investigation, the Tribunal—
    (a)   may by summons require any person to attend, at such time and place as is specified in the summons, to give evidence or to produce any books, papers and other records in his possession or under his control which the Tribunal consider it necessary for the purposes of the investigation to examine, and
    (b)   may take evidence on oath, and for the purpose administer oaths, or may, instead of administering an oath, require the person examined to make and subscribe a declaration of the truth of the matter respecting which he is examined;
but no person shall be required, in obedience to such a summons, to go more than ten miles from his place of residence, unless the necessary expenses of his attendance are paid or tendered to him.

(3)   Every person who—
    (a)   without reasonable excuse fails to attend in obedience to a summons issued under this paragraph, or refuses to give evidence, or
    (b)   intentionally alters, suppresses, conceals or destroys or refuses to produce any document which he may be required to produce for the purpose of an investigation by the Tribunal,
is liable to a fine.

(4)   Subject to the provisions of this paragraph, the Secretary of State may make rules for regulating the procedure on any investigation by the Tribunal.

(5)   In their application to Scotland, sub-paragraphs (2) and (3) above have effect as if for any reference to a summons there were substituted a reference to a notice in writing.

NOTES

    Para 1: sub-paras (1)(a)(i), (ii) substituted by the Courts and Legal Services Act 1990, s 71(2), Sch 10, para 67, as from 1 January 1991; sub-para (a)(i) further substituted, and figure in square brackets in sub-para (1)(a)(ii) substituted, by the Tribunals, Courts and Enforcement Act 2007, s 50, Sch 10, Pt 1, para 19, as from 21 July 2008; words in square brackets in sub-para (2) substituted by the Tribunals and Inquiries Act 1992, s 18(1), Sch 3, para 19, as from 1 October 1992.

    Rules: by virtue of the Interpretation Act 1978, s 17(2)(b), the Insolvency Practitioners Tribunal (Conduct of Investigations) Rules 1986, SI 1986/952 have effect as if made under this Schedule.

SCHEDULE 8
PROVISIONS CAPABLE OF INCLUSION IN COMPANY INSOLVENCY RULES
Section 411

Courts

[9.423]
1. Provision for supplementing, in relation to the insolvency or winding up of companies, any provision made by or under section 117 of this Act (jurisdiction in relation to winding up).

2. [(1)   Provision for regulating the practice and procedure of any court exercising jurisdiction for the purposes of Parts I to VII of this Act or [the Companies Acts] so far as relating to, and to matters connected with or arising out of, the insolvency or winding up of companies, being any provision that could be made by rules of court.

[(2)   Rules made by virtue of this paragraph about the consequence of failure to comply with practice or procedure may, in particular, include provision about the termination of administration.]

Notices, etc

3. Provision requiring notice of any proceedings in connection with or arising out of the insolvency or winding up of a company to be given or published in the manner prescribed by the rules.

4. Provision with respect to the form, manner of serving, contents and proof of any petition, application, order, notice, statement or other document required to be presented, made, given, published or prepared under any enactment or subordinate legislation relating to, or to matters connected with or arising out of, the insolvency or winding up of companies.

5. Provision specifying the persons to whom any notice is to be given.

Registration of voluntary arrangements

6. Provision for the registration of voluntary arrangements approved under Part I of this Act, including provision for the keeping and inspection of a register.

Provisional liquidator

7. Provision as to the manner in which a provisional liquidator appointed under section 135 is to carry out his functions.

Conduct of insolvency

8. Provision with respect to the certification of any person as, and as to the proof that a person is, the liquidator, administrator or administrative receiver of a company.

9. The following provision with respect to meetings of a company's creditors, contributories or members—
    (a)   provision as to the manner of summoning a meeting (including provision as to how any power to require a meeting is to be exercised, provision as to the manner of determining the value of any debt or contribution for the purposes of any such power and provision making the exercise of any such power subject to the deposit of a sum sufficient to cover the expenses likely to be incurred in summoning and holding a meeting);
    (b)   provision specifying the time and place at which a meeting may be held and the period of notice required for a meeting;
    (c)   provision as to the procedure to be followed at a meeting (including the manner in which decisions may be reached by a meeting and the manner in which the value of any vote at a meeting is to be determined);
    (d)   provision for requiring a person who is or has been an officer of the company to attend a meeting;
    (e)   provision creating, in the prescribed circumstances, a presumption that a meeting has been duly summoned and held;
    (f)   provision as to the manner of proving the decisions of a meeting.

10. (1)   Provision as to the functions, membership and proceedings of a committee established under [section 49, 68, 101, 141 or 142 of, or paragraph 57 of Schedule B1 to, this Act].

(2)   The following provision with respect to the establishment of a committee under section 101, 141 or 142 of this Act, that is to say—

(a) provision for resolving differences between a meeting of the company's creditors and a meeting of its contributories or members;

(b) provision authorising the establishment of the committee without a meeting of contributories in a case where a company is being wound up on grounds including its inability to pay its debts; and

(c) provision modifying the requirements of this Act with respect to the establishment of the committee in a case where a winding-up order has been made immediately upon the discharge of an administration order.

11. Provision as to the manner in which any requirement that may be imposed on a person under any of Parts I to VII of this Act by the official receiver, the liquidator, administrator or administrative receiver of a company or a special manager appointed under section 177 is to be so imposed.

12. Provision as to the debts that may be proved in a winding up, as to the manner and conditions of proving a debt and as to the manner and expenses of establishing the value of any debt or security.

13. Provision with respect to the manner of the distribution of the property of a company that is being wound up, including provision with respect to unclaimed funds and dividends.

14. Provision which, with or without modifications, applies in relation to the winding up of companies any enactment contained in Parts VIII to XI of this Act or in the Bankruptcy (Scotland) Act 1985.

[14A. Provision about the application of section 176A of this Act which may include, in particular—

(a) provision enabling a receiver to institute winding up proceedings;

(b) provision requiring a receiver to institute winding up proceedings.]

[Administration

14B. Provision which—

(a) applies in relation to administration, with or without modifications, a provision of Parts IV to VII of this Act, or

(b) serves a purpose in relation to administration similar to a purpose that may be served by the rules in relation to winding up by virtue of a provision of this Schedule.]

Financial provisions

15. Provision as to the amount, or manner of determining the amount, payable to the liquidator, administrator or administrative receiver of a company or a special manager appointed under section 177, by way of remuneration for the carrying out of functions in connection with or arising out of the insolvency or winding up of a company.

16. Provision with respect to the manner in which moneys received by the liquidator of a company in the course of carrying out his functions as such are to be invested or otherwise handled and with respect to the payment of interest on sums which, in pursuance of rules made by virtue of this paragraph, have been paid into the Insolvency Services Account.

[16A. Provision enabling the Secretary of State to set the rate of interest paid on sums which have been paid into the Insolvency Services Account.]

17. Provision as to the fees, costs, charges and other expenses that may be treated as the expenses of a winding up.

18. Provision as to the fees, costs, charges and other expenses that may be treated as properly incurred by the administrator or administrative receiver of a company.

19. Provision as to the fees, costs, charges and other expenses that may be incurred for any of the purposes of Part I of this Act or in the administration of any voluntary arrangement approved under that Part.

Information and records

20. Provision requiring registrars and other officers of courts having jurisdiction in England and Wales in relation to, or to matters connected with or arising out of, the insolvency or winding up of companies—

(a) to keep books and other records with respect to the exercise of that jurisdiction, and

(b) to make returns to the Secretary of State of the business of those courts.

21. Provision requiring a creditor, member or contributory, or such a committee as is mentioned in paragraph 10 above, to be supplied (on payment in prescribed cases of the prescribed fee) with such information and with copies of such documents as may be prescribed.

22. Provision as to the manner in which public examinations under sections 133 and 134 of this Act and proceedings under sections 236 and 237 are to be conducted, as to the circumstances in which records of such examinations or proceedings are to be made available to prescribed persons and as to the costs of such examinations and proceedings.

23. Provision imposing requirements with respect to—
(a)   the preparation and keeping by the liquidator, administrator or administrative receiver of a company, or by the supervisor of a voluntary arrangement approved under Part I of this Act, of prescribed books, accounts and other records;
(b)   the production of those books, accounts and records for inspection by prescribed persons;
(c)   the auditing of accounts kept by the liquidator, administrator or administrative receiver of a company, or the supervisor of such a voluntary arrangement; and
(d)   the issue by the administrator or administrative receiver of a company of such a certificate as is mentioned in section 22(3)(b) of the Value Added Tax Act 1983 (refund of tax in cases of bad debts) and the supply of copies of the certificate to creditors of the company.

24. Provision requiring the person who is the supervisor of a voluntary arrangement approved under Part I, when it appears to him that the voluntary arrangement has been fully implemented and that nothing remains to be done by him under the arrangement—
(a)   to give notice of that fact to persons bound by the voluntary arrangement, and
(b)   to report to those persons on the carrying out of the functions conferred on the supervisor of the arrangement.

25. Provision as to the manner in which the liquidator of a company is to act in relation to the books, papers and other records of the company, including provision authorising their disposal.

26. Provision imposing requirements in connection with the carrying out of functions under section 7(3) of the Company Directors Disqualification Act 1986 (including, in particular, requirements with respect to the making of periodic returns).

General

27. Provision conferring power on the Secretary of State [or the Treasury] to make regulations with respect to so much of any matter that may be provided for in the rules as relates to the carrying out of the functions of the liquidator, administrator or administrative receiver of a company.

28. Provision conferring a discretion on the court.

29. Provision conferring power on the court to make orders for the purpose of securing compliance with obligations imposed by or under [section 47, 66, 131, 143(2) or 235 of, or paragraph 47 of Schedule B1 to, this Act] or section 7(4) of the Company Directors Disqualification Act 1986.

30. Provision making non-compliance with any of the rules a criminal offence.

31. Provision making different provision for different cases or descriptions of cases, including different provisions for different areas.

NOTES

Para 2: sub-para (1) numbered as such, and sub-para (2) added, by the Enterprise Act 2002, s 248(3), Sch 17, paras 9, 38(1), (2), as from 15 September 2003 (for savings and transitional provisions, see the note to s 8 at **[9.105]**); words in square brackets in sub-para (1) substituted by the Companies Act 2006 (Commencement No 3, Consequential Amendments, Transitional Provisions and Savings) Order 2007, SI 2007/2194, art 10(1), (2), Sch 4, Pt 3, para 44, as from 1 October 2007.

Paras 10, 29: words in square brackets substituted by the Enterprise Act 2002, s 248(3), Sch 17, paras 9, 38(1), (3), (6), as from 15 September 2003 (for savings and transitional provisions, see the note to s 8 at **[9.105]**).

Paras 14A, 14B: inserted by the Enterprise Act 2002, s 248(3), Sch 17, paras 9, 38(1), (4), (5), as from 15 September 2003 (for savings and transitional provisions, see the note to s 8 at **[9.105]**).

Paras 16A: inserted by the Enterprise Act 2002, s 271(1), as from 18 December 2003.

Para 27: words in square brackets inserted by the Banking Act 2009, s 125(7), as from 17 February 2009.

Regulations: the Insolvency Regulations 1994, SI 1994/2507 at **[10.720]**.

SCHEDULE 10

PUNISHMENT OF OFFENCES UNDER THIS ACT

Section 430

[9.424]

Section of Act creating offence	General nature of offence	Mode of prosecution	Punishment	Daily default fine (where applicable)
[6A(1).	False representation or fraud for purpose of obtaining members' or creditors' approval of proposed voluntary arrangement.	1. On indictment.	7 years or a fine, or both.	
		2. Summary.	6 months or the statutory maximum, or both.]	
. . .			. . .	. . .
30	Body corporate acting as receiver	1. On indictment	A fine	
		2. Summary	The statutory maximum	
31	. . . bankrupt [or person in respect of whom a debt relief order is made] acting as receiver or manager	1. On indictment	2 years or a fine, or both	
		2. Summary	6 months or the statutory maximum, or both	
38(5)	Receiver failing to deliver accounts to registrar	Summary	One-fifth of the statutory maximum	One-fiftieth of the statutory maximum.
39(2)	Company and others failing to state in correspondence that receiver appointed	Summary	One-fifth of the statutory maximum	One-fiftieth of the statutory maximum.
43(6)	Administrative receiver failing to file [copy] of order permitting disposal of charged property	Summary	One-fifth of the statutory maximum	One-fiftieth of the statutory maximum.
45(5)	Administrative receiver failing to file notice of vacation of office	Summary	One-fifth of the statutory maximum	*One-fiftieth of the statutory maximum.*
46(4)	Administrative receiver failing to give notice of his appointment	Summary	One-fifth of the statutory maximum	One-fiftieth of the statutory maximum.
47(6)	Failure to comply with provisions relating to statement of affairs, where administrative receiver appointed	1. On indictment	A fine	
		2. Summary	The statutory maximum	One-tenth of the statutory maximum.

Section of Act creating offence	General nature of offence	Mode of prosecution	Punishment	Daily default fine (where applicable)
48(8)	Administrative receiver failing to comply with requirements as to his report	Summary	One-fifth of the statutory maximum	One-fiftieth of the statutory maximum.
51(4)	Body corporate or Scottish firm acting as receiver	1. On indictment 2. Summary	A fine The statutory maximum	
51(5)	Undischarged bankrupt acting as receiver (Scotland)	1. On indictment 2. Summary	2 years or a fine, or both 6 months or the statutory maximum, or both	
53(2)	Failing to deliver to registrar copy of instrument of appointment of receiver	Summary	One-fifth of the statutory maximum	*One-fiftieth of the statutory maximum.*
54(3)	Failing to deliver to registrar the court's interlocutor appointing receiver	Summary	One-fifth of the statutory maximum	*One-fiftieth of the statutory maximum.*
61(7)	Receiver failing to send to registrar certified copy of court order authorising disposal of charged property	Summary	One-fifth of the statutory maximum	One-fiftieth of the statutory maximum.
62(5)	Failing to give notice to registrar of cessation or removal of receiver	Summary	One-fifth of the statutory maximum	*One-fiftieth of the statutory maximum.*
64(2)	Company and others failing to state on correspondence etc that receiver appointed	Summary	One-fifth of the statutory maximum	
65(4)	Receiver failing to send or publish notice of his appointment	Summary	One-fifth of the statutory maximum	One-fiftieth of the statutory maximum.
66(6)	Failing to comply with provisions concerning statement of affairs, where receiver appointed	1. On indictment 2. Summary	A fine The statutory maximum	One-tenth of the statutory maximum.
67(8)	Receiver failing to comply with requirements as to his report	Summary	One-fifth of the statutory maximum	One-fiftieth of the statutory maximum.
85(2)	Company failing to give notice in Gazette of resolution for voluntary winding up	Summary	One-fifth of the statutory maximum	One-fiftieth of the statutory maximum.
89(4)	Director making statutory declaration of company's solvency without reasonable grounds for his opinion	1. On indictment	2 years or a fine, or both	

Section of Act creating offence	General nature of offence	Mode of prosecution	Punishment	Daily default fine (where applicable)
89(6)	Declaration under section 89 not delivered to registrar within prescribed time	2. Summary	6 months or the statutory maximum, or both	One-fiftieth of the statutory maximum.
[92A(2)	Liquidator failing to send progress report to members at year's end	Summary	One-fifth of the statutory maximum	One-fiftieth of the statutory maximum.
93(3)	Liquidator failing to summon general meeting of company at each year's end	Summary	Level 3 on the standard scale]	
94(4)	Liquidator failing to send to registrar a copy of account of winding up and return of final meeting	Summary	One-fifth of the statutory maximum	One-fiftieth of the statutory maximum.
94(6)	Liquidator failing to call final meeting	Summary	One-fifth of the statutory maximum	
95(8)	Liquidator failing to comply with s 95, where company insolvent	Summary	The statutory maximum	
98(6)	Company failing to comply with s 98 in respect of summoning and giving notice of creditors' meeting	1. On indictment	A fine	
		2. Summary	The statutory maximum	
99(3)	Directors failing to attend and lay statement in prescribed form before creditors' meeting	1. On indictment	A fine	
		2. Summary	The statutory maximum	
[104A(2)	Liquidator failing to send progress report to members and creditors at year's end	Summary	Level 3 on the standard scale]	
105(3)	Liquidator failing to summon company general meeting and creditors' meeting at each year's end	Summary	One-fifth of the statutory maximum	One-fiftieth of the statutory maximum.
106(4)	Liquidator failing to send to registrar account of winding up and return of final meetings	Summary	One-fifth of the statutory maximum	One-fiftieth of the statutory maximum.
106(6)	Liquidator failing to call final meeting of company or creditors	Summary	One-fifth of the statutory maximum	
109(2)	Liquidator failing to publish notice of his appointment	Summary	One-fifth of the statutory maximum	One-fiftieth of the statutory maximum.

Section of Act creating offence	General nature of offence	Mode of prosecution	Punishment	Daily default fine (where applicable)
114(4)	Directors exercising powers in breach of s 114, where no liquidator	Summary	The statutory maximum	
131(7)	Failing to comply with requirements as to statement of affairs, where liquidator appointed	1. On indictment	A fine	
		2. Summary	The statutory maximum	One-tenth of the statutory maximum.
164	Giving, offering etc corrupt inducement affecting appointment of liquidator	1. On indictment	A fine	
		2. Summary	The statutory maximum	
166(7)	Liquidator failing to comply with requirements of s 166 in creditors' voluntary winding up	Summary	The statutory maximum	
188(2)	Default in compliance with s 188 as to notification that company being wound up	Summary	One-fifth of the statutory maximum	
192(2)	Liquidator failing to notify registrar as to progress of winding up	Summary	One-fifth of the statutory maximum	One-fiftieth of the statutory maximum.
201(4)	Failing to deliver to registrar [copy] of court order deferring dissolution	Summary	One-fifth of the statutory maximum	One-fiftieth of the statutory maximum.
203(6)	Failing to deliver to registrar copy of directions or result of appeal under s 203	Summary	One-fifth of the statutory maximum	One-fiftieth of the statutory maximum.
204(7)	Liquidator failing to deliver to registrar copy of court order for early dissolution	Summary	One-fifth of the statutory maximum	One-fiftieth of the statutory maximum.
204(8)	Failing to deliver to registrar copy of court order deferring early dissolution	Summary	One-fifth of the statutory maximum	One-fiftieth of the statutory maximum.
205(7)	Failing to deliver to registrar copy of Secretary of State's directions or court order deferring dissolution	Summary	One-fifth of the statutory maximum	One-fiftieth of the statutory maximum.
206(1)	Fraud etc in anticipation of winding up	1. On indictment	7 years or a fine, or both	
		2. Summary	6 months or the statutory maximum, or both	
206(2)	Privity to fraud in anticipation of winding up; fraud, or privity to fraud, after commencement of winding up	1. On indictment	7 years or a fine, or both	

Section of Act creating offence	General nature of offence	Mode of prosecution	Punishment	Daily default fine (where applicable)
206(5)	Knowingly taking in pawn or pledge, or otherwise receiving, company property	1. On indictment	7 years or a fine, or both	
		2. Summary	6 months or the statutory maximum, or both	
207	Officer of company entering into transaction in fraud of company's creditors	1. On indictment	2 years or a fine, or both	
		2. Summary	6 months or the statutory maximum, or both	
208	Officer of company misconducting himself in course of winding up	1. On indictment	7 years or a fine, or both	
		2. Summary	6 months or the statutory maximum, or both	
209	Officer or contributory destroying, falsifying, etc company's books	1. On indictment	7 years or a fine, or both	
		2. Summary	6 months or the statutory maximum, or both	
210	Officer of company making material omission from statement relating to company's affairs	1. On indictment	7 years or a fine, or both	
		2. Summary	6 months or the statutory maximum, or both	
211	False representation or fraud for purpose of obtaining creditors' consent to an agreement in connection with winding up	1. On indictment	7 years or a fine, or both	
		2. Summary	6 months or the statutory maximum, or both	
216(4)	Contravening restrictions on re-use of name of company in insolvent liquidation	1. On indictment	2 years or a fine, or both	
		2. Summary	6 months or the statutory maximum, or both	
235(5)	Failing to co-operate with office-holder	1. On indictment	A fine	

Section of Act creating offence	General nature of offence	Mode of prosecution	Punishment	Daily default fine (where applicable)
389	Acting as insolvency practitioner when not qualified	2. Summary	The statutory maximum	One-tenth of the statutory maximum.
[Sch A1, para 9(2)].	Directors failing to notify nominee of beginning of moratorium.	1. On indictment	2 years or a fine, or both	
		2. Summary	6 months or the statutory maximum, or both	
Sch A1, para 10(3).	Nominee failing to advertise or notify beginning of moratorium.	1. On indictment.	2 years or a fine, or both.	
		2. Summary	6 months or the statutory maximum, or both.	
Sch A1, para 11(2).	Nominee failing to advertise or notify end of moratorium.	Summary.	One-fifth of the statutory maximum.	
Sch A1, para 16(2).	Company and officers failing to state in correspondence etc that moratorium in force.	Summary.	One-fifth of the statutory maximum.	
Sch A1, para 17(3)(a)	Company obtaining credit without disclosing existence of moratorium.	1. On indictment.	A fine.	
		2. Summary.	The statutory maximum.	
Sch A1, para 17(3)(b).	Obtaining credit for company without disclosing existence of moratorium.	1. On indictment.	2 years or a fine, or both.	
		2. Summary.	6 months or the statutory maximum, or both.	
Sch A1, para 18(3)(a).	Company disposing of property otherwise than in ordinary way of business.	1. On indictment.	A fine.	
		2. Summary.	The statutory maximum.	
Sch A1, para 18(3)(b).	Authorising or permitting disposal of company property.	1. On indictment.	2 years or a fine, or both.	
		2. Summary.	6 months or the statutory maximum, or both.	

Section of Act creating offence	General nature of offence	Mode of prosecution	Punishment	Daily default fine (where applicable)
Sch A1, para 19(3)(a).	Company making payments in respect of liabilities existing before beginning of moratorium.	1. On indictment. 2. Summary.	A fine. The statutory maximum.	
Sch A1, para 19(3)(b).	Authorising or permitting such a payment.	1. On indictment. 2. Summary.	2 years or a fine, or both. 6 months or the statutory maximum, or both.	
Sch A1, para 20(9).	Directors failing to send to registrar [copy] of court order permitting disposal of charged property.	Summary.	One-fifth of the statutory maximum.	
Sch A1, para 22(1).	Company disposing of charged property.	1. On indictment. 2. Summary.	A fine. The statutory maximum.	
Sch A1, para 22(2).	Authorising or permitting such a disposal.	1. On indictment. 2. Summary.	2 years or a fine, or both. 6 months or the statutory maximum, or both.	
Sch A1, para 23(1)(a).	Company entering into market contract, etc.	1. On indictment. 2. Summary.	A fine. The statutory maximum.	
Sch A1, para 23(1)(b).	Authorising or permitting company to do so.	1. On indictment. 2. Summary.	2 years or a fine, or both. 6 months or the statutory maximum, or both.	
Sch A1, para 25(6).	Nominee failing to give notice of withdrawal of consent to act.	Summary.	One-fifth of the statutory maximum.	
Sch A1, para 34(3).	Nominee failing to give notice of extension of moratorium.	Summary.	One-fifth of the statutory maximum.	

Section of Act creating offence	General nature of offence	Mode of prosecution	Punishment	Daily default fine (where applicable)
Sch A1, para 41(2).	Fraud or privity to fraud in anticipation of moratorium.	1. On indictment.	7 years or a fine, or both.	
		2. Summary.	6 months or the statutory maximum, or both.	
Sch A1, para 41(3).	Fraud or privity to fraud during moratorium.	1. On indictment.	7 years or a fine, or both.	
		2. Summary.	6 months or the statutory maximum, or both.	
Sch A1, para 42(1).	False representation or fraud for purpose of obtaining or extending moratorium.	1. On indictment.	7 years or a fine, or both.	
		2. Summary.	6 months or the statutory maximum, or both.]	
[Sch B1, para 18(7).	Making false statement in statutory declaration where administrator appointed by holder of floating charge.	1. On indictment.	2 years, or a fine or both.	
		2. Summary.	6 months, or the statutory maximum or both.	
Sch B1, para 20.	Holder of floating charge failing to notify administrator or others of commencement of appointment.	1. On indictment.	2 years, or a fine or both.	
		2. Summary.	6 months, or the statutory maximum or both.	One-tenth of the statutory maximum.
Sch B1, para 27(4).	Making false statement in statutory declaration where appointment of administrator proposed by company or directors.	1. On indictment.	2 years, or a fine or both.	
		2. Summary.	6 months, or the statutory maximum or both.	
Sch B1, para 29(7).	Making false statement in statutory declaration where administrator appointed by company or directors.	1. On indictment.	2 years, or a fine or both.	
		2. Summary.	6 months, or the statutory maximum or both.	

Section of Act creating offence	General nature of offence	Mode of prosecution	Punishment	Daily default fine (where applicable)
Sch B1, para 32.	Company or directors failing to notify administrator or others of commencement of appointment.	1. On indictment.	2 years, or a fine or both.	
		2. Summary.	6 months, or the statutory maximum, or both.	One-tenth of the statutory maximum.
Sch B1, para 45(2).	Administrator, company or officer failing to state in business document that administrator appointed.	Summary.	One-fifth of the statutory maximum.	One-fiftieth of the statutory maximum.
Sch B1, para 46(9).	Administrator failing to give notice of his appointment.	Summary.	One-fifth of the statutory maximum.	
Sch B1, para 48(4).	Failing to comply with provisions about statement of affairs where administrator appointed.	1. On indictment.	A fine.	
		2. Summary.	The statutory maximum.	One-tenth of the statutory maximum.
Sch B1, para 49(7).	Administrator failing to send out statement of his proposals.	Summary.	One-fifth of the statutory maximum.	One-fiftieth of the statutory maximum.
Sch B1, para 51(5).	Administrator failing to arrange initial creditors' meeting.	Summary.	One-fifth of the statutory maximum.	One-fiftieth of the statutory maximum.
Sch B1, para 53(3).	Administrator failing to report decision taken at initial creditors' meeting.	Summary.	One-fifth of the statutory maximum.	One-fiftieth of the statutory maximum.
Sch B1, para 54(7).	Administrator failing to report decision taken at creditors' meeting summoned to consider revised proposal.	Summary.	One-fifth of the statutory maximum.	One-fiftieth of the statutory maximum.
Sch B1, para 56(2).	Administrator failing to summon creditors' meeting.	Summary.	One-fifth of the statutory maximum.	One-fiftieth of the statutory maximum.
Sch B1, para 71(6).	Administrator failing to file court order enabling disposal of charged property.	Summary.	One-fifth of the statutory maximum.	One-fiftieth of the statutory maximum.
Sch B1, para 72(5).	Administrator failing to file court order enabling disposal of hire-purchase property.	Summary.	One-fifth of the statutory maximum.	One-fiftieth of the statutory maximum.
Sch B1, para 77(3).	Administrator failing to notify Registrar of Companies of automatic end of administration.	Summary.	One-fifth of the statutory maximum.	One-fiftieth of the statutory maximum.

Section of Act creating offence	General nature of offence	Mode of prosecution	Punishment	Daily default fine (where applicable)
Sch B1, para 78(6).	Administrator failing to give notice of extension by consent of term of office.	Summary.	One-fifth of the statutory maximum.	One-fiftieth of the statutory maximum.
Sch B1, para 80(6).	Administrator failing to give notice of termination of administration where objective achieved.	Summary.	One-fifth of the statutory maximum.	One-fiftieth of the statutory maximum.
Sch B1, para 84(9).	Administrator failing to comply with provisions where company moves to dissolution.	Summary.	One-fifth of the statutory maximum.	One-fiftieth of the statutory maximum.
Sch B1, para 86(3).	Administrator failing to notify Registrar of Companies where court terminates administration.	Summary.	One-fifth of the statutory maximum.	One-fiftieth of the statutory maximum.
Sch B1, para 89(3).	Administrator failing to give notice on ceasing to be qualified.	Summary.	One-fifth of the statutory maximum.	One-fiftieth of the statutory maximum.]
Sch 7, para 4(3)	Failure to attend and give evidence to Insolvency Practitioners Tribunal; suppressing, concealing, etc relevant documents	Summary	Level 3 on the standard scale within the meaning given by section 75 of the Criminal Justice Act 1982	

NOTES

Certain provisions outside the scope of this work have been omitted from this Schedule.

Entry relating to section 6A inserted by the Insolvency Act 2000, s 2, Sch 2, Pt I, paras 1, 12, as from 1 January 2003 (for transitional provisions see the note to s 1 at [**9.93**]).

Entries relating to ss 12(2), 15(8), 18(5), 21(3), 22(6), 23(3), 24(7), 27(6) (omitted) repealed by the Enterprise Act 2002, ss 248(3), 278(2), Sch 17, paras 9, 39(1), (3), Sch 26, as from 15 September 2003 (for savings and transitional provisions, see the note to s 8 at [**9.105**]).

Word omitted from column 2 of entry relating to s 31 repealed by the Enterprise Act 2002, s 278(2), Sch 26, as from 1 April 2004; words in square brackets in that entry inserted by the Tribunals, Courts and Enforcement Act 2007, s 108(3), Sch 20, Pt 1, paras 1, 15(1), (2), as from 6 April 2009.

Words in square brackets in the entries relating to ss 43(6), 201(4), Sch A1, para 20(9) substituted by the Companies Act 2006 (Consequential Amendments, Transitional Provisions and Savings) Order 2009, SI 2009/1941, art 2(1), Sch 1, para 80, as from 1 October 2009 (for transitional provisions see the note to s 7A at [**9.103**]).

Entries in italics in column 5 relating to ss 45(5), 53(2), 54(3), 62(5) repealed by CA 1989, s 212, Sch 24, as from a day to be appointed.

Entries relating to ss 92A(2) and 104A(2) inserted by the Legislative Reform (Insolvency) (Miscellaneous Provisions) Order 2010, SI 2010/18, arts 2, 6(5), as from 6 April 2010.

Entries relating to Schedule A1 inserted by the Insolvency Act 2000, s 1, Sch 1, paras 1, 12, as from 1 January 2003.

Entries relating to Schedule B1 inserted by the Enterprise Act 2002, s 248(3), Sch 17, paras 9, 39(1), (2), as from 15 September 2003 (for savings and transitional provisions, see the note to s 8 at [**9.105**]).

The Note to this Schedule was repealed by the Statute Law (Repeals) Act 1993, as from 5 November 1993.

COMPANY AND BUSINESS NAMES
(CHAMBER OF COMMERCE, ETC) ACT 1999

(1999 c 19)

NOTES

This Act is reproduced as amended by: the Companies Act 2006 (Consequential Amendments, Transitional Provisions and Savings) Order 2009, SI 2009/1941.

An Act to make provision concerning the approval of company or business names containing the expression "chamber of commerce" or any related expression; and for connected purposes

[27 July 1999]

[9.425]

1   Approval to be required for company or business names including the expression "chamber of commerce"

It is the duty of the Secretary of State to secure that the expression "chamber of commerce" and its Welsh equivalent ("siambr fasnach") is specified—

(a)   in regulations under [section 55 of the Companies Act 2006 (company names requiring approval of Secretary of State)], and

(b)   in regulations under [section 1194 of that Act (business names requiring approval of Secretary of State)],

as an expression for the registration of which as or as part of a company's name, or for the use of which as or as part of a business name, the approval of the Secretary of State is required.

NOTES

Words in square brackets substituted by the Companies Act 2006 (Consequential Amendments, Transitional Provisions and Savings) Order 2009, SI 2009/1941, art 2(1), Sch 1, para 176(1), (2), as from 1 October 2009.

[9.426]

2   Approval of certain company names

(1)   Before determining under [section 55 of the Companies Act 2006] whether to approve the registration of a company under a name which includes—

(a)   the expression "chamber of commerce" or "siambr fasnach", or

(b)   any other expression for the time being specified in regulations under [that section] which begins with the words "chamber of" or "chambers of" (or the Welsh equivalents),

the Secretary of State must consult at least one relevant representative body.

(2)   The Secretary of State may publish guidance with respect to factors which may be taken into account in determining whether to approve the registration of a name to which this section applies.

NOTES

Sub-s (1): words in square brackets substituted by the Companies Act 2006 (Consequential Amendments, Transitional Provisions and Savings) Order 2009, SI 2009/1941, art 2(1), Sch 1, para 176(1), (3), as from 1 October 2009.

[9.427]

3   Approval of certain business names

(1)   Before determining under [section 1194 of the Companies Act 2006] whether to approve the carrying on of a business under a name which includes—

(a)   the expression "chamber of commerce" or "siambr fasnach", or

(b)   any other expression for the time being specified in regulations under [that section] which begins with the words "chamber of" or "chambers of" (or the Welsh equivalents),

the Secretary of State must consult at least one relevant representative body.

(2)   The Secretary of State may publish guidance with respect to factors which may be taken into account in determining whether to approve the use of a business name to which this section applies.

NOTES

Sub-s (1): words in square brackets substituted by the Companies Act 2006 (Consequential Amendments, Transitional Provisions and Savings) Order 2009, SI 2009/1941, art 2(1), Sch 1, para 176(1), (4), as from 1 October 2009.

[9.428]

4   Relevant representative bodies

(1)   The relevant representative bodies for the purposes of this Act are—

(a)   British Chambers of Commerce;

(b)   the body known as Scottish Chambers of Commerce.

(2)   The Secretary of State may by order amend subsection (1) by adding to or deleting from it the name of any body (whether corporate or unincorporated).

(3)   The power to make an order under this section is exercisable by statutory instrument which shall be liable to annulment in pursuance of a resolution of either House of Parliament.

Part 9   Misc primary legislation

[9.429]

5 Citation, commencement and extent

(1) This Act may be cited as the Company and Business Names (Chamber of Commerce, Etc) Act 1999.

(2) This Act shall come into force on such day as the Secretary of State may by order made by statutory instrument appoint.

(3) This Act does not extend to Northern Ireland.

NOTES

Orders: the Company and Business Names (Chamber of Commerce, etc) Act 1999 (Commencement) Order 2001, SI 2001/258 (bringing this Act into force on 10 May 2001).

LIMITED LIABILITY PARTNERSHIPS ACT 2000

(2000 c 12)

NOTES

This Act is reproduced as amended by: the Companies (Audit, Investigations and Community Enterprise) Act 2004; the Companies Act 2006; the Income Tax Act 2007; the Corporation Tax Act 2010; the Open-Ended Investment Companies Regulations 2001, SI 2001/1228; the Limited Liability Partnerships (Particulars of Usual Residential Address) (Confidentiality Orders) Regulations 2002, SI 2002/915; the Limited Liability Partnerships (Application of Companies Act 2006) Regulations 2009, SI 2009/1804.

Application of the Banking Act 2009: s 132 of the Banking Act 2009 provides that the Lord Chancellor may, by order made with the concurrence of the Secretary of State and the Lord Chief Justice, modify provisions of Part 2 of the 2009 Act (bank insolvency) in their application to partnerships. See also s 163 of the 2009 Act which makes the same provision with regard to the application of Part 3 of that Act (bank administration). Similar provision is made with regard to Scottish partnerships by ss 133 and 164 respectively.

Fees: as to fees under this Act, see the Limited Liability Partnerships (Fees) Regulations 2004, SI 2004/2620 and the Registrar of Companies (Fees) (Companies, Overseas Companies and Limited Liability Partnerships) Regulations 2009, SI 2009/2101 at **[4.543]**.

Serious crime prevention orders: as to the winding up of an LLP on conviction of the offence of failing to comply with a serious crime prevention order, see the Serious Crime Act 2007, s 27.

ARRANGEMENT OF SECTIONS

Schedule—Names and registered offices

An Act to make provision for limited liability partnerships

[20 July 2000]

Introductory

[9.430]
1 Limited liability partnerships
(1)   There shall be a new form of legal entity to be known as a limited liability partnership.

(2)   A limited liability partnership is a body corporate (with legal personality separate from that of its members) which is formed by being incorporated under this Act; and—
- (a)   in the following provisions of this Act (except in the phrase "oversea limited liability partnership"), and
- (b)   in any other enactment (except where provision is made to the contrary or the context otherwise requires),

references to a limited liability partnership are to such a body corporate.

(3)   A limited liability partnership has unlimited capacity.

(4)   The members of a limited liability partnership have such liability to contribute to its assets in the event of its being wound up as is provided for by virtue of this Act.

(5)   Accordingly, except as far as otherwise provided by this Act or any other enactment, the law relating to partnerships does not apply to a limited liability partnership.

(6)   The Schedule (which makes provision about the names and registered offices of limited liability partnerships) has effect.

Incorporation

[9.431]
2 Incorporation document etc
(1)   For a limited liability partnership to be incorporated—
- (a)   two or more persons associated for carrying on a lawful business with a view to profit must have subscribed their names to an incorporation document,
- [(b)   the incorporation document or a copy of it must have been delivered to the registrar, and]
- (c)   there must have been so delivered a statement   . . .   made by either a solicitor engaged in the formation of the limited liability partnership or anyone who subscribed his name to the incorporation document, that the requirement imposed by paragraph (a) has been complied with.

(2)   The incorporation document must—
- (a)   . . .
- (b)   state the name of the limited liability partnership,
- (c)   state whether the registered office of the limited liability partnership is to be situated in England and Wales, in Wales[, in Scotland or in Northern Ireland],
- (d)   state the address of that registered office,
- [(e)   give the required particulars of each of the persons who are to be members of the limited liability partnership on incorporation, and]
- (f)   either specify which of those persons are to be designated members or state that every person who from time to time is a member of the limited liability partnership is a designated member.

[(2ZA)   The required particulars mentioned in subsection (2)(e) are the particulars required to be stated in the LLP's register of members and register of members' residential addresses.]

[(2A), (2B)   . . .]

(3)   If a person makes a false statement under subsection (1)(c) which he—
- (a)   knows to be false, or
- (b)   does not believe to be true,

he commits an offence.

(4)   A person guilty of an offence under subsection (3) is liable—
- (a)   on summary conviction, to imprisonment for a period not exceeding six months or a fine not exceeding the statutory maximum, or to both, or
- (b)   on conviction on indictment, to imprisonment for a period not exceeding two years or a fine, or to both.

NOTES

Sub-s (1): words omitted from para (c) repealed and para (b) substituted, by the Limited Liability Partnerships (Application of Companies Act 2006) Regulations 2009, SI 2009/1804, reg 85, Sch 3, Pt 1, para 1(1)–(3), as from 1 October 2009 (for savings see the note below).

Sub-s (2): para (a) repealed, words in square brackets in para (c) substituted, and para (e) substituted, by SI 2009/1804, reg 85, Sch 3, Pt 1, para 1(1), (4), as from 1 October 2009 (for savings see the note below).

Sub-s (2ZA): inserted by SI 2009/1804, reg 85, Sch 3, Pt 1, para 1(1), (5), as from 1 October 2009 (for savings see the note below).

Sub-ss (2A), (2B): inserted by the Limited Liability Partnerships (Particulars of Usual Residential Address) (Confidentiality Orders) Regulations 2002, SI 2002/915, reg 16, Sch 2, para 1, as from 2 April 2002, and repealed by SI 2009/1804, reg 85, Sch 3, Pt 1, para 1(1), (6), as from 1 October 2009 (for savings see the note below).

Saving provision: the Limited Liability Partnerships (Application of Companies Act 2006) Regulations 2009, SI 2009/1804, Sch 3, Pt 1, para 11 provides that the amendments made by Sch 3, Pt 1 to those Regulations do not affect an obligation arising before 1 October 2009 to deliver a document to the registrar.

[9.432]
3   Incorporation by registration
[(1)   The registrar, if satisfied that the requirements of section 2 are complied with, shall—
   (a)   register the documents delivered under that section, and
   (b)   give a certificate that the limited liability partnership is incorporated.
(1A)   The certificate must state—
   (a)   the name and registered number of the limited liability partnership,
   (b)   the date of its incorporation, and
   (c)   whether the limited liability partnership's registered office is situated in England and Wales (or in Wales), in Scotland or in Northern Ireland.]
(2)   The registrar may accept the statement delivered under paragraph (c) of subsection (1) of section 2 as sufficient evidence that the requirement imposed by paragraph (a) of that subsection has been complied with.
(3)   The certificate shall either be signed by the registrar or be authenticated by his official seal.
(4)   The certificate is conclusive evidence that the requirements of section 2 are complied with and that the limited liability partnership is incorporated by the name specified in the incorporation document.

NOTES
Sub-ss (1), (1A): substituted (for the original sub-s (1)) by the Limited Liability Partnerships (Application of Companies Act 2006) Regulations 2009, SI 2009/1804, reg 85, Sch 3, Pt 1, para 2, as from 1 October 2009, as follows (for savings see the note to s 2 at **[9.431]**).

Membership

[9.433]
4   Members
(1)   On the incorporation of a limited liability partnership its members are the persons who subscribed their names to the incorporation document (other than any who have died or been dissolved).
(2)   Any other person may become a member of a limited liability partnership by and in accordance with an agreement with the existing members.
(3)   A person may cease to be a member of a limited liability partnership (as well as by death or dissolution) in accordance with an agreement with the other members or, in the absence of agreement with the other members as to cessation of membership, by giving reasonable notice to the other members.
(4)   A member of a limited liability partnership shall not be regarded for any purpose as employed by the limited liability partnership unless, if he and the other members were partners in a partnership, he would be regarded for that purpose as employed by the partnership.

[9.434]
[4A   Minimum membership for carrying on business
(1)   This section applies where a limited liability partnership carries on business without having at least two members, and does so for more than 6 months.
(2)   A person who, for the whole or any part of the period that it so carries on business after those 6 months—
   (a)   is a member of the limited liability partnership, and
   (b)   knows that it is carrying on business with only one member,
is liable (jointly and severally with the limited liability partnership) for the payment of the limited liability partnership's debts contracted during the period or, as the case may be, that part of it.]

NOTES
Commencement: 1 October 2009.
Inserted by the Limited Liability Partnerships (Application of Companies Act 2006) Regulations 2009, SI 2009/1804, reg 85, Sch 3, Pt 1, para 3, as from 1 October 2009 (for savings see the note to s 2 at **[9.431]**).

[9.435]
5   Relationship of members etc
(1)   Except as far as otherwise provided by this Act or any other enactment, the mutual rights and duties of the members of a limited liability partnership, and the mutual rights and duties of a limited liability partnership and its members, shall be governed—
   (a)   by agreement between the members, or between the limited liability partnership and its members, or

(b)   in the absence of agreement as to any matter, by any provision made in relation to that matter by regulations under section 15(c).

(2)   An agreement made before the incorporation of a limited liability partnership between the persons who subscribe their names to the incorporation document may impose obligations on the limited liability partnership (to take effect at any time after its incorporation).

[9.436]

6   Members as agents

(1)   Every member of a limited liability partnership is the agent of the limited liability partnership.

(2)   But a limited liability partnership is not bound by anything done by a member in dealing with a person if—

(a)   the member in fact has no authority to act for the limited liability partnership by doing that thing, and

(b)   the person knows that he has no authority or does not know or believe him to be a member of the limited liability partnership.

(3)   Where a person has ceased to be a member of a limited liability partnership, the former member is to be regarded (in relation to any person dealing with the limited liability partnership) as still being a member of the limited liability partnership unless—

(a)   the person has notice that the former member has ceased to be a member of the limited liability partnership, or

(b)   notice that the former member has ceased to be a member of the limited liability partnership has been delivered to the registrar.

(4)   Where a member of a limited liability partnership is liable to any person (other than another member of the limited liability partnership) as a result of a wrongful act or omission of his in the course of the business of the limited liability partnership or with its authority, the limited liability partnership is liable to the same extent as the member.

[9.437]

7   Ex-members

(1)   This section applies where a member of a limited liability partnership has either ceased to be a member or—

(a)   has died,

(b)   has become bankrupt or had his estate sequestrated or has been wound up,

(c)   has granted a trust deed for the benefit of his creditors, or

(d)   has assigned the whole or any part of his share in the limited liability partnership (absolutely or by way of charge or security).

(2)   In such an event the former member or—

(a)   his personal representative,

(b)   his trustee in bankruptcy or permanent or interim trustee (within the meaning of the Bankruptcy (Scotland) Act 1985) or liquidator,

(c)   his trustee under the trust deed for the benefit of his creditors, or

(d)   his assignee,

may not interfere in the management or administration of any business or affairs of the limited liability partnership.

(3)   But subsection (2) does not affect any right to receive an amount from the limited liability partnership in that event.

[9.438]

8   Designated members

(1)   If the incorporation document specifies who are to be designated members—

(a)   they are designated members on incorporation, and

(b)   any member may become a designated member by and in accordance with an agreement with the other members,

and a member may cease to be a designated member in accordance with an agreement with the other members.

(2)   But if there would otherwise be no designated members, or only one, every member is a designated member.

(3)   If the incorporation document states that every person who from time to time is a member of the limited liability partnership is a designated member, every member is a designated member.

(4)   A limited liability partnership may at any time deliver to the registrar—

(a)   notice that specified members are to be designated members, or

(b)   notice that every person who from time to time is a member of the limited liability partnership is a designated member,

and, once it is delivered, subsection (1) (apart from paragraph (a)) and subsection (2), or subsection (3), shall have effect as if that were stated in the incorporation document.

(5)   . . .

(6)   A person ceases to be a designated member if he ceases to be a member.

NOTES

Sub-s (5): repealed by the Limited Liability Partnerships (Application of Companies Act 2006) Regulations 2009, SI 2009/1804, reg 85, Sch 3, Pt 1, para 4, as from 1 October 2009 (for savings see the note to s 2 at **[9.431]**).

[9.439]

9   Registration of membership changes

(1)   A limited liability partnership must ensure that—

(a)   where a person becomes or ceases to be a member or designated member, notice is delivered to the registrar within fourteen days, and

(b)   where there is any change in the [particulars contained in its register of members or its register of members' residential addresses], notice is delivered to the registrar within [14 days].

(2)   Where all the members from time to time of a limited liability partnership are designated members, subsection (1)(a) does not require notice that a person has become or ceased to be a designated member as well as a member.

[(3)   A notice delivered under subsection (1) that relates to a person becoming a member or designated member must contain—

(a)   a statement that the member or designated member consents to acting in that capacity, and

(b)   in the case of a person becoming a member, a statement of the particulars of the new member that are required to be included in the limited liability partnership's register of members and its register of residential addresses.]

[(3ZA)   Where—

(a)   a limited liability partnership gives notice of a change of a member's service address as stated in its register of members, and

(b)   the notice is not accompanied by notice of any resulting change in the particulars contained in its register of members' residential addresses,

the notice must be accompanied by a statement that no such change is required.]

[(3A), (3B)   . . .]

(4)   If a limited liability partnership fails to comply with [this section], the partnership and every designated member commits an offence.

(5)   But it is a defence for a designated member charged with an offence under subsection (4) to prove that he took all reasonable steps for securing that [this section] was complied with.

(6)   A person guilty of an offence under subsection (4) is liable on summary conviction to a fine not exceeding level 5 on the standard scale.

NOTES

Sub-ss (1), (4), (5): words in square brackets substituted by the Limited Liability Partnerships (Application of Companies Act 2006) Regulations 2009, SI 2009/1804, reg 85, Sch 3, Pt 1, para 5(1), (2), (6), as from 1 October 2009 (for savings see the note to s 2 at **[9.431]**).

Sub-s (3): substituted by SI 2009/1804, reg 85, Sch 3, Pt 1, para 5(1), (3), as from 1 October 2009 (for savings see the note to s 2 at **[9.431]**).

Sub-s (3ZA): inserted by SI 2009/1804, reg 85, Sch 3, Pt 1, para 5(1), (4), as from 1 October 2009 (for savings see the note to s 2 at **[9.431]**).

Sub-ss (3A), (3B): inserted by the Limited Liability Partnerships (Particulars of Usual Residential Address) (Confidentiality Orders) Regulations 2002, SI 2002/915, reg 16, Sch 2, para 1, as from 2 April 2002, and repealed by SI 2009/1804, reg 85, Sch 3, Pt 1, para 5(1), (5), as from 1 October 2009 (for savings see the note to s 2 at **[9.431]**).

Taxation

[9.440]

10, 11   (*S 10 amends the Income and Corporation Taxes Act 1988 and the Taxation of Chargeable Gains Act 1992, and is repealed in part by the Income Tax Act 2007, s 1031, Sch 3 and the Corporation Tax Act 2010, s 1181, Sch 3; s 11 amends the Inheritance Tax Act 1984.*)

12   Stamp duty

(1)   Stamp duty shall not be chargeable on an instrument by which property is conveyed or transferred by a person to a limited liability partnership in connection with its incorporation within the period of one year beginning with the date of incorporation if the following two conditions are satisfied.

(2)   The first condition is that at the relevant time the person—

(a)   is a partner in a partnership comprised of all the persons who are or are to be members of the limited liability partnership (and no-one else), or

(b)   holds the property conveyed or transferred as nominee or bare trustee for one or more of the partners in such a partnership.

(3)   The second condition is that—

(a)   the proportions of the property conveyed or transferred to which the persons mentioned in subsection (2)(a) are entitled immediately after the conveyance or transfer are the same as those to which they were entitled at the relevant time, or

(b)   none of the differences in those proportions has arisen as part of a scheme or arrangement of which the main purpose, or one of the main purposes, is avoidance of liability to any duty or tax.

(4)   For the purposes of subsection (2) a person holds property as bare trustee for a partner if the partner has the exclusive right (subject only to satisfying any outstanding charge, lien or other right of the trustee to resort to the property for payment of duty, taxes, costs or other outgoings) to direct how the property shall be dealt with.

(5)   In this section "the relevant time" means—

(a)   if the person who conveyed or transferred the property to the limited liability partnership acquired the property after its incorporation, immediately after he acquired the property, and

(b)   in any other case, immediately before its incorporation.

(6)   An instrument in respect of which stamp duty is not chargeable by virtue of subsection (1) shall not be taken to be duly stamped unless—

(a)   it has, in accordance with section 12 of the Stamp Act 1891, been stamped with a particular stamp denoting that it is not chargeable with any duty or that it is duly stamped, or

(b)   it is stamped with the duty to which it would be liable apart from that subsection.

13   (*Amends the Social Security Contributions and Benefits Act 1992 and the Social Security Contributions and Benefits (Northern Ireland) Act 1992.*)

Regulations

[9.441]
14   Insolvency and winding up
(1)   Regulations shall make provision about the insolvency and winding up of limited liability partnerships by applying or incorporating, with such modifications as appear appropriate[—

(a)   in relation to a limited liability partnership registered in Great Britain, Parts 1 to 4, 6 and 7 of the Insolvency Act 1986;

(b)   in relation to a limited liability partnership registered in Northern Ireland, Parts 2 to 5 and 7 of the Insolvency (Northern Ireland) Order 1989, and so much of Part 1 of that Order as applies for the purposes of those Parts.]

(2)   Regulations may make other provision about the insolvency and winding up of limited liability partnerships, and provision about the insolvency and winding up of oversea limited liability partnerships, by—

(a)   applying or incorporating, with such modifications as appear appropriate, any law relating to the insolvency or winding up of companies or other corporations which would not otherwise have effect in relation to them, or

(b)   providing for any law relating to the insolvency or winding up of companies or other corporations which would otherwise have effect in relation to them not to apply to them or to apply to them with such modifications as appear appropriate.

(3)   In this Act "oversea limited liability partnership" means a body incorporated or otherwise established outside [the United Kingdom] and having such connection with [the United Kingdom], and such other features, as regulations may prescribe.

NOTES
Sub-ss (1), (3): words in square brackets substituted by the Limited Liability Partnerships (Application of Companies Act 2006) Regulations 2009, SI 2009/1804, reg 85, Sch 3, Pt 1, para 6, as from 9 July 2009 (for the purpose of enabling the exercise of powers to make regulations or orders by statutory instrument), and as from 1 October 2009 (otherwise) (for savings see the note to s 2 at **[9.431]**).
Regulations: the Limited Liability Partnerships (Scotland) Regulations 2001, SSI 2001/128 at **[10.802]**; the Limited Liability Partnerships Regulations 2001, SI 2001/1090 at **[10.813]**.

[9.442]
15   Application of company law etc
Regulations may make provision about limited liability partnerships and oversea limited liability partnerships (not being provision about insolvency or winding up) by—

(a)   applying or incorporating, with such modifications as appear appropriate, any law relating to companies or other corporations which would not otherwise have effect in relation to them,

(b)   providing for any law relating to companies or other corporations which would otherwise have effect in relation to them not to apply to them or to apply to them with such modifications as appear appropriate, or

(c)   applying or incorporating, with such modifications as appear appropriate, any law relating to partnerships.

NOTES
Regulations: the Limited Liability Partnerships (Scotland) Regulations 2001, SSI 2001/128 at **[10.802]**; the Limited Liability Partnerships Regulations 2001, SI 2001/1090 at **[10.813]**; the Companies (Registrar, Languages and Trading Disclosures) Regulations 2006, SI 2006/3429 at **[4.2]**; the Companies (Late Filing Penalties) and Limited Liability Partnerships (Filing Periods and Late Filing Penalties) Regulations 2008, SI 2008/497 at **[4.252]**; the Limited Liability Partnerships (Accounts and Audit) (Application of Companies Act 2006) Regulations 2008, SI 2008/1911 at **[10.1003]**; the Small Limited

Liability Partnerships (Accounts) Regulations 2008, SI 2008/1912 at **[10.1061]**; the Large and Medium-sized Limited Liability Partnerships (Accounts) Regulations 2008, SI 2008/1913 at **[10.1078]**; the Limited Liability Partnerships (Application of Companies Act 2006) Regulations 2009, SI 2009/1804 at **[10.1097]**; the Companies Act 2006 and Limited Liability Partnerships (Transitional Provisions and Savings) (Amendment) Regulations 2009, SI 2009/2476 at **[4.629]**.

[9.443]
16 Consequential amendments
(1)   Regulations may make in any enactment such amendments or repeals as appear appropriate in consequence of this Act or regulations made under it.
(2)   The regulations may, in particular, make amendments and repeals affecting companies or other corporations or partnerships.

NOTES
   Regulations: the Limited Liability Partnerships (Scotland) Regulations 2001, SSI 2001/128 at **[10.802]**; the Limited Liability Partnerships Regulations 2001, SI 2001/1090 at **[10.813]**.

[9.444]
17   General
(1)   In this Act "regulations" means regulations made by the Secretary of State by statutory instrument.
(2)   Regulations under this Act may in particular—
   (a)   make provisions for dealing with non-compliance with any of the regulations (including the creation of criminal offences),
   (b)   impose fees (which shall be paid into the Consolidated Fund), and
   (c)   provide for the exercise of functions by persons prescribed by the regulations.
(3)   Regulations under this Act may—
   (a)   contain any appropriate consequential, incidental, supplementary or transitional provisions or savings, and
   (b)   make different provision for different purposes.
(4)   No regulations to which this subsection applies shall be made unless a draft of the statutory instrument containing the regulations (whether or not together with other provisions) has been laid before, and approved by a resolution of, each House of Parliament.
(5)   Subsection (4) applies to—
   (a)   regulations under section 14(2) not consisting entirely of the application or incorporation (with or without modifications) of provisions contained in or made under the Insolvency Act 1986 [or the Insolvency (Northern Ireland) Order 1989],
   [(b)   regulations under section 15 not consisting entirely of the application or incorporation (with or without modifications) of provisions contained in or made under the following provisions of the Companies Act 2006 (c 46)—
      Part 4 (a company's capacity and related matters);
      Part 5 (a company's name);
      Part 6 (a company's registered office);
      Chapters 1 and 8 of Part 10 (register of directors);
      Part 15 (accounts and reports);
      Part 16 (audit);
      Part 19 (debentures);
      Part 21 (certification and transfer of securities);
      Part 24 (a company's annual return);
      Part 25 (company charges);
      Part 26 (arrangements and reconstructions);
      Part 29 (fraudulent trading);
      Part 30 (protection of members against unfair prejudice);
      Part 31 (dissolution and restoration to the register);
      Part 35 (the registrar of companies);
      Part 36 (offences under the Companies Acts);
      Part 37 (supplementary provisions);
      Part 38 (interpretation).]
   (c)   regulations under section 14 or 15 making provision about oversea limited liability partnerships, and
   (d)   regulations under section 16.
(6)   A statutory instrument containing regulations under this Act shall (unless a draft of it has been approved by a resolution of each House of Parliament) be subject to annulment in pursuance of a resolution of either House of Parliament.

NOTES
   Sub-s (5): words in square brackets in para (a) inserted, and para (b) substituted, by the Limited Liability Partnerships (Application of Companies Act 2006) Regulations 2009, SI 2009/1804, reg 85, Sch 3, Pt 1, para 7, as from 9 July 2009 (for the purpose of enabling the exercise of powers to make regulations or orders by statutory instrument), and as from 1 October 2009 (otherwise) (for savings see the note to s 2 at **[9.431]**).

Supplementary

[9.445]
18 Interpretation
In this Act—

. . .

"business" includes every trade, profession and occupation,

"designated member" shall be construed in accordance with section 8,

"enactment" includes subordinate legislation (within the meaning of the Interpretation Act 1978),

"incorporation document" shall be construed in accordance with section 2,

"limited liability partnership" has the meaning given by section 1(2),

"member" shall be construed in accordance with section 4,

"modifications" includes additions and omissions,

"name", in relation to a member of a limited liability partnership, means—

    (a)   if an individual, his forename and surname (or, in the case of a peer or other person usually known by a title, his title instead of or in addition to either or both his forename and surname), and

    (b)   if a corporation or Scottish firm, its corporate or firm name,

"oversea limited liability partnership" has the meaning given by section 14(3),

["the registrar" means—

    (a)   if the registered office of the limited liability partnership is, or is to be, in England and Wales (or Wales), the registrar of companies for England and Wales,

    (b)   if the registered office of the limited liability partnership is, or is to be, in Scotland, the registrar of companies for Scotland, and

    (c)   if the registered office of the limited liability partnership is, or is to be, in Northern Ireland, the registrar of companies for Northern Ireland;]

"regulations" has the meaning given by section 17(1).

NOTES

Definition "address" (omitted) repealed, and definition "the registrar" substituted by the Limited Liability Partnerships (Application of Companies Act 2006) Regulations 2009, SI 2009/1804, reg 85, Sch 3, Pt 1, para 8, as from 1 October 2009 (for savings see the note to s 2 at **[9.431]**).

As to the meaning of "the registrar" and "the register", and as to the construction of references to registration in a particular part of the United Kingdom, see also the Limited Liability Partnerships (Application of Companies Act 2006) Regulations 2009, SI 2009/1804, reg 85, Sch 3, Pt 2, para 12 at **[10.1191]**.

[9.446]
19 Commencement, extent and short title
(1)   The preceding provisions of this Act shall come into force on such day as the Secretary of State may by order made by statutory instrument appoint; and different days may be appointed for different purposes.

(2)   The Secretary of State may by order made by statutory instrument make any transitional provisions and savings which appear appropriate in connection with the coming into force of any provision of this Act.

(3)   For the purposes of the Scotland Act 1998 this Act shall be taken to be a pre-commencement enactment within the meaning of that Act.

[(4)   This Act extends to the whole of the United Kingdom.]

(5)   This Act may be cited as the Limited Liability Partnerships Act 2000.

NOTES

Sub-s (4): substituted by the Limited Liability Partnerships (Application of Companies Act 2006) Regulations 2009, SI 2009/1804, reg 85, Sch 3, Pt 1, para 9, as from 1 October 2009 (for savings see the note to s 2 at **[9.431]**).

Orders: the Limited Liability Partnerships Act 2000 (Commencement) Order 2000, SI 2000/3316 (bringing this Act (with the exception of this section which came into force on Royal assent) into force on 6 April 2001).

SCHEDULE
NAMES AND REGISTERED OFFICES
Section 1

PART I
NAMES

[9.447]
1. . . .

Name to indicate status

2. (1)   The name of a limited liability partnership must end with—

(a)   the expression "limited liability partnership", or

(b)   the abbreviation "llp" or "LLP".

(2)   But if the incorporation document for a limited liability partnership states that the registered office is to be situated in Wales, its name must end with—

(a)   one of the expressions "limited liability partnership" and "partneriaeth atebolrwydd cyfyngedig", or

(b)   one of the abbreviations "llp", "LLP", "pac" and "PAC".

3.   . . .

Change of name

4. (1)   A limited liability partnership may change its name at any time.

[(2)   The name of a limited liability partnership may also be changed—

(a)   on the determination of a new name by a company names adjudicator under section 73 of the Companies Act 2006 (C 46) as applied to limited liability partnerships (powers of adjudicator on upholding objection to name);

(b)   on the determination of a new name by the court under section 74 of the Companies Act 2006 as so applied (appeal against decision of company names adjudicator);

(c)   under section 1033 as so applied (name on restoration to the register).]

Notification of change of name

5. (1)   Where a limited liability partnership changes its name it shall deliver notice of the change to the registrar.

(2)   . . .

(3)   Where the registrar receives [notice of a change of name] he shall (unless the new name is one by which a limited liability partnership may not be registered)—

[(a)   enter the new name on the register in place of the former name, and]

(b)   issue a certificate of the change of name.

(4)   The change of name has effect from the date on which the certificate is issued.

Effect of change of name

6. A change of name by a limited liability partnership does not—

(a)   affect any of its rights or duties,

(b)   render defective any legal proceedings by or against it,

and any legal proceedings that might have been commenced or continued against it by its former name may be commenced or continued against it by its new name.

Improper use of "limited liability partnership" etc

7. (1)   If any person carries on a business under a name or title which includes as the last words—

(a)   the expression "limited liability partnership" or "partneriaeth atebolrwydd cyfyngedig", or

(b)   any contraction or imitation of either of those expressions,

that person, unless a limited liability partnership or oversea limited liability partnership, commits an offence.

(2)   A person guilty of an offence under sub-paragraph (1) is liable on summary conviction to a fine not exceeding level 3 on the standard scale.

8.   . . .

NOTES

Para 1: repealed by the Companies Act 2006, s 1295, Sch 16, as from 1 October 2009.

Para 3: repealed by the Limited Liability Partnerships (Application of Companies Act 2006) Regulations 2009, SI 2009/1804, reg 85, Sch 3, Pt 1, para 10(1), (2), as from 1 October 2009 (for savings see the note to s 2 at [**9.431**]).

Para 4: sub-para (2) substituted (for the original sub-paras (2)–(9)) by SI 2009/1804, reg 85, Sch 3, Pt 1, para 10(1), (3), as from 1 October 2009 (for savings see the note to s 2 at [**9.431**]).

Para 5: sub-para (2) repealed, and words in square brackets substituted, by SI 2009/1804, reg 85, Sch 3, Pt 1, para 10(1), (4), as from 1 October 2009 (for savings see the note to s 2 at [**9.431**]).

Para 8: repealed by SI 2009/1804, reg 85, Sch 3, Pt 1, para 10(1), (5), as from 1 October 2009 (for savings see the note to s 2 at [**9.431**]).

---

*(Schedule, Pt II repealed by the Limited Liability Partnerships (Application of Companies Act 2006) Regulations 2009, SI 2009/1804, reg 85, Sch 3, Pt 1, para 10(1), (6), as from 1 October 2009 (for savings see the note to s 2 at [**9.431**].)*

FRAUD ACT 2006

(2006 c 35)

NOTES
This Act is reproduced as amended by: the Companies Act 2006 (Commencement No 3, Consequential Amendments, Transitional Provisions and Savings) Order 2007, SI 2007/2194; the Companies Act 2006 (Consequential Amendments, Transitional Provisions and Savings) Order 2009, SI 2009/1941.

ARRANGEMENT OF SECTIONS

Fraud

SCHEDULES

An Act to make provision for, and in connection with, criminal liability for fraud and obtaining services dishonestly

[8 November 2006]

Fraud

[9.448]
1   Fraud
(1)   A person is guilty of fraud if he is in breach of any of the sections listed in subsection (2) (which provide for different ways of committing the offence).
(2)   The sections are—
  (a)   section 2 (fraud by false representation),
  (b)   section 3 (fraud by failing to disclose information), and
  (c)   section 4 (fraud by abuse of position).
(3)   A person who is guilty of fraud is liable—
  (a)   on summary conviction, to imprisonment for a term not exceeding 12 months or to a fine not exceeding the statutory maximum (or to both);
  (b)   on conviction on indictment, to imprisonment for a term not exceeding 10 years or to a fine (or to both).
(4)   Subsection (3)(a) applies in relation to Northern Ireland as if the reference to 12 months were a reference to 6 months.

NOTES
Commencement: 15 January 2007.
Serious crime prevention orders: a court may make a serious crime prevention order under the Serious Crime Act 2007, ss 1, 19 if it is satisfied that a person has been involved in serious crime, and it has reasonable grounds to believe that the order would protect the public by preventing, restricting or disrupting involvement by the person in serious crime. By virtue of s 2 of, and Sch 1 to, the 2007 Act, the offence under this section (and ss 6, 7, 9, 11) is a serious crime.

[9.449]
2   Fraud by false representation
(1)   A person is in breach of this section if he—
  (a)   dishonestly makes a false representation, and
  (b)   intends, by making the representation—
    (i)   to make a gain for himself or another, or

(ii)   to cause loss to another or to expose another to a risk of loss.

(2)   A representation is false if—

(a)   it is untrue or misleading, and

(b)   the person making it knows that it is, or might be, untrue or misleading.

(3)   "Representation" means any representation as to fact or law, including a representation as to the state of mind of—

(a)   the person making the representation, or

(b)   any other person.

(4)   A representation may be express or implied.

(5)   For the purposes of this section a representation may be regarded as made if it (or anything implying it) is submitted in any form to any system or device designed to receive, convey or respond to communications (with or without human intervention).

NOTES

Commencement: 15 January 2007.

[9.450]
3   Fraud by failing to disclose information
A person is in breach of this section if he—

(a)   dishonestly fails to disclose to another person information which he is under a legal duty to disclose, and

(b)   intends, by failing to disclose the information—

(i)   to make a gain for himself or another, or

(ii)   to cause loss to another or to expose another to a risk of loss.

NOTES

Commencement: 15 January 2007.

[9.451]
4   Fraud by abuse of position
(1)   A person is in breach of this section if he—

(a)   occupies a position in which he is expected to safeguard, or not to act against, the financial interests of another person,

(b)   dishonestly abuses that position, and

(c)   intends, by means of the abuse of that position—

(i)   to make a gain for himself or another, or

(ii)   to cause loss to another or to expose another to a risk of loss.

(2)   A person may be regarded as having abused his position even though his conduct consisted of an omission rather than an act.

NOTES

Commencement: 15 January 2007.

[9.452]
5   "Gain" and "loss"
(1)   The references to gain and loss in sections 2 to 4 are to be read in accordance with this section.

(2)   "Gain" and "loss"—

(a)   extend only to gain or loss in money or other property;

(b)   include any such gain or loss whether temporary or permanent;

and "property" means any property whether real or personal (including things in action and other intangible property).

(3)   "Gain" includes a gain by keeping what one has, as well as a gain by getting what one does not have.

(4)   "Loss" includes a loss by not getting what one might get, as well as a loss by parting with what one has.

NOTES

Commencement: 15 January 2007.

[9.453]
6   Possession etc of articles for use in frauds
(1)   A person is guilty of an offence if he has in his possession or under his control any article for use in the course of or in connection with any fraud.

(2)   A person guilty of an offence under this section is liable—

(a)   on summary conviction, to imprisonment for a term not exceeding 12 months or to a fine not exceeding the statutory maximum (or to both);

(b)   on conviction on indictment, to imprisonment for a term not exceeding 5 years or to a fine (or to both).

(3)   Subsection (2)(a) applies in relation to Northern Ireland as if the reference to 12 months were a reference to 6 months.

Part 9 Misc primary legislation

NOTES
Commencement: 15 January 2007.
Serious crime prevention orders: see the note to s 1 at **[9.448]**.

[9.454]
7 Making or supplying articles for use in frauds
(1) A person is guilty of an offence if he makes, adapts, supplies or offers to supply any article—
  (a) knowing that it is designed or adapted for use in the course of or in connection with fraud, or
  (b) intending it to be used to commit, or assist in the commission of, fraud.
(2) A person guilty of an offence under this section is liable—
  (a) on summary conviction, to imprisonment for a term not exceeding 12 months or to a fine not exceeding the statutory maximum (or to both);
  (b) on conviction on indictment, to imprisonment for a term not exceeding 10 years or to a fine (or to both).
(3) Subsection (2)(a) applies in relation to Northern Ireland as if the reference to 12 months were a reference to 6 months.

NOTES
Commencement: 15 January 2007.
Serious crime prevention orders: see the note to s 1 at **[9.448]**.

[9.455]
8 "Article"
(1) For the purposes of—
  (a) sections 6 and 7, and
  (b) the provisions listed in subsection (2), so far as they relate to articles for use in the course of or in connection with fraud,
"article" includes any program or data held in electronic form.
(2) The provisions are—
  (a) section 1(7)(b) of the Police and Criminal Evidence Act 1984 (c 60),
  (b) section 2(8)(b) of the Armed Forces Act 2001 (c 19), and
  (c) Article 3(7)(b) of the Police and Criminal Evidence (Northern Ireland) Order 1989 (SI 1989/1341 (NI 12));
(meaning of "prohibited articles" for the purposes of stop and search powers).

NOTES
Commencement: 15 January 2007.

[9.456]
9 Participating in fraudulent business carried on by sole trader etc
(1) A person is guilty of an offence if he is knowingly a party to the carrying on of a business to which this section applies.
(2) This section applies to a business which is carried on—
  (a) by a person who is outside the reach of [section 993 of the Companies Act 2006] (offence of fraudulent trading), and
  (b) with intent to defraud creditors of any person or for any other fraudulent purpose.
(3) The following are within the reach of [that section]—
  (a) a company [(as defined in section 1(1) of the Companies Act 2006)];
  (b) a person to whom that section applies (with or without adaptations or modifications) as if the person were a company;
  (c) a person exempted from the application of that section.
(4) . . .
(5) "Fraudulent purpose" has the same meaning as in [that section].
(6) A person guilty of an offence under this section is liable—
  (a) on summary conviction, to imprisonment for a term not exceeding 12 months or to a fine not exceeding the statutory maximum (or to both);
  (b) on conviction on indictment, to imprisonment for a term not exceeding 10 years or to a fine (or to both).
(7) Subsection (6)(a) applies in relation to Northern Ireland as if the reference to 12 months were a reference to 6 months.

NOTES
Commencement: 15 January 2007.
Sub-ss (2), (5): words in square brackets substituted by the Companies Act 2006 (Commencement No 3, Consequential Amendments, Transitional Provisions and Savings) Order 2007, SI 2007/2194, art 10(1), Sch 4, Pt 3, para 111(1), (2), (5), (6), as from 1 October 2007 (for transitional provisions see the note below).

Sub-s (3): words in first pair of square brackets substituted by SI 2007/2194, art 10(1), Sch 4, Pt 3, para 111(1), (3)(a), (6), as from 1 October 2007 (for transitional provisions see the note below); words in square brackets in para (a) substituted by the Companies Act 2006 (Consequential Amendments, Transitional Provisions and Savings) Order 2009, SI 2009/1941, art 2(1), Sch 1, para 257, as from 1 October 2009.

Sub-s (4): repealed by SI 2007/2194, art 10(1), (3), Sch 4, Pt 3, para 111(1), (4), (6), Sch 5, as from 1 October 2007 (for transitional provisions see the note below).

Transitional provisions: with regard to the amendments made by SI 2007/2194, Sch 4, Pt 3, para 111(1)–(5) above, note that Sch 4, Pt 3, para 111(6) provides as follows—

"(6)   These amendments apply to an offence if any act, omission or other event (including any result of one or more acts or omissions) proof of which is required for conviction of the offence occurs on or after 1st October 2007.".

Serious crime prevention orders: see the note to s 1 at **[9.448]**.

10   *(Repealed by the Companies Act 2006 (Consequential Amendments, Transitional Provisions and Savings) Order 2009, SI 2009/1941, art 2(2), Sch 2, as from 1 October 2009.)*

Obtaining services dishonestly

[9.457]
11   Obtaining services dishonestly
(1)   A person is guilty of an offence under this section if he obtains services for himself or another—
    (a)   by a dishonest act, and
    (b)   in breach of subsection (2).
(2)   A person obtains services in breach of this subsection if—
    (a)   they are made available on the basis that payment has been, is being or will be made for or in respect of them,
    (b)   he obtains them without any payment having been made for or in respect of them or without payment having been made in full, and
    (c)   when he obtains them, he knows—
        (i)   that they are being made available on the basis described in paragraph (a), or
        (ii)   that they might be,
    but intends that payment will not be made, or will not be made in full.
(3)   A person guilty of an offence under this section is liable—
    (a)   on summary conviction, to imprisonment for a term not exceeding 12 months or to a fine not exceeding the statutory maximum (or to both);
    (b)   on conviction on indictment, to imprisonment for a term not exceeding 5 years or to a fine (or to both).
(4)   Subsection (3)(a) applies in relation to Northern Ireland as if the reference to 12 months were a reference to 6 months.

NOTES
Commencement: 15 January 2007.
Serious crime prevention orders: see the note to s 1 at **[9.448]**.

Supplementary

[9.458]
12   Liability of company officers for offences by company
(1)   Subsection (2) applies if an offence under this Act is committed by a body corporate.
(2)   If the offence is proved to have been committed with the consent or connivance of—
    (a)   a director, manager, secretary or other similar officer of the body corporate, or
    (b)   a person who was purporting to act in any such capacity,
he (as well as the body corporate) is guilty of the offence and liable to be proceeded against and punished accordingly.
(3)   If the affairs of a body corporate are managed by its members, subsection (2) applies in relation to the acts and defaults of a member in connection with his functions of management as if he were a director of the body corporate.

NOTES
Commencement: 15 January 2007.

[9.459]
13   Evidence
(1)   A person is not to be excused from—
    (a)   answering any question put to him in proceedings relating to property, or
    (b)   complying with any order made in proceedings relating to property,
on the ground that doing so may incriminate him or his spouse or civil partner of an offence under this Act or a related offence.
(2)   But, in proceedings for an offence under this Act or a related offence, a statement or admission made by the person in—
    (a)   answering such a question, or

Part 9 Misc primary legislation

(b)   complying with such an order,
is not admissible in evidence against him or (unless they married or became civil partners after the making of the statement or admission) his spouse or civil partner.
(3)   "Proceedings relating to property" means any proceedings for—
   (a)   the recovery or administration of any property,
   (b)   the execution of a trust, or
   (c)   an account of any property or dealings with property,
and "property" means money or other property whether real or personal (including things in action and other intangible property).
(4)   "Related offence" means—
   (a)   conspiracy to defraud;
   (b)   any other offence involving any form of fraudulent conduct or purpose.

NOTES
Commencement: 15 January 2007.

14 (*Introduces Sch 1 (minor and consequential amendments), Sch 2 (transitional provisions and savings), and Sch 3 (repeals and revocations).*)

[9.460]
15   Commencement and extent
(1)   This Act (except this section and section 16) comes into force on such day as the Secretary of State may appoint by an order made by statutory instrument; and different days may be appointed for different purposes.
(2)   Subject to subsection (3), sections 1 to 9 and 11 to 13 extend to England and Wales and Northern Ireland only.
(3)   Section 8, so far as it relates to the Armed Forces Act 2001 (c 19), extends to any place to which that Act extends.
(4)   Any amendment in section 10 or Schedule 1, and any related provision in section 14 or Schedule 2 or 3, extends to any place to which the provision which is the subject of the amendment extends.

NOTES
Commencement: 8 November 2006.
Orders: the Fraud Act 2006 (Commencement) Order 2006, SI 2006/3200.

[9.461]
16   Short title
This Act may be cited as the Fraud Act 2006.

NOTES
Commencement: 8 November 2006.

SCHEDULES

SCHEDULE 1

(*Sch 1: para 1 repeals the Theft Act 1968, s 15, 15A, 16, 20(2) (the deception offences); paras 2–38 contain minor and consequential amendments which, in so far as relevant to this work, are incorporated at the appropriate place.*)

SCHEDULE 2
TRANSITIONAL PROVISIONS AND SAVINGS
Section 14(2)

Maximum term of imprisonment for offences under this Act
[9.462]
1. In relation to an offence committed before the commencement of section 154(1) of the Criminal Justice Act 2003 (c 44), the references to 12 months in sections 1(3)(a), 6(2)(a), 7(2)(a), 9(6)(a) and 11(3)(a) are to be read as references to 6 months.

Increase in penalty for fraudulent trading
2. Section 10 does not affect the penalty for any offence committed before that section comes into force.

Abolition of deception offences
3. (1)   Paragraph 1 of Schedule 1 does not affect any liability, investigation, legal proceeding or penalty for or in respect of any offence partly committed before the commencement of that paragraph.

(2)   An offence is partly committed before the commencement of paragraph 1 of Schedule 1 if—
(a)   a relevant event occurs before its commencement, and
(b)   another relevant event occurs on or after its commencement.

(3)   "Relevant event", in relation to an offence, means any act, omission or other event (including any result of one or more acts or omissions) proof of which is required for conviction of the offence.

Scope of offences relating to stolen goods under the Theft Act 1968 (c 60)

4. Nothing in paragraph 6 of Schedule 1 affects the operation of section 24 of the Theft Act 1968 in relation to goods obtained in the circumstances described in section 15(1) of that Act where the obtaining is the result of a deception made before the commencement of that paragraph.

Dishonestly retaining a wrongful credit under the Theft Act 1968

5. Nothing in paragraph 7 of Schedule 1 affects the operation of section 24A(7) and (8) of the Theft Act 1968 in relation to credits falling within section 24A(3) or (4) of that Act and made before the commencement of that paragraph.

6–11.   (*Outside the scope of this work.*)

NOTES
Commencement: 15 January 2007.

SCHEDULE 3

(*Sch 3 (repeals and revocations) omitted.*)

BANKRUPTCY AND DILIGENCE ETC (SCOTLAND) ACT 2007

(2007 asp 3)

NOTES
Only provisions of this Act relevant to company law are reproduced (ie, Part 2 – floating charges). Provisions not reproduced are not annotated.
Commencement: by virtue of s 227 (Short title and commencement) the provisions of Part 2 come into force on such day as the Scottish Ministers may, by order, appoint. As of 1 July 2011, only s 37(7), (8) had been brought into force and only for the purpose of making Regulations (see SSI 2008/115). Section 221 in Part 17 (interpretation) was brought into force on 8 March 2007 by SSI 2007/82.
This Act is reproduced as amended by: the Child Maintenance and Other Payments Act 2008; the Banking Act 2009; the Public Services Reform (Scotland) Act 2010; the Companies Act 2006 (Consequential Amendments, Transitional Provisions and Savings) Order 2009, SI 2009/1941.
Application to bank insolvency and administration: as to the application of this Act to bank insolvency and administration, see the Banking Act 2009 (Parts 2 and 3 Consequential Amendments) Order 2009, SI 2009/317.

ARRANGEMENT OF SECTIONS

PART 2
FLOATING CHARGES

An Act of the Scottish Parliament to amend the law of sequestration and personal insolvency; to amend the law about floating charges; to establish a Scottish Civil Enforcement Commission and replace officers of court with judicial officers; to amend the law of diligence; and for connected purposes

[15 January 2007]

PART 2
FLOATING CHARGES

Registration and creation etc

[9.463]
37   Register of Floating Charges

(1)   The Keeper of the Registers of Scotland (in this Part, the "Keeper") must establish and maintain a register to be known as the Register of Floating Charges.

(2)   The Keeper must accept an application for registration of—

    (a)   any document delivered to the Keeper in pursuance of section 38, 41, 42, 43 or 44 of this Act; and

    (b)   any notice delivered to the Keeper in pursuance of section 39 or 45(2) of this Act,

provided that the application is accompanied by such information as the Keeper may require for the purposes of the registration.

(3)   On receipt of such an application, the Keeper must note the date of receipt of the application; and, where the application is accepted by the Keeper, that date is to be treated for the purposes of this Part as the date of registration of the document or notice to which the application relates.

(4)   The Keeper must, after accepting such an application, complete registration by registering in the Register of Floating Charges the document or notice to which the application relates.

(5)   The Keeper must—

    (a)   make the Register of Floating Charges available for public inspection at all reasonable times;

    (b)   provide facilities for members of the public to obtain copies of the documents in the Register; and

    (c)   supply an extract of a document in the Register, certified as a true copy of the original, to any person requesting it.

(6)   An extract certified as mentioned in subsection (5)(c) above is sufficient evidence of the original.

(7)   The Keeper may charge such fees—

    (a)   for registering a document or notice in the Register of Floating Charges; or

    (b)   in relation to anything done under subsection (5) above,

as the Scottish Ministers may by regulations prescribe.

(8)   The Scottish Ministers may by regulations make provision as to—

    (a)   the form and manner in which the Register of Floating Charges is to be maintained;

    (b)   the form of documents (including notices as mentioned in sections 39(1) and 45(2) of this Act) for registration in that Register, the particulars they are to contain and the manner in which they are to be delivered to the Keeper.

(9)   Provision under subsection (8) above may, in particular, facilitate the use—

    (a)   of electronic communication;

    (b)   of documents in electronic form (and of certified electronic signatures in documents).

NOTES

Commencement: 1 April 2008 (sub-ss (7), (8) for the purpose of making Regulations); to be appointed (otherwise).

[9.464]
38   Creation of floating charges

(1)   It continues to be competent, for the purpose of securing any obligation to which this subsection applies, for a company to grant in favour of the creditor in the obligation a charge (known as a "floating charge") over all or any part of the property which may from time to time be comprised in the company's property and undertaking.

(2)   Subsection (1) above applies to any debt or other obligation incurred or to be incurred by, or binding upon, the company or any other person.

(3)   From the coming into force of this section, a floating charge is (subject to [subsection (3A) and] section 39 of this Act) created only when a document—

    (a)   granting a floating charge; and

    (b)   subscribed by the company granting the charge,

is registered in the Register of Floating Charges.

[(3A)   If a floating charge is granted in favour of a central institution, it is created only when the document granting the floating charge is executed by the company granting the charge.]

(4)   References in this Part to a document which grants a floating charge are to a document by means of which a floating charge is granted.

NOTES

Commencement: to be appointed.

Sub-s (3): words in square brackets inserted by the Banking Act 2009, s 253(1), (2)(a), as from 21 February 2009.

Sub-s (3A): inserted by the Banking Act 2009, s 253(1), (2)(b), as from 21 February 2009.

Application in relation to floating charges which are created by, or otherwise arise under, a financial collateral arrangement: by virtue of the Financial Markets and Insolvency (Settlement Finality and Financial Collateral Arrangements) (Amendment) Regulations 2010, SI 2010/2993, reg 5(1), (2) this section applies in such circumstances with the following modification:

"(2)   In section 38 (creation of floating charges)—
   (a)   in subsection (3), after "subsection (3A)" insert ", subsection (3B)";
   (b)   after subsection (3A), insert—

"(3B)   If a floating charge is created or otherwise arises under a security financial collateral arrangement, it is created when the document granting the floating charge is executed by the company granting the charge and without registration in the Register of Floating Charges.".".

[9.465]
39   Advance notice of floating charges
(1)   Where a company proposes to grant a floating charge, the company and the person in whose favour the charge is to be granted may apply to have joint notice of the proposed charge registered in the Register of Floating Charges.
(2)   Subsection (3) below applies where—
   (a)   a notice under subsection (1) above is registered in the Register of Floating Charges; and
   (b)   within 21 days of the notice being so registered, a document—
      (i)   granting a floating charge conforming with the particulars contained in the notice; and
      (ii)   subscribed by the company granting the charge,
is registered in the Register of Floating Charges.
(3)   Where this subsection applies, the floating charge so created is to be treated as having been created when the notice under subsection (1) above was so registered.
[(4)   This section does not apply where a company proposes to grant a floating charge in favour of a central institution.]

NOTES
Commencement: to be appointed.
Sub-s (4): added by the Banking Act 2009, s 253(1), (3), as from 21 February 2009.
Application in relation to floating charges which are created by, or otherwise arise under, a financial collateral arrangement: by virtue of the Financial Markets and Insolvency (Settlement Finality and Financial Collateral Arrangements) (Amendment) Regulations 2010, SI 2010/2993, reg 5(1), (3) this section applies in such circumstances with the following modification:

"(3)   In section 39 (advance notice of floating charges), for subsection (4), substitute—

"(4)   This section does not apply—
   (a)   where a company proposes to grant a floating charge in favour of a central institution;
   (b)   where a floating charge is created or otherwise arises under a security financial collateral arrangement.".".

[9.466]
40   Ranking of floating charges
(1)   Subject to subsections (4) and (5) below, a floating charge—
   (a)   created on or after the coming into force of this section; and
   (b)   which has attached to all or any part of the property of a company,
ranks as described in subsection (2) below.
(2)   The floating charge referred to in subsection (1) above—
   (a)   ranks with—
      (i)   any other floating charge which has attached to that property or any part of it; or
      (ii)   any fixed security over that property or any part of it,
according to date of creation; and
   (b)   ranks equally with any floating charge or fixed security referred to in paragraph (a) above which was created on the same date as the floating charge referred to in subsection (1) above.
(3)   For the purposes of subsection (2) above—
   (a)   the date of creation of a fixed security is the date on which the right to the security was constituted as a real right; and
   (b)   the date of creation of a floating charge subsisting before the coming into force of this section is the date on which the instrument creating the charge was executed by the company granting the charge.
(4)   Where all or any part of the property of a company is subject to both—
   (a)   a floating charge; and
   (b)   a fixed security arising by operation of law,
the fixed security has priority over the floating charge.
(5)   Where the holder of a floating charge over all or any part of the property of a company has received intimation in writing of the subsequent creation of—
   (a)   another floating charge over the same property or any part of it; or
   (b)   a fixed security over the same property or any part of it,
the priority of ranking of the first-mentioned charge is restricted to security for the matters referred to in subsection (6) below.
(6)   Those matters are—

- (a)   the present debt incurred (whenever payable);
- (b)   any future debt which, under the contract to which the charge relates, the holder is required to allow the debtor to incur;
- (c)   any interest due or to become due on the debts referred to in paragraphs (a) and (b) above;
- (d)   any expenses or outlays which may be reasonably incurred by the holder; and
- (e)   in the case of a floating charge to secure a contingent liability (other than a liability arising under any further debts incurred from time to time), the maximum sum to which the contingent liability is capable of amounting, whether or not it is contractually limited.

(7)   Subsections (1) to (6) above, and any provision made under section 41(1) of this Act, are subject to sections 175 and 176A (provision for preferential debts and share of assets) of the Insolvency Act 1986 (c 45).

NOTES

Commencement: to be appointed.

[9.467]
41   Ranking clauses

(1)   The document granting a floating charge over all or any part of the property of a company may make provision regulating the order in which the charge ranks with any other floating charge or any fixed security (including a future floating charge or fixed security) over that property or any part of it.
(2)   Provision under subsection (1) above—
- (a)   may displace in whole or part—
  - (i)   subsections (1) and (2) of section 40 of this Act;
  - (ii)   subsections (5) and (6) of that section;
- (b)   may not affect the operation of subsection (4) of that section (whether as against subsections (1) and (2) of that section or other provision under subsection (1) above).

(3)   Accordingly, subsections (1), (2), (5) and (6) of that section have effect subject to any provision made under subsection (1) above.
(4)   Provision under subsection (1) above is not valid unless it is made with the consent of the holder of any subsisting floating charge, or any subsisting fixed security, which would be adversely affected by the provision.
(5)   A document of consent for the purpose of subsection (4) above may be registered in the Register of Floating Charges.

NOTES

Commencement: to be appointed.

[9.468]
42   Assignation of floating charges

(1)   A floating charge may be assigned (and the rights under it vested in the assignee) by the registration in the Register of Floating Charges of a document of assignation subscribed by the holder of the charge.
(2)   An assignation under subsection (1) above may be in whole or to such extent as may be specified in the document of assignation.
(3)   This section is without prejudice to any other enactment, or any rule of law, by virtue of which a floating charge may be assigned.
[(4)   This section does not apply where a floating charge is assigned (whether in whole or to a specified extent) to or by a central institution.]

NOTES

Commencement: to be appointed.
Sub-s (4): added by the Banking Act 2009, s 253(1), (4), as from 21 February 2009.
Application in relation to floating charges which are created by, or otherwise arise under, a financial collateral arrangement: by virtue of the Financial Markets and Insolvency (Settlement Finality and Financial Collateral Arrangements) (Amendment) Regulations 2010, SI 2010/2993, reg 5(1), (4) this section applies in such circumstances with the following modification:

"(4)   In section 42 (assignation of floating charges), after subsection (4), insert—

"(5)   This section does not apply to the assignation (whether in whole or to a specified extent) of a floating charge which was created or otherwise arises under a security financial collateral arrangement.".".

[9.469]
43   Alteration of floating charges

(1)   A document of alteration may alter (whether by addition, deletion or substitution of text or otherwise) the terms of a document granting a floating charge.
(2)   If (and in so far as) an alteration to the terms of a document granting a floating charge concerns—
- (a)   the ranking of the charge with any other floating charge or any fixed security; or
- (b)   the specification of—
  - (i)   the property that is subject to the charge; or

(ii)   the obligations that are secured by the charge,

the alteration is not valid unless subsection (3) below is satisfied.

(3)   This subsection is satisfied if the alteration is made by a document of alteration which is—

  (a)   subscribed by—

    (i)   the company which granted the charge;

    (ii)   the holder of the charge; and

    (iii)   the holder of any other subsisting floating charge, or any subsisting fixed security, which would be adversely affected by the alteration; and

  (b)   registered in the Register of Floating Charges.

(4)   [Paragraph] (a)(i) of subsection (3) above does not apply in respect of an alteration which—

  (a)   relates only to the ranking of the floating charge first-mentioned in that subsection with any other floating charge or any fixed security; and

  (b)   does not adversely affect the interests of the company which granted the charge.

[(4A)   Paragraph (b) of subsection (3) above does not apply in respect of an alteration if—

  (a)   the holder of the floating charge is a central institution, or

  (b)   the holder of the floating charge is not a central institution but the alteration is to be made in connection with a floating charge which is held (or which has been or is to be held) by a central institution.]

(5)   The granting, by the holder of a floating charge, of consent to the release from the scope of the charge of any particular property, or class of property, which is subject to the charge is to be treated as constituting an alteration—

  (a)   to the terms of the document granting the charge; and

  (b)   as to the specification of the property that is subject to the charge.

(6)   For the purpose of subsection (5) above, property is not to be regarded as released from the scope of a floating charge by reason only of its ceasing to be the property of the company which granted the charge.

NOTES

Commencement: to be appointed.

Sub-s (4): word in square brackets substituted by the Banking Act 2009, s 253(1), (5)(a), as from 21 February 2009.

Sub-s (4A): inserted by the Banking Act 2009, s 253(1), (5)(b), as from 21 February 2009.

Application in relation to floating charges which are created by, or otherwise arise under, a financial collateral arrangement: by virtue of the Financial Markets and Insolvency (Settlement Finality and Financial Collateral Arrangements) (Amendment) Regulations 2010, SI 2010/2993, reg 5(1), (5) this section applies in such circumstances with the following modification:

  "(5)   In section 43 (alteration of floating charges), in subsection (4A)—

    (a)   at the end of paragraph (b), insert ", or";

    (b)   after paragraph (b), insert—

      "(c)   the floating charge was created or otherwise arises under a security financial collateral arrangement.".".

[9.470]

44   Discharge of floating charges

(1)   A floating charge may be discharged by the registration in the Register of Floating Charges of a document of discharge subscribed by the holder of the charge.

(2)   A discharge under subsection (1) above may be in whole or to such extent as may be specified in the document of discharge.

(3)   This section is without prejudice to any other means by which a floating charge may be discharged or extinguished.

[(4)   This section does not apply where the floating charge to be discharged (whether in whole or to a specified extent) is or has been held by a central institution.]

NOTES

Commencement: to be appointed.

Sub-s (4): added by the Banking Act 2009, s 253(1), (6), as from 21 February 2009.

Application in relation to floating charges which are created by, or otherwise arise under, a financial collateral arrangement: by virtue of the Financial Markets and Insolvency (Settlement Finality and Financial Collateral Arrangements) (Amendment) Regulations 2010, SI 2010/2993, reg 5(1), (6) this section applies in such circumstances with the following modification:

  "(6)   In section 44 (discharge of floating charges), for subsection (4), substitute—

    "(4)   This section does not apply where the floating charge to be discharged (whether in whole or to a specified extent)—

      (a)   is or has been held by a central institution, or

      (b)   was created or otherwise arises under a security financial collateral arrangement.".".

[9.471]

45   Effect of floating charges on winding up

(1)   Where a company goes into liquidation, a floating charge created over property of the company attaches to the property to which it relates.

(2)   But, in a case mentioned in subsection (7)(a) below, there is no attachment under subsection (1) above until such time as a notice of attachment is registered in the Register of Floating Charges on the application of the holder of the charge.

(3)   The attachment of a floating charge to property under subsection (1) above is subject to the rights of any person who—

(a)   has effectually executed diligence on the property to which the charge relates or any part of it;

(b)   holds over that property or any part of it a fixed security ranking in priority to the floating charge; or

(c)   holds over that property or any part of it another floating charge so ranking.

(4)   Interest accrues in respect of a floating charge which has attached to property until payment is made of any sum due under the charge.

(5)   Part IV, except section 185, of the Insolvency Act 1986 has (subject to subsection (1) above) effect in relation to a floating charge as if the charge were a fixed security over the property to which it has attached in respect of the principal of the debt or obligation to which it relates and any interest due or to become due on it.

(6)   Subsections (1) to (5) above do not affect the operation of—

(a)   sections 53(7) and 54(6) (attachment of floating charge on appointment of receiver) of the Insolvency Act 1986;

(b)   sections 175 and 176A of that Act; or

(c)   paragraph 115(3) of Schedule B1 (attachment of floating charge on delivery of a notice by an administrator) to that Act.

(7)   For the purposes of this section, reference to a company going into liquidation—

(a)   in a case where a court of a member State has under the EC Regulation jurisdiction as respects the company which granted the relevant floating charge, means the opening of insolvency proceedings in that State;

(b)   in any other case, is to be construed in accordance with section 247(2) and (3) of the Insolvency Act 1986 (c 45).

(8)   In subsection (7)(a) above—

"the EC Regulation" is the Regulation of the Council of the European Union published as Council Regulation (EC) No 1346/2000 on insolvency proceedings;

"court" is to be construed in accordance with Article 2(d) of that Regulation;

"insolvency proceedings" is to be construed in accordance with Article 2(a) of that Regulation;

"member State" means a member State of the European Union apart from the United Kingdom.

NOTES

Commencement: to be appointed.

[9.472]
46   Repeals, savings and transitional arrangements

(1)   Part XVIII (floating charges: Scotland) of the Companies Act 1985 (c 6) is repealed.

(2)   Nothing in this Part (except sections 40 and 41 so far as they concern the ranking of floating charges subsisting immediately before the coming into force of this section) affects the validity or operation of floating charges subsisting before the coming into force of this section.

(3)   So, despite the repeal of Chapters I and III of Part XVIII of that Act by subsection (1) above, the provisions of those Chapters are to be treated as having effect for the purposes of floating charges subsisting immediately before the coming into force of this section.

(4)   In particular—

(a)   floating charges subsisting immediately before the coming into force of this section rank with each other as they ranked with each other in accordance with section 464 of the Companies Act 1985 immediately before that section was repealed by subsection (1) above; and

(b)   a floating charge subsisting immediately before the coming into force of this section ranks with a fixed security so subsisting as it ranked with the security in accordance with section 464 of the Companies Act 1985 immediately before that section was repealed by subsection (1) above.

(5)   Section 140 (floating charges (Scotland)) of the Companies Act 1989 (c 40) is repealed (but, despite being repealed, is to be treated as having effect for the purposes of subsections (3) and (4) above).

NOTES

Commencement: to be appointed.

[9.473]
47   Interpretation

In this Part—

["central institution" means—

(a)   the Bank of England,

(b)   the central bank of a country or territory outside the United Kingdom, or

(c)   the European Central Bank;]

"company" means an incorporated company (whether or not a company [as defined in section 1(1) of the Companies Act 2006]);

"fixed security", in relation to any property of a company, means any security (other than a floating charge or a charge having the character of a floating charge) which on the winding up of the company in Scotland would be treated as an effective security over that property including, in particular, a heritable security (within the meaning of section 9(8) of the Conveyancing and Feudal Reform (Scotland) Act 1970 (c 35)).

NOTES

Commencement: to be appointed.

Definition "central institution" inserted by the Banking Act 2009, s 253(1), (7), as from 21 February 2009.

Words in square brackets in the definition "company" substituted by the Companies Act 2006 (Consequential Amendments, Transitional Provisions and Savings) Order 2009, SI 2009/1941, art 2(1), Sch 1, para 267, as from 1 October 2009.

Application in relation to floating charges which are created by, or otherwise arise under, a financial collateral arrangement: by virtue of the Financial Markets and Insolvency (Settlement Finality and Financial Collateral Arrangements) (Amendment) Regulations 2010, SI 2010/2993, reg 5(1), (7) this section applies in such circumstances with the following modification:

"(7) In section 47 (interpretation), after the definition of "fixed security", insert—

"security financial collateral arrangement" has the same meaning as in regulation 3 of the Financial Collateral Arrangements (No 2) Regulations 2003;".".

48, 49 (*S 48 amends the Requirements of Writing (Scotland) Act 1995, the Conveyancing (Scotland) Act 1924, and the Law Reform (Miscellaneous Provisions) (Scotland) Act 1985; s 49 amends the Industrial and Provident Societies Act 1967 (see the Co-operative and Community Benefit Societies and Credit Unions Act 2010 which renames this Act as the Co-operative and Community Benefit Societies and Credit Unions Act 1967).*)

PART 17
GENERAL AND MISCELLANEOUS

[9.474]
221 Interpretation
In this Act—
the "1985 Act" means the Bankruptcy (Scotland) Act 1985 (c 66);
the "1987 Act" means the Debtors (Scotland) Act 1987 (c 18);
the "2002 Act" means the Debt Arrangement and Attachment (Scotland) Act 2002 (asp 17);
"certified electronic signature" is to be read in accordance with section 7(2) and (3) of the Electronic Communications Act 2000 (c 7);
. . .
"debt advice and information package" has the meaning given by section 81(8) of this Act;
"decree" means—
   (a)   a decree of the Court of Session, of the High Court of Justiciary or of the sheriff;
   (b)   a decree of the Court of Teinds;
   (c)   a summary warrant;
   (d)   a civil judgement granted outside Scotland by a court, tribunal or arbiter which, by virtue of any enactment or rule of law, is enforceable in Scotland;
   (e)   an order or determination which, by virtue of any enactment, is enforceable as if it were an extract registered decree arbitral bearing a warrant for execution granted by the sheriff;
   (f)   a warrant granted in criminal proceedings for enforcement by civil diligence;
   (g)   an order under section 114 of the Companies Clauses Consolidation (Scotland) Act 1845 (c 17);
   (h)   a determination under section 46 of the Harbours, Docks and Piers Clauses Act 1847 (c 27); or
   (i)   a liability order within the meaning of *section 33(2)* of the Child Support Act 1991 (c 48);
"document of debt" means—
   (a)   a document registered for execution in the Books of Council and Session or in the sheriff court books;
   (b)   a bill protested for non-payment by a notary public; or
   (c)   a document or settlement which, by virtue of an Order in Council made under section 13 of the Civil Jurisdiction and Judgments Act 1982 (c 27), is enforceable in Scotland;
"electronic communication" has the meaning given by section 15(1) of the Electronic Communications Act 2000 (c 7);
. . .
["officer of court" means a messenger-at-arms or a sheriff officer;]
"professional association" shall be construed in accordance with section 63(1)(a) of this Act.

NOTES
Commencement: 8 March 2007.

Definitions "the Commission" and "judicial officer" (omitted) repealed, and definition "officer of court" inserted, by the Public Services Reform (Scotland) Act 2010, s 13, Sch 4, Pt 1, paras 9, 30, Sch 4, Pt 2, para 33, as from 31 January 2011.

For the words in italics in the definition "decree" there are substituted the words "section 32M(2)" by the Child Maintenance and Other Payments Act 2008, s 57(1), Sch 7, para 6, as from a day to be appointed.

THIRD PARTIES (RIGHTS AGAINST INSURERS) ACT 2010
(NOTE)

(2010 c 10)

[9.475]

NOTES

This Act received royal assent on 25 March 2010.

Review of position prior to the passing of this Act

A party ("an insured party") that incurs a liability to another party (the "third party") may have an insurance policy to protect itself against the cost of that liability. If so, usually the insured party will make a claim under such a policy. However, if the insured party becomes insolvent before the third party is paid then, under general legal principles, the insurance money will become an asset in the insolvent estate of the insured party. As such, it becomes an asset available to other creditors.

The Third Parties (Rights against Insurers) Act 1930 (and the Third Parties (Rights against Insurers) Act (Northern Ireland) 1930) attempt to deal with this problem by transferring the insured party's rights against the insurer to the third party. However, due to deficiencies in the operation of the 1930 Acts (see the Law Commission and the Scottish Law Commission's 2001 joint report "Third Parties – Rights against Insurers" (Law Com No 272; Scot Law Com No 184)) those Acts are repealed and replaced by this Act.

Summary of Reforms made by this Act

Rights of Action for the Third Party

Multiple proceedings: Under the 1930 Acts, a third party cannot issue proceedings against an insurer without first establishing the existence and amount of the insured's liability. This Act removes the need for multiple sets of proceedings by allowing the third party to issue proceedings directly against the insurer and resolves all issues (including the insured's liability) within those proceedings. Under this Act the third party has the choice of using either the new method of single proceedings established by this Act, or the existing method of first establishing the liability of the insured before initiating proceedings against the insurer.

Defunct bodies: Under the 1930 Acts, if the insured is a defunct body which has been struck off the register of companies, the third party may first have to take proceedings to restore it to the register in order to be able to sue it. In removing the need for the third party to sue the insured, this Act also removes the need for such restoration.

Information rights: This Act improves the third party's rights to information about the insurance policy, allowing the third party to obtain information at an early stage about the rights transferred to him or her in order to enable an informed decision to be taken about whether or not to commence or continue litigation.

Insurer's Defences

This Act retains the general approach of the 1930 Acts that the rights transferred to the third party will be subject to the defences which the insurer could use against the insured. However, it introduces three exceptions which are designed to ensure that a third party is not prevented from enforcing his or her rights.

Scope

This Act updates the law to reflect changes in insolvency law since the 1930s. This includes providing for rights to be transferred to a third party where an insured is facing financial difficulties and enters into certain alternatives to insolvency such as voluntary procedures between the insured and the insured's creditors. This Act applies to voluntarily-incurred liabilities such as liabilities covered by legal expenses insurance, health insurance and car repair insurance. There was some doubt as to whether the 1930 Acts applied to such liabilities. This Act also addresses the issue of its application in cases with a cross-border element.

Commentary on Sections

Section 1: Rights against insurer of insolvent person etc

Section 1 sets out when a statutory transfer of rights occurs and specifies when the third party may enforce those rights.

Subsections (1) and (2) effect a transfer of rights of an insured under an insurance contract to a third party. Subsection (1)(a) effects a transfer where the insured, who is already subject to one of the procedures listed in ss 4, 6 or 7, incurs a liability towards the third party. Subsection (1)(b) effects a transfer where an insured, who is already subject to a liability to the third party, subsequently becomes subject to one of the procedures listed in ss 4–7.

Subsection (3) provides that the third party may initiate proceedings against the insurer without having first established the liability of the insured. This is a change from the 1930 Acts. However, sub-s (3) also states that before the third party can enforce rights transferred under s 1 against the insurer, he must establish the liability of the insured. The liability of the insured and the insurer may be established in one set of proceedings.

Subsection (4) sets out how a liability can be established.

Section 2: Establishing liability in England and Wales and Northern Ireland

This section introduces, for England and Wales and Northern Ireland, a new mechanism to enable a third party to bring proceedings against an insurer without first establishing the fact and amount of the insured's liability.

Subsections (1) and (2) entitle a third party who has received a transfer of rights, but who has not yet established that the insured is liable, or has proved that the insured is liable, but has not proved the amount of that liability, to bring proceedings against the insurer.

Subsection (2) enables a third party to seek declarations (one or both of which can be asked for by the third party) from the court in proceedings against the insurer. The first declaration (provided for in sub-s (2)(a)) will contain the court's decision on the third party's allegation that the insured is liable to him. The second declaration (provided for in sub-s (2)(b)) will contain the court's decision as to whether the insurance policy covers the liability incurred by the insured against the third party.

Subsection (3) provides that the third party is entitled to the declaration(s) requested where he has proven his or her case. In the absence of this provision, a decision on whether to grant the declarations applied for would be within the discretion of the court.

Subsection (4) enables an insurer facing a claim from a third party using the mechanism in this section and claiming a declaration as to the insured's liability (under sub-s (2)(a)) to rely on any defence which would have been available to the insured had proceedings been taken against the insured (for example, estoppel, contributory negligence etc).

Subsection (5) adjusts the operation of subsection (4) in the specific circumstances set out in s 12(1).

Subsection (6) empowers a court to give "the appropriate judgment" where the court has made a declaration the effect of which is that the insurer is liable to the third party. In many cases, this will be a judgment for a particular sum of money. However, if argument on the amount of the liability has been postponed, either to a later court hearing or to arbitration, the court might grant judgment for damages to be assessed.

Subsections (7) and (8) extend the benefit of the new mechanism to third parties who are entitled or obliged, by a provision in the insurance contract, to resolve the issue of the insurer's liability in arbitration proceedings.

Subsection (9) provides that a third party who uses the new mechanism and applies for a declaration under sub-s (2)(a) may join the insured as a defendant to the action at the outset. It will be possible to join the insured later in the proceedings in accordance with rules of court.

However, if a third party chooses not to join the insured as a defendant, the court may be required to make a declaration under sub-s (2)(a) concerning the insured's obligations, in the absence of the insured. It would be inappropriate if a declaration made in such circumstances bound the insured. Accordingly, the effect of sub-s (10) is that an insured is only bound if he is a defendant to the third party's claim.

In addition, it is intended that amended rules of court will require a third party to inform the insured of his or her action against the insurer, which will give the insured the option of applying to be joined as a defendant.

Section 3: Establishing liability in Scotland

This section introduces a new mechanism for establishing liability in Scotland. The subsections mirror those of s 2, except that there is no equivalent to s 2(3). This is because a declarator is not a discretionary remedy.

Section 4: Individuals

Subsections (1), (2) and (3) list the circumstances in which an individual is a "relevant person" for the purposes of this Act in England and Wales, Scotland and Northern Ireland respectively.

Subsection (4) provides that a person in respect of whom a debt relief order made under Part 7 of the Insolvency Act 1986 is in force is only a relevant person if the liability is incurred before he becomes subject to the order. This is because a debt relief order has no effect on liabilities incurred after the order is made.

After the recall or reduction of a sequestration award made against an insured under Scots law, the insured will no longer be subject to one of the events capable of triggering a statutory transfer. Accordingly sub-s (5) provides that the rights that were transferred under s 1 are re-transferred to the insured.

Subsection (6) states that, where an insured is discharged under Scots law, but the discharge order is subsequently recalled or reduced, then the order shall be treated as never having been made and thus will have no effect on the rights of a third party under this Act.

Section 5: Individuals who die insolvent

Subsection (1) provides that a statutory transfer from a deceased insured takes place only where the debtor dies insolvent subject to a liability against which he is insured (a transfer under s 1(1)(b)). As an insured individual cannot incur liability after death, there is no need to allow for the possibility of a transfer in these circumstances (a transfer under s 1(1)(a)). Subsection (2) lists the events that must occur after an insured's death for him or her to be regarded as having died insolvent.

Section 6: Corporate bodies etc

Subsections (1)–(4) list the circumstances in which a body corporate or an unincorporated body is a "relevant person" for the purposes of this Act. This Act brings about a statutory transfer whether the insured is a limited company, a partnership, a limited liability partnership or some other entity subject to the procedures listed in this section.

Subsections (5) and (6) limit the circumstances in which a transfer is effected in the case of some of the procedures listed in the previous subsections. These restrictions prevent transfers from occurring in cases in which the third party's position is unaffected by the procedure to which the insured is subject.

After the recall or reduction of a sequestration award made against an insured under Scots law, the insured will no longer be subject to one of the events capable of triggering a statutory transfer. Accordingly sub-s (7) provides that the rights that were transferred under s 1 are re-transferred to the insured.

Subsection (8) states that where an insured is discharged under Scots law, but the discharge order is subsequently recalled or reduced, then the order is to be deemed to have been made and thus will have no effect on the rights of a third party under this Act.

Section 7: Scottish trusts

In Scotland, the trust estate itself can be subject to sequestration, a protected trust deed or a judicial composition. These matters are provided for in s 7.

Section 8: Limit on rights transferred

This section ensures that a third party does not receive a right to recover from the insurer any amounts in excess of the insured's liability. The rights of the insured against the insurer are preserved in respect of any amount that is due under the insurance policy but not payable to the third party. An example is where the insurer is obliged by the policy not only to indemnify the insured in full but also to reimburse the insured for costs incurred in mounting a defence to a third party's claim or in seeking advice on whether a third party's claim is likely to be successful. These costs would, by virtue of s 8, be payable under the policy but not recoverable by the third party (the insured would retain the right to claim them).

Section 9: Conditions affecting transferred rights

The rights transferred to the third party are subject to all of the defences that the insurer could use against the insured, but for three exceptions in this section. These prevent an insurer from defeating a third party's claim by relying on certain technical defences, based on conditions in the insurance contract.

Subsection (2) relates to conditions in the insurance contract that require the insured to do something. Where such a condition exists and the third party, rather than the insured, has done the thing required by the condition, sub-s (2) deems that the thing required has been done for the purposes of the condition.

Subsection (3) relates to any condition in the insurance contract that requires the insured to provide continuing information and assistance to the insurer once notice has been given of the claim. Where the insured is incapable of fulfilling such a condition because it is no longer in existence (because it is an individual who has died or a company that has been dissolved), sub-s (3) provides that the transferred rights are not subject to that condition.

Subsection (4) provides, however, that a condition requiring information and assistance does not include a condition requiring the insured to give notice of a claim to the insurer. But as mentioned above, if a third party complies with such notice requirements, it will be treated as having been done by the insured.

Subsections (5) and (6) concern "pay-first" clauses, namely provisions in an insurance contract requiring the insured to pay sums due to the third party before any right to indemnity can arise. The House of Lords held in *The Fanti and the Padre Island* [1991] 2 AC 1 that a third party's claim under rights transferred by the 1930 Acts is worthless if the insurance contract contains such a section. Subsection (5) abrogates this rule, ensuring that a pay-first clause will not apply to rights transferred under this Act. Subsection (6) limits the effect of sub-s (5), preserving the rule in *The Fanti and the Padre Island* in cases of marine insurance (except in relation to death or personal injury claims).

Section 10: Insurer's right of set off
This section preserves the insurer's rights to deduct money owed to it by the insured from the monies payable to the third party. For example, this ensures that if the insured has not paid all the premiums for the insurance policy, the insurer can deduct those unpaid premiums when paying the third party's claim, to the extent to which it would have been entitled to do so had the claim been brought by the insured.

Section 11: Information and disclosure for third parties
This section introduces Schedule 1, which confers on the third party rights to obtain information about the insurance policy (see *post*).

Section 12: Limitation and prescription
This section sets out rules governing when an action to enforce rights transferred by this Act will be time-barred.

Subsections (1)–(3) govern the situation where a third party is already involved in proceedings against the insured and the limitation period or period of prescription governing those proceedings has expired. These subsections ensure that if the third party has issued proceedings against the insured in time, the third party will not be time-barred from issuing fresh proceedings against the insurer for a declaration under s 2(2)(a) (or declarator under s 3(2)(a)).

In the absence of these subsections, fresh proceedings against the insurer using the new mechanism in ss 2 or 3 would in these circumstances be time-barred. This would not matter if the third party could join the insurer to the existing proceedings against the insured. However, it is likely that this will not be possible under procedural rules which comply with s 35 of the Limitation Act 1980. These subsections therefore ensure that the new mechanism provided by this Act is available to third parties in these circumstances.

Subsection (4) applies where the insured's liability has already been established (see s 1(4)). It ensures that this Act does not alter the date on which the relevant limitation period or period of prescription for proceedings against the insurer starts.

Section 13: Jurisdiction within the United Kingdom
This section sets out what is to happen in cases in which the third party is domiciled in one part of the UK, and the insurer is domiciled in another. It provides the third party with the choice to issue proceedings either in his or her own place of domicile or in that of the insurer, regardless of any contrary provisions in the insurance contract. In the absence of this provision, proceedings brought by a third party under this Act against an insurer domiciled within the UK would be within the scope of Council Regulation (EC) 44/2001 and would therefore be governed by the Civil Jurisdiction and Judgments Act 1982, Sch 4 and any relevant clause in the insurance contract. The result might in these circumstances be that the third party is prevented from suing the insurer in the courts of his or her own place of domicile.

Section 14: Effect of transfer on insured's liability
This section sets out the effect of the statutory transfer on the third party's rights against the insured. The section seeks to remove the uncertainty under the 1930 Acts about whether a third party can recover from the insured any of his or her debt which he is entitled to recover from the insurer under transferred rights. This Act provides that the third party is not entitled to do so.

Subsection (1) provides that a third party may not seek to enforce his or her rights against the insured to the extent that there is valid insurance in place covering the liability. This is because the insured's rights against the insurer under the insurance policy have been transferred to the third party. The third party will only be able to seek payment from the insured to the extent that the insurance policy is ineffective – that is, where there is a gap between what is covered by the insurance policy (referred to as the "amount recoverable from the insurer") and the full amount of the liability.

Subsections (2) and (3) cater for the situation where an insured has become a relevant person as a result of a voluntary procedure. These provisions preserve the ability of the third party to recover from the insured the amount by which the liability exceeds the amount recoverable from the insurer. However, the voluntary procedure will apply to the amount of liability which the third party could seek to recover from the insured, so it may affect the amount which is actually recoverable.

Subsections (4) and (5) play a similar role to sub-ss (2) and (3) in respect of a liability subject to a composition approved in accordance with Schedule 4 to the Bankruptcy (Scotland) Act 1985. They remove, either partially or completely, the third party from the scope of this voluntary procedure.

Subsection (6) defines the term "amount recoverable from the insurer", used in subsections (1), (3) and (5). Subsection (6) provides that in calculating the "amount recoverable from the insurer", that amount does not include any money which cannot be recovered, because: (a) the insurer itself has also become a "relevant person", and is therefore unable to pay the debt, or (b) the contract of insurance provides for a limit on funds available to meet claims which fall in the same category as the third party's claim.

The effect of sub-s (6) is therefore to protect a third party where he is unable to recover from the insurer, due to either of the circumstances outlined above. Any amount that the third party is unable to recover for these reasons will not be treated as part of the "amount recoverable from the insurer" for the purposes of sub-ss (1)–(5), and so the third party will be entitled to recover that amount from the insured instead.

Subsection (7) relates to the Financial Services Compensation Scheme established by virtue of Part 15 of the Financial Services and Markets Act 2000. A third party may be eligible to make a claim under the scheme in respect of an amount which he cannot recover from the insurer because of the insurer's own financial difficulties. If a third party is eligible but does not make such a claim, this may reduce the amount he will be able to claim from the insured.

Section 15: Reinsurance
Section 15 provides that this Act does not apply where the liability incurred referred to in s 1(1) is itself a liability incurred by an insurer under a contract of insurance. The effect of this section is that this Act does not apply to reinsurance.

Section 16: Voluntarily-incurred liabilities
Tarbuck v Avon Plc [2001] 2 All ER 503 held that the Third Parties (Rights against Insurers) Act 1930 did not apply to claims for legal expenses insurance. The Law Commissions indicated that the same reasoning would apply to insurance for other voluntarily-incurred expenses, such as health or car repair insurance. The decision in *Tarbuck* was distinguished by the Court of Appeal in *Re OT Computers Ltd (In Administration)* [2004] EWCA Civ 653. Section 16 therefore provides that a third party will be able to make a direct claim against the insurer even if the insurance covered liabilities voluntarily-incurred by the insured.

Section 17: Avoidance

This section prevents an insurance contract from being drafted so as to nullify the effect of this Act. Any provision in an insurance contract that purports to avoid the effect of this Act will have no effect.

Section 18: Cases with a foreign element

Section 18 provides that this Act will apply irrespective of whether the case has any foreign elements (for example, if the insurer is based overseas).

Section 19: Power to amend Act

Section 19 gives the Secretary of State a power by order to amend ss 4–6 to take account of Northern Ireland legislation. The Secretary of State may update references to Northern Ireland legislation or add a reference to Northern Ireland legislation where in the opinion of the Secretary of State it corresponds with a provision of the law of England and Wales or the law of Scotland which is referred to in the section being amended.

Section 20: Amendments, transitionals, repeals, etc

This section introduces Schs 2–4 (see *post*).

Section 21: Short title, commencement and extent

Subsection (1) provides for this Act's short title. Subsection (2) provides that this Act will come into force on a day specified by the Secretary of State by order (as of 1 July 2010, no such Order had been made). Subsections (3)–(6) specify the territorial extent of this Act. Ie, this Act extends to the UK, apart from s 2 and paras 3 and 4 of Sch 1 which do not extend to Scotland, and s 3 which extends to Scotland only.

Schedule 1: Information and disclosure for third parties

It was arguable that the right to information under the 1930 Acts was restricted because it did not arise until the liability of the insured had been established. The Court of Appeal held in *Re OT Computers Ltd (In Administration)* that a third party may make a request for information under s 2 of the 1930 Acts before the insured's liability has been established. This Act allows third parties to obtain information about the rights transferred to them in order to enable an informed decision to be taken on whether or not to commence or continue litigation.

Paragraph 1 (Notices requesting information) sets out the right to request information and the information which may be requested.

Paragraph 2 (Provision of information where notice given under paragraph 1) outlines what a person receiving a notice requesting information under paragraph 1 must do.

Paragraph 3 (Notices requiring disclosure: defunct bodies) provides a mechanism similar to that under paras 1 and 2 in relation to defunct bodies. One of the purposes of this Act is to remove the need for third parties to restore a defunct body to the register of companies in order to initiate proceedings against it.

Paragraph 4 (Disclosure and inspection where notice given under paragraph 3) imposes the same duties on persons receiving a notice given under para 3 as would have been imposed by the court had the defunct body been restored to the register and orders for standard disclosure obtained.

Paragraph 5 (Avoidance) prevents the insurance contract from being drafted so as to nullify the effect of Schedule 1.

Paragraph 6 (Other rights to information etc) ensures that the rights to information outlined in paras 1 or 3 are in addition to any other such rights to information, for example rights under the Civil Procedure Rules.

Paragraph 7 (Interpretation) explains when a person is to be considered able to provide information, and when a document is to be considered to be in a person's control, for the purposes of Sch 1.

Schedule 2: Amendments

This Schedule replaces references to the 1930 Acts in other legislation with references to this Act, eg, in the Cross-Border Insolvency Regulations 2006, SI 2006/1030, Sch 1 at **[10.963]**.

Schedule 3: Transitory, Transitional and Saving Provisions

Schedule 3 sets out the provisions governing the transition from the 1930 Acts to this Act. They provide that if the insured incurs liability to the third party after the commencement day, or if the insured becomes a relevant person after the commencement day, then this Act will apply to the claim. If both of these occur before commencement day, the 1930 Acts will continue to apply. In the case of a transfer caused by the death of an insolvent insured, the 1930 Acts will apply to cases where the insured died before the commencement day, but otherwise this Act will apply.

BRIBERY ACT 2010

(2010 c 23)

ARRANGEMENT OF SECTIONS

An Act to make provision about offences relating to bribery; and for connected purposes

[8 April 2010]

General bribery offences

[9.476]
1   Offences of bribing another person
(1)   A person ("P") is guilty of an offence if either of the following cases applies.
(2)   Case 1 is where—
  (a)   P offers, promises or gives a financial or other advantage to another person, and
  (b)   P intends the advantage—
    (i)   to induce a person to perform improperly a relevant function or activity, or
    (ii)   to reward a person for the improper performance of such a function or activity.
(3)   Case 2 is where—
  (a)   P offers, promises or gives a financial or other advantage to another person, and
  (b)   P knows or believes that the acceptance of the advantage would itself constitute the improper performance of a relevant function or activity.
(4)   In case 1 it does not matter whether the person to whom the advantage is offered, promised or given is the same person as the person who is to perform, or has performed, the function or activity concerned.
(5)   In cases 1 and 2 it does not matter whether the advantage is offered, promised or given by P directly or through a third party.

NOTES
Commencement: 1 July 2010.

[9.477]
2   Offences relating to being bribed
(1)   A person ("R") is guilty of an offence if any of the following cases applies.
(2)   Case 3 is where R requests, agrees to receive or accepts a financial or other advantage intending that, in consequence, a relevant function or activity should be performed improperly (whether by R or another person).
(3)   Case 4 is where—
  (a)   R requests, agrees to receive or accepts a financial or other advantage, and
  (b)   the request, agreement or acceptance itself constitutes the improper performance by R of a relevant function or activity.
(4)   Case 5 is where R requests, agrees to receive or accepts a financial or other advantage as a reward for the improper performance (whether by R or another person) of a relevant function or activity.
(5)   Case 6 is where, in anticipation of or in consequence of R requesting, agreeing to receive or accepting a financial or other advantage, a relevant function or activity is performed improperly—
  (a)   by R, or
  (b)   by another person at R's request or with R's assent or acquiescence.
(6)   In cases 3 to 6 it does not matter—
  (a)   whether R requests, agrees to receive or accepts (or is to request, agree to receive or accept) the advantage directly or through a third party,
  (b)   whether the advantage is (or is to be) for the benefit of R or another person.
(7)   In cases 4 to 6 it does not matter whether R knows or believes that the performance of the function or activity is improper.
(8)   In case 6, where a person other than R is performing the function or activity, it also does not matter whether that person knows or believes that the performance of the function or activity is improper.

NOTES
Commencement: 1 July 2010.

[9.478]
3   Function or activity to which bribe relates

(1)   For the purposes of this Act a function or activity is a relevant function or activity if—
  (a)   it falls within subsection (2), and
  (b)   meets one or more of conditions A to C.
(2)   The following functions and activities fall within this subsection—
  (a)   any function of a public nature,
  (b)   any activity connected with a business,
  (c)   any activity performed in the course of a person's employment,
  (d)   any activity performed by or on behalf of a body of persons (whether corporate or unincorporate).
(3)   Condition A is that a person performing the function or activity is expected to perform it in good faith.
(4)   Condition B is that a person performing the function or activity is expected to perform it impartially.
(5)   Condition C is that a person performing the function or activity is in a position of trust by virtue of performing it.
(6)   A function or activity is a relevant function or activity even if it—
  (a)   has no connection with the United Kingdom, and
  (b)   is performed in a country or territory outside the United Kingdom.
(7)   In this section "business" includes trade or profession.

NOTES
Commencement: 1 July 2010.

[9.479]
4   Improper performance to which bribe relates

(1)   For the purposes of this Act a relevant function or activity—
  (a)   is performed improperly if it is performed in breach of a relevant expectation, and
  (b)   is to be treated as being performed improperly if there is a failure to perform the function or activity and that failure is itself a breach of a relevant expectation.
(2)   In subsection (1) "relevant expectation"—
  (a)   in relation to a function or activity which meets condition A or B, means the expectation mentioned in the condition concerned, and
  (b)   in relation to a function or activity which meets condition C, means any expectation as to the manner in which, or the reasons for which, the function or activity will be performed that arises from the position of trust mentioned in that condition.
(3)   Anything that a person does (or omits to do) arising from or in connection with that person's past performance of a relevant function or activity is to be treated for the purposes of this Act as being done (or omitted) by that person in the performance of that function or activity.

NOTES
Commencement: 1 July 2010.

[9.480]
5   Expectation test

(1)   For the purposes of sections 3 and 4, the test of what is expected is a test of what a reasonable person in the United Kingdom would expect in relation to the performance of the type of function or activity concerned.
(2)   In deciding what such a person would expect in relation to the performance of a function or activity where the performance is not subject to the law of any part of the United Kingdom, any local custom or practice is to be disregarded unless it is permitted or required by the written law applicable to the country or territory concerned.
(3)   In subsection (2) "written law" means law contained in—
  (a)   any written constitution, or provision made by or under legislation, applicable to the country or territory concerned, or
  (b)   any judicial decision which is so applicable and is evidenced in published written sources.

NOTES
Commencement: 1 July 2010.

Bribery of foreign public officials

[9.481]
6   Bribery of foreign public officials

(1)   A person ("P") who bribes a foreign public official ("F") is guilty of an offence if P's intention is to influence F in F's capacity as a foreign public official.
(2)   P must also intend to obtain or retain—
  (a)   business, or
  (b)   an advantage in the conduct of business.

(3)   P bribes F if, and only if—
  (a)   directly or through a third party, P offers, promises or gives any financial or other advantage—
    (i)   to F, or
    (ii)   to another person at F's request or with F's assent or acquiescence, and
  (b)   F is neither permitted nor required by the written law applicable to F to be influenced in F's capacity as a foreign public official by the offer, promise or gift.
(4)   References in this section to influencing F in F's capacity as a foreign public official mean influencing F in the performance of F's functions as such an official, which includes—
  (a)   any omission to exercise those functions, and
  (b)   any use of F's position as such an official, even if not within F's authority.
(5)   "Foreign public official" means an individual who—
  (a)   holds a legislative, administrative or judicial position of any kind, whether appointed or elected, of a country or territory outside the United Kingdom (or any subdivision of such a country or territory),
  (b)   exercises a public function—
    (i)   for or on behalf of a country or territory outside the United Kingdom (or any subdivision of such a country or territory), or
    (ii)   for any public agency or public enterprise of that country or territory (or subdivision), or
  (c)   is an official or agent of a public international organisation.
(6)   "Public international organisation" means an organisation whose members are any of the following—
  (a)   countries or territories,
  (b)   governments of countries or territories,
  (c)   other public international organisations,
  (d)   a mixture of any of the above.
(7)   For the purposes of subsection (3)(b), the written law applicable to F is—
  (a)   where the performance of the functions of F which P intends to influence would be subject to the law of any part of the United Kingdom, the law of that part of the United Kingdom,
  (b)   where paragraph (a) does not apply and F is an official or agent of a public international organisation, the applicable written rules of that organisation,
  (c)   where paragraphs (a) and (b) do not apply, the law of the country or territory in relation to which F is a foreign public official so far as that law is contained in—
    (i)   any written constitution, or provision made by or under legislation, applicable to the country or territory concerned, or
    (ii)   any judicial decision which is so applicable and is evidenced in published written sources.
(8)   For the purposes of this section, a trade or profession is a business.

NOTES
Commencement: 1 July 2010.

Failure of commercial organisations to prevent bribery
[9.482]
7   Failure of commercial organisations to prevent bribery
(1)   A relevant commercial organisation ("C") is guilty of an offence under this section if a person ("A") associated with C bribes another person intending—
  (a)   to obtain or retain business for C, or
  (b)   to obtain or retain an advantage in the conduct of business for C.
(2)   But it is a defence for C to prove that C had in place adequate procedures designed to prevent persons associated with C from undertaking such conduct.
(3)   For the purposes of this section, A bribes another person if, and only if, A—
  (a)   is, or would be, guilty of an offence under section 1 or 6 (whether or not A has been prosecuted for such an offence), or
  (b)   would be guilty of such an offence if section 12(2)(c) and (4) were omitted.
(4)   See section 8 for the meaning of a person associated with C and see section 9 for a duty on the Secretary of State to publish guidance.
(5)   In this section—
  "partnership" means—
    (a)   a partnership within the Partnership Act 1890, or
    (b)   a limited partnership registered under the Limited Partnerships Act 1907,
    or a firm or entity of a similar character formed under the law of a country or territory outside the United Kingdom,
  "relevant commercial organisation" means—
    (a)   a body which is incorporated under the law of any part of the United Kingdom and which carries on a business (whether there or elsewhere),
    (b)   any other body corporate (wherever incorporated) which carries on a business, or part of a business, in any part of the United Kingdom,

> (c)   a partnership which is formed under the law of any part of the United Kingdom and which carries on a business (whether there or elsewhere), or
>
> (d)   any other partnership (wherever formed) which carries on a business, or part of a business, in any part of the United Kingdom,

and, for the purposes of this section, a trade or profession is a business.

NOTES

Commencement: 1 July 2010.

[9.483]

8   Meaning of associated person

(1)   For the purposes of section 7, a person ("A") is associated with C if (disregarding any bribe under consideration) A is a person who performs services for or on behalf of C.

(2)   The capacity in which A performs services for or on behalf of C does not matter.

(3)   Accordingly A may (for example) be C's employee, agent or subsidiary.

(4)   Whether or not A is a person who performs services for or on behalf of C is to be determined by reference to all the relevant circumstances and not merely by reference to the nature of the relationship between A and C.

(5)   But if A is an employee of C, it is to be presumed unless the contrary is shown that A is a person who performs services for or on behalf of C.

NOTES

Commencement: 1 July 2010.

[9.484]

9   Guidance about commercial organisations preventing bribery

(1)   The Secretary of State must publish guidance about procedures that relevant commercial organisations can put in place to prevent persons associated with them from bribing as mentioned in section 7(1).

(2)   The Secretary of State may, from time to time, publish revisions to guidance under this section or revised guidance.

(3)   The Secretary of State must consult the Scottish Ministers before publishing anything under this section.

(4)   Publication under this section is to be in such manner as the Secretary of State considers appropriate.

(5)   Expressions used in this section have the same meaning as in section 7.

NOTES

Commencement: 1 July 2010.

Prosecution and penalties

[9.485]

10   Consent to prosecution

(1)   No proceedings for an offence under this Act may be instituted in England and Wales except by or with the consent of—

> (a)   the Director of Public Prosecutions,
>
> (b)   the Director of the Serious Fraud Office, or
>
> (c)   the Director of Revenue and Customs Prosecutions.

(2)   No proceedings for an offence under this Act may be instituted in Northern Ireland except by or with the consent of—

> (a)   the Director of Public Prosecutions for Northern Ireland, or
>
> (b)   the Director of the Serious Fraud Office.

(3)   No proceedings for an offence under this Act may be instituted in England and Wales or Northern Ireland by a person—

> (a)   who is acting—
>
> > (i)   under the direction or instruction of the Director of Public Prosecutions, the Director of the Serious Fraud Office or the Director of Revenue and Customs Prosecutions, or
> >
> > (ii)   on behalf of such a Director, or
>
> (b)   to whom such a function has been assigned by such a Director,

except with the consent of the Director concerned to the institution of the proceedings.

(4)   The Director of Public Prosecutions, the Director of the Serious Fraud Office and the Director of Revenue and Customs Prosecutions must exercise personally any function under subsection (1), (2) or (3) of giving consent.

(5)   The only exception is if—

> (a)   the Director concerned is unavailable, and
>
> (b)   there is another person who is designated in writing by the Director acting personally as the person who is authorised to exercise any such function when the Director is unavailable.

(6)   In that case, the other person may exercise the function but must do so personally.

(7) Subsections (4) to (6) apply instead of any other provisions which would otherwise have enabled any function of the Director of Public Prosecutions, the Director of the Serious Fraud Office or the Director of Revenue and Customs Prosecutions under subsection (1), (2) or (3) of giving consent to be exercised by a person other than the Director concerned.

(8) No proceedings for an offence under this Act may be instituted in Northern Ireland by virtue of section 36 of the Justice (Northern Ireland) Act 2002 (delegation of the functions of the Director of Public Prosecutions for Northern Ireland to persons other than the Deputy Director) except with the consent of the Director of Public Prosecutions for Northern Ireland to the institution of the proceedings.

(9) The Director of Public Prosecutions for Northern Ireland must exercise personally any function under subsection (2) or (8) of giving consent unless the function is exercised personally by the Deputy Director of Public Prosecutions for Northern Ireland by virtue of section 30(4) or (7) of the Act of 2002 (powers of Deputy Director to exercise functions of Director).

(10) Subsection (9) applies instead of section 36 of the Act of 2002 in relation to the functions of the Director of Public Prosecutions for Northern Ireland and the Deputy Director of Public Prosecutions for Northern Ireland under, or (as the case may be) by virtue of, subsections (2) and (8) above of giving consent.

NOTES

Commencement: 1 July 2010.

[9.486]

11 Penalties

(1) An individual guilty of an offence under section 1, 2 or 6 is liable—
  (a) on summary conviction, to imprisonment for a term not exceeding 12 months, or to a fine not exceeding the statutory maximum, or to both;
  (b) on conviction on indictment, to imprisonment for a term not exceeding 10 years, or to a fine, or to both.

(2) Any other person guilty of an offence under section 1, 2 or 6 is liable—
  (a) on summary conviction, to a fine not exceeding the statutory maximum,
  (b) on conviction on indictment, to a fine.

(3) A person guilty of an offence under section 7 is liable on conviction on indictment to a fine.

(4) The reference in subsection (1)(a) to 12 months is to be read—
  (a) in its application to England and Wales in relation to an offence committed before the commencement of section 154(1) of the Criminal Justice Act 2003, and
  (b) in its application to Northern Ireland,
as a reference to 6 months.

NOTES

Commencement: 1 July 2010.

Other provisions about offences

[9.487]

12 Offences under this Act: territorial application

(1) An offence is committed under section 1, 2 or 6 in England and Wales, Scotland or Northern Ireland if any act or omission which forms part of the offence takes place in that part of the United Kingdom.

(2) Subsection (3) applies if—
  (a) no act or omission which forms part of an offence under section 1, 2 or 6 takes place in the United Kingdom,
  (b) a person's acts or omissions done or made outside the United Kingdom would form part of such an offence if done or made in the United Kingdom, and
  (c) that person has a close connection with the United Kingdom.

(3) In such a case—
  (a) the acts or omissions form part of the offence referred to in subsection (2)(a), and
  (b) proceedings for the offence may be taken at any place in the United Kingdom.

(4) For the purposes of subsection (2)(c) a person has a close connection with the United Kingdom if, and only if, the person was one of the following at the time the acts or omissions concerned were done or made—
  (a) a British citizen,
  (b) a British overseas territories citizen,
  (c) a British National (Overseas),
  (d) a British Overseas citizen,
  (e) a person who under the British Nationality Act 1981 was a British subject,
  (f) a British protected person within the meaning of that Act,
  (g) an individual ordinarily resident in the United Kingdom,
  (h) a body incorporated under the law of any part of the United Kingdom,
  (i) a Scottish partnership.

(5)   An offence is committed under section 7 irrespective of whether the acts or omissions which form part of the offence take place in the United Kingdom or elsewhere.

(6)   Where no act or omission which forms part of an offence under section 7 takes place in the United Kingdom, proceedings for the offence may be taken at any place in the United Kingdom.

(7)   Subsection (8) applies if, by virtue of this section, proceedings for an offence are to be taken in Scotland against a person.

(8)   Such proceedings may be taken—
    (a)   in any sheriff court district in which the person is apprehended or in custody, or
    (b)   in such sheriff court district as the Lord Advocate may determine.

(9)   In subsection (8) "sheriff court district" is to be read in accordance with section 307(1) of the Criminal Procedure (Scotland) Act 1995.

NOTES

Commencement: 1 July 2010.

[9.488]
13   Defence for certain bribery offences etc

(1)   It is a defence for a person charged with a relevant bribery offence to prove that the person's conduct was necessary for—
    (a)   the proper exercise of any function of an intelligence service, or
    (b)   the proper exercise of any function of the armed forces when engaged on active service.

(2)   The head of each intelligence service must ensure that the service has in place arrangements designed to ensure that any conduct of a member of the service which would otherwise be a relevant bribery offence is necessary for a purpose falling within subsection (1)(a).

(3)   The Defence Council must ensure that the armed forces have in place arrangements designed to ensure that any conduct of—
    (a)   a member of the armed forces who is engaged on active service, or
    (b)   a civilian subject to service discipline when working in support of any person falling within paragraph (a),
which would otherwise be a relevant bribery offence is necessary for a purpose falling within subsection (1)(b).

(4)   The arrangements which are in place by virtue of subsection (2) or (3) must be arrangements which the Secretary of State considers to be satisfactory.

(5)   For the purposes of this section, the circumstances in which a person's conduct is necessary for a purpose falling within subsection (1)(a) or (b) are to be treated as including any circumstances in which the person's conduct—
    (a)   would otherwise be an offence under section 2, and
    (b)   involves conduct by another person which, but for subsection (1)(a) or (b), would be an offence under section 1.

(6)   In this section—
"active service" means service in—
    (a)   an action or operation against an enemy,
    (b)   an operation outside the British Islands for the protection of life or property, or
    (c)   the military occupation of a foreign country or territory,
"armed forces" means Her Majesty's forces (within the meaning of the Armed Forces Act 2006),
"civilian subject to service discipline" and "enemy" have the same meaning as in the Act of
    2006,
"GCHQ" has the meaning given by section 3(3) of the Intelligence Services Act 1994,
"head" means—
    (a)   in relation to the Security Service, the Director General of the Security Service,
    (b)   in relation to the Secret Intelligence Service, the Chief of the Secret Intelligence
        Service, and
    (c)   in relation to GCHQ, the Director of GCHQ,
"intelligence service" means the Security Service, the Secret Intelligence Service or GCHQ,
"relevant bribery offence" means—
    (a)   an offence under section 1 which would not also be an offence under section 6,
    (b)   an offence under section 2,
    (c)   an offence committed by aiding, abetting, counselling or procuring the commission
        of an offence falling within paragraph (a) or (b),
    (d)   an offence of attempting or conspiring to commit, or of inciting the commission of,
        an offence falling within paragraph (a) or (b), or
    (e)   an offence under Part 2 of the Serious Crime Act 2007 (encouraging or assisting
        crime) in relation to an offence falling within paragraph (a) or (b).

NOTES

Commencement: 1 July 2010.

[9.489]

14 Offences under sections 1, 2 and 6 by bodies corporate etc

(1) This section applies if an offence under section 1, 2 or 6 is committed by a body corporate or a Scottish partnership.

(2) If the offence is proved to have been committed with the consent or connivance of—

    (a) a senior officer of the body corporate or Scottish partnership, or

    (b) a person purporting to act in such a capacity,

the senior officer or person (as well as the body corporate or partnership) is guilty of the offence and liable to be proceeded against and punished accordingly.

(3) But subsection (2) does not apply, in the case of an offence which is committed under section 1, 2 or 6 by virtue of section 12(2) to (4), to a senior officer or person purporting to act in such a capacity unless the senior officer or person has a close connection with the United Kingdom (within the meaning given by section 12(4)).

(4) In this section—

    "director", in relation to a body corporate whose affairs are managed by its members, means a member of the body corporate,

  "senior officer" means—

    (a) in relation to a body corporate, a director, manager, secretary or other similar officer of the body corporate, and

    (b) in relation to a Scottish partnership, a partner in the partnership.

NOTES

Commencement: 1 July 2010.

[9.490]

15 Offences under section 7 by partnerships

(1) Proceedings for an offence under section 7 alleged to have been committed by a partnership must be brought in the name of the partnership (and not in that of any of the partners).

(2) For the purposes of such proceedings—

    (a) rules of court relating to the service of documents have effect as if the partnership were a body corporate, and

    (b) the following provisions apply as they apply in relation to a body corporate—

        (i) section 33 of the Criminal Justice Act 1925 and Schedule 3 to the Magistrates' Courts Act 1980,

        (ii) section 18 of the Criminal Justice Act (Northern Ireland) 1945 (c 15 (NI)) and Schedule 4 to the Magistrates' Courts (Northern Ireland) Order 1981 (SI 1981/1675 (NI 26)),

        (iii) section 70 of the Criminal Procedure (Scotland) Act 1995.

(3) A fine imposed on the partnership on its conviction for an offence under section 7 is to be paid out of the partnership assets.

(4) In this section "partnership" has the same meaning as in section 7.

NOTES

Commencement: 1 July 2010.

Supplementary and final provisions

[9.491]

16 Application to Crown

This Act applies to individuals in the public service of the Crown as it applies to other individuals.

NOTES

Commencement: 8 April 2010.

[9.492]

17 Consequential provision

(1) The following common law offences are abolished—

    (a) the offences under the law of England and Wales and Northern Ireland of bribery and embracery,

    (b) the offences under the law of Scotland of bribery and accepting a bribe.

(2) Schedule 1 (which contains consequential amendments) has effect.

(3) Schedule 2 (which contains repeals and revocations) has effect.

(4) The relevant national authority may by order make such supplementary, incidental or consequential provision as the relevant national authority considers appropriate for the purposes of this Act or in consequence of this Act.

(5) The power to make an order under this section—

    (a) is exercisable by statutory instrument,

    (b) includes power to make transitional, transitory or saving provision,

(c)   may, in particular, be exercised by amending, repealing, revoking or otherwise modifying any provision made by or under an enactment (including any Act passed in the same Session as this Act).

(6)   Subject to subsection (7), a statutory instrument containing an order of the Secretary of State under this section may not be made unless a draft of the instrument has been laid before, and approved by a resolution of, each House of Parliament.

(7)   A statutory instrument containing an order of the Secretary of State under this section which does not amend or repeal a provision of a public general Act or of devolved legislation is subject to annulment in pursuance of a resolution of either House of Parliament.

(8)   Subject to subsection (9), a statutory instrument containing an order of the Scottish Ministers under this section may not be made unless a draft of the instrument has been laid before, and approved by a resolution of, the Scottish Parliament.

(9)   A statutory instrument containing an order of the Scottish Ministers under this section which does not amend or repeal a provision of an Act of the Scottish Parliament or of a public general Act is subject to annulment in pursuance of a resolution of the Scottish Parliament.

(10)   In this section—

"devolved legislation" means an Act of the Scottish Parliament, a Measure of the National Assembly for Wales or an Act of the Northern Ireland Assembly,

"enactment" includes an Act of the Scottish Parliament and Northern Ireland legislation,

"relevant national authority" means—

(a)   in the case of provision which would be within the legislative competence of the Scottish Parliament if it were contained in an Act of that Parliament, the Scottish Ministers, and

(b)   in any other case, the Secretary of State.

NOTES

Commencement: 8 April 2010 (sub-ss (4)–(10)); 1 July 2011 (otherwise)
Orders: the Bribery Act 2010 (Consequential Amendments) Order 2011, SI 2011/1441.

[9.493]
18   Extent

(1)   Subject as follows, this Act extends to England and Wales, Scotland and Northern Ireland.

(2)   Subject to subsections (3) to (5), any amendment, repeal or revocation made by Schedule 1 or 2 has the same extent as the provision amended, repealed or revoked.

(3)   The amendment of, and repeals in, the Armed Forces Act 2006 do not extend to the Channel Islands.

(4)   The amendments of the International Criminal Court Act 2001 extend to England and Wales and Northern Ireland only.

(5)   Subsection (2) does not apply to the repeal in the Civil Aviation Act 1982.

NOTES

Commencement: 8 April 2010.

[9.494]
19   Commencement and transitional provision etc

(1)   Subject to subsection (2), this Act comes into force on such day as the Secretary of State may by order made by statutory instrument appoint.

(2)   Sections 16, 17(4) to (10) and 18, this section (other than subsections (5) to (7)) and section 20 come into force on the day on which this Act is passed.

(3)   An order under subsection (1) may—

(a)   appoint different days for different purposes,

(b)   make such transitional, transitory or saving provision as the Secretary of State considers appropriate in connection with the coming into force of any provision of this Act.

(4)   The Secretary of State must consult the Scottish Ministers before making an order under this section in connection with any provision of this Act which would be within the legislative competence of the Scottish Parliament if it were contained in an Act of that Parliament.

(5)   This Act does not affect any liability, investigation, legal proceeding or penalty for or in respect of—

(a)   a common law offence mentioned in subsection (1) of section 17 which is committed wholly or partly before the coming into force of that subsection in relation to such an offence, or

(b)   an offence under the Public Bodies Corrupt Practices Act 1889 or the Prevention of Corruption Act 1906 committed wholly or partly before the coming into force of the repeal of the Act by Schedule 2 to this Act.

(6)   For the purposes of subsection (5) an offence is partly committed before a particular time if any act or omission which forms part of the offence takes place before that time.

(7)   Subsections (5) and (6) are without prejudice to section 16 of the Interpretation Act 1978 (general savings on repeal).

NOTES

Commencement: 8 April 2010 (sub-ss (1)–(4)); 1 July 2010 (otherwise).
Orders: the Bribery Act 2010 (Commencement) Order 2011, SI 2011/1418.

[9.495]
20　Short title
This Act may be cited as the Bribery Act 2010.

NOTES

Commencement: 8 April 2010.

SCHEDULES 1 AND 2

(Sch 1 (Consequential Amendments) and Sch 2 (Repeals and Revocations) contain various amendments, repeals and revocations of enactments that are outside the scope of this work.)

FINANCIAL SERVICES ACT 2010 (NOTE)

(2010 c 28)

[9.496]

NOTES

This Act received royal assent on 8 April 2010 and provides as follows—

Section 1 (Financial stability objective): amends the Financial Services and Markets Act 2000, s 2 and inserts s 3A.

Section 2 (Enhancing public understanding of financial matters etc): amends the Financial Services and Markets Act 2000, ss 2, 5, repeals s 4 and inserts s 6A. It also makes provision for the application of the Transfer of Undertakings (Protection of Employment) Regulations 2006 to any members of staff of the FSA who are transferred to the consumer financial education body.

Section 3 (Meeting FSA's regulatory objectives): amends the Financial Services and Markets Act 2000, ss 44, 45, 138, 194.

Section 4 (Executives' remuneration reports): provides that the Treasury may make provision by regulations about the preparation, approval and disclosure of executives' remuneration reports.

Section 5 (Executives' remuneration reports: supplementary): makes further provision in relation to regulations made under s 4.

Section 6 (Rules made by FSA about remuneration): inserts the Financial Services and Markets Act 2000, s 139A.

Section 7(Rules made by FSA about recovery and resolution plans): inserts the Financial Services and Markets Act 2000, ss 139A–139F. It also provides that the Treasury may by order require the FSA to make, by a date specified in the order, recovery plan rules, or resolution plan rules, which impose requirements on authorised persons who are of a description specified in the order.

Section 8 (Power of FSA to prohibit, or require disclosure of, short selling): inserts the Financial Services and Markets Act 2000, ss 131B–131K (Part 8A: Short Selling).

Section 9 (Suspending permission to carry on regulated activities etc): inserts the Financial Services and Markets Act 2000, s 206A.

Section 10 (Removal of restriction on imposing a penalty and cancelling authorisation): repeals the Financial Services and Markets Act 2000, s 206(2).

Section 11 (Performance of controlled function without approval): inserts the Financial Services and Markets Act 2000, ss 63A–63D.

Section 12 (Approved persons guilty of misconduct): amends the Financial Services and Markets Act 2000, s 66.

Section 13 (Publication of decision notices): amends the Financial Services and Markets Act 2000, s 391.

Section 14 (Consumer redress schemes): substitutes the Financial Services and Markets Act 2000, ss 404, 404A–404G (for the original s 404). This section has effect in relation to failures occurring before the commencement of this section (as well as in relation to failures occurring at or after the commencement of this section).

Section 15 (Restrictions on provision of credit card cheques): inserts the Consumer Credit Act 1974, ss 51A, 51B, and amends Sch 1. It also provides that an offence under section 51A of the CCA 1974 is to be treated for the purposes of Part 3 of the Regulatory Enforcement and Sanctions Act 2008 (civil sanctions) as contained in the CCA 1974 immediately before the day on which that Act of 2008 was passed.

Section 16 (Contribution to costs of special resolution regime): substitutes the Financial Services and Markets Act 2000, ss 214B–214D (for the original s 214B). It also provides that ss 214B–214D (as substituted) apply to any case where a stabilisation power was exercised before the commencement of this section as if the references in ss 214B(4) and 214C(5) and (6) to any time were to any time on or after 19 November 2009.

Section 17 (Power to require FSCS manager to act in relation to other schemes): inserts the Financial Services and Markets Act 2000, ss 224B–224F (Part 15A: Power to Require FSCS Manager to Act in Relation to Other Schemes).

Section 18 (Information relating to financial stability): inserts the Financial Services and Markets Act 2000, ss 165A–165C, 169A.

Section 19 (Asset protection scheme etc): provides that the Treasury may, by notice in writing, require a person who participates (or is proposing to participate) in the asset protection scheme or a qualifying scheme: (a) to provide such information, or (b) to produce such documents, as they may reasonably require for the purposes of, or in connection with, the scheme or a relevant scheme agreement. It further provides:

—　"The asset protection scheme" means the scheme known as the Asset Protection Scheme that was the subject of a statement made by the Chancellor of the Exchequer on 26 February 2009.

—　"Qualifying scheme" means a scheme specified in an order made by the Treasury.

—　"Relevant scheme agreement" means an agreement entered into (or proposed to be entered into) under the asset protection scheme or a qualifying scheme.

— The information or documents must be provided or produced at such times, and at such place, as the Treasury may specify in the notice.

— The Treasury may require the information to be provided in such form as they may reasonably require.

— A requirement imposed on a person as a result of this section is enforceable by an injunction or, in Scotland, by an order for specific performance under s 45 of the Court of Session Act 1988.

— The Treasury may specify a scheme in an order under sub-s (3) of this section only if it appears to them that the purpose of the scheme corresponds to, or is connected with, the purpose of the asset protection scheme.

Section 20 (Services forming part of recognised inter-bank payment systems): inserts the Banking Act 2009, s 206A.

Section 21 (Minor amendments of provision made by Banking Act 2009): inserts the Banking Act 2009, s 48A, amends ss 55, 56, 84, 145, 153 of that Act, and amends the Financial Services and Markets Act 2000, s 219.

Section 22 (Administration of court funds by Director of Savings): provides that the Director of Savings ("the Director") may discharge a relevant function if appointed by the Accountant General under court funds rules to do so. A "relevant function" is a function of the Accountant General of the Senior Courts ("the Accountant General") under court funds rules (ie, rules under s 38(7) of the Administration of Justice Act 1982). The functions of the Director that are within section 69(1)(a) of the Deregulation and Contracting Out Act 1994 (contracting out of statutory functions) include any power of the Director, conferred under court funds rules, to discharge a relevant function.

Section 23 (Orders or regulations): makes provision with regard to orders and regulations made by the Treasury or the Secretary of State under this Act.

Section 24 (Minor and consequential amendments): provides for the minor and consequential amendments contained in Sch 2 to this Act. It also provides that the Treasury or the Secretary of State may by order make such other provision amending, repealing or revoking any enactment as they consider necessary or expedient in consequence of any provision made by this Act.

Section 25 (Extent): provides that this Act applies to the UK.

Section 26 (Commencement): provides for the commencement of this Act. Certain provisions came into force on 8 April 2010 and others on 8 June 2010. The remainder come into force on such day or days as the Treasury or the Secretary of State may by Order appoint.

Section 27 (Short title): provides that this Act may be cited as the Financial Services Act 2010.

Schedule 1 (Further Provision about the Consumer Financial Education Body): inserts the Financial Services and Markets Act 2000, Sch 1A. It also makes further provision with regard to rules under para 12 of the inserted Sch 1A (ie, provision with regard to taking representations and publishing a draft etc).

Schedule 2 (Minor and Consequential Amendments): contains various amendments to the Financial Services and Markets Act 2000, the Banking Act 2009, the Consumer Credit Act 1974, the Contracting Out (Functions Relating to National Savings) Order 1998, SI 1998/1449, and the Financial Services and Markets Act 2000 (Markets in Financial Instruments) (Modification of Powers) Regulations 2006, SI 2006/2975.

PART 10
MISCELLANEOUS OTHER STATUTORY INSTRUMENTS

INTRODUCTORY NOTE

The statutory instruments contained in this Part were made under the legislation included in Part 9.

INSOLVENCY RULES 1986

(SI 1986/1925)

NOTES

Made: 10 November 1986.

Authority: Insolvency Act 1986, ss 411, 412.

Commencement: These rules, as originally made, came into force on 29 December 1986; see r 0.1.

These Rules are reproduced as amended by: the Insolvency (Amendment) Rules 1987, SI 1987/1919; the Insolvency (Amendment) Rules 1989, SI 1989/397; the Insolvency (Amendment) Rules 1991, SI 1991/495; the Insolvency (Amendment) Rules 1993, SI 1993/602; the Insolvency (Amendment) Rules 1995, SI 1995/586; the Bank of England Act 1998 (Consequential Amendments of Subordinate Legislation) Order 1998, SI 1998/1129; the Insolvency (Amendment) (No 2) Rules 1999, SI 1999/1022; the Insolvency (Amendment) Rules 2001, SI 2001/763; the Financial Services and Markets Act 2000 (Consequential Amendments and Repeals) Order 2002, SI 2001/3649; the Insolvency (Amendment) Rules 2002, SI 2002/1307; the Insolvency (Amendment) (No 2) Rules 2002, SI 2002/2712; the Insolvency (Amendment) Rules 2003, SI 2003/1730; the Insolvency (Amendment) Rules 2004, SI 2004/584; the Insolvency (Amendment) Rules 2005, SI 2005/527; the Insolvency (Amendment) Rules 2006, SI 2006/1272; the Mental Capacity Act 2005 (Transitional and Consequential Provisions) Order 2007, SI 2007/1898; the Insolvency (Amendment) Rules 2007, SI 2007/1974; the Secretaries of State for Children, Schools and Families, for Innovation, Universities and Skills and for Business, Enterprise and Regulatory Reform Order 2007, SI 2007/3224; the Insolvency (Amendment) Rules 2008, SI 2008/737; the Insolvency (Amendment) Rules 2009, SI 2009/642; the Insolvency (Amendment) (No 2) Rules 2009, SI 2009/2472; the Secretary of State for Business, Innovation and Skills Order 2009, SI 2009/2748; the Insolvency (Amendment) Rules 2010, SI 2010/686.

Application of these Rules to LLPs: Limited liability partnerships: by the Limited Liability Partnerships Regulations 2001, SI 2001/1090, reg 10, Sch 6, Pt II, these Rules apply, with modifications, to limited liability partnerships (see **[10.829]**).

Other applications and miscellaneous:

As to the application of these rules to Insurers, see the Insurers (Winding Up) Rules 2001 SI 2001/3635, the Insurers (Reorganisation and Winding Up) Regulations 2004, SI 2004/353, and the Financial Services and Markets Act 2000 (Administration Orders Relating to Insurers) Order 2010, SI 2010/3023; as to their application to EEA credit institutions, see the Credit Institutions (Reorganisation and Winding up) Regulations 2004, SI 2004/1045; as to their application to railway administration proceedings, see the Railway Administration Order Rules 2001, SI 2001/3352; as to their application to EGTCs, see the European Grouping of Territorial Cooperation Regulations 2007, SI 2007/1949; as to their application to banks, see the Bank Insolvency (England and Wales) Rules 2009, SI 2009/356, and the Bank Administration (England and Wales) Rules 2009, SI 2009/357; as to their application to building societies, see the Building Society Special Administration (England and Wales) Rules 2010, SI 2010/2580.

Note that the Energy Administration Rules 2005, SI 2005/2483 and the Water Industry (Special Administration) Rules 2009, SI 2009/2477 are based upon the provisions of these Rules but are stand alone sets of rules applicable only to energy and water companies respectively.

Modification: these Rules, except rr 4.12, 4.215, 7.53, 7.54, 7.57, 9.4 (and certain other provisions that are outside the scope of this work), are modified by the Solicitors' Incorporated Practices Order 1991, SI 1991/2684, so that any reference to a solicitor or solicitors shall be construed as including a reference to a recognised body, meaning a body corporate recognised by the Council of the Law Society under the Administration of Justice Act 1985, s 9, and related expressions are to be construed accordingly.

Official receiver: as to the contracting out of certain functions of the Official receiver conferred by or under these rules, see the Contracting Out (Functions of the Official Receiver) Order 1995, SI 1995/1386 at **[10.755]**.

ARRANGEMENT OF RULES

THE FIRST GROUP OF PARTS
COMPANY INSOLVENCY; COMPANIES WINDING UP

INTRODUCTORY PROVISIONS

PART 1
COMPANY VOLUNTARY ARRANGEMENTS

CHAPTER 1
PRELIMINARY

CHAPTER 2
PROPOSAL BY DIRECTORS

CHAPTER 11
THE ADMINISTRATOR

CHAPTER 12
ENDING ADMINISTRATION

CHAPTER 13
REPLACING ADMINISTRATOR

Part 10   **Miscellaneous other SIs**

CHAPTER 6
STATEMENT OF AFFAIRS AND OTHER INFORMATION

CHAPTER 7
INFORMATION TO CREDITORS AND CONTRIBUTORIES

CHAPTER 8
MEETINGS OF CREDITORS AND CONTRIBUTORIES

Section A: Rules of General Application

Section B: Winding Up of Recognised Banks, etc

CHAPTER 9
PROOF OF DEBTS IN A LIQUIDATION

Section A: Procedure for Proving

Section B: Quantification of Claim

CHAPTER 10
SECURED CREDITORS

CHAPTER 11
THE LIQUIDATOR

Section A: Appointment and Associated Formalities

Section B: Resignation and Removal; Vacation of Office

Part 10   Miscellaneous other SIs

CHAPTER 13
THE LIQUIDATION COMMITTEE WHERE WINDING UP FOLLOWS IMMEDIATELY ON ADMINISTRATION

(No CVL Application)

CHAPTER 14
COLLECTION AND DISTRIBUTION OF COMPANY'S ASSETS BY LIQUIDATOR

CHAPTER 15
DISCLAIMER

CHAPTER 16
SETTLEMENT OF LIST OF CONTRIBUTORIES

(No CVL Application)

CHAPTER 17
CALLS

(No CVL Application)

Part 10   Miscellaneous other SIs

Part 10 Miscellaneous other SIs

INTRODUCTORY PROVISIONS

[10.1]
0.1 Citation and commencement

These Rules may be cited as the Insolvency Rules 1986 and shall come into force on 29th December 1986.

[10.2]
[0.2 Construction and interpretation

(1) In these Rules—

"the Act" means the Insolvency Act 1986 (any reference to a numbered section being to a section of that Act);

"the Companies Act" means [the Companies Act 2006];

"CPR" means the Civil Procedure Rules 1998 and "CPR" followed by a Part or rule by number means the Part or rule with that number in those Rules;

"RSC" followed by an Order by number means the Order with that number set out in Schedule 1 to the CPR; and

"the Rules" means the Insolvency Rules 1986.

(2) . . .

(3) Subject to [paragraph (1)], Part 13 of the Rules has effect for their interpretation and application.]

NOTES

Substituted by the Insolvency (Amendment) (No 2) Rules 1999, SI 1999/1022, r 3, Schedule, para 1, as from 26 April 1999.

Para (1): words in square brackets in the definition "the Companies Act" substituted by the Insolvency (Amendment) (No 2) Rules 2009, SI 2009/2472, rr 3, 4, as from 1 October 2009 (subject to transitional provisions as noted below).

Para (2): revoked by the Insolvency (Amendment) Rules 2010, SI 2010/686, r 2, Sch 1, para 2(1), (2), as from 6 April 2010, subject to transitional provisions in Sch 4, para 1 thereto, as noted to r 1.5 at **[10.7]**.

Para (3): words in square brackets substituted by SI 2010/686, r 2, Sch 1, para 2(1), (3), as from 6 April 2010, subject to transitional provisions in Sch 4, para 1 thereto, as noted to r 1.5 at **[10.7]**.

Transitional provisions: the Insolvency (Amendment) (No 2) Rules 2009, SI 2009/2472, r 2 provides as follows—

"(1) The amendments to the Insolvency Rules 1986 made by these Rules apply as follows.

(2) They apply where, in a company voluntary arrangement, a moratorium comes into force in relation to a company on or after 1st October 2009.

(3) They apply where a company enters administration on or after 1st October 2009, except where—

    (a) it enters administration by virtue of an administration order under paragraph 10 of Schedule B1 to the 1986 Act on an application made before 1st October 2009;

    (b) the administration is immediately preceded by a voluntary liquidation in respect of which the resolution to wind up was passed before 1st October 2009, or

    (c) the administration is immediately preceded by a liquidation on the making of a winding-up order on a petition which was presented before 1st October 2009.

(4) They apply where, in a receivership, a receiver or manager is appointed in respect of a company on or after 1st October 2009.

(5) They apply where a company goes into liquidation upon the passing on or after 1st October 2009 of a resolution to wind up.

(6) They apply where a company goes into voluntary liquidation under paragraph 83 of Schedule B1 to the 1986 Act, except where the preceding administration—

    (a) commenced before 1st October 2009, or

    (b) is an administration which commenced by virtue of an administration order under paragraph 10 of Schedule B1 to the 1986 Act on an application which was made before 1st October 2009.

(7) They apply where a company goes into liquidation on the making of a winding-up order on a petition presented on or after 1st October 2009, except where the liquidation is immediately preceded by—

    (a) an administration under paragraph 10 of Schedule B1 to the 1986 Act where the administration order was made on an application made before 1st October 2009;

    (b) an administration in respect of which the appointment of an administrator under paragraph 14 or 22 of Schedule B1 to the 1986 Act took effect before 1st October 2009, or

    (c) a voluntary liquidation in respect of which the resolution to wind up was passed before 1st October 2009.

(8) In this Rule, "the 1986 Act" means the Insolvency Act 1986.".

[10.3]
0.3 Extent

(1) Parts 1, 2 and 4 of the Rules, and Parts 7 to 13 as they relate to company insolvency, apply in relation to companies which the courts in England and Wales have jurisdiction to wind up.

[(2) Rule 3.1 applies to all receivers to whom Part III of the Act applies, Rule 3.39 and 3.40 apply to all receivers who are not administrative receivers, and the remainder of Part 3 of the Rules applies to administrative receivers appointed otherwise than under section 51 (Scottish Receivership).]

(3) Parts 5 and 6 of the Rules, and Parts 7 to 13 as they relate to individual insolvency, extend to England and Wales only.

NOTES

Para (2): substituted by the Insolvency (Amendment) Rules 2003, SI 2003/1730, r 3, as from 15 September 2003.

THE FIRST GROUP OF PARTS
COMPANY INSOLVENCY; COMPANIES WINDING UP

PART 1
COMPANY VOLUNTARY ARRANGEMENTS

CHAPTER 1
PRELIMINARY

[10.4]
1.1   Scope of this Part; interpretation

(1)   The Rules in this Part apply where, pursuant to Part I of the Act, it is intended to make, and there is made, a proposal to a company and its creditors for a voluntary arrangement, that is to say, a composition in satisfaction of its debts or a scheme of arrangement of its affairs.

(2)   In this Part—
  [(a)   Chapter 2 applies where the proposal for the voluntary arrangement is made by the directors of the company and
    (i)   the company is neither in liquidation nor is [the company in administration]; and
    (ii)   no steps have been taken to obtain a moratorium under Schedule A1 to the Act in connection with the proposal;]
  (b)   Chapter 3 applies where the company is in liquidation or [the company is in administration], and the proposal is made by the liquidator or (as the case may be) the administrator, he in either case being the nominee for the purposes of the proposal;
  [(c)   Chapter 4 applies in the same case as Chapter 3, but where the nominee is not the liquidator or administrator;
  (d)   Chapter 5 applies in all the three cases mentioned in sub-paragraphs (a) to (c) above;
  (e)   Chapters 7 and 8 apply to all voluntary arrangements with or without a moratorium; and
  (f)   Chapter 9 applies where the proposal is made by the directors of an eligible company with a view to obtaining a moratorium.]

(3)   In Chapters 3, 4 and 5, the liquidator or the administrator is referred to as "the responsible insolvency practitioner".

[(4)   In this Part, a reference to an "eligible company" is to a company that is eligible for a moratorium in accordance with paragraph 2 of Schedule A1 to the Act.]

NOTES

Para (2): sub-para (a) substituted, and sub-paras (c)–(f) substituted for original sub-paras (c), (d), by the Insolvency (Amendment) (No 2) Rules 2002, SI 2002/2712, r 3(1), Schedule, Pt 1, para 1, as from 1 January 2003 (subject to transitional provisions as noted below); words in square brackets in sub-paras (a), (b) substituted by the Insolvency (Amendment) Rules 2003, SI 2003/1730, r 4, Sch 1, Pt 1, para 1, as from 15 September 2003 (for transitional provisions and savings see the note preceding r 2.1 at **[10.60]**).

Para (4): added by SI 2002/2712, r 3(1), Schedule, Pt 1, para 1(c), as from 1 January 2003, subject to transitional provisions as noted below.

Transitional provisions: SI 2002/2712, r 3(2) provides as follows (note that by virtue of r 1 "the commencement date" is 1 January 2003)—

  "(2)   The amendments to Part 1 of the principal Rules set out in Part 1 of the Schedule to these Rules do not apply in relation to a voluntary arrangement under Part I of the Act where—
    (a)   a proposal is made by the directors of a company and before the commencement date the intended nominee has endorsed a copy of the written notice of the proposal under Rule 1.4(3);
    (b)   a proposal is made by the liquidator or the administrator (acting as the nominee) and before the commencement date the liquidator or administrator (as the case may be) has sent out a notice summoning the meetings under section 3 of the Act as required by Rule 1.11; or
    (c)   a proposal is made by the liquidator or the administrator of a company (not acting as the nominee) and before the commencement date the intended nominee has endorsed a copy of the written notice of the proposal under Rule 1.12(2);

  and Part 1 of the principal Rules without the amendments made in Part 1 of the Schedule to these Rules shall continue to apply in such cases.".

CHAPTER 2
PROPOSAL BY DIRECTORS

1.2   *(Revoked by the Insolvency (Amendment) Rules 2010, SI 2010/686, r 5, as from 6 April 2010, subject to transitional provisions in Sch 4, para 2 thereto, as noted to r 1.31 at **[10.34]**.)*

[10.5]
1.3   Contents of proposal

(1)   The directors' proposal shall provide a short explanation why, in their opinion, a voluntary arrangement under Part I of the Act is desirable, and give reasons why the company's creditors may be expected to concur with such an arrangement.

(2)   The following matters shall be stated, or otherwise dealt with, in the directors' proposal—

    (a)   the following matters, so far as within the directors' immediate knowledge—

       (i)   the company's assets, with an estimate of their respective values,

       (ii)   the extent (if any) to which the assets are charged in favour of creditors,

       (iii)   the extent (if any) to which particular assets are to be excluded from the voluntary arrangement;

    (b)   particulars of any property, other than assets of the company itself, which is proposed to be included in the arrangement, the source of such property and the terms on which it is to be made available for inclusion;

    (c)   the nature and amount of the company's liabilities (so far as within the directors' immediate knowledge), the manner in which they are proposed to be met, modified, postponed or otherwise dealt with by means of the arrangement, and (in particular)—

       (i)   how it is proposed to deal with preferential creditors (defined in section 4(7)) and creditors who are, or claim to be, secured,

       (ii)   how persons connected with the company (being creditors) are proposed to be treated under the arrangement, and

       (iii)   where there are, to the directors' knowledge, any circumstances giving rise to the possibility, in the event that the company should go into liquidation, of claims under—

          section 238 (transactions at an undervalue),

          section 239 (preferences),

          section 244 (extortionate credit transactions), or

          section 245 (floating charges invalid);

          and, where any such circumstances are present, whether, and if so how, it is proposed under the voluntary arrangement to make provision for wholly or partly indemnifying the company in respect of such claims;

   [(ca)   an estimate (to the best of the directors' knowledge and belief and subject to paragraph (4)) of—

       (i)   the value of the prescribed part, should the company go into liquidation if the proposal for the voluntary arrangement is not accepted, whether or not section 176A is to be disapplied; and

       (ii)   the value of the company's net property on the date that the estimate is made;]

    (d)   whether any, and if so what, guarantees have been given of the company's debts by other persons, specifying which (if any) of the guarantors are persons connected with the company;

    (e)   the proposed duration of the voluntary arrangement;

    (f)   the proposed dates of distributions to creditors, with estimates of their amounts;

   [(fa)   How it is proposed to deal with the claim of any person who is bound by the arrangement by virtue of section 5(2)(b)(ii);]

    (g)   the amount proposed to be paid to the nominee (as such) by way of remuneration and expenses;

    (h)   the manner in which it is proposed that the supervisor of the arrangement should be remunerated, and his expenses defrayed;

    (j)   whether, for the purposes of the arrangement, any guarantees are to be offered by directors, or other persons, and whether (if so) any security is to be given or sought;

    (k)   the manner in which funds held for the purposes of the arrangement are to be banked, invested or otherwise dealt with pending distribution to creditors;

    (l)   the manner in which funds held for the purpose of payment to creditors, and not so paid on the termination of the arrangement, are to be dealt with;

    (m)   the manner in which the business of the company is proposed to be conducted during the course of the arrangement;

    (n)   details of any further credit facilities which it is intended to arrange for the company, and how the debts so arising are to be paid;

    (o)   the functions which are to be undertaken by the supervisor of the arrangement;   . . .

    [(p)   the name, address and qualification of the person proposed as supervisor of the voluntary arrangement, and confirmation that he is either qualified to act as an insolvency practitioner in relation to the company or is an authorised person in relation to the company;   . . .]

    [(q)   whether the EC Regulation will apply and, if so, whether the proceedings will be main proceedings, secondary proceedings or territorial proceedings][; and

    (r)   such other matters (if any) as the directors consider appropriate for ensuring that members and creditors are enabled to reach an informed decision on the proposal.]

(3)   With the agreement in writing of the nominee, the directors' proposal may be amended at any time up to delivery of the [nominee's] report to the court under section 2(2).

Part 10   Miscellaneous other SIs

[(4) Nothing in paragraph (2)(ca) is to be taken as requiring the estimate referred to in that paragraph to include any information, the disclosure of which could seriously prejudice the commercial interests of the company. If such information is excluded from the calculation the estimate shall be accompanied by a statement to that effect.]

NOTES

Para (2): sub-para (ca) inserted by the Insolvency (Amendment) Rules 2003, SI 2003/1730, r 4, Sch 1, Pt 1, para 2(1), as from 15 September 2003 (for transitional provisions and savings see the note preceding r 2.1 at **[10.60]**); sub-para (fa) inserted, and sub-para (p) substituted, by the Insolvency (Amendment) (No 2) Rules 2002, SI 2002/2712, r 3(1), Schedule, Pt 1, para 2, as from 1 January 2003 (subject to transitional provisions as noted to r 1.1 at **[10.4]**); word omitted from sub-para (o) revoked, and sub-para (q) added, by the Insolvency (Amendment) Rules 2002, SI 2002/1307, rr 3, 4(2), as from 31 May 2002, with savings in relation to anything done under, or for the purposes of, this provision before that date; word omitted from sub-para (p) revoked, and sub-para (r) and word "and" immediately preceding it added, by the Insolvency (Amendment) Rules 2010, SI 2010/686, r 2, Sch 1, para 3(1), (2), as from 6 April 2010, where a copy of the proposal for a company voluntary arrangement is delivered to the intended nominee on or after that date (see Sch 4, para 3(1) to the 2010 Rules).

Para (3): word in square brackets substituted by SI 2010/686, r 2, Sch 1, para 3(1), (3), as from 6 April 2010, subject to transitional provisions in Sch 4, para 1 thereto, as noted to r 1.5 at **[10.7]**.

Para (4): added by SI 2003/1730, r 4, Sch 1, Pt 1, para 2(2), as from 15 September 2003 (for transitional provisions and savings see the note preceding r 2.1 at **[10.60]**).

EC Regulation: ie, Council Regulation 1346/2000/EC on insolvency proceedings.

[10.6]
1.4 Notice to intended nominee

(1) The directors shall give to the intended nominee written notice of their proposal.

(2) The notice, accompanied by a copy of the proposal, shall be delivered either to the nominee himself, or to a person authorised to take delivery of documents on his behalf.

(3) If the intended nominee agrees to act, he shall cause a copy of the notice to be endorsed to the effect that it has been received by him on a specified date; and the period of 28 days referred to in section 2(2) then runs from that date.

(4) The copy of the notice so endorsed shall be returned by the nominee [as soon as reasonably practicable] to the directors at an address specified by them in the notice for that purpose.

NOTES

Para (4): words in square brackets substituted by the Insolvency (Amendment) Rules 2009, SI 2009/642, r 5, as from 6 April 2009, subject to transitional provisions in r 3 thereof, as noted below.

Transitional provisions: SI 2009/642, r 3 (as amended by the Insolvency (Amendment) Rules 2010, SI 2010/686, r 8, as from 6 April 2010) provides as follows:

"3 Transitional provisions
(1) Subject to [paragraphs (1A) and (2)], the amendments made by Rules 5 to 31, 33 to 46, 62, 71, 73, 76 and 78 of these Rules to the principal Rules shall not apply, and the provisions of the principal Rules as unamended by these Rules shall continue to apply, where before 6th April 2009—
    (a)   in relation to a company—
        (i)   a moratorium under a company voluntary arrangement comes into force;
        (ii)   the company enters administration;
        (iii) a receiver or manager is appointed;
        (iv) a resolution for a voluntary winding up is passed; or
        (v)   a winding up petition is presented to the court; and
    (b)   in relation to an individual, a bankruptcy petition is presented to the court.
[(1A) On and after 6th April 2010, the amendment made by Rule 62 of these Rules to the principal Rules applies in respect of an advertisement appearing in the Gazette or a newspaper after that date where before 6th April 2009 the conditions contained in paragraph (1)(a) or (b) of this Rule were met.]
(2) In the case of a statutory demand, the amendments made by Rules 33, 34 and 35 of these Rules to Rules 6.3(3), 6.4(1) and 6.11(8) of the principal Rules shall not apply, and the provisions of the principal Rules as unamended by these Rules shall continue to apply where the demand is served on the debtor before 6th April 2009.".

[10.7]
1.5 Statement of affairs

(1) The directors shall, [at the same time as the] proposal is delivered to the nominee, . . . , deliver to him a statement of the company's affairs.

(2) The statement shall comprise the following particulars (supplementing or amplifying, so far as is necessary for clarifying the state of the company's affairs, those already given in the directors' proposal)—
    (a)   a list of the company's assets, divided into such categories as are appropriate for easy identification, with estimated values assigned to each category;
    (b)   in the case of any property on which a claim against the company is wholly or partly secured, particulars of the claim and its amount, and of how and when the security was created;
    (c)   the names and addresses of the company's preferential creditors (defined in section 4(7)), with the amounts of their respective claims;
    (d)   the names and addresses of the company's unsecured creditors, with the amounts of their respective claims;

(e)   particulars of any debts owed by or to the company to or by persons connected with it;

(f)   the names and addresses of the company's members, with details of their respective shareholdings;

(g)   such other particulars (if any) as the nominee may in writing require to be furnished for the purposes of making his report to the court on the directors' proposal.

(3)   The statement of affairs shall be made up to a date not earlier than 2 weeks before the date of the notice to the nominee under Rule 1.4.

However, the nominee may allow an extension of that period to the nearest practicable date (not earlier than 2 months before the date of the notice under Rule 1.4); and if he does so, he shall give his reasons in his report to the court on the directors' proposal.

[(4)   The statement must be verified by a statement of truth made by at least one director.]

NOTES

Para (1): words in square brackets substituted, and words omitted revoked, by the Insolvency (Amendment) Rules 2010, SI 2010/686, r 2, Sch 1, para 4(1), (2), as from 6 April 2010, subject to transitional provisions in Sch 4, para 1 thereto, as noted below.

Para (4): substituted by SI 2010/686, r 2, Sch 1, para 4(1), (3), as from 6 April 2010, subject to transitional provisions in Sch 4, para 1 thereto, as noted below.

Transitional provisions: SI 2010/686, Sch 4, para 1 provides as follows:

"**1   General**

(1)   The amendments to the 1986 Rules made by these Rules apply as provided in sub-paragraphs (2) to (10) except where any of paragraphs 2 to 6 provides differently.

(2)   They apply where a person agrees to act as nominee in respect of a proposal for a company voluntary arrangement on or after 6th April 2010.

(3)   They apply where a company enters administration on or after 6th April 2010, except where—

(a)   it enters administration by virtue of an administration order under paragraph 10 of Schedule B1 to the Act on an application made before 6th April 2010;

(b)   the administration is immediately preceded by a voluntary liquidation in respect of which the resolution to wind up was passed before 6th April 2010, or

(c)   the administration is immediately preceded by a liquidation on the making of a winding-up order on a petition which was presented before 6th April 2010.

(4)   They apply where, in a receivership, a receiver or manager is appointed in respect of a company on or after 6th April 2010.

(5)   They apply where a company goes into liquidation upon the passing on or after 6th April 2010 of a resolution to wind up.

(6)   They apply where a company goes into voluntary liquidation under paragraph 83 of Schedule B1 to the Act, except where the preceding administration—

(a)   commenced before 6th April 2010, or

(b)   is an administration which commenced by virtue of an administration order under paragraph 10 of Schedule B1 to the Act on an application which was made before 6th April 2010.

(7)   They apply where a company goes into liquidation on the making of a winding-up order on a petition presented on or after 6th April 2010, except where the liquidation is immediately preceded by—

(a)   an administration under paragraph 10 of Schedule B1 to the Act where the administration order was made on an application made before 6th April 2010;

(b)   an administration in respect of which the appointment of an administrator under paragraph 14 or 22 of Schedule B1 to the Act took effect before 6th April 2010, or

(c)   a voluntary liquidation in respect of which the resolution to wind up was passed before 6th April 2010.

(8)   They apply where a person agrees to act as nominee in respect of a proposal for an individual voluntary arrangement on or after 6th April 2010.

(9)   They apply where a debt relief order is made on or after 6th April 2010.

(10)   They apply where a bankruptcy order is made on a petition presented on or after 6th April 2010.".

Note also the Insolvency (Amendment) (No 2) Rules 2010, SI 2010/734, r 13 which provides as follows—

"13.   Where a company goes into voluntary liquidation under paragraph 83 of Schedule B1 to the Act in a case in which article 12(1) and (2) of the Legislative Reform (Insolvency) (Miscellaneous Provisions) Order 2010 causes section 104A of the Act and the amendments to section 105 of the Act to apply, the amendments to the Insolvency Rules 1986 made by the Insolvency (Amendment) Rules 2010 apply to the extent necessary to give effect to section 104A and the amendments to section 105 notwithstanding that by virtue of paragraph 1(6)(a) or (b) of Schedule 4 to the Insolvency (Amendment) Rules 2010 those amendments to the Insolvency Rules 1986 would otherwise not apply.".

[10.8]
1.6   Additional disclosure for assistance of nominee

(1)   If it appears to the nominee that he cannot properly prepare his report on the basis of information in the directors' proposal and statement of affairs, he may call on the directors to provide him with—

(a)   further and better particulars as to the circumstances in which, and the reasons why, the company is insolvent or (as the case may be) threatened with insolvency;

(b)   particulars of any previous proposals which have been made in respect of the company under Part I of the Act;

(c)   any further information with respect to the company's affairs which the nominee thinks necessary for the purposes of his report.

(2)   The nominee may call on the directors to inform him, with respect to any person who is, or at any time in the 2 years preceding the notice under Rule 1.4 has been, a director or officer of the company, whether and in what circumstances (in those 2 years or previously) that person—

(a)   has been concerned in the affairs of any other company (whether or not incorporated in England and Wales) which has become insolvent, or

(b)   has himself been adjudged bankrupt or entered into an arrangement with his creditors.

(3)   For the purpose of enabling the nominee to consider their proposal and prepare his report on it, the directors must give [the nominee such access to the company's accounts and records as the nominee may require].

NOTES

Para (3): words in square brackets substituted by the Insolvency (Amendment) Rules 2010, SI 2010/686, r 2, Sch 1, para 5, as from 6 April 2010, subject to transitional provisions in Sch 4, para 1 thereto, as noted to r 1.5 at **[10.7]**.

[10.9]
1.7   Nominee's report on the proposal

(1)   With his report to the court under section 2 the nominee shall deliver—

(a)   a copy of the directors' proposal (with amendments, if any, authorised under Rule 1.3(3)); and

(b)   a copy or summary of the company's statement of affairs.

(2)   If the nominee makes known his opinion [that the directors' proposal has a reasonable prospect of being approved and implemented and] that meetings of the company and its creditors should be summoned under section 3, his report shall have annexed to it his comments on the proposal.

If his opinion is otherwise, he shall give his reasons for that opinion.

(3)   The court shall cause the nominee's report to be endorsed with the date on which it is filed in court. Any director, member or creditor of the company is entitled, at all reasonable times on any business day, to inspect the file.

(4)   The nominee shall send a copy of his report, and of his comments (if any), to the company.

NOTES

Para (2): words in square brackets inserted by the Insolvency (Amendment) (No 2) Rules 2002, SI 2002/2712, r 3(1), Schedule, Pt 1, para 3, as from 1 January 2003, subject to transitional provisions as noted to r 1.1 at **[10.4]**.

[10.10]
[1.8   Replacement of nominee

(1)   Where a person other than the nominee intends to apply to the court under section 2(4) for the nominee to be replaced, (except in any case where the nominee has died) he shall give to the nominee at least [5 business] days' notice of his application.

(2)   Where the nominee intends to apply to the court under section 2(4) of the Act to be replaced, he shall give at least [5 business] days' notice of his application to the person intending to make the proposal.

(3)   No appointment of a replacement nominee shall be made by the court unless there is filed in court a statement by the replacement nominee—

(a)   indicating his consent to act, and

(b)   that he is qualified to act as an insolvency practitioner in relation to the company or is an authorised person in relation to the company.]

NOTES

Substituted by the Insolvency (Amendment) (No 2) Rules 2002, SI 2002/2712, r 3(1), Schedule, Pt 1, para 4, as from 1 January 2003, subject to transitional provisions as noted to r 1.1 at **[10.4]**.

Paras (1), (2): words in square brackets substituted by the Insolvency (Amendment) Rules 2010, SI 2010/686, r 2, Sch 1, para 6, as from 6 April 2010, subject to transitional provisions in Sch 4, para 1 thereto, as noted to r 1.5 at **[10.7]**.

See Form 1.8 at **[10.673]**.

[10.11]
1.9   Summoning of meetings under s 3

(1)   If in his report the nominee states that in his opinion meetings of the company and its creditors should be summoned to consider the directors' proposal, the date on which the meetings are to be held shall be not . . . more than 28, days from that on which the nominee's report is filed in court under Rule 1.7.

(2)   Notices calling the meetings shall be sent by the nominee, at least 14 days before the day fixed for them to be held—

(a)   in the case of the creditors' meeting, to all the creditors specified in the statement of affairs, and any other creditors of the company of [whose address the nominee] is otherwise aware; and

(b)   in the case of the meeting of members of the company, to all persons who are, to the best of the nominee's belief, members of it.

(3)   Each notice sent under this Rule shall specify the court to which the nominee's report under section 2 has been delivered and shall state the effect of [Rule 1.19(2)], (3) and (4) (requisite majorities (creditors)); and with each notice there shall be sent—
  (a)   a copy of the directors' proposal;
  (b)   a copy of the statement of affairs or, if the nominee thinks fit, a summary of it (the summary to include a list of creditors and the amount of their debts); and
  (c)   the nominee's comments on the proposal.

NOTES

Words omitted revoked, and words in square brackets substituted, by the Insolvency (Amendment) Rules 2010, SI 2010/686, r 2, Sch 1, para 7, as from 6 April 2010, subject to transitional provisions in Sch 4, para 1 thereto, as noted to r 1.5 at **[10.7]**.

CHAPTER 3
PROPOSAL BY ADMINISTRATOR OR LIQUIDATOR (HIMSELF THE NOMINEE)

[10.12]
1.10   Preparation of proposal

[(1)   The responsible insolvency practitioner's proposal must specify all such matters as under Rule 1.3 (subject to paragraph (3) below) in Chapter 2 the directors of the company would be required to include in a proposal by them, with the addition, where the company is in administration or liquidation, of the nature and amount of its preferential creditors.]

(2)   Where the company is being wound up by the court, the insolvency practitioner shall give notice of the proposal to the official receiver.

[(3)   The administrator or liquidator shall include, in place of the estimate required by Rule 1.3(2)(ca), a statement which contains—
  (a)   to the best of the administrator or liquidator's knowledge and belief—
      (i)   an estimate of the value of the prescribed part (whether or not he proposes to make an application to court under section 176A(5) or section 176A(3) applies), and
      (ii)   an estimate of the value of the company's net property, and
  (b)   whether, and, if so, why, the administrator or liquidator proposes to make an application to court under section 176A(5).

(4)   Nothing in this Rule is to be taken as requiring any such estimate to include any information, the disclosure of which could seriously prejudice the commercial interests of the company. If such information is excluded from the calculation the estimate shall be accompanied by a statement to that effect.]

NOTES

Para (1): substituted by the Insolvency (Amendment) Rules 2010, SI 2010/686, r 2, Sch 1, para 8, as from 6 April 2010, where a copy of the proposal for a company voluntary arrangement is delivered to the intended nominee on or after that date (see Sch 4, para 3(1) to the 2010 Rules).

Paras (3), (4): added by the Insolvency (Amendment) Rules 2003, SI 2003/1730, r 4, Sch 1, Pt 1, para 3(b), as from 15 September 2003 (for transitional provisions and savings see the note preceding r 2.1 at **[10.60]**).

[10.13]
1.11   Summoning of meetings under s 3

(1)   The responsible insolvency practitioner shall fix a venue for the creditors' meeting and the company meeting, and give at least 14 days' notice of the meetings—
  (a)   in the case of the creditors' meeting, to all the creditors specified in the company's statement of affairs, and to any other creditors of [whose address the insolvency practitioner is otherwise] aware; and
  (b)   in the case of the company meeting, to all persons who are, to the best of his belief, members of the company.

(2)   Each notice sent out under this Rule shall state the effect of Rule 1.19(1), (3) and (4) (requisite majorities (creditors)); and with it there shall be sent—
  (a)   a copy of the responsible insolvency practitioner's proposal, and
  (b)   a copy of the statement of affairs or, if he thinks fit, a summary of it (the summary to include a list of creditors and the amounts of their debts).

NOTES

Para (1): words in square brackets substituted by the Insolvency (Amendment) Rules 2010, SI 2010/686, r 2, Sch 1, para 9, as from 6 April 2010, subject to transitional provisions in Sch 4, para 1 thereto, as noted to r 1.5 at **[10.7]**.

Part 10   Miscellaneous other SIs

CHAPTER 4

PROPOSAL BY ADMINISTRATOR OR LIQUIDATOR

(ANOTHER INSOLVENCY PRACTITIONER THE NOMINEE)

[10.14]

1.12   Preparation of proposal and notice to nominee

(1)   The responsible insolvency practitioner shall give notice to the intended nominee, and prepare his proposal for a voluntary arrangement, in the same manner as is required of the directors, in the case of a proposal by them, under Chapter 2.

(2)   Rule 1.2 applies to the responsible insolvency practitioner as it applies to the directors; and Rule 1.4 applies as regards the action to be taken by the nominee.

(3)   The content of the proposal shall be as required by Rule 1.3 [(and, where relevant, Rule 1.10)], reading references to the directors as referring to the responsible insolvency practitioner.

(4)   Rule 1.6 applies in respect of the information to be furnished to the nominee, reading references to the directors as referring to the responsible insolvency practitioner.

(5)   With the proposal the responsible insolvency practitioner shall provide a copy of the company's statement of affairs.

(6)   Where the company is being wound up by the court, the responsible insolvency practitioner shall send a copy of the proposal to the official receiver, accompanied by the name and address of the insolvency practitioner [or authorised person] who has agreed to act as nominee.

(7)   Rules 1.7 to 1.9 apply as regards a proposal under this Chapter as they apply to a proposal under Chapter 2.

NOTES

Para (3): words in square brackets inserted by the Insolvency (Amendment) Rules 1987, SI 1987/1919, r 3(1), Schedule, Pt 1, para 4, as from 11 January 1988.

Para (6): words in square brackets added by the Insolvency (Amendment) (No 2) Rules 2002, SI 2002/2712, r 3(1), Schedule, Pt 1, para 5, as from 1 January 2003, subject to transitional provisions as noted to r 1.1 at **[10.4]**.

CHAPTER 5

PROCEEDINGS ON A PROPOSAL MADE BY THE DIRECTORS, OR BY THE ADMINISTRATOR,

OR BY THE LIQUIDATOR

Section A: Meetings of Company's Creditors and Members

[10.15]

[1.13   Summoning of meetings

(1)   Subject as follows, in fixing the venue for the creditors' meeting and the company meeting, [the nominee must] have regard primarily to the convenience of the creditors.

(2)   Meetings shall in each case be summoned for commencement between 10.00 and 16.00 hours on a business day.

(3)   The meetings may be held on the same day or on different days. If held on the same day, the meetings shall be held in the same place, but in either case the creditors' meeting shall be fixed for a time in advance of the company meeting.

(4)   Where the meetings are not held on the same day, they shall be held within [5 business] days of each other.

(5)   With every notice summoning either meeting there shall be sent out forms of proxy.]

NOTES

Substituted by the Insolvency (Amendment) Rules 2003, SI 2003/1730, r 4, Sch 1, Pt 1, para 4, as from 15 September 2003 (for transitional provisions and savings see the note preceding r 2.1 at **[10.60]**).

Paras (1), (4): words in square brackets substituted by the Insolvency (Amendment) Rules 2010, SI 2010/686, r 2, Sch 1, para 10, as from 6 April 2010, subject to transitional provisions in Sch 4, para 1 thereto, as noted to r 1.5 at **[10.7]**.

See Form 8.1 at **[10.673]**.

[10.16]

1.14   The chairman at meetings

(1)   Subject as follows, at both the creditors' meeting and the company meeting, and at any combined meeting, the [nominee must] be chairman.

(2)   If for any reason he is unable to attend, he may nominate another person to act as chairman in his place; but a person so nominated must be . . . —

   [(a)   a person qualified to act as an insolvency practitioner in relation to the company;

   (b)   an authorised person in relation to the company; or

   (c)   an employee of the [nominee] or his firm who is experienced in insolvency matters.]

NOTES

Para (1): words in square brackets substituted by the Insolvency (Amendment) Rules 2010, SI 2010/686, r 2, Sch 1, para 11(1), (2), as from 6 April 2010, subject to transitional provisions in Sch 4, para 1 thereto, as noted to r 1.5 at **[10.7]**.

Para (2): word omitted revoked, and sub-paras (a)–(c) substituted for original sub-paras (a), (b), by the Insolvency (Amendment) (No 2) Rules 2002, SI 2002/2712, r 3(1), Schedule, Pt 1, para 7, as from 1 January 2003, subject to transitional provisions as noted to r 1.1 at **[10.4]**; word in square brackets in sub-para (c) substituted by SI 2010/686, r 2, Sch 1, para 11(1), (3), as from 6 April 2010, subject to transitional provisions in Sch 4, para 1 thereto, as noted to r 1.5 at **[10.7]**.

[10.17]
1.15   The chairman as proxy-holder

The chairman shall not by virtue of any proxy held by him vote to increase or reduce the amount of the remuneration or expenses of the nominee or the supervisor of the proposed arrangement, unless the proxy specifically directs him to vote in that way.

[10.18]
1.16   Attendance by company officers

(1)   At least 14 days' notice to attend the meetings shall be given by the [nominee]—
   (a)   to all directors of the company, and
   (b)   to any persons in whose case the [nominee] thinks that their presence is required as being officers of the company, or as having been directors or officers of it at any time in the 2 years immediately preceding the date of the notice.

(2)   The chairman may, if he thinks fit, exclude any present or former director or officer from attendance at a meeting, either completely or for any part of it; and this applies whether or not a notice under this Rule has been sent to the person excluded.

NOTES

Para (1): word in square brackets substituted by the Insolvency (Amendment) Rules 2010, SI 2010/686, r 2, Sch 1, para 12, as from 6 April 2010, subject to transitional provisions in Sch 4, para 1 thereto, as noted to r 1.5 at **[10.7]**.

Section B: Voting Rights and Majorities

[10.19]
[1.17   Entitlement to vote (creditors)

(1)   Subject as follows, every creditor who has notice of the creditors' meeting is entitled to vote at the meeting or any adjournment of it.

(2)   Votes are calculated according to the amount of the creditor's debt as at the date of the meeting or, where the company is being wound up or is [in administration], the date of its going into liquidation or (as the case may be) [when the company entered administration].

(3)   A creditor may vote in respect of a debt for an unliquidated amount or any debt whose value is not ascertained and for the purposes of voting (but not otherwise) his debt shall be valued at £1 unless the chairman agrees to put a higher value on it.]

NOTES

Substituted, together with r 1.17A for original r 1.17, by the Insolvency (Amendment) (No 2) Rules 2002, SI 2002/2712, r 3(1), Schedule, Pt 1, para 8, as from 1 January 2003, subject to transitional provisions as noted to r 1.1 at **[10.4]**.

Para (2): words in square brackets substituted by the Insolvency (Amendment) Rules 2003, SI 2003/1730, r 4, Sch 1, Pt 1, para 5, as from 15 September 2003 (for transitional provisions and savings see the note preceding r 2.1 at **[10.60]**).

[10.20]
[1.17A   Procedure for admission of creditors' claims for voting purposes

(1)   Subject as follows, at any creditors' meeting the chairman shall ascertain the entitlement of persons wishing to vote and shall admit or reject their claims accordingly.

(2)   The chairman may admit or reject a claim in whole or in part.

(3)   The chairman's decision on any matter under this Rule or under paragraph (3) of Rule 1.17 is subject to appeal to the court by any creditor or member of the company.

(4)   If the chairman is in doubt whether a claim should be admitted or rejected, he shall mark it as objected to and allow votes to be cast in respect of it, subject to such votes being subsequently declared invalid if the objection to the claim is sustained.

(5)   If on an appeal the chairman's decision is reversed or varied, or votes are declared invalid, the court may order another meeting to be summoned, or make such order as it thinks just.

The court's power to make an order under this paragraph is exercisable only if it considers that the circumstances giving rise to the appeal give rise to unfair prejudice or material irregularity.

(6)   An application to the court by way of appeal against the chairman's decision shall not be made after the end of the period of 28 days beginning with the first day on which the report required by section 4(6) has been made to the court.

(7)   The chairman is not personally liable for any costs incurred by any person in respect of an appeal under this Rule.]

NOTES
Substituted as noted to r 1.17 at **[10.19]**.

[10.21]
1.18   Voting rights (members)

(1)   Subject as follows, members of the company at their meeting vote according to the rights attaching to their shares respectively in accordance with the articles.

(2)   . . .

(3)   References in this Rule to a person's shares include any other interest which he may have as a member of the company.

NOTES
Para (2): revoked by the Insolvency (Amendment) (No 2) Rules 2002, SI 2002/2712, r 3(1), Schedule, Pt 1, para 9, as from 1 January 2003, subject to transitional provisions as noted to r 1.1 at **[10.4]**.

[10.22]
1.19   Requisite majorities (creditors)

[(1)   Subject to paragraph (2), at the creditors' meeting, a resolution is passed when a majority (in value) of those present and voting in person or by proxy have voted in favour of it.

(2)   A resolution to approve the proposal or a modification is passed when a majority of three-quarters or more (in value) of those present and voting in person or by proxy have voted in favour of it.]

(3)   In the following cases there is to be left out of account a creditor's vote in respect of any claim or part of a claim—
  (a)   where written notice of the claim was not given, either at the meeting or before it, to the chairman or [nominee];
  (b)   where the claim or part is secured;
  (c)   where the claim is in respect of a debt wholly or partly on, or secured by, a current bill of exchange or promissory note, unless the creditor is willing—
      (i)   to treat the liability to him on the bill or note of every person who is liable on it antecedently to the company, and against whom a bankruptcy order has not been made (or in the case of a company, which has not gone into liquidation), as a security in his hands, and
      (ii)   to estimate the value of the security and (for the purpose of entitlement to vote, but not of any distribution under the arrangement) to deduct it from his claim.

(4)   Any resolution is invalid if those voting against it include more than half in value of the creditors, counting in these latter only those—
  (a)   to whom notice of the meeting was sent;
  (b)   whose votes are not be left out of account under paragraph (3); and
  (c)   who are not, to the best of the chairman's belief, persons connected with the company.

(5)   It is for the chairman of the meeting to decide whether under this Rule—
  (a)   a vote is to be left out of account in accordance with paragraph (3), or
  (b)   a person is a connected person for the purposes of paragraph (4)(c);
and in relation to the second of these two cases the chairman is entitled to rely on the information provided by the company's statement of affairs or otherwise in accordance with this Part of the Rules.

(6)   If the chairman uses a proxy contrary to Rule 1.15, his vote with that proxy does not count towards any majority under this Rule.

[(7)   The chairman's decision on any matter under this Rule is subject to appeal to the court by any creditor or member and paragraphs (5) to (7) of Rule 1.17A apply as regards such an appeal.]

NOTES
Paras (1), (2): substituted by the Insolvency (Amendment) Rules 2010, SI 2010/686, r 2, Sch 1, para 13(1), (2), as from 6 April 2010, subject to transitional provisions in Sch 4, para 1 thereto, as noted to r 1.5 at **[10.7]**.
Para (3): word in square brackets substituted by SI 2010/686, r 2, Sch 1, para 13(1), (3), as from 6 April 2010, subject to transitional provisions in Sch 4, para 1 thereto, as noted to r 1.5 at **[10.7]**.
Para (7): substituted by the Insolvency (Amendment) (No 2) Rules 2002, SI 2002/2712, r 3(1), Schedule, Pt 1, para 10, as from 1 January 2003, subject to transitional provisions as noted to r 1.1 at **[10.4]**.

[10.23]
1.20   Requisite majorities (members)

(1)   Subject as follows, and to any express provision made in the articles, at a company meeting any resolution is to be regarded as passed if voted for by more than one-half [in value] of the members present in person or by proxy and voting on the resolution.

[The value of members is determined by reference to the number of votes conferred on each member by the company's articles.]

(2) . . . .

(3) If the chairman uses a proxy contrary to Rule 1.15, his vote with that proxy does not count towards any majority under this Rule.

NOTES

Para (1): words in square brackets inserted by the Insolvency (Amendment) Rules 1987, SI 1987/1919, r 3(1), Schedule, Pt 1, para 5, as from 11 January 1988.

Para (2): revoked by the Insolvency (Amendment) (No 2) Rules 2002, SI 2002/2712, r 3(1), Schedule, Pt 1, para 11, as from 1 January 2003, subject to transitional provisions as noted to r 1.1 at **[10.4]**.

[10.24]
[1.21

(1) If the chairman thinks fit, the creditors' meeting and the company meeting may be held together.

(2) The chairman may, and shall if it is so resolved at the meeting in question, adjourn that meeting for not more than 14 days.

(3) If there are subsequently further adjournments, the final adjournment shall not be to a day later than 14 days after the date on which the meeting in question was originally held.

(4) In the case of a proposal by the directors, if the meetings are adjourned under paragraph (2), notice of the fact shall be given by the nominee [as soon as reasonably practicable] to the court.

[(4A) Once only in the course of a meeting the chairman may, without an adjournment, declare it suspended for any period up to 1 hour.]

(5) If following the final adjournment of the creditors' meeting the proposal (with or without modifications) has not been approved by the creditors, it is deemed rejected.]

NOTES

Substituted by the Insolvency (Amendment) (No 2) Rules 2002, SI 2002/2712, r 3(1), Schedule, Pt 1, para 12, as from 1 January 2003, subject to transitional provisions as noted to r 1.1 at **[10.4]**. Note: the substitution of this rule by SI 2002/2712 did not provide for a new rule name. Prior to its substitution this rule was named "Proceedings to obtain agreement on the proposal".

Para (4): words in square brackets substituted by the Insolvency (Amendment) Rules 2009, SI 2009/642, r 5, as from 6 April 2009, subject to transitional provisions in r 3 thereof, as noted to r 1.4 of these Rules at **[10.6]**.

Para (4A): inserted by the Insolvency (Amendment) Rules 2010, SI 2010/686, r 2, Sch 1, para 14, as from 6 April 2010, subject to transitional provisions in Sch 4, para 1 thereto, as noted to r 1.5 at **[10.7]**.

Section C: Implementation of the Arrangement

[10.25]
1.22 Resolutions to follow approval

[(1) If the voluntary arrangement is approved (with or without modifications) by the creditors' meeting, a resolution [must] be taken by the creditors, where two or more supervisors are appointed, on the question whether acts to be done in connection with the arrangement may be done by any one or more of them, or must be done by all of them.]

(2) . . .

(3) If at either meeting a resolution is moved for the appointment of some person other than the nominee to be supervisor of the arrangement, there must be produced to the chairman, at or before the meeting—

   (a) that person's written consent to act (unless he is present and then and there signifies his consent), and

   (b) his written confirmation that he is qualified to act as an insolvency practitioner in relation to the company [or is an authorised person in relation to the company].

NOTES

Para (1): substituted by the Insolvency (Amendment) (No 2) Rules 2002, SI 2002/2712, r 3(1), Schedule, Pt 1, para 13(a), as from 1 January 2003, subject to transitional provisions as noted to r 1.1 at **[10.4]**; word in square brackets substituted by the Insolvency (Amendment) Rules 2010, SI 2010/686, r 2, Sch 1, para 15, as from 6 April 2010, subject to transitional provisions in Sch 4, para 1 thereto, as noted to r 1.5 at **[10.7]**.

Para (2): revoked by SI 2002/2712, r 3(1), Schedule, Pt 1, para 13(b), as from 1 January 2003, subject to transitional provisions as noted to r 1.1 at **[10.4]**.

Para (3): words in square brackets added by SI 2002/2712, r 3(1), Schedule, Pt 1, para 13(c), as from 1 January 2003, subject to transitional provisions as noted to r 1.1 at **[10.4]**.

[10.26]
[1.22A Notice of order made under section 4A(6)

(1) This Rule applies where the court makes an order under section 4A(6).

(2) The member of the company who applied for the order shall serve sealed copies of it on—

   (a) the supervisor of the voluntary arrangement; and

   (b) the directors of the company.

(3)   Service on the directors may be effected by service of a single copy on the company at its registered office.

(4)   The directors or (as the case may be) the supervisor shall [as soon as reasonably practicable] after receiving a copy of the court's order, give notice of it to all persons who were sent notice of the creditors' or company meetings or who, not having been sent such notice, are affected by the order.

(5)   The person on whose application the order of the court was made shall, within [5 business] days of the order, deliver [a copy] to the registrar of companies.]

NOTES

Inserted by the Insolvency (Amendment) (No 2) Rules 2002, SI 2002/2712, r 3(1), Schedule, Pt 1, para 14, as from 1 January 2003, subject to transitional provisions as noted to r 1.1 at **[10.4]**.

Para (4): words in square brackets substituted by the Insolvency (Amendment) Rules 2009, SI 2009/642, r 5, as from 6 April 2009, subject to transitional provisions in r 3 thereof, as noted to r 1.4 of these Rules at **[10.6]**.

Para (5): words in first pair of square brackets substituted by the Insolvency (Amendment) Rules 2010, SI 2010/686, r 2, Sch 1, para 16, as from 6 April 2010, subject to transitional provisions in Sch 4, para 1 thereto, as noted to r 1.5 at **[10.7]**; words in second pair of square brackets substituted by the Insolvency (Amendment) (No 2) Rules 2009, SI 2009/2472, rr 3, 5, as from 1 October 2009 (for transitional provisions see the note to r 0.2 at **[10.2]**).

[10.27]
1.23   Hand-over of property etc to supervisor

(1)   [Where the decision approving the voluntary arrangement has effect under section 4A—]
   (a)   the directors, or
   (b)   where the company is in liquidation or is [in administration], and a person other than the responsible insolvency practitioner is appointed as supervisor of the voluntary arrangement, the insolvency practitioner,

shall [as soon as reasonably practicable] do all that is required for putting the supervisor into possession of the assets included in the arrangement.

(2)   Where the company is in liquidation or is [in administration], the supervisor shall on taking possession of the assets discharge any balance due to the insolvency practitioner by way of remuneration or on account of—
   (a)   fees, costs, charges and expenses properly incurred and payable under the Act or the Rules, and
   (b)   any advances made in respect of the company, together with interest on such advances at the rate specified in section 17 of the Judgments Act 1838 at the date on which the company went into liquidation or (as the case may be) [entered administration].

(3)   Alternatively, the supervisor must, before taking possession, give the responsible insolvency practitioner a written undertaking to discharge any such balance out of the first realisation of assets.

(4)   The insolvency practitioner has a charge on the assets included in the voluntary arrangement in respect of any sums due as above until they have been discharged, subject only to the deduction from realisations by the supervisor of the proper costs and expenses of such realisations.

(5)   The supervisor shall from time to time out of the realisation of assets discharge all guarantees properly given by the responsible insolvency practitioner for the benefit of the company, and shall pay all the insolvency practitioner's expenses.

(6)   References in this Rule to the responsible insolvency practitioner include, where a company is being wound up by the court, the official receiver, whether or not in his capacity as liquidator; and any sums due to the official receiver take priority over those due to a liquidator.

NOTES

Para (1): words in first pair of square brackets substituted by the Insolvency (Amendment) (No 2) Rules 2002, SI 2002/2712, r 3(1), Schedule, Pt 1, para 15, as from 1 January 2003, subject to transitional provisions as noted to r 1.1 at **[10.4]**; words in second pair of square brackets substituted by the Insolvency (Amendment) Rules 2003, SI 2003/1730, r 4, Sch 1, Pt 1, para 6(a), as from 15 September 2003 (for transitional provisions and savings see the note preceding r 2.1 at **[10.60]**); words in third pair of square brackets substituted by the Insolvency (Amendment) Rules 2009, SI 2009/642, r 5, as from 6 April 2009, subject to transitional provisions in r 3 thereof, as noted to r 1.4 of these Rules at **[10.6]**.

Para (2): words in square brackets substituted by SI 2003/1730, r 4, Sch 1, Pt 1, para 6(b), as from 15 September 2003 (for transitional provisions and savings see the note preceding r 2.1 at **[10.60]**).

[10.28]
1.24   Report of meetings

(1)   A report of the meetings shall be prepared by the person who was chairman of them.

(2)   The report shall—
   [(a)   state whether the proposal for a voluntary arrangement was approved by the creditors of the company alone or by both the creditors and members of the company and in either case whether such approval was with any modifications;]
   (b)   set out the resolutions which were taken at each meeting, and the decision on each one;
   (c)   list the creditors and members of the company (with their respective values) who were present or represented at the meetings, and how they voted on each resolution;   . . .

[(ca) state whether, in the opinion of the supervisor, (i) the EC Regulation applies to the voluntary arrangement and (ii) if so, whether the proceedings are main proceedings, secondary proceedings or territorial proceedings; and]

(d)   include such further information (if any) as the chairman thinks it appropriate to make known to the court.

(3)   A copy of the chairman's report shall, within 4 [business] days of the meetings being held, be filed in court; and the court shall cause that copy to be endorsed with the date of filing.

(4)   In respect of each of the meetings, the persons to whom notice of its result is to be sent by the chairman under section 4(6) are all those who were sent notice of the meeting under this Part of the Rules.

The notice shall be sent [as soon as reasonably practicable] after a copy of the chairman's report is filed in court under paragraph (3).

(5)   [If the decision approving the voluntary arrangement has effect under section 4A] (whether or not in the form proposed), the supervisor shall [as soon as reasonably practicable] send a copy of the chairman's report to the registrar of companies.

NOTES

Para (2): sub-para (a) substituted by the Insolvency (Amendment) (No 2) Rules 2002, SI 2002/2712, r 3(1), Schedule, Pt 1, para 16(a), as from 1 January 2003, subject to transitional provisions as noted to r 1.1 at **[10.4]**; word omitted from sub-para (c) revoked, and sub-para (ca) inserted, by the Insolvency (Amendment) Rules 2002, SI 2002/1307, rr 3, 4(3), as from 31 May 2002, with savings in relation to anything done under, or for the purposes of, this provision before that date.

Para (3): word in square brackets inserted by the Insolvency (Amendment) Rules 2010, SI 2010/686, r 2, Sch 1, para 17(1), (2), as from 6 April 2010, subject to transitional provisions in Sch 4, para 1 thereto, as noted to r 1.5 at **[10.7]**.

Para (4): words in square brackets substituted by SI 2010/686, r 2, Sch 1, para 17(1), (3), as from 6 April 2010, subject to transitional provisions in Sch 4, para 1 thereto, as noted to r 1.5 at **[10.7]**.

Para (5): words in first pair of square brackets substituted by SI 2002/2712, r 3(1), Schedule, Pt 1, para 16(b), as from 1 January 2003, subject to transitional provisions as noted to r 1.1 at **[10.4]**; words in second pair of square brackets substituted by the Insolvency (Amendment) Rules 2009, SI 2009/642, r 5, as from 6 April 2009, subject to transitional provisions in r 3 thereof, as noted to r 1.4 of these Rules at **[10.6]**.

EC Regulation: ie, Council Regulation 1346/2000/EC on insolvency proceedings.

[10.29]
1.25   Revocation or suspension of the arrangement

(1)   This Rule applies where the court makes an order of revocation or suspension under section 6.

(2)   The person who applied for the order shall serve sealed copies of it—

(a)   on the supervisor of the voluntary arrangement, and

(b)   on the directors of the company or the administrator or liquidator (according to who made the proposal for the arrangement).

Service on the directors may be effected by service of a single copy of the order on the company at its registered office.

(3)   If the order includes a direction by the court under section 6(4)(b) for any further meetings to be summoned, notice shall also be given (by the person who applied for the order) to whoever is, in accordance with the direction, required to summon the meetings.

(4)   The directors or (as the case may be) the administrator or liquidator shall—

(a)   [as soon as reasonably practicable] after receiving a copy of the court's order, give notice of it to all persons who were sent notice of the creditors' and company meetings or who, not having been sent that notice, appear to be affected by the order;

(b)   within [5 business] days of their receiving a copy of the order (or within such longer period as the court may allow), give notice to the court whether it is intended to make a revised proposal to the company and its creditors, or to invite re-consideration of the original proposal.

(5)   The person on whose application the order of revocation or suspension was made shall, within [5 business] days after the making of the order, deliver a copy of the order to the registrar of companies.

NOTES

Para (4): words in square brackets in sub-para (a) substituted by the Insolvency (Amendment) Rules 2009, SI 2009/642, r 5, as from 6 April 2009, subject to transitional provisions in r 3 thereof, as noted to r 1.4 of these Rules at **[10.6]**; words in square brackets in sub-para (b) substituted by the Insolvency (Amendment) Rules 2010, SI 2010/686, r 2, Sch 1, para 18, as from 6 April 2010, subject to transitional provisions in Sch 4, para 1 thereto, as noted to r 1.5 at **[10.7]**.

Para (5): words in square brackets substituted by SI 2010/686, r 2, Sch 1, para 18, as from 6 April 2010, subject to transitional provisions in Sch 4, para 1 thereto, as noted to r 1.5 at **[10.7]**.

[10.30]
[1.26A   Supervisor's accounts and reports

(1)   Paragraph (2) applies where the voluntary arrangement authorises or requires the supervisor—

(a)   to carry on the business of the company or trade on its behalf or in its name; or

(b)   to realise assets of the company; or

(c)   otherwise to administer or dispose of any of its funds.

(2)   The supervisor must keep accounts and records of the supervisor's acts and dealings in, and in connection with, the arrangement, including in particular records of all receipts and payments of money.

(3)   The supervisor must preserve any accounts and records in paragraph (2) which—

    (a)   were kept by any other person who has acted as supervisor of the arrangement; and

    (b)   are in the supervisor's possession.

(4)   Subject to paragraph (5), the supervisor must in respect of each period of 12 months ending with the anniversary of the commencement of the arrangement send within 2 months of the end of that period a report on the progress and prospects for the full implementation of the voluntary arrangement to—

    (a)   the registrar of companies;

    (b)   the company;

    (c)   all those of the company's creditors who are bound by the voluntary arrangement of whose address the supervisor is aware;

    (d)   subject to paragraph (7) below, the members of the company; and

    (e)   if the company is not in liquidation, the company's auditors (if any) for the time being.

(5)   The supervisor is released from an obligation to send a report under paragraph (4), if an obligation to send a final report under Rule 1.29 arises in the period of 2 months mentioned in paragraph (4).

(6)   Where the supervisor is authorised or required to do any of the things mentioned in paragraph (1)(a) to (c), the report required to be sent pursuant to paragraph (4) must include or be accompanied by—

    (a)   an abstract of receipts and payments required to be recorded by virtue of paragraph (2); or

    (b)   where there have been no such receipts and payments, a statement to that effect.

(7)   The court may, on application by the supervisor dispense with the sending under this Rule of abstracts or reports to members of the company, either altogether or on the basis that the availability of the abstract or report to members is to be advertised by the supervisor in a specified manner.]

NOTES

Commencement: 6 April 2010.

Substituted (for the original r 1.26) by the Insolvency (Amendment) Rules 2010, SI 2010/686, r 2, Sch 1, para 19, as from 6 April 2010, subject to transitional provisions in Sch 4, para 1 thereto, as noted to r 1.5 at **[10.7]**.:

[10.31]
1.27   Production of accounts and records to Secretary of State

(1)   The Secretary of State may at any time during the course of the voluntary arrangement or after its completion [or termination] require the supervisor to produce for inspection—

    (a)   his records and accounts in respect of the arrangement, and

    (b)   copies of abstracts and reports prepared in compliance with Rule [1.26A].

(2)   The Secretary of State may require production either at the premises of the supervisor or elsewhere; and it is the duty of the supervisor to comply with any requirement imposed on him under this Rule.

(3)   The Secretary of State may cause any accounts and records produced to him under this Rule to be audited; and the supervisor shall give to the Secretary of State such further information and assistance as he needs for the purposes of his audit.

NOTES

Para (1): words in first pair of square brackets added by the Insolvency (Amendment) (No 2) Rules 2002, SI 2002/2712, r 3(1), Schedule, Pt 1, para 17, as from 1 January 2003, subject to transitional provisions as noted to r 1.1 at **[10.4]**; figure in second pair of square brackets substituted by the Insolvency (Amendment) Rules 2010, SI 2010/686, r 2, Sch 1, para 20, as from 6 April 2010, subject to transitional provisions in Sch 4, para 1 thereto, as noted to r 1.5 at **[10.7]**.

[10.32]
1.28   Fees, costs, charges and expenses

(1)   The fees, costs, charges and expenses that may be incurred for any of the purposes of the voluntary arrangement are—

    (a)   any disbursements made by the nominee prior to the [decision approving the arrangement taking effect under section 4A], and any remuneration for his services as such agreed between himself and the company (or, as the case may be, the administrator or liquidator);

    (b)   any fees, costs, charges or expenses which—

        (i)   are sanctioned by the terms of the arrangement, or

        (ii)   would be payable, or correspond to those which would be payable, in an administration or winding up.

NOTES

Para (1): words in square brackets in sub-para (a) substituted by the Insolvency (Amendment) (No 2) Rules 2002, SI 2002/2712, r 3(1), Schedule, Pt 1, para 18, as from 1 January 2003, subject to transitional provisions as noted to r 1.1 at **[10.4]**.

[10.33]
**[1.29		Completion or termination of the arrangement**
(1)		Not more than 28 days after the final completion or termination of the voluntary arrangement, the supervisor shall send to creditors and members of the company who are bound by it a notice that the voluntary arrangement has been fully implemented or (as the case may be) has terminated.

(2)		With the notice there shall be sent to each creditor and member a copy of a report by the supervisor summarising all receipts and payments made by him in pursuance of the arrangement, and explaining in relation to implementation of the arrangement any departure from the proposals as they originally took effect, or (in the case of termination of the arrangement) explaining the reasons why the arrangement has terminated.

(3)		The supervisor shall, within the 28 days mentioned above, send to the registrar of companies and to the court a copy of the notice to creditors and members under paragraph (1), together with a copy of the report under paragraph (2), and the supervisor shall not vacate office until after such copies have been sent.]

[(4)		In the report under paragraph (2), the supervisor shall include a statement as to the amount paid, if any, to unsecured creditors by virtue of the application of section 176A (prescribed part).]

NOTES
	Substituted by the Insolvency (Amendment) (No 2) Rules 2002, SI 2002/2712, r 3(1), Schedule, Pt 1, para 19, as from 1 January 2003, subject to transitional provisions as noted to r 1.1 at **[10.4]**.
	Para (4): added by the Insolvency (Amendment) Rules 2003, SI 2003/1730, r 4, Sch 1, Pt 1, para 7, as from 15 September 2003 (for transitional provisions and savings see the note preceding r 2.1 at **[10.60]**).

1.30		((*Chap 6) revoked by the Insolvency (Amendment) (No 2) Rules 2002, SI 2002/2712, r 3(1), Schedule, Pt 1, para 20, as from 1 January 2003, subject to transitional provisions as noted to r 1.1 at* **[10.4]**.)

[CHAPTER 7
EC REGULATION—CONVERSION OF VOLUNTARY ARRANGEMENT INTO WINDING UP

[10.34]
**1.31		Application for conversion into winding up**
[(1)		Where a member State liquidator proposes to apply to the court for conversion of a voluntary arrangement into winding-up proceedings, a witness statement complying with Rule 1.32 must be prepared and filed in court in support of the application.

(1A)		In this Rule, and in Rules 1.32 and 1.33, "conversion into winding-up proceedings" means an order under Article 37 of the EC Regulation (conversion of earlier proceedings) that the voluntary arrangement is converted into—
	(a)		administration proceedings whose purposes are limited to the winding up of the company through administration and are to exclude the purpose contained in paragraph 3(1)(a) of Schedule B1 to the Act;
	(b)		a creditors' voluntary winding up; or
	(c)		a winding up by the court.]

(2)		An application under this Rule shall be by originating application.

(3)		The application and the [witness statement] required under this Rule shall be served upon—
	(a)		the company; and
	(b)		the supervisor.]

NOTES
	Inserted, together with preceding heading and rr 1.32–1.34 (Chaps 7, 8), by the Insolvency (Amendment) Rules 2002, SI 2002/1307, rr 3, 4(4), as from 31 May 2002.
	Paras (1), (1A): substituted for para (1) by the Insolvency (Amendment) Rules 2010, SI 2010/686, r 2, Sch 1, para 21(1), (2), as from 6 April 2010, subject to transitional provisions in Sch 4, para 1 thereto, as noted to r 1.5 at **[10.7]**.
	Para (3): words in square brackets substituted by SI 2010/686, r 2, Sch 1, para 21(1), (3), as from 6 April 2010, subject to transitional provisions in Sch 4, para 2(1)(b), (2)–(4) thereto, as noted below.
	Transitional provisions: SI 2010/686, Sch 4, para 2 (as amended by the Insolvency (Amendment) (No 2) Rules 2010, SI 2010/734, rr 2, 11, as from 6 April 2010) provides as follows (note that the words omitted are outside the scope of this work):

**"2		Revocations and amendments relating to new provisions in the Act, otiose provisions in the Rules, leave, signature, affidavits, electronic notices and court procedure**
	(1)		The following apply on and after 6th April 2010 in all cases—
	(a)		the revocation by Rule 5 of the following Rules in the 1986 Rules: 1.2, 2.73, 4.77, 4.190, 6.20, 6.36, 6.99, 6.102 and 6.235;
	[(b)		the amendments in the following paragraphs of Schedule 1 to these Rules: 1, 21(3), 22, 35, 36(2) to (4), 37, 40(3), 42, 43(4), 45(4), 66(5) and (6), 95, 97(2), 99(3), 106, 108(3), 109, 113, 114, 116(2) and (3)(a), 117, 142(2), 143, 146(2) to (5), (7) and (8)(a), 149(3), 150(2), (3)(a) and (4), 154 to 156, 161, 162(2) to (6) and (8), 165(2) and (3)(a) and (c), 166, 168(2), 169, 170(2) and (3), 171, 173, 210(2)(a) and (c), 211(2)(a) and (c), 222(4)(a) and (c), 226(2)(a) and (c), 248(2) and (3)(b), 250, 254(3), 255(4) and (5), 256, 260, . . . 440(2) and (3)(a), 441, 443 to 445, 451, 453, 456, 464(3), 465, 473(3), 478, 479, 480(3), 482, 493, 495, 499(9), 502(3) to (6), 503, 504, 505(3) and (4), 513 to 516, 518(2) and (3), 519 to 523, 525, 526, . . . 559 (so far as it relates to Forms . . . 7.1 and 7.2 and new Forms . . . 7.1A) and 560(5) and (6);]

(c)   the insertion by Rule 4 into the 1986 Rules of new Rules 12A.6 to 12A.14, 12A.30 to 12A.32 and 12A.55 as set out in Schedule 3 to these Rules.

(2)   In sub-paragraphs (3) and (4), "unamended provision" means a provision in the 1986 Rules as it has effect immediately before 6th April 2010, and "amended provision" means a provision in those Rules as amended or substituted by these Rules.

(3)   Where—
    (a)   an unamended provision refers to an affidavit, the swearing of an affidavit or the deponent to an affidavit,
    (b)   the corresponding amended provision refers to a witness statement, the making of a witness statement or a person making a witness statement, and
    (c)   the unamended provision continues to apply to any extent on or after 6th April 2010,

the references in the unamended provision to an affidavit, the swearing of an affidavit or the deponent to an affidavit are to be read as references to a witness statement, the making of a witness statement or a person making a witness statement respectively, even though the unamended provision and not the corresponding amended provision otherwise applies.

(4)   Where an amended provision ("provision A") refers to a witness statement, the making of a witness statement or a person making a witness statement as referred to or provided for in another amended provision ("provision B"), the reference in provision A includes a reference to an affidavit, the swearing of an affidavit or the deponent to an affidavit (as the case may be) as referred to or provided for in the unamended provision which corresponds to provision B.".

EC Regulation: ie, Council Regulation 1346/2000/EC on insolvency proceedings.

[10.35]
[1.32 Contents of [witness statement]

(1)   The [witness statement] shall state—
    (a)   that main proceedings have been opened in relation to the company in a member State other than the United Kingdom;
    (b)   the [belief of the person making the statement] that the conversion of the voluntary arrangement into [winding-up proceedings] would prove to be in the interests of the creditors in the main proceedings;
    [(c)   the opinion of the person making the statement as to whether the company ought to go into voluntary liquidation or be wound up by the court; and]
    (d)   all other matters that, in the opinion of the member State liquidator, would assist the court—
        (i)   in deciding whether to make such an order, and
        (ii) if the court were to do so, in considering the need for any consequential provision that would be necessary or desirable.

(2)   [A witness statement] under this Rule shall be [made] by, or on behalf of, the member State liquidator.]

NOTES

Inserted as noted to r 1.31 at **[10.34]**.

All words in square brackets (including in the rule heading) were substituted by the Insolvency (Amendment) Rules 2010, SI 2010/686, r 2, Sch 1, para 22, as from 6 April 2010, subject to transitional provisions in Sch 4, para 2 thereto, as noted to r 1.31 at **[10.34]**.

[10.36]
[1.33 Power of court

(1)   On hearing the application for conversion into [winding-up proceedings] the court may make such order as it thinks [just].

(2)   If the court makes an order for conversion into [winding-up proceedings] the order may contain all such consequential provisions as the court deems necessary or desirable.

(3)   Without prejudice to the generality of paragraph (1), an order under that paragraph may provide that the company be wound up as if a resolution for voluntary winding up under section 84 were passed on the day on which the order is made.

(4)   Where the court makes an order for conversion into [winding-up proceedings] under paragraph (1), any expenses properly incurred as expenses of the administration of the voluntary arrangement in question shall be a first charge on the company's assets.]

NOTES

Inserted as noted to r 1.31 at **[10.34]**.

Words in square brackets substituted by the Insolvency (Amendment) Rules 2010, SI 2010/686, r 2, Sch 1, paras 1, 23, as from 6 April 2010, subject to transitional provisions in Sch 4, paras 1, 2 thereto, as noted to rr 1.5, 1.31 at **[10.7]**, **[10.34]**.

[CHAPTER 8
EC REGULATION—MEMBER STATE LIQUIDATOR

[10.37]
1.34 Interpretation of creditor and notice to member State liquidator

(1)   This Rule applies where a member State liquidator has been appointed in relation to the company.

(2) Where the supervisor is obliged to give notice to, or provide a copy of a document (including an order of court) to, the court, the registrar of companies or the official receiver, the supervisor shall give notice or provide copies, as appropriate, to the member State liquidator.

(3) Paragraph (2) is without prejudice to the generality of the obligations imposed by Article 31 of the EC Regulation (duty to cooperate and communicate information).]

NOTES

Inserted as noted to r 1.31 at **[10.34]**.
EC Regulation: ie, Council Regulation 1346/2000/EC on insolvency proceedings.

[CHAPTER 9
OBTAINING A MORATORIUM
PROCEEDINGS DURING A MORATORIUM
NOMINEES
CONSIDERATION OF PROPOSALS WHERE MORATORIUM OBTAINED

Section A: Obtaining a Moratorium

[10.38]
1.35 Preparation of proposal by directors and submission to nominee

(1) The document containing the proposal referred to in paragraph 6(1)(a) of Schedule A1 to the Act shall—

   (a) be prepared by the directors;

   (b) comply with the requirements of paragraphs (1) and (2) of Rule 1.3 (save that the reference to preferential creditors shall be to preferential creditors within the meaning of paragraph 31(8) of Schedule A1 to the Act); and

   (c) state the address to which notice of the consent of the nominee to act and the documents referred to in Rule 1.38 shall be sent.

(2) With the agreement in writing of the nominee, the directors may amend the proposal at any time before submission to them by the nominee of the statement required by paragraph 6(2) of Schedule A1 to the Act.]

NOTES

Chapter 9 (rr 1.35–1.54) inserted by the Insolvency (Amendment) (No 2) Rules 2002, SI 2002/2712, r 3(1), Schedule, Pt 1, para 21, as from 1 January 2003, subject to transitional provisions as noted to r 1.1 at **[10.4]**.

[10.39]
[1.36 Delivery of documents to the intended nominee etc

(1) The documents required to be delivered to the nominee pursuant to paragraph 6(1) of Schedule A1 to the Act shall be delivered to the nominee himself or to a person authorised to take delivery of documents on his behalf.

(2) On receipt of the documents, the nominee shall [as soon as reasonably practicable] issue an acknowledgement of receipt of the documents to the directors which shall indicate the date on which the documents were received.]

NOTES

Inserted as noted to r 1.35 at **[10.38]**.
Para (2): words in square brackets substituted by the Insolvency (Amendment) Rules 2009, SI 2009/642, r 5, as from 6 April 2009, subject to transitional provisions in r 3 thereof, as noted to r 1.4 of these Rules at **[10.6]**.

[10.40]
[1.37 Statement of affairs

(1) The statement of the company's affairs required to be delivered to the nominee pursuant to paragraph 6(1)(b) of Schedule A1 to the Act shall be delivered to the nominee [at the same time as] the delivery to him of the document setting out the terms of the proposed voluntary arrangement

(2) The statement of affairs shall comprise the same particulars as required by Rule 1.5(2) (supplementing or amplifying, so far as is necessary for clarifying the state of the company's affairs, those already given in the directors' proposal).

(3) The statement of affairs shall be made up to a date not earlier than 2 weeks before the date of the delivery of the document containing the proposal for the voluntary arrangement to the nominee under Rule 1.36(1).

However, the nominee may allow an extension of that period to the nearest practicable date (not earlier than 2 months before the date of delivery of the documents referred to in Rule 1.36(1)) and if he does so, he shall give a statement of his reasons in writing to the directors.

[(4) The statement of affairs must be verified by a statement of truth made by at least one director.]]

NOTES

Inserted as noted to r 1.35 at **[10.38]**.

Para (1): words in square brackets substituted, and words omitted revoked, by the Insolvency (Amendment) Rules 2010, SI 2010/686, r 2, Sch 1, para 24(1), (2), as from 6 April 2010, subject to transitional provisions in Sch 4, para 1 thereto, as noted to r 1.5 at **[10.7]**.

Para (4): substituted by SI 2010/686, r 2, Sch 1, para 24(1), (3), as from 6 April 2010, subject to transitional provisions in Sch 4, para 1 thereto, as noted to r 1.5 at **[10.7]**.

See Form 1.6 at **[10.673]**.

[10.41]
[1.38   The nominee's statement

(1)   The nominee shall submit to the directors the statement required by paragraph 6(2) of Schedule A1 to the Act within 28 days of the submission to him of the document setting out the terms of the proposed voluntary arrangement.

(2)   The statement shall have annexed to it—
  (a)   the nominee's comments on the proposal, unless the statement contains an opinion in the negative on any of the matters referred to in paragraph 6(2)(a) and (b) of Schedule A1 to the Act, in which case he shall instead give his reasons for that opinion, and
  (b)   where he is willing to act in relation to the proposed arrangement, a statement of his consent to act.]

NOTES

Inserted as noted to r 1.35 at **[10.38]**.

See Forms 1.5, 1.8 at **[10.673]**.

[10.42]
[1.39   Documents submitted to the court to obtain moratorium

(1)   Where pursuant to paragraph 7 of Schedule A1 to the Act the directors file the document and statements referred to in that paragraph in court, those documents shall be delivered together with 4 copies of a schedule listing them within 3 [business] days of the date of the submission to them of the nominee's statement under paragraph 6(2) of Schedule A1 to the Act.

(2)   When the directors file the document and statements referred to in paragraph (1), they shall also file—
  (a)   a copy of any statement of reasons made by the nominee pursuant to Rule 1.37(3); and
  (b)   a copy of the nominee's comments on the proposal submitted to them pursuant to Rule 1.38(2).

(3)   The copies of the schedule shall be endorsed by the court with the date on which the documents were filed in court and 3 copies of the schedule sealed by the court shall be returned by the court to the person who filed the documents in court.

(4)   The statement of affairs required to be filed under paragraph 7(1)(b) of Schedule A1 to the Act shall comprise the same particulars as required by Rule 1.5(2).]

NOTES

Inserted as noted to r 1.35 at **[10.38]**.

Para (1): word in square brackets substituted by the Insolvency (Amendment) Rules 2010, SI 2010/686, r 2, Sch 1, para 25, as from 6 April 2010, subject to transitional provisions in Sch 4, para 1 thereto, as noted to r 1.5 at **[10.7]**.

See Forms 1.5 to 1.9 at **[10.673]**.

[10.43]
[1.40   Notice and advertisement of beginning of a moratorium

(1)   After receiving the copies of the schedule endorsed by the court under Rule 1.39(3), the directors shall [as soon as reasonably practicable] serve 2 of them on the nominee and one on the company.

[(2)   On receipt of the copies of the schedule pursuant to paragraph (1), the nominee—
  (a)   as soon as reasonably practicable shall cause a notice of the coming into force of the moratorium to be gazetted; and
  (b)   may advertise the notice in such other manner as the nominee thinks fit].

[(2A)   In addition to the standard contents, the notice under paragraph (2) must state—
  (a)   the nature of the business of the company;
  (b)   that a moratorium under section 1A has come into force; and
  (c)   the date upon which the moratorium came into force.]

(3)   The nominee shall [as soon as reasonably practicable] notify the registrar of companies, the company and any petitioning creditor of the company of whose [address the nominee] is aware of the coming into force of the moratorium and such notification shall specify the date on which the moratorium came into force [and the court at which the documents to obtain the moratorium were filed].

(4)   The nominee shall give notice of the coming into force of the moratorium specifying the date on which it came into force to—

(a)   any [enforcement officer] or other officer who, to his knowledge, is charged with an execution or other legal process against the company or its property; and

(b)   any person who, to his knowledge, has distrained against the company or its property.]

NOTES

Inserted as noted to r 1.35 at **[10.38]**.

Para (1): words in square brackets substituted by the Insolvency (Amendment) Rules 2009, SI 2009/642, r 5, as from 6 April 2009, subject to transitional provisions in r 3 thereof, as noted to r 1.4 of these Rules at **[10.6]**.

Para (2): substituted by SI 2009/642, rr 4, 6, as from 6 April 2009, subject to transitional provisions in r 3 thereof, as noted to r 1.4 of these Rules at **[10.6]**.

Para (2A): inserted by the Insolvency (Amendment) Rules 2010, SI 2010/686, r 2, Sch 1, para 26(1), (2), as from 6 April 2010, subject to transitional provisions in Sch 4, para 1 thereto, as noted to r 1.5 at **[10.7]**.

Para (3): words in first pair of square brackets substituted by SI 2009/642, r 5, as from 6 April 2009, subject to transitional provisions in r 3 thereof, as noted to r 1.4 of these Rules at **[10.6]**; words in second pair of square brackets substituted, and words in third pair of square brackets added, by SI 2010/686, r 2, Sch 1, para 26(1), (3), as from 6 April 2010, subject to transitional provisions in Sch 4, para 1 thereto, as noted to r 1.5 at **[10.7]**.

Para (4): words in square brackets substituted by the Insolvency (Amendment) Rules 2005, SI 2005/527, r 4, as from 1 April 2005.

See Form 1.11 at **[10.673]**.

[10.44]
[1.41   Notice of extension of moratorium

(1)   The nominee shall [as soon as reasonably practicable] notify the registrar of companies and the court of a decision taking effect pursuant to paragraph 36 of Schedule A1 to the Act to extend or further extend the moratorium and such notice shall specify the new expiry date of the moratorium.

(2)   Where an order is made by the court extending or further extending or renewing or continuing a moratorium, the nominee shall [as soon as reasonably practicable] after receiving a copy of the same give notice to the registrar of companies and with the notice shall send [a copy] of the order.]

NOTES

Inserted as noted to r 1.35 at **[10.38]**.

Para (1): words in square brackets substituted by the Insolvency (Amendment) Rules 2009, SI 2009/642, r 5, as from 6 April 2009, subject to transitional provisions in r 3 thereof, as noted to r 1.4 of these Rules at **[10.6]**.

Para (2): words in first pair of square brackets substituted by SI 2009/642, r 5, as from 6 April 2009, subject to transitional provisions in r 3 thereof, as noted to r 1.4 of these Rules at **[10.6]**; words in second pair of square brackets substituted by the Insolvency (Amendment) (No 2) Rules 2009, SI 2009/2472, rr 3, 6, as from 1 October 2009 (for transitional provisions see the note to r 0.2 at **[10.2]**).

See Form 1.13 at **[10.673]**.

[10.45]
[1.42   Notice and advertisement of end of moratorium

[(1)   After the moratorium comes to an end, the nominee—

(a)   as soon as reasonably practicable shall cause a notice of its coming to an end and the date on which it came to an end to be gazetted; and

(b)   may advertise the notice in such other manner as the nominee thinks fit.]

[(1A)   In addition to the standard contents, the notice under paragraph (1) must state—

(a)   the nature of the business of the company;

(b)   that a moratorium under section 1A has come to an end; and

(c)   the date upon which the moratorium came to an end.]

(2)   The nominee shall [as soon as reasonably practicable] give notice of the ending of the moratorium to the registrar of companies, the court, the company and any creditor of the company of whose [address the nominee] is aware and such notice shall specify the date on which the moratorium came to an end.]

NOTES

Inserted as noted to r 1.35 at **[10.38]**.

Para (1): substituted by the Insolvency (Amendment) Rules 2009, SI 2009/642, rr 4, 7, as from 6 April 2009, subject to transitional provisions in r 3 thereof, as noted to r 1.4 of these Rules at **[10.6]**.

Para (1A): inserted by the Insolvency (Amendment) Rules 2010, SI 2010/686, r 2, Sch 1, para 27(1), (2), as from 6 April 2010, subject to transitional provisions in Sch 4, para 1 thereto, as noted to r 1.5 at **[10.7]**.

Para (2): words in first pair of square brackets substituted by SI 2009/642, r 5, as from 6 April 2009, subject to transitional provisions in r 3 thereof, as noted to r 1.4 of these Rules at **[10.6]**; words in second pair of square brackets substituted by SI 2010/686, r 2, Sch 1, para 27(1), (3), as from 6 April 2010, subject to transitional provisions in Sch 4, para 1 thereto, as noted to r 1.5 at **[10.7]**.

See Forms 1.10, 1.15 at **[10.673]**.

[Section B: Proceedings During a Moratorium

[10.46]
1.43   Disposal of charged property etc during a moratorium

(1)   This Rule applies in any case where the company makes an application to the court under paragraph 20 of Schedule A1 to the Act for [permission] to dispose of property of the company which is subject to a security, or goods in possession of the company under an agreement to which that paragraph relates.

(2)   The court shall fix a venue for the hearing of the application and the company shall [as soon as reasonably practicable] give notice of the venue to the person who is the holder of the security or, as the case may be, the owner under the agreement.

(3)   If an order is made, the company shall [as soon as reasonably practicable] give notice of it to that person or owner.

(4)   The court shall send 2 sealed copies of the order to the company, who shall send one of them to that person or owner.]

NOTES

Inserted as noted to r 1.35 at **[10.38]**.
Para (1): word in square brackets substituted by the Insolvency (Amendment) Rules 2010, SI 2010/686, r 2, Sch 1, para 1, as from 6 April 2010, subject to transitional provisions in Sch 4, para 2 thereto, as noted to r 1.31 at **[10.34]**.
Paras (2), (3): words in square brackets substituted by the Insolvency (Amendment) Rules 2009, SI 2009/642, r 5, as from 6 April 2009, subject to transitional provisions in r 3 thereof, as noted to r 1.4 of these Rules at **[10.6]**.

[Section C: Nominees

[10.47]
1.44   Withdrawal of nominee's consent to act

Where the nominee withdraws his consent to act he shall, pursuant to paragraph 25(5) of Schedule A1 to the Act, [as soon as reasonably practicable] give notice of his withdrawal and the reason for withdrawing his consent to act to—

   (a)   the registrar of companies;
   (b)   the court;
   (c)   the company; and
   (d)   any creditor of the company of whose claim [and address the nominee] is aware.]

NOTES

Inserted as noted to r 1.35 at **[10.38]**.
Words in first pair of square brackets substituted by the Insolvency (Amendment) Rules 2009, SI 2009/642, r 5, as from 6 April 2009, subject to transitional provisions in r 3 thereof, as noted to r 1.4 of these Rules at **[10.6]**; words in second pair of square brackets substituted by the Insolvency (Amendment) Rules 2010, SI 2010/686, r 2, Sch 1, para 28, as from 6 April 2010, subject to transitional provisions in Sch 4, para 1 thereto, as noted to r 1.5 at **[10.7]**.
See Form 1.17 at **[10.673]**.

[10.48]
[1.45   Replacement of nominee by the court

(1)   Where the directors intend to make an application to the court under paragraph 28 of Schedule A1 to the Act for the nominee to be replaced, they shall give to the nominee at least [5 business] days' notice of their application.

(2)   Where the nominee intends to make an application to the court under that paragraph to be replaced, he shall give to the directors at least [5 business] days' notice of his application.

(3)   No appointment of a replacement nominee shall be made by the court unless there is filed in court a statement by the replacement nominee indicating [that the replacement nominee—

   (a)   consents to act; and
   (b)   is qualified to act as an insolvency practitioner in relation to the company or is an authorised person in relation to the company].]

NOTES

Inserted as noted to r 1.35 at **[10.38]**.
Words in square brackets substituted by the Insolvency (Amendment) Rules 2010, SI 2010/686, r 2, Sch 1, para 29, as from 6 April 2010, subject to transitional provisions in Sch 4, para 1 thereto, as noted to r 1.5 at **[10.7]**.
See Form 1.8 at **[10.673]**.

[10.49]
[1.46   Notification of appointment of a replacement nominee

Where a person is appointed as a replacement nominee, he shall [as soon as reasonably practicable] give notice of his appointment to—

   (a)   the registrar of companies;
   (b)   the court (in any case where he was not appointed by the court); and
   (c)   the person whom he has replaced as nominee.]

NOTES

Inserted as noted to r 1.35 at **[10.38]**.

Words in square brackets substituted by the Insolvency (Amendment) Rules 2009, SI 2009/642, r 5, as from 6 April 2009, subject to transitional provisions in r 3 thereof, as noted to r 1.4 of these Rules at **[10.6]**.

See Form 1.19 at **[10.673]**.

[10.50]

[1.47　Applications to court under paragraphs 26 or 27 of Schedule A1 to the Act

Where any person intends to make an application to the court pursuant to paragraph 26 or 27 of Schedule A1 to the Act, he shall give to the nominee at least [5 business] days' notice of his application.]

NOTES

Inserted as noted to r 1.35 at **[10.38]**.

Words in square brackets substituted by the Insolvency (Amendment) Rules 2010, SI 2010/686, r 2, Sch 1, para 30, as from 6 April 2010, subject to transitional provisions in Sch 4, para 1 thereto, as noted to r 1.5 at **[10.7]**.

[Section D: Consideration of Proposals Where Moratorium Obtained

[10.51]

1.48　Summoning of meetings; procedure at meetings etc

(1)　Where the nominee summons meetings of creditors and the company pursuant to paragraph 29(1) of Schedule A1 to the Act, each of those meetings shall be summoned for a date that is not more than 28 days from the date on which the moratorium came into force.

(2)　Notices calling the creditors' meetings shall be sent by the nominee to all creditors specified in the statement of affairs and any other creditors of the company of whose address he is aware at least 14 days before the day fixed for the meeting.

(3)　Notices calling the company meeting shall be sent by the nominee to all persons who are, to the best of the nominee's belief, members of the company at least 14 days before the day fixed for the meeting.

[(4)　Each notice sent under this Rule must—

　(a)　specify—

　　(i)　the court in which the documents relating to the obtaining of the moratorium were filed and

　　(ii)　the court reference; and

　(b)　state the effect of paragraphs (2) to (4) of Rule 1.52 (requisite majorities (creditors)).

(4A)　With each notice there must be sent—

　(a)　a copy of the directors' proposal;

　(b)　a copy of the statement of affairs or, if the nominee thinks fit, a summary of it (the summary to include a list of creditors and the amount of their debts); and

　(c)　the nominee's comments on the proposal.]

(5)　The provisions of Rules 1.13 to 1.16 shall apply.]

NOTES

Inserted as noted to r 1.35 at **[10.38]**.

Paras (4), (4A): substituted (for the original para (4)) by the Insolvency (Amendment) Rules 2010, SI 2010/686, r 2, Sch 1, para 31, as from 6 April 2010, subject to transitional provisions in Sch 4, para 1 thereto, as noted to r 1.5 at **[10.7]**.

[10.52]

[1.49　Entitlement to vote (creditors)

(1)　Subject as follows, every creditor who has notice of the creditors' meeting is entitled to vote at the meeting or any adjournment of it.

(2)　Votes are calculated according to the amount of the creditor's debt as at the beginning of the moratorium, after deducting any amounts paid in respect of that debt after that date.

(3)　A creditor may vote in respect of a debt for an unliquidated amount or any debt whose value is not ascertained and for the purposes of voting (but not otherwise) his debt shall be valued at £1 unless the chairman agrees to put a higher value on it.]

NOTES

Inserted as noted to r 1.35 at **[10.38]**.

[10.53]

[1.50　Procedure for admission of creditors' claims for voting purposes

(1)　Subject as follows, at any creditors' meeting the chairman shall ascertain the entitlement of persons wishing to vote and shall admit or reject their claims accordingly.

(2)　The chairman may admit or reject a claim in whole or in part.

(3)   The chairman's decision on any matter under this Rule or under paragraph (3) of Rule 1.49 is subject to appeal to the court by any creditor or member of the company.

(4)   If the chairman is in doubt whether a claim should be admitted or rejected, he shall mark it as objected to and allow votes to be cast in respect of it, subject to such votes being subsequently declared invalid if the objection to the claim is sustained.

(5)   If on an appeal the chairman's decision is reversed or varied, or votes are declared invalid, the court may order another meeting to be summoned, or make such order as it thinks just.

The court's power to make an order under this paragraph is exercisable only if it considers that the circumstances giving rise to the appeal are such as give rise to unfair prejudice or material irregularity.

(6)   An application to the court by way of appeal against the chairman's decision shall not be made after the end of the period of 28 days beginning with the first day on which the report required by paragraph 30(3) of Schedule A1 to the Act has been made to the court.

(7)   The chairman is not personally liable for any costs incurred by any person in respect of an appeal under this Rule.]

NOTES

Inserted as noted to r 1.35 at **[10.38]**.

[10.54]
[1.51   Voting rights (members)
Rule 1.18 shall apply.]

NOTES

Inserted as noted to r 1.35 at **[10.38]**.

[10.55]
[1.52   Requisite majorities (creditors)
[(1)   Subject to paragraph (2), at the creditors' meeting, a resolution is passed when a majority (in value) of those present and voting in person or by proxy have voted in favour of it.

(2)   A resolution to approve the proposal or a modification is passed when a majority of three-quarters or more (in value) of those present and voting in person or by proxy have voted in favour of it.]

(3)   At a meeting of the creditors for any resolution to pass extending (or further extending) a moratorium, or to bring a moratorium to an end before the end of the period of any extension, there must be a majority in excess of three quarters in value of the creditors present in person or by proxy and voting on the resolution. For this purpose paragraph (4)(b) below shall not apply and a secured creditor is entitled to vote in respect of the amount of his claim without deducting the value of his security.

(4)   In the following cases there is to be left out of account a creditor's vote in respect of any claim or part of a claim—
  (a)   where written notice of the claim was not given, either at the meeting or before it, to the chairman or [nominee];
  (b)   where the claim or part is secured;
  (c)   where the claim is in respect of a debt wholly or partly on, or secured by, a current bill of exchange or promissory note, unless the creditor is willing—
    (i)   to treat the liability to him on the bill or note of every person who is liable on it antecedently to the company, and against whom a bankruptcy order has not been made (or, in the case of a company, which has not gone into liquidation), as a security in his hands, and
    (ii)   to estimate the value of the security and (for the purpose of entitlement to vote, but not of any distribution under the arrangement) to deduct it from his claim.

(5)   Any resolution is invalid if those voting against it include more than half in value of the creditors, counting in these latter only those—
  (a)   who have notice of the meeting;
  (b)   whose votes are not to be left out of account under paragraph (4); and
  (c)   who are not, to the best of the chairman's belief, persons connected with the company.

(6)   It is for the chairman of the meeting to decide whether under this Rule—
  (a)   a vote is to be left out of account in accordance with paragraph [(4)], or
  (b)   a person is a connected person for the purposes of paragraph (5)(c);
and in relation to the second of these two cases the chairman is entitled to rely on the information provided by the statement of the company's affairs or otherwise in accordance with this Part of the Rules.

(7)   If the chairman uses a proxy contrary to Rule 1.15 as it applies by virtue of Rule [1.48(5)], his vote with that proxy does not count towards any majority under this Rule.

(8)   The chairman's decision on any matter under this Rule is subject to appeal to the court by any creditor or member and paragraphs (5) to (7) of Rule 1.50 apply as regards such an appeal.]

NOTES

Inserted as noted to r 1.35 at **[10.38]**.

Paras (1), (2): substituted by the Insolvency (Amendment) Rules 2010, SI 2010/686, r 2, Sch 1, para 32(1), (2), as from 6 April 2010, subject to transitional provisions in Sch 4, para 1 thereto, as noted to r 1.5 at **[10.7]**.

Para (4): word in square brackets substituted by SI 2010/686, r 2, Sch 1, para 32(1), (3), as from 6 April 2010, subject to transitional provisions in Sch 4, para 1 thereto, as noted to r 1.5 at **[10.7]**.

Paras (6), (7): figures in square brackets substituted by the Insolvency (Amendment) Rules 2003, SI 2003/1730, r 4, Sch 1, Pt 1, para 8, as from 15 September 2003 (for transitional provisions and savings see the note preceding r 2.1 at **[10.60]**).

[10.56]
[1.53   Requisite majorities (members) and proceedings to obtain agreement on the proposal

(1)   Rule 1.20 shall apply.

(2)   If the chairman thinks fit, the creditors' meeting and the company meeting may be held together.

(3)   The chairman may, and shall if it is so resolved at the meeting in question, adjourn that meeting, but any adjournment shall not be to a day which is more than 14 days after the date on which the moratorium (including any extension) ends.

(4)   If the meetings are adjourned under paragraph (3), notice of the fact shall be given by the nominee [as soon as reasonably practicable] to the court.

[(4A)   Once only in the course of a meeting the chairman may, without an adjournment, declare it suspended for any period up to 1 hour.]

(5)   If following the final adjournment of the creditors' meeting the proposal (with or without modifications) has not been approved by the creditors, it is deemed rejected.]

NOTES

Inserted as noted to r 1.35 at **[10.38]**.

Para (4): words in square brackets substituted by the Insolvency (Amendment) Rules 2009, SI 2009/642, r 5, as from 6 April 2009, subject to transitional provisions in r 3 thereof, as noted to r 1.4 of these Rules at **[10.6]**.

Para (4A): inserted by the Insolvency (Amendment) Rules 2010, SI 2010/686, r 2, Sch 1, para 33, as from 6 April 2010, subject to transitional provisions in Sch 4, para 1 thereto, as noted to r 1.5 at **[10.7]**.

[10.57]
[1.54   Implementation of the arrangement

(1)   Where a decision approving the arrangement has effect under paragraph 36 of Schedule A1 to the Act, the directors shall [as soon as reasonably practicable] do all that is required for putting the supervisor into possession of the assets included in the arrangement.

(2)   Subject to paragraph (3), Rules 1.22, 1.22A and 1.24 to 1.29 apply.

(3)   The provisions referred to in paragraph (2) are modified as follows—
  (a)   in paragraph (1) of Rule 1.22A the reference to section 4A(6) is to be read as a reference to paragraph 36(5) of Schedule A1 to the Act;
  (b)   in paragraph (4) of Rule 1.24 the reference to section 4(6) is to be read as a reference to paragraph 30(3) of Schedule A1 to the Act;
  (c)   in paragraph (5) of Rule 1.24 the reference to section 4A is to be read as a reference to paragraph 36 of Schedule A1 to the Act;
  (d)   in paragraph (1) of Rule 1.25 the reference to section 6 is to be read as a reference to paragraph 38 of Schedule A1 to the Act and the references in paragraphs (2) and (4) to the administrator or liquidator shall be ignored;
  (e)   in paragraph (3) of Rule 1.25 the reference to section 6(4)(b) is to be read as a reference to paragraph 38 (4)(b) of Schedule A1 to the Act; and
  (f)   in sub-paragraph (a) of paragraph (1) of Rule 1.28 the reference to section 4A is to be read as a reference to paragraph 36 of Schedule A1 to the Act.]

NOTES

Inserted as noted to r 1.35 at **[10.38]**.

Para (1): words in square brackets substituted by the Insolvency (Amendment) Rules 2009, SI 2009/642, r 5, as from 6 April 2009, subject to transitional provisions in r 3 thereof, as noted to r 1.4 of these Rules at **[10.6]**.

[CHAPTER 10
TIME RECORDING INFORMATION

[10.58]
1.55   Provision by nominee or supervisor of information about time spent on a proposal or voluntary arrangement

(1)   Subject as set out in this Rule, a person ("the relevant person") who has acted or is acting as—
  (a)   a nominee in respect of a proposed voluntary arrangement; or
  (b)   a supervisor in respect of a voluntary arrangement

must, on request in writing by any person mentioned in paragraph (2), supply free of charge to that person a statement of the kind described in paragraph (3).

(2) The persons referred to in paragraph (1) are—
  (a) any director of the company;
  (b) where the proposal has been approved, any creditor or member of the company in respect of the arrangement.

(3) The statement referred to in paragraph (1)—
  (a) must cover the period beginning with the date of the appointment of the relevant person as nominee or supervisor, as the case may be, and ending—
      (i) with the date next before the date of making the request on which the relevant person has completed any period as nominee or supervisor, or both, which is a multiple of 6 months or,
      (ii) where the relevant person has ceased to act as nominee or supervisor, the date upon which the person so ceased; and
  (b) must comprise the following details—
      (i) the total number of hours spent on the voluntary arrangement by the relevant person whether as nominee or supervisor, or both, and any staff assigned to the voluntary arrangement during that period;
      (ii) for each grade of individual so engaged, the average hourly rate at which any work carried out by individuals in that grade is charged; and
      (iii) the number of hours spent by each grade of staff during that period.

(4) No request pursuant to this Rule may be made where more than 2 years has elapsed since the relevant person ceased to act in any capacity in relation to the proposal or any voluntary arrangement arising out of the approval of the proposal.

(5) Any statement required to be provided to any person under this Rule must be supplied within 28 days of the date of the receipt of the request by the person required to supply it.]

NOTES

Commencement: 6 April 2010.

Inserted, together with r 1.56 and associated headings (Chs 10, 11), by the Insolvency (Amendment) Rules 2010, SI 2010/686, r 2, Sch 1, para 34, subject to transitional provisions in Sch 4, para 1 thereto, as noted to r 1.5 at **[10.7]**.

[CHAPTER 11
OMISSION OF INFORMATION FROM STATEMENT OF AFFAIRS

[10.59]
1.56 Omission of Information from Statement of Affairs

The court, on the application of the nominee, the directors or any person appearing to it to have an interest, may direct that specified information may be omitted from any statement of affairs required to be sent to the creditors where the disclosure of such information would be likely to prejudice the conduct of the voluntary arrangement or might reasonably be expected to lead to violence against any person.]

NOTES

Commencement: 6 April 2010.

Inserted as noted to r 1.55 at **[10.58]**.

[PART 2
ADMINISTRATION PROCEDURE

NOTES

Substitution of Pt 2: the original Pt 2 (rr 2.1–2.62) was substituted by a new Pt 2 (rr 2.1–2.133) by the Insolvency (Amendment) Rules 2003, SI 2003/1730, r 5(1), Sch 1, Pt 2, para 9, as from 15 September 2003, subject to transitional provisions and savings as noted below.

See also the note "Savings in relation to special administration regimes" to s 8 of the Insolvency Act 1986 at **[9.105]**. See also the Insolvency (Amendment) Rules 2010, SI 2010/686, r 7, Sch 5, which provide for amendments to the provisions applying to administrations which continue to be governed by the law as it stood before the Enterprise Act 2002.

Transitional provisions: the Insolvency (Amendment) Rules 2003, SI 2003/1730, r 5 provides as follows (note that by virtue of r 2(3), the "first commencement date" is 15 September 2003)—

"5   Amendments to Part 2 of the principal Rules
(1)   Subject to paragraphs (2), (3) and (4), for Part 2 of the principal Rules there are substituted the provisions set out in Part 2 of Schedule 1 to these Rules.
(2)   The provisions of Part 2 of Schedule 1 to these Rules shall not apply and Part 2 of the principal Rules as it stood before the coming into force of these Rules shall continue to apply, where a petition for an administration order has been presented to the court before the first commencement date.
(3)   The former Rules shall continue to apply (with or without modification made by or under any enactment) where a provision made by or under any enactment preserves the continuing operation (with or without modification) after the first commencement date of old Part II of the Act and in such a case the provisions of Part 2 of Schedule 1 to these Rules shall not apply.

(4)   In paragraph (3) "the former Rules" means the Insolvency Rules 1986 without the amendments made by these Rules and "old Part II" means Part II of the Act without the amendments made by the Enterprise Act 2002.".

CHAPTER 1
PRELIMINARY

[10.60]
2.1   Introductory and interpretation

(1)   In this Part—
   (a)   Chapter 2 applies in relation to the appointment of an administrator by the court;
   (b)   Chapter 3 applies in relation to the appointment of an administrator by the holder of a qualifying floating charge under paragraph 14;
   (c)   Chapter 4 applies in relation to the appointment of an administrator by the company or the directors under paragraph 22;
   (d)   The following Chapters apply in all the cases mentioned in sub-paragraphs (a)–(c) above:
   —   Chapter 5: Process of administration;
   —   Chapter 6: Meetings and reports;
   —   Chapter 7: The creditors' committee;
   —   Chapter 8: Disposal of charged property;
   —   Chapter 9: Expenses of the administration;
   —   Chapter 10: Distributions to creditors;
   —   Chapter 11: The administrator;
   —   Chapter 12: Ending administration;
   —   Chapter 13: Replacing administrator;
   —   Chapter 14: EC Regulation—conversion of administration into winding up;
   —   Chapter 15: EC Regulation—member State liquidator.

(2)   In this Part of these Rules a reference to a numbered paragraph shall, unless otherwise stated, be to the paragraph so numbered in Schedule B1 to the Act.]

NOTES
   Substituted, subject to transitional provisions, as noted above.
   EC Regulation: ie, Council Regulation 1346/2000/EC on insolvency proceedings.

[CHAPTER 2
APPOINTMENT OF ADMINISTRATOR BY COURT

[10.61]
2.2   [Witness statement] in support of administration application

(1)   Where it is proposed to apply to the court for an administration order to be made in relation to a company, the administration application shall be in Form 2.1B and [a witness statement] complying with Rule 2.4 must be prepared . . . with a view to its being filed with the court in support of the application.

(2)   If the administration application is to be made by the company or by the directors, the [witness statement] shall be made by one of the directors, or the secretary of the company, stating himself to make it on behalf of the company or, as the case may be, on behalf of the directors.

(3)   If the application is to be made by creditors, the [witness statement] shall be made by a person acting under the authority of them all, whether or not himself one of their number. In any case there must be stated in the [witness statement] the nature of his authority and the means of his knowledge of the matters to which the [witness statement] relates.

(4)   If the application is to be made by the supervisor of a voluntary arrangement under Part I of the Act, it is to be treated as if it were an application by the company.]

NOTES
   Substituted, subject to transitional provisions; see the note preceding r 2.1 at **[10.60]**.
   Words in square brackets substituted, and words omitted revoked, by the Insolvency (Amendment) Rules 2010, SI 2010/686, r 2, Sch 1, para 35, as from 6 April 2010, subject to transitional provisions in Sch 4, para 2 thereto, as noted to r 1.31 at **[10.34]**.
   See Form 2.1B at **[10.673]**.

[10.62]
[2.3   Form of application

(1)   If made by the company or by the directors, the application shall state the name of the company and its address for service, which (in the absence of special reasons to the contrary) is that of the company's registered office.

(2)   If the application is made by the directors, it shall state that it is so made under paragraph 12(1)(b); but from and after making it it is to be treated for all purposes as the application of the company.

(3)   If made by a single creditor, the application shall state his name and address for service.

(4)   If the application is made by two or more creditors, it shall state that it is so made (naming them); but from and after making it is to be treated for all purposes as the application of only one of them, named in the application as applying on behalf of himself and other creditors. An address for service for that one shall be specified.

(5)   There shall be attached to the application a written statement which shall be in Form 2.2B by each of the persons proposed to be administrator stating—

(a)   that he consents to accept appointment;

(b)   details of any prior professional relationship(s) that he has had with the company to which he is to be appointed as administrator; and

(c)   his opinion that it is reasonably likely that the purpose of administration will be achieved.]

NOTES

Substituted, subject to transitional provisions; see the note preceding r 2.1 at **[10.60]**.
See Form 2.2B at **[10.673]**.

[10.63]
[2.4   Contents of application and [witness statement] in support

(1)   The administration application shall contain a statement of the applicant's belief that the company is, or is likely to become, unable to pay its debts, except where the applicant is the holder of a qualifying floating charge and is making the application in reliance on paragraph 35.

(2)   There shall be attached to the application [a witness statement] in support which shall contain—

(a)   a statement of the company's financial position, specifying (to the best of the applicant's knowledge and belief) the company's assets and liabilities, including contingent and prospective liabilities;

(b)   details of any security known or believed to be held by creditors of the company, and whether in any case the security is such as to confer power on the holder to appoint an administrative receiver or to appoint an administrator under paragraph 14. If an administrative receiver has been appointed, that fact shall be stated;

(c)   details of any insolvency proceedings in relation to the company including any petition that has been presented for the winding up of the company so far as within the immediate knowledge of the applicant;

(d)   where it is intended to appoint a number of persons as administrators, details of the matters set out in paragraph 100(2) regarding the exercise of the function of the administrators; and

(e)   any other matters which, in the opinion of those intending to make the application for an administration order, will assist the court in deciding whether to make such an order, so far as lying within the knowledge or belief of the applicant.

(3)   Where the application is made by the holder of a qualifying floating charge in reliance on paragraph 35, he shall give sufficient details in the [witness statement] in support to satisfy the court that he is entitled to appoint an administrator under paragraph 14.

(4)   The [witness statement] shall state whether, in the opinion of the person making the application, (i) the EC Regulation will apply and (ii) if so, whether the proceedings will be main proceedings[, secondary proceedings] or territorial proceedings.]

NOTES

Substituted, subject to transitional provisions; see the note preceding r 2.1 at **[10.60]**.
Words in second pair of square brackets in para (4) inserted by the Insolvency (Amendment) Rules 2010, SI 2010/686, r 2, Sch 1, para 36(1), (5), as from 6 April 2010 (subject to transitional provisions as noted to r 1.5 at **[10.7]**).
Other words in square brackets substituted by SI 2010/686, r 2, Sch 1, para 36(1)–(4), as from 6 April 2010 (subject to transitional provisions in Sch 4, para 2 thereto, as noted to r 1.31 at **[10.34]**).
EC Regulation: ie, Council Regulation 1346/2000/EC on insolvency proceedings.

[10.64]
[2.5   Filing of application

(1)   The application (and all supporting documents) shall be filed with the court, with a sufficient number of copies for service and use as provided by Rule 2.6.

(2)   Each of the copies filed shall have applied to it the seal of the court and be issued to the applicant; and on each copy there shall be endorsed the date and time of filing.

(3)   The court shall fix a venue for the hearing of the application and this also shall be endorsed on each copy of the application issued under paragraph (2).

(4)   After the application is filed, it is the duty of the applicant to notify the court in writing of the existence of any insolvency proceedings, and any insolvency proceedings under the EC Regulation, in relation to the company, as soon as he becomes aware of them.]

NOTES

Substituted, subject to transitional provisions; see the note preceding r 2.1 at **[10.60]**.
EC Regulation: ie, Council Regulation 1346/2000/EC on insolvency proceedings.

[10.65]
[2.6 Service of application

(1) In the following paragraphs of this Rule, references to the application are to a copy of the application issued by the court under Rule 2.5(2) together with the [witness statement required by Rule 2.4] and the documents attached to the application.

(2) Notification for the purposes of paragraph 12(2) shall be by way of service in accordance with Rule 2.8, verified in accordance with Rule 2.9.

(3) The application shall be served in addition to those persons referred to in paragraph 12(2)—
- (a) if an administrative receiver has been appointed, on him;
- (b) if there is pending a petition for the winding-up of the company, on the petitioner (and also on the provisional liquidator, if any);
- (c) if a member State liquidator has been appointed in main proceedings in relation to the company, on him;
- (d) on the person proposed as administrator;
- (e) on the company, if the application is made by anyone other than the company;
- (f) if a supervisor of a voluntary arrangement under Part I of the Act has been appointed, on him.]

NOTES
Substituted, subject to transitional provisions; see the note preceding r 2.1 at **[10.60]**.
Para (1): words in square brackets substituted by the Insolvency (Amendment) Rules 2010, SI 2010/686, r 2, Sch 1, para 37, as from 6 April 2010, subject to transitional provisions in Sch 4, para 2 thereto, as noted to r 1.31 at **[10.34]**.

[10.66]
[2.7 Notice to [officers charged with execution of writs or other process], etc

The applicant shall as soon as reasonably practicable after filing the application give notice of its being made to—
- (a) any [enforcement officer] or other officer who to his knowledge is charged with an execution or other legal process against the company or its property; and
- (b) any person who to his knowledge has distrained against the company or its property.]

NOTES
Substituted, subject to transitional provisions; see the note preceding r 2.1 at **[10.60]**.
Words in square brackets substituted by the Insolvency (Amendment) Rules 2005, SI 2005/527, r 5, as from 1 April 2005.

[10.67]
[2.8 Manner in which service to be effected

(1) Service of the application in accordance with Rule 2.6 shall be effected by the applicant, or his solicitor, or by a person instructed by him or his solicitor, not less than 5 [business] days before the date fixed for the hearing.

(2) Service shall be effected as follows—
- (a) on the company (subject to paragraph (3) below), by delivering the documents to its registered office;
- (b) on any other person (subject to paragraph (4) below), by delivering the documents to his proper address;
- (c) in either case, in such other manner as the court may direct.

(3) If delivery to a company's registered office is not practicable, service may be effected by delivery to its last known principal place of business in England and Wales.

(4) Subject to paragraph (5), for the purposes of paragraph (2)(b) above, a person's proper address is any which he has previously notified as his address for service; but if he has not notified any such address, service may be effected by delivery to his usual or last known address.

(5) In the case of a person who—
- (a) is an authorised deposit-taker or former authorised deposit-taker;
- (b)
  - (i) has appointed, or is or may be entitled to appoint, an administrative receiver of the company, or
  - (ii) is, or may be, entitled to appoint an administrator of the company under paragraph 14; and
- (c) has not notified an address for service,

the proper address is the address of an office of that person where, to the knowledge of the applicant, the company maintains a bank account or, where no such office is known to the applicant, the registered office of that person, or, if there is no such office, his usual or last known address.

(6) . . .]

NOTES
Substituted, subject to transitional provisions; see the note preceding r 2.1 at **[10.60]**.
Para (1): word in square brackets inserted by the Insolvency (Amendment) Rules 2010, SI 2010/686, r 2, Sch 1, para 38(1), (2), as from 6 April 2010, subject to transitional provisions in Sch 4, para 1 thereto, as noted to r 1.5 at **[10.7]**.

Part 10   Miscellaneous other SIs

Para (6): revoked by SI 2010/686, r 2, Sch 1, para 38(1), (3), as from 6 April 2010, subject to transitional provisions in Sch 4, para 1 thereto, as noted to r 1.5 at **[10.7]**.

[10.68]
[2.9   Proof of service

[(1)   Service of the application must be verified by a certificate of service.

(1A)   The certificate of service must be sufficient to identify the application served and must specify—
(a)   the name and registered number of the company,
(b)   the address of the registered office of the company,
(c)   the name of the applicant,
(d)   the court to which the application was made and the court reference number,
(e)   the date of the application,
(f)   whether the copy served was a sealed copy,
(g)   the date on which service was effected, and
(h)   the manner in which service was effected.]

(2)   The [certificate of service] shall be filed with the court as soon as reasonably practicable after service, and in any event not less than 1 [business] day before the hearing of the application.]

NOTES
Substituted, subject to transitional provisions; see the note preceding r 2.1 at **[10.60]**.
Paras (1), (1A): substituted (for the original para (1)) by the Insolvency (Amendment) Rules 2010, SI 2010/686, r 2, Sch 1, para 39(1), (2), as from 6 April 2010, subject to transitional provisions in Sch 4, para 1 thereto, as noted to r 1.5 at **[10.7]**.
Para (2): words in first pair of square brackets substituted, and word in second pair of square brackets inserted, by SI 2010/686, r 2, Sch 1, para 39(1), (3), as from 6 April 2010, subject to transitional provisions in Sch 4, para 1 thereto, as noted to r 1.5 at **[10.7]**.

[10.69]
[2.10   Application to appoint specified person as administrator by holder of qualifying floating charge

(1)   Where the holder of a qualifying floating charge applies to the court under paragraph 36(1)(b), he shall produce to the court—
(a)   the written consent of all holders of any prior qualifying floating charge;
(b)   a written statement in the Form 2.2B made by the specified person proposed by him as administrator; and
(c)   sufficient evidence to satisfy the court that he is entitled to appoint an administrator under paragraph 14.

(2)   If an administration order is made appointing the specified person, the costs of the person who made the administration application and the applicant under paragraph 36(1)(b) shall, unless the court otherwise orders, be paid as an expense of the administration.]

NOTES
Substituted, subject to transitional provisions; see the note preceding r 2.1 at **[10.60]**.
See Form 2.2B at **[10.673]**.

[10.70]
[2.11   Application where company in liquidation

(1)   Where an administration application is made under paragraph 37 or paragraph 38, the [witness statement required by Rule 2.4] shall contain—
(a)   full details of the existing insolvency proceedings, the name and address of the liquidator, the date he was appointed and by whom;
(b)   the reasons why it has subsequently been considered appropriate that an administration application should be made;
(c)   all other matters that would, in the opinion of the applicant, assist the court in considering the need to make provisions in respect of matters arising in connection with the liquidation; and
(d)   the details required in Rules 2.4(2) and (4).

(2)   Where the application is made by the holder of a qualifying floating charge he shall set out sufficient evidence in the [witness statement required by Rule 2.4] to satisfy the court that he is entitled to appoint an administrator under paragraph 14.]

NOTES
Substituted, subject to transitional provisions; see the note preceding r 2.1 at **[10.60]**.
Para (1): words in square brackets substituted by the Insolvency (Amendment) Rules 2010, SI 2010/686, r 2, Sch 1, para 40(1), (2), as from 6 April 2010, subject to transitional provisions in Sch 4, para 1 thereto, as noted to r 1.5 at **[10.7]**.
Para (2): words in square brackets substituted by SI 2010/686, r 2, Sch 1, para 40(1), (3), as from 6 April 2010, subject to transitional provisions in Sch 4, para 2 thereto, as noted to r 1.31 at **[10.34]**.

[10.71]
[2.12 The hearing

(1) At the hearing of the administration application, any of the following may appear or be represented—

(a) the applicant;
(b) the company;
(c) one or more of the directors;
(d) if an administrative receiver has been appointed, that person;
(e) any person who has presented a petition for the winding-up of the company;
(f) the person proposed for appointment as administrator;
(g) if a member State liquidator has been appointed in main proceedings in relation to the company, that person;
(h) any person that is the holder of a qualifying floating charge;
(j) any supervisor of a voluntary arrangement under Part I of the Act;
(k) with the permission of the court, any other person who appears to have an interest justifying his appearance.

(2) If the court makes an administration order, it shall be in Form 2.4B.

(3) If the court makes an administration order, the costs of the applicant, and of any person whose costs are allowed by the court, are payable as an expense of the administration.]

NOTES

Substituted, subject to transitional provisions; see the note preceding r 2.1 at **[10.60]**.
See Form 2.4B at **[10.673]**.

[10.72]
[2.13

Where the court makes an administration order in relation to a company upon an application under paragraph 37 or 38, the court shall include in the order—

(a) in the case of a liquidator appointed in a voluntary winding-up, his removal from office;
(b) details concerning the release of the liquidator;
(c) provision for payment of the expenses of the liquidation;
(d) provisions regarding any indemnity given to the liquidator;
(e) provisions regarding the handling or realisation of any of the company's assets in the hands of or under the control of the liquidator;
(f) such provision as the court thinks [just] with respect to matters arising in connection with the liquidation; and
(g) such other provisions as the court shall think [just].]

NOTES

Substituted, subject to transitional provisions; see the note preceding r 2.1 at **[10.60]**.
Word in square brackets in sub-paras (f), (g) substituted by the Insolvency (Amendment) Rules 2010, SI 2010/686, r 2, Sch 1, para 1, as from 6 April 2010, subject to transitional provisions in Sch 4, para 2 thereto, as noted to r 1.31 at **[10.34]**.

[10.73]
[2.14 Notice of administration order

(1) If the court makes an administration order, it shall as soon as reasonably practicable send two sealed copies of the order to the person who made the application.

(2) The applicant shall send a sealed copy of the order as soon as reasonably practicable to the person appointed as administrator.

(3) If the court makes an order under paragraph 13(1)(d) or any other order under paragraph 13(1)(f), it shall give directions as to the persons to whom, and how, notice of that order is to be given.]

NOTES

Substituted, subject to transitional provisions; see the note preceding r 2.1 at **[10.60]**.

[CHAPTER 3
APPOINTMENT OF ADMINISTRATOR BY HOLDER OF FLOATING CHARGE

[10.74]
2.15 Notice of intention to appoint

(1) The prescribed form for the notice of intention to appoint for the purposes of paragraph 44(2) is Form 2.5B.

(2) For the purposes of paragraph 44(2), a copy of Form 2.5B shall be filed with the court at the same time as it is sent in accordance with paragraph 15(1) to the holder of any prior qualifying floating charge.

Part 10 Miscellaneous other SIs

(3)   The provisions of Rule 2.8(2) to 2.8(6) shall apply to the sending of a notice under this Rule as they apply to the manner in which service of an administration application is effected under that Rule.]

NOTES

Substituted, subject to transitional provisions; see the note preceding r 2.1 at **[10.60]**.
See Form 2.5B at **[10.673]**.

[10.75]
[2.16   Notice of appointment

(1)   The notice of appointment for the purposes of an appointment under paragraph 14 shall be in Form 2.6B.

(2)   The copies of the notice filed with the court, shall be accompanied by—
(a)   the administrator's written statement in Form 2.2B; and
(b)   either—
   (i)   evidence that the person making the appointment has given such notice as may be required by paragraph 15(1)(a); or
   (ii)   copies of the written consent of all those required to give consent in accordance with paragraph 15(1)(b); and
(c)   a statement of those matters provided for in paragraph 100(2), if applicable.

(3)   The statutory declaration on Form 2.6B shall be made not more than 5 business days before the form is filed with the court.

(4)   Written consent may be given by the holder of a prior qualifying floating charge where a notice of intention to appoint an administrator has been given and filed with the court in accordance with Rule 2.15 above, by completing the section provided on Form 2.5B and returning to the appointor a copy of the form.

(5)   Where the holder of a prior qualifying floating charge does not choose to complete the section provided on Form 2.5B to indicate his consent, or no such form has been sent to him, his written consent shall include—
(a)   details of the name, address of registered office and registered number of the company in respect of which the appointment is proposed to be made;
(b)   details of the charge held by him including the date it was registered and, where applicable, any financial limit and any deeds of priority;
(c)   his name and address;
(d)   the name and address of the holder of the qualifying floating charge who is proposing to make the appointment;
(e)   the date that notice of intention to appoint was given;
(f)   the name of the proposed administrator;
(g)   a statement of consent to the proposed appointment,
and it shall be [authenticated] and dated.

(6)   This Rule and the following Rule are subject to Rule 2.19, the provisions of which apply when an appointment is to be made out of court business hours.]

NOTES

Substituted, subject to transitional provisions; see the note preceding r 2.1 at **[10.60]**.
Para (5): word in square brackets substituted by the Insolvency (Amendment) Rules 2010, SI 2010/686, r 2, Sch 1, para 1, as from 6 April 2010, subject to transitional provisions in Sch 4, para 2 thereto, as noted to r 1.31 at **[10.34]**.
See Forms 2.2B, 2.5B, 2.6B at **[10.673]**.

[10.76]
[2.17

(1)   Three copies of the notice of appointment shall be filed with the court and shall have applied to them the seal of the court and be endorsed with the date and time of filing.

(2)   The court shall issue two of the sealed copies of the notice of appointment to the person making the appointment, who shall as soon as reasonably practicable send one of the sealed copies to the administrator.]

NOTES

Substituted, subject to transitional provisions; see the note preceding r 2.1 at **[10.60]**.

[10.77]
[2.18

Where, after receiving notice that an administration application has been made, the holder of a qualifying floating charge appoints an administrator in reliance on paragraph 14, he shall as soon as reasonably practicable send a copy of the notice of appointment to the person making the administration application and to the court in which the application has been made.]

NOTES

Substituted, subject to transitional provisions; see the note preceding r 2.1 at **[10.60]**.

[10.78]
[2.19 Appointment taking place out of court business hours

(1)   The holder of a qualifying floating charge may file a notice of appointment with the court, notwithstanding that the court is not open for public business. When the court is closed (and only when it is closed) a notice of appointment may be filed with the court by faxing that form [or sending it as an attachment to an e-mail in accordance with paragraphs (3) and (3A)]. The notice of appointment shall be in Form 2.7B.

(2)   The filing of a notice in accordance with this Rule shall have the same effect for all purposes as a notice of appointment filed in accordance with Rule 2.16 with the court specified in the notice as having jurisdiction in the case.

[(3)   The notice must be—
 (a)   faxed to a designated telephone number, or
 (b)   sent as an attachment by e-mail to a designated e-mail address,
which must be provided by the Court Service for that purpose.

(3A)   The Secretary of State must publish the designated telephone number and e-mail address on The Insolvency Service website and, on request to The Insolvency Service, make them available in writing.]

(4)   The appointor shall ensure that—
 [(a)   a fax transmission report detailing the time and date of the fax transmission [and the telephone number to which the notice was faxed] and containing a copy of the first page (in part or in full) of the document faxed is created by the fax machine that is used to fax the form[, or
 (b)   a hard copy of the e-mail is created detailing the time and date of the e-mail and the address to which it was sent and containing a copy of the document sent as an attachment,
as the case may be; and the appointor must retain the report or hard copy.]

(5)   The appointment shall take effect from the date and time of [the fax transmission or sending of the e-mail]. The appointor shall notify the administrator, as soon as reasonably practicable, that the notice has been filed.

(6)   The copy of the faxed notice of appointment[, or the e-mail (or a hard copy of the e-mail) containing the notice of appointment, as (in either case) received by the Court Service,] shall be forwarded as soon as reasonably practicable to the court specified in the notice as the court having jurisdiction in the case, to be placed on the relevant court file.

(7)   The appointor shall take three copies of the notice of appointment that was faxed to the designated telephone number, together with the transmission report [or hard copy required by paragraph (4)] and all the necessary supporting documents listed on Form 2.7B, to the court on the next day that the court is open for business.

(8)   The appointor shall attach to the notice a statement providing full reasons for the out of hours filing of the notice of appointment, including why it would have been damaging to the company and its creditors not to have so acted.

(9)   The copies of the notice shall be sealed by the court and shall be endorsed with the date and time when, according to the appointor's fax transmission report [or hard copy of the e-mail], the notice was faxed [or sent] and the date when the notice and accompanying documents were delivered to the court.

(10)   The administrator's appointment shall cease to have effect if the requirements of paragraph (7) are not completed within the time period indicated in that paragraph.

(11)   Where any question arises in respect of the date and time that the notice of appointment was filed with the court it shall be a presumption capable of rebuttal that the date and time shown on the appointor's fax transmission report [or hard copy of the e-mail] is the date and time at which the notice was so filed.

(12)   The court shall issue two of the sealed copies of the notice of appointment to the person making the appointment, who shall, as soon as reasonably practicable, send one of the copies to the administrator.]

NOTES

Substituted, subject to transitional provisions; see the note preceding r 2.1 at **[10.60]**.

Paras (1), (5)–(7): words in square brackets substituted by the Insolvency (Amendment) Rules 2010, SI 2010/686, r 2, Sch 1, para 41(1), (2), (5)–(7), as from 6 April 2010, subject to transitional provisions in Sch 4, para 1 thereto, as noted to r 1.5 at **[10.7]**.

Paras (3), (3A): substituted (for the original para (3)) by SI 2010/686, r 2, Sch 1, para 41(1), (3), as from 6 April 2010, subject to transitional provisions in Sch 4, para 1 thereto, as noted to r 1.5 at **[10.7]**.

Paras (4), (9), (11): words in square brackets inserted by SI 2010/686, r 2, Sch 1, para 41(1), (4), (8), (9), as from 6 April 2010, subject to transitional provisions in Sch 4, para 1 thereto, as noted to r 1.5 at **[10.7]**.

See Form 2.7B at **[10.673]**.

Part 10   Miscellaneous other SIs

[CHAPTER 4

APPOINTMENT OF ADMINISTRATOR BY COMPANY OR DIRECTORS

[10.79]
2.20   Notice of intention to appoint

(1)   The notice of intention to appoint an administrator for the purposes of paragraph 26 shall be in Form 2.8B.

(2)   A copy of the notice of intention to appoint must, in addition to the persons specified in paragraph 26, be given to—

   (a)   any [enforcement officer] who, to the knowledge of the person giving the notice, is charged with execution or other legal process against the company;

   (b)   any person who, to the knowledge of the person giving the notice, has distrained against the company or its property;

   (c)   any supervisor of a voluntary arrangement under Part I of the Act; and

   (d)   the company, if the company is not intending to make the appointment.

(3)   The provisions of Rule 2.8(2) to [2.8(5)] shall apply to the sending or giving of a notice under this Rule as they apply to the manner in which service of an administration application is effected under that Rule.]

NOTES

   Substituted, subject to transitional provisions; see the note preceding r 2.1 at **[10.60]**.

   Para (2): words in square brackets substituted by the Insolvency (Amendment) Rules 2005, SI 2005/527, r 6, as from 1 April 2005.

   Para (3): figure in square brackets substituted by the Insolvency (Amendment) Rules 2010, SI 2010/686, r 2, Sch 1, para 42, as from 6 April 2010, subject to transitional provisions in Sch 4, para 2 thereto, as noted to r 1.31 at **[10.34]**.

   See Form 2.8B at **[10.673]**.

[10.80]
[2.21

The statutory declaration on Form 2.8B shall be made not more than 5 business days before the notice is filed with the court.]

NOTES

   Substituted, subject to transitional provisions; see the note preceding r 2.1 at **[10.60]**.

   See Form 2.8B at **[10.673]**.

[10.81]
[2.22

The notice of intention to appoint shall be accompanied by either a copy of the resolution of the company to appoint an administrator (where the company intends to make the appointment) or a record of the decision of the directors (where the directors intend to make the appointment).]

NOTES

   Substituted, subject to transitional provisions; see the note preceding r 2.1 at **[10.60]**.

[10.82]
[2.23   Notice of appointment

(1)   The notice of appointment for the purposes of an appointment under paragraph 22 shall be in Form 2.9B or Form 2.10B, as appropriate.

(2)   The copies of the notice filed with the court shall be accompanied by—

   (a)   the administrator's written statement in Form 2.2B;

   (b)   the written consent of all those persons to whom notice was given in accordance with paragraph 26(1) unless the period of notice set out in paragraph 26(1) has expired; and

   (c)   a statement of the matters provided for in paragraph 100(2), where applicable.]

NOTES

   Substituted, subject to transitional provisions; see the note preceding r 2.1 at **[10.60]**.

   See Forms 2.2B, 2.9B, 2.10B at **[10.673]**.

[10.83]
[2.24

The statutory declaration on Form 2.9B or Form 2.10B shall be made not more than 5 business days before the notice is filed with the court.]

NOTES

   Substituted, subject to transitional provisions; see the note preceding r 2.1 at **[10.60]**.

   See Forms 2.9B, 2.10B at **[10.673]**.

[10.84]
[2.25

Where a notice of intention to appoint an administrator has not been given, the notice of appointment shall be accompanied by the documents specified in Rule 2.22 above.]

NOTES

Substituted, subject to transitional provisions; see the note preceding r 2.1 at **[10.60]**.

[10.85]
[2.26

(1) Three copies of the notice of appointment shall be filed with the court and shall have applied to them the seal of the court and be endorsed with the date and time of filing.

(2) The court shall issue two of the sealed copies of the notice of appointment to the person making the appointment who shall as soon as reasonably practicable send one of the sealed copies to the administrator.]

NOTES

Substituted, subject to transitional provisions; see the note preceding r 2.1 at **[10.60]**.

[CHAPTER 5
PROCESS OF ADMINISTRATION

[10.86]
2.27 Notification and advertisement of administrator's appointment

[(1) The notice of appointment to be given by the administrator as soon as reasonably practicable after appointment under paragraph 46(2)(b) shall be gazetted . . . and may be advertised in such other manner as the administrator thinks fit.]

[(1A) In addition to the standard contents, the notice under paragraph (1) must state—
  (a) that an administrator has been appointed,
  (b) the date of the appointment, and
  (c) the nature of the business of the company.]

(2) The administrator shall, as soon as reasonably practicable after the date specified in paragraph 46(6), give notice of his appointment—
  (a) if a receiver or an administrative receiver has been appointed, to him;
  (b) if there is pending a petition for the winding up of the company, to the petitioner (and also to the provisional liquidator, if any);
  (c) to any [enforcement officer] who, to the administrator's knowledge, is charged with execution or other legal process against the company;
  (d) to any person who, to the administrator's knowledge, has distrained against the company or its property; and
  (e) any supervisor of a voluntary arrangement under Part I of the Act.

(3) Where, under a provision of Schedule B1 to the Act or these Rules, the administrator is required to send a notice of his appointment to any person [other than the registrar of companies] he shall do so in Form 2.12B.]

NOTES

Substituted, subject to transitional provisions; see the note preceding r 2.1 at **[10.60]**.

Para (1): substituted by the Insolvency (Amendment) Rules 2009, SI 2009/642, rr 4, 8, as from 6 April 2009, subject to transitional provisions in r 3 thereof, as noted to r 1.4 of these Rules at **[10.6]**; words omitted revoked by the Insolvency (Amendment) Rules 2010, SI 2010/686, r 2, Sch 1, para 43(1), (2), as from 6 April 2010, subject to transitional provisions in Sch 4, para 1 thereto, as noted to r 1.5 at **[10.7]**.

Para (1A): inserted by SI 2010/686, r 2, Sch 1, para 43(1), (3), as from 6 April 2010, subject to transitional provisions in Sch 4, para 1 thereto, as noted to r 1.5 at **[10.7]**.

Para (2): words in square brackets substituted by the Insolvency (Amendment) Rules 2005, SI 2005/527, r 7, as from 1 April 2005.

Para (3): words in square brackets inserted by SI 2010/686, r 2, Sch 1, para 43(1), (4), as from 6 April 2010, subject to transitional provisions in Sch 4, para 2 thereto, as noted to r 1.31 at **[10.34]**.

See Form 2.12B at **[10.673]**.

[10.87]
[2.28 Notice requiring statement of affairs

(1) In this Chapter "relevant person" shall have the meaning given to it in paragraph 47(3).

(2) The administrator shall send notice in Form 2.13B to each relevant person whom he determines appropriate requiring him to prepare and submit a statement of the company's affairs.

(3) The notice shall inform each of the relevant persons—
  (a) of the names and addresses of all others (if any) to whom the same notice has been sent;
  (b) of the time within which the statement must be delivered;
  (c) of the effect of paragraph 48(4) (penalty for non-compliance); and

Part 10   Miscellaneous other SIs

(d) of the application to him, and to each other relevant person, of section 235 (duty to provide information, and to attend on the administrator, if required).

(4) The administrator shall furnish each relevant person to whom he has sent notice in Form 2.13B with the forms required for the preparation of the statement of affairs.]

NOTES

Substituted, subject to transitional provisions; see the note preceding r 2.1 at **[10.60]**.
See Form 2.13B at **[10.673]**.

[10.88]
[2.29 Verification and filing

(1) The statement of the company's affairs shall be in Form 2.14B, contain all the particulars required by that form and be verified by a statement of truth by the relevant person.

(2) The administrator may require any relevant person to submit a statement of concurrence in Form 2.15B stating that he concurs in the statement of affairs. Where the administrator does so, he shall inform the person making the statement of affairs of that fact.

(3) The statement of affairs shall be delivered by the relevant person making the statement of truth, together with a copy, to the administrator. The relevant person shall also deliver a copy of the statement of affairs to all those persons whom the administrator has required to make a statement of concurrence.

(4) A person required to submit a statement of concurrence shall do so before the end of the period of 5 business days (or such other period as the administrator may agree) beginning with the day on which the statement of affairs being concurred with is received by him.

(5) A statement of concurrence may be qualified in respect of matters dealt with in the statement of affairs, where the maker of the statement of concurrence is not in agreement with the relevant person, or he considers the statement of affairs to be erroneous or misleading, or he is without the direct knowledge necessary for concurring with it.

(6) Every statement of concurrence shall be verified by a statement of truth and be delivered to the administrator by the person who makes it, together with a copy of it.

(7) Subject to Rule 2.30 below, the administrator shall as soon as reasonably practicable send to the registrar of companies . . . . a copy of the statement of affairs and any statement of concurrence.]

NOTES

Substituted, subject to transitional provisions; see the note preceding r 2.1 at **[10.60]**.
Para (7): words omitted revoked by the Insolvency (Amendment) Rules 2010, SI 2010/686, r 2, Sch 1, para 44, as from 6 April 2010, subject to transitional provisions in Sch 4, para 1 thereto, as noted to r 1.5 at **[10.7]**.
See Forms 2.14B, 2.15B at **[10.673]**.

[10.89]
[2.30 Limited disclosure

(1) Where the administrator thinks that it would prejudice the conduct of the administration [or might reasonably be expected to lead to violence against any person] for the whole or part of the statement of the company's affairs to be disclosed, he may apply to the court for an order of limited disclosure in respect of the statement, or any specified part of it.

(2) The court may, on such application, order that the statement or, as the case may be, the specified part of it, shall not be filed with the registrar of companies.

(3) The administrator shall as soon as reasonably practicable send to the registrar of companies . . . a copy of the order and the statement of affairs (to the extent provided by the order) and any statement of concurrence.

(4) If a creditor seeks disclosure of a statement of affairs or a specified part of it in relation to which an order has been made under this Rule, he may apply to the court for an order that the administrator disclose it or a specified part of it. The application shall be supported by written evidence in the form of [a witness statement].

(5) The applicant shall give the administrator notice of his application at least 3 [business] days before the hearing.

(6) The court may make any order for disclosure subject to any conditions as to confidentiality, duration, the scope of the order in the event of any change of circumstances, or other matters as it sees [just].

(7) If there is a material change in circumstances rendering the limit on disclosure or any part of it unnecessary, the administrator shall, as soon as reasonably practicable after the change, apply to the court for the order or any part of it to be rescinded.

(8) The administrator shall, as soon as reasonably practicable after the making of an order under paragraph (7) above, file with the registrar of companies . . . . a copy of the statement of affairs to the extent provided by the order.

(9)   When the statement of affairs is filed in accordance with paragraph (8), the administrator shall, where he has sent a statement of proposals under paragraph 49, provide the creditors with a copy of the statement of affairs as filed, or a summary thereof.

(10)   The provisions of Part 31 of the CPR shall not apply to an application under this Rule.]

NOTES

Substituted, subject to transitional provisions; see the note preceding r 2.1 at **[10.60]**.

Paras (1), (5): words in square brackets inserted by the Insolvency (Amendment) Rules 2010, SI 2010/686, r 2, Sch 1, para 45(1), (2), (5), as from 6 April 2010, subject to transitional provisions in Sch 4, para 1 thereto, as noted to r 1.5 at **[10.7]**.

Paras (3), (8): words omitted revoked by SI 2010/686, r 2, Sch 1, para 45(1), (3), (6), as from 6 April 2010, subject to transitional provisions in Sch 4, para 1 thereto, as noted to r 1.5 at **[10.7]**.

Para (4): words in square brackets substituted by SI 2010/686, r 2, Sch 1, para 45(1), (4), as from 6 April 2010, subject to transitional provisions in Sch 4, para 2 thereto, as noted to r 1.31 at **[10.34]**.

Para (6): word in square brackets substituted by SI 2010/686, r 2, Sch 1, para 1, as from 6 April 2010, subject to transitional provisions in Sch 4, para 2 thereto, as noted to r 1.31 at **[10.34]**.

[10.90]
[2.31   Release from duty to submit statement of affairs; extension of time

(1)   The power of the administrator under paragraph 48(2) to give a release from the obligation imposed by paragraph 47(1), or to grant an extension of time, may be exercised at the administrator's own discretion, or at the request of any relevant person.

(2)   A relevant person may, if he requests a release or extension of time and it is refused by the administrator, apply to the court for it.

(3)   The court may, if it thinks that no sufficient cause is shown for the application, dismiss it without a hearing but it shall not do so without giving the relevant person at least [5 business] days' notice, upon receipt of which the relevant person may request the court to list the application for a without notice hearing. If the application is not dismissed the court shall fix a venue for it to be heard, and give notice to the relevant person accordingly.

(4)   The relevant person shall, at least 14 days before the hearing, send to the administrator a notice stating the venue and accompanied by a copy of the application and of any evidence which he (the relevant person) intends to adduce in support of it.

(5)   The administrator may appear and be heard on the application and, whether or not he appears, he may file a written report of any matters which he considers ought to be drawn to the court's attention.

If such a report is filed, a copy of it shall be sent by the administrator to the relevant person, not later than 5 [business] days before the hearing.

(6)   Sealed copies of any order made on the application shall be sent by the court to the relevant person and the administrator.

(7)   On any application under this Rule the relevant person's costs shall be paid in any event by him and, unless the court otherwise orders, no allowance towards them shall be made [as an expense of the administration].]

NOTES

Substituted, subject to transitional provisions; see the note preceding r 2.1 at **[10.60]**.

Words in square brackets substituted or inserted by the Insolvency (Amendment) Rules 2010, SI 2010/686, r 2, Sch 1, para 46, as from 6 April 2010, subject to transitional provisions in Sch 4, para 1 thereto, as noted to r 1.5 at **[10.7]**.

[10.91]
[2.32   Expenses of statement of affairs

(1)   A relevant person making the statement of [affairs of the company] or statement of concurrence shall be allowed, and paid by the administrator [as an expense of the administration], any expenses incurred by the relevant person in so doing which the administrator considers reasonable.

(2)   Any decision by the administrator under this Rule is subject to appeal to the court.

(3)   Nothing in this Rule relieves a relevant person from any obligation with respect to the preparation, verification and submission of the statement of affairs, or to the provision of information to the administrator.]

NOTES

Substituted, subject to transitional provisions; see the note preceding r 2.1 at **[10.60]**.

Para (1): words in square brackets substituted by the Insolvency (Amendment) Rules 2010, SI 2010/686, r 2, Sch 1, para 47, as from 6 April 2010, subject to transitional provisions in Sch 4, para 1 thereto, as noted to r 1.5 at **[10.7]**.

[10.92]
[2.33   Administrator's proposals

(1)   The administrator shall, under paragraph 49, make a statement which he shall send to the registrar of companies . . . .

(2)   The statement shall include, in addition to those matters set out in paragraph 49—

(a)   details of the court where the proceedings are and the relevant court reference number;

(b)   the full name, registered address, registered number and any other trading names of the company;

(c)   details relating to his appointment as administrator, including the date of appointment and the person making the application or appointment and, where there are joint administrators, details of the matters set out in paragraph 100(2);

(d)   the names of the directors and secretary of the company and details of any shareholdings in the company they may have;

(e)   an account of the circumstances giving rise to the appointment of the administrator;

(f)   if a statement of the company's affairs has been submitted, a copy or summary of it, with the administrator's comments, if any;

(g)   if an order limiting the disclosure of the statement of affairs (under Rule 2.30) has been made, a statement of that fact, as well as—
    (i)   details of who provided the statement of affairs;
    (ii)   the date of the order of limited disclosure; and
    (iii) the details or a summary of the details that are not subject to that order;

(h)   if a full statement of affairs is not provided, the names, addresses and debts of the creditors including details of any security held;

(j)   if no statement of affairs has been submitted, details of the financial position of the company at the latest practicable date (which must, unless the court otherwise orders, be a date not earlier than that on which the company entered administration), a list of the company's creditors including their names, addresses and details of their debts, including any security held, and an explanation as to why there is no statement of affairs;

(k)   the basis upon which it is proposed that the administrator's remuneration should be fixed under Rule 2.106;

[(ka) a statement complying with paragraph (2B) of any pre-administration costs charged or incurred by the administrator or, to the administrator's knowledge, by any other person qualified to act as an insolvency practitioner;]

(l)   (except where the administrator proposes a voluntary arrangement in relation to the company and subject to paragraph (3))—
    (i)   to the best of the administrator's knowledge and belief—
        (aa) an estimate of the value of the prescribed part (whether or not he proposes to make an application to court under section 176A(5) or section 176A(3) applies); and
        (bb) an estimate of the value of the company's net property; and
    (ii) whether, and, if so, why, the administrator proposes to make an application to court under section 176A(5);

(m)   [a statement (which must comply with paragraph (2C) where that paragraph applies) of] how it is envisaged the purpose of the administration will be achieved and how it is proposed that the administration shall end . . . ;

(n)   where the administrator has decided not to call a meeting of creditors, his reasons;

(o)   the manner in which the affairs and business of the company—
    (i)   have, since the date of the administrator's appointment, been managed and financed, including, where any assets have been disposed of, the reasons for such disposals and the terms upon which such disposals were made; and
    (ii) will, if the administrator's proposals are approved, continue to be managed and financed;

(p)   whether—
    (i)   the EC Regulation applies; and
    (ii) if so, whether the proceedings are main proceedings[, secondary proceedings] or territorial proceedings; and

(q)   such other information (if any) as the administrator thinks necessary to enable creditors to decide whether or not to vote for the adoption of the proposals.

[(2A)   In this Part—
(a)   "pre-administration costs" are—
    (i)   fees charged, and
    (ii) expenses incurred,
by the administrator, or another person qualified to act as an insolvency practitioner, before the company entered administration but with a view to its doing so; and

(b)   "unpaid pre-administration costs" are pre-administration costs which had not been paid when the company entered administration.

(2B)   A statement of pre-administration costs complies with this paragraph if it includes—
(a)   details of any agreement under which the fees were charged and expenses incurred, including the parties to the agreement and the date on which the agreement was made,
(b)   details of the work done for which the fees were charged and expenses incurred,
(c)   an explanation of why the work was done before the company entered administration and how it would further the achievement of an objective in sub-paragraph (1) of paragraph 3 in accordance with sub-paragraphs (2) to (4) of that paragraph,

(d)   a statement of the amount of the pre-administration costs, setting out separately—
    (i)   the fees charged by the administrator,
    (ii)   the expenses incurred by the administrator,
    (iii) the fees charged (to the administrator's knowledge) by any other person qualified to act as an insolvency practitioner (and, if more than one, by each separately), and
    (iv)   the expenses incurred (to the administrator's knowledge) by any other person qualified to act as an insolvency practitioner (and, if more than one, by each separately),

(e)   a statement of the amounts of pre-administration costs which have already been paid (set out separately as under sub-paragraph (d)),

(f)   the identity of the person who made the payment or, if more than one person made the payment, the identity of each such person and of the amounts paid by each such person set out separately as under sub-paragraph (d),

(g)   a statement of the amounts of unpaid pre-administration costs (set out separately as under sub-paragraph (d)), and

(h)   a statement that the payment of unpaid pre-administration costs as an expense of the administration is—
    (i)   subject to approval under Rule 2.67A, and
    (ii)   not part of the proposals subject to approval under paragraph 53.

(2C)   This paragraph applies where it is proposed that the administration will end by the company moving to a creditors' voluntary liquidation; and in that case, the statement required by paragraph (2)(m) must include—
(a)   details of the proposed liquidator;
(b)   where applicable, the declaration required by section 231; and
(c)   a statement that the creditors may, before the proposals are approved, nominate a different person as liquidator in accordance with paragraph 83(7)(a) and Rule 2.117A(2)(b).]

(3)   Nothing in paragraph (2)(l) is to be taken as requiring any such estimate to include any information, the disclosure of which could seriously prejudice the commercial interests of the company. If such information is excluded from the calculation the estimate shall be accompanied by a statement to that effect.

(4)   Where the court orders, upon an application by the administrator under paragraph 107, an extension of the period of time in paragraph 49(5), the administrator [must as soon as reasonably practicable after the making of the order—
(a)   notify in Form 2.18B every creditor of the company and every member of the company of whose address (in either case) the administrator is aware, and
(b)   send a copy of the notification to the registrar of companies.]

(5)   Where the administrator has made a statement under paragraph 52(1) and has not called an initial meeting of creditors, the proposals sent out under this Rule and paragraph 49 will (if no meeting has been requisitioned under paragraph 52(2) within the period set out in Rule 2.37(1)) be deemed to have been approved by the creditors.

[(5A)   Where proposals are deemed under paragraph (5) to have been approved, the administrator must, as soon as reasonably practicable after expiry of the period set out in Rule 2.37(1), give notice of the date on which they were deemed to have been approved to the registrar of companies, the court and the creditors; and a copy of the proposals must be attached to the notice given to the court and to creditors who have not previously received them.]

(6)   Where the administrator intends to apply to the court (or file a notice under paragraph 80(2)) for the administration to cease at a time before he has sent a statement of his proposals to creditors in accordance with paragraph 49, he shall, at least [7 business] days before he makes such an application (or files such a notice), send to all creditors of the company (so far as he is aware of their addresses) a report containing the information required by paragraphs (2)(a)–(p) of this Rule.

[(7)   Where the administrator wishes to publish a notice under paragraph 49(6), the notice shall be advertised in such manner as the administrator thinks fit.

[(7A)   In addition to the standard contents, the notice under paragraph (7) must state—
(a)   that members can write for a copy of the statement of proposals for achieving the purpose of administration; and
(b)   the address to which to write.]]

(8)   This notice must be published as soon as reasonably practicable after the administrator sends his statement of proposals to the company's creditors but no later than 8 weeks (or such other period as may be agreed by the creditors or as the court may order) from the date that the company entered administration.]

NOTES

Substituted, subject to transitional provisions; see the note preceding r 2.1 at **[10.60]**.

Para (1): words omitted revoked by the Insolvency (Amendment) Rules 2010, SI 2010/686, r 2, Sch 1, para 48(1), (2), as from 6 April 2010, subject to transitional provisions in Sch 4, para 1 thereto, as noted to r 1.5 at **[10.7]**.

Para (2): sub-para (ka) and words in square brackets in sub-paras (m), (p) inserted, and words omitted from sub-para (m) revoked, by SI 2010/686, r 2, Sch 1, para 48(1), (3), as from 6 April 2010, subject to transitional provisions in Sch 4, para 1 thereto, as noted to r 1.5 at **[10.7]**.

Paras (2A)–(2C), (5A): inserted by SI 2010/686, r 2, Sch 1, para 48(1), (4), (6), as from 6 April 2010, subject to transitional provisions in Sch 4, para 1 thereto, as noted to r 1.5 at **[10.7]**.

Paras (4), (6): words in square brackets substituted by SI 2010/686, r 2, Sch 1, para 48(1), (5), (7), as from 6 April 2010, subject to transitional provisions in Sch 4, para 1 thereto, as noted to r 1.5 at **[10.7]**.

Para (7): substituted, together with para (7A) for the original para (7), by the Insolvency (Amendment) Rules 2009, SI 2009/642, rr 4, 9, as from 6 April 2009, subject to transitional provisions in r 3 thereof, as noted to r 1.4 of these Rules at **[10.6]**.

Para (7A): substituted as noted to para (7) above; further substituted by SI 2010/686, r 2, Sch 1, para 48(1), (8), as from 6 April 2010, subject to transitional provisions in Sch 4, para 1 thereto, as noted to r 1.5 at **[10.7]**.

EC Regulation: ie, Council Regulation 1346/2000/EC on insolvency proceedings.

See Form 2.18B at **[10.673]**.

[10.93]
[2.33A   Limited disclosure of para 49 statement

(1)   Where the administrator thinks that it would prejudice the conduct of the administration or might reasonably be expected to lead to violence against any person for any of the matters specified in Rule 2.33(2)(h) and (j) to be disclosed, the administrator may apply to the court for an order of limited disclosure in respect of any specified part of the statement under paragraph 49.

(2)   The court may, on such application, order that some or all of the specified part of the statement must not be sent to the registrar of companies or to creditors or members of the company as otherwise required by paragraph 49(4).

(3)   The administrator must as soon as reasonably practicable send to the persons specified in paragraph 49(4) the statement under paragraph 49 (to the extent provided by the order) and an indication of the nature of the matter in relation to which the order was made.

(4)   The administrator must also send a copy of the order to the registrar of companies.

(5)   A creditor who seeks disclosure of a part of a statement under paragraph 49 in relation to which an order has been made under this Rule may apply to the court for an order that the administrator disclose it. The application must be supported by written evidence in the form of a witness statement.

(6)   The applicant must give the administrator notice of the application at least 3 business days before the hearing.

(7)   The court may make any order for disclosure subject to any conditions as to confidentiality, duration, the scope of the order in the event of any change of circumstances, or other matters as it sees just.

(8)   If there is a material change in circumstances rendering the limit on disclosure or any part of it unnecessary, the administrator must, as soon as reasonably practicable after the change, apply to the court for the order or any part of it to be rescinded.

(9)   The administrator must, as soon as reasonably practicable after the making of an order under paragraph (8), send to the persons specified in paragraph 49(4) a copy of the statement under paragraph 49 to the extent provided by the order.

(10)   The provisions of CPR Part 31 do not apply to an application under this Rule.]

NOTES
Commencement: 6 April 2010.
Inserted by the Insolvency (Amendment) Rules 2010, SI 2010/686, r 2, Sch 1, para 49, subject to transitional provisions in Sch 4, para 1 thereto, as noted to r 1.5 at **[10.7]**.

[CHAPTER 6
MEETINGS AND REPORTS

Section A: Creditors' Meetings

[10.94]
2.34   Meetings to consider administrator's proposals
[(1)   As soon as reasonably practicable after an invitation to the initial creditors' meeting has been sent to the creditors in compliance with the requirements of paragraph 51(1), the administrator [must have gazetted a notice which, in addition to the standard contents, must state—
(a)   that an initial creditors' meeting is to take place; and
(b)   the venue fixed for the meeting.]]

[(1A)   The information required to be gazetted under paragraph (1) may also be advertised in such other manner as the administrator thinks fit.]

(2)   Notice in Form 2.19B to attend the meeting shall be sent out at the same time to any directors or officers of the company (including persons who have been directors or officers in the past) whose presence at the meeting is, in the administrator's opinion, required.

(3)   Where the court orders an extension to the period set out in paragraph 51(2)(b) the administrator shall send a notice in Form 2.18B to each person to whom he is required to send notice by paragraph 49(4).

(4) If at the meeting there is not the requisite majority for approval of the administrator's proposals (with modifications, if any), the chairman may, and shall if a resolution is passed to that effect, adjourn the meeting for not more than 14 days . . . (subject to any direction by the court).

[(5) If there are subsequently further adjournments, the final adjournment must not be to a day later than 14 days after the date on which the meeting was originally held, subject to any direction of the court.

(6) Where a meeting is adjourned under this Rule, proofs and proxies may be used if lodged at any time up to 12.00 hours on the business day immediately before the adjourned meeting.]]

NOTES

Substituted, subject to transitional provisions; see the note preceding r 2.1 at **[10.60]**.
Para (1) substituted, and para (1A) inserted, by the Insolvency (Amendment) Rules 2009, SI 2009/642, rr 4, 10, as from 6 April 2009, subject to transitional provisions in r 3 thereof, as noted to r 1.4 of these Rules at **[10.6]**.
Words in square brackets in para (1) substituted by the Insolvency (Amendment) Rules 2010, SI 2010/686, r 2, Sch 1, para 50(1), (2), as from 6 April 2010, subject to transitional provisions in Sch 4, para 1 thereto, as noted to r 1.5 at **[10.7]**.
Para (4): words omitted revoked by SI 2010/686, r 2, Sch 1, para 50(1), (3), as from 6 April 2010, subject to transitional provisions in Sch 4, para 1 thereto, as noted to r 1.5 at **[10.7]**.
Paras (5), (6): added by SI 2010/686, r 2, Sch 1, para 50(1), (4), as from 6 April 2010, subject to transitional provisions in Sch 4, para 1 thereto, as noted to r 1.5 at **[10.7]**.
See Forms 2.18B, 2.19B at **[10.673]**.

[10.95]
[2.35 Creditors' meetings generally

(1) This Rule applies to creditors' meetings summoned by the administrator under—
   (a) paragraph 51 (initial creditors' meeting);
   (b) paragraph 52(2) (at the request of the creditors);
   (c) paragraph 54(2) (to consider revision to the administrator's proposals);
   (d) paragraph 56(1) (further creditors' meetings); and
   (e) paragraph 62 (general power to summon meetings of creditors).

(2) Notice of any of the meetings set out in paragraph (1) above shall be in Form 2.20B.

(3) In fixing the venue for the meeting, the administrator shall have regard to the convenience of creditors and the meeting shall be summoned for commencement between 10.00 and 16.00 hours on a business day, unless the court otherwise directs.

(4) Subject to paragraphs (6) and (7) below, at least 14 days' notice of the meeting shall be given to all creditors who are known to the administrator and had claims against the company at the date when the company entered administration unless that creditor has subsequently been paid in full; and the notice shall—
   (a) specify the purpose of the meeting;
   (b) contain a statement of the effect of Rule 2.38 (entitlement to vote); and
   (c) contain the forms of proxy.

[(4A) As soon as reasonably practicable after notice of the meeting has been given, the administrator must have gazetted a notice which, in addition to the standard contents, must state—
   (a) that a creditors' meeting is to take place;
   (b) the venue fixed for the meeting;
   (c) the purpose of the meeting; and
   (d) a statement of the effect of Rule 2.38 (entitlement to vote).]

(5) If within 30 minutes from the time fixed for commencement of the meeting there is no person present to act as chairman, the meeting stands adjourned to the same time and place in the following week or, if that is not a business day, to the business day immediately following.

[(6A) If within 30 minutes from the time fixed for the commencement of the meeting those persons attending the meeting do not constitute a quorum, the chairman may adjourn the meeting to such time and place as the chairman may appoint.

(6B) Once only in the course of the meeting the chairman may, without an adjournment, declare the meeting suspended for any period up to 1 hour.

(6C) The chairman may, and must if the meeting so resolves, adjourn the meeting to such time and place as seems to the chairman to be appropriate in the circumstances.
   An adjournment under this paragraph must not be for a period of more than 14 days, subject to the direction of the court.

(6D) If there are subsequently further adjournments, the final adjournment must not be to a day later than 14 days after the date on which the meeting was originally held.

(6E) Where a meeting is adjourned under this Rule, proofs and proxies may be used if lodged at any time up to 12.00 hours on the business day immediately before the adjourned meeting.

(6F) Paragraph (3) applies with regard to the venue fixed for a meeting adjourned under this Rule.]

(7)   . . .]

NOTES

Substituted, subject to transitional provisions; see the note preceding r 2.1 at **[10.60]**.

Para (4A): inserted by the Insolvency (Amendment) Rules 2010, SI 2010/686, r 2, Sch 1, para 51(1), (2), as from 6 April 2010, subject to transitional provisions in Sch 4, para 1 thereto, as noted to r 1.5 at **[10.7]**.

Paras (6A)–(6F): substituted for original para (6) by SI 2010/686, r 2, Sch 1, para 51(1), (3), as from 6 April 2010, subject to transitional provisions in Sch 4, para 1 thereto, as noted to r 1.5 at **[10.7]**.

Para (7): revoked by SI 2010/686, r 2, Sch 1, para 51(1), (4), as from 6 April 2010, subject to transitional provisions in Sch 4, para 1 thereto, as noted to r 1.5 at **[10.7]**.

See Form 2.20B at **[10.673]**.

[10.96]
[2.36   The chairman at meetings

(1)   At any meeting of creditors summoned by the administrator, either he shall be chairman, or a person nominated by him in writing to act in his place.

(2)   A person so nominated must be either—

   (a)   one who is qualified to act as an insolvency practitioner in relation to the company; or

   (b)   an employee of the administrator or his firm who is experienced in insolvency matters.

[(3)   Where the chairman holds a proxy which includes a requirement to vote for a particular resolution and no other person proposes that resolution—

   (a)   the chairman must propose it unless the chairman considers that there is good reason for not doing so, and

   (b)   if the chairman does not propose it, the chairman must as soon as reasonably practicable after the meeting notify the principal of the reason why not.]]

NOTES

Substituted, subject to transitional provisions; see the note preceding r 2.1 at **[10.60]**.

Para (3): added by the Insolvency (Amendment) Rules 2010, SI 2010/686, r 2, Sch 1, para 52, as from 6 April 2010, subject to transitional provisions in Sch 4, para 1 thereto, as noted to r 1.5 at **[10.7]**.

[10.97]
[2.37   Meeting requisitioned by creditors

(1)   The request for a creditors' meeting under paragraph 52(2) or 56(1) shall be in Form 2.21B. A request for an initial creditors' meeting shall be made within [8 business] days of the date on which the administrator's statement of proposals is sent out. A request under paragraph 52(2) or 56(1) shall include—

   (a)   a list of the creditors concurring with the request, showing the amounts of their respective debts in the administration;

   (b)   from each creditor concurring, written confirmation of his concurrence; and

   (c)   a statement of the purpose of the proposed meeting,

but [sub-paragraphs (a) and (b) do] not apply if the requisitioning creditor's debt is alone sufficient without the concurrence of other creditors.

(2)   A meeting requested under paragraph 52(2) or 56(1) shall be held within 28 days of the administrator's receipt of the notice requesting the meeting.

(3)   The expenses of summoning and holding a meeting at the request of a creditor shall be paid by that person, who shall deposit with the administrator security for their payment.

(4)   The sum to be deposited shall be such as the administrator may determine, and he shall not act without the deposit having been made.

(5)   The meeting may resolve that the expenses of summoning and holding it are to be payable out of the assets of the company as an expense of the administration.

(6)   To the extent that any deposit made under this Rule is not required for the payment of expenses of summoning and holding the meeting, it shall be repaid to the person who made it.]

NOTES

Substituted, subject to transitional provisions; see the note preceding r 2.1 at **[10.60]**.

Para (1): words in square brackets substituted by the Insolvency (Amendment) Rules 2010, SI 2010/686, r 2, Sch 1, para 53, as from 6 April 2010, subject to transitional provisions in Sch 4, para 1 thereto, as noted to r 1.5 at **[10.7]**.

See Form 2.21B at **[10.673]**.

[10.98]
[2.37A   Notice of meetings by advertisement only

(1)   The court may order that notice of any meeting be given by advertisement and not by individual notice to the persons concerned.

(2)   In considering whether to act under this Rule, the court must have regard to the cost of advertisement, the amount of assets available and the extent of the interest of creditors, members or any particular class of either.]

NOTES

Commencement: 6 April 2010.

Inserted by the Insolvency (Amendment) Rules 2010, SI 2010/686, r 2, Sch 1, para 54, subject to transitional provisions in Sch 4, para 1 thereto, as noted to r 1.5 at **[10.7]**.

[10.99]
[2.38   Entitlement to vote

(1)   Subject as follows, at a meeting of creditors in administration proceedings a person is entitled to vote only if—

   (a)   he has given to the administrator, not later than 12.00 hours on the business day before the day fixed for the meeting, details in writing of the debt which—

      (i)   he claims to be due to him from the company; or

      (ii)   in relation to a member State liquidator, is claimed to be due to creditors in proceedings in relation to which he holds office;

   (b)   the claim has been duly admitted under [Rule 2.39 or] this Rule; and

   (c)   there has been lodged with the administrator any proxy which he intends to be used on his behalf,

and details of the debt must include any calculation for the purposes of Rules 2.40 to 2.42.

(2)   The chairman of the meeting may allow a creditor to vote, notwithstanding that he has failed to comply with paragraph (1)(a), if satisfied that the failure was due to circumstances beyond the creditor's control.

(3)   The chairman of the meeting may call for any document or other evidence to be produced to him, where he thinks it necessary for the purpose of substantiating the whole or any part of the claim.

(4)   Votes are calculated according to the amount of a creditor's claim as at the date on which the company entered administration, less any payments that have been made to him after that date in respect of his claim and any adjustment by way of set-off in accordance with Rule 2.85 as if that Rule were applied on the date that the votes are counted.

(5)   A creditor shall not vote in respect of a debt for an unliquidated amount, or any debt whose value is not ascertained, except where the chairman agrees to put upon the debt an estimated minimum value for the purpose of entitlement to vote and admits the claim for that purpose.

(6)   No vote shall be cast by virtue of a claim more than once on any resolution put to the meeting.

(7)   Where—

   (a)   a creditor is entitled to vote under this Rule [and Rule 2.39];

   (b)   has lodged his claim in one or more sets of other proceedings; and

   (c)   votes (either in person or by proxy) on a resolution put to the meeting; and

   (d)   the member State liquidator casts a vote in respect of the same claim,

only the creditor's vote shall be counted.

(8)   Where—

   (a)   a creditor has lodged his claim in more than one set of other proceedings; and

   (b)   more than one member State liquidator seeks to vote by virtue of that claim,

the entitlement to vote by virtue of that claim is exercisable by the member State liquidator in main proceedings, whether or not the creditor has lodged his claim in the main proceedings.

(9)   For the purposes of paragraph (6), the claim of a creditor and of any member State liquidator in relation to the same debt are a single claim.

(10)   For the purposes of paragraphs (7) and (8), "other proceedings" means main proceedings, secondary proceedings or territorial proceedings in another member State.]

NOTES

Substituted, subject to transitional provisions; see the note preceding r 2.1 at **[10.60]**.

Para (1): words in square brackets substituted by the Insolvency (Amendment) Rules 2010, SI 2010/686, r 2, Sch 1, para 55(1), (2), as from 6 April 2010, subject to transitional provisions in Sch 4, para 1 thereto, as noted to r 1.5 at **[10.7]**.

Para (7): words in square brackets in sub-para (a) added by SI 2010/686, r 2, Sch 1, para 55(1), (3), as from 6 April 2010, subject to transitional provisions in Sch 4, para 1 thereto, as noted to r 1.5 at **[10.7]**.

[10.100]
[2.39   Admission and rejection of claims

(1)   At any creditors' meeting the chairman has power to admit or reject a creditor's claim for the purpose of his entitlement to vote; and the power is exercisable with respect to the whole or any part of the claim.

(2)   The chairman's decision under this Rule, or in respect of any matter arising under Rule 2.38, is subject to appeal to the court by any creditor.

(3)   If the chairman is in doubt whether a claim should be admitted or rejected, he shall mark it as objected to and allow the creditor to vote, subject to his vote being subsequently declared invalid if the objection to the claim is sustained.

Part 10   Miscellaneous other SIs

(4)   If on an appeal the chairman's decision is reversed or varied, or a creditor's vote is declared invalid, the court may order that another meeting be summoned, or make such other order as it thinks [just].

[(5)   An application to the court by way of appeal under this Rule against a decision of the chairman must be made not later than 21 days after the date of the meeting.]

(6)   Neither the administrator nor any person nominated by him to be chairman is personally liable for costs incurred by any person in respect of an appeal to the court under this Rule, unless the court makes an order to that effect.]

NOTES

Substituted, subject to transitional provisions; see the note preceding r 2.1 at **[10.60]**.

Para (4): word in square brackets substituted by the Insolvency (Amendment) Rules 2010, SI 2010/686, r 2, Sch 1, para 1, as from 6 April 2010, subject to transitional provisions in Sch 4, para 2 thereto as noted to r 1.31 at **[10.34]**.

Para (5): substituted by SI 2010/686, r 2, Sch 1, para 56, as from 6 April 2010, subject to transitional provisions in Sch 4, para 1 thereto, as noted to r 1.5 at **[10.7]**.

[10.101]
[2.40   Secured creditors

(1)   At a meeting of creditors a secured creditor is entitled to vote only in respect of the balance (if any) of his debt after deducting the value of his security as estimated by him.

(2)   However, in a case where the administrator has made a statement under paragraph 52(1)(b) and an initial creditors' meeting has been requisitioned under paragraph 52(2) then a secured creditor is entitled to vote in respect of the full value of his debt without any deduction of the value of his security.]

NOTES

Substituted, subject to transitional provisions; see the note preceding r 2.1 at **[10.60]**.

[10.102]
[2.41   Holders of negotiable instruments

A creditor shall not vote in respect of a debt on, or secured by, a current bill of exchange or promissory note, unless he is willing—

(a)   to treat the liability to him on the bill or note of every person who is liable on it antecedently to the company, and against whom a bankruptcy order has not been made (or, in the case of a company, which has not gone into liquidation), as a security in his hands; and

(b)   to estimate the value of the security and, for the purpose of his entitlement to vote [(but not for dividend)], to deduct it from his claim.]

NOTES

Substituted, subject to transitional provisions; see the note preceding r 2.1 at **[10.60]**.

Words in square brackets inserted by the Insolvency (Amendment) Rules 2010, SI 2010/686, r 2, Sch 1, para 57, as from 6 April 2010, subject to transitional provisions in Sch 4, para 1 thereto, as noted to r 1.5 at **[10.7]**.

[10.103]
[2.42   Hire-purchase, conditional sale and chattel leasing agreements

(1)   Subject as follows, an owner of goods under a hire-purchase or chattel leasing agreement, or a seller of goods under a conditional sale agreement, is entitled to vote in respect of the amount of the debt due and payable to him by the company on the date that the company entered administration.

(2)   In calculating the amount of any debt for this purpose, no account shall be taken of any amount attributable to the exercise of any right under the relevant agreement, so far as the right has become exercisable solely by virtue of the making of an administration application, a notice of intention to appoint an administrator or any matter arising as a consequence, or of the company entering administration.]

NOTES

Substituted, subject to transitional provisions; see the note preceding r 2.1 at **[10.60]**.

[10.104]
[2.43   Resolutions

(1)   Subject to paragraph (2), at a creditors' meeting in administration proceedings, a resolution is passed when a majority (in value) of those present and voting, in person or by proxy, have voted in favour of it.

(2)   Any resolution is invalid if those voting against it include more than half in value of the creditors to whom notice of the meeting was sent and who are not, to the best of the chairman's belief, persons connected with the company.]

NOTES

Substituted, subject to transitional provisions; see the note preceding r 2.1 at **[10.60]**.

[10.105]
[2.44A   Minutes

(1)   The chairman of the meeting must cause minutes of its proceedings to be kept.

(2)   The minutes must be authenticated by the chairman, and be retained by the chairman as part of the records of the administration.

(3)   The chairman must also cause to be made up and kept a list of all the creditors who attended the meeting.

(4)   The minutes must include—
  (a)   a list of the names of creditors who attended (personally or by proxy) and their claims,
  (b)   if a creditors' committee has been established, the names and addresses of those elected to be members of the committee, and
  (c)   a record of every resolution passed.]

NOTES

Commencement: 6 April 2010.

Substituted for r 2.44 by the Insolvency (Amendment) Rules 2010, SI 2010/686, r 2, Sch 1, para 58, as from 6 April 2010, subject to transitional provisions in Sch 4, para 1 thereto, as noted to r 1.5 at **[10.7]**.

[10.106]
[2.45   Revision of the administrator's proposals

(1)   The administrator shall, under paragraph 54, make a statement setting out the proposed revisions to his proposals which he shall attach to Form 2.22B and send to all those to whom he is required to send a copy of his revised proposals.

(2)   The statement of revised proposals shall include—
  (a)   details of the court where the proceedings are and the relevant court reference number;
  (b)   the full name, registered address, registered number and any other trading names of the company;
  (c)   details relating to his appointment as administrator, including the date of appointment and the person making the administration application or appointment;
  (d)   the names of the directors and secretary of the company and details of any shareholdings in the company they may have;
  (e)   a summary of the initial proposals and the reason(s) for proposing a revision;
  (f)   details of the proposed revision including details of the administrator's assessment of the likely impact of the proposed revision upon creditors generally or upon each class of creditors (as the case may be);
  (g)   where a proposed revision relates to the ending of the administration by a creditors' voluntary liquidation and the nomination of a person to be the proposed liquidator of the company—
    [(i)   details of the proposed liquidator,
    (ii)   where applicable, the declaration required by section 231, and
    (iii)   a statement that the creditors may, before the proposals are approved, nominate a different person as liquidator in accordance with paragraph 83(7)(a) and Rule 2.117A(2)(b);] and
  (h)   any other information that the administrator thinks necessary to enable creditors to decide whether or not to vote for the proposed revisions.

(3)   Subject to paragraph 54(3), within 5 [business] days of sending out the statement in paragraph (1) above, the administrator shall send a copy of the statement to every member of the company.

(4)   [Any notice to be published by the administrator acting under paragraph 54(3) shall be advertised in such manner as the administrator thinks fit.]

[(5)   The notice must be published as soon as reasonably practicable after the administrator sends the statement to the creditors and in addition to the standard contents must state—
  (a)   that members can write for a copy of the statement of revised proposals for the administration; and
  (b)   the address to which to write.]]

NOTES

Substituted, subject to transitional provisions; see the note preceding r 2.1 at **[10.60]**.

Para (2): words in square brackets in sub-para (g) substituted by the Insolvency (Amendment) Rules 2010, SI 2010/686, r 2, Sch 1, para 59(1), (2), as from 6 April 2010, subject to transitional provisions in Sch 4, para 1 thereto, as noted to r 1.5 at **[10.7]**.

Para (3): word in square brackets inserted by SI 2010/686, r 2, Sch 1, para 59(1), (3), as from 6 April 2010, subject to transitional provisions in Sch 4, para 1 thereto, as noted to r 1.5 at **[10.7]**.

Part 10   Miscellaneous other SIs

Para (4): words in square brackets substituted by the Insolvency (Amendment) Rules 2009, SI 2009/642, rr 4, 11, as from 6 April 2009, subject to transitional provisions in r 3 thereof, as noted to r 1.4 of these Rules at **[10.6]**.

Para (5): substituted for part of the original para (4) by SI 2010/686, r 2, Sch 1, para 59(1), (4), as from 6 April 2010, subject to transitional provisions in Sch 4, para 1 thereto, as noted to r 1.5 at **[10.7]**.

See Form 2.22B at **[10.673]**.

[10.107]
[2.46   Notice to creditors
As soon as reasonably practicable after the conclusion of a meeting of creditors to consider the administrator's proposals or revised proposals, the administrator shall—

[(a)   send notice in Form 2.23B of the result of the meeting to every creditor and to every other person who received a copy of the original proposals,

(b)   attach a copy of the proposals considered at the meeting to the notice sent to each creditor who did not receive notice of the meeting but of whose claim the administrator has subsequently become aware, and

(c)   file with the court a copy of the proposals considered at the meeting and notice of the result of the meeting.]]

NOTES

Substituted, subject to transitional provisions; see the note preceding r 2.1 at **[10.60]**.

Paras (a)–(c): substituted (for original paras (a), (b)) by the Insolvency (Amendment) Rules 2010, SI 2010/686, r 2, Sch 1, para 60, as from 6 April 2010, subject to transitional provisions in Sch 4, para 1 thereto, as noted to r 1.5 at **[10.7]**.

See Form 2.23B at **[10.673]**.

[10.108]
[2.47   Reports to creditors
(1)   "Progress report" means a report which includes—
    (a)   details of the court where the proceedings are and the relevant court reference number;
    (b)   full details of the company's name, address of registered office and registered number;
    (c)   full details of the administrator's name and address, date of appointment and name and address of appointor, including any changes in office-holder, and, in the case of joint administrators, their functions as set out in the statement made for the purposes of paragraph 100(2);
    (d)   details of any extensions to the initial period of appointment;
    [(da)   details of the basis fixed for the remuneration of the administrator under Rule 2.106 (or if not fixed at the date of the report, the steps taken during the period of the report to fix it);
    (db)   if the basis of remuneration has been fixed, a statement of—
        (i)   the remuneration charged by the administrator during the period of the report (subject to paragraph (2A)), and
        (ii)   where the report is the first to be made after the basis has been fixed, the remuneration charged by the administrator during the periods covered by the previous reports (subject to paragraph (2A)), together with a description of the things done by the administrator during those periods in respect of which the remuneration was charged,
    irrespective in either case of whether payment was made in respect of that remuneration during the period of the report;
    (dc)   a statement of the expenses incurred by the administrator during the period of the report, irrespective of whether payment was made in respect of them during that period;]
    (e)   details of progress during the period of the report, including a receipts and payments account (as detailed in paragraph (2) below);
    (f)   details of any assets that remain to be realised;
    [(fa)   a statement of the creditors' right to request information under Rule 2.48A and their right to challenge the administrator's remuneration and expenses under Rule 2.109; and]
    (g)   any other relevant information for the creditors.

[(2)   A receipts and payments account must be in the form of an abstract showing receipts and payments during the period of the report and, where the administrator has ceased to act, must also include a statement as to the amount paid to unsecured creditors by virtue of the application of section 176A.

(2A)   Where the basis for the remuneration is a set amount under Rule 2.106(2)(c), it may be shown as that amount without any apportionment to the period of the report.

(2B)   Where the administrator has made a statement of pre-administration costs under Rule 2.33(2)(ka)—
    (a)   if they are approved under Rule 2.67A, the first progress report after the approval must include a statement setting out the date of the approval and the amounts approved;
    (b)   each successive report, so long as any of the costs remain unapproved, must include a statement either—
        (i)   of any steps taken to get approval, or

(ii) that the administrator has decided, or (as the case may be) another insolvency practitioner entitled to seek approval has told the administrator of that practitioner's decision, not to seek approval.]

[(3) The progress report must, except where paragraph (3A) or (3B) applies, cover the period of 6 months commencing on the date on which the company entered administration and every subsequent period of 6 months.

(3A) The period to be covered by a progress report ends on the date when an administrator ceases to act, and the period to be covered by each subsequent progress report is each successive period of 6 months beginning immediately after that date (subject to the further application of this paragraph when another administrator ceases to act).

(3B) The sending of a progress report to creditors under Rule 2.112 (application for extension of administration) also satisfies paragraph (3) or (3A) of this Rule in respect of the period covered by that report; and the period to be covered by each subsequent progress report under this Rule is each successive period of 6 months beginning with the end of the period covered by the report under Rule 2.112.]

[(4) The administrator must, within 1 month of the end of the period covered by the report, send—

    (a) a copy to the creditors attached to Form 2.24B, and

    (b) a copy to the registrar of companies;

but this paragraph does not apply when the period covered by the report is that of a final progress report under Rule 2.110.]

(5) The court may, on the administrator's application, extend the period of 1 month mentioned in paragraph (4) above, or make such other order in respect of the content of the report as it thinks [just].

(6) If the administrator makes default in complying with this Rule, he is liable to a fine and, for continued contravention, to a daily default fine.]

NOTES

Substituted, subject to transitional provisions; see the note preceding r 2.1 at **[10.60]**.

Para (1): sub-paras (da)–(dc), (fa) inserted, and word omitted from sub-para (f) revoked, by the Insolvency (Amendment) Rules 2010, SI 2010/686, r 2, Sch 1, para 61(1), (2), as from 6 April 2010, subject to transitional provisions in Sch 4, para 1 thereto, as noted to r 1.5 at **[10.7]**.

Paras (2), (2A), (2B): substituted (for the original para (2)) by SI 2010/686, r 2, Sch 1, para 61(1), (3), as from 6 April 2010, subject to transitional provisions in Sch 4, para 1 thereto, as noted to r 1.5 at **[10.7]**.

Paras (3), (3A), (3B): substituted (for the original para (3)) by SI 2010/686, r 2, Sch 1, para 61(1), (4), as from 6 April 2010, subject to transitional provisions in Sch 4, para 1 thereto, as noted to r 1.5 at **[10.7]**.

Para (4): substituted by SI 2010/686, r 2, Sch 1, para 61(1), (5), as from 6 April 2010, subject to transitional provisions in Sch 4, para 1 thereto, as noted to r 1.5 at **[10.7]**.

Para (5): word in square brackets substituted by SI 2010/686, r 2, Sch 1, para 1, as from 6 April 2010, subject to transitional provisions in Sch 4, para 2 thereto, as noted to r 1.31 at **[10.34]**.

See Form 2.24B at **[10.673]**.

[10.109]
[2.48 Correspondence instead of creditors' meetings

(1) The administrator may seek to obtain the passing of a resolution by the creditors by sending a notice in Form 2.25B to every creditor who is entitled to be notified of a creditors' meeting under Rule 2.35(4).

(2) In order to be counted, votes must be received by the administrator by 12.00 hours on the closing date specified on Form 2.25B and must be accompanied by the statement in writing on entitlement to vote required by Rule 2.38 [unless it has already been given to the administrator under that Rule].

(3) If any votes are received without the statement as to entitlement, or the administrator decides that the creditor is not entitled to vote according to Rules 2.38 and 2.39, then that creditor's votes shall be disregarded.

(4) The closing date shall be set at the discretion of the administrator. In any event it must not be set less than 14 days from the date of issue of the Form 2.25B.

(5) For any business to be transacted the administrator must receive at least 1 valid Form 2.25B by the closing date specified by him.

(6) If no valid Form 2.25B is received by the closing date specified then the administrator shall call a meeting of the creditors in accordance with Rule 2.35.

(7) Any single creditor, or a group of creditors, of the company whose debt(s) amount to at least 10% of the total debts of the company may, within 5 business days from the date of the administrator sending out a resolution or proposals, require him to summon a meeting of creditors to consider the matters raised therein in accordance with Rule 2.37. Any meeting called under this Rule shall be conducted in accordance with Rule 2.35.

(8) . . .

(9)   A reference in these Rules to anything done, or required to be done, at, or in connection with, or in consequence of, a creditors' meeting includes a reference to anything done in the course of correspondence in accordance with this Rule.]

NOTES
   Substituted, subject to transitional provisions; see the note preceding r 2.1 at **[10.60]**.
   Para (2): words in square brackets inserted by the Insolvency (Amendment) Rules 2010, SI 2010/686, r 2, Sch 1, para 62(1), (2), as from 6 April 2010, subject to transitional provisions in Sch 4, para 1 thereto, as noted to r 1.5 at **[10.7]**.
   Para (8): revoked by SI 2010/686, r 2, Sch 1, para 62(1), (3), as from 6 April 2010, subject to transitional provisions in Sch 4, para 1 thereto, as noted to r 1.5 at **[10.7]**.
   See Form 2.25B at **[10.673]**.

[10.110]
[2.48A   Creditors' request for further information
(1)   If—
   (a)   within 21 days of receipt of a progress report under Rule 2.47—
      (i)   a secured creditor, or
      (ii)   an unsecured creditor with the concurrence of at least 5% in value of the unsecured creditors (including the creditor in question), or
   (b)   with the permission of the court upon an application made within that period of 21 days, any unsecured creditor,
makes a request in writing to the administrator for further information about remuneration or expenses (other than pre-administration costs) set out in a statement required by Rule 2.47(1)(db) or (dc), the administrator must, within 14 days of receipt of the request, comply with paragraph (2).
(2)   The administrator complies with this paragraph by either—
   (a)   providing all of the information asked for, or
   (b)   so far as the administrator considers that—
      (i)   the time or cost of preparation of the information would be excessive, or
      (ii)   disclosure of the information would be prejudicial to the conduct of the administration or might reasonably be expected to lead to violence against any person, or
      (iii)   the administrator is subject to an obligation of confidentiality in respect of the information,
      giving reasons for not providing all of the information.
(3)   Any creditor, who need not be the same as the creditor who requested further information under paragraph (1), may apply to the court within 21 days of—
   (a)   the giving by the administrator of reasons for not providing all of the information asked for, or
   (b)   the expiry of the 14 days provided for in paragraph (1),
and the court may make such order as it thinks just.
(4)   Without prejudice to the generality of paragraph (3), the order of the court under that paragraph may extend the period of 8 weeks provided for in Rule 2.109(1B) by such further period as the court thinks just.]

NOTES
   Commencement: 6 April 2010.
   Inserted by the Insolvency (Amendment) Rules 2010, SI 2010/686, r 2, Sch 1, para 63, subject to transitional provisions in Sch 4, para 1 thereto, as noted to r 1.5 at **[10.7]**.

[Section B: Company Meetings

[10.111]
2.49   Venue and conduct of company meeting
(1)   Where the administrator summons a meeting of members of the company, he shall fix a venue for it having regard to their convenience.
(2)   The chairman of the meeting shall be the administrator or a person nominated by him in writing to act in his place.
(3)   A person so nominated must be either—
   (a)   one who is qualified to act as an insolvency practitioner in relation to the company; or
   (b)   an employee of the administrator or his firm who is experienced in insolvency matters.
(4)   If within 30 minutes from the time fixed for commencement of the meeting there is no person present to act as chairman, the meeting stands adjourned to the same time and place in the following week or, if that is not a business day, to the business day immediately following.
[(5A)   Subject to anything to the contrary in the Act and these Rules, the meeting must be summoned and conducted—
   (a)   in the case of a company incorporated—
      (i)   in England and Wales, or in Wales, or
      (ii)   outside the United Kingdom other than in an EEA state,

in accordance with the law of England and Wales, including any applicable provision in or made under the Companies Act;

(b) in the case of a company incorporated in an EEA state other than the United Kingdom, in accordance with the law of that state applicable to meetings of the company.]

(7) The chairman of the meeting shall cause minutes of its proceedings to be entered in the company's minute book.]

NOTES

Substituted, subject to transitional provisions; see the note preceding r 2.1 at **[10.60]**.

Para (5A): substituted (for original paras (5), (6)) by the Insolvency (Amendment) Rules 2010, SI 2010/686, r 2, Sch 1, para 64, as from 6 April 2010, subject to transitional provisions in Sch 4, para 1 thereto, as noted to r 1.5 at **[10.7]**.

[CHAPTER 7
THE CREDITORS' COMMITTEE

[10.112]
2.50 Constitution of committee

(1) Where it is resolved by a creditors' meeting to establish a creditors' committee for the purposes of the administration, the committee shall consist of at least 3 and not more than 5 creditors of the company elected at the meeting.

[(2) A person claiming to be a creditor is entitled to be a member of the committee provided that—

(a) that person's claim has neither been wholly disallowed for voting purposes, nor wholly rejected for the purpose of distribution or dividend; and

(b) the claim mentioned in sub-paragraph (a) is not fully secured.]

(3) A body corporate may be a member of the committee, but it cannot act as such otherwise than by a representative appointed under Rule 2.55 below.]

NOTES

Substituted, subject to transitional provisions; see the note preceding r 2.1 at **[10.60]**.

Para (2): substituted by the Insolvency (Amendment) Rules 2010, SI 2010/686, r 2, Sch 1, para 65, as from 6 April 2010, subject to transitional provisions in Sch 4, para 1 thereto, as noted to r 1.5 at **[10.7]**.

[10.113]
[2.51 Formalities of establishment

(1) The creditors' committee does not come into being, and accordingly cannot act, until the administrator has issued a certificate in Form 2.26B of its due constitution.

[(1A) If the chairman of the creditors' meeting which resolves to establish the committee is not the administrator, the chairman must as soon as reasonably practicable give notice of the resolution to the administrator and inform the administrator of the names and addresses of the persons elected to be members of the committee.]

(2) No person may act as a member of the committee unless and until he has agreed to do so and, unless the relevant proxy or authorisation contains a statement to the contrary, such agreement may be given by his proxy-holder . . . present at the meeting establishing the committee [or, in the case of a corporation, by its duly appointed representative].

(3) The administrator's certificate of the committee's due constitution shall not be issued [before the minimum number of members set out in Rule 2.50 elected] to be members of the committee have agreed to act and shall be issued as soon as reasonably practicable thereafter.

(4) As and when the others (if any) agree to act, the administrator shall issue an amended certificate in Form 2.26B.

(5) The certificate, and any amended certificate, shall be . . . sent to the registrar of companies by the administrator, as soon as reasonably practicable.

(6) If after the first establishment of the committee there is any change in its membership, the administrator shall as soon as reasonably practicable report the change to the [registrar of companies by filing an amended certificate].]

NOTES

Substituted, subject to transitional provisions; see the note preceding r 2.1 at **[10.60]**.

Para (1A): inserted by the Insolvency (Amendment) Rules 2010, SI 2010/686, r 2, Sch 1, para 66(1), (2), as from 6 April 2010, subject to transitional provisions in Sch 4, para 1 thereto, as noted to r 1.5 at **[10.7]**.

Para (2): words omitted revoked, and words in square brackets inserted, by SI 2010/686, r 2, Sch 1, para 66(1), (3), as from 6 April 2010, subject to transitional provisions in Sch 4, para 1 thereto, as noted to r 1.5 at **[10.7]**.

Para (3): words in square brackets substituted by SI 2010/686, r 2, Sch 1, para 66(1), (4), as from 6 April 2010, subject to transitional provisions in Sch 4, para 1 thereto, as noted to r 1.5 at **[10.7]**.

Para (5): words omitted revoked by SI 2010/686, r 2, Sch 1, para 66(1), (5), as from 6 April 2010, subject to transitional provisions in Sch 4, para 2 thereto, as noted to r 1.31 at **[10.34]**.

Para (6) words in square brackets substituted by SI 2010/686, r 2, Sch 1, para 66(1), (6), as from 6 April 2010, subject to transitional provisions in Sch 4, para 2 thereto, as noted to r 1.31 at **[10.34]**.

See Form 2.26B at **[10.673]**.

[10.114]
[2.52   Functions and meetings of the committee

(1)   [In addition to any functions conferred on the creditors' committee by any provision of the Act,] the creditors' committee shall assist the administrator in discharging his functions, and act in relation to him in such manner as may be agreed from time to time.

(2)   Subject as follows, meetings of the committee shall be held when and where determined by the administrator.

[(3)   The administrator must call a first meeting of the committee to take place within 6 weeks of the committee's establishment.

(3A)   After the calling of the first meeting, the administrator must call a meeting—
   (a)   if so requested by a member of the committee or the member's representative (the meeting then to be held within 21 days of the request being received by the administrator); and
   (b)   for a specified date, if the committee has previously resolved that a meeting be held on that date.]

(4)   [Subject to paragraph (5),] the administrator shall give [5 business] days' written notice of the venue of any meeting to every member of the committee (or his representative designated for that purpose), unless in any case the requirement of notice has been waived by or on behalf of any member. Waiver may be signified either at or before the meeting.

[(5)   Where the administrator has determined that a meeting should be conducted and held in the manner referred to in Rule 12A.26(2), the notice period mentioned in paragraph (4) is 7 business days.]]

NOTES
Substituted, subject to transitional provisions; see the note preceding r 2.1 at **[10.60]**.
Para (1): words in square brackets inserted by the Insolvency (Amendment) Rules 2010, SI 2010/686, r 2, Sch 1, para 67(1), (2), as from 6 April 2010, subject to transitional provisions in Sch 4, para 1 thereto, as noted to r 1.5 at **[10.7]**.
Paras (3), (3A): substituted (for original para (3)) by SI 2010/686, r 2, Sch 1, para 67(1), (3), as from 6 April 2010, subject to transitional provisions in Sch 4, para 1 thereto, as noted to r 1.5 at **[10.7]**.
Para (4): words in first pair of square brackets inserted, and words in second pair of square brackets substituted, by SI 2010/686, r 2, Sch 1, para 67(1), (4), as from 6 April 2010, subject to transitional provisions in Sch 4, para 1 thereto, as noted to r 1.5 at **[10.7]**.
Para (5): added by SI 2010/686, r 2, Sch 1, para 67(1), (5), as from 6 April 2010, subject to transitional provisions in Sch 4, para 1 thereto, as noted to r 1.5 at **[10.7]**.

[10.115]
[2.53   The chairman at meetings

[(1)   The chairman at any meeting of the creditors' committee must be the administrator, or a person appointed by the administrator in writing to act.]

(2)   A person so [appointed] must be either—
   (a)   one who is qualified to act as an insolvency practitioner in relation to the company; or
   (b)   an employee of the administrator or his firm who is experienced in insolvency matters.]

NOTES
Substituted, subject to transitional provisions; see the note preceding r 2.1 at **[10.60]**.
Para (1): substituted by the Insolvency (Amendment) Rules 2010, SI 2010/686, r 2, Sch 1, para 68(1), (2), as from 6 April 2010, subject to transitional provisions in Sch 4, para 1 thereto, as noted to r 1.5 at **[10.7]**.
Para (2): word in square brackets substituted by SI 2010/686, r 2, Sch 1, para 68(1), (3), as from 6 April 2010, subject to transitional provisions in Sch 4, para 1 thereto, as noted to r 1.5 at **[10.7]**.

[10.116]
[2.54   Quorum

A meeting of the committee is duly constituted if due notice of it has been given to all the members, and at least 2 members are present or represented.]

NOTES
Substituted, subject to transitional provisions; see the note preceding r 2.1 at **[10.60]**.

[10.117]
[2.55   Committee-members' representatives

(1)   A member of the committee may, in relation to the business of the committee, be represented by another person duly authorised by him for that purpose.

(2)   A person acting as a committee-member's representative must hold a letter of authority entitling him so to act (either generally or specially) and [authenticated] by or on behalf of the committee-member, and for this purpose any proxy . . . in relation to any meeting of creditors of the company shall, unless it contains a statement to the contrary, be treated as a letter of authority to act generally [authenticated] by or on behalf of the committee-member.

(3)   The chairman at any meeting of the committee may call on a person claiming to act as a committee-member's representative to produce his letter of authority, and may exclude him if it appears that his authority is deficient.

[(4)   No member may be represented by—
    (a)   another member of the committee;
    (b)   a person who is at the same time representing another committee member;
    (c)   a body corporate;
    (d)   an undischarged bankrupt;
    (e)   a disqualified director; or
    (f)   a person who is subject to a bankruptcy restrictions order (including an interim order), a bankruptcy restrictions undertaking, a debt relief restrictions order (including an interim order) or a debt relief restrictions undertaking.]

(5)   . . .

(6)   Where a member's representative [authenticates] any document on the member's behalf, the fact that he so [authenticates] must be stated below his [authentication].]

NOTES

Substituted, subject to transitional provisions; see the note preceding r 2.1 at **[10.60]**.

Para (2): words in square brackets substituted, and words omitted revoked, by the Insolvency (Amendment) Rules 2010, SI 2010/686, r 2, Sch 1, paras 1, 69(1), (2), as from 6 April 2010, subject to transitional provisions in Sch 4, paras 1, 2 thereto, as noted to rr 1.5. 1.31 at **[10.7]**, **[10.34]**.

Para (4): substituted by SI 2010/686, r 2, Sch 1, para 69(1), (3), as from 6 April 2010, subject to transitional provisions in Sch 4, para 1 thereto, as noted to r 1.5 at **[10.7]**.

Para (5): revoked by SI 2010/686, r 2, Sch 1, para 69(1), (4), as from 6 April 2010, subject to transitional provisions in Sch 4, para 1 thereto, as noted to r 1.5 at **[10.7]**.

Para (6): words in square brackets substituted by SI 2010/686, r 2, Sch 1, para 1, as from 6 April 2010, subject to transitional provisions in Sch 4, para 2 thereto, as noted to r 1.31 at **[10.34]**.

[10.118]
[2.56   Resignation

A member of the committee may resign by notice in writing delivered to the administrator.]

NOTES

Substituted, subject to transitional provisions; see the note preceding r 2.1 at **[10.60]**.

[10.119]
[2.57   Termination of membership

(1)   Membership of the creditors' committee is automatically terminated if the member—
    (a)   becomes bankrupt   . . . . ; or
    (b)   at 3 consecutive meetings of the committee is neither present nor represented (unless at the third of those meetings it is resolved that this Rule is not to apply in his case); or
    [(c)   ceases to be a creditor and a period of 3 months has elapsed from the date that that member ceased to be a creditor or is found never to have been a creditor.]

(2)   However, if the cause of termination is the member's bankruptcy, his trustee in bankruptcy replaces him as a member of the committee.]

NOTES

Substituted, subject to transitional provisions; see the note preceding r 2.1 at **[10.60]**.

Para (1): words omitted revoked by the Insolvency (Amendment) Rules 2004, SI 2004/584, r 5, as from 1 April 2004; sub-para (c) substituted by the Insolvency (Amendment) Rules 2010, SI 2010/686, r 2, Sch 1, para 70, as from 6 April 2010, subject to transitional provisions in Sch 4, para 1 thereto, as noted to r 1.5 at **[10.7]**.

[10.120]
[2.58   Removal

A member of the committee may be removed by resolution at a meeting of creditors' at least 14 days' notice having been given of the intention to move that resolution.]

NOTES

Substituted, subject to transitional provisions; see the note preceding r 2.1 at **[10.60]**.

[10.121]
[2.59   Vacancies

(1)   The following applies if there is a vacancy in the membership of the creditors' committee.

(2)   The vacancy need not be filled if the administrator and a majority of the remaining members of the committee so agree, provided that the total number of members does not fall below [3].

(3)   The administrator may appoint any creditor (being qualified under the Rules to be a member of the committee) to fill the vacancy, if a majority of the other members of the committee agree to the appointment, and the creditor concerned consents to act.

[(4)   Alternatively, a meeting of creditors may resolve that a creditor be appointed (with that creditor's consent) to fill the vacancy.

(5)   Where the vacancy is filled by an appointment made by a creditors' meeting at which the administrator is not present, the chairman of the meeting must report to the administrator the appointment which has been made.]]

NOTES

Substituted, subject to transitional provisions; see the note preceding r 2.1 at **[10.60]**.

Para (2): number in square brackets substituted by the Insolvency (Amendment) Rules 2010, SI 2010/686, r 2, Sch 1, para 71(1), (2), as from 6 April 2010, subject to transitional provisions in Sch 4, para 1 thereto, as noted to r 1.5 at **[10.7]**.

Paras (4), (5): added by SI 2010/686, r 2, Sch 1, para 71(1), (3), as from 6 April 2010, subject to transitional provisions in Sch 4, para 1 thereto, as noted to r 1.5 at **[10.7]**.

[10.122]
[2.60   Procedure at meetings

(1)   At any meeting of the creditors' committee, each member of it (whether present himself, or by his representative) has one vote; and a resolution is passed when a majority of the members present or represented have voted in favour of it.

[(2)   Every resolution passed must be recorded in writing and authenticated by the chairman, either separately or as part of the minutes of the meeting, and the record must be kept with the records of the proceedings.]]

NOTES

Substituted, subject to transitional provisions; see the note preceding r 2.1 at **[10.60]**.

Para (2): substituted (for original paras (2), (3)) by the Insolvency (Amendment) Rules 2010, SI 2010/686, r 2, Sch 1, para 72, as from 6 April 2010, subject to transitional provisions in Sch 4, para 1 thereto, as noted to r 1.5 at **[10.7]**.

[10.123]
[2.61   Resolutions of creditors' committee [otherwise than at a meeting]

(1)   In accordance with this Rule, the administrator may seek to obtain the agreement of members of the creditors' committee to a resolution by sending to every member (or his representative designated for the purpose) a copy of the proposed resolution.

(2)   Where the administrator makes use of the procedure allowed by this Rule, he shall send out to members of the committee or their representatives (as the case may be) a copy of any proposed resolution on which a decision is sought, which shall be set out in such a way that agreement with or dissent from each separate resolution may be indicated by the recipient on the copy so sent.

(3)   Any member of the committee may, within 7 business days from the date of the administrator sending out a resolution, require him to summon a meeting of the committee to consider matters raised by the resolution.

(4)   In the absence of such a request, the resolution is deemed to have been passed by the committee if and when the administrator is notified in writing by a majority of the members that they concur with it.

(5)   A copy of every resolution passed under this Rule, and a note that the committee's concurrence was obtained, shall be [kept with the records of the proceedings].]

NOTES

Substituted, subject to transitional provisions; see the note preceding r 2.1 at **[10.60]**.

Words in square brackets substituted by the Insolvency (Amendment) Rules 2010, SI 2010/686, r 2, Sch 1, para 73, as from 6 April 2010, subject to transitional provisions in Sch 4, para 1 thereto, as noted to r 1.5 at **[10.7]**.

[10.124]
[2.62   Information from administrator

(1)   Where the committee resolves to require the attendance of the administrator under paragraph 57(3)(a), the notice to him shall be in writing [authenticated] by the majority of the members of the committee for the time being. A member's representative may [authenticate] for him.

(2)   The meeting at which the administrator's attendance is required shall be fixed by the committee for a business day, and shall be held at such time and place as he determines.

(3)   Where the administrator so attends, the members of the committee may elect any one of their number to be chairman of the meeting, in place of the administrator or a nominee of his.]

NOTES

Substituted, subject to transitional provisions; see the note preceding r 2.1 at **[10.60]**.

Para (1): words in square brackets substituted by the Insolvency (Amendment) Rules 2010, SI 2010/686, r 2, Sch 1, para 1, as from 6 April 2010, subject to transitional provisions in Sch 4, para 2 thereto, as noted to r 1.31 at **[10.34]**.

[10.125]
[2.63 Expenses of members

(1) Subject as follows, the administrator shall, out of the assets of the company, defray[, in the prescribed order of priority,] any reasonable travelling expenses directly incurred by members of the creditors' committee or their representatives in relation to their attendance at the committee's meetings, or otherwise on the committee's business, as an expense of the administration.

(2) Paragraph (1) does not apply to any meeting of the committee held within 6 weeks of a previous meeting, unless the meeting in question is summoned at the instance of the administrator.]

NOTES

Substituted, subject to transitional provisions; see the note preceding r 2.1 at **[10.60]**.

Para (1): words in square brackets inserted by the Insolvency (Amendment) Rules 2010, SI 2010/686, r 2, Sch 1, para 74, as from 6 April 2010, subject to transitional provisions in Sch 4, para 1 thereto, as noted to r 1.5 at **[10.7]**.

[10.126]
[2.64 Members' dealing with the company

(1) Membership of the committee does not prevent a person from dealing with the company while the company is in administration, provided that any transactions in the course of such dealings are in good faith and for value.

(2) The court may, on the application of any person interested, set aside any transaction which appears to it to be contrary to the requirements of this Rule, and may give such consequential directions as it thinks [just] for compensating the company for any loss which it may have incurred in consequence of the transaction.]

NOTES

Substituted, subject to transitional provisions; see the note preceding r 2.1 at **[10.60]**.

Para (2): word in square brackets substituted by the Insolvency (Amendment) Rules 2010, SI 2010/686, r 2, Sch 1, para 1, as from 6 April 2010, subject to transitional provisions in Sch 4, para 2 thereto, as noted to r 1.31 at **[10.34]**.

[10.127]
[2.65 Formal defects

The acts of the creditors' committee established for any administration are valid notwithstanding any defect in the appointment, election or qualifications of any member of the committee or any committee-member's representative or in the formalities of its establishment.]

NOTES

Substituted, subject to transitional provisions; see the note preceding r 2.1 at **[10.60]**.

[CHAPTER 8
DISPOSAL OF CHARGED PROPERTY

[10.128]
2.66

(1) The following applies where the administrator applies to the court under paragraphs 71 or 72 for authority to dispose of property of the company which is subject to a security (other than a floating charge), or goods in the possession of the company under a hire purchase agreement.

(2) The court shall fix a venue for the hearing of the application, and the administrator shall as soon as reasonably practicable give notice of the venue to the person who is the holder of the security or, as the case may be, the owner under the agreement.

(3) If an order is made under paragraphs 71 or 72 the court shall send two sealed copies to the administrator.

(4) The administrator shall send one of them to that person who is the holder of the security or owner under the agreement.

[(5) The administrator must send a copy of the sealed order to the registrar of companies.]]

NOTES

Substituted, subject to transitional provisions; see the note preceding r 2.1 at **[10.60]**.

Para (5): substituted by the Insolvency (Amendment) Rules 2010, SI 2010/686, r 2, Sch 1, para 75, as from 6 April 2010, subject to transitional provisions in Sch 4, para 1 thereto, as noted to r 1.5 at **[10.7]**.

[CHAPTER 9
EXPENSES OF THE ADMINISTRATION

[10.129]
2.67

(1) The expenses of the administration are payable in the following order of priority—

(a)   expenses properly incurred by the administrator in performing his functions in the administration of the company;

(b)   the cost of any security provided by the administrator in accordance with the Act or the Rules;

(c)   where an administration order was made, the costs of the applicant and any person appearing on the hearing of the application and where the administrator was appointed otherwise than by order of the court, any costs and expenses of the appointor in connection with the making of the appointment and the costs and expenses incurred by any other person in giving notice of intention to appoint an administrator;

(d)   any amount payable to a person employed or authorised, under Chapter 5 of this Part of the Rules, to assist in the preparation of a statement of affairs or statement of concurrence;

(e)   any allowance made, by order of the court, towards costs on an application for release from the obligation to submit a statement of affairs or statement of concurrence;

(f)   any necessary disbursements by the administrator in the course of the administration (including any expenses incurred by members of the creditors' committee or their representatives and allowed for by the administrator under Rule 2.63, but not including any payment of corporation tax in circumstances referred to in sub-paragraph (j) below);

(g)   the remuneration or emoluments of any person who has been employed by the administrator to perform any services for the company, as required or authorised under the Act or the Rules;

[(h)   the administrator's remuneration the basis of which has been fixed under Chapter 11 of this Part of the Rules and unpaid pre-administration costs approved under Rule 2.67A;]

(j)   the amount of any corporation tax on chargeable gains accruing on the realisation of any asset of the company (without regard to whether the realisation is effected by the administrator, a secured creditor, or a receiver or manager appointed to deal with a security).

(2)   The priorities laid down by paragraph (1) of this Rule are subject to the power of the court to make orders under paragraph (3) of this Rule where the assets are insufficient to satisfy the liabilities.

(3)   The court may, in the event of the assets being insufficient to satisfy the liabilities, make an order as to the payment out of the assets of the expenses incurred in the administration in such order of priority as the court thinks just.

[(4)   For the purposes of paragraph 99(3), the former administrator's remuneration and expenses shall comprise all those items set out in paragraph (1) of this Rule.]]

NOTES

Substituted, subject to transitional provisions; see the note preceding r 2.1 at **[10.60]**.

Para (1): sub-para (h) substituted by the Insolvency (Amendment) Rules 2010, SI 2010/686, r 2, Sch 1, para 76, as from 6 April 2010, subject to transitional provisions in Sch 4, para 1 thereto, as noted to r 1.5 at **[10.7]**.

Para (4): added by the Insolvency (Amendment) Rules 2005, SI 2005/527, r 8, as from 1 April 2005, subject to transitional provisions as noted below.

Transitional provisions: the Insolvency (Amendment) Rules 2005, SI 2005/527, r 3(1) provides as follows (note that by virtue of r 1(2) of those Rules "the commencement date" is 1 April 2005)—

"(1)   The provisions of Rules 8 to 17, 23 to 27, 43 and 44 of these Rules shall not apply, and the provisions of the principal Rules shall continue to apply without the amendments made by those Rules, in any case where a company has entered administration or gone into liquidation, or a bankruptcy order has been made, before the commencement date.".

[10.130]
[2.67A   Pre-administration costs

(1)   Where the administrator has made a statement of pre-administration costs under Rule 2.33(2)(ka), the creditors' committee may determine whether and to what extent the unpaid pre-administration costs set out in the statement are approved for payment.

(2)   But if—

(a)   there is no creditors' committee, or

(b)   there is but it does not make the necessary determination, or

(c)   it does do so but the administrator or other insolvency practitioner who has charged fees or incurred expenses as pre-administration costs considers the amount determined to be insufficient,

paragraph (3) applies.

(3)   When this paragraph applies, determination of whether and to what extent the unpaid pre-administration costs are approved for payment shall be—

(a)   by resolution of a meeting of creditors other than in a case falling in sub-paragraph (b), or

(b)   in a case where the administrator has made a statement under paragraph 52(1)(b)—

(i)   by the approval of each secured creditor of the company, or

(ii)   if the administrator has made, or intends to make, a distribution to preferential creditors, by the approval of—

(aa)   each secured creditor of the company, and

(bb)   preferential creditors whose debts amount to more than 50% of the preferential debts of the company, disregarding debts of any creditor who does not respond to an invitation to give or withhold approval.

(4) The administrator must call a meeting of the creditors' committee or of creditors if so requested for the purposes of paragraphs (1) to (3) by another insolvency practitioner who has charged fees or incurred expenses as pre-administration costs; and the administrator must give notice of the meeting within 28 days of receipt of the request.

(5) If—
- (a) there is no determination under paragraph (1) or (3), or
- (b) there is such a determination but the administrator or other insolvency practitioner who has charged fees or incurred expenses as pre-administration costs considers the amount determined to be insufficient,

the administrator (where the fees were charged or expenses incurred by the administrator) or other insolvency practitioner (where the fees were charged or expenses incurred by that practitioner) may apply to the court for a determination of whether and to what extent the unpaid pre-administration costs are approved for payment.

(6) Paragraphs (2) to (4) of Rule 2.108 apply to an application under paragraph (5) of this Rule as they do to an application under paragraph (1) of that Rule (references to the administrator being read as references to the insolvency practitioner who has charged fees or incurred expenses as pre-administration costs).

(7) Where the administrator fails to call a meeting of the creditors' committee or of creditors in accordance with paragraph (4), the other insolvency practitioner may apply to the court for an order requiring the administrator to do so.]

NOTES

Commencement: 6 April 2010.

Inserted by the Insolvency (Amendment) Rules 2010, SI 2010/686, r 2, Sch 1, para 77, subject to transitional provisions in Sch 4, para 1 thereto, as noted to r 1.5 at **[10.7]**.

[CHAPTER 10
DISTRIBUTIONS TO CREDITORS

Section A: Application of Chapter and General

[10.131]
2.68

(1) This Chapter applies where the administrator makes, or proposes to make, a distribution to any class of creditors [other than secured creditors]. Where the distribution is to a particular class of creditors, references in this Chapter to creditors shall, in so far as the context requires, be a reference to that class of creditors only.

(2) The administrator shall give notice to the creditors of his intention to declare and distribute a dividend in accordance with Rule 2.95.

(3) Where it is intended that the distribution is to be a sole or final dividend, the administrator shall, after the date specified in the notice referred to in paragraph (2)—
- (a) defray any outstanding expenses of a liquidation (including any of the items mentioned in Rule 4.218) or provisional liquidation that immediately preceded the administration;
- (b) defray any items payable in accordance with the provisions of paragraph 99;
- (c) defray any amounts (including any debts or liabilities and his own remuneration and expenses) which would, if the administrator were to cease to be the administrator of the company, be payable out of the property of which he had custody or control in accordance with the provisions of paragraph 99; and
- (d) declare and distribute that dividend without regard to the claim of any person in respect of a debt not already proved.

(4) The court may, on the application of any person, postpone the date specified in the notice.]

NOTES

Substituted, subject to transitional provisions; see the note preceding r 2.1 at **[10.60]**.

Para (1): words in square brackets inserted by the Insolvency (Amendment) Rules 2010, SI 2010/686, r 2, Sch 1, para 78, as from 6 April 2010, subject to transitional provisions in Sch 4, para 1 thereto, as noted to r 1.5 at **[10.7]**.

[10.132]
[2.69 Debts of insolvent company to rank equally

Debts other than preferential debts rank equally between themselves in the administration and, after the preferential debts, shall be paid in full unless the assets are insufficient for meeting them, in which case they abate in equal proportions between themselves.]

NOTES

Substituted, subject to transitional provisions; see the note preceding r 2.1 at **[10.60]**.

[10.133]
[2.70   Supplementary provisions as to dividend

(1)   In the calculation and distribution of a dividend the administrator shall make provision for—
   (a)   any debts which appear to him to be due to persons who, by reason of the distance of their place of residence, may not have had sufficient time to tender and establish their proofs;
   (b)   any debts which are the subject of claims which have not yet been determined; and
   (c)   disputed proofs and claims.

(2)   A creditor who has not proved his debt before the declaration of any dividend is not entitled to disturb, by reason that he has not participated in it, the distribution of that dividend or any other dividend declared before his debt was proved, but—
   (a)   when he has proved that debt he is entitled to be paid, out of any money for the time being available for the payment of any further dividend, any dividend or dividends which he has failed to receive; and
   (b)   any dividends payable under sub-paragraph (a) shall be paid before the money is applied to the payment of any such further dividend.

(3)   No action lies against the administrator for a dividend; but if he refuses to pay a dividend the court may, if it thinks [just], order him to pay it and also to pay, out of his own money—
   (a)   interest on the dividend, at the rate for the time being specified in section 17 of the Judgments Act 1838, from the time when it was withheld; and
   (b)   the costs of the proceedings in which the order to pay is made.]

NOTES
   Substituted, subject to transitional provisions; see the note preceding r 2.1 at **[10.60]**.
   Para (3): word in square brackets substituted by the Insolvency (Amendment) Rules 2010, SI 2010/686, r 2, Sch 1, para 1, as from 6 April 2010, subject to transitional provisions in Sch 4, para 2 thereto, as noted to r 1.31 at **[10.34]**.

[10.134]
[2.71   Division of unsold assets

[(1)]   The administrator may, with the permission of the creditors' committee, or if there is no creditors' committee, the creditors, divide in its existing form amongst the company's creditors, according to its estimated value, any property which from its peculiar nature or other special circumstances cannot be readily or advantageously sold.

[(2)   The administrator must—
   (a)   in the receipts and payments account included in the final progress report under Chapter 12 of this Part, state the estimated value of the property divided amongst the creditors of the company during the period to which the report relates, and
   (b)   as a note to the account, provide details of the basis of the valuation.]]

NOTES
   Substituted, subject to transitional provisions; see the note preceding r 2.1 at **[10.60]**.
   Para (1) numbered as such, and para (2) added, by the Insolvency (Amendment) Rules 2010, SI 2010/686, r 2, Sch 1, para 79, as from 6 April 2010, subject to transitional provisions in Sch 4, para 1 thereto, as noted to r 1.5 at **[10.7]**.

[Section B: Machinery of Proving a Debt

[10.135]
2.72   Proving a debt

(1)   A person claiming to be a creditor of the company and wishing to recover his debt in whole or in part must (subject to any order of the court to the contrary) submit his claim in writing to the administrator.

(2)   A creditor who claims is referred to as "proving" for his debt and a document by which he seeks to establish his claim is his "proof".

(3)   Subject to the next paragraph, a proof must—
   (a)   be made out by, or under the direction of, the creditor and [authenticated] by him or a person authorised in that behalf; and
   (b)   state the following matters—
      (i)   the creditor's name and address;
      [(ia)   if the creditor is a company, its registered number;]
      [(ii)   the total amount of the creditor's claim (including value added tax) as at the date on which the company entered administration (or, if the company was in liquidation when it entered administration, the date on which it went into liquidation), less any payments made after that date in respect of the claim, any deduction under Rule 2.84 and any adjustment by way of set-off in accordance with Rule 2.85;]
      (iii)   whether or not the claim includes outstanding uncapitalised interest;
      (iv), (v) . . .
      (vi)   particulars of how and when the debt was incurred by the company;
      (vii)   particulars of any security held, the date on which it was given and the value which the creditor puts on it;

(viii) details of any reservation of title in respect of goods to which the debt refers; and
(ix) the name, address and authority of the person [authenticating] the proof (if other than the creditor himself).

(4)   There shall be specified in the proof details of any documents by reference to which the debt can be substantiated; but (subject as follows) it is not essential that such document be attached to the proof or submitted with it.

(5)   The administrator may call for any document or other evidence to be produced to him, where he thinks it necessary for the purpose of substantiating the whole or any part of the claim made in the proof.

[(6)   Where an administration is immediately preceded by a winding up, a creditor proving in the winding up is deemed to have proved in the administration.]]

NOTES
Substituted, subject to transitional provisions; see the note preceding r 2.1 at **[10.60]**.
Para (3): word in first pair of square brackets substituted, sub-para (b)(ia) inserted, sub-para (b)(ii) substituted, sub-para (b)(iv), (v) revoked, and word in square brackets in sub-para (b)(ix) substituted, by the Insolvency (Amendment) Rules 2010, SI 2010/686, r 2, Sch 1, paras 1, 80(1), (2), as from 6 April 2010, subject to transitional provisions in Sch 4, paras 1, 2 thereto, as noted to rr 1.5, 1.31 at **[10.7]**, **[10.34]**.
Para (6): added by SI 2010/686, r 2, Sch 1, para 80(1), (3), as from 6 April 2010, subject to transitional provisions in Sch 4, para 1 thereto, as noted to r 1.5 at **[10.7]**.

2.73   (*Revoked by the Insolvency (Amendment) Rules 2010, SI 2010/686, r 5, as from 6 April 2010, subject to transitional provisions in Sch 4, para 2 thereto, as noted to r 1.31 at* **[10.34]**.)

[10.136]
[2.74   Costs of proving
Unless the court otherwise orders—
(a) every creditor bears the cost of proving his own debt, including costs incurred in providing documents or evidence under Rule 2.72(5); and
(b) costs incurred by the administrator in estimating the quantum of a debt under Rule 2.81 are payable out of the assets as an expense of the administration.]

NOTES
Substituted, subject to transitional provisions; see the note preceding r 2.1 at **[10.60]**.

[10.137]
[2.75   Administrator to allow inspection of proofs
The administrator shall, so long as proofs lodged with him are in his hands, allow them to be inspected, at all reasonable times on any business day, by any of the following persons—
(a) any creditor who has submitted a proof of debt (unless his proof has been wholly rejected for purposes of dividend or otherwise);
(b) any contributory of the company; and
(c) any person acting on behalf of either of the above.]

NOTES
Substituted, subject to transitional provisions; see the note preceding r 2.1 at **[10.60]**.

[10.138]
[2.76   New administrator appointed
(1)   If a new administrator is appointed in place of another, the former administrator [must as soon as reasonably practicable] transmit to him all proofs which he has received, together with an itemised list of them.

(2)   The new administrator shall [authenticate] the list by way of receipt for the proofs, and return it to his predecessor.

[(3)   From then on, all proofs of debt must be sent to and retained by the new administrator.]]

NOTES
Substituted, subject to transitional provisions; see the note preceding r 2.1 at **[10.60]**.
Para (1): words in square brackets substituted by the Insolvency (Amendment) Rules 2010, SI 2010/686, r 2, Sch 1, para 81(1), (2), as from 6 April 2010, subject to transitional provisions in Sch 4, para 1 thereto, as noted to r 1.5 at **[10.7]**.
Para (2): word in square brackets substituted by SI 2010/686, r 2, Sch 1, para 1, as from 6 April 2010, subject to transitional provisions in Sch 4, para 2 thereto, as noted to r 1.31 at **[10.34]**.
Para (3): added by SI 2010/686, r 2, Sch 1, para 81(1), (3), as from 6 April 2010, subject to transitional provisions in Sch 4, para 1 thereto, as noted to r 1.5 at **[10.7]**.

[10.139]
[2.77   Admission and rejection of proofs for dividend
(1)   A proof may be admitted for dividend either for the whole amount claimed by the creditor, or for part of that amount.

(2) If the administrator rejects a proof in whole or in part, he shall prepare a written statement of his reasons for doing so, and send it as soon as reasonably practicable to the creditor.]

NOTES
Substituted, subject to transitional provisions; see the note preceding r 2.1 at **[10.60]**.

[10.140]
[2.78 Appeal against decision on proof

(1) If a creditor is dissatisfied with the administrator's decision with respect to his proof (including any decision on the question of preference), he may apply to the court for the decision to be reversed or varied. The application must be made within 21 days of his receiving the statement sent under Rule 2.77(2).

(2) [A member or] any other creditor may, if dissatisfied with the administrator's decision admitting or rejecting the whole or any part of a proof, make such an application within 21 days of becoming aware of the administrator's decision.

(3) Where application is made to the court under this Rule, the court shall fix a venue for the application to be heard, notice of which shall be sent by the applicant to the creditor who lodged the proof in question (if it is not himself) and the administrator.

(4) The administrator shall, on receipt of the notice, file with the court the relevant proof, together (if appropriate) with a copy of the statement sent under Rule 2.77(2).

[(4A) Where the application is made by a member, the court must not disallow the proof (in whole or in part) unless the member shows that there is (or would be but for the amount claimed in the proof), or that it is likely that there will be (or would be but for the amount claimed in the proof), a surplus of assets to which the company would be entitled.]

(5) After the application has been heard and determined, the proof shall, unless it has been wholly disallowed, be returned by the court to the administrator.

(6) The administrator is not personally liable for costs incurred by any person in respect of an application under this Rule unless the court otherwise orders.]

NOTES
Substituted, subject to transitional provisions; see the note preceding r 2.1 at **[10.60]**.
Para (2): words in square brackets inserted by the Insolvency (Amendment) Rules 2010, SI 2010/686, r 2, Sch 1, para 82(1), (2), as from 6 April 2010, subject to transitional provisions in Sch 4, para 1 thereto, as noted to r 1.5 at **[10.7]**.
Para (4A): inserted by SI 2010/686, r 2, Sch 1, para 82(1), (3), as from 6 April 2010, subject to transitional provisions in Sch 4, para 1 thereto, as noted to r 1.5 at **[10.7]**.

[10.141]
[2.79 Withdrawal or variation of proof

A creditor's proof may at any time, by agreement between himself and the administrator, be withdrawn or varied as to the amount claimed.]

NOTES
Substituted, subject to transitional provisions; see the note preceding r 2.1 at **[10.60]**.

[10.142]
[2.80 Expunging of proof by the court

(1) The court may expunge a proof or reduce the amount claimed—
    (a) on the administrator's application, where he thinks that the proof has been improperly admitted, or ought to be reduced; or
    (b) on the application of a creditor, if the administrator declines to interfere in the matter.

(2) Where application is made to the court under this Rule, the court shall fix a venue for the application to be heard, notice of which shall be sent by the applicant—
    (a) in the case of an application by the administrator, to the creditor who made the proof; and
    (b) in the case of an application by a creditor, to the administrator and to the creditor who made the proof (if not himself).]

NOTES
Substituted, subject to transitional provisions; see the note preceding r 2.1 at **[10.60]**.

[Section C: Quantification of Claims]

[10.143]
2.81 Estimate of quantum

(1) The administrator shall estimate the value of any debt which, by reason of its being subject to any contingency or for any other reason, does not bear a certain value; and he may revise any estimate previously made, if he thinks fit by reference to any change of circumstances or to information becoming available to him. He shall inform the creditor as to his estimate and any revision of it.

(2) Where the value of a debt is estimated under this Rule, the amount provable in the administration in the case of that debt is that of the estimate for the time being.]

NOTES

Substituted, subject to transitional provisions; see the note preceding r 2.1 at **[10.60]**.

[10.144]
[2.82 Negotiable instruments, etc

Unless the administrator allows, a proof in respect of money owed on a bill of exchange, promissory note, cheque or other negotiable instrument or security cannot be admitted unless there is produced the instrument or security itself or a copy of it, certified by the creditor or his authorised representative to be a true copy.]

NOTES

Substituted, subject to transitional provisions; see the note preceding r 2.1 at **[10.60]**.

[10.145]
[2.83 Secured creditors

(1) If a secured creditor realises his security, he may prove for the balance of his debt, after deducting the amount realised.

(2) If a secured creditor voluntarily surrenders his security for the general benefit of creditors, he may prove for his whole debt, as if it were unsecured.]

NOTES

Substituted, subject to transitional provisions; see the note preceding r 2.1 at **[10.60]**.

[10.146]
[2.84 Discounts

There shall in every case be deducted from the claim all trade and other discounts which would have been available to the company but for its administration except any discount for immediate, early or cash settlement.]

NOTES

Substituted, subject to transitional provisions; see the note preceding r 2.1 at **[10.60]**.

[10.147]
[2.85 Mutual credits and set-off

(1) This Rule applies where the administrator, being authorised to make the distribution in question, has, pursuant to Rule 2.95 given notice that he proposes to make it.

(2) In this Rule "mutual dealings" means mutual credits, mutual debts or other mutual dealings between the company and any creditor of the company proving or claiming to prove for a debt in the administration but does not include any of the following—
- (a) any debt arising out of an obligation incurred after the company entered administration;
- (b) any debt arising out of an obligation incurred at a time when the creditor had notice that—
  - (i) an application for an administration order was pending; or
  - (ii) any person had given notice of intention to appoint an administrator;
- (c) any debt arising out of an obligation where—
  - (i) the administration was immediately preceded by a winding up; and
  - (ii) at the time the obligation was incurred the creditor had notice that a meeting of creditors had been summoned under section 98 or a petition for the winding up of the company was pending;
- (d) any debt arising out of an obligation incurred during a winding up which immediately preceded the administration; or
- (e) any debt which has been acquired by a creditor by assignment or otherwise, pursuant to an agreement between the creditor and any other party where that agreement was entered into—
  - (i) after the company entered administration;
  - (ii) at a time when the creditor had notice that an application for an administration order was pending;
  - (iii) at a time when the creditor had notice that any person had given notice of intention to appoint an administrator;
  - (iv) where the administration was immediately preceded by a winding up, at a time when the creditor had notice that a meeting of creditors had been summoned under section 98 or that a winding up petition was pending; or
  - (v) during a winding up which immediately preceded the administration.

(3) An account shall be taken as at the date of the notice referred to in paragraph (1) of what is due from each party to the other in respect of the mutual dealings and the sums due from one party shall be set off against the sums due from the other.

(4)   A sum shall be regarded as being due to or from the company for the purposes of paragraph (3) whether—

(a)   it is payable at present or in the future;

(b)   the obligation by virtue of which it is payable is certain or contingent; or

(c)   its amount is fixed or liquidated, or is capable of being ascertained by fixed rules or as a matter of opinion.

(5)   Rule 2.81 shall apply for the purposes of this Rule to any obligation to or from the company which, by reason of its being subject to any contingency or for any other reason, does not bear a certain value;

(6)   Rules 2.86 to 2.88 shall apply for the purposes of this Rule in relation to any sums due to the company which—

(a)   are payable in a currency other than sterling;

(b)   are of a periodical nature; or

(c)   bear interest.

(7)   Rule 2.105 shall apply for the purposes of this Rule to any sum due to or from the company which is payable in the future.

(8)   Only the balance (if any) of the account owed to the creditor is provable in the administration. Alternatively the balance (if any) owed to the company shall be paid to the administrator as part of the assets except where all or part of the balance results from a contingent or prospective debt owed by the creditor and in such a case the balance (or that part of it which results from the contingent or prospective debt) shall be paid if and when that debt becomes due and payable.

(9)   In this Rule "obligation" means an obligation however arising, whether by virtue of an agreement, rule of law or otherwise.]

NOTES

Substituted, subject to transitional provisions; see the note preceding r 2.1 at **[10.60]**.

This rule was further substituted by the Insolvency (Amendment) Rules 2005, SI 2005/527, r 9, as from 1 April 2005, subject to transitional provisions as noted to r 2.67 at **[10.129]**.

[10.148]
[2.86   Debt in foreign currency

(1)   For the purpose of proving a debt incurred or payable in a currency other than sterling, the amount of the debt shall be converted into sterling at the official exchange rate prevailing on the date when the company entered administration [or, if the administration was immediately preceded by a winding up, on the date that the company went into liquidation].

(2)   "The official exchange rate" is the middle exchange rate on the London Foreign Exchange Market at the close of business, as published for the date in question. In the absence of any such published rate, it is such rate as the court determines.]

NOTES

Substituted, subject to transitional provisions; see the note preceding r 2.1 at **[10.60]**.

Para (1): words in square brackets added by the Insolvency (Amendment) Rules 2005, SI 2005/527, r 10, as from 1 April 2005, subject to transitional provisions as noted to r 2.67 at **[10.129]**.

[10.149]
[2.87   Payments of a periodical nature

(1)   In the case of rent and other payments of a periodical nature, the creditor may prove for any amounts due and unpaid up to the date when the company entered administration [or, if the administration was immediately preceded by a winding up, up to the date that the company went into liquidation].

(2)   Where at that date any payment was accruing due, the creditor may prove for so much as would have fallen due at that date, if accruing from day to day.]

NOTES

Substituted, subject to transitional provisions; see the note preceding r 2.1 at **[10.60]**.

Para (1): words in square brackets added by the Insolvency (Amendment) Rules 2005, SI 2005/527, r 11, as from 1 April 2005, subject to transitional provisions as noted to r 2.67 at **[10.129]**.

[10.150]
[2.88   Interest

[(A1)   In this Rule, "the relevant date" means the date on which the company entered administration or, if the administration was immediately preceded by a winding up, the date on which the company went into liquidation.]

(1)   Where a debt proved in the administration bears interest, that interest is provable as part of the debt except in so far as it is payable in respect of any period after [the relevant date].

(2)   In the following circumstances the creditor's claim may include interest on the debt for periods before [the relevant date], although not previously reserved or agreed.

(3)   If the debt is due by virtue of a written instrument, and payable at a certain time, interest may be claimed for the period from that time to [the relevant date].

(4)   If the debt is due otherwise, interest may only be claimed if, before [the relevant date], a demand for payment of the debt was made in writing by or on behalf of the creditor, and notice given that interest would be payable from the date of the demand to the date of payment.

(5)   Interest under paragraph (4) may only be claimed for the period from the date of the demand to [the relevant date] and for all the purposes of the Act and the Rules shall be chargeable at a rate not exceeding that mentioned in paragraph (6).

(6)   The rate of interest to be claimed under paragraphs (3) and (4) is the rate specified in section 17 of the Judgments Act 1838 on [the relevant date].

(7)   . . . any surplus remaining after payment of the debts proved shall, before being applied for any purpose, be applied in paying interest on those debts in respect of the periods during which they have been outstanding since [the relevant date].

(8)   All interest payable under paragraph (7) ranks equally whether or not the debts on which it is payable rank equally.

(9)   The rate of interest payable under paragraph (7) is whichever is the greater of the rate specified under paragraph (6) [and] the rate applicable to the debt apart from the administration.]

NOTES

Substituted, subject to transitional provisions; see the note preceding r 2.1 at **[10.60]**.
Para (A1): inserted by the Insolvency (Amendment) Rules 2010, SI 2010/686, r 2, Sch 1, para 83(1), (2), as from 6 April 2010, subject to transitional provisions in Sch 4, para 1 thereto, as noted to r 1.5 at **[10.7]**.
Paras (1)–(6), (9): words in square brackets substituted by SI 2010/686, r 2, Sch 1, para 83(1), (3)–(8), (10), as from 6 April 2010, subject to transitional provisions in Sch 4, para 1 thereto, as noted to r 1.5 at **[10.7]**.
Para (7): words omitted revoked by SI 2005/527, r 12(b), as from 1 April 2005, subject to transitional provisions as noted to r 2.67 at **[10.129]**; words in square brackets substituted by SI 2010/686, r 2, Sch 1, para 83(1), (9), as from 6 April 2010, subject to transitional provisions in Sch 4, para 1 thereto, as noted to r 1.5 at **[10.7]**.

[10.151]
[2.89   Debt payable at future time
A creditor may prove for a debt of which payment was not yet due on the date when the company entered administration, [or, if the administration was immediately preceded by a winding up, up to the date that the company went into liquidation] subject to Rule 2.105 (adjustment of dividend where payment made before time).]

NOTES

Substituted, subject to transitional provisions; see the note preceding r 2.1 at **[10.60]**.
Words in square brackets inserted by the Insolvency (Amendment) Rules 2005, SI 2005/527, r 13, as from 1 April 2005, subject to transitional provisions as noted to r 2.67 at **[10.129]**.

[10.152]
[2.90   Value of security
(1)   A secured creditor may, with the agreement of the administrator or the [permission] of the court, at any time alter the value which he has, in his proof of debt, put upon his security.

(2)   However, if a secured creditor—
  (a)   being the applicant for an administration order or the appointor of the administrator, has in the application or the notice of appointment put a value on his security; or
  (b)   has voted in respect of the unsecured balance of his debt,
he may re-value his security only with permission of the court.]

NOTES

Substituted, subject to transitional provisions; see the note preceding r 2.1 at **[10.60]**.
Para (1): word in square brackets substituted by the Insolvency (Amendment) Rules 2010, SI 2010/686, r 2, Sch 1, para 1, as from 6 April 2010, subject to transitional provisions in Sch 4, para 2 thereto, as noted to r 1.31 at **[10.34]**.

[10.153]
[2.91   Surrender for non-disclosure
(1)   If a secured creditor omits to disclose his security in his proof of debt, he shall surrender his security for the general benefit of creditors, unless the court, on application by him, relieves him from the effect of this Rule on the ground that the omission was inadvertent or the result of honest mistake.

(2)   If the court grants that relief, it may require or allow the creditor's proof of debt to be amended, on such terms as may be just.

(3)   Nothing in this Rule or the following two Rules may affect the rights in rem of creditors or third parties protected under Article 5 of the EC Regulation (third parties' rights in rem).]

NOTES
Substituted, subject to transitional provisions; see the note preceding r 2.1 at **[10.60]**.
EC Regulation: ie, Council Regulation 1346/2000/EC on insolvency proceedings.

[10.154]
[2.92   Redemption by administrator

(1)   The administrator may at any time give notice to a creditor whose debt is secured that he proposes, at the expiration of 28 days from the date of the notice, to redeem the security at the value put upon it in the creditor's proof.

(2)   The creditor then has 21 days (or such longer period as the administrator may allow) in which, if he so wishes, to exercise his right to revalue his security (with the permission of the court, where Rule 2.90(2) applies).

If the creditor re-values his security, the administrator may only redeem at the new value.

(3)   If the administrator redeems the security, the cost of transferring it is payable out of the assets.

(4)   A secured creditor may at any time, by a notice in writing, call on the administrator to elect whether he will or will not exercise his power to redeem the security at the value then placed on it; and the administrator then has 3 months in which to exercise the power or determine not to exercise it.]

NOTES
Substituted, subject to transitional provisions; see the note preceding r 2.1 at **[10.60]**.

[10.155]
[2.93   Test of security's value

(1)   Subject as follows, the administrator, if he is dissatisfied with the value which a secured creditor puts on his security (whether in his proof or by way of re-valuation under [Rule 2.92]), may require any property comprised in the security to be offered for sale.

(2)   The terms of sale shall be such as may be agreed, or as the court may direct; and if the sale is by auction, the administrator on behalf of the company, and the creditor on his own behalf, may appear and bid.

[(3)   This Rule does not apply if the security has been revalued and the revaluation has been approved by the court.]]

NOTES
Substituted, subject to transitional provisions; see the note preceding r 2.1 at **[10.60]**.
Para (1): words in square brackets substituted by the Insolvency (Amendment) Rules 2010, SI 2010/686, r 2, Sch 1, para 84(1), (2), as from 6 April 2010, subject to transitional provisions in Sch 4, para 1 thereto, as noted to r 1.5 at **[10.7]**.
Para (3): added by SI 2010/686, r 2, Sch 1, para 84(1), (3), as from 6 April 2010, subject to transitional provisions in Sch 4, para 1 thereto, as noted to r 1.5 at **[10.7]**.

[10.156]
[2.94   Realisation of security by creditor

If a creditor who has valued his security subsequently realises it (whether or not at the instance of the administrator)—

    (a)   the net amount realised shall be substituted for the value previously put by the creditor on the security; and

    (b)   that amount shall be treated in all respects as an amended valuation made by him.]

NOTES
Substituted, subject to transitional provisions; see the note preceding r 2.1 at **[10.60]**.

[10.157]
[2.95   Notice of proposed distribution

(1)   Where an administrator is proposing to make a distribution to creditors he shall give . . . notice of that fact.

(2)   The notice given pursuant to paragraph (1) shall—

    (a)   be sent to—

        (i)   all creditors whose addresses are known to the administrator; and

        (ii)   where a member State liquidator has been appointed in relation to the company, to the member State liquidator;

    (b)   state whether the distribution is to preferential creditors or preferential creditors and unsecured creditors; and

    (c)   where the administrator proposes to make a distribution to unsecured creditors, state the value of the prescribed part, except where the court has made an order under section 176A(5).

[(3)   Subject to paragraph (5)(b), before declaring a dividend the administrator shall by notice invite the creditors to prove their debts. Such notice—
  (a)   shall be gazetted; and
  (b)   may be advertised in such other manner as the administrator thinks fit.]

(4)   A notice pursuant to [paragraph (1) or (3) must, in addition to the standard contents]—
  (a)   state that it is the intention of the administrator to make a distribution to creditors within the period of 2 months from the last date for proving;
  (b)   specify whether the proposed dividend is interim or final;
  (c)   specify a date up to which proofs may be lodged being a date which—
    (i)   is the same date for all creditors; and
    (ii)   is not less than 21 days from that of the notice.

[(5)   Where a dividend is to be declared for preferential creditors—
  (a)   the notice pursuant to paragraph (1) need only to be given to those creditors in whose case the administrator has reason to believe that their debts are preferential; and
  (b)   the notice pursuant to paragraph (3) need only be given if the administrator thinks fit.]]

NOTES
  Substituted, subject to transitional provisions; see the note preceding r 2.1 at **[10.60]**.
  Para (1): words omitted revoked by the Insolvency (Amendment) Rules 2010, SI 2010/686, r 2, Sch 1, para 85(1), (2), as from 6 April 2010, subject to transitional provisions in Sch 4, para 1 thereto, as noted to r 1.5 at **[10.7]**.
  Paras (3), (5): substituted by the Insolvency (Amendment) Rules 2009, SI 2009/642, rr 4, 12, as from 6 April 2009, subject to transitional provisions in r 3 thereof, as noted to r 1.4 of these Rules at **[10.6]**.
  Para (4): words in square brackets substituted by SI 2010/686, r 2, Sch 1, para 85(1), (3), as from 6 April 2010, subject to transitional provisions in Sch 4, para 1 thereto, as noted to r 1.5 at **[10.7]**.

[10.158]
[2.96   Admission or rejection of proofs
(1)   Unless he has already dealt with them, within [5 business] days of the last date for proving, the administrator shall—
  (a)   admit or reject [(in whole or in part)] proofs submitted to him; or
  (b)   make such provision in respect of them as he thinks fit.

(2)   The administrator is not obliged to deal with proofs lodged after the last date for proving, but he may do so, if he thinks fit.

(3)   In the declaration of a dividend no payment shall be made more than once by virtue of the same debt.

(4)   Subject to Rule 2.104, where—
  (a)   a creditor has proved; and
  (b)   a member State liquidator has proved in relation to the same debt,
payment shall only be made to the creditor.]

NOTES
  Substituted, subject to transitional provisions; see the note preceding r 2.1 at **[10.60]**.
  Para (1): words in first pair of square brackets substituted, and words in square brackets in sub-para (a) inserted, by the Insolvency (Amendment) Rules 2010, SI 2010/686, r 2, Sch 1, para 86, as from 6 April 2010, subject to transitional provisions in Sch 4, para 1 thereto, as noted to r 1.5 at **[10.7]**.

[10.159]
[2.96A   Postponement or cancellation of dividend
If in the period of 2 months referred to in Rule 2.95(4)(a)—
  (a)   the administrator has rejected a proof in whole or in part and application is made to the court for that decision to be reversed or varied, or
  (b)   application is made to the court for the administrator's decision on a proof to be reversed or varied, or for a proof to be expunged, or for a reduction of the amount claimed,
the administrator may postpone or cancel the dividend.]

NOTES
  Commencement: 6 April 2010.
  Inserted by the Insolvency (Amendment) Rules 2010, SI 2010/686, r 2, Sch 1, para 87, subject to transitional provisions in Sch 4, para 1 thereto, as noted to r 1.5 at **[10.7]**.

[10.160]
[2.97   Declaration of dividend
(1)   Subject to paragraph (2), within the 2 month period referred to in Rule 2.95(4)(a) the administrator shall proceed to declare the dividend to one or more classes of creditor of which he gave notice.

(2)   Except with the permission of the court, the administrator shall not declare a dividend so long as there is pending any application to the court to reverse or vary a decision of his on a proof, or to expunge a proof or to reduce the amount claimed.

[(3) If the court gives permission under paragraph (2), the administrator must make such provision in respect of the proof in question as the court directs.]]

NOTES

Substituted, subject to transitional provisions; see the note preceding r 2.1 at **[10.60]**.

Para (3): added by the Insolvency (Amendment) Rules 2010, SI 2010/686, r 2, Sch 1, para 88, as from 6 April 2010, subject to transitional provisions in Sch 4, para 1 thereto, as noted to r 1.5 at **[10.7]**.

[10.161]
[2.98   Notice of declaration of a dividend

(1)   Where the administrator declares a dividend he shall give notice of that fact to all creditors who have proved their debts and, where a member State liquidator has been appointed in relation to the company, to the member State liquidator.

(2)   The notice shall include the following particulars relating to the administration—

  (a)   amounts raised from the sale of assets, indicating (so far as practicable) amounts raised by the sale of particular assets;
  (b)   payments made by the administrator when acting as such;
  (c)   where the administrator proposed to make a distribution to unsecured creditors, the value of the prescribed part, except where the court has made an order under section 176A(5);
  (d)   provision (if any) made for unsettled claims, and funds (if any) retained for particular purposes;
  (e)   the total amount of dividend and the rate of dividend;
  (f)   . . . ; and
  (g)   whether, and if so when, any further dividend is expected to be declared.]

NOTES

Substituted, subject to transitional provisions; see the note preceding r 2.1 at **[10.60]**.

Para (2): sub-para (f) revoked by the Insolvency (Amendment) Rules 2010, SI 2010/686, r 2, Sch 1, para 89, as from 6 April 2010, subject to transitional provisions in Sch 4, para 1 thereto, as noted to r 1.5 at **[10.7]**.

[10.162]
[2.99   Payments of dividends and related matters

(1)   The dividend may be distributed simultaneously with the notice declaring it.

(2)   Payment of dividend may be made by post, or arrangements may be made with any creditor for it to be paid to him in another way, or held for his collection.

(3)   Where a dividend is paid on a bill of exchange or other negotiable instrument, the amount of the dividend shall be endorsed on the instrument, or on a certified copy of it, if required to be produced by the holder for that purpose.]

NOTES

Substituted, subject to transitional provisions; see the note preceding r 2.1 at **[10.60]**.

[10.163]
[2.100   Notice of no dividend, or no further dividend

If the administrator gives notice to creditors that he is unable to declare any dividend or (as the case may be) any further dividend, the notice shall contain a statement to the effect either—

  (a)   that no funds have been realised; or
  (b)   that the funds realised have already been distributed or used or allocated for defraying the expenses of administration.]

NOTES

Substituted, subject to transitional provisions; see the note preceding r 2.1 at **[10.60]**.

[10.164]
[2.101   Proof altered after payment of dividend

(1)   If after payment of dividend the amount claimed by a creditor in his proof is increased, the creditor is not entitled to disturb the distribution of the dividend; but he is entitled to be paid, out of any money for the time being available for the payment of any further dividend, any dividend or dividends which he has failed to receive.

(2)   Any dividend or dividends payable under paragraph (1) shall be paid before the money there referred to is applied to the payment of any such further dividend.

(3)   If, after a creditor's proof has been admitted, the proof is withdrawn or expunged, or the amount is reduced, the creditor is liable to repay to the administrator any amount overpaid by way of dividend.]

NOTES

Substituted, subject to transitional provisions; see the note preceding r 2.1 at **[10.60]**.

[10.165]
[2.102 Secured creditors

(1) The following applies where a creditor re-values his security at a time when a dividend has been declared.

(2) If the revaluation results in a reduction of his unsecured claim ranking for dividend, the creditor shall [as soon as reasonably practicable] repay to the administrator, for the credit of the administration, any amount received by him as dividend in excess of that to which he would be entitled having regard to the revaluation of the security.

(3) If the revaluation results in an increase of his unsecured claim, the creditor is entitled to receive from the administrator, out of any money for the time being available for the payment of a further dividend, before any such further dividend is paid, any dividend or dividends which he has failed to receive, having regard to the revaluation of the security.

However, the creditor is not entitled to disturb any dividend declared (whether or not distributed) before the date of the revaluation.]

NOTES

Substituted, subject to transitional provisions; see the note preceding r 2.1 at **[10.60]**.

Para (2): words in square brackets substituted by the Insolvency (Amendment) Rules 2009, SI 2009/642, r 5, as from 6 April 2009, subject to transitional provisions in r 3 thereof, as noted to r 1.4 of these Rules at **[10.6]**.

[10.166]
[2.103 Disqualification from dividend

If a creditor contravenes any provision of the Act or the Rules relating to the valuation of securities, the court may, on the application of the administrator, order that the creditor be wholly or partly disqualified from participation in any dividend.]

NOTES

Substituted, subject to transitional provisions; see the note preceding r 2.1 at **[10.60]**.

[10.167]
[2.104 Assignment of right to dividend

(1) If a person entitled to a dividend gives notice to the administrator that he wishes the dividend to be paid to another person, or that he has assigned his entitlement to another person, the administrator shall pay the dividend to that other accordingly.

(2) A notice given under this Rule must specify the name and address of the person to whom payment is to be made.]

NOTES

Substituted, subject to transitional provisions; see the note preceding r 2.1 at **[10.60]**.

[10.168]
[2.105 Debt payable at future time

(1) Where a creditor has proved for a debt of which payment is not due at the date of the declaration of dividend, he is entitled to dividend equally with other creditors, but subject as follows.

[(2) For the purpose of dividend (and no other purpose) the amount of the creditor's admitted proof (or, if a distribution has previously been made to him, the amount remaining outstanding in respect of his admitted proof) shall be reduced by applying the following formula—

$$X / 1.05^n$$

where—

   (a) "X" is the value of the admitted proof; and

   (b) "n" is the period beginning with the relevant date and ending with the date on which the payment of the creditor's debt would otherwise be due expressed in years and months in a decimalised form.

(3) In paragraph (2) "relevant date" means—

   (a) in the case of an administration which was not immediately preceded by a winding up, the date that the company entered administration;

   (b) in the case of an administration which was immediately preceded by a winding up, the date that the company went into liquidation.]]

NOTES

Substituted, subject to transitional provisions; see the note preceding r 2.1 at **[10.60]**.

Paras (2), (3) substituted (for the original para (2)), and the original para (3) was revoked, by the Insolvency (Amendment) Rules 2005, SI 2005/527, r 15, as from 1 April 2005, subject to transitional provisions as noted to r 2.67 at **[10.129]**.

[CHAPTER 11
THE ADMINISTRATOR

[10.169]
2.106   Fixing of remuneration

(1)   The administrator is entitled to receive remuneration for his services as such.

(2)   [The basis of remuneration] shall be fixed . . . —
   (a)   as a percentage of the value of the property with which he has to deal; or
   (b)   by reference to the time properly given by the insolvency practitioner (as administrator) and his staff in attending to matters arising in the administration[; or
   (c)   as a set amount.]

[(3A)   The basis of remuneration may be fixed as any one or more of the bases set out in paragraph (2), and different bases may be fixed in respect of different things done by the administrator.

(3B)   Where the basis of remuneration is fixed as set out in paragraph (2)(a), different percentages may be fixed in respect of different things done by the administrator.

(3C)   It is for the creditors' committee (if there is one) to determine—
   (a)   which of the bases set out in paragraph (2) are to be fixed and (where appropriate) in what combination under paragraph (3A), and
   (b)   the percentage or percentages (if any) to be fixed under paragraphs (2)(a) and (3B) and the amount (if any) to be set under paragraph (2)(c).]

(4)   In arriving at that determination, the committee shall have regard to the following matters—
   (a)   the complexity (or otherwise) of the case;
   (b)   any respects in which, in connection with the company's affairs, there falls on the administrator any responsibility of an exceptional kind or degree;
   (c)   the effectiveness with which the administrator appears to be carrying out, or to have carried out, his duties as such; and
   (d)   the value and nature of the property with which he has to deal.

(5)   If there is no creditors' committee, or the committee does not make the requisite determination, [and the case does not fall within paragraph (5A), the basis of] the administrator's remuneration may be fixed (in accordance with [paragraphs (2), (3A) and (3B)]) by a resolution of a meeting of creditors; and paragraph (4) applies to them as it does to the creditors' committee.

[(5A)   In a case where the administrator has made a statement under paragraph 52(1)(b), if there is no creditors' committee, or the committee does not make the requisite determination, [the basis of] the administrator's remuneration may be fixed (in accordance with [paragraphs (2), (3A) and (3B)]) by the approval of—
   (a)   each secured creditor of the company: or
   (b)   if the administrator has made or intends to make a distribution to preferential creditors—
      (i)   each secured creditor of the company; and
      (ii)   preferential creditors whose debts amount to more than 50% of the preferential debts of the company, disregarding debts of any creditor who does not respond to an invitation to give or withhold approval;
   and paragraph (4) applies to them as it does to the creditors' committee.]

(6)   If not fixed as above, [the basis of] the administrator's remuneration shall, on his application, be fixed by the court [and the provisions of paragraphs (2) to (4) apply as they do to the fixing of the basis of remuneration by the creditors' committee; but such an application may not be made by the administrator unless the administrator has first sought fixing of the basis in accordance with paragraph (3), (5) or (5A), and in any event may not be made more than 18 months after the date of the administrator's appointment].

(7)   Where there are joint administrators, it is for them to agree between themselves as to how the remuneration payable should be apportioned. Any dispute arising between them may be referred—
   (a)   to the court, for settlement by order; or
   (b)   to the creditors' committee or a meeting of creditors, for settlement by resolution.

(8)   If the administrator is a solicitor and employs his own firm, or any partner in it, to act on behalf of the company, profit costs shall not be paid unless this is authorised by the creditors' committee, the creditors or the court.

(9)   . . .]

NOTES

Substituted, subject to transitional provisions; see the note preceding r 2.1 at **[10.60]**.

Para (2): words in first pair of square brackets substituted, word omitted revoked, and sub-para (c) and word "or" immediately preceding it, inserted by the Insolvency (Amendment) Rules 2010, SI 2010/686, r 2, Sch 1, para 90(1), (2), as from 6 April 2010, subject to transitional provisions in Sch 4, para 1 thereto, as noted to r 1.5 at **[10.7]**.

Paras (3A)–(3C): substituted (for the original para (3)) by SI 2010/686, r 2, Sch 1, para 90(1), (3), as from 6 April 2010, subject to transitional provisions in Sch 4, para 1 thereto, as noted to r 1.5 at **[10.7]**.

Para (5): words in first pair of square brackets inserted, and words in second pair of square brackets substituted, by SI 2010/686, r 2, Sch 1, para 90(1), (4), (5), as from 6 April 2010, subject to transitional provisions in Sch 4, para 1 thereto, as noted to r 1.5 at **[10.7]**.

Para (5A): inserted by the Insolvency (Amendment) Rules 2005, SI 2005/527, r 15(1), as from 1 April 2005, subject to transitional provisions as noted to r 2.67 at **[10.129]**; words in first pair of square brackets inserted, and words in second pair of square brackets substituted, by SI 2010/686, r 2, Sch 1, para 90(1), (5), (6), as from 6 April 2010, subject to transitional provisions in Sch 4, para 1 thereto, as noted to r 1.5 at **[10.7]**.

Para (6): words in square brackets inserted by SI 2010/686, r 2, Sch 1, para 90(1), (7), (8), as from 6 April 2010, subject to transitional provisions in Sch 4, para 1 thereto, as noted to r 1.5 at **[10.7]**.

Para (9): revoked by SI 2005/527, r 15(2), as from 1 April 2005, subject to transitional provisions as noted to r 2.67 at **[10.129]**.

[10.170]
[2.107   Recourse to meeting of creditors

[(1)]   If [the basis of] the administrator's remuneration has been fixed by the creditors' committee, and he considers the rate or amount to be insufficient, [or the basis to be inappropriate, the administrator may request that the rate or amount be increased or the basis changed] by resolution of the creditors.

[(2)   In a case where the administrator has made a statement under paragraph 52(1)(b), if [the basis of] the administrator's remuneration has been fixed by the creditors' committee, and he considers the rate or amount to be insufficient, [or the basis to be inappropriate, the administrator may request that the rate or amount be increased or the basis changed] by the approval of—

(a)   each secured creditor of the company: or
(b)   if the administrator has made or intends to make a distribution to preferential creditors—
  (i)   each secured creditor of the company; and
  (ii)   preferential creditors whose debts amount to more than 50% of the preferential debts of the company, disregarding debts of any creditor who does not respond to an invitation to give or withhold approval.]]

NOTES

Substituted, subject to transitional provisions; see the note preceding r 2.1 at **[10.60]**.

Para (1): numbered as such by the Insolvency (Amendment) Rules 2005, SI 2005/527, r 16, as from 1 April 2005, subject to transitional provisions as noted to r 2.67 at **[10.129]**; words in first pair of square brackets inserted, and words in second pair of square brackets substituted, by the Insolvency (Amendment) Rules 2010, SI 2010/686, r 2, Sch 1, para 91, as from 6 April 2010, subject to transitional provisions in Sch 4, para 1 thereto, as noted to r 1.5 at **[10.7]**.

Para (2): added by SI 2005/527, r 16, as from 1 April 2005, subject to transitional provisions as noted to r 2.67 at **[10.129]**; words in first pair of square brackets inserted, and words in second pair of square brackets substituted, by SI 2010/686, r 2, Sch 1, para 91, as from 6 April 2010, subject to transitional provisions in Sch 4, para 1 thereto, as noted to r 1.5 at **[10.7]**.

[10.171]
[2.108   Recourse to the court

(1)   If the administrator considers that the [basis of] remuneration fixed for him by the creditors' committee, or by resolution of the creditors, is insufficient [or inappropriate], he may apply to the court for an order [changing it or] increasing its amount or rate.

[(1A)   In a case where the administrator has made a statement under paragraph 52(1)(b), if the administrator considers that the [basis of] remuneration fixed by the approval of the creditors in accordance with Rule 2.107(2) is insufficient [or inappropriate], he may apply to the court for an order [changing it or] increasing its amount or rate.]

[(1B)   Where an application is made under paragraph (1A), the administrator must give notice to each of the creditors whose approval was sought under Rule 2.106(5A).]

(2)   The administrator shall give at least 14 days' notice of his application to the members of the creditors' committee; and the committee may nominate one or more members to appear, or be represented, and to be heard on the application.

(3)   If there is no creditors' committee, the administrator's notice of his application shall be sent to such one or more of the company's creditors as the court may direct, which creditors may nominate one or more of their number to appear or be represented.

(4)   The court may, if it appears to be a proper case, order the costs of the administrator's application, including the costs of any member of the creditors' committee appearing or being represented on it, or any creditor so appearing or being represented, to be paid as an expense of the administration.]

NOTES

Substituted, subject to transitional provisions; see the note preceding r 2.1 at **[10.60]**.

Para (1): words in square brackets inserted by the Insolvency (Amendment) Rules 2010, SI 2010/686, r 2, Sch 1, para 92(1), (2), as from 6 April 2010, subject to transitional provisions in Sch 4, para 1 thereto, as noted to r 1.5 at **[10.7]**.

Para (1A): inserted by the Insolvency (Amendment) Rules 2005, SI 2005/527, r 17, as from 1 April 2005, subject to transitional provisions as noted to r 2.67 at **[10.129]**; words in square brackets inserted by SI 2010/686, r 2, Sch 1, para 92(1), (2), as from 6 April 2010, subject to transitional provisions in Sch 4, para 1 thereto, as noted to r 1.5 at **[10.7]**.

Para (1B): inserted by SI 2010/686, r 2, Sch 1, para 92(1), (3), as from 6 April 2010, subject to transitional provisions in Sch 4, para 1 thereto, as noted to r 1.5 at **[10.7]**.

[10.172]
[2.109   Creditors' claim that remuneration is [or other expenses are] excessive

[(1)   Any secured creditor, or any unsecured creditor with either the concurrence of at least 10% in value of the unsecured creditors (including that creditor) or the permission of the court, may apply to the court for one or more of the orders in paragraph (4).

(1A)   Application may be made on the grounds that—
   (a)   the remuneration charged by the administrator,
   (b)   the basis fixed for the administrator's remuneration under Rule 2.106, or
   (c)   expenses incurred by the administrator,
is or are, in all the circumstances, excessive or, in the case of an application under sub-paragraph (b), inappropriate.

(1B)   The application must, subject to any order of the court under Rule 2.48A(4), be made no later than 8 weeks after receipt by the applicant of the progress report which first reports the charging of the remuneration or the incurring of the expenses in question ("the relevant report").]

(2)   The court may, if it thinks that no sufficient cause is shown for a reduction, dismiss it without a hearing but it shall not do so without giving the applicant at least [5 business] days' notice, upon receipt of which the applicant may require the court to list the application for a without notice hearing. If the application is not dismissed, the court shall fix a venue for it to be heard, and give notice to the applicant accordingly.

(3)   The applicant shall, at least 14 days before the hearing, send to the administrator a notice stating the venue and accompanied by a copy of the application, and of any evidence which the applicant intends to adduce in support of it.

[(4)   If the court considers the application to be well-founded, it must make one or more of the following orders—
   (a)   an order reducing the amount of remuneration which the administrator was entitled to charge;
   (b)   an order fixing the basis of remuneration at a reduced rate or amount;
   (c)   an order changing the basis of remuneration;
   (d)   an order that some or all of the remuneration or expenses in question be treated as not being expenses of the administration;
   (e)   an order that the administrator or the administrator's personal representative pay to the company the amount of the excess of remuneration or expenses or such part of the excess as the court may specify;
and may make any other order that it thinks just; but an order under sub-paragraph (b) or (c) may be made only in respect of periods after the period covered by the relevant report.]

(5)   Unless the court orders otherwise, the costs of the application shall be paid by the applicant, and are not payable as an expense of the administration.]

NOTES
   Substituted, subject to transitional provisions; see the note preceding r 2.1 at **[10.60]**.
   Rule heading: words in square brackets inserted by the Insolvency (Amendment) Rules 2010, SI 2010/686, r 2, Sch 1, para 93(1), (2), as from 6 April 2010, subject to transitional provisions in Sch 4, para 1 thereto, as noted to r 1.5 at **[10.7]**.
   Paras (1), (1A), (1B): substituted (for original para (1)) by SI 2010/686, r 2, Sch 1, para 93(1), (3), as from 6 April 2010, subject to transitional provisions in Sch 4, para 1 thereto, as noted to r 1.5 at **[10.7]**.
   Para (2): words in square brackets substituted by SI 2010/686, r 2, Sch 1, para 93(1), (4), as from 6 April 2010, subject to transitional provisions in Sch 4, para 1 thereto, as noted to r 1.5 at **[10.7]**.
   Para (4): substituted by SI 2010/686, r 2, Sch 1, para 93(1), (5), as from 6 April 2010, subject to transitional provisions in Sch 4, para 1 thereto, as noted to r 1.5 at **[10.7]**.

[10.173]
[2.109A   Review of remuneration

(1)   Where, after the basis of the administrator's remuneration has been fixed, there is a material and substantial change in the circumstances which were taken into account in fixing it, the administrator may request that it be changed.

(2)   The request must be made—
   (a)   where the creditors' committee fixed the basis, to the committee;
   (b)   where the creditors fixed the basis, to the creditors;
   (c)   where the court fixed the basis, by application to the court;
and Rules 2.106 to 2.109 apply as appropriate.

(3)   Any change in the basis for remuneration applies from the date of the request under paragraph (2) and not for any earlier period.]

NOTES
   Commencement: 6 April 2010.
   Inserted, together with rr 2.109B, 2.109C, by the Insolvency (Amendment) Rules 2010, SI 2010/686, r 2, Sch 1, para 94, subject to transitional provisions in Sch 4, para 1 thereto, as noted to r 1.5 at **[10.7]**.

[10.174]
[2.109B   Remuneration of new administrator

If a new administrator is appointed in place of another, any determination, resolution or court order in effect under the preceding provisions of this Chapter immediately before the former administrator ceased to hold office continues to apply in respect of the remuneration of the new administrator until a further determination, resolution or court order is made in accordance with those provisions.]

NOTES
Commencement: 6 April 2010.
Inserted as noted to r 2.109A at **[10.173]**.

[10.175]
[2.109C   Apportionment of set fee remuneration

(1)   In a case in which the basis of the administrator's remuneration is a set amount under Rule 2.106(2)(c) and the administrator ("the former administrator") ceases (for whatever reason) to hold office before the time has elapsed or the work has been completed in respect of which the amount was set, application may be made for determination of what portion of the amount should be paid to the former administrator or the former administrator's personal representative in respect of the time which has actually elapsed or the work which has actually been done.

(2)   Application may be made—
   (a)   by the former administrator or the former administrator's personal representative within the period of 28 days beginning with the date upon which the former administrator ceased to hold office, or
   (b)   by the administrator for the time being in office if the former administrator or the former administrator's personal representative has not applied by the end of that period.

(3)   Application must be made—
   (a)   where the creditors' committee fixed the basis, to the committee;
   (b)   where the creditors fixed the basis, to the creditors for a resolution determining the portion;
   (c)   where the court fixed the basis, to the court for an order determining the portion.

(4)   The applicant must give a copy of the application to the administrator for the time being in office or to the former administrator or the former administrator's personal representative, as the case may be ("the recipient").

(5)   The recipient may within 21 days of receipt of the copy of the application give notice of intent to make representations to the creditors' committee or the creditors or to appear or be represented before the court, as the case may be.

(6)   No determination may be made upon the application until expiry of the 21 days referred to in paragraph (5) or, if the recipient does give notice of intent in accordance with that paragraph, until the recipient has been afforded the opportunity to make representations or to appear or be represented, as the case may be.

(7)   If the former administrator or the former administrator's personal representative (whether or not the original applicant) considers that the portion determined upon application to the creditors' committee or the creditors is insufficient, that person may apply—
   (a)   in the case of a determination by the creditors' committee, to the creditors for a resolution increasing the portion;
   (b)   in the case of a resolution of the creditors (whether under paragraph (1) or under sub-paragraph (a)), to the court for an order increasing the portion;
and paragraphs (4) to (6) apply as appropriate.]

NOTES
Commencement: 6 April 2010.
Inserted as noted to r 2.109A at **[10.173]**.

[CHAPTER 12
ENDING ADMINISTRATION

[10.176]
2.110   Final progress reports

(1)   In this Chapter reference to a progress report is to a report in the form specified in Rule 2.47.

(2)   The final progress report means a progress report which includes a summary of—
   (a)   the administrator's proposals;
   (b)   any major amendments to, or deviations from, those proposals;
   (c)   the steps taken during the administration; and
   (d)   the outcome.]

NOTES
Substituted, subject to transitional provisions; see the note preceding r 2.1 at **[10.60]**.

[10.177]
[2.111   Notice of automatic end of administration

(1)   Where the appointment of an administrator has ceased to have effect, and the administrator is not required by any other Rule to give notice of that fact, he shall, as soon as reasonably practicable, and in any event within 5 business days of the date when the appointment has ceased, file a notice of automatic end of administration in Form 2.30B with the court. The notice shall be accompanied by a final progress report.

(2)   A copy of the notice and accompanying document shall be sent as soon as reasonably practicable to the registrar of companies, and to all [other] persons who received a copy of the administrator's proposals.

(3)   If the administrator makes default in complying with this Rule, he is liable to a fine and, for continued contravention, to a daily default fine.]

NOTES
Substituted, subject to transitional provisions; see the note preceding r 2.1 at **[10.60]**.
Para (2): word in square brackets inserted by the Insolvency (Amendment) Rules 2010, SI 2010/686, r 2, Sch 1, para 95, as from 6 April 2010, subject to transitional provisions in Sch 4, para 2 thereto, as noted to r 1.31 at **[10.34]**.
See Form 2.30B at **[10.673]**.

[10.178]
[2.112   Applications for extension of administration

(1)   An application to court for an extension of administration shall be accompanied by a progress report for the period since the last progress report (if any) or the date the company entered administration.

(2)   When the administrator requests an extension of the period of the administration by consent of creditors, his request shall be accompanied by a progress report for the period since the last progress report (if any) or the date the company entered administration.

[(4)   Where the court makes an order extending the administration, the administrator must give notice of the order to the creditors as soon as reasonably practicable, together with a copy of the progress report which accompanied the application to the court.

(5)   Where the period of the administration has been extended by consent of creditors, the administrator must give notice to the creditors as soon as reasonably practicable.]]

NOTES
Substituted, subject to transitional provisions; see the note preceding r 2.1 at **[10.60]**.
Paras (4), (5): substituted (for the original para (3)) by the Insolvency (Amendment) Rules 2010, SI 2010/686, r 2, Sch 1, para 96, as from 6 April 2010, subject to transitional provisions in Sch 4, para 1 thereto, as noted to r 1.5 at **[10.7]**.

[10.179]
[2.113   Notice of end of administration

(1)   Where an administrator who was appointed under paragraph 14 or 22 gives notice that the purpose of administration has been sufficiently achieved he shall use Form 2.32B. The notice shall be accompanied by a final progress report.

(2)   The administrator shall send a copy of the notice to the registrar of companies.

(3)   Two copies of the notice shall be filed with the court and shall contain a statement that a copy of the notice has been sent to the registrar of companies. The court shall endorse each copy with the date and time of filing. The appointment shall cease to have effect from that date and time.

(4)   The court shall give a sealed copy of the notice to the administrator.

(5)   The administrator shall, as soon as reasonably practicable, and within 5 business days, send a copy of the notice of end of administration (and the accompanying report) to every creditor of the company of whose claim and address he is aware, to all those persons [(except the registrar of companies—see paragraph (2))] who were notified of his appointment and to the company.

[(6)   The requirements of paragraph 80(4) shall be taken to be complied with if, within 5 business days of filing the notice of end of administration with the court, the administrator has gazetted a notice undertaking to provide a copy of the notice of the end of administration to any creditor of the company.

(6A)   The notice under Rule 2.113(6) may be advertised in such other manner as the administrator thinks fit.]

[(7)   In addition to the standard contents, the notice under paragraph (6) must state—
    (a)   the date that the administration ended; and
    (b)   that creditors can write for a copy of the notice of end of administration and the address to which to write.]]

NOTES
Substituted, subject to transitional provisions; see the note preceding r 2.1 at **[10.60]**.
Para (5): words in square brackets inserted by the Insolvency (Amendment) Rules 2010, SI 2010/686, r 2, Sch 1, para 97(1), (2), as from 6 April 2010, subject to transitional provisions in Sch 4, para 2 thereto, as noted to r 1.31 at **[10.34]**.

Paras (6), (6A): substituted (for the original para (6)) by the Insolvency (Amendment) Rules 2009, SI 2009/642, rr 4, 13, as from 6 April 2009, subject to transitional provisions in r 3 thereof, as noted to r 1.4 of these Rules at **[10.6]**.

Para (7): substituted by SI 2010/686, r 2, Sch 1, para 97(1), (3), as from 6 April 2010, subject to transitional provisions in Sch 4, para 1 thereto, as noted to r 1.5 at **[10.7]**.

See Form 2.32B at **[10.673]**.

[10.180]
[2.114   Application to court by administrator

(1)   An application to court under paragraph 79 for an order ending an administration shall have attached to it a progress report for the period since the last progress report (if any) or the date the company entered administration and a statement indicating what the administrator thinks should be the next steps for the company (if applicable).

(2)   Where the administrator applies to the court because the creditors' meeting has required him to, he shall also attach a statement to the application in which he shall indicate (giving reasons) whether or not he agrees with the creditors' requirement to him to make the application.

(3)   When the administrator applies other than at the request of a creditors' meeting, he shall—

  (a)   give notice in writing to the applicant for the administration order under which he was appointed, or the person by whom he was appointed and the creditors of his intention to apply to court at least [5 business] days before the date that he intends to makes his application; and

  (b)   attach to his application to court a statement that he has notified the creditors, and copies of any response from creditors to that notification.

(4)   Where the administrator applies to court under paragraph 79 in conjunction with a petition under section 124 for an order to wind up the company, he shall, in addition to the requirements of paragraph (3), notify the creditors whether he intends to seek appointment as liquidator.]

NOTES

Substituted, subject to transitional provisions; see the note preceding r 2.1 at **[10.60]**.

Para (3): words in square brackets substituted by the Insolvency (Amendment) Rules 2010, SI 2010/686, r 2, Sch 1, para 98, as from 6 April 2010, subject to transitional provisions in Sch 4, para 1 thereto, as noted to r 1.5 at **[10.7]**.

[10.181]
[2.115   Application to court by creditor

(1)   Where a creditor applies to the court to end the administration a copy of the application shall be served on the administrator and the person who either made the application for the administration order or made the appointment. Where the appointment was made under paragraph 14, a copy of the application shall be served on the holder of the floating charge by virtue of which the appointment was made.

(2)   Service shall be effected not less than 5 business days before the date fixed for the hearing. The administrator, applicant or appointor, or holder of the floating charge by virtue of which the appointment was made may appear at the hearing of the application.

(3)   Where the court makes an order to end the administration, the court shall send a copy of the order to the administrator.]

NOTES

Substituted, subject to transitional provisions; see the note preceding r 2.1 at **[10.60]**.

[10.182]
[2.116   Notification by administrator of court order

[(1)]   Where the court makes an order to end the administration, the administrator [must send to the registrar of companies] a copy of the court order and a copy of his final progress report.

[(2)   As soon as reasonably practicable, the administrator must send a copy of the notice and the final progress report to all other persons who received notice of the administrator's appointment.]]

NOTES

Substituted, subject to transitional provisions; see the note preceding r 2.1 at **[10.60]**.

Para (1): numbered as such, and words in square brackets substituted, by the Insolvency (Amendment) Rules 2010, SI 2010/686, r 2, Sch 1, para 99(1)–(3), as from 6 April 2010, subject to transitional provisions in Sch 4, paras 1, 2 thereto, as noted to rr 1.5, 1.31 at **[10.7]**, **[10.34]**.

Para (2): added by SI 2010/686, r 2, Sch 1, para 99(1), (4), as from 6 April 2010, subject to transitional provisions in Sch 4, para 1 thereto, as noted to r 1.5 at **[10.7]**.

[10.183]
[2.117A   Moving from administration to creditors' voluntary liquidation

(1)   As soon as reasonably practicable after the day on which the registrar of companies registers the notice of moving from administration to creditors' voluntary liquidation sent by the administrator for the purposes of paragraph 83(3), the person who at that point ceases to be the

administrator must (whether the administrator becomes the liquidator or not) send a final progress report (which must include details of the assets to be dealt with in the liquidation) to the registrar of companies and to all those who received notice of the administrator's appointment.

(2)   For the purposes of paragraph 83(7)(a), a person is nominated by the creditors as liquidator by—

(a)   their approval of the statement of the proposed liquidator in the administrator's proposals or revised proposals, or

(b)   their nomination of a different person before their approval of the proposals or revised proposals.

(3)   Where the creditors nominate a different person, the nomination must, where applicable, include the declaration required by section 231.]

NOTES

Substituted (for the original r 2.117) by the Insolvency (Amendment) Rules 2010, SI 2010/686, r 2, Sch 1, para 100, as from 6 April 2010, subject to transitional provisions in Sch 4, para 1 thereto, as noted to r 1.5 at **[10.7]**.

[10.184]
[2.118   Moving from administration to dissolution

(1)   Where, for the purposes of paragraph 84(1), the administrator sends a notice of moving from administration to dissolution to the registrar of companies, [the administrator must] attach to that notice a final progress report.

(2)   As soon as reasonably practicable a copy of the notice and the attached document shall be sent to all [other persons] who received notice of the administrator's appointment.

(3)   Where a court makes an order under paragraph 84(7) it shall, where the applicant is not the administrator, give a copy of the order to the administrator.

(4)   . . .

NOTES

Substituted, subject to transitional provisions; see the note preceding r 2.1 at **[10.60]**.

Paras (1), (2): words in square brackets substituted by the Insolvency (Amendment) Rules 2010, SI 2010/686, r 2, Sch 1, para 101(1)–(3), as from 6 April 2010, subject to transitional provisions in Sch 4, para 1 thereto, as noted to r 1.5 at **[10.7]**.

Para (4): revoked by SI 2010/686, r 2, Sch 1, para 101(1), (4), as from 6 April 2010, subject to transitional provisions in Sch 4, para 1 thereto, as noted to r 1.5 at **[10.7]**.

[CHAPTER 13
REPLACING ADMINISTRATOR

[10.185]
2.119   Grounds for resignation

(1)   The administrator may give notice of his resignation on grounds of ill health or because—

(a)   he intends ceasing to be in practice as an insolvency practitioner; or

(b)   there is some conflict of interest, or change of personal circumstances, which precludes or makes impracticable the further discharge by him of the duties of administrator.

(2)   The administrator may, with the permission of the court, give notice of his resignation on grounds other than those specified in paragraph (1).]

NOTES

Substituted, subject to transitional provisions; see the note preceding r 2.1 at **[10.60]**.

[10.186]
[2.120   Notice of intention to resign

(1)   The administrator shall in all cases give at least [5 business] days' notice in Form 2.37B of his intention to resign, or to apply for the court's permission to do so, to the following persons—

(a)   if there is a continuing administrator of the company, to him; and

(b)   if there is a creditors' committee to it; but

(c)   if there is no such administrator and no creditors' committee, to the company and its creditors.

(2)   Where the administrator gives notice under paragraph (1), he shall also give notice to a member State liquidator, if such a person has been appointed in relation to the company.

(3)   Where the administrator was appointed by the holder of a qualifying floating charge under paragraph 14, the notice of intention to resign shall also be sent to all holders of prior qualifying floating charges, and to the person who appointed the administrator. A copy of the notice shall also be sent to the holder of the floating charge by virtue of which the appointment was made.

(4)   Where the administrator was appointed by the company or the directors of the company under paragraph 22, a copy of the notice of intention to resign shall also be sent to the appointor and all holders of a qualifying floating charge.]

NOTES

Substituted, subject to transitional provisions; see r 2.1 at **[10.60]**.

Para (1): words in square brackets substituted by the Insolvency (Amendment) Rules 2010, SI 2010/686, r 2, Sch 1, para 102, as from 6 April 2010, subject to transitional provisions in Sch 4, para 1 thereto, as noted to r 1.5 at **[10.7]**.

See Form 2.37B at **[10.673]**.

[10.187]
[2.121   Notice of resignation

(1)   The notice of resignation shall be in Form 2.38B.

(2)   Where the administrator was appointed under an administration order, the notice shall be filed with the court, and a copy sent to the registrar of companies. A copy of the notice of resignation shall be sent not more than 5 business days after it has been filed with the court to all those to whom notice of intention to resign was sent.

(3)   Where the administrator was appointed by the holder of a qualifying floating charge under paragraph 14, a copy of the notice of resignation shall be filed with the court and sent to the registrar of companies, and anyone else who received a copy of the notice of intention to resign, within 5 business days of the notice of resignation being sent to the holder of the floating charge by virtue of which the appointment was made.

(4)   Where the administrator was appointed by the company or the directors under paragraph 22, a copy of the notice of resignation shall be filed with the court and sent to the registrar of companies and to anyone else who received notice of intention to resign within 5 business days of the notice of resignation being sent to either the company or the directors that made the appointment.]

NOTES

Substituted, subject to transitional provisions; see the note preceding r 2.1 at **[10.60]**.

See Form 2.38B at **[10.673]**.

[10.188]
[2.122   Application to court to remove administrator from office

(1)   Any application under paragraph 88 shall state the grounds on which it is requested that the administrator should be removed from office.

(2)   Service of the notice of the application shall be effected on the administrator, the person who made the application for the administration order or the person who appointed the administrator, the creditors' committee (if any), the joint administrator (if any), and where there is neither a creditors' committee or joint administrator, to the company and all the creditors, including any floating charge holders not less than 5 business days before the date fixed for the application to be heard. Where the appointment was made under paragraph 14, the notice shall be served on the holder of the floating charge by virtue of which the appointment was made.

(3)   Where a court makes an order removing the administrator it shall give a copy of the order to the applicant who as soon as reasonably practicable shall send a copy to the administrator.

(4)   The applicant shall also within 5 business days of the order being made send a copy of the order to all those to whom notice of the application was sent.

(5)   A copy of the order shall also be sent to the registrar of companies   . . .   within the same time period.]

NOTES

Substituted, subject to transitional provisions; see the note preceding r 2.1 at **[10.60]**.

Para (5): words omitted revoked by the Insolvency (Amendment) Rules 2010, SI 2010/686, r 2, Sch 1, para 103, as from 6 April 2010, subject to transitional provisions in Sch 4, para 1 thereto, as noted to r 1.5 at **[10.7]**.

[10.189]
[2.123   Notice of vacation of office when administrator ceases to be qualified to act

Where the administrator who has ceased to be qualified to act as an insolvency practitioner in relation to the company gives notice in accordance with paragraph 89, he shall also give notice to the registrar of companies   . . .   ]

NOTES

Substituted, subject to transitional provisions; see the note preceding r 2.1 at **[10.60]**.

Words omitted revoked by the Insolvency (Amendment) Rules 2010, SI 2010/686, r 2, Sch 1, para 104, as from 6 April 2010, subject to transitional provisions in Sch 4, para 1 thereto, as noted to r 1.5 at **[10.7]**.

[10.190]
[2.124   Administrator deceased

(1)   Subject as follows, where the administrator has died, it is the duty of his personal representatives to give notice of the fact to the court, specifying the date of the death. This does not apply if notice has been given under either paragraph (2) or (3) of this Rule.

(2)   If the deceased administrator was a partner in [or an employee of] a firm, notice may be given by a partner in the firm who is qualified to act as an insolvency practitioner, or is a member of any body recognised by the Secretary of State for the authorisation of insolvency practitioners.

(3)   Notice of the death may be given by any person producing to the court the relevant death certificate or a copy of it.

(4)   Where a person gives notice to the court under this Rule, he shall also give notice to the registrar of companies . . .]

NOTES

Substituted, subject to transitional provisions; see the note preceding r 2.1 at **[10.60]**.

Para (2): words in square brackets inserted by the Insolvency (Amendment) Rules 2010, SI 2010/686, r 2, Sch 1, para 105(1), (2), as from 6 April 2010, subject to transitional provisions in Sch 4, para 1 thereto, as noted to r 1.5 at **[10.7]**.

Para (4): words omitted revoked by SI 2010/686, r 2, Sch 1, para 105(1), (3), as from 6 April 2010, subject to transitional provisions in Sch 4, para 1 thereto, as noted to r 1.5 at **[10.7]**.

[10.191]
[2.125   Application to replace

(1)   Where an application is made to court under paragraphs 91(1) or 95 to appoint a replacement administrator, the application shall be accompanied by a written statement in Form 2.2B by the person proposed to be the replacement administrator.

(2)   Where the original administrator was appointed under an administration order, a copy of the application shall be served, in addition to those persons listed in paragraph 12(2) and Rule 2.6(3), on the person who made the application for the administration order.

(3)   Where the application to court is made under paragraph 95, the application shall be accompanied by [a witness statement] setting out the applicant's belief as to the matters set out in that paragraph.

(4)   Rule 2.8 shall apply to the service of an application under paragraphs 91(1) and 95 as it applies to service in accordance with Rule 2.6.

(5)   Rules 2.9, 2.10, 2.12 and 2.14(1) and (2) apply to an application under paragraphs 91(1) and 95.]

NOTES

Substituted, subject to transitional provisions; see the note preceding r 2.1 at **[10.60]**.

Para (3): words in square brackets substituted by the Insolvency (Amendment) Rules 2010, SI 2010/686, r 2, Sch 1, para 106, as from 6 April 2010, subject to transitional provisions in Sch 4, para 2 thereto, as noted to r 1.31 at **[10.34]**.

See Form 2.2B at **[10.673]**.

[10.192]
[2.126   Notification and advertisement of appointment of replacement administrator

Where a replacement administrator is appointed, the same provisions apply in respect of giving notice of, and advertising, the replacement appointment as in the case of the appointment (subject to Rule 2.128), and all statements, consents etc as are required shall also be required in the case of the appointment of a replacement. All forms and notices shall clearly identify that the appointment is of a replacement administrator.]

NOTES

Substituted, subject to transitional provisions; see the note preceding r 2.1 at **[10.60]**.

[10.193]
[2.127   Notification and advertisement of appointment of joint administrator

Where, after an initial appointment has been made, an additional person or persons are to be appointed as joint administrator the same Rules shall apply in respect of giving notice of and advertising the appointment as in the case of the initial appointment, subject to Rule 2.128.]

NOTES

Substituted, subject to transitional provisions; see the note preceding r 2.1 at **[10.60]**.

[10.194]
[2.128

The replacement or additional administrator shall send notice of the appointment . . . to the registrar of companies.]

NOTES

Substituted, subject to transitional provisions; see the note preceding r 2.1 at **[10.60]**.

Words omitted revoked by the Insolvency (Amendment) Rules 2010, SI 2010/686, r 2, Sch 1, para 107, as from 6 April 2010, subject to transitional provisions in Sch 4, para 1 thereto, as noted to r 1.5 at **[10.7]**.

[10.195]
[2.129 Administrator's duties on vacating office

(1) Where the administrator ceases to be in office as such, in consequence of removal, resignation or cesser of qualification as an insolvency practitioner, he is under obligation as soon as reasonably practicable to deliver up to the person succeeding him as administrator the assets (after deduction of any expenses properly incurred and distributions made by him) and further to deliver up to that person—
- (a) the records of the administration, including correspondence, proofs and other related papers appertaining to the administration while it was within his responsibility; and
- (b) the company's books, papers and other records.

(2) If the administrator makes default in complying with this Rule, he is liable to a fine and, for continued contravention, to a daily default fine.]

NOTES

Substituted, subject to transitional provisions; see the note preceding r 2.1 at **[10.60]**.

[CHAPTER 14
EC REGULATION: CONVERSION OF ADMINISTRATION INTO WINDING UP

[10.196]
2.130 Application for conversion into winding up

[(1) Where a member State liquidator proposes to apply to the court for the conversion into winding-up proceedings of an administration, a witness statement complying with Rule 2.131 must be prepared and filed with the court in support of the application.

(1A) In this Rule, and in Rules 2.131 and 2.132, "conversion into winding-up proceedings" means an order under Article 37 of the EC Regulation (conversion of earlier proceedings) that—
- (a) the purposes of the administration are to be limited to the winding up of the company through administration and are to exclude the purpose contained in sub- paragraph (a) of paragraph 3(1);
- (b) the administration is converted into a creditors' voluntary winding up; or
- (c) the administration is converted into a winding up by the court.]

(2) An application under this Rule shall be by originating application.

(3) The application and the [witness statement] required under this Rule shall be served upon—
- (a) the company; and
- (b) the administrator.]

NOTES

Substituted, subject to transitional provisions; see the note preceding r 2.1 at **[10.60]**.

Paras (1), (1A): substituted (for the original para (1)) by the Insolvency (Amendment) Rules 2010, SI 2010/686, r 2, Sch 1, para 108(1), (2), as from 6 April 2010, subject to transitional provisions in Sch 4, para 1 thereto, as noted to r 1.5 at **[10.7]**.

Para (3): words in square brackets substituted by SI 2010/686, r 2, Sch 1, para 108(1), (3), as from 6 April 2010, subject to transitional provisions in Sch 4, para 2 thereto, as noted to r 1.31 at **[10.34]**.

EC Regulation: ie, Council Regulation 1346/2000/EC on insolvency proceedings.

[10.197]
[2.131 Contents of [witness statement]

(1) The [witness statement] shall state—
- (a) that main proceedings have been opened in relation to the company in a member State other than the United Kingdom;
- (b) the [belief of the person making the statement] that the conversion of the administration into [winding-up proceedings] would prove to be in the interests of the creditors in the main proceedings;
- [(c) the opinion of the person making the statement as to whether the company ought to go into voluntary liquidation or be wound up by the court; and]
- (d) all other matters that, in the opinion of the member State liquidator, would assist the court—
  - (i) in deciding whether to make such an order; and
  - (ii) if the court were to do so, in considering the need for any consequential provision that would be necessary or desirable.

(2) [A witness statement] under this rule shall be [made] by, or on behalf of, the member State liquidator.]

NOTES

Substituted, subject to transitional provisions; see the note preceding r 2.1 at **[10.60]**.

Words in square brackets substituted by the Insolvency (Amendment) Rules 2010, SI 2010/686, r 2, Sch 1, para 109, as from 6 April 2010, subject to transitional provisions in Sch 4, para 2 thereto, as noted to r 1.31 at **[10.34]**.

[10.198]

[2.132 Power of court

(1) On hearing the application for conversion into [winding-up proceedings] the court may make such order as it thinks [just].

(2) If the court makes an order for conversion into [winding-up proceedings] the order may contain all such consequential provisions as the court deems necessary or desirable.

(3) Without prejudice to the generality of paragraph (1), an order under that paragraph may provide that the company be wound up as if a resolution for voluntary winding up under section 84 were passed on the day on which the order is made.]

NOTES

Substituted, subject to transitional provisions; see the note preceding r 2.1 at **[10.60]**.

Para (1): words in first pair of square brackets substituted by the Insolvency (Amendment) Rules 2010, SI 2010/686, r 2, Sch 1, para 110, as from 6 April 2010, subject to transitional provisions in Sch 4, para 1 thereto, as noted to r 1.5 at **[10.7]**; word in second pair of square brackets substituted by Sch 1, para 1 of those Rules, as from 6 April 2010, subject to transitional provisions in Sch 4, para 2 thereto, as noted to r 1.31 at **[10.34]**.

Para (2): words in square brackets substituted by SI 2010/686, r 2, Sch 1, para 110, as from 6 April 2010, subject to transitional provisions in Sch 4, para 1 thereto, as noted to r 1.5 at **[10.7]**.

[CHAPTER 15
EC REGULATION: MEMBER STATE LIQUIDATOR

[10.199]

2.133 Interpretation of creditor and notice to member State liquidator

(1) This Rule applies where a member State liquidator has been appointed in relation to the company.

(2) For the purposes of the Rules referred to in paragraph (3) the member State liquidator is deemed to be a creditor.

(3) The Rules referred to in paragraph (2) are Rules 2.34 (notice of creditors' meeting), 2.35(4) (creditors' meeting), 2.37 (requisitioning of creditors' meeting), 2.38 (entitlement to vote), 2.39 (admission and rejection of claims), 2.40 (secured creditors), 2.41 (holders of negotiable instruments), 2.42 (hire-purchase, conditional sale and chattel leasing agreements), 2.46 (notice to creditors), 2.47 (reports to creditors), 2.48 (correspondence instead of creditors' meeting), 2.50(2) (creditors' committee), 2.57(1)(b) and (c) (termination of membership of creditors' committee), 2.59(3) (vacancies in creditors' committee), 2.108(3) (administrator's remuneration—recourse to court) and 2.109 (challenge to administrator's remuneration).

(4) Paragraphs (2) and (3) are without prejudice to the generality of the right to participate referred to in paragraph 3 of Article 32 of the EC Regulation (exercise of creditor's rights).

(5) Where the administrator is obliged to give notice to, or provide a copy of a document (including an order of court) to, the court, the registrar of companies or the official receiver, the administrator shall give notice or provide copies, as the case may be, to the member State liquidator.

(6) Paragraph (5) is without prejudice to the generality of the obligations imposed by Article 31 of the EC Regulation (duty to co-operate and communicate information).]

NOTES

Substituted, subject to transitional provisions; see the note preceding r 2.1 at **[10.60]**.

EC Regulation: ie, Council Regulation 1346/2000/EC on insolvency proceedings.

PART 3
ADMINISTRATIVE RECEIVERSHIP

CHAPTER 1
APPOINTMENT OF ADMINISTRATIVE RECEIVER

[10.200]

[3.1 Acceptance and confirmation of acceptance of appointment

(1) Where two or more persons are appointed as joint receivers or managers of a company's property under powers contained in an instrument, the acceptance of such an appointment shall be made by each of them in accordance with section 33 as if that person were a sole appointee, but the joint appointment takes effect only when all such persons have so accepted and is then deemed to have been made at the time at which the instrument of appointment was received by or on behalf of all such persons.

(2) Subject to the next paragraph, where a person is appointed as the sole or joint receiver of a company's property under powers contained in an instrument, the appointee shall, if he accepts the appointment, within [5 business] days confirm his acceptance in writing to the person appointing him.

(3)   Paragraph (2) does not apply where an appointment is accepted in writing.

(4)   Any acceptance or confirmation of acceptance of appointment as a receiver or manager of a company's property, whether under the Act or the Rules, may be given by any person (including, in the case of a joint appointment, any joint appointee) duly authorised for that purpose on behalf of the receiver or manager.

(5)   In confirming acceptance the appointee or person authorised for that purpose shall state—
   (a)   the time and date of receipt of the instrument of appointment, and
   (b)   the time and date of acceptance.]

NOTES
   Substituted by the Insolvency (Amendment) Rules 1987, SI 1987/1919, r 3(1), Schedule, Pt 1, para 23, as from 11 January 1988.
   Para (2): words in square brackets substituted by the Insolvency (Amendment) Rules 2010, SI 2010/686, r 2, Sch 1, para 111, as from 6 April 2010, subject to transitional provisions in Sch 4, para 1 thereto, as noted to r 1.5 at **[10.7]**.
      See Form 3.1 at **[10.673]**.

[10.201]
3.2   Notice and advertisement of appointment

(1)   This Rule relates to the notice which a person is required by section 46(1) to send and publish, when appointed as administrative receiver.

(2)   The following matters shall be stated in the [notices sent to the company and the creditors]—
   (a)   the registered name of the company, as at the date of the appointment, and its registered number;
   (b)   any other name with which the company has been registered in the 12 months preceding that date;
   (c)   any name under which the company has traded at any time in those 12 months, if substantially different from its then registered name;
   (d)   the name and address of the administrative receiver, and the date of his appointment;
   (e)   the name of the person by whom the appointment was made;
   (f)   the date of the instrument conferring the power under which the appointment was made, and a brief description of the instrument;
   (g)   a brief description of the assets of the company (if any) in respect of which the person appointed is not made the receiver.

[(3)   Subject to paragraph (4), the notice of appointment to be given by the administrative receiver under section 46(1)(a) shall be gazetted and may be advertised in such other manner as the administrative receiver thinks fit.

[(4)   In addition to the standard contents, the notice under paragraph (3) must state—
   (a)   that an administrative receiver has been appointed;
   (b)   the date of the appointment;
   (c)   the name of the person who made the appointment, and that the appointment was made by that person; and
   (d)   the nature of the business of the company.]]

NOTES
   Para (2): words in square brackets substituted by the Insolvency (Amendment) Rules 1987, SI 1987/1919, r 3(1), Schedule, Pt 1, para 24, as from 11 January 1988.
   Para (3): substituted, together with para (4), by the Insolvency (Amendment) Rules 2009, SI 2009/642, rr 4, 14, as from 6 April 2009, subject to transitional provisions in r 3 thereof, as noted to r 1.4 of these Rules at **[10.6]**.
   Para (4): substituted as noted to para (3) above; further substituted by the Insolvency (Amendment) Rules 2010, SI 2010/686, r 2, Sch 1, para 112, as from 6 April 2010, subject to transitional provisions in Sch 4, para 1 thereto, as noted to r 1.5 at **[10.7]**.
      See Form 3.1A at **[10.673]**.

CHAPTER 2
STATEMENT OF AFFAIRS AND REPORT TO CREDITORS

[10.202]
3.3   Notice requiring statement of affairs

(1)   [Where] the administrative receiver determines to require a statement of the company's affairs to be made out and submitted to him in accordance with section 47, he shall send notice to each of the persons whom he considers should be made responsible under that section, requiring them to prepare and submit the statement.

(2)   The persons to whom the notice is sent are referred to in this Chapter as "the [nominated persons]".

(3)   The notice shall inform each of the [nominated persons]—
   (a)   of the names and addresses of all others (if any) to whom the same notice has been sent;
   (b)   of the time within which the statement must be delivered;
   (c)   of the effect of section 47(6) (penalty for non-compliance); and

(d)   of the application to him, and to each of the other [nominated persons], of section 235 (duty to provide information, and to attend on the administrative receiver if required).

(4)   The administrative receiver shall, on request, furnish each [nominated person] with [the forms required for the preparation of the statement of affairs].

NOTES

Para (1): word in square brackets substituted by the Insolvency (Amendment) Rules 1987, SI 1987/1919, r 3(1), Schedule, Pt 1, para 25(1), (2), as from 11 January 1988.

Paras (2), (3): words in square brackets substituted by the Insolvency (Amendment) Rules 2010, SI 2010/686, r 2, Sch 1, para 113(1), (2), as from 6 April 2010, subject to transitional provisions in Sch 4, para 2 thereto, as noted to r 1.31 at **[10.34]**.

Para (4): words in first pair of square brackets substituted by SI 2010/686, r 2, Sch 1, para 113(1), (3), as from 6 April 2010, subject to transitional provisions in Sch 4, para 2 thereto, as noted to r 1.31 at **[10.34]**; words in second pair of square brackets substituted by SI 1987/1919, r 3(1), Schedule, Pt 1, para 25(1), (2), as from 11 January 1988.

See Form 3.1B at **[10.673]**.

[10.203]
3.4   Verification and filing

(1)   The statement of affairs shall be in Form 3.2, shall contain all the particulars required by that form and shall be verified by [a statement of truth] by the [nominated persons] (using the same form).

(2)   The administrative receiver may require any of the persons mentioned in section 47(3) to submit [a statement of concurrence], stating that he concurs [with the statement of affairs].

(3)   [A statement] of concurrence may be qualified in respect of matters dealt with in the statement of affairs, where the maker of [the statement of concurrence] is not in agreement with the [nominated persons], or he considers the statement to be erroneous or misleading, or he is without the direct knowledge necessary for concurring with it.

(4)   The statement of affairs shall be delivered to the receiver by the [nominated person] making the [statement of truth] (or by one of them, if more than one), together with a copy of the verified statement.

(5)   Every [statement] of concurrence shall be delivered by the person who makes it, together with a copy.

(6)   The administrative receiver shall retain the verified copy of the statement [of affairs] and the [statements] of concurrence (if any) as part of the records of the receivership.

NOTES

Paras (1)–(5): words in square brackets substituted by the Insolvency (Amendment) Rules 2010, SI 2010/686, r 2, Sch 1, para 114(1)–(6), as from 6 April 2010, subject to transitional provisions in Sch 4, para 2 thereto, as noted to r 1.31 at **[10.34]**.

Para (6): words in first pair of square brackets inserted, and word in second pair of square brackets substituted, by SI 2010/686, r 2, Sch 1, para 114(1), (7), as from 6 April 2010, subject to transitional provisions in Sch 4, para 2 thereto, as noted to r 1.31 at **[10.34]**.

See Form 3.2 at **[10.673]**.

[10.204]
3.5   Limited disclosure

(1)   Where the administrative receiver thinks that it would prejudice the conduct of the receivership [or might reasonably be expected to lead to violence against any person] for the whole or part of the statement of affairs to be disclosed, he may apply to the court for an order of limited disclosure in respect of the statement or a specified part of it.

(2)   The court may on the application order that the statement, or, as the case may be, the specified part of it, be not open to inspection otherwise than with [permission] of the court.

(3)   The court's order may include directions as to the delivery of documents to the registrar of companies and the disclosure of relevant information to other persons.

NOTES

Para (1): words in square brackets inserted by the Insolvency (Amendment) Rules 2010, SI 2010/686, r 2, Sch 1, para 115, as from 6 April 2010, subject to transitional provisions in Sch 4, para 1 thereto, as noted to r 1.5 at **[10.7]**.

Para (2): word in square brackets substituted by SI 2010/686, r 2, Sch 1, para 1, as from 6 April 2010, subject to transitional provisions in Sch 4, para 2 thereto, as noted to r 1.31 at **[10.34]**.

[10.205]
3.6   Release from duty to submit statement of affairs; extension of time

(1)   The power of the administrative receiver under section 47(5) to give a release from the obligation imposed by that section, or to grant an extension of time, may be exercised at the receiver's own discretion, or at the request of any [nominated person].

(2)   A [nominated person] may, if he requests a release or extension of time and it is refused by the receiver, apply to the court for it.

(3)   The court may, if it thinks that no sufficient cause is shown for the application, dismiss it; but it shall not do so unless the applicant has had an opportunity to attend the court for [a hearing without notice to any other party], of which he has been given at least [5 business] days' notice.

If the application is not dismissed under this paragraph, the court shall fix a venue for it to be heard, and give notice to the [nominated person] accordingly.

(4)   The [nominated person] shall, at least 14 days before the hearing, send to the receiver a notice stating the venue and accompanied by a copy of the application, and of any evidence which he (the [nominated person]) intends to adduce in support of it.

(5)   The receiver may appear and he heard on the application; and, whether or not he appears, he may file a written report of any matters which he considers ought to be drawn to the court's attention.

If such a report is filed, a copy of it shall be sent by the receiver to the [nominated person], not later than 5 [business] days before the hearing.

(6)   Sealed copies of any order made on the application shall be sent by the court to the [nominated person] and the receiver.

(7)   On any application under this Rule the applicant's costs shall be paid in any event by him and, unless the court otherwise orders, no allowance towards them shall be made out of the assets under the administrative receiver's control.

NOTES

Paras (1)–(4), (6): words in square brackets substituted by the Insolvency (Amendment) Rules 2010, SI 2010/686, r 2, Sch 1, para 116(1)–(3), as from 6 April 2010, subject to transitional provisions in Sch 4, paras 1, 2 thereto, as noted to rr 1.5, 1.31 at **[10.7]**, **[10.34]**.

Para (5): words in first pair of square brackets substituted, and word in second pair of square brackets inserted, by SI 2010/686, r 2, Sch 1, para 116(1), (2), (4), as from 6 April 2010, subject to transitional provisions in Sch 4, paras 1, 2 thereto, as noted to rr 1.5, 1.31 at **[10.7]**, **[10.34]**.

[10.206]
3.7   Expenses of statement of affairs

(1)   A [nominated person] making the statement of affairs and [statement of truth] shall be allowed, and paid by the administrative receiver out of his receipts, any expenses incurred by the [nominated person] is so doing which the receiver thinks reasonable.

(2)   Any decision by the receiver under this Rule is subject to appeal to the court.

(3)   Nothing in this Rule relieves a [nominated person] from any obligation with respect to the preparation, verification and submission of the statement of affairs, or to the provision of information to the receiver.

NOTES

Words in square brackets substituted by the Insolvency (Amendment) Rules 2010, SI 2010/686, r 2, Sch 1, para 117, as from 6 April 2010, subject to transitional provisions in Sch 4, para 2 thereto, as noted to r 1.31 at **[10.34]**.

[10.207]
3.8   Report to creditors

[(1)   If an administrative receiver gives notice under section 48(2)(b), the notice—
   (a)   shall be gazetted; and
   (b)   may be advertised in such other manner as the administrative receiver thinks fit.]

[(1A)   In addition to the standard contents, the notice under paragraph (1) must state that creditors can write for a copy of the report and the address to which to write.]

(2)   If he proposes to apply to the court to dispense with the holding of the meeting of unsecured creditors (otherwise required by section 48(2)), he shall in his report to creditors or (as the case may be) in the notice published as above, state the venue fixed by the court for the hearing of the application.

(3)   Subject to any order of the court under Rule 3.5, the copy of the receiver's report which under section 48(1) is to be sent to the registrar of companies shall have attached to it a copy of any statement of affairs under section 47, and copies of any [statements] of concurrence.

(4)   If the statement of affairs or [statements] of concurrence, if any, have not been submitted to the receiver by the time he sends a copy of his report to the registrar of companies, he shall send a copy of the statement [of affairs] and any [statements] of concurrence as soon thereafter as he receives them.

[(5)   The receiver's report under section 48(1) shall state, to the best of his knowledge and belief—
   (a)   an estimate of the value of the prescribed part (whether or not he proposes to make an application under section 176A(5) or whether section 176A(3) applies); and
   (b)   an estimate of the value of the company's net property.

(6)   Nothing in this Rule is to be taken as requiring any such estimate to include any information, the disclosure of which could seriously prejudice the commercial interests of the company.

If such information is excluded from the calculation the estimate shall be accompanied by a statement to that effect.

(7)   The report shall also state whether, and if so why, the receiver proposes to make an application to court under section 176A(5).]

NOTES

Para (1): substituted by the Insolvency (Amendment) Rules 2009, SI 2009/642, rr 4, 15, as from 6 April 2009, subject to transitional provisions in r 3 thereof, as noted to r 1.4 of these Rules at **[10.6]**.

Para (1A): inserted by the Insolvency (Amendment) Rules 2010, SI 2010/686, r 2, Sch 1, para 118(1), (3), as from 6 April 2010, subject to transitional provisions in Sch 4, para 1 thereto, as noted to r 1.5 at **[10.7]**.

Para (3): word in square brackets substituted by SI 2010/686, r 2, Sch 1, para 118(1), (2), as from 6 April 2010, subject to transitional provisions in Sch 4, para 1 thereto, as noted to r 1.5 at **[10.7]**.

Para (4): word in first and third pairs of square brackets substituted, and words in second pair of square brackets inserted, by SI 2010/686, r 2, Sch 1, para 118(1), (2), (4), as from 6 April 2010, subject to transitional provisions in Sch 4, para 1 thereto, as noted to r 1.5 at **[10.7]**.

Paras (5)–(7): added by the Insolvency (Amendment) Rules 2003, SI 2003/1730, r 6, Sch 1, Pt 3, para 10, as from 15 September 2003 (for transitional provisions and savings see the note preceding r 2.1 at **[10.60]**).

CHAPTER 3
CREDITORS' MEETING

[10.208]
3.9   Procedure for summoning meeting under s 48(2)

(1)   In fixing the venue for a meeting of creditors summoned under section 48(2), the administrative receiver shall have regard to the convenience of the persons who are invited to attend.

(2)   The meeting shall be summoned for commencement between 10.00 and 16.00 hours on a business day, unless the court otherwise directs.

(3)   At least 14 days' notice of the venue shall be given to all creditors of the company who   . . . are known to the receiver and had claims against the company at the date of his appointment.

(4)   With the notice summoning the meeting there shall be sent out forms of proxy.

(5)   The notice shall include a statement to the effect that creditors whose claims are wholly secured are not entitled to attend or be represented at the meeting.

[(6)   The administrative receiver—
   (a)   as soon as reasonably practicable must also have gazetted a notice of the meeting; and
   (b)   may advertise the notice of the meeting in such other manner as the administrative receiver thinks fit.

(6A)   In addition to the standard contents, the notice under paragraph (6) must—
   (a)   state that a meeting under section 48(2) is to take place;
   (b)   include the statement required by paragraph (5); and
   (c)   state the venue for the meeting.]

(7)   The notice to creditors and the [notice given under paragraph (6)] shall contain a statement of the effect of Rule 3.11(1) below (voting rights).

NOTES

Para (3): words omitted revoked by the Insolvency (Amendment) Rules 2010, SI 2010/686, r 2, Sch 1, para 119(1), (2), as from 6 April 2010, subject to transitional provisions in Sch 4, para 1 thereto, as noted to r 1.5 at **[10.7]**.

Paras (6), (6A): substituted by SI 2010/686, r 2, Sch 1, para 119(1), (3), as from 6 April 2010, subject to transitional provisions in Sch 4, para 1 thereto, as noted to r 1.5 at **[10.7]**.

Para (7): words in square brackets substituted by SI 2009/642, rr 4, 16(b), as from 6 April 2009, subject to transitional provisions in r 3 thereof, as noted to r 1.4 of these Rules at **[10.6]**.

[10.209]
3.10   The chairman at the meeting

(1)   The chairman at the creditors' meeting shall be the receiver, or a person nominated by him in writing to act in his place.

(2)   A person so nominated must be either—
   (a)   one who is qualified to act as an insolvency practitioner in relation to the company, or
   (b)   an employee of the receiver or his firm who is experienced in insolvency matters.

[10.210]
3.11   Voting rights

(1)   Subject as follows, at the creditors' meeting a person is entitled to vote only if—
   (a)   he has given to the receiver, not later than 12.00 hours on the business day before the day fixed for the meeting, details in writing of the debt that he claims to be due to him from the company, and the claim has been duly admitted under [Rule 3.12 or] this Rule, and
   (b)   there has been lodged with the administrative receiver any proxy which the creditor intends to be used on his behalf.

[and details of the debt must include any calculation for the purposes of paragraphs (6) and (7).]

(2)   The chairman of the meeting may allow a creditor to vote, notwithstanding that he has failed to comply with paragraph (1)(a), if satisfied that the failure was due to circumstances beyond the creditor's control.

(3)   The receiver or (if other) the chairman of the meeting may call for any document or other evidence to be produced to him where he thinks it necessary for the purpose of substantiating the whole or any part of the claim.

(4)   Votes are calculated according to the amount of a creditor's debt as at the date of the appointment of the receiver, after deducting any amounts paid in respect of that debt after that date.

(5)   A creditor shall not vote in respect of a debt for an unliquidated amount, or any debt whose value is not ascertained, except where the chairman agrees to put upon the debt an estimated minimum value for the purpose of entitlement to vote and admits the claim for that purpose.

[(5A)   No vote may be cast by virtue of a claim more than once on any resolution put to the meeting.]

(6)   A secured creditor is entitled to vote only in respect of the balance (if any) of his debt after deducting the value of his security as estimated by him.

(7)   A creditor shall not vote in respect of a debt on, or secured by, a current bill of exchange or promissory note, unless he is willing—

    (a)   to treat the liability to him on the bill or note of every person who is liable on it antecedently to the company, and against whom a bankruptcy order had not been made (or, in the case of a company, which has not gone into liquidation), as a security in his hands, and

    (b)   to estimate the value of the security and, for the purpose of his entitlement to vote [(but not for dividend)], to deduct it from his claim.

NOTES

Para (1): words in square brackets in sub-para (a) substituted, and words in second pair of square brackets inserted, by the Insolvency (Amendment) Rules 2010, SI 2010/686, r 2, Sch 1, para 120(1)–(3), as from 6 April 2010, subject to transitional provisions in Sch 4, para 1 thereto, as noted to r 1.5 at **[10.7]**.

Para (5A): inserted by SI 2010/686, r 2, Sch 1, para 120(1), (4), as from 6 April 2010, subject to transitional provisions in Sch 4, para 1 thereto, as noted to r 1.5 at **[10.7]**.

Para (7): words in square brackets inserted by SI 2010/686, r 2, Sch 1, para 120(1), (5), as from 6 April 2010, subject to transitional provisions in Sch 4, para 1 thereto, as noted to r 1.5 at **[10.7]**.

[10.211]
[3.11A   Contents of claim

(1)   The following matters must be stated in a creditor's claim under Rule 3.11—

    (a)   the creditor's name and address, and, if a company, its company registration number;

    (b)   the total amount of the claim (including any value added tax) as at the date of the appointment of the receiver, less all trade and other discounts available to the company, or which would have been available to the company but for the appointment, except for any discount for immediate, early or cash settlement;

    (c)   whether or not that amount includes outstanding uncapitalised interest;

    (d)   particulars of how and when the debt was incurred by the company;

    (e)   particulars of any security held, the date when it was given and the value which the creditor puts upon it;

    (f)   details of any reservation of title in respect of goods to which the debt refers; and

    (g)   the name, and address and authority of the person making out the claim (if other than the creditor himself).

(2)   The claim must specify any documents by reference to which the debt can be substantiated; but it is not essential that such documents be attached to the claim or submitted with it.]

NOTES

Commencement: 6 April 2010.

Inserted by the Insolvency (Amendment) Rules 2010, SI 2010/686, r 2, Sch 1, para 121, as from 6 April 2010, subject to transitional provisions in Sch 4, para 1 thereto, as noted to r 1.5 at **[10.7]**.

[10.212]
3.12   Admission and rejection of claim

(1)   At the creditors' meeting the chairman has power to admit or reject a creditor's claim for the purpose of his entitlement to vote; and the power is exercisable with respect to the whole or any part of the claim.

(2)   The chairman's decision under this Rule, or in respect of any matter arising under Rule 3.11, is subject to appeal to the court by any creditor.

(3)   If the chairman is in doubt whether a claim should be admitted or rejected, he shall mark it as objected to and allow the creditor to vote, subject to his vote being subsequently declared invalid if the objection to the claim is sustained.

(4)   If on an appeal the chairman's decision is reversed or varied, or a creditor's vote is declared invalid, the court may order that another meeting be summoned, or make such other order as it thinks just.

[(4A)   An application to the court by way of appeal under this Rule against a decision of the chairman must be made not later than 21 days after the date of the meeting.]

(5)   Neither the receiver nor any person nominated by him to be chairman is personally liable for costs incurred by any person in respect of an appeal to the court under this Rule, unless the court makes an order to that effect.

NOTES

Para (4A): inserted by the Insolvency (Amendment) Rules 2010, SI 2010/686, r 2, Sch 1, para 122, as from 6 April 2010, subject to transitional provisions in Sch 4, para 1 thereto, as noted to r 1.5 at **[10.7]**.

3.13   *(Revoked by the Insolvency (Amendment) Rules 1987, SI 1987/1919, r 3(1), Schedule, Pt 1, para 26, as from 11 January 1988.)*

[10.213]
3.14   Adjournment

(1)   The creditors' meeting shall not be adjourned, even if no quorum is present, unless the chairman decides that it is desirable; and in that case he shall adjourn it to such date, time and place as he thinks fit.

(2)   Rule 3.9(1) and (2) applies, with necessary modifications, to any adjourned meeting.

[(2A)   Once only in the course of a meeting the chairman may, without an adjournment, declare it suspended for any period up to 1 hour.]

(3)   If there is no quorum, and the meeting is not adjourned, it is deemed to have been duly summoned and held.

NOTES

Para (2A): inserted by the Insolvency (Amendment) Rules 2010, SI 2010/686, r 2, Sch 1, para 123, as from 6 April 2010, subject to transitional provisions in Sch 4, para 1 thereto, as noted to r 1.5 at **[10.7]**.

[10.214]
3.15   Resolutions and minutes

(1)   At the creditors' meeting, a resolution is passed when a majority (in value) of those present and voting in person or by proxy have voted in favour of it.

(2)   The chairman of the meeting shall cause a record to be made of the proceedings [(including of every resolution passed)], and kept as part of the records of the receivership.

(3)   The record shall include a list of the creditors who attended (personally or by proxy) and, if a creditors' committee has been established, the names and addresses of those elected to be members of the committee.

NOTES

Para (2): words in square brackets inserted by the Insolvency (Amendment) Rules 2010, SI 2010/686, r 2, Sch 1, para 124, as from 6 April 2010, subject to transitional provisions in Sch 4, para 1 thereto, as noted to r 1.5 at **[10.7]**.

CHAPTER 4
THE CREDITORS' COMMITTEE

[10.215]
3.16   Constitution of committee

(1)   Where it is resolved by the creditors' meeting to establish a creditors' committee, the committee shall consist of at least 3 and not more than 5 creditors of the company elected at the meeting.

[(2)   A person claiming to be a creditor is entitled to be a member of the committee provided that—

    (a)   that person's claim has not been wholly disallowed for voting purposes; and
    (b)   the claim mentioned in sub-paragraph (a) is not fully secured.]

(3)   A body corporate may be a member of the committee, but it cannot act as such otherwise than by a representative appointed under Rule 3.21 below.

NOTES

Para (2): substituted by the Insolvency (Amendment) Rules 2010, SI 2010/686, r 2, Sch 1, para 125, as from 6 April 2010, subject to transitional provisions in Sch 4, para 1 thereto, as noted to r 1.5 at **[10.7]**.

[10.216]
3.17   Formalities of establishment

(1)   The creditors' committee does not come into being, and accordingly cannot act, until the administrative receiver has issued a certificate of its due constitution.

[(1A)   If the chairman of the creditors' meeting which resolves to establish the committee is not the administrative receiver, the chairman must as soon as reasonably practicable give notice of the resolution to the receiver and inform the receiver of the names and addresses of the persons elected to be members of the committee.]

[(2)   No person may act as a member of the committee unless and until he has agreed to do so and, unless the relevant proxy or authorisation contains a statement to the contrary, such agreement may be given by his proxy-holder   . . .   present at the meeting establishing the committee [or, in the case of a corporation, by its duly appointed representative].

(2A)   The receiver's certificate of the committee's due constitution shall not [be issued before the minimum number of members set out in Rule 3.16 elected] to be members of the committee have agreed to act [and must be issued as soon as reasonably practicable thereafter].]

(3)   As and when the others (if any) agree to act, the receiver shall issue an amended certificate.

(4)   The certificate, and any amended certificate, shall be sent by the receiver to the registrar of companies [as soon as reasonably practicable].

(5)   If, after the first establishment of the committee, there is any change in its membership, [as soon as reasonably practicable] the receiver shall report the change to the registrar of companies.

NOTES

Para (1A): inserted by the Insolvency (Amendment) Rules 2010, SI 2010/686, r 2, Sch 1, para 126(1), (2), as from 6 April 2010, subject to transitional provisions in Sch 4, para 1 thereto, as noted to r 1.5 at **[10.7]**.

Para (2): substituted, together with para (2A) for original para (2), by the Insolvency (Amendment) Rules 1987, SI 1987/1919, r 3(1), Schedule, Pt 1, para 27, as from 11 January 1988; words omitted revoked, and words in square brackets added, by SI 2010/686, r 2, Sch 1, para 126(1), (3), as from 6 April 2010, subject to transitional provisions in Sch 4, para 1 thereto, as noted to r 1.5 at **[10.7]**.

Para (2A): substituted as noted to para (2) above; words in first pair of square brackets substituted, and words in second pair of square brackets inserted, by SI 2010/686, r 2, Sch 1, para 126(1), (4), as from 6 April 2010, subject to transitional provisions in Sch 4, para 1 thereto, as noted to r 1.5 at **[10.7]**.

Paras (4), (5): words in square brackets inserted by SI 2010/686, r 2, Sch 1, para 126(1), (5), (6), as from 6 April 2010, subject to transitional provisions in Sch 4, para 1 thereto, as noted to r 1.5 at **[10.7]**.

[10.217]
3.18   Functions and meetings of the committee

(1)   [In addition to any functions conferred on the creditors' committee by any provision of the Act,] the creditors' committee shall assist the administrative receiver in discharging his functions, and act in relation to him in such manner as may be agreed from time to time.

(2)   Subject as follows, meetings of the committee shall be held when and where determined by the receiver.

[(3)   The receiver must call a first meeting of the committee to take place within 6 weeks of the committee's establishment.

(3A)   After the calling of the first meeting, the receiver must call a meeting—
   (a)   if so requested by a member of the committee or the member's representative (the meeting then to be held within 21 days of the request being received by the receiver); and
   (b)   for a specified date, if the committee has previously resolved that a meeting be held on that date.]

(4)   [Subject to paragraph (5),] the receiver shall give [5 business] days' written notice of the venue of any meeting to every member (or his representative designated for that purpose), unless in any case the requirement of notice has been waived by or on behalf of any member.
  Waiver may be signified either at or before the meeting.

[(5)   Where the receiver has determined that a meeting should be conducted and held in the manner referred to in Rule 12A.26(2), the notice period mentioned in paragraph (4) is 7 business days.]

NOTES

Para (1): words in square brackets inserted by the Insolvency (Amendment) Rules 2010, SI 2010/686, r 2, Sch 1, para 127(1), (2), as from 6 April 2010, subject to transitional provisions in Sch 4, para 1 thereto, as noted to r 1.5 at **[10.7]**.

Paras (3), (3A): substituted (for the original para (3)) by SI 2010/686, r 2, Sch 1, para 127(1), (3), as from 6 April 2010, subject to transitional provisions in Sch 4, para 1 thereto, as noted to r 1.5 at **[10.7]**.

Para (4): words in first pair of square brackets inserted, and words in second pair of square brackets substituted, by SI 2010/686, r 2, Sch 1, para 127(1), (4), as from 6 April 2010, subject to transitional provisions in Sch 4, para 1 thereto, as noted to r 1.5 at **[10.7]**.

Para (5): added by SI 2010/686, r 2, Sch 1, para 127(1), (5), as from 6 April 2010, subject to transitional provisions in Sch 4, para 1 thereto, as noted to r 1.5 at **[10.7]**.

[10.218]
3.19   The chairman at meetings

[(1)   The chairman at any meeting of the creditors' committee must be the administrative receiver, or a person appointed by the receiver in writing to act.]

(2)   A person so [appointed] must be either—

(a)   one who is qualified to act as an insolvency practitioner in relation to the company, or

(b)   an employee of the receiver or his firm who is experienced in insolvency matters.

NOTES

Para (1): substituted by the Insolvency (Amendment) Rules 2010, SI 2010/686, r 2, Sch 1, para 128(1), (2), as from 6 April 2010, subject to transitional provisions in Sch 4, para 1 thereto, as noted to r 1.5 at **[10.7]**.

Para (2): word in square brackets substituted by SI 2010/686, r 2, Sch 1, para 128(1), (3), as from 6 April 2010, subject to transitional provisions in Sch 4, para 1 thereto, as noted to r 1.5 at **[10.7]**.

[10.219]
3.20   Quorum

A meeting of the committee is duly constituted if due notice has been given to all the members, and at least 2 members are present or represented.

[10.220]
3.21   Committee-members' representatives

(1)   A member of the committee may, in relation to the business of the committee, be represented by another person duly authorised by him for that purpose.

(2)   A person acting as a committee-member's representative must hold a letter of authority entitling him so to act (either generally or specially) and [authenticated] by or on behalf of the committee-member[, and for this purpose any proxy . . . in relation to any meeting of creditors of the company shall, unless it contains a statement to the contrary, be treated as a letter of authority to act generally [authenticated] by or on behalf of the committee-member].

(3)   The chairman at any meeting of the committee may call on a person claiming to act as a committee-member's representative to produce his letter of authority, and may exclude him if it appears that his authority is deficient.

[(4)   No member may be represented by—
   (a)   another member of the committee;
   (b)   a person who is at the same time representing another committee member;
   (c)   a body corporate;
   (d)   an undischarged bankrupt;
   (e)   a disqualified director; or
   (f)   a person who is subject to a bankruptcy restrictions order (including an interim order), a bankruptcy restrictions undertaking, a debt relief restrictions order (including an interim order) or a debt relief restrictions undertaking.]

(5)   . . .

(6)   Where a member's representative [authenticates] any document on the member's behalf, the fact that he so [authenticates] must be stated below his [authentication].

NOTES

Para (2): word in first and third (inner) pairs of square brackets substituted, and words omitted revoked, by the Insolvency (Amendment) Rules 2010, SI 2010/686, r 2, Sch 1, paras 1, 129(1), (2), as from 6 April 2010, subject to transitional provisions in Sch 4, paras 1, 2 thereto, as noted to rr 1.5, 1.31 at **[10.7]**, **[10.34]**; words in second (outer) pair of square brackets added by the Insolvency (Amendment) Rules 1987, SI 1987/1919, r 3(1), Schedule, Pt 1, para 28.

Para (4): substituted by SI 2010/686, r 2, Sch 1, para 129(1), (3), as from 6 April 2010, subject to transitional provisions in Sch 4, para 1 thereto, as noted to r 1.5 at **[10.7]**.

Para (5): revoked by SI 2010/686, r 2, Sch 1, para 129(1), (4), as from 6 April 2010, subject to transitional provisions in Sch 4, para 1 thereto, as noted to r 1.5 at **[10.7]**.

Para (6): words in square brackets substituted by SI 2010/686, r 2, Sch 1, para 1, as from 6 April 2010, subject to transitional provisions in Sch 4, para 2 thereto, as noted to r 1.31 at **[10.34]**.

[10.221]
3.22   Resignation

A member of the committee may resign by notice in writing delivered to the administrative receiver.

[10.222]
3.23   Termination of membership

(1)   Membership of the creditors' committee is automatically terminated if the member—
   (a)   becomes bankrupt . . . , or
   (b)   at 3 consecutive meetings of the committee is neither present nor represented (unless at the third of those meetings it is resolved that this Rule is not to apply in his case), or
   [(c)   ceases to be a creditor and a period of 3 months has elapsed from the date that that member ceased to be a creditor or is found never to have been a creditor.]

(2)   However, if the cause of termination is the member's bankruptcy, his trustee in bankruptcy replaces him as a member of the committee.

NOTES

Para (1): words omitted revoked by the Insolvency (Amendment) Rules 2004, SI 2004/584, r 7, as from 1 April 2004; sub-para (c) substituted by the Insolvency (Amendment) Rules 2010, SI 2010/686, r 2, Sch 1, para 130, as from 6 April 2010, subject to transitional provisions in Sch 4, para 1 thereto, as noted to r 1.5 at **[10.7]**.

[10.223]
3.24 Removal

A member of the committee may be removed by resolution at a meeting of creditors, at least 14 days' notice having been given of the intention to move that resolution.

[10.224]
3.25 Vacancies

(1) The following applies if there is a vacancy in the membership of the creditors' committee.

(2) The vacancy need not be filled if the administrative receiver and a majority of the remaining members of the committee so agree, provided that the total number of members does not fall below [3].

(3) The receiver may appoint any creditor (being qualified under the Rules to be a member of the committee) to fill the vacancy, if a majority of the other members of the committee agree to the appointment and the creditor concerned consents to act.

[(4) Alternatively, a meeting of creditors may resolve that a creditor be appointed (with that creditor's consent) to fill the vacancy. In this case at least 14 days' notice must have been given of a resolution to make such an appointment (whether or not of a person named in the notice).

(5) Where the vacancy is filled by an appointment made by a creditors' meeting at which the receiver is not present, the chairman of the meeting must report to the receiver the appointment which has been made.]

NOTES

Para (2): number in square brackets substituted by the Insolvency (Amendment) Rules 2010, SI 2010/686, r 2, Sch 1, para 131(1), (2), as from 6 April 2010, subject to transitional provisions in Sch 4, para 1 thereto, as noted to r 1.5 at **[10.7]**.
Paras (4), (5): added by SI 2010/686, r 2, Sch 1, para 131(1), (3), as from 6 April 2010, subject to transitional provisions in Sch 4, para 1 thereto, as noted to r 1.5 at **[10.7]**.

[10.225]
3.26 Procedure at meetings

(1) At any meeting of the committee, each member of it (whether present himself or by his representative) has one vote; and a resolution is passed when a majority of the members present or represented have voted in favour of it.

[(2) Every resolution passed must be recorded in writing and authenticated by the chairman, either separately or as part of the minutes of the meeting and the record must be kept with the records of the proceedings.]

NOTES

Para (2): substituted (for original paras (2), (3)) by the Insolvency (Amendment) Rules 2010, SI 2010/686, r 2, Sch 1, para 132, as from 6 April 2010, subject to transitional provisions in Sch 4, para 1 thereto, as noted to r 1.5 at **[10.7]**.

[10.226]
3.27 Resolutions [otherwise than at a meeting]

(1) In accordance with this Rule, the administrative receiver may seek to obtain the agreement of members of the creditors' committee to a resolution by sending to every member (or his representative designated for the purpose) a copy of the proposed resolution.

(2) Where the receiver makes use of the procedure allowed by this Rule, he shall send out to members of the committee or their representatives (as the case may be) [a copy of any proposed resolution on which a decision is sought, which shall be set out in such a way that agreement with or dissent from each separate resolution may be indicated by the recipient on the copy so sent].

(3) Any member of the committee may, within 7 business days from the date of the receiver sending out a resolution, require him to summon a meeting of the committee to consider the matters raised by the resolution.

(4) In the absence of such a request, the resolution is deemed to have been passed by the committee if and when the receiver is notified in writing by a majority of the members that they concur with it.

(5) A copy of every resolution passed under this Rule, and a note that the committee's concurrence was obtained, shall be kept with the records of the receivership.

NOTES

Rule heading: words in square brackets substituted by the Insolvency (Amendment) Rules 2010, SI 2010/686, r 2, Sch 1, para 133, as from 6 April 2010, subject to transitional provisions in Sch 4, para 1 thereto, as noted to r 1.5 at **[10.7]**.
Para (2): words in square brackets substituted by the Insolvency (Amendment) Rules 1987, SI 1987/1919, r 3(1), Schedule, Pt 1, para 29, as from 11 January 1988.

[10.227]
3.28 Information from receiver

(1)   Where the committee resolves to require the attendance of the administrative receiver under section 49(2), the notice to him shall be in writing [authenticated] by the majority of the members of the committee for the time being. A member's representative may [authenticate] for him.

(2)   The meeting at which the receiver's attendance is required shall be fixed by the committee for a business day, and shall be held at such time and place as he determines.

(3)   Where the receiver so attends, the members of the committee may elect any one of their number to be chairman of the meeting, in place of the receiver or any nominee of his.

NOTES

Para (1): words in square brackets substituted by the Insolvency (Amendment) Rules 2010, SI 2010/686, r 2, Sch 1, para 1, as from 6 April 2010, subject to transitional provisions in Sch 4, para 2 thereto, as noted to r 1.31 at **[10.34]**.

[10.228]
3.29 Expenses of members

(1)   Subject as follows, the administrative receiver shall out of the assets of the company defray[, in the prescribed order of priority,] any reasonable travelling expenses directly incurred by members of the creditors' committee or their representatives in relation to their attendance at the committee's meetings, or otherwise on the committee's business, as an expense of the receivership.

(2)   Paragraph (1) does not apply to any meeting of the committee held within 3 months of a previous meeting, unless the meeting in question is summoned at the instance of the administrative receiver.

NOTES

Para (1): words in square brackets inserted by the Insolvency (Amendment) Rules 2010, SI 2010/686, r 2, Sch 1, para 134, as from 6 April 2010, subject to transitional provisions in Sch 4, para 1 thereto, as noted to r 1.5 at **[10.7]**.

[10.229]
3.30 Members' dealings with the company

(1)   Membership of the committee does not prevent a person from dealing with the company while the receiver is acting, provided that any transactions in the course of such dealings are entered into in good faith and for value.

(2)   The court may, on the application of any person interested, set aside a transaction which appears to it to be contrary to the requirements of this Rule, and may give such consequential directions as it thinks [just] for compensating the company for any loss which it may have incurred in consequence of the transaction.

NOTES

Para (2): word in square brackets substituted by the Insolvency (Amendment) Rules 2010, SI 2010/686, r 2, Sch 1, para 1, as from 6 April 2010, subject to transitional provisions in Sch 4, para 2 thereto, as noted to r 1.31 at **[10.34]**.

[10.230]
[3.30A Formal defects

The acts of the creditors' committee established for any administrative receivership are valid notwithstanding any defect in the appointment, election or qualifications of any member of the committee or any committee-member's representative or in the formalities of its establishment.]

NOTES

Inserted by the Insolvency (Amendment) Rules 1987, SI 1987/1919, r 3(1), Schedule, Pt 1, para 30, as from 11 January 1988.

CHAPTER 5
THE ADMINISTRATIVE RECEIVER (MISCELLANEOUS)

[10.231]
3.31 Disposal of charged property

(1)   The following applies where the administrative receiver applies to the court under section 43(1) for authority to dispose of property of the company which is subject to a security.

(2)   The court shall fix a venue for the hearing of the application, and the receiver shall [as soon as reasonably practicable] give notice of the venue to the person who is the holder of the security.

[(3)   If an order is made under section 43(1), the court must send two sealed copies to the administrative receiver.

(4)   The administrative receiver must send one of them to that person who is the holder of the security.]

NOTES

Para (2): words in square brackets substituted by the Insolvency (Amendment) Rules 2009, SI 2009/642, r 5, as from 6 April 2009, subject to transitional provisions in r 3 thereof, as noted to r 1.4 of these Rules at **[10.6]**.

Paras (3), (4): substituted by the Insolvency (Amendment) Rules 2010, SI 2010/686, r 2, Sch 1, para 135, as from 6 April 2010, subject to transitional provisions in Sch 4, para 1 thereto, as noted to r 1.5 at **[10.7]**.

[10.232]
3.32　Abstract of receipts and payments

(1)　The administrative receiver shall—

   (a)　within 2 months after the end of 12 months from the date of his appointment, and of every subsequent period of 12 months, and

   (b)　within 2 months after he ceases to act as administrative receiver,

send to the registrar of companies, to the company and to the person by whom he was appointed, and to each member of the creditors' committee (if there is one), the requisite accounts of his receipts and payments as receiver.

(2)　The court may, on the receiver's application, extend the period of 2 months referred to in paragraph (1).

(3)　The accounts are to be in the form of an abstract showing—

   (a)　receipts and payments during the relevant period of 12 months, or

   (b)　where the receiver has ceased to act, receipts and payments during the period from the end of the last 12-month period to the time when he so ceased (alternatively, if there has been no previous abstract, receipts and payments in the period since his appointment as administrative receiver).

(4)　This Rule is without prejudice to the receiver's duty to render proper accounts required otherwise than as above.

(5)　If the administrative receiver makes default in complying with this Rule, he is liable to a fine and, for continued contravention, to a daily default fine.

NOTES
See Form 3.6 at **[10.673]**.

[10.233]
3.33　Resignation

(1)　Subject as follows, before resigning his office the administrative receiver shall give at least [5 business] days' notice of his intention to do so to—

   (a)　the person by whom he was appointed,

   (b)　the company or, if it is then in liquidation, its liquidator [, and

   (c)　in any case, to the members of the creditors' committee (if any)].

(2)　A notice given under this Rule shall specify the date on which the receiver intends his resignation to take effect.

(3)　. . .

NOTES
Para (1): words in first pair of square brackets substituted by the Insolvency (Amendment) Rules 2010, SI 2010/686, r 2, Sch 1, para 136(1), (2), as from 6 April 2010, subject to transitional provisions in Sch 4, para 1 thereto, as noted to r 1.5 at **[10.7]**; word omitted from sub-para (a) revoked, and sub-para (c) and the word immediately preceding it added, by SI 1987/1919, r 3(1), Schedule, Pt 1, para 31, as from 11 January 1988.
Para (3): revoked by SI 2010/686, r 2, Sch 1, para 136(1), (3), as from 6 April 2010, subject to transitional provisions in Sch 4, para 1 thereto, as noted to r 1.5 at **[10.7]**.
See Form 3.9 at **[10.673]**.

[10.234]
3.34　Receiver deceased

If the administrative receiver dies, the person by whom he was appointed shall, [as soon as reasonably practicable] on his becoming aware of the death, give notice of it to—

   (a)　the registrar of companies, . . .

   (b)　the company or, if it is in liquidation, the liquidator[, and

   (c)　in any case, to the members of the creditors' committee (if any)].

NOTES
Words in first pair of square brackets substituted by the Insolvency (Amendment) Rules 2009, SI 2009/642, r 5, as from 6 April 2009, subject to transitional provisions in r 3 thereof, as noted to r 1.4 of these Rules at **[10.6]**; word omitted from sub-para (a) revoked, and sub-para (c) and the word immediately preceding it added, by the Insolvency (Amendment) Rules 1987, SI 1987/1919, r 3(1), Schedule, Pt 1, para 32, as from 11 January 1988.

[10.235]
3.35　Vacation of office

(1)　The administrative receiver, on vacating office on completion of the receivership, or in consequence of his ceasing to be qualified as an insolvency practitioner, shall [as soon as reasonably practicable] give notice of his doing so—

   [(a)　to the company or, if it is in liquidation, the liquidator, and]

(b)   . . .   to the members of the creditors' committee (if any).

(2)   Where the receiver's office is vacated, the notice to the registrar of companies which is required by section 45(4) may be given by means of an indorsement on the notice required by [section 871(2)] of the Companies Act (notice for the purposes of the register of charges).

NOTES

Para (1): words in first pair of square brackets substituted by the Insolvency (Amendment) Rules 2009, SI 2009/642, r 5, as from 6 April 2009, subject to transitional provisions in r 3 thereof, as noted to r 1.4 of these Rules at **[10.6]**; sub-para (a) substituted, and words omitted from sub-para (b) revoked, by the Insolvency (Amendment) Rules 1987, SI 1987/1919, r 3(1), Schedule, Pt 1, para 33, as from 11 January 1988.

Para (2): words in square brackets substituted by the Insolvency (Amendment) (No 2) Rules 2009, SI 2009/2472, rr 3, 9, as from 1 October 2009 (for transitional provisions see the note to r 0.2 at **[10.2]**).

3.36–3.38   *(Rules 3.36–3.38 (Chapter 6) revoked by the Insolvency (Amendment) Rules 2010, SI 2010/686, r 5, as from 6 April 2010, subject to transitional provisions in Sch 4, para 1 thereto, as noted to r 1.5 at* **[10.7]**.*)*

[CHAPTER 7
SECTION 176A: THE PRESCRIBED PART

[10.236]
3.39   Report to creditors

(1)   This Rule applies where—
    (a)   a receiver (other than an administrative receiver) is appointed by the court or otherwise under a charge which as created was a floating charge; and
    (b)   section 176A applies.

(2)   Within 3 months (or such longer period as the court may allow) of the date of his appointment the receiver shall send to creditors, details of whose names and addresses are available to him, notice of his appointment and a report which will include the following matters—
    (a)   to the best of the receiver's knowledge and belief—
        (i)   an estimate of the value of the prescribed part (whether or not he proposes to make an application to the court under section 176A(5) or section 176A(3) applies); and
        (ii)   an estimate of the value of company's net property;
    (b)   whether, and if so, why, he proposes to make an application to court under section 176A(5); and
    (c)   whether he proposes to present a petition for the winding up of the company.

(3)   Nothing in this Rule is to be taken as requiring any such estimate to include any information, the disclosure of which could seriously prejudice the commercial interests of the company. If such information is excluded from the calculation the estimate shall be accompanied by a statement to that effect.

[(4)   Where the requirements of paragraph (5) are satisfied, the receiver may, instead of sending the report required under paragraph (2)—
    (a)   cause a notice   . . .   to be gazetted; and
    (b)   may advertise the notice in such other manner as the receiver thinks fit.

[(4A)   In addition to the standard contents, the notice under paragraph (4) must include a statement of the matters required to be included in the receiver's report under paragraph (2).]

(5)   The requirements of this paragraph are that—
    (a)   full details of the unsecured creditors of the company are not available to the receiver; or
    (b)   the receiver thinks it is otherwise impracticable to send the report.]]

NOTES

Chapter 7 (rr 3.39, 3.40) added by the Insolvency (Amendment) Rules 2003, SI 2003/1730, r 6, Sch 1, Pt 3, para 11, as from 15 September 2003 (for transitional provisions and savings see the note preceding r 2.1 at **[10.60]**).

Paras (4), (5): substituted (for the original para (4)) by the Insolvency (Amendment) Rules 2009, SI 2009/642, rr 4, 17, as from 6 April 2009, subject to transitional provisions in r 3 thereof, as noted to r 1.4 of these Rules at **[10.6]**. Words omitted from para (4) revoked by the Insolvency (Amendment) Rules 2010, SI 2010/686, r 2, Sch 1, para 137(1), (2), as from 6 April 2010, subject to transitional provisions in Sch 4, para 1 thereto, as noted to r 1.5 at **[10.7]**.

Para (4A): inserted by SI 2010/686, r 2, Sch 1, para 137(1), (3), as from 6 April 2010, subject to transitional provisions in Sch 4, para 1 thereto, as noted to r 1.5 at **[10.7]**.

[10.237]
[3.40   Receiver to deal with prescribed part

Where Rule 3.39 applies—
    (a)   the receiver may present a petition for the winding up of the company if the ground of the petition is that in section 122(1)(f);
    (b)   where a liquidator or administrator has been appointed to the company, the receiver shall deliver up the sums representing the prescribed part to him;

(c)   in any other case, the receiver shall apply to the court for directions as to the manner in which he is to discharge his duty under section 176A(2)(a) and shall act in accordance with such directions as are given by the court.]

NOTES
Added as noted to r 3.39 at **[10.236]**.

PART 4
COMPANIES WINDING UP

CHAPTER 1
THE SCHEME OF THIS PART OF THE RULES

[10.238]
4.1   Voluntary winding up; winding up by the court
[(1)   In a member's voluntary winding up, the Rules in this Part do not apply, except as follows—
  (a)   [Rules 4.3 and 4.35 apply] in the same way as [they apply] in a creditor's voluntary winding up;
  [(aa) Rules 4.49C, 4.49E and 4.49F apply except so far as it is provided (expressly or by necessary implication) that they do not apply;
  (ab)   Rule 4.49G applies only in a members' voluntary winding up, and not otherwise;]
  (b)   Rule 4.72 (additional provisions concerning meetings in relation to [the Financial Services Authority] and [the scheme manager]) applies in the winding up of [authorised deposit-takers or former authorised deposit-takers], whether members' or creditors' voluntary or by the court;
  (c)   Chapters 9 (proof of debts in a liquidation), 10 (secured creditors), 15 (disclaimer) and 18 (special manager) apply wherever, and in the same way as, they apply in a creditors' voluntary winding up;
  (d)   Section F of Chapter 11 (the liquidation) applies only in a members' voluntary winding up, and not otherwise;
  (e)   Section G of that Chapter (court's power to set aside certain transactions; rule against solicitation) applies in any winding up, whether members' or creditors' voluntary or by the court;
  (f)   [Rules 4.126A and 4.182A apply] only in a members' voluntary winding up, and not otherwise; and
  (g)   Rule 4.223-CVL (liquidator's statements) applies in the same way as it applies in a creditors' voluntary winding up.]

(2)   Subject as follows, the Rules in this Part apply both in a creditors' voluntary winding up and in a winding up by the court; and for this purpose a winding up is treated as a creditors' voluntary [winding up] if, and from the time when, the liquidator forms the opinion that the company will be unable to pay its debts in full, and determines accordingly to summon a creditors' meeting under section 95.

(3)   The following Chapters, or Sections of Chapters, of this Part do not apply in a creditors' voluntary winding up—
       Chapter 2—The statutory demand;
       Chapter 3—Petition to winding-up order;
       Chapter 4—Petition by contributories;
       Chapter 5—Provisional liquidator;
       [Chapter 11 (Section F)—The Liquidator in a members' voluntary winding up;]
       Chapter 13—The liquidation committee where winding up follows immediately on administration;
       Chapter 16—Settlement of list of contributories;
       Chapter 17—Calls;
       Chapter 19—Public examination of company officers and others; and
       Chapter 21 (Section A)—Return of capital.
       [Chapter 21 (Section C)—Dissolution after winding up

(4)   Where at the head of any Rule, or at the end of any paragraph of a Rule, there appear the words "(NO CVL APPLICATION)", this signifies that the Rule or, as the case may be, the paragraph does not apply in a creditors' voluntary winding up.

However, this does not affect the court's power to make orders under section 112 (exercise in relation to voluntary winding up of powers available in winding up by the court).

(5)   Where to any Rule or paragraph there is given a number incorporating the letters "CVL", that signifies that the Rule or (as the case may be) the paragraph applies in a creditors' voluntary winding up, and not in a winding up by the court.

[(6)   In a voluntary winding up which is commenced by the registration of a notice under paragraph 83(3) of Schedule B1 to the Act, the following provisions of this Part shall not apply—
       Rules 4.34, 4.38, 4.49, 4.51, 4.53, 4.62, 4.101, 4.103, 4.106, 4.152, 4.153, 4.206–4.210.]

Part 10   Miscellaneous other SIs

NOTES

Para (1): substituted by the Insolvency (Amendment) Rules 1987, SI 1987/1919, r 3(1), Schedule, Pt 1, para 34(1), as from 11 January 1988; words in square brackets in sub-paras (a), (f) substituted, and sub-paras (aa), (ab) inserted, by the Insolvency (Amendment) Rules 2010, SI 2010/686, r 2, Sch 1, para 138, as from 6 April 2010, subject to transitional provisions in Sch 4, para 1 thereto, as noted to r 1.5 at **[10.7]**; words in first pair of square brackets in sub-para (b) substituted by the Bank of England Act 1998 (Consequential Amendments of Subordinate Legislation) Order 1998, SI 1998/1129, art 2, Sch 1, para 4(1), (2), as from 1 June 1998; words in second and third pairs of square brackets in sub-para (b) substituted by the Financial Services and Markets Act 2000 (Consequential Amendments and Repeals) Order 2001, SI 2001/3649, arts 377(1), (3), 378(1), as from 1 December 2001.

Paras (2), (3): words in square brackets inserted by SI 1987/1919, r 3(1), Schedule, Pt 1, para 34(2), (3), as from 11 January 1988.

Para (6): added by the Insolvency (Amendment) Rules 2003, SI 2003/1730, r 7, Sch 1, Pt 4, para 12, as from 15 September 2003 (for transitional provisions and savings see the note preceding r 2.1 at **[10.60]**).

[10.239]
4.2   Winding up by the court: the various forms of petition [(NO CVL APPLICATION)]

(1)   Insofar as the Rules in this Part apply to winding up by the court, they apply (subject as follows) whether the petition for winding up is presented under any of the several paragraphs of section 122(1), namely—

  paragraph (a)—company special resolution for winding up by the court;
  paragraph (b)—public company without certificate under [section 761] of the Companies Act;
  paragraph (c)—old public company;
  paragraph (d)—company not commencing business after formation, or suspending business;
  paragraph (e)—number of company's members reduced below 2;
  paragraph (f)—company unable to pay its debts;
  [paragraph (fa)—end of moratorium without approval of voluntary arrangement;]
  paragraph (g)—court's power under the "just and equitable" rule,
or under any enactment enabling the presentation of a winding-up petition.

(2)   Except as provided by the following two paragraphs or by any particular Rule, the Rules apply whether the petition for winding up is presented by the company, the directors, one or more creditors, one or more contributories, the Secretary of State, the official receiver, or any person entitled under any enactment to present such a petition.

(3)   Chapter 2 (statutory demand) has no application except in relation to an unpaid creditor of the company satisfying section 123(1)(a) (the first of the two cases specified, in relation to England and Wales, of the company being deemed unable to pay its debts within section 122(1)(f)) or section 222(1) (the equivalent provision in relation to unregistered companies).

(4)   Chapter 3 (petition to winding-up order) has no application to a petition for winding up presented by one or more contributories; and in relation to a petition so presented Chapter 4 has effect.

NOTES

Rule heading: words in square brackets added by the Insolvency (Amendment) Rules 1987, SI 1987/1919, r 3(1), Schedule, Pt 1, para 35, as from 11 January 1988.

Para (1): words in first pair of square brackets substituted by the Insolvency (Amendment) (No 2) Rules 2009, SI 2009/2472, rr 3, 11, as from 1 October 2009 (for transitional provisions see the note to r 0.2 at **[10.2]**); sub-para (fa) inserted by the Insolvency (Amendment) (No 2) Rules 2002, SI 2002/2712, r 4(1), Schedule, Part 2, para 22, as from 1 January 2003, subject to transitional provisions as noted below.

Transitional provisions: SI 2002/2712, r 4(2) provides as follows (note that by virtue of r 1, "the commencement date" is 1 January 2003)—

  "(2)   The amendments to Part 4 of the principal Rules set out in Part 2 of the Schedule do not apply in relation to—
    (a)   a winding up by the court where the petition on which the winding-up order was made was presented prior to the commencement date; or
    (b)   a voluntary winding up where the resolution for winding up was passed prior to the commencement date;
    and Part 4 of the principal Rules without the amendments made in Part 2 of the Schedule to these Rules shall continue to apply in such cases.".

Old public companies: as to the meaning of this, see the Companies Act 2006 (Consequential Amendments and Transitional Provisions) Order 2011, SI 2011/1265, Sch 1 at **[4.651]**.

[10.240]
4.3   Time-limits

Where by any provision of the Act or the Rules about winding up, the time for doing anything is limited, the court may extend the time, either before or after it has expired, on such terms, if any, as it thinks [just].

NOTES

Word in square brackets substituted by the Insolvency (Amendment) Rules 2010, SI 2010/686, r 2, Sch 1, para 1, as from 6 April 2010, subject to transitional provisions in Sch 4, para 2 thereto, as noted to r 1.31 at **[10.34]**.

CHAPTER 2
THE STATUTORY DEMAND

(No CVL Application)

[10.241]
4.4 Preliminary

(1) This Chapter does not apply where a petition for the winding up of a company is presented under section 124 on or after the date on which the Rules come into force and the petition is based on failure to comply with a written demand served on the company before that date.

(2) A written demand served by a creditor on a company under section 123(1)(a) (registered companies) or 222(1)(a) (unregistered companies) is known . . . as "the statutory demand".

(3) The statutory demand must be dated, and be [authenticated] either by the creditor himself or by a person stating himself to be authorised to make the demand on the creditor's behalf.

NOTES

Para (2): words omitted revoked by the Insolvency (Amendment) Rules 2010, SI 2010/686, r 2, Sch 1, para 139, as from 6 April 2010, subject to transitional provisions in Sch 4, para 1 thereto, as noted to r 1.5 at **[10.7]**.

Para (3): word in square brackets substituted by SI 2010/686, r 2, Sch 1, para 1, as from 6 April 2010, subject to transitional provisions in Sch 4, para 2 thereto, as noted to r 1.31 at **[10.34]**.

[10.242]
4.5 Form and content of statutory demand

(1) The statutory demand must state the amount of the debt and the consideration for it (or, if there is no consideration, the way in which it arises).

(2) If the amount claimed in the demand includes—
   (a) any charge by way of interest not previously notified to the company as included in its liability, or
   (b) any other charge accruing from time to time,
the amount or rate of the charge must be separately identified, and the grounds on which payment of it is claimed must be stated.

   In either case the amount claimed must be limited to that which has accrued due at the date of the demand.

NOTES

See Form 4.1 at **[10.673]**.

[10.243]
4.6 Information to be given in statutory demand

(1) The statutory demand must include an explanation to the company of the following matters—
   (a) the purpose of the demand, and the fact that, if the demand is not complied with, proceedings may be instituted for the winding up of the company;
   (b) the time within which it must be complied with, if that consequence is to be avoided;
   (c) the methods of compliance which are open to the company[; and
   (d) that the company has the right to make an application to the court for an injunction restraining the creditor from presenting or advertising a petition for the winding up of the company].

(2) Information must be provided for the company as to how an officer or representative of it may enter into communication with one or more named individuals, with a view to securing or compounding for the debt to the creditor's satisfaction.

   In the case of any individual so named in the demand, his address and telephone number (if any) must be given.

NOTES

Para (1): word omitted revoked, and sub-para (d) and the word immediately preceding it added, by the Insolvency (Amendment) Rules 2010, SI 2010/686, r 2, Sch 1, para 140, as from 6 April 2010, subject to transitional provisions in Sch 4, para 1 thereto, as noted to r 1.5 at **[10.7]**.

CHAPTER 3
PETITION TO WINDING-UP ORDER

(No CVL Application)
(No Application to Petition by Contributories)

[10.244]
[4.6A   Injunction to restrain presentation or advertisement of petition

An application by a company for an injunction restraining a creditor from—

(a)   presenting a petition for the winding up of the company must be made to a court having jurisdiction to wind up the company;

(b)   advertising a petition for the winding up of a company must be made to the court in which the petition is pending.]

NOTES

Commencement: 6 April 2010.

Inserted by the Insolvency (Amendment) Rules 2010, SI 2010/686, r 2, Sch 1, para 141, subject to transitional provisions in Sch 4, para 1 thereto, as noted to r 1.5 at **[10.7]**.

[10.245]
4.7   Presentation and filing of petition

(1)   The petition, verified by [a statement of truth] in accordance with Rule 4.12 below, shall be filed in court.

[(2)   No petition shall be filed unless there is produced on presentation of the petition a receipt for the deposit payable or paragraph (2A) applies.

(2A)   This paragraph applies in any case where the Secretary of State has given written notice to the court that the petitioner has made suitable alternative arrangements for the payment of the deposit to the official receiver and such notice has not been revoked in relation to the petitioner in accordance with paragraph (2B).

(2B)   A notice of the kind referred to in paragraph (2A) may be revoked in relation to the petitioner in whose favour it is given by a further notice in writing to the court stating that the earlier notice is revoked in relation to the petitioner.]

[(3)   A petitioner who is a person other than the company must also deliver to the court one copy for service on the company.]

(4)   There shall in any case be delivered with the petition—

(a)   if the company is in course of being wound up voluntarily, and a liquidator has been appointed, one copy of the petition to be sent to him;

(b)   [if the company is in administration], one copy [. . .] to be sent to the administrator;

(c)   if an administrative receiver has been appointed in relation to the company, one copy to be sent to him;

(d)   if there is in force for the company a voluntary arrangement under Part I of the Act, one copy for the supervisor of the arrangement;   . . .

[(da)   if a member State liquidator has been appointed in main proceedings in relation to the company, one copy to be sent to him; and]

(e)   if the company is [an authorised deposit-taker or a former authorised deposit-taker], and the petitioner is not the [Financial Services Authority], one copy to be sent to the [Authority].

(5)   Each of the copies delivered shall have applied to it the seal of the court, and shall be issued to the petitioner.

(6)   The court shall fix a venue for the hearing of the petition; and this shall be endorsed on any copy issued to the petitioner under paragraph (5).

[(7)   Where a petition is filed at the instance of a company's administrator the petition shall—

(a)   be expressed to be the petition of the company by its administrator,

(b)   state the name of the administrator, [the court case number and the date that the company entered administration], and

[(c)   where applicable, contain an application under paragraph 79 of Schedule B1, requesting that the appointment of the administrator shall cease to have effect.]

[(8)   Any petition filed in relation to a company in respect of which there is in force a voluntary arrangement under Part I of the Act or which is in administration shall be presented to the court to which the nominee's report under section 2 was submitted or the court having jurisdiction for the administration.]

(9)   Any petition such as is mentioned in paragraph (7) above or presented by the supervisor of a voluntary arrangement under Part I of the Act in force for the company shall be treated as if it were a petition filed by contributories, and Chapter 4 in this Part of the Rules shall apply accordingly.

(10)   Where a petition contains a request for the appointment of a person as liquidator in accordance with section 140 (appointment of former administrator or supervisor as liquidator) the person whose appointment is sought shall, not less than 2 [business] days before the return day for the petition, file in court a report including particulars of—

(a)   a date on which he notified creditors of the company, either in writing or at a meeting of creditors, of the intention to seek his appointment as liquidator, such date to be at least [7 business] days before the day on which the report under this paragraph is filed, and

(b)   details of any response from creditors to that notification, including any objections to his appointment.]

NOTES

Para (1): words in square brackets substituted by the Insolvency (Amendment) Rules 2010, SI 2010/686, r 2, Sch 1, para 142(1), (2), as from 6 April 2010, subject to transitional provisions in Sch 4, para 2 thereto, as noted to r 1.31 at **[10.34]**.

Paras (2), (2A), (2B): substituted (for the original para (2)) by the Insolvency (Amendment) Rules 2004, SI 2004/584, r 8(a), as from 1 April 2004.

Para (3): substituted by SI 2010/686, r 2, Sch 1, para 142(1), (3), as from 6 April 2010, subject to transitional provisions in Sch 4, para 1 thereto, as noted to r 1.5 at **[10.7]**.

Para (4): words in first pair of square brackets in sub-para (b) substituted by the Insolvency (Amendment) Rules 2003, SI 2003/1730, r 7, Sch 1, Pt 4, para 13(a), as from 15 September 2003 (for transitional provisions and savings see the note preceding r 2.1 at **[10.60]**); words omitted from sub-para (b) originally inserted by SI 2003/1730, r 7, Sch 1, Pt 4, para 13(a), as from 15 September 2003, and revoked by SI 2004/584, r 8(b), as from 1 April 2004; word omitted from sub-para (d) revoked, and sub-para (da) inserted, by the Insolvency (Amendment) Rules 2002, SI 2002/1307, rr 3, 6(1), as from 31 May 2002, with savings in relation to anything done under, or for the purposes of, this provision before that date; words in first pair of square brackets in sub-para (e) substituted by the Financial Services and Markets Act 2000 (Consequential Amendments and Repeals) Order 2001, SI 2001/3649, art 377(1), (4), as from 1 December 2001; words in second and third pairs of square brackets in sub-para (e) substituted by the Bank of England Act 1998 (Consequential Amendments of Subordinate Legislation) Order 1998, SI 1998/1129, art 2, Sch 1, para 4(1), (3), as from 1 June 1998.

Para (7): added, together with paras (8)–(10), by the Insolvency (Amendment) Rules 1987, SI 1987/1919, r 3(1), Schedule, Pt 1, para 36(2), as from 11 January 1988; words in square brackets in sub-para (b) substituted by SI 2003/1730, r 7, Sch 1, Pt 4, para 13(b), as from 15 September 2003 (for transitional provisions and savings see the note preceding r 2.1 at **[10.60]**); sub-para (c) substituted by the Insolvency (Amendment) Rules 2005, SI 2005/527, r 18, as from 1 April 2005.

Para (8): added as noted above; substituted by SI 2003/1730, r 7, Sch 1, Pt 4, para 13(d), as from 15 September 2003 (for transitional provisions and savings see the note preceding r 2.1 at **[10.60]**).

Para (9): added as noted above.

Para (10): added as noted above; word in first pair of square brackets inserted, and words in second pair of square brackets substituted, by SI 2010/686, r 2, Sch 1, para 142(1), (4), as from 6 April 2010, subject to transitional provisions in Sch 4, para 1 thereto, as noted to r 1.5 at **[10.7]**.

See Form 4.2 at **[10.673]**.

[10.246]
4.8 Service of petition

(1)   The following paragraphs apply as regards service of the petition on the company (where the petitioner is other than the company itself); and references to the petition are to a copy of the petition bearing the seal of the court in which it is presented.

(2)   Subject as follows, the petition shall be served at the company's registered office, that is to say—

(a)   the place which is specified, in the company's statement delivered under [section 9] of the Companies Act as the intended situation of its registered office on incorporation, or

(b)   if notice has been given by the company to the registrar of companies under [section 87] of that Act (change of registered office), the place specified in that notice or, as the case may be, in the last such notice.

(3)   Service of the petition at the registered office may be effected in any of the following ways—

(a)   it may be handed to a person who there and then acknowledges himself to be, or to the best of the server's knowledge, information and belief is, a director or other officer, or employee, of the company; or

(b)   it may be handed to a person who there and then acknowledges himself to be authorised to accept service of documents on the company's behalf; or

(c)   in the absence of any such person as is mentioned in sub-paragraph (a) or (b), it may be deposited at or about the registered office in such a way that it is likely to come to the notice of a person attending at the office.

[(4)   If for any reason service at the registered office is not practicable, or the company has no registered office or is an unregistered company, the petition may be served on the company by leaving it at the company's last known principal place of business in such a way that it is likely to come to the attention of a person attending there, or by delivering it to the secretary or some director, manager or principal officer of the company, wherever that person may be found.]

(5)   In the case of an [overseas] company, service may be effected in any manner provided for by [section 1139(2)] of the Companies Act.

(6)   If for any reason it is impracticable to effect service as provided by paragraphs (2) to (5), the petition may be served in such other manner as the court may [approve or] direct.

(7)   Application for [permission] of the court under paragraph (6) may be made [by an application without notice to any other party], [supported by a witness statement] stating what steps have been taken to comply with paragraphs (2) to (5), and the reasons why it is impracticable to effect service as there provided.

NOTES

Paras (2), (5): words in square brackets substituted by the Insolvency (Amendment) (No 2) Rules 2009, SI 2009/2472, rr 3, 12, as from 1 October 2009 (for transitional provisions see the note to r 0.2 at **[10.2]**).

Para (4): substituted by the Insolvency (Amendment) Rules 1987, SI 1987/1919, r 3(1), Schedule, Pt 1, para 37(1), as from 11 January 1988.

Para (6): words in square brackets inserted by SI 1987/1919, r 3(1), Schedule, Pt 1, para 37(2), as from 11 January 1988.

Para (7): words in square brackets substituted by the Insolvency (Amendment) Rules 2010, SI 2010/686, r 2, Sch 1, paras 1, 143, subject to transitional provisions in Sch 4, para 2 thereto, as noted to r 1.31 at **[10.34]**.

[10.247]
[4.9A   Proof of service

(1)   Service of the petition must be proved by a certificate of service.

(2)   The certificate of service must be sufficient to identify the petition served and must specify—
  (a)   the name and registered number of the company,
  (b)   the address of the registered office of the company,
  (c)   the name of the petitioner,
  (d)   the court in which the petition was filed and the court reference number,
  (e)   the date of the petition,
  (f)   whether the copy served was a sealed copy,
  (g)   the date on which service was effected, and
  (h)   the manner in which service was effected.

(3)   Where substituted service has been ordered, the certificate of service must have attached to it a sealed copy of the order.

(4)   The certificate of service must be filed in court as soon as reasonably practicable after service, and in any event not less than 5 business days before the hearing of the petition.]

NOTES
Commencement: 6 April 2010.
Substituted (for the original r 4.9) by the Insolvency (Amendment) Rules 2010, SI 2010/686, r 2, Sch 1, para 144, as from 6 April 2010, subject to transitional provisions in Sch 4, para 1 thereto, as noted to r 1.5 at **[10.7]**.

[10.248]
4.10   Other persons to receive copies of petition

(1)   If to the petitioner's knowledge the company is in course of being wound up voluntarily, a copy of the petition shall be sent by him to the liquidator.

(2)   If to the petitioner's knowledge an administrative receiver has been appointed in relation to the company, or [the company is in administration], a copy of the petition shall be sent by him to the receiver or, as the case may be, the administrator.

(3)   If to the petitioner's knowledge there is in force for the company a voluntary arrangement under Part I of the Act, a copy of the petition shall be sent by him to the supervisor of the voluntary arrangement.

[(3A)   If to the petitioner's knowledge, there is a member State liquidator appointed in main proceedings in relation to the company, a copy of the petition shall be sent by him to that person.
This does not apply if the petitioner referred to in this paragraph is a member State liquidator.]

(4)   If the company is [an authorised institution or former authorised institution within the meaning of the Banking Act 1987], a copy of the petition shall be sent by the petitioner to the [Financial Services Authority].
This does not apply if the petitioner is the [Financial Services Authority] itself.

(5)   A copy of the petition which is required by this Rule to be sent shall be despatched on the next business day after the day on which the petition is served on the company.

NOTES
Para (2): words in square brackets substituted by the Insolvency (Amendment) Rules 2003, SI 2003/1730, r 7, Sch 1, Pt 4, para 14, as from 15 September 2003 (for transitional provisions and savings see the note preceding r 2.1 at **[10.60]**).
Para (3A): inserted by the Insolvency (Amendment) Rules 2002, SI 2002/1307, rr 3, 6(2), as from 31 May 2002, with savings in relation to anything done under, or for the purposes of, this provision before that date.
Para (4): words in first pair of square brackets substituted by the Insolvency (Amendment) Rules 1987, SI 1987/1919, r 3(1), Schedule, Pt 1, para 38, as from 11 January 1988; words in second and third pairs of square brackets substituted by the Bank of England Act 1998 (Consequential Amendments of Subordinate Legislation) Order 1998, SI 1998/1129, art 2, Sch 1, para 4(1), (4), as from 1 June 1998.
Banking Act 1987: repealed by the Financial Services and Markets Act 2000 (Consequential Amendments and Repeals) Order 2001, SI 2001/3649, art 3(1)(d), as from 1 December 2001.

[10.249]
[4.11   Advertisement of petition

(1)   Unless the court otherwise directs, the petitioner shall give notice of the petition.

(2)   The notice shall be gazetted.

(3)   Where compliance with paragraph (2) is not reasonably practicable, the court may direct that instead of the notice being gazetted, it shall be given in such other manner as the court thinks [just].

(4)   The notice must be made to appear—
  (a)   if the petitioner is the company itself, not less than 7 business days before the day appointed for the hearing; and

(b) otherwise, not less than 7 business days after service of the petition on the company, nor less than 7 business days before the day so appointed.

[(5) In addition to the standard contents, the notice under paragraph (4) must state—
   (a) that a petition has been presented for the winding up of the company;
   (b) in the case of an overseas company, the address at which service of the petition was effected;
   (c) the name and address of the petitioner;
   (d) the date on which the petition was presented;
   (e) the venue fixed for the hearing of the petition;
   (f) the name and address of the petitioner's solicitor (if any); and
   (g) that any person intending to appear at the hearing (whether to support or oppose the petition) must give notice of that intention in accordance with Rule 4.16.]

(6) If notice of the petition is not given in accordance with this Rule, the court may dismiss it.]

NOTES
Commencement: 6 April 2009.
Substituted by the Insolvency (Amendment) Rules 2009, SI 2009/642, rr 4, 18, as from 6 April 2009, subject to transitional provisions in r 3 thereof, as noted to r 1.4 of these Rules at **[10.6]**.
Para (3): word in square brackets substituted by the Insolvency (Amendment) Rules 2010, SI 2010/686, r 2, Sch 1, para 1, as from 6 April 2010, subject to transitional provisions in Sch 4, para 2 thereto, as noted to r 1.31 at **[10.34]**.
Para (5): substituted by SI 2010/686, r 2, Sch 1, para 145, as from 6 April 2010, subject to transitional provisions in Sch 4, para 1 thereto, as noted to r 1.5 at **[10.7]**.
See Form 4.6 at **[10.673]**.

[10.250]
4.12 Verification of petition

(1) The petition shall be verified by [a statement of truth].

(2) If the petition is in respect of debts due to different creditors, the debts to each creditor must be separately verified.

[(3A) A statement of truth which is not contained in or endorsed upon the petition which it verifies must be sufficient to identify the petition and must specify—
   (a) the name and registered number of the company,
   (b) the name of the petitioner, and
   (c) the court in which the petition is to be presented.]

(4) The [statement of truth must be authenticated]—
   (a) by the petitioner (or if there are two or more petitioners, any one of them), or
   (b) by some person such as a director, company secretary or similar company officer, or a solicitor, who has been concerned in the matters giving rise to the presentation of the petition, or
   (c) by some responsible person who is duly authorised to [authenticate the statement of truth] and has the requisite knowledge of those matters.

(5) Where the [person authenticating the statement of truth] is not the petitioner himself, or one of the petitioners, he must in the [statement of truth] identify himself and state—
   (a) the capacity in which, and the authority by which, he [authenticates] it, and
   (b) the means of his knowledge of the matters [verified in the statement of truth].

(6) . . .

(7) [A statement of truth] verifying more than one petition shall include in its title the names of the companies to which it relates and shall set out, in respect of each company, the statements relied on by the petitioner; and a clear and legible photocopy of the [statement of truth must be filed] with each petition which it verifies.

[(8) The [statement of truth] shall state whether, in the opinion of the person making the application, (i) the EC Regulation will apply and (ii) if so, whether the proceedings will be main proceedings[, secondary proceedings] or territorial proceedings.]

NOTES
Paras (1), (4), (5), (7): words in square brackets substituted by the Insolvency (Amendment) Rules 2010, SI 2010/686, r 2, Sch 1, para 146(1), (2), (4), (5), (7), as from 6 April 2010, subject to transitional provisions in Sch 4, para 2 thereto, as noted to r 1.31 at **[10.34]**.
Para (3A): substituted (for the original para (3)) by SI 2010/686, r 2, Sch 1, para 146(1), (3), as from 6 April 2010, subject to transitional provisions in Sch 4, para 2 thereto, as noted to r 1.31 at **[10.34]**.
Para (6): revoked by SI 2010/686, r 2, Sch 1, para 146(1), (6), as from 6 April 2010, subject to transitional provisions in Sch 4, para 1 thereto, as noted to r 1.5 at **[10.7]**.
Para (8): added by the Insolvency (Amendment) Rules 2005, SI 2005/527, r 20, as from 1 April 2005; words in first pair of square brackets substituted, and words in second pair of square brackets inserted, by SI 2010/686, r 2, Sch 1, para 146(1), (8), as from 6 April 2010, subject to transitional provisions in Sch 4, paras 1, 2 thereto, as noted to rr 1.5, 1.31 at **[10.7]**, **[10.34]**.
EC Regulation: ie, Council Regulation 1346/2000/EC on insolvency proceedings.
See Form 4.2 at **[10.673]**.

Part 10   Miscellaneous other SIs

[10.251]
4.13   Persons entitled to copy of petition

Every director, contributory or creditor of the company is entitled to be furnished by the solicitor for the petitioner (or by the petitioner himself, if acting in person) with a copy of the petition within 2 [business] days after requiring it, on payment of the appropriate fee.

NOTES

Word in square brackets inserted by the Insolvency (Amendment) Rules 2010, SI 2010/686, r 2, Sch 1, para 147, as from 6 April 2010, subject to transitional provisions in Sch 4, para 1 thereto, as noted to r 1.5 at **[10.7]**.

[10.252]
4.14   Certificate of compliance

(1)   The petitioner or his solicitor shall, at least 5 [business] days before the hearing of the petition, file in court a certificate of compliance with the Rules relating to service and advertisement.

(2)   The certificate shall show—
  (a)   the date of presentation of the petition,
  (b)   the date fixed for the hearing, and
  [(c)   the date or dates on which the petition was served and notice of it was given in compliance with the Rules.]
  (c)   the date or dates on which the petition was served and advertised in compliance with the Rules.

[A copy or, where this is not reasonably practicable, a description of the form and content of any notice given shall be filed in court with the certificate].

(3)   Non-compliance with this Rule is a ground on which the court may, if it thinks [just], dismiss the petition.

NOTES

Para (1): word in square brackets inserted by the Insolvency (Amendment) Rules 2010, SI 2010/686, r 2, Sch 1, para 148, as from 6 April 2010, subject to transitional provisions in Sch 4, para 1 thereto, as noted to r 1.5 at **[10.7]**.

Para (2): words in square brackets substituted by the Insolvency (Amendment) Rules 2009, SI 2009/642, rr 4, 19, as from 6 April 2009, subject to transitional provisions in r 3 thereof, as noted to r 1.4 of these Rules at **[10.6]**.

Para (3): word in square brackets substituted by SI 2010/686, r 2, Sch 1, para 1, as from 6 April 2010, subject to transitional provisions in Sch 4, para 2 thereto, as noted to r 1.31 at **[10.34]**.

See Form 4.7 at **[10.673]**.

[10.253]
4.15   [Permission] for petitioner to withdraw

If at least 5 [business] days before the hearing the petitioner, on an [application without notice to any other party], satisfies the court that—
  (a)   the petition has not been advertised, and
  (b)   no notices (whether in support or in opposition) have been received by him with reference to the petition, and
  (c)   the company consents to an order being made under this Rule,
the court may order that the petitioner has [permission] to withdraw the petition on such terms as to costs as the parties may agree.

NOTES

Rule heading: word in square brackets substituted by the Insolvency (Amendment) Rules 2010, SI 2010/686, r 2, Sch 1, para 1, as from 6 April 2010, subject to transitional provisions in Sch 4, para 2 thereto, as noted to r 1.31 at **[10.34]**.

Word in first pair of square brackets inserted, and other words in square brackets substituted, by SI 2010/686, r 2, Sch 1, paras 1, 149, as from 6 April 2010, subject to transitional provisions in Sch 4, paras 1, 2 thereto, as noted to rr 1.5, 1.31 at **[10.7]**, **[10.34]**.

See Form 4.8 at **[10.673]**.

[10.254]
4.16   Notice of appearance

(1)   Every person who intends to appear on the hearing of the petition shall give to the petitioner notice of his intention in accordance with this Rule.

(2)   The notice shall specify—
  (a)   the name and address of the person giving it, and any telephone number and reference which may be required for communication with him or with any other person (to be also specified in the notice) authorised to speak or act on his behalf;
  (b)   whether his intention is to support or oppose the petition; and
  (c)   the amount and nature of his debt.

(3)   The notice shall be sent to the petitioner at the address shown for him in the court records, or in the advertisement of the petition required by Rule 4.11; or it may be sent to his solicitor.

(4)   The notice shall be sent so as to reach the addressee not later than 16.00 hours on the business day before that which is appointed for the hearing (or, where the hearing has been adjourned, for the adjourned hearing).

(5)　A person failing to comply with this Rule may appear on the hearing of the petition only with the [permission] of the court.

NOTES

Para (5): word in square brackets substituted by the Insolvency (Amendment) Rules 2010, SI 2010/686, r 2, Sch 1, para 1, as from 6 April 2010, subject to transitional provisions in Sch 4, para 2 thereto, as noted to r 1.31 at **[10.34]**.

See Form 4.9 at **[10.673]**.

[10.255]
4.17　List of appearances

(1)　The petitioner shall prepare for the court a list of the persons (if any) who have given notice under Rule 4.16, specifying their names and addresses and (if known to him) their respective solicitors.

(2)　Against the name of each creditor in the list it shall be stated whether his intention is to support the petition, or to oppose it.

(3)　On the day appointed for the hearing of the petition, a copy of the list shall be handed to the court before the commencement of the hearing.

(4)　If any [permission] is given under Rule 4.16(5), the petitioner shall add to the list the same particulars in respect of the person to whom [permission] has been given.

NOTES

Para (4): words in square brackets substituted by the Insolvency (Amendment) Rules 2010, SI 2010/686, r 2, Sch 1, para 1, as from 6 April 2010, subject to transitional provisions in Sch 4, para 2 thereto, as noted to r 1.31 at **[10.34]**.

See Form 4.10 at **[10.673]**.

[10.256]
4.18　[Witness statement] in opposition

(1)　If the company intends to oppose the petition, its [witness statement] in opposition shall be filed in court not less than [5 business] days before the date fixed for the hearing.

(2)　A copy of the [witness statement] shall be sent by the company to the petitioner, [as soon as reasonably practicable] after filing.

NOTES

Rule heading, para (1): words in square brackets substituted by SI 2010/686, r 2, Sch 1, para 150(1)–(3), as from 6 April 2010, subject to transitional provisions in Sch 4, paras 1, 2 thereto, as noted to rr 1.5, 1.31 at **[10.7]**, **[10.34]**.

Para (2): words in first pair of square brackets substituted by SI 2010/686, r 2, Sch 1, para 150(1), (4), as from 6 April 2010, subject to transitional provisions in Sch 4, para 2 thereto, as noted to r 1.31 at **[10.34]**; words in second pair of square brackets substituted by the Insolvency (Amendment) Rules 2009, SI 2009/642, r 5, as from 6 April 2009, subject to transitional provisions in r 3 thereof, as noted to r 1.4 of these Rules at **[10.6]**.

[10.257]
[4.18A　Adjournment

(1)　If the court adjourns the hearing of the petition, the following applies.

(2)　Unless the court otherwise directs, the petitioning creditor must forthwith send—
- (a)　to the company, and
- (b)　where any creditor has given notice under Rule 4.16 but was not present at the hearing, to that creditor,

notice of the making of the order of adjournment. The notice must state the venue for the adjourned hearing.]

NOTES

Commencement: 6 April 2010.

Inserted by the Insolvency (Amendment) Rules 2010, SI 2010/686, r 2, Sch 1, para 151, subject to transitional provisions in Sch 4, para 1 thereto, as noted to r 1.5 at **[10.7]**.

[10.258]
4.19　Substitution of creditor or contributory for petitioner

(1)　This Rule applies where a person petitions and is subsequently found not entitled to do so, or where the petitioner—
- (a)　fails to advertise his petition within the time prescribed by the Rules or such extended time as the court may allow, or
- (b)　consents to withdraw his petition, or to allow it to be dismissed, consents to an adjournment, or fails to appear in support of his petition when it is called on in court on the day originally fixed for the hearing, or on a day to which it is adjourned, or
- (c)　appears, but does not apply for an order in the terms of the prayer of his petition.

(2)　The court may, on such terms as it thinks just, substitute as petitioner any creditor or contributory who in its opinion would have a right to present a petition, and who is desirous of prosecuting it.

[(2A)   Where a member State liquidator has been appointed in main proceedings in relation to the company, without prejudice to paragraph (2), the court may, on such terms as it thinks just, substitute the member State liquidator as petitioner, where he is desirous of prosecuting the petition.]

(3)   An order of the court under this Rule may, where a petitioner fails to advertise his petition within the time prescribed by these Rules, or consents to withdraw his petition, be made at any time.

NOTES

Para (2A): inserted by the Insolvency (Amendment) Rules 2002, SI 2002/1307, rr 3, 6(3), as from 31 May 2002, with savings in relation to anything done under, or for the purposes of, this provision before that date.

[10.259]
4.20   Notice and settling of winding-up order

(1)   When a winding-up order has been made, the court shall [as soon as reasonably practicable] give notice of the fact to the official receiver.

(2)   The petitioner and every other person who has appeared on the hearing of the petition shall, not later than the business day following that on which the order is made, leave at the court all the documents required for enabling the order to be completed [as soon as reasonably practicable].

(3)   It is not necessary for the court to appoint a venue for any person to attend to settle the order, unless in any particular case the special circumstances make an appointment necessary.

NOTES

Paras (1), (2): words in square brackets substituted by the Insolvency (Amendment) Rules 2009, SI 2009/642, r 5, as from 6 April 2009, subject to transitional provisions in r 3 thereof, as noted to r 1.4 of these Rules at **[10.6]**.
See Forms 4.11, 4.12, 4.13 at **[10.673]**.

[10.260]
4.21   Transmission and advertisement of order

(1)   When the winding-up order has been made, 3 copies of it, sealed with the seal of the court, shall be sent [as soon as reasonably practicable] by the court to the official receiver.

(2)   The official receiver shall cause a sealed copy of the order to be served on the company by prepaid letter addressed to it at its registered office (if any) or, if there is no registered office, at its principal or last known principal place of business.

Alternatively, the order may be served on such other person or persons, or in such other manner, as the court directs.

(3)   The official receiver shall forward to the registrar of companies the copy of the order which by section 130(1) is directed to be so forwarded by the company.

[(4)   The official receiver—
  (a)   as soon as reasonably practicable shall cause notice of the order to be gazetted; and
  (b)   may advertise notice of the order in such other manner as the official receiver thinks fit.]

[(5)   In addition to the standard contents a notice under paragraph (4) must state—
  (a)   that a winding-up order has been made in respect of the company; and
  (b)   the date of the order.]

NOTES

Para (1): words in square brackets substituted by the Insolvency (Amendment) Rules 2009, SI 2009/642, r 5, as from 6 April 2009, subject to transitional provisions in r 3 thereof, as noted to r 1.4 of these Rules at **[10.6]**.
Para (4): substituted by SI 2009/642, rr 4, 20, as from 6 April 2009, subject to transitional provisions in r 3 thereof, as noted to r 1.4 of these Rules at **[10.6]**.
Para (5): added by the Insolvency (Amendment) Rules 2010, SI 2010/686, r 2, Sch 1, para 152, as from 6 April 2010, subject to transitional provisions in Sch 4, para 1 thereto, as noted to r 1.5 at **[10.7]**.

[10.261]
[4.21A   Expenses of voluntary arrangement

Where a winding-up order is made and there is at the time of the presentation of the petition in force for the company a voluntary arrangement under Part I of the Act, any expenses properly incurred as expenses of the administration of the arrangement in question shall be [payable in priority to any expenses of the liquidation].

NOTES

Inserted by the Insolvency (Amendment) Rules 1987, SI 1987/1919, r 3(1), Schedule, Pt 1, para 39, as from 11 January 1988.
Words in square brackets substituted by the Insolvency (Amendment) Rules 2008, SI 2008/737, rr 3, 7(2), as from 6 April 2008, subject to transitional provisions as noted to r 4.218 at **[10.486]**.

[10.262]
[4.21B   Petition dismissed

(1)   Unless the court otherwise directs, when a petition is dismissed, as soon as reasonably practicable the petitioner shall give notice of the dismissal. Such notice shall be—
     (a)   gazetted; or
     (b)   advertised in accordance with any directions of the court.

[(2)   In addition to the standard contents, the notice published under paragraph (1) must state—
     (a)   that a petition for the winding up of the company has been dismissed;
     (b)   in the case of an overseas company, the address at which service of the petition was effected;
     (c)   the name and address of the petitioner;
     (d)   the date on which the petition was presented;
     (e)   the date on which the petition was gazetted or otherwise advertised; and
     (f)   the date of the hearing at which the petition was dismissed.]

(3)   Where—
     (a)   the petitioner is not the company itself; and
     (b)   the petitioner has not complied with paragraphs (1) and (2) within 21 days of the date of the hearing at which the petition was dismissed,
the company may give notice of the dismissal itself. Such notice shall be gazetted.]

NOTES

Commencement: 6 April 2009.

Inserted by the Insolvency (Amendment) Rules 2009, SI 2009/642, rr 4, 21, as from 6 April 2009, subject to transitional provisions in r 3 thereof, as noted to r 1.4 of these Rules at **[10.6]**.

Para (2): substituted by the Insolvency (Amendment) Rules 2010, SI 2010/686, r 2, Sch 1, para 153, as from 6 April 2010, subject to transitional provisions in Sch 4, para 1 thereto, as noted to r 1.5 at **[10.7]**.

CHAPTER 4
PETITION BY CONTRIBUTORIES

(No CVL Application)

[10.263]
4.22   Presentation and service of petition

(1)   The petition shall specify the grounds on which it is presented . . . , and shall be filed in court with one copy for service under this Rule.

[(1A)   No petition shall be filed unless there is produced with it the receipt for the deposit payable on presentation.]

(2)   The court shall fix a hearing for a day ("the return day") on which, unless the court otherwise directs, the petitioner and the company shall attend before the registrar [or district judge for—
     (a)   directions to be given in relation to the procedure on the petition; or
     (b)   where—
         (i)   the petition is presented under Rule 4.7(9), and
         (ii)   the court considers it just in all the circumstances,
the hearing of the petition.]

(3)   On fixing the return day, the court shall return to the petitioner a sealed copy of the petition for service, endorsed with the return day and time of hearing.

(4)   The petitioner shall, at least 14 days before the return day, serve a sealed copy of the petition on the company.

[(5)   Where a member State liquidator has been appointed in main proceedings in relation to the company, the petitioner shall send a copy of the petition to him.]

NOTES

Para (1): words omitted revoked by the Insolvency (Amendment) Rules 1987, SI 1987/1919, r 3(1), Schedule, Pt 1, para 40(1), as from 11 January 1988.

Para (1A): inserted by SI 1987/1919, r 3(1), Schedule, Pt 1, para 40(2), as from 11 January 1988.

Para (2): words in square brackets substituted by the Insolvency (Amendment) Rules 2010, SI 2010/686, r 2, Sch 1, para 154, as from 6 April 2010, subject to transitional provisions in Sch 4, para 2 thereto, as noted to r 1.31 at **[10.34]**.

Para (5): added by the Insolvency (Amendment) Rules 2002, SI 2002/1307, rr 3, 6(4), as from 31 May 2002, with savings in relation to anything done under, or for the purposes of, this provision before that date.

See Form 4.14 at **[10.673]**.

[10.264]
4.23   Return of petition

(1)   On the return day, or at any time after it, the court [must or, where the petition is presented under Rule 4.7(9), may] give such directions as it thinks appropriate with respect to the following matters—

    (a)   service of the petition, whether in connection with the venue for a further hearing, or for any other purpose;

    (b)   whether particulars of claim and defence are to be delivered, and generally as to the procedure on the petition;

    (c)   whether, and if so by what means, the petition is to be advertised;

    (d)   the manner in which any evidence is to be adduced at any hearing before the judge and in particular (but without prejudice to the generality of the above) as to—

        (i)   the taking of evidence wholly or in part by [witness statement] or orally;

        (ii)   the cross-examination of any [persons authenticating witness statements];

        (iii)   the matters to be dealt with in evidence;

    (e)   any other matter affecting the procedure on the petition or in connection with the hearing and disposal of the petition.

(2)   In giving directions under paragraph (1)(a), the court shall have regard to whether any of the persons specified in Rule 4.10 should be served with a copy of the petition.

NOTES

   Para (1): words in square brackets substituted by the Insolvency (Amendment) Rules 2010, SI 2010/686, r 2, Sch 1, para 155, as from 6 April 2010, subject to transitional provisions in Sch 4, para 2 thereto, as noted to r 1.31 at **[10.34]**.

[10.265]
4.24   Application of Rules in Chapter 3

The following Rules in Chapter 3 apply, with the necessary modifications—

    Rule 4.16 (notice of appearance);

    Rule 4.17 (list of appearances);

    Rule 4.20 (notice and settling of winding-up order);   . . .

    Rule 4.21 (transmission and advertisement of order)[; and

    Rule 4.21A (expenses of voluntary arrangement)].

NOTES

   Words omitted revoked, and words in square brackets added, by the Insolvency (Amendment) Rules 1987, SI 1987/1919, r 3(1), Schedule, Pt 1, para 41, as from 11 January 1988.

CHAPTER 5

PROVISIONAL LIQUIDATOR

(No CVL Application)

[10.266]
4.25   Appointment of provisional liquidator

[(1)   An application to the court for the appointment of a provisional liquidator under section 135 may be made by—

    (a)   the petitioner;

    (b)   a creditor of the company;

    (c)   a contributory;

    (d)   the company;

    (e)   the Secretary of State;

    (f)   a temporary administrator;

    (g)   a member State liquidator appointed in main proceedings; or

    (h)   any person who under any enactment would be entitled to present a petition for the winding up of the company.]

(2)   The application must be supported by [a witness statement] stating—

    (a)   the grounds on which it is proposed that a provisional liquidator should be appointed;

    (b)   if some person other than the official receiver is proposed to be appointed, that the person has consented to act and, to the best of the applicant's belief, is qualified to act as an insolvency practitioner in relation to the company;

    (c)   whether or not the official receiver has been informed of the application and, if so, has been furnished with a copy of it;

    (d)   whether to the applicant's knowledge—

        (i)   there has been proposed or is in force for the company a voluntary arrangement under Part I of the Act, or

        (ii)   an administrator or administrative receiver is acting in relation to the company, or

        (iii)   a liquidator has been appointed for its voluntary winding up; and

    (e)   the applicant's estimate of the value of the assets in respect of which the provisional liquidator is to be appointed.

(3)   The applicant shall send copies of the application and of the [witness statement] in support to the official receiver, who may attend the hearing and make any representations which he thinks appropriate.

If for any reason it is not practicable to comply with this paragraph, the official receiver must be informed of the application in sufficient time for him to be able to attend.

(4)   The court may on the application, if satisfied that sufficient grounds are shown for the appointment, make it on such terms as it thinks [just].

NOTES

Para (1): substituted by the Insolvency (Amendment) Rules 2002, SI 2002/1307, rr 3, 6(5), as from 31 May 2002, with savings in relation to anything done under, or for the purposes of, this provision before that date.

Paras (2)–(4): words in square brackets substituted by the Insolvency (Amendment) Rules 2010, SI 2010/686, r 2, Sch 1, paras 1, 156, as from 6 April 2010, subject to transitional provisions in Sch 4, para 2 thereto, as noted to r 1.31 at **[10.34]**.

[10.267]
[4.25A   Notice of appointment

(1)   Where a provisional liquidator has been appointed the court shall [as soon as reasonably practicable] give notice of the fact to the official receiver.

(2)   A copy of that notice shall at the same time be sent by the court to the provisional liquidator where he is not the official receiver.]

[(3)   Unless the court otherwise directs, on receipt of the notice of appointment, as soon as reasonably practicable the provisional liquidator shall give notice of that appointment. Such notice—
    (a)   shall be gazetted; and
    (b)   may be advertised in such other manner as the provisional liquidator thinks fit.

[(4)   In addition to the standard contents, the notice under paragraph (3) must state—
    (a)   that a provisional liquidator has been appointed; and
    (b)   the date of the appointment.]]

NOTES

Inserted by the Insolvency (Amendment) Rules 1987, SI 1987/1919, r 3(1), Schedule, Pt 1, para 42, as from 11 January 1988.

Para (1): words in square brackets substituted by the Insolvency (Amendment) Rules 2009, SI 2009/642, r 5, as from 6 April 2009, subject to transitional provisions in r 3 thereof, as noted to r 1.4 of these Rules at **[10.6]**.

Para (3): added by SI 2009/642, rr 4, 22, as from 6 April 2009, subject to transitional provisions in r 3 thereof, as noted to r 1.4 of these Rules at **[10.6]**.

Para (4): added by the Insolvency (Amendment) Rules 2010, SI 2010/686, r 2, Sch 1, para 157, as from 6 April 2010, subject to transitional provisions in Sch 4, para 1 thereto, as noted to r 1.5 at **[10.7]**.

See Form 4.14A at **[10.673]**.

[10.268]
4.26   Order of appointment

(1)   The order appointing the provisional liquidator shall specify the functions to be carried out by him in relation to the company's affairs.

(2)   The court shall, [as soon as reasonably practicable] after the order is made, send sealed copies of the order as follows—
    (a)   if the official receiver is appointed, [three] copies to him;
    (b)   if a person other than the official receiver is appointed—
        (i)   [three] copies of that person, and
        (ii)   one copy to the official receiver;
    (c)   if there is an administrative receiver acting in relation to the company, one copy to him.

[(3)   Of the three copies of the order sent to the official receiver under paragraph (2)(a), or to another person under paragraph (2)(b)(i)—
    (i)   one shall in each case be sent by the recipient to the company, or if a liquidator has been appointed for the company's voluntary winding-up, to him; and
    (ii)   one shall be sent . . .   to the registrar of companies.]

NOTES

Para (2): words in first pair of square brackets substituted by the Insolvency (Amendment) Rules 2009, SI 2009/642, r 5, as from 6 April 2009, subject to transitional provisions in r 3 thereof, as noted to r 1.4 of these Rules at **[10.6]**; word in second and third pairs of square brackets substituted by the Insolvency (Amendment) Rules 2005, SI 2005/527, r 21(a), as from 1 April 2005.

Para (3): substituted by SI 2005/527, r 21(b), as from 1 April 2005; words omitted revoked by the Insolvency (Amendment) Rules 2010, SI 2010/686, r 2, Sch 1, para 158, as from 6 April 2010, subject to transitional provisions in Sch 4, para 1 thereto, as noted to r 1.5 at **[10.7]**.

See Form 4.15 at **[10.673]**.

[10.269]
4.27   Deposit

(1)   Before an order appointing the official receiver as provisional liquidator is issued, the applicant for it shall deposit with him, or otherwise secure to his satisfaction, such sum as the court directs to cover the official receiver's remuneration and expenses.

(2)   If the sum deposited or secured subsequently proves to be insufficient, the court may, on application by the official receiver, order that an additional sum be deposited or secured. If the order is not complied with within 2 [business] days after service of it on the person to whom it is directed, the court may discharge the order appointing the provisional liquidator.

(3)   If a winding-up order is made after a provisional liquidator has been appointed, any money deposited under this Rule shall (unless it is required by reason of insufficiency of assets for payment of remuneration and expenses of the provisional liquidator) be repaid to the person depositing it (or as that person may direct) [as an expense of the liquidation], in the prescribed order of priority.

NOTES

Para (2): word in square brackets inserted by the Insolvency (Amendment) Rules 2010, SI 2010/686, r 2, Sch 1, para 159, as from 6 April 2010, subject to transitional provisions in Sch 4, para 1 thereto, as noted to r 1.5 at **[10.7]**.

Para (3): words in square brackets substituted by the Insolvency (Amendment) Rules 2008, SI 2008/737, rr 3, 7(1), as from 6 April 2008, subject to transitional provisions as noted to r 4.218 at **[10.486]**.

[10.270]
4.28   Security

(1)   The following applies where an insolvency practitioner is appointed to be provisional liquidator under section 135.

(2)   The cost of providing the security required under the Act shall be paid in the first instance by the provisional liquidator; but—

   (a)   if a winding-up order is not made, the person so appointed is entitled to be reimbursed out of the property of the company, and the court may make an order on the company accordingly, and

   (b)   if a winding-up order is made, he is entitled to be reimbursed [as an expense of the liquidation] in the prescribed order of priority.

NOTES

Para (2): words in square brackets substituted by the Insolvency (Amendment) Rules 2008, SI 2008/737, rr 3, 7(1), as from 6 April 2008, subject to transitional provisions as noted to r 4.218 at **[10.486]**.

[10.271]
4.29   Failure to give or keep up security

(1)   If the provisional liquidator fails to give or keep up his security, the court may remove him, and make such order as it thinks [just] as to costs.

(2)   If an order is made under this Rule removing the provisional liquidator, or discharging the order appointing him, the court shall give directions as to whether any, and if so what, steps should be taken for the appointment of another person in his place.

NOTES

Para (1): word in square brackets substituted by the Insolvency (Amendment) Rules 2010, SI 2010/686, r 2, Sch 1, para 1, as from 6 April 2010, subject to transitional provisions in Sch 4, para 2 thereto, as noted to r 1.31 at **[10.34]**.

[10.272]
4.30   Remuneration

(1)   The remuneration of the provisional liquidator (other than the official receiver) shall be fixed by the court from time to time on his application.

(2)   In fixing his remuneration, the court shall take into account—

   (a)   the time properly given by him (as provisional liquidator) and his staff in attending to the company's affairs;

   (b)   the complexity (or otherwise) of the case;

   (c)   any respects in which, in connection with the company's affairs, there falls on the provisional liquidator any responsibility of an exceptional kind or degree;

   (d)   the effectiveness with which the provisional liquidator appears to be carrying out, or to have carried out, his duties; and

   (e)   the value and nature of the property with which he has to deal.

(3)   [Without prejudice to any order the court may make as to costs, the provisional liquidator's remuneration (whether the official receiver or another) shall be paid to him, and the amount of any expenses incurred by him (including the remuneration and expenses of any special manager appointed under section 177) reimbursed—

   (a)   if a winding-up order is not made, out of the property of the company], and

   (b)   if a winding-up order is made, [as an expense of the liquidation], in the prescribed order of priority,

or, in either case (the relevant funds being insufficient), out of the deposit under Rule 4.27.

[(3A)   Unless the court otherwise directs, in a case falling within paragraph (3)(a) above the provisional liquidator may retain out of the company's property such sums or property as are or may be required for meeting his remuneration and expenses.]

(4)   Where a person other than the official receiver has been appointed provisional liquidator, and the official receiver has taken any steps for the purpose of obtaining a statement of affairs or has performed any other duty under the Rules, he shall pay the official receiver such sum (if any) as the court may direct.

NOTES

Para (3): words in first pair of square brackets substituted by the Insolvency (Amendment) Rules 1987, SI 1987/1919, r 3(1), Schedule, Pt 1, para 43(1), as from 11 January 1988; words in second pair of square brackets substituted by the Insolvency (Amendment) Rules 2008, SI 2008/737, rr 3, 7(1), as from 6 April 2008, subject to transitional provisions as noted to r 4.218 at **[10.486]**.

Para (3A): inserted by SI 1987/1919, r 3(1), Schedule, Pt 1, para 43(2), as from 11 January 1988.

[10.273]
4.31   Termination of appointment

(1)   The appointment of the provisional liquidator may be terminated by the court on his application, or on that of any of the persons specified in Rule 4.25(1).

(2)   If the provisional liquidator's appointment terminates, in consequence of the dismissal of the winding-up petition or otherwise, the court may give such directions as it thinks [just] with respect to the accounts of his administration or any other matters which it thinks appropriate.

[(4)   Notice of termination of the appointment of a provisional liquidator must be given by the provisional liquidator, unless the termination is on the making of a winding-up order or the court otherwise directs. Such notice—
  (a)   as soon as reasonably practicable must be sent to the registrar of companies;
  (b)   as soon as reasonably practicable must be gazetted; and
  (c)   may be advertised in such other manner as the provisional liquidator thinks fit.

(5)   In addition to the standard contents, a notice under paragraph (4)(b) or (c) must state—
  (a)   that the appointment as provisional liquidator has been terminated;
  (b)   the date of that termination; and
  (c)   that the appointment terminated otherwise than on the making of a winding-up order.]

NOTES

Para (2): word in square brackets substituted by the Insolvency (Amendment) Rules 2010, SI 2010/686, r 2, Sch 1, para 1, as from 6 April 2010, subject to transitional provisions in Sch 4, para 2 thereto, as noted to r 1.31 at **[10.34]**.

Paras (4), (5): substituted for para (3) (as added by the Insolvency (Amendment) Rules 2009, SI 2009/642, rr 4, 23, as from 6 April 2009) by SI 2010/686, r 2, Sch 1, para 160, as from 6 April 2010, subject to transitional provisions in Sch 4, para 1 thereto, as noted to r 1.5 at **[10.7]**. Note that there was an original para (3) in this rule but it was revoked by the Insolvency (Amendment) Rules 1987, SI 1987/1919, r 3(1), Schedule, Pt 1, para 44, as from 11 January 1988.

CHAPTER 6
STATEMENT OF AFFAIRS AND OTHER INFORMATION

[10.274]
4.32   Notice requiring statement of affairs (NO CVL APPLICATION)

(1)   The following applies where the official receiver determines to require a statement of the company's affairs to be made out and submitted to him in accordance with section 131.

(2)   He shall send notice to each of the persons whom he considers should be made responsible under that section, requiring them to prepare and submit the statement.

(3)   The persons to whom that notice is sent are referred to in this Chapter as "the [nominated persons]".

(4)   The notice shall inform each of the [nominated persons]—
  (a)   of the names and addresses of all others (if any) to whom the same notice has been sent;
  (b)   of the time within which the statement must be delivered;
  (c)   of the effect of section 131(7) (penalty for non-compliance); and
  (d)   of the application to him, and to each of the other [nominated persons], of section 235 (duty to provide information, and to attend on the official receiver if required).

(5)   The official receiver shall, on request, furnish a [nominated person] with instructions for the preparation of the statement and with the forms required for that purpose.

NOTES

Words in square brackets substituted by the Insolvency (Amendment) Rules 2010, SI 2010/686, r 2, Sch 1, para 161(1), (2), as from 6 April 2010, subject to transitional provisions in Sch 4, para 2 thereto, as noted to r 1.31 at **[10.34]**.

See Form 4.16 at **[10.673]**.

[10.275]
4.33   Verification and filing (NO CVL APPLICATION)

(1)   The statement of affairs shall be in Form 4.17, shall contain all the particulars required by that form and shall be verified by [a statement of truth] by the [persons making the statement of affairs] (using the same form).

(2)   The official receiver may require any of the persons mentioned in section 131(3) to submit [a statement of concurrence verified by a statement of truth], stating that he concurs in the statement of affairs.

(3)   [A statement] of concurrence made under paragraph (2) may be qualified in respect of matters dealt with in the statement of affairs, where the [maker of the statement of concurrence] is not in agreement with the [persons making the statement of affairs], or he considers the statement to be erroneous or misleading, or he is without the direct knowledge necessary for concurring in the statement.

(4)   The statement of affairs shall be delivered to the official receiver by the [nominated person] (or by one of them, if more than one), together with a copy of the verified statement.

(5)   Every [statement] of concurrence shall be delivered to the official receiver by the person who makes it, together with a copy.

[(6)   The official receiver must send the verified copy of the statement of affairs and any statements of concurrence to the registrar of companies.]

(7)   . . .

NOTES

Paras (1)–(5): words in square brackets substituted by the Insolvency (Amendment) Rules 2010, SI 2010/686, r 2, Sch 1, para 162(1)–(6), as from 6 April 2010, subject to transitional provisions in Sch 4, para 2 thereto, as noted to r 1.31 at **[10.34]**.

Para (6): substituted by SI 2010/686, r 2, Sch 1, para 162(1), (7), as from 6 April 2010, subject to transitional provisions in Sch 4, para 1 thereto, as noted to r 1.5 at **[10.7]**.

Para (7): revoked by SI 2010/686, r 2, Sch 1, para 162(1), (8), as from 6 April 2010, subject to transitional provisions in Sch 4, para 2 thereto, as noted to r 1.31 at **[10.34]**.

See Form 4.17, at **[10.673]**.

[10.276]
4.34–CVL   Statement of affairs

(1)   This Rule applies with respect to the statement of affairs made out by the liquidator under section 95(3) or (as the case may be) by the directors under section 99(1).

(2)   Where it is made out by the liquidator, the statement of affairs shall be delivered by him to the registrar of companies within [5 business] days after the creditors' meeting summoned under section 95(2).

[(3)   Where it is made out by the directors under section 99(1) the statement of affairs shall be delivered by them to the liquidator in office following the creditors' meeting summoned under section 98 [as soon as reasonably practicable] after that meeting has been held; and he shall, within [5 business] days, deliver it to the registrar of companies.

(4)   A statement of affairs under section 99(1) may be made up to a date not more than 14 days before that on which the resolution for voluntary winding up is passed by the company.]

[(5)   The liquidator may require any of the directors who has not submitted the statement of affairs to submit a statement of concurrence verified by a statement of truth, stating that that director concurs in the statement of affairs.

(6)   A statement of concurrence made under paragraph (5) may be qualified in respect of matters dealt with in the statement of affairs, where the maker of the statement of concurrence—

    (a)   is not in agreement with the persons making the statement of affairs, or

    (b)   considers the statement to be erroneous or misleading, or

    (c)   is without the direct knowledge necessary for concurring in the statement.

(7)   Every statement of concurrence must be delivered to the liquidator by the person who makes it, together with a copy.]

NOTES

Para (2): words in square brackets substituted by the Insolvency (Amendment) Rules 2010, SI 2010/686, r 2, Sch 1, para 163(1), (2), as from 6 April 2010, subject to transitional provisions in Sch 4, para 1 thereto, as noted to r 1.5 at **[10.7]**.

Para (3): substituted, together with para (4), for original para (3), by the Insolvency (Amendment) Rules 1987, SI 1987/1919, r 3(1), Schedule, Pt 1, para 45, as from 11 January 1988; words in first pair of square brackets substituted by the Insolvency (Amendment) Rules 2009, SI 2009/642, r 5, as from 6 April 2009, subject to transitional provisions in r 3 thereof, as noted to r 1.4 of these Rules at **[10.6]**; words in second pair of square brackets substituted by SI 2010/686, r 2, Sch 1, para 163(1), (2), as from 6 April 2010, subject to transitional provisions in Sch 4, para 1 thereto, as noted to r 1.5 at **[10.7]**.

Para (4): substituted as noted above.

Paras (5)–(7): added by SI 2010/686, r 2, Sch 1, para 163(1), (3), as from 6 April 2010, subject to transitional provisions in Sch 4, para 1 thereto, as noted to r 1.5 at **[10.7]**.

See Forms 4.18, 4.19 at **[10.673]**.

[10.277]
[4.34A–CVL   Copy Statement of affairs

Where a liquidator is nominated by the company at a general meeting held on a day prior to that on which the creditors' meeting summoned under section 98 is held, the directors shall [as soon as reasonably practicable] after his nomination or the making of the statement of affairs, whichever is the later, deliver to him a copy of the statement of affairs.]

NOTES

Inserted by the Insolvency (Amendment) Rules 1987, SI 1987/1919, r 3(1), Schedule, Pt 1, para 46, as from 11 January 1988.

Words in square brackets substituted by the Insolvency (Amendment) Rules 2009, SI 2009/642, r 5, as from 6 April 2009, subject to transitional provisions in r 3 thereof, as noted to r 1.4 of these Rules at **[10.6]**.

[10.278]
4.35 Limited disclosure

. . .

(1) Where the official receiver [or liquidator] thinks that it would prejudice the conduct of the liquidation [or might reasonably be expected to lead to violence against any person] for the whole or part of the statement of affairs to be disclosed, he may apply to the court for an order of limited disclosure in respect of the statement, or any specified part of it.

(2) The court may on the application order that the statement or, as the case may be, the specified part of it be not filed [with the registrar of companies].

[(3) The official receiver or liquidator must as soon as reasonably practicable send to the registrar of companies a copy of the order and the statement of affairs (to the extent provided by the order) and any statement of concurrence.

(4) In a voluntary winding up, this Rule does not apply so far as section 95, 98 or 99 does not permit limited disclosure.]

NOTES

Words omitted revoked by the Insolvency (Amendment) Rules 2010, SI 2010/686, r 2, Sch 1, para 164(1), (2), as from 6 April 2010, subject to transitional provisions in Sch 4, para 1 thereto, as noted to r 1.5 at **[10.7]**.

Para (1): words in square brackets inserted by SI 2010/686, r 2, Sch 1, para 164(1), (3), as from 6 April 2010, subject to transitional provisions in Sch 4, para 1 thereto, as noted to r 1.5 at **[10.7]**.

Para (2): words in square brackets substituted by SI 2010/686, r 2, Sch 1, para 164(1), (4), as from 6 April 2010, subject to transitional provisions in Sch 4, para 1 thereto, as noted to r 1.5 at **[10.7]**.

Paras (3), (4): added by SI 2010/686, r 2, Sch 1, para 164(1), (5), as from 6 April 2010, subject to transitional provisions in Sch 4, para 1 thereto, as noted to r 1.5 at **[10.7]**.

[10.279]
4.36 Release from duty to submit statement of affairs; extension of time
(NO CVL APPLICATION)

(1) The power of the official receiver under section 131(5) to give a release from the obligation imposed by that section, or to grant an extension of time, may be exercised at the official receiver's own discretion, or at the request of any [nominated person].

(2) A [nominated person] may, if he requests a release or extension of time and it is refused by the official receiver, apply to the court for it.

(3) The court may, if it thinks that no sufficient cause is shown for the application, dismiss it; but it shall not do so unless the applicant has had an opportunity to attend the court for [a] hearing, of which he has been given at least [5 business] days' notice [but which is without notice to any other party].

If the application is not dismissed under this paragraph, the court shall fix a venue for it to be heard, and give notice to the [nominated person] accordingly.

(4) The [nominated person] shall, at least 14 days before the hearing, send to the official receiver a notice stating the venue and accompanied by a copy of the application, and of any evidence which he (the [nominated person]) intends to adduce in support of it.

(5) The official receiver may appear and be heard on the application; and, whether or not he appears, he may file a written report of any matters which he considers ought to be drawn to the court's attention.

If such a report is filed, a copy of it shall be sent by the official receiver to the [nominated person], not later than 5 [business] days before the hearing.

(6) Sealed copies of any order made on the application shall be sent by the court to the [nominated person] and the official receiver.

(7) On any application under this Rule the applicant's costs shall be paid in any event by him and, [unless and to the extent that the court otherwise orders, shall not be an expense of the liquidation].

NOTES

Paras (1), (2), (4), (6): words in square brackets substituted by the Insolvency (Amendment) Rules 2010, SI 2010/686, r 2, Sch 1, para 165(1), (2), as from 6 April 2010, subject to transitional provisions in Sch 4, para 2 thereto, as noted to r 1.31 at **[10.34]**.

Para (3): words in third pair of square brackets inserted, and other words in square brackets substituted, by SI 2010/686, r 2, Sch 1, para 165(1)–(3), as from 6 April 2010, subject to transitional provisions in Sch 4, paras 1, 2 thereto, as noted to rr 1.5, 1.31 at **[10.7]**, **[10.34]**.

Para (5): words in first pair of square brackets substituted, and word in second pair of square brackets inserted, by SI 2010/686, r 2, Sch 1, para 165(1), (2), (4), as from 6 April 2010, subject to transitional provisions in Sch 4, paras 1, 2 thereto, as noted to rr 1.5, 1.31 at **[10.7]**, **[10.34]**.

Para (7): words in square brackets substituted by the Insolvency (Amendment) Rules 2008, SI 2008/737, rr 3, 7(3), as from 6 April 2008, subject to transitional provisions as noted to r 4.218 at **[10.486]**.

[10.280]
4.37 Expenses of statement of affairs (NO CVL APPLICATION)

(1) If any [nominated person] cannot himself prepare a proper statement of affairs, the official receiver may, [as an expense of the liquidation], employ some person or persons to assist in the preparation of the statement.

(2) At the request of any [nominated person], made on the grounds that he cannot himself prepare a proper statement, the official receiver may authorise an allowance, payable [as an expense of the liquidation], towards expenses to be incurred by the [nominated person] in employing some person or persons to assist him in preparing it.

(3) Any such request by the [nominated person] shall be accompanied by an estimate of the expenses involved; and the official receiver shall only authorise the employment of a named person or a named firm, being in either case approved by him.

(4) An authorisation given by the official receiver under this Rule shall be subject to such conditions (if any) as he thinks fit to impose with respect to the manner in which any person may obtain access to relevant books and papers.

(5) Nothing in this Rule relieves a [nominated person] from any obligation with respect to the preparation, verification and submission of the statement of affairs, or to the provision of information to the official receiver or the liquidator.

(6) Any payment [made as an expense of the liquidation] under this Rule shall be made in the prescribed order of priority.

(7) Paragraphs (2) to (6) of this Rule may be applied, on application to the official receiver by any [nominated person], in relation to the making of [a statement of concurrence verified by a statement of truth].

NOTES
Para (1): words in first pair of square brackets substituted by the Insolvency (Amendment) Rules 2010, SI 2010/686, r 2, Sch 1, para 166(1), (2), as from 6 April 2010, subject to transitional provisions in Sch 4, para 2 thereto, as noted to r 1.31 at **[10.34]**; words in second pair of square brackets substituted by SI 2008/737, rr 3, 7(4)(a), as from 6 April 2008, subject to transitional provisions as noted to r 4.218 at **[10.486]**.
Para (2): words in first and third pairs of square brackets substituted by SI 2010/686, r 2, Sch 1, para 166(1), (2), as from 6 April 2010, subject to transitional provisions in Sch 4, para 2 thereto, as noted to r 1.31 at **[10.34]**; words in second pair of square brackets substituted by SI 2008/737, rr 3, 7(1), as from 6 April 2008, subject to transitional provisions as noted to r 4.218 at **[10.486]**.
Paras (3), (5), (7): words in square brackets substituted by SI 2010/686, r 2, Sch 1, para 166(1), (2), as from 6 April 2010, subject to transitional provisions in Sch 4, para 2 thereto, as noted to r 1.31 at **[10.34]**.
Para (6): words in square brackets substituted by SI 2008/737, rr 3, 7(4)(b), as from 6 April 2008, subject to transitional provisions as noted to r 4.218 at **[10.486]**.

[10.281]
4.38–CVL Expenses of statements of affairs

(1) Payment may be made out of the company's assets, either before or after the commencement of the winding up, of any reasonable and necessary expenses of preparing the statement of affairs under section 99.

Any such payment is an expense of the liquidation.

(2) Where such a payment is made before the commencement of the winding up, the director presiding at the creditors' meeting held under section 98 shall inform the meeting of the amount of the payment and the identity of the person to whom it was made.

(3) The liquidator appointed under section 100 may make such a payment (subject to the next paragraph); but if there is a liquidation committee, he must give the committee at least [5 business] days' notice of his intention to make it.

(4) Such a payment shall not be made by the liquidator to himself, or to any associate of his, otherwise than with the approval of the liquidation committee, the creditors, or the court.

(5) This Rule is without prejudice to the powers of the court under Rule 4.219 (voluntary winding up superseded by winding up by the court).

NOTES
Para (3): words in square brackets substituted by the Insolvency (Amendment) Rules 2010, SI 2010/686, r 2, Sch 1, para 167, as from 6 April 2010, subject to transitional provisions in Sch 4, para 1 thereto, as noted to r 1.5 at **[10.7]**.

[10.282]
4.39 Submission of accounts (NO CVL APPLICATION)

(1) Any of the persons specified in section 235(3) shall, at the request of the official receiver, furnish him with accounts of the company of such nature, as at such date, and for such period, as he may specify.

(2)   The period specified may begin from a date up to 3 years preceding the date of the presentation of the winding-up petition, or from an earlier date to which audited accounts of the company were last prepared.

(3)   The court may, on the official receiver's application, require accounts for any earlier period.

(4)   Rule 4.37 applies (with the necessary modifications) in relation to accounts to be furnished under this Rule as it applies in relation to the statement of affairs.

(5)   The accounts shall, if the official receiver so requires, be verified by [a statement of truth] and (whether or not so verified) delivered to him within 21 days of the request under paragraph (1), or such longer period as he may allow.

(6)   . . .

NOTES

    Para (5): words in square brackets substituted by the Insolvency (Amendment) Rules 2010, SI 2010/686, r 2, Sch 1, para 168(1), (2), as from 6 April 2010, subject to transitional provisions in Sch 4, para 2 thereto, as noted to r 1.31 at **[10.34]**.

    Para (6): revoked by SI 2010/686, r 2, Sch 1, para 168(1), (3), as from 6 April 2010, subject to transitional provisions in Sch 4, para 1 thereto, as noted to r 1.5 at **[10.7]**.

[10.283]
4.40–CVL   Submission of accounts

(1)   Any of the persons specified in section 235(3) shall, at the request of the liquidator, furnish him with accounts of the company of such nature, as at such date, and for such period, as he may specify.

(2)   The specified period for the accounts may begin from a date up to 3 years preceding the date of the resolution for winding up, or from an earlier date to which audited accounts of the company were last prepared.

(3)   The accounts shall, if the liquidator so requires, be verified [by a statement of truth] and (whether or not so verified) delivered to him, with [the statement of truth] if required, within 21 days from the request under paragraph (1), or such longer period as he may allow.

NOTES

    Para (3): words in square brackets substituted by the Insolvency (Amendment) Rules 2010, SI 2010/686, r 2, Sch 1, para 169, as from 6 April 2010, subject to transitional provisions in Sch 4, para 2 thereto, as noted to r 1.31 at **[10.34]**.

[10.284]
4.41–CVL   Expenses of preparing accounts

(1)   Where a person is required under Rule 4.40–CVL to furnish accounts, the liquidator may, with the sanction of the liquidation committee (if there is one) and [as an expense of the liquidation], employ some person or persons to assist in the preparation of the accounts.

(2)   At the request of the person subject to the requirement, the liquidator may, with that sanction, authorise an allowance, payable [as an expense of the liquidation], towards expenses to be incurred by that person in employing others to assist him in preparing the accounts.

(3)   Any such request shall be accompanied by an estimate of the expenses involved; and the liquidator shall only authorise the employment of a named person or a named firm, being in either case approved by him.

NOTES

    Paras (1), (2): words in square brackets substituted by the Insolvency (Amendment) Rules 2008, SI 2008/737, rr 3, 7(1), (5), as from 6 April 2008, subject to transitional provisions as noted to r 4.218 at **[10.486]**.

[10.285]
4.42   Further disclosure (NO CVL APPLICATION)

(1)   The official receiver may at any time require the [nominated persons], or any one or more of them, to submit (in writing) further information amplifying, modifying or explaining any matter contained in the statement of affairs, or in accounts submitted in pursuance of the Act or the Rules.

(2)   The information shall, if the official receiver so directs, be verified by [a statement of truth], and (whether or not so verified) delivered to him within 21 days of the requirement under paragraph (1), or such longer period as he may allow.

(3)   . . .

NOTES

    Paras (1), (2): words in square brackets substituted by the Insolvency (Amendment) Rules 2010, SI 2010/686, r 2, Sch 1, para 170(1)–(3), as from 6 April 2010, subject to transitional provisions in Sch 4, para 2 thereto, as noted to r 1.31 at **[10.34]**.

    Para (3): revoked by SI 2010/686, r 2, Sch 1, para 170(1), (4), as from 6 April 2010, subject to transitional provisions in Sch 4, para 1 thereto, as noted to r 1.5 at **[10.7]**.

CHAPTER 7
INFORMATION TO CREDITORS AND CONTRIBUTORIES

[10.286]
4.43   Reports by official receiver (NO CVL APPLICATION)

[(1)]   The official receiver shall, at least once after the making of the winding-up order, send a report to creditors and contributories with respect to the proceedings in the winding up, and the state of the company's affairs.

[(1A)   The official receiver shall also include in the report under paragraph (1)—
   (a)   to the best of his knowledge and belief—
       (i)   an estimate of the value of the prescribed part (whether or not he proposes to make an application to the court under section 176A(5) or section 176A(3) applies);
       (ii)   an estimate of the value of the company's net property; and
   (b)   whether, and if so, why, he proposes to make an application to court under section 176A(5).

(1B)   Nothing in this Rule is to be taken as requiring any such estimate to include any information, the disclosure of which could seriously prejudice the commercial interests of the company. If such information is excluded from the calculation the estimate shall be accompanied by a statement to that effect.]

[(2)   . . .]

NOTES
   Para (1): numbered as such by the Insolvency (Amendment) Rules 1987, SI 1987/1919, r 3(1), Schedule, Pt 1, para 47, as from 11 January 1988.
   Paras (1A), (1B): inserted by the Insolvency (Amendment) Rules 2003, SI 2003/1730, r 7, Sch 1, Pt 4, para 15, as from 15 September 2003 (for transitional provisions and savings see the note preceding r 2.1 at **[10.60]**).
   Para (2): added by SI 1987/1919, r 3(1), Schedule, Pt 1, para 47, as from 11 January 1988; revoked by the Insolvency (Amendment) Rules 2010, SI 2010/686, r 2, Sch 1, para 171, as from 6 April 2010, subject to transitional provisions in Sch 4, para 2 thereto, as noted to r 1.31 at **[10.34]**.

[10.287]
4.44   Meaning of "creditors"

Any reference in this Chapter to creditors is to creditors of the company who are known to the official receiver or (as the case may be) the liquidator   . . .

NOTES
   Words omitted revoked by the Insolvency (Amendment) Rules 2010, SI 2010/686, r 2, Sch 1, para 172, as from 6 April 2010, subject to transitional provisions in Sch 4, para 1 thereto, as noted to r 1.5 at **[10.7]**.

[10.288]
4.45   Report where statement of affairs lodged (NO CVL APPLICATION)

(1)   Where a statement of affairs has been submitted   . . . , the official receiver shall send out to creditors and contributories a report containing a summary of the statement [(if he thinks fit, as amplified, modified or explained by virtue of Rule 4.42)] and such observations (if any) as he thinks fit to make with respect to it, or to the affairs of the company in general.

(2)   The official receiver need not comply with paragraph (1) if he has previously reported to creditors and contributories with respect to the company's affairs (so far as known to him) and he is of opinion that there are no additional matters which ought to be brought to their attention.

NOTES
   Para (1): words omitted revoked by the Insolvency (Amendment) Rules 2010, SI 2010/686, r 2, Sch 1, para 173, as from 6 April 2010, subject to transitional provisions in Sch 4, para 2 thereto, as noted to r 1.31 at **[10.34]**; words in square brackets inserted by the Insolvency (Amendment) Rules 1987, SI 1987/1919, r 3(1), Schedule, Pt 1, para 48, as from 11 January 1988.

[10.289]
4.46   Statement of affairs dispensed with (NO CVL APPLICATION)

(1)   This Rule applies where, in the company's case, release from the obligation to submit a statement of affairs has been granted by the official receiver or the court.

(2)   As soon as may be after the release has been granted, the official receiver shall send to creditors and contributories a report containing a summary of the company's affairs (so far as within his knowledge), and his observations (if any) with respect to it, or to the affairs of the company in general.

(3)   The official receiver need not comply with paragraph (2) if he has previously reported to creditors and contributories with respect to the company's affairs (so far as known to him) and he is of opinion that there are no additional matters which ought to be brought to their attention.

[10.290]
4.47   General rule as to reporting (NO CVL APPLICATION)

(1)   The court may, on the official receiver's application, relieve him of any duty imposed on him by this Chapter, or authorise him to carry out the duty in a way other than there required.

(2)   In considering whether to act under this Rule, the court shall have regard to the cost of carrying out the duty, to the amount of the assets available, and to the extent of the interest of creditors or contributories, or any particular class of them.

[10.291]
4.48   Winding up stayed (NO CVL APPLICATION)

(1)   If proceedings in the winding up are stayed by order of the court, any duty of the official receiver to send reports under the preceding Rules in this Chapter ceases.

(2)   Where the court grants a stay, it may include in its order such requirements on the company as it thinks [just] with a view to bringing the stay to the notice of creditors and contributories.

NOTES

Para (2): word in square brackets substituted by the Insolvency (Amendment) Rules 2010, SI 2010/686, r 2, Sch 1, para 1, as from 6 April 2010, subject to transitional provisions in Sch 4, para 2 thereto, as noted to r 1.31 at **[10.34]**.

[10.292]
4.49–CVL   Information to creditors and contributories

[(1)]   The liquidator shall, within 28 days of a meeting held under section 95 or 98, send to creditors and contributories of the company—
   (a)   a copy or summary of the statement of affairs, and
   (b)   a report of the proceedings at the meeting.

[(2)   The report under paragraph (1) shall also include—
   (a)   to the best of the liquidator's knowledge and belief—
      (i)   an estimate of the value of the prescribed part (whether or not he proposes to make an application to court under section 176A(5) or section 176A(3) applies); and
      (ii)   an estimate of the value of the company's net property; and
   (b)   whether, and if so, why, the liquidator proposes to make an application to court under section 176A(5).

(3)   Nothing in this Rule is to be taken as requiring any such estimate to include any information, the disclosure of which could seriously prejudice the commercial interests of the company. If such information is excluded from the calculation the estimate shall be accompanied by a statement to that effect.]

NOTES

Para (1) numbered as such, and paras (2), (3) added, by the Insolvency (Amendment) Rules 2003, SI 2003/1730, r 7, Sch 1, Pt 4, para 16, as from 15 September 2003 (for transitional provisions and savings see the note preceding r 2.1 at **[10.60]**).

[10.293]
[4.49A   Further information where liquidation follows administration

Where under section 140 the court appoints as the company's liquidator a person who was formerly its administrator [or a person is appointed as liquidator upon the registration of a notice under paragraph 83(3) of Schedule B1 to the Act] and that person becomes aware of creditors not formerly known to him in his capacity as administrator, he shall send to those creditors a copy of any statement or report sent by him to creditors under [Rule 2.33], so noted as to indicate that it is being sent under this Rule.]

NOTES

Inserted by the Insolvency (Amendment) Rules 1987, SI 1987/1919, r 3(1), Schedule, Pt 1, para 49, as from 11 January 1988.
Words in first pair of square brackets inserted, and words in second pair of square brackets substituted, by the Insolvency (Amendment) Rules 2003, SI 2003/1730, r 7, Sch 1, Pt 4, para 17, as from 15 September 2003 (for transitional provisions and savings see the note preceding r 2.1 at **[10.60]**).

[10.294]
[4.49B   Reports to creditors and members—winding up by the court
(NO CVL APPLICATION)

(1)   "Progress report" means a report which includes—
   (a)   details of the court where the proceedings are and the relevant court reference number;
   (b)   full details of the company's name, address of registered office and registered number;
   (c)   full details of the liquidator's name and address and date of appointment, including any changes in office-holder;
   (d)   details of the basis fixed for the remuneration of the liquidator under Rule 4.127 (or if not fixed at the date of the report, the steps taken during the period of the report to fix it);
   (e)   if the basis of remuneration has been fixed, a statement of—

(i)   the remuneration charged by the liquidator during the period of the report (subject to paragraph (3)), and

(ii)   where the report is the first to be made after the basis has been fixed, the remuneration charged by the liquidator during the periods covered by the previous reports (subject to paragraph (3)), together with a description of the things done by the liquidator during those periods in respect of which the remuneration was charged, irrespective in either case of whether payment was made in respect of that remuneration during that period;

(f)   a statement of the expenses incurred by the liquidator during the period of the report, irrespective of whether payment was made in respect of them during that period;

(g)   details of progress during the period of the report, including a receipts and payments account (as detailed in paragraph (2));

(h)   details of any assets that remain to be realised;

(j)   a statement of the creditors' right to request information under Rule 4.49E and their right to challenge the liquidator's remuneration and expenses under Rule 4.131; and

(k)   any other relevant information for the creditors.

(2)   A receipts and payments account must be in the form of an abstract showing receipts and payments during the period of the report and, where the liquidator has ceased to act, must also include a statement as to the amount paid to unsecured creditors by virtue of the application of section 176A.

(3)   Where the basis for the remuneration is a set amount under Rule 4.127(2)(c), it may be shown as that amount without any apportionment to the period of the report.

(4)   The progress report must, except where paragraph (5) or (6) applies, cover the period of 1 year commencing on the date on which the liquidator is appointed and every subsequent period of 1 year.

(5)   The period to be covered by a progress report ends on the date when a liquidator ceases to act, and the period to be covered by each subsequent progress report is each successive period of 1 year beginning immediately after that date (subject to the further application of this paragraph when another liquidator ceases to act).

(6)   A progress report is not required for any period which ends after the liquidator has sent a draft report to creditors under Rule 4.49D.

(7)   The liquidator must send a copy of the progress report within 2 months of the end of the period covered by the report, to the registrar of companies, to the members of the company and to the creditors.

(8)   The court may, on the liquidator's application, extend the period of 2 months mentioned in paragraph (7), or make such other order in respect of the content of the report as it thinks just.

(9)   This Rule does not apply where the liquidator is the official receiver.]

NOTES

Commencement: 6 April 2010.

Inserted, together with rr 4.49B–4.49G, by the Insolvency (Amendment) Rules 2010, SI 2010/686, r 2, Sch 1, para 174, subject to transitional provisions in Sch 4, para 1 thereto, as noted to r 1.5 at **[10.7]**.

[10.295]

[4.49C   CVL Progress reports—voluntary winding up

(1)   This Rule applies for the purposes of sections 92A and 104A.

(2)   The prescribed period for which the liquidator must produce a progress report, except when the liquidator ceases to act (in which case paragraph (3) applies) and subject to paragraph (4), is the period of 1 year commencing on the date on which the liquidator is appointed and every subsequent period of 1 year.

(3)   When a liquidator ceases to act, and subject to paragraph (4)—

(a)   the prescribed period for which the liquidator must produce a progress report ends on the date of that liquidator's ceasing to act, and

(b)   the prescribed period for which the new liquidator (if any) must produce a progress report is the period of 1 year commencing immediately after that date and every subsequent period of 1 year (subject to the further application of this paragraph when that new liquidator ceases to act).

(4)   A progress report is not required for any period which ends after the liquidator has sent a draft report to creditors under Rule 4.49D (final report to creditors).

(5)   The prescribed matters to which a progress report must relate are those set out in Rule 4.49B(1)(b) to (j), (2) and (3); and for that purpose in a members' voluntary winding up—

(a)   the reference in Rule 4.49B(1)(d) to Rule 4.127 is to be read as a reference to Rule 4.148A,

(b)   the reference in Rule 4.49B(1)(j) to—

(i)   the creditors' right to request information is to be read as a reference to the members' right to request information,

(ii)   Rule 4.131 is to be read as a reference to Rule 4.148C, and

(c)   the reference in Rule 4.49B(3) to Rule 4.127(2)(c) is to be read as a reference to Rule 4.148A(2)(c).

(6)   The prescribed person (in addition to members and creditors) to whom the liquidator must send a copy of a progress report is the registrar of companies.

(7)   The prescribed period commencing with the end of the period prescribed in sub-paragraph (a) or (b) of paragraph (3) within which the liquidator must send a copy of a progress report to members, creditors and the registrar of companies is 2 months.]

NOTES
Commencement: 6 April 2010.
Inserted as noted to r 4.49B at **[10.294]**.

[10.296]
[4.49D   Final report to creditors

(1)   The liquidator must, at least 8 weeks before holding a final meeting in accordance with section 106 or 146, send to each creditor known to the liquidator a draft of the report which the liquidator intends to lay before the meeting under Rule 4.125 or 4.126.

(2)   The draft report must—
  (a)   contain such matters and be in such terms as would comply with Rule 4.125 or 4.126, as the case may be, if the report were to be laid before a meeting as soon as reasonably practicable after the draft had been sent to creditors, and
  (b)   be accompanied by a statement of the creditors' right to request information under Rule 4.49E and their right to challenge the liquidator's remuneration and expenses under Rule 4.131.

(3)   The liquidator may not send a draft report to creditors under this Rule before giving notice under Rule 4.186 of intention to declare a final dividend or that no dividend or further dividend will be declared.

(4)   If any creditor has applied to the court under Rule 4.131 and given a copy of the application to the liquidator, the final meeting may not be held until the application (including any appeal) has been disposed of and the liquidator has complied with any order of the court.

(5)   This Rule does not apply where the liquidator is the official receiver.]

NOTES
Commencement: 6 April 2010.
Inserted as noted to r 4.49B at **[10.294]**.

[10.297]
[4.49E   Creditors' and members' request for further information

(1)   If—
  (a)   within the period mentioned in paragraph (2)—
    (i)   a secured creditor, or
    (ii)   an unsecured creditor with the concurrence of at least 5% in value of the unsecured creditors (including the creditor in question), or
    (iii)   members of the company in a members' voluntary winding up with at least 5% of the total voting rights of all the members having the right to vote at general meetings of the company, or
  (b)   with the permission of the court upon an application made within the period mentioned in paragraph (2)—
    (i)   any unsecured creditor, or
    (ii)   any member of the company in a members' voluntary winding up,
makes a request in writing to the liquidator for further information about remuneration or expenses set out in a progress report in accordance with Rule 4.49B(1)(e) or (f) (including by virtue of Rule 4.49C(5)) or in a draft report under Rule 4.49D, the liquidator must, within 14 days of receipt of the request, comply with paragraph (3) except to the extent that the request is in respect of matter in a draft report under Rule 4.49D or a progress report required by Rule 4.108 which (in either case) was previously included in a progress report not required by Rule 4.108.

(2)   The period referred to in paragraph (1)(a) and (b) is—
  (a)   7 business days of receipt (by the last of them in the case of an application by more than one member) of the progress report where it is required by Rule 4.108, and
  (b)   21 days of receipt (by the last of them in the case of an application by more than one member) of the report or draft report in any other case.

(3)   The liquidator complies with this paragraph by either—
  (a)   providing all of the information asked for, or
  (b)   so far as the liquidator considers that—
    (i)   the time or cost of preparation of the information would be excessive, or
    (ii)   disclosure of the information would be prejudicial to the conduct of the liquidation or might reasonably be expected to lead to violence against any person, or

        (iii)   the liquidator is subject to an obligation of confidentiality in respect of the information,

      giving reasons for not providing all of the information.

(4)   Any creditor, and any member of the company in a members' voluntary winding up, who need not be the same as the creditors or members who asked for the information, may apply to the court within 21 days of—

    (a)   the giving by the liquidator of reasons for not providing all of the information asked for, or

    (b)   the expiry of the 14 days provided for in paragraph (1),

and the court may make such order as it thinks just.

(5)   Without prejudice to the generality of paragraph (4), the order of the court under that paragraph may extend the period of 8 weeks or, as the case may be, 4 weeks provided for in Rule 4.131(1B) or 4.148C(2) by such further period as the court thinks just.

(6)   This Rule does not apply where the liquidator is the official receiver.]

NOTES
Commencement: 6 April 2010.
Inserted as noted to r 4.49B at **[10.294]**.

[10.298]
[4.49F   Arrangements under s 110 (acceptance of shares, etc, as consideration for sale of company property)

(1)   Where there has been an arrangement under section 110 and a distribution to members has taken place pursuant to subsection (2) or (4) of that section, the liquidator must comply with paragraph (2) in respect of any account or report which the liquidator is required to prepare pursuant to any of the following—

    (a)   section 92A (progress report to company at year's end);
    (b)   section 94 (final meeting prior to dissolution—members' voluntary winding up);
    (c)   section 104A (progress report to company and creditors at year's end);
    (d)   section 106 (final meeting prior to dissolution—creditors' voluntary winding up);
    (e)   Rule 4.49B (reports to creditors and members—winding up by the court);
    (f)   Rule 4.49D (final report to creditors);
    (g)   Rule 4.108 (creditors' meeting to receive liquidator's resignation);
    (h)   Rule 4.126 (final meeting—creditors' voluntary liquidation);
    (j)   Rule 4.142 (company meeting to receive liquidator's resignation).

(2)   The liquidator must—

    (a)   in any account or summary of receipts and payments which is required to be included in the account or report, state the estimated value of—
        (i)   the property transferred to the transferee;
        (ii)   the property received from the transferee; and
        (iii)   the property distributed to members pursuant to section 110(2) or (4),
        during the period to which the account or report relates, and
    (b)   as a note to the account or summary of receipts and payments, provide details of the basis of the valuation.]

NOTES
Commencement: 6 April 2010.
Inserted as noted to r 4.49B at **[10.294]**.

[10.299]
[4.49G   Other distributions to members in specie

(1)   In a members' voluntary winding up, where there has been a distribution of property to members in its existing form other than pursuant to an arrangement under section 110, the liquidator must comply with paragraph (2) in respect of any account or report which the liquidator is required to prepare pursuant to any of the following—

    (a)   section 92A (progress report to company at year's end);
    (b)   section 94 (final meeting prior to dissolution);
    (c)   Rule 4.142 (company meeting to receive liquidator's resignation)

(2)   The liquidator must—

    (a)   in any account or summary of receipts and payments which is required to be included in the account or report, state the estimated value of the property distributed amongst the members of the company during the period to which the account or report relates, and
    (b)   as a note to the account or summary of receipts and payments, provide details of the basis of the valuation.]

NOTES
Commencement: 6 April 2010.
Inserted as noted to r 4.49B at **[10.294]**.

CHAPTER 8
MEETINGS OF CREDITORS AND CONTRIBUTORIES

Section A: Rules of General Application

[10.300]
4.50   First meetings (NO CVL APPLICATION)
(1)   If under section 136(5) the official receiver decides to summon meetings of the company's creditors and contributories for the purpose of nominating a person to be liquidator in place of himself, he shall fix a venue for each meeting, in neither case more than 4 months from the date of the winding-up order.

(2)   When for each meeting a venue has been fixed, notice of the meetings shall be given . . . —

(a)   in the case of the creditors' meeting, to every creditor who is known to the official receiver . . . ; and

(b)   in the case of the contributories' meeting, to every person appearing (by the company's books or otherwise) to be a contributory of the company.

[(3)   Notice for each meeting must be given at least 14 days before the date fixed for it.]

[(4)   The notice to creditors must state that proofs and (if applicable) proxies must be lodged at a specified place not later than 12.00 hours on the business day before the date fixed for the meeting in order for creditors to be entitled to vote at the meeting; and the same applies in respect of contributories and their proxies.]

[(5)   Notice of the meetings shall be gazetted and may be advertised in such other manner as the official receiver thinks fit.]

[(5A)   In addition to the standard contents, a notice under paragraph (5) must state—
(a)   that a meeting of the creditors or contributories is to take place;
(b)   the venue fixed for the meeting; and
(c)   the time and date by which, and place at which, creditors must lodge proxies and hitherto unlodged proofs in order to be entitled to vote at the meeting.]

(6)   Where the official receiver receives a request by creditors under section 136(5)(c) for meetings of creditors and contributories to be summoned, and it appears to him that the request is properly made in accordance with the Act, he shall—
(a)   withdraw any notices previously given by him under section 136(5)(b) (that he has decided not to summon such meetings),
(b)   fix the venue of each meeting for not more than 3 months from his receipt of the creditors' request, and
(c)   act in accordance with paragraphs (2) to (5) above, as if he had decided under section 136 to summon the meetings.

(7)   Meetings summoned by the official receiver under this Rule are known respectively as "the first meeting of creditors" and "the first meeting of contributories", and jointly as "the first meetings in the liquidation".

(8)   Where the company is a [an authorised deposit-taker or a former authorised deposit-taker], additional notices are required by Rule 4.72.

NOTES
Para (2): words omitted revoked by the Insolvency (Amendment) Rules 2010, SI 2010/686, r 2, Sch 1, para 175(1), (2), as from 6 April 2010, subject to transitional provisions in Sch 4, para 1 thereto, as noted to r 1.5 at **[10.7]**.
Paras (3), (4): substituted by SI 2010/686, r 2, Sch 1, para 175(1), (3), (4), as from 6 April 2010, subject to transitional provisions in Sch 4, para 1 thereto, as noted to r 1.5 at **[10.7]**.
Para (5): substituted by the Insolvency (Amendment) Rules 2009, SI 2009/642, rr 4, 24, as from 6 April 2009, subject to transitional provisions in r 3 thereof, as noted to r 1.4 of these Rules at **[10.6]**.
Para (5A): inserted by SI 2010/686, r 2, Sch 1, para 175(1), (5), as from 6 April 2010, subject to transitional provisions in Sch 4, para 1 thereto, as noted to r 1.5 at **[10.7]**.
Para (8): words in square brackets substituted by the Financial Services and Markets Act 2000 (Consequential Amendments and Repeals) Order 2001, SI 2001/3649, art 377(1), (5), as from 1 December 2001.
See Form 4.21 at **[10.673]**.

[10.301]
4.51–CVL   First meeting of creditors
(1)   This Rule applies in the case of a meeting of creditors summoned by the liquidator under section 95 (where, in what starts as a members' voluntary winding up, he forms the opinion that the company will be unable to pay its debts) or a meeting under section 98 (first meeting of creditors in a creditors' voluntary winding up).

(2)   The notice summoning the meeting shall [state the name of the company and the registered number of the company, and] specify a venue for the meeting and the time (not earlier than 12.00 hours on the business day before the day fixed for the meeting) by which, and the place at which, creditors must lodge [any [proofs and] proxies necessary to entitle them to vote at the meeting].

Part 10   Miscellaneous other SIs

(3)   Where the company is [an authorised deposit-taker or a former authorised deposit-taker], additional notices are required by Rule 4.72.

NOTES

Para (2): words in first pair of square brackets inserted by the Insolvency (Amendment) Rules 2005, SI 2005/527, r 22, as from 1 April 2005; words in second (outer) pair of square brackets substituted by the Insolvency (Amendment) Rules 1987, SI 1987/1919, r 3(1), Schedule, Pt 1, para 51(1), as from 11 January 1988; words in third (inner) pair of square brackets inserted by the Insolvency (Amendment) Rules 2010, SI 2010/686, r 2, Sch 1, para 176, as from 6 April 2010, subject to transitional provisions in Sch 4, para 1 thereto, as noted to r 1.5 at **[10.7]**.

Para (3): words in square brackets substituted by the Financial Services and Markets Act 2000 (Consequential Amendments and Repeals) Order 2001, SI 2001/3649, art 377(1), (6), as from 1 December 2001.

[10.302]
4.52   Business at first meetings in the liquidation (NO CVL APPLICATION)

(1)   At the first meeting of creditors, no resolutions shall be taken other than the following—

  (a)   a resolution to appoint a named insolvency practitioner to be liquidator, or two or more insolvency practitioners as joint liquidators;

  (b)   a resolution to establish a liquidation committee;

  (c)   (unless it has been resolved to establish a liquidation committee) a resolution specifying the terms on which the liquidator is to be remunerated, or to defer consideration of that matter;

  (d)   (if, and only if, two or more persons are appointed to act jointly as liquidator) a resolution specifying whether acts are to be done by both or all of them, or by only one;

  (e)   (where the meeting has been requisitioned under section 136), a resolution authorising payment . . . as an expense of the liquidation, of the cost of summoning and holding the meeting and any meeting of contributories so requisitioned and held;

  (f)   a resolution to adjourn the meeting . . . ;

  (g)   any other resolution which the chairman thinks it right to allow for special reasons.

(2)   The same applies as regards the first meeting of contributories, but that meeting shall not pass any resolution to the effect of paragraph (1)(c) or (e).

[(3A)   The meeting may be adjourned, either in accordance with a resolution under paragraph (1)(f) or if the chairman thinks fit, but for not more than 14 days from the date on which it was fixed to commence, subject to any direction of the court.

(3B)   If there are subsequently further adjournments, the final adjournment must not be to a day later than 14 days after the date on which the meeting was originally held, subject to any direction of the court.

(3C)   Where a meeting is adjourned under this Rule, proofs and proxies may be used if lodged at any time up to 12.00 hours on the business day immediately before the adjourned meeting.]

NOTES

Para (1): words omitted from sub-para (e) revoked by the Insolvency (Amendment) Rules 2008, SI 2008/737, rr 3, 7(6), as from 6 April 2008, subject to transitional provisions as noted to r 4.218 at **[10.486]**; words omitted from sub-para (f) revoked by the Insolvency (Amendment) Rules 2010, SI 2010/686, r 2, Sch 1, para 177(1), (2), as from 6 April 2010, subject to transitional provisions in Sch 4, para 1 thereto, as noted to r 1.5 at **[10.7]**.

Paras (3A)–(3C): substituted (for the original para (3)) by SI 2010/686, r 2, Sch 1, para 177(1), (3), as from 6 April 2010, subject to transitional provisions in Sch 4, para 1 thereto, as noted to r 1.5 at **[10.7]**.

[10.303]
4.53–CVL   Business at meeting under s 95 or 98

Rule 4.52(1), except sub-paragraph (e), applies to a creditors' meeting under section 95 or 98.

[10.304]
[4.53A–CVL   Effect of adjournment of company meeting

Where a company meeting at which a resolution for voluntary winding up is to be proposed is adjourned, any resolution passed at a meeting under section 98 held before the holding of the adjourned company meeting only has effect on and from the passing by the company of a resolution for winding up.]

NOTES

Inserted, together with r 4.53B CVL, by the Insolvency (Amendment) Rules 1987, SI 1987/1919, r 3(1), Schedule, Pt 1, para 52, as from 11 January 1988.

[10.305]
[4.53B–CVL   Report by director, etc

(1)   At any meeting held under section 98 where the statement of affairs laid before the meeting does not state the company's affairs as at the date of the meeting, the directors of the company shall cause to be made to the meeting, either by the director presiding at the meeting or by another person

with knowledge of the relevant matters, a report (written or oral) on any material transactions relating to the company occurring between the date of the making of the statement of affairs and that of the meeting.

(2) Any such report shall be recorded in the minutes of the meeting kept under Rule 4.71.]

NOTES

Inserted as noted to r 4.53A CVL at **[10.304]**.

[10.306]
[4.53C–CVL Additional contents of notices gazetted or advertised under s 95

In addition to the statement of duty required under subsection (2A) of section 95, and to the standard contents, notices under paragraphs (c) and (d) of that subsection must state—
    (a)   the purpose of the meeting; and
    (b)   the venue fixed for the meeting.]

NOTES

Commencement: 6 April 2010.
Inserted, together with r 4.53D, by the Insolvency (Amendment) Rules 2010, SI 2010/686, r 2, Sch 1, para 178, subject to transitional provisions in Sch 4, para 1 thereto, as noted to r 1.5 at **[10.7]**.

[10.307]
[4.53D–CVL Additional contents of notices gazetted or advertised under s 98

In addition to the content required by section 98(2), and the standard contents, notices under section 98(1A) (c) or (d) must state—
    (a)   the purpose of the meeting; and
    (b)   the venue fixed for the meeting.]

NOTES

Commencement: 6 April 2010.
Inserted as noted to r 4.53C at **[10.306]**.

[10.308]
4.54 General power to call meetings

(1) The official receiver or the liquidator may at any time summon and conduct meetings of creditors or of contributories for the purpose of ascertaining their wishes in all matters relating to the liquidation; and in relation to any meeting summoned under the Act or the Rules, the person summoning it is referred to as "the convener".

(2) When (in either case) a venue for the meeting has been fixed, notice of it shall be given by the convener—
    (a)   in the case of a creditors' meeting, to every creditor who is known to him . . . ; and
    (b)   in the case of a meeting of contributories, to every person appearing (by the company's books or otherwise) to be a contributory of the company.

(3) Notice of the meeting shall be given at least [14] days before the date fixed for it, and shall specify the purpose of the meeting.

[(4) The notice must state that proofs and (if applicable) proxies must be lodged at a specified place not later than 12.00 hours on the business day before the date fixed for the meeting in order for creditors to be entitled to vote at the meeting; and the same applies in respect of contributories and their proxies. (NO CVL APPLICATION)]

[(5–CVL) The notice must state that proofs and (if applicable) proxies must be lodged at a specified place not later than 12.00 hours on the business day before the date fixed for the meeting in order for creditors to be entitled to vote at the meeting.]

[(6) Notice of the meeting—
    (a)   shall be gazetted; and
    (b)   may be advertised in such other manner as the convenor thinks fit.]

[(7) In addition to the standard contents, the notice under paragraph (6) must state—
    (a)   who summoned the meeting;
    (b)   if the meeting was summoned by a creditor, the fact that it was so summoned and the section of the Act under which it was summoned;
    (c)   the purpose for which the meeting was summoned;
    (d)   the venue fixed for the meeting; and
    (e)   the time and date by which, and place at which, creditors must lodge proxies and hitherto unlodged proofs in order to be entitled to vote at the meeting.]

NOTES

Para (2): words omitted revoked by the Insolvency (Amendment) Rules 2010, SI 2010/686, r 2, Sch 1, para 179(1), (2), as from 6 April 2010, subject to transitional provisions in Sch 4, para 1 thereto, as noted to r 1.5 at **[10.7]**.
Para (3): number in square brackets substituted by SI 2010/686, r 2, Sch 1, para 179(1), (3), as from 6 April 2010, subject to transitional provisions in Sch 4, para 1 thereto, as noted to r 1.5 at **[10.7]**.

Part 10 Miscellaneous other SIs

Paras (4), (5): substituted by SI 2010/686, r 2, Sch 1, para 179(1), (4), (5), as from 6 April 2010, subject to transitional provisions in Sch 4, para 1 thereto, as noted to r 1.5 at **[10.7]**.

Para (6): substituted by the Insolvency (Amendment) Rules 2009, SI 2009/642, rr 4, 25, as from 6 April 2009, subject to transitional provisions in r 3 thereof, as noted to r 1.4 of these Rules at **[10.6]**.

Para (7): added by SI 2010/686, r 2, Sch 1, para 179(1), (6), as from 6 April 2010, subject to transitional provisions in Sch 4, para 1 thereto, as noted to r 1.5 at **[10.7]**.

Disapplication: para (6)(a) is disapplied where the notice is of a meeting to be held under the Insolvency Act 1986, s 93 or s 105 (annual meetings in voluntary liquidations): see SI 2010/686, r 6(2).

See Forms 4.22, 4.23 at **[10.673]**.

[10.309]
4.55   The chairman at meetings (NO CVL APPLICATION)

(1)   This Rule applies both to a meeting of creditors and to a meeting of contributories.

(2)   Where the convener of the meeting is the official receiver, he, or a person nominated by him, shall be chairman.

A nomination under this paragraph shall be in writing, unless the nominee is another official receiver or a deputy official receiver.

(3)   Where the convener is other than the official receiver, the chairman shall be he, or a person nominated in writing by him.

A person nominated under this paragraph must be either—

   (a)   one who is qualified to act as an insolvency practitioner in relation to the company, or

   (b)   an employee of the liquidator or his firm who is experienced in insolvency matters.

[10.310]
4.56–CVL   The chairman at meetings

(1)   This Rule applies both to a meeting of creditors (except a meeting under [section 95 or 98]) and to a meeting of contributories.

(2)   The liquidator, or a person nominated by him in writing to act, shall be chairman of the meeting.

A person nominated under this paragraph must be either—

   (a)   one who is qualified to act as an insolvency practitioner in relation to the company, or

   (b)   an employee of the liquidator or his firm who is experienced in insolvency matters.

NOTES

Para (1): words in square brackets substituted by the Insolvency (Amendment) Rules 1987, SI 1987/1919, r 3(1), Schedule, Pt 1, para 53, as from 11 January 1988.

[10.311]
4.57   Requisitioned meetings

(1)   Any request by creditors to the liquidator (whether or not the official receiver) for a meeting of creditors or contributories or meetings of both, to be summoned shall be accompanied by—

   (a)   a list of the creditors concurring with the request and the amount of their respective claims in the winding up;

   (b)   from each creditor concurring, written confirmation of his concurrence; and

   (c)   a statement of the purpose of the proposed meeting.

Sub-paragraphs (a) and (b) do not apply if the requisitioning creditor's debt is alone sufficient, without the concurrence of other creditors.

(2)   The liquidator shall, if he considers the request to be properly made in accordance with the Act, fix a venue for the meeting, not more than [28] days from his receipt of the request.

(3)   The liquidator shall give [14] days' notice of the meeting, and the venue for it, to creditors.

(4)   Paragraphs (1) to (3) above apply to the requisitioning by contributories of contributories' meetings, with the following modifications—

   (a)   for the reference in paragraph (1)(a) to the creditors' respective claims substitute the contributories' respective values (being the amounts for which they may vote at any meeting); and

   (b)   the persons to be given notice under paragraph (3) are those appearing (by the company's books or otherwise) to be contributories of the company.

(NO CVL APPLICATION)

NOTES

Numbers in square brackets substituted by the Insolvency (Amendment) Rules 2010, SI 2010/686, r 2, Sch 1, para 180, as from 6 April 2010, subject to transitional provisions in Sch 4, para 1 thereto, as noted to r 1.5 at **[10.7]**.

See Forms 4.21, 4.24 at **[10.673]**.

[10.312]
4.58   Attendance at meetings of company's personnel

(1)   This Rule applies to meetings of creditors and to meetings of contributories.

(2)   Whenever a meeting is summoned, the convener shall give at least [14] days' notice to such of the company's personnel as he thinks should be told of, or be present at, the meeting.

"The company's personnel" means the persons referred to in paragraphs (a) to (d) of section 235(3) (present and past officers, employees, etc).

(3)   If the meeting is adjourned, the chairman of the meeting shall, unless for any reason he thinks it unnecessary or impracticable, give notice of the adjournment to such (if any) of the company's personnel as he considers appropriate, being persons who were not themselves present at the meeting.

(4)   The convener may, if he thinks fit, give notice to any one or more of the company's personnel that he is, or they are, required to be present at the meeting, or to be in attendance.

(5)   In the case of any meeting, any one or more of the company's personnel, and any other persons, may be admitted, but—
(a)   they must have given reasonable notice of their wish to be present, and
(b)   it is a matter for the chairman's discretion whether they are to be admitted or not, and his decision is final as to what (if any) intervention may be made by any of them.

(6)   If it is desired to put questions to any one of the company's personnel who is not present, the chairman may adjourn the meeting with a view to obtaining his attendance.

(7)   Where one of the company's personnel is present at a meeting, only such questions may be put to him as the chairman may in his discretion allow.

NOTES

Para (2): number in square brackets substituted by the Insolvency (Amendment) Rules 2010, SI 2010/686, r 2, Sch 1, para 181, as from 6 April 2010, subject to transitional provisions in Sch 4, para 1 thereto, as noted to r 1.5 at **[10.7]**.

[10.313]
4.59   Notice of meetings by advertisement only

(1)   In the case of any meeting of creditors or contributories to be held under the Act or the Rules, the court may order that notice of the meeting be given by   . . .   advertisement, and not by individual notice to the persons concerned.

(2)   In considering whether to act under this Rule, the court shall have regard to the cost of   . . . advertisement, to the amount of the assets available, and to the extent of the interest of creditors or of contributories, or any particular class of either of them.

[(3)   In addition to the standard contents, the advertisement must state—
(a)   the venue fixed for the meeting;
(b)   that proofs and (if applicable) proxies must be lodged at a specified place not later than 12.00 hours on the business day before the date fixed for the meeting;
(c)   the date of the court order or the date of the resolution to wind up.]

NOTES

Paras (1), (2): word omitted revoked by the Insolvency (Amendment) Rules 2010, SI 2010/686, r 2, Sch 1, para 182(1), (2), as from 6 April 2010, subject to transitional provisions in Sch 4, para 1 thereto, as noted to r 1.5 at **[10.7]**.

Para (3): added by SI 2010/686, r 2, Sch 1, para 182(1), (3), as from 6 April 2010, subject to transitional provisions in Sch 4, para 1 thereto, as noted to r 1.5 at **[10.7]**.

[10.314]
4.60   Venue

(1)   In fixing the venue for a meeting of creditors or contributories, the convener shall have regard to the convenience of the persons (other than whoever is to be chairman) who are invited to attend.

(2)   Meetings shall in all cases be summoned for commencement between the hours of 10.00 and 16.00 hours on a business day, unless the court otherwise directs.

(3)   With every notice summoning a meeting of creditors or contributories there shall be sent out forms of proxy.

NOTES

See Forms 8.4, 8.5 at **[10.673]**.

[10.315]
4.61   Expenses of summoning meetings

(1)   Subject as follows, the expenses of summoning and holding a meeting of creditors or contributories at the instance of any person other than the official receiver or the liquidator shall be paid by that person, who shall deposit with the liquidator security for their payment.

(2)   The sum to be deposited shall be such as the official receiver or liquidator (as the case may be) determines to be appropriate; and neither shall act without the deposit having been made.

(3)   Where a meeting of creditors is so summoned, it may vote that the expenses of summoning and holding it, and of summoning and holding any meeting of contributories requisitioned at the same time, shall be payable   . . .   as an expense of the liquidation.

(4)   Where a meeting of contributories is summoned on the requisition of contributories, it may vote that the expenses of summoning and holding it shall be payable [as an expense of the liquidation], but subject to the right of creditors to be paid in full, with interest.

(5)   To the extent that any deposit made under this Rule is not required for the payment of expenses of summoning and holding a meeting, it shall be repaid to the person who made it.

NOTES

Para (3): words omitted revoked by the Insolvency (Amendment) Rules 2008, SI 2008/737, rr 3, 7(7), as from 6 April 2008, subject to transitional provisions as noted to r 4.218 at **[10.486]**.

Para (4): words in square brackets substituted by SI 2008/737, rr 3, 7(1), as from 6 April 2008, subject to transitional provisions as noted to r 4.218 at **[10.486]**.

[10.316]
4.62–CVL   Expenses of meeting under s 98

(1)   Payment may be made   . . . , either before or after the commencement of the winding up, of any reasonable and necessary expenses incurred in connection with the summoning, advertisement and holding of a creditors' meeting under section 98.

Any such payment is an expense of the liquidation.

(2)   Where such payments are made before the commencement of the winding up, the director presiding at the creditors' meeting shall inform the meeting of their amount and the identity of the persons to whom they were made.

(3)   The liquidator appointed under section 100 may make such a payment (subject to the next paragraph); but if there is a liquidation committee, he must give the committee at least [5 business] days' notice of his intention to make the payment.

(4)   Such a payment shall not be made by the liquidator to himself, or to any associate of his, otherwise than with the approval of the liquidation committee, the creditors, or the court.

(5)   This Rule is without prejudice to the powers of the court under Rule 4.219 (voluntary winding up superseded by winding up by the court).

NOTES

Para (1): words omitted revoked by the Insolvency (Amendment) Rules 2008, SI 2008/737, rr 3, 7(8), as from 6 April 2008, subject to transitional provisions as noted to r 4.218 at **[10.486]**.

Para (3): words in square brackets substituted by the Insolvency (Amendment) Rules 2010, SI 2010/686, r 2, Sch 1, para 183, as from 6 April 2010, subject to transitional provisions in Sch 4, para 1 thereto, as noted to r 1.5 at **[10.7]**.

[10.317]
4.63   Resolutions

(1)   [Subject as follows] at a meeting of creditors or contributories, a resolution is passed when a majority (in value) of those present and voting, in person or by proxy, have voted in favour of the resolution.

The value of contributories is determined by reference to the number of votes conferred on each contributory by the company's articles.

(2)   In the case of resolution for the appointment of a liquidator—
  (a)   [. . .] if on any vote there are two nominees for appointment, the person who obtains the most support is appointed;
  (b)   if there are three or more nominees, and one of them has a clear majority over both or all the others together, that one is appointed; and
  (c)   in any other case, the chairman of the meeting shall continue to take votes (disregarding at each vote any nominee who has withdrawn and, if no nominee has withdrawn, the nominee who obtained the least support last time), until a clear majority is obtained for any one nominee.
[(2A)   . . .]

(3)   The chairman may at any time put to the meeting a resolution for the joint appointment of any two or more nominees.

(4)   Where a resolution is proposed which affects a person in respect of his remuneration or conduct as liquidator, or as proposed or former liquidator, the vote of that person, and of any partner or employee of his, shall not be reckoned in the majority required for passing the resolution.

This paragraph applies with respect to a vote given by a person [(whether personally or on his behalf by a proxy-holder)] either as creditor or contributory or as [proxy-holder] for a creditor or a contributory (but subject to Rule 8.6 in Part 8 of the Rules).

NOTES

Para (1): words in square brackets inserted by the Insolvency (Amendment) Rules 1987, SI 1987/1919, r 3(1), Schedule, Pt 1, para 54(1), (2), as from 11 January 1988.

Para (2): words omitted originally inserted by SI 1987/1919, r 3(1), Schedule, Pt 1, para 54(1), (2), and revoked by the Insolvency (Amendment) Rules 2010, SI 2010/686, r 2, Sch 1, para 184(1), (2), as from 6 April 2010, subject to transitional provisions in Sch 4, para 1 thereto, as noted to r 1.5 at **[10.7]**.

Para (2A): inserted by SI 1987/1919, r 3(1), Schedule, Pt 1, para 54(3); revoked by SI 2010/686, r 2, Sch 1, para 184(1), (3), as from 6 April 2010, subject to transitional provisions in Sch 4, para 1 thereto, as noted to r 1.5 at **[10.7]**.

Para (4): words in first pair of brackets inserted, and words in second pair of square brackets substituted, by SI 1987/1919, r 3(1), Schedule, Pt 1, para 54(4), as from 11 January 1988.

[10.318]
[4.63A   Resolutions by correspondence

(1)   The liquidator may seek to obtain the passing of a resolution by creditors or contributories without holding a meeting by giving notice of the resolution to every creditor or contributory who is entitled to be notified of a meeting at which the resolution could be passed.

(2)   In order to be counted, votes must be received by the liquidator in writing by 12.00 hours on the closing date specified in the notice, and in the case of votes cast by creditors must be accompanied by a proof of debt as required by Rule 4.67(1)(a) unless it has already been lodged under that Rule.

(3)   If any vote cast by a creditor is received without a proof of debt, or the liquidator decides that the creditor or contributory is not entitled to vote according to Rules 4.67 to 4.70, then that creditor's or contributory's vote must be disregarded.

(4)   The closing date shall be set at the discretion of the liquidator; but in any event it must not be set less than 14 days from the giving of notice provided for in paragraph (1).

(5)   For the resolution to be passed, the liquidator must receive at least one valid vote by the closing date specified in the notice.

(6)   If no valid vote is received by the closing date specified, the liquidator must call a meeting of creditors or contributories at which the resolution could be passed.

(7)   Creditors whose debts amount to at least 10% of the total debts of the company may, within 5 business days from the giving of notice provided for in paragraph (1), require the liquidator to summon a meeting of creditors to consider the resolution.

(8)   Contributories representing at least 10% of the total voting rights of all contributories having the right to vote at a meeting of contributories may, within 5 business days from the giving of notice provided for in paragraph (1), require the liquidator to summon a meeting of contributories to consider the resolution.

(9)   A reference in these Rules to a resolution passed at a creditors' or contributories' meeting includes a reference to a resolution passed under this Rule.

(10)   This Rule does not apply in respect of any resolution which the Act requires to be passed at a meeting.]

NOTES
Commencement: 6 April 2010.
Inserted by the Insolvency (Amendment) Rules 2010, SI 2010/686, r 2, Sch 1, para 185, subject to transitional provisions in Sch 4, para 1 thereto, as noted to r 1.5 at **[10.7]**.

[10.319]
4.64   Chairman of meeting as proxy-holder

Where the chairman at a meeting of creditors or contributories holds a proxy which requires him to vote for a particular resolution, and no other person proposes that resolution—
  (a)   he shall himself propose it, unless he considers that there is good reason for not doing so, and
  (b)   if he does not propose it, he shall [as soon as reasonably practicable] after the meeting notify his principal of the reason why not.

NOTES
Words in square brackets substituted by the Insolvency (Amendment) Rules 2009, SI 2009/642, r 5, as from 6 April 2009, subject to transitional provisions in r 3 thereof, as noted to r 1.4 of these Rules at **[10.6]**.

[10.320]
4.65   Suspension and adjournment

(1)   This Rule applies to meetings of creditors and to meetings of contributories.

(2)   Once only in the course of any meeting, the chairman may, in his discretion and without an adjournment, declare the meeting suspended for any period up to one hour.

(3)   The chairman at any meeting may in his discretion, and shall if the meeting so resolves, adjourn it to such time and place as seems to him to be appropriate in the circumstances.

  This is subject to Rule 4.113(3) [or, as the case may be, 4.114–CVL(3)] in case where the liquidator or his nominee is chairman, and a resolution has been proposed for the liquidator's removal.

(4)   If within a period of 30 minutes from the time appointed for the commencement of a meeting a quorum is not present, then [the chairman may, at his discretion, adjourn the meeting to such time and place as he may appoint].

(5)   An adjournment under this Rule shall not be for a period of more than [14] days; and Rule 4.60(1) and (2) applies.

[(6A)   If within 30 minutes from the time appointed for commencement of a meeting there is no person present to act as chairman, the meeting stands adjourned to the same time and place in the following week or, if that is not a business day, to the business day immediately following.

(6B)   Paragraph (6A) applies to further adjournments of a final meeting.

(6C)   In the case of any other meeting, further adjournment must be to the same time and place in the following week or, if either—

   (a)   that is not a business day, or
   (b)   whether or not it is a business day, it is later than 14 days after the date on which the meeting in question was originally held,

to the same time and place on the business day immediately preceding which is not later than 14 days after the date on which the meeting in question was originally held.]

(7)   Where a meeting is adjourned under this Rule, proofs and proxies may be used if lodged at any time up to midday on the business day immediately before the adjourned meeting.

NOTES

Para (3): words in square brackets inserted by the Insolvency (Amendment) Rules 1987, SI 1987/1919, r 3(1), Schedule, Pt 1, para 55(1), as from 11 January 1988.

Para (4): words in square brackets substituted by SI 1987/1919, r 3(1), Schedule, Pt 1, para 55(2), as from 11 January 1988.

Para (5): number in square brackets substituted by the Insolvency (Amendment) Rules 2010, SI 2010/686, r 2, Sch 1, para 186(1), (2), as from 6 April 2010, subject to transitional provisions in Sch 4, para 1 thereto, as noted to r 1.5 at **[10.7]**.

Paras (6A)–(6C): (for the original para (6)) by SI 2010/686, r 2, Sch 1, para 186(1), (3), as from 6 April 2010, subject to transitional provisions in Sch 4, para 1 thereto, as noted to r 1.5 at **[10.7]**.

4.66   *(Revoked by the Insolvency (Amendment) Rules 1987, SI 1987/1919, r 3(1), Schedule, Pt 1, para 56, as from 11 January 1988.)*

[10.321]
4.67   Entitlement to vote (creditors)

(1)   Subject as follows in this Rule and the next, at a meeting of creditors a person is entitled to vote as a creditor only if—

   (a)   there has been duly lodged (. . . by the time and date stated in the notice of the meeting) a proof of the debt—
      [(i)   claimed to be due to him from the company, or
      (ii)   in relation to a member State liquidator, is claimed to be due to creditors in proceedings in relation to which he holds office], and the claim has been admitted under Rule 4.70 for the purpose of entitlement to vote, and
   (b)   there has been lodged, by the time and date stated in the notice of the meeting, any proxy requisite for that entitlement.

(2)   The court may, in exceptional circumstances, by order declare the creditors, or any class of them, entitled to vote at creditors' meetings, without being required to prove their debts.

Where a creditor is so entitled, the court may, on the application of the liquidator, make such consequential orders as it thinks [just] (as for example an order treating a creditor as having proved his debt for the purpose of permitting payment of dividend).

(3)   A creditor shall not vote in respect of a debt for an unliquidated amount, or any debt whose value is not ascertained, except where the chairman agrees to put upon the debt an estimated minimum value for the purpose of entitlement to vote and admits his proof for that purpose.

(4)   A secured creditor is entitled to vote only in respect of the balance (if any) of his debt after deducting the value of his security as estimated by him.

(5)   A creditor shall not vote in respect of a debt on, or secured by, a current bill of exchange or promissory note, unless he is willing—

   (a)   to treat the liability to him on the bill or note of every person who is liable on it antecedently to the company, and against whom a bankruptcy order has not been made (or, in the case of a company, which has not gone into liquidation), as a security in his hands, and
   (b)   to estimate the value of the security and (for the purpose of entitlement to vote, but not for dividend) to deduct it from his proof.

[(6)   No vote shall be cast by virtue of a debt more than once on any resolution put to the meeting.

(7)   Where—

   (a)   a creditor is entitled to vote under this Rule and Rule 4.70 (admission of proof),
   (b)   has lodged his claim in one or more sets of other proceedings, and
   (c)   votes (either in person or by proxy) on a resolution put to the meeting, only the creditor's vote shall be counted.

(8)   Where—

   (a)   a creditor has lodged his claim in more than one set of other proceedings, and
   (b)   more than one member State liquidator seeks to vote by virtue of that claim,

the entitlement to vote by virtue of that claim is exercisable by the member State liquidator in main proceedings, whether or not the creditor has lodged his claim in the main proceedings.

(9)   For the purposes of paragraphs (7) and (8), "other proceedings" means main proceedings, secondary proceedings or territorial proceedings in another member State.]

NOTES

Para (1): words omitted revoked by the Insolvency (Amendment) Rules 2010, SI 2010/686, r 2, Sch 1, para 187, as from 6 April 2010, subject to transitional provisions in Sch 4, para 1 thereto, as noted to r 1.5 at **[10.7]**; words in square brackets substituted by the Insolvency (Amendment) Rules 2002, SI 2002/1307, rr 3, 6(6)(a), as from 31 May 2002, with savings in relation to anything done under, or for the purposes of, this provision before that date.

Para (2): word in square brackets substituted by SI 2010/686, r 2, Sch 1, para 1, as from 6 April 2010, subject to transitional provisions in Sch 4, para 2 thereto, as noted to r 1.31 at **[10.34]**.

Paras (6)–(9): added by SI 2002/1307, rr 3, 6(6)(b), as from 31 May 2002, with savings in relation to anything done under, or for the purposes of, this provision before that date.

[10.322]
4.68   . . .   Chairman's discretion to allow vote

At a creditors' meeting [in a creditors' voluntary winding up or a winding up by the court], the chairman may allow a creditor to vote, notwithstanding that he has failed to comply with Rule 4.67(1)(a), if satisfied that the failure was due to circumstances beyond the creditor's control.

NOTES

Rule heading: reference "CVL" (omitted) revoked by the Insolvency (Amendment) Rules 2010, SI 2010/686, r 2, Sch 1, para 188(1), (2), as from 6 April 2010, subject to transitional provisions in Sch 4, para 1 thereto, as noted to r 1.5 at **[10.7]**.

Words in square brackets inserted SI 2010/686, r 2, Sch 1, para 188(1), (3), as from 6 April 2010, subject to transitional provisions in Sch 4, para 1 thereto, as noted to r 1.5 at **[10.7]**.

[10.323]
4.69   Entitlement to vote (contributories)

At a meeting of contributories, voting rights are as at a general meeting of the company, subject to any provision in the articles affecting entitlement to vote, either generally or at a time when the company is in liquidation.

[10.324]
4.70   Admission and rejection of proof (creditors' meeting)

(1)   At any creditors' meeting the chairman has power to admit or reject a creditor's proof for the purpose of his entitlement to vote; and the power is exercisable with respect to the whole or any part of the proof.

(2)   The chairman's decision under this Rule, or in respect of any matter arising under Rule 4.67, is subject to appeal to the court by any creditor or contributory.

(3)   If the chairman is in doubt whether a proof should be admitted or rejected, he shall mark it as objected to and allow the creditor to vote, subject to his vote being subsequently declared invalid if the objection to the proof is sustained.

(4)   If on an appeal the chairman's decision is reversed or varied, or a creditor's vote is declared invalid, the court may order that another meeting be summoned, or make such other order as it thinks just.

[(4A)   An application to the court by way of appeal under this Rule against a decision of the chairman must be made not later than 21 days after the date of the meeting.]

(5)   Neither the official receiver, nor any person nominated by him to be chairman, is personally liable for costs incurred by any person in respect of an application under this Rule; and the chairman (if other than the official receiver or a person so nominated) is not so liable unless the court makes an order to that effect.

(NO CVL APPLICATION)

(6–CVL)   The liquidator or his nominee as chairman is not personally liable for costs incurred by any person in respect of an application under this Rule, unless the court makes an order to that effect.

NOTES

Para (4A): inserted by the Insolvency (Amendment) Rules 2010, SI 2010/686, r 2, Sch 1, para 189, as from 6 April 2010, subject to transitional provisions in Sch 4, para 1 thereto, as noted to r 1.5 at **[10.7]**.

[10.325]
4.71   Record of proceedings

(1)   At any meeting, the chairman shall cause minutes of the proceedings to be kept. The minutes shall be [authenticated] by him, and retained as part of the records of the liquidation.

(2)   The chairman shall also cause to be made up and kept a list of all the creditors or, as the case may be, contributories who attended the meeting.

(3)   The minutes of the meeting shall include a record of every resolution passed [and if a liquidation committee has been established, the names and addresses of those elected to be members of the committee].

(4)   . . .

NOTES

Para (1): word in square brackets substituted by the Insolvency (Amendment) Rules 2010, SI 2010/686, r 2, Sch 1, para 1, as from 6 April 2010, subject to transitional provisions in Sch 4, para 2 thereto, as noted to r 1.31 at **[10.34]**.

Para (3): words in square brackets inserted by SI 2010/686, r 2, Sch 1, para 190(1), (2) (as amended by the Insolvency (Amendment) (No 2) Rules 2010, SI 2010/734, rr 2, 4), as from 6 April 2010, subject to transitional provisions in Sch 4, para 1 thereto, as noted to r 1.5 at **[10.7]**.

Para (4): revoked by SI 2010/686, r 2, Sch 1, para 190(1), (3), as from 6 April 2010, subject to transitional provisions in Sch 4, para 1 thereto, as noted to r 1.5 at **[10.7]**.

Section B: Winding Up of Recognised Banks, etc

[10.326]
4.72   Additional provisions as regards certain meetings

(1)   This Rule applies where a company goes, or proposes to go, into liquidation and it is [an authorised deposit-taker or a former authorised deposit-taker].

(2)   Notice of any meeting of the company at which it is intended to propose a resolution for its winding up shall be given by the directors to the [Financial Services Authority] and [to the scheme manager established under section 212(1) of the Financial Services and Markets Act 2000].

(3)   Notice to the [Authority] and [the scheme manager] shall be the same as given to members of the company.

(4)   Where a creditors' meeting is summoned by the liquidator under section 95 or, in a creditors' voluntary winding up, is summoned under section 98, the same notice of the meeting must be given to the [Authority] and [the scheme manager] as is given to creditors under Rule 4.51–CVL.

(5)   Where the company is being wound up by the court, notice of the first meetings of creditors and contributories shall be given to the [Authority] and [the scheme manager] by the official receiver.

(6)   Where in the winding up (whether voluntary or by the court) a meeting of creditors or contributories or of the company is summoned for the purpose of—

   (a)   receiving the liquidator's resignation, or
   (b)   removing the liquidator, or
   (c)   appointing a new liquidator,

the person summoning the meeting and giving notice of it shall also give notice to the [Authority] and [the scheme manager].

(7)   [The scheme manager] is entitled to be represented at any meeting of which it is required by this Rule to be given notice; and Schedule 1 to the Rules has effect with respect to the voting rights of [the scheme manager] at such a meeting.

NOTES

Words "Financial Services Authority" and "Authority" in square brackets substituted by the Bank of England Act 1998 (Consequential Amendments of Subordinate Legislation) Order 1998, SI 1998/1129, art 2, Sch 1, para 4(1), (5), as from 1 June 1998; other words in square brackets substituted by the Financial Services and Markets Act 2000 (Consequential Amendments and Repeals) Order 2001, SI 2001/3649, arts 377(1), (7), 378(2), as from 1 December 2001.

CHAPTER 9
PROOF OF DEBTS IN A LIQUIDATION

Section A: Procedure for Proving

[10.327]
4.73   Meaning of "prove"

(1)   Where a company is being wound up by the court, a person claiming to be a creditor of the company and wishing to recover his debt in whole or in part must (subject to any order of the court under Rule 4.67(2)) submit his claim in writing to the liquidator. (NO CVL APPLICATION)

(2–CVL)   In a voluntary winding up (whether members' or creditors') the liquidator may require a person claiming to be a creditor of the company and wishing to recover his debt in whole or in part, to submit the claim in writing to him.

(3)   A creditor who claims (whether or not in writing) is referred to as "proving" for his debt; and a document by which he seeks to establish his claim is his "proof".

(4)   Subject to the next paragraph, a proof must be in the form known as "proof of debt" (whether the form prescribed by the Rules, or a substantially similar form), which shall be made out by or under the directions of the creditor, and [authenticated] by him or a person authorised in that behalf. (NO CVL APPLICATION)

(5)   Where a debt is due to a Minister of the Crown or a Government Department, the proof need not be in that form, provided that there are shown all such particulars of the debt as are required in the form used by other creditors, and as are relevant in the circumstances. (NO CVL APPLICATION)

(6–CVL)   The creditor's proof may be in any form.

(7)   . . .

[(8)   Where a winding up is immediately preceded by an administration, a creditor proving in the administration shall be deemed to have proved in the winding up.]

NOTES

Para (4): word in square brackets substituted by the Insolvency (Amendment) Rules 2010, SI 2010/686, r 2, Sch 1, para 1, as from 6 April 2010, subject to transitional provisions in Sch 4, para 2 thereto, as noted to r 1.31 at **[10.34]**.

Para (7): revoked by SI 2010/686, r 2, Sch 1, para 191, as from 6 April 2010, subject to transitional provisions in Sch 4, para 1 thereto, as noted to r 1.5 at **[10.7]**.

Para (8): added by the Insolvency (Amendment) Rules 2003, SI 2003/1730, r 7, Sch 1, Pt 4, para 18, as from 15 September 2003 (for transitional provisions and savings see the note preceding r 2.1 at **[10.60]**).

See Form 4.25 at **[10.673]**.

[10.328]
[4.74   Supply of Forms (NO CVL APPLICATION)
A form of proof shall be sent to any creditor of the company by the liquidator where the creditor so requests.]

NOTES

Substituted by the Insolvency (Amendment) Rules 2004, SI 2004/584, r 9, as from 1 April 2004.

[10.329]
4.75   Contents of proof (NO CVL APPLICATION)
[(1)   Subject to Rule 4.73(5), the following matters shall be stated in a creditor's proof of debt—
    (a)   the creditor's name and address, and, if a company, its company registration number;
    (b)   the total amount of his claim (including any Value Added Tax) as at the date on which the company went into liquidation [(or, if the liquidation was immediately preceded by an administration, the date on which the company entered administration), less any payments made after that date in respect of the claim and any deduction under Rule 4.89];
    (c)   whether or not that amount includes outstanding uncapitalised interest;
    (d)   particulars of how and when the debt was incurred by the company;
    (e)   particulars of any security held, the date when it was given and the value which the creditor puts upon it;
    (f)   details of any reservation of title in respect of goods to which the debt refers; and
    (g)   the name, and address and authority of the person [authenticating] the proof (if other than the creditor himself).]

(2)   There shall be specified in the proof any documents by reference to which the debt can be substantiated; but (subject as follows) it is not essential that such documents be attached to the proof or submitted with it.

(3)   The liquidator, or the chairman or convener of any meeting, may call for any document or other evidence to be produced to him, where he thinks it necessary for the purpose of substantiating the whole or any part of the claim made in the proof.

NOTES

Para (1): substituted by the Insolvency (Amendment) Rules 2004, SI 2004/584, r 10, as from 1 April 2004; words in square brackets in sub-para (b) added (subject to transitional provisions as noted to r 1.5 at **[10.7]**) and word in square brackets in sub-para (g) substituted (subject to transitional provisions as noted to r 1.31 at **[10.34]**) by the Insolvency (Amendment) Rules 2010, SI 2010/686, r 2, Sch 1, paras 1, 192, as from 6 April 2010.

Social Security Pensions Act 1975, Sch 3: repealed by the Pension Schemes Act 1993, s 188(1), Sch 5, Pt I, and replaced by Sch 4 to that Act.

[10.330]
4.76–CVL   Particulars of creditor's claim
The liquidator, or the convener or chairman of any meeting, may, if he thinks it necessary for the purpose of clarifying or substantiating the whole or any part of a creditor's claim made in his proof, call for details of any matter specified in paragraphs (a) to (h) of Rule 4.75(1), or for the production to him of such documentary or other evidence as he may require.

4.77   (*Revoked by the Insolvency (Amendment) Rules 2010, SI 2010/686, r 5, as from 6 April 2010, subject to transitional provisions in Sch 4, para 2 thereto, as noted to r 1.31 at* **[10.34]**.)

[10.331]
4.78   Cost of proving

(1)   Subject as follows, every creditor bears the cost of proving his own debt, including such as may be incurred in providing documents or evidence under Rule 4.75(3) or 4.76–CVL.

(2)   Costs incurred by the liquidator in estimating the quantum of a debt under Rule 4.86 (debts not bearing a certain value) are payable . . . as an expense of the liquidation.

(3)   Paragraphs (1) and (2) apply unless the court otherwise orders.

NOTES

Para (2): words omitted revoked by the Insolvency (Amendment) Rules 2008, SI 2008/737, rr 3, 7(9), as from 6 April 2008, subject to transitional provisions as noted to r 4.218 at **[10.486]**.

[10.332]
4.79   Liquidator to allow inspection of proofs

The liquidator shall, so long as proofs lodged with him are in his hands, allow them to be inspected, at all reasonable times on any business day, by any of the following persons—
- (a)   any creditor who has submitted his proof of debt (unless his proof has been wholly rejected for purposes of dividend or otherwise);
- (b)   any contributory of the company;
- (c)   any person acting on behalf of either of the above.

[10.333]
4.80   Transmission of proofs to liquidator (NO CVL APPLICATION)

(1)   Where a liquidator is appointed, the official receiver shall [as soon as reasonably practicable] transmit to him all the proofs which he has so far received, together with an itemised list of them.

(2)   The liquidator shall [authenticate] the list by way of receipt for the proofs, and return it to the official receiver.

(3)   From then on, all proofs of debt shall be sent to the liquidator, and retained by him.

NOTES

Para (1): words in square brackets substituted by the Insolvency (Amendment) Rules 2009, SI 2009/642, r 5, as from 6 April 2009, subject to transitional provisions in r 3 thereof, as noted to r 1.4 of these Rules at **[10.6]**.

Para (2): word in square brackets substituted by the Insolvency (Amendment) Rules 2010, SI 2010/686, r 2, Sch 1, para 1, as from 6 April 2010, subject to transitional provisions in Sch 4, para 2 thereto, as noted to r 1.31 at **[10.34]**.

[10.334]
4.81   New liquidator appointed

(1)   If a new liquidator is appointed in place of another, the former liquidator [must as soon as reasonably practicable] transmit to him all proofs which he has received, together with an itemised list of them.

(2)   The new liquidator shall [authenticate] the list by way of receipt for the proofs, and return it to his predecessor.

[(3)   From then on, all proofs of debt must be sent to and retained by the new liquidator.]

NOTES

Para (1): words in square brackets substituted by the Insolvency (Amendment) Rules 2010, SI 2010/686, r 2, Sch 1, para 193(1), (2), as from 6 April 2010, subject to transitional provisions in Sch 4, para 1 thereto, as noted to r 1.5 at **[10.7]**.

Para (2): word in square brackets substituted by SI 2010/686, r 2, Sch 1, para 1, as from 6 April 2010, subject to transitional provisions in Sch 4, para 2 thereto, as noted to r 1.31 at **[10.34]**.

Para (3): added by SI 2010/686, r 2, Sch 1, para 193(1), (3), as from 6 April 2010, subject to transitional provisions in Sch 4, para 1 thereto, as noted to r 1.5 at **[10.7]**.

[10.335]
4.82   Admission and rejection of proofs for dividend

(1)   A proof may be admitted for dividend either for the whole amount claimed by the creditor, or for part of that amount.

(2)   If the liquidator rejects a proof in whole or in part, he shall prepare a written statement of his reasons for doing so, and send it [as soon as reasonably practicable] to the creditor.

NOTES

Para (2): words in square brackets substituted by the Insolvency (Amendment) Rules 2009, SI 2009/642, r 5, as from 6 April 2009, subject to transitional provisions in r 3 thereof, as noted to r 1.4 of these Rules at **[10.6]**.

[10.336]
4.83   Appeal against decision on proof

(1)   If a creditor is dissatisfied with the liquidator's decision with respect to his proof (including any decision on the question of preference), he may apply to the court for the decision to be reversed or varied.

The application must be made within 21 days of his receiving the statement sent under Rule 4.82(2).

(2)   A contributory or any other creditor may, if dissatisfied with the liquidator's decision admitting or rejecting the whole or any part of a proof, make such an application within 21 days of becoming aware of the liquidator's decision.

(3)   Where an application is made to the court under this Rule, the court shall fix a venue for the application to be heard, notice of which shall be sent by the applicant to the creditor who lodged the proof in question (if it is not himself) and to the liquidator.

(4)   The liquidator shall, on receipt of the notice, file in court the relevant proof, together (if appropriate) with a copy of the statement sent under Rule 4.82(2).

[(4A)   Where the application is made by a contributory, the court must not disallow the proof (in whole or in part) unless the contributory shows that there is (or would be but for the amount claimed in the proof), or that it is likely that there will be (or would be but for the amount claimed in the proof), a surplus of assets to which the company would be entitled.]

(5)   After the application has been heard and determined, the proof shall, unless it has been wholly disallowed, be returned by the court to the liquidator.

(6)   The official receiver is not personally liable for costs incurred by any person in respect of an application under this Rule; and the liquidator (if other than the official receiver) is not so liable unless the court makes an order to that effect.

NOTES

Para (4A): inserted by the Insolvency (Amendment) Rules 2010, SI 2010/686, r 2, Sch 1, para 194, as from 6 April 2010, subject to transitional provisions in Sch 4, para 1 thereto, as noted to r 1.5 at **[10.7]**.

[10.337]
4.84   Withdrawal or variation of proof

A creditor's proof may at any time, by agreement between himself and the liquidator, be withdrawn or varied as to the amount claimed.

[10.338]
4.85   Expunging of proof by the court

(1)   The court may expunge a proof or reduce the amount claimed—
   (a)   on the liquidator's application, where he thinks that the proof has been improperly admitted, or ought to be reduced; or
   (b)   on the application of a creditor, if the liquidator declines to interfere in the matter.

(2)   Where application is made to the court under this Rule, the court shall fix a venue for the application to be heard, notice of which shall be sent by the applicant—
   (a)   in the case of an application by the liquidator, to the creditor who made the proof, and
   (b)   in the case of an application by a creditor, to the liquidator and to the creditor who made the proof (if not himself).

Section B: Quantification of Claim

[10.339]
4.86   Estimate of quantum

(1)   The liquidator shall estimate the value of any debt which, by reason of its being subject to any contingency or for any other reason, does not bear a certain value; and he may revise any estimate previously made, if he thinks fit by reference to any change of circumstances or to information becoming available to him.
   He shall inform the creditor as to his estimate and any revision of it.

(2)   Where the value of a debt is estimated under this Rule, or by the court under section 168(3) or (5), the amount provable in the winding up in the case of that debt is that of the estimate for the time being.

[10.340]
4.87   Negotiable instruments, etc

Unless the liquidator allows, a proof in respect of money owed on a bill of exchange, promissory note, cheque or other negotiable instrument or security cannot be admitted unless there is produced the instrument or security itself or a copy of it, certified by the creditor or his authorised representative to be a true copy.

[10.341]
4.88   Secured creditors

(1)   If a secured creditor realises his security, he may prove for the balance of his debt, after deducting the amount realised.

(2)   If a secured creditor voluntarily surrenders his security for the general benefit of creditors, he may prove for his whole debt, as if it were unsecured.

Part 10   Miscellaneous other SIs

[10.342]
4.89   Discounts

There shall in every case be deducted from the claim all trade and other discounts which would have been available to the company but for its liquidation, except any discount for immediate, early or cash settlement.

[10.343]
[4.90   Mutual credits and set-off

(1)   This Rule applies where, before the company goes into liquidation there have been mutual credits, mutual debts or other mutual dealings between the company and any creditor of the company proving or claiming to prove for a debt in the liquidation.

(2)   The reference in paragraph (1) to mutual credits, mutual debts or other mutual dealings does not include—

(a)   any debt arising out of an obligation incurred at a time when the creditor had notice that—
   (i)   a meeting of creditors had been summoned under section 98; or
   (ii)   a petition for the winding up of the company was pending;

(b)   any debt arising out of an obligation where—
   (i)   the liquidation was immediately preceded by an administration; and
   (ii)   at the time the obligation was incurred the creditor had notice that an application for an administration order was pending or a person had given notice of intention to appoint an administrator;

(c)   any debt arising out of an obligation incurred during an administration which immediately preceded the liquidation; or

(d)   any debt which has been acquired by a creditor by assignment or otherwise, pursuant to an agreement between the creditor and any other party where that agreement was entered into—
   (i)   after the company went into liquidation;
   (ii)   at a time when the creditor had notice that a meeting of creditors had been summoned under section 98;
   (iii)   at a time when the creditor had notice that a winding up petition was pending;
   (iv)   where the liquidation was immediately preceded by an administration, at a time when the creditor had notice that an application for an administration order was pending or a person had given notice of intention to appoint an administrator; or
   (v)   during an administration which immediately preceded the liquidation.

(3)   An account shall be taken of what is due from each party to the other in respect of the mutual dealings, and the sums due from one party shall be set off against the sums due from the other.

(4)   A sum shall be regarded as being due to or from the company for the purposes of paragraph (3) whether—

(a)   it is payable at present or in the future;
(b)   the obligation by virtue of which it is payable is certain or contingent; or
(c)   its amount is fixed or liquidated, or is capable of being ascertained by fixed rules or as a matter of opinion.

(5)   Rule 4.86 shall also apply for the purposes of this Rule to any obligation to or from the company which, by reason of its being subject to any contingency or for any other reason, does not bear a certain value.

(6)   Rules 4.91 to 4.93 shall apply for the purposes of this Rule in relation to any sums due to the company which—

(a)   are payable in a currency other than sterling;
(b)   are of a periodical nature; or
(c)   bear interest.

(7)   Rule 11.13 shall apply for the purposes of this Rule to any sum due to or from the company which is payable in the future.

(8)   Only the balance (if any) of the account owed to the creditor is provable in the liquidation. Alternatively the balance (if any) owed to the company shall be paid to the liquidator as part of the assets except where all or part of the balance results from a contingent or prospective debt owed by the creditor and in such a case the balance (or that part of it which results from the contingent or prospective debt) shall be paid if and when that debt becomes due and payable.

(9)   In this Rule "obligation" means an obligation however arising, whether by virtue of an agreement, rule of law or otherwise.]

NOTES

Substituted by the Insolvency (Amendment) Rules 2005, SI 2005/527, r 23, as from 1 April 2005, subject to transitional provisions as noted to r 2.67 at **[10.129]**.

[10.344]
4.91 Debt in foreign currency

(1) For the purpose of proving a debt incurred or payable in a currency other than sterling, the amount of the debt shall be converted into sterling at the official exchange rate prevailing on the date when the company went into liquidation [or, if the liquidation was immediately preceded by an administration, on the date that the company entered administration].

(2) "The official exchange rate" is the [middle exchange rate on the London Foreign Exchange Market at the close of business], as published for the date in question. In the absence of any such published rate, it is such rate as the court determines.

NOTES

Para (1): words in square brackets added by the Insolvency (Amendment) Rules 2005, SI 2005/527, r 24, as from 1 April 2005, subject to transitional provisions as noted to r 2.67 at **[10.129]**.

Para (2): words in square brackets substituted by the Insolvency (Amendment) Rules 2003, SI 2003/1730, r 7, Sch 1, Pt 4, para 20, as from 15 September 2003 (for transitional provisions and savings see the note preceding r 2.1 at **[10.60]**).

[10.345]
4.92 Payments of a periodical nature

(1) In the case of rent and other payments of a periodical nature, the creditor may prove for any amounts due and unpaid up to the date when the company went into liquidation [or, if the liquidation was immediately preceded by an administration, up to the date that the company entered administration].

(2) Where at that date any payment was accruing due, the creditor may prove for so much as would have fallen due at that date, if accruing from day to day.

NOTES

Para (1): words in square brackets added by the Insolvency (Amendment) Rules 2005, SI 2005/527, r 25, as from 1 April 2005, subject to transitional provisions as noted to r 2.67 at **[10.129]**.

[10.346]
4.93 Interest

[(A1) In this Rule, "the relevant date" means the date on which the company went into liquidation or, if the liquidation was immediately preceded by an administration, the date on which the company entered administration.]

(1) Where a debt proved in the liquidation bears interest, that interest is provable as part of the debt except in so far as it is payable in respect of any period after [the relevant date].

(2) In the following circumstances the creditor's claim may include interest on the debt for periods before [the relevant date], although not previously reserved or agreed.

(3) If the debt is due by virtue of a written instrument, and payable at a certain time, interest may be claimed for the period from that time to [the relevant date].

(4) If the debt is due otherwise, interest may only be claimed if, before [the relevant date], a demand for payment of the debt was made in writing by or on behalf of the creditor, and notice given that interest would be payable from the date of the demand to the date of payment.

(5) Interest under paragraph (4) may only be claimed for the period from the date of the demand to [the relevant date] [and for all the purposes of the Act and the Rules shall be chargeable at a rate not exceeding that mentioned in paragraph (6)].

[(6) The rate of interest to be claimed under paragraphs (3) and (4) is the rate specified in section 17 of the Judgments Act 1838 on [the relevant date].]

NOTES

Para (A1): inserted by the Insolvency (Amendment) Rules 2010, SI 2010/686, r 2, Sch 1, para 195(1), (2), as from 6 April 2010, subject to transitional provisions in Sch 4, para 1 thereto, as noted to r 1.5 at **[10.7]**.

Para (1)–(4): words in square brackets substituted by SI 2010/686, r 2, Sch 1, para 195(1)–(6), as from 6 April 2010, subject to transitional provisions in Sch 4, para 1 thereto, as noted to r 1.5 at **[10.7]**.

Para (5): words in first pair of square brackets substituted by SI 2010/686, r 2, Sch 1, para 195(1), (7), as from 6 April 2010, subject to transitional provisions in Sch 4, para 1 thereto, as noted to r 1.5 at **[10.7]**; words in second pair of square brackets added by the Insolvency (Amendment) Rules 1987, SI 1987/1919, r 3(1), Schedule, Pt 1, para 59(1), as from 11 January 1988.

Para (6): added by SI 1987/1919, r 3(1), Schedule, Pt 1, para 59(2), as from 11 January 1988; words in square brackets substituted by SI 2010/686, r 2, Sch 1, para 195(1), (8), as from 6 April 2010, subject to transitional provisions in Sch 4, para 1 thereto, as noted to r 1.5 at **[10.7]**.

[10.347]
4.94 Debt payable at future time

A creditor may prove for a debt of which payment was not yet due on the date when the company went into liquidation, [or, if the liquidation was immediately preceded by an administration, on the date that the company entered administration] but subject to Rule 11.13 in Part 11 of the Rules (adjustment of dividend where payment made before time).

NOTES

Words in square brackets added by the Insolvency (Amendment) Rules 2005, SI 2005/527, r 27, as from 1 April 2005, subject to transitional provisions as noted to r 2.67 at **[10.129]**.

CHAPTER 10
SECURED CREDITORS

[10.348]
4.95   Value of security

(1)   A secured creditor may, with the agreement of the liquidator or the [permission] of the court, at any time alter the value which he has, in his proof of debt, put upon his security.

(2)   However, if a secured creditor—
(a)   being the petitioner, has in the petition put a value on his security, or
(b)   has voted in respect of the unsecured balance of his debt,
he may re-value his security only with [permission] of the court. (NO CVL APPLICATION)

NOTES

Paras (1), (2): word in square brackets substituted by the Insolvency (Amendment) Rules 2010, SI 2010/686, r 2, Sch 1, para 1, as from 6 April 2010, subject to transitional provisions in Sch 4, para 2 thereto, as noted to r 1.31 at **[10.34]**.

[10.349]
4.96   Surrender for non-disclosure

(1)   If a secured creditor omits to disclose his security in his proof of debt, he shall surrender his security for the general benefit of creditors, unless the court, on application by him, relieves him [from] the effect of this Rule on the ground that the omission was inadvertent or the result of honest mistake.

(2)   If the court grants that relief, it may require or allow the creditor's proof of debt to be amended, on such terms as may be just.

[(3)   Nothing in this Rule or the following two Rules may affect the rights in rem of creditors or third parties protected under Article 5 of the EC Regulation (third parties' rights in rem).]

NOTES

Para (1): word in square brackets substituted by the Insolvency (Amendment) Rules 2010, SI 2010/686, r 2, Sch 1, para 196, as from 6 April 2010, subject to transitional provisions in Sch 4, para 1 thereto, as noted to r 1.5 at **[10.7]**.

Para (3): added by the Insolvency (Amendment) Rules 2002, SI 2002/1307, rr 3, 6(8), as from 31 May 2002, with savings in relation to anything done under, or for the purposes of, this provision before that date.

EC Regulation: ie, Council Regulation 1346/2000/EC on insolvency proceedings.

[10.350]
4.97   Redemption by liquidator

(1)   The liquidator may at any time give notice to a creditor whose debt is secured that he proposes, at the expiration of 28 days from the date of the notice, to redeem the security at the value put upon it in the creditor's proof.

(2)   The creditor then has 21 days (or such longer period as the liquidator may allow) in which, if he so wishes, to exercise his right to re-value his security (with the [permission] of the court, when Rule 4.95(2) applies).

If the creditor re-values his security, the liquidator may only redeem at the new value.

(3)   If the liquidator redeems the security, the cost of transferring it is payable [as an expense of the liquidation].

(4)   A secured creditor may at any time, by a notice in writing, call on the liquidator to elect whether he will or will not exercise his power to redeem the security at the value then placed on it; and the liquidator then has [3 months] in which to exercise the power or determine not to exercise it.

NOTES

Para (2): word in square brackets substituted by the Insolvency (Amendment) Rules 2010, SI 2010/686, r 2, Sch 1, para 1, as from 6 April 2010, subject to transitional provisions in Sch 4, para 2 thereto, as noted to r 1.31 at **[10.34]**.

Para (3): words in square brackets substituted by the Insolvency (Amendment) Rules 2008, SI 2008/737, rr 3, 7(1), as from 6 April 2008, subject to transitional provisions as noted to r 4.218 at **[10.486]**.

Para (4): words in square brackets substituted by SI 2010/686, r 2, Sch 1, para 197, as from 6 April 2010, subject to transitional provisions in Sch 4, para 1 thereto, as noted to r 1.5 at **[10.7]**.

[10.351]
4.98   Test of security's value

(1)   Subject as follows, the liquidator, if he is dissatisfied with the value which a secured creditor puts on his security (whether in his proof or by way of re-valuation under Rule 4.97), may require any property comprised in the security to be offered for sale.

(2)   The terms of sale shall be such as may be agreed, or as the court may direct; and if the sale is by auction, the liquidator on behalf of the company, and the creditor on his own behalf, may appear and bid.

[(3)   This Rule does not apply if the security has been revalued and the revaluation has been approved by the court.]

NOTES

Para (3): added by the Insolvency (Amendment) Rules 2010, SI 2010/686, r 2, Sch 1, para 198, as from 6 April 2010, subject to transitional provisions in Sch 4, para 1 thereto, as noted to r 1.5 at **[10.7]**.

[10.352]
4.99   Realisation of security by creditor

If a creditor who has valued his security subsequently realises it (whether or not at the instance of the liquidator)—

   (a)   the net amount realised shall be substituted for the value previously put by the creditor on the security, and

   (b)   that amount shall be treated in all respects as an amended valuation made by him.

CHAPTER 11
THE LIQUIDATOR

Section A: Appointment and Associated Formalities

[10.353]
4.100   Appointment by creditors or contributories (NO CVL APPLICATION)

(1)   This Rule applies where a person is appointed as liquidator either by a meeting of creditors or by a meeting of contributories.

(2)   The chairman of the meeting shall certify the appointment, but not unless and until the person appointed has provided him with a written statement to the effect that he is an insolvency practitioner, duly qualified under the Act to be the liquidator, and that he consents so to act.

[(3)   The liquidator's appointment, is effective from the date on which the appointment is certified, that date to be endorsed on the certificate.

(4)   The chairman of the meeting (if not himself the official receiver) shall send the certificate to the official receiver.

(5)   The official receiver shall in any case send the certificate to the liquidator   . . .]

NOTES

Paras (3), (4): substituted, together with para (5), by the Insolvency (Amendment) Rules 1987, SI 1987/1919, r 3(1), Schedule, Pt 1, para 60, as from 11 January 1988

Para (5): substituted as noted to para (3) above; words omitted revoked by the Insolvency (Amendment) Rules 2010, SI 2010/686, r 2, Sch 1, para 199, as from 6 April 2010, subject to transitional provisions in Sch 4, para 1 thereto, as noted to r 1.5 at **[10.7]**.

See Forms 4.27, 4.28 at **[10.673]**.

[10.354]
4.101–CVL   Appointment by creditors or by the company

(1)   This Rule applies where a person is appointed as liquidator either by a meeting of creditors or by a meeting of the company.

(2)   Subject as follows, the chairman of the meeting shall certify the appointment, but not unless and until the person appointed has provided him with a written statement to the effect that he is an insolvency practitioner, duly qualified under the Act to be the liquidator, and that he consents so to act; the liquidator's appointment [takes effect upon the passing of the resolution for that appointment].

(3)   The chairman shall send the certificate [as soon as reasonably practicable] to the liquidator, who shall keep it as part of the records of the liquidation.

(4)   Paragraphs (2) and (3) need not be complied with in the case of a liquidator appointed by a company meeting and replaced by another liquidator appointed on the same day by a creditors' meeting.

NOTES

Para (2): words in square brackets substituted by the Insolvency (Amendment) Rules 1987, SI 1987/1919, r 3(1), Schedule, Pt 1, para 61, as from 11 January 1988.

Para (3): words in square brackets substituted by the Insolvency (Amendment) Rules 2009, SI 2009/642, r 5, as from 6 April 2009, subject to transitional provisions in r 3 thereof, as noted to r 1.4 of these Rules at **[10.6]**.

Part 10   Miscellaneous other SIs

[10.355]
[4.101A–CVL   Power to fill vacancy in office of liquidator
Where a vacancy in the office of liquidator occurs in the manner mentioned in section 104 a meeting of creditors to fill the vacancy may be convened by any creditor or, if there were more liquidators than one, by the continuing liquidators.]

NOTES
　Inserted by the Insolvency (Amendment) Rules 1987, SI 1987/1919, r 3(1), Schedule, Pt 1, para 62, as from 11 January 1988.

[10.356]
[4.101B   Official receiver not to be appointed liquidator
The official receiver may not be appointed as liquidator by any meeting of creditors, contributories or the company.]

NOTES
　Commencement: 6 April 2010.
　Inserted by the Insolvency (Amendment) Rules 2010, SI 2010/686, r 2, Sch 1, para 200, subject to transitional provisions in Sch 4, para 1 thereto, as noted to r 1.5 at **[10.7]**.

[10.357]
4.102   Appointment by the court (NO CVL APPLICATION)
(1)   This Rule applies where the liquidator is appointed by the court under section 139(4) (different persons nominated by creditors and contributories) or section 140 (liquidation following administration or voluntary arrangement).

(2)   The court's order shall not issue unless and until the person appointed has filed in court a statement to the effect that he is an insolvency practitioner, duly qualified under the Act to be the liquidator, and that he consents so to act.

(3)   Thereafter, the court shall send 2 copies of the order to the official receiver. One of the copies shall be sealed, and this shall be sent to the person appointed as liquidator.

(4)   The liquidator's appointment takes effect from the date of the order.

[(4A)   . . .]

[(5)   Within 28 days from appointment, the liquidator shall   . . .   —
　(a)   give notice of it to all creditors and contributories of the company of whom the liquidator is aware; or
　(b)   advertise it in accordance with any directions given by the court.]

(6)   In his notice   . . .   under this Rule the liquidator shall—
　(a)   state whether he proposes to summon meetings of creditors and contributories for the purpose of establishing a liquidation committee, or proposes to summon only a meeting of creditors for that purpose, and
　(b)   if he does not propose to summon any such meeting, set out the powers of the creditors under the Act to require him to summon one.

NOTES
　Para (4A): inserted by the Insolvency (Amendment) Rules 2009, SI 2009/642, rr 4, 26(a), as from 6 April 2009, subject to transitional provisions in r 3 thereof, as noted to r 1.4 of these Rules at **[10.6]**; revoked by the Insolvency (Amendment) Rules 2010, SI 2010/686, r 2, Sch 1, para 201(1), (2), as from 6 April 2010, subject to transitional provisions in Sch 4, para 1 thereto, as noted to r 1.5 at **[10.7]**.
　Para (5) substituted by SI 2009/642, rr 4, 26(b), as from 6 April 2009, subject to transitional provisions in r 3 thereof, as noted to r 1.4 of these Rules at **[10.6]**; word omitted revoked by SI 2010/686, r 2, Sch 1, para 201(1), (3), as from 6 April 2010, subject to transitional provisions in Sch 4, para 1 thereto, as noted to r 1.5 at **[10.7]**.
　Para (6): words omitted revoked by SI 2009/642, rr 4, 26(c), as from 6 April 2009, subject to transitional provisions in r 3 thereof, as noted to r 1.4 of these Rules at **[10.6]**.
　See Forms 4.29, 4.30 at **[10.673]**.

[10.358]
4.103–CVL   Appointment by the court
(1)   This Rule applies where the liquidator is appointed by the court under section 100(3) or 108.

(2)   The court's order shall not issue unless and until the person appointed has filed in court a statement to the effect that he is an insolvency practitioner, duly qualified under the Act to be the liquidator, and that he consents so to act.

(3)   Thereafter, the court shall send a sealed copy of the order to the liquidator, whose appointment takes effect from the date of the order.

[(4)   Within 28 days from appointment, the liquidator shall—
　(a)   give notice of it to all creditors of the company of whom the liquidator is aware; or
　(b)   advertise it in accordance with any directions given by the court.]

NOTES
Para (4): substituted by the Insolvency (Amendment) Rules 2009, SI 2009/642, rr 4, 27, as from 6 April 2009, subject to transitional provisions in r 3 thereof, as noted to r 1.4 of these Rules at **[10.6]**.
See Forms 4.29, 4.30 at **[10.673]**.

[10.359]
4.104   Appointment by Secretary of State (NO CVL APPLICATION)

(1)   This Rule applies where the official receiver applies to the Secretary of State to appoint a liquidator in place of himself, or refers to the Secretary of State the need for an appointment.

(2)   If the Secretary of State makes an appointment, he shall send [a copy] of the certificate of appointment to the official receiver, who shall transmit [it] to the person appointed . . .

(3)   The certificate shall specify the date from which the liquidator's appointment is to be effective.

NOTES
Para (2): words in square brackets substituted, and words omitted revoked, by the Insolvency (Amendment) Rules 2010, SI 2010/686, r 2, Sch 1, para 202, as from 6 April 2010, subject to transitional provisions in Sch 4, para 1 thereto, as noted to r 1.5 at **[10.7]**.

[10.360]
4.105   Authentication of liquidator's appointment

A copy of the certificate of the liquidator's appointment or (as the case may be) a sealed copy of the court's order [or a copy of the notice registered in accordance with paragraph 83(3) of Schedule B1 to the Act], may in any proceedings be adduced as proof that the person appointed is duly authorised to exercise the powers and perform the duties of liquidator in the company's winding up.

NOTES
Words in square brackets inserted by the Insolvency (Amendment) Rules 2003, SI 2003/1730, r 7, Sch 1, Pt 4, para 21, as from 15 September 2003 (for transitional provisions and savings see the note preceding r 2.1 at **[10.60]**).

[10.361]
[4.106A   Appointment to be gazetted and registered

(1)   A liquidator appointed in a voluntary winding up in addition to giving notice of the appointment in accordance with section 109(1) may advertise the notice in such other manner as the liquidator thinks fit.

(2)   A liquidator appointed in a winding up by the court -
   (a)   as soon as reasonably practicable must have gazetted a notice of the appointment; and
   (b)   may advertise the notice in such other manner as the liquidator thinks fit.

(3)   In addition to the standard contents, the notice must state—
   (a)   that a liquidator has been appointed; and
   (b)   the date of the appointment.

(4)   As soon as reasonably practicable a liquidator appointed in a winding up by the court must notify the appointment to the registrar of companies.

(5)   At first instance the liquidator must bear the expense of giving notice under this Rule.

(6)   The liquidator is entitled to be reimbursed for such expenditure as an expense of the liquidation.]

NOTES
Commencement: 6 April 2010.
Substituted (for the original r 4.106) by the Insolvency (Amendment) Rules 2010, SI 2010/686, r 2, Sch 1, para 203, subject to transitional provisions in Sch 4, para 1 thereto, as noted to r 1.5 at **[10.7]**.

[10.362]
4.107   Hand-over of assets to liquidator (NO CVL APPLICATION)

(1)   This Rule applies only where the liquidator is appointed in succession to the official receiver acting as liquidator.

(2)   When the liquidator's appointment takes effect, the official receiver shall [as soon as reasonably practicable] do all that is required for putting him into possession of the assets.

(3)   On taking possession of the assets, the liquidator shall discharge any balance due to the official receiver on account of—
   (a)   expenses properly incurred by him and payable under the Act or the Rules, and
   (b)   any advances made by him in respect of the assets, together with interest on such advances at the rate specified in section 17 of the Judgments Act 1838 at the date of the winding-up order.

(4)   Alternatively, the liquidator may (before taking office) give to the official receiver a written undertaking to discharge any such balance out of the first realisation of assets.

(5)   The official receiver has a charge on the assets in respect of any sums due to him under paragraph (3). But, where the liquidator has realised assets with a view to making those payments, the official receiver's charge does not extend in respect of sums deductible by the liquidator from the proceeds of realisation, as being expenses properly incurred therein.

(6)   The liquidator shall from time to time out of the realisation of assets discharge all guarantees properly given by the official receiver for the benefit of the estate, and shall pay all the official receiver's expenses.

(7)   The official receiver shall give to the liquidator all such information relating to the affairs of the company and the course of the winding up as he (the official receiver) considers to be reasonably required for the effective discharge by the liquidator of his duties as such.

(8)   The liquidator shall also be furnished with a copy of any report made by the official receiver under Chapter 7 of this Part of the Rules.

NOTES

Para (2): words in square brackets substituted by the Insolvency (Amendment) Rules 2009, SI 2009/642, r 5, as from 6 April 2009, subject to transitional provisions in r 3 thereof, as noted to r 1.4 of these Rules at **[10.6]**.

Section B: Resignation and Removal; Vacation of Office

[10.363]
4.108   Creditors' meeting to receive liquidator's resignation

(1)   Before resigning his office, the liquidator must call a meeting of creditors for the purpose of receiving his resignation.

[(1A)   The liquidator must give at least 28 days' notice of the meeting.

(1B)   The notice summoning the meeting must—
   (a)   indicate that the purpose or one of the purposes of the meeting is to receive the liquidator's resignation; and
   (b)   draw the attention of the creditors with respect to the liquidator's release to Rule 4.121 or, as the case may be, Rule 4.122.]

(2)   A copy of the notice shall at the same time also be sent to the official receiver. (NO CVL APPLICATION)

[(3)   The notice to creditors under paragraph (1A) must be accompanied by an account of the liquidator's administration of the winding up including—
   (a)   where appropriate, a statement that the liquidator has reconciled the account with that held by the Secretary of State in respect of the winding up; and
   (b)   a progress report for the period—
      (i)   commencing with the later of the date of—
         (aa)   the appointment of the liquidator; and
         (bb)   the day immediately following the end of the period of the last progress report; and
      (ii)   ending with the date of the meeting.]

(4)   Subject as follows, the liquidator may only proceed under this Rule on grounds of ill health or because—
   (a)   he intends ceasing to be in practice as an insolvency practitioner, or
   (b)   there is some conflict of interest or change of personal circumstances which precludes or makes impracticable the further discharge by him of the duties of liquidator.

(5)   Where two or more persons are acting as liquidator jointly, any one of them may proceed under this Rule (without prejudice to the continuation in office of the other or others) on the ground that, in his opinion and that of the other or others, it is no longer expedient that there should continue to be the present number of joint liquidators.

[(6)   [Except where Rule 4.108A applies] if there is no quorum present at the meeting summoned to receive the liquidator's resignation, the meeting is deemed to have been held, a resolution is deemed to have been passed that the liquidator's resignation be accepted and the creditors are deemed not to have resolved against the liquidator having his release.

(7)   Where paragraph (6) applies any reference in the Rules to a resolution that the liquidator's resignation be accepted is replaced by a reference to the making of a written statement, [authenticated] by the person who, had there been a quorum present, would have been chairman of the meeting, that no quorum was present and that the liquidator may resign.]

NOTES

Paras (1A), (1B): substituted for part of the original para (1) by the Insolvency (Amendment) Rules 2010, SI 2010/686, r 2, Sch 1, para 204(1), (2), as from 6 April 2010, subject to transitional provisions in Sch 4, para 1 thereto, as noted to r 1.5 at **[10.7]**.

Para (3): substituted by SI 2010/686, r 2, Sch 1, para 204(1), (3) (as amended by the Insolvency (Amendment) (No 2) Rules 2010, SI 2010/734, rr 2, 5), as from 6 April 2010, subject to transitional provisions in Sch 4, para 1 thereto, as noted to r 1.5 at **[10.7]**.

Para (6): added, together with para (7), by the Insolvency (Amendment) Rules 1987, SI 1987/1919, r 3(1), Schedule, Pt 1, para 64, as from 11 January 1988; words in square brackets inserted by SI 2010/686, r 2, Sch 1, para 204(1), (4), as from 6 April 2010, subject to transitional provisions in Sch 4, para 1 thereto, as noted to r 1.5 at **[10.7]**.

Para (7): added as noted to para (6) above; word in square brackets substituted by SI 2010/686, r 2, Sch 1, para 1, as from 6 April 2010, subject to transitional provisions in Sch 4, para 2 thereto, as noted to r 1.31 at **[10.34]**.

See Form 4.22 at **[10.673]**.

[10.364]
[4.108A   Resignation (application under Rule 4.131)

(1)   This Rule applies where at the date of a meeting summoned for the purpose of receiving the liquidator's resignation, an application made to the court under Rule 4.131 (including any appeal) has not been disposed of.

(2)   At the meeting no resolution may be put regarding the liquidator's release.

(3)   If at the meeting the liquidator's resignation is accepted, the meeting must be adjourned (notwithstanding anything in Rule 4.65 (suspension and adjournment)) to a day not less than 14 days after the day on which the application under Rule 4.131 (including any appeal) has been disposed of.

(4)   The liquidator must give at least 14 days' notice of the meeting adjourned in accordance with paragraph (3) to the creditors.

(5)   At the meeting adjourned in accordance with paragraph (3)—
    (a)   a revised version of the account which accompanied the notice of the meeting must be laid showing any changes required as a result, or arising out of the application under Rule 4.131; and
    (b)   a resolution must be put for the release of the liquidator whose resignation has been accepted.

(6)   If there is no quorum present at the adjourned meeting, the meeting is deemed to have been held and the creditors are deemed to have resolved that the liquidator be released.

(7)   Where the creditors have resolved at the adjourned meeting that the liquidator be released (or are deemed to have so resolved by virtue of paragraph (5)), the chairman of the meeting (or the person who, had there been a quorum present would have been chairman of the meeting) must send as soon as reasonably practicable a certificate to that effect with a copy of the revised account to—
    (a)   the official receiver; and (NO CVL APPLICATION)
    (b)   the registrar of companies.

(8)   The official receiver must file a copy of the certificate in court.

(9)   If at the meeting the liquidator's resignation is not accepted, the liquidator must not summon any further meeting under Rule 4.108 until the application under Rule 4.131 (including any appeal) has been disposed of.

(10)   Paragraph (7) is subject to the powers of the court on an application being made to it by the liquidator under Rule 4.111 (permission to resign granted by the court).

(11)   Rule 4.108 applies to any such further meeting with the modification that the progress report required to accompany the notice of the meeting must show any changes from the report which accompanied the notice of the earlier meeting called to receive the liquidator's resignation, and in particular any changes required as a result of the application under Rule 4.131 and any further remuneration charged or expenses incurred.

(12)   The creditors' rights under Rules 4.49E and 4.131 do not apply in respect of any matter included in that report which—
    (a)   was included in the report which accompanied the notice of the earlier meeting called to receive the liquidator's resignation; or
    (b)   was the subject of the order of the court on the application made to it by the liquidator under Rule 4.131.]

NOTES
Commencement: 6 April 2010.
Inserted by the Insolvency (Amendment) Rules 2010, SI 2010/686, r 2, Sch 1, para 205, subject to transitional provisions in Sch 4, para 1 thereto, as noted to r 1.5 at **[10.7]**.

[10.365]
4.109   Action following acceptance of resignation (NO CVL APPLICATION)

(1)   This Rule applies where a meeting is summoned to receive the liquidator's resignation.

(2)   If the chairman of the meeting is other than the official receiver, and there is passed at the meeting any of the following resolutions—
    (a)   that the liquidator's resignation be accepted,
    (b)   that a new liquidator be appointed,
    (c)   that the resigning liquidator be not given his release,
the chairman shall, within 3 [business days of the date of the resolution], send to the official receiver a copy of the resolution.

If it has been resolved to accept the liquidator's resignation, the chairman shall send to the official receiver a certificate to that effect.

(3)   If the creditors have resolved to appoint a new liquidator, the certificate of his appointment shall also be sent to the official receiver within that time; and Rule 4.100 shall be complied with in respect of it.

(4)   If the liquidator's resignation is accepted, the notice of it required by section 172(6) shall be given by him [as soon as reasonably practicable] after the [resolution has been passed]; and he shall send a copy of the notice to the official receiver.

The notice shall be accompanied by a copy of the account sent to creditors under Rule 4.108(3).

(5)   The official receiver shall file a copy of the notice in court.

(6)   The liquidator's resignation is effective as from the date on which the official receiver files the copy notice in court, that date to be endorsed on the copy notice.

NOTES

Para (2): words in square brackets substituted by the Insolvency (Amendment) Rules 2010, SI 2010/686, r 2, Sch 1, para 206(1), (2), as from 6 April 2010, subject to transitional provisions in Sch 4, para 1 thereto, as noted to r 1.5 at **[10.7]**.

Para (4): words in first pair of square brackets substituted by the Insolvency (Amendment) Rules 2009, SI 2009/642, r 5, as from 6 April 2009, subject to transitional provisions in r 3 thereof, as noted to r 1.4 of these Rules at **[10.6]**; words in second pair of square brackets substituted by SI 2010/686, r 2, Sch 1, para 206(1), (3), as from 6 April 2010, subject to transitional provisions in Sch 4, para 1 thereto, as noted to r 1.5 at **[10.7]**.

See Form 4.32 at **[10.673]**.

[10.366]
4.110–CVL   Action following acceptance of resignation

(1)   This Rule applies where a meeting is summoned to receive the liquidator's resignation.

(2)   If his resignation is accepted, the notice of it required by section 171(5) shall be given by him [as soon as reasonably practicable] after the [resolution has been passed].

(3)   Where a new liquidator is appointed in place of the one who has resigned, the certificate of his appointment shall be delivered [as soon as reasonably practicable] by the chairman of the meeting to the new liquidator.

NOTES

Para (2): words in first pair of square brackets substituted by the Insolvency (Amendment) Rules 2009, SI 2009/642, r 5, as from 6 April 2009, subject to transitional provisions in r 3 thereof, as noted to r 1.4 of these Rules at **[10.6]**; words in second pair of square brackets substituted by the Insolvency (Amendment) Rules 2010, SI 2010/686, r 2, Sch 1, para 207, as from 6 April 2010, subject to transitional provisions in Sch 4, para 1 thereto, as noted to r 1.5 at **[10.7]**.

Para (3): words in square brackets substituted by SI 2009/642, r 5, as from 6 April 2009, subject to transitional provisions in r 3 thereof, as noted to r 1.4 of these Rules at **[10.6]**.

[10.367]
4.111   [Permission] to resign granted by the court

(1)   If at a creditors' meeting summoned to accept the liquidator's resignation it is resolved that it be not accepted, the court may, on the liquidator's application, make an order giving him [permission] to resign.

(2)   The court's order may include such provision as it thinks [just] with respect to matters arising in connection with the resignation, and shall determine the date from which the liquidator's release is effective.

(3)   The court shall send two sealed copies of the order to the liquidator, who shall send one of the copies [as soon as reasonably practicable] to the official receiver. (NO CVL APPLICATION)

(4–CVL)   The court shall send two sealed copies of the order to the liquidator, who shall [as soon as reasonably practicable] send one of them to the registrar of companies.

(5)   On sending notice of his resignation to the court, the liquidator shall send a copy of it to the official receiver. (NO CVL APPLICATION)

NOTES

Rule heading, paras (1), (2): word in square brackets substituted by the Insolvency (Amendment) Rules 2010, SI 2010/686, r 2, Sch 1, para 1, as from 6 April 2010, subject to transitional provisions in Sch 4, para 2 thereto, as noted to r 1.31 at **[10.34]**.

Paras (3), (4): words in square brackets substituted by the Insolvency (Amendment) Rules 2009, SI 2009/642, r 5, as from 6 April 2009, subject to transitional provisions in r 3 thereof, as noted to r 1.4 of these Rules at **[10.6]**.

See Forms 4.34, 4.36 at **[10.673]**.

[10.368]
4.112   Advertisement of resignation

Where a new liquidator is appointed in place of one who has resigned, the former shall, in giving notice of his appointment, state that his predecessor has resigned and (if it be the case) that he has been given his release.

[10.369]
4.113   Meeting of creditors to remove liquidator (NO CVL APPLICATION)

(1)   Where a meeting of creditors is summoned for the purpose of removing the liquidator, the notice summoning it shall indicate that this is the purpose, or one of the purposes, of the meeting; and the notice shall draw the attention of creditors to section 174(4) with respect to the liquidator's release.

(2)   A copy of the notice shall at the same time also be sent to the official receiver.

(3)   At the meeting, a person other than the liquidator or his nominee may be elected to act as chairman; but if the liquidator or his nominee is chairman and a resolution has been proposed for the liquidator's removal, the chairman shall not adjourn the meeting without the consent of at least one-half (in value) of the creditors present (in person or by proxy) and entitled to vote.

(4)   Where the chairman of the meeting is other than the official receiver, and there is passed at the meeting any of the following resolutions—

  (a)   that the liquidator be removed,
  (b)   that a new liquidator be appointed,
  (c)   that the removed liquidator be not given his release,

the chairman shall, within 3 [business] days, send to the official receiver a copy of the resolution.
    If it has been resolved to remove the liquidator, the chairman shall send to the official receiver a certificate to that effect.

(5)   If the creditors have resolved to appoint a new liquidator, the certificate of his appointment shall also be sent to the official receiver within that time; and Rule 4.100 above shall be complied with in respect of it.

NOTES
    Para (4): word in square brackets inserted by the Insolvency (Amendment) Rules 2010, SI 2010/686, r 2, Sch 1, para 208, as from 6 April 2010, subject to transitional provisions in Sch 4, para 1 thereto, as noted to r 1.5 at **[10.7]**.
    See Form 4.22, 4.37 at **[10.673]**.

[10.370]
4.114–CVL   Meeting of creditors to remove liquidator

(1)   A meeting held under section 171(2)(b) for the removal of the liquidator shall be summoned by him if requested by 25 per cent in value of the company's creditors, excluding those who are connected with it.

(2)   The notice summoning the meeting shall indicate that the removal of the liquidator is the purpose, or one of the purposes, of the meeting; and the notice shall draw the attention of creditors to section 173(2) with respect to the liquidator's release.

(3)   At the meeting, a person other than the liquidator or his nominee may be elected to act as chairman; but if the liquidator or his nominee is chairman and a resolution has been proposed for the liquidator's removal, the chairman shall not adjourn the meeting without the consent of at least one-half (in value) of the creditors present (in person or by proxy) and entitled to vote.

NOTES
    See Form 4.22 at **[10.673]**.

[10.371]
4.115   Court's power to regulate meetings under Rules 4.113, 4.114–CVL

Where a meeting under Rule 4.113 or 4.114–CVL is to be held, or is proposed to be summoned, the court may, on the application of any creditor, give directions as to the mode of summoning it, the sending out and return of forms of proxy, the conduct of the meeting, and any other matter which appears to the court to require regulation or control under this Rule.

[10.372]
4.116   Procedure on removal (NO CVL APPLICATION)

(1)   Where the creditors have resolved that the liquidator be removed, the official receiver shall file in court the certificate of removal.

(2)   The resolution is effective as from the date on which the official receiver files the certificate of removal in court, and that date shall be endorsed on the certificate.

[(3)   The official receiver must send a copy of the certificate, so endorsed, as soon as reasonably practicable to—

  (a)   the removed liquidator;
  (b)   the new liquidator (if appointed); and
  (c)   the registrar of companies.]

(4)   The official receiver shall not file the certificate in court unless and until the Secretary of State has certified to him that the removed liquidator has reconciled his account with that held by the Secretary of State in respect of the winding up.

NOTES

Para (3): substituted by the Insolvency (Amendment) Rules 2010, SI 2010/686, r 2, Sch 1, para 209, as from 6 April 2010, subject to transitional provisions in Sch 4, para 1 thereto, as noted to r 1.5 at **[10.7]**.

[10.373]
4.117–CVL   Procedure on removal

Where the creditors have resolved that the liquidator be removed, the chairman of the creditors' meeting shall [as soon as reasonably practicable]—

    (a)   if at the meeting another liquidator was not appointed, send the certificate of the liquidator's removal to the registrar of companies, and

    (b)   otherwise, deliver the certificate to the new liquidator, who shall send it to the registrar.

NOTES

Words in square brackets substituted by the Insolvency (Amendment) Rules 2009, SI 2009/642, r 5, as from 6 April 2009, subject to transitional provisions in r 3 thereof, as noted to r 1.4 of these Rules at **[10.6]**.

[10.374]
4.118   Advertisement of removal

Where a new liquidator is appointed in place of one removed, the former shall, in giving notice of his appointment, state that his predecessor has been removed and (if it be the case) that he has been given his release.

[10.375]
4.119   Removal of liquidator by the court (NO CVL APPLICATION)

(1)   This Rule applies where application is made to the court for the removal of the liquidator, or for an order directing the liquidator to summon a meeting of creditors for the purpose of removing him.

(2)   The court may, if it thinks that no sufficient cause is shown for the application, dismiss it; but it shall not do so unless the applicant has had an opportunity to attend the court for [a] hearing, of which he has been given at least [5 business] days' notice [but which is without notice to any other party].

    If the application is not dismissed under this paragraph, the court shall fix a venue for it to be heard.

(3)   The court may require the applicant to make a deposit or give security for the costs to be incurred by the liquidator on the application.

(4)   The applicant shall, at least 14 days before the hearing, send to the liquidator and the official receiver a notice stating the venue and accompanied by a copy of the application, and of any evidence which he intends to adduce in support of it.

(5)   Subject to any contrary order of the court, the costs of the application are not payable [as an expense of the liquidation].

(6)   Where the court removes the liquidator—

    (a)   it shall send copies of the order of removal to him and to the official receiver;

    (b)   the order may include such provision as the court thinks [just] with respect to matters arising in connection with the removal; and

    (c)   if the court appoints a new liquidator, Rule 4.102 applies.

NOTES

Para (2): word in first and second pairs of square brackets substituted, and words in third pair of square brackets added, by the Insolvency (Amendment) Rules 2010, SI 2010/686, r 2, Sch 1, para 210(1), (2), as from 6 April 2010, subject to transitional provisions in Sch 4, paras 1, 2 thereto, as noted to rr 1.5, 1.31 at **[10.7]**, **[10.34]**.

Para (5): words in square brackets substituted by the Insolvency (Amendment) Rules 2008, SI 2008/737, rr 3, 7(1), as from 6 April 2008, subject to transitional provisions as noted to r 4.218 at **[10.486]**.

Para (6): word in square brackets in sub-para (b) substituted by SI 2010/686, r 2, Sch 1, para 1, as from 6 April 2010, subject to transitional provisions in Sch 4, para 2 thereto, as noted to r 1.31 at **[10.34]**.

See Form 4.39 at **[10.673]**.

[10.376]
4.120–CVL   Removal of liquidator by the court

(1)   This Rule applies where the application is made to the court for the removal of the liquidator, or for an order directing the liquidator to summon a creditors' meeting for the purpose of removing him.

(2)   The court may, if it thinks that no sufficient cause is shown for the application, dismiss it; but it shall not do so unless the applicant has had an opportunity to attend the court for [a] hearing, of which he has been given at least [5 business] days' notice [but which is without notice to any other party].

    If the application is not dismissed under this paragraph, the court shall fix a venue for it to be heard.

(3) The court may require the applicant to make a deposit or give security for the costs to be incurred by the liquidator on the application.

(4) The applicant shall, at least 14 days before the hearing, send to the liquidator a notice stating the venue and accompanied by a copy of the application, and of any evidence which he intends to adduce in support of it.

(5) Subject to any contrary order of the court, the costs of the application are not payable [as an expense of the liquidation].

(6) Where the court removes the liquidator—
   (a) it shall send 2 copies of the order of removal to him, one to be sent by him [as soon as reasonably practicable] to the registrar of companies, with notice of his ceasing to act;
   (b) the order may include such provision as the court thinks [just] with respect to matters arising in connection with the removal; and
   (c) if the court appoints a new liquidator, Rule 4.103–CVL applies.

NOTES
   Para (2): word in first and second pairs of square brackets substituted, and words in third pair of square brackets added, by the Insolvency (Amendment) Rules 2010, SI 2010/686, r 2, Sch 1, para 211, as from 6 April 2010, subject to transitional provisions in Sch 4, paras 1, 2 thereto, as noted to rr 1.5, 1.31 at **[10.7]**, **[10.34]**.
   Para (5): words in square brackets substituted by the Insolvency (Amendment) Rules 2008, SI 2008/737, rr 3, 7(1), as from 6 April 2008, subject to transitional provisions as noted to r 4.218 at **[10.486]**.
   Para (6): words in square brackets in sub-para (a) substituted by the Insolvency (Amendment) Rules 2009, SI 2009/642, r 5, as from 6 April 2009, subject to transitional provisions in r 3 thereof, as noted to r 1.4 of these Rules at **[10.6]**; word in square brackets in sub-para (b) substituted by SI 2010/686, r 2, Sch 1, para 1, as from 6 April 2010, subject to transitional provisions in Sch 4, para 2 thereto, as noted to r 1.31 at **[10.34]**.
   See Form 4.39 at **[10.673]**.

[10.377]
4.121 Release of resigning or removed liquidator (NO CVL APPLICATION)
(1) [Subject to paragraph (1A),] where the liquidator's resignation is accepted by a meeting of creditors which has not resolved against his release, he has his release from when his resignation is effective under Rule 4.109.

[(1A) Where the liquidator's resignation is accepted under Rule 4.108A, the liquidator's release is effective as from the date on which the official receiver files the copy of the certificate under paragraph (8) of that Rule in court, that date to be endorsed on the copy certificate.]

(2) Where the liquidator is removed by a meeting of creditors which has not resolved against his release, the fact of his release shall be stated in the certificate of removal.

(3) Where—
   (a) the liquidator resigns, and the creditors' meeting called to receive his resignation has resolved against his release, or
   (b) he is removed by a creditors' meeting which has so resolved, or is removed by the court,
he must apply to the Secretary of State for his release.

(4) When the Secretary of State gives the release, he shall certify it accordingly, and send the certificate to the official receiver, to be filed in court.

(5) A copy of the certificate shall be sent by the Secretary of State to the former liquidator, whose release is effective from the date of the certificate.

NOTES
   Para (1): words in square brackets inserted by the Insolvency (Amendment) Rules 2010, SI 2010/686, r 2, Sch 1, para 212(1), (2), as from 6 April 2010, subject to transitional provisions in Sch 4, para 1 thereto, as noted to r 1.5 at **[10.7]**.
   Para (1A): inserted by SI 2010/686, r 2, Sch 1, para 212(1), (3), as from 6 April 2010, subject to transitional provisions in Sch 4, para 1 thereto, as noted to r 1.5 at **[10.7]**.
   See Form 4.41 at **[10.673]**.

[10.378]
4.122–CVL Release of resigning or removed liquidator
(1) [Subject to paragraph (1A),] where the liquidator's resignation is accepted by a meeting of creditors which has not resolved against his release, he has his release from when he gives notice of his resignation to the registrar of companies.

[(1A) Where the liquidator's resignation is accepted under Rule 4.108A, the liquidator's release is effective as from the date of the certificate.]

(2) Where the liquidator is removed by a creditors' meeting which has not resolved against his release, the fact of his release shall be stated in the certificate of removal.

(3) Where—
   (a) the liquidator resigns, and the creditors' meeting called to receive his resignation has resolved against his release, or
   (b) he is removed by a creditors' meeting which has so resolved, or is removed by the court,
he must apply to the Secretary of State for his release.

Part 10   Miscellaneous other SIs

(4) When the Secretary of State gives the release, he shall certify it accordingly, and send the certificate to the registrar of companies.

(5) A copy of the certificate shall be sent by the Secretary of State to the former liquidator, whose release is effective from the date of the certificate.

NOTES

Para (1): words in square brackets inserted by the Insolvency (Amendment) Rules 2010, SI 2010/686, r 2, Sch 1, para 213(1), (2), as from 6 April 2010, subject to transitional provisions in Sch 4, para 1 thereto, as noted to r 1.5 at **[10.7]**.

Para (1A): inserted by SI 2010/686, r 2, Sch 1, para 213(1), (3), as from 6 April 2010, subject to transitional provisions in Sch 4, para 1 thereto, as noted to r 1.5 at **[10.7]**.

See Form 4.41 at **[10.673]**.

[10.379]
4.123 Removal of liquidator by Secretary of State (NO CVL APPLICATION)

(1) If the Secretary of State decides to remove the liquidator, he shall before doing so notify the liquidator and the official receiver of his decision and the grounds of it, and specify a period within which the liquidator may make representations against implementation of the decision.

(2) If the Secretary of State directs the removal of the liquidator, he shall [as soon as reasonably practicable]—
   (a)   file notice of his decision in court, and
   (b)   send notice to the liquidator and the official receiver.
(3) If the liquidator is removed by direction of the Secretary of State—
   (a)   Rule 4.121 applies as regards the liquidator obtaining his release, as if he had been removed by the court, and
   (b)   the court may make any such order in his case as it would have power to make if he had been so removed.

NOTES

Para (2): words in square brackets substituted by the Insolvency (Amendment) Rules 2009, SI 2009/642, r 5, as from 6 April 2009, subject to transitional provisions in r 3 thereof, as noted to r 1.4 of these Rules at **[10.6]**.

Section C: Release on Completion of Administration

[10.380]
4.124 Release of official receiver (NO CVL APPLICATION)

(1) The official receiver shall, before giving notice to the Secretary of State under section 174(3) (that the winding up is for practical purposes complete), send out notice of his intention to do so to all creditors [of which he is aware].

(2) The notice shall in each case be accompanied by a summary of the official receiver's receipts and payments as liquidator.

[(2A) The summary of receipts and payments referred to in paragraph (2) shall also include a statement as to the amount paid to unsecured creditors by virtue of the application of section 176A (prescribed part).]

(3) The Secretary of State, when he has determined the date from which the official receiver is to have his release, shall give notice to the court that he has done so. The notice shall be accompanied by the summary referred to in paragraph (2).

NOTES

Para (1): words in square brackets substituted by the Insolvency (Amendment) Rules 2004, SI 2004/584, r 11, as from 1 April 2004.

Para (2A): inserted by the Insolvency (Amendment) Rules 2003, SI 2003/1730, r 7, Sch 1, Pt 4, para 22, as from 15 September 2003 (for transitional provisions and savings see the note preceding r 2.1 at **[10.60]**).

[10.381]
4.125 Final meeting (NO CVL APPLICATION)

(1) Where the liquidator is other than the official receiver, he shall give at least 28 days' notice of the final meeting of creditors to be held under section 146. The notice shall be sent to all creditors [of which he is aware] . . .

[(1A) The final meeting must not be held unless Rule 4.49D has been complied with; and if for that reason the meeting is not held—
   (a)   the liquidator must give notice of that fact as soon as reasonably practicable to all to whom notice of the meeting was given, and
   (b)   fresh notice of the meeting complying with this Rule must be given when Rule 4.49D has been complied with.

(1B)   The liquidator—
   (a)   at least 1 month before the meeting is held must have gazetted a notice of the meeting; and
   (b)   may advertise the notice in such other manner as the liquidator thinks fit.

(1C)   In addition to the standard contents, the notice under paragraph (1B) must state—

(a)   who summoned the meeting;

(b)   if the meeting was summoned at the request of a creditor, the fact that it was so summoned and the section of the Act under which it was requested;

(c)   the purpose for which the meeting is summoned;

(d)   the venue fixed for the meeting; and

(e)   the time and date by which, and place at which, creditors must lodge proxies and hitherto unlodged proofs in order to be entitled to vote at the meeting.]

(2)   The liquidator's report laid before the meeting under that section shall contain an account of the liquidator's administration of the winding up, including—

(a)   a summary of his receipts and payments, [including details of remuneration charged and expenses incurred by the liquidator,

(ab)   details of the basis fixed for the liquidator's remuneration, and]

(b)   a statement by him that he has reconciled his account with that which is held by the Secretary of State in respect of the winding up.

[(2A)   The liquidator's report shall also contain a statement as to the amount paid to unsecured creditors by virtue of the application of section 176A (prescribed part).]

[(2B)   Where the liquidator has sent a progress report to creditors in accordance with Rule 4.49B, the report to be laid at the final meeting of creditors must also—

(a)   contain a receipts and payments account in the form of an abstract showing the receipts and payments during the period since the last progress report, and

(b)   include—

(i)   details of the remuneration charged and expenses incurred by the liquidator during that period, and

(ii)   a description of the things done by the liquidator during that period in respect of which that remuneration was charged and those expenses incurred.

(2C)   In any case where the basis of the liquidator's remuneration had not been fixed by the date to which the last progress report was made up, the receipts and payments account required by paragraph (2B)(a) must also include details of the remuneration charged in the period of any preceding progress report in which details of remuneration were not included.

(2D)   Where the basis of remuneration has been fixed as a set amount only, it is sufficient compliance with paragraph (2B)(b) for the liquidator to state the amount which has been set and to supply details of the expenses charged within the period in question.]

(3)   At the final meeting, the creditors may question the liquidator with respect to any matter contained in his report, and may resolve against him having his release.

(4)   The liquidator shall give notice to the court that the final meeting has been held; and the notice shall state whether or not he has been given his release, and be accompanied by a copy of the report laid before the final meeting. A copy of the notice shall be sent by the liquidator to the [Secretary of State].

(5)   If there is no quorum present at the final meeting, the liquidator shall report to the court that a final meeting was summoned in accordance with the Rules, but there was no quorum present; and the final meeting is then deemed to have been held, and the creditors not to have resolved against the liquidator having his release.

(6)   If the creditors at the final meeting have not so resolved, the liquidator is released when the notice under paragraph (4) is filed in court. If they have so resolved, the liquidator must obtain his release from the Secretary of State and Rule 4.121 applies accordingly.

NOTES

Para (1): words in square brackets substituted by the Insolvency (Amendment) Rules 2004, SI 2004/584, r 12, as from 1 April 2004; words omitted revoked by the Insolvency (Amendment) Rules 2010, SI 2010/686, r 2, Sch 1, para 214(1), (2), as from 6 April 2010, subject to transitional provisions in Sch 4, para 1 thereto, as noted to r 1.5 at **[10.7]**.

Paras (1A)–(1C): inserted by SI 2010/686, r 2, Sch 1, para 214(1), (3), as from 6 April 2010, subject to transitional provisions in Sch 4, para 1 thereto, as noted to r 1.5 at **[10.7]**.

Para (2): words in square brackets substituted by SI 2010/686, r 2, Sch 1, para 214(1), (4), as from 6 April 2010, subject to transitional provisions in Sch 4, para 1 thereto, as noted to r 1.5 at **[10.7]**.

Para (2A): inserted by the Insolvency (Amendment) Rules 2003, SI 2003/1730, r 7, Sch 1, Pt 4, para 23, as from 15 September 2003 (for transitional provisions and savings see the note preceding r 2.1 at **[10.60]**).

Paras (2B)–(2D): inserted by SI 2010/686, r 2, Sch 1, para 214(1), (5), as from 6 April 2010, subject to transitional provisions in Sch 4, para 1 thereto, as noted to r 1.5 at **[10.7]**.

Para (4): words in square brackets substituted the Insolvency (Amendment) Rules 2005, SI 2005/527, r 28, as from 1 April 2005.

See Forms 4.22, 4.42 at **[10.673]**.

[10.382]
[4.125A   Rule as to reporting

(1)   The court may, on the liquidator or official receiver's application, relieve him of any duty imposed on him by Rule 4.124 or 4.125, or authorise him to carry out the duty in a way other than there required.

(2) In considering whether to act under this Rule, the court shall have regard to the cost of carrying out the duty, to the amount of the assets available, and to the extent of the interest of creditors or contributories, or any particular class of them.]

NOTES

Inserted by the Insolvency (Amendment) Rules 2004, SI 2004/584, r 13, as from 1 April 2004.

[10.383]
4.126–CVL   Final meeting

(1) The liquidator shall give at least 28 days' notice of the final meeting of creditors to be held under section 106. The notice shall be sent to all creditors who [are known to the liquidator].

[(1A) In addition to information required by subsection (2) of section 106 and the standard contents, the advertisement required by that subsection must state the time and date by which, and place at which, creditors must lodge proxies and hitherto unlodged proofs in order to be entitled to vote at the meeting.

(1B) In addition to the notice required by paragraph (1) and the advertisement required by section 106(2), the liquidator may advertise notice of the meeting in such other manner as the liquidator thinks fit.

(1C) In addition to the standard contents, notice under paragraph (1B) must state—
   (a)   the purpose of the meeting;
   (b)   the venue fixed for the meeting; and
   (c)   the time and date by which, and place at which, creditors must lodge proxies and hitherto unlodged proofs in order to be entitled to vote at the meeting.

(1D) The final meeting must not be held unless Rule 4.49D has been complied with; and if for that reason the meeting is not held—
   (a)   the liquidator must give notice of that fact as soon as reasonably practicable to all to whom notice of the meeting was given, and
   (b)   fresh notice of the meeting complying with this Rule must be given when Rule 4.49D has been complied with.

(1E) The liquidator's report laid before the meeting of creditors under section 106 must contain an account of the liquidator's administration of the winding up, including—
   (a)   a summary of the liquidator's receipts and payments, including at least the following items separately specified (except where the amount for an item is zero)—
      (i)   the total of all receipts, with separate specification thereunder of—
         (aa)   receipts from trading carried on by the liquidator;
         (bb)   payments made in the course of trading carried on by the liquidator;
         (cc)   the source of all other receipts;
         (dd)   payments to redeem securities;
         (ee)   costs of execution; and
         (ff)   net realisations;
      (ii)   the cost of employing a solicitor;
      (iii)   other legal costs;
      (iv)   the liquidator's remuneration;
      (v)   the cost of employing an auctioneer;
      (vi)   the cost of employing a valuer;
      (vii)   the costs of taking possession of and maintaining the company's property;
      (viii)   the cost of advertising in the Gazette and other newspapers;
      (ix)   incidental outlays;
      (x)   a statement of the total of costs and charges incurred;
      (xi)   the amount paid to holders of debentures of each class of debenture, setting out the amount paid per debenture, the nominal value of each debenture in each class and the total amount paid in respect of each class;
      (xii)   the aggregate numbers of preferential and unsecured creditors and the aggregate amounts paid out to them, the aggregates for preferential and unsecured creditors set out separately unless all creditors have been paid in full;
      (xiii)   statements of the aggregate dividend paid on each pound of preferential and of unsecured debt and of the estimate of the value of the company's net property which had been made under Rule 4.49(2)(a)(ii);
      (xiv)   the amount of interest paid under section 189;
      (xv)   the amount paid to contributories in respect of each class of share, setting out the amount per share and the nominal value of each share in each class;
      (xvi)   a statement of the total amount paid to holders of debentures, preferential and unsecured creditors and contributories;
      (xvii)   a statement of assets which have proved to be unrealisable, including the value of those assets which had been made for the purpose of Rule 4.49(2)(a)(ii);
      (xviii)   the amounts paid into the Insolvency Services Account, set out separately, in respect of—

(aa)   unclaimed dividends payable to creditors in the winding up;

(bb)   other unclaimed dividends in the winding up;

(cc)   moneys held by the company in trust in respect of dividends or other sums due before the commencement of the winding up to any person as a member of the company;

(b)   details of the basis fixed for the liquidator's remuneration and by whom it was fixed;

(c)   a statement by the liquidator that the account included in the report has been reconciled with that which is held by the Secretary of State in respect of the winding up;

(d)   any other statement which the liquidator thinks it desirable to make.]

(2)   At the final meeting, the creditors may question the liquidator with respect to any matter contained in the account required under [section 106] [or paragraph (4) of this Rule], and may resolve against the liquidator having his release.

(3)   Where the creditors have so resolved, he must obtain his release from the Secretary of State; and Rule 4.122–CVL applies accordingly.

[(4)   The account of the winding up required under section 106 shall also include a statement as to the amount paid to unsecured creditors by virtue of the application of section 176A (prescribed part).]

[(5)   Where the liquidator has sent a progress report to creditors in accordance with section 104A, the report to be laid at the final meeting of creditors must also—

(a)   contain a receipts and payments account in the form of an abstract showing the receipts and payments during the period since the last progress report, and

(b)   include—

(i)   details of the remuneration charged and expenses incurred by the liquidator during that period, and

(ii)   a description of the things done by the liquidator during that period in respect of which that remuneration was charged and those expenses incurred.

(6)   In any case where the basis of the liquidator's remuneration had not been fixed by the date to which the last progress report was made up, the receipts and payments account required by paragraph (5)(a) must also include details of the remuneration charged in the period of any preceding progress report in which details of remuneration were not included.

(7)   Where the basis of remuneration has been fixed as a set amount only, it is sufficient compliance with paragraph (5)(b) for the liquidator to state the amount which has been set and to supply details of the expenses charged within the period in question.]

NOTES

Para (1): words in square brackets substituted by the Insolvency (Amendment) Rules 2010, SI 2010/686, r 2, Sch 1, para 215(1), (2), as from 6 April 2010, subject to transitional provisions in Sch 4, para 1 thereto, as noted to r 1.5 at **[10.7]**.

Paras (1A)–(1E): inserted by SI 2010/686, r 2, Sch 1, para 215(1), (3), as from 6 April 2010, subject to transitional provisions in Sch 4, para 1 thereto, as noted to r 1.5 at **[10.7]**.

Para (2): words in first pair of square brackets substituted by SI 2010/686, r 2, Sch 1, para 215(1), (4), as from 6 April 2010, subject to transitional provisions in Sch 4, para 1 thereto, as noted to r 1.5 at **[10.7]**; words in second pair of square brackets inserted by the Insolvency (Amendment) Rules 2003, SI 2003/1730, r 7, Sch 1, Pt 4, para 24(a), as from 15 September 2003 (for transitional provisions and savings see the note preceding r 2.1 at **[10.60]**).

Para (4): added by SI 2003/1730, r 7, Sch 1, Pt 4, para 24(b), as from 15 September 2003 (for transitional provisions and savings see the note preceding r 2.1 at **[10.60]**).

Paras (5)–(7): added by SI 2010/686, r 2, Sch 1, para 215(1), (5), as from 6 April 2010, subject to transitional provisions in Sch 4, para 1 thereto, as noted to r 1.5 at **[10.7]**.

See Form 4.22 at **[10.673]**.

[10.384]
[4.126A   Final meeting in members' voluntary liquidation

(NO CVL APPLICATION)

(1)   In addition to the information required by section 94(2) and the standard contents, the advertisement required by that subsection must state the time and date by which, and place at which, members must lodge proxies in order to be entitled to vote.

(2)   In addition to the advertisement required by section 94(2), the liquidator may advertise notice of the meeting in such other manner as the liquidator thinks fit.

(3)   In addition to the standard contents, notice given under paragraph (2) must state—

(a)   the purpose of the meeting,

(b)   the venue fixed for the meeting, and

(c)   the time and date by which, and place at which, members must lodge proxies in order to be entitled to vote at the meeting.

(4)   The liquidator's report laid before the meeting of the company under section 94 must contain an account of the liquidator's administration of the winding up, including (except where the amount for an item is zero)—

(a)   a summary of the liquidator's receipts and payments, including at least the following items separately specified—

(i)   the total of all receipts, with separate specification thereunder of—

        (aa) receipts from trading carried on by the liquidator;

        (bb) payments made in the course of trading carried on by the liquidator;

        (cc) the source of all other receipts;

        (dd) payments to redeem securities;

        (ee) costs of execution; and

        (ff) net realisations;

  (ii) the cost of employing a solicitor;

  (iii) other legal costs;

  (iv) the liquidator's remuneration;

  (v) the cost of employing an auctioneer;

  (vi) the cost of employing a valuer;

  (vii) the costs of taking possession of and maintaining the company's property;

  (viii) the cost of advertising in the Gazette and other newspapers;

  (ix) incidental outlays;

  (x) a statement of the total of costs and charges incurred;

  (xi) the amount paid to holders of debentures of each class of debenture, setting out the amount paid per debenture, the nominal value of each debenture in each class and the total amount paid in respect of each class;

  (xii) the aggregate amount paid out to creditors;

  (xiii) the amount of interest paid under section 189;

  (xiv) the amount paid to contributories in respect of each class of share, setting out the amount per share and the nominal value of each share in each class;

  (xv) a statement of the total amount paid to holders of debentures, preferential and unsecured creditors and contributories;

  (xvi) a statement of assets which have proved to be unrealisable, including the value of those assets which had been made for the purpose of Rule 4.49(2)(a)(ii);

  (xvii) the amounts paid into the Insolvency Services Account, set out separately, in respect of—

        (aa) unclaimed dividends payable to creditors in the winding up;

        (bb) other unclaimed dividends in the winding up;

        (cc) moneys held by the company in trust in respect of dividends or other sums due before the commencement of the winding up to any person as a member of the company;

(b) details of the basis fixed for the liquidator's remuneration and by whom it was fixed;

(c) any other statement which the liquidator thinks it desirable to make.]

NOTES

Commencement: 6 April 2010.

Inserted by the Insolvency (Amendment) Rules 2010, SI 2010/686, r 2, Sch 1, para 216, subject to transitional provisions in Sch 4, para 1 thereto, as noted to r 1.5 at **[10.7]**.

Section D: Remuneration

[10.385]
4.127   Fixing of remuneration

(1) The liquidator is entitled to receive remuneration for his services as such.

(2) [The basis of remuneration] shall be fixed . . . —

  (a) as a percentage of the value of the assets which are realised or distributed, or of the one value and the other in combination, or

  (b) by reference to the time properly given by the insolvency practitioner (as liquidator) and his staff in attending to matters arising in the winding up[, or

  (c) as a set amount.]

[(3A) The basis of remuneration may be fixed as any one or more of the bases set out in paragraph (2), and different bases may be fixed in respect of different things done by the liquidator.

(3B) Where the basis of remuneration is fixed as set out in paragraph (2)(a), different percentages may be fixed in respect of different things done by the liquidator.

(3C) Where the liquidator is other than the official receiver, and subject to paragraph (5A), it is for the liquidation committee (if there is one) to determine—

  (a) which of the bases set out in paragraph (2) are to be fixed and (where appropriate) in what combination under paragraph (3A), and

  (b) the percentage or percentages (if any) to be fixed under paragraphs (2)(a) and (3B) and the amount (if any) to be set under paragraph (2)(c).]

(4) In arriving at that determination, the committee shall have regard to the following matters—

  (a) the complexity (or otherwise) of the case,

  (b) any respects in which, in connection with the winding up, there falls on the insolvency practitioner (as liquidator) any responsibility of an exceptional kind or degree,

(c)   the effectiveness with which the insolvency practitioner appears to be carrying out, or to have carried out, his duties as liquidator, and

(d)   the value and nature of the assets with which the liquidator has to deal.

(5)   If there is no liquidation committee, or the committee does not make the requisite determination, [and subject to paragraph (5A), the basis of] the liquidator's remuneration may be fixed (in accordance with [paragraphs (2), (3A) and (3B)]) by a resolution of a meeting of creditors; and paragraph (4) applies to them as it does to the liquidation committee.

[(5A)   Where—

(a)   a company which is in administration moves into winding up under paragraph 83 of Schedule B1 to the Act and the administrator becomes the liquidator, or

(b)   a winding-up order is made immediately upon the appointment of an administrator ceasing to have effect and the court under section 140(1) appoints as liquidator the person whose appointment as administrator has ceased to have effect,

the basis of remuneration fixed under Rule 2.106 is treated as having been fixed under this Rule and paragraphs (4) and (5) do not apply.]

[(6)   Where the liquidator is not the official receiver and [the basis of] his remuneration is not fixed as above [within 18 months after the date of the liquidator's appointment], the liquidator shall be entitled to remuneration fixed in accordance with the provisions of Rule 4.127A. [(NO CVL APPLICATION)]]

[(7–CVL)   If not fixed as above, the basis of the liquidator's remuneration shall, on application by the liquidator, be fixed by the court, and the provisions of paragraphs (2) to (4) apply as they do to the fixing of the basis of remuneration by the liquidation committee; but such an application may not be made by the liquidator unless the liquidator has first sought fixing of the basis in accordance with paragraph (3C) or (5), and in any event may not be made more than 18 months after the date of the liquidator's appointment.]

NOTES

Para (2): words in first pair of square brackets substituted, word omitted revoked, and words in second pair of square brackets added, by the Insolvency (Amendment) Rules 2010, SI 2010/686, r 2, Sch 1, para 217(1), (2), as from 6 April 2010, subject to transitional provisions in Sch 4, para 1 thereto, as noted to r 1.5 at **[10.7]**.

Paras (3A)–(3C): substituted (for the original para (3)) by SI 2010/686, r 2, Sch 1, para 217(1), (3), as from 6 April 2010, subject to transitional provisions in Sch 4, para 1 thereto, as noted to r 1.5 at **[10.7]**.

Para (5): words in first pair of square brackets inserted, and words in second pair of square brackets substituted, by SI 2010/686, r 2, Sch 1, para 217(1), (4), as from 6 April 2010, subject to transitional provisions in Sch 4, para 1 thereto, as noted to r 1.5 at **[10.7]**.

Para (5A): inserted by SI 2010/686, r 2, Sch 1, para 217(1), (5), as from 6 April 2010, subject to transitional provisions in Sch 4, para 1 thereto, as noted to r 1.5 at **[10.7]**.

Para (6): substituted by the Insolvency (Amendment) Rules 2004, SI 2004/584, r 14, as from 1 April 2004, subject to transitional provisions as noted below; words in square brackets inserted by SI 2010/686, r 2, Sch 1, para 217(1), (6), as from 6 April 2010, subject to transitional provisions in Sch 4, para 1 thereto, as noted to r 1.5 at **[10.7]**.

Para (7): added by SI 2010/686, r 2, Sch 1, para 217(1), (7), as from 6 April 2010, subject to transitional provisions in Sch 4, para 1 thereto, as noted to r 1.5 at **[10.7]**.

Transitional provisions: the Insolvency (Amendment) Rules 2004, SI 2004/584, r 3 provides as follows (note that by virtue of r 1(2) of those Rules "the commencement date" is 1 April 2004)—

"3   Transitional provisions

(1)   This Rule applies in any case where before the commencement date—

(a)   a winding-up order is made or a resolution for the winding up of the company is passed and the liquidator is entitled to remuneration by virtue of Rule 4.127(6), Rule 4.128(1) or Rule 4.148A(4); or

(b)   a bankruptcy order is made and the trustee is entitled to remuneration by virtue of Rule 6.138(6) or Rule 6.139(1).

(2)   In a case to which this Rule applies the liquidator or, as the case may be, the trustee shall continue to be entitled to remuneration on the basis that—

(a)   the amendments made to the principal Rules by these Rules do not apply; and

(b)   the amendments made to the Insolvency Regulations 1994 by the Insolvency (Amendment) Regulations 2004 had not been made.".

[10.386]

[4.127A   Liquidator's entitlement to remuneration where it is not fixed under Rule 4.127

[(NO CVL APPLICATION)]

(1)   This Rule applies where the liquidator is not the official receiver and [the basis of] his remuneration is not fixed [or treated as fixed] in accordance with Rule 4.127.

(2)   The liquidator shall be entitled by way of remuneration for his services as such, to such sum as is arrived at by—

(a)   first applying the realisation scale set out in Schedule 6 to the monies received by him from the realisation of the assets of the company (including any Value Added Tax thereon but after deducting any sums paid to secured creditors in respect of their securities and any sums spent out of money received in carrying on the business of the company); and

(b)   then by adding to the sum arrived at under sub-paragraph (a) such sum as is arrived at by applying the distribution scale set out in Schedule 6 to the value of assets distributed to creditors of the company (including payments made in respect of preferential debts) and to contributories.]

NOTES

Inserted, together with r 4.127B, by the Insolvency (Amendment) Rules 2004, SI 2004/584, r 15, as from 1 April 2004.

Rule heading, para (1): words in square brackets inserted by SI 2010/686, r 2, Sch 1, para 218, as from 6 April 2010, subject to transitional provisions in Sch 4, para 1 thereto, as noted to r 1.5 at **[10.7]**.

[10.387]
[4.127B   Liquidator's remuneration where he realises assets on behalf of chargeholder

(1)   This Rule applies where the liquidator is not the official receiver and realises assets on behalf of a secured creditor.

(2)   Where the assets realised for a secured creditor are subject to a charge which when created was a mortgage or a fixed charge, the liquidator shall be entitled to such sum by way of remuneration as is arrived at by applying the realisation scale set out in Schedule 6 to the monies received by him in respect of the assets realised (including any sums received in respect of Value Added Tax thereon but after deducting any sums spent out of money received in carrying on the business of the company).

(3)   Where the assets realised for a secured creditor are subject to a charge which when created was a floating charge, the liquidator shall be entitled to such sum by way of remuneration as is arrived at by—

(a)   first applying the realisation scale set out in Schedule 6 to monies received by him from the realisation of those assets (including any Value Added Tax thereon but ignoring any sums received which are spent in carrying on the business of the company); and

(b)   then by adding to the sum arrived at under sub-paragraph (a) such sum as is arrived at by applying the distribution scale set out in Schedule 6 to the value of the assets distributed to the holder of the charge [and payments made in respect of preferential debts].

[(4)   The sum to which the liquidator is entitled under paragraph (2) or (3) shall be taken out of the proceeds of the realisation effected under that paragraph.]]

NOTES

Inserted as noted to r 4.127A at **[10.386]**.

Para (3): words in square brackets added by the Insolvency (Amendment) Rules 2005, SI 2005/527, r 29, as from 1 April 2005, subject to transitional provisions as noted below.

Para (4): added by the Insolvency (Amendment) Rules 2010, SI 2010/686, r 2, Sch 1, para 219, as from 6 April 2010, subject to transitional provisions in Sch 4, para 1 thereto, as noted to r 1.5 at **[10.7]**.

Transitional provisions: the Insolvency (Amendment) Rules 2005, SI 2005/527, r 3(2) provides as follows (note that by virtue of r 1(2) of those Rules "the commencement date" is 1 April 2005)—

"(2)   The provisions of Rules 29, 30, 32 and 39 to these Rules shall apply in any case where, on or after 1st April 2004, a winding-up order has been made or a resolution for the winding up of a company has been passed or a bankruptcy order has been made, before the commencement date.".

[10.388]
4.128   Other matters affecting remuneration

(1)   . . .

(2)   Where there are joint liquidators, it is for them to agree between themselves as to how the remuneration payable should be apportioned. Any dispute arising between them may be referred—

(a)   to the court, for settlement by order, or

(b)   to the liquidation committee or a meeting of creditors, for settlement by resolution.

(3)   If the liquidator is a solicitor and employs his own firm, or any partner in it, to act on behalf of the company, profit costs shall not be paid unless this is authorised by the liquidation committee, the creditors or the court.

NOTES

Para (1): revoked by the Insolvency (Amendment) Rules 2004, SI 2004/584, r 16, as from 1 April 2004, subject to transitional provisions as noted to r 4.127 at **[10.385]**.

[10.389]
[4.129A   Recourse of liquidator to meeting of creditors

If the basis of the liquidator's remuneration has been fixed by the liquidation committee, or by the creditors' committee under Rule 2.106(3C) in a case falling within Rule 4.127(5A) in which the administrator had not requested an increase under Rule 2.107, and the liquidator considers the rate or amount to be insufficient or the basis to be inappropriate, the liquidator may request that the rate or amount be increased or the basis changed by resolution of the creditors.]

NOTES

Commencement: 6 April 2010.

Substituted (for the original r 4.129) by the Insolvency (Amendment) Rules 2010, SI 2010/686, r 2, Sch 1, para 220, subject to transitional provisions in Sch 4, para 1 thereto, as noted to r 1.5 at **[10.7]**.

[10.390]
4.130   Recourse to the court

[(1)   If the liquidator considers that the basis of remuneration fixed by the liquidation committee, or by resolution of the creditors, or as under Rule 4.127(5A) or (6), is insufficient or inappropriate, the liquidator may apply to the court for an order changing it or increasing its amount or rate.]

(2)   The liquidator shall give at least 14 days' notice of his application to the members of the liquidation committee; and the committee may nominate one or more members to appear or be represented, and to be heard, on the application.

(3)   If there is no liquidation committee, the liquidator's notice of his application shall be sent to such one or more of the company's creditors as the court may direct, which creditors may nominate one or more of their number to appear or be represented.

(4)   The court may, if it appears to be a proper case, order the costs of the liquidator's application, including the costs of any member of the liquidation committee appearing [or being represented] on it, or any creditor so appearing [or being represented], to be paid [as an expense of the liquidation].

NOTES
Para (1): substituted by the Insolvency (Amendment) Rules 2010, SI 2010/686, r 2, Sch 1, para 221, as from 6 April 2010, subject to transitional provisions in Sch 4, para 1 thereto, as noted to r 1.5 at **[10.7]**.
Para (4): words in first pair of square brackets inserted by the Insolvency (Amendment) Rules 1987, SI 1987/1919, r 3(1), Schedule, Pt 1, para 65, as from 11 January 1988; words in second pair of square brackets substituted by the Insolvency (Amendment) Rules 2008, SI 2008/737, rr 3, 7(1), as from 6 April 2008, subject to transitional provisions as noted to r 4.218 at **[10.486]**.

[10.391]
4.131   Creditors' claim that remuneration is [or other expenses are] excessive

[(1)   Any secured creditor, or any unsecured creditor with either the concurrence of at least 10% in value of the creditors (including that creditor) or the permission of the court, may apply to the court for one or more of the orders in paragraph (4).

(1A)   Application may be made on the grounds that—
   (a)   the remuneration charged by the liquidator,
   (b)   the basis fixed for the liquidator's remuneration under Rule 4.127, or
   (c)   expenses incurred by the liquidator,
is or are, in all the circumstances, excessive or, in the case of an application under sub-paragraph (b), inappropriate.

(1B)   The application must, subject to any order of the court under Rule 4.49E(5), be made no later than 8 weeks (or, in a case falling within Rule 4.108, 4 weeks) after receipt by the applicant of the progress report, or the draft report under Rule 4.49D, which first reports the charging of the remuneration or the incurring of the expenses in question ("the relevant report").]

(2)   The court may, if it thinks that no sufficient cause is shown for a reduction, dismiss the application; but it shall not do so unless the applicant has had an opportunity to attend the court for [a] hearing, of which he has been given at least [5 business] days' notice [but which is without notice to any other party].
   If the application is not dismissed under this paragraph, the court shall fix a venue for it to be heard, and give notice to the applicant accordingly.

(3)   The applicant shall, at least 14 days before the hearing, send to the liquidator a notice stating the venue and accompanied by a copy of the application, and of any evidence which the applicant intends to adduce in support of it.

[(4)   If the court considers the application to be well-founded, it must make one or more of the following orders—
   (a)   an order reducing the amount of remuneration which the liquidator was entitled to charge;
   (b)   an order fixing the basis of remuneration at a reduced rate or amount;
   (c)   an order changing the basis of remuneration;
   (d)   an order that some or all of the remuneration or expenses in question be treated as not being expenses of the liquidation;
   (e)   an order that the liquidator or the liquidator's personal representative pay to the company the amount of the excess of remuneration or expenses or such part of the excess as the court may specify;
and may make any other order that it thinks just; but an order under sub-paragraph (b) or (c) may be made only in respect of periods after the period covered by the relevant report.]

(5)   Unless the court orders otherwise, the costs of the application shall be paid by the applicant, and are not payable [as an expense of the liquidation].

NOTES
Rule heading: words in square brackets inserted by the Insolvency (Amendment) Rules 2010, SI 2010/686, r 2, Sch 1, para 222(1), (2), as from 6 April 2010, subject to transitional provisions in Sch 4, para 1 thereto, as noted to r 1.5 at **[10.7]**.
Paras (1), (1A), (1B): substituted (for the original para (1)) by SI 2010/686, r 2, Sch 1, para 222(1), (3), as from 6 April 2010, subject to transitional provisions in Sch 4, para 1 thereto, as noted to r 1.5 at **[10.7]**.

Part 10   Miscellaneous other SIs

Para (2): words in first and second pairs of square brackets substituted, and words in third pair of square brackets added by SI 2010/686, r 2, Sch 1, para 222(1), (4), as from 6 April 2010, subject to transitional provisions in Sch 4, paras 1, 2 thereto, as noted to rr 1.5, 1.31 at **[10.7]**, **[10.34]**.

Para (4): substituted by SI 2010/686, r 2, Sch 1, para 222(1), (5), as from 6 April 2010, subject to transitional provisions in Sch 4, para 1 thereto, as noted to r 1.5 at **[10.7]**.

Para (5): words in square brackets substituted by the Insolvency (Amendment) Rules 2008, SI 2008/737, rr 3, 7(1), as from 6 April 2008, subject to transitional provisions as noted to r 4.218 at **[10.486]**.

[10.392]
[4.131A   Review of remuneration

(1)   Where, after the basis of the liquidator's remuneration has been fixed, there is a material and substantial change in the circumstances which were taken into account in fixing it, the liquidator may request that it be changed.

(2)   The request must be made—
  (a)   where the liquidation committee fixed the basis, to the committee;
  (b)   where the creditors fixed the basis, to the creditors;
  (c)   where the court fixed the basis, by application to the court;
  (d)   where the remuneration was determined by application of the realisation scale under Rule 4.127A, to the liquidation committee if there is one or otherwise to the creditors;
and subject to paragraph (3), Rules 4.127 to 4.131 apply as appropriate.

(3)   Where Rule 4.129A is applied in accordance with paragraph (2) of this Rule, ignore the words "in which the administrator had not requested an increase under Rule 2.107".

(4)   Any change in the basis for remuneration applies from the date of the request under paragraph (2) and not for any earlier period.

(5)   This Rule does not apply where the liquidator is the official receiver.]

NOTES
Commencement: 6 April 2010.
Inserted, together with rr 4.131B, 4.131C, by the Insolvency (Amendment) Rules 2010, SI 2010/686, r 2, Sch 1, para 223, subject to transitional provisions in Sch 4, para 1 thereto, as noted to r 1.5 at **[10.7]**.

[10.393]
[4.131B   Remuneration of new liquidator

(1)   If a new liquidator is appointed in place of another, any determination, resolution or court order in effect under the preceding provisions of this Section of this Chapter immediately before the former liquidator ceased to hold office continues to apply in respect of the remuneration of the new liquidator until a further determination, resolution or court order is made in accordance with those provisions.

(2)   This Rule does not apply where the new liquidator is the official receiver.]

NOTES
Commencement: 6 April 2010.
Inserted as noted to r 4.131A at **[10.392]**.

[10.394]
[4.131C   Apportionment of set fee remuneration

(1)   In a case in which the basis of the liquidator's remuneration is a set amount under Rule 4.127(2)(c) and the liquidator ("the former liquidator") ceases (for whatever reason) to hold office before the time has elapsed or the work has been completed in respect of which the amount was set, application may be made for determination of what portion of the amount should be paid to the former liquidator or the former liquidator's personal representative in respect of the time which has actually elapsed or the work which has actually been done.

(2)   Application may be made—
  (a)   by the former liquidator or the former liquidator's personal representative within the period of 28 days beginning with the date upon which the former liquidator ceased to hold office, or
  (b)   by the liquidator for the time being in office if the former liquidator or the former liquidator's personal representative has not applied by the end of that period.

(3)   Application must be made—
  (a)   where the liquidation committee fixed the basis, to the committee;
  (b)   where the creditors fixed the basis, to the creditors for a resolution determining the portion;
  (c)   where the court fixed the basis, to the court for an order determining the portion.

(4)   The applicant must give a copy of the application to the liquidator for the time being in office or to the former liquidator or the former liquidator's personal representative, as the case may be ("the recipient").

(5)   The recipient may within 21 days of receipt of the copy of the application give notice of intent to make representations to the liquidation committee or the creditors or to appear or be represented before the court, as the case may be.

(6)   No determination may be made upon the application until expiry of the 21 days referred to in paragraph (5) or, if the recipient does give notice of intent in accordance with that paragraph, until the recipient has been afforded the opportunity to make representations or to appear or be represented, as the case may be.

(7)   If the former liquidator or the former liquidator's personal representative (whether or not the original applicant) considers that the portion determined upon application to the liquidation committee or the creditors is insufficient, that person may apply—

   (a)   in the case of a determination by the liquidation committee, to the creditors for a resolution increasing the portion;

   (b)   in the case of a resolution of the creditors (whether under paragraph (1) or under sub-paragraph (a)), to the court for an order increasing the portion;

and paragraphs (4) to (6) apply as appropriate.]

NOTES

Commencement: 6 April 2010.
Inserted as noted to r 4.131A at **[10.392]**.

Section E: Supplementary Provisions

[10.395]
4.132   Liquidator deceased (NO CVL APPLICATION)

(1)   Subject as follows, where the liquidator (other than the official receiver) has died, it is the duty of his personal representatives to give notice of the fact to the official receiver, specifying the date of the death.

This does not apply if notice has been given under any of the following paragraphs of this Rule.

(2)   If the deceased liquidator was a partner in [or an employee of] a firm, notice may be given to the official receiver by a partner in the firm who is qualified to act as an insolvency practitioner, or is a member of any body recognised by the Secretary of State for the authorisation of insolvency practitioners.

(3)   Notice of the death may be given by any person producing to the official receiver the relevant death certificate or a copy of it.

(4)   The official receiver shall give notice to the court, for the purpose of fixing the date of the deceased liquidator's release.

NOTES

Para (2): words in square brackets inserted by the Insolvency (Amendment) Rules 2010, SI 2010/686, r 2, Sch 1, para 224, as from 6 April 2010, subject to transitional provisions in Sch 4, para 1 thereto, as noted to r 1.5 at **[10.7]**.

[10.396]
4.133–CVL   Liquidator deceased

(1)   Subject as follows, where the liquidator has died, it is the duty of his personal representatives to give notice of the fact, and of the date of death, to the registrar of companies and to the liquidation committee (if any) or a member of that committee.

(2)   In the alternative, notice of the death may be given—

   (a)   if the deceased liquidator was a partner in [or an employee of] a firm, by a partner [in the firm] qualified to act as an insolvency practitioner or who is a member of any body approved by the Secretary of State for the authorisation of insolvency practitioners, or

   (b)   by any person, if he delivers with the notice a copy of the relevant death certificate.

NOTES

Para (2): words in square brackets inserted by the Insolvency (Amendment) Rules 2010, SI 2010/686, r 2, Sch 1, para 225, as from 6 April 2010, subject to transitional provisions in Sch 4, para 1 thereto, as noted to r 1.5 at **[10.7]**.

[10.397]
4.134   Loss of qualification as insolvency practitioner (NO CVL APPLICATION)

(1)   This Rule applies where the liquidator vacates office on ceasing to be qualified to act as an insolvency practitioner in relation to the company.

(2)   He shall [as soon as reasonably practicable] give notice of his doing so to the official receiver, who shall give notice to the Secretary of State.

The official receiver shall file in court a copy of his notice under this paragraph.

(3)   Rule 4.121 applies as regards the liquidator obtaining his release, as if he had been removed by the court.

NOTES

Para (2): words in square brackets substituted by the Insolvency (Amendment) Rules 2009, SI 2009/642, r 5, as from 6 April 2009, subject to transitional provisions in r 3 thereof, as noted to r 1.4 of these Rules at **[10.6]**.

See Form 4.45 at **[10.673]**.

[10.398]
4.135–CVL   Loss of qualification as insolvency practitioner

(1)   This Rule applies where the liquidator vacates office on ceasing to be qualified to act as an insolvency practitioner in relation to the company.

(2)   He shall [as soon as reasonably practicable] give notice of his doing so to the registrar of companies and the Secretary of State.

(3)   Rule 4.122–CVL applies as regards the liquidator obtaining his release, as if he had been removed by the court.

NOTES

Para (2): words in square brackets substituted by the Insolvency (Amendment) Rules 2009, SI 2009/642, r 5, as from 6 April 2009, subject to transitional provisions in r 3 thereof, as noted to r 1.4 of these Rules at **[10.6]**.

See Form 4.45 at **[10.673]**.

[10.399]
4.136–CVL   Vacation of office on making of winding-up order

Where the liquidator vacates office in consequence of the court making a winding-up order against the company, Rule 4.122-CVL applies as regards his obtaining his release, as if he had been removed by the court.

[10.400]
[4.137   Notice to official receiver of intention to vacate office (NO CVL APPLICATION)

(1)   Where the liquidator intends to vacate office, whether by resignation or otherwise, he shall give notice of his intention to the official receiver together with notice of any creditors' meeting to be held in respect of his vacation of office, including any meeting to receive his resignation.

(2)   The notice to the official receiver must be given at least 21 days before any such creditors' meeting.

(3)   Where there remains any property of the company which has not been realised, applied, distributed or otherwise fully dealt with in the winding up, the liquidator shall include in his notice to the official receiver details of the nature of that property, its value (or the fact that it has no value), its location, any action taken by the liquidator to deal with that property or any reason for his not dealing with it, and the current position in relation to it.]

NOTES

Substituted by the Insolvency (Amendment) Rules 1987, SI 1987/1919, r 3(1), Schedule, Pt 1, para 66, as from 11 January 1988.

[10.401]
4.138   Liquidator's duties on vacating office

(1)   Where the liquidator ceases to be in office as such, in consequence of removal, resignation or cesser of qualification as an insolvency practitioner, he is under obligation [as soon as reasonably practicable] to deliver up to the person succeeding him as liquidator the assets (after deduction of any expenses properly incurred, and distributions made, by him) and further to deliver up to that person—

(a)   the records of the liquidation, including correspondence, proofs and other related papers appertaining to the administration while it was within his responsibility, and

(b)   the company's books, papers and other records.

(2)   . . .

[(3)   Where the liquidator vacates office under section 172(8) (final meeting of creditors), he shall deliver up to the official receiver the company's books, papers and other records which have not already been disposed of in accordance with general regulations in the course of the liquidation. (NO CVL APPLICATION)]

NOTES

Para (1): words in square brackets substituted by the Insolvency (Amendment) Rules 2009, SI 2009/642, r 5, as from 6 April 2009, subject to transitional provisions in r 3 thereof, as noted to r 1.4 of these Rules at **[10.6]**.

Para (2): revoked by the Insolvency (Amendment) Rules 2004, SI 2004/584, r 17, as from 1 April 2004.

Para (3): added by the Insolvency (Amendment) Rules 1987, SI 1987/1919, r 3(1), Schedule, Pt 1, para 67, as from 11 January 1988.

Section F: The Liquidator in a Members' Voluntary Winding Up

[10.402]
4.139   Appointment by the company

(1)   This Rule applies where the liquidator is appointed by a meeting of the company.

(2)   Subject as follows, the chairman of the meeting shall certify the appointment, but not unless and until the person appointed has provided him with a written statement to the effect that he is an insolvency practitioner, duly qualified under the Act to be the liquidator, and that he consents so to act.

(3)   The chairman shall send the certificate [as soon as reasonably practicable] to the liquidator, who shall keep it as part of the records of the liquidation.

(4)   Not later than 28 days from his appointment, the liquidator shall give notice of it to all creditors of the company of whom he is aware in that period.

NOTES

     Para (3): words in square brackets substituted by the Insolvency (Amendment) Rules 2009, SI 2009/642, r 5, as from 6 April 2009, subject to transitional provisions in r 3 thereof, as noted to r 1.4 of these Rules at **[10.6]**.

     See Forms 4.27, 4.28 at **[10.673]**.

[10.403]
4.140   Appointment by the court

(1)   This Rule applies where the liquidator is appointed by the court under section 108.

(2)   The court's order shall not issue unless and until the person appointed has filed in court a statement to the effect that he is an insolvency practitioner, duly qualified under the Act to be the liquidator, and that he consents so to act.

(3)   Thereafter, the court shall send a sealed copy of the order to the liquidator, whose appointment takes effect from the date of the order.

(4)   Not later than 28 days from his appointment, the liquidator shall give notice of it to all creditors of the company of whom he is aware in that period.

NOTES

     See Forms 4.29, 4.30 at **[10.673]**.

[10.404]
4.141   Authentication of liquidator's appointment

A copy of the certificate of the liquidator's appointment or (as the case may be) a sealed copy of the court's order appointing him may in any proceedings be adduced as proof that the person appointed is duly authorised to exercise the powers and perform the duties of liquidator in the company's winding up.

[10.405]
4.142   Company meeting to receive liquidator's resignation

(1)   Before resigning his office, the liquidator must call a meeting of the company for the purpose of receiving his resignation. The notice summoning the meeting shall indicate that this is the purpose, or one of the purposes, of it.

(2)   The notice under paragraph (1) must be accompanied by an account of the liquidator's administration of the winding up, including—

     (a)   a summary of his receipts and payments, and

     (b)   a statement by him that he has reconciled his account with that which is held by the Secretary of State in respect of the winding up.

(3)   Subject as follows, the liquidator may only proceed under this Rule on grounds of ill health or because—

     (a)   he intends ceasing to be in practice as an insolvency practitioner, or

     (b)   there is some conflict of interest or change of personal circumstances which precludes or makes impracticable the further discharge by him of the duties of liquidator.

(4)   Where two or more persons are acting as liquidator jointly, any one of them may proceed under this Rule (without prejudice to the continuation in office of the other or others) on the ground that, in his opinion or that of the other or others, it is no longer expedient that there should continue to be the present number of joint liquidators.

[(4A)   If there is no quorum present at the meeting summoned to receive the liquidator's resignation, the meeting is deemed to have been held.]

(5)   The notice of the liquidator's resignation required by section 171(5) shall be given by him [as soon as reasonably practicable] after the meeting.

(6)   Where a new liquidator is appointed in place of one who has resigned, the former shall, in giving notice of his appointment, state that his predecessor has resigned.

NOTES

Para (4A): inserted by the Insolvency (Amendment) Rules 1987, SI 1987/1919, r 3(1), Schedule, Pt 1, para 68, as from 11 January 1988.

Para (5): words in square brackets substituted by the Insolvency (Amendment) Rules 2009, SI 2009/642, r 5, as from 6 April 2009, subject to transitional provisions in r 3 thereof, as noted to r 1.4 of these Rules at **[10.6]**.

[10.406]
4.143 Removal of liquidator by the court

(1)   This Rule applies where application is made to the court for the removal of the liquidator, or for an order directing the liquidator to summon a company meeting for the purpose of removing him.

(2)   The court may, if it thinks that no sufficient cause is shown for the application, dismiss it; but it shall not do so unless the applicant has had an opportunity to attend the court for [a] hearing, of which he has been given at least [5 business] days' notice [but which is without notice to any other party].

If the application is not dismissed under this paragraph, the court shall fix a venue for it to be heard.

(3)   The court may require the applicant to make a deposit or give security for the costs to be incurred by the liquidator on the application.

(4)   The applicant shall, at least 14 days before the hearing, send to the liquidator a notice stating the venue and accompanied by a copy of the application, and of any evidence which he intends to adduce in support of it.

Subject to any contrary order of the court, the costs of the application are not payable [as an expense of the liquidation].

(5)   Where the court removes the liquidator—
(a)   it shall send 2 copies of the order of removal to him, one to be sent by him [as soon as reasonably practicable] to the registrar of companies, with notice of his ceasing to act;
(b)   the order may include such provision as the court thinks [just] with respect to matters arising in connection with the removal; and
(c)   if the court appoints a new liquidator, Rule 4.140 applies.

NOTES

Para (2): words in first and second pairs of square brackets substituted, and words in third pair of square brackets added by the Insolvency (Amendment) Rules 2010, SI 2010/686, r 2, Sch 1, para 226, as from 6 April 2010, subject to transitional provisions in Sch 4, paras 1, 2 thereto, as noted to rr 1.5, 1.31 at **[10.7]**, **[10.34]**.

Para (4): words in square brackets substituted by the Insolvency (Amendment) Rules 2008, SI 2008/737, rr 3, 7(1), as from 6 April 2008, subject to transitional provisions as noted to r 4.218 at **[10.486]**.

Para (5): words in square brackets in sub-para (a) substituted by the Insolvency (Amendment) Rules 2009, SI 2009/642, r 5, as from 6 April 2009, subject to transitional provisions in r 3 thereof, as noted to r 1.4 of these Rules at **[10.6]**; word in square brackets in sub-para (b) substituted by SI 2010/686, r 2, Sch 1, para 1, as from 6 April 2010, subject to transitional provisions in Sch 4, para 2 thereto, as noted to r 1.31 at **[10.34]**.

See Form 4.39 at **[10.673]**.

[10.407]
4.144 Release of resigning or removed liquidator

(1)   Where the liquidator resigns, he has his release from the date on which he gives notice of his resignation to the registrar of companies.

(2)   Where the liquidator is removed by a meeting of the company, he shall [as soon as reasonably practicable] give notice to the registrar of companies of his ceasing to act.

(3)   Where the liquidator is removed by the court, he must apply to the Secretary of State for his release.

(4)   When the Secretary of State gives the release, he shall certify it accordingly, and send the certificate to the registrar of companies.

(5)   A copy of the certificate shall be sent by the Secretary of State to the former liquidator, whose release is effective from the date of the certificate.

NOTES

Para (2): words in square brackets substituted by the Insolvency (Amendment) Rules 2009, SI 2009/642, r 5, as from 6 April 2009, subject to transitional provisions in r 3 thereof, as noted to r 1.4 of these Rules at **[10.6]**.

See Form 4.41 at **[10.673]**.

[10.408]
4.145 Liquidator deceased

(1)   Subject as follows, where the liquidator has died, it is the duty of his personal representatives to give notice of the fact, and of the date of death, to the company's directors, or any one of them, and to the registrar of companies.

(2)   In the alternative, notice of the death may be given—

(a)   if the deceased liquidator was a partner in [or an employee of] a firm, by a partner [in the firm] qualified to act as an insolvency practitioner or who is a member of any body approved by the Secretary of State for the authorisation of insolvency practitioners, or

(b)   by any person, if he delivers with the notice a copy of the relevant death certificate.

NOTES

Para (2): words in square brackets inserted by the Insolvency (Amendment) Rules 2010, SI 2010/686, r 2, Sch 1, para 227, as from 6 April 2010, subject to transitional provisions in Sch 4, para 1 thereto, as noted to r 1.5 at **[10.7]**.

[10.409]
4.146   Loss of qualification as insolvency practitioner

(1)   This Rules applies where the liquidator vacates office on ceasing to be qualified to act as an insolvency practitioner in relation to the company.

(2)   He shall [as soon as reasonably practicable] give notice of his doing so to the registrar of companies and the Secretary of State.

(3)   Rule 4.144 applies as regards the liquidator obtaining his release, as if he had been removed by the court.

NOTES

Para (2): words in square brackets substituted by the Insolvency (Amendment) Rules 2009, SI 2009/642, r 5, as from 6 April 2009, subject to transitional provisions in r 3 thereof, as noted to r 1.4 of these Rules at **[10.6]**.
See Form 4.45 at **[10.673]**.

[10.410]
4.147   Vacation of office on making of winding-up order

Where the liquidator vacates office in consequence of the court making a winding-up order against the company, Rule 4.144 applies as regards his obtaining his release, as if he had been removed by the court.

[10.411]
4.148   Liquidator's duties on vacating office

Where the liquidator ceases to be in office as such, in consequence of removal, resignation or cesser of qualification as an insolvency practitioner, he is under obligation [as soon as reasonably practicable] to deliver up to the person succeeding him as liquidator the assets (after deduction of any expenses properly incurred, and distributions made, by him) and further to deliver up to that person—

(a)   the records of the liquidation, including correspondence, proofs and other related papers appertaining to the administration while it was within his responsibility, and

(b)   the company's books, papers and other records.

NOTES

Words in square brackets substituted by the Insolvency (Amendment) Rules 2009, SI 2009/642, r 5, as from 6 April 2009, subject to transitional provisions in r 3 thereof, as noted to r 1.4 of these Rules at **[10.6]**.

[10.412]
[4.148A   Remuneration of liquidator in members' voluntary winding up

(1)   The liquidator is entitled to receive remuneration for his services as such.

(2)   [The basis of remuneration shall be fixed]—

(a)   as a percentage of the value of the assets which are realised or distributed, or of the one value and the other in combination, or

(b)   by reference to the time properly given by the insolvency practitioner (as liquidator) and his staff in attending to matters arising in the winding up[, or

(c)   as a set amount.

(2A)   The basis of remuneration may be fixed as any one or more of the bases set out in paragraph (2), and different bases may be fixed in respect of different things done by the liquidator.

(2B)   Where the basis of remuneration is fixed as set out in paragraph (2)(a), different percentages may be fixed in respect of different things done by the liquidator.

(2C)   It is for the company in general meeting to determine—

(a)   which of the bases set out in paragraph (2) are to be fixed and (where appropriate) in what combination under paragraph (2A), and

(b)   the percentage or percentages (if any) to be fixed under paragraphs (2)(a) and (2B) and the amount (if any) to be set under paragraph (2)(c).]

(3)   In arriving at that determination the company in general meeting shall have regard to the matters set out in paragraph (4) of Rule 4.127.

[(4)   If not fixed as above, the basis of the liquidator's remuneration shall, on application by the liquidator, be fixed by the court, and the provisions of paragraphs (2) to (3) apply as they do to the fixing of the basis of remuneration by the company in general meeting; but such an application may not be made by the liquidator unless the liquidator has first sought fixing of the basis in accordance with paragraph (2C), and in any event may not be made more than 18 months after the date of the liquidator's appointment.]

(5)   Rule 4.128 [and Rule 4.127B] shall apply in relation to the remuneration of the liquidator in respect of the matters there mentioned and for this purpose references in that Rule to "the liquidation committee" and "a meeting of creditors" shall be read as references to the company in general meeting.

[(6)   If the liquidator considers that the basis of the remuneration fixed by the company in general meeting is insufficient or inappropriate, the liquidator may apply to the court for an order changing it or increasing its amount or rate.]

(7)   The liquidator shall give at least 14 days' notice of an application under paragraph [(4) or] (6) to the company's contributories, or such one or more of them as the court may direct, and the contributories may nominate any one or more of their number to appear or be represented.

(8)   The court may, if it appears to be a proper case, order the costs of the liquidator's application, including the costs of any contributory appearing or being represented on it, to be paid [as an expense of the liquidation].]

NOTES

Inserted by the Insolvency (Amendment) Rules 1987, SI 1987/1919, r 3(1), Schedule, Pt 1, para 69, as from 11 January 1988.

Para (2): words in first pair of square brackets substituted, and words in second pair of square brackets substituted (together with paras (2A)–(2C)), by the Insolvency (Amendment) Rules 2010, SI 2010/686, r 2, Sch 1, para 228(1)–(3), as from 6 April 2010, subject to transitional provisions in Sch 4, para 1 thereto, as noted to r 1.5 at **[10.7]**.

Paras (2A)–(2C): substituted as noted to para (2) above.

Para (4): substituted by the Insolvency (Amendment) Rules 2004, SI 2004/584, r 18, as from 1 April 2004, subject to transitional provisions as noted to r 4.127 at **[10.385]**; further substituted by SI 2010/686, r 2, Sch 1, para 228(1), (4), as from 6 April 2010, subject to transitional provisions in Sch 4, para 1 thereto, as noted to r 1.5 at **[10.7]**.

Para (5): words in square brackets inserted by the Insolvency (Amendment) Rules 2005, SI 2005/527, r 30, as from 1 April 2005, subject to transitional provisions as noted to r 4.127B at **[10.387]**.

Para (6): substituted by SI 2010/686, r 2, Sch 1, para 228(1), (5), as from 6 April 2010, subject to transitional provisions in Sch 4, para 1 thereto, as noted to r 1.5 at **[10.7]**.

Para (7): words in square brackets substituted by SI 2010/686, r 2, Sch 1, para 228(1), (6), as from 6 April 2010, subject to transitional provisions in Sch 4, para 1 thereto, as noted to r 1.5 at **[10.7]**.

Para (8): words in square brackets substituted by the Insolvency (Amendment) Rules 2008, SI 2008/737, rr 3, 7(1), as from 6 April 2008, subject to transitional provisions as noted to r 4.218 at **[10.486]**.

4.148B   *(Inserted by the Insolvency (Amendment) Rules 2004, SI 2004/584, r 19, as from 1 April 2004; revoked by the Insolvency (Amendment) Rules 2010, SI 2010/686, r 5, as from 6 April 2010, subject to transitional provisions in Sch 4, para 1 thereto, as noted to r 1.5 at **[10.7]**.)*

[10.413]
[4.148C   Members' claim that remuneration is excessive

(1)   Members of the company with at least 10% of the total voting rights of all the members having the right to vote at general meetings of the company, or any member with the permission of the court, may apply to the court for one or more of the orders in paragraph (6) on the grounds that—

    (a)   the remuneration charged by the liquidator,

    (b)   the basis fixed for the liquidator's remuneration under Rule 4.148A, or

    (c)   expenses incurred by the liquidator,

is or are, in all the circumstances, excessive or, in the case of an application under sub-paragraph (b), inappropriate.

(2)   Application must, subject to any order of the court under Rule 4.49E(5), be made no later than 8 weeks (or 4 weeks when the liquidator has resigned in accordance with Rule 4.142) after receipt by the applicant of the report or account which first reports the charging of the remuneration or the incurring of the expenses in question ("the relevant report").

(3)   The court may, if it thinks that no sufficient cause is shown for a reduction, dismiss the application; but it must not do so unless the applicant has had the opportunity to attend the court for a hearing of which the applicant has been given at least 5 business days' notice but which is without notice to any other party.

(4)   If the application is not dismissed under paragraph (3), the court must fix a venue for it to be heard and give notice to the applicant accordingly.

(5)   The applicant must at least 14 days before the hearing send to the liquidator a notice stating the venue and accompanied by a copy of the application and of any evidence which the applicant intends to adduce in support of it.

(6)   If the court considers the application to be well-founded, it must make one or more of the following orders—

    (a)   an order reducing the amount of remuneration which the liquidator was entitled to charge;

    (b)   an order fixing the basis of remuneration at a reduced rate or amount;

    (c)   an order changing the basis of remuneration;

(d)   an order that some or all of the remuneration or expenses in question be treated as not being expenses of the liquidation;

(e)   an order that the liquidator or the liquidator's personal representative pay to the company the amount of the excess of remuneration or expenses or such part of the excess as the court may specify;

and may make any other order that it thinks just; but an order under sub-paragraph (b) or (c) may be made only in respect of periods after the period covered by the relevant report.

(7)   Unless the court orders otherwise, the costs of the application must be paid by the applicant and are not payable as an expense of the liquidation.]

NOTES

Commencement: 6 April 2010.

Inserted, together with rr 4.148D, 4.148E, by the Insolvency (Amendment) Rules 2010, SI 2010/686, r 2, Sch 1, para 229, subject to transitional provisions in Sch 4, para 1 thereto, as noted to r 1.5 at **[10.7]**.

[10.414]
[4.148D   Remuneration of new liquidator

If a new liquidator is appointed in place of another, any determination or court order in effect under Rule 4.148A immediately before the former liquidator ceased to hold office continues to apply in respect of the remuneration of the new liquidator until a further determination or court order is made in accordance with that Rule.]

NOTES

Commencement: 6 April 2010.

Inserted as noted to r 4.148C at **[10.413]**.

[10.415]
[4.148E   Apportionment of fixed fee remuneration

(1)   In a case in which the basis of the liquidator's remuneration is a set amount under Rule 4.148A(2)(c) and the liquidator ("the former liquidator") ceases (for whatever reason) to hold office before the time has elapsed or the work has been completed in respect of which the amount was set, application may be made for determination of what portion of the amount should be paid to the former liquidator or the former liquidator's personal representative in respect of the time which has actually elapsed or the work which has actually been done.

(2)   Application may be made—

(a)   by the former liquidator or the former liquidator's personal representative within the period of 28 days beginning with the date upon which the former liquidator ceased to hold office, or

(b)   by the liquidator for the time being in office if the former liquidator or the former liquidator's personal representative has not applied by the end of that period.

(3)   Application must be made—

(a)   where the company in general meeting fixed the basis, to the company for a resolution determining the portion;

(b)   where the court fixed the basis, to the court for an order determining the portion.

(4)   The applicant must give a copy of the application to the liquidator for the time being in office or to the former liquidator or the former liquidator's personal representative, as the case may be ("the recipient").

(5)   The recipient may within 21 days of receipt of the copy of the application give notice of intent to make representations to the company in general meeting or to appear or be represented before the court, as the case may be.

(6)   No determination may be made upon the application until expiry of the 21 days referred to in paragraph (5) or, if the recipient does give notice of intent in accordance with that paragraph, until the recipient has been afforded the opportunity to make representations or to appear or be represented, as the case may be.

(7)   If the former liquidator or the former liquidator's personal representative (whether or not the original applicant) considers that the portion determined upon application to the company in general meeting is insufficient, that person may apply to the court for an order increasing the portion; and paragraphs (4) to (6) apply as appropriate.]

NOTES

Commencement: 6 April 2010.

Inserted as noted to r 4.148C at **[10.413]**.

Section G: Rules Applying in Every Winding Up, Whether Voluntary or by the Court

[10.416]
4.149   Power of court to set aside certain transactions

(1)   If in the administration of the estate the liquidator enters into any transaction with a person who is an associate of his, the court may, on the application of any person interested, set the transaction aside and order the liquidator to compensate the company for any loss suffered in consequence of it.

(2)   This does not apply if either—
   (a)   the transaction was entered into with the prior consent of the court, or
   (b)   it is shown to the court's satisfaction that the transaction was for value, and that it was entered into by the liquidator without knowing, or having any reason to suppose, that the person concerned was an associate.

(3)   Nothing in this Rule is to be taken as prejudicing the operation of any rule of law or equity with respect to a liquidator's dealings with trust property, or the fiduciary obligations of any person.

[10.417]
4.150   Rule against solicitation

(1)   Where the court is satisfied that any improper solicitation has been used by or on behalf of the liquidator in obtaining proxies or procuring his appointment, it may order that no remuneration [be allowed as an expense of the liquidation] to any person by whom, or on whose behalf, the solicitation was exercised.

(2)   An order of the court under this Rule overrides any resolution of the liquidation committee or the creditors, or any other provision of the Rules relating to the liquidator's remuneration.

NOTES

Para (1): words in square brackets substituted by the Insolvency (Amendment) Rules 2008, SI 2008/737, rr 3, 7(10), as from 6 April 2008, subject to transitional provisions as noted to r 4.218 at **[10.486]**.

CHAPTER 12
THE LIQUIDATION COMMITTEE

[10.418]
4.151   Preliminary (NO CVL APPLICATION)

For the purposes of this Chapter—
   (a)   an "insolvent winding up" is where the company is being wound up on grounds which include inability to pay its debts, and
   (b)   a "solvent winding up" is where the company is being wound up on grounds which do not include that one.

[10.419]
4.152   Membership of committee

(1)   Subject to Rule 4.154 below, the liquidation committee shall consist as follows—
   (a)   in any case of at least 3, and not more than 5, creditors of the company, elected by the meeting of creditors held under section 141 of the Act, and
   (b)   also, in the case of a solvent winding up, where the contributories' meeting held under that section so decides, of up to 3 contributories, elected by that meeting.

(NO CVL APPLICATION)

(2–CVL)   The committee must have at least 3 members before it can be established.

(3)   Any creditor of the company (other than one whose debt is fully secured) is eligible to be a member of the committee, so long as—
   (a)   he has lodged a proof of his debt, and
   (b)   his proof has neither been wholly disallowed for voting purposes, nor wholly rejected for purposes of distribution or dividend.

(4)   No person can be a member as both a creditor and a contributory.

(5)   A body corporate may be a member of the committee, but it cannot act as such otherwise than by a representative appointed under Rule 4.159.

(6)   Members of the committee elected or appointed to represent the creditors are called "creditor members"; and those elected or appointed to represent the contributories are called "contributory members".

[(7)   The following categories of person are to be regarded as additional creditor members—
   (a)   a representative of the Financial Services Authority who exercises the right under section 371(4)(b) of the Financial Services and Markets Act 2000 to be a member of the committee;
   (b)   a representative of the scheme manager who exercises the right under section 215(4) of that Act to be a member of the committee.]

Part 10 Miscellaneous other SIs

NOTES

Para (7): substituted by the Financial Services and Markets Act 2000 (Consequential Amendments and Repeals) Order 2001, SI 2001/3649, art 379, as from 1 December 2001.

[10.420]
4.153 Formalities of establishment

(1) The liquidation committee does not come into being, and accordingly cannot act, until the liquidator has issued a certificate of its due constitution.

(2) If the chairman of the meeting which resolves to establish the committee is not the liquidator, he shall [as soon as reasonably practicable] give notice of the resolution to the liquidator (or, as the case may be, the person appointed as liquidator by that same meeting), and inform him of the names and addresses of the persons elected to be members of the committee.

[(3) No person may act as a member of the committee unless and until he has agreed to do so and, unless the relevant proxy or authorisation contains a statement to the contrary, such agreement may be given by his proxy-holder . . . present at the meeting establishing the committee [or, in the case of a corporation, by its duly appointed representative].

(3A) The liquidator's certificate of the committee's due constitution shall not [be issued] before the minimum number of persons (in accordance with Rule 4.152) who are to be members of the committee have agreed to act [and must be issued as soon as reasonably practicable thereafter].]

(4) As and when the others (if any) agree to act, the liquidator shall issue an amended certificate.

(5) . . .

(6–CVL) The certificate, and any amended certificate, shall be sent by the liquidator to the registrar of companies [as soon as reasonably practicable].

(7) . . .

(8–CVL) If after the first establishment of the committee there is any change in its membership, [as soon as reasonably practicable] the liquidator shall report the change to the registrar of companies.

NOTES

Para (2): words in square brackets substituted by the Insolvency (Amendment) Rules 2009, SI 2009/642, r 5, as from 6 April 2009, subject to transitional provisions in r 3 thereof, as noted to r 1.4 of these Rules at **[10.6]**.

Para (3): substituted, together with para (3A) for original para (3), by the Insolvency (Amendment) Rules 1987, SI 1987/1919, r 3(1), Schedule, Pt 1, para 71, as from 11 January 1988; words omitted revoked, and words in square brackets inserted, by the Insolvency (Amendment) Rules 2010, SI 2010/686, r 2, Sch 1, para 230(1), (2), as from 6 April 2010, subject to transitional provisions in Sch 4, para 1 thereto, as noted to r 1.5 at **[10.7]**.

Para (3A): substituted as noted to para (3) above; words in first pair of square brackets substituted, and words in second pair of square brackets added, by SI 2010/686, r 2, Sch 1, para 230(1), (3), as from 6 April 2010, subject to transitional provisions in Sch 4, para 1 thereto, as noted to r 1.5 at **[10.7]**.

Paras (5), (7): revoked by SI 2010/686, r 2, Sch 1, para 230(1), (4), (6), as from 6 April 2010, subject to transitional provisions in Sch 4, para 1 thereto, as noted to r 1.5 at **[10.7]**.

Paras (6), (8); words in square brackets inserted by SI 2010/686, r 2, Sch 1, para 230(1), (5), (7), as from 6 April 2010, subject to transitional provisions in Sch 4, para 1 thereto, as noted to r 1.5 at **[10.7]**.

See Form 4.47 at **[10.673]**.

[10.421]
4.154 Committee established by contributories (NO CVL APPLICATION)

(1) The following applies where the creditors' meeting under section 141 does not decide that a liquidation committee should be established, or decides that a committee should not be established.

(2) The meeting of contributories under that section may appoint one of their number to make application to the court for an order to the liquidator that a further creditors' meeting be summoned for the purpose of establishing a liquidation committee; and—

    (a) the court may, if it thinks that there are special circumstances to justify it, make that order, and

    (b) the creditors' meeting summoned by the liquidator in compliance with the order is deemed to have been summoned under section 141.

(3) If the creditors' meeting so summoned does not establish a liquidation committee, a meeting of contributories may do so.

(4) The committee shall then consist of at least 3, and not more than 5, contributories elected by that meeting; and Rule 4.153 applies [substituting for the reference in paragraph (3A) of that Rule to Rule 4.152 a reference to this paragraph].

NOTES

Para (4): words in square brackets substituted by the Insolvency (Amendment) Rules 1987, SI 1987/1919, r 3(1), Schedule, Pt 1, para 72, as from 11 January 1988.

[10.422]
4.155 Obligations of liquidator to committee

(1) Subject as follows, it is the duty of the liquidator to report to the members of the liquidation committee all such matters as appear to him to be, or as they have indicated to him as being, of concern to them with respect to the winding up.

(2) In the case of matters so indicated to him by the committee, the liquidator need not comply with any request for information where it appears to him that—
  (a)   the request is frivolous or unreasonable, or
  (b)   the cost of complying would be excessive, having regard to the relative importance of the information, or
  (c)   there are not sufficient assets to enable him to comply.

(3) Where the committee has come into being more than 28 days after the appointment of the liquidator, he shall report to them, in summary form, what actions he has taken since his appointment, and shall answer all such questions as they may put to him regarding his conduct of the winding up hitherto.

(4) A person who becomes a member of the committee at any time after its first establishment is not entitled to require a report to him by the liquidator, otherwise than in summary form, of any matters previously arising.

(5) Nothing in this Rule disentitles the committee, or any member of it, from having access to the liquidator's records of the liquidation, or from seeking an explanation of any matter within the committee's responsibility.

[10.423]
4.156 Meetings of the committee

(1) Subject as follows, meetings of the liquidation committee shall be held when and where determined by the liquidator.

(2) The liquidator shall call a first meeting of the committee to take place within [6 weeks] of his appointment or of the committee's establishment (whichever is the later); and thereafter he shall call a meeting—
  (a)   if so requested by a creditor member of the committee or his representative (the meeting then to be held within 21 days of the request being received by the liquidator), and
  (b)   for a specified date, if the committee has previously resolved that a meeting be held on that date.

(3) [Subject to paragraph (4),] the liquidator shall give [5 business] days' written notice of the venue of a meeting to every member of the committee (or his representative, if designated for that purpose), unless in any case the requirement of the notice has been waived by or on behalf of any member.
  Waiver may be signified either at or before the meeting.

[(4) Where the liquidator has determined that a meeting should be conducted and held in the manner referred to in Rule 12A.26(2), the notice period mentioned in paragraph (3) is 7 business days.

(5) In addition to any functions conferred on a committee by any provision of the Act, a committee must assist the liquidator in discharging the liquidator's functions and act in relation to that liquidator in such manner as may from time to time be agreed.]

NOTES

Para (2): words in square brackets substituted by the Insolvency (Amendment) Rules 2010, SI 2010/686, r 2, Sch 1, para 231(1), (2), as from 6 April 2010, subject to transitional provisions in Sch 4, para 1 thereto, as noted to r 1.5 at **[10.7]**.

Para (3): words in first pair of square brackets inserted, and words in second pair of square brackets substituted, by SI 2010/686, r 2, Sch 1, para 231(1), (3), as from 6 April 2010, subject to transitional provisions in Sch 4, para 1 thereto, as noted to r 1.5 at **[10.7]**.

Paras (4), (5): added by SI 2010/686, r 2, Sch 1, para 231(1), (4), as from 6 April 2010, subject to transitional provisions in Sch 4, para 1 thereto, as noted to r 1.5 at **[10.7]**.

[10.424]
4.157 The chairman at meetings

(1) The chairman at any meetings of the liquidation committee shall be the liquidator, or a person [appointed by the liquidator in writing] to act.

(2) A person so [appointed] must be either—
  (a)   one who is qualified to act as an insolvency practitioner in relation to the company, or
  (b)   an employee of the liquidator or his firm who is experienced in insolvency matters.

NOTES

Paras (1), (2): words in square brackets substituted by the Insolvency (Amendment) Rules 2010, SI 2010/686, r 2, Sch 1, para 232, as from 6 April 2010, subject to transitional provisions in Sch 4, para 1 thereto, as noted to r 1.5 at **[10.7]**.

[10.425]
4.158   Quorum

(1)   A meeting of the committee is duly constituted if due notice of it has been given to all the members, and at least 2 creditor members are present or represented.

(NO CVL APPLICATION)

(2–CVL)   A meeting of the committee is duly constituted if due notice of it has been given to all the members, and at least 2 members are present or represented.

[10.426]
4.159   Committee-members' representatives

(1)   A member of the liquidation committee may, in relation to the business of the committee, be represented by another person duly authorised by him for that purpose.

(2)   A person acting as a committee-member's representative must hold a letter of authority entitling him so to act (either generally or specially) and [authenticated] by or on behalf of the committee-member[, and for this purpose any proxy . . . in relation to any meeting of creditors (or, as the case may be, members or contributories) of the company shall, unless it contains a statement to the contrary, be treated as such a letter of authority to act generally [authenticated] by or on behalf of the committee-member].

(3)   The chairman at any meeting of the committee may call on a person claiming to act as a committee-member's representative to produce his letter of authority, and may exclude him if it appears that his authority is deficient.

[(4)   No member may be represented by—
   (a)   another member of the committee;
   (b)   a person who is at the same time representing another committee member;
   (c)   a body corporate;
   (d)   an undischarged bankrupt;
   (e)   a disqualified director; or
   (f)   a person who is subject to a bankruptcy restrictions order (including an interim order), a bankruptcy restrictions undertaking, a debt relief restrictions order (including an interim order) or a debt relief restrictions undertaking.]

(5)   . . .

(6)   Where a member's representative [authenticates] any document on the member's behalf, the fact that he so [authenticates] must be stated below his [authentication].

NOTES

Para (2): word in first pair and third (inner) pair of square brackets substituted, and words omitted revoked by the Insolvency (Amendment) Rules 2010, SI 2010/686, r 2, Sch 1, paras 1, 233(1), (2), as from 6 April 2010, subject to transitional provisions in Sch 4, paras 1, 2 thereto, as noted to rr 1.5, 1.31 at **[10.7]**, **[10.34]**; words in second (outer) pair of square brackets added by the Insolvency (Amendment) Rules 1987, SI 1987/1919, r 3(1), Schedule, Pt 1, para 73, as from 11 January 1988.

Para (4): substituted by SI 2010/686, r 2, Sch 1, para 233(1), (3), as from 6 April 2010, subject to transitional provisions in Sch 4, para 1 thereto, as noted to r 1.5 at **[10.7]**.

Para (5): revoked by SI 2010/686, r 2, Sch 1, para 233(1), (4), as from 6 April 2010, subject to transitional provisions in Sch 4, para 1 thereto, as noted to r 1.5 at **[10.7]**.

Para (6): words in square brackets substituted by SI 2010/686, r 2, Sch 1, para 1, as from 6 April 2010, subject to transitional provisions in Sch 4, para 2 thereto, as noted to r 1.31 at **[10.34]**.

[10.427]
4.160   Resignation

A member of the liquidation committee may resign by notice in writing delivered to the liquidator.

[10.428]
4.161   Termination of membership

(1)   A person's membership of the liquidation committee is automatically terminated if—
   (a)   he becomes bankrupt . . . , or
   (b)   at 3 consecutive meetings of the committee he is neither present nor represented (unless at the third of those meetings it is resolved that this Rule is not to apply in his case).

(2)   However, if the cause of termination is the member's bankruptcy, his trustee in bankruptcy replaces him as a member of the committee.

(3)   The membership of a creditor member is also automatically terminated if he ceases to be, or is found never to have been, a creditor.

NOTES

Para (1): words omitted revoked by the Insolvency (Amendment) Rules 2004, SI 2004/584, r 21, as from 1 April 2004.

[10.429]
4.162   Removal

(1)   A creditor member of the committee may be removed by resolution at a meeting of creditors; and a contributory member may be removed by a resolution of a meeting of contributories.

(2)   In either case, 14 days' notice must be given of the intention to move the resolution.

[10.430]
4.163   Vacancy (creditor members)
(1)   The following applies if there is a vacancy among the creditor members of the committee.

(2)   The vacancy need not be filled if the liquidator and a majority of the remaining creditor members so agree, provided that the total number of members does not fall below [3].

(3)   The liquidator may appoint any creditor (being qualified under the Rules to be a member of the committee) to fill the vacancy, if a majority of the other creditor members agree to the appointment, and the creditor concerned consents to act.

(4)   Alternatively, a meeting of creditors may resolve that a creditor be appointed (with his consent) to fill the vacancy. In this case, at least 14 days' notice must have been given of the resolution to make such an appointment (whether or not of a person named in the notice).

(5)   Where the vacancy is filled by an appointment made by a creditors' meeting at which the liquidator is not present, the chairman of the meeting shall report to the liquidator the appointment which has been made.

NOTES
Para (2): number in square brackets substituted by the Insolvency (Amendment) Rules 2010, SI 2010/686, r 2, Sch 1, para 234, as from 6 April 2010, subject to transitional provisions in Sch 4, para 1 thereto, as noted to r 1.5 at **[10.7]**.

[10.431]
4.164   Vacancy (contributory members)
(1)   The following applies if there is a vacancy among the contributory members of the committee.

(2)   The vacancy need not be filled if the liquidator and a majority of the remaining contributory members so agree, provided that, in the case of a committee of contributory members only, the total number of members does not fall below [3].

(3)   The liquidator may appoint any contributory member (being qualified under the Rules to be a member of the committee) to fill the vacancy, if a majority of the other contributory members agree to the appointment, and the contributory concerned consents to act.

(4)   Alternatively, a meeting of contributories may resolve that a contributory be appointed (with his consent) to fill the vacancy. In this case, at least 14 days' notice must have been given of the resolution to make such an appointment (whether or not of a person named in the notice).

(5–CVL)   Where the contributories make an appointment under paragraph (4), the creditor members of the committee may, if they think fit, resolve that the person appointed ought not to be a member of the committee; and—
   (a)   that person is not then, unless the court otherwise directs, qualified to act as a member of the committee, and
   (b)   on any application to the court for a direction under this paragraph the court may, if it thinks [just], appoint another person (being a contributory) to fill the vacancy on the committee.

(6)   Where the vacancy is filled by an appointment made by a contributories' meeting at which the liquidator is not present, the chairman of the meeting shall report to the liquidator the appointment which has been made.

NOTES
Para (2): number in square brackets substituted by the Insolvency (Amendment) Rules 2010, SI 2010/686, r 2, Sch 1, para 235, as from 6 April 2010, subject to transitional provisions in Sch 4, para 1 thereto, as noted to r 1.5 at **[10.7]**.
Para (5): word in square brackets in sub-para (b) substituted by SI 2010/686, r 2, Sch 1, para 1, as from 6 April 2010, subject to transitional provisions in Sch 4, para 2 thereto, as noted to r 1.31 at **[10.34]**.

[10.432]
4.165   Voting rights and resolutions (NO CVL APPLICATION)
(1)   At any meeting of the committee, each member of it (whether present himself, or by his representative) has one vote; and a resolution is passed when a majority of the creditor members present or represented have voted in favour of it.

(2)   Subject to the next paragraph, the votes of contributory members do not count towards the number required for passing a resolution, but the way in which they vote on any resolution shall be recorded.

(3)   Paragraph (2) does not apply where, by virtue of Rule 4.154 or 4.171, the only members of the committee are contributories. In that case the committee is to be treated for voting purposes as if all its members were creditors.

(4)   Every resolution passed shall be recorded in writing, either separately or as part of the minutes of the meeting. The record shall be [authenticated] by the chairman and kept with the records of the liquidation.

NOTES

Para (4): word in square brackets substituted by the Insolvency (Amendment) Rules 2010, SI 2010/686, r 2, Sch 1, para 1, as from 6 April 2010, subject to transitional provisions in Sch 4, para 2 thereto, as noted to r 1.31 at **[10.34]**.

[10.433]
4.166–CVL   Voting rights and resolutions

(1)   At any meeting of the committee, each member of it (whether present himself, or by his representative) has one vote; and a resolution is passed when a majority of the members present or represented have voted in favour of it.

(2)   Every resolution passed shall be recorded in writing, either separately or as part of the minutes of the meeting. The record shall be [authenticated] by the chairman and kept with the records of the liquidation.

NOTES

Para (2): word in square brackets substituted by the Insolvency (Amendment) Rules 2010, SI 2010/686, r 2, Sch 1, para 1, as from 6 April 2010, subject to transitional provisions in Sch 4, para 2 thereto, as noted to r 1.31 at **[10.34]**.

[10.434]
4.167   Resolutions [otherwise than at a meeting]

(1)   In accordance with this Rule, the liquidator may seek to obtain the agreement of members of the liquidation committee to a resolution by sending to every member (or his representative designated for the purpose) a copy of the proposed resolution.

(2)   Where the liquidator makes use of the procedure allowed by this Rule, he shall send out to members of the committee or their representatives (as the case may be) a statement incorporating [a copy of any proposed resolution on which a decision is sought, which shall be set out in such a way that agreement with or dissent from each separate resolution may be indicated by the recipient on the copy so sent].

(3)   Any creditor member of the committee may, within 7 business days from the date of the liquidator sending out a resolution, require him to summon a meeting of the committee to consider the matters raised by the resolution. (NO CVL APPLICATION)

(4–CVL)   Any member of the committee may, within 7 business days from the date of the liquidator sending out a resolution, require him to summon a meeting of the committee to consider the matters raised by the resolution.

(5)   In the absence of such a request, the resolution is deemed to have been passed by the committee if and when the liquidator is notified in writing by a majority of the creditor members that they concur with it. (NO CVL APPLICATION)

(6–CVL)   In the absence of such a request, the resolution is deemed to have been passed by the committee if and when the liquidator is notified in writing by a majority of the members that they concur with it.

(7)   A copy of every resolution passed under this Rule, and a note that the committee's concurrence was obtained, shall be kept with the records of the liquidation.

NOTES

Rule heading: words in square brackets substituted by the Insolvency (Amendment) Rules 2010, SI 2010/686, r 2, Sch 1, para 236, as from 6 April 2010, subject to transitional provisions in Sch 4, para 1 thereto, as noted to r 1.5 at **[10.7]**.

Para (2): words in square brackets substituted by the Insolvency (Amendment) Rules 1987, SI 1987/1919, r 3(1), Schedule, Pt 1, para 74, as from 11 January 1988.

[10.435]
4.168   Liquidator's reports

(1)   The liquidator shall, as and when directed by the liquidation committee (but not more often than once in any period of 2 months), send a written report to every member of the committee setting out the position generally as regards the progress of the winding up and matters arising in connection with it, to which he (the liquidator) considers the committee's attention should be drawn.

(2)   In the absence of such directions by the committee, the liquidator shall send such a report not less often than once in every period of 6 months.

(3)   The obligations of the liquidator under this Rule are without prejudice to those imposed by Rule 4.155.

[10.436]
4.169   Expenses of members, etc

The liquidator shall defray [as an expense of the liquidation], in the prescribed order of priority, any reasonable travelling expenses directly incurred by members of the liquidation committee or their representatives in respect of their attendance at the committee's meetings, or otherwise on the committee's business.

NOTES

Words in square brackets substituted by the Insolvency (Amendment) Rules 2008, SI 2008/737, rr 3, 7(1), as from 6 April 2008, subject to transitional provisions as noted to r 4.218 at **[10.486]**.

[10.437]
4.170   Dealings by committee-members and others

(1)   This Rule applies to—
- (a)   any member of the liquidation committee,
- (b)   any committee-member's representative,
- (c)   any person who is an associate of a member of the committee or a committee-member's representative, and
- (d)   any person who has been a member of the committee at any time in the last 12 months.

(2)   Subject as follows, a person to whom this Rule applies shall not enter into any transaction whereby he—
- (a)   receives [as an expense of the liquidation] any payment for services given or goods supplied in connection with the administration, or
- (b)   obtains any profit from the administration, or
- (c)   acquires any asset forming part of the estate.

(3)   Such a transaction may be entered into by a person to whom this Rule applies—
- (a)   with the prior [permission] of the court, or
- (b)   if he does so as a matter of urgency, or by way of performance of a contract in force before the date on which the company went into liquidation, and obtains the court's [permission] for the transaction, having applied for it without undue delay, or
- (c)   with the prior sanction of the liquidation committee, where it is satisfied (after full disclosure of the circumstances) that the person will be giving full value in the transaction.

(4)   Where in the committee a resolution is proposed that sanction be accorded for a transaction to be entered into which, without that sanction or the [permission] of the court, would be in contravention of this Rule, no member of the committee, and no representative of a member, shall vote if he is to participate directly or indirectly in the transaction.

(5)   The court may, on the application of any person interested—
- (a)   set aside a transaction on the ground that it has been entered into in contravention of this Rule, and
- (b)   make with respect to it such other order as it thinks [just], including (subject to the following paragraph) an order requiring a person to whom this Rule applies to account for any profit obtained from the transaction and compensate the estate for any resultant loss.

(6)   In the case of a person to whom this Rule applies as an associate of a member of the committee or of a committee-member's representative, the court shall not make any order under paragraph (5), if satisfied that he entered into the relevant transaction without having any reason to suppose that in doing so he would contravene this Rule.

(7)   The costs of an application to the court for [permission] under this Rule are not payable [as an expense of the liquidation], unless the court so orders.

NOTES

Para (2): words in square brackets substituted by the Insolvency (Amendment) Rules 2008, SI 2008/737, rr 3, 7(11), as from 6 April 2008, subject to transitional provisions as noted to r 4.218 at **[10.486]**.

Paras (3)–(5): word in square brackets substituted by the Insolvency (Amendment) Rules 2010, SI 2010/686, r 2, Sch 1, para 1, as from 6 April 2010, subject to transitional provisions in Sch 4, para 2 thereto, as noted to r 1.31 at **[10.34]**.

Para (7): word in first pair of square brackets substituted by SI 2010/686, r 2, Sch 1, para 1, as from 6 April 2010, subject to transitional provisions in Sch 4, para 2 thereto, as noted to r 1.31 at **[10.34]**; words in second pair of square brackets substituted by SI 2008/737, rr 3, 7(1), as from 6 April 2008, subject to transitional provisions as noted to r 4.218 at **[10.486]**.

[10.438]
[4.171A   Composition of committee when creditors paid in full

(1)   Where the creditors have been paid in full together with interest in accordance with section 189, the liquidator must—
- (a)   issue a certificate to that effect; and
- (b)   send to the registrar of companies a notification to that effect together with a copy of the certificate referred to in sub-paragraph (a).

(2)   On the issue of a certificate pursuant to paragraph (1), the creditor members of the liquidation committee cease to be members of the committee.

(3)   The committee continues in existence unless—
- (a)   it is abolished by a decision of a meeting of contributories; or
- (b)   the number of members is less than 3 and 28 days have elapsed since the issue of the liquidator's certificate.

(4)   At any time in the period referred to in paragraph (3)(b) where the committee consists of less than 3 contributory members it is suspended and cannot act.

(5)   The certificate referred to in paragraph (1)(a) must include the following information—
   (a)   the name of the liquidator; and
   (b)   a statement by the liquidator certifying that the creditors of the company have been paid in full together with interest in accordance with section 189;
and must be authenticated and dated by the liquidator.]

NOTES
Commencement: 6 April 2010.
Substituted (for the original r 4.171) by the Insolvency (Amendment) Rules 2010, SI 2010/686, r 2, Sch 1, para 237, subject to transitional provisions in Sch 4, para 1 thereto, as noted to r 1.5 at **[10.7]**.

[10.439]
4.172   Committee's functions vested in Secretary of State (NO CVL APPLICATION)

(1)   At any time when the functions of the liquidation committee are vested in the Secretary of State under section 141(4) or (5), requirements of the Act or the Rules about notices to be given, or reports to be made, to the committee by the liquidator do not apply, otherwise than as enabling the committee to require a report as to any matter.

(2)   Where the committee's functions are so vested under section 141(5), they may be exercised by the official receiver.

[10.440]
[4.172A   Formal defects

The acts of the liquidation committee established for any winding up are valid notwithstanding any defect in the appointment, election or qualifications of any member of the committee or any committee-member's representative or in the formalities of its establishment.]

NOTES
Inserted by the Insolvency (Amendment) Rules 1987, SI 1987/1919, r 3(1), Schedule, Pt 1, para 75, as from 11 January 1988.

CHAPTER 13
THE LIQUIDATION COMMITTEE WHERE WINDING UP FOLLOWS IMMEDIATELY
ON ADMINISTRATION

(No CVL Application)

[10.441]
4.173   Preliminary

(1)   The rules in this Chapter apply where—
   (a)   the winding-up order has been made [by the court upon an application under paragraph 79 of Schedule B1 to the Act], . . .
   (b)   the court makes an order under section 140(1) of the Act appointing as liquidator the person who was previously the administrator,
   [(c)   a creditors' committee was established under paragraph 57 of Schedule B1 to the Act, and
   (d)   as at the date of the making of the order under section 140(1) the committee has at least three, but not more than five, members (leaving out of account any member whose debt is fully secured).]

(2)   In this Chapter, "insolvent winding up", "solvent winding up", "creditor member" and "contributory member" mean the same as in Chapter 12.

NOTES
Para (1): words in first pair of square brackets substituted by the Insolvency (Amendment) Rules 2003, SI 2003/1730, r 7, Sch 1, Pt 4, para 25, as from 15 September 2003 (for transitional provisions and savings see the note preceding r 2.1 at **[10.60]**); word omitted revoked, and sub-paras (c), (d) added, by the Insolvency (Amendment) Rules 2010, SI 2010/686, r 2, Sch 1, para 238, as from 6 April 2010, subject to transitional provisions in Sch 4, para 1 thereto, as noted to r 1.5 at **[10.7]**.

[10.442]
[4.174A   Continuation of creditors' committee

Where a committee of the kind mentioned in Rule 4.173 is in existence in the circumstances mentioned in that Rule—
   (a)   that committee is deemed to have been established under section 141;
   (b)   no action may be taken under section 141(1) to (3) to establish any other committee;
   (c)   in the case of a solvent winding up, the liquidator must, on not less than 14 days' notice summon a meeting of contributories, in order to elect (if it so wishes) contributory members of the liquidation committee, up to 3 in number; and
   (d)   pending the issue of the liquidator's certificate referred to in Rule 4.176 the committee is suspended and cannot act.]

NOTES

Commencement: 6 April 2010.

Substituted (for the original r 4.174) by the Insolvency (Amendment) Rules 2010, SI 2010/686, r 2, Sch 1, para 239, subject to transitional provisions in Sch 4, para 1 thereto, as noted to r 1.5 at **[10.7]**.

4.175   *(Revoked by the Insolvency (Amendment) Rules 2010, SI 2010/686, r 5, as from 6 April 2010, subject to transitional provisions in Sch 4, para 1 thereto, as noted to r 1.5 at* **[10.7]**.*)*

[10.443]
4.176   Liquidator's certificate

(1)   The liquidator [must ascertain whether the members of the committee agree to continue to act as members of the committee; and if the minimum number of 3 members required by Rule 4.152 to form a committee have signified their agreement so to act, the liquidator must] issue a certificate of the liquidation committee's continuance, specifying the persons who are, or are to be, members of it.

(2)   It shall be stated in the certificate whether or not the liquidator has summoned a meeting of contributories under [Rule 4.174A(c)], and whether (if so) the meeting has elected contributories to be members of the committee.

(3)   . . .

(4)   No person may act, or continue to act, as a member of the committee unless and until he has agreed to do so   . . .

(5)   As and when the others signify their agreement, the liquidator shall issue an amended certificate.

[(6)   The liquidator must send the certificate in paragraph (1) or as the case may be the amended certificate in paragraph (5) to the registrar of companies.]

(7)   If subsequently there is any change in the committee's membership, the liquidator [must send an amended certificate to the registrar of companies].

NOTES

Paras (1), (2): words in square brackets substituted by the Insolvency (Amendment) Rules 2010, SI 2010/686, r 2, Sch 1, para 240(1)–(3), as from 6 April 2010, subject to transitional provisions in Sch 4, para 1 thereto, as noted to r 1.5 at **[10.7]**.

Para (3): revoked by SI 2010/686, r 2, Sch 1, para 240(1), (4), as from 6 April 2010, subject to transitional provisions in Sch 4, para 1 thereto, as noted to r 1.5 at **[10.7]**.

Para (4): words omitted revoked by SI 2010/686, r 2, Sch 1, para 240(1), (5), as from 6 April 2010, subject to transitional provisions in Sch 4, para 1 thereto, as noted to r 1.5 at **[10.7]**.

Para (6): substituted by SI 2010/686, r 2, Sch 1, para 240(1), (6), as from 6 April 2010, subject to transitional provisions in Sch 4, para 1 thereto, as noted to r 1.5 at **[10.7]**.

Para (7): words in square brackets substituted for original words "shall report the change to the court" by SI 2010/686, r 2, Sch 1, para 240(1), (7), as from 6 April 2010, subject to transitional provisions in Sch 4, para 1 thereto, as noted to r 1.5 at **[10.7]**.

See Form 4.52 at **[10.673]**.

[10.444]
4.177   Obligations of liquidator to committee

(1)   As soon as [reasonably practicable] after the issue of the liquidator's certificate under Rule 4.176, the liquidator shall report to the liquidation committee what actions he has taken since the date on which the company went into liquidation.

(2)   A person who becomes a member of the committee after [the date of issue of the liquidator's certificate] is not entitled to require a report to him by the liquidator, otherwise than in a summary form, of any matters previously arising.

(3)   Nothing in this rule disentitles the committee, or any member of it, from having access to the records of the liquidation (whether relating to the period when he was administrator, or to any subsequent period), or from seeking an explanation of any matter within the committee's responsibility.

NOTES

Paras (1), (2): words in square brackets substituted by the Insolvency (Amendment) Rules 2010, SI 2010/686, r 2, Sch 1, para 241, as from 6 April 2010, subject to transitional provisions in Sch 4, para 1 thereto, as noted to r 1.5 at **[10.7]**.

[10.445]
4.178   Application of Chapter 12

Except as provided above in this Chapter, Rules 4.155 to [4.172A] in Chapter 12 apply to the liquidation committee following the issue of the liquidator's certificate under Rule 4.176, as if it had been established under section 141.

NOTES

Figure in square brackets substituted by the Insolvency (Amendment) Rules 1987, SI 1987/1919, r 3(1), Schedule, Pt 1, para 76, as from 11 January 1988.

CHAPTER 14

COLLECTION AND DISTRIBUTION OF COMPANY'S ASSETS BY LIQUIDATOR

[10.446]
4.179   General duties of liquidator (NO CVL APPLICATION)

(1)   The duties imposed on the court by the Act with regard to the collection of the company's assets and their application in discharge of its liabilities are discharged by the liquidator as an officer of the court subject to its control.

(2)   In the discharge of his duties the liquidator, for the purposes of acquiring and retaining possession of the company's property, has the same powers as a receiver appointed by the High Court, and the court may on his application enforce such acquisition or retention accordingly.

[10.447]
4.180   Manner of distributing assets

(1)   Whenever the liquidator has sufficient funds in hand for the purpose he shall, subject to the retention of such sums as may be necessary for the expenses of the winding up, declare and distribute dividends among the creditors in respect of the debts which they have respectively proved.

(2)   The liquidator shall give notice of his intention to declare and distribute a dividend.

(3)   Where the liquidator has declared a dividend, he shall give notice of it to the creditors, stating how the dividend is proposed to be distributed. The notice shall contain such particulars with respect to the company, and to its assets and affairs, as will enable the creditors to comprehend the calculation of the amount of the dividend and the manner of its distribution.

[10.448]
4.181   Debts of insolvent company to rank equally (NO CVL APPLICATION)

[(1)]   Debts other than preferential debts rank equally between themselves in the winding up, and, after the preferential debts, shall be paid in full unless the assets are insufficient for meeting them, in which case they abate in equal proportions between themselves.

[(2)   Paragraph (1) applies whether or not the company is unable to pay its debts.]

NOTES

Para (1) numbered as such, and para (2) added, by the Insolvency (Amendment) Rules 1987, SI 1987/1919, r 3(1), Schedule, Pt 1, para 77, as from 11 January 1988.

[10.449]
4.182   Supplementary provisions as to dividend

(1)   In the calculation and distribution of a dividend the liquidator shall make provision—
   (a)   for any debts which appear to him to be due to persons who, by reason of the distance of their place of residence, may not have had sufficient time to tender and establish their proofs,
   (b)   for any debts which are the subject of claims which have not yet been determined, and
   (c)   for disputed proofs and claims.

(2)   A creditor who has not proved his debt before the declaration of any dividend is not entitled to disturb, by reason that he has not participated in it, the distribution of that dividend or any other dividend declared before his debt was proved, but—
   (a)   when he has proved that debt he is entitled to be paid, out of any money for the time being available for the payment of any further dividend, any dividend or dividends which he has failed to receive, and
   (b)   any dividend or dividends payable under sub-paragraph (a) shall be paid before that money is applied to the payment of any such further dividend.

(3)   No action lies against the liquidator for a dividend; but if he refuses to pay a dividend the court may, if it thinks [just], order him to pay it and also to pay, out of his own money—
   (a)   interest on the dividend, at the rate for the time being specified in section 17 of the Judgments Act 1838, from the time when it was withheld, and
   (b)   the costs of the proceedings in which the order to pay is made.

NOTES

Para (3): word in square brackets substituted by the Insolvency (Amendment) Rules 2010, SI 2010/686, r 2, Sch 1, para 1, as from 6 April 2010, subject to transitional provisions in Sch 4, para 2 thereto, as noted to r 1.31 at **[10.34]**.

[10.450]
[4.182A   Distribution in members' voluntary winding up (NO CVL APPLICATION)

[(1)   In a members' voluntary winding up the liquidator may give notice of the intention to make a distribution to creditors. Such notice—
   (a)   shall be gazetted; and
   (b)   may be advertised in such other manner as the liquidator thinks fit.]

[(2)   In addition to the standard contents, the notice under paragraph (1) must—

(a)   state that the liquidator intends to make a distribution to creditors; and

(b)   specify a date ("the last date for proving") up to which proofs may be lodged at a specified place, which must be the same date for all creditors and not less than 21 days from that of the notice.]

(3)   The liquidator is not obliged to deal with proofs lodged after the last date for proving; but he may do so, if he thinks fit.

(4)   A creditor who has not proved his debt before the last date for proving or after that date increases the claim in his proof is not entitled to disturb, by reason that he has not participated in it, either at all or, as the case may be, to the extent that his increased claim would allow, that distribution or any other distribution made before his debt was proved or his claim increased; but when he has proved his debt or, as the case may be, increased his claim, he is entitled to be paid, out of any money for the time being available for the payment of any further distribution, any distribution or distributions which he has failed to receive.

(5)   Where the distribution proposed to be made is to be the only or the final distribution in that winding up, the liquidator may, subject to paragraph (6), make that distribution without regard to the claim of any person in respect of a debt not already proved.

(6)   Where the distribution proposed to be made is one specified in paragraph (5), the notice given under paragraph (1) shall state the effect of paragraph (5).]

NOTES

Inserted by the Insolvency (Amendment) Rules 1987, SI 1987/1919, r 3(1), Schedule, Pt 1, para 78, as from 11 January 1988.

Para (1): substituted by the Insolvency (Amendment) Rules 2009, SI 2009/642, rr 4, 29, as from 6 April 2009, subject to transitional provisions in r 3 thereof, as noted to r 1.4 of these Rules at **[10.6]**.

Para (2): substituted by the Insolvency (Amendment) Rules 2010, SI 2010/686, r 2, Sch 1, para 242, as from 6 April 2010, subject to transitional provisions in Sch 4, para 1 thereto, as noted to r 1.5 at **[10.7]**.

[10.451]
4.183   Division of unsold assets

[(1)]   Without prejudice to provisions of the Act about disclaimer, the liquidator may, with the permission of the liquidation committee [(or if there is no such committee, a meeting of the company's creditors)], divide in its existing form amongst the company's creditors, according to its estimated value, any property which from its peculiar nature or other special circumstances cannot be readily or advantageously sold.

[(2)   The liquidator must comply with paragraph (3) in respect of any account or report which the liquidator is required to prepare pursuant to any of the following—

(a)   section 104A (progress report to company and creditors at year's end);

(b)   section 106 (final meeting prior to dissolution—creditors' voluntary winding up);

(c)   section 146 (duty to summon final meeting—winding up by the court);

(d)   Rule 4.49B (reports to creditors and members —winding up by the court);

(e)   Rule 4.49D (final report to creditors);

(f)   Rule 4.108 (creditors' meeting to receive liquidator's resignation);

(g)   Rule 4.125 (final meeting—winding up by the court);

(h)   Rule 4.126 (final meeting—creditors' voluntary liquidation).

(3)   The liquidator must—

(a)   in any account or summary of receipts and payments which is required to be included in the account or report, state the estimated value of the property distributed amongst the creditors of the company during the period to which the account or report relates, and

(b)   as a note to the account or summary of receipts and payments, provide details of the basis of the valuation.]

NOTES

Para (1): numbered as such, and words in square brackets inserted, by the Insolvency (Amendment) Rules 2010, SI 2010/686, r 2, Sch 1, para 243(1)–(3), as from 6 April 2010, subject to transitional provisions in Sch 4, para 1 thereto, as noted to r 1.5 at **[10.7]**.

Paras (2), (3): added by SI 2010/686, r 2, Sch 1, para 243(1), (4), as from 6 April 2010, subject to transitional provisions in Sch 4, para 1 thereto, as noted to r 1.5 at **[10.7]**.

[10.452]
4.184   General powers of liquidator

(1)   Any permission given by the liquidation committee [(or if there is no such committee, a meeting of the company's creditors)] or the court under [section 165(2) or] section 167(1)(a), or under the Rules, shall not be a general permission but shall relate to a particular proposed exercise of the liquidator's power in question; and a person dealing with the liquidator in good faith and for value is not concerned to enquire whether any such permission has been given.

(2)   Where the liquidator has done anything without that permission, the court or the liquidation committee may, for the purpose of enabling him to meet his expenses out of the assets, ratify what he has done; but neither shall do so unless it is satisfied that the liquidator has acted in a case of urgency and has sought ratification without undue delay.

NOTES

Para (1): words in square brackets inserted by the Insolvency (Amendment) Rules 2005, SI 2005/527, r 31, as from 1 April 2005.

[10.453]
4.185 Enforced delivery up of company's property (NO CVL APPLICATION)

(1) The powers conferred on the court by section 234 (enforced delivery of company property) are exercisable by the liquidator or, where a provisional liquidator has been appointed, by him.

(2) Any person on whom a requirement under section 234(2) is imposed by the liquidator or provisional liquidator shall, without avoidable delay, comply with it.

[10.454]
4.186 Final distribution

(1) When the liquidator has realised all the company's assets or so much of them as can, in his opinion, be realised without needlessly protracting the liquidation, he shall give notice, under Part 11 of the Rules, either—
    (a) of his intention to declare a final dividend, or
    (b) that no dividend, or further dividend, will be declared.

(2) The notice shall contain all such particulars as are required by Part 11 of the rules and shall require claims against the assets to be established by a date specified in the notice.

(3) After that date, the liquidator shall—
    (a) defray any outstanding expenses of the winding up [as an expense of the liquidation], and
    (b) if he intends to declare a final dividend, declare and distribute that dividend without regard to the claim of any person in respect of a debt not already proved.

(4) The court may, on the application of any person, postpone the date specified in the notice.

NOTES

Para (3): words in square brackets substituted by the Insolvency (Amendment) Rules 2008, SI 2008/737, rr 3, 7(1), as from 6 April 2008, subject to transitional provisions as noted to r 4.218 at **[10.486]**.

CHAPTER 15
DISCLAIMER

[10.455]
4.187 Liquidator's notice of disclaimer

(1) Where the liquidator disclaims property under section 178, the notice of disclaimer shall contain such particulars of the property disclaimed as enable it to be easily identified.

[(2) The notice of disclaimer must be authenticated and dated by the liquidator.]

[(3A) As soon as reasonably practicable after authenticating the notice of disclaimer, the liquidator must—
    (a) send a copy of the notice to the registrar of companies; and
    (b) in any case where the disclaimer is of registered land as defined in section 132(1) of the Land Registration Act 2002, send a copy of the notice to the Chief Land Registrar.]

(4) For the purposes of section 178, the date of the prescribed notice is that [on which the liquidator authenticated it].

NOTES

Para (2): substituted by the Insolvency (Amendment) Rules 2010, SI 2010/686, r 2, Sch 1, para 244(1), (2), as from 6 April 2010, subject to transitional provisions in Sch 4, para 1 thereto, as noted to r 1.5 at **[10.7]**.

Para (3A): substituted (for the original para (3)) by SI 2010/686, r 2, Sch 1, para 244(1), (3), as from 6 April 2010, subject to transitional provisions in Sch 4, para 1 thereto, as noted to r 1.5 at **[10.7]**.

Para (4): words in square brackets substituted by SI 2010/686, r 2, Sch 1, para 244(1), (4), as from 6 April 2010, subject to transitional provisions in Sch 4, para 1 thereto, as noted to r 1.5 at **[10.7]**.

See Form 4.53A at **[10.673]**.

[10.456]
4.188 Communication of disclaimer to persons interested

[(1) Within 7 business days after the date of the notice of disclaimer, the liquidator shall send or give copies of the notice to the persons mentioned in paragraphs (2) to (4).]

(2) Where the property disclaimed is of a leasehold nature, he shall send or give a copy to every person who (to his knowledge) claims under the company as underlessee or mortgagee.

(3) He shall in any case send or give a copy of the notice to every person who (to his knowledge)—
    (a) claims an interest in the disclaimed property, or
    (b) is under any liability in respect of the property, not being a liability discharged by the disclaimer.

(4)   If the disclaimer is of an unprofitable contract, he shall send or give copies of the notice to all such persons as, to his knowledge, are parties to the contract or have interests under it.

(5)   If subsequently it comes to the liquidator's knowledge, in the case of any person, that he has such an interest in the disclaimed property as would have entitled him to receive a copy of the notice of disclaimer in pursuance of paragraphs (2) to (4), the liquidator shall then [as soon as reasonably practicable] send or give to that person a copy of the notice.

But compliance with this paragraph is not required if—
   (a)   the liquidator is satisfied that the person has already been made aware of the disclaimer and its date, or
   (b)   the court, on the liquidator's application, orders that compliance is not required in that particular case.

NOTES

Para (1): substituted by the Insolvency (Amendment) Rules 2010, SI 2010/686, r 2, Sch 1, para 245, as from 6 April 2010, subject to transitional provisions in Sch 4, para 1 thereto, as noted to r 1.5 at **[10.7]**.

Para (5): words in square brackets substituted by the Insolvency (Amendment) Rules 2009, SI 2009/642, r 5, as from 6 April 2009, subject to transitional provisions in r 3 thereof, as noted to r 1.4 of these Rules at **[10.6]**.

See Form 4.53A at **[10.673]**.

[10.457]
4.189   Additional notices

The liquidator disclaiming property may, without prejudice to his obligations under sections 178 to 180 and Rules 4.187 and 4.188, at any time [send or give copies of the] notice of the disclaimer to any persons who in his opinion ought, in the public interest or otherwise, to be informed of [the disclaimer].

NOTES

Words in square brackets substituted by the Insolvency (Amendment) Rules 2010, SI 2010/686, r 2, Sch 1, para 246, as from 6 April 2010, subject to transitional provisions in Sch 4, para 1 thereto, as noted to r 1.5 at **[10.7]**.

See Form 4.53A at **[10.673]**.

[10.458]
[4.190A   Records

The liquidator must include in the liquidator's records of the insolvency a record of—
   (a)   the persons to whom that liquidator has sent or given copies of the notice of disclaimer under the two preceding Rules, showing their names and addresses, and the nature of their respective interests;
   (b)   the dates on which the copies of the notice of disclaimer were sent or given to those persons;
   (c)   the date on which, as required by Rule 4.187(3)(a), a copy of the notice of disclaimer was sent to the registrar of companies; and
   (d)   (where applicable) the date on which, as required by Rule 4.187(3)(b), a copy of the notice was sent to the Chief Land Registrar.]

NOTES

Commencement: 6 April 2010.

Substituted, together with r 4.191A, for original rr 4.190, 4.191, by the Insolvency (Amendment) Rules 2010, SI 2010/686, r 2, Sch 1, para 247, as from 6 April 2010, subject to transitional provisions in Sch 4, para 1 thereto, as noted to r 1.5 at **[10.7]**. Note also that SI 2010/686, r 5 purports to revoke r 4.190 as from the same date.

[10.459]
[4.191A   Application to interested party under s 178(5)

(1)   The following applies where, in the case of any property, application is made to the liquidator by an interested party under section 178(5).

(2)   The application must be delivered to the liquidator—
   (a)   personally;
   (b)   by electronic means in accordance with Part 12A; or
   (c)   by any other means of delivery which enables proof of receipt of the application by the liquidator to be provided, if requested.]

NOTES

Commencement: 6 April 2010.

Substituted as noted to r 4.190A at **[10.458]**.

See Form 4.54 at **[10.673]**.

[10.460]
4.192 Interest in property to be declared on request

(1) If, in the case of property which the liquidator has the right to disclaim, it appears to him that there is some person who claims, or may claim, to have an interest in the property, he may give notice to that person calling on him to declare within 14 days whether he claims any such interest and, if so, the nature and extent of it.

(2) Failing compliance with the notice, the liquidator is entitled to assume that the person concerned has no such interest in the property as will prevent or impede its disclaimer.

NOTES

See Form 4.55 at **[10.673]**.

[10.461]
4.193 Disclaimer presumed valid and effective

Any disclaimer of property by the liquidator is presumed valid and effective, unless it is proved that he has been in breach of his duty with respect to the giving of notice of disclaimer, or otherwise under sections 178 to 180, or under this Chapter of the Rules.

[10.462]
4.194 Application for exercise of court's powers under s 181

(1) This Rule applies with respect to an application by any person under section 181 for an order of the court to vest or deliver disclaimed property.

(2) The application must be made within 3 months of the applicant becoming aware of the disclaimer, or of his receiving a copy of the liquidator's notice of disclaimer sent under Rule 4.188, whichever is the earlier.

(3) The applicant shall with his application file [a witness statement]—
  (a) stating whether he applies under paragraph (a) of section 181(2) (claim of interest in the property) or under paragraph (b) (liability not discharged);
  (b) specifying the date on which he received a copy of the liquidator's notice of disclaimer, or otherwise became aware of the disclaimer; and
  (c) specifying the grounds of his application and the order which he desires the court to make under section 181.

(4) The court shall fix a venue for the hearing of the application; and the applicant shall, not later than [5 business] days before the date fixed, give to the liquidator notice of the venue, accompanied by copies of the application and the [witness statement required by] paragraph (3).

(5) On the hearing of the application, the court may give directions as to other persons (if any) who should be sent or given notice of the application and the grounds on which it is made.

(6) Sealed copies of any order made on the application shall be sent by the court to the applicant and the liquidator.

(7) In a case where the property disclaimed is of a leasehold nature, and section 179 applies to suspend the effect of the disclaimer, there shall be included in the court's order a direction giving effect to the disclaimer.

This paragraph does not apply if, at the time when the order is issued, other applications under section 181 are pending in respect of the same property.

NOTES

Para (3): words in square brackets substituted by the Insolvency (Amendment) Rules 2010, SI 2010/686, r 2, Sch 1, para 248(1), (2), as from 6 April 2010, subject to transitional provisions in Sch 4, para 2 thereto, as noted to r 1.31 at **[10.34]**.

Para (4): words in square brackets substituted by SI 2010/686, r 2, Sch 1, para 248(1), (3), as from 6 April 2010, subject to transitional provisions in Sch 4, paras 1, 2 thereto, as noted to rr 1.5, 1.31 at **[10.7]**, **[10.34]**.

CHAPTER 16
SETTLEMENT OF LIST OF CONTRIBUTORIES

(No CVL Application)

[10.463]
4.195 Preliminary

The duties of the court with regard to the settling of the list of contributories are, by virtue of the Rules, delegated to the liquidator.

[10.464]
4.196 Duty of liquidator to settle list

(1) Subject as follows, the liquidator shall, as soon as may be after his appointment, exercise the court's power to settle a list of the company's contributories for the purposes of section 148 and, with the court's approval, rectify the register of members.

(2)   The liquidator's duties under this Rule are performed by him as an officer of the court subject to the court's control.

[10.465]
4.197   Form of list
(1)   The list shall identify—
    (a)   the several classes of the company's shares (if more than one), and
    (b)   the several classes of contributories, distinguishing between those who are contributories in their own right and those who are so as representatives of, or liable for the debts of, others.
(2)   In the case of each contributory there shall in the list be stated—
    (a)   his address,
    (b)   the number and class of shares, or the extent of any other interest to be attributed to him, and
    (c)   if the shares are not fully paid up, the amounts which have been called up and paid in respect of them (and the equivalent, if any, where his interest is other than shares).

[10.466]
4.198   Procedure for settling list
(1)   Having settled the list, the liquidator shall [as soon as reasonably practicable] give notice, to every person included in the list, that he has done so.
(2)   The notice given to each person shall state—
    (a)   in what character, and for what number of shares or what interest, he is included in the list,
    (b)   what amounts have been called up and paid up in respect of the shares or interest, and
    (c)   that in relation to any shares or interest not fully paid up, his inclusion in the list may result in the unpaid capital being called.
(3)   The notice shall inform any person to whom it is given that, if he objects to any entry in, or omission from, the list, he should so inform the liquidator in writing within 21 days from the date of the notice.
(4)   On receipt of any such objection, the liquidator shall within 14 days give notice to the objector either—
    (a)   that he has amended the list (specifying the amendment), or
    (b)   that he considers the objection to be not well-founded and declines to amend the list.
    The notice shall in either case inform the objector of the effect of Rule 4.199.

NOTES
Para (1): words in square brackets substituted by the Insolvency (Amendment) Rules 2009, SI 2009/642, r 5, as from 6 April 2009, subject to transitional provisions in r 3 thereof, as noted to r 1.4 of these Rules at **[10.6]**.

[10.467]
4.199   Application to court for variation of the list
(1)   If a person objects to any entry in, or exclusion from, the list of contributories as settled by the liquidator and, notwithstanding notice by the liquidator declining to amend the list, maintains his objection, he may apply to the court for an order removing the entry to which he objects or (as the case may be) otherwise amending the list.
(2)   The application must be made within 21 days of the service on the applicant of the liquidator's notice under Rule 4.198(4).

[10.468]
4.200   Variation of, or addition to, the list
The liquidator may from time to time vary or add to the list of contributories as previously settled by him, but subject in all respects to the preceding Rules in this Chapter.

[10.469]
4.201   Costs not to fall on official receiver
The official receiver is not personally liable for any costs incurred by a person in respect of an application to set aside or vary his act or decision in settling the list of contributories, or varying or adding to the list; and the liquidator (if other than the official receiver) is not so liable unless the court makes an order to that effect.

CHAPTER 17
CALLS

(No CVL Application)

[10.470]
4.202   Calls by liquidator
Subject as follows, the powers conferred by the Act with respect to the making of calls on contributories are exercisable by the liquidator as an officer of the court subject to the

court's control.

[10.471]
4.203 Control by liquidation committee

(1)   Where the liquidator proposes to make a call, and there is a liquidation committee, he may summon a meeting of the committee for the purpose of obtaining its sanction.

(2)   At least [5 business] days' notice of the meeting shall be given by the liquidator to each member of the committee.

(3)   The notice shall contain a statement of the proposed amount of the call, and the purpose for which it is intended to be made.

NOTES
Para (2): words in square brackets substituted by the Insolvency (Amendment) Rules 2010, SI 2010/686, r 2, Sch 1, para 249, as from 6 April 2010, subject to transitional provisions in Sch 4, para 1 thereto, as noted to r 1.5 at **[10.7]**.

[10.472]
4.204 Application to court for [permission] to make a call

(1)   For the purpose of obtaining the [permission] of the court for the making of a call on any contributories of the company, the liquidator shall apply [without notice to any other party], supporting his application by [witness statement].

(2)   There shall in the application be stated the amount of the proposed call, and the contributories on whom it is to be made.

(3)   The court may direct that notice of the order be given to the contributories concerned, or to other contributories, or may direct that the notice be publicly advertised.

NOTES
Words in square brackets substituted by the Insolvency (Amendment) Rules 2010, SI 2010/686, r 2, Sch 1, paras 1, 250, as from 6 April 2010, subject to transitional provisions in Sch 4, para 2 thereto, as noted to r 1.31 at **[10.34]**.
See Forms 4.56, 4.57 at **[10.673]**.

[10.473]
4.205 Making and enforcement of the call

(1)   Notice of the call shall be given to each of the contributories concerned, and shall specify—
   (a)   the amount or balance due from him in respect of it, and
   (b)   whether the call is made with the sanction of the court or the liquidation committee.

(2)   Payment of the amount due from any contributory may be enforced by order of the court.

NOTES
See Forms 4.58, 4.59 at **[10.673]**.

CHAPTER 18
SPECIAL MANAGER

[10.474]
4.206 Appointment and remuneration

(1)   An application made by the liquidator under section 177 for the appointment of a person to be special manager shall be supported by a report setting out the reasons for the application.
   The report shall include the applicant's estimate of the value of the [business or property] in respect of which the special manager is to be appointed.

(2)   This Chapter applies also with respect to an application by the provisional liquidator, where one has been appointed, and references to the liquidator are to be read accordingly as including the provisional liquidator. (NO CVL APPLICATION)

(3)   The court's order appointing the special manager shall specify the duration of his appointment, which may be for a period of time, or until the occurrence of a specified event. Alternatively, the order may specify that the duration of the appointment is to be subject to a further order of the court.

(4)   The appointment of a special manager may be renewed by order of the court.

(5)   The special manager's remuneration shall be fixed from time to time by the court.

(6)   The acts of the special manager are valid notwithstanding any defect in his appointment or qualifications.

NOTES
Para (1): words in square brackets substituted by the Insolvency (Amendment) Rules 2010, SI 2010/686, r 2, Sch 1, para 251, as from 6 April 2010, subject to transitional provisions in Sch 4, para 1 thereto, as noted to r 1.5 at **[10.7]**.
See Form 4.60 at **[10.673]**.

[10.475]
4.207   Security

(1)   The appointment of the special manager does not take effect until the person appointed has given (or, being allowed by the court to do so, undertaken to give) security to the person who applies for him to be appointed.

(2)   It is not necessary that security shall be given for each separate company liquidation; but it may be given either specially for a particular liquidation, or generally for any liquidation in relation to which the special manager may be employed as such.

(3)   The amount of the security shall be not less than the value of the [business or property] in respect of which he is appointed, as estimated by the applicant in his report under Rule 4.206.

(4)   When the special manager has given security to the person applying for his appointment, that person shall file in court a certificate as to the adequacy of the security.

(5)   The cost of providing the security shall be paid in the first instance by the special manager; but—
   (a)   where a winding-up order is not made, he is entitled to be reimbursed out of the property of the company, and the court may make an order on the company accordingly, and
   (b)   where a winding-up order is made, he is entitled to be reimbursed [as an expense of the liquidation] in the prescribed order of priority.

(NO CVL APPLICATION)

(6–CVL)   The cost of providing the security shall be paid in the first instance by the special manager; but he is entitled to be reimbursed [as an expense of the liquidation], in the prescribed order of priority.

NOTES

Para (3): words in square brackets substituted by the Insolvency (Amendment) Rules 2010, SI 2010/686, r 2, Sch 1, para 251, as from 6 April 2010, subject to transitional provisions in Sch 4, para 1 thereto, as noted to r 1.5 at **[10.7]**.

Paras (5), (6): words in square brackets substituted by the Insolvency (Amendment) Rules 2008, SI 2008/737, rr 3, 7(1), as from 6 April 2008, subject to transitional provisions as noted to r 4.218 at **[10.486]**.

[10.476]
4.208   Failure to give or keep up security

(1)   If the special manager fails to give the required security within the time stated for that purpose by the order appointing him, or any extension of that time that may be allowed, the liquidator shall report the failure to the court, which may thereupon discharge the order appointing the special manager.

(2)   If the special manager fails to keep up his security, the liquidator shall report his failure to the court, which may thereupon remove the special manager, and make such order as it thinks [just] as to costs.

(3)   If an order is made under this Rule removing the special manager, or discharging the order appointing him, the court shall give directions as to whether any, and if so what, steps should be taken for the appointment of another special manager in his place.

NOTES

Para (2): word in square brackets substituted by the Insolvency (Amendment) Rules 2010, SI 2010/686, r 2, Sch 1, para 1, as from 6 April 2010, subject to transitional provisions in Sch 4, para 2 thereto, as noted to r 1.31 at **[10.34]**.

[10.477]
4.209   Accounting

(1)   The special manager shall produce accounts, containing details of his receipts and payments, for the approval of the liquidator.

(2)   The accounts shall be in respect of 3–month periods for the duration of the special manager's appointment (or for a lesser period, if his appointment terminates less than 3 months from its date, or from the date to which the last accounts were made up).

(3)   When the accounts have been approved, the special manager's receipts and payments shall be added to those of the liquidator.

[10.478]
4.210   Termination of appointment

(1)   The special manager's appointment terminates if the winding-up petition is dismissed or if, a provisional liquidator having been appointed, the latter is discharged without a winding-up order having been made. (NO CVL APPLICATION)

(2)   If the liquidator is of opinion that the employment of the special manager is no longer necessary or profitable for the company, he shall apply to the court for directions, and the court may order the special manager's appointment to be terminated.

(3)   The liquidator shall make the same application if a resolution of the creditors is passed, requesting that the appointment be terminated.

CHAPTER 19

PUBLIC EXAMINATION OF COMPANY OFFICERS AND OTHERS

[10.479]
4.211 Order for public examination

(1)   If the official receiver applies to the court under section 133 for the public examination of any person, a copy of the court's order shall, [as soon as reasonably practicable] after its making, be served on that person.

(2)   Where the application relates to a person falling within section 133(1)(c) (promoters, past managers, etc), it shall be accompanied by a report by the official receiver indicating—
    (a)   the grounds on which the person is supposed to fall within that paragraph, and
    (b)   whether, in the official receiver's opinion, it is likely that service of the order on the person can be effected . . . at a known address [in accordance with Chapter 3 of Part 12A, (service of court documents), and, if so, by what means].

(3)   If in his report the official receiver gives it as his opinion that, in a case to which paragraph (2) applies, there is no reasonable certainty that service [at a known address in accordance with Chapter 3 of Part 12A] will be effective, the court may direct that the order be served by some means other than, or in [addition to, service in such manner].

(4)   In a case to which paragraphs (2) and (3) apply, the court shall rescind the order if satisfied by the person to whom it is directed that he does not fall within section 133(1)(c).

NOTES

Para (1): words in square brackets substituted by the Insolvency (Amendment) Rules 2009, SI 2009/642, r 5, as from 6 April 2009, subject to transitional provisions in r 3 thereof, as noted to r 1.4 of these Rules at **[10.6]**.

Para (2): words omitted revoked, and words in square brackets added, by the Insolvency (Amendment) Rules 2010, SI 2010/686, r 2, Sch 1, para 252(1), (2), as from 6 April 2010, subject to transitional provisions in Sch 4, para 1 thereto, as noted to r 1.5 at **[10.7]**.

Para (3): words in square brackets substituted by SI 2010/686, r 2, Sch 1, para 252(1), (3), as from 6 April 2010, subject to transitional provisions in Sch 4, para 1 thereto, as noted to r 1.5 at **[10.7]**.

See Form 4.61 at **[10.673]**.

[10.480]
4.212 Notice of hearing

(1)   The court's order shall appoint a venue for the examination of the person to whom it is directed ("the examinee"), and direct his attendance thereat.

(2)   The official receiver shall give at least 14 days' notice of the hearing—
    (a)   if a liquidator has been nominated or appointed, to him;
    (b)   if a special manager has been appointed, to him; and
    (c)   subject to any contrary direction of the court, to every creditor and contributory of the company who is known to the official receiver . . .

[(3)   Subject to paragraph (4), where the official receiver thinks fit, notice of the order—
    (a)   shall be gazetted; and
    (b)   may be advertised in such other manner as the official receiver thinks fit,
not less than 14 days before the date fixed for the hearing.]

[(3A)   In addition to the standard contents, the notice under paragraph (3) must state—
    (a)   the purpose of the hearing; and
    (b)   the venue for the hearing.]

[(4)   [Where the court's order relates to a person falling within section 133(1)(c),] unless the court otherwise directs, there shall be no publication under paragraph (3) before at least [5 business] days have elapsed since the examinee was served with the order.]

NOTES

Para (2): words omitted revoked by the Insolvency (Amendment) Rules 2010, SI 2010/686, r 2, Sch 1, para 253(1), (2), as from 6 April 2010, subject to transitional provisions in Sch 4, para 1 thereto, as noted to r 1.5 at **[10.7]**.

Para (3): substituted by the Insolvency (Amendment) Rules 2009, SI 2009/642, rr 4, 30(a), as from 6 April 2009, subject to transitional provisions in r 3 thereof, as noted to r 1.4 of these Rules at **[10.6]**.

Para (3A): inserted by SI 2010/686, r 2, Sch 1, para 253(1), (3), as from 6 April 2010, subject to transitional provisions in Sch 4, para 1 thereto, as noted to r 1.5 at **[10.7]**.

Para (4): added by SI 2009/642, rr 4, 30(b), as from 6 April 2009, subject to transitional provisions in r 3 thereof, as noted to r 1.4 of these Rules at **[10.6]**; words in first pair of square brackets inserted, and words in second pair of square brackets substituted, by SI 2010/686, r 2, Sch 1, para 253(1), (4), as from 6 April 2010, subject to transitional provisions in Sch 4, para 1 thereto, as noted to r 1.5 at **[10.7]**.

[10.481]
4.213 Order on request by creditors or contributories

(1)   A request to the official receiver by creditors or contributories under section 133(2) shall be made in writing and be accompanied by—

(a)   a list of the creditors concurring with the request and the amounts of their respective claims in the liquidation or (as the case may be) of the contributories so concurring, with their respective values, and

(b)   from each creditor or contributory concurring, written confirmation of his concurrence.

This paragraph does not apply if the requisitioning creditor's debt or, as the case may be, requisitioning contributory's shareholding is alone sufficient, without the concurrence of others.

(2)   The request must specify the name of the proposed examinee, the relationship which he has, or has had, to the company and [a statement of] the reasons why his examination is requested.

(3)   Before an application to the court is made on the request, the requisitionists shall deposit with the official receiver such sum as the latter may determine to be appropriate by way of security for the expenses of the hearing of a public examination, if ordered.

(4)   Subject as follows, the official receiver shall, within 28 days of receiving the request, make the application to the court required by section 133(2).

(5)   If the official receiver is of opinion that the request is an unreasonable one in the circumstances, he may apply to the court for an order relieving him from the obligation to make the application otherwise required by that subsection.

(6)   If the court so orders, and the application for the order was made [without notice to any other party], notice of the order shall be given [as soon as reasonably practicable] by the official receiver to the requisitionists. If the application for an order is dismissed, the official receiver's application under section 133(2) shall be made [as soon as reasonably practicable] on conclusion of the hearing of the application first mentioned.

NOTES

Para (2): words in square brackets inserted by the Insolvency (Amendment) Rules 2010, SI 2010/686, r 2, Sch 1, para 254(1), (2), as from 6 April 2010, subject to transitional provisions in Sch 4, para 1 thereto, as noted to r 1.5 at **[10.7]**.

Para (6): words in first pair of square brackets substituted by SI 2010/686, r 2, Sch 1, para 254(1), (3), as from 6 April 2010, subject to transitional provisions in Sch 4, para 2 thereto, as noted to r 1.31 at **[10.34]**; words in second and third pairs of square brackets substituted by the Insolvency (Amendment) Rules 2009, SI 2009/642, r 5, as from 6 April 2009, subject to transitional provisions in r 3 thereof, as noted to r 1.4 of these Rules at **[10.6]**.

See Forms 4.62, 4.63 at **[10.673]**.

[10.482]
4.214   [Examinee] unfit for examination

(1)   Where the examinee [is a person who lacks capacity within the meaning of the Mental Capacity Act 2005 (c 9) or] is suffering from any   . . .   physical affliction or disability rendering him unfit to undergo or attend for public examination, the court may, on [an application being made to it under this Rule], either stay the order for his public examination or direct that it shall be conducted in such manner and at such place as it thinks [just].

(2)   Application under this Rule shall be made—
   (a)   by a person who has been appointed by a court in the United Kingdom or elsewhere to manage the affairs of, or to represent, the examinee, or
   (b)   by a relative or friend of the examinee whom the court considers to be a proper person to make the application, or
   (c)   by the official receiver.

(3)   Where the application is made by a person other than the official receiver, then—
   (a)   it shall, unless the examinee is a [person who lacks capacity within the meaning of the Mental Capacity Act 2005], be supported by the [witness statement] of a registered medical practitioner as to the examinee's mental and physical condition;
   (b)   at least 7 days' notice of the application shall be given to the official receiver and the liquidator (if other than the official receiver); and
   (c)   before any order is made on the application, the applicant shall deposit with the official receiver such sum as the latter certifies to be necessary for the additional expenses of any examination that may be ordered on the application.

An order made on the application may provide that the expenses of the examination are to be payable, as to a specified proportion, out of the deposit under sub-paragraph (c), instead of [as an expense of the liquidation].

(4)   Where the application is made by the official receiver it may be made [without notice to any other party], and may be supported by evidence in the form of a report by the official receiver to the court.

NOTES

Rule heading: word in square brackets substituted by the Insolvency (Amendment) Rules 2010, SI 2010/686, r 2, Sch 1, para 255(1), (2), as from 6 April 2010, subject to transitional provisions in Sch 4, para 1 thereto, as noted to r 1.5 at **[10.7]**.

Para (1): words in first pair of square brackets inserted, and words omitted revoked, by the Mental Capacity Act 2005 (Transitional and Consequential Provisions) Order 2007, SI 2007/1898, at 6, Sch 1, para 12(1), (2)(a), as from 1 October 2007; words in second and third pairs of square brackets substituted by SI 2010/686, r 2, Sch 1, paras 1, 255(1), (3), as from 6 April 2010, subject to transitional provisions in Sch 4, paras 1, 2 thereto, as noted to rr 1.5, 1.31 at **[10.7]**, **[10.34]**.

Para (3): words in first pair of square brackets substituted by SI 2007/1898, at 6, Sch 1, para 12(1), (2)(b), as from 1 October 2007; words in second pair of square brackets substituted by SI 2010/686, r 2, Sch 1, para 255(1), (4), as from 6 April 2010, subject to transitional provisions in Sch 4, para 2 thereto, as noted to r 1.31 at **[10.34]**; words in third pair of square brackets substituted by the Insolvency (Amendment) Rules 2008, SI 2008/737, rr 3, 7(1), as from 6 April 2008, subject to transitional provisions as noted to r 4.218 at **[10.486]**.

Para (4): words in square brackets substituted by SI 2010/686, r 2, Sch 1, para 255(1), (5), as from 6 April 2010, subject to transitional provisions in Sch 4, para 2 thereto, as noted to r 1.31 at **[10.34]**.

See Form 4.64 at **[10.673]**.

[10.483]
4.215 Procedure at hearing

(1)   The examinee shall at the hearing be examined on oath; and he shall answer all such questions as the court may put, or allow to be put, to him.

(2)   Any of the persons allowed by section 133(4) to question the examinee may, with the approval of the court (made known either at the hearing or in advance of it), appear by solicitor or counsel; or he may in writing authorise another person to question the examinee on his behalf.

(3)   The examinee may at his own expense employ a solicitor with or without counsel, who may put to him such questions as the court may allow for the purpose of enabling him to explain or qualify any answers given by him, and may make representations on his behalf.

(4)   There shall be made in writing such record of the examination as the court thinks proper. The record shall be read over either to or by the examinee, [authenticated] by him, and verified by [a statement of truth] at a venue fixed by the court.

(5)   The written record may, in any proceedings (whether under the Act or otherwise) be used as evidence against the examinee of any statement made by him in the course of his public examination.

(6)   If criminal proceedings have been instituted against the examinee, and the court is of opinion that the continuance of the hearing would be calculated to prejudice a fair trial of those proceedings, the hearing may be adjourned.

NOTES

Para (4): words in square brackets substituted by the Insolvency (Amendment) Rules 2010, SI 2010/686, r 2, Sch 1, paras 1, 256, as from 6 April 2010, subject to transitional provisions in Sch 4, para 2 thereto, as noted to r 1.31 at **[10.34]**.

See Form 4.65 at **[10.673]**.

[10.484]
4.216 Adjournment

(1)   The public examination may be adjourned by the court from time to time, either to a fixed date or generally.

(2)   Where the examination has been adjourned generally, the court may at any time on the application of the official receiver or of the examinee—

(a)   fix a venue for the resumption of the examination, and

(b)   give directions as to the manner in which, and the time within which, notice of the resumed public examination is to be given to persons entitled to take part in it.

(3)   Where application under paragraph (2) is made by the examinee, the court may grant it on terms that the expenses of giving the notices required by that paragraph shall be paid by him and that, before a venue for the resumed public examination is fixed, he shall deposit with the official receiver such sum as the latter considers necessary to cover those expenses.

NOTES

See Forms 4.66, 4.67 at **[10.673]**.

[10.485]
4.217 Expenses of examination

(1)   Where a public examination of the examinee has been ordered by the court on a creditors' or contributories' requisition under Rule 4.213, the court may order that the expenses of the examination are to be paid, as to a specified proportion, out of the deposit under Rule 4.213(3), instead of [as an expense of the liquidation].

(2)   In no case do the costs and expenses of a public examination fall on the official receiver personally.

NOTES

Para (1): words in square brackets substituted by the Insolvency (Amendment) Rules 2008, SI 2008/737, rr 3, 7(1), as from 6 April 2008, subject to transitional provisions as noted to r 4.218 at **[10.486]**.

CHAPTER 20
ORDER OF PAYMENT OF COSTS, ETC, OUT OF ASSETS

[10.486]
4.218   General rule as to priority

(1)   [All fees, costs, charges and other expenses incurred in the course of the liquidation are to be regarded as expenses of the liquidation.

(2)   The expenses of the liquidation are payable out of—

   (a)   assets of the company available for the payment of general creditors, which shall be taken to include proceeds—

      (i)   of any legal action which the liquidator has power to bring in his own name or in the name of the company, or

      (ii)   arising from any award made under any arbitration or other dispute resolution procedure which the liquidator has power to bring in his own name or in the name of the company,

     which shall, for the purposes of this subparagraph, also include—

      (iii)   any payments made under any compromise or other agreement intended to avoid legal action or recourse to arbitration or to any other dispute resolution procedure, and

      (iv)   payments made as a result of a settlement of any such action, arrangement or procedure in lieu of or prior to any judgment being given or award being made;

   (b)   subject as provided in Rules 4.218A to 4.218E, property comprised in or subject to a floating charge created by the company.

(3)   Subject as provided in Rules 4.218A to 4.218E, the expenses are payable in the following order of priority—

   (a)   expenses which—

      (i)   are properly chargeable or incurred by the provisional liquidator in carrying out the functions conferred on him by the court;

      (ii)   are properly chargeable or incurred by the official receiver or the liquidator in preserving, realising or getting in any of the assets of the company or otherwise in the preparation or conduct of any legal proceedings, arbitration or other dispute resolution procedures, which he has power to bring in his own name or bring or defend in the name of the company or in the preparation or conduct of any negotiations intended to lead or leading to a settlement or compromise of any legal action or dispute to which the proceedings or procedures relate;

      (iii)   relate to the employment of a shorthand writer, if appointed by an order of the court made at the instance of the official receiver in connection with an examination; or

      (iv)   are incurred in holding an examination under Rule 4.214 (examinee unfit) where the application for it was made by the official receiver;]

   (b)   any other expenses incurred or disbursements made by the official receiver or under his authority, including those incurred or made in carrying on the business of the company;

   [(c)   the fees payable under any order made under section 414 [or section 415A], including those payable to the official receiver (other than the fee referred to in sub-paragraph (d)(i) below), and any remuneration payable to him under general regulations;

   (d)

      (i)   the fee payable under any order made under section 414 for the performance by the official receiver of his general duties as official receiver;

      (ii)   any repayable deposit lodged under any such order as security for the fee mentioned in sub-paragraph (i);]

   (e)   the cost of any security provided by a provisional liquidator, liquidator or special manager in accordance with the Act or the Rules;

   (f)   the remuneration of the provisional liquidator (if any);

   (g)   any deposit lodged on an application for the appointment of a provisional liquidator;

   (h)   the costs of the petitioner, and of any person appearing on the petition whose costs are allowed by the court;

   (j)   the remuneration of the special manager (if any);

   (k)   any amount payable to a person employed or authorised, under Chapter 6 of this Part of the Rules, to assist in the preparation of a statement of affairs or of accounts;

   (l)   any allowance made, by order of the court, towards costs on an application for release from the obligation to submit a statement of affairs, or for an extension of time for submitting such a statement;

   [(la)   the costs of employing a shorthand writer in any case other than one appointed by an order of the court at the instance of the official receiver in connection with an examination;]

   (m)   any necessary disbursements by the liquidator in the course of his administration (including any expenses incurred by members of the liquidation committee or their representatives and allowed by the liquidator under Rule 4.169, but not including any payment of [corporation] tax in circumstances referred to in sub-paragraph (p) below);

(n) the remuneration or emoluments of any person who has been employed by the liquidator to perform any services for the company, as required or authorised by or under the Act or the Rules;

(o) the remuneration of the liquidator, up to any amount not exceeding that which is payable [under Schedule 6];

(p) the amount of any corporation] tax on chargeable gains accruing on the realisation of any asset of the company (without regard to whether the realisation is effected by the liquidator, a secured creditor, or a receiver or manager appointed to deal with a security);

(q) the balance, after payment of any sums due under sub-paragraph (o) above, of any remuneration due to the liquidator[;

(r) any other expenses properly chargeable by the liquidator in carrying out his functions in the liquidation].

NOTES

The words in square brackets from "All fees, costs, charges and other expenses" (in para (1)) to the end of para (3)(a)(iv) were substituted by the Insolvency (Amendment) Rules 2008, SI 2008/737, rr 3, 4, as from 6 April 2008, subject to transitional provisions as noted below.

The original paras (2), (3) were revoked by SI 2002/2712, r 4(1), Schedule, Pt 2, para 23(d), as from 1 January 2003, subject to transitional provisions as noted to r 4.2 at **[10.239]**. The following amendments became amendments to para (3) by virtue of the substitution made by SI 2008/737 as noted above.

Sub-paras (1a), (r) inserted by the Insolvency (Amendment) (No 2) Rules 2002, SI 2002/2712, r 4(1), Schedule, Part 2, para 23, as from 1 January 2003, subject to transitional provisions as noted to r 4.2 at **[10.239]**.

Sub-paras (c), (d) substituted by the Insolvency (Amendment) Rules 1995, SI 1995/586, r 3(1), Schedule, para 1, as from 1 April 1995.

Words in square brackets in sub-para (c) inserted by the Insolvency (Amendment) Rules 2004, SI 2004/584, r 22, as from 1 April 2004.

Words in square brackets in sub-paras (m), (p) substituted by the Insolvency (Amendment) Rules 1987, SI 1987/1919, r 3(1), Schedule, Pt 1, para 79, as from 11 January 1988.

Words in square brackets in sub-para (o) substituted by the Insolvency (Amendment) Rules 2005, SI 2005/527, r 32, as from 1 April 2005, subject to transitional provisions as noted to r 4.127B at **[10.387]**.

Transitional provisions: SI 2008/737, r 2 provides as follows (note that by virtue of r 1, the "commencement date" is 6 April 2008)—

"2 Transitional provisions

The amendments to the principal Rules made by Rules 3, 4, 5, 6 and 7 of these Rules shall apply—

(a) to a creditors' voluntary winding up—
  (i) in respect of which the resolution is passed, or
  (ii) where it commenced as a members' voluntary winding up, for which the conversion to a creditors' voluntary winding up under section 96 takes effect, or
  (iii) in respect of which a notice is registered under paragraph 83 of Schedule B1 to the Act, on or after the commencement date;

(b) to a members' voluntary winding up for which the resolution is passed on or after the commencement date; and

(c) to a winding up of a company by the court where the winding up order is made on or after the commencement date except where the winding-up order is made following a resolution for a voluntary winding up passed by that company before the commencement date.".

[10.487]
[4.218A Litigation expenses and property subject to a floating charge—general provisions

(1) In this Rule and Rules 4.218B to 4.218E—

(a) "approval" and "authorisation" respectively mean:
  (i) where yet to be incurred, the approval, and
  (ii) where already incurred, the authorisation, of expenses specified in section 176ZA(3);

(b) "the creditor" means—
  (i) a preferential creditor of the company, or
  (ii) a holder of a debenture secured by, or a holder of, a floating charge created by the company;

(c) "legal proceedings" means—
  (i) proceedings under sections 212, 213, 214, 238, 239, 244 and 423 and any arbitration or other dispute resolution proceedings invoked for purposes corresponding to those to which the sections relate and any other proceedings, including arbitration or other dispute resolution procedures, which a liquidator has power to bring in his own name for the purpose of preserving, realising, or getting in any of the assets of the company;
  (ii) legal actions and proceedings, arbitration or any other dispute resolution procedures which a liquidator has power to bring or defend in the name of the company, and
  (iii) negotiations intended to lead or leading to a settlement or compromise of any action, proceeding or procedure to which subparagraphs (i) or (ii) relate;

(d) "litigation expenses" means expenses of a liquidation which—
  (i) are properly chargeable or incurred in the preparation or conduct of any legal proceedings, and

> (ii)   as expenses in the liquidation, exceed, or in the opinion of the liquidator are likely to exceed (and only in so far as they exceed or are likely to exceed), in the aggregate £5000.

(2)   Litigation expenses shall not have the priority provided by section 176ZA over any claims to property comprised in or subject to a floating charge created by the company and shall not be paid out of any such property unless and until approved or authorised in accordance with Rules 4.218B to 4.218E.]

NOTES

Commencement: 6 April 2008.

Inserted by the Insolvency (Amendment) Rules 2008, SI 2008/737, rr 3, 5, as from 6 April 2008, subject to transitional provisions as noted to r 4.218 at **[10.486]**.

[10.488]
[4.218B   Litigation expenses and property subject to a floating charge—requirement for approval or authorisation

(1)   Subject to Rules 4.218C to 4.218E, paragraphs (2) and (3) or (4) apply where, in the course of winding up a company, the liquidator—
   (a)   ascertains that property is comprised in or subject to a floating charge;
   (b)   has himself instituted or proposes to institute or continue legal proceedings or is in the process of defending or proposes to defend any legal proceeding brought or likely to be brought against the company; and
   (c)   prior to or at any stage in those proceedings, is of the opinion that—
      (i)   the assets of the company available for payment of general creditors are or will be insufficient to pay litigation expenses; and
      (ii)   in order to pay litigation expenses he will have to have recourse to property comprised in or subject to a floating charge created by the company.

(2)   As soon as reasonably practicable after the date on which he forms the opinion referred to in paragraph (1), the liquidator shall identify the creditor who, in his opinion at that time—
   (a)   has a claim to property comprised in or subject to a floating charge created by the company, and,
   (b)   taking into account the value of that claim and any subsisting property then comprised in or secured by such a charge, appears to the liquidator to be the creditor most immediately likely of any persons having such claims to receive some payment in respect of his claim but whose claim would not be paid in full ("the specified creditor").

(3)   The liquidator shall request from the specified creditor the approval or authorisation of such amount for litigation expenses as the liquidator thinks fit.

(4)   Where, in the liquidator's opinion, two or more creditors who are holders of debentures secured by, or holders of, floating charges created by the company, meet the condition in paragraph (2), the liquidator is to seek from each of them ("the specified creditors") approval or authorisation of such amount of litigation expenses as the liquidator thinks fit, apportioned between them ("the apportioned amount") according to the value of the property to the extent covered by their charges.

(5)   For so long as the conditions specified in paragraph (1) subsist, the liquidator may, in the course of a winding up, make such further requests to the specified creditor or creditors for approval or authorisation of such further amount for litigation expenses as he thinks fit to be paid out of property comprised in or subject to a floating charge created by the company, taking into account any amount for litigation expenses previously approved or authorised and the value of the property comprised in or subject to the floating charge.]

NOTES

Commencement: 6 April 2008.

Inserted by the Insolvency (Amendment) Rules 2008, SI 2008/737, rr 3, 5, as from 6 April 2008, subject to transitional provisions as noted to r 4.218 at **[10.486]**.

[10.489]
[4.218C   Litigation expenses and property subject to a floating charge—request for approval or authorisation

(1)   All requests made by the liquidator for approval or authorisation shall be in writing whether in Form 4.74 or otherwise, and shall include the following—
   (a)   a statement describing the nature of the legal proceedings, including, where relevant, the statutory provision under which proceedings are or are to be brought and the grounds upon which the liquidator relies;
   (b)   where the power to bring those proceedings is subject to sanction, a statement that the liquidator has sought and been given the relevant permissions or an undertaking that the liquidator will seek the relevant permissions upon authorisation or approval being granted;
   (c)   a statement specifying the amount or apportioned amount of litigation expenses for which approval or authorisation is sought ("the specified amount");

(d)		notice that approval or authorisation or other reply to the request must be made in writing (whether by way of Form 4.74 or otherwise) within 28 days from the date of its being received ("the specified time limit"); and

(e)		a statement explaining the consequences of a failure to reply within the specified time limit.

(2)		Where anything in paragraph (1) requires the inclusion of any information, the disclosure of which could be seriously prejudicial to the winding up of the company, the liquidator may—

(a)		exclude such information from any of the above, provided that it is accompanied by a statement to that effect; or

(b)		include it on terms—

(i)		that bind the creditor to keep the information confidential, and

(ii)		that include an undertaking on the part of the liquidator to apply to the court for an order that so much of the information as may be kept in the files of the court, not be open to public inspection.

(3)		The creditor may within the specified time limit apply to the liquidator in writing for such further particulars as is reasonable and in such a case, the time limit specified in paragraph (1)(d) shall apply from the date of the creditor's receipt of the liquidator's response to any such request.

(4)		Where the liquidator requires the approval or authorisation of two or more creditors, he shall send a request to each creditor in writing (whether by way of Form 4.74 or otherwise), containing the matters listed in paragraph (1) and also giving—

(a)		the number of creditors concerned,

(b)		the total value of their claims, or if not known, as it is estimated to be by the liquidator immediately prior to sending any such request, and

(c)		to each preferential creditor, notice that approval or authorisation of the specified amount shall be taken to be given where a majority in value of those preferential creditors who respond within the specified time limit are in favour of it, or

(d)		where Rule 4.218B(4) applies, notice to the specified creditors that the amount of litigation expenses will be apportioned between them in accordance with that rule and notice of the value of the portion allocated to, and the identity of, the specified creditors affected by that apportionment.]

NOTES

Commencement: 6 April 2008.

Inserted by the Insolvency (Amendment) Rules 2008, SI 2008/737, rr 3, 5, as from 6 April 2008, subject to transitional provisions as noted to r 4.218 at **[10.486]**.

See Form 4.74 at **[10.673]**.

[10.490]
[4.218D Litigation expenses and property subject to a floating charge—grant of approval or authorisation

(1)		Where the liquidator fails to include in his request any one of the matters, statements or notices required to be specified by paragraph (1) or paragraphs (1) and (4), of Rule 4.218C, as the case may be, the request for approval or authorisation shall be treated as not having been made.

(2)		Subject to paragraphs (3), (4) and (5), approval or authorisation shall be taken to have been given where the specified amount has been requested by the liquidator, and—

(a)		that amount is approved or authorised within the specified time limit; or

(b)		a different amount is approved or authorised within the specified time limit and the liquidator considers it sufficient.

(3)		Where the liquidator requires the approval or authorisation of two or more preferential creditors, approval or authorisation shall be taken to be given where a majority in value of those who respond within the specified time limit approve or authorise—

(a)		the specified amount, or

(b)		a different amount which the liquidator considers sufficient.

(4)		Where a majority in value of two or more preferential creditors propose an amount other than that specified by the liquidator, they shall be taken to have approved or authorised an amount equal to the lowest of the amounts so proposed.

(5)		In any case in which there is no response in writing within the specified time limit to the liquidator's request—

(a)		at all, or

(b)		at any time following the liquidator's provision of further particulars under Rule 4.218C(3),

the liquidator's request shall be taken to have been approved or authorised from the date of the expiry of that time limit.]

NOTES

Commencement: 6 April 2008.

Inserted by the Insolvency (Amendment) Rules 2008, SI 2008/737, rr 3, 5, as from 6 April 2008, subject to transitional provisions as noted to r 4.218 at **[10.486]**.

[10.491]
[4.218E   Litigation expenses and property subject to a floating charge—application to court by the liquidator

(1)   In the circumstances specified below the court may, upon the application of the liquidator, approve or authorise such amount of litigation expenses as it thinks [just].

(2)   Save as provided by paragraph (3), application to the court by a liquidator for an order approving or authorising an amount for litigation expenses may only be made where—

   (a)   the specified creditor (or, if more than one, any one of them) is or is intended to be a defendant in the legal proceedings in respect of which the litigation expenses have been or are to be incurred; or

   (b)   the specified creditor has been requested to approve or authorise the amount specified under Rule 4.218C(1)(c) and has, in any case—

      (i)   declined to approve or authorise, as the case may be, the specified amount; or

      (ii)   has approved or authorised an amount which is less than the specified amount and which lesser amount the liquidator considers insufficient, or

      (iii)   made such application for further particulars or other response to the liquidator's request as is, in the liquidator's opinion, unreasonable.

(3)   Where the liquidator is of the view that circumstances are such that he requires urgent approval or authorisation of litigation expenses, he may apply to the court for approval or authorisation either—

   (a)   without seeking approval or authorisation from the specified creditor; or

   (b)   if sought, prior to the expiry of the specified time limit.

(4)   The court may grant such application for approval or authorisation—

   (a)   provided that the liquidator satisfies it of the urgency of the case, and

   (b)   subject to such terms and conditions as it thinks [just].

(5)   The liquidator shall, at the same time as making any application to the court under this rule, send copies of it to the specified creditor or creditors, unless the court orders otherwise.

(6)   The specified creditor (including any one or all of them where there are two or more such creditors) is entitled to be heard on any such application unless the court orders otherwise.

(7)   The court may grant approval or authorisation subject to such terms and conditions as it may think [just], including terms and conditions relating to the amount or nature of the litigation expenses and as to any obligation to make further applications to the court under this Rule.

(8)   The costs of the liquidator's application under this Rule, including the costs of any specified creditor appearing or represented on it, shall be an expense of the liquidation unless the court orders otherwise.]

NOTES

Commencement: 6 April 2008.

Inserted by the Insolvency (Amendment) Rules 2008, SI 2008/737, rr 3, 5, as from 6 April 2008, subject to transitional provisions as noted to r 4.218 at **[10.486]**.

Paras (1), (4), (7): word in square brackets substituted by the Insolvency (Amendment) Rules 2010, SI 2010/686, r 2, Sch 1, para 1, as from 6 April 2010, subject to transitional provisions in Sch 4, para 2 thereto, as noted to r 1.31 at **[10.34]**.

[10.492]
4.219   Winding up commencing as voluntary

In a winding up by the court which follows immediately on a voluntary winding up (whether members' voluntary or creditors' voluntary), such remuneration of the voluntary liquidator and costs and expenses of the voluntary liquidation as the court may allow are to rank in priority with the expenses specified in Rule [4.218(3)(a)].

NOTES

Figure in square brackets substituted by the Insolvency (Amendment) Rules 2008, SI 2008/737, rr 3, 7(14), as from 6 April 2008, subject to transitional provisions as noted to r 4.218 at **[10.486]**.

[10.493]
4.220   Saving for powers of the court

(1)   In a winding up by the court, the priorities laid down by Rules 4.218 and 4.219 are subject to the power of the court to make orders under section 156, where the assets are insufficient to satisfy the liabilities.

(2)   Nothing in those Rules applies to or affects the power of any court, in proceedings by or against the company, to order costs to be paid by the company, or the liquidator; nor do they affect the rights of any person to whom such costs are ordered to be paid.

CHAPTER 21
MISCELLANEOUS RULES

Section A: Return of Capital
(No CVL Application)

[10.494]
4.221 Application to court for order authorising return

(1) This Rule applies where the liquidator intends to apply to the court for an order authorising a return of capital.

(2) The application shall be accompanied by a list of the persons to whom the return is to be made.

(3) The list shall include the same details of those persons as appears in the settled list of contributories, with any necessary alterations to take account of matters after settlement of the list, and the amount to be paid to each person.

(4) Where the court makes an order authorising the return, it shall send a sealed copy of the order to the liquidator.

[10.495]
4.222 Procedure for return

(1) The liquidator shall inform each person to whom a return is made of the rate of return per share, and whether it is expected that any further return will be made.

(2) Any payments made by the liquidator by way of the return may be sent by post, unless for any reason another method of making the payment has been agreed with the payee.

Section B: Conclusion of Winding Up

4.233 *(Revoked by the Insolvency (Amendment) Rules 2010, SI 2010/686, r 5, as from 6 April 2010, subject to transitional provisions in Sch 4, para 1 thereto, as noted to r 1.5 at* **[10.7]**.)

Section C: Dissolution after Winding Up

[10.496]
4.224 Secretary of State's directions under ss 203, 205

(1) Where the Secretary of State gives a direction under—
  (a) section 203 (where official receiver applies to registrar of companies for a company's early dissolution), or
  (b) section 205 (application by interested person for postponement of dissolution),
he shall send two copies of the direction to the applicant for it.

(2) Of those copies one shall be sent by the applicant to the registrar of companies, to comply with section 203(5) or, as the case may be, 205(6).

[10.497]
4.225 Procedure following appeal under s 203(4) or 205(4)

Following an appeal under section 203(4) or 205(4) (against a decision of the Secretary of State under the applicable section) the court shall send two sealed copies of its order to the person in whose favour the appeal was determined; and that party shall send one of the copies to the registrar of companies to comply with section 203(5) or, as the case may be, 205(6).

CHAPTER 22
[PERMISSION] TO ACT AS DIRECTOR, ETC, OF COMPANY WITH PROHIBITED NAME
(SECTION 216 OF THE ACT)

NOTES
Word in square brackets substituted in the heading above by the Insolvency (Amendment) Rules 2010, SI 2010/686, r 2, Sch 1, para 1, as from 6 April 2010, subject to transitional provisions in Sch 4, para 2 thereto, as noted to r 1.31 at **[10.34]**.

[10.498]
4.226 Preliminary

The Rules in this Chapter—
  (a) relate to the [permission] required under section 216 (restriction on re-use of name of company in insolvent liquidation) for a person to act as mentioned in section 216(3) in relation to a company with a prohibited name,
  (b) prescribe the cases excepted from that provision, that is to say, those in which a person to whom the section applies may so act without that [permission][, and
  (c) apply to all windings up to which section 216 applies, whether or not the winding up commenced before the coming into force of the Rules].

NOTES

Word in square brackets in paras (a), (b) substituted by the Insolvency (Amendment) Rules 2010, SI 2010/686, r 2, Sch 1, para 1, as from 6 April 2010, subject to transitional provisions in Sch 4, para 2 thereto, as noted to r 1.31 at **[10.34]**; word omitted from para (a) revoked, and para (c) and the word immediately preceding it added, by the Insolvency (Amendment) Rules 1987, SI 1987/1919, r 3(1), Schedule, Pt 1, para 81, as from 11 January 1988.

[10.499]
[4.227A   Application for permission under s 216(3)

(1)   At least 14 days notice of any application for permission to act in any of the circumstances which would otherwise be prohibited by section 216(3) must be given by the applicant to the Secretary of State, who may—

  (a)   appear at the hearing of the application; and

  (b)   whether or not appearing at the hearing, make representations.

(2)   When considering an application for permission under section 216, the court may call on the liquidator, or any former liquidator, of the liquidating company for a report of the circumstances in which that company became insolvent and the extent (if any) of the applicant's apparent responsibility for its doing so.]

NOTES

Commencement: 6 April 2010.

Substituted (for the original r 4.227) by the Insolvency (Amendment) Rules 2010, SI 2010/686, r 2, Sch 1, para 257, subject to transitional provisions in Sch 4, para 1 thereto, as noted to r 1.5 at **[10.7]**.

[10.500]
[4.228   First excepted case

(1)   This Rule applies where—

  (a)   a person ("the person") was within the period mentioned in section 216(1) a director, or shadow director, of an insolvent company that has gone into insolvent liquidation

  (b)   the person acts in all or any of the ways specified in section 216(3) in connection with, or for the purposes of, the carrying on (or proposed carrying on) of the whole or substantially the whole of the business of the insolvent company where that business (or substantially the whole of it) is (or is to be) acquired from the insolvent company under arrangements—

    (i)   made by its liquidator; or

    (ii)   made before the insolvent company entered into insolvent liquidation by an office-holder acting in relation to it as administrator, administrative receiver or supervisor of a voluntary arrangement under Part 1 of the Act.

(2)   The person, will not be taken to have contravened section 216 if prior to his acting in the circumstances set out in paragraph (1) a notice is, in accordance with the requirements of paragraph (3),—

  (a)   given by the person, to every creditor of the insolvent company whose name and address—

    (i)   is known by him; or

    (ii)   is ascertainable by him on the making of such enquiries as are reasonable in the circumstances; and

  (b)   published in the Gazette.

(3)   The notice referred to in paragraph (2)—

  (a)   may . . .   be given and published before the completion of the arrangements referred to in paragraph (1)(b) but must be given and published no later than 28 days after that completion;

  (b)   must state—

    (i)   the name and registered number of the insolvent company;

    (ii)   the name of the person;

    (iii)   that it is his intention to act (or, where the insolvent company has not entered insolvent liquidation, to act or continue to act) in all or any of the ways specified in section 216(3) in connection with, or for the purposes of, the carrying on of the whole or substantially the whole of the business of the insolvent company; and

    (iv)   the prohibited name or, where the company has not entered insolvent liquidation, the name under which the business is being, or is to be, carried on which would be a prohibited name in respect of the person in the event of the insolvent company entering insolvent liquidation; and

  (c)   must in the case of notice given to each creditor of the company be given using Form 4.73.

(4)   Notice may in particular be given under this Rule—

  (a)   prior to the insolvent company entering insolvent liquidation where the business (or substantially the whole of the business) is, or is to be, acquired by another company under arrangements made by an office-holder acting in relation to the insolvent company as administrator, administrative receiver or supervisor of a voluntary arrangement (whether or not at the time of the giving of the notice the director is a director of that other company); or

(b)   at a time where the person is a director of another company where—
     (i)   the other company has acquired, or is to acquire, the whole, or substantially the whole, of the business of the insolvent company under arrangements made by its liquidator; and
     (ii)   it is proposed that after the giving of the notice a prohibited name should be adopted by the other company.]

NOTES

Commencement: 6 August 2007.

Substituted by the Insolvency (Amendment) Rules 2007, SI 2007/1974, r 3(1), (2), as from 6 August 2007; for transitional provisions see the note below.

Para (3): words omitted revoked by the Insolvency (Amendment) Rules 2010, SI 2010/686, r 2, Sch 1, para 258, as from 6 April 2010, subject to transitional provisions in Sch 4, para 1 thereto, as noted to r 1.5 at **[10.7]**.

Transitional provisions: SI 2007/1974, r 2 provides as follows (the "the commencement date" is 6 August 2007)—

> **"2   Transitional provision**
>
> Rule 4.228 of the Insolvency Rules 1986 as it stands before the commencement date shall, in relation to any arrangements referred to in paragraph (1) of that Rule which have been completed before that date, continue to apply to a person who was the director or shadow director of the insolvent company the whole, or substantially the whole, of whose business is acquired.".

See Form 4.73 at **[10.673]**.

[10.501]
[4.229   Second excepted case

(1)   Where a person to whom section 216 applies as having been a director or shadow director of the liquidating company applies for [permission] of the court under that section not later than 7 [business] days from the date on which the company went into liquidation, he may, during the period specified in paragraph (2) below, act in any of the ways mentioned in section 216(3), notwithstanding that he has not the [permission] of the court under that section.

(2)   The period referred to in paragraph (1) begins with the day on which the company goes into liquidation and ends either on the day falling six weeks after that date or on the day on which the court disposes of the application for [permission] under section 216, whichever of those days occurs first.]

NOTES

Substituted by the Insolvency (Amendment) Rules 1987, SI 1987/1919, r 3(1), Schedule, Pt 1, para 82, as from 11 January 1988.

Para (1): words in first and third pairs of square brackets substituted, and word in second pair of square brackets inserted, by the Insolvency (Amendment) Rules 2010, SI 2010/686, r 2, Sch 1, paras 1, 259, as from 6 April 2010, subject to transitional provisions in Sch 4, paras 1, 2 thereto, as noted to rr 1.5, 1.31 at **[10.7]**, **[10.34]**.

Para (2): word in square brackets substituted by SI 2010/686, r 2, Sch 1, para 1, as from 6 April 2010, subject to transitional provisions in Sch 4, para 2 thereto, as noted to r 1.31 at **[10.34]**.

[10.502]
4.230   Third excepted case

The court's [permission] under section 216(3) is not required where the company there referred to, though known by a prohibited name within the meaning of the section—
   (a)   has been known by that name for the whole of the period of 12 months ending with the day before the liquidating company went into liquidation, and
   (b)   has not at any time in those 12 months been dormant within the meaning of [section 1169(1), (2) and (3)(a)] of the Companies Act.

NOTES

Word in first pair of square brackets substituted by the Insolvency (Amendment) Rules 2010, SI 2010/686, r 2, Sch 1, para 1, as from 6 April 2010, subject to transitional provisions in Sch 4, para 2 thereto, as noted to r 1.31 at **[10.34]**; words in second pair of square brackets substituted by the Insolvency (Amendment) (No 2) Rules 2009, SI 2009/2472, rr 3, 14, as from 1 October 2009 (for transitional provisions see the note to r 0.2 at **[10.2]**).

[CHAPTER 23
EC REGULATION—MEMBER STATE LIQUIDATOR

[10.503]
4.231   Interpretation of creditor and notice to member State liquidator

(1)   This Rule applies where a member State liquidator has been appointed in relation to the company.

(2)   For the purposes of the Rules referred to in paragraph (3) the member State liquidator is deemed to be a creditor.

(3)   The Rules referred to in paragraph (2) are Rules 4.43(1) (official receiver's report), 4.45(1) (report on statement of affairs), 4.46(2) (report where no statement of affairs), 4.47(2) (general rule on reporting), 4.48(2) (winding up stayed), 4.49 (information to creditors), 4.50(2) (notice of

meetings), 4.51(2) (notice of creditors' meeting—CVL), 4.54 (power to call meetings), 4.57(1) (requisitioned meetings), 4.57(3), 4.67 (entitlement to vote (creditors)), 4.68 (chairman's discretion to allow vote—CVL), 4.70 (admission and rejection of proof (creditors' meeting)), 4.73 (meaning of "prove"), 4.74 (supply of forms), 4.75 (contents of proof), 4.76 (particulars of creditor's claim) . . . , 4.78 (cost of proving), 4.79 (inspection of proofs), 4.82 (admission and rejection of proofs for dividend), 4.83(1) (appeal against decision in relation to proof), 4.83(2), 4.84 (withdrawal or variation of proof), 4.85(1) (expunging of proof), 4.86 (estimate of quantum), 4.87 (negotiable instruments, etc), 4.88 (secured creditors), 4.89 (discounts), 4.90 (mutual credit and set-off), 4.91 (debt in foreign currency), 4.92 (payment of a periodical nature), 4.93 (interest), 4.94 (debt payable at future time), 4.101A (power to fill vacancy in office of liquidator), 4.102(5) (appointment by court), 4.103(4) (appointment by court), 4.113(1) (meeting of creditors to remove liquidator), 4.114(1) (meeting of creditors to remove liquidator), 4.115 (regulation of meetings), 4.124(1) (release of official receiver), 4.125(1) (final meeting), [4.125A(2) (rule on reporting),] 4.126(1) (final meeting), 4.131(1) (challenge to liquidator's remuneration), 4.152(1) (liquidation committee), 4.152(3) (eligibility for liquidation committee), 4.163(3) (vacancy on liquidation committee), 4.175(1) (liquidation committee), 4.180 (notice of dividend) and 4.212(2) (notice of public examination hearing).

(4) Paragraphs (2) and (3) are without prejudice to the generality of the right to participate referred to in paragraph 3 of Article 32 of the EC Regulation (exercise of creditor's rights).

(5) Where the liquidator is obliged to give notice to, or provide a copy of a document (including an order of court) to, the court, the registrar of companies or the official receiver, the liquidator shall give notice or provide copies, as the case may be, to the member State liquidator.

(6) Paragraph (5) is without prejudice to the generality of the obligations imposed by Article 31 of the EC Regulation (duty to cooperate and communicate information).]

NOTES

Added, together with preceding heading, by the Insolvency (Amendment) Rules 2002, SI 2002/1307, rr 3, 6(9), as from 31 May 2002.

Para (3): words omitted revoked by the Insolvency (Amendment) Rules 2010, SI 2010/686, r 2, Sch 1, para 260, as from 6 April 2010, subject to transitional provisions in Sch 4, para 2 thereto, as noted to r 1.31 at **[10.34]**; words in square brackets inserted by the Insolvency (Amendment) Rules 2004, SI 2004/584, r 23, as from 1 April 2004.

EC Regulation: ie, Council Regulation 1346/2000/EC on insolvency proceedings.

THE SECOND GROUP OF PARTS

(The Second Group of Parts—Individual insolvency; Bankruptcy (Pts 5, 5A, 6, 6A) outside the scope of this work.)

THE THIRD GROUP OF PARTS

PART 7
COURT PROCEDURE AND PRACTICE

CHAPTER 1
APPLICATIONS

[10.504]
7.1 Preliminary
This Chapter applies to any application made to the court under the Act or Rules except . . . —
    (a)   [an application for] an administration order under Part II,
    (b)   [a petition for] a winding-up order under Part IV, or
    (c)   [a petition for] a bankruptcy order under Part IX
of the Act.

NOTES

Words omitted revoked, and words in square brackets inserted, by the Insolvency (Amendment) Rules 2003, SI 2003/1730, r 11, Sch 1, Pt 8, para 54, as from 15 September 2003 (for transitional provisions and savings see the note preceding r 2.1 at **[10.60]**).

See Form 7.1A at **[10.673]**.

7.2 *(Revoked by the Insolvency (Amendment) Rules 2010, SI 2010/686, r 5, as from 6 April 2010, subject to transitional provisions in Sch 4, para 1 thereto, as noted to r 1.5 at **[10.7]**.)*

[10.505]
7.3 Form and contents of application
(1) Each application shall be in writing and shall state—
    [(a) that the application is made under the Act;
      (aa) the names of the parties;

(ab)   the name of the bankrupt, or the debtor who or company which is the subject of the insolvency proceedings to which the application relates;

(ac)   the court (and where applicable, the division or district registry of that court) in which the application is made;

(ad)   where the court has previously allocated a number to the insolvency proceedings within which the application is made, that number;]

(b)   the nature of the [remedy] or order applied for or the directions sought from the court;

(c)   the names and addresses of the persons (if any) on whom it is intended to serve the application or that no person is intended to be served;

(d)   where the Act or Rules require that notice of the application is to be given to specified persons, the names and addresses of all those persons (so far as known to the applicant); and

(e)   the applicant's address for service.

(2)   . . .

(3)   The application must be [authenticated] by the applicant if he is acting in person or, when he is not so acting, by or on behalf of his solicitor.

NOTES

Para (1): sub-para (a) substituted, and word in square brackets in sub-para (b) substituted, by the Insolvency (Amendment) Rules 2010, SI 2010/686, r 2, Sch 1, para 439(1), (2), as from 6 April 2010, subject to transitional provisions in Sch 4, para 1 thereto, as noted to r 1.5 at **[10.7]**.

Para (2): revoked by SI 2010/686, r 2, Sch 1, para 439(1), (3), as from 6 April 2010, subject to transitional provisions in Sch 4, para 1 thereto, as noted to r 1.5 at **[10.7]**.

Para (3): word in square brackets substituted by SI 2010/686, r 2, Sch 1, para 1, as from 6 April 2010, subject to transitional provisions in Sch 4, para 2 thereto, as noted to r 1.31 at **[10.34]**.

[10.506]
[7.3A   Application under section 176A(5) to disapply section 176A

(1)   An application under section 176A(5) shall be accompanied by [a witness statement] by the liquidator, administrator or receiver.

(2)   The [witness statement] shall state—

(a)   the type of insolvency proceedings in which the application arises;

(b)   a summary of the financial position of the company;

(c)   the information substantiating the applicant's view that the cost of making a distribution to unsecured creditors would be disproportionate to the benefits; and

(d)   whether any other [office-holder] is acting in relation to the company and if so his address.]

NOTES

Inserted by the Insolvency (Amendment) Rules 2003, SI 2003/1730, r 11, Sch 1, Pt 8, para 55, as from 15 September 2003 (for transitional provisions and savings see the note preceding r 2.1 at **[10.60]**).

Words in square brackets substituted by the Insolvency (Amendment) Rules 2010, SI 2010/686, r 2, Sch 1, para 440, as from 6 April 2010, subject to transitional provisions in Sch 4, paras 1, 2 thereto, as noted to rr 1.5, 1.31 at **[10.7]**, **[10.34]**.

[10.507]
7.4   Filing and service of application

(1)   [An application must be filed with the court], accompanied by one copy and a number of additional copies equal to the number of persons who are to be served with the application.

[(2)   Where an application is filed with the court in accordance with paragraph (1), the court must fix a venue for the application to be heard unless—

(a)   it considers it is not appropriate to do so;

(b)   the Rule under which the application is brought provides otherwise; or

(c)   the case is one to which Rule 7.5A applies.]

(3)   Unless the court otherwise directs, the applicant shall serve a sealed copy of the application, endorsed with the venue for the hearing, on the respondent named in the application (or on each respondent if more than one).

(4)   The court may give any of the following directions—

(a)   that the application be served upon persons other than those specified by the relevant provision of the Act or Rules;

(b)   that the giving of notice to any person may be dispensed with;

(c)   that notice be given in some way other than that specified in paragraph (3).

[(5)   An application must be served at least 14 days before the date fixed for its hearing unless—

(a)   the provision of the Act or the Rules under which the application is made makes different provision; or

(b)   the case is one of urgency, to which paragraph (6) applies.]

(6)   Where the case is one of urgency, the court may (without prejudice to its general power to extend or abridge time limits)—

(a)   hear the application immediately, either with or without notice to, or the attendance of, other parties, or

Part 10   Miscellaneous other SIs

(b)   authorise a shorter period of service than that provided for by paragraph (5);

and any such application may be heard on terms providing for the filing or service of documents, or the carrying out of other formalities, as the court thinks [just].

NOTES

Paras (1), (6): words in square brackets substituted by the Insolvency (Amendment) Rules 2010, SI 2010/686, r 2, Sch 1, paras 1, 441(1), (2), as from 6 April 2010, subject to transitional provisions in Sch 4, para 2 thereto, as noted to r 1.31 at **[10.34]**.

Paras (2), (5): substituted by SI 2010/686, r 2, Sch 1, para 441(1), (3), (4), as from 6 April 2010, subject to transitional provisions in Sch 4, para 2 thereto, as noted to r 1.31 at **[10.34]**.

[10.508]
[7.4A   Notice of application under section 176A(5)

An application under section 176A(5) may be made without the application being served upon or notice being given to any other party, save that notice of the application shall be given to any other [office-holder who is acting] in relation to the company including any member State liquidator.]

NOTES

Inserted by the Insolvency (Amendment) Rules 2003, SI 2003/1730, r 11, Sch 1, Pt 8, para 56, as from 15 September 2003 (for transitional provisions and savings see the note preceding r 2.1 at **[10.60]**).

Words in square brackets substituted by the Insolvency (Amendment) Rules 2010, SI 2010/686, r 2, Sch 1, para 442, as from 6 April 2010, subject to transitional provisions in Sch 4, para 1 thereto, as noted to r 1.5 at **[10.7]**.

[10.509]
[7.5A   Hearings without notice

Where the relevant provisions of the Act or the Rules do not require service of the application on, or notice of it to be given to, any person—

(a)   the court may hear the application as soon as reasonably practicable without fixing a venue as required by Rule 7.4(2); or

(b)   it may fix a venue for the application to be heard in which case Rule 7.4 must apply to the extent that it is relevant;

but nothing in those provisions is to be taken as prohibiting the applicant from giving such notice if the applicant wishes to do so.]

NOTES

Commencement: 6 April 2010.

Substituted, together with rr 7.6A, 7.7A, for original rr 7.5–7.7, by the Insolvency (Amendment) Rules 2010, SI 2010/686, r 2, Sch 1, para 443, subject to transitional provisions in Sch 4, para 2 thereto, as noted to r 1.31 at **[10.34]**.

[10.510]
[7.6A   Hearing of application

(1)   Unless the court otherwise directs, the hearing of an application must be in open court.

(2)   In the county court, the jurisdiction of the court to hear and determine an application may be exercised by the district judge (to whom any application must be made in the first instance) unless—

(a)   a direction to the contrary has been given, or

(b)   it is not within the district judge's power to make the order required.

(3)   In the High Court, the jurisdiction of the court to hear and determine an application may be exercised by the registrar (to whom the application must be made in the first instance) unless—

(a)   a direction to the contrary has been given, or

(b)   it is not within the registrar's power to make the order required.

(4)   Where the application is made to the district judge in the county court or to the registrar in the High Court, the district judge or the registrar may refer to the judge any matter which the district judge or registrar thinks should properly be decided by the judge, and the judge may either dispose of the matter or refer it back to the district judge or the registrar with such directions as that judge thinks just.

(5)   Nothing in this Rule precludes an application being made directly to the judge in a proper case.]

NOTES

Commencement: 6 April 2010.

Substituted as noted to r 7.5A at **[10.509]**.

[10.511]
[7.7A   Witness statements—general

(1)   Subject to Rule 7.9, where evidence is required by the Act or the Rules as to any matter, such evidence may be provided in the form of a witness statement unless—

(a)   in any specific case a Rule or the Act makes different provision; or

(b)   the court otherwise directs.

(2) The court may, on the application of any party to the matter in question order the attendance for cross-examination of the person making the witness statement.

(3) Where, after such an order has been made, the person in question does not attend, that person's witness statement must not be used in evidence without the [permission] of the court.]

NOTES
Commencement: 6 April 2010.
Substituted as noted to r 7.5A at **[10.509]**.
Para (3): word in square brackets substituted by the Insolvency (Amendment) Rules 2010, SI 2010/686, r 2, Sch 1, para 1, as from 6 April 2010, subject to transitional provisions in Sch 4, para 2 thereto, as noted to r 1.31 at **[10.34]**.

[10.512]
7.8 Filing and service of [witness statements]

(1) Unless the provision of the Act or Rules under which the application is made provides otherwise, or the court otherwise allows—

   (a) if the applicant intends to rely at the first hearing on [evidence in a witness statement], he shall file [the witness statement with the] court and serve a copy . . . on the respondent, not less than 14 days before the date fixed for the hearing, and

   (b) where a respondent to an application intends to oppose it and to rely for that purpose on [evidence in a witness statement], he shall file [the witness statement with the] court and serve a copy . . . on the applicant, not less than [5 business] days before the date fixed for the hearing.

(2) . . .

NOTES
Rule heading: words in square brackets substituted by the Insolvency (Amendment) Rules 2010, SI 2010/686, r 2, Sch 1, para 444(1), (2), as from 6 April 2010, subject to transitional provisions in Sch 4, para 2 thereto, as noted to r 1.31 at **[10.34]**.
Para (1): words in square brackets substituted, and words omitted revoked, by SI 2010/686, r 2, Sch 1, para 444(1), (3), as from 6 April 2010, subject to transitional provisions in Sch 4, para 2 thereto, as noted to r 1.31 at **[10.34]**
Para (2): revoked by SI 2010/686, r 2, Sch 1, para 444(1), (4), as from 6 April 2010, subject to transitional provisions in Sch 4, para 2 thereto, as noted to r 1.31 at **[10.34]**.

[10.513]
7.9 Use of reports

(1) A report may be filed in court instead of [a witness statement]—

   (a) in any case, by the official receiver (whether or not he is acting in any capacity mentioned in sub-paragraph (b)), or a deputy official receiver, or

   (b) unless the application involves other parties or the court otherwise orders, by—

      (i) an administrator, a liquidator or a trustee in bankruptcy,

      (ii) a provisional liquidator or an interim receiver,

      (iii) a special manager, or

      (iv) an insolvency practitioner appointed under section 273(2).

(2) In any case where a report is filed instead of [a witness statement], the report shall be treated for the purposes of Rule 7.8(1) and any hearing before the court as if it were [a witness statement].

[(3A) Where in insolvency proceedings a witness statement is made by an office-holder, the witness statement must state—

   (a) the capacity in which that office-holder is acting, and

   (b) the address at which that office-holder works.]

NOTES
Paras (1), (2): words in square brackets substituted by the Insolvency (Amendment) Rules 2010, SI 2010/686, r 2, Sch 1, para 445(1), (2), as from 6 April 2010, subject to transitional provisions in Sch 4, para 2 thereto, as noted to r 1.31 at **[10.34]**.
Para (3A): substituted (for the original para (3)) by SI 2010/686, r 2, Sch 1, para 445(1), (3), as from 6 April 2010, subject to transitional provisions in Sch 4, para 2 thereto, as noted to r 1.31 at **[10.34]**.

[10.514]
7.10 Adjournment of hearing; directions

(1) The court may adjourn the hearing of an application on such terms . . . as it thinks [just].

(2) The court may at any time give such directions as it thinks [just] as to—

   (a) service or notice of the application on or to any person . . . ;

   (b) whether particulars of claim and defence are to be delivered and generally as to the procedure on the application [including whether a hearing is necessary];

   (c) . . .

   (d) the matters to be dealt with in evidence.

[(3) The court may give directions as to the manner in which any evidence is to be adduced at a resumed hearing and in particular as to—

   (a) the taking of evidence wholly or partly by witness statement or orally;

   (b) the cross-examination of the maker of a witness statement; or

   (c) any report to be made by an office-holder.]

Part 10 Miscellaneous other SIs

NOTES
Para (1): words omitted revoked, and word in square brackets substituted, by the Insolvency (Amendment) Rules 2010, SI 2010/686, r 2, Sch 1, paras 1, 446(1), (2), as from 6 April 2010, subject to transitional provisions in Sch 4, paras 1, 2 thereto, as noted to rr 1.5, 1.31 at **[10.7]**, **[10.34]**.
Para (2): word in first pair of square brackets substituted, words omitted from sub-para (a) revoked, words in square brackets in sub-para (b) added, and sub-para (c) revoked, by SI 2010/686, r 2, Sch 1, paras 1, 446(1), (3), as from 6 April 2010, subject to transitional provisions in Sch 4, paras 1, 2 thereto, as noted to rr 1.5, 1.31 at **[10.7]**, **[10.34]**.
Para (3): added by SI 2010/686, r 2, Sch 1, para 446(1), (4), as from 6 April 2010, subject to transitional provisions in Sch 4, para 1 thereto, as noted to r 1.5 at **[10.7]**.

7.10ZA   *(Rule (7.10ZA (Chapter 1ZA (The London Insolvency District) provides for the allocation of certain bankruptcy petitions to the London Insolvency District and is outside the scope of this work.)*

[CHAPTER 1A
BLOCK TRANSFER OF CASES WHERE INSOLVENCY PRACTITIONER HAS DIED ETC

[10.515]
7.10A   Preliminary and interpretation
(1)   The Rules in this Chapter relate to applications for a block transfer order.
(2)   In this Chapter—
"outgoing office-holder" has the meaning in Rule 7.10B(1),
"replacement office-holder" has the meaning in Rule 7.10B(1),
"block transfer order" has the meaning in Rule 7.10B(2),
"substantive application" is that part of the application in Rule 7.10C(1)(c) and (d).]

NOTES
Commencement: 6 April 2010.
Inserted, together with rr 7.10B–7.10D (Ch 1A), by the Insolvency (Amendment) Rules 2010, SI 2010/686, r 2, Sch 1, para 447, subject to transitional provisions in Sch 4, para 1 thereto, as noted to r 1.5 at **[10.7]**.

[10.516]
[7.10B   Power to make a block transfer order
(1)   This Rule applies where an individual who is acting as an office-holder ('the outgoing office-holder')—
(a)   dies,
(b)   retires from practice, or
(c)   is otherwise unable or unwilling to continue in office,
and it is expedient to transfer some or all of the cases in which the outgoing office-holder holds office to one or more office-holders ('the replacement office-holder') in a single transaction.
(2)   In a case to which this Rule applies the court has the power to make an order, ('a block transfer order'), appointing a replacement office-holder in the place of the outgoing office-holder to be—
(a)   liquidator in any winding up (including a case where the official receiver is the liquidator by virtue of section 136 of the Act),
(b)   administrator in any administration,
(c)   trustee in a bankruptcy (including a case where the official receiver is the trustee by virtue of section 300 of the Act), or
(d)   supervisor of a voluntary arrangement under Part 1 or 8 of the Act.
(3)   The replacement office-holder must be—
(a)   qualified to act as an insolvency practitioner, or
(b)   where the replacement office-holder is to be appointed supervisor of a voluntary arrangement under Part 1 or 8 of the Act—
(i)   qualified to act as an insolvency practitioner, or
(ii)   a person authorised so to act.]

NOTES
Commencement: 6 April 2010.
Inserted as noted to r 7.10A at **[10.515]**.

[10.517]
[7.10C   Application for a block transfer order
(1)   An application for a block transfer order may be made to the registrar or district judge for—
(a)   the transfer to the High Court of the cases specified in the schedule under paragraph (8);
(b)   the transfer of the cases back to the court from which they were transferred when a replacement office-holder has been appointed;
(c)   the removal of the outgoing office-holder by the exercise of any of the powers in paragraph (2);

    (d)   the appointment of a replacement office-holder by the exercise of any of the powers in paragraph (3);

    (e)   such other order or direction as may be necessary or expedient in connection with any of the matters referred to above.

(2)   The powers referred to in paragraph (1)(c) are—

    (a)   section 172(2) and Rule 7.10B(2) (winding up by the court);

    (b)   section 108 (voluntary liquidation);

    (c)   section 19, paragraph 88 of Schedule B1 to the Act and Rule 7.10B(2) (administration);

    (d)   section 298 and Rule 7.10B(2) (bankruptcy);

    (e)   section 7(5) and paragraph 39(6) of Schedule A1 to the Act (voluntary arrangement under Part 1 of the Act); and

    (f)   section 263(5) (voluntary arrangement under Part 8 of the Act).

(3)   The powers referred to in paragraph (1)(d) are—

    (a)   section 168(3) and (5) and Rule 7.10B(2) (winding up by the court);

    (b)   section 108 (voluntary liquidation);

    (c)   section 13, paragraphs 63, 91 and 95 of Schedule B1 to the Act and Rule 7.10B(2) (administration);

    (d)   sections 298 and 303(2) and Rule 7.10B(2) (bankruptcy);

    (e)   section 7(5) and paragraph 39(6) of Schedule A1 to the Act (voluntary arrangement under Part 1 of the Act); and

    (f)   section 263(5) (voluntary arrangement under Part 8 of the Act).

(4)   Subject to paragraph (5), the application may be made by any of the following—

    (a)   the outgoing office-holder (if able and willing to do so);

    (b)   any person who holds office jointly with the outgoing office-holder;

    (c)   any person who is proposed to be appointed as the replacement office-holder;

    (d)   any creditor in a case subject to the application;

    (e)   the recognised professional body or recognised body by which the outgoing office-holder is or was authorised; or

    (f)   the Secretary of State.

(5)   Where one or more outgoing office-holder in the schedule under paragraph (8) is an administrator, an application may not be made unless a person permitted to apply to replace that office-holder under section 13 or paragraph 63, 91 or 95 of Schedule B1 to the Act is the applicant or is joined as applicant in respect of the replacement of that office-holder.

(6)   An applicant (other than the Secretary of State) must give notice of the application to the Secretary of State at least 5 business days before the hearing of the application.

(7)   The following must be made a respondent to the application and served with it—

    (a)   the outgoing office-holder (if not the applicant or deceased);

    (b)   every person who holds office jointly with the outgoing office-holder; and

    (c)   such person as the registrar or district judge directs.

(8)   The application must contain a schedule setting out—

    (a)   the name of each case,

    (b)   the identity of the court having jurisdiction when the application is made,

    (c)   the case number (if any), and

    (d)   the capacity in which the outgoing office-holder was appointed.

(9)   The application must be supported by evidence—

    (a)   setting out the circumstances which gave rise to it being expedient to appoint a replacement office-holder; and

    (b)   exhibiting the written consent to act of each person who is proposed to be appointed as replacement office-holder.

(10)   Where all the cases in the schedule under paragraph (8) are in a county court or more than one county court—

    (a)   the application may be made to a district judge of a convenient county court having insolvency jurisdiction; and

    (b)   this Rule applies with appropriate modifications.]

NOTES

Commencement: 6 April 2010.

Inserted as noted to r 7.10A at **[10.515]**.

[10.518]

[7.10D   Action following application for a block transfer order

(1)   The registrar or district judge may in the first instance consider the application without a hearing and make such order as the registrar or district judge thinks just.

(2)   In the first instance, the registrar or district judge may do any of the following—

    (a)   make an order directing the transfer to the High Court of those cases not already within its jurisdiction for the purpose only of the substantive application;

(b)   if the documents are considered to be in order and that the matter is straightforward, make an order on the substantive application;

(c)   give any directions which are considered to be necessary including (if appropriate) directions for the joinder of any additional respondents or requiring the service of the application on any person or requiring additional evidence to be provided; or

(d)   if an order is not made on the substantive application, give directions for the further consideration of the substantive application by the registrar or district judge or a judge of the Chancery Division.

(3)   The applicant must ensure that a sealed copy of every order transferring any case to the High Court and of every order which is made on a substantive application is lodged with the court having jurisdiction over each case affected by such order for filing on the court file relating to that case.

(4)   In any case other than an application relating to the appointment of an administrator, in deciding to what extent (if any) the costs of making an application under this Rule should be paid as an expense of the insolvency proceedings to which the application relates, the factors to which the court must have regard include—

(a)   the reasons for the making of the application;

(b)   the number of cases to which the application relates;

(c)   the value of assets comprised in those cases; and

(d)   the nature and extent of the costs involved.

(5)   Where an application relates to the appointment of an administrator and is made by a person under section 13 or paragraph 63, 91 or 95 of Schedule B1 to the Act, the costs of making that application are to be paid as an expense of the administration to which the application relates unless the court directs otherwise.

(6)   Any appointment made under this Rule must be notified—

(a)   to the Secretary of State as soon as reasonably practicable; and

(b)   to—

(i)   the creditors, and

(ii)   such other persons as the court may direct,

in such manner as the court may direct.

(7)   Where the application was made to the district judge under Rule 7.10C(10) this Rule applies with appropriate modifications.]

NOTES

Commencement: 6 April 2010.

Inserted as noted to r 7.10A at **[10.515]**.

CHAPTER 2
TRANSFER OF PROCEEDINGS BETWEEN COURTS

[10.519]
7.11   General power of transfer

(1)   Where winding-up or bankruptcy proceedings [or proceedings relating to a debt relief order] are pending in the High Court, the court may order them to be transferred to a specified county court.

(2)   Where winding-up or bankruptcy proceedings [or proceedings relating to a debt relief order] are pending in a county court, the court may order them to be transferred either to the High Court or to another county court.

(3)   In any case where [winding-up] proceedings are transferred to a county court, the transfer must be to a court which has jurisdiction to wind up companies . . .

[(3A)   In any case where bankruptcy proceedings or proceedings relating to a debt relief order are transferred to a county court, the transfer must be to a court which has jurisdiction in bankruptcy.]

(4)   Where winding-up or bankruptcy proceedings [or proceedings relating to a debt relief order] are pending in a county court, a judge of the High Court may order them to be transferred to that Court.

[(4A)   Solely for the purposes of Rule 7.10D (action following application for a block transfer order)—

(a)   the registrar may transfer to or from the High Court; and

(b)   the district judge of the county court to which the application is made may transfer to or from that county court,

any case in the schedule under Rule 7.10C(8).]

(5)   A transfer of proceedings under this Rule may be ordered—

(a)   by the court of its own motion, or

(b)   on the application of the official receiver, or

(c)   on the application of a person appearing to the court to have an interest in the proceedings.

(6) A transfer of proceedings under this Rule may be ordered notwithstanding that the proceedings commenced before the coming into force of the Rules.

NOTES

Paras (1), (2), (4): words in square brackets inserted by the Insolvency (Amendment) Rules 2009, SI 2009/642, rr 4, 54(a), as from 6 April 2009.

Para (3): words in square brackets inserted, and words omitted revoked, by SI 2009/642, rr 4, 54(b), as from 6 April 2009.

Para (3A): inserted by SI 2009/642, rr 4, 54(c), as from 6 April 2009.

Para (4A): inserted by the Insolvency (Amendment) Rules 2010, SI 2010/686, r 2, Sch 1, para 448, as from 6 April 2010, subject to transitional provisions in Sch 4, para 1 thereto, as noted to r 1.5 at **[10.7]**.

[10.520]
7.12 Proceedings commenced in wrong court

Where winding-up or bankruptcy proceedings [or proceedings relating to a debt relief order] are commenced in a court which is, in relation to those proceedings, the wrong court, that court may—

    (a) order the transfer of the proceedings to the court in which they ought to have been commenced;

    (b) order that the proceedings be continued in the court in which they have been commenced; or

    (c) order the proceedings to be struck out.

NOTES

Words in square brackets inserted by the Insolvency (Amendment) Rules 2009, SI 2009/642, rr 4, 55, as from 6 April 2009.

[10.521]
7.13 Applications for transfer

(1) An application by the official receiver for proceedings to be transferred shall be made with a report by him—

    (a) setting out the reasons for the transfer, and

    [(b) including a statement either that—

        (i) the petitioner, or

        (ii) the debtor in proceedings relating to a debt relief order,

        consents to the transfer, or that he has been given at least 14 days' notice of the official receiver's application.]

(2) If the court is satisfied from the official receiver's report that the proceedings can be conducted more conveniently in another court, the proceedings shall be transferred to that court.

(3) Where an application for the transfer of proceedings is made otherwise than by the official receiver, at least 14 days' notice of the application shall be given by the applicant—

    (a) to the official receiver attached to the court in which the proceedings are pending, and

    (b) to the official receiver attached to the court to which it is proposed that they should be transferred.

NOTES

Para (1): sub-para (b) substituted by the Insolvency (Amendment) Rules 2009, SI 2009/642, rr 4, 56, as from 6 April 2009.

[10.522]
7.14 Procedure following order for transfer

(1) Subject as follows, the court making an order under Rule 7.11 shall [as soon as reasonably practicable] send to the transferee court a sealed copy of the order, and the file of the proceedings.

(2) On receipt of these, the transferee court shall [as soon as reasonably practicable] send notice of the transfer to the official receivers attached to that court and the transferor court respectively.

(3) Paragraph (1) does not apply where the order is made by the High Court under Rule 7.11(4). In that case—

    (a) the High Court shall send sealed copies of the order to the county court from which the proceedings are to be transferred, and to the official receivers attached to that court and the High Court respectively, and

    (b) that county court shall send the file of the proceedings to the High Court.

(4)   . . .

NOTES

Paras (1), (2): words in square brackets substituted by the Insolvency (Amendment) Rules 2009, SI 2009/642, r 5, as from 6 April 2009, subject to transitional provisions in r 3 thereof, as noted to r 1.4 of these Rules at **[10.6]**.

Para (4): revoked by the Insolvency (Amendment) Rules 2010, SI 2010/686, r 2, Sch 1, para 449, as from 6 April 2010, subject to transitional provisions in Sch 4, para 1 thereto, as noted to r 1.5 at **[10.7]**.

[10.523]
7.15 Consequential transfer of other proceedings

(1) This Rule applies where—

[(a) the High Court has—
    (i) made a bankruptcy order;
    (ii) made a winding-up order;
    (iii) appointed a provisional liquidator; or
    (iv) appointed an interim receiver; or]
(b) . . .
(c) winding-up or bankruptcy proceedings have been transferred to that Court from a county court.

(2) A judge of any Division of the High Court may, of his own motion, order the transfer to that Division of any such proceedings as are mentioned below and are pending against the company or individual concerned ("the insolvent") either in another Division of the High Court or in a court in England and Wales other than the High Court.

(3) Proceedings which may be so transferred are those brought by or against the insolvent for the purpose of enforcing a claim against the insolvent estate, or brought by a person other than the insolvent for the purpose of enforcing any such claim (including in either case proceedings of any description by a debenture-holder or mortgagee).

(4) Where proceedings are transferred under this Rule, the registrar may (subject to [the] directions of the judge) dispose of any matter arising in the proceedings which would, but for the transfer, have been disposed of in chambers or, in the case of proceedings transferred from a county court, by the [district judge].

NOTES

Para (1): sub-para (a) substituted, and sub-para (b) revoked, by the Insolvency (Amendment) Rules 2010, SI 2010/686, r 2, Sch 1, para 450(1), (2), as from 6 April 2010, subject to transitional provisions in Sch 4, para 1 thereto, as noted to r 1.5 at **[10.7]**.

Para (4): words in square brackets substituted by SI 2010/686, r 2, Sch 1, para 450(1), (3), as from 6 April 2010, subject to transitional provisions in Sch 4, para 1 thereto, as noted to r 1.5 at **[10.7]**.

CHAPTER 3
SHORTHAND WRITERS

[10.524]
7.16 Nomination and appointment of shorthand writers

(1) In the High Court the judge [or registrar] and, in a county court, [a district judge] may in writing nominate one or more persons to be official shorthand writers to the court.

(2) The court may, at any time in the course of insolvency proceedings, appoint a shorthand writer to take down the evidence of a person examined under section 133, 236, [251N,] 290 or 366.

(3) Where the official receiver applies to the court for an order appointing a shorthand writer, he shall name the person he proposes for appointment . . .

NOTES

Para (1): words in first pair of square brackets inserted, and words in second pair of square brackets substituted, by the Insolvency (Amendment) Rules 2010, SI 2010/686, r 2, Sch 1, para 451(1), (2), as from 6 April 2010, subject to transitional provisions in Sch 4, para 2 thereto, as noted to r 1.31 at **[10.34]**.

Para (2): figure in square brackets inserted by the Insolvency (Amendment) Rules 2009, SI 2009/642, rr 4, 57, as from 6 April 2009.

Para (3): words omitted revoked by SI 2010/686, r 2, Sch 1, para 451(1), (3), as from 6 April 2010, subject to transitional provisions in Sch 4, para 2 thereto, as noted to r 1.31 at **[10.34]**.

[10.525]
7.17 Remuneration

(1) The remuneration of a shorthand writer appointed in insolvency proceedings shall be paid by the party at whose instance the appointment was made, or out of the insolvent estate, or otherwise, as the court may direct.

[(2) Any question arising as to the rates of remuneration payable under this Rule shall be determined by the court in its discretion.]

NOTES

Para (2): substituted by the Insolvency (Amendment) Rules 1993, SI 1993/602, r 3, Schedule, para 1, as from 5 April 1993.

7.18 *(Revoked by the Insolvency (Amendment) Rules 2010, SI 2010/686, r 5, as from 6 April 2010, subject to transitional provisions in Sch 4, para 1 thereto, as noted to r 1.5 at* **[10.7]**.)

CHAPTER 4
ENFORCEMENT PROCEDURES

[10.526]
7.19 Enforcement of court orders

(1) In any insolvency proceedings, orders of the court may be enforced in the same manner as a judgment to the same effect.

(2) Where an order in insolvency proceedings is made, or any process is issued, by a county court ("the primary court"), the order or process may be enforced, executed and dealt with by any other county court ("the secondary court"), as if it had been made or issued for the enforcement of a judgment or order to the same effect made by the secondary court.

This applies whether or not the secondary court has jurisdiction to take insolvency proceedings.

[(3) Where a warrant for the arrest of a person is issued by the High Court, the warrant may be discharged by the county court where the person who is the subject of the warrant—

    (a)   has been brought before a county court exercising insolvency jurisdiction; and

    (b)   has given to the county court an undertaking which is satisfactory to the county court to comply with the obligations that apply to that person under the Act or the Rules.]

NOTES

Para (3): added by the Insolvency (Amendment) Rules 2010, SI 2010/686, r 2, Sch 1, para 452, as from 6 April 2010, subject to transitional provisions in Sch 4, para 1 thereto, as noted to r 1.5 at **[10.7]**.

[10.527]
7.20 Orders enforcing compliance with the Rules

(1) The court may, on application by the competent person, make such orders as it thinks necessary for the enforcement of obligations falling on any person in accordance with—

    (a)   [paragraph 47 of Schedule B1 to the Act or section] 47 or 131 (duty to submit statement of affairs in administration, administrative receivership or winding up),

    (b)   section 143(2) (liquidator to furnish information, books, papers, etc), or

    (c)   section 235 (duty of various persons to co-operate with office-holder).

(2) The competent person for this purpose is—

    (a)   under [paragraph 47 of Schedule B1 to the Act], the administrator,

    (b)   under section 47, the administrative receiver,

    (c)   under section 131 or 143(2), the official receiver, and

    (d)   under section 235, the official receiver, the administrator, the administrative receiver, the liquidator or the provisional liquidator, as the case may be.

(3) An order of the court under this Rule may provide that all costs of and incidental to the application for it shall be borne by the person against whom the order is made.

NOTES

Paras (1), (2): words in square brackets substituted by the Insolvency (Amendment) Rules 2003, SI 2003/1730, r 11, Sch 1, Pt 8, para 57, as from 15 September 2003 (for transitional provisions and savings see the note preceding r 2.1 at **[10.60]**).

[10.528]
7.21 Warrants (general provisions)

(1) A warrant issued by the court under any provision of the Act shall be addressed to such officer of the High Court or of a county court (whether or not having jurisdiction in insolvency proceedings) as the warrant specifies, or to any constable.

(2) The persons referred to in sections 134(2), 236(5), [251N(5),] 364(1), 365(3) and 366(3) (court's powers of enforcement) as the prescribed officer of the court are—

    (a)   in the case of the High Court, the tipstaff and his assistants of the court, and

    (b)   in the case of a county court, the [district judge] and the bailiffs.

(3) In this Chapter references to property include books, papers and records.

NOTES

Para (2): figure in first pair of square brackets inserted by the Insolvency (Amendment) Rules 2009, SI 2009/642, rr 4, 58, as from 6 April 2009; words in second pair of square brackets substituted by the Insolvency (Amendment) Rules 2010, SI 2010/686, r 2, Sch 1, para 453, as from 6 April 2010, subject to transitional provisions in Sch 4, para 2 thereto, as noted to r 1.31 at **[10.34]**.

[10.529]
7.22 Warrants under ss 134, 364

When a person [("the arrested person")] is arrested under a warrant issued by the court under section 134 (officer of company failing to attend for public examination), or section 364 (arrest of debtor or bankrupt)—

    [(a)   the officer apprehending the arrested person must give that person into the custody of—

        (i)   the court in a case where the court is ready and able to deal with the arrested person, or

Part 10   Miscellaneous other SIs

> (ii)   where the court is not ready and able, the governor of the prison named in the warrant (or where that prison is not able to accommodate the arrested person, the governor of such other prison with appropriate facilities which is able to accommodate the arrested person), who must keep the arrested person in custody until such time as the court otherwise orders and must produce that person before the court at its next sitting; and]
>
> (b)   any property in the arrested person's possession which may be seized shall be—
>> (i)   lodged with, or otherwise dealt with as instructed by, whoever is specified in the warrant as authorised to receive it, or
>> (ii)   kept by the officer seizing it pending the receipt of written orders from the court as to its disposal,
>
> as may be directed by the court in the warrant.

NOTES

Words in first pair of square brackets inserted, and para (a) substituted, by the Insolvency (Amendment) Rules 2010, SI 2010/686, r 2, Sch 1, para 454, as from 6 April 2010, subject to transitional provisions in Sch 4, para 1 thereto, as noted to r 1.5 at **[10.7]**.

[10.530]
7.23   Warrants under ss 236, [251N and] 366

(1)   When a person is arrested under a warrant issued under section 236 (inquiry into insolvent company's dealings)[, 251N (the equivalent in relation to debt relief orders)] or 366 (the equivalent in bankruptcy) [("the arrested person")], the officer arresting him shall [as soon as reasonably practicable] bring him before the court issuing the warrant in order that he may be examined.

(2)   If he cannot immediately be brought up for examination, the officer shall deliver him into the custody of the governor of the prison named in the warrant [(or where that prison is not able to accommodate the arrested person, the governor of such other prison with appropriate facilities which is able to accommodate the arrested person)], who shall keep him in custody and produce him before the court as it may from time to time direct.

(3)   After arresting the person named in the warrant, the officer shall [as soon as reasonably practicable] report to the court the arrest or delivery into custody (as the case may be) and apply to the court to fix a venue for the person's examination.

(4)   The court shall appoint the earliest practicable time for the examination, and shall—
   (a)   direct the governor of the prison to produce the person for examination at the time and place appointed, and
   (b)   [as soon as reasonably practicable] give notice of the venue to the person who applied for the warrant.

(5)   Any property in the arrested person's possession which may be seized shall be—
   (a)   lodged with, or otherwise dealt with as instructed by, whoever is specified in the warrant as authorised to receive it, or
   (b)   kept by the officer seizing it pending the receipt of written orders from the court as to its disposal,
as may be directed by the court.

NOTES

Rule heading: words in square brackets inserted by the Insolvency (Amendment) Rules 2009, SI 2009/642, rr 4, 59(a), as from 6 April 2009.

Para (1): words in first pair of square brackets inserted by SI 2009/642, rr 4, 59(b), as from 6 April 2009; words in second pair of square brackets inserted by the Insolvency (Amendment) Rules 2010, SI 2010/686, r 2, Sch 1, para 455(1), (2), as from 6 April 2010, subject to transitional provisions in Sch 4, para 1 thereto, as noted to r 1.5 at **[10.7]**; words in third pair of square brackets substituted by SI 2009/642, r 5, subject to transitional provisions in r 3 thereof, as noted to r 1.4 of these Rules at **[10.6]**.

Para (2): words in square brackets inserted by SI 2010/686, r 2, Sch 1, para 455(1), (3), as from 6 April 2010, subject to transitional provisions in Sch 4, para 1 thereto, as noted to r 1.5 at **[10.7]**.

Paras (3), (4): words in square brackets substituted by SI 2009/642, r 5, subject to transitional provisions in r 3 thereof, as noted to r 1.4 of these Rules at **[10.6]**.

[10.531]
7.24   Execution of warrants outside court's district

(1)   This Rule applies where a warrant for a person's arrest has been issued in insolvency proceedings by a county court ("the primary court") and is addressed to another county court ("the secondary court") for execution in its district.

(2)   The secondary court may send the warrant to the [district judge of another] county court (whether or not having jurisdiction to take insolvency proceedings) in whose district the person to be arrested is or is believed to be, with a notice to the effect that the warrant is transmitted to that court under this Rule for execution in its district at the request of the primary court.

(3)   The court receiving a warrant transmitted by the secondary court under this Rule shall apply its seal to the warrant, and secure that all such steps are taken for its execution as would be appropriate in the case of a warrant issued by itself.

NOTES

   Para (2): words in square brackets substituted by the Insolvency (Amendment) Rules 2010, SI 2010/686, r 2, Sch 1, para 456, as from 6 April 2010, subject to transitional provisions in Sch 4, para 2 thereto, as noted to r 1.31 at **[10.34]**.

[10.532]

7.25   Warrants under s 365

(1)   A warrant issued under section 365(3) (search of premises not belonging to the bankrupt) shall authorise any person executing it to seize any property of the bankrupt found as a result of the execution of the warrant.

(2)   Any property seized under a warrant issued under section 365(2) or (3) shall be—

   (a)   lodged with, or otherwise dealt with as instructed by, whoever is specified in the warrant as authorised to receive it, or

   (b)   kept by the officer seizing it pending the receipt of written orders from the court as to its disposal,

as may be directed by the warrant.

CHAPTER 5

COURT RECORDS AND RETURNS

[10.533]

[7.31A   Court file

(1)   The court must open and maintain a file in any case where documents are filed with it under the Act or the Rules.

(2)   Any documents which are filed with the court under the Act or the Rules must be placed on the file opened in accordance with paragraph (1).

(3)   The following persons may inspect or obtain from the court a copy of, or a copy of any document or documents contained in, the file opened in accordance with paragraph (1)—

   (a)   the office-holder in the proceedings;

   (b)   the Secretary of State; and

   (c)   any person who is a creditor of the company to which, or the individual to whom, the proceedings relate if that person provides the court with a statement in writing by confirming that that person is a creditor.

(4)   The same right to inspect or obtain a copy of, or a copy of any document or documents contained in, the file opened in accordance with paragraph (1) is exercisable—

   (a)   in proceedings under Parts 1 to 7 of the Act, by—

      (i)   an officer or former officer of the company to which the proceedings relate; or

      (ii)   a member of the company or a contributory in its winding up;

   (b)   in proceedings with respect to a voluntary arrangement under Part 8 of the Act, by the debtor;

   (c)   in bankruptcy proceedings, by—

      (i)   the bankrupt;

      (ii)   any person against whom a bankruptcy petition has been presented;

      (iii)   any person who has, in accordance with Chapter 1 of Part 6, been served with a statutory demand;

   (d)   in proceedings relating to a debt relief order, by the debtor.

(5)   The right to inspect or obtain a copy of, or a copy of any document or documents contained in, the file opened in accordance with paragraph (1) may be exercised on that person's behalf by a person authorised to do so by that person.

(6)   Any person who is not otherwise entitled to inspect or obtain a copy of, or a copy of any document or documents contained in, the file opened in accordance with paragraph (1) may do so if that person has the permission of the court.

(7)   The court may direct that the file, a document (or part of it) or a copy of a document (or part of it) must not be made available under paragraph (3), (4) or (5) without the permission of the court.

(8)   An application for a direction under paragraph (7) may be made by—

   (a)   the official receiver;

   (b)   the officer-holder in the proceedings; or

   (c)   any person appearing to the court to have an interest.

(9)   Where any person wishes to exercise the right to inspect the file under paragraph (3), (4), (5) or (6), that person—

   (a)   if the permission of the court is required, must file with the court an application notice in accordance with these Rules; or

   (b)   if the permission of the court is not required, may inspect the file at any reasonable time.

(10)   Where any person wishes to exercise the right to obtain a copy of a document under paragraph (3), (4), (5) or (6), that person must pay any prescribed fee and—

(a)　if the permission of the court is required, file with the court an application notice in accordance with these Rules; or

(b)　if the permission of the court is not required, file with the court a written request for the document.

(11)　An application for—

(a)　permission to inspect the file or obtain a copy of a document under paragraph (6); or

(b)　a direction under paragraph (7),

may be made without notice to any other party, but the court may direct that notice must be given to any person who would be affected by its decision.

(12)　If for the purposes of powers conferred by the Act or the Rules, the Secretary of State or the official receiver requests the transmission of the file of any insolvency proceedings, the court must comply with the request (unless the file is for the time being in use for the court's own purposes).]

NOTES

Commencement: 6 April 2010.

This rule was substituted, for the original rr 7.26–7.31, by the Insolvency (Amendment) Rules 2010, SI 2010/686, r 2, Sch 1, para 457, subject to transitional provisions in Sch 4, para 1 thereto, as noted to r 1.5 at **[10.7]**.

7.32　*(Revoked by the Insolvency (Amendment) Rules 2009, SI 2009/642, rr 4, 62, as from 6 April 2009, subject to transitional provisions in r 3 thereof, as noted to r 1.4 of these Rules at **[10.6]**.)*

[Chapter 6
Costs and Detailed Assessment

[10.534]
[7.33A　Application of Chapter 6

(1)　This chapter applies in relation to costs in connection with insolvency proceedings.

(2)　In this chapter a reference to costs includes charges and expenses.]

NOTES

Commencement: 6 April 2010.

Chapter 6 (rr 7.33–7.42) were originally substituted by the Insolvency (Amendment) (No 2) Rules 1999, SI 1999/1022, r 3, Schedule, para 3, as from 26 April 1999.

This rule was further substituted (together with r 7.34A) for rr 7.33, 7.34, by the Insolvency (Amendment) Rules 2010, SI 2010/686, r 2, Sch 1, para 458, as from 6 April 2010, subject to transitional provisions in Sch 4, para 1 thereto, as noted to r 1.5 at **[10.7]**.

[10.535]
[7.34A　Requirement to assess costs by the detailed procedure

(1)　Where the costs of any person are payable as an expense out of the insolvent estate, the amount payable must be decided by detailed assessment unless agreed between the office-holder and the person entitled to payment.

(2)　In the absence of such agreement as is mentioned in paragraph (1), the office-holder—

(a)　may serve notice requiring that person to commence detailed assessment proceedings in accordance with CPR Part 47; and

(b)　must serve such notice (except in an administrative receivership) where a liquidation or creditors' committee formed in relation to the insolvency proceedings resolves that the amount of the costs must be decided by detailed assessment.

(3)　Detailed assessment proceedings must be commenced in the court to which the insolvency proceedings are allocated or, where in relation to a company there is no such court, any court having jurisdiction to wind up the company.

(4)　Where the costs of any person employed by an office-holder in insolvency proceedings are required to be decided by detailed assessment or fixed by order of the court, the office-holder may make payments on account to such person in respect of those costs provided that person undertakes in writing—

(a)　to repay as soon as reasonably practicable any money which may, when detailed assessment is made, prove to have been overpaid; and

(b)　to pay interest on any such sum as is mentioned in sub-paragraph (a) at the rate specified in section 17 of the Judgments Act 1838 on the date payment was made and for the period beginning with the date of payment and ending with the date of repayment.

(5)　In any proceedings before the court (including proceedings on a petition), the court may order costs to be decided by detailed assessment.

(6)　Unless otherwise directed or authorised, the costs of a trustee in bankruptcy or a liquidator are to be allowed on the standard basis for which provision is made in—

(a)　CPR rule 44.4 (basis of assessment); and

(b)　CPR rule 44.5 (factors to be taken into account when deciding the amount of costs).]

NOTES

Commencement: 6 April 2010.

Substituted as noted to r 7.33A at **[10.534]**.

[10.536]
[7.35 Procedure where detailed assessment required

(1) Before making a detailed assessment of the costs of any person employed in insolvency proceedings by [the office-holder], the costs officer shall require a certificate of employment, which shall be endorsed on the bill and [authenticated] by [the office-holder].

(2) The certificate shall include—
  (a) the name and address of the person employed,
  (b) details of the functions to be carried out under the employment, and
  (c) a note of any special terms of remuneration which have been agreed.

(3) Every person whose costs in insolvency proceedings are required to be decided by detailed assessment shall, on being required in writing to do so by the [office-holder], commence detailed assessment proceedings in accordance with CPR Part 47 (procedure for detailed assessment of costs and default provisions).

(4) If that person does not commence detailed assessment proceedings within 3 months of the requirement under paragraph (3), or within such further time as the court, on application, may permit, the [office-holder] may deal with the insolvent estate without regard to any claim by that person, whose claim is forfeited by such failure to commence proceedings.

(5) Where in any such case such a claim lies additionally against an [office-holder] in his personal capacity, that claim is also forfeited by such failure to commence proceedings.

(6) Where costs have been incurred in insolvency proceedings in the High Court and those proceedings are subsequently transferred to a county court, all costs of those proceedings directed by the court or otherwise required to be assessed may nevertheless, on the application of the person who incurred the costs, be ordered to be decided by detailed assessment in the High Court.]

NOTES
Substituted as noted to r 7.33A at **[10.534]**.
Words in square brackets substituted by the Insolvency (Amendment) Rules 2010, SI 2010/686, r 2, Sch 1, paras 1, 459, as from 6 April 2010, subject to transitional provisions in Sch 4, paras 1, 2 thereto, as noted to rr 1.5, 1.31 at **[10.7]**, **[10.34]**.

[10.537]
[7.36 Costs of [officers charged with execution of writs or other process]

(1) Where [an enforcement officer, or other officer, charged with execution of the writ or other process]—
  (a) is required under section 184(2) or 346(2) to deliver up goods or money, or
  (b) has under section 184(3) or 346(3) deducted costs from the proceeds of an execution or money paid to him,
the [office-holder] may require in writing that the amount of [the enforcement officer's or other officer's] bill of costs be decided by detailed assessment.'

(2) Where such a requirement is made, Rule 7.35(4) applies.

(3) Where, in the case of a deduction under paragraph (1)(b), any amount deducted is disallowed at the conclusion of the detailed assessment proceedings, the [enforcement officer] shall [as soon as reasonably practicable] pay a sum equal to that disallowed to the [office-holder] for the benefit of the insolvent estate.]

NOTES
Substituted as noted to r 7.33A at **[10.534]**.
Rule heading: words in square brackets substituted by the Insolvency (Amendment) Rules 2005, SI 2005/527, r 42(a), as from 1 April 2005.
Para (1): words in first and third pairs of square brackets substituted by SI 2005/527, r 42(b), as from 1 April 2005; words in second pair of square brackets substituted by the Insolvency (Amendment) Rules 2010, SI 2010/686, r 2, Sch 1, para 460(1), (2), as from 6 April 2010, subject to transitional provisions in Sch 4, para 1 thereto, as noted to r 1.5 at **[10.7]**.
Para (3): words in first pair of square brackets substituted by SI 2005/527, r 42(c), as from 1 April 2005; words in second pair of square brackets substituted by the Insolvency (Amendment) Rules 2009, SI 2009/642, r 5, as from 6 April 2009, subject to transitional provisions in r 3 thereof as noted to r 1.4 of these Rules at **[10.6]**; words in third pair of square brackets substituted by SI 2010/686, r 2, Sch 1, para 460(1), (3), as from 6 April 2010, subject to transitional provisions in Sch 4, para 1 thereto, as noted to r 1.5 at **[10.7]**.

[10.538]
[7.37A Petitions presented by insolvents

(1) This Rule applies where—
  (a) a winding-up petition is presented by a company against itself;
  (b) a bankruptcy petition is presented by a debtor against that debtor,
and references in this Rule to "the insolvent" are to be read as a reference to the company or the debtor.

Part 10 **Miscellaneous other SIs**

(2)   A solicitor acting in either of the cases mentioned in paragraph (1) must in the solicitor's bill of costs give credit for any sum or security received by the solicitor as a deposit from the insolvent on account of the costs and expenses to be incurred in respect of the filing and prosecution of the petition and the deposit must be noted by the costs officer on the final costs certificate.

(3)   Where an order is made on a petition of a kind mentioned in paragraph (1) and prior to the presentation of that petition a petition had been presented by a creditor, no costs are allowed to the insolvent or that insolvent's solicitor out of that insolvent's estate unless the court considers that—
   (a)   the insolvent estate has benefited by the insolvent's conduct; or
   (b)   there are otherwise special circumstances justifying the allowance of costs.]

NOTES
   Commencement: 6 April 2010.
   Originally substituted as noted to r 7.33A at **[10.534]**.
   Further substituted (for r 7.37) by the Insolvency (Amendment) Rules 2010, SI 2010/686, r 2, Sch 1, para 461, as from 6 April 2010, subject to transitional provisions in Sch 4, para 1 thereto, as noted to r 1.5 at **[10.7]**.

[10.539]
[7.38   Costs paid otherwise than out of the insolvent estate
Where the amount of costs is decided by detailed assessment under an order of the court directing that those costs are to be paid otherwise than out of the insolvent estate, the costs officer shall note on the final costs certificate by whom, or the manner in which, the costs are to be paid.]

NOTES
   Substituted as noted to r 7.33A at **[10.534]**.

[10.540]
[7.39   Award of costs against official receiver or responsible insolvency practitioner
Without prejudice to any provision of the Act or Rules by virtue of which the official receiver is not in any event to be liable for costs and expenses, where [an office-holder or the official receiver where that official receiver is not acting as an office-holder] is made a party to any proceedings on the application of another party to the proceedings, he shall not be personally liable for costs unless the court otherwise directs.]

NOTES
   Substituted as noted to r 7.33A at **[10.534]**.
   Words in square brackets substituted by the Insolvency (Amendment) Rules 2010, SI 2010/686, r 2, Sch 1, para 462, as from 6 April 2010, subject to transitional provisions in Sch 4, para 1 thereto, as noted to r 1.5 at **[10.7]**.

[10.541]
[7.40   Applications for costs
[(1)   This Rule applies where a party to, or person affected by, any proceedings in an insolvency—
   (a)   applies to the court for an order allowing his costs, or part of them, incidental to the proceedings; and
   (b)   that application is not made at the time of the proceedings.

(2)   The person concerned shall serve a sealed copy of his or her application—
   (a)   in proceedings other than proceedings relating to a debt relief order—
       (i)   on the [office-holder], and,
       (ii)   in a winding up by the court or a bankruptcy, on the official receiver;
   (b)   in proceedings relating to a debt relief order, on the official receiver.

(3)   The [office-holder] and, where appropriate, the official receiver may appear on an application to which paragraph (2)(a) applies.

(3A)   The official receiver may appear on an application to which paragraph (2)(b) applies.]

(4)   No costs of or incidental to the application shall be allowed to the applicant unless the court is satisfied that the application could not have been made at the time of the proceedings.]

NOTES
   Substituted as noted to r 7.33A at **[10.534]**.
   Para (1): substituted together with paras (2), (3), (3A), for the original paras (1)–(3), by the Insolvency (Amendment) Rules 2009, SI 2009/642, rr 4, 63, as from 6 April 2009.
   Paras (2), (3): substituted as noted to para (1) above; words in square brackets substituted by the Insolvency (Amendment) Rules 2010, SI 2010/686, r 2, Sch 1, para 463, as from 6 April 2010, subject to transitional provisions in Sch 4, para 1 thereto, as noted to r 1.5 at **[10.7]**.
   Para (3A): substituted as noted to para (1) above.

[10.542]
[7.41   Costs and expenses of witnesses
(1)   Except as directed by the court, no allowance as a witness in any examination or other proceedings before the court shall be made to the bankrupt [or the debtor] or an officer of the insolvent company to which the proceedings relate.

(2)   A person presenting any petition in [a company insolvency or bankruptcy proceedings] shall not be regarded as a witness on the hearing of the petition, but the costs officer may allow his expenses of travelling and subsistence.]

NOTES

Substituted as noted to r 7.33A at **[10.534]**.

Para (1): words in square brackets inserted by the Insolvency (Amendment) Rules 2009, SI 2009/642, rr 4, 64(a), as from 6 April 2009.

Para (2): words in square brackets substituted by SI 2009/642, rr 4, 64(b), as from 6 April 2009.

[10.543]
[7.42   Final costs certificate

(1)   A final costs certificate of the costs officer is final and conclusive as to all matters which have not been objected to in the manner provided for under the rules of the court.

(2)   Where it is proved to the satisfaction of a costs officer that a final costs certificate has been lost or destroyed, he may issue a duplicate.]

NOTES

Substituted as noted to r 7.33A at **[10.534]**.

CHAPTER 7
[PERSONS WHO LACK CAPACITY TO MANAGE THEIR AFFAIRS]

NOTES

Chapter heading: words in square brackets substituted by the Mental Capacity Act 2005 (Transitional and Consequential Provisions) Order 2007, SI 2007/1898, art 6, Sch 1, para 12(1), (4), as from 1 October 2007.

[10.544]
7.43   Introductory

(1)   The Rules in this Chapter apply where in insolvency proceedings it appears to the court that a person affected by the proceedings is one who [lacks capacity within the meaning of the Mental Capacity Act 2005 to manage and administer his property and affairs] either—

    (a)   by reason of [lacking capacity within the meaning of the Mental Capacity Act 2005], or

    (b)   due to physical affliction or disability.

(2)   The person concerned is referred to as "the incapacitated person".

NOTES

Para (1); words in square brackets substituted by the Mental Capacity Act 2005 (Transitional and Consequential Provisions) Order 2007, SI 2007/1898, art 6, Sch 1, para 12(1), (5), as from 1 October 2007.

[10.545]
7.44   Appointment of another person to act

(1)   The court may appoint such person as it thinks [just] to appear for, represent or act for the incapacitated person.

(2)   The appointment may be made either generally or for the purpose of any particular application or proceeding, or for the exercise of particular rights or powers which the incapacitated person might have exercised but for his incapacity.

(3)   The court may make the appointment either of its own motion or on application by—

    (a)   a person who has been appointed by a court in the United Kingdom or elsewhere to manage the affairs of, or to represent, the incapacitated person, or

    (b)   any relative or friend of the incapacitated person who appears to the court to be a proper person to make the application, or

    (c)   the official receiver, or

    (d)   the person who, in relation to the proceedings, is the [office-holder].

(4)   Application under paragraph (3) may be made [without notice to any other party]; but the court may require such notice of the application as it thinks necessary to be given to the person alleged to be incapacitated, or any other person, and may adjourn the hearing of the application to enable the notice to be given.

NOTES

Para (1): word in square brackets substituted by the Insolvency (Amendment) Rules 2010, SI 2010/686, r 2, Sch 1, para 1, as from 6 April 2010, subject to transitional provisions in Sch 4, para 2 thereto, as noted to r 1.31 at **[10.34]**.

Para (3): words in square brackets substituted by SI 2010/686, r 2, Sch 1, para 464(1), (2), as from 6 April 2010, subject to transitional provisions in Sch 4, para 1 thereto, as noted to r 1.5 at **[10.7]**.

Para (4): words in square brackets substituted by SI 2010/686, r 2, Sch 1, para 464(1), (3), as from 6 April 2010, subject to transitional provisions in Sch 4, para 2 thereto, as noted to r 1.31 at **[10.34]**.

Part 10   **Miscellaneous other SIs**

[10.546]
[7.45A   Witness statement in support of application

An application under Rule 7.44(3) must be supported by a witness statement made by a registered medical practitioner as to the mental or physical condition of the incapacitated person.]

NOTES

Commencement: 6 April 2010.

Substituted (for the original r 7.45) by the Insolvency (Amendment) Rules 2010, SI 2010/686, r 2, Sch 1, para 465, subject to transitional provisions in Sch 4, para 2 thereto, as noted to r 1.31 at **[10.34]**.

[10.547]
7.46   Service of notices following appointment

Any notice served on, or sent to, a person appointed under Rule 7.44 has the same effect as if it had been served on, or given to, the incapacitated person.

CHAPTER 8
APPEALS IN INSOLVENCY PROCEEDINGS

[10.548]
7.47   Appeals and reviews of court orders [in corporate insolvency]

(1)   Every court having jurisdiction [for the purposes of Parts 1 to 4 of the Act and Parts 1 to 4 of the Rules,] may review, rescind or vary any order made by it in the exercise of that jurisdiction.

[(2)   Appeals in civil matters in proceedings under Parts 1 to 4 of the Act and Parts 1 to 4 of the Rules lie as follows—

   (a)   to a single judge of the High Court where the decision appealed against is made by the county court or the registrar;

   (b)   to the Civil Division of the Court of Appeal from a decision of a single judge of the High Court.]

(3)   A county court is not, in the exercise of its jurisdiction [for the purposes of Parts 1 to 4 of the Act and Parts 1 to 4 of the Rules], subject to be restrained by the order of any other court, and no appeal lies from its decision in the exercise of that jurisdiction except as provided by this Rule.

(4)   Any application for the rescission of a winding-up order shall be made within [5 business] days after the date on which the order was made.

NOTES

Rule heading, paras (1), (3), (4): words in square brackets substituted by the Insolvency (Amendment) Rules 2010, SI 2010/686, r 2, Sch 1, para 466(1)–(3), (5), (6), as from 6 April 2010, subject to transitional provisions in Sch 4, para 1 thereto, as noted to r 1.5 at **[10.7]**.

Para (2): substituted by SI 2010/686, r 2, Sch 1, para 466(1), (4), as from 6 April 2010, subject to transitional provisions in Sch 4, para 1 thereto, as noted to r 1.5 at **[10.7]**.

[10.549]
7.48   Appeals in bankruptcy [by the Secretary of State]

(1)   In bankruptcy proceedings, an appeal lies at the instance of the Secretary of State from any order of the court made on an application for the rescission or annulment of a bankruptcy order, or for a bankrupt's discharge.

(2)   . . .

NOTES

Rule heading: words in square brackets added by the Insolvency (Amendment) Rules 2010, SI 2010/686, r 2, Sch 1, para 467(1), (2), as from 6 April 2010, subject to transitional provisions in Sch 4, para 1 thereto, as noted to r 1.5 at **[10.7]**.

Para (2): revoked by SI 2010/686, r 2, Sch 1, para 467(1), (3), as from 6 April 2010, subject to transitional provisions in Sch 4, para 1 thereto, as noted to r 1.5 at **[10.7]**.

[10.550]
[7.49A   Procedure on appeal

(1)   An appeal against a decision at first instance may only be brought with either the permission of the court which made the decision or the permission of the court which has jurisdiction to hear the appeal.

(2)   An appellant must file an appellant's notice (within the meaning of CPR Part 52) within 21 days after the date of the decision of the court that the appellant wishes to appeal.

(3)   The procedure set out in CPR Part 52 applies to any appeal to which this Chapter applies.]

NOTES

Commencement: 6 April 2010.

Substituted (for the original r 7.49) by the Insolvency (Amendment) Rules 2010, SI 2010/686, r 2, Sch 1, para 468, as from 6 April 2010, subject to transitional provisions in Sch 4, para 1 thereto, as noted to r 1.5 at **[10.7]**.

[10.551]
7.50 Appeal against decision of Secretary of State or official receiver

[(1)] An appeal under the Act or the Rules against a decision of the Secretary of State or the official receiver shall be brought within 28 days of the notification of the decision.

[(2) In respect of a decision under Rule 6.214A(5)(b), an appeal shall be brought within 14 days of the notification of the decision.]

NOTES
Para (1) numbered as such, and para (2) added, by the Insolvency (Amendment) Rules 2003, SI 2003/1730, r 11, Sch 1, Pt 8, para 58, as from 1 April 2004 (for transitional provisions and savings see the note preceding r 2.1 at **[10.60]**).

CHAPTER 9
GENERAL

[10.552]
[7.51A Principal court rules and practice to apply

(1) The provisions of the CPR in the first column of the table in this Rule (including any related practice direction) apply to insolvency proceedings by virtue of the provisions of these Rules set out in the second column with any necessary modifications, except so far as inconsistent with these Rules.

Provisions of CPR	Provisions of these Rules
CPR Part 6 (except 6.30 to 6.51) (service of documents)	Chapter 3 of Part 12A
CPR Part 18 (further information)	Rules 7.60 and 9.2(3)(b)
CPR Part 31 (disclosure and inspection of documents)	Rules 7.60 and 9.2
CPR Part 37 (miscellaneous provisions about payments into court)	Rule 7.59
CPR Parts 44 and 47 (costs)	Chapter 6 of Part 7
CPR Part 52 (appeals)	Rule 7.49

(2) Subject to paragraph (3), the provisions of the CPR (including any related practice direction) not referred to in the table apply to proceedings under the Act and Rules with any necessary modifications, except so far as inconsistent with these Rules.

(3) All insolvency proceedings must be allocated to the multi-track for which CPR Part 29 makes provision, and accordingly those provisions of the CPR which provide for allocation questionnaires and track allocation do not apply.

(4) CPR Part 32 applies to a false statement in a document verified by a statement of truth made under these Rules as it applies to a false statement in a document verified by a statement of truth made under CPR Part 22.]

NOTES
Commencement: 6 April 2010.
Substituted (for the original r 7.51) by the Insolvency (Amendment) Rules 2010, SI 2010/686, r 2, Sch 1, para 469, subject to transitional provisions in Sch 4, para 1 thereto, as noted to r 1.5 at **[10.7]**.

[10.553]
7.52 Right of audience

(1) Official receivers and deputy official receivers have right of audience in insolvency proceedings, whether in the High Court or a county court.

(2) ...

NOTES
Para (2): revoked by the Insolvency (Amendment) Rules 2010, SI 2010/686, r 2, Sch 1, para 470, as from 6 April 2010, subject to transitional provisions in Sch 4, para 1 thereto, as noted to r 1.5 at **[10.7]**.

7.53, 7.54 (_Revoked by the Insolvency (Amendment) Rules 2010, SI 2010/686, r 5, as from 6 April 2010, subject to transitional provisions in Sch 4, para 1 thereto, as noted to r 1.5 at_ **[10.7]**.)

[10.554]
7.55 Formal defects

No insolvency proceedings shall be invalidated by any formal defect or by any irregularity, unless the court before which objection is made considers that substantial injustice has been caused by the defect or irregularity, and that the injustice cannot be remedied by any order of the court.

[10.555]
7.56 [Service of orders staying proceedings]

Where in insolvency proceedings the court makes an order staying any action, execution or other legal process against the property of a company, or against the property or person of an individual debtor or bankrupt, service of the order may be effected by sending a sealed copy of the order to whatever is the address for service of the [claimant] or other party having the carriage of the proceedings to be stayed.

NOTES

Words in square brackets substituted by the Insolvency (Amendment) Rules 2010, SI 2010/686, r 2, Sch 1, para 471, as from 6 April 2010, subject to transitional provisions in Sch 4, para 1 thereto, as noted to r 1.5 at **[10.7]**.

7.57, 7.58 *(Revoked by the Insolvency (Amendment) Rules 2010, SI 2010/686, r 5, as from 6 April 2010, subject to transitional provisions in Sch 4, para 1 thereto, as noted to r 1.5 at* **[10.7]**.*)*

[10.556]
[7.59 Payment into court

[CPR Part 37 (miscellaneous provisions about payments into court)] apply to money lodged in court under the Rules.]

NOTES

Substituted by the Insolvency (Amendment) (No 2) Rules 1999, SI 1999/1022, r 3, Schedule, para 7, as from 26 April 1999.
Words in square brackets substituted by the Insolvency (Amendment) Rules 2010, SI 2010/686, r 2, Sch 1, para 472, as from 6 April 2010, subject to transitional provisions in Sch 4, para 1 thereto, as noted to r 1.5 at **[10.7]**.

[10.557]
[7.60 Further Information and Disclosure

(1)   Any party to insolvency proceedings may apply to the court for an order—
  (a)   that any other party
      (i)   clarify any matter which is in dispute in the proceedings, or
      (ii)   give additional information in relation to any such matter;
      in accordance with CPR Part 18 (further information); or
  (b)   to obtain disclosure from any other party in accordance with CPR Part 31 (disclosure and inspection of documents).

(2)   An application under this Rule may be made without notice being served on any other party.]

NOTES

Substituted by the Insolvency (Amendment) (No 2) Rules 1999, SI 1999/1022, r 3, Schedule, para 8, as from 26 April 1999.

[10.558]
7.61 Office copies of documents

(1)   Any person who has under the Rules the right to inspect the court file of insolvency proceedings may require the court to provide him with an office copy of any document from the file.

(2)   A person's rights under this Rule may be exercised on his behalf by his solicitor.

(3)   An office copy provided by the court under this Rule shall be in such form as the registrar thinks appropriate, and shall bear the court's seal.

[CHAPTER 10
EC REGULATION—CREDITORS' VOLUNTARY WINDING UP—CONFIRMATION BY THE COURT

[10.559]
7.62 Application for confirmation

(1)   Where a company has passed a resolution for voluntary winding up, and no declaration under section 89 has been made [(or is deemed not to have been made in accordance with section 96)], the liquidator may apply to court for an order confirming the creditors' voluntary winding up for the purposes of the EC Regulation.

(2)   The application shall be in writing [supported by a witness statement] by the liquidator (using Form 7.20A the same form) and shall state—
  (a)   the name of the applicant,
  (b)   the name of the company and its registered number,
  (c)   the date on which the resolution for voluntary winding up was passed,
  (d)   that the application is accompanied by all of the documents required under paragraph (3) which are true copies of the documents required, and
  (e)   that the EC Regulation will apply to the company and whether the proceedings will be main proceedings, territorial proceedings or secondary proceedings.

(3)   The liquidator shall file in court two copies of the application, together with one copy of the following—

(a) a copy of the resolution for voluntary winding up referred to by section 84(3),
(b) evidence of his appointment as liquidator of the company, and
(c) a copy of the statement of affairs required under section 99.

(4) It shall not be necessary to serve the application on, or give notice of it to, any person.

(5) On an application under this Rule the court may confirm the creditors' voluntary winding up.

(6) If the court confirms the creditor's voluntary winding up—
(a) it may do so without a hearing,
(b) it shall affix its seal to the application.

(7) A member of the court staff may deal with an application under this Rule.]

[(8) This Rule shall also apply where a company has moved to a voluntary liquidation in accordance with paragraph 83 of Schedule B1 to the Act [except that the material to be filed with the court under paragraph (3) must be a copy of the notice of moving from administration to creditors' voluntary liquidation sent by the administrator for the purposes of paragraph 83(3) that has been registered by the registrar of companies, together with the statement of affairs required under paragraph 47 of Schedule B1 to the Act].]

NOTES
Inserted, together with preceding heading and rr 7.63, 7.64 (Chaps 10, 11) by the Insolvency (Amendment) Rules 2002, SI 2002/1307, rr 3, 9(1), as from 31 May 2002.
Para (1): words in square brackets inserted by the Insolvency (Amendment) Rules 2010, SI 2010/686, r 2, Sch 1, para 473(1), (2), as from 6 April 2010, subject to transitional provisions in Sch 4, para 1 thereto, as noted to r 1.5 at **[10.7]**.
Para (2): words in square brackets substituted by SI 2010/686, r 2, Sch 1, para 473(1), (3), as from 6 April 2010, subject to transitional provisions in Sch 4, para 2 thereto, as noted to r 1.31 at **[10.34]**. Note that the original reference in this paragraph to "Form 20" has been substituted by a reference to "Form 20A".
Para (8): added by the Insolvency (Amendment) Rules 2003, SI 2003/1730, r 11, Sch 1, Pt 8, para 60, as from 15 September 2003 (for transitional provisions and savings see the note preceding r 2.1 at **[10.60]**); words in square brackets added by SI 2010/686, r 2, Sch 1, para 473(1), (4), as from 6 April 2010, subject to transitional provisions in Sch 4, para 1 thereto, as noted to r 1.5 at **[10.7]**.
EC Regulation: ie, Council Regulation 1346/2000/EC on insolvency proceedings.
See Form 7.20A at **[10.673]**.

[10.560]
[7.63 Notice to member State liquidator and creditors in member States
Where the court has confirmed the creditors' voluntary winding up, the liquidator shall [as soon as reasonably practicable] give notice—
(a) if there is a member State liquidator in relation to the company, to the member State liquidator;
(b) in accordance with Article 40 of the EC Regulation (duty to inform creditors).]

NOTES
Inserted as noted to r 7.62 at **[10.559]**.
Words in square brackets substituted by the Insolvency (Amendment) Rules 2009, SI 2009/642, r 5, as from 6 April 2009, subject to transitional provisions in r 3 thereof, as noted to r 1.4 of these Rules at **[10.6]**.
EC Regulation: ie, Council Regulation 1346/2000/EC on insolvency proceedings.

[CHAPTER 11
EC REGULATION—MEMBER STATE LIQUIDATOR

[10.561]
7.64 Interpretation of creditor
(1) This Rule applies where a member State liquidator has been appointed in relation to a person subject to insolvency proceedings [other than proceedings relating to a debt relief order].

[(2) The member State liquidator has the same right to inspect or obtain from the court a copy of, or a copy of any document or documents contained in, the court file relating to the insolvency proceedings that is opened and maintained by the court under Rule 7.31A(1) as a creditor has under Rule 7.31A(3) and may appear at any hearing relating to those proceedings.]

(3) . . .

(4) [Paragraph (2) is] without prejudice to the generality of the right to participate referred to in paragraph 3 of Article 32 of the EC Regulation (exercise of creditor's rights).]

NOTES
Inserted as noted to r 7.62 at **[10.559]**.
Para (1): words in square brackets inserted by the Insolvency (Amendment) Rules 2009, SI 2009/642, rr 4, 65, as from 6 April 2009.
Para (2): substituted by the Insolvency (Amendment) Rules 2010, SI 2010/686, r 2, Sch 1, para 474(1), (2), as from 6 April 2010, subject to transitional provisions in Sch 4, para 1 thereto, as noted to r 1.5 at **[10.7]**.
Para (3): revoked by SI 2010/686, r 2, Sch 1, para 474(1), (3), as from 6 April 2010, subject to transitional provisions in Sch 4, para 1 thereto, as noted to r 1.5 at **[10.7]**.
Para (4): words in square brackets substituted by SI 2010/686, r 2, Sch 1, para 474(1), (4), as from 6 April 2010, subject to transitional provisions in Sch 4, para 1 thereto, as noted to r 1.5 at **[10.7]**.

EC Regulation: ie, Council Regulation 1346/2000/EC on insolvency proceedings.

PART 8
PROXIES AND COMPANY REPRESENTATION

[10.562]
8.1   Definition of "proxy"

(1)   For the purposes of the Rules, a proxy is an authority given by a person ("the principal") to another person ("the proxy-holder") to attend a meeting and speak and vote as his representative.

(2)   Proxies are for use at creditors', company or contributories' meetings [summoned or called] under the Act or the Rules.

(3)   Only one proxy may be given by a person for any one meeting at which he desires to be represented; and it may only be given to one person, being an individual aged 18 or over. But the principal may specify one or more other such individuals to be proxy-holder in the alternative, in the order in which they are named in the proxy.

(4)   Without prejudice to the generality of paragraph (3), a proxy for a particular meeting may be given to whoever is to be the chairman of the meeting; and for a meeting held as part of the proceedings in a winding up by the court, or in a bankruptcy, it may be given to the official receiver.

[(5)   A person given a proxy under paragraph (4) cannot decline to be the proxy-holder in relation to that proxy.

(6)   A proxy requires the holder to give the principal's vote on matters arising for determination at the meeting, or to abstain, or to propose, in the principal's name, a resolution to be voted on by the meeting, either as directed or in accordance with the holder's own discretion.]

NOTES

Para (2): words in square brackets inserted by the Insolvency (Amendment) Rules 1987, SI 1987/1919, r 3(1), Schedule, Pt 1, para 134(1), as from 11 January 1988.

Paras (5), (6): substituted (for the original para (5)) by SI 1987/1919, r 3(1), Schedule, Pt 1, para 134(2), as from 11 January 1988.

See Forms 8.1–8.5 at **[10.673]**.

[10.563]
8.2   Issue and use of forms

(1)   When notice is given of a meeting to be held in insolvency proceedings, and forms of proxy are sent out with the notice, no form so sent out shall have inserted in it the name or description of any person.

(2)   No form of proxy shall be used at any meeting except that which is sent out with the notice summoning the meeting, or a substantially similar form.

(3)   A form of proxy shall be [authenticated] by the principal, or by some person authorised by him (either generally or with reference to a particular meeting). If the form is [authenticated] by a person other than the principal, the nature of the person's authority shall be stated.

NOTES

Para (3): word in square brackets substituted by the Insolvency (Amendment) Rules 2010, SI 2010/686, r 2, Sch 1, para 1, as from 6 April 2010, subject to transitional provisions in Sch 4, para 2 thereto, as noted to r 1.31 at **[10.34]**.

[10.564]
8.3   Use of proxies at meetings

(1)   A proxy given for a particular meeting may be used at any adjournment of that meeting.

(2)   Where the official receiver holds proxies for use at any meeting, his deputy, or any other official receiver, may act as proxy-holder in his place.

Alternatively, the official receiver may in writing authorise another officer of the Department to act for him at the meeting and use the proxies as if that other officer were himself proxy-holder.

(3)   Where the responsible insolvency practitioner holds proxies to be used by him as chairman of a meeting, and some other person acts as chairman, the other person may use the insolvency practitioner's proxies as if he were himself proxy-holder.

[(4)   Where a proxy directs a proxy-holder to vote for or against a resolution for the nomination or appointment of a person as the responsible insolvency practitioner, the proxy-holder may, unless the proxy states otherwise, vote for or against (as he thinks fit) any resolution for the nomination or appointment of that person jointly with another or others.

(5)   A proxy-holder may propose any resolution which, if proposed by another, would be a resolution in favour of which by virtue of the proxy he would be entitled to vote.

(6)   Where a proxy gives specific directions as to voting, this does not, unless the proxy states otherwise, preclude the proxy-holder from voting at his discretion on resolutions put to the meeting which are not dealt with in the proxy.]

NOTES

Paras (4)–(6): added by the Insolvency (Amendment) Rules 1987, SI 1987/1919, r 3(1), Schedule, Pt 1, para 135, as from 11 January 1988.

[10.565]
8.4 Retention of proxies

(1) Subject as follows, proxies used for voting at any meeting shall be retained by the chairman of the meeting.

(2) The chairman shall deliver the proxies, [as soon as reasonably practicable] after the meeting, to the responsible insolvency practitioner (where that is someone other than himself).

NOTES

Para (2): words in square brackets substituted by the Insolvency (Amendment) Rules 2009, SI 2009/642, r 5, as from 6 April 2009, subject to transitional provisions in r 3 thereof, as noted to r 1.4 of these Rules at **[10.6]**.

[10.566]
8.5 Right of inspection

(1) The [office-holder] shall, so long as proxies lodged with him are in his hands, allow them to be inspected, at all reasonable times on any business day, by—
    (a) the creditors, in the case of proxies used at a meeting of creditors, and
    (b) a company's members or contributories, in the case of proxies used at a meeting of the company or of its contributories.

(2) The reference in paragraph (1) to creditors is—
    (a) in the case of a company in liquidation or of an individual's bankruptcy, those creditors who have proved their debts, and
    (b) in any other case, persons who have submitted in writing a claim to be creditors of the company or individual concerned;
but in neither case does it include a person whose proof or claim has been wholly rejected for purposes of voting, dividend or otherwise.

(3) the right of inspection given by this Rule is also exercisable—
    (a) in the case of an insolvent company, by its directors, and
    (b) in the case of an insolvent individual, by him.

(4) Any person attending a meeting in insolvency proceedings is entitled, immediately before or in the course of the meeting, to inspect proxies and associated documents [(including proofs) sent or given, in accordance with directions contained in any notice convening the meeting, to the chairman of that meeting or to any other person by a creditor, member or contributory for the purpose of that meeting.]

[(5) This Rule is subject to Rule 12A.51 (confidentiality of documents—grounds for refusing inspection).]

NOTES

Para (1): words in square brackets substituted by the Insolvency (Amendment) Rules 2010, SI 2010/686, r 2, Sch 1, para 475(1), (2), as from 6 April 2010, subject to transitional provisions in Sch 4, para 1 thereto, as noted to r 1.5 at **[10.7]**.

Para (4): words in square brackets substituted by the Insolvency (Amendment) Rules 1987, SI 1987/1919, r 3(1), Schedule, Pt 1, para 136, as from 11 January 1988.

Para (5): added by SI 2010/686, r 2, Sch 1, para 475(1), (3), as from 6 April 2010, subject to transitional provisions in Sch 4, para 1 thereto, as noted to r 1.5 at **[10.7]**.

[10.567]
8.6 Proxy-holder with financial interest

(1) A proxy-holder shall not vote in favour of any resolution which would directly or indirectly place him, or any associate of his, in a position to receive any remuneration out of the insolvent estate, unless the proxy specifically directs him to vote in that way.

[(1A) Where a proxy-holder has [authenticated] the proxy as being authorised to do so by his principal and the proxy specifically directs him to vote in the way mentioned in paragraph (1), he shall nevertheless not vote in that way unless he produces to the chairman of the meeting written authorisation from his principal sufficient to show that the proxy-holder was entitled so to [authenticate] the proxy.]

(2) This Rule applies also to any person acting as chairman of a meeting and using proxies in that capacity [under Rule 8.3]; and in its application to him, the proxy-holder is deemed an associate of his.

NOTES

Para (1A): inserted by the Insolvency (Amendment) Rules 1987, SI 1987/1919, r 3(1), Schedule, Pt 1, para 137(1), as from 11 January 1988; words in square brackets substituted by the Insolvency (Amendment) Rules 2010, SI 2010/686, r 2, Sch 1, para 1, as from 6 April 2010, subject to transitional provisions in Sch 4, para 2 thereto, as noted to r 1.31 at **[10.34]**.

Para (2): words in square brackets inserted by SI 1987/1919, r 3(1), Schedule, Pt 1, para 137(2), as from 11 January 1988.

Part 10   Miscellaneous other SIs

[10.568]
8.7   Company representation

(1)   Where a person is authorised . . .   to represent a corporation at a meeting of creditors or of the company or its contributories, he shall produce to the chairman of the meeting a copy of the resolution from which he derives his authority.

(2)   The copy resolution must be under the seal of the corporation, or certified by the secretary or a director of the corporation to be a true copy.

[(3)   Nothing in this Rule requires the authority of a person to [authenticate] a proxy on behalf of a principal which is a corporation to be in the form of a resolution of that corporation.]

NOTES

   Para (1): words omitted revoked by the Insolvency (Amendment) Rules 2010, SI 2010/686, r 2, Sch 1, para 476, as from 6 April 2010, subject to transitional provisions in Sch 4, para 1 thereto, as noted to r 1.5 at **[10.7]**.
   Para (3): added by the Insolvency (Amendment) Rules 1987, SI 1987/1919, r 3(1), Schedule, Pt 1, para 138, as from 11 January 1988; word in square brackets substituted by SI 2010/686, r 2, Sch 1, para 1, as from 6 April 2010, subject to transitional provisions in Sch 4, para 2 thereto, as noted to r 1.31 at **[10.34]**.

[10.569]
[8.8   Interpretation of creditor

(1)   This Rule applies where a member State liquidator has been appointed in relation to a person subject to insolvency proceedings.

(2)   For the purposes of rule 8.5(1) (right of inspection of proxies) a member State liquidator appointed in main proceedings is deemed to be a creditor.

(3)   Paragraph (2) is without prejudice to the generality of the right to participate referred to in paragraph 3 of Article 32 of the EC Regulation (exercise of creditor's rights).]

NOTES

   Inserted by the Insolvency (Amendment) Rules 2002, SI 2002/1307, rr 3, 9(2), as from 31 May 2002.
   EC Regulation: ie, Council Regulation 1346/2000/EC on insolvency proceedings.

PART 9

EXAMINATION OF PERSONS CONCERNED IN COMPANY AND
INDIVIDUAL INSOLVENCY

[10.570]
9.1   Preliminary

[(1)   The Rules in this Part apply to applications to the court for an order under—
   (a)   section 236 (inquiry into company's dealings),
   (b)   section 251N (debt relief orders—inquiry into dealings and property of debtor), or
   (c)   section 366 (inquiry into bankruptcy, with respect to the bankrupt's dealings—including section 366 as it applies by virtue of section 368).]

(2)   The following definitions apply—
   (a)   the person in respect of whom an order is applied for is "the respondent";
   [(b)   "the applicable section" is section 236, 251N or 366, according to whether the affairs of a company or those of a debtor in relation to a debt relief order or an application for a debt relief order or a bankrupt or (where the application under section 366 is made by virtue of section 368) a debtor in bankruptcy proceedings are in question;
   (c)   the company or, as the case may be, the debtor in relation to a debt relief order or an application for a debt relief order, the bankrupt or debtor in bankruptcy proceedings concerned is "the insolvent";
   (d)   "the applicant", in any application made under section 251N, means the official receiver].

NOTES

   Para (1): substituted by the Insolvency (Amendment) Rules 2010, SI 2010/686, r 2, Sch 1, para 477, as from 6 April 2010, subject to transitional provisions in Sch 4, para 1 thereto, as noted to r 1.5 at **[10.7]**.
   Para (2): sub-paras (b)–(d) substituted, for the original sub-para (b), (c), by SI 2009/642, rr 4, 66(b), as from 6 April 2009. See Form 9.1 at **[10.673]**.

[10.571]
9.2   Form and contents of application

(1)   The application shall be in writing [and specify] the grounds on which it is made.

[(2)   The application must specify the name of the respondent.]

(3)   It shall be stated whether the application is for the respondent—
   (a)   to be ordered to appear before the court, or
   [(b)   to be ordered to clarify any matter which is in dispute in the proceedings or to give additional information in relation to any such matter and if so CPR Part 18 (further information) shall apply to any such order, or]

   (c)   to submit [witness statements] (if so, particulars to be given of the matters to [be included]), or

   (d)   to produce books, papers or other records (if so, the items in question to be specified),

or for any two or more of those purposes.

(4)   The application may be made [without notice to any other party].

NOTES

Para (1): words in square brackets substituted by the Insolvency (Amendment) Rules 2010, SI 2010/686, r 2, Sch 1, para 478(1), (2), as from 6 April 2010, subject to transitional provisions in Sch 4, para 2 thereto, as noted to r 1.31 at **[10.34]**.

Para (2): substituted by SI 2010/686, r 2, Sch 1, para 478(1), (3), as from 6 April 2010, subject to transitional provisions in Sch 4, para 2 thereto, as noted to r 1.31 at **[10.34]**.

Para (3): sub-para (b) substituted by the Insolvency (Amendment) (No 2) Rules 1999, SI 1999/1022, r 3, Schedule, para 9, as from 26 April 1999; words in square brackets in sub-para (c) substituted by SI 2010/686, r 2, Sch 1, para 478(1), (4), as from 6 April 2010, subject to transitional provisions in Sch 4, para 2 thereto, as noted to r 1.31 at **[10.34]**.

Para (4): words in square brackets substituted by SI 2010/686, r 2, Sch 1, para 478(1), (5), as from 6 April 2010, subject to transitional provisions in Sch 4, para 2 thereto, as noted to r 1.31 at **[10.34]**.

[10.572]
9.3 Order for examination, etc

(1)   The court may, whatever the purpose of the application, make any order which it has power to make under the applicable section.

(2)   The court, if it orders the respondent to appear before it, shall specify a venue for his appearance, which shall be not less than 14 days from the date of the order.

(3)   If he is ordered to submit [witness statements], the order shall specify—

   (a)   the matters which are to be dealt with in his [witness statements], and

   (b)   the time within which they are to be submitted to the court.

(4)   If the order is to produce books, papers or other records, the time and manner of compliance shall be specified.

(5)   The order must be served [as soon as reasonably practicable] on the respondent; and it must be served personally, unless the court otherwise orders.

NOTES

Para (3): words in square brackets substituted by the Insolvency (Amendment) Rules 2010, SI 2010/686, r 2, Sch 1, para 479, as from 6 April 2010, subject to transitional provisions in Sch 4, para 2 thereto, as noted to r 1.31 at **[10.34]**.

Para (5): words in square brackets substituted by the Insolvency (Amendment) Rules 2009, SI 2009/642, r 5, as from 6 April 2009, subject to transitional provisions in r 3 thereof, as noted to r 1.4 of these Rules at **[10.6]**.

[10.573]
9.4 Procedure for examination

(1)   At any examination of the respondent, the applicant may attend in person, or be represented by a solicitor with or without counsel, and may put such questions to the respondent as the court may allow.

[(2)   Unless the applicant objects, the following persons may attend the examination with the permission of the court and may put questions to the respondent (but only through the applicant)—

   (a)   any person who could have applied for an order under the applicable section; and

   (b)   any creditor who has provided information on which the application was made under section 236 or 366.]

[(3)   If the respondent is ordered to clarify any matter or to give additional information, the court shall direct him as to the questions which he is required to answer, and as to whether his answers (if any) are to be made [in a witness statement].]

(4)   . . .

(5)   The respondent may at his own expense employ a solicitor with or without counsel, who may put to him such questions as the court may allow for the purpose of enabling him to explain or qualify any answers given by him, and may make representations on his behalf.

(6)   There shall be made in writing such record of the examination as the court thinks proper. The record shall be read over either to or by the respondent and [authenticated] by him at a venue fixed by the court.

(7)   The written record may, in any proceedings (whether under the Act or otherwise) be used as evidence against the respondent of any statement made by him in the course of his examination.

NOTES

Para (2): substituted by the Insolvency (Amendment) Rules 2010, SI 2010/686, r 2, Sch 1, para 480(1), (2), as from 6 April 2010, subject to transitional provisions in Sch 4, para 1 thereto, as noted to r 1.5 at **[10.7]**.

Para (3): substituted by the Insolvency (Amendment) (No 2) Rules 1999, SI 1999/1022, r 3, Schedule, para 10, as from 26 April 1999; words in square brackets substituted by SI 2010/686, r 2, Sch 1, para 480(1), (3), as from 6 April 2010, subject to transitional provisions in Sch 4, para 2 thereto, as noted to r 1.31 at **[10.34]**.

Para (4): revoked by SI 2010/686, r 2, Sch 1, para 480(1), (4), as from 6 April 2010, subject to transitional provisions in Sch 4, para 1 thereto, as noted to r 1.5 at **[10.7]**.

Para (6): word in square brackets substituted by SI 2010/686, r 2, Sch 1, para 1, as from 6 April 2010, subject to transitional provisions in Sch 4, para 2 thereto, as noted to r 1.31 at **[10.34]**.

[10.574]
9.5   Record of examination
[(1)   Unless the court otherwise directs, the written record of questions put to the respondent and the respondent's answers, and any witness statements submitted by the respondent in compliance with an order of the court under the applicable section, are not to be filed with the court.

(2)   The documents set out in paragraph (3) are not open to inspection without an order of the court, by any person other than—
   (a)   the applicant for an order under the applicable section, or
   (b)   any person who could have applied for such an order in respect of the affairs of the same insolvent.

(3)   The documents to which paragraph (2) applies are—
   (a)   the written record of the respondent's examination;
   (b)   copies of questions put to the respondent or proposed to be put to the respondent and answers to questions given by the respondent;
   (c)   any witness statement by the respondent; and
   (d)   any document on the court file as shows the grounds for the application for an order.]

(4)   The court may from time to time give directions as to the custody and inspection of any documents to which this Rule applies, and as to the furnishing of copies of, or extracts from, such documents.

NOTES

Paras (1)–(3): substituted by the Insolvency (Amendment) Rules 2010, SI 2010/686, r 2, Sch 1, para 481, as from 6 April 2010, subject to transitional provisions in Sch 4, para 1 thereto, as noted to r 1.5 at **[10.7]**.

[10.575]
9.6   Costs of proceedings under ss 236, [251N and] 366
(1)   Where the court has ordered an examination of any person under the applicable section, and it appears to it that the examination was made necessary because information had been unjustifiably refused by the respondent, it may order that the costs of the examination be paid by him.

(2)   Where the court makes an order against a person under—
   (a)   section 237(1) or 367(1) (to deliver up property in his possession which belongs to the insolvent), or
   (b)   section 237(2) or 367(2) (to pay any amount in discharge of a debt due to the insolvent).
the costs of the application for the order may be ordered by the court to be paid by the respondent.

(3)   Subject to paragraphs (1) and (2) above, the applicant's costs shall, unless the court otherwise orders, [be paid—
   (a)   in relation to a company insolvency, as an expense of the liquidation,
   (b)   in relation to an individual insolvency[, but not in proceedings relating to debt relief orders or applications for debt relief orders], out of the bankrupt's estate or (as the case may be) the debtor's property].

(4)   A person summoned to attend for examination under this Chapter shall be tendered a reasonable sum in respect of travelling expenses incurred in connection with his attendance. Other costs falling on him are at the court's discretion.

(5)   Where the examination is on the application of the official receiver otherwise than in the capacity of liquidator or trustee, no order shall be made for the payment of costs by him.

NOTES

Rule heading: words in square brackets inserted by the Insolvency (Amendment) Rules 2009, SI 2009/642, rr 4, 68(a), as from 6 April 2009.

Para (3): words in first (outer) pair of square brackets substituted by the Insolvency (Amendment) Rules 2008, SI 2008/737, rr 3, 7(13), as from 6 April 2008, subject to transitional provisions as noted to r 4.218 at **[10.486]**; words in second (inner) pair of square brackets inserted by SI 2009/642, rr 4, 68(b), as from 6 April 2009.

PART 10
OFFICIAL RECEIVERS

[10.576]
10.1   Appointment of official receivers
Judicial notice shall be taken of the appointment under sections 399 to 401 of official receivers and deputy official receivers.

[10.577]
10.2   Persons entitled to act on official receiver's behalf

(1)   In the absence of the official receiver authorised to act in a particular case, an officer authorised in writing for the purpose by the Secretary of State, or by the official receiver himself, may, with the [permission] of the court, act on the official receiver's behalf and in his place—
   (a)   in any examination under section 133, 236, [251N,] 290 or 366, and
   (b)   in respect of any application to the court.

(2)   In case of emergency, where there is no official receiver capable of acting, anything to be done by, to or before the official receiver may be done by, to or before the registrar [or district judge].

NOTES
Para (1): word in first pair of square brackets substituted by the Insolvency (Amendment) Rules 2010, SI 2010/686, r 2, Sch 1, para 1, as from 6 April 2010, subject to transitional provisions in Sch 4, para 2 thereto, as noted to r 1.31 at **[10.34]**; figure in second pair of square brackets inserted by the Insolvency (Amendment) Rules 2009, SI 2009/642, rr 4, 69, as from 6 April 2009.
Para (2): words in square brackets substituted by SI 2010/686, r 2, Sch 1, para 482, as from 6 April 2010, subject to transitional provisions in Sch 4, para 2 thereto, as noted to r 1.31 at **[10.34]**.

[10.578]
10.3   Application for directions

The official receiver may apply to the court for directions in relation to any matter arising in insolvency proceedings.

[10.579]
10.4   Official receiver's expenses

(1)   Any expenses incurred by the official receiver (in whatever capacity he may be acting) in connection with proceedings taken against him in insolvency proceedings are to be treated as expenses of the insolvency proceedings.
   "Expenses" includes damages.

(2)   In respect of any sums due to him under paragraph (1) [in connection with insolvency proceedings other than proceedings relating to debt relief orders or applications for debt relief orders], the official receiver has a charge on the insolvent estate.

NOTES
Para (2): words in square brackets inserted by the Insolvency (Amendment) Rules 2009, SI 2009/642, rr 4, 70, as from 6 April 2009.

PART 11
DECLARATION AND PAYMENT OF DIVIDEND (WINDING UP AND BANKRUPTCY)

[10.580]
11.1   Preliminary

(1)   The Rules in this Part relate to the declaration and payment of dividends in companies winding up and in bankruptcy.

(2)   The following definitions apply—
   (a)   "the insolvent" means the company in liquidation or, as the case may be, the bankrupt; and
   (b)   "creditors" means those creditors of the insolvent of whom the [office-holder] is aware
     . . .

[(3)   For the purposes of this Part, a member State liquidator appointed in relation to an insolvent is deemed to be a creditor.]

NOTES
Para (2): words in square brackets substituted, and words omitted revoked, by the Insolvency (Amendment) Rules 2010, SI 2010/686, r 2, Sch 1, paras 483, 484, as from 6 April 2010, subject to transitional provisions in Sch 4, para 1 thereto, as noted to r 1.5 at **[10.7]**.
Para (3): added by the Insolvency (Amendment) Rules 2002, SI 2002/1307, rr 3, 10(1), as from 31 May 2002, with savings in relation to anything done under, or for the purposes of, this provision before that date.

[10.581]
11.2   Notice of intended dividend

(1)   Before declaring a dividend, the [office-holder] shall give notice of his intention to do so—
   [(a)   to all creditors whose addresses are known to him and who have not proved their debts, and
   (b)   where a member State liquidator has been appointed in relation to the insolvent, to that person.]

[(1A)   Before declaring a first dividend the [office-holder] shall give notice of the intended dividend. As soon as reasonably practicable such notice—
   (a)   shall be gazetted; and
   (b)   may be advertised in such other manner as the [office-holder] thinks fit.]

[(1B) Paragraph (1A) shall not apply where the [office-holder] has previously, by notice [which has been gazetted], invited creditors to prove their debts.]

[(1C) In addition to the standard contents, a notice under paragraph (1A) must—

(a) state that the office-holder intends to declare a first dividend; and

(b) specify the date by which and place at which proofs must be lodged.]

(2) [Any notice under paragraph (1) and any notice of a first dividend under paragraph (1A)] shall specify a date ("the last date for proving") up to which proofs may be lodged. The date shall be the same for all creditors, and not less than 21 days from that of the notice.

(3) The [office-holder] shall in the notice state his intention to declare a dividend (specified as interim or final, as the case may be) within the period of [2] months from the last date for proving.

NOTES

Para (1): words in first pair of square brackets substituted by the Insolvency (Amendment) Rules 2010, SI 2010/686, r 2, Sch 1, para 483, as from 6 April 2010, subject to transitional provisions in Sch 4, para 1 thereto, as noted to r 1.5 at **[10.7]**; words in second pair of square brackets substituted by the Insolvency (Amendment) Rules 2002, SI 2002/1307, rr 3, 10(2), as from 31 May 2002, with savings in relation to anything done under, or for the purposes of, this provision before that date.

Para (1A): originally inserted by the Insolvency (Amendment) Rules 1987, SI 1987/1919, r 3(1), Schedule, Pt 1, para 139(2), as from 11 January 1988; subsequently substituted by the Insolvency (Amendment) Rules 2009, SI 2009/642, rr 4, 71(a), as from 6 April 2009, subject to transitional provisions in r 3 thereof, as noted to r 1.4 of these Rules at **[10.6]**; words in square brackets substituted by SI 2010/686, r 2, Sch 1, para 483, as from 6 April 2010, subject to transitional provisions in Sch 4, para 1 thereto, as noted to r 1.5 at **[10.7]**.

Para (1B): inserted by SI 2009/642, rr 4, 71(b), as from 6 April 2009, subject to transitional provisions in r 3 thereof, as noted to r 1.4 of these Rules at **[10.6]**; words in first pair of square brackets substituted, and words in second pair of square brackets inserted, by SI 2010/686, r 2, Sch 1, paras 483, 485(1), (2), as from 6 April 2010, subject to transitional provisions in Sch 4, para 1 thereto, as noted to r 1.5 at **[10.7]**.

Para (1C): inserted by SI 2010/686, r 2, Sch 1, para 485(1), (3), as from 6 April 2010, subject to transitional provisions in Sch 4, para 1 thereto, as noted to r 1.5 at **[10.7]**.

Para (2): words in square brackets substituted by SI 1987/1919, r 3(1), Schedule, Pt 1, para 139(3), as from 11 January 1988.

Para (3): words in square brackets substituted by SI 2010/686, r 2, Sch 1, paras 483, 485(1), (4), as from 6 April 2010, subject to transitional provisions in Sch 4, para 1 thereto, as noted to r 1.5 at **[10.7]**.

[10.582]
11.3 Final admission/rejection of proofs

(1) The [office-holder], shall within [5 business] days from the last date of proving, deal with every creditor's proof (in so far as not already dealt with) by admitting or rejecting it in whole or in part, or by making such provision as he thinks fit in respect of it.

(2) The [office-holder] is not obliged to deal with proofs lodged after the last date for proving; but he may do so, if he thinks fit.

[(3) In the declaration of a dividend no payment shall be made more than once by virtue of the same debt.

(4) Subject to Rule 11.11, where—

(a) a creditor has proved, and

(b) a member State liquidator has proved in relation to the same debt,

payment shall only be made to the creditor.]

NOTES

Paras (1), (2): words in square brackets substituted by the Insolvency (Amendment) Rules 2010, SI 2010/686, r 2, Sch 1, paras 483, 486, as from 6 April 2010, subject to transitional provisions in Sch 4, para 1 thereto, as noted to r 1.5 at **[10.7]**.

Paras (3), (4): added by the Insolvency (Amendment) Rules 2002, SI 2002/1307, rr 3, 10(3), as from 31 May 2002, with savings in relation to anything done under, or for the purposes of, this provision before that date.

[10.583]
11.4 Postponement or cancellation of dividend

If in the period of [2] months referred to in Rule 11.2(3)—

(a) the [office-holder] has rejected a proof in whole or in part and application is made to the court for his decision to be reversed or varied, or

(b) application is made to the court for the [office-holder's] decision on a proof to be reversed or varied, or for a proof to be expunged, or for a reduction of the amount claimed.

the [office-holder] may postpone or cancel the dividend.

NOTES

Words in square brackets substituted by the Insolvency (Amendment) Rules 2010, SI 2010/686, r 2, Sch 1, paras 483, 487, as from 6 April 2010, subject to transitional provisions in Sch 4, para 1 thereto, as noted to r 1.5 at **[10.7]**.

[10.584]
11.5 Decision to declare dividend

(1) If the [office-holder] has not, in the [2-month] period referred to in Rule 11.2(3), had cause to postpone or cancel the dividend, he shall within that period proceed to declare the dividend of which he gave notice under that Rule.

(2)　Except with the [permission] of the court, the [office-holder] shall not declare the dividend so long as there is pending any application to the court to reverse or vary a decision of his on a proof, or to expunge a proof or to reduce the amount claimed.

If the court gives [permission] under this paragraph, the [office-holder] shall make such provision in respect of the proof in question as the court directs.

NOTES

Words in square brackets substituted by the Insolvency (Amendment) Rules 2010, SI 2010/686, r 2, Sch 1, paras 1, 483, 488, as from 6 April 2010, subject to transitional provisions in Sch 4, paras 1, 2 thereto, as noted to rr 1.5, 1.31 at **[10.7]**, **[10.4]**.

[10.585]
11.6　Notice of declaration

(1)　The [office-holder] shall give notice of the dividend to—
　　[(a)　all creditors who have proved their debts, and
　　(b)　where a member State liquidator has been appointed in relation to the insolvent, to that person.]

(2)　the notice shall include the following particulars relating to the insolvency and the administration of the insolvent estate—
　　(a)　amounts realised from the sale of assets, indicating (so far as practicable) amounts raised by the sale of particular assets;
　　(b)　payments made by the [office-holder] in the administration of the insolvent estate;
　　(c)　provision (if any) made for the unsettled claims, and funds (if any) retained for particular purposes;
　　(d)　the total amount to be distributed, and the rate of dividend;
　　(e)　whether, and if so when, any further dividend is expected to be declared.

[(2A)　Where, in a winding up other than a members' voluntary winding up, the liquidator proposes to declare a dividend to unsecured creditors, the notice must also state the value of the prescribed part, except where the court has made an order under section 176A(5).]

(3)　The dividend may be distributed simultaneously with the notice declaring it.

(4)　Payment of dividend may be made by post, or arrangements may be made with any creditor for it to be paid to him in another way, or held for his collection.

(5)　Where a dividend is paid on a bill of exchange or other negotiable instrument, the amount of the dividend shall be endorsed on the instrument, or on a certified copy of it, if required to be produced by the holder for that purpose.

NOTES

Para (1): words in first pair of square brackets substituted by the Insolvency (Amendment) Rules 2010, SI 2010/686, r 2, Sch 1, para 483, as from 6 April 2010, subject to transitional provisions in Sch 4, para 1 thereto, as noted to r 1.5 at **[10.7]**; sub-paras (a), (b) substituted by the Insolvency (Amendment) Rules 2002, SI 2002/1307, rr 3, 10(4), as from 31 May 2002, with savings in relation to anything done under, or for the purposes of, this provision before that date.

Para (2): words in square brackets substituted by SI 2010/686, r 2, Sch 1, para 483, as from 6 April 2010, subject to transitional provisions in Sch 4, para 1 thereto, as noted to r 1.5 at **[10.7]**.

Para (2A): inserted by SI 2010/686, r 2, Sch 1, para 489, as from 6 April 2010, subject to transitional provisions in Sch 4, para 1 thereto, as noted to r 1.5 at **[10.7]**.

[10.586]
11.7　Notice of no, or no further, dividend

If the [office-holder] gives notice to creditors that he is unable to declare any dividend or (as the case may be) any further dividend, the notice shall contain statement to the effect either—
　　(a)　that no funds have been realised, or
　　(b)　that the funds realised have already been distributed or used or allocated for defraying the expenses of administration.

NOTES

Words in square brackets substituted by the Insolvency (Amendment) Rules 2010, SI 2010/686, r 2, Sch 1, para 483, as from 6 April 2010, subject to transitional provisions in Sch 4, para 1 thereto, as noted to r 1.5 at **[10.7]**.

[10.587]
11.8　Proof altered after payment of dividend

(1)　If after payment of dividend the amount claimed by a creditor in his proof is increased, the creditor is not entitled to disturb the distribution of the dividend; but he is entitled to be paid, out of any money for the time being available for the payment of any further dividend, any dividend or dividends which he has failed to receive.

(2)　Any dividend or dividends payable under paragraph (1) shall be paid before the money there referred to is applied to the payment of any such further dividend.

(3)　If, after a creditor's proof has been admitted, the proof is withdrawn or expunged, or the amount of it is reduced, the creditor is liable to repay to the [office-holder], for the credit of the insolvent estate, any amount overpaid by way of dividend.

NOTES

Para (3): words in square brackets substituted by the Insolvency (Amendment) Rules 2010, SI 2010/686, r 2, Sch 1, para 483, as from 6 April 2010, subject to transitional provisions in Sch 4, para 1 thereto, as noted to r 1.5 at **[10.7]**.

[10.588]
11.9   Secured creditors

(1)   The following applies where a creditor re-values his security at a time when a dividend has been declared.

(2)   If the revaluation results in a reduction of his unsecured claim ranking for dividend, the creditor shall [as soon as reasonably practicable] repay to the [office-holder], for the credit of the insolvent estate, any amount received by him as dividend in excess of that to which he would be entitled having regard to the revaluation of the security.

(3)   If the revaluation results in an increase of his unsecured claim, the creditor is entitled to receive from the [office-holder], out of any money for the time being available for the payment of a further dividend, before any such further dividend is paid, any dividend or dividends which he has failed to receive, having regard to the revaluation of the security.

However, the creditor is not entitled to disturb any dividend declared (whether or not distributed) before the date of the revaluation.

NOTES

Para (2): words in first pair of square brackets substituted by the Insolvency (Amendment) Rules 2009, SI 2009/642, r 5, as from 6 April 2009, subject to transitional provisions in r 3 thereof, as noted to r 1.4 of these Rules at **[10.6]**; words in second pair of square brackets substituted by the Insolvency (Amendment) Rules 2010, SI 2010/686, r 2, Sch 1, para 483, as from 6 April 2010, subject to transitional provisions in Sch 4, para 1 thereto, as noted to r 1.5 at **[10.7]**.

Para (3): words in square brackets substituted by SI 2010/686, r 2, Sch 1, para 483, as from 6 April 2010, subject to transitional provisions in Sch 4, para 1 thereto, as noted to r 1.5 at **[10.7]**.

[10.589]
11.10   Disqualification from dividend

If a creditor contravenes any provision of the Act or the Rules relating to the valuation of securities, the court may, on the application of the [office-holder], order that the creditor be wholly or partly disqualified from participation in any dividend.

NOTES

Words in square brackets substituted by the Insolvency (Amendment) Rules 2010, SI 2010/686, r 2, Sch 1, para 483, as from 6 April 2010, subject to transitional provisions in Sch 4, para 1 thereto, as noted to r 1.5 at **[10.7]**.

[10.590]
11.11   Assignment of right to dividend

(1)   If a person entitled to a dividend gives notice to the [office-holder] that he wishes the dividend to be paid to another person, or that he has assigned his entitlement to another person, the [office-holder] shall pay the dividend to that other accordingly.

(2)   A notice given under this Rule must specify the name and address of the person to whom payment is to be made.

NOTES

Para (1): words in square brackets substituted by the Insolvency (Amendment) Rules 2010, SI 2010/686, r 2, Sch 1, para 483, as from 6 April 2010, subject to transitional provisions in Sch 4, para 1 thereto, as noted to r 1.5 at **[10.7]**.

[10.591]
11.12   Preferential creditors

(1)   Subject as follows, the Rules in this Part apply with respect to any distribution made in the insolvency to preferential creditors, with such adaptations as are appropriate considering that such creditors are of a limited class.

(2)   The notice by the responsible [office-holder] under Rule 11.2, where a dividend is to be declared for preferential creditors, need only be given to those creditors in whose case he has reason to believe that their debts are preferential [and [notice] of the intended dividend need only be [gazetted] if the [office-holder] thinks fit].

NOTES

Para (2): words in second (outer) pair of square brackets added by the Insolvency (Amendment) Rules 1987, SI 1987/1919, r 3(1), Schedule, Pt 1, para 140, as from 11 January 1988; other words in square brackets substituted by the Insolvency (Amendment) Rules 2010, SI 2010/686, r 2, Sch 1, paras 483, 490, as from 6 April 2010, subject to transitional provisions in Sch 4, para 1 thereto, as noted to r 1.5 at **[10.7]**.

[10.592]
11.13 Debt payable at future time

(1)   Where a creditor has proved for a debt of which payment is not due at the date of the declaration of dividend, he is entitled to dividend equally with other creditors, but subject as follows.

[(2)   For the purpose of dividend (and no other purpose) the amount of the creditor's admitted proof (or, if a distribution has previously been made to him, the amount remaining outstanding in respect of his admitted proof) shall be reduced by applying the following formula—

$$X/1.05^n$$

where—
(a)   "X" is the value of the admitted proof; and
(b)   "n" is the period beginning with the relevant date and ending with the date on which the payment of the creditor's debt would otherwise be due expressed in years and months in a decimalised form.

(3)   In paragraph (2) "relevant date" means—
(a)   in the case of a winding up which was not immediately preceded by an administration, the date that the company went into liquidation;
(b)   in the case of a winding up which was immediately preceded by an administration, the date that the company entered administration; and
(c)   in the case of a bankruptcy, the date of the bankruptcy order.]

NOTES
Paras (2), (3) substituted (for the original para (2)), and the original para (3) was revoked, by the Insolvency (Amendment) Rules 2005, SI 2005/527, r 43, as from 1 April 2005, subject to transitional provisions as noted to r 2.67 at **[10.129]**.

PART 12
MISCELLANEOUS AND GENERAL

[10.593]
12.1   Power of Secretary of State to regulate certain matters

(1)   Pursuant to paragraph 27 of Schedule 8 to the Act, and paragraph 30 of Schedule 9 to the Act, the Secretary of State may[, subject to the Act and the Rules, make regulations with respect to any matter provided for in the Rules as relates to the carrying out of the functions of a liquidator, provisional liquidator, administrator or administrative receiver of a company, an interim receiver appointed under section 286, of the official receiver while acting as receiver or manager under section 287 or of a trustee of a bankrupt's estate, including, without prejudice to the generality of the foregoing provision] with respect to the following matters arising in companies winding up and individual bankruptcy—
(a)   the preparation and keeping by liquidators, trustees, provisional liquidators, interim receivers and the official receiver, of books, accounts and other records, and their production to such persons as may be authorised or required to inspect them;
(b)   the auditing of liquidators' and trustees' accounts;
(c)   the manner in which liquidators and trustees are to act in relation to the insolvent company's or bankrupt's books, papers and other records, and the manner of their disposal by the responsible [office-holder] or others;
(d)   the supply—
 (i)   in company insolvency, by the liquidator to creditors and members of the company, contributories in its winding up and the liquidation committee, and
 (ii)   in [bankruptcy], by the trustee to creditors and the creditors' committee,
 of copies of documents relating to the insolvency and the affairs of the insolvent company or individual (on payment, in such cases as may be specified by the regulations, of the specified fee);
(e)   the manner in which insolvent estates are to be distributed by liquidators and trustees, including provision with respect to unclaimed funds and dividends;
(f)   the manner in which moneys coming into the hands of a liquidator or trustee in the course of his administration are to be handled and   . . .   invested, and the payment of interest on sums which, in pursuance of regulations made by virtue of this sub-paragraph, have been paid into the Insolvency Services Account;
(g)   the amount (or the manner of determining the amount) to be paid to the official receiver by way of remuneration when acting as provisional liquidator, liquidator, interim receiver or trustee.

(2)   Any reference in paragraph (1) to a trustee includes a reference to the official receiver when acting as receiver and manager under section 287.

(3)   Regulations made pursuant to paragraph (1) may—
(a)   confer a discretion on the court;

(b) make non-compliance with any of the regulations a criminal offence;

(c) make different provision for different cases, including different provision for different areas[; and

(d) contain such incidental, supplemental and transitional provisions as may appear to the Secretary of State necessary or expedient].

NOTES

Para (1): words in first pair of square brackets substituted by the Insolvency (Amendment) Rules 1987, SI 1987/1919, r 3(1), Schedule, Pt 1, para 142(1), as from 11 January 1988; words in square brackets in sub-para (c) substituted by the Insolvency (Amendment) Rules 2010, SI 2010/686, r 2, Sch 1, para 491, as from 6 April 2010, subject to transitional provisions in Sch 4, para 1 thereto, as noted to r 1.5 at **[10.7]**; word in square brackets in sub-para (d) substituted by the Insolvency (Amendment) Rules 2009, SI 2009/642, rr 4, 72, as from 6 April 2009; words omitted from sub-para (f) revoked by the Insolvency (Amendment) Rules 2001, SI 2001/763, r 2, as from 2 April 2001.

Para (3): sub-para (d) added by SI 1987/1919, r 3(1), Schedule, Pt 1, para 142(2), as from 11 January 1988.

Regulations: the Insolvency Regulations 1994, SI 1994/2507 at **[10.720]**.

[10.594]
12.2 Costs, expenses, etc

[(1)] All fees, costs, charges and other expenses incurred in the course of winding up[, administration] or bankruptcy proceedings are to be regarded as expenses of the winding up [or the administration] or, as the case may be, of the bankruptcy.

[(2) The costs associated with the prescribed part shall be paid out of the prescribed part.]

NOTES

Para (1) numbered as such, words in square brackets in that paragraph inserted, and para (2) added, by the Insolvency (Amendment) Rules 2003, SI 2003/1730, r 12, Sch 1, Pt 9, para 61, as from 15 September 2003 (for transitional provisions and savings see the note preceding r 2.1 at **[10.60]**).

[10.595]
12.3 Provable debts

(1) Subject as follows, [in administration, winding up and bankruptcy], all claims by creditors are provable as debts against the company or, as the case may be, the bankrupt, whether they are present or future, certain or contingent, ascertained or sounding only in damages.

(2) The following are not provable—

(a) in bankruptcy, any fine imposed for an offence, and any obligation [(other than an obligation to pay a lump sum or to pay costs)] arising under an order made in family . . . proceedings [or [any obligation arising] under a maintenance assessment made under the Child Support Act 1991];

(b) in [administration,] winding up or bankruptcy, any obligation arising under a confiscation order made under section 1 of the Drug Trafficking Offences Act 1986 [or section 1 of the Criminal Justice (Scotland) Act 1987] [or section 71 of the Criminal Justice Act 1988] [or under Parts 2, 3 or 4 of the Proceeds of Crime Act 2002].

"Fine", . . . and "family proceedings" have the meanings given by section 281(8) of the Act (which applies the Magistrates' Courts Act 1980 and the Matrimonial and Family Proceedings Act 1984).

[(2A) The following are not provable except at a time when all other claims of creditors in the insolvency proceedings (other than any of a kind mentioned in this paragraph) have been paid in full with interest under section 189(2)[, Rule 2.88] or, as the case may be, section 328(4)—

[(a) in [an administration,] a winding up or a bankruptcy, any claim arising by virtue of section 382(1)(a) of the Financial Services and Markets Act 2000, not being a claim also arising by virtue of section 382(1)(b) of that Act;]

(c) in [an administration or] a winding up, any claim which by virtue of the Act or any other enactment is a claim the payment of which in a bankruptcy[, an administration] or a winding up is to be postponed.]

(3) Nothing in this Rule prejudices any enactment or rule of law under which a particular kind of debt is not provable, whether on grounds of public policy or otherwise.

NOTES

Para (1): words in square brackets substituted by the Insolvency (Amendment) Rules 2003, SI 2003/1730, r 12, Sch 1, Pt 9, para 62(a), as from 15 September 2003 (for transitional provisions and savings see the note preceding r 2.1 at **[10.60]**).

Para (2): words in first pair and third (inner) pair of square brackets in sub-para (a) inserted by the Insolvency (Amendment) Rules 2005, SI 2005/527, r 44, as from 1 April 2005; words in second (outer) pair of square brackets in sub-para (a) added, and words omitted from that sub-paragraph revoked, by the Insolvency (Amendment) Rules 1993, SI 1993/602, r 3, Schedule, para 2, as from 5 April 1993; words in first and final pairs of square brackets in sub-para (b) inserted by SI 2003/1730, r 12, Sch 1, Pt 9, para 62(b), as from 15 September 2003 (for transitional provisions and savings see the note preceding r 2.1 at **[10.60]**); words in second pair of square brackets in sub-para (b) added by the Insolvency (Amendment) Rules 1987, SI 1987/1919, r 3(1), Schedule, Pt 1, para 143(1), as from 11 January 1988, and words in third pair of square brackets in that sub-paragraph added by the Insolvency (Amendment) Rules 1989, SI 1989/397, r 3(1), Schedule, para 2, as from 3 April 1989; final words omitted revoked by SI 1993/602, r 3, Schedule, para 3, as from 5 April 1993.

Para (2A): inserted by SI 1987/1919, r 3(1), Schedule, Pt 1, para 143(2), as from 11 January 1988; sub-para (a) substituted, for original sub-paras (a), (b), by the Financial Services and Markets Act 2000 (Consequential Amendments and Repeals) Order 2001, SI 2001/3649, art 380, as from 1 December 2001; words in first pair of square brackets and words in square brackets in sub-paras (a), (c) inserted by SI 2003/1730, r 12, Sch 1, Pt 9, para 62(c)–(e), as from 15 September 2003 (for transitional provisions and savings see the note preceding r 2.1 at **[10.60]**).

Confiscation orders: the Drug Trafficking Offences Act 1986, s 1, the Criminal Justice (Scotland) Act 1987, s 1, and the Criminal Justice Act 1988, s 71 are repealed; as to the making of confiscation orders, see now the Proceeds of Crime Act 2002.

12.4–12.17 *(Revoked by the Insolvency (Amendment) Rules 2010, SI 2010/686, r 5, as from 6 April 2010, subject to transitional provisions in Sch 4, para 1 thereto, as noted to r 1.5 at* **[10.7]**.*)*

[10.596]
12.18 False claim of status as creditor, etc

(1) Where the Rules provide for creditors, members of a company or contributories in a company's winding up a right to inspect any documents, whether on the court's file or in the hands of [an office-holder] or other person, it is an offence for a person, with the intention of obtaining a sight of documents which he has not under the Rules any right to inspect, falsely to claim a status which would entitle him to inspect them.

(2) A person guilty of an offence under this Rule is liable to imprisonment or a fine, or both.

NOTES
Para (1): words in square brackets substituted by the Insolvency (Amendment) Rules 2010, SI 2010/686, r 2, Sch 1, para 492, as from 6 April 2010, subject to transitional provisions in Sch 4, para 1 thereto, as noted to r 1.5 at **[10.7]**.

12.19, 12.20 *(Revoked by the Insolvency (Amendment) Rules 2010, SI 2010/686, r 5, as from 6 April 2010, subject to transitional provisions in Sch 4, para 1 thereto, as noted to r 1.5 at* **[10.7]**.*)*

[10.597]
12.21 Punishment of offences

(1) Schedule 5 to the Rules has effect with respect to the way in which contraventions of the Rules are punishable on conviction.

(2) In relation to an offence under a provision of the Rules specified in the first column of the Schedule (the general nature of the offence being described in the second column), the third column shows whether the offence is punishable on conviction on indictment, or on summary conviction, or either in the one way or the other.

(3) The fourth column shows, in relation to an offence, the maximum punishment by way of fine or imprisonment which may be imposed on a person convicted of the offence in the way specified in relation to it in the third column (that is to say, on indictment or summarily), a reference to a period of years or months being to a term of imprisonment of that duration.

(4) The fifth column shows (in relation to an offence for which there is an entry in that column) that a person convicted of the offence after continued contravention is liable to a daily default fine; that is to say, he is liable on a second or subsequent conviction of the offence to the fine specified in that column for each day on which the contravention is continued (instead of the penalty specified for the offence in the fourth column of the Schedule).

(5) Section 431 (summary proceedings), as it applies to England and Wales, has effect in relation to offences under the Rules as to offences under the Act.

12.22 *(Revoked by the Insolvency (Amendment) Rules 2010, SI 2010/686, r 5, as from 6 April 2010, subject to transitional provisions in Sch 4, para 1 thereto, as noted to r 1.5 at* **[10.7]**.*)*

[PART 12A
PROVISIONS OF GENERAL EFFECT

CHAPTER 1
THE GIVING OF NOTICE AND THE SUPPLY OF DOCUMENTS—GENERAL

[10.598]
12A.1 Application

(1) Subject to paragraphs (2) and (3), this Chapter applies where a notice or other document is required to be given, delivered or sent under the Act or the Rules by any person, including an office-holder.

(2) This Chapter does not apply to the service of—
  (a) any petition or application to the court;
  (b) any evidence in support of that petition or application; or
  (c) any order of the court.

(3) This Chapter does not apply to the submission of documents to the registrar of companies.]

NOTES
Commencement: 6 April 2010.
Part 12A (rr 12A.1–12A.57) was inserted by the Insolvency (Amendment) Rules 2010, SI 2010/686, r 4, Sch 3. For transitional provisions in relation to the insertion of this Part, see Sch 4, paras 1, 2 to the 2010 Rules (as noted to rr 1.5, 1.31 at **[10.7]**, **[10.34]** respectively). Note also Sch 4, para 5(1), (2) to the 2010 Rules which provides that the insertion of rr 12A.22–12A.27 applies on and after 6 April 2010 in all cases, except that r 12A.22(5) applies only in cases in which r 4.49D or r 6.78B applies.

[10.599]
[12A.2   Personal delivery of documents

Personal delivery of a notice or other document is permissible in any case.]

NOTES
Commencement: 6 April 2010.
Inserted as noted to r 12A.1 at **[10.598]**.

[10.600]
[12A.3   Postal delivery of documents

Unless in any particular case some other form of delivery is required by the Act, the Rules or an order of the court, a notice or other document may be sent by post in accordance with the rules for postal service in CPR Part 6 and sending by such means has effect as specified in those rules.]

NOTES
Commencement: 6 April 2010.
Inserted as noted to r 12A.1 at **[10.598]**.

[10.601]
[12A.4   Non-receipt of notice of meeting

Where in accordance with the Act or the Rules, a meeting of creditors or other persons is summoned by notice, the meeting is presumed to have been duly summoned and held, notwithstanding that not all those to whom the notice is to be given have received it.]

NOTES
Commencement: 6 April 2010.
Inserted as noted to r 12A.1 at **[10.598]**.

[10.602]
[12A.5   Notice etc to solicitors

Where under the Act or the Rules a notice or other document is required or authorised to be given, delivered or sent to a person, it may be given, delivered or sent instead to a solicitor authorised to accept delivery on that person's behalf.]

NOTES
Commencement: 6 April 2010.
Inserted as noted to r 12A.1 at **[10.598]**.

[Chapter 2
The Giving of Notice and the Supply of Documents by or to Office-holders etc

[10.603]
12A.6   Application

(1)   Subject to paragraphs (2) to (4), this Chapter applies where a notice or other document is required to be given, delivered or sent under the Act or the Rules.

(2)   This Chapter does not apply to the submission of documents to the registrar of companies.

(3)   Rules 12A.10 to 12A.13 do not apply to—
   (a)   the filing of any notice or other document with the court; or
   (b)   the service of a statutory demand.]

NOTES
Commencement: 6 April 2010.
Inserted as noted to r 12A.1 at **[10.598]**.

[10.604]
[12A.7   The form of notices and other documents

Subject to any order of the court, any notice or other document required to be given, delivered or sent must be in writing and where electronic delivery is permitted a notice or other document in electronic form is treated as being in writing if a copy of it is capable of being produced in a legible form.]

NOTES
Commencement: 6 April 2010.
Inserted as noted to r 12A.1 at **[10.598]**.

[10.605]
[12A.8 Proof of sending etc

(1) Where in any insolvency proceedings a notice or other document is required to be given, delivered or sent by the office-holder, the giving, delivering or sending of it may be proved by means of a certificate that the notice or other document was duly given, delivered or sent.

(2) In the case of the official receiver the certificate may be given by—
(a) the official receiver; or
(b) a member of the official receiver's staff.

(3) In the case of a responsible insolvency practitioner the certificate may be given by—
(a) the practitioner;
(b) the practitioner's solicitor;
(c) a partner or an employee of either of them.

(4) In the case of a notice or other document to be given, delivered or sent by a person other than the official receiver or a responsible insolvency practitioner, the giving, delivering or sending of it may be proved by means of a certificate by that person—
(a) that the notice or document was given, delivered or sent by that person, or
(b) that another person (named in the certificate) was instructed to give, deliver or send it.

(5) A certificate under this Rule may be endorsed on a copy or specimen of the notice or document to which it relates.]

NOTES
Commencement: 6 April 2010.
Inserted as noted to r 12A.1 at **[10.598]**.

[10.606]
[12A.9 Authentication

(1) A document or information given, delivered or sent in hard copy form is sufficiently authenticated if it is signed by the person sending or supplying it.

(2) A document or information given, delivered or sent in electronic form is sufficiently authenticated—
(a) if the identity of the sender is confirmed in a manner specified by the recipient, or
(b) where no such manner has been specified by the recipient, if the communication contains or is accompanied by a statement of the identity of the sender and the recipient has no reason to doubt the truth of that statement.]

NOTES
Commencement: 6 April 2010.
Inserted as noted to r 12A.1 at **[10.598]**.

[10.607]
[12A.10 Electronic delivery in insolvency proceedings—general

(1) Unless in any particular case some other form of delivery is required by the Act or the Rules or an order of the court and subject to paragraph (3), a notice or other document may be given, delivered or sent by electronic means provided that the intended recipient of the notice or other document has—
(a) consented (whether in the specific case or generally) to electronic delivery (and has not revoked that consent); and
(b) provided an electronic address for delivery.

(2) In the absence of evidence to the contrary, a notice or other document is presumed to have been delivered where—
(a) the sender can produce a copy of the electronic message which—
(i) contained the notice or other document, or to which the notice or other document was attached, and
(ii) shows the time and date the message was sent; and
(b) that electronic message contains the address supplied under paragraph (1)(b).

(3) A message sent electronically is deemed to have been delivered to the recipient no later than 9.00am on the next business day after it was sent.]

NOTES
Commencement: 6 April 2010.
Inserted as noted to r 12A.1 at **[10.598]**.

[10.608]
[12A.11   Electronic delivery by office-holders

(1)   Where an office-holder gives, sends or delivers a notice or other document to any person by electronic means, the notice or document must contain or be accompanied by a statement that the recipient may request a hard copy of the notice or document and specifying a telephone number, e-mail address and postal address which may be used to request a hard copy.

(2)   Where a hard copy of the notice or other document is requested, it must be sent within 5 business days of receipt of the request by the office-holder.

(3)   An office-holder must not require a person making a request under paragraph (2) to pay a fee for the supply of the document.]

NOTES
Commencement: 6 April 2010.
Inserted as noted to r 12A.1 at **[10.598]**.

[10.609]
[12A.12   Use of websites by office-holder

(1)   This Rule applies for the purposes of sections 246B and 379B.

(2)   An office-holder required to give, deliver or send a document to any person may (other than in a case where personal service is required) satisfy that requirement by sending that person a notice—
   (a)   stating that the document is available for viewing and downloading on a website;
   (b)   specifying the address of that website together with any password necessary to view and download the document from that site; and
   (c)   containing a statement that the person to whom the notice is given, delivered or sent may request a hard copy of the document and specifying a telephone number, e-mail address and postal address which may be used to request a hard copy.

(3)   Where a notice to which this Rule applies is sent, the document to which it relates must—
   (a)   be available on the website for a period of not less than 3 months after the date on which the notice is sent; and
   (b)   must be in such a format as to enable it to be downloaded from the website within a reasonable time of an electronic request being made for it to be downloaded.

(4)   Where a hard copy of the document is requested it must be sent within 5 business days of the receipt of the request by the office-holder.

(5)   An office-holder must not require a person making a request under paragraph (4) to pay a fee for the supply of the document.

(6)   Where a document is given, delivered or sent to a person by means of a website in accordance with this Rule, it is deemed to have been delivered—
   (a)   when the document was first made available on the website, or
   (b)   if later, when the notice under paragraph (2) was delivered to that person.]

NOTES
Commencement: 6 April 2010.
Inserted as noted to r 12A.1 at **[10.598]**.

[10.610]
[12A.13   Special provision on account of expense as to website use

(1)   Where the court is satisfied that the expense of sending notices in accordance with Rule 12A.12 would, on account of the number of persons entitled to receive them, be disproportionate to the benefit of sending notices in accordance with that Rule, it may order that the requirement to give, deliver or send a relevant document to any person may (other than in a case where personal service is required) be satisfied by the office-holder sending each of those persons a notice—
   (a)   stating that all relevant documents will be made available for viewing and downloading on a website;
   (b)   specifying the address of that website together with any password necessary to view and download a relevant document from that site; and
   (c)   containing a statement that the person to whom the notice is given, delivered or sent may at any time request that hard copies of all, or specific, relevant documents are sent to that person, and specifying a telephone number, e-mail address and postal address which may be used to make that request.

(2)   A document to which this Rule relates must—
   (a)   be available on the website for a period of not less than 12 months from the date when it was first made available on the website or, if later, from the date upon which the notice was sent, and
   (b)   must be in such a format as to enable it to be downloaded from the website within a reasonable time of an electronic request being made for it to be downloaded.

(3)   Where hard copies of relevant documents have been requested, they must be sent by the office-holder—

   (a)   within 5 business days of the receipt by the office-holder of the request to be sent hard copies, in the case of relevant documents first appearing on the website before the request was received, or

   (b)   within 5 business days from the date a relevant document first appears on the website, in all other cases.

(4)   An office-holder must not require a person making a request under paragraph (3) to pay a fee for the supply of the document.

(5)   Where a relevant document is given, delivered or sent to a person by means of a website in accordance with this Rule, it is deemed to have been delivered—

   (a)   when the relevant document was first made available on the website, or

   (b)   if later, when the notice under paragraph (1) was delivered to that person.

(6)   In this Rule a relevant document means any document which the office-holder is first required to give, deliver or send to any person after the court has made an order under paragraph (1).]

NOTES
   Commencement: 6 April 2010.
   Inserted as noted to r 12A.1 at **[10.598]**.

[10.611]
[12A.14   Electronic delivery of insolvency proceedings to courts

(1)   Except where paragraph (2) applies or the requirements of paragraph (3) are met, no petition, application, notice or other document may be delivered or made to a court by electronic means.

(2)   This paragraph applies where electronic delivery of documents to a court is permitted by another Rule.

(3)   The requirements of this paragraph are—

   (a)   the court provides an electronic working scheme for the proceedings to which the document relates; and

   (b)   the electronic communication is—

      (i)   delivered and authenticated in a form which complies with the requirements of the scheme;

      (ii)   sent to the electronic address provided by the court for electronic delivery of those proceedings; and

      (iii) accompanied by any payment due to the court in respect of those proceedings made in a manner which complies with the requirements of the scheme.

(4)   In this Rule "an electronic working scheme" means a scheme permitting insolvency proceedings to be delivered electronically to the court set out in a practice direction.

(5)   Under paragraph (3) an electronic communication is to be treated as delivered to the court at the time it is recorded by the court as having been received.]

NOTES
   Commencement: 6 April 2010.
   Inserted as noted to r 12A.1 at **[10.598]**.

[10.612]
[12A.15   Notice etc to joint office-holders

Where there are joint office-holders in insolvency proceedings, delivery of a document to one of them is to be treated as delivery to all of them.]

NOTES
   Commencement: 6 April 2010.
   Inserted as noted to r 12A.1 at **[10.598]**.

[CHAPTER 3
SERVICE OF COURT DOCUMENTS

[10.613]
12A.16   Application

(1)   Subject to paragraph (2), this Chapter applies in relation to the service of—

   (a)   petitions,

   (b)   applications,

   (c)   documents relating to petitions or applications, and

   (d)   court orders,

which are required to be served by any provision of the Act or the Rules ("court documents").

(2)   Rules 12A.17 to 12A.19 do not apply to the service of—

   (a)   a winding-up petition,

(b)   a bankruptcy petition,

(c)   any document relating to such a petition, or

(d)   an administration, winding-up or bankruptcy order.

(3)   For the purpose of the application by this Chapter of CPR Part 6 to the service of documents in insolvency proceedings—

(a)   an application commencing insolvency proceedings (including a winding-up petition, a bankruptcy petition or an administration application), or

(b)   an application within insolvency proceedings against a respondent,

is to be treated as a claim form.]

NOTES

Commencement: 6 April 2010.

Inserted as noted to r 12A.1 at **[10.598]**.

[10.614]

[12A.17   Application of CPR Part 6 to service of court documents within the jurisdiction

Except where different provision is made in these Rules, CPR Part 6 applies in relation to the service of court documents within the jurisdiction with such modifications as the court may direct.]

NOTES

Commencement: 6 April 2010.

Inserted as noted to r 12A.1 at **[10.598]**.

[10.615]

[12A.18   Service of orders staying proceedings

(1)   This Rule applies where the court makes an order staying any action, execution or other legal process against—

(a)   the property of a company; or

(b)   the property or person of an individual debtor or bankrupt.

(2)   Service within the jurisdiction of such an order as is mentioned in paragraph (1) may be effected by sending a sealed copy of the order to the address for service of the claimant or other party having the carriage of the proceedings to be stayed.]

NOTES

Commencement: 6 April 2010.

Inserted as noted to r 12A.1 at **[10.598]**.

[10.616]

[12A.19   Service on joint office-holders

Where there are joint office-holders in insolvency proceedings, service on one of them is to be treated as service on all of them.]

NOTES

Commencement: 6 April 2010.

Inserted as noted to r 12A.1 at **[10.598]**.

[10.617]

[12A.20   Application of CPR Part 6 to service of court documents outside the jurisdiction

CPR Part 6 applies to the service of court documents outside the jurisdiction with such modifications as the court may direct.]

NOTES

Commencement: 6 April 2010.

Inserted as noted to r 12A.1 at **[10.598]**.

[CHAPTER 4
MEETINGS

[10.618]

12A.21   Quorum at meeting of creditors or contributories

(1)   Any meeting of creditors or contributories in insolvency proceedings is competent to act if a quorum is present.

(2)   Subject to the next paragraph, a quorum is—

(a)   in the case of a creditors' meeting, at least one creditor entitled to vote;

(b)   in the case of a meeting of contributories, at least two contributories so entitled, or all the contributories, if their number does not exceed two.

(3)   For the purposes of this Rule, the reference to the creditor or contributories necessary to constitute a quorum is to those persons present or represented by proxy by any person (including the chairman) and in the case of any proceedings under Parts 1 to 7 of the Act includes corporations duly represented.

(4)   Where at any meeting of creditors or contributories—
  (a)   the provisions of this Rule as to a quorum being present are satisfied by the attendance of—
    (i)   the chairman alone, or
    (ii)   one other person in addition to the chairman, and
  (b)   the chairman is aware, by virtue of proofs and proxies received or otherwise, that one or more additional persons would, if attending, be entitled to vote,
the meeting must not commence until at least the expiry of 15 minutes after the time appointed for its commencement.]

NOTES

Commencement: 6 April 2010.
Inserted as noted to r 12A.1 at **[10.598]**.

[10.619]
[12A.22   Remote attendance at meetings of creditors

(1)   This Rule applies to a request to the convener of a meeting under section 246A(9) or 379A(8) to specify a place for the meeting.

(2)   The request must be accompanied by—
  (a)   in the case of a request by creditors, a list of the creditors making or concurring with the request and the amounts of their respective debts in the insolvency proceedings in question,
  (b)   in the case of a request by contributories, a list of the contributories making or concurring with the request and their respective values (being the amounts for which they may vote at the meeting),
  (c)   in the case of a request by members, a list of the members making or concurring with the request and their voting rights, and
  (d)   from each person concurring, written confirmation of that person's concurrence.

(3)   The request must be made within 7 business days of the date on which the convener sent the notice of the meeting in question.

(4)   Where the convener considers that the request has been properly made in accordance with the Act and this Rule, the convener must—
  (a)   give notice to all those previously given notice of the meeting—
    (i)   that it is to be held at a specified place, and
    (ii)   as to whether the date and time are to remain the same or not;
  (b)   set a venue (including specification of a place) for the meeting, the date of which must be not later than 28 days after the original date for the meeting; and
  (c)   give at least 14 days' notice of that venue to all those previously given notice of the meeting;
and the notices required by sub-paragraphs (a) and (c) may be given at the same or different times.

(5)   Where—
  (a)   a request to which this Rule relates is made in respect of a final meeting under section 106, 146 or 331;
  (b)   an application is made under Rule 4.131 or 6.142 in respect of remuneration or expenses reported in the draft report for that meeting; and
  (c)   the meeting cannot be held until the application (including any appeal) has been disposed of and any order of the court complied with,
paragraph (4)(a) does not apply and the duty to set a venue (including specification of a place) for the meeting applies in relation to the meeting when it is finally held.

(6)   Where the convener has specified a place for the meeting in response to a request to which this Rule applies, the chairman of the meeting must attend the meeting by being present in person at that place.

(7)   Rules 2.37(3), (4), (5) and (6), 4.61 and 6.87 (expenses of summoning meetings) do not apply to the summoning and holding of a meeting at a place specified in accordance with section 246A(9) or 379A(8).]

NOTES

Commencement: 6 April 2010.
Inserted as noted to r 12A.1 at **[10.598]**.

[10.620]
[12A.23   Action where person excluded

(1)   In this Rule and Rules 12A.24 and 12A.25 an "excluded person" means a person who—
  (a)   has taken all steps necessary to attend a meeting under the arrangements put in place to do so by the convener of the meeting under section 246A(6) or 379A(5); and

(b)   those arrangements do not permit that person to attend the whole or part of that meeting.

(2)   Where the chairman becomes aware during the course of the meeting that there is an excluded person, the chairman may—

   (a)   continue the meeting;

   (b)   declare the meeting void and convene the meeting again;

   (c)   declare the meeting valid up to the point where the person was excluded and adjourn the meeting.

(3)   Where the chairman continues the meeting, the meeting is valid unless—

   (a)   the chairman decides in consequence of a complaint under Rule 12A.25 to declare the meeting void and hold the meeting again; or

   (b)   the court directs otherwise.

(4)   Without prejudice to paragraph (2), where the chairman becomes aware during the course of the meeting that there is an excluded person, the chairman may, in the chairman's discretion and without an adjournment, declare the meeting suspended for any period up to 1 hour.]

NOTES

Commencement: 6 April 2010.

Inserted as noted to r 12A.1 at **[10.598]**.

[10.621]
[12A.24   Indication to excluded person

(1)   A person who claims to be an excluded person may request an indication of what occurred during the period of that person's claimed exclusion (an "indication").

(2)   A request under paragraph (1) must be made as soon as reasonably practicable and, in any event, no later than 4.00 pm on the business day following the day on which the exclusion is claimed to have occurred.

(3)   A request under paragraph (1) must be made to—

   (a)   the chairman, where it is made during the course of the business of the meeting; or

   (b)   the office-holder where it is made after the conclusion of the business of the meeting.

(4)   Where satisfied that the person making the request is an excluded person, the person to whom the request is made under paragraph (3) must give the indication as soon as reasonably practicable and, in any event, no later than 4.00 pm on the business day following the day on which the request was made under paragraph (1).

(5)   In this Rule and Rule 12A.25, "office-holder" has the meaning in Rule 13.9A.]

NOTES

Commencement: 6 April 2010.

Inserted as noted to r 12A.1 at **[10.598]**.

[10.622]
[12A.25   Complaint

(1)   Any person who—

   (a)   is, or claims to be, an excluded person; or

   (b)   attends the meeting (in person or by proxy) and considers that they have been adversely affected by a person's actual, apparent or claimed exclusion,

("the complainant") may make a complaint.

(2)   The person to whom the complaint must be made ("the relevant person") is—

   (a)   the chairman, where it is made during the course of the business of the meeting; or

   (b)   the office-holder, where it is made after the meeting.

(3)   The relevant person must—

   (a)   consider whether there is an excluded person; and

   (b)   where satisfied that there is an excluded person, consider the complaint; and

   (c)   where satisfied that there has been prejudice, take such action as the relevant person considers fit to remedy the prejudice.

(4)   Paragraph (5) applies where—

   (a)   the relevant person is satisfied that the complainant is an excluded person;

   (b)   during the period of the person's exclusion—

     (i)   a resolution was put to the meeting; and

     (ii)   voted on; and

   (c)   the excluded person asserts how the excluded person intended to vote on the resolution.

(5)   Subject to paragraph (6), where satisfied that the effect of the intended vote in paragraph (4), if cast, would have changed the result of the resolution, the relevant person must—

   (a)   count the intended vote as being cast in accordance with the complainant's stated intention;

   (b)   amend the record of the result of the resolution; and

   (c)   where those entitled to attend the meeting have been notified of the result of the resolution, notify them of the change.

(6)   Where satisfied that more than one complainant in paragraph (4) is an excluded person, the relevant person must have regard to the combined effect of the intended votes.

(7)   The relevant person must notify the complainant in writing of any decision.

(8)   A complaint must be made as soon as reasonably practicable and, in any event, no later than 4pm on the business day following—

    (a)   the day on which the person was, appeared or claimed to be excluded; or

    (b)   where an indication is sought under Rule 12A.24, the day on which the complainant received the indication.

(9)   A complainant who is not satisfied by the action of the relevant person may apply to the court for directions and any application must be made no more than 2 business days from the date of receiving the decision of the relevant person.]

NOTES

Commencement: 6 April 2010.

Inserted as noted to r 12A.1 at **[10.598]**.

[10.623]

[12A.26   Remote   attendance   at   meetings   of   creditors'   committees   and liquidation committees

(1)   This Rule applies to any meeting of a creditors' committee or a liquidation committee held under these Rules.

(2)   Where the office-holder considers it appropriate, the meeting may be conducted and held in such a way that persons who are not present together at the same place may attend it.

(3)   Where a meeting is conducted and held in the manner referred to in paragraph (2), a person attends the meeting if that person is able to exercise any rights which that person may have to speak and vote at the meeting.

(4)   For the purposes of this Rule—

    (a)   a person is able to exercise the right to speak at a meeting when that person is in a position to communicate to all those attending the meeting, during the meeting, any information or opinions which that person has on the business of the meeting; and

    (b)   a person is able to exercise the right to vote at a meeting when—

        (i)   that person is able to vote, during the meeting, on resolutions or determinations put to the vote at the meeting, and

        (ii)   that person's vote can be taken into account in determining whether or not such resolutions or determinations are passed at the same time as the votes of all the other persons attending the meeting.

(5)   Where a meeting is to be conducted and held in the manner referred to in paragraph (2), the office-holder must make whatever arrangements the office-holder considers appropriate to—

    (a)   enable those attending the meeting to exercise their rights to speak or vote, and

    (b)   ensure the identification of those attending the meeting and the security of any electronic means used to enable attendance.

(6)   Where in the reasonable opinion of the office-holder—

    (a)   a meeting will be attended by persons who will not be present together at the same place, and

    (b)   it is unnecessary or inexpedient to specify a place for the meeting,

any requirement under these Rules to specify a place for the meeting may be satisfied by specifying the arrangements the office-holder proposes to enable persons to exercise their rights to speak or vote.

(7)   In making the arrangements referred to in paragraph (5) and in forming the opinion referred to in paragraph (6)(b), the office-holder must have regard to the legitimate interests of the committee members or their representatives attending the meeting in the efficient despatch of the business of the meeting.

(8)   If—

    (a)   the notice of a meeting does not specify a place for the meeting,

    (b)   the office-holder is requested in accordance with Rule 12A.27 to specify a place for the meeting, and

    (c)   that request is made by at least one member of the committee,

the office-holder must specify a place for the meeting.

(9)   In this Rule, "the committee" means the creditors' committee or the liquidation committee.]

NOTES

Commencement: 6 April 2010.

Inserted as noted to r 12A.1 at **[10.598]**.

[10.624]
[12A.27   Procedure for requests that a place for a meeting should be specified under Rule 12A.26

(1)   This Rule applies to a request to the office-holder of a meeting under Rule 12A.26 to specify a place for the meeting.

(2)   The request must be made within 5 business days of the date on which the office-holder sent the notice of the meeting in question.

(3)   Where the office-holder considers that the request has been properly made in accordance with this Rule, the office-holder must—
  (a)   give notice to all those previously given notice of the meeting—
      (i)   that it is to be held at a specified place, and
      (ii)   as to whether the date and time are to remain the same or not;
  (b)   set a venue (including specification of a place) for the meeting, the date of which must be not later than 7 business days after the original date for the meeting; and
  (c)   give 5 business days' notice of the venue to all those previously given notice of the meeting;
and the notices required by sub-paragraphs (a) and (c) may be given at the same or different times.

(4)   Where the office-holder has specified a place for the meeting in response to a request to which this Rule applies, the chairman of the meeting must attend the meeting by being present in person at that place.]

NOTES
Commencement: 6 April 2010.
Inserted as noted to r 12A.1 at **[10.598]**.

[CHAPTER 5
EFFECT OF INSOLVENCY ON EXECUTION
—SPECIFIC PROVISIONS FOR NOTICES TO ENFORCEMENT OFFICERS ETC

[10.625]
12A.28   Execution overtaken by judgment debtor's insolvency

(1)   This Rule applies where execution has been taken out against property of a judgment debtor, and notice is given to the enforcement officer or other officer charged with the execution—
  (a)   under section 184(1) (that a winding-up order has been made against the debtor, or that a provisional liquidator has been appointed, or that a resolution for voluntary winding up has been passed); or
  (b)   under section 184(4) (that a winding-up petition has been presented, or a winding-up order made, or that a meeting has been called at which there is to be proposed a resolution for voluntary winding up, or that such a resolution has been passed); or
  (c)   under section 346(2) (that a judgment debtor has been adjudged bankrupt); or
  (d)   under section 346(3)(b) (that a bankruptcy petition has been presented in respect of the debtor).

(2)   Subject to paragraph (3) and Rule 12A.29, the notice must be delivered to the office of the enforcement officer or of the officer charged with the execution—
  (a)   by hand, or
  (b)   by any other means of delivery which enables proof of receipt of the document at the relevant address.

(3)   Where the execution is in a county court and the officer in charge of it is a district judge in that court, then if—
  (a)   there is filed in that court in respect of the judgment debtor a winding-up or bankruptcy petition, or
  (b)   there is made by that court in respect of the judgment debtor a winding-up order or an order appointing a provisional liquidator, or a bankruptcy order or an order appointing an interim receiver,
section 184 or 346 is deemed satisfied as regards the requirement of a notice to be served on, or given to, the officer in charge of the execution.]

NOTES
Commencement: 6 April 2010.
Inserted as noted to r 12A.1 at **[10.598]**.

[10.626]
[12A.29   Notice to enforcement officers

(1)   This Rule applies in relation to any provision of the Act or the Rules which makes provision for the giving of notice to an enforcement officer.

(2) Any such notice as is mentioned in paragraph (1) may be given by electronic means to any person who has been authorised to receive such notice on behalf of a specified enforcement officer or on behalf of enforcement officers generally.]

NOTES
Commencement: 6 April 2010.
Inserted as noted to r 12A.1 at **[10.598]**.

[CHAPTER 6
FORMS

[10.627]
12A.30   Forms for use in insolvency proceedings
(1) Subject to the next Rule, the forms contained in Schedule 4 to these Rules must continue to be used in insolvency proceedings as provided for in specific Rules.

(2) The forms must be used with such variations, if any, as the circumstances may require.

(3) The Secretary of State, the official receiver or an insolvency practitioner may incorporate a barcode or other reference or recognition mark into any form in Schedule 4 to these Rules a copy of which is received by any of them or is sent to any person by any of them.]

NOTES
Commencement: 6 April 2010.
Inserted as noted to r 12A.1 at **[10.598]**.

[10.628]
[12A.31   Electronic submission of information instead of submission of forms to the Secretary of State, the Chief Land Registrar, office-holders, and of copies to the registrar of companies
(1) This Rule applies in any case where information in a prescribed form is required by the Rules to be sent by any person to the Secretary of State, the Chief Land Registrar, or an office-holder, or a copy of a prescribed form is to be sent to the registrar of companies.

(2) A requirement of the kind mentioned in paragraph (1) is treated as having been satisfied where—
  (a) the information is submitted electronically with the agreement of the person to whom the information is sent;
  (b) the form in which the electronic submission is made satisfies the requirements of the person to whom the information is sent (which may include a requirement that the information supplied can be reproduced in the format of the prescribed form);
  (c) that all the information required to be given in the prescribed form is provided in the electronic submission; and
  (d) the person to whom the information is sent can provide in legible form the information so submitted.

(3) Where information in a prescribed form is permitted to be sent electronically under paragraph (2), any requirement in the prescribed form that the prescribed form be accompanied by a signature is taken to be satisfied—
  (a) if the identity of the person who is supplying the information in the prescribed form and whose signature is required is confirmed in a manner specified by the recipient, or
  (b) where no such manner has been specified by the recipient, if the communication contains or is accompanied by a statement of the identity of the person who is providing the information in the prescribed form, and the recipient has no reason to doubt the truth of that statement.

(4) Where information required in prescribed form has been supplied to a person, whether or not it has been supplied electronically in accordance with paragraph (2), and a copy of that information is required to be supplied to another person falling within paragraph (1), the requirements contained in paragraph (2) apply in respect of the supply of the copy to that other person, as they apply in respect of the original.]

NOTES
Commencement: 6 April 2010.
Inserted as noted to r 12A.1 at **[10.598]**.

[10.629]
[12A.32   Electronic submission of information instead of submission of forms in all other cases
(1) Subject to paragraph (5), this Rule applies in any case where Rule 12A.31 does not apply, where information in a prescribed form is required by the Rules to be sent by any person.

(2) A requirement of the kind mentioned in paragraph (1) is treated as having been satisfied where—

(a)   the person to whom the information is sent has agreed—
  (i)   to receiving the information electronically and to the form in which it is to be sent; and
  (ii)   to the specified manner in which paragraph (3) is to be satisfied.
(b)   all the information required to be given in the prescribed form is provided in the electronic submission; and
(c)   the person to whom the information is sent can provide in legible form the information so submitted.

(3)   Any requirement in a prescribed form that it be accompanied by a signature is taken to be satisfied if the identity of the person who is supplying the information and whose signature is required, is confirmed in the specified manner.

(4)   Where information required in prescribed form has been supplied to a person, whether or not it has been supplied electronically in accordance with paragraph (2), and a copy of that information is required to be supplied to another person falling within paragraph (1), the requirements contained in paragraph (2) apply in respect of the supply of the copy to that other person, as they apply in respect of the original.

(5)   This Rule does not apply in respect of a statutory demand.]

NOTES
Commencement: 6 April 2010.
Inserted as noted to r 12A.1 at **[10.598]**.

[CHAPTER 7
GAZETTE NOTICES

[10.630]
12A.33   Contents of notices to be gazetted under the Act or Rules

(1)   Except when paragraph (3) applies, where under the Act or the Rules a notice is gazetted, in addition to any content specifically required by the Act or any other provision of the Rules, the content of such a notice must be as set out in this Chapter.

(2)   All notices published must specify insofar as it is applicable in relation to the particular notice—
(a)   the name and postal address of the office-holder acting in the proceedings;
(b)   the capacity in which the office-holder is acting and the date of appointment;
(c)   either an e-mail address, or a telephone number, through which the office-holder may be contacted;
(d)   the name of any person other than the office-holder (if any) who may be contacted regarding the proceedings;
(e)   the number assigned to the office-holder by the Secretary of State; and
(f)   the court name and any number assigned to the proceedings by the court.

(3)   This paragraph applies to notices under Rule 4.228(2) (first excepted case).]

NOTES
Commencement: 6 April 2010.
Inserted as noted to r 12A.1 at **[10.598]**.

[10.631]
[12A.34   Gazette notices relating to companies

In addition to the information required by Rule 12A.33 a notice relating to a company must specify—
(a)   the registered name of the company;
(b)   its registered number;
(c)   its registered office, or if an unregistered company, the postal address of its principal place of business;
(d)   any principal trading address if this is different from its registered office;
(e)   any name under which it was registered in the 12 months prior to the date of the commencement of the proceedings which are the subject of the Gazette notice; and
(f)   any name or style (other than its registered name) under which—
  (i)   the company carried on business; and
  (ii)   any debt owed to a creditor was incurred.]

NOTES
Commencement: 6 April 2010.
Inserted as noted to r 12A.1 at **[10.598]**.

[10.632]
[12A.35　Gazette notices relating to bankrupts

In addition to the information required by Rule 12A.33 a notice relating to a bankruptcy must state,—
(a)　the bankrupt's full name and residential address;
(b)　any other address at which the bankrupt has resided in the period of 12 months preceding the making of the bankruptcy order;
(c)　the bankrupt's date of birth;
(d)　the bankrupt's occupation;
(e)　any other name by which the bankrupt has been known;
(f)　any name or style (other than the bankrupt's own name) under which—
　　(i)　the bankrupt carried on business; and
　　(ii)　any debt owed to a creditor was incurred.]

NOTES
　　Commencement: 6 April 2010.
　　Inserted as noted to r 12A.1 at **[10.598]**.

[10.633]
[12A.36　Omission of unobtainable information

Information required under this Chapter to be included in a notice to be gazetted may be omitted if it is not reasonably practicable to obtain it.]

NOTES
　　Commencement: 6 April 2010.
　　Inserted as noted to r 12A.1 at **[10.598]**.

[10.634]
[12A.37　The Gazette—general

(1)　A copy of the Gazette containing any notice required by the Act or the Rules to be gazetted is evidence of any facts stated in the notice.

(2)　In the case of an order of the court notice of which is required by the Act or the Rules to be gazetted, a copy of the Gazette containing the notice may in any proceedings be produced as conclusive evidence that the order was made on the date specified in the notice.

(3)　Where an order of the court which is gazetted has been varied, and where any matter has been erroneously or inaccurately gazetted, the person whose responsibility it was to procure the requisite entry in the Gazette must as soon as is reasonably practicable cause the variation of the order to be gazetted or a further entry to be made in the Gazette for the purpose of correcting the error or inaccuracy.

NOTES
　　Commencement: 6 April 2010.
　　Inserted as noted to r 12A.1 at **[10.598]**.

[CHAPTER 8
NOTICES ADVERTISED OTHERWISE THAN IN THE GAZETTE

[10.635]
12A.38　Notices otherwise advertised under the Act or Rules

(1)　Where under the Act or the Rules a notice may be advertised otherwise than in the Gazette, in addition to any content specifically required by the Act or any other provision of the Rules, the content of such a notice must be as set out in this Chapter.

(2)　All notices published must specify insofar as it is applicable in relation to the particular notice—
(a)　the name and postal address of the office-holder acting in the proceedings to which the notice relates;
(b)　the capacity in which the office-holder is acting; and
(c)　either an e-mail address, or a telephone number, through which the office-holder may be contacted.]

NOTES
　　Commencement: 6 April 2010.
　　Inserted as noted to r 12A.1 at **[10.598]**.

[10.636]
[12A.39　Non-Gazette notices relating to companies

In addition to the information required by Rule 12A.38, a notice relating to a company must state—
(a)　the registered name of the company;

(b) its registered number;
(c) any name under which it was registered in the 12 months prior to the date of the commencement of the proceedings which are the subject of the notice; and
(d) any name or style (other than its registered name) under which—
  (i)   the company carried on business; and
  (ii) any debt owed to a creditor was incurred.]

NOTES
Commencement: 6 April 2010.
Inserted as noted to r 12A.1 at **[10.598]**.

[10.637]
[12A.40   Non-Gazette notices relating to bankrupts

In addition to the information required by Rule 12A.38, a notice relating to bankruptcy must state—
(a) the bankrupt's full name and address;
(b) any other address at which the bankrupt has resided in the period of 12 months preceding the making of the bankruptcy order;
(c) the bankrupt's date of birth;
(d) the bankrupt's occupation;
(e) any other name by which the bankrupt has been known;
(f) any name or style (other than the bankrupt's own name) under which—
  (i)   the bankrupt carried on business; and
  (ii) any debt owed to a creditor was incurred.]

NOTES
Commencement: 6 April 2010.
Inserted as noted to r 12A.1 at **[10.598]**.

[10.638]
[12A.41   Non-Gazette notices—other provisions

(1)   The information required to be contained in a notice to which this Chapter applies must be included in the advertisement of that notice in a manner that is reasonably likely to ensure, in relation to the form of the advertising used, that a person reading, hearing or seeing the advertisement, will be able to read, hear or see that information.

(2)   Information required under this Chapter to be included in a notice may be omitted if it is not reasonably practicable to obtain it.]

NOTES
Commencement: 6 April 2010.
Inserted as noted to r 12A.1 at **[10.598]**.

[CHAPTER 9
NOTIFICATIONS TO THE REGISTRAR OF COMPANIES

[10.639]
12A.42   Application of this Chapter

This Chapter applies where under the Act or the Rules information is to be sent or delivered to the registrar of companies.]

NOTES
Commencement: 6 April 2010.
Inserted as noted to r 12A.1 at **[10.598]**.

[10.640]
[12A.43   Information to be contained in all notifications to the registrar

Where under the Act or the Rules a return, notice, or any other document or information is to be sent to the registrar of companies, that notification must specify—
(a) the registered name of the company;
(b) its registered number;
(c) the nature of the notification;
(d) the section of the Act or the Rule under which the notification is made;
(e) the date of the notification;
(f) the name and postal address of person making the notification;
(g) the capacity in which that person is acting in respect of the company; and
the notification must be authenticated by the person making the notification.]

NOTES
Commencement: 6 April 2010.
Inserted as noted to r 12A.1 at **[10.598]**.

[10.641]
[12A.44 Notifications relating to the office of office-holders

In addition to the information required by Rule 12A.43, a notification relating to the office of the office-holder must also specify—

   (a)   the name of the office-holder;

   (b)   the nature of the appointment held by the office holder

   (c)   the date of the event notified;

   (e)   where the notification relates to an appointment, the person, body or court making the appointment;

   (f)   where the notification relates to the termination of an appointment, the reason for that termination (for example, resignation); and

   (e)   the postal address of office-holder.]

NOTES
Commencement: 6 April 2010.
Inserted as noted to r 12A.1 at **[10.598]**.

[10.642]
[12A.45 Notifications relating to documents

In addition to the information required by Rule 12A.43, a notification relating to a document (for example, a statement of affairs) must also specify—

   (a)   the nature of the document; and

   (b)   the date of the document; or

   (c)   where the document relates to a period of time (for example a report) the period of time to which the document relates.]

NOTES
Commencement: 6 April 2010.
Inserted as noted to r 12A.1 at **[10.598]**.

[10.643]
[12A.46 Notifications relating to court orders

In addition to the information required by Rule 12A.43, a notification relating to a court order must also specify—

   (a)   the nature of the court order; and

   (b)   the date of the order.]

NOTES
Commencement: 6 April 2010.
Inserted as noted to r 12A.1 at **[10.598]**.

[10.644]
[12A.47 Returns or reports of meetings

(1)   In addition to the information required by Rule 12A.43, the notification of a return or a report of a meeting must specify—

   (a)   the purpose of the meeting including the section of the Act or Rule under which it was convened;

   (b)   the venue fixed for the meeting;

   (c)   whether a required quorum was present for the meeting to take place; and

   (d)   if the meeting took place, the outcome of the meeting (including any resolutions passed at the meeting).

(2)   Where the return relates to the meeting required by section 94 or 106 (final meetings prior to dissolution), it must also specify the dates of the opening and close of the winding up.]

NOTES
Commencement: 6 April 2010.
Inserted as noted to r 12A.1 at **[10.598]**.

[10.645]
[12A.48 Notifications relating to other events

In addition to the information required by Rule 12A.43, a notification relating to any other event (for example the coming in to force of a moratorium) must specify—

   (a)   the nature of the event including the section of the Act or Rule under which it took place; and

   (b)   the date the event occurred.]

NOTES
Commencement: 6 April 2010.
Inserted as noted to r 12A.1 at **[10.598]**.

Part 10   Miscellaneous other SIs

[10.646]
[12A.49   Notifications of more than one nature

A notification which includes a notification of more than one nature must satisfy the requirements applying in respect of each of those notifications.]

NOTES
Commencement: 6 April 2010.
Inserted as noted to r 12A.1 at **[10.598]**.

[10.647]
[12A.50   Notifications made to other persons at the same time

(1)   Where under the Act or the Rules a notice or other document is to be sent to another person at the same time that it is to be sent to the registrar of companies, that requirement may be satisfied by sending to that other person a copy of the notification sent to the registrar.

(2)   Paragraph (1) does not apply—
   (a)   where a Form is prescribed for the notification to the other person; or
   (b)   where the notification to the registrar of companies is incomplete.]

NOTES
Commencement: 6 April 2010.
Inserted as noted to r 12A.1 at **[10.598]**.

[CHAPTER 10
INSPECTION OF DOCUMENTS AND THE PROVISION OF INFORMATION

[10.648]
12A.51   Confidentiality of documents—grounds for refusing inspection

(1)   Where in insolvency proceedings the office-holder considers that a document forming part of the records of those proceedings—
   (a)   should be treated as confidential, or
   (b)   is of such a nature that its disclosure would be prejudicial to the conduct of the proceedings or might reasonably be expected to lead to violence against any person,
the office-holder may decline to allow it to be inspected by a person who would otherwise be entitled to inspect it.

(2)   The persons to whom the office-holder may under this Rule refuse inspection include members of a liquidation committee or a creditors' committee.

(3)   Where under this rule the office-holder determines to refuse inspection of a document, the person wishing to inspect it may apply to the court for that determination to be overruled and the court may either overrule it altogether or sustain it subject to such conditions (if any) as it thinks just.]

NOTES
Commencement: 6 April 2010.
Inserted as noted to r 12A.1 at **[10.598]**.

[10.649]
[12A.52   Right to copy documents

Where the Act or the Rules confer a right for any person to inspect documents, the right includes that of taking copies of those documents, on payment—
   (a)   in the case of documents on the court's file of proceedings, of the fee chargeable under any order made under section 92 of the Courts Act 2003, and
   (b)   in any other case, of the appropriate fee.]

NOTES
Commencement: 6 April 2010.
Inserted as noted to r 12A.1 at **[10.598]**.

[10.650]
[12A.53   Charges for copy documents

Except where prohibited by the Rules, a responsible insolvency practitioner or the official receiver is entitled to require the payment of the appropriate fee for the supply of documents requested by a creditor, member, contributory or member of a liquidation or creditors' committee.]

NOTES
Commencement: 6 April 2010.
Inserted as noted to r 12A.1 at **[10.598]**.

[10.651]
[12A.54 Right to have list of creditors

(1) This Rule applies in the following proceedings—
   (a)   administration;
   (b)   winding up (other than a members' voluntary winding up); and
   (c)   bankruptcy.

(2) A creditor or a member State liquidator has the right to require an office-holder to provide a list of the creditors and the amounts of their respective debts unless paragraph (5) applies.

(3) The office-holder on being required to furnish the list under paragraph (2)—
   (a)   as soon as reasonably practicable must send it to the person requiring the list to be furnished; and
   (b)   may charge the appropriate fee for doing so.

(4) The name and address of any creditor may be omitted from the list furnished under paragraph (3) where the office-holder is of the view that its disclosure would be prejudicial to the conduct of the proceedings or might reasonably be expected to lead to violence against any person provided that—
   (a)   the amount of the debt in question is shown in the list; and
   (b)   a statement is included in the list that the name and address of the creditor has been omitted in respect of that debt.

(5) Paragraph (2) does not apply where a statement of affairs has been—
   (a)   delivered to the registrar of companies, in a winding up or an administration; or
   (b)   filed with the court, in bankruptcy proceedings.]

NOTES
   Commencement: 6 April 2010.
   Inserted as noted to r 12A.1 at **[10.598]**.

[CHAPTER 11
COMPUTATION OF TIME AND TIME LIMITS

[10.652]
12A.55 Time limits

(1) The provisions of CPR rule 2.8 (time) apply, as regards computation of time, to anything required or authorised to be done by the Rules.

(2) The provisions of CPR rule 3.1(2)(a) (the court's general powers of management) apply so as to enable the court to extend or shorten the time for compliance with anything required or authorised to be done by the Rules.]

NOTES
   Commencement: 6 April 2010.
   Inserted as noted to r 12A.1 at **[10.598]**.

[CHAPTER 12
SECURITY

[10.653]
12A.56 Insolvency practitioners' security

(1) Wherever under the Rules any person has to appoint, or certify the appointment of, an insolvency practitioner to any office that person must, before making or certifying the appointment, be satisfied that the person appointed or to be appointed has security for the proper performance of that office.

(2) It is the duty—
   (a)   of the creditors' committee in—
      (i)   an administration,
      (ii)   an administrative receivership,
      (iii)   a bankruptcy, and
   (b)   of the liquidation committee in a winding up,
to review from time to time the adequacy of the responsible insolvency practitioner's security.

(3) In any insolvency proceedings the cost of the responsible insolvency practitioner's security shall be defrayed as an expense of the proceedings.]

NOTES
   Commencement: 6 April 2010.
   Inserted as noted to r 12A.1 at **[10.598]**.

Part 10   Miscellaneous other SIs

[CHAPTER 13
NOTICE OF ORDER UNDER SECTION 176A(5)

[10.654]
12A.57   Notice of order under section 176A(5)

(1)   Where the court makes an order under section 176A(5), it must as soon as reasonably practicable send two sealed copies of the order to the applicant and a sealed copy to any other office-holder.

(2)   Where the court has made an order under section 176A(5), the liquidator, administrator or receiver must as soon as reasonably practicable, give notice to each creditor of whose address and claim the office-holder in question is aware.

(3)   Paragraph (2) does not apply where the court directs otherwise.

(4)   The court may direct that the requirement in paragraph (2) is complied with if a notice has been published by the liquidator, administrator or receiver which, in addition to containing the standard contents, states that the court has made an order disapplying the requirement to set aside the prescribed part. As soon as reasonably practicable the notice—
   (a)   must be gazetted; and
   (b)   may be advertised in such other manner as the liquidator, administrator, or receiver thinks fit.

(5)   The liquidator, administrator or receiver must send a copy of the order to the registrar of companies as soon as reasonably practicable after the making of the order.]

NOTES
Commencement: 6 April 2010.
Inserted as noted to r 12A.1 at **[10.598]**.

PART 13
INTERPRETATION AND APPLICATION

[10.655]
13.1   Introductory

This Part of the Rules has effect for their interpretation and application; and any definition given in this Part applies except, and in so far as, the context otherwise requires.

[10.656]
13.2   "The court"; "the registrar"

(1)   Anything to be done under or by virtue of the Act or the Rules by, to or before the court may be done by, to or before a judge[, district judge] or the registrar.

(2)   The registrar [or district judge] may authorise any act of a formal or administrative character which is not by statute his responsibility to be carried out by the chief clerk or any other officer of the court acting on his behalf, in accordance with directions given by the Lord Chancellor.

[(3A)   "The registrar" means—
   (a)   a Registrar in Bankruptcy of the High Court, or
   (b)   where the proceedings are in the District Registry of Birmingham, Bristol, Caernarfon, Cardiff, Leeds, Liverpool, Manchester, Mold, Newcastle-upon-Tyne or Preston, a district judge attached to the District Registry in question.]

NOTES
Paras (1), (2): words in square brackets inserted by the Insolvency (Amendment) Rules 2010, SI 2010/686, r 2, Sch 1, para 493(1)–(3), as from 6 April 2010, subject to transitional provisions in Sch 4, para 2 thereto, as noted to r 1.31 at **[10.34]**.
Para (3A): substituted (for the original paras (3)–(5)) by SI 2010/686, r 2, Sch 1, para 493(1), (4), as from 6 April 2010, subject to transitional provisions in Sch 4, para 2 thereto, as noted to r 1.31 at **[10.34]**.

[10.657]
13.3   "Give notice", etc

(1)–(3)   . . .

(4)   Notice of the venue fixed for an application [made to the court] may be given by service of the sealed copy of the application under Rule 7.4(3).

NOTES
Paras (1)–(3): revoked by the Insolvency (Amendment) Rules 2010, SI 2010/686, r 2, Sch 1, para 494, as from 6 April 2010, subject to transitional provisions in Sch 4, para 1 thereto, as noted to r 1.5 at **[10.7]**.
Para (4): words in square brackets inserted by the Insolvency (Amendment) Rules 2009, SI 2009/642, rr 4, 74(c), as from 6 April 2009.

[10.658]
13.4 Notice, etc to solicitors

Where under the Act or the Rules a notice or other document is required or authorised to be given to a person, it may, if he has indicated that his solicitor is authorised to accept service on his behalf, be given instead to the solicitor.

[10.659]
13.5 Notice to joint liquidators, joint trustees, etc

Where two or more persons are acting jointly as the responsible insolvency practitioner in any proceedings, delivery of a document to one of them is to be treated as delivery to them all.

[10.660]
13.6 "Venue"

References to the "venue" for any proceeding or attendance before the court, or for a meeting, are to the time, date and place for the proceeding, attendance or meeting [or to the time and date for a meeting which is held in accordance with section 246A or 379A without any place being specified for it].

NOTES

Words in square brackets added by the Insolvency (Amendment) Rules 2010, SI 2010/686, r 2, Sch 1, para 495, as from 6 April 2010, subject to transitional provisions in Sch 4, para 2 thereto, as noted to r 1.31 at **[10.34]**.

[10.661]
13.7 "Insolvency proceedings"

"Insolvency proceedings" means any proceedings under the Act or the Rules.

[10.662]
13.8 "Insolvent estate"

References to "the insolvent estate" are—
    (a)   in relation to a company insolvency, the company's assets, and
    (b)   in relation to [a bankruptcy or a petition for bankruptcy], the bankrupt's estate or (as the case may be) the debtor's property.

NOTES

Words in square brackets substituted by the Insolvency (Amendment) Rules 2009, SI 2009/642, rr 4, 75, as from 6 April 2009.

[10.663]
13.9 "Responsible insolvency practitioner", etc

(1)   In relation to any insolvency proceedings, "the responsible insolvency practitioner" means—
    (a)   the person [(other than the official receiver)] acting in a company insolvency, as supervisor of a voluntary arrangement under Part I of the Act, or as administrator, administrative receiver, liquidator or provisional liquidator;
    (b)   the person [(other than the official receiver)] acting in an individual insolvency, as the supervisor of a voluntary arrangement under Part VIII of the Act, or as trustee or interim receiver;
    (c)   . . . . .
(2)   . . . . .
[(3)   A reference to an "authorised person" is a reference to a person who is authorised pursuant to section 389A of the Act to act as nominee or supervisor of a voluntary arrangement proposed or approved under Part I or Part VIII of the Act.]

NOTES

Para (1): words in square brackets in sub-paras (a), (b) inserted, and sub-para (c) revoked, by the Insolvency (Amendment) Rules 2010, SI 2010/686, r 2, Sch 1, para 496(1), (2), as from 6 April 2010, subject to transitional provisions in Sch 4, para 1 thereto, as noted to r 1.5 at **[10.7]**.

Para (2): revoked by SI 2010/686, r 2, Sch 1, para 496(1), (3), as from 6 April 2010, subject to transitional provisions in Sch 4, para 1 thereto, as noted to r 1.5 at **[10.7]**.

Para (3): added by the Insolvency (Amendment) (No 2) Rules 2002, SI 2002/2712, r 7, as from 1 January 2003.

[10.664]
[13.9A Office-holder

"Office-holder" means in relation to insolvency proceedings any person who by virtue of any provision of the Act or the Rules holds an office in relation to those proceedings.]

NOTES

Commencement: 6 April 2010.

Inserted by the Insolvency (Amendment) Rules 2010, SI 2010/686, r 2, Sch 1, para 497, subject to transitional provisions in Sch 4, para 1 thereto, as noted to r 1.5 at **[10.7]**. Note also Sch 4, para 5(3) to the 2010 Rules which provides that this insertion applies on and after 6 April 2010 in all cases for the purposes of rr 12A.24, 12A.25 (at **[10.621]**, **[10.622]**) but otherwise applies in accordance with Sch 4, para 1 as noted above.

[10.665]
13.10   "Petitioner"

In winding up and bankruptcy, references to "the petitioner" or "the petitioning creditor" include any person who has been substituted as such, or been given carriage of the petition.

[10.666]
13.11   "The appropriate fee"

"The appropriate fee" means—
- (a)   in Rule 6.192(2) (pay or under income payments order entitled to clerical etc costs) [or Rule 6.193C(4) (payor under income payments agreement entitled to clerical etc costs)], 50 pence; and
- (b)   in other cases, 15 pence per A4 or A5 page, and 30 pence per A3 page.

NOTES

Words in square brackets inserted by the Insolvency (Amendment) Rules 2003, SI 2003/1730, r 13, Sch 1, Pt 10, para 64, as from 1 April 2004 (for transitional provisions and savings see the note preceding r 2.1 at **[10.60]**).

[10.667]
[13.12   "Debt", "liability" (winding up)

(1)   "Debt", in relation to the winding up of a company, means (subject to the next paragraph) any of the following—
- [(a)   any debt or liability to which the company is subject—
  - (i)   in the case of a winding up which was not immediately preceded by an administration, at the date on which the company went into liquidation;
  - (ii)   in the case of a winding up which was immediately preceded by an administration, at the date on which the company entered administration.]
- (b)   any debt or liability to which the company may become subject after that date by reason of any obligation incurred before that date; and
- (c)   any interest provable as mentioned in Rule 4.93(1).

(2)   For the purposes of any provision of the Act or the Rules about winding up, any liability in tort is a debt provable in the winding up, if either—
- [(a)   the cause of action has accrued—
  - (i)   in the case of a winding up which was not immediately preceded by an administration, at the date on which the company went into liquidation;
  - (ii)   in the case of a winding up which was immediately preceded by an administration, at the date on which the company entered administration.]
- (b)   all the elements necessary to establish the cause of action exist at that date except for actionable damage.

(3)   For the purposes of references in any provision of the Act or the Rules about winding up to a debt or liability, it is immaterial whether the debt or liability is present or future, whether it is certain or contingent, or whether its amount is fixed or liquidated, or is capable of being ascertained by fixed rules or as a matter of opinion; and references in any such provision to owing a debt are to be read accordingly.

(4)   In any provision of the Act or the Rules about winding up, except in so far as the context otherwise requires, "liability" means (subject to paragraph (3) above) a liability to pay money or money's worth, including any liability under an enactment, any liability for breach of trust, any liability in contract, tort or bailment, and any liability arising out of an obligation to make restitution.

(5)   This Rule shall apply where a company is in administration and shall be read as if—
- [(a)   references to winding up were references to administration,
- (b)   references to administration were references to winding up,
- (c)   references to going into liquidation were references to entering administration, and
- (d)   references to entering administration were references to going into liquidation.]]

NOTES

Substituted by the Insolvency (Amendment) Rules 2006, SI 2006/1272, r 4, as from 1 June 2006, subject to transitional provisions (see the transitional provisions note below).

Paras (1), (2), (5): words in square brackets substituted by the Insolvency (Amendment) Rules 2010, SI 2010/686, r 2, Sch 1, para 498, as from 6 April 2010, subject to transitional provisions in Sch 4, para 1 thereto, as noted to r 1.5 at **[10.7]**.

Transitional provisions: SI 2006/1272, r 3 provides for the following transitional provisions in relation to the substitution of this rule (note that by virtue of r 1(2), the "commencement date" is 1 June 2006)—

"3   Transitional provisions

The amendment to the principal Rules made by Rule 4 of these Rules shall apply in respect of a company which—
- (a)   on or after the commencement date enters administration except where—
  - (i)   it enters administration by virtue of an administration order under paragraph 10 of Schedule B1 to the Act on an application made before the commencement date;

      (ii)   the administration is immediately preceded by a voluntary liquidation in respect of which the resolution to wind up was passed before the commencement date; or

      (iii)   the administration is immediately preceded by a liquidation on the making of a winding-up order on a petition which was presented before the commencement date;

  (b)   goes into liquidation upon the passing, on or after the commencement date, of a resolution to wind up;

  (c)   goes into voluntary liquidation under paragraph 83 of Schedule B1 except where the preceding administration—

      (i)   commenced before the commencement date; or

      (ii)   is an administration which commenced by virtue of an administration order under paragraph 10 of Schedule B1 on an application which was made before the commencement date;

  (d)   goes into liquidation on the making of a winding-up order on a petition presented on or after the commencement date except where the liquidation is immediately preceded by—

      (i)   an administration under paragraph 10 of Schedule B1 to the Act where the administration order was made on an application made before the commencement date;

      (ii)   an administration in respect of which the appointment of an administrator under paragraphs 14 or 22 of Schedule B1 took effect before the commencement date; or

      (iii)   a voluntary liquidation in respect of which the resolution to wind up was passed before the commencement date.".

[10.668]
[13.12A Authorised deposit-taker and former authorised deposit-taker"

(1)   "Authorised deposit-taker" means a person with permission under Part 4 of the Financial Services and Markets Act 2000 to accept deposits.

(2)   "Former authorised deposit-taker" means a person who—

  (a)   is not an authorised deposit-taker,

  (b)   was formerly an authorised institution under the Banking Act 1987, or a recognised bank or a licensed institution under the Banking Act 1979, and

  (c)   continues to have liability in respect of any deposit for which it had a liability at a time when it was an authorised institution, recognised bank or licensed institution.

(3)   Paragraphs (1) and (2) must be read with—

  (a)   section 22 of the Financial Services and Markets Act 2000;

  (b)   any relevant order under that section; and

  (c)   Schedule 2 to that Act.]

NOTES

Inserted by the Financial Services and Markets Act 2000 (Consequential Amendments and Repeals) Order 2001, SI 2001/3649, art 381, as from 1 December 2001.

Banking Act 1987: repealed by the Financial Services and Markets Act 2000 (Consequential Amendments and Repeals) Order 2001, SI 2001/3649, art 3(1)(d), as from 1 December 2001.

[10.669]
13.13 Expressions used generally

(1)   "Business day" means any day other than a Saturday, a Sunday, Christmas Day, Good Friday or a day which is a bank holiday in any part of [England and Wales] under or by virtue of the Banking and Financial Dealings Act 1971 . . .]

(2)   "The Department" means [the Department for Business, Innovation and Skills].

[(2A)   "Duly authorised representative" means, in relation to a corporation, a person who is authorised by or under the constitution of the corporation to act on behalf of the corporation; and like expressions are to be construed accordingly.]

(3)   "File in court" [and file with the court] means deliver to the court for filing.

(4)   "The Gazette" means the London Gazette.

[(4A)   "gazetted" means [advertised] once in the Gazette.]

[(4B)   "Standard contents" means—

  (a)   in relation to a notice to be gazetted, the contents specified in Rules 12A.33 to 12A.35; and

  (b)   in relation to a notice to be advertised in any other way, the contents specified in Rules 12A.38 to 12A.40.]

(5)   "General regulations" means regulations made by the Secretary of State under Rule 12.1.

[(6)   "Practice direction" means a direction as to the practice and procedure of any court within the scope of the CPR.

(7)   "Prescribed order of priority" means the order of priority of payments laid down by Chapter 20 of Part 4 of the Rules, or Chapter 23 of Part 6.]

[(8)   "Centre of main interests" has the same meaning as in the EC Regulation.

(9)   "Establishment" has the meaning given by Article 2(h) of the EC Regulation.

(10)   "Main proceedings" means proceedings opened in accordance with Article 3(1) of the EC Regulation and falling within the definition of insolvency proceedings in Article 2(a) of the EC Regulation and

  (a)   in relation to England and Wales . . . set out in Annex A to the EC Regulation under the heading "United Kingdom", and

Part 10 Miscellaneous other SIs

(b)   in relation to another member State, set out in Annex A to the EC Regulation under the heading relating to that member State.

(11)   "Member State liquidator" means a person falling within the definition of liquidator in Article 2(b) of the EC Regulation appointed in proceedings to which it applies in a member State other than the United Kingdom.

(12)   "Secondary proceedings" means proceedings opened in accordance with Articles 3(2) and 3(3) of the EC Regulation and falling within the definition of winding-up proceedings in Article 2(c) of the EC Regulation, and

(a)   in relation to England and Wales   . . . , set out in Annex B to the EC Regulation under the heading "United Kingdom", and

(b)   in relation to another member State, set out in Annex B to the EC Regulation under the heading relating to that member State.

(13)   "Temporary administrator" means a temporary administrator referred to by Article 38 of the EC Regulation.

(14)   "Territorial proceedings" means proceedings opened in accordance with Articles 3(2) and 3(4) of the EC Regulation and falling within the definition of insolvency proceedings in Article 2(a) of the EC Regulation, and

(a)   in relation to England and Wales   . . . , set out in Annex A to the EC Regulation under the heading "United Kingdom", and

(b)   in relation to another member State, set out in Annex A to the EC Regulation under the heading relating to that member State.]

[(14A)   "Winding-up proceedings" means winding-up proceedings within the meaning of Article 2(c) of the EC Regulation as listed under the United Kingdom entry in Annex B of that Regulation, except for bankruptcy and sequestration proceedings.]

[(15)   "Prescribed part" has the same meaning as it does in section 176A(2)(a) [and the Insolvency Act 1986 (Prescribed Part) Order 2003].]

[(16)   A "certificate of service" means a certificate of service verified by a statement of truth.

(17)   A "statement of truth" means a statement of truth in accordance with CPR Part 22.

(18)   A "witness statement" means a witness statement verified by a statement of truth in accordance with CPR Part 22.

(19)   A fee or remuneration is charged when the work to which it relates is done.]

NOTES

Para (1): substituted by the Insolvency (Amendment) (No 2) Rules 1999, SI 1999/1022, r 3, Schedule, para 14(a), as from 26 April 1999; words in square brackets substituted, and words omitted revoked, by the Insolvency (Amendment) Rules 2010, SI 2010/686, r 2, Sch 1, para 499(1), (2), as from 6 April 2010, subject to transitional provisions in Sch 4, para 1 thereto, as noted to r 1.5 at **[10.7]**.

Para (2): words in square brackets substituted by the Secretary of State for Business, Innovation and Skills Order 2009, SI 2009/2748, art 8, Schedule, Pt 2, para 12, as from 13 November 2009.

Para (2A): inserted by SI 2010/686, r 2, Sch 1, para 499(1), (3), as from 6 April 2010, subject to transitional provisions in Sch 4, para 1 thereto, as noted to r 1.5 at **[10.7]**.

Para (3): words in square brackets inserted by the Insolvency (Amendment) Rules 2003, SI 2003/1730, r 13, Sch 1, Pt 10, para 66(a), as from 15 September 2003 (for transitional provisions and savings see the note preceding r 2.1 at **[10.60]**).

Para (4A): inserted by the Insolvency (Amendment) Rules 2009, SI 2009/642, rr 4, 76, as from 6 April 2009, subject to transitional provisions in r 3 thereof, as noted to r 1.4 of these Rules at **[10.6]**; word in square brackets substituted by SI 2010/686, r 2, Sch 1, para 499(1), (4), as from 6 April 2010, subject to transitional provisions in Sch 4, para 1 thereto, as noted to r 1.5 at **[10.7]**.

Para (4B): inserted by SI 2010/686, r 2, Sch 1, para 499(1), (5), as from 6 April 2010, subject to transitional provisions in Sch 4, para 1 thereto, as noted to r 1.5 at **[10.7]**.

Paras (6), (7): substituted, for original para (6), by SI 1999/1022, r 3, Schedule, para 14(b), as from 26 April 1999.

Paras (8)–(14): added by the Insolvency (Amendment) Rules 2002, SI 2002/1307, rr 3, 10(7), as from 31 May 2002, with savings in relation to anything done under, or for the purposes of, this provision before that date; words omitted from paras (10), (12), (14) revoked by SI 2010/686, r 2, Sch 1, para 499(1), (6), as from 6 April 2010, subject to transitional provisions in Sch 4, para 1 thereto, as noted to r 1.5 at **[10.7]**.

Para (14A): inserted by SI 2010/686, r 2, Sch 1, para 499(1), (7), as from 6 April 2010, subject to transitional provisions in Sch 4, para 1 thereto, as noted to r 1.5 at **[10.7]**.

Para (15): added by SI 2003/1730, r 13, Sch 1, Pt 10, para 66(b), as from 15 September 2003 (for transitional provisions and savings see the note preceding r 2.1 at **[10.60]**); words in square brackets added by SI 2010/686, r 2, Sch 1, para 499(1), (8), as from 6 April 2010, subject to transitional provisions in Sch 4, para 1 thereto, as noted to r 1.5 at **[10.7]**.

Paras (16)–(19): added by SI 2010/686, r 2, Sch 1, para 499(1), (9), as from 6 April 2010, subject to transitional provisions in Sch 4, para 2 thereto, as noted to r 1.31 at **[10.34]**.

EC Regulation: ie, Council Regulation 1346/2000/EC on insolvency proceedings.

[10.670]
13.14   Application

(1)   Subject to paragraph (2) of this Rule, and save where otherwise expressly provided, the Rules apply—

(a)   to   . . .   receivers appointed on or after the day on which the Rules come into force,

(b) to bankruptcy proceedings where the bankruptcy petition is presented on or after the day on which the Rules come into force, and

(c) to all other insolvency proceedings commenced on or after that day.

(2) The Rules also apply to winding-up and bankruptcy proceedings commenced before that day to which provisions of the Act are applied by Schedule 11 to the Act, to the extent necessary to give effect to those provisions.

NOTES

Para (1): word omitted from sub-para (a) revoked by the Insolvency (Amendment) Rules 1987, SI 1987/1919, r 3(1), Schedule, Pt 1, para 152, as from 11 January 1988.

[10.671]
[13.15 Application of Insolvency Act 1986 and Company Directors Disqualification Act 1986

For the purposes of these Rules, any reference in the Act or the Company Directors Disqualification Act 1986 to "leave" of the court is to be construed as meaning "permission" of the court.]

NOTES

Commencement: 6 April 2010.

Inserted by the Insolvency (Amendment) Rules 2010, SI 2010/686, r 2, Sch 1, para 500, as from 6 April 2010, subject to transitional provisions in Sch 4, para 1 thereto, as noted to r 1.5 at **[10.7]**.

SCHEDULES

SCHEDULE 1
[SCHEME MANAGER'S] VOTING RIGHTS

Rule 4.72(7)

[10.672]
1. This Schedule applies as does rule 4.72.

2. In relation to any meeting at which the [scheme manager] is under Rule 4.72 entitled to be represented, the [scheme manager] may submit in the liquidation, instead of a proof, a written statement of voting rights ("the statement").

3. The statement shall contain details of—
(a) the names of creditors of the company in respect of whom an obligation of the [scheme manager] has arisen or may reasonably be expected to arise as a result of the liquidation or proposed liquidation;
(b) the amount of the obligation so arising; and
(c) the total amount of all such obligations specified in the statement.

4. The [scheme manager's] statement shall, for the purpose of voting at a meeting (but for no other purpose), be treated in all respects as if it were a proof.

5. Any voting rights which a creditor might otherwise exercise at a meeting in respect of a claim against the company are reduced by a sum equal to the amount of that claim in relation to which the [scheme manager], by virtue of its having submitted a statement, is entitled to exercise voting rights at that meeting.

6. The [scheme manager] may from time to time submit a further statement, and, if it does so, that statement supersedes any statement previously submitted.

NOTES

Words in square brackets (including those in the Schedule heading) substituted by the Financial Services and Markets Act 2000 (Consequential Amendments and Repeals) Order 2001, SI 2001/3649, art 378*3), as from 1 December 2001.

SCHEDULES 2, 3

(*Sch 2 outside the scope of this work; Sch 3 revoked by the Insolvency (Amendment) Rules 1993, SI 1993/602, r 3, Schedule, para 4, as from 5 April 1993.*)

SCHEDULE 4
FORMS

[10.673]

NOTES

The actual forms are not reproduced here but details of the relevant forms are given in the table below. The forms have been amended as noted below.

Form No	Description	Status
	Part 1: Company Voluntary Arrangements	
1.1	*Notice to registrar of companies of voluntary arrangement taking effect*	*Forms 1.1–1.19 substituted for Forms 1.1–1.4 by SI 2002/2712; revoked by SI 2010/686[1]*
1.2	*Notice to registrar of companies of order of revocation or suspension of voluntary arrangement*	*Substituted as noted to Form 1.1; revoked by SI 2010/686[1]*
1.3	*Notice to registrar of companies of supervisor's abstract of receipts and payments*	*Substituted as noted to Form 1.1; revoked by SI 2010/686[1]*
1.4	*Notice to registrar of companies of completion or termination of voluntary arrangement*	*Substituted as noted to Form 1.1; revoked by SI 2010/686[1]*
1.5	Nominee's statement of opinion	Substituted as noted to Form 1.1
1.6	Statement of affairs	Substituted as noted to Form 1.1; amended by SI 2010/686[1]
1.7	Statement of eligibility for a moratorium	Substituted as noted to Form 1.1
1.8	Statement of consent to act by nominee	Substituted as noted to Form 1.1
1.9	Documents to be submitted to court to obtain moratorium	Substituted as noted to Form 1.1
1.10	Advertisement of coming into force or ending of moratorium (for Gazette and other advertising)	Substituted as noted to Form 1.1; form title substituted by SI 2009/642[2]
1.11	*Notice to registrar of companies of commencement of moratorium*	*Substituted as noted to Form 1.1; revoked by SI 2010/686[1]*
1.12	*Notice to registrar of companies of extension or further extension or renewal or continuation of moratorium*	*Substituted as noted to Form 1.1; revoked by SI 2010/686[1]*
1.13	Notice to court of extension or further extension of moratorium	Substituted as noted to Form 1.1
1.14	*Notice to the registrar of companies of ending of moratorium*	*Substituted as noted to Form 1.1; revoked by SI 2010/686[1]*
1.15	Nominee's notice to court of end of moratorium	Substituted as noted to Form 1.1
1.16	*Notice to the registrar of companies of the withdrawal of nominee's consent to act*	*Substituted as noted to Form 1.1; revoked by SI 2010/686[1]*
1.17	Notice to court by nominee of withdrawal of consent to act	Substituted as noted to Form 1.1
1.18	*Notice to the registrar of companies of the appointment of a replacement nominee*	*Substituted as noted to Form 1.1; revoked by SI 2010/686[1]*
1.19	Notice to court of appointment of replacement nominee	Substituted as noted to Form 1.1
	Part 2: Administration Procedure	
2.1B	Administration application	Forms 2.1B–2.40B substituted for Forms 2.1–2.23 by SI 2003/1730[3]. Amended by SI 2005/617, SI 2009/2472[4] and SI 2010/686[1]
2.2B	Statement of proposed administrator	Substituted as noted to Form 2.1B[3]
2.3B	*Affidavit of service of administration application*	*Substituted as noted to Form 2.1B[3]; revoked by SI 2010/686[1]*

Form No	Description	Status
2.4B	Administration order	Substituted as noted to Form 2.1B³; amended by SI 2010/686¹
2.5B	Notice of intention to appoint an administrator by holder of qualifying floating charge	Substituted as noted to Form 2.1B³; amended by SI 2010/686¹
2.6B	Notice of appointment of an administrator by holder of qualifying floating charge	Substituted as noted to Form 2.1B³; amended by SI 2010/686¹
2.7B	Notice of appointment of an administrator by holder of qualifying floating charge (For use in pursuance of Rule 2.19 of the Insolvency Rules 1986)	Substituted as noted to Form 2.1B³; amended by SI 2010/686¹
2.8B	Notice of Intention to Appoint an Administrator by Company or Director(s)	Substituted as noted to Form 2.1B³; further substituted by SI 2004/584 and SI 2005/527; amended by SI 2010/686¹
2.9B	Notice of Appointment of an Administrator by Company or Director(s)	Substituted as noted to Form 2.1B³; further substituted by SI 2004/584; amended by SI 2010/686¹
2.10B	Notice of appointment of an administrator by company or director(s) (where a notice of intention to appoint has not been issued)	Substituted as noted to Form 2.1B³; amended by SI 2010/686¹
2.11B	*Notification of appointment of administrator (for Gazette and other advertising)*	*Substituted as noted to Form 2.1B³; further substituted by SI 2004/584 and SI 2005/527; form title substituted by SI 2009/642²; revoked by SI 2010/686¹*
2.12B	Notice of administrator's appointment	Substituted as noted to Form 2.1B³; amended by SI 2010/686¹
2.13B	Notice requiring submission of a statement of affairs	Substituted as noted to Form 2.1B³; further substituted by SI 2005/527
2.14B	Statement of affairs	Substituted as noted to Form 2.1B³; further substituted by SI 2005/527
2.15B	Statement of concurrence	Substituted as noted to Form 2.1B³
2.16B	*Notice of statement of affairs*	*Substituted as noted to Form 2.1B³; revoked by SI 2010/686¹*
2.17B	*Statement of administrator's proposals*	*Substituted as noted to Form 2.1B³; revoked by SI 2010/686¹*
2.18B	Notice of extension of time period	Substituted as noted to Form 2.1B³; amended by SI 2010/686¹
2.19B	Notice to attend meeting of creditors	Substituted as noted to Form 2.1B³
2.20B	Notice of a meeting of creditors	Substituted as noted to Form 2.1B³
2.21B	Creditor's request for a meeting	Substituted as noted to Form 2.1B³
2.22B	Statement of administrator's revised proposals	Substituted as noted to Form 2.1B³; amended by SI 2010/686¹
2.23B	Notice of result of meeting of creditors	Substituted as noted to Form 2.1B³; amended by SI 2010/686¹
2.24B	Administrator's progress report	Substituted as noted to Form 2.1B³; amended by SI 2010/686¹
2.25B	Notification of Conduct of Business by Correspondence	Substituted as noted to Form 2.1B³; further substituted by SI 2004/584; amended by SI 2010/686¹
2.26B	[Amended] Certificate of constitution of creditors' committee	Substituted as noted to Form 2.1B³; amended by SI 2010/686¹
2.27B	*Notice by administrator of a change in committee membership*	*Substituted as noted to Form 2.1B³; revoked by SI 2010/686¹*
2.28B	*Notice of order to deal with charged property*	*Substituted as noted to Form 2.1B³; revoked by SI 2010/686¹*
2.29B	*Affidavit of debt*	*Substituted as noted to Form 2.1B³; revoked by SI 2010/686¹*

Part 10   Miscellaneous other SIs

Form No	Description	Status
2.30B	Notice of automatic end of administration	Substituted as noted to Form 2.1B[3]; amended by SI 2010/686[1]
2.31B	*Notice of extension of period of administration*	*Substituted as noted to Form 2.1B[3]; revoked by SI 2010/686[1]*
2.32B	Notice of end of administration	Substituted as noted to Form 2.1B[3]; amended by SI 2010/686[1]
2.33B	*Notice of court order ending administration*	*Substituted as noted to Form 2.1B[3]; revoked by SI 2010/686[1]*
2.34B	*Notice of move from administration to creditors' voluntary liquidation*	*Substituted as noted to Form 2.1B[3]; revoked by SI 2010/686[1]*
2.35B	*Notice of move from administration to dissolution*	*Substituted as noted to Form 2.1B[3]; revoked by SI 2010/686[1]*
2.36B	*Notice to registrar of companies in respect of date of dissolution*	*Substituted as noted to Form 2.1B[3]; revoked by SI 2010/686[1]*
2.37B	Notice of intention to resign as administrator	Substituted as noted to Form 2.1B[3]
2.38B	Notice of resignation by administrator	Substituted as noted to Form 2.1B[3]; amended by SI 2010/686[1]
2.39B	*Notice of vacation of office by administrator*	*Substituted as noted to Form 2.1B[3]; revoked by SI 2010/686[1]*
2.40B	*Notice of appointment of replacement/additional administrator*	*Substituted as noted to Form 2.1B[3]; revoked by SI 2010/686[1]*
	Part 3: Administrative Receivership	
3.1	Written acceptance of appointment by receiver	Inserted by SI 1987/1919
3.1A	Notice of appointment of administrative receiver (for Gazette and other advertising	Inserted by SI 1987/1919; substituted by SI 2005/527; form title substituted by SI 2009/642[2]
3.1B	Notice requiring preparation and submission of administrative receivership statement of affairs	Substituted (for Form 3.1) by SI 1987/1919
3.2	Statement of affairs	Substituted by SI 2003/1730[3]; further substituted by SI 2005/527; amended by SI 2010/686[1]
3.3	*Statement of affairs in administrative receivership following report to creditors*	*Revoked by SI 2010/686[1]*
3.4	*Certificate of constitution [amended certificate] of creditors' committee*	*Revoked by SI 2010/686[1]*
3.5	*Administrative receiver's report as to change in membership of creditors' committee*	*Revoked by SI 2010/686[1]*
3.6	Receiver or manager or administrative receiver's abstract of receipts and payments	Amended by SI 2010/686[1]
3.7	*Notice of administrative receiver's death*	*Revoked by SI 2010/686[1]*
3.8	*Notice of order to dispose of charged property*	*Amended by SI 2009/2472[4]; revoked by SI 2010/686[1]*
3.9	Notice of resignation of administrative receiver pursuant to the Insolvency Act 1986, s 45(1)	
3.10	*Administrative receiver's report*	*Revoked by SI 2010/686[1]*
	Part 4: Companies Winding Up	
4.1	Statutory demand under the Insolvency Act 1986, s 123(1)(a) or 222(1)(a)	Substituted by SI 1987/1919; amended by SI 2010/686[1]
4.2	Winding-up petition	Substituted by SI 2002/1307; amended by SI 2009/2472[4] and SI 2010/686[1]

Form No	Description	Status
4.3	*Affidavit verifying winding-up petition*	*Revoked by SI 2005/527*
4.4	*Affidavit of service of winding-up petition at registered office*	*Revoked by SI 2010/686[1]*
4.5	*Affidavit of service of winding-up petition other than at registered office or on an [overseas] company*	*Amended by SI 2009/2472[4]; revoked by SI 2010/686[1]*
4.6	Advertisement of winding-up petition	Substituted by SI 2005/527
4.7	Certificate that relevant provisions of Rules have been complied with	Amended by SI 2009/642[2]
4.8	Order for [permission] to withdraw winding-up petition	Amended by SI 2010/686[1]
4.9	Notice of intention to appear on petition	
4.10	List of persons intending to appear on the hearing of the petition	
4.11	Order for winding up by the court	Substituted by SI 2002/1307; further substituted by SI 2005/527
4.12	Order for Winding Up by the Court Following Upon the Cessation of the Appointment of an Administrator	Substituted by SI 2003/1730[3]; further substituted by SI 2005/527
4.13	Notice to Official Receiver of Winding-up Order	Substituted by SI 1987/1919; further substituted by SI 2005/527
4.14	Petition by contributory	Substituted by SI 2002/1307; further substituted by SI 2005/527; amended by SI 2009/2472[4] and SI 2010/686[1]
4.14A	Notice to official receiver of appointment of provisional liquidator	Inserted by SI 1987/1919
4.15	Order of appointment of provisional liquidator	Substituted by SI 2002/1307; amended by SI 2010/686[1]
4.15A	*Notice of appointment of provisional liquidator in winding up by the court*	*Inserted by SI 2005/527; revoked by SI 2010/686[1]*
4.16	Notice requiring preparation and submission of statement of company's affairs	Substituted by SI 1987/1919
4.17	Statement of Affairs	Substituted by SI 2003/1730[3]; further substituted by SI 2005/527; amended by SI 2010/686[1]
4.18	Statement of Affairs	Substituted by SI 2003/1730[3]; further substituted by SI 2005/527; amended by SI 2010/686[1]
4.19	Statement of Affairs	Substituted by SI 2003/1730[3]; further substituted by SI 2005/527; amended by SI 2010/686[1]
4.20	*Statement of affairs under s 95/s 99 to registrar of companies*	*Revoked by SI 2010/686[1]*
4.21	Request by creditors for a meeting of the company's creditors [and contributories]	
4.22	Notice to creditors of meeting of creditors	Amended by SI 2010/686[1]
4.23	Notice to contributories of meeting of contributories	Amended by SI 2010/686[1]
4.24	Request by contributory/contributories for a meeting of the company's contributories	
4.25	Proof of debt—general form	Substituted by SI 2004/584
4.26	*Affidavit of debt*	*Revoked by SI 2010/686[1]*
4.27	Certificate of appointment of liquidator by meeting	
4.28	Certificate of appointment of two or more liquidators by meeting	
4.29	Order of court appointing liquidator	Amended by SI 2010/686[1]

Form No	Description	Status
4.30	Order of court appointing two or more liquidators	Amended by SI 2010/686[1]
4.31	*Notice of appointment of liquidator in winding up by the court (for registrar of companies)*	*Revoked by SI 2010/686[1]*
4.32	Notice to court of resignation of liquidator following meeting of creditors	Substituted by SI 1987/1919
4.33	*Notice of resignation as voluntary liquidator under the Insolvency Act 1986, s 171(5)*	*Revoked by SI 2010/686[1]*
4.34	Order of court giving liquidator [permission] to resign	Amended by SI 2010/686[1]
4.35	*Order of court granting voluntary liquidator [permission] to resign*	*Amended and revoked by SI 2010/686[1]*
4.36	Notice to court of resignation of liquidator following leave of the court	
4.37	Certificate of removal of liquidator	
4.38	*Certificate of removal of voluntary liquidator*	*Revoked by SI 2010/686[1]*
4.39	Order of court removing liquidator or directing liquidator to summon a meeting of creditors for purpose of his removal	Amended by SI 2010/686[1]
4.40	*Notice of ceasing to act as voluntary liquidator*	*Revoked by SI 2010/686[1]*
4.41	Liquidator's application to the Secretary of State for his release	
4.42	Notice to court of final meeting of creditors	
4.43	*Notice to registrar of companies of final meeting of creditors*	*Revoked by SI 2010/686[1]*
4.44	*Notice of death of liquidator*	*Revoked by SI 2010/686[1]*
4.45	Notice to official receiver or Secretary of State by liquidator on loss of qualification as insolvency practitioner	
4.46	*Notice of vacation of office by voluntary liquidator*	*Revoked by SI 2010/686[1]*
4.47	Certificate of constitution [amended certificate] of liquidation committee	
4.48	*Notice of constitution of liquidation committee*	*Revoked by SI 2010/686[1]*
4.49	*Report by liquidator of any change in membership of liquidation committee*	*Revoked by SI 2010/686[1]*
4.50	*Liquidator's certificate that creditors paid in full*	*Revoked by SI 2010/686[1]*
4.51	*Certificate that creditors have been paid in full*	*Revoked by SI 2010/686[1]*
4.52	Liquidator's certificate of continuance of liquidation committee	Substituted by SI 2003/1730[3]
4.53A	Notice of disclaimer under the Insolvency Act 1986, s 178	Substituted (for Form 4.53) by SI 2010/686[1]
4.54	Notice to elect	
4.55	Notice of intended disclaimer to interested party	
4.56	Affidavit of liquidator in support of application for call	Amended by SI 2010/686[1]
4.57	Order giving [permission] to make a call	Amended by SI 2010/686[1]
4.58	Notice of call sanctioned by the court or the liquidation committee to be sent to contributory	

Form No	Description	Status
4.59	Order for payment of call due from contributory	
4.60	Order of appointment of special manager	Amended by SI 2010/686[1]
4.61	Order of public examination	Substituted by SI 1987/1919; amended by SI 2010/686[1]
4.62	Notice to official receiver by creditor requesting him to make application for the holding of a public examination	
4.63	Notice to official receiver by contributory requesting him to make application for the holding of a public examination	
4.64	Order as to examination of person who lacks capacity to manage and administer his property and affairs or is suffering from mental disorder or physical affliction or disability	Substituted by SI 2007/1898; amended by SI 2010/686[1]
4.65	[Statement of truth verifying] record of the public examination	Amended by SI 2010/686[1]
4.66	Order of adjournment of public examination	Substituted by SI 1987/1919; amended by SI 2010/686[1]
4.67	Order appointing time for proceeding with public examination adjourned generally	Substituted by SI 1987/1919; amended by SI 2010/686[1]
4.68	*Liquidator's Statement of Receipts and Payments*	*Substituted by SI 1987/1919; further substituted by SI 2005/527; revoked by SI 2010/686[1]*
4.69	*Order of court on appeal against Secretary of State's decision under the Insolvency Act 1986, s 203(4) or 205(4)*	*Revoked by SI 2010/686[1]*
4.70	Members' voluntary winding up declaration of solvency embodying a statement of assets and liabilities	Substituted by SI 1987/1919; amended by SI 2010/686[1]
4.71	*Return of final meeting in a members' voluntary winding up*	*Amended by SI 1991/495; further amended by SI 2009/642[2]; revoked by SI 2010/686[1]*
4.72	*Return of final meeting in creditors' voluntary winding up*	*Amended by SI 1991/495; further amended by SI 2009/642[2]; revoked by SI 2010/686[1]*
4.73	Notice to the creditors of an insolvent company of the re-use of a prohibited name	Inserted by SI 2007/1974
4.74	Request by liquidator for approval or authorisation of litigation expenses by creditor	Inserted by SI 2008/737
	Part 7: Court Procedure and Practice	
7.1A	Application notice	Substituted (for Forms 7.1, 7.2) by SI 2010/686[1]
7.3	*Declaration by official shorthand writer*	*Revoked by SI 2010/686[1]*
7.4	*Appointment of shorthand writer to take examination under the Insolvency Act 1986*	*Revoked by SI 2010/686[1]*
7.5	*Declaration by shorthand writer*	*Revoked by SI 2010/686[1]*
7.6	*Warrant for failure to attend examination under the Insolvency Act 1986, s 133*	*Revoked by SI 2010/686[1]*
7.7	*Warrant of arrest etc under the Insolvency Act 1986, s 364*	*Revoked by SI 2010/686[1]*
7.8	*Warrant of arrest etc under the Insolvency Act 1986, s 236[, 251N] or 366*	*Amended by SI 2009/2472[4]; revoked by SI 2010/686[1]*

Part 10 Miscellaneous other SIs

Form No	Description	Status
7.9	*Order for production of person arrested under warrant issued under the Insolvency Act 1986, s 134, 236[, 251N], 364 or 366*	*Substituted by SI 1987/1919; amended by SI 2009/2472[4] Revoked by SI 2010/686[1]*
7.10	*Warrant to registrar of court in whose district a person against whom a warrant of arrest has been issued is believed to be*	*Revoked by SI 2010/686[1]*
7.11	*Endorsement of warrant of arrest issued by a court to which the same has been sent for execution by the court which originally issued it*	*Revoked by SI 2010/686[1]*
7.12	*Warrant of seizure of property under the Insolvency Act 1986, s 365*	*Revoked by SI 2010/686[1]*
7.13	*Search warrant under the Insolvency Act 1986, s 365*	*Revoked by SI 2010/686[1]*
7.14	*Order of discharge from custody under the Insolvency Act 1986 [General]*	*Revoked by SI 2010/686[1]*
7.15	*Affidavit in support of application for committal for contempt of court*	*Substituted by SI 1987/1919; revoked by SI 2010/686[1]*
7.16	*Affidavit in support of application for committal of the bankrupt under section 363 of the Insolvency Act 1986*	*Revoked by SI 1987/1919*
7.17	*Warrant of committal for contempt*	*Amended by SI 1993/602; revoked by SI 2010/686[1]*
7.18	*Order of discharge from custody for contempt*	*Revoked by SI 2010/686[1]*
7.19	*Order appointing person to act for incapacitated person*	*Revoked by SI 2010/686[1]*
7.20A	Confirmation by court of creditors' voluntary winding up application and order	Substituted (for Form 7.20) by SI 2010/686[1]
	Part 8: Proxies and Company Representation	
8.1	Proxy—company or individual voluntary arrangements	
8.2	Proxy—administration	
8.3	Proxy—administrative receivership	
8.4	Proxy—winding up by the court or bankruptcy	
8.5	Proxy—members' or creditors' voluntary winding up	
	Part 9: Examination of Persons Concerned in Company and Individual Insolvency	
9.1	Order under the Insolvency Act 1986, s 236[, 251N] or 366	Amended by SI 2009/2472[4]
	Part 12: Miscellaneous and General	
12.1	*Notice to the Registrar of Companies in respect of order under section 176A*	*Inserted by SI 2003/1730[3]; revoked by SI 2010/686[1]*

NOTES

[1]   For transitional provisions in relation to the amendments made by SI 2010/686, see Sch 4, paras 1, 2 thereto as noted to rr 1.5, 1.31 of these Rules at **[10.7]**, **[10.34]**. See also Sch 4, para 6 to the 2010 Rules which provides (in relation to the amendments made by those Rules to these Rules) as follows—

"6   Forms

(1)   In this paragraph, "old Schedule 4" means Schedule 4 to the 1986 Rules as it has effect immediately before 6th April 2010.

(2)   Notwithstanding the preceding provisions of this Schedule, a form contained in old Schedule 4 may be sent to or filed with the registrar of companies without regard to an amendment, substitution or revocation provided for in these Rules only if the event which creates the obligation so to send or file it occurs before 6th April 2010.

(3)   In any other case in which the provisions of this Schedule other than this paragraph would have the effect that a form contained in old Schedule 4 should be sent to or filed with the registrar of companies without regard to an amendment, substitution or revocation provided for in these Rules, the form must not be so sent or filed but, where appropriate, that form as amended or substituted by these Rules must be sent or filed, with such variations, if any, as the circumstances may require.".

²   The substitution of the titles of Forms 1.10, 2.11B and 3.1A by SI 2009/642, rr 4, 78, Sch 2, as from 6 April 2009, and the amendment of Forms 4.7, 4.71, 4.72 are subject to the transitional provisions set out in r 3 of those Rules (see the transitional provisions note to r 1.4 of the Rules at **[10.6]**).

³   The substitution of Forms 2.1B–2.40B (for original Forms 2.1–2.23), the substitution of Forms 3.2, 4.12, 4.17, 4.18, 4.19, 4.52, and the insertion of Form 12.1, by SI 2003/1730, are subject to transitional provisions and savings (see the note preceding r 2.1 of these Rules at **[10.60]**).

⁴   For transitional provisions in relation to the amendments made by SI 2009/2472 see the note to r 0.2 of the Rules at **[10.2]**. In Form 4.5 above the word in square brackets was substituted for the original word "oversea".

Part 10   Miscellaneous other SIs

Rule 12.21

[10.674]

SCHEDULE 5

PUNISHMENT OF OFFENCES UNDER THE RULES

Note: In the fourth and fifth columns of this Schedule, "the statutory maximum" means the prescribed sum under section 32 of the Magistrates' Courts Act 1980 (c 43).

Rule creating offence.	General nature of offence.	Mode of prosecution.	Punishment.	Daily default fine (where applicable).
. . . .	. . . .	. . . .	. . . .	
In Part 2, [Rule 2.47(6)].	Administrator failing to send [a progress report].	Summary.	[Level 3 on the standard scale.]	[One-tenth of level 3 on the standard scale.]
[Rule 2.111(3).	Administrator failing to file a notice of automatic end of administration [and progress report].]	Summary.	[Level 3 on the standard scale.]	[One-tenth of level 3 on the standard scale.]]
[Rule 2.129(2)	[Failure to comply with] administrator's duties on vacating office.	Summary.	[Level 3 on the standard scale.]	[One-tenth of level 3 on the standard scale.]]
In Part 3, Rule 3.32(5).	Administrative receiver failing to send [requisite accounts of receipts and payments as receiver].	Summary.	[Level 3 on the standard scale.]	[One-tenth of level 3 on the standard scale.]
. . . .	. . . .	. . . .		
In Part 12, Rule 12.18.	False representation of status for purpose of in-specting documents.	1. On indictment.	2 years or a fine, or both.	
		2. Summary.	6 months or the statutory maximum, or both.	

NOTES

Entries omitted revoked by the Insolvency (Amendment) (No 2) Rules 2002, SI 2002/2712, r 9, as from 1 January 2003.

In entry relating to rule 2.47(6) words in square brackets in column 1 substituted, and entries relating to rules 2.111(3), 2.129(2) inserted, by the Insolvency (Amendment) Rules 2003, SI 2003/1730, r 15, as from 15 September 2003 (for transitional provisions and savings see the note preceding r 2.1 at [10.60]).

Other words in square brackets in entry relating to rule 2.47(6), and words in square brackets in entries relating to rules 2.111(3), 2.129(2), 3.32(5), inserted or substituted by the Insolvency (Amendment) Rules 2010, SI 2010/686, r 2, Sch 1, para 560, as from 6 April 2010, subject to transitional provisions in Sch 4, para 1 thereto, as noted to r 1.5 at [10.7].

Statutory maximum: by the Magistrates' Courts Act 1980, s 32(9), as amended, the statutory maximum is currently £5,000.

[SCHEDULE 6
DETERMINATION OF INSOLVENCY OFFICE HOLDER'S REMUNERATION
Rules 4.127A, 4.127B, 4.148B and 6.138A

[10.675]
As regards the determination of the remuneration of trustees and liquidators the realisation and distribution scales are as set out in the table below—

The realisation scale		
(i)	on the first £5,000 or fraction thereof	20%
(ii)	on the next £5,000 or fraction thereof	15%
(iii)	on the next £90,000 or fraction thereof	10%
(iv)	on all further sums realised	5%

The distribution scale		
(i)	on the first £5,000 or fraction thereof	10%
(ii)	on the next £5,000 or fraction thereof	7.5%
(iii)	on the next £90,000 or fraction thereof	5%
(iv)	on all further sums distributed	2.5%.]

NOTES
Inserted by the Insolvency (Amendment) Rules 2004, SI 2004/584, r 47, as from 1 April 2004.

INSOLVENT COMPANIES (DISQUALIFICATION OF UNFIT DIRECTORS) PROCEEDINGS RULES 1987

(SI 1987/2023)

NOTES
Made: 25 November 1987.
Authority: Insolvency Act 1986, s 411; Company Directors Disqualification Act 1986, s 21.
Commencement: 11 January 1988.
These Rules are reproduced as amended by: the Insolvent Companies (Disqualification of Unfit Directors) Proceedings (Amendment) Rules 1999, SI 1999/1023; the Insolvent Companies (Disqualification of Unfit Directors) Proceedings (Amendment) Rules 2001, SI 2001/765; the Insolvent Companies (Disqualification of Unfit Directors) Proceedings (Amendment) Rules 2003, SI 2003/1367; the Insolvent Companies (Disqualification of Unfit Directors) Proceedings (Amendment) Rules 2007, SI 2007/1906.
Limited liability partnerships: by the Limited Liability Partnerships Regulations 2001, SI 2001/1090, reg 10, Sch 6, Pt III, these Rules apply, with modifications, to limited liability partnerships (see **[10.830]**).
Application to bank insolvency and administration: as to the application of this SI to bank insolvency and administration, see the Banking Act 2009 (Parts 2 and 3 Consequential Amendments) Order 2009, SI 2009/317.

ARRANGEMENT OF RULES

[10.676]
1   Citation, commencement and interpretation
(1)   These Rules may be cited as the Insolvent Companies (Disqualification of Unfit Directors) Proceedings Rules 1987 and shall come into force on 11th January 1988.

[(2)   In these Rules—
   (a)   "the Companies Act" means the Companies Act 1985,
   (b)   "the Company Directors Disqualification Act" means the Company Directors Disqualification Act 1986,

Part 10   Miscellaneous other SIs

(c)   "CPR" followed by a Part or rule by number means that Part or rule with that number in the Civil Procedure Rules 1998,

(d)   "practice direction" means a direction as to the practice and procedure of any court within the scope of the Civil Procedure Rules,

(e)   "registrar" has the same meaning as in paragraphs (4) and (5) of rule 13.2 of the Insolvency Rules 1986, and

(f)   "file in court" means deliver to the court for filing.]

[(3)   These Rules apply to an application made under the Company Directors Disqualification Act on or after 6th August 2007—

(a)   for leave to commence proceedings for a disqualification order after the end of the period mentioned in section 7(2) of that Act;

(b)   to enforce any duty arising under section 7(4) of that Act;

(c)   for a disqualification order where made—

    (i)   by the Secretary of State or the official receiver under section 7(1) of that Act (disqualification of unfit directors of insolvent companies);

    (ii)   by the Secretary of State under section 8 of that Act (disqualification after investigation of company); or

    (iii)   by the Office of Fair Trading or a specified regulator under section 9A of that Act (competition disqualification order);

(d)   under section 8A of that Act (variation etc of disqualification undertaking); or—

(e)   for leave to act under—

    (i)   section 1A(1) or 9B(4) of that Act (and section 17 of that Act as it applies for the purposes of either of those sections); or

    (ii)   sections 1 and 17 as they apply for the purposes of section 6, 7(1), 8, 9A or 10 of that Act.]

NOTES

Para (2): substituted by the Insolvent Companies (Disqualification of Unfit Directors) Proceedings (Amendment) Rules 1999, SI 1999/1023, r 3, Schedule, para 2, as from 26 April 1999.

Para (3): substituted by the Insolvent Companies (Disqualification of Unfit Directors) Proceedings (Amendment) Rules 2007, SI 2007/1906, rr 1(3), 2, as from 6 August 2007, except in relation to any application made in accordance with these Rules before that date.

[10.677]
[2   Form and conduct of applications

(1)   The Civil Procedure Rules 1998, and any relevant practice direction, apply in respect of any application to which these Rules apply, except where these Rules make provision to inconsistent effect.

[(2)   Subject to paragraph (5), an application shall be made either—

(a)   by claim form as provided by the relevant practice direction and the claimant must use the CPR Part 8 (alternative procedure for claims) procedure, or

(b)   by application notice as provided for by the relevant practice direction.]

(3)   CPR rule 8.1(3) (power of the court to order the claim to continue as if the claimant had not used the Part 8 procedure), CPR rule 8.2 (contents of the claim form) and CPR rule 8.7 (Part 20 claims) do not apply.

(4)   Rule 7.47 (appeals and reviews of court orders) and rule 7.49 (procedure on appeal) of the Insolvency Rules 1986 apply.

[(5)   The Insolvency Rules 1986 shall apply to an application to enforce any duty arising under section 7(4) of the Company Directors Disqualification Act made against a person who at the date of the application is acting as liquidator, administrator or administrative receiver.]]

NOTES

Substituted by the Insolvent Companies (Disqualification of Unfit Directors) Proceedings (Amendment) Rules 1999, SI 1999/1023, r 3, Schedule, para 3, as from 26 April 1999.

Para (2): substituted by the Insolvent Companies (Disqualification of Unfit Directors) Proceedings (Amendment) Rules 2007, SI 2007/1906, rr 1(3), 3(1), (2), as from 6 August 2007, except in relation to any application made in accordance with these Rules before that date

Para (5): added by SI 2007/1906, rr 1(3), 3(1), (3), as from 6 August 2007, except in relation to any application made in accordance with these Rules before that date.

[10.678]
[2A   Application of Rules 3 to 8

Rules 3 to 8 only apply to the types of application referred to in Rule 1(3)(c).]

NOTES

Commencement: 6 August 2007.

Inserted by the Insolvent Companies (Disqualification of Unfit Directors) Proceedings (Amendment) Rules 2007, SI 2007/1906, rr 1(3), 4, as from 6 August 2007, except in relation to any application made in accordance with these Rules before that date.

[10.679]
3   The case against the [defendant]

(1)   There shall, at the time when the [claim form] is issued, be filed in court evidence in support of the application for a disqualification order; and copies of the evidence shall be served with the [claim form] on the [defendant].

(2)   The evidence shall be by one or more affidavits, except where the [claimant] is the official receiver, in which case it may be in the form of a written report (with or without affidavits by other persons) which shall be treated as if it had been verified by affidavit by him and shall be prima facie evidence of any matter contained in it.

(3)   There shall in the affidavit or affidavits or (as the case may be) the official receiver's report be included a statement of the matters by reference to which the [defendant] is alleged to be unfit to be concerned in the management of a company.

NOTES

Words in square brackets substituted by the Insolvent Companies (Disqualification of Unfit Directors) Proceedings (Amendment) Rules 1999, SI 1999/1023, r 3, Schedule, para 1, as from 26 April 1999.

[10.680]
4   Endorsement on [claim form]

There shall on the [claim form] be endorsed information to the [defendant] as follows—
   (a)   that the application is made in accordance with these Rules;
   (b)   that, in accordance with the relevant enactments, the court has power to impose disqualifications as follows—
      (i)   where the application is under section 7 of the Company Directors Disqualification Act, for a period of not less than 2, and up to 15, years; and
      (ii)   where the application is [under section 8 or 9A of that Act], for a period of up to 15 years;
   (c)   that the application for a disqualification order may, in accordance with these Rules, be heard and determined summarily, without further or other notice to the [defendant], and that, if it is so heard and determined, the court may impose disqualification for a period of up to 5 years;
   (d)   that if at the hearing of the application the court, on the evidence then before it, is minded to impose, in the [defendant]'s case, disqualification for any period longer than 5 years, it will not make a disqualification order on that occasion but will adjourn the application to be heard (with further evidence, if any) at a later date to be notified; and
   (e)   that any evidence which the [defendant] wishes to be taken into consideration by the court must be filed in court in accordance with the time limits imposed under Rule 6 (the provisions of which shall be set out on the [claim form]).

NOTES

Words in square brackets in sub-para (b)(ii) substituted by the Insolvent Companies (Disqualification of Unfit Directors) Proceedings (Amendment) Rules 2003, SI 2003/1367, r 3, Schedule, para 2, as from 20 June 2003; other words in square brackets substituted by the Insolvent Companies (Disqualification of Unfit Directors) Proceedings (Amendment) Rules 1999, SI 1999/1023, r 3, Schedule, para 1, as from 26 April 1999.

[10.681]
5   Service and acknowledgement

(1)   The [claim form] shall be served on the [defendant] by sending it by first class post to his last known address; and the date of service shall, unless the contrary is shown, be deemed to be the 7th day next following that on which the [claim form] was posted.

(2)   Where any process or order of the court or other document is required under proceedings subject to these Rules to be served on any person who is not in England and Wales, the court may order service on him of that process or order or other document to be effected within such time and in such manner as it thinks fit, and may also require such proof of service as it thinks fit.

[(3)   The claim form served on the defendant shall be accompanied by an acknowledgment of service as provided for by practice direction and CPR rule 8.3(2) (dealing with the contents of an acknowledgment of service) does not apply.]

(4)   The . . . acknowledgement of service shall state that the [defendant] should indicate—
   (a)   whether he contests the application on the grounds that, in the case of any particular company—
      (i)   he was not a director or shadow director of the company at a time when conduct of his, or of other persons, in relation to that company is in question, or
      (ii)   his conduct as director or shadow director of that company was not as alleged in support of the application for a disqualification order,
   (b)   whether, in the case of any conduct of his, he disputes the allegation that such conduct makes him unfit to be concerned in the management of a company, and
   (c)   whether he, while not resisting the application for a disqualification order, intends to adduce mitigating factors with a view to justifying only a short period of disqualification.

NOTES
Para (1): words in square brackets substituted by the Insolvent Companies (Disqualification of Unfit Directors) Proceedings (Amendment) Rules 1999, SI 1999/1023, r 3, Schedule, para 1, as from 26 April 1999.
Para (3): substituted by SI 1999/1023, r 3, Schedule, para 4(1), as from 26 April 1999.
Para (4): words omitted revoked, and word in square brackets substituted, by SI 1999/1023, r 3, Schedule, paras 1, 4(2), as from 26 April 1999.

[10.682]
6   Evidence

(1)   The [defendant] shall, within 28 days from the date of service of the [claim form], file in court any affidavit evidence in opposition to the application he wishes the court to take into consideration and shall forthwith serve upon the [claimant] a copy of such evidence.

(2)   The [claimant] shall, within 14 days from receiving the copy of the [defendant]'s evidence, file in court any further evidence in reply he wishes the court to take into consideration and shall forthwith serve a copy of that evidence upon the [defendant].

[(3)   CPR rules 8.5 (filing and serving written evidence) and 8.6(1) (requirements where written evidence is to be relied on) do not apply.]

NOTES
Paras (1), (2): words in square brackets substituted by the Insolvent Companies (Disqualification of Unfit Directors) Proceedings (Amendment) Rules 1999, SI 1999/1023, r 3, Schedule, para 1, as from 26 April 1999.
Para (3): added by SI 1999/1023, r 3, Schedule, para 5, as from 26 April 1999.

[10.683]
7   The hearing of the application

[(1)   When the claim form is issued, the court will fix a date for the first hearing of the claim which shall not be less than 8 weeks from the date of issue of the claim form.]

(2)   The hearing shall in the first instance be before the registrar in open court.

(3)   The registrar shall either determine the case on the date fixed or adjourn it.

(4)   The registrar shall adjourn the case for further consideration if—
   (a)   he forms the provisional opinion that a disqualification order ought to be made, and that a period of disqualification longer than 5 years is appropriate, or
   (b)   he is of opinion that questions of law or fact arise which are not suitable for summary determination.

(5)   If the registrar adjourns the case for further consideration he shall—
   (a)   direct whether the case is to be heard by a registrar or, if he thinks it appropriate, by the judge, for determination by him;
   (b)   state the reasons for the adjournment; and
   (c)   give directions as to the following matters—
      (i)   the manner in which and the time within which notice of the adjournment and the reasons for it are to be given to the [defendant],
      (ii)   the filing in court and the service of further evidence (if any) by the parties,
      (iii) such other matters as the registrar thinks necessary or expedient with a view to an expeditious disposal of the application, and
      (iv)   the time and place of the adjourned hearing.

(6)   Where a case is adjourned other than to the judge, it may be heard by the registrar who originally dealt with the case or by another registrar.

NOTES
Para (1): substituted by the Insolvent Companies (Disqualification of Unfit Directors) Proceedings (Amendment) Rules 1999, SI 1999/1023, r 3, Schedule, para 6, as from 26 April 1999.
Para (5): word in square brackets in sub-para (c) substituted by SI 1999/1023, r 3, Schedule, para 1, as from 26 April 1999.

[10.684]
8   Making and setting aside of disqualification order

(1)   The court may make a disqualification order against the [defendant], whether or not the latter appears, and whether or not he has completed and returned the acknowledgement of service of the [claim form], or filed evidence in accordance with Rule 6.

(2)   Any disqualification order made in the absence of the [defendant] may be set aside or varied by the court on such terms as it thinks just.

NOTES
Words in square brackets substituted by the Insolvent Companies (Disqualification of Unfit Directors) Proceedings (Amendment) Rules 1999, SI 1999/1023, r 3, Schedule, para 1, as from 26 April 1999.

9   (*Revoked by the Insolvent Companies (Disqualification of Unfit Directors) Proceedings (Amendment) Rules 2001, SI 2001/765, as from 2 April 2001.*)

[10.685]
10 Right of audience

Official receivers and deputy official receivers have right of audience in any proceedings to which these Rules apply, whether the application is made by the Secretary of State or by the official receiver at his direction, and whether made in the High Court or a county court.

[10.686]
11 Revocation and saving

(1)   . . .

(2)   Notwithstanding paragraph (1) the former Rules shall continue to apply and have effect in relation to any application described in paragraph 3(a) or (b) of Rule 1 of these Rules made before the date on which these Rules come into force.

NOTES

Para (1): revokes the Insolvent Companies (Disqualification of Unfit Directors) Proceedings Rules 1986, SI 1986/612.

DEPARTMENT OF TRADE AND INDUSTRY (FEES) ORDER 1988

(SI 1988/93)

NOTES

Made: 21 January 1988.
Authority: Finance (No 2) Act 1987, s 102.
Commencement: 22 January 1988.
This Order is reproduced as amended by: the Wireless Telegraphy Act 1998; the Department of Trade and Industry (Fees) (Amendment) Order 1995, SI 1995/1294; the Financial Services and Markets Act 2000 (Consequential Amendments and Repeals) Order 2001, SI 2001/3649.
References to "the European Community", "Community", etc: see the Treaty of Lisbon (Changes in Terminology) Order 2011, SI 2011/1043, which provides that (as from 22 April 2011) "EU" should be substituted for the word "Community" (subject to certain exceptions) in references to "Community treaties", "Community instrument", "Community obligation", "Community law", "Community legislation", etc.
Notes: (i) Rules and Regulations made under this Order (concerning patents and trade marks) are outside the scope of this work; (ii) the Department of Trade and Industry is now known as the Department for Business, Innovation & Skills.

[10.687]
1 Citation and commencement

This Order may be cited as the Department of Trade and Industry (Fees) Order 1988, and shall come into force on the day after the day on which it is made.

[10.688]
2 Interpretation

In this Order—
   (a)   "the Act" means the Finance (No 2) Act 1987;

         . . .

         "the 1985 Act" means the Companies Act 1985;
         "the 1986 Act" means the Insolvency Act 1986;

         . . .

   (b)   any reference to any provision of the 1985 Act includes any corresponding provision of any enactment repealed and re-enacted, with or without modification, by the 1985 Act.

NOTES

Definitions omitted outside the scope of this work.

[10.689]
3

(1)   In relation to the power of the Secretary of State under section 708 of the 1985 Act by regulations made by statutory instrument to require the payment to the registrar of companies of such fees as may be specified in the regulations in respect of—
   (a)   the performance by the registrar of such functions under the 1985 Act or the 1986 Act as may be so specified, including the receipt by him of any notice or other document which under either of those Acts is required to be given, delivered, sent or forwarded to him,
   (b)   the inspection of documents or other material kept by him under either of those Acts,
the functions specified for the purpose of section 102(3) of the Act shall be those specified in Part I of Schedule 1 hereto.

(2)   In relation to the power of the Secretary of State specified in paragraph (1) above, the matters specified for the purposes of section 102(4) of the Act shall be those specified in Part I of Schedule 2 hereto.

[10.690]

4

(1)   In relation to the power of the Secretary of State to fix fees under sections 53(5), 54(4) and 71(2) of the 1986 Act, the functions specified for the purposes of section 102(3) of the Act shall be those specified in Part I of Schedule 1 hereto.

(2)   In relation to the power of the Secretary of State specified in paragraph (1) above, the matters specified for the purposes of section 102(4) of the Act shall be those specified in Part I of Schedule 2 hereto.

5–8   (*Arts 5–7 outside the scope of this work; art 8 revoked by the Wireless Telegraphy Act 1998, s 7, Sch 2, Pt II.*)

[10.691]

9

(1)   In relation to the power of the Lord Chancellor to fix fees under section 133(1) of the Bankruptcy Act 1914, section 663(4) of the 1985 Act and sections 414 and 415 of the 1986 Act and in relation to the power of the Secretary of State to fix fees under sections 4 and 10 of the Insolvency Act 1985 and sections 392, 414 and 419 of the 1986 Act, the functions specified for the purposes of section 102(3) of the Act shall be those specified in Part VI of Schedule 1 hereto.

(2)   In relation to the power of the Lord Chancellor specified in paragraph (1) above and in relation to the power of the Secretary of State specified in that paragraph, the matters specified for the purposes of section 102(4) of the Act shall be those specified in Part I of Schedule 2 hereto.

[10]   (*Added by the Department of Trade and Industry (Fees) (Amendment) Order 1995, SI 1995/1294, art 2(b), as from 11 May 1995; revoked by the Financial Services and Markets Act 2000 (Consequential Amendments and Repeals) Order 2001, SI 2001/3649, art 388(1), (3), as from 1 December 2001.*)

SCHEDULES

SCHEDULE 1

PART I

[10.692]

1. Functions of the Secretary of State and the registrar of companies by virtue of the 1985 Act.

2. Functions of the registrar of companies by virtue of the 1986 Act.

3. Functions of inspectors appointed under Part XIV of the 1985 Act and of officers authorised under section 447 of that Act.

4. Functions of the Secretary of State in relation to anything done by the European Communities or any of their institutions with respect to company law, and the maintenance of relations with authorities and other persons both within the United Kingdom and abroad in respect of matters relating to company law.

5. Any other functions of the Secretary of State and the registrar of companies in relation to companies, including, without prejudice to the generality of the foregoing:—
  (a)   prosecution of offences under the 1985 Act and the taking of action with a view to ensuring compliance with any obligation arising under the 1985 Act;
  (b)   investigation of complaints relating to the conduct of the affairs of companies and consideration of requests for advice on questions of company law;
  (c)   review of the functioning of company law and consideration and development of proposals for legislation relating to companies;
  (d)   consideration, including in international fora, of accounting standards and auditing practices in relation to accounts of companies;
  (e)   the conduct of civil proceedings in relation to any of the functions specified in this part of this Schedule.

(*Pts II–V in so far as still in force, outside the scope of this work.*)

PART VI

[10.693]

16. Functions of official receivers as provisional liquidators, interim receivers of a debtor's property, receivers and managers of a bankrupt's estate, liquidators, trustees in bankruptcy and in their capacity as official receivers, under the Companies Act 1948, the 1985 Act, the

Bankruptcy Acts 1914 and 1926, the Powers of Criminal Courts Act 1973, the Insolvency Act 1976, the Insolvency Act 1985, the 1986 Act and the Company Directors Disqualification Act 1986 and subordinate legislation made under those enactments.

17. Functions of the Secretary of State, the Board of Trade and the Insolvency Practitioners Tribunal under Part V of the Companies Act 1948, Parts IX and XX of the 1985 Act, the Deeds of Arrangement Act 1914, the Bankruptcy Acts 1914 and 1926, the Insolvency Services (Accounting and Investment) Act 1970, the Insolvency Act 1976, the Insolvency Act 1985, the 1986 Act and the Company Directors Disqualification Act 1986 and subordinate legislation made under those enactments.

18. Functions of official receivers, the Secretary of State and the Board of Trade in relation to the investigation and prosecution or fraud or other malpractice in respect of the affairs of bankrupts and bodies in liquidation.

19. Functions of the Secretary of State in relation to the supervision of the operation of all the insolvency and related procedures set out in the Insolvency Act 1986, the Bankruptcy (Scotland) Act 1985, the other enactments set out in paragraphs 16 and 17 above and the Bankruptcy (Scotland) Act 1913, including the development and implementation of proposals for the modification or improvement of those procedures by primary or subordinate legislation and the consideration of and contribution to proposals for other United Kingdom legislation having an impact on those procedures.

20. Functions of the Secretary of State in relation to anything done by the European Communities or any of their institutions, or any international instruments, in relation to insolvency and the maintenance of relations with authorities and other persons both within the United Kingdom and abroad in respect of insolvency matters.

(Pt VII added by the Department of Trade and Industry (Fees) (Amendment) Order 1995, SI 1995/1294, art 2(c), as from 11 May 1995, and revoked by the Financial Services and Markets Act 2000 (Consequential Amendments and Repeals) Order 2001, SI 2001/3649, art 388(1), (4), as from 1 December 2001.)

SCHEDULE 2

PART I

[10.694]
1. All costs incurred by the Secretary of State, the registrar of companies, the Comptroller-General of Patents, Designs and Trade Marks, official receivers, the Board of Trade and the Insolvency Practitioners Tribunal which are directly attributable to the functions specified in Schedule 1 above.

2. That proportion of the costs, not falling within paragraph 1 above, incurred by, or on behalf of, any of the persons specified in paragraph 1 above, in relation to staff, equipment, premises, facilities and matters connected, whether directly or indirectly, therewith, being the proportion which falls to be attributed to any of the functions specified in Schedule 1 above.

3. A return on the resources employed in carrying out any of the functions specified in Schedule 1 above.

4. The allocation of a sum in respect of matters which would otherwise be covered by insurance, the allocation of a sum in respect of superannuation payments and provision for bad debts, in relation to any of the functions specified in Schedule 1 above.

5. The recovery of any past deficits incurred in relation to any of the functions specified in Schedule 1 above.

6. Amounts recovered in relation to any of the functions specified in Schedule 1 above other than from such fees as are referred to in this Order.

7. The allocation, over a period of years, of an initial or exceptional cost in relation to any of the functions specified in Schedule 1 above.

PART II

[10.695]
8. In respect of any function of any of the persons specified in paragraph 1 above consisting of the payment or remittance of any sum or amount, both the sum or amount in question and the cost incurred in effecting the payment or remittance.

EUROPEAN ECONOMIC INTEREST GROUPING REGULATIONS 1989

(SI 1989/638)

NOTES
Made: 10 April 1989.
Authority: European Communities Act 1972, s 2.
Commencement: 1 July 1989.
These Regulations are reproduced as amended by: the Deregulation and Contracting Out Act 1994; the Constitutional Reform Act 2005; the Companies Act 2006 (Consequential Amendments etc) Order 2008, SI 2008/948; the European Economic Interest Grouping (Amendment) Regulations 2009, SI 2009/2399.
References to "the European Community", "Community", etc: see the Treaty of Lisbon (Changes in Terminology) Order 2011, SI 2011/1043, which provides that (as from 22 April 2011) "EU" should be substituted for the word "Community" (subject to certain exceptions) in references to "Community treaties", "Community instrument", "Community obligation", "Community law", "Community legislation", etc.
Registrar of Companies: as to the contracting out of certain functions of the registrar of companies conferred by or under these regulations, see the Contracting Out (Functions in relation to the Registration of Companies) Order 1995, SI 1995/1013, arts 3, 4, Sch 1, paras 7, 8, Sch 2, para 3 at **[10.749]**, **[10.750]**, **[10.752]**, **[10.753]**.

ARRANGEMENT OF REGULATIONS

PART I
GENERAL

PART II
PROVISIONS RELATING TO ARTICLES 1–38 OF THE EC REGULATION

PART III
REGISTRATION ETC (ARTICLE 39 OF THE EC REGULATION)

PART IV
SUPPLEMENTAL PROVISIONS

SCHEDULES

PART I
GENERAL

[10.696]
1 Citation, commencement and extent

These Regulations, which extend to [the whole of the United Kingdom], may be cited as the European Economic Interest Grouping Regulations 1989 and shall come into force on 1st July 1989.

NOTES

Words in square brackets substituted by the European Economic Interest Grouping (Amendment) Regulations 2009, SI 2009/2399, regs 3, 4, as from 1 October 2009.

[10.697]
2 Interpretation

(1)   In these Regulations—
"the 1985 Act" means the Companies Act 1985;
["the 2006 Act" means the Companies Act 2006;]
["the Companies Acts" has the meaning given by section 2 of [the 2006 Act];]
"the contract" means the contract for the formation of an EEIG;
"the EC Regulation" means Council Regulation (EEC) No 2137/85 set out in Schedule 1 to these Regulations;
"EEIG" means a European Economic Interest Grouping being a grouping formed in pursuance of article 1 of the EC Regulation;
"officer", in relation to an EEIG, includes a manager, or any other person provided for in the contract as an organ of the EEIG; and
["the registrar" has the same meaning as in the Companies Acts (see section 1060 of the 2006 Act);]
and other expressions used in these Regulations and defined [for the purposes of the Companies Acts] or in relation to insolvency and winding up by the Insolvency Act 1986 [or, as regards Northern Ireland, by the Insolvency (Northern Ireland) Order 1989] have the meanings assigned to them by those provisions as if any reference to a company in any such definition were a reference to an EEIG.

[(2)   In these Regulations a reference to any Form is a reference to that Form as set out in Schedule 2 to these Regulations.]

(3)   In these Regulations, "certified translation" means a translation certified to be a correct translation—
(a)   if the translation was made in the United Kingdom, by
   (i)   a notary public in any part of the United Kingdom;
   (ii)   a solicitor (if the translation was made in Scotland), a solicitor of the Supreme Court of Judicature of England and Wales (if it was made in England or Wales), or a [solicitor of the Court of Judicature of Northern Ireland] (if it was made in Northern Ireland); or
   (iii)   a person certified by a person mentioned above to be known to him to be competent to translate the document into English; or
(b)   if the translation was made outside the United Kingdom, by—
   (i)   a notary public;
   (ii)   a person authorised in the place where the translation was made to administer an oath;
   (iii)   any of the British officials mentioned in section 6 of the Commissioners for Oaths Act 1889;
   (iv)   a person certified by a person mentioned in sub-paragraph (i), (ii) or (iii) of this paragraph to be known to him to be competent to translate the document into English.

NOTES

Para (1) is amended as follows:

Definition "the Companies Acts" inserted, and words in the penultimate pair of square brackets substituted, by the Companies Act 2006 (Consequential Amendments etc) Order 2008, SI 2008/948, art 3(1), Sch 1, Pt 2, para 161, as from 6 April 2008.

Definition "the 2006 Act" inserted, words in square brackets in the definition "the Companies Acts" substituted, definition "the registrar" substituted, and words in final pair of square brackets inserted, by the European Economic Interest Grouping (Amendment) Regulations 2009, SI 2009/2399, regs 3, 5(1), (2), as from 1 October 2009.

Para (2): substituted by SI 2009/2399, regs 3, 5(1), (3), as from 1 October 2009.

Para (3): words in square brackets substituted by the Constitutional Reform Act 2005, s 59, Sch 11, Pt 2, para 5, as from 1 October 2009.

Supreme Court of England and Wales: the Supreme Court of England and Wales is renamed the Senior Courts of England and Wales; see the Constitutional Reform Act 2005, s 59(1) (as from 1 October 2009).

PART II
PROVISIONS RELATING TO ARTICLES 1–38 OF THE EC REGULATION

[10.698]
3   Legal personality (Article 1(3) of the EC Regulation)
From the date of registration of an EEIG in [the United Kingdom] mentioned in a certificate given under regulation 9(5) below the EEIG shall, subject to regulation 11 below, be a body corporate by the name contained in the contract.

NOTES
Words in square brackets substituted by the European Economic Interest Grouping (Amendment) Regulations 2009, SI 2009/2399, regs 3, 6, as from 1 October 2009.

[10.699]
4   Transfer of official address (Article 14 of the EC Regulation)
(1)   Notice of any proposal to transfer the official address of an EEIG registered in [the United Kingdom] to any other place shall, where such transfer would result in a change in the law applicable to the contract under article 2 of the EC Regulation, be filed at the registry where the EEIG was registered by delivery of a notice in [Form EE MP01] in pursuance of [regulation 13(1B)] below.

(2)   Where the registrar, being the competent authority within the meaning of article 14(4) of the EC Regulation, receives a notice under paragraph (1) above and within the period of two months beginning with its publication in the Gazette under regulation 15(1) below opposes that transfer on the grounds of public interest, that transfer shall not take effect.

NOTES
Para (1): words in square brackets substituted by the European Economic Interest Grouping (Amendment) Regulations 2009, SI 2009/2399, regs 3, 7, as from 1 October 2009.

[10.700]
5   Managers (Article 19(2) of the EC Regulation)
(1)   A manager of an EEIG registered in [the United Kingdom] may be a legal person other than a natural person, on condition that it designates one or more natural persons to represent it and notice of particulars of each such person is sent to the registrar in [Form EE AP02] as though he were a manager.

(2)   Any natural person designated under paragraph (1) above shall be subject to the same liabilities as if he himself were a manager.

[(3)   The following must be delivered to the registrar in accordance with the provisions of regulation 13(1B) below—
  (a)   notice of appointment of any manager; and
  (b)   in respect of each manager, the particulars specified in section 163 of the 2006 Act (if the manager is an individual) or section 164 of that Act (if the manager is not).

(3A)   Subsections (2) to (4) of section 163 of the 2006 Act apply for the purposes of paragraph (3)(b) above as they apply for the purposes of that section.

(3B)   For the purposes of paragraph (3)(b) above, a person's service address may be stated to be "The EEIG's official address"]

(4)   . . .

NOTES
Para (1): words in square brackets substituted by the European Economic Interest Grouping (Amendment) Regulations 2009, SI 2009/2399, regs 3, 8(1), (2), as from 1 October 2009.
Paras (3)–(3B): substituted by SI 2009/2399, regs 3, 8(1), (3), as from 1 October 2009 (see further the final note below).
Para (4): revoked by SI 2009/2399, regs 3, 8(1), (4), as from 1 October 2009.
Note: the European Economic Interest Grouping (Amendment) Regulations 2009, SI 2009/2399, reg 8(5)–(8) provides as follows—

  "(5)   In the case of an European Economic Interest Grouping ("EEIG") which, immediately before 1st October 2009, was registered in the United Kingdom, the relevant existing address of a manager of the EEIG is deemed, on and after that date, to be a service address.
  (6)   The "relevant existing address" is the address which, immediately before 1st October 2009, was the usual residential address notified to the registrar under regulation 5(3)(a) of the European Economic Interest Grouping Regulations 1989, as they had effect before that date.
  (7)   Any notification of a change of the relevant existing address occurring before 1st October 2009 that is received by the registrar on or after that date is treated as being or, as the case may be, including notification of a change of service address.
  (8)   The registrar may make such changes to the EEIG register as the registrar considers appropriate in consequence of the operation of paragraphs (5) to (7).
  In this paragraph "the EEIG register" has the meaning given by regulation 18(4) of the European Economic Interest Grouping Regulations 1989.".

[10.701]
6 Cessation of membership (Article 28(1) of the EC Regulation)

For the purposes of national law on liquidation, winding up, insolvency or cessation of payments, a member of an EEIG registered under these Regulations shall cease to be a member if—
- (a) in the case of an individual—
  - (i) a bankruptcy order has been made against him in England and Wales [or Northern Ireland]; or
  - (ii) sequestration of his estate has been awarded by the court in Scotland under the Bankruptcy (Scotland) Act 1985;
- (b) in the case of a partnership—
  - (i) a winding up order has been made against the partnership in England and Wales [or Northern Ireland];
  - [(ii) a bankruptcy order has been made against each of the partnership's members in England and Wales on a bankruptcy petition presented under Article 11(1) of the Insolvent Partnerships Order 1994;
  - (iia) a bankruptcy order has been made against each of the partnership's members in Northern Ireland on a bankruptcy petition presented under Article 11(1) of the Insolvent Partnerships Order (Northern Ireland) 1995; or]
  - (iii) sequestration of the estate of the partnership has been awarded by the court in Scotland under the Bankruptcy (Scotland) Act 1985;
- (c) in the case of a company, the company goes into liquidation in [the United Kingdom]; or
- (d) in the case of any legal person or partnership, it is otherwise wound up or otherwise ceases to exist after the conclusion of winding up or insolvency.

NOTES

Words in first and second pairs of square brackets inserted, and other words in square brackets substituted, by the European Economic Interest Grouping (Amendment) Regulations 2009, SI 2009/2399, regs 3, 9, as from 1 October 2009.

[10.702]
7 Competent authority (Articles 32(1) and (3) and 38 of the EC Regulation)

[(1) The competent authority for the purposes of making an application to the court under Article 32(1) of the EC Regulation (winding up of EEIG in certain circumstances) shall be—
- (a) in the case of an EEIG whose official address is in Northern Ireland, the Department of Enterprise, Trade and Investment in Northern Ireland;
- (b) in any other case, the Secretary of State.]

(2) The court may, on an application by [the appropriate authority], order the winding up of an EEIG which has its official address in [the United Kingdom], if the EEIG acts contrary to the public interest and it is expedient in the public interest that the EEIG should be wound up and the court is of the opinion that it is just and equitable for it to be so.

[(2A) In paragraph (2) above "the appropriate authority" means—
- (a) in the case of an EEIG whose official address is in Great Britain, the Secretary of State;
- (b) in the case of an EEIG whose official address is in Northern Ireland, the Department of Enterprise, Trade and Investment in Northern Ireland.]

(3) The court, on an application by [the appropriate authority], shall be the competent authority for the purposes of prohibiting under article 38 of the EC Regulation any activity carried on in [the United Kingdom] by an EEIG where such an activity is in contravention of the public interest there.

[(4) In paragraph (3) above "the appropriate authority" means—
- (a) in the case of any activity carried on in Great Britain, the Secretary of State;
- (b) in the case of any activity carried on in Northern Ireland, the Department of Enterprise, Trade and Investment in Northern Ireland.]

NOTES

Para (1): substituted by the European Economic Interest Grouping (Amendment) Regulations 2009, SI 2009/2399, regs 3, 10(1), (2), as from 1 October 2009.
Paras (2), (3): words in square brackets substituted by SI 2009/2399, regs 3, 10(1), (3), (5), as from 1 October 2009.
Paras (2A), (4): inserted and added respectively by SI 2009/2399, regs 3, 10(1), (4), (6), as from 1 October 2009.

[10.703]
8 Winding up and conclusion of liquidation (Articles 35 and 36 of the EC Regulation)

(1) Where an EEIG is wound up as an unregistered company under Part V of the Insolvency Act 1986, the provisions of Part V shall apply in relation to the EEIG as if any reference in that Act . . . to a director or past director of a company included a reference to a manager of the EEIG and any other person who has or has had control or management of the EEIG's business and with the modification that in section 221(1) after the words "all the provisions" there shall be added the words "of Council Regulation (EEC) No 2137/85 and".

[(1A) Where an EEIG is wound up as an unregistered company under Part 6 of the Insolvency (Northern Ireland) Order 1989, the provisions of Part 6 shall apply in relation to the EEIG as if—

Part 10   Miscellaneous other SIs

(a)   any reference in that Order to a director or past director of a company included a reference to a manager of the EEIG and any other person who has or has had control or management of the EEIG's business; and

(b)   in Article 185(1) after "all the provisions" there were inserted "of Council Regulation (EEC) No 2137/85 and".]

(2)   At the end of the period of three months beginning with the day of receipt by the registrar of a notice of the conclusion of the liquidation of an EEIG, the EEIG shall be dissolved.

NOTES

Para (1): words omitted revoked by the Companies Act 2006 (Consequential Amendments etc) Order 2008, SI 2008/948, art 3(1), Sch 1, Pt 2, para 162, as from 6 April 2008.

Para (1A): inserted by the European Economic Interest Grouping (Amendment) Regulations 2009, SI 2009/2399, regs 3, 11, as from 1 October 2009.

PART III
REGISTRATION ETC (ARTICLE 39 OF THE EC REGULATION)

[10.704]
9   [Registration of EEIG whose official address is in the United Kingdom]

(1)   The registrar for the purposes of registration of an EEIG in [the United Kingdom] where its official address is in [the United Kingdom] shall be the registrar within the meaning of [the Companies Acts] and the contract shall be delivered—

(a)   to [the registrar of companies for England and Wales], if the contract states that the official address of the EEIG is to be situated in England and Wales, or that it is to be situated in Wales;   . . .

(b)   to [the registrar of companies for Scotland], if the contract states that the official address of the EEIG is to be situated in Scotland;

[(c)   to the registrar of companies for Northern Ireland, if the contract states that the official address of the EEIG is to be situated in Northern Ireland.]

(2)   With the contract there shall be delivered a registration form in [Form EE FM01] containing a statement of the names and the particulars set out in article 5 of the EC Regulation.

(3)   The registrar shall not register an EEIG under this regulation unless he is satisfied that all the requirements of these Regulations and of the EC Regulation in respect of registration and of matters precedent and incidental to it have been complied with but he may accept a declaration in [Form EE FM01] as sufficient evidence of compliance.

(4)   Subject to paragraph (3) above, the registrar shall retain the contract, and any certified translation, delivered to him under this regulation and register the EEIG.

(5)   On the registration of an EEIG the registrar shall give a certificate that the EEIG has been registered stating the date of registration.

(6)   The certificate may be signed by the registrar, or authenticated by his official seal.

(7)   A certificate of registration given in respect of an EEIG under this regulation is conclusive evidence that the requirements of these Regulations and of the EC Regulation in respect of registration and of matters precedent and incidental to it have been complied with, and that the EEIG is an organisation authorised to be registered, and is duly registered, under these Regulations.

(8)   Where an EEIG is to be registered with the contract written in any language other than English, the contract to be delivered under paragraph (1) above may be in the other language provided that it is accompanied by a certified translation into English.

(9)   Where an EEIG has published a proposal to transfer its official address to a place in [the United Kingdom] under article 14(1) of the EC Regulation, the registrar responsible for the registration of the EEIG with the new official address shall, where the transfer of the official address has not been opposed under paragraph (4) of that article, register the EEIG with its new official address on receipt of a registration form in [Form EE FM01] containing—

(a)   evidence of the publication of the transfer proposal; and

(b)   a statement that no competent authority has opposed the transfer under article 14(4) of the EC Regulation.

(10)   Any communication or notice may be addressed to an EEIG where its official address is in [the United Kingdom] at its official address stated on [Form EE FM01] or in the case of any change in the situation of that address at any new official address stated on [Form EE MP01].

NOTES

All amendments to this regulation were made by the European Economic Interest Grouping (Amendment) Regulations 2009, SI 2009/2399, regs 3, 12, as from 1 October 2009.

[10.705]
10   Prohibition on registration of certain names

[(1)   An EEIG shall not be registered in the United Kingdom under regulation 9 above by a name which includes—

(a)   any of the words or abbreviations specified in inverted commas in paragraph 1 of Schedule 2 to the Company and Business Names (Miscellaneous Provisions) Regulations 2009;

(b)   any word or abbreviation specified as similar to a word or abbreviation falling within sub-paragraph (a) above, within the meaning of paragraph 2 of that Schedule;

(c)   any of the expressions or abbreviations specified in inverted commas in sub-paragraphs (a) to (j) and (l) to (v) of paragraph 3 of that Schedule;

(d)   any expression or abbreviation specified as similar to an expression or abbreviation falling within sub-paragraph (c) above, within the meaning of paragraph 4 of that Schedule.

(1A)   The provisions specified in paragraph (1B) below apply to EEIGs registered or in the process of being registered under these Regulations, as if they were companies formed and registered under the 2006 Act or in the process of being registered under the 2006 Act.

(1B)   The provisions are—

(a)   section 53 of the 2006 Act (prohibited names);

(b)   section 54 of that Act (names suggesting connection with government or public authority);

(c)   section 55 of that Act (other sensitive words or expressions);

(d)   section 56 of that Act (duty to seek comments of government department or other specified body) and any regulations made by virtue of that section;

(e)   section 57(3) of that Act (permitted characters etc);

(f)   section 66(1) of that Act (name not to be the same as another in the index) and any regulations made under that section.

(1C)   The provisions specified in paragraph (1B) above have effect with the following modifications—

(a)   any reference to the 2006 Act is to be read as including a reference to these Regulations;

(b)   the reference in section 56(4)(a) to a director or secretary of the company is to be read as a reference to a manager of the EEIG;

(c)   any requirement imposed by regulations under section 66 to disregard the words "European Economic Interest Grouping" or the abbreviation "EEIG" where those words or that abbreviation appears in a name—

     (i)   is to apply wherever in the name those words or that abbreviation appears; and

     (ii)   is to be taken to include a requirement to disregard the authorised equivalents of those words or that abbreviation in official languages of the Economic Community other than English.

(2)   Schedule 3 to these Regulations sets out the authorised equivalents referred to in paragraph (1C)(c)(ii) above.]

NOTES

Commencement: 1 October 2009.

Substituted by the European Economic Interest Grouping (Amendment) Regulations 2009, SI 2009/2399, regs 3, 13, as from 1 October 2009.

[10.706]
11   Change of name

(1)   . . .

[(1A)   Sections 67(1) and 68 of the 2006 Act (power to direct change of name in case of similarity to existing name) apply to EEIGs, and their establishments, registered under these Regulations, as if they were companies formed and registered under the 2006 Act.

(1B)   In the application of section 68 of the 2006 Act to EEIGs and their establishments—

(a)   subsection (5) is to be read as if—

     (i)   the reference in paragraph (b) to an officer of the company were a reference to an officer of the EEIG, within the meaning of these Regulations; and

     (ii)   the second sentence were omitted;

(b)   subsection (6) is to be read as if the reference to a daily default fine were omitted.]

[(2)   Paragraphs (2A) and (2B) below apply where the registrar receives notice of a change of an EEIG's name.

(2A)   If the registrar is satisfied—

(a)   that the new name complies with the requirements of regulation 10(1) and the provisions applied by regulation 10(1A) above, and

(b)   that any requirements applying under or by virtue of these Regulations with respect to a change of name are complied with,

the registrar shall enter the new name on the register in place of the former name.

(2B)   On the registration of the new name, the registrar shall issue a certificate of registration altered to meet the circumstances of the case.

(3)   A change of an EEIG's name has effect from the date on which the new certificate of registration is issued.

(4)   The change does not affect any rights or obligations of the EEIG or render defective any legal proceedings by or against it.

(5)   Any legal proceedings that might have been continued or commenced against it by its former name may be continued or commenced against it by its new name.]

NOTES

Para (1): revoked by the European Economic Interest Grouping (Amendment) Regulations 2009, SI 2009/2399, regs 3, 14(1), (2), as from 1 October 2009.

Paras (1A), (1B): inserted by SI 2009/2399, regs 3, 14(1), (3), as from 1 October 2009.

Paras (2A)–(5): substituted (for the original paras (2), (3)) by SI 2009/2399, regs 3, 14(1), (4), as from 1 October 2009.

[10.707]
12   Registration of establishment of EEIG whose official address is outside the United Kingdom

(1)   The registrar for the purposes of registration under this regulation of an EEIG establishment situated in [the United Kingdom] where the EEIG's official address is outside the United Kingdom shall be the registrar within the meaning of [the Companies Acts].

(2)   For the purposes of registration under paragraph (1) above there shall be delivered, within one month of the establishment becoming so situated at any place in [the United Kingdom], to the registrar at the registration office in England and Wales[, Scotland or Northern Ireland], according to where the establishment is situated, a certified copy of the contract together with—

   (a)   a certified translation into English of the contract and other documents and particulars to be filed with it under article 10 of the EC Regulation if the contract and other documents and particulars, or any part thereof, are not in English; and

   (b)   a registration form in [Form EE FM02] containing a statement of the names and particulars set out in articles 5 and 10 of the EC Regulation.

(3)   Paragraph (2) above shall not apply where an establishment is already registered in [the United Kingdom] under paragraph (1) above.

(4)   The registrar shall not register an EEIG establishment under this regulation unless he is satisfied that all the requirements of these Regulations and of the EC Regulation in respect of registration and of matters precedent and incidental to it have been complied with but he may accept a declaration in [Form EE FM02] as sufficient evidence of compliance.

(5)   Subject to paragraph (4) above, the registrar shall retain the copy of the contract, and any certified translation, delivered to him under paragraph (2) above and register the EEIG establishment.

(6)   Any communication or notice may be addressed to an EEIG where its official address is outside the United Kingdom at any of its establishments in [the United Kingdom].

(7)   Regulation 10 above shall apply to an EEIG establishment to be registered under this regulation as it applies to an EEIG to be registered under regulation 9.

(8)   If an EEIG fails to comply with any provision of paragraph (2) above, the EEIG, and any officer of it who intentionally authorises or permits the default, is guilty of an offence and liable on summary conviction to a fine not exceeding level 3 on the standard scale and if the failure to comply with any such provision continues after conviction, the EEIG and any such officer shall be guilty of a further offence of failure to comply with that provision and shall be liable to be proceeded against and punished accordingly.

NOTES

All words in square brackets in this regulation were substituted by the European Economic Interest Grouping (Amendment) Regulations 2009, SI 2009/2399, regs 3, 15, as from 1 October 2009.

[10.708]
[12A   Registration under alternative name

(1)   This regulation applies to an EEIG—

   (a)   whose official address is outside the United Kingdom, and

   (b)   which has an establishment that is registered or is in the process of being registered under regulation 12 above.

(2)   The EEIG may at any time deliver to the registrar for registration a statement in Form EE NM01 specifying a name, other than its grouping name, under which it proposes to carry on business in the United Kingdom.

(3)   An EEIG that has registered an alternative name under paragraph (2) may at any time deliver to the registrar for registration a statement in Form EE NM02 specifying a different name under which it proposes to carry on business in the United Kingdom (which may be its grouping name or a further alternative) in substitution for the name previously registered.

(4)   The alternative name for the time being registered under this regulation is treated for all purposes of the law applying in the United Kingdom as the EEIG's grouping name.

(5)   This does not—

    (a)   affect the references in this regulation to the EEIG's grouping name,

    (b)   affect any rights or obligations of the EEIG, or

    (c)   render defective any legal proceedings by or against the EEIG.

(6)   Any legal proceedings that might have been continued or commenced against the EEIG by its grouping name, or any name previously registered under this regulation, may be continued or commenced against it by its name for the time being so registered.

(7)   Any reference in this regulation to the "grouping name" of an EEIG is a reference to the name of the EEIG referred to in the contract for its formation.]

NOTES

Commencement: 1 October 2009.

Inserted by the European Economic Interest Grouping (Amendment) Regulations 2009, SI 2009/2399, regs 3, 16, as from 1 October 2009.

[10.709]
13 Filing of documents

[(1)   This regulation applies to the documents and particulars which—

    (a)   are referred to in paragraphs (a) to (j) of Article 7 of the EC Regulation, and

    (b)   are required to be filed under that Article in the United Kingdom.

(1A)   The documents and particulars to which this regulation applies shall be filed—

    (a)   in the case of an EEIG whose official address is in the United Kingdom, within 15 days of the event to which the document in question relates;

    (b)   in the case of an EEIG whose official address is outside the United Kingdom, within 30 days of such event.

(1B)   In the case of each paragraph listed in the first column of Table 1 below, the documents and particulars referred to in that paragraph shall be filed by delivering to the registrar for registration a notice which—

    (a)   is in the Form specified in the second column of that Table, and

    (b)   contains the matters specified in the third column of that Table.

Table 1

Relevant paragraph of Article 7	Form in which notice to be given	Content of notice
Where official address of EEIG is in the United Kingdom		
Paragraphs (a), (c) and (e) to (j)	EE MP01	The documents and particulars referred to in Form EE MP01
Paragraph (b)	EE MP02	Notice of the setting up or closure of an establishment of an EEIG in the United Kingdom
Paragraph (d)	EE AP01 (in the case of any manager who is an individual) EE AP02 (in the case of any manager who is not)	The following details (the "managerial details")— (a) the names of the managers; (b) the particulars referred to in regulation 5(3) above; (c) particulars of whether the managers may act alone or must act jointly
Paragraph (d)	EE CH01 (in the case of any manager who is an individual) EE CH02 (in the case of any manager who is not)	Any changes in the managerial details
Paragraph (d)	EE TM01	Notice of the termination of any manager's appointment

Relevant paragraph of Article 7	Form in which notice to be given	Content of notice
Where official address of EEIG is outside the United Kingdom		
Paragraphs (a) and (c) to (j)	EE MP01	The documents and particulars referred to in Form EE MP01
Paragraph (b)	EE MP02	Notice of— (a) the setting up of an establishment of an EEIG in the United Kingdom, in any case where an establishment of the EEIG is already registered in the United Kingdom under regulation 12(1) above, or (b) the closure of an establishment of an EEIG in the United Kingdom

(1C)   Any notice that is delivered to the registrar in accordance with paragraph (1B) above shall be accompanied by a certified translation into English of any documents and particulars to which the notice relates, or any part of those documents and particulars, which are not in English.]

(2)   The registrar shall retain the documents and particulars and any certified translation delivered to him under this regulation.

(3)   If an EEIG fails to comply with any provision of [this regulation], the EEIG, and any officer of it who intentionally authorises or permits the default, is guilty of an offence and liable on summary conviction to a fine not exceeding level 3 on the standard scale and if the failure to comply with any such provision continues after conviction, the EEIG and any such officer shall be guilty of a further offence of failure to comply with that provision and shall be liable to be proceeded against and punished accordingly.

NOTES

Paras (1)–(1C): substituted (for the original para (1)) by the European Economic Interest Grouping (Amendment) Regulations 2009, SI 2009/2399, regs 3, 17(1), (2), as from 1 October 2009.

Para (3): words in square brackets substituted by SI 2009/2399, regs 3, 17(1), (3), as from 1 October 2009.

[10.710]
14   Inspection of documents

Any person may—
  (a)   inspect any document or particulars kept by the registrar under these Regulations or a copy thereof; and
  (b)   require the registrar to deliver or send by post to him a copy or extract of any such document or particulars or any part thereof.

[10.711]
15   Publication of documents in the Gazette and Official Journal of the Communities

(1)   The registrar shall cause to be published in the Gazette—
  (a)   the documents and particulars issued or received by him under these Regulations and referred to in article 8(a) and (b) of the EC Regulation; and
  (b)   in the case of those documents and particulars referred to in article 7(b) to (j) of the EC Regulation a notice (stating in the notice the name of the EEIG, the description of the documents or particulars and the date of receipt).

(2)   The registrar shall forward to the Office for Official Publications of the European Communities the information referred to in article 11 of the EC Regulation within one month of the publication of the relevant documents and particulars in the Gazette under paragraph (1) above.

[10.712]
16   EEIG identification

(1)   If an EEIG fails to comply with article 25 of the EC Regulation it is guilty of an offence and liable on summary conviction to a fine not exceeding level 3 on the standard scale.

(2)   If an officer of an EEIG or a person on its behalf issues or authorises the issue of any letter, order form or similar document not complying with the requirements of article 25 of the EC Regulation, he is guilty of an offence and liable on summary conviction to a fine not exceeding level 3 on the standard scale.

PART IV
SUPPLEMENTAL PROVISIONS

17   *(Revoked by the European Economic Interest Grouping (Amendment) Regulations 2009, SI 2009/2399, regs 3, 18, as from 1 October 2009.)*

[10.713]
[18   Application of provisions of the Companies Acts

(1)   The provisions of the Companies Acts specified in Schedule 4 to these Regulations apply to EEIGs, and their establishments, registered or in the process of being registered under these Regulations, as if they were companies formed and registered or in the process of being registered under [the 2006 Act].

(2)   The provisions applied have effect with the following adaptations—
- (a)   any reference to the 1985 Act[, the 2006 Act] or the Companies Acts includes a reference to these Regulations;
- (b)   any reference to a registered office includes a reference to an official address;
- [(ba) any reference to the register is to be read as a reference to the EEIG register;
- (bb) any reference to an officer of a company is to be read as a reference to an officer of an EEIG, within the meaning of these Regulations;]
- (c)   any reference to a daily default fine shall be omitted.

(3)   The provisions applied also have effect subject to any limitations mentioned in relation to those provisions in that Schedule.]

[(4)   In this regulation "the EEIG register" means—
- (a)   the documents and particulars required to be kept by the registrar under these Regulations; and
- (b)   the records falling within section 1080(1) of the 2006 Act which relate to EEIGs or their establishments.

(5)   This regulation does not affect the application of provisions of the Companies Acts to EEIGs or their establishments otherwise than by virtue of this regulation.]

NOTES
Commencement: 6 April 2008.
Substituted by the Companies Act 2006 (Consequential Amendments etc) Order 2008, SI 2008/948, art 3(1), Sch 1, Pt 2, para 163, as from 6 April 2008.
Para (1): words in square brackets substituted by the European Economic Interest Grouping (Amendment) Regulations 2009, SI 2009/2399, regs 3, 19(1), (2), as from 1 October 2009.
Para (2): words in square brackets inserted by SI 2009/2399, regs 3, 19(1), (3), as from 1 October 2009.
Paras (4), (5): added by SI 2009/2399, regs 3, 19(1), (43), as from 1 October 2009.

[10.714]
19   [Application of insolvency legislation]

(1)   Part III of the Insolvency Act 1986 shall apply to EEIGs, and their establishments, registered under these Regulations [in England and Wales or Scotland], as if they were companies registered under [the 2006 Act].

[(1A)   Part 4 of the Insolvency (Northern Ireland) Order 1989 shall apply to EEIGs, and their establishments, registered under these Regulations in Northern Ireland, as if they were companies registered under the 2006 Act.]

(2)   Section 120 of the Insolvency Act 1986 shall apply to an EEIG, and its establishments, registered under these Regulations in Scotland, as if it were a company registered in Scotland the paid-up or credited as paid-up share capital of which did not exceed £120,000 and as if in that section any reference to the Company's registered office were a reference to the official address of the EEIG.

NOTES
Regulation heading: substituted by the European Economic Interest Grouping (Amendment) Regulations 2009, SI 2009/2399, regs 3, 20(1), (4), as from 1 October 2009.
Para (1): words in first pair of square brackets inserted, and words in second pair of square brackets substituted, by SI 2009/2399, regs 3, 20(1), (2), as from 1 October 2009.
Para (1A): inserted by SI 2009/2399, regs 3, 20(1), (3), as from 1 October 2009.

[10.715]
20   [Application of legislation relating to disqualification of directors]

[(1)]   Where an EEIG is wound up as an unregistered company under Part V of the Insolvency Act 1986, the provisions of sections 1, 2, [4 to 7, 8, 9, 10, 11], 12(2), 15 to 17, 20 and 22 of, and Schedule 1 to, the Company Directors Disqualification Act 1986 shall apply in relation to the EEIG as if any reference to a director or past director of a company included a reference to a manager of the EEIG and any other person who has or has had control or management of the EEIG's business and the EEIG were a company as defined by section 22(2)(b) of that Act.

Part 10   Miscellaneous other SIs

[(2)   Where an EEIG is wound up as an unregistered company under Part 6 of the Insolvency (Northern Ireland) Order 1989 the provisions of Articles 2(2) to (6), 3, 5, 7 to 11, 13, 14, 15, 16(2), 19 to 21 and 23 of, and Schedule 1 to, the Company Directors Disqualification (Northern Ireland) Order 2002 shall apply in relation to the EEIG as if—

(a)   any reference to a director or past director of a company included a reference to a manager of the EEIG and any other person who has or has had control or management of the EEIG's business; and

(b)   the EEIG were a company as defined by Article 2(2) of that Order.]

NOTES

Regulation heading: substituted by the European Economic Interest Grouping (Amendment) Regulations 2009, SI 2009/2399, regs 3, 21(1), (5), as from 1 October 2009.

Para (1): numbered as such, and words in square brackets substituted, by SI 2009/2399, regs 3, 21(1)–(3), as from 1 October 2009.

Para (2): added by SI 2009/2399, regs 3, 21(1), (4), as from 1 October 2009.

[10.716]
21   Penalties

Nothing in these Regulations shall create any new criminal offence punishable to a greater extent than is permitted under paragraph 1(1)(d) of Schedule 2 to the European Communities Act 1972.

SCHEDULES

SCHEDULE 1

(Sch 1 reproduces the text of Council Regulation (EEC) No 2137/85 (as to which, see **[11.1]**).)

SCHEDULE 2
FORMS RELATING TO EEIGS

[10.716A]

NOTES

This sets out the forms to be used in connection with the Regulations. The forms are not reproduced here but details are given in the table below. Sch 2 was substituted by the European Economic Interest Grouping (Amendment) Regulations 2009, SI 2009/2399, regs 3, 22, Schedule, as from 1 October 2009. For transitional provisions see reg 2 of the 2009 Regulations (Transitional provision relating to forms and other documents to be delivered to registrar) which provides that in so far as relating to forms and other documents required to be delivered to the registrar, the amendments made by the 2009 Regulations do not have effect in any case where the obligation to deliver the form or other document arose before 1 October 2009.

Form No	Description
EE FM01	Statement of name, official address, members, objects and duration for EEIG whose official address is in the UK
EE FM02	Statement of name, establishment address in the UK and members of an EEIG whose official address is outside the UK
EE AP01	Appointment of manager of an EEIG where the official address of the EEIG is in the UK
EE AP02	Appointment of corporate manager of an EEIG where the official address is in the UK
EE CH01	Change of manager's details of an EEIG where the official address of the EEIG is in the UK
EE CH02	Change of corporate manager's details of an EEIG where the official address of the EEIG is in the UK
EE TM01	Termination of appointment of manager of an EEIG where the official address is in the UK
EE MP01	Notice of documents and particulars required to be filed for an EEIG
EE MP02	Notice of setting up or closure of an establishment of an EEIG
EE NM01	Statement of name, other than registered name, under which an EEIG whose official address is outside the UK proposes to carry on business in the UK
EE NM02	Statement of name, other than registered name, under which an EEIG whose official address is outside the UK, proposes to carry on business in substitution for name previously approved

SCHEDULE 3
AUTHORISED EQUIVALENTS IN OTHER COMMUNITY OFFICIAL LANGUAGES OF "EUROPEAN ECONOMIC INTEREST GROUPING" AND "EEIG"
Regulation 10(2)

[10.717]

DANISH:	Europaeiske Økonomiske Firmagruppe (EØFG)
DUTCH:	Europese Economische Samenwerkingsverbanden (EESV)
FRENCH:	Groupement Européen d'intérêt économique (GEIE)
GERMAN:	Europäische Wirtschaftliche Interessenvereinigung (EWIV)
GREEK:	Ευρωπαικος ομιλος οικονομικου σκοπου (ΕΟΟΣ) (written phonetically in letters of the Latin alphabet as "Evropaikos omilos economicou skopou (EOOS)")
IRISH:	Grupail Eorpach um Leas Eacnamaioch (GELE)
ITALIAN:	Gruppo Europeo di Interesse Economico (GEIE)
PORTUGUESE:	Agrupamento Europeu de Interesse Econômico (AEIE)
SPANISH:	Agrupación Europea de Interés Económico (AEIE)

SCHEDULE 4
PROVISIONS OF [COMPANIES ACTS] APPLYING TO EEIGS AND THEIR ESTABLISHMENTS
Regulation 18

[PART 1
PROVISIONS OF COMPANIES ACT 1985]

[10.718]

1–4. . . .

5. [section 432(1), (2) and (2A)].

6. section 434 so far as it refers to inspectors appointed under section 432 as applied by regulation 18 above and this Schedule.

7. section 436 so far as it refers to inspectors appointed under section 432, and to section 434, as applied by regulation 18 above and this Schedule.

8. sections [437 and 439].

9. section 441 so far as it applies to inspectors appointed under section 432 as applied by regulation 18 above and this Schedule.

10. [sections 447 and 447A] . . .

11. sections 448 to 452.

12. . . .

13. Part XVIII relating to floating charges and receivers (Scotland).

14–24. . . .

NOTES

The words in square brackets in the Schedule heading were substituted, the Part 1 heading was inserted, and paras 12, 24 were revoked, by the Companies Act 2006 (Consequential Amendments etc) Order 2008, SI 2008/948, art 3(1), Sch 1, Pt 2, para 164(1)–(4), as from 6 April 2008.

All other amendments were made by the European Economic Interest Grouping (Amendment) Regulations 2009, SI 2009/2399, regs 3, 23(1), (2), as from 1 October 2009.

[PART 2
PROVISIONS OF COMPANIES ACT 2006

[10.719]
[**25.** Section 75 (provision of misleading information etc), as if the second sentence of subsection (5) were omitted.

26. Part 25 (company charges).

27. Section 993 (offence of fraudulent trading).

28. Section 1066(2) to (4) (registered numbers).

29. Section 1081 (annotation of the register), as if—
(a)   after subsection (1) there were inserted—

"(1A)   Where it appears to the registrar that material on the register is misleading or confusing, the registrar may place a note in the register containing such information as appears to the registrar to be necessary to remedy, as far as possible, the misleading or confusing nature of the material.", and

(b)   subsection (5) were omitted.

30. Section 1082 (allocation of unique identifiers), as if—
(a)   the reference in subsection (1)(a) to a director of a company were a reference to a manager of an EEIG, and
(b)   paragraphs (b) and (c) of subsection (1) were omitted.

31. Section 1084 (records relating to companies that have been dissolved etc), as if subsection (4) were omitted.

32. In section 1087 (material not available for public inspection)—
(a)   subsection (1)(a) and (d), and
(b)   subsections (2) and (3), so far as relating to material falling within paragraph (a) or (d) of subsection (1).

33. Section 1089(1) (form of application for inspection or copy), as if—
(a)   the reference to inspection under section 1085 were a reference to inspection under regulation 14(a) above, and
(b)   the reference to a copy under section 1086 were a reference to a copy or extract under regulation 14(b) above.

34. Section 1090(4) (power to determine form and manner in which copies to be provided), as if—
(a)   for "the preceding provisions of this section" there were substituted "Article 39(1) of Council Regulation (EEC) No 2137/85", and
(b)   the reference to copies being provided were a reference to copies or extracts being provided under regulation 14(b) above.

35. Section 1091 (certification of copies as accurate), as if—
(a)   any reference in that section to copies were a reference to copies or extracts,
(b)   any reference to section 1086 were a reference to regulation 14(b) above,
(c)   subsections (2) and (4) were omitted, and
(d)   in subsection (5) the words preceding "copies" were omitted.

36. Section 1094 (administrative removal of material from the register), as if—
(a)   the reference in subsection (2) to section 1093 were omitted, and
(b)   in subsection (3)(a), sub-paragraphs (iii) to (vii) were omitted.

37. Section 1112 (general false statement offence).

38. Section 1117 (registrar's rules), so far as relating to sections 1066(2), 1089(1) and 1090(4).

39. The following provisions of Part 36 (offences), so far as relating to offences under sections applied by these Regulations—
(a)   section 1121 (liability of officer in default), as if subsection (2) were omitted;
(b)   section 1122 (liability of company as officer in default), as if the words ""officer" and" in subsection (3) were omitted;
(c)   sections 1126 to 1130 (consents for prosecutions, venue and time limit for summary proceedings, privilege and unincorporated bodies);
(d)   section 1132 (production and inspection of documents where offence suspected), as if the reference in subsection (3)(b) to the secretary of the company were omitted;
(e)   section 1133 (provisions not to apply to offences committed before commencement).

40. Sections 1139 to 1141 (service addresses), as if the reference in section 1140(2)(a) to a director or secretary of a company were a reference to a manager of an EEIG.]]

NOTES

Commencement: 6 April 2008.

This Part was inserted by the Companies Act 2006 (Consequential Amendments etc) Order 2008, SI 2008/948, art 3(1), Sch 1, Pt 2, para 164(1), (5), as from 6 April 2008.

The original paras 1, 2 were substituted by new paras 25–40 by the European Economic Interest Grouping (Amendment) Regulations 2009, SI 2009/2399, regs 3, 23(1), (3), as from 1 October 2009.

INSOLVENCY REGULATIONS 1994

(SI 1994/2507)

NOTES

Made: 26 September 1994.

Authority: Insolvency Rules 1986, SI 1986/1925, r 12.1; Insolvency Act 1986, ss 411, 412, Sch 8, para 27, Sch 9, para 30. Commencement: 24 October 1994.

These Regulations (as reproduced here) are printed as amended by: the Insolvency (Amendment) Regulations 2000, SI 2000/485; the Financial Services and Markets Act 2000 (Consequential Amendments and Repeals) Order 2001, SI 2001/3649; the Insolvency (Amendment) Regulations 2004, SI 2004/472; the Insolvency (Amendment) Regulations 2005, SI 2005/512; the Secretaries of State for Children, Schools and Families, for Innovation, Universities and Skills and for Business, Enterprise and Regulatory Reform Order 2007, SI 2007/3224; the Insolvency (Amendment) Regulations 2008, SI 2008/670; the Insolvency (Amendment) Regulations 2009, SI 2009/482; the Secretary of State for Business, Innovation and Skills Order 2009, SI 2009/2748.

Limited liability partnerships: by the Limited Liability Partnerships Regulations 2001, SI 2001/1090, reg 10, Sch 6, Pt II, these Regulations (and the amending Insolvency (Amendment) Regulations 2000, SI 2000/485) apply, with modifications, to limited liability partnerships (see **[10.829]**).

Application to bank insolvency and administration: as to the application of these Regulations to bank insolvency and administration, see the Banking Act 2009 (Parts 2 and 3 Consequential Amendments) Order 2009, SI 2009/317.

Note: Part 3 of these Regulations (Bankruptcy) has been omitted as outside the scope of this work.

ARRANGEMENT OF REGULATIONS

PART 1
GENERAL

[10.720]
1   Citation and commencement
These Regulations may be cited as the Insolvency Regulations 1994 and shall come into force on
24th October 1994.

[10.721]
2   Revocations
Subject to regulation 37 below, the Regulations listed in Schedule 1 to these Regulations are hereby
revoked.

[10.722]
3   Interpretation and application
(1)   In these Regulations, except where the context otherwise requires—
      ["bank" means—
      (a)   a person who has permission under Part 4 of the Financial Services and Markets
             Act 2000 to accept deposits, or
      (b)   an EEA firm of the kind mentioned in paragraph 5(b) of Schedule 3 to that Act,
             which has permission under paragraph 15 of that Schedule (as a result of qualifying
             for authorisation under paragraph 12(1) of that Schedule) to accept deposits;]
      "bankrupt" means the bankrupt or his estate;
      "company" means the company which is being wound up;
      "creditors' committee" means any committee established under section 301;
      ["electronic transfer" means transmission by any electronic means;]
      "liquidation committee" means, in the case of a winding up by the court, any committee
             established under section 141 and, in the case of a creditors' voluntary winding up, any
             committee established under section 101;
      "liquidator" includes, in the case of a company being wound up by the court, the official receiver
             when so acting;
      "local bank" means any bank in, or in the neighbourhood of, the insolvency district, or the
             district in respect of which the court has winding-up jurisdiction, in which the proceedings
             are taken, or in the locality in which any business of the company or, as the case may be,
             the bankrupt is carried on;
      "local bank account" means, in the case of a winding up by the court, a current account opened
             with a local bank under regulation 6(2) below and, in the case of a bankruptcy, a current
             account opened with a local bank under regulation 21(1) below;
      "payment instrument" means a cheque or payable order;
      "the Rules" means the Insolvency Rules 1986; and
      "trustee", subject to regulation 19(2) below, means trustee of a bankrupt's estate including the
             official receiver when so acting;
and other expressions used in these Regulations and defined by the Rules have the meanings which
they bear in the Rules.
(2)   A Rule referred to in these Regulations by number means the Rule so numbered in the Rules.
(3)   Any application to be made to the Secretary of State or to the Department or anything required
to be sent to the Secretary of State or to the Department under these Regulations shall be addressed
to [the Department for Business, Innovation and Skills], The Insolvency Service, PO Box 3690,
Birmingham B2 4UY.

(4)   Where a regulation makes provision for the use of a form obtainable from the Department, the Department may provide different forms for different cases arising under that regulation.

(5)   Subject to regulation 37 below, these Regulations [(except for regulations 3A and 36A)] apply—

    (a)   to winding-up proceedings commenced on or after 29th December 1986; and

    (b)   to bankruptcy proceedings where the bankruptcy petition is or was presented on or after that day.

[(6)   Regulation 3A applies in any case where a company entered into administration on or after 15th September 2003 other than a case where the company entered into administration by virtue of a petition presented before that date.

(7)   Regulation 36A applies in any case where an insolvency practitioner is appointed on or after 1st April 2005.]

NOTES

   Para (1): definition "bank" substituted by the Financial Services and Markets Act 2000 (Consequential Amendments and Repeals) Order 2001, SI 2001/3649, art 471, as from 1 December 2001; definition "electronic transfer" inserted by the Insolvency (Amendment) Regulations 2000, SI 2000/485, reg 3, Schedule, para 1, as from 31 March 2000.

   Para (3): words in square brackets substituted by the Secretary of State for Business, Innovation and Skills Order 2009, SI 2009/2748, art 8, Schedule, Pt 2, para 17, as from 13 November 2009.

   Para (5): words in square brackets inserted by the Insolvency (Amendment) Regulations 2005, SI 2005/512, regs 4, 5(1), (2), as from 1 April 2005.

   Paras (6), (7): added by SI 2005/512, regs 4, 5(1), (3), as from 1 April 2005.

[PART 1A
ADMINISTRATION

[10.723]
3A   Disposal of company's records and provision of information to the Secretary of State

(1)   The person who was the last administrator of a company which has been dissolved may, at any time after the expiration of a period of one year from the date of dissolution, destroy or otherwise dispose of the books, papers and other records of the company.

(2)   An administrator or former administrator shall within 14 days of a request by the Secretary of State give the Secretary of State particulars of any money in his hands or under his control representing unclaimed or undistributed assets of the company or dividends or other sums due to any person as a member or former member of the company.]

NOTES

   Inserted, together with the preceding heading, by the Insolvency (Amendment) Regulations 2005, SI 2005/512, regs 4, 6, as from 1 April 2005.

[10.724]
[3B   Payment of unclaimed dividends or other money

(1)   This regulation applies to monies which—

    (a)   are held by the former administrator of a dissolved company, and

    (b)   represent either or both of the following—

       (i)   unclaimed dividends due to creditors, or

       (ii)   sums held by the company in trust in respect of dividends or other sums due to any person as a member or former member of the company.

(2)   Any monies to which this regulation applies may be paid into the Insolvency Services Account.

(3)   Where under this regulation the former administrator pays any sums into the Insolvency Services Account, he shall at the same time give notice to the Secretary of State of—

    (a)   the name of the company,

    (b)   the name and address of the person to whom the dividend or other sum is payable,

    (c)   the amount of the dividend or other sum, and

    (d)   the date on which it was paid.

(4)   Where a dividend or other sum is paid to a person by way of a payment instrument, any payment into the Insolvency Services Account in respect of that dividend or sum pursuant to paragraph (2) may not be made earlier than on or after the expiry of 6 months from the date of the payment instrument.]

NOTES

   Commencement: 6 April 2008.

   Inserted by the Insolvency (Amendment) Regulations 2008, SI 2008/670, reg 3(1), (2), as from 6 April 2008.

[PART 1B
ADMINISTRATIVE RECEIVERSHIP

[10.725]
3C   Payment of unclaimed dividends or other money

(1)   This regulation applies to monies which—
- (a)   are held by the former administrative receiver of a dissolved company, and
- (b)   represent either or both of the following—
  - (i)   unclaimed dividends due to creditors, or
  - (ii)   sums held by the company in trust in respect of dividends or other sums due to any person as a member or former member of the company.

(2)   Any monies to which this regulation applies may be paid into the Insolvency Services Account.

(3)   Where under this regulation the former administrative receiver pays any sums into the Insolvency Services Account, he shall at the same time give notice to the Secretary of State of—
- (a)   the name of the company,
- (b)   the name and address of the person to whom the dividend or other sum is payable,
- (c)   the amount of the dividend or other sum, and
- (d)   the date on which it was paid.

(4)   Where a dividend or other sum is paid to a person by way of a payment instrument, any payment in respect of that dividend or sum into the Insolvency Services Account pursuant to paragraph (2) may not be made earlier than on or after the expiry of 6 months from the date of the payment instrument.]

NOTES

Commencement: 6 April 2008.

Inserted, together with the preceding heading, by the Insolvency (Amendment) Regulations 2008, SI 2008/670, reg 3(1), (2), as from 6 April 2008.

Note that in the Queen's Printer's copy of the 2008 Regulations there are two paragraphs numbered as paragraph (3). In the above text the second of these has been changed to paragraph (4).

PART 2
WINDING UP

[10.726]
4   Introductory

This Part of these Regulations relates to—
- (a)   voluntary winding up and
- (b)   winding up by the court

of companies which the courts in England and Wales have jurisdiction to wind up.

PAYMENT INTO AND OUT OF THE INSOLVENCY SERVICES ACCOUNT

[10.727]
5   Payments into the Insolvency Services Account

(1)   In the case of a winding up by the court, subject to regulation 6 below, the liquidator shall pay all money received by him in the course of carrying out his functions as such without any deduction into the Insolvency Services Account kept by the Secretary of State with the Bank of England to the credit of the company once every 14 days or forthwith if £5,000 or more has been received.

[(2)   In the case of a voluntary winding up, the liquidator may make payments into the Insolvency Services Account to the credit of the company.]

[(3)   Every payment of money into the Insolvency Services Account under this regulation shall be—
- (a)   made through the Bank Giro system; or
- (b)   sent direct to the Bank of England, Threadneedle Street, London EC2R 8AH by cheque drawn in favour of the "Insolvency Services Account" and crossed "A/c payee only" "Bank of England"; or
- (c)   made by electronic transfer,

and the liquidator shall on request be given by the Department a receipt for the money so paid.]

(4)   Every payment of money [made under sub-paragraph (a) or (b) of paragraph (3) above] shall be accompanied by a form obtainable from the Department for that purpose or by a form that is substantially similar.

[Every payment of money made under sub-paragraph (c) of paragraph (3) above shall specify the name of the liquidator making the payment and the name of the company to whose credit such payment is made.]

(5)   Where in a voluntary winding up a liquidator pays any unclaimed dividend into the Insolvency Services Account, he shall at the same time give notice to the Secretary of State, on a form obtainable from the Department or on one that is substantially similar, of the name and address of the person to whom the dividend is payable and the amount of the dividend.

NOTES

Para (2): substituted by the Insolvency (Amendment) Regulations 2004, SI 2004/472, reg 2, Schedule, para 1, as from 1 April 2004.

Para (3): substituted by the Insolvency (Amendment) Regulations 2000, SI 2000/485, reg 3, Schedule, para 2, as from 31 March 2000.

Para (4): words in first pair of square brackets substituted, and words in second pair of square brackets added, by SI 2000/485, reg 3, Schedule, para 3, as from 31 March 2000.

[10.728]
6   Local bank account and handling of funds not belonging to the company

(1)   This regulation does not apply in the case of a voluntary winding up.

(2)   Where the liquidator intends to exercise his power to carry on the business of the company, he may apply to the Secretary of State for authorisation to open a local bank account, and the Secretary of State may authorise him to make his payments into and out of a specified bank, subject to a limit, instead of into and out of the Insolvency Services Account if satisfied that an administrative advantage will be derived from having such an account.

(3)   Money received by the liquidator relating to the purpose for which the account was opened may be paid into the local bank account to the credit of the company to which the account relates.

(4)   Where the liquidator opens a local bank account pursuant to an authorisation granted under paragraph (2) above, he shall open and maintain the account in the name of the company.

(5)   Where money which is not an asset of the company is provided to the liquidator for a specific purpose, it shall be clearly identifiable in a separate account.

(6)   The liquidator shall keep proper records, including documentary evidence of all money paid into and out of every local bank account opened and maintained under this regulation.

(7)   The liquidator shall pay without deduction any surplus over any limit imposed by an authorisation granted under paragraph (2) above into the Insolvency Services Account in accordance with regulation 5 above as that regulation applies in the case of a winding up by the court.

(8)   As soon as the liquidator ceases to carry on the business of the company or vacates office or an authorisation given in pursuance of an application under paragraph (2) above is withdrawn, he shall close the account and pay any balance into the Insolvency Services Account in accordance with regulation 5 above as that regulation applies in the case of a winding up by the court.

[10.729]
7   Payment of disbursements etc out of the Insolvency Services Account

[(A1)   Paragraphs (1) to (3) of this regulation are subject to paragraph (3A).]

(1)   In the case of a winding up by the court, on application to the Department, the liquidator shall be repaid all necessary disbursements made by him, and expenses properly incurred by him, in the course of his administration to the date of his vacation of office out of any money standing to the credit of the company in the Insolvency Services Account.

(2)   In the case of a winding up by the court, the liquidator shall on application to the Department obtain payment instruments to the order of the payee for sums which become payable on account of the company for delivery by the liquidator to the persons to whom the payments are to be made.

(3)   In the case of a voluntary winding up, where the liquidator requires to make payments out of any money standing to the credit of the company in the Insolvency Services Account in respect of the expenses of the winding up, he shall apply to the Secretary of State who may either authorise payment to the liquidator of the sum required by him, or may direct payment instruments to be issued to the liquidator for delivery by him to the persons to whom the payments are to be made.

[(3A)   In respect of an application made by the liquidator under paragraphs (1) to (3) above, the Secretary of State, if requested to do so by the liquidator, may, at his discretion,

(a)   make the payment which is the subject of the application to the liquidator by electronic transfer; or

(b)   as an alternative to the issue of payment instruments, make payment by electronic transfer to the persons to whom the liquidator would otherwise deliver payment instruments.]

(4)   Any application under this regulation shall be made by the liquidator on a form obtainable from the Department for the purpose or on a form that is substantially similar.

(5)   In the case of a winding up by the court, on the liquidator vacating office, he shall be repaid by any succeeding liquidator out of any funds available for the purpose any necessary disbursements made by him and any expenses properly incurred by him but not repaid before he vacates office.

NOTES

Paras (A1), (3A): inserted by the Insolvency (Amendment) Regulations 2000, SI 2000/485, reg 3, Schedule, paras 4, 5, as from 31 March 2000.

DIVIDENDS TO CREDITORS AND RETURNS OF CAPITAL TO CONTRIBUTORIES OF A COMPANY

[10.730]

8   Payment

[(A1)   Paragraphs (1) to (3) of this regulation are subject to paragraph (3A).]

(1)   In the case of a winding up by the court, the liquidator shall pay every dividend by payment instruments which shall be prepared by the Department on the application of the liquidator and transmitted to him for distribution amongst the creditors.

(2)   In the case of a winding up by the court, the liquidator shall pay every return of capital to contributories by payment instruments which shall be prepared by the Department on application.

(3)   In the case of a voluntary winding up, where the liquidator requires to make payments out of any money standing to the credit of the company in the Insolvency Services Account by way of distribution, he shall apply in writing to the Secretary of State who may either authorise payment to the liquidator of the sum required by him, or may direct payment instruments to be issued to the liquidator for delivery by him to the persons to whom the payments are to be made.

[(3A)   In respect of an application made by the liquidator under paragraphs (1) to (3) above, the Secretary of State, if requested to do so by the liquidator, may, at his discretion,

    (a)   as an alternative to the issue of payment instruments, make payment by electronic transfer to the persons to whom the liquidator would otherwise deliver payment instruments; or

    (b)   make the payment which is the subject of the application to the liquidator by electronic transfer.]

(4)   Any application under this regulation for a payment instrument [or payment by electronic transfer] shall be made by the liquidator on a form obtainable from the Department for the purpose or on a form which is substantially similar.

(5)   In the case of a winding up by the court, the liquidator shall enter the total amount of every dividend and of every return to contributories that he desires to pay under this regulation in the records to be kept under regulation 10 below in one sum.

(6)   On the liquidator vacating office, he shall send to the Department any valid unclaimed or undelivered payment instruments for dividends or returns to contributories after endorsing them with the word "cancelled".

NOTES

Paras (A1), (3A): inserted by the Insolvency (Amendment) Regulations 2000, SI 2000/485, reg 3, Schedule, paras 6, 7, as from 31 March 2000.

Para (4): words in square brackets inserted by SI 2000/485, reg 3, Schedule, para 8, as from 31 March 2000.

INVESTMENT OR OTHERWISE HANDLING OF FUNDS IN WINDING UP OF COMPANIES AND PAYMENT OF INTEREST

[10.731]

9

(1)   When the cash balance standing to the credit of the company in the account in respect of that company kept by the Secretary of State is in excess of the amount which, in the opinion of the liquidator, is required for the immediate purposes of the winding up and should be invested, he may request the Secretary of State to invest the amount not so required in Government securities, to be placed to the credit of that account for the company's benefit.

(2)   When any of the money so invested is, in the opinion of the liquidator, required for the immediate purposes of the winding up, he may request the Secretary of State to raise such sum as may be required by the sale of such of those securities as may be necessary.

(3)   In cases where investments have been made at the request of the liquidator in pursuance of paragraph (1) above and additional sums to the amounts so invested, including money received under paragraph (7) below, are paid into the Insolvency Services Account to the credit of the company, a request shall be made to the Secretary of State by the liquidator if it is desired that these additional sums should be invested.

(4)   Any request relating to the investment in, or sale of, as the case may be, Treasury Bills made under paragraphs (1), (2) or (3) above shall be made on a form obtainable from the Department or on one that is substantially similar and any request relating to the purchase or sale, as the case may be, of any other type of Government security made under the provisions of those paragraphs shall be made in writing.

(5)   Any request made under paragraphs (1), (2) or (3) above shall be sufficient authority to the Secretary of State for the investment or sale as the case may be.

[(6)   Subject to paragraphs (6A) and (6B), at any time after 1st April 2004 whenever there are any monies standing to the credit of the company in the Insolvency Services Account the company shall be entitled to interest on those monies at the rate of 4.25 per cent per annum.

(6A)   Interest shall cease to accrue pursuant to paragraph (6) from the date of receipt by the Secretary of State of a notice in writing from the liquidator that in the opinion of the liquidator it is necessary or expedient in order to facilitate the conclusion of the winding up that interest should cease to accrue but interest shall start to accrue again pursuant to paragraph (6) where the liquidator gives a further notice in writing to the Secretary of State requesting that interest should start to accrue again.

(6B)   The Secretary of State may by notice published in the London Gazette vary the rate of interest prescribed by paragraph (6) and such variation shall have effect from the day after the date of publication of the notice in the London Gazette or such later date as may be specified in the notice.]

(7)   All money received in respect of investments and interest earned under this regulation shall be paid into the Insolvency Services Account to the credit of the company.

(8)   In addition to the application of paragraphs (1) to (7) above, in a voluntary winding up—
  (a)   any money invested or deposited at interest by the liquidator shall be deemed to be money under his control, and when such money forms part of the balance of funds in his hands or under his control relating to the company required to be paid into the Insolvency Services Account under regulation 5 above, the liquidator shall realise the investment or withdraw the deposit and shall pay the proceeds into that Account: Provided that where the money is invested in Government securities, such securities may, with the permission of the Secretary of State, be transferred to the control of the Secretary of State instead of being forthwith realised and the proceeds paid into the Insolvency Services Account; and
  (b)   where any of the money represented by securities transferred to the control of the Secretary of State pursuant to sub-paragraph (a) above is, in the opinion of the liquidator, required for the immediate purposes of the winding up he may request the Secretary of State to raise such sums as may be required by the sale of such of those securities as may be necessary and such request shall be sufficient authority to the Secretary of State for the sale and the Secretary of State shall pay the proceeds of the realisation into the Insolvency Services Account in accordance with paragraph (7) above and deal with them in the same way as other money paid into that Account may be dealt with.

NOTES

Paras (6), (6A), (6B): substituted, for original para (6), by the Insolvency (Amendment) Regulations 2004, SI 2004/472, reg 2, Schedule, para 2, as from 1 April 2004, subject to transitional provisions providing that where a notice that interest should cease is given pursuant to para (6)(a) as it stood immediately before that date, it shall be treated as having been given for the purposes of para (6A) above.

Treasury bills: a reference to a Treasury bill in this regulation includes a reference to uncertificated units of eligible Treasury bills; see the Uncertificated Securities (Amendment) (Eligible Debt Securities) Regulations 2003, SI 2003/1633, reg 15, Sch 2, para 2(h).

The rate of interest prescribed by para (6) above was changed from 1.25% to 0.5% with effect from 13 May 2009; the London Gazette, 12 May 2009.

RECORDS TO BE MAINTAINED BY LIQUIDATORS AND THE PROVISION
OF INFORMATION

[10.732]
10   Financial records

(1)   This regulation does not apply in the case of a members' voluntary winding up.

(2)   The liquidator shall prepare and keep—
  (a)   separate financial records in respect of each company; and
  (b)   such other financial records as are required to explain the receipts and payments entered in the records described in sub-paragraph (a) above or regulation 12(2) below, including an explanation of the source of any receipts and the destination of any payments;
and shall, subject to regulation 12(2) below as to trading accounts, from day to day enter in those records all the receipts and payments (including, in the case of a voluntary winding up, those relating to the Insolvency Services Account) made by him.

(3)   In the case of a winding up by the court, the liquidator shall obtain and keep bank statements relating to any local bank account in the name of the company.

(4)   The liquidator shall submit financial records to the liquidation committee when required for inspection.

(5)   In the case of a winding up by the court, if the liquidation committee is not satisfied with the contents of the financial records submitted under paragraph (4) above it may so inform the Secretary of State, giving the reasons for its dissatisfaction, and the Secretary of State may take such action as he thinks fit.

Part 10   Miscellaneous other SIs

[10.733]
11   Provision of information by liquidator

(1)   In the case of a winding up by the court, the liquidator shall, within 14 days of the receipt of a request for a statement of his receipts and payments as liquidator from any creditor, contributory or director of the company, supply free of charge to the person making the request, a statement of his receipts and payments as liquidator during the period of one year ending on the most recent anniversary of his becoming liquidator which preceded the request.

(2)   In the case of a voluntary winding up, the liquidator shall, on request from any creditor, contributory or director of the company for a copy of a statement for any period, including future periods, sent to the registrar of companies under section 192, send such copy free of charge to the person making the request and the copy of the statement shall be sent within 14 days of the liquidator sending the statement to the registrar or the receipt of the request whichever is the later.

[10.734]
12   Liquidator carrying on business

(1)   This regulation does not apply in the case of a members' voluntary winding up.

(2)   Where the liquidator carries on any business of the company, he shall—
   (a)   keep a separate and distinct account of the trading, including, where appropriate, in the case of a winding up by the court, particulars of all local bank account transactions; and
   (b)   incorporate in the financial records required to be kept under regulation 10 above the total weekly amounts of the receipts and payments made by him in relation to the account kept under sub-paragraph (a) above.

[10.735]
13   Retention and delivery of records

(1)   All records kept by the liquidator under regulations 10 and 12(2) and any such records received by him from a predecessor in that office shall be retained by him for a period of 6 years following—
   (a)   his vacation of office, or
   (b)   in the case of the official receiver, his release as liquidator under section 174,
unless he delivers them to another liquidator who succeeds him in office.

(2)   Where the liquidator is succeeded in office by another liquidator, the records referred to in paragraph (1) above shall be delivered to that successor forthwith, unless, in the case of a winding up by the court, the winding up is for practical purposes complete and the successor is the official receiver, in which case the records are only to be delivered to the official receiver if the latter so requests.

[10.736]
14   Provision of accounts by liquidator and audit of accounts

(1)   The liquidator shall, if required by the Secretary of State at any time, send to the Secretary of State an account in relation to the company of the liquidator's receipts and payments covering such period as the Secretary of State may direct and such account shall, if so required by the Secretary of State, be certified by the liquidator.

(2)   Where the liquidator in a winding up by the court vacates office prior to the holding of the final general meeting of creditors under section 146, he shall within 14 days of vacating office send to the Secretary of State an account of his receipts and payments as liquidator for any period not covered by an account previously so sent by him or if no such account has been sent, an account of his receipts and payments in respect of the whole period of his office.

(3)   In the case of a winding up by the court, where—
   (a)   a final general meeting of creditors has been held pursuant to section 146, or
   (b)   a final general meeting is deemed to have been held by virtue of Rule 4.125(5),
the liquidator shall send to the Secretary of State, in case (a), within 14 days of the holding of the final general meeting of creditors and, in case (b), within 14 days of his report to the court pursuant to Rule 4.125(5), an account of his receipts and payments as liquidator which are not covered by any previous account so sent by him, or if no such account has been sent an account of his receipts and payments in respect of the whole period of his office.

(4)   In the case of a winding up by the court, where a statement of affairs has been submitted under the Act, any account sent under this regulation shall be accompanied by a summary of that statement of affairs and shall show the amount of any assets realised and explain the reasons for any non-realisation of any assets not realised.

(5)   In the case of a winding up by the court, where a statement of affairs has not been submitted under the Act, any account sent under this regulation shall be accompanied by a summary of all known assets and their estimated values and shall show the amounts actually realised and explain the reasons for any non-realisation of any assets not realised.

(6)   Any account sent to the Secretary of State shall, if he so requires, be audited, but whether or not the Secretary of State requires the account to be audited, the liquidator shall send to the Secretary of State on demand any documents (including vouchers and bank statements) and any information relating to the account.

[10.737]
15   Production and inspection of records

(1)   The liquidator shall produce on demand to the Secretary of State, and allow him to inspect, any accounts, books and other records kept by him (including any passed to him by a predecessor in office), and this duty to produce and allow inspection shall extend—
    (a)   to producing and allowing inspection at the premises of the liquidator; and
    (b)   to producing and allowing inspection of any financial records of the kind described in regulation 10(2)(b) above prepared by the liquidator (or any predecessor in office of his) before 24th October 1994 and kept by the liquidator;
and any such demand may—
    (i)   require the liquidator to produce any such accounts, books or other records to the Secretary of State, and allow him to inspect them—
        (a)   at the same time as any account is sent to the Secretary of State under regulation 14 above; or
        (b)   at any time after such account is sent to the Secretary of State;
        whether or not the Secretary of State requires the account to be audited; or
    (ii) where it is made for the purpose of ascertaining whether the provisions of these Regulations relating to the handling of money received by the liquidator in the course of carrying out his functions have been or are likely to be complied with, be made at any time, whether or not an account has been sent or should have been sent to the Secretary of State under regulation 14 above and whether or not the Secretary of State has required any account to be audited.

(2)   The liquidator shall allow the Secretary of State on demand to remove and take copies of any accounts, books and other records kept by the liquidator (including any passed to him by a predecessor in office), whether or not they are kept at the premises of the liquidator.

[10.738]
16   Disposal of company's books, papers and other records

(1)   The liquidator in a winding up by the court, on the authorisation of the official receiver, during his tenure of office or on vacating office, or the official receiver while acting as liquidator, may at any time sell, destroy or otherwise dispose of the books, papers and other records of the company.

(2)   In the case of a voluntary winding up, the person who was the last liquidator of a company which has been dissolved may, at any time after the expiration of a period of one year from the date of dissolution, destroy or otherwise dispose of the books, papers and other records of the company.

[10.739]
17   Voluntary liquidator to provide information to Secretary of State

(1)   In the case of a voluntary winding up, a liquidator or former liquidator, whether the winding up has been concluded under Rule 4.223 or not, shall, within 14 days of a request by the Secretary of State, give the Secretary of State particulars of any money in his hands or under his control representing unclaimed or undistributed assets of the company or dividends or other sums due to any person as a member or former member of the company and such other particulars as the Secretary of State may require for the purpose of ascertaining or getting in any money payable into the Insolvency Services Account.

(2)   The particulars referred to in paragraph (1) above shall, if the Secretary of State so requires, be certified by the liquidator, or former liquidator, as the case may be.

[10.740]
[18   Payment of unclaimed dividends or other money

(1)   This regulation applies to monies which—
    (a)   are held by the former liquidator of a dissolved company, and
    (b)   represent either or both of the following—
        (i)   unclaimed dividends due to creditors, or
        (ii) sums held by the company in trust in respect of dividends or other sums due to any person as a member or former member of the company.

(2)   Monies to which this regulation applies—
    (a)   may in the case of a voluntary winding up,
    (b)   must in the case of a winding up by the court,
be paid into the Insolvency Services Account.

(3)   Where the former liquidator pays any sums into the Insolvency Services Account pursuant to paragraph (2), he shall at the same time give notice to the Secretary of State of—
    (a)   the name of the company,
    (b)   the name and address of the person to whom the dividend or other sum is payable,

(c)   the amount of the dividend, and

(d)   the date on which it was paid.

(4)   Where a dividend or other sum is paid to a person by way of a payment instrument, any payment into the Insolvency Services Account in respect of that dividend or sum pursuant to paragraph (2) may not be made earlier than on or after the expiry of 6 months from the date of the payment instrument.]

NOTES

Commencement: 6 April 2008.

Substituted by the Insolvency (Amendment) Regulations 2008, SI 2008/670, reg 2(1), (3), as from 6 April 2008.

19–31   *(Regs 19–31 (Part 3: Bankruptcy) outside the scope of this work.)*

PART 4
CLAIMING MONEY PAID INTO THE INSOLVENCY SERVICES ACCOUNT

[10.741]
32

(1)   Any person claiming to be entitled to any money paid into the Insolvency Services Account may apply to the Secretary of State for payment and shall provide such evidence of his claim as the Secretary of State may require.

(2)   Any person dissatisfied with the decision of the Secretary of State in respect of his claim made under this regulation may appeal to the court.

PART 5
REMUNERATION OF OFFICIAL RECEIVER

33, 34   *(Revoked by the Insolvency (Amendment) Regulations 2004, SI 2004/472, reg 2, Schedule, para 4, as from 1 April 2004.)*

[10.742]
[35   Official receiver's general remuneration while acting as interim receiver, provisional liquidator, liquidator or trustee

(1)   The official receiver shall be entitled to remuneration calculated in accordance with the applicable hourly rates set out in paragraph (2) for services provided by him (or any of his officers) in relation to—

(a)   a distribution made by him when acting as liquidator or trustee to creditors (including preferential or secured creditors or both such classes of creditor);

(b)   the realisation of assets on behalf of the holder of a fixed or floating charge or both types of those charges;

(c)   the supervision of a special manager;

(d)   the performance by him of any functions where he acts as provisional liquidator; or

(e)   the performance by him of any functions where he acts as an interim receiver.

(2)   The applicable hourly rates referred to in paragraph (1) are—

(a)   in relation to the official receiver of the London insolvency district, those set out in Table 2 in Schedule 2; and

(b)   in relation to any other official receiver, those set out in Table 3 in Schedule 2.]

NOTES

Substituted by the Insolvency (Amendment) Regulations 2005, SI 2005/512, regs 3, 4, 7, as from 1 April 2005. Note that this substitution only applies in relation to services provided by the official receiver (or any of his officers) in relation to (a) a company in respect of which a winding-up order is made on or after that date; (b) a bankruptcy where the bankruptcy order is made on or after that date; or (c) his appointment as an interim receiver or provisional liquidator where he is appointed on or after that date.

36   *(Revoked by the Insolvency (Amendment) Regulations 2004, SI 2004/472, reg 2, Schedule, para 4, as from 1 April 2004.)*

[PART 5A
INFORMATION ABOUT TIME SPENT ON A CASE TO BE PROVIDED BY INSOLVENCY PRACTITIONER TO CREDITORS ETC

[10.743]
36A

(1)   Subject as set out in this regulation, in respect of any case in which he acts, an insolvency practitioner shall on request in writing made by any person mentioned in paragraph (2), supply free of charge to that person a statement of the kind described in paragraph (3).

(2)   The persons referred to in paragraph (1) are—

(a)   any creditor in the case;

(b)   where the case relates to a company, any director or contributory of that company; and

(c)   where the case relates to an individual, that individual.

(3)   The statement referred to in paragraph (1) shall comprise in relation to the period beginning with the date of the insolvency practitioner's appointment and ending with the relevant date the following details—

    (a)   the total number of hours spent on the case by the insolvency practitioner and any staff assigned to the case during that period;

    (b)   for each grade of individual so engaged, the average hourly rate at which any work carried out by individuals in that grade is charged; and

    (c)   the number of hours spent by each grade of staff during that period.

(4)   In relation to paragraph (3) the "relevant date" means the date next before the date of the making of the request on which the insolvency practitioner has completed any period in office which is a multiple of six months or, where the insolvency practitioner has vacated office, the date that he vacated office.

(5)   Where an insolvency practitioner has vacated office, an obligation to provide information under this regulation shall only arise in relation to a request that is made within 2 years of the date he vacates office.

(6)   Any statement required to be provided to any person under this regulation shall be supplied within 28 days of the date of the receipt of the request by the insolvency practitioner.

(7)   In this regulation the expression "insolvency practitioner" shall be construed in accordance with section 388 of the Insolvency Act 1986.]

NOTES

Inserted, together with the preceding heading, by the Insolvency (Amendment) Regulations 2005, SI 2005/512, regs 4, 8, as from 1 April 2005.

PART 6
TRANSITIONAL AND SAVING PROVISIONS

[10.744]

37

The Regulations shall have effect subject to the transitional and saving provisions set out in Schedule 3 to these Regulations.

SCHEDULES
SCHEDULE 1

(Revokes the Insolvency Regulations 1986, SI 1986/1994, and the amending SI 1987/1959, SI 1988/1739, and SI 1991/380.)

SCHEDULE 2

Regulations 33 to 36

[10.745]

[TABLE 2—LONDON RATES

Grade according to the Insolvency Service grading structure/Status of Official	Total hourly rate £
D2/Official Receiver	75
C2/Deputy or Assistant Official Receiver	63
C1/Senior Examiner	58
L3/Examiner	46
L2/Examiner	42
B2/Administrator	46
L1/Examiner	40
B1/Administrator	46
A2/Administrator	40
A1/Administrator	35]

[TABLE 3—PROVINCIAL RATES

Grade according to the Insolvency Service grading structure /Status of Official	Total hourly rate £
D2/Official Receiver	69
C2/Deputy or Assistant Official Receiver	58
C1/Senior Examiner	52
L3/Examiner	46
L2 Examiner	40
B2/Administrator	43
L1/Examiner	38
B1/Administrator	42
A2/Administrator	36
A1/Administrator	31]

NOTES

Table 1: revoked by the Insolvency (Amendment) Regulations 2004, SI 2004/472, reg 2, Schedule, para 6, as from 1 April 2004.

Tables 2, 3: substituted by the Insolvency (Amendment) Regulations 2009, SI 2009/482, reg 2, as from 6 April 2009.

SCHEDULE 3

Regulation 37

[10.746]
1   Interpretation

In this Schedule the expression "the former Regulations" means the Insolvency Regulations 1986 as amended by the Insolvency (Amendment) Regulations 1987, the Insolvency (Amendment) Regulations 1988 and the Insolvency (Amendment) Regulations 1991.

2   Requests pursuant to regulation 13(1) of the former Regulations

Any request made pursuant to regulation 13(1) of the former Regulations which has not been complied with prior to 24th October 1994 shall be treated, in the case of a company that is being wound up by the court, as a request made pursuant to regulation 11(1) of these Regulations and, in the case of a bankruptcy, as a request made pursuant to regulation 25 of these Regulations and in each case the request shall be treated as if it had been made on 24th October 1994.

3   Things done under the provisions of the former Regulations

So far as anything done under, or for the purposes of, any provision of the former Regulations could have been done under, or for the purposes of, the corresponding provision of these Regulations, it is not invalidated by the revocation of that provision but has effect as if done under, or for the purposes of, the corresponding provision.

4   Time periods

Where any period of time specified in a provision of the former Regulations is current immediately before 24th October 1994, these Regulations have effect as if the corresponding provision of these Regulations had been in force when the period began to run; and (without prejudice to the foregoing) any period of time so specified and current is deemed for the purposes of these Regulations—

    (a) to run from the date or event from which it was running immediately before 24th October 1994, and

    (b) to expire whenever it would have expired if these Regulations had not been made;

and any rights, obligations, requirements, powers or duties dependent on the beginning, duration or end of such period as above-mentioned shall be under these Regulations as they were or would have been under the former Regulations.

5   References to other provisions

Where in any provision of these Regulations there is reference to another provision of these Regulations, and the first-mentioned provision operates, or is capable of operating, in relation to things done or omitted, or events occurring or not occurring, in the past (including in particular past acts of compliance with the former Regulations), the reference to that other provision is to be read as including a reference to the corresponding provision of the former Regulations.

6   Provisions of Schedule to be without prejudice to the operation of sections 16 and 17 of the Interpretation Act 1978

The provisions of this Schedule are to be without prejudice to the operation of sections 16 and 17 of the Interpretation Act 1978 (saving from, and effect of, repeals) as they are applied by section 23 of that Act.

7   Meaning of "corresponding provision"

(1)   A provision in the former Regulations, except regulation 13(1) of those Regulations, is to be regarded as the corresponding provision of a provision in these Regulations notwithstanding any modifications made to the provision as it appears in these Regulations.

(2)   Without prejudice to the generality of the term "corresponding provision" the following table shall, subject to sub-paragraph (3) below, have effect in the interpretation of that expression with a provision of these Regulations listed in the left hand column being regarded as the corresponding provision of a provision of the former Regulations listed opposite it in the right hand column and that latter provision being regarded as the corresponding provision of the first-mentioned provision—

TABLE

Provision in these Regulations	Provision in the former Regulations
5(1), 5(3), 5(4)	4
5(2), 5(3), 5(4)	24
6	6
7(1), 7(2), 7(4), 7(5)	5
7(3), 7(4)	25
8(1), 8(2), 8(4), 8(5), 8(6)	15
8(3), 8(4)	25
9	18, 34
10	9, 27
11(2)	31
12	10, 28
13	10A, 28A
15	12A, 30A
16(1)	14
16(2)	32
17	35
18	16, 33
20	4
21	6
22	5
23	15
24	9
26	10
27	10A
29	12A
30	14
31	16A
32	17, 33
33, Table 1 in Schedule 2	19
35, Tables 2 and 3 in Schedule 2	20
36, Table 1 in Schedule 2	22

(3)   Where a provision of the former Regulations is expressed in the Table in sub-paragraph (2) above to be the corresponding provision of a provision in these Regulations and the provision in the former Regulations was capable of applying to other proceedings in addition to those to which the provision in these Regulations is capable of applying, the provision in the former Regulations shall be construed as the corresponding provision of the provision in these Regulations only to the extent that they are both capable of applying to the same type of proceedings.

CONTRACTING OUT (FUNCTIONS IN RELATION TO THE REGISTRATION OF COMPANIES) ORDER 1995

(SI 1995/1013)

NOTES

Made: 4 April 1995.

Authority: Deregulation and Contracting Out Act 1994, s 69.

Commencement: 5 April 1995 (in part); 1 July 1995 (otherwise).

This Order is reproduced as amended by: the Financial Services and Markets Act 2000 (Consequential Amendments and Repeals) Order 2001, SI 2001/3649.

[10.747]
1   Citation and Commencement

(1)   This Order may be cited as the Contracting Out (Functions in relation to the Registration of Companies) Order 1995.

(2)   Save as provided in paragraph (3) below, this Order shall come into force on the day after the day on which it is made.

(3)   This Order shall come into force in relation to any functions conferred by or under sections 652A to F of the Companies Act 1985 (striking off register of non-trading private companies) immediately after those sections come into force.

NOTES

Companies Act 1985, ss 652A–652F: repealed by the Companies Act 2006, s 1295, Sch 16, as from 1 October 2009.

[10.748]
2   Interpretation

(1)   In this Order—
   "the Act" means the Companies Act 1985;
   "the Regulations" mean the European Economic Interest Grouping Regulations 1989; and
   "EEIG" means a European Economic Interest Grouping as defined in regulation 2(1) of the
      Regulations.

(2)   Any expression used in the Act, if used in this Order, bears the same meaning as it bears in the Act unless the context otherwise requires.

[10.749]
3   Contracting out of functions of the registrar in relation to England and Wales

Any function of the registrar of companies for England and Wales which is listed in Schedule 1 to this Order may be exercised by, or by employees of, such person (if any) as may be authorised in that behalf by the registrar of companies for England and Wales.

[10.750]
4   Contracting out of functions of the registrar in relation to Scotland

(1)   Subject to paragraph (2) below, any function of the registrar of companies for Scotland which is conferred by or under any enactment may be exercised by, or by employees of, such person (if any) as may be authorised in that behalf by the registrar of companies for Scotland.

(2)   Paragraph (1) above does not apply to the functions listed in Schedule 2 to this Order.

[10.751]
5   Contracting out of functions of the Secretary of State

Any function of the Secretary of State which is listed in Schedule 3 to this Order may be exercised by, or by employees of, such person (if any) as may be authorised in that behalf by the Secretary of State.

SCHEDULES

SCHEDULE 1
FUNCTIONS OF THE REGISTRAR OF COMPANIES FOR ENGLAND AND WALES ENABLED TO BE CONTRACTED OUT

Article 3

[10.752]
1. Any function of receiving any return, account or other document required to be filed with, delivered or sent, or notice of any matter required to be given, to the registrar which is conferred by or under any enactment.

2. Any functions in relation to—
   (a)   the incorporation of companies and the change of name of companies by or under Chapters I and II of Part I of the Act (company formation; company names);
   (b)   the re-registration and change of status of companies by or under Part II (re-registration as a means of altering a company's status) and sections 138 (registration of order and minute of reduction), 139 and 147 of the Act (re-registration of public companies on reduction of capital).

3. Functions conferred by or under any of the following provisions of the Act—
   (a)   sections 705 and 705A (companies' registered numbers and registration of branches of oversea companies) except insofar as they relate respectively to the determination of the form of companies' registered numbers and branches' registered numbers;
   (b)   section 706 (delivery to the registrar of documents in legible form) except insofar as they relate to specification of requirements for the purpose of enabling the copying of documents delivered to the registrar;
   (c)   section 707 (delivery to the registrar of documents other than in legible form) except insofar as they relate to the approval of the non-legible form in which information may be conveyed to the registrar;
   (d)   section 709 (inspection etc of records kept by the registrar) except insofar as they relate to the determination of the means of facilitating the exercise of the right of persons to inspect records kept by the registrar, or the form in which copies of the information contained in those records may be made available;
   (e)   section 710 (certificate of incorporation); and
   (f)   section 710A (provision and authentication by registrar of documents in non-legible form) except insofar as they relate to the approval of the means of communication to the registrar of information in non-legible form.

4. Functions conferred by or under section 13 of the Newspaper Libel and Registration Act 1881 (registrar to enter returns on register).

5. Functions conferred by or under section 16 of the Limited Partnerships Act 1907 (inspection of statements registered).

6.   . . .

7. Functions conferred by or under regulation 14 of the Regulations (inspection of documents).

8. Functions conferred by or under any provision of the Act listed in paragraphs 2 and 3 above to the extent specified in those paragraphs where any such provision is applied to EEIGs by regulation 18 of the Regulations (application of the Companies Act 1985).

NOTES
   Para 6: revoked by the Financial Services and Markets Act 2000 (Consequential Amendments and Repeals) Order 2001, SI 2001/3649, art 490, as from 1 December 2001.
   As to the repeal of most of the Companies Act 1985, see that Act at **[5.1]**.

SCHEDULE 2
FUNCTIONS OF REGISTRAR OF COMPANIES FOR SCOTLAND EXCLUDED FROM CONTRACTING OUT

Article 4

[10.753]
1. Functions conferred by or under any of the following provisions of the Act—

(a) section 242 (accounts and reports to be delivered to the registrar) so far as they relate to the making of an application to the court;

(b) sections 705 and 705A so far as they relate respectively to the determination of the form of companies' registered numbers and branches' registered numbers;

(c) section 706 so far as they relate to the specification of requirements for the purpose of enabling the copying of documents delivered to the registrar;

(d) section 707 so far as they relate to the approval of the non-legible form in which information may be conveyed to the registrar;

(e) section 707A (the keeping of company records by the registrar) so far as they relate to the determination of the form in which the information contained in documents delivered to the registrar may be recorded and kept;

(f) section 708(5) (fees payable to the registrar);

(g) section 709 so far as they relate to the determination of the means of facilitating the exercise of the right of persons to inspect records kept by the registrar, or of the form in which copies of the information contained in these records may be made available;

(h) section 710A so far as they relate to the approval of the means of communication by the registrar of information in non-legible form; and

(i) section 713 (enforcement of company's duty to make returns) so far as they relate to the making of an application to the court.

2. Functions conferred by or under any of the following provisions of the Insolvency Act 1986—

(a) section 69 (enforcement of receiver's duty to make returns etc); and

(b) section 170 (enforcement of liquidator's duty to make returns etc).

3. Functions conferred by or under regulation 4(2) of the Regulations (transfer of official address).

4. Functions conferred by or under any provision of the Act or the Insolvency Act 1986 listed in paragraphs 1 and 2(a) above to the extent specified in these paragraphs where any such provision is applied to EEIGs by regulation 18 or 19 of the Regulations.

NOTES

As to the repeal of most of the Companies Act 1985, see that Act at **[5.1]**.

SCHEDULE 3
FUNCTIONS OF THE SECRETARY OF STATE ENABLED TO BE CONTRACTED OUT

Article 5

[10.754]

1. Functions conferred by or under any of the following provisions of the Act—

(a) section 26(2) (prohibition on registration of certain names except with the approval of the Secretary of State);

(b) section 244(5) (extension by Secretary of State of the period allowed for laying and delivering accounts and reports); and

(c) section 702(5) (extension by Secretary of State of period for delivering accounts and reports of an oversea company).

2. Functions conferred by or under section 2 of the Business Names Act 1985 (prohibition of use of certain business names).

3. Functions conferred by or under section 2 of the Business Names Act 1985 as applied to EEIGs by regulation 17 of the Regulations (application of Business Names Act 1985).

NOTES

As to the repeal of most of the Companies Act 1985, see that Act at **[5.1]**.

CONTRACTING OUT (FUNCTIONS OF THE OFFICIAL RECEIVER) ORDER 1995

(SI 1995/1386)

NOTES

Made: 29 May 1995.

Authority: Deregulation and Contracting Out Act 1994, s 69.

Commencement: 30 May 1995.

Amendment: as of 1 July 2011, this Order had not been amended.

Limited liability partnerships: by the Limited Liability Partnerships Regulations 2001, SI 2001/1090, reg 10, Sch 6, Pt III, this Order applies, with modifications, to limited liability partnerships (see **[10.830]**).

[10.755]
1 Citation and commencement

(1)   This Order may be cited as the Contracting Out (Functions of the Official Receiver) Order 1995.

(2)   This Order shall come into force on the day after the day on which it is made.

[10.756]
2 Interpretation

(1)   In this Order—

"the 1986 Act" means the Insolvency Act 1986;

"the insolvency legislation" means the Insolvency Act 1986, the Companies Act 1985, the Company Directors Disqualification Act 1986, any subordinate legislation made under any of those Acts and any regulations made under rule 12.1 of the Rules;

"the Rules" means the Insolvency Rules 1986; and

"right of audience" has the meaning given to it by section 119(1) of the Courts and Legal Services Act 1990.

(2)   Any expression used in this Order other than one referred to in paragraph (1) above shall bear the same meaning as it bears in the 1986 Act.

(3)   In this Order a rule referred to by number means the rule so numbered in the Rules and, except where otherwise expressly provided, a section referred to by number means the section so numbered in the 1986 Act.

NOTES

As to the repeal of most of the Companies Act 1985, see that Act at **[5.1]**.

[10.757]
3 Contracting out of functions

(1)   Subject to paragraph (2) below, any function of the official receiver which is conferred by or under the insolvency legislation, except one which is listed in the Schedule to this Order, may be exercised by, or by employees of, such person (if any) as may be authorised in that behalf by the official receiver.

(2)   A function to which paragraph (1) above applies, and which involves the exercise of a right of audience in relation to any proceedings before a court, may only be exercised subject to the fulfilment of the condition specified in paragraph (3) below.

(3)   Such right of audience as is mentioned in paragraph (2) shall not be exercised by any person other than a person who has a right of audience in relation to the proceedings in question by virtue of the provisions of Part II of the Courts and Legal Services Act 1990.

SCHEDULE

Article 3

[10.758]

1.   The functions of the official receiver as—

(a)   a receiver appointed pursuant to section 32 (power for court to appoint official receiver);

(b)   a provisional liquidator appointed pursuant to section 135 (appointment and powers of provisional liquidator); or

(c)   an interim receiver appointed pursuant to section 286 (power to appoint interim receiver).

2.   The receipt of any deposit which relates to a bankruptcy or winding-up petition.

3.   The chairing—

(a)   by virtue of rule 4.55 of the first meeting of creditors (as defined by rule 4.50(7)) or the first meeting of contributories (as defined by rule 4.50(7)) in a winding up by the court; or

(b)   by virtue of rule 6.82 of the first meeting of creditors (as defined in rule 6.79(7)) in a bankruptcy.

4.   The making of an application to the Secretary of State—

(a)   under section 137(1) for the appointment of another person as liquidator in the place of the official receiver; or

(b)   under section 296(1) for the appointment of a person as trustee instead of the official receiver.

5.   The taking of a decision—

(a)   pursuant to section 137(2), whether or not to refer to the Secretary of State the need for an appointment of a liquidator in any case where at meetings held in pursuance of a decision under section 136(5)(a) no person is chosen to be liquidator;

(b)   pursuant to section 295(1), whether or not to refer to the Secretary of State the need for an appointment of a trustee in any case where at a meeting summoned under section 293 or 294 no appointment of a person as trustee is made.

Part 10   Miscellaneous other SIs

6. The making of a reference to the Secretary of State under section 300(4) of the need for an appointment of a trustee by the Secretary of State in the circumstances referred to in that sub-section.

7. The making of a reference to the court or the Secretary of State, as the case may be, under section 300(5) of the need to fill any vacancy in the circumstances referred to in that sub-section.

8. The functions of the official receiver—
    (a)   exercisable under rule 4.172(2) (functions of liquidation committee exercisable by official receiver) or rule 6.166(2) (functions of creditors' committee exercisable by official receiver); or
    (b)   in relation to the hearing of an application made under—
        (i)   section 280 (discharge by order of the court);
        (ii)   rule 4.36(2) (application to court for a release or extension of time in respect of statement of affairs in a winding up by the court); or
        (iii)   rule 6.62(2) (application to court by bankrupt for a release or extension of time in respect of statement of affairs).

9. The bringing or the conduct of proceedings under the Company Directors Disqualification Act 1986.

10. The giving of notice to the Secretary of State pursuant to section 174(3) (release of official receiver in winding up by the court) or section 299(2) (release of official receiver as trustee).

11. Consideration—
    (a)   pursuant to rule 4.57(2) as to whether a request by creditors for a meeting of creditors or contributories or meetings of both, or
    (b)   pursuant to rule 4.57(2) as it applies by virtue of rule 4.57(4) as to whether a request by contributories for a meeting of contributories, or
    (c)   pursuant to rule 6.83(2) as to whether a request by creditors for a meeting of creditors,
has been properly made in accordance with the 1986 Act.

12. The making or conduct of any application to the court—
    (a)   to commit a bankrupt for contempt of court for failure to comply with an obligation imposed on him by—
        (i)   section 288 (statement of affairs);
        (ii)   section 291 (duties of bankrupt in relation to official receiver);
        (iii)   section 312 (obligation to surrender control to trustee);
        (iv)   section 333 (duties of bankrupt in relation to trustee); or
        (v)   section 363 (general control of court); or
    (b)   pursuant to section 279(3) (suspension of discharge on application by official receiver).

13. The making or conduct of any application to the court to commit for contempt of court—
    (a)   a person who has failed to attend his public examination under section 133 (public examination of officers, etc); or
    (b)   a bankrupt who has failed to attend his public examination under section 290 (public examination of bankrupt).

14. The making of a report to the court pursuant to—
    (a)   section 132(1) (investigation by official receiver);
    (b)   section 289(1) (investigatory duties of official receiver);
    (c)   section 289(2) (report to the court on application by bankrupt for discharge from bankruptcy);
    (d)   rule 4.36(5) (report to court, etc on application by officers of company, etc for release from duty to submit statement of affairs or for extension of time);
    (e)   rule 6.62(5) (report to court, etc on application by bankrupt for release from duty to submit statement of affairs or for extension of time); or
    (f)   rule 6.215(2) (report in support of application for suspension of discharge).

15. The making or conduct of an application to the court for a public examination under section 133(1) or section 290(1) and the making or conduct of any application in relation to any public examination.

16. The making or conduct of an application to the court to relieve the official receiver from an obligation to make an application for a public examination requested pursuant to section 133(2) or required pursuant to section 290(2).

17. The taking part in a public examination or the questioning of a person pursuant to section 133(4)(a) or the taking part in a public examination or the questioning of a bankrupt pursuant to section 290(4)(a).

18. The making or conduct of an application to the court—

(a)   pursuant to section 134(2) for the issue of a warrant for the arrest of a person and for the seizure of any books, papers, records, money or goods in that person's possession; or

(b)   pursuant to section 364, for the issue of a warrant for the arrest of a debtor, an undischarged bankrupt or a discharged bankrupt, and for the seizure of any books, papers, records, money or goods in the debtor's or the bankrupt's possession, as the case may be.

19. The making or conduct of an application to the court pursuant to section 158 for the arrest of a contributory and for the seizure of his books, papers and movable personal property.

20. The making or conduct of an application to the court for the transfer of winding-up or bankruptcy proceedings from one court to another.

21. The taking of affidavits and declarations pursuant to rule 7.57(5) (taking of affidavits and declarations).

22. Any function of the official receiver in relation to the hearing of—

(a)   an application by a bankrupt for leave to act as a director of, or directly or indirectly to take part in or be concerned in the promotion, formation or management of, a company; or

(b)   an application by a director in respect of whom a disqualification order made under the Company Directors Disqualification Act 1986 is in force, for leave—

    (a)   to be a director of a company,

    (b)   to be a liquidator or administrator of a company,

    (c)   to be a receiver or manager of a company's property, or

    (d)   to be concerned or to take part in the promotion, formation or management of a company in any way, whether directly or indirectly.

23. The making of a report to the Secretary of State pursuant to section 7(3) of the Company Directors Disqualification Act 1986.

24. Any function corresponding to one referred to in paragraphs 1 to 23 above which is exercisable by the official receiver by virtue of the application (with or without modifications) of any provision of the insolvency legislation to insolvent partnerships or unregistered companies.

25. The presentation of a winding-up petition pursuant to section 124(5) (application by official receiver for winding up of company being wound up voluntarily).

INSOLVENT COMPANIES (REPORTS ON CONDUCT OF DIRECTORS) RULES 1996

(SI 1996/1909)

NOTES

Made: 22 July 1996.

Authority: Insolvency Act 1986, s 411; Company Directors Disqualification Act 1986, s 21(2).

Commencement: 30 September 1996.

These Rules are reproduced as amended by: the Insolvent Companies (Reports on Conduct of Directors) (Amendment) Rules 2001, SI 2001/764; the Enterprise Act 2002 (Insolvency) Order 2003, SI 2003/2096.

Limited liability partnerships: by the Limited Liability Partnerships Regulations 2001, SI 2001/1090, reg 10, Sch 6, Pt III, these Rules apply, with modifications, to limited liability partnerships (see **[10.830]**).

Application to bank insolvency and administration: as to the application of this SI to bank insolvency and administration, see the Banking Act 2009 (Parts 2 and 3 Consequential Amendments) Order 2009, SI 2009/317.

ARRANGEMENT OF RULES

[10.759]

1   Citation, commencement and interpretation

(1)   These Rules may be cited as the Insolvent Companies (Reports on Conduct of Directors) Rules 1996.

(2)   These Rules shall come into force on 30th September 1996.

(3)   In these Rules—

"the Act" means the Company Directors Disqualification Act 1986;

"the former Rules" means the Insolvent Companies (Reports on Conduct of Directors) No 2 Rules 1986; and

"the commencement date" means 30th September 1996.

[10.760]
2   Revocation

Subject to rule 7 below, the former Rules are hereby revoked.

[10.761]
3   Reports required under section 7(3) of the Act

(1)   This rule applies to any report made to the Secretary of State under section 7(3) of the Act by:—

(a)   the liquidator of a company which the courts in England and Wales have jurisdiction to wind up which passes a resolution for voluntary winding up on or after the commencement date;

(b)   an administrative receiver of a company appointed otherwise than under section 51 of the Insolvency Act 1986 (power to appoint receiver under the law of Scotland) on or after the commencement date; or

(c)   the administrator of a company which the courts in England and Wales have jurisdiction to wind up [which enters administration] on or after the commencement date.

(2)   Such a report shall be made in the Form D1 set out in the Schedule hereto, or in a form which is substantially similar, and in the manner and to the extent required by the Form D1.

NOTES

Para (1): words in square brackets substituted by the Enterprise Act 2002 (Insolvency) Order 2003, SI 2003/2096, arts 5, 6, Schedule, Pt 2, paras 68, 69, as from 15 September 2003, except in relation to any case where a petition for an administration order was presented before that date.

[10.762]
4   Return by office-holder

(1)   This rule applies where it appears to a liquidator of a company as mentioned in rule 3(1)(a), to an administrative receiver as mentioned in rule 3(1)(b), or to an administrator as mentioned in rule 3(1)(c) (each of whom is referred to hereinafter as "an office-holder") that the company has at any time become insolvent within the meaning of section 6(2) of the Act.

(2)   Subject as follows there may be furnished to the Secretary of State by an office-holder at any time during the period of 6 months from the relevant date (defined in paragraph (4) below) a return with respect to every person who:—

(a)   was, on the relevant date, a director or shadow director of the company, or

(b)   had been a director or shadow director of the company at any time in the 3 years immediately preceding that date.

(3)   The return shall be made in the Form D2 set out in the Schedule hereto, or in a form which is substantially similar, and in the manner and to the extent required by the Form D2.

(4)   For the purposes of this rule, "the relevant date" means:—

(a)   in the case of a company in creditors' voluntary winding up (there having been no declaration of solvency by the directors under section 89 of the Insolvency Act 1986), the date of the passing of the resolution for voluntary winding up,

(b)   in the case of a company in members' voluntary winding up, the date on which the liquidator forms the opinion that, at the time when the company went into liquidation, its assets were insufficient for the payment of its debts and other liabilities and the expenses of winding up,

(c)   in the case of the administrative receiver, the date of his appointment,

(d)   in the case of the administrator, the date [that the company enters administration],

and for the purposes of sub-paragraph (c) above the only appointment of an administrative receiver to be taken into account in determining the relevant date shall be that appointment which is not that of a successor in office to an administrative receiver who has vacated office either by death or pursuant to section 45 of the Insolvency Act 1986.

(5)   Subject to paragraph (6) below, it shall be the duty of an office-holder to furnish a return complying with the provisions of paragraphs (3) and (4) of this rule to the Secretary of State:—

(a)   where he is in office in relation to the company on the day one week before the expiry of the period of 6 months from the relevant date, not later than the expiry of such period;

(b)   where he vacates office (otherwise than by death) before the day one week before the expiry of the period of 6 months from the relevant date, within 14 days after his vacation of office except where he has furnished such a return on or prior to the day one week before the expiry of such period.

(6) A return need not be provided under this rule by an office-holder if he has, whilst holding that office in relation to the company, since the relevant date, made a report under rule 3 with respect to all persons falling within paragraph (2) of this rule and (apart from this paragraph) required to be the subject of a return.

(7) If an office-holder without reasonable excuse fails to comply with the duty imposed by paragraph (5) of this rule, he is guilty of an offence and—

(a) on summary conviction of the offence, is liable to a fine not exceeding level 3 on the standard scale, and

(b) after continued contravention, is liable to a daily default fine; that is to say, he is liable on a second or subsequent summary conviction of the offence to a fine of one-tenth of level 3 on the standard scale for each day on which the contravention is continued (instead of the penalty specified in sub-paragraph (a)).

(8) Section 431 of the Insolvency Act 1986 (summary proceedings), as it applies to England and Wales, has effect in relation to an offence under this rule as to offences under Parts I to VII of that Act.

NOTES

Para (4): words in square brackets substituted by the Enterprise Act 2002 (Insolvency) Order 2003, SI 2003/2096, arts 5, 6, Schedule, Pt 2, paras 68, 70, as from 15 September 2003, except in relation to any case where a petition for an administration order was presented before that date.

[10.763]
5   Forms

The forms referred to in rule 3(2) and rule 4(3) shall be used with such variations, if any, as the circumstances may require.

[10.764]
6   Enforcement of section 7(4)

(1) This rule applies where under section 7(4) of the Act (power to call on liquidators, former liquidators and others to provide information) the Secretary of State or the official receiver requires or has required a person:—

(a) to furnish him with information with respect to a person's conduct as director or shadow director of a company, and

(b) to produce and permit inspection of relevant books, papers and other records.

(2) On the application of the Secretary of State or (as the case may be) the official receiver, the court may make an order directing compliance within such period as may be specified.

(3) The court's order may provide that all costs of and incidental to the application shall be borne by the person to whom the order is directed.

[10.765]
7   Transitional and saving provisions

(1) Subject to paragraph (2) below, rules 3 and 4 of the former Rules shall continue to apply as if the former Rules had not been revoked when any of the events mentioned in sub-paragraphs (a), (b) or (c) of rule 3(1) of the former Rules (passing of resolution for voluntary winding up, appointment of administrative receiver, making of administration order) occurred on or after 29th December 1986 but before the commencement date.

(2) Until 31st December 1996—

(a) the forms contained in the Schedule to the former Rules which were required to be used for the purpose of complying with those Rules, or

(b) the Form D1 or D2 as set out in the Schedule to these Rules, as appropriate, or a form which is substantially similar thereto, with such variations, if any, as the circumstances may require,

may be used for the purpose of complying with rules 3 and 4 of the former Rules as applied by paragraph (1) above; but after that date the forms mentioned in sub-paragraph (b) of this paragraph shall be used for that purpose.

(3) When a period referred to in rule 5(2) of the former Rules is current immediately before the commencement date, these Rules have effect as if rule 6(2) of these Rules had been in force when the period began and the period is deemed to expire whenever it would have expired if these Rules had not been made and any right, obligation or power dependent on the beginning, duration or end of such period shall be under rule 6(2) of these Rules as it was or would have been under the said rule 5(2).

(4) The provisions of this rule are to be without prejudice to the operation of section 16 of the Interpretation Act 1978 (saving from repeals) as it is applied by section 23 of that Act.

SCHEDULE

[10.766]

NOTES

The Schedule sets out the forms referred to in rr 3(2) and 4(3) (see r 5 at **[10.763]**). The forms are not reproduced here but details are given in the table below. The Schedule was substituted by the Insolvent Companies (Reports on Conduct of Directors) (Amendment) Rules 2001, SI 2001/764.

Form No	Description
D1	Report under Section 7(3) of the Company Directors Disqualification Act 1986
D2	Return by Office-Holder under Rule 4 of the Insolvent Companies (Reports on Conduct of Directors) Rules 1996

INSOLVENT COMPANIES (REPORTS ON CONDUCT OF DIRECTORS) (SCOTLAND) RULES 1996

(SI 1996/1910)

NOTES

Authority: Insolvency Act 1986, s 411; Company Directors Disqualification Act 1986, s 21(2).
Made: 22 July 1996.
Commencement: 30 September 1996.
These rules are reproduced as amended by: the Insolvent Companies (Reports on Conduct of Directors) (Scotland) (Amendment) Rules 2001, SI 2001/768.
Limited liability partnerships: by the Limited Liability Partnerships Regulations 2001, SI 2001/1090, reg 10, Sch 6, Pt III, these Rules apply, with modifications, to limited liability partnerships (see **[10.830]**).

ARRANGEMENT OF RULES

[10.767]
1   Citation, commencement and interpretation

(1)   These Rules may be cited as the Insolvent Companies (Reports on Conduct of Directors) (Scotland) Rules 1996.

(2)   These Rules shall come into force on 30th September 1996.

(3)   In these Rules—
"the Act" means the Company Directors Disqualification Act 1986;
"the former Rules" means the Insolvent Companies (Reports on Conduct of Directors) (No 2) (Scotland) Rules 1986;
"the commencement date" means 30th September 1996; and
"a company" means a company which the courts in Scotland have jurisdiction to wind up.

[10.768]
2   Revocation

Subject to rule 7 below, the former Rules are hereby revoked.

[10.769]
3   Reports required under section 7(3) of the Act

(1)   This rule applies to any report made to the Secretary of State under section 7(3) of the Act by—
    (a)   the liquidator of a company which is being wound up by an order of the court made on or after the commencement date;
    (b)   the liquidator of a company which passes a resolution for voluntary winding up on or after that date;

(c)   a receiver of a company appointed under section 51 of the Insolvency Act 1986 (power to appoint receiver under the law of Scotland) on or after that date, who is an administrative receiver; or

(d)   the administrator of a company in relation to which the court makes an administration order on or after that date.

(2)   Such a report shall be made in the Form D1 (Scot) set out in the Schedule hereto, or in a form which is substantially similar, and in the manner and to the extent required by the Form D1 (Scot).

[10.770]
4   Return by office-holder

(1)   This rule applies where it appears to a liquidator of a company as mentioned in rule 3(1)(a) or (b), to an administrative receiver as mentioned in rule 3(1)(c), or to an administrator as mentioned in rule 3(1)(d) (each of whom is referred to hereinafter as "an office-holder") that the company has at any time become insolvent within the meaning of section 6(2) of the Act.

(2)   Subject as follows there may be furnished to the Secretary of State by an office-holder at any time during the period of 6 months from the relevant date (defined in paragraph (4) below) a return with respect to every person who:—

(a)   was, on the relevant date, a director or shadow director of the company, or

(b)   had been a director or shadow director of the company at any time in the 3 years immediately preceding that date.

(3)   The return shall be made in the Form D2 (Scot) set out in the Schedule hereto, or in a form which is substantially similar, and in the manner and to the extent required by the Form D2 (Scot).

(4)   For the purposes of this rule, 'the relevant date' means—

(a)   in the case of a company in liquidation (except in the case mentioned in paragraph (4)(b) below), the date on which the company goes into liquidation within the meaning of section 247(2) of the Insolvency Act 1986,

(b)   in the case of a company in members' voluntary winding up, the date on which the liquidator forms the opinion that, at the time when the company went into liquidation, its assets were insufficient for the payment of its debts and other liabilities and the expenses of winding up,

(c)   in the case of the administrative receiver, the date of his appointment,

(d)   in the case of the administrator, the date of the administration order made in relation to the company,

and for the purposes of sub-paragraph (c) above the only appointment of an administrative receiver to be taken into account in determining the relevant date shall be that appointment which is not that of a successor in office to an administrative receiver who has vacated office either by death or pursuant to section 62 of the Insolvency Act 1986.

(5)   Subject to paragraph (6) below, it shall be the duty of an office-holder to furnish a return complying with the provisions of paragraphs (3) and (4) of this rule to the Secretary of State—

(a)   where he is in office in relation to the company on the day one week before the expiry of the period of 6 months from the relevant date, not later than the expiry of such period;

(b)   where he vacates office (otherwise than by death) before the day one week before the expiry of the period of 6 months from the relevant date, within 14 days after his vacation of office except where he has furnished such a return on or prior to the day one week before the expiry of such period.

(6)   A return need not be provided under this rule by an office-holder if he has, whilst holding that office in relation to the company, since the relevant date, made a report under rule 3 with respect to all persons falling within paragraph (2) of this rule and (apart from this paragraph) required to be the subject of a return.

(7)   If an office-holder without reasonable excuse fails to comply with the duty imposed by paragraph (5) of this rule, he is guilty of an offence and—

(a)   on summary conviction of the offence, is liable to a fine not exceeding level 3 on the standard scale, and

(b)   after continued contravention, is liable to a daily default fine; that is to say, he is liable on a second or subsequent summary conviction of the offence to a fine of one-tenth of level 3 on the standard scale for each day on which the contravention is continued (instead of the penalty specified in sub-paragraph (a)).

(8)   Section 431 of the Insolvency Act 1986 (summary proceedings), as it applies to Scotland, has effect in relation to an offence under this rule as to offences under Parts I to VII of that Act.

[10.771]
5   Forms

The forms referred to in rule 3(2) and rule 4(3) shall be used with such variations, if any, as the circumstances may require.

[10.772]
6 Enforcement of section 7(4)

(1) This rule applies where under section 7(4) of the Act (power to call on liquidators, former liquidators and others to provide information) the Secretary of State requires or has required a person:—

(a) to furnish him with information with respect to a person's conduct as director or shadow director of a company, and

(b) to produce and permit inspection of relevant books, papers and other records.

(2) On the application of the Secretary of State, the court may make an order directing compliance within such period as may be specified.

(3) The court's order may provide that all expenses of and incidental to the application shall be borne by the person to whom the order is directed.

[10.773]
7 Transitional and saving provisions

(1) Subject to paragraph (2) below, rules 2 and 3 of the former Rules shall continue to apply as if the former Rules had not been revoked when any of the events mentioned in sub-paragraphs (a), (b), (c) or (d) of rule 2(1) of the former Rules (order of the court for winding up, passing of resolution for voluntary winding up, appointment of administrative receiver, making of administration order) occurred on or after 29th December 1986 but before the commencement date.

(2) Until 31st December 1996—

(a) the forms contained in the Schedule to the former Rules which were required to be used for the purpose of complying with those Rules, or

(b) the Form D1 (Scot) or D2 (Scot) as set out in the Schedule to these Rules, as appropriate, or a form which is substantially similar thereto, with such variations, if any, as the circumstances may require,

may be used for the purpose of complying with rules 2 and 3 of the former Rules as applied by paragraph (1) above; but after that date the forms mentioned in sub-paragraph (b) of this paragraph shall be used for that purpose.

(3) When a period referred to in rule 4(2) of the former Rules is current immediately before the commencement date, these Rules have effect as if rule 6(2) of these Rules had been in force when the period began and the period is deemed to expire whenever it would have expired if these Rules had not been made and any right, obligation or power dependent on the beginning, duration or end of such period shall be under rule 6(2) of these Rules as it was or would have been under the said rule 4(2).

(4) The provisions of this rule are to be without prejudice to the operation of section 16 of the Interpretation Act 1978 (saving from repeals) as it is applied by section 23 of that Act.

SCHEDULE

[10.774]

NOTES
The Schedule sets out the forms referred to in rr 3(2) and 4(3) (see r 5 at **[10.771]**). The forms are not reproduced here but details are given in the table below. The Schedule was amended by the Insolvent Companies (Reports on Conduct of Directors) (Scotland) (Amendment) Rules 2001, SI 2001/768.

Form No	Description
D1 (Scot)	Report under Section 7(3) of the Company Directors Disqualification Act 1986
D2 (Scot)	Return by Office-Holder under Rule 4 of the Insolvent Companies (Reports on Conduct of Directors) Rules (Scotland) 1996

FINANCIAL MARKETS AND INSOLVENCY (SETTLEMENT FINALITY) REGULATIONS 1999

(SI 1999/2979)

NOTES
Made: 2 November 1999.
Authority: European Communities Act 1972, s 2(2).
Commencement: 11 December 1999.
These Regulations are reproduced as amended by: the Banking Consolidation Directive (Consequential Amendments) Regulations 2000, SI 2000/2952; the Civil Jurisdiction and Judgments Order 2001, SI 2001/3929; the Electronic Money (Miscellaneous Amendments) Regulations 2002, SI 2002/765; the Financial Services and Markets Act 2000 (Consequential Amendments) Order 2002, SI 2002/1555; the Enterprise Act 2002 (Insolvency) Order 2003, SI 2003/2096; the Financial Markets and Insolvency (Settlement Finality) (Amendment) Regulations 2006, SI 2006/50; the Capital Requirements Regulations 2006, SI 2006/3221; the Financial Services (EEA State) Regulations 2007, SI 2007/108; the Financial Services and

Markets Act 2000 (Markets in Financial Instruments) Regulations 2007, SI 2007/126; the Financial Markets and Insolvency (Settlement Finality) (Amendment) Regulations 2007, SI 2007/832; the Civil Jurisdiction and Judgments Regulations 2007, SI 2007/1655; the Financial Markets and Insolvency (Settlement Finality) (Amendment) Regulations 2009, SI 2009/1972; the Financial Markets and Insolvency (Settlement Finality and Financial Collateral Arrangements) (Amendment) Regulations 2010, SI 2010/2993; the Electronic Money Regulations 2011, SI 2011/99.

References to "the European Community", "Community", etc: see the Treaty of Lisbon (Changes in Terminology) Order 2011, SI 2011/1043, which provides that (as from 22 April 2011) "EU" should be substituted for the word "Community" (subject to certain exceptions) in references to "Community treaties", "Community instrument", "Community obligation", "Community law", "Community legislation", etc.

Application to bank insolvency and administration: as to the application of these Regulations SI to bank insolvency and administration, see the Banking Act 2009 (Parts 2 and 3 Consequential Amendments) Order 2009, SI 2009/317.

ARRANGEMENT OF REGULATIONS

PART I
GENERAL

PART II
DESIGNATED SYSTEMS

PART III
TRANSFER ORDERS EFFECTED THROUGH A DESIGNATED SYSTEM
AND COLLATERAL SECURITY

Collateral security charges

General

PART I
GENERAL

[10.775]
1 Citation, commencement and extent

(1)   These Regulations may be cited as the Financial Markets and Insolvency (Settlement Finality) Regulations 1999 and shall come into force on 11th December 1999.

(2)   . . . . . .

NOTES

Para (2): revoked by the Financial Markets and Insolvency (Settlement Finality) (Amendment) Regulations 2006, SI 2006/50, reg 2(1), (2), as from 2 February 2006. Para (2) previously provided that these Regulations do not extend to Northern Ireland.

[10.776]

2 Interpretation

(1) In these Regulations—

["the 2000 Act" means the Financial Services and Markets Act 2000;]

["'business day" shall cover both day and night-time settlements and shall encompass all events happening during the business cycle of a system;]

"central bank" means a central bank of an EEA State or the European Central Bank;

"central counterparty" means a body corporate or unincorporated association interposed between the institutions in a . . . system and which acts as the exclusive counterparty of those institutions with regard to transfer orders;

"charge" means any form of security, including a mortgage and, in Scotland, a heritable security;

"clearing house" means a body corporate or unincorporated association which is responsible for the calculation of the net positions of institutions and any central counterparty or settlement agent in a . . . system;

"collateral security" means any realisable assets provided under a charge or a repurchase or similar agreement, or otherwise (including [credit claims and] money provided under a charge)—

    (a)   for the purpose of securing rights and obligations potentially arising in connection with a . . . system ("collateral security in connection with participation in a . . . system"); or

    (b)   to a central bank for the purpose of securing rights and obligations in connection with its operations in carrying out its functions as a central bank ("collateral security in connection with the functions of a central bank");

"collateral security charge" means, where collateral security consists of realisable assets (including money) provided under a charge, that charge;

["credit claims" means pecuniary claims arising out of an agreement whereby a credit institution grants credit in the form of a loan;]

["credit institution" means a credit institution as defined in [Article 4(1)] of Directive 2006/48/EC of the European Parliament and of the Council of 14 June 2006 relating to the taking up and pursuit of the business of credit institutions [(as last amended by Directive 2009/111/EC)], including the bodies set out in the list in Article 2;]

"creditors' voluntary winding-up resolution" means a resolution for voluntary winding up (within the meaning of the Insolvency Act 1986 [or the Insolvency (Northern Ireland) Order 1989]) where the winding up is a creditors' winding up (within the meaning of that Act [or that Order]);

"default arrangements" means the arrangements put in place by a designated system [or by a system which is an interoperable system in relation to that system] to limit systemic and other types of risk which arise in the event of a participant [or a system operator of an interoperable system] appearing to be unable, or likely to become unable, to meet its obligations in respect of a transfer order, including, for example, any default rules within the meaning of Part VII [or Part V] or any other arrangements for—

    (a)   netting,

    (b)   the closing out of open positions, or

    (c)   the application or transfer of collateral security;

"defaulter" means a person in respect of whom action has been taken by a designated system under its default arrangements;

"designated system" means a system which is declared by a designation order for the time being in force to be a designated system for the purposes of these Regulations;

"designating authority" means—

    (a)   in the case of a system—

        (i)   which is, or the operator of which is, a recognised investment exchange or a recognised clearing house for the purposes of [the 2000 Act],

        (ii)   which is, or the operator of which is, a listed person within the meaning of the Financial Markets and Insolvency (Money Market) Regulations 1995, or

        (iii)   through which securities transfer orders are effected (whether or not payment transfer orders are also effected through that system),

        the Financial Services Authority;

    (b)   in any other case, the Bank of England;

"designation order" has the meaning given by regulation 4;

["EEA State" has the meaning given by Schedule 1 to the Interpretation Act 1978;]

"guidance", in relation to a designated system, means guidance issued or any recommendation made by it which is intended to have continuing effect and is issued in writing or other legible form to all or any class of its participants or users or persons seeking to participate in the system or to use its facilities and which would, if it were a rule, come within the definition of a rule;

["indirect participant" means an institution, central counterparty, settlement agent, clearing house or system operator—

(a)   which has a contractual relationship with a participant in a designated system that enables the indirect participant to effect transfer orders through that system, and

(b)   the identity of which is known to the system operator;]

"institution" means—

(a)   a credit institution;

[(aa)   an electronic money institution within the meaning of Article 2.1 of Directive 2009/110/EC of the European Parliament and of the Council of 16 September 2009 on the taking up, pursuit and prudential supervision of the business of electronic money institutions amending Directives 2005/60/EC and 2006/48/EC and repealing Directive 2000/46/EC;]

(b)   an investment firm as defined in [Article 4.1.1 of Directive 2004/39/EC of the European Parliament and of the Council of 21 April 2004 on markets in financial instruments, other than a person to whom Article 2 applies];

(c)   a public authority or publicly guaranteed undertaking;

(d)   any undertaking whose head office is outside the European Community and whose functions correspond to those of a credit institution or investment firm as defined in (a) and (b) above; or

(e)   any undertaking which is treated by the designating authority as an institution in accordance with regulation 8(1),

which participates in a . . . . system and which is responsible for discharging the financial obligations arising from transfer orders which are effected through the system;

["interoperable system" in relation to a system ("the first system"), means a second system whose system operator has entered into an arrangement with the system operator of the first system that involves cross-system execution of transfer orders;]

"netting" means the conversion into one net claim or obligation of different claims or obligations between participants resulting from the issue and receipt of transfer orders between them, whether on a bilateral or multilateral basis and whether through the interposition of a clearing house, central counterparty or settlement agent or otherwise;

["Part V" means Part V of the Companies (No 2) (Northern Ireland) Order 1990;]

"Part VII" means Part VII of the Companies Act 1989;

"participant" means—

(a)   an institution;

[(aa)   a system operator;]

(b)   a body corporate or unincorporated association which carries out any combination of the functions of a central counterparty, a settlement agent or a clearing house, with respect to a system, or

(c)   an indirect participant which is treated as a participant, or is a member of a class of indirect participants which are treated as participants, in accordance with regulation 9;

"protected trust deed" and "trust deed" shall be construed in accordance with section 73(1) of the Bankruptcy (Scotland) Act 1985 (interpretation);

"relevant office-holder" means—

(a)   the official receiver;

(b)   any person acting in relation to a company as its liquidator, provisional liquidator, or administrator;

(c)   any person acting in relation to an individual (or, in Scotland, any debtor within the meaning of the Bankruptcy (Scotland) Act 1985) as his trustee in bankruptcy or interim receiver of his property or as permanent or interim trustee in the sequestration of his estate or as his trustee under a protected trust deed; . . .

(d)   any person acting as administrator of an insolvent estate of a deceased person; [or]

[(e)   any person appointed pursuant to insolvency proceedings of a country or territory outside the United Kingdom;]

and in sub-paragraph (b), "company" means any company, society, association, partnership or other body which may be wound up under the Insolvency Act 1986 [or the Insolvency (Northern Ireland) Order 1989];

"rules", in relation to a designated system, means rules or conditions governing the system with respect to the matters dealt with in these Regulations;

"securities" means (except for the purposes of the definition of "charge") any instruments referred to in section [C of Annex I to Directive 2004/39/EC of the European Parliament and of the Council of 21 April 2004 on markets in financial instruments];

"settlement account" means an account at a central bank, a settlement agent or a central counterparty used to hold funds or securities (or both) and to settle transactions between participants in a designated system;

"settlement agent" means a body corporate or unincorporated association providing settlement accounts to the institutions and any central counterparty in a designated system for the settlement of transfer orders within the system and, as the case may be, for extending credit to such institutions and any such central counterparty for settlement purposes;

["system operator" means the entity or entities legally responsible for the operation of a system. A system operator may also act as a settlement agent, central counterparty or clearing house;]

"the Settlement Finality Directive" means Directive 98/26/EC of the European Parliament and of the Council of 19th May 1998 on settlement finality in payment and securities settlement systems [as amended by Directive 2009/44/EC of the European Parliament and of the Council of 6 May 2009 amending Directive 98/26/EC on settlement finality in payment and securities settlement systems and Directive 2002/47/EC on financial collateral arrangements as regards linked systems and credit claims];

"transfer order" means—

    (a)   an instruction by a participant to place at the disposal of a recipient an amount of money by means of a book entry on the accounts of a credit institution, a central bank[, a central counterparty] or a settlement agent, or an instruction which results in the assumption or discharge of a payment obligation as defined by the rules of a designated system ("a payment transfer order"); or

    (b)   an instruction by a participant to transfer the title to, or interest in, securities by means of a book entry on a register, or otherwise ("a securities transfer order");

["winding-up" means—

    (a)   winding up by the court or creditors' voluntary winding up within the meaning of the Insolvency Act 1986 or the Insolvency (Northern Ireland) Order 1989 (but does not include members' voluntary winding up within the meaning of that Act or that Order);

    (b)   sequestration of a Scottish partnership under the Bankruptcy (Scotland) Act 1985;

    (c)   bank insolvency within the meaning of the Banking Act 2009].

(2) In these Regulations—

    (a)   references to the law of insolvency include references to every provision made by or under the Insolvency Act 1986[, the Insolvency (Northern Ireland) Order 1989] or the Bankruptcy (Scotland) Act 1985; and in relation to a building society references to insolvency law or to any provision of the Insolvency Act 1986 [or the Insolvency (Northern Ireland) Order 1989] are to that law or provision as modified by the Building Societies Act 1986;

    (b)   in relation to Scotland, references to—

        (i)   sequestration include references to the administration by a judicial factor of the insolvent estate of a deceased person,

        (ii)   an interim or permanent trustee include references to a judicial factor on the insolvent estate of a deceased person, and

        (iii)   "set off" include compensation.

(3) Subject to paragraph (1), expressions used in these Regulations which are also used in the Settlement Finality Directive have the same meaning in these Regulations as they have in the Settlement Finality Directive.

(4) References in these Regulations to things done, or required to be done, by or in relation to a designated system shall, in the case of a designated system which is neither a body corporate nor an unincorporated association, be treated as references to things done, or required to be done, by or in relation to the operator of that system.

NOTES

Para (1) is amended as follows:

Definition "the 2000 Act" substituted (for original definition "the 1986 Act"), and words in square brackets in definition "designating authority" substituted, by the Financial Services and Markets Act 2000 (Consequential Amendments) Order 2002, SI 2002/1555, art 39(1), (2), as from 3 July 2002.

Definitions "business day", "credit claims", "interoperable system", and "system operator" inserted by the Financial Markets and Insolvency (Settlement Finality and Financial Collateral Arrangements) (Amendment) Regulations 2010, SI 2010/2993, reg 2(1), (2)(a), as from 6 April 2011 (note that by virtue of reg 3 of the 2010 Regulations, nothing in those Regulations affects any designation order in force under these Regulations in relation to a designated system, and no system operator shall be required to apply for an amended designation order in consequence only of the 2010 Regulations).

Words omitted from the definitions "central counterparty", "clearing house", "settlement account" and "settlement agent" revoked by SI 2010/2993, reg 2(1), (2)(b), (c), (k), (l), as from 6 April 2011 (see further the note relating to reg 3 of the 2010 Regulations above).

In the definition of "collateral security" words omitted revoked, and words in square brackets inserted, by SI 2010/2993, reg 2(1), (2)(d), as from 6 April 2011 (see further the note relating to reg 3 of the 2010 Regulations above).

Definition "credit institution" substituted by the Capital Requirements Regulations 2006, SI 2006/3221, reg 29(4), Sch 6, para 3, as from 1 January 2007; words in first pair of square brackets substituted by SI 2010/2993, reg 2(1), (2)(e), as from 6 April 2011 (see further the note relating to reg 3 of the 2010 Regulations above); words in second pair of square brackets inserted by the Electronic Money Regulations 2011, SI 2011/99, reg 79, Sch 4, Pt 2, para 8, as from 30 April 2011.

Words in first and second pairs of square brackets in the definition "default arrangements" inserted by SI 2010/2993, reg 2(1), (2)(f), as from 6 April 2011 (see further the note relating to reg 3 of the 2010 Regulations above); words in third pair of square brackets inserted by the Financial Markets and Insolvency (Settlement Finality) (Amendment) Regulations 2006, SI 2006/50, reg 2(1), (3), as from 2 February 2006.

Words in square brackets in definitions "creditors' voluntary winding up resolution" and "winding up" inserted, and definition "Part V" inserted, by SI 2006/50, reg 2(1), (3), as from 2 February 2006.

Definition "EEA State" substituted by the Financial Services (EEA State) Regulations 2007, SI 2007/108, reg 5, as from 13 February 2007.

Definitions "indirect participant" and "winding-up" substituted by SI 2010/2993, reg 2(1), (2)(g), (o), as from 6 April 2011 (see further the note relating to reg 3 of the 2010 Regulations above).

Words in square brackets in para (b) of the definition "institution" substituted by the Financial Services and Markets Act 2000 (Markets in Financial Instruments) Regulations 2007, SI 2007/126, reg 3(6), Sch 6, Pt 2, para 14, as from 1 November 2007; para (aa) inserted, and word omitted revoked, by SI 2010/2993, reg 2(1), (2)(h), as from 6 April 2011 (see further the note relating to reg 3 of the 2010 Regulations above).

Words in square brackets in the definitions "participant", "the Settlement Finality Directive", and "transfer order" inserted by SI 2010/2993, reg 2(1), (2)(i), (m), (n), as from 6 April 2011 (see further the note relating to reg 3 of the 2010 Regulations above).

In the definition "relevant office-holder" words omitted from para (c) revoked, and para (e) (and the preceding word) inserted, by SI 2010/2993, reg 2(1), (2)(j), as from 6 April 2011 (see further the note relating to reg 3 of the 2010 Regulations above); final words in square brackets inserted by SI 2006/50, reg 2(1), (3), as from 2 February 2006.

Words in square brackets in the definition "securities" substituted by SI 2007/126, reg 3(6), Sch 6, Pt 2, para 14, as from 1 November 2007.

Para (2): words in square brackets inserted by SI 2006/50, reg 2(1), (4), as from 2 February 2006.

PART II
DESIGNATED SYSTEMS

[10.777]
3   Application for designation

(1)   Any body corporate or unincorporated association may apply to the designating authority for an order declaring it, or any system of which it is the operator, to be a designated system for the purposes of these Regulations.

(2)   Any such application—

    (a)   shall be made in such manner as the designating authority may direct; and

    (b)   shall be accompanied by such information as the designating authority may reasonably require for the purpose of determining the application.

(3)   At any time after receiving an application and before determining it, the designating authority may require the applicant to furnish additional information.

(4)   The directions and requirements given or imposed under paragraphs (2) and (3) may differ as between different applications.

(5)   Any information to be furnished to the designating authority under this regulation shall be in such form or verified in such manner as it may specify.

(6)   Every application shall be accompanied by copies of the rules of the system to which the application relates and any guidance relating to that system.

[10.778]
4   Grant and refusal of designation

(1)   Where—

    (a)   an application has been duly made under regulation 3;

    (b)   the applicant has paid any fee charged by virtue of regulation 5(1); and

    (c)   the designating authority is satisfied that the requirements of the Schedule are satisfied with respect to the system to which the application relates;

the designating authority may make an order (a "designation order") declaring the system to be a designated system [and identifying the system operator of that system] for the purposes of these Regulations.

(2)   In determining whether to make a designation order, the designating authority shall have regard to systemic risks.

(3)   Where an application has been made to the Financial Services Authority under regulation 3 in relation to a system through which both securities transfer orders and payment transfer orders are effected, the Authority shall consult the Bank of England before deciding whether to make a designation order.

(4)   A designation order shall state the date on which it takes effect.

(5)   Where the designating authority refuses an application for a designation order it shall give the applicant a written notice to that effect stating the reasons for the refusal.

NOTES

Para (1): words in square brackets inserted by the Financial Markets and Insolvency (Settlement Finality and Financial Collateral Arrangements) (Amendment) Regulations 2010, SI 2010/2993, reg 2(1), (3), as from 6 April 2011 (note that by virtue of reg 3 of the 2010 Regulations, nothing in those Regulations affects any designation order in force under these Regulations in relation to a designated system, and no system operator shall be required to apply for an amended designation order in consequence only of the 2010 Regulations).

[10.779]
5   Fees

(1)   The designating authority may charge a fee to an applicant for a designation order.

(2)   The designating authority may charge [the system operator of] a designated system a periodical fee.

(3)   Fees chargeable by the designating authority under this regulation shall not exceed an amount which reasonably represents the amount of costs incurred or likely to be incurred—

  (a)   in the case of a fee charged to an applicant for a designation order, in determining whether the designation order should be made; and

  (b)   in the case of a periodical fee, in satisfying itself that the designated [system and its system operator continue] to meet the requirements of the Schedule and [are complying] with any obligations to which [they are subject] by virtue of these Regulations.

NOTES

  Para (2): words in square brackets inserted by the Financial Markets and Insolvency (Settlement Finality and Financial Collateral Arrangements) (Amendment) Regulations 2010, SI 2010/2993, reg 2(1), (4)(a), as from 6 April 2011 (note that by virtue of reg 3 of the 2010 Regulations, nothing in those Regulations affects any designation order in force under these Regulations in relation to a designated system, and no system operator shall be required to apply for an amended designation order in consequence only of the 2010 Regulations).

  Para (3): words in square brackets substituted by SI 2010/2993, reg 2(1), (4)(b), as from 6 April 2011 (see further the note relating to reg 3 of the 2010 Regulations above).

[10.780]
6   Certain bodies deemed to satisfy requirements for designation

(1)   Subject to paragraph (2), an investment exchange or clearing house declared by an order for the time being in force to be a recognised investment exchange or recognised clearing house for the purposes of [the 2000 Act], whether that order was made before or is made after the coming into force of these Regulations, shall be deemed to satisfy the requirements in paragraphs 2 and 3 of the Schedule.

(2)   Paragraph (1) does not apply to overseas investment exchanges or overseas clearing houses within the meaning of [the 2000 Act].

NOTES

  Para (1): words in square brackets substituted by the Financial Services and Markets Act 2000 (Consequential Amendments) Order 2002, SI 2002/1555, art 39(1), (3), as from 3 July 2002.

  Para (2): words in square brackets substituted by the Financial Markets and Insolvency (Settlement Finality) (Amendment) Regulations 2009, SI 2009/1972, regs 2, 3, as from 1 October 2009.

[10.781]
7   Revocation of designation

(1)   A designation order may be revoked by a further order made by the designating authority if at any time it appears to the designating authority—

  (a)   that any requirement of the Schedule is not satisfied in the case of the system to which the designation order relates; or

  (b)   that the system [or the system operator of that system] has failed to comply with any obligation to which [they are subject] by virtue of these Regulations.

(2)   [Subsections (1) to (7) of section 298 of the 2000 Act] shall apply in relation to the revocation of a designation order under paragraph (1) as they apply in relation to the revocation of a recognition order *under* [section 297(2) of that Act]; and in those subsections as they so apply—

  [(a)   any reference to a recognised body shall be taken to be a reference to a designated system;

  (b)   any reference to members of a recognised body shall be taken to be a reference to participants in a designated system;

  (c)   references to the Authority shall, in cases where the Bank of England is the designating authority, be taken to be a reference to the Bank of England; and

  (d)   subsection (4)(a) shall have effect as if for "two months" there were substituted "three months".]

[(3)   An order revoking a designation order—

  (a)   shall state the date on which it takes effect, being no earlier than three months after the day on which the revocation order is made; and

  (b)   may contain such transitional provisions as the designating authority thinks necessary or expedient.

(4)   A designation order may be revoked at the request or with the consent of the [system operator of the] designated system, and any such revocation shall not be subject to the restriction imposed by paragraph (3)(a), or to the requirements imposed by subsections (1) to (6) of section 298 of the 2000 Act.]

NOTES

  Para (1): words in first pair of square brackets inserted, and words in second pair of square brackets substituted, by the Financial Markets and Insolvency (Settlement Finality and Financial Collateral Arrangements) (Amendment) Regulations 2010, SI 2010/2993, reg 2(1), (5), as from 6 April 2011 (note that by virtue of reg 3 of the 2010 Regulations, nothing in those Regulations affects any designation order in force under these Regulations in relation to a designated system, and no system operator shall be required to apply for an amended designation order in consequence only of the 2010 Regulations).

Para (2): words in square brackets substituted by the Financial Services and Markets Act 2000 (Consequential Amendments) Order 2002, SI 2002/1555, art 39(1), (4), as from 3 July 2002. With regard to the words in the second pair of square brackets, note that art 39(4)(b) of the 2002 Order actually provides—

"for "*under* subsection (1) of that section" substitute "section 297(2) of that Act"";

It is believed that this is an error and that the word "under" should not be removed from para (2).
Paras (3), (4): added by SI 2002/1555, art 39(1), (5), as from 3 July 2002; words in square brackets in para (4) inserted by SI 2010/2993, reg 2(1), (6), as from 6 April 2011 (see further the note relating to reg 3 of the 2010 Regulations above).

[10.782]
8   Undertakings treated as institutions

(1)   A designating authority may treat as an institution any undertaking which participates in a designated system and which is responsible for discharging financial obligations arising from transfer orders effected through that system, provided that—

  (a)   the designating authority considers such treatment to be required on grounds of systemic risk, and
  (b)   the designated system is one in which at least three institutions (other than any undertaking treated as an institution by virtue of this paragraph) participate and through which securities transfer orders are effected.

(2)   Where a designating authority decides to treat an undertaking as an institution in accordance with paragraph (1), it shall give written notice of that decision to the designated system in which the undertaking is to be treated as a participant [and to the system operator of that system].

NOTES

Para (2): words in square brackets added by the Financial Markets and Insolvency (Settlement Finality and Financial Collateral Arrangements) (Amendment) Regulations 2010, SI 2010/2993, reg 2(1), (7), as from 6 April 2011 (note that by virtue of reg 3 of the 2010 Regulations, nothing in those Regulations affects any designation order in force under these Regulations in relation to a designated system, and no system operator shall be required to apply for an amended designation order in consequence only of the 2010 Regulations).

[10.783]
9   Indirect participants treated as participants

(1)   A designating authority may treat—

  (a)   an indirect participant as a participant in a designated system, or
  (b)   a class of indirect participants as participants in a designated system,

where it considers this to be required on grounds of systemic risk, and shall give written notice of any decision to that effect to the designated system [and to the system operator of that system].

[(2)   Where a designating authority, in accordance with paragraph (1), treats an indirect participant as a participant in a designated system, the liability of the participant through which that indirect participant passes transfer orders to the designated system is not affected.]

NOTES

Words in square brackets in para (1) added, and para (2) added, by the Financial Markets and Insolvency (Settlement Finality and Financial Collateral Arrangements) (Amendment) Regulations 2010, SI 2010/2993, reg 2(1), (8), as from 6 April 2011 (note that by virtue of reg 3 of the 2010 Regulations, nothing in those Regulations affects any designation order in force under these Regulations in relation to a designated system, and no system operator shall be required to apply for an amended designation order in consequence only of the 2010 Regulations).

[10.784]
10   Provision of information by designated systems

[(1)   The system operator of a designated system shall, when that system is declared to be a designated system, provide to the designating authority in writing a list of the participants (including the indirect participants) in the designated system and shall give written notice to the designating authority of any amendment to the list within seven days of such amendment.]

(2)   The designating authority may, in writing, require [the system operator of a designated system] to furnish to it such other information relating to that designated system as it reasonably requires for the exercise of its functions under these Regulations, within such time, in such form, at such intervals and verified in such manner as the designating authority may specify.

(3)   When [the system operator of a designated system] amends, revokes or adds to its rules or its guidance, it shall within fourteen days give written notice to the designating authority of the amendment, revocation or addition.

(4)   [The system operator of a designated system] shall give the designating authority at least fourteen days' written notice of any proposal to amend, revoke or add to its default arrangements.

(5)   Nothing in this regulation shall require [the system operator of a designated system] to give any notice or furnish any information to the Financial Services Authority which it has given or furnished to the Authority pursuant to any requirement imposed by or under [section 293 of the 2000 Act] (notification requirements) or any other enactment.

Part 10   Miscellaneous other SIs

NOTES

Para (1) was substituted, the words in square brackets in paras (2)–(4) were substituted, and the words in first pair of square brackets in para (5) were substituted, by the Financial Markets and Insolvency (Settlement Finality and Financial Collateral Arrangements) (Amendment) Regulations 2010, SI 2010/2993, reg 2(1), (9)(a), as from 6 April 2011 (note that by virtue of reg 3 of the 2010 Regulations, nothing in those Regulations affects any designation order in force under these Regulations in relation to a designated system, and no system operator shall be required to apply for an amended designation order in consequence only of the 2010 Regulations).

The words in the second pair of square brackets in para (5) were substituted by the Financial Services and Markets Act 2000 (Consequential Amendments) Order 2002, SI 2002/1555, art 39(1), (6), as from 3 July 2002.

[10.785]
11   Exemption from liability in damages

(1)   Neither the designating authority nor any person who is, or is acting as, a member, officer or member of staff of the designating authority shall be liable in damages for anything done or omitted in the discharge, or purported discharge, of the designating authority's functions under these Regulations.

(2)   Paragraph (1) does not apply—
   (a)   if the act or omission is shown to have been in bad faith; or
   (b)   so as to prevent an award of damages made in respect of an act or omission on the ground that the act or omission was unlawful as a result of section 6(1) of the Human Rights Act 1998 (acts of public authorities).

[10.786]
12   Publication of information and advice

A designating authority may publish information or give advice, or arrange for the publication of information or the giving of advice, in such form and manner as it considers appropriate with respect to any matter dealt with in these Regulations.

PART III
TRANSFER ORDERS EFFECTED THROUGH A DESIGNATED SYSTEM AND COLLATERAL SECURITY

[10.787]
13   Modifications of the law of insolvency

(1)   The general law of insolvency has effect in relation to—
   (a)   transfer orders effected through a designated system and action taken under the rules of a designated system with respect to such orders; and
   (b)   collateral security,
subject to the provisions of this Part.

(2)   Those provisions apply in relation to—
   [(a)   insolvency proceedings in respect of a participant in a designated system, or of a participant in a system which is an interoperable system in relation to that designated system;]
   (b)   insolvency proceedings in respect of a provider of collateral security in connection with the functions of a central bank, in so far as the proceedings affect the rights of the central bank to the collateral security; [and]
   [(c)   insolvency proceedings in respect of a system operator of a designated system or of a system which is an interoperable system in relation to that designated system;]
but not in relation to any other insolvency proceedings, notwithstanding that rights or liabilities arising from transfer orders or collateral security fall to be dealt with in the proceedings.

(3)   Subject to regulation 21, nothing in this Part shall have the effect of disapplying Part VII [or Part V].

[(4)   References in this Part to "insolvency proceedings" shall include—
   (a)   bank insolvency under Part 2 of the Banking Act 2009; and
   (b)   bank administration under Part 3 of the Banking Act 2009.]

NOTES

Para (2): sub-para (a) substituted, word in square brackets in sub-para (b) added, and sub-para (c) added, by the Financial Markets and Insolvency (Settlement Finality and Financial Collateral Arrangements) (Amendment) Regulations 2010, SI 2010/2993, reg 2(1), (10)(a)–(c), as from 6 April 2011 (note that by virtue of reg 3 of the 2010 Regulations, nothing in those Regulations affects any designation order in force under these Regulations in relation to a designated system, and no system operator shall be required to apply for an amended designation order in consequence only of the 2010 Regulations).

Para (3): words in square brackets added by the Financial Markets and Insolvency (Settlement Finality) (Amendment) Regulations 2006, SI 2006/50, reg 2(1), (5), as from 2 February 2006.

Para (4): added by SI 2010/2993, reg 2(1), (10)(d), as from 6 April 2011 (see further the note relating to reg 3 of the 2010 Regulations above).

[10.788]

14   Proceedings of designated system take precedence over insolvency proceedings

(1)   None of the following shall be regarded as to any extent invalid at law on the ground of inconsistency with the law relating to the distribution of the assets of a person on bankruptcy, winding up, [administration,] sequestration or under a protected trust deed, or in the administration of an insolvent estate [or with the law relating to other insolvency proceedings of a country or territory outside the United Kingdom]—

  (a)   a transfer order;

  (b)   the default arrangements of a designated system;

  (c)   the rules of a designated system as to the settlement of transfer orders not dealt with under its default arrangements;

  (d)   a contract for the purpose of realising collateral security in connection with participation in a designated system [or in a system which is an interoperable system in relation to that designated system] otherwise than pursuant to its default arrangements; or

  (e)   a contract for the purpose of realising collateral security in connection with the functions of a central bank.

(2)   The powers of a relevant office-holder in his capacity as such, and the powers of the court under the Insolvency Act 1986[, the Insolvency (Northern Ireland) Order 1989] or the Bankruptcy (Scotland) Act 1985, shall not be exercised in such a way as to prevent or interfere with—

  (a)   the settlement in accordance with the rules of a designated system of a transfer order not dealt with under its default arrangements;

  (b)   any action taken under [the default arrangements of a designated system];

  (c)   any action taken to realise collateral security in connection with participation in a designated system [or in a system which is an interoperable system in relation to that designated system] otherwise than pursuant to its default arrangements; or

  (d)   any action taken to realise collateral security in connection with the functions of a central bank.
    . . .

(3)   Nothing in the following provisions of this Part shall be construed as affecting the generality of the above provisions.

(4)   A debt or other liability arising out of a transfer order which is the subject of action taken under default arrangements may not be proved in a winding up[, bankruptcy, or administration], or in Scotland claimed in a winding up, sequestration or under a protected trust deed, until the completion of the action taken under default arrangements.

    A debt or other liability which by virtue of this paragraph may not be proved or claimed shall not be taken into account for the purposes of any set-off until the completion of the action taken under default arrangements.

(5)   Paragraph (1) has the effect that the following provisions (which relate to preferential debts and the payment of expenses etc) apply subject to paragraph (6), namely—

  (a)   in the case of collateral security provided by a company (within the meaning of section [section 1 of the Companies Act 2006) or by a building society (within the meaning of section 119 of the Building Societies Act 1986)])—

    [(i)   sections 175, 176ZA and 176A of, and paragraph 65(2) of Schedule B1 to, the Insolvency Act 1986 or Articles 149, 150ZA, and 150A of, and paragraph 66(2) of Schedule B1 to, the Insolvency (Northern Ireland) Order 1989;

    (ii)   Rules 4.30(3) and 4.218(2)(b) of the Insolvency Rules 1986, Rules 4.033(3) and 4.228(2)(b) of the Insolvency Rules (Northern Ireland) 1991 and rule 4.5(3) of the Insolvency (Scotland) Rules 1986;]

    [(iii)   section 40 (or in Scotland, section 59 and 60(1)(e)) of the Insolvency Act 1986, paragraph 99(3) of Schedule B1 to that Act and section 19(4) of that Act as that section has effect by virtue of section 249(1) of the Enterprise Act 2002;

    [(iv)   paragraph 100(3) of Schedule B1 to the Insolvency (Northern Ireland) Order 1989, Article 31(4) of that Order, as it has effect by virtue of Article 4(1) of the Insolvency (Northern Ireland) Order 2005, and Article 50 of the Insolvency (Northern Ireland) Order 1989; and]

    (v)   section 754 of the Companies Act 2006 [(including that section as applied or modified by any enactment made under the Banking Act 2009)]; and]

  (b)   in the case of collateral security provided by an individual, section 328(1) and (2) of the Insolvency Act 1986[or, in Northern Ireland, Article 300(1) and (2) of the Insolvency (Northern Ireland) Order 1989] or, in Scotland, in the case of collateral security provided by an individual or a partnership, section 51 of the Bankruptcy (Scotland) Act 1985 and any like provision or rule of law affecting a protected trust deed.

(6)   The claim of a participant[, system operator] or central bank to collateral security shall be paid in priority to—

  (a)   the expenses of the winding up mentioned in sections 115 and 156 of the Insolvency Act 1986 [or Articles 100 and 134 of the Insolvency (Northern Ireland) Order 1989], the expenses of the bankruptcy within the meaning of that Act [or that Order] or, as the case may be, the remuneration and expenses of the administrator mentioned in [paragraph 99(3) of Schedule B1 to that Act] [and in section 19(4) of that Act as that section has effect by virtue of section 249(1) of the Enterprise Act 2002] [or in paragraph 100(3) to Schedule B1 to that Order] [and Article 31(4) of that Order, as that Article has effect by virtue of Article 4(1) of the Insolvency (Northern Ireland) Order 2005], and

(b)   the preferential debts of the company or the individual (as the case may be) within the meaning given by section 386 of that Act [or Article 346 of that Order], [and

(c)   the debts or liabilities arising or incurred under contracts mentioned in—

    (i)   paragraph 99(4) of Schedule B1 to the Insolvency Act 1986 and section 19(5) of that Act, as that section has effect by virtue of section 249(1) of the Enterprise Act 2002, or

    (ii) paragraph 100(4) of Schedule B1 to, the Insolvency (Northern Ireland) Order 1989 and Article 31(5) of that Order as that article has effect by virtue of Article 4(1) of the Insolvency (Northern Ireland) Order 2005,]

unless the terms on which the collateral security was provided expressly provide that such expenses, remuneration or preferential debts are to have priority.

(7)   As respects Scotland—

(a)   the reference in paragraph (6)(a) to the expenses of bankruptcy shall be taken to be a reference to the matters mentioned in paragraphs (a) to (d) of section 51(1) of the Bankruptcy (Scotland) Act 1985, or any like provision or rule of law affecting a protected trust deed; and

(b)   the reference in paragraph (6)(b) to the preferential debts of[the individual shall be taken to be a reference to the preferred debts of the debtor within the meaning of the Bankruptcy (Scotland) Act 1985, or any like definition applying with respect to a protected trust deed by virtue of any provision or rule of law affecting it.

NOTES

Para (1): word in first pair of square brackets inserted by the Financial Markets and Insolvency (Settlement Finality) (Amendment) Regulations 2009, SI 2009/1972, regs 2, 4(a), as from 1 October 2009; other words in square brackets inserted by the Financial Markets and Insolvency (Settlement Finality and Financial Collateral Arrangements) (Amendment) Regulations 2010, SI 2010/2993, reg 2(1), (11)(a), (b), as from 6 April 2011 (note that by virtue of reg 3 of the 2010 Regulations, nothing in those Regulations affects any designation order in force under these Regulations in relation to a designated system, and no system operator shall be required to apply for an amended designation order in consequence only of the 2010 Regulations).

Para (2): words in first pair of square brackets inserted by the Financial Markets and Insolvency (Settlement Finality) (Amendment) Regulations 2006, SI 2006/50, reg 2(1), (6)(a), as from 2 February 2006; words in square brackets in sub-para (b) substituted, and words in square brackets in sub-para (c) inserted, by SI 2010/2993, reg 2(1), (11)(c), (d), as from 6 April 2011 (see further the note relating to reg 3 of the 2010 Regulations above); words omitted revoked by SI 2009/1972, regs 2, 4(b), as from 1 October 2009.

Para (4): words in square brackets substituted by SI 2009/1972, regs 2, 4(c), as from 1 October 2009.

Para (5): sub-para (5)(a)(iv) substituted, and words in square brackets in (5)(a)(v) inserted, by SI 2010/2993, reg 2(1), (11)(e), (f), as from 6 April 2011 (see further the note relating to reg 3 of the 2010 Regulations above); final words in square brackets inserted by SI 2006/50, reg 2(1), (6), as from 2 February 2006; all other words in square brackets substituted by SI 2009/1972, regs 2, 4(d), as from 1 October 2009.

Para (6) is amended as follows:

Words in first pair of square brackets inserted by SI 2010/2993, reg 2(1), (11)(g), as from 6 April 2011 (see further the note relating to reg 3 of the 2010 Regulations above).

In sub-para (a) words "or Articles 100 and 134 of the Insolvency (Northern Ireland) Order 1989" and "or that Order" in square brackets inserted by SI 2006/50, reg 2(1), (6)(f), as from 2 February 2006.

In sub-para (a) words "paragraph 99(3) of Schedule B1 to that Act" in square brackets substituted by the Enterprise Act 2002 (Insolvency) Order 2003, SI 2003/2096, art 5, Schedule, Pt 2, paras 74, 75(b), as from 15 September 2003, except in relation to any case where a petition for an administration order was presented before that date.

In sub-para (a) words "and in section 19(4) of that Act as that section has effect by virtue of section 249(1) of the Enterprise Act 2002" in square brackets inserted by SI 2009/1972, regs 2, 4(e)(i)(aa), as from 1 October 2009.

In sub-para (a) words "or in paragraph 100(3) to Schedule B1 to that Order" in square brackets substituted by the Financial Markets and Insolvency (Settlement Finality) (Amendment) Regulations 2007, SI 2007/832, reg 2(1), (3), as from 6 April 2007.

In sub-para (a) words "and Article 31(4) of that Order, as that Article has effect by virtue of Article 4(1) of the Insolvency (Northern Ireland) Order 2005" in square brackets inserted by SI 2009/1972, regs 2, 4(e)(i)(bb), as from 1 October 2009.

In sub-para (b) words "or Article 346 of that Order" in square brackets inserted by SI 2006/50, reg 2(1), (6)(g), as from 2 February 2006.

Sub-para (c) and the word "and" immediately preceding it inserted by SI 2009/1972, regs 2, 4(e)(ii), as from 1 October 2009.

[10.789]
15   Net sum payable on completion of action taken under default arrangements

(1)   The following provisions apply with respect to any sum which is owed on completion of action taken under default arrangements [of a designated system] by or to a defaulter but do not apply to any sum which (or to the extent that it) arises from a transfer order which is also a market contract within the meaning of Part VII [or Part V], in which case sections 162 and 163 of the Companies Act 1989 [or Articles 85 and 86 of the Companies (No 2) (Northern Ireland) Order 1990] apply subject to the modification made by regulation 21.

(2)   If, in England and Wales [or Northern Ireland], a bankruptcy[, winding-up or administration] order has been made or a creditors' voluntary winding-up resolution has been passed, the debt—

(a)   is provable in the bankruptcy[, winding-up or administration] or, as the case may be, is payable to the relevant office-holder; and

(b)   shall be taken into account, where appropriate, under section 323 of the Insolvency Act 1986 [or Article 296 of the Insolvency (Northern Ireland) Order 1989] [or Rule 2.85 of the Insolvency Rules 1986 or Rule 2.086 of the Insolvency Rules (Northern Ireland) 1991] (mutual dealings and set-off) or the corresponding provision applicable in the case of winding up [or administration];

in the same way as a debt due before the commencement of bankruptcy, the date on which the body corporate goes into liquidation (within the meaning of section 247 of the Insolvency Act 1986 [or Article 6 of the Insolvency (Northern Ireland) Order 1989]) or [enters into administration (within the meaning of paragraph 1 of Schedule B1 to the Insolvency Act 1986 or paragraph 2 of Schedule B1 to the Insolvency (Northern Ireland) Order 1989) or], in the case of a partnership, the date of the winding-up order.

(3)   If, in Scotland, an award of sequestration or a winding-up order has been made, or a creditors' voluntary winding-up resolution has been passed, or a trust deed has been granted and it has become a protected trust deed, the debt—

(a)   may be claimed in the sequestration or winding up or under the protected trust deed or, as the case may be, is payable to the relevant office-holder; and

(b)   shall be taken into account for the purposes of any rule of law relating to set-off applicable in sequestration, winding up or in respect of a protected trust deed;

in the same way as a debt due before the date of sequestration (within the meaning of section 73(1) of the Bankruptcy (Scotland) Act 1985) or the commencement of the winding up (within the meaning of section 129 of the Insolvency Act 1986) or the grant of the trust deed.

[(4)   A reference in this regulation to "administration order" shall include—

(a)   the appointment of an administrator under paragraph 14 or 22 of Schedule B1 to the Insolvency Act 1986 or under paragraph 15 or 23 of Schedule B1 to the Insolvency (Northern Ireland) Order 1989;

(b)   the making of an order under section 8 of that Act as it has effect by virtue of section 249(1) of the Enterprise Act 2002; and

(c)   the making of an order under Article 21 of that Order as it has effect by virtue of Article 4(1) of the Insolvency (Northern Ireland) Order 2005;

and "administration" shall be construed accordingly.]

NOTES

Para (1): words in first pair of square brackets inserted by the Financial Markets and Insolvency (Settlement Finality and Financial Collateral Arrangements) (Amendment) Regulations 2010, SI 2010/2993, reg 2(1), (12), as from 6 April 2011 (note that by virtue of reg 3 of the 2010 Regulations, nothing in those Regulations affects any designation order in force under these Regulations in relation to a designated system, and no system operator shall be required to apply for an amended designation order in consequence only of the 2010 Regulations); other words in square brackets inserted by the Financial Markets and Insolvency (Settlement Finality) (Amendment) Regulations 2006, SI 2006/50, reg 2(1), (7)(a), as from 2 February 2006.

Para (2): words "or Northern Ireland", "or Article 296 of the Insolvency (Northern Ireland) Order 1989" and "or Article 6 of the Insolvency (Northern Ireland) Order 1989" in square brackets inserted by SI 2006/50, reg 2(1), (7)(b)–(d), as from 2 February 2006; all other words in square brackets inserted or substituted by the Financial Markets and Insolvency (Settlement Finality) (Amendment) Regulations 2009, SI 2009/1972, regs 2, 5(a), (b), as from 1 October 2009.

Para (4): added by SI 2009/1972, regs 2, 5(c), as from 1 October 2009.

[10.790]
16   Disclaimer of property, rescission of contracts, &c

(1)   Sections 178, 186, 315 and 345 of the Insolvency Act 1986 [or Articles 152, 157, 288 and 318 of the Insolvency (Northern Ireland) Order 1989] (power to disclaim onerous property and court's power to order rescission of contracts, &c) do not apply in relation to—

(a)   a transfer order; or

(b)   a contract for the purpose of realising collateral security.

In the application of this paragraph in Scotland, the reference to sections 178, 315 and 345 shall be construed as a reference to any rule of law having the like effect as those sections.

(2)   In Scotland, a permanent trustee on the sequestrated estate of a defaulter or a liquidator or a trustee under a protected trust deed granted by a defaulter is bound by any transfer order given by that defaulter and by any such contract as is mentioned in paragraph (1)(b) notwithstanding section 42 of the Bankruptcy (Scotland) Act 1985 or any rule of law having the like effect applying in liquidations or any like provision or rule of law affecting the protected trust deed.

(3)   [Sections 88, 127, 245 and 284 of the Insolvency Act 1986], [Articles 74, 107, 207 and 257 of the Insolvency (Northern Ireland) Order 1989] (avoidance of property dispositions effected after commencement of winding up or presentation of bankruptcy petition), section 32(8) of the Bankruptcy (Scotland) Act 1985 (effect of dealing with debtor relating to estate vested in permanent trustee) and any like provision or rule of law affecting a protected trust deed, do not apply to—

(a)   a transfer order, or any disposition of property in pursuance of such an order;

(b)   the provision of collateral security;

(c)   a contract for the purpose of realising collateral security or any disposition of property in pursuance of such a contract; or

(d) any disposition of property in accordance with the rules of a designated system as to the application of collateral security.

NOTES

Para (1): words in square brackets inserted by the Financial Markets and Insolvency (Settlement Finality) (Amendment) Regulations 2006, SI 2006/50, reg 2(1), (8), as from 2 February 2006.

Para (3): words in square brackets substituted by the Financial Markets and Insolvency (Settlement Finality) (Amendment) Regulations 2009, SI 2009/1972, regs 2, 6, as from 1 October 2009.

[10.791]
17 Adjustment of prior transactions

(1) No order shall be made in relation to a transaction to which this regulation applies under—
(a) section 238 or 339 of the Insolvency Act 1986 [or Article 202 or 312 of the Insolvency (Northern Ireland) Order 1989] (transactions at an undervalue);
(b) section 239 or 340 of that Act [or Article 203 or 313 of that Order] (preferences); or
(c) section 423 of that Act [or Article 367 of that Order] (transactions defrauding creditors).

(2) As respects Scotland, no decree shall be granted in relation to any such transaction—
(a) under section 34 or 36 of the Bankruptcy (Scotland) Act 1985 or section 242 or 243 of the Insolvency Act 1986 (gratuitous alienations and unfair preferences); or
(b) at common law on grounds of gratuitous alienations or fraudulent preferences.

(3) This regulation applies to—
(a) a transfer order, or any disposition of property in pursuance of such an order;
(b) the provision of collateral security;
(c) a contract for the purpose of realising collateral security or any disposition of property in pursuance of such a contract; or
(d) any disposition of property in accordance with the rules of a designated system as to the application of collateral security.

NOTES

Para (1): words in square brackets inserted by the Financial Markets and Insolvency (Settlement Finality) (Amendment) Regulations 2006, SI 2006/50, reg 2(1), (9), as from 2 February 2006. Note that the Queen's Printer's copy of the 2006 Regulations actually provides that the words "or Article 203 or 313 of that Order" are to be inserted after the words "section 239 or 340 of that Act" in para (2)(b) of this regulation. It is assumed that this is a drafting error.

Collateral security charges

[10.792]
18 Modifications of the law of insolvency

The general law of insolvency has effect in relation to a collateral security charge and the action taken to enforce such a charge, subject to the provisions of regulation 19.

[10.793]
19 Administration orders, &c

(1) The following provisions of [Schedule B1 to] the Insolvency Act 1986 (which relate to administration orders and administrators) do not apply in relation to a collateral security charge—
[(a) paragraph 43(2) including that provision as applied by paragraph 44; and
(b) paragraphs 70, 71 and 72 of that Schedule,]
and [paragraph 41(2) of that Schedule] (receiver to vacate office when so required by administrator) does not apply to a receiver appointed under such a charge.

[(1ZA) The following provisions of the Insolvency Act 1986 (which relate to administration orders and administrators), as they have effect by virtue of section 249(1) of the Enterprise Act 2002, do not apply in relation to a collateral security charge—
(a) sections 10(1)(b) and 11(3)(c) (restriction on enforcement of security while petition for administration order pending or order in force); and
(b) sections 15(1) and (2) (power of administrator to deal with charged property);
and section 11(2) (receiver to vacate office when so required by administrator) does not apply to a receiver appointed under such a charge.]

[(1A) The following provisions of [Schedule B1 to] the Insolvency (Northern Ireland) Order 1989 (which relate to administration orders and administrators) do not apply in relation to a collateral security charge—
[(a) paragraph 44(2), including that provision as applied by paragraph 45 (restrictions on enforcement of security where company in administration or where administration application has been made); and
(b) paragraphs 71, 72 and 73 (charged and hire purchase property);]
and [paragraph 42(2)] (receiver to vacate office when so required by administrator) does not apply to a receiver appointed under such a charge.]

[(1B) The following provisions of the Insolvency (Northern Ireland) Order 1989 (administration), as they have effect by virtue of Article 4(1) of the Insolvency (Northern Ireland) Order 2005, do not apply in relation to a collateral security charge—

- (a)   Article 23(1)(b) and Article 24(3)(c) (restriction on enforcement of security while petition for administration order pending or order in force); and
- (b)   Article 28(1) and (2) (power of administrator to deal with charged property);

and Article 24(2) of that Order (receiver to vacate office at request of administrator) shall not apply to a receiver appointed under such a charge.]

(2)   However, where a collateral security charge falls to be enforced after an administration order has been made or a petition for an administration order has been presented, and there exists another charge over some or all of the same property ranking in priority to or *pari passu* with the collateral security charge, on the application of any person interested, the court may order that there shall be taken after enforcement of the collateral security charge such steps as the court may direct for the purpose of ensuring that the chargee under the other charge is not prejudiced by the enforcement of the collateral security charge.

[(2A)   A reference in paragraph (2) to "an administration order" shall include the appointment of an administrator under paragraph 14 or 22 of Schedule B1 to the Insolvency Act 1986 [or under paragraph 15 or 23 of Schedule B1 to the Insolvency (Northern Ireland) Order 1989].]

(3)   Sections 127 and 284 of the Insolvency Act 1986 [or Articles 107 and 257 of the Insolvency (Northern Ireland) Order 1989] (avoidance of property dispositions effected after commencement of winding up or presentation of bankruptcy petition), section 32(8) of the Bankruptcy (Scotland) Act 1985 (effect of dealing with debtor relating to estate vested in permanent trustee) and any like provision or rule of law affecting a protected trust deed, do not apply to a disposition of property as a result of which the property becomes subject to a collateral security charge or any transactions pursuant to which that disposition is made.

[(4)   Paragraph 20 and paragraph 12(1)(g) of Schedule A1 to the Insolvency Act 1986, and paragraph 31 and paragraph 23(1)(g) of Schedule A1 to the Insolvency (Northern Ireland) Order 1989 (effect of moratorium on creditors) shall not apply (if they would otherwise do so) to any collateral security charge.]

NOTES

Para (1): words in first pair of square brackets inserted, words in third pair of square brackets substituted, and sub-paras (a), (b) substituted, by the Enterprise Act 2002 (Insolvency) Order 2003, SI 2003/2096, arts 5, 6, Schedule, Pt 2, paras 74, 76(a), as from 15 September 2003, except in relation to any case where a petition for an administration order was presented before that date.

Paras (1ZA), (1B), (4): inserted and added respectively by the Financial Markets and Insolvency (Settlement Finality) (Amendment) Regulations 2009, SI 2009/1972, regs 2, 7, as from 1 October 2009.

Para (1A): inserted by the Financial Markets and Insolvency (Settlement Finality) (Amendment) Regulations 2006, SI 2006/50, reg 2(1), (10)(a), as from 2 February 2006; words in square brackets substituted by the Financial Markets and Insolvency (Settlement Finality) (Amendment) Regulations 2007, SI 2007/832, reg 2(1), (4), as from 6 April 2007.

Para (2A): inserted by SI 2003/2096, arts 5, 6, Schedule, Pt 2, paras 74, 76(b), as from 15 September 2003, except in relation to any case where a petition for an administration order was presented before that date; words in square brackets inserted by SI 2007/832, reg 2(1), (5), as from 6 April 2007.

Para (3): words in square brackets inserted by SI 2006/50, reg 2(1), (10)(b), as from 2 February 2006.

General

[10.794]
20   Transfer order entered into designated system following insolvency

(1)   This Part does not apply in relation to any transfer order given by a participant which is entered into a designated system after—

- (a)   a court has made an order of a type referred to in regulation 22 [in respect of—
  - (i)   that participant;
  - (ii)   a participant in a system which is an interoperable system in relation to the designated system; or
  - (iii)   a system operator which is not a participant in the designated system, or]
- (b)   that participant[, a participant in a system which is an interoperable system in relation to the designated system or a system operator of that designated system] has passed a creditors' voluntary winding-up resolution, or
- (c)   a trust deed granted by that participant[, a participant in a system which is an interoperable system in relation to the designated system or a system operator of that designated system] has become a protected trust deed,

unless the conditions mentioned in paragraph (2) are satisfied.

(2)   The conditions referred to in paragraph (1) are that—

- (a)   the transfer order is carried out on the [same business day of the designated system] that the event specified in paragraph (1)(a), (b) or (c) occurs, and
- (b)   [the system operator] can show that it did not have notice of that event at [the time the transfer order became irrevocable].

(3)   For the purposes of paragraph (2)(b), [the relevant system operator] shall be taken to have notice of an event specified in paragraph (1)(a), (b) or (c) if it deliberately failed to make enquiries as to that matter in circumstances in which a reasonable and honest person would have done so.

NOTES

All words in square brackets in this regulation were inserted or substituted by the Financial Markets and Insolvency (Settlement Finality and Financial Collateral Arrangements) (Amendment) Regulations 2010, SI 2010/2993, reg 2(1), (13), as from 6 April 2011 (note that by virtue of reg 3 of the 2010 Regulations, nothing in those Regulations affects any designation order in force under these Regulations in relation to a designated system, and no system operator shall be required to apply for an amended designation order in consequence only of the 2010 Regulations).

[10.795]

21 Disapplication of certain provisions of Part VII [and Part V]

(1) The provisions of the Companies Act 1989 [or the Companies (No 2) (Northern Ireland) Order 1990] mentioned in paragraph (2) do not apply in relation to—

(a) a market contract which is also a transfer order effected through a designated system; or

(b) a market charge which is also a collateral security charge.

(2) The provisions referred to in paragraph (1) are as follows—

(a) section 163(4) to (6) [and Article 86(3) to (5)] (net sum payable on completion of default proceedings);

(b) section 164(4) to (6) [and Article 87(3) to (5)] (disclaimer of property, rescission of contracts, &c); and

(c) section 175(5) and (6) [and Article 97(5) and (6)] (administration orders, &c).

NOTES

Words in square brackets inserted by the Financial Markets and Insolvency (Settlement Finality) (Amendment) Regulations 2006, SI 2006/50, reg 2(1), (11), as from 2 February 2006.

[10.796]

22 Notification of insolvency order or passing of resolution for creditors' voluntary winding up

(1) Upon the making of an order for bankruptcy, sequestration, administration or winding up in respect of a participant in a designated system, the court shall forthwith notify both [the system operator of that designated system] and the designating authority that such an order has been made.

(2) Following receipt of—

(a) such notification from the court, or

(b) notification from a participant of the passing of a creditors' voluntary winding-up resolution or of a trust deed becoming a protected trust deed, pursuant to paragraph 5(4) of the Schedule,

the designating authority shall forthwith inform the Treasury of the notification.

NOTES

Para (1): words in square brackets substituted by the Financial Markets and Insolvency (Settlement Finality and Financial Collateral Arrangements) (Amendment) Regulations 2010, SI 2010/2993, reg 2(1), (14), as from 6 April 2011 (note that by virtue of reg 3 of the 2010 Regulations, nothing in those Regulations affects any designation order in force under these Regulations in relation to a designated system, and no system operator shall be required to apply for an amended designation order in consequence only of the 2010 Regulations).

[10.797]

23 Applicable law relating to securities held as collateral security

Where—

(a) securities (including rights in securities) are provided as collateral security to a participant[, a system operator] or a central bank (including any nominee, agent or third party acting on behalf of the participant[, the system operator] or the central bank), and

(b) a register, account or centralised deposit system located in an EEA State legally records the entitlement of that person to the collateral security,

the rights of that person as a holder of collateral security in relation to those securities shall be governed by the law of the EEA State or, where appropriate, the law of the part of the EEA State, where the register, account, or centralised deposit system is located.

NOTES

Words in square brackets inserted by the Financial Markets and Insolvency (Settlement Finality and Financial Collateral Arrangements) (Amendment) Regulations 2010, SI 2010/2993, reg 2(1), (15), as from 6 April 2011 (note that by virtue of reg 3 of the 2010 Regulations, nothing in those Regulations affects any designation order in force under these Regulations in relation to a designated system, and no system operator shall be required to apply for an amended designation order in consequence only of the 2010 Regulations).

[10.798]

24 Applicable law where insolvency proceedings are brought

Where insolvency proceedings are brought in any jurisdiction against a person who participates, or has participated, in a system designated for the purposes of the Settlement Finality Directive, any question relating to the rights and obligations arising from, or in connection with, that participation and falling to be determined by a court in England and Wales[, the High Court in Northern Ireland] or in Scotland shall (subject to regulation 23) be determined in accordance with the law governing that system.

NOTES

Words in square brackets inserted by the Financial Markets and Insolvency (Settlement Finality) (Amendment) Regulations 2006, SI 2006/50, reg 2(1), (12), as from 2 February 2006.

[10.799]
25 Insolvency proceedings in other jurisdictions

(1)   The references to insolvency law in section 426 of the Insolvency Act 1986 (co-operation between courts exercising jurisdiction in relation to insolvency) include, in relation to a part of the United Kingdom, this Part and, in relation to a relevant country or territory within the meaning of that section, so much of the law of that country or territory as corresponds to this Part.

(2)   A court shall not, in pursuance of that section or any other enactment or rule of law, recognise or give effect to—
  (a)   any order of a court exercising jurisdiction in relation to insolvency law in a country or territory outside the United Kingdom, or
  (b)   any act of a person appointed in such a country or territory to discharge any functions under insolvency law,
in so far as the making of the order or the doing of the act would be prohibited in the case of a court in England and Wales or Scotland[, the High Court in Northern Ireland] or a relevant office-holder by this Part.

(3)   Paragraph (2) does not affect the recognition or enforcement of a judgment required to be recognised or enforced under or by virtue of the Civil Jurisdiction and Judgments Act 1982 [or Council Regulation (EC) No 44/2001 of 22nd December 2000 on jurisdiction and the recognition and enforcement of judgments in civil and commercial matters][, as amended from time to time and as applied by the Agreement made on 19th October 2005 between the European Community and the Kingdom of Denmark on jurisdiction and the recognition and enforcement of judgments in civil and commercial matters].

NOTES

Para (2): words in square brackets inserted by the Financial Markets and Insolvency (Settlement Finality) (Amendment) Regulations 2006, SI 2006/50, reg 2(1), (13), as from 2 February 2006.

Para (3): words in first pair of square brackets added by the Civil Jurisdiction and Judgments Order 2001, SI 2001/3929, art 5, Sch 3, para 27, as from 1 March 2002; words in second pair of square brackets added by the Civil Jurisdiction and Judgments Regulations 2007, SI 2007/1655, reg 5, Schedule, Pt 2, para 32, as from 1 July 2007.

[10.800]
26 Systems designated in other EEA States . . . and Gibraltar

(1)   Where an equivalent overseas order or equivalent overseas security is subject to the insolvency law of England and Wales or Scotland [or Northern Ireland], this Part shall apply—
  (a)   in relation to the equivalent overseas order as it applies in relation to a transfer order; and
  (b)   in relation to the equivalent overseas security as it applies in relation to collateral security . . .

(2)   In paragraph (1)—
  (a)   "equivalent overseas order" means an order having the like effect as a transfer order which is effected through a system designated for the purposes of the Settlement Finality Directive in another EEA State . . . or Gibraltar; and
  [(b)   "equivalent overseas security" means any realisable assets provided under a charge or a repurchase or similar agreement, or otherwise (including credit claims and money provided under a charge)—
    (i)   for the purpose of securing rights and obligations potentially arising in connection with such a system, or
    (ii)   to a central bank for the purpose of securing rights and obligations in connection with its operations in carrying out its functions as a central bank.]

NOTES

Words omitted from para (1)(b) revoked, and para (2)(b) substituted, by the Financial Markets and Insolvency (Settlement Finality and Financial Collateral Arrangements) (Amendment) Regulations 2010, SI 2010/2993, reg 2(1), (16), as from 6 April 2011 (note that by virtue of reg 3 of the 2010 Regulations, nothing in those Regulations affects any designation order in force under these Regulations in relation to a designated system, and no system operator shall be required to apply for an amended designation order in consequence only of the 2010 Regulations).

Other words omitted revoked, and other words in square brackets inserted, by the Financial Markets and Insolvency (Settlement Finality) (Amendment) Regulations 2006, SI 2006/50, reg 2(1), (14), as from 2 February 2006.

Part 10   Miscellaneous other SIs

SCHEDULE
REQUIREMENTS FOR DESIGNATION OF SYSTEM

Regulation 4(1)

[10.801]
1 Establishment, participation and governing law

(1) The head office of at least one of the participants in the system must be in [the United Kingdom] and the law of England and Wales[, Northern Ireland] or Scotland must be the governing law of the system.

(2) There must be not less than three institutions participating in the system, unless otherwise determined by the designating authority in any case where—
- (a) there are two institutions participating in a system; and
- (b) the designating authority considers that designation is required on the grounds of systemic risk.

(3) The system must be a system through which transfer orders are effected.

(4) Where orders relating to financial instruments other than securities are effected through the system—
- (a) the system must primarily be a system through which securities transfer orders are effected; and
- (b) the designating authority must consider that designation is required on grounds of systemic risk.

[(5) An arrangement entered into between interoperable systems shall not constitute a system.]

2 Arrangements and resources

The system must have adequate arrangements and resources for the effective monitoring and enforcement of compliance with its rules or, as respects monitoring, arrangements providing for that function to be performed on its behalf (and without affecting its responsibility) by another body or person who is able and willing to perform it.

3 Financial resources

The [system operator] must have financial resources sufficient for the proper performance of its functions as a *system*.

4 Co-operation with other authorities

[The system operator] must be able and willing to co-operate, by the sharing of information and otherwise, with—
- (a) the Financial Services Authority,
- (b) the Bank of England,
- (c) any relevant office-holder, and
- (d) any authority, body or person having responsibility for any matter arising out of, or connected with, the default of a participant.

5 Specific provision in the rules

(1) The rules of the system must—
- (a) specify the point at which a transfer order takes effect as having been entered into the system,
- (b) specify the point after which a transfer order may not be revoked by a participant or any other party, and
- (c) prohibit the revocation by a participant or any other party of a transfer order from the point specified in accordance with paragraph (b).

[(1A) Where the system has one or more interoperable systems, the rules required under paragraph (1)(a) and (b) shall, as far as possible, be co-ordinated with the rules of those interoperable systems.

(1B) The rules of the system which are referred to in paragraph (1)(a) and (b) shall not be affected by any rules of that system's interoperable systems in the absence of express provision in the rules of the system and all of those interoperable systems.]

(2) The rules of the system must require each institution which participates in the system to provide upon payment of a reasonable charge the information mentioned in sub-paragraph (3) to any person who requests it, save where the request is frivolous or vexatious. The rules must require the information to be provided within fourteen days of the request being made.

(3) The information referred to in sub-paragraph (2) is as follows—
- (a) details of the systems which are designated for the purposes of the Settlement Finality Directive in which the institution participates, and
- (b) information about the main rules governing the functioning of those systems.

(4) The rules of the system must require each participant upon—
- (a) the passing of a creditors' voluntary winding up resolution, or
- (b) a trust deed granted by him becoming a protected trust deed,

to notify forthwith both the system and the designating authority that such a resolution has been passed, or, as the case may be, that such a trust deed has become a protected trust deed.

6   Default arrangements

The system must have default arrangements which are appropriate for that system in all the circumstances.

NOTES

Para 1: words in first pair of square brackets substituted, and words in second pair of square brackets inserted, by the Financial Markets and Insolvency (Settlement Finality) (Amendment) Regulations 2006, SI 2006/50, reg 2(1), (15), as from 2 February 2006; sub-para (5) added by the Financial Markets and Insolvency (Settlement Finality and Financial Collateral Arrangements) (Amendment) Regulations 2010, SI 2010/2993, reg 2(1), (17)(a), as from 6 April 2011 (note that by virtue of reg 3 of the 2010 Regulations, nothing in those Regulations affects any designation order in force under these Regulations in relation to a designated system, and no system operator shall be required to apply for an amended designation order in consequence only of the 2010 Regulations).

Paras 3, 4: words in square brackets substituted by SI 2010/2993, reg 2(1), (17)(b), (c), as from 6 April 2011 (see further the note relating to reg 3 of the 2010 Regulations above).

Para 5: sub-paras (1A), (1B) inserted by SI 2010/2993, reg 2(1), (17)(d), as from 6 April 2011 (see further the note relating to reg 3 of the 2010 Regulations above).

LIMITED LIABILITY PARTNERSHIPS (SCOTLAND) REGULATIONS 2001

(SSI 2001/128)

NOTES

Made: 28 March 2001.

Authority: Limited Liability Partnerships Act 2000, ss 14(1), (2), 15, 16, 17(1), (3).

Commencement: 6 April 2001.

These Regulations are reproduced as amended by: the Limited Liability Partnerships (Scotland) Amendment Regulations 2009, SSI 2009/310.

ARRANGEMENT OF REGULATIONS

PART I
CITATION, COMMENCEMENT EXTENT AND INTERPRETATION

[10.802]
1   Citation, commencement and extent

(1)   These Regulations may be cited as the Limited Liability Partnerships (Scotland) Regulations 2001 and shall come into force on 6th April 2001.

(2)   These Regulations extend to Scotland only.

[10.803]

2   Interpretation

In these Regulations—

"the 1985 Act" means the Companies Act 1985;

"the 1986 Act" means the Insolvency Act 1986;

"limited liability partnership agreement", in relation to a limited liability partnership, means any agreement, express or implied, made between the members of the limited liability partnership or between the limited liability partnership and the members of the limited liability partnership which determines the mutual rights and duties of the members, and their rights and duties in relation to the limited liability partnership;

"the principal Act" means the Limited Liability Partnerships Act 2000; and

"shadow member", in relation to a limited liability partnership, means a person in accordance with whose directions or instructions the members of the limited liability partnership are accustomed to act (but so that a person is not deemed a shadow member by reason only that the members of the limited liability partnership act on advice given by that person in a professional capacity).

NOTES

General note as to interpretation: as to the meaning of "the registrar" and "the register", and as to the construction of references to registration in a particular part of the United Kingdom, in any enactment relating to LLPs, see the Limited Liability Partnerships (Application of Companies Act 2006) Regulations 2009, SI 2009/1804, reg 85, Sch 3, Pt 2, para 12 at **[10.1191]**.

PART II
COMPANIES ACT

[10.804]

3   Application of the 1985 Act to limited liability partnerships

The provisions of the 1985 Act specified in the first column of Schedule 1 to these Regulations shall apply to limited liability partnerships, with the following modifications—

(a)   references to a company shall include references to a limited liability partnership;

(b)   references to the Companies Acts shall include references to the principal Act and any regulations made thereunder;

(c)   references to the 1986 Act shall include references to that Act as it applies to limited liability partnerships by virtue of Part III of these Regulations;

(d)   references in a provision of the 1985 Act to other provisions of that Act shall include references to those other provisions as they apply to limited liability partnerships by virtue of these Regulations; and

(e)   the modifications, if any, specified in the second column of Schedule 1 of the provision specified opposite them in the first column.

PART III
WINDING UP AND INSOLVENCY

[10.805]

4   Application of the 1986 Act to limited liability partnerships

(1)   Subject to paragraph (2), the provisions of the 1986 Act listed in Schedule 2 shall apply in relation to limited liability partnerships as they apply in relation to companies.

(2)   The provisions of the 1986 Act referred to in paragraph (1) shall so apply, with the following modifications—

(a)   references to a company shall include references to a limited liability partnership;

(b)   references to a director or to an officer of a company shall include references to a member of a limited liability partnership;

(c)   references to a shadow director shall include references to a shadow member;

(d)   references to the 1985 Act, the Company Directors Disqualification Act 1986, the Companies Act 1989 or to any provisions of those Acts or to any provisions of the 1986 Act shall include references to those Acts or provisions as they apply to limited liability partnerships by virtue of the principal Act or these Regulations; and

(e)   the modifications set out in Schedule 3 to these Regulations.

PART IV
MISCELLANEOUS

[10.806]

5   General and consequential amendments

The enactments referred to in Schedule 4 shall have effect subject to the amendments specified in that Schedule.

[10.807]
6   Application of subordinate legislation

(1)   The Insolvency (Scotland) Rules 1986 shall apply to limited liability partnerships with such modifications as the context requires for the purpose of giving effect to the provisions of the Insolvency Act 1986 which are applied by these Regulations.

(2)   In the case of any conflict between any provision of the subordinate legislation applied by paragraph (1) and any provision of these Regulations, the latter shall prevail.

SCHEDULES

SCHEDULE 1
MODIFICATIONS TO PROVISIONS OF THE 1985 ACT
Regulation 3
[10.808]

Formalities of Carrying on Business	
36B (execution of documents by companies)	
Floating charges and Receivers (Scotland)	
462 (power of incorporated company to create floating charge)	In subsection (1), for the words "an incorporated company (whether a company within the meaning of this Act or not)," substitute "a limited liability partnership", and the words "(including uncalled capital)" are omitted.
463 (effect of floating charge on winding up)	
466 (alteration of floating charges)	
Subsections (1), (2), (3) and (6)	
486 (interpretation for Part XVIII generally)	For the definition of "company" substitute ""company" means a limited liability partnership;"
487 (extent of Part XVIII)	

NOTES

Note that s 36B of the Companies Act 1985 was repealed by the Companies Act 2006, s 1295, Sch 16, as from 1 October 2009.

SCHEDULE 2
PROVISIONS OF THE 1986 ACT
Regulation 4(1)

[10.809]
The relevant provisions of the 1986 Act are as follows:

Sections 50 to 52;

Section 53(1) and (2), to the extent that those subsections do not relate to the requirement for a copy of the instrument and notice being delivered to the registrar of companies;

Section 53(4), (6) and (7);

Section 54(1), (2), (3) (to the extent that that subsection does not relate to the requirement for a copy of the interlocutor to be delivered to the registrar of companies), and subsections (5), (6) and (7);

Sections 55 to 58;

Section 60, other than subsection (1);

Section 61, including subsections (6) and (7) to the extent that those subsections do not relate to anything to be done or which may be sent to the registrar of companies;

Section 62, including subsection (5) to the extent that that subsection does not relate to anything to be done or which may be sent to the registrar of companies;

Sections 63 to 66;

Section 67, including subsections (1) and (8) to the extent that those subsections do not relate to anything to be sent to the registrar of companies;

Section 68;

Section 69, including subsections (1) and (2) to the extent that those subsections do not relate to anything to be done or which may be done by the registrar of companies;

Sections 70 and 71;

Subsection 84(3) to the extent that it does not concern the copy of the resolution being forwarded to the registrar of companies within 15 days;

Sections 91 to 93;

Section 94, including subsections (3) and (4) to the extent that those subsections do not relate to the liquidator being required to send to the registrar of companies a copy of the account and a return of the final meeting;

Section 95;

Section 97;

Sections 100 to 102;

Sections 104 to 105;

Section 106, including subsections (3), (4) and (5) to the extent that those subsections do not relate to the liquidator being required to send to the registrar of companies a copy of the account of winding up and a return of the final meeting/quorum;

Sections 109 to 111;

Section 112, including subsection (3) to the extent that that subsection does not relate to the liquidator being required to send to the registrar of companies a copy of the order made by the court;

Sections 113 to 115;

Sections 126 to 128;

Section 130(1) to the extent that that subsection does not relate to a copy of the order being forwarded by the court to the registrar of companies;

Section 131;

Sections 133 to 135;

Sections 138 to 140;

Sections 142 to 146;

Section 147, including subsection (3) to the extent that that subsection does not relate to a copy of the order being forwarded by the company to the registrar of companies;

Section 162 to the extent that the section concerns the matters set out in Section C 2 of Schedule 5 to the Scotland Act 1998 as being exceptions to the reservation of insolvency;

Sections 163 to 167;

Section 169;

Section 170, including subsection (2) to the extent that that subsection does not relate to an application being made by the registrar to make good the default;

Section 171;

Section 172, including subsection (8) to the extent that that subsection does not relate to the liquidator being required to give notice to the registrar of companies;

Sections 173 and 174;

Section 177;

Sections 185 to 189;

Sections 191 to 194;

Section 196;

Section 199;

Section 200;

Sections 206 to 215;

Section 218 subsections (1), (2),(4) and (6);

Sections 231 to 232 to the extent that the sections apply to administrative receivers, liquidators and provisional liquidators;

Section 233 to the extent that that section applies in the case of the appointment of an administrative receiver, of a voluntary arrangement taking effect, of a company going into liquidation or where a provisional liquidator is appointed;

Section 234 to the extent that that section applies to situations other than those where an administration [has been entered into];

Section 235 to the extent that that section applies to situations other than those where an administration [has been entered into];

Sections 236 to 237 to the extent that those sections apply to situations other than [administrations entered into] and winding up;

Sections 242 to 243;

Section 244 to the extent that that section applies in circumstances other than a company which [has entered into administration];

Section 245;

Section 251;

Section 416(1) and (4) to the extent that those subsections apply to section 206(1)(a) and (b) in connection with the offence provision relating to the winding up of a limited liability partnership;

Section 430;

Section 436;

Schedule 2;

Schedule 3;

Schedule 4;

Schedule 8 to the extent that that Schedule does not apply to voluntary arrangements or administrations within the meaning of Parts I and II of the 1986 Act;

Schedule 10 to the extent that it refers to any of the sections referred to above.

NOTES

Words in square brackets substituted by the Limited Liability Partnerships (Scotland) Amendment Regulations 2009, SSI 2009/310, reg 3, Sch 1, as from 1 October 2009.

SCHEDULE 3
MODIFICATIONS TO PROVISIONS OF THE 1986 ACT

Regulation 4(2)

[10.810]

Provisions	Modifications
Section 84 (circumstances in which company may be wound up voluntarily)	
Subsection (3)	For subsection (3) substitute the following—
	"(3) Within 15 days after a limited liability partnership has determined that it be wound up there shall be forwarded to the registrar of companies either a printed copy or a copy in some other form approved by the registrar of the determination."
	After subsection (3) insert a new subsection—
Subsection [(3A)]	"[(3A)] If a limited liability partnership fails to comply with this regulation the limited liability partnership and every designated member of it who is in default is liable on summary conviction to a fine not exceeding level 3 on the standard scale."
Section 91 (appointment of liquidator)	
Subsection (1)	Delete "in general meeting".
Subsection (2)	For subsection (2) substitute the following—
	"(2) On the appointment of a liquidator the powers of the members of the limited liability partnership shall cease except to the extent that a meeting of the members of the limited liability partnership summoned for the purpose or the liquidator sanctions their continuance."
	After subsection (2) insert—
	"(3) Subsections (3) and (4) of section 92 shall apply for the purposes of this section as they apply for the purposes of that section."
Section 92 (power to fill vacancy in office of liquidator)	
Subsection (1)	For "the company in general meeting" substitute "a meeting of the members of the limited liability partnership summoned for the purpose".
Subsection (2)	For "a general meeting" substitute "a meeting of the members of the limited liability partnership".
Subsection (3)	In subsection (3), for "articles" substitute "limited liability partnership agreement".
new subsection (4)	Add a new subsection (4) as follows—
	"(4) The quorum required for a meeting of the members of the limited liability partnership shall be any quorum required by the limited liability partnership agreement for meetings of the members of the limited liability partnership and if no requirement for a quorum has been agreed upon the quorum shall be 2 members."
Section 93 (general company meeting at each year's end)	
subsection (1)	For "a general meeting of the company" substitute "a meeting of the members of the limited liability partnership".
new subsection (4)	Add a new subsection (4) as follows—
	"(4) Subsections (3) and (4) of section 92 shall apply for the purposes of this section as they apply for the purposes of that section."

Provisions	Modifications
Section 94 *(final meeting prior to dissolution)*	
subsection (1)	For "a general meeting of the company" substitute "a meeting of the members of the limited liability partnership".
new subsection (5A)	Add a new subsection (5A) as follows—
	"(5A) Subsections (3) and (4) of section 92 shall apply for the purposes of this section as they apply for the purposes of that section."
subsection (6)	For "a general meeting of the company" substitute "a meeting of the members of the limited liability partnership".
Section 95 *(effect of company's insolvency)*	
subsection (1)	For "directors'" substitute "designated members'".
subsection (7)	For subsection (7) substitute the following—
	"(7) In this section 'the relevant period' means the period of 6 months immediately preceding the date on which the limited liability partnership determined that it be wound up voluntarily."
Section 100 *(appointment of liquidator)*	
subsection (1)	For "The creditors and the company at their respective meetings mentioned in section 98" substitute "The creditors at their meeting mentioned in section 98 and the limited liability partnership".
subsection (3)	Delete "director,".
Section 101 *(appointment of liquidation committee)*	
subsection (2)	For subsection (2) substitute the following—
	"(2) If such a committee is appointed, the limited liability partnership may, when it determines that it be wound up voluntarily or at any time thereafter, appoint such number of persons as they think fit to act as members of the committee, not exceeding 5."
Section 105 *(meetings of company and creditors at each year's end)*	
subsection (1)	For "a general meeting of the company" substitute "a meeting of the members of the limited liability partnership".
new subsection (5)	Add a new subsection (5) as follows—
	"(5) Subsections (3) and (4) of section 92 shall apply for the purposes of this section as they apply for the purposes of that section."
Section 106 *(final meeting prior to dissolution)*	
subsection (1)	For "a general meeting of the company" substitute "a meeting of the members of the limited liability partnership".
new subsection (5A)	After subsection (5) insert a new subsection (5A) as follows—
	"(5A) Subsections (3) and (4) of section 92 shall apply for the purposes of this section as they apply for the purposes of that section."
subsection (6)	For "a general meeting of the company" substitute "a meeting of the members of the limited liability partnership".
Sections 110 *(acceptance of shares, etc, as consideration for sale of company property)*	
	For the existing section substitute the following:
	"(1) This section applies, in the case of a limited liability partnership proposed to be, or being, wound up voluntarily, where the whole or part of the limited liability partnership's business or property is proposed to be transferred or sold to another company whether or not it is a company within the meaning of the Companies Act ("the transferee company") or to a limited liability partnership ("the transferee limited liability partnership").

Provisions	Modifications
	(2) With the requisite sanction, the liquidator of the limited liability partnership being, or proposed to be, wound up ("the transferor limited liability partnership") may receive, in compensation or part compensation for the transfer or sale, shares, policies or other like interests in the transferee company or the transferee limited liability partnership for distribution among the members of the transferor limited liability partnership.
	(3) The sanction required under subsection (2) is—
	(a) in the case of a members' voluntary winding up, that of a determination of the limited liability partnership at a meeting of the members of the limited liability partnership conferring either a general authority on the liquidator or an authority in respect of any particular arrangement, (subsections (3) and (4) of section 92 to apply for this purpose as they apply for the purposes of that section), and
	(b) in the case of a creditor's voluntary winding up, that of either court or the liquidation committee.
	(4) Alternatively to subsection (2), the liquidator may (with the sanction) enter into any other arrangement whereby the members of the transferor limited liability partnership may, in lieu of receiving cash, shares, policies or other like interests (or in addition thereto), participate in the profits, or receive any other benefit from the transferee company or the transferee limited liability partnership.
	(5) A sale or arrangement in pursuance of this section is binding on members of the transferor limited liability partnership.
	(6) A determination by the limited liability partnership is not invalid for the purposes of this section by reason that it is made before or concurrently with a determination by the limited liability partnership that it be wound up voluntarily or for appointing liquidators; but, if an order is made within a year for winding up the limited liability partnership by the court, the determination by the limited liability partnership is not valid unless sanctioned by the court."
Section 111 (dissent from arrangement under section 110)	
subsections (1)–(3)	For subsections (1)–(3) substitute the following—
	"(1) This section applies in the case of a voluntary winding up where, for the purposes of section 110(2) or (4), a determination of the limited liability partnership has provided the sanction requisite for the liquidator under that section.
	(2) If a member of the transferor limited liability partnership who did not vote in favour of providing the sanction required for the liquidator under section 110 expresses his dissent from it in writing addressed to the liquidator and left at the registered office of the limited liability partnership within 7 days after the date on which that sanction was given, he may require the liquidator either to abstain from carrying the arrangement so sanctioned into effect or to purchase his interest at a price to be determined by agreement or arbitration under this section.
	(3) If the liquidator elects to purchase the member's interest, the purchase money must be paid before the limited liability partnership is dissolved and be raised by the liquidator in such manner as may be determined by the limited liability partnership."
subsection (4)	Omit subsection (4).
Section 126 (power to stay or restrain proceedings against company)	
subsection (2)	Delete subsection (2).

Provisions	Modifications
Section 127 (avoidance of property dispositions, etc)	
	For "any transfer of shares" substitute "any transfer by a member of the limited liability partnership of his interest in the property of the limited liability partnership".
Section 165 (voluntary winding up)	
subsection (2)	In paragraph (a) for "an extraordinary resolution of the company" substitute "a determination by a meeting of the members of the limited liability partnership".
subsection (4)	For paragraph (c) substitute the following—
	"(c) summon meetings of the members of the limited liability partnership for the purpose of obtaining their sanction or for any other purpose he may think fit."
new subsection (4A)	Insert a new subsection (4A) as follows—
	"(4A) Subsections (3) and (4) of section 92 shall apply for the purposes of this section as they apply for the purposes of that section."
Section 166 (creditors' voluntary winding up)	
subsection (5)	In paragraph (b) for "directors" substitute "designated members".
Section 171 (removal, etc (voluntary winding up))	
subsection (2)	For paragraph (a) substitute the following—
	"(a) in the case of a members' voluntary winding up, by a meeting of the members of the limited liability partnership summoned specially for that purpose, or".
subsection (6)	In paragraph (a) for "final meeting of the company" substitute "final meeting of the members of the limited liability partnership" and in paragraph (b) for "final meetings of the company" substitute "final meetings of the members of the limited liability partnership".
new subsection (7)	Insert a new subsection (7) as follows—
	"(7) Subsections (3) and (4) of section 92 apply for the purposes of this section as they apply for the purposes of that section."
Section 173 (release (voluntary winding up))	
subsection (2)	In paragraph (a) for "a general meeting of the company" substitute "a meeting of the members of the limited liability partnership".
Section 187 (power to make over assets to employees)	
	Delete section 187
Section 194 (resolutions passed at adjourned meetings)	
	After "contributories" insert "or of the members of a limited liability partnership".
Section 206 (fraud, etc in anticipation of winding up)	
subsection (1)	For "passes a resolution for voluntary winding up" substitute "makes a determination that it be wound up voluntarily".
Section 207 (transactions in fraud of creditors)	
subsection (1)	For "passes a resolution for voluntary winding up" substitute "makes a determination that it be wound up voluntarily".
Section 210 (material omissions from statement relating to company's affairs)	
subsection (2)	For "passed a resolution for voluntary winding up" substitute "made a determination that it be wound up voluntarily".
Section 214 (wrongful trading)	
subsection (2)	Delete from "but the court shall not" to the end of the subsection.

Provisions	Modifications
After section 214	Insert the following new section 214A

"**214A Adjustment of withdrawals**

(1) This section has effect in relation to a person who is or has been a member of a limited liability partnership where, in the course of the winding up of that limited liability partnership, it appears that subsection (2) of this section applies in relation to that person.

(2) This subsection applies in relation to a person if—

    (a) within the period of two years ending with the commencement of the winding up, he was a member of the limited liability partnership who withdrew property of the limited liability partnership, whether in the form of a share of profits, salary, repayment of or payment of interest on a loan to the limited liability partnership or any other withdrawal of property, and

    (b) it is proved by the liquidator to the satisfaction of the court that at the time of the withdrawal he knew or had reasonable grounds for believing that the limited liability partnership—

        (i) was at the time of the withdrawal unable to pay its debts within the meaning of section 123 of the Act, or

        (ii) would become so unable to pay its debts after the assets of the limited liability partnership had been depleted by that withdrawal taken together with all other withdrawals (if any) made by any members contemporaneously with that withdrawal or in contemplation when that withdrawal was made.

(3) Where this section has effect in relation to any person the court, on the application of the liquidator, may declare that that person is to be liable to make such contribution (if any) to the limited liability partnership's assets as the court thinks proper.

(4) The court shall not make a declaration in relation to any person the amount of which exceeds the aggregate of the amounts or values of all the withdrawals referred to in subsection (2) made by that person within the period of 2 years referred to in that subsection.

(5) The court shall not make a declaration under this section with respect to any person unless that person knew or ought to have concluded that after each withdrawal referred to in subsection (2) there was no reasonable prospect that the limited liability partnership would avoid going into insolvent liquidation.

(6) For the purposes of subsection (5) the facts which a member ought to know or ascertain, the conclusions which he ought to reach and the steps which he ought to have taken are those which would be known or ascertained, or reached or taken, by a reasonably diligent person having both:

    (a) the general knowledge, skill and experience that may reasonably be expected of a person carrying out the same functions as are carried out by that member in relation to the limited liability partnership, and

    (b) the general knowledge, skill and experience that that member has.

(7) For the purposes of this section a limited liability partnership goes into insolvent liquidation if it goes into liquidation at a time when its assets are insufficient for the payment of its debts and other liabilities and the expenses of the winding up.

(8) In this section "member" includes a shadow member.

(9) This section is without prejudice to section 214."

Provisions	Modifications
Section 215 (proceedings under ss 213, 214)	
subsection (1)	Omit the word "or" between the words "213" and "214" and insert after "214" "or 214A".
subsection (2)	For "either section" substitute "any of those sections".
subsection (4)	For "either section" substitute "any of those sections".
subsection (5)	For "Sections 213 and 214" substitute "Sections 213, 214 or 214A".
Section 218 (prosecution of delinquent officers and members of company)	
subsection (1)	For "officer, or any member, of the company" substitute "member of the limited liability partnership"
subsections (4) and (6)	For "officer of the company, or any member of it," substitute "officer or member of the limited liability partnership".
Section 251 (expressions used generally)	
	Delete the word "and" appearing after the definition of "the rules" and insert the word "and" after the definition of "shadow director".
	After the definition of "shadow director" insert the following—
	""shadow member", in relation to a limited liability partnership, means a person in accordance with whose directions or instructions the members of the limited liability partnership are accustomed to act (but so that a person is not deemed a shadow member by reason only that the members of the limited liability partnership act on advice given by him in a professional capacity);"
Section 416 (monetary limits (companies winding up))	
subsection (1)	In subsection (1), omit the words "section 117(2) (amount of company's share capital determining whether county court has jurisdiction to wind it up);" and the words "section 120(3) (the equivalent as respects sheriff court jurisdiction in Scotland);".
Section 436 (expressions used generally)	
	The following expressions and definitions shall be added to the section—
	"designated member" has the same meaning as it has in the Limited Liability Partnerships Act 2000;
	"limited liability partnership" means a limited liability partnership formed and registered under the Limited Liability Partnership Act 2000;
	"limited liability partnership agreement", in relation to a limited liability partnership, means any agreement, express or implied, made between the members of the limited liability partnership or between the limited liability partnership and the members of the limited liability partnership which determines the mutual rights and duties of the members, and their rights and duties in relation to the limited liability partnership.
Schedule 2	
Paragraph 17	For paragraph 17 substitute the following—
	"**17.** Power to enforce any rights the limited liability partnership has against the members under the terms of the limited liability partnership agreement"
Schedule 10	
Section 93(3)	In the entry relating to section 93(3) for "general meeting of the company" substitute "meeting of members of the limited liability partnership".
Section 105(3)	In the entry relating to section 105(3) for "company general meeting" substitute "meeting of the members of the limited liability partnership".

Provisions	Modifications
Section 106(6)	In the entry relating to section 106(6) for "company" substitute "the members of the limited liability partnership"

NOTES

Figures in square brackets in the entry relating to section 84 substituted, and entry relating to section 233 (omitted) revoked, by the Limited Liability Partnerships (Scotland) Amendment Regulations 2009, SSI 2009/310, reg 4, Sch 2, as from 1 October 2009.

SCHEDULE 4
GENERAL AND CONSEQUENTIAL AMENDMENTS IN OTHER LEGISLATION
Regulation 5

[10.811]
1–5. . . . .

Culpable officer provision

6. (1)   A culpable officer provision applies in the case of a limited liability partnership as if the reference in the provision to a director (or a person purporting to act as a director) were a reference to a member (or a person purporting to act as a member) of the limited liability partnership.

(2)   A culpable officer provision is a devolved provision in any Act or subordinate legislation (within the meaning of the Interpretation Act 1978 or the Scotland Act 1998 (Transitory and Transitional Provisions) (Publication and Interpretation etc of Acts of the Scottish Parliament) Order 1999) to the effect that where—

  (a)   a body corporate is guilty of a particular offence, and
  (b)   the offence is proved to have been committed with the consent or connivance of, or to be attributable to the neglect on the part of, (among others) a director of the body corporate,

he (as well as the body corporate) is guilty of the offence.

(3)   In this paragraph "devolved provision" means any provision that would be within devolved competence for the purposes of section 101 of the Scotland Act 1998.

NOTES

Paras 1–5: amend the Insolvency Act 1986, ss 110 at **[9.199]**, the Criminal Procedure (Scotland) Act 1995, ss 70, 141, 143, and the Requirements of Writing (Scotland) Act 1995, s 7, Schs 1, 2.

LIMITED LIABILITY PARTNERSHIPS (FORMS)
REGULATIONS 2001
(AND GENERAL NOTE REGARDING FORMS)

(SI 2001/927)

[10.812]

NOTES

These Regulations were made on 9 March 2001 under the powers conferred by the Companies Act 1985, ss 190, 225, 244, 363, 391, 395, 397, 398, 400, 401, 403, 405, 410, 413, 416, 417, 419, 466, 652A, 652D (all repealed by the Companies Act 2006, with the exception of s 466 which is repealed by the Bankruptcy and Diligence etc (Scotland) Act 2007, as from a day to be appointed). The Regulations came into force on 6 April 2001, and they prescribed the forms to be used for the purposes of specified provisions of the Companies Act 1985 by limited liability partnership.

Further forms were prescribed by the Limited Liability Partnerships (Forms) Regulations 2002, SI 2002/690, made under ss 288A, 363, 706 of the 1985 Act (again, all repealed by the Companies Act 2006).

Forms in Welsh which correspond to those prescribed by SI 2001/927 and by SI 2002/690 were prescribed for use by LLPs for the purposes of the Companies Act 1985 by (i) the Limited Liability Partnerships (Welsh Language Forms) Regulations 2001, SI 2001/2917, made under the Companies Act 1985, ss 225, 363, 652A, 652D (all repealed by the Companies Act 2006), as extended by the Welsh Language Act 1993, s 26(3); and (ii) by the Limited Liability Partnerships (Welsh Language Forms) Regulations 2003, SI 2003/61, made under ss 288A, 363(2) of the 1985 Act (both repealed by the Companies Act 2006), as extended by the Welsh Language Act 1993, s 26(3).

It was provided by a number of the commencement Orders for the Companies Act 2006 that the provisions of those Orders did not affect the application to LLPs of provisions of the Companies Act 1985 (ie, as applied to LLPs by the Limited Liability Partnerships Regulations 2001, SI 2001/1090; for details see the note "Limited liability partnerships" at the beginning of the Companies Act 1985 *ante*). It should be noted that SI 2001/1090, as amended, now only applies the unrepealed provisions of the 1985 Act to LLPs. In addition, the Limited Liability Partnerships (Application of Companies Act 2006) Regulations 2009, SI 2009/1804, Sch 1, Pt 9, para 34 (at **[10.1189]**) provides: (i) that any saving in those Regulations for the effect of a provision of the 1985 Act, as applied to LLPs, requiring the use of a prescribed form extends to the form and the power under which it is prescribed; and (ii) any saving in those Regulations for the effect of a provision of the 1985 Act requiring a document to be delivered to the registrar extends to s 707B of the 1985 Act (delivery to the registrar using electronic communications) so far as relating to the provision in question and the delivery of documents under it.

Of the forms prescribed by SI 2001/927 and SI 2002/690, Form LLP466(Scot) (prescribed by SI 2001/927) continues to be used for the purposes of s 466 of the 1985 Act, the repeal of which has not yet been brought into force. It should be noted that

Part 10   Miscellaneous other SIs

forms which are no longer required have not been specifically revoked. Forms which are still relevant may be found on the Companies House website at: http://www.companieshouse.gov.uk/forms/formsOnline1985.shtml.

As to forms to be used for the purposes of the 2006 Act, see the Companies House website at: http://www.companieshouse.gov.uk/forms/formsOnline.shtml#LLPs.

LIMITED LIABILITY PARTNERSHIPS REGULATIONS 2001

(SI 2001/1090)

NOTES

Made: 19 March 2001.
Authority: Limited Liability Partnerships Act 2000, ss 14–17.
Commencement: 6 April 2001.

These Regulations are reproduced as amended by: the Financial Services and Markets Act 2000 (Consequential Amendments) Order 2004, SI 2004/355; the Limited Liability Partnerships (Amendment) Regulations 2005, SI 2005/1989; the Companies Act 1985 (Investment Companies and Accounting and Audit Amendments) Regulations 2005, SI 2005/2280; the Civil Partnership Act 2004 (Amendments to Subordinate Legislation) Order 2005, SI 2005/2114; the Companies Act 1985 (Operating and Financial Review) (Repeal) Regulations 2005, SI 2005/3442; the Companies Act 1985 (Small Companies' Accounts and Audit) Regulations 2006, SI 2006/2782; the Limited Liability Partnerships (Amendment) Regulations 2007, SI 2007/2073; the Markets in Financial Instruments Directive (Consequential Amendments) Regulations 2007, SI 2007/2932; the Companies (Late Filing Penalties) and Limited Liability Partnerships (Filing Periods and Late Filing Penalties) Regulations 2008, SI 2008/497; the Limited Liability Partnerships (Accounts and Audit) (Application of Companies Act 2006) Regulations 2008, SI 2008/1911; the Limited Liability Partnerships (Application of Companies Act 2006) Regulations 2009, SI 2009/1804; the Companies Act 2006 (Consequential Amendments, Transitional Provisions and Savings) Order 2009, SI 2009/1941.

Savings for the Companies Act 1985 as applied by these Regulations: nothing in any of the following Orders affects any provision of the Companies Act 1985 as applied by these Regulations; ie, the Companies Act 2006 (Commencement No 1, Transitional Provisions and Savings) Order 2006 (SI 2006/3428), the Companies Act 2006 (Commencement No 2, Consequential Amendments, Transitional Provisions and Savings) Order 2007 (SI 2007/1093), the Companies Act 2006 (Commencement No 3, Consequential Amendments, Transitional Provisions and Savings) Order 2007 (SI 2007/2194), the Companies Act 2006 (Commencement No 5, Transitional Provisions and Savings) Order 2007 (SI 2007/3495), the Companies Act 2006 (Commencement No 6, Saving and Commencement Nos 3 and 5 (Amendment)) Order 2008 (SI 2008/674), the Companies Act 2006 (Commencement No 7, Transitional Provisions and Savings) Order 2008 (SI 2008/1886), and the Companies Act 2006 (Consequential Amendments etc) Order 2008 (SI 2008/948); see art 8 of the fist commencement Order (at **[2.8]**), art 11 of the second commencement Order (at **[2.26]**), art 12 of the third commencement Order (at **[2.42]**), art 12 of the fifth commencement Order (at **[2.61]**), art 6 of the sixth commencement Order (at **[2.72]**), art 7 of the seventh commencement Order (at **[2.81]**), and art 11 of SI 2008/948 (at **[4.285]**). See also the Limited Liability Partnerships (Application of Companies Act 2006) Regulations 2009, SI 2009/1804 at **[10.1097]** which applies various provisions of the Companies Act 2006 to LLPs and revokes (as from 1 October 2009) most of Sch 2, Pt I to these Regulations (as noted *post*). Schedule 1 to the 2009 Regulations (at **[10.1181]** et seq) provides for detailed transitional provisions and savings in relation to the application of the 2006 Act to LLPs and the revocation of these Regulations in so far as they apply provisions of the 1985 Act to LLPs.

Contractual rights of third parties: the Contracts (Rights of Third Parties) Act 1999, s 1, confers no rights on a third party in the case of any incorporation document of a limited liability partnership or any limited liability partnership agreement as defined in these Regulations; see s 6(2A) of the 1999 Act (as inserted by Sch 5, para 20 to these Regulations).

ARRANGEMENT OF REGULATIONS

PART I
CITATION, COMMENCEMENT AND INTERPRETATION

PART III
COMPANIES ACT 1985 AND COMPANY DIRECTORS DISQUALIFICATION ACT 1986

PART IV
WINDING UP AND INSOLVENCY

PART V
FINANCIAL SERVICES AND MARKETS

PART VI
DEFAULT PROVISION AND EXPULSION

PART I
CITATION, COMMENCEMENT AND INTERPRETATION

[10.813]
1   Citation and commencement

These Regulations may be cited as the Limited Liability Partnerships Regulations 2001 and shall come into force on 6th April 2001.

[10.814]
2   Interpretation

In these Regulations—

"the 1985 Act" means the Companies Act 1985;

"the 1986 Act" means the Insolvency Act 1986;

"the 2000 Act" means the Financial Services and Markets Act 2000;

"devolved", in relation to the provisions of the 1986 Act, means the provisions of the 1986 Act which are listed in Schedule 4 and, in their application to Scotland, concern wholly or partly, matters which are set out in Section C 2 of Schedule 5 to the Scotland Act 1998 as being exceptions to the reservations made in that Act in the field of insolvency;

"limited liability partnership agreement", in relation to a limited liability partnership, means any agreement express or implied between the members of the limited liability partnership or between the limited liability partnership and the members of the limited liability partnership which determines the mutual rights and duties of the members, and their rights and duties in relation to the limited liability partnership;

"the principal Act" means the Limited Liability Partnerships Act 2000; and

"shadow member", in relation to limited liability partnerships, means a person in accordance with whose directions or instructions the members of the limited liability partnership are accustomed to act (but so that a person is not deemed a shadow member by reason only that the members of the limited partnership act on advice given by him in a professional capacity).

NOTES

General note as to interpretation: as to the meaning of "the registrar" and "the register", and as to the construction of references to registration in a particular part of the United Kingdom, in any enactment relating to LLPs, see the Limited Liability Partnerships (Application of Companies Act 2006) Regulations 2009, SI 2009/1804, reg 85, Sch 3, Pt 2, para 12 at **[10.1191]**.

[10.815]
[2A   Application of provisions

(1)   The provisions of these Regulations applying—

(a)   the Company Directors Disqualification Act 1986, or

(b)   provisions of the Insolvency Act 1986,

have effect only in relation to limited liability partnerships registered in Great Britain.

(2)   The other provisions of these Regulations have effect in relation to limited liability partnerships registered in any part of the United Kingdom.]

NOTES

Commencement: 1 October 2009.

Inserted by the Limited Liability Partnerships (Application of Companies Act 2006) Regulations 2009, SI 2009/1804, reg 85, Sch 3, Pt 2, para 13(1), (2), as from 1 October 2009.

Part 10   Miscellaneous other SIs

PART II
ACCOUNTS AND AUDIT

3 *Reg 3 (Application of the accounts and audit provisions of the 1985 Act to limited liability partnerships) was revoked by the Limited Liability Partnerships (Accounts and Audit) (Application of Companies Act 2006) Regulations 2008, SI 2008/1911, reg 58(1)(a), as from 1 October 2008, except in relation to accounts for, and otherwise as regards, financial years beginning before that date (see reg 58(3) at* **[10.1060]***).)*

PART III
COMPANIES ACT 1985 AND COMPANY DIRECTORS
DISQUALIFICATION ACT 1986

[10.816]
4 Application of [certain provisions] of the 1985 Act and of the provisions of the Company Directors Disqualification Act 1986 to limited liability partnerships

(1) The provisions of the 1985 Act specified in the first column of Part I of Schedule 2 to these Regulations shall apply to limited liability partnerships, except where the context otherwise requires, with the following modifications—
  (a) references to a company shall include references to a limited liability partnership;
  (b) . . .
  (c) references to the Insolvency Act 1986 shall include references to that Act as it applies to limited liability partnerships by virtue of Part IV of these Regulations;
  [(d) references in a provision of the 1985 Act to—
      (i) other provisions of that Act, or
      (ii) provisions of the Companies Act 2006,
      shall include references to those provisions as they apply to limited liability partnerships.]
  (e), (f). . .
  (g) references to a director of a company or to an officer of a company shall include references to a member of a limited liability partnership;
  (h) the modifications, if any, specified in the second column of Part I of Schedule 2 opposite the provision specified in the first column; and
  (i) such further modifications as the context requires for the purpose of giving effect to that legislation as applied by these Regulations.

(2) The provisions of the Company Director Disqualification Act 1986 shall apply to limited liability partnerships, except where the context otherwise requires, with the following modifications—
  (a) references to a company shall include references to a limited liability partnership;
  (b) references to the Companies Acts shall include references to the principal Act and regulations made thereunder and references to the companies legislation shall include references to the principal Act, regulations made thereunder and to any enactment applied by regulations to limited liability partnerships;
  (d) references to the Insolvency Act 1986 shall include references to that Act as it applies to limited liability partnerships by virtue of Part IV of these Regulations;
  (e) . . .
  (f) references to a shadow director shall include references to a shadow member;
  (g) references to a director of a company or to an officer of a company shall include references to a member of a limited liability partnership;
  (h) the modifications, if any, specified in the second column of Part II of Schedule 2 opposite the provision specified in the first column; and
  (i) such further modifications as the context requires for the purpose of giving effect to that legislation as applied by these Regulations.

NOTES
Regulation heading: words in square brackets substituted by the Limited Liability Partnerships (Application of Companies Act 2006) Regulations 2009, SI 2009/1804, reg 85, Sch 3, Pt 2, para 13(1), (3)(a), as from 1 October 2009.
Para (1): sub-paras (b), (e), (f) revoked, and sub-para (d) substituted, by SI 2009/1804, reg 85, Sch 3, Pt 2, para 13(1), (3)(b), as from 1 October 2009.
Para (2): sub-para (e) revoked by the Companies Act 2006 (Consequential Amendments, Transitional Provisions and Savings) Order 2009, SI 2009/1941, art 2(1), Sch 1, para 192(1), (2), as from 1 October 2009.

PART IV
WINDING UP AND INSOLVENCY

[10.817]
5 Application of the 1986 Act to limited liability partnerships
(1) Subject to paragraphs (2) and (3), the following provisions of the 1986 Act, shall apply to limited liability partnerships—

   (a)   Parts I, II, III, IV, VI and VII of the First Group of Parts (company insolvency; companies winding up),

   (b)   the Third Group of Parts (miscellaneous matters bearing on both company and individual insolvency; general interpretation; final provisions).

(2)   The provisions of the 1986 Act referred to in paragraph (1) shall apply to limited liability partnerships, except where the context otherwise requires, with the following modifications—

   (a)   references to a company shall include references to a limited liability partnership;

   (b)   references to a director or to an officer of a company shall include references to a member of a limited liability partnership;

   (c)   references to a shadow director shall include references to a shadow member;

   (d)   references to [the Companies Acts], the Company Directors Disqualification Act 1986, the Companies Act 1989 or to any provisions of those Acts or to any provisions of the 1986 Act shall include references to those Acts or provisions as they apply to limited liability partnerships by virtue of the principal Act;

   (e)   references . . . . to the articles of association of a company shall include references to the limited liability partnership agreement of a limited liability partnership;

   (f)   the modifications set out in Schedule 3 to these Regulations; and

   (g)   such further modifications as the context requires for the purpose of giving effect to that legislation as applied by these Regulations.

(3)   In the application of this regulation to Scotland, the provisions of the 1986 Act referred to in paragraph (1) shall not include the provisions listed in Schedule 4 to the extent specified in that Schedule.

NOTES

   Para (2): words in square brackets in sub-para (d) substituted, and words omitted from sub-para (e) revoked, by the Companies Act 2006 (Consequential Amendments, Transitional Provisions and Savings) Order 2009, SI 2009/1941, art 2(1), Sch 1, para 192(1), (3), as from 1 October 2009.

PART V
FINANCIAL SERVICES AND MARKETS

[10.818]
6 Application of provisions contained in Parts XV and XXIV of the 2000 Act to limited liability partnerships

(1)   Subject to paragraph (2), sections 215(3),(4) and (6), 356, 359(1) to (4), 361 to 365, 367, 370 and 371 of the 2000 Act shall apply to limited liability partnerships.

(2)   The provisions of the 2000 Act referred to in paragraph (1) shall apply to limited liability partnerships, except where the context otherwise requires, with the following modifications—

   (a)   references to a company shall include references to a limited liability partnership;

   (b)   references to body shall include references to a limited liability partnership; and

   (c)   references to the 1985 Act, the 1986 Act or to any of the provisions of those Acts shall include references to those Acts or provisions as they apply to limited liability partnerships by virtue of the principal Act.

PART VI
DEFAULT PROVISION

[10.819]
7 Default provision for limited liability partnerships

The mutual rights and duties of the members and the mutual rights and duties of the limited liability partnership and the members shall be determined, subject to the provisions of the general law and to the terms of any limited liability partnership agreement, by the following rules:

   (1)   All the members of a limited liability partnership are entitled to share equally in the capital and profits of the limited liability partnership.

   (2)   The limited liability partnership must indemnify each member in respect of payments made and personal liabilities incurred by him—

      (a)   in the ordinary and proper conduct of the business of the limited liability partnership; or

      (b)   in or about anything necessarily done for the preservation of the business or property of the limited liability partnership.

   (3)   Every member may take part in the management of the limited liability partnership.

   (4)   No member shall be entitled to remuneration for acting in the business or management of the limited liability partnership.

   (5)   No person may be introduced as a member or voluntarily assign an interest in a limited liability partnership without the consent of all existing members.

(6)   Any difference arising as to ordinary matters connected with the business of the limited liability partnership may be decided by a majority of the members, but no change may be made in the nature of the business of the limited liability partnership without the consent of all the members.

(7)   The books and records of the limited liability partnership are to be made available for inspection at the registered office of the limited liability partnership or at such other place as the members think fit and every member of the limited liability partnership may when he thinks fit have access to and inspect and copy any of them.

(8)   Each member shall render true accounts and full information of all things affecting the limited liability partnership to any member or his legal representatives.

(9)   If a member, without the consent of the limited liability partnership, carries on any business of the same nature as and competing with the limited liability partnership, he must account for and pay over to the limited liability partnership all profits made by him in that business.

(10) Every member must account to the limited liability partnership for any benefit derived by him without the consent of the limited liability partnership from any transaction concerning the limited liability partnership, or from any use by him of the property of the limited liability partnership, name or business connection.

[10.820]
8   Expulsion

No majority of the members can expel any member unless a power to do so has been conferred by express agreement between the members.

PART VII
MISCELLANEOUS

[10.821]
9   General and consequential amendments

(1)   Subject to paragraph (2), the enactments mentioned in Schedule 5 shall have effect subject to the amendments specified in that Schedule.

(2)   In the application of this regulation to Scotland—

(a)   paragraph 15 of Schedule 5 which amends section 110 of the 1986 Act shall not extend to Scotland; and

(b)   paragraph 22 of Schedule 5 which applies to limited liability partnerships the culpable officer provisions in existing primary legislation shall not extend to Scotland insofar as it relates to matters which have not been reserved by Schedule 5 to the Scotland Act 1998.

[10.822]
10   Application of subordinate legislation

(1)   The subordinate legislation specified in Schedule 6 shall apply as from time to time in force to limited liability partnerships and—

(a)   in the case of the subordinate legislation listed in Part I of that Schedule with such modifications as the context requires for the purpose of giving effect to the provisions of the Companies Act 1985 which are applied by these Regulations;

(b)   in the case of the subordinate legislation listed in Part II of that Schedule with such modifications as the context requires for the purpose of giving effect to the provisions of the Insolvency Act 1986 which are applied by these Regulations; and

(c)   in the case of the subordinate legislation listed in Part III of that Schedule with such modifications as the context requires for the purpose of giving effect to the provisions of . . .   the Company Directors Disqualification Act 1986 which are applied by these Regulations.

(2)   In the case of any conflict between any provision of the subordinate legislation applied by paragraph (1) and any provision of these Regulations, the latter shall prevail.

NOTES

Para (1): words omitted from sub-para (c) revoked by the Limited Liability Partnerships (Application of Companies Act 2006) Regulations 2009, SI 2009/1804, reg 85, Sch 3, Pt 2, para 13(1), (4), as from 1 October 2009.

SCHEDULES
SCHEDULE 1

(Sch 1 (Modifications to Provisions of Part VII of the 1985 Act Applied by these Regulations) was revoked by the Limited Liability Partnerships (Accounts and Audit) (Application of Companies Act 2006) Regulations 2008, SI 2008/1911, reg 58(1)(a), as from 1 October 2008, except in relation to accounts for, and otherwise as regards, financial years beginning before that date (see reg 58(3) at [10.1060]).)

SCHEDULE 2

PART I
MODIFICATIONS TO PROVISIONS OF THE 1985 ACT APPLIED TO LIMITED LIABILITY PARTNERSHIPS

Regulation 4
[10.823]

Provisions	Modification
. . .	
Investigation of companies and their affairs: Requisition of documents	
431 (investigation of a company on its own application or that of its members)	For subsection (2) substitute the following—
	"(2) The appointment may be made on the application of the limited liability partnership or on the application of not less than one-fifth in number of those who appear from notifications made to the registrar of companies to be currently members of the limited liability partnership."
432 (other company investigations)	
subsection (4)	For the words "but to whom shares in the company have been transferred or transmitted by operation of law" substitute "but to whom a member's share in the limited liability partnership has been transferred or transmitted by operation of law."
433 (inspectors' powers during investigation)	
434 (production of documents and evidence to inspectors)	
436 (obstruction of inspectors treated as contempt of court)	
437 (inspectors' reports)	
. . .	
439 (expenses of investigating a company's affairs)	
subsection (5)	Omit paragraph (b) together with the word "or" at the end of paragraph (a).
441 (inspectors' report to be evidence)	
[446A (general powers to give directions)	
446B (direction to terminate investigation)	
446C (resignation and revocation of appointment)	
446D (appointment of replacement inspectors)	
446E (obtaining information from former inspectors etc)]	
447 (Secretary of State's power to require production of documents)	
[447A (information provided: evidence)]	
448 (entry and search of premises)	
[448A (protection in relation to certain disclosures: information provided to Secretary of State)]	
449 (provision for security of information obtained)	
450 (punishment for destroying, mutilating etc company documents)	[Omit subsection (1A).]
451 (punishment for furnishing false information)	

Part 10   Miscellaneous other SIs

Provisions	Modification
451A (disclosure of information by Secretary of State or inspector)	[In subsection (1), for the words "sections 434 to 446E" substitute "sections 434 to 441 and 446E"]
	Omit subsection (5).
452 (privileged information)	[In subsection (1), for the words "In subsection (1), for the words "sections 431 to 446E" substitute "sections 431 to 441 and 446E"]
	In subsection (1A), for the words "sections 434, 443 or 446" substitute "section 434".
[453A (power to enter and remain on premises)	In subsection (7), for the words "section 431, 432 or 442" substitute "section 431 or 432.
453B (power to enter and remain on premises: procedural)	
453C (failure to comply with certain requirements)]	
. . .	
Floating charges and Receivers (Scotland)	
464 (ranking of floating charges)	In subsection (1), for the words "section 462" substitute "the law of Scotland".
466 (alteration of floating charges)	Omit subsections (1), (2), (3) and (6).
486 (interpretation for Part XVIII generally)	For the current definition of "company" substitute ""company" means a limited liability partnership;"
	Omit the definition of "Register of Sasines".
487 (extent of Part XVIII)	
. . .	
[Schedule 15C (Security of information obtained: specified persons)	
Schedule 15D (Security of information obtained: specified disclosures)]	
. . .	

NOTES

Entries relating to ss 384, 385, 387, 388, 388A, 389A, 390, 390A, 390B, 391, 391A, 392, 392A, 394, 394A and 742 revoked by the Limited Liability Partnerships (Accounts and Audit) (Application of Companies Act 2006) Regulations 2008, SI 2008/1911, reg 58(1)(b), as from 1 October 2008 (for transitional provisions see reg 58(3)–(11) at **[10.1060]**).

All of the other entries in this Schedule (except those relating to Part XIV (Investigation of companies and their affairs: Requisition of documents) (but including s 438) and Part XVIII (Floating charges and Receivers (Scotland))) were revoked by the Limited Liability Partnerships (Application of Companies Act 2006) Regulations 2009, SI 2009/1804, reg 85, Sch 3, Pt 2, para 13(5)(a), (b), as from 1 October 2009 (note that Sch 3, Pt 2, para 13(5)(a) was amended by the Limited Liability Partnerships (Amendment) Regulations 2009, SI 2009/1833, reg 33, as from the same date in order to correct a drafting error in the original Regulations). Note also that the revocation of the entry relating to s 438 does not affect proceedings brought under that section (as applied to LLPs) before 1 October 2009.

Entries relating to ss 446A–446E inserted by SI 2009/1804, reg 85, Sch 3, Pt 2, para 13(5)(c), as from 1 October 2009.

Entries relating to ss 447A, 448A, 453A–453C, Schs 15C, 15D inserted by the Limited Liability Partnerships (Amendment) Regulations 2007, SI 2007/2073, regs 2, 3, as from 1 October 2007.

Words in square brackets in entry relating to s 450 substituted, and words omitted from entry relating to s 460 revoked, by the Financial Services and Markets Act 2000 (Consequential Amendments) Order 2004, SI 2004/355, art 9, as from 4 March 2004.

Words in square brackets in entry relating to ss 451A, 452(1) substituted by SI 2009/1804, reg 85, Sch 3, Pt 2, para 13(5)(d), as from 1 October 2009.

PART II
MODIFICATIONS TO THE COMPANY DIRECTORS DISQUALIFICATION ACT 1986
[10.824]

Part II of Schedule I	After paragraph 8 insert—
	"8A The extent of the member's and shadow members' responsibility for events leading to a member or shadow member, whether himself or some other member or shadow member, being declared by the court to be liable to make a contribution to the assets of the limited liability partnership under section 214A of the Insolvency Act 1986."

SCHEDULE 3
MODIFICATIONS TO THE 1986 ACT

Regulation 5
[10.825]

Provisions	Modifications
Section 1 (those who may propose an arrangement)	
subsection (1)	For "The directors of a company" substitute "A limited liability partnership" and delete "to the company and".
subsection (3)	At the end add "but where a proposal is so made it must also be made to the limited liability partnership".
[Section 1A (moratorium)	
subsection (1)	For "the directors of an eligible company intend" substitute "an eligible limited liability partnership intends".
	For "they" substitute "it".]
The following modifications to sections 2 to 7 apply where a proposal under section 1 has been made by the limited liability partnership.	
Section 2 (procedure where the nominee is not the liquidator or administrator)	
[subsection (1)	[For "the directors do" substitute "the limited liability partnership does".
subsection (2)	In paragraph [(aa)] for "meetings of the company and of its creditors" substitute "a meeting of the creditors of the limited liability partnership";
	In paragraph (b) for the first "meetings" substitute "a meeting" and for the second "meetings" substitute "meeting".
subsection (3)	For "the person intending to make the proposal" substitute "the designated members of the limited liability partnership".
subsection (4)	[In paragraph (a)] for "the person intending to make the proposal" substitute "the designated members of the limited liability partnership". [In paragraph (b) for "that person" substitute "those designated members".]
Section 3 (summoning of meetings)	
subsection (1)	For "such meetings as are mentioned in section 2(2)" substitute "a meeting of creditors" and for "those meetings" substitute "that meeting".
subsection (2)	Delete subsection (2).
Section 4 (decisions of meetings)	
subsection (1)	For "meetings" substitute "meeting".
subsection (5)	For "each of the meetings" substitute "the meeting".
new subsection (5A)	Insert a new subsection (5A) as follows—

Provisions	Modifications
	"(5A) If modifications to the proposal are proposed at the meeting the chairman of the meeting shall, before the conclusion of the meeting, ascertain from the limited liability partnership whether or not it accepts the proposed modifications; and if at that conclusion the limited liability partnership has failed to respond to a proposed modification it shall be presumed not to have agreed to it."
subsection (6)	For "either" substitute "the"; after "the result of the meeting", in the first place where it occurs, insert "(including, where modifications to the proposal were proposed at the meeting, the response to those proposed modifications made by the limited liability partnership)"; and at the end add "and to the limited liability partnership".
[Section 4A (approval of arrangement)	
subsection (2)	Omit "—(a)".
	For "both meetings" substitute "the meeting".
	Omit the words from ", or" to "that section".
subsection (3)	Omit.
subsection (4)	Omit.
subsection (5)	Omit.
subsection (6)	Omit.]
Section 5 (effect of approval)	
. . .	. . .
subsection (4)	For "each of the reports" substitute "the report".
Section 6 (challenge of decisions)	
subsection (1)	For . . . "either of the meetings" substitute "the meeting".
subsection (2)	For "either of the meetings" substitute "the meeting" and after paragraph [(aa)] add a new paragraph [(ab) as follows—
	"(ab)] any member of the limited liability partnership; and".
	Omit the word "and" at the end of paragraph (b) and omit paragraph (c).
subsection (3)	For "each of the reports" substitute "the report".
subsection (4)	For subsection (4) substitute the following—
	"(4) Where on such an application the court is satisfied as to either of the grounds mentioned in subsection (1), it may do one or both of the following, namely—
	(a) revoke or suspend [any decision approving the voluntary arrangement which has effect under section 4A];
	(b) give a direction to any person for the summoning of a further meeting to consider any revised proposal the limited liability partnership may make or, in a case falling within subsection (1)(b), a further meeting to consider the original proposal.".
subsection (5)	For . . . "meetings" substitute "a meeting", for . . . and for "person who made the original proposal" substitute "limited liability partnership".
[Section 6A (false representations, etc)	
subsection (1)	Omit "members or".]
Section 7 (implementation of proposal)	
. . .	. . .
[subsection (2)	In paragraph (a) omit "one or both of" and for "meetings" substitute "meeting".]

Provisions	Modifications
The following modifications to sections 2 and 3 apply where a proposal under section 1 has been made, where [the limited liability partnership is in administration], by the administrator or, where the limited liability partnership is being wound up, by the liquidator.	
Section 2 (procedure where the nominee is not the liquidator or administrator)	
subsection (2)	In paragraph (a) for "meetings of the company" substitute "meetings of the members of the limited liability partnership".
Section 3 (summoning of meetings)	
subsection (2)	For "meetings of the company" substitute "a meeting of the members of the limited liability partnership".
. . .	. . .
. . .	. . .
. . .	. . .
. . .	. . .
. . .	. . .
Section 73 (alternative modes of winding up)	
subsection (1)	Delete ", within the meaning given to that expression by section 735 of the Companies Act,".
Section 74 (liability as contributories of present and past members)	For section 74 there shall be substituted the following—
	"74. When a limited liability partnership is wound up every present and past member of the limited liability partnership who has agreed with the other members or with the limited liability partnership that he will, in circumstances which have arisen, be liable to contribute to the assets of the limited liability partnership in the event that the limited liability partnership goes into liquidation is liable, to the extent that he has so agreed, to contribute to its assets to any amount sufficient for payment of its debts and liabilities, and the expenses of the winding up, and for the adjustment of the rights of the contributories among themselves.
	However, a past member shall only be liable if the obligation arising from such agreement survived his ceasing to be a member of the limited liability partnership."
Section 75 to 78	Delete sections 75 to 78.
Section 79 (meaning of "contributory")	
subsection (1)	In subsection (1) for "every person" substitute "(a) every present member of the limited liability partnership and (b) every past member of the limited liability partnership".
subsection (2)	After "section 214 (wrongful trading)" insert "or 214A (adjustment of withdrawals)".
subsection (3)	Delete subsection (3).
Section 83 (companies registered under Companies Act, Part XXII, Chapter II)	Delete section 83.
Section 84 (circumstances in which company may be wound up voluntarily)	
subsection (1)	For subsection (1) substitute the following—
	"(1) A limited liability partnership may be wound up voluntarily when it determines that it is to be wound up voluntarily."

Provisions	Modifications
subsection (2)	Omit subsection (2).
[subsection (2A)	For "company passes a resolution for voluntary winding up" substitute "limited liability partnership determines that it is to be wound up voluntarily" and for "resolution" where it appears for the second time substitute "determination".
subsection (2B)	For "resolution for voluntary winding up may be passed only" substitute "determination to wind up voluntarily may only be made" and in sub-paragraph (b), for "passing of the resolution" substitute "making of the determination".]
subsection (3)	For subsection (3) substitute the following—
	"(3) Within 15 days after a limited liability partnership has determined that it be wound up there shall be forwarded to the registrar of companies either a printed copy or else a copy in some other form approved by the registrar of the determination."
subsection [(5)]	After subsection [(4)] insert a new subsection [(5)]—
	"[(5)] If a limited liability partnership fails to comply with this regulation the limited liability partnership and every designated member of it who is in default is liable on summary conviction to a fine not exceeding level 3 on the standard scale."
Section 85 (notice of resolution to wind up)	
subsection (1)	For subsection (1) substitute the following—
	"(1) When a limited liability partnership has determined that it shall be wound up voluntarily, it shall within 14 days after the making of the determination give notice of the determination by advertisement in the Gazette."
Section 86 (commencement of winding up)	
	Substitute the following new section—
	"86. A voluntary winding up is deemed to commence at the time when the limited liability partnership determines that it be wound up voluntarily.".
Section 87 (effect on business and status of company)	
subsection (2)	In subsection (2), for "articles" substitute "limited liability partnership agreement".
Section 88 (avoidance of share transfers, etc after winding-up resolution)	
	For "shares" substitute "the interest of any member in the property of the limited liability partnership".
Section 89 (statutory declaration of solvency)	
	For "director(s)" wherever it appears in section 89 substitute "designated member(s)";
subsection (2)	For paragraph (a) substitute the following—
	"(a) it is made within the 5 weeks immediately preceding the date when the limited liability partnership determined that it be wound up voluntarily or on that date but before the making of the determination, and".
subsection (3)	For "the resolution for winding up is passed" substitute "the limited liability partnership determined that it be wound up voluntarily".

Provisions	Modifications
subsection (5)	For "in pursuance of a resolution passed" substitute "voluntarily".
Section 90 (distinction between "members" and "creditors" voluntary winding up)	
	For "directors'" substitute "designated members'".
Section 91 (appointment of liquidator)	
subsection (1)	Delete "in general meeting".
subsection (2)	For the existing wording substitute—
	"(2) On the appointment of a liquidator the powers of the members of the limited liability partnership shall cease except to the extent that a meeting of the members of the limited liability partnership summoned for the purpose or the liquidator sanctions their continuance."
	After subsection (2) insert—
	"(3) Subsections (3) and (4) of section 92 shall apply for the purposes of this section as they apply for the purposes of that section."
Section 92 (power to fill vacancy in office of liquidator)	
subsection (1)	For "the company in general meeting" substitute "a meeting of the members of the limited liability partnership summoned for the purpose".
subsection (2)	For "a general meeting" substitute "a meeting of the members of the limited liability partnership".
subsection (3)	In subsection (3), for "articles" substitute "limited liability partnership agreement".
new subsection (4)	Add a new subsection (4) as follows—
	"(4) The quorum required for a meeting of the members of the limited liability partnership shall be any quorum required by the limited liability partnership agreement for meetings of the members of the limited liability partnership and if no requirement for a quorum has been agreed upon the quorum shall be 2 members."
Section 93 (general company meeting at each year's end)	
subsection (1)	For "a general meeting of the company" substitute "a meeting of the members of the limited liability partnership".
new subsection (4)	Add a new subsection (4) as follows—
	"(4) subsections (3) and (4) of section 92 shall apply for the purposes of this section as they apply for the purposes of that section."
Section 94 (final meeting prior to dissolution)	
subsection (1)	For "a general meeting of the company" substitute "a meeting of the members of the limited liability partnership".
new subsection (5A)	Add a new subsection (5A) as follows
	"(5A) Subsections (3) and (4) of section 92 shall apply for the purposes of this section as they apply for the purposes of that section."
subsection (6)	For "a general meeting of the company" substitute "a meeting of the members of the limited liability partnership".
Section 95 (effect of company's insolvency)	
subsection (1)	For "directors'" substitute "designated members'".

Provisions	Modifications
subsection (7)	For subsection (7) substitute the following—
	"(7) In this section "the relevant period" means the period of 6 months immediately preceding the date on which the limited liability partnership determined that it be wound up voluntarily."
Section 96 (conversion to creditors' voluntary winding up)	
paragraph (a)	For "directors'" substitute "designated members'".
paragraph (b)	Substitute a new paragraph (b) as follows—
	"(b) the creditors' meeting was the meeting mentioned in section 98 in the next Chapter;".
Section 98 (meeting of creditors)	
subsection (1)	For paragraph (a) substitute the following—
	"(a) cause a meeting of its creditors to be summoned for a day not later than the 14th day after the day on which the limited liability partnership determines that it be wound up voluntarily;".
subsection (5)	For "were sent the notices summoning the company meeting at which it was resolved that the company be wound up voluntarily" substitute "the limited liability partnership determined that it be wound up voluntarily".
Section 99 (directors to lay statement of affairs before creditors)	
subsection (1)	For "the directors of the company" substitute "the designated members" and for "the director so appointed" substitute "the designated member so appointed".
subsection (2)	For "directors" substitute "designated members".
subsection (3)	For "directors" substitute "designated members" and for "director" substitute "designated member".
Section 100 (appointment of liquidator)	
subsection (1)	For "The creditors and the company at their respective meetings mentioned in section 98" substitute "The creditors at their meeting mentioned in section 98 and the limited liability partnership".
subsection (3)	Delete "director,".
Section 101 (appointment of liquidation committee)	
subsection (2)	For subsection (2) substitute the following—
	"(2) If such a committee is appointed, the limited liability partnership may, when it determines that it be wound up voluntarily or at any time thereafter, appoint such number of persons as they think fit to act as members of the committee, not exceeding 5."
Section 105 (meetings of company and creditors at each year's end)	
subsection (1)	For "a general meeting of the company" substitute "a meeting of the members of the limited liability partnership".
new subsection (5)	Add a new subsection (5) as follows—
	"(5) Subsections (3) and (4) of section 92 shall apply for the purposes of this section as they apply for the purposes of that section."
Section 106 (final meeting prior to dissolution)	
subsection (1)	For "a general meeting of the company" substitute "a meeting of the members of the limited liability partnership".

Provisions	Modifications
new subsection (5A)	After subsection (5) insert a new subsection (5A) as follows—
	"(5A) Subsections (3) and (4) of section 92 shall apply for the purposes of this section as they apply for the purposes of that section."
subsection (6)	For "a general meeting of the company" substitute "a meeting of the members of the limited liability partnership".
Section 110 (acceptance of shares, etc, as consideration for sale of company property)	
	For the existing section substitute the following—
	"(1) This section applies, in the case of a limited liability partnership proposed to be, or being, wound up voluntarily, where the whole or part of the limited liability partnership's business or property is proposed to be transferred or sold to another company whether or not it is a company within the meaning of the Companies Act ("the transferee company") or to a limited liability partnership ("the transferee limited liability partnership").
	(2) With the requisite sanction, the liquidator of the limited liability partnership being, or proposed to be, wound up ("the transferor limited liability partnership") may receive, in compensation or part compensation for the transfer or sale, shares, policies or other like interests in the transferee company or the transferee limited liability partnership for distribution among the members of the transferor limited liability partnership.
	(3) The sanction required under subsection (2) is—
	(a) in the case of a members' voluntary winding up, that of a determination of the limited liability partnership at a meeting of the members of the limited liability partnership conferring either a general authority on the liquidator or an authority in respect of any particular arrangement, (subsections (3) and (4) of section 92 to apply for this purpose as they apply for the purposes of that section), and
	(b) in the case of a creditor's voluntary winding up, that of either court or the liquidation committee.
	(4) Alternatively to subsection (2), the liquidator may (with the sanction) enter into any other arrangement whereby the members of the transferor limited liability partnership may, in lieu of receiving cash, shares, policies or other like interests (or in addition thereto), participate in the profits, or receive any other benefit from the transferee company or the transferee limited liability partnership.
	(5) A sale or arrangement in pursuance of this section is binding on members of the transferor limited liability partnership.

Part 10　Miscellaneous other SIs

Provisions	Modifications
	(6) A determination by the limited liability partnership is not invalid for the purposes of this section by reason that it is made before or concurrently with a determination by the limited liability partnership that it be wound up voluntarily or for appointing liquidators; but, if an order is made within a year for winding up the limited liability partnership by the court, the determination by the limited liability partnership is not valid unless sanctioned by the court."
Section 111 (dissent from arrangement under section 110)	
subsections (1)–(3)	For subsections (1)–(3) substitute the following—
	"(1) This section applies in the case of a voluntary winding up where, for the purposes of section 110(2) or (4), a determination of the limited liability partnership has provided the sanction requisite for the liquidator under that section.
	(2) If a member of the transferor limited liability partnership who did not vote in favour of providing the sanction required for the liquidator under section 110 expresses his dissent from it in writing addressed to the liquidator and left at the registered office of the limited liability partnership within 7 days after the date on which that sanction was given, he may require the liquidator either to abstain from carrying the arrangement so sanctioned into effect or to purchase his interest at a price to be determined by agreement or arbitration under this section.
	(3) If the liquidator elects to purchase the member's interest, the purchase money must be paid before the limited liability partnership is dissolved and be raised by the liquidator in such manner as may be determined by the limited liability partnership."
subsection (4)	Omit subsection (4).
Section 117 (high court and county court jurisdiction)	
subsection (2)	Delete "Where the amount of a company's share capital paid up or credited as paid up does not exceed £120,000, then (subject to this section)".
subsection (3)	Delete subsection (3).
Section 120 (court of session and sheriff court jurisdiction)	
subsection (3)	Delete "Where the amount of a company's share capital paid up or credited as paid up does not exceed £120,000,".
subsection (5)	Delete subsection (5).
Section 122 (circumstances in which company may be wound up by the court)	
subsection (1)	For subsection (1) substitute the following—
	"(1) A limited liability partnership may be wound up by the court if—
	(a) the limited liability partnership has determined that the limited liability partnership be wound up by the court,
	(b) the limited liability partnership does not commence its business within a year from its incorporation or suspends its business for a whole year,
	(c) the number of members is reduced below two,

Provisions	Modifications
	(d) the limited liability partnership is unable to pay its debts . . .
	[(da) at the time at which a moratorium for the limited liability partnership under section 1A comes to an end, no voluntary arrangement approved under Part I has effect in relation to the limited liability partnership,]
	(e) the court is of the opinion that it is just and equitable that the limited liability partnership should be wound up."
Section 124 (application for winding up)	
subsections (2), (3) and (4)(a)	Delete these subsections.
[subsection (3A)	For "122(1)(fa)" substitute "122(1)(da)".]
Section 124A (petition for winding-up on grounds of public interest)	
subsection (1)	[Omit paragraphs (b) and (bb).]
Section 126 (power to stay or restrain proceedings against company)	
subsection (2)	Delete subsection (2).
Section 127 (avoidance of property dispositions, etc)	
[subsection (1)]	For "any transfer of shares" substitute "any transfer by a member of the limited liability partnership of his interest in the property of the limited liability partnership".
Section 129 (commencement of winding up by the court)	
subsection (1)	For "a resolution has been passed by the company" substitute "a determination has been made" and for "at the time of the passing of the resolution" substitute "at the time of that determination".
Section 130 (consequences of winding-up order)	
subsection (3)	Delete subsection (3).
Section 148 (settlement of list of contributories and application of assets)	
subsection (1)	Delete ", with power to rectify the register of members in all cases where rectification is required in pursuance of the Companies Act or this Act,".
Section 149 (debts due from contributory to company)	
subsection (1)	Delete "the Companies Act or".
subsection (2)	Delete subsection (2).
subsection (3)	Delete ", whether limited or unlimited,".
Section 160 (delegation of powers to liquidator (England and Wales))	
subsection (1)	In subsection (1)(b) delete "and the rectifying of the register of members".
subsection (2)	For subsection (2) substitute the following—
	"(2) But the liquidator shall not make any call without the special leave of the court or the sanction of the liquidation committee."
Section 165 (voluntary winding up)	
subsection (2)	In paragraph (a) for "an extraordinary resolution of the company" substitute "a determination by a meeting of the members of the limited liability partnership".
subsection (4)	For paragraph (c) substitute the following—

Provisions	Modifications
	"(c) summon meetings of the members of the limited liability partnership for the purpose of obtaining their sanction or for any other purpose he may think fit."
new subsection (4A)	Insert a new subsection (4A) as follows—
	"(4A) Subsections (3) and (4) of section 92 shall apply for the purposes of this section as they apply for the purposes of that section."
Section 166 (creditors' voluntary winding up)	
subsection (5)	In paragraph (b) for "directors" substitute "designated members".
Section 171 (removal, etc (voluntary winding up))	
subsection (2)	For paragraph (a) substitute the following—
	"(a) in the case of a members' voluntary winding up, by a meeting of the members of the limited liability partnership summoned specially for that purpose, or".
subsection (6)	In paragraph (a) for "final meeting of the company" substitute "final meeting of the members of the limited liability partnership" and in paragraph (b) for "final meetings of the company" substitute "final meetings of the members of the limited liability partnership".
new subsection (7)	Insert a new subsection (7) as follows—
	"(7) Subsections (3) and (4) of section 92 are to apply for the purposes of this section as they apply for the purposes of that section."
Section 173 (release (voluntary winding up))	
subsection (2)	In paragraph (a) for "a general meeting of the company" substitute "a meeting of the members of the limited liability partnership".
Section 183 (effect of execution or attachment (England and Wales))	
subsection (2)	Delete paragraph (a).
Section 184 (duties of sheriff (England and Wales))	
subsection (1)	For "a resolution for voluntary winding up has been passed" substitute "the limited liability partnership has determined that it be wound up voluntarily".
subsection (4)	Delete "or of a meeting having been called at which there is to be proposed a resolution for voluntary winding up," and "or a resolution is passed (as the case may be)".
Section 187 (power to make over assets to employees)	
	Delete section 187.
Section 194 (resolutions passed at adjourned meetings)	
	After "contributories" insert "or of the members of a limited liability partnership".
Section 195 (meetings to ascertain wishes of creditors or contributories)	
subsection (3)	Delete "the Companies Act or".
Section 206 (fraud, etc in anticipation of winding up)	

Provisions	Modifications
subsection (1)	For "passes a resolution for voluntary winding up" substitute "makes a determination that it be wound up voluntarily".
Section 207 (transactions in fraud of creditors)	
subsection (1)	For "passes a resolution for voluntary winding up" substitute "makes a determination that it be wound up voluntarily".
Section 210 (material omissions from statement relating to company's affairs)	
subsection (2)	For "passed a resolution for voluntary winding up" substitute "made a determination that it be wound up voluntarily".
Section 214 (wrongful trading)	
subsection (2)	Delete from "but the court shall not" to the end of the subsection.
After section 214	Insert the following new section 214A—

"214A Adjustment of withdrawals

(1) This section has effect in relation to a person who is or has been a member of a limited liability partnership where, in the course of the winding up of that limited liability partnership, it appears that subsection (2) of this section applies in relation to that person.

(2) This subsection applies in relation to a person if—

(a) within the period of two years ending with the commencement of the winding up, he was a member of the limited liability partnership who withdrew property of the limited liability partnership, whether in the form of a share of profits, salary, repayment of or payment of interest on a loan to the limited liability partnership or any other withdrawal of property, and

(b) it is proved by the liquidator to the satisfaction of the court that at the time of the withdrawal he knew or had reasonable ground for believing that the limited liability partnership—

    (i) was at the time of the withdrawal unable to pay its debts within the meaning of section 123, or

    (ii) would become so unable to pay its debts after the assets of the limited liability partnership had been depleted by that withdrawal taken together with all other withdrawals (if any) made by any members contemporaneously with that withdrawal or in contemplation when that withdrawal was made.

(3) Where this section has effect in relation to any person the court, on the application of the liquidator, may declare that that person is to be liable to make such contribution (if any) to the limited liability partnership's assets as the court thinks proper.

(4) The court shall not make a declaration in relation to any person the amount of which exceeds the aggregate of the amounts or values of all the withdrawals referred to in subsection (2) made by that person within the period of two years referred to in that subsection.

Provisions	Modifications
	(5) The court shall not make a declaration under this section with respect to any person unless that person knew or ought to have concluded that after each withdrawal referred to in subsection (2) there was no reasonable prospect that the limited liability partnership would avoid going into insolvent liquidation.
	(6) For the purposes of subsection (5) the facts which a member ought to know or ascertain and the conclusions which he ought to reach are those which would be known, ascertained, or reached by a reasonably diligent person having both:
	(a) the general knowledge, skill and experience that may reasonably be expected of a person carrying out the same functions as are carried out by that member in relation to the limited liability partnership, and
	(b) the general knowledge, skill and experience that that member has.
	(7) For the purposes of this section a limited liability partnership goes into insolvent liquidation if it goes into liquidation at a time when its assets are insufficient for the payment of its debts and other liabilities and the expenses of the winding up.
	(8) In this section "member" includes a shadow member.
	(9) This section is without prejudice to section 214."
Section 215 (proceedings under ss 213, 214)	
subsection (1)	Omit the word "or" between the words "213" and "214" and insert after "214" "or 214A".
subsection (2)	For "either section" substitute "any of those sections".
subsection (4)	For "either section" substitute "any of those sections".
subsection (5)	For "Sections 213 and 214" substitute "Sections 213, 214 or 214A".
Section 218 (prosecution of delinquent officers and members of company)	
subsection (1)	For "officer, or any member, of the company" substitute "member of the limited liability partnership".
subsections (3), (4) and (6)	For "officer of the company, or any member of it," substitute "officer or member of the limited liability partnership".
Section 247 ("insolvency" and "go into liquidation")	
subsection (2)	For "passes a resolution for voluntary winding up" substitute "makes a determination that it be wound up voluntarily" and for "passing such a resolution" substitute "making such a determination".
[subsection (3)	For "resolution for voluntary winding up" substitute "determination to wind up voluntarily".]
Section 249 ("connected with a company")	For the existing words substitute—
	"For the purposes of any provision in this Group of Parts, a person is connected with a company (including a limited liability partnership) if—

Provisions	Modifications
	(a) he is a director or shadow director of a company or an associate of such a director or shadow director (including a member or a shadow member of a limited liability partnership or an associate of such a member or shadow member); or
	(b) he is an associate of the company or of the limited liability partnership."
Section 250 ("member" of a company)	Delete section 250.
Section 251 (expressions used generally)	Delete the word "and" appearing after the definition of "the rules" and insert the word "and" after the definition of "shadow director".
	After the definition of "shadow director" insert the following—
	""shadow member", in relation to a limited liability partnership, means a person in accordance with whose directions or instructions the members of the limited liability partnership are accustomed to act (but so that a person is not deemed a shadow member by reason only that the members of the limited liability partnership act on advice given by him in a professional capacity);".
Section 386 (categories of preferential debts)	
subsection (1)	In subsection (1), omit the words "or an individual".
subsection (2)	In subsection (2), omit the words "or the individual".
Section 387 ("the relevant date")	
subsection (3)	[In paragraph (ab) for "passed a resolution for voluntary winding up" substitute "made a determination that it be wound up voluntarily".]
	In paragraph (c) for "passing of the resolution for the winding up of the company" substitute "making of the determination by the limited liability partnership that it be wound up voluntarily".
subsection (5)	Omit subsection (5).
subsection (6)	Omit subsection (6).
Section 388 (meaning of "act as insolvency practitioner")	
subsection (2)	Omit subsection (2).
subsection (3)	Omit subsection (3).
subsection (4)	Delete ""company" means a company within the meaning given by section 735(1) of the Companies Act or a company which may be wound up under Part V of this Act (unregistered companies);" and delete ""interim trustee" and "permanent trustee" mean the same as the Bankruptcy (Scotland) Act 1985".
Section 389 (acting without qualification an offence)	
subsection (1)	Omit the words "or an individual".
[Section 389A (authorisation of nominees and supervisors)	
subsection (1)	Omit "or Part VIII".]
Section 402 (official petitioner)	Delete section 402.
Section 412 (individual insolvency rules (England and Wales))	Delete section 412.

Provisions	Modifications
Section 415 (Fees orders (individual insolvency proceedings in England and Wales))	Delete section 415.
Section 416 (monetary limits (companies winding up))	
subsection (1)	In subsection (1), omit the words "section 117(2) (amount of company's share capital determining whether county court has jurisdiction to wind it up);" and the words "section 120(3) (the equivalent as respects sheriff court jurisdiction in Scotland);".
subsection (3)	In subsection (3), omit the words "117(2), 120(3) or".
Section 418 (monetary limits (bankruptcy))	Delete section 418.
Section 420 (insolvent partnerships)	Delete section 420.
Section 421 (insolvent estates of deceased persons)	Delete section 421.
Section 422 (recognised banks, etc)	Delete section 422.
[Section 426A (disqualification from Parliament (England and Wales))	Omit.
Section 426B (devolution)	Omit.
Section 426C (irrelevance of privilege)	Omit.]
Section 427 (parliamentary disqualification)	Delete section 427.
Section 429 (disabilities on revocation or administration order against an individual)	Delete section 429.
Section 432 (offences by bodies corporate)	
subsection (2)	Delete "secretary or".
Section 435 (meaning of "associate")	
new subsection (3A)	Insert a new subsection (3A) as follows—
	"(3A) A member of a limited liability partnership is an associate of that limited liability partnership and of every other member of that limited liability partnership and of the husband or wife [or civil partner] or relative of every other member of that limited liability partnership.".
subsection (11)	For subsection (11) there shall be substituted—
	"(11) In this section "company" includes any body corporate (whether incorporated in Great Britain or elsewhere); and references to directors and other officers of a company and to voting power at any general meeting of a company have effect with any necessary modifications.".
Section 436 (expressions used generally)	
	The following expressions and definitions shall be added to the section—
	""designated member" has the same meaning as it has in the Limited Liability Partnerships Act 2000;
	"limited liability partnership" means a limited liability partnership formed and registered under the Limited Liability Partnerships Act 2000;

Provisions	Modifications
	"limited liability partnership agreement", in relation to a limited liability partnership, means any agreement, express or implied, made between the members of the limited liability partnership or between the limited liability partnership and the members of the limited liability partnership which determines the mutual rights and duties of the members, and their rights and duties in relation to the limited liability partnership.".
Section 437 (transitional provisions, and savings)	Delete section 437.
Section 440 (extent (Scotland))	
subsection (2)	In subsection (2), omit paragraph (b).
Section 441 (extent (Northern Ireland))	
	Delete section 441.
Section 442 (extent (other territories))	
	Delete section 442.
[Schedule A1	
Paragraph 6	
sub-paragraph (1)	For "directors of a company wish" substitute "limited liability partnership wishes".
	For "they" substitute "the designated members of the limited liability partnership".
sub-paragraph (2)	For "directors" substitute "the designated members of the limited liability partnership".
	In sub-paragraph (c), for "meetings of the company and" substitute "a meeting of".
Paragraph 7	
sub-paragraph (1)	For "directors of a company" substitute "designated members of the limited liability partnership".
	In sub-paragraph (e)(iii), for "meetings of the company and" substitute "a meeting of".
Paragraph 8	
sub-paragraph (2)	For "meetings" substitute "meeting".
	For "are" substitute "is".
	Omit the words in parenthesis.
sub-paragraph (3)	For "either of those meetings" substitute "the meeting".
	For "those meetings were" substitute "that meeting was".
	Omit the words in parenthesis.
sub-paragraph (4)	For "either" substitute "the".
sub-paragraph (6)(c)	For "one or both of the meetings" substitute "the meeting".
Paragraph 9	
sub-paragraph (1)	For "directors" substitute "designated members of the limited liability partnership".
sub-paragraph (2)	For "directors" substitute "designated members of the limited liability partnership".
Paragraph 12	
sub-paragraph (1)(b)	Omit.
sub-paragraph (1)(c)	For "resolution may be passed" substitute "determination that it may be wound up may be made".
sub-paragraph (2)	For "transfer of shares" substitute "any transfer by a member of the limited liability partnership of his interest in the property of the limited liability partnership".

Provisions	Modifications
Paragraph 20	
sub-paragraph (8)	For "directors" substitute "designated members of the limited liability partnership".
sub-paragraph (9)	For "directors" substitute "designated members of the limited liability partnership".
Paragraph 24	
sub-paragraph (2)	For "directors" substitute "designated members of the limited liability partnership".
Paragraph 25	
sub-paragraph (2)(c)	For "directors" substitute "designated members of the limited liability partnership".
Paragraph 26	
sub-paragraph (1)	Omit ", director".
Paragraph 29	
sub-paragraph (1)	For "meetings of the company and its creditors" substitute "a meeting of the creditors of the limited liability partnership".
Paragraph 30	
sub-paragraph (1)	For "meetings" substitute "meeting".
new sub-paragraph (2A)	Insert new sub-paragraph (2A) as follows—
	"(2A) If modifications to the proposal are proposed at the meeting the chairman of the meeting shall, before the conclusion of the meeting, ascertain from the limited liability partnership whether or not it accepts the proposed modifications; and if at that conclusion the limited liability partnership has failed to respond to a proposed modification it shall be presumed not to have agreed to it.".
sub-paragraph (3)	For "either" substitute "the".
	After "the result of the meeting" in the first place where it occurs insert "(including, where modifications to the proposal were proposed at the meeting, the response to those proposed modifications made by the limited liability partnership)".
	At the end add "and to the limited liability partnership".
Paragraph 31	
sub-paragraph (1)	For "meetings" substitute "meeting".
sub-paragraph (7)	For "directors of the company" substitute "designated members of the limited liability partnership".
	For "meetings (or either of them)" substitute "meeting".
	For "directors" substitute "limited liability partnership".
	For "those meetings" substitute "that meeting".
Paragraph 32	
sub-paragraph (2)	For sub-paragraphs (a) and (b) substitute "with the day on which the meeting summoned under paragraph 29 is first held.".
Paragraph 36	
sub-paragraph (2)	For sub-paragraph (2) substitute—
	"(2) The decision has effect if, in accordance with the rules, it has been taken by the creditors' meeting summoned under paragraph 29.".
sub-paragraph (3)	Omit.
sub-paragraph (4)	Omit.
sub-paragraph (5)	Omit.

Provisions	Modifications
Paragraph 37	
sub-paragraph (5)	For "each of the reports of the meetings" substitute "the report of the meeting".
Paragraph 38	
sub-paragraph (1)(a)	For "one or both of the meetings" substitute "the meeting".
sub-paragraph (1)(b)	For "either of those meetings" substitute "the meeting".
sub-paragraph (2)(a)	For "either of the meetings" substitute "the meeting".
	After sub-paragraph (2)(a) insert new (aa) as follows—
	"(aa) any member of the limited liability partnership;".
sub-paragraph (2)(b)	Omit "creditors'".
sub-paragraph (3)(a)	For "each of the reports" substitute "the report".
sub-paragraph (3)(b)	Omit "creditors'".
sub-paragraph (4)(a)(ii)	Omit "in question".
sub-paragraph (4)(b)(i)	For "further meetings" substitute "a further meeting" and for "directors" substitute "limited liability partnership".
sub-paragraph (4)(b)(ii)	Omit "company or (as the case may be) creditors'".
sub-paragraph (5)	For "directors do" substitute "limited liability partnerships does".
Paragraph 39	
sub-paragraph (1)	For "one or both of the meetings" substitute "the meeting".
Schedule B1	
Paragraph 2	
sub-paragraph (c)	For "company or its directors" substitute "limited liability partnership".
Paragraph 8	
sub-paragraph (1)(a)	For "resolution for voluntary winding up" substitute "determination to wind up voluntarily".
Paragraph 9	Omit.
Paragraph 12	
sub-paragraph (1)(b)	Omit.
Paragraph 22	For sub-paragraph (1) substitute—
	"(1) A limited liability partnership may appoint an administrator.".
	Omit sub-paragraph (2).
Paragraph 23	
sub-paragraph (1)(b)	Omit "or its directors".
Paragraph 42	
sub-paragraph (2)	For "resolution may be passed for the winding up of" substitute "determination to wind up voluntarily may be made by".
Paragraph 61	For paragraph 61 substitute—"
	"61. The administrator has power to prevent any person from taking part in the management of the business of the limited liability partnership and to appoint any person to be a manager of that business.".
Paragraph 62	At the end add the following—

Provisions	Modifications
	"Subsections (3) and (4) of section 92 shall apply for the purposes of this paragraph as they apply for the purposes of that section.".
Paragraph 83	
sub-paragraph (6)(b)	For "resolution for voluntary winding up" substitute "determination to wind up voluntarily".
sub-paragraph (8)(b)	For "passing of the resolution for voluntary winding up" substitute "determination to wind up voluntarily".
sub-paragraph (8)(e)	For "passing of the resolution for voluntary winding up" substitute "determination to wind up voluntarily".
Paragraph 87	
sub-paragraph (2)(b)	Insert at the end "or".
sub-paragraph (2)(c)	Omit ", or".
sub-paragraph (2)(d)	Omit the words from "(d)" to "company".
Paragraph 89	
sub-paragraph (2)(b)	Insert at the end "or".
sub-paragraph (2)(c)	Omit ", or".
sub-paragraph (2)(d)	Omit the words from "(d)" to "company".
Paragraph 91	
sub-paragraph (1)(c)	Omit.
Paragraph 94	Omit.
Paragraph 95	For "to 94" substitute "and 93".
Paragraph 97	
sub-paragraph (1)(a)	Omit "or directors".
Paragraph 103	
sub-paragraph (5)	Omit.
Paragraph 105	Omit.]
Schedule 1	
Paragraph 19	For paragraph 19 substitute the following—
	"19. Power to enforce any rights the limited liability partnership has against the members under the terms of the limited liability partnership agreement."
Schedule 10	
[Section 6A(1)	In the entry relating to section 6A omit "members' or".]
Section 85(2)	In the entry relating to section 85(2) for "resolution for voluntary winding up" substitute "making of determination for voluntary winding up".
Section 89(4)	In the entry relating to section 89(4) for "Director" substitute "Designated member".
Section 93(3)	In the entry relating to section 93(3) for "general meeting of the company" substitute "meeting of members of the limited liability partnership".
Section 99(3)	In the entries relating to section 99(3) for "director" and "directors" where they appear substitute "designated member" or "designated members" as appropriate.
Section 105(3)	In the entry relating to section 105(3) for "company general meeting" substitute "meeting of the members of the limited liability partnership".
Section 106(6)	In the entry relating to section 106(6) for "final meeting of the company" substitute "final meeting of the members of the limited liability partnership".

Provisions	Modifications
Sections 353(1) to 362	Delete the entries relating to sections 353(1) to 362 inclusive.
Section 429(5)	Delete the entry relating to section 429(5).
[Schedule A1, paragraph 9(2)	For "Directors" substitute "Designated Members".
Schedule A1, paragraph 20(9)	For "Directors" substitute "Designated Members".
Schedule B1, paragraph 27(4)	Omit "or directors".
Schedule B1, paragraph 29(7)	Omit "or directors".
Schedule B1, paragraph 32	Omit "or directors".]

NOTES

In entry relating to s 124A, words in square brackets substituted by the Financial Services and Markets Act 2000 (Consequential Amendments) Order 2004, SI 2004/355, art 10(1), (3), as from 4 March 2004.

In entry relating to s 435, words in square brackets inserted by the Civil Partnership Act 2004 (Amendments to Subordinate Legislation) Order 2005, SI 2005/2114, art 2(18), Sch 18, Pt 1, para 3, as from 5 December 2005.

All other words in square brackets were either inserted or substituted, and the words omitted were revoked, by the Limited Liability Partnerships (Amendment) Regulations 2005, SI 2005/1989, reg 3, Sch 2, as from 1 October 2005, except in relation to a case where a petition for an administration order has been presented before that date.

SCHEDULE 4

Regulation 5(3)

[10.826]

The provisions listed in this Schedule are not applied to Scotland to the extent specified below—

Sections 50 to 52;

Section 53(1) and (2), to the extent that those subsections do not relate to the requirement for a copy of the instrument and notice being forwarded to the registrar of companies;

Section 53(4) (6) and (7);

Section 54(1), (2), (3) (to the extent that that subsection does not relate to the requirement for a copy of the interlocutor to be sent to the registrar of companies), and subsections (5), (6) and (7);

Sections 55 to 58;

Section 60, other than subsection (1);

Section 61, including subsections (6) and (7) to the extent that those subsections do not relate to anything to be done or which may be done to or by the registrar of companies;

Section 62, including subsection (5) to the extent that that subsection does not relate to anything to be done or which may be done to or by the registrar of companies;

Sections 63 to 66;

Section 67, including subsections (1) and (8) to the extent that those subsections do not relate to anything to be done or which may be done to the registrar of companies;

Section 68;

Section 69, including subsections (1) and (2) to the extent that those subsections do not relate to anything to be done or which may be done by the registrar of companies;

Sections 70 and 71;

Subsection 84(3), to the extent that it does not concern the copy of the resolution being forwarded to the registrar of companies within 15 days;

Sections 91 to 93;

Section 94, including subsections (3) and (4) to the extent that those subsections do not relate to the liquidator being required to send to the registrar of companies a copy of the account and a return of the final meeting;

Section 95;

Section 97;

Sections 100 to 102;

Sections 104 to 105;

Section 106, including subsections (3), (4) and (5) to the extent that those subsections do not relate to the liquidator being required to send to the registrar of companies a copy of the account of winding up and a return of the final meeting/quorum;

Sections 109 to 111;

Section 112, including subsection (3) to the extent that that subsection does not relate to the liquidator being required to send to the registrar a copy of the order made by the court;

Sections 113 to 115;

Sections 126 to 128;

Section 130(1) to the extent that that subsection does not relate to a copy of the order being forwarded by the court to the registrar;

Section 131;

Sections 133 to 135;

Part 10   Miscellaneous other SIs

Sections 138 to 140;

Sections 142 to 146;

Section 147, including subsection (3) to the extent that that subsection does not relate to a copy of the order being forwarded by the company to the registrar;

Section 162 to the extent that that section concerns the matters set out in Section C.2 of Schedule 5 to the Scotland Act 1998 as being exceptions to the insolvency reservation;

Sections 163 to 167;

Section 169;

Section 170, including subsection (2) to the extent that that subsection does not relate to an application being made by the registrar to make good the default;

Section 171;

Section 172, including subsection (8) to the extent that that subsection does not relate to the liquidator being required to give notice to the registrar;

Sections 173 and 174;

Section 177;

Sections 185 to 189;

Sections 191 to 194;

Section 196 to the extent that that section applies to the specified devolved functions of Part IV of the Insolvency Act 1986;

Section 199;

Section 200 to the extent that it applies to the specified devolved functions of Part IV of the First Group of Parts of the 1986 Act;

Sections 206 to 215;

Section 218 subsections (1), (2), (4) and (6);

Section 231 to 232 to the extent that the sections apply to administrative receivers, liquidators and provisional liquidators;

Section 233, to the extent that that section applies in the case of the appointment of an administrative receiver, of a voluntary arrangement taking effect, of a company going into liquidation or where a provisional liquidator is appointed;

Section 234 to the extent that that section applies to situations other than those where an administration order applies;

Section 235 to the extent that that section applies to situations other than those where an administration order applies;

Sections 236 to 237 to the extent that those sections apply to situations other than administration orders and winding up;

Sections 242 to 243;

Section 244 to the extent that that section applies in circumstances other than a company which is subject to an administration order;

Section 245;

Section 251, to the extent that that section contains definitions which apply only to devolved matters;

Section 416(1) and (4), to the extent that those subsections apply to section 206(1)(a) and (b) in connection with the offence provision relating to the winding up of a limited liability partnership;

Schedule 2;

Schedule 3;

Schedule 4;

Schedule 8, to the extent that that Schedule does not apply to voluntary arrangements or administrations within the meaning of Parts I and II of the 1986 Act.

In addition, Schedule 10, which concerns punishment of offences under the Insolvency Act 1986, lists various sections of the Insolvency Act 1986 which create an offence. The following sections, which are listed in Schedule 10, are devolved in their application to Scotland:

Section 51(4);

Section 51(5);

Sections 53(2) to 62(5) to the extent that those subsections relate to matters other than delivery to the registrar of companies;

Section 64(2);

Section 65(4);

Section 66(6);

Section 67(8) to the extent that that subsection relates to matters other than delivery to the registrar of companies;

Section 93(3);

Section 94(4) to the extent that that subsection relates to matters other than delivery to the registrar of companies;

Section 94(6);

Section 95(8);

Section 105(3);

Section 106(4) to the extent that that subsection relates to matters other than delivery to the registrar of companies;

Section 106(6);

Section 109(2);

Section 114(4);

Section 131(7);

Section 164;

Section 166(7);

Section 188(2);

Section 192(2);

Sections 206 to 211; and

Section 235(5) to the extent that it relates to matters other than administration orders.

SCHEDULE 5
GENERAL AND CONSEQUENTIAL AMENDMENTS IN OTHER LEGISLATION
Regulation 9

[10.827]

1.–21. . . .

Culpable officer provisions

22. (1) A culpable officer provision applies in the case of a limited liability partnership as if the reference in the provision to a director (or a person purporting to act as a director) were a reference to a member (or a person purporting to act as a member) of the limited liability partnership.

(2) A culpable officer provision is a provision in any Act or subordinate legislation (within the meaning of the Interpretation Act 1978) to the effect that where—

(a)   a body corporate is guilty of a particular offence, and

(b)   the offence is proved to have been committed with the consent or connivance of, or to be attributable to the neglect on the part of, (among others) a director of the body corporate,

he (as well as the body corporate) is guilty of the offence.

NOTES

Paras 1–21: in so far as they have not been revoked, these paragraphs contain amendments which, in so far as relevant to this work, are incorporated at the appropriate place.

SCHEDULE 6
APPLICATION OF SUBORDINATE LEGISLATION
Regulation 10

PART I
REGULATIONS MADE UNDER THE 1985 ACT
[10.828]

1.–6. . . .

[7. The Companies Act 1985 (Power to Enter and Remain on Premises: Procedural) Regulations 2005.]

NOTES

Paras 1–3, 6: revoked by the Limited Liability Partnerships (Accounts and Audit) (Application of Companies Act 2006) Regulations 2008, SI 2008/1911, reg 58(1)(c), as from 1 October 2008, except in relation to accounts for, and otherwise as regards, financial years beginning before that date (see reg 58(3) at **[10.1060]**).

Paras 4, 5: revoked by the Limited Liability Partnerships (Application of Companies Act 2006) Regulations 2009, SI 2009/1804, reg 85, Sch 3, Pt 2, para 13(7)(a), as from 1 October 2009.

Para 7: added by the Limited Liability Partnerships (Amendment) Regulations 2007, SI 2007/2073, reg 4, as from 1 October 2007.

PART II
REGULATIONS MADE UNDER THE 1986 ACT
[10.829]

1. Insolvency Practitioners Regulations 1990

2. The Insolvency Practitioners (Recognised Professional Bodies) Order 1986

3. The Insolvency Rules 1986 and the Insolvency (Scotland) Rules 1986 (except in so far as they relate to the exceptions to the reserved matters specified in section C 2 of Part II of Schedule 5 to the Scotland Act 1998)

4. The Insolvency Fees Order 1986

5. The Co-operation of Insolvency Courts (Designation of Relevant Countries and Territories) Order 1986

6. The Co-operation of Insolvency Courts (Designation of Relevant Countries and Territories) Order 1996

7. The Co-operation of Insolvency Courts (Designation of Relevant Country) Order 1998

8. Insolvency Proceedings (Monetary Limits) Order 1986

9. Insolvency Practitioners Tribunal (Conduct of Investigations) Rules 1986

10. Insolvency Regulations 1994

11. Insolvency (Amendment) Regulations 2000.

NOTES
    Insolvency Practitioners Regulations 1990, SI 1990/439: revoked and replaced by the Insolvency Practitioners Regulations 2005, SI 2005/524.
    Insolvency Fees Order 1986, SI 1986/2030: revoked and replaced by the Insolvency Proceedings (Fees) Order 2004, SI 2004/593.
    Co-operation of Insolvency Courts (Designation of Relevant Countries and Territories) Order 1996: it is assumed that this refers to the Co-operation of Insolvency Courts (Designation of Relevant Countries) Order 1996, SI 1996/253.

PART III
REGULATIONS MADE UNDER OTHER LEGISLATION

[10.830]
1.   . . .

2. The Companies (Disqualification Orders) Regulations 1986

3. The Insolvent Companies (Disqualification of Unfit Directors) Proceedings Rules 1987

4. The Contracting Out (Functions of the Official Receiver) Order 1995

5. The Uncertificated Securities Regulations 1995

6. The Insolvent Companies (Reports on Conduct of Directors) Rules 1996

7. The Insolvent Companies (Reports on Conduct of Directors) (Scotland) Rules 1996.

NOTES
    Para 1: revoked by the Limited Liability Partnerships (Application of Companies Act 2006) Regulations 2009, SI 2009/1804, reg 85, Sch 3, Pt 2, para 13(7)(b), as from 1 October 2009.
    The Companies (Disqualification Orders) Regulations 1986, SI 1986/2067 were revoked and replaced by the Companies (Disqualification Orders) Regulations 2001, SI 2001/967. The 2001 Regulations were themselves revoked and replaced by the Companies (Disqualification Orders) Regulations 2009, SI 2009/2471.
    The Uncertificated Securities Regulations 1995, SI 1995/3272 were revoked and replaced by the Uncertificated Securities Regulations 2001, SI 2001/3755.

INSOLVENCY ACT 1986 (PRESCRIBED PART) ORDER 2003

(SI 2003/2097)

NOTES
    Made: 8 August 2003.
    Authority: Insolvency Act 1986, s 176A.
    Commencement: 15 September 2003.
    Amendment: as of 1 July 2011, this Order had not been amended.

[10.831]
1   Citation, Commencement and Interpretation
(1)   This Order may be cited as the Insolvency Act 1986 (Prescribed Part) Order 2003 and shall come into force on 15th September 2003.

(2)   In this order "the 1986 Act" means the Insolvency Act 1986.

[10.832]
2   Minimum value of the company's net property
For the purposes of section 176A(3)(a) of the 1986 Act the minimum value of the company's net property is £10,000.

[10.833]
3 Calculation of prescribed part

(1) The prescribed part of the company's net property to be made available for the satisfaction of unsecured debts of the company pursuant to section 176A of the 1986 Act shall be calculated as follows—

   (a) where the company's net property does not exceed £10,000 in value, 50% of that property;

   (b) subject to paragraph (2), where the company's net property exceeds £10,000 in value the sum of—

      (i) 50% of the first £10,000 in value; and

      (ii) 20% of that part of the company's net property which exceeds £10,000 in value.

(2) The value of the prescribed part of the company's net property to be made available for the satisfaction of unsecured debts of the company pursuant to section 176A shall not exceed £600,000.

INSOLVENCY PRACTITIONERS AND INSOLVENCY SERVICES ACCOUNT (FEES) ORDER 2003

(SI 2003/3363)

NOTES

Made: 30 December 2003.

Authority: Insolvency Act 1986, s 415A.

Commencement: 30 January 2004 (art 2(3)); 1 April 2004 (otherwise).

This Order is reproduced as amended by: the Insolvency Practitioners and Insolvency Services Account (Fees) (Amendment) Order 2004, SI 2004/476 the Insolvency Practitioners and Insolvency Services Account (Fees) (Amendment) Order 2005, SI 2005/523; the Insolvency Practitioners and Insolvency Services Account (Fees) (Amendment) (No 2) Order 2005, SI 2005/3524; the Insolvency Practitioners and Insolvency Services Account (Fees) (Amendment) Order 2007, SI 2007/133; the Insolvency Practitioners and Insolvency Services Account (Fees) (Amendment) (No 2) Order 2008, SI 2008/672; the Insolvency Practitioners and Insolvency Services Account (Fees) (Amendment) Order 2009, SI 2009/487; the Provision of Services (Insolvency Practitioners) Regulations 2009, SI 2009/3081.

Application to bank insolvency and administration: as to the application of this Order to bank insolvency and administration, see the Banking Act 2009 (Parts 2 and 3 Consequential Amendments) Order 2009, SI 2009/317.

ARRANGEMENT OF ARTICLES

[10.834]
1 Citation, Commencement, Interpretation and Extent

(1) This Order may be cited as the Insolvency Practitioners and Insolvency Services Account (Fees) Order 2003 and shall come into force on 1st April 2004 ("the principal commencement date") except for Article 2(3) which shall come into force on 30th January 2004.

(2) In this Order any reference to a numbered section is to the section so numbered in the Insolvency Act 1986.

(3) All the provisions of this Order except Article 5 and the Schedule to this Order extend to England and Wales and Scotland and Article 5 and the Schedule to this Order extend only to England and Wales.

[10.835]
2 Fees payable in connection with the recognition of professional bodies pursuant to section 391

(1) Every application by a body for recognition pursuant to section 391 shall be accompanied by a fee of £4,500.

[(2) On or before 6th April 2009 and on or before 6th April in each subsequent year, there shall be paid to the Secretary of State by each body recognised pursuant to section 391 in respect of the maintenance of that body's recognition pursuant to that section, a fee calculated by multiplying £300 by the number of persons who as at the 1st January in that year were authorised to act as insolvency practitioners by virtue of membership of that body.]

(3)   Each body recognised pursuant to section 391 shall on or before 31st January in each year submit to the Secretary of State a list of its members who as at 1st January in that year were authorised to act as insolvency practitioners by virtue of membership of that body.

NOTES

Para (2): substituted by the Insolvency Practitioners and Insolvency Services Account (Fees) (Amendment) Order 2009, SI 2009/487, art 3, as from 6 April 2009, subject to transitional provisions in art 4 of that Order as follows—

"**4.**—(1)   This article applies to a body recognised pursuant to section 391 of the Insolvency Act 1986 that—

(a)   pursuant to article 2(2) of the principal Order (as it stood before the coming into force of this Order) makes a payment by reference to the number of persons who as at 1st January 2009 were authorised to act as insolvency practitioners by virtue of membership of that body; and

(b)   makes that payment in the period commencing on 1st January 2009 and ending immediately before 6th April 2009.

(2)   The substitution of article 2(2) of the principal Order by article 3 of this Order shall not require a body to which this article applies to make any further payment by reference to the number of persons who as at 1st January 2009 were authorised to act as insolvency practitioners by virtue of membership of that body.".

[10.836]

3   Fees payable in connection with authorisations by the Secretary of State under section 393

(1)   [Subject to paragraph (1A), every person] who on the principal commencement date is the holder of an authorisation to act as an insolvency practitioner granted by the Secretary of State pursuant to section 393 shall within 7 days of that date pay to the Secretary of State a fee in respect of the maintenance of that authorisation calculated in accordance with paragraph (2).

[(1A)   Paragraph (1) does not apply to—

(a)   any authorisation granted on the principal commencement date; or

(b)   any authorisation granted on the 1st April in any year prior to the year 2004.]

(2)   The fee payable by virtue of paragraph (1) shall be calculated by multiplying [£2,100] by the number of days in the period starting with the principal commencement date and ending with the date immediately before the next anniversary of the granting of the authorisation or the date of expiry of the authorisation (whichever occurs first) and dividing the result by 365.

(3)   Every application made to the Secretary of State pursuant to section 392 for authorisation to act as an insolvency practitioner shall be accompanied by a fee of [£850, in connection with the grant of the application].

[(3A)   Where the application is granted, the individual to whom authorisation has been granted must pay to the Secretary of State as soon as reasonably practicable a fee of £2,400 in connection with the maintenance of the authorisation for the period of 12 months commencing with the date of the grant of the authorisation.]

(4)   Subject to paragraph (5), every person who holds an authorisation granted by the Secretary of State pursuant to section 393 to act as an insolvency practitioner shall, on each anniversary of the granting of that authorisation when it is in force, pay to the Secretary of State in connection with the maintenance of that authorisation a fee of [£3,250].

(5)   Where on the relevant anniversary the authorisation mentioned in paragraph (4) has less than a year to run, the fee shall be calculated by multiplying [£3,250] by the number of days that the authorisation has to run (starting with the day of the anniversary) and dividing the result by 365.

NOTES

Para (1): words in square brackets substituted by the Insolvency Practitioners and Insolvency Services Account (Fees) (Amendment) Order 2004, SI 2004/476, art 2(1), (2), as from 31 March 2004.

Para (1A): inserted by SI 2004/476, art 2(1), (3), as from 31 March 2004.

Para (2): sum in square brackets substituted by the Insolvency Practitioners and Insolvency Services Account (Fees) (Amendment) (No 2) Order 2005, SI 2005/3524, art 3(2), as from 1 April 2006.

Para (3): the words in square brackets were substituted (together with para (3A)) for part of this paragraph by the Provision of Services (Insolvency Practitioners) Regulations 2009, SI 2009/3081, reg 3, as from 28 December 2009 (except in relation to an application for authorisation to act as an insolvency practitioner under the Insolvency Act 1986, s 393 made or granted before that date).

Para (3A): substituted as noted above.

Paras (4), (5): sums in square brackets substituted by the Insolvency Practitioners and Insolvency Services Account (Fees) (Amendment) Order 2009, SI 2009/487, art 5, as from 6 April 2009.

[10.837]

4   Transitional cases—early applications for authorisation

(1)   This article applies to an application made to the Secretary of State pursuant to section 392 for the granting of an authorisation to act as an insolvency practitioner—

(a)   where the applicant was as at the date of its making the holder of an authorisation granted pursuant to section 393;

(b)   where the application was made—

(i)   after the date of the making of this Order but before the principal commencement date; and

(ii)   more than three months before the expiry of the authorisation mentioned in sub-paragraph (a); and

(c)   in respect of which as at the principal commencement date no decision as to whether to grant or refuse it has been taken.

(2)   In respect of an application to which this article applies, there shall be paid to the Secretary of State by the applicant within 7 days of the principal commencement date a fee of £1,500.

[10.838]
5   Fees payable in connection with the operation of the Insolvency Services Account

There shall be payable in connection with the operation of the Insolvency Services Account fees as provided for in the Schedule to this Order.

[10.839]
6   Value Added Tax

Where Value Added Tax is chargeable in respect of the provision of a service for which a fee is prescribed by any provision of this Order, there shall be payable in addition to that fee the amount of the Value Added Tax.

SCHEDULE
FEES PAYABLE IN CONNECTION WITH THE OPERATION OF THE
INSOLVENCY SERVICES ACCOUNT

Article 5

[10.840]
1   Interpretation for the purposes of the Schedule

(1)   In this Schedule a reference to a numbered regulation is to the regulation so numbered in the Insolvency Regulations 1994

(2)   In this Schedule "payment date" means any of the following dates in any year—
    (a)   1st January;
    (b)   1st April;
    (c)   1st July; and
    (d)   1st October.

[(2A)   In this Schedule "working day" means any day other than a Saturday, a Sunday, Good Friday, Christmas Day or a Bank Holiday in England and Wales in accordance with the Banking and Financial Dealings Act 1971.]

(3)   Subject to paragraphs (4) and (5), for the purposes of this Schedule an account is "maintained with the Secretary of State in respect of monies which may from time to time be paid into the Insolvency Services Account" where—
    (a)   in a winding up by the court or a bankruptcy the Secretary of State creates a record in relation to the winding up or, as the case may be, the bankruptcy for the purpose of recording payments into and out of the Insolvency Services Account relating to the winding up or, as the case may be, the bankruptcy; and
    (b)   in a voluntary winding up on the request of the liquidator the Secretary of State creates a record in relation to the winding up for the purposes of recording payments into and out of the Insolvency Services Account relating to the winding up.

[(4)   An account ceases to be maintained with the Secretary of State in the case of a winding up by the court or a bankruptcy where—
    (a)   the liquidator or the trustee has filed a receipts and payments account with the Secretary of State pursuant to regulation 14 or regulation 28;
    (b)   the account contains, or is accompanied by, a statement that it is a final receipts and payments account; and
    (c)   four working days have elapsed since the requirements of paragraphs (a) and (b) have been met,
but an account is revived in the circumstances mentioned in paragraph (5).

(4A)   An account ceases to be maintained with the Secretary of State in the case of a voluntary winding up where—
    (a)   no monies to which that account relates are held in the Insolvency Services Account (other than any unclaimed dividends or any amount that it is impracticable to distribute to creditors or is required for the payment of fees that are or will become payable while the account is maintained); and
    (b)   notice in writing has been given to the Secretary of State that the account is no longer required and four working days have elapsed since the receipt of that notice by the Secretary of State,
but an account is revived in the circumstances mentioned in paragraph (5).]

(5)   The circumstances referred to in [paragraphs (4) and (4A)] are—
    (a)   the receipt by the Secretary of State of notice in writing given by the trustee or liquidator for the revival of the account; or

(b)   the payment into the Insolvency Services Account of any sums to the credit of the company or, as the case may be, the estate of the bankrupt,

and on the occurrence of either of the circumstances mentioned above, an account is "maintained with the Secretary of State in respect of monies which may from time to time be paid into the Insolvency Services Account".

(6)   References to a bankruptcy include a bankruptcy under the Bankruptcy Act 1914 and references to a winding up include a winding up under the provisions of the Companies Act 1985.

2   Fees payable in connection with the operation of the Insolvency Services Account

Fees shall be payable in relation to the operation of the Insolvency Services Account (including payments into and out of that account) in the circumstances set out in the table below—

Fee	Description of fee and circumstances in which it is payable	Amount
1	**Banking fee; winding up by the court and bankruptcy** Where in any bankruptcy or winding up by the court an account is maintained with the Secretary of State in respect of monies which may from time to time be paid into the Insolvency Services Account, there shall be payable out of the estate of the bankrupt or, as the case may be, the assets of the company on each payment date where the liquidator or the trustee is not the official receiver, a fee of—	[£18]
2	**Banking fee; voluntary winding up** Where in a voluntary winding up an account is maintained with the Secretary of State in respect of monies which may from time to time be paid into the Insolvency Services Account there shall be payable out of the assets of the company on each payment date a fee of—	[£23]
[2A	**Payment of unclaimed dividends or other money—administration** Where any money is paid into the Insolvency Services Account pursuant to regulation 3B, that payment shall be accompanied by a fee in respect of each company to which it relates of—	£25
2B	**Payment of unclaimed dividends or other money—administrative receivership** Where any money is paid into the Insolvency Services Account pursuant to regulation 3C, that payment shall be accompanied by a fee in respect of each company to which it relates of—	£25]
[2C	**Payment of unclaimed dividends or other money—voluntary winding up** Where any money is paid into the Insolvency Services Account pursuant to regulation 18(2)(a), that payment shall be accompanied by a fee in respect of each company to which it relates of—	£25]
3	**Cheque etc issue fee** Where a cheque, money order or payable order in respect of monies in the Insolvency Services Account is issued or reissued on the application of— (a) a liquidator pursuant to regulations 7 or 8; (b) a trustee pursuant to regulations 22 or 23; or (c) any person claiming any monies in that account pursuant to regulation 32, there shall be payable out of the assets of the company, the estate of the bankrupt or, as the case may be, by the claimant— —(i) where the application is made before principal commencement date, a fee in respect of that cheque, money order or payable order of— —(ii) where the application is made on or after the principal commencement date, a fee in respect of that cheque, money order or payable order of—	 £0.65 [£1]
4	**Electronic funds systems (CHAPs and BACs etc) fees** On the making or remaking of a transfer in respect of funds held in the Insolvency Services Account on an application made by— (a) a liquidator pursuant to regulations 7 or 8; (b) a trustee pursuant to regulations 22 or 23; or (c) any person claiming pursuant to regulation 32, any monies held in the Insolvency Services Account,	

Fee	Description of fee and circumstances in which it is payable	Amount
	there shall be payable out of the assets of the company, the estate of the bankrupt or, as the case may be, by the claimant, a fee in respect of that transfer as follows:	
	(i) where it is made through the Clearing House Automated Payments System (CHAPs), a fee of—	£10
	(ii) where it is made through the Bankers' Clearing System (BACs) or any electronic funds transfer system other than CHAPs, a fee of—	£0.15]

NOTES

Para 1: sub-para (2A) inserted, sub-paras (4), (4A) substituted for original sub-para (4), and words in square brackets in sub-para (5) substituted, by the Insolvency Practitioners and Insolvency Services Account (Fees) (Amendment) Order 2005, SI 2005/523, art 2, as from 1 April 2005.

The table in para 2 is amended as follows:

Fees 2A, 2B inserted by the Insolvency Practitioners and Insolvency Services Account (Fees) (Amendment) (No 2) Order 2008, SI 2008/672, arts 2, 4, as from 6 April 2008.

Fee 2C inserted, and sums in square brackets in each of fees 1, 2, 3 substituted, by the Insolvency Practitioners and Insolvency Services Account (Fees) (Amendment) Order 2009, SI 2009/487, art 6, as from 6 April 2009.

Fee 4 substituted by the Insolvency Practitioners and Insolvency Services Account (Fees) (Amendment) Order 2007, SI 2007/133, arts 2, 4, as from 1 April 2007.

INSOLVENCY PROCEEDINGS (FEES) ORDER 2004

(SI 2004/593)

NOTES

Made: 4 March 2004.

Authority: Insolvency Act 1986, ss 414, 415; Bankruptcy Act 1914, s 133 (repealed); CA 1985, s 663(4) (repealed).

Commencement: 1 April 2004.

This Order is reproduced as amended by: the Insolvency Proceedings (Fees) (Amendment) Order 2005, SI 2005/544; the Insolvency Proceedings (Fees) (Amendment) Order 2007, SI 2007/521; the Insolvency Proceedings (Fees) (Amendment) Order 2008, SI 2008/714; the Insolvency Proceedings (Fees) (Amendment) Order 2009, SI 2009/645; the Insolvency Proceedings (Fees) (Amendment) Order 2010, SI 2010/732; the Insolvency Proceedings (Fees) (Amendment) Order 2011, SI 2011/1167.

Limited liability partnerships: this Order applies, with modifications, to limited liability partnerships; see the Limited Liability Partnerships Regulations 2001, SI 2001/1090, reg 10, Sch 6, Pt II (at **[10.829]**), and the Interpretation Act 1978, ss 17(2)(a), 23(1), (2).

ARRANGEMENT OF ARTICLES

[10.841]
1　Citation and commencement

This Order may be cited as the Insolvency Proceedings (Fees) Order 2004 and shall come into force on 1st April 2004.

[10.842]
2　Interpretation

(1)　In this Order—

"the Act" means the Insolvency Act 1986 (any reference to a numbered section being to the section so numbered in that Act);

"the commencement date" is the date referred to in Article 1;

"individual voluntary arrangement" means a voluntary arrangement pursuant to Part VIII of the Act; and

"the Rules" means the Insolvency Rules 1986 (any reference to a numbered Rule being to the Rule so numbered in the Rules).

(2)   A reference to a fee by a means of letters and a number is a reference to the fee so designated in the table in Schedule 2.

[10.843]
3   Revocations and Transitional Provisions
The instruments listed in the Schedule 1 to this Order are revoked to the extent set out in that Schedule.

[10.844]
4   Fees payable in connection with bankruptcies, [debt relief orders,] individual voluntary arrangements and winding up
(1)   Subject to paragraphs (2) and (3) and article 8, the fees payable to the Secretary of State in respect of [the costs of persons acting as approved intermediaries under Part 7A of the Act,] proceedings under Parts I to XI of the Act and the performance by the official receiver or Secretary of State of functions under those Parts shall be determined in accordance with the provisions of Schedule 2 to this Order.

(2)   Paragraph (1) and the provisions of Schedule 2 shall not apply to a bankruptcy where the bankruptcy order was made before the commencement date except insofar as is necessary to enable the charging of—
  (a)   fee INV1; or
  (b)   as regards an individual voluntary arrangement proposed by, or entered into by, the bankrupt, fees IVA1, IVA2 or IVA3.

(3)   Paragraph (1) and the provisions of Schedule 2 shall not apply to a winding up by the court where the winding-up order was made before the commencement date except insofar as is necessary to enable the charging of fee INV1.

(4)   Each request for the purchase of any government securities made by a trustee in bankruptcy under the Bankruptcy Act 1914 or a liquidator in a winding up under the provisions of the Companies Act 1985 shall be accompanied by [the appropriate amount of fee INV1].

NOTES
Words in square brackets in the article heading and in para (1) inserted by the Insolvency Proceedings (Fees) (Amendment) Order 2009, SI 2009/645, arts 3, 4(1)(a), (b), as from 6 April 2009.
Words in square brackets in para (4) substituted by SI 2009/645, arts 3, 4(1)(c), as from 6 April 2009, subject to transitional provisions as noted below.
Transitional provisions: art 7(2) to the 2009 Order provides as follows:

"(2)   The amendment made by article 4(1)(c) to article 4(4) of the principal Order increasing the fee with respect to the purchase of government securities and introducing a fee for the sale of government securities by a trustee in bankruptcy under the Bankruptcy Act 1914 or a liquidator in a winding up under the provisions of the Companies Act 1985, shall only apply where the request to purchase or sell is made on or after 6th April 2009 and, in the case of a sale, only where the request to purchase the securities which are to be sold was also made after on or after 6th April 2009.".

[10.845]
5   Fees payable to an insolvency practitioner appointed under section 273
Where a court appoints an insolvency practitioner under section 273(2) to prepare and submit a report under section 274 the court shall, on submission of the report, pay to the practitioner a fee of [£450] (that sum being inclusive of Value Added Tax).

NOTES
Sum in square brackets substituted by the Insolvency Proceedings (Fees) (Amendment) Order 2010, SI 2010/732, arts 3, 4, 8, as from 6 April 2010 (note that this amendment applies only to reports submitted to the court in respect of debtor's petitions presented on or after 6 April 2010).

[10.846]
6   Deposits—winding up by the court and bankruptcy
(1)   In this Article—
  "appropriate deposit" means—
    (a)   in relation to a winding-up petition to be presented under the Act the sum of [£1,165];
    (b)   in relation to a bankruptcy petition to be presented under section 264(1)(b) the sum of [£525]; or
    (c)   in relation to a bankruptcy petition to be presented under sections 264(1)(a), [(ba), (bb),] (c) or (d) the sum of [£700];
  "order" means a winding-up, or as the case may be, bankruptcy order;
  "petition" means a winding-up, or as the case may be, bankruptcy petition;

"relevant assets" means the assets of the company or, as the case may be the assets comprised in the estate of the bankrupt; and

"relevant fees" means in relation to winding-up proceedings fee W1 and in relation to bankruptcy proceedings fee B1 together with any fees payable under section 273.

(2) [Where a bankruptcy or winding-up petition is presented the appropriate deposit is payable by the petitioner and the deposit] shall be security for the payment of the relevant fees and shall be used to discharge those fees to the extent that the relevant assets are insufficient for that purpose.

(3) Where a deposit is paid to the court, the court shall (except to the extent that a fee is payable by virtue of Article 5) transmit the deposit paid to the official receiver attached to the court.

(4) A deposit shall be repaid to the person who made it in a case where a petition is dismissed or withdrawn except in the case of a bankruptcy petition where it is required to pay any fees arising under Article 5.

(5) In any case where an order is made (including any case where the order is subsequently annulled, rescinded or recalled), any deposit made shall be returned to the person who made it save to the extent that the relevant assets are insufficient to discharge the fees for which the deposit is security.

NOTES

Para (1) is amended as follows:

Sums in square brackets in paras (a), (b), (c) of the definition "appropriate deposit" substituted by the Insolvency Proceedings (Fees) (Amendment) Order 2011, SI 2011/1167, art 2, as from 1 June 2011, in relation to petitions presented on or after that date (the previous sums were £1000, £450, and £600 respectively)).

Words "(ba), (bb)," in square brackets in para (c) of the definition "appropriate deposit" inserted by the Insolvency Proceedings (Fees) (Amendment) Order 2005, SI 2005/544, arts 4, 5(a), as from 1 April 2005.

Para (2): words in square brackets substituted by SI 2005/544, arts 4, 5(b), as from 1 April 2005.

[10.847]
7 Deposits—official receiver acting as nominee in individual voluntary arrangement

(1) Where a proposal for an individual voluntary arrangement with the official receiver acting as nominee is notified to the official receiver, the notification shall be accompanied by a deposit of [£315] as security for fee IVA1 and fee IVA2.

(2) The deposit shall be used to discharge fee IVA1 and fee IVA2.

(3) Where the official receiver declines to act in relation to a proposal of the kind mentioned in paragraph (1) the deposit mentioned in that paragraph shall be refunded to the person entitled to it

(4) Where the official receiver agrees to act as nominee in relation to a proposal of the kind mentioned in paragraph (1) but the proposal is rejected by the bankrupt's creditors, any balance of the deposit after deducting fee IVA2 shall be returned to the person who is entitled to it.

NOTES

Para (1): sum in square brackets substituted by the Insolvency Proceedings (Fees) (Amendment) Order 2009, SI 2009/645, arts 3, 4(4), 7(5), as from 6 April 2009, in relation to notifications sent to the official receiver on or after that date.

[10.848]
8 Reduction and refund of fees—individual voluntary arrangement following bankruptcy

Where proposals made by a bankrupt for an individual voluntary arrangement with the official receiver acting as supervisor are approved by the bankrupt's creditors, fee B1 shall be reduced to [£857.50] and any payments made in respect of fee B1 which exceed that amount shall be refunded to the credit of the estate of the bankrupt.

NOTES

Sum in square brackets substituted by the Insolvency Proceedings (Fees) (Amendment) Order 2007, SI 2007/521, art 2(1), (5), 4(1), (5), as from 1 April 2007, in relation to cases in which the bankruptcy order relating to the bankrupt was made on or after that date.

[10.849]
9 Value Added Tax

Where Valued Added Tax is chargeable in respect of the provision of a service for which a fee is prescribed by virtue of any provision of this Order (other than Article 5), there shall be payable in addition to that fee the amount of the Value Added Tax.

SCHEDULES

SCHEDULE 1

(Sch 1 (Revocations) omitted.)

SCHEDULE 2
FEES PAYABLE IN INSOLVENCY PROCEEDINGS
Article 4

[10.850]

1. (1)   In this Schedule—

"the bankruptcy ceiling" means in relation to a bankruptcy, the sum which is arrived at by adding together—

    (a)   the bankruptcy debts required to be paid under the Rules

    [(b)   any interest payable by virtue of sections 328(4) and 329(2)(b); and]

    (c)   the expenses of the bankruptcy as set out in Rule 6.224 other than—

        (i)   any sums spent out of money received in carrying on the business of the bankrupt; and

        (ii)   fee B2 in the Table set out in paragraph 2;

  [. . .

   . . .]

"chargeable receipts" means those sums which are paid into the Insolvency Services Account after first deducting any amounts paid into the Insolvency Services Account which are subsequently paid out to secured creditors in respect of their securities or in carrying on the business of the company or the bankrupt; and

"the insolvency legislation" means the Insolvency Act 1986, the Insolvency Rules 1986 and the Insolvency Regulations 1994.

(2)   In this Schedule, references to the performance of the "general duties" of the official receiver on the making of a winding-up or bankruptcy order—

    (a)   include the payment by the official receiver of any fees, costs or disbursements except for those associated with the realisation of assets or the distribution of funds to creditors; but

    [(b)   does not include anything done by the official receiver in connection with or for the purposes of—

        (i)   the appointment of agents for the purposes of, or in connection with, the realisation of assets;

        (ii)   the making of a distribution to creditors (including preferential or secured creditors or both such classes of creditor);

        (iii)   the realisation of assets on behalf of the holder of a fixed or floating charge or both types of those charges; or

        (iv)   the supervision of a special manager].

2. Fees payable to the Secretary of State in respect of proceedings under Parts I to XI of the Act and the performance by the official receiver and the Secretary of State of functions under those Parts shall be determined in accordance with the provisions of the Table of Fees set out below—

TABLE OF FEES

Fees payable in relation to winding up by the court only	
Designation of Fee / *Description of fee and circumstances in which it is charged*	*Amount of fee or applicable %*
W1 Winding up by the court—official receiver's administration fee	
For the performance by the official receiver of his general duties as official receiver on the making of a winding-up order[, including his duty to investigate and report upon the affairs of bodies in liquidation,] there shall be payable a fee of—	[£2,235]

Fees payable in relation to winding up by the court only		
[W2	Winding up by the court—Secretary of State's administration fee applicable to winding up orders made on or after 6 April 2010	
	For the performance of the Secretary of State's general duties under the insolvency legislation in relation to the administration of the affairs of each company which is being wound up by the court, there shall be payable a fee calculated in accordance with the following scale as a percentage of chargeable receipts relating to the company at the rate of—	0% of the first £2,500
		100% of the next £1,700
		75% of the next £1,500
		15% of the next £396,000
		1% of the remainder, subject to a maximum of £80,000.]

Fees payable in bankruptcies and both types of winding up		
Designation of Fee	*Description of fee and circumstances in which it is charged*	*Amount of fee or applicable %*
[INV1	Investment fee on purchase or sale of government securities—	
	For each purchase or sale of any government securities made at the request of a trustee in bankruptcy or a liquidator in a compulsory or voluntary winding up—	
	(a) in respect of a purchase, where the cost of the securities (including accrued interest, if any)—	
	(i) does not exceed £5,000, a fee of—	£50
	(ii) exceeds £5,000, a fee of—	£50 plus 0.3% of the cost in excess of £5,000
	(b) in respect of a sale, where the proceeds of sale of the securities (including accrued interest, if any) exceed £5,000, a fee of—	£50 plus 0.3% of the proceeds in excess of £5,000]

Part 10 Miscellaneous other SIs

NOTES

Para 1 is amended as follows:

Para (b) of definition "the bankruptcy ceiling" substituted by the Insolvency Proceedings (Fees) (Amendment) Order 2007, SI 2007/521, art 2(1), (6), 4(1), (6), as from 1 April 2007, in relation to bankruptcy orders made on or after that date.

Definitions "excepted bankruptcy" and "excepted winding-up" (omitted) originally inserted by the Insolvency Proceedings (Fees) (Amendment) Order 2009, SI 2009/645, arts 3, 5, as from 6 April 2009, and revoked by the Insolvency Proceedings (Fees) (Amendment) Order 2010, SI 2010/732, arts 3, 7(1), 8, as from 6 April 2010, in respect of bankruptcy and winding-up orders made on or after that date

Sub-para (2)(b) substituted by the Insolvency Proceedings (Fees) (Amendment) Order 2005, SI 2005/544, arts 4, 6, as from 1 April 2005 (in relation to any case where a winding-up is made on or after that date).

Fee W1: words in square brackets in column 2 inserted by SI 2007/521, art 2(1), (7)(c), 4(1), (9), as from 1 April 2007, in respect of winding-up orders made on or after that date. Sum in square brackets in column 3 substituted by the Insolvency Proceedings (Fees) (Amendment) Order 2010, SI 2010/732, arts 3, 6(1), (2), 8, as from 6 April 2010 (note that this amendment applies only in respect of bankruptcy and winding-up orders made on or after 6 April 2010).

Fee W2: substituted by the Insolvency Proceedings (Fees) (Amendment) Order 2010, SI 2010/732, arts 3, 6(1), (4), 8, as from 6 April 2010 (note that this amendment applies only in respect of bankruptcy and winding-up orders made on or after 6 April 2010).

Fee INV1 substituted by the Insolvency Proceedings (Fees) (Amendment) Order 2009, SI 2009/645, arts 3, 6(6), as from 6 April 2009. Note that art 7(7) of the 2009 Order provides that the amendment made by art 6(6) to fee INV1, increasing the fee for the purchase of government securities and introducing a fee for the sale of government securities, shall only apply where the request to purchase or sell is made on or after 6 April 2009 and, in the case of a sale, only where the request to purchase the securities which are to be sold was also made on or after 6 April 2009.

Note: fees payable in respect of individual voluntary arrangements and debt relief orders, and fees payable in bankruptcies are omitted (outside the scope of this work).

EUROPEAN PUBLIC LIMITED-LIABILITY COMPANY REGULATIONS 2004

(SI 2004/2326)

NOTES

Made: 6 September 2004.

Authority: European Communities Act 1972, s 2(2).

Commencement: 8 October 2004.

These Regulations are reproduced as amended by: the Companies Act 2006 (Consequential Amendments etc) Order 2008, SI 2008/948; the European Public Limited-Liability Company (Amendment) Regulations 2009, SI 2009/2400.

References to "the European Community", "Community", etc: see the Treaty of Lisbon (Changes in Terminology) Order 2011, SI 2011/1043, which provides that (as from 22 April 2011) "EU" should be substituted for the word "Community" (subject to certain exceptions) in references to "Community treaties", "Community instrument", "Community obligation", "Community law", "Community legislation", etc.

ARRANGEMENT OF REGULATIONS

PART 1
GENERAL

PART 2
REGISTRATION OF SES AND THE REGISTRAR ETC

PART 4
EXERCISE OF MEMBER STATES OPTIONS UNDER THE EC REGULATION

PART 5
PROVISIONS REQUIRED BY THE EC REGULATION

PART 1
GENERAL

[10.851]
1   Citation, commencement and extent
(1)   These Regulations may be cited as the European Public Limited-Liability Company Regulations 2004.
(2)   These Regulations come into force on 8th October 2004.
(3)   These Regulations extend to [the whole of the United Kingdom].

NOTES
Para (3): words in square brackets substituted by the European Public Limited-Liability Company (Amendment) Regulations 2009, SI 2009/2400, regs 3, 4, as from 1 October 2009.

[10.852]
2   EC Directive and EC Regulation
In these Regulations—
    "the EC Directive" means Council Directive 2001/86/EC of 8 October 2001 supplementing
        the Statute for a European Company with regard to the involvement of employees;
    "the EC Regulation" means Council Regulation 2157/2001/EC of 8 October 2001 on the Statute
        for a European Company;
and references to numbered Articles are, unless otherwise specified, references to Articles in the EC Regulation.

[10.853]

3   Interpretation

(1)   In these Regulations—

. . .

the "1996 Act" means the Employment Rights Act 1996;

[the "2006 Act" means the Companies Act 2006;]

["the Companies Acts" has the meaning given by section 2 of [the 2006 Act];]

"SE" means a European Public Limited-Liability Company (or Societas Europaea) within the meaning of the EC Regulation and, except as provided in these Regulations, means an SE which is to be, or is, [registered in the United Kingdom].

(2)   Except as otherwise provided in these Regulations, words and expressions [defined for the purposes of the Companies Acts have the same meaning in these Regulations].

(3)   Except as otherwise provided in these Regulations, words and expressions which are used in the EC Regulation or the EC Directive have the same meaning as they have in that Regulation or Directive.

(4)   Where a word or expression is both[defined as mentioned] in paragraph (2) and used in the EC Regulation or the EC Directive, it has the meaning it has in that Regulation or Directive except as otherwise provided in these Regulations.

NOTES

Para (1) is amended as follows:

Definition "1985 Act" (omitted) revoked, and definition "2006 Act" inserted, by the European Public Limited-Liability Company (Amendment) Regulations 2009, SI 2009/2400, regs 3, 5(a), (b), as from 1 October 2009.

Definition "the Companies Acts" inserted by the Companies Act 2006 (Consequential Amendments etc) Order 2008, SI 2008/948, art 3(1), Sch 1, Pt 2, para 235(1), (2)(a), as from 6 April 2008; words in square brackets substituted by SI 2009/2400, regs 3, 5(c), as from 1 October 2009.

Words in square brackets in definition "SE" substituted by SI 2009/2400, regs 3, 5(d), as from 1 October 2009.

Paras (2), (4): words in square brackets substituted by SI 2008/948, art 3(1), Sch 1, Pt 2, para 235(1), (2)(b), (c), as from 6 April 2008.

PART 2
REGISTRATION OF SES AND THE REGISTRAR ETC

[10.854]

4   The registrar

The registrar has the functions conferred by this Part in relation to the registration, or the deletion of the registration, of an SE.

[10.855]

5   Registration of an SE formed by merger in accordance with Article 2(1)

Where it is proposed to register an SE formed by merger in accordance with Article 2(1) there shall be delivered to the registrar a registration form in [Form SE FM01] . . . set out in Schedule 1 together with the documents specified in respect of [that Form].

NOTES

Words in square brackets substituted, and words omitted revoked, by the European Public Limited-Liability Company (Amendment) Regulations 2009, SI 2009/2400, regs 3, 6, as from 1 October 2009.

[10.856]

6   Registration of the formation of a holding SE in accordance with Article 2(2)

Where it is proposed to register a holding SE formed in accordance with Article 2(2) there shall be delivered to the registrar a registration form in [Form SE FM02] . . . set out in Schedule 1 together with the documents specified in respect of [that Form].

NOTES

Words in square brackets substituted, and words omitted revoked, by the European Public Limited-Liability Company (Amendment) Regulations 2009, SI 2009/2400, regs 3, 7, as from 1 October 2009.

[10.857]

7   Registration of the formation of a subsidiary SE in accordance with Article 2(3)

Where it is proposed to register a subsidiary SE formed in accordance with Article 2(3) there shall be delivered to the registrar a registration form in [Form SE FM03] . . . set out in Schedule 1 together with the documents specified in respect of [that Form].

NOTES

Words in square brackets substituted, and words omitted revoked, by the European Public Limited-Liability Company (Amendment) Regulations 2009, SI 2009/2400, regs 3, 8, as from 1 October 2009.

[10.858]
8 Registration of an SE by the transformation of a public company in accordance with Article 2(4)

Where it is proposed to register an SE by the transformation of a public company in accordance with Article 2(4) there shall be delivered to the registrar a registration form in [Form SE FM04] . . . set out in Schedule 1 together with the documents specified in respect of [that Form].

NOTES
Words in square brackets substituted, and words omitted revoked, by the European Public Limited-Liability Company (Amendment) Regulations 2009, SI 2009/2400, regs 3, 9, as from 1 October 2009.

[10.859]
9 Registration of an SE formed as the subsidiary of an SE in accordance with Article 3(2)

(1) Where it is proposed to register an SE formed as the subsidiary of an SE in accordance with Article 3(2) there shall be delivered to the registrar a registration form in [Form SE FM05] . . . set out in Schedule 1 together with the documents specified in respect of [that Form].

(2) The reference to an SE, a subsidiary of which is to be registered under this regulation, includes a reference to an SE whose registered office is in another Member State.

NOTES
Para (1): words in square brackets substituted, and words omitted revoked, by the European Public Limited-Liability Company (Amendment) Regulations 2009, SI 2009/2400, regs 3, 10, as from 1 October 2009.

[10.860]
10 Registration of an SE on the transfer of its registered office to [the United Kingdom] in accordance with Article 8

Where it is proposed to transfer to [the United Kingdom] the registered office of an SE whose registered office is situated in another Member State there shall be delivered to the registrar a registration form in respect of that SE in [Form SE TR02] . . . set out in Schedule 1 together with the documents specified in respect of [that Form].

NOTES
Words in square brackets substituted, and words omitted revoked, by the European Public Limited-Liability Company (Amendment) Regulations 2009, SI 2009/2400, regs 3, 11, as from 1 October 2009.

[10.861]
11 Certificate of the competent authority under Article 8(8)

Where it is proposed to transfer the registered office of an SE from [the United Kingdom] to another Member State there shall be delivered to the Secretary of State for the purposes of applying for the issue of a certificate under Article 8(8), a transfer form in [Form SE TR03] set out in Schedule 1 together with the documents specified in that Form.

NOTES
Words in square brackets substituted by the European Public Limited-Liability Company (Amendment) Regulations 2009, SI 2009/2400, regs 3, 12, as from 1 October 2009.

[10.862]
12 Registration of an SE

The registrar shall register an SE formed or transformed under the provisions of Articles 2 and 3 or an SE whose registered office is transferred to [the United Kingdom] under Article 8 where she is satisfied that all the requirements of these Regulations and the EC Regulation in respect of such formation, transformation or transfer of an SE, as the case may be, have been complied with in respect of that SE.

NOTES
Words in square brackets substituted by the European Public Limited-Liability Company (Amendment) Regulations 2009, SI 2009/2400, regs 3, 13.

[10.863]
13 Documents sent to the registrar

[(1) The registrar shall retain any document delivered to the registrar under any provision of these Regulations or the EC Regulation.

(1A) Any reference in the 2006 Act to "the register" is to be read as including a reference to—
 (a) the documents required to be retained by the registrar under paragraph (1), and
 (b) records of the information contained in those documents.

(1B) In the application of the 2006 Act in relation to those documents and records by virtue of paragraph (1A), the provisions specified in Schedule 1A to these Regulations have effect with the modifications specified in relation to each such provision in that Schedule.]

(2)   For the purposes of this regulation documents delivered to the Secretary of State under regulation 11 shall be treated as documents delivered to the registrar on the deletion of the registration of the SE making the application under the regulation and the provisions of regulation 14 will apply accordingly.

NOTES

Paras (1)–(1B): substituted (for the original para (1)) by the European Public Limited-Liability Company (Amendment) Regulations 2009, SI 2009/2400, regs 3, 14, as from 1 October 2009.

[10.864]
[13A   Application of language requirements to documents relating to SEs
(1)   The following provisions of the 2006 Act apply in relation to documents required to be delivered to the registrar under these Regulations or the EC Regulation—
   (a)   section 1103 (documents to be drawn up and delivered in English);
   (b)   section 1105 (documents that may be drawn up and delivered in other languages);
   (c)   section 1107 (certified translations).
(2)   In the application of the provisions listed in paragraph (1) in relation to the documents referred to in that paragraph—
   (a)   section 1103 applies as if the reference to section 1104 of the 2006 Act were omitted;
   (b)   section 1105 applies as if for subsections (2) and (3) there were substituted—

   "(2)   This section applies to—
      (a)   documents specified in respect of any of the Forms mentioned in regulations 5 to 11 of the European Public Limited-Liability Company Regulations 2004 (provisions relating to registration etc);
      (b)   copies of transfer proposals required to be delivered under regulation 68(1)(a) of those Regulations (publication of terms of transfer);
      (c)   copies of draft terms required to be delivered under regulation 68(2)(a) or (3)(a) of those Regulations (publication of terms for formation of holding SE or conversion of company into SE);
      (d)   copies of amendments to statutes required to be delivered under regulation 82(1)(a) of those Regulations (notification of amendments to statutes);
      (e)   documents required to be delivered with Form SE CV01 under regulation 85 of those Regulations (registration of a public company by conversion of SE);
      (f)   copies of draft terms required to be delivered under regulation 86 of those Regulations (publication of draft terms of conversion).";

   (c)   section 1107 applies as if any reference to a company were a reference to an SE.
(3)   Section 1106(1) and (4) of the 2006 Act (voluntary filing of translations), and any provision of regulations made under section 1106(2) which specifies the languages in relation to which the facility in section 1106(1) is available, apply in relation to documents within paragraph (4), as if any reference to a company were a reference to an SE.
(4)   The documents referred to in paragraph (3) are documents that are or have been delivered to the registrar under these Regulations or the EC Regulation on or after 1st January 2007.
(5)   For the purposes of this regulation documents required to be delivered to the Secretary of State under regulation 11 shall be treated as documents required to be delivered to the registrar under that regulation.]

NOTES

Commencement: 1 October 2009.
   Inserted by the European Public Limited-Liability Company (Amendment) Regulations 2009, SI 2009/2400, regs 3, 15(1), as from 1 October 2009.

[10.865]
14   [Application of the 2006 Act to the registration of SEs]
[(1)]   The provisions of [the 2006 Act] specified in Schedule 2 to these Regulations shall apply in respect of
   (a)   the registration or the deletion of registration of SEs under these Regulations and the EC Regulation;
   (b)   the functions of the registrar in respect of such registrations or deletions.
   Those provisions shall apply under this regulation subject to any limitations or qualifications specified in relation to each such provision in that Schedule.
[(2)   This regulation does not affect the application of provisions of the 2006 Act in respect of the matters referred to in paragraph (1)(a) or (b) otherwise than by virtue of this regulation.]

NOTES

Regulation heading substituted, para (1) numbered as such, words in square brackets substituted, and para (2) added, by the European Public Limited-Liability Company (Amendment) Regulations 2009, SI 2009/2400, regs 3, 16, as from 1 October 2009.

[10.866]
15   False statements in documents sent to the registrar or the Secretary of State

Any person who makes a false statement:

(a)   in any registration form sent to the registrar under regulations 5 to 10 and regulation 85,

(b)   in any transfer form sent to the Secretary of State under regulation 11,

(c)   in any document, specified in such a form, or

(d)   in any other document required to be sent to the registrar under these Regulations,

which he knows to be false or does not believe to be true is liable, on conviction on indictment to imprisonment not exceeding two years, or to a fine, or to both, and on summary conviction to imprisonment not exceeding three months, or to a fine not exceeding the statutory maximum or to both.

16–54   *(Regs 16–54 (Part 3 – Employee Involvement) were revoked by the European Public Limited-Liability Company (Amendment) Regulations 2009, SI 2009/2400, regs 3, 17, as from 1 October 2009. The provisions formerly contained in this Part have been re-enacted, with modifications, in the European Public Limited-Liability Company (Employee Involvement) (Great Britain) Regulations 2009, SI 2009/2401 (see* **[10.1193]***) and the European Public Limited-Liability Company (Employee Involvement) (Northern Ireland) Regulations 2009, SI 2009/2402.)*

PART 4
EXERCISE OF MEMBER STATES OPTIONS UNDER THE EC REGULATION

[10.867]
55   Participation in the formation of an SE by a company formed under the law of a Member State whose head office is not in the Community (Article 2(5))

A company, formed under the law of a Member State, the head office of which is not in the Community, may participate in the formation of an SE where the company's registered office is in that Member State and it has a real and continuous link with a Member State's economy.

[10.868]
56   Additional forms of publication of transfer proposal (Article 8(2))

(1)   The SE shall notify in writing its shareholders, and every creditor of whose claim and address it is aware, of the right to examine the transfer proposal and the report drawn up under Article 8(3), at its registered office and, on request, to obtain copies of those documents free of charge, not later than one month before the general meeting called to decide on the transfer.

(2)   Every invoice, order for goods or business letter, which, at any time between the date on which the transfer proposal and report become available for inspection at the registered office of the SE and the deletion of its registration on transfer, is issued by or on behalf of the SE, shall contain a statement that the SE is proposing to transfer its registered office to another Member State under Article 8 and identifying that Member State.

(3)   If default is made in complying with [paragraph (1) or (2)] above the SE is liable on summary conviction to a fine not exceeding level 3 on the standard scale.

<hr>

NOTES

Para (3): words in square brackets substituted by the European Public Limited-Liability Company (Amendment) Regulations 2009, SI 2009/2400, regs 3, 18, as from 1 October 2009.

<hr>

[10.869]
57   Extension of protection given by Article 8(7) to liabilities incurred prior to transfer (Article 8(7))

The first sub-paragraph of Article 8(7) shall apply to liabilities that arise (or may arise) prior to the transfer.

[10.870]
58   Power of the competent authorities of a Member State to oppose a transfer on public interest grounds (Article 8(14))

If a transfer of a registered office of an SE would result in a change in the law applicable to the SE, the competent authorities may, within the two month period referred to within Article 8(6), oppose the transfer, on public interest grounds.

[10.871]
59   Power of the management or administrative organ of an SE to amend statutes where in conflict with employee involvement arrangements (Article 12(4))

Where there is a conflict between the arrangements for employee involvement and the existing statutes the management or administrative organ of the SE may amend the statutes to the extent necessary to resolve the conflict without any further decision from the general shareholders meeting.

60   *(Revoked by the European Public Limited-Liability Company (Amendment) Regulations 2009, SI 2009/2400, regs 3, 19, as from 1 October 2009.)*

[10.872]
61   Minimum number of members of the management organ (Article 39(4))
The minimum number of the members of the management organ of an SE is two.

[10.873]
62   Minimum number of members of the supervisory organ (Article 40(3))
The minimum number of the members of the supervisory organ of an SE is two.

[10.874]
63   Members of the supervisory organ to be entitled to require the management organ to provide certain information (Article 41(3))
Each member of the supervisory organ is entitled to require the management organ to provide to that member information of a kind which the supervisory organ needs to exercise supervision in accordance with Article 40(1).

[10.875]
64   Minimum number of members of an administrative organ (Article 43(2))
The minimum number of the members of the administrative organ of an SE is two.

[10.876]
65   Timing of the first general meeting of an SE (Article 54(1))
The first general meeting of an SE may be held at any time in the 18 months following an SE's incorporation.

[10.877]
66   Proportion of shareholders of an SE who may require one or more additional items to be put on the agenda of any general meeting (Article 56)
The proportion of the shareholders of an SE who may require one or more additional items put on the agenda of any general meeting is to be the holders of at least 5% of the SE's subscribed capital.

[10.878]
67   SEs subject to law on public limited liability companies as regard the expression of their capital (Article 67(1))
An SE shall be subject to the provisions of the enactments and rules of law applying to a public company as regards the expression of its capital.

PART 5
PROVISIONS REQUIRED BY THE EC REGULATION

[10.879]
68   Publication of terms of transfer, formation and conversion (Articles 8(2), 32(3) and 37(5))
(1)   Where a transfer proposal is drawn up under Article 8(2)—
  (a)   a copy of the proposal shall be delivered to the registrar together with [Form SE TR01], and
  (b)   the registrar shall cause notice of the receipt of the copy of the proposal to be published in the Gazette.

(2)   Where draft terms for the formation of a holding SE, whether or not its registered office is to be in [the United Kingdom], are drawn up under Article 32(2)—
  (a)   a copy of the draft terms shall be delivered to the registrar together with [Form SE DT01], and
  (b)   the registrar shall cause notice of the receipt of the copy of the draft terms to be published in the Gazette.

(3)   Where draft terms for the conversion of a public limited-liability company into an SE are drawn up under Article 37(4)—
  (a)   a copy of the draft terms shall be delivered to the registrar together with [Form SE DT02], and
  (b)   the registrar shall cause notice of the receipt of the copy of the draft terms to be published in the Gazette.

(4)   The Forms referred to in paragraphs (1) to (3) are those set out in Schedule 1.

NOTES
  Paras (1)–(3): words in square brackets substituted by the European Public Limited-Liability Company (Amendment) Regulations 2009, SI 2009/2400, regs 3, 20, as from 1 October 2009.

[10.880]
69 Publication of completion of merger (Article 28)

Where an SE is formed by merger, whether its registered office is in [the United Kingdom] or not, and a public company has taken part in that procedure, the registrar shall cause to be published in the Gazette notice that the merger has been completed.

NOTES

Words in square brackets substituted by the European Public Limited-Liability Company (Amendment) Regulations 2009, SI 2009/2400, regs 3, 21, as from 1 October 2009.

[10.881]
70 Publication of fulfilment of conditions for the formation of a holding SE (Article 33(3))

(1) Where, in respect of a company of a type specified in relation to the United Kingdom in Annex II to the EC Regulation, the conditions for the formation of a holding SE, whether or not it is to be [registered in the United Kingdom], are fulfilled, the company shall deliver to the registrar within 14 days of such fulfilment notice of that event in the [Form SE SC01] set out in Schedule 1 and the registrar shall cause to be published in the Gazette notice that these conditions have been fulfilled.

(2) If default is made in complying with paragraph (1), the company is liable on summary conviction to a fine not exceeding level 3 on the standard scale.

NOTES

Para (1): words in square brackets substituted by the European Public Limited-Liability Company (Amendment) Regulations 2009, SI 2009/2400, regs 3, 22, as from 1 October 2009.

[10.882]
71 Publication of other documents or information (Articles 8(12), 15(2), 59(3) and 65)

(1) Where, under the Articles of the EC Regulation listed in paragraph (2), the occurrence of an event is required to be publicised, the registrar shall cause to be published in the Gazette notice of receipt of the particulars of that event described in those Articles.

(2) The Articles referred to in paragraph (1) above are:
Article 59(3)
Article 65.

(3) Where, under the Articles listed in paragraph (4), the registration of an SE, whether on formation under Title II of the EC Regulation, or on the transfer of the registered office of an SE under Article 8 or the deletion of a registration under that Article is required to be publicised, the registrar shall cause to be published in the Gazette notice of that registration or the deletion of that registration and of the receipt of the documents and particulars related to that registration or deletion required to be delivered to the registrar by the EC Regulation or these Regulations.

(4) The Articles referred to in paragraph (3) are:
Article 8(12)
Article 15(2).

[10.883]
72 Protection of creditors and others on a transfer (Article 8(7))

(1) Where an SE proposes to transfer its registered office to another Member State under Article 8 the SE shall satisfy the Secretary of State that the interests of creditors and holders of other rights in respect of the SE (including those of public bodies) have been adequately protected in respect of any liabilities arising (or that may arise) prior to the transfer by the making of a statement of solvency in the terms set out in paragraphs (4) and (5).

(2) The statement of solvency must be made by all the members of the administrative organ in the case of an SE within the one-tier system and by all the members of the management organ in the case of an SE within the two-tier system.

(3) In the case of an SE within the two-tier system the statement of solvency may not be made unless authorised by the supervisory organ.

(4) The statement shall state that the members of the administrative or management organ, as the case may be, have formed the opinion—
  (a) as regards its financial situation immediately following the date on which the transfer is proposed to be made, that there will be no grounds on which the SE could then be found to be unable to pay its debts, and
  (b) as regards its prospects for the year immediately following that date, that, having regard to their intentions with respect to the management of the SE's business during that year and to the amount and character of the financial resources which will in their view be available to the SE during that year, the SE will be able to carry on business as a going concern (and will accordingly be able to pay its debts as they fall due throughout that year).

(5) In forming their opinion for the purposes of paragraph (4)(a), the members of the administrative or the management organ, as the case may be, shall take into account the same liabilities (including prospective and contingent liabilities) as would be relevant under section 122 of the Insolvency Act 1986 [or, as the case may be, Article 102 of the Insolvency (Northern Ireland) Order 1989] (winding up by the court) to the question whether a company is unable to pay its debts.

(6) The statement required by this regulation shall be in the [Form SE SS01] set out in Schedule 1.

(7) A member of an administrative or management organ who makes a statement under this regulation without having reasonable grounds for the opinion expressed in the statement is liable, on conviction on indictment, to imprisonment not exceeding two years, or to a fine, or to both, and on summary conviction to imprisonment not exceeding three months, or to a fine not exceeding the statutory maximum, or to both.

NOTES

Para (5): words in square brackets inserted by the European Public Limited-Liability Company (Amendment) Regulations 2009, SI 2009/2400, regs 3, 23(a), as from 1 October 2009.

Para (6): words in square brackets substituted by SI 2009/2400, regs 3, 23(b), as from 1 October 2009.

[10.884]
73 Power of Secretary of State where an SE no longer complies with the requirements of Article 7

(1) If it appears that an SE no longer complies with the requirements laid down in Article 7, the Secretary of State may direct the SE to regularise its position in accordance with Article 64(1)(a) or (b) within such period as may be specified in the direction.

(2) A direction under paragraph (1) is enforceable by the Secretary of State—
  (a) in the case of an SE whose registered office is in England and Wales, by an application to the High Court [in England and Wales] for an injunction; . . .
  (b) in the case of an SE whose registered office is in Scotland, by an application to the Court of Session for an order under section 45 of the Court of Session Act 1988;
  [(c) in the case of an SE whose registered office is in Northern Ireland, by an application to the High Court in Northern Ireland for an injunction.]

(3) (*Inserts the Insolvency Act 1986, s 124B at* **[9.215]**.)

(4) (*Amends the Insolvency Act 1986, s 124, Sch A1, Pt III, Sch B1 at* **[9.213]**, **[9.408]**, **[9.412]**.)

NOTES

Para (2): words in square brackets inserted, and word omitted revoked, by the European Public Limited-Liability Company (Amendment) Regulations 2009, SI 2009/2400, regs 3, 24, as from 1 October 2009.

[10.885]
74 Review of decisions of a competent authority (Articles 8(14) and 19)

(1) Where any competent authority or competent authorities oppose—
  (a) the transfer of the registered office of an SE under Article 8(14); or
  (b) the taking part by a company of the type specified in relation to the United Kingdom in Annex 1 to the EC Regulation in the formation of an SE by merger under Article 19 whether or not its registered office is to be in [the United Kingdom],
the provisions of paragraphs (2) to (5) shall apply.

(2) An SE, the transfer of whose registered office is opposed by a competent authority or authorities under Article 8(14) or a company whose taking part in the formation of an SE by merger, whether or not its registered office is to be in [the United Kingdom], is opposed by a competent authority or competent authorities under Article 19, may appeal to the relevant court on the grounds that the opposition:
  (a) is unlawful; or
  (b) is irrational or unreasonable; or
  (c) has been made on the basis of a procedural impropriety or otherwise contravenes the rules of natural justice.

(3) For the purposes of this regulation the "relevant court" is in the case of—
  (a) an SE, or a company, whose registered office is in England or Wales, the High Court [in England and Wales]; . . .
  (b) an SE, or a company, whose registered office is in Scotland, the Court of Session;
  [(c) an SE, or a company, whose registered office is in Northern Ireland, the High Court in Northern Ireland.]

(4) An appeal may only be brought under this regulation with the permission of the court.

(5) The court determining an appeal may—
  (a) dismiss the appeal; or
  (b) quash the opposition, and where the court quashes an opposition it may refer the matter to the opposing competent authority or authorities with a direction to reconsider it and to make a determination in accordance with the findings of the court.

NOTES

Paras (1), (2): words in square brackets substituted by the European Public Limited-Liability Company (Amendment) Regulations 2009, SI 2009/2400, regs 3, 25(1)–(3), as from 1 October 2009.

Para (3): words in square brackets inserted, and word omitted revoked, by SI 2009/2400, regs 3, 25(1), (4), as from 1 October 2009.

PART 6
PROVISIONS RELATING TO THE EFFECTIVE APPLICATION OF THE EC REGULATION

[10.886]
75   Competent authorities

The competent authorities designated under Article 68(2) are—
- (a)   in respect of Articles 8, 54, 55 and 64, the Secretary of State;
- [(b)   in respect of Article 25—
    - (i)   the High Court in England and Wales, in relation to a public company whose registered office is in England and Wales,
    - (ii)   the Court of Session, in relation to a public company whose registered office is in Scotland,
    - (iii)   the High Court in Northern Ireland, in relation to a public company whose registered office is in Northern Ireland; and]
- [(c)   in respect of Article 26—
    - (i)   the High Court in England and Wales, in relation to an SE where the registered office is proposed to be in England and Wales,
    - (ii)   the Court of Session, in relation to an SE where the registered office is proposed to be in Scotland,
    - (iii)   the High Court in Northern Ireland, in relation to an SE where the registered office is proposed to be in Northern Ireland.]

NOTES

Paras (b), (c) substituted by the European Public Limited-Liability Company (Amendment) Regulations 2009, SI 2009/2400, regs 3, 26, as from 1 October 2009.

[10.887]
76   Enforcement of obligation to amend Statutes in conflict with Arrangements for Employee Involvement

(1)   If it appears to the Secretary of State that—
- (a)   the statutes of an SE are in conflict with the arrangements for employee involvement determined in accordance with [the European Public Limited-Liability Company (Employee Involvement) (Great Britain) Regulations 2009 or, as the case may be, the European Public Limited-Liability Company (Employee Involvement) (Northern Ireland) Regulations 2009]; and
- (b)   the statutes have not, to the necessary extent, been amended she may direct the SE to amend the statutes to that extent within such period as she may specify in the direction.

(2)   A direction under this regulation is enforceable on the application of the Secretary of State—
- (a)   in respect of an SE with its registered office in England and Wales, to the High Court [in England and Wales] by injunction;   . . .
- (b)   in respect of an SE with its registered office in Scotland, to the Court of Session by an order under section 45 of the Court of Session Act 1988;
- [(c)   in respect of an SE with its registered office in Northern Ireland, to the High Court in Northern Ireland by injunction.]

NOTES

Para (1): words in square brackets substituted by the European Public Limited-Liability Company (Amendment) Regulations 2009, SI 2009/2400, regs 3, 27(1), (2), as from 1 October 2009.

Para (2): words in square brackets inserted, and word omitted revoked, by SI 2009/2400, regs 3, 27(1), (3), as from 1 October 2009.

[10.888]
77   Records of an SE transferred under Article 8(11) or a public company ceasing to exist under Article 29(1) and (2)

(1)   Where—
- (a)   the registration of an SE is deleted under Article 8(11) pursuant to a transfer of its registered office to another Member State; or
- (b)   a public company ceases to exist under Article 29(1)(c) or (2)(c), the records of that SE or public company, as the case may be, kept by the registrar shall continue to be kept by her for a period of twenty years following such a deletion or cessation of existence.

(2)   Where the registration of an SE is deleted, the Form, and the documents accompanying it, delivered to the Secretary of State under regulation 11, together with a copy of the certificate issued under Article 8(8) shall be deemed to be documents to be retained by the registrar under regulation 13 and the provisions of these Regulations apply accordingly.

[10.889]
78   Application of enactments to members of supervisory, management and administrative organs

(1)   This regulation applies to enactments relating to public companies to the extent that they are required, by the EC Regulation, in the manner described in paragraph 2, to be applied in relation to SEs.

(2)   Enactments are required to be applied for the purposes of paragraph (1) where—
  (a)   any provision of the EC Regulation, other than Article 9, requires the application of any enactment relating to public companies to determine any question or matter; or
  (b)   in the case of any matter not regulated by the EC Regulation or, where matters are partly regulated by it, of those aspects not covered by it, Article 9 requires the application of any enactment relating to public companies.

(3)   Subject to paragraphs (4), (5) and (6) references to "directors" or "board of directors" in any enactment to which this regulation applies shall have effect as if they were references—
  (a)   in a one-tier system, to the members of the administrative organ; and
  (b)   in a two-tier system, to the members of the supervisory and management organs.

(4)   Any enactment so applied in relation to a two-tier system shall be applied separately in respect of the members of the supervisory organ and the members of the management organ in relation to the functions of the organ, and in respect of the acts and omissions of the members of those organs.

(5)   Where, in a two-tier system, any function relates to the management of the SE and, by virtue of Articles 39(1) or 40(1), is a function that cannot be carried out by the supervisory organ, nothing in paragraph (3) has the effect of permitting or requiring the members of the supervisory organ to carry out any such functions.

(6)   Where, by virtue of any provision in the EC Regulation or in the statutes, any transaction or function carried out by the management organ in a two-tier system requires the authorisation of the supervisory organ, nothing in paragraph (3) affects, or removes, the requirement for such authorisation.

[10.890]
[79   Register of members of supervisory organ

(1)   Every SE which has adopted the form of a two-tier system in its statutes must keep a register of the members of its supervisory organ ("the register of SO members").

(2)   The register must contain the required particulars (see regulations 80 and 80A) of each of the members of the supervisory organ.

(3)   The register must be kept available for inspection—
  (a)   at the SE's registered office, or
  (b)   at such place as may for the time being be specified in regulations under section 1136 of the 2006 Act in the case of a company and its register of directors under section 162 of that Act.

(4)   The SE must give notice to the registrar—
  (a)   of the place at which the register is kept available for inspection, and
  (b)   of any change in that place,
unless the register has at all times been kept at the SE's registered office.

(5)   The register must be open to the inspection—
  (a)   of any shareholder of the SE without charge, and
  (b)   of any other person on payment of a fee of £3.50 for each hour or part of an hour during which the right of inspection is exercised.

(6)   If—
  (a)   default is made in complying with paragraph (1), (2) or (3),
  (b)   default is made for 14 days in complying with paragraph (4), or
  (c)   an inspection required under paragraph (5) is refused,
an offence is committed by the SE and by every officer of the SE who is in default.
  For this purpose a person who, by virtue of section 251 of the 2006 Act (shadow directors) as it applies in relation to an SE, is a shadow director of the SE is treated as an officer of the SE.

(7)   A person guilty of an offence under this regulation is liable on summary conviction to a fine not exceeding level 5 on the standard scale.

(8)   In the case of a refusal of inspection of the register, the court may by order compel an immediate inspection of it.

(9)   For the meaning of "the court" in this regulation see section 1156 of the 2006 Act.

(10)   Where an SE is required by this regulation to keep a register of SO members, the application of regulation 78 to that SE does not require particulars of members of the supervisory organ to be kept on any register under section 162 of the 2006 Act (register of directors).]

NOTES

Commencement: 1 October 2009.

This regulation (and the original reg 80) were substituted by new regs 79, 80, 80A–80E by the European Public Limited-Liability Company (Amendment) Regulations 2009, SI 2009/2400, regs 3, 28(1), as from 1 October 2009 (for transitional provisions see the note below).

Transitional provisions: the European Public Limited-Liability Company (Amendment) Regulations 2009, SI 2009/2400, reg 28(2) provides that Sch 2 to those Regulations makes transitional provision with respect to registers relating to members of the supervisory organ of an SE. That Schedule provides as follows:

"SCHEDULE 2

TRANSITIONAL PROVISION: REGISTERS RELATING TO MEMBERS OF THE SUPERVISORY ORGAN OF AN SE

1   Interpretation

(1)   In this Schedule—
   (a)   "existing SE" means an SE which, immediately before 1st October 2009, was registered in accordance with regulation 12 of the SEs Regulations or regulation 12 of the Northern Ireland SEs Regulations;
   (b)   "the SEs Regulations" means the European Public Limited-Liability Company Regulations 2004;
   (c)   "the new SEs Regulations" means the SEs Regulations, as amended by these Regulations;
   (d)   "the old SEs Regulations" means the SEs Regulations, disregarding the amendments made by these Regulations;
   (e)   "the Northern Ireland SEs Regulations" means the European Public Limited-Liability Company Regulations (Northern Ireland) 2004.

(2)   In this Schedule—
   "the Companies Acts register" means the register, within the meaning given by section 1080(2) of the Companies Act 2006, as that provision has effect in relation to SEs;
   "the old Regulations" means—
   (a)   the old SEs Regulations;
   (b)   the Northern Ireland SEs Regulations;
   "register of SO members" means the register of particulars of members of its supervisory organ which a two-tier SE is required to keep—
   (a)   by regulation 79 of the SEs Regulations, or
   (b)   by regulation 77 of the Northern Ireland SEs Regulations;
   "SE" has the same meaning as in the SEs Regulations;
   "two-tier SE" means an SE which has adopted the form of a two-tier system in its statutes.

2   Particulars to be registered

(1)   An existing SE need not comply with any provision of the new SEs Regulations which requires its register of SO members to contain particulars additional to those required by the old Regulations until the earlier of—
   (a)   the date on which the SE makes up its first annual return made up to a date on or after 1st October 2009, and
   (b)   the last date to which the SE should have made up that return.

(2)   Sub-paragraph (1) does not apply in relation to a member of whom particulars are first registered on or after 1st October 2009 (whether the member was appointed before, on or after that date).

(3)   Sub-paragraph (1) ceases to apply in relation to a member whose registered particulars fall to be altered on or after 1st October 2009 because they have changed (whether the change occurred before, on or after that date).

(4)   This paragraph does not affect the particulars required to be included in the SE's annual return.

3   Relevant existing address to be treated as service address

(1)   In the case of an existing SE—
   (a)   the relevant existing address of a member of the supervisory organ is deemed, on and after 1st October 2009, to be a service address, and
   (b)   any entry in the SE's register of SO members stating that address is treated, on and after that date, as complying with the obligation in regulation 80(1)(b) of the new SEs Regulations to state a service address.

(2)   The "relevant existing address" is—
   (a)   the address which, immediately before 1st October 2009, appeared (in accordance with regulation 80(2) of the old SEs Regulations) in the SE's register of SO members as having been notified to the SE under regulations made under sections 723B to 723F of the Companies Act 1985 (service address notified by individual applying for confidentiality order in respect of usual residential address), or
   (b)   if no such address appeared, the address which, immediately before that date, appeared in the SE's register of SO members as the member's usual residential address.

(3)   Any notification of a change of relevant existing address occurring before 1st October 2009 that is received by the SE on or after that date is treated as being or, as the case may be, including notification of a change of service address.

(4)   The operation of this paragraph does not give rise to any duty to notify the registrar under regulation 80C of the new SEs Regulations (duty to notify registrar of changes in particulars contained in the register).

4   Shadow directors

(1)   An existing SE must remove from its register of SO members on 1st October 2009 any entry relating to a person who is a shadow director of an SE by virtue of the members of the supervisory organ acting in accordance with the person's directions or instructions.

(2)   Regulation 80C of the new SEs Regulations (duty to notify registrar of changes) applies as if the shadow director had ceased to be a member of the supervisory organ on that date.

5   Removal of particulars from regulation 79 register on or after 1st October 2009

The removal by an existing SE from its register of SO members on or after 1st October 2009 of particulars required by the old Regulations but not required by the new SEs Regulations does not give rise to any duty to notify the registrar under regulation 80C of the new SEs Regulations (duty to notify registrar of changes in particulars contained in the register).

6   Register of members' usual residential addresses (regulation 80B)

(1)   The duty of a two-tier SE to keep a register under regulation 80B of the new SEs Regulations (register of residential addresses of members of its supervisory organ) has effect on and after 1st October 2009.

(2)   The entry on that register of information which, immediately before that date, was contained in the SE's register of SO members does not give rise to any duty to notify the registrar under regulation 80C of the new SEs Regulations (duty to notify registrar of changes in particulars contained in the register).

7   Duty to notify registrar of changes (Regulation 80C)

(1)   Regulation 80C of the new SEs Regulations (duty to notify registrar of changes) applies in relation to any change occurring on or after 1st October 2009—

    (a)   among the members of a two-tier SE's supervisory organ, or

    (b)   in the particulars contained in the register of SO members.

(2)   In relation to a change occurring before that date—

    (a)   regulations 79(2), (4) and (7) and 80 of the old SEs Regulations, or

    (b)   regulations 77(2), (4) and (6) and 78 of the Northern Ireland SEs Regulations,

continue to apply.

8   Members of the supervisory organ: entries on the Companies Acts register

(1)   The registrar may make such entries in the Companies Acts register as appear to be appropriate, having regard to paragraphs 2 to 6 and the information appearing on the register immediately before 1st October 2009 or notified to the registrar in accordance with paragraph 7(2).

(2)   In particular, the registrar may record as a service address—

    (a)   a relevant existing address (within the meaning of paragraph 3), or

    (b)   in the case of an SE falling within sub-paragraph (3), an address notified to the registrar in connection with that application as the usual residential address of a member of the supervisory organ.

(3)   An SE falls within this sub-paragraph if—

    (a)   it was registered on an application received by the registrar before 1st October 2009, and

    (b)   the requirements as to registration were met in relation to it before that date.

(4)   Any notification of a change of the relevant existing address occurring before 1st October 2009 that is received by the registrar on or after that date is treated as being or, as the case may be, including notification of a change of service address.

9   Residential addresses of members of the supervisory organ: protection from disclosure

Where the usual residential address of a member of the supervisory organ of an SE appears as a service address—

    (a)   in the register of SO members by virtue of paragraph 3, or

    (b)   in the Companies Acts register by virtue of paragraph 8,

that address is not protected information for the purposes of Chapter 8 of Part 10 of the Companies Act 2006.

10.   (1)   Section 242(1) of the Companies Act 2006 (duty of registrar to omit protected information from material available for inspection) does not apply—

    (a)   to material delivered to the registrar before 1st October 2009, or

    (b)   to material delivered to the registrar on or after 1st October 2009 by virtue of paragraph 7(2) (notification of change occurring before that date).

(2)   In section 242(2)(b) of the Companies Act 2006 (exclusion of material registered before commencement) the reference to things registered before Chapter 8 of Part 10 of that Act comes into force is treated as including anything registered as a result of a notification in accordance with paragraph 7(2) (notification on or after 1st October 2009 of change occurring before that date).

(3)   Sub-paragraphs (1) and (2) have effect subject to paragraph 12 (which provides for the continued protection of information formerly protected by a confidentiality order).

11.   In determining under section 245(1) of the Companies Act 2006 whether to put on the public record the usual residential address of a member of the supervisory organ of an SE, the registrar may take into account only—

    (a)   communications sent by the registrar on or after 1st October 2009, and

    (b)   evidence as to the effectiveness of service coming to the registrar's attention on or after that date.

12   Continuation of protection afforded by confidentiality orders under the Companies Act 1985

(1)   A member of the supervisory organ of an SE in relation to whom a confidentiality order under section 723B of the Companies Act 1985 was in force immediately before 1st October 2009 is treated on and after that date as if—

    (a)   the member had made an application under section 1088 of the Companies Act 2006 (application to make address unavailable for public inspection) in respect of any address which, immediately before that date, was contained in "confidential records" as defined in section 723D(3) of the Companies Act 1985, and

    (b)   that application had been determined by the registrar in the member's favour.

(2)   The provisions of regulations under section 1088 relating to decisions of the registrar in favour of an applicant (in particular, as to the duration and revocation of such a decision) apply accordingly.

(3)   In those regulations as they apply in accordance with this paragraph, any reference to an offence under section 1112 of the Companies Act 2006 (false statement) is to be read as a reference to an offence under regulations under section 723E(1)(a) of the Companies Act 1985 in relation to the application for the confidentiality order.

13.   (1)   A member of the supervisory organ of an SE in relation to whom a confidentiality order under section 723B of the Companies Act 1985 was in force immediately before 1st October 2009 is treated on and after that date as if—

    (a)   the member had made an application under section 243(4) of the Companies Act 2006 (application to prevent disclosure of protected information by registrar to credit reference agency), and

    (b)   that application had been determined by the registrar in the member's favour.

(2)   The provisions of regulations under section 243(4) relating to decisions of the registrar in favour of an applicant (in particular as to the duration and revocation of such a decision) apply accordingly.

(3)   In those regulations as they apply in accordance with this paragraph, any reference to an offence under section 1112 of the Companies Act 2006 (false statement) is to be read as a reference to an offence under regulations under section 723E(1)(a) of the Companies Act 1985 in relation to the application for the confidentiality order.

14. Where a confidentiality order under section 723B of the Companies Act 1985 was in force immediately before 1st October 2009 in relation to a member of the supervisory organ of an SE, regulation 79(5) and (8) of the new SEs Regulations (inspection of the SE's register of SO members) does not apply in relation to that part of the SE's register of SO members containing particulars of the usual residential address of the individual that before that date were protected from disclosure by regulation 79(6) of the old SEs Regulations.

15   Effect of pending application for confidentiality order
(1)   Section 723B(3) to (8) of the Companies Act 1985 (application for confidentiality order) continues to apply in relation to an application for a confidentiality order made before 1st October 2009.
(2)   Paragraphs 12 to 14 (continuation of protection afforded by confidentiality orders) apply to a person in respect of whom such an application has been made, and has not been determined or withdrawn, as to a person in relation to whom a confidentiality order was in force immediately before that date.
(3)   If the application is dismissed or withdrawn, those paragraphs cease to apply.
(4)   If the application is successful, those paragraphs continue to apply as in the case of an individual in relation to whom a confidentiality order was in force immediately before 1st October 2009.".

[10.891]
[80   Particulars of members to be registered under regulation 79: individuals
(1)   An SE's register of SO members must contain the following particulars in the case of any member of the supervisory organ who is an individual—
   (a)   name and any former name;
   (b)   a service address;
   (c)   the country or state (or part of the United Kingdom) in which the member is usually resident;
   (d)   nationality;
   (e)   business occupation (if any);
   (f)   date of birth.
(2)   For the purposes of this regulation "name" means a person's Christian name (or other forename) and surname, except that in the case of—
   (a)   a peer, or
   (b)   an individual usually known by a title,
the title may be stated instead of the person's Christian name (or other forename) and surname or in addition to either or both of them.
(3)   For the purposes of this regulation a "former name" means a name by which the individual was formerly known for business purposes.
   Where a person is or was formerly known by more than one such name, each of them must be stated.
(4)   It is not necessary for the register to contain particulars of a former name in the following cases—
   (a)   in the case of a peer or an individual normally known by a British title, where the name is one by which the person was known previous to the adoption of, or succession to, the title;
   (b)   in the case of any person, where the former name—
     (i)   was changed or disused before the person attained the age of 16 years, or
     (ii)   has been changed or disused for 20 years or more.
(5)   A person's service address may be stated to be "The SE's registered office".
(6)   For the meaning of "service address" see section 1141 of the 2006 Act.]

NOTES
Commencement: 1 October 2009.
Substituted, subject to transitional provisions, as noted to reg 79 at **[10.890]**.

[10.892]
[80A   Particulars of members to be registered under regulation 79: corporate members and firms
An SE's register of SO members must contain the following particulars in the case of a body corporate, or a firm that is a legal person under the law by which it is governed,—
   (a)   corporate or firm name;
   (b)   registered or principal office;
   (c)   in the case of an EEA company to which the First Company Law Directive (68/151/EEC) applies, particulars of—
     (i)   the register in which the company file mentioned in Article 3 of that Directive is kept (including details of the relevant state), and
     (ii)   the registration number in that register;
   (d)   in any other case, particulars of—
     (i)   the legal form of the company or firm and the law by which it is governed, and
     (ii)   if applicable, the register in which it is entered (including details of the state) and its registration number in that register.

NOTES
Commencement: 1 October 2009.

Part 10   Miscellaneous other SIs

Substituted, subject to transitional provisions, as noted to reg 79 at **[10.890]**.

[10.893]
[80B   Register of residential addresses of members of an SE's supervisory organ

(1)   Every SE which has adopted the form of a two-tier system in its statutes must keep a register of the residential addresses of the members of its supervisory organ (the "register of SO members' residential addresses").

(2)   The register must state the usual residential address of each of those members.

(3)   If a member's usual residential address is the same as the member's service address, as stated in the SE's register of SO members, the register of SO members' residential addresses need only contain an entry to that effect.
     This does not apply if the member's service address is stated to be "The SE's registered office".

(4)   If default is made in complying with this regulation, an offence is committed by—
     (a)   the SE, and
     (b)   every officer of the SE who is in default.
For this purpose a person who, by virtue of section 251 of the 2006 Act (shadow directors) as it applies in relation to an SE, is a shadow director of the SE is treated as an officer of the SE.

(5)   A person guilty of an offence under this regulation is liable on summary conviction to a fine not exceeding level 5 on the standard scale.

(6)   This regulation applies only to members who are individuals, not where the member is a body corporate or a firm that is a legal person under the law by which it is governed.

(7)   Where an SE is required by this regulation to keep a register of SO members' residential addresses, the application of regulation 78 to that SE does not require particulars of members of the supervisory organ to be kept on any register under section 165 of the 2006 Act (register of directors' usual residential addresses).]

NOTES
Commencement: 1 October 2009.
Substituted, subject to transitional provisions, as noted to reg 79 at **[10.890]**.

[10.894]
[80C   Duty to notify registrar of changes

(1)   An SE which has adopted the form of a two-tier system in its statutes must, within the period of 14 days from—
     (a)   a person becoming or ceasing to be a member of the supervisory organ of the SE, or
     (b)   the occurrence of any change in the particulars contained in its register of SO members or its register of SO members' residential addresses,
give to the registrar notice of the change, and the date when it occurred, in whichever of the Forms SE AP01, SE AP02, SE TM01, SE CH01 or SE CH02 set out in Schedule 1 is appropriate.

(2)   Notice of a person having become a member of the supervisory organ must—
     (a)   contain a statement of the particulars of the new member which are required to be included in the SE's register of SO members and those which are required to be included in its register of SO members' residential addresses,
     (b)   be accompanied by a consent by that person to act in that capacity.

(3)   Where—
     (a)   an SE gives notice of a change of a member of its supervisory organ's service address as stated in the SE's register of SO members, and
     (b)   the notice is not accompanied by notice of any resulting change in the particulars contained in the SE's register of SO members' residential addresses,
the notice must be accompanied by a statement that no such change is required.

(4)   If default is made in complying with this regulation, an offence is committed by—
     (a)   the SE, and
     (b)   every officer of the SE who is in default.
For this purpose a person who, by virtue of section 251 of the 2006 Act (shadow directors) as it applies in relation to an SE, is a shadow director of the SE is treated as an officer of the SE.

(5)   A person guilty of an offence under this regulation is liable on summary conviction to a fine not exceeding level 5 on the standard scale.

NOTES
Commencement: 1 October 2009.
Substituted, subject to transitional provisions, as noted to reg 79 at **[10.890]**.

[10.895]
[80D   Protected information: restriction on use or disclosure by SE

In the application of section 241(1)(b) of the 2006 Act in relation to an SE, the reference to any requirement of the Companies Acts includes a reference to any requirement of regulation 80C.]

Part 10   Miscellaneous other SIs

NOTES

Commencement: 1 October 2009.

Substituted, subject to transitional provisions, as noted to reg 79 at **[10.890]**.

[10.896]
[80E   Putting a member of the supervisory organ's address on the public record

(1)   In the application of section 246 of the 2006 Act (putting a director's usual residential address on the public record) in relation to a member of the supervisory organ of an SE—

(a)   the references in subsections (3)(a) and (4)(a) to the company's register of directors are references to the SE's register of SO members, and

(b)   the reference in subsection (3)(b) to the company's register of directors' residential addresses is a reference to the SE's register of SO members' residential addresses.

(2)   Paragraph (1) is without prejudice to the generality of regulation 78.]

NOTES

Commencement: 1 October 2009.

Substituted, subject to transitional provisions, as noted to reg 79 at **[10.890]**.

[10.897]
81   The SE as a body corporate

(1)   Where—

(a)   any enactment is applied in the manner described in regulation 78(2); or

(b)   any enactment applies to an SE otherwise than in the manner described in regulation 78(2) and those enactments are expressed to apply to, or in respect of, a body corporate, an SE, [whether or not registered in the United Kingdom], shall be treated for the purposes of the application of those enactments as if it were a body corporate.

(2)   Nothing in this regulation has the effect of constituting an SE as a body corporate [incorporated in, or formed under the law of, the United Kingdom (or any part of the United Kingdom)].

NOTES

Words in square brackets substituted by the European Public Limited-Liability Company (Amendment) Regulations 2009, SI 2009/2400, regs 3, 29, as from 1 October 2009.

[10.898]
82   Notification of Amendments to Statutes and Insolvency Events (Articles 59(3) and 65)

(1)   Where, under Articles 59(3) and 65, publication by the registrar in the Gazette of the events described in those Articles is required by regulation 71(1)—

(a)   in the case of Article 59(3), the amendments to the statutes shall be delivered to the registrar by the SE accompanied by [Form SE AS01] in Schedule 1 within 14 days of the adoption of those amendments; and

(b)   in the case of Article 65, notice of the relevant event set out in [Form SE WU01] in Schedule 1 shall be delivered to the registrar by the SE within 14 days of the occurrence of the event.

(2)   If default is made in complying with paragraph (1)(a) or (b) the SE is liable on summary conviction to a fine not exceeding level 3 on the standard scale.

NOTES

Para (1): words in square brackets substituted by the European Public Limited-Liability Company (Amendment) Regulations 2009, SI 2009/2400, regs 3, 30, as from 1 October 2009.

[10.899]
83   Accounting Reference Period and Financial Year of Transferring SE

(1)   Where an SE transfers its registered office to [the United Kingdom] under Article 8—

(a)   its first accounting reference period, for the purposes of [section 391 of [the 2006 Act]], is the period of twelve months beginning with its last balance sheet date before the registration of the transfer and the date on which that period ends is its accounting reference date for those purposes; and

(b)   its first financial year for the purposes of [section 390 of [the 2006 Act]] begins with the first day of its first accounting reference period and ends with the last day of that period or such other date, not more than seven days before or after the end of that period as the SE may determine.

(2)   For purposes of this regulation "the last balance sheet date" is the date as at which the balance sheet of the transferring SE was required to be drawn up under the provisions of the law of the Member State in which it had its registered office, where the balance sheet was the last one required to be drawn up before the registration of the transfer in [the United Kingdom].

(3)   Where the transferring SE has not been required to draw up a balance sheet under the provisions of the law of the Member State where it had its registered office, or, if different, of the Member State where it was first registered, before the registration of the transfer in [the United Kingdom], its accounting reference date for the purposes of [section 391 of [the 2006 Act]] is the last day of the month in which the anniversary of its registration on formation falls and its first accounting reference period is the period beginning with its date of registration on formation and ending with its accounting reference date; and paragraph (1)(b) above applies in respect of its first financial year accordingly.

NOTES

Para (1): words in first, third (inner) and fifth (inner) pairs of square brackets substituted by the European Public Limited-Liability Company (Amendment) Regulations 2009, SI 2009/2400, regs 3, 31(1), (2), as from 1 October 2009; words in second (outer) and fourth (outer) pairs of square brackets substituted by the Companies Act 2006 (Consequential Amendments etc) Order 2008, SI 2008/948, art 3(1), Sch 1, Pt 2, para 235(1), (6), as from 6 April 2008 (for savings see art 6(4) of the 2008 Order (at **[4.280]**) which provides that where by virtue of any transitional provision, a provision of the Companies Act 2006 has effect only (a) on or after a specified date, or (b) in relation to matters occurring or arising on or after a specified date, any amendment substituting or inserting a reference to that provision has effect correspondingly).

Para (2): words in square brackets substituted by SI 2009/2400, regs 3, 31(1), (3), as from 1 October 2009.

Para (3): words in first and third (inner) pairs of square brackets substituted by SI 2009/2400, regs 3, 31(1), (4), as from 1 October 2009; words in second (outer) pair of square brackets substituted by SI 2008/948, art 3(1), Sch 1, Pt 2, para 235(1), (6), as from 6 April 2008 (for savings see the para (1) note above).

[10.900]
84   Penalties for Breach of Article 11 (use of SE in name)
Where:
   (a)   an SE fails to comply with Article 11(1); or
   (b)   any person fails to comply with Article 11(2)
the SE or that person is liable on summary conviction to a fine not exceeding level 3 on the standard scale.

PART 7
PROVISIONS RELATING TO THE CONVERSION OF AN SE TO A PUBLIC COMPANY IN ACCORDANCE WITH ARTICLE 66 OF THE EC REGULATION

[10.901]
85   Registration of a public company by the conversion of an SE
[(1)]   Where it is proposed to convert an SE to a public company in accordance with Article 66 there shall be delivered to the registrar a registration form in [Form SE CV01] set out in Schedule 1 together with the documents specified in that Form;   . . .
[(2)   In this Part the SE is referred to as the "converting SE".]

NOTES

Para (1): numbered as such, words in square brackets substituted, and words omitted revoked, by the European Public Limited-Liability Company (Amendment) Regulations 2009, SI 2009/2400, regs 3, 32(1)–(3), as from 1 October 2009.

Para (2): added by SI 2009/2400, regs 3, 32(1), (4), as from 1 October 2009.

[10.902]
86   Publication of draft terms of conversion
Where under Article 66(4) draft terms of conversion are required to be publicised there shall be delivered to the registrar a copy of such draft terms accompanied by [Form SE DT03] set out in Schedule 1 and the registrar shall cause to be published in the Gazette notice of the receipt by her of the copy of the draft terms.

NOTES

Words in square brackets substituted by the European Public Limited-Liability Company (Amendment) Regulations 2009, SI 2009/2400, regs 3, 33, as from 1 October 2009.

[10.903]
87   [Registration under the 2006 Act]
[(1)   On and after the day on which Form SE CV01 is delivered to the registrar section 14 of the 2006 Act (registration) shall apply in relation to the documents delivered with Form SE CV01 as if—
   (a)   they have been delivered under section 9 of that Act (registration), and
   (b)   the requirements of that Act in respect of registration had been complied with.]
(2)   . . .
(3)   On registration of [the documents referred to in paragraph (1)] the registrar shall give a certificate—
   (a)   that the converting SE is incorporated and retains the legal personality it had when an SE;
   [(b)   that those documents are registered under the 2006 Act; and]

(c)   that it is a public company limited by shares.

(4)   The certificate is conclusive evidence—

(a)   that the requirements of [the 2006 Act] in respect of registration . . .   have been complied with, and

(b)   that on and after the registration the converting SE is a public company limited by shares.

NOTES

Regulation heading: substituted by the European Public Limited-Liability Company (Amendment) Regulations 2009, SI 2009/2400, regs 3, 34(1), (6), as from 1 October 2009.

Para (1): substituted by SI 2009/2400, regs 3, 34(1), (2), as from 1 October 2009.

Para (2): revoked by SI 2009/2400, regs 3, 34(1), (3), as from 1 October 2009.

Para (3): words in square brackets substituted by SI 2009/2400, regs 3, 34(1), (4), as from 1 October 2009.

Para (4): words in square brackets substituted, and words omitted revoked, by SI 2009/2400, regs 3, 34(1), (5), as from 1 October 2009.

[10.904]
88   Effect of registration

(1)   In its application to a converting SE on or after registration [the Companies Acts] shall have effect with the modifications set out in [paragraphs 2 to 9] of Schedule 4 to these Regulations.

(2)   On and after registration a converting SE shall be known by the name contained in [the certificate given under regulation 87(3)] (subject to [any change of name by the converting SE]).

(3)   The persons named in [Form SE CV01] shall be deemed to have been appointed as the first directors or secretaries of a converting SE on registration.

NOTES

Para (1): words in first pair of square brackets substituted the Companies Act 2006 (Consequential Amendments etc) Order 2008, SI 2008/948, art 3(1), Sch 1, Pt 2, para 235(1), (7), as from 6 April 2008; words in second pair of square brackets substituted by the European Public Limited-Liability Company (Amendment) Regulations 2009, SI 2009/2400, regs 3, 35(1), (2), as from 1 October 2009.

Paras (2), (3): words in square brackets substituted by SI 2009/2400, regs 3, 35(1), (3), (4), as from 1 October 2009.

[10.905]
89   Records of a converting SE

The records of a converting SE, when the converting SE has been registered as a public company limited by shares under the provisions of this Part, relating to any period before its registration as a public company shall be treated for the purposes of [the Companies Acts] as if they were records of that public company.

NOTES

Words in square brackets substituted the Companies Act 2006 (Consequential Amendments etc) Order 2008, SI 2008/948, art 3(1), Sch 1, Pt 2, para 235(1), (8), as from 6 April 2008.

SCHEDULES
SCHEDULE 1
FORMS RELATING TO SES

[10.906]

NOTES

Sch 1 sets out the forms prescribed for use in connection with the formation, etc of Societas Europaea. The forms are not reproduced here but their numbers and titles are given in the table below. Sch 1 was substituted by the European Public Limited-Liability Company (Amendment) Regulations 2009, SI 2009/2400, as from 1 October 2009. Regulation 2 of the 2009 Regulations (Transitional provision relating to forms and other documents to be delivered to the registrar) provided that in so far as relating to forms and other documents required to be delivered to the registrar, the amendments made by those Regulations do not have effect in any case where the obligation to deliver the form or other document arose before 1 October 2009.

Form No	Title
SE FM01	Formation by merger of Societas Europaea (SE) to be registered in the United Kingdom (UK)
SE FM02	Formation of holding Societas Europaea (SE)
SE FM03	Formation of subsidiary Societas Europaea (SE) under Article 2(3) of Council Regulation (EC) No 2157/2001
SE FM04	Transformation of Public Limited Company (PLC) to Societas Europaea (SE)
SE FM05	Formation of subsidiary Societas Europaea (SE) under Article 3(2) of Council Regulation (EC) No 2157/2001
SE TR02	Transfer to the United Kingdom (UK) of Societas Europaea (SE)

Part 10   Miscellaneous other SIs

Form No	Title
SE TR03	Transfer from the United Kingdom (UK) of Societas Europaea (SE)
SE WU01	Notice of initiation or termination of winding-up, liquidation, insolvency or cessation of payment procedures and decision to continue operating of Societas Europaea (SE)
SE CV01	Conversion of Societas Europaea (SE) to a Public Limited Company (PLC)
SE TR01	Proposed transfer from the United Kingdom (UK) of Societas Europaea (SE)
SE DT01	Draft terms of formation of holding Societas Europaea (SE) involving a United Kingdom (UK) registered company or SE
SE DT02	Draft terms of conversion of a Public Limited Company (PLC) to Societas Europaea (SE)
SE SC01	Notice of satisfaction of conditions for the formation of holding Societas Europaea (SE) by a United Kingdom (UK) registered company or SE
SE SS01	Statement of solvency by members of Societas Europaea (SE) which is proposing to transfer from the United Kingdom (UK)
SE AP01	Appointment of a member of a supervisory organ of a Societas Europaea (SE)
SE AP02	Appointment of corporate member of a supervisory organ of Societas Europaea (SE)
SE TM01	Termination of appointment of member of a supervisory organ of Societas Europaea (SE)
SE CH01	Change of member's details of a supervisory organ of a Societas Europaea (SE)
SE CH02	Change of corporate member's details of a supervisory organ of a Societas Europaea (SE)
SE AS01	Amendment of Statutes of Societas Europaea (SE)
SE DT03	Notification of draft terms of conversion of Societas Europaea (SE) to a Public Limited Company (PLC)

[SCHEDULE 1A
MODIFICATIONS OF PROVISIONS OF THE 2006 ACT APPLYING IN RELATION TO DOCUMENTS SENT TO THE REGISTRAR ETC

Regulation 13(1B)

[10.907]

1. Section 1081 (annotation of the register), as if after subsection (1) there were inserted—

"(1A) Where it appears to the registrar that material on the register is misleading or confusing, the registrar may place a note in the register containing such information as appears to the registrar to be necessary to remedy, as far as possible, the misleading or confusing nature of the material."

2. Section 1085 (inspection of the register), as if in subsection (2) the second sentence were omitted.

3. Section 1093 (registrar's notice to resolve inconsistency on the register), as if—
   (a)   any reference to a company were a reference to an SE, and
   (b)   the reference in subsection (3)(b) to an officer of a company were a reference—
      (i)   in a one-tier system, to a member of the administrative organ of an SE, and
      (ii) in a two-tier system, to a member of the supervisory or management organ of an SE.

4. Section 1094 (administrative removal of material from the register), as if—
   (a)   for paragraph (a) of subsection (3) there were substituted—

   "(a)   anything whose registration has had legal consequences in relation to the SE as regards its registration;", and

   (b)   any reference in subsection (4) to a company were a reference to an SE.

5. Section 1095 (rectification of register on application to registrar), as if any reference to a company were a reference to an SE.

6. Sections 1096(1) to (5) and 1097 (rectification of register under court order), as if any reference to a company were a reference to an SE.]

NOTES
Commencement: 1 October 2009.

Inserted by the European Public Limited-Liability Company (Amendment) Regulations 2009, SI 2009/2400, regs 3, 37, as from 1 October 2009.

[SCHEDULE 2
PROVISIONS OF THE 2006 ACT APPLYING TO THE REGISTRATION OF SES

Regulation 14

[10.908]

1. Section 1066(1) to (5) (registered numbers), as if any reference to a company were a reference to an SE.

2. Section 1082 (allocation of unique identifiers), as if—
  (a)   the reference in subsection (1)(a) to a director of a company were a reference—
      (i)   in a one-tier system, to a member of the administrative organ of an SE, and
      (ii)   in a two-tier system, to a member of the supervisory or management organ of an SE, and
  (b)   paragraphs (b) and (c) of subsection (1) were omitted.

3. Section 1084 (records relating to companies that have been dissolved etc), as if—
  (a)   any reference to a company being dissolved were a reference to an SE being dissolved,
  (b)   the reference in subsection (2) to records relating to a company included a reference to—
      (i)   the documents required to be retained by the registrar under regulation 13(1), and
      (ii)   records of the information contained in those documents, and
  (c)   subsection (4) were omitted.

4. Section 1113 (enforcement of company's filing obligations), as if—
  (a)   any reference to a company were a reference to an SE,
  (b)   any reference to an obligation under the Companies Acts were a reference to an obligation under these Regulations,
  (c)   any reference to a member of a company were a reference to a shareholder of an SE, and
  (d)   any reference to an officer of a company were a reference—
      (i)   in a one-tier system, to a member of the administrative organ of an SE, and
      (ii)   in a two-tier system, to a member of the supervisory or management organ of an SE.

5. Section 1117 (registrar's rules), so far as relating to section 1066(2).]

NOTES

Commencement: 1 October 2009.

Substituted by the European Public Limited-Liability Company (Amendment) Regulations 2009, SI 2009/2400, regs 3, 38, as from 1 October 2009.

SCHEDULE 3

(Sch 3 revoked by the European Public Limited-Liability Company (Amendment) Regulations 2009, SI 2009/2400, regs 3, 39, as from 1 October 2009. See further the note for regs 16–54 ante.)

SCHEDULE 4
[MODIFICATIONS OF THE COMPANIES ACTS ETC]

Regulations 85 and 88

Modifications applying before registration

[10.909]

1. . . .

Modifications applying on or after registration

2. A reference to a company's incorporation shall be construed as a reference to the registration of [the documents delivered with Form SE CV01 under regulation 85].

3. A reference to documents delivered under [the 2006 Act] shall be taken to include a reference to documents delivered under regulation 85.

4. (1)   A reference to a company's certificate of incorporation shall be construed as a reference to the certificate given under regulation 87(3).

(2)   A requirement for the registrar of companies to issue a certificate of incorporation to a company shall—
  (a)   be construed as a requirement to issue a certificate of registration similar to the certificate under regulation 87(3), and
  (b)   apply with such other modifications as the registrar considers necessary in consequence of paragraph (a).

[5. The converting SE is treated as if it had been formed (as well as registered) under the 2006 Act.]

Effect of registration

6. [Section 16 of the 2006 Act] (effect of registration) shall not apply.

7. [Section 112(1) of the 2006 Act] (definition of "member") shall not apply.

Use of "limited"

8. . . .

Certificate as to share capital

9. The following provisions shall not apply—
(a) [section 761 of [the 2006 Act]] (public company share capital requirements), . . .
(b) section 122(1)(b) of the Insolvency Act 1986 (winding up by the court: lack of certificate under [section 761 of [the 2006 Act]]);
[(c) Article 102(1)(b) of the Insolvency (Northern Ireland) Order 1989 (which corresponds to section 122(1)(b) of the Insolvency Act 1986).

Fees

10. . . .

Accounting Reference Date

11. No modification made under this Schedule shall affect the determination of the accounting reference date of a converting SE by the application of [section 391(4) of [the 2006 Act]], by virtue of Article 61 of the EC Regulation, or of regulation 83 prior to the registration of the converting SE under regulation 87.

NOTES
Schedule heading: words in square brackets substituted by the European Public Limited-Liability Company (Amendment) Regulations 2009, SI 2009/2400, regs 3, 40(1), (12), as from 1 October 2009.
Paras 1, 8, 10: revoked by SI 2009/2400, regs 3, 40(1), (2), (8), (10), as from 1 October 2009.
Paras 2, 3, 6, 7: words in square brackets substituted by SI 2009/2400, regs 3, 40(1), (3), (4), (6), (7), as from 1 October 2009.
Para 5: substituted by SI 2009/2400, regs 3, 40(1), (5), as from 1 October 2009.
Para 9: words in first (outer) and third (outer) pairs of square brackets substituted by the Companies Act 2006 (Consequential Amendments etc) Order 2008, SI 2008/948, art 3(1), Sch 1, Pt 2, para 235(1), (9), as from 6 April 2008; other words in square brackets inserted or substituted, and word omitted revoked, by SI 2009/2400, regs 3, 40(1), (9), as from 1 October 2009.
Para 11: words in first (outer) pair of square brackets substituted by SI 2008/948, art 3(1), Sch 1, Pt 2, para 235(1), (9)(c), as from 6 April 2008 (for savings see art 6(4) of the 2008 Order (at **[4.280]**) which provides that where by virtue of any transitional provision, a provision of the Companies Act 2006 has effect only (a) on or after a specified date, or (b) in relation to matters occurring or arising on or after a specified date, any amendment substituting or inserting a reference to that provision has effect correspondingly); words in second (inner) pair of square brackets substituted by SI 2009/2400, regs 3, 40(1), (11), as from 1 October 2009.

LIMITED LIABILITY PARTNERSHIPS (FEES) REGULATIONS 2004 (NOTE)

(SI 2004/2620)

[10.910]

NOTES
These Regulations were made under the Companies Act 1985, s 708(1) (repealed), as applied to LLPs by the Limited Liability Partnerships Regulations 2001, SI 2001/1090, reg 4, Sch 2, and came into in force on 1 February 2005. They were amended by the Secretaries of State for Children, Schools and Families, for Innovation, Universities and Skills and for Business, Enterprise and Regulatory Reform Order 2007, SI 2007/3224 (which is spent in so far as it amended these Regulations). These Regulations, which revoked and replaced the Limited Liability (Fees) (No 2) Regulations 2001, SI 2001/969 (as amended), prescribed the fees payable under the Companies Act 1985 in respect of certain functions performed by the registrar under the Limited Liability Partnerships Act 2000 and the Companies Act 1985. Section 708 of the 1985 Act was repealed by the Companies Act 2006, s 1295, Sch 16, subject to savings in the Limited Liability Partnerships (Application of Companies Act 2006) Regulations 2009, SI 2009/1804, Sch 1, Pt 9, para 36(1) at **[10.1189]**. By virtue of s 1297 of the 2006 Act and SI 2009/1804, Sch 1, Pt 9, para 36(2), any Regulations under the Companies Act 1985, s 708, as applied to LLPs, which were in force immediately before 1 October 2009 have effect on or after that date as if made under s 1063 of the 2006 Act (as applied to LLPs). These Regulations are largely revoked by SI 2009/2101. Only Fees Nos 2 and 4 in Sch 3 were not revoked. Regulations 6–8 of, and Schs 2–4 to, the 2009 Regulations (see **[4.550]** et seq) provide for a variety of transitional provisions and savings in connection with the revocation of the majority of these Regulations.
Fees Nos 2 and 4 in Sch 3 are as follows:

Matter in relation to which fee is payable	Amount of fee
2. Delivery by a limited liability partnership of all relevant documents during a relevant period, payable at the end of that period on delivery by the limited liability partnership of its annual return under section 363 of the 1985 Act, as applied to limited liability partnerships by the Limited Liability Partnerships Regulations 2001	£30.00
4. Registration of a charge under Part XII of the 1985 Act, as applied to limited liability partnerships	£13.00

EUROPEAN ECONOMIC INTEREST GROUPING (FEES) REGULATIONS 2004 (NOTE)

(SI 2004/2643)

[10.911]

NOTES

These Regulations were made under the Finance Act 1973, s 56(1), (2), and came into in force on 1 February 2005. They were amended by the Secretaries of State for Children, Schools and Families, for Innovation, Universities and Skills and for Business, Enterprise and Regulatory Reform Order 2007, SI 2007/3224 (which is spent in so far as it amended these Regulations). These Regulations, which revoked and replaced the European Economic Interest Grouping (Fees) Regulations 1999, SI 1999/268 (and the amending SI 2000/3412, SI 2002/401, and SI 2002/2928) prescribed the fees payable in connection with services and facilities provided by the (former) Department of Trade and Industry in pursuance of the Community obligations of the UK under Council Regulation (EEC) 2137/85 on the European Economic Interest Grouping. These Regulations (with the exception of Fee No 3 in Sch 2) were revoked by the European Economic Interest Grouping and European Public Limited-Liability Company (Fees) Revocation Regulations 2009, SI 2009/2492, subject to the transitional provisions in regs 2–4 of those Regulations at **[10.1242]–[10.1244]**. Fee No 3, in Sch 2 is as follows (note that 'the principal Regulations' means the European Economic Interest Grouping Regulations 1989)—

Matter in respect of which fee is payable	Amount of fee
3. Registration of a charge under paragraph 4 of Schedule 4 to the principal Regulations	£13.00

FINANCIAL SERVICES AND MARKETS ACT 2000 (MARKET ABUSE) REGULATIONS 2005 (NOTE)

(SI 2005/381)

[10.912]

NOTES

These Regulations were made on 23 February 2005 under the powers conferred by the European Communities Act 1972, s 2(2). They came into force as follows: 17 March 2005 (regs 2, 3 8, Sch 1, paras 2, 3, 6, 11); 1 July 2005 (otherwise).

These Regulations implement, in part, European Parliament and Council Directive 2003/6/EC on insider dealing and market manipulation (at **[11.259]**) and the following measures which were made under Article 17 of that Directive—

- Commission Regulation (EC) No 2273/2003 implementing Directive 2003/6/EC of the European Parliament and of the Council as regards exemptions for buy-back programmes and stabilisation of financial instruments (at **[11.347]**);
- Commission Directive 2003/124/EC implementing Directive 2003/6 of the European Parliament and of the Council as regards the definition and public disclosure of inside information and the definition of market manipulation (at **[11.325]**); and
- Commission Directive 2004/72/EC implementing Directive 2003/6 of the European Parliament and of the Council as regards accepted market practices, the definition of inside information in relation to derivatives on commodities, the drawing up of lists of insiders, the notification of managers' transactions and the notification of suspicious transactions (at **[11.384]**).

Reg 1 of these Regulations provides for citation and commencement.

Reg 2 provides for interpretation.

Reg 3 amends the Criminal Justice Act 1993, Sch 1, para 5(1) at **[5.162]**.

Reg 4 introduces Sch 1 to these Regulations (amendments of FSMA 2000, Part VI).

Reg 5 introduces Sch 2 to these Regulations (amendments of FSMA 2000, Part VIII).

Reg 6 amends FSMA 2000, s 150.

Reg 7 amends FSMA 2000, s 395.

Reg 8 amends FSMA 2000, s 397 at **[7.352]**.

Reg 9 revokes the Traded Securities (Disclosure) Regulations 1994, SI 1994/188.

Reg 10 amends the Financial Services and Markets Act 2000 (Prescribed Markets and Qualifying Investments) Order 2001, SI 2001/996 at **[8.167]**.

Reg 11 amends the Financial Services and Markets Act 2000 (Recognition Requirements for Investment Exchanges and Clearing Houses) Regulations 2001, SI 2001/995.

Sch 1 amends FSMA 2000, Pt VI (Official listing) at **[7.78]** et seq.

Sch 2 amends FSMA 2000, Pt VIII (Penalties for market abuse) at **[7.170]** et seq.

INSOLVENCY PRACTITIONERS REGULATIONS 2005

(SI 2005/524)

NOTES
Made: 8 March 2005.
Authority: IA 1986, ss 390, 392, 393, 419.
Commencement: 1 April 2005.
These Regulations are reproduced as amended by: the Secretaries of State for Children, Schools and Families, for Innovation, Universities and Skills and for Business, Enterprise and Regulatory Reform Order 2007, SI 2007/3224; the Secretary of State for Business, Innovation and Skills Order 2009, SI 2009/2748; the Provision of Services (Insolvency Practitioners) Regulations 2009, SI 2009/3081.
Application to bank insolvency and administration: as to the application of these Regulations to bank insolvency and administration, see the Banking Act 2009 (Parts 2 and 3 Consequential Amendments) Order 2009, SI 2009/317.

ARRANGEMENT OF REGULATIONS

PART 1
INTRODUCTORY

PART 2
AUTHORISATION OF INSOLVENCY PRACTITIONERS BY COMPETENT AUTHORITIES

PART 3
THE REQUIREMENTS FOR SECURITY AND CAUTION FOR THE PROPER PERFORMANCE OF THE FUNCTIONS OF AN INSOLVENCY PRACTITIONER ETC

PART 4
RECORDS TO BE MAINTAINED BY INSOLVENCY PRACTITIONERS—INSPECTION OF RECORDS

SCHEDULES

PART 1
INTRODUCTORY

[10.913]
1   Citation and commencement.

These Regulations may be cited as the Insolvency Practitioners Regulations 2005 and shall come into force on 1st April 2005.

[10.914]
2   Interpretation: general

(1)   In these Regulations—
    "the Act" means the Insolvency Act 1986;

"commencement date" means the date on which these Regulations come into force;

"initial capacity" shall be construed in accordance with regulation 3;

"insolvency practitioner" means a person who is authorised to act as an insolvency practitioner by virtue of—

    (a)   membership of a body recognised pursuant to section 391 of the Act; or

    (b)   an authorisation granted pursuant to section 393 of the Act;

"insolvent" means a person in respect of whom an insolvency practitioner is acting;

"interim trustee", "permanent trustee" and "trust deed for creditors" have the same meanings as in the Bankruptcy (Scotland) Act 1985;

"subsequent capacity" shall be construed in accordance with regulation 3.

(2)   In these Regulations a reference to the date of release or discharge of an insolvency practitioner includes—

    (a)   where the insolvency practitioner acts as nominee in relation to proposals for a voluntary arrangement under Part I or VIII of the Act, whichever is the earlier of the date on which—

        (i)   the proposals are rejected by creditors;

        (ii)   he is replaced as nominee by another insolvency practitioner; or

        (iii)   the arrangement takes effect without his becoming supervisor in relation to it; and

    (b)   where an insolvency practitioner acts as supervisor of a voluntary arrangement, whichever is the earlier of the date on which—

        (i)   the arrangement is completed or terminated; or

        (ii)   the insolvency practitioner otherwise ceases to act as supervisor in relation to the arrangement.

[10.915]

3   Interpretation—meaning of initial and subsequent capacity

(1)   In these Regulations an insolvency practitioner holds office in relation to an insolvent in a "subsequent capacity" where he holds office in relation to that insolvent in one of the capacities referred to in paragraph (3) and immediately prior to his holding office in that capacity, he held office in relation to that insolvent in another of the capacities referred to in that paragraph.

(2)   The first office held by the insolvency practitioner in the circumstances referred to in paragraph (1) is referred to in these Regulations as the "initial capacity".

(3)   The capacities referred to in paragraph (1) are, nominee in relation to proposals for a voluntary arrangement under Part I of the Act, supervisor of a voluntary arrangement under Part I of the Act, administrator, provisional liquidator, liquidator, nominee in relation to proposals for a voluntary arrangement under Part VIII of the Act, supervisor of a voluntary arrangement under Part VIII of the Act, trustee, interim trustee and permanent trustee.

[10.916]

4   Revocations and transitional and saving provisions

(1)   Subject to paragraphs (2), (3) and (4), the Regulations listed in Schedule 1 are revoked.

(2)   Parts I and II of the Insolvency Practitioners Regulations 1990 shall continue to apply in relation to an application for authorisation under section 393 of the Act to act as an insolvency practitioner made to the Secretary of State before the commencement date and accordingly nothing in these Regulations shall apply to such an application.

(3)   Parts I, III and IV of the Insolvency Practitioners Regulations 1990 shall continue to apply in relation to any case in respect of which an insolvency practitioner is appointed—

    (a)   before the commencement date; or

    (b)   in a subsequent capacity and he was appointed in an initial capacity in that case before the commencement date.

(4)   Only regulations 16 and 17 of these Regulations shall apply in relation to the cases mentioned in paragraph (3).

PART 2

AUTHORISATION OF INSOLVENCY PRACTITIONERS BY COMPETENT AUTHORITIES

[10.917]

5   Interpretation of Part

In this Part—

"advisory work experience" means experience obtained in providing advice to the office-holder in insolvency proceedings or anyone who is a party to, or whose interests are affected by, those proceedings;

"application" means an application made by an individual to the competent authority for authorisation under section 393 of the Act to act as an insolvency practitioner and "applicant" shall be construed accordingly;

"authorisation" means an authorisation to act as an insolvency practitioner granted under section 393 of the Act;

"continuing professional development" has the meaning given to it by regulation 8(3);

"higher insolvency work experience" means engagement in work in relation to insolvency proceedings where the work involves the management or supervision of the conduct of those proceedings on behalf of the office-holder acting in relation to them;

"insolvency legislation" means the provisions of, or any provision made under, the Act, the Bankruptcy (Scotland) Act 1985 or the Deeds of Arrangement Act 1914 and any other enactment past or present applying to Great Britain (or any part of it) that relates to the insolvency of any person;

"insolvency practice" means the carrying on of the business of acting as an insolvency practitioner or in a corresponding capacity under the law of any country or territory outside Great Britain, and for this purpose acting as an insolvency practitioner shall include acting as a judicial factor on the bankrupt estate of a deceased person;

"insolvency proceedings" means any proceedings in which an office-holder acts under any provision of insolvency legislation or the corresponding provision of the law of any country or territory outside Great Britain;

"insolvency work experience" means engagement in work related to the administration of insolvency proceedings—

    (a)   as the office-holder in those proceedings;

    (b)   in the employment of a firm or body whose members or employees act as insolvency practitioners; or

    (c)   in the course of employment in the Insolvency Service of the Department of Trade and Industry[, of the Department for Business, Enterprise and Regulatory Reform or of the Department for Business, Innovation and Skills].

"office-holder" means a person who acts as an insolvency practitioner or a judicial factor on the bankrupt estate of a deceased person or in a corresponding capacity under the law of any country or territory outside Great Britain and includes the official receiver acting as liquidator, provisional liquidator, trustee, interim receiver or nominee or supervisor of a voluntary arrangement; and

"regulatory work experience" means experience of work relating to the regulation of insolvency practitioners for or on behalf of a competent authority or a body recognised pursuant to section 391 of the Act or experience of work in connection with any function of the Secretary of State under that section.

NOTES

Words in square brackets in the definition "insolvency work experience" originally inserted by the Secretaries of State for Children, Schools and Families, for Innovation, Universities and Skills and for Business, Enterprise and Regulatory Reform Order 2007, SI 2007/3224, art 15, Schedule, Pt 2, para 53, as from 12 December 2007, and substituted by the Secretary of State for Business, Innovation and Skills Order 2009, SI 2009/2748, art 8, Schedule, Pt 2, para 31, as from 13 November 2009.

[10.918]
6   Matters for determining whether an applicant for an authorisation is a fit and proper person

The matters to be taken into account by a competent authority in deciding whether an individual is a fit and proper person to act as an insolvency practitioner for the purpose of section 393(2)(a) or 393(4)(a) shall include:—

    (a)   whether the applicant has been convicted of any offence involving fraud or other dishonesty or violence;

    (b)   whether the applicant has contravened any provision in any enactment contained in insolvency legislation;

    (c)   whether the applicant has engaged in any practices in the course of carrying on any trade, profession or vocation or in the course of the discharge of any functions relating to any office or employment appearing to be deceitful or oppressive or otherwise unfair or improper, whether unlawful or not, or which otherwise cast doubt upon his probity or competence for discharging the duties of an insolvency practitioner;

    (d)   whether in respect of any insolvency practice carried on by the applicant at the date of or at any time prior to the making of the application, there were established adequate systems of control of the practice and adequate records relating to the practice, including accounting records, and whether such systems of control and records have been or were maintained on an adequate basis;

    (e)   whether the insolvency practice of the applicant is, has been or, where the applicant is not yet carrying on such a practice, will be, carried on with the independence, integrity and the professional skills appropriate to the range and scale of the practice and the proper performance of the duties of an insolvency practitioner and in accordance with generally accepted professional standards, practices and principles;

    (f)   whether the applicant, in any case where he has acted as an insolvency practitioner, has failed to disclose fully to such persons as might reasonably be expected to be affected thereby circumstances where there is or appears to be a conflict of interest between his so acting and any interest of his own, whether personal, financial or otherwise, without having received such consent as might be appropriate to his acting or continuing to act despite the existence of such circumstances.

[10.919]

7   Requirements as to education and training—applicants who have never previously been authorised to act as insolvency practitioners

(1)   The requirements as to education, training and practical experience prescribed for the purposes of section 393(2)(b) of the Act in relation to an applicant who has never previously been authorised to act as an insolvency practitioner (whether by virtue of membership of a body recognised under section 391 of the Act or by virtue of an authorisation granted by a competent authority under section 393 of the Act) shall be as set out in this regulation.

(2)   An applicant must at the date of the making of his application have passed the Joint Insolvency Examination set by the Joint Insolvency Examination Board or have acquired in, or been awarded in, a country or territory outside Great Britain professional or vocational qualifications which indicate that the applicant has the knowledge and competence that is attested by a pass in that examination.

(3)   An applicant must either—

    (a)   have held office as an office-holder in not less than 30 cases during the period of 10 years immediately preceding the date on which he made his application for authorisation; or

    (b)   have acquired not less than [2000] hours of insolvency work experience of which no less than 1400 hours must have been acquired within the period of two years immediately prior to the date of the making of his application and show that he satisfies one of the three requirements set out in paragraph (4).

(4)   The three requirements referred to in paragraph (3)(b) are—

    (a)   the applicant has become an office-holder in at least 5 cases within the period of 5 years immediately prior to the date of the making of his application;

    (b)   the applicant has acquired 1,000 hours or more of higher insolvency work experience or experience as an office-holder within the period referred to in sub-paragraph (a); and

    (c)   the applicant can show that within the period referred to in sub-paragraph (a) he has achieved one of the following combinations of positions as an office-holder and hours acquired of higher insolvency work experience—

        (i)   4 cases and 200 hours;

        (ii)   3 cases and 400 hours;

        (iii)   2 cases and 600 hours; or

        (iv)   1 case and 800 hours.

(5)   Where in order to satisfy all or any of the requirements set out in paragraphs (3) and (4) an applicant relies on appointment as an office-holder or the acquisition of insolvency work experience or higher insolvency work experience in relation to cases under the laws of a country or territory outside the United Kingdom, he shall demonstrate that he has no less than 1,400 hours of insolvency work experience in cases under the law of any part of the United Kingdom acquired within the period of two years immediately prior to the date of the making of his application.

(6)   In ascertaining whether an applicant meets all or any of the requirements of paragraphs (3) and (4)—

    (a)   no account shall be taken of any case where—

        (i)   he was appointed to the office of receiver (or to a corresponding office under the law of a country or territory outside Great Britain) by or on behalf of a creditor who at the time of the appointment was an associate of the applicant; or

        (ii)   in a members' voluntary winding up or in a corresponding procedure under the laws of a country or territory outside Great Britain he was appointed liquidator at a general meeting where his associates were entitled to exercise or control the exercise of one third or more of the voting power at that general meeting;

    (b)   where the applicant has been an office-holder in relation to—

        (i)   two or more companies which were associates at the time of appointment; or

        (ii)   two or more individuals who were carrying on business in partnership with each other at the time of appointment,

    he shall be treated as having held office in only one case in respect of all offices held in relation to the companies which were associates or in respect of all offices held in relation to the individuals who were in partnership, as the case may be.

(7)   An applicant must have a good command of the English language.

NOTES

Para (3): number in square brackets substituted by the Provision of Services (Insolvency Practitioners) Regulations 2009, SI 2009/3081, reg 4, Schedule, para 3, as from 28 December 2009 (except in relation to an application for authorisation to act as an insolvency practitioner under the Insolvency Act 1986, s 393 made or granted before that date (see SI 2009/3081, reg 5)).

[10.920]

8   Requirements relating to education and training etc—applicants previously authorised to act as insolvency practitioners

(1)   The requirements prescribed for the purposes of section 393(2)(b) of the Act in relation to an applicant who has at any time been authorised to act as an insolvency practitioner (whether by virtue of membership of a body recognised under section 391 of the Act or an authorisation granted by a competent authority under section 393 of the Act) shall be as set out in this regulation.

(2)   The applicant must—

(a)   satisfy the requirements set out in regulation 7(3) to (5) or have acquired within the period of three years preceding the date of the making of his application [450] hours of any combination of the following types of experience—

(i)   experience as an office-holder;

(ii)   higher insolvency work experience;

(iii)   regulatory work experience; or

(iv)   advisory work experience; and

(b)   subject to paragraph (4), have completed at least 108 hours of continuing professional development in the period of three years ending on the day before the date of the making of his application of which—

(i)   a minimum of 12 hours must be completed in each of those years; and

(ii)   54 hours must fall into the categories in paragraphs (3)(b)(i) to (v).

(3)   "Continuing professional development" means any activities which—

(a)   relate to insolvency law or practice or the management of the practice of an insolvency practitioner; and

(b)   fall into any of the following categories—

(i)   the production of written material for publication;

(ii)   attendance at courses, seminars or conferences;

(iii)   the viewing of any recording of a course, seminar or conference;

(iv)   the giving of lectures or the presentation of papers at courses, seminars or conferences;

(v)   the completion of on-line tests; and

(vi)   the reading of books or periodical publications (including any on-line publication).

(4)   The requirement in paragraph (2)(b) shall only apply in relation to any application made on or after the third anniversary of the commencement date.

(5)   For the purposes of paragraph (3)(b)(i), "publication" includes making material available to a body recognised in pursuance of section 391 of the Act or any association or body representing the interests of those who act as insolvency practitioners.

NOTES

Para (2): number in square brackets substituted by the Provision of Services (Insolvency Practitioners) Regulations 2009, SI 2009/3081, reg 4, Schedule, para 4(1), (2), as from 28 December 2009 (except in relation to an application for authorisation to act as an insolvency practitioner under the Insolvency Act 1986, s 393 made or granted before that date (see SI 2009/3081, reg 5)).

[10.921]

[8A   Requirements relating to education and training etc—further authorisation to act as insolvency practitioners

(1)   The requirements prescribed under section 393(2)(b) of the Act in relation to further authorisation under section 393(3A) of the Act are as set out in this regulation.

(2)   The individual must—

(a)   have acquired within the period in regulation 11(1A) 150 hours of any combination of the following types of experience—

(i)   experience as an office-holder;

(ii)   higher insolvency work experience;

(iii)   regulatory work experience; or

(iv)   advisory work experience; and

(b)   have completed within the period in regulation 11(1A) at least 36 hours of continuing professional development of which 18 hours must fall into the categories in regulation 8(3)(b)(i) to (v).

(3)   In the first period after the grant of an authorisation an individual must comply with—

(a)   paragraph (2)(a) where the number of hours is 125; and

(b)   paragraph (2)(b) where the number of hours are 30 and 15 respectively.]

NOTES

Commencement: 28 December 2009.

Inserted by the Provision of Services (Insolvency Practitioners) Regulations 2009, SI 2009/3081, reg 4, Schedule, para 4(1), (3), as from 28 December 2009 (except in relation to an application for authorisation to act as an insolvency practitioner under the Insolvency Act 1986, s 393 made or granted before that date (see SI 2009/3081, reg 5)).

[10.922]
9　Records of continuing professional development activities

(1)　Every holder of an authorisation granted by the Secretary of State shall maintain a record of each continuing professional development activity undertaken by him for a period of six years from the date on which the activity was completed.

(2)　The record shall contain details of—
    (a)　which of the categories in regulation 8(3)(b) the activity comes within;
    (b)　the date that the activity was undertaken;
    (c)　the duration of the activity; and
    (d)　the topics covered by the activity.

(3)　Where the continuing professional development comprises—
    (a)　attendance at a course, seminar or conference; or
    (b)　the giving of a lecture or presentation of a paper at a course, seminar or conference,
the holder of the authorisation shall keep with the record evidence from the organiser of the course, seminar or conference of the attendance of the holder at the course, seminar or conference.

(4)　The Secretary of State may, on the giving of reasonable notice, inspect and take copies of any records or evidence maintained pursuant to this regulation.

10　*(Revoked by the Provision of Services (Insolvency Practitioners) Regulations 2009, SI 2009/3081, reg 4, Schedule, para 5, as from 28 December 2009, except in relation to an application for authorisation to act as an insolvency practitioner under the Insolvency Act 1986, s 393 made or granted before that date (see SI 2009/3081, reg 5).)*

[10.923]
11　Returns by insolvency practitioners authorised by the Secretary of State

(1)　Every holder of an authorisation granted by the Secretary of State shall make a return to the Secretary of State in respect of each period [in paragraph (1A)] during the whole or any part of which he held an authorisation granted by the Secretary of State containing the following information—
    (a)　the number of cases in respect of whom the holder of the authorisation has acted as an insolvency practitioner during the period;
    (b)　in respect of each case where the holder of the authorisation has acted as an insolvency practitioner—
        (i)　the name of the person in respect of whom the insolvency practitioner is acting,
        (ii)　the date of the appointment of the holder of the authorisation,
        (iii)　the type of proceedings involved, and
        (iv)　the number of hours worked in relation to the case by the holder of the authorisation and any person assigned to assist him in the case; *and*
    (c)　the following details of any continuing professional development undertaken activity during the period by the holder of the authorisation—
        (i)　the nature of the activity;
        (ii)　the date that the activity was undertaken;
        (iii)　the duration of the activity; and
        (iv)　the topics covered by the activity[; and
    (d)　the number of hours of any experience of the types in regulation 8A(2)(a)(i) to (iv)].

[(1A)　The period is the period of 12 months ending two months before the anniversary of the grant of the authorisation or the last further authorisation.]

(2)　Every return required to be submitted pursuant to this regulation shall be submitted [no later than 6 weeks before] of the end of the period to which it relates.

(3)　The Secretary of State may at any time request the holder of an authorisation to provide any information relating to any matters of the kind referred to in paragraph (1) and any such request shall be complied with by the holder of the authorisation within one month of its receipt or such longer period as the Secretary of State may allow.

NOTES

Para (1): words in first pair of square brackets substituted, the word omitted from sub-para (b) was revoked, and sub-para (d) (and the word immediately preceding it) was added, by the Provision of Services (Insolvency Practitioners) Regulations 2009, SI 2009/3081, reg 4, Schedule, para 6(1), (2)(a)–(c), as from 28 December 2009 (except in relation to an application for authorisation to act as an insolvency practitioner under the Insolvency Act 1986, s 393 made or granted before that date (see SI 2009/3081, reg 5)).

Para (1A): inserted by SI 2009/3081, reg 4, Schedule, para 6(1), (2)(c), as from 28 December 2009 (subject to the same exception in SI 2009/3081, reg 5 as noted above).

Para (2): words in square brackets substituted by SI 2009/3081, reg 4, Schedule, para 6(1), (3), as from 28 December 2009 (subject to the same exception in SI 2009/3081, reg 5 as noted above).

PART 3
THE REQUIREMENTS FOR SECURITY AND CAUTION FOR THE PROPER PERFORMANCE OF THE FUNCTIONS OF AN INSOLVENCY PRACTITIONER ETC

[10.924]

12

(1)   Schedule 2 shall have effect in respect of the requirements prescribed for the purposes of section 390(3)(b) in relation to security or caution for the proper performance of the functions of an insolvency practitioner and for related matters.

(2)   Where two or more persons are appointed jointly to act as insolvency practitioners in relation to any person, the provisions of this regulation shall apply to each of them individually.

[(3)   Where, in accordance with section 390(2)(c) of the Act a person is qualified to act as an insolvency practitioner by virtue of an authorisation granted by the Department of Enterprise, Trade and Investment for Northern Ireland under Article 352 of the Insolvency (Northern Ireland) Order 1989, this Part applies in relation to that person as if that authorisation had been granted pursuant to section 393 of the Act.]

NOTES

Para (3): added by the Provision of Services (Insolvency Practitioners) Regulations 2009, SI 2009/3081, reg 4, Schedule, para 7, as from 28 December 2009 (except in relation to an application for authorisation to act as an insolvency practitioner under the Insolvency Act 1986, s 393 made or granted before that date (see SI 2009/3081, reg 5)).

PART 4
RECORDS TO BE MAINTAINED BY INSOLVENCY PRACTITIONERS—INSPECTION OF RECORDS

[10.925]

13   Records to be maintained by insolvency practitioners

(1)   In respect of each case in which he acts, an insolvency practitioner shall maintain records containing at least the information specified in Schedule 3 to these Regulations as is applicable to the case.

(2)   Where at any time the records referred to in paragraph (1) do not contain all the information referred to in Schedule 3 as is applicable to the case, the insolvency practitioner shall forthwith make such changes to the records as are necessary to ensure that the records contains all such information.

(3)   References in Schedule 3 to "the Accountant in Bankruptcy" shall be construed in accordance with section 1 of the Bankruptcy (Scotland) Act 1985.

(4)   Each record maintained pursuant to paragraph (1) shall be capable of being produced by the insolvency practitioner separately from any other record.

(5)   Any records created in relation to a case pursuant to this regulation shall be preserved by the insolvency practitioner until whichever is the later of—
   (a)   the sixth anniversary of the date of the grant to the insolvency practitioner of his release or discharge in that case; or
   (b)   the sixth anniversary of the date on which any security or caution maintained in that case expires or otherwise ceases to have effect.

[10.926]

14   Notification of whereabouts of records

The insolvency practitioner shall notify the persons referred to in regulation 15(1)(a) and 15(1)(b) of the place where the records required to be maintained under this Part are so maintained and the place (if different) where they may be inspected pursuant to regulation 15.

[10.927]

15   Inspection of records

(1)   Any records maintained by an insolvency practitioner pursuant to this Part shall on the giving of reasonable notice be made available by him for inspection by—
   (a)   any professional body recognised under section 391 of the Act of which he is a member and the rules of membership of which entitle him to act as an insolvency practitioner;
   (b)   any competent authority by whom the insolvency practitioner is authorised to act pursuant to section 393 of the Act; and
   (c)   the Secretary of State.

(2)   Any person who is entitled to inspect any record pursuant to paragraph (1) shall also be entitled to take a copy of those records.

[10.928]

16   Inspection of practice records

(1)   This regulation applies to any relevant records which are held by—

(a) the holder of an authorisation to act as an insolvency practitioner granted by the Secretary of State pursuant to section 393 of the Act;

(b) his employer or former employer; or

(c) any firm or other body of which he is or was a member or partner.

(2) In this regulation "relevant records" mean any records which relate to any case where the holder of the authorisation mentioned in paragraph (1) has acted as an insolvency practitioner and which—

(a) record receipts and payments made in relation to, or in connection with, that case;

(b) record time spent on that case by the holder of the authorisation or any person assigned to assist the holder;

(c) relate to any business carried on in the case by or at the direction of the holder of the authorisation; or

(d) otherwise relate to the management of that case.

(3) The Secretary of State may, on the giving of reasonable notice to their holder, inspect and take copies of any records to which this regulation applies.

[10.929]
17 Inspection of records in administration and administrative receiverships
On the giving of reasonable notice to the insolvency practitioner, the Secretary of State shall be entitled to inspect and take copies of any records in the possession or control of that insolvency practitioner which—

(a) were required to be created by or under any provision of the Act (or any provision made under the Act); and

(b) relate to an administration or an administrative receivership.

SCHEDULES
SCHEDULE 1

(Sch 1 revokes the Insolvency Practitioners Regulations 1990, SI 1990/439, and the amending SI 1993/221, SI 2002/2710, SI 2002/2748, and SI 2004/373.)

SCHEDULE 2
REQUIREMENTS FOR SECURITY OR CAUTION AND RELATED MATTERS
Regulation 12

PART 1
INTERPRETATION

[10.930]
1 Interpretation
In this Schedule—

"cover schedule" means the schedule referred to in paragraph 3(2)(c);

"the insolvent" means the individual or company in relation to which an insolvency practitioner is acting;

"general penalty sum" shall be construed in accordance with paragraph 3(2)(b);

"insolvent's assets" means all assets comprised in the insolvent's estate together with any monies provided by a third party for the payment of the insolvent's debts or the costs and expenses of administering the insolvent's estate;

["professional liability insurance" means insurance taken out by the insolvency practitioner in respect of potential liabilities to the insolvent and third parties arising out of acting as an insolvency practitioner;]

"specific penalty sum" shall be construed in accordance with paragraph 3(2)(a).

NOTES
Definition "professional liability insurance" inserted by the Provision of Services (Insolvency Practitioners) Regulations 2009, SI 2009/3081, reg 4, Schedule, para 8(1), (2), as from 28 December 2009 (except in relation to an application for authorisation to act as an insolvency practitioner under the Insolvency Act 1986, s 393 made or granted before that date (see SI 2009/3081, reg 5)).

PART 2
REQUIREMENTS RELATING TO SECURITY AND CAUTION

[10.931]
2 Requirements in respect of security or caution
The requirements in respect of security or caution for the proper performance of the duties of insolvency practitioners prescribed for the purposes of section 390(3)(b) shall be as set out in this Part.

[2A Requirement for bond or professional liability insurance

Where an insolvency practitioner is appointed to act in respect of an insolvent there must be in force—

   (a)   a bond in a form approved by the Secretary of State which complies with paragraph 3; or

   (b)   where the insolvency practitioner is already established in another EEA state and is already covered in that state by professional liability insurance or a guarantee, professional liability insurance or a guarantee which complies with paragraph 8A.]

[3   Terms of the bond

(1)   The bond must—

   (a)   be in writing or in electronic form;

   (b)   contain provision whereby a surety or cautioner undertakes to be jointly and severally liable for losses in relation to the insolvent caused by—

      (i)   the fraud or dishonesty of the insolvency practitioner whether acting alone or in collusion with one or more persons; or

      (ii)   the fraud or dishonesty of any person committed with the connivance of the insolvency practitioner; and

   (c)   otherwise conform to the requirements of this paragraph and paragraphs 4 to 8.]

(2)   The terms of the bond shall provide—

   (a)   for the payment, in respect of each case where the insolvency practitioner acts, of claims in respect of liabilities for losses of the kind mentioned in sub-paragraph (1) up to an aggregate maximum sum in respect of that case ("the specific penalty sum") calculated in accordance with the provisions of this Schedule;

   (b)   in the event that any amounts payable under (a) are insufficient to meet all claims arising out of any case, for a further sum of £250,000 ("the general penalty sum") out of which any such claims are to be met;

   (c)   for a schedule containing the name of the insolvent and the value of the insolvent's assets to be submitted to the surety or cautioner within such period as may be specified in the bond;

   (d)   that where at any time before the insolvency practitioner obtains his release or discharge in respect of his acting in relation to an insolvent, he forms the opinion that the value of that insolvent's assets is greater than the current specific penalty sum, a revised specific penalty sum shall be applicable on the submission within such time as may be specified in the bond of a cover schedule containing a revised value of the insolvent's assets;

   (e)   for the payment of losses of the kind mentioned in sub-paragraph (1), whether they arise during the period in which the insolvency practitioner holds office in the capacity in which he was initially appointed or a subsequent period where he holds office in a subsequent capacity;

(3)   The terms of the bond may provide—

   (a)   that total claims in respect of the acts of the insolvency practitioner under all bonds relating to him are to be limited to a maximum aggregate sum (which shall not be less than £25,000,000); and

   (b)   for a time limit within which claims must be made.

4. Subject to paragraphs 5, 6 and 7, the amount of the specific penalty in respect of a case in which the insolvency practitioner acts, shall equal at least the value of the insolvent's assets as estimated by the insolvency practitioner as at the date of his appointment but ignoring the value of any assets—

   (a)   charged to a third party to the extent of any amount which would be payable to that third party; or

   (b)   held on trust by the insolvent to the extent that any beneficial interest in those assets does not belong to the insolvent.

5. In a case where an insolvency practitioner acts as a nominee or supervisor of a voluntary arrangement under Part I or Part VIII of the Act, the amount of the specific penalty shall be equal to at least the value of those assets subject to the terms of the arrangement (whether or not those assets are in his possession) including, where under the terms of the arrangement the debtor or a third party is to make payments, the aggregate of any payments to be made.

6. Where the value of the insolvent's assets is less than £5,000, the specific penalty sum shall be £5,000.

7. Where the value of the insolvent's assets is more than £5,000,000 the specific penalty sum shall be £5,000,000.

8. In estimating the value of an insolvent's assets, unless he has reason to doubt their accuracy, the insolvency practitioner may rely upon—

   (a)   any statement of affairs produced in relation to that insolvent pursuant to any provision of the Act; and

   (b)   in the case of a sequestration—

(i)   the debtor's list of assets and liabilities under section 19 of the Bankruptcy (Scotland) Act 1985;

(ii)   the preliminary statement under that Act; or

(iii) the final statement of the debtor's affairs by the interim trustee under section 23 of the Bankruptcy (Scotland) Act 1985.

[8A   Compliance of professional liability insurance cover in another EEA state

Where paragraph 2A(b) applies to an insolvency practitioner, the professional liability insurance or guarantee complies with this paragraph if the Secretary of State determines that it is equivalent or essentially comparable to the bond referred to in paragraph 3 as regards—

(a)   its purpose, and

(b)   the cover it provides in terms of—

    (i)   the risk covered,

    (ii)   the amount covered, and

    (iii) exclusions from the cover.

8B   Procedure for determining compliance of professional liability insurance or guarantee

(1)   Where an insolvency practitioner seeks a determination under paragraph 8A, the insolvency practitioner must send to the Secretary of State—

(a)   a copy of the document providing the professional liability insurance or guarantee cover in the EEA state in which the insolvency practitioner is established;

(b)   where the document in sub-paragraph (a) is not in English, a translation of it into English; and

(c)   a notice—

    (i)   where the insolvency practitioner intends to act in respect of an insolvent, specifying—

        (aa) the name of the insolvent; and

        (bb) the time and date when the insolvency practitioner intends to consent to be appointed to act; or

    (ii)   that the insolvency practitioner seeks a determination without reference to a specific appointment.

(2)   Where there is a notice sent under sub-paragraph (1)(c)(i), the documents sent under sub-paragraph (1) must be sent to the Secretary of State such that the Secretary of State receives them no later than 5 business days before the date in the notice.

(3)   Where the Secretary of State receives the documents sent under sub-paragraph (1), the Secretary of State must—

(a)   as soon as is reasonably practicable, notify the insolvency practitioner whether they were received in accordance with sub-paragraph (2);

(b)   consider them; and

(c)   determine whether the document sent under sub-paragraph (1)(a) complies with paragraph 8A.

(4)   Where the Secretary of State determines that the document sent under sub-paragraph (1)(a) complies with paragraph 8A, the Secretary of State must—

(a)   notify the insolvency practitioner that it complies with paragraph 8A; and

(b)   determine whether it contains a term equivalent or essentially comparable to a requirement to provide—

    (i)   a specific penalty sum; or

    (ii)   a cover schedule.

(5)   Where the Secretary of State determines under sub-paragraph (4)(b) that the document sent under sub-paragraph (1)(a)—

(a)   contains a term equivalent or essentially comparable to a requirement to provide a specific penalty sum or a cover schedule, the notice sent under paragraph (4)(a) must specify—

    (i)   the term equivalent or essentially comparable to a requirement to provide a specific penalty sum or a cover schedule; and

    (ii)   the thing in the term in sub-paragraph (i) which is equivalent or essentially comparable to a specific penalty sum or a cover schedule; or

(b)   does not contain a term equivalent or essentially comparable to a requirement to provide a specific penalty sum or a cover schedule, the notice sent under paragraph (4)(a) must state that determination.

(6)   Where the Secretary of State determines that the document sent under sub-paragraph (1)(a) does not comply with paragraph 8A, the Secretary of State must notify the insolvency practitioner and—

(a)   give reasons for the determination; and

(b)   specify any terms which, if included in a supplementary guarantee, will cause the Secretary of State to make a determination in accordance with paragraph 8A.

Part 10   Miscellaneous other SIs

(7)   In this paragraph a "business day" means any day other than a Saturday, a Sunday, Christmas Day, Good Friday or a day which is a bank holiday in England and Wales under or by virtue of the Banking and Financial Dealings Act 1971.

(8)   Any documents in this paragraph or paragraph 8C or 8D may be sent electronically.

8C Procedure for determining compliance of supplementary guarantee

(1)   Where the Secretary of State has made a determination under paragraph 8B(6), the insolvency practitioner may send to the Secretary of State—
- (a)   a supplementary guarantee purporting to provide for the matters specified in paragraph 8B(6)(b); and
- (b)   where the supplementary guarantee is not in English, a translation of it into English.

(2)   Where the Secretary of State receives the documents sent under sub-paragraph (1), the Secretary of State must—
- (a)   as soon as is reasonably practicable, notify the insolvency practitioner of the date and time of their receipt;
- (b)   consider them; and
- (c)   determine whether the document sent under sub-paragraph (1)(a) provides for the matters specified in paragraph 8B(6)(b).

(3)   Where the Secretary of State determines that the document sent under sub-paragraph (1)(a)—
- (a)   provides for the matters in specified in paragraph 8B(6)(b); and
- (b)   together with the document in paragraph 8B(1)(a) complies with paragraph 8A,

the Secretary of State must notify the insolvency practitioner that the documents sent under sub-paragraph (1)(a) and paragraph 8B(1)(a) together comply with paragraph 8A.

(4)   Where the Secretary of State determines in accordance with sub-paragraph (3), the Secretary of State must also determine whether the document sent under sub-paragraph (1)(a) or paragraph 8B(1)(a) contains a term equivalent or essentially comparable to a requirement to provide—
- (a)   a specific penalty sum; or
- (b)   a cover schedule.

(5)   Where the Secretary of State determines under sub-paragraph (4) that the document sent under sub-paragraph (1)(a) or paragraph 8B(1)(a)—
- (a)   contains a term equivalent or essentially comparable to a requirement to provide a specific penalty sum or a cover schedule, the notice sent under sub-paragraph (3) must specify—
  - (i)   the term equivalent or essentially comparable to a requirement to provide a specific penalty sum or a cover schedule;
  - (ii)   the thing in the term in sub-paragraph (i) which is equivalent or essentially comparable to a requirement to a specific penalty sum or a cover schedule; and
  - (iii)   the document in which the term in sub-paragraph (i) and the thing in sub-paragraph (ii) are to be found; or
- (b)   does not contain a term equivalent or essentially comparable to a requirement to provide a specific penalty sum or a cover schedule, the notice sent under sub-paragraph (3) must state that determination.

(6)   Where the Secretary of State determines that the document sent under sub-paragraph (1)(a)—
- (a)   does not provide for the matters specified in paragraph 8B(6)(b), or
- (b)   together with the document sent under paragraph 8B(1)(a) does not comply with paragraph 8A,

the Secretary of State must notify the insolvency practitioner that the documents sent under sub-paragraphs (1)(a) and paragraph 8B(1)(a) together do not comply with paragraph 8A.

8D Time for notification of determinations

(1)   The Secretary of State must notify the insolvency practitioner of the determinations under paragraph 8B or 8C in the periods set out in this paragraph.

(2)   The Secretary of State must notify the insolvency practitioner—
- (a)   where a notice under paragraph 8B(1)(c)(i) is received by the Secretary of State in accordance with paragraph 8B(2) and the determination is under—
  - (i)   paragraph 8B(4), (5) or (6), such that the insolvency practitioner receives the notice sent under paragraph 8B(4) or (6) or before the time and date in the notice sent under paragraph 8B(1)(c)(i); or
  - (ii)   paragraph 8C(4), (5) or (6), as soon as is reasonably practicable after receipt of the documents sent under paragraph 8C(1);
- (b)   where a notice sent under paragraph 8B(1)(c)(i) is received by the Secretary of State but not in accordance with paragraph 8B(2), and the determination is under—
  - (i)   paragraph 8B(4), (5) or (6), as soon as is reasonably practicable after receipt of the documents sent under paragraph 8B(1); or
  - (ii)   paragraph 8C(3), (5) or (6), as soon as is reasonably practicable after receipt of the documents sent under paragraph 8C(1); or
- (c)   where the notice is sent under paragraph 8B(1)(c)(ii), and the determination is under—

(i)   paragraph 8B(4), (5) or (6), within 28 days of receipt of the documents sent under
        paragraph 8B(1); or
(ii)   paragraph 8C(3), (5) or (6), within 14 days of receipt of the documents sent under
        paragraph 8C(1).

8E   Notification of determination out of time

(1) This paragraph applies where the insolvency practitioner—
   (a)   sends a notice under paragraph 8B(1)(c)(i);
   (b)   receives notification sent under paragraph 8B(3)(a) that the Secretary of State received the
         documents in paragraph 8B(1) in accordance with paragraph 8B(2); and
   (c)   does not receive the notifications in the time in paragraph 8D(2)(a)(i).

(2) The insolvency practitioner is qualified to act as an insolvency practitioner in respect of the
insolvent specified in the notice under paragraph 8B(1)(c)(i) until the Secretary of State notifies the
insolvency practitioner of the determination under paragraph 8B or 8C.

(3) Subject to sub-paragraph (4), where the Secretary of State notifies the insolvency practitioner
of the determination under paragraph 8B or 8C—
   (a)   the determination applies; and
   (b)   the insolvency practitioner ceases to be qualified to act as an insolvency practitioner under
         sub-paragraph (2).

(4) Where—
   (a)   the Secretary of State gives notice under paragraph 8B(6); and
   (b)   the insolvency practitioner sends the documents in paragraph 8C(1),
the insolvency practitioner is qualified to act as an insolvency practitioner under sub-paragraph (2)
until the Secretary of State determines in accordance with paragraph 8C(4) or (6).]

NOTES
Para 2A: inserted by the Provision of Services (Insolvency Practitioners) Regulations 2009, SI 2009/3081, reg 4, Schedule,
para 8(1), (3), as from 28 December 2009 (except in relation to an application for authorisation to act as an insolvency
practitioner under the Insolvency Act 1986, s 393 made or granted before that date (see SI 2009/3081, reg 5)).
Para 3: the paragraph title and sub-para (1) were substituted by SI 2009/3081, reg 4, Schedule, para 8(1), (4), as from
28 December 2009 (subject to the same exception in SI 2009/3081, reg 5 as noted above).
Paras 8A–8E: added by SI 2009/3081, reg 4, Schedule, para 8(1), (5), as from 28 December 2009 (subject to the same
exception in SI 2009/3081, reg 5 as noted above).

PART 3
RECORDS RELATING TO BONDING AND CONNECTED MATTERS

[10.932]
9   Record of specific penalty sums to be maintained by insolvency practitioner

(1) An insolvency practitioner shall maintain a record of all specific penalty sums that are
applicable in relation to any case where he is acting and such record shall contain the name of each
person to whom the specific penalty sum relates and the amount of each penalty sum that is in
force.

(2) Any record maintained by an insolvency practitioner pursuant to this paragraph shall, on the
giving of reasonable notice, be made available for inspection by—
   (a)   any professional body recognised under section 391 of the Act of which he is or was a
         member and the rules of membership of which entitle or entitled him to act as an
         insolvency practitioner;
   (b)   any competent authority by whom the insolvency practitioner is or was authorised to act
         pursuant to section 393 of the Act; and
   (c)   the Secretary of State.

[(3) Subject to sub-paragraph (4), where the Secretary of State has notified the insolvency
practitioner in accordance with paragraph 8B(5)(a) or 8C(5)(a) in relation to a specific penalty sum,
the thing notified under paragraph 8B(5)(a)(ii) or 8C(5)(a)(ii) is construed as a specific penalty sum
for the purposes of this paragraph and Schedule 3.

(4) Where the Secretary of State has notified the insolvency practitioner in accordance with
paragraph 8B(5)(b) or 8C(5)(b) in relation to a specific penalty sum, this paragraph does not apply.]

10   Retention of bond by recognised professional body or competent authority

[(1) The documents in sub-paragraph (2) or a copy must] be sent by the insolvency practitioner
to—
   (a)   any professional body recognised under section 391 of the Act of which he is a member
         and the rules of membership of which entitle him to act as an insolvency practitioner; or
   (b)   any competent authority by whom the insolvency practitioner is authorised to act pursuant
         to section 393 of the Act.

[(2) The documents in this sub-paragraph are—
   (a)   the bond referred to in paragraph 3;
   (b)   where the Secretary of State has determined under paragraph 8B(4)—

      (i)   the document in paragraph 8B(1)(a) and (b); and
      (ii)   the notice under paragraph 8B(4);
  (c)   where the Secretary of State has determined under paragraph 8C(4)
      (i)   the documents in paragraphs 8B(1)(a) and (b) and 8C(1)(a) and (b);and
      (ii)   the notice under paragraph 8C(3).

(3)   The document in sub-paragraph (2) or a copy of it may be sent electronically.]

11   Inspection and retention requirements relating to cover schedule—England and Wales

(1)   This regulation applies to an insolvency practitioner appointed in insolvency proceedings under the Act to act—
  (a)   in relation to a company which the courts in England and Wales have jurisdiction to wind up; or
  (b)   in respect of an individual.

(2)   The insolvency practitioner shall retain a copy of the cover schedule submitted by him in respect of his acting in relation to the company or, as the case may be, individual until the second anniversary of the date on which he is granted his release or discharge in relation to that company or, as the case may be, that individual.

(3)   The copy of a schedule kept by an insolvency practitioner in pursuance of sub-paragraph (2) shall be produced by him on demand for inspection by—
  (a)   any creditor of the person to whom the schedule relates;
  (b)   where the schedule relates to an insolvent who is an individual, that individual;
  (c)   where the schedule relates to an insolvent which is a company, any contributory or director or other officer of the company; and
  (d)   the Secretary of State.

[(4)   Subject to sub-paragraph (5), where the Secretary of State has notified the insolvency practitioner tin accordance with paragraph 8B(5)(a) or 8C(5)(a) in relation to a cover schedule, the thing notified under paragraph 8B(5)(a)(ii) or 8C(5)(a)(ii) is construed as a cover schedule for the purposes of this paragraph, paragraph 12, paragraph 13 and Schedule 3.

(5)   Where the Secretary of State has notified the insolvency practitioner in accordance with paragraph 8B(5)(b) or 8C(5)(b) in relation to a cover schedule, this paragraph, paragraph 12 and paragraph 13 do not apply.]

12   Inspection and retention requirements relating to the cover schedule—Scotland

(1)   Where an insolvency practitioner is appointed to act in relation to a company which the courts in Scotland have jurisdiction to wind up, he shall retain in the sederunt book kept under rule 7.33 of the Insolvency (Scotland) Rules 1986, the principal copy of any cover schedule containing entries in relation to his so acting.

(2)   Where an insolvency practitioner is appointed to act as interim trustee or permanent trustee or as a trustee under a trust deed for creditors, he shall retain in the sederunt book kept for those proceedings, the principal copy of any cover schedule containing entries in relation to his so acting.

13   Requirements to submit cover schedule to authorising body

(1)   Every insolvency practitioner shall submit to his authorising body not later than 20 days after the end of each month during which he holds office in a case—
  (a)   the information submitted to a surety or cautioner in any cover schedule related to that month;
  (b)   where no cover schedule is submitted in relation to the month, a statement either that there are no relevant particulars to be supplied or, as the case may be, that it is not practicable to supply particulars in relation to any appointments taken in that month; and
  (c)   a statement identifying any case in respect of which he has been granted his release or discharge.

(2)   In this regulation "authorising body" means in relation to an insolvency practitioner—
  (a)   any professional body recognised under section 391 of the Act of which he is a member and the rules of membership of which entitle him to act as an insolvency practitioner; or
  (b)   any competent authority by whom he is authorised to act as an insolvency practitioner pursuant to section 393 of the Act.

NOTES

   Para 9: sub-paras (3), (4) added by the Provision of Services (Insolvency Practitioners) Regulations 2009, SI 2009/3081, reg 4, Schedule, para 8(1), (6), as from 28 December 2009 (except in relation to an application for authorisation to act as an insolvency practitioner under the Insolvency Act 1986, s 393 made or granted before that date (see SI 2009/3081, reg 5)).

   Para 10: words in first pair of square brackets substituted, and sub-paras (2), (3) added, by SI 2009/3081, reg 4, Schedule, para 8(1), (7), as from 28 December 2009 (subject to the same exception in SI 2009/3081, reg 5 as noted above).

   Para 11: sub-paras (4), (5) added by SI 2009/3081, reg 4, Schedule, para 8(1), (8), as from 28 December 2009 (subject to the same exception in SI 2009/3081, reg 5 as noted above).

SCHEDULE 3
RECORDS TO BE MAINTAINED—MINIMUM REQUIREMENTS
Regulation 13

Details of the insolvency practitioner acting in the case

[10.933]
1. The name of the insolvency practitioner acting in the case.

2. The identifying number or reference issued to the insolvency practitioner by[—
   (a) a competent authority;
   (b) the Department of Enterprise, Trade and Investment for Northern Ireland; or
   (c) any body recognised under section 391 of the Act].

3. The principal business address of the insolvency practitioner.

[4. Either—
   (a) the name of—
      (i) any body by virtue of whose rules the insolvency practitioner is entitled to practise;
        or
      (ii) any competent authority by whom the insolvency practitioner is authorised; or
   (b) where the insolvency practitioner is authorised by the Department of Enterprise, Trade and Investment for Northern Ireland under Article 352 of the Insolvency (Northern Ireland) Order 1989, that such an authorisation has been granted.]

Details of the insolvent

5. The name of the person in respect of whom the insolvency practitioner is acting.

6. The type of the insolvency proceedings.

Progress of administration

7. As regards the progress of the administration of the case the following details if applicable—
   (a) the date of commencement of the proceedings;
   (b) the date of appointment of the insolvency practitioner;
   (c) the date on which the appointment was notified to—
      (i) the Registrar of Companies; or
      (ii) the Accountant in Bankruptcy.

Bonding arrangements in the case

8. As regards the arrangements for security or caution in the case—
   (a) the date of submission of the cover schedule which has the details of the specific penalty sum applicable in the case;
   (b) the amount of the specific penalty sum;
   (c) the name of the surety or cautioner;
   (d) the date of submission to surety or cautioner of a cover schedule with any increase in the amount of the specific penalty sum;
   (e) the amount of any revised specific penalty sum; and
   (f) the date of submission to the surety or cautioner of details of termination of the office held by the insolvency practitioner.

Matters relating to remuneration

9. As regards the remuneration of the insolvency practitioner—
   (a) the basis on which the remuneration of the insolvency practitioner is to be calculated; and
   (b) the date and content of any resolution of creditors in relation to the remuneration of the insolvency practitioner.

Meetings (other than any final meeting of creditors)

10. The dates of—
   (a) the meeting of members;
   (b) the date of first meeting of creditors—
      (i) to consider an administrator's proposals;
      (ii) to consider an administrative receiver's report;
      (iii) in liquidation or bankruptcy;
      (iv) to consider a voluntary arrangement proposal; or
      (v) according to a trust deed for creditors;
   (c) the date of the statutory meeting in sequestration; and
   (d) the dates and purposes of any subsequent meetings.

Disqualification of Directors

11. As regards the insolvency practitioner's duties under section 7 of the Company Directors Disqualification Act 1986 to report the conduct of directors—

(a)   the date a return under section 7 is due;

(b)   the date a return is submitted to the Secretary of State;

(c)   the date a conduct report is submitted to the Secretary of State; and

(d)   the date on which any further reports are submitted to the Secretary of State.

Vacation of office etc

12. The following details regarding the completion of the case—

(a)   the date of the final notice to, or meeting of, creditors;

(b)   the date that the insolvency practitioner vacates office; and

(c)   the date of release or discharge of the insolvency practitioner (or if there is no final meeting of creditors, the date of the final return of receipts and payments to the Secretary of State).

Distributions to creditors etc

13. As regards distributions—

(a)   in relation to each payment to preferential or preferred creditors—

(i)   the name of the person to whom the payment was made;

(ii)   the date of the payment;

(iii) the amount of the payment;

(b)   in relation to each payment to unsecured creditors—

(i)   the name of the person to whom the payment was made;

(ii)   the date of the payment;

(iii) the amount of the payment; and

(c)   in relation to each return of capital—

(i)   the name of the person to whom the return of capital was made;

(ii)   the date of the payment; and

(iii) the amount of capital returned or the value of any assets returned.

Statutory Returns

14. As regards any returns or accounts to be made to the Secretary of State, the Registrar of Companies or the Accountant in Bankruptcy—

(a)   as regards each interim return or abstract of receipts and payments;

(i)   the date the return or abstract is due;

(ii)   the date on which the return is filed; and

(b)   as regards any final return or abstract of receipts and payments—

(i)   the date that the return or abstract is due; and

(ii)   the date on which the return is filed.

Time recording

15. Records of the amount of time spent on the case by the insolvency practitioner and any persons assigned to assist in the administration of the case.

NOTES

Para 2: words in square brackets substituted by the Provision of Services (Insolvency Practitioners) Regulations 2009, SI 2009/3081, reg 4, Schedule, para 9(1), (2), as from 28 December 2009 (except in relation to an application for authorisation to act as an insolvency practitioner under the Insolvency Act 1986, s 393 made or granted before that date (see SI 2009/3081, reg 5)).

Para 4: substituted by SI 2009/3081, reg 4, Schedule, para 9(1), (3), as from 28 December 2009 (subject to the same exception in SI 2009/3081, reg 5 as noted above).

PROSPECTUS REGULATIONS 2005 (NOTE)

(SI 2005/1433)

[10.934]

NOTES

These Regulations were made on 26 May 2005 under the powers conferred by the European Communities Act 1972, s 2(2). They came into force on 1 July 2005.

These Regulations implement Directive 2003/71/EC of the European Parliament and of the Council on the prospectus to be published when securities are offered to the public or admitted to trading on a regulated market ("the prospectus directive") at **[11.284]**. They substitute FSMA 2000, ss 84–87 with new ss 84–87, 87A–87R (at **[7.91]**–**[7.112]**) and replace Sch 11 to that Act with a new Sch 11A (Transferable Securities at **[7.395]** et seq). These Regulations also revoke the Public Offers of Securities Regulations 1995 (SI 1995/1537) and the Financial Services and Markets Act 2000 (Offers of Securities) Order 2001 (SI 2001/2958), and make minor and consequential amendments to CA 1989, the Companies (Audit, Investigations and Community Enterprise) Act 2004, and the Financial Services and Markets Act 2000 (Official Listing of Securities) Regulations 2001 (SI 2001/2956). All amendments have been incorporated at the appropriate place in this Handbook.

TRANSFER OF UNDERTAKINGS (PROTECTION OF EMPLOYMENT) REGULATIONS 2006

(SI 2006/246)

NOTES

Made: 6 February 2006.

Authority: European Communities Act 1972, s 2(2); Employment Relations Act 1999, s 38.

Commencement: 6 April 2006.

These Regulations are reproduced as amended by: the Transfer of Undertakings (Protection of Employment) (Amendment) Regulations 2009, SI 2009/592; the Agency Workers Regulations 2010, SI 2010/93.

Application and modification: these Regulations (and SI 1981/1794 which they replaced) are (or were) applied and modified by a variety of other enactments for the purposes of transfer schemes made thereunder. These are generally outside the scope of this work, but for details see the Industrial Training Act 1982, the Ordnance Factories and Military Services Act 1984, the Dockyard Services Act 1986, the Dartford-Thurrock Crossing Act 1988, the Atomic Weapons Establishment Act 1991, the Export and Investment Guarantees Act 1991, the Ports Act 1991, the Coal Industry Act 1994, the Energy Act 2004, the Criminal Proceedings etc (Reform) (Scotland) Act 2007, the Transfer of Undertakings (Protection of Employment) (Rent Officer Service) Regulations 1999, SI 1999/2511, the Transfer of Undertakings (Protection of Employment) (Greater London Authority) Order 2000, SI 2000/686, the Transfer of Undertakings (Protection of Employment) (Transfer to OFCOM) Regulations 2003, SI 2003/2715, the Personal Accounts Delivery Authority Winding Up Order 2010, SI 2010/911, and the Northern Ireland Act 1998 (Devolution of Policing and Justice Functions) Order 2010, SI 2010/976; the Office of the Renewable Fuels Agency (Dissolution and Transfer of Functions) Order 2011, SI 2011/493. As to the application of these Regulations to certain individual financial institutions, see the Orders made under the Banking (Special Provisions) Act 2008 and the Banking Act 2009.

ARRANGEMENT OF REGULATIONS

[10.935]
1 Citation, commencement and extent

(1) These Regulations may be cited as the Transfer of Undertakings (Protection of Employment) Regulations 2006.

(2) These Regulations shall come into force on 6 April 2006.

(3) These Regulations shall extend to Northern Ireland, except where otherwise provided.

[10.936]
2 Interpretation

(1) In these Regulations—

"assigned" means assigned other than on a temporary basis;

"collective agreement", "collective bargaining" and "trade union" have the same meanings respectively as in the 1992 Act;

"contract of employment" means any agreement between an employee and his employer determining the terms and conditions of his employment;

references to "contractor" in regulation 3 shall include a sub-contractor;

"employee" means any individual who works for another person whether under a contract of service or apprenticeship or otherwise but does not include anyone who provides services under a contract for services and references to a person's employer shall be construed accordingly;

"insolvency practitioner" has the meaning given to the expression by Part XIII of the Insolvency Act 1986;

references to "organised grouping of employees" shall include a single employee;

"recognised" has the meaning given to the expression by section 178(3) of the 1992 Act;

"relevant transfer" means a transfer or a service provision change to which these Regulations apply in accordance with regulation 3 and "transferor" and "transferee" shall be construed accordingly and in the case of a service provision change falling within regulation 3(1)(b), "the transferor" means the person who carried out the activities prior to the service provision change and "the transferee" means the person who carries out the activities as a result of the service provision change;

"the 1992 Act" means the Trade Union and Labour Relations (Consolidation) Act 1992;

"the 1996 Act" means the Employment Rights Act 1996;

"the 1996 Tribunals Act" means the Employment Tribunals Act 1996;

"the 1981 Regulations" means the Transfer of Undertakings (Protection of Employment) Regulations 1981.

(2)   For the purposes of these Regulations the representative of a trade union recognised by an employer is an official or other person authorised to carry on collective bargaining with that employer by that trade union.

(3)   In the application of these Regulations to Northern Ireland the Regulations shall have effect as set out in Schedule 1.

[10.937]
3   A relevant transfer

(1)   These Regulations apply to—

  (a)   a transfer of an undertaking, business or part of an undertaking or business situated immediately before the transfer in the United Kingdom to another person where there is a transfer of an economic entity which retains its identity;

  (b)   a service provision change, that is a situation in which—

    (i)   activities cease to be carried out by a person ("a client") on his own behalf and are carried out instead by another person on the client's behalf ("a contractor");

    (ii)   activities cease to be carried out by a contractor on a client's behalf (whether or not those activities had previously been carried out by the client on his own behalf) and are carried out instead by another person ("a subsequent contractor") on the client's behalf; or

    (iii)   activities cease to be carried out by a contractor or a subsequent contractor on a client's behalf (whether or not those activities had previously been carried out by the client on his own behalf) and are carried out instead by the client on his own behalf,

and in which the conditions set out in paragraph (3) are satisfied.

(2)   In this regulation "economic entity" means an organised grouping of resources which has the objective of pursuing an economic activity, whether or not that activity is central or ancillary.

(3)   The conditions referred to in paragraph (1)(b) are that—

  (a)   immediately before the service provision change—

    (i)   there is an organised grouping of employees situated in Great Britain which has as its principal purpose the carrying out of the activities concerned on behalf of the client;

    (ii)   the client intends that the activities will, following the service provision change, be carried out by the transferee other than in connection with a single specific event or task of short-term duration; and

  (b)   the activities concerned do not consist wholly or mainly of the supply of goods for the client's use.

(4)   Subject to paragraph (1), these Regulations apply to—

  (a)   public and private undertakings engaged in economic activities whether or not they are operating for gain;

  (b)   a transfer or service provision change howsoever effected notwithstanding—

    (i)   that the transfer of an undertaking, business or part of an undertaking or business is governed or effected by the law of a country or territory outside the United Kingdom or that the service provision change is governed or effected by the law of a country or territory outside Great Britain;

    (ii)   that the employment of persons employed in the undertaking, business or part transferred or, in the case of a service provision change, persons employed in the organised grouping of employees, is governed by any such law;

  (c)   a transfer of an undertaking, business or part of an undertaking or business (which may also be a service provision change) where persons employed in the undertaking, business or part transferred ordinarily work outside the United Kingdom.

(5)   An administrative reorganisation of public administrative authorities or the transfer of administrative functions between public administrative authorities is not a relevant transfer.

(6)   A relevant transfer—

  (a)   may be effected by a series of two or more transactions; and

(b)   may take place whether or not any property is transferred to the transferee by the transferor.

(7)   Where, in consequence (whether directly or indirectly) of the transfer of an undertaking, business or part of an undertaking or business which was situated immediately before the transfer in the United Kingdom, a ship within the meaning of the Merchant Shipping Act 1995 registered in the United Kingdom ceases to be so registered, these Regulations shall not affect the right conferred by section 29 of that Act (right of seamen to be discharged when ship ceases to be registered in the United Kingdom) on a seaman employed in the ship.

[10.938]
4   Effect of relevant transfer on contracts of employment

(1)   Except where objection is made under paragraph (7), a relevant transfer shall not operate so as to terminate the contract of employment of any person employed by the transferor and assigned to the organised grouping of resources or employees that is subject to the relevant transfer, which would otherwise be terminated by the transfer, but any such contract shall have effect after the transfer as if originally made between the person so employed and the transferee.

(2)   Without prejudice to paragraph (1), but subject to paragraph (6), and regulations 8 and 15(9), on the completion of a relevant transfer—

     (a)   all the transferor's rights, powers, duties and liabilities under or in connection with any such contract shall be transferred by virtue of this regulation to the transferee; and

     (b)   any act or omission before the transfer is completed, of or in relation to the transferor in respect of that contract or a person assigned to that organised grouping of resources or employees, shall be deemed to have been an act or omission of or in relation to the transferee.

(3)   Any reference in paragraph (1) to a person employed by the transferor and assigned to the organised grouping of resources or employees that is subject to a relevant transfer, is a reference to a person so employed immediately before the transfer, or who would have been so employed if he had not been dismissed in the circumstances described in regulation 7(1), including, where the transfer is effected by a series of two or more transactions, a person so employed and assigned or who would have been so employed and assigned immediately before any of those transactions.

(4)   Subject to regulation 9, in respect of a contract of employment that is, or will be, transferred by paragraph (1), any purported variation of the contract shall be void if the sole or principal reason for the variation is—

     (a)   the transfer itself; or

     (b)   a reason connected with the transfer that is not an economic, technical or organisational reason entailing changes in the workforce.

(5)   Paragraph (4) shall not prevent the employer and his employee, whose contract of employment is, or will be, transferred by paragraph (1), from agreeing a variation of that contract if the sole or principal reason for the variation is—

     (a)   a reason connected with the transfer that is an economic, technical or organisational reason entailing changes in the workforce; or

     (b)   a reason unconnected with the transfer.

(6)   Paragraph (2) shall not transfer or otherwise affect the liability of any person to be prosecuted for, convicted of and sentenced for any offence.

(7)   Paragraphs (1) and (2) shall not operate to transfer the contract of employment and the rights, powers, duties and liabilities under or in connection with it of an employee who informs the transferor or the transferee that he objects to becoming employed by the transferee.

(8)   Subject to paragraphs (9) and (11), where an employee so objects, the relevant transfer shall operate so as to terminate his contract of employment with the transferor but he shall not be treated, for any purpose, as having been dismissed by the transferor.

(9)   Subject to regulation 9, where a relevant transfer involves or would involve a substantial change in working conditions to the material detriment of a person whose contract of employment is or would be transferred under paragraph (1), such an employee may treat the contract of employment as having been terminated, and the employee shall be treated for any purpose as having been dismissed by the employer.

(10)   No damages shall be payable by an employer as a result of a dismissal falling within paragraph (9) in respect of any failure by the employer to pay wages to an employee in respect of a notice period which the employee has failed to work.

(11)   Paragraphs (1), (7), (8) and (9) are without prejudice to any right of an employee arising apart from these Regulations to terminate his contract of employment without notice in acceptance of a repudiatory breach of contract by his employer.

[10.939]
5   Effect of relevant transfer on collective agreements

Where at the time of a relevant transfer there exists a collective agreement made by or on behalf of the transferor with a trade union recognised by the transferor in respect of any employee whose contract of employment is preserved by regulation 4(1) above, then—

(a)   without prejudice to sections 179 and 180 of the 1992 Act (collective agreements presumed to be unenforceable in specified circumstances) that agreement, in its application in relation to the employee, shall, after the transfer, have effect as if made by or on behalf of the transferee with that trade union, and accordingly anything done under or in connection with it, in its application in relation to the employee, by or in relation to the transferor before the transfer, shall, after the transfer, be deemed to have been done by or in relation to the transferee; and

(b)   any order made in respect of that agreement, in its application in relation to the employee, shall, after the transfer, have effect as if the transferee were a party to the agreement.

[10.940]
6   Effect of relevant transfer on trade union recognition

(1)   This regulation applies where after a relevant transfer the transferred organised grouping of resources or employees maintains an identity distinct from the remainder of the transferee's undertaking.

(2)   Where before such a transfer an independent trade union is recognised to any extent by the transferor in respect of employees of any description who in consequence of the transfer become employees of the transferee, then, after the transfer—

(a)   the trade union shall be deemed to have been recognised by the transferee to the same extent in respect of employees of that description so employed; and

(b)   any agreement for recognition may be varied or rescinded accordingly.

[10.941]
7   Dismissal of employee because of relevant transfer

(1)   Where either before or after a relevant transfer, any employee of the transferor or transferee is dismissed, that employee shall be treated for the purposes of Part X of the 1996 Act (unfair dismissal) as unfairly dismissed if the sole or principal reason for his dismissal is—

(a)   the transfer itself; or

(b)   a reason connected with the transfer that is not an economic, technical or organisational reason entailing changes in the workforce.

(2)   This paragraph applies where the sole or principal reason for the dismissal is a reason connected with the transfer that is an economic, technical or organisational reason entailing changes in the workforce of either the transferor or the transferee before or after a relevant transfer.

(3)   Where paragraph (2) applies—

(a)   paragraph (1) shall not apply;

(b)   without prejudice to the application of section 98(4) of the 1996 Act (test of fair dismissal), the dismissal shall, for the purposes of sections 98(1) and 135 of that Act (reason for dismissal), be regarded as having been for redundancy where section 98(2)(c) of that Act applies, or otherwise for a substantial reason of a kind such as to justify the dismissal of an employee holding the position which that employee held.

(4)   The provisions of this regulation apply irrespective of whether the employee in question is assigned to the organised grouping of resources or employees that is, or will be, transferred.

(5)   Paragraph (1) shall not apply in relation to the dismissal of any employee which was required by reason of the application of section 5 of the Aliens Restriction (Amendment) Act 1919 to his employment.

(6)   Paragraph (1) shall not apply in relation to a dismissal of an employee if the application of section 94 of the 1996 Act to the dismissal of the employee is excluded by or under any provision of the 1996 Act, the 1996 Tribunals Act or the 1992 Act.

[10.942]
8   Insolvency

(1)   If at the time of a relevant transfer the transferor is subject to relevant insolvency proceedings paragraphs (2) to (6) apply.

(2)   In this regulation "relevant employee" means an employee of the transferor—

(a)   whose contract of employment transfers to the transferee by virtue of the operation of these Regulations; or

(b)   whose employment with the transferor is terminated before the time of the relevant transfer in the circumstances described in regulation 7(1).

(3)   The relevant statutory scheme specified in paragraph (4)(b) (including that sub-paragraph as applied by paragraph 5 of Schedule 1) shall apply in the case of a relevant employee irrespective of the fact that the qualifying requirement that the employee's employment has been terminated is not met and for those purposes the date of the transfer shall be treated as the date of the termination and the transferor shall be treated as the employer.

(4)   In this regulation the "relevant statutory schemes" are—

(a)   Chapter VI of Part XI of the 1996 Act;

(b)   Part XII of the 1996 Act.

(5) Regulation 4 shall not operate to transfer liability for the sums payable to the relevant employee under the relevant statutory schemes.

(6) In this regulation "relevant insolvency proceedings" means insolvency proceedings which have been opened in relation to the transferor not with a view to the liquidation of the assets of the transferor and which are under the supervision of an insolvency practitioner.

(7) Regulations 4 and 7 do not apply to any relevant transfer where the transferor is the subject of bankruptcy proceedings or any analogous insolvency proceedings which have been instituted with a view to the liquidation of the assets of the transferor and are under the supervision of an insolvency practitioner.

[10.943]
9 Variations of contract where transferors are subject to relevant insolvency proceedings

(1) If at the time of a relevant transfer the transferor is subject to relevant insolvency proceedings these Regulations shall not prevent the transferor or transferee (or an insolvency practitioner) and appropriate representatives of assigned employees agreeing to permitted variations.

(2) For the purposes of this regulation "appropriate representatives" are—
  (a) if the employees are of a description in respect of which an independent trade union is recognised by their employer, representatives of the trade union; or
  (b) in any other case, whichever of the following employee representatives the employer chooses—
    (i) employee representatives appointed or elected by the assigned employees (whether they make the appointment or election alone or with others) otherwise than for the purposes of this regulation, who (having regard to the purposes for, and the method by which they were appointed or elected) have authority from those employees to agree permitted variations to contracts of employment on their behalf;
    (ii) employee representatives elected by assigned employees (whether they make the appointment or election alone or with others) for these particular purposes, in an election satisfying requirements identical to those contained in regulation 14 except those in regulation 14(1)(d).

(3) An individual may be an appropriate representative for the purposes of both this regulation and regulation 13 provided that where the representative is not a trade union representative he is either elected by or has authority from assigned employees (within the meaning of this regulation) and affected employees (as described in regulation 13(1)).

(4) (*Amends the Trade Union and Labour Relations (Consolidation) Act 1992, s 168.*)

(5) Where assigned employees are represented by non-trade union representatives—
  (a) the agreement recording a permitted variation must be in writing and signed by each of the representatives who have made it or, where that is not reasonably practicable, by a duly authorised agent of that representative; and
  (b) the employer must, before the agreement is made available for signature, provide all employees to whom it is intended to apply on the date on which it is to come into effect with copies of the text of the agreement and such guidance as those employees might reasonably require in order to understand it fully.

(6) A permitted variation shall take effect as a term or condition of the assigned employee's contract of employment in place, where relevant, of any term or condition which it varies.

(7) In this regulation—
  "assigned employees" means those employees assigned to the organised grouping of resources or employees that is the subject of a relevant transfer;
  "permitted variation" is a variation to the contract of employment of an assigned employee where—
    (a) the sole or principal reason for it is the transfer itself or a reason connected with the transfer that is not an economic, technical or organisational reason entailing changes in the workforce; and
    (b) it is designed to safeguard employment opportunities by ensuring the survival of the undertaking, business or part of the undertaking or business that is the subject of the relevant transfer;
  "relevant insolvency proceedings" has the meaning given to the expression by regulation 8(6).

[10.944]
10 Pensions

(1) Regulations 4 and 5 shall not apply—
  (a) to so much of a contract of employment or collective agreement as relates to an occupational pension scheme within the meaning of the Pension Schemes Act 1993; or
  (b) to any rights, powers, duties or liabilities under or in connection with any such contract or subsisting by virtue of any such agreement and relating to such a scheme or otherwise arising in connection with that person's employment and relating to such a scheme.

(2)   For the purposes of paragraphs (1) and (3), any provisions of an occupational pension scheme which do not relate to benefits for old age, invalidity or survivors shall not be treated as being part of the scheme.

(3)   An employee whose contract of employment is transferred in the circumstances described in regulation 4(1) shall not be entitled to bring a claim against the transferor for—

(a)   breach of contract; or

(b)   constructive unfair dismissal under section 95(1)(c) of the 1996 Act,

arising out of a loss or reduction in his rights under an occupational pension scheme in consequence of the transfer, save insofar as the alleged breach of contract or dismissal (as the case may be) occurred prior to the date on which these Regulations took effect.

[10.945]
11   Notification of Employee Liability Information

(1)   The transferor shall notify to the transferee the employee liability information of any person employed by him who is assigned to the organised grouping of resources or employees that is the subject of a relevant transfer—

(a)   in writing; or

(b)   by making it available to him in a readily accessible form.

(2)   In this regulation and in regulation 12 "employee liability information" means—

(a)   the identity and age of the employee;

(b)   those particulars of employment that an employer is obliged to give to an employee pursuant to section 1 of the 1996 Act;

(c)   information of any—

(i)   disciplinary procedure taken against an employee;

(ii)   grievance procedure taken by an employee,

within the previous two years, in circumstances where [a Code of Practice issued under Part IV of the Trade Union and Labour Relations Act 1992 which relates exclusively or primarily to the resolution of disputes applies];

(d)   information of any court or tribunal case, claim or action—

(i)   brought by an employee against the transferor, within the previous two years;

(ii)   that the transferor has reasonable grounds to believe that an employee may bring against the transferee, arising out of the employee's employment with the transferor; and

(e)   information of any collective agreement which will have effect after the transfer, in its application in relation to the employee, pursuant to regulation 5(a).

(3)   Employee liability information shall contain information as at a specified date not more than fourteen days before the date on which the information is notified to the transferee.

(4)   The duty to provide employee liability information in paragraph (1) shall include a duty to provide employee liability information of any person who would have been employed by the transferor and assigned to the organised grouping of resources or employees that is the subject of a relevant transfer immediately before the transfer if he had not been dismissed in the circumstances described in regulation 7(1), including, where the transfer is effected by a series of two or more transactions, a person so employed and assigned or who would have been so employed and assigned immediately before any of those transactions.

(5)   Following notification of the employee liability information in accordance with this regulation, the transferor shall notify the transferee in writing of any change in the employee liability information.

(6)   A notification under this regulation shall be given not less than fourteen days before the relevant transfer or, if special circumstances make this not reasonably practicable, as soon as reasonably practicable thereafter.

(7)   A notification under this regulation may be given—

(a)   in more than one instalment;

(b)   indirectly, through a third party.

NOTES

Para (2): words in square brackets substituted by the Transfer of Undertakings (Protection of Employment) (Amendment) Regulations 2009, SI 2009/592, reg 2(1), (2), as from 6 April 2009.

[10.946]
12   Remedy for failure to notify employee liability information

(1)   On or after a relevant transfer, the transferee may present a complaint to an employment tribunal that the transferor has failed to comply with any provision of regulation 11.

(2)   An employment tribunal shall not consider a complaint under this regulation unless it is presented—

(a)   before the end of the period of three months beginning with the date of the relevant transfer;

   (b)   within such further period as the tribunal considers reasonable in a case where it is satisfied that it was not reasonably practicable for the complaint to be presented before the end of that period of three months.

(3)   Where an employment tribunal finds a complaint under paragraph (1) well-founded, the tribunal—
   (a)   shall make a declaration to that effect; and
   (b)   may make an award of compensation to be paid by the transferor to the transferee.

(4)   The amount of the compensation shall be such as the tribunal considers just and equitable in all the circumstances, subject to paragraph (5), having particular regard to—
   (a)   any loss sustained by the transferee which is attributable to the matters complained of; and
   (b)   the terms of any contract between the transferor and the transferee relating to the transfer under which the transferor may be liable to pay any sum to the transferee in respect of a failure to notify the transferee of employee liability information.

(5)   Subject to paragraph (6), the amount of compensation awarded under paragraph (3) shall be not less than £500 per employee in respect of whom the transferor has failed to comply with a provision of regulation 11, unless the tribunal considers it just and equitable, in all the circumstances, to award a lesser sum.

(6)   In ascertaining the loss referred to in paragraph (4)(a) the tribunal shall apply the same rule concerning the duty of a person to mitigate his loss as applies to any damages recoverable under the common law of England and Wales, Northern Ireland or Scotland, as applicable.

(7)   Section 18 of the 1996 Tribunals Act (conciliation) shall apply to the right conferred by this regulation and to proceedings under this regulation as it applies to the rights conferred by that Act and the employment tribunal proceedings mentioned in that Act.

[10.947]
13   Duty to inform and consult representatives

(1)   In this regulation and regulations 14 and 15 references to affected employees, in relation to a relevant transfer, are to any employees of the transferor or the transferee (whether or not assigned to the organised grouping of resources or employees that is the subject of a relevant transfer) who may be affected by the transfer or may be affected by measures taken in connection with it; and references to the employer shall be construed accordingly.

(2)   Long enough before a relevant transfer to enable the employer of any affected employees to consult the appropriate representatives of any affected employees, the employer shall inform those representatives of—
   (a)   the fact that the transfer is to take place, the date or proposed date of the transfer and the reasons for it;
   (b)   the legal, economic and social implications of the transfer for any affected employees;
   (c)   the measures which he envisages he will, in connection with the transfer, take in relation to any affected employees or, if he envisages that no measures will be so taken, that fact; and
   (d)   if the employer is the transferor, the measures, in connection with the transfer, which he envisages the transferee will take in relation to any affected employees who will become employees of the transferee after the transfer by virtue of regulation 4 or, if he envisages that no measures will be so taken, that fact.

[(2A)   Where information is to be supplied under paragraph (2) by an employer—
   (a)   this must include suitable information relating to the use of agency workers (if any) by that employer; and
   (b)   "suitable information relating to the use of agency workers" means—
      (i)   the number of agency workers working temporarily for and under the supervision and direction of the employer;
      (ii)   the parts of the employer's undertaking in which those agency workers are working; and
      (iii)   the type of work those agency workers are carrying out.]

(3)   For the purposes of this regulation the appropriate representatives of any affected employees are—
   (a)   if the employees are of a description in respect of which an independent trade union is recognised by their employer, representatives of the trade union; or
   (b)   in any other case, whichever of the following employee representatives the employer chooses—
      (i)   employee representatives appointed or elected by the affected employees otherwise than for the purposes of this regulation, who (having regard to the purposes for, and the method by which they were appointed or elected) have authority from those employees to receive information and to be consulted about the transfer on their behalf;
      (ii)   employee representatives elected by any affected employees, for the purposes of this regulation, in an election satisfying the requirements of regulation 14(1).

(4)   The transferee shall give the transferor such information at such a time as will enable the transferor to perform the duty imposed on him by virtue of paragraph (2)(d).

(5)   The information which is to be given to the appropriate representatives shall be given to each of them by being delivered to them, or sent by post to an address notified by them to the employer, or (in the case of representatives of a trade union) sent by post to the trade union at the address of its head or main office.

(6)   An employer of an affected employee who envisages that he will take measures in relation to an affected employee, in connection with the relevant transfer, shall consult the appropriate representatives of that employee with a view to seeking their agreement to the intended measures.

(7)   In the course of those consultations the employer shall—
(a)   consider any representations made by the appropriate representatives; and
(b)   reply to those representations and, if he rejects any of those representations, state his reasons.

(8)   The employer shall allow the appropriate representatives access to any affected employees and shall afford to those representatives such accommodation and other facilities as may be appropriate.

(9)   If in any case there are special circumstances which render it not reasonably practicable for an employer to perform a duty imposed on him by any of paragraphs (2) to (7), he shall take all such steps towards performing that duty as are reasonably practicable in the circumstances.

(10)   Where—
(a)   the employer has invited any of the affected employee to elect employee representatives; and
(b)   the invitation was issued long enough before the time when the employer is required to give information under paragraph (2) to allow them to elect representatives by that time,
the employer shall be treated as complying with the requirements of this regulation in relation to those employees if he complies with those requirements as soon as is reasonably practicable after the election of the representatives.

(11)   If, after the employer has invited any affected employees to elect representatives, they fail to do so within a reasonable time, he shall give to any affected employees the information set out in paragraph (2).

(12)   The duties imposed on an employer by this regulation shall apply irrespective of whether the decision resulting in the relevant transfer is taken by the employer or a person controlling the employer.

NOTES

Para (2A): inserted by the Agency Workers Regulations 2010, SI 2010/93, reg 25, Sch 2, Pt 2, pars 28, 29, as from 1 October 2011.

[10.948]
14   Election of employee representatives

(1)   The requirements for the election of employee representatives under regulation 13(3) are that—
(a)   the employer shall make such arrangements as are reasonably practicable to ensure that the election is fair;
(b)   the employer shall determine the number of representatives to be elected so that there are sufficient representatives to represent the interests of all affected employees having regard to the number and classes of those employees;
(c)   the employer shall determine whether the affected employees should be represented either by representatives of all the affected employees or by representatives of particular classes of those employees;
(d)   before the election the employer shall determine the term of office as employee representatives so that it is of sufficient length to enable information to be given and consultations under regulation 13 to be completed;
(e)   the candidates for election as employee representatives are affected employees on the date of the election;
(f)   no affected employee is unreasonably excluded from standing for election;
(g)   all affected employees on the date of the election are entitled to vote for employee representatives;
(h)   the employees entitled to vote may vote for as many candidates as there are representatives to be elected to represent them or, if there are to be representatives for particular classes of employees, may vote for as many candidates as there are representatives to be elected to represent their particular class of employee;
(i)   the election is conducted so as to secure that—
(i)   so far as is reasonably practicable, those voting do so in secret; and
(ii)   the votes given at the election are accurately counted.

(2)   Where, after an election of employee representatives satisfying the requirements of paragraph (1) has been held, one of those elected ceases to act as an employee representative and as a result any affected employees are no longer represented, those employees shall elect another representative by an election satisfying the requirements of paragraph (1)(a), (e), (f) and (i).

[10.949]
15 Failure to inform or consult

(1) Where an employer has failed to comply with a requirement of regulation 13 or regulation 14, a complaint may be presented to an employment tribunal on that ground—

    (a) in the case of a failure relating to the election of employee representatives, by any of his employees who are affected employees;

    (b) in the case of any other failure relating to employee representatives, by any of the employee representatives to whom the failure related;

    (c) in the case of failure relating to representatives of a trade union, by the trade union; and

    (d) in any other case, by any of his employees who are affected employees.

(2) If on a complaint under paragraph (1) a question arises whether or not it was reasonably practicable for an employer to perform a particular duty or as to what steps he took towards performing it, it shall be for him to show—

    (a) that there were special circumstances which rendered it not reasonably practicable for him to perform the duty; and

    (b) that he took all such steps towards its performance as were reasonably practicable in those circumstances.

(3) If on a complaint under paragraph (1) a question arises as to whether or not an employee representative was an appropriate representative for the purposes of regulation 13, it shall be for the employer to show that the employee representative had the necessary authority to represent the affected employees.

(4) On a complaint under paragraph (1)(a) it shall be for the employer to show that the requirements in regulation 14 have been satisfied.

(5) On a complaint against a transferor that he had failed to perform the duty imposed upon him by virtue of regulation 13(2)(d) or, so far as relating thereto, regulation 13(9), he may not show that it was not reasonably practicable for him to perform the duty in question for the reason that the transferee had failed to give him the requisite information at the requisite time in accordance with regulation 13(4) unless he gives the transferee notice of his intention to show that fact; and the giving of the notice shall make the transferee a party to the proceedings.

(6) In relation to any complaint under paragraph (1), a failure on the part of a person controlling (directly or indirectly) the employer to provide information to the employer shall not constitute special circumstances rendering it not reasonably practicable for the employer to comply with such a requirement.

(7) Where the tribunal finds a complaint against a transferee under paragraph (1) well-founded it shall make a declaration to that effect and may order the transferee to pay appropriate compensation to such descriptions of affected employees as may be specified in the award.

(8) Where the tribunal finds a complaint against a transferor under paragraph (1) well-founded it shall make a declaration to that effect and may—

    (a) order the transferor, subject to paragraph (9), to pay appropriate compensation to such descriptions of affected employees as may be specified in the award; or

    (b) if the complaint is that the transferor did not perform the duty mentioned in paragraph (5) and the transferor (after giving due notice) shows the facts so mentioned, order the transferee to pay appropriate compensation to such descriptions of affected employees as may be specified in the award.

(9) The transferee shall be jointly and severally liable with the transferor in respect of compensation payable under sub-paragraph (8)(a) or paragraph (11).

(10) An employee may present a complaint to an employment tribunal on the ground that he is an employee of a description to which an order under paragraph (7) or (8) relates and that—

    (a) in respect of an order under paragraph (7), the transferee has failed, wholly or in part, to pay him compensation in pursuance of the order;

    (b) in respect of an order under paragraph (8), the transferor or transferee, as applicable, has failed, wholly or in part, to pay him compensation in pursuance of the order.

(11) Where the tribunal finds a complaint under paragraph (10) well-founded it shall order the transferor or transferee as applicable to pay the complainant the amount of compensation which it finds is due to him.

(12) An employment tribunal shall not consider a complaint under paragraph (1) or (10) unless it is presented to the tribunal before the end of the period of three months beginning with—

    (a) in respect of a complaint under paragraph (1), the date on which the relevant transfer is completed; or

    (b) in respect of a complaint under paragraph (10), the date of the tribunal's order under paragraph (7) or (8),

or within such further period as the tribunal considers reasonable in a case where it is satisfied that it was not reasonably practicable for the complaint to be presented before the end of the period of three months.

Part 10 Miscellaneous other SIs

[10.950]

16   Failure to inform or consult: supplemental

(1)   Section 205(1) of the 1996 Act (complaint to be sole remedy for breach of relevant rights) and section 18 of the 1996 Tribunals Act (conciliation) shall apply to the rights conferred by regulation 15 and to proceedings under this regulation as they apply to the rights conferred by those Acts and the employment tribunal proceedings mentioned in those Acts.

(2)   An appeal shall lie and shall lie only to the Employment Appeal Tribunal on a question of law arising from any decision of, or arising in any proceedings before, an employment tribunal under or by virtue of these Regulations; and section 11(1) of the Tribunals and Inquiries Act 1992 (appeals from certain tribunals to the High Court) shall not apply in relation to any such proceedings.

(3)   "Appropriate compensation" in regulation 15 means such sum not exceeding thirteen weeks' pay for the employee in question as the tribunal considers just and equitable having regard to the seriousness of the failure of the employer to comply with his duty.

(4)   Sections 220 to 228 of the 1996 Act shall apply for calculating the amount of a week's pay for any employee for the purposes of paragraph (3) and, for the purposes of that calculation, the calculation date shall be—

(a)   in the case of an employee who is dismissed by reason of redundancy (within the meaning of sections 139 and 155 of the 1996 Act) the date which is the calculation date for the purposes of any entitlement of his to a redundancy payment (within the meaning of those sections) or which would be that calculation date if he were so entitled;

(b)   in the case of an employee who is dismissed for any other reason, the effective date of termination (within the meaning of sections 95(1) and (2) and 97 of the 1996 Act) of his contract of employment;

(c)   in any other case, the date of the relevant transfer.

[10.951]

17   Employers' Liability Compulsory Insurance

(1)   Paragraph (2) applies where—

(a)   by virtue of section 3(1)(a) or (b) of the Employers' Liability (Compulsory Insurance) Act 1969 ("the 1969 Act"), the transferor is not required by that Act to effect any insurance; or

(b)   by virtue of section 3(1)(c) of the 1969 Act, the transferor is exempted from the requirement of that Act to effect insurance.

(2)   Where this paragraph applies, on completion of a relevant transfer the transferor and the transferee shall be jointly and severally liable in respect of any liability referred to in section 1(1) of the 1969 Act, in so far as such liability relates to the employee's employment with the transferor.

[10.952]

18   Restriction on contracting out

Section 203 of the 1996 Act (restrictions on contracting out) shall apply in relation to these Regulations as if they were contained in that Act, save for that section shall not apply in so far as these Regulations provide for an agreement (whether a contract of employment or not) to exclude or limit the operation of these Regulations.

19   (*Amends the Employment Rights Act 1996, s 104.*)

[10.953]

20   Repeals, revocations and amendments

(1)   Subject to regulation 21, the 1981 Regulations are revoked.

(2)   Section 33 of, and paragraph 4 of Schedule 9 to, the Trade Union Reform and Employment Rights Act 1993 are repealed.

(3)   Schedule 2 (consequential amendments) shall have effect.

[10.954]

21   Transitional provisions and savings

(1)   These Regulations shall apply in relation to—

(a)   a relevant transfer that takes place on or after 6 April 2006;

(b)   a transfer or service provision change, not falling within sub-paragraph (a), that takes place on or after 6 April 2006 and is regarded by virtue of any enactment as a relevant transfer.

(2)   The 1981 Regulations shall continue to apply in relation to—

(a)   a relevant transfer (within the meaning of the 1981 Regulations) that took place before 6 April 2006;

(b)   a transfer, not falling within sub-paragraph (a), that took place before 6 April 2006 and is regarded by virtue of any enactment as a relevant transfer (within the meaning of the 1981 Regulations).

(3)   In respect of a relevant transfer that takes place on or after 6 April 2006, any action taken by a transferor or transferee to discharge a duty that applied to them under regulation 10 or 10A of the 1981 Regulations shall be deemed to satisfy the corresponding obligation imposed by regulations 13 and 14 of these Regulations, insofar as that action would have discharged those obligations had the action taken place on or after 6 April 2006.

(4)   The duty on a transferor to provide a transferee with employee liability information shall not apply in the case of a relevant transfer that takes place on or before 19 April 2006.

(5)   Regulations 13, 14, 15 and 16 shall not apply in the case of a service provision change that is not also a transfer of an undertaking, business or part of an undertaking or business that takes place on or before 4 May 2006.

(6)   The repeal of paragraph 4 of Schedule 9 to the Trade Union Reform and Employment Rights Act 1993 does not affect the continued operation of that paragraph so far as it remains capable of having effect.

SCHEDULES 1 AND 2

(Sch 1 (Application of the Regulations to Northern Ireland), Sch 2 (Consequential Amendments) outside the scope of this work.)

CROSS-BORDER INSOLVENCY REGULATIONS 2006

(SI 2006/1030)

NOTES
   Made: 3 April 2006.
   Authority: Insolvency Act 2000, s 14.
   Commencement: 4 April 2006.
   These Regulations are reproduced as amended by: the Third Parties (Rights against Insurers) Act 2010; the Companies Act 2006 (Consequential Amendments, Transitional Provisions and Savings) Order 2009, SI 2009/1941.

ARRANGEMENT OF REGULATIONS

[10.955]
1   Citation, commencement and interpretation

(1)   These Regulations may be cited as the Cross-Border Insolvency Regulations 2006 and shall come into force on the day after the day on which they are made.

(2)   In these Regulations "the UNCITRAL Model Law" means the Model Law on cross-border insolvency as adopted by the United Nations Commission on International Trade Law on 30th May 1997.

[(3)   In these Regulations "overseas company" has the meaning given by section 1044 of the Companies Act 2006 and "establishment", in relation to such a company, has the same meaning as in the Overseas Companies Regulations 2009.]

NOTES
  Para (3): added by the Companies Act 2006 (Consequential Amendments, Transitional Provisions and Savings) Order 2009, SI 2009/1941, art 2(1), Sch 1, para 264(1), (2), as from 1 October 2009.

[10.956]
2   UNCITRAL Model Law to have force of law

(1)   The UNCITRAL Model Law shall have the force of law in Great Britain in the form set out in Schedule 1 to these Regulations (which contains the UNCITRAL Model Law with certain modifications to adapt it for application in Great Britain).

(2)   Without prejudice to any practice of the courts as to the matters which may be considered apart from this paragraph, the following documents may be considered in ascertaining the meaning or effect of any provision of the UNCITRAL Model Law as set out in Schedule 1 to these Regulations—
  (a)   the UNCITRAL Model Law;
  (b)   any documents of the United Nations Commission on International Trade Law and its working group relating to the preparation of the UNCITRAL Model Law; and
  (c)   the Guide to Enactment of the UNCITRAL Model Law (UNCITRAL document A/CN 9/442) prepared at the request of the United Nations Commission on International Trade Law made in May 1997.

[10.957]
3   Modification of British insolvency law

(1)   British insolvency law (as defined in article 2 of the UNCITRAL Model Law as set out in Schedule 1 to these Regulations) and Part 3 of the Insolvency Act 1986 shall apply with such modifications as the context requires for the purpose of giving effect to the provisions of these Regulations.

(2)   In the case of any conflict between any provision of British insolvency law or of Part 3 of the Insolvency Act 1986 and the provisions of these Regulations, the latter shall prevail.

[10.958]
4   Procedural matters in England and Wales

Schedule 2 to these Regulations (which makes provision about procedural matters in England and Wales in connection with the application of the UNCITRAL Model Law as set out in Schedule 1 to these Regulations) shall have effect.

[10.959]
5   Procedural matters in Scotland

Schedule 3 to these Regulations (which makes provision about procedural matters in Scotland in connection with the application of the UNCITRAL Model Law as set out in Schedule 1 to these Regulations) shall have effect.

[10.960]
6   Notices delivered to the registrar of companies

Schedule 4 to these Regulations (which makes provision about notices delivered to the registrar of companies under these Regulations) shall have effect.

[10.961]
7   Co-operation between courts exercising jurisdiction in relation to cross-border insolvency

(1)   An order made by a court in either part of Great Britain in the exercise of jurisdiction in relation to the subject matter of these Regulations shall be enforced in the other part of Great Britain as if it were made by a court exercising the corresponding jurisdiction in that other part.

(2)   However, nothing in paragraph (1) requires a court in either part of Great Britain to enforce, in relation to property situated in that part, any order made by a court in the other part of Great Britain.

(3) The courts having jurisdiction in relation to the subject matter of these Regulations in either part of Great Britain shall assist the courts having the corresponding jurisdiction in the other part of Great Britain.

[10.962]
8 Disapplication of section 388 of the Insolvency Act 1986

Nothing in section 388 of the Insolvency Act 1986 applies to anything done by a foreign representative—
- (a) under or by virtue of these Regulations;
- (b) in relation to relief granted or cooperation or coordination provided under these Regulations.

SCHEDULES

SCHEDULE 1
UNCITRAL MODEL LAW ON CROSS-BORDER INSOLVENCY
Regulation 2(1)

CHAPTER I
GENERAL PROVISIONS

Article 1
Scope of Application

[10.963]
1. This Law applies where—
- (a) assistance is sought in Great Britain by a foreign court or a foreign representative in connection with a foreign proceeding; or
- (b) assistance is sought in a foreign State in connection with a proceeding under British insolvency law; or
- (c) a foreign proceeding and a proceeding under British insolvency law in respect of the same debtor are taking place concurrently; or
- (d) creditors or other interested persons in a foreign State have an interest in requesting the commencement of, or participating in, a proceeding under British insolvency law.

2. This Law does not apply to a proceeding concerning—
- (a) a company holding an appointment under Chapter 1 of Part 2 of the Water Industry Act 1991 (water and sewage undertakers) or a qualifying licensed water supplier within the meaning of section 23(6) of that Act (meaning and effect of special administration order);
- (b) Scottish Water established under section 20 of the Water Industry (Scotland) Act 2002 (Scottish Water);
- (c) a protected railway company within the meaning of section 59 of the Railways Act 1993 (railway administration order) (including that section as it has effect by virtue of section 19 of the Channel Tunnel Rail Link Act 1996 (administration));
- (d) a licence company within the meaning of section 26 of the Transport Act 2000 (air traffic services);
- (e) a public private partnership company within the meaning of section 210 of the Greater London Authority Act 1999 (public-private partnership agreement);
- (f) a protected energy company within the meaning of section 154(5) of the Energy Act 2004 (energy administration orders);
- (g) a building society within the meaning of section 119 of the Building Societies Act 1986 (interpretation);
- (h) a UK credit institution or an EEA credit institution or any branch of either such institution as those expressions are defined by regulation 2 of the Credit Institutions (Reorganisation and Winding Up) Regulations 2004 (interpretation);
- (i) a third country credit institution within the meaning of regulation 36 of the Credit Institutions (Reorganisation and Winding Up) Regulations 2004 (interpretation of this Part);
- (j) a person who has permission under or by virtue of Parts 4 or 19 of the Financial Services and Markets Act 2000 to effect or carry out contracts of insurance;
- (k) an EEA insurer within the meaning of regulation 2 of the Insurers (Reorganisation and Winding Up) Regulations 2004 (interpretation);
- (l) a person (other than one included in paragraph 2(j)) pursuing the activity of reinsurance who has received authorisation for that activity from a competent authority within an EEA State; or
- (m) any of the Concessionaires within the meaning of section 1 of the Channel Tunnel Act 1987.

3. In paragraph 2 of this article—

Part 10   Miscellaneous other SIs

(a) in sub-paragraph (j) the reference to "contracts of insurance" must be construed in accordance with—
(i) section 22 of the Financial Services and Markets Act 2000 (classes of regulated activity and categories of investment);
(ii) any relevant order under that section; and
(iii) Schedule 2 to that Act (regulated activities);
(b) in sub-paragraph (1) "EEA State" means a State, other than the United Kingdom, which is a contracting party to the agreement on the European Economic Area signed at Oporto on 2 May 1992.

4. The court shall not grant any relief, or modify any relief already granted, or provide any co-operation or coordination, under or by virtue of any of the provisions of this Law if and to the extent that such relief or modified relief or cooperation or coordination would—
(a) be prohibited under or by virtue of—
(i) Part 7 of the Companies Act 1989;
(ii) Part 3 of the Financial Markets and Insolvency (Settlement Finality) Regulations 1999; or
(iii) Part 3 of the Financial Collateral Arrangements (No 2) Regulations 2003;
in the case of a proceeding under British insolvency law; or
(b) interfere with or be inconsistent with any rights of a collateral taker under Part 4 of the Financial Collateral Arrangements (No 2) Regulations 2003 which could be exercised in the case of such a proceeding.

5. Where a foreign proceeding regarding a debtor who is an insured in accordance with the provisions of the *Third Parties (Rights against Insurers) Act 1930* is recognised under this Law, any stay and suspension referred to in article 20(1) and any relief granted by the court under article 19 or 21 shall not apply to or affect—
(a) any transfer of rights of the debtor under that Act; or
(b) any claim, action, cause or proceeding by a third party against an insurer under or in respect of rights of the debtor transferred under that Act.

6. Any suspension under this Law of the right to transfer, encumber or otherwise dispose of any of the debtor's assets—
(a) is subject to section 26 of the Land Registration Act 2002 where owner's powers are exercised in relation to a registered estate or registered charge;
(b) is subject to section 52 of the Land Registration Act 2002, where the powers referred to in that section are exercised by the proprietor of a registered charge; and
(c) in any other case, shall not bind a purchaser of a legal estate in good faith for money or money's worth unless the purchaser has express notice of the suspension.

7. In paragraph 6—
(a) "owner's powers" means the powers described in section 23 of the Land Registration Act 2002 and "registered charge" and "registered estate" have the same meaning as in section 132(1) of that Act; and
(b) "legal estate" and "purchaser" have the same meaning as in section 17 of the Land Charges Act 1972.

Article 2
Definitions

For the purposes of this Law—
(a) "British insolvency law" means—
(i) in relation to England and Wales, provision extending to England and Wales and made by or under the Insolvency Act 1986 (with the exception of Part 3 of that Act) or by or under that Act as extended or applied by or under any other enactment (excluding these Regulations); and
(ii) in relation to Scotland, provision extending to Scotland and made by or under the Insolvency Act 1986 (with the exception of Part 3 of that Act), the Bankruptcy (Scotland) Act 1985 or by or under those Acts as extended or applied by or under any other enactment (excluding these Regulations);
(b) "British insolvency officeholder" means—
(i) the official receiver within the meaning of section 399 of the Insolvency Act 1986 when acting as liquidator, provisional liquidator, trustee, interim receiver or nominee or supervisor of a voluntary arrangement;
(ii) a person acting as an insolvency practitioner within the meaning of section 388 of that Act but shall not include a person acting as an administrative receiver; and
(iii) the Accountant in Bankruptcy within the meaning of section 1 of the Bankruptcy (Scotland) Act 1985 when acting as interim or permanent trustee;

(c)   "the court" except as otherwise provided in articles 14(4) and 23(6)(b), means in relation to any matter the court which in accordance with the provisions of article 4 of this Law has jurisdiction in relation to that matter;

(d)   "the EC Insolvency Regulation" means Council Regulation (EC) No 1346/2000 of 29 May 2000 on Insolvency Proceedings;

(e)   "establishment" means any place of operations where the debtor carries out a non-transitory economic activity with human means and assets or services;

(f)   "foreign court" means a judicial or other authority competent to control or supervise a foreign proceeding;

(g)   "foreign main proceeding" means a foreign proceeding taking place in the State where the debtor has the centre of its main interests;

(h)   "foreign non-main proceeding" means a foreign proceeding, other than a foreign main proceeding, taking place in a State where the debtor has an establishment within the meaning of sub-paragraph (e) of this article;

(i)   "foreign proceeding" means a collective judicial or administrative proceeding in a foreign State, including an interim proceeding, pursuant to a law relating to insolvency in which proceeding the assets and affairs of the debtor are subject to control or supervision by a foreign court, for the purpose of reorganisation or liquidation;

(j)   "foreign representative" means a person or body, including one appointed on an interim basis, authorised in a foreign proceeding to administer the reorganisation or the liquidation of the debtor's assets or affairs or to act as a representative of the foreign proceeding;

(k)   "hire-purchase agreement" includes a conditional sale agreement, a chattel leasing agreement and a retention of title agreement;

(l)   "section 426 request" means a request for assistance in accordance with section 426 of the Insolvency Act 1986 made to a court in any part of the United Kingdom;

(m)   "secured creditor" in relation to a debtor, means a creditor of the debtor who holds in respect of his debt a security over property of the debtor;

(n)   "security" means—
      (i)   in relation to England and Wales, any mortgage, charge, lien or other security; and
      (ii)   in relation to Scotland, any security (whether heritable or moveable), any floating charge and any right of lien or preference and any right of retention (other than a right of compensation or set off);

(o)   in the application of Articles 20 and 23 to Scotland, "an individual" means any debtor within the meaning of the Bankruptcy (Scotland) Act 1985;

(p)   in the application of this Law to Scotland, references howsoever expressed to—
      (i)   "filing" an application or claim are to be construed as references to lodging an application or submitting a claim respectively;
      (ii)   "relief" and "standing" are to be construed as references to "remedy" and "title and interest" respectively; and
      (iii)   a "stay" are to be construed as references to restraint, except in relation to continuation of actions or proceedings when they shall be construed as a reference to sist; and

(q)   references to the law of Great Britain include a reference to the law of either part of Great Britain (including its rules of private international law).

Article 3
International Obligations of Great Britain Under the EC Insolvency Regulation

To the extent that this Law conflicts with an obligation of the United Kingdom under the EC Insolvency Regulation, the requirements of the EC Insolvency Regulation prevail.

Article 4
Competent Court

1. The functions referred to in this Law relating to recognition of foreign proceedings and cooperation with foreign courts shall be performed by the High Court and assigned to the Chancery Division, as regards England and Wales and the Court of Session as regards Scotland.

2. Subject to paragraph 1 of this article, the court in either part of Great Britain shall have jurisdiction in relation to the functions referred to in that paragraph if—
   (a)   the debtor has—
      (i)   a place of business; or
      (ii)   in the case of an individual, a place of residence; or
      (iii)   assets,
      situated in that part of Great Britain; or
   (b)   the court in that part of Great Britain considers for any other reason that it is the appropriate forum to consider the question or provide the assistance requested.

Part 10   Miscellaneous other SIs

3. In considering whether it is the appropriate forum to hear an application for recognition of a foreign proceeding in relation to a debtor, the court shall take into account the location of any court in which a proceeding under British insolvency law is taking place in relation to the debtor and the likely location of any future proceedings under British insolvency law in relation to the debtor.

Article 5
Authorisation of British Insolvency Officeholders to Act in a Foreign State

A British insolvency officeholder is authorised to act in a foreign State on behalf of a proceeding under British insolvency law, as permitted by the applicable foreign law.

Article 6
Public Policy Exception

Nothing in this Law prevents the court from refusing to take an action governed by this Law if the action would be manifestly contrary to the public policy of Great Britain or any part of it.

Article 7
Additional Assistance under other Laws

Nothing in this Law limits the power of a court or a British insolvency officeholder to provide additional assistance to a foreign representative under other laws of Great Britain.

Article 8
Interpretation

In the interpretation of this Law, regard is to be had to its international origin and to the need to promote uniformity in its application and the observance of good faith.

CHAPTER II
ACCESS OF FOREIGN REPRESENTATIVES AND CREDITORS TO COURTS IN GREAT BRITAIN

Article 9
Right of Direct Access

A foreign representative is entitled to apply directly to a court in Great Britain.

Article 10
Limited Jurisdiction

The sole fact that an application pursuant to this Law is made to a court in Great Britain by a foreign representative does not subject the foreign representative or the foreign assets and affairs of the debtor to the jurisdiction of the courts of Great Britain or any part of it for any purpose other than the application.

Article 11
Application by a Foreign Representative to Commence a Proceeding under British Insolvency Law

A foreign representative appointed in a foreign main proceeding or foreign non-main proceeding is entitled to apply to commence a proceeding under British insolvency law if the conditions for commencing such a proceeding are otherwise met.

Article 12
Participation of a Foreign Representative in a Proceeding under British Insolvency Law

Upon recognition of a foreign proceeding, the foreign representative is entitled to participate in a proceeding regarding the debtor under British insolvency law.

Article 13
Access of Foreign Creditors to a Proceeding under British Insolvency Law

1. Subject to paragraph 2 of this article, foreign creditors have the same rights regarding the commencement of, and participation in, a proceeding under British insolvency law as creditors in Great Britain.

2. Paragraph 1 of this article does not affect the ranking of claims in a proceeding under British insolvency law, except that the claim of a foreign creditor shall not be given a lower priority than that of general unsecured claims solely because the holder of such a claim is a foreign creditor.

3. A claim may not be challenged solely on the grounds that it is a claim by a foreign tax or social security authority but such a claim may be challenged—
   (a) on the ground that it is in whole or in part a penalty, or
   (b) on any other ground that a claim might be rejected in a proceeding under British insolvency law.

Article 14
Notification to Foreign Creditors of a Proceeding under British Insolvency Law

1. Whenever under British insolvency law notification is to be given to creditors in Great Britain, such notification shall also be given to the known creditors that do not have addresses in Great Britain. The court may order that appropriate steps be taken with a view to notifying any creditor whose address is not yet known.

2. Such notification shall be made to the foreign creditors individually, unless—
   (a) the court considers that under the circumstances some other form of notification would be more appropriate; or
   (b) the notification to creditors in Great Britain is to be by advertisement only, in which case the notification to the known foreign creditors may be by advertisement in such foreign newspapers as the British insolvency officeholder considers most appropriate for ensuring that the content of the notification comes to the notice of the known foreign creditors.

3. When notification of a right to file a claim is to be given to foreign creditors, the notification shall—
   (a) indicate a reasonable time period for filing claims and specify the place for their filing;
   (b) indicate whether secured creditors need to file their secured claims; and
   (c) contain any other information required to be included in such a notification to creditors pursuant to the law of Great Britain and the orders of the court.

4. In this article "the court" means the court which has jurisdiction in relation to the particular proceeding under British insolvency law under which notification is to be given to creditors.

CHAPTER III
RECOGNITION OF A FOREIGN PROCEEDING AND RELIEF

Article 15
Application for Recognition of a Foreign Proceeding

1. A foreign representative may apply to the court for recognition of the foreign proceeding in which the foreign representative has been appointed.

2. An application for recognition shall be accompanied by—
   (a) a certified copy of the decision commencing the foreign proceeding and appointing the foreign representative; or
   (b) a certificate from the foreign court affirming the existence of the foreign proceeding and of the appointment of the foreign representative; or
   (c) in the absence of evidence referred to in sub-paragraphs (a) and (b), any other evidence acceptable to the court of the existence of the foreign proceeding and of the appointment of the foreign representative.

3. An application for recognition shall also be accompanied by a statement identifying all foreign proceedings, proceedings under British insolvency law and section 426 requests in respect of the debtor that are known to the foreign representative.

4. The foreign representative shall provide the court with a translation into English of documents supplied in support of the application for recognition.

Article 16
Presumptions Concerning Recognition

1. If the decision or certificate referred to in paragraph 2 of article 15 indicates that the foreign proceeding is a proceeding within the meaning of sub-paragraph (i) of article 2 and that the foreign representative is a person or body within the meaning of sub-paragraph (j) of article 2, the court is entitled to so presume.

2. The court is entitled to presume that documents submitted in support of the application for recognition are authentic, whether or not they have been legalised.

3. In the absence of proof to the contrary, the debtor's registered office, or habitual residence in the case of an individual, is presumed to be the centre of the debtor's main interests.

Article 17
Decision to Recognise a Foreign Proceeding

1. Subject to article 6, a foreign proceeding shall be recognised if—
   (a)   it is a foreign proceeding within the meaning of sub-paragraph (i) of article 2;
   (b)   the foreign representative applying for recognition is a person or body within the meaning of sub-paragraph (j) of article 2;
   (c)   the application meets the requirements of paragraphs 2 and 3 of article 15; and
   (d)   the application has been submitted to the court referred to in article 4.

2. The foreign proceeding shall be recognised—
   (a)   as a foreign main proceeding if it is taking place in the State where the debtor has the centre of its main interests; or
   (b)   as a foreign non-main proceeding if the debtor has an establishment within the meaning of sub-paragraph (e) of article 2 in the foreign State.

3. An application for recognition of a foreign proceeding shall be decided upon at the earliest possible time.

4. The provisions of articles 15 to 16, this article and article 18 do not prevent modification or termination of recognition if it is shown that the grounds for granting it were fully or partially lacking or have fully or partially ceased to exist and in such a case, the court may, on the application of the foreign representative or a person affected by recognition, or of its own motion, modify or terminate recognition, either altogether or for a limited time, on such terms and conditions as the court thinks fit.

Article 18
Subsequent Information

From the time of filing the application for recognition of the foreign proceeding, the foreign representative shall inform the court promptly of—
   (a)   any substantial change in the status of the recognised foreign proceeding or the status of the foreign representative's appointment; and
   (b)   any other foreign proceeding, proceeding under British insolvency law or section 426 request regarding the same debtor that becomes known to the foreign representative.

Article 19
Relief that may be Granted upon Application for Recognition of a Foreign Proceeding

1. From the time of filing an application for recognition until the application is decided upon, the court may, at the request of the foreign representative, where relief is urgently needed to protect the assets of the debtor or the interests of the creditors, grant relief of a provisional nature, including—
   (a)   staying execution against the debtor's assets;
   (b)   entrusting the administration or realisation of all or part of the debtor's assets located in Great Britain to the foreign representative or another person designated by the court, in order to protect and preserve the value of assets that, by their nature or because of other circumstances, are perishable, susceptible to devaluation or otherwise in jeopardy; and
   (c)   any relief mentioned in paragraph 1 (c), (d) or (g) of article 21.

2. Unless extended under paragraph 1(f) of article 21, the relief granted under this article terminates when the application for recognition is decided upon.

3. The court may refuse to grant relief under this article if such relief would interfere with the administration of a foreign main proceeding.

Article 20
Effects of Recognition of a Foreign Main Proceeding

1. Upon recognition of a foreign proceeding that is a foreign main proceeding, subject to paragraph 2 of this article—

    (a)   commencement or continuation of individual actions or individual proceedings concerning the debtor's assets, rights, obligations or liabilities is stayed;

    (b)   execution against the debtor's assets is stayed; and

    (c)   the right to transfer, encumber or otherwise dispose of any assets of the debtor is suspended.

2. The stay and suspension referred to in paragraph 1 of this article shall be—

    (a)   the same in scope and effect as if the debtor, in the case of an individual, had been adjudged bankrupt under the Insolvency Act 1986 or had his estate sequestrated under the Bankruptcy (Scotland) Act 1985, or, in the case of a debtor other than an individual, had been made the subject of a winding-up order under the Insolvency Act 1986; and

    (b)   subject to the same powers of the court and the same prohibitions, limitations, exceptions and conditions as would apply under the law of Great Britain in such a case,

and the provisions of paragraph 1 of this article shall be interpreted accordingly.

3. Without prejudice to paragraph 2 of this article, the stay and suspension referred to in paragraph 1 of this article, in particular, does not affect any right—

    (a)   to take any steps to enforce security over the debtor's property;

    (b)   to take any steps to repossess goods in the debtor's possession under a hire-purchase agreement;

    (c)   exercisable under or by virtue of or in connection with the provisions referred to in article 1(4); or

    (d)   of a creditor to set off its claim against a claim of the debtor,

being a right which would have been exercisable if the debtor, in the case of an individual, had been adjudged bankrupt under the Insolvency Act 1986 or had his estate sequestrated under the Bankruptcy (Scotland) Act 1985, or, in the case of a debtor other than an individual, had been made the subject of a winding-up order under the Insolvency Act 1986.

4. Paragraph 1(a) of this article does not affect the right to—

    (a)   commence individual actions or proceedings to the extent necessary to preserve a claim against the debtor; or

    (b)   commence or continue any criminal proceedings or any action or proceedings by a person or body having regulatory, supervisory or investigative functions of a public nature, being an action or proceedings brought in the exercise of those functions.

5. Paragraph 1 of this article does not affect the right to request or otherwise initiate the commencement of a proceeding under British insolvency law or the right to file claims in such a proceeding.

6. In addition to and without prejudice to any powers of the court under or by virtue of paragraph 2 of this article, the court may, on the application of the foreign representative or a person affected by the stay and suspension referred to in paragraph 1 of this article, or of its own motion, modify or terminate such stay and suspension or any part of it, either altogether or for a limited time, on such terms and conditions as the court thinks fit.

Article 21
Relief that may be Granted upon Recognition of a Foreign Proceeding

1. Upon recognition of a foreign proceeding, whether main or non-main, where necessary to protect the assets of the debtor or the interests of the creditors, the court may, at the request of the foreign representative, grant any appropriate relief, including—

    (a)   staying the commencement or continuation of individual actions or individual proceedings concerning the debtor's assets, rights, obligations or liabilities, to the extent they have not been stayed under paragraph 1(a) of article 20;

    (b)   staying execution against the debtor's assets to the extent it has not been stayed under paragraph 1(b) of article 20;

    (c)   suspending the right to transfer, encumber or otherwise dispose of any assets of the debtor to the extent this right has not been suspended under paragraph 1(c) of article 20;

    (d)   providing for the examination of witnesses, the taking of evidence or the delivery of information concerning the debtor's assets, affairs, rights, obligations or liabilities;

    (e)   entrusting the administration or realisation of all or part of the debtor's assets located in Great Britain to the foreign representative or another person designated by the court;

    (f)   extending relief granted under paragraph 1 of article 19; and

Part 10   Miscellaneous other SIs

(g)   granting any additional relief that may be available to a British insolvency officeholder under the law of Great Britain, including any relief provided under paragraph 43 of Schedule B1 to the Insolvency Act 1986.

2. Upon recognition of a foreign proceeding, whether main or non-main, the court may, at the request of the foreign representative, entrust the distribution of all or part of the debtor's assets located in Great Britain to the foreign representative or another person designated by the court, provided that the court is satisfied that the interests of creditors in Great Britain are adequately protected.

3. In granting relief under this article to a representative of a foreign non-main proceeding, the court must be satisfied that the relief relates to assets that, under the law of Great Britain, should be administered in the foreign non-main proceeding or concerns information required in that proceeding.

4. No stay under paragraph 1(a) of this article shall affect the right to commence or continue any criminal proceedings or any action or proceedings by a person or body having regulatory, supervisory or investigative functions of a public nature, being an action or proceedings brought in the exercise of those functions.

Article 22
Protection of Creditors and other Interested Persons

1. In granting or denying relief under article 19 or 21, or in modifying or terminating relief under paragraph 3 of this article or paragraph 6 of article 20, the court must be satisfied that the interests of the creditors (including any secured creditors or parties to hire-purchase agreements) and other interested persons, including if appropriate the debtor, are adequately protected.

2. The court may subject relief granted under article 19 or 21 to conditions it considers appropriate, including the provision by the foreign representative of security or caution for the proper performance of his functions.

3. The court may, at the request of the foreign representative or a person affected by relief granted under article 19 or 21, or of its own motion, modify or terminate such relief.

Article 23
Actions to Avoid Acts Detrimental to Creditors

1. Subject to paragraphs 6 and 9 of this article, upon recognition of a foreign proceeding, the foreign representative has standing to make an application to the court for an order under or in connection with sections 238, 239, 242, 243, 244, 245, 339, 340, 342A, 343, and 423 of the Insolvency Act 1986 and sections 34, 35, 36, 36A and 61 of the Bankruptcy (Scotland) Act 1985.

2. Where the foreign representative makes such an application ("an article 23 application"), the sections referred to in paragraph 1 of this article and sections 240, 241, 341, 342, 342B to 342F, 424 and 425 of the Insolvency Act 1986 and sections 36B and 36C of the Bankruptcy (Scotland) Act 1985 shall apply—
(a)   whether or not the debtor, in the case of an individual, has been adjudged bankrupt or had his estate sequestrated, or, in the case of a debtor other than an individual, is being wound up or is in administration, under British insolvency law; and
(b)   with the modifications set out in paragraph 3 of this article.

3. The modifications referred to in paragraph 2 of this article are as follows—
(a)   for the purposes of sections 241(2A)(a) and 342(2A)(a) of the Insolvency Act 1986, a person has notice of the relevant proceedings if he has notice of the opening of the relevant foreign proceeding;
(b)   for the purposes of sections 240(1) and 245(3) of that Act, the onset of insolvency shall be the date of the opening of the relevant foreign proceeding;
(c)   the periods referred to in sections 244(2), 341(1)(a) to (c) and 343(2) of that Act shall be periods ending with the date of the opening of the relevant foreign proceeding;
(d)   for the purposes of sections 242(3)(a), (3)(b) and 243(1) of that Act, the date on which the winding up of the company commences or it enters administration shall be the date of the opening of the relevant foreign proceeding; and
(e)   for the purposes of sections 34(3)(a), (3)(b), 35(1)(c), 36(1)(a) and (1)(b) and 61(2) of the Bankruptcy (Scotland) Act 1985, the date of sequestration or granting of the trust deed shall be the date of the opening of the relevant foreign proceeding.

4. For the purposes of paragraph 3 of this article, the date of the opening of the foreign proceeding shall be determined in accordance with the law of the State in which the foreign proceeding is taking place, including any rule of law by virtue of which the foreign proceeding is deemed to have opened at an earlier time.

5. When the foreign proceeding is a foreign non-main proceeding, the court must be satisfied that the article 23 application relates to assets that, under the law of Great Britain, should be administered in the foreign non-main proceeding.

6. At any time when a proceeding under British insolvency law is taking place regarding the debtor—

    (a)   the foreign representative shall not make an article 23 application except with the permission of—

        (i)   in the case of a proceeding under British insolvency law taking place in England and Wales, the High Court; or

        (ii)   in the case of a proceeding under British insolvency law taking place in Scotland, the Court of Session; and

    (b)   references to "the court" in paragraphs 1, 5 and 7 of this article are references to the court in which that proceeding is taking place.

7. On making an order on an article 23 application, the court may give such directions regarding the distribution of any proceeds of the claim by the foreign representative, as it thinks fit to ensure that the interests of creditors in Great Britain are adequately protected.

8. Nothing in this article affects the right of a British insolvency officeholder to make an application under or in connection with any of the provisions referred to in paragraph 1 of this article.

9. Nothing in paragraph 1 of this article shall apply in respect of any preference given, floating charge created, alienation, assignment or relevant contributions (within the meaning of section 342A(5) of the Insolvency Act 1986) made or other transaction entered into before the date on which this Law comes into force.

Article 24
Intervention by a Foreign Representative in Proceedings in Great Britain

Upon recognition of a foreign proceeding, the foreign representative may, provided the requirements of the law of Great Britain are met, intervene in any proceedings in which the debtor is a party.

CHAPTER IV
COOPERATION WITH FOREIGN COURTS AND FOREIGN REPRESENTATIVES

Article 25
Cooperation and Direct Communication between a Court of Great Britain and Foreign Courts or Foreign Representatives

1. In matters referred to in paragraph 1 of article 1, the court may cooperate to the maximum extent possible with foreign courts or foreign representatives, either directly or through a British insolvency officeholder.

2. The court is entitled to communicate directly with, or to request information or assistance directly from, foreign courts or foreign representatives.

Article 26
Cooperation and Direct Communication between the British Insolvency Officeholder and Foreign Courts or Foreign Representatives

1. In matters referred to in paragraph 1 of article 1, a British insolvency officeholder shall to the extent consistent with his other duties under the law of Great Britain, in the exercise of his functions and subject to the supervision of the court, cooperate to the maximum extent possible with foreign courts or foreign representatives.

2. The British insolvency officeholder is entitled, in the exercise of his functions and subject to the supervision of the court, to communicate directly with foreign courts or foreign representatives.

Article 27
Forms of Cooperation

Cooperation referred to in articles 25 and 26 may be implemented by any appropriate means, including—

    (a)   appointment of a person to act at the direction of the court;

    (b)   communication of information by any means considered appropriate by the court;

    (c)   coordination of the administration and supervision of the debtor's assets and affairs;

(d)   approval or implementation by courts of agreements concerning the coordination of proceedings;

(e)   coordination of concurrent proceedings regarding the same debtor.

CHAPTER V
CONCURRENT PROCEEDINGS

Article 28
Commencement of a Proceeding Under British Insolvency Law after Recognition of a Foreign Main Proceeding

After recognition of a foreign main proceeding, the effects of a proceeding under British insolvency law in relation to the same debtor shall, insofar as the assets of that debtor are concerned, be restricted to assets that are located in Great Britain and, to the extent necessary to implement cooperation and coordination under articles 25, 26 and 27, to other assets of the debtor that, under the law of Great Britain, should be administered in that proceeding.

Article 29
Coordination of a Proceeding Under British Insolvency Law and a Foreign Proceeding

Where a foreign proceeding and a proceeding under British insolvency law are taking place concurrently regarding the same debtor, the court may seek cooperation and coordination under articles 25, 26 and 27, and the following shall apply—

(a)   when the proceeding in Great Britain is taking place at the time the application for recognition of the foreign proceeding is filed—

    (i)   any relief granted under article 19 or 21 must be consistent with the proceeding in Great Britain; and

    (ii)   if the foreign proceeding is recognised in Great Britain as a foreign main proceeding, article 20 does not apply;

(b)   when the proceeding in Great Britain commences after the filing of the application for recognition of the foreign proceeding—

    (i)   any relief in effect under article 19 or 21 shall be reviewed by the court and shall be modified or terminated if inconsistent with the proceeding in Great Britain;

    (ii)   if the foreign proceeding is a foreign main proceeding, the stay and suspension referred to in paragraph 1 of article 20 shall be modified or terminated pursuant to paragraph 6 of article 20, if inconsistent with the proceeding in Great Britain; and

    (iii)   any proceedings brought by the foreign representative by virtue of paragraph 1 of article 23 before the proceeding in Great Britain commenced shall be reviewed by the court and the court may give such directions as it thinks fit regarding the continuance of those proceedings; and

(c)   in granting, extending or modifying relief granted to a representative of a foreign non-main proceeding, the court must be satisfied that the relief relates to assets that, under the law of Great Britain, should be administered in the foreign non-main proceeding or concerns information required in that proceeding.

Article 30
Coordination of more than one Foreign Proceeding

In matters referred to in paragraph 1 of article 1, in respect of more than one foreign proceeding regarding the same debtor, the court may seek cooperation and coordination under articles 25, 26 and 27, and the following shall apply—

(a)   any relief granted under article 19 or 21 to a representative of a foreign non-main proceeding after recognition of a foreign main proceeding must be consistent with the foreign main proceeding;

(b)   if a foreign main proceeding is recognised after the filing of an application for recognition of a foreign non-main proceeding, any relief in effect under article 19 or 21 shall be reviewed by the court and shall be modified or terminated if inconsistent with the foreign main proceeding; and

(c)   if, after recognition of a foreign non-main proceeding, another foreign non-main proceeding is recognised, the court shall grant, modify or terminate relief for the purpose of facilitating coordination of the proceedings.

Article 31
Presumption of Insolvency Based on Recognition of a Foreign Main Proceeding

In the absence of evidence to the contrary, recognition of a foreign main proceeding is, for the purpose of commencing a proceeding under British insolvency law, proof that the debtor is unable to pay its debts or, in relation to Scotland, is apparently insolvent within the meaning given to those expressions under British insolvency law.

Article 32
Rule of Payment in Concurrent Proceedings

Without prejudice to secured claims or rights in rem, a creditor who has received part payment in respect of its claim in a proceeding pursuant to a law relating to insolvency in a foreign State may not receive a payment for the same claim in a proceeding under British insolvency law regarding the same debtor, so long as the payment to the other creditors of the same class is proportionately less than the payment the creditor has already received.

NOTES

Article 1: for the words in italics in para 5 there are substituted the words "Third Parties (Rights against Insurers) Act 2010" by the Third Parties (Rights against Insurers) Act 2010, s 20, Sch 2, para 5, as from a day to be appointed (for general transitional provisions etc, see Sch 3 to that Act).

SCHEDULE 2
PROCEDURAL MATTERS IN ENGLAND AND WALES
Regulation 4

PART 1
INTRODUCTORY PROVISIONS

[10.964]
1   Interpretation

(1)   In this Schedule—
"the 1986 Act" means the Insolvency Act 1986;
"article 21 relief application" means an application to the court by a foreign representative under article 21(1) or (2) of the Model Law for relief;
"business day" means any day other than a Saturday, a Sunday, Christmas Day, Good Friday or a day which is a bank holiday in England and Wales under or by virtue of the Banking and Financial Dealings Act 1971;
"CPR" means the Civil Procedure Rules 1998 and "CPR" followed by a Part or rule by number means the Part or rule with that number in those Rules;
"enforcement officer" means an individual who is authorised to act as an enforcement officer under the Courts Act 2003;
"file in court" and "file with the court" means deliver to the court for filing;
"the Gazette" means the London Gazette;
"interim relief application" means an application to the court by a foreign representative under article 19 of the Model Law for interim relief;
"main proceedings" means proceedings opened in accordance with Article 3(1) of the EC Insolvency Regulation and falling within the definition of insolvency proceedings in Article 2(a) of the EC Insolvency Regulation;
"member State liquidator" means a person falling within the definition of liquidator in Article 2(b) of the EC Insolvency Regulation appointed in proceedings to which it applies in a member State other than the United Kingdom;
"the Model Law" means the UNCITRAL Model Law as set out in Schedule 1 to these Regulations;
"modification or termination order" means an order by the court pursuant to its powers under the Model Law modifying or terminating recognition of a foreign proceeding, the stay and suspension referred to in article 20(1) or any part of it or any relief granted under article 19 or 21 of the Model Law;
"originating application" means an application to the court which is not an application in pending proceedings before the court;
"ordinary application" means any application to the court other than an originating application;
"practice direction" means a direction as to the practice and procedure of any court within the scope of the CPR;
"recognition application" means an application to the court by a foreign representative in accordance with article 15 of the Model Law for an order recognising the foreign proceeding in which he has been appointed;
"recognition order" means an order by the court recognising a proceeding the subject of a recognition application as a foreign main proceeding or foreign non-main proceeding, as appropriate;

["relevant company" means a company that is—

- (a)   registered under the Companies Act 2006,
- (b)   subject to a requirement imposed by regulations under section 1043 of that Act 2006 (unregistered UK companies) to deliver any documents to the registrar of companies, or
- (c)   subject to a requirement imposed by regulations under section 1046 of that Act (overseas companies) to deliver any documents to the registrar of companies;]

"review application" means an application to the court for a modification or termination order;

"the Rules" means the Insolvency Rules 1986 and "Rule" followed by a number means the rule with that number in those Rules;

"secondary proceedings" means proceedings opened in accordance with Articles 3(2) and 3(3) of the EC Insolvency Regulation and falling within the definition of winding up proceedings in Article 2(c) of the EC Insolvency Regulation;

"territorial proceedings" means proceedings opened in accordance with Articles 3(2) and 3(4) of the EC Insolvency Regulation and falling within the definition of insolvency proceedings in Article 2(a) of the EC Insolvency Regulation.

(2)   Expressions defined in the Model Law have the same meaning when used in this Schedule.

(3)   In proceedings under these Regulations, "Registrar" means—

- (a)   a Registrar in Bankruptcy of the High Court; and
- (b)   where the proceedings are in a district registry, the district judge.

(4)   References to the "venue" for any proceedings or attendance before the court, are to the time, date and place for the proceedings or attendance.

(5)   References in this Schedule to ex parte hearings shall be construed as references to hearings without notice being served on any other party, and references to applications made ex parte as references to applications made without notice being served on any other party; and other references which include the expression "ex parte" shall be similarly construed.

(6)   References in this Schedule to a debtor who is of interest to the Financial Services Authority are references to a debtor who—

- (a)   is, or has been, an authorised person within the meaning of section 31 of the Financial Services and Markets Act 2000 (authorised persons);
- (b)   is, or has been, an appointed representative within the meaning of section 39 (exemption of appointed representatives) of that Act; or
- (c)   is carrying on, or has carried on, a regulated activity in contravention of the general prohibition.

(7)   In sub-paragraph (6) "the general prohibition" has the meaning given by section 19 of the Financial Services and Markets Act 2000 and the reference to a "regulated activity" must be construed in accordance with—

- (a)   section 22 of that Act (classes of regulated activity and categories of investment);
- (b)   any relevant order under that section; and
- (c)   Schedule 2 to that Act (regulated activities).

(8)   References in this Schedule to a numbered form are to the form that bears that number in Schedule 5.

NOTES

Para 1: definition "relevant company" substituted by the Companies Act 2006 (Consequential Amendments, Transitional Provisions and Savings) Order 2009, SI 2009/1941, art 2(1), Sch 1, para 264(1), (3)(a), as from 1 October 2009.

PART 2
APPLICATIONS TO COURT FOR RECOGNITION OF FOREIGN PROCEEDINGS

[10.965]
2   Affidavit in support of recognition application

A recognition application shall be in Form ML1 and shall be supported by an affidavit sworn by the foreign representative complying with paragraph 4.

3   Form and content of application

The application shall state the following matters—

- (a)   the name of the applicant and his address for service within England and Wales;
- (b)   the name of the debtor in respect of which the foreign proceeding is taking place;
- (c)   the name or names in which the debtor carries on business in the country where the foreign proceeding is taking place and in this country, if other than the name given under sub-paragraph (b);
- (d)   the principal or last known place of business of the debtor in Great Britain (if any) and, in the case of an individual, his usual or last known place of residence in Great Britain (if any);
- (e)   any registered number allocated to the debtor under [the Companies Act 2006];

(f)   brief particulars of the foreign proceeding in respect of which recognition is applied for, including the country in which it is taking place and the nature of the proceeding;

(g)   that the foreign proceeding is a proceeding within the meaning of article 2(i) of the Model Law;

(h)   that the applicant is a foreign representative within the meaning of article 2(j) of the Model Law;

(i)   the address of the debtor's centre of main interests and, if different, the address of its registered office or habitual residence, as appropriate; and

(j)   if the debtor does not have its centre of main interests in the country where the foreign proceeding is taking place, whether the debtor has an establishment within the meaning of article 2(e) of the Model Law in that country, and if so, its address.

4   Contents of affidavit in support

(1)   There shall be attached to the application an affidavit in support which shall contain or have exhibited to it—

(a)   the evidence and statement required under article 15(2) and (3) respectively of the Model Law;

(b)   any other evidence which in the opinion of the applicant will assist the court in deciding whether the proceeding the subject of the application is a foreign proceeding within the meaning of article 2(i) of the Model Law and whether the applicant is a foreign representative within the meaning of article 2(j) of the Model Law;

(c)   evidence that the debtor has its centre of main interests or an establishment, as the case may be, within the country where the foreign proceeding is taking place; and

(d)   any other matters which in the opinion of the applicant will assist the court in deciding whether to make a recognition order.

(2)   The affidavit shall state whether, in the opinion of the applicant, the EC Insolvency Regulation applies to any of the proceedings identified in accordance with article 15(3) of the Model Law and, if so, whether those proceedings are main proceedings, secondary proceedings or territorial proceedings.

(3)   The affidavit shall also have exhibited to it the translations required under article 15(4) of the Model Law and a translation in English of any other document exhibited to the affidavit which is in a language other than English.

(4)   All translations referred to in sub-paragraph (3) must be certified by the translator as a correct translation.

5   The hearing and powers of court

(1)   On hearing a recognition application the court may in addition to its powers under the Model Law to make a recognition order—

(a)   dismiss the application;

(b)   adjourn the hearing conditionally or unconditionally;

(c)   make any other order which the court thinks appropriate.

(2)   If the court makes a recognition order, it shall be in Form ML2.

6   Notification of subsequent information

(1)   The foreign representative shall set out any subsequent information required to be given to the court under article 18 of the Model Law in a statement which he shall attach to Form ML3 and file with the court.

(2)   The statement shall include—

(a)   details of the information required to be given under article 18 of the Model Law; and

(b)   in the case of any proceedings required to be notified to the court under that article, a statement as to whether, in the opinion of the foreign representative, any of those proceedings are main proceedings, secondary proceedings or territorial proceedings under the EC Insolvency Regulation.

(3)   The foreign representative shall send a copy of the Form ML3 and attached statement filed with the court to the following—

(a)   the debtor; and

(b)   those persons referred to in paragraph 26(3).

NOTES

Para 3: words in square brackets in sub-para (e) substituted by the Companies Act 2006 (Consequential Amendments, Transitional Provisions and Savings) Order 2009, SI 2009/1941, art 2(1), Sch 1, para 264(1), (3)(b), as from 1 October 2009.

PART 3
APPLICATIONS FOR RELIEF UNDER THE MODEL LAW

[10.966]
7   Application for interim relief—affidavit in support

(1)   An interim relief application must be supported by an affidavit sworn by the foreign representative stating—

   (a)   the grounds on which it is proposed that the interim relief applied for should be granted;
   (b)   details of any proceeding under British insolvency law taking place in relation to the debtor;
   (c)   whether, to the foreign representative's knowledge, an administrative receiver or receiver or manager of the debtor's property is acting in relation to the debtor;
   (d)   an estimate of the value of the assets of the debtor in England and Wales in respect of which relief is applied for;
   (e)   whether, to the best of the knowledge and belief of the foreign representative, the interests of the debtor's creditors (including any secured creditors or parties to hire-purchase agreements) and any other interested parties, including if appropriate the debtor, will be adequately protected;
   (f)   whether, to the best of the foreign representative's knowledge and belief, the grant of any of the relief applied for would interfere with the administration of a foreign main proceeding; and
   (g)   all other matters that in the opinion of the foreign representative will assist the court in deciding whether or not it is appropriate to grant the relief applied for.

8   Service of interim relief application not required

Unless the court otherwise directs, it shall not be necessary to serve the interim relief application on, or give notice of it to, any person.

9   The hearing and powers of court

On hearing an interim relief application the court may in addition to its powers under the Model Law to make an order granting interim relief under article 19 of the Model Law—

   (a)   dismiss the application;
   (b)   adjourn the hearing conditionally or unconditionally;
   (c)   make any other order which the court thinks appropriate.

10   Application for relief under article 21 of the Model Law—affidavit in support

An article 21 relief application must be supported by an affidavit sworn by the foreign representative stating—

   (a)   the grounds on which it is proposed that the relief applied for should be granted;
   (b)   an estimate of the value of the assets of the debtor in England and Wales in respect of which relief is applied for;
   (c)   in the case of an application by a foreign representative who is or believes that he is a representative of a foreign non-main proceeding, the reasons why the applicant believes that the relief relates to assets that, under the law of Great Britain, should be administered in the foreign non-main proceeding or concerns information required in that proceeding;
   (d)   whether, to the best of the knowledge and belief of the foreign representative, the interests of the debtor's creditors (including any secured creditors or parties to hire-purchase agreements) and any other interested parties, including if appropriate the debtor, will be adequately protected; and
   (e)   all other matters that in the opinion of the foreign representative will assist the court in deciding whether or not it is appropriate to grant the relief applied for.

11   The hearing and powers of court

On hearing an article 21 relief application the court may in addition to its powers under the Model Law to make an order granting relief under article 21 of the Model Law—

   (a)   dismiss the application;
   (b)   adjourn the hearing conditionally or unconditionally;
   (c)   make any other order which the court thinks appropriate.

PART 4
REPLACEMENT OF FOREIGN REPRESENTATIVE

[10.967]
12   Application for confirmation of status of replacement foreign representative

(1)   This paragraph applies where following the making of a recognition order the foreign representative dies or for any other reason ceases to be the foreign representative in the foreign proceeding in relation to the debtor.

(2)   In this paragraph "the former foreign representative" shall mean the foreign representative referred to in sub-paragraph (1).

(3)   If a person has succeeded the former foreign representative or is otherwise holding office as foreign representative in the foreign proceeding in relation to the debtor, that person may apply to the court for an order confirming his status as replacement foreign representative for the purpose of proceedings under these Regulations.

13   Contents of application and affidavit in support

(1)   An application under paragraph 12(3) shall in addition to the matters required to be stated by paragraph 19(2) state the following matters—

   (a)   the name of the replacement foreign representative and his address for service within England and Wales;

   (b)   details of the circumstances in which the former foreign representative ceased to be foreign representative in the foreign proceeding in relation to the debtor (including the date on which he ceased to be the foreign representative);

   (c)   details of his own appointment as replacement foreign representative in the foreign proceeding (including the date of that appointment).

(2)   The application shall be accompanied by an affidavit in support sworn by the applicant which shall contain or have attached to it—

   (a)   a certificate from the foreign court affirming—

      (i)   the cessation of the appointment of the former foreign representative as foreign representative; and

      (ii)   the appointment of the applicant as the foreign representative in the foreign proceeding; or

   (b)   in the absence of such a certificate, any other evidence acceptable to the court of the matters referred to in paragraph (a); and

   (c)   a translation in English of any document exhibited to the affidavit which is in a language other than English.

(3)   All translations referred to in paragraph (c) must be certified by the translator as a correct translation.

14   The hearing and powers of court

(1)   On hearing an application under paragraph 12(3) the court may—

   (a)   make an order confirming the status of the replacement foreign representative as foreign representative for the purpose of proceedings under these Regulations;

   (b)   dismiss the application;

   (c)   adjourn the hearing conditionally or unconditionally;

   (d)   make an interim order;

   (e)   make any other order which the court thinks appropriate, including in particular an order making such provision as the court thinks fit with respect to matters arising in connection with the replacement of the foreign representative.

(2)   If the court dismisses the application, it may also if it thinks fit make an order terminating recognition of the foreign proceeding and—

   (a)   such an order may include such provision as the court thinks fit with respect to matters arising in connection with the termination; and

   (b)   paragraph 15 shall not apply to such an order.

PART 5
REVIEWS OF COURT ORDERS

[10.968]
15   Reviews of court orders—where court makes order of its own motion

(1)   The court shall not of its own motion make a modification or termination order unless the foreign representative and the debtor have either—

   (a)   had an opportunity of being heard on the question; or

   (b)   consented in writing to such an order.

(2)   Where the foreign representative or the debtor desires to be heard on the question of such an order, the court shall give all relevant parties notice of a venue at which the question will be considered and may give directions as to the issues on which it requires evidence.

(3)   For the purposes of sub-paragraph (2), all relevant parties means the foreign representative, the debtor and any other person who appears to the court to have an interest justifying his being given notice of the hearing.

(4)   If the court makes a modification or termination order, the order may include such provision as the court thinks fit with respect to matters arising in connection with the modification or termination.

16   Review application—affidavit in support

A review application must be supported by an affidavit sworn by the applicant stating—

   (a)   the grounds on which it is proposed that the relief applied for should be granted;

(b)   whether, to the best of the knowledge and belief of the applicant, the interests of the debtor's creditors (including any secured creditors or parties to hire-purchase agreements) and any other interested parties, including if appropriate the debtor, will be adequately protected; and

(c)   all other matters that in the opinion of the applicant will assist the court in deciding whether or not it is appropriate to grant the relief applied for.

17   Hearing of review application and powers of the court

On hearing a review application, the court may in addition to its powers under the Model Law to make a modification or termination order—

(a)   dismiss the application;

(b)   adjourn the hearing conditionally or unconditionally;

(c)   make an interim order;

(c)   make any other order which the court thinks appropriate, including an order making such provision as the court thinks fit with respect to matters arising in connection with the modification or termination.

PART 6
COURT PROCEDURE AND PRACTICE WITH REGARD TO PRINCIPAL APPLICATIONS AND ORDERS

[10.969]
18   Preliminary and interpretation

(1)   This Part applies to—

(a)   any of the following applications made to the court under these Regulations—

(i)   a recognition application;

(ii)   an article 21 relief application;

(iii)   an application under paragraph 12(3) for an order confirming the status of a replacement foreign representative;

(iv)   a review application; and

(b)   any of the following orders made by the court under these Regulations—

(i)   a recognition order;

(ii)   an order granting interim relief under article 19 of the Model Law;

(iii)   an order granting relief under article 21 of the Model Law;

(iv)   an order confirming the status of a replacement foreign representative; and

(v)   a modification or termination order.

19   Form and contents of application

(1)   Subject to sub-paragraph (4) every application to which this Part applies shall be an ordinary application and shall be in Form ML5.

(2)   Each application shall be in writing and shall state—

(a)   the names of the parties;

(b)   the nature of the relief or order applied for or the directions sought from the court;

(c)   the names and addresses of the persons (if any) on whom it is intended to serve the application;

(d)   the names and addresses of all those persons on whom these Regulations require the application to be served (so far as known to the applicant); and

(e)   the applicant's address for service.

(3)   The application must be signed by the applicant if he is acting in person, or, when he is not so acting, by or on behalf of his solicitor.

(4)   This paragraph does not apply to a recognition application.

20   Filing of application

(1)   The application (and all supporting documents) shall be filed with the court, with a sufficient number of copies for service and use as provided by paragraph 21(2).

(2)   Each of the copies filed shall have applied to it the seal of the court and be issued to the applicant; and on each copy there shall be endorsed the date and time of filing.

(3)   The court shall fix a venue for the hearing of the application and this also shall be endorsed on each copy of the application issued under sub-paragraph (2).

21   Service of the application

(1)   In sub-paragraph (2), references to the application are to a sealed copy of the application issued by the court together with any affidavit in support of it and any documents exhibited to the affidavit.

(2)   Unless the court otherwise directs, the application shall be served on the following persons, unless they are the applicant—

(a)   on the foreign representative;

(b)   on the debtor;

(c)   if a British insolvency officeholder is acting in relation to the debtor, on him;

(d)   if any person has been appointed an administrative receiver of the debtor or, to the knowledge of the foreign representative, as a receiver or manager of the property of the debtor in England and Wales, on him;

(e)   if a member State liquidator has been appointed in main proceedings in relation to the debtor, on him;

(f)   if to the knowledge of the foreign representative a foreign representative has been appointed in any other foreign proceeding regarding the debtor, on him;

(g)   if there is pending in England and Wales a petition for the winding up or bankruptcy of the debtor, on the petitioner;

(h)   on any person who to the knowledge of the foreign representative is or may be entitled to appoint an administrator of the debtor under paragraph 14 of Schedule B1 to the 1986 Act (appointment of administrator by holder of qualifying floating charge); and

(i)   if the debtor is a debtor who is of interest to the Financial Services Authority, on that Authority.

22   Manner in which service to be effected

(1)   Service of the application in accordance with paragraph 21(2) shall be effected by the applicant, or his solicitor, or by a person instructed by him or his solicitor, not less than 5 business days before the date fixed for the hearing.

(2)   Service shall be effected by delivering the documents to a person's proper address or in such other manner as the court may direct.

(3)   A person's proper address is any which he has previously notified as his address for service within England and Wales; but if he has not notified any such address or if for any reason service at such address is not practicable, service may be effected as follows—

(a)   (subject to sub-paragraph (4)) in the case of a company incorporated in England and Wales, by delivery to its registered office;

(b)   in the case of any other person, by delivery to his usual or last known address or principal place of business in Great Britain.

(4)   If delivery to a company's registered office is not practicable, service may be effected by delivery to its last known principal place of business in Great Britain.

(5)   Delivery of documents to any place or address may be made by leaving them there or sending them by first class post in accordance with the provisions of paragraphs 70 and 75(1).

23   Proof of service

(1)   Service of the application shall be verified by an affidavit of service in Form ML6, specifying the date on which, and the manner in which, service was effected.

(2)   The affidavit of service, with a sealed copy of the application exhibited to it, shall be filed with the court as soon as reasonably practicable after service, and in any event not less than 1 business day before the hearing of the application.

24   In case of urgency

Where the case is one of urgency, the court may (without prejudice to its general power to extend or abridge time limits)—

(a)   hear the application immediately, either with or without notice to, or the attendance of, other parties; or

(b)   authorise a shorter period of service than that provided for by paragraph 22(1),

and any such application may be heard on terms providing for the filing or service of documents, or the carrying out of other formalities, as the court thinks fit.

25   The hearing

(1)   At the hearing of the application, the applicant and any of the following persons (not being the applicant) may appear or be represented—

(a)   the foreign representative;

(b)   the debtor and, in the case of any debtor other than an individual, any one or more directors or other officers of the debtor, including—

[(i)   where applicable, any person specified in particulars registered under section 1046 of the Companies Act 2006 (overseas companies) as authorised to represent the debtor;]

(ii)   in the case of a debtor which is a partnership, any person who is an officer of the partnership within the meaning of article 2 of the Insolvent Partnerships Order 1994;

(c)   if a British insolvency officeholder is acting in relation to the debtor, that person;

(d)   if any person has been appointed an administrative receiver of the debtor or as a receiver or manager of the property of the debtor in England and Wales, that person;

(e)   if a member State liquidator has been appointed in main proceedings in relation to the debtor, that person;

(f)   if a foreign representative has been appointed in any other foreign proceeding regarding the debtor, that person;

(g)   any person who has presented a petition for the winding up or bankruptcy of the debtor in England and Wales;

(h)   any person who is or may be entitled to appoint an administrator of the debtor under paragraph 14 of Schedule B1 to the 1986 Act (appointment of administrator by holder of qualifying floating charge);

(i)   if the debtor is a debtor who is of interest to the Financial Services Authority, that Authority; and

(j)   with the permission of the court, any other person who appears to have an interest justifying his appearance.

26 Notification and advertisement of order

(1)   If the court makes any of the orders referred to in paragraph 18(1)(b), it shall as soon as reasonably practicable send two sealed copies of the order to the foreign representative.

(2)   The foreign representative shall send a sealed copy of the order as soon as reasonably practicable to the debtor.

(3)   The foreign representative shall, as soon as reasonably practicable after the date of the order give notice of the making of the order—

(a)   if a British insolvency officeholder is acting in relation to the debtor, to him;

(b)   if any person has been appointed an administrative receiver of the debtor or, to the knowledge of the foreign representative, as a receiver or manager of the property of the debtor, to him;

(c)   if a member State liquidator has been appointed in main proceedings in relation to the debtor, to him;

(d)   if to his knowledge a foreign representative has been appointed in any other foreign proceeding regarding the debtor, that person;

(e)   if there is pending in England and Wales a petition for the winding up or bankruptcy of the debtor, to the petitioner;

(f)   to any person who to his knowledge is or may be entitled to appoint an administrator of the debtor under paragraph 14 of Schedule B1 to the 1986 Act (appointment of administrator by holder of qualifying floating charge);

(g)   if the debtor is a debtor who is of interest to the Financial Services Authority, to that Authority;

(h)   to such other persons as the court may direct.

(4)   In the case of an order recognising a foreign proceeding in relation to the debtor as a foreign main proceeding, or an order under article 19 or 21 of the Model Law staying execution, distress or other legal process against the debtor's assets, the foreign representative shall also, as soon as reasonably practicable after the date of the order give notice of the making of the order—

(a)   to any enforcement officer or other officer who to his knowledge is charged with an execution or other legal process against the debtor or its property; and

(b)   to any person who to his knowledge is distraining against the debtor or its property.

(5)   In the application of sub-paragraphs (3) and (4) the references to property shall be taken as references to property situated within England and Wales.

(6)   Where the debtor is a relevant company, the foreign representative shall send notice of the making of the order to the registrar of companies before the end of the period of 5 business days beginning with the date of the order. The notice to the registrar of companies shall be in Form ML7.

(7)   The foreign representative shall advertise the making of the following orders once in the Gazette and once in such newspaper as he thinks most appropriate for ensuring that the making of the order comes to the notice of the debtor's creditors—

(a)   a recognition order;

(b)   an order confirming the status of a replacement foreign representative; and

(c)   a modification or termination order which modifies or terminates recognition of a foreign proceeding,

and the advertisement shall be in Form ML8.

27 Adjournment of hearing; directions

(1)   This paragraph applies in any case where the court exercises its power to adjourn the hearing of the application.

(2)   The court may at any time give such directions as it thinks fit as to—

(a)   service or notice of the application on or to any person, whether in connection with the venue of a resumed hearing or for any other purpose;

(b)   the procedure on the application;

(c)   the manner in which any evidence is to be adduced at a resumed hearing and in particular as to—

(i)   the taking of evidence wholly or in part by affidavit or orally;

(ii)   the cross-examination on the hearing in court or in chambers, of any deponents to affidavits;

(d)   the matters to be dealt with in evidence.

NOTES

Para 25: sub-para (b)(i) substituted by the Companies Act 2006 (Consequential Amendments, Transitional Provisions and Savings) Order 2009, SI 2009/1941, art 2(1), Sch 1, para 264(1), (3)(c), as from 1 October 2009.

PART 7
APPLICATIONS TO THE CHIEF LAND REGISTRAR

[10.970]
28 Applications to Chief Land Registrar following court orders

(1) Where the court makes any order in proceedings under these Regulations which is capable of giving rise to an application or applications under the Land Registration Act 2002, the foreign representative shall, as soon as reasonably practicable after the making of the order or at the appropriate time, make the appropriate application or applications to the Chief Land Registrar.

(2) In sub-paragraph (1) an appropriate application is—
  (a) in any case where—
    (i) a recognition order in respect of a foreign main proceeding or an order suspending the right to transfer, encumber or otherwise dispose of any assets of the debtor is made, and
    (ii) the debtor is the registered proprietor of a registered estate or registered charge and holds it for his sole benefit,
    an application under section 43 of the Land Registration Act 2002 for a restriction of the kind referred to in sub-paragraph (3) to be entered in the relevant registered title; and
  (b) in any other case, an application under the Land Registration Act 2002 for such an entry in the register as shall be necessary to reflect the effect of the court order under these Regulations.

(3) The restriction referred to in sub-paragraph (2)(a) is a restriction to the effect that no disposition of the registered estate or registered charge (as appropriate) by the registered proprietor of that estate or charge is to be completed by registration within the meaning of section 27 of the Land Registration Act 2002 except under a further order of the court.

PART 8
MISFEASANCE

[10.971]
29 Misfeasance by foreign representative

(1) The court may examine the conduct of a person who—
  (a) is or purports to be the foreign representative in relation to a debtor; or
  (b) has been or has purported to be the foreign representative in relation to a debtor.

(2) An examination under this paragraph may be held only on the application of—
  (a) a British insolvency officeholder acting in relation to the debtor;
  (b) a creditor of the debtor; or
  (c) with the permission of the court, any other person who appears to have an interest justifying an application.

(3) An application under sub-paragraph (2) must allege that the foreign representative—
  (a) has misapplied or retained money or other property of the debtor;
  (b) has become accountable for money or other property of the debtor;
  (c) has breached a fiduciary or other duty in relation to the debtor; or
  (d) has been guilty of misfeasance.

(4) On an examination under this paragraph into a person's conduct the court may order him—
  (a) to repay, restore or account for money or property;
  (b) to pay interest;
  (c) to contribute a sum to the debtor's property by way of compensation for breach of duty or misfeasance.

(4) In sub-paragraph (3) "foreign representative" includes a person who purports or has purported to be a foreign representative in relation to a debtor.

PART 9
GENERAL PROVISION AS TO COURT PROCEDURE AND PRACTICE

[10.972]
30 Principal court rules and practice to apply with modifications

(1) The CPR and the practice and procedure of the High Court (including any practice direction) shall apply to proceedings under these Regulations in the High Court with such modifications as may be necessary for the purpose of giving effect to the provisions of these Regulations and in the case of any conflict between any provision of the CPR and the provisions of these Regulations, the latter shall prevail.

(2)   All proceedings under these Regulations shall be allocated to the multi-track for which CPR Part 29 (the multi-track) makes provision, and accordingly those provisions of the CPR which provide for allocation questionnaires and track allocation shall not apply.

31   Applications other than the principal applications—preliminary

Paragraphs 32 to 37 of this Part apply to any application made to the court under these Regulations, except any of the applications referred to in paragraph 18(1)(a).

32   Form and contents of application

(1)   Every application shall be in the form appropriate to the application concerned. Forms ML4 and ML5 shall be used for an originating application and an ordinary application respectively under these Regulations.

(2)   Each application shall be in writing and shall state—
   (a)   the names of the parties;
   (b)   the nature of the relief or order applied for or the directions sought from the court;
   (c)   the names and addresses of the persons (if any) on whom it is intended to serve the application or that no person is intended to be served;
   (d)   where these Regulations require that notice of the application is to be given to specified persons, the names and addresses of all those persons (so far as known to the applicant); and
   (e)   the applicant's address for service.

(3)   An originating application shall set out the grounds on which the applicant claims to be entitled to the relief or order sought.

(4)   The application must be signed by the applicant if he is acting in person or, when he is not so acting, by or on behalf of his solicitor.

33   Filing and service of application

(1)   The application shall be filed in court, accompanied by one copy and a number of additional copies equal to the number of persons who are to be served with the application.

(2)   Subject as follows in this paragraph and in paragraph 34, or unless the court otherwise orders, upon the presentation of the documents mentioned in sub-paragraph (1), the court shall fix a venue for the application to be heard.

(3)   Unless the court otherwise directs, the applicant shall serve a sealed copy of the application, endorsed with the venue of the hearing, on the respondent named in the application (or on each respondent if more than one).

(4)   The court may give any of the following directions—
   (a)   that the application be served upon persons other than those specified by the relevant provision of these Regulations;
   (b)   that the giving of notice to any person may be dispensed with;
   (c)   that notice be given in some way other than that specified in sub-paragraph (3).

(5)   Subject to sub-paragraph (6), the application must be served at least 10 business days before the date fixed for the hearing.

(6)   Where the case is one of urgency, the court may (without prejudice to its general power to extend or abridge time limits)—
   (a)   hear the application immediately, either with or without notice to, or the attendance of, other parties; or
   (b)   authorise a shorter period of service than that provided for by sub-paragraph (5);
and any such application may be heard on terms providing for the filing or service of documents, or the carrying out of other formalities, as the court thinks fit.

34   Other hearings *ex parte*

(1)   Where the relevant provisions of these Regulations do not require service of the application on, or notice of it to be given to, any person, the court may hear the application *ex parte*.

(2)   Where the application is properly made *ex parte*, the court may hear it forthwith, without fixing a venue as required by paragraph 33(2).

(3)   Alternatively, the court may fix a venue for the application to be heard, in which case paragraph 33 applies (so far as relevant).

35   Use of affidavit evidence

(1)   In any proceedings evidence may be given by affidavit unless the court otherwise directs; but the court may, on the application of any party, order the attendance for cross-examination of the person making the affidavit.

(2)   Where, after such an order has been made, the person in question does not attend, his affidavit shall not be used in evidence without the permission of the court.

36   Filing and service of affidavits

(1)   Unless the court otherwise allows—

(a) if the applicant intends to rely at the first hearing on affidavit evidence, he shall file the affidavit or affidavits (if more than one) in court and serve a copy or copies on the respondent, not less than 10 business days before the date fixed for the hearing; and

(b) where a respondent to an application intends to oppose it and to rely for that purpose on affidavit evidence, he shall file the affidavit or affidavits (if more than one) in court and serve a copy or copies on the applicant, not less than 5 business days before the date fixed for the hearing.

(2) Any affidavit may be sworn by the applicant or by the respondent or by some other person possessing direct knowledge of the subject matter of the application.

37 Adjournment of hearings; directions

The court may adjourn the hearing of an application on such terms (if any) as it thinks fit and in the case of such an adjournment paragraph 27(2) shall apply.

38 Transfer of proceedings within the High Court

(1) The High Court may, having regard to the criteria in CPR rule 30.3(2), order proceedings in the Royal Courts of Justice or a district registry, or any part of such proceedings (such as an application made in the proceedings), to be transferred—

(a) from the Royal Courts of Justice to a district registry; or

(b) from a district registry to the Royal Courts of Justice or to another district registry.

(2) The High Court may order proceedings before a district registry for the detailed assessment of costs to be transferred to another district registry if it is satisfied that the proceedings could be more conveniently or fairly taken in that other district registry.

(3) An application for an order under sub-paragraph (1) or (2) must, if the claim is proceeding in a district registry, be made to that registry.

(4) A transfer of proceedings under this paragraph may be ordered—

(a) by the court of its own motion; or

(b) on the application of a person appearing to the court to have an interest in the proceedings.

(5) Where the court orders proceedings to be transferred, the court from which they are to be transferred must give notice of the transfer to all the parties.

(6) An order made before the transfer of the proceedings shall not be affected by the order to transfer.

39 Transfer of proceedings—actions to avoid acts detrimental to creditors

(1) If—

(a) in accordance with article 23(6) of the Model Law, the court grants a foreign representative permission to make an application in accordance with paragraph 1 of that article; and

(b) the relevant proceedings under British insolvency law taking place regarding the debtor are taking place in the county court,

the court may also order those proceedings to be transferred to the High Court.

(2) Where the court makes an order transferring proceedings under sub-paragraph (1)—

(a) it shall send sealed copies of the order to the county court from which the proceedings are to be transferred, and to the official receivers attached to that court and the High Court respectively; and

(b) the county court shall send the file of the proceedings to the High Court.

(3) Following compliance with this paragraph, if the official receiver attached to the court to which the proceedings are transferred is not already, by virtue of directions given by the Secretary of State under section 399(6)(a) of the 1986 Act, the official receiver in relation to those proceedings, he becomes, in relation to those proceedings, the official receiver in place of the official receiver attached to the other court concerned.

40 Shorthand writers

(1) The judge may in writing nominate one or more persons to be official shorthand writers to the court.

(2) The court may, at any time in the course of proceedings under these Regulations, appoint a shorthand writer to take down the evidence of a person examined in pursuance of a court order under article 19 or 21 of the Model Law.

(3) The remuneration of a shorthand writer appointed in proceedings under these Regulations shall be paid by the party at whose instance the appointment was made or otherwise as the court may direct.

(4) Any question arising as to the rates of remuneration payable under this paragraph shall be determined by the court in its discretion.

41 Enforcement procedures

In any proceedings under these Regulations, orders of the court may be enforced in the same manner as a judgment to the same effect.

42   Title of proceedings

(1)   Every proceeding under these Regulations shall, with any necessary additions, be intituled "IN THE MATTER OF . . . (naming the debtor to which the proceedings relate) AND IN THE MATTER OF THE CROSS-BORDER INSOLVENCY REGULATIONS 2006".

(2)   Sub-paragraph (1) shall not apply in respect of any form prescribed under these Regulations.

43   Court records

The court shall keep records of all proceedings under these Regulations, and shall cause to be entered in the records the taking of any step in the proceedings, and such decisions of the court in relation thereto, as the court thinks fit.

44   Inspection of records

(1)   Subject as follows, the court's records of proceedings under these Regulations shall be open to inspection by any person.

(2)   If in the case of a person applying to inspect the records the Registrar is not satisfied as to the propriety of the purpose for which inspection is required, he may refuse to allow it. That person may then apply forthwith and *ex parte* to the judge, who may refuse the inspection or allow it on such terms as he thinks fit.

(3)   The decision of the judge under sub-paragraph (2) is final.

45   File of court proceedings

(1)   In respect of all proceedings under these Regulations, the court shall open and maintain a file for each case; and (subject to directions of the Registrar) all documents relating to such proceedings shall be placed on the relevant file.

(2)   No proceedings under these Regulations shall be filed in the Central Office of the High Court.

46   Right to inspect the file

(1)   In the case of any proceedings under these Regulations, the following have the right, at all reasonable times, to inspect the court's file of the proceedings—

    (a)   the Secretary of State;

    (b)   the person who is the foreign representative in relation to the proceedings;

    (c)   if a foreign representative has been appointed in any other foreign proceeding regarding the debtor to which the proceedings under these Regulations relate, that person;

    (d)   if a British insolvency officeholder is acting in relation to the debtor to which the proceedings under these Regulations relate, that person;

    (e)   any person stating himself in writing to be a creditor of the debtor to which the proceedings under these Regulations relate;

    (f)   if a member State liquidator has been appointed in relation to the debtor to which the proceedings under these Regulations relate, that person; and

    (g)   the debtor to which the proceedings under these Regulations relate, or, if that debtor is a company, corporation or partnership, every person who is, or at any time has been—

        (i)   a director or officer of the debtor;

        (ii)   a member of the debtor; or

        [(iii)   where applicable, any person specified in particulars registered under section 1046 of the Companies Act 2006 (overseas companies) as authorised to represent the debtor;]

(2)   The right of inspection conferred as above on any person may be exercised on his behalf by a person properly authorised by him.

(3)   Any person may, by leave of the court, inspect the file.

(4)   The right of inspection conferred by this paragraph is not exercisable in the case of documents, or parts of documents, as to which the court directs (either generally or specially) that they are not to be made open to inspection without the court's permission.

An application for a direction of the court under this sub-paragraph may be made by the foreign representative or by any party appearing to the court to have an interest.

(5)   If, for the purpose of powers conferred by the 1986 Act or the Rules, the Secretary of State or the official receiver wishes to inspect the file of any proceedings under these Regulations, and requests the transmission of the file, the court shall comply with such request (unless the file is for the time being in use for the court's purposes).

(6)   Paragraph 44(2) and (3) apply in respect of the court's file of any proceedings under these Regulations as they apply in respect of court records.

(7)   Where these Regulations confer a right for any person to inspect documents on the court's file of proceedings, the right includes that of taking copies of those documents on payment of the fee chargeable under any order made under section 92 of the Courts Act 2003.

47   Copies of court orders

(1)   In any proceedings under these Regulations, any person who under paragraph 46 has a right to inspect documents on the court file also has the right to require the foreign representative in relation to those proceedings to furnish him with a copy of any court order in the proceedings.

(2)   Sub-paragraph (1) does not apply if a copy of the court order has been served on that person or notice of the making of the order has been given to that person under other provisions of these Regulations.

48   Filing of Gazette notices and advertisements

(1)   In any court in which proceedings under these Regulations are pending, an officer of the court shall file a copy of every issue of the Gazette which contains an advertisement relating to those proceedings.

(2)   Where there appears in a newspaper an advertisement relating to proceedings under these Regulations pending in any court, the person inserting the advertisement shall file a copy of it in that court.

The copy of the advertisement shall be accompanied by, or have endorsed on it, such particulars as are necessary to identify the proceedings and the date of the advertisement's appearance.

(3)   An officer of any court in which proceedings under these Regulations are pending shall from time to time file a memorandum giving the dates of, and other particulars relating to, any notice published in the Gazette, and any newspaper advertisements, which relate to proceedings so pending.

The officer's memorandum is prima facie evidence that any notice or advertisement mentioned in it was duly inserted in the issue of the newspaper or the Gazette which is specified in the memorandum.

49   Persons incapable of managing their affairs—introductory

(1)   Paragraphs 50 to 52 apply where in proceedings under these Regulations it appears to the court that a person affected by the proceedings is one who is incapable of managing and administering his property and affairs either—

    (a)   by reason of mental disorder within the meaning of the Mental Health Act 1983; or

    (b)   due to physical affliction or disability.

(2)   The person concerned is referred to as "the incapacitated person".

50   Appointment of another person to act

(1)   The court may appoint such person as it thinks fit to appear for, represent or act for the incapacitated person.

(2)   The appointment may be made either generally or for the purpose of any particular application or proceeding, or for the exercise of particular rights or powers which the incapacitated person might have exercised but for his incapacity.

(3)   The court may make the appointment either of its own motion or on application by—

    (a)   a person who has been appointed by a court in the United Kingdom or elsewhere to manage the affairs of, or to represent, the incapacitated person; or

    (b)   any relative or friend of the incapacitated person who appears to the court to be a proper person to make the application; or

    (c)   in any case where the incapacitated person is the debtor, the foreign representative.

(4)   Application under sub-paragraph (3) may be made *ex parte*; but the court may require such notice of the application as it thinks necessary to be given to the person alleged to be incapacitated, or any other person, and may adjourn the hearing of the application to enable the notice to be given.

51   Affidavit in support of application

An application under paragraph 50(3) shall be supported by an affidavit of a registered medical practitioner as to the mental or physical condition of the incapacitated person.

52   Service of notices following appointment

Any notice served on, or sent to, a person appointed under paragraph 50 has the same effect as if it had been served on, or given to, the incapacitated person.

53   Rights of audience

Rights of audience in proceedings under these Regulations are the same as obtain in proceedings under British insolvency law.

54   Right of attendance

(1)   Subject as follows, in proceedings under these Regulations, any person stating himself in writing, in records kept by the court for that purpose, to be a creditor of the debtor to which the proceedings relate, is entitled at his own cost, to attend in court or in chambers at any stage of the proceedings.

(2)   Attendance may be by the person himself, or his solicitor.

(3)   A person so entitled may request the court in writing to give him notice of any step in the proceedings; and, subject to his paying the costs involved and keeping the court informed as to his address, the court shall comply with the request.

(4)   If the court is satisfied that the exercise by a person of his rights under this paragraph has given rise to costs for the estate of the debtor which would not otherwise have been incurred and ought not, in the circumstances, to fall on that estate, it may direct that the costs be paid by the person concerned, to an amount specified.

The rights of that person under this paragraph shall be in abeyance so long as those costs are not paid.

(5)   The court may appoint one or more persons to represent the creditors of the debtor to have the rights conferred by this paragraph, instead of the rights being exercised by any or all of them individually.

If two or more persons are appointed under this paragraph to represent the same interest, they must (if at all) instruct the same solicitor.

55   Right of attendance for member State liquidator

For the purposes of paragraph 54(1), a member State liquidator appointed in relation to a debtor subject to proceedings under these Regulations shall be deemed to be a creditor.

56   British insolvency officeholder's solicitor

Where in any proceedings the attendance of the British insolvency officeholder's solicitor is required, whether in court or in chambers, the British insolvency officeholder himself need not attend, unless directed by the court.

57   Formal defects

No proceedings under these Regulations shall be invalidated by any formal defect or by any irregularity, unless the court before which objection is made considers that substantial injustice has been caused by the defect or irregularity, and that the injustice cannot be remedied by any order of the court.

58   Restriction on concurrent proceedings and remedies

Where in proceedings under these Regulations the court makes an order staying any action, execution or other legal process against the property of a debtor, service of the order may be effected by sending a sealed copy of the order to whatever is the address for service of the claimant or other party having the carriage of the proceedings to be stayed.

59   Affidavits

(1)   Where in proceedings under these Regulations, an affidavit is made by any British insolvency officeholder acting in relation to the debtor, he shall state the capacity in which he makes it, the position which he holds and the address at which he works.

(2)   Any officer of the court duly authorised in that behalf, may take affidavits and declarations.

(3)   Subject to sub-paragraph (4), where these Regulations provide for the use of an affidavit, a witness statement verified by a statement of truth may be used as an alternative.

(4)   Sub-paragraph (3) does not apply to paragraphs 4 (affidavit in support of recognition application), 7 (affidavit in support of interim relief application), 10 (affidavit in support of article 21 relief application), 13 (affidavit in support of application regarding status of replacement foreign representative) and 16 (affidavit in support of review application).

60   Security in court

(1)   Where security has to be given to the court (otherwise than in relation to costs), it may be given by guarantee, bond or the payment of money into court.

(2)   A person proposing to give a bond as security shall give notice to the party in whose favour the security is required, and to the court, naming those who are to be sureties to the bond.

(3)   The court shall forthwith give notice to the parties concerned of a venue for the execution of the bond and the making of any objection to the sureties.

(4)   The sureties shall make an affidavit of their sufficiency (unless dispensed with by the party in whose favour the security is required) and shall, if required by the court, attend the court to be cross-examined.

61   Further information and disclosure

(1)   Any party to proceedings under these Regulations may apply to the court for an order—
  (a)   that any other party—
    (i)   clarify any matter which is in dispute in the proceedings; or
    (ii)   give additional information in relation to any such matter,
       in accordance with CPR Part 18 (further information); or
  (b)   to obtain disclosure from any other party in accordance with CPR Part 31 (disclosure and inspection of documents).

(2)   An application under this paragraph may be made without notice being served on any other party.

62 Office copies of documents

(1) Any person who has under these Regulations the right to inspect the court file of proceedings may require the court to provide him with an office copy of any document from the file.

(2) A person's right under this paragraph may be exercised on his behalf by his solicitor.

(3) An office copy provided by the court under this paragraph shall be in such form as the Registrar thinks appropriate, and shall bear the court's seal.

63 "The court"

(1) Anything to be done in proceedings under these Regulations by, to or before the court may be done by, to or before a judge of the High Court or a Registrar.

(2) Where these Regulations require or permit the court to perform an act of a formal or administrative character, that act may be performed by a court officer.

NOTES

Para 46: sub-para (1)(g)(iii) substituted by the Companies Act 2006 (Consequential Amendments, Transitional Provisions and Savings) Order 2009, SI 2009/1941, art 2(1), Sch 1, para 264(1), (3)(d), as from 1 October 2009.

PART 10
COSTS AND DETAILED ASSESSMENT

[10.973]

64 Requirement to assess costs by the detailed procedure

In any proceedings before the court, the court may order costs to be decided by detailed assessment.

65 Costs of officers charged with execution of writs or other process

(1) Where by virtue of article 20 of the Model Law or a court order under article 19 or 21 of the Model Law an enforcement officer, or other officer, charged with execution of the writ or other process—

(a) is required to deliver up goods or money; or

(b) has deducted costs from the proceeds of an execution or money paid to him,

the foreign representative may require in writing that the amount of the enforcement officer's or other officer's bill of costs be decided by detailed assessment.

(2) Where such a requirement is made, if the enforcement officer or other officer does not commence detailed assessment proceedings within 3 months of the requirement under sub-paragraph (1), or within such further time as the court, on application, may permit, any claim by the enforcement officer or other officer in respect of his costs is forfeited by such failure to commence proceedings.

(3) Where, in the case of a deduction of costs by the enforcement officer or other officer, any amount deducted is disallowed at the conclusion of the detailed assessment proceedings, the enforcement officer or other officer shall forthwith pay a sum equal to that disallowed to the foreign representative for the benefit of the debtor.

66 Final costs certificate

(1) A final costs certificate of the costs officer is final and conclusive as to all matters which have not been objected to in the manner provided for under the rules of the court.

(2) Where it is proved to the satisfaction of a costs officer that a final costs certificate has been lost or destroyed, he may issue a duplicate.

PART 11
APPEALS IN PROCEEDINGS UNDER THESE REGULATIONS

[10.974]

67 Appeals from court orders

(1) An appeal from a decision of a Registrar of the High Court in proceedings under these Regulations lies to a single judge of the High Court; and an appeal from a decision of that judge on such an appeal lies, with the permission of the Court of Appeal, to the Court of Appeal.

(2) An appeal from a decision of a judge of the High Court in proceedings under these Regulations which is not a decision on an appeal made to him under sub-paragraph (1) lies, with the permission of that judge or the Court of Appeal, to the Court of Appeal.

68 Procedure on appeals

(1) Subject as follows, CPR Part 52 (appeals to the Court of Appeal) and its practice direction apply to appeals in proceedings under these Regulations.

(2) The provisions of Part 4 of the practice direction on Insolvency Proceedings supporting CPR Part 49 relating to first appeals (as defined in that Part) apply in relation to any appeal to a single judge of the High Court under paragraph 67, with any necessary modifications.

(3)   In proceedings under these Regulations, the procedure under CPR Part 52 is by ordinary application and not by appeal notice.

PART 12
GENERAL

[10.975]
69   Notices

(1)   All notices required or authorised by or under these Regulations to be given must be in writing, unless it is otherwise provided, or the court allows the notice to be given in some other way.

(2)   Where in proceedings under these Regulations a notice is required to be sent or given by any person, the sending or giving of it may be proved by means of a certificate by that person that he posted the notice, or instructed another person (naming him) to do so.

(3)   A certificate under this paragraph may be endorsed on a copy or specimen of the notice to which it relates.

70   "Give notice" etc

(1)   A reference in these Regulations to giving notice, or to delivering, sending or serving any document, means that the notice or document may be sent by post.

(2)   Subject to paragraph 75, any form of post may be used.

(3)   Personal service of a document is permissible in all cases.

(4)   Notice of the venue fixed for an application may be given by service of the sealed copy of the application under paragraph 33(3).

71   Notice, etc to solicitors

Where in proceedings under these Regulations a notice or other document is required or authorised to be given to a person, it may, if he has indicated that his solicitor is authorised to accept service on his behalf, be given instead to the solicitor.

72   Notice to joint British insolvency officeholders

Where two or more persons are acting jointly as the British insolvency officeholder in proceedings under British insolvency law, delivery of a document to one of them is to be treated as delivery to them all.

73   Forms for use in proceedings under these Regulations

(1)   The forms contained in Schedule 5 to these Regulations shall be used in, and in connection with, proceedings under these Regulations.

(2)   The forms shall be used with such variations, if any, as the circumstances may require.

74   Time limits

(1)   The provisions of CPR Rule 2.8 (time) apply, as regards computation of time, to anything required or authorised to be done by these Regulations.

(2)   The provisions of CPR rule 3.1(2)(a) (the court's general powers of management) apply so as to enable the court to extend or shorten the time for compliance with anything required or authorised to be done by these Regulations.

75   Service by post

(1)   For a document to be properly served by post, it must be contained in an envelope addressed to the person on whom service is to be effected, and pre-paid for first class post.

(2)   A document to be served by post may be sent to the last known address of the person to be served.

(3)   Where first class post is used, the document is treated as served on the second business day after the date of posting, unless the contrary is shown.

(4)   The date of posting is presumed, unless the contrary is shown, to be the date shown in the post-mark on the envelope in which the document is contained.

76   General provisions as to service and notice

Subject to paragraphs 22, 75 and 77, CPR Part 6 (service of documents) applies as regards any matter relating to the service of documents and the giving of notice in proceedings under these Regulations.

77   Service outside the jurisdiction

(1)   Sections III and IV of CPR Part 6 (service out of the jurisdiction and service of process of foreign court) do not apply in proceedings under these Regulations.

(2)   Where for the purposes of proceedings under these Regulations any process or order of the court, or other document, is required to be served on a person who is not in England and Wales, the court may order service to be effected within such time, on such person, at such place and in such manner as it thinks fit, and may also require such proof of service as it thinks fit.

(3)   An application under this paragraph shall be supported by an affidavit stating—
  (a)   the grounds on which the application is made; and
  (b)   in what place or country the person to be served is, or probably may be found.

78   False claim of status as creditor

(1)   Rule 12.18 (false claim of status as creditor, etc) shall apply with any necessary modifications in any case where a person falsely claims the status of a creditor of a debtor, with the intention of obtaining a sight of documents whether on the court's file or in the hands of the foreign representative or other person, which he has not under these Regulations any right to inspect.

(2)   Rule 21.21 and Schedule 5 of the Rules shall apply to an offence under Rule 12.18 as applied by sub-paragraph (1) as they apply to an offence under Rule 12.18.

79   The Gazette

(1)   A copy of the Gazette containing any notice required by these Regulations to be gazetted is evidence of any fact stated in the notice.

(2)   In the case of an order of the court notice of which is required by these Regulations to be gazetted, a copy of the Gazette containing the notice may in any proceedings be produced as conclusive evidence that the order was made on the date specified in the notice.

SCHEDULE 3
PROCEDURAL MATTERS IN SCOTLAND
Regulation 5

PART 1
INTERPRETATION

[10.976]
1   Interpretation

(1)   In this Schedule—
  "the 1986 Act" means the Insolvency Act 1986;
  "article 21 remedy application" means an application to the court by a foreign representative
      under article 21(1) or (2) of the Model Law for remedy;
  "business day" means any day other than a Saturday, a Sunday, Christmas Day, Good Friday or
      a day which is a bank holiday in Scotland under or by virtue of the Banking and Financial
      Dealings Act 1971;
  "the Gazette" means the Edinburgh Gazette;
  "main proceedings" means proceedings opened in accordance with Article 3(1) of the EC
      Insolvency Regulation and falling within the definition of insolvency proceedings in
      Article 2(a) of the EC Insolvency Regulation;
  "member State liquidator" means a person falling within the definition of liquidator in
      Article 2(b) of the EC Insolvency Regulation appointed in proceedings to which it applies
      in a member State other than the United Kingdom;
  "the Model Law" means the UNCITRAL Model Law as set out in Schedule 1 to these
      Regulations;
  "modification or termination order" means an order by the court pursuant to its powers under the
      Model Law modifying or terminating recognition of a foreign proceeding, the sist, restraint
      or suspension referred to in article 20(1) or any part of it or any remedy granted under
      article 19 or 21 of the Model Law;
  "recognition application" means an application to the court by a foreign representative in
      accordance with article 15 of the Model Law for an order recognising the foreign
      proceeding in which he has been appointed;
  "recognition order" means an order by the court recognising a proceeding the subject of a
      recognition application as a foreign main proceeding or foreign non-main proceeding, as
      appropriate;
  ["relevant company" means a company that is—
    (a)   registered under the Companies Act 2006,
    (b)   subject to a requirement imposed by regulations under section 1043 of that Act
        (unregistered UK companies) to deliver any documents to the registrar of companies,
        or
    (c)   subject to a requirement imposed by regulations under section 1046 of that Act
        (overseas companies) to deliver any documents to the registrar of companies;]
  "review application" means an application to the court for a modification or termination order.

(2)   Expressions defined in the Model Law have the same meaning when used in this Schedule.

(3)   References in this Schedule to a debtor who is of interest to the Financial Services Authority are references to a debtor who—

(a)   is, or has been, an authorised person within the meaning of section 31 of the Financial Services and Markets Act 2000 (authorised persons);

(b)   is, or has been, an appointed representative within the meaning of section 39 (exemption of appointed representatives) of that Act; or

(c)   is carrying, or has carried on, a regulated activity in contravention of the general prohibition.

(4)   In sub-paragraph (3) "the general prohibition" has the meaning given by section 19 of the Financial Services and Markets Act 2000 and the reference to a "regulated activity" must be construed in accordance with—

(a)   section 22 of that Act (classes of regulated activity and categories of investment);

(b)   any relevant order under that section; and

(c)   Schedule 2 to that Act (regulated activities).

(4)   References in this Schedule to a numbered form are to the form that bears that number in Schedule 5.

NOTES

Para 1: definition "relevant company" in sub-para (1) substituted by the Companies Act 2006 (Consequential Amendments, Transitional Provisions and Savings) Order 2009, SI 2009/1941, art 2(1), Sch 1, para 264(1), (4)(a), as from 1 October 2009. This Part is reproduced as it appears in the Queen's Printer's copy (ie, with two sub-paras (4)).

PART 2
THE FOREIGN REPRESENTATIVE

[10.977]

2   Application for confirmation of status of replacement foreign representative

(1)   This paragraph applies where following the making of a recognition order the foreign representative dies or for any other reason ceases to be the foreign representative in the foreign proceedings in relation to the debtor.

(2)   In this paragraph "the former foreign representative" means the foreign representative referred to in sub-paragraph (1).

(3)   If a person has succeeded the former foreign representative or is otherwise holding office as foreign representative in the foreign proceeding in relation to the debtor, that person may apply to the court for an order confirming his status as replacement foreign representative for the purpose of proceedings under these Regulations.

(4)   If the court dismisses an application under sub-paragraph (3) then it may also, if it thinks fit, make an order terminating recognition of the foreign proceeding and—

(a)   such an order may include such provision as the court thinks fit with respect to matters arising in connection with the termination; and

(b)   paragraph 5 shall not apply to such an order.

3   Misfeasance by a foreign representative

(1)   The court may examine the conduct of a person who—

(a)   is or purports to be the foreign representative in relation to a debtor, or

(b)   has been or has purported to be the foreign representative in relation to a debtor.

(2)   An examination under this paragraph may be held only on the application of—

(a)   a British insolvency officeholder acting in relation to the debtor,

(b)   a creditor of the debtor, or

(c)   with the permission of the court, any other person who appears to have an interest justifying an application.

(3)   An application under sub-paragraph (2) must allege that the foreign representative—

(a)   has misapplied or retained money or other property of the debtor,

(b)   has become accountable for money or other property of the debtor,

(c)   has breached a fiduciary duty or other duty in relation to the debtor, or

(d)   has been guilty of misfeasance.

(4)   On an examination under this paragraph into a person's conduct the court may order him—

(a)   to repay, restore or account for money or property;

(b)   to pay interest;

(c)   to contribute a sum to the debtor's property by way of compensation for breach of duty or misfeasance.

(5)   In sub-paragraph (3), "foreign representative" includes a person who purports or has purported to be a foreign representative in relation to a debtor.

PART 3
COURT PROCEDURE AND PRACTICE

[10.978]
4   Preliminary and interpretation

(1)   This Part applies to—
- (a)   any of the following applications made to the court under these Regulations—
  - (i)   a recognition application;
  - (ii)   an article 21 remedy application;
  - (iii)   an application under paragraph 2(3) for an order confirming the status of a replacement foreign representative;
  - (iv)   a review application; and
- (b)   any of the following orders made by the court under these Regulations—
  - (i)   a recognition order;
  - (ii)   an order granting interim remedy under article 19 of the Model Law;
  - (iii)   an order granting remedy under article 21 of the Model Law;
  - (iv)   an order confirming the status of a replacement foreign representative; or
  - (v)   a modification or termination order.

5   Reviews of court orders—where court makes order of its own motion

(1)   The court shall not of its own motion make a modification or termination order unless the foreign representative and the debtor have either—
- (a)   had an opportunity of being heard on the question, or
- (b)   consented in writing to such an order.

(2)   If the court makes a modification or termination order, the order may include such provision as the court thinks fit with respect to matters arising in connection with the modification or termination.

6   The hearing

(1)   At the hearing of the application, the applicant and any of the following persons (not being the applicant) may appear or be represented—
- (a)   the foreign representative;
- (b)   the debtor and, in the case of any debtor other than an individual, any one or more directors or other officers of the debtor, including—
  - [(i)   where applicable, any person specified in particulars registered under section 1046 of the Companies Act 2006 (overseas companies) as authorised to represent the debtor;]
  - (ii)   in the case of a debtor which is a partnership, any person who is a member of the partnership;
- (c)   if a British insolvency officeholder is acting in relation to the debtor, that person;
- (d)   if any person has been appointed an administrative receiver of the debtor or as a receiver or manager of the property of the debtor, that person;
- (e)   if a member State liquidator has been appointed in main proceedings in relation to the debtor, that person;
- (f)   if a foreign representative has been appointed in any other foreign proceeding regarding the debtor, that person;
- (g)   any person who has presented a petition for the winding up or sequestration of the debtor in Scotland;
- (h)   any person who is or may be entitled to appoint an administrator of the debtor under paragraph 14 of Schedule B1 to the 1986 Act (appointment of administrator by holder of qualifying floating charge);
- (i)   if the debtor is a debtor who is of interest to the Financial Services Authority, that Authority; and
- (j)   with the permission of the court, any other person who appears to have an interest justifying his appearance.

7   Notification and advertisement of order

(1)   This paragraph applies where the court makes any of the orders referred to in paragraph 4(1)(b).

(2)   The foreign representative shall send a certified copy of the interlocutor as soon as reasonably practicable to the debtor.

(3)   The foreign representative shall, as soon as reasonably practicable after the date of the order, give notice of the making of the order—
- (a)   if a British insolvency officeholder is acting in relation to the debtor, to him;
- (b)   if any person has been appointed an administrative receiver of the debtor or, to the knowledge of the foreign representative, as a receiver or manager of the property of the debtor, to him;
- (c)   if a member State liquidator has been appointed in main proceedings in relation to the debtor, to him;

(d)   if to his knowledge a foreign representative has been appointed in any other foreign proceeding regarding the debtor, that person;

(e)   if there is pending in Scotland a petition for the winding up or sequestration of the debtor, to the petitioner;

(f)   to any person who to his knowledge is or may be entitled to appoint an administrator of the debtor under paragraph 14 of Schedule B1 to the 1986 Act (appointment of administrator by holder of qualifying floating charge);

(g)   if the debtor is a debtor who is of interest to the Financial Services Authority, to that Authority; and

(h)   to such persons as the court may direct.

(4)   Where the debtor is a relevant company, the foreign representative shall send notice of the making of the order to the registrar of companies before the end of the period of 5 business days beginning with the date of the order. The notice to the registrar of companies shall be in Form ML7.

(5)   The foreign representative shall advertise the making of the following orders once in the Gazette and once in such newspaper as he thinks most appropriate for ensuring that the making of the order comes to the notice of the debtor's creditors—

(a)   a recognition order,

(b)   an order confirming the status of a replacement foreign representative, and

(c)   a modification or termination order which modifies or terminates recognition of a foreign proceeding,

and the advertisement shall be in Form ML8.

8   Registration of court order

(1)   Where the court makes a recognition order in respect of a foreign main proceeding or an order suspending the right to transfer, encumber or otherwise dispose of any assets of the debtor being heritable property, the clerk of the court shall send forthwith a certified copy of the order to the keeper of the register of inhibitions and adjudications for recording in that register.

(2)   Recording under sub-paragraph (1) or (3) shall have the effect as from the date of the order of an inhibition and of a citation in an adjudication of the debtor's heritable estate at the instance of the foreign representative.

(3)   Where the court makes a modification or termination order, the clerk of the court shall send forthwith a certified copy of the order to the keeper of the register of inhibitions and adjudications for recording in that register.

(4)   The effect mentioned in sub-paragraph (2) shall expire—

(a)   on the recording of a modification or termination order under sub-paragraph (3); or

(b)   subject to sub-paragraph (5), if the effect has not expired by virtue of paragraph (a), at the end of the period of 3 years beginning with the date of the order.

(5)   The foreign representative may, if recognition of the foreign proceeding has not been modified or terminated by the court pursuant to its powers under the Model Law, before the end of the period of 3 years mentioned in sub-paragraph (4)(b), send a memorandum in a form prescribed by the Court of Session by act of sederunt to the keeper of the register of inhibitions and adjudications for recording in that register, and such recording shall renew the effect mentioned in sub-paragraph (2); and thereafter the said effect shall continue to be preserved only if such memorandum is so recorded before the expiry of every subsequent period of 3 years.

9   Right to inspect court process

(1)   In the case of any proceedings under these Regulations, the following have the right, at all reasonable times, to inspect the court process of the proceedings—

(a)   the Secretary of State;

(b)   the person who is the foreign representative in relation to the proceedings;

(c)   if a foreign representative has been appointed in any other foreign proceeding regarding the debtor, that person;

(d)   if a British insolvency officeholder is acting in relation to the debtor, that person;

(e)   any person stating himself in writing to be a creditor of the debtor to which the proceedings under these Regulations relate;

(f)   if a member State liquidator has been appointed in relation to a debtor which is subject to proceedings under these Regulations, that person; and

(g)   the debtor to which the proceedings under these Regulations relate, or, if that debtor is a company, corporation or partnership, every person who is, or at any time has been—

   (i)   a director or officer of the debtor,

   (ii)   a member of the debtor, or

   [(iii)   where applicable, any person specified in particulars registered under section 1046 of the Companies Act 2006 (overseas companies) as authorised to represent the debtor;]

(2)   The right of inspection conferred as above on any person may be exercised on his behalf by a person properly authorised by him.

10   Copies of court orders

(1)   In any proceedings under these Regulations, any person who under paragraph 9 has a right to inspect documents in the court process also has the right to require the foreign representative in relation to those proceedings to furnish him with a copy of any court order in the proceedings.

(2)   Sub-paragraph (1) does not apply if a copy of the court order has been served on that person or notice of the making of the order has been given to that person under other provisions of these Regulations.

11   Transfer of proceedings—actions to avoid acts detrimental to creditors

If, in accordance with article 23(6) of the Model Law, the court grants a foreign representative permission to make an application in accordance with paragraph (1) of that article, it may also order the relevant proceedings under British insolvency law taking place regarding the debtor to be transferred to the Court of Session if those proceedings are taking place in Scotland and are not already in that court.

NOTES

    Para 6: sub-para (1)(b)(i) substituted by the Companies Act 2006 (Consequential Amendments, Transitional Provisions and Savings) Order 2009, SI 2009/1941, art 2(1), Sch 1, para 264(1), (4)(b), as from 1 October 2009.

    Para 9: sub-para (1)(g)(iii) substituted by SI 2009/1941, art 2(1), Sch 1, para 264(1), (4)(c), as from 1 October 2009.

PART 4

GENERAL

NOTES

    It is assumed that this Part should be Part 4 but it was numbered as a second Part 3 in the original Queen's Printer's copy.

[10.979]

12   Giving of notices, etc

(1)   All notices required or authorised by or under these Regulations to be given, sent or delivered must be in writing, unless it is otherwise provided, or the court allows the notice to be sent or given in some other way.

(2)   Any reference in these Regulations to giving, sending or delivering a notice or any such document means, without prejudice to any other way and unless it is otherwise provided, that the notice or document may be sent by post, and that, subject to paragraph 13, any form of post may be used. Personal service of the notice or document is permissible in all cases.

(3)   Where under these Regulations a notice or other document is required or authorised to be given, sent or delivered by a person ("the sender") to another ("the recipient"), it may be given, sent or delivered by any person duly authorised by the sender to do so to any person duly authorised by the recipient to receive or accept it.

(4)   Where two or more persons are acting jointly as the British insolvency officeholder in proceedings under British insolvency law, the giving, sending or delivering of a notice or document to one of them is to be treated as the giving, sending or delivering of a notice or document to each or all.

13   Sending by post

(1)   For a document to be properly sent by post, it must be contained in an envelope addressed to the person to whom it is to be sent, and pre-paid for either first or second class post.

(2)   Any document to be sent by post may be sent to the last known address of the person to whom the document is to be sent.

(3)   Where first class post is used, the document is to be deemed to be received on the second business day after the date of posting, unless the contrary is shown.

(4)   Where second class post is used, the document is to be deemed to be received on the fourth business day after the date of posting, unless the contrary is shown.

14   Certificate of giving notice, etc

(1)   Where in any proceedings under these Regulations a notice or document is required to be given, sent or delivered by any person, the date of giving, sending or delivery of it may be proved by means of a certificate by that person that he gave, posted or otherwise sent or delivered the notice or document on the date stated in the certificate, or that he instructed another person (naming him) to do so.

(2)   A certificate under this paragraph may be endorsed on a copy of the notice to which it relates.

(3)   A certificate purporting to be signed by or on behalf of the person mentioned in sub-paragraph (1) shall be deemed, unless the contrary is shown, to be sufficient evidence of the matters stated therein.

15 Forms for use in proceedings under these Regulations

(1) Forms ML7 and ML8 contained in Schedule 5 to these Regulations shall be used in, and in connection with, proceedings under these Regulations.

(2) The forms shall be used with such variations, if any, as the circumstances may require.

SCHEDULE 4
NOTICES DELIVERED TO THE REGISTRAR OF COMPANIES
Regulation 6

[10.980]
1 Interpretation

(1) In this Schedule—

"electronic communication" means the same as in the Electronic Communications Act 2000;
"Model Law notice" means a notice delivered to the registrar of companies under paragraph 26(6) of Schedule 2 or paragraph 7(4) of Schedule 3.

(2) Expressions defined in the Model Law or Schedule 2 or 3, as appropriate, have the same meaning when used in this Schedule.

(3) References in this Schedule to delivering a notice include sending, forwarding, producing or giving it.

2 Functions of the registrar of companies

(1) Where a Model Law notice is delivered to the registrar of companies in respect of a relevant company, the registrar shall enter a note in the register relating to that company.

(2) The note referred to in sub-paragraph (1) shall contain the following particulars, in each case as stated in the notice delivered to the registrar—

  (a)   brief details of the court order made;
  (b)   the date of the court order; and
  (c)   the name and address for service of the person who is the foreign representative in relation to the company.

3. . . .

4 Delivery to registrar of notices

(1) Electronic communications may be used for the delivery of any Model Law notice, provided that such delivery is in such form and manner as is directed by the registrar.

(2) Where the Model Law notice is required to be signed, it shall instead be authenticated in such manner as is directed by the registrar.

(3) If a Model Law notice is delivered to the registrar which does not comply with the requirements of these Regulations, he may serve on the person by whom the notice was delivered (or, if there are two or more such persons, on any of them) a notice (a non-compliance notice) indicating the respect in which the Model Law notice does not comply.

(4) Where the registrar serves a non-compliance notice, then, unless a replacement Model Law notice—

  (a)   is delivered to him within 14 days after the service of the non-compliance notice, and
  (b)   complies with the requirements of these Regulations or is not rejected by him for failure to comply with those requirements,

the original Model Law notice shall be deemed not to have been delivered to him.

5 Enforcement of foreign representative's duty to give notice to registrar

(1) If a foreign representative, having made default in complying with paragraph 26(6) of Schedule 2 or paragraph 7(4) of Schedule 3 fails to make good the default within 14 days after the service of a notice on the foreign representative requiring him to do so, the court may, on an application made to it by any creditor, member, director or other officer of the debtor or by the registrar of companies, make an order directing the foreign representative to make good the default within such time as may be specified in the order.

(2) The court's order may provide that all costs of and incidental to the application shall be borne by the foreign representative.

6 Rectification of the register under court order

(1) The registrar shall remove from the register any note, or part of a note—

  (a)   that relates to or is derived from a court order that the court has declared to be invalid or ineffective, or
  (b)   that the court declares to be factually inaccurate or derived from something that is factually inaccurate or forged,

and that the court directs should be removed from the register.

(2)   The court order must specify what is to be removed from the register and indicate where on the register it is and the registrar shall carry out his duty under sub-paragraph (1) within a reasonable time of receipt by him of the relevant court order.

NOTES

Para 1: definition "the 1985 Act" (omitted) revoked by the Companies Act 2006 (Consequential Amendments, Transitional Provisions and Savings) Order 2009, SI 2009/1941, art 2(1), Sch 1, para 264(1), (5)(a), as from 1 October 2009.

Para 3: revoked by SI 2009/1941, art 2(1), Sch 1, para 264(1), (5)(b), as from 1 October 2009.

SCHEDULE 5
FORMS

[10.981]

NOTES

This Schedule sets out the forms prescribed for use in connection with proceedings under these Regulations. The forms are not reproduced here but details are given in the table below. The forms have been amended as noted below.

Form No	Description	Prescribed by
ML1	Recognition application	Sch 2, para 2; amended by SI 2009/1941
ML2	Recognition order	Sch 2, para 5(2)
ML3	Statement of subsequent information	Sch 2, para 6
ML4	Originating application	Sch 2, para 32
ML5	Ordinary application	Sch 2, paras 19, 32
ML6	Affidavit of service of application under the Cross-Border Insolvency Regulations 2006	Sch 2, para 23
ML7	Notice to registrar of companies of order under the Cross-Border Insolvency Regulations 2006	Sch 2, para 26(6) Sch 3, para 7(4); amended by SI 2009/1941
ML8	Notification of order under the Cross-Border Insolvency Regulations 2006 (for newspaper and London or Edinburgh Gazette)	Sch 2, para 26(7) Sch 3, para 7(5)

INSURANCE ACCOUNTS DIRECTIVE (MISCELLANEOUS INSURANCE UNDERTAKINGS) REGULATIONS 2008 (NOTE)

(SI 2008/565)

[10.982]

NOTES

These Regulations were made on 26 February 2008 under the powers conferred by the European Communities Act 1972, s 2(2).

They apply to the insurance undertakings specified in reg 2(2)–(4) which are incorporated in or formed under the law of any part of the UK. They replace the Insurance Accounts Directive (Miscellaneous Insurance Undertakings) Regulations 1993 (SI 1993/3245) which applied to such undertakings incorporated in or formed under the law of GB, and the Insurance Accounts Directive (Miscellaneous Insurance Undertakings) Regulations (Northern Ireland) 1994 (SR 1994/429) which applied to such undertakings formed or incorporated under the law of Northern Ireland.

The Regulations continue the implementation of Council Directive 91/674/EEC on the annual accounts and consolidated accounts of insurance undertakings. They also implement, in part, Directive 2006/43/EC on statutory audits of annual accounts and consolidated accounts ("the Audit Directive").

The Regulations came into force on 6 April 2008 and apply to financial years of the insurance undertakings to which they relate beginning on or after that date and auditors appointed in respect of those financial years (reg 1(2)).

Regulation 2(2)–(4) re-enacts the provisions of the 1993 and 1994 Regulations defining the insurance undertakings which are subject to the accounting requirements of these Regulations. Those provisions read as follows—

"(2)   Subject to paragraph (3), a body incorporated in or formed under the law of any part of the United Kingdom is an insurance undertaking for the purposes of these Regulations if it—

(a)   is incorporated by or registered under any public general Act of Parliament,

(b)   requires permission under Part 4 of the Financial Services and Markets Act 2000 to effect or carry out contracts of insurance without contravening the prohibition imposed by section 19 of that Act, and

(c)   is not required by any enactment to prepare accounts under Part 15 of the Companies Act 2006 (accounts and reports).

(3)   Paragraph (2)(b) must be read with—

(a)   section 22 of the Financial Services and Markets Act 2000,

(b)   the Financial Services and Markets Act 2000 (Regulated Activities) Order 2001,

    (c)   Schedule 2 to that Act.

(4)   A body is not an insurance undertaking for the purposes of these Regulations if it—

    (a)   is excluded from the scope of Council Directive 73/239/EEC by Article 3 of that Directive,

    (b)   is referred to in Article 3(2) to (6) of Directive 2002/83/EC of the European Parliament and of the Council of 5th November 2002 concerning life assurance, or

    (c)   is a friendly society.".

Regulation 3 re-enacts the requirements of the 1993 and 1994 Regulations that insurance undertakings prepare accounts and directors' reports, and cause to be prepared auditors' reports, as if they were insurance companies or parent companies of insurance groups (within the meaning of the Companies Act 2006). The accounts are to comply with the provisions set out in reg 3(3) and are to be prepared within the period of 6 months from the end of the relevant financial year, which is a reduction of the period for such preparation from 7 months as provided for in the 1993 and 1994 Regulations. This reflects the new time limit in s 442(2)(b) of the Companies Act 2006.

Regulation 3(5) applies the relevant provisions of the Companies (Disclosure of Auditor Remuneration and Liability Limitation Agreements) Regulations 2008 (SI 2008/489) to insurance undertakings. This implements Article 49 of the Audit Directive on the disclosure of auditor remuneration.

Regulation 4 re-enacts the requirements of the 1993 and 1994 Regulations relating to publication of the accounts. Regulation 5 re-enacts the penalties for non-compliance with the provisions of regs 3 and 4.

Regulation 6 implements Article 37 of the Audit Directive, which requires the auditor to be appointed by the general meeting of shareholders or members of the audited entity. It does so by applying ss 485–488 of the Companies Act 2006. Regulation 7 imposes equivalent functions on auditors to those imposed by the Companies Act 2006, and reg 8 implements Article 28(1) of the Audit Directive on signature of the auditor's report.

Regulation 9 implements Article 38(1) of the Audit Directive, which requires Member States to ensure that auditors may be dismissed only where there are proper grounds. It creates a new right to apply to the High Court, which may be exercised by a member of the insurance undertaking or by the FSA.

Regulations 10 and 11 implement Article 38(2) of the Audit Directive, which requires Member States to ensure that the audited entity and the auditor inform the authorities responsible for public oversight of the resignation or dismissal of the auditor. Regulation 12 contains penalties for non-compliance with regs 10 and 11.

Regulation 14 and Schs 1, 2 modify the Friendly and Industrial and Provident Societies Act 1968 and the Industrial and Provident Societies (Northern Ireland) Act 1969 and regulation 15 makes consequential amendments to these enactments. Regulation 15 also makes a consequential amendment to the Companies Act 2006, s 1210. Note that the Friendly and Industrial and Provident Societies Act 1968 is renamed as the Co-operative and Community Benefit Societies and Credit Unions Act 1968 by the Co-operative and Community Benefit Societies and Credit Unions Act 2010.

Regulation 16 revokes the 1993 and 1994 Regulations and makes transitional provision for the continued application of those regulations after revocation in respect of financial years beginning before 6 April 2008.

BANK ACCOUNTS DIRECTIVE (MISCELLANEOUS BANKS) REGULATIONS 2008 (NOTE)

(SI 2008/567)

[10.983]

NOTES

These Regulations were made on 26 February 2008 under the powers conferred by the European Communities Act 1972, s 2(2). They replace the Bank Accounts Directive (Miscellaneous Banks) Regulations 1991 (SI 1991/2704) and continue the implementation of Council Directive 86/635/EEC on the annual and consolidated accounts of banks and other financial institutions. They also implement, in part, Directive 2006/43/EC on statutory audits of annual accounts and consolidated accounts ("the Audit Directive").

The Regulations came into force on 6 April 2008, and apply to financial years beginning on or after that date, and auditors appointed in respect of those financial years (reg 1(2)). They extend to the whole of the UK. They apply to the undertakings specified in reg 3 which have their principal place of business in the UK. That provision reads as follows—

"3   Meaning of "qualifying bank"

(1)   Any body of persons, whether incorporated or unincorporated, which—

    (a)   is incorporated or formed by or established under any public general Act of Parliament passed before the year 1837,

    (b)   has a principal place of business within the United Kingdom,

    (c)   is an authorised deposit taker, and

    (d)   is not required by any enactment to prepare accounts under Part 15 of the Companies Act 2006,

is a qualifying bank for the purposes of these Regulations.

(2)   In paragraph (1), "authorised deposit taker" means a person with permission under Part 4 of the Financial Services and Markets Act 2000 to accept deposits, but excludes—

    (a)   a building society, within the meaning of section 119 of the Building Societies Act 1986,

    (b)   a credit union, within the meaning of the Credit Unions Act 1979 or the Credit Unions (Northern Ireland) Order 1985,

    (c)   a specially authorised friendly society, within the meaning of section 7(1)(f) of the Friendly Societies Act 1974, and

    (d)   a person who has permission to accept deposits only in the course of effecting or carrying out contracts of insurance in accordance with that permission.

(3)   References in paragraph (2) to—

    (a)   accepting deposits, and

    (b)   effecting and carrying out contracts of insurance,

must be read with section 22 of the Financial Services and Markets Act 2000, the Financial Services and Markets Act 2000 (Regulated Activities) Order 2001, and Schedule 2 to that Act.".

Regulation 4 re-enacts the requirements of the 1991 Regulations that qualifying banks prepare accounts and a directors' report, and cause to be prepared an auditor's report, as if they were banking companies or parent companies of banking groups (within the meaning of the Companies Act 2006). Relevant provisions of the Companies Act 2006 and of the Large and Medium-sized Companies and Groups (Accounts and Reports) Regulations 2008 (SI 2008/410) are applied to the accounts and reports of such banks. Some of those provisions are modified by the Schedule to the Regulations. Regulation 4(2) applies the relevant provisions of the Companies (Disclosure of Auditor Remuneration and Liability Limitation Agreements) Regulations 2008 (SI 2008/489) to qualifying banks. This implements Article 49 of the Audit Directive on the disclosure of auditor remuneration.

The requirement of the 1991 Regulations that the accounts of qualifying banks should be prepared within 7 months of the end of the relevant year is replaced by a requirement that the accounts should be prepared within 6 months of that date (reg 4(3)), reflecting the new time limit in the Companies Act 2006, s 442(2)(b).

Regulation 5 re-enacts the provisions of the 1991 Regulations for the publication of the accounts required by these Regulations. Regulation 6 contains penalties for non-compliance with regs 4 and 5.

Regulation 7 implements Article 37 of the Audit Directive, which requires the auditor to be appointed by the general meeting of shareholders or members of the audited entity. It does so by applying ss 485–488 of the Companies Act 2006. Regulation 8 imposes equivalent functions on auditors to those imposed by the Companies Act 2006, and reg 9 implements Article 28(1) of the Audit Directive on signature of the auditor's report.

Regulation 10 implements Article 38(1) of the Audit Directive, which requires Member States to ensure that auditors may be dismissed only where there are proper grounds. It creates a new right to apply to the High Court, which may be exercised by a member of the qualifying bank or by the FSA.

Regulations 11 and 12 implement Article 38(2) of the Audit Directive, which requires Member States to ensure that the audited entity and the auditor inform the authorities responsible for public oversight of the resignation or dismissal of the auditor. Regulation 13 contains penalties for non-compliance with regs 11 and 12.

Regulation 14 makes a consequential amendment to the Companies Act 2006.

Regulation 15 revokes the 1991 Regulations and makes transitional provision for the continued application of those regulations in respect of financial years of qualifying banks beginning before 6 April 2008.

PARTNERSHIPS (ACCOUNTS) REGULATIONS 2008

(SI 2008/569)

NOTES
Made: 26 February 2008.
Authority: European Communities Act 1972, s 2(2), Companies Act 2006, ss 1210(1)(h), 1292(2).
Commencement: 6 April 2008.
Amendment: as of 1 July 2011 these Regulations had not been amended.

ARRANGEMENT OF REGULATIONS

PART 1
INTRODUCTION

PART 2
PARTNERSHIP ACCOUNTS

PART 3
AUDITORS

PART 4
OFFENCES

PART 5
FINAL PROVISIONS

SCHEDULE

PART 1
INTRODUCTION

[10.984]
1   Citation, commencement and application

(1)   These Regulations may be cited as the Partnerships (Accounts) Regulations 2008.

(2)   These Regulations come into force on 6th April 2008 and apply in relation to—

    (a)   qualifying partnerships' financial years beginning on or after that date, and

    (b)   auditors appointed in respect of those financial years.

NOTES
Commencement: 6 April 2008.

[10.985]
2   Interpretation

(1)   In these Regulations—

"the accounts", in relation to a qualifying partnership, means the annual accounts, the directors' report and the auditor's report required by regulation 4,

"dealt with on a consolidated basis" means dealt with by the method of full consolidation, the method of proportional consolidation or the equity method of accounting,

"financial year", in relation to a qualifying partnership, means any period of not more than 18 months in respect of which a profit and loss account of the partnership is required to be made up by or in accordance with its constitution or, failing any such requirement, each period of 12 months beginning with 1st April,

"the Fourth Directive" means the Fourth Council Directive (78/660/EEC) of 25th July 1978 on the annual accounts of certain types of companies,

"general partner" has the same meaning as in the Limited Partnerships Act 1907,

"the Large and Medium-sized Companies Accounts Regulations" means the Large and Medium-sized Companies and Groups (Accounts and Reports) Regulations 2008,

"limited company" means a company limited by shares or limited by guarantee,

"limited partnership" means a partnership formed in accordance with the Limited Partnerships Act 1907,

"qualifying partnership" has the meaning given by regulation 3,

"the Seventh Directive" means the Seventh Council Directive (83/349/EEC) of 13th June 1983 on consolidated accounts,

"the Small Companies Accounts Regulations" means the Small Companies and Groups (Accounts and Directors' Report) Regulations 2008,

and except as otherwise provided in these Regulations, words and expressions used in the Companies Act 2006 have the same meaning in these Regulations as they have in that Act.

(2)   Any reference in these Regulations to the members of a qualifying partnership is to be construed, in relation to a limited partnership, as a reference to its general partner or partners.

NOTES
Commencement: 6 April 2008.

[10.986]
3   Qualifying partnerships

(1)   A partnership which is formed under the law of any part of the United Kingdom is a qualifying partnership for the purposes of these Regulations if each of its members is—

    (a)   a limited company, or

    (b)   an unlimited company, or a Scottish partnership, each of whose members is a limited company.

(2)   Where the members of a qualifying partnership include—

    (a)   an unlimited company, or a Scottish partnership, each of whose members is a limited company, or

    (b)   a member of another partnership each of whose members is—

        (i)   a limited company, or

        (ii)   an unlimited company, or a Scottish partnership, each of whose members is a limited company,

any reference in these Regulations to the members of the qualifying partnership includes a reference to the members of that company or other partnership.

(3)   The requirements of these Regulations apply without regard to any change in the members of a qualifying partnership which does not result in it ceasing to be such a partnership.

(4)   Any reference in paragraph (1) or (2) to a limited company, an unlimited company or a partnership includes a reference to any comparable undertaking incorporated in or formed under the law of any country or territory outside the United Kingdom.

NOTES

Commencement: 6 April 2008.

PART 2
PARTNERSHIP ACCOUNTS

[10.987]

4   Preparation of accounts of qualifying partnerships

(1)   Subject to regulation 7, the persons who are members of a qualifying partnership at the end of any financial year of the partnership must, in respect of that year—

    (a)   prepare the like annual accounts and directors' report, and

    (b)   cause to be prepared such an auditor's report,

as would be required, if the partnership were a company, under Part 15 (accounts and reports) and Chapter 1 of Part 16 (requirement for audited accounts) of the Companies Act 2006, and under the Small Companies Accounts Regulations or the Large and Medium-sized Companies Accounts Regulations (as the case may be).

(2)   Regulations 4 to 6 of the Companies (Disclosure of Auditor Remuneration and Liability Limitation Agreements) Regulations 2008 apply in relation to the accounts required by this regulation as they apply in relation to the annual accounts of a company or group.

(3)   The accounts required by this regulation must—

    (a)   be prepared within the period of 9 months beginning immediately after the end of the partnership's financial year, and

    (b)   state that they are prepared under this regulation.

(4)   Part 1 of the Schedule to these Regulations sets out certain modifications and adaptations for the purposes of this regulation.

NOTES

Commencement: 6 April 2008.

[10.988]

5   Delivery of accounts of qualifying partnerships to registrar etc

(1)   Subject to regulation 7, each limited company which is a member of a qualifying partnership at the end of any financial year of the partnership must append to the copy of its accounts and reports which is next delivered to the registrar in accordance with section 441(1) of the Companies Act 2006 (duty to file accounts and reports with the registrar) a copy of the accounts of the partnership prepared for that year under regulation 4.

(2)   Subject to regulation 7, a limited company which is a member of a qualifying partnership must supply to any person upon request—

    (a)   the name of each member of the partnership which is to deliver, or has delivered, a copy of the latest accounts of the partnership to the registrar under paragraph (1), and

    (b)   the name of each member of the partnership incorporated in a member State other than the United Kingdom which is to publish, or has published, the latest accounts for the partnership in accordance with the provisions of the Fourth or Seventh Directive.

NOTES

Commencement: 6 April 2008.

[10.989]

6   Publication of accounts of qualifying partnerships at head office

(1)   Subject to paragraph (2) and regulation 7, this regulation applies where a qualifying partnership's head office is in the United Kingdom and each of its members is—

    (a)   an undertaking comparable to a limited company which is incorporated in a country or territory outside the United Kingdom, or

    (b)   an undertaking comparable to an unlimited company or partnership—

        (i)   which is incorporated in or formed under the law of such a country or territory, and

        (ii)   each of whose members is such an undertaking as is mentioned in sub-paragraph (a).

(2)   This regulation does not apply where any member of a qualifying partnership is—

    (a)   an undertaking comparable to a limited company which is incorporated in a member State other than the United Kingdom, or

    (b)   an undertaking comparable to an unlimited company or partnership—

        (i)   which is incorporated in or formed under the law of such a State, and

        (ii)   each of whose members is such an undertaking as is mentioned in sub-paragraph (a), and (in either case) the latest accounts of the qualifying partnership have been or are to be appended to the accounts of any member of the partnership and published under the law of that State and in accordance with the provisions of the Fourth or Seventh Directive.

(3)   The members of the qualifying partnership—
  (a)   must make the latest accounts of the partnership available for inspection by any person, without charge and during business hours, at the head office of the partnership, and
  (b)   if any document comprised in those accounts is in a language other than English, must annex to that document a translation of it into English, certified as an accurate translation—
    (i)   if the translation was made in the United Kingdom, by—
      (aa)   a notary public in any part of the United Kingdom;
      (bb)   a solicitor (if the translation was made in Scotland), a solicitor of the Supreme Court of Judicature of England and Wales (if it was made in England or Wales), or a solicitor of the Supreme Court of Judicature of Northern Ireland (if it was made in Northern Ireland); or
      (cc)   a person certified by a person mentioned above to be known to be competent to translate the document into English; or
    (ii)   if the translation was made outside the United Kingdom, by—
      (aa)   a notary public;
      (bb)   a person authorised in the place where the translation was made to administer an oath;
      (cc)   any of the British officials mentioned in section 6 of the Commissioners for Oaths Act 1889;
      (dd)   a person certified by a person mentioned above to be known to be competent to translate the document into English.

(4)   A member of the qualifying partnership must supply to any person upon request—
  (a)   a copy of the accounts required by paragraph (3)(a) to be made available for inspection, and
  (b)   a copy of any translation required by paragraph (3)(b) to be annexed to any document comprised in those accounts,
at a price not exceeding the administrative cost of making the copy.

NOTES
Commencement: 6 April 2008.

[10.990]
7   Exemption from regulations 4 to 6 where accounts consolidated
(1)   The members of a qualifying partnership are exempt from the requirements of regulations 4 to 6 if the partnership is dealt with on a consolidated basis in group accounts prepared by—
  (a)   a member of the partnership which is established under the law of a member State, or
  (b)   a parent undertaking of such a member which parent undertaking is so established,
and (in either case) the conditions mentioned in paragraph (2) are complied with.
(2)   The conditions are—
  (a)   that the group accounts are prepared and audited under the law of the member State concerned in accordance with the provisions of the Seventh Directive or of international accounting standards, and
  (b)   the notes to those accounts disclose that advantage has been taken of the exemption conferred by this regulation.
(3)   Where advantage is taken of the exemption conferred by this regulation, any member of the qualifying partnership which is a limited company must disclose on request the name of at least one member or parent undertaking in whose group accounts the partnership has been or is to be dealt with on a consolidated basis.

NOTES
Commencement: 6 April 2008.

PART 3
AUDITORS

[10.991]
8   Appointment of auditor
An auditor may be appointed for the purposes of regulation 4(1)(b) only by the members of a qualifying partnership.

NOTES
Commencement: 6 April 2008.

[10.992]
9 Functions of auditor

(1) The following provisions of the Companies Act 2006 apply to the auditor of a qualifying partnership as they apply to an auditor of a company—
- (a) section 495 (auditor's report on company's annual accounts);
- (b) section 498 (duties of auditor);
- (c) section 499 (auditor's general right to information).

(2) The auditor of a qualifying partnership must supply the members of the qualifying partnership with such information as is necessary to enable any disclosure required by regulation 4(2) to be made.

NOTES
Commencement: 6 April 2008.

[10.993]
10 Signature of auditor's report

Sections 503 to 506 of the Companies Act 2006 (signature of auditor's report) apply in relation to the auditor's report required by regulation 4(1)(b), subject to—
- (a) any necessary modifications to take account of the fact that the qualifying partnership is unincorporated, and
- (b) the modification set out in Part 2 of the Schedule to these Regulations.

NOTES
Commencement: 6 April 2008.

[10.994]
11 Removal of auditors on improper grounds

(1) Where the auditor of a qualifying partnership is removed from office an application may be made to the High Court under this regulation.

(2) The persons who may make such an application are—
- (a) any member of the qualifying partnership who was also a member at the time of the removal, and
- (b) the Secretary of State.

(3) If the court is satisfied that the removal was—
- (a) on grounds of divergence of opinion on accounting treatments or audit procedures, or
- (b) on any other improper grounds,

it may make such order as it thinks fit for giving relief in respect of the removal.

(4) The court may, in particular—
- (a) declare that any decision of the qualifying partnership removing an auditor, or appointing a new auditor in his place, is void;
- (b) require the members of the qualifying partnership to re-appoint the dismissed auditor;
- (c) give directions as to the conduct of the qualifying partnership's affairs in the future.

(5) In the application of this regulation to a qualifying partnership formed under the law of Scotland or Northern Ireland, references to the High Court are to be read as references to the Court of Session or, as the case may be, the High Court in Northern Ireland.

NOTES
Commencement: 6 April 2008.

[10.995]
12 Duty of auditor to notify supervisory body

(1) Where an auditor of a qualifying partnership ceases to hold office before the end of his term of office, he must notify the supervisory body of which he is a member.

(2) The notice must—
- (a) inform the supervisory body that he has ceased to hold office, and
- (b) be accompanied by a statement of any circumstances connected with his ceasing to hold office.

(3) The auditor must notify the supervisory body not more than 14 days after the date on which he ceases to hold office.

(4) In this regulation and regulation 13, "supervisory body" has the same meaning as in Part 42 of the Companies Act 2006 (statutory auditors) (see section 1217).

NOTES
Commencement: 6 April 2008.

[10.996]
13   Duty of members of qualifying partnership to notify supervisory body

(1)   Where an auditor of a qualifying partnership ceases to hold office before the end of his term of office, the members of the partnership must notify the supervisory body of which the auditor is a member.

(2)   The notice must—
  (a)   inform the supervisory body that the auditor has ceased to hold office, and
  (b)   be accompanied by a statement by the body of the reasons for his ceasing to hold office.

(3)   The members of the qualifying partnership must notify the supervisory body not more than 14 days after the date on which the auditor ceases to hold office.

NOTES
  Commencement: 6 April 2008.

[10.997]
14   Statutory auditors

For the purposes of section 1210(1)(h) of the Companies Act 2006 (meaning of "statutory auditor")—
  (a)   a qualifying partnership is a prescribed person, and
  (b)   regulation 4(1)(b) is a prescribed enactment,
and accordingly a person appointed as auditor of a qualifying partnership for the purposes of regulation 4(1)(b) is a statutory auditor.

NOTES
  Commencement: 6 April 2008.

PART 4
OFFENCES

[10.998]
15   Penalties for non-compliance by members of qualifying partnership

(1)   If, in respect of a financial year of a qualifying partnership, the requirements of paragraph (1) of regulation 4 are not complied with within the period referred to in paragraph (3) of that regulation, every person who was a member of the partnership or a director of such a member at the end of that year is liable on summary conviction to a fine not exceeding level 5 on the standard scale.

(2)   If the accounts of a qualifying partnership—
  (a)   a copy of which is delivered to the registrar under regulation 5, or
  (b)   which are made available for inspection under regulation 6,
do not comply with the requirements of regulation 4(1), every person who, at the time when the copy was so delivered or (as the case may be) the accounts were first made available for inspection, was a member of the partnership or a director of such a member is liable on summary conviction to a fine not exceeding level 5 on the standard scale.

(3)   If a member of a qualifying partnership fails to comply with regulation 5, 6, 7(3) or 13, that member and any director of that member is liable on summary conviction to a fine not exceeding level 5 on the standard scale.

(4)   In proceedings for an offence under this section it is a defence for the person charged to show that he took all reasonable steps and exercised all due diligence to avoid the commission of the offence.

(5)   The following provisions of the Companies Act 2006, namely—
  (a)   sections 1127 and 1128 (summary proceedings: venue and time limit for proceedings), and
  (b)   section 1130 (proceedings against unincorporated bodies),
apply to an offence under this regulation.

NOTES
  Commencement: 6 April 2008.

[10.999]
16   Penalties for non-compliance by auditors of qualifying partnerships

(1)   If a person ceasing to hold office as auditor fails to comply with regulation 12, an offence is committed by—
  (a)   that person, and
  (b)   if that person is a firm, every officer of the firm who is in default.

(2)   In proceedings for an offence under this section it is a defence for the person charged to show that he took all reasonable steps and exercised all due diligence to avoid the commission of the offence.

(3)   A person guilty of an offence under this regulation is liable—

(a)   on conviction on indictment, to a fine, and

(b)   on summary conviction, to a fine not exceeding the statutory maximum.

(4)   The following provisions of the Companies Act 2006, namely—
   (a)   sections 1121 to 1123 (liability of officer in default),
   (b)   sections 1127 and 1128 (summary proceedings: venue and time limit for proceedings), and
   (c)   section 1130 (proceedings against unincorporated bodies),
apply to an offence under this regulation.

NOTES

Commencement: 6 April 2008.

PART 5
FINAL PROVISIONS

[10.1000]

17   *(Amends the Small Companies and Groups (Accounts and Directors' Report) Regulations 2008, SI 2008/409, Sch 2, Pt 1, Sch 6, Pt 2 at* **[4.158]**, **[4.165]**, *and the Large and Medium-sized Companies and Groups (Accounts and Reports) Regulations 2008, SI 2008/410, Sch 4, Pt 1 at* **[4.196]**.*)*

18   Revocation and transitional provisions etc

(1)   The Partnerships and Unlimited Companies (Accounts) Regulations 1993 and the Partnerships and Unlimited Companies (Accounts) Regulations (Northern Ireland) 1994 are revoked.

(2)   The regulations specified in paragraph (1) continue to apply to any financial year of a qualifying partnership beginning before 6th April 2008.

NOTES

Commencement: 6 April 2008.

SCHEDULE

Regulations 4(4) and 10(b)

PART 1
MODIFICATIONS AND ADAPTATIONS FOR PURPOSES OF REGULATION 4

[10.1001]

1. (1)   Accounts prepared under regulation 4 of these Regulations must comply with the requirements of Part 15 and Chapter 1 of Part 16 of the Companies Act 2006, and with the Small Companies Accounts Regulations or the Large and Medium-sized Companies Accounts Regulations (as the case may be) subject to—
   (a)   the provisions of section 1161(2) and (3) of that Act (how to construe "shares" and other expressions appropriate to companies),
   (b)   the omission of the provisions of the Small Companies Accounts Regulations mentioned in paragraph 2(1) below,
   (c)   the omission of the provisions of the Large and Medium-sized Companies Accounts Regulations mentioned in paragraph 2(2) below, and
   (d)   any necessary modifications to take account of the fact that partnerships are unincorporated.

(2)   For the purposes of the provisions of Part 15 and Chapter 1 of Part 16 of the Companies Act 2006 and of the Small Companies Accounts Regulations and the Large and Medium-sized Companies Accounts Regulations as applied to the accounts and report so prepared, these Regulations are to be regarded as part of the requirements of that Act and those regulations.

2. (1)   The provisions of the Small Companies Accounts Regulations referred to in paragraph 1(1)(b) are—
   (a)   in Part 1 of Schedule 1—
      (i)   in paragraph 3(2), the words from "used" to the end, and
      (ii)   paragraph 6,
   (b)   in Part 2 of Schedule 1, paragraph 21,
   (c)   in Part 3 of Schedule 1, paragraphs 49 and 50,
   (d)   in Part 1 of Schedule 2, paragraph 10,
   (e)   in Part 1 of Schedule 3, paragraph 3,
   (f)   Schedule 5, and
   (g)   in Part 1 of Schedule 6, paragraphs 13(3) and (4), 14 and 15, and in Part 2 of that Schedule, paragraph 36.

(2)   The provisions of the Large and Medium-sized Companies Accounts Regulations referred to in paragraph 1(1)(c) are—
   (a)   in Part 1 of Schedule 1—

       (i)   in paragraph 3(2), the words from "used" to the end, and
       (ii)   paragraph 6,
  (b)   in Part 2 of Schedule 1, paragraph 21,
  (c)   in Part 3 of Schedule 1, paragraphs 45, 50, 52, 53, 54, 64(2), 66 and 67,
  (d)   in Part 1 of Schedule 4, paragraph 9, and in Part 2 paragraph 12,
  (e)   in Schedule 5, paragraphs 2, 4 and 5,
  (f)   in Part 1 of Schedule 6 to those Regulations, paragraphs 13(3) and (4), 14 and 15, and
  (g)   Schedule 7 to those Regulations except paragraph 7.

(3)   Sub-paragraphs (1) and (2) are not to be construed as affecting the requirement to give a true and fair view under sections 393, 396 and 404 of the Companies Act 2006.

NOTES

Commencement: 6 April 2008.

PART 2
MODIFICATION FOR PURPOSES OF REGULATION 10

[10.1002]

3. In section 506(1)(b) of the Companies Act 2006 the reference to the copy of the report delivered to the registrar under Chapter 10 of Part 15 (filing of accounts and reports) is treated as a reference to the copy of the accounts required to be delivered to the registrar under regulation 5(1).

NOTES

Commencement: 6 April 2008.

LIMITED LIABILITY PARTNERSHIPS (ACCOUNTS AND AUDIT) (APPLICATION OF COMPANIES ACT 2006) REGULATIONS 2008

(SI 2008/1911)

NOTES

Made: 17 July 2008.
Authority: Limited Liability Partnerships Act 2000, ss 15, 17; Companies Act 2006, ss 1210(1)(h), 1292(2).
Commencement: 1 October 2008.
These Regulations are reproduced as amended by: the Financial Services and Markets Act 2000 (Regulated Activities) (Amendment) Order 2009, SI 2009/1342; the Limited Liability Partnerships (Application of Companies Act 2006) Regulations 2009, SI 2009/1804; the Electronic Money Regulations 2011, SI 2011/99.
References to "the European Community", "Community", etc: see the Treaty of Lisbon (Changes in Terminology) Order 2011, SI 2011/1043, which provides that (as from 22 April 2011) "EU" should be substituted for the word "Community" (subject to certain exceptions) in references to "Community treaties", "Community instrument", "Community obligation", "Community law", "Community legislation", etc.

ARRANGEMENT OF REGULATIONS

PART 1
GENERAL INTRODUCTORY PROVISIONS

PART 2
LLPS QUALIFYING AS SMALL

PART 3
ACCOUNTING RECORDS

PART 4
FINANCIAL YEARS

PART 5
ANNUAL ACCOUNTS

PART 1
GENERAL INTRODUCTORY PROVISIONS

[10.1003]
1   Citation and commencement

These Regulations may be cited as the Limited Liability Partnerships (Accounts and Audit) (Application of Companies Act 2006) Regulations 2008 and come into force on 1st October 2008.

NOTES

Commencement: 1 October 2008.

[10.1004]
2   Application

(1)   Subject to paragraphs (2) to (11), these Regulations apply to accounts for financial years beginning on or after 1st October 2008.

(2)   Any question whether—
  (a)   for the purposes of section 382, 383, 384(3) or 467(3) of the Companies Act 2006, as applied to limited liability partnerships by regulations 5 and 26, a limited liability partnership or group qualified as small in a financial year beginning before 1st October 2008, or
  (b)   for the purposes of section 465 or 466 of that Act, as applied to limited liability partnerships by regulation 26, a limited liability partnership or group qualified as medium-sized in any such financial year,

is to be determined by reference to the corresponding provisions of the Companies Act 1985 or the Companies (Northern Ireland) Order 1986 as applied to limited liability partnerships by the Limited Liability Partnerships Regulations 2001 or the Limited Liability Partnerships Regulations (Northern Ireland) 2004.

(3)   Sections 485 to 488 of the Companies Act 2006, as applied to limited liability partnerships by regulation 36, apply in relation to appointments of auditors for financial years beginning on or after 1st October 2008.

(4)   Sections 492, 494 and 499 to 501 of the Companies Act 2006, as applied to limited liability partnerships by regulations 37, 38 and 40, apply to auditors appointed for financial years beginning on or after 1st October 2008.

(5)   Section 502 of the Companies Act 2006, as applied to limited liability partnerships by regulation 40, applies to auditors appointed on or after 1st October 2008.

(6)   Sections 495, 498 and 503 to 509 of the Companies Act 2006, as applied to limited liability partnerships by regulations 39 to 42, apply to auditors' reports on accounts for financial years beginning on or after 1st October 2008.

(7)   Sections 510 to 513 of the Companies Act 2006, as applied to limited liability partnerships by regulations 43 and 44, apply where notice of the proposed removal is given to the auditor on or after 1st October 2008.

(8)   Section 515 of the Companies Act 2006, as applied to limited liability partnerships by regulation 45, applies to appointments of auditors for financial years beginning on or after 1st October 2008.

(9)   Sections 516 to 518 of the Companies Act 2006, as applied to limited liability partnerships by regulation 45, apply to resignations occurring on or after 1st October 2008.

(10)   Sections 519 to 525 of the Companies Act 2006, as applied to limited liability partnerships by regulation 46, apply where the auditor ceases to hold office on or after 1st October 2008.

(11)   Section 526 of the Companies Act 2006, as applied to limited liability partnerships by regulation 46, applies where the vacancy occurs on or after 1st October 2008.

NOTES

Commencement: 1 October 2008.

[10.1005]

3 Interpretation

(1)   In these Regulations—

"1985 Act" means the Companies Act 1985,

"1986 Order" means the Companies (Northern Ireland) Order 1986, and

"LLP" means a limited liability partnership [registered under the Limited Liability Partnerships Act 2000].

(2)   In these Regulations, unless the context otherwise requires—

(a)   any reference to a numbered Part, section or Schedule is to the Part, section or Schedule so numbered in the Companies Act 2006,

(b)   references in provisions applied to LLPs to other provisions of the Companies Act 2006 are to those provisions as applied to LLPs by these Regulations, and

(c)   references in provisions applied to LLPs to provisions of the Insolvency Act 1986 or the Insolvency (Northern Ireland) Order 1989 are to those provisions as applied to LLPs by the Limited Liability Partnerships Regulations 2001 or the Limited Liability Partnerships Regulations (Northern Ireland) 2004.

NOTES

Commencement: 1 October 2008.

Para (1): words in square brackets substituted by the Limited Liability Partnerships (Application of Companies Act 2006) Regulations 2009, SI 2009/1804, reg 85, Sch 3, Pt 2, para 15(1), (2), as from 1 October 2009.

General note as to interpretation: as to the meaning of "the registrar" and "the register", and as to the construction of references to registration in a particular part of the United Kingdom, in any enactment relating to LLPs, see the Limited Liability Partnerships (Application of Companies Act 2006) Regulations 2009, SI 2009/1804, reg 85, Sch 3, Pt 2, para 12 at **[10.1191]**.

[10.1006]

4 Scheme of Part 15 as applied to LLPs

Section 380 applies to LLPs, modified so that it reads as follows—

"380 Scheme of this Part

(1)   The requirements of this Part as to accounts and auditors' reports apply in relation to each financial year of an LLP.

(2)   In certain respects different provisions apply to different kinds of LLP.

(3)   The main distinctions for this purpose are between LLPs subject to the small LLPs regime (see section 381) and LLPs that are not subject to that regime.

(4)   In this Part, where provisions do not apply to all kinds of LLP, provisions applying to LLPs subject to the small LLPs regime appear before the provisions applying to other LLPs."

NOTES

Commencement: 1 October 2008.

PART 2
LLPS QUALIFYING AS SMALL

[10.1007]

5 LLPs subject to the small LLPs regime

Sections 381 to 384 apply to LLPs, modified so that they read as follows—

"381 LLPs subject to the small LLPs regime

The small LLPs regime applies to an LLP for a financial year in relation to which the LLP—

(a)   qualifies as small (see sections 382 and 383), and

(b)   is not excluded from the regime (see section 384).

382 LLPs qualifying as small: general

(1)   An LLP qualifies as small in relation to its first financial year if the qualifying conditions are met in that year.

(2)   An LLP qualifies as small in relation to a subsequent financial year—

(a)   if the qualifying conditions are met in that year and the preceding financial year;

(b)   if the qualifying conditions are met in that year and the LLP qualified as small in relation to the preceding financial year;

(c)   if the qualifying conditions were met in the preceding financial year and the LLP qualified as small in relation to that year.

(3)   The qualifying conditions are met by an LLP in a year in which it satisfies two or more of the following requirements—

1. Turnover	Not more than £6.5 million
2. Balance sheet total	Not more than £3.26 million
3. Number of employees	Not more than 50

(4)   For a period that is an LLP's financial year but not in fact a year the maximum figures

for turnover must be proportionately adjusted.

(5)   The balance sheet total means the aggregate of the amounts shown as assets in the LLP's balance sheet.

(6)   The number of employees means the average number of persons employed by the LLP in the year, determined as follows—

    (a)   find for each month in the financial year the number of persons employed under contracts of service by the LLP in that month (whether throughout the month or not),

    (b)   add together the monthly totals, and

    (c)   divide by the number of months in the financial year.

(7)   This section is subject to section 383 (LLPs qualifying as small: parent LLPs).

383 LLPs qualifying as small: parent LLPs

(1)   A parent LLP qualifies as a small LLP in relation to a financial year only if the group headed by it qualifies as a small group.

(2)   A group qualifies as small in relation to the parent LLP's first financial year if the qualifying conditions are met in that year.

(3)   A group qualifies as small in relation to a subsequent financial year of the parent LLP—

    (a)   if the qualifying conditions are met in that year and the preceding financial year;

    (b)   if the qualifying conditions are met in that year and the group qualified as small in relation to the preceding financial year;

    (c)   if the qualifying conditions were met in the preceding financial year and the group qualified as small in relation to that year.

(4)   The qualifying conditions are met by a group in a year in which it satisfies two or more of the following requirements—

1. Aggregate turnover	Not more than £6.5 million net (or £7.8 million gross)
2. Aggregate balance sheet total	Not more than £3.26 million net (or £3.9 million gross)
3. Aggregate number of employees	Not more than 50

(5)   The aggregate figures are ascertained by aggregating the relevant figures determined in accordance with section 382 for each member of the group.

(6)   In relation to the aggregate figures for turnover and balance sheet total—

    "net" means after any set-offs and other adjustments made to eliminate group transactions—

        (a)   in the case of non-IAS accounts in accordance with Part 1 of Schedule 4 to the Small Limited Liability Partnerships (Accounts) Regulations 2008 (SI 2008/1912) or Schedule 3 to the Large and Medium-sized Limited Liability Partnerships (Accounts) Regulations 2008 (SI 2008/1913),

        (b)   in the case of IAS accounts, in accordance with international accounting standards; and

    "gross" means without those set-offs and other adjustments.

An LLP may satisfy any relevant requirement on the basis of either the net or the gross figure.

(7)   The figures for each subsidiary undertaking shall be those included in its individual accounts for the relevant financial year, that is—

    (a)   if its financial year ends with that of the parent LLP, that financial year, and

    (b)   if not, its financial year ending last before the end of the financial year of the parent LLP.

If those figures cannot be obtained without disproportionate expense or undue delay, the latest available figures shall be taken.

384 LLPs excluded from the small LLPs regime

(1)   The small LLPs regime does not apply to an LLP that is, or was at any time within the financial year to which the accounts relate—

    (a)   an LLP whose securities are admitted to trading on a regulated market in an EEA State,

    (b)   an LLP that—

        (i)   is an authorised insurance company, a banking LLP, an e-money issuer, a MiFID investment firm or a UCITS management company, or

        (ii)   carries on insurance market activity, or

    (c)   a member of an ineligible group.

(2)   A group is ineligible if any of its members is—

    (a)   a public company,

    (b)   a body corporate (other than a company) whose shares are admitted to trading on a regulated market in an EEA State,

(c)   a person (other than a small company or small LLP) who has permission under Part 4 of the Financial Services and Markets Act 2000 (c.8) to carry on a regulated activity,

(d)   a small company or small LLP that is an authorised insurance company, a banking company or banking LLP, an e-money issuer, a MiFID investment firm or a UCITS management company, or

(e)   a person who carries on insurance market activity.

(3)   A company or LLP is a small company or small LLP for the purposes of subsection (2) if it qualified as small in relation to its last financial year ending on or before the end of the financial year to which the accounts relate."

NOTES

Commencement: 1 October 2008.

PART 3
ACCOUNTING RECORDS

[10.1008]
6   LLP's accounting records

Sections 386 to 389 apply to LLPs, modified so that they read as follows—

"386   Duty to keep accounting records

(1)   Every LLP must keep adequate accounting records.

(2)   Adequate accounting records means records that are sufficient—

(a)   to show and explain the LLP's transactions,

(b)   to disclose with reasonable accuracy, at any time, the financial position of the LLP at that time, and

(c)   to enable the members of the LLP to ensure that any accounts required to be prepared comply with the requirements of this Act.

(3)   Accounting records must, in particular, contain—

(a)   entries from day to day of all sums of money received and expended by the LLP and the matters in respect of which the receipt and expenditure takes place, and

(b)   a record of the assets and liabilities of the LLP.

(4)   If the LLP's business involves dealing in goods, the accounting records must contain—

(a)   statements of stock held by the LLP at the end of each financial year of the LLP,

(b)   all statements of stocktakings from which any statement of stock as is mentioned in paragraph (a) has been or is to be prepared, and

(c)   except in the case of goods sold by way of ordinary retail trade, statements of all goods sold and purchased, showing the goods and the buyers and sellers in sufficient detail to enable all these to be identified.

(5)   A parent LLP that has a subsidiary undertaking in relation to which the above requirements do not apply must take reasonable steps to secure that the undertaking keeps such accounting records as to enable the members of the parent LLP to ensure that any accounts required to be prepared under this Part comply with the requirements of this Act.

387   Duty to keep accounting records: offence

(1)   If an LLP fails to comply with any provision of section 386 (duty to keep accounting records), an offence is committed by every member of the LLP who is in default.

(2)   It is a defence for a person charged with such an offence to show that he acted honestly and that in the circumstances in which the LLP's business was carried on the default was excusable.

(3)   A person guilty of an offence under this section is liable—

(a)   on conviction on indictment, to imprisonment for a term not exceeding two years or a fine (or both);

(b)   on summary conviction—

(i)   in England and Wales [or Scotland], to imprisonment for a term not exceeding twelve months or to a fine not exceeding the statutory maximum (or both);

(ii)   in . . . Northern Ireland, to imprisonment for a term not exceeding six months, or to a fine not exceeding the statutory maximum (or both).

388   Where and for how long records to be kept

(1)   An LLP's accounting records—

(a)   must be kept at its registered office or such other place as the members think fit, and

(b)   must at all times be open to inspection by the members of the LLP.

(2)   If accounting records are kept at a place outside the United Kingdom, accounts and returns with respect to the business dealt with in the accounting records so kept must be sent to, and kept at, a place in the United Kingdom, and must at all times be open to such inspection.

(3)   The accounts and returns to be sent to the United Kingdom must be such as to—

(a)   disclose with reasonable accuracy the financial position of the business in question at intervals of not more than six months, and

(b)   enable the members of the LLP to ensure that the accounts required to be prepared under this Part comply with the requirements of this Act.

(4)   Accounting records that an LLP is required by section 386 to keep must be preserved by it for three years from the date on which they are made.

(5)   Subsection (4) is subject to any provision contained in rules made under section 411 of the Insolvency Act 1986 (c.45) (company insolvency rules) or Article 359 of the Insolvency (Northern Ireland) Order 1989 (SI 1989/2405 (NI 19)).

389 Where and for how long records to be kept: offences

(1)   If an LLP fails to comply with any provision of subsections (1) to (3) of section 388 (requirements as to keeping of accounting records), an offence is committed by every member of the LLP who is in default.

(2)   It is a defence for a person charged with such an offence to show that he acted honestly and that in the circumstances in which the LLP's business was carried on the default was excusable.

(3)   A member of an LLP commits an offence if he—

(a)   fails to take all reasonable steps for securing compliance by the LLP with subsection (4) of that section (period for which records to be preserved), or

(b)   intentionally causes any default by the LLP under that subsection.

(4)   A person guilty of an offence under this section is liable—

(a)   on conviction on indictment, to imprisonment for a term not exceeding two years or a fine (or both);

(b)   on summary conviction—

(i)   in England and Wales [or Scotland], to imprisonment for a term not exceeding twelve months or to a fine not exceeding the statutory maximum (or both);

(ii)   in . . . Northern Ireland, to imprisonment for a term not exceeding six months, or to a fine not exceeding the statutory maximum (or both)."

NOTES

Commencement: 1 October 2008.

In ss 387(3)(b), 389(4)(b) as set out above, the words in square brackets were inserted, and the words omitted were revoked, by the Limited Liability Partnerships (Application of Companies Act 2006) Regulations 2009, SI 2009/1804, reg 85, Sch 3, Pt 2, para 16, as from 1 October 2009.

PART 4
FINANCIAL YEARS

[10.1009]
7 An LLP's financial year

(1)   Sections 390 to 392 apply to LLPs, modified so that they read as follows—

"390 An LLP's financial year

(1)   An LLP's financial year is determined as follows.

(2)   Its first financial year—

(a)   begins with the first day of its first accounting reference period, and

(b)   ends with the last day of that period or such other date, not more than seven days before or after the end of that period, as the members of the LLP may determine.

(3)   Subsequent financial years—

(a)   begin with the day immediately following the end of the LLP's previous financial year, and

(b)   end with the last day of its next accounting reference period or such other date, not more than seven days before or after the end of that period, as the members of the LLP may determine.

(4)   In relation to an undertaking that is not an LLP, references in this Act to its financial year are to any period in respect of which a profit and loss account of the undertaking is required to be made up (by its constitution or by the law under which it is established), whether that period is a year or not.

(5)   The members of a parent LLP must secure that, except where in their opinion there are good reasons against it, the financial year of each of its subsidiary undertakings coincides with the LLP's own financial year.

391 Accounting reference periods and accounting reference date

(1)   An LLP's accounting reference periods are determined according to its accounting reference date in each calendar year.

(2)   The accounting reference date of an LLP is the last day of the month in which the anniversary of its incorporation falls.

(3)   An LLP's first accounting reference period is the period of more than six months, but not more than 18 months, beginning with the date of its incorporation and ending with its

accounting reference date.

(4)   Its subsequent accounting reference periods are successive periods of twelve months beginning immediately after the end of the previous accounting reference period and ending with its accounting reference date.

(5)   This section has effect subject to the provisions of section 392 (alteration of accounting reference date).

392 Alteration of accounting reference date

(1)   An LLP may by notice given to the registrar specify a new accounting reference date having effect in relation to—

(a)   the LLP's current accounting reference period and subsequent periods, or

(b)   the LLP's previous accounting reference period and subsequent periods.

An LLP's "previous accounting reference period" means the one immediately preceding its current accounting reference period.

(2)   The notice must state whether the current or previous accounting reference period—

(a)   is to be shortened, so as to come to an end on the first occasion on which the new accounting reference date falls or fell after the beginning of the period, or

(b)   is to be extended, so as to come to an end on the second occasion on which that date falls or fell after the beginning of the period.

(3)   A notice extending an LLP's current or previous accounting reference period is not effective if given less than five years after the end of an earlier accounting reference period of the LLP that was extended under this section.

This does not apply—

(a)   to a notice given by an LLP that is a subsidiary undertaking or parent undertaking of another EEA undertaking if the new accounting reference date coincides with that of the other EEA undertaking or, where that undertaking is not a company or an LLP, with the last day of its financial year, or

(b)   where the LLP is in administration under Part 2 of the Insolvency Act 1986 (c.45) or Part 3 of the Insolvency (Northern Ireland) Order 1989 (SI 1989/2405 (NI 19)), or

(c)   where the Secretary of State directs that it should not apply, which he may do with respect to a notice that has been given or that may be given.

(4)   A notice under this section may not be given in respect of a previous accounting reference period if the period for filing the accounts and auditor's report for the financial year determined by reference to that accounting reference period has already expired.

(5)   An accounting reference period may not be extended so as to exceed 18 months and a notice under this section is ineffective if the current or previous accounting reference period as extended in accordance with the notice would exceed that limit.

This does not apply where the LLP is in administration under Part 2 of the Insolvency Act 1986 (c.45) or Part 3 of the Insolvency (Northern Ireland) Order 1989 (SI 1989/2405 (NI 19)).

(6)   In this section "EEA undertaking" means an undertaking established under the law of any part of the United Kingdom or the law of any other EEA State."

(2)   Until section 1068(1) comes fully into force, the notice referred to in section 392 (notice of alteration of accounting reference date) as applied to LLPs by paragraph (1) must be given in the form prescribed for the purposes of—

(a)   section 225(1) of the 1985 Act as applied to LLPs by regulation 3 of, and Schedule 1 to, the Limited Liability Partnerships Regulations 2001, or

(b)   Article 233(1) of the 1986 Order as applied to LLPs by regulation 3 of, and Schedule 1 to, the Limited Liability Partnerships Regulations (Northern Ireland) 2004.

NOTES

Commencement: 1 October 2008.

PART 5
ANNUAL ACCOUNTS

[10.1010]
8 Annual accounts to give true and fair view

Section 393 applies to LLPs, modified so that it reads as follows—

"393 Accounts to give true and fair view

(1)   The members of an LLP must not approve accounts for the purposes of this Chapter unless they are satisfied that they give a true and fair view of the assets, liabilities, financial position and profit or loss—

(a)   in the case of the LLP's individual accounts, of the LLP;

(b)   in the case of the LLP's group accounts, of the undertakings included in the consolidation as a whole, so far as concerns members of the LLP.

(2)   The auditor of an LLP in carrying out his functions under this Act in relation to the LLP's annual accounts must have regard to the members' duty under subsection (1)."

NOTES
Commencement: 1 October 2008.

[10.1011]
9   Individual accounts

Sections 394 to 397 apply to LLPs, modified so that they read as follows—

"394   Duty to prepare individual accounts

The members of every LLP must prepare accounts for the LLP for each of its financial years.
Those accounts are referred to as the LLP's "individual accounts".

395   Individual accounts: applicable accounting framework

(1)   An LLP's individual accounts may be prepared—

(a)   in accordance with section 396 ("non-IAS individual accounts"), or

(b)   in accordance with international accounting standards ("IAS individual accounts").

This is subject to the following provisions of this section and to section 407 (consistency of financial reporting within group).

(2)   After the first financial year in which the members of an LLP prepare IAS individual accounts ("the first IAS year"), all subsequent individual accounts of the LLP must be prepared in accordance with international accounting standards unless there is a relevant change of circumstance.

(3)   There is a relevant change of circumstance if, at any time during or after the first IAS year—

(a)   the LLP becomes a subsidiary undertaking of another undertaking that does not prepare IAS individual accounts,

(b)   the LLP ceases to be a subsidiary undertaking,

(c)   the LLP ceases to be an LLP with securities admitted to trading on a regulated market in an EEA State, or

(d)   a parent undertaking of the LLP ceases to be an undertaking with securities admitted to trading on a regulated market in an EEA State.

(4)   If, having changed to preparing non-IAS individual accounts following a relevant change of circumstance, the members again prepare IAS individual accounts for the LLP, subsections (2) and (3) apply again as if the first financial year for which such accounts are again prepared were the first IAS year.

396   Non-IAS individual accounts

(1)   Non-IAS individual accounts must comprise—

(a)   a balance sheet as at the last day of the financial year, and

(b)   a profit and loss account.

(2)   The accounts must—

(a)   in the case of the balance sheet, give a true and fair view of the state of affairs of the LLP as at the end of the financial year, and

(b)   in the case of the profit and loss account, give a true and fair view of the profit or loss of the LLP for the financial year.

(3)   The accounts must comply with the provisions of—

(a)   regulation 3 of the Small Limited Liability Partnerships (Accounts) Regulations 2008 (non-IAS individual accounts of LLP subject to the small LLPs regime) (SI 2008/1912), or

(b)   regulations 3 and 4 of the Large and Medium-sized Limited Liability Partnerships (Accounts) Regulations 2008 (non-IAS individual accounts of large and medium-sized LLPs) (SI 2008/1913),

as to the form and content of the balance sheet and profit and loss account, and additional information to be provided by way of notes to the accounts..

(4)   If compliance with the regulations specified in subsection (3), and any other provision made by or under this Act as to the matters to be included in an LLP's individual accounts or in notes to those accounts, would not be sufficient to give a true and fair view, the necessary additional information must be given in the accounts or in a note to them.

(5)   If in special circumstances compliance with any of those provisions is inconsistent with the requirement to give a true and fair view, the members must depart from that provision to the extent necessary to give a true and fair view.

Particulars of any such departure, the reasons for it and its effect must be given in a note to the accounts.

397   IAS individual accounts

Where the members of an LLP prepare IAS individual accounts, they must state in the notes to the accounts that the accounts have been prepared in accordance with international accounting standards."

NOTES
  Commencement: 1 October 2008.

[10.1012]
10   Group accounts

Sections 398 to 408 apply to LLPs, modified so that they read as follows—

"398 Option to prepare group accounts

If at the end of a financial year an LLP subject to the small LLPs regime is a parent LLP the members, as well as preparing individual accounts for the year, may prepare group accounts for the year.

399 Duty to prepare group accounts

(1)   This section applies to LLPs that are not subject to the small LLPs regime.

(2)   If at the end of a financial year the LLP is a parent LLP the members, as well as preparing individual accounts for the year, must prepare group accounts for the year unless the LLP is exempt from that requirement.

(3)   There are exemptions under—

    (a)   section 400 (LLP included in EEA accounts of larger group),

    (b)   section 401 (LLP included in non-EEA accounts of larger group), and

    (c)   section 402 (LLP none of whose subsidiary undertakings need be included in the consolidation).

(4)   An LLP to which this section applies but which is exempt from the requirement to prepare group accounts, may do so.

400 Exemption for LLP included in EEA group accounts of larger group

(1)   An LLP is exempt from the requirement to prepare group accounts if it is itself a subsidiary undertaking and its immediate parent undertaking is established under the law of an EEA State, in the following cases—

    (a)   where the LLP is a wholly-owned subsidiary of that parent undertaking;

    (b)   where that parent undertaking holds more than 50% of the shares in the LLP and notice requesting the preparation of group accounts has not been served on the LLP by members holding in aggregate—

        (i)   more than half of the remaining shares in the LLP, or

        (ii)   5% of the total shares in the LLP.

Such notice must be served not later than six months after the end of the financial year before that to which it relates.

(2)   Exemption is conditional upon compliance with all of the following conditions—

    (a)   the LLP must be included in consolidated accounts for a larger group drawn up to the same date, or to an earlier date in the same financial year, by a parent undertaking established under the law of an EEA State;

    (b)   those accounts must be drawn up and audited, and that parent undertaking's annual report must be drawn up, according to that law—

        (i)   in accordance with the provisions of the Seventh Directive (83/349/EEC) (as modified, where relevant, by the provisions of the Bank Accounts Directive (86/635/EEC) or the Insurance Accounts Directive (91/674/EEC)), or

        (ii)   in accordance with international accounting standards;

    (c)   the LLP must disclose in its individual accounts that it is exempt from the obligation to prepare and deliver group accounts;

    (d)   the LLP must state in its individual accounts the name of the parent undertaking that draws up the group accounts referred to above and—

        (i)   if it is incorporated outside the United Kingdom, the country in which it is incorporated, or

        (ii)   if it is unincorporated, the address of its principal place of business;

    (e)   the LLP must deliver to the registrar, within the period for filing its accounts and auditor's report for the financial year in question, copies of those group accounts, together with the auditor's report on them;

    (f)   any requirement of Part 35 of this Act as to the delivery to the registrar of a certified translation into English must be met in relation to any document comprised in the accounts and reports delivered in accordance with paragraph (e).

(3)   For the purposes of subsection (1)(b) shares held by a wholly-owned subsidiary of the parent undertaking, or held on behalf of the parent undertaking or a wholly-owned subsidiary, shall be attributed to the parent undertaking.

(4)   The exemption does not apply to an LLP any of whose securities are admitted to trading on a regulated market in an EEA State.

(5)   In subsection (4) "securities" includes—

    (a)   debentures, including debenture stock, loan stock, bonds, certificates of deposit and other instruments creating or acknowledging indebtedness,

    (b)   warrants or other instruments entitling the holder to subscribe for securities falling within paragraph (a), and

    (c)   certificates or other instruments that confer—

        (i)   property rights in respect of a security falling within paragraph (a) or (b),

        (ii)   any right to acquire, dispose of, underwrite or convert a security, being a right to which the holder would be entitled if he held any such security to which the certificate or other instrument relates, or

        (iii)   a contractual right (other than an option) to acquire any such security otherwise than by subscription.

401 Exemption for LLP included in non-EEA group accounts of larger group

(1)   An LLP is exempt from the requirement to prepare group accounts if it is itself a subsidiary undertaking and its parent undertaking is not established under the law of an EEA State, in the following cases—

    (a)   where the LLP is a wholly-owned subsidiary of that parent undertaking;

    (b)   where that parent undertaking holds more than 50% of the shares in the LLP and notice requesting the preparation of group accounts has not been served on the LLP by members holding in aggregate—

        (i)   more than half of the remaining shares in the LLP, or

        (ii)   5% of the total shares in the LLP.

Such notice must be served not later than six months after the end of the financial year before that to which it relates.

(2)   Exemption is conditional upon compliance with all of the following conditions—

    (a)   the LLP and all of its subsidiary undertakings must be included in consolidated accounts for a larger group drawn up to the same date, or to an earlier date in the same financial year, by a parent undertaking;

    (b)   those accounts must be drawn up—

        (i)   in accordance with the provisions of the Seventh Directive (83/349/EEC) (as modified, where relevant, by the provisions of the Bank Accounts Directive (86/635/EEC) or the Insurance Accounts Directive (91/674/EEC)), or

        (ii)   in a manner equivalent to consolidated accounts so drawn up;

    (c)   the group accounts must be audited by one or more persons authorised to audit accounts under the law under which the parent undertaking which draws them up is established;

    (d)   the LLP must disclose in its individual accounts that it is exempt from the obligation to prepare and deliver group accounts;

    (e)   the LLP must state in its individual accounts the name of the parent undertaking which draws up the group accounts referred to above and—

        (i)   if it is incorporated outside the United Kingdom, the country in which it is incorporated, or

        (ii)   if it is unincorporated, the address of its principal place of business;

    (f)   the LLP must deliver to the registrar, within the period for filing its accounts and auditor's report for the financial year in question, copies of the group accounts, together with the auditor's report on them;

    (g)   any requirement of Part 35 of this Act as to the delivery to the registrar of a certified translation into English must be met in relation to any document comprised in the accounts and reports delivered in accordance with paragraph (f).

(3)   For the purposes of subsection (1)(b) shares held by a wholly-owned subsidiary of the parent undertaking, or held on behalf of the parent undertaking or a wholly-owned subsidiary, shall be attributed to the parent undertaking.

(4)   The exemption does not apply to an LLP any of whose securities are admitted to trading on a regulated market in an EEA State.

(5)   In subsection (4) "securities" includes—

    (a)   debentures, including debenture stock, loan stock, bonds, certificates of deposit and other instruments creating or acknowledging indebtedness,

    (b)   warrants or other instruments entitling the holder to subscribe for securities falling within paragraph (a), and

    (c)   certificates or other instruments that confer—

        (i)   property rights in respect of a security falling within paragraph (a) or (b),

        (ii)   any right to acquire, dispose of, underwrite or convert a security, being a right to which the holder would be entitled if he held any such security to which the certificate or other instrument relates, or

        (iii)   a contractual right (other than an option) to acquire any such security otherwise than by subscription.

402 Exemption if no subsidiary undertakings need be included in the consolidation

A parent LLP is exempt from the requirement to prepare group accounts if under section 405 all of its subsidiary undertakings could be excluded from consolidation in non-IAS group accounts.

403 Group accounts: applicable accounting framework

(1)   The group accounts of a parent LLP may be prepared—
-   (a)   in accordance with section 404 ("non-IAS group accounts"), or
-   (b)   in accordance with international accounting standards ("IAS group accounts").

This is subject to the following provisions of this section.

(2)   After the first financial year in which the members of a parent LLP prepare IAS group accounts ("the first IAS year"), all subsequent group accounts of the LLP must be prepared in accordance with international accounting standards unless there is a relevant change of circumstance.

(3)   There is a relevant change of circumstance if, at any time during or after the first IAS year—
-   (a)   the LLP becomes a subsidiary undertaking of another undertaking that does not prepare IAS group accounts,
-   (b)   the LLP ceases to be an LLP with securities admitted to trading on a regulated market in an EEA State, or
-   (c)   a parent undertaking of the LLP ceases to be an undertaking with securities admitted to trading on a regulated market in an EEA State.

(4)   If, having changed to preparing non-IAS group accounts following a relevant change of circumstance, the members again prepare IAS group accounts for the LLP, subsections (2) and (3) apply again as if the first financial year for which such accounts are again prepared were the first IAS year.

404 Non-IAS group accounts

(1)   Non-IAS group accounts must comprise—
-   (a)   a consolidated balance sheet dealing with the state of affairs of the parent LLP and its subsidiary undertakings, and
-   (b)   a consolidated profit and loss account dealing with the profit or loss of the parent LLP and its subsidiary undertakings.

(2)   The accounts must give a true and fair view of the state of affairs as at the end of the financial year, and the profit or loss for the financial year, of the undertakings included in the consolidation as a whole, so far as concerns members of the LLP.

(3)   The accounts must comply with the provisions of—
-   (a)   regulation 6 of the Small Limited Liability Partnerships (Accounts) Regulations 2008 (non-IAS group accounts of small parent LLP opting to prepare group accounts) (SI 2008/1912), or
-   (b)   regulation 6 of the Large and Medium-sized Limited Liability Partnerships (Accounts) Regulations 2008 (non-IAS group accounts of large and medium-sized parent LLPs) (SI 2008/1913),

as to the form and content of the consolidated balance sheet and consolidated profit and loss account, and additional information to be provided by way of notes to the accounts.

(4)   If compliance with the regulations specified in subsection (3), and any other provision made by or under this Act as to the matters to be included in an LLP's group accounts or in notes to those accounts, would not be sufficient to give a true and fair view, the necessary additional information must be given in the accounts or in a note to them.

(5)   If in special circumstances compliance with any of those provisions is inconsistent with the requirement to give a true and fair view, the members must depart from that provision to the extent necessary to give a true and fair view.

Particulars of any such departure, the reasons for it and its effect must be given in a note to the accounts.

405 Non-IAS group accounts: subsidiary undertakings included in the consolidation

(1)   Where a parent LLP prepares non-IAS group accounts, all the subsidiary undertakings of the LLP must be included in the consolidation, subject to the following exceptions.

(2)   A subsidiary undertaking may be excluded from consolidation if its inclusion is not material for the purpose of giving a true and fair view (but two or more undertakings may be excluded only if they are not material taken together).

(3)   A subsidiary undertaking may be excluded from consolidation where—
-   (a)   severe long-term restrictions substantially hinder the exercise of the rights of the parent LLP over the assets or management of that undertaking, or
-   (b)   the information necessary for the preparation of group accounts cannot be obtained without disproportionate expense or undue delay, or
-   (c)   the interest of the parent LLP is held exclusively with a view to subsequent resale.

(4)   The reference in subsection (3)(a) to the rights of the parent LLP and the reference in subsection (3)(c) to the interest of the parent LLP are, respectively, to rights and interests held by or attributed to the LLP for the purposes of the definition of "parent undertaking" (see section 1162) in the absence of which it would not be the parent LLP.

Part 10   Miscellaneous other SIs

406 IAS group accounts

Where the members of an LLP prepare IAS group accounts, they must state in the notes to those accounts that the accounts have been prepared in accordance with international accounting standards.

407 Consistency of financial reporting within group

(1)   The members of a parent LLP must secure that the individual accounts of—

(a)   the parent LLP, and

(b)   each of its subsidiary undertakings,

are all prepared using the same financial reporting framework, except to the extent that in their opinion there are good reasons for not doing so.

(2)   Subsection (1) does not apply if the members do not prepare group accounts for the parent LLP.

(3)   Subsection (1) only applies to accounts of subsidiary undertakings that are required to be prepared under this Part.

(4)   Subsection (1)(a) does not apply where the members of a parent LLP prepare IAS group accounts and IAS individual accounts.

408 Individual profit and loss account where group accounts prepared

(1)   This section applies where—

(a)   an LLP prepares group accounts in accordance with this Act, and

(b)   the notes to the LLP's individual balance sheet show the LLP's profit or loss for the financial year determined in accordance with this Act

(2)   The LLP's individual profit and loss account need not contain the information specified in section 411 (information about employee numbers and costs).

(3)   The LLP's individual profit and loss account must be approved in accordance with section 414(1) (approval by members) but may be omitted from the LLP's annual accounts for the purposes of the other provisions of this Act.

(4)   The exemption conferred by this section is conditional upon its being disclosed in the LLP's annual accounts that the exemption applies."

NOTES

Commencement: 1 October 2008.

[10.1013]

11 Information to be given in notes to accounts

Section 409 to 411 apply to LLPs, modified so that they read as follows—

"409 Information about related undertakings

(1)   The notes to the LLP's annual accounts must contain the information about related undertakings required by—

(a)   regulations 4 and 7 of the Small Limited Liability Partnerships (Accounts) Regulations 2008 (information about related undertakings: non-IAS or IAS individual or group accounts) (SI 2008/1912), or

(b)   regulation 5 of the Large and Medium-sized Limited Liability Partnerships (Accounts) Regulations 2008 (information about related undertakings: non-IAS or IAS individual or group accounts) (SI 2008/1913).

(2)   That information need not be disclosed with respect to an undertaking that—

(a)   is established under the law of a country outside the United Kingdom, or

(b)   carries on business outside the United Kingdom,

if the following conditions are met.

(4)   The conditions are—

(a)   that in the opinion of the members of the LLP the disclosure would be seriously prejudicial to the business of—

(i)   that undertaking,

(ii)   the LLP,

(iii)   any of the LLP's subsidiary undertakings, or

(iv)   any other undertaking which is included in the consolidation;

(b)   that the Secretary of State agrees that the information need not be disclosed.

(5)   Where advantage is taken of any such exemption, that fact must be stated in a note to the LLP's annual accounts.

410 Information about related undertakings: alternative compliance

(1)   This section applies where the members of an LLP are of the opinion that the number of undertakings in respect of which the LLP is required to disclose information under any provision of the regulations specified in section 409(1) (related undertakings) is such that compliance with that provision would result in information of excessive length being given in notes to the LLP's annual accounts.

(2)   The information need only be given in respect of—

(a)   the undertakings whose results or financial position, in the opinion of the members, principally affected the figures shown in the LLP's annual accounts, and

(b)   where the LLP prepares group accounts, undertakings excluded from consolidation under section 405(3) (undertakings excluded on grounds other than materiality).

(3)   If advantage is taken of subsection (2)—

(a)   there must be included in the notes to the LLP's annual accounts a statement that the information is given only with respect to such undertakings as are mentioned in that subsection, and

(b)   the full information (both that which is disclosed in the notes to the accounts and that which is not) must be annexed to the LLP's next annual return.

For this purpose the "next annual return" means that next delivered to the registrar after the accounts in question have been approved under section 414.

(4)   If an LLP fails to comply with subsection (3)(b), an offence is committed by—

(a)   the LLP, and

(b)   every member of the LLP who is in default.

(5)   A person guilty of an offence under subsection (4) is liable on summary conviction to a fine not exceeding level 3 on the standard scale and, for continued contravention, a daily default fine not exceeding one-tenth of level 3 on the standard scale.

410A Information about off-balance sheet arrangements

(1)   In the case of an LLP that is not subject to the small LLPs regime, if in any financial year—

(a)   the LLP is or has been party to arrangements that are not reflected in its balance sheet, and

(b)   at the balance sheet date the risks or benefits arising from those arrangements are material,

the information required by this section must be given in notes to the LLP's annual accounts.

(2)   The information required is—

(a)   the nature and business purpose of the arrangements, and

(b)   the financial impact of the arrangements on the LLP.

(3)   The information need only be given to the extent necessary for enabling the financial position of the LLP to be assessed.

(4)   If the LLP qualifies as medium-sized in relation to the financial year (see sections 465 to 467) it need not comply with subsection (2)(b).

(5)   This section applies in relation to group accounts as if the undertakings included in the consolidation were a single LLP.

411 Information about employee numbers and costs

(1)   In the case of an LLP not subject to the small LLPs regime, the following information with respect to the employees of the LLP must be given in notes to the LLP's annual accounts—

(a)   the average number of persons employed by the LLP in the financial year, and

(b)   the average number of persons so employed within each category of persons employed by the LLP.

(2)   The categories by reference to which the number required to be disclosed by subsection (1)(b) is to be determined must be such as the members may select having regard to the manner in which the LLP's activities are organised.

(3)   The average number required by subsection (1)(a) or (b) is determined by dividing the relevant annual number by the number of months in the financial year.

(4)   The relevant annual number is determined by ascertaining for each month in the financial year—

(a)   for the purposes of subsection (1)(a), the number of persons employed under contracts of service by the LLP in that month (whether throughout the month or not);

(b)   for the purposes of subsection (1)(b), the number of persons in the category in question of persons so employed;

and adding together all the monthly numbers.

(5)   In respect of all persons employed by the LLP during the financial year who are taken into account in determining the relevant annual number for the purposes of subsection (1)(a) there must also be stated the aggregate amounts respectively of—

(a)   wages and salaries paid or payable in respect of that year to those persons;

(b)   social security costs incurred by the LLP on their behalf; and

(c)   other pension costs so incurred.

This does not apply in so far as those amounts, or any of them, are stated elsewhere in the LLP's accounts.

(6)   In subsection (5)—

"pension costs" includes any costs incurred by the LLP in respect of—

(a)   any pension scheme established for the purpose of providing pensions for persons currently or formerly employed by the LLP,

Part 10   Miscellaneous other SIs

(b)   any sums set aside for the future payment of pensions directly by the LLP to current or former employees, and

(c)   any pensions paid directly to such persons without having first been set aside;

"social security costs" means any contributions by the LLP to any state social security or pension scheme, fund or arrangement.

(7)   This section applies in relation to group accounts as if the undertakings included in the consolidation were a single LLP."

NOTES

Commencement: 1 October 2008.

[10.1014]

12   Approval and signing of accounts

Section 414 applies to LLPs, modified so that it reads as follows—

"414   Approval and signing of accounts

(1)   An LLP's annual accounts must be approved by the members, and signed on behalf of all the members by a designated member.

(2)   The signature must be on the LLP's balance sheet.

(3)   If the accounts are prepared in accordance with the provisions applicable to LLPs subject to the small LLPs regime, the balance sheet must contain a statement to that effect in a prominent position above the signature.

(4)   If annual accounts are approved that do not comply with the requirements of this Act, every member of the LLP who—

(a)   knew that they did not comply, or was reckless as to whether they complied, and

(b)   failed to take reasonable steps to secure compliance with those requirements or, as the case may be, to prevent the accounts from being approved,

commits an offence.

(5)   A person guilty of an offence under this section is liable—

(a)   on conviction on indictment, to a fine;

(b)   on summary conviction, to a fine not exceeding the statutory maximum."

NOTES

Commencement: 1 October 2008.

PART 6
PUBLICATION OF ACCOUNTS AND AUDITOR'S REPORT

[10.1015]

13   Publication of accounts and auditor's report

Section 423 applies to LLPs, modified so that it reads as follows—

"423   Duty to circulate copies of annual accounts and auditor's report

(1)   Every LLP must send a copy of its annual accounts and auditor's report for each financial year to—

(a)   every member of the LLP, and

(b)   every holder of the LLP's debentures,

not later than the end of the period for filing accounts and the auditor's report on them, or, if earlier, the date on which it actually delivers its accounts and the auditor's report on those accounts to the registrar.

(2)   Copies need not be sent to a person for whom the LLP does not have a current address.

(3)   An LLP has a "current address" for a person if—

(a)   an address has been notified to the LLP by the person as one at which documents may be sent to him, and

(b)   the LLP has no reason to believe that documents sent to him at that address will not reach him.

(4)   Where copies are sent out over a period of days, references in this Act to the day on which copies are sent out shall be read as references to the last day of that period."

NOTES

Commencement: 1 October 2008.

[10.1016]

14   Default in sending out copies of accounts and auditor's report

Section 425 applies to LLPs, modified so that it reads as follows—

"425   Default in sending out copies of accounts and auditor's report: offences

(1)   If default is made in complying with section 423, an offence is committed by—

(a)   the LLP, and

(b)   every member of the LLP who is in default.

(2)   A person guilty of an offence under this section is liable—
  (a)   on conviction on indictment, to a fine;
  (b)   on summary conviction, to a fine not exceeding the statutory maximum."

NOTES
Commencement: 1 October 2008.

[10.1017]
15   Right of member or debenture holder to copies of accounts and auditor's report
Section 431 applies to LLPs, modified so that it reads as follows—

"431   Right of member or debenture holder to copies of accounts and auditor's report
(1)   A member of, or holder of debentures of, an LLP is entitled to be provided, on demand and without charge, with a copy of—
  (a)   the LLP's last annual accounts, and
  (b)   the auditor's report on those accounts.
(2)   The entitlement under this section is to a single copy of those documents, but that is in addition to any copy to which a person may be entitled under section 423.
(3)   If a demand made under this section is not complied with within seven days of receipt by the LLP, an offence is committed by—
  (a)   the LLP, and
  (b)   every member of the LLP who is in default.
(4)   A person guilty of an offence under this section is liable on summary conviction to a fine not exceeding level 3 on the standard scale and, for continued contravention, a daily default fine not exceeding one-tenth of level 3 on the standard scale."

NOTES
Commencement: 1 October 2008.

[10.1018]
16   Requirements in connection with publication of accounts and auditor's report
Sections 433 to 436 apply to LLPs, modified so that they read as follows—

"433   Name of signatory to be stated in published copies of accounts
(1)   Every copy of the LLP's balance sheet that is published by or on behalf of the LLP must state the name of the person who signed it on behalf of the members of the LLP.
(2)   If a copy is published without the required statement of the signatory's name, an offence is committed by—
  (a)   the LLP, and
  (b)   every member of the LLP who is in default.
(3)   A person guilty of an offence under this section is liable on summary conviction to a fine not exceeding level 3 on the standard scale.

434   Requirements in connection with publication of statutory accounts
(1)   If an LLP publishes any of its statutory accounts, they must be accompanied by the auditor's report on those accounts (unless the LLP is exempt from audit and the members have taken advantage of that exemption).
(2)   An LLP that prepares statutory group accounts for a financial year must not publish its statutory individual accounts for that year without also publishing with them its statutory group accounts.
(3)   An LLP's "statutory accounts" are its accounts for a financial year as required to be delivered to the registrar under section 441.
(4)   If an LLP contravenes any provision of this section, an offence is committed by—
  (a)   the LLP, and
  (b)   every member of the LLP who is in default.
(5)   A person guilty of an offence under this section is liable on summary conviction to a fine not exceeding level 3 on the standard scale.

435   Requirements in connection with publication of non-statutory accounts
(1)   If an LLP publishes non-statutory accounts, it must publish with them a statement indicating—
  (a)   that they are not the LLP's statutory accounts,
  (b)   whether statutory accounts dealing with any financial year with which the non-statutory accounts purport to deal have been delivered to the registrar, and
  (c)   whether an auditor's report has been made on the LLP's statutory accounts for any such financial year, and if so whether the report—
    (i)   was qualified or unqualified, or included a reference to any matters to which the auditor drew attention by way of emphasis without qualifying the report, or
    (ii)   contained a statement under section 498(2) (accounting records or returns inadequate or accounts not agreeing with records and returns), or

section 498(3) (failure to obtain necessary information and explanations).

(2)   The LLP must not publish with non-statutory accounts the auditor's report on the LLP's statutory accounts.

(3)   References in this section to the publication by an LLP of "non-statutory accounts" are to the publication of—

(a)   any balance sheet or profit and loss account relating to, or purporting to deal with, a financial year of the LLP, or

(b)   an account in any form purporting to be a balance sheet or profit and loss account for a group headed by the LLP relating to, or purporting to deal with, a financial year of the LLP,

otherwise than as part of the LLP's statutory accounts.

(4)   In subsection (3)(b) "a group headed by the LLP" means a group consisting of the LLP and any other undertaking (regardless of whether it is a subsidiary undertaking of the LLP) other than a parent undertaking of the LLP.

(5)   If an LLP contravenes any provision of this section, an offence is committed by—

(a)   the LLP, and

(b)   every member of the LLP who is in default.

(6)   A person guilty of an offence under this section is liable on summary conviction to a fine not exceeding level 3 on the standard scale.

436   Meaning of "publication" in relation to accounts and auditor's report

(1)   This section has effect for the purposes of—

•   section 433 (name of signatory to be stated in published copies of accounts),

•   section 434 (requirements in connection with publication of statutory accounts), and

•   section 435 (requirements in connection with publication of non-statutory accounts).

(2)   For the purposes of those sections an LLP is regarded as publishing a document if it publishes, issues or circulates it or otherwise makes it available for public inspection in a manner calculated to invite members of the public generally, or any class of members of the public, to read it."

NOTES

Commencement: 1 October 2008.

PART 7
FILING OF ACCOUNTS AND AUDITOR'S REPORT

[10.1019]
17   Duty to file accounts and reports

(1)   Sections 441 to 444 apply to LLPs, modified so that they read as follow—

"441   Duty to file accounts and auditor's report with the registrar

The designated members of an LLP must deliver to the registrar for each financial year the accounts and auditor's report required by—

•   section 444 (filing obligations of LLPs subject to small LLPs regime),

•   section 445 (filing obligations of medium-sized LLPs), or

•   section 446 (filing obligations of large LLPs).

442   Period allowed for filing accounts

(1)   This section specifies the period allowed for the designated members of an LLP to comply with their obligation under section 441 to deliver accounts and the auditor's report for a financial year to the registrar.

This is referred to in this Act as the "period for filing" those accounts and that report.

(2)   The period is nine months after the end of the relevant accounting reference period.

This is subject to the following provisions of this section.

(3)   If the relevant accounting reference period is the LLP's first and is a period of more than twelve months, the period is—

(a)   nine months from the first anniversary of the incorporation of the LLP, or

(b)   three months after the end of the accounting reference period,

whichever last expires.

(4)   If the relevant accounting reference period is treated as shortened by virtue of a notice given by the LLP under section 392 (alteration of accounting reference date), the period is—

(a)   that applicable in accordance with the above provisions, or

(b)   three months from the date of the notice under that section,

whichever last expires.

(5)   If for any special reason the Secretary of State thinks fit he may, on an application made before the expiry of the period otherwise allowed, by notice in writing to an LLP extend that period by such further period as may be specified in the notice.

(6)   In this section "the relevant accounting reference period" means the accounting reference period by reference to which the financial year for the accounts in question was determined.

443 Calculation of period allowed

(1)   This section applies for the purposes of calculating the period for filing an LLP's accounts and auditor's report which is expressed as a specified number of months from a specified date or after the end of a specified previous period.

(2)   Subject to the following provisions, the period ends with the date in the appropriate month corresponding to the specified date or the last day of the specified previous period.

(3)   If the specified date, or the last day of the specified previous period, is the last day of a month, the period ends with the last day of the appropriate month (whether or not that is the corresponding date).

(4)   If—

    (a)   the specified date, or the last day of the specified previous period, is not the last day of a month but is the 29th or 30th, and

    (b)   the appropriate month is February,

the period ends with the last day of February.

(5)   "The appropriate month" means the month that is the specified number of months after the month in which the specified date, or the end of the specified previous period, falls.

444 Filing obligations of LLPs subject to small LLPs regime

(1)   The designated members of an LLP subject to the small LLPs regime—

    (a)   must deliver to the registrar for each financial year a copy of a balance sheet drawn up as at the last day of that year, and

    (b)   may also deliver to the registrar a copy of the LLP's profit and loss account for that year.

(2)   The designated members must also deliver to the registrar a copy of the auditor's report on the accounts that they deliver.

This does not apply if the LLP is exempt from audit and the members have taken advantage of that exemption.

(3)   The copies of accounts and auditors' reports delivered to the registrar must be copies of the LLP's annual accounts and auditor's report, except that where the LLP prepares non-IAS accounts the designated members may deliver to the registrar a copy of a balance sheet drawn up in accordance with regulation 5 of the Small Limited Liability Partnerships (Accounts) Regulations 2008 (non-IAS individual accounts for delivery to registrar of companies) (SI 2008/1912).

These are referred to in this Part as "abbreviated accounts".

(4)   If abbreviated accounts are delivered to the registrar the obligation to deliver a copy of the auditor's report on the accounts is to deliver a copy of the special auditor's report required by section 449.

(5)   Where the designated members of an LLP subject to the small LLPs regime deliver to the registrar IAS accounts, or non-IAS accounts that are not abbreviated accounts, and in accordance with this section do not deliver to the registrar a copy of the LLP's profit and loss account, the copy of the balance sheet delivered to the registrar must contain in a prominent position a statement that the LLP's annual accounts have been delivered in accordance with the provisions applicable to LLPs subject to the small LLPs regime.

(6)   The copy of the balance sheet delivered to the registrar under this section must state the name of the person who signed it on behalf of the members.

(7)   The copy of the auditor's report delivered to the registrar under this section must—

    (a)   state the name of the auditor and (where the auditor is a firm) the name of the person who signed it as senior statutory auditor, or

    (b)   if the conditions in section 506 (circumstances in which names may be omitted) are met, state that a determination has been made and notified to the Secretary of State in accordance with that section."

(2)   Until section 1068 comes fully into force, for subsections (6) and (7) of section 444 as applied to LLPs by paragraph (1) substitute—

    "(6)   The copy of the balance sheet delivered to the registrar under this section must—

    (a)   state the name of the person who signed it on behalf of the members under section 414, and

    (b)   be signed on behalf of the members by a designated member.

    (7)   The copy of the auditor's report delivered to the registrar under this section must—

    (a)   state the name of the auditor and (where the auditor is a firm) the name of the person who signed it as senior statutory auditor, and

    (b)   be signed by the auditor or (where the auditor is a firm) in the name of the firm by a person authorised to sign on its behalf,

or, if the conditions in section 506 (circumstances in which names may be omitted) are met, state that a determination has been made and notified to the Secretary of State in accordance with that section."

NOTES

Commencement: 1 October 2008.

[10.1020]
18   Filing obligations of medium-sized LLPs

(1)   Section 445 applies to LLPs, modified so that it reads as follows—

"445   Filing obligations of medium-sized LLPs

(1)   The designated members of an LLP that qualifies as a medium-sized LLP in relation to a financial year (see sections 465 to 467) must deliver a copy of the LLP's annual accounts to the registrar.

(2)   They must also deliver to the registrar a copy of the auditor's report on those accounts.

(3)   Where the LLP prepares non-IAS accounts, the designated members may deliver to the registrar a copy of the LLP's annual accounts for the financial year—

    (a)   that includes a profit and loss account in which items are combined in accordance with regulation 4 of the Large and Medium-sized Limited Liability Partnerships (Accounts) Regulations 2008 (exemptions for non-IAS individual accounts of medium-sized LLPs) (SI 2008/1913), and

    (b)   that does not contain items whose omission is authorised by that regulation.

    These are referred to in this Part as "abbreviated accounts".

(4)   If abbreviated accounts are delivered to the registrar the obligation to deliver a copy of the auditor's report on the accounts is to deliver a copy of the special auditor's report required by section 449.

(5)   The copy of the balance sheet delivered to the registrar under this section must state the name of the person who signed it on behalf of the members.

(6)   The copy of the auditor's report delivered to the registrar under this section must—

    (a)   state the name of the auditor and (where the auditor is a firm) the name of the person who signed it as senior statutory auditor, or

    (b)   if the conditions in section 506 (circumstances in which names may be omitted) are met, state that a determination has been made and notified to the Secretary of State in accordance with that section.

(7)   This section does not apply to LLPs within section 444 (filing obligations of LLPs subject to the small LLPs regime)."

(2)   Until section 1068 comes fully into force, for subsections (5) and (6) of section 445 as applied to LLPs by paragraph (1) substitute—

"(5)   The copy of the balance sheet delivered to the registrar under this section must—

    (a)   state the name of the person who signed it on behalf of the members under section 414, and

    (b)   be signed on behalf of the members by a designated member.

(6)   The copy of the auditor's report delivered to the registrar under this section must—

    (a)   state the name of the auditor and (where the auditor is a firm) the name of the person who signed it as senior statutory auditor, and

    (b)   be signed by the auditor or (where the auditor is a firm) in the name of the firm by a person authorised to sign on its behalf,

or, if the conditions in section 506 (circumstances in which names may be omitted) are met, state that a determination has been made and notified to the Secretary of State in accordance with that section."

NOTES

Commencement: 1 October 2008.

[10.1021]
19   Filing obligations of large LLPs

(1)   Section 446 applies to LLPs, modified so as to read as follows—

"446   Filing obligations of large LLPs

(1)   The designated members of an LLP that does not qualify as small or medium-sized must deliver to the registrar for each financial year of the LLP a copy of the LLP's annual accounts.

(2)   The designated members must also deliver to the registrar a copy of the auditor's report on those accounts.

(3)   The copy of the balance sheet delivered to the registrar under this section must state the name of the person who signed it on behalf of the members.

(4)   The copy of the auditor's report delivered to the registrar under this section must—

    (a)   state the name of the auditor and (where the auditor is a firm) the name of the person who signed it as senior statutory auditor, or

    (b)   if the conditions in section 506 (circumstances in which names may be omitted) are met, state that a determination has been made and notified to the Secretary of State in accordance with that section.

(5)   This section does not apply to LLPs within—

    (a)   section 444 (filing obligations of LLPs subject to the small LLPs regime), or

    (b)   section 445 (filing obligations of medium-sized LLPs)."

(2) Until section 1068 comes fully into force, for subsections (3) and (4) of section 446 as applied to LLPs by paragraph (1) substitute—

> "(3) The copy of the balance sheet delivered to the registrar under this section must—
> (a) state the name of the person who signed it on behalf of the members under section 414, and
> (b) be signed on behalf of the members by a designated member.
> (4) The copy of the auditor's report delivered to the registrar under this section must—
> (a) state the name of the auditor and (where the auditor is a firm) the name of the person who signed it as senior statutory auditor, and
> (b) be signed by the auditor or (where the auditor is a firm) in the name of the firm by a person authorised to sign on its behalf,
> or, if the conditions in section 506 (circumstances in which names may be omitted) are met, state that a determination has been made and notified to the Secretary of State in accordance with that section."

NOTES
Commencement: 1 October 2008.

[10.1022]
20   Requirements where abbreviated accounts delivered

(1) Section 449 applies to LLPs, modified so that it reads as follow—

> **"449   Special auditor's report where abbreviated accounts delivered**
> (1) This section applies where—
> (a) the designated members of an LLP deliver abbreviated accounts to the registrar, and
> (b) the LLP is not exempt from audit (or the members have not taken advantage of any such exemption).
> (2) The designated members must also deliver to the registrar a copy of a special report of the LLP's auditor stating that in his opinion—
> (a) the LLP is entitled to deliver abbreviated accounts in accordance with the section in question, and
> (b) the abbreviated accounts to be delivered are properly prepared in accordance with—
> (i) regulation 5 of the Small Limited Liability Partnerships (Accounts) Regulations 2008 (SI 2008/1912), or
> (ii) regulation 4 of the Large and Medium-sized Limited Liability Partnerships (Accounts) Regulations 2008 (SI 2008/1913).
> (3) The auditor's report on the LLP's annual accounts need not be delivered, but—
> (a) if that report was qualified, the special report must set out that report in full together with any further material necessary to understand the qualification, and
> (b) if that report contained a statement under—
> (i) section 498(2)(a) or (b) (accounts, records or returns inadequate or accounts not agreeing with records and returns), or
> (ii) section 498(3) (failure to obtain necessary information and explanations), the special report must set out that statement in full.
> (4) The provisions of—
> • sections 503 to 506 (signature of auditor's report), and
> • sections 507 to 509 (offences in connection with auditor's report),
> apply to a special report under this section as they apply to an auditor's report on the LLP's annual accounts prepared under Part 16.
> (5) If abbreviated accounts are delivered to the registrar, the references in section 434 or 435 (requirements in connection with publication of accounts) to the auditor's report on the LLP's annual accounts shall be read as references to the special auditor's report required by this section."

(2) Until section 1068 comes fully into force, after subsection (4) of section 449 as applied to LLPs by paragraph (1) insert—

> "(4A) The copy of the special report delivered to the registrar under this section must—
> (a) be signed by the auditor or (where the auditor is a firm) in the name of the firm by a person authorised to sign on its behalf, or
> (b) if the conditions in section 506 (circumstances in which names may be omitted) are met, state that a determination has been made and notified to the Secretary of State in accordance with that section."

NOTES
Commencement: 1 October 2008.

[10.1023]
21   Approval and signing of abbreviated accounts

Section 450 is applied to LLPs, modified so as to read as follows—

"450   Approval and signing of abbreviated accounts
(1)   Abbreviated accounts must be approved by the members and signed on behalf of all the members by a designated member.
(2)   The signature must be on the balance sheet.
(3)   The balance sheet must contain in a prominent position above the signature a statement to the effect that it is prepared in accordance with the special provisions of this Act relating (as the case may be) to LLPs subject to the small LLPs regime or to medium-sized LLPs.
(4)   If abbreviated accounts are approved that do not comply with the requirements of regulation 5 of the Small Limited Liability Partnerships (Accounts) Regulations 2008 (SI 2008/1912), or (as the case may be) regulation 4 of the Large and Medium-sized Limited Liability Partnerships (Accounts) Regulations 2008 (SI 2008/1913), every member of the LLP who—
   (a)   knew that they did not comply, or was reckless as to whether they complied, and
   (b)   failed to take reasonable steps to prevent them from being approved,
commits an offence.
(5)   A person guilty of an offence under subsection (4) is liable—
   (a)   on conviction on indictment, to a fine;
   (b)   on summary conviction, to a fine not exceeding the statutory maximum."

NOTES
Commencement: 1 October 2008.

[10.1024]
22   Failure to file accounts and auditor's report
(1)   Sections 451 to 453 apply to LLPs, modified so that they read as follow—

"451   Default in filing accounts and auditor's report: offences
(1)   If the requirements of section 441 (duty to file accounts and auditor's report) are not complied with in relation to an LLP's accounts for a financial year and the auditor's report on those accounts before the end of the period for filing those accounts and that report, every person who immediately before the end of that period was a designated member of the LLP commits an offence.
(2)   It is a defence for a person charged with such an offence to prove that he took all reasonable steps for securing that those requirements would be complied with before the end of that period.
(3)   It is not a defence to prove that the documents in question were not in fact prepared as required by this Part.
(4)   A person guilty of an offence under this section is liable on summary conviction to a fine not exceeding level 5 on the standard scale and, for continued contravention, a daily default fine not exceeding one-tenth of level 5 on the standard scale.

452   Default in filing accounts and auditor's report: court order
(1)   If—
   (a)   the requirements of section 441 (duty to file accounts and auditor's report) are not complied with in relation to an LLP's accounts for a financial year and the auditor's report on those accounts before the end of the period for filing those accounts and that report, and
   (b)   the designated members of the LLP fail to make good the default within 14 days after the service of a notice on them requiring compliance,
the court may, on the application of any member or creditor of the LLP or of the registrar, make an order directing the designated members (or any of them) to make good the default within such time as may be specified in the order.
(2)   The court's order may provide that all costs (in Scotland, expenses) of and incidental to the application are to be borne by the members.

453   Civil penalty for failure to file accounts and auditor's report
(1)   Where the requirements of section 441 are not complied with in relation to an LLP's accounts for a financial year and the auditor's report on those accounts before the end of the period for filing those accounts and that report, the LLP is liable to a civil penalty.
   This is in addition to any liability of the designated members under section 451.
(2)   Regulations 1(3) and 4(2) and (3) of the Companies (Late Filing Penalties) and Limited Liability Partnerships (Filing Periods and Late Filing Penalties) Regulations 2008 (SI 2008/497) apply to LLPs with the following modifications—
   (a)   references to a company or private company include references to an LLP;
   (b)   references to 6th April 2008 are to be read as references to 1st October 2008; and
   (c)   the second column of the table in regulation 4(2) (penalties for public companies) is

omitted.

(3)   The penalty may be recovered by the registrar and is to be paid into the Consolidated Fund.

(4)   It is not a defence in proceedings under this section to prove that the documents in question were not in fact prepared as required by this Part."

(2)   *(Amends the Companies (Late Filing Penalties) and Limited Liability Partnerships (Filing Periods and Late Filing Penalties) Regulations 2008, SI 2008/497, reg 6 at* **[4.255]**.*)*

NOTES

Commencement: 1 October 2008.

PART 8
REVISION OF DEFECTIVE ACCOUNTS

[10.1025]
23   Revision of defective accounts

Sections 454 to 456 apply to LLPs, modified so that they read as follows—

"**454** (1)   If it appears to the members of an LLP that the LLP's annual accounts did not comply with the requirements of this Act, they may prepare revised accounts.

(2)   Where copies of the previous accounts have been sent out to members or delivered to the registrar, the revisions must be confined to—

(a)   the correction of those respects in which the previous accounts did not comply with the requirements of this Act, and

(b)   the making of any necessary consequential alterations.

(3)   The Companies (Revision of Defective Accounts and Reports) Regulations 2008 (SI 2008/373) apply for the purposes of this section with the following modifications—

(a)   references to a company include references to an LLP; and

(b)   references to a director or to an officer of a company include references to a member of an LLP.

455 Secretary of State's notice in respect of accounts

(1)   This section applies where copies of an LLP's annual accounts have been delivered to the registrar, and it appears to the Secretary of State that there is, or may be, a question whether the accounts comply with the requirements of this Act.

(2)   The Secretary of State may give notice to the members of the LLP indicating the respects in which it appears that such a question arises or may arise.

(3)   The notice must specify a period of not less than one month for the members to give an explanation of the accounts or prepare revised accounts.

(4)   If at the end of the specified period, or such longer period as the Secretary of State may allow, it appears to the Secretary of State that the members have not—

(a)   given a satisfactory explanation of the accounts, or

(b)   revised the accounts so as to comply with the requirements of this Act,

the Secretary of State may apply to the court.

(5)   The provisions of this section apply equally to revised annual accounts, in which case they have effect as if the references to revised accounts were references to further revised accounts.

456 Application to court in respect of defective accounts

(1)   An application may be made to the court—

(a)   by the Secretary of State, after having complied with section 455, or

(b)   by the Financial Reporting Review Panel,

for a declaration (in Scotland, a declarator) that the annual accounts of an LLP do not comply with the requirements of this Act and for an order requiring the members of the LLP to prepare revised accounts.

(2)   Notice of the application, together with a general statement of the matters at issue in the proceedings, shall be given by the applicant to the registrar for registration.

(3)   If the court orders the preparation of revised accounts, it may give directions as to—

(a)   the auditing of the accounts, and

(b)   the taking of steps by the members to bring the making of the order to the notice of persons likely to rely on the previous accounts,

and such other matters as the court thinks fit.

(4)   If the court finds that the accounts did not comply with the requirements of this Act it may order that all or part of—

(a)   the costs (in Scotland, expenses) of and incidental to the application, and

(b)   any reasonable expenses incurred by the LLP in connection with or in consequence of the preparation of revised accounts,

are to be borne by such of the members as were party to the approval of the defective accounts.

For this purpose every member of the LLP at the time of the approval of the accounts shall be taken to have been a party to the approval unless he shows that he took all reasonable steps to prevent that approval.

(5)   Where the court makes an order under subsection (4) it shall have regard to whether the members party to the approval of the defective accounts knew or ought to have known that the accounts did not comply with the requirements of this Act, and it may exclude one or more members from the order or order the payment of different amounts by different members.

(6)   On the conclusion of proceedings on an application under this section, the applicant must send to the registrar for registration a copy of the court order or, as the case may be, give notice to the registrar that the application has failed or been withdrawn.

(7)   The provisions of this section apply equally to revised annual accounts, in which case they have effect as if the references to revised accounts were references to further revised accounts."

NOTES

Commencement: 1 October 2008.

[10.1026]
24   Disclosure of information

Sections 458 to 461 apply to LLPs, modified so that they read as follows—

"458 Disclosure of information by tax authorities

(1)   The Commissioners for Her Majesty's Revenue and Customs may disclose information to the Financial Reporting Review Panel for the purpose of facilitating—

    (a)   the taking of steps by the Financial Reporting Review Panel to discover whether there are grounds for an application to the court under section 456 (application in respect of defective accounts etc), or

    (b)   a decision by the Financial Reporting Review Panel whether to make such an application.

(2)   This section applies despite any statutory or other restriction on the disclosure of information.

Provided that, in the case of personal data within the meaning of the Data Protection Act 1998 (c.29), information is not to be disclosed in contravention of that Act.

(3)   Information disclosed to the Financial Reporting Review Panel under this section—

    (a)   may not be used except in or in connection with—

        (i)   taking steps to discover whether there are grounds for an application to the court under section 456, or

        (ii)   deciding whether or not to make such an application,

    or in, or in connection with, proceedings on such an application; and

    (b)   must not be further disclosed except—

        (i)   to the person to whom the information relates, or

        (ii)   in, or in connection with, proceedings on any such application to the court.

(4)   A person who contravenes subsection (3) commits an offence unless—

    (a)   he did not know, and had no reason to suspect, that the information had been disclosed under this section, or

    (b)   he took all reasonable steps and exercised all due diligence to avoid the commission of the offence.

(5)   A person guilty of an offence under subsection (4) is liable—

    (a)   on conviction on indictment, to imprisonment for a term not exceeding two years or a fine (or both);

    (b)   on summary conviction—

        (i)   in England and Wales [or Scotland], to imprisonment for a term not exceeding twelve months or to a fine not exceeding the statutory maximum (or both);

        (ii)   in . . . Northern Ireland, to imprisonment for a term not exceeding six months, or to a fine not exceeding the statutory maximum (or both).

(6)   Where an offence under this section is committed by a body corporate, every officer of the body who is in default also commits the offence.

For this purpose—

    (a)   any person who purports to act as director, manager or secretary of the body is treated as an officer of the body, and

    (b)   if the body is a company, any shadow director is treated as an officer of the company.

459 Power of the Financial Reporting Review Panel to require documents, information and explanations

(1)   This section applies where it appears to the Financial Reporting Review Panel that there is, or may be, a question whether an LLP's annual accounts comply with the requirements of this Act.

(2)   The Financial Reporting Review Panel may require any of the persons mentioned in subsection (3) to produce any document, or to provide him with any information or explanations, that he may reasonably require for the purpose of—
  (a)   discovering whether there are grounds for an application to the court under section 456, or
  (b)   deciding whether to make such an application.
(3)   Those persons are—
  (a)   the LLP;
  (b)   any member, employee, or auditor of the LLP;
  (c)   any persons who fell within paragraph (b) at a time to which the document or information required by the Financial Reporting Review Panel relates.
(4)   If a person fails to comply with such a requirement, the Financial Reporting Review Panel may apply to the court.
(5)   If it appears to the court that the person has failed to comply with a requirement under subsection (2), it may order the person to take such steps as it directs for securing that the documents are produced or the information or explanations are provided.
(6)   A statement made by a person in response to a requirement under subsection (2) or an order under subsection (5) may not be used in evidence against him in any criminal proceedings.
(7)   Nothing in this section compels any person to disclose documents or information in respect of which a claim to legal professional privilege (in Scotland, to confidentiality of communications) could be maintained in legal proceedings.
(8)   In this section "document" includes information recorded in any form.

460   Restrictions on disclosure of information obtained under compulsory powers
(1)   This section applies to information (in whatever form) obtained in pursuance of a requirement or order under section 459 (power of Financial Reporting Review Panel to require documents etc) that relates to the private affairs of an individual or to any particular business.
(2)   No such information may, during the lifetime of that individual or so long as that business continues to be carried on, be disclosed without the consent of that individual or the person for the time being carrying on that business.
(3)   This does not apply—
  (a)   to disclosure permitted by section 461 (permitted disclosure of information obtained under compulsory powers), or
  (b)   to the disclosure of information that is or has been available to the public from another source.
(4)   A person who discloses information in contravention of this section commits an offence, unless—
  (a)   he did not know, and had no reason to suspect, that the information had been disclosed under section 459, or
  (b)   he took all reasonable steps and exercised all due diligence to avoid the commission of the offence.
(5)   A person guilty of an offence under this section is liable—
  (a)   on conviction on indictment, to imprisonment for a term not exceeding two years or a fine (or both);
  (b)   on summary conviction—
    (i)   in England and Wales [or Scotland], to imprisonment for a term not exceeding twelve months or to a fine not exceeding the statutory maximum (or both);
    (ii)   in . . . Northern Ireland, to imprisonment for a term not exceeding six months, or to a fine not exceeding the statutory maximum (or both).
(6)   Where an offence under this section is committed by a body corporate, every officer of the body who is in default also commits the offence.
  For this purpose—
  (a)   any person who purports to act as director, manager or secretary of the body is treated as an officer of the body, and
  (b)   if the body is a company, any shadow director is treated as an officer of the company.

461   Permitted disclosure of information obtained under compulsory powers
(1)   The prohibition in section 460 of the disclosure of information obtained in pursuance of a requirement or order under section 459 (power of Financial Reporting Review Panel to require documents etc) that relates to the private affairs of an individual or to any particular business has effect subject to the following exceptions.
(2)   It does not apply to the disclosure of information for the purpose of facilitating the carrying out by the Financial Reporting Review Panel of its functions under section 456.
(3)   It does not apply to disclosure to—
  (a)   the Secretary of State,
  (b)   the Department of Enterprise, Trade and Investment for Northern Ireland,

    (c)   the Treasury,

    (d)   the Bank of England,

    (e)   the Financial Services Authority, or

    (f)   the Commissioners for Her Majesty's Revenue and Customs.

(4) It does not apply to disclosure—

    (a)   for the purpose of assisting the body known as the Professional Oversight Board established under the articles of association of the Financial Reporting Council Limited (registered number 02486368) to exercise its functions under Part 42 of this Act;

    (b)   with a view to the institution of, or otherwise for the purposes of, disciplinary proceedings relating to the performance by an accountant or auditor of his professional duties;

    (c)   for the purpose of enabling or assisting the Secretary of State or the Treasury to exercise any of their functions under any of the following—

        (i)   the Companies Acts,

        (ii) Part 5 of the Criminal Justice Act 1993 (c.36) (insider dealing),

        (iii) the Insolvency Act 1986 (c.45) or the Insolvency (Northern Ireland) Order 1989 (SI 1989/2405 (NI 19)),

        (iv) the Company Directors Disqualification Act 1986 (c.46) or the Company Directors Disqualification (Northern Ireland) Order 2002 (SI 2002/3150 (NI 4)),

        (v) the Financial Services and Markets Act 2000 (c.8);

    (d)   for the purpose of enabling or assisting the Department of Enterprise, Trade and Investment for Northern Ireland to exercise any powers conferred on it by the enactments relating to companies, directors' disqualification or insolvency;

    (e)   for the purpose of enabling or assisting the Bank of England to exercise its functions;

    (f)   for the purpose of enabling or assisting the Commissioners for Her Majesty's Revenue and Customs to exercise their functions;

    (g)   for the purpose of enabling or assisting the Financial Services Authority to exercise its functions under any of the following—

        (i)   the legislation relating to friendly societies or to industrial and provident societies,

        (ii) the Building Societies Act 1986 (c.53),

        (iii) Part 7 of the Companies Act 1989 (c.40),

        (iv) the Financial Services and Markets Act 2000; or

    (h)   in pursuance of any Community obligation.

(5) It does not apply to disclosure to a body exercising functions of a public nature under legislation in any country or territory outside the United Kingdom that appear to the Financial Reporting Review Panel to be similar to its functions under section 456 for the purpose of enabling or assisting that body to exercise those functions.

(6) In determining whether to disclose information to a body in accordance with subsection (5), the Financial Reporting Review Panel must have regard to the following considerations—

    (a)   whether the use which the body is likely to make of the information is sufficiently important to justify making the disclosure;

    (b)   whether the body has adequate arrangements to prevent the information from being used or further disclosed other than—

        (i)   for the purposes of carrying out the functions mentioned in that subsection, or

        (ii) for other purposes substantially similar to those for which information disclosed to the Financial Reporting Review Panel could be used or further disclosed.

(7) Nothing in this section authorises the making of a disclosure in contravention of the Data Protection Act 1998 (c.29)."

NOTES

Commencement: 1 October 2008.

In ss 458(5)(b), 460(5)(b) as set out above, the words in square brackets were inserted, and the words omitted were revoked, by the Limited Liability Partnerships (Application of Companies Act 2006) Regulations 2009, SI 2009/1804, reg 85, Sch 3, Pt 2, para 16, as from 1 October 2009.

PART 9
ACCOUNTS: SUPPLEMENTARY PROVISIONS

[10.1027]
25 Accounting standards

Section 464 applies to LLPs, modified so that it reads as follows—

"464 Accounting standards

(1)   In this Part "accounting standards" means statements of standard accounting practice issued by the body known as the Accounting Standards Board, as prescribed by the Accounting Standards (Prescribed Body) Regulations 2008 (SI 2008/651).

(2)   References in this Part to accounting standards applicable to an LLP's annual accounts are to such standards as are, in accordance with their terms, relevant to the LLP's circumstances and to the accounts."

NOTES

Commencement: 1 October 2008.

[10.1028]
26   Medium-sized LLPs

Sections 465 to 467 apply to LLPs, modified so that they read as follows—

"465 LLPs qualifying as medium-sized: general

(1)   An LLP qualifies as medium-sized in relation to its first financial year if the qualifying conditions are met in that year.

(2)   An LLP qualifies as medium-sized in relation to a subsequent financial year—

(a)   if the qualifying conditions are met in that year and the preceding financial year;

(b)   if the qualifying conditions are met in that year and the LLP qualified as medium-sized in relation to the preceding financial year;

(c)   if the qualifying conditions were met in the preceding financial year and the LLP qualified as medium-sized in relation to that year.

(3)   The qualifying conditions are met by an LLP in a year in which it satisfies two or more of the following requirements—

1. Turnover	Not more than £25.9 million
2. Balance sheet total	Not more than £12.9 million
3. Number of employees	Not more than 250

(4)   For a period that is an LLP's financial year but not in fact a year the maximum figures for turnover must be proportionately adjusted.

(5)   The balance sheet total means the aggregate of the amounts shown as assets in the LLP's balance sheet.

(6)   The number of employees means the average number of persons employed by the LLP in the year, determined as follows—

(a)   find for each month in the financial year the number of persons employed under contracts of service by the LLP in that month (whether throughout the month or not),

(b)   add together the monthly totals, and

(c)   divide by the number of months in the financial year.

(7)   This section is subject to section 466 (LLPs qualifying as medium-sized: parent LLPs).

466 LLPs qualifying as medium-sized: parent LLPs

(1)   A parent LLP qualifies as a medium-sized LLP in relation to a financial year only if the group headed by it qualifies as a medium-sized group.

(2)   A group qualifies as medium-sized in relation to the parent LLP's first financial year if the qualifying conditions are met in that year.

(3)   A group qualifies as medium-sized in relation to a subsequent financial year of the parent LLP—

(a)   if the qualifying conditions are met in that year and the preceding financial year;

(b)   if the qualifying conditions are met in that year and the group qualified as medium-sized in relation to the preceding financial year;

(c)   if the qualifying conditions were met in the preceding financial year and the group qualified as medium-sized in relation to that year.

(4)   The qualifying conditions are met by a group in a year in which it satisfies two or more of the following requirements—

1. Aggregate turnover	Not more than £25.9 million net (or £31.1 million gross)
2. Aggregate balance sheet total	Not more than £12.9 million net (or £15.5 million gross)
3. Aggregate number of employees	Not more than 250

(5)   The aggregate figures are ascertained by aggregating the relevant figures determined in accordance with section 465 for each member of the group.

(6)   In relation to the aggregate figures for turnover and balance sheet total—

"net" means after any set-offs and other adjustments made to eliminate group transactions—

Part 10   Miscellaneous other SIs

(a)   in the case of non-IAS accounts, in accordance with Schedule 3 to the Large and Medium-sized Limited Liability Partnerships (Accounts) Regulations 2008 (SI 2008/1913),

(b)   in the case of IAS accounts, in accordance with international accounting standards; and

"gross" means without those set-offs and other adjustments.

An LLP may satisfy any relevant requirement on the basis of either the net or the gross figure.

(7)   The figures for each subsidiary undertaking shall be those included in its individual accounts for the relevant financial year, that is—

(a)   if its financial year ends with that of the parent LLP, that financial year, and

(b)   if not, its financial year ending last before the end of the financial year of the parent LLP.

If those figures cannot be obtained without disproportionate expense or undue delay, the latest available figures shall be taken.

467 LLPs excluded from being treated as medium-sized

(1)   An LLP is not entitled to take advantage of any of the provisions of this Part relating to LLPs qualifying as medium-sized if it was at any time within the financial year in question—

(a)   an LLP whose securities are admitted to trading on a regulated market in an EEA State,

(b)   an LLP that—

(i)   has permission under Part 4 of the Financial Services and Markets Act 2000 (c.8) to carry on a regulated activity, or

(ii)   carries on insurance market activity, or

(c)   a member of an ineligible group.

(2)   A group is ineligible if any of its members is—

(a)   a public company,

(b)   a body corporate (other than a company) whose shares are admitted to trading on a regulated market,

(c)   a person (other than a small company or small LLP) who has permission under Part 4 of the Financial Services and Markets Act 2000 to carry on a regulated activity,

(d)   a small company or small LLP that is an authorised insurance company, a banking company or banking LLP, an e-money issuer, a MiFID investment firm or a UCITS management company, or

(e)   a person who carries on insurance market activity.

(3)   An LLP is a small LLP for the purposes of subsection (2) if it qualified as small in relation to its last financial year ending on or before the end of the financial year in question."

NOTES

Commencement: 1 October 2008.

[10.1029]
27 General power to make further provision about accounts

Section 468 applies to LLPs, modified so that it reads as follows—

"468 General power to make further provision about accounts

(1)   The Secretary of State may make provision by regulations about—

(a)   the accounts that LLPs are required to prepare;

(b)   the categories of LLPs required to prepare accounts of any description;

(c)   the form and content of the accounts that LLPs are required to prepare;

(d)   the obligations of LLPs and others as regards—

(i)   the approval of accounts,

(ii)   the sending of accounts to members and others,

(iii) the delivery of copies of accounts to the registrar, and

(iv)   the publication of accounts.

(2)   The regulations may amend this Part by adding, altering or repealing provisions.

(3)   But they must not amend (other than consequentially)—

(a)   section 393 (accounts to give true and fair view), or

(b)   the provisions of Chapter 11 (revision of defective accounts and reports).

(4)   The regulations may create criminal offences in cases corresponding to those in which an offence is created by an existing provision of this Part.

The maximum penalty for any such offence may not be greater than is provided in relation to an offence under the existing provision.

(5)   The regulations may provide for civil penalties in circumstances corresponding to those within section 453(1) (civil penalty for failure to file accounts and reports).

The provisions of section 453(3) and (4) apply in relation to any such penalty."

NOTES
Commencement: 1 October 2008.

[10.1030]
28   Other supplementary provisions

Section 469 applies to LLPs, modified so that it reads as follows—

"469   Preparation and filing of accounts in euros

(1)   The amounts set out in the annual accounts of an LLP may also be shown in the same accounts translated into euros.

(2)   When complying with section 441 (duty to file accounts and auditor's report), the designated members of an LLP may deliver to the registrar an additional copy of the LLP's annual accounts in which the amounts have been translated into euros.

(3)   In both cases—

   (a)   the amounts must have been translated at the exchange rate prevailing on the date to which the balance sheet is made up, and

   (b)   that rate must be disclosed in the notes to the accounts.

(4)   For the purposes of sections 434 and 435 (requirements in connection with published accounts) any additional copy of the LLP's annual accounts delivered to the registrar under subsection (2) above shall be treated as statutory accounts of the LLP.

In the case of such a copy, references in those sections to the auditor's report on the LLP's annual accounts shall be read as references to the auditor's report on the annual accounts of which it is a copy."

NOTES
Commencement: 1 October 2008.

[10.1031]
29   Meaning of "annual accounts"

Section 471 applies to LLPs, modified so that it reads as follows—

"471   Meaning of "annual accounts" and related expressions

(1)   In this Part an LLP's "annual accounts", in relation to a financial year, means—

   (a)   the LLP's individual accounts for that year (see section 394), and

   (b)   any group accounts prepared by the LLP for that year (see sections 398 and 399).

This is subject to section 408 (option to omit individual profit and loss account from annual accounts where information given in group accounts).

(2)   In this Part an LLP's "annual accounts and auditor's report" for a financial year are—

   (a)   its annual accounts,

   (b)   the auditor's report on those accounts (unless the LLP is exempt from audit)."

NOTES
Commencement: 1 October 2008.

[10.1032]
30   Notes to the accounts

Section 472 applies to LLPs, modified so that it reads as follows—

"472   Notes to the accounts

(1)   Information required by this Part to be given in notes to an LLP's annual accounts may be contained in the accounts or in a separate document annexed to the accounts.

(2)   References in this Part to an LLP's annual accounts, or to a balance sheet or profit and loss account, include notes to the accounts giving information which is required by any provision of this Act or international accounting standards, and required or allowed by any such provision to be given in a note to LLP accounts."

NOTES
Commencement: 1 October 2008.

[10.1033]
31   Parliamentary procedure for regulations under section 468

Section 473 applies to LLPs, modified so that it reads as follows—

"473   Parliamentary procedure for regulations under section 468

(1)   This section applies to regulations under section 468 (general power to make further provision about accounts).

(2)   Any such regulations may make consequential amendments or repeals in other provisions of this Act, or in other enactments.

(3)   Regulations that—

(a)   restrict the classes of LLP which have the benefit of any exemption, exception or special provision,

(b)   require additional matter to be included in a document of any class, or

(c)   otherwise render the requirements of this Part more onerous,

are subject to affirmative resolution procedure.

(4)   Otherwise, the regulations are subject to negative resolution procedure."

NOTES

Commencement: 1 October 2008.

[10.1034]

32   Minor definitions

Section 474 applies to LLPs, modified so that it reads as follows—

"474   Minor definitions

(1)   In this Part—

"authorised insurance company" means a person (whether incorporated or not) who has permission under Part 4 of the Financial Services and Markets Act 2000 (c.8) to effect or carry out contracts of insurance, but does not include a friendly society within the meaning of the Friendly Societies Act 1992 (c.40);

"banking company" means a person who has permission under Part 4 of the Financial Services and Markets Act 2000 to accept deposits, other than—

(a)   a person who is not a company, and

(b)   a person who has such permission only for the purpose of carrying on another regulated activity in accordance with permission under that Part;

"banking LLP" means an LLP which has permission under Part 4 of the Financial Services and Markets Act 2000 to accept deposits (but does not include such an LLP which has permission to accept deposits only for the purpose of carrying on another regulated activity in accordance with that permission);

"e-money issuer" means a person [who is registered as an authorised electronic money institution or a small electronic money institution within the meaning of the Electronic Money Regulations 2011 or] who has permission under Part 4 of the Financial Services and Markets Act 2000 to carry on the activity of issuing electronic money within the meaning of article 9B of the Financial Services and Markets Act 2000 (Regulated Activities) Order 2001 (SI 2001/544);

"Financial Reporting Review Panel" means the body known as the Financial Reporting Review Panel established under the articles of association of the Financial Reporting Council Limited (registered number 02486368);

"group" means a parent undertaking and its subsidiary undertakings;

"IAS Regulation" means EC Regulation No. 1606/2002 of the European Parliament and of the Council of 19 July 2002 on the application of international accounting standards;

"included in the consolidation", in relation to group accounts, or "included in consolidated group accounts", means that the undertaking is included in the accounts by the method of full (and not proportional) consolidation, and references to an undertaking excluded from consolidation shall be construed accordingly;

"insurance company" means—

(a)   an authorised insurance company, or

(b)   any other person (whether incorporated or not) who—

(i)   carries on insurance market activity (within the meaning of section 316(3) of the Financial Services and Markets Act 2000), or

(ii)   may effect or carry out contracts of insurance under which the benefits provided by that person are exclusively or primarily benefits in kind in the event of accident to or breakdown of a vehicle,

but does not include a friendly society within the meaning of the Friendly Societies Act 1992;

"international accounting standards" means the international accounting standards, within the meaning of the IAS Regulation, adopted from time to time by the European Commission in accordance with that Regulation;

"LLP" means a limited liability partnership [registered under the Limited Liability Partnerships Act 2000];

"MiFID investment firm" means an investment firm within the meaning of Article 4.1.1 of Directive 2004/39/EC of the European Parliament and of the Council of 21 April 2004 on markets in financial instruments other than—

(a)   an LLP to which that Directive does not apply by virtue of Article 2 of that Directive,

(b)   an LLP which is an exempt investment firm within the meaning of regulation 4A(3) of the Financial Services and Markets Act 2000 (Markets in Financial Instruments) Regulations 2007 (SI 2007/126), and

(c)   any other LLP which fulfils all the requirements set out in regulation 4C(3) of those Regulations;

"profit and loss account", in relation to an LLP that prepares IAS accounts, includes an income statement or other equivalent financial statement required to be prepared by international accounting standards;

"regulated activity" has the meaning given in section 22 of the Financial Services and Markets Act 2000, except that it does not include activities of the kind specified in any of the following provisions of the Financial Services and Markets Act 2000 (Regulated Activities) Order 2001 (SI 2001/544)—

(a)   article 25A (arranging regulated mortgage contracts),
(b)   article 25B (arranging regulated home reversion plans),
(c)   article 25C (arranging regulated home purchase plans),
[(ca) article 25E (arranging regulated sale and rent back agreements),]
(d)   article 39A (assisting administration and performance of a contract of insurance),
(e)   article 53A (advising on regulated mortgage contracts),
(f)   article 53B (advising on regulated home reversion plans),
(g)   article 53C (advising on regulated home purchase plans),
[(ga) article 53D (advising on regulated sale and rent back agreements),]
(h)   article 21 (dealing as agent), article 25 (arranging deals in investments) or article 53 (advising on investments) where the activity concerns relevant investments that are not contractually based investments (within the meaning of article 3 of that Order), or
(i)   article 64 (agreeing to carry on a regulated activity of the kind mentioned in paragraphs (a) to (h));

"turnover", in relation to an LLP, means the amounts derived from the provision of goods and services falling within the LLP's ordinary activities, after deduction of—

(a)   trade discounts,
(b)   value added tax, and
(c)   any other taxes based on the amounts so derived;

"UCITS management company" has the meaning given by the Glossary forming part of the Handbook made by the Financial Services Authority under the Financial Services and Markets Act 2000 (c.8);

"wholly-owned subsidiary" has the meaning given in section 1159(2) of this Act.

(2) In subsection (1)—

(a)   the definitions of "banking company" and "banking LLP", and
(b)   references in the definition of "insurance company" to contracts of insurance and to the effecting or carrying out of such contracts,

must be read with—

(i)   section 22 of the Financial Services and Markets Act 2000,
(ii)   the Financial Services and Markets Act 2000 (Regulated Activities) Order 2001 (SI 2001/544), and
(iii) Schedule 2 to that Act."

NOTES

Commencement: 1 October 2008.

Words in square brackets in the definition "e-money issuer" in s 474 as set out above inserted by the Electronic Money Regulations 2011, SI 2011/99, reg 79, Sch 4, Pt 2, para 20, as from 30 April 2011.

Words in square brackets in the definition "LLP" in s 474 as set out above substituted by the Limited Liability Partnerships (Application of Companies Act 2006) Regulations 2009, SI 2009/1804, reg 85, Sch 3, Pt 2, para 15(3), as from 1 October 2009.

Paras (ca), (ga) of the definition "regulated activity" in s 474 as set out above were inserted by the Financial Services and Markets Act 2000 (Regulated Activities) (Amendment) Order 2009, SI 2009/1342, art 31, as from 1 July 2009 (certain purposes), and as from 30 June 2010 (otherwise).

PART 10
AUDIT REQUIREMENT

[10.1035]
33 Requirement for audited accounts

Section 475 applies to LLPs, modified so that it reads as follows—

"475 Requirement for audited accounts

(1) An LLP's annual accounts for a financial year must be audited in accordance with this Part unless the LLP is exempt from audit under—

(a)   section 477 (small LLPs), or
(b)   section 480 (dormant LLPs).

(2) An LLP is not entitled to any such exemption unless its balance sheet contains a statement by the members to that effect.

(3) An LLP is not entitled to exemption under any of the provisions mentioned in subsection (1)(a) unless its balance sheet contains a statement by the members to the effect that the members acknowledge their responsibilities for complying with the requirements of

Part 10   Miscellaneous other SIs

this Act with respect to accounting records and the preparation of accounts.

(4)   The statement required by subsection (2) or (3) must appear on the balance sheet above the signature required by section 414."

NOTES

Commencement: 1 October 2008.

[10.1036]

34   Exemption from audit: small LLPs

Sections 477 to 479 apply to LLPs, modified so that they read as follows—

"477   Small LLPs: conditions for exemption from audit

(1)   An LLP that meets the following conditions in respect of a financial year is exempt from the requirements of this Act relating to the audit of accounts for that year.

(2)   The conditions are—

    (a)   that the LLP qualifies as a small LLP in relation to that year,

    (b)   that its turnover in that year is not more than £6.5 million, and

    (c)   that its balance sheet total for that year is not more than £3.26 million.

(3)   For a period which is an LLP's financial year but not in fact a year the maximum figure for turnover shall be proportionately adjusted.

(4)   For the purposes of this section—

    (a)   whether an LLP qualifies as a small LLP shall be determined in accordance with section 382(1) to (6), and

    (b)   "balance sheet total" has the same meaning as in that section.

(5)   This section has effect subject to—

    •   section 475(2) and (3) (requirements as to statements to be contained in balance sheet),

    •   section 478 (LLPs excluded from small LLPs exemption), and

    •   section 479 (availability of small LLPs exemption in case of group LLP).

478   LLPs excluded from small LLPs exemption

An LLP is not entitled to the exemption conferred by section 477 (small LLPs) if it was at any time within the financial year in question—

    (a)   an LLP whose securities are admitted to trading on a regulated market in an EEA State,

    (b)   an LLP that—

        (i)   is an authorised insurance company, a banking LLP, an e-money issuer, a MiFID investment firm or a UCITS management company, or

        (ii)   carries on insurance market activity, or

    (c)   an employers' association as defined in section 122 of the Trade Union and Labour Relations (Consolidation) Act 1992 (c.52) or Article 4 of the Industrial Relations (Northern Ireland) Order 1992 (SI 1992/807 (NI 5)).

479   Availability of small LLPs exemption in case of group LLP

(1)   An LLP is not entitled to the exemption conferred by section 477 (small LLPs) in respect of a financial year during any part of which it was a group LLP unless—

    (a)   the conditions specified in subsection (2) below are met, or

    (b)   subsection (3) applies.

(2)   The conditions are—

    (a)   that the group—

        (i)   qualifies as a small group in relation to that financial year, and

        (ii)   was not at any time in that year an ineligible group;

    (b)   that the group's aggregate turnover in that year is not more than £6.5 million net (or £7.8 million gross);

    (c)   that the group's aggregate balance sheet total for that year is not more than £3.26 million net (or £3.9 million gross).

(3)   An LLP is not excluded by subsection (1) if, throughout the whole of the period or periods during the financial year when it was a group LLP, it was both a subsidiary undertaking and dormant.

(4)   In this section—

    (a)   "group LLP" means an LLP that is a parent LLP or a subsidiary undertaking, and

    (b)   "the group", in relation to a group LLP, means that LLP together with all its associated undertakings.

For this purpose undertakings are associated if one is a subsidiary undertaking of the other or both are subsidiary undertakings of a third undertaking.

(5)   For the purposes of this section—

    (a)   whether a group qualifies as small shall be determined in accordance with section 383 (LLPs qualifying as small: parent LLPs);

    (b)   "ineligible group" has the meaning given by section 384(2) and (3);

(c)   a group's aggregate turnover and aggregate balance sheet total shall be determined as for the purposes of section 383;

(d)   "net" and "gross" have the same meaning as in that section;

(e)   an LLP may meet any relevant requirement on the basis of either the gross or the net figure.

(6)   The provisions mentioned in subsection (5) apply for the purposes of this section as if all the bodies corporate in the group were LLPs or companies."

NOTES
Commencement: 1 October 2008.

[10.1037]
35   Exemption from audit: dormant LLPs

Sections 480 and 481 apply to LLPs, modified so that they read as follows—

"480   Dormant LLPS: conditions for exemption from audit

(1)   An LLP is exempt from the requirements of this Act relating to the audit of accounts in respect of a financial year if—

(a)   it has been dormant since its formation, or

(b)   it has been dormant since the end of the previous financial year and the following conditions are met.

(2)   The conditions are that the LLP—

(a)   as regards its individual accounts for the financial year in question—

(i)   is entitled to prepare accounts in accordance with the small LLPs regime (see sections 381 to 384), or

(ii)   would be so entitled but for having been a member of an ineligible group, and

(b)   is not required to prepare group accounts for that year.

(3)   This section has effect subject to—

•   section 475(2) and (3) (requirements as to statements to be contained in balance sheet), and

•   section 481 (LLPs excluded from dormant LLPs exemption).

481   LLPs excluded from dormant LLPs exemption

An LLP is not entitled to the exemption conferred by section 480 (dormant LLPs) if it was at any time within the financial year in question an LLP that—

(a)   is an authorised insurance company, a banking LLP, an e-money issuer, a MiFID investment firm or a UCITS management company, or

(b)   carries on insurance market activity."

NOTES
Commencement: 1 October 2008.

PART 11
APPOINTMENT OF AUDITORS

[10.1038]
36   Appointment of auditors

Sections 485 to 488 apply to LLPs, modified so that they read as follows—

"485   Appointment of auditors: general

(1)   An auditor or auditors of an LLP must be appointed for each financial year of the LLP, unless the designated members reasonably determine otherwise on the ground that audited accounts are unlikely to be required.

(2)   For each financial year for which an auditor or auditors is or are to be appointed (other than the LLP's first financial year), the appointment must be made before the end of the period of 28 days beginning with—

(a)   the end of the time allowed for sending out copies of the LLP's annual accounts and auditor's report for the previous financial year (see section 423), or

(b)   if earlier, the day on which copies of the LLP's annual accounts and auditor's report for the previous financial year are sent out under section 423.

This is the "period for appointing auditors".

(3)   The designated members may appoint an auditor or auditors—

(a)   at any time before the LLP's first period for appointing auditors,

(b)   following a period during which the LLP (being exempt from audit) did not have any auditor, at any time before the LLP's next period for appointing auditors, or

(c)   to fill a casual vacancy in the office of auditor.

(4)   The members may appoint an auditor or auditors—

(a)   during a period for appointing auditors,

(b)   if the LLP should have appointed an auditor or auditors during a period for appointing auditors but failed to do so, or

Part 10   Miscellaneous other SIs

(c)   where the designated members had power to appoint under subsection (3) but have failed to make an appointment.

(5)   An auditor or auditors of an LLP may only be appointed—
  (a)   in accordance with this section, or
  (b)   in accordance with section 486 (default power of Secretary of State).
This is without prejudice to any deemed re-appointment under section 487.

486   Appointment of auditor: default power of Secretary of State

(1)   If an LLP fails to appoint an auditor or auditors in accordance with section 485, the Secretary of State may appoint one or more persons to fill the vacancy.

(2)   Where subsection (2) of that section applies and the LLP fails to make the necessary appointment before the end of the period for appointing auditors, the LLP must within one week of the end of that period give notice to the Secretary of State of his power having become exercisable.

(3)   If an LLP fails to give the notice required by this section, an offence is committed by—
  (a)   the LLP, and
  (b)   every designated member who is in default.

(4)   A person guilty of an offence under this section is liable on summary conviction to a fine not exceeding level 3 on the standard scale and, for continued contravention, a daily default fine not exceeding one-tenth of level 3 on the standard scale.

487   Term of office of auditors

(1)   An auditor or auditors of an LLP hold office in accordance with the terms of their appointment, subject to the requirements that—
  (a)   they do not take office until any previous auditor or auditors cease to hold office, and
  (b)   they cease to hold office at the end of the next period for appointing auditors unless re-appointed.

(2)   Where no auditor has been appointed by the end of the next period for appointing auditors, any auditor in office immediately before that time is deemed to be re-appointed at that time, unless—
  (a)   the LLP agreement requires actual re-appointment, or
  (b)   the deemed re-appointment is prevented by the members under section 488, or
  (c)   the members have determined that he should not be re-appointed, or
  (d)   the designated members have determined that no auditor or auditors should be appointed for the financial year in question.

(3)   This is without prejudice to the provisions of this Part as to removal and resignation of auditors.

(4)   No account shall be taken of any loss of the opportunity of deemed reappointment under this section in ascertaining the amount of any compensation or damages payable to an auditor on his ceasing to hold office for any reason.

488   Prevention by members of deemed re-appointment of auditor

(1)   An auditor of an LLP is not deemed to be re-appointed under section 487(2) if the LLP has received notices under this section from members representing at least the requisite percentage of the total voting rights in the LLP that the auditor should not be re-appointed.

(2)   The "requisite percentage" is 5%, or such lower percentage as is specified for this purpose in the LLP agreement.

(3)   A notice under this section—
  (a)   may be in hard copy or electronic form,
  (b)   must be authenticated by the person or persons giving it, and
  (c)   must be received by the LLP before the end of the accounting reference period immediately preceding the time when the deemed reappointment would have effect."

NOTES

Commencement: 1 October 2008.

[10.1039]

37   Fixing of auditor remuneration

Section 492 applies to LLPs, modified so that it reads as follows—

"492   Fixing of auditor's remuneration

(1)   The remuneration of an auditor appointed by the LLP must be fixed by the designated members or in such manner as the members of the LLP may determine.

(2)   The remuneration of an auditor appointed by the Secretary of State must be fixed by the Secretary of State.

(3)   For the purposes of this section "remuneration" includes sums paid in respect of expenses.

(4)   This section applies in relation to benefits in kind as to payments of money."

NOTES
Commencement: 1 October 2008.

[10.1040]
38   Disclosure of auditor remuneration

Section 494 applies to LLPs, modified so that it reads as follows—

> **"494   Disclosure of services provided by auditor or associates and related remuneration**
> Parts 1 and 2 of the Companies (Disclosure of Auditor Remuneration and Liability Limitation Agreements) Regulations 2008 (SI 2008/489) apply to LLPs with the following modifications—
>
> (a)   in regulation 3(1), omit the definition of "principal terms";
> (b)   references to 6th April 2008 are to be read as references to 1st October 2008;
> (c)   references to a company include references to an LLP; and
> (d)   except in paragraph 3 of Schedule 1, references to a director or to an officer of a company include references to a member of an LLP."

NOTES
Commencement: 1 October 2008.

PART 12
FUNCTIONS OF AUDITOR

[10.1041]
39   Auditor's report

Section 495 applies to LLPs, modified so that it reads as follows—

> **"495   Auditor's report on LLP's annual accounts**
> (1)   An LLP's auditor must make a report to the LLP's members on all annual accounts of the LLP of which copies are, during his tenure of office to be sent out to members under section 423.
> (2)   The auditor's report must include—
> (a)   an introduction identifying the annual accounts that are the subject of the audit and the financial reporting framework that has been applied in their preparation, and
> (b)   a description of the scope of the audit identifying the auditing standards in accordance with which the audit was conducted.
> (3)   The report must state clearly whether, in the auditor's opinion, the annual accounts—
> (a)   give a true and fair view—
>   (i)   in the case of an individual balance sheet, of the state of affairs of the LLP as at the end of the financial year,
>   (ii)   in the case of an individual profit and loss account, of the profit or loss of the LLP for the financial year,
>   (iii)   in the case of group accounts, of the state of affairs as at the end of the financial year and of the profit or loss for the financial year of the undertakings included in the consolidation as a whole, so far as concerns members of the LLP;
> (b)   have been properly prepared in accordance with the relevant financial reporting framework; and
> (c)   have been prepared in accordance with the requirements of this Act.
> Expressions used in this subsection that are defined for the purposes of Part 15 (see section 474) have the same meaning as in that Part.
> (4)   The auditor's report—
> (a)   must be either unqualified or qualified, and
> (b)   must include a reference to any matters to which the auditor wishes to draw attention by way of emphasis without qualifying the report."

NOTES
Commencement: 1 October 2008.

[10.1042]
40   Duties and rights of auditors

Sections 498 to 502 apply to LLPs, modified so that they read as follows—

> **"498   Duties of auditor**
> (1)   An LLP's auditor, in preparing his report, must carry out such investigations as will enable him to form an opinion as to—
> (a)   whether adequate accounting records have been kept by the LLP and returns adequate for their audit have been received from branches not visited by him, and
> (b)   whether the LLP's individual accounts are in agreement with the accounting records

and returns.

(2)   If the auditor is of the opinion—

(a)   that adequate accounting records have not been kept, or that returns adequate for their audit have not been received from branches not visited by him, or

(b)   that the LLP's individual accounts are not in agreement with the accounting records and returns,

the auditor shall state that fact in his report.

(3)   If the auditor fails to obtain all the information and explanations which, to the best of his knowledge and belief, are necessary for the purposes of his audit, he shall state that fact in his report.

(4)   If the members of the LLP have prepared accounts in accordance with the small LLPs regime and in the auditor's opinion they were not entitled so to do, the auditor shall state that fact in his report.

499   Auditor's general right to information

(1)   An auditor of an LLP—

(a)   has a right of access at all times to the LLP's books, accounts and vouchers (in whatever form they are held), and

(b)   may require any of the following persons to provide him with such information or explanations as he thinks necessary for the performance of his duties as auditor.

(2)   Those persons are—

(a)   any member or employee of the LLP;

(b)   any person holding or accountable for any of the LLP's books, accounts or vouchers;

(c)   any subsidiary undertaking of the LLP which is a body corporate incorporated in the United Kingdom;

(d)   any officer, employee or auditor of any such subsidiary undertaking or any person holding or accountable for any books, accounts or vouchers of any such subsidiary undertaking;

(e)   any person who fell within any of paragraphs (a) to (d) at a time to which the information or explanations required by the auditor relates or relate.

(3)   A statement made by a person in response to a requirement under this section may not be used in evidence against him in criminal proceedings except proceedings for an offence under section 501.

(4)   Nothing in this section compels a person to disclose information in respect of which a claim to legal professional privilege (in Scotland, to confidentiality of communications) could be maintained in legal proceedings.

500   Auditor's right to information from overseas subsidiaries

(1)   Where a parent LLP has a subsidiary undertaking that is not a body corporate incorporated in the United Kingdom, the auditor of the parent LLP may require it to obtain from any of the following persons such information or explanations as he may reasonably require for the purposes of his duties as auditor.

(2)   Those persons are—

(a)   the undertaking;

(b)   any officer, employee or auditor of the undertaking;

(c)   any person holding or accountable for any of the undertaking's books, accounts or vouchers;

(d)   any person who fell within paragraph (b) or (c) at a time to which the information or explanations relates or relate.

(3)   If so required, the parent LLP must take all such steps as are reasonably open to it to obtain the information or explanations from the person concerned.

(4)   A statement made by a person in response to a requirement under this section may not be used in evidence against him in criminal proceedings except proceedings for an offence under section 501.

(5)   Nothing in this section compels a person to disclose information in respect of which a claim to legal professional privilege (in Scotland, to confidentiality of communications) could be maintained in legal proceedings.

501   Auditor's right to information: offences

(1)   A person commits an offence who knowingly or recklessly makes to an auditor of an LLP a statement (oral or written) that—

(a)   conveys or purports to convey any information or explanations which the auditor requires, or is entitled to require, under section 499, and

(b)   is misleading, false or deceptive in a material particular.

(2)   A person guilty of an offence under subsection (1) is liable—

(a)   on conviction on indictment, to imprisonment for a term not exceeding two years or a fine (or both);

(b)   on summary conviction—

    (i)   in England and Wales [or Scotland], to imprisonment for a term not exceeding twelve months or to a fine not exceeding the statutory maximum (or both);

    (ii) in . . . Northern Ireland, to imprisonment for a term not exceeding six months or to a fine not exceeding the statutory maximum (or both).

(3) A person who fails to comply with a requirement under section 499 without delay commits an offence unless it was not reasonably practicable for him to provide the required information or explanations.

(4) If a parent LLP fails to comply with section 500, an offence is committed by—

    (a)   the LLP, and

    (b)   every member of the LLP who is in default.

(5) A person guilty of an offence under subsection (3) or (4) is liable on summary conviction to a fine not exceeding level 3 on the standard scale.

(6) Nothing in this section affects any right of an auditor to apply for an injunction (in Scotland, an interdict or an order for specific performance) to enforce any of his rights under section 499 or 500.

502 Auditor's rights in relation to meetings

(1) An LLP's auditor is entitled—

    (a)   to receive all notices of, and other communications relating to, any meeting which a member of the LLP is entitled to receive, where any part of the business of the meeting concerns them as auditors,

    (b)   to attend any meeting of the LLP where any part of the business of the meeting concerns them as auditors, and

    (c)   to be heard at any meeting which he attends on any part of the business of the meeting which concerns him as auditor.

(2) Where the auditor is a firm, the right to attend or be heard at a meeting is exercisable by an individual authorised by the firm in writing to act as its representative at the meeting."

NOTES

Commencement: 1 October 2008.

In s 501(2)(b) as set out above, the words in square brackets were inserted, and the words omitted were revoked, by the Limited Liability Partnerships (Application of Companies Act 2006) Regulations 2009, SI 2009/1804, reg 85, Sch 3, Pt 2, para 16, as from 1 October 2009.

[10.1043]
41   Signature of auditor's report

Sections 503 to 506 apply to LLPs, modified so that they read as follows—

"503 Signature of auditor's report

(1) The auditor's report must state the name of the auditor and be signed and dated.

(2) Where the auditor is an individual, the report must be signed by him.

(3) Where the auditor is a firm, the report must be signed by the senior statutory auditor in his own name, for and on behalf of the auditor.

504 Senior statutory auditor

(1) The senior statutory auditor means the individual identified by the firm as senior statutory auditor in relation to the audit in accordance with—

    (a)   standards issued by the European Commission, or

    (b)   if there is no applicable standard so issued, any relevant guidance issued by—

        (i)   the Secretary of State, or

        (ii) a body appointed by order of the Secretary of State.

(2) The person identified as senior statutory auditor must be eligible for appointment as auditor of the LLP in question (see Chapter 2 of Part 42 of this Act).

(3) The senior statutory auditor is not, by reason of being named or identified as senior statutory auditor or by reason of his having signed the auditor's report, subject to any civil liability to which he would not otherwise be subject.

(4) An order appointing a body for the purpose of subsection (1)(b)(ii) is subject to negative resolution procedure.

505 Names to be stated in published copies of auditor's report

(1) Every copy of the auditor's report that is published by or on behalf of the LLP must—

    (a)   state the name of the auditor and (where the auditor is a firm) the name of the person who signed it as senior statutory auditor, or

    (b)   if the conditions in section 506 (circumstances in which names may be omitted) are met, state that a determination has been made and notified to the Secretary of State in accordance with that section.

(2) For the purposes of this section an LLP is regarded as publishing the report if it publishes, issues or circulates it or otherwise makes it available for public inspection in a manner calculated to invite members of the public generally, or any class of members of the public, to read it.

(3) If a copy of the auditor's report is published without the statement required by this section, an offence is committed by—
   (a)   the LLP, and
   (b)   every designated member of the LLP who is in default.

(4) A person guilty of an offence under this section is liable on summary conviction to a fine not exceeding level 3 on the standard scale.

506 Circumstances in which names may be omitted

(1) The auditor's name and, where the auditor is a firm, the name of the person who signed the report as senior statutory auditor, may be omitted from—
   (a)   published copies of the report, and
   (b)   the copy of the report delivered to the registrar under Chapter 10 of Part 15 (filing of accounts and reports),
if the following conditions are met.

(2) The conditions are that the LLP—
   (a)   considering on reasonable grounds that statement of the name would create or be likely to create a serious risk that the auditor or senior statutory auditor, or any other person, would be subject to violence or intimidation, has determined that the name should not be stated, and
   (b)   has given notice of the determination to the Secretary of State, stating—
      (i)   the name and registered number of the LLP,
      (ii)   the financial year of the LLP to which the report relates, and
      (iii)   the name of the auditor and (where the auditor is a firm) the name of the person who signed the report as senior statutory auditor."

NOTES
Commencement: 1 October 2008.

[10.1044]
42   Offences in connection with auditor's report
Sections 507 to 509 apply to LLPs, modified so that they read as follows—

"507 Offences in connection with auditor's report
(1) A person to whom this section applies commits an offence if he knowingly or recklessly causes a report under section 495 (auditor's report on LLP's annual accounts) to include any matter that is misleading, false or deceptive in a material particular.

(2) A person to whom this section applies commits an offence if he knowingly or recklessly causes such a report to omit a statement required by—
   (a)   section 498(2)(b) (statement that LLP's accounts do not agree with accounting records and returns),
   (b)   section 498(3) (statement that necessary information and explanations not obtained), or
   (c)   section 498(4) (statement that members wrongly prepared accounts in accordance with the small LLPs regime).

(3) This section applies to—
   (a)   where the auditor is an individual, that individual and any employee or agent of his who is eligible for appointment as auditor of the LLP;
   (b)   where the auditor is a firm, any director, member, employee or agent of the firm who is eligible for appointment as auditor of the LLP.

(4) A person guilty of an offence under this section is liable—
   (a)   on conviction on indictment, to a fine;
   (b)   on summary conviction, to a fine not exceeding the statutory maximum.

508 Guidance for regulatory and prosecuting authorities: England, Wales and Northern Ireland
(1) The Secretary of State may issue guidance for the purpose of helping relevant regulatory and prosecuting authorities to determine how they should carry out their functions in cases where behaviour occurs that—
   (a)   appears to involve the commission of an offence under section 507 (offences in connection with auditor's report), and
   (b)   has been, is being or may be investigated pursuant to arrangements—
      (i)   under paragraph 15 of Schedule 10 (investigation of complaints against auditors and supervisory bodies), or
      (ii)   of a kind mentioned in paragraph 24 of that Schedule (independent investigation for disciplinary purposes of public interest cases).

(2) The Secretary of State must obtain the consent of the Attorney General before issuing any such guidance.

(3) In this section "relevant regulatory and prosecuting authorities" means—
   (a)   supervisory bodies within the meaning of Part 42 of this Act,

(b)   bodies to which the Secretary of State may make grants under section 16(1) of the Companies (Audit, Investigations and Community Enterprise) Act 2004 (c.27) (bodies concerned with accounting standards etc),

(c)   the Director of the Serious Fraud Office,

(d)   the Director of Public Prosecutions or the Director of Public Prosecutions for Northern Ireland, and

(e)   the Secretary of State.

(4)   This section does not apply to Scotland.

509 Guidance for regulatory authorities: Scotland

(1)   The Lord Advocate may issue guidance for the purpose of helping relevant regulatory authorities to determine how they should carry out their functions in cases where behaviour occurs that—

(a)   appears to involve the commission of an offence under section 507 (offences in connection with auditor's report), and

(b)   has been, is being or may be investigated pursuant to arrangements—

(i)   under paragraph 15 of Schedule 10 (investigation of complaints against auditors and supervisory bodies), or

(ii)   of a kind mentioned in paragraph 24 of that Schedule (independent investigation for disciplinary purposes of public interest cases).

(2)   The Lord Advocate must consult the Secretary of State before issuing any such guidance.

(3)   In this section "relevant regulatory authorities" means—

(a)   supervisory bodies within the meaning of Part 42 of this Act,

(b)   bodies to which the Secretary of State may make grants under section 16(1) of the Companies (Audit, Investigations and Community Enterprise) Act 2004 (c.27) (bodies concerned with accounting standards etc), and

(c)   the Secretary of State.

(4)   This section applies only to Scotland."

NOTES

Commencement: 1 October 2008.

PART 13
REMOVAL, RESIGNATION, ETC OF AUDITORS

[10.1045]

43   Removal, resignation, etc of auditors

(1)   Sections 510 to 512 apply to LLPs, modified so that they read as follows—

"510 Removal of auditor

(1)   The members of an LLP may remove an auditor from office at any time.

(2)   Nothing in this section is to be taken as depriving the person removed of compensation or damages payable to him in respect of the termination—

(a)   of his appointment as auditor, or

(b)   of any appointment terminating with that as auditor.

(3)   An auditor may not be removed from office before the expiration of his term of office except under this section.

511 Notice of removal of auditor

(1)   No determination to remove an auditor before the expiration of his term of office may be made under section 510 unless the LLP has given 7 days' prior notice to any auditor whom it is proposed to remove

(2)   The auditor proposed to be removed may make with respect to the proposal representations in writing to the LLP (not exceeding a reasonable length) and request their notification to members of the LLP.

(3)   The LLP must upon receipt send a copy of the representations to every member.

(4)   Copies of the representations need not be sent out if, on the application either of the LLP or of any other person claiming to be aggrieved, the court is satisfied that the auditor is using the provisions of this section to secure needless publicity for defamatory matter.

The court may order the LLP's costs (in Scotland, expenses) on the application to be paid in whole or in part by the auditor, notwithstanding that he is not a party to the application.

512 Notice to registrar of determination removing auditor from office

(1)   Where the members of an LLP have removed an auditor from office under section 510, the LLP must give notice of that fact to the registrar within 14 days.

(2)   If the LLP fails to give the notice required by this section, an offence is committed by the LLP and every designated member who is in default.

(3) A person guilty of an offence under this section is liable on summary conviction to a fine not exceeding level 3 on the standard scale and, for continued contravention, a daily default fine not exceeding one-tenth of level 3 on the standard scale."

(2) Until section 1068(1) comes into force, the notice referred to in section 512(1) as applied to LLPs by paragraph (1) must be in the form prescribed for the purposes of section 391(2) of the 1985 Act or Article 399(2) of the 1986 Order as applied to LLPs.

NOTES
  Commencement: 1 October 2008.

[10.1046]
44 Rights of auditor removed from office
(1) Section 513 applies to LLPs, modified so that it reads as follows—

"513 Rights of auditor who has been removed from office
  (1) An auditor who has been removed has, notwithstanding his removal, the rights conferred by section 502(1) in relation to any meeting of the LLP—
    (a) at which his term of office would otherwise have expired, or
    (b) at which it is proposed to fill the vacancy caused by his removal.
  (2) In such a case the references in that section to matters concerning the auditor as auditor shall be construed as references to matters concerning him as a former auditor."

(2) In section 513 (applied to LLPs by paragraph (1)) as it applies in relation to an auditor appointed before 1st October 2008, the reference to rights under section 502(1) shall be read as a reference to rights under section 390(1) of the 1985 Act or Article 398(1) of the 1986 Order as applied to LLPs.

NOTES
  Commencement: 1 October 2008.

[10.1047]
45 Rights of auditor not re-appointed
(1) Sections 515 to 518 apply to LLPs, modified so that they read as follows—

"515 Failure to re-appoint auditor: rights of auditor who is not re-appointed
  (1) No person may be appointed as auditor in place of a person (the "outgoing auditor") whose term of office has ended or is to end at the end of the period for appointing auditors unless the LLP has given 7 days' prior notice to the outgoing auditor.
  (2) The outgoing auditor may make with respect to the proposal representations in writing to the LLP (not exceeding a reasonable length) and request their notification to members of the LLP.
  (3) The LLP must upon receipt send a copy of the representations to every member.
  (4) Copies of the representations need not be sent out if, on the application either of the LLP or of any other person claiming to be aggrieved, the court is satisfied that the auditor is using the provisions of this section to secure needless publicity for defamatory matter.
      The court may order the LLP's costs (in Scotland, expenses) on the application to be paid in whole or in part by the auditor, notwithstanding that he is not a party to the application.

516 Resignation of auditor
  (1) An auditor of an LLP may resign his office by depositing a notice in writing to that effect at the LLP's registered office.
  (2) The notice is not effective unless it is accompanied by the statement required by section 519.
  (3) An effective notice of resignation operates to bring the auditor's term of office to an end as of the date on which the notice is deposited or on such later date as may be specified in it.

517 Notice to registrar of resignation of auditor
  (1) Where an auditor resigns the LLP must within 14 days of the deposit of a notice of resignation send a copy of the notice to the registrar of companies.
  (2) If default is made in complying with this section, an offence is committed by—
    (a) the LLP, and
    (b) every designated member of the LLP who is in default.
  (3) A person guilty of an offence under this section is liable—
    (a) on conviction on indictment, to a fine;
    (b) on summary conviction, to a fine not exceeding the statutory maximum and, for continued contravention, a daily default fine not exceeding one-tenth of the statutory maximum.

518 Rights of resigning auditor
  (1) This section applies where an auditor's notice of resignation is accompanied by a

statement of the circumstances connected with his resignation (see section 519).

(2)   He may deposit with the notice a signed requisition calling on the designated members of the LLP forthwith duly to convene a meeting of the members of the LLP for the purpose of receiving and considering such explanation of the circumstances connected with his resignation as he may wish to place before the meeting.

(3)   He may request the LLP to circulate to its members before the meeting convened on his requisition, a statement in writing (not exceeding a reasonable length) of the circumstances connected with his resignation.

(4)   The LLP must (unless the statement is received too late for it to comply)—

    (a)   in any notice of the meeting given to members of the LLP, state the fact of the statement having been made, and

    (b)   send a copy of the statement to every member of the LLP to whom notice of the meeting is or has been sent.

(5)   The designated members must within 21 days from the date of the deposit of a requisition under this section proceed duly to convene a meeting for a day not more than 28 days after the date on which the notice convening the meeting is given.

(6)   If default is made in complying with subsection (5), every designated member who failed to take all reasonable steps to secure that a meeting was convened commits an offence.

(7)   A person guilty of an offence under this section is liable—

    (a)   on conviction on indictment, to a fine;

    (b)   on summary conviction to a fine not exceeding the statutory maximum.

(8)   If a copy of the statement mentioned above is not sent out as required because received too late or because of the LLP's default, the auditor may (without prejudice to his right to be heard orally) require that the statement be read out at the meeting.

(9)   Copies of a statement need not be sent out and the statement need not be read out at the meeting if, on the application either of the LLP or of any other person who claims to be aggrieved, the court is satisfied that the auditor is using the provisions of this section to secure needless publicity for defamatory matter.

The court may order the LLP's costs (in Scotland, expenses) on such an application to be paid in whole or in part by the auditor, notwithstanding that he is not a party to the application.

(10)   An auditor who has resigned has, notwithstanding his resignation, the rights conferred by section 502(1) in relation to any such meeting of the LLP as is mentioned in subsection (3).

In such a case the references in that section to matters concerning the auditor as auditor shall be construed as references to matters concerning him as a former auditor."

(2)   In section 518 (applied to LLPs by paragraph (1)) as it applies in relation to an auditor appointed before 1st October 2008, the reference to rights under section 502(1) shall be read as a reference to rights under section 390(1) of the 1985 Act or Article 398(1) of the 1986 Order as applied to LLPs.

NOTES

Commencement: 1 October 2008.

[10.1048]
46   Auditor statements

Sections 519 to 526 apply to LLPs, modified so that they read as follows—

"519 Statement by auditor to be deposited with LLP

(1)   Where an auditor of an LLP ceases for any reason to hold office, he must deposit at the LLP's registered office a statement of the circumstances connected with his ceasing to hold office, unless he considers that there are no circumstances in connection with his ceasing to hold office that need to be brought to the attention of members or creditors of the LLP.

(2)   If he considers that there are no circumstances in connection with his ceasing to hold office that need to be brought to the attention of members or creditors of the LLP, he must deposit at the LLP's registered office a statement to that effect.

(3)   The statement required by this section must be deposited—

    (a)   in the case of resignation, along with the notice of resignation;

    (b)   in the case of failure to seek re-appointment, not less than 14 days before the end of the time allowed for next appointing an auditor;

    (c)   in any other case, not later than the end of the period of 14 days beginning with the date on which he ceases to hold office.

(4)   A person ceasing to hold office as auditor who fails to comply with this section commits an offence.

(5)   In proceedings for such an offence it is a defence for the person charged to show that he took all reasonable steps and exercised all due diligence to avoid the commission of the offence.

(6)   A person guilty of an offence under this section is liable—

    (a)   on conviction on indictment, to a fine;

(b)   on summary conviction, to a fine not exceeding the statutory maximum.

(7)   Where an offence under this section is committed by a body corporate, every officer of the body who is in default also commits the offence.

For this purpose—

(a)   any person who acts as director, manager or secretary of the body is treated as an officer of the body, and

(b)   if the body is a company, any shadow director is treated as an officer of the company.

520   LLP's duties in relation to statement

(1)   This section applies where the statement deposited under section 519 states the circumstances connected with the auditor's ceasing to hold office.

(2)   The LLP must within 14 days of the deposit of the statement either—

(a)   send a copy of it to every person who under section 423 is entitled to be sent copies of the accounts, or

(b)   apply to the court.

(3)   If it applies to the court, the LLP must notify the auditor of the application.

(4)   If the court is satisfied that the auditor is using the provisions of section 519 to secure needless publicity for defamatory matter—

(a)   it shall direct that copies of the statement need not be sent out, and

(b)   it may further order the LLP's costs (in Scotland, expenses) on the application to be paid in whole or in part by the auditor, even if he is not a party to the application.

The LLP must within 14 days of the court's decision send to the persons mentioned in subsection (2)(a) a statement setting out the effect of the order.

(5)   If no such direction is made the LLP must send copies of the statement to the persons mentioned in subsection (2)(a) within 14 days of the court's decision or, as the case may be, of the discontinuance of the proceedings.

(6)   In the event of default in complying with this section an offence is committed by every designated member of the LLP who is in default.

(7)   In proceedings for such an offence it is a defence for the person charged to show that he took all reasonable steps and exercised all due diligence to avoid the commission of the offence.

(8)   A person guilty of an offence under this section is liable—

(a)   on conviction on indictment, to a fine;

(b)   on summary conviction, to a fine not exceeding the statutory maximum.

521   Copy of statement to be sent to registrar

(1)   Unless within 21 days beginning with the day on which he deposited the statement under section 519 the auditor receives notice of an application to the court under section 520, he must within a further seven days send a copy of the statement to the registrar.

(2)   If an application to the court is made under section 520 and the auditor subsequently receives notice under subsection (5) of that section, he must within seven days of receiving the notice send a copy of the statement to the registrar.

(3)   An auditor who fails to comply with subsection (1) or (2) commits an offence.

(4)   In proceedings for such an offence it is a defence for the person charged to show that he took all reasonable steps and exercised all due diligence to avoid the commission of the offence.

(5)   A person guilty of an offence under this section is liable—

(a)   on conviction on indictment, to a fine;

(b)   on summary conviction, to a fine not exceeding the statutory maximum.

(6)   Where an offence under this section is committed by a body corporate, every officer of the body who is in default also commits the offence.

For this purpose—

(a)   any person who acts as director, manager or secretary of the body is treated as an officer of the body, and

(b)   if the body is a company, any shadow director is treated as an officer of the company.

522   Duty of auditor to notify appropriate audit authority

(1)   Where—

(a)   in the case of a major audit, an auditor ceases for any reason to hold office, or

(b)   in the case of an audit that is not a major audit, an auditor ceases to hold office before the end of his term of office,

the auditor ceasing to hold office must notify the appropriate audit authority.

(2)   The notice must—

(a)   inform the appropriate audit authority that he has ceased to hold office, and

(b)   be accompanied by a copy of the statement deposited by him at the LLP's registered office in accordance with section 519.

(3)   If the statement so deposited is to the effect that he considers that there are no circumstances in connection with his ceasing to hold office that need to be brought to the attention of members or creditors of the LLP, the notice must also be accompanied by a statement of the reasons for his ceasing to hold office.

(4)   The auditor must comply with this section—

(a)   in the case of a major audit, at the same time as he deposits a statement at the LLP's registered office in accordance with section 519;

(b)   in the case of an audit that is not a major audit, at such time (not being earlier than the time mentioned in paragraph (a)) as the appropriate audit authority may require.

(5)   A person ceasing to hold office as auditor who fails to comply with this section commits an offence.

(6)   If that person is a firm an offence is committed by—

(a)   the firm, and

(b)   every officer of the firm who is in default.

(7)   In proceedings for an offence under this section it is a defence for the person charged to show that he took all reasonable steps and exercised all due diligence to avoid the commission of the offence.

(8)   A person guilty of an offence under this section is liable—

(a)   on conviction on indictment, to a fine;

(b)   on summary conviction, to a fine not exceeding the statutory maximum.

523 Duty of LLP to notify appropriate audit authority

(1)   Where an auditor ceases to hold office before the end of his term of office, the LLP must notify the appropriate audit authority.

(2)   The notice must—

(a)   inform the appropriate audit authority that the auditor has ceased to hold office, and

(b)   be accompanied by—

(i)   a statement by the LLP of the reasons for his ceasing to hold office, or

(ii)   if the copy of the statement deposited by the auditor at the LLP's registered office in accordance with section 519 contains a statement of circumstances in connection with his ceasing to hold office that need to be brought to the attention of members or creditors of the LLP, a copy of that statement.

(3)   The LLP must give notice under this section not later than 14 days after the date on which the auditor's statement is deposited at the LLP's registered office in accordance with section 519.

(4)   If an LLP fails to comply with this section, an offence is committed by—

(a)   the LLP, and

(b)   every designated member of the LLP who is in default.

(5)   In proceedings for such an offence it is a defence for the person charged to show that he took all reasonable steps and exercised all due diligence to avoid the commission of the offence.

(6)   A person guilty of an offence under this section is liable—

(a)   on conviction on indictment, to a fine;

(b)   on summary conviction, to a fine not exceeding the statutory maximum.

524 Information to be given to accounting authorities

(1)   The appropriate audit authority on receiving notice under section 522 or 523 of an auditor's ceasing to hold office—

(a)   must inform the accounting authorities, and

(b)   may if it thinks fit forward to those authorities a copy of the statement or statements accompanying the notice.

(2)   The accounting authorities are—

(a)   the Secretary of State, and

(b)   the body known as the Financial Reporting Review Panel established under the articles of association of the Financial Reporting Council Limited (registered number 02486368).

(3)   If either of the accounting authorities is also the appropriate audit authority it is only necessary to comply with this section as regards any other accounting authority.

(4)   If the court has made an order under section 520(4) directing that copies of the statement need not be sent out by the LLP, sections 460 and 461 (restriction on further disclosure) apply in relation to the copies sent to the accounting authorities as they apply to information obtained under section 459 (power to require documents etc).

525 Meaning of "appropriate audit authority" and "major audit"

(1)   In sections 522, 523 and 524 "appropriate audit authority" means—

(a)   in the case of a major audit (other than one conducted by an Auditor General), the body known as the Professional Oversight Board established under the articles of association of the Financial Reporting Council Limited (registered number 02486368);

(b)   in the case of an audit (other than one conducted by an Auditor General) that is not a major audit, the relevant supervisory body;

(c)   in the case of an audit conducted by an Auditor General, the Independent Supervisor.

"Supervisory body" and "Independent Supervisor" have the same meaning as in Part 42 (statutory auditors) (see sections 1217 and 1228).

(2)   In section 522 and this section "major audit" means a statutory audit conducted in respect of—

(a)   an LLP any of whose securities have been admitted to the official list (within the meaning of Part 6 of the Financial Services and Markets Act 2000 (c.8)), or

(b)   any other person in whose financial condition there is a major public interest.

(3)   In determining whether an audit is a major audit within subsection (2)(b), regard shall be had to any guidance issued by any of the authorities mentioned in subsection (1).

526 Effect of casual vacancies

If an auditor ceases to hold office for any reason, any surviving or continuing auditor or auditors may continue to act."

NOTES

Commencement: 1 October 2008.

PART 14
LLP AUDIT: SUPPLEMENTARY PROVISIONS

[10.1049]
47   Minor definitions

Section 539 applies to LLPs, modified so that it reads as follows—

"539 Minor definitions

In this Part—

"e-money issuer" means a person [who is registered as an authorised electronic money institution or a small electronic money institution within the meaning of the Electronic Money Regulations 2011 or] who has permission under Part 4 of the Financial Services and Markets Act 2000 (c 8) to carry on the activity of issuing electronic money within the meaning of article 9B of the Financial Services and Markets Act 2000 (Regulated Activities) Order 2001 (SI 2001/544);

"LLP agreement" means any agreement express or implied between the members of the LLP or between the LLP and the members of the LLP which determines the mutual rights and duties of the members, and their rights and duties in relation to the LLP;

"MiFID investment firm" means an investment firm within the meaning of Article 4.1.1 of Directive 2004/39/EEC of the European Parliament and of the Council of 21 April 2004 on markets in financial instruments, other than—

(a)   an LLP to which that Directive does not apply by virtue of Article 2 of that Directive,

(b)   an LLP which is an exempt investment firm within the meaning of regulation 4A(3) of the Financial Services and Markets Act 2000 (Markets in Financial Instruments) Regulations 2007, and

(c)   any other LLP which fulfils all the requirements set out in regulation 4C(3) of those Regulations;

"qualified", in relation to an auditor's report (or a statement contained in an auditor's report), means that the report or statement does not state the auditor's unqualified opinion that the accounts have been properly prepared in accordance with this Act or, in the case of an undertaking not required to prepare accounts in accordance with this Act, under any corresponding legislation under which it is required to prepare accounts;

"turnover", in relation to an LLP, means the amounts derived from the provision of goods and services falling within the LLP's ordinary activities, after deduction of—

(a)   trade discounts,

(b)   value added tax, and

(c)   any other taxes based on the amounts so derived;

"UCITS management company" has the meaning given by the Glossary forming part of the Handbook made by the Financial Services Authority under the Financial Services and Markets Act 2000."

NOTES

Commencement: 1 October 2008.

Words in square brackets in the definition "e-money issuer" in s 539 as set out above inserted by the Electronic Money Regulations 2011, SI 2011/99, reg 79, Sch 4, Pt 2, para 20, as from 30 April 2011.

PART 15
STATUTORY AUDITORS

[10.1050]
48　Extension of Part 42

For the purposes of section 1210(1)(h) (meaning of "statutory auditor")—

    (a)　an LLP is a prescribed person, and

    (b)　Part 16 of the Companies Act 2006 as applied to LLPs is a prescribed enactment,

(and accordingly a person appointed as auditor of an LLP under Part 16 of that Act as applied to LLPs by these Regulations is a statutory auditor).

NOTES

  Commencement: 1 October 2008.

PART 16
OFFENCES

[10.1051]
49　Liability of member in default

Sections 1121 and 1122 apply to LLPs [for the purposes of these Regulations], modified so that they read as follows—

> **"1121　Liability of member in default**
>
> (1)　This section has effect for the purposes of any provision of the Companies Acts to the effect that, in the event of contravention of an enactment in relation to an LLP, an offence is committed by every member or, as the case may be, every designated member of the LLP who is in default.
>
> (2)　A member or designated member is "in default" for the purposes of the provision if he authorises or permits, participates in, or fails to take all reasonable steps to prevent, the contravention.
>
> **1122　Liability of company as member in default**
>
> (1)　Where a company is a member or designated member of an LLP, it does not commit an offence as a member or designated member in default unless one of its officers is in default.
>
> (2)　Where any such offence is committed by a company the officer in question also commits the offence and is liable to be proceeded against and punished accordingly.
>
> (3)　In this section—
>
>   (a)　officer" includes any director, manager or secretary, and
>
>   (b)　an officer is "in default" for the purposes of the provision if he authorises or permits, participates in, or fails to take all reasonable steps to prevent, the contravention."

NOTES

  Commencement: 1 October 2008.

  Words in square brackets inserted by the Limited Liability Partnerships (Application of Companies Act 2006) Regulations 2009, SI 2009/1804, reg 85, Sch 3, Pt 2, para 15(4), as from 1 October 2009.

[10.1052]
50　General provisions

Sections 1125 to 1132 apply to LLPs [for the purposes of these Regulations], modified so that they read as follows—

> **"1125　Meaning of "daily default fine"**
>
> (1)　This section defines what is meant in the Companies Acts where it is provided that a person guilty of an offence is liable on summary conviction to a fine not exceeding a specified amount "and, for continued contravention, a daily default fine" not exceeding a specified amount.
>
> (2)　This means that the person is liable on a second or subsequent summary conviction of the offence to a fine not exceeding the latter amount for each day on which the contravention is continued (instead of being liable to a fine not exceeding the former amount).
>
> **1126　Consents required for certain prosecutions**
>
> (1)　This section applies to proceedings for an offence under section 458 or 460 of this Act.
>
> (2)　No such proceedings are to be brought in England and Wales except by or with the consent of the Secretary of State or the Director of Public Prosecutions.
>
> (3)　No such proceedings are to be brought in Northern Ireland except by or with the consent of the Secretary of State or the Director of Public Prosecutions for Northern Ireland.
>
> **1127　Summary proceedings: venue**
>
> (1)　Summary proceedings for any offence under the Companies Acts may be taken—
>
>   (a)　against a body corporate, at any place at which the body has a place of business, and
>
>   (b)　against any other person, at any place at which he is for the time being.

(2)   This is without prejudice to any jurisdiction exercisable apart from this section.

1128 Summary proceedings: time limit for proceedings

(1)   An information relating to an offence under the Companies Acts that is triable by a magistrates' court in England and Wales may be so tried if it is laid—
- (a)   at any time within three years after the commission of the offence, and
- (b)   within twelve months after the date on which evidence sufficient in the opinion of the Director of Public Prosecutions or the Secretary of State (as the case may be) to justify the proceedings comes to his knowledge.

(2)   Summary proceedings in Scotland for an offence under the Companies Acts—
- (a)   must not be commenced after the expiration of three years from the commission of the offence;
- (b)   subject to that, may be commenced at any time—
  - (i)   within twelve months after the date on which evidence sufficient in the Lord Advocate's opinion to justify the proceedings came to his knowledge, or
  - (ii)   where such evidence was reported to him by the Secretary of State, within twelve months after the date on which it came to the knowledge of the latter.

Section 136(3) of the Criminal Procedure (Scotland) Act 1995 (c.46) (date when proceedings deemed to be commenced) applies for the purposes of this subsection as for the purposes of that section.

(3)   A magistrates' court in Northern Ireland has jurisdiction to hear and determine a complaint charging the commission of a summary offence under the Companies Acts provided that the complaint is made—
- (a)   within three years from the time when the offence was committed, and
- (b)   within twelve months from the date on which evidence sufficient in the opinion of the Director of Public Prosecutions for Northern Ireland or the Secretary of State (as the case may be) to justify the proceedings comes to his knowledge.

(4)   For the purposes of this section a certificate of the Director of Public Prosecutions, the Lord Advocate, the Director of Public Prosecutions for Northern Ireland or the Secretary of State (as the case may be) as to the date on which such evidence as is referred to above came to his notice is conclusive evidence.

1129 Legal professional privilege

In proceedings against a person for an offence under the Companies Acts, nothing in those Acts is to be taken to require any person to disclose any information that he is entitled to refuse to disclose on grounds of legal professional privilege (in Scotland, confidentiality of communications).

1130 Proceedings against unincorporated bodies

(1)   Proceedings for an offence under the Companies Acts alleged to have been committed by an unincorporated body must be brought in the name of the body (and not in that of any of its members).

(2)   For the purposes of such proceedings—
- (a)   any rules of court relating to the service of documents have effect as if the body were a body corporate, and
- (b)   the following provisions apply as they apply in relation to a body corporate—
  - (i)   in England and Wales, section 33 of the Criminal Justice Act 1925 (c.86) and Schedule 3 to the Magistrates' Courts Act 1980 (c.43),
  - (ii)   in Scotland, sections 70 and 143 of the Criminal Procedure (Scotland) Act 1995 (c.46),
  - (iii) in Northern Ireland, section 18 of the Criminal Justice Act (Northern Ireland) 1945 (c.15 (NI)) and Article 166 of and Schedule 4 to the Magistrates' Courts (Northern Ireland) Order 1981 (SI 1981/1675 (NI 26)).

(3)   A fine imposed on an unincorporated body on its conviction of an offence under the Companies Acts must be paid out of the funds of the body.

1131 Imprisonment on summary conviction in England and Wales: transitory provision

(1)   This section applies to any provision of the Companies Acts that provides that a person guilty of an offence is liable on summary conviction in England and Wales to imprisonment for a term not exceeding twelve months.

(2)   In relation to an offence committed before the commencement of section 154(1) of the Criminal Justice Act 2003 (c.44), for "twelve months" substitute "six months".

1132 Production and inspection of documents where offence suspected

(1)   An application under this section may be made—
- (a)   in England and Wales, to a judge of the High Court by the Director of Public Prosecutions, the Secretary of State or a chief officer of police;
- (b)   in Scotland, to one of the Lords Commissioners of Justiciary by the Lord Advocate;
- (c)   in Northern Ireland, to the High Court by the Director of Public Prosecutions for Northern Ireland, the Department of Enterprise, Trade and Investment or a chief superintendent of the Police Service of Northern Ireland.

(2) If on an application under this section there is shown to be reasonable cause to believe—

    (a)   that any person has, while a member of an LLP, committed an offence in connection with the management of the LLP's affairs, and

    (b)   that evidence of the commission of the offence is to be found in any documents in the possession or control of the LLP, an order under this section may be made.

(3) The order may—

    (a)   authorise any person named in it to inspect the documents in question, or any of them, for the purpose of investigating and obtaining evidence of the offence, or

    (b)   require such member of the LLP as may be named in the order, to produce the documents (or any of them) to a person named in the order at a place so named.

(4) This section applies also in relation to documents in the possession or control of a person carrying on the business of banking, so far as they relate to the LLP's affairs, as it applies to documents in the possession or control of the LLP, except that no such order as is referred to in subsection (3)(b) may be made by virtue of this subsection."

The decision under this section of a judge of the High Court, any of the Lords Commissioners of Justiciary or the High Court is not appealable.

In this section "document" includes information recorded in any form.

NOTES

Commencement: 1 October 2008.

Words in square brackets inserted by the Limited Liability Partnerships (Application of Companies Act 2006) Regulations 2009, SI 2009/1804, reg 85, Sch 3, Pt 2, para 15(4), as from 1 October 2009.

PART 17
LLPS: SUPPLEMENTARY AND INTERPRETATION

[10.1053]
51 Courts and legal proceedings

Section 1157 applies to LLPs [for the purposes of these Regulations], modified so that it reads as follows—

"1157 Power of court to grant relief in certain cases

(1) If in proceedings for negligence, default, breach of duty or breach of trust against—

    (a)   a member of an LLP, or

    (b)   a person employed by an LLP as auditor,

it appears to the court hearing the case that the member or person is or may be liable but that he acted honestly and reasonably, and that having regard to all the circumstances of the case (including those connected with his appointment) he ought fairly to be excused, the court may relieve him, either wholly or in part, from his liability on such terms as it thinks fit.

(2) If any such member or person has reason to apprehend that a claim will or might be made against him in respect of negligence, default, breach of duty or breach of trust—

    (a)   he may apply to the court for relief, and

    (b)   the court has the same power to relieve him as it would have had if it had been a court before which proceedings against him for negligence, default, breach of duty or breach of trust had been brought.

(3) Where a case to which subsection (1) applies is being tried by a judge with a jury, the judge, after hearing the evidence, may, if he is satisfied that the defendant (in Scotland, the defender) ought in pursuance of that subsection to be relieved either in whole or in part from the liability sought to be enforced against him, withdraw the case from the jury and forthwith direct judgment to be entered for the defendant (in Scotland, grant decree of absolvitor) on such terms as to costs (in Scotland, expenses) or otherwise as the judge may think proper."

NOTES

Commencement: 1 October 2008.

Words in square brackets inserted by the Limited Liability Partnerships (Application of Companies Act 2006) Regulations 2009, SI 2009/1804, reg 85, Sch 3, Pt 2, para 15(4), as from 1 October 2009. Note that Sch 3, Pt 2, para 15(4) actually provides that these words should be inserted after the words "apply to LLPs" in this regulation; it is assumed that this is a drafting error and the words have been inserted above.

[10.1054]
52 Meaning of "undertaking" and related expressions

Sections 1161 and 1162 and Schedule 7 apply to LLPs, modified so that they read as follows—

"1161 Meaning of "undertaking" and related expressions

(1) In this Act "undertaking" means—

    (a)   a body corporate or partnership, or

    (b)   an unincorporated association carrying on a trade or business, with or without a view to profit.

(2) In this Act references to shares—

    (a)   in relation to an undertaking with capital but no share capital, are to rights to share in the capital of the undertaking; and

    (b)   in relation to an undertaking without capital, are to interests—

        (i)   conferring any right to share in the profits or liability to contribute to the losses of the undertaking, or

        (ii) giving rise to an obligation to contribute to the debts or expenses of the undertaking in the event of a winding up.

(3) Other expressions appropriate to companies shall be construed, in relation to an undertaking which is not a company, as references to the corresponding persons, officers, documents or organs, as the case may be, appropriate to undertakings of that description.

    This is subject to provision in any specific context providing for the translation of such expressions.

(4) References in this Act to "fellow subsidiary undertakings" are to undertakings which are subsidiary undertakings of the same parent undertaking but are not parent undertakings or subsidiary undertakings of each other.

(5) In this Act "group undertaking", in relation to an undertaking, means an undertaking which is—

    (a)   a parent undertaking or subsidiary undertaking of that undertaking, or

    (b)   a subsidiary undertaking of any parent undertaking of that undertaking.

1162 Parent and subsidiary undertakings

(1) This section (together with Schedule 7) defines "parent undertaking" and "subsidiary undertaking" for the purposes of this Act.

(2) An undertaking is a parent undertaking in relation to another undertaking, a subsidiary undertaking, if—

    (a)   it holds a majority of the voting rights in the undertaking, or

    (b)   it is a member of the undertaking and has the right to appoint or remove a majority of its board of directors, or

    (c)   it has the right to exercise a dominant influence over the undertaking—

        (i)   by virtue of provisions contained in the undertaking's articles or in an LLP Agreement, or

        (ii) by virtue of a control contract, or

    (d)   it is a member of the undertaking and controls alone, pursuant to an agreement with other shareholders or members, a majority of the voting rights in the undertaking.

(3) For the purposes of subsection (2) an undertaking shall be treated as a member of another undertaking—

    (a)   if any of its subsidiary undertakings is a member of that undertaking, or

    (b)   if any shares in that other undertaking are held by a person acting on behalf of the undertaking or any of its subsidiary undertakings.

(4) An undertaking is also a parent undertaking in relation to another undertaking, a subsidiary undertaking, if—

    (a)   it has the power to exercise, or actually exercises, dominant influence or control over it, or

    (b)   it and the subsidiary undertaking are managed on a unified basis.

(5) A parent undertaking shall be treated as the parent undertaking of undertakings in relation to which any of its subsidiary undertakings are, or are to be treated as, parent undertakings; and references to its subsidiary undertakings shall be construed accordingly.

(6) Schedule 7 contains provisions explaining expressions used in this section and otherwise supplementing this section.

(7) In this section and that Schedule references to shares, in relation to an undertaking, are to allotted shares."

"SCHEDULE 7

PARENT AND SUBSIDIARY UNDERTAKINGS: SUPPLEMENTARY PROVISIONS

Introduction

1. The provisions of this Schedule explain expressions used in section 1162 (parent and subsidiary undertakings) and otherwise supplement that section.

Voting rights in an undertaking

2. (1) In section 1162(2)(a) and (d) the references to the voting rights in an undertaking are to the rights conferred on shareholders in respect of their shares or, in the case of an undertaking not having a share capital, on members, to vote at general meetings of the undertaking on all, or substantially all, matters.

(2) In relation to an undertaking which does not have general meetings at which matters are decided by the exercise of voting rights the references to holding a majority of the voting rights in the undertaking are to be construed as references to having the right under the constitution of the undertaking to direct the overall policy of the undertaking or to alter the terms of its constitution.

Right to appoint or remove a majority of members or directors

3. (1)   In section 1162(2)(b) the reference to the right to appoint or remove a majority of the board of directors is to the right to appoint or remove directors holding a majority of the voting rights at meetings of the board on all, or substantially all, matters.

(2)   An undertaking shall be treated as having the right to appoint to a directorship if—

(a)   a person's appointment to it follows necessarily from his appointment as director of the undertaking, or

(b)   the directorship is held by the undertaking itself.

(3)   A right to appoint or remove which is exercisable only with the consent or concurrence of another person shall be left out of account unless no other person has a right to appoint or, as the case may be, remove in relation to that directorship.

(4)   (4) In relation to an undertaking the business of which is managed by the members, references to the board of directors or directors are to be construed as references to members.

Right to exercise dominant influence

4. (1)   For the purposes of section 1162(2)(c) an undertaking shall not be regarded as having the right to exercise a dominant influence over another undertaking unless it has a right to give directions with respect to the operating and financial policies of that other undertaking which its directors are obliged to comply with whether or not they are for the benefit of that other undertaking.

(2)   A "control contract" means a contract in writing conferring such a right which—

(a)   is of a kind authorised by the articles of the undertaking or by the LLP agreement of the LLP in relation to which the right is exercisable, and

(b)   is permitted by the law under which that undertaking is established.

(3)   In relation to an undertaking the business of which is managed by the members, references to directors are to be construed as references to members.

(4)   This paragraph shall not be read as affecting the construction of section 1162(4)(a).

Rights exercisable only in certain circumstances or temporarily incapable of exercise

5. (1)   Rights which are exercisable only in certain circumstances shall be taken into account only—

(a)   when the circumstances have arisen, and for so long as they continue to obtain, or

(b)   when the circumstances are within the control of the person having the rights.

(2)   Rights which are normally exercisable but are temporarily incapable of exercise shall continue to be taken into account.

Rights held by one person on behalf of another

6. Rights held by a person in a fiduciary capacity shall be treated as not held by him.

7. (1)   Rights held by a person as nominee for another shall be treated as held by the other.

(2)   Rights shall be regarded as held as nominee for another if they are exercisable only on his instructions or with his consent or concurrence.

Rights attached to shares held by way of security

8. Rights attached to shares held by way of security shall be treated as held by the person providing the security—

(a)   where apart from the right to exercise them for the purpose of preserving the value of the security, or of realising it, the rights are exercisable only in accordance with his instructions, and

(b)   where the shares are held in connection with the granting of loans as part of normal business activities and apart from the right to exercise them for the purpose of preserving the value of the security, or of realising it, the rights are exercisable only in his interests.

Rights attributed to parent undertaking

9. (1)   Rights shall be treated as held by a parent undertaking if they are held by any of its subsidiary undertakings.

(2)   Nothing in paragraph 7 or 8 shall be construed as requiring rights held by a parent undertaking to be treated as held by any of its subsidiary undertakings.

(3)   For the purposes of paragraph 8 rights shall be treated as being exercisable in accordance with the instructions or in the interests of an undertaking if they are exercisable in accordance with the instructions of or, as the case may be, in the interests of any group undertaking.

Disregard of certain rights

10. The voting rights in an undertaking shall be reduced by any rights held by the undertaking itself.

Supplementary

11. References in any provision of paragraphs 6 to 10 to rights held by a person include rights falling to be treated as held by him by virtue of any other provision of those paragraphs but not rights which by virtue of any such provision are to be treated as not held by him."

NOTES
Commencement: 1 October 2008.

[10.1055]
53 Meaning of "dormant"
Section 1169 applies to LLPs, modified so that it reads as follows—

"1169 Dormant LLPs
(1)   For the purposes of this Act an LLP is "dormant" during any period in which it has no significant accounting transaction.
(2)   A "significant accounting transaction" means a transaction that is required by section 386 to be entered in the LLP's accounting records.
(3)   In determining whether or when an LLP is dormant, there shall be disregarded any transaction consisting of the payment of—
    (a)   a fee to the registrar on a change of the LLP's name,
    (b)   a penalty under section 453 (penalty for failure to file accounts), or
    (c)   a fee to the registrar for the registration of an annual return."

NOTES
Commencement: 1 October 2008.

[10.1056]
54 Requirements of this Act
Section 1172 applies to LLPs [for the purposes of these Regulations], modified so that it reads as follows—

"1172 References to requirements of this Act
References in the provisions of this Act applied to LLPs to the requirements of this Act include the requirements of regulations and orders made under it."

NOTES
Commencement: 1 October 2008.
Words in square brackets inserted by the Limited Liability Partnerships (Application of Companies Act 2006) Regulations 2009, SI 2009/1804, reg 85, Sch 3, Pt 2, para 15(4), as from 1 October 2009. Note that Sch 3, Pt 2, para 15(4) actually provides that these words should be inserted after the words "apply to LLPs" in this regulation; it is assumed that this is a drafting error and the words have been inserted above.

[10.1057]
55 Minor definitions
Section 1173 applies to LLPs [for the purposes of these Regulations], modified so that it reads as follows—

"1173 Minor definitions: general
(1)   In this Act—
    "body corporate" includes a body incorporated outside the United Kingdom, but does not include—
        (a)   a corporation sole, or
        (b)   a partnership that, whether or not a legal person, is not regarded as a body corporate under the law by which it is governed;
    "EEA undertaking" means an undertaking governed by the law of an EEA State.
    ["firm" means any entity, whether or not a legal person, that is not an individual and includes a body corporate, a corporation sole and a partnership or other unincorporated association;]
    "parent LLP" means an LLP that is a parent undertaking (see section 1162 and Schedule 7);
    "regulated activity" has the meaning given by section 22 of the Financial Services and Markets Act 2000 (c.8);
    "regulated market" has the same meaning as in Directive 2004/39/EC of the European Parliament and of the Council on markets in financial instruments (see Article 4.1(14)).
(2)   In relation to an EEA State that has not implemented Directive 2004/39/EC of the European Parliament and of the Council on markets in financial instruments, the following definition of "regulated market" has effect in place of that in subsection (1)—
    "regulated market" has the same meaning as it has in Council Directive 93/22/EEC on investment services in the securities field."

NOTES

Commencement: 1 October 2008.

First words in square brackets inserted by the Limited Liability Partnerships (Application of Companies Act 2006) Regulations 2009, SI 2009/1804, reg 85, Sch 3, Pt 2, para 15(4), as from 1 October 2009. Note that Sch 3, Pt 2, para 15(4) actually provides that these words should be inserted after the words "apply to LLPs" in this regulation; it is assumed that this is a drafting error and the words have been inserted above.

Definition "firm" as set out in s 1173 above inserted by SI 2009/1804, reg 85, Sch 3, Pt 2, para 15(5), as from 1 October 2009.

[10.1058]
56   Regulations

Sections 1288 to 1290 apply to LLPs [for the purposes of these Regulations], modified so that they read as follows—

"1288   Regulations: statutory instrument
Except as otherwise provided, regulations under this Act shall be made by statutory instrument.

1289   Regulations: negative resolution procedure
Where regulations under this Act are subject to "negative resolution procedure" the statutory instrument containing the regulations or order shall be subject to annulment in pursuance of a resolution of either House of Parliament.

1290   Regulations: affirmative resolution procedure
Where regulations under this Act are subject to "affirmative resolution procedure" the regulations must not be made unless a draft of the statutory instrument containing them has been laid before Parliament and approved by a resolution of each House of Parliament."

NOTES

Commencement: 1 October 2008.

Words in square brackets inserted by the Limited Liability Partnerships (Application of Companies Act 2006) Regulations 2009, SI 2009/1804, reg 85, Sch 3, Pt 2, para 15(4), as from 1 October 2009.

[10.1059]
57

Section 1292 applies to LLPs [for the purposes of these Regulations], modified so that it reads as follows—

"1292   Regulations and orders: supplementary
(1)   Regulations under this Act may—
   (a)   make different provision for different cases or circumstances,
   (b)   include supplementary, incidental and consequential provision, and
   (c)   make transitional provision and savings.
(2)   Any provision that may be made by regulations under this Act subject to negative resolution procedure may be made by regulations subject to affirmative resolution procedure."

NOTES

Commencement: 1 October 2008.

Words in square brackets inserted by the Limited Liability Partnerships (Application of Companies Act 2006) Regulations 2009, SI 2009/1804, reg 85, Sch 3, Pt 2, para 15(4), as from 1 October 2009. Note that Sch 3, Pt 2, para 15(4) actually provides that these words should be inserted after the words "apply to LLPs" in this regulation; it is assumed that this is a drafting error and the words have been inserted above.

PART 18
FINAL PROVISIONS

[10.1060]
58   Revocation and transitional provisions

(1)   Subject to paragraphs (3) to (11), the following provisions of the Limited Liability Partnerships Regulations 2001 are revoked—
   (a)   regulation 3 and Schedule 1,
   (b)   in Schedule 2, the entries relating to sections 384, 385, 387, 388, 388A, 389A, 390, 390A, 390B, 391, 391A, 392, 392A, 394, 394A and 742, and
   (c)   entries 1, 2, 3 and 6 in Part I of Schedule 6.

(2)   Subject to paragraphs (3) to (11), the following provisions of the Limited Liability Partnerships Regulations (Northern Ireland) 2004 are revoked—
   (a)   regulation 3 and Schedule 1,
   (b)   in Schedule 2, the entries relating to Articles 10, 392, 393, 395, 396, 396A, 397A, 398, 398A, 398B, 399, 399A, 400, 400A, 401A and 401B, and
   (c)   entries 1, 2, 3 and 6 in Part I of Schedule 5.

(3)   The provisions specified in paragraphs (1)(a) and (c) and (2)(a) and (c), and the entries specified in paragraphs (1)(b) and (2)(b) relating to section 742 of the 1985 Act or Article 10 of the 1986 Order, continue to apply to accounts for, and otherwise as regards, financial years beginning before 1st October 2008.

(4)   The entries specified in paragraphs (1)(b) and (2)(b) relating to sections 384, 385, 387, 388 and 388A of the 1985 Act or Articles 392, 393, 395, 396 and 396A of the 1986 Order continue to apply in relation to appointments of auditors for financial years beginning before 1st October 2008, and section 388(2) of the 1985 Act or Article 396(2) of the 1986 Order as applied to LLPs continues to apply where the vacancy occurs before that date.

(5)   The entries specified in paragraphs (1)(b) and (2)(b) relating to section 389A of the 1985 Act or Article 397A of the 1986 Order continue to apply as regards financial years beginning before 1st October 2008.

(6)   The entries specified in paragraphs (1)(b) and (2)(b) relating to section 390 of the 1985 Act or Article 398 of the 1986 Order continue to apply to auditors appointed before 1st October 2008.

(7)   The entries specified in paragraphs (1)(b) and (2)(b) relating to sections 390A and 390B of the 1985 Act or Articles 398A and 398B of the 1986 Order continue to apply to auditors appointed for financial years beginning before 1st October 2008.

(8)   The entries specified in paragraphs (1)(b) and (2)(b) relating to sections 391 and 391A of the 1985 Act or Articles 399 and 399A of the 1986 Order continue to apply as respects removal of auditors where notice is given to the auditor before 1st October 2008.

(9)   The entries specified in paragraphs (1)(b) and (2)(b) relating to section 391A of the 1985 Act or Article 399A of the 1986 Order continue to apply as regards failure to re-appoint an auditor to appointments for financial years beginning before 1st October 2008.

(10)   The entries specified in paragraphs (1)(b) and (2)(b) relating to sections 392 and 392A of the 1985 Act or Articles 400 and 400A of the 1986 Order continue to apply to resignations occurring before 1st October 2008.

(11)   The entries specified in paragraphs (1)(b) and (2)(b) relating to sections 394 and 394A of the 1985 Act or Articles 401A and 401B of the 1986 Order continue to apply where the auditor ceases to hold office before 1st October 2008.

NOTES

Commencement: 1 October 2008.

SMALL LIMITED LIABILITY PARTNERSHIPS (ACCOUNTS) REGULATIONS 2008

(SI 2008/1912)

NOTES

Made: 17 July 2008.

Authority: Limited Liability Partnerships Act 2000, ss 15, 17.

Commencement: 1 October 2008.

Amendment: as of 1 July 2011, these Regulations had not been amended.

ARRANGEMENT OF REGULATIONS

PART 1
INTRODUCTION

PART 2
FORM AND CONTENT OF INDIVIDUAL ACCOUNTS

PART 3
FORM AND CONTENT OF GROUP ACCOUNTS

PART 4
INTERPRETATION

PART 1
INTRODUCTION

[10.1061]
1 Citation and interpretation

(1)   These Regulations may be cited as the Small Limited Liability Partnerships (Accounts) Regulations 2008.

(2)   In these Regulations—
    "the 2006 Act" means the Companies Act 2006;
    "LLP" means a limited liability partnership formed under the Limited Liability Partnerships Act 2000 or the Limited Liability Partnerships Act (NI) 2002;
    "the Small Companies Accounts Regulations" means the Small Companies and Groups (Accounts and Directors' Report) Regulations 2008.

(3)   Any reference in these Regulations to a numbered Part or section of the 2006 Act is a reference to that Part or section as applied to LLPs by the Limited Liability Partnerships (Accounts and Audit) (Application of Companies Act 2006) Regulations 2008.

NOTES
Commencement: 1 October 2008.
General note as to interpretation: as to the meaning of "the registrar" and "the register", and as to the construction of references to registration in a particular part of the United Kingdom, in any enactment relating to LLPs, see the Limited Liability Partnerships (Application of Companies Act 2006) Regulations 2009, SI 2009/1804, reg 85, Sch 3, Pt 2, para 12 at **[10.1191]**.

[10.1062]
2 Commencement and application

(1)   These Regulations come into force on 1st October 2008.

(2)   They apply in relation to financial years beginning on or after 1st October 2008.

(3)   They apply to LLPs which are subject to the small LLPs regime under Part 15 of the 2006 Act (see section 381 of that Act) provisions of the Small Companies Accounts Regulations, with modifications.

NOTES
Commencement: 1 October 2008.

PART 2
FORM AND CONTENT OF INDIVIDUAL ACCOUNTS

[10.1063]
3 Non-IAS individual accounts

(1)   Regulation 3 of the Small Companies Accounts Regulations applies to LLPs, modified so that it reads as follows—

"3 Non-IAS individual accounts
(1)   Non-IAS individual accounts under section 396 of the 2006 Act (non-IAS individual accounts) must comply with the provisions of Schedule 1 to the Small Limited Liability Partnerships (Accounts) Regulations 2008 as to the form and content of the balance sheet and profit and loss account, and additional information to be provided by way of notes to the accounts.

(2)   The profit and loss account of an LLP that falls within section 408 of the 2006 Act (individual profit and loss account where group accounts prepared) need not contain the information specified in paragraphs 57 to 59 of Schedule 1 to the Small Limited Liability Partnerships (Accounts) Regulations 2008 (information supplementing the profit and loss account).

(3)   Accounts are treated as having complied with any provision of Schedule 1 to the Small Limited Liability Partnerships (Accounts) Regulations 2008 if they comply instead with the corresponding provision of Schedule 1 to the Large and Medium-sized Limited Liability Partnerships (Accounts) Regulations 2008.".

(2)   The provisions of Schedule 1 to the Small Companies Accounts Regulations apply to LLPs, modified so that they are the provisions set out in Schedule 1 to these Regulations.

NOTES
Commencement: 1 October 2008.

[10.1064]
4   Information about related undertakings (non-IAS or IAS individual accounts)
(1)   Regulation 4 of the Small Companies Accounts Regulations applies to LLPs, modified so that it reads as follows—

> **"4   Information about related undertakings (non-IAS or IAS individual accounts)**
> (1)   Non-IAS or IAS individual accounts must comply with the provisions of Schedule 2 to the Small Limited Liability Partnerships (Accounts) Regulations 2008 as to information about related undertakings to be given in notes to the LLP's accounts.
> (2)   Information otherwise required to be given by Schedule 2 to the Small Limited Liability Partnerships (Accounts) Regulations 2008 need not be disclosed with respect to an undertaking that—
> (a)   is established under the law of a country outside the United Kingdom, or
> (b)   carries on business outside the United Kingdom,
> if the conditions specified in section 409(4) of the 2006 Act are met (see section 409(5) of the 2006 Act for disclosure required where advantage taken of this exemption).".

(2)   The provisions of Schedule 2 to the Small Companies Accounts Regulations apply to LLPs, modified so that they are the provisions set out in Schedule 2 to these Regulations.

NOTES
Commencement: 1 October 2008.

[10.1065]
5   Accounts for delivery to registrar of companies (non-IAS individual accounts)
(1)   Regulation 6 of the Small Companies Accounts Regulations applies to LLPs, modified so that it reads as follows—

> **"6   Accounts for delivery to registrar of companies (non-IAS individual accounts)**
> The designated members of an LLP for which non-IAS individual accounts are being prepared may deliver to the registrar of companies under section 444 of the 2006 Act (filing obligations of LLPs subject to small LLPs regime) a copy of a balance sheet which complies with Schedule 3 to the Small Limited Liability Partnerships (Accounts) Regulations 2008 rather than Schedule 1 to those Regulations.".

(2)   The provisions of Schedule 4 to the Small Companies Accounts Regulations apply to LLPs, modified so that they are the provisions set out in Schedule 3 to these Regulations.

NOTES
Commencement: 1 October 2008.

PART 3
FORM AND CONTENT OF GROUP ACCOUNTS

[10.1066]
6   Non-IAS group accounts
(1)   Regulation 8 of the Small Companies Accounts Regulations applies to LLPs, modified so that it reads as follows—

> **"8   Non-IAS group accounts**
> (1)   Where the members of a parent LLP which—
> (a)   is subject to the small LLPs regime, and
> (b)   has prepared non-IAS individual accounts in accordance with regulation 3,
> prepare non-IAS group accounts under section 398 of the 2006 Act (option to prepare group accounts), those accounts must comply with the provisions of Part 1 of Schedule 4 to the

Small Limited Liability Partnerships (Accounts) Regulations 2008 as to the form and content of the consolidated balance sheet and consolidated profit and loss account, and additional information to be provided by way of notes to the accounts.

(2)   Accounts are treated as having complied with any provision of Part 1 of Schedule 4 to the Small Limited Liability Partnerships (Accounts) Regulations 2008 if they comply instead with the corresponding provision of Schedule 3 to the Large and Medium-sized Limited Liability Partnerships (Accounts) Regulations 2008.".

(2)   The provisions of Part 1 of Schedule 6 to the Small Companies Accounts Regulations apply to LLPs, modified so that they are the provisions set out in Part 1 of Schedule 4 to these Regulations.

NOTES

Commencement: 1 October 2008.

[10.1067]
7   Information about related undertakings (Non-IAS or IAS group accounts)

(1)   Regulation 10 of the Small Companies Accounts Regulations applies to LLPs, modified so that it reads as follows—

"10   Information about related undertakings (Non-IAS or IAS group accounts)
(1)   Non-IAS or IAS group accounts must comply with the provisions of Part 2 of Schedule 4 to the Small Limited Liability Partnerships (Accounts) Regulations 2008 as to information about related undertakings to be given in notes to the LLP's accounts.
(2)   Information otherwise required to be given by Part 2 of Schedule 4 to the Small Limited Liability Partnerships (Accounts) Regulations 2008 need not be disclosed with respect to an undertaking that—
   (a)   is established under the law of a country outside the United Kingdom, or
   (b)   carries on business outside the United Kingdom,
if the conditions specified in section 409(4) of the 2006 Act are met (see section 409(5) of the 2006 Act for disclosure required where advantage taken of this exemption).".

(2)   The provisions of Part 2 of Schedule 6 to the Small Companies Accounts Regulations apply to LLPs, modified so that they are the provisions set out in Part 2 of Schedule 4 to these Regulations.

NOTES

Commencement: 1 October 2008.

PART 4
INTERPRETATION

[10.1068]
8   General interpretation

(1)   Regulation 13 of the Small Companies Accounts Regulations applies to LLPs, modified so that it reads as follows—

"13   General interpretation
Schedule 5 to the Small Limited Liability Partnerships (Accounts) Regulations 2008 contains general definitions for the purposes of these Regulations.".

(2)   The provisions of Schedule 8 to the Small Companies Accounts Regulations apply to LLPs, modified so that they are the provisions set out in Schedule 5 to these Regulations.

NOTES

Commencement: 1 October 2008.

SCHEDULES

SCHEDULE 1
NON-IAS INDIVIDUAL ACCOUNTS

Regulation 3

PART 1
GENERAL RULES AND FORMATS

SECTION A
GENERAL RULES

[10.1069]
1. (1)   Subject to the following provisions of this Schedule—
   (a)   every balance sheet of an LLP must show the items listed in either of the balance sheet formats in Section B of this Part, and

    (b)   every profit and loss account must show the items listed in either of the profit and loss account formats in Section B.

(2)   References in this Schedule to the items listed in any of the formats in Section B are to those items read together with any of the notes following the formats which apply to those items.

(3)   The items must be shown in the order and under the headings and sub-headings given in the particular format used, but—

    (a)   the notes to the formats may permit alternative positions for any particular items, and

    (b)   the heading or sub-heading for any item does not have to be distinguished by any letter or number assigned to that item in the format used.

2. (1)   Where in accordance with paragraph 1 an LLP's balance sheet or profit and loss account for any financial year has been prepared by reference to one of the formats in Section B, the members of the LLP must use the same format in preparing non-IAS individual accounts for subsequent financial years, unless in their opinion there are special reasons for a change.

(2)   Particulars of any such change must be given in a note to the accounts in which the new format is first used, and the reasons for the change must be explained.

3. (1)   Any item required to be shown in an LLP's balance sheet or profit and loss account may be shown in greater detail than required by the particular format used.

(2)   The balance sheet or profit and loss account may include an item representing or covering the amount of any asset or liability, income or expenditure not otherwise covered by any of the items listed in the format used, save that none of the following may be treated as assets in any balance sheet—

    (a)   preliminary expenses,

    (b)   expenses of, and commission on, any issue of debentures,

    (c)   costs of research.

4. (1)   Where the special nature of the LLP's business requires it, the members of the LLP must adapt the arrangement, headings and sub-headings otherwise required in respect of items given an Arabic number in the balance sheet or profit and loss account format used.

(2)   The members may combine items to which Arabic numbers are given in any of the formats set out in Section B if—

    (a)   their individual amounts are not material to assessing the state of affairs or profit or loss of the LLP for the financial year in question, or

    (b)   the combination facilitates that assessment.

(3)   Where sub-paragraph (2)(b) applies, the individual amounts of any items which have been combined must be disclosed in a note to the accounts.

5. (1)   Subject to sub-paragraph (2), the members must not include a heading or sub-heading corresponding to an item in the balance sheet or profit and loss account format used if there is no amount to be shown for that item for the financial year to which the balance sheet or profit and loss account relates.

(2)   Where an amount can be shown for the item in question for the immediately preceding financial year that amount must be shown under the heading or sub-heading required by the format for that item.

6. Every profit and loss account must show the amount of an LLP's profit or loss on ordinary activities before taxation.

7. (1)   For every item shown in the balance sheet or profit and loss account the corresponding amount for the immediately preceding financial year must also be shown.

(2)   Where that corresponding amount is not comparable with the amount to be shown for the item in question in respect of the financial year to which the balance sheet or profit and loss account relates, the former amount may be adjusted, and particulars of the non-comparability and of any adjustment must be disclosed in a note to the accounts.

8. Amounts in respect of items representing assets or income may not be set off against amounts in respect of items representing liabilities or expenditure (as the case may be), or vice versa.

9. The members of the LLP must, in determining how amounts are presented within items in the profit and loss account and balance sheet, have regard to the substance of the reported transaction or arrangement, in accordance with generally accepted accounting principles or practice.

SECTION B
THE REQUIRED FORMATS FOR ACCOUNTS

Balance sheet formats

Format 1

A. Fixed assets
    I.   Intangible assets
        1.   Goodwill [1]
        2.   Other intangible assets [2]
    II.   Tangible assets
        1.   Land and buildings
        2.   Plant and machinery etc.
    III.   Investments
        1.   Shares in group undertakings and participating interests
        2.   Loans to group undertakings and undertakings in which the LLP has a participating interest
        3.   Other investments other than loans
        4.   Other investments

B. Current assets
    I.   Stocks
        1.   Stocks
        2.   Payments on account
    II.   Debtors [3]
        1.   Trade debtors
        2.   Amounts owed by group undertakings and undertakings in which the LLP has a participating interest
        3.   Other debtors
    III.   Investments
        1.   Shares in group undertakings
        2.   Other investments
    IV.   Cash at bank and in hand

C. Prepayments and accrued income [4]

D. Creditors: amounts falling due within one year
        1.   Bank loans and overdrafts
        2.   Trade creditors
        3.   Amounts owed to group undertakings and undertakings in which the LLP has a participating interest
        4.   Other creditors [5]

E. Net current assets (liabilities) [6]

F. Total assets less current liabilities

G. Creditors: amounts falling due after more than one year
        1.   Bank loans and overdrafts
        2.   Trade creditors
        3.   Amounts owed to group undertakings and undertakings in which the LLP has a participating interest
        4.   Other creditors [5]

H. Provisions for liabilities

I. Accruals and deferred income [5]

J. Loans and other debts due to members [7]

K. Members' other interests
    I.   Members' capital
    II.   Revaluation reserve
    III.   Other reserves

Part 10   Miscellaneous other SIs

Balance sheet formats

Format 2

ASSETS

A. Fixed assets
  I.   Intangible assets
      1.   Goodwill [1]
      2.   Other intangible assets [2]
  II. Tangible assets
      1.   Land and buildings
      2.   Plant and machinery etc.
  III. Investments
      1.   Shares in group undertakings and participating interests
      2.   Loans to group undertakings and undertakings in which the LLP has a participating interest
      3.   Other investments other than loans
      4.   Other investments

B. Current assets
  I.   Stocks
      1.   Stocks
      2.   Payments on account
  II. Debtors [3]
      1.   Trade debtors
      2.   Amounts owed by group undertakings and undertakings in which the LLP has a participating interest
      3.   Other debtors
  III. Investments
      1.   Shares in group undertakings
      2.   Other investments
  IV. Cash at bank and in hand

C. Prepayments and accrued income [4]

LIABILITIES

A. Loans and other debts due to members [7]

B. Members' other interests
  I.   Members' capital [7]
  II. Revaluation reserve
  III. Other reserves

C. Provisions for liabilities

D. Creditors [8]
      1.   Bank loans and overdrafts
      2.   Trade creditors
      3.   Amounts owed to group undertakings and undertakings in which the LLP has a participating interest
      4.   Other creditors [5]

E. Accruals and deferred income [5]

Notes on the balance sheet formats

(1)   Goodwill
(Formats 1 and 2, item A.I.1.)
Amounts representing goodwill must only be included to the extent that the goodwill was acquired for valuable consideration.

(2)   Other intangible assets
(Formats 1 and 2, item A.I.2.)
Amounts in respect of concessions, patents, licences, trade marks and similar rights and assets must only be included in an LLP's balance sheet under this item if either—
  (a)   the assets were acquired for valuable consideration and are not required to be shown under goodwill, or
  (b)   the assets in question were created by the LLP itself.

(3)   Debtors
(Formats 1 and 2, items B.II.1 to 3.)

The amount falling due after more than one year must be shown separately for each item included under debtors unless the aggregate amount of debtors falling due after more than one year is disclosed in the notes to the accounts.

(4)   Prepayments and accrued income
(Formats 1 and 2, item C.)
   This item may alternatively be included under item B.II.3 in Format 1 or 2.

(5)   Other creditors
(Format 1, items D.4, G.4 and I and Format 2, items D.4 and E.)
   There must be shown separately—
   (a)   the amount of any convertible loans, and
   (b)   the amount for creditors in respect of taxation and social security.
Payments received on account of orders must be included in so far as they are not shown as deductions from stocks.
   In Format 1, accruals and deferred income may be shown under item I or included under item D.4 or G.4, or both (as the case may require). In Format 2, accruals and deferred income may be shown under item E or within item D.4 under Liabilities.

(6)   Net current assets (liabilities)
(Format 1, item E.)
   In determining the amount to be shown under this item any prepayments and accrued income must be taken into account wherever shown.

(7)   Loans and other debts due to members
(Format 1, item J and Format 2, Liabilities item A)
   The following amounts must be shown separately under this item—
   (a)   the aggregate amount of money advanced to the LLP by the members by way of loan,
   (b)   the aggregate amount of money owed to members by the LLP in respect of profits,
   (c)   any other amounts.

(8)   Creditors
(Format 2, Liabilities items D.1 to 4.)
   Amounts falling due within one year and after one year must be shown separately for each of these items and for the aggregate of all of these items unless the aggregate amount of creditors falling due within one year and the aggregate amount of creditors falling due after more than one year is disclosed in the notes to the accounts.

Profit and loss account formats

Format 1
(see note (12) below)

1.   Turnover

2.   Cost of sales [(9)]

3.   Gross profit or loss

4.   Distribution costs [(9)]

5.   Administrative expenses [(9)]

6.   Other operating income

7.   Income from shares in group undertakings

8.   Income from participating interests

9.   Income from other fixed asset investments [(10)]

10.   Other interest receivable and similar income [(10)]

11.   Amounts written off investments

12.   Interest payable and similar charges [(11)]

13.   Tax on profit or loss on ordinary activities

14.   Profit or loss on ordinary activities after taxation

15.   Extraordinary income

16.   Extraordinary charges

17.   Extraordinary profit or loss

18.   Tax on extraordinary profit or loss

19.   Other taxes not shown under the above items

20.   Profit or loss for the financial year before members' remuneration and profit shares

Profit and loss account formats

Format 2

1.   Turnover

2.   Change in stocks of finished goods and in work in progress

3.   Own work capitalised

4.   Other operating income

5.
   (a)   Raw materials and consumables
   (b)   Other external charges

6.   Staff costs
   (a)   wages and salaries
   (b)   social security costs
   (c)   other pension costs

7.
   (a)   Depreciation and other amounts written off tangible and intangible fixed assets
   (b)   Exceptional amounts written off current assets

8.   Other operating charges

9.   Income from shares in group undertakings

10.   Income from participating interests

11.   Income from other fixed asset investments [(10)]

12.   Other interest receivable and similar income [(10)]

13.   Amounts written off investments

14.   Interest payable and similar charges [(11)]

15.   Tax on profit or loss on ordinary activities

16.   Profit or loss on ordinary activities after taxation

17.   Extraordinary income

18.   Extraordinary charges

19.   Extraordinary profit or loss

20.   Tax on extraordinary profit or loss

21.   Other taxes not shown under the above items

22.   Profit or loss for the financial year before members' remuneration and profit shares

Notes on the profit and loss account formats

(9)   Cost of sales: distribution costs: administrative expenses

(Format 1, items 2, 4 and 5.)
   These items must be stated after taking into account any necessary provisions for depreciation or diminution in value of assets.

(10)   Income from other fixed asset investments: other interest receivable and similar income

(Format 1, items 9 and 10; Format 2, items 11 and 12.)
   Income and interest derived from group undertakings must be shown separately from income and interest derived from other sources. Interest receivable from members must not be included under this item.

(11)   Interest payable and similar charges

(Format 1, item 12; Format 2, item 14.)

The amount payable to group undertakings must be shown separately. Interest payable to members must not be included under this item.

(12)   Format 1

The amount of any provisions for depreciation and diminution in value of tangible and intangible fixed assets falling to be shown under item 7(a) in Format 2 must be disclosed in a note to the accounts in any case where the profit and loss account is prepared using Format 1.

NOTES

Commencement: 1 October 2008.

PART 2
ACCOUNTING PRINCIPLES AND RULES

SECTION A
ACCOUNTING PRINCIPLES

Preliminary

[10.1070]

10. (1)   The amounts to be included in respect of all items shown in an LLP's accounts must be determined in accordance with the principles set out in this Section.

(2)   But if it appears to the members of the LLP that there are special reasons for departing from any of those principles in preparing the LLP's accounts in respect of any financial year they may do so, in which case particulars of the departure, the reasons for it and its effect must be given in a note to the accounts.

Accounting principles

11. The LLP is presumed to be carrying on business as a going concern.

12. Accounting policies must be applied consistently within the same accounts and from one financial year to the next.

13. The amount of any item must be determined on a prudent basis, and in particular—
   (a)   only profits realised at the balance sheet date must be included in the profit and loss account, and
   (b)   all liabilities which have arisen in respect of the financial year to which the accounts relate or a previous financial year must be taken into account, including those which only become apparent between the balance sheet date and the date on which it is signed on behalf of the members in accordance with section 414 of the 2006 Act (approval and signing of accounts).

14. All income and charges relating to the financial year to which the accounts relate must be taken into account, without regard to the date of receipt or payment.

15. In determining the aggregate amount of any item, the amount of each individual asset or liability that falls to be taken into account must be determined separately.

SECTION B
HISTORICAL COST ACCOUNTING RULES

Preliminary

16. Subject to Sections C and D of this Part of this Schedule, the amounts to be included in respect of all items shown in an LLP's accounts must be determined in accordance with the rules set out in this Section.

Fixed assets

General rules

17. (1)   The amount to be included in respect of any fixed asset must be its purchase price or production cost.

(2)   This is subject to any provision for depreciation or diminution in value made in accordance with paragraphs 18 to 20.

Rules for depreciation and diminution in value

18. In the case of any fixed asset which has a limited useful economic life, the amount of—
   (a)   its purchase price or production cost, or
   (b)   where it is estimated that any such asset will have a residual value at the end of the period of its useful economic life, its purchase price or production cost less that estimated residual value,

must be reduced by provisions for depreciation calculated to write off that amount systematically over the period of the asset's useful economic life.

19. (1)   Where a fixed asset investment of a description falling to be included under item A.III of either of the balance sheet formats set out in Part 1 of this Schedule has diminished in value, provisions for diminution in value may be made in respect of it and the amount to be included in respect of it may be reduced accordingly.

(2)   Provisions for diminution in value must be made in respect of any fixed asset which has diminished in value if the reduction in its value is expected to be permanent (whether its useful economic life is limited or not), and the amount to be included in respect of it must be reduced accordingly.

(3)   Any provisions made under sub-paragraph (1) or (2) which are not shown in the profit and loss account must be disclosed (either separately or in aggregate) in a note to the accounts.

20. (1)   Where the reasons for which any provision was made in accordance with paragraph 19 have ceased to apply to any extent, that provision must be written back to the extent that it is no longer necessary.

(2)   Any amounts written back in accordance with sub-paragraph (1) which are not shown in the profit and loss account must be disclosed (either separately or in aggregate) in a note to the accounts.

Development costs

21. (1)   Notwithstanding that an item in respect of "development costs" is included under "fixed assets" in the balance sheet formats set out in Part 1 of this Schedule, an amount may only be included in an LLP's balance sheet in respect of development costs in special circumstances.

(2)   If any amount is included in an LLP's balance sheet in respect of development costs the following information must be given in a note to the accounts—
  (a)   the period over which the amount of those costs originally capitalised is being or is to be written off, and
  (b)   the reasons for capitalising the development costs in question.

Goodwill

22. (1)   The application of paragraphs 17 to 20 in relation to goodwill (in any case where goodwill is treated as an asset) is subject to the following.

(2)   Subject to sub-paragraph (3), the amount of the consideration for any goodwill acquired by an LLP must be reduced by provisions for depreciation calculated to write off that amount systematically over a period chosen by the members of the LLP.

(3)   The period chosen must not exceed the useful economic life of the goodwill in question.

(4)   In any case where any goodwill acquired by an LLP is shown or included as an asset in the LLP's balance sheet there must be disclosed in a note to the accounts—
  (a)   the period chosen for writing off the consideration for that goodwill, and
  (b)   the reasons for choosing that period.

Current assets

23.   Subject to paragraph 24, the amount to be included in respect of any current asset must be its purchase price or production cost.

24. (1)   If the net realisable value of any current asset is lower than its purchase price or production cost, the amount to be included in respect of that asset must be the net realisable value.

(2)   Where the reasons for which any provision for diminution in value was made in accordance with sub-paragraph (1) have ceased to apply to any extent, that provision must be written back to the extent that it is no longer necessary.

Miscellaneous and supplementary provisions

Excess of money owed over value received as an asset item

25. (1)   Where the amount repayable on any debt owed by an LLP is greater than the value of the consideration received in the transaction giving rise to the debt, the amount of the difference may be treated as an asset.

(2)   Where any such amount is so treated—
  (a)   it must be written off by reasonable amounts each year and must be completely written off before repayment of the debt, and
  (b)   if the current amount is not shown as a separate item in the LLP's balance sheet, it must be disclosed in a note to the accounts.

Assets included at a fixed amount

26. (1)   Subject to sub-paragraph (2), assets which fall to be included—
  (a)   amongst the fixed assets of an LLP under the item "tangible assets", or

(b)   amongst the current assets of an LLP under the item "raw materials and consumables", may be included at a fixed quantity and value.

(2)   Sub-paragraph (1) applies to assets of a kind which are constantly being replaced where—

     (a)   their overall value is not material to assessing the LLP's state of affairs, and

     (b)   their quantity, value and composition are not subject to material variation.

Determination of purchase price or production cost

27.   (1)   The purchase price of an asset is to be determined by adding to the actual price paid any expenses incidental to its acquisition.

(2)   The production cost of an asset is to be determined by adding to the purchase price of the raw materials and consumables used the amount of the costs incurred by the LLP which are directly attributable to the production of that asset.

(3)   In addition, there may be included in the production cost of an asset—

     (a)   a reasonable proportion of the costs incurred by the LLP which are only indirectly attributable to the production of that asset, but only to the extent that they relate to the period of production, and

     (b)   interest on capital borrowed to finance the production of that asset, to the extent that it accrues in respect of the period of production,

provided, however, in a case within paragraph (b), that the inclusion of the interest in determining the cost of that asset and the amount of the interest so included is disclosed in a note to the accounts.

(4)   In the case of current assets distribution costs may not be included in production costs.

28.   (1)   The purchase price or production cost of—

     (a)   any assets which fall to be included under any item shown in an LLP's balance sheet under the general item "stocks", and

     (b)   any assets which are fungible assets (including investments),

may be determined by the application of any of the methods mentioned in sub-paragraph (2) in relation to any such assets of the same class, provided that the method chosen is one which appears to the members to be appropriate in the circumstances of the LLP.

(2)   Those methods are—

     (a)   the method known as "first in, first out" (FIFO),

     (b)   the method known as "last in, first out" (LIFO),

     (c)   a weighted average price, and

     (d)   any other method similar to any of the methods mentioned above.

(3)   For the purposes of this paragraph, assets of any description must be regarded as fungible if assets of that description are substantially indistinguishable one from another.

Substitution of original stated amount where price or cost unknown

29.   (1)   This paragraph applies where—

     (a)   there is no record of the purchase price or production cost of any asset of an LLP or of any price, expenses or costs relevant for determining its purchase price or production cost in accordance with paragraph 27, or

     (b)   any such record cannot be obtained without unreasonable expense or delay.

(2)   In such a case, the purchase price or production cost of the asset must be taken, for the purposes of paragraphs 17 to 24, to be the value ascribed to it in the earliest available record of its value made on or after its acquisition or production by the LLP.

SECTION C
ALTERNATIVE ACCOUNTING RULES

Preliminary

30.   (1)   The rules set out in Section B are referred to below in this Schedule as the historical cost accounting rules.

(2)   Those rules, with the omission of paragraphs 16, 22 and 26 to 29, are referred to below in this Part of this Schedule as the depreciation rules; and references below in this Schedule to the historical cost accounting rules do not include the depreciation rules as they apply by virtue of paragraph 33.

31.   Subject to paragraphs 33 to 35, the amounts to be included in respect of assets of any description mentioned in paragraph 32 may be determined on any basis so mentioned.

Alternative accounting rules

32.   (1)   Intangible fixed assets, other than goodwill, may be included at their current cost.

(2)   Tangible fixed assets may be included at a market value determined as at the date of their last valuation or at their current cost.

(3) Investments of any description falling to be included under item A.III of either of the balance sheet formats set out Part 1 of this Schedule may be included either—

    (a)   at a market value determined as at the date of their last valuation, or

    (b)   at a value determined on any basis which appears to the members to be appropriate in the circumstances of the LLP.

But in the latter case particulars of the method of valuation adopted and of the reasons for adopting it must be disclosed in a note to the accounts.

(4) Investments of any description falling to be included under item B.III of either of the balance sheet formats set out in Part 1 of this Schedule may be included at their current cost.

(5) Stocks may be included at their current cost.

Application of the depreciation rules

33. (1) Where the value of any asset of an LLP is determined on any basis mentioned in paragraph 32, that value must be, or (as the case may require) be the starting point for determining, the amount to be included in respect of that asset in the LLP's accounts, instead of its purchase price or production cost or any value previously so determined for that asset.

The depreciation rules apply accordingly in relation to any such asset with the substitution for any reference to its purchase price or production cost of a reference to the value most recently determined for that asset on any basis mentioned in paragraph 32.

(2) The amount of any provision for depreciation required in the case of any fixed asset by paragraphs 18 to 20 as they apply by virtue of sub-paragraph (1) is referred to below in this paragraph as the adjusted amount, and the amount of any provision which would be required by any of those paragraphs in the case of that asset according to the historical cost accounting rules is referred to as the historical cost amount.

(3) Where sub-paragraph (1) applies in the case of any fixed asset the amount of any provision for depreciation in respect of that asset—

    (a)   included in any item shown in the profit and loss account in respect of amounts written off assets of the description in question, or

    (b)   taken into account in stating any item so shown which is required by note (9) of the notes on the profit and loss account formats set out in Part 1 of this Schedule to be stated after taking into account any necessary provision for depreciation or diminution in value of assets included under it,

may be the historical cost amount instead of the adjusted amount, provided that the amount of any difference between the two is shown separately in the profit and loss account or in a note to the accounts.

Additional information to be provided in case of departure from historical cost accounting rules

34. (1) This paragraph applies where the amounts to be included in respect of assets covered by any items shown in an LLP's accounts have been determined on any basis mentioned in paragraph 32.

(2) The items affected and the basis of valuation adopted in determining the amounts of the assets in question in the case of each such item must be disclosed in a note to the accounts.

(3) In the case of each balance sheet item affected (except stocks) either—

    (a)   the comparable amounts determined according to the historical cost accounting rules, or

    (b)   the differences between those amounts and the corresponding amounts actually shown in the balance sheet in respect of that item,

must be shown separately in the balance sheet or in a note to the accounts.

(4) In sub-paragraph (3), references in relation to any item to the comparable amounts determined as there mentioned are references to—

    (a)   the aggregate amount which would be required to be shown in respect of that item if the amounts to be included in respect of all the assets covered by that item were determined according to the historical cost accounting rules, and

    (b)   the aggregate amount of the cumulative provisions for depreciation or diminution in value which would be permitted or required in determining those amounts according to those rules.

Revaluation reserve

35. (1) With respect to any determination of the value of an asset of an LLP on any basis mentioned in paragraph 32, the amount of any profit or loss arising from that determination (after allowing, where appropriate, for any provisions for depreciation or diminution in value made otherwise than by reference to the value so determined and any adjustments of any such provisions made in the light of that determination) must be credited or (as the case may be) debited to a separate reserve ("the revaluation reserve").

(2)   The amount of the revaluation reserve must be shown in the LLP's balance sheet under a separate sub-heading in the position given for the item "revaluation reserve" in Format 1 or 2 of the balance sheet formats set out in Part 1 of this Schedule, but need not be shown under that name.

(3)   The treatment for taxation purposes of amounts credited or debited to the revaluation reserve must be disclosed in a note to the accounts.

SECTION D
FAIR VALUE ACCOUNTING

Inclusion of financial instruments at fair value

36. (1)   Subject to sub-paragraphs (2) to (5), financial instruments (including derivatives) may be included at fair value.

(2)   Sub-paragraph (1) does not apply to financial instruments that constitute liabilities unless—
  (a)   they are held as part of a trading portfolio,
  (b)   they are derivatives, or
  (c)   they are financial instruments falling within sub-paragraph (4).

(3)   Unless they are financial instruments falling within sub-paragraph (4), sub-paragraph (1) does not apply to—
  (a)   financial instruments (other than derivatives) held to maturity,
  (b)   loans and receivables originated by the LLP and not held for trading purposes,
  (c)   interests in subsidiary undertakings, associated undertakings and joint ventures,
  (d)   equity instruments issued by the LLP,
  (e)   contracts for contingent consideration in a business combination, or
  (f)   other financial instruments with such special characteristics that the instruments, according to generally accepted accounting principles or practice, should be accounted for differently from other financial instruments.

(4)   Financial instruments that, under international accounting standards adopted by the European Commission on or before 5th September 2006 in accordance with the IAS Regulation, may be included in accounts at fair value, may be so included, provided that the disclosures required by such accounting standards are made.

(5)   If the fair value of a financial instrument cannot be determined reliably in accordance with paragraph 37, sub-paragraph (1) does not apply to that financial instrument.

(6)   In this paragraph—
   "associated undertaking" has the meaning given by paragraph 19 of Schedule 4 to these Regulations;
   "joint venture" has the meaning given by paragraph 18 of that Schedule.

Determination of fair value

37. (1)   The fair value of a financial instrument is its value determined in accordance with this paragraph.

(2)   If a reliable market can readily be identified for the financial instrument, its fair value is to be determined by reference to its market value.

(3)   If a reliable market cannot readily be identified for the financial instrument but can be identified for its components or for a similar instrument, its fair value is determined by reference to the market value of its components or of the similar instrument.

(4)   If neither sub-paragraph (2) nor (3) applies, the fair value of the financial instrument is a value resulting from generally accepted valuation models and techniques.

(5)   Any valuation models and techniques used for the purposes of sub-paragraph (4) must ensure a reasonable approximation of the market value.

Hedged items

38. An LLP may include any assets and liabilities, or identified portions of such assets or liabilities, that qualify as hedged items under a fair value hedge accounting system at the amount required under that system.

Other assets that may be included at fair value

39. (1)   This paragraph applies to—
  (a)   investment property, and
  (b)   living animals and plants,
that, under international accounting standards, may be included in accounts at fair value.

(2)   Such investment property and such living animals and plants may be included at fair value, provided that all such investment property or, as the case may be, all such living animals and plants are so included where their fair value can reliably be determined.

(3)   In this paragraph, "fair value" means fair value determined in accordance with relevant international accounting standards.

Accounting for changes in value

40. (1) This paragraph applies where a financial instrument is valued in accordance with paragraph 36 or 38 or an asset is valued in accordance with paragraph 39.

(2) Notwithstanding paragraph 13 in this Part of this Schedule, and subject to sub-paragraphs (3) and (4), a change in the value of the financial instrument or of the investment property or living animal or plant must be included in the profit and loss account.

(3) Where—

   (a)   the financial instrument accounted for is a hedging instrument under a hedge accounting system that allows some or all of the change in value not to be shown in the profit and loss account, or

   (b)   the change in value relates to an exchange difference arising on a monetary item that forms part of an LLP's net investment in a foreign entity,

the amount of the change in value must be credited to or (as the case may be) debited from a separate reserve ("the fair value reserve").

(4) Where the instrument accounted for—

   (a)   is an available for sale financial asset, and

   (b)   is not a derivative,

the change in value may be credited to or (as the case may be) debited from the fair value reserve.

The fair value reserve

41. (1) The fair value reserve must be adjusted to the extent that the amounts shown in it are no longer necessary for the purposes of paragraph 40(3) or (4).

(2) The treatment for taxation purposes of amounts credited or debited to the fair value reserve must be disclosed in a note to the accounts.

NOTES

Commencement: 1 October 2008.

PART 3
NOTES TO THE ACCOUNTS

Preliminary

[10.1071]

42. Any information required in the case of any LLP by the following provisions of this Part of this Schedule must (if not given in the LLP's accounts) be given by way of a note to those accounts.

Reserves

43. Any amount set aside or proposed to be set aside to, or withdrawn or proposed to be withdrawn from, reserves must be stated.

Disclosure of accounting policies

44. The accounting policies adopted by the LLP in determining the amounts to be included in respect of items shown in the balance sheet and in determining the profit or loss of the LLP must be stated (including such policies with respect to the depreciation and diminution in value of assets).

Information supplementing the balance sheet

45. Paragraphs 46 to 56 require information which either supplements the information given with respect to any particular items shown in the balance sheet or is otherwise relevant to assessing the LLP's state of affairs in the light of the information so given.

Loans and other debts due to members

46. The following information must be given—

   (a)   the aggregate amount of loans and other debts due to members as at the date of the beginning of the financial year,

   (b)   the aggregate amounts contributed by members during the financial year,

   (c)   the aggregate amounts transferred to or from the profit and loss account during that year,

   (d)   the aggregate amounts withdrawn by members or applied on behalf of members during that year,

   (e)   the aggregate amount of loans and other debts due to members as at the balance sheet date, and

   (f)   the aggregate amount of loans and other debts due to members that fall due after one year.

Fixed assets

47. (1) In respect of each item which is or would but for paragraph 4(2)(b) be shown under the general item "fixed assets" in the LLP's balance sheet the following information must be given—

   (a)   the appropriate amounts in respect of that item as at the date of the beginning of the financial year and as at the balance sheet date respectively,

   (b)   the effect on any amount shown in the balance sheet in respect of that item of—

    (i)   any revision of the amount in respect of any assets included under that item made during that year on any basis mentioned in paragraph 32,

    (ii)   acquisitions during that year of any assets,

    (iii) disposals during that year of any assets, and

    (iv) any transfers of assets of the LLP to and from that item during that year.

(2)   The reference in sub-paragraph (1)(a) to the appropriate amounts in respect of any item as at any date there mentioned is a reference to amounts representing the aggregate amounts determined, as at that date, in respect of assets falling to be included under that item on either of the following bases, that is to say—

    (a)   on the basis of purchase price or production cost (determined in accordance with paragraphs 27 and 28), or

    (b)   on any basis mentioned in paragraph 32,

(leaving out of account in either case any provisions for depreciation or diminution in value).

(3)   In respect of each item within sub-paragraph (1) there must also be stated—

    (a)   the cumulative amount of provisions for depreciation or diminution in value of assets included under that item as at each date mentioned in sub-paragraph (1)(a),

    (b)   the amount of any such provisions made in respect of the financial year,

    (c)   the amount of any adjustments made in respect of any such provisions during that year in consequence of the disposal of any assets, and

    (d)   the amount of any other adjustments made in respect of any such provisions during that year.

48. Where any fixed assets of the LLP (other than listed investments) are included under any item shown in the LLP's balance sheet at an amount determined on any basis mentioned in paragraph 32, the following information must be given—

    (a)   the years (so far as they are known to the members) in which the assets were severally valued and the several values, and

    (b)   in the case of assets that have been valued during the financial year, the names of the persons who valued them or particulars of their qualifications for doing so and (whichever is stated) the bases of valuation used by them.

Investments

49. (1) In respect of the amount of each item which is or would but for paragraph 4(2)(b) be shown in the LLP's balance sheet under the general item "investments" (whether as fixed assets or as current assets) there must be stated how much of that amount is ascribable to listed investments.

(2)   Where the amount of any listed investments is stated for any item in accordance with sub-paragraph (1), the following amounts must also be stated—

    (a)   the aggregate market value of those investments where it differs from the amount so stated, and

    (b)   both the market value and the stock exchange value of any investments of which the former value is, for the purposes of the accounts, taken as being higher than the latter.

Information about fair value of assets and liabilities

50. (1) This paragraph applies where financial instruments have been valued in accordance with paragraph 36 or 38.

(2)   There must be stated—

    (a)   the significant assumptions underlying the valuation models and techniques used where the fair value of the instruments has been determined in accordance with paragraph 37(4),

    (b)   for each category of financial instrument, the fair value of the instruments in that category and the changes in value—

        (i)   included in the profit and loss account, or

        (ii)   credited to or (as the case may be) debited from the fair value reserve,

    in respect of those instruments, and

    (c)   for each class of derivatives, the extent and nature of the instruments, including significant terms and conditions that may affect the amount, timing and certainty of future cash flows.

(3)   Where any amount is transferred to or from the fair value reserve during the financial year, there must be stated in tabular form—

    (a)   the amount of the reserve as at the date of the beginning of the financial year and as at the balance sheet date respectively,

    (b)   the amount transferred to or from the reserve during that year, and

    (c)   the source and application respectively of the amounts so transferred.

51. (1) This paragraph applies if—

    (a)   the LLP has financial fixed assets that could be included at fair value by virtue of paragraph 36,

    (b)   the amount at which those items are included under any item in the LLP's accounts is in excess of their fair value, and

    (c)   the LLP has not made provision for diminution in value of those assets in accordance with paragraph 19(1) of this Schedule.

(2)   There must be stated—
-   (a)   the amount at which either the individual assets or appropriate groupings of those individual assets are included in the LLP's accounts,
-   (b)   the fair value of those assets or groupings, and
-   (c)   the reasons for not making a provision for diminution in value of those assets, including the nature of the evidence that provides the basis for the belief that the amount at which they are stated in the accounts will be recovered.

Information where investment property and living animals and plants included at fair value
52. (1)   This paragraph applies where the amounts to be included in an LLP's accounts in respect of investment property or living animals and plants have been determined in accordance with paragraph 39.

(2)   The balance sheet items affected and the basis of valuation adopted in determining the amounts of the assets in question in the case of each such item must be disclosed in a note to the accounts.

(3)   In the case of investment property, for each balance sheet item affected there must be shown, either separately in the balance sheet or in a note to the accounts—
-   (a)   the comparable amounts determined according to the historical cost accounting rules, or
-   (b)   the differences between those amounts and the corresponding amounts actually shown in the balance sheet in respect of that item.

(4)   In sub-paragraph (3), references in relation to any item to the comparable amounts determined in accordance with that sub-paragraph are to—
-   (a)   the aggregate amount which would be required to be shown in respect of that item if the amounts to be included in respect of all the assets covered by that item were determined according to the historical cost accounting rules, and
-   (b)   the aggregate amount of the cumulative provisions for depreciation or diminution in value which would be permitted or required in determining those amounts according to those rules.

Reserves and provisions
53. (1)   This paragraph applies where any amount is transferred—
-   (a)   to or from any reserves, or
-   (b)   to any provision for liabilities, or
-   (c)   from any provision for liabilities otherwise than for the purpose for which the provision was established,

and the reserves or provisions are or would but for paragraph 4(2)(b) be shown as separate items in the LLP's balance sheet.

(2)   The following information must be given in respect of the aggregate of reserves or provisions included in the same item—
-   (a)   the amount of the reserves or provisions as at the date of the beginning of the financial year and as at the balance sheet date respectively,
-   (b)   any amounts transferred to or from the reserves or provisions during that year, and
-   (c)   the source and application respectively of any amounts so transferred.

(3)   Particulars must be given of each provision included in the item "other provisions" in the LLP's balance sheet in any case where the amount of that provision is material.

Details of indebtedness
54. (1)   For the aggregate of all items shown under "creditors" in the LLP's balance sheet there must be stated the aggregate of the following amounts—
-   (a)   the amount of any debts included under "creditors" which are payable or repayable otherwise than by instalments and fall due for payment or repayment after the end of the period of five years beginning with the day next following the end of the financial year, and
-   (b)   in the case of any debts so included which are payable or repayable by instalments, the amount of any instalments which fall due for payment after the end of that period.

(2)   In respect of each item shown under "creditors" in the LLP's balance sheet there must be stated the aggregate amount of any debts included under that item in respect of which any security has been given by the LLP.

(3)   References above in this paragraph to an item shown under "creditors" in the LLP's balance sheet include references, where amounts falling due to creditors within one year and after more than one year are distinguished in the balance sheet—
-   (a)   in a case within sub-paragraph (1), to an item shown under the latter of those categories,
-   (b)   in a case within sub-paragraph (2), to an item shown under either of those categories.

References to items shown under "creditors" include references to items which would but for paragraph 4(2)(b) be shown under that heading.

Guarantees and other financial commitments
55. (1)   Particulars must be given of any charge on the assets of the LLP to secure the liabilities of any other person, including, where practicable, the amount secured.

(2)   The following information must be given with respect to any other contingent liability not provided for—

    (a)   the amount or estimated amount of that liability,

    (b)   its legal nature, and

    (c)   whether any valuable security has been provided by the LLP in connection with that liability and if so, what.

(3)   There must be stated, where practicable, the aggregate amount or estimated amount of contracts for capital expenditure, so far as not provided for.

(4)   Particulars must be given of—

    (a)   any pension commitments included under any provision shown in the LLP's balance sheet, and

    (b)   any such commitments for which no provision has been made,

and where any such commitment relates wholly or partly to pensions payable to past members of the LLP separate particulars must be given of that commitment so far as it relates to such pensions.

(5)   Particulars must also be given of any other financial commitments that—

    (a)   have not been provided for, and

    (b)   are relevant to assessing the LLP's state of affairs.

(6)   Commitments within any of sub-paragraphs (1) to (5) which are undertaken on behalf of or for the benefit of—

    (a)   any parent undertaking or fellow subsidiary undertaking, or

    (b)   any subsidiary undertaking of the LLP,

must be stated separately from the other commitments within that sub-paragraph, and commitments within paragraph (a) must also be stated separately from those within paragraph (b).

Miscellaneous matters
56.   Particulars must be given of any case where the purchase price or production cost of any asset is for the first time determined under paragraph 29.

Information supplementing the profit and loss account
57.   Paragraphs 58 and 59 require information which either supplements the information given with respect to any particular items shown in the profit and loss account or otherwise provides particulars of income or expenditure of the LLP or of circumstances affecting the items shown in the profit and loss account (see regulation 3 for exemption for LLP falling within section 408 of the 2006 Act).

Particulars of turnover
58.   (1)   If the LLP has supplied geographical markets outside the United Kingdom during the financial year in question, there must be stated the percentage of its turnover that, in the opinion of the members, is attributable to those markets.

(2)   In analysing for the purposes of this paragraph the source of turnover, the members of the LLP must have regard to the manner in which the LLP's activities are organised.

Miscellaneous matters
59.   (1)   Where any amount relating to any preceding financial year is included in any item in the profit and loss account, the effect must be stated.

(2)   Particulars must be given of any extraordinary income or charges arising in the financial year.

(3)   The effect must be stated of any transactions that are exceptional by virtue of size or incidence though they fall within the ordinary activities of the LLP.

Sums denominated in foreign currencies
60.   Where sums originally denominated in foreign currencies have been brought into account under any items shown in the balance sheet or profit and loss account, the basis on which those sums have been translated into sterling (or the currency in which the accounts are drawn up) must be stated.

Dormant LLPs acting as agents
61.   Where the members of an LLP take advantage of the exemption conferred by section 480 of the 2006 Act (dormant LLPs: exemption from audit), and the LLP has during the financial year in question acted as an agent for any person, the fact that it has so acted must be stated.

NOTES
  Commencement: 1 October 2008.

SCHEDULE 2
INFORMATION ABOUT RELATED UNDERTAKINGS WHERE LLP NOT PREPARING GROUP ACCOUNTS (NON-IAS OR IAS INDIVIDUAL ACCOUNTS)
Regulation 4

Subsidiary undertakings

[10.1072]
1. (1)   The following information must be given where at the end of the financial year the LLP has subsidiary undertakings.

(2)   The name of each subsidiary undertaking must be stated.

(3)   There must be stated with respect to each subsidiary undertaking—
   (a)   if it is incorporated outside the United Kingdom, the country in which it is incorporated,
   (b)   if it is unincorporated, the address of its principal place of business.

Holdings in subsidiary undertakings
2. (1)   There must be stated in relation to shares of each class held by the LLP in a subsidiary undertaking—
   (a)   the identity of the class, and
   (b)   the proportion of the nominal value of the shares of that class represented by those shares.

(2)   The shares held by or on behalf of the LLP itself must be distinguished from those attributed to the LLP which are held by or on behalf of a subsidiary undertaking.

Financial information about subsidiary undertakings
3. (1)   There must be disclosed with respect to each subsidiary undertaking—
   (a)   the aggregate amount of its capital and reserves as at the end of its relevant financial year, and
   (b)   its profit or loss for that year.

(2)   That information need not be given if the LLP would (if it were not subject to the small LLP regime) be exempt by virtue of section 400 or 401 of the 2006 Act (parent LLP included in accounts of larger group) from the requirement to prepare group accounts.

(3)   That information need not be given if the LLP's investment in the subsidiary undertaking is included in the LLP's accounts by way of the equity method of valuation.

(4)   That information need not be given if—
   (a)   the subsidiary undertaking is not required by any provision of the 2006 Act to deliver a copy of its balance sheet for its relevant financial year and does not otherwise publish that balance sheet in the United Kingdom or elsewhere, and
   (b)   the LLP's holding is less than 50% of the nominal value of the shares in the undertaking.

(5)   Information otherwise required by this paragraph need not be given if it is not material.

(6)   For the purposes of this paragraph the "relevant financial year" of a subsidiary undertaking is—
   (a)   if its financial year ends with that of the LLP, that year, and
   (b)   if not, its financial year ending last before the end of the LLP's financial year.

Significant holdings in undertakings other than subsidiary undertakings
4. (1)   The information required by paragraphs 5 and 6 must be given where at the end of the financial year the LLP has a significant holding in an undertaking which is not a subsidiary undertaking of the LLP.

(2)   A holding is significant for this purpose if—
   (a)   it amounts to 20% or more of the nominal value of any class of shares in the undertaking, or
   (b)   the amount of the holding (as stated or included in the LLP's accounts) exceeds 20% of the amount (as so stated) of the LLP's assets.

5. (1)   The name of the undertaking must be stated.

(2)   There must be stated—
   (a)   if the undertaking is incorporated outside the United Kingdom, the country in which it is incorporated,
   (b)   if it is unincorporated, the address of its principal place of business.

(3)   There must also be stated—
   (a)   the identity of each class of shares in the undertaking held by the LLP, and
   (b)   the proportion of the nominal value of the shares of that class represented by those shares.

6. (1)   There must also be stated—
   (a)   the aggregate amount of the capital and reserves of the undertaking as at the end of its relevant financial year, and
   (b)   its profit or loss for that year.

(2)   That information need not be given if—

(a)   the LLP would (if it were not subject to the small LLP regime) be exempt by virtue of section 400 or 401 of the 2006 Act (parent LLP included in accounts of larger group) from the requirement to prepare group accounts, and

(b)   the investment of the LLP in all undertakings in which it has such a holding as is mentioned in sub-paragraph (1) is shown, in aggregate, in the notes to the accounts by way of the equity method of valuation.

(3)   That information need not be given in respect of an undertaking if—

(a)   the undertaking is not required by any provision of the 2006 Act to deliver to the registrar a copy of its balance sheet for its relevant financial year and does not otherwise publish that balance sheet in the United Kingdom or elsewhere, and

(b)   the LLP's holding is less than 50% of the nominal value of the shares in the undertaking.

(4)   Information otherwise required by this paragraph need not be given if it is not material.

(5)   For the purposes of this paragraph the "relevant financial year" of an undertaking is—

(a)   if its financial year ends with that of the LLP, that year, and

(b)   if not, its financial year ending last before the end of the LLP's financial year.

Parent undertaking drawing up accounts for larger group

7. (1)   Where the LLP is a subsidiary undertaking, the following information must be given with respect to the parent undertaking of—

(a)   the largest group of undertakings for which group accounts are drawn up and of which the LLP is a member, and

(b)   the smallest such group of undertakings.

(2)   The name of the parent undertaking must be stated.

(3)   There must be stated—

(a)   if the undertaking is incorporated outside the United Kingdom, the country in which it is incorporated,

(b)   if it is unincorporated, the address of its principal place of business.

(4)   If copies of the group accounts referred to in sub-paragraph (1) are available to the public, there must also be stated the addresses from which copies of the accounts can be obtained.

Identification of ultimate parent

8. (1)   Where the LLP is a subsidiary undertaking, the following information must be given with respect to the body corporate (if any) regarded by the members as being the LLP's ultimate parent.

(2)   The name of that body corporate must be stated.

(3)   If that body corporate is incorporated outside the United Kingdom, the country in which it is incorporated must be stated (if known to the members).

Construction of references to shares held by LLP

9. (1)   References in this Part of this Schedule to shares held by an LLP are to be construed as follows.

(2)   For the purposes of paragraphs 2 and 3 (information about subsidiary undertakings)—

(a)   there must be attributed to the LLP any shares held by a subsidiary undertaking, or by a person acting on behalf of the LLP or a subsidiary undertaking; but

(b)   there must be treated as not held by the LLP any shares held on behalf of a person other than the LLP or a subsidiary undertaking.

(3)   For the purposes of paragraphs 4 to 6 (information about undertakings other than subsidiary undertakings)—

(a)   there must be attributed to the LLP shares held on its behalf by any person; but

(b)   there must be treated as not held by an LLP shares held on behalf of a person other than the LLP.

(4)   For the purposes of any of those provisions, shares held by way of security must be treated as held by the person providing the security—

(a)   where apart from the right to exercise them for the purpose of preserving the value of the security, or of realising it, the rights attached to the shares are exercisable only in accordance with his instructions, and

(b)   where the shares are held in connection with the granting of loans as part of normal business activities and apart from the right to exercise them for the purpose of preserving the value of the security, or of realising it, the rights attached to the shares are exercisable only in his interests.

NOTES

Commencement: 1 October 2008.

SCHEDULE 3
NON-IAS ABBREVIATED ACCOUNTS FOR DELIVERY TO REGISTRAR
OF COMPANIES

Regulation 5

PART 1
THE REQUIRED BALANCE SHEET FORMATS

[10.1073]

1. (1) An LLP may deliver to the registrar a copy of the balance sheet showing the items listed in either of the balance sheet formats set out below, in the order and under the headings and sub-headings given in the format adopted, but in other respects corresponding to the full balance sheet.

(2)   The copy balance sheet must contain in a prominent position a statement that it has been prepared in accordance with the provisions applicable to LLP subject to the small LLP regime.

Balance sheet formats

Format 1

A.   Fixed assets
   I.   Intangible assets
   II.   Tangible assets
   III.   Investments

B.   Current assets
   I.   Stocks
   II.   Debtors [(1)]
   III.   Investments
   IV.   Cash at bank and in hand

C.   Prepayments and accrued income

D.   Creditors: amounts falling due within one year

E.   Net current assets (liabilities)

F.   Total assets less current liabilities

G.   Creditors: amounts falling due after more than one year

H.   Provisions for liabilities

I.   Accruals and deferred income

J.   Loans and other debts due to members

K.   Members' other interests
   I.   Members' capital
   II.   Revaluation reserve
   III.   Other reserves

Balance sheet formats

Format 2

ASSETS

A.   Fixed assets
   I.   Intangible assets
   II.   Tangible assets
   III.   Investments

B.   Current assets
   I.   Stocks
   II.   Debtors [(1)]
   III.   Investments
   IV.   Cash at bank and in hand

C.   Prepayments and accrued income

LIABILITIES

A.   Loans and other debts due to members

B. Members' other interests
    I.   Members' capital
    II.   Revaluation reserve
    III. Other reserves

C. Provisions for liabilities

D. Creditors ⁽²⁾

E. Accruals and deferred income

Notes on the balance sheet formats

(1) Debtors

(Formats 1 and 2, items B.II.)

    The aggregate amount of debtors falling due after more than one year must be shown separately, unless it is disclosed in the notes to the accounts.

(2) Creditors

(Format 2, Liabilities item D.)

    The aggregate amount of creditors falling due within one year and of creditors falling due after more than one year must be shown separately, unless it is disclosed in the notes to the accounts.

NOTES
Commencement: 1 October 2008.

PART 2
NOTES TO THE ACCOUNTS

Preliminary

[10.1074]
2. Any information required in the case of any LLP by the following provisions of this Part of this Schedule must (if not given in the LLP's accounts) be given by way of a note to those accounts.

Disclosure of accounting policies
3. The accounting policies adopted by the LLP in determining the amounts to be included in respect of items shown in the balance sheet and in determining the profit or loss of the LLP must be stated (including such policies with respect to the depreciation and diminution in value of assets).

Information supplementing the balance sheet

Fixed assets
4. (1) In respect of each item to which a letter or Roman number is assigned under the general item "fixed assets" in the LLP's balance sheet the following information must be given—
    (a)   the appropriate amounts in respect of that item as at the date of the beginning of the financial year and as at the balance sheet date respectively,
    (b)   the effect on any amount shown in the balance sheet in respect of that item of—
        (i)   any revision of the amount in respect of any assets included under that item made during that year on any basis mentioned in paragraph 32 of Schedule 1 to these Regulations,
        (ii)   acquisitions during that year of any assets,
        (iii) disposals during that year of any assets, and
        (iv) any transfers of assets of the LLP to and from that item during that year.
(2) The reference in sub-paragraph (1)(a) to the appropriate amounts in respect of any item as at any date there mentioned is a reference to amounts representing the aggregate amounts determined, as at that date, in respect of assets falling to be included under that item on either of the following bases, that is to say—
    (a)   on the basis of purchase price or production cost (determined in accordance with paragraphs 27 and 28 of Schedule 1 to these Regulations), or
    (b)   on any basis mentioned in paragraph 32 of that Schedule,
(leaving out of account in either case any provisions for depreciation or diminution in value).
(3) In respect of each item within sub-paragraph (1) there must also be stated—
    (a)   the cumulative amount of provisions for depreciation or diminution in value of assets included under that item as at each date mentioned in sub-paragraph (1)(a),
    (b)   the amount of any such provisions made in respect of the financial year,
    (c)   the amount of any adjustments made in respect of any such provisions during that year in consequence of the disposal of any assets, and

(d)   the amount of any other adjustments made in respect of any such provisions during that year.

Financial fixed assets

5. (1)   This paragraph applies if—
(a)   the LLP has financial fixed assets that could be included at fair value by virtue of paragraph 36 of Schedule 1 to these Regulations,
(b)   the amount at which those items are included under any item in the LLP's accounts is in excess of their fair value, and
(c)   the LLP has not made provision for diminution in value of those assets in accordance with paragraph 19(1) of that Schedule.

(2)   There must be stated—
(a)   the amount at which either the individual assets or appropriate groupings of those individual assets are included in the LLP's accounts,
(b)   the fair value of those assets or groupings, and
(c)   the reasons for not making a provision for diminution in value of those assets, including the nature of the evidence that provides the basis for the belief that the amount at which they are stated in the accounts will be recovered.

Details of indebtedness

6. (1)   For the aggregate of all items shown under "creditors" in the LLP's balance sheet there must be stated the aggregate of the following amounts—
(a)   the amount of any debts included under "creditors" which are payable or repayable otherwise than by instalments and fall due for payment or repayment after the end of the period of five years beginning with the day next following the end of the financial year, and
(b)   in the case of any debts so included which are payable or repayable by instalments, the amount of any instalments which fall due for payment after the end of that period.

(2)   In respect of each item shown under "creditors" in the LLP's balance sheet there must be stated the aggregate amount of any debts included under that item in respect of which any security has been given by the LLP.

Sums denominated in foreign currencies

7.   Where sums originally denominated in foreign currencies have been brought into account under any items shown in the balance sheet or profit and loss account, the basis on which those sums have been translated into sterling (or the currency in which the accounts are drawn up) must be stated.

Dormant LLPs acting as agents

8.   Where the members of an LLP take advantage of the exemption conferred by section 480 of the 2006 Act (dormant LLPs: exemption from audit), and the LLP has during the financial year in question acted as an agent for any person, the fact that it has so acted must be stated.

NOTES

Commencement: 1 October 2008.

SCHEDULE 4
GROUP ACCOUNTS

Regulations 6 and 7

PART 1
FORM AND CONTENT OF NON-IAS GROUP ACCOUNTS

General rules

[10.1075]

1. (1)   Subject to sub-paragraphs (1) and (2), group accounts must comply so far as practicable with the provisions of Schedule 1 to these Regulations (non-IAS individual accounts) as if the undertakings included in the consolidation ("the group") were a single LLP.

(2)   For item A.III in each balance sheet format set out in that Schedule substitute—

"A.III.   Investments
1.   Shares in group undertakings
2.   Interests in associated undertakings
3.   Other participating interests
4.   Loans to group undertakings and undertakings in which a participating interest is held
5.   Other investments other than loans
6.   Others".

(3)   In the profit and loss account formats replace the items headed "Income from participating interests", that is—

    (a)   in Format 1, item 8, and

    (b)   in Format 2, item 10,

by two items: "Income from interests in associated undertakings" and "Income from other participating interests".

2. (1)   The consolidated balance sheet and profit and loss account must incorporate in full the information contained in the individual accounts of the undertakings included in the consolidation, subject to the adjustments authorised or required by the following provisions of this Schedule and to such other adjustments (if any) as may be appropriate in accordance with generally accepted accounting principles or practice.

(2)   If the financial year of a subsidiary undertaking included in the consolidation does not end with that of the parent LLP, the group accounts must be made up—

    (a)   from the accounts of the subsidiary undertaking for its financial year last ending before the end of the parent LLP's financial year, provided that year ended no more than three months before that of the parent LLP, or

    (b)   from interim accounts prepared by the subsidiary undertaking as at the end of the parent LLP's financial year.

3. (1)   Where assets and liabilities to be included in the group accounts have been valued or otherwise determined by undertakings according to accounting rules differing from those used for the group accounts, the values or amounts must be adjusted so as to accord with the rules used for the group accounts.

(2)   If it appears to the members of the parent LLP that there are special reasons for departing from sub-paragraph (1) they may do so, but particulars of any such departure, the reasons for it and its effect must be given in a note to the accounts.

(3)   The adjustments referred to in this paragraph need not be made if they are not material for the purpose of giving a true and fair view.

4.   Any differences of accounting rules as between a parent LLP's individual accounts for a financial year and its group accounts must be disclosed in a note to the latter accounts and the reasons for the difference given.

5.   Amounts that in the particular context of any provision of this Schedule are not material may be disregarded for the purposes of that provision.

Elimination of group transactions

6. (1)   Debts and claims between undertakings included in the consolidation, and income and expenditure relating to transactions between such undertakings, must be eliminated in preparing the group accounts.

(2)   Where profits and losses resulting from transactions between undertakings included in the consolidation are included in the book value of assets, they must be eliminated in preparing the group accounts.

(3)   The elimination required by sub-paragraph (2) may be effected in proportion to the group's interest in the shares of the undertakings.

(4)   Sub-paragraphs (1) and (2) need not be complied with if the amounts concerned are not material for the purpose of giving a true and fair view.

Acquisition and merger accounting

7. (1)   The following provisions apply where an undertaking becomes a subsidiary undertaking of the parent LLP.

(2)   That event is referred to in those provisions as an "acquisition", and references to the "undertaking acquired" are to be construed accordingly.

8.   An acquisition must be accounted for by the acquisition method of accounting unless the conditions for accounting for it as a merger are met and the merger method of accounting is adopted.

9. (1)   The acquisition method of accounting is as follows.

(2)   The identifiable assets and liabilities of the undertaking acquired must be included in the consolidated balance sheet at their fair values as at the date of acquisition.

(3)   The income and expenditure of the undertaking acquired must be brought into the group accounts only as from the date of the acquisition.

(4)   There must be set off against the acquisition cost of the interest in the shares of the undertaking held by the parent LLP and its subsidiary undertakings the interest of the parent LLP and its subsidiary undertakings in the adjusted capital and reserves of the undertaking acquired.

(5)   The resulting amount if positive must be treated as goodwill, and if negative as a negative consolidation difference.

10. The conditions for accounting for an acquisition as a merger are that adoption of the merger method of accounting accords with generally accepted accounting principles or practice.

11. (1)   Where an LLP adopts the merger method of accounting, it must comply with this paragraph, and with generally accepted accounting principles or practice.

(2)   The assets and liabilities of the undertaking acquired must be brought into the group accounts at the figures at which they stand in the undertaking's accounts, subject to any adjustment authorised or required by this Schedule.

(3)   The income and expenditure of the undertaking acquired must be included in the group accounts for the entire financial year, including the period before the acquisition.

(4)   The group accounts must show corresponding amounts relating to the previous financial year as if the undertaking acquired had been included in the consolidation throughout that year.

12. (1)   Where a group is acquired, paragraphs 9 to 11 apply with the following adaptations.

(2)   References to shares of the undertaking acquired are to be construed as references to shares of the parent undertaking of the group.

(3)   Other references to the undertaking acquired are to be construed as references to the group; and references to the assets and liabilities, income and expenditure and capital and reserves of the undertaking acquired must be construed as references to the assets and liabilities, income and expenditure and capital and reserves of the group after making the set-offs and other adjustments required by this Schedule in the case of group accounts.

13. (1)   The following information with respect to acquisitions taking place in the financial year must be given in a note to the accounts.

(2)   There must be stated—
  (a)   the name of the undertaking acquired or, where a group was acquired, the name of the parent undertaking of that group, and
  (b)   whether the acquisition has been accounted for by the acquisition or the merger method of accounting;
and in relation to an acquisition which significantly affects the figures shown in the group accounts, the following further information must be given.

(3)   The composition and fair value of the consideration for the acquisition given by the parent LLP and its subsidiary undertakings must be stated.

(4)   Where the acquisition method of accounting has been adopted, the book values immediately prior to the acquisition, and the fair values at the date of acquisition, of each class of assets and liabilities of the undertaking or group acquired must be stated in tabular form, including a statement of the amount of any goodwill or negative consolidation difference arising on the acquisition, together with an explanation of any significant adjustments made.

(5)   In ascertaining for the purposes of sub-paragraph (4) the profit or loss of a group, the book values and fair values of assets and liabilities of a group or the amount of the assets and liabilities of a group, the set-offs and other adjustments required by this Schedule in the case of group accounts must be made.

14. (1)   There must also be stated in a note to the accounts the cumulative amount of goodwill resulting from acquisitions in that and earlier financial years which has been written off otherwise than in the consolidated profit and loss account for that or any earlier financial year.

(2)   That figure must be shown net of any goodwill attributable to subsidiary undertakings or businesses disposed of prior to the balance sheet date.

15. Where during the financial year there has been a disposal of an undertaking or group which significantly affects the figures shown in the group accounts, there must be stated in a note to the accounts—
  (a)   the name of that undertaking or, as the case may be, of the parent undertaking of that group, and
  (b)   the extent to which the profit or loss shown in the group accounts is attributable to profit or loss of that undertaking or group.

16. The information required by paragraph 13, 14 or 15 need not be disclosed with respect to an undertaking which—
  (a)   is established under the law of a country outside the United Kingdom, or
  (b)   carries on business outside the United Kingdom,
if in the opinion of the members of the parent LLP the disclosure would be seriously prejudicial to the business of that undertaking or to the business of the parent LLP or any of its subsidiary undertakings and the Secretary of State agrees that the information should not be disclosed.

Minority interests
17. (1)   The formats set out in Schedule 1 to these Regulations have effect in relation to group accounts with the following additions.

(2) In the Balance Sheet Formats there must be shown, as a separate item and under an appropriate heading, the amount of capital and reserves attributable to shares in subsidiary undertakings included in the consolidation held by or on behalf of persons other than the parent LLP and its subsidiary undertakings.

(3) In the Profit and Loss Account Formats there must be shown, as a separate item and under an appropriate heading—

    (a) the amount of any profit or loss on ordinary activities, and

    (b) the amount of any profit or loss on extraordinary activities,

attributable to shares in subsidiary undertakings included in the consolidation held by or on behalf of persons other than the parent LLP and its subsidiary undertakings.

(4) For the purposes of paragraph 4 of Schedule 1 (power to adapt or combine items)—

    (a) the additional item required by sub-paragraph (2) above is treated as one to which a letter is assigned, and

    (b) the additional items required by sub-paragraph (3)(a) and (b) above are treated as ones to which an Arabic number is assigned.

Joint ventures

18. (1) Where an undertaking included in the consolidation manages another undertaking jointly with one or more undertakings not included in the consolidation, that other undertaking ("the joint venture") may, if it is not—

    (a) a body corporate, or

    (b) a subsidiary undertaking of the parent LLP,

be dealt with in the group accounts by the method of proportional consolidation.

(2) The provisions of this Schedule relating to the preparation of consolidated accounts apply, with any necessary modifications, to proportional consolidation under this paragraph.

Associated undertakings

19. (1) An "associated undertaking" means an undertaking in which an undertaking included in the consolidation has a participating interest and over whose operating and financial policy it exercises a significant influence, and which is not—

    (a) a subsidiary undertaking of the parent LLP, or

    (b) a joint venture dealt with in accordance with paragraph 18.

(2) Where an undertaking holds 20% or more of the voting rights in another undertaking, it is presumed to exercise such an influence over it unless the contrary is shown.

(3) The voting rights in an undertaking means the rights conferred on shareholders in respect of their shares or, in the case of an undertaking not having a share capital, on members, to vote at general meetings of the undertaking on all, or substantially all, matters.

(4) The provisions of paragraphs 5 to 11 of Schedule 7 to the 2006 Act (parent and subsidiary undertakings: rights to be taken into account and attribution of rights) apply in determining for the purposes of this paragraph whether an undertaking holds 20% or more of the voting rights in another undertaking.

20. (1) The interest of an undertaking in an associated undertaking, and the amount of profit or loss attributable to such an interest, must be shown by the equity method of accounting (including dealing with any goodwill arising in accordance with paragraphs 17 to 20 and 22 of Schedule 1 to these Regulations).

(2) Where the associated undertaking is itself a parent undertaking, the net assets and profits or losses to be taken into account are those of the parent and its subsidiary undertakings (after making any consolidation adjustments).

(3) The equity method of accounting need not be applied if the amounts in question are not material for the purpose of giving a true and fair view.

NOTES

Commencement: 1 October 2008.

PART 2

INFORMATION ABOUT RELATED UNDERTAKINGS WHERE LLP PREPARING GROUP ACCOUNTS (NON-IAS OR IAS GROUP ACCOUNTS)

Introduction and interpretation

[10.1076]

21. In this Part of this Schedule "the group" means the group consisting of the parent LLP and its subsidiary undertakings.

Subsidiary undertakings

22. (1) The following information must be given with respect to the undertakings that are subsidiary undertakings of the parent LLP at the end of the financial year.

(2)   The name of each undertaking must be stated.

(3)   There must be stated—

    (a)   if the undertaking is incorporated outside the United Kingdom, the country in which it is incorporated,

    (b)   if it is unincorporated, the address of its principal place of business.

(4)   It must also be stated whether the subsidiary undertaking is included in the consolidation and, if it is not, the reasons for excluding it from consolidation must be given.

(5)   It must be stated with respect to each subsidiary undertaking by virtue of which of the conditions specified in section 1162(2) or (4) of the 2006 Act it is a subsidiary undertaking of its immediate parent undertaking.

That information need not be given if the relevant condition is that specified in subsection (2)(a) of that section (holding of a majority of the voting rights) and the immediate parent undertaking holds the same proportion of the shares in the undertaking as it holds voting rights.

Holdings in subsidiary undertakings

23.   (1)   The following information must be given with respect to the shares of a subsidiary undertaking held—

    (a)   by the parent LLP, and

    (b)   by the group,

and the information under paragraphs (a) and (b) must (if different) be shown separately.

(2)   There must be stated—

    (a)   the identity of each class of shares held, and

    (b)   the proportion of the nominal value of the shares of that class represented by those shares.

Financial information about subsidiary undertakings not included in the consolidation

24.   (1)   There must be shown with respect to each subsidiary undertaking not included in the consolidation—

    (a)   the aggregate amount of its capital and reserves as at the end of its relevant financial year, and

    (b)   its profit or loss for that year.

(2)   That information need not be given if the group's investment in the undertaking is included in the accounts by way of the equity method of valuation or if—

    (a)   the undertaking is not required by any provision of the 2006 Act to deliver a copy of its balance sheet for its relevant financial year and does not otherwise publish that balance sheet in the United Kingdom or elsewhere, and

    (b)   the holding of the group is less than 50% of the nominal value of the shares in the undertaking.

(3)   Information otherwise required by this paragraph need not be given if it is not material.

(4)   For the purposes of this paragraph the "relevant financial year" of a subsidiary undertaking is—

    (a)   if its financial year ends with that of the LLP, that year, and

    (b)   if not, its financial year ending last before the end of the LLP's financial year.

Joint ventures

25.   (1)   The following information must be given where an undertaking is dealt with in the consolidated accounts by the method of proportional consolidation in accordance with paragraph 18 of this Schedule (joint ventures)—

    (a)   the name of the undertaking,

    (b)   the address of the principal place of business of the undertaking,

    (c)   the factors on which joint management of the undertaking is based, and

    (d)   the proportion of the capital of the undertaking held by undertakings included in the consolidation.

(2)   Where the financial year of the undertaking did not end with that of the LLP, there must be stated the date on which a financial year of the undertaking last ended before that date.

Associated undertakings

26.   (1)   The following information must be given where an undertaking included in the consolidation has an interest in an associated undertaking.

(2)   The name of the associated undertaking must be stated.

(3)   There must be stated—

    (a)   if the undertaking is incorporated outside the United Kingdom, the country in which it is incorporated,

    (b)   if it is unincorporated, the address of its principal place of business.

(4)   The following information must be given with respect to the shares of the undertaking held—

    (a)   by the parent LLP, and

    (b)   by the group,

and the information under paragraphs (a) and (b) must be shown separately.

(5)   There must be stated—
  (a)   the identity of each class of shares held, and
  (b)   the proportion of the nominal value of the shares of that class represented by those shares.

(6)   In this paragraph "associated undertaking" has the meaning given by paragraph 19 of this Schedule; and the information required by this paragraph must be given notwithstanding that paragraph 20(3) of this Schedule (materiality) applies in relation to the accounts themselves.

Other significant holdings of parent LLP or group

27. (1)   The information required by paragraphs 28 and 29 must be given where at the end of the financial year the parent LLP has a significant holding in an undertaking which is not one of its subsidiary undertakings and does not fall within paragraph 25 (joint ventures) or paragraph 26 (associated undertakings).

(2)   A holding is significant for this purpose if—
  (a)   it amounts to 20% or more of the nominal value of any class of shares in the undertaking, or
  (b)   the amount of the holding (as stated or included in the LLP's individual accounts) exceeds 20% of the amount of its assets (as so stated).

28. (1)   The name of the undertaking must be stated.

(2)   There must be stated—
  (a)   if the undertaking is incorporated outside the United Kingdom, the country in which it is incorporated,
  (b)   if it is unincorporated, the address of its principal place of business.

(3)   The following information must be given with respect to the shares of the undertaking held by the parent LLP.

(4)   There must be stated—
  (a)   the identity of each class of shares held, and
  (b)   the proportion of the nominal value of the shares of that class represented by those shares.

29. (1)   There must also be stated—
  (a)   the aggregate amount of the capital and reserves of the undertaking as at the end of its relevant financial year, and
  (b)   its profit or loss for that year.

(2)   That information need not be given in respect of an undertaking if—
  (a)   the undertaking is not required by any provision of the 2006 Act to deliver a copy of its balance sheet for its relevant financial year and does not otherwise publish that balance sheet in the United Kingdom or elsewhere, and
  (b)   the LLP's holding is less than 50% of the nominal value of the shares in the undertaking.

(3)   Information otherwise required by this paragraph need not be given if it is not material.

(4)   For the purposes of this paragraph the "relevant financial year" of an undertaking is—
  (a)   if its financial year ends with that of the LLP, that year, and
  (b)   if not, its financial year ending last before the end of the LLP's financial year.

30. (1)   The information required by paragraphs 31 and 32 must be given where at the end of the financial year the group has a significant holding in an undertaking which is not a subsidiary undertaking of the parent LLP and does not fall within paragraph 25 (joint ventures) or paragraph 26 (associated undertakings).

(2)   A holding is significant for this purpose if—
  (a)   it amounts to 20% or more of the nominal value of any class of shares in the undertaking, or
  (b)   the amount of the holding (as stated or included in the group accounts) exceeds 20% of the amount of the group's assets (as so stated).

31. (1)   The name of the undertaking must be stated.

(2)   There must be stated—
  (a)   if the undertaking is incorporated outside the United Kingdom, the country in which it is incorporated,
  (b)   if it is unincorporated, the address of its principal place of business.

(3)   The following information must be given with respect to the shares of the undertaking held by the group.

(4)   There must be stated—
  (a)   the identity of each class of shares held, and
  (b)   the proportion of the nominal value of the shares of that class represented by those shares.

32. (1)   There must also be stated—
  (a)   the aggregate amount of the capital and reserves of the undertaking as at the end of its relevant financial year, and
  (b)   its profit or loss for that year.

(2) That information need not be given if—
- (a) the undertaking is not required by any provision of the 2006 Act to deliver a copy of its balance sheet for its relevant financial year and does not otherwise publish that balance sheet in the United Kingdom or elsewhere, and
- (b) the holding of the group is less than 50% of the nominal value of the shares in the undertaking.

(3) Information otherwise required by this paragraph need not be given if it is not material.

(4) For the purposes of this paragraph the "relevant financial year" of an outside undertaking is—
- (a) if its financial year ends with that of the parent LLP, that year, and
- (b) if not, its financial year ending last before the end of the parent LLP's financial year.

Parent undertaking drawing up accounts for larger group

33. (1) Where the parent LLP is itself a subsidiary undertaking, the following information must be given with respect to that parent undertaking of the LLP which heads—
- (a) the largest group of undertakings for which group accounts are drawn up and of which that LLP is a member, and
- (b) the smallest such group of undertakings.

(2) The name of the parent undertaking must be stated.

(3) There must be stated—
- (a) if the undertaking is incorporated outside the United Kingdom, the country in which it is incorporated,
- (b) if it is unincorporated, the address of its principal place of business.

(4) If copies of the group accounts referred to in sub-paragraph (1) are available to the public, there must also be stated the addresses from which copies of the accounts can be obtained.

Identification of ultimate parent

34. (1) Where the parent LLP is itself a subsidiary undertaking, the following information must be given with respect to the body corporate (if any) regarded by the members as being that LLP's ultimate parent.

(2) The name of that body corporate must be stated.

(3) If that body corporate is incorporated outside the United Kingdom, the country in which it is incorporated must be stated (if known to the members).

Construction of references to shares held by parent LLP or group

35. (1) References in this Part of this Schedule to shares held by the parent LLP or the group are to be construed as follows.

(2) For the purposes of paragraphs 23, 26(4) and (5) and 27 to 29 (information about holdings in subsidiary and other undertakings)—
- (a) there must be attributed to the parent LLP shares held on its behalf by any person; but
- (b) there must be treated as not held by the parent LLP shares held on behalf of a person other than the LLP.

(3) References to shares held by the group are to any shares held by or on behalf of the parent LLP or any of its subsidiary undertakings; but any shares held on behalf of a person other than the parent LLP or any of its subsidiary undertakings are not to be treated as held by the group.

(4) Shares held by way of security must be treated as held by the person providing the security—
- (a) where apart from the right to exercise them for the purpose of preserving the value of the security, or of realising it, the rights attached to the shares are exercisable only in accordance with his instructions, and
- (b) where the shares are held in connection with the granting of loans as part of normal business activities and apart from the right to exercise them for the purpose of preserving the value of the security, or of realising it, the rights attached to the shares are exercisable only in his interests.

NOTES

Commencement: 1 October 2008.

SCHEDULE 5
GENERAL INTERPRETATION

Regulation 8

Financial instruments

[10.1077]

1. References to "derivatives" include commodity-based contracts that give either contracting party the right to settle in cash or in some other financial instrument, except where such contracts—
- (a) were entered into for the purpose of, and continue to meet, the LLP's expected purchase, sale or usage requirements,
- (b) were designated for such purpose at their inception, and

(c)   are expected to be settled by delivery of the commodity.

2. (1)   The expressions listed in sub-paragraph (2) have the same meaning as they have in Council Directive 78/660/EEC on the annual accounts of certain types of companies.

(2)   Those expressions are "available for sale financial asset", "business combination", "commodity-based contracts", "derivative", "equity instrument", "exchange difference", "fair value hedge accounting system", "financial fixed asset", "financial instrument", "foreign entity", "hedge accounting", "hedge accounting system", "hedged items", "hedging instrument", "held for trading purposes", "held to maturity", "monetary item", "receivables", "reliable market" and "trading portfolio".

Fixed and current assets
3. "Fixed assets" means assets of an LLP which are intended for use on a continuing basis in the LLP's activities, and "current assets" means assets not intended for such use.

Historical cost accounting rules
4. References to the historical cost accounting rules are to be read in accordance with paragraph 30 of Schedule 1 to these Regulations.

Listed investments
5. (1)   "Listed investment" means an investment as respects which there has been granted a listing on—

     (a)   a recognised investment exchange other than an overseas investment exchange, or

     (b)   a stock exchange of repute outside the United Kingdom.

(2)   "Recognised investment exchange" and "overseas investment exchange" have the meaning given in Part 18 of the Financial Services and Markets Act 2000.

Loans
6. A loan is treated as falling due for repayment, and an instalment of a loan is treated as falling due for payment, on the earliest date on which the lender could require repayment or (as the case may be) payment, if he exercised all options and rights available to him.

Materiality
7. Amounts which in the particular context of any provision of Schedule 1 to these Regulations are not material may be disregarded for the purposes of that provision.

Participating interests
8. (1)   A "participating interest" means an interest held by an undertaking in the shares of another undertaking which it holds on a long-term basis for the purpose of securing a contribution to its activities by the exercise of control or influence arising from or related to that interest.

(2)   A holding of 20% or more of the shares of the undertaking is to be presumed to be a participating interest unless the contrary is shown.

(3)   The reference in sub-paragraph (1) to an interest in shares includes—

     (a)   an interest which is convertible into an interest in shares, and

     (b)   an option to acquire shares or any such interest,

and an interest or option falls within paragraph (a) or (b) notwithstanding that the shares to which it relates are, until the conversion or the exercise of the option, unissued.

(4)   For the purposes of this paragraph an interest held on behalf of an undertaking is to be treated as held by it.

(5)   In the balance sheet and profit and loss formats set out in Part 1 of Schedule 1 and Part 1 of Schedule 3 to these Regulations, "participating interest" does not include an interest in a group undertaking.

(6)   For the purpose of this paragraph as it applies in relation to the expression "participating interest"—

     (a)   in those formats as they apply in relation to group accounts, and

     (b)   in paragraph 19 of Schedule 4 (group accounts: undertakings to be accounted for as associated undertakings),

the references in sub-paragraphs (1) to (4) to the interest held by, and the purposes and activities of, the undertaking concerned are to be construed as references to the interest held by, and the purposes and activities of, the group (within the meaning of paragraph 1 of that Schedule).

Provisions
9. (1)   References to provisions for depreciation or diminution in value of assets are to any amount written off by way of providing for depreciation or diminution in value of assets.

(2)   Any reference in the profit and loss account formats set out in Part 1 of Schedule 1 to these Regulations to the depreciation of, or amounts written off, assets of any description is to any provision for depreciation or diminution in value of assets of that description.

10. References to provisions for liabilities are to any amount retained as reasonably necessary for the purpose of providing for any liability the nature of which is clearly defined and which is either likely to be incurred, or certain to be incurred but uncertain as to amount or as to the date on which it will arise.

Purchase price
11. "Purchase price", in relation to an asset of an LLP or any raw materials or consumables used in the production of such an asset, includes any consideration (whether in cash or otherwise) given by the LLP in respect of that asset or those materials or consumables, as the case may be.

Staff costs
12. (1) "Social security costs" means any contributions by the LLP to any state social security or pension scheme, fund or arrangement.

(2) "Pension costs" includes—
- (a) any costs incurred by the LLP in respect of any pension scheme established for the purpose of providing pensions for persons currently or formerly employed by the LLP,
- (b) any sums set aside for the future payment of pensions directly by the LLP to current or former employees, and
- (c) any pensions paid directly to such persons without having first been set aside.

(3) Any amount stated in respect of the item "social security costs" or in respect of the item "wages and salaries" in the LLP's profit and loss account must be determined by reference to payments made or costs incurred in respect of all persons employed by the LLP during the financial year under contracts of service.

NOTES
Commencement: 1 October 2008.

LARGE AND MEDIUM-SIZED LIMITED LIABILITY PARTNERSHIPS (ACCOUNTS) REGULATIONS 2008

(SI 2008/1913)

NOTES
Made: 17 July 2008.
Authority: Limited Liability Partnerships Act 2000, ss 15, 17.
Commencement: 1 October 2008.
Amendment: as of 1 July 2011, these Regulations had not been amended.

ARRANGEMENT OF REGULATIONS

PART 1
INTRODUCTION

[10.1078]
1 Citation and interpretation

(1) These Regulations may be cited as the Large and Medium-sized Limited Liability Partnerships (Accounts) Regulations 2008.

(2) In these Regulations—
 "the 2006 Act" means the Companies Act 2006;
 "the Large and Medium-sized Companies Accounts Regulations" means the Large and Medium-sized Companies and Groups (Accounts and Reports) Regulations 2008;
 "LLP" means a limited liability partnership formed under the Limited Liability Partnerships Act 2000 or the Limited Liability Partnerships Act (NI) 2002.

(3) Any reference in these Regulations to a numbered Part or section of the 2006 Act is a reference to that Part or section as applied to LLPs by the Limited Liability Partnerships (Accounts and Audit) (Application of Companies Act 2006) Regulations 2008.

NOTES
Commencement: 1 October 2008.
 General note as to interpretation: as to the meaning of "the registrar" and "the register", and as to the construction of references to registration in a particular part of the United Kingdom, in any enactment relating to LLPs, see the Limited Liability Partnerships (Application of Companies Act 2006) Regulations 2009, SI 2009/1804, reg 85, Sch 3, Pt 2, para 12 at **[10.1191]**.

[10.1079]
2 Commencement and application

(1) These Regulations come into force on 1st October 2008.

(2) They apply in relation to financial years beginning on or after 1st October 2008.

(3) They apply to LLPs, with modifications, provisions of the Large and Medium-sized Companies Accounts Regulations.

(4) They do not apply to LLPs which are subject to the small LLPs regime under Part 15 of the 2006 Act.

NOTES
Commencement: 1 October 2008.

PART 2
FORM AND CONTENT OF ACCOUNTS

[10.1080]
3 Non-IAS individual accounts

(1) Regulation 3 of the Large and Medium-sized Companies Accounts Regulations applies to LLPs, modified so that it reads as follows—

 "3 Non-IAS individual accounts
 (1) Subject to regulation 4, non-IAS individual accounts under section 396 of the 2006 Act (non-IAS individual accounts) must comply with the provisions of Schedule 1 to the Large and Medium-sized Limited Liability Partnerships (Accounts) Regulations 2008 as to the form and content of the balance sheet and profit and loss account, and additional information to be provided by way of notes to the accounts.
 (2) The profit and loss account of an LLP that falls within section 408 of the 2006 Act (individual profit and loss account where group accounts prepared) need not contain the information specified in paragraphs 62 to 67 of Schedule 1 to the Large and Medium-sized Limited Liability Partnerships (Accounts) Regulations 2008 (information supplementing the profit and loss account).".

(2) The provisions of Schedule 1 to the Large and Medium-sized Companies Accounts Regulations apply to LLPs, modified so that they are the provisions set out in Schedule 1 to these Regulations.

NOTES
Commencement: 1 October 2008.

[10.1081]
4 Medium-sized LLPs: exemptions for non-IAS individual accounts

Regulation 4 of the Large and Medium-sized Companies Accounts Regulations applies to LLPs, modified so that it reads as follows—

 "4 Medium-sized LLPs: exemptions for non-IAS individual accounts
 (1) This regulation applies to an LLP—

(a)   which qualifies as medium-sized in relation to a financial year under section 465 of the 2006 Act, and

(b)   the members of which are preparing non-IAS individual accounts under section 396 of that Act for that year.

(2)   The individual accounts for the year need not comply with the following provisions of Schedule 1 to the Large and Medium-sized Limited Liability Partnerships (Accounts) Regulations 2008—

(a)   paragraph 45 (disclosure with respect to compliance with accounting standards), and

(b)   paragraph 70 (related party transactions).

(3)   The members of the LLP may deliver to the registrar of companies a copy of the accounts for the year—

(a)   which includes a profit and loss account in which the following items listed in the profit and loss account formats set out in Schedule 1 to the Large and Medium-sized Limited Liability Partnerships (Accounts) Regulations 2008 are combined as one item—

- items 2, 3 and 6 in format 1;
- items 2 to 5 in format 2;

(b)   which does not contain the information required by paragraph 65 of Schedule 1 to those Regulations (particulars of turnover).".

NOTES

Commencement: 1 October 2008.

[10.1082]

5   Information about related undertakings (non-IAS or IAS individual or group accounts)

(1)   Regulation 7 of the Large and Medium-sized Companies Accounts Regulations applies to LLPs, modified so that it reads as follows—

"7   Information about related undertakings (non-IAS or IAS individual or group accounts

(1)   Non-IAS or IAS individual or group accounts must comply with the provisions of Schedule 2 to the Large and Medium-sized Limited Liability Partnerships (Accounts) Regulations 2008 as to information about related undertakings to be given in notes to the LLP's accounts.

(2)   In Schedule 2 to the Large and Medium-sized Limited Liability Partnerships (Accounts) Regulations 2008—

- Part 1 contains provisions applying to all LLPs
- Part 2 contains provisions applying only to LLPs not required to prepare group accounts
- Part 3 contains provisions applying only to LLPs required to prepare group accounts.

(3)   Information otherwise required to be given by Schedule 2 need not be disclosed with respect to an undertaking that—

(a)   is established under the law of a country outside the United Kingdom, or

(b)   carries on business outside the United Kingdom,

if the conditions specified in section 409(4) of the 2006 Act are met (see section 409(5) of the 2006 Act for disclosure required where advantage taken of this exemption).".

(2)   The provisions of Schedule 4 to the Large and Medium-sized Companies Accounts Regulations apply to LLPs, modified so that they are the provisions set out in Schedule 2 to these Regulations.

NOTES

Commencement: 1 October 2008.

[10.1083]

6   Non-IAS group accounts

(1)   Regulation 9 of the Large and Medium-sized Companies Accounts Regulations applies to LLPs, modified so that it reads as follows—

"9   Non-IAS group accounts

Where the members of a parent LLP prepare non-IAS group accounts under section 403 of the 2006 Act (group accounts: applicable accounting framework), those accounts must comply with the provisions of Schedule 3 to the Large and Medium-sized Limited Liability Partnerships (Accounts) Regulations 2008 as to the form and content of the consolidated balance sheet and consolidated profit and loss account, and additional information to be provided by way of notes to the accounts.".

(2)   The provisions of Part 1 of Schedule 6 to the Large and Medium-sized Companies Accounts Regulations apply to LLPs, modified so that they are the provisions set out in Schedule 3 to these Regulations.

NOTES
Commencement: 1 October 2008.

PART 3
INTERPRETATION

[10.1084]
7   General interpretation

(1)   Regulation 13 of the Large and Medium-sized Companies Accounts Regulations applies to LLPs, modified so that it reads as follows—

"13   General interpretation
Schedule 4 to the Large and Medium-sized Limited Liability Partnerships (Accounts) Regulations 2008 contains general definitions for the purposes of these Regulations as applied to LLPs.".

(2)   The provisions of Schedule 10 to the Large and Medium-sized Companies Accounts Regulations apply to LLPs, modified so that they are the provisions set out in Schedule 4 to these Regulations.

NOTES
Commencement: 1 October 2008.

SCHEDULES

SCHEDULE 1
NON-IAS INDIVIDUAL ACCOUNTS

Regulation 3

PART 1
GENERAL RULES AND FORMATS

SECTION A
GENERAL RULES

[10.1085]
1.   (1)   Subject to the following provisions of this Schedule—
   (a)   every balance sheet of an LLP must show the items listed in either of the balance sheet formats in Section B of this Part, and
   (b)   every profit and loss account must show the items listed in either of the profit and loss account formats in Section B.

(2)   References in this Schedule to the items listed in any of the formats in Section B are to those items read together with any of the notes following the formats which apply to those items.

(3)   The items must be shown in the order and under the headings and sub-headings given in the particular format used, but—
   (a)   the notes to the formats may permit alternative positions for any particular items, and
   (b)   the heading or sub-heading for any item does not have to be distinguished by any letter or number assigned to that item in the format used.

2.   (1)   Where in accordance with paragraph 1 an LLP's balance sheet or profit and loss account for any financial year has been prepared by reference to one of the formats in Section B, the members of the LLP must use the same format in preparing non-IAS individual accounts for subsequent financial years, unless in their opinion there are special reasons for a change.

(2)   Particulars of any such change must be given in a note to the accounts in which the new format is first used, and the reasons for the change must be explained.

3.   (1)   Any item required to be shown in an LLP's balance sheet or profit and loss account may be shown in greater detail than required by the particular format used.

(2)   The balance sheet or profit and loss account may include an item representing or covering the amount of any asset or liability, income or expenditure not otherwise covered by any of the items listed in the format used, save that none of the following may be treated as assets in any balance sheet—
   (a)   preliminary expenses,
   (b)   expenses of, and commission on, any issue of debentures, and
   (c)   costs of research.

4. (1)　Where the special nature of the LLP's business requires it, the members of the LLP must adapt the arrangement, headings and sub-headings otherwise required in respect of items given an Arabic number in the balance sheet or profit and loss account format used.

(2)　The members may combine items to which Arabic numbers are given in any of the formats in Section B if—

  (a)　their individual amounts are not material to assessing the state of affairs or profit or loss of the LLP for the financial year in question, or

  (b)　the combination facilitates that assessment.

(3)　Where sub-paragraph (2)(b) applies, the individual amounts of any items which have been combined must be disclosed in a note to the accounts.

5. (1)　Subject to sub-paragraph (2), the members must not include a heading or sub-heading corresponding to an item in the balance sheet or profit and loss account format used if there is no amount to be shown for that item for the financial year to which the balance sheet or profit and loss account relates.

(2)　Where an amount can be shown for the item in question for the immediately preceding financial year that amount must be shown under the heading or sub-heading required by the format for that item.

6. Every profit and loss account must show the amount of an LLP's profit or loss on ordinary activities before taxation.

7. (1)　For every item shown in the balance sheet or profit and loss account the corresponding amount for the immediately preceding financial year must also be shown.

(2)　Where that corresponding amount is not comparable with the amount to be shown for the item in question in respect of the financial year to which the balance sheet or profit and loss account relates, the former amount may be adjusted, and particulars of the non-comparability and of any adjustment must be disclosed in a note to the accounts.

8. Amounts in respect of items representing assets or income may not be set off against amounts in respect of items representing liabilities or expenditure (as the case may be), or vice versa.

9. The members of the LLP must, in determining how amounts are presented within items in the profit and loss account and balance sheet, have regard to the substance of the reported transaction or arrangement, in accordance with generally accepted accounting principles or practice.

SECTION B

THE REQUIRED FORMATS FOR ACCOUNTS

Balance sheet formats

Format 1

A.　Fixed assets

　　I.　　Intangible assets

　　　　1.　　Development costs

　　　　2.　　Concessions, patents, licences, trade marks and similar rights and assets[1]

　　　　3.　　Goodwill[2]

　　　　4.　　Payments on account

　　II.　　Tangible assets

　　　　1.　　Land and buildings

　　　　2.　　Plant and machinery

　　　　3.　　Fixtures, fittings, tools and equipment

　　　　4.　　Payments on account and assets in course of construction

　　III.　　Investments

　　　　1.　　Shares in group undertakings

　　　　2.　　Loans to group undertakings

　　　　3.　　Participating interests

　　　　4.　　Loans to undertakings in which the LLP has a participating interest

　　　　5.　　Other investments other than loans

　　　　6.　　Other loans

B.　Current assets

　　I.　　Stocks

　　　　1.　　Raw materials and consumables

　　　　2.　　Work in progress

　　　　3.　　Finished goods and goods for resale

　　　　4.　　Payments on account

　　II.　　Debtors[3]

　　　　1.　　Trade debtors

    2.   Amounts owed by group undertakings

    3.   Amounts owed by undertakings in which the LLP has a participating interest

    4.   Other debtors

    5.   Prepayments and accrued income[4]

  III. Investments

    1.   Shares in group undertakings

    2.   Other investments

  IV. Cash at bank and in hand

C. Prepayments and accrued income[4]

D. Creditors: amounts falling due within one year

    1.   Debenture loans[5]

    2.   Bank loans and overdrafts

    3.   Payments received on account[6]

    4.   Trade creditors

    5.   Bills of exchange payable

    6.   Amounts owed to group undertakings

    7.   Amounts owed to undertakings in which the LLP has a participating interest

    8.   Other creditors including taxation and social security[7]

    9.   Accruals and deferred income[8]

E. Net current assets (liabilities)[9]

F. Total assets less current liabilities

G. Creditors: amounts falling due after more than one year

    1.   Debenture loans[5]

    2.   Bank loans and overdrafts

    3.   Payments received on account[6]

    4.   Trade creditors

    5.   Bills of exchange payable

    6.   Amounts owed to group undertakings

    7.   Amounts owed to undertakings in which the LLP has a participating interest

    8.   Other creditors including taxation and social security[7]

    9.   Accruals and deferred income[8]

H. Provisions for liabilities

    1.   Pensions and similar obligations

    2.   Taxation, including deferred taxation

    3.   Other provisions

I. Accruals and deferred income[8]

J. Loans and other debts due to members[10]

K. Members' other interests

  I.   Members' capital

  II.   Revaluation reserve

  III.   Other reserves

Balance sheet formats

Format 2

ASSETS

A. Fixed assets

  I.   Intangible assets

    1.   Development costs

    2.   Concessions, patents, licences, trade marks and similar rights and assets[1]

    3.   Goodwill[2]

    4.   Payments on account

  II.   Tangible assets

    1.   Land and buildings

    2.   Plant and machinery

    3.   Fixtures, fittings, tools and equipment

    4.   Payments on account and assets in course of construction

  III. Investments

    1.   Shares in group undertakings

    2.   Loans to group undertakings

    3.   Participating interests

    4.   Loans to undertakings in which the LLP has a participating interest
    5.   Other investments other than loans
    6.   Other loans

B. Current assets
   I.   Stocks
        1.   Raw materials and consumables
        2.   Work in progress
        3.   Finished goods and goods for resale
        4.   Payments on account
  II.   Debtors[3]
        1.   Trade debtors
        2.   Amounts owed by group undertakings
        3.   Amounts owed by undertakings in which the LLP has a participating interest
        4.   Other debtors
        5.   Prepayments and accrued income[4]
 III. Investments
        1.   Shares in group undertakings
        2.   Other investments
  IV. Cash at bank and in hand

C. Prepayments and accrued income[4]

LIABILITIES

A. Loans and other debts due to members[10]

B. Members' other interests
   I.   Members' capital
  II.   Revaluation reserve
 III. Other reserves

C. Provisions for liabilities
        1.   Pensions and similar obligations
        2.   Taxation, including deferred taxation
        3.   Other provisions

D. Creditors[11]
        1.   Debenture loans[5]
        2.   Bank loans and overdrafts
        3.   Payments received on account[6]
        4.   Trade creditors
        5.   Bills of exchange payable
        6.   Amounts owed to group undertakings
        7.   Amounts owed to undertakings in which the LLP has a participating interest
        8.   Other creditors including taxation and social security[7]
        9.   Accruals and deferred income[8]

E. Accruals and deferred income[8]

Notes on the balance sheet formats

(1) Concessions, patents, licences, trade marks and similar rights and assets

(Formats 1 and 2, item A.I.2.)
   Amounts in respect of assets are only to be included in an LLP's balance sheet under this item if either—
   (a) the assets were acquired for valuable consideration and are not required to be shown under goodwill, or
   (b) the assets in question were created by the LLP itself.

(2) Goodwill

(Formats 1 and 2, item A.I.3.)
   Amounts representing goodwill are only to be included to the extent that the goodwill was acquired for valuable consideration.

(3) Debtors

(Formats 1 and 2, items B.II.1 to 5.)
   The amount falling due after more than one year must be shown separately for each item included under debtors.

(4) Prepayments and accrued income

(Formats 1 and 2, items B.II.5 and C.)
This item may be shown in either of the two positions given in Formats 1 and 2.

(5)   Debenture loans

(Format 1, items D.1 and G.1 and Format 2, item D.1.)
The amount of any convertible loans must be shown separately.

(6)   Payments received on account

(Format 1, items D.3 and G.3 and Format 2, item D.3.)
Payments received on account of orders must be shown for each of these items in so far as they are not shown as deductions from stocks.

(7)   Other creditors including taxation and social security

(Format 1, items D.8 and G.8 and Format 2, item D.8.)

The amount for creditors in respect of taxation and social security must be shown separately from the amount for other creditors.

(8)   Accruals and deferred income

(Format 1, items D.9, G.9 and I and Format 2, items D.9 and E.)
The two positions given for this item in Format 1 at D.9 and G.9 are an alternative to the position at I, but if the item is not shown in a position corresponding to that at I it may be shown in either or both of the other two positions (as the case may require).
The two positions given for this item in Format 2 are alternatives.

(9)   Net current assets (liabilities)

(Format 1, item E.)
In determining the amount to be shown for this item any amounts shown under "prepayments and accrued income" must be taken into account wherever shown.

(10)   Loans and other debts due to members

(Format 1, item J and Format 2, Liabilities item A.)
The following amounts must be shown separately under this item—
(a)   the aggregate amount of money advanced to the LLP by the members by way of loan,
(b)   the aggregate amount of money owed to members by the LLP in respect of profits,
(c)   any other amounts.

(11)   Creditors

(Format 2, items D.1 to 9.)
Amounts falling due within one year and after one year must be shown separately for each of these items and for the aggregate of all of these items.

Profit and loss account formats

Format 1
(see note (15) below)

1.   Turnover

2.   Cost of sales[12]

3.   Gross profit or loss

4.   Distribution costs[12]

5.   Administrative expenses[12]

6.   Other operating income

7.   Income from shares in group undertakings

8.   Income from participating interests

9.   Income from other fixed asset investments[13]

10.   Other interest receivable and similar income[13]

11.   Amounts written off investments

12.   Interest payable and similar charges[14]

13. Tax on profit or loss on ordinary activities

14. Profit or loss on ordinary activities after taxation

15. Extraordinary income

16. Extraordinary charges

17. Extraordinary profit or loss

18. Tax on extraordinary profit or loss

19. Other taxes not shown under the above items

20. Profit or loss for the financial year before members' remuneration and profit shares

Profit and loss account formats

Format 2

1. Turnover

2. Change in stocks of finished goods and in work in progress

3. Own work capitalised

4. Other operating income

5.
  (a) Raw materials and consumables
  (b) Other external charges

6. Staff costs
  (a) wages and salaries
  (b) social security costs
  (c) other pension costs

7.
  (a) Depreciation and other amounts written off tangible and intangible fixed assets
  (b) Exceptional amounts written off current assets

8. Other operating charges

9. Income from shares in group undertakings

10. Income from participating interests

11. Income from other fixed asset investments[13]

12. Other interest receivable and similar income[13]

13. Amounts written off investments

14. Interest payable and similar charges[14]

15. Tax on profit or loss on ordinary activities

16. Profit or loss on ordinary activities after taxation

17. Extraordinary income

18. Extraordinary charges

19. Extraordinary profit or loss

20. Tax on extraordinary profit or loss

21. Other taxes not shown under the above items

22. Profit or loss for the financial year before members' remuneration and profit shares

Notes on the profit and loss account formats

(12)   Cost of sales: distribution costs: administrative expenses

(Format 1, items 2, 4 and 5.)
   These items must be stated after taking into account any necessary provisions for depreciation or diminution in value of assets.

(13)   Income from other fixed asset investments: other interest receivable and similar income

(Format 1, items 9 and 10; Format 2, items 11 and 12.)

Income and interest derived from group undertakings must be shown separately from income and interest derived from other sources. Interest receivable from members must not be included under this item.

(14)   Interest payable and similar charges

(Format 1, item 12; Format 2, item 14.)

The amount payable to group undertakings must be shown separately. Interest payable to members must not be included under this item.

(15)   Format 1

The amount of any provisions for depreciation and diminution in value of tangible and intangible fixed assets falling to be shown under item 7(a) in Format 2 must be disclosed in a note to the accounts in any case where the profit and loss account is prepared using Format 1.

NOTES
Commencement: 1 October 2008.

PART 2
ACCOUNTING PRINCIPLES AND RULES

SECTION A
ACCOUNTING PRINCIPLES

Preliminary
[10.1086]
10. (1)   The amounts to be included in respect of all items shown in an LLP's accounts must be determined in accordance with the principles set out in this Section.

(2)   But if it appears to the LLP's members that there are special reasons for departing from any of those principles in preparing the LLP's accounts in respect of any financial year they may do so, in which case particulars of the departure, the reasons for it and its effect must be given in a note to the accounts.

Accounting principles
11.   The LLP is presumed to be carrying on business as a going concern.

12.   Accounting policies must be applied consistently within the same accounts and from one financial year to the next.

13.   The amount of any item must be determined on a prudent basis, and in particular—
   (a)   only profits realised at the balance sheet date are to be included in the profit and loss account, and
   (b)   all liabilities which have arisen in respect of the financial year to which the accounts relate or a previous financial year must be taken into account, including those which only become apparent between the balance sheet date and the date on which it is signed on behalf of the members in accordance with section 414 of the 2006 Act (approval and signing of accounts).

14.   All income and charges relating to the financial year to which the accounts relate must be taken into account, without regard to the date of receipt or payment.

15.   In determining the aggregate amount of any item, the amount of each individual asset or liability that falls to be taken into account must be determined separately.

SECTION B
HISTORICAL COST ACCOUNTING RULES

Preliminary
16.   Subject to Sections C and D of this Part of this Schedule, the amounts to be included in respect of all items shown in an LLP's accounts must be determined in accordance with the rules set out in this Section.

Fixed assets

General rules
17. (1)   The amount to be included in respect of any fixed asset must be its purchase price or production cost.

(2)   This is subject to any provision for depreciation or diminution in value made in accordance with paragraphs 18 to 20.

Rules for depreciation and diminution in value

18. In the case of any fixed asset which has a limited useful economic life, the amount of—

(a)   its purchase price or production cost, or

(b)   where it is estimated that any such asset will have a residual value at the end of the period of its useful economic life, its purchase price or production cost less that estimated residual value,

must be reduced by provisions for depreciation calculated to write off that amount systematically over the period of the asset's useful economic life.

19. (1)   Where a fixed asset investment falling to be included under item A.III of either of the balance sheet formats set out in Part 1 of this Schedule has diminished in value, provisions for diminution in value may be made in respect of it and the amount to be included in respect of it may be reduced accordingly.

(2)   Provisions for diminution in value must be made in respect of any fixed asset which has diminished in value if the reduction in its value is expected to be permanent (whether its useful economic life is limited or not), and the amount to be included in respect of it must be reduced accordingly.

(3)   Any provisions made under sub-paragraph (1) or (2) which are not shown in the profit and loss account must be disclosed (either separately or in aggregate) in a note to the accounts.

20. (1)   Where the reasons for which any provision was made in accordance with paragraph 19 have ceased to apply to any extent, that provision must be written back to the extent that it is no longer necessary.

(2)   Any amounts written back in accordance with sub-paragraph (1) which are not shown in the profit and loss account must be disclosed (either separately or in aggregate) in a note to the accounts.

Development costs

21. (1)   Notwithstanding that an item in respect of "development costs" is included under "fixed assets" in the balance sheet formats set out in Part 1 of this Schedule, an amount may only be included in an LLP's balance sheet in respect of development costs in special circumstances.

(2)   If any amount is included in an LLP's balance sheet in respect of development costs the following information must be given in a note to the accounts—

(a)   the period over which the amount of those costs originally capitalised is being or is to be written off, and

(b)   the reasons for capitalising the development costs in question.

Goodwill

22. (1)   The application of paragraphs 17 to 20 in relation to goodwill (in any case where goodwill is treated as an asset) is subject to the following.

(2)   Subject to sub-paragraph (3), the amount of the consideration for any goodwill acquired by an LLP must be reduced by provisions for depreciation calculated to write off that amount systematically over a period chosen by the members of the LLP.

(3)   The period chosen must not exceed the useful economic life of the goodwill in question.

(4)   In any case where any goodwill acquired by an LLP is shown or included as an asset in the LLP's balance sheet there must be disclosed in a note to the accounts—

(a)   the period chosen for writing off the consideration for that goodwill, and

(b)   the reasons for choosing that period.

Current assets

23. Subject to paragraph 24, the amount to be included in respect of any current asset must be its purchase price or production cost.

24. (1)   If the net realisable value of any current asset is lower than its purchase price or production cost, the amount to be included in respect of that asset must be the net realisable value.

(2)   Where the reasons for which any provision for diminution in value was made in accordance with sub-paragraph (1) have ceased to apply to any extent, that provision must be written back to the extent that it is no longer necessary.

Miscellaneous and supplementary provisions

Excess of money owed over value received as an asset item

25. (1)   Where the amount repayable on any debt owed by an LLP is greater than the value of the consideration received in the transaction giving rise to the debt, the amount of the difference may be treated as an asset.

(2)   Where any such amount is so treated—

(a)   it must be written off by reasonable amounts each year and must be completely written off before repayment of the debt, and

(b)   if the current amount is not shown as a separate item in the LLP's balance sheet, it must be disclosed in a note to the accounts.

Assets included at a fixed amount

26. (1)   Subject to sub-paragraph (2), assets which fall to be included—
 (a)   amongst the fixed assets of an LLP under the item "tangible assets", or
 (b)   amongst the current assets of an LLP under the item "raw materials and consumables", may be included at a fixed quantity and value.

(2)   Sub-paragraph (1) applies to assets of a kind which are constantly being replaced where—
 (a)   their overall value is not material to assessing the LLP's state of affairs, and
 (b)   their quantity, value and composition are not subject to material variation.

Determination of purchase price or production cost

27. (1)   The purchase price of an asset is to be determined by adding to the actual price paid any expenses incidental to its acquisition.

(2)   The production cost of an asset is to be determined by adding to the purchase price of the raw materials and consumables used the amount of the costs incurred by the LLP which are directly attributable to the production of that asset.

(3)   In addition, there may be included in the production cost of an asset—
 (a)   a reasonable proportion of the costs incurred by the LLP which are only indirectly attributable to the production of that asset, but only to the extent that they relate to the period of production, and
 (b)   interest on capital borrowed to finance the production of that asset, to the extent that it accrues in respect of the period of production,
provided, however, in a case within paragraph (b), that the inclusion of the interest in determining the cost of that asset and the amount of the interest so included is disclosed in a note to the accounts.

(4)   In the case of current assets distribution costs may not be included in production costs.

28. (1)   The purchase price or production cost of—
 (a)   any assets which fall to be included under any item shown in an LLP's balance sheet under the general item "stocks", and
 (b)   any assets which are fungible assets (including investments),
may be determined by the application of any of the methods mentioned in sub-paragraph (2) in relation to any such assets of the same class, provided that the method chosen is one which appears to the members to be appropriate in the circumstances of the LLP.

(2)   Those methods are—
 (a)   the method known as "first in, first out" (FIFO),
 (b)   the method known as "last in, first out" (LIFO),
 (c)   a weighted average price, and
 (d)   any other method similar to any of the methods mentioned above.

(3)   Where in the case of any LLP—
 (a)   the purchase price or production cost of assets falling to be included under any item shown in the LLP's balance sheet has been determined by the application of any method permitted by this paragraph, and
 (b)   the amount shown in respect of that item differs materially from the relevant alternative amount given below in this paragraph,
the amount of that difference must be disclosed in a note to the accounts.

(4)   Subject to sub-paragraph (5), for the purposes of sub-paragraph (3)(b), the relevant alternative amount, in relation to any item shown in an LLP's balance sheet, is the amount which would have been shown in respect of that item if assets of any class included under that item at an amount determined by any method permitted by this paragraph had instead been included at their replacement cost as at the balance sheet date.

(5)   The relevant alternative amount may be determined by reference to the most recent actual purchase price or production cost before the balance sheet date of assets of any class included under the item in question instead of by reference to their replacement cost as at that date, but only if the former appears to the members of the LLP to constitute the more appropriate standard of comparison in the case of assets of that class.

(6)   "Fungible assets" means assets of any description which are substantially indistinguishable one from another.

Substitution of original stated amount where price or cost unknown

29. (1)   This paragraph applies where—
 (a)   there is no record of the purchase price or production cost of any asset of an LLP or of any price, expenses or costs relevant for determining its purchase price or production cost in accordance with paragraph 27, or
 (b)   any such record cannot be obtained without unreasonable expense or delay.

(2)   In such a case, the purchase price or production cost of the asset must be taken, for the purposes of paragraphs 17 to 24, to be the value ascribed to it in the earliest available record of its value made on or after its acquisition or production by the LLP.

SECTION C
ALTERNATIVE ACCOUNTING RULES

Preliminary

30. (1)   The rules set out in Section B are referred to below in this Schedule as the historical cost accounting rules.

(2)   Those rules, with the omission of paragraphs 16, 22 and 26 to 29, are referred to below in this Part of this Schedule as the depreciation rules; and references below in this Schedule to the historical cost accounting rules do not include the depreciation rules as they apply by virtue of paragraph 33.

31.   Subject to paragraphs 33 to 35, the amounts to be included in respect of assets of any description mentioned in paragraph 32 may be determined on any basis so mentioned.

Alternative accounting rules

32. (1)   Intangible fixed assets, other than goodwill, may be included at their current cost.

(2)   Tangible fixed assets may be included at a market value determined as at the date of their last valuation or at their current cost.

(3)   Investments of any description falling to be included under item A III of either of the balance sheet formats set out in Part 1 of this Schedule may be included either—

    (a)   at a market value determined as at the date of their last valuation, or

    (b)   at a value determined on any basis which appears to the members to be appropriate in the circumstances of the LLP.

But in the latter case particulars of the method of valuation adopted and of the reasons for adopting it must be disclosed in a note to the accounts.

(4)   Investments of any description falling to be included under item B III of either of the balance sheet formats set out in Part 1 of this Schedule may be included at their current cost.

(5)   Stocks may be included at their current cost.

Application of the depreciation rules

33. (1)   Where the value of any asset of an LLP is determined on any basis mentioned in paragraph 32, that value must be, or (as the case may require) be the starting point for determining, the amount to be included in respect of that asset in the LLP's accounts, instead of its purchase price or production cost or any value previously so determined for that asset.

The depreciation rules apply accordingly in relation to any such asset with the substitution for any reference to its purchase price or production cost of a reference to the value most recently determined for that asset on any basis mentioned in paragraph 32.

(2)   The amount of any provision for depreciation required in the case of any fixed asset by paragraphs 18 to 20 as they apply by virtue of sub-paragraph (1) is referred to below in this paragraph as the adjusted amount, and the amount of any provision which would be required by any of those paragraphs in the case of that asset according to the historical cost accounting rules is referred to as the historical cost amount.

(3)   Where sub-paragraph (1) applies in the case of any fixed asset the amount of any provision for depreciation in respect of that asset—

    (a)   included in any item shown in the profit and loss account in respect of amounts written off assets of the description in question, or

    (b)   taken into account in stating any item so shown which is required by note (12) of the notes on the profit and loss account formats set out in Part 1 of this Schedule to be stated after taking into account any necessary provision for depreciation or diminution in value of assets included under it,

may be the historical cost amount instead of the adjusted amount, provided that the amount of any difference between the two is shown separately in the profit and loss account or in a note to the accounts.

Additional information to be provided in case of departure from historical cost accounting rules

34. (1)   This paragraph applies where the amounts to be included in respect of assets covered by any items shown in an LLP's accounts have been determined on any basis mentioned in paragraph 32.

(2)   The items affected and the basis of valuation adopted in determining the amounts of the assets in question in the case of each such item must be disclosed in a note to the accounts.

(3)   In the case of each balance sheet item affected (except stocks) either—

(a)   the comparable amounts determined according to the historical cost accounting rules, or

(b)   the differences between those amounts and the corresponding amounts actually shown in the balance sheet in respect of that item,

must be shown separately in the balance sheet or in a note to the accounts.

(4)   In sub-paragraph (3), references in relation to any item to the comparable amounts determined as there mentioned are references to—

(a)   the aggregate amount which would be required to be shown in respect of that item if the amounts to be included in respect of all the assets covered by that item were determined according to the historical cost accounting rules, and

(b)   the aggregate amount of the cumulative provisions for depreciation or diminution in value which would be permitted or required in determining those amounts according to those rules.

Revaluation reserve

35. (1)   With respect to any determination of the value of an asset of an LLP on any basis mentioned in paragraph 32, the amount of any profit or loss arising from that determination (after allowing, where appropriate, for any provisions for depreciation or diminution in value made otherwise than by reference to the value so determined and any adjustments of any such provisions made in the light of that determination) must be credited or (as the case may be) debited to a separate reserve ("the revaluation reserve").

(2)   The amount of the revaluation reserve must be shown in the LLP's balance sheet under a separate sub-heading in the position given for the item "revaluation reserve" in Format 1 or 2 of the balance sheet formats set out in Part 1 of this Schedule, but need not be shown under that name.

(3)   The treatment for taxation purposes of amounts credited or debited to the revaluation reserve must be disclosed in a note to the accounts.

<h2 style="text-align:center">Section D
Fair Value Accounting</h2>

Inclusion of financial instruments at fair value

36. (1)   Subject to sub-paragraphs (2) to (5), financial instruments (including derivatives) may be included at fair value.

(2)   Sub-paragraph (1) does not apply to financial instruments that constitute liabilities unless—

(a)   they are held as part of a trading portfolio,

(b)   they are derivatives, or

(c)   they are financial instruments falling within sub-paragraph (4).

(3)   Unless they are financial instruments falling within sub-paragraph (4), sub-paragraph (1) does not apply to—

(a)   financial instruments (other than derivatives) held to maturity,

(b)   loans and receivables originated by the LLP and not held for trading purposes,

(c)   interests in subsidiary undertakings, associated undertakings and joint ventures,

(d)   equity instruments issued by the LLP,

(e)   contracts for contingent consideration in a business combination, or

(f)   other financial instruments with such special characteristics that the instruments, according to generally accepted accounting principles or practice, should be accounted for differently from other financial instruments.

(4)   Financial instruments that, under international accounting standards adopted by the European Commission on or before 5th September 2006 in accordance with the IAS Regulation, may be included in accounts at fair value, may be so included, provided that the disclosures required by such accounting standards are made.

(5)   If the fair value of a financial instrument cannot be determined reliably in accordance with paragraph 37, sub-paragraph (1) does not apply to that financial instrument.

(6)   In this paragraph—

"associated undertaking" has the meaning given by paragraph 19 of Schedule 3 to these Regulations;

"joint venture" has the meaning given by paragraph 18 of that Schedule.

Determination of fair value

37. (1)   The fair value of a financial instrument is its value determined in accordance with this paragraph.

(2)   If a reliable market can readily be identified for the financial instrument, its fair value is determined by reference to its market value.

(3)   If a reliable market cannot readily be identified for the financial instrument but can be identified for its components or for a similar instrument, its fair value is determined by reference to the market value of its components or of the similar instrument.

Part 10   Miscellaneous other SIs

(4)   If neither sub-paragraph (2) nor (3) applies, the fair value of the financial instrument is a value resulting from generally accepted valuation models and techniques.

(5)   Any valuation models and techniques used for the purposes of sub-paragraph (4) must ensure a reasonable approximation of the market value.

Hedged items

38. An LLP may include any assets and liabilities, or identified portions of such assets or liabilities, that qualify as hedged items under a fair value hedge accounting system at the amount required under that system.

Other assets that may be included at fair value

39. (1)   This paragraph applies to—
   (a)   investment property, and
   (b)   living animals and plants,
that, under international accounting standards, may be included in accounts at fair value.

(2)   Such investment property and such living animals and plants may be included at fair value, provided that all such investment property or, as the case may be, all such living animals and plants are so included where their fair value can reliably be determined.

(3)   In this paragraph, "fair value" means fair value determined in accordance with relevant international accounting standards.

Accounting for changes in value

40. (1)   This paragraph applies where a financial instrument is valued in accordance with paragraph 36 or 38 or an asset is valued in accordance with paragraph 39.

(2)   Notwithstanding paragraph 13 in this Part of this Schedule, and subject to sub-paragraphs (3) and (4), a change in the value of the financial instrument or of the investment property or living animal or plant must be included in the profit and loss account.

(3)   Where—
   (a)   the financial instrument accounted for is a hedging instrument under a hedge accounting system that allows some or all of the change in value not to be shown in the profit and loss account, or
   (b)   the change in value relates to an exchange difference arising on a monetary item that forms part of an LLP's net investment in a foreign entity,
the amount of the change in value must be credited to or (as the case may be) debited from a separate reserve ("the fair value reserve").

(4)   Where the instrument accounted for—
   (a)   is an available for sale financial asset, and
   (b)   is not a derivative,
the change in value may be credited to or (as the case may be) debited from the fair value reserve.

The fair value reserve

41. (1)   The fair value reserve must be adjusted to the extent that the amounts shown in it are no longer necessary for the purposes of paragraph 40(3) or (4).

(2)   The treatment for taxation purposes of amounts credited or debited to the fair value reserve must be disclosed in a note to the accounts.

NOTES
   Commencement: 1 October 2008.

PART 3
NOTES TO THE ACCOUNTS

Preliminary

[10.1087]

42. Any information required in the case of any LLP by the following provisions of this Part of this Schedule must (if not given in the LLP's accounts) be given by way of a note to the accounts.

General

Reserves

43. Any amount set aside or proposed to be set aside to, or withdrawn or proposed to be withdrawn from, reserves must be stated.

Disclosure of accounting policies

44. The accounting policies adopted by the LLP in determining the amounts to be included in respect of items shown in the balance sheet and in determining the profit or loss of the LLP must be stated (including such policies with respect to the depreciation and diminution in value of assets).

45. It must be stated whether the accounts have been prepared in accordance with applicable accounting standards and particulars of any material departure from those standards and the reasons for it must be given (see regulation 4 for exemption for medium-sized LLPs).

Information supplementing the balance sheet

46. Paragraphs 47 to 61 require information which either supplements the information given with respect to any particular items shown in the balance sheet or is otherwise relevant to assessing the LLP's state of affairs in the light of the information so given.

Loans and other debts due to members

47. The following information must be given—
- (a)   the aggregate amount of loans and other debts due to members as at the date of the beginning of the financial year,
- (b)   the aggregate amounts contributed by members during the financial year,
- (c)   the aggregate amounts transferred to or from the profit and loss account during that year,
- (d)   the aggregate amounts withdrawn by members or applied on behalf of members during that year,
- (e)   the aggregate amount of loans and other debts due to members as at the balance sheet date, and
- (f)   the aggregate amount of loans and other debts due to members that fall due after one year.

Debentures

48. (1) If the LLP has issued any debentures during the financial year to which the accounts relate, the following information must be given—
- (a)   the classes of debentures issued, and
- (b)   as respects each class of debentures, the amount issued and the consideration received by the LLP for the issue.

(2)   Where any of the LLP's debentures are held by a nominee of or trustee for the LLP, the nominal amount of the debentures and the amount at which they are stated in the accounting records kept by the LLP in accordance with section 386 of the 2006 Act (duty to keep accounting records) must be stated.

Fixed assets

49. (1)   In respect of each item which is or would but for paragraph 4(2)(b) be shown under the general item "fixed assets" in the LLP's balance sheet the following information must be given—
- (a)   the appropriate amounts in respect of that item as at the date of the beginning of the financial year and as at the balance sheet date respectively,
- (b)   the effect on any amount shown in the balance sheet in respect of that item of—
  - (i)   any revision of the amount in respect of any assets included under that item made during that year on any basis mentioned in paragraph 32,
  - (ii)   acquisitions during that year of any assets,
  - (iii) disposals during that year of any assets, and
  - (iv)   any transfers of assets of the LLP to and from that item during that year.

(2)   The reference in sub-paragraph (1)(a) to the appropriate amounts in respect of any item as at any date there mentioned is a reference to amounts representing the aggregate amounts determined, as at that date, in respect of assets falling to be included under that item on either of the following bases, that is to say—
- (a)   on the basis of purchase price or production cost (determined in accordance with paragraphs 27 and 28), or
- (b)   on any basis mentioned in paragraph 32,

(leaving out of account in either case any provisions for depreciation or diminution in value).

(3)   In respect of each item within sub-paragraph (1) there must also be stated—
- (a)   the cumulative amount of provisions for depreciation or diminution in value of assets included under that item as at each date mentioned in sub-paragraph (1)(a),
- (b)   the amount of any such provisions made in respect of the financial year,
- (c)   the amount of any adjustments made in respect of any such provisions during that year in consequence of the disposal of any assets, and
- (d)   the amount of any other adjustments made in respect of any such provisions during that year.

50. Where any fixed assets of the LLP (other than listed investments) are included under any item shown in the LLP's balance sheet at an amount determined on any basis mentioned in paragraph 32, the following information must be given—
- (a) the years (so far as they are known to the members) in which the assets were severally valued and the several values, and
- (b) in the case of assets that have been valued during the financial year, the names of the persons who valued them or particulars of their qualifications for doing so and (whichever is stated) the bases of valuation used by them.

51. (1) In relation to any amount which is or would but for paragraph 4(2)(b) be shown in respect of the item "land and buildings" in the LLP's balance sheet there must be stated—
- (a) how much of that amount is ascribable to land of freehold tenure and how much to land of leasehold tenure, and
- (b) how much of the amount ascribable to land of leasehold tenure is ascribable to land held on long lease and how much to land held on short lease.

(2) In this paragraph—
- (a) "long lease" means a lease in the case of which the portion of the term for which it was granted remaining unexpired at the end of the financial year is not less than 50 years,
- (b) "short lease" means a lease which is not a long lease, and
- (c) "lease" includes an agreement for a lease.

(3) In the application of this regulation to Scotland, "land of freehold tenure" means land in respect of which the LLP is the owner; "land of leasehold tenure" means land of which the company is the tenant under a lease.

Investments

52. (1) In respect of the amount of each item which is or would but for paragraph 4(2)(b) be shown in the LLP's balance sheet under the general item "investments" (whether as fixed assets or as current assets) there must be stated how much of that amount is ascribable to listed investments.

(2) Where the amount of any listed investments is stated for any item in accordance with sub-paragraph (1), the following amounts must also be stated—
- (a) the aggregate market value of those investments where it differs from the amount so stated, and
- (b) both the market value and the stock exchange value of any investments of which the former value is, for the purposes of the accounts, taken as being higher than the latter.

Information about fair value of assets and liabilities

53. (1) This paragraph applies where financial instruments have been valued in accordance with paragraph 36 or 38.

(2) There must be stated—
- (a) the significant assumptions underlying the valuation models and techniques used where the fair value of the instruments has been determined in accordance with paragraph 37(4),
- (b) for each category of financial instrument, the fair value of the instruments in that category and the changes in value—
  - (i) included in the profit and loss account, or
  - (ii) credited to or (as the case may be) debited from the fair value reserve,
  - in respect of those instruments, and
- (c) for each class of derivatives, the extent and nature of the instruments, including significant terms and conditions that may affect the amount, timing and certainty of future cash flows.

(3) Where any amount is transferred to or from the fair value reserve during the financial year, there must be stated in tabular form—
- (a) the amount of the reserve as at the date of the beginning of the financial year and as at the balance sheet date respectively,
- (b) the amount transferred to or from the reserve during that year, and
- (c) the source and application respectively of the amounts so transferred.

54. Where the LLP has derivatives that it has not included at fair value, there must be stated for each class of such derivatives—
- (a) the fair value of the derivatives in that class, if such a value can be determined in accordance with paragraph 37, and
- (b) the extent and nature of the derivatives.

55. (1) This paragraph applies if—
- (a) the LLP has financial fixed assets that could be included at fair value by virtue of paragraph 36,
- (b) the amount at which those items are included under any item in the LLP's accounts is in excess of their fair value, and
- (c) the LLP has not made provision for diminution in value of those assets in accordance with paragraph 19(1) of this Schedule.

(2)   There must be stated—
  (a)   the amount at which either the individual assets or appropriate groupings of those individual assets are included in the LLP's accounts,
  (b)   the fair value of those assets or groupings, and
  (c)   the reasons for not making a provision for diminution in value of those assets, including the nature of the evidence that provides the basis for the belief that the amount at which they are stated in the accounts will be recovered.

Information where investment property and living animals and plants included at fair value

56.   (1)   This paragraph applies where the amounts to be included in an LLP's accounts in respect of investment property or living animals and plants have been determined in accordance with paragraph 39.

(2)   The balance sheet items affected and the basis of valuation adopted in determining the amounts of the assets in question in the case of each such item must be disclosed in a note to the accounts.

(3)   In the case of investment property, for each balance sheet item affected there must be shown, either separately in the balance sheet or in a note to the accounts—
  (a)   the comparable amounts determined according to the historical cost accounting rules, or
  (b)   the differences between those amounts and the corresponding amounts actually shown in the balance sheet in respect of that item.

(4)   In sub-paragraph (3), references in relation to any item to the comparable amounts determined in accordance with that sub-paragraph are to—
  (a)   the aggregate amount which would be required to be shown in respect of that item if the amounts to be included in respect of all the assets covered by that item were determined according to the historical cost accounting rules, and
  (b)   the aggregate amount of the cumulative provisions for depreciation or diminution in value which would be permitted or required in determining those amounts according to those rules.

Reserves and provisions

57.   (1)   This paragraph applies where any amount is transferred—
  (a)   to or from any reserves, or
  (b)   to any provision for liabilities, or
  (c)   from any provision for liabilities otherwise than for the purpose for which the provision was established,
and the reserves or provisions are or would but for paragraph 4(2)(b) be shown as separate items in the LLP's balance sheet.

(2)   The following information must be given in respect of the aggregate of reserves or provisions included in the same item—
  (a)   the amount of the reserves or provisions as at the date of the beginning of the financial year and as at the balance sheet date respectively,
  (b)   any amounts transferred to or from the reserves or provisions during that year, and
  (c)   the source and application respectively of any amounts so transferred.

(3)   Particulars must be given of each provision included in the item "other provisions" in the LLP's balance sheet in any case where the amount of that provision is material.

Provision for taxation

58.   The amount of any provision for deferred taxation must be stated separately from the amount of any provision for other taxation.

Details of indebtedness

59.   (1)   For the aggregate of all items shown under "creditors" in the LLP's balance sheet there must be stated the aggregate of the following amounts—
  (a)   the amount of any debts included under "creditors" which are payable or repayable otherwise than by instalments and fall due for payment or repayment after the end of the period of five years beginning with the day next following the end of the financial year, and
  (b)   in the case of any debts so included which are payable or repayable by instalments, the amount of any instalments which fall due for payment after the end of that period.

(2)   Subject to sub-paragraph (3), in relation to each debt falling to be taken into account under sub-paragraph (1), the terms of payment or repayment and the rate of any interest payable on the debt must be stated.

(3)   If the number of debts is such that, in the opinion of the members, compliance with sub-paragraph (2) would result in a statement of excessive length, it is sufficient to give a general indication of the terms of payment or repayment and the rates of any interest payable on the debts.

(4)   In respect of each item shown under "creditors" in the LLP's balance sheet there must be stated—

(a)   the aggregate amount of any debts included under that item in respect of which any security has been given by the LLP, and

(b)   an indication of the nature of the securities so given.

(5)   References above in this paragraph to an item shown under "creditors" in the LLP's balance sheet include references, where amounts falling due to creditors within one year and after more than one year are distinguished in the balance sheet—

(a)   in a case within sub-paragraph (1), to an item shown under the latter of those categories, and

(b)   in a case within sub-paragraph (4), to an item shown under either of those categories.

References to items shown under "creditors" include references to items which would but for paragraph 4(2)(b) be shown under that heading.

Guarantees and other financial commitments

60.   (1)   Particulars must be given of any charge on the assets of the LLP to secure the liabilities of any other person, including, where practicable, the amount secured.

(2)   The following information must be given with respect to any other contingent liability not provided for—

(a)   the amount or estimated amount of that liability,

(b)   its legal nature, and

(c)   whether any valuable security has been provided by the LLP in connection with that liability and if so, what.

(3)   There must be stated, where practicable, the aggregate amount or estimated amount of contracts for capital expenditure, so far as not provided for.

(4)   Particulars must be given of—

(a)   any pension commitments included under any provision shown in the LLP's balance sheet, and

(b)   any such commitments for which no provision has been made,

and where any such commitment relates wholly or partly to pensions payable to past members of the LLP separate particulars must be given of that commitment so far as it relates to such pensions.

(5)   Particulars must also be given of any other financial commitments that—

(a)   have not been provided for, and

(b)   are relevant to assessing the LLP's state of affairs.

Miscellaneous matters

61.   Particulars must be given of any case where the purchase price or production cost of any asset is for the first time determined under paragraph 29.

Information supplementing the profit and loss account

62.   Paragraphs 63 to 67 require information which either supplements the information given with respect to any particular items shown in the profit and loss account or otherwise provides particulars of income or expenditure of the LLP or of circumstances affecting the items shown in the profit and loss account (see regulation 3 for exemption for LLP falling within section 408 of the 2006 Act (individual profit and loss account where group accounts prepared)).

Separate statement of certain items of income and expenditure

63.   (1)   Subject to sub-paragraph (2), there must be stated the amount of the interest on or any similar charges in respect of bank loans and overdrafts, and loans of any other kind made to the LLP.

(2)   Sub-paragraph (1) does not apply to interest or charges on loans to the LLP from group undertakings, but, with that exception, it applies to interest or charges on all loans, whether made on the security of debentures or not.

Particulars of tax

64.   (1)   Particulars must be given of any special circumstances which affect liability in respect of taxation of profits, income or capital gains for the financial year or liability in respect of taxation of profits, income or capital gains for succeeding financial years.

(2)   The following amounts must be stated—

(a)   the amount of the charge for United Kingdom corporation tax,

(b)   if that amount would have been greater but for relief from double taxation, the amount which it would have been but for such relief,

(c)   the amount of the charge for United Kingdom income tax, and

(d)   the amount of the charge for taxation imposed outside the United Kingdom of profits, income and (so far as charged to revenue) capital gains.

These amounts must be stated separately in respect of each of the amounts which is or would but for paragraph 4(2)(b) be shown under the items "tax on profit or loss on ordinary activities" and "tax on extraordinary profit or loss" in the profit and loss account.

Particulars of turnover

65. (1) If in the course of the financial year the LLP has carried on business of two or more classes that, in the opinion of the members, differ substantially from each other, the amount of the turnover attributable to each class must be stated and the class described (see regulation 4(3)(b) for exemption for medium-sized LLP in accounts delivered to registrar).

(2) If in the course of the financial year the LLP has supplied markets that, in the opinion of the members, differ substantially from each other, the amount of the turnover attributable to each such market must also be stated.

In this paragraph "market" means a market delimited by geographical bounds.

(3) In analysing for the purposes of this paragraph the source (in terms of business or in terms of market) of turnover, the members of the LLP must have regard to the manner in which the LLP's activities are organised.

(4) For the purposes of this paragraph—

    (a)   classes of business which, in the opinion of the members, do not differ substantially from each other must be treated as one class, and

    (b)   markets which, in the opinion of the members, do not differ substantially from each other must be treated as one market,

and any amounts properly attributable to one class of business or (as the case may be) to one market which are not material may be included in the amount stated in respect of another.

(5) Where in the opinion of the members the disclosure of any information required by this paragraph would be seriously prejudicial to the interests of the LLP, that information need not be disclosed, but the fact that any such information has not been disclosed must be stated.

Particulars of members

66. (1) Particulars must be given of the average number of members of the LLP in the financial year, which number is to be determined by dividing the relevant annual number by the number of months in the financial year.

(2) The relevant annual number is to be determined by ascertaining for each month in the financial year the number of members of the LLP for all or part of that month, and adding together all the monthly numbers.

(3) Where the amount of the profit of the LLP for the financial year before members' remuneration and profit shares exceeds £200,000, there must be disclosed the amount of profit (including remuneration) which is attributable to the member with the largest entitlement to profit (including remuneration).

(4) For the purpose of determining the amount to be disclosed under sub-paragraph (3), "remuneration" includes any emoluments specified in paragraph 1(1)(a), (c) or (d) of Schedule 5 to the Large and Medium-sized Companies and Groups (Accounts and Reports) Regulations 2008(12) receivable from—

    (a)   the LLP,

    (b)   the LLP's subsidiary undertakings, and

    (c)   any other person.

Miscellaneous matters

67. (1) Where any amount relating to any preceding financial year is included in any item in the profit and loss account, the effect must be stated.

(2) Particulars must be given of any extraordinary income or charges arising in the financial year.

(3) The effect must be stated of any transactions that are exceptional by virtue of size or incidence though they fall within the ordinary activities of the LLP.

Sums denominated in foreign currencies

68. Where any sums originally denominated in foreign currencies have been brought into account under any items shown in the balance sheet format or profit and loss account formats, the basis on which those sums have been translated into sterling (or the currency in which the accounts are drawn up) must be stated.

Dormant LLPs acting as agents

69. Where the members of an LLP take advantage of the exemption conferred by section 480 of the 2006 Act (dormant LLPs: exemption from audit), and the LLP has during the financial year in question acted as an agent for any person, the fact that it has so acted must be stated.

Related party transactions

70. (1) Particulars may be given of transactions which the LLP has entered into with related parties, and must be given if such transactions are material and have not been concluded under normal market conditions (see regulation 4 for exemption for medium-sized LLPs).

(2) The particulars of transactions required to be disclosed by sub-paragraph (1) must include—

    (a)   the amount of such transactions,

(b)   the nature of the related party relationship, and

(c)   other information about the transactions necessary for an understanding of the financial position of the LLP.

(3)   Information about individual transactions may be aggregated according to their nature, except where separate information is necessary for an understanding of the effects of related party transactions on the financial position of the LLP.

(4)   Particulars need not be given of transactions entered into between two or more members of a group, provided that any subsidiary undertaking which is a party to the transaction is wholly-owned by such a member.

(5)   In this paragraph, "related party" has the same meaning as in international accounting standards.

NOTES
Commencement: 1 October 2008.

PART 4
SPECIAL PROVISION WHERE LLP IS A PARENT LLP OR SUBSIDIARY UNDERTAKING

LLP's own accounts: guarantees and other financial commitments in favour of group undertakings

[10.1088]

71.   Commitments within any of sub-paragraphs (1) to (5) of paragraph 60 (guarantees and other financial commitments) which are undertaken on behalf of or for the benefit of—

(a)   any parent undertaking or fellow subsidiary undertaking, or

(b)   any subsidiary undertaking of the LLP,

must be stated separately from the other commitments within that paragraph, and commitments within paragraph (a) must also be stated separately from those within paragraph (b).

NOTES
Commencement: 1 October 2008.

SCHEDULE 2
INFORMATION ON RELATED UNDERTAKINGS REQUIRED WHETHER PREPARING NON-IAS OR IAS ACCOUNTS
Regulation 5

PART 1
PROVISIONS APPLYING TO ALL LLPS

Subsidiary undertakings

[10.1089]

1.   (1)   The following information must be given where at the end of the financial year the LLP has subsidiary undertakings.

(2)   The name of each subsidiary undertaking must be stated.

(3)   There must be stated with respect to each subsidiary undertaking—

(a)   if it is incorporated outside the United Kingdom, the country in which it is incorporated,

(b)   if it is unincorporated, the address of its principal place of business.

Financial information about subsidiary undertakings

2.   (1)   There must be disclosed with respect to each subsidiary undertaking not included in consolidated accounts by the LLP—

(a)   the aggregate amount of its capital and reserves as at the end of its relevant financial year, and

(b)   its profit or loss for that year.

(2)   That information need not be given if the LLP is exempt by virtue of section 400 or 401 of the 2006 Act from the requirement to prepare group accounts (parent LLP included in accounts of larger group).

(3)   That information need not be given if the LLP's investment in the subsidiary undertaking is included in the LLP's accounts by way of the equity method of valuation.

(4)   That information need not be given if—

(a)   the subsidiary undertaking is not required by any provision of the 2006 Act to deliver a copy of its balance sheet for its relevant financial year and does not otherwise publish that balance sheet in the United Kingdom or elsewhere, and

(b)   the LLP's holding is less than 50% of the nominal value of the shares in the undertaking.

(5)   Information otherwise required by this paragraph need not be given if it is not material.

(6)   For the purposes of this paragraph the "relevant financial year" of a subsidiary undertaking is—
- (a)   if its financial year ends with that of the LLP, that year, and
- (b)   if not, its financial year ending last before the end of the LLP's financial year.

Significant holdings in undertakings other than subsidiary undertakings
3. (1)   The information required by paragraphs 4 and 5 must be given where at the end of the financial year the LLP has a significant holding in an undertaking which is not a subsidiary undertaking of the LLP, and which does not fall within paragraph 16 (joint ventures) or 17 (associated undertakings).

(2)   A holding is significant for this purpose if—
- (a)   it amounts to 20% or more of the nominal value of any class of shares in the undertaking, or
- (b)   the amount of the holding (as stated or included in the LLP's individual accounts) exceeds one-fifth of the amount (as so stated) of the LLP's assets.

4. (1)   The name of the undertaking must be stated.

(2)   There must be stated—
- (a)   if the undertaking is incorporated outside the United Kingdom, the country in which it is incorporated,
- (b)   if it is unincorporated, the address of its principal place of business.

(3)   There must also be stated—
- (a)   the identity of each class of shares in the undertaking held by the LLP, and
- (b)   the proportion of the nominal value of the shares of that class represented by those shares.

5. (1)   Subject to paragraph 12, there must also be stated—
- (a)   the aggregate amount of the capital and reserves of the undertaking as at the end of its relevant financial year, and
- (b)   its profit or loss for that year.

(2)   That information need not be given in respect of an undertaking if—
- (a)   the undertaking is not required by any provision of the 2006 Act to deliver a copy of its balance sheet for its relevant financial year and does not otherwise publish that balance sheet in the United Kingdom or elsewhere, and
- (b)   the LLP's holding is less than 50% of the nominal value of the shares in the undertaking.

(3)   Information otherwise required by this paragraph need not be given if it is not material.

(4)   For the purposes of this paragraph the "relevant financial year" of an undertaking is—
- (a)   if its financial year ends with that of the LLP, that year, and
- (b)   if not, its financial year ending last before the end of the LLP's financial year.

Parent undertaking drawing up accounts for larger group
6. (1)   Where the LLP is a subsidiary undertaking, the following information must be given with respect to the parent undertaking of—
- (a)   the largest group of undertakings for which group accounts are drawn up and of which the LLP is a member, and
- (b)   the smallest such group of undertakings.

(2)   The name of the parent undertaking must be stated.

(3)   There must be stated—
- (a)   if the undertaking is incorporated outside the United Kingdom, the country in which it is incorporated,
- (b)   if it is unincorporated, the address of its principal place of business.

(4)   If copies of the group accounts referred to in sub-paragraph (1) are available to the public, there must also be stated the addresses from which copies of the accounts can be obtained.

Identification of ultimate parent
7. (1)   Where the LLP is a subsidiary undertaking, the following information must be given with respect to the body corporate (if any) regarded by the members as being the LLP's ultimate parent.

(2)   The name of that body corporate must be stated.

(3)   If that body corporate is incorporated outside the United Kingdom, the country in which it is incorporated must be stated (if known to the members).

NOTES

Commencement: 1 October 2008.

(Right margin, vertical:) **Part 10   Miscellaneous other SIs**

PART 2
LLP NOT REQUIRED TO PREPARE GROUP ACCOUNTS

Reason for not preparing group accounts

[10.1090]
8. (1)   The reason why the LLP is not required to prepare group accounts must be stated.

(2)   If the reason is that all the subsidiary undertakings of the LLP fall within the exclusions provided for in section 405 of the 2006 Act (non-IAS group accounts: subsidiary undertakings included in the consolidation), it must be stated with respect to each subsidiary undertaking which of those exclusions applies.

Holdings in subsidiary undertakings

9. (1)   There must be stated in relation to shares of each class held by the LLP in a subsidiary undertaking—
   (a)   the identity of the class, and
   (b)   the proportion of the nominal value of the shares of that class represented by those shares.

(2)   The shares held by or on behalf of the LLP itself must be distinguished from those attributed to the LLP which are held by or on behalf of a subsidiary undertaking.

Financial years of subsidiary undertakings

10.   Where—
   (a)   disclosure is made under paragraph 2(1) with respect to a subsidiary undertaking, and
   (b)   that undertaking's financial year does not end with that of the LLP,

there must be stated in relation to that undertaking the date on which its last financial year ended (last before the end of the LLP's financial year).

Exemption from giving information about significant holdings in non-subsidiary undertakings

11.   The information otherwise required by paragraph 3 (significant holdings in undertakings other than subsidiary undertaking) need not be given if—
   (a)   the LLP is exempt by virtue of section 400 or 401 of the 2006 Act from the requirement to prepare group accounts (parent LLP included in accounts of larger group), and
   (b)   the investment of the LLP in all undertakings in which it has such a holding as is mentioned in sub-paragraph (1) is shown, in aggregate, in the notes to the accounts by way of the equity method of valuation.

Construction of references to shares held by LLP

12. (1)   References in Parts 1 and 2 of this Schedule to shares held by an LLP are to be construed as follows.

(2)   For the purposes of paragraphs 2, 9 and 10 (information about subsidiary undertakings)—
   (a)   there must be attributed to the LLP any shares held by a subsidiary undertaking, or by a person acting on behalf of the LLP or a subsidiary undertaking; but
   (b)   there must be treated as not held by the LLP any shares held on behalf of a person other than the LLP or a subsidiary undertaking.

(3)   For the purposes of paragraphs 3 to 5 (information about undertakings other than subsidiary undertakings)—
   (a)   there must be attributed to the LLP shares held on its behalf by any person; but
   (b)   there must be treated as not held by an LLP shares held on behalf of a person other than the LLP.

(4)   For the purposes of any of those provisions, shares held by way of security must be treated as held by the person providing the security—
   (a)   where apart from the right to exercise them for the purpose of preserving the value of the security, or of realising it, the rights attached to the shares are exercisable only in accordance with that person's instructions, and
   (b)   where the shares are held in connection with the granting of loans as part of normal business activities and apart from the right to exercise them for the purpose of preserving the value of the security, or of realising it, the rights attached to the shares are exercisable only in that person's interests.

NOTES
Commencement: 1 October 2008.

PART 3
LLP REQUIRED TO PREPARE GROUP ACCOUNTS

Introductory

[10.1091]

13. In this Part of this Schedule "the group" means the group consisting of the parent LLP and its subsidiary undertakings.

Subsidiary undertakings

14. (1)   In addition to the information required by paragraph 2, the following information must also be given with respect to the undertakings which are subsidiary undertakings of the parent LLP at the end of the financial year.

(2)   It must be stated whether the subsidiary undertaking is included in the consolidation and, if it is not, the reasons for excluding it from consolidation must be given.

(3)   It must be stated with respect to each subsidiary undertaking by virtue of which of the conditions specified in section 1162(2) or (4) of the 2006 Act it is a subsidiary undertaking of its immediate parent undertaking.

That information need not be given if the relevant condition is that specified in subsection (2)(a) of that section (holding of a majority of the voting rights) and the immediate parent undertaking holds the same proportion of the shares in the undertaking as it holds voting rights.

Holdings in subsidiary undertakings

15. (1)   The following information must be given with respect to the shares of a subsidiary undertaking held—

    (a)   by the parent LLP, and

    (b)   by the group,

and the information under paragraphs (a) and (b) must (if different) be shown separately.

(2)   There must be stated—

    (a)   the identity of each class of shares held, and

    (b)   the proportion of the nominal value of the shares of that class represented by those shares.

Joint ventures

16. (1)   The following information must be given where an undertaking is dealt with in the consolidated accounts by the method of proportional consolidation in accordance with paragraph 18 of Schedule 3 to these Regulations (joint ventures)—

    (a)   the name of the undertaking,

    (b)   the address of the principal place of business of the undertaking,

    (c)   the factors on which joint management of the undertaking is based, and

    (d)   the proportion of the capital of the undertaking held by undertakings included in the consolidation.

(2)   Where the financial year of the undertaking did not end with that of the LLP, there must be stated the date on which a financial year of the undertaking last ended before that date.

Associated undertakings

17. (1)   The following information must be given where an undertaking included in the consolidation has an interest in an associated undertaking.

(2)   The name of the associated undertaking must be stated.

(3)   There must be stated—

    (a)   if the undertaking is incorporated outside the United Kingdom, the country in which it is incorporated,

    (b)   if it is unincorporated, the address of its principal place of business.

(4)   The following information must be given with respect to the shares of the undertaking held—

    (a)   by the parent LLP, and

    (b)   by the group,

and the information under paragraphs (a) and (b) must be shown separately.

(5)   There must be stated—

    (a)   the identity of each class of shares held, and

    (b)   the proportion of the nominal value of the shares of that class represented by those shares.

(6)   In this paragraph "associated undertaking" has the meaning given by paragraph 19 of Schedule 3 to these Regulations; and the information required by this paragraph must be given notwithstanding that paragraph 21(3) of that Schedule (materiality) applies in relation to the accounts themselves.

Requirement to give information about other significant holdings of parent LLP or group

18. (1) The information required by paragraphs 4 and 5 must also be given where at the end of the financial year the group has a significant holding in an undertaking which is not a subsidiary undertaking of the parent LLP and does not fall within paragraph 16 (joint ventures) or 17 (associated undertakings), as though the references to the LLP in those paragraphs were a reference to the group.

(2) A holding is significant for this purpose if—
   (a) it amounts to 20% or more of the nominal value of any class of shares in the undertaking, or
   (b) the amount of the holding (as stated or included in the group accounts) exceeds one-fifth of the amount of the group's assets (as so stated).

(3) For the purposes of those paragraphs as applied to a group the "relevant financial year" of an outside undertaking is—
   (a) if its financial year ends with that of the parent LLP, that year, and
   (b) if not, its financial year ending last before the end of the parent LLP's financial year.

Construction of references to shares held by parent LLP or group

19. (1) References in Parts 1 and 3 of this Schedule to shares held by that parent LLP or group are to be construed as follows.

(2) For the purposes of paragraphs 3 to 5, 15 and 17(4) and (5) (information about holdings in subsidiary and other undertakings)—
   (a) there must be attributed to the parent LLP shares held on its behalf by any person; but
   (b) there must be treated as not held by the parent LLP shares held on behalf of a person other than the LLP.

(3) References to shares held by the group are to any shares held by or on behalf of the parent LLP or any of its subsidiary undertakings; but any shares held on behalf of a person other than the parent LLP or any of its subsidiary undertakings are not to be treated as held by the group.

(4) Shares held by way of security must be treated as held by the person providing the security—
   (a) where apart from the right to exercise them for the purpose of preserving the value of the security, or of realising it, the rights attached to the shares are exercisable only in accordance with his instructions, and
   (b) where the shares are held in connection with the granting of loans as part of normal business activities and apart from the right to exercise them for the purpose of preserving the value of the security, or of realising it, the rights attached to the shares are exercisable only in his interests.

NOTES

Commencement: 1 October 2008.

SCHEDULE 3
NON-IAS GROUP ACCOUNTS

Regulation 6

General rules

[10.1092]
1. Group accounts must comply so far as practicable with the provisions of Schedule 1 to these Regulations as if the undertakings included in the consolidation ("the group") were a single LLP.

2. (1) The consolidated balance sheet and profit and loss account must incorporate in full the information contained in the individual accounts of the undertakings included in the consolidation, subject to the adjustments authorised or required by the following provisions of this Schedule and to such other adjustments (if any) as may be appropriate in accordance with generally accepted accounting principles or practice.

(2) If the financial year of a subsidiary undertaking included in the consolidation does not end with that of the parent LLP, the group accounts must be made up—
   (a) from the accounts of the subsidiary undertaking for its financial year last ending before the end of the parent LLP's financial year, provided that year ended no more than three months before that of the parent LLP, or
   (b) from interim accounts prepared by the subsidiary undertaking as at the end of the parent LLP's financial year.

3. (1) Where assets and liabilities to be included in the group accounts have been valued or otherwise determined by undertakings according to accounting rules differing from those used for the group accounts, the values or amounts must be adjusted so as to accord with the rules used for the group accounts.

(2) If it appears to the members of the parent LLP that there are special reasons for departing from sub-paragraph (1) they may do so, but particulars of any such departure, the reasons for it and its effect must be given in a note to the accounts.

(3)   The adjustments referred to in this paragraph need not be made if they are not material for the purpose of giving a true and fair view.

4. Any differences of accounting rules as between a parent LLP's individual accounts for a financial year and its group accounts must be disclosed in a note to the latter accounts and the reasons for the difference given.

5. Amounts that in the particular context of any provision of this Schedule are not material may be disregarded for the purposes of that provision.

Elimination of group transactions

6. (1)   Debts and claims between undertakings included in the consolidation, and income and expenditure relating to transactions between such undertakings, must be eliminated in preparing the group accounts.

(2)   Where profits and losses resulting from transactions between undertakings included in the consolidation are included in the book value of assets, they must be eliminated in preparing the group accounts.

(3)   The elimination required by sub-paragraph (2) may be effected in proportion to the group's interest in the shares of the undertakings.

(4)   Sub-paragraphs (1) and (2) need not be complied with if the amounts concerned are not material for the purpose of giving a true and fair view.

Acquisition and merger accounting

7. (1)   The following provisions apply where an undertaking becomes a subsidiary undertaking of the parent LLP.

(2)   That event is referred to in those provisions as an "acquisition", and references to the "undertaking acquired" are to be construed accordingly.

8. An acquisition must be accounted for by the acquisition method of accounting unless the conditions for accounting for it as a merger are met and the merger method of accounting is adopted.

9. (1)   The acquisition method of accounting is as follows.

(2)   The identifiable assets and liabilities of the undertaking acquired must be included in the consolidated balance sheet at their fair values as at the date of acquisition.

(3)   The income and expenditure of the undertaking acquired must be brought into the group accounts only as from the date of the acquisition.

(4)   There must be set off against the acquisition cost of the interest in the shares of the undertaking held by the parent LLP and its subsidiary undertakings the interest of the parent LLP and its subsidiary undertakings in the adjusted capital and reserves of the undertaking acquired.

(5)   The resulting amount if positive must be treated as goodwill, and if negative as a negative consolidation difference.

10. The conditions for accounting for an acquisition as a merger are that adoption of the merger method of accounting accords with generally accepted accounting principles or practice.

11. (1)   Where an LLP adopts the merger method of accounting it must comply with this paragraph, and with generally accepted accounting principles or practice.

(2)   The assets and liabilities of the undertaking acquired must be brought into the group accounts at the figures at which they stand in the undertaking's accounts, subject to any adjustment authorised or required by this Schedule.

(3)   The income and expenditure of the undertaking acquired must be included in the group accounts for the entire financial year, including the period before the acquisition.

(4)   The group accounts must show corresponding amounts relating to the previous financial year as if the undertaking acquired had been included in the consolidation throughout that year.

12. (1)   Where a group is acquired, paragraphs 9 to 11 apply with the following adaptations.

(2)   References to shares of the undertaking acquired are to be construed as references to shares of the parent undertaking of the group.

(3)   Other references to the undertaking acquired are to be construed as references to the group; and references to the assets and liabilities, income and expenditure and capital and reserves of the undertaking acquired must be construed as references to the assets and liabilities, income and expenditure and capital and reserves of the group after making the set-offs and other adjustments required by this Schedule in the case of group accounts.

13. (1)   The following information with respect to acquisitions taking place in the financial year must be given in a note to the accounts.

(2)   There must be stated—

(a) the name of the undertaking acquired or, where a group was acquired, the name of the parent undertaking of that group, and

(b) whether the acquisition has been accounted for by the acquisition or the merger method of accounting;

and in relation to an acquisition which significantly affects the figures shown in the group accounts, the following further information must be given.

(3) The composition and fair value of the consideration for the acquisition given by the parent LLP and its subsidiary undertakings must be stated.

(4) Where the acquisition method of accounting has been adopted, the book values immediately prior to the acquisition, and the fair values at the date of acquisition, of each class of assets and liabilities of the undertaking or group acquired must be stated in tabular form, including a statement of the amount of any goodwill or negative consolidation difference arising on the acquisition, together with an explanation of any significant adjustments made.

(5) In ascertaining for the purposes of sub-paragraph (4) the profit or loss of a group, the book values and fair values of assets and liabilities of a group or the amount of the assets and liabilities of a group, the set-offs and other adjustments required by this Schedule in the case of group accounts must be made.

14. (1) There must also be stated in a note to the accounts the cumulative amount of goodwill resulting from acquisitions in that and earlier financial years which has been written off otherwise than in the consolidated profit and loss account for that or any earlier financial year.

(2) That figure must be shown net of any goodwill attributable to subsidiary undertakings or businesses disposed of prior to the balance sheet date.

15. Where during the financial year there has been a disposal of an undertaking or group which significantly affects the figure shown in the group accounts, there must be stated in a note to the accounts—

(a) the name of that undertaking or, as the case may be, of the parent undertaking of that group, and

(b) the extent to which the profit or loss shown in the group accounts is attributable to profit or loss of that undertaking or group.

16. The information required by paragraph 13, 14 or 15 need not be disclosed with respect to an undertaking which—

(a) is established under the law of a country outside the United Kingdom, or

(b) carries on business outside the United Kingdom,

if in the opinion of the members of the parent LLP the disclosure would be seriously prejudicial to the business of that undertaking or to the business of the parent LLP or any of its subsidiary undertakings and the Secretary of State agrees that the information should not be disclosed.

Minority interests

17. (1) The formats set out in Schedule 1 to these Regulations have effect in relation to group accounts with the following additions.

(2) In the balance sheet formats there must be shown, as a separate item and under an appropriate heading, the amount of capital and reserves attributable to shares in subsidiary undertakings included in the consolidation held by or on behalf of persons other than the parent LLP and its subsidiary undertakings.

(3) In the profit and loss account formats there must be shown, as a separate item and under an appropriate heading—

(a) the amount of any profit or loss on ordinary activities, and

(b) the amount of any profit or loss on extraordinary activities,

attributable to shares in subsidiary undertakings included in the consolidation held by or on behalf of persons other than the parent LLP and its subsidiary undertakings.

(4) For the purposes of paragraph 4 of Schedule 1 (power to adapt or combine items)—

(a) the additional item required by sub-paragraph (2) above is treated as one to which a letter is assigned, and

(b) the additional items required by sub-paragraph (3)(a) and (b) above are treated as ones to which an Arabic number is assigned.

Joint ventures

18. (1) Where an undertaking included in the consolidation manages another undertaking jointly with one or more undertakings not included in the consolidation, that other undertaking ("the joint venture") may, if it is not—

(a) a body corporate, or

(b) a subsidiary undertaking of the parent LLP,

be dealt with in the group accounts by the method of proportional consolidation.

(2) The provisions of this Schedule relating to the preparation of consolidated accounts apply, with any necessary modifications, to proportional consolidation under this paragraph.

Associated undertakings

19. (1) An "associated undertaking" means an undertaking in which an undertaking included in the consolidation has a participating interest and over whose operating and financial policy it exercises a significant influence, and which is not—

(a)   a subsidiary undertaking of the parent LLP, or

(b)   a joint venture dealt with in accordance with paragraph 18.

(2) Where an undertaking holds 20% or more of the voting rights in another undertaking, it is presumed to exercise such an influence over it unless the contrary is shown.

(3) The voting rights in an undertaking means the rights conferred on shareholders in respect of their shares or, in the case of an undertaking not having a share capital, on members, to vote at general meetings of the undertaking on all, or substantially all, matters.

(4) The provisions of paragraphs 5 to 11 of Schedule 7 to the 2006 Act (parent and subsidiary undertakings: rights to be taken into account and attribution of rights) apply in determining for the purposes of this paragraph whether an undertaking holds 20% or more of the voting rights in another undertaking.

20. (1) The formats set out in Schedule 1 to these Regulations have effect in relation to group accounts with the following modifications.

(2) In the balance sheet formats replace the items headed "Participating interests", that is—

(a)   in format 1, item A.III.3, and

(b)   in format 2, item A.III.3 under the heading "ASSETS",

by two items: "Interests in associated undertakings" and "Other participating interests".

(3) In the profit and loss account formats replace the items headed "Income from participating interests", that is—

(a)   in format 1, item 8, and

(b)   in format 2, item 10,

by two items: "Income from interests in associated undertakings" and "Income from other participating interests".

21. (1) The interest of an undertaking in an associated undertaking, and the amount of profit or loss attributable to such an interest, must be shown by the equity method of accounting (including dealing with any goodwill arising in accordance with paragraphs 17 to 20 and 22 of Schedule 1 to these Regulations).

(2) Where the associated undertaking is itself a parent undertaking, the net assets and profits or losses to be taken into account are those of the parent and its subsidiary undertakings (after making any consolidation adjustments).

(3) The equity method of accounting need not be applied if the amounts in question are not material for the purpose of giving a true and fair view.

Related party transactions

22. Paragraph 70 of Schedule 1 to these Regulations applies to transactions which the parent LLP, or other undertakings included in the consolidation, have entered into with related parties, unless they are intra group transactions.

NOTES

Commencement: 1 October 2008.

SCHEDULE 4
GENERAL INTERPRETATION

Regulation 7

Financial instruments

[10.1093]

1. References to "derivatives" include commodity-based contracts that give either contracting party the right to settle in cash or in some other financial instrument, except where such contracts—

(a)   were entered into for the purpose of, and continue to meet, the LLP's expected purchase, sale or usage requirements,

(b)   were designated for such purpose at their inception, and

(c)   are expected to be settled by delivery of the commodity.

2. (1) The expressions listed in sub-paragraph (2) have the same meaning as they have in Council Directive 78/660/EEC on the annual accounts of certain types of companies(13).

(2) Those expressions are "available for sale financial asset", "business combination", "commodity-based contracts", "derivative", "equity instrument", "exchange difference", "fair value hedge accounting system", "financial fixed asset", "financial instrument", "foreign entity", "hedge accounting", "hedge accounting system", "hedged items", "hedging instrument", "held for trading purposes", "held to maturity", "monetary item", "receivables", "reliable market" and "trading portfolio".

Fixed and current assets

3. "Fixed assets" means assets of an LLP which are intended for use on a continuing basis in the LLP's activities, and "current assets" means assets not intended for such use.

Historical cost accounting rules

4. References to the historical cost accounting rules are to be read in accordance with paragraph 30 of Schedule 1 to these Regulations.

Listed investments

5. (1) "Listed investment" means an investment as respects which there has been granted a listing on—

    (a)   a recognised investment exchange other than an overseas investment exchange, or

    (b)   a stock exchange of repute outside the United Kingdom.

(2) "Recognised investment exchange" and "overseas investment exchange" have the meaning given in Part 18 of the Financial Services and Markets Act 2000(14).

Loans

6. A loan or advance (including a liability comprising a loan or advance) is treated as falling due for repayment, and an instalment of a loan or advance is treated as falling due for payment, on the earliest date on which the lender could require repayment or (as the case may be) payment, if he exercised all options and rights available to him.

Materiality

7. Amounts which in the particular context of any provision of Schedule 1 to these Regulations are not material may be disregarded for the purposes of that provision.

Participating interests

8. (1) A "participating interest" means an interest held by an undertaking in the shares of another undertaking which it holds on a long-term basis for the purpose of securing a contribution to its activities by the exercise of control or influence arising from or related to that interest.

(2) A holding of 20% or more of the shares of the undertaking is to be presumed to be a participating interest unless the contrary is shown.

(3) The reference in sub-paragraph (1) to an interest in shares includes—

    (a)   an interest which is convertible into an interest in shares, and

    (b)   an option to acquire shares or any such interest,

and an interest or option falls within paragraph (a) or (b) notwithstanding that the shares to which it relates are, until the conversion or the exercise of the option, unissued.

(4) For the purposes of this paragraph an interest held on behalf of an undertaking is to be treated as held by it.

(5) In the balance sheet and profit and loss formats set out in Schedule 1 to these Regulations, "participating interest" does not include an interest in a group undertaking.

(6) For the purpose of this paragraph as it applies in relation to the expression "participating interest"—

    (a)   in those formats as they apply in relation to group accounts, and

    (b)   in paragraph 19 of Schedule 3 (group accounts: undertakings to be accounted for as associated undertakings),

the references in sub-paragraphs (1) to (4) to the interest held by, and the purposes and activities of, the undertaking concerned are to be construed as references to the interest held by, and the purposes and activities of, the group (within the meaning of paragraph 1 of that Schedule).

Provisions

9. (1) References to provisions for depreciation or diminution in value of assets are to any amount written off by way of providing for depreciation or diminution in value of assets.

(2) Any reference in the profit and loss account formats set out in Schedule 1 to these Regulations to the depreciation of, or amounts written off, assets of any description is to any provision for depreciation or diminution in value of assets of that description.

10. References to provisions for liabilities are to any amount retained as reasonably necessary for the purpose of providing for any liability the nature of which is clearly defined and which is either likely to be incurred, or certain to be incurred but uncertain as to amount or as to the date on which it will arise.

Purchase price

11. "Purchase price", in relation to an asset of an LLP or any raw materials or consumables used in the production of such an asset, includes any consideration (whether in cash or otherwise) given by the LLP in respect of that asset or those materials or consumables, as the case may be.

Staff costs

12. (1) "Social security costs" means any contributions by the LLP to any state social security or pension scheme, fund or arrangement.

(2) "Pension costs" includes—

    (a)   any costs incurred by the LLP in respect of any pension scheme established for the purpose of providing pensions for persons currently or formerly employed by the LLP,

    (b)   any sums set aside for the future payment of pensions directly by the LLP to current or former employees, and

    (c)   any pensions paid directly to such persons without having first been set aside.

(3) Any amount stated in respect of the item "social security costs" or in respect of the item "wages and salaries" in the LLP's profit and loss account must be determined by reference to payments made or costs incurred in respect of all persons employed by the LLP during the financial year under contracts of service.

NOTES

Commencement: 1 October 2008.

TAKEOVER CODE (CONCERT PARTIES) REGULATIONS 2008

(SI 2008/3073)

NOTES

Made: 28 November 2008 (10.00am).

Authority: European Communities Act 1972, s 2(2).

Commencement: 28 November 2008 (12.00pm).

Amendment: as of 1 July 2011, these Regulations had not been amended.

[10.1094]

1 Citation, commencement and interpretation

(1) These Regulations may be cited as the Takeover Code (Concert Parties) Regulations 2008 and come into force 12.00 pm on 28th November 2008.

(2) In these Regulations—

    (a)   "the Takeover Code" means the rules made by the Panel on Takeovers and Mergers under section 943 of the Companies Act 2006 otherwise known as the City Code on Takeovers and Mergers;

    (b)   "shares" means equity securities within the meaning of section 560 of the Companies Act 2006 and other transferable securities carrying voting rights;

    (c)   "recapitalisation scheme" means the facility announced by the Chancellor of the Exchequer on 8 October 2008 to make available capital to certain financial institutions in order to strengthen their resources in the interests of financial stability;

    (d)   "UKFI" means UK Financial Investments Limited, company registered number 06720891.

NOTES

Commencement: 28 November 2008 (12.00pm).

[10.1095]

2 Application of Rule 9 of the Takeover Code

(1) For the purposes of Rule 9 of the Takeover Code the following persons are not to be regarded as acting in concert with each other or the Treasury or the Secretary of State or UKFI by virtue of the Treasury holding (through a nominee or otherwise) shares in each of those persons—

    (a)   a person some or all of the shares in which are held by a nominee of the Treasury or a company wholly owned by the Treasury as a result of the exercise of powers under the Banking (Special Provisions) Act 2008;

    (b)   a person participating in the recapitalisation scheme.

(2) For the purposes of Rule 9 of the Takeover Code, the Treasury, the Secretary of State and UKFI are not to be regarded as acting in concert with each other by virtue of the Treasury's relationship with, and the Secretary of State's and UKFI's functions in relation to, a person listed in paragraph (1)(a) or (b).

NOTES

Commencement: 28 November 2008 (12.00pm).

COMPANIES (SHAREHOLDERS' RIGHTS) REGULATIONS 2009 (NOTE)

(SI 2009/1632)

[10.1096]

NOTES

These Regulations were made on 2 July 2009 under the powers conferred by the European Communities Act 1972, s 2(2). They come into force on 3 August 2009 and apply in relation to meetings of which notice is given, or first given, on or after that date (see reg 1). These Regulations implement Directive 2007/36/EC of the European Parliament and of the Council on the exercise of certain rights of shareholders in listed companies (at **[11.542]**) so far as it is not already given effect in UK law. Except in one respect (reg 22), they do so by amendment of Part 13 (Resolutions and Meetings) of the Companies Act 2006 at **[1.281]** et seq.

Part 2 of these Regulations (Amendments of General application) provides as follows. Regulation 2 enables Article 10 of the Directive (proxy voting) and Article 13(4) (split votes by nominee shareholders) to be implemented by clarifying the relationship between the general voting rules in ss 282–284 of the 2006 Act and the rules about nominee shareholders, proxies, split votes and corporate representatives in ss 152, 285, 322, 322A and 323. Regulation 3 implements Article 10(1) (shareholders' rights are the same whether exercised in person or by proxy) and Article 10(5) (proxies for more than one shareholder may split their votes) by replacing the existing s 285 with two new sections, ie, ss 285 and 285A. Regulation 4 implements Article 6(2) (minimum stake to require a meeting to be called must not exceed 5%) by providing a single percentage, 5%, of the members of any type of company who may require the directors to call a general meeting. Regulation 5 implements Article 12 (voting by correspondence) by providing for votes to be cast in advance. Regulation 6 implements Article 13(4) (split votes by nominee shareholders) by enabling corporate representatives to vote in different ways from one another in respect of different blocks of shares. Regulation 7 implements Article 10(4) (proxies to vote in accordance with instructions). Regulation 8 implements Article 8 (participation in general meetings by electronic means) by preventing anything in Part 13 of CA 2006 from being an obstacle to meetings being held electronically. Regulation 9 implements Article 5(1) (period of notice for general meetings) by amending ss 307 and 360 and inserting a new s 307A. The changes from existing s 307 are that annual general meetings of private companies with traded shares require 21 days' notice, and that other general meetings of companies (public and private) with traded shares also require 21 days' notice unless electronic voting is available and a resolution reducing the period to not less than 14 days was passed at the previous AGM or at a general meeting held since then.

Part 3 of these Regulations (Amendments relating to Traded Companies) provides as follows. Regulations 10 and 11 implement Article 5(3), (4) (contents of notices of, and website publication of advance information about, general meetings of companies with traded shares). Regulation 12 implements Article 9 (right to ask questions at general meetings). Regulation 13 implements Article 11 (formalities for proxy holder appointment and notification). Regulation 14 makes consequential provision in respect of class meetings. Regulation 15 requires private companies with traded shares to hold AGMs. This implements the obligation to apply the provisions of the Directive about annual general meetings to such companies which arises from the scope of the Directive provided for in Article 1(1). Regulation 16 implements Article 5(3)(b)(i) (notice of rights under Article 6) in respect of annual general meetings by providing for notice to be given of the right to require a company with traded shares to circulate a resolution to be moved at its AGM or to include something on the AGM agenda. Regulation 17 implements Article 6(1)(a), (2), (3) (right to put items other than resolutions on the agenda of a general meeting) in respect of annual general meetings. Regulation 18 implements Article 6(4) (revised agenda to be circulated when right to put items other than resolutions on the agenda of a general meeting exercised) in respect of annual general meetings and ensures that there is no obstacle to enjoyment of Article 6 rights by placing on the company the cost of circulating resolutions for the annual general meeting of a company with traded shares. Regulation 19 implements Article 14 (determination of voting results and publication on website). Regulation 20 implements Article 7 (requirements for participation and voting at general meetings). Regulation 21 defines a company with traded voting shares as a "traded company", if the shares are admitted to trading by or with consent of the company. Regulation 22 implements Article 4 (equal treatment of shareholders) by excluding traded companies from the operation of the provision in the amended Companies Act 2006 (Commencement No 3, Consequential Amendments, Transitional Provisions and Savings) Order 2007 (SI 2007/2194) preserving articles in force before 1 October 2007 which provide for the chairman of a company general meeting to have a casting vote. Regulation 23 makes transitional provisions in connection with the new s 307A of the 2006 Act.

LIMITED LIABILITY PARTNERSHIPS (APPLICATION OF COMPANIES ACT 2006) REGULATIONS 2009

(SI 2009/1804)

NOTES

Made: 8 July 2009.

Authority: Limited Liability Partnerships Act 2000, ss 15, 17; Companies Act 2006, ss 1101, 1292, 1294, 1296.

Commencement: 9 July 2009 (regs 8, 64, 77, 80, 81, Sch 3, paras 6, 7 for the purpose of enabling the exercise of powers to make regulations or orders by statutory instrument); 1 October 2009 (otherwise).

These Regulations are reproduced as amended by: the Limited Liability Partnerships (Amendment) Regulations 2009, SI 2009/1833; the Companies Act 2006 and Limited Liability Partnerships (Transitional Provisions and Savings) (Amendment) Regulations 2009, SI 2009/2476; the Limited Liability Partnerships (Amendment) (No 2) Regulations 2009, SI 2009/2995.

ARRANGEMENT OF REGULATIONS

PART 1
GENERAL INTRODUCTORY PROVISIONS

PART 1
GENERAL INTRODUCTORY PROVISIONS

[10.1097]
1   Citation
These Regulations may be cited as the Limited Liability Partnerships (Application of Companies Act 2006) Regulations 2009.

NOTES
Commencement: 1 October 2009.

[10.1098]
2   Commencement
(1)   The provisions of these Regulations come into force as follows.

(2)   Regulations 8, 64, 77, 80 and 81 of, and paragraphs 6 and 7 of Schedule 3 to, these Regulations come into force on the day after the Regulations are made for the purpose of enabling the exercise of powers to make regulations or orders by statutory instrument.

(3)   Otherwise, the Regulations come into force on 1st October 2009.

NOTES
Commencement: 1 October 2009.

[10.1099]
3   Interpretation
(1)   In these Regulations "LLP" means a limited liability partnership registered under the Limited Liability Partnerships Act 2000.

(2)   In these Regulations, unless the context otherwise requires—
    (a)   any reference to a numbered Part, section or Schedule is to the Part, section or Schedule so numbered in the Companies Act 2006;
    (b)   references in provisions applied to LLPs—
        (i)   to provisions of the Companies Act 2006, or
        (ii)   to provisions of instruments made under that Act,
        are to those provisions as applied to LLPs by these Regulations or by the Limited Liability

Partnerships (Accounts and Audit) (Application of Companies Act 2006) Regulations 2008;

(c)   references in provisions applied to LLPs to provisions of the Insolvency Act 1986 or the Insolvency (Northern Ireland) Order 1989 are to those provisions as applied to LLPs by the Limited Liability Partnerships Regulations 2001 or the Limited Liability Partnerships Regulations (Northern Ireland) 2004.

NOTES
Commencement: 1 October 2009.

PART 2
FORMALITIES OF DOING BUSINESS

[10.1100]
4   Formalities of doing business under the law of England and Wales or Northern Ireland
Sections 43 to 47 apply to LLPs, modified so that they read as follows—

"43 LLP contracts
(1)   Under the law of England and Wales or Northern Ireland a contract may be made—
    (a)   by an LLP, by writing under its common seal, or
    (b)   on behalf of an LLP, by a person acting under its authority, express or implied.
(2)   This is without prejudice to section 6 of the Limited Liability Partnerships Act 2000 (c 12) (members as agents).
(3)   Any formalities required by law in the case of a contract made by an individual also apply, unless a contrary intention appears, to a contract made by or on behalf of an LLP.

44 Execution of documents
(1)   Under the law of England and Wales or Northern Ireland a document is executed by an LLP—
    (a)   by the affixing of its common seal, or
    (b)   by signature in accordance with the following provisions.
(2)   A document is validly executed by an LLP if it is signed on behalf of the LLP—
    (a)   by two members, or
    (b)   by a member of the LLP in the presence of a witness who attests the signature.
(3)   A document signed in accordance with subsection (2) and expressed, in whatever words, to be executed by the LLP has the same effect as if executed under the common seal of the LLP.
(4)   In favour of a purchaser a document is deemed to have been duly executed by an LLP if it purports to be signed in accordance with subsection (2).
A "purchaser" means a purchaser in good faith for valuable consideration and includes a lessee, mortgagee or other person who for valuable consideration acquires an interest in property.
(5)   Where a document is to be signed by a person on behalf of more than one LLP, or on behalf of an LLP and a company, it is not duly signed by that person for the purposes of this section unless he signs it separately in each capacity.
(6)   References in this section to a document being (or purporting to be) signed by a member are to be read, in a case where that member is a firm, as references to its being (or purporting to be) signed by an individual authorised by the firm to sign on its behalf.
(7)   This section applies to a document that is (or purports to be) executed by an LLP in the name of or on behalf of another person whether or not that person is also an LLP.

45 Common seal
(1)   An LLP may have a common seal, but need not have one.
(2)   An LLP which has a common seal shall have its name engraved in legible characters on the seal.
(3)   If an LLP fails to comply with subsection (2) an offence is committed by—
    (a)   the LLP, and
    (b)   every member of the LLP who is in default.
(4)   A member of an LLP, or a person acting on behalf of an LLP, commits an offence if he uses, or authorises the use of, a seal purporting to be a seal of the LLP on which its name is not engraved as required by subsection (2).
(5)   A person guilty of an offence under this section is liable on summary conviction to a fine not exceeding level 3 on the standard scale.
(6)   This section does not form part of the law of Scotland.

46 Execution of deeds
(1)   A document is validly executed by an LLP as a deed for the purposes of section 1(2)(b) of the Law of Property (Miscellaneous Provisions) Act 1989 (c 34) and for the purposes of the law of Northern Ireland if, and only if—
    (a)   it is duly executed by the LLP, and

(b)   it is delivered as a deed.

(2)   For the purposes of subsection (1)(b) a document is presumed to be delivered upon its being executed, unless a contrary intention is proved.

47 Execution of deeds or other documents by attorney

(1)   Under the law of England and Wales or Northern Ireland an LLP may, by instrument executed as a deed, empower a person, either generally or in respect of specified matters, as its attorney to execute deeds or other documents on its behalf.

(2)   A deed or other document so executed, whether in the United Kingdom or elsewhere, has effect as if executed by the LLP.".

NOTES

Commencement: 1 October 2009.

[10.1101]

5   Formalities of doing business under the law of Scotland

Section 48 applies to LLPs, modified so that it reads as follows—

"48 Execution of documents by LLPs: Scotland

(1)   The following provisions form part of the law of Scotland only.

(2)   Notwithstanding the provisions of any enactment, an LLP need not have a common seal.

(3)   For the purposes of any enactment—

    (a)   providing for a document to be executed by an LLP by affixing its common seal, or

    (b)   referring (in whatever terms) to a document so executed,

a document signed or subscribed by or on behalf of the LLP in accordance with the provisions of the Requirements of Writing (Scotland) Act 1995 (c 7) has effect as if so executed.".

NOTES

Commencement: 1 October 2009.

[10.1102]

6   Official seal for use abroad

Section 49 applies to LLPs, modified so that it reads as follows—

"49 Official seal for use abroad

(1)   An LLP that has a common seal may have an official seal for use outside the United Kingdom.

(2)   The official seal must be a facsimile of the LLP's common seal, with the addition on its face of the place or places where it is to be used.

(3)   The official seal when duly affixed to a document has the same effect as the LLP's common seal.

    This subsection does not extend to Scotland.

(4)   An LLP having an official seal for use outside the United Kingdom may—

    (a)   by writing under its common seal, or

    (b)   as respects Scotland, by writing subscribed in accordance with the Requirements of Writing (Scotland) Act 1995,

authorise any person appointed for the purpose to affix the official seal to any deed or other document to which the LLP is party.

(5)   As between the LLP and a person dealing with such an agent, the agent's authority continues—

    (a)   during the period mentioned in the instrument conferring the authority, or

    (b)   if no period is mentioned, until notice of the revocation or termination of the agent's authority has been given to the person dealing with him.

(6)   The person affixing the official seal must certify in writing on the deed or other document to which the seal is affixed the date on which, and place at which, it is affixed.".

NOTES

Commencement: 1 October 2009.

[10.1103]

7   Other matters

Sections 51 and 52 apply to LLPs, modified so that they read as follows—

"51 Pre-incorporation contracts, deeds and obligations

(1)   A contract that purports to be made by or on behalf of an LLP at a time when the LLP has not been formed has effect, subject to any agreement to the contrary, as one made with the person purporting to act for the LLP or as agent for it, and he is personally liable on the contract accordingly.

(2)   Subsection (1) applies—

> (a)   to the making of a deed under the law of England and Wales or Northern Ireland, and
>
> (b)   to the undertaking of an obligation under the law of Scotland,
>
> as it applies to the making of a contract.

52 Bills of exchange and promissory notes

A bill of exchange or promissory note is deemed to have been made, accepted or endorsed on behalf of an LLP if made, accepted or endorsed in the name of, or by or on behalf or on account of, the LLP by a person acting under its authority.".

NOTES

Commencement: 1 October 2009.

PART 3
AN LLP'S NAME

CHAPTER 1
GENERAL REQUIREMENTS

[10.1104]

8 Prohibited names and sensitive words and expressions

Sections 53 to 56 apply to LLPs, modified so that they read as follows—

"53 Prohibited names

An LLP must not be registered under the Limited Liability Partnerships Act 2000 (c 12) by a name if, in the opinion of the Secretary of State—

> (a)   its use by the LLP would constitute an offence, or
>
> (b)   it is offensive.

54 Names suggesting connection with government or public authority

(1)   The approval of the Secretary of State is required for an LLP to be registered under the Limited Liability Partnerships Act 2000 (c 12) by a name that would be likely to give the impression that the LLP is connected with—

> (a)   Her Majesty's Government, any part of the Scottish Administration[, the Welsh Assembly Government] or Her Majesty's Government in Northern Ireland,
>
> (b)   a local authority, or
>
> (c)   any public authority specified for the purposes of this section by regulations made by the Secretary of State.

(2)   For the purposes of this section—

"local authority" means—

> (a)   a local authority within the meaning of the Local Government Act 1972 (c 70), the Common Council of the City of London or the Council of the Isles of Scilly,
>
> (b)   a council constituted under section 2 of the Local Government etc (Scotland) Act 1994 (c 39), or
>
> (c)   a district council in Northern Ireland;

"public authority" includes any person or body having functions of a public nature.

(3)   Regulations under this section are subject to affirmative resolution procedure.

55 Other sensitive words or expressions

(1)   The approval of the Secretary of State is required for an LLP to be registered under the Limited Liability Partnerships Act 2000 (c 12) by a name that includes a word or expression for the time being specified in regulations made by the Secretary of State under this section.

(2)   Regulations under this section are subject to approval after being made.

56 Duty to seek comments of government department or other specified body

(1)   The Secretary of State may by regulations under—

> (a)   section 54 (name suggesting connection with government or public authority), or
>
> (b)   section 55 (other sensitive words or expressions),

require that, in connection with an application for the approval of the Secretary of State under that section, the applicant must seek the view of a specified Government department or other body.

(2)   Where such a requirement applies, the applicant must request the specified department or other body (in writing) to indicate whether (and if so why) it has any objections to the proposed name.

(3)   Where a request under this section is made in connection with an application for the registration of an LLP under the Limited Liability Partnerships Act 2000 (c 12), the application must—

> (a)   include a statement that a request under this section has been made, and
>
> (b)   be accompanied by a copy of any response received.

(4)   Where a request under this section is made in connection with a change in an LLP's name, the notice of the change sent to the registrar must—

(a)　　include a statement by a designated member of the LLP that a request under this section has been made, and

(b)　　be accompanied by a copy of any response received.

(5)　In this section "specified" means specified in the regulations.".

NOTES

Commencement: 9 July 2009 (for the purpose of enabling the exercise of powers to make regulations or orders by statutory instrument); 1 October 2009 (otherwise).

Words in square brackets in s 54(1)(a) as set out above inserted by the Limited Liability Partnerships (Amendment) (No 2) Regulations 2009, SI 2009/2995, reg 2, as from 14 December 2009.

[10.1105]

9　Permitted characters etc

Section 57 applies to LLPs, modified so that it reads as follows—

"57　Permitted characters etc

(1)　The provisions of the Company and Business Names (Miscellaneous Provisions) Regulations 2009 (SI 2009/1085) relating to the characters, signs or symbols and punctuation that may be used in a registered name apply to LLPs.

(2)　Those provisions are—

(a)　　regulation 2 and Schedule 1, and

(b)　　any other provisions of those Regulations having effect for the purpose of those provisions.

(3)　In those provisions as they apply to LLPs—

(a)　　for "company" substitute "LLP", and

(b)　　for "the Act" substitute "the Limited Liability Partnerships Act 2000".

(4)　An LLP may not be registered under the Limited Liability Partnerships Act 2000 (c 12) by a name that consists of or includes anything that is not permitted in accordance with the provisions applied by this section.".

NOTES

Commencement: 1 October 2009.

[10.1106]

10　Inappropriate use of indications of company type or legal form

Section 65 applies to LLPs, modified so that it reads as follows—

"65　Inappropriate use of indications of company type or legal form

(1)　The provisions of the Company and Business Names (Miscellaneous Provisions) Regulations 2009 (SI 2009/1085) relating to inappropriate use of indications of company type or legal form apply to LLPs.

(2)　Those provisions are—

(a)　　regulation 4 and Schedule 2, and

(b)　　any other provisions of those Regulations having effect for the purpose of those provisions.

(3)　As applied to LLPs regulation 4 is modified so as to read as follows—

"4.—(1)　An LLP must not be registered under the Limited Liability Partnerships Act 2000 (c 12) by a name that includes in any part of the name—

(a)　　an expression or abbreviation specified in inverted commas in paragraph 3(a) to (o) or (r) to (v) in Schedule 2 (other than the abbreviation "LLP" or "PAC" (with or without full stops) at the end of its name), or

(b)　　an expression or abbreviation specified as similar.

(2)　An LLP must not be registered under the Limited Liability Partnerships Act 2000 by a name that includes immediately before the expression "LIMITED LIABILITY PARTNERSHIP" OR "PARTNERIAETH ATEBOLRWYDD CYFYNGEDIG" or the abbreviations "LLP" or "PAC" an abbreviation specified in inverted commas in paragraph 3(v) of that Schedule (or any abbreviation specified as similar)".

NOTES

Commencement: 1 October 2009.

Note: the Company, Limited Liability Partnership and Business Names (Miscellaneous Provisions) (Amendment) Regulations 2009, SI 2009/2404, reg 2(1), (3) amends the Company and Business Names (Miscellaneous Provisions) Regulations 2009, SI 2009/1085, Sch 2, including that Schedule as applied to LLPs.

CHAPTER 2
SIMILARITY TO OTHER NAMES

[10.1107]
11 Similarity to other name on registrar's index
Sections 66 to 68 apply to LLPs, modified so that they read as follows—

"66 Name not to be the same as another in the index
(1) An LLP must not be registered under the Limited Liability Partnerships Act 2000 (c 12) by a name that is the same as another name appearing in the registrar's index of company names.
(2) The provisions of the Company and Business Names (Miscellaneous Provisions) Regulations 2009 (SI 2009/1085) supplementing this section apply to LLPs.
(3) Those provisions are—
    (a)   regulation 7 and Schedule 3 (matters that are to be disregarded and words, expressions, signs and symbols that are to be regarded as the same),
    (b)   regulation 8 (consent to registration of a name which is the same as another in the registrar's index of company names), and
    (c)   any other provisions of those Regulations having effect for the purpose of those provisions.
(4) In regulation 8 as applied to LLPs—
    (a)   for "a company" or "the company" substitute "an LLP" or "the LLP",
    (b)   for "Company Y" substitute "LLP Y", and
    (c)   in paragraph (1), for "the Act" substitute "the Limited Liability Partnerships Act 2000".

67 Power to direct change of name in case of similarity to existing name
The Secretary of State may direct an LLP to change its name if it has been registered in a name that is the same as or, in the opinion of the Secretary of State, too like—
    (a)   a name appearing at the time of the registration in the registrar's index of company names, or
    (b)   a name that should have appeared in that index at that time.

68 Direction to change names: supplementary provisions
(1) The following provisions have effect in relation to a direction under section 67 (power to direct change of name in case of similarity to existing name).
(2) Any such direction—
    (a)   must be given within twelve months of the LLP's registration by the name in question, and
    (b)   must specify the period within which the LLP is to change its name.
(3) The Secretary of State may by a further direction extend that period.
    Any such direction must be given before the end of the period for the time being specified.
(4) A direction under section 67 or this section must be in writing.
(5) If an LLP fails to comply with the direction, an offence is committed by—
    (a)   the LLP, and
    (b)   every designated member of the LLP who is in default.
(6) A person guilty of an offence under this section is liable on summary conviction to a fine not exceeding level 3 on the standard scale and, for continued contravention, a daily default fine not exceeding one-tenth of level 3 on the standard scale.".

NOTES
Commencement: 1 October 2009.

[10.1108]
12 Similarity to other name in which person has goodwill
Sections 69 to 74 apply to LLPs, modified so that they read as follows—

"69 Objection to LLP's registered name
(1) A person ("the applicant") may object to an LLP's registered name on the ground—
    (a)   that it is the same as a name associated with the applicant in which he has goodwill, or
    (b)   that it is sufficiently similar to such a name that its use in the United Kingdom would be likely to mislead by suggesting a connection between the LLP and the applicant.
(2) The objection must be made by application to a company names adjudicator (see section 70).
(3) The LLP concerned shall be the primary respondent to the application.
    Any of its members may be joined as respondents.
(4) If the ground specified in subsection (1)(a) or (b) is established, it is for the respondents to show—

    (a)   that the name was registered before the commencement of the activities on which the applicant relies to show goodwill; or

    (b)   that the LLP—

        (i)   is operating under the name, or

        (ii) is proposing to do so and has incurred substantial start-up costs in preparation, or

        (iii) was formerly operating under the name and is now dormant; or

    (c)   that the name was registered in the ordinary course of an LLP formation business and the LLP is available for sale to the applicant on the standard terms of that business; or

    (d)   that the name was adopted in good faith; or

    (e)   that the interests of the applicant are not adversely affected to any significant extent.

If none of those is shown, the objection shall be upheld.

(5)   If the facts mentioned in subsection (4)(a), (b) or (c) are established, the objection shall nevertheless be upheld if the applicant shows that the main purpose of the respondents (or any of them) in registering the name was to obtain money (or other consideration) from the applicant or prevent him from registering the name.

(6)   If the objection is not upheld under subsection (4) or (5), it shall be dismissed.

(7)   In this section "goodwill" includes reputation of any description.

70 Company names adjudicators

(1)   The Secretary of State shall appoint persons to be company names adjudicators.

(2)   The persons appointed must have such legal or other experience as, in the Secretary of State's opinion, makes them suitable for appointment.

(3)   An adjudicator—

    (a)   holds office in accordance with the terms of his appointment,

    (b)   is eligible for re-appointment when his term of office ends,

    (c)   may resign at any time by notice in writing given to the Secretary of State, and

    (d)   may be dismissed by the Secretary of State on the ground of incapacity or misconduct.

(4)   One of the adjudicators shall be appointed Chief Adjudicator.

He shall perform such functions as the Secretary of State may assign to him.

(5)   The other adjudicators shall undertake such duties as the Chief Adjudicator may determine.

(6)   The Secretary of State may—

    (a)   appoint staff for the adjudicators;

    (b)   pay remuneration and expenses to the adjudicators and their staff;

    (c)   defray other costs arising in relation to the performance by the adjudicators of their functions;

    (d)   compensate persons for ceasing to be adjudicators.

71 Procedural rules

(1)   The Company Names Adjudicator Rules 2008 (SI 2008/1738) apply to LLPs.

(2)   As they apply to LLPs, omit—

    (a)   in rule 3(6) (persons joined as respondent), the reference to a director of the primary respondent;

    (b)   rule 13(2) (registered office treated as address for service).

72 Decision of adjudicator to be made available to public

(1)   A company names adjudicator must, within 90 days of determining an application under section 69, make his decision and his reasons for it available to the public.

(2)   He may do so by means of a website or by such other means as appear to him to be appropriate.

73 Order requiring name to be changed

(1)   If an application under section 69 is upheld, the adjudicator shall make an order—

    (a)   requiring the respondent LLP to change its name to one that is not an offending name, and

    (b)   requiring all the respondents—

        (i)   to take all such steps as are within their power to make, or facilitate the making, of that change, and

        (ii) not to cause or permit any steps to be taken calculated to result in another LLP being registered with a name that is an offending name.

(2)   An "offending name" means a name that, by reason of its similarity to the name associated with the applicant in which he claims goodwill, would be likely—

    (a)   to be the subject of a direction under section 67 (power of Secretary of State to direct change of name), or

    (b)   to give rise to a further application under section 69.

(3)   The order must specify a date by which the respondent LLP's name is to be changed and may be enforced—

    (a)   in England and Wales or Northern Ireland, in the same way as an order of the High Court;

    (b)   in Scotland, in the same way as a decree of the Court of Session.

(4)   If the respondent LLP's name is not changed in accordance with the order by the specified date, the adjudicator may determine a new name for the LLP.

(5)   If the adjudicator determines a new name for the respondent LLP he must give notice of his determination—

    (a)   to the applicant,

    (b)   to the respondents, and

    (c)   to the registrar.

(6)   For the purposes of this section an LLP's name is changed when the change takes effect in accordance with paragraph 5(4) in Part 1 of the Schedule to the Limited Liability Partnerships Act 2000 (c 12) (on the issue of the certificate of the change of name).

74 Appeal from adjudicator's decision

(1)   An appeal lies to the court from any decision of a company names adjudicator to uphold or dismiss an application under section 69.

(2)   Notice of appeal against a decision upholding an application must be given before the date specified in the adjudicator's order by which the respondent LLP's name is to be changed.

(3)   If notice of appeal is given against a decision upholding an application, the effect of the adjudicator's order is suspended.

(4)   If on appeal the court—

    (a)   affirms the decision of the adjudicator to uphold the application, or

    (b)   reverses the decision of the adjudicator to dismiss the application,

the court may (as the case may require) specify the date by which the adjudicator's order is to be complied with, remit the matter to the adjudicator or make any order or determination that the adjudicator might have made.

(5)   If the court determines a new name for the LLP it must give notice of the determination—

    (a)   to the parties to the appeal, and

    (b)   to the registrar.".

NOTES

Commencement: 1 October 2009.

CHAPTER 3
OTHER POWERS OF THE SECRETARY OF STATE

[10.1109]
13 Provision of misleading information etc

Sections 75 and 76 apply to LLPs, modified so that they read as follows—

"75 Provision of misleading information etc

(1)   If it appears to the Secretary of State—

    (a)   that misleading information has been given for the purposes of an LLP's registration by a particular name, or

    (b)   that an undertaking or assurance has been given for that purpose and has not been fulfilled,

the Secretary of State may direct the LLP to change its name.

(2)   Any such direction—

    (a)   must be given within five years of the LLP's registration by that name, and

    (b)   must specify the period within which the LLP is to change its name.

(3)   The Secretary of State may by a further direction extend the period within which the LLP is to change its name.

Any such direction must be given before the end of the period for the time being specified.

(4)   A direction under this section must be in writing.

(5)   If an LLP fails to comply with a direction under this section, an offence is committed by—

    (a)   the LLP, and

    (b)   every designated member of the LLP who is in default.

(6)   A person guilty of an offence under this section is liable on summary conviction to a fine not exceeding level 3 on the standard scale and, for continued contravention, a daily default fine not exceeding one-tenth of level 3 on the standard scale.

76 Misleading indication of activities

(1)   If in the opinion of the Secretary of State the name by which an LLP is registered gives so misleading an indication of the nature of its activities as to be likely to cause harm to the public, the Secretary of State may direct the LLP to change its name.

(2)   The direction must be in writing.

(3) The direction must be complied with within a period of six weeks from the date of the direction or such longer period as the Secretary of State may think fit to allow.

This does not apply if an application is duly made to the court under the following provisions.

(4) The LLP may apply to the court to set the direction aside.

The application must be made within the period of three weeks from the date of the direction.

(5) The court may set the direction aside or confirm it.

If the direction is confirmed, the court shall specify the period within which the direction is to be complied with.

(6) If an LLP fails to comply with a direction under this section, an offence is committed by—

(a) the LLP, and
(b) every designated member of the LLP who is in default.

(7) A person guilty of an offence under this section is liable on summary conviction to a fine not exceeding level 3 on the standard scale and, for continued contravention, a daily default fine not exceeding one-tenth of level 3 on the standard scale.".

NOTES

Commencement: 1 October 2009.

CHAPTER 4
TRADING DISCLOSURES

Requirement to disclose LLP name etc

[10.1110]
14

Sections 82 and 83 apply to LLPs, modified so that they read as follows—

"82 Requirement to disclose LLP name etc
(1) The Companies (Trading Disclosures) Regulations 2008 (SI 2008/495) apply to LLPs.
(2) As they apply to LLPs—
(a) read references to a company as references to an LLP;
(b) read references to a director as references to a member of an LLP;
(c) read references to an officer of a company as references to a designated member of an LLP;
(d) in regulation 7 (further particulars to appear in business letters, order forms and websites), for paragraphs (2)(d) to (f) and (3) substitute—
"(d) in the case of an LLP whose name ends with the abbreviation "llp", "LLP", "pac" or "PAC", the fact that it is an LLP or a partneriaeth atebolrwydd cyfyngedig".";
(e) in regulation 8 (disclosure of names of members)—
(i) at the beginning of paragraph (1) insert "Subject to paragraph (3)," and
(ii) after paragraph (2) insert—
"(3) Paragraph (1) does not apply in relation to any document issued by an LLP with more than 20 members which maintains at its principal place of business a list of the names of all the members if the document states in legible characters the address of the principal place of business of the LLP and that the list of the members' names is open to inspection at that place.
(4) Where an LLP maintains a list of the members' names for the purposes of paragraph (3), any person may inspect the list during office hours.";
(f) omit regulation 10(3) (offences: shadow directors).

83 Civil consequences of failure to make required disclosure
(1) This section applies to any legal proceedings brought by an LLP to which section 82 applies (requirement to disclose LLP name etc) to enforce a right arising out of a contract made in the course of a business in respect of which the LLP was, at the time the contract was made, in breach of the Companies (Trading Disclosures) Regulations 2008 (SI 2008/495).
(2) The proceedings shall be dismissed if the defendant (in Scotland, the defender) to the proceedings shows—
(a) that he has a claim against the claimant (pursuer) arising out of the contract that he has been unable to pursue by reason of the latter's breach of the regulations, or
(b) that he has suffered some financial loss in connection with the contract by reason of the claimant's (pursuer's) breach of the regulations,
unless the court before which the proceedings are brought is satisfied that it is just and equitable to permit the proceedings to continue.
(3) This section does not affect the right of any person to enforce such rights as he may have against another person in any proceedings brought by that person.".

NOTES
Commencement: 1 October 2009.

[10.1111]
15

Section 85 applies to LLPs, modified so that it reads as follows—

"85 Minor variations in form of name to be left out of account
(1)   For the purposes of this Chapter, in considering an LLP's name no account is to be taken of—

(a)   whether upper or lower case characters (or a combination of the two) are used,

(b)   whether diacritical marks or punctuation are present or absent,

provided there is no real likelihood of names differing only in those respects being taken to be different names.

(2)   This does not affect the operation of provisions of the Company and Business Names (Miscellaneous Provisions) Regulations 2009 (SI 2009/1085) permitting only specified characters or punctuation.".

NOTES
Commencement: 1 October 2009.

PART 4
AN LLP'S REGISTERED OFFICE

[10.1112]
16   General

Sections 86 and 87 apply to LLPs, modified so that they read as follows—

"86 An LLP's registered office
(1)   An LLP must at all times have a registered office situated in England and Wales (or in Wales), in Scotland or in Northern Ireland, to which all communications and notices may be addressed.

(2)   On the incorporation of an LLP the situation of its registered office shall be that stated in the incorporation document.

87 Change of address of registered office
(1)   An LLP may change the address of its registered office by giving notice to the registrar.

(2)   The change takes effect upon the notice being registered by the registrar, but until the end of the period of 14 days beginning with the date on which it is registered a person may validly serve any document on the LLP at the address previously registered.

(3)   For the purposes of any duty of an LLP—

(a)   to keep available for inspection at its registered office any register, index or other document, or

(b)   to mention the address of its registered office in any document,

an LLP that has given notice to the registrar of a change in the address of its registered office may act on the change as from such date, not more than 14 days after the notice is given, as it may determine.

(4)   Where an LLP unavoidably ceases to perform at its registered office any such duty as is mentioned in subsection (3)(a) in circumstances in which it was not practicable to give prior notice to the registrar of a change in the address of its registered office, but—

(a)   resumes performance of that duty at other premises as soon as practicable, and

(b)   gives notice accordingly to the registrar of a change in the situation of its registered office within 14 days of doing so,

it is not to be treated as having failed to comply with that duty.".

NOTES
Commencement: 1 October 2009.

[10.1113]
17   Welsh LLPs

Section 88 applies to LLPs, modified so that it reads as follows—

"88 Welsh LLPs
(1)   In this Act a "Welsh LLP" means an LLP as to which it is stated in the register that its registered office is to be situated in Wales.

(2)   An LLP—

(a)   whose registered office is in Wales, and

(b)   as to which it is stated in the register that its registered office is to be situated in England and Wales, may determine that the register be amended so that it states that the LLP's registered office is to be situated in Wales.

(3)   An LLP—
    (a)   whose registered office is in Wales, and
    (b)   as to which it is stated in the register that its registered office is to be situated in Wales,

may determine that the register be amended so that it states that the LLP's registered office is to be situated in England and Wales.

(4)   Where an LLP makes a determination under this section it must give notice to the registrar, who shall—
    (a)   amend the register accordingly, and
    (b)   issue a new certificate of incorporation altered to meet the circumstances of the case.".

NOTES
Commencement: 1 October 2009.

PART 5
AN LLP'S MEMBERS

CHAPTER 1
REGISTER OF MEMBERS

[10.1114]
18   Requirements for register of members
Sections 162 to 165 apply to LLPs, modified so that they read as follows—

"162 Register of members
(1)   Every LLP must keep a register of its members.
(2)   The register must contain the required particulars (see sections 163 and 164) of each person who is a member of the LLP.
(3)   The register must be kept available for inspection—
    (a)   at the LLP's registered office, or
    (b)   at a place specified in Part 2 of the Companies (Company Records) Regulations 2008 (SI 2008/3006).
(4)   The LLP must give notice to the registrar—
    (a)   of the place at which the register is kept available for inspection, and
    (b)   of any change in that place,
unless it has at all times been kept at the LLP's registered office.
(5)   The register must be open to the inspection—
    (a)   of any member of the LLP without charge, and
    (b)   of any other person on payment of the fee prescribed by regulation 2(a) of the Companies (Fees for Inspection of Company Records) Regulations 2008 (SI 2008/3007).
(6)   If default is made in complying with subsection (1), (2) or (3) or if default is made for 14 days in complying with subsection (4), or if an inspection required under subsection (5) is refused, an offence is committed by—
    (a)   the LLP, and
    (b)   every designated member of the LLP who is in default.
(7)   A person guilty of an offence under this section is liable on summary conviction to a fine not exceeding level 5 on the standard scale and, for continued contravention, a daily default fine not exceeding one-tenth of level 5 on the standard scale.
(8)   In the case of a refusal of inspection of the register, the court may by order compel an immediate inspection of it.

163 Particulars of members to be registered: individuals
(1)   An LLP's register of members must contain the following particulars in the case of an individual—
    (a)   name and any former name;
    (b)   a service address;
    (c)   the country or state (or part of the United Kingdom) in which he is usually resident;
    (d)   date of birth;
    (e)   whether he is a designated member.
(2)   For the purposes of this section "name" means a person's Christian name (or other forename) and surname, except that in the case of—
    (a)   a peer, or
    (b)   an individual usually known by a title,
the title may be stated instead of his Christian name (or other forename) and surname or in addition to either or both of them.

(3)   For the purposes of this section a "former name" means a name by which the individual was formerly known for business purposes.

Where a person is or was formerly known by more than one such name, each of them must be stated.

(4)   It is not necessary for the register to contain particulars of a former name in the following cases—

- (a)   in the case of a peer or an individual normally known by a British title, where the name is one by which the person was known previous to the adoption of or succession to the title;
- (b)   in the case of any person, where the former name—
  - (i)   was changed or disused before the person attained the age of 16 years, or
  - (ii)   has been changed or disused for 20 years or more.

(5)   A person's service address may be stated to be "The LLP's registered office".

164 Particulars of members to be registered: corporate members and firms

An LLP's register of members must contain the following particulars in the case of a body corporate, or a firm that is a legal person under the law by which it is governed—

- (a)   corporate or firm name;
- (b)   registered or principal office;
- (c)   in the case of an EEA company to which the First Company Law Directive (68/151/EEC) applies, particulars of—
  - (i)   the register in which the company file mentioned in Article 3 of that Directive is kept (including details of the relevant state), and
  - (ii)   the registration number in that register;
- (d)   in any other case, particulars of—
  - (i)   the legal form of the company or firm and the law by which it is governed, and
  - (ii)   if applicable, the register in which it is entered (including details of the state) and its registration number in that register;
- (e)   whether it is a designated member.

165 Register of members' residential addresses

(1)   Every LLP must keep a register of members' residential addresses.

(2)   The register must state the usual residential address of each of the LLP's members.

(3)   If a member's usual residential address is the same as his service address (as stated in the LLP's register of members), the register of members' residential addresses need only contain an entry to that effect.

This does not apply if his service address is stated to be "The LLP's registered office".

(4)   If default is made in complying with this section, an offence is committed by—

- (a)   the LLP, and
- (b)   every designated member of the LLP who is in default.

(5)   A person guilty of an offence under this section is liable on summary conviction to a fine not exceeding level 5 on the standard scale and, for continued contravention, a daily default fine not exceeding one-tenth of level 5 on the standard scale.

(6)   This section applies only to members who are individuals, not where the member is a body corporate or a firm that is a legal person under the law by which it is governed.".

NOTES

Commencement: 1 October 2009.

CHAPTER 2
MEMBERS' RESIDENTIAL ADDRESSES: PROTECTION FROM DISCLOSURE

[10.1115]
19   Members' residential addresses: protection from disclosure

Sections 240 to 246 apply to LLPs, modified so that they read as follows—

"240 Protected information

(1)   This Chapter makes provision for protecting, in the case of an LLP member who is an individual—

- (a)   information as to his usual residential address;
- (b)   the information that his service address is his usual residential address.

(2)   That information is referred to in this Chapter as "protected information".

(3)   Information does not cease to be protected information on the individual ceasing to be a member of the LLP.

References in this Chapter to a member include, to that extent, a former member.

241 Protected information: restriction on use or disclosure by LLP

(1)   An LLP must not use or disclose protected information about any of its members, except—

- (a)   for communicating with the member concerned,

(b)   in order to comply with any requirement of this Act or of the Limited Liability
Partnerships Act 2000 (c 12) as to particulars to be sent to the registrar, or
(c)   in accordance with section 244 (disclosure under court order).
(2)   Subsection (1) does not prohibit any use or disclosure of protected information with the
consent of the member concerned.

242 Protected information: restriction on use or disclosure by registrar
(1)   The registrar must omit protected information from the material on the register that is
available for inspection where—
(a)   it is contained in a document delivered to him in which such information is required
to be stated, and
(b)   in the case of a document having more than one part, it is contained in a part of the
document in which such information is required to be stated.
(2)   The registrar is not obliged—
(a)   to check other documents or (as the case may be) other parts of the document to
ensure the absence of protected information, or
(b)   to omit from the material that is available for public inspection anything registered
before 1st October 2009.
(3)   The registrar must not use or disclose protected information except—
(a)   as permitted by section 243 (permitted use or disclosure by registrar), or
(b)   in accordance with section 244 (disclosure under court order).

243 Permitted use or disclosure by the registrar
(1)   The registrar may use protected information for communicating with the member in
question.
(2)   The registrar may disclose protected information—
(a)   to a public authority specified for the purposes of this section, or
(b)   to a credit reference agency.
(3)   The provisions of the Companies (Disclosure of Address) Regulations 2009
(SI 2009/214) relating to disclosure of protected information under this section apply to LLPs.
(4)   The provisions are—
(a)   Part 2 (disclosure of protected information),
(b)   Part 4 (matters relating to applications), so far as relating to disclosure under this
section, and
(c)   any other provisions of the Regulations having effect for the purposes of those
provisions.
(5)   As those provisions apply to LLPs—
(a)   references to provisions of the Companies Act 1985 (c 6), the Insolvency Act 1986
(c 45), the Companies (Northern Ireland) Order 1986 (SI 1986/1032 (NI 6)) or the
Insolvency (Northern Ireland) Order 1989 (SI 1989/2405 (NI 9)) are to those
provisions as applied to LLPs by the Limited Liability Partnerships
Regulations 2001 (SI 2001/1090) or the Limited Liability Partnerships Regulations
(Northern Ireland) 2004 (SR (NI) 2004 No 307);
(b)   read references to a company or proposed company as references to an LLP or
proposed LLP;
(c)   read references to a director as references to a member of an LLP;
(d)   read references to a subscriber to a memorandum of association as references to a
proposed member of a proposed LLP;
(e)   in regulation 1(2), for the definition of "former name" substitute—
""former name" means a name by which an individual was formerly known and
which has been notified to the registrar under section 2 or 9 of the Limited Liability
Partnerships Act 2000;".
(6)   In this section—
"credit reference agency" means a person carrying on a business comprising the furnishing
of information relevant to the financial standing of individuals, being information
collected by the agency for that purpose; and
"public authority" includes any person or body having functions of a public nature.

244 Disclosure under court order
(1)   The court may make an order for the disclosure of protected information by the LLP or
by the registrar if—
(a)   there is evidence that service of documents at a service address other than the
member's usual residential address is not effective to bring them to the notice of the
member, or
(b)   it is necessary or expedient for the information to be provided in connection with the
enforcement of an order or decree of the court,
and the court is otherwise satisfied that it is appropriate to make the order.
(2)   An order for disclosure by the registrar is to be made only if the LLP—
(a)   does not have the member's usual residential address, or
(b)   has been dissolved.

(3)   The order may be made on the application of a liquidator, creditor or member of the LLP, or any other person appearing to the court to have a sufficient interest.

(4)   The order must specify the persons to whom, and purposes for which, disclosure is authorised.

245 Circumstances in which registrar may put address on the public record

(1)   The registrar may put a member's usual residential address on the public record if—

    (a)   communications sent by the registrar to the member and requiring a response within a specified period remain unanswered, or

    (b)   there is evidence that service of documents at a service address provided in place of the member's usual residential address is not effective to bring them to the notice of the member.

(2)   The registrar must give notice of the proposal—

    (a)   to the member, and

    (b)   to every LLP of which the registrar has been notified that the individual is a member.

(3)   The notice must—

    (a)   state the grounds on which it is proposed to put the member's usual residential address on the public record, and

    (b)   specify a period within which representations may be made before that is done.

(4)   It must be sent to the member at his usual residential address, unless it appears to the registrar that service at that address may be ineffective to bring it to the individual's notice, in which case it may be sent to any service address provided in place of that address.

(5)   The registrar must take account of any representations received within the specified period.

(6)   What is meant by putting the address on the public record is explained in section 246.

246 Putting the address on the public record

(1)   The registrar, on deciding in accordance with section 245 that a member's usual residential address is to be put on the public record, shall proceed as if notice of a change of registered particulars had been given—

    (a)   stating that address as the member's service address, and

    (b)   stating that the member's usual residential address is the same as his service address.

(2)   The registrar must give notice of having done so—

    (a)   to the member, and

    (b)   to the LLP.

(3)   On receipt of the notice the LLP must—

    (a)   enter the member's usual residential address in its register of members as his service address, and

    (b)   state in its register of members' residential addresses that his usual residential address is the same as his service address.

(4)   If the LLP has been notified by the member in question of a more recent address as his usual residential address, it must—

    (a)   enter that address in its register of members as the member's service address, and

    (b)   give notice to the registrar as on a change of registered particulars.

(5)   If an LLP fails to comply with subsection (3) or (4), an offence is committed by—

    (a)   the LLP, and

    (b)   every designated member of the LLP who is in default.

(6)   A person guilty of an offence under subsection (5) is liable on summary conviction to a fine not exceeding level 5 on the standard scale and, for continued contravention, a daily default fine not exceeding one-tenth of level 5 on the standard scale.

(7)   A member whose usual residential address has been put on the public record by the registrar under this section may not register a service address other than his usual residential address for a period of five years from the date of the registrar's decision.".

NOTES

Commencement: 1 October 2009.

PART 6
DEBENTURES

[10.1116]
20   General provisions

Sections 738 to 742 apply to LLPs, modified so that they read as follows—

"738 Meaning of "debenture"

In this Act "debenture" includes debenture stock, bonds and any other securities of an LLP, whether or not constituting a charge on the assets of the LLP.

739 Perpetual debentures

(1)   A condition contained in debentures, or in a deed for securing debentures, is not invalid by reason only that the debentures are made—
  (a)   irredeemable, or
  (b)   redeemable only—
    (i)   on the happening of a contingency (however remote), or
    (ii)   on the expiration of a period (however long),
any rule of equity to the contrary notwithstanding.

(2)   Subsection (1) applies to debentures whenever issued and to deeds whenever executed.

740 Enforcement of contract to subscribe for debentures

A contract with an LLP to take up and pay for debentures of the LLP may be enforced by an order for specific performance.

741 Registration of allotment of debentures

(1)   An LLP must register an allotment of debentures as soon as practicable and in any event within two months after the date of the allotment.

(2)   If an LLP fails to comply with this section, an offence is committed by—
  (a)   the LLP, and
  (b)   every member of the LLP who is in default.

(3)   A person guilty of an offence under this section is liable on summary conviction to a fine not exceeding level 3 on the standard scale and, for continued contravention, a daily default fine not exceeding one-tenth of level 3 on the standard scale.

(4)   For the duties of the LLP as to the issue of the debentures, or certificates of debenture stock, see Part 21 (certification and transfer of securities).

742 Debentures to bearer (Scotland)

Notwithstanding anything in the statute of the Scots Parliament of 1696, chapter 25, debentures to bearer issued in Scotland are valid and binding according to their terms.".

NOTES
  Commencement: 1 October 2009.

[10.1117]
21   Register of debenture holders

Sections 743 to 748 apply to LLPs, modified so that they read as follows—

"743 Register of debenture holders

(1)   Any register of debenture holders of an LLP that is kept by the LLP must be kept available for inspection—
  (a)   at the LLP's registered office, or
  (b)   at a place specified in Part 2 of the Companies (Company Records) Regulations 2008 (SI 2008/3006).

(2)   An LLP must give notice to the registrar of the place where any such register is kept available for inspection and of any change in that place.

(3)   No such notice is required if the register has, at all times since it came into existence, been kept available for inspection at the LLP's registered office.

(4)   If an LLP makes default for 14 days in complying with subsection (2), an offence is committed by—
  (a)   the LLP, and
  (b)   every member of the LLP who is in default.

(5)   A person guilty of an offence under this section is liable on summary conviction to a fine not exceeding level 3 on the standard scale and, for continued contravention, a daily default fine not exceeding one-tenth of level 3 on the standard scale.

(6)   References in this section to a register of debenture holders include a duplicate—
  (a)   of a register of debenture holders that is kept outside the United Kingdom, or
  (b)   of any part of such a register.

744 Register of debenture holders: right to inspect and require copy

(1)   Every register of debenture holders of an LLP must, except when duly closed, be open to the inspection—
  (a)   of the registered holder of any such debentures, or any member of the LLP, without charge, and
  (b)   of any other person on payment of the fee prescribed by regulation 2 of the Companies (Fees for Inspection and Copying of Company Records) (No 2) Regulations 2007 (SI 2007/3535).

(2)   Any person may require a copy of the register, or any part of it, on payment of the fee prescribed by regulation 3 of the Companies (Fees for Inspection and Copying of Company Records) (No 2) Regulations 2007 (SI 2007/3535).

(3)   A person seeking to exercise either of the rights conferred by this section must make a request to the LLP to that effect.

(4)   The request must contain the following information—
- (a)   in the case of an individual, his name and address;
- (b)   in the case of an organisation, the name and address of an individual responsible for making the request on behalf of the organisation;
- (c)   the purpose for which the information is to be used; and
- (d)   whether the information will be disclosed to any other person, and if so—
  - (i)   where that person is an individual, his name and address,
  - (ii)   where that person is an organisation, the name and address of an individual responsible for receiving the information on its behalf, and
  - (iii)   the purpose for which the information is to be used by that person.

(5)   For the purposes of this section a register is "duly closed" if it is closed in accordance with provision contained—
- (a)   in the debentures,
- (b)   in the case of debenture stock in the stock certificates, or
- (c)   in the trust deed or other document securing the debentures or debenture stock.

The total period for which a register is closed in any year must not exceed 30 days.

(6)   References in this section to a register of debenture holders include a duplicate—
- (a)   of a register of debenture holders that is kept outside the United Kingdom, or
- (b)   of any part of such a register.

745 Register of debenture holders: response to request for inspection or copy

(1)   Where an LLP receives a request under section 744 (register of debenture holders: right to inspect and require copy), it must within five working days either—
- (a)   comply with the request, or
- (b)   apply to the court.

(2)   If it applies to the court it must notify the person making the request.

(3)   If on an application under this section the court is satisfied that the inspection or copy is not sought for a proper purpose—
- (a)   it shall direct the LLP not to comply with the request, and
- (b)   it may further order that the LLP's costs (in Scotland, expenses) on the application be paid in whole or in part by the person who made the request, even if he is not a party to the application.

(4)   If the court makes such a direction and it appears to the court that the LLP is or may be subject to other requests made for a similar purpose (whether made by the same person or different persons), it may direct that the LLP is not to comply with any such request.

The order must contain such provision as appears to the court appropriate to identify the requests to which it applies.

(5)   If on an application under this section the court does not direct the LLP not to comply with the request, the LLP must comply with the request immediately upon the court giving its decision or, as the case may be, the proceedings being discontinued.

746 Register of debenture holders: refusal of inspection or default in providing copy

(1)   If an inspection required under section 744 (register of debenture holders: right to inspect and require copy) is refused or default is made in providing a copy required under that section, otherwise than in accordance with an order of the court, an offence is committed by—
- (a)   the LLP, and
- (b)   every member of the LLP who is in default.

(2)   A person guilty of an offence under this section is liable on summary conviction to a fine not exceeding level 3 on the standard scale and, for continued contravention, a daily default fine not exceeding one-tenth of level 3 on the standard scale.

(3)   In the case of any such refusal or default the court may by order compel an immediate inspection or, as the case may be, direct that the copy required be sent to the person requesting it.

747 Register of debenture holders: offences in connection with request for or disclosure of information

(1)   It is an offence for a person knowingly or recklessly to make in a request under section 744 (register of debenture holders: right to inspect and require copy) a statement that is misleading, false or deceptive in a material particular.

(2)   It is an offence for a person in possession of information obtained by exercise of either of the rights conferred by that section—
- (a)   to do anything that results in the information being disclosed to another person, or
- (b)   to fail to do anything with the result that the information is disclosed to another person,

knowing, or having reason to suspect, that person may use the information for a purpose that is not a proper purpose.

(3)   A person guilty of an offence under this section is liable—
- (a)   on conviction on indictment, to imprisonment for a term not exceeding two years or a fine (or both);
- (b)   on summary conviction—

     (i)   in England and Wales or Scotland, to imprisonment for a term not exceeding twelve months or to a fine not exceeding the statutory maximum (or both);

     (ii)   in Northern Ireland, to imprisonment for a term not exceeding six months, or to a fine not exceeding the statutory maximum (or both).

748 Time limit for claims arising from entry in register

(1)   Liability incurred by an LLP—

   (a)   from the making or deletion of an entry in the register of debenture holders, or

   (b)   from a failure to make or delete any such entry,

is not enforceable more than ten years after the date on which the entry was made or deleted or, as the case may be, the failure first occurred.

(2)   This is without prejudice to any lesser period of limitation (and, in Scotland, to any rule that the obligation giving rise to the liability prescribes before the expiry of that period).".

NOTES

Commencement: 1 October 2009.

Supplementary provisions

[10.1118]

22

Sections 749 and 750 apply to LLPs, modified so that they read as follows—

"749 Right of debenture holder to copy of deed

(1)   Any holder of debentures of an LLP is entitled, on request and on payment of the fee prescribed by regulation 4 of the Companies (Fees for Inspection and Copying of Company Records) (No 2) Regulations 2007 (SI 2007/3535), to be provided with a copy of any trust deed for securing the debentures.

(2)   If default is made in complying with this section, an offence is committed by every member of the LLP who is in default.

(3)   A person guilty of an offence under this section is liable on summary conviction to a fine not exceeding level 3 on the standard scale and, for continued contravention, a daily default fine not exceeding one-tenth of level 3 on the standard scale.

(4)   In the case of any such default the court may direct that the copy required be sent to the person requiring it.

750 Liability of trustees of debentures

(1)   Any provision contained in—

   (a)   a trust deed for securing an issue of debentures, or

   (b)   any contract with the holders of debentures secured by a trust deed,

is void in so far as it would have the effect of exempting a trustee of the deed from, or indemnifying him against, liability for breach of trust where he fails to show the degree of care and diligence required of him as trustee, having regard to the provisions of the trust deed conferring on him any powers, authorities or discretions.

(2)   Subsection (1) does not invalidate—

   (a)   a release otherwise validly given in respect of anything done or omitted to be done by a trustee before the giving of the release;

   (b)   any provision enabling such a release to be given—

     (i)   on being agreed to by a majority of not less than 75% in value of the debenture holders present and voting in person or, where proxies are permitted, by proxy at a meeting summoned for the purpose, and

     (ii)   either with respect to specific acts or omissions or on the trustee dying or ceasing to act.".

NOTES

Commencement: 1 October 2009.

[10.1119]

23

Sections 752 to 754 apply to LLPs, modified so that they read as follows—

"752 Power to re-issue redeemed debentures

(1)   Where an LLP has redeemed debentures previously issued, then unless—

   (a)   provision to the contrary (express or implied) is contained in any contract made by the LLP, or

   (b)   the LLP has, by making a determination to that effect or by some other act, manifested its intention that the debentures shall be cancelled,

the LLP may re-issue the debentures, either by re-issuing the same debentures or by issuing new debentures in their place.

This subsection is deemed always to have had effect.

(2)   On a re-issue of redeemed debentures the person entitled to the debentures has (and is

deemed always to have had) the same priorities as if the debentures had never been redeemed.

(3) The re-issue of a debenture or the issue of another debenture in its place under this section is treated as the issue of a new debenture for the purposes of stamp duty.

It is not so treated for the purposes of any provision limiting the amount or number of debentures to be issued.

(4) A person lending money on the security of a debenture re-issued under this section which appears to be duly stamped may give the debenture in evidence in any proceedings for enforcing his security without payment of the stamp duty or any penalty in respect of it, unless he had notice (or, but for his negligence, might have discovered) that the debenture was not duly stamped.

In that case the LLP is liable to pay the proper stamp duty and penalty.

753 Deposit of debentures to secure advances

Where an LLP has deposited any of its debentures to secure advances from time to time on current account or otherwise, the debentures are not treated as redeemed by reason only of the LLP's account having ceased to be in debit while the debentures remained so deposited.

754 Priorities where debentures secured by floating charge

(1) This section applies where debentures of an LLP registered in England and Wales or Northern Ireland are secured by a charge that, as created, was a floating charge.

(2) If possession is taken, by or on behalf of the holders of the debentures, of any property comprised in or subject to the charge, and the LLP is not at that time in the course of being wound up, the LLP's preferential debts shall be paid out of assets coming to the hands of the persons taking possession in priority to any claims for principal or interest in respect of the debentures.

(3) "Preferential debts" means the categories of debts listed in Schedule 6 to the Insolvency Act 1986 (c 45) or Schedule 4 to the Insolvency (Northern Ireland) Order 1989 (SI 1989/2405 (NI 19)).

For the purposes of those Schedules "the relevant date" is the date of possession being taken as mentioned in subsection (2).

(4) Payments under this section shall be recouped, as far as may be, out of the assets of the LLP available for payment of general creditors.".

NOTES

Commencement: 1 October 2009.

PART 7
CERTIFICATION AND TRANSFER OF DEBENTURES

[10.1120]
24 Issue of certificates etc on allotment

Section 769 applies to LLPs, modified so that it reads as follows—

"769 Duty of LLP as to issue of certificates etc on allotment

(1) An LLP must, within two months after the allotment of any of its debentures or debenture stock, complete and have ready for delivery—
  (a) the debentures allotted, or
  (b) the certificates of the debenture stock allotted.

(2) Subsection (1) does not apply—
  (a) if the conditions of issue of the debentures or debenture stock provide otherwise, or
  (b) in the case of allotment to a financial institution (see section 778).

(3) If default is made in complying with subsection (1) an offence is committed by every member of the LLP who is in default.

(4) A person guilty of an offence under subsection (3) is liable on summary conviction to a fine not exceeding level 3 on the standard scale and, for continued contravention, a daily default fine not exceeding one-tenth of level 3 on the standard scale.".

NOTES

Commencement: 1 October 2009.

[10.1121]
25 Transfer of debentures

Sections 770 and 771 apply to LLPs, modified so that they read as follows—

"770 Registration of transfer

(1) An LLP may not register a transfer of debentures of the LLP unless—
  (a) a proper instrument of transfer has been delivered to it, or
  (b) the transfer is an exempt transfer within the Stock Transfer Act 1982 (c 41).

(2)   Subsection (1) does not affect any power of the LLP to register as debenture holder a person to whom the right to any debentures of the LLP has been transmitted by operation of law.

771 Procedure on transfer being lodged

(1)   When a transfer of debentures of an LLP has been lodged with the LLP, the LLP must either—

    (a)   register the transfer, or

    (b)   give the transferee notice of refusal to register the transfer, together with its reasons for the refusal,

as soon as practicable and in any event within two months after the date on which the transfer is lodged with it.

(2)   If the LLP refuses to register the transfer, it must provide the transferee with such further information about the reasons for the refusal as the transferee may reasonably request.

    This does not include copies of minutes of meetings of members.

(3)   If an LLP fails to comply with this section, an offence is committed by—

    (a)   the LLP, and

    (b)   every member of the LLP who is in default.

(4)   A person guilty of an offence under this section is liable on summary conviction to a fine not exceeding level 3 on the standard scale and, for continued contravention, a daily default fine not exceeding one-tenth of level 3 on the standard scale.

(5)   This section does not apply in relation to the transmission of debentures by operation of law.".

NOTES

Commencement: 1 October 2009.

[10.1122]

26 Other matters

Sections 774 and 775 apply to LLPs, modified so that they read as follows—

"774 Evidence of grant of probate etc

The production to an LLP of any document that is by law sufficient evidence of the grant of—

    (a)   probate of the will of a deceased person,

    (b)   letters of administration of the estate of a deceased person, or

    (c)   confirmation as executor of a deceased person,

shall be accepted by the LLP as sufficient evidence of the grant.

775 Certification of instrument of transfer

(1)   The certification by an LLP of an instrument of transfer of any debentures of the LLP is to be taken as a representation by the LLP to any person acting on the faith of the certification that there have been produced to the LLP such documents as on their face show a prima facie title to the debentures in the transferor named in the instrument.

(2)   The certification is not to be taken as a representation that the transferor has any title to the debentures.

(3)   Where a person acts on the faith of a false certification by an LLP made negligently, the LLP is under the same liability to him as if the certification had been made fraudulently.

(4)   For the purposes of this section—

    (a)   an instrument of transfer is certificated if it bears the words "certificate lodged" (or words to the like effect);

    (b)   the certification of an instrument of transfer is made by an LLP if—

        (i)   the person issuing the instrument is a person authorised to issue certificated instruments of transfer on the LLP's behalf, and

        (ii)   the certification is signed by a person authorised to certificate transfers on the LLP's behalf or by a member or employee of the LLP or by an officer or employee of a body corporate so authorised;

    (c)   a certification is treated as signed by a person if—

        (i)   it purports to be authenticated by his signature or initials (whether handwritten or not), and

        (ii)   it is not shown that the signature or initials was or were placed there neither by himself nor by a person authorised to use the signature or initials for the purpose of certificating transfers on the LLP's behalf.".

NOTES

Commencement: 1 October 2009.

[10.1123]
27 Issue of certificates etc on transfer

Section 776 applies to LLPs, modified so that it reads as follows—

> **"776 Duty of LLP as to issue of certificates etc on transfer**
> (1) An LLP must, within two months after the date on which a transfer of any of its debentures or debenture stock is lodged with the LLP, complete and have ready for delivery—
>> (a) the debentures transferred, or
>> (b) the certificates of the debenture stock transferred.
> (2) For this purpose a "transfer" means—
>> (a) a transfer duly stamped and otherwise valid, or
>> (b) an exempt transfer within the Stock Transfer Act 1982 (c 41),
> but does not include a transfer that the LLP is for any reason entitled to refuse to register and does not register.
> (3) Subsection (1) does not apply—
>> (a) if the conditions of issue of the debentures or debenture stock provide otherwise, or
>> (b) in the case of a transfer to a financial institution (see section 778).
> (4) If default is made in complying with subsection (1) an offence is committed by every member of the LLP who is in default.
> (5) A person guilty of an offence under this section is liable on summary conviction to a fine not exceeding level 3 on the standard scale and, for continued contravention, a daily default fine not exceeding one-tenth of level 3 on the standard scale.".

NOTES
Commencement: 1 October 2009.

[10.1124]
28 Issue of certificates etc on allotment or transfer to financial institution

Section 778 applies to LLPs, modified so that it reads as follows—

> **"778 Issue of certificates etc: allotment or transfer to financial institution**
> (1) An LLP—
>> (a) of which debentures are allotted to a financial institution,
>> (b) of which debenture stock is allotted to a financial institution, or
>> (c) with which a transfer for transferring debentures or debenture stock to a financial institution is lodged,
> is not required in consequence of that allotment or transfer to comply with section 769(1) or 776(1) (duty of LLP as to issue of certificates etc).
> (2) A "financial institution" means—
>> (a) a recognised clearing house acting in relation to a recognised investment exchange, or
>> (b) a nominee of—
>>> (i) a recognised clearing house acting in that way, or
>>> (ii) a recognised investment exchange,
> designated for the purposes of this section in the rules of the recognised investment exchange in question.
> (3) Expressions used in subsection (2) have the same meaning as in Part 18 of the Financial Services and Markets Act 2000 (c 8).".

NOTES
Commencement: 1 October 2009.

[10.1125]
29 Supplementary provisions

Section 782 is applied to LLPs, modified so that it reads as follows—

> **"782 Issue of certificates etc: court order to make good default**
> (1) If an LLP on which a notice has been served requiring it to make good any default in complying with—
>> (a) section 769(1) (duty of LLP as to issue of certificates etc on allotment), or
>> (b) section 776(1) (duty of LLP as to issue of certificates etc on transfer),
> fails to make good the default within ten days after service of the notice, the person entitled to have the certificates or the debentures delivered to him may apply to the court.
> (2) The court may on such an application make an order directing the LLP and any member of it to make good the default within such time as may be specified in the order.
> (3) The order may provide that all costs (in Scotland, expenses) of and incidental to the application are to be borne by the LLP or by a member of it responsible for the default.".

NOTES
Commencement: 1 October 2009.

PART 8
AN LLP'S ANNUAL RETURN

Contents and delivery of LLP's annual return

[10.1126]
30
Sections 854, 855 and 855A apply to LLPs, modified so that they read as follows—

"854 Duty to deliver annual returns
(1) Every LLP must deliver to the registrar successive annual returns each of which is made up to a date not later than the date that is from time to time the LLP's return date.
(2) The LLP's return date is—
   (a)   the anniversary of the LLP's incorporation, or
   (b)   if the LLP's last return delivered in accordance with this Part was made up to a different date, the anniversary of that date.
(3) Each return must—
   (a)   contain the information required by or under the following provisions of this Part, and
   (b)   be delivered to the registrar within 28 days after the date to which it is made up.

855 Contents of annual return: general
(1) Every annual return must state the date to which it is made up and contain the following information—
   (a)   the address of the LLP's registered office;
   (b)   the required particulars of the members of the LLP (see section 855A);
   (c)   if any LLP records are kept at a place other than the LLP's registered office, the address of that place and the records that are kept there.
(2) In this Part, "return period", in relation to an annual return, means the period beginning immediately after the date to which the last return was made up (or, in the case of the first return, with the incorporation of the LLP) and ending with the date to which the return is made up.

855A Required particulars of members
(1) For the purposes of section 855(1)(b) the required particulars of a member are—
   (a)   where the member is an individual, the particulars required by section 163 to be entered in the register of members (subject to subsection (2) below); and
   (b)   where the member is a body corporate or a firm that is a legal person under the law by which it is governed, the particulars required by section 164 to be entered in the register of members.
(2) The former name of a member who is an individual is a required particular in relation to an annual return only if the member was known by the name for business purposes during the return period.".

NOTES
Commencement: 1 October 2009.

[10.1127]
31
Section 858 applies to LLPs, modified so that it reads as follows—

"858 Failure to deliver annual return
(1) If an LLP fails to deliver an annual return before the end of the period of 28 days after a return date, an offence is committed by—
   (a)   the LLP, and
   (b)   subject to subsection (4), every designated member of the LLP.
(2) A person guilty of an offence under subsection (1) is liable on summary conviction to a fine not exceeding level 5 on the standard scale and, for continued contravention, a daily default fine not exceeding one-tenth of level 5 on the standard scale.
(3) The contravention continues until such time as an annual return made up to that return date is delivered by the LLP to the registrar.
(4) It is a defence for a designated member charged with an offence under subsection (1)(b) to prove that he took all reasonable steps to avoid the commission or continuation of the offence.

Part 10   Miscellaneous other SIs

(5)   In the case of continued contravention, an offence is also committed by every designated member of the LLP who did not commit an offence under subsection (1) in relation to the initial contravention but is in default in relation to the continued contravention.

A person guilty of an offence under this subsection is liable on summary conviction to a fine not exceeding one-tenth of level 5 on the standard scale for each day on which the contravention continues and he is in default.".

NOTES

Commencement: 1 October 2009.

PART 9
LLP CHARGES

CHAPTER 1
LLPS REGISTERED IN ENGLAND AND WALES OR IN NORTHERN IRELAND

[10.1128]
32   Requirement to register LLP charges
Sections 860 to 862 apply to LLPs, modified so that they read as follows—

"860   Charges created by an LLP
(1)   An LLP that creates a charge to which this section applies must deliver the required particulars of the charge, together with the instrument (if any) by which the charge is created or evidenced, to the registrar for registration before the end of the period allowed for registration.
(2)   The required particulars are those prescribed by regulation 2 of the Companies (Particulars of Company Charges) Regulations 2008 (SI 2008/2996).
(3)   Registration of a charge to which this section applies may instead be effected on the application of a person interested in it.
(4)   Where registration is effected on the application of some person other than the LLP, that person is entitled to recover from the LLP the amount of any fees properly paid by him to the registrar on registration.
(5)   If an LLP fails to comply with subsection (1), an offence is committed by—
  (a)   the LLP, and
  (b)   every member of it who is in default.
(6)   A person guilty of an offence under this section is liable—
  (a)   on conviction on indictment, to a fine;
  (b)   on summary conviction, to a fine not exceeding the statutory maximum.
(7)   Subsection (5) does not apply if registration of the charge has been effected on the application of some other person.
(8)   This section applies to the following charges—
  (a)   a charge on land or any interest in land, other than a charge for any rent or other periodical sum issuing out of land,
  (b)   a charge created or evidenced by an instrument which, if executed by an individual, would require registration as a bill of sale,
  (c)   a charge for the purposes of securing any issue of debentures,
  (d)   a charge on book debts of the LLP,
  (e)   a floating charge on the LLP's property or undertaking,
  (f)   a charge on a ship or aircraft, or any share in a ship,
  (g)   a charge on goodwill or on any intellectual property.

861   Charges which have to be registered: supplementary
(1)   The holding of debentures entitling the holder to a charge on land is not, for the purposes of section 860(8)(a), an interest in the land.
(2)   It is immaterial for the purposes of this Chapter where land subject to a charge is situated.
(3)   The deposit by way of security of a negotiable instrument given to secure the payment of book debts is not, for the purposes of section 860(8)(d), a charge on those book debts.
(4)   For the purposes of section 860(8)(g), "intellectual property" means—
  (a)   any patent, trade mark, registered design, copyright or design right;
  (b)   any licence under or in respect of any such right.
(5)   In this Chapter—
    "charge" includes mortgage, and
    "LLP" means an LLP registered in England and Wales or in Northern Ireland.

862   Charges existing on property acquired
(1)   This section applies where an LLP acquires property which is subject to a charge of a kind which would, if it had been created by the LLP after the acquisition of the property, have been required to be registered under this Chapter.

(2) The LLP must deliver the required particulars of the charge, together with a certified copy of the instrument (if any) by which the charge is created or evidenced, to the registrar for registration.

(3) The required particulars are those prescribed by regulation 4 of the Companies (Particulars of Company Charges) Regulations 2008 (SI 2008/2996).

(4) Subsection (2) must be complied with before the end of the period allowed for registration.

(5) If default is made in complying with this section, an offence is committed by—

    (a)   the LLP, and

    (b)   every member of it who is in default.

(6) A person guilty of an offence under this section is liable—

    (a)   on conviction on indictment, to a fine;

    (b)   on summary conviction, to a fine not exceeding the statutory maximum.".

NOTES

Commencement: 1 October 2009.

[10.1129]

33   Special rules about debentures

Sections 863 to 865 apply to LLPs, modified so that they read as follows—

"863   Charge in series of debentures

(1) Where a series of debentures containing, or giving by reference to another instrument, any charge to the benefit of which debenture holders of that series are entitled *pari passu* is created by an LLP, it is for the purposes of section 860(1) sufficient if the required particulars, together with the deed containing the charge (or, if there is no such deed, one of the debentures of the series), are delivered to the registrar before the end of the period allowed for registration.

(2) The following are the required particulars—

    (a)   the total amount secured by the whole series, and

    (b)   the dates of the determinations of the LLP authorising the issue of the series and the date of the covering deed (if any) by which the series is created or defined, and

    (c)   a general description of the property charged, and

    (d)   the names of the trustees (if any) for the debenture holders.

(3) Particulars of the date and amount of each issue of debentures of a series of the kind mentioned in subsection (1) must be sent to the registrar for entry in the register of charges.

(4) Failure to comply with subsection (3) does not affect the validity of the debentures issued.

(5) Subsections (3) to (7) of section 860 apply for the purposes of this section as they apply for the purposes of that section, but as if references to the registration of a charge were references to the registration of a series of debentures.

864   Additional registration requirement for commission etc in relation to debentures

(1) Where any commission, allowance or discount has been paid or made either directly or indirectly by an LLP to a person in consideration of his—

    (a)   subscribing or agreeing to subscribe, whether absolutely or conditionally, for debentures in an LLP, or

    (b)   procuring or agreeing to procure subscriptions, whether absolute or conditional, for such debentures,

the particulars required to be sent for registration under section 860 shall include particulars as to the amount or rate per cent. of the commission, discount or allowance so paid or made.

(2) The deposit of debentures as security for a debt of the LLP is not, for the purposes of this section, treated as the issue of debentures at a discount.

(3) Failure to comply with this section does not affect the validity of the debentures issued.

865   Endorsement of certificate on debentures

(1) The LLP shall cause a copy of every certificate of registration given under section 869 to be endorsed on every debenture or certificate of debenture stock which is issued by the LLP, and the payment of which is secured by the charge so registered.

(2) But this does not require an LLP to cause a certificate of registration of any charge so given to be endorsed on any debenture or certificate of debenture stock issued by the LLP before the charge was created.

(3) If a person knowingly and wilfully authorises or permits the delivery of a debenture or certificate of debenture stock which under this section is required to have endorsed on it a copy of a certificate of registration, without the copy being so endorsed upon it, he commits an offence.

(4) A person guilty of an offence under this section is liable on summary conviction to a fine not exceeding level 3 on the standard scale.".

NOTES
Commencement: 1 October 2009.

[10.1130]
34 Charges in other jurisdictions

Sections 866 and 867 apply to LLPs, modified so that they read as follows—

"866 Charges created in, or over property in, jurisdictions outside the United Kingdom
(1) Where a charge is created outside the United Kingdom comprising property situated outside the United Kingdom, the delivery to the registrar of a verified copy of the instrument by which the charge is created or evidenced has the same effect for the purposes of this Chapter as the delivery of the instrument itself.
(2) Where a charge is created in the United Kingdom but comprises property outside the United Kingdom, the instrument creating or purporting to create the charge may be sent for registration under section 860 even if further proceedings may be necessary to make the charge valid or effectual according to the law of the country in which the property is situated.

867 Charges created in, or over property in, another United Kingdom jurisdiction
(1) Subsection (2) applies where—
    (a) a charge comprises property situated in a part of the United Kingdom other than the part in which the LLP is registered, and
    (b) registration in that other part is necessary to make the charge valid or effectual under the law of that part of the United Kingdom.
(2) The delivery to the registrar of a verified copy of the instrument by which the charge is created or evidenced, together with a certificate stating that the charge was presented for registration in that other part of the United Kingdom on the date on which it was so presented has, for the purposes of this Chapter, the same effect as the delivery of the instrument itself.".

NOTES
Commencement: 1 October 2009.

[10.1131]
35 Orders charging land: Northern Ireland

Section 868 applies to LLPs, modified so that it reads as follows—

"868 Northern Ireland: registration of certain charges etc affecting land
(1) Where a charge imposed by an order under Article 46 of the 1981 Order or notice of such a charge is registered in the Land Registry against registered land or any estate in registered land of an LLP, the Registrar of Titles shall as soon as may be cause two copies of the order made under Article 46 of that Order or of any notice under Article 48 of that Order to be delivered to the registrar.
(2) Where a charge imposed by an order under Article 46 of the 1981 Order is registered in the Registry of Deeds against any unregistered land or estate in land of an LLP, the Registrar of Deeds shall as soon as may be cause two copies of the order to be delivered to the registrar.
(3) On delivery of copies under this section, the registrar shall—
    (a) register one of them in accordance with section 869, and
    (b) not later than 7 days from that date of delivery, cause the other copy together with a certificate of registration under section 869(5) to be sent to the LLP against which judgment was given.
(4) Where a charge to which subsection (1) or (2) applies is vacated, the Registrar of Titles or, as the case may be, the Registrar of Deeds shall cause a certified copy of the certificate of satisfaction lodged under Article 132(1) of the 1981 Order to be delivered to the registrar for entry of a memorandum of satisfaction in accordance with section 872.
(5) In this section—
    "the 1981 Order" means the Judgments Enforcement (Northern Ireland) Order 1981 (SI 1981/226 (NI 6));
    "the Registrar of Deeds" means the registrar appointed under the Registration of Deeds Act (Northern Ireland) 1970 (c 25);
    "Registry of Deeds" has the same meaning as in the Registration of Deeds Acts;
    "Registration of Deeds Acts" means the Registration of Deeds Act (Northern Ireland) 1970 and every statutory provision for the time being in force amending that Act or otherwise relating to the registry of deeds, or the registration of deeds, orders or other instruments or documents in such registry;
    "the Land Registry" and "the Registrar of Titles" are to be construed in accordance with section 1 of the Land Registration Act (Northern Ireland) 1970 (c 18);
    "registered land" and "unregistered land" have the same meaning as in Part 3 of the Land Registration Act (Northern Ireland) 1970.".

NOTES
Commencement: 1 October 2009.

[10.1132]
36 The register of charges

Sections 869 to 873 apply to LLPs, modified so that they read as follows—

"869 Register of charges to be kept by registrar

(1)   The registrar shall keep, with respect to each LLP, a register of all the charges requiring registration under this Chapter.

(2)   In the case of a charge to the benefit of which holders of a series of debentures are entitled, the registrar shall enter in the register the required particulars specified in section 863(2).

(3)   In the case of a charge imposed by the Enforcement of Judgments Office under Article 46 of the Judgments Enforcement (Northern Ireland) Order 1981, the registrar shall enter in the register the date on which the charge became effective.

(4)   In the case of any other charge, the registrar shall enter in the register the following particulars—

(a)   if it is a charge created by an LLP, the date of its creation and, if it is a charge which was existing on property acquired by the LLP, the date of the acquisition,

(b)   the amount secured by the charge,

(c)   short particulars of the property charged, and

(d)   the persons entitled to the charge.

(5)   The registrar shall give a certificate of the registration of any charge registered in pursuance of this Chapter, stating the amount secured by the charge.

(6)   The certificate—

(a)   shall be signed by the registrar or authenticated by the registrar's official seal, and

(b)   is conclusive evidence that the requirements of this Chapter as to registration have been satisfied.

(7)   The register kept in pursuance of this section shall be open to inspection by any person.

870 The period allowed for registration

(1)   The period allowed for registration of a charge created by an LLP is—

(a)   21 days beginning with the day after the day on which the charge is created, or

(b)   if the charge is created outside the United Kingdom, 21 days beginning with the day after the day on which the instrument by which the charge is created or evidenced (or a copy of it), could, in due course of post (and if despatched with due diligence) have been received in the United Kingdom.

(2)   The period allowed for registration of a charge to which property acquired by an LLP is subject is—

(a)   21 days beginning with the day after the day on which the acquisition is completed, or

(b)   if the property is situated and the charge was created outside the United Kingdom, 21 days beginning with the day after the day on which the instrument by which the charge is created or evidenced (or a copy of it) could, in due course of post (and if despatched with due diligence) have been received in the United Kingdom.

(3)   The period allowed for registration of particulars of a series of debentures as a result of section 863 is—

(a)   if there is a deed containing the charge mentioned in section 863(1), 21 days beginning with the day after the day on which that deed is executed, or

(b)   if there is no such deed, 21 days beginning with the day after the day on which the first debenture of the series is executed.

871 Registration of enforcement of security

(1)   If a person obtains an order for the appointment of a receiver or manager of an LLP's property, or appoints such a receiver or manager under powers contained in an instrument, he shall within 7 days of the order or of the appointment under those powers, give notice of the fact to the registrar.

(2)   Where a person appointed receiver or manager of an LLP's property under powers contained in an instrument ceases to act as such receiver or manager, he shall, on so ceasing, give the registrar notice to that effect.

(3)   The registrar must enter a fact of which he is given notice under this section in the register of charges.

(4)   A person who makes default in complying with the requirements of this section commits an offence.

(5)   A person guilty of an offence under this section is liable on summary conviction to a fine not exceeding level 3 on the standard scale and, for continued contravention, a daily default fine not exceeding one-tenth of level 3 on the standard scale.

Part 10   Miscellaneous other SIs

872   Entries of satisfaction and release

(1)   Subsection (2) applies if a statement is delivered to the registrar verifying with respect to a registered charge—

    (a)   that the debt for which the charge was given has been paid or satisfied in whole or in part, or

    (b)   that part of the property or undertaking charged has been released from the charge or has ceased to form part of the LLP's property or undertaking.

(2)   The registrar may enter on the register a memorandum of satisfaction in whole or in part, or of the fact part of the property or undertaking has been released from the charge or has ceased to form part of the LLP's property or undertaking (as the case may be).

(3)   Where the registrar enters a memorandum of satisfaction in whole, the registrar shall if required send the LLP a copy of it.

873   Rectification of register of charges

(1)   Subsection (2) applies if the court is satisfied—

    (a)   that the failure to register a charge before the end of the period allowed for registration, or the omission or mis-statement of any particular with respect to any such charge or in a memorandum of satisfaction—

        (i)   was accidental or due to inadvertence or to some other sufficient cause, or

        (ii) is not of a nature to prejudice the position of creditors of the LLP, or

    (b)   that on other grounds it is just and equitable to grant relief.

(2)   The court may, on the application of the LLP or a person interested, and on such terms and conditions as seem to the court just and expedient, order that the period allowed for registration shall be extended or, as the case may be, that the omission or mis-statement shall be rectified.".

NOTES

Commencement: 1 October 2009.

[10.1133]

37   Avoidance of certain charges

Section 874 applies to LLPs, modified so that it reads as follows—

"874   Consequence of failure to register charges created by an LLP

(1)   If an LLP creates a charge to which section 860 applies, the charge is void (so far as any security on the LLP's property or undertaking is conferred by it) against—

    (a)   a liquidator of the LLP,

    (b)   an administrator of the LLP, and

    (c)   a creditor of the LLP,

unless that section is complied with.

(2)   Subsection (1) is subject to the provisions of this Chapter.

(3)   Subsection (1) is without prejudice to any contract or obligation for repayment of the money secured by the charge; and when a charge becomes void under this section, the money secured by it immediately becomes payable.".

NOTES

Commencement: 1 October 2009.

[10.1134]

38   LLPs' records and registers

Sections 875 to 877 apply to LLPs, modified so that they read as follows—

"875   LLPs to keep copies of instruments creating charges

(1)   An LLP must keep available for inspection a copy of every instrument creating a charge requiring registration under this Chapter, including any document delivered to the LLP under section 868(3)(b) (Northern Ireland: orders imposing charges affecting land).

(2)   In the case of a series of uniform debentures, a copy of one of the debentures of the series is sufficient.

876   LLP's register of charges

(1)   Every LLP shall keep available for inspection a register of charges and enter in it—

    (a)   all charges specifically affecting property of the LLP, and

    (b)   all floating charges on the whole or part of the LLP's property or undertaking.

(2)   The entry shall in each case give a short description of the property charged, the amount of the charge and, except in the cases of securities to bearer, the names of the persons entitled to it.

(3)   If a member of the LLP knowingly and wilfully authorises or permits the omission of an entry required to be made in pursuance of this section, he commits an offence.

(4)   A person guilty of an offence under this section is liable—

    (a)   on conviction on indictment, to a fine;

(b)   on summary conviction, to a fine not exceeding the statutory maximum.

877 Instruments creating charges and register of charges to be available for inspection
(1)   This section applies to—
(a)   documents required to be kept available for inspection under section 875 (copies of instruments creating charges), and
(b)   an LLP's register of charges kept in pursuance of section 876.
(2)   The documents and register must be kept available for inspection—
(a)   at the LLP's registered office, or
(b)   at a place specified in Part 2 of the Companies (Company Records) Regulations 2008 (SI 2008/3006).
(3)   The LLP must give notice to the registrar—
(a)   of the place at which the documents and register are kept available for inspection, and
(b)   of any change in that place,
unless they have at all times been kept at the LLP's registered office.
(4)   The documents and register shall be open to the inspection—
(a)   of any creditor or member of the LLP without charge, and
(b)   of any other person on payment of the fee prescribed by regulation 2(c) of the Companies (Fees for Inspection of Company Records) Regulations 2008 (SI 2008/3007).
(5)   If default is made for 14 days in complying with subsection (3) or an inspection required under subsection (4) is refused, an offence is committed by—
(a)   the LLP, and
(b)   every member of the LLP who is in default.
(6)   A person guilty of an offence under this section is liable on summary conviction to a fine not exceeding level 3 on the standard scale and, for continued contravention, a daily default fine not exceeding one-tenth of level 3 on the standard scale.
(7)   If an inspection required under subsection (4) is refused the court may by order compel an immediate inspection.".

NOTES
Commencement: 1 October 2009.

CHAPTER 2
LLPS REGISTERED IN SCOTLAND

[10.1135]
39   Charges requiring registration
Sections 878 to 881 apply to LLPs, modified so that they read as follows—

"878 Charges created by an LLP
(1)   An LLP that creates a charge to which this section applies must deliver the required particulars of the charge, together with a copy certified as a correct copy of the instrument (if any) by which the charge is created or evidenced, to the registrar for registration before the end of the period allowed for registration.
(2)   The required particulars are those prescribed by regulation 3 of the Companies (Particulars of Company Charges) Regulations 2008 (SI 2008/2996).
(3)   Registration of a charge to which this section applies may instead be effected on the application of a person interested in it.
(4)   Where registration is effected on the application of some person other than the LLP, that person is entitled to recover from the LLP the amount of any fees properly paid by him to the registrar on the registration.
(5)   If an LLP fails to comply with subsection (1), an offence is committed by—
(a)   the LLP, and
(b)   every member of the LLP who is in default.
(6)   A person guilty of an offence under this section is liable—
(a)   on conviction on indictment, to a fine;
(b)   on summary conviction, to a fine not exceeding the statutory maximum.
(7)   Subsection (5) does not apply if registration of the charge has been effected on the application of some other person.
(8)   This section applies to the following charges—
(a)   a charge on land or any interest in such land, other than a charge for any rent or other periodical sum payable in respect of the land,
(b)   a security over incorporeal moveable property of any of the following categories—
(i)   goodwill,
(ii)   a patent or a licence under a patent,
(iii)   a trade mark,
(iv)   a copyright or a licence under a copyright,

Part 10   Miscellaneous other SIs

(v)   a registered design or a licence in respect of such a design,

(vi)   a design right or a licence under a design right, and

(vii)   the book debts (whether book debts of the LLP or assigned to it),

(c)   a security over a ship or aircraft or any share in a ship,

(d)   a floating charge.

879   Charges which have to be registered: supplementary

(1)   A charge on land, for the purposes of section 878(8)(a), includes a charge created by a heritable security within the meaning of section 9(8) of the Conveyancing and Feudal Reform (Scotland) Act 1970 (c 35).

(2)   The holding of debentures entitling the holder to a charge on land is not, for the purposes of section 878(8)(a), deemed to be an interest in land.

(3)   It is immaterial for the purposes of this Chapter where land subject to a charge is situated.

(4)   The deposit by way of security of a negotiable instrument given to secure the payment of book debts is not, for the purposes of section 878(8)(b)(vii), to be treated as a charge on those book debts.

(5)   References in this Chapter to the date of the creation of a charge are—

(a)   in the case of a floating charge, the date on which the instrument creating the floating charge was executed by the LLP creating the charge, and

(b)   in any other case, the date on which the right of the person entitled to the benefit of the charge was constituted as a real right.

(6)   In this Chapter "LLP" means an LLP registered in Scotland.

880   Duty to register charges existing on property acquired

(1)   Subsection (2) applies where an LLP acquires any property which is subject to a charge of any kind as would, if it had been created by the LLP after the acquisition of the property, have been required to be registered under this Chapter.

(2)   The LLP must deliver the required particulars of the charge, together with a copy (certified to be a correct copy) of the instrument (if any) by which the charge was created or is evidenced, to the registrar for registration before the end of the period allowed for registration.

(3)   The required particulars are those prescribed by regulation 4 of the Companies (Particulars of Company Charges) Regulations 2008 (SI 2008/2996).

(4)   If default is made in complying with this section, an offence is committed by—

(a)   the LLP, and

(b)   every member of it who is in default.

(5)   A person guilty of an offence under this section is liable—

(a)   on conviction on indictment, to a fine;

(b)   on summary conviction, to a fine not exceeding the statutory maximum.

881   Charge by way of ex facie absolute disposition, etc

(1)   For the avoidance of doubt, it is hereby declared that, in the case of a charge created by way of an ex facie absolute disposition or assignation qualified by a back letter or other agreement, or by a standard security qualified by an agreement, compliance with section 878(1) does not of itself render the charge unavailable as security for indebtedness incurred after the date of compliance.

(2)   Where the amount secured by a charge so created is purported to be increased by a further back letter or agreement, a further charge is held to have been created by the ex facie absolute disposition or assignation or (as the case may be) by the standard security, as qualified by the further back letter or agreement.

(3)   In that case, the provisions of this Chapter apply to the further charge as if—

(a)   references in this Chapter (other than in this section) to a charge were references to the further charge, and

(b)   references to the date of the creation of a charge were references to the date on which the further back letter or agreement was executed.".

NOTES

Commencement: 1 October 2009.

[10.1136]
40   Special rules about debentures

Sections 882 and 883 apply to LLPs, modified so that they read as follows—

"882   Charge in series of debentures

(1)   Where a series of debentures containing, or giving by reference to any other instrument, any charge to the benefit of which the debenture-holders of that series are entitled *pari passu*, is created by an LLP, it is sufficient for purposes of section 878 if the required particulars, together with a copy of the deed containing the charge (or, if there is no such deed, of one of the debentures of the series) are delivered to the registrar before the end of the period allowed

for registration.

(2)   The following are the required particulars—

(a)   the total amount secured by the whole series,

(b)   the dates of the determinations of the LLP authorising the issue of the series and the date of the covering deed (if any) by which the security is created or defined,

(c)   a general description of the property charged,

(d)   the names of the trustees (if any) for the debenture-holders, and

(e)   in the case of a floating charge, a statement of any provisions of the charge and of any instrument relating to it which prohibit or restrict or regulate the power of the LLP to grant further securities ranking in priority to, or *pari passu* with, the floating charge, or which vary or otherwise regulate the order of ranking of the floating charge in relation to subsisting securities.

(3)   Where more than one issue is made of debentures in the series, particulars of the date and amount of each issue of debentures of the series must be sent to the registrar for entry in the register of charges.

(4)   Failure to comply with subsection (3) does not affect the validity of any of those debentures.

(5)   Subsections (3) to (7) of section 878 apply for the purposes of this section as they apply for the purposes of that section but as if for the reference to the registration of the charge there was substituted a reference to the registration of the series of debentures.

883 Additional registration requirement for commission etc in relation to debentures

(1)   Where any commission, allowance or discount has been paid or made either directly or indirectly by an LLP to a person in consideration of his—

(a)   subscribing or agreeing to subscribe, whether absolutely or conditionally, for debentures in an LLP, or

(b)   procuring or agreeing to procure subscriptions, whether absolute or conditional, for such debentures,

the particulars required to be sent for registration under section 878 shall include particulars as to the amount or rate per cent. of the commission, discount or allowance so paid or made.

(2)   The deposit of debentures as security for a debt of the LLP is not, for the purposes of this section, treated as the issue of debentures at a discount.

(3)   Failure to comply with this section does not affect the validity of the debentures issued.".

NOTES

Commencement: 1 October 2009.

[10.1137]

41   Charges on property outside the United Kingdom

Section 884 applies to LLPs, modified so that it reads as follows—

"884 Charges on property outside United Kingdom

Where a charge is created in the United Kingdom but comprises property outside the United Kingdom, the copy of the instrument creating or purporting to create the charge may be sent for registration under section 878 even if further proceedings may be necessary to make the charge valid or effectual according to the law of the country in which the property is situated.".

NOTES

Commencement: 1 October 2009.

[10.1138]

42   The register of charges

Sections 885 to 888 apply to LLPs, modified so that they read as follows—

"885 Register of charges to be kept by registrar

(1)   The registrar shall keep, with respect to each LLP, a register of all the charges requiring registration under this Chapter.

(2)   In the case of a charge to the benefit of which holders of a series of debentures are entitled, the registrar shall enter in the register the required particulars specified in section 882(2).

(3)   In the case of any other charge, the registrar shall enter in the register the following particulars—

(a)   if it is a charge created by an LLP, the date of its creation and, if it is a charge which was existing on property acquired by the LLP, the date of the acquisition,

(b)   the amount secured by the charge,

(c)   short particulars of the property charged,

(d)   the persons entitled to the charge, and

(e)   in the case of a floating charge, a statement of any of the provisions of the charge and of any instrument relating to it which prohibit or restrict or regulate the LLP's power to grant further securities ranking in priority to, or *pari passu* with, the floating charge, or which vary or otherwise regulate the order of ranking of the floating charge in relation to subsisting securities.

(4)   The registrar shall give a certificate of the registration of any charge registered in pursuance of this Chapter, stating—

(a)   the name of the LLP and the person first-named in the charge among those entitled to the benefit of the charge (or, in the case of a series of debentures, the name of the holder of the first such debenture issued), and

(b)   the amount secured by the charge.

(5)   The certificate—

(a)   shall be signed by the registrar or authenticated by the registrar's official seal, and

(b)   is conclusive evidence that the requirements of this Chapter as to registration have been satisfied.

(6)   The register kept in pursuance of this section shall be open to inspection by any person.

886 The period allowed for registration

(1)   The period allowed for registration of a charge created by an LLP is—

(a)   21 days beginning with the day after the day on which the charge is created, or

(b)   if the charge is created outside the United Kingdom, 21 days beginning with the day after the day on which a copy of the instrument by which the charge is created or evidenced could, in due course of post (and if despatched with due diligence) have been received in the United Kingdom.

(2)   The period allowed for registration of a charge to which property acquired by an LLP is subject is—

(a)   21 days beginning with the day after the day on which the transaction is settled, or

(b)   if the property is situated and the charge was created outside the United Kingdom, 21 days beginning with the day after the day on which a copy of the instrument by which the charge is created or evidenced could, in due course of post (and if despatched with due diligence) have been received in the United Kingdom.

(3)   The period allowed for registration of particulars of a series of debentures as a result of section 882 is—

(a)   if there is a deed containing the charge mentioned in section 882(1), 21 days beginning with the day after the day on which that deed is executed, or

(b)   if there is no such deed, 21 days beginning with the day after the day on which the first debenture of the series is executed.

887 Entries of satisfaction and relief

(1)   Subsection (2) applies if a statement is delivered to the registrar verifying with respect to any registered charge—

(a)   that the debt for which the charge was given has been paid or satisfied in whole or in part, or

(b)   that part of the property charged has been released from the charge or has ceased to form part of the LLP's property.

(2)   If the charge is a floating charge, the statement must be accompanied by either—

(a)   a statement by the creditor entitled to the benefit of the charge, or a person authorised by him for the purpose, verifying that the statement mentioned in subsection (1) is correct, or

(b)   a direction obtained from the court, on the ground that the statement by the creditor mentioned in paragraph (a) could not be readily obtained, dispensing with the need for that statement.

(3)   The registrar may enter on the register a memorandum of satisfaction (in whole or in part) regarding the fact contained in the statement mentioned in subsection (1).

(4)   Where the registrar enters a memorandum of satisfaction in whole, he shall, if required, furnish the LLP with a copy of the memorandum.

(5)   Nothing in this section requires the LLP to submit particulars with respect to the entry in the register of a memorandum of satisfaction where the LLP, having created a floating charge over all or any part of its property, disposes of part of the property subject to the floating charge.

888 Rectification of register of charges

(1)   Subsection (2) applies if the court is satisfied—

(a)   that the failure to register a charge before the end of the period allowed for registration, or the omission or mis-statement of any particular with respect to any such charge or in a memorandum of satisfaction—

(i)   was accidental or due to inadvertence or to some other sufficient cause, or

(ii)   is not of a nature to prejudice the position of creditors of the LLP, or

(b)   that on other grounds it is just and equitable to grant relief.

(2)   The court may, on the application of the LLP or a person interested, and on such terms and conditions as seem to the court just and expedient, order that the period allowed for registration shall be extended or, as the case may be, that the omission or mis-statement shall be rectified.".

NOTES
Commencement: 1 October 2009.

[10.1139]
43   Avoidance of certain charges

Section 889 applies to LLPs, modified so that it reads as follows—

"889   Charges void unless registered
(1)   If an LLP creates a charge to which section 878 applies, the charge is void (so far as any security on the LLP's property or any part of it is conferred by the charge) against—
    (a)   the liquidator of the LLP,
    (b)   an administrator of the LLP, and
    (c)   any creditor of the LLP,
unless that section is complied with.
(2)   Subsection (1) is without prejudice to any contract or obligation for repayment of the money secured by the charge; and when a charge becomes void under this section the money secured by it immediately becomes payable.".

NOTES
Commencement: 1 October 2009.

[10.1140]
44   LLPs' records and registers

Sections 890 to 892 apply to LLPs, modified so that they read as follows—

"890   Copies of instruments creating charges to be kept by LLP
(1)   Every LLP shall cause a copy of every instrument creating a charge requiring registration under this Chapter to be kept available for inspection.
(2)   In the case of a series of uniform debentures, a copy of one debenture of the series is sufficient.

891   LLP's register of charges
(1)   Every LLP shall keep available for inspection a register of charges and enter in it all charges specifically affecting property of the LLP, and all floating charges on any property of the LLP.
(2)   There shall be given in each case a short description of the property charged, the amount of the charge and, except in the case of securities to bearer, the names of the persons entitled to it.
(3)   If a member of the LLP knowingly and wilfully authorises or permits the omission of an entry required to be made in pursuance of this section, he commits an offence.
(4)   A person guilty of an offence under this section is liable—
    (a)   on conviction on indictment, to a fine;
    (b)   on summary conviction, to a fine not exceeding the statutory maximum.

892   Instruments creating charges and register of charges to be available for inspection
(1)   This section applies to—
    (a)   documents required to be kept available for inspection under section 890 (copies of instruments creating charges), and
    (b)   an LLP's register of charges kept in pursuance of section 891.
(2)   The documents and register must be kept available for inspection—
    (a)   at the LLP's registered office, or
    (b)   at a place specified in Part 2 of the Companies (Company Records) Regulations 2008 (SI 2008/3006).
(3)   The LLP must give notice to the registrar—
    (a)   of the place at which the documents and register are kept available for inspection, and
    (b)   of any change in that place,
unless they have at all times been kept at the LLP's registered office.
(4)   The documents and register shall be open to the inspection—
    (a)   of any creditor or member of the LLP without charge, and
    (b)   of any other person on payment of the fee prescribed by regulation 2(d) of the Companies (Fees for Inspection of Company Records) Regulations (SI 2008/3007).
(5)   If default is made for 14 days in complying with subsection (3) or an inspection required under subsection (4) is refused, an offence is committed by—

(a)   the LLP, and

(b)   every member of the LLP who is in default.

(6)   A person guilty of an offence under this section is liable on summary conviction to a fine not exceeding level 3 on the standard scale and, for continued contravention, a daily default fine not exceeding one-tenth of level 3 on the standard scale.

(7)   If an inspection required under subsection (4) is refused the court may by order compel an immediate inspection.".

NOTES

Commencement: 1 October 2009.

PART 10
ARRANGEMENTS, RECONSTRUCTIONS AND CROSS-BORDER MERGERS

[10.1141]
45   Arrangements and reconstructions

(1)   Sections 895 to 900 apply to LLPs, modified so that they read as follows—

"895 Application of this Part

The provisions of this Part apply where a compromise or arrangement is proposed between an LLP and—

(a)   its creditors, or any class of them, or

(b)   its members, or any class of them.

896 Court order for holding of meeting

(1)   The court may, on an application under this section, order a meeting of the creditors or class of creditors, or of the members of the LLP or class of members (as the case may be), to be summoned in such manner as the court directs.

(2)   An application under this section may be made by—

(a)   the LLP,

(b)   any creditor or member of the LLP,

(c)   if the LLP is being wound up, the liquidator, or

(d)   if the LLP is in administration, the administrator.

897 Statement to be circulated or made available

(1)   Where a meeting is summoned under section 896—

(a)   every notice summoning the meeting that is sent to a creditor or member must be accompanied by a statement complying with this section, and

(b)   every notice summoning the meeting that is given by advertisement must either—

(i)   include such a statement, or

(ii)   state where and how creditors or members entitled to attend the meeting may obtain copies of such a statement.

(2)   The statement must—

(a)   explain the effect of the compromise or arrangement, and

(b)   in particular, state—

(i)   any material interests of the members of the LLP (whether as members or as creditors of the LLP or otherwise), and

(ii)   the effect on those interests of the compromise or arrangement, in so far as it is different from the effect on the like interests of other persons.

(3)   Where the compromise or arrangement affects the rights of debenture holders of the LLP, the statement must give the like explanation as respects the trustees of any deed for securing the issue of the debentures as it is required to give as respects the LLP's members.

(4)   Where a notice given by advertisement states that copies of an explanatory statement can be obtained by creditors or members entitled to attend the meeting, every such creditor or member is entitled, on making application in the manner indicated by the notice, to be provided by the LLP with a copy of the statement free of charge.

(5)   If an LLP makes default in complying with any requirement of this section, an offence is committed by—

(a)   the LLP, and

(b)   every member of the LLP who is in default.

This is subject to subsection (7) below.

(6)   For this purpose the following are treated as members of the LLP—

(a)   a liquidator or administrator of the LLP, and

(b)   a trustee of a deed for securing the issue of debentures of the LLP.

(7)   A person is not guilty of an offence under this section if he shows that the default was due to the refusal of a member or trustee for debenture holders to supply the necessary particulars of his interests.

(8)   A person guilty of an offence under this section is liable—

(a)   on conviction on indictment, to a fine;

(b)   on summary conviction, to a fine not exceeding the statutory maximum.

898 Duty of members and trustees to provide information

(1) It is the duty of—
- (a)   any member of the LLP, and
- (b)   any trustee for its debenture holders,

to give notice to the LLP of such matters relating to himself as may be necessary for the purposes of section 897 (explanatory statement to be circulated or made available).

(2)   Any person who makes default in complying with this section commits an offence.

(3)   A person guilty of an offence under this section is liable on summary conviction to a fine not exceeding level 3 on the standard scale.

899 Court sanction for compromise or arrangement

(1)   If a majority in number representing 75% in value of the creditors or class of creditors or members or class of members (as the case may be), present and voting either in person or by proxy at the meeting summoned under section 896, agree a compromise or arrangement, the court may, on an application under this section, sanction the compromise or arrangement.

(2)   An application under this section may be made by—
- (a)   the LLP,
- (b)   any creditor or member of the LLP,
- (c)   if the LLP is being wound up, the liquidator, or
- (d)   if the LLP is in administration, the administrator.

(3)   A compromise or agreement sanctioned by the court is binding on—
- (a)   all creditors or the class of creditors or on the members or class of members (as the case may be), and
- (b)   the LLP or, in the case of an LLP in the course of being wound up, the liquidator and contributories of the LLP.

(4)   The court's order has no effect until a copy of it has been delivered to the registrar.

900 Powers of court to facilitate reconstruction or amalgamation

(1)   This section applies where application is made to the court under section 899 to sanction a compromise or arrangement and it is shown that—
- (a)   the compromise or arrangement is proposed for the purposes of, or in connection with, a scheme for the reconstruction of any LLP or LLPs, or the amalgamation of any two or more relevant bodies corporate (where one or more of them is an LLP), and
- (b)   under the scheme the whole or any part of the undertaking or the property of any LLP concerned in the scheme ("a transferor LLP") is to be transferred to another relevant body corporate ("the transferee body corporate").

(2)   The court may, either by the order sanctioning the compromise or arrangement or by a subsequent order, make provision for all or any of the following matters—
- (a)   the transfer to the transferee body corporate of the whole or any part of the undertaking and of the property or liabilities of any transferor LLP;
- (b)   the allotting or appropriation by the transferee body corporate of any shares, debentures, policies or other like interests in that body corporate which under the compromise or arrangement are to be allotted or appropriated by that body corporate to or for any person;
- (c)   the continuation by or against the transferee body corporate of any legal proceedings pending by or against any transferor LLP;
- (d)   the dissolution, without winding up, of any transferor LLP;
- (e)   the provision to be made for any persons who, within such time and in such manner as the court directs, dissent from the compromise or arrangement;
- (f)   such incidental, consequential and supplemental matters as are necessary to secure that the reconstruction or amalgamation is fully and effectively carried out.

(3)   If an order under this section provides for the transfer of property or liabilities—
- (a)   the property is by virtue of the order transferred to, and vests in, the transferee body corporate, and
- (b)   the liabilities are, by virtue of the order, transferred to and become liabilities of that body corporate.

(4)   The property (if the order so directs) vests freed from any charge that is by virtue of the compromise or arrangement to cease to have effect.

(5)   In this section—

"relevant body corporate" means an LLP or a company;

"property" includes property, rights and powers of every description; and

"liabilities" includes duties.

(6)   Every body corporate in relation to which an order is made under this section must cause a copy of the order to be delivered to the registrar within seven days after its making.

(7)   If default is made in complying with subsection (6) an offence is committed by—
- (a)   the LLP, and every member of the LLP who is in default, and
- (b)   the company, and every officer of the company who is in default.

Part 10   Miscellaneous other SIs

(8)   A person guilty of an offence under subsection (7) is liable on summary conviction to a fine not exceeding level 3 on the standard scale and, for continued contravention, a daily default fine not exceeding one-tenth of level 3 on the standard scale.".

(2)   Section 323 of the Companies Act 2006 (representation of corporations at meetings) applies to a meeting of creditors of the LLP under section 896 or 899 of that Act.

NOTES

Commencement: 1 October 2009.

[10.1142]
46   Cross-border mergers
(1)   Parts 1 to 3 and 5 of the Companies (Cross-Border Mergers) Regulations 2007 apply to LLPs with the following modifications.
(2)   The modifications are—
   (a)   for references to a company substitute references to an LLP (or other EEA body corporate);
   (b)   for references to a UK company, substitute references to a UK LLP;
   (c)   for references to an EEA company substitute references to an EEA body corporate;
   (d)   references to a transferor or transferee LLP include references to an EEA body corporate which is the transferor or transferee in a cross-border merger with a UK LLP;
   (e)   for references to the directors or officers of a company substitute references to the members of an LLP;
   (f)   for "share exchange ratio" substitute "the rights to be given to transferor members";
   (g)   in regulation 2 (meaning of "cross-border merger")—
      (i)   for paragraph (2)(f) substitute—

         "(f)   the consideration for the transfer is—
            (i)   members of the transferor LLP becoming members of the transferee LLP, and
            (ii)   if so agreed, a cash payment receivable by members of the transferor LLP.",

      (ii)   for paragraph (3)(a) to (c) substitute—

         "(a)   there is one transferor LLP, of which the only member is an existing transferee LLP;",

      (iii)   for paragraph (4)(c) substitute—

         "(c)   the consideration for the transfer is—
            (i)   members of the transferor LLP becoming members of the transferee LLP, and
            (ii)   if so agreed, a cash payment receivable by members of the transferor LLP.";

   (h)   in regulation 3(1) (interpretation)—
      (i)   for the definitions of "EEA company", "member" and "members' report" substitute respectively—

         ""EEA body corporate" means a body corporate governed by the law of an EEA State other than the United Kingdom;"
         ""member", in relation to a UK LLP, has the same meaning as in section 4 of the Limited Liability Partnerships Act 2000 (c 12);"
         ""members' report" means a report prepared and adopted in accordance with regulation 8 (members' report);",

      (ii)   omit the definitions of "the 1996 Act", "the Appeal Tribunal", "the CAC", "director", "dismissed" and "dismissal", "employee", "employee participation", "employee representatives", "share exchange ratio", "standard rules of employee participation", "treasury shares", "UK employee" and "UK members of the special negotiating body",
      (iii)   for the definition of "UK company" substitute—

         ""UK LLP" means a limited liability partnership registered and incorporated under the Limited Liability Partnerships Act 2000 other than a limited liability partnership which is being wound up;";

   (i)   omit regulation 5 (unregistered companies);
   (j)   in regulation 7 (draft terms of merger)—
      (i)   omit paragraphs (2)(c), (g) and (j) and (4),
      (ii)   for paragraph (2)(e) substitute—

         "(e)   the date from which being a member of the transferee LLP will entitle the member to participate in profits, and any special conditions affecting that entitlement;", and

      (iii)   paragraph (2)(i) only applies where the transferee body corporate is a company;
   (k)   in regulation 8 (members' report)—
      (i)   in paragraph (2)(b)(ii), omit "or as members", and

(ii)   omit paragraphs (5) and (6);
(l)   in regulation 9 (independent expert's report)—
   (i)   in paragraph (1)(b) for "90% or more (but not all) of the relevant securities" substitute "90% or more (but not all) of the voting rights at meetings of members",
   (ii)   omit paragraph (9);
(m)   in regulation 10 (inspection of documents)—
   (i)   in paragraph (1), omit "and its employee representatives (or if there are no such representatives, the employees)", and
   (ii)   in paragraph (2), omit ", or any class of members,";
(n)   in regulation 11 (power of court to summon meeting of members or creditors), in paragraphs (1)(a) and (2)(b) omit "or a class of members";
(o)   in regulation 12 (public notice of receipt of registered documents)—
   (i)   omit paragraph (1)(c)(v),
   (ii)   in paragraph (1)(c)(vi) omit "other";
(p)   in regulation 13 (approval of members in meeting)—
   (i)   in paragraph (1), for "75% in value, of each class of members of the UK merging company" substitute " 75% of the voting rights of the members of the UK merging LLP";
   (ii)   omit paragraph (2),
   (iii)   in paragraph (4)(c)(i)—
      (aa)   for "the paid up capital of the company which carried the right to vote at general meetings of the company (excluding any shares held as treasury shares)" substitute "the voting rights at meetings of members of the LLP", and
      (bb)   omit "each class of members";
(q)   in regulation 16 (court approval of cross-border merger), omit paragraph (1)(f);
(r)   omit regulation 19(2)(b) and the word "other" in regulation 19(2)(c);
(s)   omit regulation 20 (obligations of transferee company with respect to articles etc);
(t)   omit regulation 21(1)(a) and in regulation 21(1)(b) the word "other".

NOTES
Commencement: 1 October 2009.

PART 11
FRAUDULENT TRADING

[10.1143]
47   Offence of fraudulent trading
Section 993 applies to LLPs, modified so that it reads as follows—

"993 Offence of fraudulent trading
(1)   If any business of an LLP is carried on with intent to defraud creditors of the LLP or creditors of any other person, or for any fraudulent purpose, every person who is knowingly a party to the carrying on of the business in that manner commits an offence.
(2)   This applies whether or not the LLP has been, or is in the course of being, wound up.
(3)   A person guilty of an offence under this section is liable—
   (a)   on conviction on indictment, to imprisonment for a term not exceeding ten years or a fine (or both);
   (b)   on summary conviction—
      (i)   in England and Wales or Scotland, to imprisonment for a term not exceeding twelve months or a fine not exceeding the statutory maximum (or both);
      (ii)   in Northern Ireland, to imprisonment for a term not exceeding six months or a fine not exceeding the statutory maximum (or both).".

NOTES
Commencement: 1 October 2009.

PART 12
PROTECTION OF MEMBERS AGAINST UNFAIR PREJUDICE

[10.1144]
48   Main provisions
Sections 994 to 996 apply to LLPs, modified so that they read as follows—

"994 Petition by LLP member
(1)   A member of an LLP may apply to the court by petition for an order under this Part on the ground—
   (a)   that the LLP's affairs are being or have been conducted in a manner that is unfairly prejudicial to the interests of members generally or of some part of its members (including at least himself), or

(b)   that an actual or proposed act or omission of the LLP (including an act or omission on its behalf) is or would be so prejudicial.

(2) For the purposes of subsection (1)(a), a removal of the LLP's auditor from office—

    (a)   on grounds of divergence of opinions on accounting treatments or audit procedures, or

    (b)   on any other improper grounds,

shall be treated as being unfairly prejudicial to the interests of some part of the LLP's members.

(3) The members of an LLP may by unanimous agreement exclude the right contained in subsection (1) either indefinitely or for such period as is specified in the agreement. The agreement must be recorded in writing.

995 Petition by Secretary of State

(1) This section applies to an LLP in respect of which—

    (a)   the Secretary of State has received a report under section 437 of the Companies Act 1985 (c 6) (inspector's report);

    (b)   the Secretary of State has exercised his powers under section 447 or 448 of that Act (powers to require documents and information or to enter and search premises);

    (c)   the Secretary of State or the Financial Services Authority has exercised his or its powers under Part 11 of the Financial Services and Markets Act 2000 (c 8) (information gathering and investigations); or

    (d)   the Secretary of State has received a report from an investigator appointed by him or the Financial Services Authority under that Part.

(2) If it appears to the Secretary of State that in the case of such an LLP—

    (a)   the LLP's affairs are being or have been conducted in a manner that is unfairly prejudicial to the interests of members generally or of some part of its members, or

    (b)   an actual or proposed act or omission of the LLP (including an act or omission on its behalf) is or would be so prejudicial,

he may apply to the court by petition for an order under this Part.

(3) The Secretary of State may do this in addition to, or instead of, presenting a petition for the winding up of the LLP.

996 Powers of the court under this Part

(1) If the court is satisfied that a petition under this Part is well founded, it may make such order as it thinks fit for giving relief in respect of the matters complained of.

(2) Without prejudice to the generality of subsection (1), the court's order may—

    (a)   regulate the conduct of the LLP's affairs in the future;

    (b)   require the LLP—

        (i)   to refrain from doing or continuing an act complained of, or

        (ii) to do an act that the petitioner has complained it has omitted to do;

    (c)   authorise civil proceedings to be brought in the name and on behalf of the LLP by such person or persons and on such terms as the court may direct;

    (d)   require the LLP or the members of the LLP not to make any, or any specified, alterations in the LLP agreement without the leave of the court;

    (e)   provide for the purchase of the rights and interests of any members in the LLP by other members or by the LLP itself.".

NOTES

Commencement: 1 October 2009.

[10.1145]

49 Supplementary provision

Section 997 applies to LLPs as follows—

"997 Application of general rule-making powers

The power to make rules under section 411 of the Insolvency Act 1986 (c 45) or Article 359 of the Insolvency (Northern Ireland) Order 1989 (SI 1989/2405 (NI 19)), so far as relating to a winding-up petition, applies for the purposes of a petition under this Part.".

NOTES

Commencement: 1 October 2009.

PART 13
DISSOLUTION AND RESTORATION TO THE REGISTER

CHAPTER 1
STRIKING OFF

[10.1146]
50   Registrar's power to strike off defunct LLP

Sections 1000 to 1002 apply to LLPs, modified so that they read as follows—

"1000   Power to strike off LLP not carrying on business or in operation

(1)   If the registrar has reasonable cause to believe that an LLP is not carrying on business or in operation, the registrar may send to the LLP by post a letter inquiring whether the LLP is carrying on business or in operation.

(2)   If the registrar does not within one month of sending the letter receive any answer to it, the registrar must within 14 days after the expiration of that month send to the LLP by post a registered letter referring to the first letter, and stating—

   (a)   that no answer to it has been received, and

   (b)   that if an answer is not received to the second letter within one month from its date, a notice will be published in the Gazette with a view to striking the LLP's name off the register.

(3)   If the registrar—

   (a)   receives an answer to the effect that the LLP is not carrying on business or in operation, or

   (b)   does not within one month after sending the second letter receive any answer,

the registrar may publish in the Gazette, and send to the LLP by post, a notice that at the expiration of three months from the date of the notice the name of the LLP mentioned in it will, unless cause is shown to the contrary, be struck off the register and the LLP will be dissolved.

(4)   At the expiration of the time mentioned in the notice the registrar may, unless cause to the contrary is previously shown by the LLP, strike its name off the register.

(5)   The registrar must publish notice in the Gazette of the LLP's name having been struck off the register.

(6)   On the publication of the notice in the Gazette the LLP is dissolved.

(7)   However—

   (a)   the liability (if any) of every member of the LLP continues and may be enforced as if the LLP had not been dissolved, and

   (b)   nothing in this section affects the power of the court to wind up an LLP the name of which has been struck off the register.

1001   Duty to act in case of LLP being wound up

(1)   If, in a case where an LLP is being wound up—

   (a)   the registrar has reasonable cause to believe—

      (i)   that no liquidator is acting, or

      (ii)   that the affairs of the LLP are fully wound up, and

   (b)   the returns required to be made by the liquidator have not been made for a period of six consecutive months,

       the registrar must publish in the Gazette and send to the LLP or the liquidator (if any) a notice that at the expiration of three months from the date of the notice the name of the LLP mentioned in it will, unless cause is shown to the contrary, be struck off the register and the LLP will be dissolved.

(2)   At the expiration of the time mentioned in the notice the registrar may, unless cause to the contrary is previously shown by the LLP, strike its name off the register.

(3)   The registrar must publish notice in the Gazette of the LLP's name having been struck off the register.

(4)   On the publication of the notice in the Gazette the LLP is dissolved.

(5)   However—

   (a)   the liability (if any) of every member of the LLP continues and may be enforced as if the LLP had not been dissolved, and

   (b)   nothing in this section affects the power of the court to wind up an LLP the name of which has been struck off the register.

1002   Supplementary provisions as to service of letter or notice

(1)   A letter or notice to be sent under section 1000 or 1001 to an LLP may be addressed to the LLP at its registered office or, if no office has been registered, to the care of some member of the LLP.

(2)   If there is no member of the LLP whose name and address are known to the registrar, the letter or notice may be sent to each of the persons who subscribed the incorporation document (if their addresses are known to the registrar).

(3)   A notice to be sent to a liquidator under section 1001 may be addressed to him at his last known place of business.".

NOTES

Commencement: 1 October 2009.

[10.1147]
51   Voluntary striking off

Sections 1003 to 1011 apply to LLPs, modified so that they read as follows—

"1003 Striking off on application by LLP

(1)   The registrar of companies may strike the LLP's name off the register on application by—

    (a)   a majority of the members of an LLP, or

    (b)   if there are only two such members, by both of them, or

    (c)   if there is only one remaining member of an LLP, by that member.

(2)   The application must contain a declaration by the member or members making the application that neither section 1004 nor 1005 prevents the application from being made.

(3)   The registrar may not strike an LLP off under this section until after the expiration of three months from the publication by the registrar in the Gazette of a notice—

    (a)   stating that the registrar may exercise the power under this section in relation to the LLP, and

    (b)   inviting any person to show cause why that should not be done.

(4)   The registrar must publish notice in the Gazette of the LLP's name having been struck off.

(5)   On the publication of the notice in the Gazette the LLP is dissolved.

(6)   However—

    (a)   the liability (if any) of every member of the LLP continues and may be enforced as if the LLP had not been dissolved, and

    (b)   nothing in this section affects the power of the court to wind up an LLP the name of which has been struck off the register.

1004 Circumstances in which application not to be made: activities of LLP

(1)   An application under section 1003 (application for voluntary striking off) on behalf of an LLP must not be made if, at any time in the previous three months, the LLP has—

    (a)   changed its name,

    (b)   traded or otherwise carried on business,

    (c)   made a disposal for value of property or rights that, immediately before ceasing to trade or otherwise carry on business, it held for the purpose of disposal for gain in the normal course of trading or otherwise carrying on business, or

    (d)   engaged in any other activity, except one which is—

        (i)   necessary or expedient for the purpose of making an application under that section, or deciding whether to do so,

        (ii)   necessary or expedient for the purpose of concluding the affairs of the LLP, or

        (iii)   necessary or expedient for the purpose of complying with any statutory requirement.

(2)   For the purposes of this section, an LLP is not to be treated as trading or otherwise carrying on business by virtue only of the fact that it makes a payment in respect of a liability incurred in the course of trading or otherwise carrying on business.

(3)   It is an offence for a person to make an application in contravention of this section.

(4)   In proceedings for such an offence it is a defence for the accused to prove that he did not know, and could not reasonably have known, of the existence of the facts that led to the contravention.

(5)   A person guilty of an offence under this section is liable—

    (a)   on conviction on indictment, to a fine;

    (b)   on summary conviction, to a fine not exceeding the statutory maximum.

1005 Circumstances in which application not to be made: proceedings pending

(1)   An application under section 1003 (application for voluntary striking off) on behalf of an LLP must not be made at a time when—

    (a)   an application to the court under Part 26 has been made on behalf of the LLP for the sanctioning of a compromise or arrangement and the matter has not been finally concluded;

    (b)   a voluntary arrangement in relation to the LLP has been proposed under Part 1 of the Insolvency Act 1986 (c 45) or Part 2 of the Insolvency (Northern Ireland) Order 1989 (SI 1989/2405 (NI 19)) and the matter has not been finally concluded;

    (c)   the LLP is in administration under Part 2 of that Act or Part 3 of that Order;

(d)   paragraph 44 of Schedule B1 to that Act or paragraph 45 of Schedule B1 to that Order applies (interim moratorium on proceedings where application to the court for an administration order has been made or notice of intention to appoint administrator has been filed);

(e)   the LLP is being wound up under Part 4 of that Act or Part 5 of that Order, whether voluntarily or by the court, or a petition under that Part for winding up of the LLP by the court has been presented and not finally dealt with or withdrawn;

(f)   there is a receiver or manager of the LLP's property;

(g)   the LLP's estate is being administered by a judicial factor.

(2) For the purposes of subsection (1)(a), the matter is finally concluded if—

(a)   the application has been withdrawn,

(b)   the application has been finally dealt with without a compromise or arrangement being sanctioned by the court, or

(c)   a compromise or arrangement has been sanctioned by the court and has, together with anything required to be done under any provision made in relation to the matter by order of the court, been fully carried out.

(3) For the purposes of subsection (1)(b), the matter is finally concluded if—

(a)   no meeting is to be summoned under section 3 of the Insolvency Act 1986 (c 45) or Article 16 of the Insolvency (Northern Ireland) Order 1989,

(b)   the meeting summoned under that section or Article fails to approve the arrangement with no, or the same, modifications,

(c)   an arrangement approved by a meeting summoned under that section, or in consequence of a direction under section 6(4)(b) of that Act or Article 19(4)(b) of that Order, has been fully implemented, or

(d)   the court makes an order under section 6(5) of that Act or Article 19(5) of that Order revoking approval given at a previous meeting and, if the court gives any directions under section 6(6) of that Act or Article 19(6) of that Order, the LLP has done whatever it is required to do under those directions.

(4) It is an offence for a person to make an application in contravention of this section.

(5) In proceedings for such an offence it is a defence for the accused to prove that he did not know, and could not reasonably have known, of the existence of the facts that led to the contravention.

(6) A person guilty of an offence under this section is liable—

(a)   on conviction on indictment, to a fine;

(b)   on summary conviction, to a fine not exceeding the statutory maximum.

1006 Copy of application to be given to members, employees etc

(1) A person who makes an application under section 1003 (application for voluntary striking off) on behalf of an LLP must secure that, within seven days from the day on which the application is made, a copy of it is given to every person who at any time on that day is—

(a)   a member of the LLP,

(b)   an employee of the LLP,

(c)   a creditor of the LLP, or

(d)   a manager or trustee of any pension fund established for the benefit of employees of the LLP.

(2) Subsection (1) does not require a copy of the application to be given to a member who is a party to the application.

(3) The duty imposed by this section ceases to apply if the application is withdrawn before the end of the period for giving the copy application.

(4) A person who fails to perform the duty imposed on him by this section commits an offence.

If he does so with the intention of concealing the making of the application from the person concerned, he commits an aggravated offence.

(5) In proceedings for an offence under this section it is a defence for the accused to prove that he took all reasonable steps to perform the duty.

(6) A person guilty of an offence under this section (other than an aggravated offence) is liable—

(a)   on conviction on indictment, to a fine;

(b)   on summary conviction, to a fine not exceeding the statutory maximum.

(7) A person guilty of an aggravated offence under this section is liable—

(a)   on conviction on indictment, to imprisonment for a term not exceeding seven years or a fine (or both);

(b)   on summary conviction—

(i)   in England and Wales or Scotland, to imprisonment for a term not exceeding twelve months or to a fine not exceeding the statutory maximum (or both);

(ii) in Northern Ireland, to imprisonment for a term not exceeding six months, or to a fine not exceeding the statutory maximum (or both).

Part 10   Miscellaneous other SIs

1007 Copy of application to be given to new members, employees, etc

(1) This section applies in relation to any time after the day on which an LLP makes an application under section 1003 (application for voluntary striking off) and before the day on which the application is finally dealt with or withdrawn.

(2) A person who is a member of the LLP at the end of a day on which a person (other than himself) becomes—

    (a)   a member of the LLP,

    (b)   an employee of the LLP,

    (c)   a creditor of the LLP, or

    (d)   a manager or trustee of any pension fund established for the benefit of employees of the LLP,

must secure that a copy of the application is given to that person within seven days from that day.

(3) The duty imposed by this section ceases to apply if the application is finally dealt with or withdrawn before the end of the period for giving the copy application.

(4) A person who fails to perform the duty imposed on him by this section commits an offence.

If he does so with the intention of concealing the making of the application from the person concerned, he commits an aggravated offence.

(5) In proceedings for an offence under this section it is a defence for the accused to prove—

    (a)   that at the time of the failure he was not aware of the fact that the LLP had made an application under section 1003, or

    (b)   that he took all reasonable steps to perform the duty.

(6) A person guilty of an offence under this section (other than an aggravated offence) is liable—

    (a)   on conviction on indictment, to a fine;

    (b)   on summary conviction, to a fine not exceeding the statutory maximum.

(7) A person guilty of an aggravated offence under this section is liable—

    (a)   on conviction on indictment, to imprisonment for a term not exceeding seven years or a fine (or both);

    (b)   on summary conviction—

        (i)   in England and Wales or Scotland, to imprisonment for a term not exceeding twelve months or to a fine not exceeding the statutory maximum (or both);

        (ii)   in Northern Ireland, to imprisonment for a term not exceeding six months, or to a fine not exceeding the statutory maximum (or both).

1008 Copy of application: provisions as to service of documents

(1) The following provisions have effect for the purposes of—

section 1006 (copy of application to be given to members, employees, etc), and

section 1007 (copy of application to be given to new members, employees, etc).

(2) A document is treated as given to a person if it is—

    (a)   delivered to him, or

    (b)   left at his proper address, or

    (c)   sent by post to him at that address.

(3) For the purposes of subsection (2) and section 7 of the Interpretation Act 1978 (c 30) (service of documents by post) as it applies in relation to that subsection, the proper address of a person is—

    (a)   in the case of a firm incorporated or formed in the United Kingdom, its registered or principal office;

    (b)   in the case of a firm incorporated or formed outside the United Kingdom—

        (i)   if it has a place of business in the United Kingdom, its principal office in the United Kingdom, or

        (ii)   if it does not have a place of business in the United Kingdom, its registered or principal office;

    (c)   in the case of an individual, his last known address.

(4) In the case of a creditor of the LLP a document is treated as given to him if it is left or sent by post to him—

    (a)   at the place of business of his with which the LLP has had dealings by virtue of which he is a creditor of the LLP, or

    (b)   if there is more than one such place of business, at each of them.

1009 Circumstances in which application to be withdrawn

(1) This section applies where, at any time on or after the day on which an LLP makes an application under section 1003 (application for voluntary striking off) and before the day on which the application is finally dealt with or withdrawn—

    (a)   the LLP—

        (i)   changes its name,

        (ii)   trades or otherwise carries on business,

         (iii) makes a disposal for value of any property or rights other than those which it was necessary or expedient for it to hold for the purpose of making, or proceeding with, an application under that section, or

         (iv) engages in any activity, except one to which subsection (4) applies;

  (b)   an application is made to the court under Part 26 on behalf of the LLP for the sanctioning of a compromise or arrangement;

  (c)   a voluntary arrangement in relation to the LLP is proposed under Part 1 of the Insolvency Act 1986 (c 45) or Part 2 of the Insolvency (Northern Ireland) Order 1989 (SI 1989/2405 (NI 19));

  (d)   an application to the court for an administration order in respect of the LLP is made under paragraph 12 of Schedule B1 to that Act or paragraph 13 of Schedule B1 to that Order;

  (e)   an administrator is appointed in respect of the LLP under paragraph 14 or 22 of Schedule B1 to that Act or paragraph 15 or 23 of Schedule B1 to that Order, or a copy of notice of intention to appoint an administrator of the LLP under any of those provisions is filed with the court;

  (f)   there arise any of the circumstances in which, under section 84(1) of that Act or Article 70 of that Order, the LLP may be voluntarily wound up;

  (g)   a petition is presented for the winding up of the LLP by the court under Part 4 of that Act or Part 5 of that Order;

  (h)   a receiver or manager of the LLP's property is appointed; or

  (i)   a judicial factor is appointed to administer the LLP's estate.

(2) A person who, at the end of a day on which any of the events mentioned in subsection (1) occurs, is a member of the LLP must secure that the LLP's application is withdrawn forthwith.

(3) For the purposes of subsection (1)(a), an LLP is not treated as trading or otherwise carrying on business by virtue only of the fact that it makes a payment in respect of a liability incurred in the course of trading or otherwise carrying on business.

(4) The excepted activities referred to in subsection (1)(a)(iv) are any activity necessary or expedient for the purposes of—

  (a)   making, or proceeding with, an application under section 1003 (application for voluntary striking off),

  (b)   concluding affairs of the LLP that are outstanding because of what has been necessary or expedient for the purpose of making, or proceeding with, such an application, or

  (c)   complying with any statutory requirement.

(5) A person who fails to perform the duty imposed on him by this section commits an offence.

(6) In proceedings for an offence under this section it is a defence for the accused to prove—

  (a)   that at the time of the failure he was not aware of the fact that the LLP had made an application under section 1003, or

  (b)   that he took all reasonable steps to perform the duty.

(7) A person guilty of an offence under this section is liable—

  (a)   on conviction on indictment, to a fine;

  (b)   on summary conviction, to a fine not exceeding the statutory maximum.

1010 Withdrawal of application

An application under section 1003 is withdrawn by notice to the registrar.

1011 Meaning of "creditor"

In this Chapter "creditor" includes a contingent or prospective creditor.".

NOTES

Commencement: 1 October 2009.

CHAPTER 2
PROPERTY OF DISSOLVED LLP

[10.1148]

52 Property of dissolved LLP vesting as bona vacantia

Sections 1012 to 1014 apply to LLPs, modified so that they read as follows—

"1012 Property of dissolved LLP to be bona vacantia

(1) When an LLP is dissolved, all property and rights whatsoever vested in or held on trust for the LLP immediately before its dissolution (including leasehold property, but not including property held by the LLP on trust for another person) are deemed to be *bona vacantia* and—

  (a)   accordingly belong to the Crown, or to the Duchy of Lancaster or to the Duke of Cornwall for the time being (as the case may be), and

  (b)   vest and may be dealt with in the same manner as other *bona vacantia* accruing to the Crown, to the Duchy of Lancaster or to the Duke of Cornwall.

(2) Subsection (1) has effect subject to the possible restoration of the LLP to the register under Chapter 3 (see section 1034).

1013 Crown disclaimer of property vesting as bona vacantia

(1) Where property vests in the Crown under section 1012, the Crown's title to it under that section may be disclaimed by a notice signed by the Crown representative, that is to say the Treasury Solicitor, or, in relation to property in Scotland, the Queen's and Lord Treasurer's Remembrancer.

(2) The right to execute a notice of disclaimer under this section may be waived by or on behalf of the Crown either expressly or by taking possession.

(3) A notice of disclaimer must be executed within three years after—

- (a) the date on which the fact that the property may have vested in the Crown under section 1012 first comes to the notice of the Crown representative, or
- (b) if ownership of the property is not established at that date, the end of the period reasonably necessary for the Crown representative to establish the ownership of the property.

(4) If an application in writing is made to the Crown representative by a person interested in the property requiring him to decide whether he will or will not disclaim, any notice of disclaimer must be executed within twelve months after the making of the application or such further period as may be allowed by the court.

(5) A notice of disclaimer under this section is of no effect if it is shown to have been executed after the end of the period specified by subsection (3) or (4).

(6) A notice of disclaimer under this section must be delivered to the registrar and retained and registered by him.

(7) Copies of it must be published in the Gazette and sent to any persons who have given the Crown representative notice that they claim to be interested in the property.

(8) This section applies to property vested in the Duchy of Lancaster or the Duke of Cornwall under section 1012 as if for references to the Crown and the Crown representative there were respectively substituted references to the Duchy of Lancaster and to the Solicitor to that Duchy, or to the Duke of Cornwall and to the Solicitor to the Duchy of Cornwall, as the case may be.

1014 Effect of Crown disclaimer

(1) Where notice of disclaimer is executed under section 1013 as respects any property, that property is deemed not to have vested in the Crown under section 1012.

(2) The following sections contain provisions as to the effect of the Crown disclaimer—
sections 1015 to 1019 apply in relation to property in England and Wales or Northern Ireland;
sections 1020 to 1022 apply in relation to property in Scotland.".

NOTES

Commencement: 1 October 2009.

[10.1149]

53 Effect of Crown disclaimer: England and Wales and Northern Ireland

Sections 1015 to 1019 apply to LLPs, modified so that they read as follows—

"1015 General effect of disclaimer

(1) The Crown's disclaimer operates so as to terminate, as from the date of the disclaimer, the rights, interests and liabilities of the LLP in or in respect of the property disclaimed.

(2) It does not, except so far as is necessary for the purpose of releasing the LLP from any liability, affect the rights or liabilities of any other person.

1016 Disclaimer of leaseholds

(1) The disclaimer of any property of a leasehold character does not take effect unless a copy of the disclaimer has been served (so far as the Crown representative is aware of their addresses) on every person claiming under the LLP as underlessee or mortgagee, and either—

- (a) no application under section 1017 (power of court to make vesting order) is made with respect to that property before the end of the period of 14 days beginning with the day on which the last notice under this paragraph was served, or
- (b) where such an application has been made, the court directs that the disclaimer shall take effect.

(2) Where the court gives a direction under subsection (1)(b) it may also, instead of or in addition to any order it makes under section 1017, make such order as it thinks fit with respect to fixtures, tenant's improvements and other matters arising out of the lease.

(3) In this section the "Crown representative" means—

- (a) in relation to property vested in the Duchy of Lancaster, the Solicitor to that Duchy;
- (b) in relation to property vested in the Duke of Cornwall, the Solicitor to the Duchy of Cornwall;
- (c) in relation to property in Scotland, the Queen's and Lord Treasurer's Remembrancer;

(d)   in relation to other property, the Treasury Solicitor.

1017 Power of court to make vesting order
(1)   The court may on application by a person who—
  (a)   claims an interest in the disclaimed property, or
  (b)   is under a liability in respect of the disclaimed property that is not discharged by the disclaimer,
make an order under this section in respect of the property.
(2)   An order under this section is an order for the vesting of the disclaimed property in, or its delivery to—
  (a)   a person entitled to it (or a trustee for such a person), or
  (b)   a person subject to such a liability as is mentioned in subsection (1)(b) (or a trustee for such a person).
(3)   An order under subsection (2)(b) may only be made where it appears to the court that it would be just to do so for the purpose of compensating the person subject to the liability in respect of the disclaimer.
(4)   An order under this section may be made on such terms as the court thinks fit.
(5)   On a vesting order being made under this section, the property comprised in it vests in the person named in that behalf in the order without conveyance, assignment or transfer.

1018 Protection of persons holding under a lease
(1)   The court must not make an order under section 1017 vesting property of a leasehold nature in a person claiming under the LLP as underlessee or mortgagee except on terms making that person—
  (a)   subject to the same liabilities and obligations as those to which the LLP was subject under the lease, or
  (b)   if the court thinks fit, subject to the same liabilities and obligations as if the lease had been assigned to him.
(2)   Where the order relates to only part of the property comprised in the lease, subsection (1) applies as if the lease had comprised only the property comprised in the vesting order.
(3)   A person claiming under the LLP as underlessee or mortgagee who declines to accept a vesting order on such terms is excluded from all interest in the property.
(4)   If there is no person claiming under the LLP who is willing to accept an order on such terms, the court has power to vest the LLP's estate and interest in the property in any person who is liable (whether personally or in a representative character, and whether alone or jointly with the LLP) to perform the lessee's covenants in the lease.
(5)   The court may vest that estate and interest in such a person freed and discharged from all estates, incumbrances and interests created by the LLP.

1019 Land subject to rentcharge
Where in consequence of the disclaimer land that is subject to a rentcharge vests in any person, neither he nor his successors in title are subject to any personal liability in respect of sums becoming due under the rentcharge, except sums becoming due after he, or some person claiming under or through him, has taken possession or control of the land or has entered into occupation of it.".

NOTES
Commencement: 1 October 2009.

[10.1150]
54   Effect of Crown disclaimer: Scotland
Sections 1020 to 1022 apply to LLPs, modified so that they read as follows—

"1020 General effect of disclaimer
(1)   The Crown's disclaimer operates to determine, as from the date of the disclaimer, the rights, interests and liabilities of the LLP, and the property of the LLP, in or in respect of the property disclaimed.
(2)   It does not (except so far as is necessary for the purpose of releasing the LLP and its property from liability) affect the rights or liabilities of any other person.

1021 Power of court to make vesting order
(1)   The court may—
  (a)   on application by a person who either claims an interest in disclaimed property or is under a liability not discharged by this Act in respect of disclaimed property, and
  (b)   on hearing such persons as it thinks fit,
make an order for the vesting of the property in or its delivery to any persons entitled to it, or to whom it may seem just that the property should be delivered by way of compensation for such liability, or a trustee for him.
(2)   The order may be made on such terms as the court thinks fit.

(3)   On a vesting order being made under this section, the property comprised in it vests accordingly in the person named in that behalf in the order, without conveyance or assignation for that purpose.

1022 Protection of persons holding under a lease
(1)   Where the property disclaimed is held under a lease the court must not make a vesting order in favour of a person claiming under the LLP, whether—
   (a)   as sub-lessee, or
   (b)   as creditor in a duly registered or (as the case may be) recorded heritable security over a lease,
except on the following terms.
(2)   The person must by the order be made subject—
   (a)   to the same liabilities and obligations as those to which the LLP was subject under the lease in respect of the property, or
   (b)   if the court thinks fit, only to the same liabilities and obligations as if the lease had been assigned to him.
   In either event (if the case so requires) the liabilities and obligations must be as if the lease had comprised only the property comprised in the vesting order.
(3)   A sub-lessee or creditor declining to accept a vesting order on such terms is excluded from all interest in and security over the property.
(4)   If there is no person claiming under the LLP who is willing to accept an order on such terms, the court has power to vest the LLP's estate and interest in the property in any person liable (either personally or in a representative character, and either alone or jointly with the LLP) to perform the lessee's obligations under the lease.
(5)   The court may vest that estate and interest in such a person freed and discharged from all interests, rights and obligations created by the LLP in the lease or in relation to the lease.
(6)   For the purposes of this section a heritable security—
   (a)   is duly recorded if it is recorded in the Register of Sasines, and
   (b)   is duly registered if registered in accordance with the Land Registration (Scotland) Act 1979 (c 33).".

NOTES
Commencement: 1 October 2009.

[10.1151]
55 Supplementary provisions
Section 1023 applies to LLPs, modified so that it reads as follows—

"1023 Liability for rentcharge on LLP's land after dissolution
(1)   This section applies where on the dissolution of an LLP land in England and Wales or Northern Ireland that is subject to a rentcharge vests by operation of law in the Crown or any other person ("the proprietor").
(2)   Neither the proprietor nor his successors in title are subject to any personal liability in respect of sums becoming due under the rentcharge, except sums becoming due after the proprietor, or some person claiming under or through him, has taken possession or control of the land or has entered into occupation of it.".

NOTES
Commencement: 1 October 2009.

CHAPTER 3
RESTORATION TO THE REGISTER

[10.1152]
56 Administrative restoration to the register
Sections 1024 to 1028 apply to LLPs, modified so that they read as follows—

"1024 Application for administrative restoration to the register
(1)   An application may be made to the registrar to restore to the register an LLP that has been struck off the register under section 1000 or 1001 (power of registrar to strike off defunct LLP).
(2)   An application under this section may be made whether or not the LLP has in consequence been dissolved.
(3)   An application under this section may only be made by a former member of the LLP.
(4)   An application under this section may not be made after the end of the period of six years from the date of the dissolution of the LLP.
   For this purpose an application is made when it is received by the registrar.

1025 Requirements for administrative restoration
(1)   On an application under section 1024 the registrar shall restore the LLP to the register if,

and only if, the following conditions are met.

(2)   The first condition is that the LLP was carrying on business or in operation at the time of its striking off.

(3)   The second condition is that, if any property or right previously vested in or held on trust for the LLP has vested as *bona vacantia*, the Crown representative has signified to the registrar in writing consent to the LLP's restoration to the register.

(4)   It is the applicant's responsibility to obtain that consent and to pay any costs (in Scotland, expenses) of the Crown representative—

(a)   in dealing with the property during the period of dissolution, or

(b)   in connection with the proceedings on the application,

that may be demanded as a condition of giving consent.

(5)   The third condition is that the applicant has—

(a)   delivered to the registrar such documents relating to the LLP as are necessary to bring up to date the records kept by the registrar, and

(b)   paid any penalties under section 453 or corresponding earlier provisions (civil penalty for failure to deliver accounts) that were outstanding at the date of dissolution or striking off.

(6)   The fourth condition is that the applicant has sent notice of the application under section 1024 to all those who were members of the LLP at the time of its striking off.

(7)   In this section the "Crown representative" means—

(a)   in relation to property vested in the Duchy of Lancaster, the Solicitor to that Duchy;

(b)   in relation to property vested in the Duke of Cornwall, the Solicitor to the Duchy of Cornwall;

(c)   in relation to property in Scotland, the Queen's and Lord Treasurer's Remembrancer;

(d)   in relation to other property, the Treasury Solicitor.

1026 Application to be accompanied by statement of compliance

(1)   An application under section 1024 (application for administrative restoration to the register) must be accompanied by a statement of compliance.

(2)   The statement of compliance required is a statement—

(a)   that the person making the application has standing to apply (see subsection (3) of that section), and

(b)   that the requirements for administrative restoration (see section 1025) are met.

(3)   The registrar may accept the statement of compliance as sufficient evidence of those matters.

1027 Registrar's decision on application for administrative restoration

(1)   The registrar must give notice to the applicant of the decision on an application under section 1024 (application for administrative restoration to the register).

(2)   If the decision is that the LLP should be restored to the register, the restoration takes effect as from the date that notice is sent.

(3)   In the case of such a decision, the registrar must—

(a)   enter on the register a note of the date as from which the LLP's restoration to the register takes effect, and

(b)   cause notice of the restoration to be published in the Gazette.

(4)   The notice under subsection (3)(b) must state—

(a)   the name of the LLP or, if the LLP is restored to the register under a different name (see section 1033), that name and its former name,

(b)   the LLP's registered number, and

(c)   the date as from which the restoration of the LLP to the register takes effect.

1028 Effect of administrative restoration

(1)   The general effect of administrative restoration to the register is that the LLP is deemed to have continued in existence as if it had not been dissolved or struck off the register.

(2)   The LLP is not liable to a penalty under section 453 or any corresponding earlier provision (civil penalty for failure to deliver accounts) for a financial year in relation to which the period for filing accounts and reports ended—

(a)   after the date of dissolution or striking off, and

(b)   before the restoration of the LLP to the register.

(3)   The court may give such directions and make such provision as seems just for placing the LLP and all other persons in the same position (as nearly as may be) as if the LLP had not been dissolved or struck off the register.

(4)   An application to the court for such directions or provision may be made any time within three years after the date of restoration of the LLP to the register.".

NOTES

Commencement: 1 October 2009.

Part 10   Miscellaneous other SIs

[10.1153]
57 Restoration to the register by the court

Sections 1029 to 1032 apply to LLPs, modified so that they read as follows—

"1029 Application to court for restoration to the register

(1) An application may be made to the court to restore to the register an LLP—

    (a)   that has been dissolved under Chapter 9 of Part 4 of the Insolvency Act 1986 (c 45) or Chapter 9 of Part 5 of the Insolvency (Northern Ireland) Order 1989 (SI 1989/2405 (NI 19)) (dissolution of LLP after winding up),

    (b)   that is deemed to have been dissolved under paragraph 84(6) of Schedule B1 to that Act or paragraph 85(6) of Schedule B1 to that Order (dissolution of LLP following administration), or

    (c)   that has been struck off the register—

        (i)   under section 1000 or 1001 (power of registrar to strike off defunct LLP), or

        (ii) under section 1003 (voluntary striking off),

    whether or not the LLP has in consequence been dissolved.

(2) An application under this section may be made by—

    (a)   the Secretary of State,

    (b)   any person having an interest in land in which the LLP had a superior or derivative interest,

    (c)   any person having an interest in land or other property—

        (i)   that was subject to rights vested in the LLP, or

        (ii) that was benefited by obligations owed by the LLP,

    (d)   any person who but for the LLP's dissolution would have been in a contractual relationship with it,

    (e)   any person with a potential legal claim against the LLP,

    (f)   any manager or trustee of a pension fund established for the benefit of employees of the LLP,

    (g)   any former member of the LLP (or the personal representatives of such a person),

    (h)   any person who was a creditor of the LLP at the time of its striking off or dissolution,

    (i)   any former liquidator of the LLP,

or by any other person appearing to the court to have an interest in the matter.

1030 When application to the court may be made

(1) An application to the court for restoration of an LLP to the register may be made at any time for the purpose of bringing proceedings against the LLP for damages for personal injury.

(2) No order shall be made on such an application if it appears to the court that the proceedings would fail by virtue of any enactment as to the time within which proceedings must be brought.

(3) In making that decision the court must have regard to its power under section 1032(3) (power to give consequential directions etc) to direct that the period between the dissolution (or striking off) of the LLP and the making of the order is not to count for the purposes of any such enactment.

(4) In any other case an application to the court for restoration of an LLP to the register may not be made after the end of the period of six years from the date of the dissolution of the LLP, subject as follows.

(5) In a case where—

    (a)   the LLP has been struck off the register under section 1000 or 1001 (power of registrar to strike off defunct LLP),

    (b)   an application to the registrar has been made under section 1024 (application for administrative restoration to the register) within the time allowed for making such an application, and

    (c)   the registrar has refused the application,

an application to the court under this section may be made within 28 days of notice of the registrar's decision being issued by the registrar, even if the period of six years mentioned in subsection (4) above has expired.

(6) For the purposes of this section—

    (a)   "personal injury" includes any disease and any impairment of a person's physical or mental condition; and

    (b)   references to damages for personal injury include—

        (i)   any sum claimed by virtue of section 1(2)(c) of the Law Reform (Miscellaneous Provisions) Act 1934 (c 41) or section 14(2)(c) of the Law Reform (Miscellaneous Provisions) Act (Northern Ireland) 1937 (1937 C 9 (NI)) (funeral expenses), and

        (ii) damages under the Fatal Accidents Act 1976 (c 30), the Damages (Scotland) Act 1976 (c 13) or the Fatal Accidents (Northern Ireland) Order 1977 (SI 1977/1251 (NI 18)).

1031 Decision on application for restoration by the court

(1)   On an application under section 1029 the court may order the restoration of the LLP to the register—

  (a)   if the LLP was struck off the register under section 1000 or 1001 (power of registrar to strike off defunct LLPs) and the LLP was, at the time of the striking off, carrying on business or in operation;

  (b)   if the LLP was struck off the register under section 1003 (voluntary striking off) and any of the requirements of sections 1004 to 1009 was not complied with;

  (c)   if in any other case the court considers it just to do so.

(2)   If the court orders restoration of the LLP to the register, the restoration takes effect on a copy of the court's order being delivered to the registrar.

(3)   The registrar must cause to be published in the Gazette notice of the restoration of the LLP to the register.

(4)   The notice must state—

  (a)   the name of the LLP or, if the LLP is restored to the register under a different name (see section 1033), that name and its former name,

  (b)   the LLP's registered number, and

  (c)   the date on which the restoration took effect.

1032 Effect of court order for restoration to the register

(1)   The general effect of an order by the court for restoration to the register is that the LLP is deemed to have continued in existence as if it had not been dissolved or struck off the register.

(2)   The LLP is not liable to a penalty under section 453 or any corresponding earlier provision (civil penalty for failure to deliver accounts) for a financial year in relation to which the period for filing accounts and reports ended—

  (a)   after the date of dissolution or striking off, and

  (b)   before the restoration of the LLP to the register.

(3)   The court may give such directions and make such provision as seems just for placing the LLP and all other persons in the same position (as nearly as may be) as if the LLP had not been dissolved or struck off the register.

(4)   The court may also give directions as to—

  (a)   the delivery to the registrar of such documents relating to the LLP as are necessary to bring up to date the records kept by the registrar,

  (b)   the payment of the costs (in Scotland, expenses) of the registrar in connection with the proceedings for the restoration of the LLP to the register,

  (c)   where any property or right previously vested in or held on trust for the LLP has vested as *bona vacantia*, the payment of the costs (in Scotland, expenses) of the Crown representative—

    (i)   in dealing with the property during the period of dissolution, or

    (ii)   in connection with the proceedings on the application.

(5)   In this section the "Crown representative" means—

  (a)   in relation to property vested in the Duchy of Lancaster, the Solicitor to that Duchy;

  (b)   in relation to property vested in the Duke of Cornwall, the Solicitor to the Duchy of Cornwall;

  (c)   in relation to property in Scotland, the Queen's and Lord Treasurer's Remembrancer;

  (d)   in relation to other property, the Treasury Solicitor.".

NOTES

Commencement: 1 October 2009.

[10.1154]
58 Supplementary provisions

Sections 1033 and 1034 apply to LLPs, modified so that they read as follows—

"1033 LLP's name on restoration

(1)   An LLP is restored to the register with the name it had before it was dissolved or struck off the register, subject to the following provisions.

(2)   If at the date of restoration the LLP could not be registered under its former name without contravening section 66 (name not to be the same as another in the registrar's index of names), it must be restored to the register—

  (a)   under another name specified—

    (i)   in the case of administrative restoration, in the application to the registrar, or

    (ii)   in the case of restoration under a court order, in the court's order, or

  (b)   as if its registered number was also its name.

References to an LLP's being registered in a name, and to registration in that context, shall be read as including the LLP's being restored to the register.

(3) If an LLP is restored to the register under a name specified in the application to the registrar, the provisions of—

paragraph 5 of the Schedule to the Limited Liability Partnerships Act 2000 (c 12) (change of name: registration and issue of certificate of change of name), and

paragraph 6 of that Schedule (change of name: effect),

apply as if the application to the registrar were notice of a change of name.

(4) If an LLP is restored to the register under a name specified in the court's order, the provisions of—

paragraph 5 of the Schedule to the Limited Liability Partnerships Act 2000 (c 12) (change of name: registration and issue of certificate of change of name), and

paragraph 6 of that Schedule (change of name: effect),

apply as if the copy of the court order delivered to the registrar were notice of a change a name.

(5) If the LLP is restored to the register as if its registered number was also its name—

- (a) the LLP must change its name within 14 days after the date of the restoration,
- (b) the change may be made by determination of the members,
- (c) the LLP must give notice to the registrar of the change, and
- (d) paragraphs 5 and 6 of the Schedule to the Limited Liability Partnerships Act 2000 (c 12) apply as regards the registration and effect of the change.

(6) If the LLP fails to comply with subsection (5)(a) or (c) an offence is committed by—

- (a) the LLP, and
- (b) every designated member of the LLP who is in default.

(7) A person guilty of an offence under subsection (6) is liable on summary conviction to a fine not exceeding level 5 on the standard scale and, for continued contravention, a daily default fine not exceeding one-tenth of level 5 on the standard scale.

1034 Effect of restoration to the register where property has vested as bona vacantia

(1) The person in whom any property or right is vested by section 1012 (property of dissolved LLP to be *bona vacantia*) may dispose of, or of an interest in, that property or right despite the fact that the LLP may be restored to the register under this Chapter.

(2) If the LLP is restored to the register—

- (a) the restoration does not affect the disposition (but without prejudice to its effect in relation to any other property or right previously vested in or held on trust for the LLP), and
- (b) the Crown or, as the case may be, the Duke of Cornwall shall pay to the LLP an amount equal to—
  - (i) the amount of any consideration received for the property or right or, as the case may be, the interest in it, or
  - (ii) the value of any such consideration at the time of the disposition,

  or, if no consideration was received an amount equal to the value of the property, right or interest disposed of, as at the date of the disposition.

(3) There may be deducted from the amount payable under subsection (2)(b) the reasonable costs of the Crown representative in connection with the disposition (to the extent that they have not been paid as a condition of administrative restoration or pursuant to a court order for restoration).

(4) Where a liability accrues under subsection (2) in respect of any property or right which before the restoration of the LLP to the register had accrued as *bona vacantia* to the Duchy of Lancaster, the Attorney General of that Duchy shall represent Her Majesty in any proceedings arising in connection with that liability.

(5) Where a liability accrues under subsection (2) in respect of any property or right which before the restoration of the LLP to the register had accrued as *bona vacantia* to the Duchy of Cornwall, such persons as the Duke of Cornwall (or other possessor for the time being of the Duchy) may appoint shall represent the Duke (or other possessor) in any proceedings arising out of that liability.

(6) In this section the "Crown representative" means—

- (a) in relation to property vested in the Duchy of Lancaster, the Solicitor to that Duchy;
- (b) in relation to property vested in the Duke of Cornwall, the Solicitor to the Duchy of Cornwall;
- (c) in relation to property in Scotland, the Queen's and Lord Treasurer's Remembrancer;
- (d) in relation to other property, the Treasury Solicitor.".

NOTES

Commencement: 1 October 2009.

PART 14
OVERSEAS LLPS

[10.1155]
59 Trading disclosures

Section 1051 applies to LLPs, modified so that it reads as follows—

"1051 Trading disclosures
(1) The following provisions of Part 7 of the Overseas Companies Regulations 2009 (SI 2009/1801) (trading disclosures) apply to LLPs—
   (a)   regulation 58(2);
   (b)   regulation 59;
   (c)   regulations 61 and 62;
   (d)   regulation 66;
   (e)   regulation 67(1) and (2).
(2) As those provisions apply to LLPs—
   (a)   for references to an overseas company substitute references to an overseas LLP;
   (b)   for references to an officer of a company substitute references to a member of an LLP;
   (c)   for regulation 61(1) substitute—
"(1) Every overseas LLP must display the name of the LLP and the country in which it is incorporated or otherwise established at every location where it carries on business in the United Kingdom.";
   (d)   for the introductory words to regulation 62 substitute—
"Every overseas LLP must state the LLP's name and the country in which it is incorporated on all—".
(3) For the purposes of paragraph (2)(a) above, "overseas LLP" means a body incorporated or otherwise established outside the United Kingdom whose name under its law of incorporation or establishment includes (or when translated into English includes) the words "limited liability partnership" or the abbreviation "llp" or "LLP".".

NOTES
Commencement: 1 October 2009.

PART 15
THE REGISTRAR OF COMPANIES

[10.1156]
60 Provisions of general application

(1) The application to LLPs by the following regulations of certain provisions of Part 35 of the Companies Act 2006 is without prejudice to the application in relation to LLPs of the provisions of that Part that are of general application.
(2) Those provisions are—
sections 1060(1) and (2) and 1061 to 1063 (the registrar),
sections 1068 to 1071 (delivery of documents to the registrar),
sections 1072 to 1076 (requirements for proper delivery),
sections 1080(1), (4) and (5) and 1092 (keeping and production of records),
section 1083 (preservation of original documents),
sections 1108 to 1110 (language requirements: transliteration),
sections 1111 and 1114 to 1119 (supplementary provisions).

NOTES
Commencement: 1 October 2009.

[10.1157]
61 Certificates of incorporation

Sections 1064 and 1065 apply to LLPs, modified so that they read as follows—

"1064 Public notice of issue of certificate of incorporation
(1) The registrar must cause to be published—
   (a)   in the Gazette, or
   (b)   in accordance with section 1116 (alternative means of giving public notice),
notice of the issue by the registrar of any certificate of incorporation of an LLP.
(2) The notice must state the name and registered number of the LLP and the date of issue of the certificate.
(3) This section applies to a certificate issued under—
   (a)   paragraph 5 of the Schedule to the Limited Liability Partnerships Act 2000 (c 12) (change of name: registration and issue of certificate of change of name), or
   (b)   section 88(4) of this Act (Welsh LLPs),

as well as to the certificate issued on an LLP's formation.

1065 Right to certificate of incorporation

Any person may require the registrar to provide him with a copy of any certificate of incorporation of an LLP, signed by the registrar or authenticated by the registrar's seal.".

NOTES

Commencement: 1 October 2009.

[10.1158]
62   Registered numbers

Section 1066 applies to LLPs, modified so that it reads as follows—

"1066 LLP's registered numbers

(1)   The registrar shall allocate to every LLP a number, which shall be known as the LLP's registered number.

(2)   LLPs' registered numbers shall be in such form, consisting of one or more sequences of figures or letters, as the registrar may determine.

(3)   The registrar may on adopting a new form of registered number make such changes of existing registered numbers as appear necessary.

(4)   A change of an LLP's registered number has effect from the date on which the LLP is notified by the registrar of the change.

(5)   For a period of three years beginning with that date any requirement to disclose the LLP's registered number imposed by section 82 or section 1051 (trading disclosures) is satisfied by the use of either the old number or the new.".

NOTES

Commencement: 1 October 2009.

[10.1159]
63   Public notice of receipt of certain documents

Sections 1077 to 1079 apply to LLPs, modified so that they read as follows—

"1077 Public notice of receipt of certain documents

(1)   The registrar must cause to be published—
   (a)   in the Gazette, or
   (b)   in accordance with section 1116 (alternative means of giving public notice),
notice of the receipt by the registrar of any document specified in section 1078.

(2)   The notice must state the name and registered number of the LLP, the description of document and the date of receipt.

(3)   The registrar is not required to cause notice of the receipt of a document to be published before the date of incorporation of the LLP to which the document relates.

1078 The section 1077 documents

The following documents are specified for the purposes of section 1077—
Constitutional documents
1.   The LLP's incorporation document.
2.   Any notice delivered under section 8(4) of the Limited Liability Partnerships Act 2000 (c 12).
3.   Any notice of the change of the LLP's name.
Members
1.   Notification of any change in the membership of the LLP.
2.   Notification of any change in the particulars of members required to be delivered to the registrar.
Accounts and returns
1.   All documents required to be delivered to the registrar under section 441 (annual accounts).
2.   The LLP's annual return.
Registered office
Notification of any change of the LLP's registered office.
Winding up
1.   Copy of any winding-up order in respect of the LLP.
2.   Notice of the appointment of liquidators.
3.   Order for the dissolution of an LLP on a winding up.
4.   Return by a liquidator of the final meeting of an LLP on a winding up.

1079 Effect of failure to give public notice

(1)   An LLP is not entitled to rely against other persons on the happening of any event to which this section applies unless—
   (a)   the event has been officially notified at the material time, or
   (b)   the LLP shows that the person concerned knew of the event at the material time.

(2)   The events to which this section applies are—

- (a)   (as regards service of any document on the LLP) a change of the LLP's registered office,
- (b)   the making of a winding-up order in respect of the LLP, or
- (c)   the appointment of a liquidator in a voluntary winding up of the LLP.

(3)   If the material time falls—

- (a)   on or before the 15th day after the date of official notification, or
- (b)   where the 15th day was not a working day, on or before the next day that was,

the LLP is not entitled to rely on the happening of the event as against a person who shows that he was unavoidably prevented from knowing of the event at that time.

(4)   "Official notification" means—

- (a)   in relation to anything stated in a document specified in section 1078, notification of that document in accordance with section 1077;
- (b)   in relation to the appointment of a liquidator in a voluntary winding up, notification of that event in accordance with section 109 of the Insolvency Act 1986 (c 45) or Article 95 of the Insolvency (Northern Ireland) Order 1989 (SI 1989/2405 (NI 19)).".

NOTES

Commencement: 1 October 2009.

[10.1160]
64   The register

Sections 1081 and 1082 apply to LLPs, modified so that they read as follows—

"1081   Annotation of the register

(1)   The registrar must place a note in the register recording—

- (a)   the date on which a document is delivered to the registrar;
- (b)   if a document is corrected under section 1075, the nature and date of the correction;
- (c)   if a document is replaced (whether or not material derived from it is removed), the fact that it has been replaced and the date of delivery of the replacement;
- (d)   if material is removed—
  - (i)   what was removed (giving a general description of its contents),
  - (ii)   under what power, and
  - (iii)   the date on which that was done.

(2)   Regulation 3 of the Registrar of Companies and Applications for Striking Off Regulations 2009 (SI 2009/1803) applies to LLPs as regards—

- (a)   other circumstances in which the registrar is required or authorised to annotate the register, and
- (b)   the contents of any such annotation.

(3)   No annotation is required in the case of a document that by virtue of section 1072(2) (documents not meeting requirements for proper delivery) is treated as not having been delivered.

(4)   A note may be removed if it no longer serves any useful purpose.

(5)   Any duty or power of the registrar with respect to annotation of the register is subject to the court's power under section 1097 (powers of court on ordering removal of material from the register) to direct—

- (a)   that a note be removed from the register, or
- (b)   that no note shall be made of the removal of material that is the subject of the court's order.

(6)   Notes placed in the register in accordance with subsection (1), or in pursuance of the provision referred to in subsection (2), are part of the register for all purposes of the Companies Acts and the Limited Liability Partnerships Act 2000.

1082   Allocation of unique identifiers

(1)   The Secretary of State may make provision for the use, in connection with the register, of reference numbers ("unique identifiers") to identify each person who is a member of an LLP.

(2)   The regulations may—

- (a)   provide that a unique identifier may be in such form, consisting of one or more sequences of letters or numbers, as the registrar may from time to time determine;
- (b)   make provision for the allocation of unique identifiers by the registrar;
- (c)   require there to be included, in any specified description of documents delivered to the registrar, as well as a statement of the person's name—
  - (i)   a statement of the person's unique identifier, or
  - (ii)   a statement that the person has not been allocated a unique identifier;
- (d)   enable the registrar to take steps where a person appears to have more than one unique identifier to discontinue the use of all but one of them.

(3)   The regulations may contain provision for the application of the scheme in relation to

persons appointed, and documents registered, before the commencement of this Act.

(4)   The regulations may make different provision for different descriptions of person and different descriptions of document.

(5)   Regulations under this section are subject to affirmative resolution procedure.".

NOTES
Commencement: 9 July 2009 (for the purpose of enabling the exercise of powers to make regulations or orders by statutory instrument); 1 October 2009 (otherwise).

[10.1161]
65   Records relating to dissolved LLPs

Section 1084 applies to LLPs, modified so that it reads as follows—

"1084   Records relating to LLPs that have been dissolved

(1)   This section applies where an LLP is dissolved.

(2)   At any time after two years from the date on which it appears to the registrar that the LLP has been dissolved, the registrar may direct that records relating to the LLP may be removed to the Public Record Office or, as the case may be, the Public Record Office of Northern Ireland.

(3)   Records in respect of which such a direction is given shall be disposed of under the enactments relating to that Office and the rules made under them.

(4)   This section does not extend to Scotland.".

NOTES
Commencement: 1 October 2009.

[10.1162]
66   Inspection etc of the register

Sections 1085 to 1091 apply to LLPs, modified so that they read as follows—

"1085   Inspection of the register

(1)   Any person may inspect the register.

(2)   The right of inspection extends to the originals of documents delivered to the registrar in hard copy form if, and only if, the record kept by the registrar of the contents of the document is illegible or unavailable.

The period for which such originals are to be kept is limited by section 1083(1).

(3)   This section has effect subject to section 1087 (material not available for public inspection).

1086   Right to copy of material not on the register

(1)   Any person may require a copy of any material on the register.

(2)   The fee for any such copy of material derived from a document specified for the purposes of section 1077, whether in hard copy or electronic form, must not exceed the administrative cost of providing it.

(3)   This section has effect subject to section 1087 (material not available for public inspection).

1087   Material not available for public inspection

(1)   The following material must not be made available by the registrar for public inspection—

    (a)   the contents of any document sent to the registrar containing views expressed pursuant to section 56 (comments on proposal by LLP to use certain words or expressions in LLP name);

    (b)   protected information within section 242(1) (members' residential addresses: restriction on disclosure by registrar);

    (c)   representations received by the registrar in response to a notice under section 245(2) (notice of proposal to put member's usual residential address on the public record);

    (d)   any application to the registrar under section 1024 (application for administrative restoration to the register) that has not yet been determined or was not successful;

    (e)   any document received by the registrar in connection with the giving or withdrawal of consent under section 1075 (informal correction of documents);

    (f)   any application or other document delivered to the registrar under section 1088 (application to make address unavailable for public inspection) and any address in respect of which such an application is successful;

    (g)   any application or other document delivered to the registrar under section 1095 (application for rectification of register);

    (h)   any court order under section 1096 (rectification of the register under court order) that the court has directed under section 1097 (powers of court on ordering removal of material from the register) is not to be made available for public inspection;

    (i)   the contents of—

       (i)   any instrument creating or evidencing a charge, or

(ii)   any certified or verified copy of an instrument creating or evidencing a charge, delivered to the registrar under Part 25 (LLP charges);

(j)   any e-mail address, identification code or password deriving from a document delivered for the purpose of authorising or facilitating electronic filing procedures or providing information by telephone;

(k)   any other material excluded from public inspection by or under any other enactment.

(2)   A restriction applying by reference to material deriving from a particular description of document does not affect the availability for public inspection of the same information contained in material derived from another description of document in relation to which no such restriction applies.

(3)   Material to which this section applies need not be retained by the registrar for longer than appears to the registrar reasonably necessary for the purposes for which the material was delivered to the registrar.

1088 Application to registrar to make address unavailable for public inspection

(1)   The provisions of the Companies (Disclosure of Address) Regulations 2009 (SI 2009/214) relating to applications to make an address unavailable for inspection under this section apply to LLPs.

(2)   The provisions are—

(a)   Part 3 (disclosure of protected information),

(b)   Part 4 (matters relating to applications), so far as relating to applications to make an address unavailable for inspection under this section, and

(c)   any other provisions of the Regulations having effect for the purposes of those provisions.

(3)   As those provisions apply to LLPs—

(a)   references in the regulations to provisions of the Companies Act 1985 (c 6) or the Companies (Northern Ireland) Order 1986 (SI 1986/1032 (NI 6)) are to those provisions as applied to LLPs by the Limited Liability Partnerships Regulations 2001 (SI 2001/1090) or the Limited Liability Partnerships Regulations (Northern Ireland) 2004 (SR (NI) 2004 No 307);

(b)   read references to a company as references to an LLP;

(c)   read references to a director as references to a member of an LLP;

(d)   omit all references to secretaries or permanent representatives;

(e)   in regulation 1(2) for the definition of "former name" substitute—

""former name" means a name by which the individual was formerly known and which has been notified to the registrar under section 2 or 9 of the Limited Liability Partnerships Act 2000;";

(f)   in regulation 9, for paragraph (1) substitute—

"(1)   A section 1088 application may be made to the registrar by an individual whose usual residential address was placed on the register either—

(a)   under section 288 (register of members) or 363 (duty to deliver annual returns) of the 1985 Act;

(b)   under Article 296 or 371 of the 1986 Order;

(c)   under section 2 (incorporation document etc) or 9 (registration of membership changes) of the Limited Liability Partnerships Act 2000; or

(d)   as a service address under section 855 (contents of annual return) of the Act,

in respect of that usual residential address where it was placed on the register on or after 1st January 2003;"; and

(g)   omit regulation 10.

1089 Form of application for inspection or copy

The registrar may specify the form and manner in which application is to be made for—

(a)   inspection under section 1085, or

(b)   a copy under section 1086.

1090 Form and manner in which copies to be provided

The registrar may determine the form and manner in which copies are to be provided.

1091 Certification of copies as accurate

(1)   Copies provided under section 1086 in hard copy form must be certified as true copies unless the applicant dispenses with such certification.

(2)   Copies so provided in electronic form must not be certified as true copies unless the applicant expressly requests such certification.

(3)   A copy provided under section 1086, certified by the registrar (whose official position it is unnecessary to prove) to be an accurate record of the contents of the original document, is in all legal proceedings admissible in evidence—

(a)   as of equal validity with the original document, and

(b)   as evidence (in Scotland, sufficient evidence) of any fact stated in the original document of which direct oral evidence would be admissible.

(4) Regulation 2 of the Companies (Registrar, Languages and Trading Disclosures) Regulations 2006 (SI 2006/3429) (certification of electronic copies by registrar) applies where the copy is provided in electronic form.

(5) Copies provided by the registrar may, instead of being certified in writing to be an accurate record, be sealed with the registrar's official seal.".

NOTES
Commencement: 1 October 2009.

[10.1163]
67 Correction or removal of material on the register
Sections 1093 to 1098 apply to LLPs, modified so that they read as follows—

"1093 Registrar's notice to resolve inconsistency on the register
(1) Where it appears to the registrar that the information contained in a document delivered to the registrar is inconsistent with other information on the register, the registrar may give notice to the LLP to which the document relates—

    (a)   stating in what respects the information contained in it appears to be inconsistent with other information on the register, and

    (b)   requiring the LLP to take steps to resolve the inconsistency.

(2) The notice must—

    (a)   state the date on which it is issued, and

    (b)   require the delivery to the registrar, within 14 days after that date, of such replacement or additional documents as may be required to resolve the inconsistency.

(3) If the necessary documents are not delivered within the period specified, an offence is committed by—

    (a)   the LLP, and

    (b)   every member of the LLP who is in default.

(4) A person guilty of an offence under subsection (3) is liable on summary conviction to a fine not exceeding level 5 on the standard scale and, for continued contravention, a daily default fine not exceeding one-tenth of level 5 on the standard scale.

1094 Administrative removal of material from the register
(1) The registrar may remove from the register anything that there was power, but no duty, to include.

(2) This power is exercisable, in particular, so as to remove—

    (a)   unnecessary material within the meaning of section 1074, and

    (b)   material derived from a document that has been replaced under—

section 1076 (replacement of document not meeting requirements for proper delivery), or section 1093 (notice to remedy inconsistency on the register).

(3) This section does not authorise the removal from the register of—

    (a)   anything whose registration has had legal consequences in relation to the LLP as regards—

        (i)   its formation,

        (ii) a change of name,

        (iii) a change of registered office,

        (iv) a change in the situation of a registered office,

        (v)   the registration of a charge, or

        (vi) its dissolution;

    (b)   an address that is a person's registered address for the purposes of section 1140 (service of documents on members and others).

(4) On or before removing any material under this section (otherwise than at the request of the LLP) the registrar must give notice—

    (a)   to the person by whom the material was delivered (if the identity, and name and address of that person are known), or

    (b)   to the LLP to which the material relates (if notice cannot be given under paragraph (a) and the identity of that LLP is known).

(5) The notice must—

    (a)   state what material the registrar proposes to remove, or has removed, and on what grounds, and

    (b)   state the date on which it is issued.

1095 Rectification of register on application to registrar
(1) The provisions of the Registrar of Companies and Applications for Striking Off Regulations 2009 (SI 2009/1803) requiring the registrar, on application, to remove from the register material that—

    (a)   derives from anything invalid or ineffective or that was done without authority, or

    (b)   is factually inaccurate, or is derived from something that is factually inaccurate or forged,

apply to LLPs.
(2) Those provisions are—
    (a)   regulations 4 and 5, and
    (b)   any other provisions of the regulations having effect for the purposes of those provisions.
(2A) In those provisions as they apply to LLPs—
    (a)   for "company" substitute "LLP", and for "relevant company form" substitute "relevant LLP form";
    (b)   omit all references to overseas companies and overseas company forms;
    (c)   omit all references to secretaries;
    (d)   in regulation 4—
        (i)   for paragraph (3) substitute—
"(3)   A "relevant LLP form" is—
        (a)   a standard form required for giving notice under section 87 of the Companies Act 2006 (change of address of registered office) or section 9 of the Limited Liability Partnerships Act 2000 (c 12) (changes relating to members); or
        (b)   so much of a standard form required for delivering an application under section 2 of the Limited Liability Partnerships Act 2000 (incorporation document etc) as is required for the statement of those who are to be members of the LLP referred to in section 2(2)(e).",
        (ii)   omit paragraphs (4) and (6),
        (iii)   in paragraph (7) omit "or (6)", and
        (iv)   in paragraph (8)(a), for "(2), (3), (4) or (5)" substitute "(2) or (3)";
    (e)   in regulation 5—
        (i)   in paragraph (1)(b), omit "or (6)",
        (ii)   in paragraphs (2)(b) and (3)(b), for "director or secretary of the company" substitute "designated member of the LLP",
        (iii)   omit paragraphs (4) to (7) and (16),
        (iv)   in paragraphs (8), (11), (12) and (14)(c), for "(2), (3), (4) or (5)" substitute "(2) or (3)"; and
        (v)   omit paragraph (8)(b) and (c).
(3)   An application must—
    (a)   specify what is to be removed from the register and indicate where on the register it is, and
    (b)   be accompanied by a statement that the material specified in the application complies with this section and the regulations.
(4)   If no objections are made to the application, the registrar may accept the statement as sufficient evidence that the material specified in the application should be removed from the register.
(5)   Where anything is removed from the register under this section the registration of which had legal consequences as mentioned in section 1094(3), any person appearing to the court to have a sufficient interest may apply to the court for such consequential orders as appear just with respect to the legal effect (if any) to be accorded to the material by virtue of its having appeared on the register.

1096 Rectification of the register under court order
(1)   The registrar shall remove from the register any material—
    (a)   that derives from anything that the court has declared to be invalid or ineffective, or to have been done without the authority of the LLP, or
    (b)   that a court declares to be factually inaccurate, or to be derived from something that is factually inaccurate, or forged,
and that the court directs should be removed from the register.
(2)   The court order must specify what is to be removed from the register and indicate where on the register it is.
(3)   The court must not make an order for the removal from the register of anything the registration of which had legal consequences as mentioned in section 1094(3) unless satisfied—
    (a)   that the presence of the material on the register has caused, or may cause, damage to the LLP, and
    (b)   that the LLP's interest in removing the material outweighs any interest of other persons in the material continuing to appear on the register.
(4)   Where in such a case the court does make an order for removal, it may make such consequential orders as appear just with respect to the legal effect (if any) to be accorded to the material by virtue of its having appeared on the register.
(5)   A copy of the court's order must be sent to the registrar for registration.
(6)   This section does not apply where the court has other, specific, powers to deal with the matter, for example under—
    (a)   the provisions of Part 15 relating to the revision of defective accounts, or
    (b)   section 873 or 888 (rectification of the register of charges).

1097 Powers of court on ordering removal of material from the register

(1)   Where the court makes an order for the removal of anything from the register under section 1096 (rectification of the register), it may give directions under this section.

(2)   It may direct that any note on the register that is related to the material that is the subject of the court's order shall be removed from the register.

(3)   It may direct that its order shall not be available for public inspection as part of the register.

(4)   It may direct—
   (a)   that no note shall be made on the register as a result of its order, or
   (b)   that any such note shall be restricted to such matters as may be specified by the court.

(5)   The court shall not give any direction under this section unless it is satisfied—
   (a)   that—
      (i)   the presence on the register of the note or, as the case may be, of an unrestricted note, or
      (ii)   the availability for public inspection of the court's order,
      may cause damage to the LLP, and
   (b)   that the LLP's interest in non-disclosure outweighs any interest of other persons in disclosure.

1098 Public notice of removal of certain material from the register

(1)   The registrar must cause to be published—
   (a)   in the Gazette, or
   (b)   in accordance with section 1116 (alternative means of giving public notice),
notice of the removal from the register of any document specified in section 1078 or of any material derived from such a document.

(2)   The notice must state the name and registered number of the LLP, the description of document and the date of receipt.".

NOTES
Commencement: 1 October 2009.

[10.1164]
68   Language requirements: translation

Sections 1103 to 1107 apply to LLPs, modified so that they read as follows—

"1103 Documents to be drawn up and delivered in English

(1)   The general rule is that all documents required to be delivered to the registrar must be drawn up and delivered in English.

(2)   This is subject to—
section 1104 (documents relating to Welsh LLPs) and
section 1105 (documents that may be drawn up and delivered in other languages).

1104 Documents relating to Welsh LLPs

(1)   Documents relating to a Welsh LLP may be drawn up and delivered to the registrar in Welsh.

(2)   On delivery to the registrar any such document must be accompanied by a certified translation into English, unless they are—
   (a)   annual accounts and auditors' reports required to be delivered to the registrar under Part 15,
   (b)   revised accounts, and any auditor's report on such revised accounts, required to be delivered to the registrar by the Companies (Revision of Defective Accounts and Reports) Regulations 2008 (SI 2008/373), or
   (c)   in a form prescribed in Welsh (or partly in Welsh and partly in English) by virtue of section 26 of the Welsh Language Act 1993 (c 38).

(3)   Where a document is properly delivered to the registrar in Welsh without a certified translation into English, the registrar must obtain such a translation if the document is to be available for public inspection.
   The translation is treated as if delivered to the registrar in accordance with the same provision as the original.

(4)   A Welsh LLP may deliver to the registrar a certified translation into Welsh of any document in English that relates to the LLP and is or has been delivered to the registrar.

(5)   Section 1105 (which requires certified translations into English of documents delivered to the registrar in another language) does not apply to a document relating to a Welsh LLP that is drawn up and delivered in Welsh.

1105 Documents that may be drawn up and delivered in other languages

(1)   Documents to which this section applies may be drawn up and delivered to the registrar in a language other than English, but when delivered to the registrar they must be accompanied by a certified translation into English.

(2)   This section applies to—
  (a)   documents required to be delivered under section 400(2)(e) or section 401(2)(f) (LLP included in accounts of larger group: required to deliver copy of group accounts);
  (b)   instruments or copy instruments required to be delivered under Part 25 (LLP charges);
  (c)   any order made by a competent court in the United Kingdom or elsewhere.

1106 Voluntary filing of translations
(1)   An LLP may deliver to the registrar one or more certified translations of any document relating to the LLP that is or has been delivered to the registrar.
(2)   The facility described in subsection (1) is available in relation to—
  (a)   all the official languages of the European Union, and
  (b)   all the documents specified by section 1078.
(3)   The power of the registrar to impose requirements as to the form and manner of delivery includes power to impose requirements as to the identification of the original document and the delivery of the translation in a form and manner enabling it to be associated with the original.
(4)   This section does not apply where the original document was delivered to the registrar before this section came into force.

1107 Certified translations
(1)   In this Part a "certified translation" means a translation certified to be a correct translation.
(2)   In the case of any discrepancy between the original language version of a document and a certified translation—
  (a)   the LLP may not rely on the translation as against a third party, but
  (b)   a third party may rely on the translation unless the LLP shows that the third party had knowledge of the original.
(3)   A "third party" means a person other than the LLP or the registrar.".

NOTES
Commencement: 1 October 2009.

[10.1165]
69   Supplementary provisions
Sections 1112 and 1113 apply to LLPs, modified so that they read as follows—

"1112 General false statement offence
(1)   It is an offence for a person knowingly or recklessly—
  (a)   to deliver or cause to be delivered to the registrar, for any purpose of this Act or the Limited Liability Partnerships Act 2000 (c 12), a document, or
  (b)   to make to the registrar, for any such purpose, a statement,
that is misleading, false or deceptive in a material particular.
(2)   A person guilty of an offence under this section is liable—
  (a)   on conviction on indictment, to imprisonment for a term not exceeding two years or a fine (or both);
  (b)   on summary conviction—
    (i)   in England and Wales or Scotland, to imprisonment for a term not exceeding twelve months or to a fine not exceeding the statutory maximum (or both);
    (ii)   in Northern Ireland, to imprisonment for a term not exceeding six months, or to a fine not exceeding the statutory maximum (or both).

1113 Enforcement of LLP's filing obligations
(1)   This section applies where an LLP has made default in complying with any obligation under this Act or the Limited Liability Partnerships Act 2000 (c 12)—
  (a)   to deliver a document to the registrar, or
  (b)   to give notice to the registrar of any matter.
(2)   The registrar, or any member or creditor of the LLP, may give notice to the LLP requiring it to comply with the obligation.
(3)   If the LLP fails to make good the default within 14 days after service of the notice, the registrar, or any member or creditor of the LLP, may apply to the court for an order directing the LLP, and any specified member of it, to make good the default within a specified time.
(4)   The court's order may provide that all costs (in Scotland, expenses) of or incidental to the application are to be borne by the LLP or by any members of it responsible for the default.
(5)   This section does not affect the operation of any enactment making it an offence, or imposing a civil penalty, for the default.".

NOTES
Commencement: 1 October 2009.

PART 16
OFFENCES

[10.1166]
70   Liability of member in default
Sections 1121 and 1122 apply to LLPs for the purposes of these Regulations, modified so that they read as follows—

> **"1121   Liability of member in default**
> (1)   This section has effect for the purposes of any provision of the Companies Acts to the effect that, in the event of contravention of an enactment in relation to an LLP, an offence is committed by every member or, as the case may be, every designated member of the LLP who is in default.
> (2)   A member or designated member is "in default" for the purposes of the provision if he authorises or permits, participates in, or fails to take all reasonable steps to prevent, the contravention.
>
> **1122   Liability of company or LLP as member in default**
> (1)   Where a company or an LLP is a member or designated member of an LLP, it does not commit an offence as a member or designated member in default unless (in the case of a company) one of its officers is in default, or (in the case of a member LLP) one of its members is in default.
> (2)   Where any such offence is committed by a company or LLP the officer or member in question also commits the offence and is liable to be proceeded against and punished accordingly.
> (3)   In this section an officer or member is "in default" for the purposes of the provision if he authorises or permits, participates in, or fails to take all reasonable steps to prevent, the contravention.".

NOTES
   Commencement: 1 October 2009.

[10.1167]
71   Daily default fine
Section 1125 applies to LLPs for the purposes of these Regulations as follows—

> **"1125   Meaning of "daily default fine"**
> (1)   This section defines what is meant in the Companies Acts where it is provided that a person guilty of an offence is liable on summary conviction to a fine not exceeding a specified amount "and, for continued contravention, a daily default fine" not exceeding a specified amount.
> (2)   This means that the person is liable on a second or subsequent summary conviction of the offence to a fine not exceeding the latter amount for each day on which the contravention is continued (instead of being liable to a fine not exceeding the former amount).".

NOTES
   Commencement: 1 October 2009.

[10.1168]
72   Consents for certain prosecutions
Section 1126 applies to LLPs, modified so that it reads as follows—

> **"1126   Consents required for certain prosecutions**
> (1)   This section applies to proceedings for an offence under section 448, 449, 450, 451 or 453A of the Companies Act 1985, as applied to LLPs.
> (2)   No such proceedings are to be brought in England and Wales except by or with the consent of the Secretary of State or the Director of Public Prosecutions.
> (3)   No such proceedings are to be brought in Northern Ireland except by or with the consent of the Secretary of State or the Director of Public Prosecutions for Northern Ireland.".

NOTES
   Commencement: 1 October 2009.

[10.1169]
73   General provisions
Sections 1127 to 1133 apply to LLPs for the purposes of these Regulations, modified so that they read as follows—

> **"1127   Summary proceedings: venue**
> (1)   Summary proceedings for any offence under the Companies Acts may be taken—
>   (a)   against a body corporate, at any place at which the body has a place of business, and

(b)   against any other person, at any place at which he is for the time being.

(2)   This is without prejudice to any jurisdiction exercisable apart from this section.

1128 Summary proceedings: time limit for proceedings

(1)   An information relating to an offence under the Companies Acts that is triable by a magistrates' court in England and Wales may be so tried if it is laid—

(a)   at any time within three years after the commission of the offence, and

(b)   within twelve months after the date on which evidence sufficient in the opinion of the Director of Public Prosecutions or the Secretary of State (as the case may be) to justify the proceedings comes to his knowledge.

(2)   Summary proceedings in Scotland for an offence under the Companies Acts—

(a)   must not be commenced after the expiration of three years from the commission of the offence;

(b)   subject to that, may be commenced at any time—

(i)   within twelve months after the date on which evidence sufficient in the Lord Advocate's opinion to justify the proceedings came to his knowledge, or

(ii)   where such evidence was reported to him by the Secretary of State, within twelve months after the date on which it came to the knowledge of the latter.

Section 136(3) of the Criminal Procedure (Scotland) Act 1995 (c 46) (date when proceedings deemed to be commenced) applies for the purposes of this subsection as for the purposes of that section.

(3)   A magistrates' court in Northern Ireland has jurisdiction to hear and determine a complaint charging the commission of a summary offence under the Companies Acts provided that the complaint is made—

(a)   within three years from the time when the offence was committed, and

(b)   within twelve months from the date on which evidence sufficient in the opinion of the Director of Public Prosecutions for Northern Ireland or the Secretary of State (as the case may be) to justify the proceedings comes to his knowledge.

(4)   For the purposes of this section a certificate of the Director of Public Prosecutions, the Lord Advocate, the Director of Public Prosecutions for Northern Ireland or the Secretary of State (as the case may be) as to the date on which such evidence as is referred to above came to his notice is conclusive evidence.

1129 Legal professional privilege

In proceedings against a person for an offence under the Companies Acts, nothing in those Acts is to be taken to require any person to disclose any information that he is entitled to refuse to disclose on grounds of legal professional privilege (in Scotland, confidentiality of communications).

1130 Proceedings against unincorporated bodies

(1)   Proceedings for an offence under the Companies Acts alleged to have been committed by an unincorporated body must be brought in the name of the body (and not in that of any of its members).

(2)   For the purposes of such proceedings—

(a)   any rules of court relating to the service of documents have effect as if the body were a body corporate, and

(b)   the following provisions apply as they apply in relation to a body corporate—

(i)   in England and Wales, section 33 of the Criminal Justice Act 1925 (c 86) and Schedule 3 to the Magistrates' Courts Act 1980 (c 43),

(ii)   in Scotland, sections 70 and 143 of the Criminal Procedure (Scotland) Act 1995 (c 46),

(iii) in Northern Ireland, section 18 of the Criminal Justice Act (Northern Ireland) 1945 (c 15 (NI)) and Article 166 of and Schedule 4 to the Magistrates' Courts (Northern Ireland) Order 1981 (SI 1981/1675 (NI 26)).

(3)   A fine imposed on an unincorporated body on its conviction of an offence under the Companies Acts must be paid out of the funds of the body.

1131 Imprisonment on summary conviction in England and Wales: transitory provision

(1)   This section applies to any provision of the Companies Acts that provides that a person guilty of an offence is liable on summary conviction in England and Wales to imprisonment for a term not exceeding twelve months.

(2)   In relation to an offence committed before the commencement of section 154(1) of the Criminal Justice Act 2003 (c 44), for "twelve months" substitute "six months".

1132 Production and inspection of documents where offence suspected

(1)   An application under this section may be made—

(a)   in England and Wales, to a judge of the High Court by the Director of Public Prosecutions, the Secretary of State or a chief officer of police;

(b)   in Scotland, to one of the Lords Commissioners of Justiciary by the Lord Advocate;

(c)   in Northern Ireland, to the High Court by the Director of Public Prosecutions for Northern Ireland, the Department of Enterprise, Trade and Investment or a chief superintendent of the Police Service of Northern Ireland.

(2)   If on an application under this section there is shown to be reasonable cause to believe—

(a)   that any person has, while a member of an LLP, committed an offence in connection with the management of the LLP's affairs, and

(b)   that evidence of the commission of the offence is to be found in any documents in the possession or control of the LLP,

an order under this section may be made.

(3)   The order may—

(a)   authorise any person named in it to inspect the documents in question, or any of them, for the purpose of investigating and obtaining evidence of the offence, or

(b)   require such member of the LLP as may be named in the order, to produce the documents (or any of them) to a person named in the order at a place so named.

(4)   This section applies also in relation to documents in the possession or control of a person carrying on the business of banking, so far as they relate to the LLP's affairs, as it applies to documents in the possession or control of the LLP, except that no such order as is referred to in subsection (3)(b) may be made by virtue of this subsection.

(5)   The decision under this section of a judge of the High Court, any of the Lords Commissioners of Justiciary or the High Court is not appealable.

(6)   In this section "document" includes information recorded in any form.

1133 Transitional provision
The provisions of this Part except section 1132 do not apply to offences committed before 1st October 2009.".

NOTES
Commencement: 1 October 2009.

PART 17
SUPPLEMENTARY PROVISIONS AND INTERPRETATION

[10.1170]
74   LLP records
Sections 1134 to 1138 apply to LLPs, modified so that they read as follows—

"1134 Meaning of "LLP records"
In this Part "LLP records" means—

(a)   any register, index, accounting records, agreement, memorandum, minutes or other document required by this Act to be kept by an LLP, and

(b)   any register kept by an LLP of its debenture holders.

1135 Form of LLP records
(1)   LLP records—

(a)   may be kept in hard copy or electronic form, and

(b)   may be arranged in such manner as the members of the LLP think fit,

provided the information in question is adequately recorded for future reference.

(2)   Where the records are kept in electronic form, they must be capable of being reproduced in hard copy form.

(3)   If an LLP fails to comply with this section, an offence is committed by every member of the LLP who is in default.

(4)   A person guilty of an offence under this section is liable on summary conviction to a fine not exceeding level 3 on the standard scale and, for continued contravention, a daily default fine not exceeding one-tenth of level 3 on the standard scale.

1136 Where certain LLP records to be kept available for inspection
(1)   The provisions of the Companies (Company Records) Regulations 2008 (SI 2008/3006) relating to places other than the registered office at which records required to be kept available for inspection under a relevant provision may be so kept in compliance with that provision apply to LLPs.

(2)   The "relevant provisions" are—

section 162 (register of members);

section 743 (register of debenture holders);

section 877 (instruments creating charges and register of charges: England and Wales);

section 892 (instruments creating charges and register of charges: Scotland).

(3)   The provisions applied by subsection (1) are—

(a)   regulation 3, and

(b)   any other provision of the regulations having effect for the purposes of that provision.

(4)   In the application of those provisions to LLPs for "company" substitute "LLP".

1137 Inspection of records and provision of copies

(1)   The provisions of the Companies (Company Records) Regulations 2008 (SI 2008/3006) as to the obligations of an LLP that is required by any provision of this Act or of the Limited Liability Partnerships Act 2000 (c 12)—

    (a)   to keep available for inspection any LLP records, or

    (b)   to provide copies of any LLP records,

apply to LLPs.

(2)   Those provisions are—

    (a)   Part 3 (inspection of records),

    (b)   Part 4 (provision of copies of records), and

    (c)   any other provision of the regulations having effect for the purposes of those provisions.

(3)   As those provisions apply to LLPs—

    (a)   for "a company" or "the company" substitute "an LLP" or "the LLP";

    (b)   for "company record" substitute "LLP record";

    (c)   in regulation 4 (inspection: private company)—

        (i)   for the reference in paragraph (1) to a private company substitute a reference to an LLP,

        (ii)   for sub-paragraph (b) substitute—

            "(b)   that person gives the LLP at least 10 working days' notice of the specified day.";

    (d)   omit paragraphs (2) and (3); and

    (e)   omit regulation 5 (inspection: public company).

(4)   An LLP that fails to comply with the regulations is treated as having refused inspection or, as the case may be, having failed to provide a copy.

(5)   Nothing in any provision of this Act or in the regulations shall be read as preventing an LLP—

    (a)   from affording more extensive facilities than are required by the regulations, or

    (b)   where a fee may be charged, from charging a lesser fee than that prescribed or none at all.

1138 Duty to take precautions against falsification

(1)   Where LLP records are kept otherwise than in bound books, adequate precautions must be taken—

    (a)   to guard against falsification, and

    (b)   to facilitate the discovery of falsification.

(2)   If an LLP fails to comply with this section, an offence is committed by every member of the LLP who is in default.

(3)   A person guilty of an offence under this section is liable on summary conviction to a fine not exceeding level 3 on the standard scale and, for continued contravention, a daily default fine not exceeding one-tenth of level 3 on the standard scale.".

NOTES

Commencement: 1 October 2009.

[10.1171]
75   Service addresses

Sections 1139 to 1142 apply to LLPs, modified so that they read as follows—

"1139   Service of documents on LLP

(1)   A document may be served on an LLP by leaving it at, or sending it by post to, the LLP's registered office.

(2)   Where an LLP registered in Scotland or Northern Ireland carries on business in England and Wales, the process of any court in England and Wales may be served on the LLP by leaving it at, or sending it by post to, the LLP's principal place of business in England and Wales, addressed to the manager or a designated member in England and Wales of the LLP.

    Where process is served on an LLP under this subsection, the person issuing out the process must send a copy of it by post to the LLP's registered office.

1140   Service of documents on members and others

(1)   A document may be served on—

    (a)   a member of an LLP, or

    (b)   a person appointed in relation to an LLP as a judicial factor (in Scotland),

by leaving it at, or sending it by post to, the member's or factor's registered address.

(2)   This section applies whatever the purpose of the document in question.

(3)   For the purposes of this section a person's "registered address" means any address for the time being shown as a current address in relation to that person in the part of the register available for public inspection.

(4)   If notice of a change of that address is given to the registrar, a person may validly serve a document at the address previously registered until the end of the period of 14 days beginning with the date on which notice of the change is registered.

(5)   Service may not be effected by virtue of this section at an address if notice has been registered of the cessation of the membership or (as the case may be) termination of the appointment in relation to which the address was registered and the address is not a registered address of the person concerned in relation to any other appointment.

(6)   Nothing in this section shall be read as affecting any enactment or rule of law under which permission is required for service out of the jurisdiction.

1141   Service addresses

(1)   In this Act a "service address", in relation to a person, means an address at which documents may be effectively served on that person.

(2)   The service address must be a place where—
  (a)   the service of documents can be effected by physical delivery; and
  (b)   the delivery of documents is capable of being recorded by the obtaining of an acknowledgment of delivery.

1142   Requirement to give service address

Any obligation under this Act to give a person's address is, unless otherwise expressly provided, to give a service address for that person.".

NOTES
Commencement: 1 October 2009.

[10.1172]
76   Notice of appointment of judicial factor

Sections 1154 and 1155 apply to LLPs, modified so that they read as follows—

"1154   Duty to notify registrar of appointment of judicial factor

(1)   Notice must be given to the registrar of the appointment in relation to an LLP of a judicial factor (in Scotland).

(2)   The notice must be given by the judicial factor.

(3)   The notice must specify an address at which service of documents (including legal process) may be effected on the judicial factor.
  Notice of a change in the address for service may be given to the registrar by the judicial factor.

(4)   Where notice has been given under this section of the appointment of a judicial factor, notice must also be given to the registrar by the judicial factor of the termination of the appointment.

1155   Offence of failure to give notice

(1)   If a judicial factor fails to give notice of his appointment in accordance with section 1154 within the period of 14 days after the appointment he commits an offence.

(2)   A person guilty of an offence under this section is liable on summary conviction to a fine not exceeding level 5 on the standard scale and, for continued contravention, a daily default fine not exceeding one-tenth of level 5 on the standard scale.".

NOTES
Commencement: 1 October 2009.

[10.1173]
77   Courts and legal proceedings

Sections 1156 and 1157 apply to LLPs for the purposes of these Regulations, modified so that they read as follows—

"1156   Meaning of "the court"

(1)   Except as otherwise provided, in this Act "the court" means—
  (a)   in England and Wales, the High Court or (subject to subsection (3)) a county court;
  (b)   in Scotland, the Court of Session or the sheriff court;
  (c)   in Northern Ireland, the High Court.

(2)   The provisions of the Companies Acts conferring jurisdiction on "the court" as defined above have effect subject to any enactment or rule of law relating to the allocation of jurisdiction or distribution of business between courts in any part of the United Kingdom.

(3)   The Lord Chancellor may, with the concurrence of the Lord Chief Justice, by order—
  (a)   exclude a county court from having jurisdiction under this Act, and
  (b)   for the purposes of that jurisdiction attach that court's district, or any part of it, to another county court.

(4)   The Lord Chief Justice may nominate a judicial office holder (as defined in section 109(4) of the Constitutional Reform Act 2005 (c 4)) to exercise his functions under subsection (3).

1157   Power of court to grant relief in certain cases

(1)   If in proceedings for negligence, default, breach of duty or breach of trust against—

   (a)   a member of an LLP, or

   (b)   a person employed by an LLP as auditor,

it appears to the court hearing the case that the member or person is or may be liable but that he acted honestly and reasonably, and that having regard to all the circumstances of the case (including those connected with his appointment) he ought fairly to be excused, the court may relieve him, either wholly or in part, from his liability on such terms as it thinks fit.

(2)   If any such member or person has reason to apprehend that a claim will or might be made against him in respect of negligence, default, breach of duty or breach of trust—

   (a)   he may apply to the court for relief, and

   (b)   the court has the same power to relieve him as it would have had if it had been a court before which proceedings against him for negligence, default, breach of duty or breach of trust had been brought.

(3)   Where a case to which subsection (1) applies is being tried by a judge with a jury, the judge, after hearing the evidence, may, if he is satisfied that the defendant (in Scotland, the defender) ought in pursuance of that subsection to be relieved either in whole or in part from the liability sought to be enforced against him, withdraw the case from the jury and forthwith direct judgment to be entered for the defendant (in Scotland, grant decree of absolvitor) on such terms as to costs (in Scotland, expenses) or otherwise as the judge may think proper.".

NOTES

Commencement: 9 July 2009 (for the purpose of enabling the exercise of powers to make regulations or orders by statutory instrument); 1 October 2009 (otherwise).

[10.1174]
78   Requirements of this Act

Section 1172 applies to LLPs for the purposes of these Regulations, modified so that it reads as follows—

> **"1172 References to requirements of this Act**
>
> References in the provisions of this Act applied to LLPs to the requirements of this Act include the requirements of regulations and orders made under it.".

NOTES

Commencement: 1 October 2009.

[10.1175]
79   Minor definitions

Section 1173 applies to LLPs for the purposes of these Regulations, modified so that it reads as follows—

> **"1173 Minor definitions: general**
>
> (1)   In this Act—
>
> "body corporate" and "corporation" include a body incorporated outside the United Kingdom, but do not include—
>
>   (a)   a corporation sole, or
>
>   (b)   a partnership that, whether or not a legal person, is not regarded as a body corporate under the law by which it is governed;
>
> "the Companies Acts" is to be construed in accordance with section 2;
>
> "firm" means any entity, whether or not a legal person, that is not an individual and includes a body corporate, a corporation sole and a partnership or other unincorporated association;
>
> "the Gazette" means—
>
>   (a)   as respects LLPs registered in England and Wales, the London Gazette,
>
>   (b)   as respects LLPs registered in Scotland, the Edinburgh Gazette, and
>
>   (c)   as respects LLPs registered in Northern Ireland, the Belfast Gazette;
>
> "LLP" means a limited liability partnership registered under the Limited Liability Partnerships Act 2000 (c 12);
>
> "LLP agreement" means any agreement, express or implied, between the members of the LLP or between the LLP and the members of the LLP which determines the mutual rights and duties of the members, and their rights and duties in relation to the LLP;
>
> "officer", in relation to a body corporate, includes a director, manager or secretary;
>
> "working day", in relation to an LLP, means a day that is not a Saturday or Sunday, Christmas Day, Good Friday or any day that is a bank holiday under the Banking and Financial Dealings Act 1971 (c 80) in the part of the United Kingdom where the LLP is registered.
>
> (2)   In this Act, unless the context otherwise requires, "enactment" includes—
>
>   (a)   an enactment contained in subordinate legislation within the meaning of the Interpretation Act 1978 (c 30),
>
>   (b)   an enactment contained in, or in an instrument made under, an Act of the Scottish Parliament, and

Part 10   Miscellaneous other SIs

(c)   an enactment contained in, or in an instrument made under, Northern Ireland legislation within the meaning of the Interpretation Act 1978.".

NOTES
Commencement: 1 October 2009.

Regulations and orders

[10.1176]
80
Sections 1288 to 1290 apply to LLPs for the purposes of these Regulations, modified so that they read as follows—

"1288 Regulations and orders: statutory instrument
Except as otherwise provided, regulations and orders under this Act shall be made by statutory instrument.

1289 Regulations: negative resolution procedure
Where regulations under this Act are subject to "negative resolution procedure" the statutory instrument containing the regulations shall be subject to annulment in pursuance of a resolution of either House of Parliament.

1290 Regulations: affirmative resolution procedure
Where regulations under this Act are subject to "affirmative resolution procedure" the regulations must not be made unless a draft of the statutory instrument containing them has been laid before Parliament and approved by a resolution of each House of Parliament.".

NOTES
Commencement: 9 July 2009 (for the purpose of enabling the exercise of powers to make regulations or orders by statutory instrument); 1 October 2009 (otherwise).

[10.1177]
81
Section 1292 applies to LLPs for the purposes of these Regulations, modified so that it reads as follows—

"1292 Regulations and orders: supplementary
(1)   Regulations or orders under this Act may—
   (a)   make different provision for different cases or circumstances,
   (b)   include supplementary, incidental and consequential provision, and
   (c)   make transitional provision and savings.
(2)   Any provision that may be made by regulations under this Act may be made by order; and any provision that may be made by order under this Act may be made by regulations.
(3)   Any provision that may be made by regulations or order under this Act for which no Parliamentary procedure is prescribed may be made by regulations subject to negative or affirmative resolution procedure.
(4)   Any provision that may be made by regulations under this Act subject to negative resolution procedure may be made by regulations subject to affirmative resolution procedure.".

NOTES
Commencement: 9 July 2009 (for the purpose of enabling the exercise of powers to make regulations or orders by statutory instrument); 1 October 2009 (otherwise).

[10.1178]
82   Continuity of the law
Section 1297 applies to LLPs, modified so that it reads as follows—

"1297 Continuity of the law
(1)   This section applies where any provision of this Act applied to LLPs re-enacts (with or without modification) an enactment repealed by this Act which was applied to LLPs.
(2)   The repeal and re-enactment does not affect the continuity of the law.
(3)   Anything done (including subordinate legislation made and applied to LLPs), or having effect as if done, under or for the purposes of the repealed provision as applied to LLPs that could have been done under or for the purposes of the corresponding provision of this Act as applied to LLPs, if in force or effective immediately before the commencement of that corresponding provision, has effect thereafter as if done under or for the purposes of that corresponding provision.
(4)   Any reference (express or implied) in this Act or any other enactment, instrument or document to a provision of this Act as applied to LLPs shall be construed (so far as the context permits) as including, as respects times, circumstances or purposes in relation to which the

corresponding repealed provision had effect, a reference to that corresponding provision.

(5)   Any reference (express or implied) in any enactment, instrument or document to a repealed provision which was applied to LLPs shall be construed (so far as the context permits), as respects times, circumstances and purposes in relation to which the corresponding provision of this Act applied to LLPs has effect, as being or (according to the context) including a reference to the corresponding provision of this Act.

(6)   This section has effect subject to any specific transitional provision or saving contained in this Act as applied to LLPs.

(7)   References in this section to this Act as applied to LLPs include subordinate legislation made under this Act as so applied.

(8)   In this section "subordinate legislation" has the same meaning as in the Interpretation Act 1978 (c 30).".

NOTES

Commencement: 1 October 2009.

PART 18
TRANSITIONAL AND CONSEQUENTIAL PROVISIONS

[10.1179]
83   Transitional provisions: application of provisions of Companies Act 2006

Schedule 1 to these Regulations contains transitional and savings provisions in connection with the application to LLPs of provisions of the Companies Act 2006.

NOTES

Commencement: 1 October 2009.

84   *(Reg 84 (Transitional provisions: Northern Ireland LLPs) outside the scope of this work.)*

[10.1180]
85   Consequential amendments and revocations

Schedule 3 to these Regulations contains consequential amendments and revocations.

NOTES

Commencement: 1 October 2009.

SCHEDULES

SCHEDULE 1
TRANSITIONAL PROVISIONS: APPLICATION OF PROVISIONS OF COMPANIES ACT 2006

Regulation 83

PART 1
INTRODUCTORY

[10.1181]
1   Introduction

(1)   This Schedule contains transitional provisions and savings in connection with the coming into force of the provisions of these Regulations applying provisions of the Companies Act 2006 to LLPs.

(2)   In this Schedule—
   "the 1985 Act" means the Companies Act 1985, and
   "the 1986 Order" means the Companies (Northern Ireland) Order 1986.

(3)   References in this Schedule to an LLP in relation to times before 1st October 2009 include a limited liability partnership registered under the Limited Liability Partnerships Act (Northern Ireland) 2002.

(4)   References in this Schedule to an LLP registered immediately before 1st October 2009 include a limited liability partnership registered under that Act on an application made before, but not determined before, that date (see paragraph 2 of Schedule 2 below).

NOTES

Commencement: 1 October 2009.

PART 2
FORMALITIES OF DOING BUSINESS

[10.1182]
2   Execution of deeds etc

(1)   Section 47 of the Companies Act 2006 (execution of deeds or other documents by attorney), as applied to LLPs by regulation 4, applies where the instrument empowering a person to act as an LLP's attorney is executed on or after 1st October 2009.

(2)   Section 38 of the 1985 Act or Article 48 of the 1986 Order, as applied to LLPs, continues to have effect where the power to act as an LLP's attorney was conferred before that date (including in relation to instruments executed by the attorney on behalf of the LLP on or after that date).

NOTES
Commencement: 1 October 2009.

PART 3
AN LLP'S NAME

An LLP's name

[10.1183]
3. (1)   The following provisions of the Companies Act 2006, as applied to LLPs by regulations 8 to 11, do not affect the continued registration of an LLP by a name by which it was duly registered immediately before 1st October 2009.

(2)   The provisions are—
    (a)   section 54 (name suggesting connection with government or public authority);
    (b)   section 55 (other sensitive words or expressions);
    (c)   section 57 (permitted characters etc);
    (d)   section 65 (inappropriate use of indications of company type or legal form);
    (e)   section 66 (name not to be the same as another in registrar's index).

4. Sections 54 to 56 of the Companies Act 2006 (sensitive words and expressions), as applied to LLPs by regulation 8, apply to applications for approval received by the Secretary of State on or after 1st October 2009.

NOTES
Commencement: 1 October 2009.

PART 4
AN LLP'S MEMBERS

Particulars to be registered

[10.1184]
5. (1)   The duty of an LLP to keep a register of members under section 162 of the Companies Act 2006 (register of members), as applied to LLPs by regulation 18, has effect on and after 1st October 2009.

(2)   In the case of an LLP that was registered immediately before 1st October 2009—
    (a)   the address of a member notified under—
        (i)   section 2(2)(e) or 9(1)(b) of the Limited Liability Partnerships Act 2000, or
        (ii)   Article 2(2)(e) or 9(1)(b) of the Limited Liability Partnerships Act (Northern Ireland) 2002,
        is to be treated, on and after 1st October 2009, as a service address, and
    (b)   any entry in the LLP's register of members stating that address is treated as complying with the obligation in section 163(1)(b) of the Companies Act 2006, as applied to LLPs by regulation 18, to state a service address.

(3)   The operation of this paragraph does not give rise to any obligation to notify the registrar under section 9(1)(b) of the Limited Liability Partnerships Act 2000.

Register of members' residential addresses
6. (1)   The duty of an LLP to keep a register of members' residential addresses under section 165 of the Companies Act 2006 (register of residential addresses), as applied to LLPs by regulation 18, has effect on and after 1st October 2009.

(2)   The entry on that register of information does not give rise to any duty to notify the registrar under section 9 of the Limited Liability Partnerships Act 2000 (registration of membership changes).

Members: entries on the register of companies
7. (1)   The registrar may make such entries in the register as appear to be appropriate having regard to paragraphs 5 and 6 above and the information appearing on the register immediately before 1st October 2009 or notified to the registrar in pursuance of an obligation arising before that date.

(2)   In particular, the registrar may record an address falling within paragraph 5 as a service address.

(3)   Any notification of a change of an address of a member occurring before 1st October 2009 that is received by the registrar on or after that date is treated as being or including notification of a change of service address.

Members' residential addresses: protection from disclosure
8.   Where a member's usual residential address appears as a service address—
  (a)   in the LLP's register of members by virtue of paragraph 5 above, or
  (b)   in the register of LLPs by virtue of paragraph 7,
that address is not protected information for the purposes of sections 240 to 246 of the Companies Act 2006, as applied to LLPs by regulation 19.

9. (1)   Section 242(1) of the Companies Act 2006 (duty of registrar to omit protected information from material available for inspection), as applied to LLPs by regulation 19, does not apply—
  (a)   to material delivered to the registrar before 1st October 2009, or
  (b)   to material delivered to the registrar on or after 1st October 2009 by virtue of paragraph 7(3) (notification of change occurring before that date).

(2)   Sub-paragraph (1) above has effect subject to paragraph 11 below (which provides for the continued protection of information formerly protected by a confidentiality order).

10.   In determining under section 245(1) of the Companies Act 2006, as applied to LLPs by regulation 19, whether to put a member's usual residential address on the public record, the registrar may take into account only—
  (a)   communications sent by the registrar on or after 1st October 2009, and
  (b)   evidence as to the effectiveness of service coming to the registrar's attention on or after that date.

Continuation of protection afforded by confidentiality orders under the 1985 Act
11. (1)   A member in relation to whom a confidentiality order under section 723B of the 1985 Act, as applied to LLPs, was in force immediately before 1st October 2009 is treated on and after that date as if—
  (a)   the member had made an application under section 1088 of the Companies Act 2006 (application to make address unavailable for public inspection), as applied to LLPs, in respect of any address that immediately before that date was contained in "confidential records" as defined in section 723D(3) of the 1985 Act, and
  (b)   that application had been determined by the registrar in the member's favour.

(2)   The provisions of Parts 1, 3 and 4 of the Companies (Disclosure of Address) Regulations 2009 relating to decisions of the registrar in favour of an applicant (in particular, as to the duration and revocation of such a decision) apply accordingly.

(3)   As those regulations apply in accordance with this paragraph any reference to an offence under section 1112 of the Companies Act 2006 (false statement) as applied to LLPs by regulation 69 shall be read as a reference to an offence under the Limited Liability Partnerships (Particulars of Usual Residential Address) (Confidentiality Orders) Regulations 2002 in relation to the application for the confidentiality order.

12. (1)   A member in relation to whom a confidentiality order under section 723B of the 1985 Act as applied to LLPs was in force immediately before 1st October 2009 is treated on and after that date as if—
  (a)   the member had made an application under section 243(5) of the Companies Act 2006 (application to prevent disclosure of protected information by registrar to credit reference agency), as applied to LLPs by regulation 19, and
  (b)   that application had been determined by the registrar in the member's favour.

(2)   The provisions of Parts 1, 2 and 4 of the Companies (Disclosure of Address) Regulations 2009 relating to decisions of the registrar in favour of an applicant (in particular, as to the duration and revocation of such a decision) apply accordingly.

(3)   As those regulations apply in accordance with this paragraph any reference to an offence under section 1112 (false statement) as applied to LLPs by regulation 69 shall be read as a reference to an offence under the Limited Liability Partnerships (Particulars of Usual Residential Address) (Confidentiality Orders) Regulations 2002 in relation to the application for the confidentiality order.

Part 10   Miscellaneous other SIs

13. Where a confidentiality order under section 723B of the 1985 Act as applied to LLPs was in force immediately before 1st October 2009 in relation to a member, section 162(5) and (8) of the Companies Act 2006 as applied to LLPs by regulation 18 do not apply in relation to the part of the LLP's register containing particulars of the usual residential address of the individual that before that date were protected from disclosure.

Effect of pending application for confidentiality order
14. (1) The Limited Liability Partnerships (Particulars of Usual Residential Address) (Confidentiality Orders) Regulations 2002 continue to apply in relation to an application for a confidentiality order made before 1st October 2009.

(2) Paragraphs 11 to 13 above (continuity of protection afforded by confidentiality orders) apply to a person in respect of whom such an application has been made, and has not been determined or withdrawn, as to a person in relation to whom a confidentiality order was in force immediately before that date.

(3) If the application is dismissed or withdrawn, those paragraphs cease to apply.

(4) If the application is successful those paragraphs continue to apply as in the case of an individual in relation to whom a confidentiality order was in force immediately before 1st October 2009.

NOTES
Commencement: 1 October 2009.

PART 5
AN LLP'S ANNUAL RETURN

[10.1185]
15   Annual returns
(1) Sections 854, 855, 855A and 858 of the Companies Act 2006 (annual returns), as applied to LLPs by regulations 30 and 31, apply to annual returns made up to a date on or after 1st October 2009.

(2) Sections 363 and 364 of the 1985 Act or Articles 371 and 372 of the 1986 Order, as applied to LLPs, continue to apply to annual returns made up to a date before 1st October 2009.

(3) Any reference in the Companies Act 2006 (as applied to LLPs) to an LLP's last return, or to a return delivered in accordance with Part 24 of that Act, shall be read as including (so far as necessary to ensure the continuity of the law) a return made up to a date before 1st October 2009 or delivered in accordance with the 1985 Act or the 1986 Order (as applied to LLPs).

NOTES
Commencement: 1 October 2009.

PART 6
LLP CHARGES

LLP charges

[10.1186]
16. (1) Sections 860 and 878 of the Companies Act 2006 (charges created by LLP), as applied to LLPs by regulations 32 and 39, apply to charges created on or after 1st October 2009.

(2) The corresponding provisions of the 1985 Act or 1986 Order, as applied to LLPs, continue to apply to charges created before that date.

17. (1) Sections 862 and 880 of the Companies Act 2006 (charges existing on property acquired), as applied to LLPs by regulations 32 and 39, apply to property acquired on or after 1st October 2009.

(2) Sections 400 and 416 of the 1985 Act or Article 407 of the 1986 Order, as applied to LLPs, continue to apply to property acquired before that date.

18. (1) Sections 863 and 882 of the Companies Act 2006 (charge in series of debentures), as applied to LLPs by regulations 33 and 40, apply where the first debenture of the series is executed on or after 1st October 2009.

(2) The corresponding provisions of the 1985 Act or the 1986 Order, as applied to LLPs, continue to apply where the first debenture of the series is executed before that date.

19. (1) Section 868 of the Companies Act 2006 (Northern Ireland: registration of certain charges etc affecting land), as applied to LLPs by regulation 35, applies where the date of registration of the charge in the Land Registry is on or after 1st October 2009.

(2) Article 408 of the 1986 Order, as applied to LLPs, continues to apply where the date of registration of the charge in the Land Registry is before that date.

20. (1)   Section 871 of the Companies Act 2006 (notice to registrar of appointment of receiver or manager etc), as applied to LLPs by regulation 36, applies where the order or appointment is made, or the receiver or manager ceases to act, on or after 1st October 2009.

(2)   Section 405 of the 1985 Act or Article 413 of the 1986 Order, as applied to LLPs, continues to apply where the order or appointment is made, or the receiver or manager ceases to act, before that date.

21. (1)   Sections 872 and 887 of the Companies Act 2006 (entries of satisfaction and release), as applied to LLPs by regulations 36 and 42, apply to statements delivered to the registrar on or after 1st October 2009.

(2)   Section 403 or 419 of the 1985 Act or Article 411 of the 1986 Order, as applied to LLPs, continues to apply where the relevant statutory declaration, statement or application and statutory declaration or statement is received by the registrar before that date.

NOTES
Commencement: 1 October 2009.

PART 7
DISSOLUTION AND RESTORATION TO THE REGISTER

[Property of dissolved LLP

[10.1187]
22. (1)   Sections 1012 to 1023 of the Companies Act 2006 (property of dissolved LLP), as applied to LLPs by regulations 52 to 55, apply in relation to the property of an LLP dissolved on or after 1st October 2009.

(2)   Subject to paragraph 22A, the corresponding provisions of the 1985 Act or 1986 Order, as applied to LLPs, continue to apply in relation to the property of an LLP dissolved before that date.

22A. (1)   Section 1013 of the Companies Act 2006 (Crown disclaimer of property vesting as bona vacantia), as applied to LLPs by regulation 52, applies in relation to property of an LLP dissolved before 1st October 2009 if at that date—
  (a)   no period has begun to run in relation to the property under section 656(3)(a) or (b) of the 1985 Act or Article 607(3)(a) or (b) of the 1986 Order (period within which notice of disclaimer must be executed), as applied to LLPs, and
  (b)   the right to disclaim has not ceased to be exercisable in relation to the property by virtue of section 656(2) of the 1985 Act or Article 607(2) of the 1986 Order (waiver of right to disclaim), as applied to LLPs.

(2)   In section 1013, as applied to LLPs and as it applies by virtue of this paragraph, the references to property vesting under section 1012 (as applied to LLPs by regulation 52) shall be read as references to its vesting under section 654 of the 1985 Act or Article 605 of the 1986 Order as applied to LLPs.

(3)   Where section 1013 (as applied to LLPs by regulation 52) applies by virtue of this paragraph—
  (a)   the other provisions of sections 1012 to 1022 of the Companies Act 2006 (as applied to LLPs by regulations 52 to 54) apply accordingly, and
  (b)   the corresponding provisions of the 1985 Act or 1986 Order (as applied to LLPs) do not apply.]

Saving for applications to court made before 1st October 2009
23. The repeal of the following provisions, as applied to LLPs—
  (a)   section 651 of the 1985 Act or Article 602 of the 1986 Order (power of court to declare dissolution of LLP void), or
  (b)   section 653 of the 1985 Act or Article 604 of the 1986 Order (objection to striking off by person aggrieved),
does not affect an application made under that section or Article before 1st October 2009.

Application to court for restoration to the register
24. Sections 1029 to 1032 of the Companies Act 2006 (restoration to register by the court), as applied to LLPs by regulation 57, apply whether the LLP was dissolved or struck off the register before, on or after 1st October 2009.

25. (1)   The following provisions apply where the LLP was dissolved or struck off the register before 1st October 2009.

(2)   In section 1029 (application to court for restoration to register), as applied to LLPs, the references in subsection (1) to enactments under which an LLP may have been dissolved or struck off include corresponding earlier enactments as applied to LLPs (and for this purpose sections 1000 and 1003 of the Companies Act 2006 are regarded as corresponding to sections 652 and 652A of the 1985 Act and Articles 603 and 603A of the 1986 Order).

(3)   No application under section 1029 as applied to LLPs may be made if an application in respect of the same dissolution or striking off has been made under section 653 of the 1985 Act or Article 604 of the 1986 Order (objection to striking off by person aggrieved) as applied to LLPs, and has not been withdrawn.

(4)   Section 1030(4) (general time limit of six years) as applied to LLPs does not enable an application to be made in respect of an LLP dissolved before 1st October 2007, subject to sub-paragraphs (5) and (6).

(5)   If the LLP was struck off under section 652 or 652A of the 1985 Act or Article 603 or 603A of the 1986 Order as applied to LLPs, section 1030(4) as applied to LLPs does not prevent an application being made at any time before—

    (a)   1st October 2015 (that is, six years after commencement), or

    (b)   the expiration of the period of 20 years from publication in the Gazette of notice under the relevant section or Article,

whichever occurs first.

(6)   Section 1030(5) (extension of period for application where application for administrative restoration refused), as applied to LLPs, applies in relation to the time limit under sub-paragraph (5) above as in relation to the time limit in section 1030(4).

Effect of restoration to the register where property has vested as bona vacantia

26. (1)   Section 1034 of the Companies Act 2006 (effect of restoration to the register where property has vested as *bona vacantia*), as applied to LLPs by regulation 58, applies whenever the LLP was dissolved.

(2)   The following provisions apply where the LLP was dissolved before 1st October 2009.

(3)   The reference in section 1034(1) to section 1012 (property of dissolved LLP to be *bona vacantia*) shall be read as a reference to section 654 of the 1985 Act or Article 605 of the 1986 Order as applied to LLPs.

(4)   No deduction is to be made under section 1034(3) (deduction of reasonable costs of Crown representative from amount payable to LLP) as applied to LLPs from consideration realised before 1st October 2009.

NOTES

  Commencement: 1 October 2009.

  Paras 22, 22A: substituted, for the original para 22, by the Companies Act 2006 and Limited Liability Partnerships (Transitional Provisions and Savings) (Amendment) Regulations 2009, SI 2009/2476, reg 3, as from 1 October 2009.

PART 8
THE REGISTRAR OF COMPANIES

[10.1188]
27 Provisions of general application

The general provisions of Part 35 of the Companies Act 2006 mentioned in regulation 60 apply to LLPs subject to relevant transitional provisions and savings in Schedule 2 to the Companies Act 2006 (Commencement No 8, Transitional Provisions and Savings) Order 2008 and in the Schedule to the Companies Act 2006 (Part 35) (Consequential Amendments, Transitional Provisions and Savings) Order 2009.

28 Certificates of incorporation

Sections 1064 and 1065 of the Companies Act 2006 (certificates of incorporation), as applied to LLPs by regulation 61, apply to certificates of incorporation whenever issued.

29 Annotation of the register

(1)   Section 1081 of the Companies Act 2006 (annotation of the register), as applied to LLPs by regulation 64, applies in relation to—

    (a)   documents delivered to the registrar on or after 1st October 2009 other than those delivered in pursuance of an obligation arising before that date, and

    (b)   certificates issued by the registrar on or after 1st October 2009 other than those issued in response to a document delivered to the registrar before that date or in pursuance of an obligation arising before that date,

and in relation to the content of, and material derived from, such documents and certificates.

(2)   The provisions applicable before 1st October 2009 (and the registrar's former practice with respect to annotation of the register) continue to apply in relation to—

    (a)   documents delivered to the registrar before that date, or in pursuance of an obligation arising before that date, and

    (b)   certificates issued by the registrar before that date or in response to a document delivered to the registrar before that date or in pursuance of an obligation arising before that date,

and in relation to the content of, and material derived from, such documents and certificates.

30 Registrar's notice to resolve inconsistency on the register

(1) Section 1093 of the Companies Act 2006 (registrar's notice to resolve inconsistency on the register), as applied to LLPs by regulation 67, applies where—

   (a) a document is delivered to the registrar on or after 1st October 2009 otherwise than in pursuance of an obligation arising before that date, and

   (b) it appears to the registrar that the information contained in the document is inconsistent with other information on the register.

(2) The provisions applicable before 1st October 2009 (and the registrar's former practice with respect to inconsistencies on the register) continue to apply in relation to documents delivered to the registrar before that date or in pursuance of an obligation arising before that date.

31 Removal of material from the register

(1) This paragraph applies to—

   (a) sections 1094 to 1097 of the Companies Act 2006 (removal of material from the register), as applied to LLPs by regulation 67, and

   (b) section 1098 of that Act (public notice of removal of certain material from the register), as so applied.

(2) Those provisions apply in relation to—

   (a) documents delivered to the registrar on or after 1st October 2009 other than those delivered in pursuance of an obligation arising before that date, and

   (b) certificates issued by the registrar on or after 1st October 2009, other than those issued in response to a document delivered to the registrar before that date or in pursuance of an obligation arising before that date,

and in relation to the content of, and material derived from, such documents and certificates.

(3) The provisions applicable before 1st October 2009 (and the registrar's former practice with respect to removal of material from the register) continue to apply in relation to—

   (a) documents delivered to the registrar before that date, or in pursuance of an obligation arising before that date, and

   (b) certificates issued by the registrar before that date or in response to a document delivered to the registrar before that date or in pursuance of an obligation arising before that date,

and in relation to the content of, and material derived from, such documents or certificates.

32 General false statement offence

Section 1112 of the Companies Act 2006 (general false statement offence), as applied to LLPs by regulation 69, applies to all documents delivered, and statements made, on or after 1st October 2009.

33 Provision and authentication by registrar of documents sent by electronic means

The repeal of section 710A of the 1985 Act or Article 659A of the 1986 Order (provision and authentication by registrar of documents in non-legible form) does not affect the application of those provisions as applied to LLPs on or after 1st October 2009 in relation to saved provisions of that Act or Order as applied to LLPs.

NOTES

Commencement: 1 October 2009.

PART 9
SUPPLEMENTARY

[10.1189]
34 Forms

(1) Any saving in these Regulations for the effect of a provision of the 1985 Act or the 1986 Order, as applied to LLPs, requiring the use of a prescribed form extends to the form and the power under which it is prescribed.

(2) Any saving in these Regulations for the effect of a provision of the 1985 Act or the 1986 Order requiring a document to be delivered to the registrar extends to section 707B of the 1985 Act or Article 656B of the 1986 Order (delivery to the registrar using electronic communications) so far as relating to the provision in question and the delivery of documents under it.

35 Offences

Any saving in—

   (a) this Schedule, or

   (b) the Limited Liability Partnerships (Accounts and Audit) (Application of Companies Act 2006) Regulations 2008,

for the effect of a provision of the 1985 Act or the 1986 Order as applied to LLPs that creates an offence extends to the entry relating to that provision in Schedule 24 to that Act or Schedule 23 to that Order (punishment of offences) as applied to LLPs.

36 Fees

(1)   The repeal of section 708 of the 1985 Act or Article 657 of the 1986 Order, as applied to LLPs, shall not prevent the registrar from continuing to charge fees under that section or Article, as applied to LLPs, of which notice had before the repeal been given to those to whom the services in question have been, are being or are to be provided (including notice by publication of a list of fees in respect of services provided to any person who seeks their provisions).

(2)   Any regulations under section 708 of the 1985 Act or Article 657 of the 1986 Order as applied to LLPs (fees payable to registrar) that are in force immediately before 1st October 2009 have effect on or after that date as if made under section 1063 of the Companies Act 2006.

NOTES

Commencement: 1 October 2009.

SCHEDULE 2

(Sch 2 (Transitional Provisions: Northern Ireland LLPs) outside the scope of this work.)

SCHEDULE 3
CONSEQUENTIAL AMENDMENTS AND REVOCATIONS

Regulation 85

PART 1
CONSEQUENTIAL AMENDMENTS OF THE LIMITED LIABILITY PARTNERSHIPS ACT 2000

[10.1190]
1–10.   *(Amend the Limited Liability Partnerships Act 2000, ss 2, 3, 8, 9, 14, 17–19, Schedule, and add s 4A (see the 2000 Act at* **[9.430]** *et seq).)*

11 Saving

The amendments made by this Part of this Schedule do not affect an obligation arising before 1st October 2009 to deliver a document to the registrar.

NOTES

Commencement: 9 July 2009 (paras 6, 7 for the purpose of enabling the exercise of powers to make regulations or orders by statutory instrument); 1 October 2009 (otherwise). Note that paras 6, 7 amend ss 14, 17 of the 2000 Act.

PART 2
OTHER CONSEQUENTIAL AMENDMENTS AND REVOCATIONS

[10.1191]
12 General

(1)   In any enactment relating to LLPs—
  (a)   "the registrar" has the meaning given by section 18 of the Limited Liability Partnerships Act 2000,
  (b)   "the register" means the records kept by the registrar relating to LLPs, and
  (c)   references to registration in a particular part of the United Kingdom are to registration by the registrar for that part of the United Kingdom.

(2)   In sub-paragraph (1) "enactment" includes—
  (a)   an enactment contained in subordinate legislation within the meaning of the Interpretation Act 1978,
  (b)   an enactment contained in, or in an instrument made under, an Act of the Scottish Parliament,
  (c)   an enactment contained in, or in an instrument made under, Northern Ireland legislation, and
  (d)   an enactment contained in, or in an instrument made under, a Measure or Act of the National Assembly for Wales.

13–17.   *(Para 13 amends the Limited Liability Partnerships Regulations 2001, SI 2001/1090, regs 4, 10, Sch 2, Pt I, Sch 5, Sch 6, Pts I, III, and inserts reg 2A (see the 2001 Regulations at* **[10.813]** *et seq); para 14 amends the Limited Liability Partnerships Regulations (Northern Ireland) 2004, SR 2004/307 (outside the scope of this work); paras 15, 16 amend the Limited Liability Partnerships (Accounts and Audit) (Application of Companies Act 2006) Regulations 2008, SI 2008/1911, regs 3, 6, 24, 32, 40, 49–51, 54–57 (see the 2008 Regulations at* **[10.1003]** *et seq); para 17 revokes the Limited Liability Partnerships (No 2) Regulations 2002, SI 2002/913, and the Limited Liability Partnerships (Particulars of Usual Residential Address) (Confidentiality Orders) Regulations 2002, SI 2002/915.)*

NOTES

Commencement: 1 October 2009.

Note that para 13(5) of this Schedule (amendment of Sch 2, Pt I to the Limited Liability Partnerships Regulations 2001, SI 2001/1090) was amended by the Limited Liability Partnerships (Amendment) Regulations 2009, SI 2009/1833 to correct a drafting error.

LIMITED PARTNERSHIPS (FORMS) RULES 2009 (NOTE)

(SI 2009/2160)

[10.1192]

NOTES

These Rules were made on 31 July 2009 under the powers conferred by the Limited Partnerships Act 1907, s 17, and came into force on 1 October 2009.

These Rules replace most of the provisions of the Limited Partnerships Rules 1907.

These Rules do not re-enact r 2 of the 1907 Rules, which provided for the division of responsibilities between the offices of the registrar of joint stock companies. Such provision is unnecessary as a result of amendments made to ss 15 and 16 of the 1907 Act by paragraph 3 of Schedule 1 to the Companies Act 2006 (Consequential Amendments, Transitional Provisions and Savings) Order 2009 (SI 2009/1941).

Regulation 3 of the 1907 Rules provided for fees payable to the registrar. The powers to set fees under the 1907 Act were repealed on 6 April 2007 by s 1063(7) of the Companies Act 2006. But savings in paragraph 6 of Schedule 1 to the Companies Act 2006 (Commencement No 1, Transitional Provisions and Savings) Order 2006 (SI 2006/3428) preserved the fees set under s 16 of the 1907 Act (inspection of statements registered) and saved r 3(a) of the 1907 Rules (fee for original registration). These Rules revoke neither r 3(a) of the 1907 Rules nor the savings for limited partnerships fees in the First Commencement Order. They do, however, revoke the rest of the 1907 Rules.

These Rules replace the forms which are to be used for registering limited partnerships, and for registering changes to existing limited partnerships, under the Limited Partnerships Act 1907. The Schedule to these Rules prescribes:

(i)   the form that must be used for any application for the registration of a limited partnership under the 1907 Act (Form for Registration of Limited Partnerships (LP5));

(ii)   the form that must be used for any statement sent or delivered to the registrar under section 9 of the 1907 Act (Form for Registering Changes to Limited Partnerships (LP6)).

EUROPEAN PUBLIC LIMITED-LIABILITY COMPANY (EMPLOYEE INVOLVEMENT) (GREAT BRITAIN) REGULATIONS 2009

(SI 2009/2401)

NOTES

Made: 9 September 2009.
Authority: European Communities Act 1972, s 2(2).
Commencement: 1 October 2009.
These Regulations are reproduced as amended by: the Agency Workers Regulations 2010, SI 2010/93.

ARRANGEMENT OF REGULATIONS

PART 1
INTRODUCTORY PROVISIONS

PART 2
PARTICIPATING COMPANIES AND THE SPECIAL NEGOTIATING BODY

PART 3
ELECTION OR APPOINTMENT OF UK MEMBERS OF THE SPECIAL NEGOTIATING BODY

PART 1
INTRODUCTORY PROVISIONS

[10.1193]
1   Citation, commencement and extent

(1)   These Regulations may be cited as the European Public Limited-Liability Company
(Employee Involvement) (Great Britain) Regulations 2009.

(2)   These Regulations come into force on 1st October 2009.

(3)   These Regulations extend to the whole of Great Britain.

NOTES

Commencement: 1 October 2009.

[10.1194]
2   EC Directive and EC Regulation

(1)   In these Regulations—

"the EC Directive" means Council Directive 2001/86/EC of 8 October 2001 supplementing
the Statute for a European Company with regard to the involvement of employees;

"the EC Regulation" means Council Regulation 2157/2001/EC of 8 October 2001 on the Statute
for a European Company.

(2) References in these Regulations to numbered Articles are, unless otherwise specified, references to Articles in the EC Regulation.

NOTES

Commencement: 1 October 2009.

[10.1195]
3 Interpretation

(1) In these Regulations—

"absolute majority vote" means a vote passed by a majority of the total membership of the special negotiating body where the members voting with that majority represent the majority of the employees of the participating companies and their concerned subsidiaries and establishments employed in the EEA states;

["agency worker" has the same meaning as in regulation 3 of the Agency Workers Regulations 2010;]

"Appeal Tribunal" means the Employment Appeal Tribunal;

"CAC" means the Central Arbitration Committee;

"dismissed" and "dismissal", in relation to an employee, have the same meaning as in Part 10 of the Employment Rights Act 1996;

"employee" means an individual who has entered into or works under a contract of employment and includes, where the employment has ceased, an individual who worked under a contract of employment;

"employee involvement agreement" means an agreement reached between the special negotiating body and the competent organs of the participating companies governing the arrangements for the involvement of employees within the SE;

"employees' representatives" means—

    (a) if the employees are of a description in respect of which an independent trade union is recognised by their employer for the purpose of collective bargaining, representatives of the trade union who normally take part as negotiators in the collective bargaining process, and

    (b) any other employees of their employer who are elected or appointed as employee representatives to positions in which they are expected to receive, on behalf of the employees, information—

        (i) which is relevant to the terms and conditions of employment of the employees, or

        (ii) about the activities of the undertaking which may significantly affect the interests of the employees,

but excluding representatives who are expected to receive information relevant only to a specific aspect of the terms and conditions or interests of the employees, such as health and safety or collective redundancies;

"information and consultation representative" has the meaning given to it in regulation 15(5);

"participation" means the influence of the representative body and the employees' representatives in the SE or a participating company by way of the right to—

    (a) elect or appoint some of the members of the SE's or the participating company's supervisory or administrative organ, or

    (b) recommend or oppose the appointment of some or all of the members of the SE's or the participating company's supervisory or administrative organ;

"representative body" means the persons elected or appointed under the employee involvement agreement or under the standard rules on employee involvement;

"SE" means a European Public Limited-Liability Company (or Societas Europaea) within the meaning of the EC Regulation;

"SE established by merger" means an SE established in accordance with Article 2(1);

"SE established by formation of a holding company or subsidiary company" means an SE established in accordance with Article 2(2) or 2(3), as the case may be;

"SE established by transformation" means an SE established in accordance with Article 2(4);

"standard rules on employee involvement" means the rules in the Schedule to these Regulations;

["suitable information relating to the use of agency workers" means—

    (a) the number of agency workers working temporarily for and under the supervision and direction of the undertaking;

    (b) the parts of the undertaking in which those agency workers are working; and

    (c) the type of work those agency workers are carrying out;]

"two thirds majority vote" means a vote passed by a majority of at least two thirds of the total membership of the special negotiating body where the members voting with that majority—

    (a) represent at least two thirds of the employees of the participating companies and their concerned subsidiaries and establishments employed in the EEA states, and

    (b) include members representing employees employed in at least two EEA states;

"UK employee" means an employee employed to work in the United Kingdom;

"UK members of the special negotiating body" means members of the special negotiating body elected or appointed by UK employees.

(2)   In these Regulations the following expressions have the meaning given by Article 2 of the EC Directive—

"participating companies",
"subsidiary",
"special negotiating body",
"involvement of employees",
"information",
"consultation",

and references to a "concerned subsidiary" or a "concerned establishment" are to be construed in accordance with the definition of "concerned subsidiary or establishment" in the EC Directive.

(3)   Except as otherwise provided, words and expressions used in the EC Regulation or the EC Directive have the same meaning in these Regulations as they have in that Regulation or Directive.

(4)   Except as otherwise provided, references in these Regulations to an SE are to an SE that is to be, or is, registered in Great Britain.

NOTES
Commencement: 1 October 2009.
Para (1): definitions "agency worker" and "suitable information relating to the use of agency workers" inserted by the Agency Workers Regulations 2010, SI 2010/93, reg 25, Sch 2, Pt 2, paras 47, 48, as from 1 October 2011.

[10.1196]
4   Application of these Regulations
(1)   These Regulations apply where—
   (a)   a participating company intends to establish an SE whose registered office is to be in Great Britain, or
   (b)   an SE has its registered office in Great Britain.

(2)   Where there are UK employees, Part 3 also applies (regardless of where the registered office is to be situated) in relation to the election or appointment of UK members of the special negotiating body, unless the majority of those employees is employed to work in Northern Ireland.

(3)   Parts 6 to 9 also apply (regardless of where the registered office of the SE is, or is intended to be situated) if any of the following is registered or, as the case may be, situated in Great Britain—
   (a)   a participating company, its concerned subsidiaries or establishments;
   (b)   a subsidiary of an SE;
   (c)   an establishment of an SE;
   (d)   an employee or an employees' representative.

NOTES
Commencement: 1 October 2009.

PART 2
PARTICIPATING COMPANIES AND THE SPECIAL NEGOTIATING BODY

[10.1197]
5   Duty on participating company to provide information
(1)   When the competent organ of a participating company decides to form an SE, that organ must, as soon as possible after—
   (a)   publishing the draft terms of merger,
   (b)   creating a holding company, or
   (c)   agreeing a plan to form a subsidiary or to transform into an SE,
provide information to the employees' representatives of the participating company, its concerned subsidiaries and establishments or, if no such representatives exist, the employees themselves.

(2)   The information referred to in paragraph (1) must include, as a minimum, information—
   (a)   identifying the participating companies, concerned subsidiaries and establishments,
   (b)   giving the number of employees employed by each participating company and concerned subsidiary and at each concerned establishment, *and*
   (c)   giving the number of employees employed to work in each EEA State;
   [(d)   the number of agency workers working temporarily for and under the supervision and direction of the undertaking;
   (e)   the parts of the undertaking in which those agency workers are working; and
   (f)   the type of work those agency workers are carrying out].

(3)   When a special negotiating body has been formed in accordance with regulation 8, the competent organs of each participating company must provide that body with such information as is necessary to keep it informed of the plan and progress of establishing the SE up to the time the SE has been registered.

NOTES
Commencement: 1 October 2009.
Para (2): the word "and" in italics in sub-para (b) is revoked, and sub-paras (d)–(f) are added, by the Agency Workers Regulations 2010, SI 2010/93, reg 25, Sch 2, Pt 2, paras 47, 49, as from 1 October 2011.

[10.1198]
6 Complaint of failure to provide information

(1)   An employees' representative, or an employee for whom there is no such representative, may present a complaint to the CAC that—
  (a)   the competent organ of a participating company has failed to provide the information referred to in regulation 5, or
  (b)   the information provided by the competent organ of a participating company for the purpose of complying with regulation 5 is false or incomplete in a material particular.
(2)   If the CAC finds the complaint well-founded, it must make an order requiring the competent organ to disclose information to the complainant.
(3)   The order must specify—
  (a)   the information in respect of which the CAC finds that the complaint is well-founded and which is to be disclosed to the complainant, and
  (b)   a date (not less than one week after the date of the order) by which the competent organ must disclose the information specified in the order.

NOTES
Commencement: 1 October 2009.

[10.1199]
7 Function of the special negotiating body

The special negotiating body and the competent organs of the participating companies have the task of reaching an employee involvement agreement.

NOTES
Commencement: 1 October 2009.

[10.1200]
8 Composition of the special negotiating body

(1)   The competent organs of the participating companies must make arrangements for the establishment of a special negotiating body constituted in accordance with the following provisions of this regulation.
(2)   In each EEA state in which employees of a participating company or concerned subsidiary are employed to work, those employees must be given an entitlement to elect or appoint one member of the special negotiating body for each 10%, or fraction of 10%, which those employees represent of the total workforce. These members are the "ordinary members".
(3)   If, in the case of an SE to be established by merger, following an election or appointment under paragraph (2), the members elected or appointed to the special negotiating body do not include at least one eligible member in respect of each relevant company, the employees of any relevant company in respect of which there is no eligible member must be given an entitlement, subject to paragraph (4), to elect or appoint an additional member to the special negotiating body.
(4)   The number of additional members which the employees are entitled to elect or appoint under paragraph (3) must not exceed 20% of the number of ordinary members elected or appointed under paragraph (2). If the number of additional members under paragraph (3) would exceed that percentage, the employees who are entitled to appoint or elect the additional members are—
  (a)   if one additional member is to be appointed or elected, those employed by the company not represented under paragraph (3) having the highest number of employees;
  (b)   if more than one additional member is to be appointed or elected, those employed by the companies in each EEA state that are not represented under paragraph (3) having the highest number of employees in descending order, starting with the company with the highest number, followed by those employed by the companies in each EEA state that are not so represented having the second highest number of employees in descending order, starting with the company (among those companies) with the highest number.
(5)   The competent organs of the participating companies must, as soon as reasonably practicable and in any event no later than one month after the establishment of the special negotiating body, inform their employees and those of their concerned subsidiaries of the identity of the members of the special negotiating body.
(6)   If, following the appointment or election of members to the special negotiating body in accordance with this regulation, changes to the participating companies, concerned subsidiaries or concerned establishments result in the number of ordinary or additional members which employees would be entitled to elect or appoint under this regulation either increasing or decreasing—

(a)   the original appointment or election of members of the special negotiating body ceases to have effect, and

(b)   those employees are entitled to elect or appoint the new number of members in accordance with the provisions of these Regulations.

(7)   If a member of the special negotiating body is no longer willing or able to continue serving as such a member, the employees whom the member represents are entitled to elect or appoint a new member in place of that member.

(8)   In this regulation—

"eligible member" means a person who is—

(a)   in the case of a relevant company registered in an EEA state whose legislation allows representatives of trade unions who are not employees to be elected to the special negotiating body, an employee of the relevant company or a trade union representative;

(b)   in the case of a relevant company not registered in such an EEA state, an employee of the relevant company;

"relevant company" means a participating company which has employees in the EEA state in which it is registered and which it is proposed will cease to exist on or following the registration of the SE;

"the total workforce" means the total number of employees employed by all participating companies and concerned subsidiaries throughout all EEA states.

NOTES
Commencement: 1 October 2009.

[10.1201]
9   Complaint about establishment of special negotiating body

(1)   An application may be presented to the CAC for a declaration that the special negotiating body has not been established at all or has not been established properly in accordance with regulation 8.

(2)   An application may be presented under this regulation by any of the following—

(a)   a person elected or appointed to be a member of the special negotiating body;

(b)   an employees' representative;

(c)   where there is no employees' representative in respect of a participating company or concerned subsidiary, an employee of that participating company or concerned subsidiary;

(d)   the competent organ of a participating company or concerned subsidiary.

(3)   The CAC may only consider an application made under paragraph (1) if it is made within a period of one month following the date or, if more than one, the last date on which the participating companies complied or should have complied with the obligation to inform their employees under regulation 8(5).

(4)   If the CAC finds the application well-founded—

(a)   it must make a declaration that the special negotiating body has not been established at all or has not been established properly, and

(b)   the competent organs of the participating companies continue to be under the obligation in regulation 8(1).

NOTES
Commencement: 1 October 2009.

PART 3
ELECTION OR APPOINTMENT OF UK MEMBERS OF THE SPECIAL NEGOTIATING BODY

[10.1202]
10   Ballot arrangements

(1)   Subject to regulation 11, the UK members of the special negotiating body must be elected by balloting the UK employees.

(2)   The management of the participating companies that employ UK employees ("the management") must arrange for the holding of a ballot or ballots of those employees in accordance with the requirements specified in paragraph (3).

(3)   The requirements are—

(a)   in relation to the election of ordinary members under regulation 8(2), that—

(i)   if the number of members which UK employees are entitled to elect to the special negotiating body is equal to the number of participating companies which have UK employees, there must be separate ballots of the UK employees in each participating company;

(ii)   if the number of members which the UK employees are entitled to elect to the special negotiating body is greater than the number of participating companies which have

UK employees, there must be separate ballots of the UK employees in each participating company and the management must ensure, as far as practicable, that at least one member representing each such participating company is elected to the special negotiating body and that the number of members representing each company is proportionate to the number of employees in that company;

  (iii) if the number of members which the UK employees are entitled to elect to the special negotiating body is smaller than the number of participating companies which have employees in the United Kingdom—

  (aa) the number of ballots held must be equivalent to the number of members to be elected,

  (bb) a separate ballot must be held in respect of each of the participating companies with the higher or highest number of employees, and

  (cc) it must be ensured that any employees of a participating company in respect of which a ballot does not have to be held are entitled to vote in a ballot held in respect of one of the other participating companies;

  (iv) if there are any UK employees employed by a concerned subsidiary or establishment of non-UK participating companies, the management must ensure that those employees are entitled to vote in a ballot held pursuant to this regulation;

  (b) that in relation to the ballot of additional members under regulation 8(3) the management must hold a separate ballot in respect of each participating company entitled to elect an additional member;

  (c) that, in a ballot in respect of a particular participating company, all UK employees employed by that participating company or by its concerned subsidiaries or at its concerned establishments are entitled to vote;

  (d) that a person is entitled to stand as a candidate for election as a member of the special negotiating body in a ballot in respect of a particular participating company if, immediately before the latest time at which a person may become a candidate, the person is—

  (i) a UK employee employed by that participating company, by any of its concerned subsidiaries or at any of its concerned establishments, or

  (ii) if the management of that participating company so permits, a representative of a trade union who is not an employee of that participating company or any of its concerned subsidiaries;

  (e) that the management must appoint in accordance with paragraph (7) a person (a "ballot supervisor")—

  (i) to supervise the conduct of the ballot of UK employees, or

  (ii) where there is to be more than one ballot, to supervise the conduct of each of the separate ballots,

  and, in a case falling within paragraph (ii), may appoint different persons to supervise the conduct of such different separate ballots as the management may determine;

  (f) that after the management has formulated proposals as to the arrangements for the ballot of UK employees and before it has published the final arrangements under sub-paragraph (g) it must, so far as reasonably practicable, consult the UK employees' representatives on the proposed arrangements for the ballot of UK employees; and

  (g) that the management must publish the final arrangements for the ballot of UK employees in such manner as to bring them to the attention of, so far as reasonably practicable, all UK employees and the UK employees' representatives.

(4) Any UK employee or UK employees' representative who believes that the arrangements for the ballot of the UK employees do not comply with the requirements of paragraph (3) may, within a period of 21 days beginning on the date on which the management published the final arrangements under sub-paragraph (g) of that paragraph, present a complaint to the CAC.

(5) If the CAC finds the complaint well-founded, it must make a declaration to that effect and may make an order requiring the management to modify the arrangements it has made for the ballot of UK employees or to satisfy the requirements in sub-paragraph (f) or (g) of paragraph (3).

(6) An order under paragraph (5) must specify—

  (a) the modifications to the arrangements which the management is required to make, and

  (b) the requirements it must satisfy.

(7) The management may appoint a person to be a ballot supervisor for the purposes of paragraph (3)(e) only if the management—

  (a) reasonably believes that the person will carry out competently any functions conferred on the person in relation to the ballot, and

  (b) has no reasonable grounds for believing that the person's independence in relation to the ballot might reasonably be called into question.

NOTES

Commencement: 1 October 2009.

Part 10   Miscellaneous other SIs

[10.1203]
11 Conduct of the ballot

(1) The management must—

   (a) ensure that a ballot supervisor appointed under regulation 10(3)(e) carries out the functions conferred or imposed on the ballot supervisor under this regulation;

   (b) ensure that there is no interference from the management with the ballot supervisor's carrying out of those functions;

   (c) comply with all reasonable requests made by a ballot supervisor for the purposes of, or in connection with, the carrying out of those functions.

(2) A ballot supervisor's appointment must require that the ballot supervisor—

   (a) supervises the conduct of the ballot, or the separate ballots, that the ballot supervisor is being appointed to supervise, in accordance with the arrangements for the ballot of UK employees published by the management under regulation 10(3)(g) or, where appropriate, in accordance with the arrangements as required to be modified by an order made as a result of a complaint presented under regulation 10(4);

   (b) does not conduct the ballot or any of the separate ballots before the management has satisfied the requirement specified in regulation 10(3)(g) and—

      (i) where no complaint has been presented under regulation 10(4), before the expiry of a period of 21 days beginning on the date on which the management published its arrangements under regulation 10(3)(g), or

      (ii) where a complaint has been presented under regulation 10(4), before the complaint has been determined and, where appropriate, the arrangements have been modified as required by an order made as a result of that complaint;

   (c) conducts the ballot, or each separate ballot, so as to secure that—

      (i) so far as reasonably practicable, those entitled to vote are given the opportunity to vote,

      (ii) so far as reasonably practicable, those entitled to stand as candidates are given the opportunity to stand,

      (iii) so far as reasonably practicable, those voting are able to do so in secret, and

      (iv) the votes given in the ballot are fairly and accurately counted.

(3) As soon as reasonably practicable after the holding of the ballot, the ballot supervisor must publish the results of the ballot in such manner as to make them available to the management and, so far as reasonably practicable, to the UK employees entitled to vote in the ballot and the persons who stood as candidates.

(4) If a ballot supervisor considers (whether on the basis of representations made to the ballot supervisor by another person or otherwise)—

   (a) that any of the requirements referred to in paragraph (2) was not satisfied, with the result that the outcome of the ballot would have been different, or

   (b) that there was interference with the carrying out of the ballot supervisor's functions, or a failure by the management to comply with all reasonable requests made by the ballot supervisor, with the result that the ballot supervisor was unable to form a proper judgement as to whether each of the requirements referred to in paragraph (2) was satisfied in the ballot,

the ballot supervisor must publish a report ("an ineffective ballot report").

(5) Where a ballot supervisor publishes an ineffective ballot report, the report must be published within a period of one month commencing on the date on which the ballot supervisor publishes the results of the ballot under paragraph (3).

(6) A ballot supervisor must publish an ineffective ballot report in such manner as to make it available to the management and, so far as reasonably practicable, to the UK employees entitled to vote in the ballot and the persons who stood as candidates in the ballot.

(7) Where a ballot supervisor publishes an ineffective ballot report, then—

   (a) if there has been a single ballot, or if an ineffective ballot report has been published in respect of every separate ballot, the outcome of the ballot or ballots has no effect and the management is again under the obligation in regulation 10(2);

   (b) if there have been separate ballots and sub-paragraph (a) does not apply—

      (i) the management must arrange for the separate ballot or ballots in respect of which an ineffective ballot report was published to be re-held in accordance with regulation 10 and this regulation, and

      (ii) no such ballot has effect until it has been re-held and no ineffective ballot report has been published in respect of it.

(8) All costs relating to the holding of a ballot, including payments made to a ballot supervisor for supervising the conduct of the ballot, must be borne by the management (whether or not an ineffective ballot report has been published).

NOTES
Commencement: 1 October 2009.

[10.1204]

12   Appointment of UK members by a consultative committee

(1)   This regulation applies where—

  (a)   regulation 10(3)(a)(i) or (ii) or (b) would (apart from this regulation) require a ballot to be held, but

  (b)   there exists in the participating company in respect of which a ballot would be held under regulation 10, a consultative committee.

(2)   Where this regulation applies—

  (a)   the election provided for in regulation 10 must not take place;

  (b)   the consultative committee is entitled to appoint the UK member or members of the special negotiating body who would otherwise be elected pursuant to regulation 10;

  (c)   any such appointment by the consultative committee must comply with paragraph (3).

(3)   The consultative committee may appoint as a member of the special negotiating body—

  (a)   one of their number, or

  (b)   if the management of the participating company in respect of which the consultative committee exists so permits, a trade union representative who is not an employee of that company.

(4)   In this regulation a "consultative committee" means a body of persons—

  (a)   whose normal functions include or comprise the carrying out of an information and consultation function,

  (b)   which is able to carry out its information and consultation function without interference from the management of the participating company,

  (c)   which, in carrying out its information and consultation function, represents all the employees of the participating company, and

  (d)   which consists wholly of persons who are employees of the participating company or its concerned subsidiaries.

(5)   In paragraph (4) "information and consultation function" means the function of—

  (a)   receiving, on behalf of all the employees of the participating company, information which may significantly affect the interests of the employees of that company, but excluding information which is relevant only to a specific aspect of the interests of the employees, such as health and safety or collective redundancies, and

  (b)   being consulted by the management of the participating company on the information referred to in sub-paragraph (a).

(6)   The consultative committee must publish the names of the persons whom it has appointed to be members of the special negotiating body in such a manner as to bring them to the attention of the management of the participating company and, so far as reasonably practicable, the employees and the employees' representatives of that company and its concerned subsidiaries.

(7)   Where the management of the participating company, or an employee or an employees' representative, believes that—

  (a)   the consultative committee does not satisfy the requirements in paragraph (4), or

  (b)   any of the persons appointed by the consultative committee is not entitled to be appointed, the management of the participating company or, as the case may be, the employee or the employees' representative may present a complaint to the CAC within a period of 21 days beginning on the date on which the consultative committee published under paragraph (6) the names of the persons appointed.

(8)   If the CAC finds the complaint well-founded it must make a declaration to that effect.

(9)   Where the CAC has made a declaration under paragraph (8)—

  (a)   any appointment made by the consultative committee is ineffective, and

  (b)   the members of the special negotiating body must be elected by a ballot of the employees in accordance with regulation 10.

(10)   Where the consultative committee appoints any person to be a member of the special negotiating body, that appointment has effect—

  (a)   where no complaint has been presented under paragraph (7), after the expiry of a period of 21 days beginning on the date on which the consultative committee published under paragraph (6) the names of the persons appointed;

  (b)   where a complaint has been presented under paragraph (7), as from the day on which the complaint has been determined without a declaration under paragraph (8) being made.

NOTES

Commencement: 1 October 2009.

[10.1205]

13   Representation of employees

(1)   A member elected in a ballot in accordance with regulation 8(2) is treated as representing the employees for the time being of the participating company and of any concerned subsidiary or establishment whose employees were entitled to vote in the ballot in which the member was elected.

(2)   If an additional member is elected in accordance with regulation 8(3) and (4), that additional member, and not any member elected in accordance with regulation 8(2), is treated as representing the employees for the time being of the participating company and of any concerned subsidiary or establishment whose employees were entitled to vote in the ballot in which the additional member was elected.

(3)   When a member of the special negotiating body is appointed by a consultative committee in accordance with regulation 12, the employees whom the consultative committee represents and the employees of any concerned subsidiary are treated as being represented by the member so appointed.

NOTES
Commencement: 1 October 2009.

PART 4
NEGOTIATION OF THE EMPLOYEE INVOLVEMENT AGREEMENT

[10.1206]
14   Negotiations to reach an employee involvement agreement

(1)   In this regulation and in regulation 15 the competent organs of the participating companies and the special negotiating body are referred to as "the parties".

(2)   The parties are under a duty to negotiate in a spirit of cooperation with a view to reaching an employee involvement agreement.

(3)   The duty referred to in paragraph (2) commences one month after the date or, if more than one, the last date on which the members of the special negotiating body were elected or appointed and applies—
  (a)   for the period of six months starting with the day on which the duty commenced or, where an employee involvement agreement is successfully negotiated within that period, until the completion of the negotiations;
  (b)   where the parties agree before the end of that six month period that it is to be extended, for the period of twelve months starting with the day on which the duty commenced or, where an employee involvement agreement is successfully negotiated within the twelve month period, until the completion of the negotiations.

NOTES
Commencement: 1 October 2009.

[10.1207]
15   The employee involvement agreement

(1)   The employee involvement agreement must be in writing.

(2)   The employee involvement agreement must specify each of the following—
  (a)   the scope of the agreement;
  (b)   the composition, number of members and allocation of seats on the representative body;
  (c)   the functions and the procedure for the information and consultation of the representative body;
  (d)   the frequency of meetings of the representative body;
  (e)   the financial and material resources to be allocated to the representative body;
  (f)   if, during negotiations, the parties decide to establish one or more information and consultation procedures instead of a representative body, the arrangements for implementing those procedures;
  (g)   if, during negotiations, the parties decide to establish arrangements for participation, the substance of those arrangements including (if applicable) the number of members in the SE's administrative or supervisory body which the employees will be entitled to elect, appoint, recommend or oppose, the procedures as to how these members may be elected, appointed, recommended or opposed by the employees, and their rights;
  (h)   the date of entry into force of the agreement and its duration, the circumstances, if any, in which the agreement is required to be re-negotiated and the procedure for its re-negotiation.
  This paragraph is without prejudice to the autonomy of the parties and is subject to paragraph (4).

(3)   The employee involvement agreement is not subject to the standard rules on employee involvement, unless it contains a provision to the contrary.

[(3A)   Where under the employee involvement agreement the competent organ of the SE is to provide information on the employment situation in that company, such information must include suitable information relating to the use of agency workers (if any) in that company.]

(4)   In relation to an SE to be established by way of transformation, the employee involvement agreement must provide for the elements of employee involvement at all levels to be at least as favourable as those which exist in the company to be transformed into an SE.

(5)   If—

(a)   the parties decide, in accordance with paragraph (2)(f), to establish one or more information and consultation procedures instead of a representative body, and

(b)   those procedures include a provision for representatives to be elected or appointed to act in relation to information and consultation,

those representatives are "information and consultation representatives".

NOTES

Commencement: 1 October 2009.

Para (3A): inserted by the Agency Workers Regulations 2010, SI 2010/93, reg 25, Sch 2, Pt 2, paras 47, 50, as from 1 October 2011.

[10.1208]

16   Decisions of the special negotiating body

(1)   Each member of the special negotiating body has one vote.

(2)   The special negotiating body must take decisions by an absolute majority vote, except in those cases where paragraph (3) or regulation 17 provides otherwise.

(3)   In the following circumstances any decision which would result in a reduction of participation rights must be taken by a two thirds majority vote—

(a)   where an SE is to be established by merger and at least 25% of the employees employed to work in the EEA states by the participating companies which are due to merge have participation rights;

(b)   where an SE is to be established by formation of a holding company or of a subsidiary company and at least 50% of the total number of employees employed to work in the EEA states by the participating companies have participation rights.

In this paragraph, "reduction of participation rights" means that the body representative of the employees has participation rights in relation to a smaller proportion of members of the supervisory or administrative organs of the SE than the employees' representatives had in the participating company which gave participation rights in relation to the highest proportion of such members in that company.

(4)   Where the special negotiating body takes a decision under this regulation or under regulation 17—

(a)   it must publish the details of the decision in such a manner as to bring the decision, so far as reasonably practicable, to the attention of the employees whom it represents, and

(b)   such publication must take place as soon as reasonably practicable and, in any event, no later than 14 days after the decision has been taken.

(5)   For the purpose of negotiations, the special negotiating body may be assisted by experts of its choice.

(6)   The participating company or companies must pay for—

(a)   any reasonable expenses of the functioning of the special negotiating body, and

(b)   any reasonable expenses relating to the negotiations that are necessary to enable the special negotiating body to carry out its functions in an appropriate manner,

but where the special negotiating body is assisted by more than one expert the participating company is not required to pay such expenses in respect of more than one of them.

NOTES

Commencement: 1 October 2009.

[10.1209]

17   Decision not to open, or to terminate, negotiations

(1)   The special negotiating body may decide, by a two thirds majority vote,—

(a)   not to open negotiations with the competent organs of the participating companies, or

(b)   to terminate any such negotiations.

(2)   The special negotiating body cannot take the decision referred to in paragraph (1) in relation to an SE to be established by transformation if any employees of the company to be transformed have participation rights.

(3)   Any decision made under paragraph (1) has the following effects—

(a)   the duty in regulation 14(2) to negotiate with a view to reaching an employee involvement agreement ceases as from the date of the decision;

(b)   any rules relating to the information and consultation of employees in an EEA state in which employees of the SE are employed apply to the employees of the SE in that EEA state;

(c)   the special negotiating body is to be reconvened only if a request that meets the conditions in paragraph (4) is made by employees or employees' representatives.

(4)   The conditions are that the request is made—

(a)   in writing;

(b)   by at least 10% of the employees of—

(i)   the participating companies and their concerned subsidiaries, or (ii)　where the SE has been registered, the SE and its subsidiaries,

or by employees' representatives representing at least that percentage of those employees;

(c)　no earlier than two years after the decision made under paragraph (1) was or should have been published in accordance with regulation 16(4) unless—

(i)　the special negotiating body, and

(ii)　the competent organs of every participating company or, where the SE has been registered, the SE,

agree to the special negotiating body being reconvened earlier.

NOTES

Commencement: 1 October 2009.

[10.1210]
18　Complaint about decisions of special negotiating body

(1)　If a person who is a member of the special negotiating body, or who is an employees' representative or an employee for whom there is no such representative, believes that the special negotiating body has taken a decision referred to in regulation 16 or 17 and—

(a)　that the decision was not taken by the majority required by regulation 16 or 17, as the case may be, or

(b)　that the special negotiating body failed to publish the decision in accordance with regulation 16(4),

the person may present a complaint to the CAC within 21 days after the date on which the special negotiating body published their decision in accordance with regulation 16(4) or, if they have not done so, the date by which they should have so published their decision.

(2)　Where the CAC finds the complaint well-founded, it must make a declaration that the decision was not taken properly and that it is of no effect.

NOTES

Commencement: 1 October 2009.

PART 5
STANDARD RULES ON EMPLOYEE INVOLVEMENT

[10.1211]
19　Standard rules on employee involvement

(1)　Where this regulation applies, the competent organ of the SE and its subsidiaries and establishments must make arrangements for the involvement of employees of the SE and its subsidiaries and establishments in accordance with the standard rules on employee involvement.

This paragraph is without prejudice to paragraph (3).

(2)　This regulation applies in the following circumstances—

(a)　where the parties agree that the standard rules on employee involvement are to apply; or

(b)　where the period specified in regulation 14(3)(a) or, where applicable, (b) has expired without the parties reaching an employee involvement agreement and—

(i)　the competent organs of each of the participating companies agree that the standard rules on employee involvement are to apply and so continue with the registration of the SE, and

(ii)　the special negotiating body has not taken any decision under regulation 17(1) either not to open, or to terminate, the negotiations referred to in that regulation.

(3)　The standard rules set out in Part 3 of the Schedule to these Regulations (standard rules on participation) apply only in the following circumstances—

(a)　in the case of an SE established by merger if, before registration of the SE, one or more forms of participation existed in at least one of the participating companies and either—

(i)　that participation applied to at least 25% of the total number of employees of the participating companies employed in the EEA states, or

(ii)　that participation applied to less than 25% of the total number of employees of the participating companies employed in the EEA states but the special negotiating body has decided that the standard rules on participation will apply to the employees of the SE; or

(b)　in the case of an SE established by formation of a holding company or subsidiary company if, before registration of the SE, one or more forms of employee participation existed in at least one of the participating companies and either—

(i)　that participation applied to at least 50% of the total number of employees of the participating companies employed in the EEA states, or

(ii)　that participation applied to less than 50% of the total number of employees of the participating companies employed in the EEA states but the special negotiating body has decided that the standard rules on participation will apply to the employees of the SE.

[(3A)   This paragraph applies to an agency worker whose contract within regulation 3(1)(b) of the Agency Workers Regulations 2010 (contract with the temporary work agency) is not a contract of employment—

    (a)   for the purposes of paragraph (3)(a) and (b), any agency worker who has a contract with a temporary work agency, which was at the relevant time a participating company, is to be treated as having been employed by that temporary work agency for the duration of their assignment with a hirer, and

    (b)   in this paragraph "assignment" and "hirer" have the same meaning as in regulation 2, and "temporary work agency" has the same meaning as in regulation 4, of the Agency Workers Regulations 2010.]

(4)   Where—

    (a)   the standard rules on participation apply, and

    (b)   more than one form of employee participation exists in the participating companies,

the special negotiating body must decide which of the existing forms of participation is to exist in the SE and must inform the competent organs of the participating companies accordingly.

NOTES

    Commencement: 1 October 2009.

    Para (3A): inserted by the Agency Workers Regulations 2010, SI 2010/93, reg 25, Sch 2, Pt 2, paras 47, 51, as from 1 October 2011.

PART 6

COMPLIANCE AND ENFORCEMENT

[10.1212]

20   Disputes about the operation of an employee involvement agreement or the standard rules on employee involvement

(1)   Where—

    (a)   an employee involvement agreement has been agreed, or

    (b)   the standard rules on employee involvement apply,

a complaint may be presented to the CAC by a relevant applicant who considers that the competent organ of a participating company or of the SE has failed to comply with the terms of the employee involvement agreement or, as the case may be, one or more of the standard information and consultation provisions.

(2)   A complaint brought under paragraph (1) must be brought within the period of 3 months commencing with—

    (a)   the date of the alleged failure, or

    (b)   where the failure takes place over a period, the last day of that period.

(3)   In this regulation—

"failure" means an act or omission;

"relevant applicant" means—

    (a)   in a case where a representative body has been appointed or elected, a member of that body;

    (b)   in a case where no representative body has been elected or appointed, an information and consultation representative or an employee of the SE.

(4)   Where it finds the complaint well-founded, the CAC—

    (a)   must make a declaration to that effect, and

    (b)   may make an order requiring the SE to take such steps as are necessary to comply with the terms of the employee involvement agreement or, as the case may be, the standard rules on employee involvement.

(5)   An order made under paragraph (4) must specify—

    (a)   the steps which the SE is required to take;

    (b)   the date of the failure;

    (c)   the period within which the order must be complied with.

(6)   If the CAC makes a declaration under paragraph (4), the relevant applicant may, within the period of three months beginning with the day on which the decision is made, make an application to the Appeal Tribunal for a penalty notice to be issued.

(7)   Where such an application is made, the Appeal Tribunal must issue a written penalty notice to the SE requiring it to pay a penalty to the Secretary of State in respect of the failure, unless the Appeal Tribunal is satisfied, on hearing representations from the SE,—

    (a)   that the failure resulted from a reason beyond its control, or

    (b)   that it has some other reasonable excuse for its failure.

(8)   Regulation 21 applies in respect of a penalty notice issued under this regulation.

(9)   No order of the CAC under this regulation has the effect of suspending or altering the effect of any act done or of any agreement made by the participating company or the SE.

NOTES
Commencement: 1 October 2009.

[10.1213]
21   Penalties

(1)   A penalty notice issued under regulation 20 must specify—
(a)   the amount of the penalty which is payable;
(b)   the date before which the penalty must be paid;
(c)   the failure and period to which the penalty relates.

(2)   No penalty set by the Appeal Tribunal under this regulation may exceed £75,000.

(3)   When setting the amount of the penalty, the Appeal Tribunal must take into account—
(a)   the gravity of the failure;
(b)   the period of time over which the failure occurred;
(c)   the reason for the failure;
(d)   the number of employees affected by the failure;
(e)   the number of employees employed by the undertaking.

(4)   The date specified under paragraph (1)(b) must not be earlier than the end of the period within which an appeal against a decision or order made by the CAC under regulation 20 may be made.

(5)   If the specified date in a penalty notice has passed and —
(a)   the period during which an appeal may be made has expired without an appeal having been made, or
(b)   such an appeal has been made and determined,
the Secretary of State may recover from the SE, as a civil debt due to the Secretary of State, any amount payable under the penalty notice which remains outstanding.

(6)   The making of an appeal suspends the effect of the penalty notice.

(7)   Any sums received by the Secretary of State under regulation 20 or this regulation must be paid into the Consolidated Fund.

NOTES
Commencement: 1 October 2009.

[10.1214]
22   Misuse of procedures

(1)   If an employees' representative, or an employee for whom there is no such representative, believes that a participating company or an SE is misusing or intending to misuse the SE or the powers in these Regulations for the purpose of—
(a)   depriving the employees of that participating company or of any of its concerned subsidiaries or, as the case may be, of the SE or of any of its subsidiaries of their rights to employee involvement, or
(b)   withholding rights from any of the employees referred to in sub-paragraph (a),
the representative or, as the case may be, the employee may make a complaint to the CAC.

(2)   Where a complaint is made to the CAC under paragraph (1)—
(a)   before registration of the SE, or
(b)   within the period of 12 months following the date of its registration,
the CAC must uphold the complaint unless the respondent proves that it did not misuse or intend to misuse the SE or the powers in these Regulations for a purpose specified in sub-paragraph (a) or (b) of paragraph (1).

(3)   If it finds the complaint to be well founded, the CAC—
(a)   must make a declaration to that effect, and
(b)   may make an order requiring the participating company or the SE, as the case may be, to take such action as is specified in the order to ensure that the employees referred to in paragraph (1)(a) are not deprived of their rights to employee involvement or that such rights are not withheld from them,
and the provisions of regulations 20(6) to (9) and 21 apply where the CAC makes a declaration or order under this paragraph as they apply where it makes a declaration or order under regulation 20(4).

NOTES
Commencement: 1 October 2009.

[10.1215]
23   Exclusivity of remedy

The remedy for infringement of the rights conferred by these Regulations is by way of complaint to the CAC in accordance with these Regulations and not otherwise.

NOTES
Commencement: 1 October 2009.

PART 7
CONFIDENTIAL INFORMATION

[10.1216]
24   Breach of statutory duty

(1)   Where a body which is—
- (a)   an SE,
- (b)   a subsidiary of an SE,
- (c)   a participating company, or
- (d)   a concerned subsidiary,

entrusts a person, pursuant to the provisions of these Regulations, with any information or document on terms requiring it to be held in confidence, the person must not disclose that information or document except in accordance with the terms on which it was disclosed to the person.

(2)   In this regulation a person referred to in paragraph (1) to whom information or a document is entrusted is referred to as a "recipient".

(3)   Where paragraph (1) applies—
- (a)   the obligation to comply with that paragraph is a duty owed to the body that disclosed the information or document to the recipient, and
- (b)   a breach of the duty is actionable accordingly (subject to the defences and other incidents applying to actions for breach of statutory duty).

(4)   Paragraph (3) does not affect—
- (a)   any legal liability which any person may incur otherwise than under this regulation by disclosing the information or document, or
- (b)   any right which any person may have in relation to such disclosure otherwise than under this regulation.

(5)   No action lies under paragraph (3) where the recipient reasonably believed the disclosure to be a "protected disclosure" within the meaning given by section 43A of the Employment Rights Act 1996.

(6)   A recipient to whom a body mentioned in paragraph (1) has, pursuant to the provisions of these Regulations, entrusted any information or document on terms requiring it to be held in confidence may apply to the CAC for a declaration as to whether it was reasonable for the body to require the recipient to hold the information or document in confidence.

(7)   If the CAC considers that the disclosure of the information or the document by the recipient would not, or would not be likely to, harm the legitimate interests of the undertaking, it must make a declaration that it was not reasonable for the body to require the recipient to hold the information or document in confidence.

(8)   If a declaration is made under paragraph (7), the information or document is not at any time after the making of the declaration to be regarded as having been entrusted to the recipient who made the application under paragraph (6), or to any other recipient, on terms requiring it to be held in confidence.

NOTES
Commencement: 1 October 2009.

[10.1217]
25   Withholding of information

(1)   Neither an SE nor a participating company is required to disclose any information or document to a person for the purposes of these Regulations where the nature of the information or document is such that, according to objective criteria, the disclosure of the information or document would seriously harm the functioning of, or would be prejudicial to,—
- (a)   the SE or any subsidiary or establishment of the SE, or
- (b)   the participating company or any subsidiary or establishment of the participating company.

(2)   Where there is a dispute between the SE or a participating company and—
- (a)   where a representative body has been appointed or elected, a member of that body, or
- (b)   where a representative body has not been appointed or elected, an information and consultation representative or an employee,

and the dispute is as to whether the nature of the information or document which the SE or the participating company has failed to provide is such as is described in paragraph (1), the SE or participating company, or a person referred to in sub-paragraph (a) or (b), may apply to the CAC for a declaration as to whether the information or document is of such a nature.

(3)   If the CAC makes a declaration that the disclosure of the information or document in question would not, according to objective criteria, be seriously harmful or prejudicial as mentioned in paragraph (1), the CAC must order the company to disclose the information or document.

(4)   An order under paragraph (3) must specify—
   (a)   the information or document to be disclosed;
   (b)   the person or persons to whom the information or document is to be disclosed;
   (c)   any terms on which the information or document is to be disclosed;
   (d)   the date before which the information or document is to be disclosed.

NOTES
Commencement: 1 October 2009.

PART 8
PROTECTION FOR MEMBERS OF SPECIAL NEGOTIATING BODY ETC

[10.1218]
26   Right to time off for members of special negotiating body etc
(1)   Where an employee is any of the following—
   (a)   a member of a special negotiating body,
   (b)   a member of a representative body,
   (c)   an information and consultation representative,
   (d)   an employee member on a supervisory or administrative organ,
   (e)   a candidate in an election in which any person elected will, on being elected, be such a member or a representative,
the employee is entitled to be permitted by the employer to take reasonable time off during working hours in order to perform functions as such a member, representative or candidate.

(2)   In this regulation "working hours" means any time when, in accordance with the employee's contract of employment, the employee is required to be at work.

NOTES
Commencement: 1 October 2009.

[10.1219]
27   Right to remuneration for time off under regulation 26
(1)   An employee who is permitted to take time off under regulation 26 is entitled to be paid remuneration by the employer for the time taken off at the appropriate hourly rate.

(2)   Chapter 2 of Part 14 of the Employment Rights Act 1996 (a week's pay) applies in relation to this regulation as it applies in relation to section 62 of that Act.

(3)   The appropriate hourly rate, in relation to an employee, is the amount of one week's pay divided by the number of normal working hours in a week for that employee when employed under the contract of employment in force on the day when the time is taken.

(4)   But where the number of normal working hours differs from week to week or over a longer period, the amount of one week's pay is to be divided instead by—
   (a)   the average number of normal working hours calculated by dividing by twelve the total number of the employee's normal working hours during the period of twelve weeks ending with the last complete week before the day on which the time off is taken, or
   (b)   where the employee has not been employed for a sufficient period to enable the calculation to be made under sub-paragraph (a), a number which fairly represents the number of normal working hours in a week having regard to such of the considerations specified in paragraph (5) as are appropriate in the circumstances.

(5)   The considerations are—
   (a)   the average number of normal working hours in a week which the employee could expect in accordance with the terms of the contract;
   (b)   the average number of normal working hours of other employees engaged in relevant comparable employment with the same employer.

(6)   A right to any amount under paragraph (1) does not affect any right of an employee in relation to remuneration under the employee's contract of employment.

(7)   But—
   (a)   any contractual remuneration paid to an employee in respect of a period of time off under regulation 26 goes towards discharging any liability of the employer to pay remuneration under paragraph (1) in respect of that period, and
   (b)   conversely, any payment of remuneration under paragraph (1) in respect of a period goes towards discharging any liability of the employer to pay contractual remuneration in respect of that period.

NOTES
Commencement: 1 October 2009.

[10.1220]
28   Right to time off: complaints to tribunals

(1)   An employee may present a complaint to an employment tribunal that the employer—
- (a)   has unreasonably refused to permit the employee to take time off as required under regulation 26, or
- (b)   has failed to pay the whole or any part of any amount to which the employee is entitled under regulation 27.

(2)   A tribunal must not consider a complaint under this regulation unless it is presented—
- (a)   before the end of the period of three months beginning with the day on which the time off was taken or on which it is alleged the time off should have been permitted, or
- (b)   within such further period as the tribunal considers reasonable in a case where it is satisfied that it was not reasonably practicable for the complaint to be presented before the end of that period of three months.

(3)   Where a tribunal finds a complaint under this regulation well-founded, the tribunal must make a declaration to that effect.

(4)   If the complaint is that the employer has unreasonably refused to permit the employee to take time off, the tribunal must also order the employer to pay to the employee an amount equal to the remuneration to which the employee would have been entitled under regulation 27 if the employer had not refused.

(5)   If the complaint is that the employer has failed to pay the employee the whole or part of any amount to which the employee is entitled under regulation 27, the tribunal must also order the employer to pay to the employee the amount which it finds is due to the employee.

NOTES

Commencement: 1 October 2009.

[10.1221]
29   Unfair dismissal

(1)   An employee who is dismissed is to be regarded as unfairly dismissed for the purposes of Part 10 of the Employment Rights Act 1996 if—
- (a)   paragraph (2) applies to the employee and the reason (or, if more than one, the principal reason) for the dismissal is a reason specified in paragraph (3), or
- (b)   paragraph (5) applies to the employee and the reason (or, if more than one, the principal reason) for the dismissal is a reason specified in paragraph (6).

(2)   This paragraph applies to an employee who is any of the following—
- (a)   a member of a special negotiating body;
- (b)   a member of a representative body;
- (c)   an information and consultation representative;
- (d)   an employee member in a supervisory or administrative organ;
- (e)   a candidate in an election in which any person elected will, on being elected, be such a member or a representative.

(3)   The reasons are—
- (a)   that the employee performed, or proposed to perform, any functions or activities as such a member, representative or candidate (but see paragraph (4));
- (b)   that the employee, or a person acting on behalf of the employee, made or proposed to make a request to exercise an entitlement conferred on the employee by regulation 26 or 27.

(4)   Paragraph (3)(a) does not apply if—
- (a)   the reason (or principal reason) for the dismissal is that, in the performance or purported performance of the employee's functions or activities, the employee has disclosed any information or document in breach of the duty in regulation 24, and
- (b)   the case is not one where the employee reasonably believed the disclosure to be a "protected disclosure" within the meaning given by section 43A of the Employment Rights Act 1996.

(5)   This paragraph applies to any employee (whether or not paragraph (2) also applies).

(6)   The reasons are that the employee did any of the following—
- (a)   took, or proposed to take, any proceedings before an employment tribunal to enforce any right conferred on the employee by these Regulations;
- (b)   exercised, or proposed to exercise, any entitlement to apply or complain to the CAC or the Appeal Tribunal conferred by these Regulations or exercised, or proposed to exercise, the right to appeal in connection with any rights conferred by these Regulations;
- (c)   acted with a view to securing that a special negotiating body, a representative body or an information and consultation procedure did or did not come into existence;
- (d)   indicated that the employee did or did not support the coming into existence of a special negotiating body, a representative body or an information and consultation procedure;

    (e)   stood as a candidate in an election in which any person elected would, on being elected, be a member of a special negotiating body or a representative body, an employee member on a supervisory or administrative organ, or an information and consultation representative;

    (f)   influenced, or sought to influence, by lawful means the way in which votes were to be cast by other employees in a ballot arranged under these Regulations;

    (g)   voted in such a ballot;

    (h)   expressed doubts, whether to a ballot supervisor or otherwise, as to whether such a ballot had been properly conducted;

    (i)   proposed to do, failed to do, or proposed to decline to do, any of the things mentioned in sub-paragraphs (d) to (h).

(7)   It is immaterial for the purposes of sub-paragraph (a) of paragraph (6)—

    (a)   whether or not the employee has the right, or

    (b)   whether or not the right has been infringed,

but for that sub-paragraph to apply, the claim to the right and, if applicable, the claim that it has been infringed must be made in good faith.

NOTES

   Commencement: 1 October 2009.

---

30   *(Amends the Employment Rights Act 1996 (outside the scope of this work).)*

[10.1222]
31   Detriment

(1)   An employee to whom paragraph (2) or (5) applies has the right not to be subjected to any detriment by any act, or deliberate failure to act, by the employer, done on a ground specified in, respectively, paragraph (3) or (6).

(2)   This paragraph applies to an employee who is any of the following—

    (a)   a member of a special negotiating body;

    (b)   a member of a representative body;

    (c)   an information and consultation representative;

    (d)   an employee member on a supervisory or administrative organ;

    (e)   a candidate in an election in which any person elected will, on being elected, be such a member or representative.

(3)   The grounds are—

    (a)   that the employee performed or proposed to perform any functions or activities as such a member, representative or candidate (but see paragraph (4));

    (b)   that the employee, or a person acting on behalf of the employee, made or proposed to make a request to exercise an entitlement conferred on the employee by regulation 26 or 27.

(4)   Paragraph (3)(a) does not apply if—

    (a)   the ground for the subjection to detriment is that in the performance, or purported performance, of the employee's functions or activities the employee has disclosed any information or document in breach of the duty in regulation 24, and

    (b)   the case is not one where the employee reasonably believed the disclosure to be a "protected disclosure" within the meaning given by section 43A of the Employment Rights Act 1996.

(5)   This paragraph applies to any employee (whether or not paragraph (2) also applies).

(6)   The grounds are that the employee did any of the following—

    (a)   took, or proposed to take, any proceedings before an employment tribunal to enforce any right conferred on the employee by these Regulations;

    (b)   exercised, or proposed to exercise, any entitlement to apply or complain to the CAC or the Appeal Tribunal conferred by these Regulations or exercised, or proposed to exercise, the right to appeal in connection with any rights conferred by these Regulations;

    (c)   acted with a view to securing that a special negotiating body, a representative body or an information and consultation procedure did or did not come into existence;

    (d)   indicated that the employee did or did not support the coming into existence of a special negotiating body, a representative body or an information and consultation procedure;

    (e)   stood as a candidate in an election in which any person elected would, on being elected, be a member of a special negotiating body or a representative body, an employee member on a supervisory or administrative organ, or an information and consultation representative;

    (f)   influenced, or sought to influence, by lawful means the way in which votes were to be cast by other employees in a ballot arranged under these Regulations;

    (g)   voted in such a ballot;

    (h)   expressed doubts, whether to a ballot supervisor or otherwise, as to whether such a ballot had been properly conducted;

    (i)   proposed to do, failed to do, or proposed to decline to do, any of the things mentioned in sub-paragraphs (d) to (h).

(7)   It is immaterial for the purposes of sub-paragraph (a) of paragraph (6)—

(a)   whether or not the employee has the right, or

(b)   whether or not the right has been infringed,

but for that sub-paragraph to apply, the claim to the right and, if applicable, the claim that it has been infringed must be made in good faith.

(8)   This regulation does not apply where the detriment in question amounts to dismissal.

NOTES
Commencement: 1 October 2009.

[10.1223]
32   Detriment: enforcement and subsidiary provisions

(1)   An employee may present a complaint to an employment tribunal that the employee has been subjected to a detriment in contravention of regulation 31.

(2)   The provisions of section 48(2) to (4) of the Employment Rights Act 1996 (complaints to employment tribunals) apply in relation to a complaint under this regulation as they apply in relation to a complaint under section 48 of that Act but taking references in those provisions to the employer as references to the employer within the meaning of regulation 31(1).

(3)   The provisions of section 49(1) to (5) of the Employment Rights Act 1996 (remedies) apply in relation to a complaint under this regulation.

NOTES
Commencement: 1 October 2009.

33   *(Amends the Employment Tribunals Act 1996 (outside the scope of this work).)*

PART 9
MISCELLANEOUS

[10.1224]
34   CAC proceedings

(1)   Where under these Regulations a person presents a complaint or makes an application to the CAC, the complaint or application must be in writing and in such form as the CAC may require.

(2)   In its consideration of a complaint or application under these Regulations, the CAC must—

(a)   make such enquiries as it sees fit, and

(b)   give any person whom it considers has a proper interest in the complaint or application an opportunity to be heard.

(3)   Where the participating company, concerned subsidiary or establishment or the SE has its registered office in England and Wales—

(a)   a declaration made by the CAC under these Regulations may be relied on as if it were a declaration or order made by the High Court in England and Wales, and

(b)   an order made by the CAC under these Regulations may be enforced in the same way as an order of the High Court in England and Wales.

(4)   Where a participating company or concerned subsidiary or an SE has its registered office in Scotland—

(a)   a declaration or order made by the CAC under these Regulations may be relied on as if it were a declaration or order made by the Court of Session, and

(b)   an order made by the CAC under these Regulations may be enforced in the same way as an order of the Court of Session.

(5)   A declaration or order made by the CAC under these Regulations must be in writing and state the reasons for the CAC's findings.

(6)   An appeal lies to the Appeal Tribunal on any question of law arising from any declaration or order of, or arising in any proceedings before, the CAC under these Regulations.

NOTES
Commencement: 1 October 2009.

[10.1225]
35   Appeal Tribunal: location of certain proceedings under these Regulations

(1)   Any proceedings before the Appeal Tribunal under these Regulations, other than appeals under paragraph (w) of section 21(1) of the Employment Tribunals Act 1996 (appeals from employment tribunals on questions of law), must—

(a)   where the registered office of the participating company, concerned subsidiary or the SE is situated in England and Wales, be held in England and Wales, and

(b)   where the registered office of the participating company, concerned subsidiary or the SE is situated in Scotland, be held in Scotland.

(2)   *(Amends the Employment Tribunals Act 1996 (outside the scope of this work).)*

NOTES
Commencement: 1 October 2009.

36   *(Amends the Employment Tribunals Act 1996 (outside the scope of this work).)*

[10.1226]
37   ACAS

(1)   If, on receipt of an application or complaint under these Regulations, the CAC is of the opinion that it is reasonably likely to be settled by conciliation, it must—

(a)   refer the application or complaint to the Advisory, Conciliation and Arbitration Service ("ACAS"), and

(b)   notify the applicant or complainant and any persons whom it considers have a proper interest in the application or complaint accordingly,

and ACAS must seek to promote a settlement of the matter.

(2)   If—

(a)   an application or complaint so referred is not settled or withdrawn, and

(b)   ACAS is of the opinion that further attempts at conciliation are unlikely to result in a settlement,

ACAS must inform the CAC of that opinion.

(3)   If—

(a)   the application or complaint is not referred to ACAS, or

(b)   it is so referred, but ACAS informs the CAC of its opinion that further attempts at conciliation are unlikely to result in a settlement,

the CAC must proceed to hear and determine the application or complaint.

NOTES
Commencement: 1 October 2009.

[10.1227]
38   Restrictions on contracting out: general

(1)   Any provision in any agreement (whether an employee's contract or not) is void in so far as it purports—

(a)   to exclude or limit the operation of any provision of these Regulations, other than a provision of Part 8, or

(b)   to preclude a person from bringing any proceedings before the CAC under any provision of these Regulations other than a provision of that Part.

(2)   Paragraph (1) does not apply to any agreement to refrain from continuing any proceedings referred to in sub-paragraph (b) of that paragraph made after the proceedings have been instituted.

NOTES
Commencement: 1 October 2009.

[10.1228]
39   Restrictions on contracting out: Part 8

(1)   Any provision in any agreement (whether an employee's contract or not) is void in so far as it purports—

(a)   to exclude or limit the operation of any provision of Part 8 of these Regulations, or

(b)   to preclude a person from bringing any proceedings before an employment tribunal under that Part.

(2)   Paragraph (1) does not apply to any agreement to refrain from instituting or continuing proceedings before an employment tribunal where a conciliation officer has taken action under section 18 of the Employment Tribunals Act 1996 (conciliation).

(3)   Paragraph (1) does not apply to any agreement to refrain from instituting or continuing before an employment tribunal proceedings within section 18(1)(v) of the Employment Tribunals Act 1996 (proceedings under these Regulations where conciliation is available) if the conditions regulating compromise agreements under these Regulations are satisfied in relation to the agreement.

(4)   For the purposes of paragraph (3) the conditions regulating compromise agreements are as follows—

(a)   the agreement must be in writing;

(b)   the agreement must relate to the particular proceedings;

(c)   the employee must have received advice from a relevant independent adviser as to the terms and effect of the proposed agreement and, in particular, its effect on the ability of the employee to pursue the employee's rights before an employment tribunal;

(d)   there must be in force, when the adviser gives the advice, a contract of insurance, or an indemnity provided for members of a profession or professional body, covering the risk of a claim by the employee in respect of loss arising in consequence of the advice;

(e)   the agreement must identify the adviser;

(f)   the agreement must state that the conditions in sub-paragraphs (a) to (e) are satisfied.

(5)   For the purposes of paragraph (4)(c) a "relevant independent adviser" is a person who is any of the following—

    (a)   a qualified lawyer;

    (b)   an officer, official, employee or member of an independent trade union who has been certified in writing by the trade union as competent to give advice and authorised to do so on behalf of the trade union;

    (c)   a person who works at an advice centre (whether as an employee or as a volunteer) and has been certified in writing by the centre as competent to give advice and authorised to do so on behalf of the centre;

but this is subject to paragraph (6).

(6)   A person is not a relevant independent adviser for the purposes of paragraph (4)(c) in relation to the employee in any of the following cases—

    (a)   if the person is, is employed by, or is acting in the matter for, the employer or an associated employer;

    (b)   in the case of a person within paragraph (5)(b) or (c), if the trade union or advice centre is the employer or an associated employer;

    (c)   in the case of a person within paragraph (5)(c), if the employee makes a payment for the advice received.

(7)   In paragraph (5)(a) "qualified lawyer" means any of the following—

    (a)   as respects England and Wales—

       (i)   a barrister (whether in practice as such or employed to give legal advice);

       (ii)   a solicitor who holds a practising certificate;

       (iii)   a person, other than a barrister or solicitor, who is an authorised advocate or authorised litigator (within the meaning of the Courts and Legal Services Act 1990);

    (b)   as respects Scotland—

       (i)   an advocate (whether in practice as such or employed to give legal advice); or

       (ii)   a solicitor who holds a practising certificate.

(8)   For the purposes of paragraph (6) any two employers are "associated" if—

    (a)   one is a company of which the other (directly or indirectly) has control, or

    (b)   both are companies of which a third person (directly or indirectly) has control,

and "associated employer" is to be construed accordingly.

NOTES

Commencement: 1 October 2009.

40   *(Amends the Transnational Information and Consultation of Employees Regulations 1999, SI 1999/3323 (outside the scope of this work).)*

[10.1229]
41   Existing employee involvement rights

(1)   Nothing in these Regulations affects involvement rights of employees of an SE, its subsidiaries or establishments provided for by law or practice in the EEA state in which they were employed immediately prior to the registration of the SE.

(2)   Paragraph (1) does not apply to rights to participation.

NOTES

Commencement: 1 October 2009.

SCHEDULE
STANDARD RULES ON EMPLOYEE INVOLVEMENT

Regulation 19(3)

PART 1
COMPOSITION OF THE REPRESENTATIVE BODY

[10.1230]
1. (1)   The management of the SE must arrange for the establishment of a representative body in accordance with the following provisions.

(2)   The representative body must be composed of employees of the SE and its subsidiaries and establishments.

(3)   The representative body must be composed of one member for each 10%, or fraction of 10%, of employees of the SE, its subsidiaries and establishments employed for the time being in each EEA state.

(4)   The members of the representative body must be elected or appointed by the members of the special negotiating body.

(5)   The election or appointment is to be carried out by whatever method the special negotiating body decides.

2. Where its size so warrants, the representative body must elect a select committee from among its members comprising at most 3 members.

3. The representative body must adopt rules of procedure.

4. The representative body must inform the competent organ of the SE of the composition of the representative body and any changes in its composition.

5. (1)   Four years after its establishment, the representative body must decide—
   (a)   whether to open negotiations with the competent organ of the SE to reach an employee involvement agreement, or
   (b)   whether the standard rules in Part 2 of this Schedule and, where applicable, Part 3 of this Schedule are to continue to apply.

(2)   Where a decision is taken under sub-paragraph (1) to open negotiations, regulations 14 to 16 and 18 apply to the representative body as they apply to the special negotiating body.

NOTES
Commencement: 1 October 2009.

PART 2
STANDARD RULES FOR INFORMATION AND CONSULTATION

[10.1231]
6. (1)   The competence of the representative body is limited to—
   (a)   questions which concern the SE itself and any of its subsidiaries or establishments in another EEA state, and
   (b)   questions which exceed the powers of the decision-making organ in a single EEA state.

(2)   For the purpose of informing and consulting under sub-paragraph (1), the competent organ of the SE must—
   (a)   prepare and provide to the representative body regular reports on the progress of the business of the SE and the SE's prospects;
   (b)   provide the representative body with the agenda for meetings of the administrative or, where appropriate, the management or supervisory organs and copies of all documents submitted to the general meeting of its shareholders;
   (c)   inform the representative body when there are exceptional circumstances affecting the employees' interests to a considerable extent, particularly in the event of relocations, transfers, the closure of establishments or undertakings or collective redundancies.

7. (1)   The competent organ must, if the representative body so desires, meet with that body at least once a year to discuss the reports referred to in paragraph 6(2)(a).
   This sub-paragraph is without prejudice to paragraph 8.

(2)   The meetings must relate in particular to the structure, economic and financial situation, the probable development of business and of production and sales, the situation and probable trend of employment, investments and substantial changes concerning organisation, introduction of new working methods or production processes, transfers of production, mergers, cut-backs or closures of undertakings or establishments, or important parts of undertakings or establishments, and collective redundancies.

8. (1)   In the circumstances set out in paragraph 6(2)(c), the representative body may decide, for reasons of urgency, to allow the select committee to meet the competent organ and it has the right to meet a more appropriate level of management within the SE rather than the competent organ itself.

(2)   In the event of the competent organ not acting in accordance with the opinion expressed by the representative body, the two bodies must meet again to seek an agreement, if the representative body so wishes.

(3)   In the circumstances set out in sub-paragraph (1), if the select committee attends the meeting, any other members of the representative body who represent employees who are directly concerned by the measures being discussed also have the right to participate in the meeting.

(4)   Before any meeting referred to in this paragraph, the members of the representative body or the select committee, as the case may be, are entitled to meet without the representatives of the competent organ being present.

[8A.   Where under the provisions of this Part, the competent organ of the SE is to provide information on the employment situation in that company, such information must include suitable information relating to the use of agency workers (if any) in that company.]

9. Without prejudice to regulations 24 and 25, the members of the representative body must inform the employees' representatives or, if no such representatives exist, the employees of the SE and its subsidiaries and establishments, of the content and outcome of the information and consultation procedures.

10. The representative body and the select committee may each be assisted by experts of its choice.

11. (1)   The costs of the representative body must be borne by the SE which must also provide the members of that body with financial and material resources needed to enable them to perform their duties in an appropriate manner, including (unless agreed otherwise) the cost of organising meetings, providing interpretation facilities and accommodation and travelling expenses.

(2)   However, where the representative body or the select committee is assisted by more than one expert, the SE is not required to pay the expenses of more than one of them.

NOTES

Commencement: 1 October 2009.

Para 8A: inserted by the Agency Workers Regulations 2010, SI 2010/93, reg 25, Sch 2, Pt 2, paras 47, 52, as from 1 October 2011.

PART 3
STANDARD RULES FOR PARTICIPATION

[10.1232]

12. (1)   In the case of an SE established by transformation, if the rules of a Member State relating to employee participation in the administrative or supervisory body applied before registration, all aspects of employee participation continue to apply to the SE.

(2)   Paragraph 13 applies to that end with the necessary modifications.

13. (1)   In the case where—
   (a)   an SE is established otherwise than by transformation, and
   (b)   the employees or their representatives of at least one of the participating companies had
        participation rights,
the representative body has the right to elect, appoint, recommend or oppose the appointment of a number of members of the administrative or supervisory body of the SE.

(2)   Their number must be equal to the highest proportion in force in the participating companies concerned before the registration of the SE.

14. (1)   The representative body must decide on the allocation of seats within the administrative or supervisory body.

(2)   In doing so, the representative body must take into account the proportion of employees of the SE employed in each EEA state.

(3)   If the employees of one or more EEA states are not covered by that proportional criterion, the representative body, in making its decision under sub-paragraph (1), must appoint a member from one of those EEA states including one from the EEA state in which the SE is registered, if appropriate.

(4)   Every member of the administrative body or, where appropriate, the supervisory body of the SE who has been elected, appointed or recommended by the representative body or the employees is to be a full member with the same rights and obligations as the members representing shareholders, including the right to vote.

NOTES

Commencement: 1 October 2009.

COMPANIES (UNFAIR PREJUDICE APPLICATIONS) PROCEEDINGS RULES 2009

(SI 2009/2469)

NOTES

Made: 8 September 2009.

Authority: Insolvency Act 1986, s 411.

Commencement: 1 October 2009 (see r 1 at **[10.1233]**).

Amendment: as of 1 July 2011 these Rules had not been amended.

ARRANGEMENT OF RULES

[10.1233]
1 Citation, commencement, interpretation and revocation
(1)   These Rules may be cited as the Companies (Unfair Prejudice Applications) Proceedings Rules 2009 and come into force on 1st October 2009.

(2)   In these Rules "the Act" means the Companies Act 2006.

(3)   The Companies (Unfair Prejudice Applications) Proceedings Rules 1986 ("the 1986 Rules") are hereby revoked.

NOTES
Commencement: 1 October 2009.

[10.1234]
2 Preliminary
(1)   These Rules apply in relation to petitions presented to the court under Part 30 of the Act (protection of company's members against unfair prejudice) by a member of a company under section 994(1), by a person treated as a member under section 994(2) or by the Secretary of State under section 995.

(2)   Except so far as inconsistent with the Act and these Rules, the Civil Procedure Rules 1998 apply to proceedings under Part 30 of the Act with any necessary modifications.

NOTES
Commencement: 1 October 2009.

[10.1235]
3 Presentation of petition
(1)   The petition shall be in the form set out in the Schedule to these Rules, with such variations, if any, as the circumstances may require.

(2)   The petition shall specify the grounds on which it is presented and the nature of the relief which is sought by the petitioner, and shall be delivered to the court for filing with sufficient copies for service under Rule 4.

(3)   The court shall fix a hearing for a day ("the return day") on which, unless the court otherwise directs, the petitioner and any respondent (including the company) shall attend before the registrar or District Judge for directions to be given in relation to the procedure on the petition.

(4)   On fixing the return day, the court shall return to the petitioner sealed copies of the petition for service, each endorsed with the return day and the time of hearing.

NOTES
Commencement: 1 October 2009.

[10.1236]
4 Service of petition
(1)   The petitioner shall, at least 14 days before the return day, serve a sealed copy of the petition on the company.

(2)   In the case of a petition based upon section 994 of the Act, the petitioner shall also, at least 14 days before the return day, serve a sealed copy of the petition on every respondent named in the petition.

NOTES
Commencement: 1 October 2009.

[10.1237]
5 Return of petition
On the return day, or at any time after it, the court shall give such directions as it thinks appropriate with respect to the following matters—
    (a)   service of the petition on any person, whether in connection with the time, date and place of a further hearing, or for any other purpose;
    (b)   whether points of claim and defence are to be delivered;
    (c)   whether, and if so by what means, the petition is to be advertised;

(d) the manner in which any evidence is to be adduced at any hearing before the judge and in particular (but without prejudice to the generality of the above) as to—
    (i) the taking of evidence wholly or in part by witness statement or orally;
    (ii) the cross-examination of any persons making a witness statement;
    (iii) the matters to be dealt with in evidence;
(e) any other matter affecting the procedure on the petition or in connection with the hearing and disposal of the petition; and
(f) such orders, if any, including a stay for any period, as the court thinks fit, with a view to mediation or other alternative dispute resolution.

NOTES

Commencement: 1 October 2009.

[10.1238]
6   Advertisement of the order

If the court considers that the order should be advertised, it shall give directions as to the manner and time of advertisement.

NOTES

Commencement: 1 October 2009.

[10.1239]
7   Transitional provision

These Rules shall not apply, and the provisions of the 1986 Rules shall continue to apply, to any petition presented to the court under Part XVII of the Companies Act 1985 before 1st October 2009.

NOTES

Commencement: 1 October 2009.

SCHEDULE

Rule 3
[10.1240]

(a) Insert title of court	To (a). . . . .
(b) Insert full name(s) and address(es) of petitioner(s)	The petition of (b) . . . .
(c) Insert full name and registered no of company subject to petition	1 (c) . . . . ("the company") was incorporated on
(d) Insert date of incorporation	(d). . . . . under the Companies Act . . . .
(e) Insert address of registered office	2 The registered office of the company is at (e) . . . .
(f) Insert amount of nominal capital and how it is divided	3 The nominal capital of the company is (f) £ . . divided into . .shares of £.each. The amount of the capital paid up or credited as paid up is (g) £.
(g) Insert amount of capital paid up or credited as paid up	The petitioner is the holder of . . . . .shares of £ . . . . .each
	4 The principal business which is carried on by the company is: . . . . . .

(h) Set out the grounds on which the petition is presented	5 (h) . . . .
Delete as applicable	In these circumstances your petitioner submits that the affairs of the company are being conducted in a manner which is unfairly prejudicial to the interests of [some part of the members (including your petitioner)]/[your petitioner].
	or
Delete as applicable	[The act or omission]/[the proposed act or omission referred to in part 5 above [is]/[would be] unfairly prejudicial to the interests of [some part of the members (including your petitioner)]/[your petitioner].
(i) Set out the nature of the relief sought	The petitioner therefore prays as follows: (i) . . . .
	or
	that such other order may be made as the court thinks fit.
Insert the name or names of the intended respondents	It is intended to serve this petition on. . . . .

Endorsement to be completed by the court

This petition having been presented to the court on . . . .

all parties should attend before [The Registrar]/[District Judge] on

(Date). . . . . at

(Time) . . . . hours

(Place) . . . .

for directions to be given.

The solicitor(s) for the petitioner is/are:—

Name. . . . .

Address . . . .
Telephone No: . . . .
Reference . . . .
[Whose Agents are:— . . . .
Name. . . . .

Address . . . .

NOTES
Commencement: 1 October 2009.

EUROPEAN ECONOMIC INTEREST GROUPING AND EUROPEAN PUBLIC LIMITED-LIABILITY COMPANY (FEES) REVOCATION REGULATIONS 2009

(SI 2009/2492)

NOTES

Made: 10 September 2009.

Authority: Finance Act 1973, s 56(1), (2).

Commencement: 1 October 2009 (see reg 1 at **[10.1241]**).

Amendment: as of 1 July 2011 these Regulations had not been amended.

[10.1241]

1 Citation, commencement and interpretation

(1) These Regulations may be cited as the European Economic Interest Grouping and European Public Limited-Liability Company (Fees) Revocation Regulations 2009 and come into force on 1st October 2009.

(2) In these Regulations—

"the continuing provisions" mean the provisions of the Revoked Regulations excepted from revocation in Schedule 2;

"EEIG" means a European Economic Interest Grouping formed in pursuance of article 1 of the Council Regulation (EEC) No 2137/85 of 25 July 1985 on the European Economic Interest Grouping;

"the EEIG Regulations" means the European Economic Interest Grouping Regulations 1989;

"the Fees Regulations" means the Registrar of Companies (Fees) (European Economic Interest Grouping and European Public Limited-Liability Company) Regulations 2009; and

"the Revoked Regulations" means the Regulations listed in Schedule 2.

(3) In these Regulations words and expressions used in the Fees Regulations have the same meaning when used in these Regulations.

NOTES

Commencement: 1 October 2009.

Transitional Provisions

[10.1242]

2

Where any document delivered to the registrar on or before 30th September 2009, to which any of the Revoked Regulations apply, is registered on or after 1st October 2009, the fee prescribed in Schedule 1 to the Fees Regulations shall not apply and any fee payable in respect of that document by virtue of the Revoked Regulations shall apply.

NOTES

Commencement: 1 October 2009.

[10.1243]

3

Where any document to which the Revoked Regulations apply is delivered to the registrar on or after 1st October 2009 under a provision specified in Schedule 1 in the circumstances specified there, the fee prescribed in Schedule 1 to the Fees Regulations shall not apply and any fee payable in respect of that document by virtue of the continuing provisions shall apply.

NOTES

Commencement: 1 October 2009.

[10.1244]

4

Where any application to which the Revoked Regulations apply is made to the registrar on or before 30th September 2009 in respect of the inspection of, or the provision of copies of, material kept by the registrar the fee prescribed in Schedule 2 to the Fees Regulations or determined by the registrar in the exercise of his power under section 1063(5) of the Companies Act 2006 in respect of that application shall not apply and any fee payable under the Revoked Regulations shall apply.

NOTES

Commencement: 1 October 2009.

[10.1245]

5

Subject to regulations 2, 3 and 4, the Regulations listed in Schedule 2 are revoked to the extent specified.

NOTES

Commencement: 1 October 2009.

SCHEDULES

SCHEDULE 1

Regulation 3

[10.1246]

1. Listed below are the circumstances when a fee required by the continuing provisions is payable—

(a) where the documents required for the registration of a charge by an EEIG under Part 12 of the Companies Act 1985, as applied to EEIGs by the EEIG Regulations, are delivered to the registrar on or after 1st October 2009, and the charge was created, the property subject to the charge acquired or the first in a series of debentures was executed, on or before the 30th September 2009;

(b) where the documents required for the registration of a charge of the type described in sub-paragraph (a) above are not delivered to the registrar within the time prescribed for their delivery and the documents are subsequently delivered pursuant to an order of the court under the enactment specified in that sub-paragraph.

2. In this Schedule words or expressions defined or used in the Companies Act 1985 have the same meaning when so used.

NOTES

Commencement: 1 October 2009.

SCHEDULE 2

Regulations 2, 4 and 5

[10.1247]

Regulation	Extent of Revocation
The European Public-Limited Liability Company (Fees) Regulations 2004	The whole Regulations
The European Economic Interest Grouping (Fees) Regulations 2004	The whole Regulations with the exception of Fee No 3 in Schedule 2

NOTES

Commencement: 1 October 2009.

PART 11
EU LEGISLATION

COUNCIL REGULATION
(2137/85/EEC)
of 25 July 1985
on the European Economic Interest Grouping (EEIG)

NOTES

Date of publication in OJ: OJ L199, 31.7.85, p 1. Notes are as in the original OJ version.
As at 1 July 2011, this Regulation had not been amended.

[11.1]
THE COUNCIL OF THE EUROPEAN COMMUNITIES,

Having regard to the Treaty establishing the European Economic Community, and in particular Article 235 thereof,

Having regard to the proposal from the Commission,[1]

Having regard to the opinion of the European Parliament,[2]

Having regard to the opinion of the Economic and Social Committee,[3]

Whereas a harmonious development of economic activities and a continuous and balanced expansion throughout the Community depend on the establishment and smooth functioning of a common market offering conditions analogous to those of a national market; whereas to bring about this single market and to increase its unity a legal framework which facilitates the adaptation of their activities to the economic conditions of the Community should be created for natural persons, companies, firms and other legal bodies in particular; whereas to that end it is necessary that those natural persons, companies, firms and other legal bodies should be able to co-operate effectively across frontiers;

Whereas co-operation of this nature can encounter legal, fiscal or psychological difficulties; whereas the creation of an appropriate Community legal instrument in the form of a European Economic Interest Grouping would contribute to the achievement of the above-mentioned objectives and therefore proves necessary;

Whereas the Treaty does not provide the necessary powers for the creation of such a legal instrument;

Whereas a grouping's ability to adapt to economic conditions must be guaranteed by the considerable freedom for its members in their contractual relations and the internal organisation of the grouping;

Whereas a grouping differs from a firm or company principally in its purpose, which is only to facilitate or develop the economic activities of its members to enable them to improve their own results; whereas, by reason of that ancillary nature, a grouping's activities must be related to the economic activities of its members but not replace them so that, to that extent, for example, a grouping may not itself, with regard to third parties, practise a profession, the concept of economic activities being interpreted in the widest sense;

Whereas access to grouping form must be made as widely available as possible to natural persons, companies, firms and other legal bodies, in keeping with the aims of this Regulation; whereas this Regulation shall not, however, prejudice the application at national level of legal rules and/or ethical codes concerning the conditions for the pursuit of business and professional activities;

Whereas this Regulation does not itself confer on any person the right to participate in a grouping, even where the conditions it lays down are fulfilled;

Whereas the power provided by this Regulation to prohibit or restrict participation in a grouping on grounds of public interest is without prejudice to the laws of Member States which govern the pursuit of activities and which may provide further prohibitions or restrictions or otherwise control or supervise participation in a grouping by any natural person, company, firm or other legal body or any class of them;

Whereas, to enable a grouping to achieve its purpose, it should be endowed with legal capacity and provision should be made for it to be represented vis-à-vis third parties by an organ legally separate from its membership;

Whereas the protection of third parties requires widespread publicity; whereas the members of a grouping have unlimited joint and several liability for the grouping's debts and other liabilities, including those relating to tax or social security, without, however, that principle's affecting the freedom to exclude or restrict the liability of one or more of its members in respect of a particular debt or other liability by means of a specific contract between the grouping and a third party;

Whereas matters relating to the status or capacity of natural persons and to the capacity of legal persons are governed by national law;

Whereas the grounds for winding up which are peculiar to the grouping should be specific while referring to national law for its liquidation and the conclusion thereof;

Whereas groupings are subject to national laws relating to insolvency and cessation of payments; whereas such laws may provide other grounds for the winding up of groupings;

Whereas this Regulation provides that the profits or losses resulting from the activities of a grouping shall be taxable only in the hands of its members; whereas it is understood that otherwise national tax laws apply, particularly as regards the apportionment of profits, tax procedures and any obligations imposed by national tax law;

Whereas in matters not covered by this Regulation the laws of the Member States and Community law are applicable, for example with regard to—
— social and labour laws,
— competition law,
— intellectual property law;

Whereas the activities of groupings are subject to the provisions of Member States' laws on the pursuit and supervision of activities; whereas in the event of abuse or circumvention of the laws of a Member State by a grouping or its members that Member State may impose appropriate sanctions;

Whereas the Member States are free to apply or to adopt any laws, regulations or administrative measures which do not conflict with the scope or objectives of this Regulation;

Whereas this Regulation must enter into force immediately in its entirety; whereas the implementation of some provisions must nevertheless be deferred in order to allow the Member States first to set up the necessary machinery for the registration of groupings in their territories and the disclosure of certain matters relating to groupings; whereas, with effect from the date of implementation of this Regulation, groupings set up may operate without territorial restrictions,

NOTES

1   OJ C14, 15.2.74, p 30; OJ C103, 28.4.78, p 4.

2   OJ C163, 11.7.77, p 17.

3   OJ C108, 15.5.75, p 46.

HAS ADOPTED THIS REGULATION—

[11.2]
Article 1
1.   European Economic Interest Groupings shall be formed upon the terms, in the manner and with the effects laid down in this Regulation.

Accordingly, parties intending to form a grouping must conclude a contract and have the registration provided for in Article 6 carried out.

2.   A grouping so formed shall, from the date of its registration as provided for in Article 6, have the capacity, in its own name, to have rights and obligations of all kinds, to make contracts or accomplish other legal acts, and to sue and be sued.

3.   The Member States shall determine whether or not groupings registered at their registries, pursuant to Article 6, have legal personality.

[11.3]
Article 2
1.   Subject to the provisions of this Regulation, the law applicable, on the one hand, to the contract for the formation of a grouping, except as regards matters relating to the status or capacity of natural persons and to the capacity of legal persons and, on the other hand, to the internal organisation of a grouping shall be the internal law of the State in which the official address is situated, as laid down in the contract for the formation of the grouping.

2.   Where a State comprises several territorial units, each of which has its own rules of law applicable to the matters referred to in paragraph 1, each territorial unit shall be considered as a State for the purposes of identifying the law applicable under this Article.

[11.4]
Article 3
1.   The purpose of a grouping shall be to facilitate or develop the economic activities of its members and to improve or increase the results of those activities; its purpose is not to make profits for itself.

Its activity shall be related to the economic activities of its members and must not be more than ancillary to those activities.

2.   Consequently, a grouping may not—
   (a)   exercise, directly or indirectly, a power of management or supervision over its members' own activities or over the activities of another undertaking, in particular in the fields of personnel, finance and investment;

(b)   directly or indirectly, on any basis whatsoever, hold shares of any kind in a member undertaking; the holding of shares in another undertaking shall be possible only in so far as it is necessary for the achievement of the grouping's objects and if it is done on its members' behalf;

(c)   employ more than 500 persons;

(d)   be used by a company to make a loan to a director of a company, or any person connected with him, when the making of such loans is restricted or controlled under the Member States' laws governing companies. Nor must a grouping be used for the transfer of any property between a company and a director, or any person connected with him, except to the extent allowed by the Member States' laws governing companies. For the purposes of this provision the making of a loan includes entering into any transaction or arrangement of similar effect, and property includes moveable and immoveable property;

(e)   be a member of another European Economic Interest Grouping.

[11.5]
Article 4

1.   Only the following may be members of a grouping—

(a)   companies or firms within the meaning of the second paragraph of Article 58 of the Treaty and other legal bodies governed by public or private law, which have been formed in accordance with the law of a Member State and which have their registered or statutory office and central administration in the Community; where, under the law of a Member State, a company, firm or other legal body is not obliged to have a registered or statutory office, it shall be sufficient for such a company, firm or other legal body to have its central administration in the Community;

(b)   natural persons who carry on any industrial, commercial, craft or agricultural activity or who provide professional or other services in the Community.

2.   A grouping must comprise at least—

(a)   two companies, firms or other legal bodies, within the meaning of paragraph 1, which have their central administrations in different Member States, or

(b)   two natural persons, within the meaning of paragraph 1, who carry on their principal activities in different Member States, or

(c)   a company, firm or other legal body within the meaning of paragraph 1 and a natural person, of which the first has its central administration in one Member State and the second carries on his principal activity in another Member State.

3.   A Member State may provide that groupings registered at its registries in accordance with Article 6 may have no more than 20 members. For this purpose, that Member State may provide that, in accordance with its laws, each member of a legal body formed under its laws, other than a registered company, shall be treated as a separate member of a grouping.

4.   Any Member State may, on grounds of that State's public interest, prohibit or restrict participation in groupings by certain classes of natural persons, companies, firms, or other legal bodies.

[11.6]
Article 5

A contract for the formation of a grouping shall include at least—

(a)   the name of the grouping preceded or followed either by the words "European Economic Interest Grouping" or by the initials "EEIG", unless those words or initials already form part of the name;

(b)   the official address of the grouping;

(c)   the objects for which the grouping is formed;

(d)   the name, business name, legal form, permanent address or registered office, and the number and place of registration, if any, of each member of the grouping;

(e)   the duration of the grouping, except where this is indefinite.

[11.7]
Article 6

A grouping shall be registered in the State in which it has its official address, at the registry designated pursuant to Article 39(1).

[11.8]
Article 7

A contract for the formation of a grouping shall be filed at the registry referred to in Article 6.
The following documents and particulars must also be filed at that registry;

(a)   any amendment to the contract for the formation of a grouping, including any change in the composition of a grouping;

(b)   notice of the setting up or closure of any establishment of the grouping;

(c)   any judicial decision establishing or declaring the nullity of a grouping, in accordance with Article 15;

    (d)   notice of the appointment of the manager or managers of a grouping, their names and any other identification particulars required by the law of the Member State in which the register is kept, notification that they may act alone or must act jointly, and the termination of any manager's appointment;

    (e)   notice of a member's assignment of his participation in a grouping or a proportion thereof, in accordance with Article 22(1);

    (f)   any decision by members ordering or establishing the winding up of a grouping, in accordance with Article 31, or any judicial decision ordering such winding up, in accordance with Articles 31 or 32;

    (g)   notice of the appointment of the liquidator or liquidators of a grouping, as referred to in Article 35, their names and any other identification particulars required by the law of the Member State in which the register is kept, and the termination of any liquidator's appointment;

    (h)   notice of the conclusion of a grouping's liquidation, as referred to in Article 35(2);

    (i)   any proposal to transfer the official address, as referred to in Article 14(1);

    (j)   any clause exempting a new member from the payment of debts and other liabilities which originated prior to his admission, in accordance with Article 26(2).

[11.9]
Article 8
The following must be published, as laid down in Article 39, in the gazette referred to in paragraph 1 of that Article—

    (a)   the particulars which must be included in the contract for the formation of a grouping pursuant to Article 5, and any amendments thereto;

    (b)   the number, date and place of registration as well as notice of the termination of that registration;

    (c)   the documents and particulars referred to in Article 7(b) to (j).

The particulars referred to in (a) and (b) must be published in full. The documents and particulars referred to in (c) may be published either in full or in extract form or by means of a reference to their filing at the registry, in accordance with the national legislation applicable.

[11.10]
Article 9
1.   The documents and particulars which must be published pursuant to this Regulation may be relied on by a grouping as against third parties under the conditions laid down by the national law applicable pursuant to Article 3(5) and (7) of Council Directive 68/151/EEC of 9 March 1968 on co-ordination of safeguards which, for the protection of the interests of members and others, are required by Member States of companies within the meaning of the second paragraph of Article 58 of the Treaty, with a view to making such safeguards equivalent throughout the Community.

2.   If activities have been carried on on behalf of a grouping before its registration in accordance with Article 6 and if the grouping does not, after its registration, assume the obligations arising out of such activities, the natural persons, companies, firms or other legal bodies which carried on those activities shall bear unlimited joint and several liability for them.

[11.11]
Article 10
Any grouping establishment situated in a Member State other than that in which the official address is situated shall be registered in that State. For the purpose of such registration, a grouping shall file, at the appropriate registry in that Member State, copies of the documents which must be filed at the registry of the Member State in which the official address is situated, together, if necessary, with a translation which conforms with the practice of the registry where the establishment is registered.

[11.12]
Article 11
Notice that a grouping has been formed or that the liquidation of a grouping has been concluded stating the number, date and place of registration and the date, place and title of publication, shall be given in the *Official Journal of the European Communities* after it has been published in the gazette referred to in Article 39(1).

[11.13]
Article 12
The official address referred to in the contract for the formation of a grouping must be situated in the Community.

    The official address must be fixed either—

    (a)   where the grouping has its central administration, or

    (b)   where one of the members of the grouping has its central administration or, in the case of a natural person, his principal activity, provided that the grouping carries on an activity there.

[11.14]
Article 13
The official address of a grouping may be transferred within the Community.

When such a transfer does not result in a change in the law applicable pursuant to Article 2, the decision to transfer shall be taken in accordance with the conditions laid down in the contract for the formation of the grouping.

[11.15]
Article 14
1. When the transfer of the official address results in a change in the law applicable pursuant to Article 2, a transfer proposal must be drawn up, filed and published in accordance with the conditions laid down in Articles 7 and 8.

No decision to transfer may be taken for two months after publication of the proposal. Any such decision must be taken by the members of the grouping unanimously. The transfer shall take effect on the date on which the grouping is registered, in accordance with Article 6, at the registry for the new official address. That registration may not be effected until evidence has been produced that the proposal to transfer the official address has been published.

2. The termination of a grouping's registration at the registry for its old official address may not be effected until evidence has been produced that the grouping has been registered at the registry for its new official address.

3. Upon publication of a grouping's new registration the new official address may be relied on as against third parties in accordance with the conditions referred to in Article 9(1); however, as long as the termination of the grouping's registration at the registry for the old official address has not been published, third parties may continue to rely on the old official address unless the grouping proves that such third parties were aware of the new official address.

4. The laws of a Member State may provide that, as regards groupings registered under Article 6 in that Member State, the transfer of an official address which would result in a change of the law applicable shall not take effect if, within the two-month period referred to in paragraph 1, a competent authority in that Member State opposes it. Such opposition may be based only on grounds of public interest. Review by a judicial authority must be possible.

[11.16]
Article 15
1. Where the law applicable to a grouping by virtue of Article 2 provides for the nullity of that grouping, such nullity must be established or declared by judicial decision. However, the court to which the matter is referred must, where it is possible for the affairs of the grouping to be put in order, allow time to permit that to be done.

2. The nullity of a grouping shall entail its liquidation in accordance with the conditions laid down in Article 35.

3. A decision establishing or declaring the nullity of a grouping may be relied on as against third parties in accordance with the conditions laid down in Article 9(1).

Such a decision shall not of itself affect the validity of liabilities, owed by or to a grouping, which originated before it could be relied on as against third parties in accordance with the conditions laid down in the previous subparagraph.

[11.17]
Article 16
1. The organs of a grouping shall be the members acting collectively and the manager or managers.

A contract for the formation of a grouping may provide for other organs; if it does it shall determine their powers.

2. The members of a grouping, acting as a body, may take any decision for the purpose of achieving the objects of the grouping.

[11.18]
Article 17
1. Each member shall have one vote. The contract for the formation of a grouping may, however, give more than one vote to certain members, provided that no one member holds a majority of the votes.

2. A unanimous decision by the members shall be required to—
  (a)   alter the objects of a grouping;
  (b)   alter the number of votes allotted to each member;
  (c)   alter the conditions for the taking of decisions;
  (d)   extend the duration of a grouping beyond any period fixed in the contract for the formation of the grouping;
  (e)   alter the contribution by every member or by some members to the grouping's financing;
  (f)   alter any other obligation of a member, unless otherwise provided by the contract for the formation of the grouping;

(g) make any alteration to the contract for the formation of the grouping not covered by this paragraph, unless otherwise provided by that contract.

3.   Except where this Regulation provides that decisions must be taken unanimously, the contract for the formation of a grouping may prescribe the conditions for a quorum and for a majority, in accordance with which the decisions, or some of them, shall be taken. Unless otherwise provided for by the contract, decisions shall be taken unanimously.

4.   On the initiative of a manager or at the request of a member, the manager or managers must arrange for the members to be consulted so that the latter can take a decision.

[11.19]
Article 18
Each member shall be entitled to obtain information from the manager or managers concerning the grouping's business and to inspect the grouping's books and business records.

[11.20]
Article 19
1.   A grouping shall be managed by one or more natural persons appointed in the contract for the formation of the grouping or by decision of the members.

No person may be a manager of a grouping if—
—   by virtue of the law applicable to him, or
—   by virtue of the internal law of the State in which the grouping has its official address, or
—   following a judicial or administrative decision made or recognised in a Member State
he may not belong to the administrative or management body of a company, may not manage an undertaking or may not act as manager of a European Economic Interest Grouping.

2.   A Member State may, in the case of groupings registered at their registries pursuant to Article 6, provide that legal persons may be managers on condition that such legal persons designate one or more natural persons, whose particulars shall be the subject of the filing provisions of Article 7(d) to represent them.

If a Member State exercises this option, it must provide that the representative or representatives shall be liable as if they were themselves managers of the groupings concerned.

The restrictions imposed in paragraph 1 shall also apply to those representatives.

3.   The contract for the formation of a grouping or, failing that, a unanimous decision by the members shall determine the conditions for the appointment and removal of the manager or managers and shall lay down their powers.

[11.21]
Article 20
1.   Only the manager or, where there are two or more, each of the managers shall represent a grouping in respect of dealings with third parties.

Each of the managers shall bind the grouping as regards third parties when he acts on behalf of the grouping, even where his acts do not fall within the objects of the grouping, unless the grouping proves that the third party knew or could not, under the circumstances, have been unaware that the act fell outside the objects of the grouping; publication of the particulars referred to in Article 5(c) shall not of itself be proof thereof.

No limitation on the powers of the manager or managers, whether deriving from the contract for the formation of the grouping or from a decision by the members, may be relied on as against third parties even if it is published.

2.   The contract for the formation of the grouping may provide that the grouping shall be validly bound only by two or more managers acting jointly. Such a clause may be relied on as against third parties in accordance with the conditions referred to in Article 9(1) only if it is published in accordance with Article 8.

[11.22]
Article 21
1.   The profits resulting from a grouping's activities shall be deemed to be the profits of the members and shall be apportioned among them in the proportions laid down in the contract for the formation of the grouping or, in the absence of any such provision, in equal shares.

2.   The members of a grouping shall contribute to the payment of the amount by which expenditure exceeds income in the proportions laid down in the contract for the formation of the grouping or, in the absence of any such provision, in equal shares.

[11.23]
Article 22
1.   Any member of a grouping may assign his participation in the grouping, or a proportion thereof, either to another member or to a third party; the assignment shall not take effect without the unanimous authorisation of the other members.

2. A member of a grouping may use his participation in the grouping as security only after the other members have given their unanimous authorisation, unless otherwise laid down in the contract for the formation of the grouping. The holder of the security may not at any time become a member of the grouping by virtue of that security.

[11.24]
Article 23
No grouping may invite investment by the public.

[11.25]
Article 24
1. The members of a grouping shall have unlimited joint and several liability for its debts and other liabilities of whatever nature. National law shall determine the consequences of such liability.
2. Creditors may not proceed against a member for payment in respect of debts and other liabilities, in accordance with the conditions laid down in paragraph 1, before the liquidation of a grouping is concluded, unless they have first requested the grouping to pay and payment has not been made within an appropriate period.

[11.26]
Article 25
Letters, order forms and similar documents must indicate legibly—
    (a)   the name of the grouping preceded or followed either by the words "European Economic Interest Grouping" or by the initials "EEIG", unless those words or initials already occur in the name;
    (b)   the location of the registry referred to in Article 6, in which the grouping is registered, together with the number of the grouping's entry at the registry;
    (c)   the grouping's official address;
    (d)   where applicable, that the managers must act jointly;
    (e)   where applicable, that the grouping is in liquidation, pursuant to Article 15, 31, 32 or 36.
Every establishment of a grouping, when registered in accordance with Article 10, must give the above particulars, together with those relating to its own registration, on the documents referred to in the first paragraph of this Article uttered by it.

[11.27]
Article 26
1. A decision to admit new members shall be taken unanimously by the members of the grouping.
2. Every new member shall be liable, in accordance with the conditions laid down in Article 24, for the grouping's debts and other liabilities, including those arising out of the grouping's activities before his admission.

He may, however, be exempted by a clause in the contract for the formation of the grouping or in the instrument of admission from the payment of debts and other liabilities which originated before his admission. Such a clause may be relied on as against third parties, under the conditions referred to in Article 9(1), only if it is published in accordance with Article 8.

[11.28]
Article 27
1. A member of a grouping may withdraw in accordance with the conditions laid down in the contract for the formation of a grouping or, in the absence of such conditions, with the unanimous agreement of the other members.

Any member of a grouping may, in addition, withdraw on just and proper grounds.
2. Any member of a grouping may be expelled for the reasons listed in the contract for the formation of the grouping and, in any case, if he seriously fails in his obligations or if he causes or threatens to cause serious disruption in the operation of the grouping.

Such expulsion may occur only by the decision of a court to which joint application has been made by a majority of the other members, unless otherwise provided by the contract for the formation of a grouping.

[11.29]
Article 28
1. A member of a grouping shall cease to belong to it on death or when he no longer complies with the conditions laid down in Article 4(1).

In addition, a Member State may provide, for the purposes of its liquidation, winding up, insolvency or cessation of payments laws, that a member shall cease to be a member of any grouping at the moment determined by those laws.
2. In the event of the death of a natural person who is a member of a grouping, no person may become a member in his place except under the conditions laid down in the contract for the formation of the grouping or, failing that, with the unanimous agreement of the remaining members.

[11.30]
Article 29
As soon as a member ceases to belong to a grouping, the manager or managers must inform the other members of that fact; they must also take the steps required as listed in Articles 7 and 8. In addition, any person concerned may take those steps.

[11.31]
Article 30
Except where the contract for the formation of a grouping provides otherwise and without prejudice to the rights acquired by a person under Articles 22(1) or 28(2), a grouping shall continue to exist for the remaining members after a member has ceased to belong to it, in accordance with the conditions laid down in the contract for the formation of the grouping or determined by unanimous decision of the members in question.

[11.32]
Article 31
1. A grouping may be wound up by a decision of its members ordering its winding up. Such a decision shall be taken unanimously, unless otherwise laid down in the contract for the formation of the grouping.
2. A grouping must be wound up by a decision of its members—
    (a) noting the expiry of the period fixed in the contract for the formation of the grouping or the existence of any other cause for winding up provided for in the contract, or
    (b) noting the accomplishment of the grouping's purpose or the impossibility of pursuing it further.
Where, three months after one of the situations referred to in the first subparagraph has occurred, a members' decision establishing the winding up of the grouping has not been taken, any member may petition the court to order winding up.
3. A grouping must also be wound up by a decision of its members or of the remaining member when the conditions laid down in Article 4(2) are no longer fulfilled.
4. After a grouping has been wound up by decision of its members, the manager or managers must take the steps required as listed in Articles 7 and 8. In addition, any person concerned may take those steps.

[11.33]
Article 32
1. On application by any person concerned or by a competent authority, in the event of the infringement of Articles 3, 12 or 31(3), the court must order a grouping to be wound up, unless its affairs can be and are put in order before the court has delivered a substantive ruling.
2. On application by a member, the court may order a grouping to be wound up on just and proper grounds.
3. A Member State may provide that the court may, on application by a competent authority, order the winding up of a grouping which has its official address in the State to which that authority belongs, wherever the grouping acts in contravention of that State's public interest, if the law of that State provides for such a possibility in respect of registered companies or other legal bodies subject to it.

[11.34]
Article 33
When a member ceases to belong to a grouping for any reason other than the assignment of his rights in accordance with the conditions laid down in Article 22(1), the value of his rights and obligations shall be determined taking into account the assets and liabilities of the grouping as they stand when he ceases to belong to it.
The value of the rights and obligations of a departing member may not be fixed in advance.

[11.35]
Article 34
Without prejudice to Article 37(1), any member who ceases to belong to a grouping shall remain answerable, in accordance with the conditions laid down in Article 24, for the debts and other liabilities arising out of the grouping's activities before he ceased to be a member.

[11.36]
Article 35
1. The winding up of a grouping shall entail its liquidation.
2. The liquidation of a grouping and the conclusion of its liquidation shall be governed by national law.
3. A grouping shall retain its capacity, within the meaning of Article 1(2), until its liquidation is concluded.
4. The liquidator or liquidators shall take the steps required as listed in Articles 7 and 8.

[11.37]
Article 36
Groupings shall be subject to national laws governing insolvency and cessation of payments. The commencement of proceedings against a grouping on grounds of its insolvency or cessation of payments shall not by itself cause the commencement of such proceedings against its members.

[11.38]
Article 37
1. A period of limitation of five years after the publication, pursuant to Article 8, of notice of a member's ceasing to belong to a grouping shall be substituted for any longer period which may be laid down by the relevant national law for actions against that member in connection with debts and other liabilities arising out of the grouping's activities before he ceased to be a member.
2. A period of limitation of five years after the publication, pursuant to Article 8, of notice of the conclusion of the liquidation of a grouping shall be substituted for any longer period which may be laid down by the relevant national law for actions against a member of the grouping in connection with debts and other liabilities arising out of the grouping's activities.

[11.39]
Article 38
Where a grouping carries on any activity in a Member State in contravention of that State's public interest, a competent authority of that State may prohibit that activity. Review of that competent authority's decision by a judicial authority shall be possible.

[11.40]
Article 39
1. The Member States shall designate the registry or registries responsible for effecting the registration referred to in Articles 6 and 10 and shall lay down the rules governing registration. They shall prescribe the conditions under which the documents referred to in Articles 7 and 10 shall be filed. They shall ensure that the documents and particulars referred to in Article 8 are published in the appropriate official gazette of the Member State in which the grouping has its official address, and may prescribe the manner of publication of the documents and particulars referred to in Article 8(c).

The Member States shall also ensure that anyone may, at the appropriate registry pursuant to Article 6 or, where appropriate, Article 10, inspect the documents referred to in Article 7 and obtain, even by post, full or partial copies thereof.

The Member States may provide for the payment of fees in connection with the operations referred to in the preceding subparagraphs; those fees may not, however, exceed the administrative cost thereof.
2. The Member States shall ensure that the information to be published in the *Official Journal of the European Communities* pursuant to Article 11 is forwarded to the Office for Official Publications of the European Communities within one month of its publication in the official gazette referred to in paragraph 1.
3. The Member States shall provide for appropriate penalties in the event of failure to comply with the provisions of Articles 7, 8 and 10 on disclosure and in the event of failure to comply with Article 25.

[11.41]
Article 40
The profits or losses from the activities of a grouping shall be taxable only in the hands of its members.

[11.42]
Article 41
1. The Member States shall take the measures required by virtue of Article 39 before 1 July 1989. They shall immediately communicate them to the Commission.
2. For information purposes, the Member States shall inform the Commission of the classes of natural persons, companies, firms and other legal bodies which they prohibit from participating in groupings pursuant to Article 4(4). The Commission shall inform the other Member States.

[11.43]
Article 42
1. Upon the adoption of this Regulation, a Contact Committee shall be set up under the auspices of the Commission. Its function shall be—
   (a)   to facilitate, without prejudice to Articles 169 and 170 of the Treaty, application of this Regulation through regular consultation dealing in particular with practical problems arising in connection with its application;
   (b)   to advise the Commission, if necessary, on additions or amendments to this Regulation.
2. The Contact Committee shall be composed of representatives of the Member States and representatives of the Commission. The chairman shall be a representative of the Commission. The Commission shall provide the secretariat.

3.   The Contact Committee shall be convened by its chairman either on his own initiative or at the request of one of its members.

[11.44]
Article 43
This Regulation shall enter into force on the third day following its publication in the *Official Journal of the European Communities*.

It shall apply from 1 July 1989, with the exception of Articles 39, 41 and 42 which shall apply as from the entry into force of the Regulation.

This Regulation shall be binding in its entirety and directly applicable in all Member States.

COUNCIL REGULATION

(1103/97/EC)

of 17 June 1997

on certain provisions relating to the introduction of the euro

NOTES
Date of publication in OJ: OJ L162, 19.6.1997, p 1. Notes are as in the original OJ version.
This Regulation is reproduced as amended by: Council Regulation 2595/2000/EC.

[11.45]
THE COUNCIL OF THE EUROPEAN UNION,
Having regard to the Treaty establishing the European Community, and in particular Article 235 thereof,
Having regard to the proposal of the Commission,[1]
Having regard to the opinion of the European Parliament,[2]
Having regard to the opinion of the European Monetary Institute,[3]

(1)   Whereas, at its meeting held in Madrid on 15 and 16 December 1995, the European Council confirmed that the third stage of Economic and Monetary Union will start on 1 January 1999 as laid down in Article 109j(4) of the Treaty; whereas the Member States which will adopt the euro as the single currency in accordance with the Treaty will be defined for the purposes of this Regulation as the "participating Member States";

(2)   Whereas, at the meeting of the European Council in Madrid, the decision was taken that the term "ECU" used by the Treaty to refer to the European currency unit is a generic term; whereas the Governments of the fifteen Member States have achieved the common agreement that this decision is the agreed and definitive interpretation of the relevant Treaty provisions; whereas the name given to the European currency shall be the "euro"; whereas the euro as the currency of the participating Member States will be divided into one hundred sub-units with the name "cent"; whereas the European Council furthermore considered that the name of the single currency must be the same in all the official languages of the European Union, taking into account the existence of different alphabets;

(3)   Whereas a Regulation on the introduction of the euro will be adopted by the Council on the basis of the third sentence of Article 109l(4) of the Treaty as soon as the participating Member States are known in order to define the legal framework of the euro; whereas the Council, when acting at the starting date of the third stage in accordance with the first sentence of Article 109l(4) of the Treaty, shall adopt the irrevocably fixed conversion rates;

(4)   Whereas it is necessary, in the course of the operation of the common market and for the changeover to the single currency, to provide legal certainty for citizens and firms in all Member States on certain provisions relating to the introduction of the euro well before the entry into the third stage; whereas this legal certainty at an early stage will allow preparations by citizens and firms to proceed under good conditions;

(5)   Whereas the third sentence of Article 109l(4) of the Treaty, which allows the Council, acting with the unanimity of participating Member States, to take other measures necessary for the rapid introduction of the single currency is available as a legal basis only when it has been confirmed, in accordance with Article 109j(4) of the Treaty, which Member States fulfil the necessary conditions for the adoption of a single currency; whereas it is therefore necessary to have recourse to Article 235 of the Treaty as a legal basis for those provisions where there is an urgent need for legal certainty; whereas therefore this Regulation and the aforesaid Regulation on the introduction of the euro will together provide the legal framework for the euro, the principles of which legal framework were agreed by the European Council in Madrid; whereas the introduction of the euro concerns day-to-day operations of the whole population in participating Member States; whereas measures other than those in this Regulation and in the Regulation which will be adopted under the third sentence of Article 109l(4) of the Treaty should be examined to ensure a balanced changeover, in particular for consumers;

(6)   Whereas the ECU as referred to in Article 109g of the Treaty and as defined in Council Regulation (EC) No 3320/94 of 22 December 1994 on the consolidation of the existing Community legislation on the definition of the ECU following the entry into force of the Treaty on European

Union[4] will cease to be defined as a basket of component currencies on 1 January 1999 and the euro will become a currency in its own right; whereas the decision of the Council regarding the adoption of the conversion rates shall not in itself modify the external value of the ECU; whereas this means that one ECU in its composition as a basket of component currencies will become one euro; whereas Regulation (EC) No 3320/94 therefore becomes obsolete and should be repealed; whereas for references in legal instruments to the ECU, parties shall be presumed to have agreed to refer to the ECU as referred to in Article 109g of the Treaty and as defined in the aforesaid Regulation; whereas such presumption should be rebuttable taking into account the intentions of the parties;

(7)   Whereas it is a generally accepted principle of law that the continuity of contracts and other legal instruments is not affected by the introduction of a new currency; whereas the principle of freedom of contract has to be respected; whereas the principle of continuity should be compatible with anything which parties might have agreed with reference to the introduction of the euro; whereas, in order to reinforce legal certainty and clarity, it is appropriate explicitly to confirm that the principle of continuity of contracts and other legal instruments shall apply between the former national currencies and the euro and between the ECU as referred to in Article 109g of the Treaty and as defined in Regulation (EC) No 3320/94 and the euro; whereas this implies, in particular, that in the case of fixed interest rate instruments the introduction of the euro does not alter the nominal interest rate payable by the debtor; whereas the provisions on continuity can fulfil their objective to provide legal certainty and transparency to economic agents, in particular for consumers, only if they enter into force as soon as possible;

(8)   Whereas the introduction of the euro constitutes a change in the monetary law of each participating Member State; whereas the recognition of the monetary law of a State is a universally accepted principle; whereas the explicit confirmation of the principle of continuity should lead to the recognition of continuity of contracts and other legal instruments in the jurisdictions of third countries;

(9)   Whereas the term "contract used for the definition of legal instruments is meant to include all types of contracts, irrespective of the way in which they are concluded;

(10)   Whereas the Council, when acting in accordance with the first sentence of Article 109l(4) of the Treaty, shall define the conversion rates of the euro in terms of each of the national currencies of the participating Member States; whereas these conversion rates should be used for any conversion between the euro and the national currency units or between the national currency units; whereas for any conversion between national currency units, a fixed algorithm should define the result; whereas the use of inverse rates for conversion would imply rounding of rates and could result in significant inaccuracies, notably if large amounts are involved;

(11)   Whereas the introduction of the euro requires the rounding of monetary amounts; whereas an early indication of rules for rounding is necessary in the course of the operation of the common market and to allow a timely preparation and a smooth transition to Economic and Monetary Union; whereas these rules do not affect any rounding practice, convention or national provisions providing a higher degree of accuracy for intermediate computations;

(12)   Whereas, in order to achieve a high degree of accuracy in conversion operations, the conversion rates should be defined with six significant figures; whereas a rate with six significant figures means a rate which, counted from the left and starting by the first non-zero figure, has six figures,

---

NOTES

[1]   OJ C369, 7.12.96, p 8.

[2]   OJ C380, 16.12.96, p 49.

[3]   Opinion delivered on 29 November 1996.

[4]   OJ L350, 31.12.94, p 27.

HAS ADOPTED THIS REGULATION—

[11.46]
Article 1
For the purpose of this Regulation—
—   "legal instruments" shall mean legislative and statutory provisions, acts of administration, judicial decisions, contracts, unilateral legal acts, payment instruments other than banknotes and coins, and other instruments with legal effect,
—   "participating Member States" shall mean those Member States which adopt the single currency in accordance with the Treaty,
—   "conversion rates" shall mean the irrevocably fixed conversion rates which the Council adopts in accordance with the first sentence of Article 109l(4) of the Treaty [or in accordance with paragraph 5 of that Article],
—   "national currency units" shall mean the units of the currencies of participating Member States, as those units are defined on the day before the start of the third stage of Economic and Monetary Union [or, as the case may be, on the day before the euro is substituted for the currency of a member state which adopts the euro at a later date],
—   "euro unit" shall mean the unit of the single currency as defined in the Regulation on the introduction of the euro which will enter into force at the starting date of the third stage of Economic and Monetary Union.

NOTES

Words in square brackets inserted by Council Regulation 2595/2000/EC, Art 1, as from 1 January 2001.

[11.47]
Article 2
1. Every reference in a legal instrument to the ECU, as referred to in Article 109g of the Treaty and as defined in Regulation (EC) No 3320/94, shall be replaced by a reference to the euro at a rate of one euro to one ECU. References in a legal instrument to the ECU without such a definition shall be presumed, such presumption being rebuttable taking into account the intentions of the parties, to be references to the ECU as referred to in Article 109g of the Treaty and as defined in Regulation (EC) No 3320/94.
2. (*Repeals Regulation 3320/94/EC.*)
3. This Article shall apply as from 1 January 1999 in accordance with the decision pursuant to Article 109j(4) of the Treaty.

[11.48]
Article 3
The introduction of the euro shall not have the effect of altering any term of a legal instrument or of discharging or excusing performance under any legal instrument, nor give a party the right unilaterally to alter or terminate such an instrument. This provision is subject to anything which parties may have agreed.

[11.49]
Article 4
1. The conversion rates shall be adopted as one euro expressed in terms of each of the national currencies of the participating Member States. They shall be adopted with six significant figures.
2. The conversion rates shall not be rounded or truncated when making conversions.
3. The conversion rates shall be used for conversions either way between the euro unit and the national currency units. Inverse rates derived from the conversion rates shall not be used.
4. Monetary amounts to be converted from one national currency unit into another shall first be converted into a monetary amount expressed in the euro unit, which amount may be rounded to not less than three decimals and shall then be converted into the other national currency unit. No alternative method of calculation may be used unless it produces the same results.

[11.50]
Article 5
Monetary amounts to be paid or accounted for when a rounding takes place after a conversion into the euro unit pursuant to Article 4 shall be rounded up or down to the nearest cent. Monetary amounts to be paid or accounted for which are converted into a national currency unit shall be rounded up or down to the nearest sub-unit or in the absence of a sub-unit to the nearest unit, or according to national law or practice to a multiple or fraction of the sub-unit or unit of the national currency unit. If the application of the conversion rate gives a result which is exactly half-way, the sum shall be rounded up.

[11.51]
Article 6
This Regulation shall enter into force on the day following that of its publication in the *Official Journal of the European Communities*.
This Regulation shall be binding in its entirety and directly applicable in all Member States.

COUNCIL REGULATION

(974/98/EC)

of 3 May 1998

on the introduction of the euro

NOTES

Date of publication in OJ: OJ L139, 11.5.98, p 1. Notes are as in the original OJ version.
This Regulation is reproduced as amended by: Council Regulation 2169/2005/EC; Council Regulation 1647/2006/EC; Council Regulation 835/2007/EC; Council Regulation 836/2007/EC; Council Regulation 693/2008/EC; Council Regulation 670/2010/EU.

[11.52]
THE COUNCIL OF THE EUROPEAN UNION,
Having regard to the Treaty establishing the European Community, and in particular Article 109l(4), third sentence thereof,

Having regard to the proposal from the Commission,[1]

Having regard to the opinion of the European Monetary Institute,[2]

Having regard to the opinion of the European Parliament,[3]

(1)   Whereas this Regulation defines monetary law provisions of the Member States which have adopted the euro; whereas provisions on continuity of contracts, the replacement of references to the ecu in legal instruments by references to the euro and rounding have already been laid down in Council Regulation (EC) No 1103/97 of 17 June 1997 on certain provisions relating to the introduction of the euro;[4] whereas the introduction of the euro concerns day-to-day operations of the whole population in participating Member States; whereas measures other than those in this Regulation and in Regulation (EC) No 1103/97 should be examined to ensure a balanced changeover, in particular for consumers;

(2)   Whereas, at the meeting of the European Council in Madrid on 15 and 16 December 1995, the decision was taken that the term "ecu" used by the Treaty to refer to the European currency unit is a generic term; whereas the Governments of the 15 Member States have reached the common agreement that this decision is the agreed and definitive interpretation of the relevant Treaty provisions; whereas the name given to the European currency shall be the "euro"; whereas the euro as the currency of the participating Member States shall be divided into one hundred sub-units with the name "cent"; whereas the definition of the name "cent" does not prevent the use of variants of this term in common usage in the Member States; whereas the European Council furthermore considered that the name of the single currency must be the same in all the official languages of the European Union, taking into account the existence of different alphabets;

(3)   Whereas the Council when acting in accordance with the third sentence of Article 109l(4) of the Treaty shall take the measures necessary for the rapid introduction of the euro other than the adoption of the conversion rates;

(4)   Whereas whenever under Article 109k(2) of the Treaty a Member State becomes a participating Member State, the Council shall according to Article 109l(5) of the Treaty take the other measures necessary for the rapid introduction of the euro as the single currency of this Member State;

(5)   Whereas according to the first sentence of Article 109l(4) of the Treaty the Council shall at the starting date of the third stage adopt the conversion rates at which the currencies of the participating Member States shall be irrevocably fixed and at which irrevocably fixed rate the euro shall be substituted for these currencies;

(6)   Whereas given the absence of exchange rate risk either between the euro unit and the national currency units or between these national currency units, legislative provisions should be interpreted accordingly;

(7)   Whereas the term "contract" used for the definition of legal instruments is meant to include all types of contracts, irrespective of the way in which they are concluded;

(8)   Whereas in order to prepare a smooth changeover to the euro a transitional period is needed between the substitution of the euro for the currencies of the participating Member States and the introduction of euro banknotes and coins; whereas during this period the national currency units will be defined as sub-divisions of the euro; whereas thereby a legal equivalence is established between the euro unit and the national currency units;

(9)   Whereas in accordance with Article 109g of the Treaty and with Regulation (EC) No 1103/97, the euro will replace the ECU as from 1 January 1999 as the unit of account of the institutions of the European Communities; whereas the euro should also be the unit of account of the European Central Bank (ECB) and of the central banks of the participating Member States; whereas, in line with the Madrid conclusions, monetary policy operations will be carried out in the euro unit by the European System of Central Banks (ESCB); whereas this does not prevent national central banks from keeping accounts in their national currency unit during the transitional period, in particular for their staff and for public administrations;

(10)   Whereas each participating Member State may allow the full use of the euro unit in its territory during the transitional period;

(11)   Whereas during the transitional period contracts, national laws and other legal instruments can be drawn up validly in the euro unit or in the national currency unit; whereas during this period, nothing in this Regulation should affect the validity of any reference to a national currency unit in any legal instrument;

(12)   Whereas, unless agreed otherwise, economic agents have to respect the denomination of a legal instrument in the performance of all acts to be carried out under that instrument;

(13)   Whereas the euro unit and the national currency units are units of the same currency; whereas it should be ensured that payments inside a participating Member State by crediting an account can be made either in the euro unit or the respective national currency unit; whereas the provisions on payments by crediting an account should also apply to those cross-border payments, which are denominated in the euro unit or the national currency unit of the account of the creditor; whereas it is necessary to ensure the smooth functioning of payment systems by laying down provisions dealing with the crediting of accounts by payment instruments credited through those systems; whereas the provisions on payments by crediting an account should not imply that financial intermediaries are obliged to make available either other payment facilities or products denominated in any particular unit of the euro; whereas the provisions on payments by crediting an account do not prohibit financial intermediaries from coordinating the introduction of payment facilities denominated in the euro unit which rely on a common technical infrastructure during the transitional period;

(14)   Whereas in accordance with the conclusions reached by the European Council at its meeting held in Madrid, new tradeable public debt will be issued in the euro unit by the participating Member States as from 1 January 1999; whereas it is desirable to allow issuers of debt to redenominate outstanding debt in the euro unit; whereas the provisions on redenomination should be such that they can also be applied in the jurisdictions of third countries; whereas issuers should be enabled to redenominate outstanding debt if the debt is denominated in a national currency unit of a Member State which has redenominated part or all of the outstanding debt of its general government; whereas these provisions do not address the introduction of additional measures to amend the terms of outstanding debt to alter, among other things, the nominal amount of outstanding debt, these being matters subject to relevant national law; whereas it is desirable to allow Member States to take appropriate measures for changing the unit of account of the operating procedures of organised markets;

(15)   Whereas further action at the Community level may also be necessary to clarify the effect of the introduction of the euro on the application of existing provisions of Community law, in particular concerning netting, set-off and techniques of similar effect;

(16)   Whereas any obligation to use the euro unit can only be imposed on the basis of Community legislation; whereas in transactions with the public sector participating Member States may allow the use of the euro unit; whereas in accordance with the reference scenario decided by the European Council at its meeting held in Madrid, the Community legislation laying down the time frame for the generalisation of the use of the euro unit might leave some freedom to individual Member States;

(17)   Whereas in accordance with Article 105a of the Treaty the Council may adopt measures to harmonise the denominations and technical specifications of all coins;

(18)   Whereas banknotes and coins need adequate protection against counterfeiting;

(19)   Whereas banknotes and coins denominated in the national currency units lose their status of legal tender at the latest six months after the end of the transitional period; whereas limitations on payments in notes and coins, established by Member States for public reasons, are not incompatible with the status of legal tender of euro banknotes and coins, provided that other lawful means for the settlement of monetary debts are available;

(20)   Whereas as from the end of the transitional period references in legal instruments existing at the end of the transitional period will have to be read as references to the euro unit according to the respective conversion rates; whereas a physical redenomination of existing legal instruments is therefore not necessary to achieve this result; whereas the rounding rules defined in Regulation (EC) No 1103/97 shall also apply to the conversions to be made at the end of the transitional period or after the transitional period; whereas for reasons of clarity it may be desirable that the physical redenomination will take place as soon as appropriate;

(21)   Whereas paragraph 2 of Protocol 11 on certain provisions relating to the United Kingdom of Great Britain and Northern Ireland stipulates that, *inter alia*, paragraph 5 of that Protocol shall have effect if the United Kingdom notifies the Council that it does not intend to move to the third stage; whereas the United Kingdom gave notice to the Council on 30 October 1997 that it does not intend to move to the third stage; whereas paragraph 5 stipulates that, *inter alia*, Article 109l(4) of the Treaty shall not apply to the United Kingdom;

(22)   Whereas Denmark, referring to paragraph 1 of Protocol 12 on certain provisions relating to Denmark has notified, in the context of the Edinburgh decision of 12 December 1992, that it will not participate in the third stage; whereas, therefore, in accordance with paragraph 2 of the said Protocol, all Articles and provisions of the Treaty and the Statute of the ESCB referring to a derogation shall be applicable to Denmark;

(23)   Whereas, in accordance with Article 109l(4) of the Treaty, the single currency will be introduced only in the Member States without a derogation;

(24)   Whereas this Regulation, therefore, shall be applicable pursuant to Article 189 of the Treaty, subject to Protocols 11 and 12 and Article 109k(1),

NOTES

[1]   OJ C369, 7.12.96, p 10.

[2]   OJ C205, 5.7.97, p 18.

[3]   OJ C380, 16.12.96, p 50.

[4]   OJ L162, 19.6.97, p 1.

HAS ADOPTED THIS REGULATION—

PART I
DEFINITIONS

[11.53]
[Article 1
For the purpose of this Regulation:
  (a)   "participating Member States" shall mean the Member States listed in the table in the Annex;
  (b)   "legal instruments" shall mean legislative and statutory provisions, acts of administration, judicial decisions, contracts, unilateral legal acts, payment instruments other than banknotes and coins, and other instruments with legal effect;

(c)   "conversion rate" shall mean the irrevocably fixed conversion rate adopted for the currency of each participating Member State by the Council in accordance with the first sentence of Article 123(4) of the Treaty or with paragraph 5 of that Article;

(d)   "euro adoption date" shall mean either the date on which the respective Member State enters the third stage under Article 121(3) of the Treaty or the date on which the abrogation of the respective Member State's derogation under Article 122(2) of the Treaty enters into force, as the case may be;

(e)   "cash changeover date" shall mean the date on which euro banknotes and coins acquire the status of legal tender in a given participating Member State;

(f)   "euro unit" shall mean the currency unit as referred to in the second sentence of Article 2;

(g)   "national currency units" shall mean the units of the currency of a participating Member State, as those units are defined on the day before the adoption of the euro in that Member State;

(h)   "transitional period" shall mean a period of three years at the most beginning at 00.00 hours on the euro adoption date and ending at 00.00 hours on the cash changeover date;

(i)   "phasing-out period" shall mean a period of one year at the most beginning on the euro adoption date, which can only apply to Member States where the euro adoption date and the cash changeover date fall on the same day;

(j)   "redenominate" shall mean changing the unit in which the amount of outstanding debt is stated from a national currency unit to the euro unit, but which does not have through the act of redenomination the effect of altering any other term of the debt, this being a matter subject to relevant national law;

(k)   "credit institutions" shall mean credit institutions as defined in Article 1(1) of Directive 2000/12/EC of the European Parliament and of the Council of 20 March 2000 relating to the taking up and pursuit of the business of credit institutions.[1] For the purpose of this Regulation, the institutions listed in Article 2(3) of that Directive with the exception of post office giro institutions shall not be considered as credit institutions.]

NOTES

Substituted by Council Regulation 2169/2005/EC, Art 1, as from 18 January 2006.

[1]   OJ L126, 26.5.2000, p 1. Directive as last amended by Directive 2005/1/EC of the European Parliament and of the Council (OJ L79, 24.3.2005, p 9).

[11.54]
[Article 1a
The euro adoption date, the cash changeover date, and the phasing-out period, if applicable, for each participating Member State shall be as set out in the Annex.]

NOTES

Inserted by Council Regulation 2169/2005/EC, Art 2, as from 18 January 2006.

PART II
SUBSTITUTION OF THE EURO FOR THE CURRENCIES OF THE PARTICIPATING MEMBER STATES

[11.55]
[Article 2
With effect from the respective euro adoption dates, the currency of the participating Member States shall be the euro. The currency unit shall be one euro. One euro shall be divided into one hundred cents.]

NOTES

Substituted by Council Regulation 2169/2005/EC, Art 3, as from 18 January 2006.

[11.56]
Article 3
The euro shall be substituted for the currency of each participating Member State at the conversion rate.

[11.57]
Article 4
The euro shall be the unit of account of the European Central Bank (ECB) and of the central banks of the participating Member States.

PART III
TRANSITIONAL PROVISIONS

[11.58]
Article 5
Articles 6, 7, 8 and 9 shall apply during the transitional period.

Part 11   EU Legislation

[11.59]
Article 6
1.   The euro shall also be divided into the national currency units according to the conversion rates. Any subdivision thereof shall be maintained. Subject to the provisions of this Regulation the monetary law of the participating Member States shall continue to apply.
2.   Where in a legal instrument reference is made to a national currency unit, this reference shall be as valid as if reference were made to the euro unit according to the conversion rates.

[11.60]
Article 7
The substitution of the euro for the currency of each participating Member State shall not in itself have the effect of altering the denomination of legal instruments in existence on the date of substitution.

[11.61]
Article 8
1.   Acts to be performed under legal instruments stipulating the use of or denominated in a national currency unit shall be performed in that national currency unit. Acts to be performed under legal instruments stipulating the use of or denominated in the euro unit shall be performed in that unit.
2.   The provisions of paragraph 1 are subject to anything which parties may have agreed.
3.   Notwithstanding the provisions of paragraph 1, any amount denominated either in the euro unit or in the national currency unit of a given participating Member State and payable within that Member State by crediting an account of the creditor, can be paid by the debtor either in the euro unit or in that national currency unit. The amount shall be credited to the account of the creditor in the denomination of his account, with any conversion being effected at the conversion rates.
4.   Notwithstanding the provisions of paragraph 1, each participating Member State may take measures which may be necessary in order to—
—   redenominate in the euro unit outstanding debt issued by that Member State's general government, as defined in the European system of integrated accounts, denominated in its national currency unit and issued under its own law. If a Member State has taken such a measure, issuers may redenominate in the euro unit debt denominated in that Member State's national currency unit unless redenomination is expressly excluded by the terms of the contract; this provision shall apply to debt issued by the general government of a Member State as well as to bonds and other forms of securitised debt negotiable in the capital markets, and to money market instruments, issued by other debtors,
—   enable the change of the unit of account of their operating procedures from a national currency unit to the euro unit by—
    (a)   markets for the regular exchange, clearing and settlement of any instrument listed in section B of the Annex to Council Directive 93/22/EEC of 10 May 1993 on investment services in the securities field[1] and of commodities; and
    (b)   systems for the regular exchange, clearing and settlement of payments.
5.   Provisions other than those of paragraph 4 imposing the use of the euro unit may only be adopted by the participating Member States in accordance with any time-frame laid down by Community legislation.
6.   National legal provisions of participating Member States which permit or impose netting, set-off or techniques with similar effects shall apply to monetary obligations, irrespective of their currency denomination, if that denomination is in the euro unit or in a national currency unit, with any conversion being effected at the conversion rates.

NOTES
[1]   OJ L141, 11.6.93, p 27. Directive as amended by Directive 95/26/EC of the European Parliament and of the Council (OJ L168, 18.7.95, p 7).

[11.62]
[Article 9
Banknotes and coins denominated in a national currency unit shall retain their status as legal tender within their territorial limits as from the day before the euro adoption date in the participating Member State concerned.]

NOTES
Substituted by Council Regulation 2169/2005/EC, Art 4, as from 18 January 2006.

[11.63]
[Article 9a
The following shall apply in a Member State with a "phasing-out" period. In legal instruments created during the phasing-out period and to be performed in that Member State, reference may continue to be made to the national currency unit. These references shall be read as references to the

euro unit according to the respective conversion rates. Without prejudice to Article 15, the acts performed under these legal instruments shall be performed only in the euro unit. The rounding rules laid down in Regulation (EC) No 1103/97 shall apply.

The Member State concerned shall limit the application of the first subparagraph to certain types of legal instrument, or to legal instruments adopted in certain fields.

The Member State concerned may shorten the period.]

NOTES

Inserted by Council Regulation 2169/2005/EC, Art 5, as from 18 January 2006.

PART IV
EURO BANKNOTES AND COINS

[11.64]
[Article 10
With effect from the respective cash changeover dates, the ECB and the central banks of the participating Member States shall put into circulation banknotes denominated in euro in the participating Member States.

Without prejudice to Article 15, these banknotes denominated in euro shall be the only banknotes which have the status of legal tender in participating Member States.]

NOTES

Substituted by Council Regulation 2169/2005/EC, Art 6, as from 18 January 2006.

[11.65]
[Article 11
With effect from the respective cash changeover date, the participating Member States shall issue coins denominated in euro or in cent and complying with the denominations and technical specifications which the Council may lay down in accordance with the second sentence of Article 106(2) of the Treaty. Without prejudice to Article 15 and to the provisions of any agreement under Article 111(3) of the Treaty concerning monetary matters, those coins shall be the only coins which have the status of legal tender in participating Member States. Except for the issuing authority and for those persons specifically designated by the national legislation of the issuing Member State, no party shall be obliged to accept more than 50 coins in any single payment.]

NOTES

Substituted by Council Regulation 2169/2005/EC, Art 6, as from 18 January 2006.

[11.66]
Article 12
Participating Member States shall ensure adequate sanctions against counterfeiting and falsification of euro banknotes and coins.

PART V
FINAL PROVISIONS

[11.67]
[Article 13
Articles 10, 11, 14, 15 and 16 shall apply with effect from the respective cash changeover date in each participating Member State.]

NOTES

Substituted by Council Regulation 2169/2005/EC, Art 7, as from 18 January 2006.

[11.68]
[Article 14
Where, in legal instruments existing on the day before the cash changeover date, reference is made to the national currency units, these references shall be read as references to the euro unit according to the respective conversion rates. The rounding rules laid down in Regulation (EC) No 1103/97 shall apply.]

NOTES

Substituted by Council Regulation 2169/2005/EC, Art 7, as from 18 January 2006.

[11.69]
Article 15
1. Banknotes and coins denominated in a national currency unit as referred to in Article 6(1) shall remain legal tender within their territorial limits until six months [from the respective cash changeover date] at the latest; this period may be shortened by national law.

2. Each participating Member State may, for a period of up to six months [from the respective cash changeover date], lay down rules for the use of the banknotes and coins denominated in its national currency unit as referred to in Article 6(1) and take any measures necessary to facilitate their withdrawal.

[3. During the period referred to in paragraph 1, credit institutions in participating Member States adopting the euro after 1 January 2002 shall exchange their customers' banknotes and coins denominated in the national currency unit of that Member State for banknotes and coins in euro, free of charge, up to a ceiling which may be set by national law. Credit institutions may require that notice be given if the amount to be exchanged exceeds a ceiling set by national law or, in the absence of such provisions, by themselves and corresponding to a household amount.

The credit institutions referred to in the first subparagraph shall exchange banknotes and coins denominated in the national currency unit of that Member State of persons other than their customers, free of charge up to a ceiling set by national law or, in the absence of such provisions, by themselves.

National law may limit the obligation under the preceding two subparagraphs to specific types of credit institutions. National law may also extend this obligation upon other persons.]

NOTES
Words in square brackets in paras 1, 2 substituted, and para 3 added, by Council Regulation 2169/2005/EC, Art 8, as from 18 January 2006.

[11.70]
Article 16
In accordance with the laws or practices of participating Member States, the respective issuers of banknotes and coins shall continue to accept, against euro at the conversion rate, the banknotes and coins previously issued by them.

PART VI
ENTRY INTO FORCE

[11.71]
Article 17
This Regulation shall enter into force on 1 January 1999.

This Regulation shall be binding in its entirety and directly applicable in all Member States, in accordance with the Treaty, subject to Protocols 11 and 12 and Article 109k(1).

[ANNEX

[11.72]

Member State	Euro adoption date	Cash changeover date	Member State with a "phasing-out" period
Belgium	1 January 1999	1 January 2002	n/a
Germany	1 January 1999	1 January 2002	n/a
[Estonia	1 January 2011	1 January 2011	No]
Greece	1 January 2001	1 January 2002	n/a
Spain	1 January 1999	1 January 2002	n/a
France	1 January 1999	1 January 2002	n/a
Ireland	1 January 1999	1 January 2002	n/a
Italy	1 January 1999	1 January 2002	n/a
[Cyprus	1 January 2008	1 January 2008	No]
[Malta	1 January 2008	1 January 2008	No]
Luxembourg	1 January 1999	1 January 2002	n/a
Netherlands	1 January 1999	1 January 2002	n/a
Austria	1 January 1999	1 January 2002	n/a
Portugal	1 January 1999	1 January 2002	n/a
[Slovenia	1 January 2007	1 January 2007	No]
[Slovakia	1 January 2009	1 January 2009	No]
Finland	1 January 1999	1 January 2002	n/a]

NOTES
Added by Council Regulation 2169/2005/EC, Art 9, as from 18 January 2006.
Entry relating to Estonia inserted by Council Regulation 670/2010/EU, Art 1, Annex, as from 1 January 2011.
Entry relating to Cyprus inserted by Council Regulation 835/2007/EC, Art 1, Annex, as from 1 January 2008.
Entry relating to Malta inserted by Council Regulation 836/2007/EC, Art 1, Annex, as from 1 January 2008.

Entry relating to Slovenia inserted by Council Regulation 1647/2006/EC, Art 1, Annex, as from 1 January 2007.
Entry relating to Slovakia inserted by Council Regulation 693/2008/EC, Art 1, Annex, as from 1 January 2009.

COUNCIL REGULATION

(1346/2000/EC)

of 29 May 2000

on insolvency proceedings

NOTES

Date of publication in OJ: OJ L160, 30.06.2000, p 1. Notes are as in the original OJ version.

This Regulation is reproduced as amended by: AA5 (Act of Accession of the Czech Republic, Estonia, Cyprus, Latvia, Lithuania, Hungary, Malta, Poland, Slovenia and Slovakia); Council Regulation 1791/2006/EC; Council Regulation 210/2010/EC; Council Regulation 583/2011/EU. Note that other amendments made to the Annexes have been superseded by Council Regulation 210/2010/EC which codifies them.

[11.73]

THE COUNCIL OF THE EUROPEAN UNION,

Having regard to the Treaty establishing the European Community, and in particular Articles 61(c) and 67(1) thereof,

Having regard to the initiative of the Federal Republic of Germany and the Republic of Finland,

Having regard to the opinion of the European Parliament,[1]

Having regard to the opinion of the Economic and Social Committee,[2]

Whereas:

(1) The European Union has set out the aim of establishing an area of freedom, security and justice.

(2) The proper functioning of the internal market requires that cross-border insolvency proceedings should operate efficiently and effectively and this Regulation needs to be adopted in order to achieve this objective which comes within the scope of judicial cooperation in civil matters within the meaning of Article 65 of the Treaty.

(3) The activities of undertakings have more and more cross-border effects and are therefore increasingly being regulated by Community law. While the insolvency of such undertakings also affects the proper functioning of the internal market, there is a need for a Community act requiring coordination of the measures to be taken regarding an insolvent debtor's assets.

(4) It is necessary for the proper functioning of the internal market to avoid incentives for the parties to transfer assets or judicial proceedings from one Member State to another, seeking to obtain a more favourable legal position (forum shopping).

(5) These objectives cannot be achieved to a sufficient degree at national level and action at Community level is therefore justified.

(6) In accordance with the principle of proportionality this Regulation should be confined to provisions governing jurisdiction for opening insolvency proceedings and judgments which are delivered directly on the basis of the insolvency proceedings and are closely connected with such proceedings. In addition, this Regulation should contain provisions regarding the recognition of those judgments and the applicable law which also satisfy that principle.

(7) Insolvency proceedings relating to the winding-up of insolvent companies or other legal persons, judicial arrangements, compositions and analogous proceedings are excluded from the scope of the 1968 Brussels Convention on Jurisdiction and the Enforcement of Judgments in Civil and Commercial Matters,[3] as amended by the Conventions on Accession to this Convention.[4]

(8) In order to achieve the aim of improving the efficiency and effectiveness of insolvency proceedings having cross-border effects, it is necessary, and appropriate, that the provisions on jurisdiction, recognition and applicable law in this area should be contained in a Community law measure which is binding and directly applicable in Member States.

(9) This Regulation should apply to insolvency proceedings, whether the debtor is a natural person or a legal person, a trader or an individual. The insolvency proceedings to which this Regulation applies are listed in the Annexes. Insolvency proceedings concerning insurance undertakings, credit institutions, investment undertakings holding funds or securities for third parties and collective investment undertakings should be excluded from the scope of this Regulation. Such undertakings should not be covered by this Regulation since they are subject to special arrangements and, to some extent, the national supervisory authorities have extremely wide-ranging powers of intervention.

(10) Insolvency proceedings do not necessarily involve the intervention of a judicial authority; the expression "court" in this Regulation should be given a broad meaning and include a person or body empowered by national law to open insolvency proceedings. In order for this Regulation to apply, proceedings (comprising acts and formalities set down in law) should not only have to comply with the provisions of this Regulation, but they should also be officially recognised and legally effective in the Member State in which the insolvency proceedings are opened and should be

collective insolvency proceedings which entail the partial or total divestment of the debtor and the appointment of a liquidator.

(11) This Regulation acknowledges the fact that as a result of widely differing substantive laws it is not practical to introduce insolvency proceedings with universal scope in the entire Community. The application without exception of the law of the State of opening of proceedings would, against this background, frequently lead to difficulties. This applies, for example, to the widely differing laws on security interests to be found in the Community. Furthermore, the preferential rights enjoyed by some creditors in the insolvency proceedings are, in some cases, completely different. This Regulation should take account of this in two different ways. On the one hand, provision should be made for special rules on applicable law in the case of particularly significant rights and legal relationships (eg rights in rem and contracts of employment). On the other hand, national proceedings covering only assets situated in the State of opening should also be allowed alongside main insolvency proceedings with universal scope.

(12) This Regulation enables the main insolvency proceedings to be opened in the Member State where the debtor has the centre of his main interests. These proceedings have universal scope and aim at encompassing all the debtor's assets. To protect the diversity of interests, this Regulation permits secondary proceedings to be opened to run in parallel with the main proceedings. Secondary proceedings may be opened in the Member State where the debtor has an establishment. The effects of secondary proceedings are limited to the assets located in that State. Mandatory rules of coordination with the main proceedings satisfy the need for unity in the Community.

(13) The "centre of main interests" should correspond to the place where the debtor conducts the administration of his interests on a regular basis and is therefore ascertainable by third parties.

(14) This Regulation applies only to proceedings where the centre of the debtor's main interests is located in the Community.

(15) The rules of jurisdiction set out in this Regulation establish only international jurisdiction, that is to say, they designate the Member State the courts of which may open insolvency proceedings. Territorial jurisdiction within that Member State must be established by the national law of the Member State concerned.

(16) The court having jurisdiction to open the main insolvency proceedings should be enabled to order provisional and protective measures from the time of the request to open proceedings. Preservation measures both prior to and after the commencement of the insolvency proceedings are very important to guarantee the effectiveness of the insolvency proceedings. In that connection this Regulation should afford different possibilities. On the one hand, the court competent for the main insolvency proceedings should be able also to order provisional protective measures covering assets situated in the territory of other Member States. On the other hand, a liquidator temporarily appointed prior to the opening of the main insolvency proceedings should be able, in the Member States in which an establishment belonging to the debtor is to be found, to apply for the preservation measures which are possible under the law of those States.

(17) Prior to the opening of the main insolvency proceedings, the right to request the opening of insolvency proceedings in the Member State where the debtor has an establishment should be limited to local creditors and creditors of the local establishment or to cases where main proceedings cannot be opened under the law of the Member State where the debtor has the centre of his main interest. The reason for this restriction is that cases where territorial insolvency proceedings are requested before the main insolvency proceedings are intended to be limited to what is absolutely necessary. If the main insolvency proceedings are opened, the territorial proceedings become secondary.

(18) Following the opening of the main insolvency proceedings, the right to request the opening of insolvency proceedings in a Member State where the debtor has an establishment is not restricted by this Regulation. The liquidator in the main proceedings or any other person empowered under the national law of that Member State may request the opening of secondary insolvency proceedings.

(19) Secondary insolvency proceedings may serve different purposes, besides the protection of local interests. Cases may arise where the estate of the debtor is too complex to administer as a unit or where differences in the legal systems concerned are so great that difficulties may arise from the extension of effects deriving from the law of the State of the opening to the other States where the assets are located. For this reason the liquidator in the main proceedings may request the opening of secondary proceedings when the efficient administration of the estate so requires.

(20) Main insolvency proceedings and secondary proceedings can, however, contribute to the effective realisation of the total assets only if all the concurrent proceedings pending are coordinated. The main condition here is that the various liquidators must cooperate closely, in particular by exchanging a sufficient amount of information. In order to ensure the dominant role of the main insolvency proceedings, the liquidator in such proceedings should be given several possibilities for intervening in secondary insolvency proceedings which are pending at the same time. For example, he should be able to propose a restructuring plan or composition or apply for realisation of the assets in the secondary insolvency proceedings to be suspended.

(21) Every creditor, who has his habitual residence, domicile or registered office in the Community, should have the right to lodge his claims in each of the insolvency proceedings pending in the Community relating to the debtor's assets. This should also apply to tax authorities and social insurance institutions. However, in order to ensure equal treatment of creditors, the distribution of proceeds must be coordinated. Every creditor should be able to keep what he has received in the course of insolvency proceedings but should be entitled only to participate in the distribution of total assets in other proceedings if creditors with the same standing have obtained the same proportion of their claims.

(22) This Regulation should provide for immediate recognition of judgments concerning the opening, conduct and closure of insolvency proceedings which come within its scope and of

judgments handed down in direct connection with such insolvency proceedings. Automatic recognition should therefore mean that the effects attributed to the proceedings by the law of the State in which the proceedings were opened extend to all other Member States. Recognition of judgments delivered by the courts of the Member States should be based on the principle of mutual trust. To that end, grounds for non-recognition should be reduced to the minimum necessary. This is also the basis on which any dispute should be resolved where the courts of two Member States both claim competence to open the main insolvency proceedings. The decision of the first court to open proceedings should be recognised in the other Member States without those Member States having the power to scrutinise the court's decision.

(23) This Regulation should set out, for the matters covered by it, uniform rules on conflict of laws which replace, within their scope of application, national rules of private international law. Unless otherwise stated, the law of the Member State of the opening of the proceedings should be applicable (lex concursus). This rule on conflict of laws should be valid both for the main proceedings and for local proceedings; the lex concursus determines all the effects of the insolvency proceedings, both procedural and substantive, on the persons and legal relations concerned. It governs all the conditions for the opening, conduct and closure of the insolvency proceedings.

(24) Automatic recognition of insolvency proceedings to which the law of the opening State normally applies may interfere with the rules under which transactions are carried out in other Member States. To protect legitimate expectations and the certainty of transactions in Member States other than that in which proceedings are opened, provisions should be made for a number of exceptions to the general rule.

(25) There is a particular need for a special reference diverging from the law of the opening State in the case of rights in rem, since these are of considerable importance for the granting of credit. The basis, validity and extent of such a right in rem should therefore normally be determined according to the lex situs and not be affected by the opening of insolvency proceedings. The proprietor of the right in rem should therefore be able to continue to assert his right to segregation or separate settlement of the collateral security. Where assets are subject to rights in rem under the lex situs in one Member State but the main proceedings are being carried out in another Member State, the liquidator in the main proceedings should be able to request the opening of secondary proceedings in the jurisdiction where the rights in rem arise if the debtor has an establishment there. If a secondary proceeding is not opened, the surplus on sale of the asset covered by rights in rem must be paid to the liquidator in the main proceedings.

(26) If a set-off is not permitted under the law of the opening State, a creditor should nevertheless be entitled to the set-off if it is possible under the law applicable to the claim of the insolvent debtor. In this way, set-off will acquire a kind of guarantee function based on legal provisions on which the creditor concerned can rely at the time when the claim arises.

(27) There is also a need for special protection in the case of payment systems and financial markets. This applies for example to the position-closing agreements and netting agreements to be found in such systems as well as to the sale of securities and to the guarantees provided for such transactions as governed in particular by Directive 98/26/EC of the European Parliament and of the Council of 19 May 1998 on settlement finality in payment and securities settlement systems.[5] For such transactions, the only law which is material should thus be that applicable to the system or market concerned. This provision is intended to prevent the possibility of mechanisms for the payment and settlement of transactions provided for in the payment and set-off systems or on the regulated financial markets of the Member States being altered in the case of insolvency of a business partner. Directive 98/26/EC contains special provisions which should take precedence over the general rules in this Regulation.

(28) In order to protect employees and jobs, the effects of insolvency proceedings on the continuation or termination of employment and on the rights and obligations of all parties to such employment must be determined by the law applicable to the agreement in accordance with the general rules on conflict of law. Any other insolvency-law questions, such as whether the employees' claims are protected by preferential rights and what status such preferential rights may have, should be determined by the law of the opening State.

(29) For business considerations, the main content of the decision opening the proceedings should be published in the other Member States at the request of the liquidator. If there is an establishment in the Member State concerned, there may be a requirement that publication is compulsory. In neither case, however, should publication be a prior condition for recognition of the foreign proceedings.

(30) It may be the case that some of the persons concerned are not in fact aware that proceedings have been opened and act in good faith in a way that conflicts with the new situation. In order to protect such persons who make a payment to the debtor because they are unaware that foreign proceedings have been opened when they should in fact have made the payment to the foreign liquidator, it should be provided that such a payment is to have a debt-discharging effect.

(31) This Regulation should include Annexes relating to the organisation of insolvency proceedings. As these Annexes relate exclusively to the legislation of Member States, there are specific and substantiated reasons for the Council to reserve the right to amend these Annexes in order to take account of any amendments to the domestic law of the Member States.

(32) The United Kingdom and Ireland, in accordance with Article 3 of the Protocol on the position of the United Kingdom and Ireland annexed to the Treaty on European Union and the Treaty establishing the European Community, have given notice of their wish to take part in the adoption and application of this Regulation.

(33) Denmark, in accordance with Articles 1 and 2 of the Protocol on the position of Denmark annexed to the Treaty on European Union and the Treaty establishing the European Community, is

not participating in the adoption of this Regulation, and is therefore not bound by it nor subject to its application,

NOTES

1   Opinion delivered on 2 March 2000 (not yet published in the Official Journal).

2   Opinion delivered on 26 January 2000 (not yet published in the Official Journal).

3   OJ L299, 31.12.1972, p 32.

4   OJ L204, 2.8.1975, p 28; OJ L304, 30.10.1978, p 1; OJ L388, 31.12.1982, p 1; OJ L285, 3.10.1989, p 1; OJ C15, 15.1.1997, p 1.

5   OJ L166, 11.6.1998, p 45.

HAS ADOPTED THIS REGULATION—

CHAPTER I
GENERAL PROVISIONS

[11.74]
Article 1
Scope
1.   This Regulation shall apply to collective insolvency proceedings which entail the partial or total divestment of a debtor and the appointment of a liquidator.
2.   This Regulation shall not apply to insolvency proceedings concerning insurance undertakings, credit institutions, investment undertakings which provide services involving the holding of funds or securities for third parties, or to collective investment undertakings.

[11.75]
Article 2
Definitions
For the purposes of this Regulation—
   (a)   "insolvency proceedings" shall mean the collective proceedings referred to in Article 1(1). These proceedings are listed in Annex A;
   (b)   "liquidator" shall mean any person or body whose function is to administer or liquidate assets of which the debtor has been divested or to supervise the administration of his affairs. Those persons and bodies are listed in Annex C;
   (c)   "winding-up proceedings" shall mean insolvency proceedings within the meaning of point (a) involving realising the assets of the debtor, including where the proceedings have been closed by a composition or other measure terminating the insolvency, or closed by reason of the insufficiency of the assets. Those proceedings are listed in Annex B;
   (d)   "court" shall mean the judicial body or any other competent body of a Member State empowered to open insolvency proceedings or to take decisions in the course of such proceedings;
   (e)   "judgment" in relation to the opening of insolvency proceedings or the appointment of a liquidator shall include the decision of any court empowered to open such proceedings or to appoint a liquidator;
   (f)   "the time of the opening of proceedings" shall mean the time at which the judgment opening proceedings becomes effective, whether it is a final judgment or not;
   (g)   "the Member State in which assets are situated" shall mean, in the case of:
         —   tangible property, the Member State within the territory of which the property is situated,
         —   property and rights ownership of or entitlement to which must be entered in a public register, the Member State under the authority of which the register is kept,
         —   claims, the Member State within the territory of which the third party required to meet them has the centre of his main interests, as determined in Article 3(1);
   (h)   "establishment" shall mean any place of operations where the debtor carries out a non-transitory economic activity with human means and goods.

[11.76]
Article 3
International jurisdiction
1.   The courts of the Member State within the territory of which the centre of a debtor's main interests is situated shall have jurisdiction to open insolvency proceedings. In the case of a company or legal person, the place of the registered office shall be presumed to be the centre of its main interests in the absence of proof to the contrary.
2.   Where the centre of a debtor's main interests is situated within the territory of a Member State, the courts of another Member State shall have jurisdiction to open insolvency proceedings against that debtor only if he possesses an establishment within the territory of that other Member State. The effects of those proceedings shall be restricted to the assets of the debtor situated in the territory of the latter Member State.

3. Where insolvency proceedings have been opened under paragraph 1, any proceedings opened subsequently under paragraph 2 shall be secondary proceedings. These latter proceedings must be winding-up proceedings.

4. Territorial insolvency proceedings referred to in paragraph 2 may be opened prior to the opening of main insolvency proceedings in accordance with paragraph 1 only:

    (a) where insolvency proceedings under paragraph 1 cannot be opened because of the conditions laid down by the law of the Member State within the territory of which the centre of the debtor's main interests is situated; or

    (b) where the opening of territorial insolvency proceedings is requested by a creditor who has his domicile, habitual residence or registered office in the Member State within the territory of which the establishment is situated, or whose claim arises from the operation of that establishment.

[11.77]
Article 4
Law applicable

1. Save as otherwise provided in this Regulation, the law applicable to insolvency proceedings and their effects shall be that of the Member State within the territory of which such proceedings are opened, hereafter referred to as the "State of the opening of proceedings".

2. The law of the State of the opening of proceedings shall determine the conditions for the opening of those proceedings, their conduct and their closure. It shall determine in particular:

    (a) against which debtors insolvency proceedings may be brought on account of their capacity;

    (b) the assets which form part of the estate and the treatment of assets acquired by or devolving on the debtor after the opening of the insolvency proceedings;

    (c) the respective powers of the debtor and the liquidator;

    (d) the conditions under which set-offs may be invoked;

    (e) the effects of insolvency proceedings on current contracts to which the debtor is party;

    (f) the effects of the insolvency proceedings on proceedings brought by individual creditors, with the exception of lawsuits pending;

    (g) the claims which are to be lodged against the debtor's estate and the treatment of claims arising after the opening of insolvency proceedings;

    (h) the rules governing the lodging, verification and admission of claims;

    (i) the rules governing the distribution of proceeds from the realisation of assets, the ranking of claims and the rights of creditors who have obtained partial satisfaction after the opening of insolvency proceedings by virtue of a right in rem or through a set-off;

    (j) the conditions for and the effects of closure of insolvency proceedings, in particular by composition;

    (k) creditors' rights after the closure of insolvency proceedings;

    (l) who is to bear the costs and expenses incurred in the insolvency proceedings;

    (m) the rules relating to the voidness, voidability or unenforceability of legal acts detrimental to all the creditors.

[11.78]
Article 5
Third parties' rights in rem

1. The opening of insolvency proceedings shall not affect the rights in rem of creditors or third parties in respect of tangible or intangible, moveable or immoveable assets—both specific assets and collections of indefinite assets as a whole which change from time to time—belonging to the debtor which are situated within the territory of another Member State at the time of the opening of proceedings.

2. The rights referred to in paragraph 1 shall in particular mean:

    (a) the right to dispose of assets or have them disposed of and to obtain satisfaction from the proceeds of or income from those assets, in particular by virtue of a lien or a mortgage;

    (b) the exclusive right to have a claim met, in particular a right guaranteed by a lien in respect of the claim or by assignment of the claim by way of a guarantee;

    (c) the right to demand the assets from, and/or to require restitution by, anyone having possession or use of them contrary to the wishes of the party so entitled;

    (d) a right in rem to the beneficial use of assets.

3. The right, recorded in a public register and enforceable against third parties, under which a right in rem within the meaning of paragraph 1 may be obtained, shall be considered a right in rem.

4. Paragraph 1 shall not preclude actions for voidness, voidability or unenforceability as referred to in Article 4(2)(m).

[11.79]
Article 6
Set-off

1. The opening of insolvency proceedings shall not affect the right of creditors to demand the set-off of their claims against the claims of the debtor, where such a set-off is permitted by the law applicable to the insolvent debtor's claim.

2.   Paragraph 1 shall not preclude actions for voidness, voidability or unenforceability as referred to in Article 4(2)(m).

[11.80]
Article 7
Reservation of title
1.   The opening of insolvency proceedings against the purchaser of an asset shall not affect the seller's rights based on a reservation of title where at the time of the opening of proceedings the asset is situated within the territory of a Member State other than the State of opening of proceedings.
2.   The opening of insolvency proceedings against the seller of an asset, after delivery of the asset, shall not constitute grounds for rescinding or terminating the sale and shall not prevent the purchaser from acquiring title where at the time of the opening of proceedings the asset sold is situated within the territory of a Member State other than the State of the opening of proceedings.
3.   Paragraphs 1 and 2 shall not preclude actions for voidness, voidability or unenforceability as referred to in Article 4(2)(m).

[11.81]
Article 8
Contracts relating to immoveable property
The effects of insolvency proceedings on a contract conferring the right to acquire or make use of immoveable property shall be governed solely by the law of the Member State within the territory of which the immoveable property is situated.

[11.82]
Article 9
Payment systems and financial markets
1.   Without prejudice to Article 5, the effects of insolvency proceedings on the rights and obligations of the parties to a payment or settlement system or to a financial market shall be governed solely by the law of the Member State applicable to that system or market.
2.   Paragraph 1 shall not preclude any action for voidness, voidability or unenforceability which may be taken to set aside payments or transactions under the law applicable to the relevant payment system or financial market.

[11.83]
Article 10
Contracts of employment
The effects of insolvency proceedings on employment contracts and relationships shall be governed solely by the law of the Member State applicable to the contract of employment.

[11.84]
Article 11
Effects on rights subject to registration
The effects of insolvency proceedings on the rights of the debtor in immoveable property, a ship or an aircraft subject to registration in a public register shall be determined by the law of the Member State under the authority of which the register is kept.

[11.85]
Article 12
Community patents and trade marks
For the purposes of this Regulation, a Community patent, a Community trade mark or any other similar right established by Community law may be included only in the proceedings referred to in Article 3(1).

[11.86]
Article 13
Detrimental acts
Article 4(2)(m) shall not apply where the person who benefited from an act detrimental to all the creditors provides proof that:
—   the said act is subject to the law of a Member State other than that of the State of the opening of proceedings, and
—   that law does not allow any means of challenging that act in the relevant case.

[11.87]
Article 14
Protection of third-party purchasers
Where, by an act concluded after the opening of insolvency proceedings, the debtor disposes, for consideration, of:
—   an immoveable asset, or
—   a ship or an aircraft subject to registration in a public register, or
—   securities whose existence presupposes registration in a register laid down by law,

the validity of that act shall be governed by the law of the State within the territory of which the immoveable asset is situated or under the authority of which the register is kept.

[11.88]
Article 15
Effects of insolvency proceedings on lawsuits pending
The effects of insolvency proceedings on a lawsuit pending concerning an asset or a right of which the debtor has been divested shall be governed solely by the law of the Member State in which that lawsuit is pending.

CHAPTER II
RECOGNITION OF INSOLVENCY PROCEEDINGS

[11.89]
Article 16
Principle
1. Any judgment opening insolvency proceedings handed down by a court of a Member State which has jurisdiction pursuant to Article 3 shall be recognised in all the other Member States from the time that it becomes effective in the State of the opening of proceedings.

This rule shall also apply where, on account of his capacity, insolvency proceedings cannot be brought against the debtor in other Member States.
2. Recognition of the proceedings referred to in Article 3(1) shall not preclude the opening of the proceedings referred to in Article 3(2) by a court in another Member State. The latter proceedings shall be secondary insolvency proceedings within the meaning of Chapter III.

[11.90]
Article 17
Effects of recognition
1. The judgment opening the proceedings referred to in Article 3(1) shall, with no further formalities, produce the same effects in any other Member State as under this law of the State of the opening of proceedings, unless this Regulation provides otherwise and as long as no proceedings referred to in Article 3(2) are opened in that other Member State.
2. The effects of the proceedings referred to in Article 3(2) may not be challenged in other Member States. Any restriction of the creditors' rights, in particular a stay or discharge, shall produce effects vis-à-vis assets situated within the territory of another Member State only in the case of those creditors who have given their consent.

[11.91]
Article 18
Powers of the liquidator
1. The liquidator appointed by a court which has jurisdiction pursuant to Article 3(1) may exercise all the powers conferred on him by the law of the State of the opening of proceedings in another Member State, as long as no other insolvency proceedings have been opened there nor any preservation measure to the contrary has been taken there further to a request for the opening of insolvency proceedings in that State. He may in particular remove the debtor's assets from the territory of the Member State in which they are situated, subject to Articles 5 and 7.
2. The liquidator appointed by a court which has jurisdiction pursuant to Article 3(2) may in any other Member State claim through the courts or out of court that moveable property was removed from the territory of the State of the opening of proceedings to the territory of that other Member State after the opening of the insolvency proceedings. He may also bring any action to set aside which is in the interests of the creditors.
3. In exercising his powers, the liquidator shall comply with the law of the Member State within the territory of which he intends to take action, in particular with regard to procedures for the realisation of assets. Those powers may not include coercive measures or the right to rule on legal proceedings or disputes.

[11.92]
Article 19
Proof of the liquidator's appointment
The liquidator's appointment shall be evidenced by a certified copy of the original decision appointing him or by any other certificate issued by the court which has jurisdiction.

A translation into the official language or one of the official languages of the Member State within the territory of which he intends to act may be required. No legalisation or other similar formality shall be required.

Part 11   EU Legislation

[11.93]
Article 20
Return and imputation
1. A creditor who, after the opening of the proceedings referred to in Article 3(1) obtains by any means, in particular through enforcement, total or partial satisfaction of his claim on the assets belonging to the debtor situated within the territory of another Member State, shall return what he has obtained to the liquidator, subject to Articles 5 and 7.
2. In order to ensure equal treatment of creditors a creditor who has, in the course of insolvency proceedings, obtained a dividend on his claim shall share in distributions made in other proceedings only where creditors of the same ranking or category have, in those other proceedings, obtained an equivalent dividend.

[11.94]
Article 21
Publication
1. The liquidator may request that notice of the judgment opening insolvency proceedings and, where appropriate, the decision appointing him, be published in any other Member State in accordance with the publication procedures provided for in that State. Such publication shall also specify the liquidator appointed and whether the jurisdiction rule applied is that pursuant to Article 3(1) or Article 3(2).
2. However, any Member State within the territory of which the debtor has an establishment may require mandatory publication. In such cases, the liquidator or any authority empowered to that effect in the Member State where the proceedings referred to in Article 3(1) are opened shall take all necessary measures to ensure such publication.

[11.95]
Article 22
Registration in a public register
1. The liquidator may request that the judgment opening the proceedings referred to in Article 3(1) be registered in the land register, the trade register and any other public register kept in the other Member States.
2. However, any Member State may require mandatory registration. In such cases, the liquidator or any authority empowered to that effect in the Member State where the proceedings referred to in Article 3(1) have been opened shall take all necessary measures to ensure such registration.

[11.96]
Article 23
Costs
The costs of the publication and registration provided for in Articles 21 and 22 shall be regarded as costs and expenses incurred in the proceedings.

[11.97]
Article 24
Honouring of an obligation to a debtor
1. Where an obligation has been honoured in a Member State for the benefit of a debtor who is subject to insolvency proceedings opened in another Member State, when it should have been honoured for the benefit of the liquidator in those proceedings, the person honouring the obligation shall be deemed to have discharged it if he was unaware of the opening of proceedings.
2. Where such an obligation is honoured before the publication provided for in Article 21 has been effected, the person honouring the obligation shall be presumed, in the absence of proof to the contrary, to have been unaware of the opening of insolvency proceedings; where the obligation is honoured after such publication has been effected, the person honouring the obligation shall be presumed, in the absence of proof to the contrary, to have been aware of the opening of proceedings.

[11.98]
Article 25
Recognition and enforceability of other judgments
1. Judgments handed down by a court whose judgment concerning the opening of proceedings is recognised in accordance with Article 16 and which concern the course and closure of insolvency proceedings, and compositions approved by that court shall also be recognised with no further formalities. Such judgments shall be enforced in accordance with Articles 31 to 51, with the exception of Article 34(2), of the Brussels Convention on Jurisdiction and the Enforcement of Judgments in Civil and Commercial Matters, as amended by the Conventions of Accession to this Convention.
   The first subparagraph shall also apply to judgments deriving directly from the insolvency proceedings and which are closely linked with them, even if they were handed down by another court.
   The first subparagraph shall also apply to judgments relating to preservation measures taken after the request for the opening of insolvency proceedings.

2.   The recognition and enforcement of judgments other than those referred to in paragraph 1 shall be governed by the Convention referred to in paragraph 1, provided that that Convention is applicable.

3.   The Member States shall not be obliged to recognise or enforce a judgment referred to in paragraph 1 which might result in a limitation of personal freedom or postal secrecy.

[11.99]
Article 26[1]
Public policy
Any Member State may refuse to recognise insolvency proceedings opened in another Member State or to enforce a judgment handed down in the context of such proceedings where the effects of such recognition or enforcement would be manifestly contrary to that State's public policy, in particular its fundamental principles or the constitutional rights and liberties of the individual.

NOTES

   [1]   Note the Declaration by Portugal concerning the application of Articles 26 and 37 (OJ C183, 30.6.2000, p 1).

CHAPTER III
SECONDARY INSOLVENCY PROCEEDINGS

[11.100]
Article 27
Opening of proceedings
The opening of the proceedings referred to in Article 3(1) by a court of a Member State and which is recognised in another Member State (main proceedings) shall permit the opening in that other Member State, a court of which has jurisdiction pursuant to Article 3(2), of secondary insolvency proceedings without the debtor's insolvency being examined in that other State. These latter proceedings must be among the proceedings listed in Annex B. Their effects shall be restricted to the assets of the debtor situated within the territory of that other Member State.

[11.101]
Article 28
Applicable law
Save as otherwise provided in this Regulation, the law applicable to secondary proceedings shall be that of the Member State within the territory of which the secondary proceedings are opened.

[11.102]
Article 29
Right to request the opening of proceedings
The opening of secondary proceedings may be requested by:
    (a)   the liquidator in the main proceedings;
    (b)   any other person or authority empowered to request the opening of insolvency proceedings under the law of the Member State within the territory of which the opening of secondary proceedings is requested.

[11.103]
Article 30
Advance payment of costs and expenses
Where the law of the Member State in which the opening of secondary proceedings is requested requires that the debtor's assets be sufficient to cover in whole or in part the costs and expenses of the proceedings, the court may, when it receives such a request, require the applicant to make an advance payment of costs or to provide appropriate security.

[11.104]
Article 31
Duty to cooperate and communicate information
1.   Subject to the rules restricting the communication of information, the liquidator in the main proceedings and the liquidators in the secondary proceedings shall be duty bound to communicate information to each other. They shall immediately communicate any information which may be relevant to the other proceedings, in particular the progress made in lodging and verifying claims and all measures aimed at terminating the proceedings.

2.   Subject to the rules applicable to each of the proceedings, the liquidator in the main proceedings and the liquidators in the secondary proceedings shall be duty bound to cooperate with each other.

3.   The liquidator in the secondary proceedings shall give the liquidator in the main proceedings an early opportunity of submitting proposals on the liquidation or use of the assets in the secondary proceedings.

[11.105]
Article 32
Exercise of creditors' rights
1.   Any creditor may lodge his claim in the main proceedings and in any secondary proceedings.
2.   The liquidators in the main and any secondary proceedings shall lodge in other proceedings claims which have already been lodged in the proceedings for which they were appointed, provided that the interests of creditors in the latter proceedings are served thereby, subject to the right of creditors to oppose that or to withdraw the lodgement of their claims where the law applicable so provides.
3.   The liquidator in the main or secondary proceedings shall be empowered to participate in other proceedings on the same basis as a creditor, in particular by attending creditors' meetings.

[11.106]
Article 33
Stay of liquidation
1.   The court, which opened the secondary proceedings, shall stay the process of liquidation in whole or in part on receipt of a request from the liquidator in the main proceedings, provided that in that event it may require the liquidator in the main proceedings to take any suitable measure to guarantee the interests of the creditors in the secondary proceedings and of individual classes of creditors. Such a request from the liquidator may be rejected only if it is manifestly of no interest to the creditors in the main proceedings. Such a stay of the process of liquidation may be ordered for up to three months. It may be continued or renewed for similar periods.
2.   The court referred to in paragraph 1 shall terminate the stay of the process of liquidation:
   —   at the request of the liquidator in the main proceedings,
   —   of its own motion, at the request of a creditor or at the request of the liquidator in the secondary proceedings if that measure no longer appears justified, in particular, by the interests of creditors in the main proceedings or in the secondary proceedings.

[11.107]
Article 34
Measures ending secondary insolvency proceedings
1.   Where the law applicable to secondary proceedings allows for such proceedings to be closed without liquidation by a rescue plan, a composition or a comparable measure, the liquidator in the main proceedings shall be empowered to propose such a measure himself.
   Closure of the secondary proceedings by a measure referred to in the first subparagraph shall not become final without the consent of the liquidator in the main proceedings; failing his agreement, however, it may become final if the financial interests of the creditors in the main proceedings are not affected by the measure proposed.
2.   Any restriction of creditors' rights arising from a measure referred to in paragraph 1 which is proposed in secondary proceedings, such as a stay of payment or discharge of debt, may not have effect in respect of the debtor's assets not covered by those proceedings without the consent of all the creditors having an interest.
3.   During a stay of the process of liquidation ordered pursuant to Article 33, only the liquidator in the main proceedings or the debtor, with the former's consent, may propose measures laid down in paragraph 1 of this Article in the secondary proceedings; no other proposal for such a measure shall be put to the vote or approved.

[11.108]
Article 35
Assets remaining in the secondary proceedings
If by the liquidation of assets in the secondary proceedings it is possible to meet all claims allowed under those proceedings, the liquidator appointed in those proceedings shall immediately transfer any assets remaining to the liquidator in the main proceedings.

[11.109]
Article 36
Subsequent opening of the main proceedings
Where the proceedings referred to in Article 3(1) are opened following the opening of the proceedings referred to in Article 3(2) in another Member State, Articles 31 to 35 shall apply to those opened first, in so far as the progress of those proceedings so permits.

[11.110]
Article 37[1]
Conversion of earlier proceedings
The liquidator in the main proceedings may request that proceedings listed in Annex A previously opened in another Member State be converted into winding-up proceedings if this proves to be in the interests of the creditors in the main proceedings.
   The court with jurisdiction under Article 3(2) shall order conversion into one of the proceedings listed in Annex B.

NOTES

[1]   Note the Declaration by Portugal concerning the application of Articles 26 and 37 (OJ C183, 30.6.2000, p 1).

[11.111]
Article 38
Preservation measures
Where the court of a Member State which has jurisdiction pursuant to Article 3(1) appoints a temporary administrator in order to ensure the preservation of the debtor's assets, that temporary administrator shall be empowered to request any measures to secure and preserve any of the debtor's assets situated in another Member State, provided for under the law of that State, for the period between the request for the opening of insolvency proceedings and the judgment opening the proceedings.

CHAPTER IV
PROVISION OF INFORMATION FOR CREDITORS AND LODGEMENT OF THEIR CLAIMS

[11.112]
Article 39
Right to lodge claims
Any creditor who has his habitual residence, domicile or registered office in a Member State other than the State of the opening of proceedings, including the tax authorities and social security authorities of Member States, shall have the right to lodge claims in the insolvency proceedings in writing.

[11.113]
Article 40
Duty to inform creditors
1. As soon as insolvency proceedings are opened in a Member State, the court of that State having jurisdiction or the liquidator appointed by it shall immediately inform known creditors who have their habitual residences, domiciles or registered offices in the other Member States.
2. That information, provided by an individual notice, shall in particular include time limits, the penalties laid down in regard to those time limits, the body or authority empowered to accept the lodgement of claims and the other measures laid down. Such notice shall also indicate whether creditors whose claims are preferential or secured in rem need lodge their claims.

[11.114]
Article 41
Content of the lodgement of a claim
A creditor shall send copies of supporting documents, if any, and shall indicate the nature of the claim, the date on which it arose and its amount, as well as whether he alleges preference, security in rem or a reservation of title in respect of the claim and what assets are covered by the guarantee he is invoking.

[11.115]
Article 42
Languages
1. The information provided for in Article 40 shall be provided in the official language or one of the official languages of the State of the opening of proceedings. For that purpose a form shall be used bearing the heading "Invitation to lodge a claim. Time limits to be observed" in all the official languages of the institutions of the European Union.
2. Any creditor who has his habitual residence, domicile or registered office in a Member State other than the State of the opening of proceedings may lodge his claim in the official language or one of the official languages of that other State. In that event, however, the lodgement of his claim shall bear the heading "Lodgement of claim" in the official language or one of the official languages of the State of the opening of proceedings. In addition, he may be required to provide a translation into the official language or one of the official languages of the State of the opening of proceedings.

CHAPTER V
TRANSITIONAL AND FINAL PROVISIONS

[11.116]
Article 43
Applicability in time
The provisions of this Regulation shall apply only to insolvency proceedings opened after its entry into force. Acts done by a debtor before the entry into force of this Regulation shall continue to be governed by the law which was applicable to them at the time they were done.

[11.117]
Article 44
Relationship to Conventions
1.   After its entry into force, this Regulation replaces, in respect of the matters referred to therein, in the relations between Member States, the Conventions concluded between two or more Member States, in particular:

(a)   the Convention between Belgium and France on Jurisdiction and the Validity and Enforcement of Judgments, Arbitration Awards and Authentic Instruments, signed at Paris on 8 July 1899;

(b)   the Convention between Belgium and Austria on Bankruptcy, Winding-up, Arrangements, Compositions and Suspension of Payments (with Additional Protocol of 13 June 1973), signed at Brussels on 16 July 1969;

(c)   the Convention between Belgium and the Netherlands on Territorial Jurisdiction, Bankruptcy and the Validity and Enforcement of Judgments, Arbitration Awards and Authentic Instruments, signed at Brussels on 28 March 1925;

(d)   the Treaty between Germany and Austria on Bankruptcy, Winding-up, Arrangements and Compositions, signed at Vienna on 25 May 1979;

(e)   the Convention between France and Austria on Jurisdiction, Recognition and Enforcement of Judgments on Bankruptcy, signed at Vienna on 27 February 1979;

(f)   the Convention between France and Italy on the Enforcement of Judgments in Civil and Commercial Matters, signed at Rome on 3 June 1930;

(g)   the Convention between Italy and Austria on Bankruptcy, Winding-up, Arrangements and Compositions, signed at Rome on 12 July 1977;

(h)   the Convention between the Kingdom of the Netherlands and the Federal Republic of Germany on the Mutual Recognition and Enforcement of Judgments and other Enforceable Instruments in Civil and Commercial Matters, signed at The Hague on 30 August 1962;

(i)   the Convention between the United Kingdom and the Kingdom of Belgium providing for the Reciprocal Enforcement of Judgments in Civil and Commercial Matters, with Protocol, signed at Brussels on 2 May 1934;

(j)   the Convention between Denmark, Finland, Norway, Sweden and Iceland on Bankruptcy, signed at Copenhagen on 7 November 1933;

(k)   the European Convention on Certain International Aspects of Bankruptcy, signed at Istanbul on 5 June 1990;

[(l)   the Convention between the Federative People's Republic of Yugoslavia and the Kingdom of Greece on the Mutual Recognition and Enforcement of Judgments, signed at Athens on 18 June 1959;

(m)   the Agreement between the Federative People's Republic of Yugoslavia and the Republic of Austria on the Mutual Recognition and Enforcement of Arbitral Awards and Arbitral Settlements in Commercial Matters, signed at Belgrade on 18 March 1960;

(n)   the Convention between the Federative People's Republic of Yugoslavia and the Republic of Italy on Mutual Judicial Cooperation in Civil and Administrative Matters, signed at Rome on 3 December 1960;

(o)   the Agreement between the Socialist Federative Republic of Yugoslavia and the Kingdom of Belgium on Judicial Cooperation in Civil and Commercial Matters, signed at Belgrade on 24 September 1971;

(p)   the Convention between the Governments of Yugoslavia and France on the Recognition and Enforcement of Judgments in Civil and Commercial Matters, signed at Paris on 18 May 1971;

(q)   the Agreement between the Czechoslovak Socialist Republic and the Hellenic Republic on Legal Aid in Civil and Criminal Matters, signed at Athens on 22 October 1980, still in force between the Czech Republic and Greece;

(r)   the Agreement between the Czechoslovak Socialist Republic and the Republic of Cyprus on Legal Aid in Civil and Criminal Matters, signed at Nicosia on 23 April 1982, still in force between the Czech Republic and Cyprus;

(s)   the Treaty between the Government of the Czechoslovak Socialist Republic and the Government of the Republic of France on Legal Aid and the Recognition and Enforcement of Judgments in Civil, Family and Commercial Matters, signed at Paris on 10 May 1984, still in force between the Czech Republic and France;

(t)   the Treaty between the Czechoslovak Socialist Republic and the Italian Republic on Legal Aid in Civil and Criminal Matters, signed at Prague on 6 December 1985, still in force between the Czech Republic and Italy;

(u)   the Agreement between the Republic of Latvia, the Republic of Estonia and the Republic of Lithuania on Legal Assistance and Legal Relationships, signed at Tallinn on 11 November 1992;

(v)   the Agreement between Estonia and Poland on Granting Legal Aid and Legal Relations on Civil, Labour and Criminal Matters, signed at Tallinn on 27 November 1998;

(w)   the Agreement between the Republic of Lithuania and the Republic of Poland on Legal Assistance and Legal Relations in Civil, Family, Labour and Criminal Matters, signed in Warsaw on 26 January 1993;]

[(x)   the Convention between Socialist Republic of Romania and the Hellenic Republic on legal assistance in civil and criminal matters and its Protocol, signed at Bucharest on 19 October 1972;

(y)   the Convention between Socialist Republic of Romania and the French Republic on legal assistance in civil and commercial matters, signed at Paris on 5 November 1974;

(z)   the Agreement between the People's Republic of Bulgaria and the Hellenic Republic on Legal Assistance in Civil and Criminal Matters, signed at Athens on 10 April 1976;

(aa)   the Agreement between the People's Republic of Bulgaria and the Republic of Cyprus on Legal Assistance in Civil and Criminal Matters, signed at Nicosia on 29 April 1983;

(ab)   the Agreement between the Government of the People's Republic of Bulgaria and the Government of the French Republic on Mutual Legal Assistance in Civil Matters, signed at Sofia on 18 January 1989;

(ac)   the Treaty between Romania and the Czech Republic on judicial assistance in civil matters, signed at Bucharest on 11 July 1994;

(ad)   the Treaty between Romania and Poland on legal assistance and legal relations in civil cases, signed at Bucharest on 15 May 1999.]

2.   The Conventions referred to in paragraph 1 shall continue to have effect with regard to proceedings opened before the entry into force of this Regulation.

3.   This Regulation shall not apply:

(a)   in any Member State, to the extent that it is irreconcilable with the obligations arising in relation to bankruptcy from a convention concluded by that State with one or more third countries before the entry into force of this Regulation;

(b)   in the United Kingdom of Great Britain and Northern Ireland, to the extent that is irreconcilable with the obligations arising in relation to bankruptcy and the winding-up of insolvent companies from any arrangements with the Commonwealth existing at the time this Regulation enters into force.

NOTES

Para 1: sub-paras (l)–(w) added by AA5, as from 1 May 2004; sub-paras (x)–(ad) added by Council Regulation 1791/2006/EC, Art 1, Annex, as from 1 January 2007.

[11.118]
Article 45
Amendment of the Annexes

The Council, acting by qualified majority on the initiative of one of its members or on a proposal from the Commission, may amend the Annexes.

[11.119]
Article 46
Reports

No later than 1 June 2012, and every five years thereafter, the Commission shall present to the European Parliament, the Council and the Economic and Social Committee a report on the application of this Regulation. The report shall be accompanied if need be by a proposal for adaptation of this Regulation.

[11.120]
Article 47
Entry into force

This Regulation shall enter into force on 31 May 2002.

This Regulation shall be binding in its entirety and directly applicable in the Member States in accordance with the Treaty establishing the European Community.

ANNEXES

[ANNEX A
INSOLVENCY PROCEEDINGS REFERRED TO IN ARTICLE 2(A)

[11.121]

. . .

UNITED KINGDOM

—   Winding-up by or subject to the supervision of the court

—   Creditors' voluntary winding-up (with confirmation by the court)

—   Administration, including appointments made by filing prescribed documents with the court

—   Voluntary arrangements under insolvency legislation

—   Bankruptcy or sequestration]

NOTES

Note: entries other than for the UK have been omitted. Note also that this Annex was substituted by virtue of Council Regulation 210/2010/EC, Art 1(1), Annex I, as from 2 April 2010, and further amended by Council Regulation 583/2011/EU (in relation to the other entries in this Annex).

[ANNEX B
WINDING-UP PROCEEDINGS REFERRED TO IN ARTICLE 2(C)

[11.122]

UNITED KINGDOM

— Winding-up by or subject to the supervision of the court

— Winding-up through administration, including appointments made by filing prescribed documents with the court

— Creditors' voluntary winding-up (with confirmation by the court)

— Bankruptcy or sequestration]

NOTES

Note: entries other than for the UK have been omitted. Note also that this Annex was substituted by virtue of Council Regulation 210/2010/EC, Art 1(2), Annex II, as from 2 April 2010, and further amended by Council Regulation 583/2011/EU (in relation to the other entries in this Annex).

[ANNEX C
LIQUIDATORS REFERRED TO IN ARTICLE 2(B)

[11.123]

UNITED KINGDOM

— Liquidator

— Supervisor of a voluntary arrangement

— Administrator

— Official receiver

— Trustee

— Provisional liquidator

— Judicial factor]

NOTES

Note: entries other than for the UK have been omitted. Note also that this Annex was substituted by virtue of Council Regulation 210/2010/EC, Art 1(3), Annex III, as from 2 April 2010, and further amended by Council Regulation 583/2011/EU (in relation to the other entries in this Annex).

DIRECTIVE OF THE EUROPEAN PARLIAMENT
AND OF THE COUNCIL

(2001/34/EC)

of 28 May 2001

on the admission of securities to official stock exchange listing and on information to be published on those securities

NOTES

Date of publication in OJ: OJ L184, 6.7.2001, p 1. Notes are as in the original OJ version.

This Directive is reproduced as amended by: European Parliament and Council Directive 2003/71/EC; European Parliament and Council Directive 2004/109/EC; European Parliament and Council Directive 2005/1/EC.

[11.124]

THE EUROPEAN PARLIAMENT AND THE COUNCIL OF THE EUROPEAN UNION,

Having regard to the Treaty establishing the European Economic Community, and in particular Articles 44 and 95 thereof,

Having regard to the proposal from the Commission,

Having regard to the Opinion of the Economic and Social Committee,[1]

Acting in accordance with the procedure laid down in Article 251 of the Treaty,[2]

Whereas—

(1) Council Directive 79/279/EEC of 5 March 1979 coordinating the conditions for the admission of securities to official stock exchange listing,[3] Council Directive 80/390/EEC of 17 March 1980 coordinating the requirements for the drawing up, scrutiny and distribution of the listing particulars to be published for the admission of securities to official stock exchange listing,[4] Council Directive 82/121/EEC of 15 February 1982 on information to be published on a regular basis by companies the shares of which have been admitted to official stock-exchange listing[5] and Council Directive 88/627/EEC of 12 December 1988 on the information to be published when a major holding in a listed company is acquired or disposed of[6] have been substantially amended several times. In the interests of clarity and rationality, the said Directives should therefore be codified by grouping them together in a single text.

(2) The coordination of the conditions for the admission of securities to official listing on stock exchanges situated or operating in the Member States is likely to provide equivalent protection for investors at Community level, because of the more uniform guarantees offered to investors in the various Member States, it will facilitate both the admission to official stock exchange listing, in each such State, of securities from other Member States and the listing of any given security on a number of stock exchanges in the Community; it will accordingly make for greater interpenetration of national securities markets by removing those obstacles that may prudently be removed and therefore contribute to the prospect of establishing a European capital market.

(3) Such coordination must therefore apply to securities, independently of the legal status of their issuers, and must therefore also apply to securities issued by non-member States or their regional or local authorities or international public bodies; this Directive therefore covers entities not covered by the second paragraph of Article 48 of the Treaty.

(4) There should be the possibility of a right to apply to the courts against decisions by the competent national authorities in respect of the application of this Directive, concerning the admission of securities to official listing, although such right to apply must not be allowed to restrict the discretion of these authorities.

(5) Initially, this coordination of the conditions for admission of securities to official listing should be sufficiently flexible to enable account to be taken of present differences in the structures of securities markets in the Member States and to enable the Member States to take account of any specific situations with which they may be confronted.

(6) For this reason, coordination should first be limited to the establishment of minimum conditions for the admission of securities to official listing on stock exchanges situated or operating in the Member States, without however giving issuers any right to listing.

(7) This partial coordination of the conditions for admission to official listing constitutes a first step towards subsequent closer alignment of the rules of Member States in this field.

(8) The market in which undertakings operate has been enlarged to embrace the whole Community and this enlargement involves a corresponding increase in their financial requirements and extension of the capital markets on which they must call to satisfy them; admission to official listing on stock exchanges of Member States of securities issued by undertakings constitutes an important means of access to these capital markets; furthermore exchange restrictions on the purchase of securities traded on the stock exchanges of another Member State have been eliminated as part of the liberalisation of capital movements.

(9) Safeguards for the protection of the interests of actual and potential investors are required in most Member States of undertakings offering their securities to the public, either at the time of their offer or of their admission to official stock exchange listing; such safeguards require the provision of information which is sufficient and as objective as possible concerning the financial circumstances of the issuer and particulars of the securities for which admission to official listing is requested; the form under which this information is required usually consists of the publication of listing particulars.

(10) The safeguards required differ from Member State to Member State, both as regards the contents and the layout of the listing particulars and the efficacy, methods and timing of the check on the information given therein; the effect of these differences is not only to make it more difficult for undertakings to obtain admission of securities to official listing on stock exchanges of several Member States but also to hinder the acquisition by investors residing in one Member State of securities listed on stock exchanges of other Member States and thus to inhibit the financing of the undertakings and investment throughout the Community.

(11) These differences should be eliminated by coordinating the rules and regulations without necessarily making them completely uniform, in order to achieve an adequate degree of equivalence in the safeguards required in each Member State to ensure the provision of information which is sufficient and as objective as possible for actual or potential security holders.

(12) Such coordination must apply to securities independently of the legal status of the issuing undertaking; this Directive applies to entities to which no reference is made in the second paragraph of Article 48 of the Treaty.

(13) Mutual recognition of listing particulars to be published for the admission of securities to official listing represents an important step forward in the creation of the Community's internal market.

(14) In this connection, it is necessary to specify which authorities are competent to check and

approve listing particulars to be published for the admission of securities to official listing in the event of simultaneous applications for admission to official listing in two or more Member States.

(15)   Article 21 of Council Directive 89/298/EEC of 17 April 1989 coordinating the requirements for the drawing-up, scrutiny and distribution of the prospectus to be published when transferable securities are offered to the public[7] provides that where public offers are made simultaneously or within short intervals of one another in two or more Member States, a public-offer prospectus drawn up and approved in accordance with Article 7, 8 or 12 of that Directive must be recognised as a public-offer prospectus in the other Member States concerned on the basis of mutual recognition.

(16)   It is also desirable to provide the recognition of a public-offer prospectus as listing particulars where admission to official stock-exchange listing is requested within a short period of the public offer.

(17)   The mutual recognition of a public-offer prospectus and admission to official listings does not in itself confer a right to admissions.

(18)   It is advisable to provide for the extension, by means of agreements to be concluded by the Community with non-member countries, of the recognition of listing particulars for admission to official listings from those countries on a reciprocal basis.

(19)   It seems appropriate to provide for the possibility for the Member State in which admission to official listing is sought in certain cases to grant partial or complete exemption from the obligation to publish listing particulars for admission to official listings to issuers the securities of which have already been admitted to official stock-exchange listing in another Member State.

(20)   Companies which have already been listed in the Community for some time and are of high quality and international standing are the most likely candidates for cross-border listing. Those companies are generally well known in most Member States: information concerning them is widely circulated and available.

(21)   The aim of this Directive is to ensure that sufficient information is provided for investors; therefore, when such a company seeks to have its securities admitted to listing in a host Member State, investors operating on the market in that country may be sufficiently protected by receiving only simplified information rather than full listing particulars.

(22)   Member States may find it useful to establish non-discriminatory minimum quantitative criteria, such as the current equity market capitalisation, which issuers must fulfil to be eligible to benefit from the possibilities for exemption provided for in this Directive; given the increasing integration of securities markets, it should equally be open to the competent authorities to give smaller companies similar treatment.

(23)   Furthermore, many stock exchanges have second-tier markets in order to deal in shares of companies not admitted to official listing; in some cases the second-tier markets are regulated and supervised by authorities recognised by public bodies that impose on companies disclosure requirements equivalent in substance to those imposed on officially listed companies; therefore, the principle underlying Article 23 of this Directive could also be applied when such companies seek to have their securities admitted to official listing.

(24)   In order to protect investors the documents intended to be made available to the public must first be sent to the competent authorities in the Member State in which admission to official listing is sought; it is for that Member State to decide whether those documents should be scrutinised by its competent authorities and to determine, if necessary, the nature and the manner in which that scrutiny should be carried out.

(25)   In the case of securities admitted to official stock-exchange listing, the protection of investors requires that the latter be supplied with appropriate regular information throughout the entire period during which the securities are listed; coordination of requirements for this regular information has similar objectives to those envisaged for the listing particulars, namely to improve such protection and to make it more equivalent, to facilitate the listing of these securities on more than one stock exchange in the Community, and in so doing to contribute towards the establishment of a genuine Community capital market by permitting a fuller inter-penetration of securities markets.

(26)   Under this Directive, listed companies must as soon as possible make available to investors their annual accounts and report giving information on the company for the whole of the financial year; whereas the Fourth Council Directive 78/660/EEC[8] has coordinated the laws, regulations and administrative provisions of the Member States concerning the annual accounts of certain types of companies.

(27)   Companies should also, at least once during each financial year, make available to investors reports on their activities; this Directive can, consequently, be confined to coordinating the content and distribution of a single report covering the first six months of the financial year.

(28)   However, in the case of ordinary debentures, because of the rights they confer on their holders, the protection of investors by means of the publication of a half-yearly report is not essential; by virtue of this Directive, convertible or exchangeable debentures and debentures with warrants may be admitted to official listing only if the related shares are already listed on the same stock exchange or on another regulated, regularly operating, recognised open market or are so admitted simultaneously; the Member States may derogate from this principle only if their competent authorities are satisfied that holders have at their disposal all the information necessary to form an opinion concerning the value of the shares to which these debentures relate; consequently, regular information needs to be coordinated only for companies whose shares are admitted to official stock-exchange listing.

(29)   The half-yearly report must enable investors to make an informed appraisal of the general development of the company's activities during the period covered by the report; however, this

report need contain only the essential details on the financial position and general progress of the business of the company in question.

(30)   So as to ensure the effective protection of investors and the proper operation of stock exchanges, the rules relating to regular information to be published by companies, the shares of which are admitted to official stock-exchange listing within the Community, should apply not only to companies from Member States, but also to companies from non-member countries.

(31)   A policy of adequate information of investors in the field of transferable securities is likely to improve investor protection, to increase investors' confidence in securities markets and thus to ensure that securities markets function correctly.

(32)   By making such protection more equivalent, coordination of that policy at Community level is likely to make for greater inter-penetration of the Member States' transferable securities markets and therefore help to establish a true European capital market.

(33)   To that end investors should be informed of major holdings and of changes in those holdings in Community companies the shares of which are officially listed on stock exchanges situated or operating within the Community.

(34)   Coordinated rules should be laid down concerning the detailed content and the procedure for applying that requirement.

(35)   Companies, the shares of which are officially listed on a Community stock exchange, can inform the public of changes in major holdings only if they have been informed of such changes by the holders of those holdings.

(36)   Most Member States do not subject holders to such a requirement and where such a requirement exists there are appreciable differences in the procedures for applying it; coordinated rules should therefore be adopted at Community level in this field.

(37)   This Directive should not affect the obligations of the Member States concerning the deadlines for transposition set out in Annex II, Part B,

---

NOTES

[1]   OJ C116, 20.4.2001, p 69.

[2]   Opinion of the European Parliament of 14 March 2001 (not yet published in the Official Journal) and Council Decision of 7 May 2001.

[3]   OJ L66, 16.3.1979, p 21. Directive as last amended by Directive 88/627/EEC (OJ L348, 17.12.1988, p 62).

[4]   OJ L100, 17.4.1980, p 1. Directive as last amended by European Parliament and Council Directive 94/18/EC (OJ L135, 31.5.1994, p 1).

[5]   OJ L48, 20.2.1982, p 26.

[6]   OJ L348, 17.12.1988, p 62.

[7]   OJ L124, 5.5.1989, p 8.

[8]   OJ L222, 14.8.1978, p 11. Directive as last amended by Directive 1999/60/EC (OJ L162, 26.6.1999, p 65).

HAVE ADOPTED THIS DIRECTIVE—

TITLE I
DEFINITIONS AND SCOPE OF APPLICATION

CHAPTER I
DEFINITIONS

[11.125]
Article 1
For the purposes of this Directive—
   (a)   "issuers" shall mean companies and other legal persons and any undertaking whose securities are the subject of an application for admission to official listing on a stock exchange;
   (b)   "collective investment undertakings other than the closed-end type" shall mean unit trusts and investment companies—
      (i)   the object of which is the collective investment of capital provided by the public, and which operate on the principle of risk spreading, and
      (ii)   the units of which are, at the holders' request, repurchased or redeemed, directly or indirectly, out of the assets of these undertakings. Action taken by such undertakings to ensure that the stock exchange value of its units does not significantly vary from their net asset value shall be regarded as equivalent to such repurchase or redemption;
   (c)   for the purposes of this Directive "investment companies other than those of the closed-end type" shall mean investment companies—
      (i)   the object of which is the collective investment of capital provided by the public, and which operate on the principle of risk spreading, and
      (ii)   the shares of which are, at the holders' request, repurchased or redeemed, directly or indirectly, out of those companies' assets. Action taken by such companies to ensure

that the stock exchange value operating of their shares does not significantly vary from their net asset value shall be regarded as equivalent to such repurchase or redemption;

(d) "credit institution" shall mean an undertaking whose business is to receive deposits or other repayable funds from the public and to grant credits for its own account;

(e) "units of a collective investment undertaking" shall mean securities issued by a collective investment undertaking as representing the rights of participants in the assets of such undertaking;

(f) "participating interest" shall mean rights in the capital of other undertakings, whether or not represented by certificates, which, by creating a durable link with those undertakings, are intended to contribute to the activities of the undertaking which holds these rights;

(g), (h) . . .

NOTES

Points (g), (h) repealed by European Parliament and Council Directive 2004/109/EC, Art 32(1), as from 20 January 2007.

CHAPTER II
SCOPE OF APPLICATION

[11.126]
Article 2
1. Articles 5 to 19, 42 to 69, and 78 to 84 shall apply to securities which are admitted to official listing or are the subject of an application for admission to official listing on a stock exchange situated or operating within a Member State.
2. Member States may decide not to apply the provisions mentioned in paragraph 1 to—
    (a) units issued by collective investment undertakings other than the closed-end type,
    (b) securities issued by a Member State or its regional or local authorities.

Articles 3, 4   *(Article 3 repealed by European Parliament and Council Directive 2003/71/EC, Art 27(2), as from 1 July 2005; Article 4 repealed by European Parliament and Council Directive 2004/109/EC, Art 32(2), as from 20 January 2007.)*

TITLE II
GENERAL PROVISIONS CONCERNING THE OFFICIAL LISTING OF SECURITIES

CHAPTER I
GENERAL CONDITIONS FOR ADMISSION

[11.127]
Article 5
Member States shall ensure—
    (a) securities may not be admitted to official listing on any stock exchange situated or operating within their territory unless the conditions laid down by this Directive are satisfied, and
    (b) that issuers of securities admitted to such official listing, to regardless of the date on which this admission takes place, are subject to the obligations provided for by this Directive.

[11.128]
Article 6
1. The admission of securities to official listing shall be subject to the conditions set out in Articles 42 to 51, or 52 to 63, relating to shares and debt securities respectively.
2. . . .
3. Certificates representing shares may be admitted to official listing only if the issuer of the shares represented fulfils the conditions set out in Articles 42 to 44 and the obligations set out in Articles 64 to 69 and if the certificates fulfil the conditions set out in Articles 45 to 50.

NOTES

Para 2: repealed by European Parliament and Council Directive 2004/109/EC, Art 32(3), as from 20 January 2007.

[11.129]
Article 7
Member States may not make the admission to official listing of securities issued by companies or other legal persons which are nationals of another Member State subject to the condition that the securities must already have been admitted to official listing on a stock exchange situated or operating in one of the Member States.

CHAPTER II
MORE STRINGENT OR ADDITIONAL CONDITIONS AND OBLIGATIONS

[11.130]
Article 8
1.   Subject to the prohibitions provided for in Article 7 and in Articles 42 to 63, the Member States may make the admission of securities to official listing subject to more stringent conditions than those set out in Articles 42 to 63 or to additional conditions, provided that these more stringent and additional conditions apply generally for all issuers or for individual classes of issuer and that they have been published before application for admission of such securities is made.
[2.   Member States may make the issuers of securities admitted to official listing subject to additional obligations, provided that those additional obligations apply generally for all issuers or for individual classes of issuers.]
3.   Member States may, under the same conditions as those laid down in Article 9, authorise derogations from the additional or more stringent conditions and obligations referred to in paragraphs 1 and 2 hereof.
4.   Member States may, in accordance with the applicable national rules require issuers of securities admitted to official listing to inform the public on a regular basis of their financial position and the general course of their business.

NOTES

Para 2: substituted by European Parliament and Council Directive 2004/109/EC, Art 32(4), as from 20 January 2007.

CHAPTER III
DEROGATIONS

[11.131]
Article 9
Any derogations from the conditions for the admission of securities to official listing which may be authorised in accordance with Articles 42 to 63 must apply generally for all issuers where the circumstances justifying them are similar.

[11.132]
Article 10
Member States may decide not to apply the conditions set out in Articles 52 to 63 and the obligations set out in Article 81(1) and (3) in respect of applications for admission to official listing of debt securities issued by companies and other legal persons which are nationals of a Member State and which are set up by, governed by or managed pursuant to a special law where repayments and interest payments in respect of those securities are guaranteed by a Member State or one of its federal states.

CHAPTER IV
POWERS OF THE NATIONAL COMPETENT AUTHORITIES

SECTION 1
DECISION OF ADMISSION

[11.133]
Article 11
1.   The competent authorities referred to in Article 105 shall decide on the admission of securities to official listing on a stock exchange situated or operating within their territories.
2.   Without prejudice to the other powers conferred upon them, the competent authorities may reject an application for the admission of a security to official listing if, in their opinion, the issuer's situation is such that admission would be detrimental to investors' interests.

[11.134]
Article 12
By way of derogation from Article 8, Member States may, solely in the interests of protecting the investors, give the competent authorities power to make the admission of a security to official listing subject to any special condition which the competent authorities consider appropriate and of which they have explicitly informed the applicant.

[11.135]
Article 13
1.   Where applications are to be made simultaneously or within short intervals of one another for admission of the same securities to official listing on stock exchanges situated or operating in more than one Member State, or where an application for admission is made in respect of a security already listed on a stock exchange in another Member State, the competent authorities shall

communicate with each other and make such arrangements as may be necessary to expedite the procedure and simplify as far as possible the formalities and any additional conditions required for admission of the security concerned.

2. In order to facilitate the work of the competent authorities, any application for the admission of a security to official listing on a stock exchange situated or operating in a Member State must state whether a similar application is being or has been made in another Member State, or will be made in the near future.

[11.136]
Article 14
The competent authorities may refuse to admit to official listing a security already officially listed in another Member State where the issuer fails to comply with the obligations resulting from admission in that Member State.

[11.137]
Article 15
Where an application for admission to official listing relates to certificates representing shares, the application shall be considered only if the competent authorities are of the opinion that the issuer of the certificates is offering adequate safeguards for the protection of investors.

SECTION 2
INFORMATION REQUESTED BY THE COMPETENT AUTHORITIES

[11.138]
Article 16
1. An issuer whose securities are admitted to official listing shall provide the competent authorities with all the information which the latter consider appropriate in order to protect investors or ensure the smooth operation of the market.

2. Where protection of investors or the smooth operation of the market so requires, an issuer may be required by the competent authorities to publish such information in such a form and within such time limits as they consider appropriate. Should the issuer fail to comply with such requirement, the competent authorities may themselves publish such information after having heard the issuer.

SECTION 3
ACTION AGAINST AN ISSUER FAILING TO COMPLY WITH THE OBLIGATIONS
RESULTING FROM ADMISSION

[11.139]
Article 17
Without prejudice to any other action or penalties which they may contemplate in the event of failure on the part of the issuer to comply with the obligations resulting from admission to official listing, the competent authorities may make public the fact that an issuer is failing to comply with those obligations.

SECTION 4
SUSPENSION AND DISCONTINUANCE

[11.140]
Article 18
1. The competent authorities may decide to suspend the listing of a security where the smooth operation of the market is, or may be, temporarily jeopardised or where protection of investors so requires.

2. The competent authorities may decide that the listing of the security be discontinued where they are satisfied that, owing to special circumstances, normal regular dealings in a security are no longer possible.

SECTION 5
RIGHT TO APPLY TO THE COURTS IN CASE OF REFUSAL OF ADMISSION
OR DISCONTINUANCE

[11.141]
Article 19
1. Member States shall ensure decisions of the competent authorities refusing the admission of a security to official listing or discontinuing such a listing shall be subject to the right to apply to the courts.

2. An applicant shall be notified of a decision regarding his application for admission to official listing within six months of receipt of the application or, should the competent authority require any further information within that period, within six months of the applicant's supplying such information.

3.   Failure to give a decision within the time limit specified in paragraph 2 shall be deemed a rejection of the application. Such rejection shall give rise to the right to apply to the courts provided for in paragraph 1.

TITLE III
PARTICULAR CONDITIONS RELATING TO OFFICIAL LISTINGS OF SECURITIES

Articles 20–41   (*Articles 20–41 (Chapter 1) repealed by European Parliament and Council Directive 2003/71/EC, Art 27(1), as from 1 July 2005.*)

CHAPTER II
SPECIFIC CONDITIONS FOR THE ADMISSION OF SHARES

SECTION 1
CONDITIONS RELATING TO COMPANIES FOR THE SHARES OF WHICH ADMISSION TO OFFICIAL LISTING IS SOUGHT

[11.142]
Article 42
The legal position of the company must be in conformity with the laws and Regulations to which it is subject, as regards both its formation and its operation under its statutes.

[11.143]
Article 43
1.   The foreseeable market capitalisation of the shares for which admission to official listing is sought or, if this cannot be assessed, the company's capital and reserves, including profit or loss, from the last financial year, must be at least one million euro.
2.   Member States may provide for admission to official listing, even when this condition is not fulfilled, provided that the competent authorities are satisfied that there will be an adequate market for the shares concerned.
3.   A higher foreseeable market capitalisation or higher capital and reserves may be required by a Member State for admission to official listing only if another regulated, regularly operating, recognised open market exists in that State and the requirements for it are equal to or less than those referred to in paragraph 1.
4.   The condition set out in paragraph 1 shall not be applicable for the admission to official listing of a further block of shares of the same class as those already admitted.
5.   The equivalent in national currency of one million euro shall initially be the equivalent in national currency of one million European units of account that were applicable on 5 March 1979.
6.   If, as a result of adjustment of the equivalent of the euro in national currency, the market capitalisation expressed in national currency remains for a period of one year at least 10% more or less than the value of one million euro the Member state must, within the 12 months following the expiry of that period, adjust its laws, regulations or administrative provisions to comply with paragraph 1.

[11.144]
Article 44
A company must have published or filed its annual accounts in accordance with national law for the three financial years preceding the application for official listing. By way of exception, the competent authorities may derogate from this condition where such derogation is desirable in the interests of the company or of investors and where the competent authorities are satisfied that investors have the necessary information available to be able to arrive at an informed judgement on the company and the shares for which admission to official listing is sought.

SECTION 2
CONDITIONS RELATING TO THE SHARES FOR WHICH ADMISSION IS SOUGHT

[11.145]
Article 45
The legal position of the shares must be in conformity with the laws and regulations to which they are subject.

[11.146]
Article 46
1.   The shares must be freely negotiable.
2.   The competent authorities may treat shares which are not fully paid up as freely negotiable, if arrangements have been made to ensure that the negotiability of such shares is not restricted and that dealing is made open and proper by providing the public with all appropriate information.
3.   The competent authorities may, in the case of the admission to official listing of shares which may be acquired only subject to approval, derogate from paragraph 1 only if the use of the approval clause does not disturb the market.

Part 11   EU Legislation

[11.147]
Article 47
Where public issue precedes admission to official listing, the first listing may be made only after the end of the period during which subscription applications may be submitted.

[11.148]
Article 48
1. A sufficient number of shares must be distributed to the public in one or more Member States not later than the time of admission.
2. The condition set out in paragraph 1 shall not apply where shares are to be distributed to the public through the stock exchange. In that event, admission to official listing may be granted only if the competent authorities are satisfied that a sufficient number of shares will be distributed through the stock exchange within a short period.
3. Where admission to official listing is sought for a further block of shares of the same class, the competent authorities may assess whether a sufficient number of shares has been distributed to the public in relation to all the shares issued and not only in relation to this further block.
4. By way of derogation from paragraph 1, if the shares are admitted to official listing in one or more non-member countries, the competent authorities may provide for their admission to official listing if a sufficient number of shares is distributed to the public in the non-Member State or States where they are listed.
5. A sufficient number of shares shall be deemed to have been distributed either when the shares in respect of which application for admission has been made are in the hands of the public to the extent of at least 25% of the subscribed capital represented by the class of shares concerned or when, in view of the large number of shares of the same class and the extent of their distribution to the public, the market will operate properly with a lower percentage.

[11.149]
Article 49
1. The application for admission to official listing must cover all the shares of the same class already issued.
2. Member States may provide that this condition shall not apply to applications for admission not covering all the shares of the same class already issued where the shares of that class for which admission is not sought belong to blocks serving to maintain control of the company or are not negotiable for a certain time under agreements, provided that the public is informed of such situations and that there is no danger of such situations prejudicing the interests of the holders of the shares for which admission to official listing is sought.

[11.150]
Article 50
1. For the admission to official listing of shares issued by companies which are nationals of another Member State and which shares have a physical form it is necessary and sufficient that their physical form comply with the standards laid down in that other Member State. Where the physical form does not conform to the standards in force in the Member State in which admission to official listing is applied for, the competent authorities of that state shall make that fact known to the public.
2. The physical form of shares issued by companies which are nationals of a non-member country must afford sufficient safeguard for the protection of the investors.

[11.151]
Article 51
If the shares issued by a company which is a national of a non-member country are not listed in either the country of origin or in the country in which the major proportion of the shares is held, they may not be admitted to official listing unless the competent authorities are satisfied that the absence of a listing the in the country of origin or in the country in which the major proportion is held is not due to the need to protect investors.

CHAPTER III
PARTICULAR CONDITIONS RELATING TO THE ADMISSION TO OFFICIAL LISTING OF DEBT SECURITIES ISSUED BY AN UNDERTAKING

SECTION 1
CONDITIONS RELATING TO UNDERTAKINGS FOR THE DEBT SECURITIES OF WHICH ADMISSION TO OFFICIAL LISTING IS SOUGHT

[11.152]
Article 52
The legal position of the undertaking must be in conformity with the laws and regulations to which it is subject, as regards both its formation and its operation under its statutes.

Part 11   EU Legislation

SECTION 2

CONDITIONS RELATING TO THE DEBT SECURITIES FOR WHICH ADMISSION TO OFFICIAL LISTING IS SOUGHT

[11.153]
Article 53
The legal position of the debt securities must be in conformity with the laws and regulations to which they are subject.

[11.154]
Article 54
1. The debt securities must be freely negotiable.
2. The competent authorities may treat debt securities which are not fully paid up as freely negotiable if arrangements have been made to ensure that the negotiability of these debt securities is not restricted and that dealing is made open and proper by providing the public with all appropriate information.

[11.155]
Article 55
Where public issue precedes admission to official listing, the first listing may be made only after the end of the period during which subscription applications may be submitted. This provision shall not apply in the case of tap issues of debt securities when the closing date for subscription is not fixed.

[11.156]
Article 56
The application for admission to official listing must cover all debt securities ranking *pari passu*.

[11.157]
Article 57
1. For the admission to official listing of debt securities issued by undertakings which are nationals of another Member State and which debt securities have a physical form, it is necessary and sufficient that their physical form comply with the standards laid down in that other Member State. Where the physical form does not conform to the standards in force in the Member State in which admission to official listing is applied for, the competent authorities of that State shall make that fact known to the public.
2. The physical form of debt securities issued in a single Member State must conform to the standards in force in that State.
3. The physical form of debt securities issued by undertakings which are nationals of a non-member country must afford sufficient safeguard for the protection of the investors.

SECTION 3

OTHER CONDITIONS

[11.158]
Article 58
1. The amount of the loan may not be less than EUR 200,000. This provision shall not be applicable in the case of tap issues where the amount of the loan is not fixed.
2. Member States may provide for admission to official listing even when this condition is not fulfilled, where the competent authorities are satisfied that there will be a sufficient market for the debt securities concerned.
3. The equivalent in national currency of EUR 200,000 shall initially be the equivalent in national currency of 200,000 units of account that were applicable on 5 March 1979.
4. If as a result of adjustment of the equivalent of the euro in national currency the minimum amount of the loan expressed in national currency remains, for a period of one year, at least 10% less than the value of EUR 200,000 the Member State must, within the 12 months following the expiry of that period, amend its laws, regulations and administrative provisions to comply with paragraph 1.

[11.159]
Article 59
1. Convertible or exchangeable debentures and debentures with warrants may be admitted to official listing only if the related shares are already listed on the same stock exchange or on another regulated, regularly operating, recognised open market or are so admitted simultaneously.
2. Member States may, by way of derogation from paragraph 1, provide for the admission to official listing of convertible or exchangeable debentures or debentures with warrants, if the competent authorities are satisfied that holders have at their disposal all the information necessary to form an opinion concerning the value of the shares to which these debt securities relate.

CHAPTER IV

PARTICULAR CONDITIONS RELATING TO THE ADMISSION TO OFFICIAL LISTING
OF DEBT SECURITIES ISSUED BY A STATE, ITS REGIONAL OR LOCAL AUTHORITIES
OR A PUBLIC INTERNATIONAL BODY

[11.160]
Article 60
The debt securities must be freely negotiable.

[11.161]
Article 61
Where public issue precedes admission to official listing, the first listing may be made only after the end of the period during which subscription applications may be submitted. This provision shall not apply where the closing date for subscription is not fixed.

[11.162]
Article 62
The application for admission to official listing must cover all the securities ranking *pari passu*.

[11.163]
Article 63
1. For the admission to official listing of debt securities which are issued by a Member State or its regional or local authorities in a physical form, it is necessary and sufficient that such physical form comply with the standards in force in that Member State. Where the physical form does not comply with the standards in force in the Member State where admission to official listing is applied for, the competent authorities of that state shall bring this situation to the attention of the public.
2. The physical form of debt securities issued by non-member countries or their regional or local authorities or by public international bodies must afford sufficient safeguard for the protection of the investors.

TITLE IV

OBLIGATIONS RELATING TO SECURITIES ADMITTED TO OFFICIAL LISTING

CHAPTER I

OBLIGATIONS OF COMPANIES WHOSE SHARES ARE ADMITTED TO
OFFICIAL LISTING

SECTION 1

LISTING OF NEWLY ISSUED SHARES OF THE SAME CLASS

[11.164]
Article 64
Without prejudice to Article 49(2), in the case of a new public issue of shares of the same class as those already officially listed, the company shall be required, where the new shares are not automatically admitted, to apply for their admission to the same listing, either not more than a year after their issue or when they become freely negotiable.

Articles 65–104   *(Articles 65–97 (Title IV, Chapter I, Sections 2–8, and Chapters II, III) repealed by European Parliament and Council Directive 2004/109/EC, Art 32(5), as from 20 January 2007; Articles 98–104 (Title V): Arts 98–101, 104 repealed by European Parliament and Council Directive 2003/71/EC, Art 27(2), as from 1 July 2005; Arts 102, 103 repealed by European Parliament and Council Directive 2004/109/EC, Art 32(6), as from 20 January 2007.)*

TITLE VI

COMPETENT AUTHORITIES AND COOPERATION BETWEEN MEMBER STATES

[11.165]
Article 105
1. Member States shall ensure that this Directive is applied and shall appoint one or more competent authorities for the purposes of the Directive. They shall notify the Commission thereof, giving details of any division of powers among them.
2. Member States shall ensure that the competent authorities have the powers necessary for them to carry out their task.
3. This Directive shall not affect the competent authorities' liability, which shall continue to be governed solely by national law.

[11.166]
Article 106
The competent authorities shall cooperate whenever necessary for the purpose of carrying out their duties and shall exchange any information useful for that purpose.

[11.167]
Article 107
1.   Member States shall provide that all persons employed or formerly employed by the competent authorities shall be bound by professional secrecy. This means that any confidential information received in the course of their duties may not be divulged to any person or authority except by virtue of provisions laid down by law.
2.   Paragraph 1 shall not, however, preclude the competent authorities of the various Member States from exchanging information as provided for in this Directive. Information thus exchanged shall be covered by the obligation of professional secrecy to which the persons employed or formerly employed by the competent authorities receiving the information are subject.
3.   . . .

NOTES

Para 3: repealed by a combination of European Parliament and Council Directive 2003/71/EC, Art 27(2), as from 1 July 2005, and European Parliament and Council Directive 2004/109/EC, Art 32(7), as from 20 January 2007.

TITLE VII
CONTACT COMMITTEE

CHAPTER I
COMPOSITION, WORKING AND TASKS OF THE COMMITTEE

Article 108   (*Repealed by European Parliament and Council Directive 2005/1/EC, Art 10(1), as from 13 April 2005.*)

CHAPTER II
ADAPTATION OF THE AMOUNT OF EQUITY MARKET CAPITALISATION

[11.168]
[Article 109
1.   For the purpose of adjusting, in the light of the requirements of the economic situation, the minimum amount of the foreseeable market capitalisation laid down in Article 43(1), the Commission shall submit to the European Securities Committee instituted by Commission Decision 2001/528/EC of 6 June 2001[1] a draft of the measures to be taken.
2.   Where reference is made to this paragraph, Articles 5 and 7 of Council Decision 1999/468/EC of 28 June 1999 laying down the procedures for the exercise of implementing powers conferred on the Commission[2] shall apply, having regard to Article 8 thereof.
    The period laid down in Article 5(6) of Decision 1999/468/EC shall be set at three months.
3.   The Committee shall adopt its rules of procedure.]

NOTES

Substituted by European Parliament and Council Directive 2005/1/EC, Art 10(2), as from 13 April 2005.
[1]   OJ L191, 13.7.2001, p 45. Decision as amended by Decision 2004/8/EC (OJ L3, 7.1.2004, p 33).
[2]   OJ L184, 17.7.1999, p 23.

TITLE VIII
FINAL PROVISIONS

[11.169]
Article 110
The Member States shall communicate to the Commission the texts of the main laws, regulations and administrative provisions which they adopt in the field covered by this Directive.

[11.170]
Article 111
1.   Directives 79/279/EEC, 80/390/EEC, 82/121/EEC and 88/627/EEC, as amended by the acts listed in Annex II Part A, are hereby repealed without prejudice to the obligations of the Member States concerning the time-limits for transposition set out in Annex II Part B.
2.   References to the repealed Directives shall be construed as references to this Directive and should be read in accordance with the correlation table shown in Annex III.

[11.171]
Article 112
This Directive shall enter into force the twentieth day following that of its publication in the *Official Journal of the European Communities*.

[11.172]
Article 113
This Directive is addressed to the Member States.

ANNEXES

ANNEX I

(Annex I repealed by European Parliament and Council Directive 2003/71/EC, Art 27(4), as from 1 July 2005.)

ANNEX II

PART A
REPEALED DIRECTIVES AND THEIR SUCCESSIVE AMENDMENTS
(REFERRED TO IN ARTICLE 111)

[11.173]

Council Directive 79/279/EEC	(OJ L66, 16.3.1979, p 21)
Council Directive 82/148/EEC	(OJ L62, 5.3.1982, p 22)
Council Directive 88/627/EEC	(OJ L348, 17.12.1988, p 62)
Council Directive 80/390/EEC	(OJ L100, 17.4.1980, p 1)
Council Directive 82/148/EEC	(OJ L62, 5.3.1982, p 22)
Council Directive 87/345/EEC	(OJ L185, 4.7.1987, p 81)
Council Directive 90/211/EEC	(OJ L112, 3.5.1990, p 24)
European Parliament and Council Directive 94/18/EC	(OJ L135, 31.5.1994, p 1)
Council Directive 82/121/EEC	(OJ L48, 20.2.1982, p 26)
Council Directive 88/627/EEC	(OJ L348, 17.12.1988, p 62)

PART B
TIME-LIMITS FOR TRANSPOSITION INTO NATIONAL LAW
(REFERRED TO IN ARTICLE 111)

Directive	*Time-limit for transposition*
79/279/EEC	8 March 1981[1, 2]
80/390/EEC	19 September 1982[2]
82/121/EEC; 82/148/EEC	30 June 1983[3]
87/345/EEC	1 January 1990
	1 January 1991 for Spain
	1 January 1992 for Portugal
88/627/EEC	1 January 1991
90/211/EEC; 94/18/EC	17 April 1991

NOTES

[1]   8.3.1982 for the Member States which introduce simultaneously Directives 79/279/EEC and 80/390/EEC.

[2]   30.6.1983 for the Member States which introduce simultaneously Directives 79/279/EEC, 80/390/EEC and 82/121/EEC.

[3]   Time-limit for application: 30.6.1986.

ANNEX III

(Annex III (Correlation Table) outside the scope of this work.)

COUNCIL REGULATION

(2157/2001/EC)

of 8 October 2001

on the Statute for a European company (SE)

NOTES

Date of publication in OJ: OJ L294, 10.11.2001, p 1. Notes are as in the original OJ version.

This Regulation is reproduced as amended by: Council Regulation 885/2004/EC; Council Regulation 1791/2006/EC.

[11.174]

THE COUNCIL OF THE EUROPEAN UNION,

Having regard to the Treaty establishing the European Community, and in particular Article 308 thereof,

Having regard to the proposal from the Commission,[1]

Having regard to the opinion of the European Parliament,[2]

Having regard to the opinion of the Economic and Social Committee,[3]

Whereas:

(1) The completion of the internal market and the improvement it brings about in the economic and social situation throughout the Community mean not only that barriers to trade must be removed, but also that the structures of production must be adapted to the Community dimension. For that purpose it is essential that companies the business of which is not limited to satisfying purely local needs should be able to plan and carry out the reorganisation of their business on a Community scale.

(2) Such reorganisation presupposes that existing companies from different Member States are given the option of combining their potential by means of mergers. Such operations can be carried out only with due regard to the rules of competition laid down in the Treaty.

(3) Restructuring and cooperation operations involving companies from different Member States give rise to legal and psychological difficulties and tax problems. The approximation of Member States' company law by means of Directives based on Article 44 of the Treaty can overcome some of those difficulties. Such approximation does not, however, release companies governed by different legal systems from the obligation to choose a form of company governed by a particular national law.

(4) The legal framework within which business must be carried on in the Community is still based largely on national laws and therefore no longer corresponds to the economic framework within which it must develop if the objectives set out in Article 18 of the Treaty are to be achieved. That situation forms a considerable obstacle to the creation of groups of companies from different Member States.

(5) Member States are obliged to ensure that the provisions applicable to European companies under this Regulation do not result either in discrimination arising out of unjustified different treatment of European companies compared with public limited-liability companies or in disproportionate restrictions on the formation of a European company or on the transfer of its registered office.

(6) It is essential to ensure as far as possible that the economic unit and the legal unit of business in the Community coincide. For that purpose, provision should be made for the creation, side by side with companies governed by a particular national law, of companies formed and carrying on business under the law created by a Community Regulation directly applicable in all Member States.

(7) The provisions of such a Regulation will permit the creation and management of companies with a European dimension, free from the obstacles arising from the disparity and the limited territorial application of national company law.

(8) The Statute for a European public limited-liability company (hereafter referred to as "SE") is among the measures to be adopted by the Council before 1992 listed in the Commission's White Paper on completing the internal market, approved by the European Council that met in Milan in June 1985. The European Council that met in Brussels in 1987 expressed the wish to see such a Statute created swiftly.

(9) Since the Commission's submission in 1970 of a proposal for a Regulation on the Statute for a European public limited-liability company, amended in 1975, work on the approximation of national company law has made substantial progress, so that on those points where the functioning of an SE does not need uniform Community rules reference may be made to the law governing public limited-liability companies in the Member State where it has its registered office.

(10) Without prejudice to any economic needs that may arise in the future, if the essential objective of legal rules governing SEs is to be attained, it must be possible at least to create such a company as a means both of enabling companies from different Member States to merge or to create a holding company and of enabling companies and other legal persons carrying on economic activities and governed by the laws of different Member States to form joint subsidiaries.

(11) In the same context it should be possible for a public limited-liability company with a registered office and head office within the Community to transform itself into an SE without going into liquidation, provided it has a subsidiary in a Member State other than that of its registered office.

(12) National provisions applying to public limited-liability companies that offer their securities to the public and to securities transactions should also apply where an SE is formed by means of an offer of securities to the public and to SEs wishing to utilise such financial instruments.

(13) The SE itself must take the form of a company with share capital, that being the form most suited, in terms of both financing and management, to the needs of a company carrying on business on a European scale. In order to ensure that such companies are of reasonable size, a minimum amount of capital should be set so that they have sufficient assets without making it difficult for small and medium-sized undertakings to form SEs.

(14) An SE must be efficiently managed and properly supervised. It must be borne in mind that there are at present in the Community two different systems for the administration of public limited-liability companies. Although an SE should be allowed to choose between the two systems,

the respective responsibilities of those responsible for management and those responsible for supervision should be clearly defined.

(15)   Under the rules and general principles of private international law, where one undertaking controls another governed by a different legal system, its ensuing rights and obligations as regards the protection of minority shareholders and third parties are governed by the law governing the controlled undertaking, without prejudice to the obligations imposed on the controlling undertaking by its own law, for example the requirement to prepare consolidated accounts.

(16)   Without prejudice to the consequences of any subsequent coordination of the laws of the Member States, specific rules for SEs are not at present required in this field. The rules and general principles of private international law should therefore be applied both where an SE exercises control and where it is the controlled company.

(17)   The rule thus applicable where an SE is controlled by another undertaking should be specified, and for this purpose reference should be made to the law governing public limited-liability companies in the Member State in which the SE has its registered office.

(18)   Each Member State must be required to apply the sanctions applicable to public limited-liability companies governed by its law in respect of infringements of this Regulation.

(19)   The rules on the involvement of employees in the European company are laid down in Directive 2001/86/EC,[4] and those provisions thus form an indissociable complement to this Regulation and must be applied concomitantly.

(20)   This Regulation does not cover other areas of law such as taxation, competition, intellectual property or insolvency. The provisions of the Member States' law and of Community law are therefore applicable in the above areas and in other areas not covered by this Regulation.

(21)   Directive 2001/86/EC is designed to ensure that employees have a right of involvement in issues and decisions affecting the life of their SE. Other social and labour legislation questions, in particular the right of employees to information and consultation as regulated in the Member States, are governed by the national provisions applicable, under the same conditions, to public limited-liability companies.

(22)   The entry into force of this Regulation must be deferred so that each Member State may incorporate into its national law the provisions of Directive 2001/86/EC and set up in advance the necessary machinery for the formation and operation of SEs with registered offices within its territory, so that the Regulation and the Directive may be applied concomitantly.

(23)   A company the head office of which is not in the Community should be allowed to participate in the formation of an SE provided that company is formed under the law of a Member State, has its registered office in that Member State and has a real and continuous link with a Member State's economy according to the principles established in the 1962 General Programme for the abolition of restrictions on freedom of establishment. Such a link exists in particular if a company has an establishment in that Member State and conducts operations therefrom.

(24)   The SE should be enabled to transfer its registered office to another Member State. Adequate protection of the interests of minority shareholders who oppose the transfer, of creditors and of holders of other rights should be proportionate. Such transfer should not affect the rights originating before the transfer.

(25)   This Regulation is without prejudice to any provision which may be inserted in the 1968 Brussels Convention or in any text adopted by Member States or by the Council to replace such Convention, relating to the rules of jurisdiction applicable in the case of transfer of the registered offices of a public limited-liability company from one Member State to another.

(26)   Activities by financial institutions are regulated by specific directives and the national law implementing those directives and additional national rules regulating those activities apply in full to an SE.

(27)   In view of the specific Community character of an SE, the "real seat" arrangement adopted by this Regulation in respect of SEs is without prejudice to Member States' laws and does not pre-empt any choices to be made for other Community texts on company law.

(28)   The Treaty does not provide, for the adoption of this Regulation, powers of action other than those of Article 308 thereof.

(29)   Since the objectives of the intended action, as outlined above, cannot be adequately attained by the Member States in as much as a European public limited-liability company is being established at European level and can therefore, because of the scale and impact of such company, be better attained at Community level, the Community may take measures in accordance with the principle of subsidiarity enshrined in Article 5 of the Treaty. In accordance with the principle of proportionality as set out in the said Article, this Regulation does not go beyond what is necessary to attain these objectives,

NOTES

[1]   OJ C263, 16.10.1989, p 41 and OJ C176, 8.7.1991, p 1.

[2]   Opinion of 4 September 2001 (not yet published in the Official Journal).

[3]   OJ C124, 21.5.1990, p 34.

[4]   See p 22 of this Official Journal.

HAS ADOPTED THIS REGULATION:

TITLE I
GENERAL PROVISIONS

[11.175]
Article 1

1. A company may be set up within the territory of the Community in the form of a European public limited-liability company (Societas Europaea or SE) on the conditions and in the manner laid down in this Regulation.

2. The capital of an SE shall be divided into shares. No shareholder shall be liable for more than the amount he has subscribed.

3. An SE shall have legal personality.

4. Employee involvement in an SE shall be governed by the provisions of Directive 2001/86/EC.

[11.176]
Article 2

1. Public limited-liability companies such as referred to in Annex I, formed under the law of a Member State, with registered offices and head offices within the Community may form an SE by means of a merger provided that at least two of them are governed by the law of different Member States.

2. Public and private limited-liability companies such as referred to in Annex II, formed under the law of a Member State, with registered offices and head offices within the Community may promote the formation of a holding SE provided that each of at least two of them:

    (a) is governed by the law of a different Member State, or

    (b) has for at least two years had a subsidiary company governed by the law of another Member State or a branch situated in another Member State.

3. Companies and firms within the meaning of the second paragraph of Article 48 of the Treaty and other legal bodies governed by public or private law, formed under the law of a Member State, with registered offices and head offices within the Community may form a subsidiary SE by subscribing for its shares, provided that each of at least two of them:

    (a) is governed by the law of a different Member State, or

    (b) has for at least two years had a subsidiary company governed by the law of another Member State or a branch situated in another Member State.

4. A public limited-liability company, formed under the law of a Member State, which has its registered office and head office within the Community may be transformed into an SE if for at least two years it has had a subsidiary company governed by the law of another Member State.

5. A Member State may provide that a company the head office of which is not in the Community may participate in the formation of an SE provided that company is formed under the law of a Member State, has its registered office in that Member State and has a real and continuous link with a Member State's economy.

[11.177]
Article 3

1. For the purposes of Article 2(1), (2) and (3), an SE shall be regarded as a public limited-liability company governed by the law of the Member State in which it has its registered office.

2. An SE may itself set up one or more subsidiaries in the form of SEs. The provisions of the law of the Member State in which a subsidiary SE has its registered office that require a public limited-liability company to have more than one shareholder shall not apply in the case of the subsidiary SE. The provisions of national law implementing the twelfth Council Company Law Directive (89/667/EEC) of 21 December 1989 on single-member private limited-liability companies[1] shall apply to SEs mutatis mutandis.

NOTES

    [1]   OJ L395, 30.12.1989, p 40. Directive as last amended by the 1994 Act of Accession.

[11.178]
Article 4

1. The capital of an SE shall be expressed in euro.

2. The subscribed capital shall not be less than EUR 120,000.

3. The laws of a Member State requiring a greater subscribed capital for companies carrying on certain types of activity shall apply to SEs with registered offices in that Member State.

[11.179]
Article 5

Subject to Article 4(1) and (2), the capital of an SE, its maintenance and changes thereto, together with its shares, bonds and other similar securities shall be governed by the provisions which would apply to a public limited-liability company with a registered office in the Member State in which the SE is registered.

[11.180]
Article 6
For the purposes of this Regulation, "the statutes of the SE" shall mean both the instrument of incorporation and, where they are the subject of a separate document, the statutes of the SE.

[11.181]
Article 7
The registered office of an SE shall be located within the Community, in the same Member State as its head office. A Member State may in addition impose on SEs registered in its territory the obligation of locating their head office and their registered office in the same place.

[11.182]
Article 8
1. The registered office of an SE may be transferred to another Member State in accordance with paragraphs 2 to 13. Such a transfer shall not result in the winding up of the SE or in the creation of a new legal person.
2. The management or administrative organ shall draw up a transfer proposal and publicise it in accordance with Article 13, without prejudice to any additional forms of publication provided for by the Member State of the registered office. That proposal shall state the current name, registered office and number of the SE and shall cover:
    (a)   the proposed registered office of the SE;
    (b)   the proposed statutes of the SE including, where appropriate, its new name;
    (c)   any implication the transfer may have on employees' involvement;
    (d)   the proposed transfer timetable;
    (e)   any rights provided for the protection of shareholders and/or creditors.
3. The management or administrative organ shall draw up a report explaining and justifying the legal and economic aspects of the transfer and explaining the implications of the transfer for shareholders, creditors and employees.
4. An SE's shareholders and creditors shall be entitled, at least one month before the general meeting called upon to decide on the transfer, to examine at the SE's registered office the transfer proposal and the report drawn up pursuant to paragraph 3 and, on request, to obtain copies of those documents free of charge.
5. A Member State may, in the case of SEs registered within its territory, adopt provisions designed to ensure appropriate protection for minority shareholders who oppose a transfer.
6. No decision to transfer may be taken for two months after publication of the proposal. Such a decision shall be taken as laid down in Article 59.
7. Before the competent authority issues the certificate mentioned in paragraph 8, the SE shall satisfy it that, in respect of any liabilities arising prior to the publication of the transfer proposal, the interests of creditors and holders of other rights in respect of the SE (including those of public bodies) have been adequately protected in accordance with requirements laid down by the Member State where the SE has its registered office prior to the transfer.

    A Member State may extend the application of the first subparagraph to liabilities that arise (or may arise) prior to the transfer.

    The first and second subparagraphs shall be without prejudice to the application to SEs of the national legislation of Member States concerning the satisfaction or securing of payments to public bodies.
8. In the Member State in which an SE has its registered office the court, notary or other competent authority shall issue a certificate attesting to the completion of the acts and formalities to be accomplished before the transfer.
9. The new registration may not be effected until the certificate referred to in paragraph 8 has been submitted, and evidence produced that the formalities required for registration in the country of the new registered office have been completed.
10. The transfer of an SE's registered office and the consequent amendment of its statutes shall take effect on the date on which the SE is registered, in accordance with Article 12, in the register for its new registered office.
11. When the SE's new registration has been effected, the registry for its new registration shall notify the registry for its old registration. Deletion of the old registration shall be effected on receipt of that notification, but not before.
12. The new registration and the deletion of the old registration shall be publicised in the Member States concerned in accordance with Article 13.
13. On publication of an SE's new registration, the new registered office may be relied on as against third parties. However, as long as the deletion of the SE's registration from the register for its previous registered office has not been publicised, third parties may continue to rely on the previous registered office unless the SE proves that such third parties were aware of the new registered office.
14. The laws of a Member State may provide that, as regards SEs registered in that Member State, the transfer of a registered office which would result in a change of the law applicable shall not take effect if any of that Member State's competent authorities opposes it within the two-month period referred to in paragraph 6. Such opposition may be based only on grounds of public interest.

Where an SE is supervised by a national financial supervisory authority according to Community directives the right to oppose the change of registered office applies to this authority as well.

Review by a judicial authority shall be possible.

15. An SE may not transfer its registered office if proceedings for winding up, liquidation, insolvency or suspension of payments or other similar proceedings have been brought against it.

16. An SE which has transferred its registered office to another Member State shall be considered, in respect of any cause of action arising prior to the transfer as determined in paragraph 10, as having its registered office in the Member States where the SE was registered prior to the transfer, even if the SE is sued after the transfer.

[11.183]
Article 9
1. An SE shall be governed:
  (a) by this Regulation,
  (b) where expressly authorised by this Regulation, by the provisions of its statutes
       or
  (c) in the case of matters not regulated by this Regulation or, where matters are partly regulated by it, of those aspects not covered by it, by:
       (i)   the provisions of laws adopted by Member States in implementation of Community measures relating specifically to SEs;
       (ii) the provisions of Member States' laws which would apply to a public limited-liability company formed in accordance with the law of the Member State in which the SE has its registered office;
       (iii) the provisions of its statutes, in the same way as for a public limited-liability company formed in accordance with the law of the Member State in which the SE has its registered office.
2. The provisions of laws adopted by Member States specifically for the SE must be in accordance with Directives applicable to public limited-liability companies referred to in Annex I.
3. If the nature of the business carried out by an SE is regulated by specific provisions of national laws, those laws shall apply in full to the SE.

[11.184]
Article 10
Subject to this Regulation, an SE shall be treated in every Member State as if it were a public limited-liability company formed in accordance with the law of the Member State in which it has its registered office.

[11.185]
Article 11
1. The name of an SE shall be preceded or followed by the abbreviation SE.
2. Only SEs may include the abbreviation SE in their name.
3. Nevertheless, companies, firms and other legal entities registered in a Member State before the date of entry into force of this Regulation in the names of which the abbreviation SE appears shall not be required to alter their names.

[11.186]
Article 12
1. Every SE shall be registered in the Member State in which it has its registered office in a register designated by the law of that Member State in accordance with Article 3 of the first Council Directive (68/151/EEC) of 9 March 1968 on coordination of safeguards which, for the protection of the interests of members and others, are required by Member States of companies within the meaning of the second paragraph of Article 58 of the Treaty, with a view to making such safeguards equivalent throughout the Community.[1]
2. An SE may not be registered unless an agreement on arrangements for employee involvement pursuant to Article 4 of Directive 2001/86/EC has been concluded, or a decision pursuant to Article 3(6) of the Directive has been taken, or the period for negotiations pursuant to Article 5 of the Directive has expired without an agreement having been concluded.
3. In order for an SE to be registered in a Member State which has made use of the option referred to in Article 7(3) of Directive 2001/86/EC, either an agreement pursuant to Article 4 of the Directive must have been concluded on the arrangements for employee involvement, including participation, or none of the participating companies must have been governed by participation rules prior to the registration of the SE.
4. The statutes of the SE must not conflict at any time with the arrangements for employee involvement which have been so determined. Where new such arrangements determined pursuant to the Directive conflict with the existing statutes, the statutes shall to the extent necessary be amended.

In this case, a Member State may provide that the management organ or the administrative organ of the SE shall be entitled to proceed to amend the statutes without any further decision from the general shareholders meeting.

NOTES

    ¹ OJ L65, 14.3.1968, p 8. Directive as last amended by the 1994 Act of Accession.

[11.187]
Article 13
Publication of the documents and particulars concerning an SE which must be publicised under this Regulation shall be effected in the manner laid down in the laws of the Member State in which the SE has its registered office in accordance with Directive 68/151/EEC.

[11.188]
Article 14
1.   Notice of an SE's registration and of the deletion of such a registration shall be published for information purposes in the Official Journal of the European Communities after publication in accordance with Article 13. That notice shall state the name, number, date and place of registration of the SE, the date and place of publication and the title of publication, the registered office of the SE and its sector of activity.
2.   Where the registered office of an SE is transferred in accordance with Article 8, notice shall be published giving the information provided for in paragraph 1, together with that relating to the new registration.
3.   The particulars referred to in paragraph 1 shall be forwarded to the Office for Official Publications of the European Communities within one month of the publication referred to in Article 13.

TITLE II
FORMATION

SECTION 1
GENERAL

[11.189]
Article 15
1.   Subject to this Regulation, the formation of an SE shall be governed by the law applicable to public limited-liability companies in the Member State in which the SE establishes its registered office.
2.   The registration of an SE shall be publicised in accordance with Article 13.

[11.190]
Article 16
1.   An SE shall acquire legal personality on the date on which it is registered in the register referred to in Article 12.
2.   If acts have been performed in an SE's name before its registration in accordance with Article 12 and the SE does not assume the obligations arising out of such acts after its registration, the natural persons, companies, firms or other legal entities which performed those acts shall be jointly and severally liable therefor, without limit, in the absence of agreement to the contrary.

SECTION 2
FORMATION BY MERGER

[11.191]
Article 17
1.   An SE may be formed by means of a merger in accordance with Article 2(1).
2.   Such a merger may be carried out in accordance with:
   (a)   the procedure for merger by acquisition laid down in Article 3(1) of the third Council Directive (78/855/EEC) of 9 October 1978 based on Article 54(3)(g) of the Treaty concerning mergers of public limited-liability companies¹ or
   (b)   the procedure for merger by the formation of a new company laid down in Article 4(1) of the said Directive.
In the case of a merger by acquisition, the acquiring company shall take the form of an SE when the merger takes place. In the case of a merger by the formation of a new company, the SE shall be the newly formed company.

NOTES

    ¹ OJ L295, 20.10.1978, p 36. Directive as last amended by the 1994 Act of Accession.

[11.192]
Article 18
For matters not covered by this section or, where a matter is partly covered by it, for aspects not covered by it, each company involved in the formation of an SE by merger shall be governed by the provisions of the law of the Member State to which it is subject that apply to mergers of public limited-liability companies in accordance with Directive 78/855/EEC.

[11.193]
Article 19
The laws of a Member State may provide that a company governed by the law of that Member State may not take part in the formation of an SE by merger if any of that Member State's competent authorities opposes it before the issue of the certificate referred to in Article 25(2).

Such opposition may be based only on grounds of public interest. Review by a judicial authority shall be possible.

[11.194]
Article 20
1. The management or administrative organs of merging companies shall draw up draft terms of merger. The draft terms of merger shall include the following particulars:
   (a)   the name and registered office of each of the merging companies together with those proposed for the SE;
   (b)   the share-exchange ratio and the amount of any compensation;
   (c)   the terms for the allotment of shares in the SE;
   (d)   the date from which the holding of shares in the SE will entitle the holders to share in profits and any special conditions affecting that entitlement;
   (e)   the date from which the transactions of the merging companies will be treated for accounting purposes as being those of the SE;
   (f)   the rights conferred by the SE on the holders of shares to which special rights are attached and on the holders of securities other than shares, or the measures proposed concerning them;
   (g)   any special advantage granted to the experts who examine the draft terms of merger or to members of the administrative, management, supervisory or controlling organs of the merging companies;
   (h)   the statutes of the SE;
   (i)   information on the procedures by which arrangements for employee involvement are determined pursuant to Directive 2001/86/EC.
2. The merging companies may include further items in the draft terms of merger.

[11.195]
Article 21
For each of the merging companies and subject to the additional requirements imposed by the Member State to which the company concerned is subject, the following particulars shall be published in the national gazette of that Member State:
   (a)   the type, name and registered office of every merging company;
   (b)   the register in which the documents referred to in Article 3(2) of Directive 68/151/EEC are filed in respect of each merging company, and the number of the entry in that register;
   (c)   an indication of the arrangements made in accordance with Article 24 for the exercise of the rights of the creditors of the company in question and the address at which complete information on those arrangements may be obtained free of charge;
   (d)   an indication of the arrangements made in accordance with Article 24 for the exercise of the rights of minority shareholders of the company in question and the address at which complete information on those arrangements may be obtained free of charge;
   (e)   the name and registered office proposed for the SE.

[11.196]
Article 22
As an alternative to experts operating on behalf of each of the merging companies, one or more independent experts as defined in Article 10 of Directive 78/855/EEC, appointed for those purposes at the joint request of the companies by a judicial or administrative authority in the Member State of one of the merging companies or of the proposed SE, may examine the draft terms of merger and draw up a single report to all the shareholders.

The experts shall have the right to request from each of the merging companies any information they consider necessary to enable them to complete their function.

[11.197]
Article 23
1. The general meeting of each of the merging companies shall approve the draft terms of merger.
2. Employee involvement in the SE shall be decided pursuant to Directive 2001/86/EC. The general meetings of each of the merging companies may reserve the right to make registration of the SE conditional upon its express ratification of the arrangements so decided.

[11.198]
Article 24

1. The law of the Member State governing each merging company shall apply as in the case of a merger of public limited-liability companies, taking into account the cross-border nature of the merger, with regard to the protection of the interests of:

(a) creditors of the merging companies;

(b) holders of bonds of the merging companies;

(c) holders of securities, other than shares, which carry special rights in the merging companies.

2. A Member State may, in the case of the merging companies governed by its law, adopt provisions designed to ensure appropriate protection for minority shareholders who have opposed the merger.

[11.199]
Article 25

1. The legality of a merger shall be scrutinised, as regards the part of the procedure concerning each merging company, in accordance with the law on mergers of public limited-liability companies of the Member State to which the merging company is subject.

2. In each Member State concerned the court, notary or other competent authority shall issue a certificate conclusively attesting to the completion of the pre-merger acts and formalities.

3. If the law of a Member State to which a merging company is subject provides for a procedure to scrutinise and amend the share-exchange ratio, or a procedure to compensate minority shareholders, without preventing the registration of the merger, such procedures shall only apply if the other merging companies situated in Member States which do not provide for such procedure explicitly accept, when approving the draft terms of the merger in accordance with Article 23(1), the possibility for the shareholders of that merging company to have recourse to such procedure. In such cases, the court, notary or other competent authorities may issue the certificate referred to in paragraph 2 even if such a procedure has been commenced. The certificate must, however, indicate that the procedure is pending. The decision in the procedure shall be binding on the acquiring company and all its shareholders.

[11.200]
Article 26

1. The legality of a merger shall be scrutinised, as regards the part of the procedure concerning the completion of the merger and the formation of the SE, by the court, notary or other authority competent in the Member State of the proposed registered office of the SE to scrutinise that aspect of the legality of mergers of public limited-liability companies.

2. To that end each merging company shall submit to the competent authority the certificate referred to in Article 25(2) within six months of its issue together with a copy of the draft terms of merger approved by that company.

3. The authority referred to in paragraph 1 shall in particular ensure that the merging companies have approved draft terms of merger in the same terms and that arrangements for employee involvement have been determined pursuant to Directive 2001/86/EC.

4. That authority shall also satisfy itself that the SE has been formed in accordance with the requirements of the law of the Member State in which it has its registered office in accordance with Article 15.

[11.201]
Article 27

1. A merger and the simultaneous formation of an SE shall take effect on the date on which the SE is registered in accordance with Article 12.

2. The SE may not be registered until the formalities provided for in Articles 25 and 26 have been completed.

[11.202]
Article 28

For each of the merging companies the completion of the merger shall be publicised as laid down by the law of each Member State in accordance with Article 3 of Directive 68/151/EEC.

[11.203]
Article 29

1. A merger carried out as laid down in Article 17(2)(a) shall have the following consequences ipso jure and simultaneously:

(a) all the assets and liabilities of each company being acquired are transferred to the acquiring company;

(b) the shareholders of the company being acquired become shareholders of the acquiring company;

(c) the company being acquired ceases to exist;

(d) the acquiring company adopts the form of an SE.

2.   A merger carried out as laid down in Article 17(2)(b) shall have the following consequences ipso jure and simultaneously:
  (a)   all the assets and liabilities of the merging companies are transferred to the SE;
  (b)   the shareholders of the merging companies become shareholders of the SE;
  (c)   the merging companies cease to exist.

3.   Where, in the case of a merger of public limited-liability companies, the law of a Member State requires the completion of any special formalities before the transfer of certain assets, rights and obligations by the merging companies becomes effective against third parties, those formalities shall apply and shall be carried out either by the merging companies or by the SE following its registration.

4.   The rights and obligations of the participating companies on terms and conditions of employment arising from national law, practice and individual employment contracts or employment relationships and existing at the date of the registration shall, by reason of such registration be transferred to the SE upon its registration.

[11.204]
Article 30
A merger as provided for in Article 2(1) may not be declared null and void once the SE has been registered.

The absence of scrutiny of the legality of the merger pursuant to Articles 25 and 26 may be included among the grounds for the winding-up of the SE.

[11.205]
Article 31
1.   Where a merger within the meaning of Article 17(2)(a) is carried out by a company which holds all the shares and other securities conferring the right to vote at general meetings of another company, neither Article 20(1)(b), (c) and (d), Article 29(1)(b) nor Article 22 shall apply. National law governing each merging company and mergers of public limited-liability companies in accordance with Article 24 of Directive 78/855/EEC shall nevertheless apply.

2.   Where a merger by acquisition is carried out by a company which holds 90% or more but not all of the shares and other securities conferring the right to vote at general meetings of another company, reports by the management or administrative body, reports by an independent expert or experts and the documents necessary for scrutiny shall be required only to the extent that the national law governing either the acquiring company or the company being acquired so requires.

Member States may, however, provide that this paragraph may apply where a company holds shares conferring 90% or more but not all of the voting rights.

SECTION 3
FORMATION OF A HOLDING SE

[11.206]
Article 32
1.   A holding SE may be formed in accordance with Article 2(2).

A company promoting the formation of a holding SE in accordance with Article 2(2) shall continue to exist.

2.   The management or administrative organs of the companies which promote such an operation shall draw up, in the same terms, draft terms for the formation of the holding SE. The draft terms shall include a report explaining and justifying the legal and economic aspects of the formation and indicating the implications for the shareholders and for the employees of the adoption of the form of a holding SE. The draft terms shall also set out the particulars provided for in Article 20(1)(a), (b), (c), (f), (g), (h) and (i) and shall fix the minimum proportion of the shares in each of the companies promoting the operation which the shareholders must contribute to the formation of the holding SE. That proportion shall be shares conferring more than 50% of the permanent voting rights.

3.   For each of the companies promoting the operation, the draft terms for the formation of the holding SE shall be publicised in the manner laid down in each Member State's national law in accordance with Article 3 of Directive 68/151/EEC at least one month before the date of the general meeting called to decide thereon.

4.   One or more experts independent of the companies promoting the operation, appointed or approved by a judicial or administrative authority in the Member State to which each company is subject in accordance with national provisions adopted in implementation of Directive 78/855/EEC, shall examine the draft terms of formation drawn up in accordance with paragraph 2 and draw up a written report for the shareholders of each company. By agreement between the companies promoting the operation, a single written report may be drawn up for the shareholders of all the companies by one or more independent experts, appointed or approved by a judicial or administrative authority in the Member State to which one of the companies promoting the operation or the proposed SE is subject in accordance with national provisions adopted in implementation of Directive 78/855/EEC.

Part 11   EU Legislation

5.   The report shall indicate any particular difficulties of valuation and state whether the proposed share-exchange ratio is fair and reasonable, indicating the methods used to arrive at it and whether such methods are adequate in the case in question.

6.   The general meeting of each company promoting the operation shall approve the draft terms of formation of the holding SE.

   Employee involvement in the holding SE shall be decided pursuant to Directive 2001/86/EC. The general meetings of each company promoting the operation may reserve the right to make registration of the holding SE conditional upon its express ratification of the arrangements so decided.

7.   These provisions shall apply mutatis mutandis to private limited-liability companies.

[11.207]
Article 33

1.   The shareholders of the companies promoting such an operation shall have a period of three months in which to inform the promoting companies whether they intend to contribute their shares to the formation of the holding SE. That period shall begin on the date upon which the terms for the formation of the holding SE have been finally determined in accordance with Article 32.

2.   The holding SE shall be formed only if, within the period referred to in paragraph 1, the shareholders of the companies promoting the operation have assigned the minimum proportion of shares in each company in accordance with the draft terms of formation and if all the other conditions are fulfilled.

3.   If the conditions for the formation of the holding SE are all fulfilled in accordance with paragraph 2, that fact shall, in respect of each of the promoting companies, be publicised in the manner laid down in the national law governing each of those companies adopted in implementation of Article 3 of Directive 68/151/EEC.

   Shareholders of the companies promoting the operation who have not indicated whether they intend to make their shares available to the promoting companies for the purpose of forming the holding SE within the period referred to in paragraph 1 shall have a further month in which to do so.

4.   Shareholders who have contributed their securities to the formation of the SE shall receive shares in the holding SE.

5.   The holding SE may not be registered until it is shown that the formalities referred to in Article 32 have been completed and that the conditions referred to in paragraph 2 have been fulfilled.

[11.208]
Article 34

A Member State may, in the case of companies promoting such an operation, adopt provisions designed to ensure protection for minority shareholders who oppose the operation, creditors and employees.

SECTION 4
FORMATION OF A SUBSIDIARY SE

[11.209]
Article 35

An SE may be formed in accordance with Article 2(3).

[11.210]
Article 36

Companies, firms and other legal entities participating in such an operation shall be subject to the provisions governing their participation in the formation of a subsidiary in the form of a public limited-liability company under national law.

SECTION 5
CONVERSION OF AN EXISTING PUBLIC LIMITED-LIABILITY COMPANY
INTO AN SE

[11.211]
Article 37

1.   An SE may be formed in accordance with Article 2(4).

2.   Without prejudice to Article 12 the conversion of a public limited-liability company into an SE shall not result in the winding up of the company or in the creation of a new legal person.

3.   The registered office may not be transferred from one Member State to another pursuant to Article 8 at the same time as the conversion is effected.

4.   The management or administrative organ of the company in question shall draw up draft terms of conversion and a report explaining and justifying the legal and economic aspects of the conversion and indicating the implications for the shareholders and for the employees of the adoption of the form of an SE.

5. The draft terms of conversion shall be publicised in the manner laid down in each Member State's law in accordance with Article 3 of Directive 68/151/EEC at least one month before the general meeting called upon to decide thereon.

6. Before the general meeting referred to in paragraph 7 one or more independent experts appointed or approved, in accordance with the national provisions adopted in implementation of Article 10 of Directive 78/855/EEC, by a judicial or administrative authority in the Member State to which the company being converted into an SE is subject shall certify in compliance with Directive 77/91/EEC[1] mutatis mutandis that the company has net assets at least equivalent to its capital plus those reserves which must not be distributed under the law or the Statutes.

7. The general meeting of the company in question shall approve the draft terms of conversion together with the statutes of the SE. The decision of the general meeting shall be passed as laid down in the provisions of national law adopted in implementation of Article 7 of Directive 78/855/EEC.

8. Member States may condition a conversion to a favourable vote of a qualified majority or unanimity in the organ of the company to be converted within which employee participation is organised.

9. The rights and obligations of the company to be converted on terms and conditions of employment arising from national law, practice and individual employment contracts or employment relationships and existing at the date of the registration shall, by reason of such registration be transferred to the SE.

NOTES

[1] Second Council Directive 77/91/EEC of 13 December 1976 on coordination of safeguards which, for the protection of the interests of members and others, are required by Member States of companies within the meaning of the second paragraph of Article 58 of the Treaty, in respect of the formation of public limited liability companies and the maintenance and alteration of their capital, with a view to making such safeguards equivalent (OJ L26, 31.1.1977, p 1). Directive as last amended by the 1994 Act of Accession.

TITLE III
STRUCTURE OF THE SE

[11.212]
Article 38

Under the conditions laid down by this Regulation an SE shall comprise:
(a) a general meeting of shareholders and
(b) either a supervisory organ and a management organ (two-tier system) or an administrative organ (one-tier system) depending on the form adopted in the statutes.

SECTION 1
TWO-TIER SYSTEM

[11.213]
Article 39

1. The management organ shall be responsible for managing the SE. A Member State may provide that a managing director or managing directors shall be responsible for the current management under the same conditions as for public limited-liability companies that have registered offices within that Member State's territory.

2. The member or members of the management organ shall be appointed and removed by the supervisory organ.

A Member State may, however, require or permit the statutes to provide that the member or members of the management organ shall be appointed and removed by the general meeting under the same conditions as for public limited-liability companies that have registered offices within its territory.

3. No person may at the same time be a member of both the management organ and the supervisory organ of the same SE. The supervisory organ may, however, nominate one of its members to act as a member of the management organ in the event of a vacancy. During such a period the functions of the person concerned as a member of the supervisory organ shall be suspended. A Member State may impose a time limit on such a period.

4. The number of members of the management organ or the rules for determining it shall be laid down in the SE's statutes. A Member State may, however, fix a minimum and/or a maximum number.

5. Where no provision is made for a two-tier system in relation to public limited-liability companies with registered offices within its territory, a Member State may adopt the appropriate measures in relation to SEs.

[11.214]
Article 40

1. The supervisory organ shall supervise the work of the management organ. It may not itself exercise the power to manage the SE.

Part 11 EU Legislation

2. The members of the supervisory organ shall be appointed by the general meeting. The members of the first supervisory organ may, however, be appointed by the statutes. This shall apply without prejudice to Article 47(4) or to any employee participation arrangements determined pursuant to Directive 2001/86/EC.

3. The number of members of the supervisory organ or the rules for determining it shall be laid down in the statutes. A Member State may, however, stipulate the number of members of the supervisory organ for SEs registered within its territory or a minimum and/or a maximum number.

[11.215]
Article 41

1. The management organ shall report to the supervisory organ at least once every three months on the progress and foreseeable development of the SE's business.

2. In addition to the regular information referred to in paragraph 1, the management organ shall promptly pass the supervisory organ any information on events likely to have an appreciable effect on the SE.

3. The supervisory organ may require the management organ to provide information of any kind which it needs to exercise supervision in accordance with Article 40(1). A Member State may provide that each member of the supervisory organ also be entitled to this facility.

4. The supervisory organ may undertake or arrange for any investigations necessary for the performance of its duties.

5. Each member of the supervisory organ shall be entitled to examine all information submitted to it.

[11.216]
Article 42

The supervisory organ shall elect a chairman from among its members. If half of the members are appointed by employees, only a member appointed by the general meeting of shareholders may be elected chairman.

SECTION 2
THE ONE-TIER SYSTEM

[11.217]
Article 43

1. The administrative organ shall manage the SE. A Member State may provide that a managing director or managing directors shall be responsible for the day-to-day management under the same conditions as for public limited-liability companies that have registered offices within that Member State's territory.

2. The number of members of the administrative organ or the rules for determining it shall be laid down in the SE's statutes. A Member State may, however, set a minimum and, where necessary, a maximum number of members.

The administrative organ shall, however, consist of at least three members where employee participation is regulated in accordance with Directive 2001/86/EC.

3. The member or members of the administrative organ shall be appointed by the general meeting. The members of the first administrative organ may, however, be appointed by the statutes. This shall apply without prejudice to Article 47(4) or to any employee participation arrangements determined pursuant to Directive 2001/86/EC.

4. Where no provision is made for a one-tier system in relation to public limited-liability companies with registered offices within its territory, a Member State may adopt the appropriate measures in relation to SEs.

[11.218]
Article 44

1. The administrative organ shall meet at least once every three months at intervals laid down by the statutes to discuss the progress and foreseeable development of the SE's business.

2. Each member of the administrative organ shall be entitled to examine all information submitted to it.

[11.219]
Article 45

The administrative organ shall elect a chairman from among its members. If half of the members are appointed by employees, only a member appointed by the general meeting of shareholders may be elected chairman.

SECTION 3
RULES COMMON TO THE ONE-TIER AND TWO-TIER SYSTEMS

[11.220]
Article 46
1. Members of company organs shall be appointed for a period laid down in the statutes not exceeding six years.
2. Subject to any restrictions laid down in the statutes, members may be reappointed once or more than once for the period determined in accordance with paragraph 1.

[11.221]
Article 47
1. An SE's statutes may permit a company or other legal entity to be a member of one of its organs, provided that the law applicable to public limited-liability companies in the Member State in which the SE's registered office is situated does not provide otherwise.

That company or other legal entity shall designate a natural person to exercise its functions on the organ in question.
2. No person may be a member of any SE organ or a representative of a member within the meaning of paragraph 1 who:
   (a) is disqualified, under the law of the Member State in which the SE's registered office is situated, from serving on the corresponding organ of a public limited-liability company governed by the law of that Member State, or
   (b) is disqualified from serving on the corresponding organ of a public limited-liability company governed by the law of a Member State owing to a judicial or administrative decision delivered in a Member State.
3. An SE's statutes may, in accordance with the law applicable to public limited-liability companies in the Member State in which the SE's registered office is situated, lay down special conditions of eligibility for members representing the shareholders.
4. This Regulation shall not affect national law permitting a minority of shareholders or other persons or authorities to appoint some of the members of a company organ.

[11.222]
Article 48
1. An SE's statutes shall list the categories of transactions which require authorisation of the management organ by the supervisory organ in the two-tier system or an express decision by the administrative organ in the one-tier system.

A Member State may, however, provide that in the two-tier system the supervisory organ may itself make certain categories of transactions subject to authorisation.
2. A Member State may determine the categories of transactions which must at least be indicated in the statutes of SEs registered within its territory.

[11.223]
Article 49
The members of an SE's organs shall be under a duty, even after they have ceased to hold office, not to divulge any information which they have concerning the SE the disclosure of which might be prejudicial to the company's interests, except where such disclosure is required or permitted under national law provisions applicable to public limited-liability companies or is in the public interest.

[11.224]
Article 50
1. Unless otherwise provided by this Regulation or the statutes, the internal rules relating to quorums and decision-taking in SE organs shall be as follows:
   (a) quorum: at least half of the members must be present or represented;
   (b) decision-taking: a majority of the members present or represented.
2. Where there is no relevant provision in the statutes, the chairman of each organ shall have a casting vote in the event of a tie. There shall be no provision to the contrary in the statutes, however, where half of the supervisory organ consists of employees' representatives.
3. Where employee participation is provided for in accordance with Directive 2001/86/EC, a Member State may provide that the supervisory organ's quorum and decision-making shall, by way of derogation from the provisions referred to in paragraphs 1 and 2, be subject to the rules applicable, under the same conditions, to public limited-liability companies governed by the law of the Member State concerned.

[11.225]
Article 51
Members of an SE's management, supervisory and administrative organs shall be liable, in accordance with the provisions applicable to public limited-liability companies in the Member State in which the SE's registered office is situated, for loss or damage sustained by the SE following any breach on their part of the legal, statutory or other obligations inherent in their duties.

SECTION 4
GENERAL MEETING

[11.226]
Article 52
The general meeting shall decide on matters for which it is given sole responsibility by:
  (a)   this Regulation or
  (b)   the legislation of the Member State in which the SE's registered office is situated adopted
         in implementation of Directive 2001/86/EC.
  Furthermore, the general meeting shall decide on matters for which responsibility is given to the
general meeting of a public limited-liability company governed by the law of the Member State in
which the SE's registered office is situated, either by the law of that Member State or by the
SE's statutes in accordance with that law.

[11.227]
Article 53
Without prejudice to the rules laid down in this section, the organisation and conduct of general
meetings together with voting procedures shall be governed by the law applicable to public limited-
liability companies in the Member State in which the SE's registered office is situated.

[11.228]
Article 54
1.   An SE shall hold a general meeting at least once each calendar year, within six months of the
end of its financial year, unless the law of the Member State in which the SE's registered office is
situated applicable to public limited-liability companies carrying on the same type of activity as the
SE provides for more frequent meetings. A Member State may, however, provide that the first
general meeting may be held at any time in the 18 months following an SE's incorporation.
2.   General meetings may be convened at any time by the management organ, the administrative
organ, the supervisory organ or any other organ or competent authority in accordance with the
national law applicable to public limited-liability companies in the Member State in which the
SE's registered office is situated.

[11.229]
Article 55
1.   One or more shareholders who together hold at least 10% of an SE's subscribed capital may
request the SE to convene a general meeting and draw up the agenda therefor; the SE's statutes or
national legislation may provide for a smaller proportion under the same conditions as those
applicable to public limited-liability companies.
2.   The request that a general meeting be convened shall state the items to be put on the agenda.
3.   If, following a request made under paragraph 1, a general meeting is not held in due time and,
in any event, within two months, the competent judicial or administrative authority within the
jurisdiction of which the SE's registered office is situated may order that a general meeting be
convened within a given period or authorise either the shareholders who have requested it or their
representatives to convene a general meeting. This shall be without prejudice to any national
provisions which allow the shareholders themselves to convene general meetings.

[11.230]
Article 56
One or more shareholders who together hold at least 10% of an SE's subscribed capital may request
that one or more additional items be put on the agenda of any general meeting. The procedures and
time limits applicable to such requests shall be laid down by the national law of the Member State
in which the SE's registered office is situated or, failing that, by the SE's statutes. The above
proportion may be reduced by the statutes or by the law of the Member State in which the
SE's registered office is situated under the same conditions as are applicable to public limited-
liability companies.

[11.231]
Article 57
Save where this Regulation or, failing that, the law applicable to public limited-liability companies
in the Member State in which an SE's registered office is situated requires a larger majority, the
general meeting's decisions shall be taken by a majority of the votes validly cast.

[11.232]
Article 58
The votes cast shall not include votes attaching to shares in respect of which the shareholder has not
taken part in the vote or has abstained or has returned a blank or spoilt ballot paper.

[11.233]
Article 59
1. Amendment of an SE's statutes shall require a decision by the general meeting taken by a majority which may not be less than two thirds of the votes cast, unless the law applicable to public limited-liability companies in the Member State in which an SE's registered office is situated requires or permits a larger majority.
2. A Member State may, however, provide that where at least half of an SE's subscribed capital is represented, a simple majority of the votes referred to in paragraph 1 shall suffice.
3. Amendments to an SE's statutes shall be publicised in accordance with Article 13.

[11.234]
Article 60
1. Where an SE has two or more classes of shares, every decision by the general meeting shall be subject to a separate vote by each class of shareholders whose class rights are affected thereby.
2. Where a decision by the general meeting requires the majority of votes specified in Article 59(1) or (2), that majority shall also be required for the separate vote by each class of shareholders whose class rights are affected by the decision.

TITLE IV
ANNUAL ACCOUNTS AND CONSOLIDATED ACCOUNTS

[11.235]
Article 61
Subject to Article 62 an SE shall be governed by the rules applicable to public limited-liability companies under the law of the Member State in which its registered office is situated as regards the preparation of its annual and, where appropriate, consolidated accounts including the accompanying annual report and the auditing and publication of those accounts.

[11.236]
Article 62
1. An SE which is a credit or financial institution shall be governed by the rules laid down in the national law of the Member State in which its registered office is situated in implementation of Directive 2000/12/EC of the European Parliament and of the Council of 20 March 2000 relating to the taking up and pursuit of the business of credit institutions[1] as regards the preparation of its annual and, where appropriate, consolidated accounts, including the accompanying annual report and the auditing and publication of those accounts.
2. An SE which is an insurance undertaking shall be governed by the rules laid down in the national law of the Member State in which its registered office is situated in implementation of Council Directive 91/674/EEC of 19 December 1991 on the annual accounts and consolidated accounts of insurance undertakings[2] as regards the preparation of its annual and, where appropriate, consolidated accounts including the accompanying annual report and the auditing and publication of those accounts.

NOTES
[1]   OJ L126, 26.5.2000, p 1.
[2]   OJ L374, 31.12.1991, p 7.

TITLE V
WINDING UP, LIQUIDATION, INSOLVENCY AND CESSATION OF PAYMENTS

[11.237]
Article 63
As regards winding up, liquidation, insolvency, cessation of payments and similar procedures, an SE shall be governed by the legal provisions which would apply to a public limited-liability company formed in accordance with the law of the Member State in which its registered office is situated, including provisions relating to decision-making by the general meeting.

[11.238]
Article 64
1. When an SE no longer complies with the requirement laid down in Article 7, the Member State in which the SE's registered office is situated shall take appropriate measures to oblige the SE to regularise its position within a specified period either:
(a) by re-establishing its head office in the Member State in which its registered office is situated or
(b) by transferring the registered office by means of the procedure laid down in Article 8.
2. The Member State in which the SE's registered office is situated shall put in place the measures necessary to ensure that an SE which fails to regularise its position in accordance with paragraph 1 is liquidated.

3. The Member State in which the SE's registered office is situated shall set up a judicial remedy with regard to any established infringement of Article 7. That remedy shall have a suspensory effect on the procedures laid down in paragraphs 1 and 2.

4. Where it is established on the initiative of either the authorities or any interested party that an SE has its head office within the territory of a Member State in breach of Article 7, the authorities of that Member State shall immediately inform the Member State in which the SE's registered office is situated.

[11.239]
Article 65

Without prejudice to provisions of national law requiring additional publication, the initiation and termination of winding up, liquidation, insolvency or cessation of payment procedures and any decision to continue operating shall be publicised in accordance with Article 13.

[11.240]
Article 66

1. An SE may be converted into a public limited-liability company governed by the law of the Member State in which its registered office is situated. No decision on conversion may be taken before two years have elapsed since its registration or before the first two sets of annual accounts have been approved.

2. The conversion of an SE into a public limited-liability company shall not result in the winding up of the company or in the creation of a new legal person.

3. The management or administrative organ of the SE shall draw up draft terms of conversion and a report explaining and justifying the legal and economic aspects of the conversion and indicating the implications of the adoption of the public limited-liability company for the shareholders and for the employees.

4. The draft terms of conversion shall be publicised in the manner laid down in each Member State's law in accordance with Article 3 of Directive 68/151/EEC at least one month before the general meeting called to decide thereon.

5. Before the general meeting referred to in paragraph 6, one or more independent experts appointed or approved, in accordance with the national provisions adopted in implementation of Article 10 of Directive 78/855/EEC, by a judicial or administrative authority in the Member State to which the SE being converted into a public limited-liability company is subject shall certify that the company has assets at least equivalent to its capital.

6. The general meeting of the SE shall approve the draft terms of conversion together with the statutes of the public limited-liability company. The decision of the general meeting shall be passed as laid down in the provisions of national law adopted in implementation of Article 7 of Directive 78/855/EEC.

TITLE VI
ADDITIONAL AND TRANSITIONAL PROVISIONS

[11.241]
Article 67

1. If and so long as the third phase of economic and monetary union (EMU) does not apply to it each Member State may make SEs with registered offices within its territory subject to the same provisions as apply to public limited-liability companies covered by its legislation as regards the expression of their capital. An SE may, in any case, express its capital in euro as well. In that event the national currency/euro conversion rate shall be that for the last day of the month preceding that of the formation of the SE.

2. If and so long as the third phase of EMU does not apply to the Member State in which an SE has its registered office, the SE may, however, prepare and publish its annual and, where appropriate, consolidated accounts in euro. The Member State may require that the SE's annual and, where appropriate, consolidated accounts be prepared and published in the national currency under the same conditions as those laid down for public limited-liability companies governed by the law of that Member State. This shall not prejudge the additional possibility for an SE of publishing its annual and, where appropriate, consolidated accounts in euro in accordance with Council Directive 90/604/EEC of 8 November 1990 amending Directive 78/60/EEC on annual accounts and Directive 83/349/EEC on consolidated accounts as concerns the exemptions for small and medium-sized companies and the publication of accounts in ecu.[1]

NOTES

[1] OJ L317, 16.11.1990, p 57.

TITLE VII
FINAL PROVISIONS

[11.242]
Article 68
1.   The Member States shall make such provision as is appropriate to ensure the effective application of this Regulation.
2.   Each Member State shall designate the competent authorities within the meaning of Articles 8, 25, 26, 54, 55 and 64. It shall inform the Commission and the other Member States accordingly.

[11.243]
Article 69
Five years at the latest after the entry into force of this Regulation, the Commission shall forward to the Council and the European Parliament a report on the application of the Regulation and proposals for amendments, where appropriate. The report shall, in particular, analyse the appropriateness of:
(a)   allowing the location of an SE's head office and registered office in different Member States;
(b)   broadening the concept of merger in Article 17(2) in order to admit also other types of merger than those defined in Articles 3(1) and 4(1) of Directive 78/855/EEC;
(c)   revising the jurisdiction clause in Article 8(16) in the light of any provision which may have been inserted in the 1968 Brussels Convention or in any text adopted by Member States or by the Council to replace such Convention;
(d)   allowing provisions in the statutes of an SE adopted by a Member State in execution of authorisations given to the Member States by this Regulation or laws adopted to ensure the effective application of this Regulation in respect to the SE which deviate from or are complementary to these laws, even when such provisions would not be authorised in the statutes of a public limited-liability company having its registered office in the Member State.

[11.244]
Article 70
This Regulation shall enter into force on 8 October 2004.
   This Regulation shall be binding in its entirety and directly applicable in all Member States.

ANNEXES

ANNEX I
PUBLIC LIMITED-LIABILITY COMPANIES REFERRED TO IN ARTICLE 2(1)

[11.245]
BELGIUM:

la société anonyme/de naamloze vennootschap

[BULGARIA:

акционерно дружество]

[CZECH REPUBLIC:

akciová společnost]

DENMARK:

aktieselskaber

GERMANY:

die Aktiengesellschaft

[ESTONIA:

aktsiaselts]

GREECE:

ανώνυμη εταιρία

SPAIN:

la sociedad anónima

FRANCE:

la société anonyme

Part 11   EU Legislation

IRELAND:

public companies limited by shares

public companies limited by guarantee having a share capital

ITALY:

società per azioni

[CYPRUS:

Δημόσια Εταιρεία περιορισμένης ευθύνης με μετοχές, Δημόσια Εταιρεία περιορισμένης ευθύνης με εγγύηση

LATVIA:

akciju sabiedrība

LITHUANIA:

akcin s bendrov s]

LUXEMBOURG:

la société anonyme

[HUNGARY:

részvénytársaság

MALTA:

kumpaniji pubbliċi / public limited liability companies]

NETHERLANDS:

de naamloze vennootschap

AUSTRIA:

die Aktiengesellschaft

[POLAND:

spółka akcyjna]

PORTUGAL:

a sociedade anónima de responsabilidade limitada

[ROMANIA:

societate pe ac iuni]

[SLOVENIA:

delniška družba

SLOVAKIA:

akciová spoločnos]

FINLAND:

julkinen osakeyhtiö/publikt aktiebolag

SWEDEN:

publikt aktiebolag

UNITED KINGDOM:

public companies limited by shares

public companies limited by guarantee having a share capital

NOTES

Entries relating to Bulgaria and Romania inserted by Council Regulation 1791/2006/EC, Art 1, Annex, as from 1 January 2007; other entries in square brackets inserted by Council Regulation 885/2004/EC, Annex, as from 1 May 2004.

ANNEX II
PUBLIC AND PRIVATE LIMITED-LIABILITY COMPANIES REFERRED TO IN ARTICLE 2(2)

[11.246]
BELGIUM:

la société anonyme/de naamloze vennootschap,

la société privée à responsabilité limitée/besloten vennootschap met beperkte aansprakelijkheid

[BULGARIA:

акционерно дружество, дружество с ограничена отговорност]

[CZECH REPUBLIC:

akciová společnost,

společnost s ručením omezeným]

DENMARK:

aktieselskaber,

anpartsselskaber

GERMANY:

die Aktiengesellschaft,

die Gesellschaft mit beschränkter Haftung

[ESTONIA:

aktsiaselts ja osaühing]

GREECE:

ανώνυμη εταιρία

εταιρία περιορισμένης ευθύνης

SPAIN:

la sociedad anónima,

la sociedad de responsabilidad limitada

FRANCE:

la société anonyme,

la société à responsabilité limitée

IRELAND:

public companies limited by shares,

public companies limited by guarantee having a share capital,

private companies limited by shares,

private companies limited by guarantee having a share capital

ITALY:

società per azioni,

società a responsabilità limitata

[CYPRUS:

Δημόσια εταιρεία περιορισμένης ευθύνης με μετοχές,

δημόσια Εταιρεία περιορισμένης ευθύνης με εγγύηση,

ιδιωτική εταιρεία

LATVIA:

akciju sabiedriba,

Part 11   EU Legislation

un sabiedrība ar ierobežotu atbildību

LITHUANIA:

akcin s bendrov s,

uždarosios akcin s bendrov s]

LUXEMBOURG:

la société anonyme,

la société à responsabilité limitée

[HUNGARY:

részvénytársaság,

korlátolt felelősségû társaság

MALTA:

kumpaniji pubbliċi / public limited liability companies

kumpaniji privati / private limited liability companies]

NETHERLANDS:

de naamloze vennootschap,

de besloten vennootschap met beperkte aansprakelijkheid

AUSTRIA:

die Aktiengesellschaft,

die Gesellschaft mit beschränkter Haftung

[POLAND:

spółka akcyjna,

spółka z ograniczon odpowiedzialności]

PORTUGAL:

a sociedade anónima de responsabilidade limitada,

a sociedade por quotas de responsabilidade limitada

[ROMANIA:

societate pe ac iuni, societate cu răspundere limitată]

[SLOVENIA:

delniška družba,

družba z omejeno odgovornostjo

SLOVAKIA:

akciová spoločnos',

spoločnost' s ručením obmedzeným]

FINLAND:

osakeyhtiö

aktiebolag

SWEDEN:

aktiebolag

UNITED KINGDOM:

public companies limited by shares,

public companies limited by guarantee having a share capital,

private companies limited by shares,

private companies limited by guarantee having a share capital

NOTES

Entries relating to Bulgaria and Romania inserted by Council Regulation 1791/2006/EC, Art 1, Annex, as from 1 January 2007; other entries in square brackets inserted by Council Regulation 885/2004/EC, Annex, as from 1 May 2004.

EUROPEAN PARLIAMENT AND COUNCIL REGULATION

(1606/2002/EC)

of 19 July 2002

on the application of international accounting standards

NOTES

Date of publication in OJ: OJ L243, 11.9.2002, p 1. Notes are as in the original OJ version.

This Regulation is reproduced as amended by: European Parliament and Council Regulation 297/2008/EC.

[11.247]

THE EUROPEAN PARLIAMENT AND THE COUNCIL OF THE EUROPEAN UNION,

Having regard to the Treaty establishing the European Community, and in particular Article 95(1) thereof,

Having regard to the proposal from the Commission,[1]

Having regard to the opinion of the Economic and Social Committee,[2]

Acting in accordance with the procedure laid down in Article 251 of the Treaty,[3]

Whereas:

(1) The Lisbon European Council of 23 and 24 March 2000 emphasised the need to accelerate completion of the internal market for financial services, set the deadline of 2005 to implement the Commission's Financial Services Action Plan and urged that steps be taken to enhance the comparability of financial statements prepared by publicly traded companies.

(2) In order to contribute to a better functioning of the internal market, publicly traded companies must be required to apply a single set of high quality international accounting standards for the preparation of their consolidated financial statements. Furthermore, it is important that the financial reporting standards applied by Community companies participating in financial markets are accepted internationally and are truly global standards. This implies an increasing convergence of accounting standards currently used internationally with the ultimate objective of achieving a single set of global accounting standards.

(3) Council Directive 78/660/EEC of 25 July 1978 on the annual accounts of certain types of companies,[4] Council Directive 83/349/EEC of 13 June 1983 on consolidated accounts,[5] Council Directive 86/635/EEC of 8 December 1986 on the annual accounts and consolidated accounts of banks and other financial institutions[6] and Council Directive 91/674/EEC of 19 December 1991 on the annual accounts and consolidated accounts of insurance companies[7] are also addressed to publicly traded Community companies. The reporting requirements set out in these Directives cannot ensure the high level of transparency and comparability of financial reporting from all publicly traded Community companies which is a necessary condition for building an integrated capital market which operates effectively, smoothly and efficiently. It is therefore necessary to supplement the legal framework applicable to publicly traded companies.

(4) This Regulation aims at contributing to the efficient and cost-effective functioning of the capital market. The protection of investors and the maintenance of confidence in the financial markets is also an important aspect of the completion of the internal market in this area. This Regulation reinforces the freedom of movement of capital in the internal market and helps to enable Community companies to compete on an equal footing for financial resources available in the Community capital markets, as well as in world capital markets.

(5) It is important for the competitiveness of Community capital markets to achieve convergence of the standards used in Europe for preparing financial statements, with international accounting standards that can be used globally, for cross-border transactions or listing anywhere in the world.

(6) On 13 June 2000, the Commission published its Communication on "EU Financial Reporting Strategy: the way forward" in which it was proposed that all publicly traded Community companies prepare their consolidated financial statements in accordance with one single set of accounting standards, namely International Accounting Standards (IAS), at the latest by 2005.

(7) International Accounting Standards (IASs) are developed by the International Accounting Standards Committee (IASC), whose purpose is to develop a single set of global accounting standards. Further to the restructuring of the IASC, the new Board on 1 April 2001, as one of its first decisions, renamed the IASC as the International Accounting Standards Board (IASB) and, as far as future international accounting standards are concerned, renamed IAS as International Financial Reporting Standards (IFRS). These standards should, wherever possible and provided that they ensure a high degree of transparency and comparability for financial reporting in the Community, be made obligatory for use by all publicly traded Community companies.

(8) The measures necessary for the implementation of this Regulation should be adopted in accordance with Council Decision 1999/468/EC of 28 June 1999 laying down the procedures for the

Part 11   EU Legislation

exercise of implementing powers conferred on the Commission[8] and with due regard to the declaration made by the Commission in the European Parliament on 5 February 2002 concerning the implementation of financial services legislation.

(9) To adopt an international accounting standard for application in the Community, it is necessary firstly that it meets the basic requirement of the aforementioned Council Directives, that is to say that its application results in a true and fair view of the financial position and performance of an enterprise – this principle being considered in the light of the said Council Directives without implying a strict conformity with each and every provision of those Directives; secondly that, in accordance with the conclusions of the Council of 17 July 2000, it is conducive to the European public good and lastly that it meets basic criteria as to the quality of information required for financial statements to be useful to users.

(10) An accounting technical committee should provide support and expertise to the Commission in the assessment of international accounting standards.

(11) The endorsement mechanism should act expeditiously on proposed international accounting standards and also be a means to deliberate, reflect and exchange information on international accounting standards among the main parties concerned, in particular national accounting standard setters, supervisors in the fields of securities, banking and insurance, central banks including the ECB, the accounting profession and users and preparers of accounts. The mechanism should be a means to foster common understanding of adopted international accounting standards in the Community.

(12) In accordance with the principle of proportionality, the measures provided for in this Regulation, in requiring that a single set of international accounting standards be applied to publicly traded companies, are necessary to achieve the objective of contributing to the efficient and cost-effective functioning of Community capital markets and thereby to the completion of the internal market.

(13) In accordance with the same principle, it is necessary, as regards annual accounts, to leave to Member States the option to permit or require publicly traded companies to prepare them in conformity with international accounting standards adopted in accordance with the procedure laid down in this Regulation. Member States may decide as well to extend this permission or this requirement to other companies as regards the preparation of their consolidated accounts and/or their annual accounts.

(14) In order to facilitate an exchange of views and to allow Member States to coordinate their positions, the Commission should periodically inform the accounting regulatory committee about active projects, discussion papers, point outlines and exposure drafts issued by the IASB and about the consequential technical work of the accounting technical committee. It is also important that the accounting regulatory committee is informed at an early stage if the Commission intends not to propose to adopt an international accounting standard.

(15) In its deliberations on and in elaborating positions to be taken on documents and papers issued by the IASB in the process of developing international accounting standards (IFRS and SIC-IFRIC), the Commission should take into account the importance of avoiding competitive disadvantages for European companies operating in the global marketplace, and, to the maximum possible extent, the views expressed by the delegations in the Accounting Regulatory Committee. The Commission will be represented in constituent bodies of the IASB.

(16) A proper and rigorous enforcement regime is key to underpinning investors' confidence in financial markets. Member States, by virtue of Article 10 of the Treaty, are required to take appropriate measures to ensure compliance with international accounting standards. The Commission intends to liaise with Member States, notably through the Committee of European Securities Regulators (CESR), to develop a common approach to enforcement.

(17) Further, it is necessary to allow Member States to defer the application of certain provisions until 2007 for those companies publicly traded both in the Community and on a regulated third-country market which are already applying another set of internationally accepted standards as the primary basis for their consolidated accounts as well as for companies which have only publicly traded debt securities. It is nonetheless crucial that by 2007 at the latest a single set of global international accounting standards, the IAS, apply to all Community companies publicly traded on a Community regulated market.

(18) In order to allow Member States and companies to carry out the necessary adaptations to make the application of international accounting standards possible, it is necessary to apply certain provisions only in 2005. Appropriate provisions should be put in place for the first-time application of IAS by companies as a result of the entry into force of the present regulation. Such provisions should be drawn up at international level in order to ensure international recognition of the solutions adopted,

---

NOTES

[1]   OJ C154E, 29.5.2001, p 285.

[2]   OJ C260, 17.9.2001, p. 86.

[3]   Opinion of the European Parliament of 12 March 2002 (not yet published in the Official Journal) and Decision of the Council of 7 June 2002.

[4]   OJ L222, 14.8.1978, p. 11. Directive as last amended by European Parliament and Council Directive 2001/65/EC (OJ L283, 27.10.2001, p 28).

[5]   OJ L193, 18.7.1983, p 1. Directive as last amended by European Parliament and Council Directive 2001/65/EC.

[6]   OJ L372, 31.12.1986, p 1. Directive as last amended by European Parliament and Council Directive 2001/65/EC.

⁷   OJ L374, 31.12.1991, p 7.

⁸   OJ L184, 17.7.1999, p 23.

HAVE ADOPTED THIS REGULATION:

[11.248]
Article 1
Aim
This Regulation has as its objective the adoption and use of international accounting standards in the Community with a view to harmonising the financial information presented by the companies referred to in Article 4 in order to ensure a high degree of transparency and comparability of financial statements and hence an efficient functioning of the Community capital market and of the Internal Market.

[11.249]
Article 2
Definitions
For the purpose of this Regulation, "international accounting standards" shall mean International Accounting Standards (IAS), International Financial Reporting Standards (IFRS) and related Interpretations (SIC-IFRIC interpretations), subsequent amendments to those standards and related interpretations, future standards and related interpretations issued or adopted by the International Accounting Standards Board (IASB).

[11.250]
Article 3
Adoption and use of international accounting standards
[1.   The Commission shall decide on the applicability within the Community of international accounting standards. Those measures, designed to amend non-essential elements of this Regulation by supplementing it, shall be adopted in accordance with the regulatory procedure with scrutiny referred to in Article 6(2).]
2.   The international accounting standards can only be adopted if:
—   they are not contrary to the principle set out in Article 2(3) of Directive 78/660/EEC and in Article 16(3) of Directive 83/349/EEC and are conducive to the European public good and,
—   they meet the criteria of understandability, relevance, reliability and comparability required of the financial information needed for making economic decisions and assessing the stewardship of management.
3.   At the latest by 31 December 2002, the Commission shall, in accordance with the procedure laid down in Article 6(2), decide on the applicability within the Community of the international accounting standards in existence upon entry into force of this Regulation.
4.   Adopted international accounting standards shall be published in full in each of the official languages of the Community, as a Commission Regulation, in the Official Journal of the European Communities.

NOTES
Para 1: substituted by European Parliament and Council Regulation 297/2008/EC, Art 1(1), as from 10 April 2008.

[11.251]
Article 4
Consolidated accounts of publicly traded companies
For each financial year starting on or after 1 January 2005, companies governed by the law of a Member State shall prepare their consolidated accounts in conformity with the international accounting standards adopted in accordance with the procedure laid down in Article 6(2) if, at their balance sheet date, their securities are admitted to trading on a regulated market of any Member State within the meaning of Article 1(13) of Council Directive 93/22/EEC of 10 May 1993 on investment services in the securities field.¹

NOTES
¹   OJ L141, 11.6.1993, p 27. Directive as last amended by European Parliament and Council Directive 2000/64/EC (OJ L290, 17.11.2000, p 27).

[11.252]
Article 5
Options in respect of annual accounts and of non publicly-traded companies
Member States may permit or require:
  (a)   the companies referred to in Article 4 to prepare their annual accounts,
  (b)   companies other than those referred to in Article 4 to prepare their consolidated accounts and/or their annual accounts,
in conformity with the international accounting standards adopted in accordance with the procedure laid down in Article 6(2).

[11.253]
Article 6
Committee procedure
1. The Commission shall be assisted by an accounting regulatory committee hereinafter referred to as "the Committee".
[2. Where reference is made to this paragraph, Article 5a(1) to (4) and Article 7 of Decision 1999/468/EC shall apply, having regard to the provisions of Article 8 thereof.]
3. . . .

NOTES
Para 2 substituted, and para 3 repealed, by European Parliament and Council Regulation 297/2008/EC, Art 1(2), as from 10 April 2008.

[11.254]
Article 7
Reporting and coordination
1. The Commission shall liaise on a regular basis with the Committee about the status of active IASB projects and any related documents issued by the IASB in order to coordinate positions and to facilitate discussions concerning the adoption of standards that might result from these projects and documents.
2. The Commission shall duly report to the Committee in a timely manner if it intends not to propose the adoption of a standard.

[11.255]
Article 8
Notification
Where Member States take measures by virtue of Article 5, they shall immediately communicate these to the Commission and to other Member States.

[11.256]
Article 9
Transitional provisions
By way of derogation from Article 4, Member States may provide that the requirements of Article 4 shall only apply for each financial year starting on or after January 2007 to those companies:
  (a) whose debt securities only are admitted on a regulated market of any Member State within the meaning of Article 1(13) of Directive 93/22/EEC; or
  (b) whose securities are admitted to public trading in a non-member State and which, for that purpose, have been using internationally accepted standards since a financial year that started prior to the publication of this Regulation in the *Official Journal of the European Communities*.

[11.257]
Article 10
Information and review
The Commission shall review the operation of this Regulation and report thereon to the European Parliament and to the Council by 1 July 2007 at the latest.

[11.258]
Article 11
Entry into force
This Regulation shall enter into force on the third day following that of its publication in the *Official Journal of the European Communities*.
  This Regulation shall be binding in its entirety and directly applicable in all Member States.

DIRECTIVE OF THE EUROPEAN PARLIAMENT AND OF THE COUNCIL

(2003/6/EC)
of 28 January 2003

on insider dealing and market manipulation (market abuse)

NOTES
Date of publication in OJ: OJ L096, 12.4.2003, p 16. Notes are as in the original OJ version.
This Directive is reproduced as amended by: European Parliament and Council Directive 2008/26/EC; European Parliament and Council Directive 2010/78/EU.

[11.259]
THE EUROPEAN PARLIAMENT AND THE COUNCIL OF THE EUROPEAN UNION,

Having regard to the Treaty establishing the European Community, and in particular Article 95 thereof,

Having regard to the proposal from the Commission,[1]

Having regard to the opinion of the European Economic and Social Committee,[2]

Having regard to the opinion of the European Central Bank,[3]

Acting in accordance with the procedure laid down in Article 251,[4]

Whereas:

(1) A genuine Single Market for financial services is crucial for economic growth and job creation in the Community.

(2) An integrated and efficient financial market requires market integrity. The smooth functioning of securities markets and public confidence in markets are prerequisites for economic growth and wealth. Market abuse harms the integrity of financial markets and public confidence in securities and derivatives.

(3) The Commission Communication of 11 May 1999 entitled "Implementing the framework for financial markets: action plan" identifies a series of actions that are needed in order to complete the single market for financial services. The Lisbon European Council of April 2000 called for the implementation of that action plan by 2005. The action plan stresses the need to draw up a Directive against market manipulation.

(4) At its meeting on 17 July 2000, the Council set up the Committee of Wise Men on the Regulation of European Securities Markets. In its final report, the Committee of Wise Men proposed the introduction of new legislative techniques based on a four-level approach, namely framework principles, implementing measures, cooperation and enforcement. Level 1, the Directive, should confine itself to broad general "framework" principles while Level 2 should contain technical implementing measures to be adopted by the Commission with the assistance of a committee.

(5) The Resolution adopted by the Stockholm European Council of March 2001 endorsed the final report of the Committee of Wise Men and the proposed four-level approach to make the regulatory process for Community securities legislation more efficient and transparent.

(6) The Resolution of the European Parliament of 5 February 2002 on the implementation of financial services legislation also endorsed the Committee of Wise Men's report, on the basis of the solemn declaration made before Parliament the same day by the Commission and the letter of 2 October 2001 addressed by the Internal Market Commissioner to the chairman of Parliament's Committee on Economic and Monetary Affairs with regard to the safeguards for the European Parliament's role in this process.

(7) The measures necessary for the implementation of this Directive should be adopted in accordance with Council Decision 1999/468/EC of 28 June 1999 laying down the procedures for the exercise of implementing powers conferred on the Commission.[5]

(8) According to the Stockholm European Council, Level 2 implementing measures should be used more frequently, to ensure that technical provisions can be kept up to date with market and supervisory developments, and deadlines should be set for all stages of Level 2 work.

(9) The European Parliament should be given a period of three months from the first transmission of draft implementing measures to allow it to examine them and to give its opinion. However, in urgent and duly justified cases, this period may be shortened. If, within that period, a resolution is passed by the European Parliament, the Commission should re-examine the draft measures.

(10) New financial and technical developments enhance the incentives, means and opportunities for market abuse: through new products, new technologies, increasing cross-border activities and the Internet.

(11) The existing Community legal framework to protect market integrity is incomplete. Legal requirements vary from one Member State to another, leaving economic actors often uncertain over concepts, definitions and enforcement. In some Member States there is no legislation addressing the issues of price manipulation and the dissemination of misleading information.

(12) Market abuse consists of insider dealing and market manipulation. The objective of legislation against insider dealing is the same as that of legislation against market manipulation: to ensure the integrity of Community financial markets and to enhance investor confidence in those markets. It is therefore advisable to adopt combined rules to combat both insider dealing and market manipulation. A single Directive will ensure throughout the Community the same framework for allocation of responsibilities, enforcement and cooperation.

(13) Given the changes in financial markets and in Community legislation since the adoption of Council Directive 89/592/EEC of 13 November 1989 coordinating regulations on insider dealing,[6] that Directive should now be replaced, to ensure consistency with legislation against market manipulation. A new Directive is also needed to avoid loopholes in Community legislation which could be used for wrongful conduct and which would undermine public confidence and therefore prejudice the smooth functioning of the markets.

(14) This Directive meets the concerns expressed by the Member States following the terrorist attacks on 11 September 2001 as regards the fight against financing terrorist activities.

(15) Insider dealing and market manipulation prevent full and proper market transparency, which is a prerequisite for trading for all economic actors in integrated financial markets.

(16) Inside information is any information of a precise nature which has not been made public, relating, directly or indirectly, to one or more issuers of financial instruments or to one or more financial instruments. Information which could have a significant effect on the evolution and forming

of the prices of a regulated market as such could be considered as information which indirectly relates to one or more issuers of financial instruments or to one or more related derivative financial instruments.

(17) As regards insider dealing, account should be taken of cases where inside information originates not from a profession or function but from criminal activities, the preparation or execution of which could have a significant effect on the prices of one or more financial instruments or on price formation in the regulated market as such.

(18) Use of inside information can consist in the acquisition or disposal of financial instruments by a person who knows, or ought to have known, that the information possessed is inside information. In this respect, the competent authorities should consider what a normal and reasonable person would know or should have known in the circumstances. Moreover, the mere fact that market-makers, bodies authorised to act as counterparties, or persons authorised to execute orders on behalf of third parties with inside information confine themselves, in the first two cases, to pursuing their legitimate business of buying or selling financial instruments or, in the last case, to carrying out an order dutifully, should not in itself be deemed to constitute use of such inside information.

(19) Member States should tackle the practice known as "front running", including "front running" in commodity derivatives, where it constitutes market abuse under the definitions contained in this Directive.

(20) A person who enters into transactions or issues orders to trade which are constitutive of market manipulation may be able to establish that his reasons for entering into such transactions or issuing orders to trade were legitimate and that the transactions and orders to trade were in conformity with accepted practice on the regulated market concerned. A sanction could still be imposed if the competent authority established that there was another, illegitimate, reason behind these transactions or orders to trade.

(21) The competent authority may issue guidance on matters covered by this Directive, eg definition of inside information in relation to derivatives on commodities or implementation of the definition of accepted market practices relating to the definition of market manipulation. This guidance should be in conformity with the provisions of the Directive and the implementing measures adopted in accordance with the comitology procedure.

(22) Member States should be able to choose the most appropriate way to regulate persons producing or disseminating research concerning financial instruments or issuers of financial instruments or persons producing or disseminating other information recommending or suggesting investment strategy, including appropriate mechanisms for self-regulation, which should be notified to the Commission.

(23) Posting of inside information by issuers on their internet sites should be in accordance with the rules on transfer of personal data to third countries as laid down in Directive 95/46/EC of the European Parliament and of the Council of 24 October 1995 on the protection of individuals with regard to the processing of personal data and on the movement of such data.[7]

(24) Prompt and fair disclosure of information to the public enhances market integrity, whereas selective disclosure by issuers can lead to a loss of investor confidence in the integrity of financial markets. Professional economic actors should contribute to market integrity by various means. Such measures could include, for instance, the creation of "grey lists", the application of "window trading" to sensitive categories of personnel, the application of internal codes of conduct and the establishment of "Chinese walls". Such preventive measures may contribute to combating market abuse only if they are enforced with determination and are dutifully controlled. Adequate enforcement control would imply for instance the designation of compliance officers within the bodies concerned and periodic checks conducted by independent auditors.

(25) Modern communication methods make it possible for financial market professionals and private investors to have more equal access to financial information, but also increase the risk of the spread of false or misleading information.

(26) Greater transparency of transactions conducted by persons discharging managerial responsibilities within issuers and, where applicable, persons closely associated with them, constitutes a preventive measure against market abuse. The publication of those transactions on at least an individual basis can also be a highly valuable source of information to investors.

(27) Market operators should contribute to the prevention of market abuse and adopt structural provisions aimed at preventing and detecting market manipulation practices. Such provisions may include requirements concerning transparency of transactions concluded, total disclosure of price-regularisation agreements, a fair system of order pairing, introduction of an effective atypical-order detection scheme, sufficiently robust financial instrument reference price-fixing schemes and clarity of rules on the suspension of transactions.

(28) This Directive should be interpreted, and implemented by Member States, in a manner consistent with the requirements for effective regulation in order to protect the interests of holders of transferable securities carrying voting rights in a company (or which may carry such rights as a consequence of the exercise of rights or conversion) when the company is subject to a public take-over bid or other proposed change of control. In particular, this Directive does not in any way prevent a Member State from putting or having in place such measures as it sees fit for these purposes.

(29) Having access to inside information relating to another company and using it in the context of a public take-over bid for the purpose of gaining control of that company or proposing a merger with that company should not in itself be deemed to constitute insider dealing.

(30) Since the acquisition or disposal of financial instruments necessarily involves a prior decision to acquire or dispose taken by the person who undertakes one or other of these operations,

the carrying out of this acquisition or disposal should not be deemed in itself to constitute the use of inside information.

(31) Research and estimates developed from publicly available data should not be regarded as inside information and, therefore, any transaction carried out on the basis of such research or estimates should not be deemed in itself to constitute insider dealing within the meaning of this Directive.

(32) Member States and the European System of Central Banks, national central banks or any other officially designated body, or any person acting on their behalf, should not be restricted in carrying out monetary, exchange-rate or public debt management policy.

(33) Stabilisation of financial instruments or trading in own shares in buy-back programmes can be legitimate, in certain circumstances, for economic reasons and should not, therefore, in themselves be regarded as market abuse. Common standards should be developed to provide practical guidance.

(34) The widening scope of financial markets, the rapid change and the range of new products and developments require a wide application of this Directive to financial instruments and techniques involved, in order to guarantee the integrity of Community financial markets.

(35) Establishing a level playing field in Community financial markets requires wide geographical application of the provisions covered by this Directive. As regards derivative instruments not admitted to trading but falling within the scope of this Directive, each Member State should be competent to sanction actions carried out on its territory or abroad which concern underlying financial instruments admitted to trading on a regulated market situated or operating within its territory or for which a request for admission to trading on such a regulated market has been made. Each Member State should also be competent to sanction actions carried out on its territory which concern underlying financial instruments admitted to trading on a regulated market in a Member State or for which a request for admission to trading on such a market has been made.

(36) A variety of competent authorities in Member States, having different responsibilities, may create confusion among economic actors. A single competent authority should be designated in each Member State to assume at least final responsibility for supervising compliance with the provisions adopted pursuant to this Directive, as well as international collaboration. Such an authority should be of an administrative nature guaranteeing its independence of economic actors and avoiding conflicts of interest. In accordance with national law, Member States should ensure appropriate financing of the competent authority. That authority should have adequate arrangements for consultation concerning possible changes in national legislation such as a consultative committee composed of representatives of issuers, financial services providers and consumers, so as to be fully informed of their views and concerns.

(37) A common minimum set of effective tools and powers for the competent authority of each Member State will guarantee supervisory effectiveness. Market undertakings and all economic actors should also contribute at their level to market integrity. In this sense, the designation of a single competent authority for market abuse does not exclude collaboration links or delegation under the responsibility of the competent authority, between that authority and market undertakings with a view to guaranteeing efficient supervision of compliance with the provisions adopted pursuant to this Directive.

(38) In order to ensure that a Community framework against market abuse is sufficient, any infringement of the prohibitions or requirements laid down pursuant to this Directive will have to be promptly detected and sanctioned. To this end, sanctions should be sufficiently dissuasive and proportionate to the gravity of the infringement and to the gains realised and should be consistently applied.

(39) Member States should remain alert, in determining the administrative measures and sanctions, to the need to ensure a degree of uniformity of regulation from one Member State to another.

(40) Increasing cross-border activities require improved cooperation and a comprehensive set of provisions for the exchange of information between national competent authorities. The organisation of supervision and of investigatory powers in each Member State should not hinder cooperation between the competent national authorities.

(41) Since the objective of the proposed action, namely to prevent market abuse in the form of insider dealing and market manipulation, cannot be sufficiently achieved by the Member States and can therefore, by reason of the scale and effects of the measures, be better achieved at Community level, the Community may adopt measures, in accordance with the principle of subsidiarity as set out in Article 5 of the Treaty. In accordance with the principle of proportionality, as set out in that Article, this Directive does not go beyond what is necessary in order to achieve that objective.

(42) Technical guidance and implementing measures for the rules laid down in this Directive may from time to time be necessary to take account of new developments on financial markets. The Commission should accordingly be empowered to adopt implementing measures, provided that these do not modify the essential elements of this Directive and the Commission acts according to the principles set out in this Directive, after consulting the European Securities Committee established by Commission Decision 2001/528/EC.[8]

(43) In exercising its implementing powers in accordance with this Directive, the Commission should respect the following principles:
— the need to ensure confidence in financial markets among investors by promoting high standards of transparency in financial markets,

Part 11   EU Legislation

— the need to provide investors with a wide range of competing investments and a level of disclosure and protection tailored to their circumstances,

— the need to ensure that independent regulatory authorities enforce the rules consistently, especially as regards the fight against economic crime,

— the need for high levels of transparency and consultation with all market participants and with the European Parliament and the Council,

— the need to encourage innovation in financial markets if they are to be dynamic and efficient,

— the need to ensure market integrity by close and reactive monitoring of financial innovation,

— the importance of reducing the cost of, and increasing access to, capital,

— the balance of costs and benefits to market participants on a long-term basis (including small and medium-sized businesses and small investors) in any implementing measures,

— the need to foster the international competitiveness of EU financial markets without prejudice to a much-needed extension of international cooperation,

— the need to achieve a level playing field for all market participants by establishing EU-wide regulations every time it is appropriate,

— the need to respect differences in national markets where these do not unduly impinge on the coherence of the single market,

— the need to ensure coherence with other Community legislation in this area, as imbalances in information and a lack of transparency may jeopardise the operation of the markets and above all harm consumers and small investors.

(44) This Directive respects the fundamental rights and observes the principles recognised in particular by the Charter of Fundamental Rights of the European Union and in particular by Article 11 thereof and Article 10 of the European Convention on Human Rights. In this regard, this Directive does not in any way prevent Member States from applying their constitutional rules relating to freedom of the press and freedom of expression in the media,

NOTES

[1] OJ C240E, 28.8.2001, p 265.

[2] OJ C80, 3.4.2002, p 61.

[3] OJ C24, 26.1.2002, p 8.

[4] Opinion of the European Parliament of 14 March 2002 (not yet published in the Official Journal), Council Common Position of 19 July 2002 (OJ C228E, 25.9.2002, p 19) and Decision of the European Parliament of 24 October 2002 (not yet published in the Official Journal).

[5] OJ L184, 17.7.1999, p 23.

[6] OJ L334, 18.11.1989, p 30.

[7] OJ L281, 23.11.1995, p 31.

[8] OJ L191, 13.7.2001, p 45.

HAVE ADOPTED THIS DIRECTIVE:

[11.260]
Article 1
For the purposes of this Directive:

1. "Inside information" shall mean information of a precise nature which has not been made public, relating, directly or indirectly, to one or more issuers of financial instruments or to one or more financial instruments and which, if it were made public, would be likely to have a significant effect on the prices of those financial instruments or on the price of related derivative financial instruments.

In relation to derivatives on commodities, "inside information" shall mean information of a precise nature which has not been made public, relating, directly or indirectly, to one or more such derivatives and which users of markets on which such derivatives are traded would expect to receive in accordance with accepted market practices on those markets.

For persons charged with the execution of orders concerning financial instruments, "inside information" shall also mean information conveyed by a client and related to the client's pending orders, which is of a precise nature, which relates directly or indirectly to one or more issuers of financial instruments or to one or more financial instruments, and which, if it were made public, would be likely to have a significant effect on the prices of those financial instruments or on the price of related derivative financial instruments.

2. "Market manipulation" shall mean:

(a) transactions or orders to trade:

— which give, or are likely to give, false or misleading signals as to the supply of, demand for or price of financial instruments, or

— which secure, by a person, or persons acting in collaboration, the price of one or several financial instruments at an abnormal or artificial level,

unless the person who entered into the transactions or issued the orders to trade establishes that his reasons for so doing are legitimate and that these transactions or orders to trade conform to accepted market practices on the regulated market concerned;

(b) transactions or orders to trade which employ fictitious devices or any other form of deception or contrivance;

(c) dissemination of information through the media, including the Internet, or by any other means, which gives, or is likely to give, false or misleading signals as to financial instruments, including the dissemination of rumours and false or misleading news, where the person who made the dissemination knew, or ought to have known, that the information was false or misleading. In respect of journalists when they act in their professional capacity such dissemination of information is to be assessed, without prejudice to Article 11, taking into account the rules governing their profession, unless those persons derive, directly or indirectly, an advantage or profits from the dissemination of the information in question.

In particular, the following instances are derived from the core definition given in points (a), (b) and (c) above:

— conduct by a person, or persons acting in collaboration, to secure a dominant position over the supply of or demand for a financial instrument which has the effect of fixing, directly or indirectly, purchase or sale prices or creating other unfair trading conditions,

— the buying or selling of financial instruments at the close of the market with the effect of misleading investors acting on the basis of closing prices,

— taking advantage of occasional or regular access to the traditional or electronic media by voicing an opinion about a financial instrument (or indirectly about its issuer) while having previously taken positions on that financial instrument and profiting subsequently from the impact of the opinions voiced on the price of that instrument, without having simultaneously disclosed that conflict of interest to the public in a proper and effective way.

The definitions of market manipulation shall be adapted so as to ensure that new patterns of activity that in practice constitute market manipulation can be included.

3. "Financial instrument" shall mean:

— transferable securities as defined in Council Directive 93/22/EEC of 10 May 1993 on investment services in the securities field,[1]

— units in collective investment undertakings,

— money-market instruments,

— financial-futures contracts, including equivalent cash-settled instruments,

— forward interest-rate agreements,

— interest-rate, currency and equity swaps,

— options to acquire or dispose of any instrument falling into these categories, including equivalent cash-settled instruments. This category includes in particular options on currency and on interest rates,

— derivatives on commodities,

— any other instrument admitted to trading on a regulated market in a Member State or for which a request for admission to trading on such a market has been made.

4. "Regulated market" shall mean a market as defined by Article 1(13) of Directive 93/22/EEC.

[5. "Accepted market practices" shall mean practices that are reasonably expected in one or more financial markets and are accepted by the competent authority in accordance with guidelines adopted by the Commission in accordance with the regulatory procedure with scrutiny laid down in Article 17(2a).

[The European Supervisory Authority (European Securities and Markets Authority) (hereinafter "ESMA"), established by Regulation (EU) No 1095/2010 of the European Parliament and of the Council[2] may develop draft implementing technical standards to ensure uniform conditions of application of the acts adopted by the Commission in accordance with this Article in relation to accepted market practices.

Power is conferred on the Commission to adopt the implementing technical standards referred to in the second subparagraph in accordance with Article 15 of Regulation (EU) No 1095/2010.]]

6. "Person" shall mean any natural or legal person.

7. "Competent authority" shall mean the competent authority designated in accordance with Article 11.

In order to take account of developments on financial markets and to ensure uniform application of this Directive in the Community, the Commission, . . . shall adopt implementing measures concerning points 1, 2 and 3 of this Article. [Those measures, designed to amend non-essential elements of this Directive by supplementing it, shall be adopted in accordance with the regulatory procedure with scrutiny referred to in Article 17(2a).]

NOTES

Para 5 substituted, words omitted from the final subparagraph of para 7 repealed, and words in square brackets in that subparagraph inserted, by European Parliament and Council Directive 2008/26/EC, Art 1(1), as from 21 March 2008.

The second and third subparagraphs of para 5 were added by European Parliament and Council Directive 2010/78/EU, Art 3(1), as from 4 January 2011.

 ¹ OJ L141, 11.6.1993, p 27. Directive as last amended by European Parliament and Council Directive 2000/64/EC (OJ L290, 17.11.2000, p. 27).

² OJ L331, 15.12.2010,p 84.

[11.261]
Article 2

1. Member States shall prohibit any person referred to in the second subparagraph who possesses inside information from using that information by acquiring or disposing of, or by trying to acquire or dispose of, for his own account or for the account of a third party, either directly or indirectly, financial instruments to which that information relates.

The first subparagraph shall apply to any person who possesses that information:

  (a)   by virtue of his membership of the administrative, management or supervisory bodies of the issuer; or

  (b)   by virtue of his holding in the capital of the issuer; or

  (c)   by virtue of his having access to the information through the exercise of his employment, profession or duties; or

  (d)   by virtue of his criminal activities.

2. Where the person referred to in paragraph 1 is a legal person, the prohibition laid down in that paragraph shall also apply to the natural persons who take part in the decision to carry out the transaction for the account of the legal person concerned.

3. This Article shall not apply to transactions conducted in the discharge of an obligation that has become due to acquire or dispose of financial instruments where that obligation results from an agreement concluded before the person concerned possessed inside information.

[11.262]
Article 3

Member States shall prohibit any person subject to the prohibition laid down in Article 2 from:

  (a)   disclosing inside information to any other person unless such disclosure is made in the normal course of the exercise of his employment, profession or duties;

  (b)   recommending or inducing another person, on the basis of inside information, to acquire or dispose of financial instruments to which that information relates.

[11.263]
Article 4

Member States shall ensure that Articles 2 and 3 also apply to any person, other than the persons referred to in those Articles, who possesses inside information while that person knows, or ought to have known, that it is inside information.

[11.264]
Article 5

Member States shall prohibit any person from engaging in market manipulation.

[11.265]
Article 6

1. Member States shall ensure that issuers of financial instruments inform the public as soon as possible of inside information which directly concerns the said issuers.

Without prejudice to any measures taken to comply with the provisions of the first subparagraph, Member States shall ensure that issuers, for an appropriate period, post on their Internet sites all inside information that they are required to disclose publicly.

2. An issuer may under his own responsibility delay the public disclosure of inside information, as referred to in paragraph 1, such as not to prejudice his legitimate interests provided that such omission would not be likely to mislead the public and provided that the issuer is able to ensure the confidentiality of that information. Member States may require that an issuer shall without delay inform the competent authority of the decision to delay the public disclosure of inside information.

3. Member States shall require that, whenever an issuer, or a person acting on his behalf or for his account, discloses any inside information to any third party in the normal exercise of his employment, profession or duties, as referred to in Article 3(a), he must make complete and effective public disclosure of that information, simultaneously in the case of an intentional disclosure and promptly in the case of a non-intentional disclosure.

The provisions of the first subparagraph shall not apply if the person receiving the information owes a duty of confidentiality, regardless of whether such duty is based on a law, on regulations, on articles of association or on a contract.

Member States shall require that issuers, or persons acting on their behalf or for their account, draw up a list of those persons working for them, under a contract of employment or otherwise, who have access to inside information. Issuers and persons acting on their behalf or for their account shall regularly update this list and transmit it to the competent authority whenever the latter requests it.

4. Persons discharging managerial responsibilities within an issuer of financial instruments and, where applicable, persons closely associated with them, shall, at least, notify to the competent authority the existence of transactions conducted on their own account relating to shares of the said issuer, or to derivatives or other financial instruments linked to them. Member States shall ensure that public access to information concerning such transactions, on at least an individual basis, is readily available as soon as possible.

5. Member States shall ensure that there is appropriate regulation in place to ensure that persons who produce or disseminate research concerning financial instruments or issuers of financial instruments and persons who produce or disseminate other information recommending or suggesting investment strategy, intended for distribution channels or for the public, take reasonable care to ensure that such information is fairly presented and disclose their interests or indicate conflicts of interest concerning the financial instruments to which that information relates. Details of such regulation shall be notified to the Commission.

6. Member States shall ensure that market operators adopt structural provisions aimed at preventing and detecting market manipulation practices.

7. With a view to ensuring compliance with paragraphs 1 to 5, the competent authority may take all necessary measures to ensure that the public is correctly informed.

8. Public institutions disseminating statistics liable to have a significant effect on financial markets shall disseminate them in a fair and transparent way.

9. Member States shall require that any person professionally arranging transactions in financial instruments who reasonably suspects that a transaction might constitute insider dealing or market manipulation shall notify the competent authority without delay.

10. In order to take account of technical developments on financial markets and to ensure uniform application of this Directive, the Commission shall adopt, . . . implementing measures concerning:

— the technical modalities for appropriate public disclosure of inside information as referred to in paragraphs 1 and 3,
— the technical modalities for delaying the public disclosure of inside information as referred to in paragraph 2,
— the technical modalities designed to favour a common approach in the implementation of the second sentence of paragraph 2,
— the conditions under which issuers, or entities acting on their behalf, are to draw up a list of those persons working for them and having access to inside information, as referred to in paragraph 3, together with the conditions under which such lists are to be updated,
— the categories of persons who are subject to a duty of disclosure as referred to in paragraph 4 and the characteristics of a transaction, including its size, which trigger that duty, and the technical arrangements for disclosure to the competent authority,
— technical arrangements, for the various categories of person referred to in paragraph 5, for fair presentation of research and other information recommending investment strategy and for disclosure of particular interests or conflicts of interest as referred to in paragraph 5. Such arrangements shall take into account the rules, including self-regulation, governing the profession of journalist,
— technical arrangements governing notification to the competent authority by the persons referred to in paragraph 9.

[Those measures, designed to amend non-essential elements of this Directive by supplementing it, shall be adopted in accordance with the regulatory procedure with scrutiny referred to in Article 17(2a).]

[11. ESMA may develop draft implementing technical standards to ensure uniform conditions of application of the acts adopted by the Commission in accordance with the sixth indent of the first subparagraph of paragraph 10.

Power is conferred on the Commission to adopt the implementing technical standards referred to in the first subparagraph in accordance with Article 15 of Regulation (EU) No 1095/2010.]

NOTES

Para 10: words omitted repealed, and words in square brackets inserted, by European Parliament and Council Directive 2008/26/EC, Art 1(2), as from 21 March 2008.

Para 11: added by European Parliament and Council Directive 2010/78/EU, Art 3(2), as from 4 January 2011.

[11.266]
Article 7

This Directive shall not apply to transactions carried out in pursuit of monetary, exchange-rate or public debt-management policy by a Member State, by the European System of Central Banks, by a national central bank or by any other officially designated body, or by any person acting on their behalf. Member States may extend this exemption to their federated States or similar local authorities in respect of the management of their public debt.

[11.267]
Article 8
[1.] The prohibitions provided for in this Directive shall not apply to trading in own shares in "buy-back" programmes or to the stabilisation of a financial instrument provided such trading is carried out in accordance with implementing measures . . .

[Those measures, designed to amend non-essential elements of this Directive by supplementing it, shall be adopted in accordance with the regulatory procedure with scrutiny referred to in Article 17(2a).]

[2. ESMA may develop draft implementing technical standards to ensure uniform conditions of application of acts adopted by the Commission in accordance with paragraph 1.

Power is conferred on the Commission to adopt the implementing technical standards referred to in the first subparagraph in accordance with Article 15 of Regulation (EU) No 1095/2010.]

NOTES

Para 1 numbered as such, and para 2 added, by European Parliament and Council Directive 2010/78/EU, Art 3(3), as from 4 January 2011.

In para 1 (as so numbered) words omitted repealed, and words in square brackets inserted, by European Parliament and Council Directive 2008/26/EC, Art 1(3), as from 21 March 2008.

[11.268]
Article 9
This Directive shall apply to any financial instrument admitted to trading on a regulated market in at least one Member State, or for which a request for admission to trading on such a market has been made, irrespective of whether or not the transaction itself actually takes place on that market.

Articles 2, 3 and 4 shall also apply to any financial instrument not admitted to trading on a regulated market in a Member State, but whose value depends on a financial instrument as referred to in paragraph 1.

Article 6(1) to (3) shall not apply to issuers who have not requested or approved admission of their financial instruments to trading on a regulated market in a Member State.

[11.269]
Article 10
Each Member State shall apply the prohibitions and requirements provided for in this Directive to:
(a) actions carried out on its territory or abroad concerning financial instruments that are admitted to trading on a regulated market situated or operating within its territory or for which a request for admission to trading on such market has been made;
(b) actions carried out on its territory concerning financial instruments that are admitted to trading on a regulated market in a Member State or for which a request for admission to trading on such market has been made.

[11.270]
Article 11
Without prejudice to the competences of the judicial authorities, each Member State shall designate a single administrative authority competent to ensure that the provisions adopted pursuant to this Directive are applied.

Member States shall establish effective consultative arrangements and procedures with market participants concerning possible changes in national legislation. These arrangements may include consultative committees within each competent authority, the membership of which should reflect as far as possible the diversity of market participants, be they issuers, providers of financial services or consumers.

[11.271]
Article 12
1. The competent authority shall be given all supervisory and investigatory powers that are necessary for the exercise of its functions. It shall exercise such powers:
(a) directly; or
(b) in collaboration with other authorities or with the market undertakings; or
(c) under its responsibility by delegation to such authorities or to the market undertakings; or
(d) by application to the competent judicial authorities.
2. Without prejudice to Article 6(7), the powers referred to in paragraph 1 of this Article shall be exercised in conformity with national law and shall include at least the right to:
(a) have access to any document in any form whatsoever, and to receive a copy of it;
(b) demand information from any person, including those who are successively involved in the transmission of orders or conduct of the operations concerned, as well as their principals, and if necessary, to summon and hear any such person;
(c) carry out on-site inspections;
(d) require existing telephone and existing data traffic records;
(e) require the cessation of any practice that is contrary to the provisions adopted in the implementation of this Directive;

(f) suspend trading of the financial instruments concerned;
(g) request the freezing and/or sequestration of assets;
(h) request temporary prohibition of professional activity.
3. This Article shall be without prejudice to national legal provisions on professional secrecy.

[11.272]
Article 13
The obligation of professional secrecy shall apply to all persons who work or who have worked for the competent authority or for any authority or market undertaking to whom the competent authority has delegated its powers, including auditors and experts instructed by the competent authority. Information covered by professional secrecy may not be disclosed to any other person or authority except by virtue of provisions laid down by law.

[11.273]
Article 14
1. Without prejudice to the right of Member States to impose criminal sanctions, Member States shall ensure, in conformity with their national law, that the appropriate administrative measures can be taken or administrative sanctions be imposed against the persons responsible where the provisions adopted in the implementation of this Directive have not been complied with. Member States shall ensure that these measures are effective, proportionate and dissuasive.
2. In accordance with the procedure laid down in Article 17(2), the Commission shall, for information, draw up a list of the administrative measures and sanctions referred to in paragraph 1.
3. Member States shall determine the sanctions to be applied for failure to cooperate in an investigation covered by Article 12.
4. Member States shall provide that the competent authority may disclose to the public every measure or sanction that will be imposed for infringement of the provisions adopted in the implementation of this Directive, unless such disclosure would seriously jeopardise the financial markets or cause disproportionate damage to the parties involved.
[5. Member States shall provide ESMA annually with aggregated information regarding all administrative measures and sanctions imposed in accordance with paragraphs 1 and 2.
    Where the competent authority has disclosed an administrative measure or a sanction to the public, it shall contemporaneously report that fact to ESMA.
    Where a published sanction relates to an investment firm authorised in accordance with Directive 2004/39/EC, ESMA shall add a reference to the published sanction in the register of investment firms established under Article 5(3) of Directive 2004/39/EC.]

NOTES
Para 5: added by European Parliament and Council Directive 2010/78/EU, Art 3(4), as from 4 January 2011. Note that this provision has a transposition date of 31 December 2011.

[11.274]
Article 15
Member States shall ensure that an appeal may be brought before a court against the decisions taken by the competent authority.

[11.275]
[Article 15a
1. The competent authorities shall cooperate with ESMA for the purposes of this Directive, in accordance with Regulation (EU) No 1095/2010.
2. The competent authorities shall, without delay, provide ESMA with all information necessary to carry out its duties, in accordance with Article 35 of Regulation (EU) No 1095/2010.]

NOTES
Inserted by European Parliament and Council Directive 2010/78/EU, Art 3(5), as from 4 January 2011.

[11.276]
Article 16
1. Competent authorities shall cooperate with each other whenever necessary for the purpose of carrying out their duties, making use of their powers whether set out in this Directive or in national law. Competent authorities shall render assistance to competent authorities of other Member States. In particular, they shall exchange information and cooperate in investigation activities.
2. Competent authorities shall, on request, immediately supply any information required for the purpose referred to in paragraph 1. Where necessary, the competent authorities receiving any such request shall immediately take the necessary measures in order to gather the required information. If the requested competent authority is not able to supply the required information immediately, it shall notify the requesting competent authority of the reasons. Information thus supplied shall be covered by the obligation of professional secrecy to which the persons employed or formerly employed by the competent authorities receiving the information are subject.
    The competent authorities may refuse to act on a request for information where:

— communication might adversely affect the sovereignty, security or public policy of the Member State addressed,

— judicial proceedings have already been initiated in respect of the same actions and against the same persons before the authorities of the Member State addressed, or

— where a final judgment has already been delivered in relation to such persons for the same actions in the Member State addressed.

In any such case, they shall notify the requesting competent authority accordingly, providing as detailed information as possible on those proceedings or the judgment.

Without prejudice to Article 226 of the Treaty, a competent authority whose request for information is not acted upon within a reasonable time or whose request for information is rejected may bring that non-compliance to the attention of the Committee of European Securities Regulators, where discussion will take place in order to reach a rapid and effective solution.

[Without prejudice to Article 258 of the Treaty on the Functioning of the European Union (TFEU), a competent authority whose request for information is not acted upon within a reasonable time or whose request for information is rejected may refer that rejection or absence of action within a reasonable timeframe to ESMA. In the situations referred to in the first sentence, ESMA may act in accordance with Article 19 of Regulation (EU) No 1095/2010, without prejudice to the possibilities for refusing to act on a request for information provided for in the second subparagraph of this paragraph and to the possibility of ESMA acting in accordance with Article 17 of Regulation (EU) No 1095/2010.]

3. Where a competent authority is convinced that acts contrary to the provisions of this Directive are being, or have been, carried out on the territory of another Member State or that acts are affecting financial instruments traded on a regulated market situated in another Member State, it shall give notice of that fact in as specific a manner as possible to the competent authority of the other Member State. The competent authority of the other Member State shall take appropriate action. It shall inform the notifying competent authority of the outcome and, so far as possible, of significant interim developments. This paragraph shall not prejudice the competences of the competent authority that has forwarded the information. The competent authorities of the various Member States that are competent for the purposes of Article 10 shall consult each other on the proposed follow-up to their action.

4. A competent authority of one Member State may request that an investigation be carried out by the competent authority of another Member State, on the latter's territory.

It may further request that members of its own personnel be allowed to accompany the personnel of the competent authority of that other Member State during the course of the investigation.

The investigation shall, however, be subject throughout to the overall control of the Member State on whose territory it is conducted.

The competent authorities may refuse to act on a request for an investigation to be conducted as provided for in the first subparagraph, or on a request for its personnel to be accompanied by personnel of the competent authority of another Member State as provided for in the second subparagraph, where such an investigation might adversely affect the sovereignty, security or public policy of the State addressed, or where judicial proceedings have already been initiated in respect of the same actions and against the same persons before the authorities of the State addressed or where a final judgment has already been delivered in relation to such persons for the same actions in the State addressed. In such case, they shall notify the requesting competent authority accordingly, providing information, as detailed as possible, on those proceedings or judgment.

[Without prejudice to Article 258 TFEU, a competent authority whose application to open an inquiry or whose request for authorisation for its officials to accompany those of the other Member State's competent authority is not acted upon within a reasonable time or is rejected may refer that rejection or absence of action within a reasonable timeframe to ESMA. In the situations referred to in the first sentence, ESMA may act in accordance with Article 19 of Regulation (EU) No 1095/2010, without prejudice to the possibilities for refusing to act on a request for information provided in the fourth subparagraph of this paragraph and to the possibility of ESMA acting in accordance with Article 17 of Regulation (EU) No 1095/2010.]

[5. In order to ensure uniform conditions of application of paragraphs 2 and 4, ESMA may develop draft implementing technical standards on the procedures and forms for exchange of information and for cross-border inspections as referred to in this Article.

Power is conferred on the Commission to adopt the implementing technical standards referred to in the first subparagraph in accordance with Article 15 of Regulation (EU) No 1095/2010.]

NOTES

Para 2: words in square brackets substituted by European Parliament and Council Directive 2010/78/EU, Art 3(6)(a), as from 4 January 2011. Note that this provision has a transposition date of 31 December 2011, and that the original text read as follows—

"Without prejudice to the obligations to which they are subject in judicial proceedings under criminal law, the competent authorities which receive information pursuant to paragraph 1 may use it only for the exercise of their functions within the scope of this Directive and in the context of administrative or judicial proceedings specifically related to the exercise of those functions. However, where the competent authority communicating information consents thereto, the authority receiving the information may use it for other purposes or forward it to other States' competent authorities.".

Para 4: words in square brackets substituted by European Parliament and Council Directive 2010/78/EU, Art 3(6)(b), as from 4 January 2011. Note that this provision has a transposition date of 31 December 2011, and that the original text read as follows—

"Without prejudice to the provisions of Article 226 of the Treaty, a competent authority whose application to open an inquiry or whose request for authorisation for its officials to accompany those of the other Member State's competent authority is not acted upon within a reasonable time or is rejected may bring that non-compliance to the attention of the Committee of European Securities Regulators, where discussion will take place in order to reach a rapid and effective solution.".

Para 5: substituted by European Parliament and Council Directive 2010/78/EU, Art 3(6)(c), as from 4 January 2011.

[11.277]
Article 17
1.   The Commission shall be assisted by the European Securities Committee instituted by Decision 2001/528/EC (hereinafter referred to as the "Committee").
2.   Where reference is made to this paragraph, Articles 5 and 7 of Decision 1999/468/EC shall apply, having regard to the provisions of Article 8 thereof, provided that the implementing measures adopted according to this procedure do not modify the essential provisions of this Directive.
  The period laid down in Article 5(6) of Decision 1999/468/EC shall be set at three months.
[2a.   Where reference is made to this paragraph, Article 5a(1) to (4) and Article 7 of Decision 1999/468/EC shall apply, having regard to the provisions of Article 8 thereof.]
[3.   By 31 December 2010, and, thereafter, at least every three years, the Commission shall review the provisions concerning its implementing powers and present a report to the European Parliament and to the Council on the functioning of those powers. The report shall examine, in particular, the need for the Commission to propose amendments to this Directive in order to ensure the appropriate scope of the implementing powers conferred on the Commission. The conclusion as to whether or not amendment is necessary shall be accompanied by a detailed statement of reasons. If necessary, the report shall be accompanied by a legislative proposal to amend the provisions conferring implementing powers on the Commission.]

NOTES
  Para 2a inserted, and para 3 substituted (for original paras 3, 4), by European Parliament and Council Directive 2008/26/EC, Art 1(5), as from 21 March 2008.

[11.278]
[Article 17a
By 1 December 2011 the Commission shall review Articles 1,6, 8, 14, and 16 and present any appropriate legislative proposals in order to allow the full application of the delegated acts under Article 290 TFEU and implementing acts under Article 291 TFEU in respect of this Directive. Without prejudice to implementing measures already adopted, the powers conferred on the Commission in Article 17 to adopt implementing measures that remain after the entry into force of the Lisbon Treaty shall cease to apply on 1 December 2012.]

NOTES
  Inserted by European Parliament and Council Directive 2010/78/EU, Art 3(7), as from 4 January 2011.

[11.279]
Article 18
Member States shall bring into force the laws, regulations and administrative provisions necessary to comply with this Directive not later than 12 October 2004. They shall forthwith inform the Commission thereof.
  When Member States adopt those measures, they shall contain a reference to this Directive or be accompanied by such a reference on the occasion of their official publication. Member States shall determine how such reference is to be made.

[11.280]
Article 19
Article 11 shall not prejudice the possibility for a Member State to make separate legal and administrative arrangements for overseas European territories for whose external relations that Member State is responsible.

[11.281]
Article 20
Directive 89/592/EEC and Article 68(1) and Article 81(1) of Directive 2001/34/EC of the European Parliament and of the Council of 28 May 2001 on the admission of securities to official stock exchange listing and on information to be published on those securities[1] shall be repealed with effect from the date of entry into force of this Directive.

Part 11   EU Legislation

NOTES

[1] OJ L184, 6.7.2001, p 1.

[11.282]
Article 21
This Directive shall enter into force on the day of its publication in the *Official Journal of the European Union*.

[11.283]
Article 22
This Directive is addressed to the Member States.

DIRECTIVE OF THE EUROPEAN PARLIAMENT AND OF THE COUNCIL

(2003/71/EC)

of 4 November 2003

on the prospectus to be published when securities are offered to the public or admitted to trading and amending Directive 2001/34/EC

(Text with EEA relevance)

NOTES

Date of publication in OJ: OJ L345, 31.12.2003, p 64. Notes are as in the original OJ version.

This Directive is reproduced as amended by: European Parliament and Council Directive 2008/11/EC; European Parliament and Council Directive 2010/73/EU; European Parliament and Council Directive 2010/78/EU.

[11.284]
THE EUROPEAN PARLIAMENT AND THE COUNCIL OF THE EUROPEAN UNION,
Having regard to the Treaty establishing the European Community, and in particular Articles 44 and 95 thereof,
Having regard to the proposal from the Commission,[1]
Having regard to the opinion of the European Economic and Social Committee,[2]
Having regard to the opinion of the European Central Bank,[3]
Acting in accordance with the procedure laid down in Article 251 of the Treaty,[4]
Whereas:

(1) Council Directives 80/390/EEC of 17 March 1980 coordinating the requirements for the drawing up, scrutiny and distribution of the listing particulars to be published for the admission of securities to official stock exchange listing[5] and 89/298/EEC of 17 April 1989 coordinating the requirements for the drawing up, scrutiny and distribution of the prospectus to be published when transferable securities are offered to the public[6] were adopted several years ago introducing a partial and complex mutual recognition mechanism which is unable to achieve the objective of the single passport provided for by this Directive. Those directives should be upgraded, updated and grouped together into a single text.

(2) Meanwhile, Directive 80/390/EEC was integrated into Directive 2001/34/EC of the European Parliament and of the Council of 28 May 2001 on the admission of securities to official stock exchange listing and on information to be published on those securities,[7] which codifies several directives in the field of listed securities.

(3) For reasons of consistency, however, it is appropriate to regroup the provisions of Directive 2001/34/EC which stem from Directive 80/390/EEC together with Directive 89/298/EEC and to amend Directive 2001/34/EC accordingly.

(4) This Directive constitutes an instrument essential to the achievement of the internal market as set out in timetable form in the Commission communications 'Risk capital action plan' and 'Implementing the framework for financial market: Action Plan' facilitating the widest possible access to investment capital on a Community-wide basis, including for small and medium-sized enterprises (SMEs) and start-ups, by granting a single passport to the issuer.

(5) On 17 July 2000, the Council set up the Committee of Wise Men on the regulation of European securities markets. In its initial report of 9 November 2000 the Committee stresses the lack of an agreed definition of public offer of securities, with the result that the same operation is regarded as a private placement in some Member States and not in others; the current system discourages firms from raising capital on a Community-wide basis and therefore from having real access to a large, liquid and integrated financial market.

(6) In its final report of 15 February 2001 the Committee of Wise Men proposed the introduction of new legislative techniques based on a four-level approach, namely framework principles, implementing measures, cooperation and enforcement. Level 1, the directive, should confine itself to broad, general 'framework' principles, while Level 2 should contain technical implementing

measures to be adopted by the Commission with the assistance of a committee.

(7) The Stockholm European Council of 23 and 24 March 2001 endorsed the final report of the Committee of Wise Men and the proposed four-level approach to make the regulatory process for Community securities legislation more efficient and transparent.

(8) The resolution of the European Parliament of 5 February 2002 on the implementation of financial services legislation also endorsed the Committee of Wise Men's final report, on the basis of the solemn declaration made before Parliament the same day by the Commission and the letter of 2 October 2001 addressed by the Internal Market Commissioner to the chairman of Parliament's Committee on Economic and Monetary Affairs with regard to the safeguards for the European Parliament's role in this process.

(9) According to the Stockholm European Council, Level 2 implementing measures should be used more frequently to ensure that technical provisions can be kept up to date with market and supervisory developments and deadlines should be set for all stages of Level 2.

(10) The aim of this Directive and its implementing measures is to ensure investor protection and market efficiency, in accordance with high regulatory standards adopted in the relevant international fora.

(11) Non-equity securities issued by a Member State or by one of a Member State's regional or local authorities, by public international bodies of which one or more Member States are members, by the European Central Bank or by the central banks of the Member States are not covered by this Directive and thus remain unaffected by this Directive; the abovementioned issuers of such securities may, however, if they so choose, draw up a prospectus in accordance with this Directive.

(12) Full coverage of equity and non-equity securities offered to the public or admitted to trading on regulated markets as defined by Council Directive 93/22/EEC of 10 May 1993 on investment services in the securities field,[8] and not only securities which have been admitted to the official lists of stock exchanges, is also needed to ensure investor protection. The wide definition of securities in this Directive, which includes warrants and covered warrants and certificates, is only valid for this Directive and consequently in no way affects the various definitions of financial instruments used in national legislation for other purposes, such as taxation. Some of the securities defined in this Directive entitle the holder to acquire transferable securities or to receive a cash amount through a cash settlement determined by reference to other instruments, notably transferable securities, currencies, interest rates or yields, commodities or other indices or measures. Depositary receipts and convertible notes, eg securities convertible at the option of the investor, fall within the definition of non-equity securities set out in this Directive.

(13) Issuance of securities having a similar type and/or class in the case of non-equity securities issued on the basis of an offering programme, including warrants and certificates in any form, as well as the case of securities issued in a continuous or repeated manner, should be understood as covering not only identical securities but also securities that belong in general terms to one category. These securities may include different products, such as debt securities, certificates and warrants, or the same product under the same programme, and may have different features notably in terms of seniority, types of underlying, or the basis on which to determine the redemption amount or coupon payment.

(14) The grant to the issuer of a single passport, valid throughout the Community, and the application of the country of origin principle require the identification of the home Member State as the one best placed to regulate the issuer for the purposes of this Directive.

(15) The disclosure requirements of the present Directive do not prevent a Member State or a competent authority or an exchange through its rule book to impose other particular requirements in the context of admission to trading of securities on a regulated market (notably regarding corporate governance). Such requirements may not directly or indirectly restrict the drawing up, the content and the dissemination of a prospectus approved by a competent authority.

(16) One of the objectives of this Directive is to protect investors. It is therefore appropriate to take account of the different requirements for protection of the various categories of investors and their level of expertise. Disclosure provided by the prospectus is not required for offers limited to qualified investors. In contrast, any resale to the public or public trading through admission to trading on a regulated market requires the publication of a prospectus.

(17) Issuers, offerors or persons asking for the admission to trading on a regulated market of securities which are exempted from the obligation to publish a prospectus will benefit from the single passport if they comply with this Directive.

(18) The provision of full information concerning securities and issuers of those securities promotes, together with rules on the conduct of business, the protection of investors. Moreover, such information provides an effective means of increasing confidence in securities and thus of contributing to the proper functioning and development of securities markets. The appropriate way to make this information available is to publish a prospectus.

(19) Investment in securities, like any other form of investment, involves risk. Safeguards for the protection of the interests of actual and potential investors are required in all Member States in order to enable them to make an informed assessment of such risks and thus to take investment decisions in full knowledge of the facts.

(20) Such information, which needs to be sufficient and as objective as possible as regards the financial circumstances of the issuer and the rights attaching to the securities, should be provided in an easily analysable and comprehensible form. Harmonisation of the information contained in the prospectus should provide equivalent investor protection at Community level.

(21) Information is a key factor in investor protection; a summary conveying the essential

Part 11   EU Legislation

characteristics of, and risks associated with, the issuer, any guarantor and the securities should be included in the prospectus. To ensure easy access to this information, the summary should be written in non-technical language and normally should not exceed 2,500 words in the language in which the prospectus was originally drawn up.

(22) Best practices have been adopted at international level in order to allow cross-border offers of equities to be made using a single set of disclosure standards established by the International Organisation of Securities Commissions (IOSCO); the IOSCO disclosure standards[9] will upgrade information available for the markets and investors and at the same time will simplify the procedure for Community issuers wishing to raise capital in third countries. The Directive also calls for tailored disclosure standards to be adopted for other types of securities and issuers.

(23) Fast-track procedures for issuers admitted to trading on a regulated market and frequently raising capital on these markets require the introduction at Community level of a new format of prospectuses for offering programmes or mortgage bonds and a new registration document system. Issuers may choose not to use those formats and therefore to draft the prospectus as a single document.

(24) The content of a base prospectus should, in particular, take into account the need for flexibility in relation to the information to be provided about the securities.

(25) Omission of sensitive information to be included in a prospectus should be allowed through a derogation granted by the competent authority in certain circumstances in order to avoid detrimental situations for an issuer.

(26) A clear time limit should be set for the validity of a prospectus in order to avoid outdated information.

(27) Investors should be protected by ensuring publication of reliable information. The issuers whose securities are admitted to trading on a regulated market are subject to an ongoing disclosure obligation but are not required to publish updated information regularly. Further to this obligation, issuers should, at least annually, list all relevant information published or made available to the public over the preceding 12 months, including information provided to the various reporting requirements laid down in other Community legislation. This should make it possible to ensure the publication of consistent and easily understandable information on a regular basis. To avoid excessive burdens for certain issuers, issuers of non-equity securities with high minimum denomination should not be required to meet this obligation.

(28) It is necessary for the annual information to be provided by issuers whose securities are admitted to trading on a regulated market to be appropriately monitored by Member States in accordance with their obligations under the provisions of Community and national law concerning the regulation of securities, issuers of securities and securities markets.

(29) The opportunity of allowing issuers to incorporate by reference documents containing the information to be disclosed in a prospectus—provided that the documents incorporated by reference have been previously filed with or accepted by the competent authority—should facilitate the procedure of drawing up a prospectus and lower the costs for the issuers without endangering investor protection.

(30) Differences regarding the efficiency, methods and timing of the checking of the information given in a prospectus not only make it more difficult for undertakings to raise capital or to obtain admission to trading on a regulated market in more than one Member State but also hinder the acquisition by investors established in one Member State of securities offered by an issuer established in another Member State or admitted to trading in another Member State. These differences should be eliminated by harmonising the rules and regulations in order to achieve an adequate degree of equivalence of the safeguards required in each Member State to ensure the provision of information which is sufficient and as objective as possible for actual or potential securities holders.

(31) To facilitate circulation of the various documents making up the prospectus, the use of electronic communication facilities such as the Internet should be encouraged. The prospectus should always be delivered in paper form, free of charge to investors on request.

(32) The prospectus should be filed with the relevant competent authority and be made available to the public by the issuer, the offeror or the person asking for admission to trading on a regulated market, subject to European Union provisions relating to data protection.

(33) It is also necessary, in order to avoid loopholes in Community legislation which would undermine public confidence and therefore prejudice the proper functioning of financial markets, to harmonise advertisements.

(34) Any new matter liable to influence the assessment of the investment, arising after the publication of the prospectus but before the closing of the offer or the start of trading on a regulated market, should be properly evaluated by investors and therefore requires the approval and dissemination of a supplement to the prospectus.

(35) The obligation for an issuer to translate the full prospectus into all the relevant official languages discourages cross-border offers or multiple trading. To facilitate cross-border offers, where the prospectus is drawn up in a language that is customary in the sphere of international finance, the host or home Member State should only be entitled to require a summary in its official language(s).

(36) The competent authority of the host Member State should be entitled to receive a certificate from the competent authority of the home Member State which states that the prospectus has been drawn up in accordance with this Directive. In order to ensure that the purposes of this Directive will

be fully achieved, it is also necessary to include within its scope securities issued by issuers governed by the laws of third countries.

(37) A variety of competent authorities in Member States, having different responsibilities, may create unnecessary costs and overlapping of responsibilities without providing any additional benefit. In each Member State one single competent authority should be designated to approve prospectuses and to assume responsibility for supervising compliance with this Directive. Under strict conditions, a Member State should be allowed to designate more than one competent authority, but only one will assume the duties for international cooperation. Such an authority or authorities should be established as an administrative authority and in such a form that their independence from economic actors is guaranteed and conflicts of interest are avoided. The designation of a competent authority for prospectus approval should not exclude cooperation between that authority and other entities, with a view to guaranteeing efficient scrutiny and approval of prospectuses in the interest of issuers, investors, markets participants and markets alike. Any delegation of tasks relating to the obligations provided for in this Directive and in its implementing measures should be reviewed, in accordance with Article 31, five years after the date of entry into force of this Directive and should, except for publication on the Internet of approved prospectuses, and the filing of prospectuses as mentioned in Article 14, end eight years after the entry into force of this Directive.

(38) A common minimum set of powers for the competent authorities will guarantee the effectiveness of their supervision. The flow of information to the markets required by Directive 2001/34/EC should be ensured and action against breaches should be taken by competent authorities.

(39) For the purposes of carrying out their duties, cooperation between competent authorities of the Member States is required.

(40) Technical guidance and implementing measures for the rules laid down in this Directive may from time to time be necessary to take into account developments on financial markets. The Commission should accordingly be empowered to adopt implementing measures, provided that these do not modify the essential elements of this Directive and provided that the Commission acts in accordance with the principles set out in this Directive, after consulting the European Securities Committee established by Commission Decision 2001/528/EC.[10]

(41) In exercising its implementing powers in accordance with this Directive, the Commission should respect the following principles:
— the need to ensure confidence in financial markets among small investors and small and medium-sized enterprises (SMEs) by promoting high standards of transparency in financial markets,
— the need to provide investors with a wide range of competing investment opportunities and a level of disclosure and protection tailored to their circumstances,
— the need to ensure that independent regulatory authorities enforce the rules consistently, especially as regards the fight against white-collar crime,
— the need for a high level of transparency and consultation with all market participants and with the European Parliament and the Council,
— the need to encourage innovation in financial markets if they are to be dynamic and efficient,
— the need to ensure systemic stability of the financial system by close and reactive monitoring of financial innovation,
— the importance of reducing the cost of, and increasing access to, capital,
— the need to balance, on a long-term basis, the costs and benefits to market participants (including SMEs and small investors) of any implementing measures,
— the need to foster the international competitiveness of the Community's financial markets without prejudice to a much-needed extension of international cooperation,
— the need to achieve a level playing field for all market participants by establishing Community legislation every time it is appropriate,
— the need to respect differences in national financial markets where these do not unduly impinge on the coherence of the single market,
— the need to ensure coherence with other Community legislation in this area, as imbalances in information and a lack of transparency may jeopardise the operation of the markets and above all harm consumers and small investors.

(42) The European Parliament should be given a period of three months from the first transmission of draft implementing measures to allow it to examine them and to give its opinion. However, in urgent and duly justified cases, this period may be shortened. If, within that period, a resolution is passed by the European Parliament, the Commission should re-examine the draft measures.

(43) Member States should lay down a system of sanctions for breaches of the national provisions adopted pursuant to this Directive and should take all the measures necessary to ensure that these sanctions are applied. The sanctions thus provided for should be effective, proportional and dissuasive.

(44) Provision should be made for the right of judicial review of decisions taken by Member States' competent authorities in respect of the application of this Directive.

(45) In accordance with the principle of proportionality, it is necessary and appropriate for the achievement of the basic objective of ensuring the completion of a single securities market to lay down rules on a single passport for issuers. This Directive does not go beyond what is necessary in order to achieve the objectives pursued in accordance with the third paragraph of Article 5 of the Treaty.

(46) The assessment made by the Commission of the application of this Directive should focus in particular on the process of approval of prospectuses by the competent authorities of the Member States, and more generally on the application of the home-country principle, and whether or not problems of investor protection and market efficiency might result from this application; the Commission should also examine the functioning of Article 10.

(47) For future developments of this Directive, consideration should be given to the matter of deciding which approval mechanism should be adopted to enhance further the uniform application of Community legislation on prospectuses, including the possible establishment of a European Securities Unit.

(48) This Directive respects the fundamental rights and observes the principles recognised in particular by the Charter of Fundamental Rights of the European Union.

(49) The measures necessary for the implementation of this Directive should be adopted in accordance with Council Decision 1999/468/EC of 28 June 1999 laying down the procedures for the exercise of implementing powers conferred on the Commission,[11]

NOTES

1. OJ C240E, 28.8.2001, p 272 and OJ C20E, 28.1.2003, p 122.
2. OJ C80, 3.4.2002, p 52.
3. OJ C344, 6.12.2001, p 4.
4. Opinion of the European Parliament of 14 March 2002 (OJ C47E, 27.2.2003, p 417), Council Common Position of 24 March 2003 (OJ C125E, 27.5.2003, p 21) and Position of the European Parliament of 2 July 2003 (not yet published in the Official Journal). Decision of the Council of 15 July 2003.
5. OJ L100, 17.4.1980, p 1. Directive as last amended by Directive of the European Parliament and of the Council 94/18/EC (OJ L135, 31.5.1994, p 1).
6. OJ L124, 5.5.1989, p 8.
7. OJ L184, 6.7.2001, p 1.
8. OJ L141, 11.6.1993, p 27. Directive as last amended by Directive 2000/64/EC of the European Parliament and of the Council (OJ L290, 17.11.2000, p 27).
9. International disclosure standards for cross-border offering and initial listings by foreign issuers, Part I, International Organisation of Securities Commissions, September 1998.
10. OJ L191, 13.7.2001, p 45.
11. OJ L184, 17.7.1999, p 23.

HAVE ADOPTED THIS DIRECTIVE:

CHAPTER I
GENERAL PROVISIONS

[11.285]
Article 1
Purpose and scope
1. The purpose of this Directive is to harmonise requirements for the drawing up, approval and distribution of the prospectus to be published when securities are offered to the public or admitted to trading on a regulated market situated or operating within a Member State.
2. This Directive shall not apply to:
    (a) units issued by collective investment undertakings other than the closed-end type;
    (b) non-equity securities issued by a Member State or by one of a Member State's regional or local authorities, by public international bodies of which one or more Member States are members, by the European Central Bank or by the central banks of the Member States;
    (c) shares in the capital of central banks of the Member States;
    (d) securities unconditionally and irrevocably guaranteed by a Member State or by one of a Member State's regional or local authorities;
    (e) securities issued by associations with legal status or non-profit-making bodies, recognised by a Member State, with a view to their obtaining the means necessary to achieve their non-profit-making objectives;
    (f) non-equity securities issued in a continuous or repeated manner by credit institutions provided that these securities:
        (i) are not subordinated, convertible or exchangeable;
        (ii) do not give a right to subscribe to or acquire other types of securities and that they are not linked to a derivative instrument;
        (iii) materialise reception of repayable deposits;
        (iv) are covered by a deposit guarantee scheme under Directive 94/19/EC of the European Parliament and of the Council on deposit-guarantee schemes;[1]
    (g) non-fungible shares of capital whose main purpose is to provide the holder with a right to occupy an apartment, or other form of immovable property or a part thereof and where the shares cannot be sold on without this right being given up;
    [(h) securities included in an offer where the total consideration for the offer in the Union is less than EUR 5,000,000, which shall be calculated over a period of 12 months;]

   (i)   'bostadsobligationer' issued repeatedly by credit institutions in Sweden whose main purpose is to grant mortgage loans, provided that

      (i)   the 'bostadsobligationer' issued are of the same series;

      (ii)   the 'bostadsobligationer' are issued on tap during a specified issuing period;

      (iii)   the terms and conditions of the 'bostadsobligationer' are not changed during the issuing period;

      (iv)   the sums deriving from the issue of the said 'bostadsobligationer', in accordance with the articles of association of the issuer, are placed in assets which provide sufficient coverage for the liability deriving from securities;

  [(j)   non-equity securities issued in a continuous or repeated manner by credit institutions where the total consideration for the offer in the Union is less than EUR 75,000,000, which shall be calculated over a period of 12 months, provided that those securities:

      (i)   are not subordinated, convertible or exchangeable;

      (ii)   do not give a right to subscribe to or acquire other types of securities and that they are not linked to a derivative instrument.]

3.   Notwithstanding paragraph 2(b), (d), (h), (i) and (j), an issuer, an offeror or a person asking for admission to trading on a regulated market shall be entitled to draw up a prospectus in accordance with this Directive when securities are offered to the public or admitted to trading.

[4.   In order to take account of technical developments on financial markets, including inflation, the Commission shall adopt, by means of delegated acts in accordance with Article 24a, and subject to the conditions of Articles 24b and 24c, measures concerning the adjustment of the limits referred to in points (h) and (j) of paragraph 2 of this Article.]

NOTES

Para 2: points (h), (j) substituted by European Parliament and Council Directive 2010/73/EU, Art 1(1)(a), as from 31 December 2010. Note that Directive 2010/73/EU has a transposition date of 1 July 2012, and that the original text read as follows—

    "(h)   securities included in an offer where the total consideration of the offer is less than EUR 2,500,000, which limit shall be calculated over a period of 12 months;";

    "(j)   non-equity securities issued in a continuous or repeated manner by credit institutions where the total consideration of the offer is less than EUR 50,000,000, which limit shall be calculated over a period of 12 months, provided that these securities:

      (i)   are not subordinated, convertible or exchangeable;

      (ii)   do not give a right to subscribe to or acquire other types of securities and that they are not linked to a derivative instrument.".

Para 4: added by European Parliament and Council Directive 2010/73/EU, Art 1(1)(b), as from 31 December 2010. Note that Directive 2010/73/EU has a transposition date of 1 July 2012.

¹   OJ L135, 31.5.1994, p 5.

[11.286]
Article 2
Definitions

1.   For the purposes of this Directive, the following definitions shall apply:

   (a)   'securities' means transferable securities as defined by Article 1(4) of Directive 93/22/EEC with the exception of money market instruments as defined by Article 1(5) of Directive 93/22/EEC, having a maturity of less than 12 months. For these instruments national legislation may be applicable;

   (b)   'equity securities' means shares and other transferable securities equivalent to shares in companies, as well as any other type of transferable securities giving the right to acquire any of the aforementioned securities as a consequence of their being converted or the rights conferred by them being exercised, provided that securities of the latter type are issued by the issuer of the underlying shares or by an entity belonging to the group of the said issuer;

   (c)   'non-equity securities' means all securities that are not equity securities;

   (d)   'offer of securities to the public' means a communication to persons in any form and by any means, presenting sufficient information on the terms of the offer and the securities to be offered, so as to enable an investor to decide to purchase or subscribe to these securities. This definition shall also be applicable to the placing of securities through financial intermediaries;

  [(e)   "qualified investors" means persons or entities that are described in points (1) to (4) of Section I of Annex II to Directive 2004/39/EC of the European Parliament and of the Council of 21 April 2004 on markets in financial instruments,* and persons or entities who are, on request, treated as professional clients in accordance with Annex II to Directive 2004/39/EC, or recognised as eligible counterparties in accordance with Article 24 of Directive 2004/39/EC unless they have requested that they be treated as non-professional clients. Investment firms and credit institutions shall communicate their classification on request to the issuer without prejudice to the relevant legislation on data protection. Investment firms authorised to continue considering existing professional clients as such in accordance with Article 71(6) of Directive 2004/39/EC shall be authorised to treat those clients as qualified investors under this Directive;]

Part 11   EU Legislation

(f) 'small and medium-sized enterprises' means companies, which, according to their last annual or consolidated accounts, meet at least two of the following three criteria: an average number of employees during the financial year of less than 250, a total balance sheet not exceeding EUR 43,000,000 and an annual net turnover not exceeding EUR 50,000,000;

(g) 'credit institution' means an undertaking as defined by Article 1(1)(a) of Directive 2000/12/EC of the European Parliament and of the Council of 20 March 2000 relating to the taking up and pursuit of the business of credit institutions;[1]

(h) 'issuer' means a legal entity which issues or proposes to issue securities;

(i) 'person making an offer' (or 'offeror') means a legal entity or individual which offers securities to the public;

(j) 'regulated market' means a market as defined by Article 1(13) of Directive 93/22/EEC;

(k) 'offering programme' means a plan which would permit the issuance of non-equity securities, including warrants in any form, having a similar type and/or class, in a continuous or repeated manner during a specified issuing period;

(l) 'securities issued in a continuous or repeated manner' means issues on tap or at least two separate issues of securities of a similar type and/or class over a period of 12 months;

(m) 'home Member State' means:

    (i) for all Community issuers of securities which are not mentioned in (ii), the Member State where the issuer has its registered office;

    (ii) for any issues of non-equity securities whose denomination per unit amounts to at least EUR 1,000, and for any issues of non-equity securities giving the right to acquire any transferable securities or to receive a cash amount, as a consequence of their being converted or the rights conferred by them being exercised, provided that the issuer of the non-equity securities is not the issuer of the underlying securities or an entity belonging to the group of the latter issuer, the Member State where the issuer has its registered office, or where the securities were or are to be admitted to trading on a regulated market or where the securities are offered to the public, at the choice of the issuer, the offeror or the person asking for admission, as the case may be. The same regime shall be applicable to non-equity securities in a currency other than euro, provided that the value of such minimum denomination is nearly equivalent to EUR 1,000;

    (iii) for all issuers of securities incorporated in a third country, which are not mentioned in (ii), the Member State where the securities are intended to be offered to the public for the first time after the date of entry into force of this Directive or where the first application for admission to trading on a regulated market is made, at the choice of the issuer, the offeror or the person asking for admission, as the case may be, subject to a subsequent election by issuers incorporated in a third country if the home Member State was not determined by their choice;

(n) 'host Member State' means the State where an offer to the public is made or admission to trading is sought, when different from the home Member State;

(o) 'collective investment undertaking other than the closed-end type' means unit trusts and investment companies:

    (i) the object of which is the collective investment of capital provided by the public, and which operate on the principle of risk-spreading;

    (ii) the units of which are, at the holder's request, repurchased or redeemed, directly or indirectly, out of the assets of these undertakings;

(p) 'units of a collective investment undertaking' mean securities issued by a collective investment undertaking as representing the rights of the participants in such an undertaking over its assets;

(q) 'approval' means the positive act at the outcome of the scrutiny of the completeness of the prospectus by the home Member State's competent authority including the consistency of the information given and its comprehensibility;

(r) 'base prospectus' means a prospectus containing all relevant information as specified in Articles 5, 7 and 16 in case there is a supplement, concerning the issuer and the securities to be offered to the public or admitted to trading, and, at the choice of the issuer, the final terms of the offering;

[(s) "key information" means essential and appropriately structured information which is to be provided to investors with a view to enabling them to understand the nature and the risks of the issuer, guarantor and the securities that are being offered to them or admitted to trading on a regulated market and, without prejudice to Article 5(2)(b), to decide which offers of securities to consider further. In light of the offer and securities concerned, the key information shall include the following elements:

    (i) a short description of the risks associated with and essential characteristics of the issuer and any guarantor, including the assets, liabilities and financial position;

    (ii) a short description of the risk associated with and essential characteristics of the investment in the relevant security, including any rights attaching to the securities;

    (iii) general terms of the offer, including estimated expenses charged to the investor by the issuer or the offeror;

(iv)   details of the admission to trading;
(v)   reasons for the offer and use of proceeds;
(t)   "company with reduced market capitalisation" means a company listed on a regulated market that had an average market capitalisation of less than EUR 100,000,000 on the basis of end-year quotes for the previous three calendar years.]
2.   *For the purposes of paragraph 1(e)(iv) the criteria are as follows:*
(a)   *the investor has carried out transactions of a significant size on securities markets at an average frequency of, at least, 10 per quarter over the previous four quarters;*
(b)   *the size of the investor's securities portfolio exceeds EUR 0.5 million;*
(c)   *the investor works or has worked for at least one year in the financial sector in a professional position which requires knowledge of securities investment.*
3.   *For the purposes of paragraphs 1(e)(iv) and (v) the following shall apply:*
   Each competent authority shall ensure that appropriate mechanisms are in place for a register of natural persons and SMEs considered as qualified investors, taking into account the need to ensure an adequate level of data protection. The register shall be available to all issuers. Each natural person or SME wishing to be considered as a qualified investor shall register and each registered investor may decide to opt out at any moment.
[4.   In order to take account of technical developments on financial markets and to specify the requirements laid down in this Article, the Commission shall adopt, by means of delegated acts in accordance with Article 24a, and subject to the conditions of Articles 24b and 24c, the definitions referred to in paragraph 1, including the adjustment of the figures used for the definition of SMEs, and the thresholds for reduced market capitalisation, taking into account the situation on different national markets, including the classification used by the operators of regulated markets, Union legislation and recommendations as well as economic developments.]

NOTES

Para 1: point (e) substituted, and points (s), (t) added, by European Parliament and Council Directive 2010/73/EU, Art 1(2)(a), as from 31 December 2010. Note that Directive 2010/73/EU has a transposition date of 1 July 2012, and that the original point (e) read as follows—

"(e)   'qualified investors' means:
   (i)   legal entities which are authorised or regulated to operate in the financial markets, including: credit institutions, investment firms, other authorised or regulated financial institutions, insurance companies, collective investment schemes and their management companies, pension funds and their management companies, commodity dealers, as well as entities not so authorised or regulated whose corporate purpose is solely to invest in securities;
   (ii)   national and regional governments, central banks, international and supranational institutions such as the International Monetary Fund, the European Central Bank, the European Investment Bank and other similar international organisations;
   (iii) other legal entities which do not meet two of the three criteria set out in paragraph (f);
   (iv)   certain natural persons: subject to mutual recognition, a Member State may choose to authorise natural persons who are resident in the Member State and who expressly ask to be considered as qualified investors if these persons meet at least two of the criteria set out in paragraph 2;
   (v)   certain SMEs: subject to mutual recognition, a Member State may choose to authorise SMEs which have their registered office in that Member State and who expressly ask to be considered as qualified investors;".

Paras 2, 3: repealed by European Parliament and Council Directive 2010/73/EU, Art 1(2)(b), as from 31 December 2010. Note that Directive 2010/73/EU has a transposition date of 1 July 2012.
Para 4: substituted by European Parliament and Council Directive 2010/73/EU, Art 1(2)(c), as from 31 December 2010. Note that Directive 2010/73/EU has a transposition date of 1 July 2012, and that the original para 4 (as amended by European Parliament and Council Directive 2008/11/EC, Art 1(1)) read as follows—

"4.   In order to take account of technical developments on financial markets and to ensure uniform application of this Directive, the Commission shall . . . adopt implementing measures concerning the definitions referred to in paragraph 1, including adjustment of the figures used for the definition of SMEs, taking into account Community legislation and recommendations as well as economic developments and disclosure measures relating to the registration of individual qualified investors. [Those measures, designed to amend non-essential elements of this Directive by supplementing it, shall be adopted in accordance with the regulatory procedure with scrutiny referred to in Article 24(2a).]".

*   OJ L145, 30.4.2004, p 1.

1   OJ L126, 26.5.2000, p 1. Directive as last amended by Directive 2000/28/EC (OJ L275, 27.10.2000, p 37).

[11.287]
Article 3
Obligation to publish a prospectus
1.   Member States shall not allow any offer of securities to be made to the public within their territories without prior publication of a prospectus.
[2.   The obligation to publish a prospectus shall not apply to the following types of offer:
   (a)   an offer of securities addressed solely to qualified investors; and/or
   (b)   an offer of securities addressed to fewer than 150 natural or legal persons per Member State, other than qualified investors; and/or
   (c)   an offer of securities addressed to investors who acquire securities for a total consideration of at least EUR 100,000 per investor, for each separate offer; and/or

(d)   an offer of securities whose denomination per unit amounts to at least EUR 100,000; and/or

(e)   an offer of securities with a total consideration in the Union of less than EUR 100,000, which shall be calculated over a period of 12 months.]

However, any subsequent resale of securities which were previously the subject of one or more of the types of offer mentioned in this paragraph shall be regarded as a separate offer and the definition set out in Article 2(1)(d) shall apply for the purpose of deciding whether that resale is an offer of securities to the public. The placement of securities through financial intermediaries shall be subject to publication of a prospectus if none of the conditions (a) to (e) are met for the final placement.

[Member States shall not require another prospectus in any such subsequent resale of securities or final placement of securities through financial intermediaries as long as a valid prospectus is available in accordance with Article 9 and the issuer or the person responsible for drawing up such prospectus consents to its use by means of a written agreement.]

3.   Member States shall ensure that any admission of securities to trading on a regulated market situated or operating within their territories is subject to the publication of a prospectus.

[4.   In order to take account of technical developments on financial markets, including inflation, the Commission shall adopt, by means of delegated acts in accordance with Article 24a, and subject to the conditions of Articles 24b and 24c, measures concerning the thresholds in points (c) to (e) of paragraph 2 of this Article.]

NOTES

The first subparagraph of para 2 was substituted, and the final subparagraph in para 2 and all of para 4 were added, by European Parliament and Council Directive 2010/73/EU, Art 1(3), as from 31 December 2010. Note that Directive 2010/73/EU has a transposition date of 1 July 2012, and that the original text of para 2 read as follows—

"2.   The obligation to publish a prospectus shall not apply to the following types of offer:

(a)   an offer of securities addressed solely to qualified investors; and/or

(b)   an offer of securities addressed to fewer than 100 natural or legal persons per Member State, other than qualified investors; and/or

(c)   an offer of securities addressed to investors who acquire securities for a total consideration of at least EUR 50,000 per investor, for each separate offer; and/or

(d)   an offer of securities whose denomination per unit amounts to at least EUR 50,000; and/or

(e)   an offer of securities with a total consideration of less than EUR 100,000, which limit shall be calculated over a period of 12 months.".

[11.288]
Article 4
Exemptions from the obligation to publish a prospectus

1.   The obligation to publish a prospectus shall not apply to offers of securities to the public of the following types of securities:

(a)   shares issued in substitution for shares of the same class already issued, if the issuing of such new shares does not involve any increase in the issued capital;

(b)   securities offered in connection with a takeover by means of an exchange offer, provided that a document is available containing information which is regarded by the competent authority as being equivalent to that of the prospectus, taking into account the requirements of Community legislation;

[(c)   securities offered, allotted or to be allotted in connection with a merger or division, provided that a document is available containing information which is regarded by the competent authority as being equivalent to that of the prospectus, taking into account the requirements of Union legislation;

(d)   dividends paid out to existing shareholders in the form of shares of the same class as the shares in respect of which such dividends are paid, provided that a document is made available containing information on the number and nature of the shares and the reasons for and details of the offer;

(e)   securities offered, allotted or to be allotted to existing or former directors or employees by their employer or by an affiliated undertaking provided that the company has its head office or registered office in the Union and provided that a document is made available containing information on the number and nature of the securities and the reasons for and details of the offer.]

[Point (e) shall also apply to a company established outside the Union whose securities are admitted to trading either on a regulated market or on a third-country market. In the latter case, the exemption shall apply provided that adequate information, including the document referred to in point (e), is available at least in a language customary in the sphere of international finance and provided that the Commission has adopted an equivalence decision regarding the third-country market concerned.

On the request of the competent authority of a Member State, the Commission shall adopt equivalence decisions in accordance with the procedure referred to in Article 24(2), stating whether the legal and supervisory framework of a third country ensures that a regulated market authorised in that third country complies with legally binding requirements which are, for the purpose of the application of the exemption under point (e), equivalent to the requirements resulting from Directive 2003/6/EC of the European Parliament and of the Council of 28 January 2003 on insider dealing and market manipulation (market abuse),[1] from Title III of Directive 2004/39/EC and from Directive 2004/109/EC of the European Parliament and of the Council of 15 December 2004 on the harmonisation of transparency requirements in relation to information about issuers whose securities are admitted to trading on a regulated market,[2] and which are subject to effective supervision and enforcement in that third country. That competent authority shall indicate why it considers that the legal and supervisory framework of the third country concerned is to be considered equivalent and shall provide relevant information to this end.

Such a third-country legal and supervisory framework may be considered equivalent where that framework fulfils at least the following conditions:

(i)   the markets are subject to authorisation and to effective supervision and enforcement on an ongoing basis;

(ii)   the markets have clear and transparent rules regarding admission of securities to trading so that such securities are capable of being traded in a fair, orderly and efficient manner, and are freely negotiable;

(iii)   security issuers are subject to periodic and ongoing information requirements ensuring a high level of investor protection; and

(iv)   market transparency and integrity are ensured by the prevention of market abuse in the form of insider dealing and market manipulation.

As regards point (e), in order to take into account the developments of financial markets, the Commission may adopt by means of delegated acts in accordance with Article 24a, and subject to the conditions of Articles 24b and 24c, measures to specify the above criteria or to add further ones to be applied in the assessment of the equivalence.]

2.   The obligation to publish a prospectus shall not apply to the admission to trading on a regulated market of the following types of securities:

(a)   shares representing, over a period of 12 months, less than 10 per cent of the number of shares of the same class already admitted to trading on the same regulated market;

(b)   shares issued in substitution for shares of the same class already admitted to trading on the same regulated market, if the issuing of such shares does not involve any increase in the issued capital;

(c)   securities offered in connection with a takeover by means of an exchange offer, provided that a document is available containing information which is regarded by the competent authority as being equivalent to that of the prospectus, taking into account the requirements of Community legislation;

[(d)   securities offered, allotted or to be allotted in connection with a merger or a division, provided that a document is available containing information which is regarded by the competent authority as being equivalent to that of the prospectus, taking into account the requirements of Union legislation;]

(e)   shares offered, allotted or to be allotted free of charge to existing shareholders, and dividends paid out in the form of shares of the same class as the shares in respect of which such dividends are paid, provided that the said shares are of the same class as the shares already admitted to trading on the same regulated market and that a document is made available containing information on the number and nature of the shares and the reasons for and details of the offer;

(f)   securities offered, allotted or to be allotted to existing or former directors or employees by their employer or an affiliated undertaking, provided that the said securities are of the same class as the securities already admitted to trading on the same regulated market and that a document is made available containing information on the number and nature of the securities and the reasons for and detail of the offer;

(g)   shares resulting from the conversion or exchange of other securities or from the exercise of the rights conferred by other securities, provided that the said shares are of the same class as the shares already admitted to trading on the same regulated market;

(h)   securities already admitted to trading on another regulated market, on the following conditions:

(i)   that these securities, or securities of the same class, have been admitted to trading on that other regulated market for more than 18 months;

(ii)   that, for securities first admitted to trading on a regulated market after the date of entry into force of this Directive, the admission to trading on that other regulated market was associated with an approved prospectus made available to the public in conformity with Article 14;

(iii)   that, except where (ii) applies, for securities first admitted to listing after 30 June 1983, listing particulars were approved in accordance with the requirements of Directive 80/390/EEC or Directive 2001/34/EC;

(iv)   that the ongoing obligations for trading on that other regulated market have been fulfilled;

(v)   that the person seeking the admission of a security to trading on a regulated market under this exemption makes a summary document available to the public in a language accepted by the competent authority of the Member State of the regulated market where admission is sought;

(vi)   that the summary document referred to in (v) is made available to the public in the Member State of the regulated market where admission to trading is sought in the manner set out in Article 14(2); and

(vii)   that the contents of the summary document shall comply with Article 5(2). Furthermore the document shall state where the most recent prospectus can be obtained and where the financial information published by the issuer pursuant to his ongoing disclosure obligations is available.

[3.   In order to ensure consistent harmonisation of this Directive, the European Supervisory Authority (European Securities and Markets Authority) (hereinafter "ESMA")established by Regulation (EU) No 1095/2010 of the European Parliament and of the Council[3] may develop draft regulatory technical standards to specify the exemptions concerning the points (a) to (e) of paragraph 1 and points (a)to (h) of paragraph 2.

Power is delegated to the Commission to adopt the regulatory technical standards referred to in the first subparagraph in accordance with the procedure laid down in Articles 10 to 14 of Regulation (EU) No 1095/2010.]

NOTES

Para 1: points (c)–(e) substituted, and other words in square brackets added, by European Parliament and Council Directive 2010/73/EU, Art 1(4)(a), as from 31 December 2010. Note that Directive 2010/73/EU has a transposition date of 1 July 2012, and that the original points (c)–(e) read as follows—

"(c)   securities offered, allotted or to be allotted in connection with a merger, provided that a document is available containing information which is regarded by the competent authority as being equivalent to that of the prospectus, taking into account the requirements of Community legislation;

(d)   shares offered, allotted or to be allotted free of charge to existing shareholders, and dividends paid out in the form of shares of the same class as the shares in respect of which such dividends are paid, provided that a document is made available containing information on the number and nature of the shares and the reasons for and details of the offer;

(e)   securities offered, allotted or to be allotted to existing or former directors or employees by their employer which has securities already admitted to trading on a regulated market or by an affiliated undertaking, provided that a document is made available containing information on the number and nature of the securities and the reasons for and details of the offer.".

Para 2: point (d) substituted, and other words in square brackets added, by European Parliament and Council Directive 2010/73/EU, Art 1(4)(b), as from 31 December 2010. Note that Directive 2010/73/EU has a transposition date of 1 July 2012, and that the original text read as follows—

"(d)   securities offered, allotted or to be allotted in connection with a merger, provided that a document is available containing information which is regarded by the competent authority as being equivalent to that of the prospectus, taking into account the requirements of Community legislation;".

Para 3: substituted by European Parliament and Council Directive 2010/78/EU, Art 5(1), as from 4 January 2011.

1   OJ L96, 12.4.2003, p 16.

2   OJ L390, 31.12.2004, p 38.

3   OJ L331, 15.12.2010,p 84.

CHAPTER II
DRAWING UP OF THE PROSPECTUS

[11.289]
Article 5
The prospectus

1.   Without prejudice to Article 8(2), the prospectus shall contain all information which, according to the particular nature of the issuer and of the securities offered to the public or admitted to trading on a regulated market, is necessary to enable investors to make an informed assessment of the assets and liabilities, financial position, profit and losses, and prospects of the issuer and of any guarantor, and of the rights attaching to such securities. This information shall be presented in an easily analysable and comprehensible form.

[2.   The prospectus shall contain information concerning the issuer and the securities to be offered to the public or to be admitted to trading on a regulated market. It shall also include a summary that, in a concise manner and in non- technical language, provides key information in the language in which the prospectus was originally drawn up. The format and content of the summary of the prospectus shall provide, in conjunction with the prospectus, appropriate information about essential elements of the securities concerned in order to aid investors when considering whether to invest in such securities.

The summary shall be drawn up in a common format in order to facilitate comparability of the summaries of similar securities and its content should convey the key information of the securities

concerned in order to aid investors when considering whether to invest in such securities. The summary shall also contain a warning that:]
- (a) it should be read as an introduction to the prospectus;
- (b) any decision to invest in the securities should be based on consideration of the prospectus as a whole by the investor;
- (c) where a claim relating to the information contained in a prospectus is brought before a court, the plaintiff investor might, under the national legislation of the Member States, have to bear the costs of translating the prospectus before the legal proceedings are initiated; and
- (d) civil liability attaches to those persons who have tabled the summary including any translation thereof, and applied for its notification, but only if the summary is misleading, inaccurate or inconsistent when read together with the other parts of the prospectus.

[Where the prospectus relates to the admission to trading on a regulated market of non-equity securities having a denomination of at least EUR 100,000, there shall be no requirement to provide a summary, save where a Member State so requires in accordance with Article 19(4).]

[In order to ensure uniform conditions of application of this Directive and of the delegated acts adopted by the Commission in accordance with paragraph 5, ESMA shall develop draft implementing technical standards in order to ensure uniform conditions of application of the delegated acts adopted by the Commission in accordance with paragraph 5 in relation to a uniform template for the presentation of the summary and to allow investors to compare the security concerned with other relevant products.

Power is conferred on the Commission to adopt the implementing technical standards referred to in the first subparagraph in accordance with Article 15 of Regulation (EU) No 1095/2010.]

[3. The issuer, offeror or person asking for the admission to trading on a regulated market may draw up the prospectus as a single document or separate documents. A prospectus composed of separate documents shall divide the required information into a registration document, a securities note and a summary note. The registration document shall contain the information relating to the issuer. The securities note shall contain the information concerning the securities offered to the public or to be admitted to trading on a regulated market.]

4. For the following types of securities, the prospectus can, at the choice of the issuer, offeror or person asking for the admission to trading on a regulated market consist of a base prospectus containing all relevant information concerning the issuer and the securities offered to the public or to be admitted to trading on a regulated market:
- (a) non-equity securities, including warrants in any form, issued under an offering programme;
- (b) non-equity securities issued in a continuous or repeated manner by credit institutions,
    - (i) where the sums deriving from the issue of the said securities, under national legislation, are placed in assets which provide sufficient coverage for the liability deriving from securities until their maturity date;
    - (ii) where, in the event of the insolvency of the related credit institution, the said sums are intended, as a priority, to repay the capital and interest falling due, without prejudice to the provisions of Directive 2001/24/EC of the European Parliament and of the Council of 4 April 2001 on the reorganisation and winding up of credit institutions.[1]

The information given in the base prospectus shall be supplemented, if necessary, in accordance with Article 16, with updated information on the issuer and on the securities to be offered to the public or to be admitted to trading on a regulated market.

[Where the final terms of the offer are neither included in the base prospectus nor in a supplement, the final terms shall be made available to investors, filed with the competent authority of the home Member State and communicated, by the issuer, to the competent authority of the host Member State(s) when each public offer is made as soon as practicable and, if possible, in advance of the beginning of the public offer or admission to trading. The final terms shall contain only information that relates to the securities note and shall not be used to supplement the base prospectus. Article 8(1)(a) shall apply in those cases.]

[5. In order to take account of technical developments on financial markets and to specify the requirements laid down in this Article, the Commission shall adopt, by means of delegated acts in accordance with Article 24a and subject to the conditions of Articles 24b and 24c, measures relating to the following:
- (a) the format of the prospectus or base prospectus, the summary, final terms and supplements; and
- (b) the detailed content and specific form of the key information to be included in the summary.

Those delegated acts shall be adopted by 1 July 2012.]

NOTES

Para 2 is amended as follows:

The introductory words of the first subparagraph, and all of the antepenultimate subparagraph, were substituted by European Parliament and Council Directive 2010/73/EU, Art 1(5)(a), as from 31 December 2010. Note that Directive 2010/73/EU has a transposition date of 1 July 2012, and that the original text read as follows—

Part 11 EU Legislation

"2.   The prospectus shall contain information concerning the issuer and the securities to be offered to the public or to be admitted to trading on a regulated market. It shall also include a summary. The summary shall, in a brief manner and in non-technical language, convey the essential characteristics and risks associated with the issuer, any guarantor and the securities, in the language in which the prospectus was originally drawn up. The summary shall also contain a warning that:";

"Where the prospectus relates to the admission to trading on a regulated market of non-equity securities having a denomination of at least EUR 50,000, there shall be no requirement to provide a summary except when requested by a Member State as provided for in Article 19(4).".

The final two subparagraphs were added by European Parliament and Council Directive 2010/78/EU, Art 5(2), as from 4 January 2011.

Para 3: substituted by European Parliament and Council Directive 2010/73/EU, Art 1(5)(c), as from 31 December 2010. Note that Directive 2010/73/EU has a transposition date of 1 July 2012, and that the original text read as follows—

"3.   Subject to paragraph 4, the issuer, offeror or person asking for the admission to trading on a regulated market may draw up the prospectus as a single document or separate documents. A prospectus composed of separate documents shall divide the required information into a registration document, a securities note and a summary note. The registration document shall contain the information relating to the issuer. The securities note shall contain the information concerning the securities offered to the public or to be admitted to trading on a regulated market.".

Para 4: final subparagraph substituted by European Parliament and Council Directive 2010/73/EU, Art 1(5)(c), as from 31 December 2010. Note that Directive 2010/73/EU has a transposition date of 1 July 2012, and that the original text read as follows—

"If the final terms of the offer are not included in either the base prospectus or a supplement, the final terms shall be provided to investors and filed with the competent authority when each public offer is made as soon as practicable and if possible in advance of the beginning of the offer. The provisions of Article 8(1)(a) shall be applicable in any such case.".

Para 5: substituted by European Parliament and Council Directive 2010/73/EU, Art 1(5)(c), as from 31 December 2010. Note that Directive 2010/73/EU has a transposition date of 1 July 2012, and that the original text (as amended by European Parliament and Council Directive 2008/11/EC, Art 1(1)) read as follows—

"5.   In order to take account of technical developments on financial markets and to ensure uniform application of this Directive, the Commission shall . . . adopt implementing measures concerning the format of the prospectus or base prospectus and supplements. [Those measures, designed to amend non-essential elements of this Directive by supplementing it, shall be adopted in accordance with the regulatory procedure with scrutiny referred to in Article 24(2a).]".

¹   OJ L125, 5.5.2001, p 15.

[11.290]
Article 6
Responsibility attaching to the prospectus
1.   Member States shall ensure that responsibility for the information given in a prospectus attaches at least to the issuer or its administrative, management or supervisory bodies, the offeror, the person asking for the admission to trading on a regulated market or the guarantor, as the case may be. The persons responsible shall be clearly identified in the prospectus by their names and functions or, in the case of legal persons, their names and registered offices, as well as declarations by them that, to the best of their knowledge, the information contained in the prospectus is in accordance with the facts and that the prospectus makes no omission likely to affect its import.
2.   Member States shall ensure that their laws, regulation and administrative provisions on civil liability apply to those persons responsible for the information given in a prospectus.

[However, Member States shall ensure that no civil liability shall attach to any person solely on the basis of the summary, including any translation thereof, unless it is misleading, inaccurate or inconsistent, when read together with the other parts of the prospectus, or it does not provide, when read together with the other parts of the prospectus, key information in order to aid investors when considering whether to invest in such securities. The summary shall contain a clear warning to that effect.]

NOTES

Para 2: second subparagraph substituted by European Parliament and Council Directive 2010/73/EU, Art 1(6), as from 31 December 2010. Note that Directive 2010/73/EU has a transposition date of 1 July 2012, and that the original text read as follows—

"However, Member States shall ensure that no civil liability shall attach to any person solely on the basis of the summary, including any translation thereof, unless it is misleading, inaccurate or inconsistent when read together with the other parts of the prospectus.".

[11.291]
Article 7
Minimum information
[1.   Detailed delegated acts regarding the specific information which must be included in a prospectus, avoiding duplication of information when a prospectus is composed of separate documents, shall be adopted by the Commission in accordance with Article 24a and subject to the conditions of Articles 24b and 24c.]
2.   In particular, for the elaboration of the various models of prospectuses, account shall be taken of the following:

(a) the various types of information needed by investors relating to equity securities as compared with non-equity securities; a consistent approach shall be taken with regard to information required in a prospectus for securities which have a similar economic rationale, notably derivative securities;

[(b) the various types and characteristics of offers and admissions to trading on a regulated market of non-equity securities. The information required in a prospectus shall be appropriate from the point of view of the investors concerned for non-equity securities having a denomination per unit of at least EUR 100,000;]

(c) the format used and the information required in prospectuses relating to non-equity securities, including warrants in any form, issued under an offering programme;

(d) the format used and the information required in prospectuses relating to non-equity securities, in so far as these securities are not subordinated, convertible, exchangeable, subject to subscription or acquisition rights or linked to derivative instruments, issued in a continuous or repeated manner by entities authorised or regulated to operate in the financial markets within the European Economic Area;

[(e) the various activities and size of the issuer, in particular credit institutions issuing non-equity securities referred to in Article 1(2)(j), companies with reduced market capitalisation and SMEs. For such companies the information shall be adapted to their size and, where appropriate, to their shorter track record;]

(f) if applicable, the public nature of the issuer;

[(g) a proportionate disclosure regime shall apply to offers of shares by companies whose shares of the same class are admitted to trading on a regulated market or a multilateral trading facility as defined in Article 4(1)(15) of Directive 2004/39/EC, which are subject to appropriate ongoing disclosure requirements and rules on market abuse, provided that the issuer has not disapplied the statutory pre-emption rights.]

[3. The delegated acts referred to in paragraph 1 shall be based on the standards in the field of financial and non-financial information set out by international securities commission organisations, in particular by IOSCO and on the indicative Annexes to this Directive.]

[4. ESMA may develop draft implementing technical standards in order to ensure uniform conditions of application of the delegated acts adopted by the Commission in accordance with paragraph 1.

Power is conferred on the Commission to adopt the implementing technical standards referred to in the first subparagraph in accordance with Article 15 of Regulation (EU) No 1095/2010.]

NOTES

Para 1: substituted by European Parliament and Council Directive 2010/73/EU, Art 1(7)(a), as from 31 December 2010. Note that Directive 2010/73/EU has a transposition date of 1 July 2012, and that the original text (as amended by European Parliament and Council Directive 2008/11/EC, Art 1(1)) read as follows—

"1. Detailed implementing measures regarding the specific information which must be included in a prospectus, avoiding duplication of information when a prospectus is composed of separate documents, shall be adopted by the Commission . . . . The first set of implementing measures shall be adopted by 1 July 2004. [Those measures, designed to amend non-essential elements of this Directive by supplementing it, shall be adopted in accordance with the regulatory procedure with scrutiny referred to in Article 24(2a).]".

Para 2: points (b), (e) substituted, and point (g) added, by European Parliament and Council Directive 2010/73/EU, Art 1(7)(b), as from 31 December 2010. Note that Directive 2010/73/EU has a transposition date of 1 July 2012, and that the original points (b), (e) read as follows—

"(b) the various types and characteristics of offers and admissions to trading on a regulated market of non-equity securities. The information required in a prospectus shall be appropriate from the point of view of the investors concerned for non-equity securities having a denomination per unit of at least EUR 50,000;";

"(e) the various activities and size of the issuer, in particular SMEs. For such companies the information shall be adapted to their size and, where appropriate, to their shorter track record;".

Para 3: substituted by European Parliament and Council Directive 2010/73/EU, Art 1(7)(c), as from 31 December 2010. Note that Directive 2010/73/EU has a transposition date of 1 July 2012, and that the original text read as follows—

"3. The implementing measures referred to in paragraph 1 shall be based on the standards in the field of financial and non-financial information set out by international securities commission organisations, and in particular by IOSCO and on the indicative Annexes to this Directive.".

Para 4: added by European Parliament and Council Directive 2010/78/EU, Art 5(3), as from 4 January 2011.

[11.292]
Article 8
Omission of information

1. Member States shall ensure that where the final offer price and amount of securities which will be offered to the public cannot be included in the prospectus:

(a) the criteria, and/or the conditions in accordance with which the above elements will be determined or, in the case of price, the maximum price, are disclosed in the prospectus; or

(b) the acceptances of the purchase or subscription of securities may be withdrawn for not less than two working days after the final offer price and amount of securities which will be offered to the public have been filed.

The final offer price and amount of securities shall be filed with the competent authority of the home Member State and published in accordance with the arrangements provided for in Article 14(2).

2.   The competent authority of the home Member State may authorise the omission from the prospectus of certain information provided for in this Directive or in the [delegated acts] referred to in Article 7(1), if it considers that:

(a)   disclosure of such information would be contrary to the public interest; or

(b)   disclosure of such information would be seriously detrimental to the issuer, provided that the omission would not be likely to mislead the public with regard to facts and circumstances essential for an informed assessment of the issuer, offeror or guarantor, if any, and of the rights attached to the securities to which the prospectus relates; or

(c)   such information is of minor importance only for a specific offer or admission to trading on a regulated market and is not such as will influence the assessment of the financial position and prospects of the issuer, offeror or guarantor, if any.

3.   Without prejudice to the adequate information of investors, where, exceptionally, certain information required by [delegated acts] referred to in Article 7(1) to be included in a prospectus is inappropriate to the issuer's sphere of activity or to the legal form of the issuer or to the securities to which the prospectus relates, the prospectus shall contain information equivalent to the required information. If there is no such information, this requirement shall not apply.

[3a.   Where securities are guaranteed by a Member State, an issuer, an offeror or a person asking for admission to trading on a regulated market, when drawing up a prospectus in accordance with Article 1(3), shall be entitled to omit information about such guarantor.]

[4.   In order to take account of technical developments on financial markets and to specify the requirements laid down in this Article, the Commission shall adopt, by means of delegated acts in accordance with Article 24a and subject to the conditions of Articles 24b and 24c, measures concerning paragraph 2.]

[5.   ESMA may develop draft implementing technical standards to ensure uniform conditions of application of the delegated acts adopted by the Commission in accordance with paragraph 4.

Power is conferred on the Commission to adopt the implementing technical standards referred to in the first subparagraph in accordance with Article 15 of Regulation (EU) No 1095/2010.]

NOTES

Words in square brackets in paras 2, 3 substituted (for the original words "implementing measures"), para 3a inserted, and para 4 substituted, by European Parliament and Council Directive 2010/73/EU, Art 1(8), as from 31 December 2010. Note that Directive 2010/73/EU has a transposition date of 1 July 2012, and that the original para 4 (as amended by European Parliament and Council Directive 2008/11/EC, Art 1(1)) read as follows—

"4.   In order to take account of technical developments on financial markets and to ensure uniform application of this Directive, the Commission shall . . . adopt implementing measures concerning paragraph 2. [Those measures, designed to amend non-essential elements of this Directive by supplementing it, shall be adopted in accordance with the regulatory procedure with scrutiny referred to in Article 24(2a).]".

Para 5: added by European Parliament and Council Directive 2010/78/EU, Art 5(4), as from 4 January 2011.

[11.293]
Article 9
Validity of a prospectus, base prospectus and registration document

[1.   A prospectus shall be valid for 12 months after its approval for offers to the public or admissions to trading on a regulated market, provided that the prospectus is completed by any supplements required pursuant to Article 16.]

2.   In the case of an offering programme, the base prospectus, previously filed, shall be valid for a period of up to 12 months.

3.   In the case of non-equity securities referred to in Article 5(4)(b), the prospectus shall be valid until no more of the securities concerned are issued in a continuous or repeated manner.

[4.   A registration document, as referred to in Article 5(3), previously filed and approved, shall be valid for a period of up to 12 months. The registration document, updated in accordance with Article 12(2) or Article 16, accompanied by the securities note and the summary note shall be considered to constitute a valid prospectus.]

NOTES

Paras 1, 4: substituted by European Parliament and Council Directive 2010/73/EU, Art 1(9), as from 31 December 2010. Note that Directive 2010/73/EU has a transposition date of 1 July 2012, and that the original paragraphs read as follows—

"1.   A prospectus shall be valid for 12 months after its publication for offers to the public or admissions to trading on a regulated market, provided that the prospectus is completed by any supplements required pursuant to Article 16.";

"4.   A registration document, as referred to in Article 5(3), previously filed, shall be valid for a period of up to 12 months provided that it has been updated in accordance with Article 10(1). The registration document accompanied by the securities note, updated if applicable in accordance with Article 12, and the summary note shall be considered to constitute a valid prospectus.".

[11.294]
Article 10
Information

1.   *Issuers whose securities are admitted to trading on a regulated market shall at least annually provide a document that contains or refers to all information that they have published or made available to the public over the preceding 12 months in one or more Member States and in third countries in compliance with their obligations under Community and national laws and rules dealing with the regulation of securities, issuers of securities and securities markets. Issuers shall refer at least to the information required pursuant to company law directives, Directive 2001/34/EC and Regulation (EC) No 1606/2002 of the European Parliament and of the Council of 19 July 2002 on the application of international accounting standards.[1]*

2.   *The document shall be filed with the competent authority of the home Member State after the publication of the financial statement. Where the document refers to information, it shall be stated where the information can be obtained.*

3.   *The obligation set out in paragraph 1 shall not apply to issuers of non-equity securities whose denomination per unit amounts to at least EUR 50,000.*

4.   *In order to take account of technical developments on financial markets and to ensure uniform application of this Directive, the Commission may, in accordance with the procedure referred to in Article 24(2), adopt implementing measures concerning paragraph 1. These measures will relate only to the method of publication of the disclosure requirements mentioned in paragraph 1 and will not entail new disclosure requirements. The first set of implementing measures shall be adopted by 1 July 2004.*

NOTES

Repealed by European Parliament and Council Directive 2010/73/EU, Art 1(10), as from 31 December 2010. Note that Directive 2010/73/EU has a transposition date of 1 July 2012.

[1]   OJ L243, 11.9.2002, p 1.

[11.295]
Article 11
Incorporation by reference

[1.   Member States shall allow information to be incorporated in the prospectus by reference to one or more previously or simultaneously published documents that have been approved by the competent authority of the home Member State or filed with it in accordance with this Directive or Directive 2004/109/EC. Such information shall be the most recent available to the issuer. The summary shall not incorporate information by reference.]

2.   When information is incorporated by reference, a cross-reference list must be provided in order to enable investors to identify easily specific items of information.

[3.   In order to take account of technical developments on financial markets and to specify the requirements laid down in this Article, the Commission shall adopt, by means of delegated acts in accordance with Article 24a and subject to the conditions of Articles 24b and 24c, measures concerning the information to be incorporated by reference.]

NOTES

Paras 1, 3: substituted by European Parliament and Council Directive 2010/73/EU, Art 1(11), as from 31 December 2010. Note that Directive 2010/73/EU has a transposition date of 1 July 2012, and that the original paragraphs (as amended in the case of para 3 by European Parliament and Council Directive 2008/11/EC, Art 1(1)) read as follows—

"1.   Member States shall allow information to be incorporated in the prospectus by reference to one or more previously or simultaneously published documents that have been approved by the competent authority of the home Member State or filed with it in accordance with this Directive, in particular pursuant to Article 10, or with Titles IV and V of Directive 2001/34/EC. This information shall be the latest available to the issuer. The summary shall not incorporate information by reference.";

"3.   In order to take account of technical developments on financial markets and to ensure uniform application of this Directive, the Commission shall . . . . adopt implementing measures concerning the information to be incorporated by reference. The first set of implementing measures shall be adopted by 1 July 2004. [Those measures, designed to amend non-essential elements of this Directive by supplementing it, shall be adopted in accordance with the regulatory procedure with scrutiny referred to in Article 24(2a).]".

[11.296]
Article 12
Prospectuses consisting of separate documents

1.   An issuer which already has a registration document approved by the competent authority shall be required to draw up only the securities note and the summary note when securities are offered to the public or admitted to trading on a regulated market.

[2.   In this case, the securities note shall provide information that would normally be provided in the registration document, where there has been a material change or recent development which could affect investors' assessments since the latest updated registration document, unless such information is provided in a supplement in accordance with Article 16. The securities and summary notes shall be subject to a separate approval.]

3. Where an issuer has only filed a registration document without approval, the entire documentation, including updated information, shall be subject to approval.

NOTES

Para 2: substituted by European Parliament and Council Directive 2010/73/EU, Art 1(12), as from 31 December 2010. Note that Directive 2010/73/EU has a transposition date of 1 July 2012, and that the original paragraph read as follows—

"2. In this case, the securities note shall provide information that would normally be provided in the registration document if there has been a material change or recent development which could affect investors' assessments since the latest updated registration document or any supplement as provided for in Article 16 was approved. The securities and summary notes shall be subject to a separate approval.".

CHAPTER III
ARRANGEMENTS FOR APPROVAL AND PUBLICATION OF THE PROSPECTUS

[11.297]
Article 13
Approval of the prospectus
1. No prospectus shall be published until it has been approved by the competent authority of the home Member State.
2. This competent authority shall notify the issuer, the offeror or the person asking for admission to trading on a regulated market, as the case may be, of its decision regarding the approval of the prospectus within 10 working days of the submission of the draft prospectus.

If the competent authority fails to give a decision on the prospectus within the time limits laid down in this paragraph and paragraph 3, this shall not be deemed to constitute approval of the application.

[The competent authority shall notify ESMA of the approval of the prospectus and any supplement thereto at the same time as that approval is notified to the issuer, the offeror or the person asking for admission to trading on a regulated market, as the case may be. The competent authorities shall at the same time provide ESMA with a copy of the prospectus and any supplement thereto.]
3. The time limit referred to in paragraph 2 shall be extended to 20 working days if the public offer involves securities issued by an issuer which does not have any securities admitted to trading on a regulated market and who has not previously offered securities to the public.
4. If the competent authority finds, on reasonable grounds, that the documents submitted to it are incomplete or that supplementary information is needed, the time limits referred to in paragraphs 2 and 3 shall apply only from the date on which such information is provided by the issuer, the offeror or the person asking for admission to trading on a regulated market.

In the case referred to in paragraph 2 the competent authority should notify the issuer if the documents are incomplete within 10 working days of the submission of the application.
[5. The competent authority of the home Member State may transfer the approval of a prospectus to the competent authority of another Member State, subject to prior notification to ESMA and the agreement of the competent authority. Such a transfer shall be notified to the issuer, the offeror or the person asking for admission to trading on a regulated market within three working days from the date of the decision taken by the competent authority of the home Member State. The time limit referred to in paragraph 2 shall apply from that date. Article 28(4) of Regulation (EU) No 1095/2010 shall not apply to the transfer of the approval of the prospectus in accordance with this paragraph.

In order to ensure uniform conditions of application of this Directive and to facilitate communication between the competent authorities and between the competent authorities and ESMA, ESMA may develop draft implementing technical standards to establish standard forms, templates and procedures for the notifications provided for in this paragraph.

Power is conferred on the Commission to adopt the implementing technical standards referred to in the second subparagraph in accordance with Article 15 of Regulation (EU) No 1095/2010.]
6. This Directive shall not affect the competent authority's liability, which shall continue to be governed solely by national law.

Member States shall ensure that their national provisions on the liability of competent authorities apply only to approvals of prospectuses by their competent authority or authorities.
[7. In order to take account of technical developments on financial markets and to specify the requirements laid down in this Article, the Commission shall adopt, by means of delegated acts in accordance with Article 24a and subject to the conditions of Articles 24b and 24c, measures concerning the conditions in accordance with which time limits may be adjusted.]

NOTES

Para 2: words in square brackets added by European Parliament and Council Directive 2010/78/EU, Art 5(5)(a), as from 4 January 2011. Note that this provision has a transposition date of 31 December 2011.

Para 5: substituted by European Parliament and Council Directive 2010/78/EU, Art 5(5)(b), as from 4 January 2011. Note that this provision has a transposition date of 31 December 2011 in so far as relating to the first subparagraph, and that the original text read as follows—

"5. The competent authority of the home Member State may transfer the approval of a prospectus to the competent authority of another Member State, subject to the agreement of that authority. Furthermore, this transfer shall be notified to the issuer, the offeror or the person asking for admission to trading on a regulated market within three working days from the date of the decision taken by the competent authority of the home Member State. The time limit referred to in paragraph 2 shall apply from that date.".

Para 7: substituted by European Parliament and Council Directive 2010/73/EU, Art 1(13), as from 31 December 2010. Note that Directive 2010/73/EU has a transposition date of 1 July 2012, and that the original paragraph (as amended by European Parliament and Council Directive 2008/11/EC, Art 1(1)) read as follows—

"7. In order to take account of technical developments on financial markets and to ensure uniform application of this Directive, the Commission may . . . . adopt implementing measures concerning the conditions in accordance with which time limits may be adjusted. [Those measures, designed to amend non-essential elements of this Directive by supplementing it, shall be adopted in accordance with the regulatory procedure with scrutiny referred to in Article 24(2a).]".

[11.298]
Article 14
Publication of the prospectus
[1. Once approved, the prospectus shall be filed with the competent authority of the home Member State, shall be accessible to ESMA through the competent authority and shall be made available to the public by the issuer, the offeror or the person asking for admission to trading on a regulated market as soon as practicable and, in any event, at a reasonable time in advance of, and at the latest at the beginning of, the offer to the public or the admission to trading of the securities involved. In addition, in the case of an initial public offer of a class of shares not already admitted to trading on a regulated market that is to be admitted to trading for the first time, the prospectus shall be available at least six working days before the end of the offer.]
2. The prospectus shall be deemed available to the public when published either:
    (a)   by insertion in one or more newspapers circulated throughout, or widely circulated in, the Member States in which the offer to the public is made or the admission to trading is sought; or
    (b)   in a printed form to be made available, free of charge, to the public at the offices of the market on which the securities are being admitted to trading, or at the registered office of the issuer and at the offices of the financial intermediaries placing or selling the securities, including paying agents; or
    [(c)   in electronic form on the issuer's website or, if applicable, on the website of the financial intermediaries placing or selling the securities, including paying agents; or']
    (d)   in an electronic form on the website of the regulated market where the admission to trading is sought; or
    (e)   in electronic form on the website of the competent authority of the home Member State if the said authority has decided to offer this service.
[Member States shall require issuers or the persons responsible for drawing up a prospectus that publish their prospectus in accordance with point (a) or (b) also to publish their prospectus electronically in accordance with point (c).]
3. In addition, a home Member State may require publication of a notice stating how the prospectus has been made available and where it can be obtained by the public.
4. The competent authority of the home Member State shall publish on its website over a period of 12 months, at its choice, all the prospectuses approved, or at least the list of prospectuses approved in accordance with Article 13, including, if applicable, a hyperlink to the prospectus published on the website of the issuer, or on the website of the regulated market.
[4a. ESMA shall publish on its website the list of prospectuses approved in accordance with Article 13, including, if applicable, a hyperlink to the prospectus published on the website of the competent authority of the home Member State, or on the website of the issuer, or on the website of the regulated market. The published list shall be kept up-to-date and each item shall remain on the website for a period of at least 12 months.]
5. In the case of a prospectus comprising several documents and/or incorporating information by reference, the documents and information making up the prospectus may be published and circulated separately provided that the said documents are made available, free of charge, to the public, in accordance with the arrangements established in paragraph 2. Each document shall indicate where the other constituent documents of the full prospectus may be obtained.
6. The text and the format of the prospectus, and/or the supplements to the prospectus, published or made available to the public, shall at all times be identical to the original version approved by the competent authority of the home Member State.
7. Where the prospectus is made available by publication in electronic form, a paper copy must nevertheless be delivered to the investor, upon his request and free of charge, by the issuer, the offeror, the person asking for admission to trading or the financial intermediaries placing or selling the securities.
[8. In order to take account of technical developments on financial markets and to specify the requirements laid down in this Article, the Commission shall adopt, by means of delegated acts in accordance with Article 24a and subject to the conditions of Articles 24b and 24c, measures concerning paragraphs 1 to 4 of this Article.]

NOTES

Para 1 was substituted, and para 4a was inserted, by European Parliament and Council Directive 2010/78/EU, Art 5(6), as from 4 January 2011. Note that this provision has a transposition date of 31 December 2011, and that the original para 1 read as follows—

"1.   Once approved, the prospectus shall be filed with the competent authority of the home Member State and shall be made available to the public by the issuer, offeror or person asking for admission to trading on a regulated market as soon as practicable and in any case, at a reasonable time in advance of, and at the latest at the beginning of, the offer to the public or the admission to trading of the securities involved. In addition, in the case of an initial public offer of a class of shares not already admitted to trading on a regulated market that is to be admitted to trading for the first time, the prospectus shall be available at least six working days before the end of the offer.".

Point (c) of para 2, the second subparagraph in para 2, and all of para 8, were substituted by European Parliament and Council Directive 2010/73/EU, Art 1(14), as from 31 December 2010. Note that Directive 2010/73/EU has a transposition date of 1 July 2012, and that the original text (as amended in the case of para 8 by European Parliament and Council Directive 2008/11/EC, Art 1(1)) read as follows—

"(c)   in an electronic form on the issuer's website and, if applicable, on the website of the financial intermediaries placing or selling the securities, including paying agents; or";

"A home Member State may require issuers which publish their prospectus in accordance with (a) or (b) also to publish their prospectus in an electronic form in accordance with (c).";

"8.   In order to take account of technical developments on financial markets and to ensure uniform application of the Directive, the Commission shall   . . .   adopt implementing measures concerning paragraphs 1, 2, 3 and 4. The first set of implementing measures shall be adopted by 1 July 2004. [Those measures, designed to amend non-essential elements of this Directive by supplementing it, shall be adopted in accordance with the regulatory procedure with scrutiny referred to in Article 24(2a).]".

[11.299]
Article 15
Advertisements

1.   Any type of advertisements relating either to an offer to the public of securities or to an admission to trading on a regulated market shall observe the principles contained in paragraphs 2 to 5. Paragraphs 2 to 4 shall apply only to cases where the issuer, the offeror or the person applying for admission to trading is covered by the obligation to draw up a prospectus.

2.   Advertisements shall state that a prospectus has been or will be published and indicate where investors are or will be able to obtain it.

3.   Advertisements shall be clearly recognisable as such. The information contained in an advertisement shall not be inaccurate, or misleading. This information shall also be consistent with the information contained in the prospectus, if already published, or with the information required to be in the prospectus, if the prospectus is published afterwards.

4.   In any case, all information concerning the offer to the public or the admission to trading on a regulated market disclosed in an oral or written form, even if not for advertising purposes, shall be consistent with that contained in the prospectus.

5.   When according to this Directive no prospectus is required, material information provided by an issuer or an offeror and addressed to qualified investors or special categories of investors, including information disclosed in the context of meetings relating to offers of securities, shall be disclosed to all qualified investors or special categories of investors to whom the offer is exclusively addressed. Where a prospectus is required to be published, such information shall be included in the prospectus or in a supplement to the prospectus in accordance with Article 16(1).

6.   The competent authority of the home Member State shall have the power to exercise control over the compliance of advertising activity, relating to a public offer of securities or an admission to trading on a regulated market, with the principles referred to in paragraphs 2 to 5.

[7.   In order to take account of technical developments on financial markets and to specify the requirements laid down in this Article, the Commission shall adopt, by means of delegated acts in accordance with Article 24a and subject to the conditions of Articles 24b and 24c, measures concerning the dissemination of advertisements announcing the intention to offer securities to the public or the admission to trading on a regulated market, in particular before the prospectus has been made available to the public or before the opening of the subscription, and concerning paragraph 4 of this Article.]

NOTES

Para 7: substituted by European Parliament and Council Directive 2010/73/EU, Art 1(15), as from 31 December 2010. Note that Directive 2010/73/EU has a transposition date of 1 July 2012, and that the original paragraph (as amended by European Parliament and Council Directive 2008/11/EC, Art 1(1)) read as follows—

"7.   In order to take account of technical developments on financial markets and to ensure uniform application of this Directive, the Commission shall   . . .   adopt implementing measures concerning the dissemination of advertisements announcing the intention to offer securities to the public or the admission to trading on a regulated market, in particular before the prospectus has been made available to the public or before the opening of the subscription, and concerning paragraph 4. The first set of implementing measures shall be adopted by the Commission by 1 July 2004. [Those measures, designed to amend non-essential elements of this Directive by supplementing it, shall be adopted in accordance with the regulatory procedure with scrutiny referred to in Article 24(2a).]".

[11.300]
[Article 16
Supplements to the prospectus
1. Every significant new factor, material mistake or inaccuracy relating to the information included in the prospectus which is capable of affecting the assessment of the securities and which arises or is noted between the time when the prospectus is approved and the final closing of the offer to the public or, as the case may be, the time when trading on a regulated market begins, whichever occurs later, shall be mentioned in a supplement to the prospectus. Such a supplement shall be approved in the same way in a maximum of seven working days and published in accordance with at least the same arrangements as were applied when the original prospectus was published. The summary, and any translations thereof, shall also be supplemented, if necessary, to take into account the new information included in the supplement.
2. Where the prospectus relates to an offer of securities to the public, investors who have already agreed to purchase or subscribe for the securities before the supplement is published shall have the right, exercisable within two working days after the publication of the supplement, to withdraw their acceptances, provided that the new factor, mistake or inaccuracy referred to in paragraph 1 arose before the final closing of the offer to the public and the delivery of the securities. That period may be extended by the issuer or the offeror. The final date of the right of withdrawal shall be stated in the supplement.
[3. In order to ensure consistent harmonisation, to specify the requirements laid down in this Article and to take account of technical developments on financial markets, ESMA shall develop draft regulatory technical standards to specify situations where a significant new factor, material mistake or inaccuracy relating to the information included in the prospectus requires a supplement to the prospectus to be published. ESMA shall submit those draft regulatory technical standards to the Commission by 1 January 2014.
Power is delegated to the Commission to adopt the regulatory technical standards referred to in the first subparagraph in accordance with the procedure laid down in Articles 10 to 14 of Regulation (EU) No 1095/2010.]]

NOTES
Substituted by European Parliament and Council Directive 2010/73/EU, Art 1(16), as from 31 December 2010. Note that Directive 2010/73/EU has a transposition date of 1 July 2012, and that the original Article read as follows—

"**Article 16**
Supplements to the prospectus
1. Every significant new factor, material mistake or inaccuracy relating to the information included in the prospectus which is capable of affecting the assessment of the securities and which arises or is noted between the time when the prospectus is approved and the final closing of the offer to the public or, as the case may be, the time when trading on a regulated market begins, shall be mentioned in a supplement to the prospectus. Such a supplement shall be approved in the same way in a maximum of seven working days and published in accordance with at least the same arrangements as were applied when the original prospectus was published. The summary, and any translations thereof, shall also be supplemented, if necessary to take into account the new information included in the supplement.
2. Investors who have already agreed to purchase or subscribe for the securities before the supplement is published shall have the right, exercisable within a time limit which shall not be shorter than two working days after the publication of the supplement, to withdraw their acceptances.".

Para 3: added by European Parliament and Council Directive 2010/78/EU, Art 5(7), as from 4 January 2011.

CHAPTER IV
CROSS-BORDER OFFERS AND ADMISSION TO TRADING

[11.301]
Article 17
Community scope of approvals of prospectuses
[1. Without prejudice to Article 23, where an offer to the public or admission to trading on a regulated market is provided for in one or more Member States, or in a Member State other than the home Member State, the prospectus approved by the home Member State and any supplements thereto shall be valid for the public offer or the admission to trading in any number of host Member States, provided that ESMA and the competent authority of each host Member State are notified in accordance with Article 18. Competent authorities of host Member States shall not undertake any approval or administrative procedures relating to prospectuses.]
[2. If significant new factors, material mistakes or inaccuracies come to light after approval of the prospectus, as referred to in Article 16, the competent authority of the home Member State shall require the publication of a supplement to be approved in accordance with Article 13(1). ESMA and the competent authority of the host Member State may inform the competent authority of the home Member State of the need for new information.]

NOTES
Paras 1, 2: substituted by European Parliament and Council Directive 2010/78/EU, Art 5(8)(a), (b), as from 4 January 2011. Note that this provision has a transposition date of 31 December 2011, and that the original text read as follows—

Part 11   EU Legislation

"1.   Without prejudice to Article 23, where an offer to the public or admission to trading on a regulated market is provided for in one or more Member States, or in a Member State other than the home Member State, the prospectus approved by the home Member State and any supplements thereto shall be valid for the public offer or the admission to trading in any number of host Member States, provided that the competent authority of each host Member State is notified in accordance with Article 18. Competent authorities of host Member States shall not undertake any approval or administrative procedures relating to prospectuses.

2.   If there are significant new factors, material mistakes or inaccuracies, as referred to in Article 16, arising since the approval of the prospectus, the competent authority of the home Member State shall require the publication of a supplement to be approved as provided for in Article 13(1). The competent authority of the host Member State may draw the attention of the competent authority of the home Member State to the need for any new information.".

[11.302]
Article 18
Notification

[1.   The competent authority of the home Member State shall, at the request of the issuer or the person responsible for drawing up the prospectus and within three working days following receipt of that request or, where the request is submitted together with the draft prospectus, within one working day after the approval of the prospectus, notify the competent authority of the host Member State with a certificate of approval attesting that the prospectus has been drawn up in accordance with this Directive and with a copy of that prospectus. If applicable, that notification shall be accompanied by a translation of the summary produced under the responsibility of the issuer or person responsible for drawing up the prospectus. The same procedure shall be followed for any supplement to the prospectus. The issuer or the person responsible for drawing up the prospectus shall also be notified of the certificate of approval at the same time as the competent authority of the host Member State.]

2.   The application of the provisions of Article 8(2) and (3) shall be stated in the certificate, as well as its justification.

[3.   The competent authority of the home Member State shall notify ESMA of the certificate of approval of the prospectus at the same time as it is notified to the competent authority of the host Member State.

ESMA and the competent authority of the host Member State shall publish on their websites the list of certificates of approval of prospectuses and any supplements thereto, which are notified in accordance with this Article, including, if applicable, a hyperlink to those documents published on the website of the competent authority of the home Member State, on the website of the issuer, or on the website of the regulated market. The published list shall be kept up-to-date and each item shall remain on the websites for a period of at least 12 months.

4.   In order to ensure uniform conditions of application of this Directive and to take account of technical developments on financial markets, ESMA may develop draft implementing technical standards to establish standard forms, templates and procedures for the notification of the certificate of approval, the copy of the prospectus, the supplement of the prospectus and the translation of the summary.

Power is conferred on the Commission to adopt the implementing technical standards referred to in the first subparagraph in accordance with Article 15 of Regulation (EU) No 1095/2010.]

NOTES

Para 1: substituted by European Parliament and Council Directive 2010/73/EU, Art 1(17), as from 31 December 2010. Note that Directive 2010/73/EU has a transposition date of 1 July 2012, and that the original text read as follows—

"1.   The competent authority of the home Member State shall, at the request of the issuer or the person responsible for drawing up the prospectus and within three working days following that request or, if the request is submitted together with the draft prospectus, within one working day after the approval of the prospectus provide the competent authority of the host Member State with a certificate of approval attesting that the prospectus has been drawn up in accordance with this Directive and with a copy of the said prospectus. If applicable, this notification shall be accompanied by a translation of the summary produced under the responsibility of the issuer or person responsible for drawing up the prospectus. The same procedure shall be followed for any supplement to the prospectus.".

Paras 3, 4: added by European Parliament and Council Directive 2010/78/EU, Art 5(9), as from 4 January 2011. Note that this provision has a transposition date of 31 December 2011 in so far as relating to para 3.

CHAPTER V
USE OF LANGUAGES AND ISSUERS INCORPORATED IN THIRD COUNTRIES

[11.303]
Article 19
Use of languages

1.   Where an offer to the public is made or admission to trading on a regulated market is sought only in the home Member State, the prospectus shall be drawn up in a language accepted by the competent authority of the home Member State.

2.   Where an offer to the public is made or admission to trading on a regulated market is sought in one or more Member States excluding the home Member State, the prospectus shall be drawn up either in a language accepted by the competent authorities of those Member States or in a language

customary in the sphere of international finance, at the choice of the issuer, offeror or person asking for admission, as the case may be. The competent authority of each host Member State may only require that the summary be translated into its official language(s).

For the purpose of the scrutiny by the competent authority of the home Member State, the prospectus shall be drawn up either in a language accepted by this authority or in a language customary in the sphere of international finance, at the choice of the issuer, offeror or person asking for admission to trading, as the case may be.

3.   Where an offer to the public is made or admission to trading on a regulated market is sought in more than one Member State including the home Member State, the prospectus shall be drawn up in a language accepted by the competent authority of the home Member State and shall also be made available either in a language accepted by the competent authorities of each host Member State or in a language customary in the sphere of international finance, at the choice of the issuer, offeror, or person asking for admission to trading, as the case may be. The competent authority of each host Member State may only require that the summary referred to in Article 5(2) be translated into its official language(s).

[4.   Where admission to trading on a regulated market of non-equity securities whose denomination per unit amounts to at least EUR 100,000 is sought in one or more Member States, the prospectus shall be drawn up either in a language accepted by the competent authorities of the home and host Member States or in a language customary in the sphere of international finance, at the choice of the issuer, offeror or person asking for admission to trading, as the case may be. Member States may choose to require in their national legislation that a summary be drawn up in their official language(s).]

NOTES

Para 4: substituted by European Parliament and Council Directive 2010/73/EU, Art 1(18), as from 31 December 2010. Note that Directive 2010/73/EU has a transposition date of 1 July 2012, and that the original text read as follows—

"4.   Where admission to trading on a regulated market of non-equity securities whose denomination per unit amounts to at least EUR 50,000 is sought in one or more Member States, the prospectus shall be drawn up either in a language accepted by the competent authorities of the home and host Member States or in a language customary in the sphere of international finance, at the choice of the issuer, offeror or person asking for admission to trading, as the case may be. Member States may choose to require in their national legislation that a summary be drawn up in their official language(s).".

[11.304]
Article 20
Issuers incorporated in third countries

1.   The competent authority of the home Member State of issuers having their registered office in a third country may approve a prospectus for an offer to the public or for admission to trading on a regulated market, drawn up in accordance with the legislation of a third country, provided that:

(a)   the prospectus has been drawn up in accordance with international standards set by international securities commission organisations, including the IOSCO disclosure standards;

(b)   the information requirements, including information of a financial nature, are equivalent to the requirements under this Directive.

2.   In the case of an offer to the public or admission to trading on a regulated market of securities, issued by an issuer incorporated in a third country, in a Member State other than the home Member State, the requirements set out in Articles 17, 18 and 19 shall apply.

[[3.   The Commission shall adopt, by means of delegated acts in accordance with Article 24a and subject to the conditions of Articles 24b and 24c, measures to establish general equivalence criteria, based on the requirements laid down in Articles 5 and 7.]

On the basis of the above criteria, the Commission may adopt implementing measures in accordance with the regulatory procedure referred to in Article 24(2), stating that a third country ensures the equivalence of prospectuses drawn up in that country with this Directive by reason of its national law or of practices or procedures based on international standards set by international organisations, including the IOSCO disclosure standards.]

NOTES

Para 3: originally substituted by European Parliament and Council Directive 2008/11/EC, Art 1(2) as from 20 March 2008; the first subparagraph was again substituted by European Parliament and Council Directive 2010/73/EU, Art 1(19), as from 31 December 2010; note that Directive 2010/73/EU has a transposition date of 1 July 2012, and that the original text read as follows—

"3.   In order to ensure uniform application of this Directive, the Commission shall adopt implementing measures aimed at establishing general equivalence criteria, based on the requirements laid down in Articles 5 and 7. Those measures, designed to amend non-essential elements of this Directive by supplementing it, shall be adopted in accordance with the regulatory procedure with scrutiny referred to in Article 24(2a).".

Part 11   EU Legislation

CHAPTER VI
COMPETENT AUTHORITIES

[11.305]
Article 21
Powers

1. Each Member State shall designate a central competent administrative authority responsible for carrying out the obligations provided for in this Directive and for ensuring that the provisions adopted pursuant to this Directive are applied.

However, a Member State may, if so required by national law, designate other administrative authorities to apply Chapter III.

These competent authorities shall be completely independent from all market participants.

If an offer of securities is made to the public or admission to trading on a regulated market is sought in a Member State other than the home Member State, only the central competent administrative authority designated by each Member State shall be entitled to approve the prospectus.

[1a. The competent authorities shall cooperate with ESMA for the purposes of this Directive, in accordance with Regulation (EU) No 1095/2010.

1b. The competent authorities shall without delay provide ESMA with all information necessary to carry out its duties, in accordance with Article 35 of Regulation (EU) No 1095/2010.]

2. Member States may allow their competent authority or authorities to delegate tasks. Except for delegation of the publication on the Internet of approved prospectuses and the filing of prospectuses as mentioned in Article 14, any delegation of tasks relating to the obligations provided for in this Directive and in its implementing measures shall be reviewed, in accordance with Article 31 by 31 December 2008, and shall end on 31 December 2011. Any delegation of tasks to entities other than the authorities referred to in paragraph 1 shall be made in a specific manner stating the tasks to be undertaken and the conditions under which they are to be carried out.

These conditions shall include a clause obliging the entity in question to act and be organised in such a manner as to avoid conflict of interest and so that information obtained from carrying out the delegated tasks is not used unfairly or to prevent competition. In any case, the final responsibility for supervising compliance with this Directive and with its implementing measures and for approving the prospectus shall lie with the competent authority or authorities designated in accordance with paragraph 1.

[The Member States shall inform the Commission, ESMA and the competent authorities of other Member States of any arrangements entered into with regard to delegation of tasks, including the precise conditions regulating such delegation.]

3. Each competent authority shall have all the powers necessary for the performance of its functions. A competent authority that has received an application for approving a prospectus shall be empowered at least to:

(a) require issuers, offerors or persons asking for admission to trading on a regulated market to include in the prospectus supplementary information, if necessary for investor protection;

(b) require issuers, offerors or persons asking for admission to trading on a regulated market, and the persons that control them or are controlled by them, to provide information and documents;

(c) require auditors and managers of the issuer, offeror or person asking for admission to trading on a regulated market, as well as financial intermediaries commissioned to carry out the offer to the public or ask for admission to trading, to provide information;

(d) suspend a public offer or admission to trading for a maximum of 10 consecutive working days on any single occasion if it has reasonable grounds for suspecting that the provisions of this Directive have been infringed;

(e) prohibit or suspend advertisements for a maximum of 10 consecutive working days on any single occasion if it has reasonable grounds for believing that the provisions of this Directive have been infringed;

(f) prohibit a public offer if it finds that the provisions of this Directive have been infringed or if it has reasonable grounds for suspecting that they would be infringed;

(g) suspend or ask the relevant regulated markets to suspend trading on a regulated market for a maximum of 10 consecutive working days on any single occasion if it has reasonable grounds for believing that the provisions of this Directive have been infringed;

(h) prohibit trading on a regulated market if it finds that the provisions of this Directive have been infringed;

(i) make public the fact that an issuer is failing to comply with its obligations.

Where necessary under national law, the competent authority may ask the relevant judicial authority to decide on the use of the powers referred to in points (d) to (h) above.

4. Each competent authority shall also, once the securities have been admitted to trading on a regulated market, be empowered to:

(a)   require the issuer to disclose all material information which may have an effect on the assessment of the securities admitted to trading on regulated markets in order to ensure investor protection or the smooth operation of the market;

(b)   suspend or ask the relevant regulated market to suspend the securities from trading if, in its opinion, the issuer's situation is such that trading would be detrimental to investors' interests;

(c)   ensure that issuers whose securities are traded on regulated markets comply with the obligations provided for in Articles 102 and 103 of Directive 2001/34/EC and that equivalent information is provided to investors and equivalent treatment is granted by the issuer to all securities holders who are in the same position, in all Member States where the offer to the public is made or the securities are admitted to trading;

(d)   carry out on-site inspections in its territory in accordance with national law, in order to verify compliance with the provisions of this Directive and [the delegated acts referred to therein]. Where necessary under national law, the competent authority or authorities may use this power by applying to the relevant judicial authority and/or in cooperation with other authorities.

[In accordance with Article 21 of Regulation (EU) No 1095/2010, ESMA shall be entitled to participate in on-site inspections referred to in point (d) where they are carried out jointly by two or more competent authorities.]

5.   Paragraphs 1 to 4 shall be without prejudice to the possibility for a Member State to make separate legal and administrative arrangements for overseas European territories for whose external relations that Member State is responsible.

NOTES

Paras 1a, 1b: inserted by European Parliament and Council Directive 2010/78/EU, Art 5(10)(a), as from 4 January 2011. Note that this provision has a transposition date of 31 December 2011.

Para 2: words in square brackets substituted by European Parliament and Council Directive 2010/78/EU, Art 5(10)(b), as from 4 January 2011. Note that this provision has a transposition date of 31 December 2011, and that the original text read as follows—

"Member States shall inform the Commission and the competent authorities of other Member States of any arrangements entered into with regard to delegation of tasks, including the precise conditions regulating such delegation.".

Para 4: words in first pair of square brackets substituted (for the original words "its implementing measures") by European Parliament and Council Directive 2010/73/EU, Art 1(20), as from 31 December 2010 (note that Directive 2010/73/EU has a transposition date of 1 July 2012); final words in square brackets added by European Parliament and Council Directive 2010/78/EU, Art 5(10)(c), as from 4 January 2011 (note that this provision has a transposition date of 31 December 2011).

[11.306]
Article 22
Professional secrecy and cooperation between authorities

1.   The obligation of professional secrecy shall apply to all persons who work or have worked for the competent authority and for entities to which competent authorities may have delegated certain tasks. Information covered by professional secrecy may not be disclosed to any other person or authority except in accordance with provisions laid down by law.

2.   Competent authorities of Member States shall cooperate with each other whenever necessary for the purpose of carrying out their duties and making use of their powers. Competent authorities shall render assistance to competent authorities of other Member States. In particular, they shall exchange information and cooperate when an issuer has more than one home competent authority because of its various classes of securities, or where the approval of a prospectus has been transferred to the competent authority of another Member State pursuant to Article 13(5). They shall also closely cooperate when requiring suspension or prohibition of trading for securities traded in various Member States in order to ensure a level playing field between trading venues and protection of investors. Where appropriate, the competent authority of the host Member State may request the assistance of the competent authority of the home Member State from the stage at which the case is scrutinised, in particular as regards a new type or rare forms of securities. The competent authority of the home Member State may ask for information from the competent authority of the host Member State on any items specific to the relevant market.

Without prejudice to Article 21, the competent authorities of Member States may consult with operators of regulated markets as necessary and, in particular, when deciding to suspend, or to ask a regulated market to suspend or prohibit trading.

[The competent authorities may refer to ESMA situations where a request for cooperation, in particular to exchange information, has been rejected or has not been acted upon within a reasonable time. Without prejudice to Article 258 of the Treaty on the Functioning of the European Union (TFEU), ESMA may, in the situations referred to in the first sentence, act in accordance with the power conferred on it under Article 19 of Regulation (EU) No 1095/2010.]

[3.   Paragraph 1 shall not prevent the competent authorities from exchanging confidential information or from transmitting confidential information to ESMA or the European Systemic Risk Board (hereinafter the "ESRB"), subject to constraints relating to firm-specific information and effects on third countries as provided for in Regulation (EU) No 1095/2010 and Regulation(EU)

No 1092/2010 of the European Parliament and of the Council of 24 November 2010 on European Union macro-prudential oversight of the financial system and establishing a European Systemic Risk Board[1] respectively. Information exchanged between competent authorities and ESMA or the ESRB shall be covered by the obligation of professional secrecy, to which the persons employed or formerly employed by the competent authorities receiving the information are subject.]

[4.   In order to ensure consistent harmonisation of this Article and to take account of technical developments on financial markets, ESMA shall develop draft regulatory technical standards to specify the information required in paragraph 2.

Power is delegated to the Commission to adopt the regulatory technical standards referred to in the first subparagraph in accordance with Articles 10 to 14 of Regulation (EU) No 1095/2010.

In order to ensure uniform conditions of application of paragraph 2, and to take account of technical developments on financial markets, ESMA may develop draft implementing technical standards to establish standard forms, templates and procedures for the cooperation and exchange of information between competent authorities.

Power is conferred on the Commission to adopt the implementing technical standards referred to in the third subparagraph in accordance with Article 15 of Regulation (EU) No 1095/2010.]

NOTES

Words in square brackets in para 2 added, and para 3 substituted, by European Parliament and Council Directive 2010/78/EU, Art 5(11)(a), (b), as from 4 January 2011. Note that these provisions have a transposition date of 31 December 2011, and that the original para 3 read as follows—

"3.   Paragraph 1 shall not prevent the competent authorities from exchanging confidential information. Information thus exchanged shall be covered by the obligation of professional secrecy, to which the persons employed or formerly employed by the competent authorities receiving the information are subject.".

Para 4: added by European Parliament and Council Directive 2010/78/EU, Art 5(11)(c), as from 4 January 2011.

[1]   OJ L331, 15.12.2010,p 1.

[11.307]
[Article 23
Precautionary measures
1.   Where the competent authority of the host Member State finds that irregularities have been committed by the issuer or by the financial institutions in charge of the public offer or that the issuer has breached its obligations by reason of the fact that securities are admitted to trading on a regulated market, it shall refer those findings to the competent authority of the home Member State and to ESMA.
2.   If, despite the measures taken by the competent authority of the home Member State or because such measures prove inadequate, the issuer or the financial institution in charge of the public offer persists in breaching the relevant legal or regulatory provisions, the competent authority of the host Member State, after informing the competent authority of the home Member State and ESMA, shall take all appropriate measures in order to protect investors and shall inform the Commission and ESMA thereof at the earliest opportunity.]

NOTES

Substituted by European Parliament and Council Directive 2010/78/EU, Art 5(12), as from 4 January 2011. Note that this provision has a transposition date of 31 December 2011, and that the original text read as follows—

"**Article 23**
Precautionary measures
1.   Where the competent authority of the host Member State finds that irregularities have been committed by the issuer or by the financial institutions in charge of the public offer or that breaches have been committed of the obligations attaching to the issuer by reason of the fact that the securities are admitted to trading on a regulated market, it shall refer these findings to the competent authority of the home Member State.
2.   If, despite the measures taken by the competent authority of the home Member State or because such measures prove inadequate, the issuer or the financial institution in charge of the public offer persists in breaching the relevant legal or regulatory provisions, the competent authority of the host Member State, shall take all the appropriate measures in order to protect investors. The Commission shall be informed of such measures at the earliest opportunity.".

CHAPTER VII
IMPLEMENTING MEASURES

[11.308]
Article 24
Committee procedure
1.   The Commission shall be assisted by the European Securities Committee, instituted by Decision 2001/528/EC (hereinafter referred to as 'the Committee').
2.   Where reference is made to this paragraph, Articles 5 and 7 of Decision 1999/468/EC shall apply, having regard to the provisions of Article 8 thereof and provided that the implementing measures adopted in accordance with this procedure do not modify the essential provisions of this Directive.

The period laid down in Article 5(6) of Decision 1999/468/EC shall be set at three months.

[2a. Where reference is made to this paragraph, Article 5a(1) to (4) and Article 7 of Decision 1999/468/EC shall apply, having regard to the provisions of Article 8 thereof.]

[3. By 31 December 2010 and, thereafter, at least every three years, the Commission shall review the provisions concerning its implementing powers and present a report to the European Parliament and to the Council on the functioning of those powers. The report shall examine, in particular, the need for the Commission to propose amendments to this Directive in order to ensure the appropriate scope of the implementing powers conferred on the Commission. The conclusion as to whether or not amendment is necessary shall be accompanied by a detailed statement of reasons. If necessary, the report shall be accompanied by a legislative proposal to amend the provisions conferring implementing powers on the Commission.]

NOTES

    Para 2a inserted, and para 3 substituted (for original paras 3, 4) by European Parliament and Council Directive 2008/11/EC, Art 1(3) as from 20 March 2008.

[11.309]
[Article 24a
Exercise of the delegation

1. The power to adopt delegated acts referred to in Article 1(4), Article 2(4), Article 3(4), the fifth subparagraph of Article 4(1), Article 5(5), Article 7(1), Article 8(4), Article 11(3), Article 13(7), Article 14(8), Article 15(7) and the first subparagraph of Article 20(3) shall be conferred on the Commission for a period of 4 years from 31 December 2010. The Commission shall draw up a report in respect of the delegated power at the latest 6 months before the end of the four-year period. The delegation of power shall be automatically extended for periods of an identical duration, unless the European Parliament or the Council revokes it in accordance with Article 24b.

2. As soon as it adopts a delegated act, the Commission shall notify it simultaneously to the European Parliament and to the Council.

3. The power to adopt delegated acts is conferred on the Commission subject to the conditions laid down in Articles 24b and 24c.]

NOTES

    Inserted, together with Articles 24b, 24c, by European Parliament and Council Directive 2010/73/EU, Art 1(21), as from 31 December 2010. Note that Directive 2010/73/EU has a transposition date of 1 July 2012.

[11.310]
Article 24b
Revocation of the delegation

1. The delegation of power referred to in Article 1(4), Article 2(4), Article 3(4), the fifth subparagraph of Article 4(1), Article 5(5), Article 7(1), Article 8(4), Article 11(3), Article 13(7), Article 14(8), Article 15(7) or the first subparagraph of Article 20(3) may be revoked at any time by the European Parliament or by the Council.

2. The institution which has commenced an internal procedure for deciding whether to revoke a delegation of power shall endeavour to inform the other institution and the Commission within a reasonable time before the final decision is taken, indicating the delegated power which could be subject to revocation.

3. The decision of revocation shall put an end to the delegation of the power specified in that decision. It shall take effect immediately or at a later date specified therein. It shall not affect the validity of the delegated acts already in force. It shall be published in the *Official Journal of the European Union.*

NOTES

    Inserted as noted to Article 24a at **[11.309]**.

[11.311]
[Article 24c
Objections to delegated acts

1. The European Parliament or the Council may object to a delegated act within a period of 3 months from the date of notification.

    At the initiative of the European Parliament or the Council that period shall be extended by 3 months.

2. If, on expiry of the period referred to in paragraph 1, neither the European Parliament nor the Council has objected to the delegated act, it shall be published in the *Official Journal of the European Union* and shall enter into force on the date stated therein.

    The delegated act may be published in the *Official Journal of the European Union* and enter into force before the expiry of that period if the European Parliament and the Council have both informed the Commission of their intention not to raise objections.

3. If either the European Parliament or the Council objects to the delegated act within the period referred to in paragraph 1, it shall not enter into force. In accordance with Article 296 of the Treaty on the Functioning of the European Union, the institution which objects shall state the reasons for objecting to the delegated act.]

NOTES
Inserted as noted to Article 24a at [11.309].

[11.312]
Article 25
Sanctions
1. Without prejudice to the right of Member States to impose criminal sanctions and without prejudice to their civil liability regime, Member States shall ensure, in conformity with their national law, that the appropriate administrative measures can be taken or administrative sanctions be imposed against the persons responsible, where the provisions adopted in the implementation of this Directive have not been complied with. Member States shall ensure that these measures are effective, proportionate and dissuasive.
2. Member States shall provide that the competent authority may disclose to the public every measure or sanction that has been imposed for infringement of the provisions adopted pursuant to this Directive, unless the disclosure would seriously jeopardise the financial markets or cause disproportionate damage to the parties involved.

[11.313]
Article 26
Right of appeal
Member States shall ensure that decisions taken pursuant to laws, regulations and administrative provisions adopted in accordance with this Directive are subject to the right to appeal to the courts.

CHAPTER VIII
TRANSITIONAL AND FINAL PROVISIONS

[11.314]
Article 27
Amendments
With effect from the date set out in Article 29, Directive 2001/34/EC is hereby amended as follows:
1. Articles 3, 20 to 41, 98 to 101, 104 and 108(2)(c)(ii) shall be deleted;
2. in Article 107(3), the first subparagraph shall be deleted;
3. in Article 108(2)(a), the words 'the conditions of establishment, the control and circulation of listing particulars to be published for admission' shall be deleted;
4. Annex I shall be deleted.

[11.315]
Article 28
Repeal
With effect from the date indicated in Article 29, Directive 89/298/EEC shall be repealed. References to the repealed Directive shall be construed as references to this Directive.

[11.316]
Article 29
Transposition
Member States shall bring into force the laws, regulations and administrative provisions necessary to comply with this Directive not later than 1 July 2005. They shall forthwith inform the Commission thereof. When Member States adopt those measures they shall contain a reference to this Directive or shall be accompanied by such a reference on the occasion of their official publication. The methods for making such reference shall be laid down by Member States.

[11.317]
Article 30
Transitional provision
1. Issuers which are incorporated in a third country and whose securities have already been admitted to trading on a regulated market shall choose their competent authority in accordance with Article 2(1)(m)(iii) and notify their decision to the competent authority of their chosen home Member State by 31 December 2005.
2. By way of derogation from Article 3, Member States which have used the exemption in Article 5(a) of Directive 89/298/EEC may continue to allow credit institutions or other financial institutions equivalent to credit institutions which are not covered by Article 1(2)(j) of this Directive to offer debt securities or other transferable securities equivalent to debt securities issued in a continuous or repeated manner within their territory for five years following the date of entry into force of this Directive.

3. By way of derogation from Article 29, the Federal Republic of Germany shall comply with Article 21(1) by 31 December 2008.

[11.318]
Article 31
Review
Five years after the date of entry into force of this Directive, the Commission shall make an assessment of the application of this Directive and present a report to the European Parliament and the Council, accompanied where appropriate by proposals for its review.

[11.319]
Article 32
Entry into force
This Directive shall enter into force on the day of its publication in the *Official Journal of the European Union.*

[11.320]
Article 33
Addressees
This Directive is addressed to the Member States.

ANNEXES

ANNEX I
PROSPECTUS

I.
SUMMARY

[11.321]
The summary shall provide in a few pages the most important information included in the prospectus, covering at least the following items:
  A.   identity of directors, senior management, advisers and auditors
  B.   offer statistics and expected timetable
  C.   [essential information] concerning selected financial data; capitalisation and indebtedness; reasons for the offer and use of proceeds; risk factors
  D.   information concerning the issuer
       —   history and development of the issuer
       —   business overview
  E.   operating and financial review and prospects
       —   research and development, patents and licences, etc
       —   trends
  F.   directors, senior management and employees
  G.   major shareholders and related-party transactions
  H.   financial information
       —   consolidated statement and other financial information
       —   significant changes
  I.   details of the offer and admission to trading
       —   offer and admission to trading
       —   plan for distribution
       —   markets
       —   selling shareholders
       —   dilution (equity securities only)
       —   expenses of the issue
  J.   additional information
       —   share capital
       —   memorandum and articles of association
       —   documents on display

II.
IDENTITY OF DIRECTORS, SENIOR MANAGEMENT, ADVISERS AND AUDITORS

The purpose is to identify the company representatives and other individuals involved in the company's offer or admission to trading; these are the persons responsible for drawing up the prospectus as required by Article 5 of the Directive and those responsible for auditing the financial statements.

III.
OFFER STATISTICS AND EXPECTED TIMETABLE

The purpose is to provide [essential information] regarding the conduct of any offer and the identification of important dates relating to that offer.

A. Offer statistics
B. Method and expected timetable

IV.
[ESSENTIAL INFORMATION]

The purpose is to summarise [essential information] about the company's financial condition, capitalisation and risk factors. If the financial statements included in the document are restated to reflect material changes in the company's group structure or accounting policies, the selected financial data must also be restated.

A. Selected financial data
B. Capitalisation and indebtedness
C. Reasons for the offer and use of proceeds
D. Risk factors

V.
INFORMATION ON THE COMPANY

The purpose is to provide information about the company's business operations, the products it makes or the services it provides, and the factors which affect the business. It is also intended to provide information regarding the adequacy and suitability of the company's properties, plant and equipment, as well as its plans for future capacity increases or decreases.

A. History and development of the company
B. Business overview
C. Organisational structure
D. Property, plant and equipment

VI.
OPERATING AND FINANCIAL REVIEW AND PROSPECTS

The purpose is to provide the management's explanation of factors that have affected the company's financial condition and results of operations for the historical periods covered by the financial statements, and management's assessment of factors and trends which are expected to have a material effect on the company's financial condition and results of operations in future periods.

A. Operating results
B. Liquidity and capital resources
C. Research and development, patents and licences, etc
D. Trends

VII.
DIRECTORS, SENIOR MANAGEMENT AND EMPLOYEES

The purpose is to provide information concerning the company's directors and managers that will allow investors to assess their experience, qualifications and levels of remuneration, as well as their relationship with the company.

A. Directors and senior management
B. Remuneration
C. Board practices
D. Employees
E. Share ownership

VIII.
MAJOR SHAREHOLDERS AND RELATED-PARTY TRANSACTIONS

The purpose is to provide information regarding the major shareholders and others that may control or have an influence on the company. It also provides information regarding transactions the company has entered into with persons affiliated with the company and whether the terms of such transactions are fair to the company.

A. Major shareholders
B. Related-party transactions
C. Interests of experts and advisers

IX.
FINANCIAL INFORMATION

The purpose is to specify which financial statements must be included in the document, as well as the periods to be covered, the age of the financial statements and other information of a financial nature. The accounting and auditing principles that will be accepted for use in preparation and audit of the financial statements will be determined in accordance with international accounting and auditing standards.

    A.   Consolidated statements and other financial information

    B.   Significant changes

X.
DETAILS OF THE OFFER AND ADMISSION TO TRADING DETAILS

The purpose is to provide information regarding the offer and the admission to trading of securities, the plan for distribution of the securities and related matters.

    A.   Offer and admission to trading

    B.   Plan for distribution

    C.   Markets

    D.   Holders of securities who are selling

    E.   Dilution (for equity securities only)

    F.   Expenses of the issue

XI.
ADDITIONAL INFORMATION

The purpose is to provide information, most of which is of a statutory nature, that is not covered elsewhere in the prospectus.

    A.   Share capital

    B.   Memorandum and articles of association

    C.   Material contracts

    D.   Exchange controls

    E.   Taxation

    F.   Dividends and paying agents

    G.   Statement by experts

    H.   Documents on display

    I.   Subsidiary information

NOTES

    Words "essential information" in square brackets substituted (for the original words "key information") by European Parliament and Council Directive 2010/73/EU, Art 1(22), as from 31 December 2010. Note that Directive 2010/73/EU has a transposition date of 1 July 2012.

ANNEX II
REGISTRATION DOCUMENT

I.
IDENTITY OF DIRECTORS, SENIOR MANAGEMENT, ADVISERS AND AUDITORS

[11.322]

The purpose is to identify the company representatives and other individuals involved in the company's offer or admission to trading; these are the persons responsible for drawing up the prospectus and those responsible for auditing the financial statements.

II.
[ESSENTIAL INFORMATION] ABOUT THE ISSUER

The purpose is to summarise [essential information] about the company's financial condition, capitalisation and risk factors. If the financial statements included in the document are restated to reflect material changes in the company's group structure or accounting policies, the selected financial data must also be restated.

    A.   Selected financial data

    B.   Capitalisation and indebtedness

    C.   Risk factors

III.
INFORMATION ON THE COMPANY

The purpose is to provide information about the company's business operations, the products it makes or the services it provides and the factors which affect the business. It is also intended to provide information regarding the adequacy and suitability of the company's properties, plants and equipment, as well as its plans for future capacity increases or decreases.

A. History and development of the company
B. Business overview
C. Organisational structure
D. Property, plants and equipment

IV.
OPERATING AND FINANCIAL REVIEW AND PROSPECTS

The purpose is to provide the management's explanation of factors that have affected the company's financial condition and results of operations for the historical periods covered by the financial statements, and management's assessment of factors and trends which are expected to have a material effect on the company's financial condition and results of operations in future periods.

A. Operating results
B. Liquidity and capital resources
C. Research and development, patents and licences, etc
D. Trends

V.
DIRECTORS, SENIOR MANAGEMENT AND EMPLOYEES

The purpose is to provide information concerning the company's directors and managers that will allow investors to assess their experience, qualifications and levels of remuneration, as well as their relationship with the company.

A. Directors and senior management
B. Remuneration
C. Board practices
D. Employees
E. Share ownership

VI.
MAJOR SHAREHOLDERS AND RELATED-PARTY TRANSACTIONS

The purpose is to provide information regarding the major shareholders and others that may control or have an influence on the company. It also provides information regarding transactions the company has entered into with persons affiliated with the company and whether the terms of such transactions are fair to the company.

A. Major shareholders
B. Related-party transactions
C. Interests of experts and advisers

VII.
FINANCIAL INFORMATION

The purpose is to specify which financial statements must be included in the document, as well as the periods to be covered, the age of the financial statements and other information of a financial nature. The accounting and auditing principles that will be accepted for use in preparation and audit of the financial statements will be determined in accordance with international accounting and auditing standards.

A. Consolidated statements and other financial information
B. Significant changes

VIII.
ADDITIONAL INFORMATION

The purpose is to provide information, most of which is of a statutory nature, that is not covered elsewhere in the prospectus.

A. Share capital
B. Memorandum and articles of association
C. Material contracts
D. Statement by experts
E. Documents on display
F. Subsidiary information

NOTES

Words "essential information" in square brackets substituted (for the original words "key information") by European Parliament and Council Directive 2010/73/EU, Art 1(22), as from 31 December 2010. Note that Directive 2010/73/EU has a transposition date of 1 July 2012.

ANNEX III
SECURITIES NOTE

I.
IDENTITY OF DIRECTORS, SENIOR MANAGEMENT, ADVISERS AND AUDITORS

[11.323]
The purpose is to identify the company representatives and other individuals involved in the company's offer or admission to trading; these are the persons responsible for drawing up the prospectus and those responsible for auditing the financial statements.

II.
OFFER STATISTICS AND EXPECTED TIMETABLE

The purpose is to provide [essential information] regarding the conduct of any offer and the identification of important dates relating to that offer.
A.   Offer statistics
B.   Method and expected timetable

III.
[ESSENTIAL INFORMATION] ABOUT THE ISSUER

The purpose is to summarise [essential information] about the company's financial condition, capitalisation and risk factors. If the financial statements included in the document are restated to reflect material changes in the company's group structure or accounting policies, the selected financial data must also be restated.
A.   Capitalisation and indebtedness
B.   Reasons for the offer and use of proceeds
C.   Risk factors

IV.
INTERESTS OF EXPERTS

The purpose is to provide information regarding transactions the company has entered into with experts or advisers employed on a contingent basis.

V.
DETAILS OF THE OFFER AND ADMISSION TO TRADING

The purpose is to provide information regarding the offer and the admission to trading of securities, the plan for distribution of the securities and related matters.
A.   Offer and admission to trading
B.   Plan for distribution
C.   Markets
D.   Selling securities holders
E.   Dilution (for equity securities only)
F.   Expenses of the issue

VI.
ADDITIONAL INFORMATION

The purpose is to provide information, most of which is of a statutory nature, that is not covered elsewhere in the prospectus.
A.   Exchange controls
B.   Taxation
C.   Dividends and paying agents
D.   Statement by experts
E.   Documents on display

NOTES

Words "essential information" in square brackets substituted (for the original words "key information") by European Parliament and Council Directive 2010/73/EU, Art 1(22), as from 31 December 2010. Note that Directive 2010/73/EU has a transposition date of 1 July 2012.

ANNEX IV
SUMMARY NOTE

[11.324]

The summary note shall provide in a few pages the most important information included in the prospectus, covering at least the following items:

— identity of directors, senior management, advisers and auditors
— offer statistics and expected timetable
— [essential information] concerning selected financial data; capitalisation and indebtedness; reasons for the offer and use of proceeds; risk factors
— information concerning the issuer
    — history and development of the issuer
    — business overview
— operating and financial review and prospects
    — research and development, patents and licences, etc
    — trends
— directors, senior management and employees
— major shareholders and related-party transactions
— financial information
    — consolidated statement and other financial information
    — significant changes
— details on the offer and admission to trading
    — offer and admission to trading
    — plan for distribution
    — markets
    — selling shareholders
    — dilution (for equity securities only)
    — expenses of the issue
— additional information
    — share capital
    — memorandum and articles of incorporation
    — documents available for inspection

NOTES

Words "essential information" in square brackets substituted (for the original words "key information") by European Parliament and Council Directive 2010/73/EU, Art 1(22), as from 31 December 2010. Note that Directive 2010/73/EU has a transposition date of 1 July 2012.

COMMISSION DIRECTIVE

(2003/124/EC)

of 22 December 2003

implementing Directive 2003/6/EC of the European Parliament and of the Council as regards the definition and public disclosure of inside information and the definition of market manipulation

(Text with EEA relevance)

NOTES

Date of publication in OJ: OJ L339, 24.12.2003, p 70. Notes are as in the original OJ version.
As at 1 July 2011, this Directive had not been amended.

[11.325]

THE COMMISSION OF THE EUROPEAN COMMUNITIES,

Having regard to the Treaty establishing the European Community,

Having regard to Directive 2003/6/EC of the European Parliament and of the Council of 28 January 2003 on insider dealing and market manipulation (market abuse),[1] and in particular the second paragraph of Article 1 and the first, second and third indents of Article 6(10) thereof,

After consulting the Committee of European Securities Regulators (CESR)[2] for technical advice,

Whereas:

(1) Reasonable investors base their investment decisions on information already available to them, that is to say, on *ex ante* available information. Therefore, the question whether, in making an investment decision, a reasonable investor would be likely to take into account a particular piece of information should be appraised on the basis of the *ex ante* available information. Such an assessment has to take into consideration the anticipated impact of the information in light of the totality of the related issuer's activity, the reliability of the source of information and any other

market variables likely to affect the related financial instrument or derivative financial instrument related thereto in the given circumstances.

(2)   *Ex post* information may be used to check the presumption that the *ex ante* information was price sensitive, but should not be used to take action against someone who drew reasonable conclusions from *ex ante* information available to him.

(3)   Legal certainty for market participants should be enhanced through a closer definition of two of the elements essential to the definition of inside information, namely the precise nature of that information and the significance of its potential effect on the prices of financial instruments or related derivative financial instruments.

(4)   Not only does the protection of investors require timely public disclosure of inside information by issuers, it also requires such disclosure to be as fast and as synchronised as possible between all categories of investors in all Member States in which the issuer has requested or approved admission of its financial instruments to trading on a regulated market, in order to guarantee at Community level equal access of investors to such information and to prevent insider dealing. To this end Member States may officially appoint mechanisms to be used for such disclosure.

(5)   In order to protect the legitimate interests of issuers, it should be permissible, in closely defined specific circumstances, to delay public disclosure of inside information. However, the protection of investors requires that in such cases the information be kept confidential in order to prevent insider dealing.

(6)   In order to guide both market participants and competent authorities, signals have to be taken into account when examining possibly manipulative behaviours.

(7)   The measures provided for in this Directive are in accordance with the opinion of the European Securities Committee,

NOTES

[1]   OJ L96, 12.4.2003, p 16.

[2]   CESR was established by Commission Decision 2001/527/EC (OJ L191,13.7.2001, p 43).

HAS ADOPTED THIS DIRECTIVE:

[11.326]
Article 1
Inside information
1.   For the purposes of applying point 1 of Article 1 of Directive 2003/6/EC, information shall be deemed to be of a precise nature if it indicates a set of circumstances which exists or may reasonably be expected to come into existence or an event which has occurred or may reasonably be expected to do so and if it is specific enough to enable a conclusion to be drawn as to the possible effect of that set of circumstances or event on the prices of financial instruments or related derivative financial instruments.
2.   For the purposes of applying point 1 of Article 1 of Directive 2003/6/EC, 'information which, if it were made public, would be likely to have a significant effect on the prices of financial instruments or related derivative financial instruments' shall mean information a reasonable investor would be likely to use as part of the basis of his investment decisions.

[11.327]
Article 2
Means and time-limits for public disclosure of inside information
1.   For the purposes of applying Article 6(1) of Directive 2003/6/EC, Articles 102(1) and Article 103 of Directive 2001/34/EC of the European Parliament and of the Council[1] shall apply.

Furthermore, Member States shall ensure that the inside information is made public by the issuer in a manner which enables fast access and complete, correct and timely assessment of the information by the public.

In addition, Member States shall ensure that the issuer does not combine, in a manner likely to be misleading, the provision of inside information to the public with the marketing of its activities.
2.   Member States shall ensure that issuers are deemed to have complied with the first subparagraph of Article 6(1) of Directive 2003/6/EC where, upon the coming into existence of a set of circumstances or the occurrence of an event, albeit not yet formalised, the issuers have promptly informed the public thereof.
3.   Any significant changes concerning already publicly disclosed inside information shall be publicly disclosed promptly after these changes occur, through the same channel as the one used for public disclosure of the original information.
4.   Member States shall require issuers to take reasonable care to ensure that the disclosure of inside information to the public is synchronised as closely as possible between all categories of investors in all Member States in which those issuers have requested or approved the admission to trading of their financial instruments on a regulated market.

NOTES

[1]   OJ L184, 6.7.2001, p 1.

[11.328]
Article 3
Legitimate interests for delaying public disclosure and confidentiality

1. For the purposes of applying Article 6(2) of Directive 2003/6/EC, legitimate interests may, in particular, relate to the following non-exhaustive circumstances:

    (a)   negotiations in course, or related elements, where the outcome or normal pattern of those negotiations would be likely to be affected by public disclosure. In particular, in the event that the financial viability of the issuer is in grave and imminent danger, although not within the scope of the applicable insolvency law, public disclosure of information may be delayed for a limited period where such a public disclosure would seriously jeopardise the interest of existing and potential shareholders by undermining the conclusion of specific negotiations designed to ensure the long-term financial recovery of the issuer;

    (b)   decisions taken or contracts made by the management body of an issuer which need the approval of another body of the issuer in order to become effective, where the organisation of such an issuer requires the separation between these bodies, provided that a public disclosure of the information before such approval together with the simultaneous announcement that this approval is still pending would jeopardise the correct assessment of the information by the public.

2. For the purposes of applying Article 6(2) of Directive 2003/6/EC, Member States shall require that, in order to be able to ensure the confidentiality of inside information, an issuer controls access to such information and, in particular, that:

    (a)   the issuer has established effective arrangements to deny access to such information to persons other than those who require it for the exercise of their functions within the issuer;

    (b)   the issuer has taken the necessary measures to ensure that any person with access to such information acknowledges the legal and regulatory duties entailed and is aware of the sanctions attaching to the misuse or improper circulation of such information;

    (c)   the issuer has in place measures which allow immediate public disclosure in case the issuer was not able to ensure the confidentiality of the relevant inside information, without prejudice to the second subparagraph of Article 6(3) of Directive 2003/6/EC.

[11.329]
Article 4
Manipulative behaviour related to false or misleading signals and to price securing

For the purposes of applying point 2(a) of Article 1 of Directive 2003/6/EC, and without prejudice to the examples set out in the second paragraph of point 2 thereof, Member States shall ensure that the following non-exhaustive signals, which should not necessarily be deemed in themselves to constitute market manipulation, are taken into account when transactions or orders to trade are examined by market participants and competent authorities:

    (a)   the extent to which orders to trade given or transactions undertaken represent a significant proportion of the daily volume of transactions in the relevant financial instrument on the regulated market concerned, in particular when these activities lead to a significant change in the price of the financial instrument;

    (b)   the extent to which orders to trade given or transactions undertaken by persons with a significant buying or selling position in a financial instrument lead to significant changes in the price of the financial instrument or related derivative or underlying asset admitted to trading on a regulated market;

    (c)   whether transactions undertaken lead to no change in beneficial ownership of a financial instrument admitted to trading on a regulated market;

    (d)   the extent to which orders to trade given or transactions undertaken include position reversals in a short period and represent a significant proportion of the daily volume of transactions in the relevant financial instrument on the regulated market concerned, and might be associated with significant changes in the price of a financial instrument admitted to trading on a regulated market;

    (e)   the extent to which orders to trade given or transactions undertaken are concentrated within a short time span in the trading session and lead to a price change which is subsequently reversed;

    (f)   the extent to which orders to trade given change the representation of the best bid or offer prices in a financial instrument admitted to trading on a regulated market, or more generally the representation of the order book available to market participants, and are removed before they are executed;

    (g)   the extent to which orders to trade are given or transactions are undertaken at or around a specific time when reference prices, settlement prices and valuations are calculated and lead to price changes which have an effect on such prices and valuations.

[11.330]
Article 5
Manipulative behaviours related to the employment of fictitious devices or any other form of deception or contrivance
For the purposes of applying point 2(b) of Article 1 of Directive 2003/6/EC, and without prejudice to the examples set out in the second paragraph of point 2 thereof, Member States shall ensure that the following non-exhaustive signals, which should not necessarily be deemed in themselves to constitute market manipulation, are taken into account when transactions or orders to trade are examined by market participants and competent authorities:

(a) whether orders to trade given or transactions undertaken by persons are preceded or followed by dissemination of false or misleading information by the same persons or persons linked to them;

(b) whether orders to trade are given or transactions are undertaken by persons before or after the same persons or persons linked to them produce or disseminate research or investment recommendations which are erroneous or biased or demonstrably influenced by material interest.

[11.331]
Article 6
Transposition
1. Member States shall bring into force the laws, regulations and administrative provisions necessary to comply with this Directive by 12 October 2004 at the latest. They shall forthwith communicate to the Commission the text of the provisions and a correlation table between those provisions and this Directive.

When Member States adopt those provisions, they shall contain a reference to this Directive or be accompanied by such a reference on the occasion of their official publication. Member States shall determine how such reference is to be made.
2. Member States shall communicate to the Commission the text of the main provisions of national law which they adopt in the field covered by this Directive.

[11.332]
Article 7
Entry into force
This Directive shall enter into force on the day of its publication in the *Official Journal of the European Union*.

[11.333]
Article 8
Addressees
This Directive is addressed to the Member States.

COMMISSION DIRECTIVE

(2003/125/EC)

of 22 December 2003

implementing Directive 2003/6/EC of the European Parliament and of the Council as regards the fair presentation of investment recommendations and the disclosure of conflicts of interest

(Text with EEA relevance)

NOTES
Date of publication in OJ: OJ L339, 24.12.2003, p 73. Notes are as in the original OJ version.
As at 1 July 2011, this Directive had not been amended.

[11.334]
THE COMMISSION OF THE EUROPEAN COMMUNITIES,
Having regard to the Treaty establishing the European Community,
Having regard to Directive 2003/6/EC of the European Parliament and of the Council of 28 January 2003 on insider dealing and market manipulation (market abuse),[1] and in particular the sixth indent of Article 6(10) thereof,
After consulting the Committee of European Securities Regulators (CESR)[2] for technical advice, Whereas:

(1) Harmonised standards are necessary for the fair, clear and accurate presentation of information and disclosure of interests and conflicts of interest, to be complied with by persons producing or disseminating information recommending or suggesting an investment strategy, intended for distribution channels or for the public. In particular, market integrity requires high

standards of fairness, probity and transparency when information recommending or suggesting an investment strategy is presented.

(2) Recommending or suggesting an investment strategy is either done explicitly (such as 'buy', 'hold' or 'sell' recommendations) or implicitly (by reference to a price target or otherwise).

(3) Investment advice, through the provision of a personal recommendation to a client in respect of one or more transactions relating to financial instruments (in particular informal short-term investment recommendations originating from inside the sales or trading departments of an investment firm or a credit institution expressed to their clients), which are not likely to become publicly available, should not be considered in themselves as recommendations within the meaning of this Directive.

(4) Investment recommendations that constitute a possible basis for investment decisions should be produced and disseminated in accordance with high standards of care in order to avoid misleading market participants.

(5) The identity of the producer of investment recommendations, his conduct of business rules and the identity of his competent authority should be disclosed, since it may be a valuable piece of information for investors to consider in relation to their investment decisions.

(6) Recommendations should be presented clearly and accurately.

(7) Own interests or conflicts of interest of persons recommending or suggesting investment strategy may influence the opinion that they express in investment recommendations. In order to ensure that the objectivity and reliability of the information can be evaluated, appropriate disclosure should be made of significant financial interests in any financial instrument which is the subject of the information recommending investment strategies, or of any conflicts of interest or control relationship with respect to the issuer to whom the information relates, directly or indirectly. However, this Directive should not require relevant persons producing investment recommendations to breach effective information barriers put in place in order to prevent and avoid conflicts of interest.

(8) Investment recommendations may be disseminated in unaltered, altered or summarised form by a person other than the producer. The way in which disseminators handle such recommendations may have an important impact on the evaluation of those recommendations by investors. In particular, the knowledge of the identity of the disseminator of investment recommendations, his conduct of business rules or the extent of alteration of the original recommendation can be a valuable piece of information for investors when considering their investment decisions.

(9) Posting of investment recommendations on internet sites should be in accordance with the rules on transfer of personal data to third countries as laid down in Directive 95/46/EC of the European Parliament and of the Council of 24 October 1995 on the protection of individuals with regard to the processing of personal data and on the movement of such data.[3]

(10) Credit rating agencies issue opinions on the creditworthiness of a particular issuer or financial instrument as of a given date. As such, these opinions do not constitute a recommendation within the meaning of this Directive. However, credit rating agencies should consider adopting internal policies and procedures designed to ensure that credit ratings published by them are fairly presented and that they appropriately disclose any significant interests or conflicts of interest concerning the financial instruments or the issuers to which their credit ratings relate.

(11) This Directive respects the fundamental rights and observes the principles recognised in particular by the Charter of Fundamental Rights of the European Union and in particular by Article 11 thereof and Article 10 of the European Convention on Human Rights. In this regard, this Directive does not in any way prevent Member States from applying their constitutional rules relating to freedom of the press and freedom of expression in the media.

(12) The measures provided for in this Directive are in accordance with the opinion of the European Securities Committee,

NOTES

[1]   OJ L96, 12.4.2003, p 16.

[2]   CESR was established by Commission Decision 2001/527/EC (OJ L191,13.7.2001, p 43).

[3]   OJ L281, 23.11.1995, p 31.

HAS ADOPTED THIS DIRECTIVE:

CHAPTER I
DEFINITIONS

[11.335]
Article 1
Definitions

For the purposes of this Directive, the following definitions shall apply in addition to those laid down in Directive 2003/6/EC:

1.   'investment firm' means any person as defined in Article 1(2) of Council Directive 93/22/EEC;[1]

2.   'credit institution' means any person as defined in Article 1(1) of Directive 2000/12/EC of the European Parliament and of the Council;[2]

3.   'recommendation' means research or other information recommending or suggesting an investment strategy, explicitly or implicitly, concerning one or several financial instruments or the issuers of financial instruments, including any opinion as to the present or future value or price of such instruments, intended for distribution channels or for the public;

4.   'research or other information recommending or suggesting investment strategy' means:
   (a)   information produced by an independent analyst, an investment firm, a credit institution, any other person whose main business is to produce recommendations or a natural person working for them under a contract of employment or otherwise, that, directly or indirectly, expresses a particular investment recommendation in respect of a financial instrument or an issuer of financial instruments;
   (b)   information produced by persons other than the persons referred to in (a) which directly recommends a particular investment decision in respect of a financial instrument;

5.   'relevant person' means a natural or legal person producing or disseminating recommendations in the exercise of his profession or the conduct of his business;

6.   'issuer' means the issuer of a financial instrument to which a recommendation relates, directly or indirectly;

7.   'distribution channels' shall mean a channel through which information is, or is likely to become, publicly available. 'Likely to become publicly available information' shall mean information to which a large number of persons have access;

8.   'appropriate regulation' shall mean any regulation, including self-regulation, in place in Member States as referred to by Directive 2003/6/EC.

NOTES

¹   OJ L141, 11.6.1993, p 27.
²   OJ L126, 26.5.2000, p 1.

CHAPTER II
PRODUCTION OF RECOMMENDATIONS

[11.336]
Article 2
Identity of producers of recommendations

1.   Member States shall ensure that there is appropriate regulation in place to ensure that any recommendation discloses clearly and prominently the identity of the person responsible for its production, in particular, the name and job title of the individual who prepared the recommendation and the name of the legal person responsible for its production.

2.   Where the relevant person is an investment firm or a credit institution, Member States shall require that the identity of the relevant competent authority be disclosed.

Where the relevant person is neither an investment firm nor a credit institution, but is subject to self-regulatory standards or codes of conduct, Member States shall ensure that a reference to those standards or codes is disclosed.

3.   Member States shall ensure that there is appropriate regulation in place to ensure that the requirements laid down in paragraphs 1 and 2 are adapted in order not to be disproportionate in the case of non-written recommendations. Such adaptation may include a reference to the place where such disclosures can be directly and easily accessed by the public, such as an appropriate internet site of the relevant person.

4.   Paragraphs 1 and 2 shall not apply to journalists subject to equivalent appropriate regulation, including equivalent appropriate self regulation, in the Member States, provided that such regulation achieves similar effects as those of paragraphs 1 and 2.

[11.337]
Article 3
General standard for fair presentation of recommendations

1.   Member States shall ensure that there is appropriate regulation in place to ensure that all relevant persons take reasonable care to ensure that:
   (a)   facts are clearly distinguished from interpretations, estimates, opinions and other types of non-factual information;
   (b)   all sources are reliable or, where there is any doubt as to whether a source is reliable, this is clearly indicated;
   (c)   all projections, forecasts and price targets are clearly labelled as such and that the material assumptions made in producing or using them are indicated.

2.   Member States shall ensure that there is appropriate regulation in place to ensure that the requirements laid down in paragraph 1 are adapted in order not to be disproportionate in the case of non-written recommendations.

3.   Member States shall require that all relevant persons take reasonable care to ensure that any recommendation can be substantiated as reasonable, upon request by the competent authorities.

4. Paragraphs 1 and 3 shall not apply to journalists subject to equivalent appropriate regulation in the Member States, including equivalent appropriate self regulation, provided that such regulation achieves similar effects as those of paragraphs 1 and 3.

[11.338]
Article 4
Additional obligations in relation to fair presentation of recommendations

1. In addition to the obligations laid down in Article 3, where the relevant person is an independent analyst, an investment firm, a credit institution, any related legal person, any other relevant person whose main business is to produce recommendations, or a natural person working for them under a contract of employment or otherwise, Member States shall ensure that there is appropriate regulation in place to ensure that person to take reasonable care to ensure that at least:

(a) all substantially material sources are indicated, as appropriate, including the relevant issuer, together with the fact whether the recommendation has been disclosed to that issuer and amended following this disclosure before its dissemination;

(b) any basis of valuation or methodology used to evaluate a financial instrument or an issuer of a financial instrument, or to set a price target for a financial instrument, is adequately summarised;

(c) the meaning of any recommendation made, such as buy, sell or hold, which may include the time horizon of the investment to which the recommendation relates, is adequately explained and any appropriate risk warning, including a sensitivity analysis of the relevant assumptions, indicated;

(d) reference is made to the planned frequency, if any, of updates of the recommendation and to any major changes in the coverage policy previously announced;

(e) the date at which the recommendation was first released for distribution is indicated clearly and prominently, as well as the relevant date and time for any financial instrument price mentioned;

(f) where a recommendation differs from a recommendation concerning the same financial instrument or issuer, issued during the 12-month period immediately preceding its release, this change and the date of the earlier recommendation are indicated clearly and prominently.

2. Member States shall ensure that, where the requirements laid down in points (a), (b) or (c) of paragraph 1 would be disproportionate in relation to the length of the recommendation distributed, it shall suffice to make clear and prominent reference in the recommendation itself to the place where the required information can be directly and easily accessed by the public, such as a direct Internet link to that information on an appropriate internet site of the relevant person, provided that there has been no change in the methodology or basis of valuation used.

3. Member States shall ensure that there is appropriate regulation in place to ensure that, in the case of non-written recommendations, the requirements of paragraph 1 are adapted so that they are not disproportionate.

[11.339]
Article 5
General standard for disclosure of interests and conflicts of interest

1. Member States shall ensure that there is appropriate regulation in place to ensure that relevant persons disclose all relationships and circumstances that may reasonably be expected to impair the objectivity of the recommendation, in particular where relevant persons have a significant financial interest in one or more of the financial instruments which are the subject of the recommendation, or a significant conflict of interest with respect to an issuer to which the recommendation relates.

Where the relevant person is a legal person, that requirement shall apply also to any legal or natural person working for it, under a contract of employment or otherwise, who was involved in preparing the recommendation.

2. Where the relevant person is a legal person, the information to be disclosed in accordance with paragraph 1 shall at least include the following:

(a) any interests or conflicts of interest of the relevant person or of related legal persons that are accessible or reasonably expected to be accessible to the persons involved in the preparation of the recommendation;

(b) any interests or conflicts of interest of the relevant person or of related legal persons known to persons who, although not involved in the preparation of the recommendation, had or could reasonably be expected to have access to the recommendation prior to its dissemination to customers or the public.

3. Member States shall ensure that there is appropriate regulation in place to ensure that the recommendation itself shall include the disclosures provided for in paragraphs 1 and 2. Where such disclosures would be disproportionate in relation to the length of the recommendation distributed, it shall suffice to make clear and prominent reference in the recommendation itself to the place where such disclosures can be directly and easily accessed by the public, such as a direct Internet link to the disclosure on an appropriate internet site of the relevant person.

4.   Member States shall ensure that there is appropriate regulation in place to ensure that the requirements laid down in paragraph 1 are adapted in order not to be disproportionate in the case of non-written recommendations.

5.   Paragraphs 1 to 3 shall not apply to journalists subject to equivalent appropriate regulation, including equivalent appropriate self regulation, in the Member States, provided that such regulation achieves similar effects as those of paragraphs 1 to 3.

[11.340]
Article 6
Additional obligations in relation to disclosure of interests or conflicts of interest

1.   In addition to the obligations laid down in Article 5, Member States shall require that any recommendation produced by an independent analyst, an investment firm, a credit institution, any related legal person, or any other relevant person whose main business is to produce recommendations, discloses clearly and prominently the following information on their interests and conflicts of interest:

(a)   major shareholdings that exist between the relevant person or any related legal person on the one hand and the issuer on the other hand. These major shareholdings include at least the following instances:

   —   when shareholdings exceeding 5% of the total issued share capital in the issuer are held by the relevant person or any related legal person, or

   —   when shareholdings exceeding 5% of the total issued share capital of the relevant person or any related legal person are held by the issuer.

   Member States may provide for lower thresholds than the 5% threshold as provided for in these two instances;

(b)   other significant financial interests held by the relevant person or any related legal person in relation to the issuer;

(c)   where applicable, a statement that the relevant person or any related legal person is a market maker or liquidity provider in the financial instruments of the issuer;

(d)   where applicable, a statement that the relevant person or any related legal person has been lead manager or co-lead manager over the previous 12 months of any publicly disclosed offer of financial instruments of the issuer;

(e)   where applicable, a statement that the relevant person or any related legal person is party to any other agreement with the issuer relating to the provision of investment banking services, provided that this would not entail the disclosure of any confidential commercial information and that the agreement has been in effect over the previous 12 months or has given rise during the same period to the payment of a compensation or to the promise to get a compensation paid;

(f)   where applicable, a statement that the relevant person or any related legal person is party to an agreement with the issuer relating to the production of the recommendation.

2.   Member States shall require disclosure, in general terms, of the effective organisational and administrative arrangements set up within the investment firm or the credit institution for the prevention and avoidance of conflicts of interest with respect to recommendations, including information barriers.

3.   Member States shall require that for natural or legal persons working for an investment firm or a credit institution, under a contract of employment or otherwise, and who were involved in preparing the recommendation, the requirement under the second subparagraph of paragraph 1 of Article 5 shall include, in particular, disclosure of whether the remuneration of such persons is tied to investment banking transactions performed by the investment firm or credit institution or any related legal person.

Where those natural persons receive or purchase the shares of the issuers prior to a public offering of such shares, the price at which the shares were acquired and the date of acquisition shall also be disclosed.

4.   Member States shall require that investment firms and credit institutions disclose, on a quarterly basis, the proportion of all recommendations that are 'buy', 'hold', 'sell' or equivalent terms, as well as the proportion of issuers corresponding to each of these categories to which the investment firm or the credit institution has supplied material investment banking services over the previous 12 months.

5.   Member States shall ensure that the recommendation itself includes the disclosures required by paragraphs 1 to 4. Where the requirements under paragraphs 1 to 4 would be disproportionate in relation to the length of the recommendation distributed, it shall suffice to make clear and prominent reference in the recommendation itself to the place where such disclosure can be directly and easily accessed by the public, such as a direct Internet link to the disclosure on an appropriate internet site of the investment firm or credit institution.

6.   Member States shall ensure that there is appropriate regulation in place to ensure that, in the case of non-written recommendations, the requirements of paragraph 1 are adapted so that they are not disproportionate.

CHAPTER III
DISSEMINATION OF RECOMMENDATIONS PRODUCED BY THIRD PARTIES

[11.341]
Article 7
Identity of disseminators of recommendations
Member States shall ensure that there is appropriate regulation in place to ensure that, whenever a relevant person under his own responsibility disseminates a recommendation produced by a third party, the recommendation indicates clearly and prominently the identity of that relevant person.

[11.342]
Article 8
General standard for dissemination of recommendations
Member States shall ensure that there is appropriate regulation in place to ensure that whenever a recommendation produced by a third party is substantially altered within disseminated information, that information clearly indicates the substantial alteration in detail. Member States shall ensure that whenever the substantial alteration consists of a change of the direction of the recommendation (such as changing a 'buy' recommendation into a 'hold' or 'sell' recommendation or vice versa), the requirements laid down in Articles 2 to 5 on producers are met by the disseminator, to the extent of the substantial alteration.

In addition, Member States shall ensure that there is appropriate regulation in place to ensure that relevant legal persons who themselves, or through natural persons, disseminate a substantially altered recommendation have a formal written policy so that the persons receiving the information may be directed to where they can have access to the identity of the producer of the recommendation, the recommendation itself and the disclosure of the producer's interests or conflicts of interest, provided that these elements are publicly available.

The first and second paragraphs do not apply to news reporting on recommendations produced by a third party where the substance of the recommendation is not altered.

In case of dissemination of a summary of a recommendation produced by a third party, the relevant persons disseminating such summary shall ensure that the summary is clear and not misleading, mentioning the source document and where the disclosures related to the source document can be directly and easily accessed by the public provided that they are publicly available.

[11.343]
Article 9
Additional obligations for investment firms and credit institutions
In addition to the obligations laid down in Articles 7 and 8, whenever the relevant person is an investment firm, a credit institution or a natural person working for such persons under a contract of employment or otherwise, and disseminates recommendations produced by a third party, Member States shall require that:

(a)   the name of the competent authority of the investment firm or credit institution is clearly and prominently indicated;

(b)   if the producer of the recommendation has not already disseminated it through a distribution channel, the requirements laid down in Article 6 on producers are met by the disseminator;

(c)   if the investment firm or credit institution has substantially altered the recommendation, the requirements laid down in Articles 2 to 6 on producers are met.

CHAPTER IV
FINAL PROVISIONS

[11.344]
Article 10
Transposition
1.   Member States shall bring into force the laws, regulations and administrative provisions necessary to comply with this Directive by 12 October 2004 at the latest. They shall forthwith communicate to the Commission the text of those provisions and a correlation table between these provisions and this Directive.

When Member States adopt those provisions, they shall contain a reference to this Directive or be accompanied by such a reference on the occasion of their official publication. Member States shall determine how such reference is to be made.

2.   Member States shall communicate to the Commission the text of the main provisions of national law which they adopt in the field covered by this Directive.

[11.345]
Article 11
Entry into force
This Directive shall enter into force on the day of its publication in the *Official Journal of the European Union.*

[11.346]
Article 12
Addressees
This Directive is addressed to the Member States.

COMMISSION REGULATION

(2273/2003/EC)

of 22 December 2003

implementing Directive 2003/6/EC of the European Parliament and of the Council as regards exemptions for buy-back programmes and stabilisation of financial instruments

(Text with EEA relevance)

NOTES
  Date of publication in OJ: OJ L336, 23.12.2003, p 33. Notes are as in the original OJ version.
  As at 1 July 2011, this Regulation had not been amended.

[11.347]
THE COMMISSION OF THE EUROPEAN COMMUNITIES,
  Having regard to the Treaty establishing the European Community,
  Having regard to Directive 2003/6/EC of the European Parliament and the Council of 28 January 2003 on insider dealing and market manipulation (market abuse),[1] and in particular Article 8 thereof,
  After consulting the Committee of European Securities Regulators (CESR)[2] for technical advice,
  Whereas:

  (1)   Article 8 of Directive 2003/6/EC provides that the prohibitions provided therein shall not apply to trading in own shares in 'buy back' programmes or to the stabilisation of a financial instrument, provided such trading is carried out in accordance with implementing measures adopted to that effect.

  (2)   Activities of trading in own shares in 'buy-back' programmes and of stabilisation of a financial instrument which would not benefit from the exemption of the prohibitions of Directive 2003/6/EC as provided for by Article 8 thereof, should not in themselves be deemed to constitute market abuse.

  (3)   On the other hand, the exemptions created by this Regulation only cover behaviour directly related to the purpose of the buy-back and stabilisation activities. Behaviour which is not directly related to the purpose of the buy-back and stabilisation activities shall therefore be considered as any other action covered by Directive 2003/6/EC and may be the object of administrative measures or sanctions, if the competent authority establishes that the action in question constitutes market abuse.

  (4)   As regards trading in own shares in 'buy-back' programmes, the rules provided for by this Regulation are without prejudice to the application of Council Directive 77/91/EEC on coordination of safeguards which, for the protection of the interests of members and others, are required by Member States of companies within the meaning of the second paragraph of Article 58 of the Treaty, in respect of the formation of public limited liability companies and the maintenance and alteration of their capital, with a view to making such safeguards equivalent.[3]

  (5)   Allowable 'buy back' activities in order to benefit from the exemption of the prohibitions of Directive 2003/6/EC include issuers needing the possibility to reduce their capital, to meet obligations arising from debt financial instruments exchangeable into equity instruments, and to meet obligations arising from allocations of shares to employees.

  (6)   Transparency is a prerequisite for prevention of market abuse. To this end Member States may officially appoint mechanisms to be used for public disclosure of information required to be publicly disclosed under this Regulation.

  (7)   Issuers having adopted 'buy-back' programmes shall inform their competent authority and, wherever required, the public.

  (8)   Trading in own shares in 'buy-back' programmes may be carried out through derivative financial instruments.

  (9)   In order to prevent market abuse, the daily volume of trading in own shares in 'buy-back' programmes shall be limited. However, some flexibility is necessary in order to respond to given market conditions such as a low level of transactions.

  (10)   Particular attention has to be paid to the selling of own shares during the life of a 'buy-back' programme, to the possible existence of closed periods within issuers during which transactions are

prohibited and to the fact that an issuer may have legitimate reasons to delay public disclosure of inside information.

(11) Stabilisation transactions mainly have the effect of providing support for the price of an offering of relevant securities during a limited time period if they come under selling pressure, thus alleviating sales pressure generated by short term investors and maintaining an orderly market in the relevant securities. This is in the interest of those investors having subscribed or purchased those relevant securities in the context of a significant distribution, and of issuers. In this way, stabilisation can contribute to greater confidence of investors and issuers in the financial markets.

(12) Stabilisation activity may be carried out either on or off a regulated market and may be carried out by use of financial instruments other than those admitted or to be admitted to the regulated market which may influence the price of the instrument admitted or to be admitted to trading on a regulated market.

(13) Relevant securities shall include financial instruments that become fungible after an initial period because they are substantially the same, although they have different initial dividend or interest payment rights.

(14) In relation to stabilisation, block trades shall not be considered as a significant distribution of relevant securities as they are strictly private transactions.

(15) When Member States permit, in the context of an initial public offer, trading prior to the beginning of the official trading on a regulated market, the permission covers 'when issued trading'.

(16) Market integrity requires the adequate public disclosure of stabilisation activity by issuers or by entities undertaking stabilisation, acting or not on behalf of these issuers. Methods used for adequate public disclosure of such information should be efficient and can take into account market practices accepted by competent authorities.

(17) There should be adequate coordination in place between all investment firms and credit institutions undertaking stabilisation. During stabilisation, one investment firm or credit institution shall act as a central point of inquiry for any regulatory intervention by the competent authority in each Member State concerned.

(18) In order to avoid confusion of market participants, stabilisation activity should be carried out by taking into account the market conditions and the offering price of the relevant security and transactions to liquidate positions established as a result of stabilisation activity should be undertaken to minimise market impact having due regard to prevailing market conditions.

(19) Overallotment facilities and 'greenshoe options' are closely related to stabilisation, by providing resources and hedging for stabilisation activity.

(20) Particular attention should be paid to the exercise of an overallotment facility by an investment firm or a credit institution for the purpose of stabilisation when it results in a position uncovered by the 'greenshoe option'.

(21) The measures provided for in this Regulation are in accordance with the opinion of the European Securities Committee,

NOTES

[1]   OJ L96, 12.4.2003, p 16.

[2]   CESR was established by Commission Decision 2001/527/EC (OJ L191,13.7.2001, p 43).

[3]   OJ L26, 31.1.1977, p 1.

HAS ADOPTED THIS REGULATION:

CHAPTER I
DEFINITIONS

[11.348]
Article 1
Subject matter
This Regulation lays down the conditions to be met by buyback programmes and the stabilisation of financial instruments in order to benefit from the exemption provided for in Article 8 of Directive 2003/6/EC.

[11.349]
Article 2
Definitions
For the purposes of this Regulation, the following definitions shall apply in addition to those laid down in Directive 2003/6/EC:

1.   'investment firm' means any legal person as defined in point (2) of Article 1 of Council Directive 93/22/EEC;[1]
2.   'credit institution' means a legal person as defined in Article 1(1) of Directive 2000/12/EC of the European Parliament and the Council;[2]
3.   'buy-back programmes' means trading in own shares in accordance with Articles 19 to 24 of Council Directive 77/91/EEC;

4.   'time-scheduled "buy-back" programme' means a 'buy-back' programme where the dates and quantities of securities to be traded during the time period of the programme are set out at the time of the public disclosure of the 'buy-back' programme;

5.   'adequate public disclosure' means disclosure made in accordance with the procedure laid down in Articles 102(1) and 103 of Directive 2001/34/EC of the European Parliament and of the Council;[3]

6.   'relevant securities' means transferable securities as defined in Directive 93/22/EEC, which are admitted to trading on a regulated market or for which a request for admission to trading on such a market has been made, and which are the subject of a significant distribution;

7.   'stabilisation' means any purchase or offer to purchase relevant securities, or any transaction in associated instruments equivalent thereto, by investment firms or credit institutions, which is undertaken in the context of a significant distribution of such relevant securities exclusively for supporting the market price of these relevant securities for a predetermined period of time, due to a selling pressure in such securities;

8.   'associated instruments' means the following financial instruments (including those which are not admitted to trading on a regulated market, or for which a request for admission to trading on such a market has not been made, provided that the relevant competent authorities have agreed to standards of transparency for transactions in such financial instruments):

     (a)   contracts or rights to subscribe for, acquire or dispose of relevant securities;

     (b)   financial derivatives on relevant securities;

     (c)   where the relevant securities are convertible or exchangeable debt instruments, the securities into which such convertible or exchangeable debt instruments may be converted or exchanged;

     (d)   instruments which are issued or guaranteed by the issuer or guarantor of the relevant securities and whose market price is likely to materially influence the price of the relevant securities, or vice versa;

     (e)   where the relevant securities are securities equivalent to shares, the shares represented by those securities (and any other securities equivalent to those shares).

9.   'significant distribution' means an initial or secondary offer of relevant securities, publicly announced and distinct from ordinary trading both in terms of the amount in value of the securities offered and the selling methods employed;

10.   'offeror' means the prior holders of, or the entity issuing, the relevant securities;

11.   'allotment' means the process or processes by which the number of relevant securities to be received by investors who have previously subscribed or applied for them is determined;

12.   'ancillary stabilisation' means the exercise of an overallotment facility or of a greenshoe option by investment firms or credit institutions, in the context of a significant distribution of relevant securities, exclusively for facilitating stabilisation activity;

13.   'overallotment facility' means a clause in the underwriting agreement or lead management agreement which permits acceptance of subscriptions or offers to purchase a greater number of relevant securities than originally offered;

14.   'greenshoe option' means an option granted by the offeror in favour of the investment firm(s) or credit institution(s) involved in the offer for the purpose of covering overallotments, under the terms of which such firm(s) or institution(s) may purchase up to a certain amount of relevant securities at the offer price for a certain period of time after the offer of the relevant securities.

NOTES

[1]   OJ L141, 11.6.1993, p 27.

[2]   OJ L126, 26.5.2000, p 1.

[3]   OJ L184, 6.7.2001, p 1.

CHAPTER II
'BUY-BACK' PROGRAMMES

[11.350]
Article 3
Objectives of buy-back programmes

In order to benefit from the exemption provided for in Article 8 of Directive 2003/6/EC, a buy-back programme must comply with Articles 4, 5 and 6 of this Regulation and the sole purpose of that buy-back programme must be to reduce the capital of an issuer (in value or in number of shares) or to meet obligations arising from any of the following:

     (a)   debt financial instruments exchangeable into equity instruments;

     (b)   employee share option programmes or other allocations of shares to employees of the issuer or of an associate company.

[11.351]
Article 4
Conditions for 'buy-back' programmes and disclosure
1. The 'buy-back' programme must comply with the conditions laid down by Article 19(1) of Directive 77/91/EEC.
2. Prior to the start of trading, full details of the programme approved in accordance with Article 19(1) of Directive 77/91/EEC must be adequately disclosed to the public in Member States in which an issuer has requested admission of its shares to trading on a regulated market.

Those details must include the objective of the programme as referred to in Article 3, the maximum consideration, the maximum number of shares to be acquired and the duration of the period for which authorisation for the programme has been given.

Subsequent changes to the programme must be subject to adequate public disclosure in Member States.
3. The issuer must have in place the mechanisms ensuring that it fulfils trade reporting obligations to the competent authority of the regulated market on which the shares have been admitted to trading. These mechanisms must record each transaction related to 'buy-back' programmes, including the information specified in Article 20(1) of Directive 93/22/EEC.
4. The issuer must publicly disclose details of all transactions as referred to in paragraph 3 no later than the end of the seventh daily market session following the date of execution of such transactions.

[11.352]
Article 5
Conditions for trading
1. In so far as prices are concerned, the issuer must not, when executing trades under a 'buy-back' programme, purchase shares at a price higher than the higher of the price of the last independent trade and the highest current independent bid on the trading venues where the purchase is carried out.

If the trading venue is not a regulated market, the price of the last independent trade or the highest current independent bid taken in reference shall be the one of the regulated market of the Member State in which the purchase is carried out.

Where the issuer carries out the purchase of own shares through derivative financial instruments, the exercise price of those derivative financial instruments shall not be above the higher of the price of the last independent trade and the highest current independent bid.
2. In so far as volume is concerned, the issuer must not purchase more than 25% of the average daily volume of the shares in any one day on the regulated market on which the purchase is carried out.

The average daily volume figure must be based on the average daily volume traded in the month preceding the month of public disclosure of that programme and fixed on that basis for the authorised period of the programme.

Where the programme makes no reference to that volume, the average daily volume figure must be based on the average daily volume traded in the 20 trading days preceding the date of purchase.
3. For the purposes of paragraph 2, in cases of extreme low liquidity on the relevant market, the issuer may exceed the 25% limit, provided that the following conditions are met:
(a)   the issuer informs the competent authority of the relevant market, in advance, of its intention to deviate from the 25% limit;
(b)   the issuer discloses adequately to the public the fact that it may deviate from the 25% limit;
(c)   the issuer does not exceed 50% of the average daily volume.

[11.353]
Article 6
Restrictions
1. In order to benefit from the exemption provided by Article 8 of Directive 2003/6/EC, the issuer shall not, during its participation in a buy-back programme, engage in the following trading:
(a)   selling of own shares during the life of the programme;
(b)   trading during a period which, under the law of the Member State in which trading takes place, is a closed period;
(c)   trading where the issuer has decided to delay the public disclosure of inside information in accordance with Article 6(2) of Directive 2003/6/EC.
2. Paragraph 1(a) shall not apply if the issuer is an investment firm or credit institution and has established effective information barriers (Chinese Walls) subject to supervision by the competent authority, between those responsible for the handling of inside information related directly or indirectly to the issuer and those responsible for any decision relating to the trading of own shares (including the trading of own shares on behalf of clients), when trading in own shares on the basis of such any decision.

Paragraphs 1(b) and (c) shall not apply if the issuer is an investment firm or credit institution and has established effective information barriers (Chinese Walls) subject to supervision by the competent authority, between those responsible for the handling of inside information related directly or indirectly to the issuer (including trading decisions under the 'buy-back' programme) and those responsible for the trading of own shares on behalf of clients, when trading in own shares on behalf of those clients.

3. Paragraph 1 shall not apply if:
- (a) the issuer has in place a time-scheduled 'buy-back' programme; or
- (b) the 'buy-back' programme is lead-managed by an investment firm or a credit institution which makes its trading decisions in relation to the issuer's shares independently of, and without influence by, the issuer with regard to the timing of the purchases.

CHAPTER III
STABILISATION OF A FINANCIAL INSTRUMENT

[11.354]
Article 7
Conditions for stabilisation
In order to benefit from the exemption provided for in Article 8 of Directive 2003/6/EC, stabilisation of a financial instrument must be carried out in accordance with Articles 8, 9 and 10 of this Regulation.

[11.355]
Article 8
Time-related conditions for stabilisation
1. Stabilisation shall be carried out only for a limited time period.
2. In respect of shares and other securities equivalent to shares, the time period referred to in paragraph 1 shall, in the case of an initial offer publicly announced, start on the date of commencement of trading of the relevant securities on the regulated market and end no later than 30 calendar days thereafter.

Where the initial offer publicly announced takes place in a Member State that permits trading prior to the commencement of trading on a regulated market, the time period referred to in paragraph 1 shall start on the date of adequate public disclosure of the final price of the relevant securities and end no later than 30 calendar days thereafter, provided that any such trading is carried out in compliance with the rules, if any, of the regulated market on which the relevant securities are to be admitted to trading, including any rules concerning public disclosure and trade reporting.
3. In respect of shares and other securities equivalent to shares, the time period referred to in paragraph 1 shall, in the case of a secondary offer, start on the date of adequate public disclosure of the final price of the relevant securities and end no later than 30 calendar days after the date of allotment.
4. In respect of bonds and other forms of securitised debt (which are not convertible or exchangeable into shares or into other securities equivalent to shares), the time period referred to in paragraph 1 shall start on the date of adequate public disclosure of the terms of the offer of the relevant securities(ie including the spread to the benchmark, if any, once it has been fixed) and end, whatever is earlier, either no later than 30 calendar days after the date on which the issuer of the instruments received the proceeds of the issue, or no later than 60 calendar days after the date of allotment of the relevant securities.
5. In respect of securitised debt convertible or exchangeable into shares or into other securities equivalent to shares, the time period referred to in paragraph 1 shall start on the date of adequate public disclosure of the final terms of the offer of the relevant securities and end, whatever is earlier, either no later than 30 calendar days after the date on which the issuer of the instruments received the proceeds of the issue, or no later than 60 calendar days after the date of allotment of the relevant securities.

[11.356]
Article 9
Disclosure and reporting conditions for stabilisation
1. The following information shall be adequately publicly disclosed by issuers, offerors, or entities undertaking the stabilisation acting, or not, on behalf of such persons, before the opening of the offer period of the relevant securities:
- (a) the fact that stabilisation may be undertaken, that there is no assurance that it will be undertaken and that it may be stopped at any time;
- (b) the fact that stabilisation transactions are aimed to support the market price of the relevant securities;
- (c) the beginning and end of the period during which stabilisation may occur;
- (d) the identity of the stabilisation manager, unless this is not known at the time of publication in which case it must be publicly disclosed before any stabilisation activity begins;
- (e) the existence and maximum size of any overallotment facility or greenshoe option, the exercise period of the greenshoe option and any conditions for the use of the overallotment facility or exercise of the greenshoe option.

The application of the provisions of this paragraph shall be suspended for offers under the scope of application of the measures implementing Directive 2004/ . . . /EC (prospectus Directive), from the date of application of these measures.

2. Without prejudice to Article 12(1)(c) of Directive 2003/6/EC, the details of all stabilisation transactions must be notified by issuers, offerors, or entities undertaking the stabilisation acting, or not, on behalf of such persons, to the competent authority of the relevant market no later than the end of the seventh daily market session following the date of execution of such transactions.

3. Within one week of the end of the stabilisation period, the following information must be adequately disclosed to the public by issuers, offerors, or entities undertaking the stabilisation acting, or not, on behalf of such persons:

(a) whether or not stabilisation was undertaken;
(b) the date at which stabilisation started;
(c) the date at which stabilisation last occurred;
(d) the price range within which stabilisation was carried out, for each of the dates during which stabilisation transactions were carried out.

4. Issuers, offerors, or entities undertaking the stabilisation, acting or not, on behalf of such persons, must record each stabilisation order or transaction with, as a minimum, the information specified in Article 20(1) of Directive 93/22/EEC extended to financial instruments other than those admitted or going to be admitted to the regulated market.

5. Where several investment firms or credit institutions undertake the stabilisation acting, or not, on behalf of the issuer or offeror, one of those persons shall act as central point of inquiry for any request from the competent authority of the regulated market on which the relevant securities have been admitted to trading.

[11.357]
Article 10
Specific price conditions
1. In the case of an offer of shares or other securities equivalent to shares, stabilisation of the relevant securities shall not in any circumstances be executed above the offering price.
2. In the case of an offer of securitised debt convertible or exchangeable into instruments as referred to in paragraph 1, stabilisation of those instruments shall not in any circumstances be executed above the market price of those instruments at the time of the public disclosure of the final terms of the new offer.

[11.358]
Article 11
Conditions for ancillary stabilisation
In order to benefit from the exemption provided for in Article 8 of Directive 2003/6/EC, ancillary stabilisation must be undertaken in accordance with Article 9 of this Regulation and with the following:

(a) relevant securities may be overallotted only during the subscription period and at the offer price;
(b) a position resulting from the exercise of an overallotment facility by an investment firm or credit institution which is not covered by the greenshoe option may not exceed 5% of the original offer;
(c) the greenshoe option may be exercised by the beneficiaries of such an option only where relevant securities have been overallotted;
(d) the greenshoe option may not amount to more than 15% of the original offer;
(e) the exercise period of the greenshoe option must be the same as the stabilisation period required under Article 8;
(f) the exercise of the greenshoe option must be disclosed to the public promptly, together with all appropriate details, including in particular the date of exercise and the number and nature of relevant securities involved.

CHAPTER IV
FINAL PROVISION

[11.359]
Article 12
Entry into force
This Regulation shall enter into force in Member States on the day of its publication in the *Official Journal of the European Union.*

This Regulation shall be binding in its entirety and directly applicable in all Member States.

DIRECTIVE OF THE EUROPEAN PARLIAMENT AND OF THE COUNCIL

(2004/25/EC)

of 21 April 2004

on takeover bids

(Text with EEA relevance)

NOTES

Date of publication in OJ: OJ L142, 30.4.2004, p 12. Notes are as in the original OJ version.
This Directive is reproduced as amended by: European Parliament and Council Regulation 219/2009/EC.

[11.360]

THE EUROPEAN PARLIAMENT AND THE COUNCIL OF THE EUROPEAN UNION,

Having regard to the Treaty establishing the European Community, and in particular Article 44(1) thereof,

Having regard to the proposal from the Commission,[1]

Having regard to the opinion of the European Economic and Social Committee,[2]

Acting in accordance with the procedure laid down in Article 251 of the Treaty,[3]

Whereas:

(1)   In accordance with Article 44(2)(g) of the Treaty, it is necessary to coordinate certain safeguards which, for the protection of the interests of members and others, Member States require of companies governed by the law of a Member State the securities of which are admitted to trading on a regulated market in a Member State, with a view to making such safeguards equivalent throughout the Community.

(2)   It is necessary to protect the interests of holders of the securities of companies governed by the law of a Member State when those companies are the subject of takeover bids or of changes of control and at least some of their securities are admitted to trading on a regulated market in a Member State.

(3)   It is necessary to create Community-wide clarity and transparency in respect of legal issues to be settled in the event of takeover bids and to prevent patterns of corporate restructuring within the Community from being distorted by arbitrary differences in governance and management cultures.

(4)   In view of the public-interest purposes served by the central banks of the Member States, it seems inconceivable that they should be the targets of takeover bids. Since, for historical reasons, the securities of some of those central banks are listed on regulated markets in Member States, it is necessary to exclude them explicitly from the scope of this Directive.

(5)   Each Member State should designate an authority or authorities to supervise those aspects of bids that are governed by this Directive and to ensure that parties to takeover bids comply with the rules made pursuant to this Directive. All those authorities should cooperate with one another.

(6)   In order to be effective, takeover regulation should be flexible and capable of dealing with new circumstances as they arise and should accordingly provide for the possibility of exceptions and derogations. However, in applying any rules or exceptions laid down or in granting any derogations, supervisory authorities should respect certain general principles.

(7)   Self-regulatory bodies should be able to exercise supervision.

(8)   In accordance with general principles of Community law, and in particular the right to a fair hearing, decisions of a supervisory authority should in appropriate circumstances be susceptible to review by an independent court or tribunal. However, Member States should be left to determine whether rights are to be made available which may be asserted in administrative or judicial proceedings, either in proceedings against a supervisory authority or in proceedings between parties to a bid.

(9)   Member States should take the necessary steps to protect the holders of securities, in particular those with minority holdings, when control of their companies has been acquired. The Member States should ensure such protection by obliging the person who has acquired control of a company to make an offer to all the holders of that company's securities for all of their holdings at an equitable price in accordance with a common definition. Member States should be free to establish further instruments for the protection of the interests of the holders of securities, such as the obligation to make a partial bid where the offeror does not acquire control of the company or the obligation to announce a bid at the same time as control of the company is acquired.

(10)   The obligation to make a bid to all the holders of securities should not apply to those controlling holdings already in existence on the date on which the national legislation transposing this Directive enters into force.

(11)   The obligation to launch a bid should not apply in the case of the acquisition of securities which do not carry the right to vote at ordinary general meetings of shareholders. Member States should, however, be able to provide that the obligation to make a bid to all the holders of securities relates not only to securities carrying voting rights but also to securities which carry voting rights only in specific circumstances or which do not carry voting rights.

(12) To reduce the scope for insider dealing, an offeror should be required to announce his/her decision to launch a bid as soon as possible and to inform the supervisory authority of the bid.

(13) The holders of securities should be properly informed of the terms of a bid by means of an offer document. Appropriate information should also be given to the representatives of the company's employees or, failing that, to the employees directly.

(14) The time allowed for the acceptance of a bid should be regulated.

(15) To be able to perform their functions satisfactorily, supervisory authorities should at all times be able to require the parties to a bid to provide information concerning themselves and should cooperate and supply information in an efficient and effective manner, without delay, to other authorities supervising capital markets.

(16) In order to prevent operations which could frustrate a bid, the powers of the board of an offeree company to engage in operations of an exceptional nature should be limited, without unduly hindering the offeree company in carrying on its normal business activities.

(17) The board of an offeree company should be required to make public a document setting out its opinion of the bid and the reasons on which that opinion is based, including its views on the effects of implementation on all the company's interests, and specifically on employment.

(18) In order to reinforce the effectiveness of existing provisions concerning the freedom to deal in the securities of companies covered by this Directive and the freedom to exercise voting rights, it is essential that the defensive structures and mechanisms envisaged by such companies be transparent and that they be regularly presented in reports to general meetings of shareholders.

(19) Member States should take the necessary measures to afford any offeror the possibility of acquiring majority interests in other companies and of fully exercising control of them. To that end, restrictions on the transfer of securities, restrictions on voting rights, extraordinary appointment rights and multiple voting rights should be removed or suspended during the time allowed for the acceptance of a bid and when the general meeting of shareholders decides on defensive measures, on amendments to the articles of association or on the removal or appointment of board members at the first general meeting of shareholders following closure of the bid. Where the holders of securities have suffered losses as a result of the removal of rights, equitable compensation should be provided for in accordance with the technical arrangements laid down by Member States.

(20) All special rights held by Member States in companies should be viewed in the framework of the free movement of capital and the relevant provisions of the Treaty. Special rights held by Member States in companies which are provided for in private or public national law should be exempted from the 'breakthrough' rule if they are compatible with the Treaty.

(21) Taking into account existing differences in Member States' company law mechanisms and structures, Member States should be allowed not to require companies established within their territories to apply the provisions of this Directive limiting the powers of the board of an offeree company during the time allowed for the acceptance of a bid and those rendering ineffective barriers, provided for in the articles of association or in specific agreements. In that event Member States should at least allow companies established within their territories to make the choice, which must be reversible, to apply those provisions. Without prejudice to international agreements to which the European Community is a party, Member States should be allowed not to require companies which apply those provisions in accordance with the optional arrangements to apply them when they become the subject of offers launched by companies which do not apply the same provisions, as a consequence of the use of those optional arrangements.

(22) Member States should lay down rules to cover the possibility of a bid's lapsing, the offeror's right to revise his/her bid, the possibility of competing bids for a company's securities, the disclosure of the result of a bid, the irrevocability of a bid and the conditions permitted.

(23) The disclosure of information to and the consultation of representatives of the employees of the offeror and the offeree company should be governed by the relevant national provisions, in particular those adopted pursuant to Council Directive 94/45/EC of 22 September 1994 on the establishment of a European Works Council or a procedure in Community-scale undertakings and Community-scale groups of undertakings for the purposes of informing and consulting employees,[4] Council Directive 98/59/EC of 20 July 1998 on the approximation of the laws of the Member States relating to collective redundancies,[5] Council Directive 2001/86/EC of 8 October 2001 supplementing the statute for a European Company with regard to the involvement of employees[6] and Directive 2002/14/EC of the European Parliament and of the Council of 11 March 2002 establishing a general framework for informing and consulting employees in the European Community — Joint declaration of the European Parliament, the Council and the Commission on employee representation.[7] The employees of the companies concerned, or their representatives, should nevertheless be given an opportunity to state their views on the foreseeable effects of the bid on employment. Without prejudice to the rules of Directive 2003/6/EC of the European Parliament and of the Council of 28 January 2003 on insider dealing and market manipulation (market abuse),[8] Member States may always apply or introduce national provisions concerning the disclosure of information to and the consultation of representatives of the employees of the offeror before an offer is launched.

(24) Member States should take the necessary measures to enable an offeror who, following a takeover bid, has acquired a certain percentage of a company's capital carrying voting rights to require the holders of the remaining securities to sell him/her their securities. Likewise, where, following a takeover bid, an offeror has acquired a certain percentage of a company's capital carrying voting rights, the holders of the remaining securities should be able to require him/her to buy their securities. These squeeze-out and sell-out procedures should apply only under specific conditions linked to takeover bids. Member States may continue to apply national rules to squeeze-out and sell-out procedures in other circumstances.

(25) Since the objectives of the action envisaged, namely to establish minimum guidelines for the conduct of takeover bids and ensure an adequate level of protection for holders of securities throughout the Community, cannot be sufficiently achieved by the Member States because of the need for transparency and legal certainty in the case of cross-border takeovers and acquisitions of control, and can therefore, by reason of the scale and effects of the action, be better achieved at Community level, the Community may adopt measures, in accordance with the principle of subsidiarity as set out in Article 5 of the Treaty. In accordance with the principle of proportionality as set out in that Article, this Directive does not go beyond what is necessary to achieve those objectives.

(26) The adoption of a Directive is the appropriate procedure for the establishment of a framework consisting of certain common principles and a limited number of general requirements which Member States are to implement through more detailed rules in accordance with their national systems and their cultural contexts.

(27) Member States should, however, provide for sanctions for any infringement of the national measures transposing this Directive.

(28) Technical guidance and implementing measures for the rules laid down in this Directive may from time to time be necessary, to take account of new developments on financial markets. For certain provisions, the Commission should accordingly be empowered to adopt implementing measures, provided that these do not modify the essential elements of this Directive and the Commission acts in accordance with the principles set out in this Directive, after consulting the European Securities Commission established by Commission Directive 2001/528/EC.[9] The measures necessary for the implementation of this Directive should be adopted in accordance with the Council Decision 1999/468/EC of 28 June 1999 laying down the procedures for the exercise of implementing powers conferred on the Commission[10] and with due regard to the declaration made by the Commission in the European Parliament on 5 February 2002 concerning the implementation of financial services legislation. For the other provisions, it is important to entrust a contact committee with the task of assisting Member States and the supervisory authorities in the implementation of this Directive and of advising the Commission, if necessary, on additions or amendments to this Directive. In so doing, the contact committee may make use of the information which Member States are to provide on the basis of this Directive concerning takeover bids that have taken place on their regulated markets.

(29) The Commission should facilitate movement towards the fair and balanced harmonisation of rules on takeovers in the European Union. To that end, the Commission should be able to submit proposals for the timely revision of this Directive,

NOTES

[1]   OJ C45E, 25.2.2003, p 1.

[2]   OJ C208, 3.9.2003, p 55.

[3]   Opinion of the European Parliament of 16 December 2003 (not yet published in the Official Journal) and Council decision of 30 March 2004.

[4]   OJ L254, 30.9.1994, p 64. Directive as amended by Directive 97/74/EC (OJ L10, 16.1.1998, p 22).

[5]   OJ L225, 12.8.1998, p 16.

[6]   OJ L294, 10.11.2001, p 22.

[7]   OJ L80, 23.3.2002, p 29.

[8]   OJ L96, 12.4.2003, p 16.

[9]   OJ L191, 13.7.2001, p 45. Decision as amended by Decision 2004/8/EC (OJ L3, 7.1.2004, p 33).

[10]   OJ L184, 17.7.1999, p 23.

HAVE ADOPTED THIS DIRECTIVE:

[11.361]
Article 1
Scope
1.   This Directive lays down measures coordinating the laws, regulations, administrative provisions, codes of practice and other arrangements of the Member States, including arrangements established by organisations officially authorised to regulate the markets (hereinafter referred to as 'rules'), relating to takeover bids for the securities of companies governed by the laws of Member States, where all or some of those securities are admitted to trading on a regulated market within the meaning of Directive 93/22/EEC[1] in one or more Member States (hereinafter referred to as a 'regulated market').
2.   This Directive shall not apply to takeover bids for securities issued by companies, the object of which is the collective investment of capital provided by the public, which operate on the principle of risk-spreading and the units of which are, at the holders' request, repurchased or redeemed, directly or indirectly, out of the assets of those companies. Action taken by such companies to ensure that the stock exchange value of their units does not vary significantly from their net asset value shall be regarded as equivalent to such repurchase or redemption.
3.   This Directive shall not apply to takeover bids for securities issued by the Member States' central banks.

NOTES

[1] Council Directive 93/22/EEC of 10 May 1993 on investment services in the securities field (OJ L141, 11.6.1993, p 27). Directive as last amended by Directive 2002/87/EC of the European Parliament and of the Council (OJ L35, 11.2.2003, p 1).

[11.362]
Article 2
Definitions

1. For the purposes of this Directive:
    (a) 'takeover bid' or 'bid' shall mean a public offer (other than by the offeree company itself) made to the holders of the securities of a company to acquire all or some of those securities, whether mandatory or voluntary, which follows or has as its objective the acquisition of control of the offeree company in accordance with national law;
    (b) 'offeree company' shall mean a company, the securities of which are the subject of a bid;
    (c) 'offeror' shall mean any natural or legal person governed by public or private law making a bid;
    (d) 'persons acting in concert' shall mean natural or legal persons who cooperate with the offeror or the offeree company on the basis of an agreement, either express or tacit, either oral or written, aimed either at acquiring control of the offeree company or at frustrating the successful outcome of a bid;
    (e) 'securities' shall mean transferable securities carrying voting rights in a company;
    (f) 'parties to the bid' shall mean the offeror, the members of the offeror's board if the offeror is a company, the offeree company, holders of securities of the offeree company and the members of the board of the offeree company, and persons acting in concert with such parties;
    (g) 'multiple vote securities' shall mean securities included in a distinct and separate class and carrying more than one vote each.
2. For the purposes of paragraph 1(d), persons controlled by another person within the meaning of Article 87 of Directive 2001/34/EC[1] shall be deemed to be persons acting in concert with that other person and with each other.

NOTES

[1] Directive 2001/34/EC of the European Parliament and of the Council of 28 May 2001 on the admission of securities to official stock exchange listing and on information to be published on those securities (OJ L184, 6.7.2001, p 1). Directive as last amended by Directive 2003/71/EC (OJ L345, 31.12.2003, p 64).

[11.363]
Article 3
General Principles

1. For the purpose of implementing this Directive, Member States shall ensure that the following principles are complied with:
    (a) all holders of the securities of an offeree company of the same class must be afforded equivalent treatment; moreover, if a person acquires control of a company, the other holders of securities must be protected;
    (b) the holders of the securities of an offeree company must have sufficient time and information to enable them to reach a properly informed decision on the bid; where it advises the holders of securities, the board of the offeree company must give its views on the effects of implementation of the bid on employment, conditions of employment and the locations of the company's places of business;
    (c) the board of an offeree company must act in the interests of the company as a whole and must not deny the holders of securities the opportunity to decide on the merits of the bid;
    (d) false markets must not be created in the securities of the offeree company, of the offeror company or of any other company concerned by the bid in such a way that the rise or fall of the prices of the securities becomes artificial and the normal functioning of the markets is distorted;
    (e) an offeror must announce a bid only after ensuring that he/she can fulfil in full any cash consideration, if such is offered, and after taking all reasonable measures to secure the implementation of any other type of consideration;
    (f) an offeree company must not be hindered in the conduct of its affairs for longer than is reasonable by a bid for its securities.
2. With a view to ensuring compliance with the principles laid down in paragraph 1, Member States:
    (a) shall ensure that the minimum requirements set out in this Directive are observed;
    (b) may lay down additional conditions and provisions more stringent than those of this Directive for the regulation of bids.

[11.364]
Article 4
Supervisory authority and applicable law
1. Member States shall designate the authority or authorities competent to supervise bids for the purposes of the rules which they make or introduce pursuant to this Directive. The authorities thus designated shall be either public authorities, associations or private bodies recognised by national law or by public authorities expressly empowered for that purpose by national law. Member States shall inform the Commission of those designations, specifying any divisions of functions that may be made. They shall ensure that those authorities exercise their functions impartially and independently of all parties to a bid.
2.

(a) The authority competent to supervise a bid shall be that of the Member State in which the offeree company has its registered office if that company's securities are admitted to trading on a regulated market in that Member State.

(b) If the offeree company's securities are not admitted to trading on a regulated market in the Member State in which the company has its registered office, the authority competent to supervise the bid shall be that of the Member State on the regulated market of which the company's securities are admitted to trading.

  If the offeree company's securities are admitted to trading on regulated markets in more than one Member State, the authority competent to supervise the bid shall be that of the Member State on the regulated market of which the securities were first admitted to trading.

(c) If the offeree company's securities were first admitted to trading on regulated markets in more than one Member State simultaneously, the offeree company shall determine which of the supervisory authorities of those Member States shall be the authority competent to supervise the bid by notifying those regulated markets and their supervisory authorities on the first day of trading.

  If the offeree company's securities have already been admitted to trading on regulated markets in more than one Member State on the date laid down in Article 21(1) and were admitted simultaneously, the supervisory authorities of those Member States shall agree which one of them shall be the authority competent to supervise the bid within four weeks of the date laid down in Article 21(1). Otherwise, the offeree company shall determine which of those authorities shall be the competent authority on the first day of trading following that four-week period.

(d) Member States shall ensure that the decisions referred to in (c) are made public.

(e) In the cases referred to in (b) and (c), matters relating to the consideration offered in the case of a bid, in particular the price, and matters relating to the bid procedure, in particular the information on the offeror's decision to make a bid, the contents of the offer document and the disclosure of the bid, shall be dealt with in accordance with the rules of the Member State of the competent authority. In matters relating to the information to be provided to the employees of the offeree company and in matters relating to company law, in particular the percentage of voting rights which confers control and any derogation from the obligation to launch a bid, as well as the conditions under which the board of the offeree company may undertake any action which might result in the frustration of the bid, the applicable rules and the competent authority shall be those of the Member State in which the offeree company has its registered office.

3. Member States shall ensure that all persons employed or formerly employed by their supervisory authorities are bound by professional secrecy. No information covered by professional secrecy may be divulged to any person or authority except under provisions laid down by law.
4. The supervisory authorities of the Member States for the purposes of this Directive and other authorities supervising capital markets, in particular in accordance with Directive 93/22/EEC, Directive 2001/34/EC, Directive 2003/6/EC and Directive 2003/71/EC of the European Parliament and of the Council of 4 November 2003 on the prospectus to be published when securities are offered to the public or admitted to trading shall cooperate and supply each other with information wherever necessary for the application of the rules drawn up in accordance with this Directive and in particular in cases covered by paragraph 2(b), (c) and (e). Information thus exchanged shall be covered by the obligation of professional secrecy to which persons employed or formerly employed by the supervisory authorities receiving the information are subject. Cooperation shall include the ability to serve the legal documents necessary to enforce measures taken by the competent authorities in connection with bids, as well as such other assistance as may reasonably be requested by the supervisory authorities concerned for the purpose of investigating any actual or alleged breaches of the rules made or introduced pursuant to this Directive.
5. The supervisory authorities shall be vested with all the powers necessary for the purpose of carrying out their duties, including that of ensuring that the parties to a bid comply with the rules made or introduced pursuant to this Directive.

Provided that the general principles laid down in Article 3(1) are respected, Member States may provide in the rules that they make or introduce pursuant to this Directive for derogations from those rules:

Part 11 EU Legislation

(i)   by including such derogations in their national rules, in order to take account of circumstances determined at national level
and/or

(ii) by granting their supervisory authorities, where they are competent, powers to waive such national rules, to take account of the circumstances referred to in (i) or in other specific circumstances, in which case a reasoned decision must be required.

6.   This Directive shall not affect the power of the Member States to designate judicial or other authorities responsible for dealing with disputes and for deciding on irregularities committed in the course of bids or the power of Member States to regulate whether and under which circumstances parties to a bid are entitled to bring administrative or judicial proceedings. In particular, this Directive shall not affect the power which courts may have in a Member State to decline to hear legal proceedings and to decide whether or not such proceedings affect the outcome of a bid. This Directive shall not affect the power of the Member States to determine the legal position concerning the liability of supervisory authorities or concerning litigation between the parties to a bid.

[11.365]
Article 5
Protection of minority shareholders, the mandatory bid and the equitable price
1.   Where a natural or legal person, as a result of his/her own acquisition or the acquisition by persons acting in concert with him/her, holds securities of a company as referred to in Article 1(1) which, added to any existing holdings of those securities of his/hers and the holdings of those securities of persons acting in concert with him/her, directly or indirectly give him/her a specified percentage of voting rights in that company, giving him/her control of that company, Member States shall ensure that such a person is required to make a bid as a means of protecting the minority shareholders of that company. Such a bid shall be addressed at the earliest opportunity to all the holders of those securities for all their holdings at the equitable price as defined in paragraph 4.
2.   Where control has been acquired following a voluntary bid made in accordance with this Directive to all the holders of securities for all their holdings, the obligation laid down in paragraph 1 to launch a bid shall no longer apply.
3.   The percentage of voting rights which confers control for the purposes of paragraph 1 and the method of its calculation shall be determined by the rules of the Member State in which the company has its registered office.
4.   The highest price paid for the same securities by the offeror, or by persons acting in concert with him/her, over a period, to be or determined by Member States, of not less than six months and not more than 12 before the bid referred to in paragraph 1 shall be regarded as the equitable price. If, after the bid has been made public and before the offer closes for acceptance, the offeror or any person acting in concert with him/her purchases securities at a price higher than the offer price, the offeror shall increase his/her offer so that it is not less than the highest price paid for the securities so acquired.

Provided that the general principles laid down in Article 3(1) are respected, Member States may authorise their supervisory authorities to adjust the price referred to in the first subparagraph in circumstances and in accordance with criteria that are clearly determined. To that end, they may draw up a list of circumstances in which the highest price may be adjusted either upwards or downwards, for example where the highest price was set by agreement between the purchaser and a seller, where the market prices of the securities in question have been manipulated, where market prices in general or certain market prices in particular have been affected by exceptional occurrences, or in order to enable a firm in difficulty to be rescued. They may also determine the criteria to be applied in such cases, for example the average market value over a particular period, the break-up value of the company or other objective valuation criteria generally used in financial analysis.

Any decision by a supervisory authority to adjust the equitable price shall be substantiated and made public.
5.   By way of consideration the offeror may offer securities, cash or a combination of both.

However, where the consideration offered by the offeror does not consist of liquid securities admitted to trading on a regulated market, it shall include a cash alternative.

In any event, the offeror shall offer a cash consideration at least as an alternative where he/she or persons acting in concert with him/her, over a period beginning at the same time as the period determined by the Member State in accordance with paragraph 4 and ending when the offer closes for acceptance, has purchased for cash securities carrying 5% or more of the voting rights in the offeree company.

Member States may provide that a cash consideration must be offered, at least as an alternative, in all cases.
6.   In addition to the protection provided for in paragraph 1, Member States may provide for further instruments intended to protect the interests of the holders of securities in so far as those instruments do not hinder the normal course of a bid.

[11.366]
Article 6
Information concerning bids

1.   Member States shall ensure that a decision to make a bid is made public without delay and that the supervisory authority is informed of the bid. They may require that the supervisory authority must be informed before such a decision is made public. As soon as the bid has been made public, the boards of the offeree company and of the offeror shall inform the representatives of their respective employees or, where there are no such representatives, the employees themselves.

2.   Member States shall ensure that an offeror is required to draw up and make public in good time an offer document containing the information necessary to enable the holders of the offeree company's securities to reach a properly informed decision on the bid. Before the offer document is made public, the offeror shall communicate it to the supervisory authority. When it is made public, the boards of the offeree company and of the offeror shall communicate it to the representatives of their respective employees or, where there are no such representatives, to the employees themselves.

Where the offer document referred to in the first subparagraph is subject to the prior approval of the supervisory authority and has been approved, it shall be recognised, subject to any translation required, in any other Member State on the market of which the offeree company's securities are admitted to trading, without its being necessary to obtain the approval of the supervisory authorities of that Member State. Those authorities may require the inclusion of additional information in the offer document only if such information is specific to the market of a Member State or Member States on which the offeree company's securities are admitted to trading and relates to the formalities to be complied with to accept the bid and to receive the consideration due at the close of the bid as well as to the tax arrangements to which the consideration offered to the holders of the securities will be subject.

3.   The offer document referred to in paragraph 2 shall state at least:

   (a)   the terms of the bid;
   (b)   the identity of the offeror and, where the offeror is a company, the type, name and registered office of that company;
   (c)   the securities or, where appropriate, the class or classes of securities for which the bid is made;
   (d)   the consideration offered for each security or class of securities and, in the case of a mandatory bid, the method employed in determining it, with particulars of the way in which that consideration is to be paid;
   (e)   the compensation offered for the rights which might be removed as a result of the breakthrough rule laid down in Article 11(4), with particulars of the way in which that compensation is to be paid and the method employed in determining it;
   (f)   the maximum and minimum percentages or quantities of securities which the offeror undertakes to acquire;
   (g)   details of any existing holdings of the offeror, and of persons acting in concert with him/her, in the offeree company;
   (h)   all the conditions to which the bid is subject;
   (i)   the offeror's intentions with regard to the future business of the offeree company and, in so far as it is affected by the bid, the offeror company and with regard to the safeguarding of the jobs of their employees and management, including any material change in the conditions of employment, and in particular the offeror's strategic plans for the two companies and the likely repercussions on employment and the locations of the companies' places of business;
   (j)   the time allowed for acceptance of the bid;
   (k)   where the consideration offered by the offeror includes securities of any kind, information concerning those securities;
   (l)   information concerning the financing for the bid;
   (m)   the identity of persons acting in concert with the offeror or with the offeree company and, in the case of companies, their types, names, registered offices and relationships with the offeror and, where possible, with the offeree company;
   (n)   the national law which will govern contracts concluded between the offeror and the holders of the offeree company's securities as a result of the bid and the competent courts.

[4.   The Commission may adopt rules modifying the list in paragraph 3. Those measures, designed to amend non-essential elements of this Directive, shall be adopted in accordance with the regulatory procedure with scrutiny referred to in Article 18(2).]

5.   Member States shall ensure that the parties to a bid are required to provide the supervisory authorities of their Member State at any time on request with all the information in their possession concerning the bid that is necessary for the supervisory authority to discharge its functions.

NOTES

Para 4: substituted by European Parliament and Council Regulation 219/2009/EC, Annex, para 5(1), as from 20 April 2009.

[11.367]
Article 7
Time allowed for acceptance
1. Member States shall provide that the time allowed for the acceptance of a bid may not be less than two weeks nor more than 10 weeks from the date of publication of the offer document. Provided that the general principle laid down in Article 3(1)(f) is respected, Member States may provide that the period of 10 weeks may be extended on condition that the offeror gives at least two weeks' notice of his/her intention of closing the bid.
2. Member States may provide for rules changing the period referred to in paragraph 1 in specific cases. A Member State may authorise a supervisory authority to grant a derogation from the period referred to in paragraph 1 in order to allow the offeree company to call a general meeting of shareholders to consider the bid.

[11.368]
Article 8
Disclosure
1. Member States shall ensure that a bid is made public in such a way as to ensure market transparency and integrity for the securities of the offeree company, of the offeror or of any other company affected by the bid, in particular in order to prevent the publication or dissemination of false or misleading information.
2. Member States shall provide for the disclosure of all information and documents required by Article 6 in such a manner as to ensure that they are both readily and promptly available to the holders of securities at least in those Member States on the regulated markets of which the offeree company's securities are admitted to trading and to the representatives of the employees of the offeree company and the offeror or, where there are no such representatives, to the employees themselves.

[11.369]
Article 9
Obligations of the board of the offeree company
1. Member States shall ensure that the rules laid down in paragraphs 2 to 5 are complied with.
2. During the period referred to in the second subparagraph, the board of the offeree company shall obtain the prior authorisation of the general meeting of shareholders given for this purpose before taking any action, other than seeking alternative bids, which may result in the frustration of the bid and in particular before issuing any shares which may result in a lasting impediment to the offeror's acquiring control of the offeree company.
Such authorisation shall be mandatory at least from the time the board of the offeree company receives the information referred to in the first sentence of Article 6(1) concerning the bid and until the result of the bid is made public or the bid lapses. Member States may require that such authorisation be obtained at an earlier stage, for example as soon as the board of the offeree company becomes aware that the bid is imminent.
3. As regards decisions taken before the beginning of the period referred to in the second subparagraph of paragraph 2 and not yet partly or fully implemented, the general meeting of shareholders shall approve or confirm any decision which does not form part of the normal course of the company's business and the implementation of which may result in the frustration of the bid.
4. For the purpose of obtaining the prior authorisation, approval or confirmation of the holders of securities referred to in paragraphs 2 and 3, Member States may adopt rules allowing a general meeting of shareholders to be called at short notice, provided that the meeting does not take place within two weeks of notification's being given.
5. The board of the offeree company shall draw up and make public a document setting out its opinion of the bid and the reasons on which it is based, including its views on the effects of implementation of the bid on all the company's interests and specifically employment, and on the offeror's strategic plans for the offeree company and their likely repercussions on employment and the locations of the company's places of business as set out in the offer document in accordance with Article 6(3)(i). The board of the offeree company shall at the same time communicate that opinion to the representatives of its employees or, where there are no such representatives, to the employees themselves. Where the board of the offeree company receives in good time a separate opinion from the representatives of its employees on the effects of the bid on employment, that opinion shall be appended to the document.
6. For the purposes of paragraph 2, where a company has a two-tier board structure 'board' shall mean both the management board and the supervisory board.

[11.370]
Article 10
Information on companies as referred to in Article 1(1)
1. Member States shall ensure that companies as referred to in Article 1(1) publish detailed information on the following:

(a)   the structure of their capital, including securities which are not admitted to trading on a regulated market in a Member State, where appropriate with an indication of the different classes of shares and, for each class of shares, the rights and obligations attaching to it and the percentage of total share capital that it represents;

(b)   any restrictions on the transfer of securities, such as limitations on the holding of securities or the need to obtain the approval of the company or other holders of securities, without prejudice to Article 46 of Directive 2001/34/EC;

(c)   significant direct and indirect shareholdings (including indirect shareholdings through pyramid structures and cross-shareholdings) within the meaning of Article 85 of Directive 2001/34/EC;

(d)   the holders of any securities with special control rights and a description of those rights;

(e)   the system of control of any employee share scheme where the control rights are not exercised directly by the employees;

(f)   any restrictions on voting rights, such as limitations of the voting rights of holders of a given percentage or number of votes, deadlines for exercising voting rights, or systems whereby, with the company's cooperation, the financial rights attaching to securities are separated from the holding of securities;

(g)   any agreements between shareholders which are known to the company and may result in restrictions on the transfer of securities and/or voting rights within the meaning of Directive 2001/34/EC;

(h)   the rules governing the appointment and replacement of board members and the amendment of the articles of association;

(i)   the powers of board members, and in particular the power to issue or buy back shares;

(j)   any significant agreements to which the company is a party and which take effect, alter or terminate upon a change of control of the company following a takeover bid, and the effects thereof, except where their nature is such that their disclosure would be seriously prejudicial to the company; this exception shall not apply where the company is specifically obliged to disclose such information on the basis of other legal requirements;

(k)   any agreements between the company and its board members or employees providing for compensation if they resign or are made redundant without valid reason or if their employment ceases because of a takeover bid.

2.   The information referred to in paragraph 1 shall be published in the company's annual report as provided for in Article 46 of Directive 78/660/EEC[1] and Article 36 of Directive 83/349/EEC.[2]

3.   Member States shall ensure, in the case of companies the securities of which are admitted to trading on a regulated market in a Member State, that the board presents an explanatory report to the annual general meeting of shareholders on the matters referred to in paragraph 1.

NOTES

[1]   Fourth Council Directive 78/660/EEC of 25 July 1978 on the annual accounts of certain types of companies (OJ L222, 14.8.1978, p 11). Directive as last amended by Directive 2003/51/EC of the European Parliament and of the Council (OJ L178, 17.7.2003, p 16).

[2]   Seventh Council Directive 83/349/EEC of 13 June 1983 on consolidated accounts (OJ L193, 18.7.1983, p 1). Directive as last amended by Directive 2003/51/EC.

[11.371]
Article 11
Breakthrough

1.   Without prejudice to other rights and obligations provided for in Community law for the companies referred to in Article 1(1), Member States shall ensure that the provisions laid down in paragraphs 2 to 7 apply when a bid has been made public.

2.   Any restrictions on the transfer of securities provided for in the articles of association of the offeree company shall not apply vis-à-vis the offeror during the time allowed for acceptance of the bid laid down in Article 7(1).

Any restrictions on the transfer of securities provided for in contractual agreements between the offeree company and holders of its securities, or in contractual agreements between holders of the offeree company's securities entered into after the adoption of this Directive, shall not apply vis-à-vis the offeror during the time allowed for acceptance of the bid laid down in Article 7(1).

3.   Restrictions on voting rights provided for in the articles of association of the offeree company shall not have effect at the general meeting of shareholders which decides on any defensive measures in accordance with Article 9.

Restrictions on voting rights provided for in contractual agreements between the offeree company and holders of its securities, or in contractual agreements between holders of the offeree company's securities entered into after the adoption of this Directive, shall not have effect at the general meeting of shareholders which decides on any defensive measures in accordance with Article 9.

Multiple-vote securities shall carry only one vote each at the general meeting of shareholders which decides on any defensive measures in accordance with Article 9.

Part 11   EU Legislation

4.   Where, following a bid, the offeror holds 75% or more of the capital carrying voting rights, no restrictions on the transfer of securities or on voting rights referred to in paragraphs 2 and 3 nor any extraordinary rights of shareholders concerning the appointment or removal of board members provided for in the articles of association of the offeree company shall apply; multiple-vote securities shall carry only one vote each at the first general meeting of shareholders following closure of the bid, called by the offeror in order to amend the articles of association or to remove or appoint board members.

To that end, the offeror shall have the right to convene a general meeting of shareholders at short notice, provided that the meeting does not take place within two weeks of notification.

5.   Where rights are removed on the basis of paragraphs 2, 3, or 4 and/or Article 12, equitable compensation shall be provided for any loss suffered by the holders of those rights. The terms for determining such compensation and the arrangements for its payment shall be set by Member States.

6.   Paragraphs 3 and 4 shall not apply to securities where the restrictions on voting rights are compensated for by specific pecuniary advantages.

7.   This Article shall not apply either where Member States hold securities in the offeree company which confer special rights on the Member States which are compatible with the Treaty, or to special rights provided for in national law which are compatible with the Treaty or to cooperatives.

[11.372]
Article 12
Optional arrangements

1.   Member States may reserve the right not to require companies as referred to in Article 1(1) which have their registered offices within their territories to apply Article 9(2) and (3) and/or Article 11.

2.   Where Member States make use of the option provided for in paragraph 1, they shall nevertheless grant companies which have their registered offices within their territories the option, which shall be reversible, of applying Article 9(2) and (3) and/or Article 11, without prejudice to Article 11(7).

The decision of the company shall be taken by the general meeting of shareholders, in accordance with the law of the Member State in which the company has its registered office in accordance with the rules applicable to amendment of the articles of association. The decision shall be communicated to the supervisory authority of the Member State in which the company has its registered office and to all the supervisory authorities of Member States in which its securities are admitted to trading on regulated markets or where such admission has been requested.

3.   Member States may, under the conditions determined by national law, exempt companies which apply Article 9(2) and (3) and/or Article 11 from applying Article 9(2) and (3) and/or Article 11 if they become the subject of an offer launched by a company which does not apply the same Articles as they do, or by a company controlled, directly or indirectly, by the latter, pursuant to Article 1 of Directive 83/349/EEC.

4.   Member States shall ensure that the provisions applicable to the respective companies are disclosed without delay.

5.   Any measure applied in accordance with paragraph 3 shall be subject to the authorisation of the general meeting of shareholders of the offeree company, which must be granted no earlier than 18 months before the bid was made public in accordance with Article 6(1).

[11.373]
Article 13
Other rules applicable to the conduct of bids

Member States shall also lay down rules which govern the conduct of bids, at least as regards the following:

   (a)   the lapsing of bids;
   (b)   the revision of bids;
   (c)   competing bids;
   (d)   the disclosure of the results of bids;
   (e)   the irrevocability of bids and the conditions permitted.

[11.374]
Article 14
Information for and consultation of employees' representatives

This Directive shall be without prejudice to the rules relating to information and to consultation of representatives of and, if Member States so provide, co-determination with the employees of the offeror and the offeree company governed by the relevant national provisions, and in particular those adopted pursuant to Directives 94/45/EC, 98/59/EC, 2001/86/EC and 2002/14/EC.

[11.375]
Article 15
The right of squeeze-out
1. Member States shall ensure that, following a bid made to all the holders of the offeree company's securities for all of their securities, paragraphs 2 to 5 apply.
2. Member States shall ensure that an offeror is able to require all the holders of the remaining securities to sell him/her those securities at a fair price. Member States shall introduce that right in one of the following situations:

    (a)   where the offeror holds securities representing not less than 90% of the capital carrying voting rights and 90% of the voting rights in the offeree company,
           or
    (b)   where, following acceptance of the bid, he/she has acquired or has firmly contracted to acquire securities representing not less than 90% of the offeree company's capital carrying voting rights and 90% of the voting rights comprised in the bid.

In the case referred to in (a), Member States may set a higher threshold that may not, however, be higher than 95% of the capital carrying voting rights and 95% of the voting rights.
3. Member States shall ensure that rules are in force that make it possible to calculate when the threshold is reached.

Where the offeree company has issued more than one class of securities, Member States may provide that the right of squeeze- out can be exercised only in the class in which the threshold laid down in paragraph 2 has been reached.
4. If the offeror wishes to exercise the right of squeeze-out he/she shall do so within three months of the end of the time allowed for acceptance of the bid referred to in Article 7.
5. Member States shall ensure that a fair price is guaranteed. That price shall take the same form as the consideration offered in the bid or shall be in cash. Member States may provide that cash shall be offered at least as an alternative.

Following a voluntary bid, in both of the cases referred to in paragraph 2(a) and (b), the consideration offered in the bid shall be presumed to be fair where, through acceptance of the bid, the offeror has acquired securities representing not less than 90% of the capital carrying voting rights comprised in the bid.

Following a mandatory bid, the consideration offered in the bid shall be presumed to be fair.

[11.376]
Article 16
The right of sell-out
1. Member States shall ensure that, following a bid made to all the holders of the offeree company's securities for all of their securities, paragraphs 2 and 3 apply.
2. Member States shall ensure that a holder of remaining securities is able to require the offeror to buy his/her securities from him/her at a fair price under the same circumstances as provided for in Article 15(2).
3. Article 15(3) to (5) shall apply *mutatis mutandis.*

[11.377]
Article 17
Sanctions
Member States shall determine the sanctions to be imposed for infringement of the national measures adopted pursuant to this Directive and shall take all necessary steps to ensure that they are put into effect. The sanctions thus provided for shall be effective, proportionate and dissuasive. Member States shall notify the Commission of those measures no later than the date laid down in Article 21(1) and of any subsequent change thereto at the earliest opportunity.

[11.378]
Article 18
Committee procedure
1. The Commission shall be assisted by the European Securities Committee established by Decision 2001/528/EC (hereinafter referred to as 'the Committee').
[2. Where reference is made to this paragraph, Article 5a(1) to (4) and Article 7 of Decision 1999/468/EC shall apply, having regard to the provisions of Article 8 thereof.]
3. . . .

NOTES
    Para 2 substituted, and para 3 repealed, by European Parliament and Council Regulation 219/2009/EC, Annex, para 5(2), (3), as from 20 April 2009.

[11.379]
Article 19
Contact committee
1. A contact committee shall be set up which has as its functions:

Part 11   EU Legislation

(a) to facilitate, without prejudice to Articles 226 and 227 of the Treaty, the harmonised application of this Directive through regular meetings dealing with practical problems arising in connection with its application;

(b) to advise the Commission, if necessary, on additions or amendments to this Directive.

2.   It shall not be the function of the contact committee to appraise the merits of decisions taken by the supervisory authorities in individual cases.

[11.380]
Article 20
Revision

Five years after the date laid down in Article 21(1), the Commission shall examine this Directive in the light of the experience acquired in applying it and, if necessary, propose its revision. That examination shall include a survey of the control structures and barriers to takeover bids that are not covered by this Directive.

To that end, Member States shall provide the Commission annually with information on the takeover bids which have been launched against companies the securities of which are admitted to trading on their regulated markets. That information shall include the nationalities of the companies involved, the results of the offers and any other information relevant to the understanding of how takeover bids operate in practice.

[11.381]
Article 21
Transposition

1.   Member States shall bring into force the laws, regulations and administrative provisions necessary to comply with this Directive no later than 20 May 2006. They shall forthwith inform the Commission thereof.

When Member States adopt those provisions, they shall contain a reference to this Directive or shall be accompanied by such reference on the occasion of their official publication. The methods of making such reference shall be laid down by the Member States.

2.   Member States shall communicate to the Commission the text of the main provisions of national law that they adopt in the fields covered by this Directive.

[11.382]
Article 22
Entry into force

This Directive shall enter into force on the 20th day after that of its publication in the *Official Journal of the European Union*.

[11.383]
Article 23
Addressees

This Directive is addressed to Member States.

COMMISSION DIRECTIVE

(2004/72/EC)

of 29 April 2004

implementing Directive 2003/6/EC of the European Parliament and of the Council as regards accepted market practices, the definition of inside information in relation to derivatives on commodities, the drawing up of lists of insiders, the notification of managers' transactions and the notification of suspicious transactions

(Text with EEA relevance)

NOTES

Date of publication in OJ: OJ L162, 30.4.2004, p 70. Notes are as in the original OJ version.
As at 1 July 2011, this Directive had not been amended.

[11.384]

THE COMMISSION OF THE EUROPEAN COMMUNITIES,

Having regard to the Treaty establishing the European Community,

Having regard to Directive 2003/6/EC of the European Parliament and of the Council of 28 January 2003 on insider dealing and market manipulation (market abuse)[1], and in particular the second paragraph of point 1 and point 2(a) of Article 1 and the fourth, fifth and seventh indents of Article 6(10) thereof,

After consulting the Committee of European Securities Regulators (CESR)[2] for technical advice,

Whereas:

(1)   Practising fairness and efficiency by market participants is required in order not to create prejudice to normal market activity and market integrity. In particular, market practices inhibiting the interaction of supply and demand by limiting the opportunities for other market participants to respond to transactions can create higher risks for market integrity and are, therefore, less likely to be accepted by competent authorities. On the other hand, market practices which enhance liquidity are more likely to be accepted than those practices reducing them. Market practices breaching rules and regulations designed to prevent market abuse, or codes of conduct, are less likely to be accepted by competent authorities. Since market practices change rapidly in order to meet investors' needs, competent authorities need to be alert to new and emerging market practice.

(2)   Transparency of market practices by market participants is crucial for considering whether a particular market practice can be accepted by competent authorities. The less transparent a practice is, the more likely it is not to be accepted. However, practices on non regulated markets might for structural reasons be less transparent than similar practices on regulated markets. Such practices should not be in themselves considered as unacceptable by competent authorities.

(3)   Particular market practices in a given market should not put at risk market integrity of other, directly or indirectly, related markets throughout the Community, whether those markets be regulated or not. Therefore, the higher the risk for market integrity on such a related market within the Community, the less those practices are likely to be accepted by competent authorities.

(4)   Competent authorities, while considering the acceptance of a particular market practice, should consult other competent authorities, particularly for cases where there exist comparable markets to the one under scrutiny. However, there might be circumstances in which a market practice can be deemed to be acceptable on one particular market and unacceptable on another comparable market within the Community. In case of discrepancies between market practices which are accepted in one Member State and not in another one, discussion could take place in the Committee of European Securities Regulators in order to find a solution. With regard to their decisions about such acceptance, competent authorities should ensure a high degree of consultation and transparency vis-à-vis market participants and end-users.

(5)   It is essential for market participants on derivative markets the underlying of which is not a financial instrument, to get greater legal certainty on what constitutes inside information.

(6)   The establishment, by issuers or persons acting on their behalf or for their account, of lists of persons working for them under a contract of employment or otherwise and having access to inside information relating, directly or indirectly, to the issuer, is a valuable measure for protecting market integrity. These lists may serve issuers or such persons to control the flow of such inside information and thereby manage their confidentiality duties. Moreover, these lists may also constitute a useful tool for competent authorities when monitoring the application of market abuse legislation. Identifying inside information to which any insider has access and the date on which it gained access thereto is necessary for issuers and competent authorities. Access to inside information relating, directly or indirectly, to the issuer by persons included on such a list is without prejudice to their duty to refrain from insider dealing on the basis of any inside information as defined in Directive 2003/6/EC.

(7)   The notification of transactions conducted by persons discharging managerial responsibilities within an issuer on their own account, or by persons closely associated with them, is not only a valuable information for market participants, but also constitutes an additional means for competent authorities to supervise markets. The obligation by senior executives to notify transactions is without prejudice to their duty to refrain from insider dealing on the basis of any inside information as defined in Directive 2003/6/EC.

(8)   Notification of transactions should be in accordance with the rules on transfer of personal data laid down in Directive 95/46/EC[3] of the European Parliament and of the Council of 24 October 1995 on the protection of individuals with regard to the processing of personal data and on the movement of such data.

(9)   Notification of suspicious transactions by persons professionally arranging transactions in financial instruments to the competent authority requires sufficient indications that the transactions might constitute market abuse, ie transactions which give reasonable ground for suspecting that insider dealing or market manipulation is involved. Certain transactions by themselves may seem completely void of anything suspicious, but might deliver such indications of possible market abuse, when seen in perspective with other transactions, certain behaviour or other information.

(10)   This Directive respects the fundamental rights and observes the principles recognised in particular by the Charta of Fundamental Rights of the European Union and in particular by Article 8 of the European Convention on Human Rights.

(11)   The measures provided for in this Directive are in accordance with the opinion of the European Securities Committee,

NOTES

[1]   OJ L96, 12.4.2003, p 16.

[2]   CESR was established by Commission Decision 2001/527/EC of 6 June 2001 (OJ L191, 13.7.2001, p 43).

[3]   OJ L281, 23.11.1995, p 31.

HAVE ADOPTED THIS DIRECTIVE—

[11.385]
Article 1
Definitions
For the purpose of applying Article 6(10) of Directive 2003/6/EC:

1. 'Person discharging managerial responsibilities within an issuer' shall mean a person who is
    (a) a member of the administrative, management or supervisory bodies of the issuer;
    (b) a senior executive, who is not a member of the bodies as referred to in point (a), having regular access to inside information relating, directly or indirectly, to the issuer, and the power to make managerial decisions affecting the future developments and business prospects of this issuer.

2. 'Person closely associated with a person discharging managerial responsibilities within an issuer of financial instruments' shall mean:
    (a) the spouse of the person discharging managerial responsibilities, or any partner of that person considered by national law as equivalent to the spouse;
    (b) according to national law, dependent children of the person discharging managerial responsibilities;
    (c) other relatives of the person discharging managerial responsibilities, who have shared the same household as that person for at least one year on the date of the transaction concerned;
    (d) any legal person, trust or partnership, whose managerial responsibilities are discharged by a person referred to in point 1 of this Article or in letters (a), (b) and (c) of this point, or which is directly or indirectly controlled by such a person, or that is set up for the benefit of such a person, or whose economic interests are substantially equivalent to those of such person.

3. 'Person professionally arranging transactions' shall mean at least an investment firm or a credit institution.

4. 'Investment firm' shall mean any person as defined in Article 1(2) of Council Directive 93/22/EEC;[1]

5. 'Credit institution' shall mean any person as defined in Article 1(1) of Directive 2000/12/EC of the European Parliament and of the Council;[2]

6. 'Competent authority' shall mean the competent authority as defined in Article 1(7) of Directive 2003/6/EC.

NOTES
[1] OJ L141, 11.6.1993, p 27.
[2] OJ L126, 26.5.2000, p 1.

[11.386]
Article 2
Factors to be taken into account when considering market practices
1. For the purposes of applying paragraph 2 of point 1 and point 2(a) of Article 1 of Directive 2003/6/EC, Member States shall ensure that the following non exhaustive factors are taken into account by competent authorities, without prejudice to collaboration with other authorities, when assessing whether they can accept a particular market practice:
    (a) the level of transparency of the relevant market practice to the whole market;
    (b) the need to safeguard the operation of market forces and the proper interplay of the forces of supply and demand;
    (c) the degree to which the relevant market practice has an impact on market liquidity and efficiency;
    (d) the degree to which the relevant practice takes into account the trading mechanism of the relevant market and enables market participants to react properly and in a timely manner to the new market situation created by that practice;
    (e) the risk inherent in the relevant practice for the integrity of, directly or indirectly, related markets, whether regulated or not, in the relevant financial instrument within the whole Community;
    (f) the outcome of any investigation of the relevant market practice by any competent authority or other authority mentioned in Article 12(1) of Directive 2003/6/EC, in particular whether the relevant market practice breached rules or regulations designed to prevent market abuse, or codes of conduct, be it on the market in question or on directly or indirectly related markets within the Community;
    (g) the structural characteristics of the relevant market including whether it is regulated or not, the types of financial instruments traded and the type of market participants, including the extent of retail investors participation in the relevant market.

Member States shall ensure that competent authorities shall, when considering the need for safeguard referred to in point (b) of the first subparagraph, in particular analyse the impact of the relevant market practice against the main market parameters, such as the specific market conditions before carrying out the relevant market practice, the weighted average price of a single session or the daily closing price.

2. Member States shall ensure that practices, in particular new or emerging market practices are not assumed to be unacceptable by the competent authority simply because they have not been previously accepted by it.

3. Member States shall ensure that competent authorities review regularly the market practices they have accepted, in particular taking into account significant changes to the relevant market environment, such as changes to trading rules or to market infrastructure.

[11.387]
Article 3
Consultation procedures and disclosure of decisions

1. For the purposes of applying paragraph 2 of point 1 and point 2(a) of Article 1 of Directive 2003/6/EC, Member States shall ensure that the procedures set out in paragraphs 2 and 3 of this Article are observed by competent authorities when considering whether to accept or continue to accept a particular market practice.

2. Without prejudice to Article 11(2) of Directive 2003/6/EC, Member States shall ensure that competent authorities, before accepting or not the market practice concerned, consult as appropriate relevant bodies such as representatives of issuers, financial services providers, consumers, other authorities and market operators.

The consultation procedure shall include consultation of other competent authorities, in particular where there exist comparable markets, ie in structures, volume, type of transactions.

3. Member States shall ensure that competent authorities publicly disclose their decisions regarding the acceptability of the market practice concerned, including appropriate descriptions of such practices. Member States shall further ensure that competent authorities transmit their decisions as soon as possible to the Committee of European Securities Regulators which shall make them immediately available on its website.

The disclosure shall include a description of the factors taken into account in determining whether the relevant practice is regarded as acceptable, in particular where different conclusions have been reached regarding the acceptability of the same practice on different Member States markets.

4. When investigatory actions on specific cases have already started, the consultation procedures set out in paragraphs 1 to 3 may be delayed until the end of such investigation and possible related sanctions.

5. A market practice which was accepted following the consultation procedures set out in paragraphs 1 to 3 shall not be changed without using the same consultation procedures.

[11.388]
Article 4
Inside information in relation to derivatives on commodities

For the purposes of applying the second paragraph of point 1 of Article 1 of Directive 2003/6/EC, users of markets on which derivatives on commodities are traded, are deemed to expect to receive information relating, directly or indirectly, to one or more such derivatives which is:

    (a)   routinely made available to the users of those markets, or

    (b)   required to be disclosed in accordance with legal or regulatory provisions, market rules, contracts or customs on the relevant underlying commodity market or commodity derivatives market.

[11.389]
Article 5
Lists of insiders

1. For the purposes of applying the third subparagraph of Article 6(3) of Directive 2003/6/EC, Member States shall ensure that lists of insiders include all persons covered by that Article who have access to inside information relating, directly or indirectly, to the issuer, whether on a regular or occasional basis.

2. Lists of insiders shall state at least:

    (a)   the identity of any person having access to inside information;

    (b)   the reason why any such person is on the list;

    (c)   the date at which the list of insiders was created and updated.

3. Lists of insiders shall be promptly updated:

    (a)   whenever there is a change in the reason why any person is already on the list;

    (b)   whenever any new person has to be added to the list;

    (c)   by mentioning whether and when any person already on the list has no longer access to inside information.

4. Member States shall ensure that lists of insiders will be kept for at least five years after being drawn up or updated.

Part 11   EU Legislation

5.   Member States shall ensure that the persons required to draw up lists of insiders take the necessary measures to ensure that any person on such a list that has access to inside information acknowledges the legal and regulatory duties entailed and is aware of the sanctions attaching to the misuse or improper circulation of such information.

[11.390]
Article 6
Managers' Transactions
1.   For the purposes of applying Article 6(4) of Directive 2003/6/EC, and without prejudice to the right of Member States to provide for other notification obligations than those covered by that Article, Member States shall ensure that all transactions related to shares admitted to trading on a regulated market, or to derivatives or other financial instruments linked to them, conducted on the own account of persons referred to in Article 1 points 1 and 2 above, are notified to the competent authorities. The rules of notification to which those persons have to comply with shall be those of the Member State where the issuer is registered. The notification shall be made within five working days of the transaction date to the competent authority of that Member State. When the issuer is not registered in a Member State, this notification shall be made to the competent authority of the Member State in which it is required to file the annual information in relation to the shares in accordance with Article 10 of Directive 2003/71/EC.
2.   Member States may decide that, until the total amount of transactions has reached five thousand Euros at the end of a calendar year, no notification is required or notification may be delayed until the 31 January of the following year. The total amount of transactions shall be computed by summing up the transactions conducted on the own account of persons referred to in Article 1 point 1 with the transactions conducted on the own account of persons referred to in Article 1 point 2.
3.   The notification shall contain the following information:
 (a)   name of the person discharging managerial responsibilities within the issuer, or, where applicable, name of the person closely associated with such a person,
 (b)   reason for responsibility to notify,
 (c)   name of the relevant issuer,
 (d)   description of the financial instrument,
 (e)   nature of the transaction (eg acquisition or disposal),
 (f)   date and place of the transaction
 (g)   price and volume of the transaction.

[11.391]
Article 7
Suspicious transactions to be notified
For the purposes of applying Article 6(9) of Directive 2003/6/EC, Member States shall ensure that persons referred to in Article 1 point 3 above shall decide on a case-by-case basis whether there are reasonable grounds for suspecting that a transaction involves insider dealing or market manipulation, taking into account the elements constituting insider dealing or market manipulation, referred to in Articles 1 to 5 of Directive 2003/6/EC, in Commission Directive 2003/124/EC[1] implementing Directive 2003/6/EC as regards the definition and public disclosure of inside information and the definition of market manipulation, and in Article 4 of this Directive. Without prejudice to Article 10 of Directive 2003/6/EC, persons professionally arranging transactions shall be subject to the rules of notification of the Member State in which they are registered or have their head office, or in the case of a branch, the Member State where the branch is situated. The notification shall be addressed to the competent authority of this Member State.
   Member States shall ensure that competent authorities receiving the notification of suspicious transactions transmit such information immediately to the competent authorities of the regulated markets concerned.

NOTES
¹   OJ L339, 24.12.2003, p 70.

[11.392]
Article 8
Timeframe for notification
Member States shall ensure that in the event that persons, as referred to in Article 1 point 3, become aware of a fact or information that gives reasonable ground for suspicion concerning the relevant transaction, make a notification without delay.

[11.393]
Article 9
Content of notification
1.   Member States shall ensure that persons subject to the notification obligation transmit to the competent authority the following information:

(a)   description of the transactions, including the type of order (such as limit order, market order or other characteristics of the order) and the type of trading market (such as block trade);

(b)   reasons for suspicion that the transactions might constitute market abuse;

(c)   means for identification of the persons on behalf of whom the transactions have been carried out, and of other persons involved in the relevant transactions;

(d)   capacity in which the person subject to the notification obligation operates (such as for own account or on behalf of third parties);

(e)   any information which may have significance in reviewing the suspicious transactions.

2.   Where that information is not available at the time of notification, the notification shall include at least the reasons why the notifying persons suspect that the transactions might constitute insider dealing or market manipulation. All remaining information shall be provided to the competent authority as soon as it becomes available.

[11.394]
Article 10
Means of notification

Member States shall ensure that notification to the competent authority can be done by mail, electronic mail, telecopy or telephone, provided that in the latter case confirmation is notified by any written form upon request by the competent authority.

[11.395]
Article 11
Liability and professional secrecy

1.   Member States shall ensure that the person notifying to the competent authority as referred to in Articles 7 to 10 shall not inform any other person, in particular the persons on behalf of whom the transactions have been carried out or parties related to those persons, of this notification, except by virtue of provisions laid down by law. The fulfilment of this requirement shall not involve the notifying person in liability of any kind, providing the notifying person acts in good faith.

2.   Member States shall ensure that competent authorities do not disclose to any person the identity of the person having notified these transactions, if disclosure would, or would be likely to harm the person having notified the transactions. This provision is without prejudice to the requirements of the enforcement and the sanctioning regimes under Directive 2003/6/EC and to the rules on transfer of personal data laid down in Directive 95/46/EC.

3.   The notification in good faith to the competent authority as referred to in Articles 7 to 10 shall not constitute a breach of any restriction on disclosure of information imposed by contract or by any legislative, regulatory or administrative provision, and shall not involve the person notifying in liability of any kind related to such notification.

[11.396]
Article 12
Transposition

1.   Member States shall bring into force the laws, regulations and administrative provisions necessary to comply with this Directive by 12 October 2004 at the latest. They shall forthwith communicate to the Commission the text of the provisions and a correlation table between those provisions and this Directive.

When Member States adopt those provisions, they shall contain a reference to this Directive or be accompanied by such a reference on the occasion of their official publication. Member States shall determine how such reference is to be made.

2.   Member States shall communicate to the Commission the text of the main provisions of national law which they adopt in the field covered by this Directive.

[11.397]
Article 13
Entry into force

This Directive shall enter into force on the day of its publication in the *Official Journal of the European Union.*

[11.398]
Article 14
Addressees

This Directive is addressed to the Member States.

COMMISSION REGULATION

(809/2004/EC)

of 29 April 2004

implementing Directive 2003/71/EC of the European Parliament and of the Council as regards information contained in prospectuses as well as the format, incorporation by reference and publication of such prospectuses and dissemination of advertisements

(Text with EEA relevance)

NOTES

Date of publication in OJ: this Regulation was originally published in OJ L149, 30.4.2004, p 1. Note that a corrigendum was published in OJ L215, 16.6.2004, p 3; that corrigendum set out the whole of this Regulation (with changes incorporated) and it is the version from that corrigendum that is reproduced here. Notes are as in the OJ version.

This Regulation is reproduced as amended by: Commission Regulation 1787/2006/EC; Commission Regulation 211/2007/EC; Commission Regulation 1289/2008/EC.

[11.399]

THE COMMISSION OF THE EUROPEAN COMMUNITIES,

Having regard to the Treaty establishing the European Community,

Having regard to Directive 2003/71/EC of the European Parliament and the Council of 4 November 2003 on the prospectus to be published when securities are offered to the public or admitted to trading and amending Directive 2001/34/EC,[1] and in particular Article 5(5), Article 7, Article 10(4), Article 11(3), Article 14(8) and Article 15(7) thereof,

After consulting the Committee of European Securities Regulators (CESR)[2] for technical advice,

Whereas:

(1) Directive 2003/71/EC lays down principles to be observed when drawing up prospectuses. These principles need to be supplemented as far as the information to be given therein, the format and aspects of publication, the information to be incorporated by reference in a prospectus and dissemination of advertisements are concerned.

(2) Depending on the type of issuer and securities involved, a typology of minimum information requirements should be established corresponding to those schedules that are in practice most frequently applied. The schedules should be based on the information items required in the IOSCO "Disclosure Standards for cross-border offering and initial listings" (part I) and on the existing schedules of Directive 2001/34/EC of the European Parliament and of the Council of 28 May on the admission of securities to official stock exchange listing and on information to be published on those securities.[3]

(3) Information given by the issuer, the offeror or the person asking for admission to trading on a regulated market, according to this Regulation, should be subject to European Union provisions relating to data protection.

(4) Care should be taken that, in those cases where a prospectus is composed of separate documents, duplication of information is avoided; to this end separate detailed schedules for the registration document and for the securities note, adapted to the particular type of issuer and securities concerned, should be laid down in order to cover each type of security.

(5) The issuer, the offeror or the person asking for admission to trading on a regulated market are entitled to include in a prospectus or base prospectus additional information going beyond the information items provided for in the schedules and building blocks. Any additional information provided should be appropriate to the type of securities or the nature of the issuer involved.

(6) In most cases, given the variety of issuers, the types of securities, the involvement or not of a third party as a guarantor, whether or not there is a listing etc, one single schedule will not give the appropriate information for an investor to make his investment decision. Therefore the combination of various schedules should be possible. A non exhaustive table of combinations, providing for different possible combinations of schedules and "building blocks" for most of the different type of securities, should be set up in order to assist issuers when drafting their prospectus.

(7) The share registration document schedule should be applicable to shares and other transferable securities equivalent to shares but also to other securities giving access to the capital of the issuer by way of conversion or exchange. In the latter case this schedule should not be used where the underlying shares to be delivered have already been issued before the issuance of the securities giving access to the capital of the issuer; however this schedule should be used where the underlying shares to be delivered have already been issued but are not yet admitted to trading on a regulated market.

(8) Voluntary disclosure of profit forecasts in a share registration document should be presented in a consistent and comparable manner and accompanied by a statement prepared by independent accountants or auditors. This information should not be confused with the disclosure of known trends or other factual data with material impact on the issuers' prospects. Moreover, they should provide an explanation of any changes in disclosure policy relating to profit forecasts when supplementing a prospectus or drafting a new prospectus.

(9) Pro forma financial information is needed in case of significant gross change, i. e. a variation

of more than 25% relative to one or more indicators of the size of the issuer's business, in the situation of an issuer due to a particular transaction, with the exception of those situations where merger accounting is required.

(10) The schedule for the share securities note should be applicable to any class of share since it considers information regarding a description of the rights attached to the securities and the procedure for the exercise of any rights attached to the securities.

(11) Some debt securities such as structured bonds incorporate certain elements of a derivative security, therefore additional disclosure requirements related to the derivative component in the interest payment should be included in the securities note schedule for debt securities.

(12) The additional "building block" related to guarantee should apply to any obligation in relation to any kind of security.

(13) The asset backed securities registration document should not apply to mortgage bonds as provided for in Article 5(4)(b) of Directive 2003/71/EC and other covered bonds. The same should apply for the asset backed securities additional "building block" that has to be combined with the securities note for debt securities.

(14) Wholesale investors should be able to make their investment decision on other elements than those taken into consideration by retail investors. Therefore a differentiated content of prospectus is necessary for debt and derivative securities aimed at those investors who purchase debt or derivative securities with a denomination per unit of at least EUR 50,000 or a denomination in another currency provided that the value of such minimum denomination when converted to EURO amounts to at least EURO 50,000.

(15) In the context of depository receipts, emphasis should be put on the issuer of the underlying shares and not on the issuer of the depository receipt. Where there is legal recourse to the depository over and above a breach of its fiduciary or agency duties, the risk factors section in the prospectus should contain full information on this fact and on the circumstances of such recourse. Where a prospectus is drafted as a tripartite document (i.e. registration document, securities note and summary), the registration document should be limited to the information on the depository.

(16) The banks registration document schedule should be applicable to banks from third countries which do not fall under the definition of credit institution provided for in Article 1(1)(a) of Directive 2000/12/EC of the European Parliament and of the Council of 20 March 2000 relating to the taking up and pursuit of the business of credit institutions[4] but have their registered office in a state which is a member of the OECD.

(17) If a special purpose vehicle issues debt and derivative securities guaranteed by a bank, it should not use the banks registration document schedule.

(18) The schedule "securities note for derivative securities" should be applicable to securities which are not covered by the other schedules and building blocks. The scope of this schedule is determined by reference to the other two generic categories of shares and debt securities. In order to provide a clear and comprehensive explanation to help investors understand how the value of their investment is affected by the value of the underlying, issuers should be able to use appropriate examples on a voluntary basis. For instance, for some complex derivatives securities, examples might be the most effective way to explain the nature of those securities.

(19) The additional information "building block" on the underlying share for certain equity securities should be added to the securities note for debt securities or substitute the item referring to "information required in respect of the underlying" of the schedule securities note for derivative securities, depending on the characteristics of the securities being issued.

(20) Member States and their regional or local authorities are outside the scope of Directive 2003/71/EC. However, they may choose to produce a prospectus in accordance with this Directive. Third country sovereign issuers and their regional or local authorities are not outside the scope of Directive 2003/71/EC and are obliged to produce a prospectus if they wish to make a public offer of securities in the Community or wish their securities to be admitted to trading on a regulated market. For those cases, particular schedules should be used for the securities issued by States, their regional and local authorities and by public international bodies.

(21) A base prospectus and its final terms should contain the same information as a prospectus. All the general principles applicable to a prospectus are applicable also to the final terms. Nevertheless, where the final terms are not included in the base prospectus they do not have to be approved by the competent authority.

(22) For some categories of issuers the competent authority should be entitled to require adapted information going beyond the information items included in the schedules and building blocks because of the particular nature of the activities carried out by those issuers. A precise and restrictive list of issuers for which adapted information may be required is necessary. The adapted information requirements for each category of issuers included in this list should be appropriate and proportionate to the type of business involved. The Committee of European Securities Regulators could actively try to reach convergence on these information requirements within the Community. Inclusion of new categories in the list should be restricted to those cases where this can be duly justified.

(23) In the case of completely new types of securities which cannot be covered by the existing schedules or any of their combinations, the issuer should still have the possibility to apply for approval for a prospectus. In those cases he should be able to discuss the content of the information to be provided with the competent authority. The prospectus approved by the competent authority under those circumstances should benefit from the single passport established in Directive 2003/71/EC. The competent authority should always try to find similarities and make use as much as possible of existing schedules. Any additional information requirements should be proportionate

and appropriate to the type of securities involved.

(24) Certain information items required in the schedules and building blocks or equivalent information items are not relevant to a particular security and thus may be inapplicable in some specific cases; in those cases the issuer should have the possibility to omit this information.

(25) The enhanced flexibility in the articulation of the base prospectus with its final terms compared to a single issue prospectus should not hamper the easy access to material information for investors.

(26) With respect to base prospectuses, it should be set out in an easily identifiable manner which kind of information will have to be included as final terms. This requirement should be able to be satisfied in a number of different ways, for example, if the base prospectus contains blanks for any information to be inserted in the final terms or if the base prospectus contains a list of the missing information.

(27) Where a single document includes more than one base prospectus and each base prospectus would require approval by a different home competent authority, the respective competent authorities should act in cooperation and, where appropriate, transfer the approval of the prospectus in accordance with Article 13(5) of Directive 2003/71/EC, so that the approval by only one competent authority is sufficient for the entire document.

(28) Historical financial information as required in the schedules should principally be presented in accordance with Regulation (EC) No 1606/2002 of the European Parliament and of the Council of 19 July 2002 on the application of international accounting standard[5] or Member States' accounting standards. Specific requirements should, however, be laid down for third country issuers.

(29) For the purposes of publication of the document referred to in Article 10 of Directive 2003/71/EC, issuers should be allowed to choose the method of publication they consider adequate among those referred to in Article 14 of that Directive. In selecting the method of publication they should consider the objective of the document and that it should permit investors a fast and cost-efficient access to that information.

(30) The aim of incorporation by reference, as provided for in Article 11 of Directive 2003/71/EC, is to simplify and reduce the costs of drafting a prospectus; however this aim should not be achieved to the detriment of other interests the prospectus is meant to protect. For instance, the fact that the natural location of the information required is the prospectus, and that the information should be presented in an easily and comprehensible form, should also be considered. Particular attention should be granted to the language used for information incorporated by reference and its consistency with the prospectus itself. Information incorporated by reference may refer to historical data, however if this information is no more relevant due to material change, this should be clearly stated in the prospectus and the updated information should also be provided.

(31) Where a prospectus is published in electronic form, additional safety measures compared to traditional means of publication, using best practices available, are necessary in order to maintain the integrity of the information, to avoid manipulation or modification from unauthorised persons, to avoid altering its comprehensibility and to escape from possible adverse consequences from different approaches on offer of securities to the public in third countries.

(32) The newspaper chosen for the publication of a prospectus should have a wide area of distribution and a high circulation.

(33) A home Member State should be able to require publication of a notice stating how the prospectus has been made available and where it can be obtained by the public. Where a home Member State requires publication of notices in its legislation, the content of such a notice should be kept to the necessary items information to avoid duplication with the summary. These home Member States may also require that an additional notice in relation to the final terms of a base prospectus is to be published.

(34) In order to facilitate centralising useful information for investors a mention should be included in the list of approved prospectuses posted in the web-site of the competent authority of the home Member State, indicating how a prospectus has been published and where it can be obtained.

(35) Member States should ensure effective compliance of advertising rules concerning public offers and admission to trading on a regulated market. Proper co-ordination between competent authorities should be achieved in cross-border offerings or cross-border admission to trading.

(36) In view of the interval between the entry into force of Regulation (EC) No 1606/2002 and the production of certain of its effects, a number of transitional arrangements for historical financial information to be included in a prospectus should be provided for, in order to prevent excessive burden on issuers and enable them to adapt the way they prepare and present historical financial information within a reasonable period of time after the entry into force of Directive 2003/71/EC.

(37) The obligation to restate in a prospectus historical financial information according to Regulation (EC) No 1606/2002 does not cover securities with a denomination per unit of at least EUR 50,000; consequently such transitional arrangements are not necessary for such securities.

(38) For reasons of coherence it is appropriate that this Regulation applies from the date of transposition of Directive 2003/71/EC.

(39) Whereas the measures provided for in this Regulation are in accordance with the opinion of the European Securities Committee,

---

NOTES

[1]   OJ L345, 31.12.2003, p 64.

[2]   CESR was established by Commission Decision 2001/527/EC of 6 June 2001, OJ L191, 13 July 2001, p 43.

³   OJ L184, 6.7.2001, p 1. Directive as last amended by Directive 2003/71/EC.

⁴   OJ L126, 26.5.2000, p 1. Directive as last amended by the 2003 Act of Accession.

⁵   OJ L243, 11.9.2002, p 1.

HAS ADOPTED THIS REGULATION:

CHAPTER I
SUBJECT MATTER AND DEFINITIONS

[11.400]
Article 1
Subject matter
This Regulation lays down:
1.   the format of prospectus referred to in Article 5 of Directive 2003/71/EC;
2.   the minimum information requirements to be included in a prospectus provided for in Article 7 of Directive 2003/71/EC;
3.   the method of publication referred to in Article 10 of Directive 2003/71/EC;
4.   the modalities according to which information can be incorporated by reference in a prospectus provided for in Article 11 of Directive 2003/71/EC;
5.   the publication methods of a prospectus in order to ensure that a prospectus is publicly available according to Article 14 of Directive 2003/71/EC;
6.   the methods of dissemination of advertisements referred to in Article 15 of Directive 2003/71/EC.

[11.401]
Article 2
Definitions
For the purposes of this Regulation, the following definitions shall apply in addition to those laid down in Directive 2003/71/EC:
1.   "schedule" means a list of minimum information requirements adapted to the particular nature of the different types of issuers and/or the different securities involved;
2.   "building block" means a list of additional information requirements, not included in one of the schedules, to be added to one or more schedules, as the case may be, depending on the type of instrument and/or transaction for which a prospectus or base prospectus is drawn up;
3.   "risk factors" means a list of risks which are specific to the situation of the issuer and/or the securities and which are material for taking investment decisions;
4.   "special purpose vehicle" means an issuer whose objects and purposes are primarily the issue of securities;
5.   "asset backed securities" means securities which:
    (a)   represent an interest in assets, including any rights intended to assure servicing, or the receipt or timeliness of receipts by holders of assets of amounts payable there under; or
    (b)   are secured by assets and the terms of which provide for payments which relate to payments or reasonable projections of payments calculated by reference to identified or identifiable assets;
6.   "umbrella collective investment undertaking" means a collective investment undertaking invested in one or more collective investment undertakings, the asset of which is composed of separate class(es) or designation(s) of securities;
7.   "property collective investment undertaking" means a collective investment undertaking whose investment objective is the participation in the holding of property in the long term;
8.   "public international body" means a legal entity of public nature established by an international treaty between sovereign States and of which one or more Member States are members;
9.   "advertisement" means announcements:
    (a)   relating to an specific offer to the public of securities or to an admission to trading on a regulated market; and
    (b)   aiming to specifically promote the potential subscription or acquisition of securities.
10.   "profit forecast" means a form of words which expressly states or by implication indicates a figure or a minimum or maximum figure for the likely level of profits or losses for the current financial period and/or financial periods subsequent to that period, or contains data from which a calculation of such a figure for future profits or losses may be made, even if no particular figure is mentioned and the word "profit" is not used.
11.   "profit estimate" means a profit forecast for a financial period which has expired and for which results have not yet been published.
12.   "regulated information" means all information which the issuer, or any person who has applied for the admission of securities to trading on a regulated market without the issuer's consent, is required to disclose under Directive 2001/34/EC or under Article 6 of Directive 2003/6/EC of the European Parliament and of the Council.[1]

NOTES
1   OJ L96, 12.4.2003, p 16.

CHAPTER II
MINIMUM INFORMATION

[11.402]
Article 3
Minimum information to be included in a prospectus
A prospectus shall be drawn up by using one or a combination of the following schedules and building blocks set out in Articles 4 to 20, according to the combinations for various types of securities provided for in Article 21.

A prospectus shall contain the information items required in Annexes I to XVII depending on the type of issuer and securities involved, provided for in the schedules and building blocks set out in Articles 4 to 20. [Subject to Article 4a(1), a competent authority shall not request that a prospectus contain information items which are not included in Annexes I to XVII.]

In order to ensure conformity with the obligation referred to in Article 5(1) of Directive 2003/71/EC, the competent authority of the home Member State, when approving a prospectus in accordance with Article 13 of that Directive, may require that the information provided by the issuer, the offeror or the person asking for admission to trading on a regulated market be completed, for each of the information items, on a case by case basis.

NOTES
Words in square brackets substituted by Commission Regulation 211/2007/EC, Art 1(1), as from 1 March 2007.

[11.403]
Article 4
Share registration document schedule
1.   For the share registration document information shall be given in accordance with the schedule set out in Annex I.
2.   The schedule set out in paragraph 1 shall apply to the following:
   (1)   shares and other transferable securities equivalent to shares;
   (2)   other securities which comply with the following conditions:
      (a)   they can be converted or exchanged into shares or other transferable securities equivalent to shares, at the issuer's or at the investor's discretion, or on the basis of the conditions established at the moment of the issue, or give, in any other way, the possibility to acquire shares or other transferable securities equivalent to shares; and
      (b)   provided that these shares or other transferable securities equivalent to shares are or will be issued by the issuer of the security and are not yet traded on a regulated market or an equivalent market outside the Community at the time of the approval of the prospectus covering the securities, and that the underlying shares or other transferable securities equivalent to shares can be delivered with physical settlement.

[11.404]
[Article 4a
Share registration document schedule in cases of complex financial history or significant financial commitment
1.   Where the issuer of a security covered by Article 4(2) has a complex financial history, or has made a significant financial commitment, and in consequence the inclusion in the registration document of certain items of financial information relating to an entity other than the issuer is necessary in order to satisfy the obligation laid down in Article 5(1) of Directive 2003/71/EC, those items of financial information shall be deemed to relate to the issuer. The competent authority of the home Member State shall in such cases request that the issuer, the offeror or the person asking for admission to trading include those items of information in the registration document.

Those items of financial information may include pro forma information prepared in accordance with Annex II. In this context, where the issuer has made a significant financial commitment any such pro forma information shall illustrate the anticipated effects of the transaction that the issuer has agreed to undertake, and references in Annex II to "the transaction" shall be read accordingly.
2.   The competent authority shall base any request pursuant to paragraph 1 on the requirements set out in item 20.1 of Annex I as regards the content of financial information and the applicable accounting and auditing principles, subject to any modification which is appropriate in view of any of the following factors:
   (a)   the nature of the securities;
   (b)   the nature and range of information already included in the prospectus, and the existence of financial information relating to an entity other than the issuer in a form that might be included in a prospectus without modification;

(c)　the facts of the case, including the economic substance of the transactions by which the issuer has acquired or disposed of its business undertaking or any part of it, and the specific nature of that undertaking;

(d)　the ability of the issuer to obtain financial information relating to another entity with reasonable effort.

Where, in the individual case, the obligation laid down in Article 5(1) of Directive 2003/71/EC may be satisfied in more than one way, preference shall be given to the way that is the least costly or onerous.

3.　Paragraph 1 is without prejudice to the responsibility under national law of any other person, including the persons referred to in Article 6(1) of Directive 2003/71/EC, for the information contained in the prospectus. In particular, those persons shall be responsible for the inclusion in the registration document of any items of information requested by the competent authority pursuant to paragraph 1.

4.　For the purposes of paragraph 1, an issuer shall be treated as having a complex financial history if all of the following conditions apply:

(a)　its entire business undertaking at the time that the prospectus is drawn up is not accurately represented in the historical financial information which it is required to provide under item 20.1 of Annex I;

(b)　that inaccuracy will affect the ability of an investor to make an informed assessment as mentioned in Article 5(1) of Directive 2003/71/EC; and

(c)　information relating to its business undertaking that is necessary for an investor to make such an assessment is included in financial information relating to another entity.

5.　For the purposes of paragraph 1, an issuer shall be treated as having made a significant financial commitment if it has entered into a binding agreement to undertake a transaction which, on completion, is likely to give rise to a significant gross change.

In this context, the fact that an agreement makes completion of the transaction subject to conditions, including approval by a regulatory authority, shall not prevent that agreement from being treated as binding if it is reasonably certain that those conditions will be fulfilled.

In particular, an agreement shall be treated as binding where it makes the completion of the transaction conditional on the outcome of the offer of the securities that are the subject matter of the prospectus or, in the case of a proposed takeover, if the offer of securities that are the subject matter of the prospectus has the objective of funding that takeover.

6.　For the purposes of paragraph 5 of this Article, and of item 20.2 of Annex I, a significant gross change means a variation of more than 25%, relative to one or more indicators of the size of the issuer's business, in the situation of an issuer.]

NOTES

Inserted by Commission Regulation 211/2007/EC, Art 1(2), as from 1 March 2007.

[11.405]
Article 5
Pro-forma financial information building block

For pro forma financial information, information shall be given in accordance with the building block set out in Annex II.

Pro forma financial information should be preceded by an introductory explanatory paragraph that states in clear terms the purpose of including this information in the prospectus.

[11.406]
Article 6
Share securities note schedule

1.　For the share securities note information is necessary to be given in accordance with the schedule set out in Annex III.

2.　The schedule shall apply to shares and other transferable securities equivalent to shares.

[11.407]
Article 7
Debt and derivative securities registration document schedule for securities with a denomination per unit of less than EUR 50,000

For the debt and derivative securities registration document concerning securities which are not covered in Article 4 with a denomination per unit of less than EUR 50,000 or, where there is no individual denomination, securities that can only be acquired on issue for less than EUR 50,000 per security, information shall be given in accordance with the schedule set out in Annex IV.

[11.408]
Article 8
Securities note schedule for debt securities with a denomination per unit of less than EUR 50,000

1.　For the securities note for debt securities with a denomination per unit of less than EUR 50,000 information shall be given in accordance with the schedule set out in Annex V.

2. The schedule shall apply to debt where the issuer has an obligation arising on issue to pay the investor 100% of the nominal value in addition to which there may be also an interest payment.

[11.409]
Article 9
Guarantees building block
For guarantees information shall be given in accordance with the building block set out in Annex VI.

[11.410]
Article 10
Asset backed securities registration document schedule
For the asset backed securities registration document information shall be given in accordance with the schedule set out in Annex VII.

[11.411]
Article 11
Asset backed securities building block
For the additional information building block to the securities note for asset backed securities information shall be given in accordance with the building block set out in Annex VIII.

[11.412]
Article 12
Debt and derivative securities registration document schedule for securities with a denomination per unit of at least EUR 50,000
For the debt and derivative securities registration document concerning securities which are not covered in Article 4 with a denomination per unit of at least EUR 50,000 or, where there is no individual denomination, securities that can only be acquired on issue for at least EUR 50,000 per security, information shall be given in accordance with the schedule set out in Annex IX.

[11.413]
Article 13
Depository receipts schedule
For depository receipts issued over shares information shall be given in accordance with the schedule set out in Annex X.

[11.414]
Article 14
Banks registration document schedule
1. For the banks registration document for debt and derivative securities and those securities which are not covered by Article 4 information shall be given in accordance with the schedule set out in Annex XI.
2. The schedule set out in paragraph 1 shall apply to credit institutions as defined in point (a) of Article 1(1) of Directive 2000/12/EC as well as to third country credit institutions which do not fall under that definition but have their registered office in a state which is a member of the OECD.
   These entities may also use alternatively the registration document schedules provided for under in Articles 7 and 12.

[11.415]
Article 15
Securities note schedule for derivative securities
1. For the securities note for derivative securities information shall be given in accordance with the schedule set out in Annex XII.
2. The schedule shall apply to securities which are not in the scope of application of the other securities note schedules referred to in Articles 6, 8 and 16, including certain securities where the payment and/or delivery obligations are linked to an underlying.

[11.416]
Article 16
Securities note schedule for debt securities with a denomination per unit of at least EUR 50,000
1. For the securities note for debt securities with a denomination per unit of at least EUR 50,000 information shall be given in accordance with the schedule set out in Annex XIII.
2. The schedule shall apply to debt where the issuer has an obligation arising on issue to pay the investor 100% of the nominal value in addition to which there may be also an interest payment.

[11.417]
Article 17
Additional information building block on the underlying share
1. For the additional information on the underlying share, the description of the underlying share shall be given in accordance with the building block set out in Annex XIV.

In addition, if the issuer of the underlying share is an entity belonging to the same group, the information required by the schedule referred to in Article 4 shall be given in respect of that issuer.
2.   The additional information referred to in the first subparagraph of paragraph 1 shall only apply to those securities which comply with both of the following conditions:
(1)   they can be converted or exchanged into shares or other transferable securities equivalent to shares, at the issuer's or at the investor's discretion, or on the basis of the conditions established at the moment of the issue or give, in any other way, the possibility to acquire shares or other transferable securities equivalent to shares; and
(2)   provided that these shares or other transferable securities equivalent to shares are or will be issued by the issuer of the security or by an entity belonging to the group of that issuer and are not yet traded on a regulated market or an equivalent market outside the Community at the time of the approval of the prospectus covering the securities, and that the underlying shares or other transferable securities equivalent to shares can be delivered with physical settlement.

[11.418]
Article 18
Registration document schedule for collective investment undertakings of the closed-end type
1.   In addition to the information required pursuant to items 1, 2, 3, 4, 5.1, 7, 9.1, 9.2.1, 9.2.3, 10.4, 13, 14, 15, 16, 17.2, 18, 19, 20, 21, 22, 23, 24, 25 of Annex I, for the registration document for securities issued by collective investment undertakings of the closed-end type information shall be given in accordance with the schedule set out in Annex XV.
2.   The schedule shall apply to collective investment undertakings of the closed-end type holding a portfolio of assets on behalf of investors that:
(1)   are recognised by national law in the Member State in which it is incorporated as a collective investment undertaking of the closed end type; or
(2)   do not take or seek to take legal or management control of any of the issuers of its underlying investments. In such a case, legal control and/or participation in the administrative, management or supervisory bodies of the underlying issuer(s) may be taken where such action is incidental to the primary investment objective, necessary for the protection of shareholders and only in circumstances where the collective investment undertaking will not exercise significant management control over the operations of that underlying issuer(s).

[11.419]
Article 19
Registration document schedule for Member States, third countries and their regional and local authorities
1.   For the registration document for securities issued by Member States, third countries and their regional and local authorities information shall be given in accordance with the schedule set out in Annex XVI.
2.   The schedule shall apply to all types of securities issued by Member States, third countries and their regional and local authorities.

[11.420]
Article 20
Registration document schedule for public international bodies and for issuers of debt securities guaranteed by a member state of the OECD
1.   For the registration document for securities issued by public international bodies and for securities unconditionally and irrevocably guaranteed, on the basis of national legislation, by a state which is member of the OECD information shall be given in accordance with the schedule set out in Annex XVII.
2.   The schedule shall apply to:
—   all types of securities issued by public international bodies,
—   to debt securities unconditionally and irrevocably guaranteed, on the basis of national legislation, by a state which is member of the OECD.

[11.421]
Article 21
Combination of schedules and building blocks
1.   The use of the combinations provided for in the table set out in Annex XVIII shall be mandatory when drawing up prospectuses for the types of securities to which those combinations correspond according to this table.
However, for securities not covered by those combinations further combinations may be used.
2.   The most comprehensive and stringent registration document schedule, ie the most demanding schedule in term of number of information items and the extent of the information included in them, may always be used to issue securities for which a less comprehensive and stringent registration document schedule is provided for, according to the following ranking of schedules:
(1)   share registration document schedule;

(2) debt and derivative securities registration document schedule for securities with a denomination per unit of less than EUR 50,000;

(3) debt and derivative securities registration document schedule for securities with a denomination per unit at least EUR 50,000.

[11.422]
Article 22
Minimum information to be included in a base prospectus and its related final terms

1. A base prospectus shall be drawn up by using one or a combination of schedules and building blocks provided for in Articles 4 to 20 according to the combinations for various types of securities set out in Annex XVIII.

A base prospectus shall contain the information items required in Annexes I to XVII depending on the type of issuer and securities involved, provided for in the schedules and building blocks set out in Articles 4 to 20. A competent authority shall not request that a base prospectus contains information items which are not included in Annexes I to XVII.

In order to ensure conformity with the obligation referred to in Article 5(1) of Directive 2003/71/EC, the competent authority of the home Member State, when approving a base prospectus in accordance with Article 13 of that Directive, may require that the information provided by the issuer, the offeror or the person asking for admission to trading on a regulated market be completed, for each of the information items, on a case by case basis.

2. The issuer, the offeror or the person asking for admission to trading on a regulated market may omit information items which are not known when the base prospectus is approved and which can only be determined at the time of the individual issue.

3. The use of the combinations provided for in the table in Annex XVIII shall be mandatory when drawing up base prospectuses for the types of securities to which those combinations correspond according to this table.

However, for securities not covered by those combinations further combinations may be used.

4. The final terms attached to a base prospectus shall only contain the information items from the various securities note schedules according to which the base prospectus is drawn up.

5. In addition to the information items set out in the schedules and building blocks referred to in Articles 4 to 20 the following information shall be included in a base prospectus:

(1) indication on the information that will be included in the final terms;

(2) the method of publication of the final terms; if the issuer is not in a position to determine, at the time of the approval of the prospectus, the method of publication of the final terms, an indication of how the public will be informed about which method will be used for the publication of the final terms;

(3) in the case of issues of non equity securities according to point (a) of Article 5(4) of Directive 2003/71/EC, a general description of the programme.

6. Only the following categories of securities may be contained in a base prospectus and its related final terms covering issues of various types of securities:

(1) asset backed securities;

(2) warrants falling under Article 17;

(3) non-equity securities provided for under point (b) of Article 5(4) of Directive 2003/71/EC;

(4) all other non-equity securities including warrants with the exception of those mentioned in (2).

In drawing up a base prospectus the issuer, the offeror or the person asking for admission to trading on a regulated market shall clearly segregate the specific information on each of the different securities included in these categories.

7. Where an event envisaged under Article 16(1) of Directive 2003/71/EC occurs between the time that the base prospectus has been approved and the final closing of the offer of each issue of securities under the base prospectus or, as the case may be, the time that trading on a regulated market of those securities begins, the issuer, the offeror or the person asking for admission to trading on a regulated market shall publish a supplement prior to the final closing of the offer or the admission of those securities to trading.

[11.423]
Article 23
Adaptations to the minimum information given in prospectuses and base prospectuses

1. Notwithstanding Articles 3 second paragraph and 22(1) second subparagraph, where the issuer's activities fall under one of the categories included in Annex XIX, the competent authority of the home Member State, taking into consideration the specific nature of the activities involved, may ask for adapted information, in addition to the information items included in the schedules and building blocks set out in Articles 4 to 20, including, where appropriate, a valuation or other expert's report on the assets of the issuer, in order to comply with the obligation referred to in Article 5(1) of Directive 2003/71/EC. The competent authority shall forthwith inform the Commission thereof.

In order to obtain the inclusion of a new category in Annex XIX a Member State shall notify its request to the Commission. The Commission shall update this list following the Committee procedure provided for in Article 24 of Directive 2003/71/EC.

2.   By way of derogation of Articles 3 to 22, where an issuer, an offeror or a person asking for admission to trading on a regulated market applies for approval of a prospectus or a base prospectus for a security which is not the same but comparable to the various types of securities mentioned in the table of combinations set out in Annex XVIII, the issuer, the offeror or the person asking for admission to trading on a regulated market shall add the relevant information items from another securities note schedule provided for in Articles 4 to 20 to the main securities note schedule chosen. This addition shall be done in accordance with the main characteristics of the securities being offered to the public or admitted to trading on a regulated market.

3.   By way of derogation of Articles 3 to 22, where an issuer, an offeror or a person asking for admission to trading on a regulated market applies for approval of a prospectus or a base prospectus for a new type of security, the issuer, the offeror or the person asking for admission to trading on a regulated market shall notify a draft prospectus or base prospectus to the competent authority of the home Member State.

The competent authority shall decide, in consultation with the issuer, the offeror or the person asking for admission to trading on a regulated market, what information shall be included in the prospectus or base prospectus in order to comply with the obligation referred to in Article 5(1) of Directive 2003/71/EC. The competent authority shall forthwith inform the Commission thereof.

The derogation referred to in the first subparagraph shall only apply in case of a new type of security which has features completely different from the various types of securities mentioned in Annex XVIII, if the characteristics of this new security are such that a combination of the different information items referred to in the schedules and building blocks provided for in Articles 4 to 20 is not pertinent.

4.   By way of derogation of Articles 3 to 22, in the cases where one of the information items required in one of the schedules or building blocks referred to in 4 to 20 or equivalent information is not pertinent to the issuer, to the offer or to the securities to which the prospectus relates, that information may be omitted.

[11.424]
Article 24
Content of the summary of prospectus and base prospectus
The issuer, the offeror or the person asking for admission to trading on a regulated market shall determine on its own the detailed content of the summary to the prospectus or base prospectus referred to in Article 5(2) of Directive 2003/71/EC.

CHAPTER III
FORMAT OF THE PROSPECTUS, BASE PROSPECTUS
AND SUPPLEMENTS

[11.425]
Article 25
Format of the prospectus
1.   Where an issuer, an offeror or a person asking for the admission to trading on a regulated market chooses, according to Article 5(3) of Directive 2003/71/EC to draw up a prospectus as a single document, the prospectus shall be composed of the following parts in the following order:

    (1)   a clear and detailed table of contents;
    (2)   the summary provided for in Article 5 (2) of Directive 2003/71/EC;
    (3)   the risk factors linked to the issuer and the type of security covered by the issue;
    (4)   the other information items included in the schedules and building blocks according to which the prospectus is drawn up.

2.   Where an issuer, an offeror or a person asking for the admission to trading on a regulated market chooses, according to in Article 5(3) of Directive 2003/71/EC, to draw up a prospectus composed of separate documents, the securities note and the registration document shall be each composed of the following parts in the following order:

    (1)   a clear and detailed table of content;
    (2)   as the case may be, the risk factors linked to the issuer and the type of security covered by the issue;
    (3)   the other information items included in the schedules and building blocks according to which the prospectus is drawn up.

3.   In the cases mentioned in paragraphs 1 and 2, the issuer, the offeror or the person asking for admission to trading on a regulated market shall be free in defining the order in the presentation of the required information items included in the schedules and building blocks according to which the prospectus is drawn up.

4.   Where the order of the items does not coincide with the order of the information provided for in the schedules and building blocks according to which the prospectus is drawn up, the competent authority of the home Member State may ask the issuer, the offeror or the person asking for the

Part 11   EU Legislation

admission to trading on a regulated market to provide a cross reference list for the purpose of checking the prospectus before its approval. Such list shall identify the pages where each item can be found in the prospectus.

5. Where the summary of a prospectus must be supplemented according to Article 16(1) of Directive 2003/71/EC, the issuer, the offeror or the person asking for admission to trading on a regulated market shall decide on a case-by-case basis whether to integrate the new information in the original summary by producing a new summary, or to produce a supplement to the summary.

If the new information is integrated in the original summary, the issuer, the offeror or the person asking for admission to trading on a regulated market shall ensure that investors can easily identify the changes, in particular by way of footnotes.

[11.426]
Article 26
Format of the base prospectus and its related final terms
1. Where an issuer, an offeror or a person asking for the admission to trading on a regulated market chooses, according to Article 5 (4) of Directive 2003/71/EC to draw up a base prospectus, the base prospectus shall be composed of the following parts in the following order:
(1) a clear and detailed table of contents;
(2) the summary provided for in Article 5 (2) of Directive 2003/71/EC;
(3) the risk factors linked to the issuer and the type of security or securities covered by the issue(s);
(4) the other information items included in the schedules and building blocks according to which the prospectus is drawn up.
2. Notwithstanding paragraph 1, the issuer, the offeror or the person asking for admission to trading on a regulated market shall be free in defining the order in the presentation of the required information items included in the schedules and building blocks according to which the prospectus is drawn up. The information on the different securities contained in the base prospectus shall be clearly segregated.
3. Where the order of the items does not coincide with the order of the information provided for by the schedules and building blocks according to which the prospectus is drawn up, the home competent authority may ask the issuer, the offeror or the person asking for admission to trading on a regulated market to provide a cross reference list for the purpose of checking the prospectus before its approval. Such list should identify the pages where each item can be found in the prospectus.
4. In case the issuer, the offeror or the person asking for admission to trading on a regulated market has previously filed a registration document for a particular type of security and, at a later stage, chooses to draw up base prospectus in conformity with the conditions provided for in points (a) and (b) of Article 5(4) of Directive 2003/71/EC, the base prospectus shall contain:
(1) the information contained in the previously or simultaneously filed and approved registration document which shall be incorporated by reference, following the conditions provided for in Article 28 of this Regulation;
(2) the information which would otherwise be contained in the relevant securities note less the final terms where the final terms are not included in the base prospectus.
5. The final terms attached to a base prospectus shall be presented in the form of a separate document containing only the final terms or by inclusion of the final terms into the base prospectus.

In the case that the final terms are included in a separate document containing only the final terms, they may replicate some information which has been included in the approved base prospectus according to the relevant securities note schedule that has been used for drawing up the base prospectus. In this case the final terms have to be presented in such a way that they can be easily identified as such.

A clear and prominent statement shall be inserted in the final terms indicating that the full information on the issuer and on the offer is only available on the basis of the combination of base prospectus and final terms and where the base prospectus is available.
6. Where a base prospectus relates to different securities, the issuer, the offeror or the person asking for admission to trading on a regulated market shall include a single summary in the base prospectus for all securities. The information on the different securities contained in the summary, however, shall be clearly segregated.
7. Where the summary of a base prospectus must be supplemented according to Article 16(1) of Directive 2003/71/EC, the issuer, the offeror or the person asking for admission to trading on a regulated market shall decide on a case-by-case basis whether to integrate the new information in the original summary by producing a new summary, or by producing a supplement to the summary.

If the new information is integrated in the original summary of the base prospectus by producing a new summary, the issuer, the offeror or the person asking for admission to trading on a regulated market shall ensure that investors can easily identify the changes, in particular by way of footnotes.
8. Issuers, offerors or persons asking for admission to trading on a regulated market may compile in one single document two or more different base prospectuses.

CHAPTER IV
INFORMATION AND INCORPORATION BY REFERENCE

[11.427]
Article 27
Publication of the document referred to in Article 10(1) of Directive 2003/71/EC
1.   The document referred to in Article 10(1) of Directive 2003/71/EC shall be made available to the public, at the choice of the issuer, the offeror or the person asking for admission to trading on a regulated market, through one of the means permitted under Article 14 of that Directive in the home Member State of the issuer.
2.   The document shall be filed with the competent authority of the home Member State and made available to the public at the latest 20 working days after the publication of the annual financial statements in the home Member State.
3.   The document shall include a statement indicating that some information may be out-of-date, if such is the case.

[11.428]
Article 28
Arrangements for incorporation by reference
1.   Information may be incorporated by reference in a prospectus or base prospectus, notably if it is contained in one the following documents:
   (1)   annual and interim financial information;
   (2)   documents prepared on the occasion of a specific transaction such as a merger or de-merger;
   (3)   audit reports and financial statements;
   (4)   memorandum and articles of association;
   (5)   earlier approved and published prospectuses and/or base prospectuses;
   (6)   regulated information;
   (7)   circulars to security holders.
2.   The documents containing information that may be incorporated by reference in a prospectus or base prospectus or in the documents composing it shall be drawn up following the provisions of Article 19 of Directive 2003/71/EC.
3.   If a document which may be incorporated by reference contains information which has undergone material changes, the prospectus or base prospectus shall clearly state such a circumstance and shall give the updated information.
4.   The issuer, the offeror or the person asking for admission to trading on a regulated market may incorporate information in a prospectus or base prospectus by making reference only to certain parts of a document, provided that it states that the non-incorporated parts are either not relevant for the investor or covered elsewhere in the prospectus.
5.   When incorporating information by reference, issuers, offerors or persons asking for admission to trading on a regulated market shall endeavour not to endanger investor protection in terms of comprehensibility and accessibility of the information.

CHAPTER V
PUBLICATION AND DISSEMINATION OF ADVERTISEMENTS

[11.429]
Article 29
Publication in electronic form
1.   The publication of the prospectus or base prospectus in electronic form, either pursuant to points (c) (d) and (e) of Article 14(2) of Directive 2003/71/EC, or as an additional means of availability, shall be subject to the following requirements:
   (1)   the prospectus or base prospectus shall be easily accessible when entering the web-site;
   (2)   the file format shall be such that the prospectus or base prospectus cannot be modified;
   (3)   the prospectus or base prospectus shall not contain hyper-links, with exception of links to the electronic addresses where information incorporated by reference is available;
   (4)   the investors shall have the possibility of downloading and printing the prospectus or base prospectus.
The exception referred to in point 3 of the first subparagraph shall only be valid for documents incorporated by reference; those documents shall be available with easy and immediate technical arrangements.
2.   If a prospectus or base prospectus for offer of securities to the public is made available on the web-sites of issuers and financial intermediaries or of regulated markets, these shall take measures, to avoid targeting residents in Members States or third countries where the offer of securities to the public does not take place, such as the insertion of a disclaimer as to who are the addressees of the offer.

Part 11   EU Legislation

[11.430]
Article 30
Publication in newspapers
1.   In order to comply with point (a) of Article 14(2) of Directive 2003/71/EC the publication of a prospectus or a base prospectus shall be made in a general or financial information newspaper having national or supra-regional scope;
2.   If the competent authority is of the opinion that the newspaper chosen for publication does not comply with the requirements set out in paragraph 1, it shall determine a newspaper whose circulation is deemed appropriate for this purpose taking into account, in particular, the geographic area, number of inhabitants and reading habits in each Member State.

[11.431]
Article 31
Publication of the notice
1.   If a Member State makes use of the option, referred to in Article 14(3) of Directive 2003/71/EC, to require the publication of a notice stating how the prospectus or base prospectus has been made available and where it can be obtained by the public, that notice shall be published in a newspaper that fulfils the requirements for publication of prospectuses according to Article 30 of this Regulation.
   If the notice relates to a prospectus or base prospectus published for the only purpose of admission of securities to trading on a regulated market where securities of the same class are already admitted, it may alternatively be inserted in the gazette of that regulated market, irrespective of whether that gazette is in paper copy or electronic form.
2.   The notice shall be published no later than the next working day following the date of publication of the prospectus or base prospectus pursuant to Article 14(1) of Directive 2003/71/EC.
3.   The notice shall contain the following information:
   (1)   the identification of the issuer;
   (2)   the type, class and amount of the securities to be offered and/or in respect of which admission to trading is sought, provided that these elements are known at the time of the publication of the notice;
   (3)   the intended time schedule of the offer/admission to trading;
   (4)   a statement that a prospectus or base prospectus has been published and where it can be obtained;
   (5)   if the prospectus or base prospectus has been published in a printed form, the addresses where and the period of time during which such printed forms are available to the public;
   (6)   if the prospectus or base prospectus has been published in electronic form, the addresses to which investors shall refer to ask for a paper copy;
   (7)   the date of the notice.

[11.432]
Article 32
List of approved prospectuses
The list of the approved prospectuses and base prospectuses published on the web-site of the competent authority, in accordance with Article 14(4) of Directive 2003/71/EC, shall mention how such prospectuses have been made available and where they can be obtained.

[11.433]
Article 33
Publication of the final terms of base prospectuses
The publication method for final terms related to a base prospectus does not have to be the same as the one used for the base prospectus as long as the publication method used is one of the publication methods indicated in Article 14 of the Directive 2003/71/EC.

[11.434]
Article 34
Dissemination of advertisements
Advertisements related to an offer to the public of securities or to an admission to trading on a regulated market may be disseminated to the public by interested parties, such as issuer, offeror or person asking for admission, the financial intermediaries that participate in the placing and/or underwriting of securities, notably by one of the following means of communication:
   (1)   addressed or unaddressed printed matter;
   (2)   electronic message or advertisement received via a mobile telephone or pager;
   (3)   standard letter;
   (4)   Press advertising with or without order form;
   (5)   catalogue;
   (6)   telephone with or without human intervention;
   (7)   seminars and presentations;
   (8)   radio;
   (9)   videophone;

(10) videotext;
(11) electronic mail;
(12) facsimile machine (fax);
(13) television;
(14) notice;
(15) bill;
(16) poster;
(17) brochure;
(18) web posting including internet banners.

CHAPTER VI
TRANSITIONAL AND FINAL PROVISIONS

[11.435]
Article 35
Historical financial information
1. The obligation for Community issuers to restate in a prospectus historical financial information according to Regulation (EC) No 1606/2002, set out in Annex I item 20.1, Annex IV item 13.1, Annex VII items 8.2, Annex X items 20.1 and Annex XI item 11.1 shall not apply to any period earlier than 1 January 2004 or, where an issuer has securities admitted to trading on a regulated market on 1 July 2005, until the issuer has published its first consolidated annual accounts with accordance with Regulation (EC) No 1606/2002.
2. Where a Community issuer is subject to transitional national provisions adopted pursuant Article 9 of Regulation (EC) No 1606/2002, the obligation to restate in a prospectus historical financial information does not apply to any period earlier than 1 January 2006 or, where an issuer has securities admitted to trading on a regulated market on 1 July 2005, until the issuer has published its first consolidated annual accounts with accordance with Regulation (EC) No 1606/2002.
3. Until 1 January 2007 the obligation to restate in a prospectus historical financial information according to Regulation (EC) No 1606/2002, set out in Annex I item 20.1, Annex IV item 13.1, Annex VII items 8.2, Annex X items 20.1 and Annex XI item 11.1 shall not apply to issuers from third countries:
   (1) who have their securities admitted to trading on a regulated market on 1 January 2007; and
   (2) who have presented and prepared historical financial information according to the national accounting standards of a third country.
In this case, historical financial information shall be accompanied with more detailed and/or additional information if the financial statements included in the prospectus do not give a true and fair view of the issuer's assets and liabilities, financial position and profit and loss.
4. Third country issuers having prepared historical financial information according to internationally accepted standards as referred to in Article 9 of Regulation (EC) No 1606/2002 may use that information in any prospectus filed before 1 January 2007, without being subject to restatement obligations.
[5. From 1 January 2009, third country issuers shall present their historical financial information in accordance either with one of the following accounting standards:
   (a) International Financial Reporting Standards adopted pursuant to Regulation (EC) No 1606/2002;
   (b) International Financial Reporting Standards provided that the notes to the audited financial statements that form part of the historical financial information contain an explicit and unreserved statement that these financial statements comply with International Financial Reporting Standards in accordance with IAS 1 Presentation of Financial Statements;
   (c) Generally Accepted Accounting Principles of Japan;
   (d) Generally Accepted Accounting Principles of the United States of America.
5a. Third country issuers are not subject to a requirement, under Annex I, item 20.1; Annex IV, item 13.1; Annex VII, item 8.2; Annex X, item 20.1 or Annex XI, item 11.1, to restate historical financial information, included in a prospectus and relevant for the financial years prior to financial years starting on or after 1 January 2012, or to a requirement under Annex VII, item 8.2.bis; Annex IX, item 11.1; or Annex X, item 20.1.bis, to provide a narrative description of the differences between International Financial Reporting Standards adopted pursuant to Regulation (EC) No 1606/2002 and the accounting principles in accordance with which such information is drawn up relating to the financial years prior to financial years starting on or after 1 January 2012, provided that the historical financial information is prepared in accordance with the Generally Accepted Accounting Principles of the People's Republic of China, Canada, the Republic of Korea or the Republic of India.]
[5b.–5e.   . . .]
6. The provisions of this Article shall also apply to Annex VI, item 3.

NOTES
  Paras 5, 5a: substituted by Commission Regulation 1289/2008/EC, Art 1(1), as from 1 January 2009 (para 5a was previously inserted by Commission Regulation 1787/2006/EC, Art 1, as from 8 December 2006).

Paras 5b–5e: inserted by Commission Regulation 1787/2006/EC, Art 1, as from 8 December 2006, and repealed by Commission Regulation 1289/2008/EC, Art 1(2), as from 1 January 2009.

[11.436]
Article 36
Entry into force
This Regulation shall enter into force in Member States on the twentieth day after its publication in the *Official Journal of the European Union.*
   It shall apply from 1 July 2005.
   This Regulation shall be binding in its entirety and directly applicable in all Member States.

ANNEXES

ANNEX I
MINIMUM DISCLOSURE REQUIREMENTS FOR THE SHARE REGISTRATION DOCUMENT (SCHEDULE)

[11.437]
1. Persons responsible
1.1.   All persons responsible for the information given in the Registration Document and, as the case may be, for certain parts of it, with, in the latter case, an indication of such parts. In the case of natural persons including members of the issuer's administrative, management or supervisory bodies indicate the name and function of the person; in case of legal persons indicate the name and registered office.
1.2.   A declaration by those responsible for the registration document that, having taken all reasonable care to ensure that such is the case, the information contained in the registration document is, to the best of their knowledge, in accordance with the facts and contains no omission likely to affect its import. As the case may be, a declaration by those responsible for certain parts of the registration document that, having taken all reasonable care to ensure that such is the case, the information contained in the part of the registration document for which they are responsible is, to the best of their knowledge, in accordance with the facts and contains no omission likely to affect its import.

2. Statutory auditors
2.1.   Names and addresses of the issuer's auditors for the period covered by the historical financial information (together with their membership in a professional body).
2.2.   If auditors have resigned, been removed or not been re-appointed during the period covered by the historical financial information, indicate details if material.

3. Selected financial information
3.1.   Selected historical financial information regarding the issuer, presented for each financial year for the period covered by the historical financial information, and any subsequent interim financial period, in the same currency as the financial information.
   The selected historical financial information must provide the key figures that summarise the financial condition of the issuer.
3.2.   If selected financial information for interim periods is provided, comparative data from the same period in the prior financial year must also be provided, except that the requirement for comparative balance sheet information is satisfied by presenting the year end balance sheet information.

4. Risk factors
Prominent disclosure of risk factors that are specific to the issuer or its industry in a section headed "Risk Factors".

5. Information about the issuer
5.1.   *History and development of the issuer*
5.1.1.   The legal and commercial name of the issuer
5.1.2.   The place of registration of the issuer and its registration number
5.1.3.   The date of incorporation and the length of life of the issuer, except where indefinite
5.1.4.   The domicile and legal form of the issuer, the legislation under which the issuer operates, its country of incorporation, and the address and telephone number of its registered office (or principal place of business if different from its registered office)
5.1.5.   The important events in the development of the issuer's business.
5.2.   *Investments*
5.2.1.   A description, (including the amount) of the issuer's principal investments for each financial year for the period covered by the historical financial information up to the date of the registration document

5.2.2.   A description of the issuer's principal investments that are in progress, including the geographic distribution of these investments (home and abroad) and the method of financing (internal or external)

5.2.3.   Information concerning the issuer's principal future investments on which its management bodies have already made firm commitments.

6.   Business overview

6.1.   *Principal Activities*

6.1.1.   A description of, and key factors relating to, the nature of the issuer's operations and its principal activities, stating the main categories of products sold and/or services performed for each financial year for the period covered by the historical financial information; and

6.1.2.   An indication of any significant new products and/or services that have been introduced and, to the extent the development of new products or services has been publicly disclosed, give the status of development.

6.2.   *Principal Markets*

A description of the principal markets in which the issuer competes, including a breakdown of total revenues by category of activity and geographic market for each financial year for the period covered by the historical financial information.

6.3.   Where the information given pursuant to items 6.1 and 6.2 has been influenced by exceptional factors, mention that fact.

6.4.   If material to the issuer's business or profitability, a summary information regarding the extent to which the issuer is dependent, on patents or licences, industrial, commercial or financial contracts or new manufacturing processes.

6.5.   The basis for any statements made by the issuer regarding its competitive position.

7.   Organisational structure

7.1.   If the issuer is part of a group, a brief description of the group and the issuer's position within the group.

7.2.   A list of the issuer's significant subsidiaries, including name, country of incorporation or residence, proportion of ownership interest and, if different, proportion of voting power held.

8.   Property, plants and equipment

8.1.   Information regarding any existing or planned material tangible fixed assets, including leased properties, and any major encumbrances thereon.

8.2.   A description of any environmental issues that may affect the issuer's utilisation of the tangible fixed assets.

9.   Operating and financial review

9.1.   *Financial condition*

To the extent not covered elsewhere in the registration document, provide a description of the issuer's financial condition, changes in financial condition and results of operations for each year and interim period, for which historical financial information is required, including the causes of material changes from year to year in the financial information to the extent necessary for an understanding of the issuer's business as a whole.

9.2.   *Operating results*

9.2.1.   Information regarding significant factors, including unusual or infrequent events or new developments, materially affecting the issuer's income from operations, indicating the extent to which income was so affected.

9.2.2.   Where the financial statements disclose material changes in net sales or revenues, provide a narrative discussion of the reasons for such changes.

9.2.3.   Information regarding any governmental, economic, fiscal, monetary or political policies or factors that have materially affected, or could materially affect, directly or indirectly, the issuer's operations.

10.   Capital resources

10.1.   Information concerning the issuer's capital resources (both short and long term);

10.2.   An explanation of the sources and amounts of and a narrative description of the issuer's cash flows;

10.3.   Information on the borrowing requirements and funding structure of the issuer;

10.4.   Information regarding any restrictions on the use of capital resources that have materially affected, or could materially affect, directly or indirectly, the issuer's operations.

10.5.   Information regarding the anticipated sources of funds needed to fulfil commitments referred to in items 5.2.3 and 8.1.

11. Research and development, patents and licences

Where material, provide a description of the issuer's research and development policies for each financial year for the period covered by the historical financial information, including the amount spent on issuer-sponsored research and development activities.

12. Trend information

12.1. The most significant recent trends in production, sales and inventory, and costs and selling prices since the end of the last financial year to the date of the registration document.

12.2. Information on any known trends, uncertainties, demands, commitments or events that are reasonably likely to have a material effect on the issuer's prospects for at least the current financial year.

13. Profit forecasts or estimates

If an issuer chooses to include a profit forecast or a profit estimate the registration document must contain the information set out in items 13.1 and 13.2:

13.1. A statement setting out the principal assumptions upon which the issuer has based its forecast, or estimate.

There must be a clear distinction between assumptions about factors which the members of the administrative, management or supervisory bodies can influence and assumptions about factors which are exclusively outside the influence of the members of the administrative, management or supervisory bodies; the assumptions must be readily understandable by investors, be specific and precise and not relate to the general accuracy of the estimates underlying the forecast.

13.2. A report prepared by independent accountants or auditors stating that in the opinion of the independent accountants or auditors the forecast or estimate has been properly compiled on the basis stated and that the basis of accounting used for the profit forecast or estimate is consistent with the accounting policies of the issuer.

13.3. The profit forecast or estimate must be prepared on a basis comparable with the historical financial information.

13.4. If a profit forecast in a prospectus has been published which is still outstanding, then provide a statement setting out whether or not that forecast is still correct as at the time of the registration document, and an explanation of why such forecast is no longer valid if that is the case.

14. Administrative, management, and supervisory bodies and senior management

14.1. Names, business addresses and functions in the issuer of the following persons and an indication of the principal activities performed by them outside that issuer where these are significant with respect to that issuer:

(a) members of the administrative, management or supervisory bodies;

(b) partners with unlimited liability, in the case of a limited partnership with a share capital;

(c) founders, if the issuer has been established for fewer than five years; and

(d) any senior manager who is relevant to establishing that the issuer has the appropriate expertise and experience for the management of the issuer's business.

The nature of any family relationship between any of those persons.

In the case of each member of the administrative, management or supervisory bodies of the issuer and of each person mentioned in points (b) and (d) of the first subparagraph, details of that person's relevant management expertise and experience and the following information:

(a) the names of all companies and partnerships of which such person has been a member of the administrative, management or supervisory bodies or partner at any time in the previous five years, indicating whether or not the individual is still a member of the administrative, management or supervisory bodies or partner. It is not necessary to list all the subsidiaries of an issuer of which the person is also a member of the administrative, management or supervisory bodies;

(b) any convictions in relation to fraudulent offences for at least the previous five years;

(c) details of any bankruptcies, receiverships or liquidations with which a person described in (a) and (d) of the first subparagraph who was acting in the capacity of any of the positions set out in (a) and (d) of the first subparagraph was associated for at least the previous five years;

(d) details of any official public incrimination and/or sanctions of such person by statutory or regulatory authorities (including designated professional bodies) and whether such person has ever been disqualified by a court from acting as a member of the administrative, management or supervisory bodies of an issuer or from acting in the management or conduct of the affairs of any issuer for at least the previous five years.

If there is no such information to be disclosed, a statement to that effect is to be made.

14.2. Administrative, management, and supervisory bodies' and senior management conflicts of interests

Potential conflicts of interests between any duties to the issuer, of the persons referred to in item 14.1 and their private interests and or other duties must be clearly stated. In the event that there are no such conflicts, a statement to that effect must be made.

Any arrangement or understanding with major shareholders, customers, suppliers or others, pursuant to which any person referred to in item 14.1 was selected as a member of the administrative, management or supervisory bodies or member of senior management.

Details of any restrictions agreed by the persons referred to in item 14.1 on the disposal within a certain period of time of their holdings in the issuer's securities.

15. Remuneration and benefits
In relation to the last full financial year for those persons referred to in points (a) and (d) of the first subparagraph of item 14.1:

15.1. The amount of remuneration paid (including any contingent or deferred compensation), and benefits in kind granted to such persons by the issuer and its subsidiaries for services in all capacities to the issuer and its subsidiaries by any person.

That information must be provided on an individual basis unless individual disclosure is not required in the issuer's home country and is not otherwise publicly disclosed by the issuer.

15.2. The total amounts set aside or accrued by the issuer or its subsidiaries to provide pension, retirement or similar benefits.

16. Board practices
In relation to the issuer's last completed financial year, and unless otherwise specified, with respect to those persons referred to in point (a) of the first subparagraph of 14.1:

16.1. Date of expiration of the current term of office, if applicable, and the period during which the person has served in that office.

16.2. Information about members of the administrative, management or supervisory bodies' service contracts with the issuer or any of its subsidiaries providing for benefits upon termination of employment, or an appropriate negative statement.

16.3. Information about the issuer's audit committee and remuneration committee, including the names of committee members and a summary of the terms of reference under which the committee operates.

16.4. A statement as to whether or not the issuer complies with its country's of incorporation corporate governance regime(s). In the event that the issuer does not comply with such a regime, a statement to that effect must be included together with an explanation regarding why the issuer does not comply with such regime.

17. Employees
17.1. Either the number of employees at the end of the period or the average for each financial year for the period covered by the historical financial information up to the date of the registration document (and changes in such numbers, if material) and, if possible and material, a breakdown of persons employed by main category of activity and geographic location. If the issuer employs a significant number of temporary employees, include disclosure of the number of temporary employees on average during the most recent financial year.

17.2. Shareholdings and stock options

With respect to each person referred to in points (a) and (d) of the first subparagraph of item 14.1. provide information as to their share ownership and any options over such shares in the issuer as of the most recent practicable date.

17.3. Description of any arrangements for involving the employees in the capital of the issuer.

18. Major shareholders
18.1. In so far as is known to the issuer, the name of any person other than a member of the administrative, management or supervisory bodies who, directly or indirectly, has an interest in the issuer's capital or voting rights which is notifiable under the issuer's national law, together with the amount of each such person's interest or, if there are no such persons, an appropriate negative statement.

18.2. Whether the issuer's major shareholders have different voting rights, or an appropriate negative statement.

18.3. To the extent known to the issuer, state whether the issuer is directly or indirectly owned or controlled and by whom and describe the nature of such control and describe the measures in place to ensure that such control is not abused.

18.4. A description of any arrangements, known to the issuer, the operation of which may at a subsequent date result in a change in control of the issuer.

Part 11 EU Legislation

19. Related party transactions

Details of related party transactions (which for these purposes are those set out in the Standards adopted according to the Regulation (EC) No 1606/2002), that the issuer has entered into during the period covered by the historical financial information and up to the date of the registration document, must be disclosed in accordance with the respective standard adopted according to Regulation (EC) No 1606/2002 if applicable.

If such standards do not apply to the issuer the following information must be disclosed:

(a)   the nature and extent of any transactions which are – as a single transaction or in their entirety – material to the issuer. Where such related party transactions are not concluded at arm's length provide an explanation of why these transactions were not concluded at arm's length. In the case of outstanding loans including guarantees of any kind indicate the amount outstanding;

(b)   the amount or the percentage to which related party transactions form part of the turnover of the issuer.

20.   Financial information concerning the issuer's assets and liabilities, financial position and profits and losses

20.1.   *Historical financial information*

Audited historical financial information covering the latest three financial years (or such shorter period that the issuer has been in operation), and the audit report in respect of each year. [If the issuer has changed its accounting reference date during the period for which historical financial information is required, the audited historical information shall cover at least 36 months, or the entire period for which the issuer has been in operation, whichever is the shorter.] Such financial information must be prepared according to Regulation (EC) No 1606/2002, or if not applicable to a Member State national accounting standards for issuers from the Community. For third country issuers, such financial information must be prepared according to the international accounting standards adopted pursuant to the procedure of Article 3 of Regulation (EC) No 1606/2002 or to a third country's national accounting standards equivalent to these standards. If such financial information is not equivalent to these standards, it must be presented in the form of restated financial statements.

The last two years audited historical financial information must be presented and prepared in a form consistent with that which will be adopted in the issuer's next published annual financial statements having regard to accounting standards and policies and legislation applicable to such annual financial statements.

If the issuer has been operating in its current sphere of economic activity for less than one year, the audited historical financial information covering that period must be prepared in accordance with the standards applicable to annual financial statements under the Regulation (EC) No 1606/2002, or if not applicable to a Member State national accounting standards where the issuer is an issuer from the Community. For third country issuers, the historical financial information must be prepared according to the international accounting standards adopted pursuant to the procedure of Article 3 of Regulation (EC) No 1606/2002 or to a third country's national accounting standards equivalent to these standards. This historical financial information must be audited.

If the audited financial information is prepared according to national accounting standards, the financial information required under this heading must include at least:

(a)   balance sheet;

(b)   income statement;

(c)   a statement showing either all changes in equity or changes in equity other than those arising from capital transactions with owners and distributions to owners;

(d)   cash flow statement;

(e)   accounting policies and explanatory notes.

The historical annual financial information must be independently audited or reported on as to whether or not, for the purposes of the registration document, it gives a true and fair view, in accordance with auditing standards applicable in a Member State or an equivalent standard.

20.2.   *Pro forma financial information*

In the case of a significant gross change, a description of how the transaction might have affected the assets and liabilities and earnings of the issuer, had the transaction been undertaken at the commencement of the period being reported on or at the date reported.

This requirement will normally be satisfied by the inclusion of pro forma financial information.

This pro forma financial information is to be presented as set out in Annex II and must include the information indicated therein.

Pro forma financial information must be accompanied by a report prepared by independent accountants or auditors.

20.3.   *Financial statements*

If the issuer prepares both own and consolidated annual financial statements, include at least the consolidated annual financial statements in the registration document.

20.4.   *Auditing of historical annual financial information*

20.4.1.   A statement that the historical financial information has been audited. If audit reports on the historical financial information have been refused by the statutory auditors or if they contain qualifications or disclaimers, such refusal or such qualifications or disclaimers must be reproduced in full and the reasons given.

20.4.2.   Indication of other information in the registration document which has been audited by the auditors.

20.4.3.   Where financial data in the registration document is not extracted from the issuer's audited financial statements state the source of the data and state that the data is unaudited.

20.5.   *Age of latest financial information*

20.5.1. The last year of audited financial information may not be older than one of the following:
  (a)   18 months from the date of the registration document if the issuer includes audited interim financial statements in the registration document;
  (b)   15 months from the date of the registration document if the issuer includes unaudited interim financial statements in the registration document.

20.6.   *Interim and other financial information*

20.6.1.   If the issuer has published quarterly or half yearly financial information since the date of its last audited financial statements, these must be included in the registration document. If the quarterly or half yearly financial information has been reviewed or audited, the audit or review report must also be included. If the quarterly or half yearly financial information is unaudited or has not been reviewed state that fact.

20.6.2.   If the registration document is dated more than nine months after the end of the last audited financial year, it must contain interim financial information, which may be unaudited (in which case that fact must be stated) covering at least the first six months of the financial year.

The interim financial information must include comparative statements for the same period in the prior financial year, except that the requirement for comparative balance sheet information may be satisfied by presenting the years end balance sheet.

20.7.   *Dividend policy*

A description of the issuer's policy on dividend distributions and any restrictions thereon.

20.7.1.   The amount of the dividend per share for each financial year for the period covered by the historical financial information adjusted, where the number of shares in the issuer has changed, to make it comparable.

20.8.   *Legal and arbitration proceedings*

Information on any governmental, legal or arbitration proceedings (including any such proceedings which are pending or threatened of which the issuer is aware), during a period covering at least the previous 12 months which may have, or have had in the recent past significant effects on the issuer and/or group's financial position or profitability, or provide an appropriate negative statement.

20.9.   *Significant change in the issuer's financial or trading position*

A description of any significant change in the financial or trading position of the group which has occurred since the end of the last financial period for which either audited financial information or interim financial information have been published, or provide an appropriate negative statement.

21.   Additional information

21.1.   *Share capital*

The following information as of the date of the most recent balance sheet included in the historical financial information:

21.1.1.   The amount of issued capital, and for each class of share capital:
  (a)   the number of shares authorised;
  (b)   the number of shares issued and fully paid and issued but not fully paid;
  (c)   the par value per share, or that the shares have no par value; and
  (d)   a reconciliation of the number of shares outstanding at the beginning and end of the year. If more than 10% of capital has been paid for with assets other than cash within the period covered by the historical financial information, state that fact.

21.1.2.   If there are shares not representing capital, state the number and main characteristics of such shares.

21.1.3.   The number, book value and face value of shares in the issuer held by or on behalf of the issuer itself or by subsidiaries of the issuer.

21.1.4.   The amount of any convertible securities, exchangeable securities or securities with warrants, with an indication of the conditions governing and the procedures for conversion, exchange or subscription.

21.1.5.   Information about and terms of any acquisition rights and or obligations over authorised but unissued capital or an undertaking to increase the capital.

21.1.6.   Information about any capital of any member of the group which is under option or agreed conditionally or unconditionally to be put under option and details of such options including those persons to whom such options relate.

21.1.7.   A history of share capital, highlighting information about any changes, for the period covered by the historical financial information.

21.2.   *Memorandum and Articles of Association*

21.2.1.   A description of the issuer's objects and purposes and where they can be found in the memorandum and articles of association.

21.2.2.   A summary of any provisions of the issuer's articles of association, statutes, charter or bylaws with respect to the members of the administrative, management and supervisory bodies.

21.2.3.   A description of the rights, preferences and restrictions attaching to each class of the existing shares.

21.2.4.   A description of what action is necessary to change the rights of holders of the shares, indicating where the conditions are more significant than is required by law.

21.2.5.   A description of the conditions governing the manner in which annual general meetings and extraordinary general meetings of shareholders are called including the conditions of admission.

21.2.6.   A brief description of any provision of the issuer's articles of association, statutes, charter or bylaws that would have an effect of delaying, deferring or preventing a change in control of the issuer.

21.2.7.   An indication of the articles of association, statutes, charter or bylaw provisions, if any, governing the ownership threshold above which shareholder ownership must be disclosed.

21.2.8.   A description of the conditions imposed by the memorandum and articles of association statutes, charter or bylaw governing changes in the capital, where such conditions are more stringent than is required by law.

22.   Material contracts

A summary of each material contract, other than contracts entered into in the ordinary course of business, to which the issuer or any member of the group is a party, for the two years immediately preceding publication of the registration document.

A summary of any other contract (not being a contract entered into in the ordinary course of business) entered into by any member of the group which contains any provision under which any member of the group has any obligation or entitlement which is material to the group as at the date of the registration document.

23.   Third party information and statement by experts and declarations of any interest

23.1.   Where a statement or report attributed to a person as an expert is included in the registration document, provide such person's name, business address, qualifications and material interest if any in the issuer. If the report has been produced at the issuer's request a statement to the effect that such statement or report is included, in the form and context in which it is included, with the consent of the person who has authorised the contents of that part of the registration document.

23.2.   Where information has been sourced from a third party, provide a confirmation that this information has been accurately reproduced and that as far as the issuer is aware and is able to ascertain from information published by that third party, no facts have been omitted which would render the reproduced information inaccurate or misleading. In addition, identify the source(s) of the information.

24.   Documents on display

A statement that for the life of the registration document the following documents (or copies thereof), where applicable, may be inspected:
   (a)   the memorandum and articles of association of the issuer;
   (b)   all reports, letters, and other documents, historical financial information, valuations and statements prepared by any expert at the issuer's request any part of which is included or referred to in the registration document;
   (c)   the historical financial information of the issuer or, in the case of a group, the historical financial information for the issuer and its subsidiary undertakings for each of the two financial years preceding the publication of the registration document.

An indication of where the documents on display may be inspected, by physical or electronic means.

25.   Information on holdings

Information relating to the undertakings in which the issuer holds a proportion of the capital likely to have a significant effect on the assessment of its own assets and liabilities, financial position or profits and losses.

NOTES

Words in square brackets in item 20.1 inserted by Commission Regulation 211/2007/EC, Art 1(3), as from 1 March 2007.

ANNEX II
PRO FORMA FINANCIAL INFORMATION BUILDING BLOCK

[11.438]

1. The pro forma information must include a description of the transaction, the businesses or entities involved and the period to which it refers, and must clearly state the following:
   (a) the purpose to which it has been prepared;
   (b) the fact that it has been prepared for illustrative purposes only;
   (c) the fact that because of its nature, the pro forma financial information addresses a hypothetical situation and, therefore, does not represent the company's actual financial position or results.

2. In order to present pro forma financial information, a balance sheet and profit and loss account, and accompanying explanatory notes, depending on the circumstances may be included.

3. Pro forma financial information must normally be presented in columnar format, composed of:
   (a) the historical unadjusted information;
   (b) the pro forma adjustments; and
   (c) the resulting pro forma financial information in the final column.
   The sources of the pro forma financial information have to be stated and, if applicable, the financial statements of the acquired businesses or entities must be included in the prospectus

4. The pro forma information must be prepared in a manner consistent with the accounting policies adopted by the issuer in its last or next financial statements and shall identify the following:
   (a) the basis upon which it is prepared;
   (b) the source of each item of information and adjustment.

5. Pro forma information may only be published in respect of:
   (a) the current financial period;
   (b) the most recently completed financial period; and/or
   (c) the most recent interim period for which relevant unadjusted information has been or will be published or is being published in the same document.

6. Pro forma adjustments related to the pro forma financial information must be:
   (a) clearly shown and explained;
   (b) directly attributable to the transaction;
   (c) factually supportable.
   In addition, in respect of a pro forma profit and loss or cash flow statement, they must be clearly identified as to those expected to have a continuing impact on the issuer and those which are not.

7. The report prepared by the independent accountants or auditors must state that in their opinion:
   (a) the pro forma financial information has been properly compiled on the basis stated;
   (b) that basis is consistent with the accounting policies of the issuer.

ANNEX III
MINIMUM DISCLOSURE REQUIREMENTS FOR THE SHARE SECURITIES NOTE
(SCHEDULE)

[11.439]

1. Persons responsible

1.1. All persons responsible for the information given in the prospectus and, as the case may be, for certain parts of it, with, in the latter case, an indication of such parts. In the case of natural persons including members of the issuer's administrative, management or supervisory bodies indicate the name and function of the person; in case of legal persons indicate the name and registered office.

1.2. A declaration by those responsible for the prospectus that, having taken all reasonable care to ensure that such is the case the information contained in the prospectus is, to the best of their knowledge, in accordance with the facts and contains no omission likely to affect its import. As the case may be, declaration by those responsible for certain parts of the prospectus that, having taken all reasonable care to ensure that such is the case the information contained in the part of the prospectus for which they are responsible is, to the best of their knowledge, in accordance with the facts and contains no omission likely to affect its import.

2. Risk factors

Prominent disclosure of risk factors that are material to the securities being offered and/or admitted to trading in order to assess the market risk associated with these securities in a section headed "Risk Factors".

3. Key information

3.1. *Working capital statement*

Statement by the issuer that, in its opinion, the working capital is sufficient for the issuer's present requirements or, if not, how it proposes to provide the additional working capital needed.

3.2. *Capitalisation and indebtedness*

A statement of capitalisation and indebtedness (distinguishing between guaranteed and unguaranteed, secured and unsecured indebtedness) as of a date no earlier than 90 days prior to the date of the document. Indebtedness also includes indirect and contingent indebtedness.

3.3. *Interest of natural and legal persons involved in the issue/offer*

A description of any interest, including conflicting ones that is material to the issue/offer, detailing the persons involved and the nature of the interest.

3.4. *Reasons for the offer and use of proceeds*

Reasons for the offer and, where applicable, the estimated net amount of the proceeds broken into each principal intended use and presented by order of priority of such uses. If the issuer is aware that the anticipated proceeds will not be sufficient to fund all the proposed uses, state the amount and sources of other funds needed. Details must be given with regard to the use of the proceeds, in particular when they are being used to acquire assets, other than in the ordinary course of business, to finance announced acquisitions of other business, or to discharge, reduce or retire indebtedness.

4. Information concerning the securities to be offered/admitted to trading

4.1.   A description of the type and the class of the securities being offered and/or admitted to trading, including the ISIN (international security identification number) or other such security identification code.

4.2.   Legislation under which the securities have been created.

4.3.   An indication whether the securities are in registered form or bearer form and whether the securities are in certificated form or book-entry form. In the latter case, name and address of the entity in charge of keeping the records.

4.4.   Currency of the securities issue.

4.5.   A description of the rights attached to the securities, including any limitations of those rights, and procedure for the exercise of those rights.

    Dividend rights:
— fixed date(s) on which the entitlement arises,
— time limit after which entitlement to dividend lapses and an indication of the person in whose favour the lapse operates,
— dividend restrictions and procedures for non-resident holders,
— rate of dividend or method of its calculation, periodicity and cumulative or non-cumulative nature of payments.

    Voting rights.
    Pre-emption rights in offers for subscription of securities of the same class.
    Right to share in the issuer's profits.
    Rights to share in any surplus in the event of liquidation.
— Redemption provisions.
— Conversion provisions.

4.6.   In the case of new issues, a statement of the resolutions, authorisations and approvals by virtue of which the securities have been or will be created and/or issued.

4.7.   In the case of new issues, the expected issue date of the securities.

4.8.   A description of any restrictions on the free transferability of the securities.

4.9.   An indication of the existence of any mandatory takeover bids and/or squeeze-out and sell-out rules in relation to the securities.

4.10.   An indication of public takeover bids by third parties in respect of the issuer's equity, which have occurred during the last financial year and the current financial year. The price or exchange terms attaching to such offers and the outcome thereof must be stated.

4.11.   In respect of the country of registered office of the issuer and the country(ies) where the offer is being made or admission to trading is being sought:
— information on taxes on the income from the securities withheld at source,
— indication as to whether the issuer assumes responsibility for the withholding of taxes at the source.

5. Terms and conditions of the offer

5.1. *Conditions, offer statistics, expected timetable and action required to apply for the offer*

5.1.1. Conditions to which the offer is subject.

5.1.2. Total amount of the issue/offer, distinguishing the securities offered for sale and those offered for subscription; if the amount is not fixed, description of the arrangements and time for announcing to the public the definitive amount of the offer.

5.1.3. The time period, including any possible amendments, during which the offer will be open and description of the application process.

5.1.4. An indication of when, and under which circumstances, the offer may be revoked or suspended and whether revocation can occur after dealing has begun.

5.1.5. A description of the possibility to reduce subscriptions and the manner for refunding excess amount paid by applicants.

5.1.6. Details of the minimum and/or maximum amount of application (whether in number of securities or aggregate amount to invest).

5.1.7. An indication of the period during which an application may be withdrawn, provided that investors are allowed to withdraw their subscription.

5.1.8. Method and time limits for paying up the securities and for delivery of the securities.

5.1.9. A full description of the manner and date in which results of the offer are to be made public.

5.1.10. The procedure for the exercise of any right of pre-emption, the negotiability of subscription rights and the treatment of subscription rights not exercised.

5.2. *Plan of distribution and allotment*

5.2.1. The various categories of potential investors to which the securities are offered. If the offer is being made simultaneously in the markets of two or more countries and if a tranche has been or is being reserved for certain of these, indicate any such tranche.

5.2.2. To the extent known to the issuer, an indication of whether major shareholders or members of the issuer's management, supervisory or administrative bodies intended to subscribe in the offer, or whether any person intends to subscribe for more than five per cent of the offer.

5.2.3. Pre-allotment disclosure:
- (a) the division into tranches of the offer including the institutional, retail and issuer's employee tranches and any other tranches;
- (b) the conditions under which the clawback may be used, the maximum size of such claw back and any applicable minimum percentages for individual tranches;
- (c) the allotment method or methods to be used for the retail and issuer's employee tranche in the event of an over-subscription of these tranches;
- (d) a description of any pre-determined preferential treatment to be accorded to certain classes of investors or certain affinity groups (including friends and family programmes) in the allotment, the percentage of the offer reserved for such preferential treatment and the criteria for inclusion in such classes or groups;
- (e) whether the treatment of subscriptions or bids to subscribe in the allotment may be determined on the basis of which firm they are made through or by;
- (f) a target minimum individual allotment if any within the retail tranche;
- (g) the conditions for the closing of the offer as well as the date on which the offer may be closed at the earliest;
- (h) whether or not multiple subscriptions are admitted, and where they are not, how any multiple subscriptions will be handled.

5.2.4. Process for notification to applicants of the amount allotted and indication whether dealing may begin before notification is made.

5.2.5. Over-allotment and "green shoe":
- (a) the existence and size of any over-allotment facility and/or "green shoe".
- (b) the existence period of the over-allotment facility and/or "green shoe".
- (c) any conditions for the use of the over-allotment facility or exercise of the "green shoe".

5.3. *Pricing*

5.3.1. An indication of the price at which the securities will be offered. If the price is not known or if there is no established and/or liquid market for the securities, indicate the method for determining the offer price, including a statement as to who has set the criteria or is formally responsible for the determination. Indication of the amount of any expenses and taxes specifically charged to the subscriber or purchaser.

5.3.2. Process for the disclosure of the offer price.

5.3.3. If the issuer's equity holders have pre-emptive purchase rights and this right is restricted or withdrawn, indication of the basis for the issue price if the issue is for cash, together with the reasons for and beneficiaries of such restriction or withdrawal.

Part 11   EU Legislation

5.3.4. Where there is or could be a material disparity between the public offer price and the effective cash cost to members of the administrative, management or supervisory bodies or senior management, or affiliated persons, of securities acquired by them in transactions during the past year, or which they have the right to acquire, include a comparison of the public contribution in the proposed public offer and the effective cash contributions of such persons.

5.4. *Placing and underwriting*

5.4.1. Name and address of the coordinator(s) of the global offer and of single parts of the offer and, to the extend known to the issuer or to the offeror, of the placers in the various countries where the offer takes place.

5.4.2. Name and address of any paying agents and depository agents in each country.

5.4.3. Name and address of the entities agreeing to underwrite the issue on a firm commitment basis, and name and address of the entities agreeing to place the issue without a firm commitment or under "best efforts" arrangements. Indication of the material features of the agreements, including the quotas. Where not all of the issue is underwritten, a statement of the portion not covered. Indication of the overall amount of the underwriting commission and of the placing commission.

5.4.4. When the underwriting agreement has been or will be reached.

6. Admission to trading and dealing arrangements

6.1. An indication as to whether the securities offered are or will be the object of an application for admission to trading, with a view to their distribution in a regulated market or other equivalent markets with indication of the markets in question. This circumstance must be mentioned, without creating the impression that the admission to trading will necessarily be approved. If known, the earliest dates on which the securities will be admitted to trading.

6.2. All the regulated markets or equivalent markets on which, to the knowledge of the issuer, securities of the same class of the securities to be offered or admitted to trading are already admitted to trading.

6.3. If simultaneously or almost simultaneously with the creation of the securities for which admission to a regulated market is being sought securities of the same class are subscribed for or placed privately or if securities of other classes are created for public or private placing, give details of the nature of such operations and of the number and characteristics of the securities to which they relate.

6.4. Details of the entities which have a firm commitment to act as intermediaries in secondary trading, providing liquidity through bid and offer rates and description of the main terms of their commitment.

6.5. Stabilisation: where an issuer or a selling shareholder has granted an over-allotment option or it is otherwise proposed that price stabilising activities may be entered into in connection with an offer:

6.5.1. The fact that stabilisation may be undertaken, that there is no assurance that it will be undertaken and that it may be stopped at any time,

6.5.2. The beginning and the end of the period during which stabilisation may occur,

6.5.3. The identity of the stabilisation manager for each relevant jurisdiction unless this is not known at the time of publication,

6.5.4. The fact that stabilisation transactions may result in a market price that is higher than would otherwise prevail.

7. Selling securities holders

7.1. Name and business address of the person or entity offering to sell the securities, the nature of any position office or other material relationship that the selling persons has had within the past three years with the issuer or any of its predecessors or affiliates.

7.2. The number and class of securities being offered by each of the selling security holders.

7.3. Lock-up agreements
The parties involved.
Content and exceptions of the agreement.
Indication of the period of the lock up.

8. Expense of the issue/offer

8.1. The total net proceeds and an estimate of the total expenses of the issue/offer.

9. Dilution

9.1. The amount and percentage of immediate dilution resulting from the offer.

9.2. In the case of a subscription offer to existing equity holders, the amount and percentage of immediate dilution if they do not subscribe to the new offer.

10. Additional information

10.1. If advisors connected with an issue are mentioned in the Securities Note, a statement of the capacity in which the advisors have acted.

10.2. An indication of other information in the Securities Note which has been audited or reviewed by statutory auditors and where auditors have produced a report. Reproduction of the report or, with permission of the competent authority, a summary of the report.

10.3. Where a statement or report attributed to a person as an expert is included in the Securities Note, provide such persons' name, business address, qualifications and material interest if any in the issuer. If the report has been produced at the issuer's request a statement to the effect that such statement or report is included, in the form and context in which it is included, with the consent of the person who has authorised the contents of that part of the Securities Note.

10.4. Where information has been sourced from a third party, provide a confirmation that this information has been accurately reproduced and that as far as the issuer is aware and is able to ascertain from information published by that third party, no facts have been omitted which would render the reproduced information inaccurate or misleading. In addition, identify the source(s) of the information.

ANNEX IV
MINIMUM DISCLOSURE REQUIREMENTS FOR THE DEBT AND DERIVATIVE SECURITIES REGISTRATION DOCUMENT (SCHEDULE)

(Debt and derivative securities with a denomination per unit of less than EUR 50,000)

[11.440]

1. Persons responsible

1.1. All persons responsible for the information given in the registration document and, as the case may be, for certain parts of it, with, in the latter case, an indication of such parts. In the case of natural persons including members of the issuer's administrative, management or supervisory bodies indicate the name and function of the person; in case of legal persons indicate the name and registered office.

1.2. A declaration by those responsible for the registration document that, having taken all reasonable care to ensure that such is the case the information contained in the registration document is, to the best of their knowledge, in accordance with the facts and contains no omission likely to affect its import. As the case may be, declaration by those responsible for certain parts of the registration document that, having taken all reasonable care to ensure that such is the case, the information contained in the part of the registration document for which they are responsible is, to the best of their knowledge, in accordance with the facts and contains no omission likely to affect its import.

2. Statutory auditors

2.1. Names and addresses of the issuer's auditors for the period covered by the historical financial information (together with their membership in a professional body).

2.2. If auditors have resigned, been removed or not been re-appointed during the period covered by the historical financial information, details if material.

3. Selected financial information

3.1. Selected historical financial information regarding the issuer, presented, for each financial year for the period covered by the historical financial information, and any subsequent interim financial period, in the same currency as the financial information.

The selected historical financial information must provide key figures that summarise the financial condition of the issuer.

3.2. If selected financial information for interim periods is provided, comparative data from the same period in the prior financial year must also be provided, except that the requirement for comparative balance sheet data is satisfied by presenting the year end balance sheet information.

4. Risk factors

Prominent disclosure of risk factors that may affect the issuer's ability to fulfil its obligations under the securities to investors in a section headed "Risk Factors".

5. Information about the issuer

5.1. *History and development of the issuer*

5.1.1. the legal and commercial name of the issuer;

5.1.2. the place of registration of the issuer and its registration number;

5.1.3. the date of incorporation and the length of life of the issuer, except where indefinite;

5.1.4. the domicile and legal form of the issuer, the legislation under which the issuer operates, its country of incorporation, and the address and telephone number of its registered office (or principal place of business if different from its registered office);

5.1.5. any recent events particular to the issuer which are to a material extent relevant to the evaluation of the issuer's solvency.

5.2. *Investments*

5.2.1. A description of the principal investments made since the date of the last published financial statements.

5.2.2. Information concerning the issuer's principal future investments, on which its management bodies have already made firm commitments.

5.2.3. Information regarding the anticipated sources of funds needed to fulfil commitments referred to in item 5.2.2.

6. Business overview

6.1. *Principal activities*

6.1.1. A description of the issuer's principal activities stating the main categories of products sold and/or services performed; and

6.1.2. an indication of any significant new products and/or activities.

6.2. *Principal markets*

A brief description of the principal markets in which the issuer competes.

6.3. The basis for any statements made by the issuer regarding its competitive position.

7. Organisational structure

7.1. If the issuer is part of a group, a brief description of the group and of the issuer's position within it.

7.2. If the issuer is dependent upon other entities within the group, this must be clearly stated together with an explanation of this dependence.

8. Trend information

8.1. Include a statement that there has been no material adverse change in the prospects of the issuer since the date of its last published audited financial statements.

In the event that the issuer is unable to make such a statement, provide details of this material adverse change.

8.2. Information on any known trends, uncertainties, demands, commitments or events that are reasonably likely to have a material effect on the issuer's prospects for at least the current financial year.

9. Profit forecasts or estimates

If an issuer chooses to include a profit forecast or a profit estimate, the registration document must contain the information items 9.1 and 9.2:

9.1. A statement setting out the principal assumptions upon which the issuer has based its forecast, or estimate.

There must be a clear distinction between assumptions about factors which the members of the administrative, management or supervisory bodies can influence and assumptions about factors which are exclusively outside the influence of the members of the administrative, management or supervisory bodies; the assumptions must be readily understandable by investors, be specific and precise and not relate to the general accuracy of the estimates underlying the forecast.

9.2. A report prepared by independent accountants or auditors must be included stating that in the opinion of the independent accountants or auditors the forecast or estimate has been properly compiled on the basis stated and that the basis of accounting used for the profit forecast or estimate is consistent with the accounting policies of the issuer.

9.3. The profit forecast or estimate must be prepared on a basis comparable with the historical financial information.

10. Administrative, management, and supervisory bodies

10.1. Names, business addresses and functions in the issuer of the following persons, and an indication of the principal activities performed by them outside the issuer where these are significant with respect to that issuer:

    (a)   members of the administrative, management or supervisory bodies;

    (b)   partners with unlimited liability, in the case of a limited partnership with a share capital.

10.2. Administrative, management, and supervisory bodies' conflicts of interests

Potential conflicts of interests between any duties to the issuing entity of the persons referred to in item 10.1 and their private interests and or other duties must be clearly stated. In the event that there are no such conflicts, make a statement to that effect.

11. Board practices

11.1. Details relating to the issuer's audit committee, including the names of committee members and a summary of the terms of reference under which the committee operates.

11.2.   A statement as to whether or not the issuer complies with its country's of incorporation corporate governance regime(s). In the event that the issuer does not comply with such a regime a statement to that effect must be included together with an explanation regarding why the issuer does not comply with such regime.

12.   Major shareholders

12.1.   To the extent known to the issuer, state whether the issuer is directly or indirectly owned or controlled and by whom and describe the nature of such control, and describe the measures in place to ensure that such control is not abused.

12.2.   A description of any arrangements, known to the issuer, the operation of which may at a subsequent date result in a change in control of the issuer.

13.   Financial information concerning the issuer's assets and liabilities, financial position and profits and losses

13.1. *Historical financial information*

Audited historical financial information covering the latest 2 financial years (or such shorter period that the issuer has been in operation), and the audit report in respect of each year. [If the issuer has changed its accounting reference date during the period for which historical financial information is required, the audited historical information shall cover at least 24 months, or the entire period for which the issuer has been in operation, whichever is the shorter.] Such financial information must be prepared according to Regulation (EC) No 1606/2002, or if not applicable to a Member States national accounting standards for issuers from the Community. For third country issuers, such financial information must be prepared according to the international accounting standards adopted pursuant to the procedure of Article 3 of Regulation (EC) No 1606/2002 or to a third country's national accounting standards equivalent to these standards. If such financial information is not equivalent to these standards, it must be presented in the form of restated financial statements.

The most recent year's historical financial information must be presented and prepared in a form consistent with that which will be adopted in the issuer's next published annual financial statements having regard to accounting standards and policies and legislation applicable to such annual financial statements.

If the issuer has been operating in its current sphere of economic activity for less than one year, the audited historical financial information covering that period must be prepared in accordance with the standards applicable to annual financial statements under the Regulation (EC) No 1606/2002, or if not applicable to a Member States national accounting standards where the issuer is an issuer from the Community. For third country issuers, the historical financial information must be prepared according to the international accounting standards adopted pursuant to the procedure of Article 3 of Regulation (EC) No 1606/2002 or to a third country's national accounting standards equivalent to these standards. This historical financial information must be audited.

If the audited financial information is prepared according to national accounting standards, the financial information required under this heading must include at least:

    (a)   balance sheet;
    (b)   income statement;
    (c)   cash flow statement; and
    (d)   accounting policies and explanatory notes

The historical annual financial information must have been independently audited or reported on as to whether or not, for the purposes of the registration document, it gives a true and fair view, in accordance with auditing standards applicable in a Member State or an equivalent standard.

13.2. *Financial statements*

If the issuer prepares both own and consolidated financial statements, include at least the consolidated financial statements in the registration document.

13.3. *Auditing of historical annual financial information*

13.3.1.   A statement that the historical financial information has been audited. If audit reports on the historical financial information have been refused by the statutory auditors or if they contain qualifications or disclaimers, such refusal or such qualifications or disclaimers must be reproduced in full and the reasons given.

13.3.2.   An indication of other information in the registration document which has been audited by the auditors.

13.3.3.   Where financial data in the registration document is not extracted from the issuer's audited financial statements state the source of the data and state that the data is unaudited.

13.4. *Age of latest financial information*

13.4.1.   The last year of audited financial information may not be older than 18 months from the date of the registration document.

13.5. *Interim and other financial information*

13.5.1. If the issuer has published quarterly or half yearly financial information since the date of its last audited financial statements, these must be included in the registration document. If the quarterly or half yearly financial information has been reviewed or audited the audit or review report must also be included. If the quarterly or half yearly financial information is unaudited or has not been reviewed state that fact.

13.5.2. If the registration document is dated more than nine months after the end of the last audited financial year, it must contain interim financial information, covering at least the first six months of the financial year. If the interim financial information is un-audited state that fact.

The interim financial information must include comparative statements for the same period in the prior financial year, except that the requirement for comparative balance sheet information may be satisfied by presenting the years end balance sheet.

13.6. *Legal and arbitration proceedings*

Information on any governmental, legal or arbitration proceedings (including any such proceedings which are pending or threatened of which the issuer is aware), during a period covering at least the previous 12 months which may have, or have had in the recent past, significant effects on the issuer and/or group's financial position or profitability, or provide an appropriate negative statement.

13.7. *Significant change in the issuer's financial or trading position*

A description of any significant change in the financial or trading position of the group which has occurred since the end of the last financial period for which either audited financial information or interim financial information have been published, or an appropriate negative statement.

14. Additional information

14.1. *Share capital*

14.1.1. The amount of the issued capital, the number and classes of the shares of which it is composed with details of their principal characteristics, the part of the issued capital still to be paid up, with an indication of the number, or total nominal value, and the type of the shares not yet fully paid up, broken down where applicable according to the extent to which they have been paid up.

14.2. *Memorandum and Articles of Association*

14.2.1. The register and the entry number therein, if applicable, and a description of the issuer's objects and purposes and where they can be found in the memorandum and articles of association.

15. Material contracts

A brief summary of all material contracts that are not entered into in the ordinary course of the issuer's business, which could result in any group member being under an obligation or entitlement that is material to the issuer's ability to meet its obligation to security holders in respect of the securities being issued.

16. Third party information and statement by experts and declarations of any interest

16.1. Where a statement or report attributed to a person as an expert is included in the registration document, provide such person's name, business address, qualifications and material interest if any in the issuer. If the report has been produced at the issuer's request a statement to that effect that such statement or report is included, in the form and context in which it is included, with the consent of that person who has authorised the contents of that part of the registration document.

16.2. Where information has been sourced from a third party, provide a confirmation that this information has been accurately reproduced and that as far as the issuer is aware and is able to ascertain from information published by that third party, no facts have been omitted which would render the reproduced information inaccurate or misleading. In addition, the issuer shall identify the source(s) of the information.

17. Documents on display

A statement that for the life of the registration document the following documents (or copies thereof), where applicable, may be inspected:

(a) the memorandum and articles of association of the issuer;

(b) all reports, letters, and other documents, historical financial information, valuations and statements prepared by any expert at the issuer's request any part of which is included or referred to in the registration document;

(c) the historical financial information of the issuer or, in the case of a group, the historical financial information of the issuer and its subsidiary undertakings for each of the two financial years preceding the publication of the registration document.

An indication of where the documents on display may be inspected, by physical or electronic means.

NOTES
    Words in square brackets in item 13.1 inserted by Commission Regulation 211/2007/EC, Art 1(4), as from 1 March 2007.

ANNEX V
MINIMUM DISCLOSURE REQUIREMENTS FOR THE SECURITIES NOTE RELATED TO DEBT SECURITIES (SCHEDULE)

(Debt securities with a denomination per unit of less than EUR 50,000)

[11.441]
1. Persons responsible

1.1. All persons responsible for the information given in the prospectus and, as the case may be, for certain parts of it, with, in the latter case, an indication of such parts. In the case of natural persons including members of the issuer's administrative, management or supervisory bodies indicate the name and function of the person; in case of legal persons indicate the name and registered office.

1.2. A declaration by those responsible for the prospectus that, having taken all reasonable care to ensure that such is the case, the information contained in the prospectus is, to the best of their knowledge, in accordance with the facts and contains no omission likely to affect its import. As the case may be, declaration by those responsible for certain parts of the prospectus that the information contained in the part of the prospectus for which they are responsible is, to the best of their knowledge, in accordance with the facts and contains no omission likely to affect its import.

2. Risk factors

2.1. Prominent disclosure of risk factors that are material to the securities being offered and/or admitted to trading in order to assess the market risk associated with these securities in a section headed "Risk Factors".

3. Key information

3.1. *Interest of natural and legal persons involved in the issue/offer*
    A description of any interest, including conflicting ones, that is material to the issue/offer, detailing the persons involved and the nature of the interest.

3.2. *Reasons for the offer and use of proceeds*
    Reasons for the offer if different from making profit and/or hedging certain risks. Where applicable, disclosure of the estimated total expenses of the issue/offer and the estimated net amount of the proceeds. These expenses and proceeds shall be broken into each principal intended use and presented by order of priority of such uses. If the issuer is aware that the anticipated proceeds will not be sufficient to fund all the proposed uses, state the amount and sources of other funds needed.

4. Information concerning the securities to be offered/admitted to trading

4.1. A description of the type and the class of the securities being offered and/or admitted to trading, including the ISIN (International Security Identification Number) or other such security identification code.

4.2. Legislation under which the securities have been created.

4.3. An indication of whether the securities are in registered form or bearer form and whether the securities are in certificated form or book-entry form. In the latter case, name and address of the entity in charge of keeping the records.

4.4. Currency of the securities issue.

4.5. Ranking of the securities being offered and/or admitted to trading, including summaries of any clauses that are intended to affect ranking or subordinate the security to any present or future liabilities of the issuer.

4.6. A description of the rights attached to the securities, including any limitations of those rights, and procedure for the exercise of those rights.

4.7. The nominal interest rate and provisions relating to interest payable.
    —   The date from which interest becomes payable and the due dates for interest
    —   The time limit on the validity of claims to interest and repayment of principal.
    Where the rate is not fixed, description of the underlying on which it is based and of the method used to relate the two and an indication where information about the past and the further performance of the underlying and its volatility can be obtained.
    —   A description of any market disruption or settlement disruption events that affect the underlying
    —   Adjustment rules with relation to events concerning the underlying
    —   Name of the calculation agent.

If the security has a derivative component in the interest payment, provide a clear and comprehensive explanation to help investors understand how the value of their investment is affected by the value of the underlying instrument(s), especially under the circumstances when the risks are most evident.

4.8.   Maturity date and arrangements for the amortisation of the loan, including the repayment procedures. Where advance amortisation is contemplated, on the initiative of the issuer or of the holder, it shall be described, stipulating amortisation terms and conditions.

4.9.   An indication of yield. Describe the method whereby that yield is calculated in summary form.

4.10.   Representation of debt security holders including an identification of the organisation representing the investors and provisions applying to such representation. Indication of where the public may have access to the contracts relating to these forms of representation.

4.11.   In the case of new issues, a statement of the resolutions, authorisations and approvals by virtue of which the securities have been or will be created and/or issued.

4.12.   In the case of new issues, the expected issue date of the securities.

4.13.   A description of any restrictions on the free transferability of the securities.

4.14.   In respect of the country of registered office of the issuer and the country(ies) where the offer being made or admission to trading is being sought:
— information on taxes on the income from the securities withheld at source;
— indication as to whether the issuer assumes responsibility for the withholding of taxes at the source.

5.   Terms and conditions of the offer

5.1.   *Conditions, offer statistics, expected timetable and action required to apply for the offer*

5.1.1.   Conditions to which the offer is subject.

5.1.2.   Total amount of the issue/offer; if the amount is not fixed, description of the arrangements and time for announcing to the public the definitive amount of the offer.

5.1.3.   The time period, including any possible amendments, during which the offer will be open and description of the application process.

5.1.4.   A description of the possibility to reduce subscriptions and the manner for refunding excess amount paid by applicants.

5.1.5.   Details of the minimum and/or maximum amount of application, (whether in number of securities or aggregate amount to invest).

5.1.6.   Method and time limits for paying up the securities and for delivery of the securities.

5.1.7.   A full description of the manner and date in which results of the offer are to be made public.

5.1.8.   The procedure for the exercise of any right of pre-emption, the negotiability of subscription rights and the treatment of subscription rights not exercised.

5.2.   *Plan of distribution and allotment*

5.2.1.   The various categories of potential investors to which the securities are offered. If the offer is being made simultaneously in the markets of two or more countries and if a tranche has been or is being reserved for certain of these, indicate any such tranche.

5.2.2.   Process for notification to applicants of the amount allotted and indication whether dealing may begin before notification is made.

5.3.   *Pricing*

5.3.1.   An indication of the expected price at which the securities will be offered or the method of determining the price and the process for its disclosure. Indicate the amount of any expenses and taxes specifically charged to the subscriber or purchaser.

5.4.   *Placing and underwriting*

5.4.1.   Name and address of the co-ordinator(s) of the global offer and of single parts of the offer and, to the extend known to the issuer or to the offeror, of the placers in the various countries where the offer takes place.

5.4.2.   Name and address of any paying agents and depository agents in each country.

5.4.3.   Name and address of the entities agreeing to underwrite the issue on a firm commitment basis, and name and address of the entities agreeing to place the issue without a firm commitment or under "best efforts" arrangements. Indication of the material features of the agreements, including the quotas. Where not all of the issue is underwritten, a statement of the portion not covered. Indication of the overall amount of the underwriting commission and of the placing commission.

5.4.4.   When the underwriting agreement has been or will be reached.

6. Admission to trading and dealing arrangements

6.1. An indication as to whether the securities offered are or will be the object of an application for admission to trading, with a view to their distribution in a regulated market or other equivalent markets with indication of the markets in question. This circumstance must be mentioned, without creating the impression that the admission to trading will necessarily be approved. If known, give the earliest dates on which the securities will be admitted to trading.

6.2. All the regulated markets or equivalent markets on which, to the knowledge of the issuer, securities of the same class of the securities to be offered or admitted to trading are already admitted to trading.

6.3. Name and address of the entities which have a firm commitment to act as intermediaries in secondary trading, providing liquidity through bid and offer rates and description of the main terms of their commitment.

7. Additional information

7.1. If advisors connected with an issue are mentioned in the Securities Note, a statement of the capacity in which the advisors have acted.

7.2. An indication of other information in the Securities Note which has been audited or reviewed by statutory auditors and where auditors have produced a report. Reproduction of the report or, with permission of the competent authority, a summary of the report.

7.3. Where a statement or report attributed to a person as an expert is included in the Securities Note, provide such persons' name, business address, qualifications and material interest if any in the issuer. If the report has been produced at the issuer's request a statement to that effect that such statement or report is included, in the form and context in which it is included, with the consent of that person who has authorised the contents of that part of the Securities Note.

7.4. Where information has been sourced from a third party, provide a confirmation that this information has been accurately reproduced and that as far as the issuer is aware and is able to ascertain from information published by that third party, no facts have been omitted which would render the reproduced information inaccurate or misleading. In addition, identify the source(s) of the information.

7.5. Credit ratings assigned to an issuer or its debt securities at the request or with the co-operation of the issuer in the rating process. A brief explanation of the meaning of the ratings if this has previously been published by the rating provider.

ANNEX VI
MINIMUM DISCLOSURE REQUIREMENTS FOR GUARANTEES
(ADDITIONAL BUILDING BLOCK)

[11.442]
1. Nature of the guarantee

A description of any arrangement intended to ensure that any obligation material to the issue will be duly serviced, whether in the form of guarantee, surety, Keep well Agreement, Mono-line Insurance policy or other equivalent commitment (hereafter referred to generically as "guarantees" and their provider as "guarantor" for convenience).

Without prejudice to the generality of the foregoing, such arrangements encompass commitments to ensure obligations to repay debt securities and/or the payment of interest and the description shall set out how the arrangement is intended to ensure that the guaranteed payments will be duly serviced.

2. Scope of the guarantee

Details shall be disclosed about the terms and conditions and scope of the guarantee. Without prejudice to the generality of the foregoing, these details should cover any conditionality on the application of the guarantee in the event of any default under the terms of the security and the material terms of any mono-line insurance or keep well agreement between the issuer and the guarantor. Details must also be disclosed of any guarantor's power of veto in relation to changes to the security holder's rights, such as is often found in Mono-line Insurance.

3. Information to be disclosed about the guarantor

The guarantor must disclose information about itself as if it were the issuer of that same type of security that is the subject of the guarantee.

4. Documents on display

Indication of the places where the public may have access to the material contracts and other documents relating to the guarantee.

Part 11   EU Legislation

ANNEX VII
MINIMUM DISCLOSURE REQUIREMENTS FOR ASSET BACKED SECURITIES
REGISTRATION DOCUMENT (SCHEDULE)

[11.443]
1. Persons responsible

1.1. All persons responsible for the information given in the registration document and, as the case may be, for certain parts of it, with, in the latter case, an indication of such parts. In the case of natural persons including members of the issuer's administrative, management or supervisory bodies indicate the name and function of the person; in case of legal persons indicate the name and registered office.

1.2. A declaration by those responsible for the registration document that, having taken all reasonable care to ensure that such is the case, the information given in the registration document is, to the best of their knowledge, in accordance with the facts and does not omit anything likely to affect its import. As the case may be, declaration by those responsible for certain parts of the registration document that having taken all reasonable care to ensure that such is the case, the information contained in that part of the registration document for which they are responsible is, to the best of their knowledge, in accordance with the facts and contains no omission likely to affect its import.

2. Statutory auditors

2.1. Names and addresses of the issuer's auditors for the period covered by the historical financial information (together with any membership of any relevant professional body).

3. Risk factors

3.1. The document must prominently disclose risk factors in a section headed "Risk Factors" that are specific to the issuer and its industry.

4. Information about the issuer:

4.1. A statement whether the issuer has been established as a special purpose vehicle or entity for the purpose of issuing asset backed securities;

4.2. The legal and commercial name of the issuer;

4.3. The place of registration of the issuer and its registration number;

4.4. The date of incorporation and the length of life of the issuer, except where indefinite;

4.5. The domicile and legal form of the issuer, the legislation under which the issuer operates its country of incorporation and the address and telephone number of its registered office (or principal place of business if different from its registered office).

4.6. Description of the amount of the issuer's authorised and issued capital and the amount of any capital agreed to be issued, the number and classes of the securities of which it is composed.

5. Business overview

5.1. A brief description of the issuer's principal activities.

5.2. A global overview of the parties to the securitisation program including information on the direct or indirect ownership or control between those parties.

6. Administrative, management and supervisory bodies

6.1. Names, business addresses and functions in the issuer of the following persons, and an indication of the principal activities performed by them outside the issuer where these are significant with respect to that issuer:

    (a)   members of the administrative, management or supervisory bodies;

    (b)   partners with unlimited liability, in the case of a limited partnership with a share capital.

7. Major shareholders

7.1. To the extent known to the issuer, state whether the issuer is directly or indirectly owned or controlled and by whom, and describe the nature of such control and describe the measures in place to ensure that such control is not abused.

8. Financial information concerning the issuer's assets and liabilities, financial position, and profits and losses

8.1. Where, since the date of incorporation or establishment, an issuer has not commenced operations and no financial statements have been made up as at the date of the registration document, a statement to that effect shall be provided in the registration document.

8.2. *Historical financial information*

Where, since the date of incorporation or establishment, an issuer has commenced operations and financial statements have been made up, the registration document must contain audited historical financial information covering the latest 2 financial years (or shorter period that the issuer has been in operation) and the audit report in respect of each year. [If the issuer has changed its accounting reference date during the period for which historical financial information is required, the audited historical information shall cover at least 24 months, or the entire period for which the issuer has been in operation, whichever is the shorter.] Such financial information must be prepared according to Regulation (EC) No 1606/2002, or if not applicable to a Member's State national accounting standards for issuers from the Community. For third country issuers, such financial information must be prepared according to the international accounting standards adopted pursuant to the procedure of Article 3 of Regulation (EC) No 1606/2002 or to a third country's national accounting standards equivalent to these standards. If such financial information is not equivalent to these standards, it must be presented in the form of restated financial statements.

The most recent year's historical financial information must be presented and prepared in a form consistent with that which will be adopted in the issuer's next annual published financial statements having regard to accounting standards and policies and legislation applicable to such annual financial statements.

If the issuer has been operating in its current sphere of economic activity for less than one year, the audited historical financial information covering that period must be prepared in accordance with the standards applicable to annual financial statements under Regulation (EC) No 1606/2002, or if not applicable to a Member States national accounting standards where the issuer is from the Community. For third country issuers, the historical financial information must be prepared according to the international accounting standards adopted pursuant to the procedure of Article 3 of Regulation (EC) No 1606/2002 or to a third country's national accounting standards equivalent to these standards. This historical financial information must be audited.

If the audited financial information is prepared according to national accounting standards, the financial information required under this heading must include at least the following:

   (a)   the balance sheet;
   (b)   the income statement;
   (c)   the accounting policies and explanatory notes.

The historical annual financial information must be independently audited or reported on as to whether or not, for the purposes of the registration document, it gives a true and fair view, in accordance with auditing standards applicable in a Member State or an equivalent standard.

8.2a. This paragraph may be used only for issues of asset backed securities having a denomination per unit of at least EUR 50,000.

Where, since the date of incorporation or establishment, an issuer has commenced operations and financial statements have been made up, the registration document must contain audited historical financial information covering the latest 2 financial years (or shorter period that the issuer has been in operation) and the audit report in respect of each year. [If the issuer has changed its accounting reference date during the period for which historical financial information is required, the audited historical information shall cover at least 24 months, or the entire period for which the issuer has been in operation, whichever is the shorter.] Such financial information must be prepared according to Regulation (EC) No 1606/2002 or, if not applicable, to a Member's State national accounting standards for issuers from the Community. For third country issuers, such financial information must be prepared according to the international accounting standards adopted pursuant to the procedure of Article 3 of Regulation (EC) No 1606/2002 or to a third country's national accounting standards equivalent to these standards. Otherwise, the following information must be included in the registration document:

   (a)   a prominent statement that the financial information included in the registration document has not been prepared in accordance with the international accounting standards adopted pursuant to the procedure of Article 3 of Regulation (EC) No 1606/2002 and that there may be material differences in the financial information had Regulation (EC) No 1606/2002 been applied to the historical financial information;

   (b)   immediately following the historical financial information a narrative description of the differences between the international accounting standards adopted pursuant to the procedure of Article 3 of Regulation (EC) No 1606/2002 and the accounting principles adopted by the issuer in preparing its annual financial statements.

The most recent year's historical financial information must be presented and prepared in a form consistent with that which will be adopted in the issuer's next annual financial statements having regard to accounting standards and policies and legislation applicable to such annual financial statements.

If the audited financial information is prepared according to national accounting standards, the financial information required under this heading must include at least the following:

   (a)   the balance sheet;
   (b)   the income statement;
   (c)   the accounting policies and explanatory notes.

The historical annual financial information must be independently audited or reported on as to whether or not, for the purposes of the registration document, it gives a true and fair view, in accordance with auditing standards applicable in a Member State or an equivalent standard. Otherwise, the following information must be included in the registration document:

(a) a prominent statement disclosing which auditing standards have been applied;

(b) an explanation of any significant departures from International Standards on Auditing.

8.3. *Legal and arbitration proceedings*

Information on any governmental, legal or arbitration proceedings (including any such proceedings which are pending or threatened of which the company is aware), during a period covering at least the previous 12 months, which may have, or have had in the recent past, significant effects on the issuer and/or group's financial position or profitability, or provide an appropriate negative statement.

8.4. *Material adverse change in the issuer's financial position*

Where an issuer has prepared financial statements, include a statement that there has been no material adverse change in the financial position or prospects of the issuer since the date of its last published audited financial statements. Where a material adverse change has occurred, this must be disclosed in the registration document.

9. Third party information and statement by experts and declarations of any interest

9.1. Where a statement or report attributed to a person as an expert is included in the registration document, provide such person's name, business address, qualifications and material interest if any in the issuer. If the report has been produced at the issuer's request a statement to that effect that such statement or report is included, in the form and context in which it is included, with the consent of that person who has authorised the contents of that part of the registration document.

9.2. Where information has been sourced from a third party, provide a confirmation that this information has been accurately reproduced and that as far as the issuer is aware and is able to ascertain from information published by that third party, no facts have been omitted which would render the reproduced information inaccurate or misleading In addition, the issuer shall identify the source(s) of the information.

10. Documents on display

10.1. A statement that for the life of the registration document the following documents (or copies thereof), where applicable, may be inspected:

(a) the memorandum and articles of association of the issuer;

(b) all reports, letters, and other documents, historical financial information, valuations and statements prepared by any expert at the issuer's request any part of which is included or referred to in the registration document;

(c) the historical financial information of the issuer or, in the case of a group, the historical financial information of the issuer and its subsidiary undertakings for each of the two financial years preceding the publication of the registration document.

An indication of where the documents on display may be inspected, by physical or electronic means.

NOTES

Words in square brackets in items 8.2, 8.2a inserted by Commission Regulation 211/2007/EC, Art 1(4), as from 1 March 2007.

ANNEX VIII
MINIMUM DISCLOSURE REQUIREMENTS FOR THE ASSET-BACKED SECURITIES ADDITIONAL BUILDING BLOCK

[11.444]

1. The securities

1.1. The minimum denomination of an issue.

1.2. Where information is disclosed about an undertaking/obligor which is not involved in the issue, provide a confirmation that the information relating to the undertaking/obligor has been accurately reproduced from information published by the undertaking/obligor. So far as the issuer is aware and is able to ascertain from information published by the undertaking/obligor no facts have been omitted which would render the reproduced information misleading.

In addition, identify the source(s) of information in the Securities Note that has been reproduced from information published by an undertaking/obligor.

2. The underlying assets

2.1. Confirmation that the securitised assets backing the issue have characteristics that demonstrate capacity to produce funds to service any payments due and payable on the securities.

2.2. In respect of a pool of discrete assets backing the issue:

2.2.1. The legal jurisdiction by which the pool of assets is governed

2.2.2.
- (a) In the case of a small number of easily identifiable obligors, a general description of each obligor.
- (b) In all other cases, a description of: the general characteristics of the obligors; and the economic environment, as well as global statistical data referred to the securitised assets.

2.2.3. The legal nature of the assets;

2.2.4. the expiry or maturity date(s) of the assets;

2.2.5. the amount of the assets;

2.2.6. loan to value ratio or level of collateralisation;

2.2.7. the method of origination or creation of the assets, and for loans and credit agreements, the principal lending criteria and an indication of any loans which do not meet these criteria and any rights or obligations to make further advances;

2.2.8. an indication of significant representations and collaterals given to the issuer relating to the assets;

2.2.9. any rights to substitute the assets and a description of the manner in which and the type of assets which may be so substituted; if there is any capacity to substitute assets with a different class or quality of assets a statement to that effect together with a description of the impact of such substitution;

2.2.10. a description of any relevant insurance policies relating to the assets. Any concentration with one insurer must be disclosed if it is material to the transaction.

2.2.11. Where the assets comprise obligations of 5 or fewer obligors which are legal persons or where an obligor accounts for 20% or more of the assets, or where an obligor accounts for a material portion of the assets, so far as the issuer is aware and/or is able to ascertain from information published by the obligor(s) indicate either of the following:
- (a) information relating to each obligor as if it were an issuer drafting a registration document for debt and derivative securities with an individual denomination of at least EUR 50,000;
- (b) if an obligor or guarantor has securities already admitted to trading on a regulated or equivalent market or the obligations are guaranteed by an entity admitted to trading on a regulated or equivalent market, the name, address, country of incorporation, nature of business and name of the market in which its securities are admitted.

2.2.12. If a relationship exists that is material to the issue, between the issuer, guarantor and obligor, details of the principal terms of that relationship.

2.2.13. Where the assets comprise obligations that are not traded on a regulated or equivalent market, a description of the principal terms and conditions of the obligations.

2.2.14. Where the assets comprise equity securities that are admitted to trading on a regulated or equivalent market indicate the following:
- (a) a description of the securities;
- (b) a description of the market on which they are traded including its date of establishment, how price information is published, an indication of daily trading volumes, information as to the standing of the market in the country and the name of the market's regulatory authority;
- (c) the frequency with which prices of the relevant securities, are published.

2.2.15. Where more than ten (10) per cent of the assets comprise equity securities that are not traded on a regulated or equivalent market, a description of those equity securities and equivalent information to that contained in the schedule for share registration document in respect of each issuer of those securities.

2.2.16. Where a material portion of the assets are secured on or backed by real property, a valuation report relating to the property setting out both the valuation of the property and cash flow/income streams.

Compliance with this disclosure is not required if the issue is of securities backed by mortgage loans with property as security, where there has been no revaluation of the properties for the purpose of the issue, and it is clearly stated that the valuations quoted are as at the date of the original initial mortgage loan origination.

2.3. In respect of an actively managed pool of assets backing the issue:

2.3.1. equivalent information to that contained in items 2.1 and 2.2 to allow an assessment of the type, quality, sufficiency and liquidity of the asset types in the portfolio which will secure the issue;

2.3.2. the parameters within which investments can be made, the name and description of the entity responsible for such management including a description of that entity's expertise and experience, a summary of the provisions relating to the termination of the appointment of such entity and the appointment of an alternative management entity, and a description of that entity's relationship with any other parties to the issue.

2.4. Where an issuer proposes to issue further securities backed by the same assets, a prominent statement to that effect and unless those further securities are fungible with or are subordinated to those classes of existing debt, a description of how the holders of that class will be informed.

3. Structure and cash flow

3.1.   Description of the structure of the transaction, including, if necessary, a structure diagram.

3.2.   Description of the entities participating in the issue and description of the functions to be performed by them.

3.3.   Description of the method and date of the sale, transfer, novation or assignment of the assets or of any rights and/or obligations in the assets to the issuer or, where applicable, the manner and time period in which the proceeds from the issue will be fully invested by the issuer.

3.4.   An explanation of the flow of funds including:

3.4.1.   how the cash flow from the assets will meet the issuer's obligations to holders of the securities, including, if necessary, a financial service table and a description of the assumptions used in developing the table;

3.4.2.   information on any credit enhancements, an indication of where material potential liquidity shortfalls may occur and the availability of any liquidity supports and indication of provisions designed to cover interest/principal shortfall risks;

3.4.3.   without prejudice to item 3.4.2, details of any subordinated debt finance;

3.4.4.   an indication of any investment parameters for the investment of temporary liquidity surpluses and description of the parties responsible for such investment;

3.4.5.   how payments are collected in respect of the assets;

3.4.6.   the order of priority of payments made by the issuer to the holders of the class of securities in question;

3.4.7.   details of any other arrangements upon which payments of interest and principal to investors are dependent.

3.5.   The name, address and significant business activities of the originators of the securitised assets.

3.6.   Where the return on, and/or repayment of the security is linked to the performance or credit of other assets which are not assets of the issuer, items 2.2 and 2.3 are necessary.

3.7.   The name, address and significant business activities of the administrator, calculation agent or equivalent, together with a summary of the administrator's/calculation agents responsibilities, their relationship with the originator or the creator of the assets and a summary of the provisions relating to the termination of the appointment of the administrator/calculation agent and the appointment of an alternative administrator/calculation agent.

3.8.   The names and addresses and brief description of:

(a)   any swap counterparties and any providers of other material forms of credit/liquidity enhancement;

(b)   the banks with which the main accounts relating to the transaction are held.

4. Post issuance reporting

4.1.   Indication in the prospectus whether or not it intends to provide post-issuance transaction information regarding securities to be admitted to trading and the performance of the underlying collateral. Where the issuer has indicated that it intends to report such information, specify in the prospectus what information will be reported, where such information can be obtained, and the frequency with which such information will be reported.

ANNEX IX
MINIMUM DISCLOSURE REQUIREMENTS FOR THE DEBT AND DERIVATIVE SECURITIES REGISTRATION DOCUMENT (SCHEDULE)

(Debt and derivative securities with a denomination per unit of at least EUR 50,000)

[11.445]
1. Persons responsible

1.1.   All persons responsible for the information given in the registration document and, as the case may be, for certain parts of it, with, in the latter case, an indication of such parts. In the case of natural persons including members of the issuer's administrative, management or supervisory bodies indicate the name and function of the person; in case of legal persons indicate the name and registered office.

1.2.   A declaration by those responsible for the registration document that, having taken all reasonable care to ensure that such is the case, the information contained in the registration document is, to the best of their knowledge, in accordance with the facts and contains no omission likely to affect its import. As the case may be, declaration by those responsible for certain parts of the registration document that, having taken all reasonable care to ensure that such is the case, the information contained in the part of the registration document for which they are responsible is, to the best of their knowledge, in accordance with the facts and contains no omission likely to affect its import.

2. Statutory auditors

2.1. Names and addresses of the issuer's auditors for the period covered by the historical financial information (together with their membership in a professional body).

2.2. If auditors have resigned, been removed or not been re-appointed during the period covered by the historical financial information, details if material.

3. Risk factors

3.1. Prominent disclosure of risk factors that may affect the issuer's ability to fulfil its obligations under the securities to investors in a section headed "Risk Factors".

4. Information about the issuer

4.1. *History and development of the issuer*

4.1.1. the legal and commercial name of the issuer;

4.1.2. the place of registration of the issuer and its registration number;

4.1.3. the date of incorporation and the length of life of the issuer, except where indefinite;

4.1.4. the domicile and legal form of the issuer, the legislation under which the issuer operates, its country of incorporation, and the address and telephone number of its registered office (or principal place of business if different from its registered office;

4.1.5. any recent events particular to the issuer and which are to a material extent relevant to the evaluation of the issuer's solvency.

5. Business overview

5.1. *Principal activities:*

5.1.1. A brief description of the issuer's principal activities stating the main categories of products sold and/or services performed;

5.1.2. The basis for any statements in the registration document made by the issuer regarding its competitive position.

6. Organisational structure

6.1. If the issuer is part of a group, a brief description of the group and of the issuer's position within it.

6.2. If the issuer is dependent upon other entities within the group, this must be clearly stated together with an explanation of this dependence.

7. Trend information

7.1. Include a statement that there has been no material adverse change in the prospects of the issuer since the date of its last published audited financial statements.

In the event that the issuer is unable to make such a statement, provide details of this material adverse change.

8. Profit forecasts or estimates

If an issuer chooses to include a profit forecast or a profit estimate, the registration document must contain the information items 8.1 and 8.2 the following:

8.1. A statement setting out the principal assumptions upon which the issuer has based its forecast, or estimate.

There must be a clear distinction between assumptions about factors which the members of the administrative, management or supervisory bodies can influence and assumptions about factors which are exclusively outside the influence of the members of the administrative, management or supervisory bodies; be readily understandable by investors; be specific and precise; and not relate to the general accuracy of the estimates underlying the forecast.

8.2. Any profit forecast set out in the registration document must be accompanied by a statement confirming that the said forecast has been properly prepared on the basis stated and that the basis of accounting is consistent with the accounting policies of the issuer.

8.3. The profit forecast or estimate must be prepared on a basis comparable with the historical financial information.

9. Administrative, management, and supervisory bodies

9.1. Names, business addresses and functions in the issuer of the following persons, and an indication of the principal activities performed by them outside the issuer where these are significant with respect to that issuer:

    (a) members of the administrative, management or supervisory bodies;

    (b) partners with unlimited liability, in the case of a limited partnership with a share capital.

9.2. *Administrative, management, and supervisory bodies' conflicts of interests*

Potential conflicts of interests between any duties to the issuing entity of the persons referred to in item 9.1 and their private interests and or other duties must be clearly stated. In the event that there are no such conflicts, a statement to that effect.

10. Major shareholders

10.1. To the extent known to the issuer, state whether the issuer is directly or indirectly owned or controlled and by whom, and describe the nature of such control, and describe the measures in place to ensure that such control is not abused.

10.2. A description of any arrangements, known to the issuer, the operation of which may at a subsequent date result in a change in control of the issuer.

11. Financial information concerning the issuer's assets and liabilities, financial position and profits and losses

11.1. *Historical financial information*

Audited historical financial information covering the latest two financial years (or such shorter period that the issuer has been in operation), and the audit report in respect of each year. [If the issuer has changed its accounting reference date during the period for which historical financial information is required, the audited historical information shall cover at least 24 months, or the entire period for which the issuer has been in operation, whichever is the shorter.] Such financial information must be prepared according to Regulation (EC) No 1606/2002, or if not applicable to a Member's State national accounting standards for issuers from the Community. For third country issuers, such financial information must be prepared according to the international accounting standards adopted pursuant to the procedure of Article 3 of Regulation (EC) No 1606/2002 or to a third country's national accounting standards equivalent to these standards. Otherwise, the following information must be included in the registration document:

(a)   a prominent statement that the financial information included in the registration document has not been prepared in accordance with the international accounting standards adopted pursuant to the procedure of Article 3 of Regulation (EC) No 1606/2002 and that there may be material differences in the financial information had Regulation (EC) No 1606/2002 been applied to the historical financial information;

(b)   immediately following the historical financial information a narrative description of the differences between the international accounting standards adopted pursuant to the procedure of Article 3 of Regulation (EC) No 1606/2002 and the accounting principles adopted by the issuer in preparing its annual financial statements.

The most recent year's historical financial information must be presented and prepared in a form consistent with that which will be adopted in the issuer's next published annual financial statements having regard to accounting standards and policies and legislation applicable to such annual financial statements.

If the audited financial information is prepared according to national accounting standards, the financial information required under this heading must include at least the following:

(a)   the balance sheet;

(b)   the income statement;

(c)   the accounting policies and explanatory notes.

The historical annual financial information must be independently audited or reported on as to whether or not, for the purposes of the registration document, it gives a true and fair view, in accordance with auditing standards applicable in a Member State or an equivalent standard. Otherwise, the following information must be included in the registration document:

(a)   a prominent statement disclosing which auditing standards have been applied;

(b)   an explanation of any significant departures from international standards on auditing.

11.2. *Financial statements*

If the issuer prepares both own and consolidated financial statements, include at least the consolidated financial statements in the registration document.

11.3. *Auditing of historical annual financial information*

11.3.1. A statement that the historical financial information has been audited. If audit reports on the historical financial information have been refused by the statutory auditors or if they contain qualifications or disclaimers, such refusal or such qualifications or disclaimers must be reproduced in full and the reasons given.

11.3.2. An indication of other information in the registration document which has been audited by the auditors.

11.3.3. Where financial data in the registration document is not extracted from the issuer's audited financial statements, state the source of the data and state that the data is unaudited.

11.4. *Age of latest financial information*

11.4.1. The last year of audited financial information may not be older than 18 months from the date of the registration document.

11.5. *Legal and arbitration proceedings*

Information on any governmental, legal or arbitration proceedings (including any such proceedings which are pending or threatened of which the issuer is aware), during a period covering at least the previous 12 months which may have, or have had in the recent past, significant effects on the issuer and/or group's financial position or profitability, or provide an appropriate negative statement.

11.6. *Significant change in the issuer's financial or trading position*

A description of any significant change in the financial or trading position of the group which has occurred since the end of the last financial period for which either audited financial information or interim financial information have been published, or an appropriate negative statement.

12. Material contracts

A brief summary of all material contracts that are not entered into in the ordinary course of the issuer's business, which could result in any group member being under an obligation or entitlement that is material to the issuer's ability to meet its obligation to security holders in respect of the securities being issued.

13. Third party information and statement by experts and declarations of any interest

13.1. Where a statement or report attributed to a person as an expert is included in the registration document, provide such person's name, business address, qualifications and material interest if any in the issuer. If the report has been produced at the issuer's request a statement to that effect that such statement or report is included, in the form and context in which it is included, with the consent of that person who has authorised the contents of that part of the registration document.

13.2. *Third party information*

Where information has been sourced from a third party, provide a confirmation that this information has been accurately reproduced and that as far as the issuer is aware and is able to ascertain from information published by that third party, no facts have been omitted which would render the reproduced information inaccurate or misleading; in addition, identify the source(s) of the information.

14. Documents on display

A statement that for the life of the registration document the following documents (or copies thereof), where applicable, may be inspected:
  (a) the memorandum and articles of association of the issuer;
  (b) all reports, letters, and other documents, historical financial information, valuations and statements prepared by any expert at the issuer's request any part of which is included or referred to in the registration document;
  (c) the historical financial information of the issuer or, in the case of a group, the historical financial information of the issuer and its subsidiary undertakings for each of the two financial years preceding the publication of the registration document.

An indication of where the documents on display may be inspected, by physical or electronic means.

NOTES

Words in square brackets in item 11.1 inserted by Commission Regulation 211/2007/EC, Art 1(4), as from 1 March 2007.

ANNEX X
MINIMUM DISCLOSURE REQUIREMENTS FOR THE DEPOSITORY RECEIPTS ISSUED OVER SHARES (SCHEDULE)

Information about the Issuer of the Underlying Shares

[11.446]
1. Persons responsible

1.1. All persons responsible for the information given in the prospectus and, as the case may be, for certain parts of it, with, in the latter case, an indication of such parts. In the case of natural persons including members of the issuer's administrative, management or supervisory bodies indicate the name and function of the person; in case of legal persons indicate the name and registered office.

1.2. A declaration by those responsible for the prospectus that, having taken all reasonable care to ensure that such is the case, the information contained in the prospectus is, to the best of their knowledge, in accordance with the facts and contains no omission likely to affect its import. As the case may be, declaration by those responsible for certain parts of the prospectus that, having taken all reasonable care to ensure that such is the case, the information contained in the part of the prospectus for which they are responsible is, to the best of their knowledge, in accordance with the facts and contains no omission likely to affect its import.

2. Statutory auditors

2.1. Names and addresses of the issuer's auditors for the period covered by the historical financial information (together with their membership in a professional body).

2.2. If auditors have resigned, been removed or not been re-appointed during the period covered by the historical financial information, indicate details if material.

3. Selected financial information

3.1. Selected historical financial information regarding the issuer, presented for each financial year for the period covered by the historical financial information, and any subsequent interim financial period, in the same currency as the financial information.

The selected historical financial information must provide the key figures that summarise the financial condition of the issuer.

3.2. If selected financial information for interim periods is provided, comparative data from the same period in the prior financial year shall also be provided, except that the requirement for comparative balance sheet information is satisfied by presenting the year end balance sheet information.

4. Risk factors

Prominent disclosure of risk factors that are specific to the issuer or its industry in a section headed "Risk Factors".

5. Information about the issuer

5.1. *History and development of the issuer*

5.1.1. the legal and commercial name of the issuer;

5.1.2. the place of registration of the issuer and its registration number;

5.1.3. the date of incorporation and the length of life of the issuer, except where indefinite;

5.1.4. the domicile and legal form of the issuer, the legislation under which the issuer operates, its country of incorporation, and the address and telephone number of its registered office (or principal place of business if different from its registered office);

5.1.5. the important events in the development of the issuer's business.

5.2. *Investments*

5.2.1. A description, (including the amount) of the issuer's principal investments for each financial year for the period covered by the historical financial information up to the date of the prospectus;

5.2.2. A description of the issuer's principal investments that are currently in progress, including the distribution of these investments geographically (home and abroad) and the method of financing (internal or external);

5.2.3. Information concerning the issuer's principal future investments on which its management bodies have already made firm commitments.

6. Business overview

6.1. *Principal activities*

6.1.1. A description of, and key factors relating to, the nature of the issuer's operations and its principal activities, stating the main categories of products sold and/or services performed for each financial year for the period covered by the historical financial information.

6.1.2. An indication of any significant new products and/or services that have been introduced and, to the extent the development of new products or services has been publicly disclosed, give the status of development.

6.2. *Principal markets*

A description of the principal markets in which the issuer competes, including a breakdown of total revenues by category of activity and geographic market for each financial year for the period covered by the historical financial information.

6.3. Where the information given pursuant to items 6.1 and 6.2 has been influenced by exceptional factors, mention that fact.

6.4. If material to the issuer's business or profitability, disclose summary information regarding the extent to which the issuer is dependent, on patents or licences, industrial, commercial or financial contracts or new manufacturing processes.

6.5. The basis for any statements made by the issuer regarding its competitive position.

7. Organisational structure

7.1. If the issuer is part of a group, a brief description of the group and the issuer's position within the group.

7.2. A list of the issuer's significant subsidiaries, including name, country of incorporation or residence, proportion of ownership interest and, if different, proportion of voting power held.

8. Property, plants and equipment

8.1. Information regarding any existing or planned material tangible fixed assets, including leased properties, and any major encumbrances thereon.

8.2.   A description of any environmental issues that may affect the issuer's utilisation of the tangible fixed assets.

9.   Operating and financial review

9.1.   *Financial condition*

To the extent not covered elsewhere in the prospectus, provide a description of the issuer's financial condition, changes in financial condition and results of operations for each year and interim period, for which historical financial information is required, including the causes of material changes from year to year in the financial information to the extent necessary for an understanding of the issuer's business as a whole.

9.2.   *Operating results*

9.2.1.   Information regarding significant factors, including unusual or infrequent events or new developments, materially affecting the issuer's income from operations, indicating the extent to which income was so affected.

9.2.2.   Where the financial statements disclose material changes in net sales or revenues, provide a narrative discussion of the reasons for such changes.

9.2.3.   Information regarding any governmental, economic, fiscal, monetary or political policies or factors that have materially affected, or could materially affect, directly or indirectly, the issuer's operations.

10.   Capital resources

10.1.   Information concerning the issuer's capital resources (both short and long term).

10.2.   An explanation of the sources and amounts of and a narrative description of the issuer's cash flows.

10.3.   Information on the borrowing requirements and funding structure of the issuer.

10.4.   Information regarding any restrictions on the use of capital resources that have materially affected, or could materially affect, directly or indirectly, the issuer's operations.

10.5.   Information regarding the anticipated sources of funds needed to fulfil commitments referred to in items 5.2.3 and 8.1.

11.   Research and development, patents and licences

Where material, provide a description of the issuer's research and development policies for each financial year for the period covered by the historical financial information, including the amount spent on issuer-sponsored research and development activities.

12.   Trend information

12.1.   The most significant recent trends in production, sales and inventory, and costs and selling prices since the end of the last financial year to the date of the prospectus.

12.2.   Information on any known trends, uncertainties, demands, commitments or events that are reasonably likely to have a material effect on the issuer's prospects for at least the current financial year.

13.   Profit forecasts or estimates

If an issuer chooses to include a profit forecast or a profit estimate the prospectus must contain the information items 13.1 and 13.2.

13.1.   A statement setting out the principal assumptions upon which the issuer has based its forecast, or estimate.

There must be a clear distinction between assumptions about factors which the members of the administrative, management or supervisory bodies can influence and assumptions about factors which are exclusively outside the influence of the members of the administrative, management or supervisory bodies; the assumptions must be readily understandable by investors, be specific and precise and not relate to the general accuracy of the estimates underlying the forecast.

13.2.   A report prepared by independent accountants or auditors stating that in the opinion of the independent accountants or auditors the forecast or estimate has been properly compiled on the basis stated and that the basis of accounting used for the profit forecast or estimate is consistent with the accounting policies of the issuer.

13.3.   The profit forecast or estimate prepared on a basis comparable with the historical financial information.

13.4.   If the issuer has published a profit forecast in a prospectus which is still outstanding, provide a statement setting out whether or not that forecast is still correct as at the time of the prospectus, and an explanation of why such forecast is no longer valid if that is the case.

14.   Administrative, management, and supervisory bodies and senior management

14.1.   Names, business addresses and functions in the issuer of the following persons and an indication of the principal activities performed by them outside that issuer where these are significant with respect to that issuer:

(a)　members of the administrative, management or supervisory bodies;
(b)　partners with unlimited liability, in the case of a limited partnership with a share capital;
(c)　founders, if the issuer has been established for fewer than five years;
(d)　any senior manager who is relevant to establishing that the issuer has the appropriate expertise and experience for the management of the issuer's business.

The nature of any family relationship between any of those persons.

In the case of each member of the administrative, management or supervisory bodies of the issuer and person described in points (b) and (d) of the first subparagraph, details of that person's relevant management expertise and experience and the following information:

(a)　the names of all companies and partnerships of which such person has been a member of the administrative, management or supervisory bodies or partner at any time in the previous five years, indicating whether or not the individual is still a member of the administrative, management or supervisory bodies or partner. It is not necessary to list all the subsidiaries of an issuer of which the person is also a member of the administrative, management or supervisory bodies;
(b)　any convictions in relation to fraudulent offences for at least the previous five years;
(c)　details of any bankruptcies, receiverships or liquidations with which a person described in points (a) and (d) of the first subparagraph who was acting in the capacity of any of the positions set out in points (a) and (d) of the first subparagraph member of the administrative, management or supervisory bodies was associated for at least the previous five years;
(d)　details of any official public incrimination and/or sanctions of such person by statutory or regulatory authorities (including designated professional bodies) and whether such person has ever been disqualified by a court from acting as a member of the administrative, management or supervisory bodies of an issuer or from acting in the management or conduct of the affairs of any issuer for at least the previous five years.

If there is no such information to be disclosed, a statement to that effect must be made.

14.2.　*Administrative, management, and supervisory bodies' and senior management conflicts of interests*

Potential conflicts of interests between any duties to the issuer of the persons referred to in the first subparagraph of item 14.1 and their private interests and or other duties must be clearly stated. In the event that there are no such conflicts, make a statement to that effect.

Any arrangement or understanding with major shareholders, customers, suppliers or others, pursuant to which any person referred to in the first subparagraph of item 14.1 was selected as a member of the administrative, management or supervisory bodies or member of senior management.

15.　Remuneration and benefits

In relation to the last full financial year for those persons referred to in points (a) and (d) of the first subparagraph of item 14.1:

15.1.　The amount of remuneration paid (including any contingent or deferred compensation), and benefits in kind granted, to such persons by the issuer and its subsidiaries for services in all capacities to the issuer and its subsidiaries by any person.

This information must be provided on an individual basis unless individual disclosure is not required in the issuer's home country and is not otherwise publicly disclosed by the issuer.

15.2.　The total amounts set aside or accrued by the issuer or its subsidiaries to provide pension, retirement or similar benefits.

16.　Board practices

In relation to the issuer's last completed financial year, and unless otherwise specified, with respect to those persons referred to in point (a) of the first subparagraph of item 14.1.

16.1.　Date of expiration of the current term of office, if applicable, and the period during which the person has served in that office.

16.2.　Information about members of the administrative, management or supervisory bodies' service contracts with the issuer or any of its subsidiaries providing for benefits upon termination of employment, or an appropriate negative statement.

16.3.　Information about the issuer's audit committee and remuneration committee, including the names of committee members and a summary of the terms of reference under which the committee operates.

16.4.　A statement as to whether or not the issuer complies with its country's of incorporation corporate governance regime(s). In the event that the issuer does not comply with such a regime, a statement to that effect together with an explanation regarding why the issuer does not comply with such regime.

17. Employees

17.1. Either the number of employees at the end of the period or the average for each financial year for the period covered by the historical financial information up to the date of the prospectus (and changes in such numbers, if material) and, if possible and material, a breakdown of persons employed by main category of activity and geographic location. If the issuer employs a significant number of temporary employees, include disclosure of the number of temporary employees on average during the most recent financial year.

17.2. Shareholdings and stock options

With respect to each person referred to in points (a) and (b) of the first subparagraph of item 14.1, provide information as to their share ownership and any options over such shares in the issuer as of the most recent practicable date.

17.3. Description of any arrangements for involving the employees in the capital of the issuer.

18. Major shareholders

18.1. In so far as is known to the issuer, the name of any person other than a member of the administrative, management or supervisory bodies who, directly or indirectly, has an interest notifiable under the issuer's national law in the issuer's capital or voting rights, together with the amount of each such person's interest or, if there are no such persons, an appropriate negative statement.

18.2. Whether the issuer's major shareholders have different voting rights, or an appropriate negative statement.

18.3. To the extent known to the issuer, state whether the issuer is directly or indirectly owned or controlled and by whom and describe the nature of such control and describe the measures in place to ensure that such control is not abused.

18.4. A description of any arrangements, known to the issuer, the operation of which may at a subsequent date result in a change in control of the issuer.

19. Related party transactions

Details of related party transactions (which for these purposes are those set out in the Standards adopted according to Regulation (EC) No 1606/2002), that the issuer has entered into during the period covered by the historical financial information and up to the date of the prospectus must be disclosed in accordance with the respective standard adopted according to Regulation (EC) No 1606/2002 if applicable.

If such standards do not apply to the issuer the following information must be disclosed:

(a) the nature and extent of any transactions which are – as a single transaction or in their entirety – material to the issuer. Where such related party transactions are not concluded at arm's length provide an explanation of why these transactions were not concluded at arm's length. In the case of outstanding loans including guarantees of any kind indicate the amount outstanding;

(b) the amount or the percentage to which related party transactions form part of the turnover of the issuer.

20. Financial information concerning the issuer's assets and liabilities, financial position and profits and losses

20.1. *Historical financial information*

Audited historical financial information covering the latest 3 financial years (or such shorter period that the issuer has been in operation), and the audit report in respect of each year. [If the issuer has changed its accounting reference date during the period for which historical financial information is required, the audited historical information shall cover at least 36 months, or the entire period for which the issuer has been in operation, whichever is the shorter.] Such financial information must be prepared according to Regulation (EC) No 1606/2002, or if not applicable to a Member States national accounting standards for issuers from the Community. For third country issuers, such financial information must be prepared according to the international accounting standards adopted pursuant to the procedure of Article 3 of Regulation (EC) No 1606/2002 or to a third country's national accounting standards equivalent to these standards. If such financial information is not equivalent to these standards, it must be presented in the form of restated financial statements.

The last two years audited historical financial information must be presented and prepared in a form consistent with that which will be adopted in the issuer's next published annual financial statements having regard to accounting standards and policies and legislation applicable to such annual financial statements.

If the issuer has been operating in its current sphere of economic activity for less than one year, the audited historical financial information covering that period must be prepared in accordance with the standards applicable to annual financial statements under Regulation (EC) No 1606/2002, or if not applicable to a Member States national accounting standards where the issuer is an issuer from the Community. For third country issuers, the historical financial information must be prepared according to the international accounting standards adopted pursuant to the procedure of Article 3 of Regulation (EC) No 1606/2002 or to a third country's national accounting standards equivalent to these standards. This historical financial information must be audited.

If the audited financial information is prepared according to national accounting standards, the financial information required under this heading must include at least the following:

(a) the balance sheet;

(b) the income statement;

(c) a statement showing either all changes in equity or changes in equity other than those arising from capital transactions with owners and distributions to owners;

(d) the cash flow statement;

(e) the accounting policies and explanatory notes.

The historical annual financial information must be independently audited or reported on as to whether or not, for the purposes of the prospectus, it gives a true and fair view, in accordance with auditing standards applicable in a Member State or an equivalent standard.

20.1a. *This paragraph may be used only for issues of depository receipts having a denomination per unit of at least EUR 50,000.*

Audited historical financial information covering the latest three financial years (or such shorter period that the issuer has been in operation), and the audit report in respect of each year. [If the issuer has changed its accounting reference date during the period for which historical financial information is required, the audited historical information shall cover at least 36 months, or the entire period for which the issuer has been in operation, whichever is the shorter.] Such financial information must be prepared according to Regulation (EC) No 1606/2002, or if not applicable to a Member State's national accounting standards for issuers from the Community. For third country issuers, such financial information must be prepared according to the international accounting standards adopted pursuant to the procedure of Article 3 of Regulation (EC) No 1606/2002 or to a third country's national accounting standards equivalent to these standards. Otherwise, the following information must be included in the prospectus:

(a) a prominent statement that the financial information included in the registration document has not been prepared in accordance with the international accounting standards adopted pursuant to the procedure of Article 3 of Regulation (EC) No 1606/2002 and that there may be material differences in the financial information had Regulation (EC) No 1606/2002 been applied to the historical financial information;

(b) immediately following the historical financial information a narrative description of the differences between the international accounting standards adopted pursuant to the procedure of Article 3 of Regulation (EC) No 1606/2002 and the accounting principles adopted by the issuer in preparing its annual financial statements.

The last two years audited historical financial information must be presented and prepared in a form consistent with that which will be adopted in the issuer's next published annual financial statements having regard to accounting standards and policies and legislation applicable to such annual financial statements.

If the audited financial information is prepared according to national accounting standards, the financial information required under this heading must include at least the following:

(a) the balance sheet;

(b) the income statement;

(c) a statement showing either all changes in equity or changes in equity other than those arising from capital transactions with owners and distributions to owners;

(d) the cash flow statement;

(e) the accounting policies and explanatory notes.

The historical annual financial information must be independently audited or reported on as to whether or not, for the purposes of the prospectus, it gives a true and fair view, in accordance with auditing standards applicable in a Member State or an equivalent standard. Otherwise, the following information must be included in the prospectus:

(a) a prominent statement disclosing which auditing standards have been applied;

(b) an explanation of any significant departures from international standards on auditing.

20.2. *Financial statements*

If the issuer prepares both own and consolidated annual financial statements, include at least the consolidated annual financial statements in the prospectus.

20.3. *Auditing of historical annual financial information*

20.3.1. A statement that the historical financial information has been audited. If audit reports on the historical financial information have been refused by the statutory auditors or if they contain qualifications or disclaimers, such refusal or such qualifications or disclaimers must be reproduced in full and the reasons given.

20.3.2. Indication of other information in the prospectus which has been audited by the auditors.

20.3.3. Where financial data in the prospectus is not extracted from the issuer's audited financial statements state the source of the data and state that the data is unaudited.

20.4. *Age of latest financial information*

20.4.1.   The last year of audited financial information may not be older than:
- (a) 18 months from the date of the prospectus if the issuer includes audited interim financial statements in the prospectus;
- (b) 15 months from the date of the prospectus if the issuer includes unaudited interim financial statements in the prospectus.

20.5. *Interim and other financial information*

20.5.1.   If the issuer has published quarterly or half yearly financial information since the date of its last audited financial statements, these must be included in the prospectus. If the quarterly or half yearly financial information has been reviewed or audited the audit or review report must also be included. If the quarterly or half yearly financial information is unaudited or has not been reviewed, state that fact.

20.5.2.   If the prospectus is dated more than nine months after the end of the last audited financial year, it must contain interim financial information, which may be unaudited (in which case that fact shall be stated) covering at least the first six months of the financial year.

The interim financial information must include comparative statements for the same period in the prior financial year, except that the requirement for comparative balance sheet information may be satisfied by presenting the years end balance sheet.

20.6. *Dividend policy*

A description of the issuer's policy on dividend distributions and any restrictions thereon.

20.6.1.   The amount of the dividend per share for each financial year for the period covered by the historical financial information adjusted, where the number of shares in the issuer has changed, to make it comparable.

20.7. *Legal and arbitration proceedings*

Information on any governmental, legal or arbitration proceedings (including any such proceedings which are pending or threatened of which the issuer is aware), during a period covering at least the previous 12 months which may have, or have had in the recent past significant effects on the issuer and/or group's financial position or profitability, or provide an appropriate negative statement.

20.8. *Significant change in the issuer's financial or trading position*

A description of any significant change in the financial or trading position of the group which has occurred since the end of the last financial period for which either audited financial information or interim financial information have been published, or provide an appropriate negative statement.

21.   Additional information

21.1. *Share capital*

The following information as of the date of the most recent balance sheet included in the historical financial information:

21.1.1.   The amount of issued capital, and for each class of share capital:
- (a) the number of shares authorised;
- (b) the number of shares issued and fully paid and issued but not fully paid;
- (c) the par value per share, or that the shares have no par value;
- (d) a reconciliation of the number of shares outstanding at the beginning and end of the year. If more than 10% of capital has been paid for with assets other than cash within the period covered by the historical financial information, state that fact.

21.1.2.   If there are shares not representing capital, state the number and main characteristics of such shares.

21.1.3.   The number, book value and face value of shares in the issuer held by or on behalf of the issuer itself or by subsidiaries of the issuer.

21.1.4.   The amount of any convertible securities, exchangeable securities or securities with warrants, with an indication of the conditions governing and the procedures for conversion, exchange or subscription.

21.1.5.   Information about and terms of any acquisition rights and or obligations over authorised but unissued capital or an undertaking to increase the capital.

21.1.6.   Information about any capital of any member of the group which is under option or agreed conditionally or unconditionally to be put under option and details of such options including those persons to whom such options relate.

21.1.7.   A history of share capital, highlighting information about any changes, for the period covered by the historical financial information.

21.2. *Memorandum and Articles of Association*

21.2.1.   A description of the issuer's objects and purposes and where they can be found in the memorandum and articles of association.

21.2.2.   A summary of any provisions of the issuer's articles of association, statutes or charter and bylaws with respect to the members of the administrative, management and supervisory bodies.

21.2.3.   A description of the rights, preferences and restrictions attaching to each class of the existing shares.

21.2.4.   A description of what action is necessary to change the rights of holders of the shares, indicating where the conditions are more significant than is required by law.

21.2.5.   A description of the conditions governing the manner in which annual general meetings and extraordinary general meetings of shareholders are called including the conditions of admission.

21.2.6.   A brief description of any provision of the issuer's articles of association, statutes, charter or bylaws that would have an effect of delaying, deferring or preventing a change in control of the issuer.

21.2.7.   An indication of the articles of association, statutes, charter or bylaws provisions, if any, governing the ownership threshold above which shareholder ownership must be disclosed.

21.2.8.   A description of the conditions imposed by the memorandum and articles of association statutes, charter or bylaws governing changes in the capital, where such conditions are more stringent than is required by law.

22.   Material contracts

A summary of each material contract, other than contracts entered into in the ordinary course of business, to which the issuer or any member of the group is a party, for the two years immediately preceding publication of the prospectus.

A summary of any other contract (not being a contract entered into in the ordinary course of business) entered into by any member of the group which contains any provision under which any member of the group has any obligation or entitlement which is material to the group as at the date of the prospectus.

23.   Third party information, statement by experts and declarations of any interest

23.1.   Where a statement or report attributed to a person as an expert is included in the prospectus provide such person's name, business address, qualifications and material interest if any in the issuer. If the report has been produced at the issuer's request a statement to that effect that such statement or report is included, in the form and context in which it is included, with the consent of that person who has authorised the contents of that part of the prospectus.

23.2.   Where information has been sourced from a third party, provide a confirmation that this information has been accurately reproduced and that as far as the issuer is aware and is able to ascertain from information published by that third party, no facts have been omitted which would render the reproduced information inaccurate or misleading. In addition, the issuer shall identify the source(s) of the information.

24.   Documents on display

A statement that for the life of the prospectus the following documents (or copies thereof), where applicable, may be inspected:
  (a)   the memorandum and articles of association of the issuer;
  (b)   all reports, letters, and other documents, historical financial information, valuations and statements prepared by any expert at the issuer's request any part of which is included or referred to in the prospectus;
  (c)   the historical financial information of the issuer or, in the case of a group, the historical financial information for the issuer and its subsidiary undertakings for each of the two financial years preceding the publication of the prospectus.
An indication of where the documents on display may be inspected, by physical or electronic means.

25.   Information on holdings

25.1.   Information relating to the undertakings in which the issuer holds a proportion of the capital likely to have a significant effect on the assessment of its own assets and liabilities, financial position or profits and losses.

26.   Information about the issuer of the depository receipts

26.1.   Name, registered office and principal administrative establishment if different from the registered office.

26.2.   Date of incorporation and length of life of the issuer, except where indefinite.

26.3.   Legislation under which the issuer operates and legal form which it has adopted under that legislation.

27.   Information about the underlying shares

27.1.   A description of the type and the class of the underlying shares, including the ISIN (International Security Identification Number) or other such security identification code.

27.2.   Legislation under which the underlying shares have been created.

27.3.   An indication whether the underlying shares are in registered form or bearer form and whether the underlying shares are in certificated form or book-entry form. In the latter case, name and address of the entity in charge of keeping the records.

27.4.   Currency of the underlying shares.

27.5.   A description of the rights, including any limitations of these, attached to the underlying shares and procedure for the exercise of said rights.

27.6.   Dividend rights:
- (a)   fixed date(s) on which the entitlement arises;
- (b)   time limit after which entitlement to dividend lapses and an indication of the person in whose favour the lapse operates;
- (c)   dividend restrictions and procedures for non-resident holders;
- (d)   rate of dividend or method of its calculation, periodicity and cumulative or non-cumulative nature of payments.

27.7.   Voting rights
Pre-emption rights in offers for subscription of securities of the same class
Right to share in the issuer's profits
Rights to share in any surplus in the event of liquidation
Redemption provisions
Conversion provisions.

27.8.   The issue date of the underlying shares if new underlying shares are being created for the issue of the depository receipts and they are not in existence at the time of issue of the depository receipts.

27.9.   If new underlying shares are being created for the issue of the depository receipts, state the resolutions, authorisations and approvals by virtue of which the new underlying shares have been or will be created and/or issued.

27.10.   A description of any restrictions on the free transferability of the underlying shares.

27.11.   In respect of the country of registered office of the issuer and the country(ies) where the offer is being made or admission to trading is being sought:
- (a)   information on taxes on the income from the underlying shares withheld at source;
- (b)   indication as to whether the issuer assumes responsibility for the withholding of taxes at the source.

27.12.   An indication of the existence of any mandatory takeover bids and/or squeeze-out and sell-out rules in relation to the underlying shares.

27.13.   An indication of public takeover bids by third parties in respect of the issuer's equity, which have occurred during the last financial year and the current financial year. The price or exchange terms attaching to such offers and the outcome thereof must be stated.

27.14.   Lock up agreements:
- —   the parties involved,
- —   content and exceptions of the agreement,
- —   indication of the period of the lock up.

27.15.   *Information about selling share holders if any*

27.15.1.   Name and business address of the person or entity offering to sell the underlying shares, the nature of any position office or other material relationship that the selling persons has had within the past three years with the issuer of the underlying shares or any of its predecessors or affiliates.

27.16.   *Dilution*

27.16.1.   Amount and percentage of immediate dilution resulting from the offer of the depository receipts.

27.16.2.   In the case of a subscription offer of the depository receipts to existing shareholders, disclose the amount and percentage of immediate dilutions if they do not subscribe to the offer of depository receipts.

27.17.   *Additional information where there is a simultaneous or almost simultaneous offer or admission to trading of the same class of underlying shares as those underlying shares over which the depository receipts are being issued.*

27.17.1.   If simultaneously or almost simultaneously with the creation of the depository receipts for which admission to a regulated market is being sought underlying shares of the same class as those over which the depository receipts are being issued are subscribed for or placed privately, details are to be given of the nature of such operations and of the number and characteristics of the underlying shares to which they relate.

27.17.2.   Disclose all regulated markets or equivalent markets on which, to the knowledge of the issuer of the depository receipts, underlying shares of the same class of those over which the depository receipts are being issued are offered or admitted to trading.

27.17.3. To the extent known to the issuer of the depository receipts, indicate whether major shareholders, members of the administrative, management or supervisory bodies intended to subscribe in the offer, or whether any person intends to subscribe for more than five per cent of the offer.

28. Information regarding the depository receipts

28.1. A description of the type and class of depository receipts being offered and/or admitted to trading.

28.2. Legislation under which the depository receipts have been created.

28.3. An indication whether the depository receipts are in registered or bearer form and whether the depository receipts are in certificated or book-entry form. In the latter case, include the name and address of the entity in charge of keeping the records.

28.4. Currency of the depository receipts.

28.5. Describe the rights attaching to the depository receipts, including any limitations of these attached to the depository receipts and the procedure if any for the exercise of these rights.

28.6. If the dividend rights attaching to depository receipts are different from the dividend rights disclosed in relation to the underlying disclose the following about the dividend rights:
- (a) fixed date(s) on which the entitlement arises;
- (b) time limit after which entitlement to dividend lapses and an indication of the person in whose favour the lapse operates;
- (c) dividend restrictions and procedures for non-resident holders;
- (d) rate of dividend or method of its calculation, periodicity and cumulative or non-cumulative nature of payments.

28.7. If the voting rights attaching to the depository receipts are different from the voting rights disclosed in relation to the underlying shares disclose the following about those rights:
- voting rights.
- pre-emption rights in offers for subscription of securities of the same class.
- right to share in the issuer's profits.
- rights to share in any surplus in the event of liquidation.
- redemption provisions.
- conversion provisions.

28.8. Describe the exercise of and benefit from the rights attaching to the underlying shares, in particular voting rights, the conditions on which the issuer of the depository receipts may exercise such rights, and measures envisaged to obtain the instructions of the depository receipt holders – and the right to share in profits and any liquidation surplus which are not passed on to the holder of the depository receipt.

28.9. The expected issue date of the depository receipts.

28.10. A description of any restrictions on the free transferability of the depository receipts.

28.11. In respect of the country of registered office of the issuer and the country(ies) where the offer is being made or admission to trading is being sought:
- (a) information on taxes on the income from the depository receipts withheld at source;
- (b) indication as to whether the issuer assumes responsibility for the withholding of taxes at the source.

28.12. Bank or other guarantees attached to the depository receipts and intended to underwrite the issuer's obligations.

28.13. Possibility of obtaining the delivery of the depository receipts into original shares and procedure for such delivery.

29. Information about the terms and conditions of the offer of the depository receipts

29.1. *Conditions, offer statistics, expected timetable and action required to apply for the offer*

29.1.1. Total amount of the issue/offer, distinguishing the securities offered for sale and those offered for subscription; if the amount is not fixed, description of the arrangements and time for announcing to the public the definitive amount of the offer.

29.1.2. The time period, including any possible amendments, during which the offer will be open and description of the application process.

29.1.3. An indication of when, and under what circumstances, the offer may be revoked or suspended and whether revocation can occur after dealing has begun.

29.1.4. A description of the possibility to reduce subscriptions and the manner for refunding excess amount paid by applicants.

29.1.5. Details of the minimum and/or maximum amount of application (whether in number of securities or aggregate amount to invest).

29.1.6. An indication of the period during which an application may be withdrawn, provided that investors are allowed to withdraw their subscription.

29.1.7. Method and time limits for paying up the securities and for delivery of the securities.

29.1.8. A full description of the manner and date in which results of the offer are to be made public.

29.1.9. The procedure for the exercise of any right of pre-emption, the negotiability of subscription rights and the treatment of subscription rights not exercised.

29.2. *Plan of distribution and allotment*

29.2.1. The various categories of potential investors to which the securities are offered. If the offer is being made simultaneously in the markets of two or more countries and if a tranche has been or is being reserved for certain of these, indicate any such tranche.

29.2.2. To the extent known to the issuer, indicate whether major shareholders or members of the issuer's management, supervisory or administrative bodies intended to subscribe in the offer, or whether any person intends to subscribe for more than five per cent of the offer.

29.2.3. Pre-allotment disclosure:

29.2.3.1. The division into tranches of the offer including the institutional, retail and issuer's employee tranches and any other tranches.

29.2.3.2. The conditions under which the claw-back may be used, the maximum size of such claw back and any applicable minimum percentages for individual tranches.

29.2.3.3. The allotment method or methods to be used for the retail and issuer's employee tranche in the event of an over-subscription of these tranches.

29.2.3.4. A description of any pre-determined preferential treatment to be accorded to certain classes of investors or certain affinity groups (including friends and family programmes) in the allotment, the percentage of the offer reserved for such preferential treatment and the criteria for inclusion in such classes or groups.

29.2.3.5. Whether the treatment of subscriptions or bids to subscribe in the allotment may be determined on the basis of which firm they are made through or by.

29.2.3.6. A target minimum individual allotment if any within the retail tranche.

29.2.3.7. The conditions for the closing of the offer as well as the date on which the offer may be closed at the earliest;

29.2.3.8. Whether or not multiple subscriptions are admitted, and where they are not, how any multiple subscriptions will be handled.

29.2.3.9. Process for notification to applicants of the amount allotted and indication whether dealing may begin before notification is made.

29.2.4. Over-allotment and "green shoe":

29.2.4.1. The existence and size of any over-allotment facility and/or "green shoe".

29.2.4.2. The existence period of the over-allotment facility and/or "green shoe".

29.2.4.3. Any conditions for the use of the over-allotment facility or exercise of the "green shoe".

29.3. *Pricing*

29.3.1. An indication of the price at which the securities will be offered. When the price is not known or when there is not an established and/or liquid market for the securities, indicate the method for determination of the offer price, including who has set the criteria or is formally responsible for its determination. Indication of the amount of any expenses and taxes specifically charged to the subscriber or purchaser.

29.3.2. Process for the disclosure of the offer price.

29.3.3. Where there is or could be a material disparity between the public offer price and the effective cash cost to members of the administrative, management or supervisory bodies or senior management, or affiliated persons, of securities acquired by them in transactions during the past year, or which they have the right to acquire, include a comparison of the public contribution in the proposed public offer and the effective cash contributions of such persons.

29.4. *Placing and underwriting*

29.4.1. Name and address of the co-coordinator(s) of the global offer and of single parts of the offer and, to the extend known to the issuer, of the placers in the various countries where the offer takes place.

29.4.2. Name and address of any paying agents and depository agents in each country.

29.4.3. Name and address of the entities agreeing to underwrite the issue on a firm commitment basis, and name and address of the entities agreeing to place the issue without a firm commitment or under "best efforts" arrangements. Indication of the material features of the agreements, including the quotas. Where not all of the issue is underwritten, a statement of the portion not covered. Indication of the overall amount of the underwriting commission and of the placing commission.

29.4.4. When the underwriting agreement has been or will be reached.

30. Admission to trading and dealing arrangements in the depository receipts

30.1.   An indication as to whether the securities offered are or will be the object of an application for admission to trading, with a view to their distribution in a regulated market or other equivalent markets with indication of the markets in question. This circumstance must be mentioned, without creating the impression that the admission to trading necessarily will be approved. If known, the earliest dates on which the securities will be admitted to trading must be given.

30.2.   All the regulated markets or equivalent markets on which, to the knowledge of the issuer, securities of the same class of the securities to be offered or admitted to trading are already admitted to trading.

30.3.   If simultaneously or almost simultaneously with the creation of the securities for which admission to a regulated market is being sought securities of the same class are subscribed for or placed privately or if securities of other classes are created for public or private placing, details must be given of the nature of such operations and of the number and characteristics of the securities to which they relate.

30.4.   Name and address of the entities which have a firm commitment to act as intermediaries in secondary trading, providing liquidity through bid and offer rates and description of the main terms of their commitment.

30.5.   Stabilisation: where an issuer or a selling shareholder has granted an over-allotment option or it is otherwise proposed that price stabilising activities may be entered into in connection with an offer:

30.6.   The fact that stabilisation may be undertaken, that there is no assurance that it will be undertaken and that it may be stopped at any time.

30.7.   The beginning and the end of the period during which stabilisation may occur.

30.8.   The identity of the stabilisation manager for each relevant jurisdiction unless this is not known at the time of publication.

30.9.   The fact that stabilisation transactions may result in a market price that is higher than would otherwise prevail.

31. Key information about the issue of the depository receipts

31.1.   *Reasons for the offer and use of proceeds*

31.1.1.   Reasons for the offer and, where applicable, the estimated net amount of the proceeds broken into each principal intended use and presented by order of priority of such uses. If the issuer is aware that the anticipated proceeds will not be sufficient to fund all the proposed uses, state the amount and sources of other funds needed. Details must be given with regard to the use of the proceeds, in particular when they are being used to acquire assets, other than in the ordinary course of business, to finance announced acquisitions of other business, or to discharge, reduce or retire indebtedness.

31.2.   *Interest of natural and legal persons involved in the issue/offer*

31.2.1.   A description of any interest, including conflicting ones, that is material to the issue/offer, detailing the persons involved and the nature of the interest.

31.3.   *Risk factors*

31.3.1.   Prominent disclosure of risk factors that are material to the securities being offered and/or admitted to trading in order to assess the market risk associated with these securities in a section headed "Risk factors".

32. Expense of the issue/offer of the depository receipts

32.1.   The total net proceeds and an estimate of the total expenses of the issue/offer.

NOTES

Words in square brackets in items 20.1, 20.1a inserted by Commission Regulation 211/2007/EC, Art 1(3), as from 1 March 2007.

ANNEX XI
MINIMUM DISCLOSURE REQUIREMENTS FOR THE BANKS REGISTRATION DOCUMENT (SCHEDULE)

[11.447]
1. Persons responsible

1.1.   All persons responsible for the information given in the registration document and, as the case may be, for certain parts of it, with, in the latter case, an indication of such parts. In the case of natural persons including members of the issuer's administrative, management or supervisory bodies indicate the name and function of the person; in case of legal persons indicate the name and registered office.

1.2.   A declaration by those responsible for the registration document that, having taken all reasonable care to ensure that such is the case, the information contained in the registration document is, to the best of their knowledge, in accordance with the facts and contains no omission likely to affect its import. As the case may be, declaration by those responsible for certain parts of the registration document that, having taken all reasonable care to ensure that such is the case, the information contained in the part of the registration document for which they are responsible is, to the best of their knowledge, in accordance with the facts and contains no omission likely to affect its import.

2. Statutory auditors

2.1. Names and addresses of the issuer's auditors for the period covered by the historical financial information (together with their membership in a professional body).

2.2. If auditors have resigned, been removed or not been reappointed during the period covered by the historical financial information, details if material.

3. Risk factors

3.1. Prominent disclosure of risk factors that may affect the issuer's ability to fulfil its obligations under the securities to investors in a section headed "Risk factors".

4. Information about the issuer

4.1. *History and development of the Issuer*

4.1.1. the legal and commercial name of the issuer;

4.1.2. the place of registration of the issuer and its registration number;

4.1.3. the date of incorporation and the length of life of the issuer, except where indefinite;

4.1.4. the domicile and legal form of the issuer, the legislation under which the issuer operates, its country of incorporation, and the address and telephone number of its registered office (or principal place of business if different from its registered office);

4.1.5. any recent events particular to the issuer which are to a material extent relevant to the evaluation of the issuer's solvency.

5. Business overview

5.1. *Principal activities:*

5.1.1. A brief description of the issuer's principal activities stating the main categories of products sold and/or services performed;

5.1.2. An indication of any significant new products and/or activities.

5.1.3. Principal markets
A brief description of the principal markets in which the issuer competes.

5.1.4. The basis for any statements in the registration document made by the issuer regarding its competitive position.

6. Organisational structure

6.1. If the issuer is part of a group, a brief description of the group and of the issuer's position within it.

6.2. If the issuer is dependent upon other entities within the group, this must be clearly stated together with an explanation of this dependence.

7. Trend information

7.1. Include a statement that there has been no material adverse change in the prospects of the issuer since the date of its last published audited financial statements.

In the event that the issuer is unable to make such a statement, provide details of this material adverse change.

7.2. Information on any known trends, uncertainties, demands, commitments or events that are reasonably likely to have a material effect on the issuer's prospects for at least the current financial year.

8. Profit forecasts or estimates

If an issuer chooses to include a profit forecast or a profit estimate the registration document must contain the information items 8.1 and 8.2.

8.1. A statement setting out the principal assumptions upon which the issuer has based its forecast, or estimate.

There must be a clear distinction between assumptions about factors which the members of the administrative, management or supervisory bodies can influence and assumptions about factors which are exclusively outside the influence of the members of the administrative, management or supervisory bodies; be readily understandable by investors; be specific and precise; and not relate to the general accuracy of the estimates underlying the forecast.

8.2. A report prepared by independent accountants or auditors stating that in the opinion of the independent accountants or auditors the forecast or estimate has been properly compiled on the basis stated and that the basis of accounting used for the profit forecast or estimate is consistent with the accounting policies of the issuer.

8.3. The profit forecast or estimate must be prepared on a basis comparable with the historical financial information.

9. Administrative, management, and supervisory bodies

9.1. Names, business addresses and functions in the issuer of the following persons, and an indication of the principal activities performed by them outside the issuer where these are significant with respect to that issuer:

- (a) members of the administrative, management or supervisory bodies;
- (b) partners with unlimited liability, in the case of a limited partnership with a share capital.

9.2. *Administrative, Management, and Supervisory bodies conflicts of interests*

Potential conflicts of interests between any duties to the issuing entity of the persons referred to in item 9.1 and their private interests and or other duties must be clearly stated. In the event that there are no such conflicts, make a statement to that effect.

10. Major shareholders

10.1. To the extent known to the issuer, state whether the issuer is directly or indirectly owned or controlled and by whom, and describe the nature of such control, and describe the measures in place to ensure that such control is not abused.

10.2. A description of any arrangements, known to the issuer, the operation of which may at a subsequent date result in a change in control of the issuer.

11. Financial information concerning the issuer's assets and liabilities, financial position and profits and losses

11.1. *Historical Financial Information*

Audited historical financial information covering the latest two financial years (or such shorter period that the issuer has been in operation), and the audit report in respect of each year. [If the issuer has changed its accounting reference date during the period for which historical financial information is required, the audited historical information shall cover at least 24 months, or the entire period for which the issuer has been in operation, whichever is the shorter.] Such financial information must be prepared according to Regulation (EC) No 1606/2002, or if not applicable to a Member State national accounting standards for issuers from the Community. For third country issuers, such financial information must be prepared according to the international accounting standards adopted pursuant to the procedure of Article 3 of Regulation (EC) No 1606/2002 or to a third country's national accounting standards equivalent to these standards. If such financial information is not equivalent to these standards, it must be presented in the form of restated financial statements.

The most recent year's audited historical financial information must be presented and prepared in a form consistent with that which will be adopted in the issuer's next published annual financial statements having regard to accounting standards and policies and legislation applicable to such annual financial statements.

If the issuer has been operating in its current sphere of economic activity for less than one year, the audited historical financial information covering that period must be prepared in accordance with the standards applicable to annual financial statements under Regulation (EC) No 1606/2002, or if not applicable to a Member State national accounting standards where the issuer is an issuer from the Community. For third country issuers, the historical financial information must be prepared according to the international accounting standards adopted pursuant to the procedure of Article 3 of Regulation (EC) No 1606/2002 or to a third country's national accounting standards equivalent to these standards. This historical financial information must be audited.

If the audited financial information is prepared according to national accounting standards, the financial information required under this heading must include at least the following:

- (a) the balance sheet;
- (b) the income statement;
- (c) in the case of an admission of securities to trading on a regulated market only, a cash flow statement;
- (d) the accounting policies and explanatory notes.

The historical annual financial information must be independently audited or reported on as to whether or not, for the purposes of the registration document, it gives a true and fair view, in accordance with auditing standards applicable in a Member State or an equivalent standard.

11.2. *Financial statements*

If the issuer prepares both own and consolidated financial statements, include at least the consolidated financial statements in the registration document.

11.3.   *Auditing of historical annual financial information*

11.3.1.   A statement that the historical financial information has been audited. If audit reports on the historical financial information have been refused by the statutory auditors or if they contain qualifications or disclaimers, such refusal or such qualifications or disclaimers must be reproduced in full and the reasons given.

11.3.2.   An indication of other information in the registration document which has been audited by the auditors.

11.3.3.   Where financial data in the registration document is not extracted from the issuer's audited financial statements state the source of the data and state that the data is unaudited.

11.4.   *Age of latest financial information*

11.4.1.   The last year of audited financial information may not be older than 18 months from the date of the registration document.

11.5.   *Interim and other financial information*

11.5.1.   If the issuer has published quarterly or half yearly financial information since the date of its last audited financial statements, these must be included in the registration document. If the quarterly or half yearly financial information has been reviewed or audited the audit or review report must also be included. If the quarterly or half yearly financial information is unaudited or has not been reviewed state that fact.

11.5.2.   If the registration document is dated more than nine months after the end of the last audited financial year, it must contain interim financial information, covering at least the first six months of the financial year. If the interim financial information is un-audited state that fact.

The interim financial information must include comparative statements for the same period in the prior financial year, except that the requirement for comparative balance sheet information may be satisfied by presenting the years-end balance sheet.

11.6.   *Legal and arbitration proceedings*

Information on any governmental, legal or arbitration proceedings (including any such proceedings which are pending or threatened of which the issuer is aware), during a period covering at least the previous 12 months which may have, or have had in the recent past, significant effects on the issuer and/or group's financial position or profitability, or provide an appropriate negative statement.

11.7.   *Significant change in the issuer's financial position*

A description of any significant change in the financial position of the group which has occurred since the end of the last financial period for which either audited financial information or interim financial information have been published, or an appropriate negative statement.

12.   Material contracts

A brief summary of all material contracts that are not entered into in the ordinary course of the issuer's business, which could result in any group member being under an obligation or entitlement that is material to the issuer's ability to meet its obligation to security holders in respect of the securities being issued.

13.   Third party information and statement by experts and declarations of any interest

13.1.   Where a statement or report attributed to a person as an expert is included in the registration document, provide such person's name, business address, qualifications and material interest if any in the issuer. If the report has been produced at the issuer's request a statement to that effect that such statement or report is included, in the form and context in which it is included, with the consent of that person who has authorised the contents of that part of the registration document.

13.2.   Where information has been sourced from a third party, provide a confirmation that this information has been accurately reproduced and that as far as the issuer is aware and is able to ascertain from information published by that third party, no facts have been omitted which would render the reproduced information inaccurate or misleading In addition, the issuer shall identify the source(s) of the information.

14.   Documents on display

A statement that for the life of the registration document the following documents (or copies thereof), where applicable, may be inspected:

   (a)   the memorandum and articles of association of the issuer;
   (b)   all reports, letters, and other documents, historical financial information, valuations and statements prepared by any expert at the issuer's request any part of which is included or referred to in the registration document;
   (c)   the historical financial information of the issuer or, in the case of a group, the historical financial information of the issuer and its subsidiary undertakings for each of the two financial years preceding the publication of the registration document.

An indication of where the documents on display may be inspected, by physical or electronic means.

NOTES

Words in square brackets in item 11.1 inserted by Commission Regulation 211/2007/EC, Art 1(4), as from 1 March 2007.

ANNEX XII
MINIMUM DISCLOSURE REQUIREMENTS FOR THE SECURITIES NOTE FOR DERIVATIVE SECURITIES (SCHEDULE)

[11.448]
1. Persons responsible

1.1.   All persons responsible for the information given in the prospectus and, as the case may be, for certain parts of it, with, in the latter case, an indication of such parts. In the case of natural persons including members of the issuer's administrative, management or supervisory bodies indicate the name and function of the person; in case of legal persons indicate the name and registered office.

1.2.   A declaration by those responsible for the prospectus that, having taken all reasonable care to ensure that such is the case, the information contained in the prospectus is, to the best of their knowledge, in accordance with the facts and contains no omission likely to affect its import. As the case may be, declaration by those responsible for certain parts of the prospectus that, having taken all reasonable care to ensure that such is the case, the information contained in the part of the prospectus for which they are responsible is, to the best of their knowledge, in accordance with the facts and contains no omission likely to affect its import.

2. Risk factors

Prominent disclosure of risk factors that are material to the securities being offered and/or admitted to trading in order to assess the market risk associated with these securities in a section headed "risk factors". This must include a risk warning to the effect that investors may lose the value of their entire investment or part of it, as the case may be, and/or, if the investor's liability is not limited to the value of his investment, a statement of that fact, together with a description of the circumstances in which such additional liability arises and the likely financial effect.

3. Key information

3.1.   *Interest of natural and legal persons involved in the issue/offer*

A description of any interest, including conflicting ones that is material to the issue/offer, detailing the persons involved and the nature of the interest.

3.2.   *Reasons for the offer and use of proceeds when different from making profit and/or hedging certain risks*

If reasons for the offer and use of proceeds are disclosed provide the total net proceeds and an estimate of the total expenses of the issue/offer.

4. Information concerning the securities to be offered/admitted to trading

4.1.   *Information concerning the securities*

4.1.1.   A description of the type and the class of the securities being offered and/or admitted to trading, including the ISIN (International security identification number) or other such security identification code.

4.1.2.   A clear and comprehensive explanation to help investors understand how the value of their investment is affected by the value of the underlying instrument(s), especially under the circumstances when the risks are most evident unless the securities have a denomination per unit of at least EUR 50,000 or can only be acquired for at least EUR 50,000 per security.

4.1.3.   Legislation under which the securities have been created.

4.1.4.   An indication whether the securities are in registered form or bearer form and whether the securities are in certificated form or book-entry form. In the latter case, name and address of the entity in charge of keeping the records.

4.1.5.   Currency of the securities issue.

4.1.6.   Ranking of the securities being offered and/or admitted to trading, including summaries of any clauses that are intended to affect ranking or subordinate the security to any present or future liabilities of the issuer.

4.1.7.   A description of the rights, including any limitations of these, attached to the securities and procedure for the exercise of said rights.

4.1.8.   In the case of new issues, a statement of the resolutions, authorisations and approvals by virtue of which the securities have been or will be created and/or issued.

4.1.9.   The issue date of the securities.

4.1.10.   A description of any restrictions on the free transferability of the securities.

4.1.11.

—   The expiration or maturity date of the derivative securities.

—   The exercise date or final reference date.

4.1.12.   A description of the settlement procedure of the derivative securities.

4.1.13.   A description of how any return on derivative securities takes place, the payment or delivery date, and the way it is calculated.

4.1.14.   In respect of the country of registered office of the issuer and the country(ies) where the offer is being made or admission to trading is being sought:

    (a)   information on taxes on the income from the securities withheld at source;

    (b)   indication as to whether the issuer assumes responsibility for the withholding of taxes at the source.

4.2.   *Information concerning the underlying*

4.2.1.   The exercise price or the final reference price of the underlying.

4.2.2.   A statement setting out the type of the underlying and details of where information on the underlying can be obtained:

—   an indication where information about the past and the further performance of the underlying and its volatility can be obtained,

—   where the underlying is a security,

    —   the name of the issuer of the security,

    —   the ISIN (international security identification number) or other such security identification code,

—   where the underlying is an index,

    —   the name of the index and a description of the index if it is composed by the issuer. If the index is not composed by the issuer, where information about the index can be obtained,

—   where the underlying is an interest rate,

    —   a description of the interest rate,

—   others:

    —   Where the underlying does not fall within the categories specified above the securities note shall contain equivalent information.

—   where the underlying is a basket of underlyings,

    —   disclosure of the relevant weightings of each underlying in the basket.

4.2.3.   A description of any market disruption or settlement disruption events that affect the underlying.

4.2.4.   Adjustment rules with relation to events concerning the underlying.

5.   Terms and conditions of the offer

5.1.   *Conditions, offer statistics, expected timetable and action required to apply for the offer*

5.1.1.   Conditions to which the offer is subject.

5.1.2.   Total amount of the issue/offer; if the amount is not fixed, description of the arrangements and time for announcing to the public the amount of the offer.

5.1.3.   The period of time, including any possible amendments, during which the offer will be open and description of the application process.

5.1.4.   Details of the minimum and/or maximum amount of application, (whether in number of securities or aggregate amount to invest).

5.1.5.   Method and time limits for paying up the securities and for delivery of the securities.

5.1.6.   A full description of the manner and date in which results of the offer are to be made public.

5.2.   *Plan of distribution and allotment*

5.2.1.   The various categories of potential investors to which the securities are offered. If the offer is being made simultaneously in the markets of two or more countries and if a tranche has been or is being reserved for certain of these, indicate any such tranche.

5.2.2.   Process for notification to applicants of the amount allotted and indication whether dealing may begin before notification is made.

5.3.   *Pricing*

Indication of the expected price at which the securities will be offered or the method of determining the price and the process for its disclosure. Indicate the amount of any expenses and taxes specifically charged to the subscriber or purchaser.

5.4.   *Placing and underwriting*

5.4.1.   Name and address of the coordinator(s) of the global offer and of single parts of the offer and, to the extend known to the issuer or to the offeror, of the placers in the various countries where the offer takes place.

5.4.2.   Name and address of any paying agents and depository agents in each country.

5.4.3.   Entities agreeing to underwrite the issue on a firm commitment basis, and entities agreeing to place the issue without a firm commitment or under "best efforts" arrangements. Where not all of the issue is underwritten, a statement of the portion not covered.

5.4.4.   When the underwriting agreement has been or will be reached.

5.4.5.   Name and address of a calculation agent.

6.   Admission to trading and dealing arrangements

6.1.   An indication as to whether the securities offered are or will be the object of an application for admission to trading, with a view to their distribution in a regulated market or other equivalent markets with indication of the markets in question. This circumstance shall be mentioned, without creating the impression that the admission to trading necessarily will be approved. If known, the earliest dates on which the securities will be admitted to trading shall be given.

6.2.   All the regulated markets or equivalent markets on which, to the knowledge of the issuer, securities of the same class of the securities to be offered or admitted to trading are already admitted to trading.

6.3.   Name and address of the entities which have a firm commitment to act as intermediaries in secondary trading, providing liquidity through bid and offer rates and description of the main terms of their commitment.

7.   Additional information

7.1.   If advisors connected with an issue are mentioned in the Securities Note, a statement of the capacity in which the advisors have acted.

7.2.   An indication of other information in the Securities Note which has been audited or reviewed by statutory auditors and where auditors have produced a report. Reproduction of the report or, with permission of the competent authority, a summary of the report.

7.3.   Where a statement or report attributed to a person as an expert is included in the Securities Note, provide such person's name, business address, qualifications and material interest, if any, in the issuer. If the report has been produced at the issuer's request a statement to that effect that such statement or report is included, in the form and context in which it is included, with the consent of that person who has authorised the contents of that part of the Securities Note.

7.4.   Where information has been sourced from a third party, provide a confirmation that this information has been accurately reproduced and that as far as the issuer is aware and is able to ascertain from information published by that third party, no facts have been omitted which would render the reproduced information inaccurate or misleading. In addition, the issuer shall identify the source(s) of the information.

7.5.   An indication in the prospectus whether or not the issuer intends to provide post-issuance information. Where the issuer has indicated that it intends to report such information, the issuer shall specify in the prospectus what information will be reported and where such information can be obtained.

ANNEX XIII
MINIMUM DISCLOSURE REQUIREMENTS FOR THE SECURITIES NOTE FOR DEBT SECURITIES WITH A DENOMINATION PER UNIT OF AT LEAST EUR 50,000 (SCHEDULE)

[11.449]
1.   Persons responsible

1.1.   All persons responsible for the information given in the prospectus and, as the case may be, for certain parts of it, with, in the latter case, an indication of such parts. In case of natural persons including members of the issuer's administrative, management or supervisory bodies indicate the name and function of the person; in case of legal persons indicate the name and registered office.

1.2.   A declaration by those responsible for the prospectus that, having taken all reasonable care to ensure that such is the case, the information contained in the prospectus is, to the best of their knowledge, in accordance with the facts and contains no omission likely to affect its import. As the case may be, declaration by those responsible for certain parts of the prospectus that the information contained in the part of the prospectus for which they are responsible is, to the best of their knowledge, in accordance with the facts and contains no omission likely to affect its import.

2.   Risk factors

Prominent disclosure of risk factors that are material to the securities admitted to trading in order to assess the market risk associated with these securities in a section headed "Risk factors".

3.   Key information

Interest of natural and legal persons involved in the issue

A description of any interest, including conflicting ones, that is material to the issue, detailing the persons involved and the nature of the interest.

4.   Information concerning the securities to be admitted to trading

4.1.   Total amount of securities being admitted to trading.

4.2.   A description of the type and the class of the securities being admitted to trading, including the ISIN (international security identification number) or other such security identification code.

4.3.   Legislation under which the securities have been created.

4.4. An indication of whether the securities are in registered or bearer form and whether the securities are in certificated or book-entry form. In the latter case, name and address of the entity in charge of keeping the records.

4.5. Currency of the securities issue.

4.6. Ranking of the securities being admitted to trading, including summaries of any clauses that are intended to affect ranking or subordinate the security to any present or future liabilities of the issuer.

4.7. A description of the rights, including any limitations of these, attached to the securities and procedure for the exercise of said rights.

4.8. The nominal interest rate and provisions relating to interest payable:
— The date from which interest becomes payable and the due dates for interest.
— The time limit on the validity of claims to interest and repayment of principal.

Where the rate is not fixed, description of the underlying on which it is based and of the method used to relate the two:
— A description of any market disruption or settlement disruption events that affect the underlying.
— Adjustment rules with relation to events concerning the underlying.
— Name of the calculation agent.

4.9. Maturity date and arrangements for the amortisation of the loan, including the repayment procedures. Where advance amortisation is contemplated, on the initiative of the issuer or of the holder, it must be described, stipulating amortisation terms and conditions.

4.10. An indication of yield.

4.11. Representation of debt security holders including an identification of the organisation representing the investors and provisions applying to such representation. Indication of where investors may have access to the contracts relating to these forms of representation.

4.12. A statement of the resolutions, authorisations and approvals by virtue of which the securities have been created and/or issued.

4.13. The issue date of the securities.

4.14. A description of any restrictions on the free transferability of the securities.

5. Admission to trading and dealing arrangements

5.1. Indication of the market where the securities will be traded and for which prospectus has been published. If known, give the earliest dates on which the securities will be admitted to trading.

5.2. Name and address of any paying agents and depository agents in each country.

6. Expense of the admission to trading

An estimate of the total expenses related to the admission to trading.

7. Additional information

7.1. If advisors are mentioned in the Securities Note, a statement of the capacity in which the advisors have acted.

7.2. An indication of other information in the Securities Note which has been audited or reviewed by auditors and where auditors have produced a report. Reproduction of the report or, with permission of the competent authority, a summary of the report.

7.3. Where a statement or report attributed to a person as an expert is included in the Securities Note, provide such person's name, business address, qualifications and material interest if any in the issuer. If the report has been produced at the issuer's request a statement to that effect that such statement or report is included, in the form and context in which it is included, with the consent of that person who has authorised the contents of that part of the Securities Note.

7.4. Where information has been sourced from a third party, provide a confirmation that this information has been accurately reproduced and that as far as the issuer is aware and is able to ascertain from information published by that third party, no facts have been omitted which would render the reproduced information inaccurate or misleading. In addition, identify the source(s) of the information.

7.5. Credit ratings assigned to an issuer or its debt securities at the request or with the cooperation of the issuer in the rating process.

ANNEX XIV
ADDITIONAL INFORMATION BUILDING BLOCK ON UNDERLYING SHARE FOR SOME EQUITY SECURITIES

[11.450]
1. Description of the underlying share
   1.1. Describe the type and the class of the shares
   1.2. Legislation under which the shares have been or will be created

1.3. Indication whether the securities are in registered form or bearer form and whether the securities are in certificated form or book-entry form. In the latter case, name and address of the entity in charge of keeping the records

1.4. Indication of the currency of the shares issue

1.5. A description of the rights, including any limitations of these, attached to the securities and procedure for the exercise of those rights:
   — Dividend rights:
      — fixed date(s) on which the entitlement arises,
      — time limit after which entitlement to dividend lapses and an indication of the person in whose favour the lapse operates,
      — dividend restrictions and procedures for non resident holders,
      — rate of dividend or method of its calculation, periodicity and cumulative or non-cumulative nature of payments.
   — Voting rights.
   — pre-emption rights in offers for subscription of securities of the same class.
   — right to share in the issuer's profits.
   — rights to share in any surplus in the event of liquidation.
   — redemption provisions.
   — conversion provisions.

1.6. In the case of new issues, a statement of the resolutions, authorisations and approvals by virtue of which the shares have been or will be created and/or issued and indication of the issue date.

1.7. Where and when the shares will be or have been admitted to trading.

1.8. Description of any restrictions on the free transferability of the shares.

1.9. Indication of the existence of any mandatory takeover bids/or squeeze-out and sell-out rules in relation to the shares.

1.10. Indication of public takeover bids by third parties in respect of the issuer's equity, which have occurred during the last financial year and the current financial year. The price or exchange terms attaching to such offers and the outcome thereof must be stated.

1.11. Impact on the issuer of the underlying share of the exercise of the right and potential dilution effect for the shareholders.

2.   When the issuer of the underlying is an entity belonging to the same group, the information to provide on this issuer is the one required by the share registration document schedule.

ANNEX XV
MINIMUM DISCLOSURE REQUIREMENTS FOR THE REGISTRATION DOCUMENT FOR SECURITIES ISSUED BY COLLECTIVE INVESTMENT UNDERTAKINGS OF THE CLOSED-END TYPE (SCHEDULE)

[11.451]
In addition to the information required in this schedule, the collective investment undertaking must provide the following information as required under paragraphs and items 1, 2, 3, 4, 5.1, 7, 9.1, 9.2.1, 9.2.3, 10.4, 13, 14, 15, 16, 17.2, 18, 19, 20, 21, 22, 23, 24, 25 in Annex I (minimum disclosure requirements for the share registration document schedule).

1. Investment objective and policy

1.1.   A detailed description of the investment objective and policy which the collective investment undertaking will pursue and a description of how that investment objectives and policy may be varied including any circumstances in which such variation requires the approval of investors. A description of any techniques and instruments that may be used in the management of the collective investment undertaking.

1.2.   The borrowing and/or leverage limits of the collective investment undertaking. If there are no such limits, include a statement to that effect.

1.3.   The regulatory status of the collective investment undertaking together with the name of any regulator in its country of incorporation.

1.4.   The profile of a typical investor for whom the collective investment undertaking is designed.

2. Investment restrictions

2.1.   A statement of the investment restrictions which apply to the collective investment undertaking, if any, and an indication of how the holders of securities will be informed of the actions that the investment manager will take in the event of a breach.

2.2.   Where more than 20% of the gross assets of any collective investment undertaking (except where items 2.3 or 2.5 apply) may be:
   (a)   invested in, either directly or indirectly, or lent to any single underlying issuer (including the underlying issuer's subsidiaries or affiliates); or
   (b)   invested in one or more collective investment undertakings which may invest in excess of 20% of its gross assets in other collective investment undertakings (open-end and/or closed-end type); or

(c)   exposed to the creditworthiness or solvency of any one counterparty (including its subsidiaries or affiliates);

the following information must be disclosed:

(i)   information relating to each underlying issuer/collective investment undertaking/counterparty as if it were an issuer for the purposes of the minimum disclosure requirements for the share registration document schedule (in the case of (a)) or minimum disclosure requirements for the registration document schedule for securities issued by collective investment undertaking of the closed-end type (in the case of (b)) or the minimum disclosure requirements for the debt and derivative securities with an individual denomination per unit of at least EUR 50,000 registration document schedule (in the case of (c)); or

(ii)   if the securities issued by the underlying issuer/collective investment undertaking/counterparty have already been admitted to trading on a regulated or equivalent market or the obligations are guaranteed by an entity admitted to trading on a regulated or equivalent market, the name, address, country of incorporation, nature of business and name of the market in which its securities are admitted.

This requirement shall not apply where the 20% is exceeded due to appreciations or depreciations, changes in exchange rates, or by reason of the receipt of rights, bonuses, benefits in the nature of capital or by reason of any other action affecting every holder of that investment, provided the investment manager has regard to the threshold when considering changes in the investment portfolio.

2.3.   Where a collective investment undertaking may invest in excess of 20% of its gross assets in other collective investment undertakings (open ended and/or closed ended), a description of if and how risk is spread in relation to those investments. In addition, item 2.2 shall apply, in aggregate, to its underlying investments as if those investments had been made directly.

2.4.   With reference to point (c) of item 2.2, if collateral is advanced to cover that portion of the exposure to any one counterparty in excess of 20% of the gross assets of the collective investment undertaking, details of such collateral arrangements.

2.5.   Where a collective investment undertaking may invest in excess of 40% of its gross assets in another collective investment undertaking either of the following must be disclosed:

(a)   information relating to each underlying collective investment undertaking as if it were an issuer under minimum disclosure requirements for the registration document schedule for securities issued by collective investment undertaking of the closed-end type;

(b)   if securities issued by an underlying collective investment undertaking have already been admitted to trading on a regulated or equivalent market or the obligations are guaranteed by an entity admitted to trading on a regulated or equivalent market, the name, address, country of incorporation, nature of business and name of the market in which its securities are admitted.

2.6. *Physical commodities*

Where a collective investment undertaking invests directly in physical commodities a disclosure of that fact and the percentage that will be so invested.

2.7. *Property collective investment undertakings*

Where a collective investment undertaking is a property collective investment undertaking, disclosure of that fact, the percentage of the portfolio that is to be invested in the property, as well as a description of the property and any material costs relating to the acquisition and holding of such property. In addition, a valuation report relating to the properties must be included.

Disclosure of item 4.1. applies to:

(a)   the valuation entity;

(b)   any other entity responsible for the administration of the property.

2.8. *Derivatives financial instruments/money market instruments/currencies*

Where a collective investment undertaking invests in derivatives financial instruments, money market instruments or currencies other than for the purposes of efficient portfolio management (i.e. solely for the purpose of reducing, transferring or eliminating investment risk in the underlying investments of a collective investment undertaking, including any technique or instrument used to provide protection against exchange and credit risks), a statement whether those investments are used for hedging or for investment purposes, and a description of if and how risk is spread in relation to those investments.

2.9.   Item 2.2 does not apply to investment in securities issued or guaranteed by a government, government agency or instrumentality of any Member State, its regional or local authorities, or OECD Member State.

2.10.   Point (a) of item 2.2 does not apply to a collective investment undertaking whose investment objective is to track, without material modification, that of a broadly based and recognised published index. A description of the composition of the index must be provided.

3. The applicant's service providers

3.1. The actual or estimated maximum amount of all material fees payable directly or indirectly by the collective investment undertaking for any services under arrangements entered into on or prior to the date of the registration document and a description of how these fees are calculated.

3.2. A description of any fee payable directly or indirectly by the collective investment undertaking which cannot be quantified under item 3.1 and which is or may be material.

3.3. If any service provider to the collective investment undertaking is in receipt of any benefits from third parties (other than the collective investment undertaking) by virtue of providing any services to the collective investment undertaking, and those benefits may not accrue to the collective investment undertaking, a statement of that fact, the name of that third party, if available, and a description of the nature of the benefits.

3.4. The name of the service provider which is responsible for the determination and calculation of the net asset value of the collective investment undertaking.

3.5. A description of any material potential conflicts of interest which any of the service providers to the collective investment undertaking may have as between their duty to the collective investment undertaking and duties owed by them to third parties and their other interests. A description of any arrangements which are in place to address such potential conflicts.

4. Investment manager/advisers

4.1. In respect of any investment manager such information as is required to be disclosed under items 5.1.1 to 5.1.4 and, if material, under item 5.1.5 of Annex I together with a description of its regulatory status and experience.

4.2. In respect of any entity providing investment advice in relation to the assets of the collective investment undertaking, the name and a brief description of such entity.

5. Custody

5.1. A full description of how the assets of the collective investment undertaking will be held and by whom and any fiduciary or similar relationship between the collective investment undertaking and any third party in relation to custody:

Where a custodian, trustee, or other fiduciary is appointed:

  (a) such information as is required to be disclosed under items 5.1.1 to 5.1.4 and, if material, under item 5.1.5 of Annex I;

  (b) a description of the obligations of such party under the custody or similar agreement;

  (c) any delegated custody arrangements;

  (d) the regulatory status of such party and delegates.

5.2. Where any entity other than those entities mentioned in item 5.1, holds any assets of the collective investment undertaking, a description of how these assets are held together with a description of any additional risks.

6. Valuation

6.1. A description of how often, and the valuation principles and the method by which, the net asset value of the collective investment undertaking will be determined, distinguishing between categories of investments and a statement of how such net asset value will be communicated to investors.

6.2. Details of all circumstances in which valuations may be suspended and a statement of how such suspension will be communicated or made available to investors.

7. Cross liabilities

7.1. In the case of an umbrella collective investment undertaking, a statement of any cross liability that may occur between classes or investments in other collective investment undertakings and any action taken to limit such liability.

8. Financial information

8.1. Where, since the date of incorporation or establishment, a collective investment undertaking has not commenced operations and no financial statements have been made up as at the date of the registration document, a statement to that effect.

Where a collective investment undertaking has commenced operations, the provisions of item 20 of Annex I on the Minimum Disclosure Requirements for the share registration document apply.

8.2. A comprehensive and meaningful analysis of the collective investment undertaking's portfolio (if unaudited, clearly marked as such).

8.3. An indication of the most recent net asset value per security must be included in the securities note schedule (and, if un-audited, clearly marked as such).

ANNEX XVI
MINIMUM DISCLOSURE REQUIREMENTS FOR THE REGISTRATION DOCUMENT FOR SECURITIES ISSUED BY MEMBER STATES, THIRD COUNTRIES AND THEIR REGIONAL AND LOCAL AUTHORITIES (SCHEDULE)

[11.452]

1. Persons responsible

1.1. All persons responsible for the information given in the registration document and, as the case may be, for certain parts of it, with, in the latter case, an indication of such parts. In the case of natural persons including members of the issuer's administrative, management or supervisory bodies indicate the name and function of the person; in case of legal persons indicate the name and registered office.

1.2. A declaration by those responsible for the registration document that, having taken all reasonable care to ensure that such is the case, the information contained in the registration document is, to the best of their knowledge in accordance with the facts and contains no omission likely to affect its import. As the case may be, declaration by those responsible for certain parts of the registration document that, having taken all reasonable care to ensure that such is the case the information contained in the part of the registration document for which they are responsible is, to the best of their knowledge, in accordance with the facts and contains no omission likely to affect its import.

2. Risk factors

Prominent disclosure of risk factors that may affect the issuer's ability to fulfil its obligations under the securities to investors in a section headed "Risk factors".

3. Information about the issuer

3.1. The legal name of the issuer and a brief description of the issuer's position within the national governmental framework.

3.2. The domicile or geographical location and legal form of the issuer and its contact address and telephone number.

3.3. Any recent events relevant to the evaluation of the issuer's solvency.

3.4. A description of the issuer's economy including:
  (a) the structure of the economy with details of the main sectors of the economy;
  (b) gross domestic product with a breakdown by the issuer's economic sectors over for the previous two fiscal years.

3.5. A general description of the issuer's political system and government including details of the governing body of the issuer.

4. Public finance and trade

Information on the following for the two fiscal years prior to the date of the registration document:
  (a) the tax and budgetary systems;
  (b) gross public debt including a summary of the debt, the maturity structure of outstanding debt (particularly noting debt with a residual maturity of less than one year) and debt payment record, and of the parts of debt denominated in the domestic currency of the issuer and in foreign currencies;
  (c) foreign trade and balance of payment figures;
  (d) foreign exchange reserves including any potential encumbrances to such foreign exchange reserves as forward contracts or derivatives;
  (e) financial position and resources including liquid deposits available in domestic currency;
  (f) income and expenditure figures.
  Description of any auditing or independent review procedures on the accounts of the issuer.

5. Significant change

5.1. Details of any significant changes to the information provided pursuant to item 4 which have occurred since the end of the last fiscal year, or an appropriate negative statement.

6. Legal and arbitration proceedings

6.1. Information on any governmental, legal or arbitration proceedings (including any such proceedings which are pending or threatened of which the issuer is aware), during a period covering at least the previous 12 months which may have, or have had in the recent past, significant effects on the issuer financial position, or provide an appropriate negative statement.

6.2. Information on any immunity the issuer may have from legal proceedings.

7. Statement by experts and declarations of any interest

Where a statement or report attributed to a person as an expert is included in the registration document, provide such person's name, business address and qualifications. If the report has been produced at the issuer's request a statement to that effect, that such statement or report is included, in the form and context in which it is included, with the consent of that person, who has authorised the contents of that part of the registration document.

To the extent known to the issuer, provide information in respect of any interest relating to such expert which may have an effect on the independence of the expert in the preparation of the report.

8. Documents on display

A statement that for the life of the registration document the following documents (or copies thereof), where applicable, may be inspected:

(a) financial and audit reports for the issuer covering the last two fiscal years and the budget for the current fiscal year;

(b) all reports, letters, and other documents, valuations and statements prepared by any expert at the issuer's request any part of which is included or referred to in the registration document.

An indication of where the documents on display may be inspected, by physical or electronic means.

ANNEX XVII
MINIMUM DISCLOSURE REQUIREMENTS FOR THE REGISTRATION DOCUMENT FOR SECURITIES ISSUED BY PUBLIC INTERNATIONAL BODIES AND FOR DEBT SECURITIES GUARANTEED BY A MEMBER STATE OF THE OECD (SCHEDULE)

[11.453]
1. Persons responsible

1.1. All persons responsible for the information given in the registration document and, as the case may be, for certain parts of it, with, in the latter case, an indication of such parts. In the case of natural persons including members of the issuer's administrative, management or supervisory bodies indicate the name and function of the person; in case of legal persons indicate the name and registered office.

1.2. A declaration by those responsible for the registration document, that, having taken all reasonable care to ensure that such is the case, the information contained in the registration document is, to the best of their knowledge, in accordance with the facts and contains no omission likely to materially affect its import. As the case may be, declaration by those responsible for certain parts of the registration document that, having taken all reasonable care to ensure that such is the case the information contained in the part of the registration document for which they are responsible is, to the best of their knowledge, in accordance with the facts and contains no omission likely to affect its import.

2. Risk factors

Prominent disclosure of risk factors that may affect the issuer's ability to fulfil its obligations under the securities to investors in a section headed "Risk factors".

3. Information about the issuer

3.1. The legal name of the issuer and a brief description of the issuer's legal status.

3.2. The location of the principal office and the legal form of the issuer and its contact address and telephone number.

3.3. Details of the governing body of the issuer and a description of its governance arrangements, if any.

3.4. A brief description of the issuer's purpose and functions.

3.5. The sources of funding, guarantees and other obligations owed to the issuer by its members.

3.6. Any recent events relevant to the evaluation of the issuer's solvency.

3.7. A list of the issuer's members.

4. Financial information

4.1. The two most recently published audited annual financial statements prepared in accordance with the accounting and auditing principles adopted by the issuer, and a brief description of those accounting and auditing principles.

Details of any significant changes to the issuer's financial position which has occurred since the end of the latest published audited annual financial statement, or an appropriate negative statement.

5. Legal and arbitration proceedings

5.1. Information on any governmental, legal or arbitration proceedings (including any such proceedings which are pending or threatened of which the issuer is aware), during a period covering at least the previous 12 months which are likely to have, or have had in the recent past, significant effects on the issuer's financial position, or provide an appropriate negative statement.

5.2. Information on any immunity the issuer may have from legal proceedings pursuant to its constituent document.

6. Statement by experts and declaration of any interests

Where a statement or report attributed to a person as an expert is included in the registration document, provide such person's name, business address and qualifications. If the report has been produced at the issuer's request a statement to that effect, that such statement or report is included, in the form and context in which it is included, with the consent of that person.

To the extent known to the issuer, provide information in respect of any conflict of interests relating to such expert which may have an effect on the independence of the expert in the preparation of the report.

7. Document on display

A statement that for the life of the registration document the following documents (or copies thereof), where applicable, will be made available on request:

   (a)   annual and audit reports of the issuer for each of the last two financial years prepared in accordance with the accounting and auditing principles adopted by the issuer;

   (b)   all reports, letters, and other documents, valuations and statements prepared by any expert at the issuer's request any part of which is included or referred to in the registration document;

   (c)   the issuer's constituent document.

An indication of where the documents on display may be inspected, by physical or electronic means.

ANNEX XVIII
TABLE OF COMBINATIONS

[11.454]

ANNEX XVIII TYPES OF SECURITIES	REGISTRATION DOCUMENT					BUILDING BLOCK
	SHARE	SCHEDULES				PRO FORMA INFORMATION
		DEBT and DERIVATIVE (<EUR 50000)	DEBT and DERIVATIVE (> or = EUR 50000)	ASSET BACKED SEC.	BANKS DEBT and DERIVATIVE	
Shares (preference shares, redeemable shares, shares with preferential subscription rights; etc…)						
Bonds (vanilla bonds, income bonds, structured bonds, etc …) with a denomination of less than EUR 50 000		OR			OR	
Bonds (vanilla bonds, income bonds, structured bonds, etc …) with a denomination of at least EUR 50 000			OR		OR	
Debt securities guaranteed by a third party		OR	OR		OR	
Derivative sec. guaranteed by a third party		OR	OR		OR	
Asset backed securities						
Bonds exchangeable or convertible into third party shares or issuers' or group shares which are admitted on a regulated market		OR	OR		OR	
Bonds exchangeable or convertible into the issuer's shares not admitted on a regulated market						
Bonds exchangeable or convertible into group's shares not admitted on a regulated market		OR	OR		OR	
Bonds with warrants to acquire the issuer's shares not admitted to trading on a regulated market						
Shares with warrants to acquire the issuer's shares not admitted to trading on a regulated market						
Derivatives sec. giving the right to subscribe or to acquire the issuer's shares not admitted on a regulated market						
Derivatives sec. giving the right to acquire group's shares not admitted on a regulated market		OR	OR		OR	
Derivatives sec. giving the right to subscribe or to acquire issuer's or group shares which are admitted on a regulated market and derivatives sec. linked to any other underlying than issuer's or group shares which are not admitted on a regulated market (including any derivatives sec. entitling to cash settlement)		OR	OR		OR	

ANNEX XVIII	REGISTRATION DOCUMENT		
	SCHEDULES		
TYPES OF SECURITIES	COLLECTIVE INVESTMENT UNDERTAKING OF THE CLOSED-END TYPE	STATES AND THEIR REGIONAL AND LOCAL AUTHORITIES	PUBLIC INTERNATIONAL BODIES/Debt Securities guaranteed by a Member State of the OECD
Shares (preference shares, redeemable shares, shares with preferential subscription rights; etc…)			
Bonds (vanilla bonds, income bonds, structured bonds, etc …) with a denomination of less than EUR 50 000			
Bonds (vanilla bonds, income bonds, structured bonds, etc …) with a denomination of at least EUR 50 000			
Debt securities guaranteed by a third party			
Derivative sec. guaranteed by a third party			
Asset backed securities			
Bonds exchangeable or convertible into third party shares or issuers' or group shares which are admitted on a regulated market			
Bonds exchangeable or convertible into the issuer's shares not admitted on a regulated market			
Bonds exchangeable or convertible into group's shares not admitted on a regulated market			
Bonds with warrants to acquire the issuer's shares not admitted to trading on a regulated market			
Shares with warrants to acquire the issuer's shares not admitted to trading on a regulated market			
Derivatives sec. giving the right to subscribe or to acquire the issuer's shares not admitted on a regulated market			
Derivatives sec, giving the right to acquire group's shares not admitted on a regulated market			
Derivatives sec. giving the right to subscribe or to acquire issuer's or group shares which are admitted on a regulated market and derivatives sec. linked to any other underlying than issuer's or group shares which are not admitted on a regulated market (including any derivatives sec. entitling to cash settlement)			

ANNEX XVIII	SECURITIES NOTE						
	SCHEDULES				ADDITIONAL BUILDING BLOCKS		
TYPES OF SECURITIES	SHARE	DEBT (<EUR 50000)	DEBT (> or = EUR 50000)	DERIVATIVES SEC.	GUARANTEES	ASSET BACKED SEC.	UNDERLYING SHARE
Shares (preference shares, redeemable shares, shares with preferential subscription rights; etc…)	■						
Bonds (vanilla bonds, income bonds, structured bonds, etc …) with a denomination of less than EUR 50 000		■					
Bonds (vanilla bonds, income bonds, structured bonds, etc …) with a denomination of at least EUR 50 000			■				
Debt securities guaranteed by a third party		OR	OR		■		
Derivative sec. guaranteed by a third party				■	■		
Asset backed securities		OR	OR			■	
Bonds exchangeable or convertible into third party shares or issuers' or group shares which are admitted on a regulated market		OR	OR	only item 4.2.2			
Bonds exchangeable or convertible into the issuer's shares not admitted on a regulated market		OR	OR				■
Bonds exchangeable or convertible into group's shares not admitted on a regulated market		OR	OR				■
Bonds with warrants to acquire the issuer's shares not admitted to trading on a regulated market		OR	OR	AND except item 4.2.2			■
Shares with warrants to acquire the issuer's shares not admitted to trading on a regulated market	■			AND except item 4.2.2			■
Derivatives sec. giving the right to subscribe or to acquire the issuer's shares not admitted on a regulated market				except item 4.2.2			■
Derivatives sec, giving the right to acquire group's shares not admitted on a regulated market				except item 4.2.2			■
Derivatives sec. giving the right to subscribe or to acquire issuer's or group shares which are admitted on a regulated market and derivatives sec. linked to any other underlying than issuer's or group shares which are not admitted on a regulated market (including any derivatives sec. entitling to cash settlement)				■			

ANNEX XIX
LIST OF SPECIALIST ISSUERS

[11.455]
— Property companies

— Mineral companies

— Investment companies

— Scientific research based companies

— Companies with less than three years of existence (start-up companies)

— Shipping companies.

DIRECTIVE OF THE EUROPEAN PARLIAMENT
AND OF THE COUNCIL

(2004/109/EC)

of 15 December 2004

on the harmonisation of transparency requirements in relation to information about issuers whose securities are admitted to trading on a regulated market and amending Directive 2001/34/EC

NOTES
　　Date of publication in OJ: OJ L390, 31.12.2004, p 38. Notes are as in the original OJ version.
　　This Directive is reproduced as amended by: European Parliament and Council Directive 2008/22/EC; European Parliament and Council Directive 2010/73/EU; European Parliament and Council Directive 2010/78/EU.

[11.456]
THE EUROPEAN PARLIAMENT AND THE COUNCIL OF THE EUROPEAN UNION,

Having regard to the Treaty establishing the European Community, and in particular Articles 44 and 95 thereof,

Having regard to the proposal from the Commission,

Having regard to the opinion of the European Economic and Social Committee,[1]

Having regard to the opinion of the European Central Bank,[2]

Acting in accordance with the procedure laid down in Article 251 of the Treaty,[3]

Whereas:

(1)　Efficient, transparent and integrated securities markets contribute to a genuine single market in the Community and foster growth and job creation by better allocation of capital and by reducing costs. The disclosure of accurate, comprehensive and timely information about security issuers builds sustained investor confidence and allows an informed assessment of their business performance and assets. This enhances both investor protection and market efficiency.

(2)　To that end, security issuers should ensure appropriate transparency for investors through a regular flow of information. To the same end, shareholders, or natural persons or legal entities holding voting rights or financial instruments that result in an entitlement to acquire existing shares with voting rights, should also inform issuers of the acquisition of or other changes in major holdings in companies so that the latter are in a position to keep the public informed.

(3)　The Commission Communication of 11 May 1999, entitled "Implementing the framework for financial markets: Action Plan", identifies a series of actions that are needed in order to complete the single market for financial services. The Lisbon European Council of March 2000 calls for the implementation of that Action Plan by 2005. The Action Plan stresses the need to draw up a Directive upgrading transparency requirements. That need was confirmed by the Barcelona European Council of March 2002.

(4)　This Directive should be compatible with the tasks and duties conferred upon the European System of Central Banks (ESCB) and the Member States' central banks by the Treaty and the Statute of the European System of Central Banks and of the European Central Bank; particular attention in this regard needs to be given to the Member States' central banks whose shares are currently admitted to trading on a regulated market, in order to guarantee the pursuit of primary Community law objectives.

(5)　Greater harmonisation of provisions of national law on periodic and ongoing information requirements for security issuers should lead to a high level of investor protection throughout the Community. However, this Directive does not affect existing Community legislation on units issued by collective investment undertakings other than the closed-end type, or on units acquired or disposed of in such undertakings.

(6)　Supervision of an issuer of shares, or of debt securities the denomination per unit of which is less than EUR 1000, for the purposes of this Directive, would be best effected by the Member State in which the issuer has its registered office. In that respect, it is vital to ensure consistency with Directive 2003/71/EC of the European Parliament and of the Council of 4 November 2003 on the prospectus to be published when securities are offered to the public or admitted to trading.[4] Along the same lines, some flexibility should be introduced allowing third country issuers and Community companies issuing only securities other than those mentioned above a choice of home Member State.

(7)   A high level of investor protection throughout the Community would enable barriers to the admission of securities to regulated markets situated or operating within a Member State to be removed. Member States other than the home Member State should no longer be allowed to restrict admission of securities to their regulated markets by imposing more stringent requirements on periodic and ongoing information about issuers whose securities are admitted to trading on a regulated market.

(8)   The removal of barriers on the basis of the home Member State principle under this Directive should not affect areas not covered by this Directive, such as rights of shareholders to intervene in the management of an issuer. Nor should it affect the home Member State's right to request the issuer to publish, in addition, parts of or all regulated information through newspapers.

(9)   Regulation (EC) No 1606/2002 of the European Parliament and of the Council of 19 July 2002 on the application of international accounting standards[5] has already paved the way for a convergence of financial reporting standards throughout the Community for issuers whose securities are admitted to trading on a regulated market and who are required to prepare consolidated accounts. Thus, a specific regime for security issuers beyond the general system for all companies, as laid down in the Company Law Directives, is already established. This Directive builds on this approach with regard to annual and interim financial reporting, including the principle of providing a true and fair view of an issuer's assets, liabilities, financial position and profit or loss. A condensed set of financial statements, as part of a half-yearly financial report, also represents a sufficient basis for giving such a true and fair view of the first six months of an issuer's financial year.

(10)   An annual financial report should ensure information over the years once the issuer's securities have been admitted to a regulated market. Making it easier to compare annual financial reports is only of use to investors in securities markets if they can be sure that this information will be published within a certain time after the end of the financial year. As regards debt securities admitted to trading on a regulated market prior to 1 January 2005 and issued by issuers incorporated in a third country, the home Member State may under certain conditions allow issuers not to prepare annual financial reports in accordance with the standards required under this Directive.

(11)   This Directive introduces more comprehensive half-yearly financial reports for issuers of shares admitted to trading on a regulated market. This should allow investors to make a more informed assessment of the issuer's situation.

(12)   A home Member State may provide for exemptions from half-yearly reporting by issuers of debt securities in the case of:

—   credit institutions acting as small-size issuers of debt securities, or
—   issuers already existing on the date of the entry into force of this Directive who exclusively issue debt securities unconditionally and irrevocably guaranteed by the home Member State or by one of its regional or local authorities, or
—   during a transitional period of ten years, only in respect of those debt securities admitted to trading on a regulated market prior to 1 January 2005 which may be purchased by professional investors only. If such an exemption is given by the home Member State, it may not be extended in respect of any debt securities admitted to a regulated market thereafter.

(13)   The European Parliament and the Council welcome the Commission's commitment rapidly to consider enhancing the transparency of the remuneration policies, total remuneration paid, including any contingent or deferred compensation, and benefits in kind granted to each member of administrative, management or supervisory bodies under its Action Plan for "Modernising Company Law and Enhancing Corporate Governance in the European Union" of 21 May 2003 and the Commission's intention to make a Recommendation on this topic in the near future.

(14)   The home Member State should encourage issuers whose shares are admitted to trading on a regulated market and whose principal activities lie in the extractive industry to disclose payments to governments in their annual financial report. The home Member State should also encourage an increase in the transparency of such payments within the framework established at various international financial fora.

(15)   This Directive will also make half-yearly reporting mandatory for issuers of only debt securities on regulated markets. Exemptions should only be provided for wholesale markets on the basis of a denomination per unit starting at EUR 50,000, as under Directive 2003/71/EC. Where debt securities are issued in another currency, exemptions should only be possible where the denomination per unit in such a currency is, at the date of the issue, at least equivalent to EUR 50,000.

(16)   More timely and more reliable information about the share issuer's performance over the financial year also requires a higher frequency of interim information. A requirement should therefore be introduced to publish an interim management statement during the first six months and a second interim management statement during the second six months of a financial year. Share issuers who already publish quarterly financial reports should not be required to publish interim management statements.

(17)   Appropriate liability rules, as laid down by each Member State under its national law or regulations, should be applicable to the issuer, its administrative, management or supervisory bodies, or persons responsible within the issuer. Member States should remain free to determine the extent of the liability.

(18) The public should be informed of changes to major holdings in issuers whose shares are traded on a regulated market situated or operating within the Community. This information should enable investors to acquire or dispose of shares in full knowledge of changes in the voting structure; it should also enhance effective control of share issuers and overall market transparency of important capital movements. Information about shares or financial instruments as determined by Article 13, lodged as collateral, should be provided in certain circumstances.

(19) Articles 9 and 10(c) should not apply to shares provided to or by the members of the ESCB in carrying out their functions as monetary authorities provided that the voting rights attached to such shares are not exercised; the reference to a "short period" in Article 11 should be understood with reference to credit operations carried out in accordance with the Treaty and the European Central Bank (ECB) legal acts, in particular the ECB Guidelines on monetary policy instruments and procedures and TARGET, and to credit operations for the purpose of performing equivalent functions in accordance with national provisions.

(20) In order to avoid unnecessary burdens for certain market participants and to clarify who actually exercises influence over an issuer, there is no need to require notification of major holdings of shares, or other financial instruments as determined by Article 13 that result in an entitlement to acquire shares with regard to market makers or custodians, or of holdings of shares or such financial instruments acquired solely for clearing and settlement purposes, within limits and guarantees to be applied throughout the Community. The home Member State should be allowed to provide limited exemptions as regards holdings of shares in trading books of credit institutions and investment firms.

(21) In order to clarify who is actually a major holder of shares or other financial instruments in the same issuer throughout the Community, parent undertakings should not be required to aggregate their own holdings with those managed by undertakings for collective investment in transferable securities (UCITS) or investment firms, provided that such undertakings or firms exercise voting rights independently from their parent undertakings and fulfil certain further conditions.

(22) Ongoing information to holders of securities admitted to trading on a regulated market should continue to be based on the principle of equal treatment. Such equal treatment only relates to shareholders in the same position and does not therefore prejudice the issue of how many voting rights may be attached to a particular share. By the same token, holders of debt securities ranking pari passu should continue to benefit from equal treatment, even in the case of sovereign debt. Information to holders of shares and/or debt securities in general meetings should be facilitated. In particular, holders of shares and/or debt securities situated abroad should be more actively involved in that they should be able to mandate proxies to act on their behalf. For the same reasons, it should be decided in a general meeting of holders of shares and/or debt securities whether the use of modern information and communication technologies should become a reality. In that case, issuers should put in place arrangements in order effectively to inform holders of their shares and/or debt securities, insofar as it is possible for them to identify those holders.

(23) Removal of barriers and effective enforcement of new Community information requirements also require adequate control by the competent authority of the home Member State. This Directive should at least provide for a minimum guarantee for the timely availability of such information. For this reason, at least one filing and storage system should exist in each Member State.

(24) Any obligation for an issuer to translate all ongoing and periodic information into all the relevant languages in all the Member States where its securities are admitted to trading does not foster integration of securities markets, but has deterrent effects on cross-border admission of securities to trading on regulated markets. Therefore, the issuer should in certain cases be entitled to provide information drawn up in a language that is customary in the sphere of international finance. Since a particular effort is needed to attract investors from other Member States and third countries, Member States should no longer prevent shareholders, persons exercising voting rights, or holders of financial instruments, from making the required notifications to the issuer in a language that is customary in the sphere of international finance.

(25) Access for investors to information about issuers should be more organised at a Community level in order to actively promote integration of European capital markets. Investors who are not situated in the issuer's home Member State should be put on an equal footing with investors situated in the issuer's home Member State, when seeking access to such information. This could be achieved if the home Member State ensures compliance with minimum quality standards for disseminating information throughout the Community, in a fast manner on a non-discriminatory basis and depending on the type of regulated information in question. In addition, information which has been disseminated should be available in the home Member State in a centralised way allowing a European network to be built up, accessible at affordable prices for retail investors, while not leading to unnecessary duplication of filing requirements for issuers. Issuers should benefit from free competition when choosing the media or operators for disseminating information under this Directive.

(26) In order to further simplify investor access to corporate information across Member States, it should be left to the national supervisory authorities to formulate guidelines for setting up electronic networks, in close consultation with the other parties concerned, in particular security issuers, investors, market participants, operators of regulated markets and financial information providers.

(27) So as to ensure the effective protection of investors and the proper operation of regulated markets, the rules relating to information to be published by issuers whose securities are admitted to trading on a regulated market should also apply to issuers which do not have a registered office in a Member State and which do not fall within the scope of Article 48 of the Treaty. It should also be ensured that any additional relevant information about Community issuers or third country

issuers, disclosure of which is required in a third country but not in a Member State, is made available to the public in the Community.

(28) A single competent authority should be designated in each Member State to assume final responsibility for supervising compliance with the provisions adopted pursuant to this Directive, as well as for international cooperation. Such an authority should be of an administrative nature, and its independence from economic players should be ensured in order to avoid conflicts of interest. Member States may however designate another competent authority for examining that information referred to in this Directive is drawn up in accordance with the relevant reporting framework and taking appropriate measures in case of discovered infringements; such an authority need not be of an administrative nature.

(29) Increasing cross-border activities require improved cooperation between national competent authorities, including a comprehensive set of provisions for the exchange of information and for precautionary measures. The organisation of the regulatory and supervisory tasks in each Member State should not hinder efficient cooperation between the competent national authorities.

(30) At its meeting on 17 July 2000, the Council set up the Committee of Wise Men on the Regulation of European securities markets. In its final report, that Committee proposed the introduction of new legislative techniques based on a four-level approach, namely essential principles, technical implementing measures, cooperation amongst national securities regulators, and enforcement of Community law. This Directive should confine itself to broad "framework" principles, while implementing measures to be adopted by the Commission with the assistance of the European Securities Committee established by Commission Decision 2001/528/EC[6] should lay down the technical details.

(31) The Resolution adopted by the Stockholm European Council of March 2001 endorsed the final report of the Committee of Wise Men and the proposed four-level approach to make the regulatory process for Community securities legislation more efficient and transparent.

(32) According to that Resolution, implementing measures should be used more frequently, to ensure that technical provisions can be kept up to date with market and supervisory developments, and deadlines should be set for all stages of implementing rules.

(33) The Resolution of the European Parliament of 5 February 2002 on the implementation of financial services legislation also endorsed the Committee of Wise Men's report, on the basis of the solemn declaration made before the European Parliament the same day by the President of the Commission and the letter of 2 October 2001 addressed by the Internal Market Commissioner to the Chairman of the Parliament's Committee on Economic and Monetary Affairs with regard to safeguards for the European Parliament's role in this process.

(34) The European Parliament should be given a period of three months from the first transmission of draft implementing measures to allow it to examine them and to give its opinion. However, in urgent and duly justified cases, that period may be shortened. If, within that period, a Resolution is passed by the European Parliament, the Commission should re-examine the draft measures.

(35) Technical implementing measures for the rules laid down in this Directive may be necessary to take account of new developments on securities markets. The Commission should accordingly be empowered to adopt implementing measures, provided that they do not modify the essential elements of this Directive and provided that the Commission acts in accordance with the principles set out therein, after consulting the European Securities Committee.

(36) In exercising its implementing powers in accordance with this Directive, the Commission should respect the following principles:
— the need to ensure confidence in financial markets among investors by promoting high standards of transparency in financial markets;
— the need to provide investors with a wide range of competing investments and a level of disclosure and protection tailored to their circumstances;
— the need to ensure that independent regulatory authorities enforce the rules consistently, especially as regards the fight against economic crime;
— the need for high levels of transparency and consultation with all market participants and with the European Parliament and the Council;
— the need to encourage innovation in financial markets if they are to be dynamic and efficient;
— the need to ensure market integrity by close and reactive monitoring of financial innovation;
— the importance of reducing the cost of, and increasing access to, capital;
— the balance of costs and benefits to market participants on a long-term basis, including small and medium-sized businesses and small investors, in any implementing measures;
— the need to foster the international competitiveness of Community financial markets without prejudice to a much-needed extension of international cooperation;
— the need to achieve a level playing field for all market participants by establishing Community-wide regulations wherever appropriate;
— the need to respect differences in national markets where these do not unduly impinge on the coherence of the single market;
— the need to ensure coherence with other Community legislation in this area, as imbalances in information and a lack of transparency may jeopardise the operation of the markets and above all harm consumers and small investors.

(37) In order to ensure that the requirements set out in this Directive or the measures implementing this Directive are fulfilled, any infringement of those requirements or measures should be promptly detected and, if necessary, subject to penalties. To that end, measures and penalties should be sufficiently dissuasive, proportionate and consistently enforced. Member States should ensure that decisions taken by the competent national authorities are subject to the right of appeal to the courts.

(38) This Directive aims to upgrade the current transparency requirements for security issuers and investors acquiring or disposing of major holdings in issuers whose shares are admitted to trading on a regulated market. This Directive replaces some of the requirements set out in Directive 2001/34/EC of the European Parliament and of the Council of 28 May 2001 on the admission of securities to official stock exchange listing and on information to be published on those securities.[7] In order to gather transparency requirements in a single act it is necessary to amend it accordingly. Such an amendment however should not affect the ability of Member States to impose additional requirements under Articles 42 to 63 of Directive 2001/34/EC, which remain valid.

(39) This Directive is in line with Directive 95/46/EC of the European Parliament and of the Council of 24 October 1995 on the protection of individuals with regard to the processing of personal data and on the free movement of such data.[8]

(40) This Directive respects fundamental rights and observes the principles recognised in particular by the Charter of the Fundamental Rights of the European Union.

(41) Since the objectives of this Directive, namely to ensure investor confidence through equivalent transparency throughout the Community and thereby to complete the internal market, cannot be sufficiently achieved by the Member States on the basis of the existing Community legislation and can therefore be better achieved at Community level, the Community may adopt measures, in accordance with the principle of subsidiarity as set out in Article 5 of the Treaty. In accordance with the principle of proportionality, as set out in that Article, this Directive does not go beyond what is necessary in order to achieve these objectives.

(42) The measures necessary for implementing this Directive should be adopted in accordance with Council Decision 1999/468/EC of 28 June 1999 laying down the procedures for the exercise of implementing powers conferred on the Commission,[9]

NOTES

[1]   OJ C80, 30.3.2004, p 128.

[2]   OJ C242, 9.10.2003, p 6.

[3]   Opinion of the European Parliament of 30 March 2004 (not yet published in the Official Journal) and Council Decision of 2 December 2004.

[4]   OJ L345, 31.12.2003, p 64.

[5]   OJ L243, 11.9.2002, p 1.

[6]   OJ L191, 13.7.2001, p 45. Decision as amended by Decision 2004/8/EC (OJ L3, 7.1.2004, p 33).

[7]   OJ L184, 6.7.2001, p 1. Directive as last amended by Directive 2003/71/EC.

[8]   OJ L281, 23.11.1995, p 31. Directive as amended by Regulation (EC) No 1882/2003 (OJ L284, 31.10.2003, p 1).

[9]   OJ L184, 17.7.1999, p 23.

HAVE ADOPTED THIS DIRECTIVE:

CHAPTER I
GENERAL PROVISIONS

[11.457]
Article 1
Subject matter and scope
1. This Directive establishes requirements in relation to the disclosure of periodic and ongoing information about issuers whose securities are already admitted to trading on a regulated market situated or operating within a Member State.
2. This Directive shall not apply to units issued by collective investment undertakings other than the closed-end type, or to units acquired or disposed of in such collective investment undertakings.
3. Member States may decide not to apply the provisions mentioned in Article 16(3) and in paragraphs 2, 3 and 4 of Article 18 to securities which are admitted to trading on a regulated market issued by them or their regional or local authorities.
4. Member States may decide not to apply Article 17 to their national central banks in their capacity as issuers of shares admitted to trading on a regulated market if this admission took place before 20 January 2005.

[11.458]
Article 2
Definitions
1. For the purposes of this Directive the following definitions shall apply:
(a)   "securities" means transferable securities as defined in Article 4(1), point 18, of Directive 2004/39/EC of the European Parliament and of the Council of 21 April 2004 on markets in

financial instruments[1] with the exception of money-market instruments, as defined in Article 4(1), point 19, of that Directive having a maturity of less than 12 months, for which national legislation may be applicable;

(b) "debt securities" means bonds or other forms of transferable securitised debts, with the exception of securities which are equivalent to shares in companies or which, if converted or if the rights conferred by them are exercised, give rise to a right to acquire shares or securities equivalent to shares;

(c) "regulated market" means a market as defined in Article 4(1), point 14, of Directive 2004/39/EC;

(d) "issuer" means a legal entity governed by private or public law, including a State, whose securities are admitted to trading on a regulated market, the issuer being, in the case of depository receipts representing securities, the issuer of the securities represented;

(e) "shareholder" means any natural person or legal entity governed by private or public law, who holds, directly or indirectly:

   (i) shares of the issuer in its own name and on its own account;

   (ii) shares of the issuer in its own name, but on behalf of another natural person or legal entity;

   (iii) depository receipts, in which case the holder of the depository receipt shall be considered as the shareholder of the underlying shares represented by the depository receipts;

(f) "controlled undertaking" means any undertaking

   (i) in which a natural person or legal entity has a majority of the voting rights; or

   (ii) of which a natural person or legal entity has the right to appoint or remove a majority of the members of the administrative, management or supervisory body and is at the same time a shareholder in, or member of, the undertaking in question; or

   (iii) of which a natural person or legal entity is a shareholder or member and alone controls a majority of the shareholders' or members' voting rights, respectively, pursuant to an agreement entered into with other shareholders or members of the undertaking in question; or

   (iv) over which a natural person or legal entity has the power to exercise, or actually exercises, dominant influence or control;

(g) "collective investment undertaking other than the closed-end type" means unit trusts and investment companies:

   (i) the object of which is the collective investment of capital provided by the public, and which operate on the principle of risk spreading; and

   (ii) the units of which are, at the request of the holder of such units, repurchased or redeemed, directly or indirectly, out of the assets of those undertakings;

(h) "units of a collective investment undertaking" means securities issued by a collective investment undertaking and representing rights of the participants in such an undertaking over its assets;

(i) "home Member State" means

   [(i) in the case of an issuer of debt securities the denomination per unit of which is less than EUR 1000 or an issuer of shares:

    — where the issuer is incorporated in the Union, the Member State in which it has its registered office,

    — where the issuer is incorporated in a third country, the Member State referred to in point (iii) of Article 2(1)(m) of Directive 2003/71/EC.

    The definition of "home" Member State shall be applicable to debt securities in a currency other than euro, provided that the value of such denomination per unit is, at the date of the issue, less than EUR 1000, unless it is nearly equivalent to EUR 1000;]

   (ii) for any issuer not covered by (i), the Member State chosen by the issuer from among the Member State in which the issuer has its registered office and those Member States which have admitted its securities to trading on a regulated market on their territory. The issuer may choose only one Member State as its home Member State. Its choice shall remain valid for at least three years unless its securities are no longer admitted to trading on any regulated market in the Community;

(j) "host Member State" means a Member State in which securities are admitted to trading on a regulated market, if different from the home Member State;

(k) "regulated information" means all information which the issuer, or any other person who has applied for the admission of securities to trading on a regulated market without the issuer's consent, is required to disclose under this Directive, under Article 6 of Directive 2003/6/EC of the European Parliament and of the Council of 28 January 2003 on insider dealing and market manipulation (market abuse),[2] or under the laws, regulations or administrative provisions of a Member State adopted under Article 3(1) of this Directive;

(l)   "electronic means" are means of electronic equipment for the processing (including digital compression), storage and transmission of data, employing wires, radio, optical technologies, or any other electromagnetic means;

(m)   "management company" means a company as defined in Article 1a(2) of Council Directive 85/611/EEC of 20 December 1985 on the coordination of laws, regulations and administrative provisions relating to undertakings for collective investment in transferable securities (UCITS);[3]

(n)   "market maker" means a person who holds himself out on the financial markets on a continuous basis as being willing to deal on own account by buying and selling financial instruments against his proprietary capital at prices defined by him;

(o)   "credit institution" means an undertaking as defined in Article 1(1)(a) of Directive 2000/12/EC of the European Parliament and of the Council of 20 March 2000 relating to the taking up and pursuit of the business of credit institutions;[4]

(p)   "securities issued in a continuous or repeated manner" means debt securities of the same issuer on tap or at least two separate issues of securities of a similar type and/or class.

2.   For the purposes of the definition of "controlled undertaking" in paragraph 1(f)(ii), the holder's rights in relation to voting, appointment and removal shall include the rights of any other undertaking controlled by the shareholder and those of any natural person or legal entity acting, albeit in its own name, on behalf of the shareholder or of any other undertaking controlled by the shareholder.

[[3.   In order to take account of technical developments on financial markets, to specify the requirements and to ensure the uniform application of paragraph 1, the Commission shall adopt, in accordance with Article 27(2a), (2b) and (2c), and subject to the conditions of Articles 27a and 27b, measures concerning the definitions set out in paragraph 1.]

The Commission shall, in particular:

(a)   establish, for the purposes of paragraph 1(i)(ii), the procedural arrangements in accordance with which an issuer may make the choice of the home Member State;

(b)   adjust, where appropriate for the purposes of the choice of the home Member State referred to in paragraph 1(i)(ii), the three-year period in relation to the issuer's track record in the light of any new requirement under Community law concerning admission to trading on a regulated market; and

(c)   establish, for the purposes of paragraph 1(l), an indicative list of means which are not to be considered as electronic means, thereby taking into account Annex V to Directive 98/34/EC of the European Parliament and of the Council of 22 June 1998 laying down a procedure for the provision of information in the field of technical standards and regulations and of rules on Information Society services[5] in accordance with the regulatory procedure referred to in Article 27(2).

[The measures referred to in points (a) and (b) of the second subparagraph shall be laid down by means of delegated acts in accordance with Article 27(2a), (2b) and (2c), and subject to the conditions of Articles 27a and 27b.]]

NOTES

Para 3: substituted by European Parliament and Council Directive 2008/22/EC, Art 1(1), as from 20 March 2008.

[1]   OJ L145, 30.4.2004, p 1.

[2]   OJ L96, 12.4.2003, p 16.

[3]   OJ L375, 31.12.1985, p 3. Directive as last amended by Directive 2004/39/EC.

[4]   OJ L126, 26.5.2000, p 1. Directive as last amended by Commission Directive 2004/69/EC (OJ L125, 28.4.2004, p 44).

[5]   OJ L 204, 21.7.1998, p. 37. Directive as last amended by Council Directive 2006/96/EC (OJ L 363, 20.12.2006, p. 81).

[11.459]
Article 3
Integration of securities markets

1.   The home Member State may make an issuer subject to requirements more stringent than those laid down in this Directive.

The home Member State may also make a holder of shares, or a natural person or legal entity referred to in Articles 10 or 13, subject to requirements more stringent than those laid down in this Directive.

2.   A host Member State may not:

(a)   as regards the admission of securities to a regulated market in its territory, impose disclosure requirements more stringent than those laid down in this Directive or in Article 6 of Directive 2003/6/EC;

(b)   as regards the notification of information, make a holder of shares, or a natural person or legal entity referred to in Articles 10 or 13, subject to requirements more stringent than those laid down in this Directive.

CHAPTER II
PERIODIC INFORMATION

[11.460]
Article 4
Annual financial reports

1. The issuer shall make public its annual financial report at the latest four months after the end of each financial year and shall ensure that it remains publicly available for at least five years.

2. The annual financial report shall comprise:
   (a) the audited financial statements;
   (b) the management report; and
   (c) statements made by the persons responsible within the issuer, whose names and functions shall be clearly indicated, to the effect that, to the best of their knowledge, the financial statements prepared in accordance with the applicable set of accounting standards give a true and fair view of the assets, liabilities, financial position and profit or loss of the issuer and the undertakings included in the consolidation taken as a whole and that the management report includes a fair review of the development and performance of the business and the position of the issuer and the undertakings included in the consolidation taken as a whole, together with a description of the principal risks and uncertainties that they face.

3. Where the issuer is required to prepare consolidated accounts according to the Seventh Council Directive 83/349/EEC of 13 June 1983 on consolidated accounts,[1] the audited financial statements shall comprise such consolidated accounts drawn up in accordance with Regulation (EC) No 1606/2002 and the annual accounts of the parent company drawn up in accordance with the national law of the Member State in which the parent company is incorporated.

   Where the issuer is not required to prepare consolidated accounts, the audited financial statements shall comprise the accounts prepared in accordance with the national law of the Member State in which the company is incorporated.

4. The financial statements shall be audited in accordance with Articles 51 and 51a of the Fourth Council Directive 78/660/EEC of 25 July 1978 on the annual accounts of certain types of companies[2] and, if the issuer is required to prepare consolidated accounts, in accordance with Article 37 of Directive 83/349/EEC.

   The audit report, signed by the person or persons responsible for auditing the financial statements, shall be disclosed in full to the public together with the annual financial report.

5. The management report shall be drawn up in accordance with Article 46 of Directive 78/660/EEC and, if the issuer is required to prepare consolidated accounts, in accordance with Article 36 of Directive 83/349/EEC.

6. The Commission shall, in accordance with the procedure referred to in Article 27(2), adopt implementing measures in order to take account of technical developments in financial markets and to ensure the uniform application of paragraph 1. The Commission shall in particular specify the technical conditions under which a published annual financial report, including the audit report, is to remain available to the public. Where appropriate, the Commission may also adapt the five-year period referred to in paragraph 1.

NOTES

[1] OJ L193, 18.7.1983, p 1. Directive as last amended by Directive 2003/51/EC of the European Parliament and of the Council (OJ L178, 17.7.2003, p 16).

[2] OJ L222, 14.8.1978, p 11. Directive as last amended by Directive 2003/51/EC.

[11.461]
Article 5
Half-yearly financial reports

1. The issuer of shares or debt securities shall make public a half-yearly financial report covering the first six months of the financial year as soon as possible after the end of the relevant period, but at the latest two months thereafter. The issuer shall ensure that the half-yearly financial report remains available to the public for at least five years.

2. The half-yearly financial report shall comprise:
   (a) the condensed set of financial statements;
   (b) an interim management report; and
   (c) statements made by the persons responsible within the issuer, whose names and functions shall be clearly indicated, to the effect that, to the best of their knowledge, the condensed set of financial statements which has been prepared in accordance with the applicable set of accounting standards gives a true and fair view of the assets, liabilities, financial position and profit or loss of the issuer, or the undertakings included in the consolidation as a whole as required under paragraph 3, and that the interim management report includes a fair review of the information required under paragraph 4.

3.   Where the issuer is required to prepare consolidated accounts, the condensed set of financial statements shall be prepared in accordance with the international accounting standard applicable to the interim financial reporting adopted pursuant to the procedure provided for under Article 6 of Regulation (EC) No 1606/2002.

Where the issuer is not required to prepare consolidated accounts, the condensed set of financial statements shall at least contain a condensed balance sheet, a condensed profit and loss account and explanatory notes on these accounts. In preparing the condensed balance sheet and the condensed profit and loss account, the issuer shall follow the same principles for recognising and measuring as when preparing annual financial reports.

4.   The interim management report shall include at least an indication of important events that have occurred during the first six months of the financial year, and their impact on the condensed set of financial statements, together with a description of the principal risks and uncertainties for the remaining six months of the financial year. For issuers of shares, the interim management report shall also include major related parties transactions.

5.   If the half-yearly financial report has been audited, the audit report shall be reproduced in full. The same shall apply in the case of an auditors' review. If the half-yearly financial report has not been audited or reviewed by auditors, the issuer shall make a statement to that effect in its report.

[6.   The Commission shall adopt, in accordance with Article 27(2) or Article 27(2a), (2b) and (2c), in order to take account of technical developments on financial markets, measures to specify the requirements and ensure the uniform application of paragraphs 1 to 5 of this Article.]

The Commission shall, in particular:

(a)   specify the technical conditions under which a published half-yearly financial report, including the auditors' review, is to remain available to the public;

(b)   clarify the nature of the auditors' review;

(c)   specify the minimum content of the condensed balance sheet and profit and loss accounts and explanatory notes on these accounts, where they are not prepared in accordance with the international accounting standards adopted pursuant to the procedure provided for under Article 6 of Regulation (EC) No 1606/2002.

[The measures referred to in point (a) shall be adopted in accordance with the regulatory procedure referred to in Article 27(2). The measures referred to in points (b) and (c) shall be laid down by means of delegated acts in accordance with Article 27(2a), (2b) and (2c), and subject to the conditions of Articles 27a and 27b.]

[Where appropriate, the Commission may also adapt the five-year period referred to in paragraph 1 by means of a delegated act in accordance with Article 27(2a), (2b) and (2c), and subject to the conditions of Articles 27a and 27b.]

NOTES

Para 6: words in square brackets substituted by European Parliament and Council Directive 2010/78/EU, Art 7(2), as from 4 January 2011.

[11.462]
Article 6
Interim management statements

1.   Without prejudice to Article 6 of Directive 2003/6/EC, an issuer whose shares are admitted to trading on a regulated market shall make public a statement by its management during the first six-month period of the financial year and another statement by its management during the second six-month period of the financial year. Such statement shall be made in a period between ten weeks after the beginning and six weeks before the end of the relevant six-month period. It shall contain information covering the period between the beginning of the relevant six-month period and the date of publication of the statement. Such a statement shall provide:

—   an explanation of material events and transactions that have taken place during the relevant period and their impact on the financial position of the issuer and its controlled undertakings, and

—   a general description of the financial position and performance of the issuer and its controlled undertakings during the relevant period.

2.   Issuers which, under either national legislation or the rules of the regulated market or of their own initiative, publish quarterly financial reports in accordance with such legislation or rules shall not be required to make public statements by the management provided for in paragraph 1.

3.   The Commission shall provide a report to the European Parliament and the Council by 20 January 2010 on the transparency of quarterly financial reporting and statements by the management of issuers to examine whether the information provided meets the objective of allowing investors to make an informed assessment of the financial position of the issuer. Such a report shall include an impact assessment on areas where the Commission considers proposing amendments to this Article.

[11.463]
Article 7
Responsibility and liability
Member States shall ensure that responsibility for the information to be drawn up and made public in accordance with Articles 4, 5, 6 and 16 lies at least with the issuer or its administrative, management or supervisory bodies and shall ensure that their laws, regulations and administrative provisions on liability apply to the issuers, the bodies referred to in this Article or the persons responsible within the issuers.

[11.464]
Article 8
Exemptions
1. Articles 4, 5 and 6 shall not apply to the following issuers:
   (a) a State, a regional or local authority of a State, a public international body of which at least one Member State is a member, the ECB, and Member States' national central banks whether or not they issue shares or other securities; and
   [(b) an issuer exclusively of debt securities admitted to trading on a regulated market, the denomination per unit of which is at least EUR 100,000 or, in the case of debt securities denominated in a currency other than euro, the value of such denomination per unit is, at the date of the issue, equivalent to at least EUR 100,000.]
2. The home Member State may choose not to apply Article 5 to credit institutions whose shares are not admitted to trading on a regulated market and which have, in a continuous or repeated manner, only issued debt securities provided that the total nominal amount of all such debt securities remains below EUR 100,000,000 and that they have not published a prospectus under Directive 2003/71/EC.
3. The home Member State may choose not to apply Article 5 to issuers already existing at the date of the entry into force of Directive 2003/71/EC which exclusively issue debt securities unconditionally and irrevocably guaranteed by the home Member State or by one of its regional or local authorities, on a regulated market.
[4. By way of derogation from paragraph (1)(b), Articles 4, 5 and 6 shall not apply to issuers of exclusively debt securities the denomination per unit of which is at least EUR 50,000 or, in the case of debt securities denominated in a currency other than euro, the value of such denomination per unit is, at the date of the issue, equivalent to at least EUR 50,000, which have already been admitted to trading on a regulated market in the Union before 31 December 2010, for as long as such debt securities are outstanding.]

Para 1: point (b) substituted by European Parliament and Council Directive 2010/73/EU, Art 2(2)(a), as from 31 December 2010. Note that Directive 2010/73/EU has a transposition date of 1 July 2012, and that the original text read as follows—

"(b)   an issuer exclusively of debt securities admitted to trading on a regulated market, the denomination per unit of which is at least EUR 50,000 or, in the case of debt securities denominated in a currency other than Euro, the value of such denomination per unit is, at the date of the issue, equivalent to at least EUR 50,000.".

Para 4: added by European Parliament and Council Directive 2010/73/EU, Art 2(2)(b), as from 31 December 2010. Note that Directive 2010/73/EU has a transposition date of 1 July 2012.

CHAPTER III
ONGOING INFORMATION

SECTION I
INFORMATION ABOUT MAJOR HOLDINGS

[11.465]
Article 9
Notification of the acquisition or disposal of major holdings
1. The home Member State shall ensure that, where a shareholder acquires or disposes of shares of an issuer whose shares are admitted to trading on a regulated market and to which voting rights are attached, such shareholder notifies the issuer of the proportion of voting rights of the issuer held by the shareholder as a result of the acquisition or disposal where that proportion reaches, exceeds or falls below the thresholds of 5%, 10%, 15%, 20%, 25%, 30%, 50% and 75%.
The voting rights shall be calculated on the basis of all the shares to which voting rights are attached even if the exercise thereof is suspended. Moreover this information shall also be given in respect of all the shares which are in the same class and to which voting rights are attached.
2. The home Member States shall ensure that the shareholders notify the issuer of the proportion of voting rights, where that proportion reaches, exceeds or falls below the thresholds provided for in paragraph 1, as a result of events changing the breakdown of voting rights, and on the basis of the information disclosed pursuant to Article 15. Where the issuer is incorporated in a third country, the notification shall be made for equivalent events.
3. The home Member State need not apply:
   (a) the 30% threshold, where it applies a threshold of one-third;

(b)   the 75% threshold, where it applies a threshold of two-thirds.

4.   This Article shall not apply to shares acquired for the sole purpose of clearing and settling within the usual short settlement cycle, or to custodians holding shares in their custodian capacity provided such custodians can only exercise the voting rights attached to such shares under instructions given in writing or by electronic means.

5.   This Article shall not apply to the acquisition or disposal of a major holding reaching or crossing the 5% threshold by a market maker acting in its capacity of a market maker, provided that:

(a)   it is authorised by its home Member State under Directive 2004/39/EC; and

(b)   it neither intervenes in the management of the issuer concerned nor exerts any influence on the issuer to buy such shares or back the share price.

6.   Home Member States under Article 2(1)(i) may provide that voting rights held in the trading book, as defined in Article 2(6) of Council Directive 93/6/EEC of 15 March 1993 on the capital adequacy of investment firms and credit institutions,[1] of a credit institution or investment firm shall not be counted for the purposes of this Article provided that:

(a)   the voting rights held in the trading book do not exceed 5%, and

(b)   the credit institution or investment firm ensures that the voting rights attaching to shares held in the trading book are not exercised nor otherwise used to intervene in the management of the issuer.

[[7.   The Commission shall adopt, by means of delegated acts in accordance with Article 27(2a), (2b) and (2c), and subject to the conditions of Articles 27a and 27b, measures in order to take account of technical developments on financial markets and to specify the requirements laid down in paragraphs 2, 4 and 5.]

[The Commission shall specify, by means of delegated acts in accordance with Article 27(2a), (2b) and (2c), and subject to the conditions of Articles 27a and 27b, the maximum length of the "short settlement cycle" referred to in paragraph 4 of this Article, as well as the appropriate control mechanisms by the competent authority of the home Member State.]

In addition, the Commission may draw up a list of the events referred to in paragraph 2 of this Article, in accordance with the regulatory procedure referred to in Article 27(2).]

NOTES

Para 7: substituted by European Parliament and Council Directive 2008/22/EC, Art 1(3), as from 20 March 2008; the first and second subparagraphs were further substituted by European Parliament and Council Directive 2010/78/EU, Art 7(3), as from 4 January 2011.

[1]   OJ L141, 11.6.1993, p 1. Directive as last amended by Directive 2004/39/EC.

[11.466]
Article 10
Acquisition or disposal of major proportions of voting rights

The notification requirements defined in paragraphs 1 and 2 of Article 9 shall also apply to a natural person or legal entity to the extent it is entitled to acquire, to dispose of, or to exercise voting rights in any of the following cases or a combination of them:

(a)   voting rights held by a third party with whom that person or entity has concluded an agreement, which obliges them to adopt, by concerted exercise of the voting rights they hold, a lasting common policy towards the management of the issuer in question;

(b)   voting rights held by a third party under an agreement concluded with that person or entity providing for the temporary transfer for consideration of the voting rights in question;

(c)   voting rights attaching to shares which are lodged as collateral with that person or entity, provided the person or entity controls the voting rights and declares its intention of exercising them;

(d)   voting rights attaching to shares in which that person or entity has the life interest;

(e)   voting rights which are held, or may be exercised within the meaning of points (a) to (d), by an undertaking controlled by that person or entity;

(f)   voting rights attaching to shares deposited with that person or entity which the person or entity can exercise at its discretion in the absence of specific instructions from the shareholders;

(g)   voting rights held by a third party in its own name on behalf of that person or entity;

(h)   voting rights which that person or entity may exercise as a proxy where the person or entity can exercise the voting rights at its discretion in the absence of specific instructions from the shareholders.

[11.467]
Article 11

1.   Articles 9 and 10(c) shall not apply to shares provided to or by the members of the ESCB in carrying out their functions as monetary authorities, including shares provided to or by members of the ESCB under a pledge or repurchase or similar agreement for liquidity granted for monetary policy purposes or within a payment system.

2.   The exemption shall apply to the above transactions lasting for a short period and provided that the voting rights attaching to such shares are not exercised.

[11.468]
Article 12
Procedures on the notification and disclosure of major holdings
1. The notification required under Articles 9 and 10 shall include the following information:
   (a) the resulting situation in terms of voting rights;
   (b) the chain of controlled undertakings through which voting rights are effectively held, if applicable;
   (c) the date on which the threshold was reached or crossed; and
   (d) the identity of the shareholder, even if that shareholder is not entitled to exercise voting rights under the conditions laid down in Article 10, and of the natural person or legal entity entitled to exercise voting rights on behalf of that shareholder.
2. The notification to the issuer shall be effected as soon as possible, but not later than four trading days, the first of which shall be the day after the date on which the shareholder, or the natural person or legal entity referred to in Article 10,
   (a) learns of the acquisition or disposal or of the possibility of exercising voting rights, or on which, having regard to the circumstances, should have learned of it, regardless of the date on which the acquisition, disposal or possibility of exercising voting rights takes effect; or
   (b) is informed about the event mentioned in Article 9(2).
3. An undertaking shall be exempted from making the required notification in accordance with paragraph 1 if the notification is made by the parent undertaking or, where the parent undertaking is itself a controlled undertaking, by its own parent undertaking.
4. The parent undertaking of a management company shall not be required to aggregate its holdings under Articles 9 and 10 with the holdings managed by the management company under the conditions laid down in Directive 85/611/EEC, provided such management company exercises its voting rights independently from the parent undertaking.

However, Articles 9 and 10 shall apply where the parent undertaking, or another controlled undertaking of the parent undertaking, has invested in holdings managed by such management company and the management company has no discretion to exercise the voting rights attached to such holdings and may only exercise such voting rights under direct or indirect instructions from the parent or another controlled undertaking of the parent undertaking.
5. The parent undertaking of an investment firm authorised under Directive 2004/39/EC shall not be required to aggregate its holdings under Articles 9 and 10 with the holdings which such investment firm manages on a client-by-client basis within the meaning of Article 4(1), point 9, of Directive 2004/39/EC, provided that:
   — the investment firm is authorised to provide such portfolio management under point 4 of Section A of Annex I to Directive 2004/39/EC;
   — it may only exercise the voting rights attached to such shares under instructions given in writing or by electronic means or it ensures that individual portfolio management services are conducted independently of any other services under conditions equivalent to those provided for under Directive 85/611/EEC by putting into place appropriate mechanisms; and
   — the investment firm exercises its voting rights independently from the parent undertaking.

However, Articles 9 and 10 shall apply where the parent undertaking, or another controlled undertaking of the parent undertaking, has invested in holdings managed by such investment firm and the investment firm has no discretion to exercise the voting rights attached to such holdings and may only exercise such voting rights under direct or indirect instructions from the parent or another controlled undertaking of the parent undertaking.
6. Upon receipt of the notification under paragraph 1, but no later than three trading days thereafter, the issuer shall make public all the information contained in the notification.
7. A home Member State may exempt issuers from the requirement in paragraph 6 if the information contained in the notification is made public by its competent authority, under the conditions laid down in Article 21, upon receipt of the notification, but no later than three trading days thereafter.
[8. In order to take account of technical developments on financial markets and to specify the requirements laid down in paragraphs 1, 2, 4, 5 and 6 of this Article, the Commission shall adopt, in accordance with Article 27(2a), (2b) and (2c), and subject to the conditions of Articles 27a and 27b, measures:]
   (a)   . . .
   (b) to determine a calendar of "trading days" for all Member States;
   (c) to establish in which cases the shareholder, or the natural person or legal entity referred to in Article 10, or both, shall effect the necessary notification to the issuer;
   (d) to clarify the circumstances under which the shareholder, or the natural person or legal entity referred to in Article 10, should have learned of the acquisition or disposal;
   (e) to clarify the conditions of independence to be complied with by management companies and their parent undertakings or by investment firms and their parent undertakings to benefit from the exemptions in paragraphs 4 and 5.

   . . .

[9. In order to ensure the uniform conditions of application of this Article and to take account of technical developments on financial markets, the European Supervisory Authority (European Securities and Markets Authority) (hereinafter "ESMA"), established by Regulation (EU) No 1095/2010 of the European Parliament and of the Council[1] may develop draft implementing technical standards to establish standard forms, templates and procedures to be used when notifying the required information to the issuer under paragraph 1 of this Article or when filing information under Article 19(3).

Power is conferred on the Commission to adopt the implementing technical standards referred to in the first subparagraph in accordance with Article 15 of Regulation (EU) No 1095/2010.]

NOTES
Words in square brackets in para 8 substituted, words omitted from that paragraph repealed, and para 9 added, by European Parliament and Council Directive 2010/78/EU, Art 7(4), as from 4 January 2011.
    [1]   OJ L331, 15.12.2010, p 84.

[11.469]
Article 13
1. The notification requirements laid down in Article 9 shall also apply to a natural person or legal entity who holds, directly or indirectly, financial instruments that result in an entitlement to acquire, on such holder's own initiative alone, under a formal agreement, shares to which voting rights are attached, already issued, of an issuer whose shares are admitted to trading on a regulated market.
[2. The Commission shall adopt, by means of delegated acts in accordance with Article 27(2a), (2b) and (2c), and subject to the conditions of Articles 27a and 27b, measures in order to take account of technical developments on financial markets and to specify the requirements laid down in paragraph 1. It shall in particular determine:]
    (a)   the types of financial instruments referred to in paragraph 1 and their aggregation;
    (b)   the nature of the formal agreement referred to in paragraph 1;
    [(c)   the contents of the notification to be made;]
    (d)   the notification period;
    (e)   to whom the notification is to be made.
    . . .
[3. In order to ensure uniform conditions of application of paragraph 1 of this Article and to take account of technical developments on financial markets, ESMA may develop draft implementing technical standards to establish standard forms, templates and procedures to be used when notifying the required information to the issuer under paragraph 1 of this Article or when filing information under Article 19(3).

Power is conferred on the Commission to adopt the implementing technical standards referred to in the first subparagraph in accordance with Article 15 of Regulation (EU) No 1095/2010.]

NOTES
Words in square brackets in para 2 substituted, words omitted from that paragraph repealed, and para 3 added, by European Parliament and Council Directive 2010/78/EU, Art 7(5), as from 4 January 2011.

[11.470]
Article 14
1. Where an issuer of shares admitted to trading on a regulated market acquires or disposes of its own shares, either itself or through a person acting in his own name but on the issuer's behalf, the home Member State shall ensure that the issuer makes public the proportion of its own shares as soon as possible, but not later than four trading days following such acquisition or disposal where that proportion reaches, exceeds or falls below the thresholds of 5% or 10% of the voting rights. The proportion shall be calculated on the basis of the total number of shares to which voting rights are attached.
[2. The Commission shall adopt, by means of delegated acts in accordance with Article 27(2a), (2b) and (2c), and subject to the conditions of Articles 27a and 27b, measures in order to take account of technical developments on financial markets and to specify the requirements laid down in paragraph 1.]

NOTES
Para 2: substituted by European Parliament and Council Directive 2010/78/EU, Art 7(6), as from 4 January 2011.

[11.471]
Article 15
For the purpose of calculating the thresholds provided for in Article 9, the home Member State shall at least require the disclosure to the public by the issuer of the total number of voting rights and capital at the end of each calendar month during which an increase or decrease of such total number has occurred.

[11.472]
Article 16
Additional information

1.   The issuer of shares admitted to trading on a regulated market shall make public without delay any change in the rights attaching to the various classes of shares, including changes in the rights attaching to derivative securities issued by the issuer itself and giving access to the shares of that issuer.

2.   The issuer of securities, other than shares admitted to trading on a regulated market, shall make public without delay any changes in the rights of holders of securities other than shares, including changes in the terms and conditions of these securities which could indirectly affect those rights, resulting in particular from a change in loan terms or in interest rates.

3.   The issuer of securities admitted to trading on a regulated market shall make public without delay of new loan issues and in particular of any guarantee or security in respect thereof. Without prejudice to Directive 2003/6/EC, this paragraph shall not apply to a public international body of which at least one Member State is member.

SECTION II

INFORMATION FOR HOLDERS OF SECURITIES ADMITTED TO TRADING
ON A REGULATED MARKET

[11.473]
Article 17
Information requirements for issuers whose shares are admitted to trading on a regulated market

1.   The issuer of shares admitted to trading on a regulated market shall ensure equal treatment for all holders of shares who are in the same position.

2.   The issuer shall ensure that all the facilities and information necessary to enable holders of shares to exercise their rights are available in the home Member State and that the integrity of data is preserved. Shareholders shall not be prevented from exercising their rights by proxy, subject to the law of the country in which the issuer is incorporated. In particular, the issuer shall:

   (a)   provide information on the place, time and agenda of meetings, the total number of shares and voting rights and the rights of holders to participate in meetings;

   (b)   make available a proxy form, on paper or, where applicable, by electronic means, to each person entitled to vote at a shareholders' meeting, together with the notice concerning the meeting or, on request, after an announcement of the meeting;

   (c)   designate as its agent a financial institution through which shareholders may exercise their financial rights; and

   (d)   publish notices or distribute circulars concerning the allocation and payment of dividends and the issue of new shares, including information on any arrangements for allotment, subscription, cancellation or conversion.

3.   For the purposes of conveying information to shareholders, the home Member State shall allow issuers the use of electronic means, provided such a decision is taken in a general meeting and meets at least the following conditions:

   (a)   the use of electronic means shall in no way depend upon the location of the seat or residence of the shareholder or, in the cases referred to in Article 10(a) to (h), of the natural persons or legal entities;

   (b)   identification arrangements shall be put in place so that the shareholders, or the natural persons or legal entities entitled to exercise or to direct the exercise of voting rights, are effectively informed;

   (c)   shareholders, or in the cases referred to in Article 10(a) to (e) the natural persons or legal entities entitled to acquire, dispose of or exercise voting rights, shall be contacted in writing to request their consent for the use of electronic means for conveying information and, if they do not object within a reasonable period of time, their consent shall be deemed to be given. They shall be able to request, at any time in the future, that information be conveyed in writing, and

   (d)   any apportionment of the costs entailed in the conveyance of such information by electronic means shall be determined by the issuer in compliance with the principle of equal treatment laid down in paragraph 1.

[4.   The Commission shall adopt, by means of delegated acts in accordance with Article 27(2a), (2b) and (2c), and subject to the conditions of Articles 27a and 27b, measures in order to take account of technical developments on financial markets, to take account of developments in information and communication technology and to specify the requirements laid down in paragraphs 1, 2 and 3. The Commission shall, in particular, specify the types of financial institution through which a shareholder may exercise the financial rights provided for in paragraph 2(c).]

NOTES

Para 4: substituted by European Parliament and Council Directive 2010/78/EU, Art 7(7), as from 4 January 2011.

[11.474]
Article 18
Information requirements for issuers whose debt securities are admitted to trading on a regulated market
1.   The issuer of debt securities admitted to trading on a regulated market shall ensure that all holders of debt securities ranking pari passu are given equal treatment in respect of all the rights attaching to those debt securities.

2.   The issuer shall ensure that all the facilities and information necessary to enable debt securities holders to exercise their rights are publicly available in the home Member State and that the integrity of data is preserved. Debt securities holders shall not be prevented from exercising their rights by proxy, subject to the law of country in which the issuer is incorporated. In particular, the issuer shall:

     (a)   publish notices, or distribute circulars, concerning the place, time and agenda of meetings of debt securities holders, the payment of interest, the exercise of any conversion, exchange, subscription or cancellation rights, and repayment, as well as the right of those holders to participate therein;

     (b)   make available a proxy form on paper or, where applicable, by electronic means, to each person entitled to vote at a meeting of debt securities holders, together with the notice concerning the meeting or, on request, after an announcement of the meeting; and

     (c)   designate as its agent a financial institution through which debt securities holders may exercise their financial rights.

[3.   Where only holders of debt securities whose denomination per unit amounts to at least EUR 100,000 or, in the case of debt securities denominated in a currency other than euro whose denomination per unit is, at the date of the issue, equivalent to at least EUR 100,000, are to be invited to a meeting, the issuer may choose as venue any Member State, provided that all the facilities and information necessary to enable such holders to exercise their rights are made available in that Member State.

The choice referred to in the first subparagraph shall also apply with regard to holders of debt securities whose denomination per unit amounts to at least EUR 50,000 or, in the case of debt securities denominated in a currency other than euro, the value of such denomination per unit is, at the date of the issue, equivalent to at least EUR 50,000, which have already been admitted to trading on a regulated market in the Union before 31 December 2010, for as long as such debt securities are outstanding, provided that all the facilities and information necessary to enable such holders to exercise their rights are made available in the Member State chosen by the issuer.]

4.   For the purposes of conveying information to debt securities holders, the home Member State, or the Member State chosen by the issuer pursuant to paragraph 3, shall allow issuers the use of electronic means, provided such a decision is taken in a general meeting and meets at least the following conditions:

     (a)   the use of electronic means shall in no way depend upon the location of the seat or residence of the debt security holder or of a proxy representing that holder;

     (b)   identification arrangements shall be put in place so that debt securities holders are effectively informed;

     (c)   debt securities holders shall be contacted in writing to request their consent for the use of electronic means for conveying information and if they do not object within a reasonable period of time, their consent shall be deemed to be given. They shall be able to request, at any time in the future, that information be conveyed in writing; and

     (d)   any apportionment of the costs entailed in the conveyance of information by electronic means shall be determined by the issuer in compliance with the principle of equal treatment laid down in paragraph 1.

[5.   The Commission shall adopt, by means of delegated acts in accordance with Article 27(2a), (2b) and (2c), and subject to the conditions of Articles 27a and 27b, measures in order to take account of technical developments on financial markets, to take account of developments in information and communication technology and to specify the requirements laid down in paragraphs 1 to 4. The Commission shall, in particular, specify the types of financial institution through which a debt security holder may exercise the financial rights provided for in paragraph 2(c).]

Part 11   EU Legislation

NOTES

   Para 3: substituted by European Parliament and Council Directive 2010/73/EU, Art 2(3), as from 31 December 2010. Note that Directive 2010/73/EU has a transposition date of 1 July 2012, and that the original text read as follows—

     "3.   If only holders of debt securities whose denomination per unit amounts to at least EUR 50,000 or, in the case of debt securities denominated in a currency other than Euro whose denomination per unit is, at the date of the issue, equivalent to at least EUR 50,000, are to be invited to a meeting, the issuer may choose as venue any Member State, provided that all the facilities and information necessary to enable such holders to exercise their rights are made available in that Member State.".

   Para 5: substituted by European Parliament and Council Directive 2010/78/EU, Art 7(8), as from 4 January 2011.

CHAPTER IV
GENERAL OBLIGATIONS

[11.475]
Article 19
Home Member State control
1.   Whenever the issuer, or any person having requested, without the issuer's consent, the admission of its securities to trading on a regulated market, discloses regulated information, it shall at the same time file that information with the competent authority of its home Member State. That competent authority may decide to publish such filed information on its Internet site.

Where an issuer proposes to amend its instrument of incorporation or statutes, it shall communicate the draft amendment to the competent authority of the home Member State and to the regulated market to which its securities have been admitted to trading. Such communication shall be effected without delay, but at the latest on the date of calling the general meeting which is to vote on, or be informed of, the amendment.

2.   The home Member State may exempt an issuer from the requirement under paragraph 1 in respect of information disclosed in accordance with Article 6 of Directive 2003/6/EC or Article 12(6) of this Directive.

3.   Information to be notified to the issuer in accordance with Articles 9, 10, 12 and 13 shall at the same time be filed with the competent authority of the home Member State.

[4.   The Commission shall adopt, by means of delegated acts in accordance with Article 27(2a), (2b) and (2c), and subject to the conditions of Articles 27a and 27b, measures in order to specify the requirements laid down in paragraphs 1, 2 and 3.

The Commission shall, in particular, specify the procedure in accordance with which an issuer, a holder of shares or other financial instruments, or a person or entity referred to in Article 10, is to file information with the competent authority of the home Member State under paragraph 1 or 3, respectively, in order to enable filing by electronic means in the home Member State.]

NOTES

Para 4: substituted by European Parliament and Council Directive 2010/78/EU, Art 7(9), as from 4 January 2011.

[11.476]
Article 20
Languages
1.   Where securities are admitted to trading on a regulated market only in the home Member State, regulated information shall be disclosed in a language accepted by the competent authority in the home Member State.

2.   Where securities are admitted to trading on a regulated market both in the home Member State and in one or more host Member States, regulated information shall be disclosed:
   (a)   in a language accepted by the competent authority in the home Member State; and
   (b)   depending on the choice of the issuer, either in a language accepted by the competent authorities of those host Member States or in a language customary in the sphere of international finance.

3.   Where securities are admitted to trading on a regulated market in one or more host Member States, but not in the home Member State, regulated information shall, depending on the choice of the issuer, be disclosed either in a language accepted by the competent authorities of those host Member States or in a language customary in the sphere of international finance.

In addition, the home Member State may lay down in its law, regulations or administrative provisions that the regulated information shall, depending on the choice of the issuer, be disclosed either in a language accepted by its competent authority or in a language customary in the sphere of international finance.

4.   Where securities are admitted to trading on a regulated market without the issuer's consent, the obligations under paragraphs 1, 2 and 3 shall be incumbent not upon the issuer, but upon the person who, without the issuer's consent, has requested such admission.

5.   Member States shall allow shareholders and the natural person or legal entity referred to in Articles 9, 10 and 13 to notify information to an issuer under this Directive only in a language customary in the sphere of international finance. If the issuer receives such a notification, Member States may not require the issuer to provide a translation into a language accepted by the competent authorities.

[6.   By way of derogation from paragraphs 1 to 4, where securities whose denomination per unit amounts to at least EUR 100,000 or, in the case of debt securities denominated in a currency other than euro equivalent to at least EUR 100,000 at the date of the issue, are admitted to trading on a regulated market in one or more Member States, regulated information shall be disclosed to the public either in a language accepted by the competent authorities of the home and host Member States or in a language customary in the sphere of international finance, at the choice of the issuer or of the person who, without the issuer's consent, has requested such admission.

The derogation referred to in the first subparagraph shall also apply to debt securities the denomination per unit of which is at least EUR 50,000 or, in the case of debt securities denominated in a currency other than euro, the value of such denomination per unit is, at the date of the issue, equivalent to at least EUR 50,000, which have already been admitted to trading on a regulated market in one or more Member States before 31 December 2010, for as long as such debt securities are outstanding.]

7. If an action concerning the content of regulated information is brought before a court or tribunal in a Member State, responsibility for the payment of costs incurred in the translation of that information for the purposes of the proceedings shall be decided in accordance with the law of that Member State.

NOTES

Para 6: substituted by European Parliament and Council Directive 2010/73/EU, Art 2(4), as from 31 December 2010. Note that Directive 2010/73/EU has a transposition date of 1 July 2012, and that the original text read as follows—

"6. By way of derogation from paragraphs 1 to 4, where securities whose denomination per unit amounts to at least EUR 50,000 or, in the case of debt securities denominated in a currency other than Euro equivalent to at least EUR 50,000 at the date of the issue, are admitted to trading on a regulated market in one or more Member States, regulated information shall be disclosed to the public either in a language accepted by the competent authorities of the home and host Member States or in a language customary in the sphere of international finance, at the choice of the issuer or of the person who, without the issuer's consent, has requested such admission.".

[11.477]
Article 21
Access to regulated information
1. The home Member State shall ensure that the issuer, or the person who has applied for admission to trading on a regulated market without the issuer's consent, discloses regulated information in a manner ensuring fast access to such information on a non-discriminatory basis and makes it available to the officially appointed mechanism referred to in paragraph 2. The issuer, or the person who has applied for admission to trading on a regulated market without the issuer's consent, may not charge investors any specific cost for providing the information. The home Member State shall require the issuer to use such media as may reasonably be relied upon for the effective dissemination of information to the public throughout the Community. The home Member State may not impose an obligation to use only media whose operators are established on its territory.
2. The home Member State shall ensure that there is at least one officially appointed mechanism for the central storage of regulated information. These mechanisms should comply with minimum quality standards of security, certainty as to the information source, time recording and easy access by end users and shall be aligned with the filing procedure under Article 19(1).
3. Where securities are admitted to trading on a regulated market in only one host Member State and not in the home Member State, the host Member State shall ensure disclosure of regulated information in accordance with the requirements referred to in paragraph 1.
[4. The Commission shall adopt, by means of delegated acts in accordance with Article 27(2a), (2b) and (2c), and subject to the conditions of Articles 27a and 27b, measures to take account of technical developments on financial markets, to take account of developments in information and communication technology and to specify the requirements laid down in paragraphs 1, 2 and 3.
The Commission shall, in particular, specify:
(a) minimum standards for the dissemination of regulated information, as referred to in paragraph 1;
(b) minimum standards for the central storage mechanism as referred to in paragraph 2.
The Commission may also specify and update a list of media for the dissemination of information to the public.]

NOTES

Para 4: substituted by European Parliament and Council Directive 2010/78/EU, Art 7(10), as from 4 January 2011.

[11.478]
Article 22
Guidelines
[1. ESMA shall draw up guidelines, in accordance with Article 16 of Regulation (EU) No 1095/2010, with a view to further facilitating public access to information to be disclosed under Directive 2003/6/EC, Directive 2003/71/EC and under this Directive.]
The aim of those guidelines shall be the creation of:
(a) an electronic network to be set up at national level between national securities regulators, operators of regulated markets and national company registers covered by the First Council Directive 68/151/EEC of 9 March 1968 on coordination of safeguards which, for the protection of the interests of members and others, are required by Member States of companies within the meaning of the second paragraph of Article 48[1] of the Treaty, with a view to making such safeguards equivalent throughout the Community;[2] and
(b) a single electronic network, or a platform of electronic networks across Member States.

2. The Commission shall review the results achieved under paragraph 1 by 31 December 2006 and may, in accordance with the procedure referred to in Article 27(2), adopt implementing measures to facilitate compliance with Articles 19 and 21.

NOTES

Para 1: words in square brackets substituted by European Parliament and Council Directive 2010/78/EU, Art 7(11), as from 4 January 2011.

¹ The title has been adjusted to take account of the renumbering of the Articles of the Treaty establishing the European Community in accordance with Article 12 of the Treaty of Amsterdam; the original reference was to Article 58 of the Treaty.

² OJ L65, 14.3.1968, p 8. Directive as last amended by Directive 2003/58/EC of the European Parliament and of the Council (OJ L221, 4.9.2003, p 13).

[11.479]
Article 23
Third countries
[1. Where the registered office of an issuer is situated in a third country, the competent authority of the home Member State may exempt that issuer from requirements under Articles 4 to 7, Article 12(6) and Articles 14 to 18, provided that the law of the third country in question lays down equivalent requirements or such an issuer complies with requirements of the law of a third country that the competent authority of the home Member State considers as equivalent.

The competent authority shall then inform ESMA of the exemption granted.]

2. By way of derogation from paragraph 1, an issuer whose registered office is in a third country shall be exempted from preparing its financial statement in accordance with Article 4 or Article 5 prior to the financial year starting on or after 1 January 2007, provided such issuer prepares its financial statements in accordance with internationally accepted standards referred to in Article 9 of Regulation (EC) No 1606/2002.

3. The competent authority of the home Member State shall ensure that information disclosed in a third country which may be of importance for the public in the Community is disclosed in accordance with Articles 20 and 21, even if such information is not regulated information within the meaning of Article 2(1)(k).

[4. In order to ensure the uniform conditions of application of paragraph 1, the Commission shall adopt, in accordance with the procedure referred to in Article 27(2), implementing measures:

   (i)   setting up a mechanism ensuring the establishment of equivalence of information required under this Directive, including financial statements and information, required under the law, regulations or administrative provisions of a third country;

   (ii) stating that, by reason of its domestic law, regulations, administrative provisions, or of the practices or procedures based on the international standards set by international organisations, the third country where the issuer is registered ensures the equivalence of the information requirements provided for in this Directive.

In the context of point (ii) of the first subparagraph, the Commission shall also adopt, by means of delegated acts in accordance with Article 27(2a), (2b) and (2c), and subject to the conditions of Articles 27a and 27b, measures concerning the assessment of standards relevant to the issuers of more than one country.

The Commission shall, in accordance with the procedure referred to in Article 27(2), take the necessary decisions on the equivalence of accounting standards which are used by third-country issuers under the conditions set out in Article 30(3). If the Commission decides that the accounting standards of a third country are not equivalent, it may allow the issuers concerned to continue using such accounting standards during an appropriate transitional period.

In the context of the third subparagraph, the Commission shall also adopt, by means of delegated acts in accordance with Article 27(2a), (2b) and (2c), and subject to the conditions of Articles 27a and 27b, measures aimed at establishing general equivalence criteria regarding accounting standards relevant to issuers of more than one country.]

[5. In order to specify the requirements laid down in paragraph 2, the Commission may adopt, by means of delegated acts in accordance with Article 27(2a), (2b) and (2c), and subject to the conditions of Articles 27a and 27b, measures defining the type of information disclosed in a third country that is of importance to the public in the Union.]

6. Undertakings whose registered office is in a third country which would have required an authorisation in accordance with Article 5(1) of Directive 85/611/EEC or, with regard to portfolio management under point 4 of section A of Annex I to Directive 2004/39/EC if it had its registered office or, only in the case of an investment firm, its head office within the Community, shall also be exempted from aggregating holdings with the holdings of its parent undertaking under the requirements laid down in Article 12(4) and (5) provided that they comply with equivalent conditions of independence as management companies or investment firms.

7. In order to take account of technical developments in financial markets and to ensure the uniform application of paragraph 6, the Commission shall, in accordance with the procedure referred to in Article 27(2), adopt implementing measures stating that, by reason of its domestic law, regulations, or administrative provisions, a third country ensures the equivalence of the independence requirements provided for under this Directive and its implementing measures.

[The Commission shall also adopt, by means of delegated acts in accordance with Article 27(2a), (2b) and (2c), and subject to the conditions of Articles 27a and 27b, measures aimed at establishing general equivalence criteria for the purpose of the first subparagraph.]

[8. ESMA shall assist the Commission in carrying out its tasks under this Article in accordance with Article 33 of Regulation (EU) No 1095/2010.]

NOTES

Para 1: substituted by European Parliament and Council Directive 2010/78/EU, Art 7(12)(a), as from 4 January 2011. Note that this provision has a transposition date of 31 December 2011, and that the original text read as follows—

"1.   Where the registered office of an issuer is in a third country, the competent authority of the home Member State may exempt that issuer from requirements under Articles 4 to 7 and Articles 12(6), 14, 15 and 16 to 18, provided that the law of the third country in question lays down equivalent requirements or such an issuer complies with requirements of the law of a third country that the competent authority of the home Member State considers as equivalent.

However, the information covered by the requirements laid down in the third country shall be filed in accordance with Article 19 and disclosed in accordance with Articles 20 and 21."

Paras 4, 5 substituted, words in square brackets in para 7 substituted, and para 8 added, by European Parliament and Council Directive 2010/78/EU, Art 7(12)(b)–(e), as from 4 January 2011.

CHAPTER V
COMPETENT AUTHORITIES

[11.480]
Article 24
Competent authorities and their powers
[1.   Each Member State shall designate the central authority referred to in Article 21(1) of Directive 2003/71/EC as the central competent administrative authority responsible for carrying out the obligations provided for in this Directive and for ensuring that the provisions adopted pursuant to this Directive are applied. Member States shall inform the Commission and ESMA accordingly.]

However, for the purpose of paragraph 4(h) Member States may designate a competent authority other than the central competent authority referred to in the first subparagraph.

2.   Member States may allow their central competent authority to delegate tasks. Except for the tasks referred to in paragraph 4(h), any delegation of tasks relating to the obligations provided for in this Directive and in its implementing measures shall be reviewed five years after the entry into force of this Directive and shall end eight years after the entry into force of this Directive. Any delegation of tasks shall be made in a specific manner stating the tasks to be undertaken and the conditions under which they are to be carried out.

Those conditions shall include a clause requiring the entity in question to be organised in a manner such that conflicts of interest are avoided and information obtained from carrying out the delegated tasks is not used unfairly or to prevent competition. In any case, the final responsibility for supervising compliance with the provisions of this Directive and implementing measures adopted pursuant thereto shall lie with the competent authority designated in accordance with paragraph 1.

[3.   Member States shall inform the Commission, ESMA in accordance with Article 28(4) of Regulation(EU) No 1095/2010, and competent authorities of other Member States of any arrangements entered into with regard to the delegation of tasks, including the precise conditions for regulating the delegations.]

4.   Each competent authority shall have all the powers necessary for the performance of its functions. It shall at least be empowered to:
(a)   require auditors, issuers, holders of shares or other financial instruments, or persons or entities referred to in Articles 10 or 13, and the persons that control them or are controlled by them, to provide information and documents;
(b)   require the issuer to disclose the information required under point (a) to the public by the means and within the time limits the authority considers necessary. It may publish such information on its own initiative in the event that the issuer, or the persons that control it or are controlled by it, fail to do so and after having heard the issuer;
(c)   require managers of the issuers and of the holders of shares or other financial instruments, or of persons or entities referred to in Articles 10 or 13, to notify the information required under this Directive, or under national law adopted in accordance with this Directive, and, if necessary, to provide further information and documents;
(d)   suspend, or request the relevant regulated market to suspend, trading in securities for a maximum of ten days at a time if it has reasonable grounds for suspecting that the provisions of this Directive, or of national law adopted in accordance with this Directive, have been infringed by the issuer;

(e) prohibit trading on a regulated market if it finds that the provisions of this Directive, or of national law adopted in accordance with this Directive, have been infringed, or if it has reasonable grounds for suspecting that the provisions of this Directive have been infringed;

(f) monitor that the issuer discloses timely information with the objective of ensuring effective and equal access to the public in all Member States where the securities are traded and take appropriate action if that is not the case;

(g) make public the fact that an issuer, or a holder of shares or other financial instruments, or a person or entity referred to in Articles 10 or 13, is failing to comply with its obligations;

(h) examine that information referred to in this Directive is drawn up in accordance with the relevant reporting framework and take appropriate measures in case of discovered infringements; and

(i) carry out on-site inspections in its territory in accordance with national law, in order to verify compliance with the provisions of this Directive and its implementing measures. Where necessary under national law, the competent authority or authorities may use this power by applying to the relevant judicial authority and/or in cooperation with other authorities.

5.   Paragraphs 1 to 4 shall be without prejudice to the possibility for a Member State to make separate legal and administrative arrangements for overseas European territories for whose external relations that Member State is responsible.

6.   The disclosure to competent authorities by the auditors of any fact or decision related to the requests made by the competent authority under paragraph (4)(a) shall not constitute a breach of any restriction on disclosure of information imposed by contract or by any law, regulation or administrative provision and shall not involve such auditors in liability of any kind.

NOTES

The first subparagraph of para 1, and all of para 3, were substituted by European Parliament and Council Directive 2010/78/EU, Art 7(13), as from 4 January 2011. Note that this provision has a transposition date of 31 December 2011, and that the original text read as follows—

"1.   Each Member State shall designate the central authority referred to in Article 21(1) of Directive 2003/71/EC as central competent administrative authority responsible for carrying out the obligations provided for in this Directive and for ensuring that the provisions adopted pursuant to this Directive are applied. Member States shall inform the Commission accordingly.";

"3.   Member States shall inform the Commission and competent authorities of other Member States of any arrangements entered into with regard to the delegation of tasks, including the precise conditions for regulating the delegations.".

[11.481]
Article 25
Professional secrecy and cooperation between Member States
1.   The obligation of professional secrecy shall apply to all persons who work or who have worked for the competent authority and for entities to which competent authorities may have delegated certain tasks. Information covered by professional secrecy may not be disclosed to any other person or authority except by virtue of the laws, regulations or administrative provisions of a Member State.

2.   Competent authorities of the Member States shall cooperate with each other, whenever necessary, for the purpose of carrying out their duties and making use of their powers, whether set out in this Directive or in national law adopted pursuant to this Directive. Competent authorities shall render assistance to competent authorities of other Member States.

[2a.   The competent authorities may refer to ESMA situations where a request for cooperation has been rejected or has not been acted upon within a reasonable time. Without prejudice to the Article 258 of the Treaty on the Functioning of the European Union (TFEU), ESMA may, in situations referred to in the first sentence, act in accordance with the powers conferred on it under Article 19 of Regulation (EU) No 1095/2010.

2b.   The competent authorities shall cooperate with ESMA for the purposes of this Directive, in accordance with Regulation (EU) No 1095/2010.

2c.   The competent authorities shall without delay provide ESMA with all information necessary to carry out its duties under this Directive and under Regulation (EU) No 1095/2010, in accordance with Article 35 of that Regulation.]

3.   [Paragraph 1 shall not prevent the competent authorities from exchanging confidential information with, or from transmitting information to, other competent authorities, ESMA and the European Systemic Risk Board (ESRB) established by Regulation (EU) No 1092/2010 of the European Parliament and of the Council of 24 November 2010 on European Union macroprudential oversight of the financial system and establishing a European Systemic Risk Board.[1]] Information thus exchanged shall be covered by the obligation of professional secrecy to which the persons employed or formerly employed by the competent authorities receiving the information are subject.

[4.   Member States and ESMA in accordance with Article 33 of Regulation (EU) No 1095/2010, may conclude cooperation agreements providing for the exchange of information with the competent authorities or bodies of third countries enabled by their respective legislation to carry out any tasks under this Directive in accordance with Article 24. Member States shall notify ESMA when they conclude cooperation agreements. Such an exchange of information is subject to guarantees of professional secrecy at least equivalent to those referred to in this Article. Such an exchange of information shall be intended for the performance of the supervisory task of the authorities or bodies mentioned. Where the information originates in another Member State, it shall not be disclosed without the express agreement of the competent authorities which disclosed it and, where appropriate, solely for the purposes for which those authorities gave their agreement.]

NOTES

Paras 2a–2c inserted, words in square brackets in para 3 substituted (for the original words "Paragraph 1 shall not prevent the competent authorities from exchanging confidential information"), and para 4 substituted, by European Parliament and Council Directive 2010/78/EU, Art 7(14), as from 4 January 2011. Note that this provision has a transposition date of 31 December 2011, and that para 4 previously read as follows—

"4. Member States may conclude cooperation agreements providing for the exchange of information with the competent authorities or bodies of third countries enabled by their respective legislation to carry out any of the tasks assigned by this Directive to the competent authorities in accordance with Article 24. Such an exchange of information is subject to guarantees of professional secrecy at least equivalent to those referred to in this Article. Such exchange of information shall be intended for the performance of the supervisory task of the authorities or bodies mentioned. Where the information originates in another Member State, it may not be disclosed without the express agreement of the competent authorities which have disclosed it and, where appropriate, solely for the purposes for which those authorities gave their agreement.".

 [1] OJ L331, 15.12.2010,p 1.

[11.482]
[Article 26
Precautionary measures

1. Where the competent authority of a host Member State finds that the issuer or the holder of shares or other financial instruments, or the person or entity referred to in Article 10, has committed irregularities or infringed its obligations, it shall refer its findings to the competent authority of the home Member State and to ESMA.

2. If, despite the measures taken by the competent authority of the home Member State, or because such measures prove inadequate, the issuer or the security holder persists in infringing the relevant legal or regulatory provisions, the competent authority of the host Member State shall, after informing the competent authority of the home Member State, take, in accordance with Article 3(2), all the appropriate measures in order to protect investors, informing the Commission and ESMA thereof at the earliest opportunity.]

NOTES

 Substituted by European Parliament and Council Directive 2010/78/EU, Art 7(15), as from 4 January 2011. Note that this provision has a transposition date of 31 December 2011, and that the original text read as follows—

"Article 26
Precautionary measures

1. Where the competent authority of a host Member State finds that the issuer or the holder of shares or other financial instruments, or the person or entity referred to in Article 10, has committed irregularities or infringed its obligations, it shall refer its findings to the competent authority of the home Member State.

2. If, despite the measures taken by the competent authority of the home Member State, or because such measures prove inadequate, the issuer or the security holder persists in infringing the relevant legal or regulatory provisions, the competent authority of the host Member State shall, after informing the competent authority of the home Member State, take, in accordance with Article 3(2), all the appropriate measures in order to protect investors. The Commission shall be informed of such measures at the earliest opportunity.".

CHAPTER VI
[DELEGATED ACTS AND IMPLEMENTING MEASURES]

NOTES

 Words in square brackets in the preceding heading substituted (for the original words "Implementing Measures") by European Parliament and Council Directive 2010/78/EU, Art 7(16), as from 4 January 2011. Note that this provision has a transposition date of 31 December 2011.

[11.483]
Article 27
Committee procedure

1. The Commission shall be assisted by the European Securities Committee, instituted by Article 1 of Decision 2001/528/EC.

2. Where reference is made to this paragraph, Articles 5 and 7 of Decision 1999/468/EC shall apply, having regard to the provisions of Article 8 thereof, provided that the implementing measures adopted in accordance with that procedure do not modify the essential provisions of this Directive.

 The period laid down in Article 5(6) of Decision 1999/468/EC shall be set at three months.

[2a. The power to adopt the delegated acts referred to in Article 2(3), Article 5(6), Article 9(7), Article 12(8), Article 13(2), Article 14(2), Article 17(4), Article 18(5), Article 19(4), Article 21(4), Article 23(4), Article 23(5) and Article 23(7) shall be conferred on the Commission for a period of 4 years from 4 January 2011. The Commission shall draw up a report in respect of delegated power at the latest 6 months before the end of the four-year period. The delegation of power shall be automatically extended for periods of an identical duration, unless the European Parliament or the Council revokes it in accordance with Article 27a.]

[2b.   As soon as it adopts a delegated act, the Commission shall notify it simultaneously to the European Parliament and to the Council.

2c.   The power to adopt delegated acts is conferred on the Commission subject to the conditions laid down in Articles 27a and 27b.]

[3.   By 31 December 2010, and, thereafter, at least every three years, the Commission shall review the provisions concerning its implementing powers and present a report to the European Parliament and to the Council on the functioning of those powers. The report shall examine, in particular, the need for the Commission to propose amendments to this Directive in order to ensure the appropriate scope of the implementing powers conferred on the Commission. The conclusion as to whether or not amendment is necessary shall be accompanied by a detailed statement of reasons. If necessary, the report shall be accompanied by a legislative proposal to amend the provisions conferring implementing powers on the Commission.]

NOTES

Para 2a originally inserted, and para 3 substituted (for original paras 3, 4), by European Parliament and Council Directive 2008/22/EC, Art 1(10), as from 20 March 2008.

Para 2a subsequently substituted, and paras 2b, 2c inserted, by European Parliament and Council Directive 2010/78/EU, Art 7(17), as from 4 January 2011.

[11.484]
[Article 27a
Revocation of the delegation
1.   The delegation of power referred to in Article 2(3), Article 5(6), Article 9(7), Article 12(8), Article 13(2), Article 14(2), Article 17(4), Article 18(5), Article 19(4) article 21(4), Article 23(4), Article 23(5) and Article 23(7)may be revoked at any time by the European Parliament or by the Council.

2.   The institution which has commenced an internal procedure for deciding whether to revoke a delegation of power shall endeavour to inform the other institution and the Commission within a reasonable time before the final decision is taken, indicating the delegated power which could be subject to revocation.

3.   The decision of revocation shall put an end to the delegation of the power specified in that decision. It shall take effect immediately or at a later date specified therein. It shall not affect the validity of the delegated acts already in force. It shall be published in the Official Journal of the European Union.]

NOTES

Inserted, together with Article 27b, by European Parliament and Council Directive 2010/78/EU, Art 7(18), as from 4 January 2011.

[11.485]
[Article 27b
Objections to delegated acts
1.   The European Parliament or the Council may object to a delegated act within a period of 3 months from the date of notification. At the initiative of the European Parliament or the Council that period shall be extended by 3 months.

2.   If, on the expiry of the period referred to in paragraph 1, neither the European Parliament nor the Council has objected to the delegated act, it shall be published in the *Official Journal of the European Union* and shall enter into force on the date stated therein.

The delegated act may be published in the *Official Journal of the European Union* and enter into force before the expiry of that period if the European Parliament and the Council have both informed the Commission of their intention not to raise objections.

3.   If either the European Parliament or the Council objects to a delegated act within the period referred to in paragraph 1, it shall not enter into force. In accordance with Article 296 TFEU, the institution which objects shall state the reasons for objecting to the delegated act.]

NOTES

Inserted as noted to Article 27a at **[11.484]**.

[11.486]
Article 28
Penalties
1.   Without prejudice to the right of Member States to impose criminal penalties, Member States shall ensure, in conformity with their national law, that at least the appropriate administrative measures may be taken or civil and/or administrative penalties imposed in respect of the persons responsible, where the provisions adopted in accordance with this Directive have not been complied with. Member States shall ensure that those measures are effective, proportionate and dissuasive.

2.   Member States shall provide that the competent authority may disclose to the public every measure taken or penalty imposed for infringement of the provisions adopted in accordance with this Directive, save where such disclosure would seriously jeopardise the financial markets or cause disproportionate damage to the parties involved.

[11.487]
Article 29
Right of appeal
Member States shall ensure that decisions taken under laws, regulations, and administrative provisions adopted in accordance with this Directive are subject to the right of appeal to the courts.

CHAPTER VII
TRANSITIONAL AND FINAL PROVISIONS

[11.488]
Article 30
Transitional provisions
1.   By way of derogation from Article 5(3) of this Directive, the home Member State may exempt from disclosing financial statements in accordance with Regulation (EC) No 1606/2002 issuers referred to in Article 9 of that Regulation for the financial year starting on or after 1 January 2006.
2.   Notwithstanding Article 12(2), a shareholder shall notify the issuer at the latest two months after the date in Article 31(1) of the proportion of voting rights and capital it holds, in accordance with Articles 9, 10 and 13, with issuers at that date, unless it has already made a notification containing equivalent information before that date.
     Notwithstanding Article 12(6), an issuer shall in turn disclose the information received in those notifications no later than three months after the date in Article 31(1).
3.   Where an issuer is incorporated in a third country, the home Member State may exempt such issuer only in respect of those debt securities which have already been admitted to trading on a regulated market in the Community prior to 1 January 2005 from drawing up its financial statements in accordance with Article 4(3) and its management report in accordance with Article 4(5) as long as
     (a)   the competent authority of the home Member State acknowledges that annual financial statements prepared by issuers from such a third country give a true and fair view of the issuer's assets and liabilities, financial position and results;
     (b)   the third country where the issuer is incorporated has not made mandatory the application of international accounting standards referred to in Article 2 of Regulation (EC) No 1606/2002; and
     (c)   the Commission has not taken any decision in accordance with Article 23(4)(ii) as to whether there is an equivalence between the abovementioned accounting standards and
           —   the accounting standards laid down in the law, regulations or administrative provisions of the third country where the issuer is incorporated, or
           —   the accounting standards of a third country such an issuer has elected to comply with.
4.   The home Member State may exempt issuers only in respect of those debt securities which have already been admitted to trading on a regulated market in the Community prior to 1 January 2005 from disclosing half-yearly financial report in accordance with Article 5 for 10 years following 1 January 2005, provided that the home Member State had decided to allow such issuers to benefit from the provisions of Article 27 of Directive 2001/34/EC at the point of admission of those debt securities.

[11.489]
Article 31
Transposition
1.   Member States shall take the necessary measures to comply with this Directive by 20 January 2007. They shall forthwith inform the Commission thereof.
     When Member States adopt these measures, they shall contain a reference to this Directive or shall be accompanied by such reference on the occasion of their official publication. The methods of making such reference shall be laid down by Member States.
2.   Where Member States adopt measures pursuant to Articles 3(1), 8(2), 8(3), 9(6) or 30, they shall immediately communicate those measures to the Commission and to the other Member States.

Article 32   *(Amends Directive 2001/34/EC at* **[11.124]** *et seq.)*

[11.490]
Article 33
Review
The Commission shall by 30 June 2009 report on the operation of this Directive to the European Parliament and to the Council including the appropriateness of ending the exemption for existing debt securities after the 10-year period as provided for by Article 30(4) and its potential impact on the European financial markets.

Part 11   EU Legislation

[11.491]
Article 34
Entry into force
This Directive shall enter into force on the twentieth day following that of its publication in the Official Journal of the European Union.

[11.492]
Article 35
Addressees
This Directive is addressed to the Member States.

DIRECTIVE OF THE EUROPEAN PARLIAMENT AND OF THE COUNCIL

(2005/56/EC)

of 26 October 2005

on cross-border mergers of limited liability companies

(Text with EEA relevance)

NOTES
Date of publication in OJ: OJ L310, 25.11.2005, p 1. Notes are as in the original OJ version.
This Directive is reproduced as amended by: European Parliament and Council Directive 2009/109/EC.

[11.493]
THE EUROPEAN PARLIAMENT AND THE COUNCIL OF THE EUROPEAN UNION,
Having regard to the Treaty establishing the European Community, and in particular Article 44 thereof,
Having regard to the proposal from the Commission,
Having regard to the opinion of the European Economic and Social Committee,[1]
Acting in accordance with the procedure laid down in Article 251 of the Treaty,[2]
Whereas:

(1) There is a need for cooperation and consolidation between limited liability companies from different Member States. However, as regards cross-border mergers of limited liability companies, they encounter many legislative and administrative difficulties in the Community. It is therefore necessary, with a view to the completion and functioning of the single market, to lay down Community provisions to facilitate the carrying-out of cross-border mergers between various types of limited liability company governed by the laws of different Member States.

(2) This Directive facilitates the cross-border merger of limited liability companies as defined herein. The laws of the Member States are to allow the cross-border merger of a national limited liability company with a limited liability company from another Member State if the national law of the relevant Member States permits mergers between such types of company.

(3) In order to facilitate cross-border merger operations, it should be laid down that, unless this Directive provides otherwise, each company taking part in a cross-border merger, and each third party concerned, remains subject to the provisions and formalities of the national law which would be applicable in the case of a national merger. None of the provisions and formalities of national law, to which reference is made in this Directive, should introduce restrictions on freedom of establishment or on the free movement of capital save where these can be justified in accordance with the case-law of the Court of Justice and in particular by requirements of the general interest and are both necessary for, and proportionate to, the attainment of such overriding requirements.

(4) The common draft terms of the cross-border merger are to be drawn up in the same terms for each of the companies concerned in the various Member States. The minimum content of such common draft terms should therefore be specified, while leaving the companies free to agree on other items.

(5) In order to protect the interests of members and others, both the common draft terms of cross-border mergers and the completion of the cross-border merger are to be publicised for each merging company via an entry in the appropriate public register.

(6) The laws of all the Member States should provide for the drawing-up at national level of a report on the common draft terms of the cross-border merger by one or more experts on behalf of each of the companies that are merging. In order to limit experts' costs connected with cross-border mergers, provision should be made for the possibility of drawing up a single report intended for all members of companies taking part in a cross-border merger operation. The common draft terms of the cross-border merger are to be approved by the general meeting of each of those companies.

(7) In order to facilitate cross-border merger operations, it should be provided that monitoring of the completion and legality of the decision-making process in each merging company should be carried out by the national authority having jurisdiction over each of those companies, whereas monitoring of the completion and legality of the cross-border merger should be carried out by the national authority having jurisdiction over the company resulting from the cross-border merger. The

national authority in question may be a court, a notary or any other competent authority appointed by the Member State concerned. The national law determining the date on which the cross-border merger takes effect, this being the law to which the company resulting from the cross-border merger is subject, should also be specified.

(8)   In order to protect the interests of members and others, the legal effects of the cross-border merger, distinguishing as to whether the company resulting from the cross-border merger is an acquiring company or a new company, should be specified. In the interests of legal certainty, it should no longer be possible, after the date on which a cross-border merger takes effect, to declare the merger null and void.

(9)   This Directive is without prejudice to the application of the legislation on the control of concentrations between undertakings, both at Community level, by Regulation (EC) No 139/2004,[3] and at the level of Member States.

(10)   This Directive does not affect Community legislation regulating credit intermediaries and other financial undertakings and national rules made or introduced pursuant to such Community legislation.

(11)   This Directive is without prejudice to a Member State's legislation demanding information on the place of central administration or the principal place of business proposed for the company resulting from the cross-border merger.

(12)   Employees' rights other than rights of participation should remain subject to the national provisions referred to in Council Directive 98/59/EC of 20 July 1998 on collective redundancies,[4] Council Directive 2001/23/EC of 12 March 2001 on the safeguarding of employees' rights in the event of transfers of undertakings, businesses or parts of undertakings or businesses,[5] Directive 2002/14/EC of the European Parliament and of the Council of 11 March 2002 establishing a general framework for informing and consulting employees in the European Community[6] and Council Directive 94/45/EC of 22 September 1994 on the establishment of a European Works Council or a procedure in Community-scale undertakings and Community-scale groups of undertakings for the purposes of informing and consulting employees.[7]

(13)   If employees have participation rights in one of the merging companies under the circumstances set out in this Directive and, if the national law of the Member State in which the company resulting from the cross-border merger has its registered office does not provide for the same level of participation as operated in the relevant merging companies, including in committees of the supervisory board that have decision-making powers, or does not provide for the same entitlement to exercise rights for employees of establishments resulting from the cross-border merger, the participation of employees in the company resulting from the cross-border merger and their involvement in the definition of such rights are to be regulated. To that end, the principles and procedures provided for in Council Regulation (EC) No 2157/2001 of 8 October 2001 on the Statute for a European company (SE)[8] and in Council Directive 2001/86/EC of 8 October 2001 supplementing the Statute for a European company with regard to the involvement of employees,[9] are to be taken as a basis, subject, however, to modifications that are deemed necessary because the resulting company will be subject to the national laws of the Member State where it has its registered office. A prompt start to negotiations under Article 16 of this Directive, with a view to not unnecessarily delaying mergers, may be ensured by Member States in accordance with Article 3(2)(b) of Directive 2001/86/EC.

(14)   For the purpose of determining the level of employee participation operated in the relevant merging companies, account should also be taken of the proportion of employee representatives amongst the members of the management group, which covers the profit units of the companies, subject to employee participation.

(15)   Since the objective of the proposed action, namely laying down rules with common features applicable at transnational level, cannot be sufficiently achieved by the Member States and can therefore, by reason of the scale and impact of the proposed action, be better achieved at Community level, the Community may adopt measures in accordance with the principle of subsidiarity as set out in Article 5 of the Treaty. In accordance with the principle of proportionality as set out in that Article, this Directive does not go beyond what is necessary to achieve that objective.

(16)   In accordance with paragraph 34 of the Interinstitutional Agreement on better law-making,[10] Member States should be encouraged to draw up, for themselves and in the interest of the Community, their own tables which will, as far as possible, illustrate the correlation between this Directive and the transposition measures and to make them public,

---

NOTES

[1]   OJ C117, 30.4.2004, p 43.

[2]   Opinion of the European Parliament of 10 May 2005 (not yet published in the Official Journal) and Council Decision of 19 September 2005.

[3]   Council Regulation (EC) No 139/2004 of 20 January 2004 on the control of concentrations between undertakings (the EC Merger Regulation) (OJ L24, 29.1.2004, p 1).

[4]   OJ L225, 12.8.1998, p 16.

[5]   OJ L82, 22.3.2001, p 16.

[6]   OJ L80, 23.3.2002, p 29.

[7]   OJ L254, 30.9.1994, p 64. Directive as amended by Directive 97/74/EC (OJ L10, 16.1.1998, p 22).

[8]   OJ L294, 10.11.2001, p 1. Regulation as amended by Regulation (EC) No 885/2004 (OJ L168, 1.5.2004, p 1).

[9]   OJ L294, 10.11.2001, p 22.

Part 11   EU Legislation

[10]   OJ C321, 31.12.2003, p 1.

HAVE ADOPTED THIS DIRECTIVE:

[11.494]
Article 1
Scope
This Directive shall apply to mergers of limited liability companies formed in accordance with the law of a Member State and having their registered office, central administration or principal place of business within the Community, provided at least two of them are governed by the laws of different Member States (hereinafter referred to as cross-border mergers).

[11.495]
Article 2
Definitions
For the purposes of this Directive:
1)   "limited liability company", hereinafter referred to as "company", means:
    (a)   a company as referred to in Article 1 of Directive 68/151/EEC,[1] or
    (b)   a company with share capital and having legal personality, possessing separate assets which alone serve to cover its debts and subject under the national law governing it to conditions concerning guarantees such as are provided for by Directive 68/151/EEC for the protection of the interests of members and others;
2.   "merger" means an operation whereby:
    (a)   one or more companies, on being dissolved without going into liquidation, transfer all their assets and liabilities to another existing company, the acquiring company, in exchange for the issue to their members of securities or shares representing the capital of that other company and, if applicable, a cash payment not exceeding 10% of the nominal value, or, in the absence of a nominal value, of the accounting par value of those securities or shares; or
    (b)   two or more companies, on being dissolved without going into liquidation, transfer all their assets and liabilities to a company that they form, the new company, in exchange for the issue to their members of securities or shares representing the capital of that new company and, if applicable, a cash payment not exceeding 10% of the nominal value, or in the absence of a nominal value, of the accounting par value of those securities or shares; or
    (c)   a company, on being dissolved without going into liquidation, transfers all its assets and liabilities to the company holding all the securities or shares representing its capital.

NOTES
[1]   First Council Directive 68/151/EEC of 9 March 1968 on coordination of safeguards which, for the protection of the interests of members and others, are required by Member States of companies within the meaning of the second paragraph of Article 58 of the Treaty, with a view to making such safeguards equivalent throughout the Community (OJ L65, 14.3.1968, p 8). Directive as last amended by the 2003 Act of Accession.

[11.496]
Article 3
Further provisions concerning the scope
1.   Notwithstanding Article 2(2), this Directive shall also apply to cross-border mergers where the law of at least one of the Member States concerned allows the cash payment referred to in points (a) and (b) of Article 2(2) to exceed 10% of the nominal value, or, in the absence of a nominal value, of the accounting par value of the securities or shares representing the capital of the company resulting from the cross-border merger.
2.   Member States may decide not to apply this Directive to cross-border mergers involving a cooperative society even in the cases where the latter would fall within the definition of "limited liability company" as laid down in Article 2(1).
3.   This Directive shall not apply to cross-border mergers involving a company the object of which is the collective investment of capital provided by the public, which operates on the principle of risk-spreading and the units of which are, at the holders' request, repurchased or redeemed, directly or indirectly, out of the assets of that company. Action taken by such a company to ensure that the stock exchange value of its units does not vary significantly from its net asset value shall be regarded as equivalent to such repurchase or redemption.

[11.497]
Article 4
Conditions relating to cross-border mergers
1.   Save as otherwise provided in this Directive,
    (a)   cross-border mergers shall only be possible between types of companies which may merge under the national law of the relevant Member States, and

(b)   a company taking part in a cross-border merger shall comply with the provisions and formalities of the national law to which it is subject. The laws of a Member State enabling its national authorities to oppose a given internal merger on grounds of public interest shall also be applicable to a cross-border merger where at least one of the merging companies is subject to the law of that Member State. This provision shall not apply to the extent that Article 21 of Regulation (EC) No 139/2004 is applicable.

2.   The provisions and formalities referred to in paragraph 1(b) shall, in particular, include those concerning the decision-making process relating to the merger and, taking into account the cross-border nature of the merger, the protection of creditors of the merging companies, debenture holders and the holders of securities or shares, as well as of employees as regards rights other than those governed by Article 16. A Member State may, in the case of companies participating in a cross-border merger and governed by its law, adopt provisions designed to ensure appropriate protection for minority members who have opposed the cross-border merger.

[11.498]
Article 5
Common draft terms of cross-border mergers

The management or administrative organ of each of the merging companies shall draw up the common draft terms of cross-border merger. The common draft terms of cross-border merger shall include at least the following particulars:

(a)   the form, name and registered office of the merging companies and those proposed for the company resulting from the cross-border merger;

(b)   the ratio applicable to the exchange of securities or shares representing the company capital and the amount of any cash payment;

(c)   the terms for the allotment of securities or shares representing the capital of the company resulting from the cross-border merger;

(d)   the likely repercussions of the cross-border merger on employment;

(e)   the date from which the holding of such securities or shares representing the company capital will entitle the holders to share in profits and any special conditions affecting that entitlement;

(f)   the date from which the transactions of the merging companies will be treated for accounting purposes as being those of the company resulting from the cross-border merger;

(g)   the rights conferred by the company resulting from the cross-border merger on members enjoying special rights or on holders of securities other than shares representing the company capital, or the measures proposed concerning them;

(h)   any special advantages granted to the experts who examine the draft terms of the cross-border merger or to members of the administrative, management, supervisory or controlling organs of the merging companies;

(i)   the statutes of the company resulting from the cross-border merger;

(j)   where appropriate, information on the procedures by which arrangements for the involvement of employees in the definition of their rights to participation in the company resulting from the cross-border merger are determined pursuant to Article 16;

(k)   information on the evaluation of the assets and liabilities which are transferred to the company resulting from the cross-border merger;

(l)   dates of the merging companies' accounts used to establish the conditions of the cross-border merger.

[11.499]
Article 6
Publication

1.   The common draft terms of the cross-border merger shall be published in the manner prescribed by the laws of each Member State in accordance with Article 3 of Directive 68/151/EEC for each of the merging companies at least one month before the date of the general meeting which is to decide thereon.

[Any of the merging companies shall be exempt from the publication requirement laid down in Article 3 of Directive 68/151/EEC if, for a continuous period beginning at least one month before the day fixed for the general meeting which is to decide on the common draft terms of cross-border merger and ending not earlier than the conclusion of that meeting, it makes the common draft terms of such merger available on its website free of charge for the public. Member States shall not subject that exemption to any requirements or constraints other than those which are necessary in order to ensure the security of the website and the authenticity of the documents and may impose such requirements or constraints only to the extent that they are proportionate in order to achieve those objectives.

By way of derogation from the second subparagraph, Member States may require that publication be effected via the central electronic platform referred to in Article 3(4) of Directive 68/151/EEC. Member States may alternatively require that such publication be made on any other website designated by them for that purpose. Where Member States avail themselves of one of those possibilities, they shall ensure that companies are not charged a specific fee for such publication.

Where a website other than the central electronic platform is used, a reference giving access to that website shall be published on the central electronic platform at least one month before the day fixed for the general meeting. That reference shall include the date of publication of the common draft terms of cross-border merger on the website and shall be accessible to the public free of charge. Companies shall not be charged a specific fee for such publication.

The prohibition precluding the charging to companies of a specific fee for publication, laid down in the third and fourth subparagraphs, shall not affect the ability of Member States to pass on to companies the costs in respect of the central electronic platform.

Member States may require companies to maintain the information for a specific period after the general meeting on their website or, where applicable, on the central electronic platform or the other website designated by the Member State concerned. Member States may determine the consequences of temporary disruption of access to the website or to the central electronic platform, caused by technical or other factors.]

2. For each of the merging companies and subject to the additional requirements imposed by the Member State to which the company concerned is subject, the following particulars shall be published in the national gazette of that Member State:

(a) the type, name and registered office of every merging company;
(b) the register in which the documents referred to in Article 3(2) of Directive 68/151/EEC are filed in respect of each merging company, and the number of the entry in that register;
(c) an indication, for each of the merging companies, of the arrangements made for the exercise of the rights of creditors and of any minority members of the merging companies and the address at which complete information on those arrangements may be obtained free of charge.

NOTES

Para 1: words in square brackets added by European Parliament and Council Directive 2009/109/EC, Art 4(1), as from 22 October 2009.

[11.500]
Article 7
Report of the management or administrative organ
The management or administrative organ of each of the merging companies shall draw up a report intended for the members explaining and justifying the legal and economic aspects of the cross-border merger and explaining the implications of the cross-border merger for members, creditors and employees.

The report shall be made available to the members and to the representatives of the employees or, where there are no such representatives, to the employees themselves, not less than one month before the date of the general meeting referred to in Article 9.

Where the management or administrative organ of any of the merging companies receives, in good time, an opinion from the representatives of their employees, as provided for under national law, that opinion shall be appended to the report.

[11.501]
Article 8
Independent expert report
1. An independent expert report intended for members and made available not less than one month before the date of the general meeting referred to in Article 9 shall be drawn up for each merging company. Depending on the law of each Member State, such experts may be natural persons or legal persons.

2. As an alternative to experts operating on behalf of each of the merging companies, one or more independent experts, appointed for that purpose at the joint request of the companies by a judicial or administrative authority in the Member State of one of the merging companies or of the company resulting from the cross-border merger or approved by such an authority, may examine the common draft terms of cross-border merger and draw up a single written report to all the members.

3. The expert report shall include at least the particulars provided for by Article 10(2) of Council Directive 78/855/EEC of 9 October 1978 concerning mergers of public limited liability companies.[1] The experts shall be entitled to secure from each of the merging companies all information they consider necessary for the discharge of their duties.

4. Neither an examination of the common draft terms of cross-border merger by independent experts nor an expert report shall be required if all the members of each of the companies involved in the cross-border merger have so agreed.

NOTES

[1] OJ L295, 20.10.1978, p 36. Directive as last amended by the 2003 Act of Accession.

[11.502]
Article 9
Approval by the general meeting
1. After taking note of the reports referred to in Articles 7 and 8, the general meeting of each of the merging companies shall decide on the approval of the common draft terms of cross-border merger.
2. The general meeting of each of the merging companies may reserve the right to make implementation of the cross-border merger conditional on express ratification by it of the arrangements decided on with respect to the participation of employees in the company resulting from the cross-border merger.
3. The laws of a Member State need not require approval of the merger by the general meeting of the acquiring company if the conditions laid down in Article 8 of Directive 78/855/EEC are fulfilled.

[11.503]
Article 10
Pre-merger certificate
1. Each Member State shall designate the court, notary or other authority competent to scrutinise the legality of the cross-border merger as regards that part of the procedure which concerns each merging company subject to its national law.
2. In each Member State concerned the authority referred to in paragraph 1 shall issue, without delay to each merging company subject to that State's national law, a certificate conclusively attesting to the proper completion of the pre-merger acts and formalities.
3. If the law of a Member State to which a merging company is subject provides for a procedure to scrutinise and amend the ratio applicable to the exchange of securities or shares, or a procedure to compensate minority members, without preventing the registration of the cross-border merger, such procedure shall only apply if the other merging companies situated in Member States which do not provide for such procedure explicitly accept, when approving the draft terms of the cross-border merger in accordance with Article 9(1), the possibility for the members of that merging company to have recourse to such procedure, to be initiated before the court having jurisdiction over that merging company. In such cases, the authority referred to in paragraph 1 may issue the certificate referred to in paragraph 2 even if such procedure has commenced. The certificate must, however, indicate that the procedure is pending. The decision in the procedure shall be binding on the company resulting from the cross-border merger and all its members.

[11.504]
Article 11
Scrutiny of the legality of the cross-border merger
1. Each Member State shall designate the court, notary or other authority competent to scrutinise the legality of the cross-border merger as regards that part of the procedure which concerns the completion of the cross-border merger and, where appropriate, the formation of a new company resulting from the cross-border merger where the company created by the cross-border merger is subject to its national law. The said authority shall in particular ensure that the merging companies have approved the common draft terms of cross-border merger in the same terms and, where appropriate, that arrangements for employee participation have been determined in accordance with Article 16.
2. To that end each merging company shall submit to the authority referred to in paragraph 1 the certificate referred to in Article 10(2) within six months of its issue together with the common draft terms of cross-border merger approved by the general meeting referred to in Article 9.

[11.505]
Article 12
Entry into effect of the cross-border merger
The law of the Member State to whose jurisdiction the company resulting from the cross-border merger is subject shall determine the date on which the cross-border merger takes effect. That date must be after the scrutiny referred to in Article 11 has been carried out.

[11.506]
Article 13
Registration
The law of each of the Member States to whose jurisdiction the merging companies were subject shall determine, with respect to the territory of that State, the arrangements, in accordance with Article 3 of Directive 68/151/EEC, for publicising completion of the cross-border merger in the public register in which each of the companies is required to file documents.
The registry for the registration of the company resulting from the cross-border merger shall notify, without delay, the registry in which each of the companies was required to file documents that the cross-border merger has taken effect. Deletion of the old registration, if applicable, shall be effected on receipt of that notification, but not before.

Part 11   EU Legislation

[11.507]
Article 14
Consequences of the cross-border merger
1.   A cross-border merger carried out as laid down in points (a) and (c) of Article 2(2) shall, from the date referred to in Article 12, have the following consequences:
   (a)   all the assets and liabilities of the company being acquired shall be transferred to the acquiring company;
   (b)   the members of the company being acquired shall become members of the acquiring company;
   (c)   the company being acquired shall cease to exist.
2.   A cross-border merger carried out as laid down in point (b) of Article 2(2) shall, from the date referred to in Article 12, have the following consequences:
   (a)   all the assets and liabilities of the merging companies shall be transferred to the new company;
   (b)   the members of the merging companies shall become members of the new company;
   (c)   the merging companies shall cease to exist.
3.   Where, in the case of a cross-border merger of companies covered by this Directive, the laws of the Member States require the completion of special formalities before the transfer of certain assets, rights and obligations by the merging companies becomes effective against third parties, those formalities shall be carried out by the company resulting from the cross-border merger.
4.   The rights and obligations of the merging companies arising from contracts of employment or from employment relationships and existing at the date on which the cross-border merger takes effect shall, by reason of that cross-border merger taking effect, be transferred to the company resulting from the cross-border merger on the date on which the cross-border merger takes effect.
5.   No shares in the acquiring company shall be exchanged for shares in the company being acquired held either:
   (a)   by the acquiring company itself or through a person acting in his or her own name but on its behalf;
   (b)   by the company being acquired itself or through a person acting in his or her own name but on its behalf.

[11.508]
Article 15
Simplified formalities
1.   Where a cross-border merger by acquisition is carried out by a company which holds all the shares and other securities conferring the right to vote at general meetings of the company or companies being acquired:
   —   Articles 5, points (b), (c) and (e), 8 and 14(1), point (b) shall not apply,
   —   Article 9(1) shall not apply to the company or companies being acquired.
[2.   Where a cross-border merger by acquisition is carried out by a company which holds 90% or more, but not all, of the shares and other securities conferring the right to vote at general meetings of the company or companies being acquired, reports by an independent expert or experts and the documents necessary for scrutiny shall be required only to the extent that the national law governing either the acquiring company or the company or companies being acquired so requires, in accordance with Directive 78/855/EEC.]

NOTES
   Para 2: substituted by European Parliament and Council Directive 2009/109/EC, Art 4(2), as from 22 October 2009.

[11.509]
Article 16
Employee participation
1.   Without prejudice to paragraph 2, the company resulting from the cross-border merger shall be subject to the rules in force concerning employee participation, if any, in the Member State where it has its registered office.
2.   However, the rules in force concerning employee participation, if any, in the Member State where the company resulting from the cross-border merger has its registered office shall not apply, where at least one of the merging companies has, in the six months before the publication of the draft terms of the cross-border merger as referred to in Article 6, an average number of employees that exceeds 500 and is operating under an employee participation system within the meaning of Article 2(k) of Directive 2001/86/EC, or where the national law applicable to the company resulting from the cross-border merger does not
   (a)   provide for at least the same level of employee participation as operated in the relevant merging companies, measured by reference to the proportion of employee representatives amongst the members of the administrative or supervisory organ or their committees or of the management group which covers the profit units of the company, subject to employee representation, or

(b)   provide for employees of establishments of the company resulting from the cross-border merger that are situated in other Member States the same entitlement to exercise participation rights as is enjoyed by those employees employed in the Member State where the company resulting from the cross-border merger has its registered office.

3.   In the cases referred to in paragraph 2, the participation of employees in the company resulting from the cross-border merger and their involvement in the definition of such rights shall be regulated by the Member States, *mutatis mutandis* and subject to paragraphs 4 to 7 below, in accordance with the principles and procedures laid down in Article 12(2), (3) and (4) of Regulation (EC) No 2157/2001 and the following provisions of Directive 2001/86/EC:

(a)   Article 3(1), (2) and (3), (4) first subparagraph, first indent, and second subparagraph, (5) and (7);

(b)   Article 4(1), (2), points (a), (g) and (h), and (3);

(c)   Article 5;

(d)   Article 6;

(e)   Article 7(1), (2) first subparagraph, point (b), and second subparagraph, and (3). However, for the purposes of this Directive, the percentages required by Article 7(2), first subparagraph, point (b) of Directive 2001/86/EC for the application of the standard rules contained in part 3 of the Annex to that Directive shall be raised from 25 to 33⅓%;

(f)   Articles 8, 10 and 12;

(g)   Article 13(4);

(h)   part 3 of the Annex, point (b).

4.   When regulating the principles and procedures referred to in paragraph 3, Member States:

(a)   shall confer on the relevant organs of the merging companies the right to choose without any prior negotiation to be directly subject to the standard rules for participation referred to in paragraph 3(h), as laid down by the legislation of the Member State in which the company resulting from the cross-border merger is to have its registered office, and to abide by those rules from the date of registration;

(b)   shall confer on the special negotiating body the right to decide, by a majority of two thirds of its members representing at least two thirds of the employees, including the votes of members representing employees in at least two different Member States, not to open negotiations or to terminate negotiations already opened and to rely on the rules on participation in force in the Member State where the registered office of the company resulting from the cross-border merger will be situated;

(c)   may, in the case where, following prior negotiations, standard rules for participation apply and notwithstanding these rules, determine to limit the proportion of employee representatives in the administrative organ of the company resulting from the cross-border merger. However, if in one of the merging companies employee representatives constituted at least one third of the administrative or supervisory board, the limitation may never result in a lower proportion of employee representatives in the administrative organ than one third.

5.   The extension of participation rights to employees of the company resulting from the cross-border merger employed in other Member States, referred to in paragraph 2(b), shall not entail any obligation for Member States which choose to do so to take those employees into account when calculating the size of workforce thresholds giving rise to participation rights under national law.

6.   When at least one of the merging companies is operating under an employee participation system and the company resulting from the cross-border merger is to be governed by such a system in accordance with the rules referred to in paragraph 2, that company shall be obliged to take a legal form allowing for the exercise of participation rights.

7.   When the company resulting from the cross-border merger is operating under an employee participation system, that company shall be obliged to take measures to ensure that employees' participation rights are protected in the event of subsequent domestic mergers for a period of three years after the cross-border merger has taken effect, by applying *mutatis mutandis* the rules laid down in this Article.

[11.510]
Article 17
Validity
A cross-border merger which has taken effect as provided for in Article 12 may not be declared null and void.

[11.511]
Article 18
Review
Five years after the date laid down in the first paragraph of Article 19, the Commission shall review this Directive in the light of the experience acquired in applying it and, if necessary, propose its amendment.

[11.512]
Article 19
Transposition
Member States shall bring into force the laws, regulations and administrative provisions necessary to comply with this Directive by 15 December 2007.

When Member States adopt these measures, they shall contain a reference to this Directive or shall be accompanied by such reference on the occasion of their official publication. The methods of making such reference shall be laid down by Member States.

[11.513]
Article 20
Entry into force
This Directive shall enter into force on the 20th day following its publication in the *Official Journal of the European Union.*

[11.514]
Article 21
Addressees
This Directive is addressed to the Member States.

COMMISSION DIRECTIVE

(2007/14/EC)

of 8 March 2007

laying down detailed rules for the implementation of certain provisions of Directive 2004/109/EC on the harmonisation of transparency requirements in relation to information about issuers whose securities are admitted to trading on a regulated market

NOTES
Date of publication in OJ: OJ L69, 9.3.2007, p 27. Notes are as in the original OJ version.
As at 1 July 2011, this Directive had not been amended.

[11.515]
THE COMMISSION OF THE EUROPEAN COMMUNITIES,
  Having regard to the Treaty establishing the European Community,
  Having regard to Directive 2004/109/EC of the European Parliament and of the Council of 15 December 2004 on the harmonisation of transparency requirements in relation to information about issuers whose securities are admitted to trading on a regulated market and amending Directive 2001/34/EC,[1] and in particular Articles 2(3)(a), 5(6), first subparagraph, and 5(6)(c), 9(7), 12(8)(b) to (e), 13(2), 14(2), 21(4)(a), 23(4)(ii) and 23(7) thereof,
  After consulting the Committee of European Securities Regulators (CESR)[2] for technical advice, Whereas:

(1) Directive 2004/109/EC establishes the general principles for the harmonisation of transparency requirements in respect of the holding of voting rights or financial instruments that result in an entitlement to acquire existing shares with voting rights. It seeks to ensure that, through the disclosure of accurate, comprehensive and timely information about security issuers, investor confidence is built up and sustained. By the same token, by requiring issuers to be informed of movements affecting major holdings in companies, it seeks to ensure that the latter are in a position to keep the public informed.

(2) The rules for the implementation of the rules governing transparency requirements should likewise be designed to ensure a high level of investor protection, to enhance market efficiency, and to be applied in a uniform manner.

(3) As regards the procedural arrangements in accordance with which investors are to be informed of the issuer's choice of home Member State, it is appropriate that such choices be disclosed in accordance with the same procedure as regulated information under Directive 2004/109/EC.

(4) As regards the minimum content of the condensed set of half-yearly financial statements, where that set is not prepared in accordance with international accounting standards, this should be such as to avoid giving a misleading view of the assets, liabilities, financial position and profit or loss of the issuer. The content of half-yearly reports should be such as to ensure appropriate transparency for investors through a regular flow of information about the performance of the issuer, and that information should be presented in such a way that it is easy to compare it with the information provided in the annual report of the preceding year.

(5) Issuers of shares who prepare consolidated accounts in accordance with International Accounting Standards (IAS) and International Financial Reporting Standards (IFRS) should apply the same definition of related party transactions in annual and half-yearly reports under Directive 2004/109/EC. Issuers of shares who do not prepare consolidated accounts and are not required to

apply IAS and IFRS should, in their half-yearly reports under Directive 2004/109/EC, apply the definition of related party transactions set out in Council Directive 78/660/EEC of 25 July 1978 based on Article 54(3)(g) of the Treaty on the annual accounts of certain types of companies.[3]

(6) For the purposes of benefiting from the exemption from the notification of major holdings under Directive 2004/109/EC in the case of shares acquired for the sole purpose of clearing and settling, the maximum length of the "short settlement cycle" should be as short as possible.

(7) In order for the relevant competent authority to be able to monitor compliance as regards the derogation for market makers with respect to the notification of information about major holdings, the market maker seeking to benefit from that derogation should make known that it is acting or intends to act as market maker and for which shares or financial instruments.

(8) Conducting market making activities in full transparency is particularly important. Thus, the market maker should be capable upon request from the relevant competent authority of identifying the activities conducted in relation to the issuer in question, and in particular the shares or financial instruments held for market making activities purposes.

(9) As regards the calendar of trading days, it is appropriate, for the sake of ease of operation, that time limits be calculated by reference to the trading days in the Member State of the issuer. However, in order to enhance transparency, provision should be made for each competent authority to inform investors and market participants of the calendar of trading days applicable for the various regulated markets situated or operating on its territory.

(10) As regards the circumstances in which notification of major holdings is to be made, it is appropriate to determine when that obligation is triggered either individually or collectively, and how that obligation is to be complied with in the case of proxies.

(11) It is reasonable to assume that natural persons or legal entities exercise a high duty of care when acquiring or disposing of major holdings. It follows that such persons or entities will very quickly become aware of such acquisitions or disposals, or of the possibility to exercise voting rights, and it is therefore appropriate to specify only a very short period following the relevant transaction as the period after which they are deemed to have knowledge.

(12) The exemption from the obligation to aggregate major holdings should be available only to parent undertakings that can demonstrate that their subsidiary management companies or investment firms fulfil adequate conditions of independence. To ensure full transparency, a statement to that effect should be notified ex ante to the relevant competent authority. In this regard, it is important that the notification mentions the competent authority supervising the management companies' activities under the conditions laid down pursuant to Council Directive 85/611/EEC of 20 December 1985 on the coordination of laws, regulations and administrative provisions relating to undertakings for collective investment in transferable securities (UCITS),[4] irrespective of whether or not they are authorised under that Directive, provided in the latter case that they are supervised under national legislation.

(13) For the purposes of Directive 2004/109/EC, financial instruments should be taken into account in the context of notifying major holdings, to the extent that such instruments give the holder an unconditional right to acquire the underlying shares or discretion as to whether to acquire the underlying shares or cash on maturity. Consequently, financial instruments should not be considered to include instruments entitling the holder to receive shares depending on the price of the underlying share reaching a certain level at a certain moment in time. Nor should they be considered to cover those instruments that allow the instrument issuer or a third party to give shares or cash to the instrument holder on maturity.

(14) The financial instruments in Section C of Annex I of Directive 2004/39/EC of the European Parliament and of the Council[5] which are not mentioned in Article 11(1) of this Commission directive do not qualify as financial instruments within the meaning of Article 13(1) of Directive 2004/109/EC.

(15) Directive 2004/109/EC sets high-level requirements in the area of dissemination of regulated information. The mere availability of information, which means that investors must actively seek it out, is therefore not sufficient for the purposes of that Directive. Accordingly, dissemination should involve the active distribution of information from the issuers to the media, with a view to reaching investors.

(16) Minimum quality standards for the dissemination of regulated information are necessary to ensure that investors, even if situated in a Member State other than that of the issuer, have equal access to regulated information. Issuers should ensure that those minimum standards are met, whether by disseminating the regulated information themselves or by entrusting a third party to do so on their behalf. In the latter case, the third party should be capable of dissemination in adequate conditions and have adequate mechanisms in place to ensure that the regulated information it receives emanates from the relevant issuer and that there is no significant risk of data corruption or of unauthorised access to unpublished inside information. Where the third party provides other services or performs other functions, such as media, competent authorities, stock exchanges or the entity in charge of the officially appointed storage mechanism, such services or functions should be kept clearly separated from the services and functions relating to the dissemination of regulated information. When communicating information to the media, issuers or third parties should give priority to the use of electronic means and industry standard formats so as to facilitate and accelerate the processing of the information.

(17) Additionally, by way of minimum standards, regulated information should be disseminated in a way that ensures the widest possible public access, and where possible reaching the public simultaneously inside and outside the issuer's home Member State. That is without prejudice to the right of Member States to request issuers to publish parts or all regulated information through

newspapers, and to the possibility for issuers to make regulated information available on their own or other websites accessible to investors.

(18) Equivalence should be able to be declared when general disclosure rules of third countries provide users with understandable and broadly equivalent assessment of issuers' position that enable them to make similar decisions as if they were provided with the information according to requirements under Directive 2004/109/EC, even if the requirements are not identical. However, equivalence should be limited to the substance of the relevant information and no exception as regards the time limits set by Directive 2004/109/EC should be accepted.

(19) In order to establish whether or not a third country issuer is meeting equivalent requirements to those laid down in Article 4(3) of Directive 2004/109/EC, it is important to ensure that there is consistency with Commission Regulation (EC) No 809/2004 of 29 April 2004 implementing Directive 2003/71/EC of the European Parliament and of the Council as regards information contained in prospectuses as well as the format, incorporation by reference and publication of such prospectuses and dissemination of advertisements,[6] in particular the items dealing with Historical Financial Information to be included in a prospectus.

(20) As regards the equivalence of independence requirements, a parent undertaking of a management company or investment firm registered in a third country should be able to benefit from the exemption under Article 12(4) or (5) of Directive 2004/109/EC, independently of whether the authorisation is required by the law of the third country for the controlled management company or investment firm to conduct management activities or portfolio management activities, provided that certain conditions of independence are respected.

(21) The measures provided for in this Directive are in accordance with the opinion of the European Securities Committee,

---

NOTES

[1] OJ L390, 31.12.2004, p 38.

[2] CESR was established by Commission Decision 2001/527/EC of 6 June 2001 (OJ L191, 13.7.2001, p 43).

[3] OJ L222, 14.8.1978, p 11. Directive as last amended by Directive 2006/46/EC of the European Parliament and of the Council (OJ L224, 16.8.2006, p 1).

[4] OJ L375, 31.12.1985, p 3, Directive as last amended by Directive 2005/1/EC of the European Parliament and of the Council (OJ L79, 24.3.2005, p 9).

[5] OJ L145, 30.4.2004, p 1. Directive as amended by Directive 2006/31/EC (OJ L114, 27.4.2006, p 60).

[6] OJ L149, 30.4.2004, p 1, as corrected by OJ L215, 16.6.2004, p 3. Regulation as amended by Regulation (EC) No 1787/2006 (OJ L337, 5.12.2006, p 17).

HAS ADOPTED THIS DIRECTIVE:

[11.516]
Article 1
Subject matter
This Directive lays down detailed rules for the implementation of Article 2(1)(i)(ii), the second subparagraph of Article 5(3), the second sentence of Article 5(4), Article 9(1), (2) and (4), Article 10, Article 12(1), (2), (4), (5) and (6), Article 12(2)(a), Article 13(1), Article 21(1), Article 23(1) and (6) of Directive 2004/109/EC.

[11.517]
Article 2
Procedural arrangements for the choice of the home Member State
(Article 2(1)(i)(ii) of Directive 2004/109/EC)
Where the issuer makes a choice of home Member State, that choice shall be disclosed in accordance with the same procedure as regulated information.

[11.518]
Article 3
Minimum content of half-yearly non-consolidated financial statements
(Article 5(3), second subparagraph, of Directive 2004/109/EC)
1. The minimum content of the condensed set of half-yearly financial statements, where that set is not prepared in accordance with international accounting standards adopted pursuant to the procedure provided for under Article 6 of Regulation (EC) No 1606/2002, shall be in accordance with paragraphs 2 and 3 of this Article.
2. The condensed balance sheet and the condensed profit and loss account shall show each of the headings and subtotals included in the most recent annual financial statements of the issuer. Additional line items shall be included if, as a result of their omission, the half-yearly financial statements would give a misleading view of the assets, liabilities, financial position and profit or loss of the issuer.

In addition, the following comparative information shall be included:
   (a) balance sheet as at the end of the first six months of the current financial year and comparative balance sheet as at the end of the immediate preceding financial year;

(b)　profit and loss account for the first six months of the current financial year with, from two years after the date of entry into force of this Directive, comparative information for the comparable period for the preceding financial year.

3.　The explanatory notes shall include the following:

(a)　sufficient information to ensure the comparability of the condensed half-yearly financial statements with the annual financial statements;

(b)　sufficient information and explanations to ensure a user's proper understanding of any material changes in amounts and of any developments in the half-year period concerned, which are reflected in the balance sheet and the profit and loss account.

[11.519]
Article 4
Major related parties' transactions
(Article 5(4), second sentence, of Directive 2004/109/EC)

1.　In the interim management reports, issuers of shares shall disclose as major related parties' transactions, as a minimum, the following:

(a)　related parties' transactions that have taken place in the first six months of the current financial year and that have materially affected the financial position or the performance of the enterprise during that period;

(b)　any changes in the related parties' transactions described in the last annual report that could have a material effect on the financial position or performance of the enterprise in the first six months of the current financial year.

2.　Where the issuer of shares is not required to prepare consolidated accounts, it shall disclose, as a minimum, the related parties' transactions referred to in Article 43(1)(7b) of Directive 78/660/EEC.

[11.520]
Article 5
Maximum length of the usual "short settlement cycle"
(Article 9(4) of Directive 2004/109/EC)

The maximum length of the usual "short settlement cycle" shall be three trading days following the transaction.

[11.521]
Article 6
Control mechanisms by competent authorities as regards market makers
(Article 9(5) of Directive 2004/109/EC)

1.　The market maker seeking to benefit from the exemption provided for in Article 9(5) of Directive 2004/109/EC shall notify to the competent authority of the Home Member State of the issuer, at the latest within the time limit laid down in Article 12(2) of Directive 2004/109/EC, that it conducts or intends to conduct market making activities on a particular issuer.

Where the market maker ceases to conduct market making activities on the issuer concerned, it shall notify that competent authority accordingly.

2.　Without prejudice to the application of Article 24 of Directive 2004/109/EC, where in case the market maker seeking to benefit from the exemption provided for in Article 9(5) of that Directive is requested by the competent authority of the issuer to identify the shares or financial instruments held for market making activity purposes, that market maker shall be allowed to make such identification by any verifiable means. Only if the market maker is not able to identify the shares or financial instruments concerned, he may be required to hold them in a separate account for the purposes of that identification.

3.　Without prejudice to the application of Article 24(4)(a) of Directive 2004/109/EC, if a market-making agreement between the market maker and the stock exchange and/or the issuer is required under national law, the market maker shall upon request of the relevant competent authority provide the agreement to such authority.

[11.522]
Article 7
Calendar of trading days
(Article 12(2) and (6), and Article 14(1), of Directive 2004/109/EC)

1.　For the purposes of Article 12(2) and (6), and Article 14(1), of Directive 2004/109/EC, the calendar of trading days of the home Member State of the issuer shall apply.

2.　Each competent authority shall publish in its Internet site the calendar of trading days of the different regulated markets situated or operating on the territory within its jurisdiction.

[11.523]
Article 8
Shareholders and natural persons or legal entities referred to in Article 10 of the Transparency Directive required to make the notification of major holdings
(Article 12(2) of Directive 2004/109/EC)
1.   For the purposes of Article 12(2) of Directive 2004/109/EC, the notification obligation which arises as soon as the proportion of voting rights held reaches, exceeds or falls below the applicable thresholds following transactions of the type referred to in Article 10 of Directive 2004/109/EC shall be an individual obligation incumbent upon each shareholder, or each natural person or legal entity as referred to in Article 10 of that Directive, or both in case the proportion of voting rights held by each party reaches, exceeds or falls below the applicable threshold.

In the circumstances referred to in point (a) of Article 10 of the Directive 2004/109/EC, the notification obligation shall be a collective obligation shared by all parties to the agreement.
2.   In the circumstances referred to in point (h) of Article 10 of Directive 2004/109/EC, if a shareholder gives the proxy in relation to one shareholder meeting, notification may be made by means of a single notification at the moment of giving the proxy provided that it is made clear in the notification what the resulting situation in terms of voting rights will be when the proxy may no longer exercise the voting rights at its discretion.

If, in the circumstances referred to in point (h) of Article 10, the proxy holder receives one or several proxies in relation to one shareholder meeting, notification may be made by means of a single notification at the moment of receiving the proxies provided that it is made clear in the notification what the resulting situation in terms of voting rights will be when the proxy may no longer exercise the voting rights at its discretion.
3.   Where the duty to make a notification lies with more than one natural person or legal entity, notification may be made by means of a single common notification.

However, use of a single common notification may not be deemed to release any of the natural persons or legal entities concerned from their responsibility in relation to notification.

[11.524]
Article 9
Circumstances under which the notifying person should have learned of acquisition or disposal or of possibility to exercise voting rights
(Article 12(2) of Directive 2004/109/EC)
For the purposes of point (a) of Article 12(2) of Directive 2004/109/EC, the shareholder, or the natural person or legal entity referred to in Article 10 of that Directive, shall be deemed to have knowledge of the acquisition, disposal or possibility to exercise voting rights no later than two trading days following the transaction.

[11.525]
Article 10
Conditions of independence to be complied with by management companies and investment firms involved in individual portfolio management
(Article 12(4), first subparagraph, and Article 12(5), first subparagraph, of Directive 2004/109/EC)
1.   For the purposes of the exemption to the aggregation of holdings provided for in the first subparagraphs of Article 12(4) and (5) of Directive 2004/109/EC, a parent undertaking of a management company or of an investment firm shall comply with the following conditions:
   (a)   it must not interfere by giving direct or indirect instructions or in any other way in the exercise of the voting rights held by that management company or investment firm;
   (b)   that management company or investment firm must be free to exercise, independently of the parent undertaking, the voting rights attached to the assets it manages.
2.   A parent undertaking which wishes to make use of the exemption shall, without delay, notify the following to the competent authority of the home Member State of issuers whose voting rights are attached to holdings managed by the management companies or investment firms:
   (a)   a list of the names of those management companies and investment firms, indicating the competent authorities that supervise them or that no competent authority supervises them, but with no reference to the issuers concerned;
   (b)   a statement that, in the case of each such management company or investment firm, the parent undertaking complies with the conditions laid down in paragraph 1.
The parent undertaking shall update the list referred to in point (a) on an ongoing basis.
3.   Where the parent undertaking intends to benefit from the exemptions only in relation to the financial instruments referred to in Article 13 of Directive 2004/109/EC, it shall notify to the competent authority of the home Member State of the issuer only the list referred to in point (a) of paragraph 2.
4.   Without prejudice to the application of Article 24 of Directive 2004/109/EC, a parent undertaking of a management company or of an investment firm shall be able to demonstrate to the competent authority of the home Member State of the issuer on request that:

(a) the organisational structures of the parent undertaking and the management company or investment firm are such that the voting rights are exercised independently of the parent undertaking;

(b) the persons who decide how the voting rights are to be exercised act independently;

(c) if the parent undertaking is a client of its management company or investment firm or has holding in the assets managed by the management company or investment firm, there is a clear written mandate for an arms-length customer relationship between the parent undertaking and the management company or investment firm.

The requirement in point (a) shall imply as a minimum that the parent undertaking and the management company or investment firm must established written policies and procedures reasonably designed to prevent the distribution of information between the parent undertaking and the management company or investment firm in relation to the exercise of voting rights.

5. For the purposes of point (a) of paragraph 1, "direct instruction" means any instruction given by the parent undertaking, or another controlled undertaking of the parent undertaking, specifying how the voting rights are to be exercised by the management company or investment firm in particular cases.

"Indirect instruction" means any general or particular instruction, regardless of the form, given by the parent undertaking, or another controlled undertaking of the parent undertaking, that limits the discretion of the management company or investment firm in relation to the exercise of the voting rights in order to serve specific business interests of the parent undertaking or another controlled undertaking of the parent undertaking.

[11.526]
Article 11
Types of financial instruments that result in an entitlement to acquire, on the holder's own initiative alone, shares to which voting rights are attached
(Article 13(1) of Directive 2004/109/EC)
1. For the purposes of Article 13(1) of Directive 2004/109/EC, transferable securities; and options, futures, swaps, forward rate agreements and any other derivative contracts, as referred to in Section C of Annex I of Directive 2004/39/EC, shall be considered to be financial instruments, provided that they result in an entitlement to acquire, on the holder's own initiative alone, under a formal agreement, shares to which voting rights are attached, already issued, of an issuer whose shares are admitted to trading on a regulated market.

The instrument holder must enjoy, on maturity, either the unconditional right to acquire the underlying shares or the discretion as to his right to acquire such shares or not.

A formal agreement means an agreement which is binding under the applicable law.

2. For the purposes of Article 13(1) of Directive 2004/109/EC, the holder shall aggregate and notify all financial instruments within the meaning of paragraph 1 relating to the same underlying issuer.

3. The notification required under Article 13(1) of Directive 2004/109/EC shall include the following information:

(a) the resulting situation in terms of voting rights;

(b) if applicable, the chain of controlled undertakings through which financial instruments are effectively held;

(c) the date on which the threshold was reached or crossed;

(d) for instruments with an exercise period, an indication of the date or time period where shares will or can be acquired, if applicable;

(e) date of maturity or expiration of the instrument;

(f) identity of the holder;

(g) name of the underlying issuer.

For the purposes of point (a), the percentage of voting rights shall be calculated by reference to the total number of voting rights and capital as last disclosed by the issuer under Article 15 of Directive 2004/109/EC.

4. The notification period shall be the same as laid down in Article 12(2) of Directive 2004/109/EC and the related implementing provisions.

5. The notification shall be made to the issuer of the underlying share and to the competent authority of the home Member States of such issuer.

If a financial instrument relates to more than one underlying share, a separate notification shall be made to each issuer of the underlying shares.

[11.527]
Article 12
Minimum Standards
(Article 21(1) of Directive 2004/109/EC)
1. The dissemination of regulated information for the purposes of Article 21(1) of Directive 2004/109/EC shall be carried out in compliance with the minimum standards set out in paragraphs 2 to 5.

2. Regulated information shall be disseminated in a manner ensuring that it is capable of being disseminated to as wide a public as possible, and as close to simultaneously as possible in the home Member State, or the Member State referred to in Article 21(3) of Directive 2004/109/EC, and in the other Member States.

3. Regulated information shall be communicated to the media in unedited full text.

However, in the case of the reports and statements referred to in Articles 4, 5 and 6 of Directive 2004/109/EC, this requirement shall be deemed fulfilled if the announcement relating to the regulated information is communicated to the media and indicates on which website, in addition to the officially appointed mechanism for the central storage of regulated information referred to in Article 21 of that Directive, the relevant documents are available.

4. Regulated information shall be communicated to the media in a manner which ensures the security of the communication, minimises the risk of data corruption and unauthorised access, and provides certainty as to the source of the regulated information.

Security of receipt shall be ensured by remedying as soon as possible any failure or disruption in the communication of regulated information.

The issuer or the person who has applied for admission to trading on a regulated market without the issuer's consent shall not be responsible for systemic errors or shortcomings in the media to which the regulated information has been communicated.

5. Regulated information shall be communicated to the media in a way which makes clear that the information is regulated information, identifies clearly the issuer concerned, the subject matter of the regulated information and the time and date of the communication of the information by the issuer or the person who has applied for admission to trading on a regulated market without the issuer's consent.

Upon request, the issuer or the person who has applied for admission to trading on a regulated market without the issuer's consent shall be able to communicate to the competent authority, in relation to any disclosure of regulated information, the following:

(a) the name of the person who communicated the information to the media;

(b) the security validation details;

(c) the time and date on which the information was communicated to the media;

(d) the medium in which the information was communicated;

(e) if applicable, details of any embargo placed by the issuer on the regulated information.

[11.528]
Article 13
Requirements equivalent to Article 4(2)(b) of Directive 2004/109/EC
(Article 23(1) of Directive 2004/109/EC)

A third country shall be deemed to set requirements equivalent to those set out in Article 4(2)(b) of Directive 2004/109/EC where, under the law of that country, the annual management report is required to include at least the following information:

(a) a fair review of the development and performance of the issuer's business and of its position, together with a description of the principal risks and uncertainties that it faces, such that the review presents a balanced and comprehensive analysis of the development and performance of the issuer's business and of its position, consistent with the size and complexity of the business;

(b) an indication of any important events that have occurred since the end of the financial year;

(c) indications of the issuer's likely future development.

The analysis referred to in point (a) shall, to the extent necessary for an understanding of the issuer's development, performance or position, include both financial and, where appropriate, non-financial key performance indicators relevant to the particular business.

[11.529]
Article 14
Requirements equivalent to Article 5(4) of Directive 2004/109/EC
(Article 23(1) of Directive 2004/109/EC)

A third country shall be deemed to set requirements equivalent to those set out in Article 5(4) of Directive 2004/109/EC where, under the law of that country, a condensed set of financial statements is required in addition to the interim management report, and the interim management report is required to include at least the following information:

(a) review of the period covered;

(b) indications of the issuer's likely future development for the remaining six months of the financial year;

(c) for issuers of shares and if already not disclosed on an ongoing basis, major related parties transactions.

[11.530]
Article 15
Requirements equivalent to Articles 4(2) and 5(2)(c) of Directive 2004/109/EC
(Article 23(1) of Directive 2004/109/EC)
A third country shall be deemed to set requirements equivalent to those set out in Articles 4(2)(c) and 5(2)(c) of Directive 2004/109/EC where, under the law of that country, a person or persons within the issuer are responsible for the annual and half-yearly financial information, and in particular for the following:
    (a)   the compliance of the financial statements with the applicable reporting framework or set of accounting standards;
    (b)   the fairness of the management review included in the management report.

[11.531]
Article 16
Requirements equivalent to Article 6 of Directive 2004/109/EC
(Article 23(1) of Directive 2004/109/EC)
A third country shall be deemed to set requirements equivalent to those set out in Article 6 of Directive 2004/109/EC where, under the law of that country, an issuer is required to publish quarterly financial reports.

[11.532]
Article 17
Requirements equivalent to Article 4(3) of Directive 2004/109/EC
(Article 23(1) of Directive 2004/109/EC)
A third country shall be deemed to set requirements equivalent to those set out in the first subparagraph of Article 4(3) of Directive 2004/109/EC where, under the law of that country, the provision of individual accounts by the parent company is not required but the issuer whose registered office is in that third country is required, in preparing consolidated accounts, to include the following information:
    (a)   for issuers of shares, dividends computation and ability to pay dividends;
    (b)   for all issuers, where applicable, minimum capital and equity requirements and liquidity issues.
    For the purposes of equivalence, the issuer must also be able to provide the competent authority of the home Member State with additional audited disclosures giving information on the individual accounts of the issuer as a standalone, relevant to the elements of information referred to under points (a) and (b). Those disclosures may be prepared under the accounting standards of the third country.

[11.533]
Article 18
Requirements equivalent to Article 4(3), second subparagraph, of Directive 2004/109/EC
(Article 23(1) of Directive 2004/109/EC)
A third country shall be deemed to set requirements equivalent to those set out in the second subparagraph of Article 4(3) of Directive 2004/109/EC in relation to individual accounts where, under the law of a third country, an issuer whose registered office is in that third country is not required to prepare consolidated accounts but is required to prepare its individual accounts in accordance with international accounting standards recognised pursuant to Article 3 of Regulation (EC) No 1606/2002 of the European Parliament and of the Council[1] as applicable within the Community or with third country national accounting standards equivalent to those standards.
    For the purposes of equivalence, if such financial information is not in line with those standards, it must be presented in the form of restated financial statements.
    In addition, the individual accounts must be audited independently.

NOTES
    [1]   OJ L243, 11.9.2002, p 1.

[11.534]
Article 19
Requirements equivalent to Article 12(6) of Directive 2004/109/EC
(Article 23(1) of Directive 2004/109/EC)
A third country shall be deemed to set requirements equivalent to those set out in Article 12(6) of Directive 2004/109/EC where, under the law of that country, the time period within which an issuer whose registered office is in that third country must be notified of major holdings and within which it must disclose to the public those major holdings is in total equal to or shorter than seven trading days.
    The time frames for the notification to the issuer and for the subsequent disclosure to the public by the issuer may be different from those set out in Articles 12(2) and 12(6) of Directive 2004/109/EC.

[11.535]
Article 20
Requirements equivalent to Article 14 of Directive 2004/109/EC
(Article 23(1) of Directive 2004/109/EC)
A third country shall be deemed to set requirements equivalent to those set out in Article 14 of Directive 2004/109/EC where, under the law of that country, an issuer whose registered office is in that third country is required to comply with the following conditions:
  (a)   in the case of an issuer allowed to hold up to a maximum of 5% of its own shares to which voting rights are attached, it must make a notification whenever that threshold is reached or crossed;
  (b)   in the case of an issuer allowed to hold up to a maximum of between 5% and 10% of its own shares to which voting rights are attached, it must make a notification whenever a 5% threshold or that maximum threshold is reached or crossed;
  (c)   in the case of an issuer allowed to hold more than 10% of its own shares to which voting rights are attached, it must make a notification whenever the 5% threshold or the 10% threshold is reached or crossed.
  For the purposes of equivalence, notification above the 10% threshold need not be required.

[11.536]
Article 21
Requirements equivalent to Article 15 of Directive 2004/109/EC
(Article 23(1) of Directive 2004/109/EC)
A third country shall be deemed to set requirements equivalent to those set out in Article 15 of Directive 2004/109/EC where, under the law of that country, an issuer whose registered office is in that third country is required to disclose to the public the total number of voting rights and capital within 30 calendar days after an increase or decrease of such total number has occurred.

[11.537]
Article 22
Requirements equivalent to Articles 17(2)(a) and 18(2)(a) of Directive 2004/109/EC
(Article 23(1) of Directive 2004/109/EC)
A third country shall be deemed to set requirements equivalent to those set out in Article 17(2)(a) and 18(2)(a) of Directive 2004/109/EC, as far as the content of the information about meetings is concerned, where, under the law of that country, an issuer whose registered office is in that third country is required to provide at least information on the place, time and agenda of meetings.

[11.538]
Article 23
Equivalence in relation to the test of independence for parent undertakings of management companies and investment firms
(Article 23(6) of Directive 2004/109/EC)
1.   A third country shall be deemed to set conditions of independence equivalent to those set out in Article 12(4) and (5) of that Directive where, under the law of that country, a management company or investment firm as referred to in Article 23(6) of Directive 2004/109/EC is required to meet the following conditions:
  (a)   the management company or investment firm must be free in all situations to exercise, independently of its parent undertaking, the voting rights attached to the assets it manages;
  (b)   the management company or investment firm must disregard the interests of the parent undertaking or of any other controlled undertaking of the parent undertaking whenever conflicts of interest arise.
2.   The parent undertaking shall comply with the notification requirements laid down in Article 10(2)(a) and (3) of this Directive.
  In addition, it shall make a statement that, in the case of each management company or investment firm concerned, the parent undertaking complies with the conditions laid down in paragraph 1 of this Article.
3.   Without prejudice to the application of Article 24 of Directive 2004/109/EC, the parent undertaking shall be able to demonstrate to the competent authority of the home Member State of the issuer on request that the requirements laid down in Article 10(4) of this Directive are respected.

[11.539]
Article 24
Transposition
1.   Member States shall bring into force the laws, regulations and administrative provisions necessary to comply with this Directive by 12 months after date of adoption at the latest. They shall forthwith communicate to the Commission the text of those provisions and a correlation table between those provisions and this Directive.
  When Member States adopt those provisions, they shall contain a reference to this Directive or be accompanied by such a reference on the occasion of their official publication. Member States shall determine how such reference is to be made.

2. Member States shall communicate to the Commission the text of the main provisions of national law which they adopt in the field covered by this Directive.

[11.540]
Article 25
This Directive shall enter into force on the 20th day following its publication in the Official Journal of the European Union.

[11.541]
Article 26
This Directive is addressed to the Member States.

DIRECTIVE OF THE EUROPEAN PARLIAMENT AND OF THE COUNCIL

(2007/36/EC)

of 11 July 2007

on the exercise of certain rights of shareholders in listed companies

NOTES
Date of publication in OJ: OJ L184, 14.07.2007, p 17. Notes are as in the original OJ version.
As at 1 July 2011, this Directive had not been amended.

[11.542]
THE EUROPEAN PARLIAMENT AND THE COUNCIL OF THE EUROPEAN UNION,

Having regard to the Treaty establishing the European Community, and in particular Articles 44 and 95 thereof,

Having regard to the proposal from the Commission,

Having regard to the opinion of the European Economic and Social Committee,[1]

Acting in accordance with the procedure laid down in Article 251 of the Treaty,[2]

Whereas:

(1) In its Communication to the Council and the European Parliament of 21 May 2003, entitled "Modernising Company Law and enhancing Corporate Governance in the European Union — A Plan to Move Forward", the Commission indicated that new tailored initiatives should be taken with a view to enhancing shareholders' rights in listed companies and that problems relating to cross-border voting should be solved as a matter of urgency.

(2) In its Resolution of 21 April 2004,[3] the European Parliament expressed its support for the Commission's intention to strengthen shareholders' rights, in particular through the extension of the rules on transparency, proxy voting rights, the possibility of participating in general meetings via electronic means and ensuring that cross-border voting rights are able to be exercised.

(3) Holders of shares carrying voting rights should be able to exercise those rights given that they are reflected in the price that has to be paid at the acquisition of the shares. Furthermore, effective shareholder control is a pre-requisite to sound corporate governance and should, therefore, be facilitated and encouraged. It is therefore necessary to adopt measures to approximate the laws of the Member States to this end. Obstacles which deter shareholders from voting, such as making the exercise of voting rights subject to the blocking of shares during a certain period before the general meeting, should be removed. However, this Directive does not affect existing Community legislation on units issued by collective investment undertakings or on units acquired or disposed of in such undertakings.

(4) The existing Community legislation is not sufficient to achieve this objective. Directive 2001/34/EC of the European Parliament and of the Council of 28 May 2001 on the admission of securities to official stock exchange listing and on information to be published on those securities[4] focuses on the information issuers have to disclose to the market and accordingly does not deal with the shareholder voting process itself. Moreover, Directive 2004/109/EC of the European Parliament and of the Council of 15 December 2004 on the harmonisation of transparency requirements in relation to information about issuers whose securities are admitted to trading on a regulated market[5] imposes on issuers an obligation to make available certain information and documents relevant to general meetings, but such information and documents are to be made available in the issuer's home Member State. Therefore, certain minimum standards should be introduced with a view to protecting investors and promoting the smooth and effective exercise of shareholder rights attaching to voting shares. As regards rights other than the right to vote, Member States are free to extend the application of these minimum standards also to non-voting shares, to the extent that those shares do not enjoy such standards already.

(5) Significant proportions of shares in listed companies are held by shareholders who do not reside in the Member State in which the company has its registered office. Non-resident shareholders should be able to exercise their rights in relation to the general meeting as easily as shareholders who reside in the Member State in which the company has its registered office. This requires that existing obstacles which hinder the access of non-resident shareholders to the information relevant to the general meeting and the exercise of voting rights without physically attending the general meeting

be removed. The removal of these obstacles should also benefit resident shareholders who do not or cannot attend the general meeting.

(6)   Shareholders should be able to cast informed votes at, or in advance of, the general meeting, no matter where they reside. All shareholders should have sufficient time to consider the documents intended to be submitted to the general meeting and determine how they will vote their shares. To this end, timely notice should be given of the general meeting, and shareholders should be provided with the complete information intended to be submitted to the general meeting. The possibilities which modern technologies offer to make information instantly accessible should be exploited. This Directive presupposes that all listed companies already have an Internet site.

(7)   Shareholders should, in principle, have the possibility to put items on the agenda of the general meeting and to table draft resolutions for items on the agenda. Without prejudice to different time-frames and modalities which are currently in use across the Community, the exercise of those rights should be made subject to two basic rules, namely that any threshold required for the exercise of those rights should not exceed 5% of the company's share capital and that all shareholders should in every case receive the final version of the agenda in sufficient time to prepare for the discussion and voting on each item on the agenda.

(8)   Every shareholder should, in principle, have the possibility to ask questions related to items on the agenda of the general meeting and to have them answered, while the rules on how and when questions are to be asked and answered should be left to be determined by Member States.

(9)   Companies should face no legal obstacles in offering to their shareholders any means of electronic participation in the general meeting. Voting without attending the general meeting in person, whether by correspondence or by electronic means, should not be subject to constraints other than those necessary for the verification of identity and the security of electronic communications. However, this should not prevent Member States from adopting rules aimed at ensuring that the results of the voting reflect the intentions of the shareholders in all circumstances, including rules aimed at addressing situations where new circumstances occur or are revealed after a shareholder has cast his vote by correspondence or by electronic means.

(10)   Good corporate governance requires a smooth and effective process of proxy voting. Existing limitations and constraints which make proxy voting cumbersome and costly should therefore be removed. But good corporate governance also requires adequate safeguards against a possible abuse of proxy voting. The proxy holder should therefore be bound to observe any instructions he may have received from the shareholder and Member States should be able to introduce appropriate measures ensuring that the proxy holder does not pursue any interest other than that of the shareholder, irrespective of the reason that has given rise to the conflict of interests. Measures against possible abuse may, in particular, consist of regimes which Member States may adopt in order to regulate the activity of persons who actively engage in the collection of proxies or who have in fact collected more than a certain significant number of proxies, notably to ensure an adequate degree of reliability and transparency. Shareholders have an unfettered right under this Directive to appoint such persons as proxy holders to attend and vote at general meetings in their name. This Directive does not, however, affect any rules or sanctions that Member States may impose on such persons where votes have been cast by making fraudulent use of proxies collected. Moreover, this Directive does not impose any obligation on companies to verify that proxy holders cast votes in accordance with the voting instructions of the appointing shareholders.

(11)   Where financial intermediaries are involved, the effectiveness of voting upon instructions relies, to a great extent, on the efficiency of the chain of intermediaries, given that investors are frequently unable to exercise the voting rights attached to their shares without the cooperation of every intermediary in the chain, who may not have an economic stake in the shares. In order to enable the investor to exercise his voting rights in cross-border situations, it is therefore important that intermediaries facilitate the exercise of voting rights. Further consideration should be given to this issue by the Commission in the context of a Recommendation, with a view to ensuring that investors have access to effective voting services and that voting rights are exercised in accordance with the instructions given by those investors.

(12)   While the timing of disclosure to the administrative, management or supervisory body as well as to the public of votes cast in advance of the general meeting electronically or by correspondence is an important matter of corporate governance, it can be determined by Member States.

(13)   Voting results should be established through methods that reflect the voting intentions expressed by shareholders, and they should be made transparent after the general meeting at least through the company's Internet site.

(14)   Since the objective of this Directive, namely to allow shareholders effectively to make use of their rights throughout the Community, cannot be sufficiently achieved by the Member States on the basis of the existing Community legislation and can therefore, by reason of the scale and effects of the measures, be better achieved at Community level, the Community may adopt measures, in accordance with the principle of subsidiarity as set out in Article 5 of the Treaty. In accordance with the principle of proportionality, as set out in that Article, this Directive does not go beyond what is necessary in order to achieve that objective.

(15)   In accordance with paragraph 34 of the Interinstitutional Agreement on better law-making,[6] Member States are encouraged to draw up, for themselves and in the interests of the Community, their own tables illustrating, as far as possible, the correlation between this Directive and the transposition measures, and to make them public,

NOTES

1   OJ C318, 23.12.2006, p 42.

2   Opinion of the European Parliament of 15 February 2007 (not yet published in the Official Journal) and Council Decision of 12 June 2007.

3   OJ C104E, 30.4.2004, p 714.

4   OJ L184, 6.7.2001, p 1. Directive as last amended by Directive 2005/1/EC (OJ L79, 24.3.2005, p 9).

5   OJ L390, 31.12.2004, p 38.

6   OJ C321, 31.12.2003, p 1.

HAVE ADOPTED THIS DIRECTIVE:

CHAPTER I
GENERAL PROVISIONS

[11.543]
Article 1
Subject-matter and scope
1.   This Directive establishes requirements in relation to the exercise of certain shareholder rights attaching to voting shares in relation to general meetings of companies which have their registered office in a Member State and whose shares are admitted to trading on a regulated market situated or operating within a Member State.
2.   The Member State competent to regulate matters covered in this Directive shall be the Member State in which the company has its registered office, and references to the "applicable law" are references to the law of that Member State.
3.   Member States may exempt from this Directive the following types of companies:
   (a)   collective investment undertakings within the meaning of Article 1(2) of Council Directive 85/611/EEC of 20 December 1985 on the coordination of laws, regulations and administrative provisions relating to undertakings for collective investment in transferable securities (UCITS);[1]
   (b)   undertakings the sole object of which is the collective investment of capital provided by the public, which operate on the principle of risk spreading and which do not seek to take legal or management control over any of the issuers of their underlying investments, provided that these collective investment undertakings are authorised and subject to the supervision of competent authorities and that they have a depositary exercising functions equivalent to those under Directive 85/611/EEC;
   (c)   cooperative societies.

NOTES

1   OJ L375, 31.12.1985, p 3.

[11.544]
Article 2
Definitions
For the purposes of this Directive the following definitions shall apply:
   (a)   "regulated market" means a market as defined in Article 4(1), point 14, of Directive 2004/39/EC of the European Parliament and of the Council of 21 April 2004 on markets in financial instruments;[1]
   (b)   "shareholder" means the natural or legal person that is recognised as a shareholder under the applicable law;
   (c)   "proxy" means the empowerment of a natural or legal person by a shareholder to exercise some or all rights of that shareholder in the general meeting in his name.

NOTES

1   OJ L145, 30.4.2004, p 1.

[11.545]
Article 3
Further national measures
This Directive shall not prevent Member States from imposing further obligations on companies or from otherwise taking further measures to facilitate the exercise by shareholders of the rights referred to in this Directive.

Part 11   EU Legislation

CHAPTER II
GENERAL MEETINGS OF SHAREHOLDERS

[11.546]
Article 4
Equal treatment of shareholders
The company shall ensure equal treatment for all shareholders who are in the same position with regard to participation and the exercise of voting rights in the general meeting.

[11.547]
Article 5
Information prior to the general meeting
1. Without prejudice to Articles 9(4) and 11(4) of Directive 2004/25/EC of the European Parliament and of the Council of 21 April 2004 on takeover bids,[1] Member States shall ensure that the company issues the convocation of the general meeting in one of the manners specified in paragraph 2 of this Article not later than on the 21st day before the day of the meeting.

Member States may provide that, where the company offers the facility for shareholders to vote by electronic means accessible to all shareholders, the general meeting of shareholders may decide that it shall issue the convocation of a general meeting which is not an annual general meeting in one of the manners specified in paragraph 2 of this Article not later than on the 14th day before the day of the meeting. This decision is to be taken by a majority of not less than two thirds of the votes attaching to the shares or the subscribed capital represented and for a duration not later than the next annual general meeting.

Member States need not apply the minimum periods referred to in the first and second subparagraphs for the second or subsequent convocation of a general meeting issued for lack of a quorum required for the meeting convened by the first convocation, provided that this Article has been complied with for the first convocation and no new item is put on the agenda, and that at least 10 days elapse between the final convocation and the date of the general meeting.

2. Without prejudice to further requirements for notification or publication laid down by the competent Member State as defined in Article 1(2), the company shall be required to issue the convocation referred to in paragraph 1 of this Article in a manner ensuring fast access to it on a non-discriminatory basis. The Member State shall require the company to use such media as may reasonably be relied upon for the effective dissemination of information to the public throughout the Community. The Member State may not impose an obligation to use only media whose operators are established on its territory.

The Member State need not apply the first subparagraph to companies that are able to identify the names and addresses of their shareholders from a current register of shareholders, provided that the company is under an obligation to send the convocation to each of its registered shareholders.

In either case the company may not charge any specific cost for issuing the convocation in the prescribed manner.

3. The convocation referred to in paragraph 1 shall at least:
   (a) indicate precisely when and where the general meeting is to take place, and the proposed agenda for the general meeting;
   (b) contain a clear and precise description of the procedures that shareholders must comply with in order to be able to participate and to cast their vote in the general meeting. This includes information concerning:
       (i) the rights available to shareholders under Article 6, to the extent that those rights can be exercised after the issuing of the convocation, and under Article 9, and the deadlines by which those rights may be exercised; the convocation may confine itself to stating only the deadlines by which those rights may be exercised, provided it contains a reference to more detailed information concerning those rights being made available on the Internet site of the company;
       (ii) the procedure for voting by proxy, notably the forms to be used to vote by proxy and the means by which the company is prepared to accept electronic notifications of the appointment of proxy holders; and
       (iii) where applicable, the procedures for casting votes by correspondence or by electronic means;
   (c) where applicable, state the record date as defined in Article 7(2) and explain that only those who are shareholders on that date shall have the right to participate and vote in the general meeting;
   (d) indicate where and how the full, unabridged text of the documents and draft resolutions referred to in points (c) and (d) of paragraph 4 may be obtained;
   (e) indicate the address of the Internet site on which the information referred to in paragraph 4 will be made available.

4. Member States shall ensure that, for a continuous period beginning not later than on the 21 day before the day of the general meeting and including the day of the meeting, the company shall make available to its shareholders on its Internet site at least the following information:
   (a) the convocation referred to in paragraph 1;

(b)　the total number of shares and voting rights at the date of the convocation (including separate totals for each class of shares where the company's capital is divided into two or more classes of shares);

(c)　the documents to be submitted to the general meeting;

(d)　a draft resolution or, where no resolution is proposed to be adopted, a comment from a competent body within the company, to be designated by the applicable law, for each item on the proposed agenda of the general meeting; moreover, draft resolutions tabled by shareholders shall be added to the Internet site as soon as practicable after the company has received them;

(e)　where applicable, the forms to be used to vote by proxy and to vote by correspondence, unless those forms are sent directly to each shareholder.

Where the forms referred to in point (e) cannot be made available on the Internet for technical reasons, the company shall indicate on its Internet site how the forms can be obtained on paper. In this case the company shall be required to send the forms by postal services and free of charge to every shareholder who so requests.

Where, pursuant to Articles 9(4) or 11(4) of Directive 2004/25/EC, or to the second subparagraph of paragraph 1 of this Article, the convocation of the general meeting is issued later than on the 21st day before the meeting, the period specified in this paragraph shall be shortened accordingly.

NOTES

[1]　　OJ L142, 30.4.2004, p 12.

[11.548]
Article 6
Right to put items on the agenda of the general meeting and to table draft resolutions

1.　Member States shall ensure that shareholders, acting individually or collectively:

(a)　have the right to put items on the agenda of the general meeting, provided that each such item is accompanied by a justification or a draft resolution to be adopted in the general meeting; and

(b)　have the right to table draft resolutions for items included or to be included on the agenda of a general meeting.

Member States may provide that the right referred to in point (a) may be exercised only in relation to the annual general meeting, provided that shareholders, acting individually or collectively, have the right to call, or to require the company to call, a general meeting which is not an annual general meeting with an agenda including at least all the items requested by those shareholders.

Member States may provide that those rights shall be exercised in writing (submitted by postal services or electronic means).

2.　Where any of the rights specified in paragraph 1 is subject to the condition that the relevant shareholder or shareholders hold a minimum stake in the company, such minimum stake shall not exceed 5% of the share capital.

3.　Each Member State shall set a single deadline, with reference to a specified number of days prior to the general meeting or the convocation, by which shareholders may exercise the right referred to in paragraph 1, point (a). In the same manner each Member State may set a deadline for the exercise of the right referred to in paragraph 1, point (b).

4.　Member States shall ensure that, where the exercise of the right referred to in paragraph 1, point (a) entails a modification of the agenda for the general meeting already communicated to shareholders, the company shall make available a revised agenda in the same manner as the previous agenda in advance of the applicable record date as defined in Article 7(2) or, if no record date applies, sufficiently in advance of the date of the general meeting so as to enable other shareholders to appoint a proxy or, where applicable, to vote by correspondence.

[11.549]
Article 7
Requirements for participation and voting in the general meeting

1.　Member States shall ensure:

(a)　that the rights of a shareholder to participate in a general meeting and to vote in respect of any of his shares are not subject to any requirement that his shares be deposited with, or transferred to, or registered in the name of, another natural or legal person before the general meeting; and

(b)　that the rights of a shareholder to sell or otherwise transfer his shares during the period between the record date, as defined in paragraph 2, and the general meeting to which it applies are not subject to any restriction to which they are not subject at other times.

2.　Member States shall provide that the rights of a shareholder to participate in a general meeting and to vote in respect of his shares shall be determined with respect to the shares held by that shareholder on a specified date prior to the general meeting (the record date).

Member States need not apply the first subparagraph to companies that are able to identify the names and addresses of their shareholders from a current register of shareholders on the day of the general meeting.

3.   Each Member State shall ensure that a single record date applies to all companies. However, a Member State may set one record date for companies which have issued bearer shares and another record date for companies which have issued registered shares, provided that a single record date applies to each company which has issued both types of shares. The record date shall not lie more than 30 days before the date of the general meeting to which it applies. In implementing this provision and Article 5(1), each Member State shall ensure that at least eight days elapse between the latest permissible date for the convocation of the general meeting and the record date. In calculating that number of days those two dates shall not be included. In the circumstances described in Article 5(1), third subparagraph, however, a Member State may require that at least six days elapse between the latest permissible date for the second or subsequent convocation of the general meeting and the record date. In calculating that number of days those two dates shall not be included.

4.   Proof of qualification as a shareholder may be made subject only to such requirements as are necessary to ensure the identification of shareholders and only to the extent that they are proportionate to achieving that objective.

[11.550]
Article 8
Participation in the general meeting by electronic means
1.   Member States shall permit companies to offer to their shareholders any form of participation in the general meeting by electronic means, notably any or all of the following forms of participation:

(a)   real-time transmission of the general meeting;
(b)   real-time two-way communication enabling shareholders to address the general meeting from a remote location;
(c)   a mechanism for casting votes, whether before or during the general meeting, without the need to appoint a proxy holder who is physically present at the meeting.

2.   The use of electronic means for the purpose of enabling shareholders to participate in the general meeting may be made subject only to such requirements and constraints as are necessary to ensure the identification of shareholders and the security of the electronic communication, and only to the extent that they are proportionate to achieving those objectives.

This is without prejudice to any legal rules which Member States have adopted or may adopt concerning the decision-making process within the company for the introduction or implementation of any form of participation by electronic means.

[11.551]
Article 9
Right to ask questions
1.   Every shareholder shall have the right to ask questions related to items on the agenda of the general meeting. The company shall answer the questions put to it by shareholders.
2.   The right to ask questions and the obligation to answer are subject to the measures which Member States may take, or allow companies to take, to ensure the identification of shareholders, the good order of general meetings and their preparation and the protection of confidentiality and business interests of companies. Member States may allow companies to provide one overall answer to questions having the same content.

Member States may provide that an answer shall be deemed to be given if the relevant information is available on the company's Internet site in a question and answer format.

[11.552]
Article 10
Proxy voting
1.   Every shareholder shall have the right to appoint any other natural or legal person as a proxy holder to attend and vote at a general meeting in his name. The proxy holder shall enjoy the same rights to speak and ask questions in the general meeting as those to which the shareholder thus represented would be entitled.

Apart from the requirement that the proxy holder possess legal capacity, Member States shall abolish any legal rule which restricts, or allows companies to restrict, the eligibility of persons to be appointed as proxy holders.

2.   Member States may limit the appointment of a proxy holder to a single meeting, or to such meetings as may be held during a specified period.

Without prejudice to Article 13(5), Member States may limit the number of persons whom a shareholder may appoint as proxy holders in relation to any one general meeting. However, if a shareholder has shares of a company held in more than one securities account, such limitation shall not prevent the shareholder from appointing a separate proxy holder as regards shares held in each securities account in relation to any one general meeting. This does not affect rules prescribed by the applicable law that prohibit the casting of votes differently in respect of shares held by one and the same shareholder.

3. Apart from the limitations expressly permitted in paragraphs 1 and 2, Member States shall not restrict or allow companies to restrict the exercise of shareholder rights through proxy holders for any purpose other than to address potential conflicts of interest between the proxy holder and the shareholder, in whose interest the proxy holder is bound to act, and in doing so Member States shall not impose any requirements other than the following:

(a) Member States may prescribe that the proxy holder disclose certain specified facts which may be relevant for the shareholders in assessing any risk that the proxy holder might pursue any interest other than the interest of the shareholder;

(b) Member States may restrict or exclude the exercise of shareholder rights through proxy holders without specific voting instructions for each resolution in respect of which the proxy holder is to vote on behalf of the shareholder;

(c) Member States may restrict or exclude the transfer of the proxy to another person, but this shall not prevent a proxy holder who is a legal person from exercising the powers conferred upon it through any member of its administrative or management body or any of its employees.

A conflict of interest within the meaning of this paragraph may in particular arise where the proxy holder:

(i) is a controlling shareholder of the company, or is another entity controlled by such shareholder;

(ii) is a member of the administrative, management or supervisory body of the company, or of a controlling shareholder or controlled entity referred to in point (i);

(iii) is an employee or an auditor of the company, or of a controlling shareholder or controlled entity referred to in (i);

(iv) has a family relationship with a natural person referred to in points (i) to (iii).

4. The proxy holder shall cast votes in accordance with the instructions issued by the appointing shareholder.

Member States may require proxy holders to keep a record of the voting instructions for a defined minimum period and to confirm on request that the voting instructions have been carried out.

5. A person acting as a proxy holder may hold a proxy from more than one shareholder without limitation as to the number of shareholders so represented. Where a proxy holder holds proxies from several shareholders, the applicable law shall enable him to cast votes for a certain shareholder differently from votes cast for another shareholder.

[11.553]
Article 11
Formalities for proxy holder appointment and notification
1. Member States shall permit shareholders to appoint a proxy holder by electronic means. Moreover, Member States shall permit companies to accept the notification of the appointment by electronic means, and shall ensure that every company offers to its shareholders at least one effective method of notification by electronic means.
2. Member States shall ensure that proxy holders may be appointed, and that such appointment be notified to the company, only in writing. Beyond this basic formal requirement, the appointment of a proxy holder, the notification of the appointment to the company and the issuance of voting instructions, if any, to the proxy holder may be made subject only to such formal requirements as are necessary to ensure the identification of the shareholder and of the proxy holder, or to ensure the possibility of verifying the content of voting instructions, respectively, and only to the extent that they are proportionate to achieving those objectives.
3. The provisions of this Article shall apply mutatis mutandis for the revocation of the appointment of a proxy holder.

[11.554]
Article 12
Voting by correspondence
Member States shall permit companies to offer their shareholders the possibility to vote by correspondence in advance of the general meeting. Voting by correspondence may be made subject only to such requirements and constraints as are necessary to ensure the identification of shareholders and only to the extent that they are proportionate to achieving that objective.

[11.555]
Article 13
Removal of certain impediments to the effective exercise of voting rights
1. This Article applies where a natural or legal person who is recognised as a shareholder by the applicable law acts in the course of a business on behalf of another natural or legal person (the client).

2.   Where the applicable law imposes disclosure requirements as a prerequisite for the exercise of voting rights by a shareholder referred to in paragraph 1, such requirements shall not go beyond a list disclosing to the company the identity of each client and the number of shares voted on his behalf.

3.   Where the applicable law imposes formal requirements on the authorisation of a shareholder referred to in paragraph 1 to exercise voting rights, or on voting instructions, such formal requirements shall not go beyond what is necessary to ensure the identification of the client, or the possibility of verifying the content of voting instructions, respectively, and is proportionate to achieving those objectives.

4.   A shareholder referred to in paragraph 1 shall be permitted to cast votes attaching to some of the shares differently from votes attaching to the other shares.

5.   Where the applicable law limits the number of persons whom a shareholder may appoint as proxy holders in accordance with Article 10(2), such limitation shall not prevent a shareholder referred to in paragraph 1 of this Article from granting a proxy to each of his clients or to any third party designated by a client.

[11.556]
Article 14
Voting results

1.   The company shall establish for each resolution at least the number of shares for which votes have been validly cast, the proportion of the share capital represented by those votes, the total number of votes validly cast as well as the number of votes cast in favour of and against each resolution and, where applicable, the number of abstentions.

However, Member States may provide or allow companies to provide that if no shareholder requests a full account of the voting, it shall be sufficient to establish the voting results only to the extent needed to ensure that the required majority is reached for each resolution.

2.   Within a period of time to be determined by the applicable law, which shall not exceed 15 days after the general meeting, the company shall publish on its Internet site the voting results established in accordance with paragraph 1.

3.   This Article is without prejudice to any legal rules that Member States have adopted or may adopt concerning the formalities required in order for a resolution to become valid or the possibility of a subsequent legal challenge to the voting result.

CHAPTER III
FINAL PROVISIONS

[11.557]
Article 15
Transposition

Member States shall bring into force the laws, regulations and administrative provisions necessary to comply with this Directive by 3 August 2009 at the latest. They shall forthwith communicate to the Commission the text of those measures.

Notwithstanding the first paragraph, Member States which on 1 July 2006 had in force national measures restricting or prohibiting the appointment of a proxy holder in the case of Article 10(3), second subparagraph, point (ii), shall bring into force the laws, regulations and administrative provisions necessary in order to comply with Article 10(3) as concerns such restriction or prohibition by 3 August 2012 at the latest.

Member States shall forthwith communicate the number of days specified under Articles 6(3) and 7(3), and any subsequent changes thereof, to the Commission, which shall publish this information in the Official Journal of the European Union.

When Member States adopt the measures referred to in the first paragraph, they shall contain a reference to this Directive or shall be accompanied by such reference on the occasion of their official publication. The methods of making such reference shall be laid down by the Member States.

[11.558]
Article 16
Entry into force

This Directive shall enter into force on the 20th day following its publication in the Official Journal of the European Union.

[11.559]
Article 17
Addressees

This Directive is addressed to the Member States.

that these statements be placed on any company website.

(9) The protection of third parties should be ensured by provisions which restrict to the greatest possible extent the grounds on which obligations entered into in the name of the company are not valid.

(10) It is necessary, in order to ensure certainty in the law as regards relations between the company and third parties, and also between members, to limit the cases in which nullity can arise and the retroactive effect of a declaration of nullity, and to fix a short time limit within which third parties may enter objection to any such declaration.

(11) This Directive should be without prejudice to the obligations of the Member States relating to the time limits for transposition into national law of the Directives set out in Annex I, Part B,

NOTES

¹   OJ 2, 15.1.1962, p 36/62.

²   OJ C204, 9.8.2008, p 25.

³   Opinion of the European Parliament of 17 June 2008 (not yet published in the Official Journal) and Council Decision of 13 July 2009.

⁴   OJ L65, 14.3.1968, p 8.

⁵   See Annex I, Part A.

HAVE ADOPTED THIS DIRECTIVE:

CHAPTER 1
SCOPE

[11.566]
Article 1
The coordination measures prescribed by this Directive shall apply to the laws, regulations and administrative provisions of the Member States relating to the following types of company:

— **Belgium:**
naamloze vennootschap, société anonyme, commanditaire vennootschap op aandelen, société en commandite par actions, personenvennootschap met beperkte aansprakelijkheid, société de personnes à responsabilité limitée;

— **Bulgaria:**
акционерно дружество, дружество с ограничена отговорност, командитно дружество с акции;

— **Czech Republic:**
společnost s ručením omezeným, akciová společnost;

— **Denmark:**
aktieselskab, kommanditaktieselskab, anpartsselskab;

— **Germany:**
die Aktiengesellschaft, die Kommanditgesellschaft auf Aktien, die Gesellschaft mit beschränkter Haftung;

— **Estonia:**
aktsiaselts, osaühing;

— **Ireland:**
Companies incorporated with limited liability;

— **Greece:**
ανώνυμη εταιρία, εταιρία περιωρισμένης ευθύνης, ετερόρρυθμη κατά μετοχές εταιρία;

— **Spain:**
la sociedad anónima, la sociedad comanditaria por acciones, la sociedad de responsabilidad limitada;

— **France:**
société anonyme, société en commandite par actions, société à responsabilité limitée, société par actions simplifiée;

— **Italy:**
società per azioni, società in accomandita per azioni, società a responsabilità limitata;

— **Cyprus:**
δημόσιες εταιρείες περιορισμένης ευθύνης με μετοχές ή με εγγύηση, ιδιωτικές εταιρείες περιορισμένης ευθύνης με μετοχές ή με εγγύηση;

— **Latvia:**
akciju sabiedrība, sabiedrība ar ierobežotu atbildību, komandītsabiedrība;

— **Lithuania:**
akcin bendrov , uždaroji akcin bendrov ;

Part II   EU Legislation

— **Luxembourg:**

société anonyme, société en commandite par actions, société à responsabilité limitée;

— **Hungary:**

részvénytársaság, korlátolt felelősségű társaság;

— **Malta:**

kumpannija pubblika/public limited liability company, kumpannija privata/private limited liability company;

— **The Netherlands:**

naamloze vennootschap, besloten vennootschap met beperkte aansprakelijkheid;

— **Austria:**

die Aktiengesellschaft, die Gesellschaft mit beschränkter Haftung;

— **Poland:**

spółka z ograniczon odpowiedzialności , spółka komandytowo-akcyjna, spółka akcyjna;

— **Portugal:**

a sociedade anónima de responsabilidade limitada, a sociedade em comandita por acções, a sociedade por quotas de responsabilidade limitada;

— **Romania:**

societate pe actiuni, societate cu răspundere limitată, societate în comandită pe actiuni;

— **Slovenia:**

delniška družba, družba z omejeno odgovornostjo, komaditna delniška družba;

— **Slovakia:**

akciová spoločnos , spoločnos s ručením obmedzeným;

— **Finland:**

yksityinen osakeyhtiö/privat aktiebolag, julkinen osakeyhtiö/publikt aktiebolag;

— **Sweden:**

aktiebolag;

— **United Kingdom:**

Companies incorporated with limited liability.

CHAPTER 2
DISCLOSURE

[11.567]
Article 2

Member States shall take the measures required to ensure compulsory disclosure by companies as referred to in Article 1 of at least the following documents and particulars:

(a) the instrument of constitution, and the statutes if they are contained in a separate instrument;

(b) any amendments to the instruments mentioned in point (a), including any extension of the duration of the company;

(c) after every amendment of the instrument of constitution or of the statutes, the complete text of the instrument or statutes as amended to date;

(d) the appointment, termination of office and particulars of the persons who either as a body constituted pursuant to law or as members of any such body:

    (i) are authorised to represent the company in dealings with third parties and in legal proceedings; it must be apparent from the disclosure whether the persons authorised to represent the company may do so alone or must act jointly;

    (ii) take part in the administration, supervision or control of the company;

(e) at least once a year, the amount of the capital subscribed, where the instrument of constitution or the statutes mention an authorised capital, unless any increase in the capital subscribed necessitates an amendment of the statutes;

(f) the accounting documents for each financial year which are required to be published in accordance with Council Directives 78/660/EEC,[1] 83/349/EEC,[2] 86/635/EEC[3] and 91/674/EEC;[4]

(g) any change of the registered office of the company;

(h) the winding-up of the company;

(i) any declaration of nullity of the company by the courts;

(j) the appointment of liquidators, particulars concerning them, and their respective powers, unless such powers are expressly and exclusively derived from law or from the statutes of the company;

(k) the termination of the liquidation and, in Member States where striking off the register entails legal consequences, the fact of any such striking off.

NOTES

1   Fourth Council Directive 78/660/EEC of 25 July 1978 based on Article 54(3)(g) of the Treaty on the annual accounts of certain types of companies (OJ L222, 14.8.1978, p 11).

2   Seventh Council Directive 83/349/EEC of 13 June 1983 based on the Article 54(3)(g) of the Treaty on consolidated accounts (OJ L193, 18.7.1983, p 1).

3   Council Directive 86/635/EEC of 8 December 1986 on the annual accounts and consolidated accounts of banks and other financial institutions (OJ L372, 31.12.1986, p 1).

4   Council Directive 91/674/EEC of 19 December 1991 on the annual accounts and consolidated accounts of insurance undertakings (OJ L374, 31.12.1991, p 7).

[11.568]
Article 3

1. In each Member State, a file shall be opened in a central register, commercial register or companies register, for each of the companies registered therein.

2. For the purposes of this Article, "by electronic means" shall mean that the information is sent initially and received at its destination by means of electronic equipment for the processing (including digital compression) and storage of data, and entirely transmitted, conveyed and received in a manner to be determined by Member States by wire, by radio, by optical means or by other electromagnetic means.

3. All documents and particulars which must be disclosed pursuant to Article 2 shall be kept in the file, or entered in the register; the subject matter of the entries in the register must in every case appear in the file.

Member States shall ensure that the filing by companies, as well as by other persons and bodies required to make or assist in making notifications, of all documents and particulars which must be disclosed pursuant to Article 2 is possible by electronic means. In addition, Member States may require all, or certain categories of, companies to file all, or certain types of, such documents and particulars by electronic means.

All documents and particulars referred to in Article 2 which are filed, whether by paper means or by electronic means, shall be kept in the file, or entered in the register, in electronic form. To this end, Member States shall ensure that all such documents and particulars which are filed by paper means are converted by the register to electronic form.

The documents and particulars referred to in Article 2 that have been filed by paper means up to 31 December 2006 shall not be required to be converted automatically into electronic form by the register. Member States shall nevertheless ensure that they are converted into electronic form by the register upon receipt of an application for disclosure by electronic means submitted in accordance with the measures adopted to give effect to paragraph 4.

4. A copy of the whole or any part of the documents or particulars referred to in Article 2 must be obtainable on application. Applications may be submitted to the register by paper means or by electronic means as the applicant chooses.

Copies as referred to in the first subparagraph must be obtainable from the register by paper means or by electronic means as the applicant chooses. This shall apply in the case of all documents and particulars already filed. However, Member States may decide that all, or certain types of, documents and particulars filed by paper means on or before a date which may not be later than 31 December 2006 shall not be obtainable from the register by electronic means if a specified period has elapsed between the date of filing and the date of the application submitted to the register. Such specified period may not be less than 10 years.

The price of obtaining a copy of the whole or any part of the documents or particulars referred to in Article 2, whether by paper means or by electronic means, shall not exceed the administrative cost thereof.

Paper copies supplied shall be certified as "true copies", unless the applicant dispenses with such certification. Electronic copies supplied shall not be certified as "true copies", unless the applicant explicitly requests such a certification.

Member States shall take the necessary measures to ensure that certification of electronic copies guarantees both the authenticity of their origin and the integrity of their contents, by means at least of an advanced electronic signature within the meaning of Article 2(2) of Directive 1999/93/EC.[1]

5. Disclosure of the documents and particulars referred to in paragraph 3 shall be effected by publication in the national gazette designated for that purpose by the Member State, either of the full text or of a partial text, or by means of a reference to the document which has been deposited in the file or entered in the register. The national gazette designated for that purpose may be kept in electronic form.

Member States may decide to replace publication in the national gazette with equally effective means, which shall entail at least the use of a system whereby the information disclosed can be accessed in chronological order through a central electronic platform.

6.   The documents and particulars may be relied on by the company as against third parties only after they have been disclosed in accordance with paragraph 5, unless the company proves that the third parties had knowledge thereof.

However, with regard to transactions taking place before the sixteenth day following the disclosure, the documents and particulars shall not be relied on as against third parties who prove that it was impossible for them to have had knowledge thereof.

7.   Member States shall take the necessary measures to avoid any discrepancy between what is disclosed in accordance with paragraph 5 and what appears in the register or file.

However, in cases of discrepancy, the text disclosed in accordance with paragraph 5 may not be relied on as against third parties; such third parties may nevertheless rely thereon, unless the company proves that they had knowledge of the texts deposited in the file or entered in the register.

Third parties may, moreover, always rely on any documents and particulars in respect of which the disclosure formalities have not yet been completed, save where non-disclosure causes them not to have effect.

NOTES

¹   Directive 1999/93/EC of the European Parliament and of the Council of 13 December 1999 on a Community framework for electronic signatures (OJ L13, 19.1.2000, p 12).

[11.569]
Article 4

1.   Documents and particulars which must be disclosed pursuant to Article 2 shall be drawn up and filed in one of the languages permitted by the language rules applicable in the Member State in which the file referred to in Article 3(1) is opened.

2.   In addition to the mandatory disclosure referred to in Article 3, Member States shall allow documents and particulars referred to in Article 2 to be disclosed voluntarily in accordance with Article 3 in any official language(s) of the Community.

Member States may prescribe that the translation of such documents and particulars be certified.

Member States shall take the necessary measures to facilitate access by third parties to the translations voluntarily disclosed.

3.   In addition to the mandatory disclosure referred to in Article 3, and to the voluntary disclosure provided for under paragraph 2 of this Article, Member States may allow the documents and particulars concerned to be disclosed, in accordance with Article 3, in any other language(s).

Member States may prescribe that the translation of such documents and particulars be certified.

4.   In cases of discrepancy between the documents and particulars disclosed in the official languages of the register and the translation voluntarily disclosed, the latter may not be relied upon as against third parties. Third parties may nevertheless rely on the translations voluntarily disclosed, unless the company proves that the third parties had knowledge of the version which was the subject of the mandatory disclosure.

[11.570]
Article 5

Member States shall prescribe that letters and order forms, whether they are in paper form or use any other medium, are to state the following particulars:

(a)   the information necessary in order to identify the register in which the file mentioned in Article 3 is kept, together with the number of the company in that register;

(b)   the legal form of the company, the location of its registered office and, where appropriate, the fact that the company is being wound up.

Where, in those documents, mention is made of the capital of the company, the reference shall be to the capital subscribed and paid up.

Member States shall prescribe that company websites are to contain at least the particulars mentioned in the first paragraph and, if applicable, a reference to the capital subscribed and paid up.

[11.571]
Article 6

Each Member State shall determine by which persons the disclosure formalities are to be carried out.

[11.572]
Article 7

Member States shall provide for appropriate penalties at least in the case of:

(a)   failure to disclose accounting documents as required by Article 2(f);

(b)   omission from commercial documents or from any company website of the compulsory particulars provided for in Article 5.

CHAPTER 3
VALIDITY OF OBLIGATIONS ENTERED INTO BY THE COMPANY

[11.573]
Article 8
If, before a company being formed has acquired legal personality, action has been carried out in its name and the company does not assume the obligations arising from such action, the persons who acted shall, without limit, be jointly and severally liable therefor, unless otherwise agreed.

[11.574]
Article 9
Completion of the formalities of disclosure of the particulars concerning the persons who, as an organ of the company, are authorised to represent it shall constitute a bar to any irregularity in their appointment being relied upon as against third parties unless the company proves that such third parties had knowledge thereof.

[11.575]
Article 10
1. Acts done by the organs of the company shall be binding upon it even if those acts are not within the objects of the company, unless such acts exceed the powers that the law confers or allows to be conferred on those organs.

However, Member States may provide that the company shall not be bound where such acts are outside the objects of the company, if it proves that the third party knew that the act was outside those objects or could not in view of the circumstances have been unaware of it; disclosure of the statutes shall not of itself be sufficient proof thereof.

2. The limits on the powers of the organs of the company, arising under the statutes or from a decision of the competent organs, may not be relied on as against third parties, even if they have been disclosed.

3. If the national law provides that authority to represent a company may, in derogation from the legal rules governing the subject, be conferred by the statutes on a single person or on several persons acting jointly, that law may provide that such a provision in the statutes may be relied on as against third parties on condition that it relates to the general power of representation; the question whether such a provision in the statutes can be relied on as against third parties shall be governed by Article 3.

CHAPTER 4
NULLITY OF THE COMPANY

[11.576]
Article 11
In all Member States whose laws do not provide for preventive, administrative or judicial control, at the time of formation of a company, the instrument of constitution, the company statutes and any amendments to those documents shall be drawn up and certified in due legal form.

[11.577]
Article 12
The laws of the Member States may not provide for the nullity of companies otherwise than in accordance with the following provisions:
  (a)   nullity must be ordered by decision of a court of law;
  (b)   nullity may be ordered only on the grounds:
      (i)   that no instrument of constitution was executed or that the rules of preventive control or the requisite legal formalities were not complied with;
      (ii)   that the objects of the company are unlawful or contrary to public policy;
      (iii) that the instrument of constitution or the statutes do not state the name of the company, the amount of the individual subscriptions of capital, the total amount of the capital subscribed or the objects of the company;
      (iv) of failure to comply with the provisions of the national law concerning the minimum amount of capital to be paid up;
      (v)   of the incapacity of all the founder members;
      (vi) that, contrary to the national law governing the company, the number of founder members is less than two.

Apart from the foregoing grounds of nullity, a company shall not be subject to any cause of non-existence, absolute nullity, relative nullity or declaration of nullity.

[11.578]
Article 13
1. The question whether a decision of nullity pronounced by a court of law may be relied on as against third parties shall be governed by Article 3. Where the national law entitles a third party to challenge the decision, he may do so only within six months of public notice of the decision of the court being given.

2.   Nullity shall entail the winding-up of the company, as may dissolution.

3.   Nullity shall not of itself affect the validity of any commitments entered into by or with the company, without prejudice to the consequences of the company's being wound up.

4.   The laws of each Member State may make provision for the consequences of nullity as between members of the company.

5.   Holders of shares in the capital shall remain obliged to pay up the capital agreed to be subscribed by them but which has not been paid up, to the extent that commitments entered into with creditors so require.

CHAPTER 5
GENERAL PROVISIONS

[11.579]
Article 14
Member States shall communicate to the Commission the text of the main provisions of national law which they adopt in the field covered by this Directive.

[11.580]
Article 15
The Commission shall present to the European Parliament and to the Council, by no later than 1 January 2012, a report, together with a proposal, if appropriate, for amendment of the provisions of Article 2(f) and Articles 3, 4, 5 and 7 in the light of the experience acquired in applying those provisions, of their aims and of the technological developments observed at the time.

[11.581]
Article 16
Directive 68/151/EEC, as amended by the acts listed in Annex I, Part A, is hereby repealed, without prejudice to the obligations of the Member States relating to the time limits for transposition into national law of the Directives set out in Annex I, Part B.

   References to the repealed Directive shall be construed as references to this Directive and shall be read in accordance with the correlation table in Annex II.

[11.582]
Article 17
This Directive shall enter into force on the 20th day following its publication in the Official Journal of the European Union.

[11.583]
Article 18
This Directive is addressed to the Member States.

ANNEXES

ANNEX I

PART A
REPEALED DIRECTIVE WITH LIST OF ITS SUCCESSIVE AMENDMENTS
(referred to in Article 16)

[11.584]
Council Directive 68/151/EEC (OJ L65, 14.3.1968, p 8)
   Point III.H of Annex I to the 1972 Act of Accession (OJ L73, 27.3.1972, p 89)
   Point III.C of Annex I to the 1979 Act of Accession (OJ L291, 19.11.1979, p 89)
   Point II.D of Annex I to the 1985 Act of Accession (OJ L302, 15.11.1985, p 157)
   Point XI.A of Annex I to the 1994 Act of Accession (OJ C241, 29.8.1994, p 194)
   Directive 2003/58/CE of the European Parliament and of the Council (OJ L221, 4.9.2003, p 13)
   Point 1.4.A of Annex II to the 2003 Act of Accession (OJ L236, 23.9.2003, p 338)
   Council Directive 2006/99/EC (OJ L363, 20.12.2006, p 137). Only point A.1 of the Annex

PART B
LIST OF TIME LIMITS FOR TRANSPOSITION INTO NATIONAL LAW
(referred to in Article 16)

Directive	Time limit for transposition
68/151/EEC	11 September 1969
2003/58/EC	30 December 2006
2006/99/EC	1 January 2007

ANNEX II
CORRELATION TABLE

[11.585]

Directive 68/151/EEC	This Directive
Article 1	Article 1
Article 2	Article 2
Article 3(1)	Article 3(1)
Article 3(2)	Article 3(3)
Article 3(3)	Article 3(4)
Article 3(4)	Article 3(5)
Article 3(5)	Article 3(6)
Article 3(6), first and second subparagraphs	Article 3(7), first and second subparagraphs
Article 3(7)	Article 3(7), third subparagraph
Article 3(8)	Article 3(2)
Article 3a	Article 4
Article 4	Article 5
Article 5	Article 6
Article 6	Article 7
Article 7	Article 8
Article 8	Article 9
Article 9	Article 10
Article 10	Article 11
Article 11, introductory wording	Article 12, introductory wording
Article 11, point 1	Article 12, point (a)
Article 11, point 2, introductory wording	Article 12, point (b), introductory wording
Article 11, point 2, points (a) to (f)	Article 12, point (b), points (i) to (vi)
Article 12	Article 13
Article 13, first, second and third paragraphs	—
Article 13, fourth paragraph	Article 14
Article 14	Article 18
—	Article 15
—	Article 16
—	Article 17
—	Annex I
—	Annex II

Part 11   EU Legislation

DIRECTIVE OF THE EUROPEAN PARLIAMENT AND OF THE COUNCIL

(2009/102/EC)

of 16 September 2009

in the area of company law on single-member private limited liability companies

(Codified version)

(Text with EEA relevance)

NOTES

Date of publication in OJ: OJ L258, 1.10.2009, p 20. Notes are as in the original OJ version.
As at 1 July 2011, this Directive had not been amended.

[11.586]

THE EUROPEAN PARLIAMENT AND THE COUNCIL OF THE EUROPEAN UNION,

Having regard to the Treaty establishing the European Community, and in particular Article 44 thereof,

Having regard to the proposal from the Commission,

Having regard to the opinion of the European Economic and Social Committee,[1]

Acting in accordance with the procedure laid down in Article 251 of the Treaty,[2]

Whereas:

(1) Twelfth Council Company Law Directive 89/667/EEC of 21 December 1989 on single-member private limited-liability[3] has been substantially amended several times.[4] In the interests of clarity and rationality the said Directive should be codified.

(2) Certain safeguards which, for the protection of the interests of members and others, are required by Member States of companies and firms within the meaning of the second paragraph of Article 48 of the Treaty should be coordinated with a view to making such safeguards equivalent throughout the Community.

(3) In this field, First Council Directive 68/151/EEC of 9 March 1968 on coordination of safeguards which, for the protection of the interests of members and others, are required by Member States of companies within the meaning of the second paragraph of Article 58 of the Treaty, with a view to making such safeguards equivalent throughout the Community,[5] Fourth Council Directive 78/660/EEC of 25 July 1978 based on Article 54(3)(g) of the Treaty on the annual accounts of certain types of companies[6] and Seventh Council Directive 83/349/EEC of 13 June 1983 based on Article 54(3)(g) of the Treaty on consolidated accounts,[7] respectively concerning disclosure, the validity of commitments, nullity, annual accounts and consolidated accounts, apply to all share-capital companies. However, Second Council Directive 77/91/EEC of 13 December 1976 on coordination of safeguards which, for the protection of the interests of members and others, are required by Member States of companies within the meaning of the second paragraph of Article 58 of the Treaty, in respect of the formation of public limited liability companies and the maintenance and alteration of their capital, with a view to making such safeguards equivalent,[8] Third Council Directive 78/855/EEC of 9 October 1978 based on Article 54(3)(g) of the Treaty concerning mergers of public limited liability companies,[9] and Sixth Council Directive 82/891/EEC of 17 December 1982 based on Article 54(3)(g) of the Treaty, concerning the division of public limited liability companies,[10] relating respectively to formation and capital, mergers and divisions, apply only to public limited liability companies.

(4) A legal instrument is required allowing the limitation of liability of the individual entrepreneur throughout the Community, without prejudice to the laws of the Member States, which, in exceptional circumstances, require that entrepreneur to be liable for the obligations of his undertaking.

(5) A private limited liability company may be a single-member company from the time of its formation, or may become one because its shares have come to be held by a single shareholder. Pending the coordination of national provisions on the laws relating to groups, Member States may lay down certain special provisions and penalties for cases where a natural person is the sole member of several companies or where a single-member company or any other legal person is the sole member of a company. The sole aim of this power is to take account of the differences which exist in certain national laws. For that purpose, Member States may in specific cases lay down restrictions on the use of single-member companies or remove the limits on the liabilities of sole members. Member States are free to lay down rules to cover the risks that single-member companies may present as a consequence of having single members, particularly in order to ensure that the subscribed capital is paid.

(6) The fact that all the shares have come to be held by a single shareholder and the identity of the sole member should be disclosed by an entry in a register accessible to the public.

(7) Decisions taken by the sole member exercising the powers of the general meeting should be recorded in writing.

(8) Contracts between a sole member and his company as represented by him should likewise be recorded in writing, in so far as such contracts do not relate to current operations concluded under normal conditions.

(9) This Directive should be without prejudice to the obligations of the Member States relating to the time limits for transposition into national law and application of the Directives set out in Annex II, Part B,

---

NOTES

[1] OJ C77, 31.3.2009, p 42.

[2] Opinion of the European Parliament of 18 November 2008 (not yet published in the Official Journal) and Council Decision of 13 July 2009.

[3] OJ L395, 30.12.1989, p 40.

[4] See Annex II, Part A.

[5] OJ L65, 14.3.1968, p 8.

[6] OJ L222, 14.8.1978, p 11.

[7] OJ L193, 18.7.1983, p 1.

[8] OJ L26, 31.1.1977, p 1.

[9] OJ L295, 20.10.1978, p 36.

[10] OJ L378, 31.12.1982, p 47.

HAVE ADOPTED THIS DIRECTIVE:

[11.587]
Article 1
The coordination measures prescribed by this Directive shall apply to the laws, regulations and administrative provisions of the Member States relating to the types of company listed in Annex I.

[11.588]
Article 2
1.   A company may have a sole member when it is formed and also when all its shares come to be held by a single person (single-member company).
2.   Member States may, pending coordination of national laws relating to groups, lay down special provisions or penalties for cases where:
    (a)   a natural person is the sole member of several companies; or
    (b)   a single-member company or any other legal person is the sole member of a company.

[11.589]
Article 3
Where a company becomes a single-member company because all its shares come to be held by a single person, that fact, together with the identity of the sole member, must either be recorded in the file or entered in the register as referred to in Article 3(1) and (2) of Directive 68/151/EEC or be entered in a register kept by the company and accessible to the public.

[11.590]
Article 4
1.   The sole member shall exercise the powers of the general meeting of the company.
2.   Decisions taken by the sole member in the field referred to in paragraph 1 shall be recorded in minutes or drawn up in writing.

[11.591]
Article 5
1.   Contracts between the sole member and his company as represented by him shall be recorded in minutes or drawn up in writing.
2.   Member States need not apply paragraph 1 to current operations concluded under normal conditions.

[11.592]
Article 6
Where a Member State allows single-member companies as defined by Article 2(1) in the case of public limited companies as well, this Directive shall apply.

[11.593]
Article 7
A Member State need not allow the formation of single-member companies where its legislation provides that an individual entrepreneur may set up an undertaking the liability of which is limited to a sum dedicated to a stated activity, on condition that safeguards are laid down for such undertakings which are equivalent to those imposed by this Directive or by any other Community provisions applicable to the companies referred to in Article 1.

[11.594]
Article 8
Member States shall communicate to the Commission the texts of the main provisions of national law which they adopt in the field covered by this Directive.

[11.595]
Article 9
Directive 89/667/EEC, as amended by the acts listed in Annex II, Part A, is repealed, without prejudice to the obligations of the Member States relating to the time limits for transposition into national law and application of the Directives set out in Annex II, Part B.

    References to the repealed Directive shall be construed as references to this Directive and shall be read in accordance with the correlation table in Annex III.

[11.596]
Article 10
This Directive shall enter into force on the 20th day following its publication in the Official Journal of the European Union.

[11.597]
Article 11
This Directive is addressed to the Member States.

ANNEXES

ANNEX I
TYPES OF COMPANIES REFERRED TO IN ARTICLE 1

[11.598]

— Belgium:
"société privée à responsabilité limitée/besloten vennootschap met beperkte aansprakelijkheid",

— **Bulgaria:**
"дружество с ограничена отговорност, акционерно дружество",

— **Czech Republic:**
"společnost s ručením omezeným",

— **Denmark:**
"anpartsselskaber",

— **Germany:**
"Gesellschaft mit beschränkter Haftung",

— **Estonia:**
"aktsiaselts, osaühing",

— **Ireland:**
"private company limited by shares or by guarantee",

— **Greece:**
"εταιρεία περιορισμένης ευθύνης",

— **Spain:**
"sociedad de responsabilidad limitada",

— **France:**
"société à responsabilité limitée",

— **Italy:**
"società a responsabilità limitata",

— **Cyprus:**
"ιδιωτική εταιρεία περιορισμένης ευθύνης με μετοχές ή με εγγύηση",

— **Latvia:**
"sabiedrība ar ierobežotu atbildību",

— **Lithuania:**
"uždaroji akcin bendrov ",

— **Luxembourg:**
"société à responsabilité limitée",

— **Hungary:**
"korlátolt felelősségű társaság, részvénytársaság",

— **Malta:**
"kumpannija privata/Private limited liability company",

— **The Netherlands:**
"besloten vennootschap met beperkte aansprakelijkheid",

— **Austria:**
"Aktiengesellschaft, Gesellschaft mit beschränkter Haftung",

— **Poland:**
"spółka z ograniczon odpowiedzialności ",

— **Portugal:**
"sociedade por quotas",

— **Romania:**
"societate cu răspundere limitată",

— **Slovenia:**
"družba z omejeno odgovornostjo",

— **Slovakia:**
"spoločnos s ručením obmedzeným",

— **Finland:**
"osakeyhtiö/aktiebolag",

— **Sweden:**
"aktiebolag",

— **United Kingdom:**
"private company limited by shares or by guarantee".

APPENDICES

COMMISSION REGULATION

(1126/2008/EC)

of 3 November 2008

adopting certain international accounting standards in accordance with Regulation (EC) No 1606/2002 of the European Parliament and of the Council

NOTES

Date of publication in OJ: OJ L320, 29.11.2008, p 1.

As to the amendment of this Regulation, see the note to the Annex *post*.

[11.560]

THE COMMISSION OF THE EUROPEAN COMMUNITIES,

Having regard to the Treaty establishing the European Community, Having regard to Regulation (EC) No 1606/2002 of the European Parliament and of the Council of 19 July 2002 on the application of international accounting standards,[1] and in particular Article 3(1) thereof,

Whereas:

(1) Regulation (EC) No 1606/2002 requires that for each financial year starting on or after 1 January 2005, publicly traded companies governed by the law of a Member State are, under certain conditions, to prepare their consolidated accounts in conformity with international accounting standards as defined in Article 2 of that Regulation.

(2) By Commission Regulation (EC) No 1725/2003 of 29 September 2003 adopting certain international accounting standards in accordance with Regulation (EC) No 1606/2002 of the European Parliament and of the Council,[2] certain international standards and interpretations that were in existence at 14 September 2002 were adopted. The Commission, having considered the advice provided by the Technical Expert Group (TEG) of the European Financial Reporting Advisory Group (EFRAG), has amended that Regulation in order to include all standards presented by the International Accounting Standards Board (IASB) as well as all interpretations presented by the International Financial Reporting Interpretations Committee (IFRIC) and adopted within the Community by 15 October 2008 in full, except for IAS 39 (related to recognition and measurement of financial instruments), of which limited parts have been omitted.

(3) The different international standards have been adopted by a number of amending regulations. This causes legal uncertainty and difficulty in correctly applying international accounting standards in the Community. In order to simplify Community legislation on accounting standards, it is appropriate, for the sake of clarity and transparency, to incorporate in a single text the standards presently contained in Regulation (EC) No 1725/2003 and the acts amending it.

(4) Regulation (EC) No 1725/2003 should therefore be replaced by this Regulation.

(5) The measures provided for in this Regulation are in accordance with the opinion of the Accounting Regulatory Committee,

NOTES

[1]   OJ L243, 11.9.2002, p 1.

[2]   OJ L261, 13.10.2003, p 1.

HAS ADOPTED THIS REGULATION,

[11.561]
Article 1
The international accounting standards, as defined in Article 2 of Regulation (EC) No 1606/2002, shall be adopted as set out in the Annex hereto.

[11.562]
Article 2
Regulation (EC) No 1725/2003 is hereby repealed.

References to the repealed Regulation shall be construed as references to this Regulation.

[11.563]
Article 3
This Regulation shall enter into force on the third day following its publication in the Official Journal of the European Union.

This Regulation shall be binding in its entirety and directly applicable in all Member States.

ANNEX

The Annex sets out the international accounting standards introduced by Article 1 and, due to its size, has been omitted. The full version (in PDF format and consolidated as of 27 July 2010) is available on the EUR-Lex website at:

http://eur-lex.europa.eu/LexUriServ/LexUriServ.do?uri=CONSLEG:2008R1126:20100727:EN:PDF

Note also that since that date the Annex has been amended by the following Regulations:
— Commission Regulation (EU) No 149/2011 of 18 February 2011 amending Regulation (EC) No 1126/2008 adopting certain international accounting standards in accordance with Regulation (EC) No 1606/2002 of the European Parliament and of the Council as regards Improvements to International Financial Reporting Standards (IFRSs) 1 (with effect from 22 February 2011).

DIRECTIVE OF THE EUROPEAN PARLIAMENT AND OF THE COUNCIL

(2009/101/EC)

of 16 September 2009

on coordination of safeguards which, for the protection of the interests of members and third parties, are required by Member States of companies within the meaning of the second paragraph of Article 48 of the Treaty, with a view to making such safeguards equivalent (Codified version)

(Text with EEA relevance)

NOTES
Date of publication in OJ: OJ L258, 1.10.2009, p 11. Notes are as in the original OJ version.
As at 1 July 2011, this Directive had not been amended.

[11.565]
THE EUROPEAN PARLIAMENT AND THE COUNCIL OF THE EUROPEAN UNION,
Having regard to the Treaty establishing the European Community, and in particular Article 44(2)(g) thereof,
Having regard to the General Programme for the abolition of restrictions on freedom of establishment,[1] and in particular Title VI thereof,
Having regard to the proposal from the Commission,
Having regard to the opinion of the European Economic and Social Committee,[2]
Acting in accordance with the procedure laid down in Article 251 of the Treaty,[3]
Whereas:

(1) First Council Directive 68/151/EEC of 9 March 1968 on coordination of safeguards which, for the protection of the interests of members and others, are required by Member States of companies within the meaning of the second paragraph of Article 58 of the Treaty, with a view to making such safeguards equivalent throughout the Community[4] has been substantially amended several times.[5] In the interests of clarity and rationality that Directive should be codified.

(2) The coordination of national provisions concerning disclosure, the validity of obligations entered into by, and the nullity of, companies limited by shares or otherwise having limited liability is of special importance, particularly for the purpose of protecting the interests of third parties.

(3) The basic documents of the company should be disclosed in order that third parties may be able to ascertain their contents and other information concerning the company, especially particulars of the persons who are authorised to bind the company.

(4) Without prejudice to substantive requirements and formalities established by the national law of the Member States, companies should be able to choose to file their compulsory documents and particulars by paper means or by electronic means.

(5) Interested parties should be able to obtain from the register a copy of such documents and particulars by paper means as well as by electronic means.

(6) Member States should be allowed to decide to keep the national gazette, designated for publication of compulsory documents and particulars, in paper form or electronic form, or to provide for disclosure by equally effective means.

(7) Cross-border access to company information should be facilitated by allowing, in addition to the mandatory disclosure made in one of the languages permitted in the company's Member State, voluntary registration in additional languages of the required documents and particulars. Third parties acting in good faith should be able to rely on the translations thereof.

(8) It is appropriate to clarify that the statement of the compulsory particulars set out in this Directive should be included in all company letters and order forms, whether they are in paper form or use any other medium. In the light of technological developments, it is also appropriate to provide

ANNEX II

PART A
REPEALED DIRECTIVE WITH LIST OF ITS SUCCESSIVE AMENDMENTS

(referred to in Article 9)

[11.599]
Council Directive 89/667/EEC (OJ L395, 30.12.1989, p 40)
  Annex I, point XI.A of the 1994 Act of Accession (OJ C241, 29.8.1994, p 194)
  Annex II, point 4.A of the 2003 Act of Accession (OJ L236, 23.9.2003, p 338)
  Council Directive 2006/99/EC (OJ L363, 20.12.2006, p 137). Only point A.4 of the Annex

PART B
LIST OF TIME LIMITS FOR TRANSPOSITION INTO NATIONAL LAW AND APPLICATION

(referred to in Article 9)

Directive	Time limit for transposition	Date of Application
89/667/EEC	31 December 1991	1 January 1993 in the case of companies already in existence on 1 January 1992
2006/99/EC	1 January 2007	

ANNEX III
CORRELATION TABLE

[11.600]

Directive 89/667/EEC	This Directive
Article 1, introductory wording	Article 1
Article 1, first to 27th indent	Annex I
Articles 2 to 7	Articles 2 to 7
Article 8(1)	—
Article 8(2)	—
Article 8(3)	Article 8
—	Article 9
—	Article 10
Article 9	Article 11
—	Annex I
—	Annex II
—	Annex III

Appendix 1:
Companies Act 2006 Model Articles

[A1]

NOTES

These model articles are prescribed by the Secretary of State under the Companies Act 2006, s 19(1) at **[1.19]**. They are contained in Schs 1–3 to the Companies (Model Articles) Regulations 2008, SI 2008/3229 at **[4.340]** et seq, and have effect from 1 October 2009.

By virtue of s 19(1), (2) of the 2006 Act, a company may adopt all or any of the provisions of model articles and any amendment of model articles by Regulations made under s 19 does not affect a company registered before the amendment takes effect. As of 1 July 2011 the Model Articles had not been amended.

By s 20 of the 2006 Act (at **[1.20]**) on the formation of a limited company (a) if articles are not registered, or (b) if articles are registered, in so far as they do not exclude or modify the relevant model articles, then the relevant model articles (so far as applicable) form part of the company's articles in the same manner and to the same extent as if articles in the form of those articles had been duly registered.

Sch 1 (Model Articles for Private Companies Limited by Shares), Sch 2 (Model Articles for Private Companies Limited by Guarantee), and Sch 3 (Model Articles for Public Companies) are reproduced here at **[A1.1]**, **[A1.2]**, and **[A1.3]** respectively.

MODEL ARTICLES FOR PRIVATE COMPANIES LIMITED BY SHARES

[A1.1]

NOTES

These are set out in Schedule 1 to the Companies (Model Articles) Regulations 2008.

INDEX TO THE ARTICLES

PART 1
INTERPRETATION AND LIMITATION OF LIABILITY

1   Defined terms

In the articles, unless the context requires otherwise—

"articles" means the company's articles of association;

"bankruptcy" includes individual insolvency proceedings in a jurisdiction other than England and Wales or Northern Ireland which have an effect similar to that of bankruptcy;

"chairman" has the meaning given in article 12;

"chairman of the meeting" has the meaning given in article 39;

"Companies Acts" means the Companies Acts (as defined in section 2 of the Companies Act 2006), in so far as they apply to the company;

"director" means a director of the company, and includes any person occupying the position of director, by whatever name called;

"distribution recipient" has the meaning given in article 31;

"document" includes, unless otherwise specified, any document sent or supplied in electronic form;

"electronic form" has the meaning given in section 1168 of the Companies Act 2006;

"fully paid" in relation to a share, means that the nominal value and any premium to be paid to the company in respect of that share have been paid to the company;

"hard copy form" has the meaning given in section 1168 of the Companies Act 2006;

"holder" in relation to shares means the person whose name is entered in the register of members as the holder of the shares;

"instrument" means a document in hard copy form;

"ordinary resolution" has the meaning given in section 282 of the Companies Act 2006;

"paid" means paid or credited as paid;

"participate", in relation to a directors' meeting, has the meaning given in article 10;

"proxy notice" has the meaning given in article 45;

"shareholder" means a person who is the holder of a share;

"shares" means shares in the company;

"special resolution" has the meaning given in section 283 of the Companies Act 2006;

"subsidiary" has the meaning given in section 1159 of the Companies Act 2006;

"transmittee" means a person entitled to a share by reason of the death or bankruptcy of a shareholder or otherwise by operation of law; and

"writing" means the representation or reproduction of words, symbols or other information in a visible form by any method or combination of methods, whether sent or supplied in electronic form or otherwise.

Unless the context otherwise requires, other words or expressions contained in these articles bear the same meaning as in the Companies Act 2006 as in force on the date when these articles become binding on the company.

2 Liability of members

The liability of the members is limited to the amount, if any, unpaid on the shares held by them.

PART 2

DIRECTORS

Directors' Powers and Responsibilities

3 Directors' general authority

Subject to the articles, the directors are responsible for the management of the company's business, for which purpose they may exercise all the powers of the company.

4 Shareholders' reserve power

(1) The shareholders may, by special resolution, direct the directors to take, or refrain from taking, specified action.

(2) No such special resolution invalidates anything which the directors have done before the passing of the resolution.

5 Directors may delegate

(1) Subject to the articles, the directors may delegate any of the powers which are conferred on them under the articles—

(a) to such person or committee;

(b) by such means (including by power of attorney);

(c) to such an extent;

(d) in relation to such matters or territories; and

(e) on such terms and conditions;

as they think fit.

(2) If the directors so specify, any such delegation may authorise further delegation of the directors' powers by any person to whom they are delegated.

(3) The directors may revoke any delegation in whole or part, or alter its terms and conditions.

6 Committees

(1) Committees to which the directors delegate any of their powers must follow procedures which are based as far as they are applicable on those provisions of the articles which govern the taking of decisions by directors.

(2) The directors may make rules of procedure for all or any committees, which prevail over rules derived from the articles if they are not consistent with them.

Decision-Making by Directors

7 Directors to take decisions collectively

(1) The general rule about decision-making by directors is that any decision of the directors must be either a majority decision at a meeting or a decision taken in accordance with article 8.

(2) If—

(a) the company only has one director, and

(b) no provision of the articles requires it to have more than one director,

the general rule does not apply, and the director may take decisions without regard to any of the provisions of the articles relating to directors' decision-making.

8 Unanimous decisions

(1) A decision of the directors is taken in accordance with this article when all eligible directors indicate to each other by any means that they share a common view on a matter.

(2) Such a decision may take the form of a resolution in writing, copies of which have been signed by each eligible director or to which each eligible director has otherwise indicated agreement in writing.

Appendices

(3)   References in this article to eligible directors are to directors who would have been entitled to vote on the matter had it been proposed as a resolution at a directors' meeting.

(4)   A decision may not be taken in accordance with this article if the eligible directors would not have formed a quorum at such a meeting.

9   Calling a directors' meeting

(1)   Any director may call a directors' meeting by giving notice of the meeting to the directors or by authorising the company secretary (if any) to give such notice.

(2)   Notice of any directors' meeting must indicate—
  (a)   its proposed date and time;
  (b)   where it is to take place; and
  (c)   if it is anticipated that directors participating in the meeting will not be in the same place, how it is proposed that they should communicate with each other during the meeting.

(3)   Notice of a directors' meeting must be given to each director, but need not be in writing.

(4)   Notice of a directors' meeting need not be given to directors who waive their entitlement to notice of that meeting, by giving notice to that effect to the company not more than 7 days after the date on which the meeting is held. Where such notice is given after the meeting has been held, that does not affect the validity of the meeting, or of any business conducted at it.

10   Participation in directors' meetings

(1)   Subject to the articles, directors participate in a directors' meeting, or part of a directors' meeting, when—
  (a)   the meeting has been called and takes place in accordance with the articles, and
  (b)   they can each communicate to the others any information or opinions they have on any particular item of the business of the meeting.

(2)   In determining whether directors are participating in a directors' meeting, it is irrelevant where any director is or how they communicate with each other.

(3)   If all the directors participating in a meeting are not in the same place, they may decide that the meeting is to be treated as taking place wherever any of them is.

11   Quorum for directors' meetings

(1)   At a directors' meeting, unless a quorum is participating, no proposal is to be voted on, except a proposal to call another meeting.

(2)   The quorum for directors' meetings may be fixed from time to time by a decision of the directors, but it must never be less than two, and unless otherwise fixed it is two.

(3)   If the total number of directors for the time being is less than the quorum required, the directors must not take any decision other than a decision—
  (a)   to appoint further directors, or
  (b)   to call a general meeting so as to enable the shareholders to appoint further directors.

12   Chairing of directors' meetings

(1)   The directors may appoint a director to chair their meetings.

(2)   The person so appointed for the time being is known as the chairman.

(3)   The directors may terminate the chairman's appointment at any time.

(4)   If the chairman is not participating in a directors' meeting within ten minutes of the time at which it was to start, the participating directors must appoint one of themselves to chair it.

13   Casting vote

(1)   If the numbers of votes for and against a proposal are equal, the chairman or other director chairing the meeting has a casting vote.

(2)   But this does not apply if, in accordance with the articles, the chairman or other director is not to be counted as participating in the decision-making process for quorum or voting purposes.

14   Conflicts of interest

(1)   If a proposed decision of the directors is concerned with an actual or proposed transaction or arrangement with the company in which a director is interested, that director is not to be counted as participating in the decision-making process for quorum or voting purposes.

(2)   But if paragraph (3) applies, a director who is interested in an actual or proposed transaction or arrangement with the company is to be counted as participating in the decision-making process for quorum and voting purposes.

(3)   This paragraph applies when—
  (a)   the company by ordinary resolution disapplies the provision of the articles which would otherwise prevent a director from being counted as participating in the decision-making process;
  (b)   the director's interest cannot reasonably be regarded as likely to give rise to a conflict of interest; or

(c)   the director's conflict of interest arises from a permitted cause.

(4)   For the purposes of this article, the following are permitted causes—

(a)   a guarantee given, or to be given, by or to a director in respect of an obligation incurred by or on behalf of the company or any of its subsidiaries;

(b)   subscription, or an agreement to subscribe, for shares or other securities of the company or any of its subsidiaries, or to underwrite, sub-underwrite, or guarantee subscription for any such shares or securities; and

(c)   arrangements pursuant to which benefits are made available to employees and directors or former employees and directors of the company or any of its subsidiaries which do not provide special benefits for directors or former directors.

(5)   For the purposes of this article, references to proposed decisions and decision-making processes include any directors' meeting or part of a directors' meeting.

(6)   Subject to paragraph (7), if a question arises at a meeting of directors or of a committee of directors as to the right of a director to participate in the meeting (or part of the meeting) for voting or quorum purposes, the question may, before the conclusion of the meeting, be referred to the chairman whose ruling in relation to any director other than the chairman is to be final and conclusive.

(7)   If any question as to the right to participate in the meeting (or part of the meeting) should arise in respect of the chairman, the question is to be decided by a decision of the directors at that meeting, for which purpose the chairman is not to be counted as participating in the meeting (or that part of the meeting) for voting or quorum purposes.

15   Records of decisions to be kept

The directors must ensure that the company keeps a record, in writing, for at least 10 years from the date of the decision recorded, of every unanimous or majority decision taken by the directors.

16   Directors' discretion to make further rules

Subject to the articles, the directors may make any rule which they think fit about how they take decisions, and about how such rules are to be recorded or communicated to directors.

Appointment of Directors

17   Methods of appointing directors

(1)   Any person who is willing to act as a director, and is permitted by law to do so, may be appointed to be a director—

(a)   by ordinary resolution, or

(b)   by a decision of the directors.

(2)   In any case where, as a result of death, the company has no shareholders and no directors, the personal representatives of the last shareholder to have died have the right, by notice in writing, to appoint a person to be a director.

(3)   For the purposes of paragraph (2), where 2 or more shareholders die in circumstances rendering it uncertain who was the last to die, a younger shareholder is deemed to have survived an older shareholder.

18   Termination of director's appointment

A person ceases to be a director as soon as—

(a)   that person ceases to be a director by virtue of any provision of the Companies Act 2006 or is prohibited from being a director by law;

(b)   a bankruptcy order is made against that person;

(c)   a composition is made with that person's creditors generally in satisfaction of that person's debts;

(d)   a registered medical practitioner who is treating that person gives a written opinion to the company stating that that person has become physically or mentally incapable of acting as a director and may remain so for more than three months;

(e)   by reason of that person's mental health, a court makes an order which wholly or partly prevents that person from personally exercising any powers or rights which that person would otherwise have;

(f)   notification is received by the company from the director that the director is resigning from office, and such resignation has taken effect in accordance with its terms.

19   Directors' remuneration

(1)   Directors may undertake any services for the company that the directors decide.

(2)   Directors are entitled to such remuneration as the directors determine—

(a)   for their services to the company as directors, and

(b)   for any other service which they undertake for the company.

(3)   Subject to the articles, a director's remuneration may—

(a)   take any form, and

Appendices

(b) include any arrangements in connection with the payment of a pension, allowance or gratuity, or any death, sickness or disability benefits, to or in respect of that director.

(4) Unless the directors decide otherwise, directors' remuneration accrues from day to day.

(5) Unless the directors decide otherwise, directors are not accountable to the company for any remuneration which they receive as directors or other officers or employees of the company's subsidiaries or of any other body corporate in which the company is interested.

20 Directors' expenses

The company may pay any reasonable expenses which the directors properly incur in connection with their attendance at—

(a) meetings of directors or committees of directors,

(b) general meetings, or

(c) separate meetings of the holders of any class of shares or of debentures of the company,

or otherwise in connection with the exercise of their powers and the discharge of their responsibilities in relation to the company.

PART 3
SHARES AND DISTRIBUTIONS

Shares

21 All shares to be fully paid up

(1) No share is to be issued for less than the aggregate of its nominal value and any premium to be paid to the company in consideration for its issue.

(2) This does not apply to shares taken on the formation of the company by the subscribers to the company's memorandum.

22 Powers to issue different classes of share

(1) Subject to the articles, but without prejudice to the rights attached to any existing share, the company may issue shares with such rights or restrictions as may be determined by ordinary resolution.

(2) The company may issue shares which are to be redeemed, or are liable to be redeemed at the option of the company or the holder, and the directors may determine the terms, conditions and manner of redemption of any such shares.

23 Company not bound by less than absolute interests

Except as required by law, no person is to be recognised by the company as holding any share upon any trust, and except as otherwise required by law or the articles, the company is not in any way to be bound by or recognise any interest in a share other than the holder's absolute ownership of it and all the rights attaching to it.

24 Share certificates

(1) The company must issue each shareholder, free of charge, with one or more certificates in respect of the shares which that shareholder holds.

(2) Every certificate must specify—

(a) in respect of how many shares, of what class, it is issued;

(b) the nominal value of those shares;

(c) that the shares are fully paid; and

(d) any distinguishing numbers assigned to them.

(3) No certificate may be issued in respect of shares of more than one class.

(4) If more than one person holds a share, only one certificate may be issued in respect of it.

(5) Certificates must—

(a) have affixed to them the company's common seal, or

(b) be otherwise executed in accordance with the Companies Acts.

25 Replacement share certificates

(1) If a certificate issued in respect of a shareholder's shares is—

(a) damaged or defaced, or

(b) said to be lost, stolen or destroyed,

that shareholder is entitled to be issued with a replacement certificate in respect of the same shares.

(2) A shareholder exercising the right to be issued with such a replacement certificate—

(a) may at the same time exercise the right to be issued with a single certificate or separate certificates;

(b) must return the certificate which is to be replaced to the company if it is damaged or defaced; and

(c) must comply with such conditions as to evidence, indemnity and the payment of a reasonable fee as the directors decide.

26   Share transfers

(1)   Shares may be transferred by means of an instrument of transfer in any usual form or any other form approved by the directors, which is executed by or on behalf of the transferor.

(2)   No fee may be charged for registering any instrument of transfer or other document relating to or affecting the title to any share.

(3)   The company may retain any instrument of transfer which is registered.

(4)   The transferor remains the holder of a share until the transferee's name is entered in the register of members as holder of it.

(5)   The directors may refuse to register the transfer of a share, and if they do so, the instrument of transfer must be returned to the transferee with the notice of refusal unless they suspect that the proposed transfer may be fraudulent.

27   Transmission of shares

(1)   If title to a share passes to a transmittee, the company may only recognise the transmittee as having any title to that share.

(2)   A transmittee who produces such evidence of entitlement to shares as the directors may properly require—

  (a)   may, subject to the articles, choose either to become the holder of those shares or to have them transferred to another person, and

  (b)   subject to the articles, and pending any transfer of the shares to another person, has the same rights as the holder had.

(3)   But transmittees do not have the right to attend or vote at a general meeting, or agree to a proposed written resolution, in respect of shares to which they are entitled, by reason of the holder's death or bankruptcy or otherwise, unless they become the holders of those shares.

28   Exercise of transmittees' rights

(1)   Transmittees who wish to become the holders of shares to which they have become entitled must notify the company in writing of that wish.

(2)   If the transmittee wishes to have a share transferred to another person, the transmittee must execute an instrument of transfer in respect of it.

(3)   Any transfer made or executed under this article is to be treated as if it were made or executed by the person from whom the transmittee has derived rights in respect of the share, and as if the event which gave rise to the transmission had not occurred.

29   Transmittees bound by prior notices

If a notice is given to a shareholder in respect of shares and a transmittee is entitled to those shares, the transmittee is bound by the notice if it was given to the shareholder before the transmittee's name has been entered in the register of members.

Dividends and Other Distributions

30   Procedure for declaring dividends

(1)   The company may by ordinary resolution declare dividends, and the directors may decide to pay interim dividends.

(2)   A dividend must not be declared unless the directors have made a recommendation as to its amount. Such a dividend must not exceed the amount recommended by the directors.

(3)   No dividend may be declared or paid unless it is in accordance with shareholders' respective rights.

(4)   Unless the shareholders' resolution to declare or directors' decision to pay a dividend, or the terms on which shares are issued, specify otherwise, it must be paid by reference to each shareholder's holding of shares on the date of the resolution or decision to declare or pay it.

(5)   If the company's share capital is divided into different classes, no interim dividend may be paid on shares carrying deferred or non-preferred rights if, at the time of payment, any preferential dividend is in arrear.

(6)   The directors may pay at intervals any dividend payable at a fixed rate if it appears to them that the profits available for distribution justify the payment.

(7)   If the directors act in good faith, they do not incur any liability to the holders of shares conferring preferred rights for any loss they may suffer by the lawful payment of an interim dividend on shares with deferred or non-preferred rights.

31   Payment of dividends and other distributions

(1)   Where a dividend or other sum which is a distribution is payable in respect of a share, it must be paid by one or more of the following means—

  (a)   transfer to a bank or building society account specified by the distribution recipient either in writing or as the directors may otherwise decide;

   (b)   sending a cheque made payable to the distribution recipient by post to the distribution recipient at the distribution recipient's registered address (if the distribution recipient is a holder of the share), or (in any other case) to an address specified by the distribution recipient either in writing or as the directors may otherwise decide;

   (c)   sending a cheque made payable to such person by post to such person at such address as the distribution recipient has specified either in writing or as the directors may otherwise decide; or

   (d)   any other means of payment as the directors agree with the distribution recipient either in writing or by such other means as the directors decide.

(2)   In the articles, "the distribution recipient" means, in respect of a share in respect of which a dividend or other sum is payable—

   (a)   the holder of the share; or

   (b)   if the share has two or more joint holders, whichever of them is named first in the register of members; or

   (c)   if the holder is no longer entitled to the share by reason of death or bankruptcy, or otherwise by operation of law, the transmittee.

32 No interest on distributions

The company may not pay interest on any dividend or other sum payable in respect of a share unless otherwise provided by—

   (a)   the terms on which the share was issued, or

   (b)   the provisions of another agreement between the holder of that share and the company.

33 Unclaimed distributions

(1)   All dividends or other sums which are—

   (a)   payable in respect of shares, and

   (b)   unclaimed after having been declared or become payable,

may be invested or otherwise made use of by the directors for the benefit of the company until claimed.

(2)   The payment of any such dividend or other sum into a separate account does not make the company a trustee in respect of it.

(3)   If—

   (a)   twelve years have passed from the date on which a dividend or other sum became due for payment, and

   (b)   the distribution recipient has not claimed it,

the distribution recipient is no longer entitled to that dividend or other sum and it ceases to remain owing by the company.

34 Non-cash distributions

(1)   Subject to the terms of issue of the share in question, the company may, by ordinary resolution on the recommendation of the directors, decide to pay all or part of a dividend or other distribution payable in respect of a share by transferring non-cash assets of equivalent value (including, without limitation, shares or other securities in any company).

(2)   For the purposes of paying a non-cash distribution, the directors may make whatever arrangements they think fit, including, where any difficulty arises regarding the distribution—

   (a)   fixing the value of any assets;

   (b)   paying cash to any distribution recipient on the basis of that value in order to adjust the rights of recipients; and

   (c)   vesting any assets in trustees.

35 Waiver of distributions

Distribution recipients may waive their entitlement to a dividend or other distribution payable in respect of a share by giving the company notice in writing to that effect, but if—

   (a)   the share has more than one holder, or

   (b)   more than one person is entitled to the share, whether by reason of the death or bankruptcy of one or more joint holders, or otherwise,

the notice is not effective unless it is expressed to be given, and signed, by all the holders or persons otherwise entitled to the share.

Capitalisation of Profits

36 Authority to capitalise and appropriation of capitalised sums

(1)   Subject to the articles, the directors may, if they are so authorised by an ordinary resolution—

   (a)   decide to capitalise any profits of the company (whether or not they are available for distribution) which are not required for paying a preferential dividend, or any sum standing to the credit of the company's share premium account or capital redemption reserve; and

   (b)   appropriate any sum which they so decide to capitalise (a "capitalised sum") to the persons who would have been entitled to it if it were distributed by way of dividend (the "persons entitled") and in the same proportions.

(2)   Capitalised sums must be applied—

(a)   on behalf of the persons entitled, and

(b)   in the same proportions as a dividend would have been distributed to them.

(3)   Any capitalised sum may be applied in paying up new shares of a nominal amount equal to the capitalised sum which are then allotted credited as fully paid to the persons entitled or as they may direct.

(4)   A capitalised sum which was appropriated from profits available for distribution may be applied in paying up new debentures of the company which are then allotted credited as fully paid to the persons entitled or as they may direct.

(5)   Subject to the articles the directors may—

(a)   apply capitalised sums in accordance with paragraphs (3) and (4) partly in one way and partly in another;

(b)   make such arrangements as they think fit to deal with shares or debentures becoming distributable in fractions under this article (including the issuing of fractional certificates or the making of cash payments); and

(c)   authorise any person to enter into an agreement with the company on behalf of all the persons entitled which is binding on them in respect of the allotment of shares and debentures to them under this article.

PART 4
DECISION-MAKING BY SHAREHOLDERS

Organisation of General Meetings

37   Attendance and speaking at general meetings

(1)   A person is able to exercise the right to speak at a general meeting when that person is in a position to communicate to all those attending the meeting, during the meeting, any information or opinions which that person has on the business of the meeting.

(2)   A person is able to exercise the right to vote at a general meeting when—

(a)   that person is able to vote, during the meeting, on resolutions put to the vote at the meeting, and

(b)   that person's vote can be taken into account in determining whether or not such resolutions are passed at the same time as the votes of all the other persons attending the meeting.

(3)   The directors may make whatever arrangements they consider appropriate to enable those attending a general meeting to exercise their rights to speak or vote at it.

(4)   In determining attendance at a general meeting, it is immaterial whether any two or more members attending it are in the same place as each other.

(5)   Two or more persons who are not in the same place as each other attend a general meeting if their circumstances are such that if they have (or were to have) rights to speak and vote at that meeting, they are (or would be) able to exercise them.

38   Quorum for general meetings

No business other than the appointment of the chairman of the meeting is to be transacted at a general meeting if the persons attending it do not constitute a quorum.

39   Chairing general meetings

(1)   If the directors have appointed a chairman, the chairman shall chair general meetings if present and willing to do so.

(2)   If the directors have not appointed a chairman, or if the chairman is unwilling to chair the meeting or is not present within ten minutes of the time at which a meeting was due to start—

(a)   the directors present, or

(b)   (if no directors are present), the meeting,

must appoint a director or shareholder to chair the meeting, and the appointment of the chairman of the meeting must be the first business of the meeting.

(3)   The person chairing a meeting in accordance with this article is referred to as "the chairman of the meeting".

40   Attendance and speaking by directors and non-shareholders

(1)   Directors may attend and speak at general meetings, whether or not they are shareholders.

(2)   The chairman of the meeting may permit other persons who are not—

(a)   shareholders of the company, or

(b)   otherwise entitled to exercise the rights of shareholders in relation to general meetings,

to attend and speak at a general meeting.

41   Adjournment

(1)   If the persons attending a general meeting within half an hour of the time at which the meeting was due to start do not constitute a quorum, or if during a meeting a quorum ceases to be present, the chairman of the meeting must adjourn it.

(2) The chairman of the meeting may adjourn a general meeting at which a quorum is present if—

    (a) the meeting consents to an adjournment, or

    (b) it appears to the chairman of the meeting that an adjournment is necessary to protect the safety of any person attending the meeting or ensure that the business of the meeting is conducted in an orderly manner.

(3) The chairman of the meeting must adjourn a general meeting if directed to do so by the meeting.

(4) When adjourning a general meeting, the chairman of the meeting must—

    (a) either specify the time and place to which it is adjourned or state that it is to continue at a time and place to be fixed by the directors, and

    (b) have regard to any directions as to the time and place of any adjournment which have been given by the meeting.

(5) If the continuation of an adjourned meeting is to take place more than 14 days after it was adjourned, the company must give at least 7 clear days' notice of it (that is, excluding the day of the adjourned meeting and the day on which the notice is given)—

    (a) to the same persons to whom notice of the company's general meetings is required to be given, and

    (b) containing the same information which such notice is required to contain.

(6) No business may be transacted at an adjourned general meeting which could not properly have been transacted at the meeting if the adjournment had not taken place.

Voting at General Meetings

42 Voting: general

A resolution put to the vote of a general meeting must be decided on a show of hands unless a poll is duly demanded in accordance with the articles.

43 Errors and disputes

(1) No objection may be raised to the qualification of any person voting at a general meeting except at the meeting or adjourned meeting at which the vote objected to is tendered, and every vote not disallowed at the meeting is valid.

(2) Any such objection must be referred to the chairman of the meeting, whose decision is final.

44 Poll votes

(1) A poll on a resolution may be demanded—

    (a) in advance of the general meeting where it is to be put to the vote, or

    (b) at a general meeting, either before a show of hands on that resolution or immediately after the result of a show of hands on that resolution is declared.

(2) A poll may be demanded by—

    (a) the chairman of the meeting;

    (b) the directors;

    (c) two or more persons having the right to vote on the resolution; or

    (d) a person or persons representing not less than one tenth of the total voting rights of all the shareholders having the right to vote on the resolution.

(3) A demand for a poll may be withdrawn if—

    (a) the poll has not yet been taken, and

    (b) the chairman of the meeting consents to the withdrawal.

(4) Polls must be taken immediately and in such manner as the chairman of the meeting directs.

45 Content of proxy notices

(1) Proxies may only validly be appointed by a notice in writing (a "proxy notice") which—

    (a) states the name and address of the shareholder appointing the proxy;

    (b) identifies the person appointed to be that shareholder's proxy and the general meeting in relation to which that person is appointed;

    (c) is signed by or on behalf of the shareholder appointing the proxy, or is authenticated in such manner as the directors may determine; and

    (d) is delivered to the company in accordance with the articles and any instructions contained in the notice of the general meeting to which they relate.

(2) The company may require proxy notices to be delivered in a particular form, and may specify different forms for different purposes.

(3) Proxy notices may specify how the proxy appointed under them is to vote (or that the proxy is to abstain from voting) on one or more resolutions.

(4) Unless a proxy notice indicates otherwise, it must be treated as—

    (a) allowing the person appointed under it as a proxy discretion as to how to vote on any ancillary or procedural resolutions put to the meeting, and

    (b) appointing that person as a proxy in relation to any adjournment of the general meeting to which it relates as well as the meeting itself.

46   Delivery of proxy notices

(1)   A person who is entitled to attend, speak or vote (either on a show of hands or on a poll) at a general meeting remains so entitled in respect of that meeting or any adjournment of it, even though a valid proxy notice has been delivered to the company by or on behalf of that person.

(2)   An appointment under a proxy notice may be revoked by delivering to the company a notice in writing given by or on behalf of the person by whom or on whose behalf the proxy notice was given.

(3)   A notice revoking a proxy appointment only takes effect if it is delivered before the start of the meeting or adjourned meeting to which it relates.

(4)   If a proxy notice is not executed by the person appointing the proxy, it must be accompanied by written evidence of the authority of the person who executed it to execute it on the appointor's behalf.

47   Amendments to resolutions

(1)   An ordinary resolution to be proposed at a general meeting may be amended by ordinary resolution if—

  (a)   notice of the proposed amendment is given to the company in writing by a person entitled to vote at the general meeting at which it is to be proposed not less than 48 hours before the meeting is to take place (or such later time as the chairman of the meeting may determine), and

  (b)   the proposed amendment does not, in the reasonable opinion of the chairman of the meeting, materially alter the scope of the resolution.

(2)   A special resolution to be proposed at a general meeting may be amended by ordinary resolution, if—

  (a)   the chairman of the meeting proposes the amendment at the general meeting at which the resolution is to be proposed, and

  (b)   the amendment does not go beyond what is necessary to correct a grammatical or other non-substantive error in the resolution.

(3)   If the chairman of the meeting, acting in good faith, wrongly decides that an amendment to a resolution is out of order, the chairman's error does not invalidate the vote on that resolution.

PART 5
ADMINISTRATIVE ARRANGEMENTS

48   Means of communication to be used

(1)   Subject to the articles, anything sent or supplied by or to the company under the articles may be sent or supplied in any way in which the Companies Act 2006 provides for documents or information which are authorised or required by any provision of that Act to be sent or supplied by or to the company.

(2)   Subject to the articles, any notice or document to be sent or supplied to a director in connection with the taking of decisions by directors may also be sent or supplied by the means by which that director has asked to be sent or supplied with such notices or documents for the time being.

(3)   A director may agree with the company that notices or documents sent to that director in a particular way are to be deemed to have been received within a specified time of their being sent, and for the specified time to be less than 48 hours.

49   Company seals

(1)   Any common seal may only be used by the authority of the directors.

(2)   The directors may decide by what means and in what form any common seal is to be used.

(3)   Unless otherwise decided by the directors, if the company has a common seal and it is affixed to a document, the document must also be signed by at least one authorised person in the presence of a witness who attests the signature.

(4)   For the purposes of this article, an authorised person is—

  (a)   any director of the company;
  (b)   the company secretary (if any); or
  (c)   any person authorised by the directors for the purpose of signing documents to which the common seal is applied.

50   No right to inspect accounts and other records

Except as provided by law or authorised by the directors or an ordinary resolution of the company, no person is entitled to inspect any of the company's accounting or other records or documents merely by virtue of being a shareholder.

Appendices

51   Provision for employees on cessation of business

The directors may decide to make provision for the benefit of persons employed or formerly employed by the company or any of its subsidiaries (other than a director or former director or shadow director) in connection with the cessation or transfer to any person of the whole or part of the undertaking of the company or that subsidiary.

Directors' Indemnity and Insurance

52   Indemnity

(1)   Subject to paragraph (2), a relevant director of the company or an associated company may be indemnified out of the company's assets against—

   (a)   any liability incurred by that director in connection with any negligence, default, breach of duty or breach of trust in relation to the company or an associated company,

   (b)   any liability incurred by that director in connection with the activities of the company or an associated company in its capacity as a trustee of an occupational pension scheme (as defined in section 235(6) of the Companies Act 2006),

   (c)   any other liability incurred by that director as an officer of the company or an associated company.

(2)   This article does not authorise any indemnity which would be prohibited or rendered void by any provision of the Companies Acts or by any other provision of law.

(3)   In this article—

   (a)   companies are associated if one is a subsidiary of the other or both are subsidiaries of the same body corporate, and

   (b)   a "relevant director" means any director or former director of the company or an associated company.

53   Insurance

(1)   The directors may decide to purchase and maintain insurance, at the expense of the company, for the benefit of any relevant director in respect of any relevant loss.

(2)   In this article—

   (a)   a "relevant director" means any director or former director of the company or an associated company,

   (b)   a "relevant loss" means any loss or liability which has been or may be incurred by a relevant director in connection with that director's duties or powers in relation to the company, any associated company or any pension fund or employees' share scheme of the company or associated company, and

   (c)   companies are associated if one is a subsidiary of the other or both are subsidiaries of the same body corporate.

MODEL ARTICLES FOR PRIVATE COMPANIES LIMITED BY GUARANTEE
[A1.2]

NOTES

These are set out in Schedule 2 to the Companies (Model Articles) Regulations 2008.

INDEX TO THE ARTICLES

Appendices

PART 1
PART 1
INTERPRETATION AND LIMITATION OF LIABILITY

1 Defined terms

In the articles, unless the context requires otherwise—

"articles" means the company's articles of association;

"bankruptcy" includes individual insolvency proceedings in a jurisdiction other than England and Wales or Northern Ireland which have an effect similar to that of bankruptcy;

"chairman" has the meaning given in article 12;

"chairman of the meeting" has the meaning given in article 25;

"Companies Acts" means the Companies Acts (as defined in section 2 of the Companies Act 2006), in so far as they apply to the company;

"director" means a director of the company, and includes any person occupying the position of director, by whatever name called;

"document" includes, unless otherwise specified, any document sent or supplied in electronic form;

"electronic form" has the meaning given in section 1168 of the Companies Act 2006;

"member" has the meaning given in section 112 of the Companies Act 2006;

"ordinary resolution" has the meaning given in section 282 of the Companies Act 2006;

"participate", in relation to a directors' meeting, has the meaning given in article 10;

"proxy notice" has the meaning given in article 31;

"special resolution" has the meaning given in section 283 of the Companies Act 2006;

"subsidiary" has the meaning given in section 1159 of the Companies Act 2006; and

"writing" means the representation or reproduction of words, symbols or other information in a visible form by any method or combination of methods, whether sent or supplied in electronic form or otherwise.

Unless the context otherwise requires, other words or expressions contained in these articles bear the same meaning as in the Companies Act 2006 as in force on the date when these articles become binding on the company.

2 Liability of members

The liability of each member is limited to £1, being the amount that each member undertakes to contribute to the assets of the company in the event of its being wound up while he is a member or within one year after he ceases to be a member, for—

(a) payment of the company's debts and liabilities contracted before he ceases to be a member,

(b) payment of the costs, charges and expenses of winding up, and

(c) adjustment of the rights of the contributories among themselves.

PART 2
DIRECTORS

Directors' Powers and Responsibilities

3 Directors' general authority

Subject to the articles, the directors are responsible for the management of the company's business, for which purpose they may exercise all the powers of the company.

4 Members' reserve power

(1) The members may, by special resolution, direct the directors to take, or refrain from taking, specified action.

(2) No such special resolution invalidates anything which the directors have done before the passing of the resolution.

5 Directors may delegate

(1) Subject to the articles, the directors may delegate any of the powers which are conferred on them under the articles—

(a) to such person or committee;

(b) by such means (including by power of attorney);

(c) to such an extent;

(d) in relation to such matters or territories; and

(e) on such terms and conditions;

as they think fit.

(2) If the directors so specify, any such delegation may authorise further delegation of the directors' powers by any person to whom they are delegated.

(3) The directors may revoke any delegation in whole or part, or alter its terms and conditions.

6   Committees

(1)   Committees to which the directors delegate any of their powers must follow procedures which are based as far as they are applicable on those provisions of the articles which govern the taking of decisions by directors.

(2)   The directors may make rules of procedure for all or any committees, which prevail over rules derived from the articles if they are not consistent with them.

Decision-Making by Directors

7   Directors to take decisions collectively

(1)   The general rule about decision-making by directors is that any decision of the directors must be either a majority decision at a meeting or a decision taken in accordance with article 8.

(2)   If—
  (a)   the company only has one director, and
  (b)   no provision of the articles requires it to have more than one director,
the general rule does not apply, and the director may take decisions without regard to any of the provisions of the articles relating to directors' decision-making.

8   Unanimous decisions

(1)   A decision of the directors is taken in accordance with this article when all eligible directors indicate to each other by any means that they share a common view on a matter.

(2)   Such a decision may take the form of a resolution in writing, copies of which have been signed by each eligible director or to which each eligible director has otherwise indicated agreement in writing.

(3)   References in this article to eligible directors are to directors who would have been entitled to vote on the matter had it been proposed as a resolution at a directors' meeting.

(4)   A decision may not be taken in accordance with this article if the eligible directors would not have formed a quorum at such a meeting.

9   Calling a directors' meeting

(1)   Any director may call a directors' meeting by giving notice of the meeting to the directors or by authorising the company secretary (if any) to give such notice.

(2)   Notice of any directors' meeting must indicate—
  (a)   its proposed date and time;
  (b)   where it is to take place; and
  (c)   if it is anticipated that directors participating in the meeting will not be in the same place, how it is proposed that they should communicate with each other during the meeting.

(3)   Notice of a directors' meeting must be given to each director, but need not be in writing.

(4)   Notice of a directors' meeting need not be given to directors who waive their entitlement to notice of that meeting, by giving notice to that effect to the company not more than 7 days after the date on which the meeting is held. Where such notice is given after the meeting has been held, that does not affect the validity of the meeting, or of any business conducted at it.

10   Participation in directors' meetings

(1)   Subject to the articles, directors participate in a directors' meeting, or part of a directors' meeting, when—
  (a)   the meeting has been called and takes place in accordance with the articles, and
  (b)   they can each communicate to the others any information or opinions they have on any particular item of the business of the meeting.

(2)   In determining whether directors are participating in a directors' meeting, it is irrelevant where any director is or how they communicate with each other.

(3)   If all the directors participating in a meeting are not in the same place, they may decide that the meeting is to be treated as taking place wherever any of them is.

11   Quorum for directors' meetings

(1)   At a directors' meeting, unless a quorum is participating, no proposal is to be voted on, except a proposal to call another meeting.

(2)   The quorum for directors' meetings may be fixed from time to time by a decision of the directors, but it must never be less than two, and unless otherwise fixed it is two.

(3)   If the total number of directors for the time being is less than the quorum required, the directors must not take any decision other than a decision—
  (a)   to appoint further directors, or
  (b)   to call a general meeting so as to enable the members to appoint further directors.

12   Chairing of directors' meetings

(1)   The directors may appoint a director to chair their meetings.

(2)   The person so appointed for the time being is known as the chairman.

(3)   The directors may terminate the chairman's appointment at any time.

(4)   If the chairman is not participating in a directors' meeting within ten minutes of the time at which it was to start, the participating directors must appoint one of themselves to chair it.

13   Casting vote

(1)   If the numbers of votes for and against a proposal are equal, the chairman or other director chairing the meeting has a casting vote.

(2)   But this does not apply if, in accordance with the articles, the chairman or other director is not to be counted as participating in the decision-making process for quorum or voting purposes.

14   Conflicts of interest

(1)   If a proposed decision of the directors is concerned with an actual or proposed transaction or arrangement with the company in which a director is interested, that director is not to be counted as participating in the decision-making process for quorum or voting purposes.

(2)   But if paragraph (3) applies, a director who is interested in an actual or proposed transaction or arrangement with the company is to be counted as participating in the decision-making process for quorum and voting purposes.

(3)   This paragraph applies when—
  (a)   the company by ordinary resolution disapplies the provision of the articles which would otherwise prevent a director from being counted as participating in the decision-making process;
  (b)   the director's interest cannot reasonably be regarded as likely to give rise to a conflict of interest; or
  (c)   the director's conflict of interest arises from a permitted cause.

(4)   For the purposes of this article, the following are permitted causes—
  (a)   a guarantee given, or to be given, by or to a director in respect of an obligation incurred by or on behalf of the company or any of its subsidiaries;
  (b)   subscription, or an agreement to subscribe, for securities of the company or any of its subsidiaries, or to underwrite, sub-underwrite, or guarantee subscription for any such securities; and
  (c)   arrangements pursuant to which benefits are made available to employees and directors or former employees and directors of the company or any of its subsidiaries which do not provide special benefits for directors or former directors.

(5)   For the purposes of this article, references to proposed decisions and decision-making processes include any directors' meeting or part of a directors' meeting.

(6)   Subject to paragraph (7), if a question arises at a meeting of directors or of a committee of directors as to the right of a director to participate in the meeting (or part of the meeting) for voting or quorum purposes, the question may, before the conclusion of the meeting, be referred to the chairman whose ruling in relation to any director other than the chairman is to be final and conclusive.

(7)   If any question as to the right to participate in the meeting (or part of the meeting) should arise in respect of the chairman, the question is to be decided by a decision of the directors at that meeting, for which purpose the chairman is not to be counted as participating in the meeting (or that part of the meeting) for voting or quorum purposes.

15   Records of decisions to be kept

The directors must ensure that the company keeps a record, in writing, for at least 10 years from the date of the decision recorded, of every unanimous or majority decision taken by the directors.

16   Directors' discretion to make further rules

Subject to the articles, the directors may make any rule which they think fit about how they take decisions, and about how such rules are to be recorded or communicated to directors.

Appointment of Directors

17   Methods of appointing directors

(1)   Any person who is willing to act as a director, and is permitted by law to do so, may be appointed to be a director—
  (a)   by ordinary resolution, or
  (b)   by a decision of the directors.

(2)   In any case where, as a result of death, the company has no members and no directors, the personal representatives of the last member to have died have the right, by notice in writing, to appoint a person to be a director.

(3)   For the purposes of paragraph (2), where 2 or more members die in circumstances rendering it uncertain who was the last to die, a younger member is deemed to have survived an older member.

18 Termination of director's appointment

A person ceases to be a director as soon as—

(a) that person ceases to be a director by virtue of any provision of the Companies Act 2006 or is prohibited from being a director by law;

(b) a bankruptcy order is made against that person;

(c) a composition is made with that person's creditors generally in satisfaction of that person's debts;

(d) a registered medical practitioner who is treating that person gives a written opinion to the company stating that that person has become physically or mentally incapable of acting as a director and may remain so for more than three months;

(e) by reason of that person's mental health, a court makes an order which wholly or partly prevents that person from personally exercising any powers or rights which that person would otherwise have;

(f) notification is received by the company from the director that the director is resigning from office, and such resignation has taken effect in accordance with its terms.

19 Directors' remuneration

(1) Directors may undertake any services for the company that the directors decide.

(2) Directors are entitled to such remuneration as the directors determine—

(a) for their services to the company as directors, and

(b) for any other service which they undertake for the company.

(3) Subject to the articles, a director's remuneration may—

(a) take any form, and

(b) include any arrangements in connection with the payment of a pension, allowance or gratuity, or any death, sickness or disability benefits, to or in respect of that director.

(4) Unless the directors decide otherwise, directors' remuneration accrues from day to day.

(5) Unless the directors decide otherwise, directors are not accountable to the company for any remuneration which they receive as directors or other officers or employees of the company's subsidiaries or of any other body corporate in which the company is interested.

20 Directors' expenses

The company may pay any reasonable expenses which the directors properly incur in connection with their attendance at—

(a) meetings of directors or committees of directors,

(b) general meetings, or

(c) separate meetings of the holders of debentures of the company,

or otherwise in connection with the exercise of their powers and the discharge of their responsibilities in relation to the company.

PART 3
MEMBERS

Becoming and Ceasing to be a Member

21 Applications for membership

No person shall become a member of the company unless—

(a) that person has completed an application for membership in a form approved by the directors, and

(b) the directors have approved the application.

22 Termination of membership

(1) A member may withdraw from membership of the company by giving 7 days' notice to the company in writing.

(2) Membership is not transferable.

(3) A person's membership terminates when that person dies or ceases to exist.

Organisation of General Meetings

23 Attendance and speaking at general meetings

(1) A person is able to exercise the right to speak at a general meeting when that person is in a position to communicate to all those attending the meeting, during the meeting, any information or opinions which that person has on the business of the meeting.

(2) A person is able to exercise the right to vote at a general meeting when—

(a) that person is able to vote, during the meeting, on resolutions put to the vote at the meeting, and

(b) that person's vote can be taken into account in determining whether or not such resolutions are passed at the same time as the votes of all the other persons attending the meeting.

(3)   The directors may make whatever arrangements they consider appropriate to enable those attending a general meeting to exercise their rights to speak or vote at it.

(4)   In determining attendance at a general meeting, it is immaterial whether any two or more members attending it are in the same place as each other.

(5)   Two or more persons who are not in the same place as each other attend a general meeting if their circumstances are such that if they have (or were to have) rights to speak and vote at that meeting, they are (or would be) able to exercise them.

24   Quorum for general meetings

No business other than the appointment of the chairman of the meeting is to be transacted at a general meeting if the persons attending it do not constitute a quorum.

25   Chairing general meetings

(1)   If the directors have appointed a chairman, the chairman shall chair general meetings if present and willing to do so.

(2)   If the directors have not appointed a chairman, or if the chairman is unwilling to chair the meeting or is not present within ten minutes of the time at which a meeting was due to start—

(a)   the directors present, or

(b)   (if no directors are present), the meeting,

must appoint a director or member to chair the meeting, and the appointment of the chairman of the meeting must be the first business of the meeting.

(3)   The person chairing a meeting in accordance with this article is referred to as "the chairman of the meeting".

26   Attendance and speaking by directors and non-members

(1)   Directors may attend and speak at general meetings, whether or not they are members.

(2)   The chairman of the meeting may permit other persons who are not members of the company to attend and speak at a general meeting.

27   Adjournment

(1)   If the persons attending a general meeting within half an hour of the time at which the meeting was due to start do not constitute a quorum, or if during a meeting a quorum ceases to be present, the chairman of the meeting must adjourn it.

(2)   The chairman of the meeting may adjourn a general meeting at which a quorum is present if—

(a)   the meeting consents to an adjournment, or

(b)   it appears to the chairman of the meeting that an adjournment is necessary to protect the safety of any person attending the meeting or ensure that the business of the meeting is conducted in an orderly manner.

(3)   The chairman of the meeting must adjourn a general meeting if directed to do so by the meeting.

(4)   When adjourning a general meeting, the chairman of the meeting must—

(a)   either specify the time and place to which it is adjourned or state that it is to continue at a time and place to be fixed by the directors, and

(b)   have regard to any directions as to the time and place of any adjournment which have been given by the meeting.

(5)   If the continuation of an adjourned meeting is to take place more than 14 days after it was adjourned, the company must give at least 7 clear days' notice of it (that is, excluding the day of the adjourned meeting and the day on which the notice is given)—

(a)   to the same persons to whom notice of the company's general meetings is required to be given, and

(b)   containing the same information which such notice is required to contain.

(6)   No business may be transacted at an adjourned general meeting which could not properly have been transacted at the meeting if the adjournment had not taken place.

Voting at General Meetings

28   Voting: general

A resolution put to the vote of a general meeting must be decided on a show of hands unless a poll is duly demanded in accordance with the articles.

29   Errors and disputes

(1)   No objection may be raised to the qualification of any person voting at a general meeting except at the meeting or adjourned meeting at which the vote objected to is tendered, and every vote not disallowed at the meeting is valid.

(2)   Any such objection must be referred to the chairman of the meeting whose decision is final.

30   Poll votes

(1)   A poll on a resolution may be demanded—

(a) in advance of the general meeting where it is to be put to the vote, or

(b) at a general meeting, either before a show of hands on that resolution or immediately after the result of a show of hands on that resolution is declared.

(2) A poll may be demanded by—

(a) the chairman of the meeting;

(b) the directors;

(c) two or more persons having the right to vote on the resolution; or

(d) a person or persons representing not less than one tenth of the total voting rights of all the members having the right to vote on the resolution.

(3) A demand for a poll may be withdrawn if—

(a) the poll has not yet been taken, and

(b) the chairman of the meeting consents to the withdrawal.

(4) Polls must be taken immediately and in such manner as the chairman of the meeting directs.

31 Content of proxy notices

(1) Proxies may only validly be appointed by a notice in writing (a "proxy notice") which—

(a) states the name and address of the member appointing the proxy;

(b) identifies the person appointed to be that member's proxy and the general meeting in relation to which that person is appointed;

(c) is signed by or on behalf of the member appointing the proxy, or is authenticated in such manner as the directors may determine; and

(d) is delivered to the company in accordance with the articles and any instructions contained in the notice of the general meeting to which they relate.

(2) The company may require proxy notices to be delivered in a particular form, and may specify different forms for different purposes.

(3) Proxy notices may specify how the proxy appointed under them is to vote (or that the proxy is to abstain from voting) on one or more resolutions.

(4) Unless a proxy notice indicates otherwise, it must be treated as—

(a) allowing the person appointed under it as a proxy discretion as to how to vote on any ancillary or procedural resolutions put to the meeting, and

(b) appointing that person as a proxy in relation to any adjournment of the general meeting to which it relates as well as the meeting itself.

32 Delivery of proxy notices

(1) A person who is entitled to attend, speak or vote (either on a show of hands or on a poll) at a general meeting remains so entitled in respect of that meeting or any adjournment of it, even though a valid proxy notice has been delivered to the company by or on behalf of that person.

(2) An appointment under a proxy notice may be revoked by delivering to the company a notice in writing given by or on behalf of the person by whom or on whose behalf the proxy notice was given.

(3) A notice revoking a proxy appointment only takes effect if it is delivered before the start of the meeting or adjourned meeting to which it relates.

(4) If a proxy notice is not executed by the person appointing the proxy, it must be accompanied by written evidence of the authority of the person who executed it to execute it on the appointor's behalf.

33 Amendments to resolutions

(1) An ordinary resolution to be proposed at a general meeting may be amended by ordinary resolution if—

(a) notice of the proposed amendment is given to the company in writing by a person entitled to vote at the general meeting at which it is to be proposed not less than 48 hours before the meeting is to take place (or such later time as the chairman of the meeting may determine), and

(b) the proposed amendment does not, in the reasonable opinion of the chairman of the meeting, materially alter the scope of the resolution.

(2) A special resolution to be proposed at a general meeting may be amended by ordinary resolution, if—

(a) the chairman of the meeting proposes the amendment at the general meeting at which the resolution is to be proposed, and

(b) the amendment does not go beyond what is necessary to correct a grammatical or other non-substantive error in the resolution.

(3) If the chairman of the meeting, acting in good faith, wrongly decides that an amendment to a resolution is out of order, the chairman's error does not invalidate the vote on that resolution.

PART 4
ADMINISTRATIVE ARRANGEMENTS

34   Means of communication to be used

(1)   Subject to the articles, anything sent or supplied by or to the company under the articles may be sent or supplied in any way in which the Companies Act 2006 provides for documents or information which are authorised or required by any provision of that Act to be sent or supplied by or to the company.

(2)   Subject to the articles, any notice or document to be sent or supplied to a director in connection with the taking of decisions by directors may also be sent or supplied by the means by which that director has asked to be sent or supplied with such notices or documents for the time being.

(3)   A director may agree with the company that notices or documents sent to that director in a particular way are to be deemed to have been received within a specified time of their being sent, and for the specified time to be less than 48 hours.

35   Company seals

(1)   Any common seal may only be used by the authority of the directors.

(2)   The directors may decide by what means and in what form any common seal is to be used.

(3)   Unless otherwise decided by the directors, if the company has a common seal and it is affixed to a document, the document must also be signed by at least one authorised person in the presence of a witness who attests the signature.

(4)   For the purposes of this article, an authorised person is—
   (a)   any director of the company;
   (b)   the company secretary (if any); or
   (c)   any person authorised by the directors for the purpose of signing documents to which the common seal is applied.

36   No right to inspect accounts and other records

Except as provided by law or authorised by the directors or an ordinary resolution of the company, no person is entitled to inspect any of the company's accounting or other records or documents merely by virtue of being a member.

37   Provision for employees on cessation of business

The directors may decide to make provision for the benefit of persons employed or formerly employed by the company or any of its subsidiaries (other than a director or former director or shadow director) in connection with the cessation or transfer to any person of the whole or part of the undertaking of the company or that subsidiary.

Directors' Indemnity and Insurance

38   Indemnity

(1)   Subject to paragraph (2), a relevant director of the company or an associated company may be indemnified out of the company's assets against—
   (a)   any liability incurred by that director in connection with any negligence, default, breach of duty or breach of trust in relation to the company or an associated company,
   (b)   any liability incurred by that director in connection with the activities of the company or an associated company in its capacity as a trustee of an occupational pension scheme (as defined in section 235(6) of the Companies Act 2006),
   (c)   any other liability incurred by that director as an officer of the company or an associated company.

(2)   This article does not authorise any indemnity which would be prohibited or rendered void by any provision of the Companies Acts or by any other provision of law.

(3)   In this article—
   (a)   companies are associated if one is a subsidiary of the other or both are subsidiaries of the same body corporate, and
   (b)   a "relevant director" means any director or former director of the company or an associated company.

39   Insurance

(1)   The directors may decide to purchase and maintain insurance, at the expense of the company, for the benefit of any relevant director in respect of any relevant loss.

(2)   In this article—
   (a)   a "relevant director" means any director or former director of the company or an associated company,

(b) a "relevant loss" means any loss or liability which has been or may be incurred by a relevant director in connection with that director's duties or powers in relation to the company, any associated company or any pension fund or employees' share scheme of the company or associated company, and

(c) companies are associated if one is a subsidiary of the other or both are subsidiaries of the same body corporate.

MODEL ARTICLES FOR PUBLIC COMPANIES

[A1.3]

NOTES

These are set out in Schedule 3 to the Companies (Model Articles) Regulations 2008.

INDEX TO THE ARTICLES

PART 1
INTERPRETATION AND LIMITATION OF LIABILITY

PART 2
DIRECTORS

Directors' Powers and Responsibilities

Decision-Making by Directors

Appointment of Directors

Alternate Directors

PART 3
DECISION-MAKING BY MEMBERS

Organisation of General Meetings

Voting at General Meetings

Restrictions on Member Rights

Directors' Indemnity and Insurance

85 Indemnity
86 Insurance

PART 1
INTERPRETATION AND LIMITATION OF LIABILITY

1 Defined terms

In the articles, unless the context requires otherwise—

"alternate" or "alternate director" has the meaning given in article 25;

"appointor" has the meaning given in article 25;

"articles" means the company's articles of association;

"bankruptcy" includes individual insolvency proceedings in a jurisdiction other than England and Wales or Northern Ireland which have an effect similar to that of bankruptcy;

"call" has the meaning given in article 54;

"call notice" has the meaning given in article 54;

"certificate" means a paper certificate (other than a share warrant) evidencing a person's title to specified shares or other securities;

"certificated" in relation to a share, means that it is not an uncertificated share or a share in respect of which a share warrant has been issued and is current;

"chairman" has the meaning given in article 12;

"chairman of the meeting" has the meaning given in article 31;

"Companies Acts" means the Companies Acts (as defined in section 2 of the Companies Act 2006), in so far as they apply to the company;

"company's lien" has the meaning given in article 52;

"director" means a director of the company, and includes any person occupying the position of director, by whatever name called;

"distribution recipient" has the meaning given in article 72;

"document" includes, unless otherwise specified, any document sent or supplied in electronic form;

"electronic form" has the meaning given in section 1168 of the Companies Act 2006;

"fully paid" in relation to a share, means that the nominal value and any premium to be paid to the company in respect of that share have been paid to the company;

"hard copy form" has the meaning given in section 1168 of the Companies Act 2006;

"holder" in relation to shares means the person whose name is entered in the register of members as the holder of the shares, or, in the case of a share in respect of which a share warrant has been issued (and not cancelled), the person in possession of that warrant;

"instrument" means a document in hard copy form;

"lien enforcement notice" has the meaning given in article 53;

"member" has the meaning given in section 112 of the Companies Act 2006;

"ordinary resolution" has the meaning given in section 282 of the Companies Act 2006;

"paid" means paid or credited as paid;

"participate", in relation to a directors' meeting, has the meaning given in article 9;

"partly paid" in relation to a share means that part of that share's nominal value or any premium at which it was issued has not been paid to the company;

"proxy notice" has the meaning given in article 38;

"securities seal" has the meaning given in article 47;

"shares" means shares in the company;

"special resolution" has the meaning given in section 283 of the Companies Act 2006;

"subsidiary" has the meaning given in section 1159 of the Companies Act 2006;

"transmittee" means a person entitled to a share by reason of the death or bankruptcy of a shareholder or otherwise by operation of law;

"uncertificated" in relation to a share means that, by virtue of legislation (other than section 778 of the Companies Act 2006) permitting title to shares to be evidenced and transferred without a certificate, title to that share is evidenced and may be transferred without a certificate; and

"writing" means the representation or reproduction of words, symbols or other information in a visible form by any method or combination of methods, whether sent or supplied in electronic form or otherwise.

Unless the context otherwise requires, other words or expressions contained in these articles bear the same meaning as in the Companies Act 2006 as in force on the date when these articles become binding on the company.

2 Liability of members

The liability of the members is limited to the amount, if any, unpaid on the shares held by them.

PART 2
DIRECTORS

Directors' Powers and Responsibilities

3 Directors' general authority

Subject to the articles, the directors are responsible for the management of the company's business, for which purpose they may exercise all the powers of the company.

4 Members' reserve power

(1) The members may, by special resolution, direct the directors to take, or refrain from taking, specified action.

(2) No such special resolution invalidates anything which the directors have done before the passing of the resolution.

5 Directors may delegate

(1) Subject to the articles, the directors may delegate any of the powers which are conferred on them under the articles—
  (a) to such person or committee;
  (b) by such means (including by power of attorney);
  (c) to such an extent;
  (d) in relation to such matters or territories; and
  (e) on such terms and conditions;
as they think fit.

(2) If the directors so specify, any such delegation may authorise further delegation of the directors' powers by any person to whom they are delegated.

(3) The directors may revoke any delegation in whole or part, or alter its terms and conditions.

6 Committees

(1) Committees to which the directors delegate any of their powers must follow procedures which are based as far as they are applicable on those provisions of the articles which govern the taking of decisions by directors.

(2) The directors may make rules of procedure for all or any committees, which prevail over rules derived from the articles if they are not consistent with them.

Decision-Making by Directors

7 Directors to take decisions collectively

Decisions of the directors may be taken—
  (a) at a directors' meeting, or
  (b) in the form of a directors' written resolution.

8 Calling a directors' meeting

(1) Any director may call a directors' meeting.

(2) The company secretary must call a directors' meeting if a director so requests.

(3) A directors' meeting is called by giving notice of the meeting to the directors.

(4) Notice of any directors' meeting must indicate—
  (a) its proposed date and time;
  (b) where it is to take place; and
  (c) if it is anticipated that directors participating in the meeting will not be in the same place, how it is proposed that they should communicate with each other during the meeting.

(5) Notice of a directors' meeting must be given to each director, but need not be in writing.

(6) Notice of a directors' meeting need not be given to directors who waive their entitlement to notice of that meeting, by giving notice to that effect to the company not more than 7 days after the date on which the meeting is held. Where such notice is given after the meeting has been held, that does not affect the validity of the meeting, or of any business conducted at it.

9 Participation in directors' meetings

(1) Subject to the articles, directors participate in a directors' meeting, or part of a directors' meeting, when—
  (a) the meeting has been called and takes place in accordance with the articles, and
  (b) they can each communicate to the others any information or opinions they have on any particular item of the business of the meeting.

(2) In determining whether directors are participating in a directors' meeting, it is irrelevant where any director is or how they communicate with each other.

(3) If all the directors participating in a meeting are not in the same place, they may decide that the meeting is to be treated as taking place wherever any of them is.

10 Quorum for directors' meetings

(1)   At a directors' meeting, unless a quorum is participating, no proposal is to be voted on, except a proposal to call another meeting.

(2)   The quorum for directors' meetings may be fixed from time to time by a decision of the directors, but it must never be less than two, and unless otherwise fixed it is two.

11 Meetings where total number of directors less than quorum

(1)   This article applies where the total number of directors for the time being is less than the quorum for directors' meetings.

(2)   If there is only one director, that director may appoint sufficient directors to make up a quorum or call a general meeting to do so.

(3)   If there is more than one director—

(a)   a directors' meeting may take place, if it is called in accordance with the articles and at least two directors participate in it, with a view to appointing sufficient directors to make up a quorum or calling a general meeting to do so, and

(b)   if a directors' meeting is called but only one director attends at the appointed date and time to participate in it, that director may appoint sufficient directors to make up a quorum or call a general meeting to do so.

12 Chairing directors' meetings

(1)   The directors may appoint a director to chair their meetings.

(2)   The person so appointed for the time being is known as the chairman.

(3)   The directors may appoint other directors as deputy or assistant chairmen to chair directors' meetings in the chairman's absence.

(4)   The directors may terminate the appointment of the chairman, deputy or assistant chairman at any time.

(5)   If neither the chairman nor any director appointed generally to chair directors' meetings in the chairman's absence is participating in a meeting within ten minutes of the time at which it was to start, the participating directors must appoint one of themselves to chair it.

13 Voting at directors' meetings: general rules

(1)   Subject to the articles, a decision is taken at a directors' meeting by a majority of the votes of the participating directors.

(2)   Subject to the articles, each director participating in a directors' meeting has one vote.

(3)   Subject to the articles, if a director has an interest in an actual or proposed transaction or arrangement with the company—

(a)   that director and that director's alternate may not vote on any proposal relating to it, but

(b)   this does not preclude the alternate from voting in relation to that transaction or arrangement on behalf of another appointor who does not have such an interest.

14 Chairman's casting vote at directors' meetings

(1)   If the numbers of votes for and against a proposal are equal, the chairman or other director chairing the meeting has a casting vote.

(2)   But this does not apply if, in accordance with the articles, the chairman or other director is not to be counted as participating in the decision-making process for quorum or voting purposes.

15 Alternates voting at directors' meetings

A director who is also an alternate director has an additional vote on behalf of each appointor who is—

(a)   not participating in a directors' meeting, and

(b)   would have been entitled to vote if they were participating in it.

16 Conflicts of interest

(1)   If a directors' meeting, or part of a directors' meeting, is concerned with an actual or proposed transaction or arrangement with the company in which a director is interested, that director is not to be counted as participating in that meeting, or part of a meeting, for quorum or voting purposes.

(2)   But if paragraph (3) applies, a director who is interested in an actual or proposed transaction or arrangement with the company is to be counted as participating in a decision at a directors' meeting, or part of a directors' meeting, relating to it for quorum and voting purposes.

(3)   This paragraph applies when—

(a)   the company by ordinary resolution disapplies the provision of the articles which would otherwise prevent a director from being counted as participating in, or voting at, a directors' meeting;

(b)   the director's interest cannot reasonably be regarded as likely to give rise to a conflict of interest; or

(c)   the director's conflict of interest arises from a permitted cause.

(4)   For the purposes of this article, the following are permitted causes—
  (a)   a guarantee given, or to be given, by or to a director in respect of an obligation incurred by or on behalf of the company or any of its subsidiaries;
  (b)   subscription, or an agreement to subscribe, for shares or other securities of the company or any of its subsidiaries, or to underwrite, sub-underwrite, or guarantee subscription for any such shares or securities; and
  (c)   arrangements pursuant to which benefits are made available to employees and directors or former employees and directors of the company or any of its subsidiaries which do not provide special benefits for directors or former directors.

(5)   Subject to paragraph (6), if a question arises at a meeting of directors or of a committee of directors as to the right of a director to participate in the meeting (or part of the meeting) for voting or quorum purposes, the question may, before the conclusion of the meeting, be referred to the chairman whose ruling in relation to any director other than the chairman is to be final and conclusive.

(6)   If any question as to the right to participate in the meeting (or part of the meeting) should arise in respect of the chairman, the question is to be decided by a decision of the directors at that meeting, for which purpose the chairman is not to be counted as participating in the meeting (or that part of the meeting) for voting or quorum purposes.

17   Proposing directors' written resolutions

(1)   Any director may propose a directors' written resolution.

(2)   The company secretary must propose a directors' written resolution if a director so requests.

(3)   A directors' written resolution is proposed by giving notice of the proposed resolution to the directors.

(4)   Notice of a proposed directors' written resolution must indicate—
  (a)   the proposed resolution, and
  (b)   the time by which it is proposed that the directors should adopt it.

(5)   Notice of a proposed directors' written resolution must be given in writing to each director.

(6)   Any decision which a person giving notice of a proposed directors' written resolution takes regarding the process of adopting that resolution must be taken reasonably in good faith.

18   Adoption of directors' written resolutions

(1)   A proposed directors' written resolution is adopted when all the directors who would have been entitled to vote on the resolution at a directors' meeting have signed one or more copies of it, provided that those directors would have formed a quorum at such a meeting.

(2)   It is immaterial whether any director signs the resolution before or after the time by which the notice proposed that it should be adopted.

(3)   Once a directors' written resolution has been adopted, it must be treated as if it had been a decision taken at a directors' meeting in accordance with the articles.

(4)   The company secretary must ensure that the company keeps a record, in writing, of all directors' written resolutions for at least ten years from the date of their adoption.

19   Directors' discretion to make further rules

Subject to the articles, the directors may make any rule which they think fit about how they take decisions, and about how such rules are to be recorded or communicated to directors.

Appointment of Directors

20   Methods of appointing directors

Any person who is willing to act as a director, and is permitted by law to do so, may be appointed to be a director—
  (a)   by ordinary resolution, or
  (b)   by a decision of the directors.

21   Retirement of directors by rotation

(1)   At the first annual general meeting all the directors must retire from office.

(2)   At every subsequent annual general meeting any directors—
  (a)   who have been appointed by the directors since the last annual general meeting, or
  (b)   who were not appointed or reappointed at one of the preceding two annual general meetings,
must retire from office and may offer themselves for reappointment by the members.

22   Termination of director's appointment

A person ceases to be a director as soon as—
  (a)   that person ceases to be a director by virtue of any provision of the Companies Act 2006 or is prohibited from being a director by law;
  (b)   a bankruptcy order is made against that person;

(c)   a composition is made with that person's creditors generally in satisfaction of that person's debts;

(d)   a registered medical practitioner who is treating that person gives a written opinion to the company stating that that person has become physically or mentally incapable of acting as a director and may remain so for more than three months;

(e)   by reason of that person's mental health, a court makes an order which wholly or partly prevents that person from personally exercising any powers or rights which that person would otherwise have;

(f)   notification is received by the company from the director that the director is resigning from office as director, and such resignation has taken effect in accordance with its terms.

23   Directors' remuneration

(1)   Directors may undertake any services for the company that the directors decide.

(2)   Directors are entitled to such remuneration as the directors determine—
    (a)   for their services to the company as directors, and
    (b)   for any other service which they undertake for the company.

(3)   Subject to the articles, a director's remuneration may—
    (a)   take any form, and
    (b)   include any arrangements in connection with the payment of a pension, allowance or gratuity, or any death, sickness or disability benefits, to or in respect of that director.

(4)   Unless the directors decide otherwise, directors' remuneration accrues from day to day.

(5)   Unless the directors decide otherwise, directors are not accountable to the company for any remuneration which they receive as directors or other officers or employees of the company's subsidiaries or of any other body corporate in which the company is interested.

24   Directors' expenses

The company may pay any reasonable expenses which the directors properly incur in connection with their attendance at—
    (a)   meetings of directors or committees of directors,
    (b)   general meetings, or
    (c)   separate meetings of the holders of any class of shares or of debentures of the company,
or otherwise in connection with the exercise of their powers and the discharge of their responsibilities in relation to the company.

Alternate Directors

25   Appointment and removal of alternates

(1)   Any director (the "appointor") may appoint as an alternate any other director, or any other person approved by resolution of the directors, to—
    (a)   exercise that director's powers, and
    (b)   carry out that director's responsibilities,
in relation to the taking of decisions by the directors in the absence of the alternate's appointor.

(2)   Any appointment or removal of an alternate must be effected by notice in writing to the company signed by the appointor, or in any other manner approved by the directors.

(3)   The notice must—
    (a)   identify the proposed alternate, and
    (b)   in the case of a notice of appointment, contain a statement signed by the proposed alternate that the proposed alternate is willing to act as the alternate of the director giving the notice.

26   Rights and responsibilities of alternate directors

(1)   An alternate director has the same rights, in relation to any directors' meeting or directors' written resolution, as the alternate's appointor.

(2)   Except as the articles specify otherwise, alternate directors—
    (a)   are deemed for all purposes to be directors;
    (b)   are liable for their own acts and omissions;
    (c)   are subject to the same restrictions as their appointors; and
    (d)   are not deemed to be agents of or for their appointors.

(3)   A person who is an alternate director but not a director—
    (a)   may be counted as participating for the purposes of determining whether a quorum is participating (but only if that person's appointor is not participating), and
    (b)   may sign a written resolution (but only if it is not signed or to be signed by that person's appointor).
No alternate may be counted as more than one director for such purposes.

(4)   An alternate director is not entitled to receive any remuneration from the company for serving as an alternate director except such part of the alternate's appointor's remuneration as the appointor may direct by notice in writing made to the company.

27 Termination of alternate directorship

An alternate director's appointment as an alternate terminates—

(a) when the alternate's appointor revokes the appointment by notice to the company in writing specifying when it is to terminate;

(b) on the occurrence in relation to the alternate of any event which, if it occurred in relation to the alternate's appointor, would result in the termination of the appointor's appointment as a director;

(c) on the death of the alternate's appointor; or

(d) when the alternate's appointor's appointment as a director terminates, except that an alternate's appointment as an alternate does not terminate when the appointor retires by rotation at a general meeting and is then re-appointed as a director at the same general meeting.

PART 3
DECISION-MAKING BY MEMBERS
Organisation of General Meetings

28 Members can call general meeting if not enough directors

If—

(a) the company has fewer than two directors, and

(b) the director (if any) is unable or unwilling to appoint sufficient directors to make up a quorum or to call a general meeting to do so,

then two or more members may call a general meeting (or instruct the company secretary to do so) for the purpose of appointing one or more directors.

29 Attendance and speaking at general meetings

(1) A person is able to exercise the right to speak at a general meeting when that person is in a position to communicate to all those attending the meeting, during the meeting, any information or opinions which that person has on the business of the meeting.

(2) A person is able to exercise the right to vote at a general meeting when—

(a) that person is able to vote, during the meeting, on resolutions put to the vote at the meeting, and

(b) that person's vote can be taken into account in determining whether or not such resolutions are passed at the same time as the votes of all the other persons attending the meeting.

(3) The directors may make whatever arrangements they consider appropriate to enable those attending a general meeting to exercise their rights to speak or vote at it.

(4) In determining attendance at a general meeting, it is immaterial whether any two or more members attending it are in the same place as each other.

(5) Two or more persons who are not in the same place as each other attend a general meeting if their circumstances are such that if they have (or were to have) rights to speak and vote at that meeting, they are (or would be) able to exercise them.

30 Quorum for general meetings

No business other than the appointment of the chairman of the meeting is to be transacted at a general meeting if the persons attending it do not constitute a quorum.

31 Chairing general meetings

(1) If the directors have appointed a chairman, the chairman shall chair general meetings if present and willing to do so.

(2) If the directors have not appointed a chairman, or if the chairman is unwilling to chair the meeting or is not present within ten minutes of the time at which a meeting was due to start—

(a) the directors present, or

(b) (if no directors are present), the meeting,

must appoint a director or member to chair the meeting, and the appointment of the chairman of the meeting must be the first business of the meeting.

(3) The person chairing a meeting in accordance with this article is referred to as "the chairman of the meeting".

32 Attendance and speaking by directors and non-members

(1) Directors may attend and speak at general meetings, whether or not they are members.

(2) The chairman of the meeting may permit other persons who are not—

(a) members of the company, or

(b) otherwise entitled to exercise the rights of members in relation to general meetings,

to attend and speak at a general meeting.

33 Adjournment

(1) If the persons attending a general meeting within half an hour of the time at which the meeting was due to start do not constitute a quorum, or if during a meeting a quorum ceases to be present, the chairman of the meeting must adjourn it.

(2) The chairman of the meeting may adjourn a general meeting at which a quorum is present if—
- (a) the meeting consents to an adjournment, or
- (b) it appears to the chairman of the meeting that an adjournment is necessary to protect the safety of any person attending the meeting or ensure that the business of the meeting is conducted in an orderly manner.

(3) The chairman of the meeting must adjourn a general meeting if directed to do so by the meeting.

(4) When adjourning a general meeting, the chairman of the meeting must—
- (a) either specify the time and place to which it is adjourned or state that it is to continue at a time and place to be fixed by the directors, and
- (b) have regard to any directions as to the time and place of any adjournment which have been given by the meeting.

(5) If the continuation of an adjourned meeting is to take place more than 14 days after it was adjourned, the company must give at least 7 clear days' notice of it (that is, excluding the day of the adjourned meeting and the day on which the notice is given)—
- (a) to the same persons to whom notice of the company's general meetings is required to be given, and
- (b) containing the same information which such notice is required to contain.

(6) No business may be transacted at an adjourned general meeting which could not properly have been transacted at the meeting if the adjournment had not taken place.

Voting at General Meetings

34 Voting: general

A resolution put to the vote of a general meeting must be decided on a show of hands unless a poll is duly demanded in accordance with the articles.

35 Errors and disputes

(1) No objection may be raised to the qualification of any person voting at a general meeting except at the meeting or adjourned meeting at which the vote objected to is tendered, and every vote not disallowed at the meeting is valid.

(2) Any such objection must be referred to the chairman of the meeting whose decision is final.

36 Demanding a poll

(1) A poll on a resolution may be demanded—
- (a) in advance of the general meeting where it is to be put to the vote, or
- (b) at a general meeting, either before a show of hands on that resolution or immediately after the result of a show of hands on that resolution is declared.

(2) A poll may be demanded by—
- (a) the chairman of the meeting;
- (b) the directors;
- (c) two or more persons having the right to vote on the resolution; or
- (d) a person or persons representing not less than one tenth of the total voting rights of all the members having the right to vote on the resolution.

(3) A demand for a poll may be withdrawn if—
- (a) the poll has not yet been taken, and
- (b) the chairman of the meeting consents to the withdrawal.

37 Procedure on a poll

(1) Subject to the articles, polls at general meetings must be taken when, where and in such manner as the chairman of the meeting directs.

(2) The chairman of the meeting may appoint scrutineers (who need not be members) and decide how and when the result of the poll is to be declared.

(3) The result of a poll shall be the decision of the meeting in respect of the resolution on which the poll was demanded.

(4) A poll on—
- (a) the election of the chairman of the meeting, or
- (b) a question of adjournment,
must be taken immediately.

(5) Other polls must be taken within 30 days of their being demanded.

(6) A demand for a poll does not prevent a general meeting from continuing, except as regards the question on which the poll was demanded.

(7) No notice need be given of a poll not taken immediately if the time and place at which it is to be taken are announced at the meeting at which it is demanded.

(8) In any other case, at least 7 days' notice must be given specifying the time and place at which the poll is to be taken.

38 Content of proxy notices

(1) Proxies may only validly be appointed by a notice in writing (a "proxy notice") which—
- (a) states the name and address of the member appointing the proxy;
- (b) identifies the person appointed to be that member's proxy and the general meeting in relation to which that person is appointed;
- (c) is signed by or on behalf of the member appointing the proxy, or is authenticated in such manner as the directors may determine; and
- (d) is delivered to the company in accordance with the articles and any instructions contained in the notice of the general meeting to which they relate.

(2) The company may require proxy notices to be delivered in a particular form, and may specify different forms for different purposes.

(3) Proxy notices may specify how the proxy appointed under them is to vote (or that the proxy is to abstain from voting) on one or more resolutions.

(4) Unless a proxy notice indicates otherwise, it must be treated as—
- (a) allowing the person appointed under it as a proxy discretion as to how to vote on any ancillary or procedural resolutions put to the meeting, and
- (b) appointing that person as a proxy in relation to any adjournment of the general meeting to which it relates as well as the meeting itself.

39 Delivery of proxy notices

(1) Any notice of a general meeting must specify the address or addresses ("proxy notification address") at which the company or its agents will receive proxy notices relating to that meeting, or any adjournment of it, delivered in hard copy or electronic form.

(2) A person who is entitled to attend, speak or vote (either on a show of hands or on a poll) at a general meeting remains so entitled in respect of that meeting or any adjournment of it, even though a valid proxy notice has been delivered to the company by or on behalf of that person.

(3) Subject to paragraphs (4) and (5), a proxy notice must be delivered to a proxy notification address not less than 48 hours before the general meeting or adjourned meeting to which it relates.

(4) In the case of a poll taken more than 48 hours after it is demanded, the notice must be delivered to a proxy notification address not less than 24 hours before the time appointed for the taking of the poll.

(5) In the case of a poll not taken during the meeting but taken not more than 48 hours after it was demanded, the proxy notice must be delivered—
- (a) in accordance with paragraph (3), or
- (b) at the meeting at which the poll was demanded to the chairman, secretary or any director.

(6) An appointment under a proxy notice may be revoked by delivering a notice in writing given by or on behalf of the person by whom or on whose behalf the proxy notice was given to a proxy notification address.

(7) A notice revoking a proxy appointment only takes effect if it is delivered before—
- (a) the start of the meeting or adjourned meeting to which it relates, or
- (b) (in the case of a poll not taken on the same day as the meeting or adjourned meeting) the time appointed for taking the poll to which it relates.

(8) If a proxy notice is not signed by the person appointing the proxy, it must be accompanied by written evidence of the authority of the person who executed it to execute it on the appointor's behalf.

40 Amendments to resolutions

(1) An ordinary resolution to be proposed at a general meeting may be amended by ordinary resolution if—
- (a) notice of the proposed amendment is given to the company secretary in writing by a person entitled to vote at the general meeting at which it is to be proposed not less than 48 hours before the meeting is to take place (or such later time as the chairman of the meeting may determine), and
- (b) the proposed amendment does not, in the reasonable opinion of the chairman of the meeting, materially alter the scope of the resolution.

(2) A special resolution to be proposed at a general meeting may be amended by ordinary resolution, if—
- (a) the chairman of the meeting proposes the amendment at the general meeting at which the resolution is to be proposed, and
- (b) the amendment does not go beyond what is necessary to correct a grammatical or other non-substantive error in the resolution.

(3)   If the chairman of the meeting, acting in good faith, wrongly decides that an amendment to a resolution is out of order, the chairman's error does not invalidate the vote on that resolution.

Restrictions on Members' Rights

41   No voting of shares on which money owed to company

No voting rights attached to a share may be exercised at any general meeting, at any adjournment of it, or on any poll called at or in relation to it, unless all amounts payable to the company in respect of that share have been paid.

Application of Rules to Class Meetings

42   Class meetings

The provisions of the articles relating to general meetings apply, with any necessary modifications, to meetings of the holders of any class of shares.

PART 4
SHARES AND DISTRIBUTIONS

Issue of Shares

43   Powers to issue different classes of share

(1)   Subject to the articles, but without prejudice to the rights attached to any existing share, the company may issue shares with such rights or restrictions as may be determined by ordinary resolution.

(2)   The company may issue shares which are to be redeemed, or are liable to be redeemed at the option of the company or the holder, and the directors may determine the terms, conditions and manner of redemption of any such shares.

44   Payment of commissions on subscription for shares

(1)   The company may pay any person a commission in consideration for that person—
   (a)   subscribing, or agreeing to subscribe, for shares, or
   (b)   procuring, or agreeing to procure, subscriptions for shares.
(2)   Any such commission may be paid—
   (a)   in cash, or in fully paid or partly paid shares or other securities, or partly in one way and partly in the other, and
   (b)   in respect of a conditional or an absolute subscription.

Interests in Shares

45   Company not bound by less than absolute interests

Except as required by law, no person is to be recognised by the company as holding any share upon any trust, and except as otherwise required by law or the articles, the company is not in any way to be bound by or recognise any interest in a share other than the holder's absolute ownership of it and all the rights attaching to it.

Share Certificates

46   Certificates to be issued except in certain cases

(1)   The company must issue each member with one or more certificates in respect of the shares which that member holds.
(2)   This article does not apply to—
   (a)   uncertificated shares;
   (b)   shares in respect of which a share warrant has been issued; or
   (c)   shares in respect of which the Companies Acts permit the company not to issue a certificate.
(3)   Except as otherwise specified in the articles, all certificates must be issued free of charge.
(4)   No certificate may be issued in respect of shares of more than one class.
(5)   If more than one person holds a share, only one certificate may be issued in respect of it.

47   Contents and execution of share certificates

(1)   Every certificate must specify—
   (a)   in respect of how many shares, of what class, it is issued;
   (b)   the nominal value of those shares;
   (c)   the amount paid up on them; and
   (d)   any distinguishing numbers assigned to them.
(2)   Certificates must—
   (a)   have affixed to them the company's common seal or an official seal which is a facsimile of the company's common seal with the addition on its face of the word "Securities" (a "securities seal"), or

(b)   be otherwise executed in accordance with the Companies Acts.

48   Consolidated share certificates

(1)   When a member's holding of shares of a particular class increases, the company may issue that member with—

    (a)   a single, consolidated certificate in respect of all the shares of a particular class which that member holds, or

    (b)   a separate certificate in respect of only those shares by which that member's holding has increased.

(2)   When a member's holding of shares of a particular class is reduced, the company must ensure that the member is issued with one or more certificates in respect of the number of shares held by the member after that reduction. But the company need not (in the absence of a request from the member) issue any new certificate if—

    (a)   all the shares which the member no longer holds as a result of the reduction, and

    (b)   none of the shares which the member retains following the reduction,

were, immediately before the reduction, represented by the same certificate.

(3)   A member may request the company, in writing, to replace—

    (a)   the member's separate certificates with a consolidated certificate, or

    (b)   the member's consolidated certificate with two or more separate certificates representing such proportion of the shares as the member may specify.

(4)   When the company complies with such a request it may charge such reasonable fee as the directors may decide for doing so.

(5)   A consolidated certificate must not be issued unless any certificates which it is to replace have first been returned to the company for cancellation.

49   Replacement share certificates

(1)   If a certificate issued in respect of a member's shares is—

    (a)   damaged or defaced, or

    (b)   said to be lost, stolen or destroyed,

that member is entitled to be issued with a replacement certificate in respect of the same shares.

(2)   A member exercising the right to be issued with such a replacement certificate—

    (a)   may at the same time exercise the right to be issued with a single certificate or separate certificates;

    (b)   must return the certificate which is to be replaced to the company if it is damaged or defaced; and

    (c)   must comply with such conditions as to evidence, indemnity and the payment of a reasonable fee as the directors decide.

Shares not Held in Certificated Form

50   Uncertificated shares

(1)   In this article, "the relevant rules" means—

    (a)   any applicable provision of the Companies Acts about the holding, evidencing of title to, or transfer of shares other than in certificated form, and

    (b)   any applicable legislation, rules or other arrangements made under or by virtue of such provision.

(2)   The provisions of this article have effect subject to the relevant rules.

(3)   Any provision of the articles which is inconsistent with the relevant rules must be disregarded, to the extent that it is inconsistent, whenever the relevant rules apply.

(4)   Any share or class of shares of the company may be issued or held on such terms, or in such a way, that—

    (a)   title to it or them is not, or must not be, evidenced by a certificate, or

    (b)   it or they may or must be transferred wholly or partly without a certificate.

(5)   The directors have power to take such steps as they think fit in relation to—

    (a)   the evidencing of and transfer of title to uncertificated shares (including in connection with the issue of such shares);

    (b)   any records relating to the holding of uncertificated shares;

    (c)   the conversion of certificated shares into uncertificated shares; or

    (d)   the conversion of uncertificated shares into certificated shares.

(6)   The company may by notice to the holder of a share require that share—

    (a)   if it is uncertificated, to be converted into certificated form, and

    (b)   if it is certificated, to be converted into uncertificated form,

to enable it to be dealt with in accordance with the articles.

(7)   If—

    (a)   the articles give the directors power to take action, or require other persons to take action, in order to sell, transfer or otherwise dispose of shares, and

(b)   uncertificated shares are subject to that power, but the power is expressed in terms which assume the use of a certificate or other written instrument,

the directors may take such action as is necessary or expedient to achieve the same results when exercising that power in relation to uncertificated shares.

(8)   In particular, the directors may take such action as they consider appropriate to achieve the sale, transfer, disposal, forfeiture, re-allotment or surrender of an uncertificated share or otherwise to enforce a lien in respect of it.

(9)   Unless the directors otherwise determine, shares which a member holds in uncertificated form must be treated as separate holdings from any shares which that member holds in certificated form.

(10)   A class of shares must not be treated as two classes simply because some shares of that class are held in certificated form and others are held in uncertificated form.

51   Share warrants

(1)   The directors may issue a share warrant in respect of any fully paid share.

(2)   Share warrants must be—
    (a)   issued in such form, and
    (b)   executed in such manner,
as the directors decide.

(3)   A share represented by a share warrant may be transferred by delivery of the warrant representing it.

(4)   The directors may make provision for the payment of dividends in respect of any share represented by a share warrant.

(5)   Subject to the articles, the directors may decide the conditions on which any share warrant is issued. In particular, they may—
    (a)   decide the conditions on which new warrants are to be issued in place of warrants which are damaged or defaced, or said to have been lost, stolen or destroyed;
    (b)   decide the conditions on which bearers of warrants are entitled to attend and vote at general meetings;
    (c)   decide the conditions subject to which bearers of warrants may surrender their warrant so as to hold their shares in certificated or uncertificated form instead; and
    (d)   vary the conditions of issue of any warrant from time to time,
and the bearer of a warrant is subject to the conditions and procedures in force in relation to it, whether or not they were decided or specified before the warrant was issued.

(6)   Subject to the conditions on which the warrants are issued from time to time, bearers of share warrants have the same rights and privileges as they would if their names had been included in the register as holders of the shares represented by their warrants.

(7)   The company must not in any way be bound by or recognise any interest in a share represented by a share warrant other than the absolute right of the bearer of that warrant to that warrant.

Partly Paid Shares

52   Company's lien over partly paid shares

(1)   The company has a lien ("the company's lien") over every share which is partly paid for any part of—
    (a)   that share's nominal value, and
    (b)   any premium at which it was issued,
which has not been paid to the company, and which is payable immediately or at some time in the future, whether or not a call notice has been sent in respect of it.

(2)   The company's lien over a share—
    (a)   takes priority over any third party's interest in that share, and
    (b)   extends to any dividend or other money payable by the company in respect of that share and (if the lien is enforced and the share is sold by the company) the proceeds of sale of that share.

(3)   The directors may at any time decide that a share which is or would otherwise be subject to the company's lien shall not be subject to it, either wholly or in part.

53   Enforcement of the company's lien

(1)   Subject to the provisions of this article, if—
    (a)   a lien enforcement notice has been given in respect of a share, and
    (b)   the person to whom the notice was given has failed to comply with it,
the company may sell that share in such manner as the directors decide.

(2)   A lien enforcement notice—
    (a)   may only be given in respect of a share which is subject to the company's lien, in respect of which a sum is payable and the due date for payment of that sum has passed;
    (b)   must specify the share concerned;
    (c)   must require payment of the sum payable within 14 days of the notice;

(d)   must be addressed either to the holder of the share or to a person entitled to it by reason of the holder's death, bankruptcy or otherwise; and

(e)   must state the company's intention to sell the share if the notice is not complied with.

(3)   Where shares are sold under this article—

(a)   the directors may authorise any person to execute an instrument of transfer of the shares to the purchaser or a person nominated by the purchaser, and

(b)   the transferee is not bound to see to the application of the consideration, and the transferee's title is not affected by any irregularity in or invalidity of the process leading to the sale.

(4)   The net proceeds of any such sale (after payment of the costs of sale and any other costs of enforcing the lien) must be applied—

(a)   first, in payment of so much of the sum for which the lien exists as was payable at the date of the lien enforcement notice,

(b)   second, to the person entitled to the shares at the date of the sale, but only after the certificate for the shares sold has been surrendered to the company for cancellation or a suitable indemnity has been given for any lost certificates, and subject to a lien equivalent to the company's lien over the shares before the sale for any money payable in respect of the shares after the date of the lien enforcement notice.

(5)   A statutory declaration by a director or the company secretary that the declarant is a director or the company secretary and that a share has been sold to satisfy the company's lien on a specified date—

(a)   is conclusive evidence of the facts stated in it as against all persons claiming to be entitled to the share, and

(b)   subject to compliance with any other formalities of transfer required by the articles or by law, constitutes a good title to the share.

54   Call notices

(1)   Subject to the articles and the terms on which shares are allotted, the directors may send a notice (a "call notice") to a member requiring the member to pay the company a specified sum of money (a "call") which is payable in respect of shares which that member holds at the date when the directors decide to send the call notice.

(2)   A call notice—

(a)   may not require a member to pay a call which exceeds the total sum unpaid on that member's shares (whether as to the share's nominal value or any amount payable to the company by way of premium);

(b)   must state when and how any call to which it relates it is to be paid; and

(c)   may permit or require the call to be paid by instalments.

(3)   A member must comply with the requirements of a call notice, but no member is obliged to pay any call before 14 days have passed since the notice was sent.

(4)   Before the company has received any call due under a call notice the directors may—

(a)   revoke it wholly or in part, or

(b)   specify a later time for payment than is specified in the notice,

by a further notice in writing to the member in respect of whose shares the call is made.

55   Liability to pay calls

(1)   Liability to pay a call is not extinguished or transferred by transferring the shares in respect of which it is required to be paid.

(2)   Joint holders of a share are jointly and severally liable to pay all calls in respect of that share.

(3)   Subject to the terms on which shares are allotted, the directors may, when issuing shares, provide that call notices sent to the holders of those shares may require them—

(a)   to pay calls which are not the same, or

(b)   to pay calls at different times.

56   When call notice need not be issued

(1)   A call notice need not be issued in respect of sums which are specified, in the terms on which a share is issued, as being payable to the company in respect of that share (whether in respect of nominal value or premium)—

(a)   on allotment;

(b)   on the occurrence of a particular event; or

(c)   on a date fixed by or in accordance with the terms of issue.

(2)   But if the due date for payment of such a sum has passed and it has not been paid, the holder of the share concerned is treated in all respects as having failed to comply with a call notice in respect of that sum, and is liable to the same consequences as regards the payment of interest and forfeiture.

57   Failure to comply with call notice: automatic consequences

(1)   If a person is liable to pay a call and fails to do so by the call payment date—

(a)   the directors may issue a notice of intended forfeiture to that person, and
(b)   until the call is paid, that person must pay the company interest on the call from the call payment date at the relevant rate.

(2)   For the purposes of this article—
(a)   the "call payment date" is the time when the call notice states that a call is payable, unless the directors give a notice specifying a later date, in which case the "call payment date" is that later date;
(b)   the "relevant rate" is—
(i)   the rate fixed by the terms on which the share in respect of which the call is due was allotted;
(ii)   such other rate as was fixed in the call notice which required payment of the call, or has otherwise been determined by the directors; or
(iii) if no rate is fixed in either of these ways, 5 per cent per annum.

(3)   The relevant rate must not exceed by more than 5 percentage points the base lending rate most recently set by the Monetary Policy Committee of the Bank of England in connection with its responsibilities under Part 2 of the Bank of England Act 1998.

(4)   The directors may waive any obligation to pay interest on a call wholly or in part.

58   Notice of intended forfeiture

A notice of intended forfeiture—
(a)   may be sent in respect of any share in respect of which a call has not been paid as required by a call notice;
(b)   must be sent to the holder of that share or to a person entitled to it by reason of the holder's death, bankruptcy or otherwise;
(c)   must require payment of the call and any accrued interest by a date which is not less than 14 days after the date of the notice;
(d)   must state how the payment is to be made; and
(e)   must state that if the notice is not complied with, the shares in respect of which the call is payable will be liable to be forfeited.

59   Directors' power to forfeit shares

If a notice of intended forfeiture is not complied with before the date by which payment of the call is required in the notice of intended forfeiture, the directors may decide that any share in respect of which it was given is forfeited, and the forfeiture is to include all dividends or other moneys payable in respect of the forfeited shares and not paid before the forfeiture.

60   Effect of forfeiture

(1)   Subject to the articles, the forfeiture of a share extinguishes—
(a)   all interests in that share, and all claims and demands against the company in respect of it, and
(b)   all other rights and liabilities incidental to the share as between the person whose share it was prior to the forfeiture and the company.

(2)   Any share which is forfeited in accordance with the articles—
(a)   is deemed to have been forfeited when the directors decide that it is forfeited;
(b)   is deemed to be the property of the company; and
(c)   may be sold, re-allotted or otherwise disposed of as the directors think fit.

(3)   If a person's shares have been forfeited—
(a)   the company must send that person notice that forfeiture has occurred and record it in the register of members;
(b)   that person ceases to be a member in respect of those shares;
(c)   that person must surrender the certificate for the shares forfeited to the company for cancellation;
(d)   that person remains liable to the company for all sums payable by that person under the articles at the date of forfeiture in respect of those shares, including any interest (whether accrued before or after the date of forfeiture); and
(e)   the directors may waive payment of such sums wholly or in part or enforce payment without any allowance for the value of the shares at the time of forfeiture or for any consideration received on their disposal.

(4)   At any time before the company disposes of a forfeited share, the directors may decide to cancel the forfeiture on payment of all calls and interest due in respect of it and on such other terms as they think fit.

61   Procedure following forfeiture

(1)   If a forfeited share is to be disposed of by being transferred, the company may receive the consideration for the transfer and the directors may authorise any person to execute the instrument of transfer.

(2)   A statutory declaration by a director or the company secretary that the declarant is a director or the company secretary and that a share has been forfeited on a specified date—

(a)   is conclusive evidence of the facts stated in it as against all persons claiming to be entitled to the share, and

(b)   subject to compliance with any other formalities of transfer required by the articles or by law, constitutes a good title to the share.

(3)   A person to whom a forfeited share is transferred is not bound to see to the application of the consideration (if any) nor is that person's title to the share affected by any irregularity in or invalidity of the process leading to the forfeiture or transfer of the share.

(4)   If the company sells a forfeited share, the person who held it prior to its forfeiture is entitled to receive from the company the proceeds of such sale, net of any commission, and excluding any amount which—

(a)   was, or would have become, payable, and

(b)   had not, when that share was forfeited, been paid by that person in respect of that share, but no interest is payable to such a person in respect of such proceeds and the company is not required to account for any money earned on them.

62   Surrender of shares

(1)   A member may surrender any share—

(a)   in respect of which the directors may issue a notice of intended forfeiture;

(b)   which the directors may forfeit; or

(c)   which has been forfeited.

(2)   The directors may accept the surrender of any such share.

(3)   The effect of surrender on a share is the same as the effect of forfeiture on that share.

(4)   A share which has been surrendered may be dealt with in the same way as a share which has been forfeited.

Transfer and Transmission of Shares

63   Transfers of certificated shares

(1)   Certificated shares may be transferred by means of an instrument of transfer in any usual form or any other form approved by the directors, which is executed by or on behalf of—

(a)   the transferor, and

(b)   (if any of the shares is partly paid) the transferee.

(2)   No fee may be charged for registering any instrument of transfer or other document relating to or affecting the title to any share.

(3)   The company may retain any instrument of transfer which is registered.

(4)   The transferor remains the holder of a certificated share until the transferee's name is entered in the register of members as holder of it.

(5)   The directors may refuse to register the transfer of a certificated share if—

(a)   the share is not fully paid;

(b)   the transfer is not lodged at the company's registered office or such other place as the directors have appointed;

(c)   the transfer is not accompanied by the certificate for the shares to which it relates, or such other evidence as the directors may reasonably require to show the transferor's right to make the transfer, or evidence of the right of someone other than the transferor to make the transfer on the transferor's behalf;

(d)   the transfer is in respect of more than one class of share; or

(e)   the transfer is in favour of more than four transferees.

(6)   If the directors refuse to register the transfer of a share, the instrument of transfer must be returned to the transferee with the notice of refusal unless they suspect that the proposed transfer may be fraudulent.

64   Transfer of uncertificated shares

A transfer of an uncertificated share must not be registered if it is in favour of more than four transferees.

65   Transmission of shares

(1)   If title to a share passes to a transmittee, the company may only recognise the transmittee as having any title to that share.

(2)   Nothing in these articles releases the estate of a deceased member from any liability in respect of a share solely or jointly held by that member.

66   Transmittees' rights

(1)   A transmittee who produces such evidence of entitlement to shares as the directors may properly require—

(a)   may, subject to the articles, choose either to become the holder of those shares or to have them transferred to another person, and

(b)   subject to the articles, and pending any transfer of the shares to another person, has the same rights as the holder had.

(2)   But transmittees do not have the right to attend or vote at a general meeting in respect of shares to which they are entitled, by reason of the holder's death or bankruptcy or otherwise, unless they become the holders of those shares

67   Exercise of transmittees' rights

(1)   Transmittees who wish to become the holders of shares to which they have become entitled must notify the company in writing of that wish.

(2)   If the share is a certificated share and a transmittee wishes to have it transferred to another person, the transmittee must execute an instrument of transfer in respect of it.

(3)   If the share is an uncertificated share and the transmittee wishes to have it transferred to another person, the transmittee must—

(a)   procure that all appropriate instructions are given to effect the transfer, or

(b)   procure that the uncertificated share is changed into certificated form and then execute an instrument of transfer in respect of it.

(4)   Any transfer made or executed under this article is to be treated as if it were made or executed by the person from whom the transmittee has derived rights in respect of the share, and as if the event which gave rise to the transmission had not occurred.

68   Transmittees bound by prior notices

If a notice is given to a member in respect of shares and a transmittee is entitled to those shares, the transmittee is bound by the notice if it was given to the member before the transmittee's name has been entered in the register of members.

Consolidation of Shares

69   Procedure for disposing of fractions of shares

(1)   This article applies where—

(a)   there has been a consolidation or division of shares, and

(b)   as a result, members are entitled to fractions of shares.

(2)   The directors may—

(a)   sell the shares representing the fractions to any person including the company for the best price reasonably obtainable;

(b)   in the case of a certificated share, authorise any person to execute an instrument of transfer of the shares to the purchaser or a person nominated by the purchaser; and

(c)   distribute the net proceeds of sale in due proportion among the holders of the shares.

(3)   Where any holder's entitlement to a portion of the proceeds of sale amounts to less than a minimum figure determined by the directors, that member's portion may be distributed to an organisation which is a charity for the purposes of the law of England and Wales, Scotland or Northern Ireland.

(4)   The person to whom the shares are transferred is not obliged to ensure that any purchase money is received by the person entitled to the relevant fractions.

(5)   The transferee's title to the shares is not affected by any irregularity in or invalidity of the process leading to their sale.

Distributions

70   Procedure for declaring dividends

(1)   The company may by ordinary resolution declare dividends, and the directors may decide to pay interim dividends.

(2)   A dividend must not be declared unless the directors have made a recommendation as to its amount. Such a dividend must not exceed the amount recommended by the directors.

(3)   No dividend may be declared or paid unless it is in accordance with members' respective rights.

(4)   Unless the members' resolution to declare or directors' decision to pay a dividend, or the terms on which shares are issued, specify otherwise, it must be paid by reference to each member's holding of shares on the date of the resolution or decision to declare or pay it.

(5)   If the company's share capital is divided into different classes, no interim dividend may be paid on shares carrying deferred or non-preferred rights if, at the time of payment, any preferential dividend is in arrear.

(6)   The directors may pay at intervals any dividend payable at a fixed rate if it appears to them that the profits available for distribution justify the payment.

(7)   If the directors act in good faith, they do not incur any liability to the holders of shares conferring preferred rights for any loss they may suffer by the lawful payment of an interim dividend on shares with deferred or non-preferred rights.

71   Calculation of dividends

(1)   Except as otherwise provided by the articles or the rights attached to shares, all dividends must be—

   (a)   declared and paid according to the amounts paid up on the shares on which the dividend is paid, and

   (b)   apportioned and paid proportionately to the amounts paid up on the shares during any portion or portions of the period in respect of which the dividend is paid.

(2)   If any share is issued on terms providing that it ranks for dividend as from a particular date, that share ranks for dividend accordingly.

(3)   For the purposes of calculating dividends, no account is to be taken of any amount which has been paid up on a share in advance of the due date for payment of that amount.

72   Payment of dividends and other distributions

(1)   Where a dividend or other sum which is a distribution is payable in respect of a share, it must be paid by one or more of the following means—

   (a)   transfer to a bank or building society account specified by the distribution recipient either in writing or as the directors may otherwise decide;

   (b)   sending a cheque made payable to the distribution recipient by post to the distribution recipient at the distribution recipient's registered address (if the distribution recipient is a holder of the share), or (in any other case) to an address specified by the distribution recipient either in writing or as the directors may otherwise decide;

   (c)   sending a cheque made payable to such person by post to such person at such address as the distribution recipient has specified either in writing or as the directors may otherwise decide; or

   (d)   any other means of payment as the directors agree with the distribution recipient either in writing or by such other means as the directors decide.

(2)   In the articles, "the distribution recipient" means, in respect of a share in respect of which a dividend or other sum is payable—

   (a)   the holder of the share; or

   (b)   if the share has two or more joint holders, whichever of them is named first in the register of members; or

   (c)   if the holder is no longer entitled to the share by reason of death or bankruptcy, or otherwise by operation of law, the transmittee.

73   Deductions from distributions in respect of sums owed to the company

(1)   If—

   (a)   a share is subject to the company's lien, and

   (b)   the directors are entitled to issue a lien enforcement notice in respect of it,

they may, instead of issuing a lien enforcement notice, deduct from any dividend or other sum payable in respect of the share any sum of money which is payable to the company in respect of that share to the extent that they are entitled to require payment under a lien enforcement notice.

(2)   Money so deducted must be used to pay any of the sums payable in respect of that share.

(3)   The company must notify the distribution recipient in writing of—

   (a)   the fact and amount of any such deduction;

   (b)   any non-payment of a dividend or other sum payable in respect of a share resulting from any such deduction; and

   (c)   how the money deducted has been applied.

74   No interest on distributions

The company may not pay interest on any dividend or other sum payable in respect of a share unless otherwise provided by—

   (a)   the terms on which the share was issued, or

   (b)   the provisions of another agreement between the holder of that share and the company.

75   Unclaimed distributions

(1)   All dividends or other sums which are—

   (a)   payable in respect of shares, and

   (b)   unclaimed after having been declared or become payable,

may be invested or otherwise made use of by the directors for the benefit of the company until claimed.

(2)   The payment of any such dividend or other sum into a separate account does not make the company a trustee in respect of it.

(3)   If—

   (a)   twelve years have passed from the date on which a dividend or other sum became due for payment, and

   (b)   the distribution recipient has not claimed it,

the distribution recipient is no longer entitled to that dividend or other sum and it ceases to remain owing by the company.

76   Non-cash distributions

(1)   Subject to the terms of issue of the share in question, the company may, by ordinary resolution on the recommendation of the directors, decide to pay all or part of a dividend or other distribution payable in respect of a share by transferring non-cash assets of equivalent value (including, without limitation, shares or other securities in any company).

(2)   If the shares in respect of which such a non-cash distribution is paid are uncertificated, any shares in the company which are issued as a non-cash distribution in respect of them must be uncertificated.

(3)   For the purposes of paying a non-cash distribution, the directors may make whatever arrangements they think fit, including, where any difficulty arises regarding the distribution—
(a)   fixing the value of any assets;
(b)   paying cash to any distribution recipient on the basis of that value in order to adjust the rights of recipients; and
(c)   vesting any assets in trustees.

77   Waiver of distributions

Distribution recipients may waive their entitlement to a dividend or other distribution payable in respect of a share by giving the company notice in writing to that effect, but if—
(a)   the share has more than one holder, or
(b)   more than one person is entitled to the share, whether by reason of the death or bankruptcy of one or more joint holders, or otherwise,
the notice is not effective unless it is expressed to be given, and signed, by all the holders or persons otherwise entitled to the share.

Capitalisation of Profits

78   Authority to capitalise and appropriation of capitalised sums

(1)   Subject to the articles, the directors may, if they are so authorised by an ordinary resolution—
(a)   decide to capitalise any profits of the company (whether or not they are available for distribution) which are not required for paying a preferential dividend, or any sum standing to the credit of the company's share premium account or capital redemption reserve; and
(b)   appropriate any sum which they so decide to capitalise (a "capitalised sum") to the persons who would have been entitled to it if it were distributed by way of dividend (the "persons entitled") and in the same proportions.

(2)   Capitalised sums must be applied—
(a)   on behalf of the persons entitled, and
(b)   in the same proportions as a dividend would have been distributed to them.

(3)   Any capitalised sum may be applied in paying up new shares of a nominal amount equal to the capitalised sum which are then allotted credited as fully paid to the persons entitled or as they may direct.

(4)   A capitalised sum which was appropriated from profits available for distribution may be applied—
(a)   in or towards paying up any amounts unpaid on existing shares held by the persons entitled, or
(b)   in paying up new debentures of the company which are then allotted credited as fully paid to the persons entitled or as they may direct.

(5)   Subject to the articles the directors may—
(a)   apply capitalised sums in accordance with paragraphs (3) and (4) partly in one way and partly in another;
(b)   make such arrangements as they think fit to deal with shares or debentures becoming distributable in fractions under this article (including the issuing of fractional certificates or the making of cash payments); and
(c)   authorise any person to enter into an agreement with the company on behalf of all the persons entitled which is binding on them in respect of the allotment of shares and debentures to them under this article.

PART 5
MISCELLANEOUS PROVISIONS

Communications

79   Means of communication to be used

(1)   Subject to the articles, anything sent or supplied by or to the company under the articles may be sent or supplied in any way in which the Companies Act 2006 provides for documents or information which are authorised or required by any provision of that Act to be sent or supplied by or to the company.

(2)   Subject to the articles, any notice or document to be sent or supplied to a director in connection with the taking of decisions by directors may also be sent or supplied by the means by which that director has asked to be sent or supplied with such notices or documents for the time being.

(3)   A director may agree with the company that notices or documents sent to that director in a particular way are to be deemed to have been received within a specified time of their being sent, and for the specified time to be less than 48 hours.

80   Failure to notify contact details

(1)   If—
- (a)   the company sends two consecutive documents to a member over a period of at least 12 months, and
- (b)   each of those documents is returned undelivered, or the company receives notification that it has not been delivered,

that member ceases to be entitled to receive notices from the company.

(2)   A member who has ceased to be entitled to receive notices from the company becomes entitled to receive such notices again by sending the company—
- (a)   a new address to be recorded in the register of members, or
- (b)   if the member has agreed that the company should use a means of communication other than sending things to such an address, the information that the company needs to use that means of communication effectively.

Administrative Arrangements

81   Company seals

(1)   Any common seal may only be used by the authority of the directors.

(2)   The directors may decide by what means and in what form any common seal or securities seal is to be used.

(3)   Unless otherwise decided by the directors, if the company has a common seal and it is affixed to a document, the document must also be signed by at least one authorised person in the presence of a witness who attests the signature.

(4)   For the purposes of this article, an authorised person is—
- (a)   any director of the company;
- (b)   the company secretary; or
- (c)   any person authorised by the directors for the purpose of signing documents to which the common seal is applied.

(5)   If the company has an official seal for use abroad, it may only be affixed to a document if its use on that document, or documents of a class to which it belongs, has been authorised by a decision of the directors.

(6)   If the company has a securities seal, it may only be affixed to securities by the company secretary or a person authorised to apply it to securities by the company secretary.

(7)   For the purposes of the articles, references to the securities seal being affixed to any document include the reproduction of the image of that seal on or in a document by any mechanical or electronic means which has been approved by the directors in relation to that document or documents of a class to which it belongs.

82   Destruction of documents

(1)   The company is entitled to destroy—
- (a)   all instruments of transfer of shares which have been registered, and all other documents on the basis of which any entries are made in the register of members, from six years after the date of registration;
- (b)   all dividend mandates, variations or cancellations of dividend mandates, and notifications of change of address, from two years after they have been recorded;
- (c)   all share certificates which have been cancelled from one year after the date of the cancellation;
- (d)   all paid dividend warrants and cheques from one year after the date of actual payment; and
- (e)   all proxy notices from one year after the end of the meeting to which the proxy notice relates.

(2)   If the company destroys a document in good faith, in accordance with the articles, and without notice of any claim to which that document may be relevant, it is conclusively presumed in favour of the company that—
- (a)   entries in the register purporting to have been made on the basis of an instrument of transfer or other document so destroyed were duly and properly made;
- (b)   any instrument of transfer so destroyed was a valid and effective instrument duly and properly registered;
- (c)   any share certificate so destroyed was a valid and effective certificate duly and properly cancelled; and

(d) any other document so destroyed was a valid and effective document in accordance with its recorded particulars in the books or records of the company.

(3) This article does not impose on the company any liability which it would not otherwise have if it destroys any document before the time at which this article permits it to do so.

(4) In this article, references to the destruction of any document include a reference to its being disposed of in any manner.

83 No right to inspect accounts and other records

Except as provided by law or authorised by the directors or an ordinary resolution of the company, no person is entitled to inspect any of the company's accounting or other records or documents merely by virtue of being a member.

84 Provision for employees on cessation of business

The directors may decide to make provision for the benefit of persons employed or formerly employed by the company or any of its subsidiaries (other than a director or former director or shadow director) in connection with the cessation or transfer to any person of the whole or part of the undertaking of the company or that subsidiary.

Directors' Indemnity and Insurance

85 Indemnity

(1) Subject to paragraph (2), a relevant director of the company or an associated company may be indemnified out of the company's assets against—

(a) any liability incurred by that director in connection with any negligence, default, breach of duty or breach of trust in relation to the company or an associated company,

(b) any liability incurred by that director in connection with the activities of the company or an associated company in its capacity as a trustee of an occupational pension scheme (as defined in section 235(6) of the Companies Act 2006),

(c) any other liability incurred by that director as an officer of the company or an associated company.

(2) This article does not authorise any indemnity which would be prohibited or rendered void by any provision of the Companies Acts or by any other provision of law.

(3) In this article—

(a) companies are associated if one is a subsidiary of the other or both are subsidiaries of the same body corporate, and

(b) a "relevant director" means any director or former director of the company or an associated company.

86 Insurance

(1) The directors may decide to purchase and maintain insurance, at the expense of the company, for the benefit of any relevant director in respect of any relevant loss.

(2) In this article—

(a) a "relevant director" means any director or former director of the company or an associated company,

(b) a "relevant loss" means any loss or liability which has been or may be incurred by a relevant director in connection with that director's duties or powers in relation to the company, any associated company or any pension fund or employees' share scheme of the company or associated company, and

(c) companies are associated if one is a subsidiary of the other or both are subsidiaries of the same body corporate.

Appendix 2:
Companies Act 1985, Table A

[A2]

NOTES

The Companies Act 1985, Table A is set out in the Schedule to the Companies (Tables A to F) Regulations 1985.

The Companies Act 1985, s 8(2), (3) (repealed by CA 2006, but see further the note relating to SI 2008/2860 below) provide as follows—

"(2)   In the case of a company limited by shares, if articles are not registered or, if articles are registered, in so far as they do not exclude or modify Table A, that Table (so far as applicable, and as in force at the date of the company's registration) constitutes the company's articles, in the same manner and to the same extent as if articles in the form of that Table had been duly registered.

(3)   If in consequence of regulations under this section Table A is altered, the alteration does not affect a company registered before the alteration takes effect, or repeal as respects that company any portion of the Table.".

Following amendments by regulations made under s 8 of the 1985 Act, this table is set out below both in its original form and in its form as amended at different dates.

Note also that this Table A was also amended by the Companies Act 1985 (Electronic Communications) Order 2000, SI 2000/3373. The 2000 Order was made under the powers conferred by the Electronic Communications Act 2000, ss 8, 9. It is assumed that these amendments (which do not fall within s 8(3) of the 1985 Act) are generally applicable.

Note that the Companies Act 2006 (Commencement No 8, Transitional Provisions and Savings) Order 2008, SI 2008/2860, Sch 2, para 1(1) (at **[2.91]**) provides that nothing in the Companies Act 2006 affects (a) the registration or re-registration of a company under the former Companies Acts, or the continued existence of a company by virtue of such registration or re-registration, or (b) the application in relation to an existing company of (i) Table B in the Joint Stock Companies Act 1856, (ii) Table A in any of the former Companies Acts, or (iii) the Companies (Tables A to F) Regulations 1985 or the Companies (Tables A to F) Regulations (Northern Ireland) 1986.

TABLE A
REGULATIONS FOR MANAGEMENT OF A COMPANY LIMITED BY SHARES

INTERPRETATION

1. In these regulations—

    ["the Act" means the Companies Act 1985 including any statutory modification or re-enactment thereof for the time being in force and any provisions of the Companies Act 2006 for the time being in force;]

    "the articles" means the articles of the company.

    "clear days" in relation to the period of a notice means that period excluding the day when the notice is given or deemed to be given and the day for which it is given or on which it is to take effect.

    ["communication" means the same as in the Electronic Communications Act 2000.]

    ["electronic communication" means the same as in the Electronic Communications Act 2000.]

    "executed" includes any mode of execution.

    "office" means the registered office of the company.

    "the holder" in relation to shares means the member whose name is entered in the register of members as the holder of the shares.

    "the seal" means the common seal of the company.

    "secretary" means the secretary of the company or any other person appointed to perform the duties of the secretary of the company, including a joint, assistant or deputy secretary.

    "the United Kingdom" means Great Britain and Northern Ireland.

    Unless the context otherwise requires, words or expressions contained in these regulations bear the same meaning as in the Act but excluding any statutory modification thereof not in force when these regulations become binding on the company.

NOTES

Definition "the Act" substituted by the Companies (Tables A to F) (Amendment) Regulations 2007, SI 2007/2541, reg 3, as from 1 October 2007; the original definition read as follows—

    "the Act" means the Companies Act 1985 including any statutory modification or re-enactment thereof for the time being in force.".

Definitions "communication" and "electronic communication" inserted by the Companies Act 1985 (Electronic Communications) Order 2000, SI 2000/3373, art 32(1), Sch 1, para 1, as from 22 December 2000.

SHARE CAPITAL

2. Subject to the provisions of the Act and without prejudice to any rights attached to any existing shares, any share may be issued with such rights or restrictions as the company may by ordinary resolution determine.

Appendices

3. Subject to the provisions of the Act, shares may be issued which are to be redeemed or are to be liable to be redeemed at the option of the company or the holder on such terms and in such manner as may be provided by the articles.

4. The company may exercise the powers of paying commissions conferred by the Act. Subject to the [provisions] of the Act, any such commission may be satisfied by the payment of cash or by the allotment of fully or partly paid shares or partly in one way and partly in the other.

NOTES

Word in square brackets substituted for the original word "provision" by the Companies (Tables A to F) (Amendment) Regulations 1985, SI 1985/1052, reg 2, as from 1 August 1985.

5. Except as required by law, no person shall be recognised by the company as holding any share upon any trust and (except as otherwise provided by the articles or by law) the company shall not be bound by or recognise any interest in any share except an absolute right to the entirety thereof in the holder.

SHARE CERTIFICATES

6. Every member, upon becoming the holder of any shares, shall be entitled without payment to one certificate for all the shares of each class held by him (and, upon transferring a part of his holding of shares of any class, to a certificate for the balance of such holding) or several certificates each for one or more of his shares upon payment for every certificate after the first of such reasonable sum as the directors may determine. Every certificate shall be sealed with the seal and shall specify the number, class and distinguishing numbers (if any) of the shares to which it relates and the amount or respective amounts paid up thereon. The company shall not be bound to issue more than one certificate for shares held jointly by several persons and delivery of a certificate to one joint holder shall be a sufficient delivery to all of them.

7. If a share certificate is defaced, worn-out, lost or destroyed, it may be renewed on such terms (if any) as to evidence and indemnity and payment of the expenses reasonably incurred by the company in investigating evidence as the directors may determine but otherwise free of charge, and (in the case of defacement or wearing-out) on delivery up of the old certificate.

LIEN

8. The company shall have a first and paramount lien on every share (not being a fully paid share) for all moneys (whether presently payable or not) payable at a fixed time or called in respect of that share. The directors may at any time declare any share to be wholly or in part exempt from the provisions of this regulation. The company's lien on a share shall extend to any amount payable in respect of it.

9. The company may sell in such manner as the directors determine any shares on which the company has a lien if a sum in respect of which the lien exists is presently payable and is not paid within fourteen clear days after notice has been given to the holder of the share or to the person entitled to it in consequence of the death or bankruptcy of the holder, demanding payment and stating that if the notice is not complied with the shares may be sold.

10. To give effect to a sale the directors may authorise some person to execute an instrument of transfer of the shares sold to, or in accordance with the directions of, the purchaser. The title of the transferee to the shares shall not be affected by any irregularity in or invalidity of the proceedings in reference to the sale.

11. The net proceeds of the sale, after payment of the costs, shall be applied in payment of so much of the sum for which the lien exists as is presently payable, and any residue shall (upon surrender to the company for cancellation of the certificate for the shares sold and subject to a like lien for any moneys not presently payable as existed upon the shares before the sale) be paid to the person entitled to the shares at the date of the sale.

CALLS ON SHARES AND FORFEITURE

12. Subject to the terms of allotment, the directors may make calls upon the members in respect of any moneys unpaid on their shares (whether in respect of nominal value or premium) and each member shall (subject to receiving at least fourteen clear days' notice specifying when and where payment is to be made) pay to the company as required by the notice the amount called on his shares. A call may be required to be paid by instalments. A call may, before receipt by the company of any sum due thereunder, be revoked in whole or part and payment of a call may be postponed in whole or part. A person upon whom a call is made shall remain liable for calls made upon him notwithstanding the subsequent transfer of the shares in respect whereof the call was made.

13. A call shall be deemed to have been made at the time when the resolution of the directors authorising the call was passed.

14. The joint holders of a share shall be jointly and severally liable to pay all calls in respect thereof.

15. If a call remains unpaid after it has become due and payable the person from whom it is due and payable shall pay interest on the amount unpaid from the day it became due and payable until it is paid at the rate fixed by the terms of allotment of the share or in the notice of the call or, if no rate is fixed, at the appropriate rate (as defined by the Act) but the directors may waive payment of the interest wholly or in part.

16. An amount payable in respect of a share on allotment or at any fixed date, whether in respect of nominal value or premium or as an instalment of a call, shall be deemed to be a call and if it is not paid the provisions of the articles shall apply as if that amount had become due and payable by virtue of a call.

17. Subject to the terms of allotment, the directors may make arrangements on the issue of shares for a difference between the holders in the amounts and times of payment of calls on their shares.

18. If a call remains unpaid after it has become due and payable the directors may give to the person from whom it is due not less than fourteen clear days' notice requiring payment of the amount unpaid together with any interest which may have accrued. The notice shall name the place where payment is to be made and shall state that if the notice is not complied with the shares in respect of which the call was made will be liable to be forfeited.

19. If the notice is not complied with any share in respect of which it was given may, before the payment required by the notice has been made, be forfeited by a resolution of the directors and the forfeiture shall include all dividends or other moneys payable in respect of the forfeited shares and not paid before the forfeiture.

20. Subject to the provisions of the Act, a forfeited share may be sold, re-allotted or otherwise disposed of on such terms and in such manner as the directors determine either to the person who was before the forfeiture the holder or to any other person and at any time before sale, re-allotment or other disposition, the forfeiture may be cancelled on such terms as the directors think fit. Where for the purposes of its disposal a forfeited share is to be transferred to any person the directors may authorise some person to execute an instrument of transfer of the share to that person.

21. A person any of whose shares have been forfeited shall cease to be a member in respect of them and shall surrender to the company for cancellation the certificate for the shares forfeited but shall remain liable to the company for all moneys which at the date of forfeiture were presently payable by him to the company in respect of those shares with interest at the rate at which interest was payable on those moneys before the forfeiture or, if no interest was so payable, at the appropriate rate (as defined in the Act) from the date of forfeiture until payment but the directors may waive payment wholly or in part or enforce payment without any allowance for the value of the shares at the time of forfeiture or for any consideration received on their disposal.

22. A statutory declaration by a director or the secretary that a share has been forfeited on a specified date shall be conclusive evidence of the facts stated in it as against all persons claiming to be entitled to the share and the declaration shall (subject to the execution of an instrument of transfer if necessary) constitute a good title to the share and the person to whom the share is disposed of shall not be bound to see to the application of the consideration, if any, nor shall his title to the share be affected by any irregularity in or invalidity of the proceedings in reference to the forfeiture or disposal of the share.

TRANSFER OF SHARES

23. The instrument of transfer of a share may be in any usual form or in any other form which the directors may approve and shall be executed by or on behalf of the transferor and, unless the share is fully paid, by or on behalf of the transferee.

24. The directors may refuse to register the transfer of a share which is not fully paid to a person of whom they do not approve and they may refuse to register the transfer of a share on which the company has a lien. They may also refuse to register a transfer unless—

   (a)   it is lodged at the office or at such other place as the directors may appoint and is accompanied by the certificate for the shares to which it relates and such other evidence as the directors may reasonably require to show the right of the transferor to make the transfer;

   (b)   it is in respect of only one class of shares; and

   (c)   it is in favour of not more than four transferees.

25. If the directors refuse to register a transfer of a share, they shall within two months after the date on which the transfer was lodged with the company send to the transferee notice of the refusal.

26. The registration of transfers of shares or of transfers of any class of shares may be suspended at such times and for such periods (not exceeding thirty days in any year) as the directors may determine.

27. No fee shall be charged for the registration of any instrument of transfer or other document relating to or affecting the title to any share.

28. The company shall be entitled to retain any instrument of transfer which is registered, but any instrument of transfer which the directors refuse to register shall be returned to the person lodging it when notice of the refusal is given.

TRANSMISSION OF SHARES

29. If a member dies the survivor or survivors where he was a joint holder, and his personal representatives where he was a sole holder or the only survivor of joint holders, shall be the only persons recognised by the company as having any title to his interest; but nothing herein contained shall release the estate of a deceased member from any liability in respect of any share which had been jointly held by him.

30. A person becoming entitled to a share in consequence of the death or bankruptcy of a member may, upon such evidence being produced as the directors may properly require, elect either to become the holder of the share or to have some person nominated by him registered as the transferee. If he elects to become the holder he shall give notice to the company to that effect. If he elects to have another person registered he shall execute an instrument of transfer of the share to that person. All the articles relating to the transfer of shares shall apply to the notice or instrument of transfer as if it were an instrument of transfer executed by the member and the death or bankruptcy of the member had not occurred.

31. A person becoming entitled to a share in consequence of the death or bankruptcy of a member shall have the rights to which he would be entitled if he were the holder of the share, except that he shall not, before being registered as the holder of the share, be entitled in respect of it to attend or vote at any meeting of the company or at any separate meeting of the holders of any class of shares in the company.

ALTERATION OF SHARE CAPITAL

32. The company may by ordinary resolution—
- (a) increase its share capital by new shares of such amount as the resolution prescribes;
- (b) consolidate and divide all or any of its share capital into shares of larger amount than its existing shares;
- (c) subject to the provisions of the Act, sub-divide its shares, or any of them, into shares of smaller amount and the resolution may determine that, as between the shares resulting from the sub-division, any of them may have any preference or advantage as compared with the others; and
- (d) cancel shares which, at the date of the passing of the resolution, have not been taken or agreed to be taken by any person and diminish the amount of its share capital by the amount of the shares so cancelled.

33. Whenever as a result of a consolidation of shares any members would become entitled to fractions of a share, the directors may, on behalf of those members, sell the shares representing the fractions for the best price reasonably obtainable to any person (including, subject to the provisions of the Act, the company) and distribute the net proceeds of sale in due proportion among those members, and the directors may authorise some person to execute an instrument of transfer of the shares to, or in accordance with the directions of, the purchaser. The transferee shall not be bound to see to the application of the purchase money nor shall his title to the shares be affected by any irregularity in or invalidity of the proceedings in reference to the sale.

34. Subject to the provisions of the Act, the company may by special resolution reduce its share capital, any capital redemption reserve and any share premium account in any way.

PURCHASE OF OWN SHARES

35. Subject to the provisions of the Act, the company may purchase its own shares (including any redeemable shares) and, if it is a private company, make a payment in respect of the redemption or purchase of its own shares otherwise than out of distributable profits of the company or the proceeds of a fresh issue of shares.

GENERAL MEETINGS

36. All general meetings other than annual general meetings shall be called extraordinary general meetings.

NOTES

Revoked by the Companies (Tables A to F) (Amendment) Regulations 2007, SI 2007/2541, reg 4, as from 1 October 2007.

37. The directors may call general meetings and, on the requisition of members pursuant to the provisions of the Act, shall forthwith proceed to convene [a] general meeting [in accordance with the provisions of the Act]. If there are not within the United Kingdom sufficient directors to call a general meeting, any director or any member of the company may call a general meeting.

NOTES

Words in square brackets substituted for the original words "an extraordinary" and "for a date not later than eight weeks after receipt of the requisition" respectively, by the Companies (Tables A to F) (Amendment) Regulations 2007, SI 2007/2541, reg 5, as from 1 October 2007.

NOTICE OF GENERAL MEETINGS

38. *An annual general meeting and an extraordinary general meeting called for the passing of a special resolution or a resolution appointing a person as a director shall be called by at least twenty-one clear days' notice. All other extraordinary* general meetings shall be called by at least fourteen clear days' notice but a general meeting may be called by shorter notice if it is so agreed—

    (a)   *in the case of an annual general meeting, by all the members entitled to attend and vote thereat; and*

    (b)   in the case of any other meeting by a majority in number of the members having a right to attend and vote being a majority together holding not less than ninety-*five* per cent in nominal value of the shares giving that right.

The notice shall specify the time and place of the meeting and the general nature of the business to be transacted *and, in the case of an annual general meeting, shall specify the meeting as such.*

Subject to the provisions of the articles and to any restrictions imposed on any shares, the notice shall be given to all the members, to all persons entitled to a share in consequence of the death or bankruptcy of a member and to the directors and auditors.

NOTES

The Companies (Tables A to F) (Amendment) Regulations 2007, SI 2007/2541, regs 8, 9, provide that the following amendments apply (as from 1 October 2007) in so far as this regulation relates to private companies limited by shares—

    (i)   Omit the words "An annual general meeting and an extraordinary general meeting called for the passing of a special resolution or a resolution appointing a person as a director shall be called by at least twenty-one clear days' notice. All other extraordinary".

    (ii)   Omit paragraph (a).

    (iii) In paragraph (b), omit the words "in the case of any other meeting" and "-five".

    (iv) Omit the words "and, in the case of an annual general meeting, shall specify the meeting as such".

Regulations 19, 20 of the 2007 Regulations further provide that the following amendments apply (as from 1 October 2007) in so far as this regulation relates to public companies limited by shares—

    (i)   After the words "annual general meeting" omit the words "and an extraordinary general meeting called for the passing of a special resolution or a resolution appointing a person as a director".

    (ii)   After the words "All other" omit the word "extraordinary".

39. The accidental omission to give notice of a meeting to, or the non-receipt of notice of a meeting by, any person entitled to receive notice shall not invalidate the proceedings at that meeting.

PROCEEDINGS AT GENERAL MEETINGS

40. No business shall be transacted at any meeting unless a quorum is present. Two persons entitled to vote upon the business to be transacted, each being a member or a proxy for a member or a duly authorised representative of a corporation, shall be a quorum.

NOTES

The Companies (Tables A to F) (Amendment) Regulations 2007, SI 2007/2541, regs 8, 10, provide that the following amendment applies (as from 1 October 2007) in so far as this regulation relates to private companies limited by shares—

At the beginning of the second sentence insert the words "Save in the case of a company with a single member".

41. If such a quorum is not present within half an hour from the time appointed for the meeting, or if during a meeting such a quorum ceases to be present, the meeting shall stand adjourned to the same day in the next week at the same time and place or [to] such time and place as the directors may determine.

NOTES

Word in square brackets inserted by the Companies (Tables A to F) (Amendment) Regulations 1985, SI 1985/1052, reg 2, as from 1 August 1985.

42. The chairman, if any, of the board of directors or in his absence some other director nominated by the directors shall preside as chairman of the meeting, but if neither the chairman nor such other director (if any) be present within fifteen minutes after the time appointed for holding the meeting and willing to act, the directors present shall elect one of their number to be chairman and, if there is only one director present and willing to act, he shall be chairman.

43. If no director is willing to act as chairman, or if no director is present within fifteen minutes after the time appointed for holding the meeting, the members present and entitled to vote shall choose one of their number to be chairman.

44. A director shall, notwithstanding that he is not a member, be entitled to attend and speak at any general meeting and at any separate meeting of the holders of any class of shares in the company.

45. The chairman may, with the consent of a meeting at which a quorum is present (and shall if so directed by the meeting), adjourn the meeting from time to time and from place to place, but no business shall be transacted at an adjourned meeting other than business which might properly have been transacted at the meeting had the adjournment not taken place. When a meeting is adjourned for fourteen days or more, at least seven clear days' notice shall be given specifying the time and place of the adjourned meeting and the general nature of the business to be transacted. Otherwise it shall not be necessary to give any such notice.

46. A resolution put to the vote of a meeting shall be decided on a show of hands unless before, or on the declaration of the result of, the show of hands a poll is duly demanded. Subject to the provisions of the Act, a poll may be demanded—
- (a) by the chairman; or
- (b) by at least two members having the right to vote at the meeting; or
- (c) by a member or members representing not less than one-tenth of the total voting rights of all the members having the right to vote at the meeting; or
- (d) by a member or members holding shares conferring a right to vote at the meeting being shares on which an aggregate sum has been paid up equal to not less than one-tenth of the total sum paid up on all the shares conferring that right;

and a demand by a person as proxy for a member shall be the same as a demand by the member.

47. Unless a poll is duly demanded a declaration by the chairman that a resolution has been carried or carried unanimously, or by a particular majority, or lost, or not carried by a particular majority and an entry to that effect in the minutes of the meeting shall be conclusive evidence of the fact without proof of the number or proportion of the votes recorded in favour of or against the resolution.

48. The demand for a poll may, before the poll is taken, be withdrawn but only with the consent of the chairman and a demand so withdrawn shall not be taken to have invalidated the result of a show of hands declared before the demand was made.

49. A poll shall be taken as the chairman directs and he may appoint scrutineers (who need not be members) and fix a time and place for declaring the result of the poll. The result of the poll shall be deemed to be the resolution of the meeting at which the poll was demanded.

50. *In the case of an equality of votes, whether on a show of hands or on a poll, the chairman shall be entitled to a casting vote in addition to any other vote he may have.*

NOTES

Revoked by the Companies (Tables A to F) (Amendment) (No 2) Regulations 2007, SI 2007/2826, reg 3, as from 1 October 2007.

51. A poll demanded on the election of a chairman or on a question of adjournment shall be taken forthwith. A poll demanded on any other question shall be taken either forthwith or at such time and place as the chairman directs not being more than thirty days after the poll is demanded. The demand for a poll shall not prevent the continuance of a meeting for the transaction of any business other than the question on which the poll was demanded. If a poll is demanded before the declaration of the result of a show of hands and the demand is duly withdrawn, the meeting shall continue as if the demand had not been made.

52. No notice need be given of a poll not taken forthwith if the time and place at which it is to be taken are announced at the meeting at which it is demanded. In any other case at least seven clear days' notice shall be given specifying the time and place at which the poll is to be taken.

53. *A resolution in writing executed by or on behalf of each member who would have been entitled to vote upon it if it had been proposed at a general meeting at which he was present shall be as effectual as if it had been passed at a general meeting duly convened and held and may consist of several instruments in the like form each executed by or on behalf of one or more members.*

NOTES

Revoked by the Companies (Tables A to F) (Amendment) Regulations 2007, SI 2007/2541, reg 6, as from 1 October 2007.

VOTES OF MEMBERS

54. Subject to any rights or restrictions attached to any shares, on a show of hands every member who (being an individual) is present in person [or by proxy] or (being a corporation) is present by a duly authorised representative [or by proxy], [unless the proxy (in either case) or the representative is] himself a member entitled to vote, shall have one vote and on a poll every member shall have one vote for every share of which he is the holder.

NOTES

Words in first and second pairs of square brackets inserted, and words in third pair of square brackets substituted for the original words "not being", by the Companies (Tables A to F) (Amendment) (No 2) Regulations 2007, SI 2007/2826, reg 4, as from 1 October 2007.

55. In the case of joint holders the vote of the senior who tenders a vote, whether in person or by proxy, shall be accepted to the exclusion of the votes of the other joint holders; and seniority shall be determined by the order in which the names of the holders stand in the register of members.

56. A member in respect of whom an order has been made by any court having jurisdiction (whether in the United Kingdom or elsewhere) in matters concerning mental disorder may vote, whether on a show of hands or on a poll, by his receiver, curator bonis or other person authorised in that behalf appointed by that court, and any such receiver, curator bonis or other person may, on a poll, vote by proxy. Evidence to the satisfaction of the directors of the authority of the person claiming to exercise the right to vote shall be deposited at the office, or at such other place as is specified in accordance with the articles for the deposit of instruments of proxy, not less than 48 hours before the time appointed for holding the meeting or adjourned meeting at which the right to vote is to be exercised and in default the right to vote shall not be exercisable.

57. No member shall vote at any general meeting or at any separate meeting of the holders of any class of shares in the company, either in person or by proxy, in respect of any share held by him unless all moneys presently payable by him in respect of that share have been paid.

58. No objection shall be raised to the qualification of any voter except at the meeting or adjourned meeting at which the vote objected to is tendered, and every vote not disallowed at the meeting shall be valid. Any objection made in due time shall be referred to the chairman whose decision shall be final and conclusive.

59. On a poll votes may be given either personally or by proxy. A member may appoint more than one proxy to attend on the same occasion.

60. [The appointment of] a proxy shall be *in writing* executed by or on behalf of the appointor and shall be in the following form (or in a form as near thereto as circumstances allow or in any other form which is usual or which the directors may approve)—

". . . . . PLC/Limited

I/We, ... of . . . .

being a member/members of the above-named company,

hereby appoint . . . . of . . . . ,

or failing him, ... of . . . . ,

as my/our proxy to vote in my/our name[s] and on my/our behalf at the *annual/extraordinary* general meeting of the company, to be held on

. . . . 19. . . . . , and at any adjournment thereof.

Signed on . . . . 19. . . . . "

NOTES

Words in square brackets substituted for the original words "An instrument appointing", and words "in writing" in italics revoked, by the Companies Act 1985 (Electronic Communications) Order 2000, SI 2000/3373, art 32(1), Sch 1, para 2, as from 22 December 2000.

The Companies (Tables A to F) (Amendment) Regulations 2007, SI 2007/2541, regs 8, 11, provide that the following amendment applies (as from 1 October 2007) in so far as this regulation relates to private companies limited by shares—

After the words "our behalf at the" omit the words "annual/extraordinary".

Regulations 19, 21 of the 2007 Regulations further provide that the following amendment applies (as from 1 October 2007) in so far as this regulation relates to public companies limited by shares—

After the words "our behalf at the annual/" omit the word "extraordinary" and insert the words "any other".

61. Where it is desired to afford members an opportunity of instructing the proxy how he shall act the [appointment of] a proxy shall be in the following form (or in a form as near thereto as circumstances allow or in any other form which is usual or which the directors may approve)—

". . . . . PLC/Limited

I/We, ... of . . . .

being a member/members of the above-named company,

hereby appoint . . . . of . . . . ,

or failing him, ... of . . . . ,

as my/our proxy to vote in my/our name[s] and on my/our behalf at the *annual/extraordinary* general meeting of the company, to be held on

. . . . 19. . . . ., and at any adjournment thereof.

This form is to be used in respect of the resolutions mentioned below as follows:

Resolution No 1 *for *against

Resolution No 2 *for *against.

* Strike out whichever is not desired.

Unless otherwise instructed, the proxy may vote as he thinks fit or abstain from voting.

Signed this . . . . day of . . . . 19. . . . . ”

NOTES

Words in square brackets substituted for the original words "instrument appointing" by the Companies Act 1985 (Electronic Communications) Order 2000, SI 2000/3373, art 32(1), Sch 1, para 3, as from 22 December 2000.

The Companies (Tables A to F) (Amendment) Regulations 2007, SI 2007/2541, regs 8, 12, provide that the following amendment applies (as from 1 October 2007) in so far as this regulation relates to private companies limited by shares—
After the words "our behalf at the" omit the words "annual/extraordinary".

Regulations 19, 22 of the 2007 Regulations further provide that the following amendment applies (as from 1 October 2007) in so far as this regulation relates to public companies limited by shares—
After the words "our behalf at the annual/" omit the word "extraordinary" and insert the words "any other".

62. [The appointment of] a proxy and any authority under which it is executed or a copy of such authority certified notarially or in some other way approved by the directors may—

(a) [in the case of an instrument in writing] be deposited at the office or at such other place within the United Kingdom as is specified in the notice convening the meeting or in any instrument of proxy sent out by the company in relation to the meeting not less than 48 hours before the time for holding the meeting or adjourned meeting at which the person named in the instrument proposes to vote; or

[(aa) in the case of an appointment contained in an electronic communication, where an address has been specified for the purpose of receiving electronic communications—
    (i) in the notice convening the meeting, or
    (ii) in any instrument of proxy sent out by the company in relation to the meeting, or
    (iii) in any invitation contained in an electronic communication to appoint a proxy issued by the company in relation to the meeting,
be received at such address not less than 48 hours before the time for holding the meeting or adjourned meeting at which the person named in the appointment proposes to vote;]

(b) in the case of a poll taken more than 48 hours after it is demanded, be deposited [or received] as aforesaid after the poll has been demanded and not less than 24 hours before the time appointed for the taking of the poll; or

(c) where the poll is not taken forthwith but is taken not more than 48 hours after it was demanded, be delivered at the meeting at which the poll was demanded to the chairman or to the secretary or to any director;

[and an appointment of proxy which is not deposited, delivered or received] in a manner so permitted shall be invalid.

[In this regulation and the next, "address", in relation to electronic communications, includes any number or address used for the purposes of such communications.]

NOTES

Words in first pair of square brackets substituted for the original words "The instrument appointing", words in fifth pair of square brackets substituted for the original words "and an instrument of proxy which is not deposited or delivered", and other words in square brackets inserted, by the Companies Act 1985 (Electronic Communications) Order 2000, SI 2000/3373, art 32(1), Sch 1, para 4, as from 22 December 2000.

63. A vote given or poll demanded by proxy or by the duly authorised representative of a corporation shall be valid notwithstanding the previous determination of the authority of the person voting or demanding a poll unless notice of the determination was received by the company at the office or at such other place at which the instrument of proxy was duly deposited [or, where the appointment of the proxy was contained in an electronic communication, at the address at which such appointment was duly received] before the commencement of the meeting or adjourned meeting at which the vote is given or the poll demanded or (in the case of a poll taken otherwise than on the same day as the meeting or adjourned meeting) the time appointed for taking the poll.

NOTES

Words in square brackets inserted by the Companies Act 1985 (Electronic Communications) Order 2000, SI 2000/3373, art 32(1), Sch 1, para 5, as from 22 December 2000.

NUMBER OF DIRECTORS

64. Unless otherwise determined by ordinary resolution, the number of directors (other than alternate directors) shall not be subject to any maximum but shall be not less than two.

ALTERNATE DIRECTORS

65. Any director (other than an alternate director) may appoint any other director, or any other person approved by resolution of the directors and willing to act, to be an alternate director and may remove from office an alternate director so appointed by him.

66. An alternate director shall be entitled to receive notice of all meetings of directors and of all meetings of committees of directors of which his appointor is a member, to attend and vote at any such meeting at which the director appointing him is not personally present, and generally to perform all the functions of his appointor as a director in his absence but shall not be entitled to receive any remuneration from the company for his services as an alternate director. But it shall not be necessary to give notice of such a meeting to an alternate director who is absent from the United Kingdom.

67. An alternate director shall cease to be an alternate director if his appointor ceases to be a director; but, if a director retires by rotation or otherwise but is reappointed or deemed to have been reappointed at the meeting at which he retires, any appointment of an alternate director made by him which was in force immediately prior to his retirement shall continue after his reappointment.

68. Any appointment or removal of an alternate director shall be by notice to the company signed by the director making or revoking the appointment or in any other manner approved by the directors.

69. Save as otherwise provided in the articles, an alternate director shall be deemed for all purposes to be a director and shall alone be responsible for his own acts and defaults and he shall not be deemed to be the agent of the director appointing him.

POWERS OF DIRECTORS

70. Subject to the provisions of the Act, the memorandum and the articles and to any directions given by special resolution, the business of the company shall be managed by the directors who may exercise all the powers of the company. No alteration of the memorandum or articles and no such direction shall invalidate any prior act of the directors which would have been valid if that alteration had not been made or that direction had not been given. The powers given by this regulation shall not be limited by any special power given to the directors by the articles and a meeting of directors at which a quorum is present may exercise all powers exercisable by the directors.

71. The directors may, by power of attorney or otherwise, appoint any person to be the agent of the company for such purposes and on such conditions as they determine, including authority for the agent to delegate all or any of his powers.

DELEGATION OF DIRECTORS' POWERS

72. The directors may delegate any of their powers to any committee consisting of one or more directors. They may also delegate to any managing director or any director holding any other executive office such of their powers as they consider desirable to be exercised by him. Any such delegation may be made subject to any conditions the directors may impose, and either collaterally with or to the exclusion of their own powers and may be revoked or altered. Subject to any such conditions, the proceedings of a committee with two or more members shall be governed by the articles regulating the proceedings of directors so far as they are capable of applying.

APPOINTMENT AND RETIREMENT OF DIRECTORS

73. *At the first annual general meeting all the directors shall retire from office, and at every subsequent annual general meeting one-third of the directors who are subject to retirement by rotation or, if their number is not three or a multiple of three, the number nearest to one-third shall retire from office; but, if there is only one director who is subject to retirement by rotation, he shall retire.*

NOTES

The Companies (Tables A to F) (Amendment) Regulations 2007, SI 2007/2541, regs 8, 13, provide that this regulation is revoked (as from 1 October 2007) in so far as it relates to private companies limited by shares.

74. *Subject to the provisions of the Act, the directors to retire by rotation shall be those who have been longest in office since their last appointment or reappointment, but as between persons who became or were last reappointed directors on the same day those to retire shall (unless they otherwise agree among themselves) be determined by lot.*

NOTES

The Companies (Tables A to F) (Amendment) Regulations 2007, SI 2007/2541, regs 8, 13, provide that this regulation is revoked (as from 1 October 2007) in so far as it relates to private companies limited by shares.

75. *If the company, at the meeting at which a director retires by rotation, does not fill the vacancy the retiring director shall, if willing to act, be deemed to have been reappointed unless at the meeting it is resolved not to fill the vacancy or unless a resolution for the reappointment of the director is put to the meeting and lost.*

NOTES

The Companies (Tables A to F) (Amendment) Regulations 2007, SI 2007/2541, regs 8, 13, provide that this regulation is revoked (as from 1 October 2007) in so far as it relates to private companies limited by shares.

76. No person *other than a director retiring by rotation* shall be appointed or reappointed a director at any general meeting unless—

    (a)   he is recommended by the directors; or

    (b)   not less than fourteen nor more than thirty-five clear days before the date appointed for the meeting, notice executed by a member qualified to vote at the meeting has been given to the company of the intention to propose that person for appointment or reappointment stating the particulars which would, if he were so appointed or reappointed, be required to be included in the company's register of directors together with notice executed by that person of his willingness to be appointed or reappointed.

NOTES

The Companies (Tables A to F) (Amendment) Regulations 2007, SI 2007/2541, regs 8, 14, provide that the following amendment applies (as from 1 October 2007) in so far as this Regulation relates to private companies limited by shares—
After the words "No person" omit the words "other than a director retiring by rotation".

77. Not less than seven nor more than twenty-eight clear days before the date appointed for holding a general meeting notice shall be given to all who are entitled to receive notice of the meeting of any person *(other than a director retiring by rotation at the meeting)* who is recommended by the directors for appointment or reappointment as a director at the meeting or in respect of whom notice has been duly given to the company of the intention to propose him at the meeting for appointment or reappointment as a director. The notice shall give the particulars of that person which would, if he were so appointed or reappointed, be required to be included in the company's register of directors.

NOTES

The Companies (Tables A to F) (Amendment) Regulations 2007, SI 2007/2541, regs 8, 15, provide that the following amendment applies (as from 1 October 2007) in so far as this Regulation relates to private companies limited by shares—
After the words "meeting of any person" omit the words "(other than a director retiring by rotation at the meeting)".

78. *Subject as aforesaid,* the company may by ordinary resolution appoint a person who is willing to act to be a director either to fill a vacancy or as an additional director and may also determine the rotation in which any additional directors are to retire.

NOTES

The Companies (Tables A to F) (Amendment) Regulations 2007, SI 2007/2541, regs 8, 16, provide that the following amendment applies (as from 1 October 2007) in so far as this Regulation relates to private companies limited by shares—
Omit the words "Subject as aforesaid,".

79. The directors may appoint a person who is willing to act to be a director, either to fill a vacancy or as an additional director, provided that the appointment does not cause the number of directors to exceed any number fixed by or in accordance with the articles as the maximum number of directors. *A director so appointed shall hold office only until the next following annual general meeting and shall not be taken into account in determining the directors who are to retire by rotation at the meeting. If not reappointed at such annual general meeting, he shall vacate office at the conclusion thereof.*

NOTES

The Companies (Tables A to F) (Amendment) Regulations 2007, SI 2007/2541, regs 8, 17, provide that the following amendment applies (as from 1 October 2007) in so far as this Regulation relates to private companies limited by shares—
Omit the second and third sentences.

80. *Subject as aforesaid, a director who retires at an annual general meeting may, if willing to act, be reappointed. If he is not reappointed, he shall retain office until the meeting appoints someone in his place, or if it does not do so, until the end of the meeting.*

NOTES

The Companies (Tables A to F) (Amendment) Regulations 2007, SI 2007/2541, regs 8, 18, provide that this regulation is revoked (as from 1 October 2007) in so far as it relates to private companies limited by shares.

DISQUALIFICATION AND REMOVAL OF DIRECTORS

81. The office of a director shall be vacated if—

    (a)   he ceases to be a director by virtue of any provision of the Act or he becomes prohibited by law from being a director; or

    (b)   he becomes bankrupt or makes any arrangement or composition with his creditors generally; or

    (c)   he is, or may be, suffering from mental disorder and either—

        (i)   he is admitted to hospital in pursuance of an application for admission for treatment under the Mental Health Act 1983 or, in Scotland, an application for admission under the Mental Health (Scotland) Act 1960, or

        (ii)   an order is made by a court having jurisdiction (whether in the United Kingdom or elsewhere) in matters concerning mental disorder for his detention or for the appointment of a receiver, curator bonis or other person to exercise powers with respect to his property or affairs; or

    (d)   he resigns his office by notice to the company; or

    (e)   he shall for more than six consecutive months have been absent without permission of the directors from meetings of directors held during that period and the directors resolve that his office be vacated.

REMUNERATION OF DIRECTORS

82. The directors shall be entitled to such remuneration as the company may by ordinary resolution determine and, unless the resolution provides otherwise, the remuneration shall be deemed to accrue from day to day.

DIRECTORS' EXPENSES

83. The directors may be paid all travelling, hotel, and other expenses properly incurred by them in connection with their attendance at meetings of directors or committees of directors or general meetings or separate meetings of the holders of any class of shares or of debentures of the company or otherwise in connection with the discharge of their duties.

DIRECTORS' APPOINTMENTS AND INTERESTS

84. Subject to the provisions of the Act, the directors may appoint one or more of their number to the office of managing director or to any other executive office under the company and may enter into an agreement or arrangement with any director for his employment by the company or for the provision by him of any services outside the scope of the ordinary duties of a director. Any such appointment, agreement or arrangement may be made upon such terms as the directors determine and they may remunerate any such director for his services as they think fit. Any appointment of a director to an executive office shall terminate if he ceases to be a director but without prejudice to any claim to damages for breach of the contract of service between the director and the company. A managing director and a director holding any other executive office shall not be subject to retirement by rotation.

85. Subject to the provisions of the Act, and provided that he has disclosed to the directors the nature and extent of any material interest of his, a director notwithstanding his office—

    (a)   may be a party to, or otherwise interested in, any transaction or arrangement with the company or in which the company is otherwise interested;

    (b)   may be a director or other officer of, or employed by, or a party to any transaction or arrangement with, or otherwise interested in, any body corporate promoted by the company or in which the company is otherwise interested; and

    (c)   shall not, by reason of his office, be accountable to the company for any benefit which he derives from any such office or employment or from any such transaction or arrangement or from any interest in any such body corporate and no such transaction or arrangement shall be liable to be avoided on the ground of any such interest or benefit.

86. For the purposes of regulation 85—

    (a)   a general notice given to the directors that a director is to be regarded as having an interest of the nature and extent specified in the notice in any transaction or arrangement in which a specified person or class of persons is interested shall be deemed to be a disclosure that the director has an interest in any such transaction of the nature and extent so specified; and

    (b)   an interest of which a director has no knowledge and of which it is unreasonable to expect him to have knowledge shall not be treated as an interest of his.

DIRECTORS' GRATUITIES AND PENSIONS

87. The directors may provide benefits, whether by the payment of gratuities or pensions or by insurance or otherwise, for any director who has held but no longer holds any executive office or employment with the company or with any body corporate which is or has been a subsidiary of the company or a predecessor in business of the company or of any such subsidiary, and for any member of his family (including a spouse and a former spouse) or any person who is or was dependent on him, and may (as well before as after he ceases to hold such office or employment) contribute to any fund and pay premiums for the purchase or provision of any such benefit.

PROCEEDINGS OF DIRECTORS

88. Subject to the provisions of the articles, the directors may regulate their proceedings as they think fit. A director may, and the secretary at the request of a director shall, call a meeting of the directors. It shall not be necessary to give notice of a meeting to a director who is absent from the United Kingdom. Questions arising at a meeting shall be decided by a majority of votes. In the case of an equality of votes, the chairman shall have a second or casting vote. A director who is also an alternate director shall be entitled in the absence of his appointor to a separate vote on behalf of his appointor in addition to his own vote.

89. The quorum for the transaction of the business of the directors may be fixed by the directors and unless so fixed at any other number shall be two. A person who holds office only as an alternate director shall, if his appointor is not present, be counted in the quorum.

90. The continuing directors or a sole continuing director may act notwithstanding any vacancies in their number, but, if the number of directors is less than the number fixed as the quorum, the continuing directors or director may act only for the purpose of filling vacancies or of calling a general meeting.

91. The directors may appoint one of their number to be the chairman of the board of directors and may at any time remove him from that office. Unless he is unwilling to do so, the director so appointed shall preside at every meeting of directors at which he is present. But if there is no director holding that office, or if the director holding it is unwilling to preside or is not present within five minutes after the time appointed for the meeting, the directors present may appoint one of their number to be chairman of the meeting.

92. All acts done by a meeting of directors, or of a committee of directors, or by a person acting as a director shall, notwithstanding that it be afterwards discovered that there was a defect in the appointment of any director or that any of them were disqualified from holding office, or had vacated office, or were not entitled to vote, be as valid as if every such person had been duly appointed and was qualified and had continued to be a director and had been entitled to vote.

93. A resolution in writing signed by all the directors entitled to receive notice of a meeting of directors or of a committee of directors shall be as valid and effectual as if it had been passed at a meeting of directors or (as the case may be) a committee of directors duly convened and held and may consist of several documents in the like form each signed by one or more directors; but a resolution signed by an alternate director need not also be signed by his appointor and, if it is signed by a director who has appointed an alternate director, it need not be signed by the alternate director in that capacity.

94. Save as otherwise provided by the articles, a director shall not vote at a meeting of directors or of a committee of directors on any resolution concerning a matter in which he has, directly or indirectly, an interest or duty which is material and which conflicts or may conflict with the interests of the company unless his interest or duty arises only because the case falls within one or more of the following paragraphs—

(a) the resolution relates to the giving to him of a guarantee, security, or indemnity in respect of money lent to, or an obligation incurred by him for the benefit of, the company or any of its subsidiaries;

(b) the resolution relates to the giving to a third party of a guarantee, security, or indemnity in respect of an obligation of the company or any of its subsidiaries for which the director has assumed responsibility in whole or part and whether alone or jointly with others under a guarantee or indemnity or by the giving of security;

(c) his interest arises by virtue of his subscribing or agreeing to subscribe for any shares, debentures or other securities of the company or any of its subsidiaries, or by virtue of his being, or intending to become, a participant in the underwriting or sub-underwriting of an offer of any such shares, debentures, or other securities by the company or any of its subsidiaries for subscription, purchase or exchange;

(d) the resolution relates in any way to a retirement benefits scheme which has been approved, or is conditional upon approval, by the Board of Inland Revenue for taxation purposes.

For the purposes of this regulation, an interest of a person who is, for any purpose of the Act (excluding any statutory modification thereof not in force when this regulation becomes binding on the company), connected with a director shall be treated as an interest of the director and, in relation to an alternate director, an interest of his appointor shall be treated as an interest of the alternate director without prejudice to any interest which the alternate director has otherwise.

95. A director shall not be counted in the quorum present at a meeting in relation to a resolution on which he is not entitled to vote.

96. The company may by ordinary resolution suspend or relax to any extent, either generally or in respect of any particular matter, any provision of the articles prohibiting a director from voting at a meeting of directors or of a committee of directors.

97. Where proposals are under consideration concerning the appointment of two or more directors to offices or employments with the company or any body corporate in which the company is interested the proposals may be divided and considered in relation to each director separately and (provided he is not for another reason precluded from voting) each of the directors concerned shall be entitled to vote and be counted in the quorum in respect of each resolution except that concerning his own appointment.

98. If a question arises at a meeting of directors or of a committee of directors as to the right of a director to vote, the question may, before the conclusion of the meeting, be referred to the chairman of the meeting and his ruling in relation to any director other than himself shall be final and conclusive.

SECRETARY

99. Subject to the provisions of the Act, the secretary shall be appointed by the directors for such term, at such remuneration and upon such conditions as they may think fit; and any secretary so appointed may be removed by them.

MINUTES

100. The directors shall cause minutes to be made in books kept for the purpose—
     (a)   of all appointments of officers made by the directors; and
     (b)   of all proceedings at meetings of the company, of the holders of any class of shares in the company, and of the directors, and of committees of directors, including the names of the directors present at each such meeting.

THE SEAL

101. The seal shall only be used by the authority of the directors or of a committee of directors authorised by the directors. The directors may determine who shall sign any instrument to which the seal is affixed and unless otherwise so determined it shall be signed by a director and by the secretary or by a second director.

DIVIDENDS

102. Subject to the provisions of the Act, the company may by ordinary resolution declare dividends in accordance with the respective rights of the members, but no dividend shall exceed the amount recommended by the directors.

103. Subject to the provisions of the Act, the directors may pay interim dividends if it appears to them that they are justified by the profits of the company available for distribution. If the share capital is divided into different classes, the directors may pay interim dividends on shares which confer deferred or non-preferred rights with regard to dividend as well as on shares which confer preferential rights with regard to dividend, but no interim dividend shall be paid on shares carrying deferred or non-preferred rights if, at the time of payment, any preferential dividend is in arrear. The directors may also pay at intervals settled by them any dividend payable at a fixed rate if it appears to them that the profits available for distribution justify the payment. Provided the directors act in good faith they shall not incur any liability to the holders of shares conferring preferred rights for any loss they may suffer by the lawful payment of an interim dividend on any shares having deferred or non-preferred rights.

104. Except as otherwise provided by the rights attached to shares, all dividends shall be declared and paid according to the amounts paid up on the shares on which the dividend is paid. All dividends shall be apportioned and paid proportionately to the amounts paid up on the shares during any portion or portions of the period in respect of which the dividend is paid; but, if any share is issued on terms providing that it shall rank for dividend as from a particular date, that share shall rank for dividend accordingly.

105. A general meeting declaring a dividend may, upon the recommendation of the directors, direct that it shall be satisfied wholly or partly by the distribution of assets and, where any difficulty arises in regard to the distribution, the directors may settle the same and in particular may issue fractional certificates and fix the value for distribution of any assets and may determine that cash shall be paid to any member upon the footing of the value so fixed in order to adjust the rights of members and may vest any assets in trustees.

106. Any dividend or other moneys payable in respect of a share may be paid by cheque sent by post to the registered address of the person entitled or, if two or more persons are the holders of the share or are jointly entitled to it by reason of the death or bankruptcy of the holder, to the registered address of that one of those persons who is first named in the register of members or to such person and to such address as the person or persons entitled may in writing direct. Every cheque shall be made payable to the order of the person or persons entitled or to such other person as the person or persons entitled may in writing direct and payment of the cheque shall be a good discharge to the company. Any joint holder or other person jointly entitled to a share as aforesaid may give receipts for any dividend or other moneys payable in respect of the share.

107. No dividend or other moneys payable in respect of a share shall bear interest against the company unless otherwise provided by the rights attached to the share.

108. Any dividend which has remained unclaimed for twelve years from the date when it became due for payment shall, if the directors so resolve, be forfeited and cease to remain owing by the company.

ACCOUNTS

109. No member shall (as such) have any right of inspecting any accounting records or other book or document of the company except as conferred by statute or authorised by the directors or by ordinary resolution of the company.

CAPITALISATION OF PROFITS

110. The directors may with the authority of an ordinary resolution of the company—
(a)   subject as hereinafter provided, resolve to capitalise any undivided profits of the company not required for paying any preferential dividend (whether or not they are available for distribution) or any sum standing to the credit of the company's share premium account or capital redemption reserve;
(b)   appropriate the sum resolved to be capitalised to the members who would have been entitled to it if it were distributed by way of dividend and in the same proportions and apply such sum on their behalf either in or towards paying up the amounts, if any, for the time being unpaid on any shares held by them respectively, or in paying up in full unissued shares or debentures of the company of a nominal amount equal to that sum, and allot the shares or debentures credited as fully paid to those members, or as they may direct, in those proportions, or partly in one way and partly in the other: but the share premium account, the capital redemption reserve, and any profits which are not available for distribution may, for the purposes of this regulation, only be applied in paying up unissued shares to be allotted to members credited as fully paid;
(c)   make such provision by the issue of fractional certificates or by payment in cash or otherwise as they determine in the case of shares or debentures becoming distributable under this regulation in fractions; and
(d)   authorise any person to enter on behalf of all the members concerned into an agreement with the company providing for the allotment to them respectively, credited as fully paid, of any shares or debentures to which they are entitled upon such capitalisation, any agreement made under such authority being binding on all such members.

NOTICES

[**111.**   Any notice to be given to or by any person pursuant to the articles (other than a notice calling a meeting of the directors) shall be in writing or shall be given using electronic communications to an address for the time being notified for that purpose to the person giving the notice.

In this regulation, "address", in relation to electronic communications, includes any number or address used for the purposes of such communications.]

NOTES

Substituted by the Companies Act 1985 (Electronic Communications) Order 2000, SI 2000/3373, art 32(1), Sch 1, para 6, as from 22 December 2000. The original reg 111 read as follows—

"111. Any notice to be given to or by any person pursuant to the articles shall be in writing except that a notice calling a meeting of the directors need not be in writing.".

---

112. The company may give any notice to a member either personally or by sending it by post in a prepaid envelope addressed to the member at his registered address or by leaving it at that address [or by giving it using electronic communications to an address for the time being notified to the company by the member]. In the case of joint holders of a share, all notices shall be given to the joint holder whose name stands first in the register of members in respect of the joint holding and notice so given shall be sufficient notice to all the joint holders. A member whose registered address is not within the United Kingdom and who gives to the company an address within the United Kingdom at which notices may be given to him[, or an address to which notices may be sent using electronic communications,] shall be entitled to have notices given to him at that address, but otherwise no such member shall be entitled to receive any notice from the company.

[In this regulation and the next, "address", in relation to electronic communications, includes any number or address used for the purposes of such communications.]

NOTES

Words in square brackets inserted by the Companies Act 1985 (Electronic Communications) Order 2000, SI 2000/3373, art 32(1), Sch 1, para 7, as from 22 December 2000.

113. A member present, either in person or by proxy, at any meeting of the company or of the holders of any class of shares in the company shall be deemed to have received notice of the meeting and, where requisite, of the purposes for which it was called.

114. Every person who becomes entitled to a share shall be bound by any notice in respect of that share which, before his name is entered in the register of members, has been duly given to a person from whom he derives his title.

115. Proof that an envelope containing a notice was properly addressed, prepaid and posted shall be conclusive evidence that the notice was given. [Proof that a notice contained in an electronic communication was sent in accordance with guidance issued by the Institute of Chartered Secretaries and Administrators shall be conclusive evidence that the notice was given.] A notice shall, *unless the contrary is proved,* be deemed to be given at the expiration of 48 hours after the envelope containing it was posted [or, in the case of a notice contained in an electronic communication, at the expiration of 48 hours after the time it was sent].

NOTES

Words in square brackets inserted by the Companies Act 1985 (Electronic Communications) Order 2000, SI 2000/3373, art 32(1), Sch 1, para 8, as from 22 December 2000; words in italics revoked by the Companies (Tables A to F) (Amendment) Regulations 1985, SI 1985/1052, reg 2, as from 1 August 1985.

116. A notice may be given by the company to the persons entitled to a share in consequence of the death or bankruptcy of a member by sending or delivering it, in any manner authorised by the articles for the giving of notice to a member, addressed to them by name, or by the title of representatives of the deceased, or trustee of the bankrupt or by any like description at the address, if any, within the United Kingdom supplied for that purpose by the persons claiming to be so entitled. Until such an address has been supplied, a notice may be given in any manner in which it might have been given if the death or bankruptcy had not occurred.

WINDING UP

117. If the company is wound up, the liquidator may, with the sanction of [a special] resolution of the company and any other sanction required by the Act, divide among the members in specie the whole or any part of the assets of the company and may, for that purpose, value any assets and determine how the division shall be carried out as between the members or different classes of members. The liquidator may, with the like sanction, vest the whole or any part of the assets in trustees upon such trusts for the benefit of the members as he with the like sanction determines, but no member shall be compelled to accept any assets upon which there is a liability.

NOTES

Words in square brackets substituted for the original words "an extraordinary" by the Companies (Tables A to F) (Amendment) Regulations 2007, SI 2007/2541, reg 7, as from 1 October 2007.

INDEMNITY

118. Subject to the provisions of the Act but without prejudice to any indemnity to which a director may otherwise be entitled, every director or other officer or auditor of the company shall be indemnified out of the assets of the company against any liability incurred by him in defending any proceedings, whether civil or criminal, in which judgment is given in his favour or in which he is acquitted or in connection with any application in which relief is granted to him by the court from liability for negligence, default, breach of duty or breach of trust in relation to the affairs of the company.

Appendix 3:
Companies Act 1948, Table A

[A3]

NOTES

Table A was contained in the First Schedule to the Companies Act 1948.

Generally, the Table A which applies to any company is the Table A in force at the date of the company's registration, and if Table A is altered, the alteration does not affect a company registered before the alteration takes effect; see CA 1985, s 8(2), (3) and the introductory notes to the 1985 Table A at **[A2]**. Note that CA 1985, s 8 was repealed by CA 2006, but see further the note relating to SI 2008/2860 below.

Accordingly, Table A to the 1948 Act, which was specifically preserved by the Companies Consolidation (Consequential Provisions) Act 1985, s 31(8), is set out below both in its original form and in its form as amended at different dates. Note that the Companies Consolidation (Consequential Provisions) Act 1985 was repealed by the Companies Act 2006 (Consequential Amendments and Transitional Provisions) Order 2011, SI 2011/1265, art 2, as from 12 May 2011. Article 5 of the 2011 Order (at **[4.650]**) provides, inter alia, that the repeal of the 1985 Act does not affect the operation of any saving that remains capable of having effect in relation to the repeal of an enactment by that Act.

Part I of Table A applies (subject to the savings set out in CA 1980, s 88(4)) in relation to private companies limited by shares as it applies in relation to public companies so limited (CA 1980, Sch 3, para 36(1)).

Note that the Companies Act 2006 (Commencement No 8, Transitional Provisions and Savings) Order 2008, SI 2008/2860, Sch 2, para 1(1) (at **[2.91]**) provides that nothing in the Companies Act 2006 affects (a) the registration or re-registration of a company under the former Companies Acts, or the continued existence of a company by virtue of such registration or re-registration, or (b) the application in relation to an existing company of (i) Table B in the Joint Stock Companies Act 1856, (ii) Table A in any of the former Companies Acts, or (iii) the Companies (Tables A to F) Regulations 1985 or the Companies (Tables A to F) Regulations (Northern Ireland) 1986.

TABLE A

PART I

REGULATIONS FOR MANAGEMENT OF A COMPANY LIMITED BY SHARES, NOT BEING A PRIVATE COMPANY

Interpretation

1. In these regulations:—

"the Act" means the Companies Act, 1948.

"the seal" means the common seal of the company.

"secretary" means any person appointed to perform the duties of the secretary of the company.

"the United Kingdom" means Great Britain and Northern Ireland.

Expressions referring to writing shall, unless the contrary intention appears, be construed as including references to printing, lithography, photography, and other modes of representing or reproducing words in a visible form.

Unless the context otherwise requires, words or expressions contained in these regulations shall bear the same meaning as in the Act or any statutory modification thereof in force at the date at which these regulations become binding on the company.

Share Capital and Variation of Rights

2. Without prejudice to any special rights previously conferred on the holders of any existing shares or class of shares, any share in the company may be issued with such preferred, deferred or other special rights or such restrictions, whether in regard to dividend, voting, return of capital or otherwise as the company may from time to time by ordinary resolution determine.

3. Subject to the provisions of *section 58 of the Act*, *any preference shares* may, with the sanction of an ordinary resolution, be issued on the terms that they are, or at the option of the company are liable, to be redeemed on such terms and in such manner as the company before the issue of the shares may by special resolution determine.

NOTES

Reg 3: for the words in italics there are substituted the words "Part III of CA 1981, any shares" by CA 1981, Sch 3, in relation to any company registered on or after 3 December 1981.

4. If at any time the share capital is divided into different classes of shares, the rights attached to any class (*unless otherwise provided by the terms of issue of the shares of that class*) may, whether or not the company is being wound up, be varied with the consent in writing of the holders of three-fourths of the issued shares of that class, or with the sanction of an extraordinary resolution passed at a separate general meeting of the holders of the shares of the class. *To every such separate* *general meeting the provisions of these regulations relating to general meetings shall apply, but so that the necessary quorum shall be two persons at least holding or representing by proxy one-third of the issued shares of the class and that any holder of shares of the class present in person or by proxy may demand a poll.*

NOTES

Words in italics repealed by CA 1980, Sch 4, in relation to any company registered on or after 22 December 1980.

5. The rights conferred upon the holders of the shares of any class issued with preferred or other rights shall not, unless otherwise expressly provided by the terms of issue of the shares of that class, be deemed to be varied by the creation or issue of further shares ranking pari passu therewith.

6. The company may exercise the powers of paying commissions conferred by section 53 of the Act, provided that the rate per cent or amount of the commission paid or agreed to be paid shall be disclosed in the manner required by the said section and the rate of the commission shall not exceed the rate of 10 per cent of the price at which the shares in respect whereof the same is paid are issued or an amount equal to 10 per cent of such price (as the case may be). Such commission may be satisfied by the payment of cash or the allotment of fully or partly paid shares or partly in one way and partly in the other. The company may also on any issue of shares pay such brokerage as may be lawful.

7. Except as required by law, no person shall be recognised by the company as holding any share upon any trust, and the company shall not be bound by or be compelled in any way to recognise (even when having notice thereof) any equitable, contingent, future or partial interest in any share or any interest in any fractional part of a share or (except only as by these regulations or by law otherwise provided) any other rights in respect of any share except an absolute right to the entirety thereof in the registered holder.

8. Every person whose name is entered as a member in the register of members shall be entitled without payment to receive within two months after allotment or lodgment of transfer (or within such other period as the conditions of issue shall provide) one certificate for all his shares or several certificates each for one or more of his shares upon payment of 2s 6d for every certificate after the first or such less sum as the directors shall from time to time determine. Every certificate shall be under the seal [or under the official seal kept by the company by virtue of section 2 of the Stock Exchange (Completion of Bargains) Act 1976] and shall specify the shares to which it relates and the amount paid up thereon. Provided that in respect of a share or shares held jointly by several persons the company shall not be bound to issue more than one certificate, and delivery of a certificate for a share to one of several joint holders shall be sufficient delivery to all such holders.

NOTES

Reg 8: words in square brackets inserted by the Stock Exchange (Completion of Bargains) Act 1976, s 2(3), in relation to any company registered on or after 2 February 1979.

9. If a share certificate be defaced, lost or destroyed, it may be renewed on payment of a fee of 2s 6d or such less sum and on such terms (if any) as to evidence and indemnity and the payment of out-of-pocket expenses of the company of investigating evidence as the directors think fit.

10. *The company shall not give, whether directly or indirectly, and whether by means of a loan, guarantee, the provision of security or otherwise, any financial assistance for the purpose of or in connection with a purchase or subscription made or to be made by any person of or for any shares in the company or in its holding company nor shall the company make a loan for any purpose whatsoever on the security of its shares or those of its holding company, but nothing in this regulation shall prohibit transactions mentioned in the proviso to section 54(1) of the Act.*

NOTES

Reg 10: repealed by CA 1981, Sch 4, in relation to any company registered on or after 3 December 1981.

Lien

11. The company shall have a first and paramount lien on every share (not being a fully paid share) for all moneys (whether presently payable or not) called or payable at a fixed time in respect of that share, *and the company shall also have a first and paramount lien on all shares (other than fully paid shares) standing registered in the name of a single person for all moneys presently payable by him or his estate to the company*; but the directors may at any time declare any share to be wholly or in part exempt from the provisions of this regulation. The company's lien, if any, on a share shall extend to all dividends payable thereon.

NOTES

Words in italics repealed by CA 1980, Sch 4, in relation to any company registered on or after 22 December 1980.

12. The company may sell, in such manner as the directors think fit, any shares on which the company has a lien, but no sale shall be made unless a sum in respect of which the lien exists is presently payable, nor until the expiration of fourteen days after a notice in writing, stating and demanding payment of such part of the amount in respect of which the lien exists as is presently payable, has been given to the registered holder for the time being of the share, or the person entitled thereto by reason of his death or bankruptcy.

13. To give effect to any such sale the directors may authorise some person to transfer the shares sold to the purchaser thereof. The purchaser shall be registered as the holder of the shares comprised in any such transfer, and he shall not be bound to see to the application of the purchase money, nor shall his title to the shares be affected by any irregularity or invalidity in the proceedings in reference to the sale.

14. The proceeds of the sale shall be received by the company and applied in payment of such part of the amount in respect of which the lien exists as is presently payable, and the residue, if any, shall (subject to a like lien for sums not presently payable as existed upon the shares before the sale) be paid to the person entitled to the shares at the date of the sale.

Calls on Shares

15. The directors may from time to time make calls upon the members in respect of any moneys unpaid on their shares (whether on account of the nominal value of the shares or by way of premium) and not by the conditions of allotment thereof made payable at fixed times, provided that no call shall exceed one-fourth of the nominal value of the share or be payable at less than one month from the date fixed for the payment of the last preceding call, and each member shall (subject to receiving at least fourteen days' notice specifying the time or times and place of payment) pay to the company at the time or times and place so specified the amount called on his shares. A call may be revoked or postponed as the directors may determine.

16. A call shall be deemed to have been made at the time when the resolution of the directors authorising the call was passed and may be required to be paid by instalments.

17. The joint holders of a share shall be jointly and severally liable to pay all calls in respect thereof.

18. If a sum called in respect of a share is not paid before or on the day appointed for payment thereof, the person from whom the sum is due shall pay interest on the sum from the day appointed for payment thereof to the time of actual payment at such rate not exceeding 5 per cent per annum as the directors may determine, but the directors shall be at liberty to waive payment of such interest wholly or in part.

19. Any sum which by the terms of issue of a share becomes payable on allotment or at any fixed date, whether on account of the nominal value of the share or by way of premium, shall for the purposes of these regulations be deemed to be a call duly made and payable on the date on which by the terms of issue the same becomes payable, and in case of non-payment all the relevant provisions of these regulations as to payment of interest and expenses, forfeiture or otherwise shall apply as if such sum had become payable by virtue of a call duly made and notified.

20. The directors may, on the issue of shares, differentiate between the holders as to the amount of calls to be paid and the times of payment.

21. The directors may, if they think fit, receive from any member willing to advance the same, all or any part of the moneys uncalled and unpaid upon any shares held by him, and upon all or any of the moneys so advanced may (until the same would, but for such advance, become payable) pay interest at such rate not exceeding (unless the company in general meeting shall otherwise direct) 5 per cent per annum, as may be agreed upon between the directors and the member paying such sum in advance.

Transfer of Shares

22. The instrument of transfer of any share shall be executed by or on behalf of the transferor and transferee, and, *except as provided by sub-paragraph (a) of paragraph 2 of the Seventh Schedule to the Act*, the transferor shall be deemed to remain a holder of the share until the name of the transferee is entered in the register of members in respect thereof.

NOTES

Words in italics repealed by CA 1967, Sch 8, Pt III, in relation to any company registered on or after 27 January 1968.

23. Subject to such of the restrictions of these regulations as may be applicable, any member may transfer all or any of his shares by instrument in writing in any usual or common form or any other form which the directors may approve.

24. The directors may decline to register the transfer of a share (not being a fully paid share) to a person of whom they shall not approve, and they may also decline to register the transfer of a share on which the company has a lien.

25. The directors may also decline to recognise any instrument of transfer unless:—

(a)   a fee of 2s 6d or such lesser sum as the directors may from time to time require is paid to the company in respect thereof;

(b)   the instrument of transfer is accompanied by the certificate of the shares to which it relates, and such other evidence as the directors may reasonably require to show the right of the transferor to make the transfer; and

(c)   the instrument of transfer is in respect of only one class of share.

26. If the directors refuse to register a transfer they shall within two months after the date on which the transfer was lodged with the company send to the transferee notice of the refusal.

27. The registration of transfers may be suspended at such times and for such periods as the directors may from time to time determine, provided always that such registration shall not be suspended for more than thirty days in any year.

28. The company shall be entitled to charge a fee not exceeding 2s 6d on the registration of every probate, letters of administration, certificate of death or marriage, power of attorney, notice in lieu of distringas, or other instrument.

Transmission of Shares

29. In case of the death of a member the survivor or survivors where the deceased was a joint holder, and the legal personal representatives of the deceased where he was a sole holder, shall be the only persons recognised by the company as having any title to his interest in the shares; but nothing herein contained shall release the estate of a deceased joint holder from any liability in respect of any share which had been jointly held by him with other persons.

30. Any person becoming entitled to a share in consequence of the death or bankruptcy of a member may, upon such evidence being produced as may from time to time properly be required by the directors and subject as hereinafter provided, elect either to be registered himself as holder of the share or to have some person nominated by him registered as the transferee thereof, but the directors shall, in either case, have the same right to decline or suspend registration as they would have had in the case of a transfer of the share by that member before his death or bankruptcy, as the case may be.

31. If the person so becoming entitled shall elect to be registered himself, he shall deliver or send to the company a notice in writing signed by him stating that he so elects. If he shall elect to have another person registered he shall testify his election by executing to that person a transfer of the share. All the limitations, restrictions and provisions of these regulations relating to the right to transfer and the registration of transfers of shares shall be applicable to any such notice or transfer as aforesaid as if the death or bankruptcy of the member had not occurred and the notice or transfer were a transfer signed by that member.

32. A person becoming entitled to a share by reason of the death or bankruptcy of the holder shall be entitled to the same dividends and other advantages to which he would be entitled if he were the registered holder of the share, except that he shall not, before being registered as a member in respect of the share, be entitled in respect of it to exercise any right conferred by membership in relation to meetings of the company:

Provided always that the directors may at any time give notice requiring any such person to elect either to be registered himself or to transfer the share, and if the notice is not complied with within ninety days the directors may thereafter withhold payment of all dividends, bonuses or other moneys payable in respect of the share until the requirements of the notice have been complied with.

Forfeiture of Shares

33. If a member fails to pay any call or instalment of a call on the day appointed for payment thereof, the directors may, at any time thereafter during such time as any part of the call or instalment remains unpaid, serve a notice on him requiring payment of so much of the call or instalment as is unpaid, together with any interest which may have accrued.

34. The notice shall name a further day (not earlier than the expiration of fourteen days from the date of service of the notice) on or before which the payment required by the notice is to be made, and shall state that in the event of non-payment at or before the time appointed the shares in respect of which the call was made will be liable to be forfeited.

35. If the requirements of any such notice as aforesaid are not complied with, any share in respect of which the notice has been given may at any time thereafter, before the payment required by the notice has been made, be forfeited by a resolution of the directors to that effect.

36. A forfeited share may be sold or otherwise disposed of on such terms and in such manner as the directors think fit, and at any time before a sale or disposition the forfeiture may be cancelled on such terms as the directors think fit.

37. A person whose shares have been forfeited shall cease to be a member in respect of the forfeited shares, but shall, notwithstanding, remain liable to pay to the company all moneys which, at the date of forfeiture, were payable by him to the company in respect of the shares, but his liability shall cease if and when the company shall have received payment in full of all such moneys in respect of the shares.

38. A statutory declaration in writing that the declarant is a director or the secretary of the company, and that a share in the company has been duly forfeited on a date stated in the declaration, shall be conclusive evidence of the facts therein stated as against all persons claiming to be entitled to the share. The company may receive the consideration, if any, given for the share on any sale or disposition thereof and may execute a transfer of the share in favour of the person to whom the share is sold or disposed of and he shall thereupon be registered as the holder of the share, and shall not be bound to see to the application of the purchase money, if any, nor shall his title to the share be affected by any irregularity or invalidity in the proceedings in reference to the forfeiture, sale or disposal of the share.

39. The provisions of these regulations as to forfeiture shall apply in the case of non-payment of any sum which, by the terms of issue of a share, becomes payable at a fixed time, whether on account of the nominal value of the share or by way of premium, as if the same had been payable by virtue of a call duly made and notified.

Conversion of Shares into Stock

40. The company may by ordinary resolution convert any paid-up shares into stock, and reconvert any stock into paid-up shares of any denomination.

41. The holders of stock may transfer the same, or any part thereof, in the same manner, and subject to the same regulations, as and subject to which the shares from which the stock arose might previously to conversion have been transferred, or as near thereto as circumstances admit; and the directors may from time to time fix the minimum amount of stock transferable but so that such minimum shall not exceed the nominal amount of the shares from which the stock arose.

42. The holders of stock shall, according to the amount of stock held by them, have the same rights, privileges and advantages as regards dividends, voting at meetings of the company and other matters as if they held the shares from which the stock arose, but no such privilege or advantage (except participation in the dividends and profits of the company and in the assets on winding up) shall be conferred by an amount of stock which would not, if existing in shares, have conferred that privilege or advantage.

43. Such of the regulations of the company as are applicable to paid-up shares shall apply to stock, and words "share" and "shareholder" therein shall include "stock" and "stockholder".

Alteration of Capital

44. The company may from time to time by ordinary resolution increase the share capital by such sum, to be divided into shares of such amount, as the resolution shall prescribe.

45. The company may by ordinary resolution—
- (a) consolidate and divide all or any of its share capital to shares of larger amount than its existing shares;
- (b) sub-divide its existing shares, or any of them, into shares of smaller amount than is fixed by the memorandum of association subject, nevertheless, to the provisions of section 61(1)(d) of the Act;
- (c) cancel any shares which, at the date of the passing of the resolution, have not been taken or agreed to be taken by any person.

46. The company may by special resolution reduce its share capital, any capital redemption reserve fund or any share premium account in any manner and with, and subject to, any incident authorised, and consent required, by law.

General Meetings

47. The company shall in each year hold a general meeting as its annual general meeting in addition to any other meetings in that year, and shall specify the meeting as such in the notices calling it; and not more than fifteen months shall elapse between the date of one annual general meeting of the company and that of the next. Provided that so long as the company holds its first annual general meeting within eighteen months of its incorporation, it need not hold it in the year of its incorporation or in the following year. The annual general meeting shall be held at such time and place as the directors shall appoint.

48. All general meetings other than annual general meetings shall be called extraordinary general meetings.

49. The directors may, whenever they think fit, convene an extraordinary general meeting, and extraordinary general meetings shall also be convened on such requisition, or, in default, may be convened by such requisitionists, as provided by section 132 of the Act. If at any time there are not within the United Kingdom sufficient directors capable of acting to form a quorum, any director or any two members of the company may convene an extraordinary general meeting in the same manner as nearly as possible as that in which meetings may be convened by the directors.

Notice of General Meetings

50. An annual general meeting and a meeting called for the passing of a special resolution shall be called by twenty-one days' notice in writing at the least, and a meeting of the company other than an annual general meeting or a meeting for the passing of a special resolution shall be called by fourteen days' notice in writing at the least. The notice shall be exclusive of the day on which it is served or deemed to be served and of the day for which it is given, and shall specify the place, the day and the hour of meeting and, in case of special business, the general nature of that business, and shall be given, in manner hereinafter mentioned or in such other manner, if any, as may be prescribed by the company in general meeting, to such persons as are, under the regulations of the company, entitled to receive such notices from the company:

Provided that a meeting of the company shall, notwithstanding that it is called by shorter notice than that specified in this regulation, be deemed to have been duly called if it is so agreed—

- (a) in the case of a meeting called as the annual general meeting, by all the members entitled to attend and vote thereat; and
- (b) in the case of any other meeting, by a majority in number of the members having a right to attend and vote at the meeting, being a majority together holding not less than 95 per cent in nominal value of the shares giving that right.

51. The accidental omission to give notice of a meeting to, or the non-receipt of notice of a meeting by, any person entitled to receive notice shall not invalidate the proceedings at that meeting.

Proceedings at General Meetings

52. All business shall be deemed special that is transacted at an extraordinary general meeting, and also all that is transacted at an annual general meeting, with the exception of declaring a dividend, the consideration of the accounts, balance sheets, and the reports of the directors and auditors, the election of directors in the place of those retiring and the appointment of, and the fixing of the remuneration of, the auditors.

53. No business shall be transacted at any general meeting unless a quorum of members is present at the time when the meeting proceeds to business; save as herein otherwise provided *three members present in person shall be a quorum.*

NOTES

For the words in italics there are substituted the words "two members present in person or by proxy shall be a quorum" by CA 1980, Sch 3, in relation to any company registered on or after 22 December 1980.

---

54. If within half an hour from the time appointed for the meeting a quorum is not present, the meeting, if convened upon the requisition of members, shall be dissolved; in any other case it shall stand adjourned to the same day in the next week, at the same time and place or to such other day and at such other time and place as the directors may determine, *and if at the adjourned meeting a quorum is not present within half an hour from the time appointed for the meeting, the members present shall be a quorum.*

NOTES

Words in italics repealed by CA 1980, Sch 4, in relation to any company registered on or after 22 December 1980.

---

55. The chairman, if any, of the board of directors shall preside as chairman at every general meeting of the company, or if there is no such chairman, or if he shall not be present within fifteen minutes after the time appointed for the holding of the meeting or is unwilling to act the directors present shall elect one of their number to be chairman of the meeting.

56. If at any meeting no director is willing to act as chairman or if no director is present within fifteen minutes after the time appointed for holding the meeting, the members present shall choose one of their number to be chairman of the meeting.

57. The chairman may, with the consent of any meeting at which a quorum is present (and shall if so directed by the meeting), adjourn the meeting from time to time and from place to place, but no business shall be transacted at any adjourned meeting other than the business left unfinished at the meeting from which the adjournment took place. When a meeting is adjourned for thirty days or more, notice of the adjourned meeting shall be given as in the case of an original meeting. Save as aforesaid it shall not be necessary to give any notice of an adjournment or of the business to be transacted at an adjourned meeting.

58. At any general meeting a resolution put to the vote of the meeting shall be decided on a show of hands unless a poll is (before or on the declaration of the result of the show of hands) demanded—
- (a) by the chairman; or
- (b) by at least *three* members present in person or by proxy; or
- (c) by any member or members present in person or by proxy and representing not less than one-tenth of the total voting rights of all the members having the right to vote at the meeting; or
- (d) by a member or members holding shares in the company conferring a right to vote at the meeting being shares on which an aggregate sum has been paid up equal to not less than one-tenth of the total sum paid up on all the shares conferring that right.

Unless a poll be so demanded a declaration by the chairman that a resolution has on a show of hands been carried or carried unanimously, or by a particular majority, or lost and an entry to that effect in the book containing the minutes of the proceedings of the company shall be conclusive evidence of the fact without proof of the number or proportion of the votes recorded in favour of or against such resolution.

The demand for a poll may be withdrawn.

NOTES

For the word in italics there is substituted the word "two" by CA 1980, Sch 3, in relation to any company registered on or after 22 December 1980.

59. Except as provided in regulation 61, if a poll is duly demanded it shall be taken in such manner as the chairman directs, and the result of the poll shall be deemed to be the resolution of the meeting at which the poll was demanded.

60. In the case of an equality of votes, whether on a show of hands or on a poll, the chairman of the meeting at which the show of hands takes place or at which the poll is demanded, shall be entitled to a second or casting vote.

61. A poll demanded on the election of a chairman or on a question of adjournment shall be taken forthwith. A poll demanded on any other question shall be taken at such time as the chairman of the meeting directs, and any business other than that upon which a poll has been demanded may be proceeded with pending the taking of the poll.

Votes of Members

62. Subject to any rights or restrictions for the time being attached to any class or classes of shares, on a show of hands every member present in person shall have one vote, and on a poll every member shall have one vote for each share of which he is the holder.

63. In the case of joint holders the vote of the senior who tenders a vote, whether in person or by proxy, shall be accepted to the exclusion of the votes of the other joint holders; and for this purpose seniority shall be determined by the order in which the names stand in the register of members.

64. A member of unsound mind, or in respect of whom an order has been made by any court having jurisdiction in lunacy, may vote, whether on a show of hands or on a poll, by his committee, receiver, curator bonis, or other person in the nature of a committee, receiver or curator bonis appointed by that court, and any such committee, receiver, curator bonis or other person may, on a poll, vote by proxy.

65. No member shall be entitled to vote at any general meeting unless all calls or other sums presently payable by him in respect of shares in the company have been paid.

66. No objection shall be raised to the qualification of any voter except at the meeting or adjourned meeting at which the vote objected to is given or tendered, and every vote not disallowed at such meeting shall be valid for all purposes. Any such objection made in due time shall be referred to the chairman of the meeting whose decision shall be final and conclusive.

67. On a poll votes may be given either personally or by proxy.

68. The instrument appointing a proxy shall be in writing under the hand of the appointer or of his attorney duly authorised in writing, or, if the appointer is a corporation, either under seal, or under the hand of an officer or attorney duly authorised. A proxy need not be a member of the company.

69. The instrument appointing a proxy and the power of attorney or other authority if any, under which it is signed or a notarially certified copy of that power or authority shall be deposited at the registered office of the company or at such other place within the United Kingdom as is specified for that purpose in the notice convening the meeting, not less than 48 hours before the time for holding the meeting or adjourned meeting, at which the person named in the instrument proposes to vote, or, in the case of a poll, not less than 24 hours before the time appointed for the taking of the poll, and in default the instrument of proxy shall not be treated as valid.

70. An instrument appointing a proxy shall be in the following form or a form as near thereto as circumstances admit—

". . . . . Limited

I/We, ... of . . . .

in the county of . . . .

being a member/members of the above-named company,

hereby appoint . . . . of . . . . ,

or failing him, ... of . . . . ,

as my/our proxy to vote for me/us on my/our behalf at the [annual or extraordinary, as the case may be] general meeting of the company, to be held on

the . . . . day of . . . . 19. . . . . , and at any adjournment thereof.

Signed this . . . . day of . . . . 19. . . . ."

71. Where it is desired to afford members an opportunity of voting for or against a resolution the instrument appointing a proxy shall be in the following form or a form as near thereto as circumstances admit—

". . . . . Limited

I/We, ... of . . . .

in the county of . . . . ,

being a member/members of the above-named company,

hereby appoint . . . . of . . . . ,

or failing him, ... of . . . . ,

as my/our proxy to vote for me/us on my/our behalf at the [annual or extraordinary, as the case may be] general meeting of the company, to be held on

the . . . . day of . . . . 19. . . . . , and at any adjournment thereof.

Signed this . . . . day of . . . . 19. . . . . "

This form is to be used *in favour of/against the resolution. Unless otherwise instructed, the proxy will vote as he thinks fit.

* Strike out whichever is not desired."

72. The instrument appointing a proxy shall be deemed to confer authority to demand or join in demanding a poll.

73. A vote given in accordance with the terms of an instrument of proxy shall be valid notwithstanding the previous death or insanity of the principal or revocation of the proxy or of the authority under which the proxy was executed, on the transfer of the share in respect of which the proxy is given, provided that no intimation in writing of such death, insanity, revocation or transfer as aforesaid shall have been received by the company at the office before the commencement of the meeting or adjourned meeting at which the proxy is used.

[**73A.** Subject to the provisions of CAs 1948 to *1980* a resolution in writing signed by all the members for the time being entitled to receive notice of and to attend and vote at general meetings (or being corporations by their duly authorised representatives) shall be as valid and effective as if the same had been passed at a general meeting of the company duly convened and held.]

NOTES

Added by CA 1980, Sch 3, in relation to any company registered on or after 22 December 1980; for the year in italics there is substituted the year "1981" by CA 1981, Sch 3, in relation to any company registered on or after 3 December 1981.

Corporations acting by Representatives at Meetings

74. Any corporation which is a member of the company may by resolution of its directors or other governing body authorise such person as it thinks fit to act as its representative at any meeting of the company or of any class of members of the company, and the person so authorised shall be entitled to exercise the same powers on behalf of the corporation which he represents as that corporation could exercise if it were an individual member of the company.

Directors

75. The number of the directors and the names of the first directors shall be determined in writing by the subscribers of the memorandum of association or a majority of them.

76. The remuneration of the directors shall from time to time be determined by the company in general meeting. Such remuneration shall be deemed to accrue from day to day. The directors may also be paid all travelling, hotel and other expenses properly incurred by them in attending and returning from meetings of the directors or any committee of the directors or general meetings of the company or in connection with the business of the company.

77. The shareholding qualification for directors may be fixed by the company in general meeting, and unless and until so fixed no qualification shall be required.

78. A director of the company may be or become a director or other officer of, or otherwise interested in, any company promoted by the company or in which the company may be interested as shareholder or otherwise, and no such director shall be accountable to the company for any remuneration or other benefits received by him as a director or officer of, or from his interest in, such other company unless the company otherwise direct.

Borrowing Powers

79. The directors may exercise all the powers of the company to borrow money, and to mortgage or charge its undertaking, property and uncalled capital or any part thereof, and[, subject to section 14 of CA 1980] to issue debentures, debenture stock, and other securities whether outright or as security for any debt, liability or obligation of the company or of any third party:

Provided that the amount for the time being remaining undischarged of moneys borrowed or secured by the directors as aforesaid (apart from temporary loans obtained from the company's bankers in the ordinary course of business) shall not at any time, without the previous sanction of the company in general meeting, exceed the nominal amount of the share capital of the company for the time being issued, but nevertheless no lender or other person dealing with the company shall be concerned to see or inquire whether this limit is observed. No debt incurred or security given in excess of such limit shall be invalid or ineffectual except in the case of express notice to the lender or the recipient of the security at the time when the debt was incurred or security given that the limit hereby imposed had been or was thereby exceeded.

NOTES

Words in square brackets inserted by CA 1980, Sch 3, in relation to any company registered on or after 22 December 1980.

Powers and Duties of Directors

80. The business of the company shall be managed by the directors, who may pay all expenses incurred in promoting and registering the company, and may exercise all such powers of the company as are not, by the *Act* or by these regulations, required to be exercised by the company in general meeting, subject, nevertheless, to any of these regulations, to the provisions of the *Act* and to such regulations being not inconsistent with the aforesaid regulations or provisions, as may be prescribed by the company in general meeting; but no regulation made by the company in general meeting shall invalidate any prior act of the directors which would have been valid if that regulation had not been made.

NOTES

For the words in italics there are substituted the words "Companies Acts 1948 to 1980" in both places by CA 1980, Sch 3, in relation to companies registered on or after 22 December 1980; in the text as substituted the year "1980" is substituted by the year "1981" by CA 1981, Sch 3, in relation to companies registered on or after 3 December 1981.

81. The directors may from time to time and at any time by power of attorney appoint any company, firm or person or body of persons, whether nominated directly or indirectly by the directors, to be the attorney or attorneys of the company for such purposes and with such powers, authorities and discretions (not exceeding those vested in or exercisable by the directors under these regulations) and for such period and subject to such conditions as they may think fit, and any such powers of attorney may contain such provisions for the protection and convenience of persons dealing with any such attorney as the directors may think fit and may also authorise any such attorney to delegate all or any of the powers, authorities and discretions vested in him.

82. The company may exercise the powers conferred by section 35 of the Act with regard to having an official seal for use abroad, and such powers shall be vested in the directors.

83. The company may exercise the powers conferred upon the company by sections 119 to 123 (both inclusive) of the Act with regard to the keeping of a dominion register, and the directors may (subject to the provisions of those sections) make and vary such regulations as they may think fit respecting the keeping of any such register.

84. (1)   A director who is in any way, whether directly or indirectly, interested in a contract or proposed contract with the company shall declare the nature of his interest at a meeting of the directors in accordance with section 199 of the Act.

(2)   A director shall not vote in respect of any contract or arrangement in which he is interested, and if he shall do so his vote shall not be counted, nor shall he be counted in the quorum present at the meeting, but neither of these prohibitions shall apply to—

- (a)   any arrangement for giving any director any security or indemnity in respect of money lent by him to or obligations undertaken by him for the benefit of the company; or
- (b)   to any arrangement for the giving by the company of any security to a third party in respect of a debt or obligation of the company for which the director himself has assumed responsibility in whole or in part under a guarantee or indemnity or by the deposit of a security; or
- (c)   any contract by a director to subscribe for or underwrite shares or debentures of the company; or
- (d)   any contract or arrangement with any other company in which he is interested only as an officer of the company or as holder of shares or other securities;

and these prohibitions may at any time be suspended or relaxed to any extent, and either generally or in respect of any particular contract, arrangement or transaction, by the company in general meeting.

(3)   A director may hold any other office or place of profit under the company (other than the office of auditor) in conjunction with his office of director for such period and on such terms (as to remuneration and otherwise) as the directors may determine and no director or intending director shall be disqualified by his office from contracting with the company either with regard to his tenure of any such other office or place of profit or as vendor, purchaser or otherwise, nor shall any such contract, or any contract or arrangement entered into by or on behalf of the company in which any director is in any way interested, be liable to be avoided, nor shall any director so contracting or being so interested be liable to account to the company for any profit realised by any such contract or arrangement by reason of such director holding that office or of the fiduciary relation thereby established.

(4)   A director, notwithstanding his interest, may be counted in the quorum present at any meeting whereat he or any other director is appointed to hold any such office or place of profit under the company or whereat the terms of any such appointment are arranged, and he may vote on any such appointment or arrangement other than his own appointment or the arrangement of the terms thereof.

(5)   Any director may act by himself or his firm in a professional capacity for the company, and he or his firm shall be entitled to remuneration for professional services as if he were not a director; provided that nothing herein contained shall authorise a director or his firm to act as auditor to the company.

85.   All cheques, promissory notes, drafts, bills of exchange and other negotiable instruments, and all receipts for moneys paid to the company, shall be signed, drawn, accepted, endorsed, or otherwise executed, as the case may be, in such manner as the directors shall from time to time by resolution determine.

86.   The directors shall cause minutes to be made in books provided for the purpose—

- (a)   of all appointments of officers made by the directors;
- (b)   of the names of the directors present at each meeting of the directors and of any committee of the directors;
- (c)   of all resolutions and proceedings at all meetings of the company, and of the directors, and of committees of directors;

and every director present at any meeting of directors or committee of directors shall sign his name in a book to be kept for that purpose.

87.   The directors on behalf of the company may pay a gratuity or pension or allowance on retirement to any director who has held any other salaried office or place of profit with the company or to his widow or dependants and may make contributions to any fund and pay premiums for the purchase or provision of any such gratuity, pension or allowance.

Disqualification of Directors

88.   The office of director shall be vacated if the director—

- (a)   ceases to be a director by virtue of section 182 or 185 of the Act; or
- (b)   becomes bankrupt or makes any arrangement or composition with his creditors generally; or
- (c)   becomes prohibited from being a director by reason of any order made under section 188 of the Act [*or under section 28 of CA 1976*]; or
- (d)   becomes of unsound mind; or
- (e)   resigns his office by notice in writing to the company; or

(f)   shall for more than six months have been absent without permission of the directors from meetings of the directors held during that period.

NOTES

Words in square brackets inserted by CA 1976, in relation to any company registered on or after 1 June 1977, and repealed by CA 1981, Sch 4, in relation to any company registered on or after 3 December 1981.

Rotation of Directors

89. At the first annual general meeting of the company all the directors shall retire from office, and at the annual general meeting in every subsequent year one-third of the directors for the time being, or, if their number is not three or a multiple of three, then the number nearest one-third, shall retire from office.

90. The directors to retire in every year shall be those who have been longest in office since their last election, but as between persons who became directors on the same day those to retire shall (unless they otherwise agree among themselves) be determined by lot.

91. A retiring director shall be eligible for re-election.

92. The company at the meeting at which a director retires in manner aforesaid may fill the vacated office by electing a person thereto, and in default the retiring director shall if offering himself for re-election be deemed to have been re-elected, unless at such meeting it is expressly resolved not to fill such vacated office or unless a resolution for the re-election of such director shall have been put to the meeting and lost.

93. No person other than a director retiring at the meeting shall unless recommended by the directors be eligible for election to the office of director at any general meeting unless not less than three nor more than twenty-one days before the date appointed for the meeting there shall have been left at the registered office of the company notice in writing, signed by a member duly qualified to attend and vote at the meeting for which such notice is given, of his intention to propose such person for election, and also notice in writing signed by that person of his willingness to be elected.

94. The company may from time to time by ordinary resolution increase or reduce the number of directors, and may also determine in what rotation the increased or reduced number is to go out of office.

95. The directors shall have power at any time, and from time to time, to appoint any person to be a director, either to fill a casual vacancy or as an addition to the existing directors, but so that the total number of directors shall not at any time exceed the number fixed in accordance with these regulations. Any director so appointed shall hold office only until the next following annual general meeting, and shall then be eligible for re-election but shall not be taken into account in determining the directors who are to retire by rotation at such meeting.

96. The company may by ordinary resolution, of which special notice has been given in accordance with section 142 of the Act, remove any director before the expiration of his period of office notwithstanding anything in these regulations or in any agreement between the company and such director. Such removal shall be without prejudice to any claim such director may have for damages for breach of any contract of service between him and the company.

97. The company may by ordinary resolution appoint another person in place of a director removed from office under the immediately preceding regulation, and without prejudice to the powers of the directors under regulation 95 the company in general meeting may appoint any person to be a director either to fill a casual vacancy or as an additional director. A person appointed in place of a director so removed or to fill such a vacancy shall be subject to retirement at the same time as if he had become a director on the day on which the director in whose place he is appointed was last elected a director.

Proceedings of Directors

98. The directors may meet together for the despatch of business, adjourn, and otherwise regulate their meetings, as they think fit. Questions arising at any meeting shall be decided by a majority of votes. In case of an equality of votes, the chairman shall have a second or casting vote. A director may, and the secretary on the requisition of a director shall, at any time summon a meeting of the directors. It shall not be necessary to give notice of a meeting of directors to any director for the time being absent from the United Kingdom.

99. The quorum necessary for the transaction of the business of the directors may be fixed by the directors, and unless so fixed shall be two.

100. The continuing directors may act notwithstanding any vacancy in their body, but, if and so long as their number is reduced below the number fixed by or pursuant to the regulations of the company as the necessary quorum of directors, the continuing directors or director may act for the purpose of increasing the number of directors to that number, or of summoning a general meeting of the company, but for no other purpose.

101. The directors may elect a chairman of their meetings and determine the period for which he is to hold office; but if no such chairman is elected, or if at any meeting the chairman is not present within five minutes after the time appointed for holding the same, the directors present may choose one of their number to be chairman of the meeting.

102. The directors may delegate any of their powers to committees consisting of such member or members of their body as they think fit; any committee so formed shall in the exercise of the powers so delegated conform to any regulations that may be imposed on it by the directors.

103. A committee may elect a chairman of its meetings; if no such chairman is elected, or if at any meeting the chairman is not present within five minutes after the time appointed for holding the same, the members present may choose one of their number to be chairman of the meeting.

104. A committee may meet and adjourn as it thinks proper. Questions arising at any meeting shall be determined by a majority of votes of the members present, and in the case of an equality of votes the chairman shall have a second or casting vote.

105. All acts done by any meeting of the directors or of a committee of directors or by any person acting as a director shall, notwithstanding that it be afterwards discovered that there was some defect in the appointment of any such director or person acting as aforesaid, or that they or any of them were disqualified, be as valid as if every such person had been duly appointed and was qualified to be a director.

106. A resolution in writing, signed by all the directors for the time being entitled to receive notice of a meeting of the directors, shall be as valid and effectual as if it had been passed at a meeting of the directors duly convened and held.

Managing Director

107. The directors may from time to time appoint one of more of their body to the office of managing director for such period and on such terms as they think fit, and, subject to the terms of any agreement entered into in any particular case, may revoke such appointment. A director so appointed shall not, whilst holding that office, be subject to retirement by rotation or be taken into account in determining the rotation of retirement of directors, but his appointment shall be automatically determined if he cease from any cause to be a director.

108. A managing director shall receive such remuneration (whether by way of salary, commission or participation in profits, or partly in one way and partly in another) as the directors may determine.

109. The directors may entrust to and confer upon a managing director any of the powers exercisable by them upon such terms and conditions and with such restrictions as they may think fit, and either collaterally with or to the exclusion of their own powers and may from time to time revoke, withdraw, alter or vary all or any of such powers.

Secretary

110. [Subject to Section 21(5) of CA 1976] the secretary shall be appointed by the directors for such term, at such remuneration and upon such conditions as they may think fit; and any secretary so appointed may be removed by them.

NOTES

Words in square brackets inserted by CA 1976, Sch 2, in relation to any company registered on or after 18 April 1977.

111. No person shall be appointed or hold office as secretary who is—
  (a) the sole director of the company; or
  (b) a corporation the sole director of which is the sole director of the company; or
  (c) the sole director of a corporation which is the sole director of the company.

112. A provision of the Act or these regulations requiring or authorising a thing to be done by or to a director and the secretary shall not be satisfied by its being done by or to the same person acting both as director and as, or in place of, the secretary.

The Seal

113. The directors shall provide for the safe custody of the seal, which shall only be used by the authority of the directors or of a committee of the directors authorised by the directors in that behalf, and every instrument to which the seal shall be affixed shall be signed by a director and shall be countersigned by the secretary or by a second director or by some other person appointed by the directors for the purpose.

Dividends and Reserve

114. The company in general meeting may declare dividends, but no dividend shall exceed the amount recommended by the directors.

115. The directors may from time to time pay to the members such interim dividends as appear to the directors to be justified by the profits of the company.

116. *No dividend shall be paid otherwise than out of profits.*

NOTES
  Substituted by CA 1980, Sch 3, in relation to any company registered on or after 22 December 1980, as follows—
  "No dividend or interim dividend shall be paid otherwise than in accordance with the provisions of Part III of CA 1980 which apply to the company.".

117. The directors may, before recommending any dividend, set aside out of the profits of the company such sums as they think proper as a reserve or reserves which shall, at the discretion of the directors, be applicable for any purpose to which the profits of the company may be properly applied, and pending such application may, at the like discretion, either be employed in the business of the company or be invested in such investments (other than shares of the company) as the directors may from time to time think fit. The directors may also without placing the same to reserve carry forward any profits which they may think prudent not to divide.

118. Subject to the rights of persons, if any, entitled to shares with special rights as to dividend, all dividends shall be declared and paid according to the amounts paid or credited as paid on the shares in respect whereof the dividend is paid, but no amount paid or credited as paid on a share in advance of calls shall be treated for the purposes of this regulation as paid on the share. All dividends shall be apportioned and paid proportionately to the amounts paid or credited as paid on the shares during any portion or portions of the period in respect of which the dividend is paid; but if any share is issued on terms providing that it shall rank for dividend as from a particular date such share shall rank for dividend accordingly.

119. The directors may deduct from any dividend payable to any member all sums of money (if any) presently payable by him to the company on account of calls or otherwise in relation to the shares of the company.

120. Any general meeting declaring a dividend or bonus may direct payment of such dividend or bonus wholly or partly by the distribution of specific assets and in particular of paid up shares, debentures or debenture stock of any other company or in any one or more of such ways, and the directors shall give effect to such resolution, and where any difficulty arises in regard to such distribution, the directors may settle the same as they think expedient, and in particular may issue fractional certificates and fix the value for distribution of such specific assets or any part thereof and may determine that cash payments shall be made to any members upon the footing of the value so fixed in order to adjust the rights of all parties, and may vest any such specific assets in trustees as may seem expedient to the directors.

121. Any dividend, interest or other moneys payable in cash in respect of shares may be paid by cheque or warrant sent through the post directed to the registered address of the holder or, in the case of joint holders, to the registered address of that one of the joint holders who is first named on the register of members or to such person and to such address as the holder or joint holders may in writing direct. Every such cheque or warrant shall be made payable to the order of the person to whom it is sent. Any one of two or more joint holders may give effectual receipts for any dividends, bonuses or other moneys payable in respect of the shares held by them as joint holders.

122. No dividend shall bear interest against the company.

Accounts

123. The directors *shall cause proper books of account to be kept with respect to—*
  (a) all sums of money received and expended by the company and the matters in respect of which the receipt and expenditure takes place;
  (b) all sales and purchases of goods by the company; and
  (c) the assets and liabilities of the company.

Proper books shall not be deemed to be kept if there are not kept such books of account as are necessary to give a true and fair view of the state of the company's affairs and to explain its transactions.

NOTES

For the words in italics there are substituted the words "shall cause accounting records to be kept in accordance with section 12 of CA 1976" by CA 1976, Sch 2, in relation to any company registered on or after 1 October 1977.

124. *The books of account shall be kept at the registered office of the Company, or, subject to section 147(3) of the Act, at such other place or places as the directors think fit, and shall always be open to the inspection of the directors.*

NOTES

Substituted by CA 1976, Sch 2, in relation to any company registered on or after 1 October 1977, as follows—

"The accounting records shall be kept at the registered office of the company or, subject to section 12(6) and (7) of CA 1976, at such other place or places as the directors think fit, and shall always be open to the inspection of the officers of the company.".

125. The directors shall from time to time determine whether and to what extent and at what times and places and under what conditions or regulations the accounts and books of the company or any of them shall be open to the inspection of members not being directors, and no member (not being a director) shall have any right of inspecting any account or book or document of the company except as conferred by statute or authorised by the directors or by the company in general meeting.

126. The directors shall from time to time, in accordance with *sections 148, 150 and 157 of the Act,* cause to be prepared and to be laid before the company in general meeting such profit and loss accounts, balance sheets, group accounts (if any) and reports as are referred to in those sections.

NOTES

For the words in italics there are substituted the words "sections 150 and 157 of the Act and sections 1, 6 and 7 of CA 1976" by CA 1976, Sch 2, in relation to any company registered on or after 1 October 1977.

127. A copy of every balance sheet (including every document required by law to be annexed thereto) which is to be laid before the company in general meeting, together with a copy of the auditors' report [and directors' report], shall not less than twenty-one days before the date of the meeting be sent to every member of, and every holder of debentures of, the company and to every person registered under regulation 31. Provided that this regulation shall not require a copy of those documents to be sent to any person of whose address the company is not aware or to more than one of the joint holders of any shares or debentures.

NOTES

Words in square brackets inserted by CA 1976, Sch 2, in relation to any company registered on or after 1 October 1977.

Capitalisation of Profits

128. The company in general meeting may upon the recommendation of the directors resolve that it is desirable to capitalise any part of the amount for the time being standing to the credit of any of the company's reserve accounts or to the credit of the profit and loss account or otherwise available for distribution, and accordingly that such sum be set free for distribution amongst the members who would have been entitled thereto if distributed by way of dividend and in the same proportions on condition that the same be not paid in cash but be applied either in or towards paying up any amounts for the time being unpaid on any shares held by such members respectively or paying up in full unissued shares or debentures of the company to be allotted and distributed credited as fully paid up to and amongst such members in the proportion aforesaid, or partly in the one way and partly in the other, and the directors shall give effect to such resolution:

Provided that a share premium account and a capital redemption reserve fund may, for the purposes of this regulation, only be applied in the paying up of unissued shares to be issued to members of the company as fully paid bonus shares.

NOTES

For the word in italics there is substituted the word "allotted" by CA 1980, Sch 3, in relation to any company registered on or after 22 December 1980.

[128A. The company in general meeting may on the recommendation of the directors resolve that it is desirable to capitalise any part of the amount for the time being standing to the credit of any of the company's reserve accounts or to the credit of the profit and loss account which is not available for distribution by applying such sum in paying up in full unissued shares to be allotted as fully paid bonus shares to those members of the company who would have been entitled to that sum if it were distributed by way of dividend (and in the same proportions), and the directors shall give effect to such resolution.]

NOTES

Added by CA 1980, Sch 3, in relation to any company registered on or after 22 December 1980.

129. *Whenever such a resolution as aforesaid shall have been passed* the directors shall make all appropriations and applications of the undivided profits resolved to be capitalised thereby, and all allotments and issues of fully-paid shares or debentures, if any, and generally shall do all acts and things required to give effect thereto, with full power to the directors to make such provision by the issue of fractional certificates or by payment in cash or otherwise as they think fit for the case of shares or debentures becoming distributable in fractions, and also to authorise any person to enter on behalf of all members entitled thereto into an agreement with the company providing for the allotment to them respectively, credited as fully paid up, of any further shares or debentures to which they may be entitled upon such capitalisation, or (as the case may require) for the payment up by the company on their behalf, by the application thereto of their respective proportions of the profits resolved to be capitalised, of the amounts or any part of the amounts remaining unpaid on their existing shares, and any agreement made under such authority shall be effective and binding on all such members.

NOTES

For the words in italics there are substituted the words "Whenever a resolution is passed in pursuance of regulation 128 or 128A above" by CA 1980, Sch 3, in relation to any company registered on or after 22 December 1980.

Audit

130. Auditors shall be appointed and their duties regulated in accordance with *sections 159 to 162 of the Act.*

NOTES

The regulation set out above applies to any company registered before 27 January 1968.

For the words in italics there are substituted the words "sections 159 to 161 of the Act and section 14 of the Companies Act 1967" by CA 1967, in relation to any company registered between 27 January 1968 and 17 April 1977; for the words in italics there are substituted the words "section 161 of the Act, section 14 of CA 1967 and sections 13 to 18 of CA 1976" by CA 1976, in relation to any company registered between 18 April 1977 and 2 December 1981, and for the words in italics there are substituted the words "section 161 of the Act, sections 14 and 23A of CA 1967, sections 13 to 18 of CA 1976 and sections 7 and 12 of CA 1981" by CA 1981, in relation to any company registered between 3 December 1981 and 30 June 1985.

Notices

131. A notice may be given by the company to any member either personally or by sending it by post to him or to his registered address, or (if he has no registered address within the United Kingdom) to the address, if any, within the United Kingdom supplied by him to the company for the giving of notice to him. Where a notice is sent by post, service of the notice shall be deemed to be effected by properly addressing, prepaying, and posting a letter containing the notice, and to have been effected in the case of a notice of a meeting at the expiration of 24 hours after the letter containing the same is posted, and in any other case at the time at which the letter would be delivered in the ordinary course of post.

132. A notice may be given by the company to the joint holders of a share by giving the notice to the joint holder first named in the register of members in respect of the share.

133. A notice may be given by the company to the persons entitled to a share in consequence of the death or bankruptcy of a member by sending it through the post in a prepaid letter addressed to them by name, or by the title of representatives of the deceased, or trustee of the bankrupt, or any like description, at the address, if any, within the United Kingdom supplied for the purpose by the persons claiming to be so entitled, or (until such an address has been so supplied) by giving the notice in any manner in which the same might have been given if the death or bankruptcy had not occurred.

134. Notice of every general meeting shall be given in any manner hereinbefore authorised to—
  (a)   every member except those members who (having no registered address within the United Kingdom) have not supplied to the company an address within the United Kingdom for the giving of notices to them;
  (b)   every person upon whom the ownership of a share devolves by reason of his being a legal personal representative or a trustee in bankruptcy of a member where the member but for his death or bankruptcy would be entitled to receive notice of the meeting; and
  (c)   the auditor for the time being of the company.
No other person shall be entitled to receive notices of general meetings.

Winding up

135. If the company shall be wound up the liquidator may, with the sanction of an extraordinary resolution of the company and any other sanction required by the Act, divide amongst the members in specie or kind the whole or any part of the assets of the company (whether they shall consist of property of the same kind or not) and may, for such purpose set such value as he deems fair upon any property to be divided as aforesaid and may determine how such division shall be carried out as between the members or different classes of members. The liquidator may, with the like sanction, vest the whole or any part of such assets in trustees upon such trusts for the benefit of the contributories as the liquidator, with the like sanction, shall think fit, but so that no member shall be compelled to accept any shares or other securities whereon there is any liability.

Indemnity

136. Every director, managing director, agent, auditor, secretary and other officer for the time being of the company shall be indemnified out of the assets of the company against any liability incurred by him in defending any proceedings, whether civil or criminal, in which judgment is given in his favour or in which he is acquitted or in connection with any application under section 448 of the Act in which relief is granted to him by the court.

PART II
REGULATIONS FOR THE MANAGEMENT OF A PRIVATE COMPANY LIMITED BY SHARES

1. The regulations contained in Part I of Table A (with the exception of regulations 24 and 53) shall apply.

2. The company is a private company and accordingly—
  (a) the right to transfer shares is restricted in manner hereinafter prescribed;
  (b) the number of members of the company (exclusive of persons who are in the employment of the company and of persons who having been formerly in the employment of the company were while in such employment and have continued after the determination of such employment to be members of the company) is limited to fifty. Provided that where two or more persons hold one or more shares in the company jointly they shall for the purpose of this regulation be treated as a single member;
  (c) any invitation to the public to subscribe for any shares or debentures of the company is prohibited;
  (d) the company shall not have power to issue share warrants to bearer.

3. The directors may, in their absolute discretion and without assigning any reason therefor, decline to register any transfer of any share, whether or not it is a fully paid share.

4. No business shall be transacted at any general meeting unless a quorum of members is present at the time when the meeting proceeds to business; save as herein otherwise provided two members present in person or by proxy shall be a quorum.

5. Subject to the provisions of the Act, a resolution in writing signed by all the members for the time being entitled to receive notice of and to attend and vote at general meetings (or being corporations by their duly authorised representatives) shall be as valid and effective as if the same had been passed at a general meeting of the company duly convened and held.

6. The directors may at any time require any person whose name is entered in the register of members of the company to furnish them with any information, supported (if the directors so require) by a statutory declaration, which they may consider necessary for the purpose of determining whether or not the company is an exempt private company within the meaning of subsection (4) of section 129 of the Act.
  Note. Regulations 3 and 4 of this Part are alternative to regulations 24 and 53 respectively of Part I.

NOTES
  Pt II repealed by CA 1980, Sch 3, in relation to any company registered on or after 22 December 1980.
  Reg 6 repealed by CA 1967, Sch 8, Pt III, in relation to any company registered on or after 27 January 1968.

Index